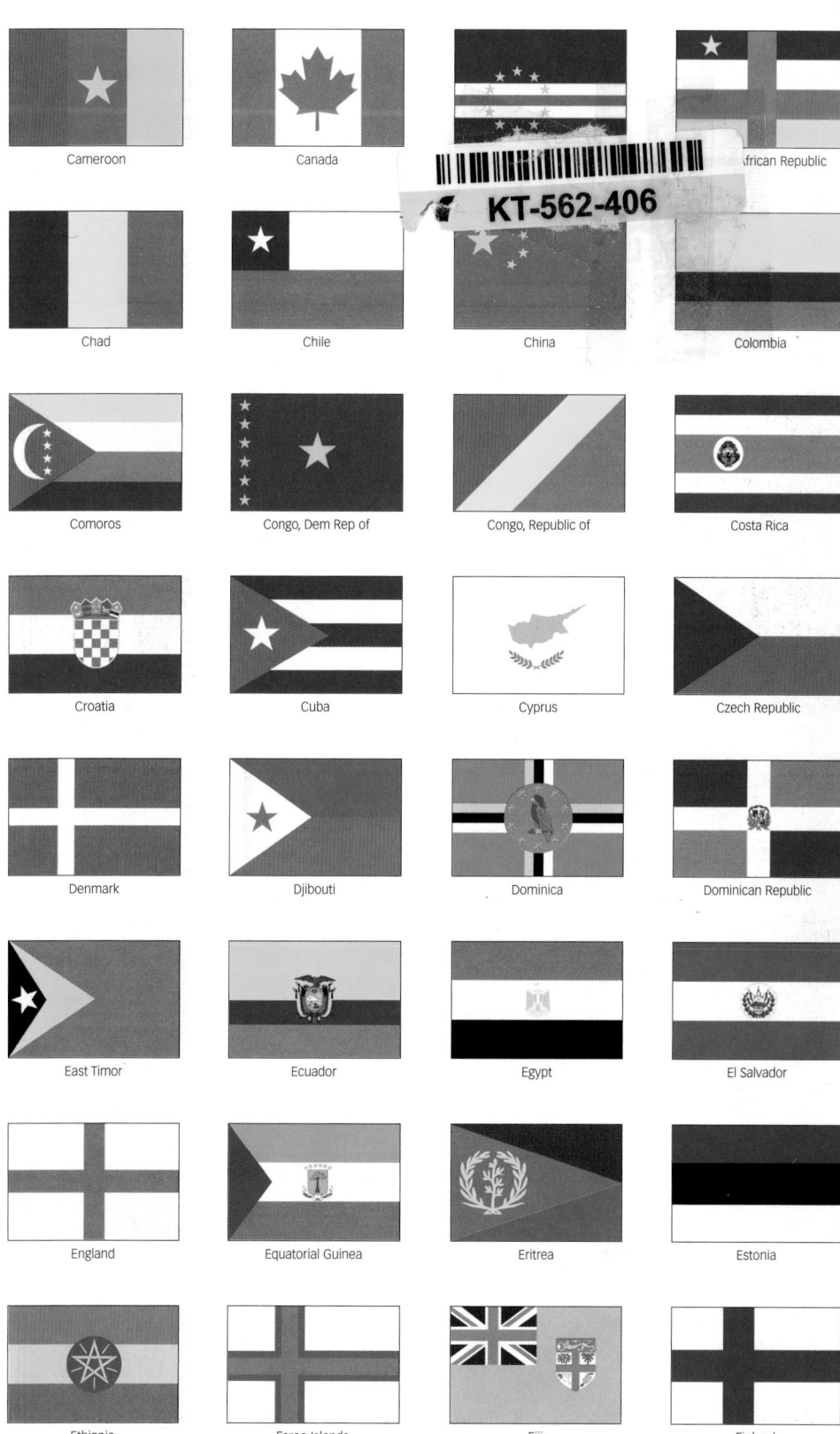

Cameroon

Canada

KT-562-406

...frican Republic

Chad

Chile

China

Colombia

Comoros

Congo, Dem Rep of

Congo, Republic of

Costa Rica

Croatia

Cuba

Cyprus

Czech Republic

Denmark

Djibouti

Dominica

Dominican Republic

East Timor

Ecuador

Egypt

El Salvador

England

Equatorial Guinea

Eritrea

Estonia

Ethiopia

Faroe Islands

Fiji

Finland

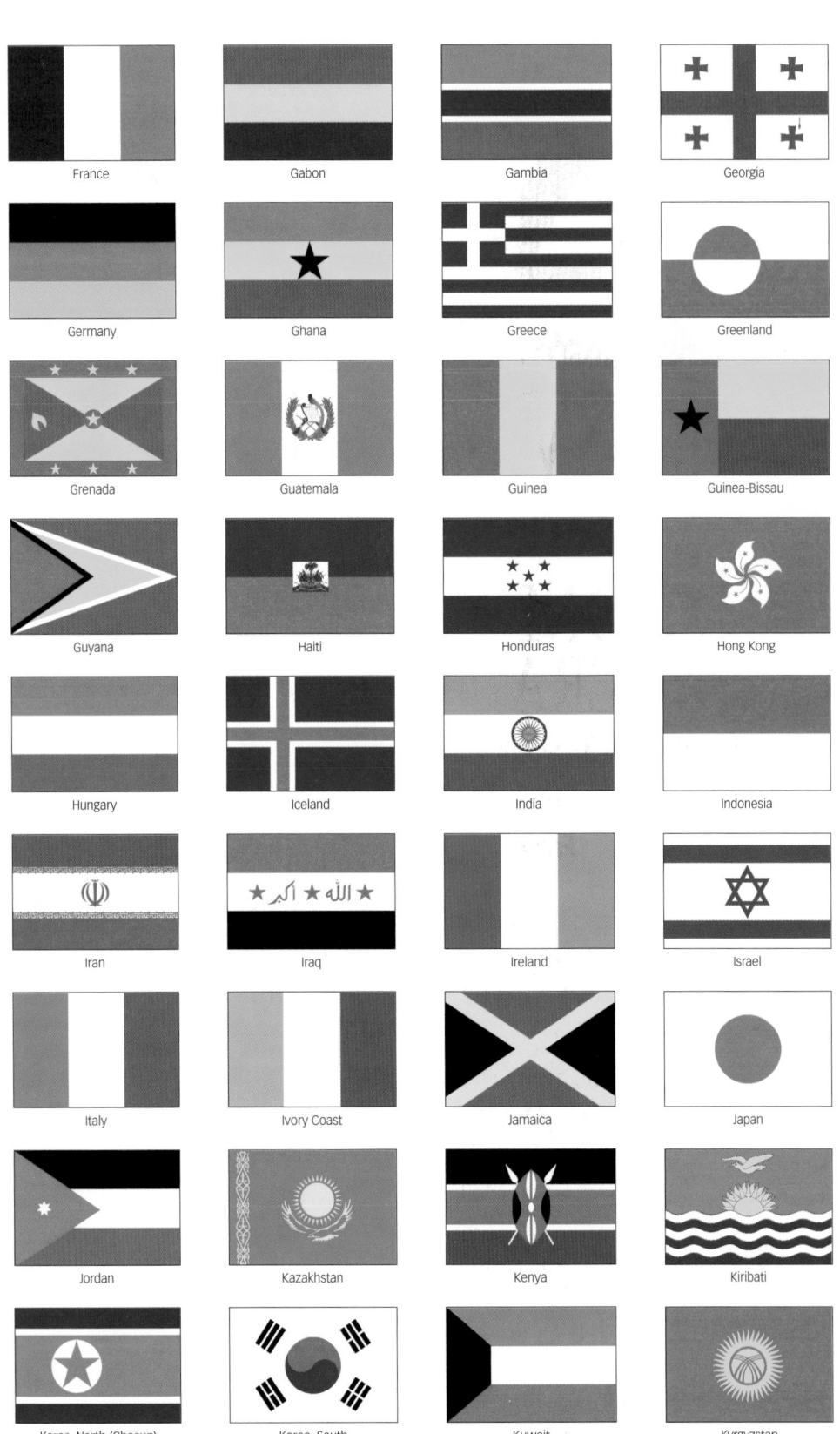

France   Gabon   Gambia   Georgia

Germany   Ghana   Greece   Greenland

Grenada   Guatemala   Guinea   Guinea-Bissau

Guyana   Haiti   Honduras   Hong Kong

Hungary   Iceland   India   Indonesia

Iran   Iraq   Ireland   Israel

Italy   Ivory Coast   Jamaica   Japan

Jordan   Kazakhstan   Kenya   Kiribati

Korea, North (Chosun)   Korea, South   Kuwait   Kyrgyzstan

A TO Z
almost
OF EVERYTHING

A COMPENDIUM OF
GENERAL KNOWLEDGE

TREVOR MONTAGUE

Revised and updated

ALSO BY TREVOR MONTAGUE

A to Z of Sport

LITTLE, BROWN

LITTLE, BROWN

First published in Great Britain in 2001 by Little, Brown
Second edition published in 2003
This edition published in 2005

A CIP catalogue record for this book
is available from the British Library.

ISBN 0 316 73137 4

Typeset in Helvetica by M Rules
Printed and bound in Great Britain by
The Bath Press, Bath

Little, Brown
An imprint of
Time Warner Book Group UK
Brettenham House
Lancaster Place
London WC2E 7EN

www.twbg.co.uk

CONTENTS

Acknowledgements

I would like to thank the following people for their help in the compilation of this work: Kevin Ashman, Mike Billson, Mark Bytheway, Eric Carden, Peter Chitty, Bob Collier, Patricia Cowley, Andy Curtis, Peter Ediss, Robert Edwards, Brian Ennis, Keith Fawdry, Gavin Fuller, Gavin Gaughan, Phillida Grantham, Paul Henderson, Christopher Hughes, June Humphries, Ann Kelly, Phil Lewis, Magnus Magnusson, Angelita March, Christine Moorcroft, Mike O'Sullivan, Anita Oxley, Fiona Redmond, Craig Scott, Leo Stevenson, Rob Sutherland, Geoff Thomas, Gordon Troughton, Ritchie Venner, Tim Westcott, Neil White and John Wilson.

Author's note

This third edition of the *A to Z of Everything* has been completely revised with the latest abbreviations and biographies of contemporary artists and architects, newly discovered planetary satellites, recent film releases and marriages, more pseudonyms and middle names of famous people, the most fashionable fashion designers, the latest foreign cuisine and population figures, new musicians, novelists, pop groups and playwrights, plus updated military battles, politics (including the 2005 General Election results), sports (including Athens Olympic results), radio and television programmes, and transport.

New sections include, by popular demand, the derivation of commonly used phrases, county flowers, the 1000 UK No. 1 hit records (sorted chronologically and by artist), and a comprehensive biographical list of Jane Austen characters across her six completed novels.

Readers will note that I have not replaced the sporting current affairs, which is more appropriate to the *A to Z of Sport*. Instead I have included much of the sporting news within the general sporting record section.

As ever, I hope the reader will be edified and entertained. I have done my utmost to achieve 100 per cent accuracy, but with a project of this magnitude, covering such a wide range of subjects, it seems unavoidable that mistakes will be made – for which I apologise. I would be delighted to have any errors pointed out to me so that I can ensure future editions of the *A to Z of Everything* are as correct as possible. If you would like to offer a correction, or to suggest a new topic for the book, please write to me c/o the Time Warner Book Group UK.

Introduction to the First Edition by Magnus Magnusson KBE

Trevor Montague is a Masterminder. That is to say, in 1995 he became one of the 1,231 bravehearts who appeared on the television *Mastermind* during its twenty-five-year run. But Trevor Montague is much more than that: he is that not-quite-so-rare-now animal, a quiz addict.

Trevor is also a begetter of quiz-teams. There is an unofficial *Mastermind* mafia which meets every month in the Grape Street wine bar in London, and from its regulars Trevor puts together formidable scratch teams of veteran Masterminders to take part in all and any quiz challenges. Trevor is also the question-setter of the fledgling British Quiz Championship which is a part of the annual Mind Sports Olympiad at London's Olympia.

That in itself is a sign of the immense and growing popularity of quizzes of all kinds on television, on radio, in pubs, in the Civil Service, and now even on the Internet. And it has given rise to Trevor's most ambitious project yet – *An A–Z of Almost Everything*: a massive factfile of information calculated to be of value to anyone and everyone interested in quizzes.

But how does one define 'General Knowledge' as opposed to 'Specialised Knowledge'? Indeed, when does 'Specialised Knowledge' become 'General Knowledge'? With the staggering growth of pub quiz-teams and television game-shows over recent years, the reservoir of what used to be considered 'General Knowledge' has expanded out of all recognition. Over the twenty-five years of *Mastermind*, for instance, questions which would once have come into the specialised category became demoted to the General Knowledge sets. I tried to make that very point, as subtly as possible, in the last round of the last Final of the last *Mastermind* series (in Kirkwall Cathedral, Orkney, in 1997): the last question echoed the very first question I had asked, in the University of Liverpool back in 1972:

Q: During the Spanish Civil War, which town in the Basque country was destroyed by German bombers, an event which was commemorated in a painting by Picasso?

A: Guernica

When that question was first asked in 1972, it was in a set of specialised questions on 'The Visual Arts'; in 1997 it was in a General Knowledge set.

So, what exactly makes up an A–Z of Everything? For Trevor, everything is grist to his insatiable mill. He has produced a monster factfile on an astonishing array of subjects from abbreviations to zodiac, embracing Americanisms, animal adjectives, assassination attempts, *Carry On* films, dubbed singing voices, famous dogs, gestation periods, London postal areas, middle names, nursery rhymes, obituaries, pub names, quantum theory, Schrödinger's cat, sculptors, trains, Visigoth rulers and zip codes.

I can think of few subjects which have been omitted, except perhaps for some of the classic *Mastermind* offerings which never made it to the screen: 'orthopaedic bone cement in total hip-replacement'; 'self-service petrol stations from 1963–68'; 'perfect squares from 992–9801'; and 'motorway routes to anywhere in mainland Britain from Letchworth'.

To put together this weighty tome, Trevor called upon his network of friends and colleagues in the Mastermind Club – that remarkable association of survivors of the Black Chair. The Club membership represents an astonishing reservoir of knowledge which its owners are always ready to impart to others. Many is the time I found myself marooned in a hotel without reference books and phoned friends in the Club to check on some vital detail which I needed for an occasion in the next morning.

The quiz cognoscenti who will avidly devour this book may well start off feeling superior ('I know that, of course!'), but I am pretty sure that even they will find much to intrigue them in this shrine of serendipity.

Abbreviations

A & E   Accident and Emergency
A & P   Advertising and Promotion
A & R   Artists and Repertoire / Recording
AA   Automobile Association; Alcoholics Anonymous
AAA   Amateur Athletic Association; Anti-Aircraft Artillery
AAM   Air-to-Air Missile
ABC   Atomic, Biological and Chemical; American Broadcasting Company; Australian Broadcasting Commission
ABH   Actual Bodily Harm
ABM   Anti-Ballistic Missile
ABRACADABRA   ABbreviations and Related ACronyms Associated with Defense, Astronautics, Business and RAdio-electronics
ABS   Anti-lock Braking System
ABTA   Association of British Travel Agents
AC   Alternating Current; Audit Commission
A/C   Account
ACAS   Advisory Conciliation and Arbitration Service
ACCA   Association of Certified and Corporate Accountants
ACLU   American Civil Liberties Union
ACM   Air Chief Marshal
ACPO   Association of Chief Police Officers
ACPOS   Association of Chief Police Officers in Scotland
ACT   Advance Corporation Tax
ACTT   Association of Cinematograph, Television and Allied Technicians
ACV   Air-Cushion Vehicle
AD   Anno Domini
ADC   Aide-De-Camp
ADCM   Archbishop of Canterbury's Diploma in Church Music
ADSL   Asymmetric Digital Subscriber Line
AEEU   Amalgamated Engineering and Electrical Union
AEGIS   Aid for the Elderly in Government InstitutionS
AEU   Amalgamated Engineering Union
AFP   Agence France Press
AFR   Automatic Fingerprint Recognition
AFV   Armoured Fighting Vehicle
AG   Attorney General; Adjutant General
AGM   Air-to-Ground Missile; Annual General Meeting
AGR   Advanced Gas-cooled Reactor
AH   Anno Hegirae (from 622 AD, the start of the Muslim calendar)
AI   Artificial Intelligence; Amnesty International; Artificial Insemination
AID   Artificial Insemination by Donor
AIDS   Acquired Immune Deficiency Syndrome
AIM   Alternative Investment Market
AKA   Also Known As
ALGOL   ALGOrithmic Language
ALICE   Autistic and Language-Impaired Children's Education
ALWR   Advanced Light Water Reactor
AM   Ante Meridiem; Amplitude Modulation

AMCST   Associate, Manchester College of Science and Technology
AMICE   Associate Member of the Institute of Civil Engineers
ANC   African National Congress
ANPR   Automatic Number Plate Recognition
ANZAC   Australian and New Zealand Army Corps
AOL   America On Line
AONB   Area of Outstanding Natural Beauty
AP   Associated Press; Artist's Proof
APEX   Advance Purchase EXcursion; Association of Professional, EXecutive, Clerical and Computer Staff
APR   Annual / Annualised Percentage Rate
APT   Advanced Passenger Train
APWR   Advanced Pressurised Water Reactor
ARCO   Associate of the Royal College of Organists
ARCS   Associate of the Royal College of Science
ARP   Association of Retired Persons; Air-Raid Precautions
AS   Advanced Subsidiary (Education)
ASA   Advertising Standards Authority; Amateur Swimming Association
ASAP   As Soon As Possible
ASB   Alternative Service Book
ASBM   Air-to-Surface Ballistic Missile
ASBO   Anti-Social Behaviour Order
ASCII   American Standard Code for Information Interchange
ASDA   ASsociated DAiries
ASDE   Airport Surface Detection Equipment
ASDIC   Anti-Submarine Detection Investigation Committee
ASEAN   Association of South East Asian Nations
ASH   Action on Smoking and Health
ASLEF   Associated Society of Locomotive Engineers and Firemen
ASSC   Accounting Standards Steering Committee
ASSR   Autonomous Soviet Socialist Republic
ASTMS   Association of Scientific, Technical and Managerial Staff
AT & T   American Telephone and Telegraph Company
ATC   Air Traffic Control; Air Training Corps
ATOL   Air Travel Organisers Licence
ATS   Auxiliary Territorial Service; Automated Traffic Signal
ATV   Associated TeleVision
AUC   Anno Urbis Conditae (in the year of the founding of the city); Ab Urbe Condita (years since the foundation of Rome)
AUEW   Amalgamated Union of Engineering Workers (now AEU)
AUT   Association of University Teachers
AVR   Army Volunteer Reserve
AWACS   Airborne Warning And Control System
AWOL   Absent WithOut Leave / Absent Without Official Leave
AWP   Amusement With Prizes
AWRE   Atomic Weapons Research Establishment

BA   Bachelor of Arts; British Airways
BAA   British Airports Authority
BAC   British Aircraft Corporation
BACS   Bankers' Automated Clearing Service
BACUP   British Association of Cancer-United Patients
BAF   British Athletics Federation
BAFTA   British Academy of Film and Television Arts
BALPA   British AirLine Pilots' Association
BANANA   Build Absolutely Nothing Anywhere Near Anyone
BAOR   British Army Of the Rhine
BARB   British Audience Research Bureau; Broadcasters' Audience Research Board
BART   Baronet
BART   Bay Area Rapid Transit
BASIC   Beginners All-Purpose Symbolic Instruction Code
BAT   British American Tobacco Company
BBBC   British Boxing Board of Control
BBC   British Broadcasting Corporation
BBFC   British Board of Film Censors / Classification (new title)
BC   Before Christ; British Colombia
BCC   British Chamber of Commerce
BCE   Before Common / Christian Era
BCh(D) / BDS   Bachelor of Dental Surgery
BEC   Building Employers' Confederation
BECTU   Broadcasting, Entertainment and Cinematograph Technicians Union
BEF   British Expeditionary Force
BEM   British Empire Medal
BES   Business Expansion Scheme
BEST   British Expertise in Science and Technology
BFI   British Film Institute
BFPO   British Forces Post Office
BHF   British Heart Foundation
BHI   British Horological Institute
BIFU   Banking, Insurance and Finance Union
BIM   British Institute of Management
BIT   BInary DigiT
BLitt   Bachelor of Letters
BMA   British Medical Association
BMJ   British Medical Journal
BMR   Basal Metabolic Rate
BMX   Bicycle Motocross
BOAC   British Overseas Airways Corporation
BPD   Barrels Per Day
BPS   Bits Per Second; Bytes Per Second
BRCS   British Red Cross Society
BSA   Birmingham Small Arms
BSAD   British Sports Association for the Disabled
BSB   British Satellite Broadcasting
BSc   Bachelor of Science
BSE   Bovine Spongiform Encephalopathy
BSI   British Standards Institution
BSL   British Sign Language
BST   British Summer Time
BSW   British Standard Whitworth
Bt   Baronet
BTEC   Business and Technology Education Council
BTP   British Transport Police
BUNA   BUtadiene and NAtrium (synthetic rubber)
BUPA   British United Provident Association
BUS   Broadcast and Unknown Server

BVM   Blessed Virgin Mary
BWIA   British West Indian Airways
BWR   Boiling Water Reactor
BYO   Bring Your Own

CAA   Civil Aviation Authority
CAB   Citizens Advice Bureau
CAD   Computer Aided Design
CADD   Computer Aided Design and Drafting
CAFOD   CAtholic Fund for Overseas Development
CAL   Computer Aided Learning
CAMRA   CAMpaign for Real Ale
CAN   Christian Advertising Network
Cantab   Cantabrigiensis (of Cambridge)
CAP   Computer Aided Publishing; Common Agricultural Policy
CARE   Co-operative for American Relief Everywhere
CAT   Computerised Axial Tomography
CB   Companion of the order of the Bath
CBC   Canadian Broadcasting Corporation
CBE   Commander of the Order of the British Empire
CBI   Confederation of British Industry
CBS   Columbia Broadcasting System
CCRC   Criminal Cases Review Commission
CCTV   Closed Circuit TeleVision
CDI   Compact Disc Interactive
CDS   Chief of the Defence Staff
CE   Christian Era; Common Era
CERN   Conseil Européen pour la Recherche Nucléaire
CET   Central European Time; Common External Tariff
CFC   ChloroFluoroCarbon
CFS   Chronic Fatigue Syndrome (see ME)
CGM   Conspicuous Gallantry Medal
CGS   Centimetre-Gramme-Second; Chief of General Staff
CH   Companion of Honour
CHP   Combined Heat and Power
CIA   Central Intelligence Agency
CICB   Criminal Injuries Compensation Board
CID   Criminal Investigations Department
CIPFA   Chartered Institute of Public Finance and Accountancy
CIS   Commonwealth of Independent States (former Soviet republics)
CITES   Convention on International Trade in Endangered Species
CIWF   Compassion In World Farming
CJD   Creutzfeldt-Jakob Disease
CLA   Country Landowners' Association
CM   Chirurgiae Magister (Master of Surgery)
CMEA   Council for Mutual Economic Assistance
CND   Campaign for Nuclear Disarmament
CNN   Cable News Network
COBOL   COmmon Business-Oriented Language
COD   Cash On Delivery
COHSE   Confederation Of Health Service Employees (Now UNISON)
COI   Central Office of Information
COMECON   COuncil for Mutual ECONomic aid / assistance
COMINTERN   COMmunist INTERNational
CPRE   Council for the Protection of Rural England
CPS   Crown Prosecution Service; Characters Per Second

CPSA Civil and Public Services Association
CPU Central Processing Unit
CRE Commission for Racial Equality
CRT Cathode Ray Tube
CS (gas) Carson and Staughton
CSA Child Support Agency
CSE Certificate of Secondary Education
CSO Central Statistical Office
CTO Cancelled To Order (Philately)
CTS Counter Terrorist Search
CTT Capital Transfer Tax
CURE Care, Understanding, REsearch
CV Curriculum Vitae; Cardio Vascular
CVD Compact Video Disc
CVO Commander of the Royal Victorian Order
CVP Climate, Vegetation and Productivity
CWU Communication Workers' Union
CYP Children and Young Persons

DA District Attorney
DAB Digital Audio Broadcasting
DAGMAR Defining Advertising Goals for Measured Advertising Results
D & C Dilatation and Curettage
DAR Daughters of the American Revolution
DAT Digital Audio Tape
DBE Dame Commander of the Order of the British Empire
DBS Direct Broadcasting by Satellite
DC Direct Current; District of Columbia
DCL Doctor of Civil Law
DCM Distinguished Conduct Medal
DCMG Dame Commander of the Order of St Michael and St George
DCMS Department for Culture, Media and Sport
DD Doctor of Divinity
DDS Doctor of Dental Surgery
DDT DichloroDiphenylTrichloroethane
DEFRA Department for Environment, Food and Rural Affairs
DERV Diesel-Engined-Road Vehicle
DFC Distinguished Flying Cross
DFM Distinguished Flying Medal
DHTML Dynamic HyperText Mark-up Language
DINKY Double Income No Kids Yet
DipSW Diploma in Social Work
DLitt Doctor of Letters
DLR Docklands Light Railway
DNA DeoxyriboNucleic Acid
DOA Dead On Arrival
DORA Defence Of the Realm Act (1914)
DOS Disc Operating System
DPA Data Protection Act
DPP Director of Public Prosecutions
DQL Data Query Language
DSA Driving Standards Agency
DSC Distinguished Service Cross
DSL Digital Subscriber Line
DSM Distinguished Service Medal
DSO Distinguished Service Order
DSS Department of Social Security
DTI Department of Trade and Industry
DTLR Department of Transport, Local Government and the Regions
DTP Desk-Top Publishing

DVD Digital Versatile / Video Disc
DVLA Driver Vehicle Licensing Authority
DVM Doctor of Veterinary Medicine
DWI Drinking Water Inspectorate
DWP Department for Work and Pensions
DWT Denarius WeighT (pennyweight); Dead Weight Tonnage

EAROM Electrically Alterable Read Only Memory
EBRD European Bank for Reconstruction and Development
EBV Epstein-Barr Virus
EC European Commission/Community
ECG ElectroCardioGram / Graph
ECGD Export Credit Guarantee Department
ECHR European Court of Human Rights; European Convention on Human Rights
ECJ European Court of Justice
ECO English Chamber Orchestra
ECSC European Coal and Steel Community
ECT Electro-Convulsive Therapy
ECU European Currency Unit
EDM Early Day Motion
EDP Electronic Data Processing
EEC European Economic Community
EEG ElectroEncephaloGram / Graph
EFA European Fighter Aircraft; Extended File Attribute
EFTA European Free Trade Association
EFTS Electronic Funds Transfer System
e.g. exempli gratia (for example)
EHF Extremely High Frequency
EIB European Investment Bank
EIS Educational Institute of Scotland
E-Mail Electronic Mail
EMF Electro-Motive Force; European Monetary Fund
EMI Electro-Magnetic Interference
EMS European Monetary System
EMU ElectroMagnetic Unit; European Monetary Union
ENEA European Nuclear Energy Agency
ENG Electronic News Gathering
ENIAC Electronic Numerical Integrator Analyser and Computer
ENO English National Opera
ENSA Entertainments National Service Association
ENT Ear, Nose and Throat
EOC Equal Opportunities Commission
EPCOT Experimental Prototype Community Of Tomorrow
ER Elizabeth Regina
ERA Engine Room Artificer (navy)
ERM Exchange Rate Mechanism
ERNIE Electronic Random Number Indicator Equipment
EROM Erasable Read Only Memory
ESA European Space Agency
ESF European Social Fund
ESP ExtraSensory Perception
ESSO Standard Oil
et seq. et sequentia (and the following)
ETA Estimated Time of Arrival; Euzkadi Ta Askatasuna (Basque separatist organisation)
ETD Estimated Time of Departure
EU European Union

EVA   ExtraVehicular Activity
EWCB   England and Wales Cricket Board
E-ZINE   Electronic magaZINE

FANY   First Aid Nursing Yeomanry
FAO   Food and Agriculture Organisation
FAP   File Access Protocol
FAQ   Frequently Asked Questions
Fax   Facsimile transmission
FBI   Federal Bureau of Investigation
FBOU   Fellow of the British Ornithologists' Union
FCO   Foreign and Commonwealth Office
FGS   Fellow of the Geographical Society
FHS   Fellow of the Heraldry Society
FIA   Fellow of the Institute of Actuaries
FICE   Fellow of the Institution of Civil Engineers
FIFA   Fédération Internationale de Football Association
FIFO   First In, First Out
FILO   First In, Last Out
FIRST   Fixed Interest Rate Savings Tax free
FMCG   Fast Moving Consumer Goods
FOIA   Freedom Of Information Act
FOREST   Freedom Organisation for the Right to Enjoy Smoking Tobacco
FORTRAN   Formula Translation
FPN   Fixed Penalty Notice
FRAM   Fellow of the Royal Academy of Music
FRAS   Fellow of the Royal Astronomical Society
FRBS   Fellow of the Royal Botanical Society
FRCGP   Fellow of the Royal College of General Practitioners
FRCM   Fellow of the Royal College of Music
FRCOG   Fellow of the Royal College of Obstetricians and Gynaecologists
FRCP   Fellow of the Royal College of Physicians
FRHS   Fellow of the Royal Horticultural Society
FTP   File Transfer Protocol
FTSE   Financial Times Stock Exchange
FWTK   FireWall Tool Kit
FYI   For Your Information

GAA   Gaelic Athletic Association
GATT   General Agreement on Tariffs and Trade
GBE   Knight or Dame Grand Cross of the Order of the British Empire
GBH   Grievous Bodily Harm
GC   George Cross
GCB   Knight or Dame Grand Cross of the Order of the Bath
GCHQ   Government Communications Headquarters
GCSE   General Certificate of Secondary Education
GCVO   Knight or Dame Grand Cross of the Royal Victorian Order
GDBA   Guide Dogs for the Blind Association
GDP   Gross Domestic Product
Gestapo   GEheime STAatsPOlizei
GIF   Graphics Interchange Format
GIFT   Gamete IntraFallopian Transfer
GMB   Grand Master Bowman
GMT   Greenwich Mean Time
GNP   Gross National Product
GNVQ   General National Vocational Qualification
GPMU   Graphical, Paper and Media Union
GPS   Global Positioning System

GRAS   Generally Regarded As Safe
GRU   Glavnoye Razvedyvatelnoye Upravleniye (military counterpart of KGB in former Soviet Union)

HB   Hard Black (pencil)
HBM   Her / His Britannic Majesty
HCF   Highest Common Factor
HDRA   Henry Doubleday Research Association (Gardening)
HDTV   High-Definition TeleVision
HF   High Frequency
HGV   Heavy Goods Vehicle
HIV   Human Immunodeficiency Virus
HJ   Hic Jacet (here lies, seen on gravestones)
HMCE   Her/His Majesty's Customs and Excise
HMSO   Her / His Majesty's Stationery Office
HNC   Higher National Certificate
HND   Higher National Diploma
HOLMES   Home Office Large Major Enquiry System (police computer system)
HOTOL   HOrizontal Take-Off and Landing
HRH   Her/His Royal Highness
HSH   Her / His Serene Highness
HSV   Herpes Simplex Virus
HTHL   Horizontal Take-Off Horizontal Landing
HTML   HyperText Mark-up Language
HTTP   HyperText Transfer Protocol
HTVL   Horizontal Take-Off Vertical Landing
HWM   High Water Mark

IATA   International Air Transport Association
ib.   ibidem (in the same place)
IBA   International Broadcasting Authority
ibid.   Ibidem (in the same place)
ICAEW   Institute of Chartered Accountants of England and Wales
ICAO   International Civil Aviation Organisation
ICBM   InterContinental Balistic Missile
ICU   Intensive Care Unit
IDDS   Insulin Dependent Diabetic Syndrome
i.e.   id est (that is)
IFAW   International Fund for Animal Welfare
IFOR   Implementation FORce
IFS   Institute for Fiscal Studies
IGC   Inter-Governmental Conference
IGY   International Geophysical Year
ILO   International Labour Organisation
IMO   International Maritime Organisation
INRI   Iesus Nazarenus Rex Iudaeorum (Jesus of Nazareth King of the Jews)
INSET   INSErvice Training
INST   INSTant (current month)
INTEGRAL   INTErnational Gamma-Ray Astrophysics Laboratory
INTERPOL   INTERnational Criminal POLice Organisation
IOM   Isle Of Man
IOTA   Infrared-Optical Telescope Array; International Occultation Timing Association
IOW   Isle Of Wight
IPA   International Phonetic Alphabet
IQ   Intelligence Quotient
IRC   International Red Cross
IRS   Internal Revenue Service
IRSF   Inland Revenue Staff Federation

ISBN International Standard Book Number
ISH Information Super Highway
ISP Internet Service Provider
ISY International Space Year
IT Information Technology
ITA Initial Teaching Alphabet
ITC Independent Television Commission
ITU International Telecommunications Union; Intensive Therapy Unit
ITV Independent TeleVision
IV Intra Vires (within power); IntraVenous
IVF In Vitro Fertilisation
IWC International Whaling Commission

J & B Justerini and Brooks
JCR Junior Common Room
JCS Joint Chiefs of Staff
JP Justice of the Peace
JPEG Joint Photographic Experts Group
JPL Jet Propulsion Laboratory
JRDF Joint Rapid Deployment Force

KBE Knight Commander of the Order of the British Empire
KCVO Knight Commander of the Royal Victorian Order
KG Knight of the Order of the Garter
KGB Komitet Gosudarstvennoi Bezopasnosti (State Security Committee in former Soviet Union)
KT Knight of the Order of the Thistle

LACS League Against Cruel Sports
LAN Local Area Net (computer Internet)
LASER Light Amplification by Stimulated Emission of Radiation
LAUTRO Life Assurance and Unit Trust Regulatory Organisation
LBO Leveraged BuyOut
LCE London Commodities Exchange
LCJ Lord Chief Justice
LCM Lowest Common Multiple
LDOS Lord's Day Observance Society
LDV Local Defence Volunteers (Home Guard)
LED Light Emitting Diode
LEM Lunar Excursion Module
LGV Light Goods Vehicle
LH Liquid Hydrogen
LIDAR LIght Detection And Ranging
LIFFE London International Financial Futures and options Exchange
LIFO Last In, First Out
LIFT London International Festival Theatre
LILO Last In, Last Out
LLD Doctor of Laws
LMS / LMSR London, Midland and Scottish Railway
LNER London and North Eastern Railway
LORAN Long RAnge Navigation
LOX Liquid OXygen
LSD Librae Solidi Denarii; LySergic Acid Diethylamide
LSE London School of Economics
LSO London Symphony Orchestra
LULU Locally Unacceptable Land Use
LWM Low Water Mark

M & B May and Baker (forerunner of antibiotics)
MAD Mutually Assured Destruction
MADD Mothers Against Drunk Driving
MAFF Ministry of Agriculture Fisheries and Food
MANWEB Merseyside And North Wales Electricity Board
MASER Microwave Amplification by Stimulated Emission of Radiation
MBA Master of Business Administration
MBE Member of the Order of the British Empire
MBO Management BuyOut
MBR Master Boot Record
MCC Marylebone Cricket Club
MCS Marine Conservation Society
ME Myalgic Encephalomyelitis (see CFS)
MEP Member of the European Parliament
MFH Master of Fox Hounds
MFN Most Favoured Nation
M. ft. mistura fiat (let a mixture be made)
MIDAS Missile Defence Alarm System
MIG Mortgage Indemnity Guarantee
MIPS Millions of Instructions Per Second
MIRAS Mortgage Income Relief At Source
MIRV Multiple Independently targeted Re-entry Vehicle
MIT Massachusetts Institute of Technology
MKS Metre Kilogram Second
MLR Minimum Lending Rate
MM Messieurs; Military Medal
MMR Measles, Mumps, Rubella
MNR Marine Nature Reserve
MO Modus Operandi
MOBO MOther BOard; Music Of Black Origin
MOMA Museum Of Modern Art
MOD Ministry Of Defence
MOMI Museum Of Moving Image
MORI Market and Opinion Research Institute
MoT Ministry of Transport
MP Member of Parliament; Military Police
MPLA Movimento Popular de Libertação de Angola (Popular Movement for the Liberation of Angola)
MPV Multi-Purpose Vehicle
MRSA Methicillin Resistant Staphylococcus Aureus
MSF Manufacturing, Science and Finance (Union)
MSP Member of Scottish Parliament
MST Mountain Standard Time
MWA Member of the Welsh Assembly
MWGM Most Worthy Grand Master (Masons)

NAACP National Association for the Advancement of Colored People
NAAFI Navy, Army, and Air Force Institutes
NACODS National Association of Colliery Overmen, Deputies and Shotfirers
NACRO National Association for the Care and Resettlement of Offenders
NALGO National Association of Local Government Officers (now UNISON)
NAO National Audit Office
NARAS National Academy of Recording Arts and Sciences
NASA National Aeronautics and Space Administration
NASDAQ National Association of Securities Dealers Automatic Quotation

NAS / UWT National Association of Schoolmasters / Union of Women Teachers
NATO North Atlantic Treaty Organisation
NB Nota Bene (note well)
NBC National Broadcasting Company
NBL National Book League
NCCL National Council for Civil Liberties
NCDL National Canine Defence League
NCIS National Criminal Intelligence Service
NCVO National Council for Voluntary Organisations
NCVQ National Council for Vocational Qualifications
NEDC National Economic Development Council (Neddy)
NFT National Film Theatre
NFU National Farmers' Union
NGA National Graphical Association (now merged with SOGAT to form GPMU)
NHI National Health Insurance
NIDDS Non-Insulin-Dependent Diabetic Syndrome
NIMBY Not In My Back Yard
NIREX Nuclear Industry Radioactive waste EXecutive
NORWICH (K)Nickers Off Ready When I Come Home
NP Notary Public
NPT Non-Proliferation Treaty
NRA National Rifle Association; National Rivers Authority
NSPCC National Society for the Prevention of Cruelty to Children
NUCPS National Union of Civil and Public Servants (now the PCS)
NUJ National Union of Journalists
NUMAST National Union of Marine, Aviation and Shipping Transport Officers
NUPE National Union of Public Employees (now UNISON)
NUS National Union of Students
NUT National Union of Teachers
NVQ National Vocational Qualification
NW Neighbourhood Watch
NYO National Youth Orchestra
NYT National Youth Theatre

O & M Organisation and Method
OAPEC Organisation of Arab Petroleum-Exporting Countries
OAS Organisation of American States
OAU Organisation of African Unity
OBE Officer of the Order of the British Empire; Out-of-Body Experience
OBO Ore Bulk Oil (carrier)
OCR Optical Character Recognition
OECD Organisation for Economic Co-operation and Development
OED Oxford English Dictionary
OFFER OFFice of Electricity Regulation
OFGAS OFfice of GAS Supply
OFSTED OFfice for STandards in EDucation
OFTEL OFfice of TELecommunications
OFWAT Office of Water Services
OHMS On Her / His Majesty's Service
OM Order of Merit
OMOV One Member One Vote
ONO Or Near Offer

OP Opposite Prompt side (theatre); Out of Print (publishing)
OPCS Office of Population Censuses and Surveys
OPEC Organisation of Petroleum-Exporting Countries
OS Old Style; Ordnance Survey
OST Office of Science and Technology
OT Old Testament
OUDS Oxford University Dramatic Society
OXFAM OXford Committee for FAMine Relief
Oxon Oxoniensis (of Oxford)

P & O Peninsular and Oriental Steamship Company
PABX Private Automatic Branch eXchange
PACE Police And Criminal Evidence act
parSec parallax second (3.26 light-years)
PAS Power-Assisted Steering
PAYE Pay As You Earn
PBX Private Branch eXchange
PC Personal Computer; Privy Council; Police Constable; Prince Consort; Politically Correct
PCA Police Complaints Authority
PCB Printed Circuit Board
PCS Public and Commercial Services Union
PDF Portable Document File; Package Definition File
PDSA People's Dispensary for Sick Animals
PEP Personal Equity Plan
pH potential of Hydrogen ions
PIA Personal Investment Authority (replaced LAUTRO)
PIN Personal Identification Number
PIPO Parallel In, Parallel Out
Pixel Picture Element
PLA Port of London Authority
PLC Public Limited Company
PLO Palestine Liberation Organisation
PLR Public Lending Rights
PM Post Mortem
PMT Pre-Menstrual Tension
PNMPB Police National Missing Persons Bureau
POS Point Of Sale
POW Prisoner Of War
PP Per Procurationem (by proxy); Parallel Port
PPS Parliamentary Private Secretary
PPV Pay Per View
pro tem. pro tempore (for the time being)
PROM Programmable Read Only Memory
PRP Profit-Related Pay
PRS Performing Rights Society
PS Post Scriptum
PSBR Public Sector Borrowing Requirement
PSDR Public Sector Debt Repayment
PSV Public Service Vehicle
PTI Physical Training Instructor
PTO Please Turn Over
PTSD Post-Traumatic Stress Disorder
PVC PolyVinylChloride

QA Quantitative Analysis; Quality Assurance
QANTAS Queensland And Northern Territory Aerial Service
QARANC Queen Alexandra's Royal Army Nursing Corps
QARNNS Queen Alexandra's Royal Naval Nursing Service

QBD Queen's Bench Division
QC Queen's Counsel; Quality Control
QED Quod Erat Demonstrandum (which was to be demonstrated)
QGM Queen's Gallantry Medal
QMG QuarterMaster General
QMV Qualified Majority Voting
QPM Queen's Police Medal; Quality and Performance Management
QSO Quasi-Stellar Object (quasar)
QUANGO QUasi-Autonomous Non-Governmental Organisation
qv quod vide (which see)

RAC Royal Automobile Club
RADA Royal Academy of Dramatic Art
RADAR RAdio Detection And Ranging
RAEC Royal Army Educational Corps
RAFVR Royal Air Force Voluntary Reserve
RAM Random-Access Memory
RAMC Royal Army Medical Corps
RAOC Royal Army Ordnance Corps
RAVC Royal Army Veterinary Corps
RBA Royal Society of British Artists
RC Roman Catholic; Red Cross
RCA Radio Corporation of America
RCM Royal College of Music
RCMP Royal Canadian Mounted Police
RCN Royal College of Nursing
REM Rapid Eye Movement
REME Royal Electrical and Mechanical Engineers
RFA Royal Fleet Auxiliary
RFDS Royal Flying Doctor Service
RH Relative Humidity
RHA Regional Health Authority
RHS Royal Historical / Horticultural / Humane Society
RIBA Royal Institute of British Architects
RKO Radio-Keith-Orpheum
RMT (National Union of) Rail, Maritime and Transport Workers
RNA RiboNucleic Acid
RNAS Royal Naval Air Service
RNIB Royal National Institute for the Blind
RNID Royal National Institute for the Deaf
RNLI Royal National Lifeboat Institution
RNR Royal Naval Reserve
ROC Royal Observer Corps
ROI Return On Investment
ROM Read-Only Memory
ROSPA ROyal Society for the Prevention of Accidents
RP Received Pronunciation
RPI Retail Price Index
RRP Recommended Retail Price
RSC Royal Shakespeare Company
RSI Repetitive Stress Injury
RSM Regimental Sergeant Major
RSPB Royal Society for the Protection of Birds
RSPCA Royal Society for the Prevention of Cruelty to Animals
RSV Revised Standard Version (Bible)
RSVP Répondez S'il Vous Plaît
RTA Road Traffic Accident
RTE Radio Telefis Eireann

RTS Royal Television Society
RTZ Rio Tinto Zinc Corporation Ltd
RUC Royal Ulster Constabulary
RYS Royal Yacht Squadron

SA Sociedad Anónima (Spanish: limited company); Société Anonyme (French: limited company)
SAD Seasonal Affective Disorder
SAE Stamped Addressed Envelope
SAFE Saving Animals From Extinction
SALT Strategic Arms Limitation Talks
SANE Schizophrenia – A National Emergency
SARS Severe Acute Respiratory Syndrome
SAS Special Air Service
SATB Soprano, Alto, Tenor, Bass
SBS Special Boat Squadron; Sick Building Syndrome
SCM State Certified Midwife
SCO Scottish Chamber Orchestra
SCR Senior Common Room
SCREAM Society for the Control and Registration of Estate Agents and Mortgage brokers
SCUBA Self-Contained Underwater Breathing Apparatus
SDA Severe Disability Allowance
SDI Strategic Defence Initiative
SDLP Social Democratic and Labour Party
SDP Social Democratic Party
SEA Single European Act
SEC Securities Exchange Commission
SEN Special Educational Needs; State Enrolled Nurse
SERPS State Earnings-Related Pension Scheme
SETI Search for Extra-Terrestrial Intelligence
SFO Serious Fraud Office
SHAPE Supreme Headquarters Allied Powers in Europe
SHF Super High Frequency
SI Système International (of units); Statutory Instrument
SIB Securities and Investments Board
SIG Special Interest Group
SIM Subscriber Identity Module
SJ Society of Jesus (Jesuits)
SLBM Submarine-Launched Ballistic Missile
SLDP Social and Liberal Democratic Party
SLR Single Lens Reflex
SMMT Society of Motor Manufacturers and Traders
SMP Statutory Maternity Pay
SMS Short Message Service
SNAFU Situation Normal All Fouled / Fucked Up
SNCF Société Nationale des Chemins de Fer français
SNP Scottish National Party
SOCO Scene Of Crime Officer
SOGAT Society Of Graphical and Allied Trades (now merged with NGA to form GPMU)
SOM Start Of Message
SONAR SOund Navigation And Ranging
SOS Save Our Souls
SOWETO SOuth WEstern TOwnships (South Africa)
SP Sine Prole (without issue)
SPCK Society for Promoting Christian Knowledge
SPF Sun Protection Factor
SPG Special Patrol Group

ABBREVIATIONS

SPQR Senatus PopulusQue Romanus (the Senate and People of Rome)
SRA Squash Rackets Association
SRN State Registered Nurse
SS SchutzStaffel
SSP Statutory Sick Pay
SSSI Site of Special Scientific Interest
SST SuperSonic Travel
START STrategic Arms Reduction Talks
STD Subscriber Trunk Dialling; Sexually Transmitted Disease
STOL Short TakeOff and Landing
STRIVE Society for The Preservation of Rural Industrial and Village Enterprises
STROBE Satellite TRacking Of Balloons and Emergencies
STV Single Transferable Vote
SVQ Scottish Vocational Qualification
SWALK Sealed With A Loving Kiss
SWAPO South West African People's Organisation
SWAT Special Weapons And Tactics

TA Territorial Army
TAMBA Twins And Multiple Births Association
TASS Technical, Administrative and Supervisory Section (of AUEW); Telegrafnoye Agentsvo Sovetshkovo Soyuza (news agency)
TAURUS Transfer and AUtomated Registration of Uncertified Stock
TAVR Territorial and Army Volunteer Reserve
TAVRA Territorial Auxiliary and Volunteer Reserve Association
TBA To Be Advised / Agreed / Announced / Arranged
TCCB Test and County Cricket Board
TEC Training and Enterprise Corporation
TEFL Teaching English as a Foreign Language
TELEX TELeprinter EXchange
TES Times Educational Supplement
TGWU Transport and General Workers Union
3GL Third Generation Language
TIFF Tag Image File Format (computing)
TIROS Television and InfraRed Observation Satellite
TLD Top Level Domain
TLR Twin Lens Reflex
TLS Times Literary Supplement
TM Transcendental Meditation; Trade Mark
TNT TriNitroToluene
Toc H Talbot House (Christian aid organisation)
TT Tuberculin Tested; Tourist Trophy
TUC Trades Union Congress
TVP Textured Vegetable Protein
TWAIN Technology Without Any Interesting Name
24/7 Twenty-Four Hours a Day, Seven Days a Week
TWOC Take WithOut Consent

UA Unitary Authority
UAE United Arab Emirates
UCAS Universities and Colleges Admissions Service (replaced UCCA in 1993)
UCATT Union of Construction, Allied Trades and Technicians
UCCA Universities Central Council on Admissions (replaced by UCAS in 1993)
UCLA University of California Los Angeles
UDA Ulster Defence Association

UDC Urban Development Corporation (e.g. Docklands) Urban District Council
UDI Unilateral Declaration of Independence
UDM Union of Democratic Mineworkers
UDP United Democratic Party; Ulster Democratic Party
UDR Ulster Defence Regiment
UEFA Union of European Football Associations
UFC Universities' Funding Council
UFO Unidentified Flying Object
UGC University Grants Committee
UHF Ultra High Frequency
UHT Ultra High Temperature; Ultra Heat Treatment
UKAEA United Kingdom Atomic Energy Authority
ULCC Ultra Large Crude Carrier
ULTRA Unrelated Live Transplant Regulatory Authority
UMIST University of Manchester Institute of Science and Technology
UNCTAD United Nations Conference on Trade And Development
UNESCO United Nations Educational, Scientific and Cultural Organisation
UNHCR United Nations High Commission for Refugees
UNICEF United Nations Children's Fund
UNITA União Nacional para a Independencia Total de Angola (National Union for the Total Independence of Angola)
UNITAR United Nations Institute for Training And Research
UNPROFOR United Nations Protection Force
UNRRA United Nations Relief and Rehabilitation Administration
UPC Universal Product Code
UPU Universal Postal Union
URL Uniform Resource Locator
USB Universal Serial Bus
USDAW Union of Shop, Distributive and Allied Workers
USM Unlisted Securities Market
USSR Union of Soviet Socialist Republics
UUP Ulster Unionist Party
UV Ultra Violet
UVF Ulster Volunteer Force

VASCAR Visual Average Speed Computer And Recorder
VAT Value Added Tax
VC Victoria Cross
VDU Video / Visual Display Unit
VHF Very High Frequency
VHS Video Home System
vix. vixit (she / he lived)
viz. videlicet (namely)
VLF Very Low Frequency
VLT Very Large Telescope
VOD Video On Demand
VR Virtual Reality
VRY ViceRoY
VSO Voluntary Service Overseas
VSOP Very Special Old Pale
VTOL Vertical TakeOff and Landing

WAN Wide Area Net (computer Internet)
WAP Wireless Application Protocol

WASP White Anglo-Saxon Protestant
WCC World Council of Churches
WDCS Whales and Dolphins Conservation Society
WEA Workers' Educational Association
WEU Western European Union
WFP World Food Programme
WFTU World Federation of Trade Unions
WHAM Winning Hearts And Minds (Vietnam propaganda slogan)
WHO World Health Organisation
WIBF Women's International Boxing Federation
WIMP Windows Icons Menus Pointing (computing); Weakly Interacting Massive Particle
WMD Weapons of Mass Destruction
WMO World Meteorological Organisation
WOMAN World Organisation for Mothers of All Nations
WORM Write Once Read Many (times)
WPBSA World Professional Billiards and Snooker Association
WRAC Women's Royal Army Corps
WRAF Women's Royal Air Force
WRNS Women's Royal Naval Service
WRP Worker's Revolutionary Party
WRVS Women's Royal Voluntary Service
WSPA World Society for the Protection of Animals
WTO World Trade Organisation

WVS Women's Voluntary Service
WWF World Wide Fund for Nature (formerly World Wildlife Fund)
WWW World Weather Watch; World Wide Web
WYSBYGI What You See Before You Get It
WYSIWYG What You See Is What You Get

YCNAC Young Conservative National Advisory Committee
YHA Youth Hostels Association
YMCA Young Men's Christian Association
YOC Young Ornithologists' Club
Y2K Year 2000
YTD Year To Date
YUPPIE Young Upwardly mobile / Urban Professional
YWCA Young Women's Christian Association

ZANU Zimbabwe African National Union
ZAPU Zimbabwe African People's Union
ZEBRA Zero-Energy Breeder-Reactor Assembly
ZEG Zero Economic Growth
ZENITH Zero-Energy NITrogen-Heated thermal reactor
ZIP Zone Improvement Plan; Zigzag In-line Package
ZPG Zero Population Growth

NB: For Internet chat-room abbreviations please see the Computer section.

ARCHITECTURE
Famous Architects

Aalto, Alvar (1898–1976) Finnish architect and designer whose work included the Hall of Residence, Massachusetts Institute of Technology, the Finlandia Concert Hall, Helsinki and Nordic Centre in Reykjavik. He also invented bent plywood furniture in 1932.

Abercrombie, (Sir) Patrick (1879–1957) English architect and pioneer of town planning in Britain, brother of the poet Lascelles Abercrombie. His major work was the replanning of London (County of London Plan, 1943, and Greater London Plan, 1944).

Adam, Robert (1728–92) Scottish architect and interior designer, leader of the British Neo-Classical revival. Famous works include the interiors of Harewood House, Luton Hoo, Syon House and Osterley Park. He worked with his brother James Adam, on the Adelphi near Charing Cross, largely rebuilt in 1936.

Archer, Thomas (1668–1743) Along with Vanbrugh and Hawksmoor, the third member of the great triumvirate of English Baroque architects. The north elevation at Chatsworth with its pilastered bow front is his best-known remaining work. Born in Tamworth, Archer's work was chiefly in ecclesiastical architecture. He designed the church of St Paul's, Deptford (1712-30), the church of St John's, Westminster (1714-28) and Birmingham Cathedral (1709-15).

Barry, (Sir) Charles (1795–1860) British architect of the Neo-Gothic Houses of Parliament (1840–60), which were completed after his death by his son Edward Middleton Barry. Other works included the church of St Peter, Brighton; Travellers' Club, Pall Mall; the Reform Club, London; King Edward's School, Birmingham, and the Manchester Athenaeum. His fifth son Sir John Wolfe-Barry (1836–1918) was engineer of Tower Bridge and Barry Docks.

Bramante, Donato (1444–1514) Italian High Renaissance architect, born near Urbano. Designed the new Basilica of St Peter's as well as the Belvedere courtyard, the Tempietto di S Pietro in Montorio and the Palazzo Caprini.

Brown, Lancelot (1716–83) English landscape-gardener and architect, nicknamed 'Capability' due to his stock reply to clients that their gardens had 'excellent capabilities'. Works include the gardens at Blenheim, Kew, Stowe, and Warwick Castle.

Brunel, Isambard Kingdom (1806–59) English engineer and inventor, born in Portsmouth, son of Sir Marc Isambard Brunel. His numerous works include the original Thames Tunnel, Clifton and Hungerford Suspension Bridges, and the Saltash Bridge over the Tamar. His ship designs include the *Great Western* (1838), the *Great Britain* (1845) and the *Great Eastern*, in collaboration with John Scott Russell.

Chambers, (Sir) William (1723–96) Swedish-born, Scottish architect. He popularised Chinese influence (Kew Garden pagoda) and designed Somerset House, London (1776).

Cockerell, Charles Robert (1788–1863) English architect, son of Samuel Pepys Cockerell. He designed the Taylorian Institute at Oxford, Fitzwilliam Museum at Cambridge, and Ashmolean Museum, Oxford.

Foster, Norman (Lord Foster of Thames Bank) (1935–) British architect of the high-tech school. His best-known buildings include the Willis Faber office, Ipswich (1975), the Sainsbury Centre for the visual arts, Norwich (1978), the Hong Kong and Shanghai Bank, Hong Kong (1986), the Stansted Airport Terminal Building (1991), the American Air Museum, Duxford, Cambridgeshire (1998), the Millennium Footbridge, London (1999), 30 St Mary Axe (Swiss Reinsurers), London (2004) and the Millau Viaduct, France (2004).

Fuller, Richard Buckminster (1895–1983) American architect who invented the Geodesic Dome. Examples of his works are at the Union Tank Car Repair Shop, Louisiana (1958), and the US Pavilion, Montreal Exhibition (1967).

Gaudí, Antonio (1852–1926) Spanish architect, noted for his flamboyant style. His work on the Church of the Holy Family in Barcelona begun in 1883 was unfinished at his death.

Gehry, Frank (1929–) Toronto-born architect who moved to California when he was 17 and became a naturalised American citizen. Known for his curvaceous free-form sculptural style, often encompassing titanium sheathing for his buildings. His best-known buildings include the Frederick Weisman Museum of Art, University of Minnesota (1990), the Guggenheim Museum, Bilbao, Spain (1997), and the Walt Disney Concert Hall, Los Angeles (2003).

Gibbs, James (1682–1754) Scottish Neo-Classical architect whose works include St Martin-in-the-Fields, London (1722), and the Radcliffe Camera, Oxford (1737).

Hadid, Zaha (1950–) British architect born in Baghdad, Iraq. Became the first woman to win the $100,000 Pritzker Architecture Prize, in 2004. Her projects to date include the Vitra Fire Station (1994) and the LFone pavilion (1999), in Weil am Rhein, Germany, the Mind Zone at the Millennium Dome, London (1999), a ski jump in Innsbruck, Austria (2002) and the Contemporary Arts Centre, Cincinnati (2003).

Hawksmoor, Nicholas (1661–1736) English Baroque architect born in Nottingham. He designed many London churches including St George's, Bloomsbury, and Christ Church, Spitalfields. Assisted Vanbrugh at Blenheim Palace and Castle Howard and was clerk to Wren.

Jones, Inigo (1573–1652) English architect, born in London. The founder of Classical English architecture whose innovations include the introduction of the proscenium arch and movable scenery to the English stage. In 1616 he designed the Queen's House at Greenwich. Other commissions included the rebuilding of the Banqueting Hall at Whitehall, the nave and transepts and a large Corinthian portico of old St Paul's, Marlborough Chapel, the Double-Cube room at Wilton, and possibly the York Water Gate. Jones also laid out Covent Garden and Lincoln's Inn Fields.

Kent, William (1684–1748) Born in Yorkshire. After studying painting in Rome became a leading light in the introduction of the Palladian style of architecture into Britain. He designed many public buildings in

London, including the Royal Mews in Trafalgar Square, the Treasury buildings and the Horse Guards block in Whitehall (1745). An example of his gardens is at Stowe House in Buckinghamshire and his artistry is visible in the Gothic screens at Westminster Hall and Gloucester Cathedral. He also designed the interiors of Burlington House and Chiswick House in London.

Lasdun, (Sir) Denys Louis (1914–2001) English architect whose works include the Royal College of Physicians, London; University of East Anglia, Norwich; National Theatre, London; and the European Investment Bank in Luxembourg.

Le Corbusier (1887–1965) Pseudonym of Charles Édouard Jeanneret, Swiss-born French architect, famous for his proclamation that the house is a habitable machine to be designed to functional criteria. His works include the Palace of the Nations, Geneva; and Cité Radieuse, Marseilles; as well as the town plan for Chandigarh, India.

Lutyens, (Sir) Edwin Landseer (1869–1944) English architect whose designs ranged from the picturesque of his early country houses, including Marsh Court, Stockbridge, and the restoration of Lindisfarne Castle, which owed much to the Arts and Crafts movement, to those in the Renaissance style such as Heathcote, Ilkley and Salutation, Sandwich. He finally evolved a classical style exhibited in the Cenotaph, Whitehall, which reached its height in his design – never built – for Liverpool Roman Catholic Cathedral. Other works include the Viceroy's House, New Delhi, and the British Embassy in Washington.

Mackintosh, Charles Rennie (1868–1928) Scottish architect, designer, and water colourist. Outstanding exponent of the Art Nouveau style in Scotland. Born in Glasgow, the son of a police superintendent, he married Margaret Mackintosh in 1900. His output included the Glasgow School of Art, Cranston tearooms, and houses such as Hill House in Helensburgh. By the end of World War I he had given up architecture for a career in water colours, mainly in France.

Mies Van Der Rohe, Ludwig (1886–1969) German-born American architect, born in Aachen. A pioneer of glass skyscrapers and high-rise flats, he also designed tubular-steel furniture, particularly the 'Barcelona Chair'. Became professor of architecture at the Illinois Institute of Technology in Chicago and designed two glass apartment towers on Lake Shore Drive, and the Seagram Building in New York. He also designed the Washington DC Public Library and two art galleries in Berlin.

Nash, John (1752–1835) British architect who designed Regent's Park and its terraces, Regent Street and Marble Arch. He also recreated Buckingham Palace from old Buckingham House and rebuilt Brighton Pavilion in oriental style. Trafalgar Square and St James's Park were also laid out by Nash.

Paxton, (Sir) Joseph (1801–65) British architect and garden superintendent to the Duke of Devonshire. By far his most famous work was the design of the Great Exhibition Building of 1851, the Crystal Palace, the first example of a prefabricated industrialised building on a large scale.

Pei, Ieoh Meng (1917–) Chinese-born American architect whose works include the John Hancock Tower, Boston; the Mile High Center, Denver and the glass pyramid at the Louvre.

Piano, Renzo (1937–) Born in Genoa, Italy, and graduated from the University of Milan in 1964. The Italian designer and lecturer is best-known for his partnership with Richard Rogers (1970–78) during which time they designed the Pompidou Centre in Paris. He received the Pritzker Prize in 1998 and has designed buildings in Italy, France, the United States, Germany, Japan, and notably Dakar, Senegal.

Rogers, Richard (Lord Rogers of Riverside) (1933–) Florence-born British architect whose works include the Pompidou Centre in Paris (1977), the Lloyd's building, London (1986) the Channel 4 Headquarters, London (1994), the European Court of Human Rights, Strasbourg (1995), and the Millennium Dome (1999). He is presently working on Terminal 5 at Heathrow Airport, London, and Barajas Airport, Madrid. He was created a life peer in 1996. Founder member with Norman Foster and their wives of 'Team 4'.

Saarinen, Eero (1910–61) Finnish-born American architect whose works include the American Embassy in London and Dulles Airport near Washington DC.

Scott, (Sir) George Gilbert (1811–78) English architect, born in Gawcott, Bucks. His works include the Albert Memorial, St Pancras station, and the Episcopal Cathedral in Edinburgh.

Scott, (Sir) Giles Gilbert (1880–1960) English architect, grandson of Sir George Gilbert Scott. Won a competition in 1903 for the design of the Anglican Cathedral in Liverpool (consecrated 1924). Other works include the new Bodleian Library at Oxford and the new Cambridge University Library. He also planned the new Waterloo Bridge and was responsible for the rebuilding of the House of Commons after World War II.

Shaw, Norman (1831–1912) English architect born in Edinburgh. Worked with his partner William Eden Nesfield (1835–88) in many styles ranging from Gothic Revival to Neo-Baroque, but became an acknowledged leader in the trend away from the Victorian style back to traditional Georgian design, leading to the English Domestic Revival. His major buildings include the Old Swan House, Chelsea (1876), New Scotland Yard (1888), the Gaiety Theatre, Aldwych (1902, now demolished), and Piccadilly Hotel (1905). He also designed the garden suburb at Bedford Park, London.

Smirke, (Sir) Robert (1781–1867) English architect, son of Robert Smirke (1752–1845) the painter and book illustrator. His works in London include Covent Garden Theatre (destroyed), British Museum, King's College and the Royal College of Physicians (now Canada House).

Soane, (Sir) John (1753–1837) English architect, born near Reading, the son of a mason. His works included the Bank of England, the Dulwich Picture Gallery and his own house in Lincoln's Inn Fields, London which he bequeathed to the nation.

Spence, (Sir) Basil Urwin (1907–76) Scottish architect, born in India. His works include the conversions at Queen's College, Cambridge; the pavilions for the Festival of Britain and the British Embassy in Rome. His best-known work is his prize design for the new Coventry Cathedral (1951).

Sullivan, Louis (1856–1924) Architect born in Boston, Massachusetts but studied in Paris. Won the New Exposition building contract (1886) with Dankmar Adler (1844–1900). Sullivan was an early pioneer of the skyscraper: e.g. the Wainwright building in St Louis (1891). His experimental, functional skeleton constructions of skyscrapers and office blocks, particularly the Stock Exchange, Chicago, earned him the title 'Father of Modernism'.

A
R
C
H
I
T
E
C
T
U
R
E

Tange, Kenzo (1913–2005)   Japanese architect who designed the National Gymnasium for the Tokyo Olympics and the city plan for the new Nigerian capital of Abuja (completed 1986).

Utzon, Jørn (1918–)   Danish architect born in Copenhagen. Came to prominence after winning a competition to design Sydney Opera House in 1956. The building, completed between 1957 and 1973, is one of the most famous landmarks of the 20th century. Other works include the Municipal Theatre in Zurich (1964) and the Kuwait Parliamentary Building (1983). His awards include the gold medal of the Royal Institute of British Architects (1978), the Alvar Aalto medal (1982), the Fritz Schumacher prize (1988) and the Pritzker Prize (2003).

Vanbrugh, (Sir) John (1664–1726)   English playwright and Baroque architect, born in London, the son of a tradesman. Educated in France and commissioned into Lord Huntingdon's regiment, he suffered imprisonment in the Bastille as a suspected spy. His major architectural work was Blenheim Palace at Woodstock, Oxfordshire, which was so disliked by the Duchess of Marlborough that she refused to pay him for some time.

Wilkins, William (1778–1839)   Son of an architect, he was educated at Cambridge and established a reputation as an enthusiastic Greek revivalist with the publication of his *Antiquities of Magna Graecia*. In London he built St George's Hospital at Hyde Park Corner (1827–8) and the National Gallery in Trafalgar Square (1832).

Wren, Christopher (1632–1723)   Wren was educated at Westminster School and Wadham College, Oxford, and became a fellow of All Souls, Oxford. He became professor of astronomy at Gresham College, London, 1657, before returning to Oxford to take up a similar position. The chapel at Pembroke College, Cambridge, 1663, was the first design of Wren's to be built and later that year he began designs for Sheldonian Theatre at Oxford. Following the Great Fire he designed over 50 London churches including St Paul's (1675–1710). Other works included the Ashmolean Museum at Oxford, Chelsea Hospital, Greenwich Observatory, parts of Hampton Court Palace, Royal Exchange, and parts of the Royal Naval College, Greenwich. Wren was a founder of the Royal Society, was knighted in 1673, and became MP for Plympton in 1685, Windsor in 1689, and finally, Weymouth in 1701.

Wright, Frank Lloyd (1867–1959)   American architect, born in Richland Center, Wisconsin. Studied civil engineering at Wisconsin University, but the collapse of a newly-built wing of the Wisconsin State Capitol caused him to apply engineering principles to architecture. After setting up in practice in Chicago he became known for low-built prairie-style bungalows like Robie House. His best-known public buildings include the Imperial Hotel in Tokyo (1916–20), the 'Falling Water' weekend retreat at Mill Run in Pennsylvania (1936), the Johnson Wax office block in Racine, Wisconsin (1936), Florida Southern College (1940) and the Guggenheim Museum of Art in New York (1959), in which the exhibits line the walls of a continuous spiral ramp.

Wyatt, James (1746–1813)   Born in Staffordshire, he closely followed the style of Robert Adam in his early days, so much so that Adam accused him of plagiarism. Wyatt won a competition to redesign the Pantheon in Oxford Street (1772) and his reputation was made. Fonthill Abbey in Wiltshire displays the extravagant Gothic Revival country house he built for William Thomas Beckford.

Architectural Terms

Abacus   The top member of a capital, usually a square or rounded slab of stone or marble

Acanthus   Conventionalised acanthus leaf used to decorate Corinthian and Composite capitals

Adobe   Sun-dried brick mainly of clay; also the name of buildings constructed of such bricks

Architrave   Lowest part of an entablature, resting immediately upon the abacus (flat slab) on the capital of a column. The term also describes the moulding around the exterior of an arch or the various parts surrounding a door or window

Art Deco   Popular design style of the 1920s and at its height in the 1930s, characterised by geometrical shapes, bold outlines and zigzag forms

Ashlar   Hewn and squared stones prepared for building

Astragal   Small convex moulding usually with a semi-circular cross-section

Atrium   Inner courtyard of a home or other building that is open to the sky or covered by a skylight

Baluster   Short post or pillar in a series that supports a rail, thus forming a balustrade

Bauhaus   German school of architecture and design founded by Walter Gropius in 1919 and closed in 1933

Bay, bow and oriel windows   These windows project out from the front or side of a house. Oriel windows generally project from an upper storey, supported by a bracket. Bay windows are angled projections that rise up from the ground on the first floor. Bow windows are rounded projections, often formed of the window glass itself

Brickwork: Types   English Bond: Bricklaying with alternate courses of headers and stretchers. Flemish Bond: Bricklaying with courses of alternate headers and stretcher. Monk Bond: Bricklaying with courses alternating with pairs of stretchers

Buildings, New   Bridgewater Hall, Manchester: International concert hall opened in September 1996. Experimental Office Building for Building Research Establishment, Garston, near Watford, Herts: latest addition to the BRE site. River and Rowing Museum, Henley, Oxfordshire: opened in 1997. St Barnabas Church, Dulwich, London: rebuilding of Victorian church destroyed by fire in 1992. Waterfront Hall, Lanyon Place, Laganside Belfast: conference centre opened 17 Jan 1997. Greater London Authority Headquarters, Southwark, London, opened by The Queen on 23 July 2002 and designed by Foster and Partners

Buttress   Structure of wood, stone or brick built against a wall to strengthen or support it

Campanile   A free-standing bell-tower

Cantilever   Horizontal projection from a building, such as a step, beam, balcony or canopy, that is without external bracing and appears self-supporting

Capital   Head of a column, usually featuring mouldings or carvings

Cartouche   Scroll-shaped ornament or corbel. Term also describes a tablet representing a scroll with rolled-up ends or edges, with or without an inscription

Caryatid   Female figure used as a pillar to support an entablature

Clerestory   Row of windows in the upper part of the wall of a church that divides the nave from the aisle, set above the aisle roof

Column   Tall, often slightly tapering, cylinder usually surmounted by an entablature and forming part of an arcade or colonnade, or standing alone as a monument

Console   Ornamental flat-sided bracket or corbel, usually incorporating a volute at each end

Corbel   Projection of stone or timber jutting out from a wall to support weight

Corinthian Column   One of the five classical orders of architecture, characterised by a bell-shaped capital having carved ornamental decorations of acanthus leaves

Cornice   Horizontal, usually moulded projection crowning the outside of a building or structure, especially the uppermost part of an entablature, above the frieze. Term also applies to an ornamental moulding running round the wall of a room near the ceiling

Cupola   Rounded vault or dome forming part of a roof of a building. Term also describes the ceiling of a dome

Curtain Wall   External non-loadbearing wall composed of repeated modular elements generally of glass in metal framing. These are prefabricated then erected on site.

Cyma   Moulding in a section of two contrasting curves, either cyma recta or cyma reversa

Dado   The plain portion of a pedestal between the base and the cornice. Term also describes the lower part of an interior wall when faced or coloured differently from the upper part

Dome: Geodesic   Invented by Richard Buckminster Fuller, the geodesic dome, built with lightweight rods arranged as linked hexagons, is the only practical kind of building that has no limiting dimensions, i.e. beyond which the structural strength must be insufficient

Doric Column   Greek-style column with only a simple decoration around the top, usually a smooth or slightly rounded band of wood, stone or plaster

Dormer Window   Window placed vertically in a sloping roof that has a tiny roof of its own. Most often seen in second-floor bedrooms

Ell   Single-storey extension to a building, usually at right angles

Engaged Column   Column that is attached to the wall so that only a half to three-quarters of its circumference stands visible

Entablature   The part of a classical temple above the columns, having an architrave, a frieze, and a cornice

Fanlight   Fan-shaped window over a door or other window

Flute   Vertical channelling in the shaft of a column

Flying Buttress   Buttress, usually on an arch, which slants upwards to a wall from a pier or other support

Frieze   Central member of the classical entablature

Gable   Triangular upper portion of a wall at the end of a pitched roof

Gargoyle   Grotesque carving, usually in the form of a human or real or fantastic animal mouth, head, or body projecting from the gutter of a building,

especially in Gothic architecture, and used as a spout to drain off rainwater

Gazebo   Building or structure that commands a view, i.e. a summer-house or balcony

Gothic   Style of architecture prevalent in western Europe from the 12th to the 16th century, of which familiar features include the pointed arch and the flying buttress

Greek Orders   The three original classical orders of architecture, i.e. Doric, Ionic and Corinthian

Groin   The edge formed by the intersection of two vaults. Term also describes an arch supporting a vault

Hammerbeam   Horizontal beam in timber roof situated as a tie beam but in two sections with main opening in the centre

Hypocaust   Hollow space under the floor where hot air was sent from a furnace to provide heating in Roman houses

Keystone   The wedge-shaped block or central voussoir at the summit of an arch built of stone

Kouros   Sculptured representation of a youth on Ionic architecture

Lancet   High, narrow window with a lancet arch

Lancet Arch   An arch with a head resembling the blade of a lancet (surgical knife)

Lintel   Horizontal stone slab or timber beam spanning an opening and supported on columns or walls

Loggia   Covered area on the side of a building that opens on one or more sides

Lunette   Semicircular panel, often ornamented in the form of stone, wood or glass

Mansard   Roof in which each face has two slopes, the lower one steeper than the upper

Mezzanine   Low storey between two others in a building, usually between the ground floor and the floor above. Term also describes the floor beneath the stage in a theatre, from which the traps are worked

Mullion   Vertical bar dividing the lights in a window, especially in Gothic architecture

Niche   Artificially constructed wall recess often holding a statue or urn

Ogee   Moulding consisting of a continuous double curve, especially with the upper part concave and the lower part convex

Ogee Arch   Arch formed by two contrasted ogees which meet at its apex, often called a pointed or Gothic arch

Ogive   The diagonal groin or rib of a vault, two of which cross each other at the vault's centre; or any pointed arch

Oriel   Porch or balcony at the head of an outdoor staircase

Oriel Window   Large polygonal recess with a window, projecting from upper storey of a building, and supported from the ground or on corbels

Palladian Window   A window with three openings, the central one arched and wider than the others

Pediment   Triangular part crowning the front of a building in the classical style, usually situated over a portico and consisting of a flat recessed field, framed by a cornice and often ornamented with sculptures

Pergola   Covered walk in a garden, usually formed by a double row of posts or pillars with joists above and covered by climbing plants

Pier   Solid support designed to sustain vertical pressure, e.g. a doorpost or gatepost; also a massive supporting column, holding up a nave or a bridge

Porte-cochere   Large covered entrance for vehicles leading into a courtyard

Portico   Formal entrance to a classical temple, church, or other building, consisting of columns at regular intervals supporting a roof often in the form of a pediment, a covered walkway

Porticus   Addition on north or south side of a church of the Anglo-Saxon period, resembling an aisle or transept and containing a chapel

Prefabrication   The manufacture of whole buildings or components cast in a factory or on site before being placed in position

Purlin   Horizontal beam along the length of a roof, resting on principals (pairs of angled supporting beams that meet at the top) and supporting the common rafters

Quoin   Dressed stones at the corners of a building

Rib   A curved member supporting a vault or defining its form. The term also describes the curved pieces of stone, timber or metal strips forming the framework of a dome or the arched or flat beam or girder supporting a bridge

Roman Orders   The two classical orders of architecture, i.e. Tuscan and Composite, which were added to the earlier Greek orders

Rotunda   Building with a circular interior and plan, especially one with a dome, e.g. the Pantheon in Rome

Rustication   Style of masonry in which the surface of the blocks is roughened. Rustication also refers to masonry cut in massive blocks separated from each other by deep joints

Soffit   Underside of any architectural element such as an arch, beam or stair

Spandrel   Originally, a space between timbers supporting a building, but now refers to the almost triangular space between one side of the outer curve of an arch and the rectangle formed by the mouldings enclosing it. The term also applies to the area of support between a set of steps and the ground

Stucco   Fine plaster usually made from gypsum and pulverised marble, for covering walls and ceilings

Stupa   Domed structure erected as a Buddhist burial mound

Styles   Regency, Baroque, Palladian, Rococo, International

Telamon   Male figure used as a pillar to support an entablature or other structure

Terrazzo   Floor or wall finish made by setting marble or other stone chips into a layer of mortar and polishing the surface

Tracery   Ornamentation in the upper part of a Gothic window, consisting of a perforated design or of an intersecting pattern, formed by the elaboration of the mullions. Tracery also refers to the interlaced work of a vault or panel

Transom   Horizontal supporting or strengthening crossbar in any structure but usually refers to a window frame

Tuscan Order   Simplest of the five classical orders of architecture, resembling the Doric, but devoid of all ornaments

Tympanum   Triangular space between the sloping and horizontal cornices of a classical pediment

Vault   Continuous arch, or a series of arches radiating from a central point or line, used to form a roof over a space inside a building

Venetian Window   Composite window with three separate openings, the central one being arched and taller than the others

Volute   Spiral scroll characteristic of Ionic capitals and also used in Corinthian and Composite capitals

Voussoir   Each of the wedge-shaped or tapered stones forming an arch or vaulting

Wainscoting   Decorative panelling applied to the lower half of an interior wall; usually wood in a plain design but may be painted

Wattle-and-Daub   Walling made from vertical timber stakes woven horizontally with branches and reeds. The whole is then surfaced with mud

Wonders of the World: Ancient   Colossus of Rhodes: bronze statue of Apollo erected c 280 BC; Hanging Gardens of Babylon: adjoining Nebuchadnezzar's palace 60 miles south of Baghdad; Pharos of Alexandria: lighthouse erected c 270 BC; Pyramids of Gizeh (Giza) near Cairo: Zoser, at Saqqara built c 2650 BC; Cheops built c 2580 BC (both still standing); Statue of Zeus: marble statue, built by Phidias c 430 BC, in the plains of Elis, Olympia; Temple of Artemis at Ephesus: Ionic temple built c 350 BC and burned by the Goths in AD 262; Tomb of Mausolus at Halicarnassus: built by the widowed Queen Artemisia c 350 BC

Wonders of the World: Modern   The seven modern wonders of the world are the Colosseum of Rome; Catacombs of Alexandria; Great Wall of China; Stonehenge; Leaning Tower of Pisa; Porcelain Tower of Nanking; Mosque of St Sophia at Constantinople

Pritzker Architecture Prize

The most prestigious award in the world of architecture is the Pritzker Architecture Prize, often referred to as 'architecture's Nobel'. Inaugurated in 1979 by the wealthy Pritzker family of Chicago through their Hyatt Foundation, and awarded each year to a living architect for lifetime achievement. The presentation ceremonies move around the world each year, paying homage to the architecture of other eras and also to works of previous winners. The bronze medallion awarded to each Laureate is based on the designs of Chicago architect Louis H Sullivan, widely acknowledged as the father of the skyscraper. On one side is the name of the prize and the winner's name and on the other the words 'firmness, commodity and delight'. These are the three conditions for good architecture referred to by Henry Wotton, England's first ambassador to Venice, in his 1624 treatise, *The Elements of Architecture*, which was a translation of Marcus Vitruvius' work, *Ten Books of Architecture*, dedicated to the Roman Emperor Augustus. The panel of judges (usually between six and ten) consists of internationally respected architects and design experts.

The complete list of Pritzker Architecture Prize winners is as follows:

1979	Philip Johnson (USA) presented at Dumbarton Oaks, Washington, DC
1980	Luis Barragán (Mexico) presented at Dumbarton Oaks, Washington, DC
1981	James Stirling (Great Britain) presented at the National Building Museum, Washington, DC
1982	Kevin Roche (USA) presented at the Art Institute, Chicago, Illinois
1983	Ieoh Ming Pei (USA) presented at the Metropolitan Museum of Art, New York
1984	Richard Meier (USA) presented at the National Gallery of Art, Washington, DC
1985	Hans Hollein (Austria) presented at the Huntington Library, Art Collections and Botanical Gardens, San Marino, California
1986	Gottfried Boehm (Germany) presented at Goldsmiths' Hall, London, England
1987	Kenzo Tange (Japan) presented at the Kimbell Art Museum, Fort Worth, Texas
1988	Gordon Bunshaft (USA) and Oscar Niemeyer (Brazil) presented at the Art Institute, Chicago, Illinois
1989	Frank Gehry (USA) presented at Todaiji Buddhist Temple, Nara, Japan
1990	Aldo Rossi (Italy) presented at Palazzo Grassi, Venice, Italy
1991	Robert Venturi (USA) presented at Palacio de Iturbide, Mexico City, Mexico
1992	Alvaro Siza (Portugal) presented at the Harold Washington Library Center, Chicago, Illinois
1993	Fumihiko Maki (Japan) presented at Prague Castle, Czech Republic
1994	Christian de Portzamparc (France) presented at The Commons, Columbus, Indiana
1995	Tadao Ando (Japan) presented at the Grand Trianon and Chateau of Versailles, France
1996	Rafael Moneo (Spain) presented at the construction site of the Getty Center, Los Angeles, California
1997	Sverre Fehn (Norway) presented at the construction site of the Guggenheim Museum, Bilbao, Spain
1998	Renzo Piano (Italy) presented at the White House, Washington, DC
1999	Lord Foster of Thames Bank (Great Britain) presented at the Altes Museum, Berlin, Germany
2000	Rem Koolhaas (Netherlands) presented at the Jerusalem Archaeological Park, Israel
2001	Jacques Herzog and Pierre de Meuron (Switzerland) presented at Thomas Jefferson's Monticello, Virginia
2002	Glenn Murcutt (Australia) presented at Michelangelo's Campidoglio, Rome, Italy
2003	Jørn Utzon (Denmark) presented at the Royal Academy of Fine Arts of San Fernando, Madrid, Spain
2004	Zaha Hadid (Great Britain) presented at the State Hermitage Museum of St Petersburg, Russia
2005	Thom Mayne (USA) presented at the Jay Pritzker Pavilion, Millennium Park, Chicago, Illinois

ARCHITECTURE

ART

Famous Artists

Abbate, Niccolo dell' (c1512–71)   Italian Mannerist landscapist.

  Selected work: *Rape of Proserpine* (Louvre, Paris).

Albers, Josef (1888–1976)   German Bauhaus painter who founded the American Bauhaus in 1933 and took US citizenship in 1939.

  Selected work: *Homage to the Square* series (Museum of Modern Art, New York).

Alma-Tadema, (Sir) Lawrence (1836–1912)   Dutch-born British painter of Classical genre paintings.

  Selected works: *The Visit* (Victoria and Albert Museum, London); *Pheidias and the Frieze of the Parthenon, Athens* (Birmingham City Gallery).

Altdorfer, Albrecht (c1480–1538)   German landscape painter and engraver, a pioneer of copperplate etching.

  Selected works: *Landscape with a Bridge* (National Gallery, London); *St George* (Alte Pinakothek, Munich).

Andrea del Sarto (1486–1530) Florentine High Renaissance painter. His original name was Andrea D'Agnolo, but his father's family (from Lanfranchi) were tailors, hence del Sarto.

  Selected works: *Madonna of the Harpies* (Uffizi, Florence); *St John the Baptist* (Pitti Palace, Florence); *A Young Man* (National Gallery, London).

Angelico, Fra (c1387–1455)   Florentine religious painter and Dominican (monastic name Giovanni da Fiesole).

  Selected works: *Annunciation* (Convent of San Marco, Florence); *St Lawrence Receiving the Treasure of the Church* (Vatican Museum, Rome).

Antonello da Messina (c1430–79)   Sicilian Renaissance landscapist and master of the oil-painting rather than tempera.

  Selected works: *St Sebastian* (Gemäldegalerie, Dresden); *Salvator Mundi* his first dated work (1465); *A Man* (both National Gallery, London).

Appel, Karel (1921–)   Dutch Abstract Expressionist who founded the CoBrA group.

  Selected work: *The Horseman* (Stedelijk Van Abbe-Museum, Eindhoven).

Avercamp, Hendrick (1585–1634)   Deaf and dumb Dutch landscapist who specialised in winter scenes.

  Selected works: *Ice Skating in a Village* (Rijksmuseum Kröller-Müller, Otterlo); *Winter Landscape with Ice Skaters* (Rijksmuseum, Amsterdam); *Winter Scene* (National Gallery, London).

Bacon, Francis (1909–92)   Dublin-born figurative painter, influenced by Surrealism and violent imagery; studied under Graham Sutherland. A good collection of his work is in the Tate Gallery, London, including *Three Studies for a Crucifixion*.

  Selected work: triptych inspired by the *Oresteia* trilogy of Aeschylus (Scottish National Gallery of Modern Art, Edinburgh).

Baldung (aka Grien), Hans (1484–1545)   German religious painter of the macabre.

  Selected works: *A Man* (National Gallery, London); *Allegorical Figure* (Alte Pinakothek, Munich).

Balla, Giacomo (1871–1958)   Italian Futurist who signed the Futurist Manifesto (1910) but by 1930 adopted a more conventional style of painting.

  Selected work: *Dynamism of a Dog on a Leash* (Museum of Modern Art, New York).

Barocci, Federico (1530–1612)   Religious painter from Urbino who developed a very personal colour scheme of vivid reds and yellows.

  Selected works: *The Circumcision* (Louvre, Paris); *Madonna of the Rosary* (Ashmolean Museum, Oxford); *Ecce Homo* (Pinacoteca di Brera, Milan).

Bassano, Jacopo (c1510/17–92)   Italian Mannerist and specialist in religious scenes. An important collection of his works and those of his followers is in the Museo Civico, Bassano del Grappa.

  Selected works: *The Holy Family* (Castle Howard, North Yorkshire); *The Adoration of the Magi* (National Gallery of Scotland, Edinburgh); *The Good Samaritan* (National Gallery, London).

Beardsley, Aubrey Vincent (1872–98)   English illustrator, born in Brighton. Became famous for his fantastic posters and illustrations for *Morte d'Arthur*, Wilde's *Salome*, *Pope's Rape of the Lock*, as well as for the *Yellow Book* magazine (1894–6) and his own *Book of Fifty Drawings*. With Wilde he is regarded as leader of the 'Decadents' of the 1890s. Died of TB at Menton, France, having embraced Catholicism.

Beckmann, Max (1884–1950)   German Expressionist figurative painter and draughtsman who emigrated to the USA in 1947.

  Selected work: *Night* (Kunstsammlung Nordrhein-Westfalen, Düsseldorf).

Bellini Family (fifteenth-century)   Jacopo (c1400–70) was founder of Venetian Renaissance art. His sons were Gentile (1429–1507), a portrait and panorama painter, and Giovanni (c1430–1516), the first Renaissance master of Venetian art, who taught both Giorgione and Titian.

  Selected works (Giovanni):   *Descent into Limbo* (City of Bristol Art Gallery); *Doge Leonardo Loredan* (National Gallery, London); *Pietà* (Brera, Milan).

Bellotto, Bernardo (1720–80)   Venetian topographical artist, nephew of Canaletto. Painted a masterly interior of King's College Chapel, Cambridge.

  Selected work: *View of Dresden* (Gemäldegalerie, Dresden).

Bernini, Gian Lorenzo (1598–1680)   Italian sculptor, architect and painter, born in Naples. Patronised by Cardinal Scipione Borghese. He designed the monumental baldacchino (choir canopy) for Saint Peter's in the Vatican. Although frequently used by Pope Urban VIII he was less popular with Innocent X, who preferred Alessandro Algardi. His most famous works include the Cornaro Chapel in the church of Santa Maria della Vittoria, the tomb of Alexander VII in Saint Peter's and the small Jesuit church of San Andrea al Quirinale, all in Rome. He was buried in Rome in the church of Santa Maria Maggiore.

Bewick, Thomas (1753–1828)   English wood engraver, born a farmer's son in Ovingham, Northumberland. His *History of British Birds* (1797–1804) was his masterpiece and the Bewick's Swan was named in his honour shortly after his death.

Blake, Peter (1932–) British Pop artist during the 1960s and now more conventional. His best-known work is the cover for The Beatles' album *Sergeant Pepper's Lonely Hearts Club Band* (1967).

Selected work: *Toy Shop* (Tate Gallery, London).

Blake, William (1757–1827) English Romantic painter, poet and visionary.

Selected works: 20 illustrations to Dante's *Divine Comedy* (Tate Gallery, London); *Heads of the Poets* (18 pictures) (Manchester City Art Gallery); *The Circle of the Lustful* (Birmingham City Art Gallery).

Bonington, Richard Parkes (1802–28) English topographical watercolourist.

Selected work: *View of Normandy* (Tate Gallery, London).

Bonnard, Pierre (1867–1947) French landscape painter who also specialised in domestic scenes. Bonnard joined the Nabis, who included Denis and Vuillard, with whom he formed the Intimiste group.

Selected work: *Women with a Dog* (Phillips Collection, Washington DC).

Bosch, Hieronymus (c1450–1516) Netherlandish painter of the macabre and master of fantasy.

Selected works: *The Ship of Fools* (Louvre, Paris); *Christ Mocked* (National Gallery, London); altarpiece *The Garden of Earthly Delights* (Prado, Madrid).

Botticelli, Sandro (1445–1510) Florentine Renaissance allegorical painter with distinctive linear style.

Selected works: *Mars and Venus* (National Gallery, London); *La Primavera*; *The Birth of Venus* (both Uffizi, Florence).

Boucher, François (1703–70) French Rococo court painter and decorator to Louis XV; also director of the famous French tapestry workshop the Gobelins.

Selected works: *Diana after her Bath* (Louvre, Paris); *Reclining Girl* (Alte Pinakothek, Munich); *Madame de Pompadour* (Wallace Collection, London).

Boudin, Eugène Louis (1824–98) French 'plein-airiste', painting in particular the fashionable French resorts of Trouville and Deauville in the 1860s. Collections of his work are in the Musée de Doctor Faure, Aix-les-Bains, and the Musée des Beaux-Arts Jules Chéret, Nice.

Selected works: *Deauville* (Tate Gallery, London); *Harbour of Trouville* (National Gallery, London); *Corvette Russe* (Luxembourg, Paris); *Beach Scene* (Leeds Castle, Kent).

Bourgeois, Louise (1911–) Born in Paris and studied under Léger before moving to New York in 1938. Regarded as one of the most important artists working today, she has explored her ideas in painting, sculpture, printmaking, installation and performance, using various media from wood and stone to latex and rubber. In 2000 she was commissioned to exhibit the first of the annual Unilever Series at the Turbine Hall of Tate Modern. The installation consists of three steel towers, entitled *I Do, I Undo* and *I Redo*. Each tower is 9m high; *I Do* and *I Redo* are encircled by spiral staircases while *I Undo* has an additional staircase in its core.

Brancusi, Constantin (1876–1957) Romanian sculptor, born in Pestisani, near Turgujiu. In his youth he was a shepherd boy in the Carpathians. Brancusi worked in Rodin's atelier and produced his *The Kiss* (1908) 22 years after Rodin's. His *Sleeping Muse* (1910) also shows Rodin's influence, but is the first of his characteristic highly polished egg-shaped carvings. The *Prodigal Son* (1925) shows the influence of African sculpture. Brancusi was a pioneer of modern abstract sculpture.

Selected works: *Adam and Eve*; *Flying Turtle* (both Guggenheim Museum, New York).

Brangwyn, Sir Frank (1867–1956) Welsh painter, initially apprenticed to the Socialist designer William Morris. He presented a collection of his work to the city of Bruges in 1936 which is now housed in the Brangwyn Museum, and there is a substantial collection in the McManus Gallery, Dundee, and Brangwyn Hall, Swansea.

Selected work: *British Empire Panels* (Swansea Guildhall).

Braque, Georges (1882–1963) French pioneer of Cubism, with Picasso, who designed scenes for two Diaghilev ballets, *Les Fâcheux* and *Zéphyr et Flore*. Braque was a Grand Officier of the Légion d'Honneur and was awarded an honorary doctorate by Oxford University in 1956. He was the first man to have his work exhibited in the Louvre during his lifetime.

Selected works: *Still Life* (Musée National d'Art Moderne, Paris); *Still Life with Playing Cards* (Rijksmuseum Kröller-Müller, Otterlo); *The Woman Musician* (Kunstmuseum, Basel); *The Candlestick* (Scottish National Gallery of Modern Art, Edinburgh).

Bronzino, Agnolo (1503–72) Florentine Mannerist and portraitist.

Selected works: *Noli Me Tangere* (Louvre, Paris); *Venus, Cupid, Folly and Time* (National Gallery, London); *Portrait of Don Garzia de Medici* (Ashmolean Museum, Oxford); *Eleanora da Toledo with Her Son*; *Christ in Limbo* (both Uffizi, Florence).

Brouwer, Adriaen (c1605–38) Flemish-born low-life painter who studied at Haarlem under Frans Hals and is regarded as 'culturally' Dutch, although eventually settling in Antwerp, where he died of the plague.

Selected works: *A Boor Asleep* (Wallace Collection, London); *Interior of an Alehouse* (Dulwich Picture Gallery, London); *Man with a Pointed Hat* (Museum Boymans-van Beuningen, Rotterdam).

Brown, Ford Madox (1821–93) French-born British painter associated with Pre-Raphaelites and William Morris in particular. He completed twelve frescoes for Manchester Town Hall, just before his death. His most famous picture, *Work,* was first exhibited at a retrospective exhibition held in London but is now hung in Manchester. Brown was the early tutor of Dante Gabriel Rossetti.

Selected work: *The Last of England* (Birmingham Museum & Art Gallery).

Brueghel, Jan (1568–1625) Flemish landscape and flower painter; son of 'Peasant' Brueghel.

Selected works: *The Tower of Babel* (Koninklijk Museum voor Schone Kunsten, Antwerp); *Still Life with Garland of Flowers* (Musées Royaux des Beaux Arts, Brussels); *Vase of Flowers* (Ashmolean Museum, Oxford).

Brueghel the Elder, Pieter (c1520–69) Flemish allegorical and religious painter, nicknamed 'Peasant' Brueghel.

Selected works: *Adoration of the Magi* (National Gallery, London); *Peasant Dance* (Kunsthistorisches Museum, Vienna).

Brueghel the Younger (c1564–1638) Flemish painter nicknamed 'Hell' because he painted scenes of diablerie; son of Pieter 'Peasant' Brueghel.

ART

Burne-Jones, Sir Edward Coley (1833–98) British painter associated with Pre-Raphaelites and the Arts and Crafts Movement.

Selected works: *Perseus* series (Southampton Art Gallery); *The Legend of the Briar Rose* series (Buscot Park, Oxfordshire); *King Cophetua and the Beggar Maid* (Tate Gallery, London).

Canaletto, Antonio (1697–1768) Venetian topographical artist who was the uncle of Bellotto. Canaletto was associated with his views of London and Venice, where the entrepreneur Joseph Smith was responsible for popularising his work.

Selected works: *View of the Grand Canal*, Venice (Uffizi, Florence); *View of the City of London from Richmond House* (Goodwood House, Sussex); *Stonemason's Yard* (National Gallery, London).

Caravaggio, Michelangelo Merisi da (c1573–1610) Italian Baroque painter who specialised in painting chiaroscuro. He fled Rome in 1606 after killing a man and spent the rest of his life as a refugee, moving between Naples, Sicily and Malta.

Selected works: *The Young Bacchus* (Uffizi, Florence); *Beheading of St John* (Cathedral of St John, Valletta, Malta); *Supper at Emmaus* (National Gallery, London).

Caro, (Sir) Anthony (1924–) English sculptor. Assistant to Henry Moore between 1951 and 1953 and specialising in clay figures. From 1953 he was influenced by the American sculptor David Smith and began to use steel as his medium. He was knighted in 1987.

Selected work: *The Tower of Discovery* (Tate Gallery, London).

Carpaccio, Vittore (c1450–1525) Venetian early Renaissance religious painter. His most characteristic work is seen in the nine subjects from the life of St Ursula, and in his masterpiece, *the Presentation in the Temple*, both now in the Accademia, Venice.

Selected works: *The Preaching of St Stephen* (Louvre, Paris); *Courtesans* (Civico Museo Correr, Venice).

Carrà, Carlo (1881–1966) Italian Futurist who founded the Metaphysical School with de Chirico in 1917.

Carracci, Annibale (1560–1609) Most important of the family of Bolognese Mannerists.

Selected works: *The Butcher's Shop* (Christchurch Picture Gallery, Oxford); *Bacchus and Silenus* (National Gallery, London); *Coronation of the Virgin* (Staatliche Museen, Berlin).

Castagno, Andrea del (c1420–57) Florentine Early Renaissance fresco painter.

Selected works: *Dante* (Convent of S. Apollonia, Florence); *The Youthful David* (National Gallery of Art, Washington DC).

Cézanne, Paul (1839–1906) French Post-Impressionist who married Hortense Fiquet (subject of many of his paintings) in 1886, the year his friendship with Émile Zola ended, due to the publication of Zola's *L'Oeuvre*, in which the central figure is unflatteringly Cézanne.

Selected works: *Self portrait* (National Gallery, London); *The Lake at Annecy* (Courtauld Institute Galleries, London); *Card Players* (Metropolitan Museum of Art, New York).

Chagall, Marc (1887–1985) Russian-born figurative painter, active in France and the USA. The Musée Marc Chagall in Nice is entirely devoted to his work.

Selected works: *The Dead Man* (Marc Chagall Collection, Saint-Paul, France); *I and the Village* (Museum of Modern Art, New York); *Self Portrait with Seven Fingers* (Stedelijk Museum, Amsterdam).

Champaigne, Philippe de (1602–74) Brussels-born, French Baroque court painter to Louis XIII who was patronised by Cardinal Richelieu. After 1647 he was associated with the Jansenists, a strict Roman Catholic sect.

Selected works: *Ex Voto of 1662*; *Cardinal Richelieu* (both Louvre, Paris).

Chardin, Jean-Baptiste Siméon (1699–1779) French still-life genre painter.

Selected works: *Grace before Meat*; *Housewife* (both Louvre, Paris); *The Young Schoolmistress* (National Gallery, London); *Still Life* (Badische Kunsthalle, Karlsruhe).

Chirico, Giorgio de (1888–1978) Italian Surrealist and co-founder of Metaphysical School with Carlo Carrà.

Selected work: *The Pink Tower* (Guggenheim Foundation, Venice).

Cimabue, Giovanni (c1240–1302) Florentine fresco painter who is accepted as the teacher of Giotto.

Selected work: *Madonna and Child* (Louvre, Paris).

Claude (le) Lorrain (1600–82) French Classical landscapist (born Claude Gellée).

Selected works: *Village Fête* (Louvre, Paris); *Aeneas at Delos* (National Gallery, London); *Ascanius Shooting the Stag of Sylvia* (Ashmolean Museum, Oxford).

Clouet the Younger, Jean (c1485–1541) French court painter to François I.

Selected work: *Guillaume Budé* (Metropolitan Museum of Art, New York).

Clouet, François (c1510–72) French court painter to Francis I, Henri II, Francis II, and Charles IX.

Selected works: *Elizabeth of Austria* (Louvre, Paris); *Mary Queen of Scots* (Scottish National Portrait Gallery, Edinburgh); *Portrait of Henri II* (Uffizi, Florence).

Constable, John (1776–1837) English landscapist, born in East Bergholt, Suffolk, the county where many of his most famous works are set.

Selected works: *Dedham Vale* (National Gallery of Scotland, Edinburgh); *The Haywain* (National Gallery, London); *Harnham Ridge from Archdeacon Fisher's House, Salisbury* (National Gallery of Ireland, Dublin).

Copley, John Singleton (1738–1815) American portraitist and history painter working in England from 1775.

Selected works: *Hugh Montgomery, 12th Earl of Eglinton* (Scottish National Portrait Gallery, Edinburgh); *The Siege of Gibraltar* (Guildhall Art Gallery, London); *The Copley Family* (National Gallery of Art, Washington DC); *Brook Watson and the Shark* (National Gallery of Art, Washington DC).

Corot, Jean-Baptiste Camille (1796–1875) French landscapist.

Selected works: *Louis Robert as a Child* (Louvre, Paris); *Avignon* (National Gallery, London).

Correggio, Antonio Allegri da (c1490–1534) Italian High Renaissance painter, active mainly in Parma.

Selected works: *Ecce Homo* (National Gallery, London); *The Agony in the Garden* (Wellington Museum, London); *St Mary Magdalen* (National Gallery, London); *Danae* (Borghese Gallery, Rome).

Cortona, Pietro Berrettini da (1596–1669) Italian

painter and architect, creator of Roman High Baroque.

Selected works: *The Rape of the Sabines* (Capitoline Gallery, Rome); *Allegory of Divine Providence and Barbarian Power* (ceiling frescoe in the Galleria Nazionale, Rome).

Cotman, John Sell (1782–1842) English landscapist, co-founder of the Norwich School.

Selected works: *The Devil's Elbow* (Castle Museum, Norwich); *Greta Bridge* (British Museum, London); *Seashore with Boats* (Tate Gallery, London).

Courbet, Gustave (1819–77) French Realist who joined the Paris Commune, was imprisoned for his part in the destruction of the Vendôme Column and died in exile in Switzerland.

Selected works: *Studio of the Painter: an Allegory of Realism* (Louvre, Paris); *Les Demoiselles de Village* (Leeds City Art Gallery); *Bonjour, Monsieur Courbet* (Musée Fabre, Montpellier); *Stream in a Ravine* (Louvre, Paris); *Young Women on the Banks of the Seine* (Musée du Petit Palais, Paris).

Craig-Martin, Michael (1941–) Dublin-born conceptual artist who influenced many of the so-called 'Young British Artists' while teaching at Goldsmiths College, London (1974–88). In 1989 a major retrospective of his work was held at the Whitechapel Art Gallery, London. He has done installations for the Projects exhibition series at the Museum of Modern Art, New York (1991) and at the Centre Pompidou in Paris (1994). He was a Trustee of the Tate Gallery, London, from 1989 to 1999.

Selected work: *An Oak Tree* (Tate Modern, London)

Cranach the Elder, Lucas (1472–1553) German court painter to the Elector of Saxony. A number of his works are in the collection at Jagdschloss Grunewald, Berlin. He had three sons, one of them Lucas the Younger (1515–86), whose works are hard to distinguish from his father's.

Selected works: *A Young Girl* (Louvre, Paris); *Adam and Eve* (Courtauld Institute Galleries, London); *A Crucifixion* (Stadtkirche, Weimar); *Martin Luther* (Bristol City Art Gallery).

Crome, John (1768–1821) English topographical artist and founding member of the Norwich Society (1803), now known as the Norwich School.

Selected works: *Yarmouth Jetty* (Castle Museum, Norwich); *The Beaters* (National Gallery of Scotland, Edinburgh); *Marlingford Grove* (Lady Lever Art Gallery, Port Sunlight).

Cuyp, Aelbert (1620–91) Dutch landscapist who was greatly influenced by Jan van Goyen. He also painted animals, seascapes and still lifes.

Selected works: *River Scene with a View of Dordrecht* (Manchester City Art Gallery); *River Scene with a View of Dordrecht* (Wallace Collection, London); *Sunset after Rain* (Fitzwilliam Museum, Cambridge); *Resting Horsemen in a Landscape* (Dordrecht Museum).

Daddi, Bernardo (c1290–1348) Florentine Early Renaissance contemporary of Giotto.

Selected work: *Virgin and Child* (Museu de Arte de São Paolo 'Assis Chateaubriand', Brazil).

Dali, Salvador (1904–89) Spanish Surrealist. Born in Figueras but lived in Paris and, from 1940, in the USA. Dali collaborated with Luis Buñuel on such Surrealist films as *Le Chien Andalou* (1928) and *L'Age d'Or* (1930). His painting *The Persistence of Memory* in New York's Museum of Modern Art was known as 'The Limp Watches'.

Selected works: *Christ of St John of the Cross* (Glasgow Art Gallery & Museum); *Inventions of the Monsters* (Art Institute of Chicago); *Galacidalacideoxyribonucleicacid* (New England Merchant Bank, Boston, Mass.).

Daubigny, Charles-François (1817–78) French landscapist of the Barbizon School who was a pupil of Paul Delaroche.

Selected work: *Evening Landscape* (Metropolitan Museum of Art, New York).

David, Gerard (c1460–1523) Netherlandish painter who became dean of the Painters' Guild of Bruges in 1501.

Selected works: *The Transfiguration* (Lieve Vrouwkerk, Bruges); *The Marriage at Cana* (Louvre, Paris); *The Tree of Jesse* (Musée des Beaux-Arts, Lyons).

David, Jacques-Louis (1748–1825) French Neo-classicist who voted in the National Convention for the death of Louis XVI and after Robespierre's death was twice imprisoned. He produced his masterpiece *The Rape of the Sabines* in 1799 and in 1804 became court painter to Napoleon, but was eventually banished as a regicide after the Bourbon restoration.

Selected works: *The Death of Marat* (Musées Royaux des Beaux Arts, Brussels); *Death of Socrates* (Metropolitan Museum of Art, New York); *Madame Récamier* (Louvre, Paris); *Napoleon Crowning Josephine* (Musée de l'Histoire de la France, Versailles).

Degas, Edgar (1834–1917) French Impressionist painter and sculptor who specialised in dancers.

Selected works: *Miss La La at the Cirque Fernando* (National Gallery, London); *The Dancing Class* (Musée du Jeu de Paume, Paris); *L'Absinthe* (Louvre, Paris).

Delacroix, Eugène (1798–1863) French Romantic painter. Delacroix's Paris studio-apartment is now a museum for his work.

Selected works: *The Death of Sardanapalus* (Louvre, Paris); *Battle of Taillebourg* (Galerie des Batailles, Versailles); Baron Schwiter (National Gallery, London); *The Massacre at Chios* (Louvre, Paris); *The Execution of Faliero* (Wallace Collection, London); *Liberty Leading the People* (Louvre, Paris).

Delaunay, Robert (1885–1941) French Cubist and exponent of Orphism, husband of the pioneer abstract painter Sonia Delaunay Terk (1885–1979).

Selected works: *La Tour Eiffel (*Kunstmuseum, Basel); *L'Equipe de Cardiff* (Scottish National Gallery of Modern Art, Edinburgh).

Delvaux, Paul (1897–1994) Belgian Neo-Impressionist, Expressionist and Surrealist.

Selected work: *Sleeping Venus* (Tate Gallery, London).

Denis, Maurice (1870–1943) French painter, founder of the 'Nabis' group.

Selected work: *Hommage à Cézanne* (Musée d'Art Moderne, Paris).

Derain, André (1880–1954) French Fauvist painter and sculptor.

Selected works: *Mountains at Collioure* (Scottish National Gallery of Modern Art, Edinburgh); *Blackfriars* (Glasgow Art Gallery & Museum).

Dix, Otto (1891–1969) German Expressionist painter, a leader of the Neue Sachlichkeit group.

Selected works: *Sylvia von Harden* (Musée

ART

National d'Art Moderne, Paris); *Nude Girl in a Fur* (Scottish National Gallery of Modern Art, Edinburgh).

Dobson, William (c1610–46)   English portrait painter who succeeded Van Dyck as painter to the exiled Charles I (1641).

Selected work: *Endymion Porter* (Tate Gallery, London).

Doesburg, Theo van (1883–1931)   Dutch artist and architect. Leader of De Stijl movement with Mondrian and devotee of a severe form of geometrical abstraction known as Neo-Plasticism. He was originally called Christian Emil Marie Kupper.

Domenichino (1581–1641)   Bolognese landscapist and portrait painter.

Selected works: *Portrait of Monsignor Agucchi* (York Art Gallery); *Sibyl* (Borghese Gallery, Rome); *Last Communion of St Jerome* (Vatican Palace, Rome); *Tobias* (National Gallery, London).

Domenico Veneziano (c1400–61)   Florentine Early Renaissance painter.

Selected work: *St Lucy Altarpiece* (Uffizi, Florence).

Dongen, Kees van (1877–1968)   Dutch painter active in Paris. Fauvist and member of Die Brücke (The Bridge).

Selected work: *Women on the Balcony* (Musée del'Annonciade, St Tropez).

Dossi, Dosso (c1479–1542)   Ferrarese fresco painter.

Selected works: *The Christ Child Learning to Walk* (Nottingham Castle); *The Sorceress Circe* (Borghese Gallery, Rome).

Dou, Gerrit (or Gerard) (1613–75)   Dutch painter and former collaborator with Rembrandt. Started the 'Fijnschilder' (fine painter) School in Leiden.

Selected works: *A Woman at a Window* (Fitzwilliam Museum, Cambridge); *Rembrandt's Mother*, *Self Portrait* (both Rijksmuseum, Amsterdam); *A Poulterer's Shop* (National Gallery, London); *The Astronomer* (Stedtlijk Museum 'De Lakenhal', Leiden).

Duccio di Buoninsegna (c1260–c1318)   Sienese painter.

Selected works: *Maestà* (Cathedral Museum, Siena); *Rucellai Madonna* (Uffizi, Florence); *Christ Healing the Blind Man*; *The Annunciation* (both National Gallery, London).

Duchamp, Marcel (1887–1968)   French-born American painter and sculptor, brother of Jacques Villon. Inventor of the 'Ready-Made' and leader of the New York Dadaists.

Selected work: *The Bride Stripped Bare by her Bachelors, Even*, also known as *The Large Glass* (1923) (Philadelphia Museum of Art).

Dufy, Raoul (1877–1953)   French artist and designer, born in Le Havre. Dufy played a big part in popularising Fauvism. In 1911 he illustrated Guillaume Apollinaire's *Bestiary*.

Selected work: *Château and Horses* (Philips Collection, Washington DC).

Dürer, Albrecht (1471–1528)   German painter and graphic artist, born in Nuremberg, the son of a Hungarian goldsmith. Dürer is often considered the inventor of etching and was a supreme master of the woodcut.

Selected works: *Self Portrait in a Fur-collared Robe* (Alte Pinakothek, Munich); *A Young Man* (Hampton Court Palace, London); *Adoration of the Magi* (Uffizi, Florence).

Dyck, (Sir) Anthony van (1599–1641)   Anglo-Flemish court painter to Charles I of England and pupil of Rubens.

Selected works: *Triple Portrait of Charles I* (Windsor Castle); *Portrait of the Earl of Strafford* (Petworth House, Sussex); *The Lornellini Family* (National Gallery of Scotland, Edinburgh).

Eakins, Thomas (1844–1916)   American painter and photographer, born in Philadelphia. His composite plates inspired Duchamp's *Nude Descending a Staircase*.

Selected works: *Max Schmitt in a Single Scull*; *Chess Players* (both Metropolitan Museum of Art, New York).

Eliasson, Olafur (1967–)   Born in Copenhagen, Denmark and attended the Royal Academy of Arts in Copenhagen from 1989 to 1995. He specialises in large installation works and *The Weather Project* is the fourth in the annual Unilever Series of commissions for the Turbine Hall at Tate Modern. Currently based in Berlin.

Elsheimer, Adam (1578–1610)   German painter on copper, of night scenes and landscapes.

Selected works: *St Paul on Malta* (National Gallery, London); *Judith and Holofernes* (Wellington Museum, London); *Tobias and the Angel* (Historisches Museum, Frankfurt am Main).

Emin, Tracey (1963–)   British modern artist, who may be best described as Controversialist. Typical work includes *The Hut* and *My Bed*. Her best-selling autobiography was entitled *Exploration of the Soul*.

Selected work: *Every Part of Me's Bleeding* (Lehman Maupin Gallery, New York).

Ensor, James (1860–1949)   Belgian painter of the macabre and precursor of Surrealism.

Selected work: *Entry of Christ into Brussels* (Casino Communal, Belgium).

Epstein, (Sir) Jacob (1880–1959)   American-born British sculptor, born a Russian-Polish Jew in New York. His early commissions included 18 nude figures for the façade of the British Medical Association building in the Strand (1907–8) and *Night and Day* (1929) for the London Transport Building in Westminster. These and later symbolic sculptures, such as the marble *Genesis* (1930), the *Ecce Homo* (1934) and the alabaster *Adam* (1939), resulted in accusations of indecency and blasphemy. His last two large commissioned works were *Christ in Majesty* (Llandaff Cathedral) and *St Michael and the Devil* (Coventry Cathedral).

Ernst, Max (1891–1976)   German painter and sculptor who was a founder of the Surrealist movement. He invented the technique of frottage (pencil rubbings on canvas).

Selected works: *The Elephant Celebes* (Tate Gallery, London); *Le Grand Amoureux* (Scottish National Gallery of Modern Art, Edinburgh).

Etty, William (1787–1849)   English portrait painter who specialised in nudes.

Selected works: *Monk Bar, York* (York City Art Gallery); *The Combat* (National Gallery of Scotland, Edinburgh); *Somnolency* (Aberdeen Art Gallery); *The Fairy of the Fountain* (Tate Gallery, London).

Eyck, Jan van (c1389–1441)   Netherlands painter, probably born near Maastricht; successively in the service of John of Bavaria, the Count of Holland and Philip the Good of Burgundy.

Selected works: *The Arnolfini Wedding* (National Gallery, London); *Adoration of the Lamb* (Church of St Bavo, Ghent); *The Madonna with Chancellor*

Rolin (Louvre, Paris); *Man in a Red Turban* (National Gallery, London).

Fabritius, Carel (1622–54)   Dutch painter of still lifes and street-scenes. Worked under Rembrandt around 1641 and lived mainly at Delft, where he was killed in the explosion of the municipal ammunition depot.

Selected works: *View of Delft* (National Gallery, London); *An Old Man* (Walker Art Gallery, Liverpool); *The Goldfinch* (Mauritshuis, The Hague); *Self-portrait* (Museum Boymans-van Beuningen, Rotterdam).

Fantin-Latour, Henri (1836–1904)   French genre, still-life and Symbolist painter, born in Grenoble.

Selected works: *Flowers and Fruit* (Louvre, Paris); *Homage to Delacroix* (Musé du Jeu de Paume, Paris).

Feininger, Lyonel (1871–1956)   American artist and cartoonist, born in New York of German immigrant parents. Taught at the Bauhaus at Weimar and Dessau, but when the Nazis came to power he returned to the USA and, with Gropius and Mies van der Rohe, founded the Chicago Bauhaus.

Selected works: *Sailing Boats* (Collection Tannahill, Detroit); *Gelmeroda III* (Scottish National Gallery of Modern Art, Edinburgh).

Fouquet, Jean (c1420–81)   French court painter to Louis I. Pope Eugenius IV commissioned a portrait from him, now lost.

Selected works: *Etienne Chevalier with St Stephen* (Staatliche Museen, Berlin); *Madonna and Child* (Musée des Beaux Arts, Antwerp); *Charles VII* (Louvre, Paris).

Fragonard, Jean-Honoré (1732–1806)   French Rococo painter.

Selected works: *The Swing* (Wallace Collection, London); *Bathers* (Louvre, Paris).

Frankenthaler, Helen (1928–)   American Abstract Expressionist painter, who devised a technique for staining unprimed canvases with washes of colour.

Selected work: *Blue Territory* (Whitney Museum, New York City).

Freud, Lucian (1922–)   German-born, English figurative painter. In his early years he was one of the Neo-Romantic group along with Minton, Craxton, Sutherland and Piper; but from the 1950s he developed a realist style. One of the most respected artists since World War II. Freud's work does not lend itself to be pigeon-holed in any particular style and includes portraits ranging from *Francis Bacon* in the Tate (stolen in 1988 whilst on exhibition in Germany) to the painting of a man in a raincoat with a yucca – *Interior in Paddington* (Walker Art Gallery, Liverpool). Sigmund Freud was the artist's grandfather. In 1948 he married Kitty Garman, the daughter of Jacob Epstein, and after the marriage was annulled in 1952 he married Lady Caroline Maureen Blackwood (marriage dissolved in 1957; she died in 1996).

Friedrich, Caspar David (1774–1840)   German Romantic painter of nature, and particularly forest scenes. His works are included in the German Romantic collection in the Schinkel Pavilion at Schloss Charlottenburg and in the Neue National Galerie, both in Berlin.

Selected works: *Man and Woman Gazing at the Moon* (Staatliche Museen, Berlin); *Wreck of the Hope* (Kunsthalle, Hamburg).

(Dame) Elizabeth Frink (1930–1993)   English sculptress. The horror of war ran through her entire oeuvre and is best depicted in *Gogglehead*.

Selected works: *Arrival at Canterbury* (Royal Museum and Art Gallery, Canterbury).

Frith, William Powell (1819–1909)   English genre painter who became the wealthiest painter of his time by selling both paintings and their copyright.

Selected works: *The Derby Day* (Tate Gallery, London); *The Railway Station* (Royal Holloway College, Egham, Surrey).

Fuseli, Henry (1741–1825)   Swiss Romantic fantasy painter who took British citizenship and became professor of painting at the Royal Academy, and Keeper in 1804.

Selected works: *Lady Macbeth Sleepwalking* (Louvre, Paris); *Titania and Bottom* (Tate Gallery, London); *The Three Witches from Macbeth* (Kunsthaus, Zurich); *The Nightmare* (Detroit Institute of Art).

Gaddi, Taddeo (c1300–66)   Florentine painter and mosaicist who was Giotto's best pupil and also his godson.

Selected work: *Life of the Virgin* (Baroncelli Chapel, Church of S. Croce, Florence).

Gainsborough, Thomas (1727–88)   English portrait and landscape painter, born in Sudbury, Suffolk. Married Margaret Burr, the illegitimate daughter of the 4th Duke of Beaufort.

Selected works: *Harvest Wagon* (Barber Institute, University of Birmingham); *Self Portrait* (National Portrait Gallery, London); *Portrait of Mary, Countess Howe* (Iveagh Bequest, Kenwood House, London); *The Watering Place* (Tate Gallery, London); *Mrs Graham* (National Gallery of Scotland, Edinburgh); *George III and Queen Charlotte* (Windsor Castle).

Gaudier-Brzeska, Henri (1891–1915)   French Cubist sculptor born in St Jean de Braye. Henri Gaudier came to England in 1911 with his childhood sweetheart Sophie Brzeska and founded the London Group of Sculpture. In 1914 he signed the Vorticist Manifesto. He joined the French army at the outbreak of WWI and was killed in action.

Selected work: *Armour* (Tate Gallery, London).

Gauguin, Paul (1848–1903)   French Post-Impressionist who gave up a stockbroking career to devote himself to painting. He evolved a style known as 'Synthetism' in a reaction against Impressionism. Lived in Tahiti 1891–1901 and then the Marquesas Islands. Fell out with his friend Van Gogh at Arles in 1888.

Selected works: *The Vision after the Sermon* (National Gallery of Scotland, Edinburgh); *Tahitian Women* (Metropolitan Museum of Art, New York); *La Seine au Pont d'Iéna* (Louvre, Paris).

Gentile da Fabriano (c1370–1427)   Italian International Gothic painter (properly, Niccolo di Giovanni di Massio).

Selected work: *Adoration of the Magi* (Uffizi, Florence).

Gentileschi, Artemisia (c1597–c1651)   Italian painter, daughter of the Bolognese painter Orazio Gentileschi.

Selected works: *Self-portrait as Pittura* (Kensington Palace, London); *Susannah and the Elders* (Schloss Eisenstein, Pommersfelden).

Géricault, Théodore (1791–1824)   French Romantic history painter. He died following a fall from his horse. His tomb in Père Lachaise cemetery, Paris, has a brass relief of *The Raft of the Medusa*.

Selected works: *The Raft of the Medusa*; *The Wounded Cuirassier* (both Louvre, Paris); *Mad*

A
R
T

Woman with a Mania of Envy (Musée des Beaux Arts, Lyons).

Gheeraerts, Marcus, the Younger (c1561–1636) Flemish portraitist. Court painter to Elizabeth I and James I of England (VI of Scotland). Portrait of Arabella Stuart in the Scottish National Portrait Gallery is possibly by Gheeraerts.

Selected works: *The Ditchley Portrait of Elizabeth I* (National Portrait Gallery, London); *Sir Thomas Lee* (Tate Gallery, London); *William Camden* (Bodleian Library, Oxford).

Ghirlandaio, Domenico (1449–94) Florentine Renaissance fresco painter (properly, Domenico di Tommaso Bigordi).

Selected works: *Life of the Virgin* (Strozzi Chapel, S. Maria Novella, Florence); *Visitation of the Virgin* (Louvre, Paris); *Old Man and His Grandson* (Louvre, Paris).

Gilbert, (Sir) Alfred (1854–1934) English sculptor and goldsmith who was a leader of the New Sculpture movement. The Clarence Memorial in Windsor is considered the climax of his work. Other works include the Alexandra Memorial in Marlborough Road, London, and the *Queen Victoria* statue in Winchester.

Selected works: *Eros* (Piccadilly Circus, London); *Perseus Arming* (Victoria and Albert Museum, London); *Joule* (Manchester Town Hall).

Gill, Eric (1882–1940) English sculptor, engraver, writer and typographer, born in Brighton, the son of a clergyman. In 1909 he carved his first stone figure *The Madonna and Child*. Through the influence of Augustus John he exhibited at the Chenil Galleries, Chelsea (1911). He maintained a steady output for the rest of his life, during which he designed the classic typeface Gill. Joined the Fabian movement and eventually became Catholic.

Selected works: *Mankind* (Tate Gallery, London); *Stations of the Cross* (Westminster Cathedral, London); *Prospero and Ariel* (BBC Broadcasting House, London).

Gillray, James (1756–1815) English political and social caricaturist and printmaker, born in Chelsea, the son of a Lanark trooper. Gillray had a life-long partnership with the publisher Mrs Humphrey. From 1810 until his death he was hopelessly insane.

Giordano, Luca (1634–1705) Neapolitan decorative painter, precursor of Rococo and court painter to Charles II of Spain. Renowned for his speed of working, hence his nickname 'Luca Fa Presto' (Luke Go Quickly).

Selected work: *Apotheosis of the Medici* (ballroom ceiling, Palazzo Medici-Riccardi, Florence).

Giorgione (c1478–1510) Venetian Renaissance painter (properly, Giorgio Barbarelli).

Selected works: *The Adulteress before Christ* (Glasgow Art Gallery & Museum); *The Adoration of the Magi* (National Gallery, London); *The Tempest* (Galleria dell'Accademia, Venice).

Giotto di Bondone (c1266–1337) Florentine painter who introduced sculptural solidity into painting and heralded the Renaissance. He was a pupil of Cimabue, but because of confusion as to his early life it is not known for sure if the St Francis of Assisi frescoes were attributable to him. Often called the 'Father of Modern Painting'. Both he and Cimabue are mentioned by Dante. Legend says he drew a perfect circle freehand for the Pope.

Selected works: the Arena Chapel murals (S. Maria Annunziata dell'Arena, Padua); *Ognissanti Madonna* (Uffizi, Florence).

Giulio Romano (1492–1546) Roman Mannerist painter and architect. An indication of his fame is a mention in Shakespeare's *Winter's Tale*.

Selected works: *Isabella d'Este* (Hampton Court Palace, London); *Allegory of Immortality* (Alnwick Castle, Northumberland); fresco decorations at the Palazzo del Te, Mantua.

Goes, Hugo van der (c1440–82) Flemish master painter, mostly of religious subjects.

Selected works: *Adoration of the Shepherds* (Uffizi, Florence); *Death of the Virgin* (Musée Communal, Bruges); *Adoration of the Magi* (Museum Dahlem, Berlin).

Gogh, Vincent van (1853–90) Dutch Post-Impressionist. The Rijksmuseum Vincent van Gogh in Amsterdam houses over 700 of his paintings and drawings.

Selected works: *Cornfield and Cypress Trees* (National Gallery, London); *Self Portrait* (Saint-Rémy, 1889: Louvre, Paris); *The Potato Eaters* (Rijksmuseum Vincent van Gogh, Amsterdam); *Sunflowers* (Tate Gallery, London).

Gore, Spencer Frederick (1878–1914) English painter, born in Epsom, Surrey. Gore was a founder member and first president of the Camden Town Group (1911).

Selected work: *From a Window in Cambrian Road, Richmond* (Tate Gallery, London).

Gorky, Arshile (1904–48) Armenian-born US painter influenced by Cubism, Surrealism and Abstract Expressionism. Original name: Vosdanig Manoog Adoian.

Selected work: *The Liver Is the Cock's Comb* (Albright-Knox Art Gallery, Buffalo, NY State).

Gormley, Antony (1950–) At the forefront of a generation of British artists who emerged during the 1980s. He has exhibited work around the world and has major public works in Australia, Ireland, Japan, Norway and the USA. Public work in Britain can be seen in locations as diverse as the crypt at Winchester Cathedral and Birmingham city centre. In 1994 he won the Turner Prize and in 1997 was awarded the OBE for services to sculpture. His best-known work is *The Angel of the North* in Gateshead, a 20m high steel structure with a 54m wingspan. In May 2003 his latest sculpture was unveiled at the Baltic Arts Centre in Gateshead. *Domain Field* is a room full of life-size depictions of the human form made out of stainless steel rods.

Goya y Lucientes, Francisco (1746–1828) Spanish Romantic artist who was court painter to Charles IV of Spain. His series of etchings, *The Disasters of War*, describe the horrors of the Penninsular war in Spain.

Selected works: *Family of Charles IV*; *The Naked Maja* (both Prado, Madrid); *The Duke of Wellington* (National Gallery, London).

Goyen, Jan van (1596–1656) Dutch realistic landscapist.

Selected works: *Cottages and Fishermen by a River* (Glasgow City Art Gallery); *Leiden from the North-East* (Stedelijk Museum 'De Lakenhal', Leiden); *View of Dordrecht from Papendrecht* (Mauritshuis, The Hague).

Gozzoli, Benozzo (c1421–97) Florentine fresco painter, a pupil of Fra Angelico.

Selected works: frescoes (Medici Palace, Florence); *Journey of the Magi* (chapel of the Palazzo Medici-Riccardi, Florence).

Greco, El (1541–1614) Cretan-born Spanish Mannerist (properly, Domenico Theotocopoulos).

Selected works: *The Saviour* (National Gallery of Scotland, Edinburgh); *The Tears of St Peter* (Bowes Museum, Barnard Castle, Durham); *The Disrobing of Christ* (Toledo Cathedral).

Greuze, Jean-Baptiste (1725–1805) French genre and portrait painter.

Selected works: *The Broken Pitcher* (Louvre, Paris); *Girl with Doves* (Wallace Collection, London).

Gris, Juan (1887–1927) Spanish Cubist (properly, José Victoriano González).

Selected works: *Still Life with Dice* (Musée National d'Art Moderne, Paris); *The Glass* (Glasgow Art Gallery & Museum).

Grosz, George (1893–1959) German-born American Expressionist and Dadaist whose depictions of the depravity of war were so graphic that the Nazis called him 'Cultural Bolshevist Number One'. Although starting as a Dadaist, he was a co-founder of the Neue Sachlichkeit movement.

Selected works: *Kristallnacht* (Leicester Museum & Art Gallery, Leicester); *To Oskar Panizza* (Staatsgalerie, Stuttgart).

Grünewald, Matthias (c1470/80–1528) German visionary artist (properly, Mathis Gothardt – although he occasionally added his wife's surname Neithardt to his own). Grünewald is the 'Mathis der Maler' of Hindemith's opera of that name.

Selected works: *The Isenheim Altarpiece* (Musée d'Unterlinden, Colmar, France); *The Mocking of Christ* (Alte Pinakothek, Munich); *The Miracle of the Snow* (Aschaffenburg Altarpiece, Augustinermuseum, Freiburg-in-Breisgau).

Guardi, Francesco (1712–93) Italian topographical artist, born in Pinzolo. Pupil of Canaletto, and like his master famous for his views of Venice.

Selected works: *Ascent in a Balloon* (Staatliche Museen, Berlin); *The Doge Embarking on the Bucintoro* (Louvre, Paris); *The Doge's Palace* (National Gallery, London).

Guercino (1591–1666) Bolognese early Baroque painter (properly, Gian-Francesco Barbieri).

Selected works: *The Incredulity of St Thomas* (National Gallery, London); *Susanna Bathing* (Prado, Madrid).

Hals, Frans (c1580–1666) Dutch genre and portrait painter, born in Antwerp.

Selected works: *The Laughing Cavalier* (Wallace Collection, London); *Married Couple in a Garden* (Rijksmuseum, Amsterdam); *Aletta Hannemans* (Mauritshuis, The Hague); *The Merry Toper* (Rijksmuseum, Amsterdam).

Hamilton, Richard (1922–) English artist who became a pioneer of Pop Art after attending the *This is Tomorrow* exhibition in Whitechapel Art Gallery, London, in 1956. He reconstructed Duchamp's *Bride Stripped Bare by her Bachelors, Even*, by consulting the original notes and studies by the artist (Tate Gallery, London).

Selected work: *Just What Is It That Makes Today's Homes So Different, So Appealing* (Private Collection, California).

Hepworth, (Dame) Jocelyn Barbara (1903–75) English sculptor, born in Wakefield, West Yorkshire. Her first marriage was to fellow sculptor John Skeaping and her second to painter Ben Nicholson. Hepworth was noted for the strength and formal discipline of her carving, e.g. *Contrapuntal Forms*, exhibited at the Festival of Britain, 1951. Such pieces as *Wave* (1944) and *Mr & Mrs Ashley* (Havinden Collection, England) became increasingly open, hollowed out and variously perforated, so that the interior space became as important as the mass surrounding it.

Selected works: *Pelagos* (Tate Gallery); *Pendour* (Hirshhorn Museum, Washington DC).

Hilliard, Nich (1537–1619) English miniature-painter at the courts of Elizabeth I and James I of England.

Selected works: *Young Man among Roses* (Vicoria and Albert Museum, London); *Elizabeth I Playing a Lute* (Berkeley Castle, Gloucester); *Self-portrait Aged 31* (Drumlanrig Castle, Dumfriesshire).

Hirst, Damien (1965–) Avant-garde artist, born in Bristol. Following a disappointing 'D' in his A-Level art exam went on to train at Goldsmiths College, London. Became known for his works which made use of parts or all of dead animals preserved in formaldehyde, such as *I Want You Because I Can't Have You* (1992), a series of fish behind a perspex casing enclosed within a steel, melamine and wood exterior, and *Mother and Child Divided* (1993) – four tanks containing the severed halves of a cow and calf. His 1994 exhibition contained a dead lamb *Away from the Flock*, suspended within a tank. In 1995 he was awarded the Turner Prize and in 1996 his New York exhibition 'No Sense of Absolute Corruption' (Gagosian Gallery), contained several large paintings, as well as earlier works including an 8.3ins porcelain ashtray full of cigarette butts entitled *Home Sweet Home*.

Hobbema, Meindert (1638–1709) Dutch landscapist and pupil of Jacob von Ruysdael.

Selected works: *The Avenue at Middleharnis* (National Gallery, London); *A Watermill* (Rijksmuseum, Amsterdam); *A Peasant Cottage on a Water* Course (Historisches Museum, Amsterdam).

Hockney, David (1937–) Versatile Bradford-born artist often considered a pop artist, although not delighting in this tag himself. Californian swimming pools were prolifically painted in his early career, notably *A Bigger Splash* (1967). In the Seventies his style became more traditional with a series of portraits of couples such as *Mr and Mrs Clark and Percy* (1970, Percy being a white cat) and *My Parents* (1977), both displayed in Tate Britain, London. Hockney is also a celebrated graphic artist, photographer and stage designer of operatic productions.

Selected works: *Le Plongeur* (1978, Cartwright Hall Art Gallery, Bradford); *Rocky Mountains and Tired Indians* (1965, Scottish National Gallery of Modern Art, Edinburgh).

Hogarth, William (1697–1764) English painter and satirist, born in Smithfield, the son of a teacher. Studied under Sir James Thornhill and married Thornhill's daughter in 1729.

Selected works: *Lord George Graham in His Cabin* (National Maritime Museum, London); *The Rake's Progress* series (Sir John Soane's Museum, London); *Self-portrait with His Pug* (Tate Gallery, London).

Hokusai, Katsushika (1760–1849) Japanese engraver and watercolourist whose work became extremely popular in England after the Anglo-Japanese trade agreements of the 1880s. His work influenced Whistler.

Selected work: *Thirty-six Views of Mount Fuji* series (Art Institute of Chicago).

ART

Holbein the Younger, Hans (c1497–1543) German realist portraitist who was court painter to Henry VIII. His father, Hans Holbein the Elder (c1460–1524), was also a painter of note.

Selected works: *The Ambassadors* (National Gallery, London); *Sir Thomas Moore* (Frick Collection, New York); *Jane Seymour* (Mauritshuis, The Hague).

Homer, Winslow (1836–1910) American painter, born in Boston. Began as an illustrator for magazines such as *Harper's Weekly* and *Ballou's Pictorial*. Worked for many years at his Prouts Neck studio in Maine, where the local sea area became a favourite subject for depiction.

Selected works: *Fog Warning* (Museum of Fine Arts, Boston, Mass.); *Pitching Quoits* (Fogg Art Museum, Cambridge, Mass.).

Honthorst, Gerrit van (1590–1656) Dutch genre and night-scene painter who was the court painter to the Stadholder of Holland and Charles I of England.

Selected works: *Winter Queen* (Elizabeth of Bohemia) (National Portrait Gallery, London); *Willem II, Prince of Orange* (Mauritshuis, The Hague); *The Death of Seneca* (Centraal Museum, Utrecht).

Hooch (or Hoogh), Pieter de (1629–84) Dutch genre painter.

Selected works: *A Musical Party* (Wellington Museum, Apsley House, London); *Interior with a Woman Delousing a Child's Hair* (Rijksmuseum, Amsterdam); *A Courtyard in Delft* (Mauritshuis, The Hague).

Hopper, Edward (1882–1967) American realist painter, mostly of urban scenes, born in New York.

Selected works: *Early Sunday Morning* (Whitney Museum of American Art, New York); *Room in Brooklyn* (Museum of Fine Arts, Boston, Mass.).

Hunt, William Holman (1827–1910) English painter and founder member of the Pre-Raphaelite Brotherhood.

Selected works: *The Scapegoat* (Lady Lever Gallery, Port Sunlight); *Claudio and Isabella* (Tate Gallery, London); *The Light of the World* (Keble College, Oxford).

Hunt, William Morris (1824–79) American Romantic painter who created a fashion in the USA for the luminous, atmospheric painting of the Barbizon School.

Selected work: *Girl at a Fountain* (Metropolitan Museum of Art, New York).

Huysum, Jan van (1682–1749) Dutch still-life painter.

Selected work: *Fruit, Flowers and Insects* (Alte Pinakothek, Munich).

Ingres, Jean Auguste Dominique (1780–1867) French Classical painter of portraits and history pictures. Ingres bequeathed much of his work to his home town of Montauban, and the collection is now housed in the town's Musée Ingres. His motto was 'A thing well drawn is well enough painted'. Ingres was awarded the Légion d'Honneur and made a senator in 1862.

Selected works: *Madame Moitessier* (National Gallery, London); *The Turkish Bath* (Louvre, Paris).

Inness, George (1825–94) American landscapist, later influenced by the Barbizon School.

Selected works: *The Delaware Valley* (Metropolitan Museum of Art, New York); *Rainbow after a Storm* (Chicago Art Institute).

Jawlensky, Alexej von (1864–1941) Russian Expressionist working in Munich from 1896 and France from 1905. In 1924 he co-founded Der Blaue Vier (Blue Four group) with Kandinsky, Klee and Feininger.

Selected work: *Head of a Woman* (Scottish National Gallery of Modern Art, Edinburgh).

John, Augustus Edwin (1878–1961) Welsh painter, born in Tenby. Graduated from the Slade School of Art, London, with his elder sister, Gwen John. His favourite themes were gypsies, fishing folk and wild, lovely, yet regal women.

Selected works: *Smiling Woman* (Tate Gallery, London); *Richard Hughes* (Tenby Museum & Picture Gallery).

John, Gwen (1876–1939) Welsh painter and elder sister of Augustus John. Worked as an artist's model and became Rodin's mistress.

Selected works: *Self-portrait* (Tate Gallery, London); *A Corner of the Artist's Room* (Cannon Hall, Barnsley).

Johns, Jasper (1930–) American Neo-Dadaist painter and sculptor, a strong influence on Pop Art, whose sculptures are of everyday items. Throughout his career he has specialised in numerous drawings and prints of flags in various media. His 1987 etching with aquatint, *The Seasons (Summer)* is highly acclaimed.

Selected work: *Zero Through Nine* (Tate Gallery, London).

Jordaens, Jacob (1593–1678) Flemish low-life and religious painter. Pupil of Rubens.

Selected works: *Commerce and Industry Protecting the Fine Arts* (Koninklijk Museum voor Schone Kunsten, Antwerp); *Presentation in the Temple* (Rubenshuis, Antwerp); *The Fruit Seller* (Glasgow City Art Gallery).

Jorn, Asger Oluf (1914–73) Danish Expressionist (properly, Asger Jorgensen). Founded the CoBrA group, which was named after COpenhagen, BRussels, Amsterdam.

Selected work: *The Lost World* (Stedelijk Van Abbe-Museum, Eindhoven).

Kandinsky, Wassily (1866–1944) Russian pioneer of abstract art who was influenced by the Fauves, Bauhaus, and Surrealists. He founded Der Blaue Reiter group with Franz Marc.

Selected works: *First Abstract Watercolour* (Nina Kandinsky Collection, Neuilly-sur-Seine); *First Abstract Watercolour* (Musée National d'Art Moderne, Paris); *Blue Mountain* (Solomon R. Guggenheim Museum, New York).

Kapoor, Anish (1954–) Born in Bombay but lives and works in London. Renowned for his enigmatic sculptural forms that permeate physical and psychological space. His versatility and inventiveness have resulted in works ranging from powdered pigment sculptures and site-specific interventions on wall or floor, to gigantic installations both in and outdoors. Throughout, he has explored what he sees as deep-rooted metaphysical polarities: presence and absence, being and non-being, place and non-place and the solid and the intangible.

Best-known work to date is *Marsyas*, the third in the Unilever series of commissions for the Turbine Hall at the Tate Modern. He was awarded the CBE in 2003.

Kauffmann, Angelica (1741–1807) Swiss Neo-classical painter in England who co-founded the Royal Academy (1768). She married the Venetian painter Antonio Zucchi.

Selected works: *Self Portraits* (National Portrait Gallery & Tate Gallery, London); *Rinaldo and Armida* (Kenwood House, London); *Euphrosyne Complains to Venus of the Wounds of Cupid* (Attingham Park, Shropshire).

Kirchner, Ernst Ludwig (1880–1938) German Expressionist, influenced by Neo-Impressionism, Fauvism and Primitive art.

Selected works: Die Brücke painters – portraits of Otto Muller, Erich Heckel, Schmidt-Rotluff and Kirchner (Wallraf-Richartz Museum / Museum Ludwig, Cologne); *Japanisches Theater* (Scottish National Gallery of Modern Art, Edinburgh).

Kitaj, Ron B. (1932–) American Pop artist, introducing cultural and political elements. Active in the UK.

Selected work: *If Not . . . Not* (Scottish National Gallery of Modern Art, Edinburgh).

Klee, Paul (1879–1940) Swiss painter and etcher. Blaue Reiter member and teacher at the Bauhaus. Described his work as 'taking a line for a walk'. A large collection of his work from 1906 to 1938 is housed in the Kunstsammlung Nordrhein-Westfalen at Düsseldorf.

Selected works: *Death and Fire* (Kunstmuseum, Berne); *Around the Fish* (Museum of Modern Art, New York), *Ad Marginem* (Kunstmuseum, Basel).

Klein, Yves (1928–62) French revolutionary Minimalist, painting only in blue. Klein was a celebrated exponent of judo and lived in Japan in 1952–3.

Selected work: *ANT 143 The Handsome Teuton* (London Arts Gallery).

Klimt, Gustav (1862–1918) Austrian Art Nouveau painter, founder member of the Vienna Secession, 1898, artists who resigned as a group from conventional academic bodies.

Selected works: *Salome* (Galleria d'Arte Moderna, Ca' Pesaro, Venice); *The Kiss* (Österreichische Galerie, Vienna).

Kneller, (Sir) Godfrey (1646–1723) German portrait painter in England, court painter to William III and George I. Famous for painting 42 portraits of the members of the literary association called the Kit-Kat Club, now in the National Portrait Gallery, London. These pictures were painted between 1700 and 1720 and are of a size (36" x 28") now known as 'Kit-Kat' size.

Selected works: *Isaac Newton* (National Gallery, London); *James, Duke of Monmouth* (Goodwood House, Sussex).

Knight, (Dame) Laura (1877–1970) British artist best known for her beautifully tranquil beach and seaside paintings, paintings of the circus and of ballet. She was elected a Royal Academician in 1936. Dame Laura was an official war artist who was sent to make portraits at the Nuremberg Trials.

Kokoschka, Oskar (1886–1980) Austrian Expressionist working in England and Switzerland.

Selected works: *Still Life with Tortoise and Hyacinth* (Österreichische Galerie, Vienna); *The Tempest* (Kunstmuseum, Basel).

Koninck, Philips de (1619–88) Dutch panoramic landscapist.

Selected work: *Landscape* (Hunterian Art Gallery, Glasgow).

Kooning, Willem de (1904–97) Dutch-born American Abstract Expressionist.

Selected work: *Woman I* (Museum of Modern Art, New York).

La Tour, Georges de (1593–1652) French painter of candle-lit scenes, active entirely in Lorraine.

Selected works: *St Joseph the Carpenter* (Louvre, Paris); *The Dice Players* (Middlesbrough Art Gallery); *St Jerome* (Musée de Grenoble).

La Tour, Maurice Quentin de (1704–88) French pastellist and portrait painter whose works are celebrated in the Musée Antoine Lecuyer in Saint-Quentin, France.

Selected works: *Mr and Mrs Angerstein*; *Madame de Pompadour* (both Louvre, Paris).

Lancret, Nicholas (1690–1743) French Rococo genre and *fêtes galantes* painter in the style of Watteau.

Selected work: *Mademoiselle Camargo Dancing* (Wallace Collection, London).

Landseer, (Sir) Edwin Henry (1802–73) English animal painter and engraver – a favourite of Queen Victoria. Landseer is famous for his *Monarch of the Glen* and for sculpting the lions at the foot of Nelson's Column. Buried in St Paul's Cathedral, London.

Selected works: *Dignity and Impudence*; *The Rout of Comus* (both Tate Gallery, London).

Lawrence, (Sir) Thomas (1769–1830) English painter, born in Bristol, the son of an innkeeper. In 1792 he became painter to George III.

Selected work: *Queen Charlotte* (National Gallery, London).

Le Nain Brothers Antoine (c1588–1648), Louis (c1593–1648) and Mathieu (c1607–77). French painters, born in Laon. All painted scenes of peasant life but did not sign work with their initials, thus making attributions almost impossible.

Selected works: *Peasant Children* (Burrell Collection, Glasgow); *A Blacksmith in His Forge* (Louvre, Paris).

Léger, Fernand (1881–1955) French Cubist who has a museum dedicated to him at Boit on the Côte d'Azur.

Selected works: *Homage to David* (Musée National d'Art Moderne, Paris); *Woman and Still Life* (Scottish National Gallery of Modern Art, Edinburgh).

Leighton, (Lord) Frederick (1830–96) English painter of classical subjects, who became the 1st Baron Leighton of Stretton, the first British artist to be awarded a peerage; Leighton is buried in St Paul's Cathedral, London.

Selected work: *The Garden of the Hesperides* (Lady Lever Gallery, Port Sunlight).

Lely, (Sir) Peter (1618–80) Dutch portrait painter working in England. Court painter to Charles II.

Selected works: *Ladies of the Lake Family* (Tate Gallery, London); *The Windsor Beauties* (Hampton Court Palace, London).

Leonardo da Vinci (1452–1519) Italian painter, sculptor, scientist and creator of the High Renaissance style. Worked in the pay of Cesare Borgia, son of Pope Alexander VI, as senior military architect and general engineer, and then for François I of France.

Selected works: *Mona Lisa* (aka *La Gioconda*) (Louvre, Paris); *The Virgin of the Rocks* (National Gallery, London); *The Last Supper* (Convent of S. Maria delle Grazie, Milan).

Leyster, Judith (1609–60) Dutch genre and portrait painter, pupil of Hals. She married and worked with the painter Jan Molenaer (c1609–68).

Selected work: *The Lute-Playing Fool* (Rijksmuseum, Amsterdam).

A
R
T

Lichtenstein, Roy (1923–97)   American Pop artist, whose works were inspired by comic strips.
  Selected works: *Whaam!* (Tate Gallery, London); *In the Car* (Scottish National Gallery of Modern Art, Edinburgh).

Limbourg Brothers (early 15th-century)   Flemish family of miniature painters in the International Gothic style. The three brothers were Pol, Jehanequin and Hermann de Limbourg.
  Selected work: *Les Très Riches Heures* (Musée Condé, Chantilly).

Lippi, Filippino (c1457–1504)   Florentine painter of the transition from Early to High Renaissance. Son of Fra Filippo Lippi.
  Selected work: *Vision of St Bernard* (Badia, Florence).

Lippi, Fra Filippo (c1406–69)   Florentine fresco painter, influenced by Masaccio and Gothic art. Aka 'Fra Lippo Lippi'.
  Selected works: *Annunciation* (Church of S. Lorenzo, Florence); *The Adoration of the Magi* (National Gallery, Washington DC).

Lissitzky, Eleazar M (1890–1941)   Russian Constructivist painter, influenced by Malevich.
  Selected work: *Victory over the Sun* (Tate Gallery, London).

Lorenzetti, Ambrogio (c1290/1300–c1348)   Sienese landscapist and realist.
  Selected work: frescoes in the Palazzo Pubblico, Siena.

Lotto, Lorenzo (c1480–1556)   Italian Renaissance painter.
  Selected works: *Portrait of Andreas Odoni* (Hampton Court Palace, London); *Madonna and Child with Saints* (National Gallery, Rome); *A Gentleman in His Study* (Galleria dell'Accademia, Venice).

Louis, Morris (1912–62)   American Cubist until 1952 and then influenced by Jackson Pollock. He pioneered Colorfield painting, using bands of colour. Louis was further influenced by Helen Frankenthaler's *Mountains and Sea*, which prompted him to throw acrylic paint onto unprimed canvases to create brilliant patches of abstract colour.
  Selected work: *Alpha-Phi* (Tate Gallery, London).

Low, (Sir) David (1891–1963)   New Zealand-born British political cartoonist. Joined the *Evening Standard* in 1927. His most famous creation was 'Colonel Blimp', an embodiment of the die-hard British bigot.

Lowry, Laurence Stephen (1887–1976)   Salford painter famous for his matchstick-like men and women. Lowry was only ever a part-time painter and worked most of his life as a clerk.
  Selected work: *The Pond* (Tate Gallery, London).

Lucas, Sarah (1962–)   British modern artist who works with a variety of materials and media, including photographs, sculpture and installations. Her work often features images of herself in a confrontational stance, eg *Self Portrait: Eating a Banana* (1990) and *Divine* (1991). In 1993 she opened a shop with Tracy Emin in Bethnal Green (simply named 'The Shop') and shares a similar level of notoriety in her work.

Mabuse, Jan (c1478–1532)   Flemish Mannerist allegorical painter (properly, Jan Gossaert).
  Selected work: *The Adoration of the Kings*; *Little Girl* (both National Gallery, London).

Maes, Nicolaes (1634–93)   Dutch portrait and genre painter, pupil of Rembrandt.

Selected works: *The Idle Servant* (National Gallery, London).

Magritte, René (1898–1967)   Belgian Surrealist, influenced by de Chirico.
  Selected work: *Black Flag* (Scottish National Gallery of Modern Art, Edinburgh).

Malevich, Kasimir (1878–1935)   Russian Suprematist, producing the first strictly geometrical art of the 20th century.
  Selected work: *Woman with Water Pails* (Museum of Modern Art, New York).

Manet, Edouard (1832–83)   French precursor of Impressionism.
  Selected works: *Music in the Tuileries Garden* (Hugh Lane Municipal Gallery, Dublin); *A Bar at the Folies Bergère* (Courtauld Institute Galleries, London); *Olympia* (Musée du Jeu de Paume, Paris); *Déjeuner sur l'herbe* (Louvre, Paris).

Mantegna, Andrea (1431–1506)   Italian Renaissance painter working in Padua and Mantua. Mantegna married a daughter of Jacopo Bellini.
  Selected works: *The Triumph of Caesar* (Hampton Court Palace, London); *Crucifixion* (Louvre, Paris); frescoes in the Camera degli Sposi, Palazzo Ducale, Mantua.

Marc, Franz (1880–1916)   German Expressionist and leading member of Der Blaue Reiter. Marc was killed at Verdun.
  Selected works: *Large Blue Horses* (Walker Art Center, Minneapolis); *Red Woman* (Leicester Museum and Art Gallery).

Martini, Simone (c1280–1344)   Artist of the Sienese School.
  Selected works: *Madonna with Angels and Saints, Maesta* (Palazzo Pubblico, Siena); *Christ Returns to his Parents* (Walker Art Gallery, Liverpool).

Masaccio (1401–28)   Florentine painter (properly Tommaso di Ser Giovanni di Simone dei Guidi), whose nickname literally means 'Hulking Tom'.
  Selected works: frescoes in the Brancacci Chapel, S. Maria del Carmine, Florence; *Madonna and Child* (National Gallery, London); *Crucifixion* (Capodimonte, Naples).

Massys, Quentin (c1465–1530)   Netherlandish portrait and religious-subject painter, influenced by Italian art.
  Selected works: *Jesus and the Infant St John Embracing* (Chatsworth House, Derbyshire); *The Virgin and Child with Angels* (National Gallery, London); *Altarpiece of the Lamentation* (Koninklijk Museum voor Schone Kunsten, Antwerp).

Matisse, Henri (1869–1954)   French painter who was leader of the Fauves, 1905–6, before changing his style. The Chapelle de Rosaire in Vence, France, was entirely designed and decorated by him. The Musée Matisse in Nice houses a collection donated by the artist's family.
  Selected works: *The Painting Lesson* (Scottish National Gallery of Modern Art, Edinburgh); *Interior with Aubergines* (Musée de Peinture, Grenoble).

Memling, Hans (c1430–94)   Flemish biblical and portrait painter. A good collection of his work is housed in the Memlingmuseum in Bruges.
  Selected works: *Bathsheba* (Staatsgalerie, Stuttgart); *St John* (National Gallery, London); *The Adoration of the Magi* (Memlingmuseum, Bruges).

Mengs, Anton-Raphael (1728–79)   German painter, born in Bohemia, the son of a Danish artist. Precursor of Neo-Classicism.

Selected works: *Maria Luisa of Parma* (Prado, Madrid); *Richard Wilson* (National Museum of Wales, Cardiff).

Metsu, Gabriel (1629–67) Dutch genre painter, particularly of domestic scenes, a pupil of Dou.

Selected works: *The Sick Child* (Rijksmuseum, Amsterdam); *The Music Lesson* (National Gallery, London); *Woman at the Spinet* (Museum Boymans-van Beuningen, Rotterdam).

Michelangelo Buonarotti (1475–1564) High Renaissance and later Mannerist painter, sculptor and architect, born near Florence, where he grew up. Patronised by Pope Julius II, for whom he decorated the ceiling of Sistine Chapel (1508–12).

Selected works: *The Last Judgement* (Sistine Chapel, Vatican Palace, Rome); *Holy Family* (Uffizi, Florence); *The Entombment* (National Gallery, London); *David* (Accademia, Florence).

Millais, (Sir) John Everett (1829–96) English co-founder of the Pre-Raphaelite Brotherhood. Born in Southampton. In 1840 he became the youngest ever student at the Royal Academy, and in 1896 its President.

Selected works: *The Blind Girl* (Birmingham City Museum & Art Gallery); *Christ in the House of His Parents* (Tate Gallery, London); *The Return of the Dove to the Ark* (Ashmolean Museum, Oxford); *Ophelia* (Tate Gallery, London); *Autumn Leaves* (Manchester City Art Gallery).

Millet, Jean François (1814–75) French realist painter of peasant life. Worked at Barbizon from 1849.

Selected works: *The Gleaners* (Louvre, Paris); *La Famille du Paysan* (National Museum of Wales, Cardiff).

Miró, Joan (1893–1983) Spanish Abstract painter, sculptor and ceramicist, influenced by Cubism and Surrealism.

Selected works: *Samurai* (Cannon Hall, Barnsley); *The Egg* (Fondation Maeght, Saint-Paul-de Vence).

Modigliani, Amedeo (1884–1920) Italian painter and sculptor, working in Paris from 1906.

Selected work: *Seated Nude* (Courtauld Institute, London).

Moholy-Nagy, László (1895–1946) Hungarian-born, American experimental artist and photographer, influenced by Lissitzky and Constructivism. He developed kinetic art and taught at the Bauhaus and in Chicago.

Selected work: *Z IV* (Marlborough Gallery, London).

Mondrian, Piet (1872–1944) Dutch member of De Stijl and developer of Neo-Plasticism, who influenced the Bauhaus School.

Selected works: *Broadway Boogie Woogie* (Museum of Modern Art, New York); *Composition in Black and White* (Rijksmuseum Kröller-Müller, Otterlo); *The Grey Tree* (Haags Gemeentemuseum, The Hague).

Monet, Claude (1840–1926) Father of Impressionism, whose *Impression: Sunrise* gave its name to the movement. Monet's *Déjeuner sur l'herbe* (Luncheon on the Grass) should not be confused with Manet's.

Selected works: *Field with Poppies* (Louvre, Paris); *The Beach at Trouville* (Tate Gallery, London); *Rouen Cathedral: Sunset* (Museum of Fine Arts, Boston, Mass.).

Moore, Henry Spencer (1898–1986) English sculptor, born in Castleford, Yorkshire, the son of a coal-miner. Moore is best known for his reclining female figures, carved in wood and stone or cast in bronze. He was an official war artist 1940–42, during which time he produced a famous series of drawings of air-raid shelter scenes. His principal commissions included the *Madonna and Child* in St Matthew's Church, Northampton; the decorative frieze on the Time-Life building, London; and the massive reclining figures for the UNESCO building in Paris and the Lincoln Center in New York. Moore was awarded the Order of Merit in 1963.

Moreau, Gustave (1826–98) French Symbolist painter whose Paris home and studio is now the Musée Gustave Moreau.

Selected work: *The Apparition* (Louvre, Paris).

Morisot, Berthe (1841–95) French Impressionist, granddaughter of Fragonard, who married Eugène, the brother of Manet.

Selected work: *Cradle* (Louvre, Paris).

Moro, Antonio (c1519–76) Dutch court painter to the Habsburgs and Mary I of England, who knighted him as Sir Anthony More.

Selected works: *Queen Anna of Spain* (Kunsthistorisches Museum, Vienna); *Sir Henry Lee* (National Portrait Gallery, London).

Morse, Samuel (1791–1872) American painter and first President of the National Academy (1826), but better known for his invention of the electric telegraph.

Selected works: *House of Representatives* (Corcoran, Washington DC); *Lafayette* (Brooklyn Museum, New York).

Motherwell, Robert Burns (1915–91) American Abstract Expressionist who married fellow Expressionist Helen Frankenthaler in 1955.

Selected works: *Elegy to the Spanish Republic XXXIV* (Albright-Knox Art Gallery, Buffalo, NY).

Mucha, Alphonse (1860–1939) Czech painter, graphic artist and designer, chiefly known for his Art Nouveau illustration style, especially the posters for the actress Sarah Bernhardt.

Selected work: *Job and Lorenzaccio* (Victoria and Albert Museum, London).

Munch, Edvard (1863–1944) Norwegian Expressionist. Important collections of his work are at the Rasmus Meyers Samlinger, Bergen, and the Munch Museum and the National Gallery, Oslo.

Selected works: *The Scream* (Nasjonalgalleriet, Oslo); *Vampire* (Munch-Museet, Oslo); *Ashes* (Nasjonalgalleriet, Oslo).

Muñoz, Juan (1953–2001) Born in Madrid, Spain, and studied at the Central School of Art in London and the Pratt Centre in New York. A leading exponent of installation sculpture, he was commissioned to submit the second of the Unilever Series at the Turbine Hall at Tate Modern. The work, entitled *Double Bind* consisted of a series of optical illusions and spectacular follies. He died of a stomach haemorrhage in August 2001.

Murillo, Bartolomé Esteban (c1618–82) Spanish Baroque painter of religious and genre subjects. Born in Seville, Murillo fell from a scaffold when painting an altarpiece at Cadiz, and died shortly afterwards in Seville.

Selected works: *Virgin of the Rosary* (Archbishop's Palace, Seville); *The Two Trinities*, aka *The Holy Family* (National Gallery, London); *Boys with Fruit* (Alte Pinakothek, Munich).

Nash, Paul (1889–1946) English painter and co-founder of the Modern Movement. Nash was an official war artist in both world wars.

Selected works: *Landscape of the Vernal Equinox* (Scottish National Gallery of Modern Art, Edinburgh); *Pillar and Moon*); *Totes Meer* (Dead Sea) (both Tate Gallery, London).

Nauman, Bruce (1941–) Born in Indiana, USA. After studying mathematics at university he has established himself as a leading installation artist. His large-scale video installation *Mapping the Studio II* (2001) has been acquired by the Tate and *Raw Materials*, consisting of 22 spoken texts from existing works to create an aural collage, is the fifth in the Unilever Series of commissions for the Turbine Hall at Tate Modern. He currently lives and works in New Mexico.

Nicholson, Ben (1894–1982) English Abstract painter who used a restricted palette of greys and muted tones. Married three times; his second wife was the sculptor Barbara Hepworth.

Selected works: *Still Life* (Glasgow Art Gallery & Museum); *White Relief* (Tate Gallery, London).

Nolde, Emil (1867–1956) German Expressionist and printmaker (properly, Emil Hansen). His Art Nouveau house in Seebull, Germany, is now a museum.

Selected works: *Doubting Thomas* (Nolde-Museum, Seebull); *Death of Mary* (Museum Folkwang, Essen); *The Flower Garden* (Wallraf-Richartz Museum, Cologne).

Ofili, Chris (1968–) Born in Manchester but heavily influenced by his African roots. His controversial collage *The Holy Virgin Mary*, which featured a black Virgin Mary with elephant dung on one breast and cutouts from pornographic magazines glued in the background, created a stir when exhibited in New York.

Selected work: *The Adoration of Captain Shit and the Legend of the Black Stars* Part 2 (1998, Museum of Contemporary Art, Sydney).

O'Keeffe, Georgia (1887–1986) American Surrealist and Abstract painter who married photographer Alfred Stieglitz. In May 2001 her 1928 painting *Calla Lilies with Red Anemone* was sold at Christie's, New York, for $6,166,000, the top auction price for a work by a woman artist.

Selected work: *Black Iris* (Metropolitan Museum of Art, New York).

Oliver, Isaac (c1560–1617) French-born English miniaturist who married the half-sister of Marcus Gheeraerts the Younger. Oliver's work included a famous miniature of Elizabeth I of England that displeased her immensely.

Selected work: *Self Portrait* (National Portrait Gallery, London).

Opie, John (1761–1807) Cornish portrait and history painter, son of a carpenter. Nicknamed the 'Cornish Wonder'.

Patronised by John Wolcot (the political satirist Peter Pindar). His first exhibited historical work was *The Assassination of James I of Scotland* (1786), followed by *The Murder of Rizzio* (1787), both destroyed by bombing in 1941.

Selected work: *Mary Wollstonecraft* (Tate Gallery, London).

Oudry, Jean-Baptiste (1686–1755) French still-life painter.

Selected works: *The Dog* (Burrell Collection, Glasgow); *The Calling of the Hounds* (tapestry) (Pitti Palace, Florence).

Palma Vecchio (c1480–1528) Venetian painter of *sacra conversazione* altarpieces (properly, Jacopo Palma).

Selected works: *Venus and Cupid* (Fitzwilliam Museum, Cambridge); *Polyptych of St Barbara* (S. Maria Formosa, Venice); *The Assumption* (Galleria dell'Accademia, Venice).

Palmer, Samuel (1805–81) English landscapist and etcher, influenced by William Blake.

Selected work: *Coming from Evening Church* (Tate Gallery, London).

Parmigianino, Il (1503–40) Italian early Mannerist (properly, Girolamo Francesco Maria Mazzola).

Selected works: *The Marriage of St Catherine* (National Gallery, London); *Madonna with the Long Neck* (Uffizi, Florence); frescoes in S. Maria della Steccata, Parma.

Pasmore, Victor (1908–98) English portrait, still-life and landscape painter. Co-founder of the Euston Road School. In the late 1940s he turned towards abstract art.

Selected works: *Inland Sea* (Tate Gallery, London); *Wine Red* (Bristol City Art Gallery).

Pechstein, Max Hermann (1881–1955) Co-founder of German Expressionism and member of Die Brücke from 1906 before helping to found the rival Neue Sezession (New Secession).

Selected work: *Indian and Woman* (Morton D. May Collection).

Perugino, Pietro (c1445–1523) Umbrian Renaissance painter (properly, Pietro di Cristoforo Vannucci). Perugino was the master of Raphael.

Selected work: *Virgin and Child* (National Gallery, London).

Piazzetta, Giovanni Battista (1682–1754) Venetian painter, illustrator and designer.

Selected works: *Fortune Teller* (Galleria dell' Accademia, Venice); fresco *The Crucifixion* (Church of S. Maddalena de' Pazzi, Florence).

Picabia, Francis (1879–1953) French Cubist, Dadaist and Surrealist who also dabbled in Futurism. Married Gabrielle Buffet in 1909.

Selected work: *Udnie* (Musée d'art Moderne, Paris).

Picasso, Pablo (1881–1973) Spanish painter and sculptor who embraced Cubism, Surrealism and Expressionism. Born in Malaga, Picasso, along with Braque, pioneered Cubism. Picasso's blue period was from 1902 to 1904, followed by his pink period (1904–6) and a short brown period (1905–6). He was director of the Prado during the Spanish Civil War and joined the Communist Party in 1944. Picasso died in Mougins, France. The Musée Picasso in Antibes was decorated by him in 1946, and many works are in the Musée Picasso, Paris. His mural *War and Peace* is housed in the Musée National Picasso in Vallauris, and *Man with a Lamb* is in the public square. The Museo Pablo Picasso in Barcelona holds early works donated by the painter in 1970.

Selected works: *Three Dancers* (Tate Gallery, London); *Les Demoiselles d'Avignon* (Museum of Modern Art, New York); *Guernica* (Prado, Madrid).

Piero della Francesca (c1419–92) Umbrian painter, scientist and mathematician.

Selected works: *The Nativity* (National Gallery, London); *Constantine's Dream* (Legend of the Holy Cross) (S. Francesco, Arezzo); *Federigo da Montefeltro* (Uffizi, Florence).

Piper, John (1903–92) English artist, born in Epsom, Surrey. Originally an abstract painter, he turned to Romantic realism under the influence of Palmer and the earlier English topographical painters. As an official war artist (1940–42), he painted many successful war pictures, but his design of the stained glass windows for Coventry Cathedral and Eton are his best-known works.

Pisanello, Antonio (c1390–1455)   Italian painter and follower of the International Gothic style of Gentile da Fabriano.

Selected works: *The Vision of St Eustace* (National Gallery, London); *Lionello d'Este* (Accademia Carrara, Bergamo); *St George and the Princess* (Church of S. Anastasia, Verona).

Pisano, Andrea (c1290–c1349)   Italian sculptor born in Pontadera and trained in Pisa. Considered the founder of the Florentine School of sculpture. Best known for his relief panels on the bronze south door of the Florence Baptistry.

Selected works: *Weaver* (Campanile, Florence cathedral); *Noah* (Museo dell'Opere del Duomo, Florence).

Pissarro, Camille (1830–1903)   French Impressionist and Pointillist, born in St Thomas, West Indies.

Selected works: *Boulevard Montmartre by Night*, *Lower Norwood, London, Snow* (both National Gallery, London).

Pollaiuolo, Antonio (c1431–c1498)   Florentine painter, sculptor, goldsmith and engraver, properly Antonio di Jacopo d'Antonio Benci, but took his name from his father's profession as a poulterer. Collaborated with his brother Piero (c1443–c1496) on the bronze tomb of Sixtus IV and the monument to Pope Innocent VIII, both in Saint Peter's, Rome. Other notable works include the bronze statuette *Hercules and Antaeus* in the Bargello, Florence, and the signed engraving *Battle of the Ten Nude Gods*. It is not always clear which brother should be credited with some of their oeuvre, but Piero, principally a painter, is thought to be responsible for at least three of the *Seven Virtues* in the Uffizi, Florence; three others were probably collaborations with Antonio, and the seventh by Botticelli.

Pollock, Jackson (1912–56)   American Abstract Expressionist and early exponent of tachisme (action painting). *Full Fathom Five* was probably the first work of this controversial 'poured painting' style. Alcoholism and his death in a car crash added to Pollock's notoriety.

Selected works: *Enchanted Wood* (Guggenheim Foundation, Venice); *Summertime: Number 9a* (Tate Gallery, London).

Pontormo, Jacopo Carrucci (1494–1557)   Florentine early Mannerist.

Selected works: *Four Scenes from the Life of Joseph* (National Gallery, London); frescoes in S. Felicità, Florence; *Cosimo I de Medici* (Uffizi, Florence).

Poussin, Nicolas (1594–1665)   French Classical landscapist who was court painter to Louis XIII. His oeuvre included mythological works and biblical subjects; he was an early exponent of history painting.

Selected works: *The Nurture of Jupiter* (Dulwich Gallery, London); *Tancred and Erminia* (Barber Institute, University of Birmingham); *Inspiration of the Poet* (Louvre, Paris); *The Adoration of the Golden Calf* (National Gallery, London).

Primaticcio, Francesco (1504–70)   Italian Mannerist painter, sculptor and architect. A collection of his drawings is in the Louvre.

Selected works: *The Rape of Helen* (Bowes Museum, Barnard Castle); Fontainebleau Palace decorations, France.

Puvis de Chavannes, Pierre (1824–98)   French decorative, symbolic painter, noted for his murals. A number of huge canvases are set in to the walls of the grand staircase of the Musée de Picardie, Amiens.

Selected work: *Poor Fisherman* (Louvre, Paris).

Raeburn, (Sir) Henry (1756–1823)   Scottish portraitist, elected to the Royal Academy in 1815 and Selected works: *Reverend Robert Walker Skating on Duddingston Loch* (National Gallery of Scotland, Edinburgh); *Self Portrait* (National Gallery of Scotland, Edinburgh); *Lady Dalrymple* (Tate Gallery, London).

Raphael (1483–1520)   Italian High Renaissance painter who worked on a number of Papal commissions. Raphael (properly, Raffaello Santi or Sanzio) was born in Urbino. Leo X selected him to succeed Donato Bramante (a relative) as architect of St Peter's in 1514. His last work, the *Transfiguration* was left unfinished when he died.

Selected works: *Pope Julius II* (National Gallery, London); *The Madonna of the Goldfinch* (Uffizi, Florence); frescoes in the Vatican Palace, Rome.

Redon, Odilon (1840–1916)   French Symbolist painter and graphic artist; a precursor of Surrealism.

Selected work: *Violette Heyman* (Cleveland Museum of Art, Ohio).

Rembrandt Harmenszoon van Rijn (1606–69)   Dutch painter, etcher and graphic artist whose home is now a museum in Amsterdam. Born in Leiden, the son of a prosperous miller, his first wife was Saskia van Ulenburgh (d. 1642). He failed to achieve financial security and, despite being the most famous painter of his time, died a pauper.

Selected works: *Self Portrait* (Walker Art Gallery, Liverpool); *Portrait of Titus* (Wallace Collection, London); *The Night Watch – The Militia Company of Captain Frans Banning Cocq* (Rijksmuseum, Amsterdam).

Reni, Guido (1575–1642)   Bolognese Classical painter of Baroque religious works.

Selected work: *St John the Baptist* (Dulwich Gallery , London).

Renoir, Pierre Auguste (1841–1919)   French Impressionist, born in Limoges. He visited Italy in 1880 and during the next few years painted a series of *Bathers* in a colder, more classical style, influenced by Ingres and Raphael. He then returned to hot reds, orange and gold to portray nudes in sunlight. Renoir's hands were crippled by arthritis in later years. His son Jean (1894–1979) became a great film director.

Selected works: *Umbrellas* (Hugh Lane Municipal Gallery of Modern Art, Dublin); *Umbrellas* (National Gallery, London); *Moulin de la Galette* (Louvre, Paris); *Madame Charpentier and Her Children* (Metropolitan Museum of Art, New York).

Reynolds, (Sir) Joshua (1723–92)   English portraitist and art theorist. Co-founder and first President of the Royal Academy, 1768. Principal painter to George III of England, 1784.

Selected works: *Self-portrait*, c1753 (National Portrait Gallery, London); *Three Ladies Adorning a Term of Hymen: The Montgomerie Sisters* (Tate Gallery, London); *Admiral Lord Anson* (Shugborough, Staffordshire).

Ribera, Jusepe de (c1591–1652)   Spanish Baroque painter, known as Lo Spagnoletto (The Little Spaniard).

Selected work: *Martyrdom of St Bartholomew* (Prado, Madrid).

ART

Richter, Hans (1888–1976) American painter, sculptor and film-maker, born in Berlin. Member of the Zurich Dadaists, 1917.

Rigaud, Hyacinthe (1659–1743) French Rococo painter. Portraitist to Louis XIV and Louis XV of France. A small collection of his works is housed in the Musée Rigaud, Perpignan.

Selected works: *Cardinal de Bouillon* (Musée Rigaud, Perpignan); *Louis XIV; Louis XV* (both Musée de l'Histoire de la France, Versailles).

Riley, Bridget (1931–) English Op artist since the early 1960s.

Selected work: *Crest* (Rowan Gallery, London).

Rodin, Auguste (1840–1917) French sculptor, born in Paris, the son of a clerk. Produced his first great work in 1864, *L'Homme au nez cassé*. In 1877 he made a tour of the French cathedrals and published *Les Cathédrales de la France* in 1914. From 1886 to 1895 he worked on *Les Bourgeois de Calais*. His statues include a nude Victor Hugo and Balzac in a dressing gown. His works are represented in the Musée Rodin, Paris; the Rodin Museum, Philadelphia; and the Victoria and Albert Museum, London, where there is a collection of his bronzes that he presented to the British nation in 1914.

Selected works: *Le Penseur* (The Thinker) (Musée Rodin, Paris); *Le Baiser* (The Kiss) (Tate Gallery, London).

Romney, George (1734–1802) English portraitist and history painter, born in Lancashire. At the height of his fame he rivalled both Reynolds and Gainsborough and his later history paintings and portraits of Emma Hart (later Lady Hamilton) enhanced his reputation, but he eventually died insane.

Selected work: *Self-portrait* (National Gallery, London).

Rosa, Salvator (1615–73) Neapolitan Baroque and macabre painter.

Selected work: *Landscape* (National Gallery, London).

Rossetti, Dante Gabriel (1828–1882) Anglo-Italian painter and poet, brother of the poet Christina Rossetti. DG Rossetti was born in London and his mother was Frances Mary Lavinia Polidori, daughter of Gaetano Polidori and sister of Lord Byron's physician, Dr John Polidori. Rossetti was fascinated by the Middle Ages and was a co-founder of the Pre-Raphaelite Brotherhood.

Selected works: *St George and the Princess Sabra; Ecce Ancilla Domini* (both Tate Gallery, London); *The Blessed Damozel* (Lady Lever Art Gallery, Port Sunlight).

Rothko, Mark (1903–70) American Abstract Expressionist and co-founder of Colorfield painting. Latvian-born (properly, Marcus Rothkovitch).

Selected work: *Two Openings in Black over Wine* (Tate Gallery, London).

Rouault, Georges (1871–1958) French Expressionist painter often on religious themes. Many of his works were acquired by the art dealer Ambroise Vollard.

Selected works: *Head of Christ* (Musée National d'Art Moderne, Paris); *Two Nudes* (Metropolitan Museum of Art, New York).

Rousseau, Henri (1844–1910) French Primitive painter, known as 'Le Douanier' due to his early occupation as a tax collector in the Paris customs office.

Selected works: *The Child among Rocks* (Philadelphia Museum of Art); *The Sleeping Gypsy* (Museum of Modern Art, New York).

Rubens, (Sir) Peter Paul (1577–1640) Enormously successful and productive Flemish Baroque painter and diplomat. Rubens's Antwerp home is now a museum. He married his first wife, Isabella Brandt, in 1609 (d. 1626) and his second, Helen Fourment, in 1630.

Selected works: *The Judgement of Paris* (National Gallery, London); *Descent from the Cross* (Antwerp Cathedral); *Peace and War* (National Gallery, London); *Portrait of Isabella Brandt* (Wallace Collection, London); *Apotheosis of James I* (Whitehall Banqueting House, London); *Helen Fourment with Two of Her Children* (Louvre, Paris).

Ruysdael, Jacob van (1628–82) Dutch landscapist whose work was only appreciated after his death.

Selected works: *The Jewish Cemetery* (Gemäldegalerie, Dresden); *View on the Amstel Looking toward Amsterdam* (Fitzwilliam Museum, Cambs); *The Windmill at Wijk bij Duurstede* (Rijksmuseum, Amsterdam).

Ruysdael, Salomon van (c1600–70) Dutch realist landscapist, properly, Salomon de Goyer. Uncle of Jacob van Ruysdael.

Selected works: *River Scene* (Leicester City Art Gallery); *River Scene near Utrecht* (Gemeentemuseum, Arnhem); *Landscape with a Carriage and Horsemen at a Pool* (National Gallery, London).

Saenredam, Pieter Janszoon (1597–1665) Dutch architectural painter.

Selected works: *Interior of the Grote Kerk at Haarlem* (National Gallery, London); *Interior of the Nieuwe Kerk* (Frans Hals Museum, Haarlem); *Interior of the Janskerk*, Utrecht (Centraal Museum, Utrecht).

Sargent, John Singer (1856–1925) American portraitist of fashionable London society from 1884. Born in Florence, Sargent was an official war artist during World War I.

Selected works: *Carnation, Lily, Lily, Rose* (Tate Gallery, London); *Madame Gautreau* (Metropolitan Museum of Art, New York); *The Three Vickers Sisters* (Mappin Art Gallery, Sheffield); *Gassed* (Imperial War Museum, London).

Sassetta, Stefano di Giovanni (c1392–1450) Sienese painter of large altarpieces.

Selected works: *St Francis Renounces His Earthly Father* (National Gallery, London); *Journey of the Magi* (Metropolitan Museum of Art, New York).

Sebastiano del Piombo (c1485–1547) Venetian painter influenced by Giorgione and Michelangelo.

Selected works: *The Raising of Lazarus* (National Gallery, London); *The Madonna and Child with SS. Catherine and John the Baptist* (Galleria dell'Accademia, Venice).

Seurat, Georges Pierre (1859–91) French Neo-Impressionist and developer of Pointillism.

Selected works: *Sunday Afternoon on the Island of the Grande Jatte* (Art Institute of Chicago); *Circus* (Louvre, Paris); *Bathers at Asnières* (National Gallery, London).

Sickert, Walter Richard (1860–1942) German-born, English painter, influenced by Degas and Whistler. Co-founder of the Camden Town Group.

Selected works: *The Lion of St Mark* (Fitzwilliam Museum, Cambridge); *View at Ramsgate* (Huddersfield Art Gallery).

Sisley, Alfred (1839–99)   French landscape Impressionist of British parentage, noted for his subtle treatment of skies.

Selected works: *Flood at Port Marly*; *The Boat during the Flood* (both Louvre, Paris).

Snyders, Frans (1579–1657)   Flemish painter, born in Antwerp. Pupil of Pieter Brueghel the Younger. He specialised in still life and animals, often assisting Rubens in hunting scenes. In 1611 he married Margaretha de Vos, the sister of the Flemish painters Cornelis and Paul de Vos.

Selected work: *Stag Hunt* (Prado, Madrid).

Soutine, Chaim (1893–1943)   Lithuanian painter, in Paris from 1913, influenced by Cézanne and Die Brücke group.

Selected work: *Les Gorges du Loup sur Vence* (Scottish National Gallery of Modern Art, Edinburgh).

Spencer, (Sir) Stanley (1891–1959)   English painter of portraits, landscapes and religious works. Born in Cookham, Berkshire. Spencer was an official war artist in World War II.

Selected works: Sandham Memorial Chapel murals, Burghclere; *The Garden at Cookham Rise* (Huddersfield Art Gallery).

Steen, Jan (c1626–79)   Dutch painter of low-life scenes and still-life subjects.

Selected works: *The Effects of Intemperance* (National Gallery, London); *Self-portrait* (Rijksmuseum, Amsterdam); *Romping Couple* (Stedelijk Museum 'De Lakenhal', Leiden).

Steer, Philip Wilson (1860–1942)   English landscapist. Member of the New English Art Club.

Selected works: *Mrs Cyprian Williams and Her Daughters* (Tate Gallery, London); *The Last Chapter* (Cartwright Hall, Bradford); *Self Portrait*, *The Music Room* (Tate Gallery, London).

Stella, Frank (1936–)   American Abstract Expressionist and Minimalist.

Selected work: *Hyena Stomp* (Tate Gallery, London).

Streeter, Robert (1624–79)   Pepys's famous history painter who became Charles II's serjeant-painter in 1660. The ceiling of Oxford's Sheldonian Theatre is one of his few remaining decorative works.

Stubbs, George (1724–1806)   English animal painter and engraver, born in Liverpool. Stubbs specialised in painting horses.

Selected works: *Mares and Foals in a River Landscape* (Tate Gallery, London); *Self-portrait* (National Portrait Gallery, London); *Molly Long Legs with a Jockey* (Walker Art Gallery, Liverpool).

Sutherland, Graham Vivian (1903–80)   English portraitist and official war artist, WW2. His official portrait of Sir Winston Churchill was destroyed by Lady Churchill, as she detested it. The Graham Sutherland Gallery in Haverfordwest was devoted almost entirely to his work until 1996, when it was closed, and the nearly 800 works have been displayed at Tenby Art Gallery (1996), Bodelwyddan Castle (1997) and the Turner House Gallery, Penarth (1998 and 2000-1). At time of writing Pembrokeshire Coast National Park is pursuing a new home near its visitors centre at St Davids.

Selected work: *Somerset Maugham* (Tate Gallery, London); *Christ in Majesty* (tapestry in Coventry Cathedral).

Tanguy, Yves (1900–55)   French Surrealist in the USA from 1939, influenced by de Chirico.

Selected work: *The Furniture of Time* (Collection Soby, New Canaan, Connecticut).

Teniers the Younger, David (1610–90)   Flemish genre painter. Curator of Archduke Leopold Wilhelm's picture gallery in Brussels, and copyist of many of its masterpieces.

Selected works: *Archduke Leopold Wilhelm in His Gallery* (Musées Royaux des Beaux Arts, Brussels); *The Dentist* (Manchester City Art Gallery); *Interior with a Peasant* (Nottingham Castle Museum).

Terborch, Gerard (1617–81)   Dutch genre painter of domestic scenes.

Selected works: *A Man* (Museum de Waag, Deventer); *A Woman Playing a Theorbo to Two Men* (National Gallery, London); *Woman at a Mirror* (Rijksmuseum, Amsterdam).

Terbrugghen, Hendrick (c1588–1629)   Dutch religious and genre painter, influenced by Caravaggio.

Selected work: *Jacob, Laban and Leah* (National Gallery, London).

Thornhill, (Sir) James (1675–1734)   English Baroque painter, born in Melcombe Regis, Dorset. His paintings for the dome of St Paul's (1707), the hall at Blenheim Palace, Hampton Court and the Painted Hall at Greenwich Hospital – on a scale unrivalled in Britain in the 15th century – made his reputation. He was the father-in-law of William Hogarth. Knighted by George I (1720) and appointed serjeant-painter; from 1722 became MP for Melcombe Regis.

Thornycroft, (Sir) William Hamo (1850–1925)   English sculptor, born in London.

Selected works: public statues of General Gordon in Trafalgar Square; John Bright in Rochdale; and Cromwell outside the Houses of Parliament.

Tiepolo, Giambattista (1696–1770)   Venetian Rococo decorative painter. His work is prominent in palaces and churches throughout Europe.

Selected works: *Finding of Moses* (National Gallery of Scotland, Edinburgh); frescoes in the Residenz, Würzburg, and the Royal Palace, Madrid.

Tintoretto (1518–94)   Venetian Mannerist (properly, Jacopo Robusti). The son of a silk dyer (*tintore*), hence his nickname of Tintoretto (Little Dyer).

Selected works: *St George Killing the Dragon* (National Gallery, London); *Miracle of S. Marco* (Galleria dell'Accademia, Venice); *The Washing of the Feet* (Wilton House, Wiltshire).

Titian (c1487–1576)   Venetian painter (properly, Tiziano Vecellio); renowned for his use of colour. The Prado in Madrid has a superb collection of his work, particularly the paintings done under the patronage of the Holy Roman Emperor, Charles V. Titian was buried in the Church of S. Maria dei Frari, Venice.

Selected works: *The Three Ages of Man* (National Gallery of Scotland, Edinburgh); *Venus, Cupid and a Lute Player* (Fitzwilliam Museum, Cambridge); *Ecce Homo* (National Gallery of Ireland); *The Assumption* (S. Maria dei Frari, Venice).

Toulouse-Lautrec, Henri de (1864–1901)   French painter, graphic artist and lithographer who forsook his noble origins for the cafés of Montmartre. He was influenced by Degas and by Japanese prints. Much of his work is housed in the Musée Toulouse-Lautrec et Galerie d'Art Moderne, Albi, France.

Selected works: *Jane Avril at the Moulin Rouge* (Courtauld Institute, London); *La Toilette* (Louvre, Paris); *The Artist's Mother* (Musée Toulouse-Lautrec, Albi); *At the Moulin Rouge*; *In the Circus Fernando: The Ringmaster* (both Art Institute of Chicago); *At the Moulin de la Galette* (Stedelijk Museum, Amsterdam); *Jane Avril Dansant* (Louvre, Paris).

A
R
T

Turner, Joseph Mallord William (1775–1851) English Romantic landscapist and precursor of Impressionism. A superb collection of Turner's work is in the Clore Gallery, attached to the Tate Gallery, London. Turner entered the Royal Academy at the age of 14 and was patronised by Lord Egremont of Petworth. He died in temporary lodgings in Chelsea under the assumed name of Booth.

Selected works: *Battle of Trafalgar* (National Maritime Museum, London); *Norham Castle, Sunrise* (Tate Gallery, London); *The Fall of the Clyde* (Lady Lever Art Gallery, Port Sunlight).

Uccello, Paolo (1397–1475) Florentine painter noted for his sophisticated use of perspective.

Selected works: *The Hunt* (Ashmolean Museum, Oxford); *The Battle of San Romano* (National Gallery, London); *The Deluge* (Church of S. Maria Novella, Florence).

Utrillo, Maurice (1883–1955) French painter, born in Montmartre, Paris, the illegitimate son of painter Suzanne Valadon. Adopted by the Spanish writer Miguel Utrillo, he began to paint at Montmagny in 1902. Utrillo specialised in Paris street scenes. Despite acute alcoholism and drug addiction, his output was astonishing. His 'White Period' paintings of about 1908–14 are much sought after. He signed his works 'Maurice Utrillo V', incorporating the initial of his mother's family name.

Vasarely, Victor (1908–97) Hungarian-born, French precursor of Op art. The 16th-century Château de Gordes in Vaucluse, France, is now the Musée Didactique Vasarely.

Selected works: *Sirius II* (Galerie Denise René, Paris); *Ondho* (Museum of Modern Art, New York); *Supernovae* (Tate Gallery, London).

Vasari, Giorgio (1511–74) Italian Mannerist fresco painter, architect and biographer. His *Lives of the Artists* was first published in Florence in 1550. The Casa Vasari in Arezzo was decorated by him.

Selected works: *Allegory of the Immaculate Conception* (Ashmolean Museum, Oxford); *Lorenzo the Magnificent* (Uffizi, Florence).

Velazquez, Diego Rodriguez de Silva y (1599–1660) Spanish Baroque genre and royal portrait painter to Philip IV of Spain. Born in Seville and pupil of Francisco Pacheco, whose daughter he married in 1618.

Selected works: *Las Meninas* (aka *Maids of Honour*) (Prado, Madrid); *An Old Woman Cooking Eggs* (National Gallery of Scotland, Edinburgh); *The Toilet of Venus*, known as *The Rokeby Venus* (National Gallery, London).

Velde, Esaias van de (c1591–1630) Dutch realistic landscapist who was the master of Jan van Goyen.

Selected work: *Ice Scene* (Alte Pinakothek, Munich).

Vermeer, Jan (1632–75) Dutch genre painter of domestic scenes. Born in Delft, the son of an art dealer, he married Caterina Bolnes, who was to bear him eleven children. Fewer than 40 of his paintings are known. During World War II, forged Vermeers were produced by Jan Van Meegeren, who for some time deceived the experts.

Selected works: *A Young Woman Standing at a Virginal* (National Gallery, London); *A Lady Reading a Letter* (Rijksmuseum, Amsterdam); *Head of Girl with a Pearl Earring* (Mauritshuis, The Hague).

Veronese (c1528–88) Venetian biblical and allegorical painter (properly, Paolo Caliari).

Selected works: *Hermes, Herse and Aglauros* (Fitzwilliam Museum, Cambridge); *Mars and Venus* (National Gallery of Scotland, Edinburgh); frescoes in the Palazzo Ducale, Venice.

Vigée-Lebrun, Elisabeth Louise (1755–1842) French painter famous for her female subjects such as Marie Antoinette. She did paint male subjects, notably the Prince of Wales and Lord Byron.

Villon, Jacques (1875–1963) French painter (real name Gaston Duchamp) who specialised in Cubist works.

Vlaminck, Maurice de (1876–1958) French Fauve who was also a noted violinist, author and racing cyclist.

Selected work: *Woody River Scene* (Glasgow Art Gallery and Museum).

Vouet, Simon (1590–1649) French Baroque history and portrait painter who was influenced by Caravaggio. Court painter to Louis XIII.

Selected work: *La Richesse* (Louvre, Paris).

Vuillard, Edouard (1868–1940) French portrait and domestic genre painter. Member of the Nabis in the 1890s.

Selected works: *The Mantelpiece* (National Gallery, London); *The Open Window* (Scottish National Gallery of Modern Art, Edinburgh).

Warhol, Andy (1928–87) American Pop Art painter, graphic artist and film-maker who was famous for the Campbell soup-can labels and magazine illustrations directly reproduced by silk-screen. His controversial films included *Sleep* (1963) and *Chelsea Girls* (1966). In 1968 he was shot and wounded by Valerie Solanis, an actress in one of his films.

Selected work: *Green Coca-Cola Bottles* (Whitney Museum of American Art, New York).

Watteau, Jean-Antoine (1684–1721) French Rococo painter of *fêtes galantes*.

Selected works: *The Music Party* (Wallace Collection, London); *Gilles* (Louvre, Paris); *Mezzetin* (Metropolitan Museum of Art, New York); *L'Enseigne de Gerseint* (Gerseint's Signboard) (Schloss Charlottenburg, Berlin).

Watts, George Frederick (1817–1904) English portrait and allegorical painter who first drew attention with his cartoon of Caractacus in the competition for murals for the new Houses of Parliament. In 1864 he married actress Ellen Terry but parted from her within a year.

Selected works: *Found Drowned* (Watts Gallery, Compton, Surrey); *Hope* (Tate Gallery, London).

West, Benjamin (1738–1820) American Neo-classical painter, in England from 1763. Founding member of the Royal Academy and its President in 1792. Court painter to George III of England, who patronised him for 40 years.

Selected works: *The Death of General Wolfe* (National Gallery of Canada, Ottawa); *The Apotheosis of Lord Nelson* (National Maritime Museum, London); *Mrs Worrall as Hebe* (Tate Gallery, London).

Westmacott, (Sir) Richard (1775–1856) A leading Neo-classical sculptor of public monuments and statues. After studying in Italy he returned to London and became a favourite sculptor of the Committee of Taste. His most accomplished monument was a public subscription commission commemorating Charles James Fox, in Westminster Abbey. His bronze public monuments include the *Achilles* at Hyde Park Corner, Park Lane.

Weyden, Rogier van der (c1399–1464) Netherlandish painter of portraits and altarpieces, noted for his technical brilliance and emotional intensity.

Selected works: *Lamentation (Pietà) over the dead Christ* (National Gallery, London); *Antoine de Bourgogne* (Musées Royaux des Beaux Arts, Brussels); *Deposition* (Prado, Madrid); *Bladelin Altarpiece* (Museum Dahlem, Berlin).

Whistler, James Abbott McNeill (1834–1903) American painter who lived in London and Paris. The critic John Ruskin's vitriolic criticism of his contributions to the Grosvenor Gallery exhibition of 1877, accusing him of 'flinging a pot of paint in the public's face', provoked the famous lawsuit in which Whistler was awarded a farthing's damages. Famous for his evening scenes, called nocturnes, such as the well-known impression of Battersea Bridge in the Tate Gallery, London. Whistler often dressed as the typical stereotype of an artist.

Selected works: *Thomas Carlyle* (Glasgow Art Gallery); *Little White Girl: Symphony in White No. II* (Tate Gallery, London); *Arrangement in Grey and Black, No. I: The Artist's Mother* (Louvre, Paris).

Wilson, Richard (1714–82) Welsh Classical landscapist, influenced by Claude and Poussin. The National Museum of Wales, Cardiff, holds an important collection of his British and Italian landscapes. In 1776 he became librarian to the Royal Academy.

Selected works: *Caernarvon Castle* (National Museum of Wales, Cardiff); *Flora Macdonald* (Scottish National Portrait Gallery, Edinburgh); *Hadrian's Villa* (Tate Gallery, London, and Manchester City Art Gallery).

Wright, Joseph (1734–97) English genre and portrait painter who specialised in fireside portraits and industrial scenes. A large number of his works are in his home town at Derby Art Gallery; he is known as Wright of Derby.

Selected works: *A Philosopher Giving a Lecture on the Orrery* (Derby Museum & Art Gallery); *An Experiment on a Bird in the Air Pump* (National Gallery, London); *Sir Brooke Boothby* (Tate Gallery, London).

Wyeth, Andrew Newell (1917–97) American figurative painter of scenes in Pennsylvania. His *Christina's World* in the Museum of Modern Art, New York, is probably the most famous American picture of the 20th century.

Selected work: *Young America* (Pennsylvania Academy of Fine Arts, Philadelphia).

Yeats, Jack Butler (1870–1957) Irish painter, born in London, brother of the poet William Butler Yeats. Jack Yeats is considered as his country's greatest modern artist.

Selected works: *Grief* (National Gallery of Ireland, Dublin); *The Two Travellers* (Tate Gallery, London).

Zoffany, Johann (1733–1810) German portraitist working in England from 1758, Italy from 1772 and India from 1783. Patronised by George III of England and a founder member of the Royal Academy.

Selected works: *Garrick, Ackman and Bransby in Lethe* (Birmingham City Art Gallery); *Self Portrait* (National Portrait Gallery, London); *The Bradshaw Family* (Tate Gallery, London); *Charles Towneley among His Marbles* (Towneley Hall Art Gallery, Burnley).

Zurbarán, Francisco de (1598–1664) Spanish Baroque religious painter whose earliest known painting, *Immaculate Conception* dated 1616, suggests he was schooled in the same naturalistic style as his contemporary Velazquez.

Selected works: *The Vision of St Peter Nolasco* (Prado, Madrid); *Death of St Bonaventure* (Louvre, Paris).

ART

Painting Movements and Terms

Abstract Art Non-representational forms, relying on line, form and colour, rather than realistic depiction. Originally formulated by Kandinsky c1912, the art form was embraced by all media, including sculpture. The early years of English Abstract art are represented in the Jim Ede collection at Kettle's Yard, Cambridge, which includes a large collection by Henri Gaudier-Brzeska and works by Nicholson and Brancusi.

Abstract Expressionism American painting movement developed in the 1940s from Surrealism, in which the idea is to make painting a spontaneous act, devoid of premeditation. Jackson Pollock and Willem de Kooning are the foremost exponents of Action Painting (or Tachisme, as it is called in France), using riotous swirls and splatters of colour. Rothko, Motherwell and Gorky were also Abstract Expressionists.

Academic Painting Traditional and figurative painting, often representing the work of a school or academy.

Action Painting see Abstract Expressionism.

Alla Prima Describes the technique, general since the 19th century but considered freakish and slapdash before then, of completing the picture surface in one session in full colour and with such opacity that neither any previous drawing nor underpainting (if in existence) modifies the final effect. The French term is 'Au Premier Coup'.

Altarpiece Decorated screen or panel placed behind an altar. The number of panels is indicated by the words diptych (2), triptych (3) or polyptych (many).

Armory Show, 1913 This exhibition introduced New York to modern European painting and sculpture, including the work of Marcel Duchamp.

Arts and Crafts English aesthetic movement that grew out of disenchantment at the mass-produced and trite decorative arts that followed the Industrial Revolution. By 1861, the social reformer, poet and designer William Morris had co-founded a firm of interior decorators dedicated to recapturing the essence and quality of medieval craftmanship. Together with artists Edward Burne-Jones and Ford Madox Brown, and architect Philip Webb, Morris set out to produce hand-crafted jewellery, wallpaper, textiles, furniture and books. Many of Morris's wallpaper and furniture designs continue to be popular today.

Art Brut (Raw Art) Term coined by Jean Dubuffet, referring to spontaneous and untrained artworks, often by criminals or the mentally ill.

Art Nouveau (New Art) Art and design style developed at the end of the 19th century, incorporating angular or sinuous vegetable forms into furniture and architecture. The style had its roots in the Arts and Crafts Movement and was popular all over Europe and North America. Samuel Bing coined the term when he opened his Paris gallery under the name L'Art Nouveau in 1895, although in Germany it was known as 'Jugendstil', in Italy as 'Stile Floreale' or 'Stile Liberty', in Spain as 'Modernismo' and in Austria as 'Sezession'. Leading exponents included René Lalique (glassware), Louis Comfort Tiffany (lamps and jewellery), Alphonse Mucha (graphic design), Alfred Gilbert (sculpture), Charles Rennie Mackintosh (interiors, buildings, furniture), Victor Horta and Hector Guimard (architecture), and Klimt, Beardsley, Jan Toorop and Ferdinand Hodler (art).

Ashcan School Painting group preoccupied with depicting the low-life of New York in the early 20th century. George Wesley Bellows and his master, Robert Henri, were leading exponents.

Attribution An artwork is 'attributed' to an artist when its provenance has not been proven.

Au Premier Coup see Alla Prima.

Automatism The method of producing a painting spontaneously and without conscious control. Used by Surrealists such as Miró and Abstract Expressionists such as Pollock.

Avant-garde Literally 'Vanguard'. In the forefront of artistic development, often with a conscious rejection of traditional methods or prior art forms.

Barbizon School Mid-19th-century French school of landscape painting based in the village of Barbizon, near Fontainebleau. Members included Théodore Rousseau, Narcisse Diaz, Daubigny and Millet. As the precursors of Impressionism they painted *en plein air* observing light.

Baroque European style of art and architecture following the High Renaissance and Mannerism, c1600–1740. It was a particularly Catholic style, popular in Italy, France and Spain in churches and public buildings, and encouraged as an integral part of the Counter-Reformation to appeal to the emotions and the senses of a still largely illiterate population. It was also eminently suitable for dramatising the idea of the divine right of kingship, and was fostered by many monarchs, such as Louis XIV of France. Exponents included the sculptor Bernini and the painters Rubens and da Cortona.

Bauhaus School of modern art and design originally based in Weimar, founded and headed by the architect Walter Gropius in 1919. Its policy was to explore the avant-garde and to reforge the link between art and design and industry, which the Arts and Crafts Movement had largely surrendered. The Bauhaus moved to Dessau in 1925, and then to Berlin, where it was closed by the Nazis in 1933. The new Bauhaus was set up by László Moholy-Nagy in Chicago in 1937.

Blaue Reiter, Der (Blue Rider) German Expressionist group that exhibited in Munich in 1911 and 1912. Among its members was the Russian émigré Kandinsky, who developed one of the earliest forms of abstract painting, and Franz Marc. It was an early titlework of Kandinsky's which provided the name. Other key members were Georges Braque, Robert Delaunay, André Derain, Paul Klee, August Macke, Henri Rousseau and Maurice de Vlaminck. Representative works are at the Kunsthalle, Bielefeld, Germany.

Bloomsbury Group British group of the 1920s and 1930s, influenced by French Post-Impressionism and later developments. Members included Vanessa Bell, Roger Fry and Duncan Grant. Roger Fry staged the first Post-Impressionist exhibition in London in 1910.

Brücke, Die (The Bridge) Among the earliest of the German Expressionist groups, Die Brücke was founded in Dresden in 1905, and included the artists van Dongen, Erich Heckel, Kirchner, Nolde and Karl Schmidt-Rottluff. The group disbanded in 1913. Two of the best collections of artworks by Die Brücke are housed in the Brücke-Museum, Berlin, and the Kunsthalle at Bielefeld. Kirchner's portrait series of the Die Brücke members is in the Wallraf-Richartz Museum / Ludwig Museum, Cologne.

Cabinet Picture Small easel picture, usually not more than about 3 or 4 feet across, and often much less. The minor Dutch masters were the principal painters of this type of furniture picture at its best.

Camera Obscura Mechanical means of securing accuracy in drawing, particularly of topographical detail. Invented in the 16th century and consisting of an arrangement of lenses and mirrors in a darkened tent or box. The view seen through the lens is reflected through the mirrors on to a sheet of paper, so that all the observer has to do is to trace round the edges. Canaletto is known to have used the device in making studies for his 'Vedute' (views). Camera Lucida is a more sophisticated optical instrument incorporating a prism.

Camden Town Group British group formed in 1911 and influenced by the Post-Impressionists. Members included Sickert, Gore, Augustus John, Harold Gilman, Charles Ginner, Lucien Pissaro and Robert Bevan.

Capriccio A picture in which real scenes, forms and figures are rearranged to suit a particular composition.

Caravaggisti Those artists heavily influenced by the style of Caravaggio, particularly in his use of chiaroscuro – contrasting light and dark. A strong Dutch Caravaggist school in the 17th century included van Honthorst, Terborch and Dirk van Baburen.

Cartoon Originally a full-size preparatory drawing of an intended artwork (painting, fresco or tapestry).

Chiaroscuro (Italian, light and dark) Defined contrast of light and dark most particularly in candle-lit scenes. Term used to describe works by Rembrandt and Caravaggio.

Classicism The imitation of Classical art, i.e. the style of Ancient Greece or Rome. An ordered style based on the harmony of perspective and composition, devised in the early Renaissance period by Filippo Brunelleschi. Classicism influenced thinking in the Renaissance period, leading to the philosophies of Platonism and Humanism, and the stories of Homer and other ancients provided a host of popular subjects which were applied to portraits, history subjects (Titian, Jacques-Louis David) and landscape (Poussin, Claude) into the 18th century. The Stoicism of ancient Rome provided the inspiration for the Neo-classical reaction to the Rococo style in the 1780s. In the 19th century the more mundane details of life in ancient Greece or Rome became the vehicle for finely executed decorative works by Leighton, Alma-Tadema and Albert Moore.

CoBrA Painting group that drew members from Copenhagen, Brussels and Amsterdam, including Appel and Jorn; founded in 1948. Their style incorporated violent figurative forms with Action Painting. Collections are in the Stedelijk Museum,

Amsterdam, the Stedelijk Van Abbe-Museum, Eindhoven, and the Museum voor Schone Kunsten, Ghent.

Collage   Picture built up wholly or partly from pieces of paper, cloth or other material stuck on to the canvas or other ground. The word comes from the French *coller* (to stick). The device was much used by the early Cubists and by the Dadaists, such as Kurt Schwitters. In his last years Matisse used pieces of coloured paper as a complete substitute for painting.

Colorfield Painting   American offshoot of Abstract Expressionism and Minimalism, exploring monochromes or restricted contrasts in paint. The original of this idea was Malevich's *Black Square* of 1913. Rothko and Klein were typical exponents.

Constructivism   Russian abstract sculptural and architectural movement from 1917 to 1921, founded by Vladimir Tatlin and developed by Naum Gabo and Antoine Pevsner, whose interest centred on movement in space and a reflection of the modern age.

Counterproof   Mirror-image reproduction made by damping an original drawing or engraving, laying a damp sheet of clean paper on it, and then running both through a press. It is sometimes done by an artist in order to bring a fresh eye to his/her work by seeing it in reverse, but it is also the commonest method of faking 'original' drawings. Such fakes are obviously easily detectable because of the reversal. An offset is the same as a counterproof but has a wider meaning, for example in printing.

Cubism   In 1907 Picasso and Braque began what was perhaps the first major development in painting away from figurative art. They were influenced by African tribal masks and by Cézanne, who looked at the world in terms of subtle coloured planes. This was the basis of Facet Cubism (1907–9). Analytical Cubism (1910–12) further fragmented basic shapes from all angles, and Synthetic Cubism (1913–14) totally recreated new objects. Delaunay (see Orphism), Léger and Gris were prominent Cubists. Although, as a particular style of art, Cubism developed into other things, it changed forever the way objects, and even the human form, were looked at.

Dada   Formulated as an anarchic form of Expressionism during World War I in Zurich, 1916, possibly by the poet Tristan Tzara. The main centres of Dada in Germany were in Berlin, Hanover and Cologne. Its purpose was to discomfit and enrage the viewer. One of its major exponents was Kurt Schwitters, whose *Elterwater Merz* is in the Hatton Gallery at the University of Newcastle upon Tyne. Other exponents included Man Ray, Jean Arp, Duchamp, Ernst, Hannah Hoch and Picabia. Dada eventually developed into Surrealism.

Euston Road School   Originally known as the Fitzroy Street School, this was a London-based school of painting and drawing, 1937–9, established by Pasmore, Claude Rogers and William Coldstream. It aimed to counteract the tendencies of Surrealism and abstract art by returning to more figurative and natural forms of expression. Exponents included Vanessa Bell, Eric Gill, Duncan Grant, Augustus John, Kenneth Martin, John Nash and Fred Uhlman.

Expressionism   Early 20th-century painting movement that expressed highly charged emotions and thoughts through colour, violence, distortion and exaggeration. The German Expressionist groups were among the first so to characterise their work, which itself developed further into Dada and Abstract Expressionism.

Fauves (Wild Beasts)   An initially derogatory label applied by the critics of artists such as Derain, Matisse, Rouault and Vlaminck when their work was exhibited in one room at the Paris Salon d'Automne of 1905. The distortion and flat patterns, along with the intensity of the colour, created a furore, and the Fauves were born. Matisse came to be regarded as their leader, although the movement itself had fallen apart by 1908 as a number of its members defected to Cubism.

Fête champêtre   Typical Rococo scene of lovers in an ideal setting, as epitomised by Lancret and Fragonard.

Fête galante   Pastoral masquerade in dreamlike setting, as painted by Lancret and Watteau.

Figurative Art   Artworks that contain recognisable objects.

Found Object (objet trouvé)   A Dadaist and Surrealist technique of taking any given object and displaying it as an art form, as in *Bicycle Wheel*.

Fresco   Wall-painting using water-based paints on damp plaster, particularly in European churches and ancient Greek and Egyptian temples. Giotto was one of the masters of fresco painting.

Futurism   Italian art movement developed in Venice c1909–15, embracing the machine and new technology. Balla, Carrà, Umberto Boccioni and Gino Severini were its leading exponents. The term was born in Paris, in an article in *Le Figaro* by the poet Filippo Marinetti (1876–1944). Although Futurism is sometimes used to mean any art more recent than 1900, as a discrete aesthetic movement it died early in World War I.

Genre   Type of subject painting or, more particularly, paintings of everyday life in a naturalistic style, reported without idealisation. Extremely popular in 17th-century Holland.

German Expressionism   Much of German Expressionism grew out of a painterly reaction to modernity, but most particularly to the horrors of World War I. Die Brücke was one of the first Expressionist groups, and the movement also embraced Der Blaue Reiter and Dada. Representative artists include Ernst Barlach, Beckmann, Grosz, Kirchner and Nolde.

German Romantic Painting   Early 19th-century forerunner of the English Pre-Raphaelite school. Artists were inspired by the collection of 14th and 15th century painting at the home of Bernhard August von Lindenau, now the Staatliches Lindenau-Museum, Altenburg. Friedrich, Philip Otto Runge and the Nazarenes are typical exponents.

Gothic   A generic term first used in the Renaissance period to describe the style of the 11th to 15th centuries. It was initially a critical term implying barbarism because the style made no reference to Classical precedents. In the 19th century medieval architecture and painting 'pre-Raphael' became the inspiration for a Victorian resurgence, led by the critic John Ruskin and the architect-designer A. W. Pugin, which produced 'Gothic' fantasies far removed from the original inspiration. William Morris, whilst also taking the medieval Gothic period for inspiration, went back to basics and developed the culture of craftsmanship and simple forms.

Grisaille   A painting done in tones of grey to define shadows or modelling. Often used in *trompe l'oeil*.

A
R
T

Happening An art form developed from the 1960s in which an artist participates in an action that encompasses the whole purpose of the piece, and once over is gone. Similar to Performance Art. Largely developed by Joseph Beuys.

High Victorian Art The British art of the 1870s until the turn of the century, epitomised by the languid classical beauties of Albert Moore, Leighton and Alma-Tadema – fabulously painted, very beautiful and often low on meaning. Fine collections are in the Lady Lever Art Gallery, Port Sunlight; Birmingham Museum and Art Gallery; and the Tate Gallery, London, as well as at Leighton's House in Holland Park Road, London.

History Painting After portraiture, the painting of uplifting scenes from history, the Bible or allegory was the highest form of art according to Reynolds. It was also used very effectively for propaganda purposes by the Neo-Classical painters such as Jacques-Louis David. (See his *Death of Marat*.)

Hudson River School 19th-century American landscape painting school, highly Romantic in feeling and glorifying the wonders of nature. The name is properly applied to the period after 1825 when leading exponent Thomas Cole, painter of *The Voyage of Life*, settled in New York. Other members include Albert Bierstadt, Asher B. Osmond and Frederick Church.

Impasto Word used to describe the thickness of the paint applied to a canvas or panel. When the paint is so heavily applied that it stands up in lumps, with the tracks of the brush clearly evident, it is said to be 'heavily' impasted.

Impressionism Essentially the painting of light and its effects on nature and objects. Developed in France in the late 19th century and influential all over Europe. Monet's *Impression: Sunrise* (Musée Marmottan, Paris) of 1872 was the work that suggested the name of the movement. Other leading protagonists included Cézanne, Degas, Morisot, Pissarro, Renoir and Sisley. The Impressionist exhibitions were held between 1874 and 1886. Seurat and Paul Signac took Impressionism a stage further with Pointillism.

International Gothic Late 14th-century form of Gothic which spread throughout Europe. Leading exponents were Gentile da Fabriano and Pisanello.

Kinetic Art Art that relies on real or apparent movement.

Land Art, Earth Art Arrangements of earth mounds or natural elements in situ, often in rural areas. Developed in the USA from the 1960s as a reaction to materialistic Pop Art. Richard Long is a leading exponent. Grizedale Forest in Cumbria is one of the foremost sculpture parks here, specialising in sculpture within natural settings.

Maestà (Majesty) A term used to describe a painting of the Virgin and Child enthroned, with saints or angels.

Mannerism The style that succeeded the High Renaissance, c1520–1600, exemplified by exaggerated figure drawing. Bronzino, El Greco, Michelangelo, Parmigianino and Pontormo were all Mannerists.

Metaphysical School Surrealist art group formed in Ferrara in 1917 by de Chirico and Carrà, which survived until 1920.

Minimalism American art movement in painting and sculpture, essentially paring ideas down to bare essentials. Exponents include Carl André and Richard Serra.

Mobile A form of sculpture invented in 1932 by Alexander Calder, and named by Marcel Duchamp. Usually a mobile consists of a number of shapes cut from wood, cardboard, plastic or metal, connected by wires or rods and suspended so that a gentle touch will cause the whole to revolve and produce transforming 3D patterns of planes, solids and colours, and sometimes sounds.

Modern Art Accepted as the course of art in the 20th century from Impressionism up to the present day, embracing all major artistic developments including Cubism, Expressionism, Surrealism, Abstract Art, Pop Art, Minimalism and Performance Art. Excellent British public collections are in the Tate Galleries in London, Liverpool and St Ives; and the Scottish National Gallery of Modern Art in Edinburgh.

Nabis (Prophets) French anti-Impressionist art group inspired by Paul Gauguin's use of outline and flat colour which exhibited from 1892 to 1899. Members included Bonnard, Denis, Paul Sérusier and Vuillard.

Nazarenes Group of early 19th-century German and Austrian Romantic religious painters, founded by Friedrich Overbeck and Franz Pforr.

Neo-classicism Often described as the art of the French Revolution, it was a late 18th-century reaction to the fussiness of the Rococo, embracing noble simplicity and stoic grandeur. Jacques-Louis David was its leading exponent in painting, and Antonio Canova in sculpture.

Neo-Impressionism A pre-Cubist movement which examined Impressionism from a scientific standpoint rather than an aesthetic one. An offshoot of Neo-Impressionism was Pointillism.

Neo-Plasticism Mondrian's term for his style of pure abstract art, first used in *De Stijl* magazine in 1917.

Neue Sachlichkeit An inter-war German brutal realism art style represented by Dix, Grosz and Christian Schad. The literal meaning is 'New Objectivity'.

Newlyn School Group of British painters based in the fishing village near Penzance, Cornwall, and dedicated to Plein air, following the lead in France. The school was founded by Stanhope Forbes (1857-1947) and his wife Elizabeth (1857–1912). Other members included Walter Langley (1852–1922) and Laura Knight (née Johnson) and her husband Harold.

New English Art Club British art group founded in 1886, which included George Clausen, Stanhope Forbes, Sargent, Steer and Edward Stott's work. The Club is well represented in the collection at Cartwright Hall, Bradford.

Norwich School A group of early 19th-century landscape painters led by Cotman and Crome.

Objet trouvé see Found Object.

Omega Workshops Co-operative workshop-cum-showroom at 33 Fitzroy Square, London, run by Roger Fry from 1913 to 1919, for the production of painted furniture, textiles, artefacts and decorative commissions.

Op Art (short for Optical Art) is a style of painting which manipulates overall patterns, using repeated shapes or undulating lines which give an optical illusion of movement and often dazzles the beholder. Victor Vasarely (1908–97) is often considered a precursor of the op art movement with his black and white geometrical paintings but the movement became established in the early 1960s by Bridget Riley when she began to use colour in her optical paintings. The term became popularised following the 1965 New York City exhibition 'The Responsive Eye' at the Museum of Modern Art.

Perspective   Quasi-mathematical system for the representation of three-dimensional objects in spatial recession on a two-dimensional surface, i.e. for the creation of an independent pictorial space as a microcosm of nature. The basic assumption of all perspective systems is that parallel lines never meet, but they appear to do so; and that, further, all parallel lines going in any one direction meet at a single point on the horizon, known as a vanishing point.

Pietà (Pity)   Painting or sculpture showing the dead Christ cradled in the lap of the Virgin Mary.

Plein air   19th- and 20th-century landscape painting carried out in the open air, depicting nature and light as realistically as possible, as opposed to the deliberate Classicism of Old Masters such as Claude Lorrain and Poussin. Plein airists included the Barbizon School, the Impressionists, the Pre-Raphaelites, Millais, Ford Madox Brown and William Holman Hunt.

Pointillism   Also known as 'Divisionism'. Seurat developed the Neo-Impressionist technique of using tiny dots of colour to build up form and subject; most notably used in his *Sunday Afternoon on the Island of the Grand Jatte*.

Pop Art   American-formulated art form embracing painting, graphic design and sculpture, and preoccupied with modern technology, materialism and advertising. Exponents included Warhol, Blake, Johns, Robert Rauschenberg, Hamilton, Hockney, Lichtenstein and Claes Oldenburg.

Post-Impressionism   Roger Fry of the Bloomsbury Group coined the term when he staged the 'Manet and the Post-Impressionists' Exhibition in London in 1910. They were artists whose chief feature in common was that they had rejected naturalism in various ways, through form, colour and subject, and included Cézanne, Denis, Gauguin, van Gogh, Picasso, Rouault, Seurat, Paul Sérusier, and Vlaminck.

Pre-Raphaelite Brotherhood   The dream of a new generation to return art to its original purity of form and colour by preferring truth to nature to the stylised ideals of the Royal Academy and the ground rules laid down by its first president, Reynolds. The group was formed in London in 1848 by the painters Dante Gabriel Rossetti, William Holman Hunt, Millais and James Collinson, the art critics William Michael Rossetti and Frederick Stephens, and the sculptor Thomas Woolner. The group itself was shortlived, as its members were following separate artistic paths by 1853, but its impact on contemporary Victorian art was far more long-lasting. Pre-Raphaelitism strongly influenced Ford Madox Brown, Burne-Jones, Augustus Egg, Frith, Hubert Herkomer, Watts, among others, and formed the basis of High Victorian Art. It was also a foundation stone of the Arts and Crafts Movement, led by William Morris, and the English Art Nouveau of Charles Rennie Mackintosh and the Glasgow School, Scottish painters of the late 19th century. The style also opened the way for a new class of art collectors in the form of major industrialists based in the north, important contemporary art galleries such as the Grosvenor Gallery, and satire in the form of Gilbert and Sullivan's *Patience* and the cartoons in *Punch*. Subject matter varies from the willowy and lush allegorical beauties of Rossetti and Burne-Jones to the real-life and religious subjects of Holman Hunt and Ford Madox Brown. Major collections of Pre-Raphaelite art are in the Tate Gallery, London; Walker Art Gallery, Liverpool; Lady Lever Art Gallery, Port Sunlight; Birmingham Museum and Art Gallery, and Manchester City Art Gallery.

Primitive   Term applied to pre-Renaissance art and provincial or naive art by untrained artists.

Provenance   The documented history – and hence authenticity – of an artwork: who created it, who owned it, etc.

Ready-Made   Term coined by Duchamp for his found objects, such as the urinal he exhibited at the 1913 Armory Show, signed 'R. Mutt'.

Realism   Term applied to the realistic painting of artists such as Courbet, using a precision of detail and natural colour without idealisation.

Renaissance   The 'rebirth' of art and ideas in Italy after the Dark Ages and Gothic art, starting in the 14th century. It had repercussions around the European world on artistic expression, intellectual discussion, religious thought and scientific experiment. It was inspired by the rediscovery of the Classicism of the ancient civilisations of Rome and Greece in Italy and the rise of humanism. The Early Renaissance period, up to c1500, includes the artists Giotto, Duccio and Uccello, and the first experiments in art with perspective and painterly modelling. The High Renaissance saw the development of architecture, sculpture and painting by men such as Michelangelo, Leonardo, Raphael and Titian, leading to Mannerism and the late Renaissance of Correggio, Veronese and the sculptor Benvenuto Cellini. Dürer was responsible for introducing new ideas into Germany, and Holbein the Younger into England. France embraced Renaissance ideals following the rise of Italian influence after the marriage of Catherine de' Medici to the future Henri II in 1533.

Rococo   18th-century French decorative style, epitomised by the paintings of Rigaud, Boucher, Fragonard and Watteau. It illustrated the dream world in which the nobility wished to live, of sunlit *fêtes galantes*, garden swings, cherry-picking and whimsical shepherdesses. The French Revolution forced them to face an unpleasant reality. Rococo also influenced painters, architects and sculptors in Austria , Germany and Italy.

Romanticism   The early 19th-century reaction to the cold formality of Neo-classicism, the style introduced a new depth of colour, expression and passion into painting not seen since Titian, particularly in the works of Delacroix and Géricault. Stylistically different Romanticists were William Blake, Constable, Friedrich, Fuseli, Turner, the Nazarenes and the Pre-Raphaelites.

Sacra conversazione   A painting of the Virgin and Child, often with saints or family in an informal setting, first depicted by Fra Angelico in the 15th-century. The term literally means 'Holy Conversation'.

Slade School of Art   London art school, founded 1871, that in the 1890s and under the professorship in 1918–30 of Henry Tonks produced some of the most important painters of British 20th-century art. Slade teachers and graduates included David Bomberg, Mark Gertler, Harold Gilman, Spencer Gore, Duncan Grant, Augustus John, Gwen John, Wyndham Lewis, Ambrose McEvoy, Paul Nash, C.R.W. Nevinson, Ben Nicholson, William Orpen, William Rothenstein, Matthew Smith, Stanley Spencer and Edward Wadsworth.

Socialist Realism   A realistic if stylised art form officially sponsored and sanctioned for propaganda purposes in the Soviet Union, where it was first defined in 1932, and later in China and Cuba.

A
R
T

Stijl, De ('The style') Dutch 20th-century art movement which embraced painting, sculpture, graphic design, interior design and architecture. Exponents include Mondrian, van Doesburg, Bart van der Leck and the architects Rietveld and Jacobus Oud. De Stijl architecture includes the Zonnestraal Sanatorium by Johannes Duiker, and Rietveld's Schröder house at Utrecht.

Suprematism Malevich produced his first non-representational Suprematist painting in 1913, *Black Square*, exploring elementary forms and restricted contrasts of colour which in turn influenced Expressionism, Abstract Art and Colorfield Painting.

Surrealism Art of the inner reality, of objects out of context, and spontaneous writing, developed from Dada, founded in 1924 by the poet André Breton and influenced by Sigmund Freud's ideas. Exponents included de Chirico, Dali, Duchamp, Ernst, Klee, Magritte, Miró, Man Ray and Tanguy.

Symbolism Late figurative style of painting, associated with the Art Nouveau period. Jan Toorop, Johan Thorn Prikker, Munch, Arnold Böcklin, Redon, Puvis de Chavannes, Rouault and Moreau were all exponents.

Tempera Although this term actually means any kind of binder which will serve to 'temper' powder colour and make it workable, in practice it is confined to egg tempera (using the yolk of the egg), which was until the late 15th century the commonest technique of painting easel pictures.

Tenebrism Sombrely atmospheric painting particularly as seen in the works of those early 17th-century painters, mostly Neapolitan and Spanish, who were much influenced by Caravaggio. The term literally means 'Dark colouring'.

Trompe l'oeil Illusionistic painting effect, such as painting a ceiling to look as if it is open to the sky. The term literally means 'Deceive the eye'.

Veduta (View) Detailed topographical painting of an existing place. Leading 'Vedutisti' were Guardi and Canaletto.

Vernissage The practice – once common, now discontinued – by which painters would enter an exhibition after the pictures had been hung but before it was open to the public, so that they could varnish and also retouch their pictures. Turner would often submit his pictures incomplete and take advantage of Vernissage (Varnishing Day). Nowadays the custom is merely to invite favoured patrons to see the pictures before the public are allowed in.

Vorticism Brief English movement from 1914 with similar influences to Futurism, led by Percy Wyndham Lewis.

Watercolour The English landscapists were particularly strong in their use of watercolour, especially the artists of the Norwich School, William Blake, Girtin, Bonington and Turner. Dante Gabriel Rossetti brought a new jewel-like richness to watercolour painting in the 1850s, which raised the medium from insipidity.

Young British Artists Movement having its foundation in the exhibition 'Freeze', organised while he was a student at Goldsmiths College, London, in 1988 by Damien Hirst, who became the most celebrated of the YBAs. Goldsmiths, which numbered Michael Craig-Martin among its most influential teachers, encouraged new forms of creativity. Leading artists have preserved dead animals (Hirst), presented her own bed (Tracey Emin) and made sculpture from women's tights (Sarah Lucas).

Artists (not listed in main table)

Amigoni, Jacopo (c1682–1752) Venetian history and portrait painter. The altarpiece of Emmanuel College, Cambridge, is his.

André, Carl (1935–) American Minimalist sculptor famous for his 120 bricks (*Equivalent VIII*) in the Tate.

Arp, Jean (1887–1966) French artist and co-founder of Dadaism.

Avercamp, Hendrick (1585–1634) Dutch landscape painter who specialised in winter scenes.

Baily, Edward Hodges (1788–1867) English sculptor whose most famous work is his *Nelson* for the column in Trafalgar Square.

Beechey, Sir William (1753–1839) English portraitist who was knighted for *George III and the Prince of Wales Reviewing Troops*.

Beerbohm, Max (1872–1956) English writer and caricaturist famous for his watercolours of Oscar Wilde and Edward VII.

Bell, Vanessa (1879–1961) English painter and decorative designer, sister of the writer Virginia Woolf.

Calder, Alexander (1898–1976) American kinetic sculptor, abstract painter and illustrator of children's books. Calder invented the mobile.

Canova, Antonio (1757–1822) Venetian Neoclassicist sculptor whose work includes *The Three Graces* and *Daedalus and Icarus*.

Christo (1935–) Bulgarian-born, American sculptor famous for his 'wrappings', e.g. of the Reichstag building. His full name is Javacheff Christo.

Cooper, Samuel (c1608–72) English miniaturist whose *Oliver Cromwell* (Buccleuch College) was his most famous work.

Cuyp, Jacob (1594–1651) Dutch landscape and animal painter, many of whose works are housed in the Dulwich Gallery, London.

Dadd, Richard (1817–86) English literary painter whose *Fairy Feller's Master-Stroke* is in the Tate. He murdered his father and was confined in an asylum.

Daumier, Honoré (1808–79) French caricaturist and political satirist.

Delaroche, Paul (1797–1859) French history painter whose *Children of King Edward* is housed in the Louvre.

Donatello (c1386–1466) Florentine sculptor whose work included his *David* and *St George Killing the Dragon* (properly, Donato di Niccolò.)

Dyce, William (1806–64) Scottish painter and pioneer of state art education in Great Britain.

Eyck, Hubert van (c1366–1426) Flemish painter; the brother of Jan van Eyck.

Gabo, Naum (1890–1977) Russian born, US artist; the brother of Antoine Pevsner, with whom he founded Constructivism.

Gérard, Baron François (1770–1837) French artist, born in Rome; his *Cupid and Psyche* is housed in the Louvre.

Giacometti, Alberto (1901–66) Swiss sculptor and painter best known for his attenuated sculptures of solitary figures.

Gibson, John (1790–1866) Welsh Neo-classical sculptor whose *Tinted Venus* is in the Walker Art Gallery, Liverpool.

Gilbert & George (1943– / 1942–) English avant-garde artists, noted for painting their faces gold and wearing identical outfits. Their full names are Gilbert Proesch and George Passmore.

Guardi, Giovanni (1699–1760) Venetian painter, born in Vienna, brother of Francesco Guardi.

Hamilton, Gavin (1723–98) Scottish painter in Rome, who pioneered the depiction of Homeric subjects in a severe manner.

Heartfield, John (1891–1968) German painter, originally Helmut Herzfelde, a leading member of Berlin Dada and a lifelong pacifist.

Hoppner, John (1758–1810) English portraitist whose masterpiece was *The Countess of Oxford*.

Hughes, Arthur (1830–1915) English painter associated with the Pre-Raphaelite Brotherhood, although never formally.

Ibbetson, Julius Caesar (1759–1817) English landscapist who specialised in the scenery of the Lakes and his native Yorkshire.

Judd, Donald (1928–1994) American Minimalist artist and sculptor who has geometric boxes built especially to use in his work.

Kiefer, Anselm (1945–) German avant-garde artist whose work tends to concentrate on German history.

Kline, Franz Joseph (1910–62) American artist who became an Abstract Expressionist around 1950, using black shapes on white canvas.

Le Brun, Charles (1619–90) French historical painter; the first director of the Gobelins tapestry works (1662).

Lear, Edward (1812–88) English landscape painter, youngest of 21 children, famous for his nonsense verse.

Liebermann, Max (1847–1935) German painter and etcher, leader of the German Impressionist school.

Lorenzo, Monaco (the Monk) (c1370–1425) Sienese painter in the International Gothic style who took holy orders in 1391.

Macke, August (1887–1914) German painter and leader of Der Blaue Reiter group killed in action in WWI.

Masson, André (1896–1987) French Surrealist painter and graphic artist who was famous for working whilst in a state of trance.

Moses, Anna Mary ('Grandma') (1860–1961) American Primitive artist who did not start to paint until she was 75 years old.

Newman, Barnett (1905–70) American painter who founded the 'subject of the Artist' school with William Baziotes, Rothko and Motherwell.

Nolan, (Sir) Sidney (1917–92) Australian artist noted for his series of Ned Kelly paintings, begun in 1946.

Oldenburg, Claes Thure (1929–) Swedish-born, US sculptor specialising in representing giant foodstuffs, such as hamburgers.

Pevsner, Antoine (1886–1962) Russian-born French Constructivist painter, brother of Naum Gabo.

Quelling, Arnold (1653–1686) English sculptor who collaborated with Grinling Gibbons on many works.

Rackham, Arthur (1867–1939) English artist best known for his illustrations of *Peter Pan* and of Hans Christian Andersen's fairy tales.

Ramsay, Allan (1713–84) Scottish portrait painter to George III of England.

Rauschenberg, Robert (1925–) American avant-garde artist specialising in works constructed from everyday rubbish. Also a noted Pop silk-screenist.

Ray, Man (1890–1976) American painter, photographer and film-maker; he co-founded the New York Dadaist movement.

Rousseau, Théodore (1812–67) French landscape painter whose best known work was *The Forest of Compiègne*.

Schiele, Egon (1890–1918) Austrian Expressionist painter who died in the influenza epidemic of 1918.

Signac, Paul (1863–1935) French painter akin to Seurat, but using mosaic-like patches of colour as opposed to dots.

Smith, David Roland (1906–65) American sculptor who specialised in welded metal pieces.

Tàpies, Antoni (1923–) Spanish painter; a founder member of the Dau al Set (Die with the Seven) and El Paso groups.

Tatlin, Vladimir (1885–1953) Russian painter and designer, the founder of Constructivism, whose model *Monument to the Third International* was never built.

Teniers, the Elder, David (1582–1649) Flemish genre painter whose best-known work is *Temptation of St Anthony*.

Tenniel, (Sir) John (1820–1914) English illustrator and political satirist (especially in *Punch*), best known for his illustrations of Lewis Carroll's *Alice in Wonderland* and *Through the Looking Glass*.

Tinguely, Jean (1925–91) Swiss sculptor who pioneered kinetic and auto-destructive art.

Twygge, Richard (1476–1510) English painter on glass whose work can be seen in many Malvern buildings.

Van Loo, Charles André (Carle) (1705–65) Prolific French artist and Rococo decorator; principle painter to Louis XV from 1762; the most talented of the artistic Van Loo family.

Van Loo, Jean-Baptiste (1684–1745) French portrait painter in England also notable for historical subjects. Brother of Charles André.

Wilkie, (Sir) David (1785–1841) Scottish painter famous for his genre pictures in the Dutch style, eg, *Card Players*, and *Penny Wedding*.

Zincke, Christian Frederick (c1683–1767) German enamel portraitist in London from 1714.

ART

Famous Works of Art

Paintings	Artist	Location
Abduction of Rebecca, The	Delacroix	Louvre, Paris
Absinthe Drinker, The	Manet	Copenhagen
Accommodations of Desire	Dali	Mr & Mrs Julien Levy Collection, Bridgewater, Connecticut
Adam and Eve	Dürer	Prado, Madrid
Adam and Eve in Paradise	Brueghel	Mauritshuis, The Hague
Adonis in Y-Fronts	Hamilton, Richard	Wolverhampton Art Gallery
Adoration of the Kings, The	Brueghel the Elder (Pieter)	Musées Royaux des Beaux-Arts, Brussels
Adoration of the Kings, The	Correggio	Brera, Milan
Adoration of the Kings, The	Veronese	National Gallery, London
Adoration of the Lamb, The	Jan van Eyck	Altarpiece of St Bavo Cathedral, Ghent
Adoration of the Magi, The	Bassano	Kunsthistorisches Museum, Vienna
Adoration of the Magi, The	Bosch	Johnson Collection, Philadelphia
Adoration of the Magi, The	Botticelli	Uffizi, Florence (1475) & Washington National Gallery, DC (1482)
Adoration of the Magi, The (1500)	Dürer	Uffizi, Florence
Adoration of the Magi, The	Leonardo da Vinci	Uffizi, Florence
Adoration of the Magi, The (1446)	Lippi	National Gallery, Washington DC
Adoration of the Magi, The (1479)	Memling	Memling Museum, Bruges
Adoration of the Magi, The	Velazquez	Prado, Madrid
Adoration of the Magi, The (tapestry)	Burne-Jones	Exeter College, Oxford
Adoration of the Shepherds, The	Bassano	Hampton Court Palace, London
Adoration of the Shepherds, The	Caravaggio	Museo Nazionale, Messina
Allegory of Fortitude and Wisdom	Tiepolo	Ca' Rezzonico, Venice
Allegory of Spring (aka La Prima vera)	Botticelli	Uffizi, Florence
Ambassadors, The	Holbein the Younger	National Gallery, London
Anatomy Lesson of Dr Jan Deyman	Rembrandt	Rijksmuseum, Amsterdam
Anatomy Lesson of Dr Nicolaes Tulp	Rembrandt	Mauritshuis, The Hague
Andromeda	Rembrandt	Mauritshuis, The Hague
Angelus, The	Millet	Louvre, Paris
Anna Selbdritt	Dürer	Metropolitan Museum of Art, New York
Anne of Cleves	Holbein the Younger	Victoria and Albert Museum, London
Annunciation, The	Duccio di Buoninsegna	National Gallery, London
Annunciation, The	Jan van Eyck	National Gallery, Washington DC
Annunciation, The	Goya	Private Spanish Collection
Annunciation, The	Leonardo da Vinci	Versions in the Uffizi, Florence and Louvre, Paris
Anthony and Cleopatra	Steen	Kunstsammlung der Universität, Göttingen, Germany
Antibes	Monet	Toledo Museum of Art
Aristotle Contemplating the Bust of Homer	Rembrandt	Metropolitan Museum of Art, New York
Arnolfini Wedding, The	van Eyck, Jan	National Gallery, London
Around the Fish	Klee	Museum of Modern Art, New York
Arrangement in Grey and Black; No. 1: The Artist's Mother	Whistler	Louvre, Paris
Arrangement in Grey and Black; No. 2: Thomas Carlyle	Whistler	Glasgow Art Gallery
Artist and His Wife, The	Metsu	Metropolitan Museum of Art, New York
Ascension of Christ, The	Correggio	San Giovanni Church, Parma
Assumption	Titian	S. Maria dei Frara, Venice
Assumption of the Virgin	Correggio	Parma Cathedral
Assumption of the Virgin	El Greco	Church of Santo Domingo el Antiguo, Toledo, Spain
At the Bar	Toulouse-Lautrec	Kunsthaus, Zurich
At the Linen Closet	Hooch	Rijksmuseum, Amsterdam
At the Moulin Rouge	Toulouse-Lautrec	Art Institute of Chicago
At the Nouveau Cirque: Five Stuffed Shirts	Toulouse-Lautrec	Philadelphia Museum of Art
At the Races	Degas	Fogg Art Museum, Cambridge, Mass.
Avenue at Middelharnis, The	Hobbema	National Gallery, London

Paintings	Artist	Location
Backgammon Players	de Hooch	National Gallery of Ireland, Dublin
Balaam's Ass and the Angel	Rembrandt	Cognacq-Jay Museum, Paris
Ballet Scene, The	Degas	National Gallery, Washington DC
Banker Jabach and His Family, The	Le Brun	Staatliche Museen Preussischer Kulturbesitz, Berlin
Banks of the Seine, The	Henri Rousseau	Private Collection, Paris
Banquet of Anthony and Cleopatra	Tiepolo	Palazzo Labia, Venice
Baptism of Christ, The	Piero della Francesca	National Gallery, London
Bar at the Folies-Bergère, A	Manet	Courtauld Institute Galleries, London
Baron Schwiter	Delacroix	National Gallery, London
Bather	Renoir	Albright-Knox Art Gallery, Buffalo, NY (1879–90) and Sterling and Francine Clark Art Institute, Williamstown, Mass. (1881)
Bather, The	Cézanne	Museum of Modern Art, New York
Bathers	Renoir	Tyson Collection, Philadelphia
Bathsheba	Rembrandt	Louvre, Paris
Battle between Two Stags	Courbet	Louvre, Paris
Battle of Austerlitz	François Gérard	Versailles
Beach at Trouville, The	Monet	Tate Gallery, London
Beggar's Opera, The	Hogarth	Tate Gallery, London
Belle Jardinière, La	Raphael	Louvre, Paris
Belshazzar's Feast	Rembrandt	National Gallery, London
Bentheim Castle	Jacob van Ruysdael	National Gallery of Ireland, Dublin
Bicycle Wheel	Duchamp	Museum of Modern Art
Birth of Venus, The	Botticelli	Uffizi, Florence
Blind Girl, The	Millais	Birmingham City Museum & Art Gallery
Blonde with Bare Breasts	Manet	Louvre, Paris
Blue Boy, The	Gainsborough	Huntington Library & Gallery, San Marino, California
Blue Mountain	Kandinsky	Guggenheim Museum, New York
Blue Rider, The	Kandinsky	Ernst Bührle Collection, Zürich
Blue Vase, The	Cézanne	Louvre, Paris
Boat during the Flood, The	Sisley	Louvre, Paris
Boatbuilding near Flatford Mill	Constable	Victoria and Albert Museum, London
Boy Bitten by a Lizard	Caravaggio	Louvre, Paris
Boy in a Red Waist-Coat	Cézanne	Mr & Mrs Paul Mellon Collection, Upperville, Vancouver
Boyhood of Raleigh, The	Millais	Tate Gallery, London
Breaking Wave of Kanagawa, The	Hokusai	One of 36 Views of Mt Fuji series, Art Institute of Chicago
Broadway Boogie Woogie	Mondrian	Museum of Modern Art, New York
Bubbles	Millais	Lever Foundation Collection
Burial of the Count de Orgaz	El Greco	Church of Santo Tomé, Toledo, Spain
Calling of St Matthew, The	Caravaggio	Contarelli Chapel, S. Luigi dei Francesci, Rome
Calvary	Bassano	Fitzwilliam Museum, Cambridge
Capt Woodes Rogers and Family	Hogarth	National Maritime Museum, Greenwich
Capture of Samson	Rembrandt	Dahlem Museums, Berlin
Card Players	Cézanne	Metropolitan Museum of Art, New York
Cardinal Richelieu	Champaigne	Louvre, Paris
Carrying of the Cross	Van Dyck	St Paul's, Antwerp
Cascade, The	Henri Rousseau	Art Institute of Chicago
Chair and the Pipe, The (aka Van Gogh's Chair)	Van Gogh	Tate Gallery, London
Chancellor Séguier, The	Le Brun	Louvre, Paris
Charge of the Mamelukes, The	Goya	Prado, Madrid
Charging Chasseur, The	Géricault	Louvre, Paris
Charles Brandon	Holbein the Younger	Windsor Castle
Charles I and Henrietta Maria with Their Children	Van Dyck	Windsor Castle
Charles I, King of England	Van Dyck	Louvre, Paris
Charles VII	Fouquet	Louvre, Paris
Chess Players, The	Duchamp	Philadelphia Museum of Art
Child among Rocks, The	Henri Rousseau	Philadelphia Museum of Art
Children of Edward	Delaroche	Louvre, Paris

ART

Paintings	Artist	Location
Christ among the Doctors	Veronese	Prado, Madrid
Christ before Pilate	Rembrandt	National Gallery, London
Christ Crowned With Thorns	Titian	Louvre, Paris
Christ Healing the Blind Man	Duccio	National Gallery, London
Christ in the House of His Parents	Millais	Tate Gallery, London
Christ Nailed to the Cross	Gerard David	National Gallery, London
Christ on the Cross	Goya	Prado, Madrid
Christ on the Cross	Velazquez	Prado, Madrid
Christ Taking Leave of His Mother	Correggio	National Gallery, London
Christina of Denmark, Duchess of Milan	Holbein the Younger	National Gallery, London
Church at Auvers, The	Van Gogh	Louvre, Paris
Church at Blainville	Duchamp	Philadelphia Museum of Art
Close Together	Appel	Rosenbaum Contemporary, Florida
Clothed Maja, The	Goya	Prado, Madrid
Colossus, The	Goya	Prado, Madrid
Composition in Black and White	Mondrian	Rijksmuseum Kröller-Müller, Otterlo, Netherlands
Composition in Diamond Shape	Mondrian	Rijksmuseum Kröller-Müller, Otterlo, Netherlands
Composition II	Kandinsky	State Tretyakov Gallery, Moscow
Conversion of St Paul, The	Michelangelo	Pauline Chapel, Vatican
Conversion of St Paul, The	Caravaggio	Sta Maria del Popolo, Rome
Conversion of St Paul, The	Brueghel the Elder (Pieter)	Kunsthistorisches Museum, Vienna
Cornfield (etching)	Jacob van Ruysdael	Petit-Palais, Paris
Cornfield, The	Constable	National Gallery, London
Coronation of the Virgin, The	Fra Angelico	Uffizi, Florence
Coronation of the Virgin, The	Raphael	Vatican Museum, Rome
Country Festival near Antwerp	Teniers the Younger	National Gallery, London
Cripples, The	Brueghel the Elder (Pieter)	Louvre, Paris
Crowning with Thorns, The	Bosch	Versions in the National Gallery, London & Escorial, Madrid
Crucifixion of St Peter	Caravaggio	Sta Maria del Popolo, Rome
Crucifixion of St Peter	Michelangelo	Pauline Chapel, Vatican
Cupid and Psyche	Van Dyck	Buckingham Palace, London
Cupid and Psyche	François Gérard	Louvre, Paris
Cure of Folly, The	Bosch	Prado, Madrid
Danae	Correggio	Borghese Gallery, Rome
Danae	Rembrandt	Hermitage, St Petersburg
Dance of Four Breton Women	Gauguin	Neue Pinakothek, Munich
Dancer	Renoir	National Gallery of Art, Washington DC
Dancers, The	Degas	Toledo Museum of Art, Toledo, Ohio
Dead Man, The	Chagall	Marc Chagall Collection, Saint-Paul, France
Dead Marat, The	Jacques-Louis David	Louvre, Paris
Death and Fire	Klee	Kunstmuseum, Berne
Death of the Virgin	Brueghel the Elder (Pieter)	National Gallery, London
Death of the Virgin	Caravaggio	Louvre, Paris
Dedham Lock and Mill	Constable	Victoria and Albert Museum, London
Déjeuner sur l'herbe, Le	Manet	Louvre, Paris
Demoiselles d'Avignon, Les	Picasso	Museum of Modern Art, New York
Deposition in the Tomb, The	Weyden	Uffizi, Florence
Descent from the Cross	Rembrandt	Alte Pinakothek, Munich
Descent from the Cross	Rubens	Antwerp Cathedral
Dignity and Impudence	Landseer	Tate Gallery, London
Dinner Table, The	Matisse	Stavros Niarchos Collection, London
Duchess of Cleveland	Lely	Courtauld Institute, London
Duet, The	Metsu	National Gallery, London
Duke of Wellington, The	Goya	National Gallery, London
Dunes	Jacob van Ruysdael	Louvre, Paris
Early Sunday Morning	Hopper	Whitney Museum of American Art, New York
Ecce Homo	Bosch	Stadelsches Kunstinstitut, Frankfurt-am-Main
Ecce Homo	Caravaggio	Galleria di Palazzo Rosso, Genoa
Ecce Homo	Correggio	National Gallery, London
Ecstasy of St Diego of Alcalá	Murillo	Louvre, Paris
Education of Cupid	Correggio	National Gallery, London
Emmanuel Philibert	Van Dyck	Dulwich Gallery, London

Paintings	Artist	Location
Entombment of the Lord, The	Massys	Musée Royal des Beaux-Arts, Antwerp
Entry into Jerusalem, The	Van Dyck	Herron Museum of Art, Indianapolis
Erasmus	Holbein the Younger	Louvre, Paris
Erasmus in the Roundel	Holbein the Younger	Kunstmuseum, Basel,
(L') Estaque, l'embarcadère	Braque	Musée National d'Art Moderne, Paris
Evening Hour, The	Munch	Munch Museet, Oslo
Ex Voto of 1662	Champaigne	Louvre, Paris
Execution of Faliero	Delacroix	Wallace Collection, London
Fable of Arachne, The (aka The Spinners)	Velazquez	Prado, Madrid
Feast of the Rose Garlands, The	Dürer	St Bartholomew Church, Venice
Field of Waterloo, The	Turner	Tate Gallery, London
Fight between Carnival and Lent, The	Brueghel the Elder (Pieter)	Kunsthistorisches Museum, Vienna
Fighting Temeraire, The	Turner	National Gallery, London
First Abstract Watercolour	Kandinsky	Nina Kandinsky Collection, Neuilly-sur-Seine
Fishing Party, A	Hogarth	Dulwich Gallery, London
Flatford Mill on the River Stour	Constable	Tate Gallery, London
Flight into Egypt	Bassano	Bassano, Italy
Football Players	Henri Rousseau	Guggenheim Museum, New York
Fortune-Teller (aka La Zingara)	Caravaggio	Louvre, Paris
Four Saints	Correggio	Metropolitan Museum of Art, New York
Frau Adele Bloch-Bauer	Klimt	Österreichische Galerie, Vienna
Frau Fritza Riedler	Klimt	Österreichische Galerie, Vienna
From the Week of Hell '94	Emin	Tate Britain, London
Fuji in Spring	Hokusai	Art Institute of Chicago
Galacidalacideoxyribonucleicacid	Dali	New England Merchant Bank, Boston, Mass.
Garden of Earthly Delights, The	Bosch	Prado, Madrid
Gardener, The	Cézanne	Tate Gallery, London
Garrick in the Character of Richard III	Hogarth	Earl of Feversham Collection
Gilles and His Family	Watteau	Wallace Collection, London
Gioconda, La (aka Mona Lisa)	Leonardo da Vinci	Louvre, Paris
Girl Asleep, A	Vermeer	Metropolitan Museum of Art, New York
Girl Balancing on a Ball	Picasso	Pushkin Museum, Moscow
Girl Drinking Wine with a Gentleman	Vermeer	Staatliche Museen Preussischer Kulturbesitz, Berlin
Girl in the Artist's Studio	Toulouse-Lautrec	Kunsthalle, Bremen
Girl With a White Dog	Freud	Tate Britain, London
Girl with Bare Feet	Picasso	Picasso Museum, Paris
Gleaners, The	Millet	Louvre, Paris
Golconda	Magritte	D and J de Menil Collection, Houston, Texas
Goldfish and Sculpture	Matisse	Museum of Modern Art, New York
Good Samaritan, The	Hogarth	St Bartholomew's Hospital, London
Graham Children, The	Hogarth	National Gallery, London
Greenwich Hospital from the North Bank of the Thames	Canaletto	National Maritime Museum, Greenwich
Grey Tree, The	Mondrian	Haags Gemeentemuseum, The Hague
Guernica	Picasso	Prado, Madrid
Guillaume Budé	Clouet the Younger	Metropolitan Museum of Art, New York
Gypsy Girl	Hals	Louvre, Paris
Half-Past Three	Chagall	Philadelphia Museum of Art
Hamlet (aka Young Man Holding a Skull)	Hals	Richard Proby Collection, Peterborough
Hay Wain, The	Bosch	Prado, Madrid
Haywain, The	Constable	National Gallery, London
Haystacks at Giverny	Monet	Josef Rosensaft Collection, New York
Henry VIII	Holbein the Younger	Thyssen-Bornemisza Collection, Castagnola, Switzerland
Hercules and Antaeus	Cranach the Elder	Private Collection, Garmisch-Partenkirchen, Germany
Hercules Killing the Stymphalian Birds	Dürer	Germanisches Nationalmuseum, Nürnberg

ART

Paintings	Artist	Location
Holy Family	Michelangelo	Uffizi, Florence
Holy Family	Turner	Tate Gallery, London
Holy Family on the Steps	Poussin	National Gallery, Washington DC
Holy Family with St James	Correggio	Hampton Court Palace, London
Holy Family (aka The Two Trinities)	Murillo	National Gallery, London
Home Sweet Home	Hirst	Gagosian Gallery, New York
Hope	Watts	Tate Gallery, London
Horatius Cocles Defending Rome	Le Brun	Dulwich Gallery, London
House by the Railroad	Hopper	Museum of Modern Art, New York
Hunters in the Snow	Brueghel the Elder (Pieter)	Kunsthistorisches Museum, Vienna
Hyde Park, London	Monet	Philadelphia Museum of Art
I and the Village	Chagall	Museum of Modern Art, New York
I Want You Because I Can't Have You	Hirst	Private Collection
L'île de Cythère	Watteau	J Heugel Collection, Paris
Impression: Sunrise	Monet	Musée Marmottan, Paris
In the Circus Fernando: The Ringmaster	Toulouse-Lautrec	Art Institute of Chicago
In the Field	Van Gogh	Rijksmuseum, Vincent Van Gogh, Amsterdam
Inventions of the Monsters	Dali, Salvador	Art Institute of Chicago
Jane Seymour	Holbein the Younger	Kunsthistorisches Museum, Vienna
Jewish Bride, The	Rembrandt	Rijksmuseum, Amsterdam
Jewish Cemetery	Jacob van Ruysdael	Gemäldegalerie, Dresden
Job and His Wife	Dürer	Wallraf-Richartz-Museum, Cologne
Josephine Bonaparte	François Gérard	Louvre, Paris
Judgement of Paris, The	Cranach the Elder	Kunsthalle, Karlsruhe,
Judgement of Paris, The	Rubens	National Gallery, London
Judgement of Solomon	Giorgione	Uffizi, Florence
Juggler, The	Chagall	Art Institute of Chicago
Jupiter and Io	Correggio	Kunsthistorisches Museum, Vienna
King Charles on Horseback	Van Dyck	National Gallery, London
King Cophetua and the Beggar Maid	Burne-Jones	Tate Gallery, London
King's Wife, The (aka Women with Mangoes)	Gauguin	Pushkin Museum, Moscow
Kiss, The	Klimt	Österreichische Galerie, Vienna
Kitchen-Maid, The (1658)	Vermeer	Rijksmuseum, Amsterdam
Lady Reading a Letter at an Open Window, A	Vermeer	Gemäldegalerie, Dresden
Lamentation	Giotto	S. Maria Annunziata dell'Arena, Padua
Lamentation for Christ	Van Dyck	Alte Pinakothek, Munich
Lamentation over St Sebastian	La Tour	Staatliche Museen Preussischer Kulturbesitz, Berlin
Landscape with a Bridge	Altdorfer	National Gallery, London
Large Glass, The	Duchamp	Philadelphia Museum of Art; replica by Richard Hamilton in the Tate Gallery, London
Last Judgement, The	Michelangelo	Sistine Chapel, Vatican
Last Supper, The	Dali	National Gallery, Washington DC
Last Supper, The	Holbein the Younger	Kunstmuseum, Basel, Switzerland
Last Supper, The (mural)	Leonardo da Vinci	Convent of S. Maria delle Grazie, Milan
Laughing Cavalier, The	Hals	Wallace Collection, London
Le Plongeur	Hockney	Cartwright Hall Art Gallery, Bradford
Leaping Horse, The	Constable	Royal Academy of Arts, London
Leda	Correggio	Berlin Museum
Liberty Leading the People	Delacroix	Louvre, Paris
Light of the World, The	Holman Hunt	Keble College, Oxford
Linlithgow Palace	Turner	Walker Gallery, Liverpool
Little Street, The	Vermeer	Rijksmuseum, Amsterdam
Loge, La (aka The Theatre Box)	Renoir	Courtauld Institute, London
Lucretia	Dürer	Alte Pinakothek, Munich
Luncheon, The	Manet	Neue Staatsgalerie, Munich
Luncheon of the Boating Party, The	Renoir	Phillips Collection, Washington DC
Lute Player, The	Caravaggio	Hermitage, St Petersburg
MacNab, The	Raeburn	John Dewar & Sons Collection
Mad Woman with a Mania of Envy	Géricault	Musée des Beaux-Arts, Lyons
Madame Charpentier and Her Children	Renoir	Metropolitan Museum of Art, New York
Mademoiselle Gachet at the Piano	Van Gogh	Kunstmuseum, Basel
Madhouse, The	Goya	Dallas, Texas

Paintings	Artist	Location
Madonna in Glory, The	Giotto	Uffizi, Florence
Madonna of St Jerome, The	Correggio	National Gallery, Parma
Madonna of the Basket, The	Correggio	National Gallery, London
Madonna of the Goldfinch, The	Raphael	Uffizi, Florence
Madonna of the Rosary	Van Dyck	Oratorio del Rosario, Palermo
Madonna of the Star	Fra Angelico	Museo di San Marco, Florence
Madonna with Angels and Saints	Gerard David	Musée des Beaux-Arts, Rouen
Madonna with Chancellor Rolin, The	Jan van Eyck	Louvre, Paris
Madonna with Musical Angels	Dürer	Staatliche Museen Preussischer Kulturbesitz, Berlin
Madonna with the Carnation	Leonardo da Vinci	Alte Pinakothek, Munich
Maestà	Duccio di Buoninsegna	Cathedral Museum, Siena
Maids of Honour, The (aka Las Meninas)	Velazquez	Prado, Madrid
Man with a Straw Hat, The	Cézanne	Metropolitan Museum of Art, New York
Market Cart, The	Gainsborough	Tate Gallery, London
Marriage at Cana	Veronese	Louvre, Paris
Marriage of Isaac and Rebecca, The (aka The Mill)	Claude Lorrain	National Gallery, London
Mars and Venus	Botticelli	National Gallery, London
Marsh in the Woods	Jacob van Ruysdael	Hermitage, St Petersburg
Massacre at Chios, The	Delacroix	Louvre, Paris
Massacre of the Innocents, The	Brueghel the Elder (Pieter)	Hampton Court Palace, London
Meninas, Las (aka Maids of Honour)	Velazquez	Prado, Madrid
Merlin and Nimue	Burne-Jones	Victoria and Albert Museum, London
Merry Company, The	Hals	Metropolitan Museum of Art, New York
Merry Drinker, The	Hals	Rijksmuseum, Amsterdam
Militia Company of Captain Frans Banning Cocq, The (aka Night Watch)	Rembrandt	Rijksmuseum, Amsterdam
Milkmaid, The (1844)	Millet	Louvre, Paris
Milkmaid of Bordeaux, The	Goya	Prado, Madrid
Mill, The (aka The Marriage of Isaac and Rebecca)	Claude Lorrain	National Gallery, London
Miracle of St Bavo	Rubens	St Bavo Cathedral, Ghent
Miss Cicely Alexander: Harmony in Grey and Green	Whistler	Tate Gallery, London
Miss Harriet Cholmondeley	Hoppner	Tate Gallery, London
Mocker Mocked, The	Klee	Museum of Modern Art, New York
Model Reading	Hopper	Art Institute of Chicago
Mona Lisa (aka La Gioconda)	Leonardo da Vinci	Louvre, Paris
Mona Lisa with Moustache and Goatee	Duchamp	Ready Made (photograph) – various venues
Money Changer and His Wife, The	Massys	Louvre, Paris
Montgomery Clift was a Twin	Blake, Peter	Bilbao Fine Arts Museum
Morning Walk, The	Gainsborough	National Gallery, London
Mother and Child, Divided	Hirst	Astrup Fearnley Museum, Oslo
Mother beside a Cradle, A	Hooch	Staatliche Museen Preussischer Kulturbesitz, Berlin
Moulin Rouge, The	Toulouse-Lautrec	Národni Gallery, Prague
Mr and Mrs Andrews	Gainsborough	National Gallery, London
Mr and Mrs Clark and Percy	Hockney	Tate Britain, London
Mrs Robinson (aka Perdita)	Gainsborough	Wallace Collection, London
Mrs Siddons	Gainsborough	National Gallery, London
Mrs Siddons as the Tragic Muse	Reynolds	Henry E. Huntington Library, San Marino, California
Music Lesson, The	Metsu	Metropolitan Museum of Art, New York
My Parents	Hockney	Tate Britain, London
Naked Maja, The	Goya	Prado, Madrid
Nativity	Correggio	Brera, Milan
Night-School	Gerrit Dou	Rijksmuseum, Amsterdam
Night Watch, The (aka The Militia)	Rembrandt	Rijksmuseum, Amsterdam
Nighthawks	Hopper	Art Institute of Chicago
Nocturne in Black and Gold: The Falling Rocket	Whistler	Detroit Institute of Arts
Nocturne in Blue and Gold: Old Battersea Bridge	Whistler	Tate Gallery, London
Nude Descending a Staircase, Nos 1–4	Duchamp	Philadelphia Museum of Art (No. 2 is most famous)
Nurse and Child	Hals	Staatliche Museen Preussischer Kulturbesitz, Berlin

A
R
T

Paintings	Artist	Location
Oath of the Tennis Court	David	Louvre, Paris
Odalisque	Renoir	National Gallery of Art, Washington DC
Oedipus and the Sphinx	Ingres	Louvre, Paris
Officer and Laughing Girl	Vermeer	Frick Collection, New York
Old Man and the Courtesan, The	Massys	Pourtalès Collection, Paris
Old Walton Bridge	Canaletto	Dulwich Gallery, London
Old Woman Cooking Eggs, An	Velázquez	National Gallery of Scotland, Edinburgh
Old Woman Praying	Rembrandt	Residenz Gallery, Salzburg
Old Women of Arles	Gauguin	Art Institute of Chicago
Open Window	Matisse	John Hay Whitney Collection, New York
Order of Release, The	Millais	Tate Gallery, London
Oswolt Krel	Dürer	Alte Pinakothek, Munich
Owl and the Pussycat, The	Blake, Peter	Bristol Museum and Art Gallery
Painter's Daughters Chasing a Butterfly, The	Gainsborough	National Gallery, London
Pantry, The	Hooch	Rijksmuseum, Amsterdam
Paradise	Cranach the Elder	Kunsthistorisches Museum, Vienna
Parapluies, Les (aka Umbrellas)	Renoir	National Gallery, London
Paris through the Window	Chagall	Guggenheim Museum, New York
Parting of Hero and Leander, The	Turner	National Gallery, London
Pastoral	Bassano	Lugano, Switzerland
Payment, The	Cranach the Elder, Lucas	Nationalmuseum, Stockholm
Peasant Wedding	Brueghel the Elder (Pieter)	Kunsthistorisches Museum, Vienna
Peasant Woman in a Red Bonnet	Van Gogh, Vincent	Rijksmuseum Vincent Van Gogh, Amsterdam
Peasants Playing Music	Teniers the Younger	Alte Pinakothek, Munich
Peasants Returning from Market	Gainsborough	Toledo Museum of Art, Ohio
Pembroke Family, The	Reynolds	Wilton House, Wiltshire
People Like You Need to Fuck People Like Me	Emin	Lehmann Maupin Gallery, New York
Perdita (aka Mrs Robinson)	Gainsborough	Wallace Collection, London
Peter Denying Christ	Rembrandt	Rijksmuseum, Amsterdam
Pheidias and the Frieze of the Parthenon, Athens	Alma-Tadema	Birmingham City Gallery
Piano and Lute	Braque	Guggenheim Museum, New York
Piazza San Marco and the Colonnade of the Procuratie Nuove	Canaletto	National Gallery, London
Piazza San Marco Looking East from South of the Central Line	Canaletto	Fogg Art Museum, Cambridge, Mass.
Pipe and Bandaged Ear (Self-portrait)	Van Gogh	Leigh B. Block Collection, Chicago
Pluto and Proserpina	Rembrandt	Dahlem Museums, Berlin
Portrait of a Young Man	Dürer	Alte Pinakothek, Munich
Portrait of David Hockney in a Hollywood Spanish Interior	Blake, Peter	Tate Britain, London
Potato Eaters, The	Van Gogh	Rijksmuseum Vincent Van Gogh, Amsterdam
Poulterer's Shop, A	Dou	National Gallery, London
Primavera, La (aka Allegory of Spring)	Botticelli	Uffizi, Florence
Princess Charlotte and her Two Sisters (aka Three Eldest Princesses)	Gainsborough	Buckingham Palace, London
Punjab	Riley	Kelvingrove Art Gallery, Glasgow
Rabbi of Vitebsk (aka The Praying Jew)	Chagall	Art Institute of Chicago
Raft of the Medusa, The	Géricault	Louvre, Paris
Rain, Steam and Speed	Turner	National Gallery, London
Raising of Lazarus	Rembrandt	Los Angeles County Museum of Art
Raisng the Cross	Rubens	Antwerp Cathedral
Rake's Progress, The	Hogarth	Sir John Soane's Museum, London
Rape of Proserpine	dell Abbate	Louvre, Paris
Rape of the Sabine Women, The	Poussin	Louvre, Paris
Red Cloud, The	Mondrian	Haags Gemeentemuseum, The Hague
Red Tree, The	Mondrian	Haags Gemeentemuseum, The Hague
Rembrandt's Mother	Dou	Rijksmuseum, Amsterdam
Republic, The	Daumier	Louvre, Paris
Repudiation of Hagar	Tiepolo	Rasini Collection, Milan

Paintings	Artist	Location
Rest on the Flight into Egypt	Bassano	Milan
Return of the Dove to the Ark, The	Millais	Ashmolean Museum, Oxford
Return of the Prodigal Son	Rembrandt	Hermitage, St Petersburg
Rio dei Mendicanti	Guardi	Accademia Carrara, Bergamo
River, The	Monet	Art Institute of Chicago
Rocky Mountains and Tired Indians	Hockney	Scottish National Gallery of Modern Art, Edinburgh
Roffey Family	Reynolds	City of Birmingham Museum and Art Gallery
Rokeby Venus, The (aka The Toilet of Venus)	Velázquez	National Gallery, London
Room in Brooklyn	Hopper	Museum of Fine Arts, Boston, Mass.
Rouen Cathedral: Sunset	Monet	Museum of Fine Arts, Boston, Mass.
Rout of Comus, The	Landseer	Tate Gallery, London
Rout of San Romano, The	Uccello	National Gallery, London
Rucellai Madonna	Ducio	Uffizi, Florence
Ruins of Brederode Castle, The	Hobbema	National Gallery, London
Sabines, Les	Jacques-Louis David	Louvre, Paris
Sacrifice of Abraham (aka Sacrifice of Isaac)	Tiepolo	S. Maria dei Derelitti, Venice
Sacrifice of Isaac	Caravaggio	Uffizi, Florence
Sacrifice of Isaac	Rembrandt	Hermitage St Petersburg, and Alte Pinakothek, Munich
Sacrifice of Isaac (aka Sacrifice of Abraham)	Tiepolo	S. Maria dei Derelitti, Venice
Sad Shower in New York	Emin	Tate Britain, London
Sad Young Man in a Train	Duchamp	Peggy Guggenheim Collection, Venice
St Ildefonso	El Greco	Hospital de la Caridad, Illescas, Spain
St Jerome Curing the Lion	Dürer	Kunstmuseum, Basel
St Joseph the Carpenter	La tour	Louvre, Paris
St Lawrence Receiving the Treasure of the Church	Fra Angelico	Vatican Museum, Rome
St Luke Painting the Virgin	Weyden	Museum of Fine Arts, Boston, Mass.
St Mawes at the Pilchard Season	Turner	Tate Gallery, London
St Michael Vanquishing Satan	Raphael	Louvre, Paris
Salisbury Cathedral from the Bishop's Grounds	Constable	Victoria and Albert Museum, London
Salisbury Cathedral from the Meadows	Constable	Lord Ashton of Hyde Collection, Moreton-in-Marsh
Salvator Mundi	Antonello da Messina	National Gallery, London
Samson and Delilah	Van Dyck	Kunsthistorisches Museum, Vienna
School of Athens	Raphael	Stanza della Segnatura, the Vatican, Rome
School of Love, The	Correggio	National Gallery, London
Scream, The	Munch	Nasjonalgalleriet, Oslo
Seine au Pont d'Iéna, La	Gauguin	Louvre, Paris
Self Portrait with Badges	Blake, Peter	Tate Gallery, London
Self Portrait with Seven Fingers	Chagall	Stedelijk Museum, Amsterdam
Semiramis Founding Babylon	Degas	Louvre, Paris
Serenade	Steen	Národní Galerie, Prague
Seven Deadly Sins, The	Boschs	Prado, Madrid
Shoeing	Landseer	Tate Gallery, London
Shrimp Girl, The	Hogarth	National Gallery, London
Sick Child, The	Munch	Nasjonalgalleriet, Oslo
Sir Stanley Unwin	Kokoschka	Allen and Unwin Collection, London
Sir Thomas More	Holbein the Younger	Frick Collection, New York
Sistine Chapel ceiling	Michelangelo	Sistine Chapel, Vatican
Skating	Manet	Fogg Art Museum, Cambridge, Mass.
Skittle Players outside an Inn	Steen	National Gallery, London
Skull with a Cigarette	Van Gogh	Rijksmuseum Vincent Van Gogh, Amsterdam
Sleeping Gypsy, The	Henri Rousseau	Museum of Modern Art, New York
Smiling Woman	Augustus John	Tate Gallery, London
Snow, Moon and Flowers	Hokusai	Art Institute of Chicago
Sojourn in Egypt, The	Correggio	Uffizi, Florence
Soldier Drinks, The	Chagall	Guggenheim Museum, New York
Solitude	Chagall	Tel Aviv Museum

ART

Paintings	Artist	Location
Soup, The	Picasso	Art Gallery of Ontario, Toronto
Sower, The	Millet	Various locations
Spanish Singer	Manet	Metropolitan Museum of Art, New York
Spinners, The (aka The Fable of Arachne)	Velázquez	Prado, Madrid
Stag Hunt of the Elector Frederick the Wise	Cranach the Elder	Kunsthistorisches Museum, Vienna
Standing by the Rags	Freud	Tate Modern, London
Starry Night, The	van Gogh	Museum of Modern Art, New York
Still Life with Gingerpot	Mondrian	Haags Gemeentemuseum, The Hague
Still Life with Playing Cards	Braque	Rijksmuseum Kröller-Müller, Otterlo
Still Life with Tortoise and Hyacinth	Kokoschka	Österreichische Galerie, Vienna
Stoning of St Stephen	Rembrandt	Museum of Fine Arts, Lyons
Storm at Sea, The	Bruege the Elder (Pieter)	Kunsthistorisches Museum, Vienna
Street in Tahiti	Gauguin	Toledo Museum of Art, Ohio
Street Singer, The	Manet	Museum of Fine Arts, Boston, Mass.
Suicide's House, The	Cézanne	Louvre, Paris
Sunday Afternoon on the Island of La Grande Jatte	Seurat	Art Institute of Chicago
Sunflowers and Pears	Gauguin	Private Collection, Paris
Susannah and the Elders	Bassano	Bassano, Italy
Swineherd, The	Gauguin	N. Simon Collection, Los Angeles
Symphony in Grey and Green: The Ocean	Whistler	Frick Collection, New York
Symphony in White No. 1: The White Girl	Whistler	National Gallery, Washington DC
Taking of Christ, The	Van Dyck	Prado, Madrid
Tempered Elan	Kandinsky	Nina Kandinsky Collection, Neuilly-sur-Seine
Tempest, The	Kokoschka	Kunstmuseum, Basel
Tête-à-Tête Supper, The	Toulouse-Lautrec	Courtauld Institute, London
Theatre Box, The (aka La Loge)	Renoir	Courtauld Institute, London
Thirty-Six Views of Mt Fuji (series)	Hokusai	Art Institute of Chicago
Threatening Weather	Magritte	Penrose Collection, London
Three Dancers	Picasso	Tate Gallery, London
Three Eldest Princesses (aka Princess Charlotte and Her Two Sisters)	Gainsborough	Buckingham Palace, London
Three Flags	Johns	Whitney Museum of Art, New York
Three Graces	Raphael	Musée Condé, Chantilly
Three Lawyers in Conversation	Daumier	Phillips Collection, Washington DC
Three Women of Ghent	Jacques-Louis David	Louvre, Paris
Toilet of Venus, The (aka The Rokeby Venus)	Velázquez	National Gallery, London
Toilette, La	Toulouse-Lautrec	Louvre, Paris
Topers, The (aka Triumph of Bacchus)	Velázquez	Prado, Madrid
Tour Eiffel, La	Delaunay	Kunstmuseum, Basel
Tower of Babel	Brueghel the Elder (Pieter)	Kunsthistorisches Museum, Vienna
Transfiguration	Duccio	National Gallery, London
Trial of Moses	Giorgione	Uffizi, Florence
Trinity	El Greco	Prado, Madrid
Triumph of Bacchus (aka The Topers)	Velázquez	Prado, Madrid
Triumph of the Innocents, The	Holman Hunt	Tate Gallery, London
Tropical Forest with Monkeys	Rousseau, Henri	John Hay Whitney Collection, New York
Tuna Fishing	Dali	Paul Ricard Collection, Paris
Turkish Bath, The	Ingres	Louvre, Paris
Twittering Machine	Klee	Museum of Modern Art, New York
Two Haystacks	Monet	Art Institute of Chicago
Two Trinities, The (aka Holy Family)	Murillo	National Gallery, London
Ugolino	Reynolds	Knole House, Sevenoaks, Kent
Umbrellas (aka Les Parapluies)	Renoir	National Gallery, London
Uncle Dominic as a Monk	Cézanne	Private Collection, New York
Vampire	Munch	Munch-Museet, Oslo
Van Gogh's Chair	Van Gogh	National Gallery, London
Venus and Adonis	Titian	Prado, Madrid
Venus and Adonis	Turner	Tate Gallery, London
Venus and Cupid	Cranach the Elder	Staatliche Museen Preussischer

Paintings	Artist	Location
		Kulturbesitz, Berlin
Venus of Urbino	Titian	Uffizi, Florence
Victory Boogie Woogie	Mondrian	Burton Tremaine Collection, Meriden, Conn.
View of Delft	Vermeer	Mauritshuis, The Hague
View of Naples	Brueghel the Elder (Pieter)	Galleria Doria-Pamphili, Rome
Village Fête, The	Teniers the Younger, David	Hermitage, St Petersburg
Violin and Jug	Braque	Kunstmuseum, Basel
Virgin and Child with Saints	Duccio di Buoninsegna	National Gallery, London
Virgin and Child with Saints and Donor	Gerard David	National Gallery, London
Virgin in Prayer, The	Massys	Musée Royal des Beaux-Arts, Antwerp
Virgin of the Rocks	Leonardo da Vinci	Louvre, Paris and National Gallery, London
Virgin of the Rosary	Murillo	Archbishop's Palace, Seville
Vision of St Bernard	Lippi, Filippino	Badia, Florence
Visit, The	Alma-Tadema	Victoria and Albert Museum, London
Washerwoman, The	Daumier, Honoré	Louvre, Paris
Water-Lily Pool	Monet	Louvre, Paris
Water Mill, The	Hobbema	Wallace Collection, London
Way to Calvary, The	Brueghel the Elder, Pieter	Kunsthistorisches Museum, Vienna
Wedding Dance, The	Brueghel the Elder, Pieter	Detroit Institute of Arts
Wedding of Stephen Beckingham & Mary Cox	Hogarth	Metropolitan Museum of Art, New York
Whaam!	Lichtenstein	Tate Gallery, London
Wheatfields	van Ruysdael, Jacob	Metropolitan Museum of Art, New York
When Shall We Be Married	Gauguin	Kunstmuseum, Basel
Whistler's Mother (aka Arrangement in Grey and Black No. 1)	Whistler	Louvre, Paris
White Crucifixion	Chagall	Art Institute of Chicago
White Line	Kandinsky	Nina Kandinsky Collection, Neuilly-sur-Seine
Wild Poppies	Monet	Louvre, Paris
William Warham, Archbishop of Canterbury	Holbein the Younger	Louvre, Paris
Windmill in Sunlight	Mondrian	Haags Gemeentemuseum, The Hague
Windsor Beauties, The	Lely	Hampton Court Palace, London
Winter Palace	Riley	Leeds City Art Gallery
Woman and Her Maid in a Court	Hooch	National Gallery, London
Woman in an Armchair	Picasso	Picasso Museum, Paris
Woman Musician, The	Braque	Kunstmuseum, Basel
Woman Weighing Gold, A	Vermeer	National Gallery of Art, Washington DC
Woman with Pears	Picasso	Pushkin Museum, Moscow
Woman with the Hat	Matisse	Walter A Haas Collection, San Francisco
Women in a Brothel	Toulouse-Lautrec	Szépmüvészeti Museum, Budapest
Women of Algiers in Their Apartment	Delacroix	Louvre, Paris
Women with Mangoes (aka The King's Wife)	Gauguin	Pushkin Museum, Moscow
Woodcutter Courting a Milkmaid, The	Gainsborough	Woburn Abbey, Bedfordshire
Woods near Oele	Mondrian	Haags Gemeentemuseum, The Hague
World Upside-down, The	Steen	Kunsthistorisches Museum, Vienna
Wounded Cuirassier, The	Géricault	Louvre, Paris
Wounded Heron, The	Watts	Watts Gallery, Compton, Surrey
Wreck of a Transport Ship	Turner	Gulbenkian Foundation, Lisbon
Young Bacchus, The	Caravaggio	Uffizi, Florence
Young Lady with a Pearl Necklace	Vermeer	Staatliche Museen Preussischer Kulturbesitz, Berlin
Young Man Holding a Skull (aka Hamlet)	Hals	Richard Proby Collection, Peterborough
Young Man in a Garden	Hilliard	Victoria and Albert Museum, London
Young Mother, The	Dou	Mauritshuis, The Hague
Young Virgin Auto-Sodomized by Her Own Chastity	Dali	Carlos B Alemany Collection, New York

Paintings	Artist	Location
Young Woman Holding a Powder-Puff	Seurat	Courtauld Institute, London
Young Woman Standing at a Virginal, A	Vermeer	National Gallery, London
Yellow Christ, The	Gauguin	Albright-Knox Art Gallery, Buffalo, NY
Young Woman with a Water Jug, A	Vermeer	Metropolitan Museum of Art, New York
Young Women on the Banks of the Seine	Courbet	Musée du Petit Palais, Paris
Zingara, La (aka *The Fortune-Teller*)	Caravaggio	Louvre, Paris
Zoological Garden	Klee	Klee Foundation, Berne

NB: There are a number of points to be considered with reference to this section. The history of art is a complex subject and although it is traditional to fix a label on artists and their works, in fact not only is it often impossible to identify a painter with any one group, it is also just as precarious to attach one term to the whole oeuvre of an artist. Even the historical styles overlap in many instances. The problem is that painters do not like to be pigeonholed, as styles and moods change and very often one style or school may become defunct or develop into something else. In researching this section I have also found that the nationalities of artists, especially those of the Low Countries, are open to interpretation, dependent not only on place of birth or naturalisation but also on style. I have endeavoured to qualify any contentious entries so as to give a more complete picture of the nature of the artist and his or her work.

A problem when listing artworks is that not only are particular subjects covered as 'stock' pieces by numerous artists (such as *The Adoration of the Magi*) but also many individual artists often paint more than one version of a particular work – for example, Cézanne painted several versions of *The Card Players* and Millet painted several versions of *The Sower*. The final observation I have to offer in this web of intrigue is that when I came to list paintings in alphabetical order it occurred to me that many have alternative titles. For instance Vermeer's *The Kitchen-Maid* is listed in reputable sources with the alternative titles of *The Milkmaid*, *The Maid with a Milk Jug*, *The Cook*, *The Maid-Servant Pouring Milk* and *The Servant Pouring Milk*. I have listed only the most common variants in the table.

Art Movements and Schools: Some Members and Founders

Members / Founders (F)	Art Movements & Schools	Members / Founders (F)	Art Movements & Schools
Arp, Jean (F)	Dada	van Doesburg, Theo	Neo-Plasticism
Ball, Hugo	Dada	van Dongen, Kees	Post-Impressionism
Beardsley, Aubrey	Art Nouveau	Duccio di Buoninsegna (F)	Sienese School
Bell, Vanessa	Omega Workshops	Duchamp, Marcel	Dada
Bellows, George	Ashcan School	van Dyck, Anthony	Antwerp School
Blake, Peter	Pop Art	Emin, Tracey	Young British Artists
Bleyl, Fritz (F)	Die Brücke (The Bridge)	Ernst, Max	Dada
Bomberg, David	Kitchen Sink School	Ernst, Max	Surrealism
Bonnard, Pierre	Nabis	Forbes, Stanhope	Newlyn School
Braque, Georges (F)	Cubism	Fry, Roger (F)	Omega Workshops
Braque, Georges (F)	Fauvism	Funi, Achille	Novecento Italiano
Bratby, John	Kitchen Sink School	Gauguin, Paul	Pont-Aven School
Brown, Ford Madox	Pre-Raphaelite Brotherhood	Gauguin, Paul	Post-Impressionism
Brueghel the Elder, Pieter	Antwerp School	Gilman, Harold (F)	Camden Town Group
Burne-Jones, Edward	Arts and Crafts Movement	Ginner, Charles (F)	Camden Town Group
Burne-Jones, Edward	Pre-Raphaelite Brotherhood	Giulio Romano	Mannerism
Carrà, Carlo (F)	Metaphysical school	van Gogh, Vincent	Post-Impressionism
Cézanne, Paul	Impressionism	Goncharova, Natalia	Rayonnism
Cézanne, Paul	Post-Impressionism	Gore, Spencer (F)	Camden Town Group
de Chirico, Giorgio	Metaphysical School	Gowing, Lawrence	Euston Road School
Church, F. E.	Hudson River School	'Grandma' Moses	Primitivism
Coldstream, William (F)	Euston Road School	Grant, Duncan	Omega Workshops
Cole, Thomas	Hudson River School	El Greco	Mannerism
Cotman, John (F)	Norwich School	Grosz, George	Neue Sachlichkeit
Crome, John (F)	Norwich School	Hamilton, Richard	Pop Art
Dali, Salvador	Surrealism	Heckel, Erich (F)	Die Brücke (The Bridge)
Degas, Edgar	Impressionism	Hepworth, Barbara	St Ives Painters
Delaunay, Robert (F)	Orphism	Hirst, Damien (F)	Young British Artists
Delaunay, Robert	Synchronism	Hunt, William Holman (F)	Pre-Raphaelite Brotherhood
Delaunay Terk, Sonia (F)	Orphism	Kandinsky, Wassily (F)	Blaue Reiter (Blue Rider)
Denis, Maurice (F)	Nabis	Kirchner, Ernst Ludwig (F)	Die Brücke (The Bridge)
Derain, André (F)	Fauvism	Klee, Paul	Blaue Reiter (Blue Rider)
Dix, Otto	Neue Sachlichkeit	Knight, Laura	Newlyn School
van Doesburg, Theo (F)	De Stijl	Kokoschka, Oscar	Expressionism

Members / Founders (F)	Art Movements & Schools	Members / Founders (F)	Art Movements & Schools
Kooning, Willem de (F)	Abstract Expressionism	Picasso, Pablo (F)	Cubism
Ladbrooke, Robert	Norwich School	Piper, John	Neo-Romanticism
Larionov, Mikhail (F)	Rayonism	Pissarro, Camille	Impressionism
Léger, Fernand	Cubism	Pollock, Jackson (F)	Abstract Expressionism
Lewis, Wyndham (F)	Vorticism	Puvis de Chavannes	Symbolism
Lichtenstein, Roy (F)	Pop Art	Redon, Odilon	Symbolism
Lucas, Sarah	Young British Artists	Renoir, Pierre	Impressionism
Mackintosh, Charles Rennie (F)	Glasgow School	Riley, Bridget (F)	Op Art
		Rossetti, Dante Gabriel (F)	Pre-Raphaelite Brotherhood
Magritte, René	Surrealism	Rothko, Mark	Abstract Expressionism
Malevich, Kasimir (F)	Suprematism	Rouault, Georges	Expressionism
Manet, Edouard	Impressionism	Rouault, Georges (F)	Fauvism
Marc, Franz (F)	Blaue Reiter (Blue Rider)	Rousseau, Henri	Primitivism
Matisse, Henri (F)	Fauvism	Rousseau, Théodore	Barbizon School
Millais, John Everett (F)	Pre-Raphaelite Brotherhood	Rubens, Peter Paul	Antwerp School
Mondrian, Piet	Cubism	Schmidt-Rottluff, Karl (F)	Die Brücke (The Bridge)
Mondrian, Piet (F)	De Stijl	Seurat, Georges (F)	Pointillism
Mondrian, Piet (F)	Neo-Plasticism	Sickert, Walter (F)	Camden Town Group
Monet, Claude (F)	Impressionism	Sisley, Alfred	Impressionism
Moreau, Gustave	Symbolism	Sluijters, Jan	Post-Impressionism
Morris, William	Arts and Crafts Movement	Stella, Frank	Post-Painterly Abstraction
Morris, William	Pre-Raphaelite Brotherhood	Stokes, Adrian	St Ives Painters
Munch, Edvard	Expressionism	Sutherland, Graham	Neo-Romanticism
Nicholson, Ben	St Ives Painters	Tatlin, Vladimir (F)	Constructivism
Overbeck, Friedrich (F)	Nazarenes	Tintoretto	Mannerism
Parmigianino, Francesco	Mannerism	de Vlaminck, Maurice (F)	Fauvism
Pasmore, Victor (F)	Euston Road School	Vuillard, Edouard	Nabis
Pechstein, Max	Expressionism	Warhol, Andy (F)	Pop Art
Pforr, Franz	Nazarenes	Watteau, Jean-Antoine	Rococo

NB: The table above should be taken as a quick reference for identifying artists and groups. As has been stated previously, there is a distinct grey area in attempting to categorise painters – e.g. although Peter Blake was certainly identified with Pop Art in his early career, whether he would consider himself as such nowadays is debatable.

A
R
T

Art: General Information

Action Painting: aka	Abstract Expressionism
Adoration of the Magi (Botticelli)	The Medici family are depicted as the Magi
Angel of the North: details	Sculpted by Antony Gormley and situated on the site of an old coal mine next to the A1 at Eighton Banks, Gateshead, Tyne and Wear. The 20m (65ft) high figure in steel with a copper mixture has a wingspan of 54m (175ft), a weight of 200 tonnes (100 tonnes for the body and 50 tonnes per wing), and cost £800,000 to construct, largely funded by National Lottery donations. As the surface oxidises to form a patina the sculpture has become a rich brown colour
Arrangement in Grey and Black: nickname	Whistler's Mother
Art Deco	Refers to a decorative style of the 1920s and 1930s
Art Gallery: largest	The Hermitage in St Petersburg
Beggarstaff Brothers	Sir William Nicholson (1872–1949) and James Pryde (1866–1941), still-life and poster painters
Blue Boy: depiction of	Master Jonathan Buttall, a friend of the artist Gainsborough
Blue Period: Picasso	Between 1901 and mid-1904
Brueg(h)el: nicknames	Pieter (The Elder) – Peasant, Pieter (The Younger) – Hell, Jan – Velvet
Brueg(h)el: spelling	Pieter the Elder spelt the name with an 'H' until 1559 and his children resorted back to original spelling
Bubbles: subject	Millais' grandson, the future Admiral William James
Churchill Portrait (Sutherland)	Destroyed by Churchill's wife
Cire Perdue	Modern bronzes are made either in sand moulds or by the 'cire perdue' (lost wax) method, which consists of a model smaller than the mould, the space between being filled with wax and vent pipes inserted. The molten bronze is poured in the top and takes the place of the wax which has been melted out
Claude Lorrain Glass	Black convex glass used by artists to reflect the landscape in miniature and, in doing so, to merge details and reduce the strength of colour so that the artist is presented with a broad picture of the scene
Collage	Objects such as newspaper, string or cloth which are pasted onto

	paper or canvas. Picasso's *Still Life with Chair Caning* may have been the first example of collage
Constructivism	Russian art movement initiated by Vladimir Tatlin in 1913 and favouring the use of a 'Culture of Materials' which resulted in an art which had social purpose
Correggio	Named from the town in Modena where he was born
Cranach the Elder, Lucas: epitaph	Pictor Celerrimus (swiftest of painters) is how Cranach is described on his tombstone
Cubism: first picture	*Les Demoiselles d'Avignon* by Picasso
Customs Officer: former	Henri Rousseau (hence his byname 'Le Douanier')
Dada: formed where	In a nightclub in Zurich (Cabaret Voltaire) 1916
Duke of Wellington (Goya)	Stolen in 1961 but later found
Fakers: famous	Tom Keating faked Samuel Palmer paintings; Hans van Meegeren faked Vermeers
Frottage	Technique employed by Surrealists such as Max Ernst, which involves placing a piece of paper over an object and rubbing the paper with chalk or charcoal
Hay-Wain, The: farm	Willy Lott's farm
I Want You: Recruiting Poster	James Montgomery Flagg
Intaglio	Term used to describe types of printing such as etching and engraving whereby the design is incised as opposed to relief printing, such as wood cutting, where the raised portion creates the design
Killed a man in argument	Caravaggio in 1606 forced to flee Rome after killing a man in fit of temper
Knighted by Britain & Spain	Sir Peter Paul Rubens
Libel Action Against John Ruskin	James Whistler, for Ruskin's attack on his *Falling Rocket* (won the case but received only one farthing)
Madonna Rucellai	Now attributed to Duccio Di Buoninsegna: formerly thought to be a work of Cimabue (Vasari's attribution)
Magic Realism	Refers to a type of painting which combines a realistic technique with fanciful designs, as in the paintings of René Magritte and other surrealists. In its strict sense it refers to German realist art of the 1920s
Marsyas: details	The title refers to a satyr in Greek mythology who was flayed alive by the god Apollo. The PVC membrane has a fleshy quality and the dark red colour suggests something 'of the physical, of the earthly, of the bodily'. *Marsyas* confounds spatial perception, immersing the viewer in a monochromatic field of colour. It is impossible to view the entire sculpture from any one position. The sculpture comprises three steel rings joined together by a single span. The flute-shaped structure is 500ft long and 10 storeys high, filling the entire space of the Tate Modern's Turbine Hall
Montage	Form of collage but refers specifically to the use of components which are complete in themselves
Murdered His Father	Richard Dadd
Myra (Hindley): painter	Marcus Harvey painted this controversial painting on display at the 'Sensations' exhibition of 1997
Neo-Expressionism	Refers to an International art movement of the late 1970s and 1980s involving revival of expressionist concerns
Neo-Plasticism	Name used by Mondrian & van Doesburg for a type of art which avoids representation in favour of abstraction
Neo-Romanticism	British art movement existing before the Second World War which revived the interest in the Romantic landscapes of William Blake and Samuel Palmer
New Objectivity	Name coined by G.F. Artlaub to describe a group of German artists who rejected abstract culture of the 1920s
Novecento Italiano	Italian art movement of the 1920s which encouraged a return to the renaissance art
Novembergruppe	Formed in Berlin 1918 and advocating art for the masses
Obscene: exhibition closed as	Modigliani
Old Masters: highest prices at auction	1 Rubens *(Massacre of the Innocents)* £49.5m ($76.6m)
	2 Pontormo *(Portrait of Duke Cosimo I, de Medici)* $35.2m
	3 Rembrandt *(Portrait of a Lady aged 62, perhaps AP Uylenburgh)* $29.04m
	4 Canaletto *(The Old Horse Guards)* $17.6m
	5 Guardi *(Veduta della Giudecca e della Zattere a Venezia)* $15.3m
	6 Titian *(Venus & Adonis)* $13.61m

7   Hals *(Portrait of Tieleman Roosterman)* $12.7m
8   Rembrandt *(Portrait of a Bearded Man in a Red Doublet)* $12.6m
9   Canaletto *(Le Retour du Bucentaure Ader)* $12.43m
10   Michelangelo *(The Risen Christ* – drawing) $12.28m

Orphism	Term coined by poet Apollinaire in 1912 to distinguish the fragmented use of colour from the Cubist approach
Painting: highest price at auction	Van Gogh's *Portrait of Dr Gachet* fetched £44,378,696 in May 1990 when sold to Japanese businessman Ryoei Saito. It was subsequently repurchased by Christie's for one-eighth the price
Patina	Term used to describe the beautiful greenish surface alteration on a bust or statue caused by age
Pears Soap Advertisement	*Bubbles* by Sir John Everett Millais
Pentimento	Phenomenon of earlier painting showing through a layer or layers of paint on a canvas
Pop Art: term coined by	The critic Lawrence Alloway
Post-Painterly Abstraction	Term coined by the critic Clement Greenberg in 1964 to refer to non-objective artists who were not members of the Abstract Expressionist movement
Primary Colours	The colours from which all other colours are made up i.e. Blue, Yellow and Red
Purism	Term coined in 1918 by Amédée Ozenfant in 'Après le Cubisme' which rejected decorative qualities of Cubism
Putto	A plump naked boy used as a decorative addition to painting and sculpture, especially in the Baroque
Quattrocento	The 15th century, especially with reference to Renaissance Italian Art (literally four hundred, i.e. short for 14 hundred)
Rayonism	Russian art movement described as a combination of Cubism, Futurism and Orphism
Renoir's Nude Sitter	Renoir's maid, Gabrielle, would often sit as nude model for his paintings
Rheumatism Sufferer	In later life Renoir was forced to paint with the brush tied to his fingers
Rokeby Venus (Velázquez)	Slashed by suffragette in the National Gallery
Rose Period: Picasso	Late 1904 to 1906
Saturday Evening Post	Norman Rockwell was famous for the covers
Scumbling	Term used to describe the effect when an opaque colour is applied over another colour but allows the original colour to show through
Secondary Colours	Aka Complementary Colours; produced when two primary colours are mixed together, i.e. Green, Orange & Violet
Sensation	Charles Saatchi's controversial 1997 exhibition at the Royal Academy which includes such items as Damien Hirst's *Tiger Shark, Bisected Pig* & *Thousand Years*; Marcus Harvey's *Myra*, and Tracey Emin's *Everyone I have ever slept with*
Signed Paintings 'OK'	Oscar Kokoschka signed many of his paintings 'OK' making them look like they had been vandalised
Stole Mona Lisa 1914	Vincenzo Perugia (sentenced to one year, 15 days imprisonment)
Stolen from National Gallery	*The Scream* (stolen in 1994 but returned 2 months later)
Surrealism	Term coined in 1922 by André Breton to describe the real and unreal world of waking and dreaming as depicted by the artist. Breton chose term from earlier description of a Chagall work by Guillaume Apollinaire
Tachisme	Term often used synonymously with Abstract Expressionism, but it strictly refers to a French movement of the 1950s which consisted of paintings composed of large blobs of colour
Tempest, The (Kokoschka)	Depicts the artist and Alma Mahler resting in a huge cockleshell in the midst of a raging sea
Thousand Years	Damien Hirst's rotting cow head in a smear of blood, beset by flies
Turner Prize winners	Sponsored by Channel 4 and awarded to a British artist under 50. Inaugurated in 1984, the prize is worth £20,000 to the winner and is awarded at a ceremony at Tate Britain where an exhibition of the short-listed artists is on display for several months before the prize is announced. The full list of previous winners are Malcolm Morley (1984), Howard Hodgkin (1985), Gilbert and George (1986), Richard Deacon (1987), Tony Cragg (1988), Richard Long (1989), Prize suspended (1990), Anish Kapoor (1991), Grenville Davey (1992), Rachel Whiteread (1993), Antony Gormley (1994), Damien Hirst (1995), Douglas Gordon (1996), Gillian Wearing (1997), Chris Ofili (1998), Steve McQueen (1999), Wolfgang Tillmans (2000), Martin Creed (2001), Keith Tyson (2002), Grayson Perry (2003), Jeremy Deller (2004)
Van Gogh: only painting sold	*Red Vineyard* was the only painting he sold in his lifetime

A
R
T

ASTRONOMY

Constellations

Latin name	English name	Latin name	English name	Latin name	English name
Andromeda	Andromeda	Crux	Southern Cross	Orion	Orion
Antlia	Air Pump			Pavo	Peacock
Apus	Bird of Paradise	Cygnus	Swan	Pegasus	Winged Horse
		Delphinus	Dolphin	Perseus	Perseus
Aquarius	Water Bearer	Dorado	Swordfish or Goldfish	Phoenix	Phoenix
Aquila	Eagle			Pictor	Painter
Ara	Altar	Draco	Dragon	Pisces	Fishes
Aries	Ram	Equuleus	Foal	Piscis Austrinus	Southern Fish
Auriga	Charioteer	Eridanus	River Eridanus	Puppis	Poop or Stern
Boötes	Herdsman	Fornax	Furnace	Pyxis	Mariner's Compass
Caelum	Chisel	Gemini	Twins		
Camelopardalis	Giraffe	Grus	Crane	Reticulum	Net
Cancer	Crab	Hercules	Hercules	Sagitta	Arrow
Canes Venatici	Hunting Dogs	Horologium	Clock	Sagittarius	Archer
Canis Major	Great Dog	Hydra	Sea Serpent	Scorpius	Scorpion
Canis Minor	Little Dog	Hydrus	Water Snake	Sculptor	Sculptor
Capricornus	Sea Goat	Indus	Indian	Scutum	Shield
Carina	Keel	Lacerta	Lizard	Serpens	Serpent
Cassiopeia	Cassiopeia	Leo	Lion	Sextans	Sextant
Centaurus	Centaur	Leo Minor	Little Lion	Taurus	Bull
Cepheus	Cepheus	Lepus	Hare	Telescopium	Telescope
Cetus	Whale	Libra	Scales	Triangulum	Triangle
Chamaeleon	Chameleon	Lupus	Wolf	Triangulum Australe	Southern Triangle
Circinus	Compasses	Lynx	Lynx		
Columba	Dove	Lyra	Lyre	Tucana	Toucan
Coma Berenices	Berenice's Hair	Mensa	Table	Ursa Major	Great Bear
		Microscopium	Microscope	Ursa Minor	Little Bear
Corona Australis	Southern Crown	Monoceros	Unicorn	Vela	Sails
		Musca	Fly	Virgo	Virgin
Corona Borealis	Northern Crown	Norma	Level	Volans	Flying Fish
		Octans	Octant	Vulpecula	Fox
Corvus	Crow	Ophiuchus	Serpent Bearer		
Crater	Cup				

The Planets

Planetary data	Diameter km	miles	Maximum distance from Sun (millions) km	miles	Minimum distance from Sun (millions) km	miles	Sidereal period	Axial rotation period
Mercury	4878	3031	69.4	43	46.8	29	88 days	58d 16h
Venus	12104	7521	109	67.6	107.6	66.7	224.7 days	243 days
Earth	12756	7927	152.6	94.6	147.4	91.4	365.26 days	23h 56m
Mars	6794	4222	249.2	154.5	207.3	128.5	687 days	24h 37m 23s
Jupiter	142800	88700	817.4	506.8	741.6	459.8	11.86 years	9h 50m 30s
Saturn	120000	74600	1512	937.6	1346	834.6	29.46 years	10h 14m
Uranus	52000	32300	3011	1867	2740	1699.0	84.01 years	16-28 hours
Neptune	48400	30000	4543	2817	4466	2769.0	164.79 years	18-20 hours
Pluto	2300	1430	7364	4566	4461	2766.0	248.5 years	6d 9h

Astronomers Royal

John Flamsteed	1675–1719	Sir Frank Dyson	1910–1933	Until 1972 the title of Astronomer Royal was given to the director of Greenwich Observatory. It is now an honorary title for an outstanding astronomer, who receives a stipend of approximately £100 per year.
Edmund Halley	1720–1742	Sir Harold Jones	1933–1955	
James Bradley	1742–1762	Sir Richard Woolley	1956–1971	
Nathaniel Bliss	1762–1764	Sir Martin Ryle	1972–1982	
Nevil Maskelyne	1765–1811	Sir Francis Graham–Smith	1982–1990	
John Pond	1811–1835	Sir Arnold Wolfendale	1991–1995	
Sir George Airy	1835–1881	Sir Martin Rees	1995–	
Sir William Christie	1881–1910			

Planetary Satellites (Named)

		Discovered	Diameter km	Diameter miles			Discovered	Diameter km	Diameter miles
Earth	Moon		3476	2160		Telesto	1980	24	15
Mars	Phobos	1877	27	17		Prometheus	1980	10	6
	Deimos	1877	15	9		Pan	1990	20	12
Jupiter	Ganymede	1610	5260	3270	**Uranus**	Oberon	1787	1600	1000
	Callisto	1610	4800	3000		Titania	1787	1600	1000
	Io	1610	3650	2268		Ariel	1851	1300	800
	Europa	1610	3138	1950		Umbriel	1851	1100	700
	Amalthea	1892	270	168		Miranda	1948	400	250
	Himalia	1904	180	110		Puck	1986	170	105
	Elara	1905	80	50		Portia	1986	90	55
	Pasiphae	1908	50	30		Cressida	1986	70	40
	Sinope	1914	40	25		Juliet	1986	70	40
	Carme	1938	40	25		Belinda	1986	50	30
	Lysithea	1938	40	25		Bianca	1986	50	30
	Metis	1979	40	25		Desdemona	1986	50	30
	Ananke	1951	30	19		Rosalind	1986	50	30
	Adrastea	1979	24	15		Ophelia	1986	20	12
	Leda	1974	20	12		Cordelia	1986	15	9
	Thebe	1979	100	62		Caliban	1997	80	50
Saturn	Titan	1655	5150	3200		Sycorax	1997	160	100
	Rhea	1672	1530	950		Prospero	1999	30	19
	Iapetus	1671	1440	900		Setebos	1999	30	19
	Dione	1684	1120	700		Stephano	1999	20	12
	Tethys	1684	1050	650		Trinculo	2001	20	12
	Enceladus	1789	500	310	**Neptune**	Triton	1846	2700	1678
	Hyperion	1848	400	250		Proteus	1989	415	260
	Mimas	1789	390	240		Nereid	1949	300	190
	Phoebe	1898	220	135		Larissa	1989	190	118
	Janus	1966	200	120		Galatea	1989	160	100
	Epimetheus	1980	140	90		Despina	1989	150	95
	Helene	1980	100	60		Naiad	1989	50	30
	Pandora	1980	100	60		Thalassa	1989	50	30
	Atlas	1980	40	25	**Pluto**	Charon	1978	1000	620
	Calypso	1980	30	19					

Astronomy and Space: Selected Data

Albedo Reflecting power of a planet or other non-luminous body

American in Space: 1st Alan Shepard in Freedom 7 (5 May 1961); duration of flight 15 minutes 28 seconds

American to Orbit the Earth: 1st John Glenn in Friendship 7 (20 Feb 1962); for 3 orbits, duration of flight 4 hrs 55 mins 23 secs

Animals in Space Laika (meaning 'barker' in Russian) the dog was the first animal in space aboard *Sputnik 2* (3 November 1957). The first monkey in space was Gordo aboard the US Army rocket *Jupiter AM-13* (13 December 1958). Both animals survived the flight but died during re-entry.

Aphelion Furthest distance of a planet from the Sun

Apogee Furthest point of the Moon from the Earth

Apollo 13: Crew James Lovell, Jack Swigert and Fred Haise. The service module exploded 55 hrs into the mission to the Moon, but the lunar module was used to reach home safely on 17 Apr 1970

Appleton Layer Highest region of the Ionosphere, extending from a height of about 150 to about 1,000 kilometres. It contains the highest proportion of free electrons and is the most useful region for long-range radio transmission. The layer is also called the F-region

Artificial Satellite: 1st Sputnik 1, launched by Soviet Union on 4 October 1957. Sputnik was an 83.6 kg metal sphere, transmitting signals for three weeks before failing batteries caused it to fall to Earth on 4 January 1958

Asteroid Another name for a minor planet. Eros, discovered in 1898, comes closer to the Earth (every 37 years) than anything except the Moon

Asteroid: brightest Vesta

Asteroid: largest 1. Ceres 2. Pallas 3. Vesta 4. Hygeia

Asteroid Belt The 4,000-plus minor planets (asteroids) that orbit the Sun between Mars and Jupiter

Astrolabe Ancient instrument used to measure altitudes of celestial bodies

Astronomical Unit Mean distance between the Earth and the Sun: 149,598,500 km

Baikonur Launch site for manned Soviet space flights in Kazakhstan

Baily's Beads Brilliant points seen around the Moon just before and after a total solar eclipse

Big Bang Theory First advanced by Georges Lemaître: the idea that the universe began, around 15 to 17 billion years ago, as a point of superdense matter that exploded and has been expanding ever since

Black Hole   Region of immense gravitational pull around a massive collapsed star from which not even light can escape

Bolide   A brilliant exploding meteor

Brightest Stars in the celestial sphere   1. Sirius 2. Canopus 3. Alpha Centauri 4. Arcturus 5. Vega. It is traditional to omit our own sun from this list although it is easily the brightest object in the sky.

British National Space Centre   Head Office at 151 Buckingham Palace Road, London SW1 9SS

Cassini-Huygens **Probe**   Launched from Cape Canaveral, Florida, October 1997, to seek out the moons of Saturn. The probe flew by the moon Phoebe on 11 June 2004. Several new moons were discovered, giving a total of 37

Cassini's Division   Dark gap between rings A and B of Saturn discovered by Gian Domenico Cassini, among others

Celestial Equator   Projection of the Earth's equator on to the celestial sphere

Celestial Sphere   Imaginary sphere surrounding the Earth on which all heavenly bodies appear to move, and whose centre is the same as that of the Earth's globe

Challenger   US space shuttle exploded 72 seconds after lift-off on 28 Jan 1986, killing all 7 crew members, including schoolteacher Christa McAuliffe

Chinaman in Space: 1st   Lt Col Yang Liwei (October 2003)

Chromosphere   Part of the Sun's atmosphere that lies above the Photosphere

Coldest Planet   Pluto

Comet: Shortest known orbital period Encke's Comet, 3.3 years

Comet: meaning   From the Latin 'Coma', which means hair

Constellations   31 in Northern and 52 in Southern hemisphere, with 5 'floaters' overlapping. **Largest**: Hydra. **Smallest**: Crux Australis

Corona   Outermost part of the Sun's atmosphere visible with the naked eye only during a total solar eclipse

Cosmogony   Study of the origin and evolution of the universe

Cosmology   Study of the universe considered as a whole

Declination   Angular distance of celestial body north or south of celestial equator, corresponding to latitude on the Earth

Doppler Effect   Apparent change in wavelength of the light from a luminous body in motion relative to the observer

D-region   Lowest layer of the Ionosphere. Extends from a height of about 60 to about 90 kilometres, contains a low concentration of free electrons, and reflects low-frequency radio waves

Earth: mean distance from Sun   150 million kms (93 million miles)

Ecliptic   Apparent yearly path of the Sun among the stars

Ephemeris   Table showing the predicted positions of a celestial body such as a planet, comet or asteroid

Equinox   Equinoxes are two points at which the ecliptic cuts the celestial equator; vernal equinox 21 Mar, autumnal 22 Sep

European Space Agency   Created 1975 by merger of European Space Research Organisation and European Launcher Development Organisation. Members are Austria, Belgium, Denmark, Finland, France, Germany, Ireland, Italy, Netherlands, Norway, Spain, Sweden, Switzerland and the UK. Canada being non-European

is deemed a co-operating state. Head Office is at 8–10 Rue Mario Nikis, 75738 Paris, France

Exosphere   Outermost part of a planet's atmosphere

Expanding Universe   Observation made by Edwin Hubble in 1929 that the universe appears to be expanding; this confirms the Big Bang Theory

Flocculi   Patches on the Sun's surface: bright (calcium) and dark (hydrogen)

Galaxies   Systems made up of stars, nebulae and interstellar matter, forming star families held together by their own gravitational pull and separate from other such galaxies

Gibbous Phase   Phase of the Moon or planet when between half and full

Golf Shot on the Moon   Alan Shepard made the first-ever golf shot on the moon on 6 February 1971, using a six-iron head attached to the handle of a rock sample collector

Great Red Spot   Enormous red feature in the atmosphere of Jupiter, visible since the 17th century

Heaviside Layer   Region of the Ionosphere, extending from a height of 90 to about 150 kilometres. It reflects radio waves of medium wavelength. This layer is also called the E-region

Hertzsprung-Russell Diagram   Diagram in which stars are plotted according to their spectral types and their absolute magnitudes

Hottest Planet   Venus

Hubble Space Telescope   Placed in the Earth's orbit by the space shuttle *Discovery* (24 April 1990)

Inferior Planets   Mercury and Venus: closer to the Sun than the Earth is

Inner Planets   The 4 planets that orbit the Sun within the Asteroid Belt; i.e. Mercury, Venus, Earth, Mars

Ionosphere   Region of the Earth's atmosphere lying above the Stratosphere

Jupiter   Mean distance from Sun: 778.34 million km (486 million miles). Galileo discovered satellites Callisto, Europa, Ganymede and Io. Atmosphere: hydrogen, ammonia and methane. Temperature can be as low as -200º C. Probes: *Pioneer 10* and *11* (1973/4); *Voyager 1* and *2* (1979); *Galileo* (1995). Although there are 16 named moons there are in excess of 47 additional minor moons

Largest Planet   Jupiter

Light Year   Distance travelled by light in one year: 9.4607 million million km. Light travels at 186,000 miles per second (7 1/2 times round the Earth)

Local Group   Group of more than two dozen galaxies, including our own galaxy. Largest member is the Andromeda Galaxy, M.31

Lunar Eclipse   Passage of the Moon through the shadow cast by the Earth

Magnitude   Measurement unit for the brightness of a star or planet

Mariner 9   US space probe to Mars in 1971

Mars   Mean distance from the Sun: 227.94 million km (142 million miles). Atmosphere nearest to our own, but there is no water on Mars. Probes: *Mariner 4, 6, 7, 8, 9* (1965–71); and *1* and *2* landed 1976; *Pathfinder* landed 1997

Mercury   Mean distance from the Sun: 57.9 million kms (36.2 million miles). Atmosphere: non-existent – burnt off by closeness to Sun. Probe: *Mariner 10* (1974 & 1975)

Mesosphere   Region of the Earth's atmosphere between the Stratosphere and the Thermosphere, sometimes called the D-region and characterised by a rapid decrease in temperature with height

Messier, Charles (1730–1817)   French astronomer nicknamed the 'comet ferret' who between 1760 and 1784 compiled the first catalogue of galaxies, nebulae, and star clusters. The 103 items on his list were assigned 'Messier' numbers. Although these were replaced by New General Catalogue (NGC) numbers from 1888, galaxies discovered prior to the change are identified by both 'M' and 'NGC' numbers

Meteor   Particle or small rock moving around Sun and destroyed when entering atmosphere

Meteorite   Larger object that reaches the ground without being destroyed

Milky Way   The galaxy of which our Sun is a member. It contains approximately 100,000 million stars, of which 5,776 are visible to the naked eye

Mir   Advanced type of space station 1st launched by the Soviet Union in 1986

Moon   Mean distance from Earth: 384,000 km (239,900 miles). Diameter: 3,476 km (2,160 miles). Revolves around the Earth from west to east. First soft landing by Soviet *Luna 9*, launched on 31 Jan 1966, landed 3 Feb. First manned flight around the Moon: *Apollo 8* in Dec 1968. First manned landing and walk: *Apollo 11* on 20 Jul 1969. Last man on the Moon was Eugene Cernan in *Apollo 17* on 11 Dec 1972

Moon Walks   12 men, all American, have walked on the surface of the Moon, Neil Armstrong and Buzz Aldrin *(Apollo 11)*, Charles Conrad Jr and Alan Bean *(Apollo 12)*, Alan Shepard and Edgar Mitchell *(Apollo 14)*, David Scott and James Irwin *(Apollo 15)*, John Young and Charles Duke *(Apollo 16)*, Eugene Cernan and Harrison Schmitt *(Apollo 17)*

Moon's Rotation   Rotates about its own axis in 29 1/2 days, which is about the same time it takes to orbit the Earth. Hence the same face of the Moon is always presented to the Earth

Nadir   Point on the celestial sphere directly below the observer, diametrically opposite the zenith

Nearest Galaxy   Andromeda (2.3 million light years)

Nearest Planet to Earth   Venus

Nearest Star to Earth   Sun

Nearest Stars to Sun   1. Proxima Centauri (4.26 light years) 2. Alpha Centauri (4.34) 3. Barnard's Star (5.88)

Nebula   Cloud of gas and dust in space

Neptune   Mean distance from the Sun: 4,496.7 million km (2,810 million miles). Discovered by JG Galle in 1846. Atmosphere: hydrogen, helium, methane, ammonia. First suggested name was 'Janus'. Probe: *Voyager 2* (1989). To date 13 moons have been discovered

Neutron Star   Remnant of a massive star that once exploded as a supernova

Nova   Star that suddenly flares up to many times its normal brilliancy and then fades back to obscurity

Occultation   The obscuring of one celestial body by another

Ophiuchus   Often called the 13th constellation of the Zodiac

Orbit of the Earth: 1st   Yuri Gagarin (12 April 1961). 1st American, John Glenn in *Mercury Friendship 7* (20 February 1962). Glenn also became the oldest man in space, aged 77 (6 November 1998)

Orrery   Model showing the Sun and the orbiting planets, capable of being moved mechanically to scale

Outer Planets   The 5 planets that orbit the Sun beyond the Asteroid belt; i.e. Jupiter, Saturn, Uranus, Neptune, Pluto

Ozone Layer   Located in the Stratosphere, between c19 and 30 km above the surface of the Earth. Ozone is created when energetic solar radiation strikes molecules of oxygen and causes the oxygen atoms to split apart. These atoms can then reform with O_2 molecules to form ozone (O_3) – a process known as photolysis. Ozone absorbs most of the incoming solar UV radiation which can be harmful to life on Earth

Parsec   Basic unit used to measure large astronomic distances: 3.26 light years

Perigee   Position of the Moon in its orbit when closest to the Earth

Perihelion   Position in orbit of a planet when closest to the Sun

Photosphere   The bright surface of the Sun

Planet   Large body orbiting a star; the name means 'Wanderer' in Greek

Pluto   Mean distance from the Sun: 5,900 million km (3,687 million miles). Atmosphere: tenuous. Discovered by Clyde Tombaugh 1930; named by Venetia Burney

Polaris   Also called the Pole Star, it is 680 light years from the Earth

Quadrant   Ancient astronomical instrument used for measuring the apparent positions of celestial bodies

Reversing Layer   Gaseous layer above the Sun's photosphere

Rings of Saturn   Discs composed of ice and rock, in sizes ranging from tiny particles to massive boulders, orbiting Jupiter, Neptune and Uranus, and most spectaculary Saturn

Rotating Backwards   Venus (east to west)

Saturn   Mean distance from the Sun: 1,427 million km (891 million miles). Atmosphere: mostly hydrogen and helium, some methane and ammonia. Christiaan Huygens discovered the rings in 1655. Cassini discovered 4 of the satellites. The satellite Phoebe revolves in the opposite direction to the others. Probes: *Voyager 1* and *2*, 1980–81; *Cassini-Huygens*, 1997–present. Saturn is now thought to have 49 moons. Three moons discovered in 2004 were named Methone, Pallene and Polydeuces in February 2005; 12 moons were discovered in May 2005, all approx 5km in diameter

Second Space Flight   Virgil 'Gus' Grissom became the second American in space aboard *Liberty Bell 7* (21 July 1961) and became the first person to make two space flights aboard *Gemini 3* (23 March 1965)

Sirius   Also called the 'Dog Star', it is 8.7 light years from the Earth

Solar Cycle   Discovered by H. Schwabe in 1826. He found that there is an 11-year solar cycle of sunspot activity

Solar Eclipse   Blotting out of the Sun by the Moon, so that the Moon is directly between the Earth and the Sun

Solar Flares   Brilliant eruptions of hydrogen in outer part of Sun's atmosphere

Solar Wind   Flow of ionised hydrogen and helium from the Sun

Solstices   Times when Sun is at its maximum declination of 23 1/2 degrees

Space Flight: 1st   Yuri Gagarin in *Vostok 1* (12 Apr 1961); duration of flight 1 hr 48 mins. 2nd, Alan Shepard in *Freedom 7* (5 May 1961), the first American in space

Space Flight: 1st Briton   Helen Sharman (18 May 1991)

Space Station: 1st   *Salyut 1*, launched on 19 April 1971 from Baikonur and orbited for 179.93 days

ASTRONOMY

Space Walk: 1st American   Ed White (June 1965 from *Gemini IV*)

Space Walk: 1st American Woman   Dr Kathryn Sullivan (Oct 1984 from *Challenger*)

Space Walk: 1st Briton   Michael Foale

Space Walk: 1st Untethered   Bruce McCandless of the USA (3 Feb 1984)

Space Walk: 1st Woman   Svetlana Savitskaya of the USSR (17 Jul 1984)

Stratosphere   Region of the Earth's atmosphere lying above the Troposphere and below the Ionosphere

Sun   Distance from the Earth: 149,597,900 km on average. Diameter: 1,392,000 km. Light takes 8 minutes 14.2 seconds to reach the Earth. Most common elements in the sun 1. Hydrogen 2. Helium 3. Oxygen

Sunspot   Region of lower temperature and therefore less brilliance, on the surface of the Sun

Superior Planets   Those whose orbits lie outside the Earth's: Mars, Jupiter, Saturn, Uranus, Neptune, Pluto.

Supernova   Cataclysmic explosion of a very massive star, which ends its career as a patch of expanding gas with a neutron star at its centre

Syzygy   Position of the Moon in its orbit when new or full

Telescope: Largest   Mount Semirodriki, Caucasus, with a 600 cm (236.2 in) reflector

Troposphere   Lowest part of the Earth's atmosphere, reaching to about 11km

Umbra   Main cone of shadow cast by Earth. Also darkest part of a sunspot

Unmanned Moon Landing: 1st   *Lunik 2* (USSR) 1959. First US landing, *Ranger 4* in 1962, although this was a crash-landing

Uranus   Mean distance from Sun: 2,869.6 million km (1,793 million miles). Atmosphere: hydrogen and helium. Discovered by William Herschel 1781. Probe:

Voyager 2 (1986). Currently there are 21 named moons and six unnamed

Van Allen Radiation Belts   Zones of charged particles around the Earth, held captive by the Earth's magnetic field

Venera Space Probes   Russian series commencing with *Venera 4* in 1967 to explore Venus, the first planetary probe

Venus   Mean distance from Sun: 108.2 million km (67.2 million miles). Atmosphere is largely carbon dioxide. Probes: Russian *Venera* series (1962–71); US *Mariners 2, 5,* and 10; *Magellan* (1990). Other names: Hesperus (evening star), Phosphorus (morning star)

Voyager   A pair of unmanned US interplanetary probes launched to observe and transmit to Earth data about the outer planetary system. *Voyager* runs out of power around 2020. *Voyager 1* was Launched on 5 Sep 1977, flew by Jupiter in March 1979, reached Saturn in Nov 1980, then proceeded out of the solar system. *Voyager 2* was launched on 20 Aug 1977. It flew by Jupiter (Jul 1979), Saturn (Aug 1981), Uranus (Jan 1986) and Neptune (Aug 1989), then on into interstellar space

Walk in Space: 1st   Alexei Leonov (18 Mar 1965)

Woman in Space: 1st   Valentina Tereshkova (16 June 1963) 1st American woman, Sally Ride aboard the space shuttle *Challenger* (18 June 1983)

Youngest Man in Space   Gherman Titor, aged 25yrs 10 months 25 days (6 August 1961)

Zenith   Point on the celestial sphere directly above the observer (altitude 90 degrees)

Zodiac   Belt stretching around the sky 8 degrees to either side of ecliptic. The constellations Aries, Taurus, Gemini, Cancer, Leo, Virgo, Libra, Scorpius, Sagittarius, Capricornus, Aquarius and Pisces lies within this belt, and so do the apparent paths of the Sun and all the planets except Pluto, which sometimes moves outside it

United Kingdom: Administration Centres

A restructure of the old County boundaries has been ongoing throughout the UK. Formerly there were 46 English County Councils, but this has been reduced to 34, all of which have the same Administrative Headquarters as before.
The other twelve Counties, along with parts of still existing Counties, have been restructured and are now known officially as Unitary Authorities. There are 82 such authorities at present, plus the 32 London Boroughs and the City of London Corporation.
A similar position exists in Scotland, Wales and Northern Ireland.
Northern Ireland's six Counties have been rationalised across 26 districts (the same number as there are Counties of the Irish Republic), although at present only the traditional six Counties plus Belfast City and Londonderry City have Lord-Lieutenants.

English County Councils (as at 31 December 2004)

County	Admin Headquarters	County	Admin Headquarters
Bedfordshire	Bedford	Lincolnshire	Lincoln
Buckinghamshire	Aylesbury	Norfolk	Norwich
Cambridgeshire	Cambridge	Northamptonshire	Northampton
Cheshire	Chester	Northumberland	Morpeth
Cornwall	Truro	North Yorkshire	Northallerton
Cumbria	Carlisle	Nottinghamshire	Nottingham
Derbyshire	Matlock	Oxfordshire	Oxford
Devon	Exeter	Shropshire	Shrewsbury
Dorset	Dorchester	Somerset	Taunton
Durham	Durham	Staffordshire	Stafford
East Sussex	Lewes	Suffolk	Ipswich
Essex	Chelmsford	Surrey	Kingston-upon-Thames
Gloucestershire	Gloucester		
Hampshire	Winchester	Warwickshire	Warwick
Hertfordshire	Hertford	West Sussex	Chichester
Kent	Maidstone	Wiltshire	Trowbridge
Lancashire	Preston	Worcestershire	Worcester
Leicestershire	Leicester		

NB: The five inhabited islands of the Scillies, i.e. St Mary's (Admin HQ), Tresco, Bryher, St Agnes and St Martin's, although not constituting a separate County, do however have their own Council.

London Boroughs

(these are also Unitary Authorities)

Council	Admin Headquarters	Council	Admin Headquarters
Barking & Dagenham	Dagenham	Hounslow	Hounslow
Barnet	Hendon	* Islington	Islington
Bexley	Bexleyheath	* Kensington and Chelsea #	Kensington
Brent	Wembley	Kingston-upon-Thames #	Kingston-upon-Thames
Bromley	Bromley		
* Camden	Camden	* Lambeth	Brixton
City of London	Guildhall, London	* Lewisham	Catford
Croydon	Croydon	Merton	Morden
Ealing	Ealing	Newham	East Ham
Enfield	Enfield	Redbridge	Ilford
* Greenwich	Woolwich	Richmond-upon-Thames	Twickenham
* Hackney	Hackney	* Southwark	Southwark
* Hammersmith & Fulham	Hammersmith	Sutton	Sutton
Haringey	Wood Green	* Tower Hamlets	Tower Hamlets
Harrow	Harrow	Waltham Forest	Walthamstow
Havering	Romford	* Wandsworth	Wandsworth
Hillingdon	Uxbridge	* Westminster City	Westminster

* denotes Inner London Borough

# denotes Royal Borough

Unitary Authorities (as at 31 December 2004)

Authority	Headquarters	Authority	Headquarters
Barnsley*	Barnsley	Oldham*	Oldham
Bath and North East Somerset	Bath	Peterborough	Peterborough
Birmingham*	Birmingham	Plymouth	Plymouth
Blackburn with Darwen	Blackburn	Poole	Poole
Blackpool	Blackpool	Portsmouth	Portsmouth
Bolton*	Bolton	Reading	Reading
Bournemouth	Bournemouth	Redcar and Cleveland	Redcar
Bracknell Forest	Bracknell	Rochdale*	Rochdale
Bradford*	Bradford	Rotherham*	Rotherham
Brighton and Hove	Brighton	Rutland	Oakham
Bristol	Bristol	St Helens*	St Helens
Bury*	Bury	Salford*	Swinton
Calderdale*	Halifax	Sandwell*	West Bromwich
Coventry*	Coventry	Sefton*	Southport
Darlington	Darlington	Sheffield*	Sheffield
Derby	Derby	Slough	Slough
Doncaster*	Doncaster	Solihull*	Solihull
Dudley*	Dudley	Southampton	Southampton
East Riding of Yorkshire	Beverley	Southend	Southend
Gateshead*	Gateshead	South Gloucestershire	Thornbury
Halton	Widnes	South Tyneside*	South Shields
Hartlepool	Hartlepool	Stockport*	Stockport
Herefordshire	Hereford	Stockton-on-Tees	Stockton-on-Tees
Isle of Wight	Newport		
Kingston-upon-Hull	Kingston-upon-Hull	Stoke-on-Trent	Stoke-on-Trent
Kirklees*	Huddersfield	Sunderland*	Sunderland
Knowsley*	Huyton	Swindon	Swindon
Leeds*	Leeds	Tameside*	Ashton-under-Lyme
Leicester	Leicester		
Liverpool*	Liverpool	Telford and Wrekin	Telford
Luton	Luton	Thurrock	Grays
Manchester*	Manchester	Torbay	Torquay
Medway Towns	Rochester	Trafford*	Stretford
Middlesbrough	Middlesbrough	Wakefield*	Wakefield
Milton Keynes	Milton Keynes	Walsall*	Walsall
Newcastle-upon-Tyne*	Newcastle-upon-Tyne	Warrington	Warrington
		West Berkshire	Newbury
North East Lincolnshire	Grimsby	Windsor and Maidenhead	Maidenhead
North Lincolnshire	Brigg	Wigan*	Wigan
North Somerset	Weston-Super-Mare	Wirral*	Wallasey
		Wokingham	Wokingham
North Tyneside*	North Shields	Wolverhampton*	Wolverhampton
Nottingham	Nottingham	York	York

* denotes Metropolitan Authority

Scottish Districts (Unitary Authorities)

Council	Admin Headquarters	Council	Admin Headquarters
Aberdeen	Aberdeen	Highland	Inverness
Aberdeenshire	Aberdeen	Inverclyde	Greenock
Angus	Forfar	Midlothian	Dalkeith
Argyll and Bute	Lochgilphead	Moray	Elgin
Clackmannanshire	Alloa	North Ayrshire	Irvine
Comhairlenan Eilean Siar	Stornoway	North Lanarkshire	Motherwell
Dumfries and Galloway	Dumfries	Orkney	Kirkwall
Dundee	Dundee	Perth and Kinrosshire	Perth
East Ayrshire	Kilmarnock	Renfrewshire	Paisley
East Dunbartonshire	Kirkintilloch	Scottish Borders	Melrose
East Lothian	Haddington	Shetland	Lerwick
East Renfrewshire	Glasgow	South Ayrshire	Ayr
Edinburgh	Edinburgh	South Lanarkshire	Hamilton
Falkirk	Falkirk	Stirling	Stirling
Fife	Glenrothes	West Dunbartonshire	Dumbarton
Glasgow City	Glasgow	West Lothian	Livingston

Welsh Districts
(Unitary Authorities)

District Council	Admin Headquarters	District Council	Admin Headquarters
Anglesey	Llangefni	Merthyr Tydfil	Merthyr Tydfil
Blaenau Gwent	Ebbw Vale	Monmouth	Cwmbran
Bridgend	Bridgend	Neath Port Talbot	Port Talbot
Caerphilly	Hengoed	Newport	Newport
Cardiff	Cardiff	Pembrokeshire	Haverfordwest
Carmarthenshire	Carmarthen	Powys	Llandrindod Wells
Ceredigion	Aberystwyth	Rhondda, Cynon, Taff	Cardiff
Conwy	Conwy	Swansea, City and County	Swansea
Denbighshire	Ruthin	Torfaen	Pontypool
Flintshire	Mold	Vale of Glamorgan	Barry
Gwynedd	Caernarfon	Wrexham	Wrexham

Northern Irish Districts
(Unitary Authorities)

District Council	Admin Headquarters	District Council	Admin Headquarters
Antrim	Antrim	Down	Downpatrick
Ards	Newtownards	Dungannon	Dungannon
Armagh	Armagh	Fermanagh	Enniskillen
Ballymena	Ballymena	Larne	Larne
Ballymoney	Ballymoney	Limavady	Limavady
Banbridge	Banbridge	Lisburn	Lisburn
Belfast	Belfast	Magherafelt	Magherafelt
Carrickfergus	Carrickfergus	Moyle	Ballycastle
Castlereagh	Castlereagh	Newry and Mourne	Newry
Coleraine	Coleraine	Newtownabbey	Newtownabbey
Cookstown	Cookstown	North Down	Bangor
Craigavon	Craigavon	Omagh	Omagh
Derry	Derry	Strabane	Strabane

Shopping Centres
by Towns and Cities

Town	Centre
Aberdeen	Bredero; The Academy
Aldershot	The Arcade
Ashford	Park Mall
Aylesbury	Hale Leys
Banbury	Castle Quay
Barnstaple, Devon	Green Lanes
Basildon	Eastgate Centre
Basingstoke	Festival Place
Bath	Green Park
Bayswater	Whiteleys Centre
Bedford	Harpur
Belfast	Castle Court
Bexleyheath	Broadway
Bideford	Atlantic Village
Birmingham	Bull Ring; City Plaza
Blackpool	Hounds Hill
Bolton	Crompton Place
Bradford	Kirkgate Mall
Brighton	Churchill Square
Bristol	Galleries; Clifton Arcade; Broadmead
Bromley	Glades
Burgess Hill	The Martletts
Burnley	Charter Walk
Bury	Millgate
Cambridge	Grafton Centre; Castle Mall
Cardiff	St Davids
Carlisle	The Lanes
Caterham	Church Walk
Chelmsford	Meadows
Cheltenham	Regent Arcade; Beechwood Arcade
Chester	Grosvenor; The Forum
Colchester	Culver Square; St John's Walk
Coventry	Cannon Park; West Orchard
Crawley	County Mall
Croydon	Whitgift Centre
Darlington	Cornmill Centre
Dartford	Orchards
Derby	Eagle Centre
Dorking	St Martin's Walk
Dudley	Trident
Dundee	Wellgate Centre
Durham	Milburngate
Eastbourne	Arndale Centre
Eastleigh	Swan
Edgware	Broad Walk
Edinburgh	Cameron Toll; Gyle
Ellesmere Port	Cheshire Oaks
Epsom	Ashley Centre
Exeter	Guildhall
Farnborough	Kingsmead
Gateshead	MetroCentre
Glasgow	St Enoch; Sauchiehall Centre; Braehead Centre; Forge Centre

BRITAIN

Gloucester	Kings Square	Poole	Dolphin
Greenhithe, Kent	Bluewater	Portsmouth	Bridge; Cascades
Grimsby	Freshney Place	Preston	Fishergate
Guildford	Friary, White Lion Walk	Reading	Oracle
Halifax	Woolshops	Redditch	Kingfisher Centre
Hanley	The Potteries	Redhill	Belfry
Harlow	Harvey Centre	Romford	Liberty 2
Hartlepool	Middleton Grange	Scarborough	Brunswick; Balmoral
Hatfield	Galleria Outlet Centre	Scunthorpe	The Parishes
Havant	Meridian Centre	Sheffield	Forum; Meadowhall; Crystal
Hemel Hempstead	The Marlowes		Peaks; The Moor
Hereford	Maylord; The Atrium	Shrewsbury	Darwin; Pride Hill
High Wycombe	Chilterns	Skegness	Hildreds Centre
Hinckley, Leics	Britannia	Skipton, North Yorks	Craven Court
Horsham	Swan Walk; Piries Place	Slough	Queensmere; Observatory
Hounslow	Treaty Centre		Centre
Hull	North Point; Princess Quay	Solihull	Mell Square
Ilford	Exchange	Southampton	Marlands; WestQuay
Ipswich	Tower Ramparts	Southend	Victoria Plaza, Royals
Kingston Upon		Southport	Marble Place
Thames	Bentalls	St Albans	Christopher Place; The Maltings
Lancaster	St Nicholas; Markgate	Stevenage	Westgate
Leatherhead	Swan Centre	St Helens	St Mary's Arcade; Church
Leeds	Bramley Centre; Crossgates;		Square
	Merrion Centre; White Rose;	Stockton	Teeside Park
	The Light	Stoke-on-Trent	Potteries
Leicester	Shires	Street, Somerset	Clarks Village
Lincoln	Waterside	Sunderland	Bridges
Liverpool	Clayton Square; St John's	Sutton Coldfield	Sainsbury Centre; Gracechurch
	Precinct		Centre
Lowestoft	The Britten Centre	Sutton (Surrey)	St Nicholas; Times Square
Luton	Arndale Centre	Swansea	St Davids
Maidenhead	The Nicholsons Centre	Swindon	Brunel Centre
Maidstone	The Corn Exchange	Thurrock	Lakeside
Manchester	Arndale Centre; Trafford Centre	Torquay	Fleet Walk
Mansfield	Four Seasons	Tunbridge Wells	Royal Victoria Place
Morecambe	Arndale	Uxbridge	The Chimes
Newcastle	Eldon Gardens; Metro Centre	Wakefield	The Ridings
Northampton	Grosvenor Centre; Weston	Wandsworth	Arndale
	Favell; Peacock Place	Warrington	Cockhedge; Golden Square
Norwich	Castle Mall; Dixons	Watford	Harlequin Centre
Nottingham	Broadmarsh; Victoria	Wellingborough	Swansgate
Nuneaton	Abbey Gate	Welwyn Garden City	Howard Centre
Oldham	Spindles	Weston-super-Mare	Sovereign
Oxford	Westgate	Wigan	Galleries
Penzance	Wharfside	Winchester	Brooks
Peterborough	Queensgate	Worcester	Crowngate
Piccadilly, London	The London Pavilion	York	Coppergate; Swinegate;
Plymouth	The Armada Centre		Monks Cross

Pub Names

Bear & Ragged Staff	Heraldic sign of the Earl of Warwick.
Blind Beggar	Situated in Whitechapel Road, London and famous as the site of Ronald Kray's murder of George Cornell.
Crown	Most popular pub name in Britain. For a long time second to the Red Lion but currently No. 1 (March 2005)
Five Alls	Sign depicts a king with the caption 'I rule for all', a parson with 'I pray for all', a lawyer with 'I plead for all' a soldier with 'I fight for all' and a labourer with 'I work for all'.
Greyhound	Situated in Tinsley Green, Crawley and famous for hosting the World Marbles Championships at Easter.
Marquis of Granby	Named after John Manners, Marquis of Granby (1721–70). C-in-C of the British army in 1766.
Nutshell	Situated in Bury St Edmunds, the smallest pub in England.
Red Lion	Second most popular pub name in Britain, it was the badge of John of Gaunt. James I (VI of Scotland) ordered Red Lions to be displayed outside all public places as it is part of the Royal Arms of Scotland.
Royal Oak	Named after the oak tree that Charles II hid in after the battle of Worcester in 1651, the third most popular pub name in Britain.
Tan Hill Inn	Situated in Arkengarthdale, near Reeth, N. Yorks, the highest pub in Britain.

Trip to Jerusalem	Situated in the Brewhouse Yard, Nottingham, possibly the oldest pub in Britain.
White Hart	Named after Richard II's heraldic symbol.
White Lion	Named after Edward IV's heraldic symbol.

There are approximately 60,000 pubs in Britain. Since 1988 they can remain open any time between 11am and 11pm, although new legislation is to permit 24-hour opening on application.

National Parks

	sq. miles		sq. miles
Brecon Beacons (1957)	519	New Forest (2005)	224
Broads (1989)	117	Northumberland (1956)	405
Cairngorms (2003)	1,461	North York Moors (1952)	554
Dartmoor (1951)	368	Peak District (1951)	555
Exmoor (1954)	268	Pembrokeshire Coast (1952)	240
Lake District (1951)	885	Snowdonia (1951)	835
Loch Lomond and the Trossachs (2002)	720	Yorkshire Dales (1954)	683

The Peak District was the first British National Park to be established. The New Forest became the latest on 1 March 2005. Scotland has two National Parks, the first established in July 2002.

Prisons

Name	Location	Name	Location
* Aberdeen	Aberdeen	Downview	Sutton, Surrey
Acklington	Morpeth, Northumberland	* Drake Hall	Eccleshall, Staffs
Albany	Newport, Isle of Wight	* Dumfries	Dumfries
Aldington	Ashford, Kent	Dungavel	Strathaven, Lanark
** Altcourse	Liverpool	* Durham	Old Elvet, Durham
Armley	Leeds	* East Sutton Park	Maidstone, Kent
Ashfield	Bristol	* Eastwood Park	Falfield
Ashwell	Oakham, Leics	Edinburgh	Edinburgh
* Askham Grange	Askham Richard, York	Edmunds Hill	Newmarket, Suffolk
Aylesbury	Aylesbury, Bucks	Elmley	Sheerness, Kent
Barlinnie	Glasgow	Erlestoke House	Devizes, Wilts
	(holds the most prisoners in	Everthorpe	Brough, Yorks
	Scotland, approx 1,300)	Exeter	Exeter
Bedford	Bedford	Featherstone	Featherstone,
Belmarsh	Thamesmead, London		Wolverhampton
** Blakenhurst	Redditch, Worcs	Ford	Arundel, West Sussex
Blantyre House	Cranbrook, Kent	Forest Bank	Pendlebury, Manchester
Blundeston	Lowestoft, Suffolk	* Foston Hall	Ashbourne, Derby
Brinsford	Wolverhampton	Frankland	Brasside, Durham
Bristol	Bristol	Friarton	Perth
Brixton	Brixton, London	Full Sutton	Full Sutton, Yorks
* Brockhill	Redditch, Worcs	Garth	Preston, Lancs
* Bronzefield	Ashford	Gartree	Market Harborough, Leics
** Buckley Hall	Rochdale, Lancs	Gateside	Greenock
Bullingdon	Bicester, Oxon	Glenochil	Clackmannanshire
* Bullwood Hall	Hockley, Essex	Glen Parva	Leicester
Camp Hill	Newport, Isle of Wight	Gloucester	Barrack Square,
Cardiff	Cardiff, South Wales		Gloucester
Castington	Morpeth	Grendon	Aylesbury, Bucks
Castle Huntly	Longforgan, nr Dundee	Guys Marsh	Shaftesbury, Dorset
Channings Wood	Newton Abbott, Devon	Haslar	Gosport, Hants
* Chelmsford	Chelmsford, Essex	Hatfield	Hatfield, Doncaster
Coldingley	Woking, Surrey	Haverigg	Millom, Cumbria
* Cookham Wood	Rochester, Kent	Hewell Grange	Redditch, Worcs
* Cornton Vale	Stirling	High Down	Sutton, Surrey
Crumlin Road	Belfast	* Highpoint	Newmarket, Suffolk
Dartmoor	Princetown, Yelverton,	Hindley	Wigan, Lancs
	Devon	Hollesley Bay	Woodbridge, Suffolk
Deerbolt	Barnard Castle	* Holloway	Parkhurst Rd, London
** Doncaster	Marshgate, Doncaster	Holme House	Stockton-on-Tees
Dorchester	North Square, Dorchester	Hull	Hull, Yorks
** Dovegate	Uttoxeter	Hydebank Wood	Belfast
Dover	Dover, Kent	** Kilmarnock	Kilmarnock

BRITAIN

Name	Location	Name	Location
Kingston	Portsmouth	Portland	Portland, Dorset
Kirkham	Preston, Lancs	Prescoed	Pontypool
Kirklevington Grange	Yarm, Cleveland	Preston	Preston, Lancs
Lancaster	Lancaster	Ranby	Retford, Notts
Lancaster Farms	Lancaster	Reading	Reading
Latchmere House	Richmond, Surrey	* Risley	Warrington
Leicester	Leicester	Rochester	Rochester, Kent
Lewes	Lewes, East Sussex	** Rye Hill	Rugby, Warwickshire
Leyhill	Wotton-under-Edge, Glos	Send	Woking, Surrey
Lincoln	Lincoln	Shepton Mallet	Somerset
Lindholme	Doncaster	Shotts	Shotts, Lanarkshire
Littlehey	Huntingdon	Shrewsbury	The Dana, Shrewsbury
Liverpool	Liverpool (holds on average most prisoners in Europe, approx 1,476)	Spring Hill	Buckinghamshire
		Stafford	Gaol Rd, Stafford
		Standford Hill	Sheerness, Kent
Long Lartin	Evesham, Worcs	Stocken	Stretton, Leics
Longport	Canterbury, Kent	Stoke Heath	Market Drayton, Shrops
Longriggend	Airdrie	* Styal	Wilmslow, Cheshire
** Lowdham Grange	Lowdham, Notts	Sudbury	Sudbury, Derbyshire
Low Moss	Glasgow	Swaleside	Isle of Sheppey, Kent
* Low Newton	Brasside, Durham	Swansea	Swansea
Maghaberry	Lisburn, Co Antrim	Swinfen Hall	Lichfield, Staffs
Magilligan	Londonderry	Thorn Cross	Warrington
Maidstone	Maidstone	Usk	Usk, Gwent
Manchester	Manchester	Verne, The	Portland, Dorset
Maze (formerly 'Long Kesh')	Lisburn, Co Antrim	Wakefield	Wakefield, Yorks
		Wandsworth	London
Moorland	Doncaster	Wayland	Thetford, Norfolk
Morton Hall	Lincoln	Wealston	Wetherby, W. Yorks
Mount	Hemel Hempstead	Weare	Portland Harbour, Dorset
Mountjoy	Dublin		
Mousehold	Norwich	Wellingborough	Wellingborough, Northants
* New Hall	Wakefield, Yorks		
Noranside	Angus	Werrington	Stoke-on-Trent
Northallerton	Northallerton, N. Yorks	Wetherby	Wetherby, Yorks
North Sea Camp	Boston, Lincs	Whatton	Notts
Norwich	Norwich	Whitemoor	March, Cambs
Nottingham	Nottingham	* Winchester	Winchester, Hants
Onley	Rugby, Warks	Winson Green	Birmingham
** Parc	Bridgend, S. Wales	** Wolds, The	Brough, Yorks
Parkhurst	Newport, Isle of Wight	Woodhill	Milton Keynes
Penninghame	Newton Stewart	Wormwood Scrubs	DuCane Rd, London (built in 1874, the Scrubs is the largest prison in GB)
Pentonville	London		
Perth	Perth		
Peterhead	Aberdeenshire		
Polmont	Falkirk	Wymott	Preston, Lancs
* Porterfield	Inverness		

* denotes women's prison (or women's wing attached)
** denotes private prison

British Castles

Name	Location	General Information
Abergavenny	Gwent	Norman Motte & Bailey castle founded by Hamelin of Ballon between 1087 & 1100, rebuilt in stone C12, captured by Welsh. c1172, recaptured by William de Braose c1175, ordered to be destroyed by Charles I in 1645.
Aberystwyth	Dyfed	Edwardian concentric castle erected 1277–90 under aegis of Edmund Crouchback and Master Giles of St George (after destruction in 1282 by Welsh). Held by Glyndwr 1404–9, slighted by Parliament in 1649.
Abinger	Surrey	Norman Motte & Bailey castle erected c1100. Wooden Donjon on stilts, excavated 1947–9.
Aboyne	Grampian	Motte castle erected C13, stone additions by 1300.
Acton Burnell	Shropshire	Fortified manor founded by Bishop Burnell c1284–90.
Airlie	Tayside	Enclosure castle founded by Ogilvy family c1432.
Allington	Kent	Founded by Stephen of Penchester 1281 beside site of Norman Motte & Bailey. Altered at end of C15 by Sir Henry Wyatt, restored by Lord Conway 1905–30. Now a Carmelite nunnery.

Name	Location	General Information
Alnwick	Northumberland	Norman castle founded by Gilbert de Tesson, C12 shell keep, seat of Percy family since 1309, remodelled by Salvin C19.
Amberley	West Sussex	Built for the Bishops of Chichester, licence to crenellate 1377. Partially ruined, now a private residence.
Anstey	Herts	C12 Motte & Bailey, now lost.
Appleby	Cumbria	Norman castle erected C12 by Henry II, restored by Lady Anne Clifford 1651.
Ardrossan	Strathclyde	Courtyard castle founded late C13, gatehouse improved C15/16.
Arundel	West Sussex	Norman castle, founded 1069 by Roger of Montgomery, C12 shell keep, seat of Dukes of Norfolk.
Ashby de la Zouch	Leicestershire	Norman hall founded C12 by Zouch family. Converted into a castle 1474 by Lord Hastings, slighted by Parliament 1648. Now owned by English Heritage.
Auchen	Dumfries & Galloway	Castle founded C13, slighted by Bruce, rebuilt C14 as quadrangular castle.
Ayr	Strathclyde	Castle founded C12 by William the Lion, besieged by English 1298.
Balvenie	Grampian	Enclosure castle founded late C13 by Douglases, remodelled C16 by 4th Earl of Atholl.
Bamburgh	Northumberland	Norman castle with C12 tower keep erected by Henry II, besieged in 1095, 1462 and 1464, 'restored' by Lord Armstrong 1894–1905.
Bampton	Oxfordshire	Quadrangular castle founded 1315 by Aymer de Valence, now lost.
Banbury	Oxfordshire	Norman castle built early C12 by Bishops of Lincoln, extended 1400 into concentric plan, now lost.
Barnard Castle	Durham	Norman castle erected by Guy de Balliol c1100, C13 round keep, dismantled 1630 by Sir Henry Vane, now owned by English Heritage.
Barnstaple	Devon	Norman Motte & Bailey castle erected C11 by Judhael, C12 shell keep now lost.
Barnwell	Northants	Norman castle founded 1132 by Reginald de Moine. Rebuilt c1265, now ruined.
Bass of Inverurie	Grampian	Motte & Bailey castle founded c1180 by David, Earl of Huntingdon.
Beaumaris	Gwynedd	Concentric Edwardian castle erected by Master James of St George 1295–1330.
Bedford	Bedfordshire	Norman Motte & Bailey castle founded late C11, modified and enlarged C12, besieged by Henry III 1224 and destroyed shortly after.
Beeston	Cheshire	Built by Ranulf of Chester c1220, slighted in Civil War, owned by English Heritage.
Belvoir	Lincolnshire	Gothic style C19 castle, seat of Dukes of Rutland on site of Norman Motte & Bailey castle founded by Robert de Todeni C11, destroyed by King John.
Berkeley	Gloucestershire	Norman castle founded by William Fitz Osbern pre-1086, current building erected 1154 by Robert Fitzhardinge.
Berkhamsted	Hertfordshire	Norman Motte & Bailey castle founded by Robert of Mortain, rebuilt by Thomas Becket 1155–65 and King John, rare double moat, now owned by English Heritage.
Berry Pomeroy	Devon	Norman castle probably founded C12.
Bickleigh	Devon	Norman Motte & Bailey castle dismantled mid-C12; Courtenay family built fortified mansion on site C14.
Bishop's Stortford	Hertfordshire	Norman Motte & Bailey castle, now lost.
Blackness	Lothian	Tower castle founded C15, extended C16 with plan resembling that of a ship.
Blair	Tayside	Tower founded c1270, last castle to be besieged (1746), C18 mansion, seat of Dukes of Atholl.
Bodiam	East Sussex	Quadrangular moated castle built by Edward Dalyngrigge 1386, restored by Lord Curzon. National Trust property.
Bolingbroke	Lincolnshire	Built by Ranulf, Earl of Chester, c1220, now ruined.
Bolsover	Derbyshire	Norman castle founded by William Peverel, rebuilt by Smythson in Jacobean Romantic style, owned by English Heritage.
Bolton	North Yorkshire	Quadrangular castle built by Lord Scrope c1381–99, slighted during Civil War.
Bothwell	Strathclyde	Castle founded in 1270s by Moravia family, captured by Scots 1297, English 1301 & 1331, dismantled by Sir Andrew de Moravia 1337, rebuilt by Black Douglas in 1360s.
Bowes	County Durham	Tower castle built by the Earl of Richmond 1170–87, now owned by English Heritage.
Bramber	West Sussex	Norman castle founded by William de Braose c1070, slighted during Civil War, now owned by National Trust.

Name	Location	General Information
Brecon	Powys	Norman castle founded 1090 by Bernard de Neufmarche, extended and fortified in stone C12, unsuccessfully besieged by Welsh 1216, 1233 & 1404.
Bridgnorth	Shropshire	Norman castle founded by Robert de Belleme C11, C12 keep erected by Henry II, slighted during Civil War.
Bristol	Avon	Norman Motte & Bailey castle founded after Conquest; Tower Keep erected C12 by Stephen, destroyed in 1650s.
Bronllys	Powys	Norman Motte & Bailey castle founded C12, cylindrical tower added c1176 after a fire.
Brough	Cumbria	Norman castle founded by William Rufus c1095 in ruins of a Roman fort, destroyed 1174 by William the Lion, rebuilt by Theobald de Valoires, restored C17 by Lady Anne Clifford. Now owned by English Heritage.
Brougham	Cumbria	Norman castle built C12 by Hugh d'Albini, pulled down c1700, now owned by English Heritage.
Buckingham	Buckinghamshire	Norman Motte & Bailey castle now covered by a church.
Builth	Powys	Norman Motte & Bailey castle founded by Philip de Braose c1100, destroyed by Llywelyn ap Gruffyd 1260, rebuilt 1277–82 by Edward I under direction of Master James of St George, severely damaged by Glyndwr.
Bungay	Suffolk	Norman castle founded by Roger Bigod c1105, demolished 1176, shell keep & bailey erected c1295 by Roger Bigod.
Caerlaverock	Dumfries	Built c1280 to a triangular plan, captured by Edward I 1300, slighted by Bruce, rebuilt C15, now owned by Historic Scotland.
Caerleon	Gwent	Norman Motte & Bailey castle erected c1086, great tower added. 1158–73.
Caernarvon	Gwynedd	Norman Motte & Bailey castle erected 1093 by Earl Hugh of Chester, destroyed by Welsh 1115, Edwardian castle on site constructed by Master James of St George 1283–1330, designed to resemble walls of Constantinople.
Caerphilly	Mid Glamorgan	Built by Gilbert de Clare, Earl of Gloucester, 1271–80 after original castle of 1267–70 destroyed by Llywelyn, now owned by Welsh Historic Mons.
Cainhoe	Bedfordshire	Norman castle founded by Nigel d'Albini, motte and 3 bailleys.
Caister	Norfolk	Built by Sir John Fastolf 1432–36, made of brick and surrounded by a moat.
Caldicot	Gwent	Norman Motte & Bailey castle founded by Walter Fitzroger early C12, developed by de Bohun Earls of Hereford late C12/early C13, gatehouse extended c1385, repaired late C19.
Cambridge	Cambs	Norman castle founded by William I 1068, rebuilt 1284–98, slighted in 1647.
Canterbury	Kent	Norman Motte & Bailey castle founded by William I 1066, Keep erected early C12.
Cardiff	South Glamorgan	Norman Motte built C1080 by Robert Fitzhamon on site of Roman fort, shell keep erected C12, further additions by Gilbert de Clare C13, castle remodelled by William Burges for 3rd Marquess of Bute C19.
Cardigan	Dyfed	Norman castle founded c1093, captured by Welsh c1170 and converted to stone, sold to John 1199, destroyed by Llywelyn the Great 1231, new castle built near original site by English in 1240s.
Carew	Dyfed	Norman Motte & Bailey castle founded by Gerald de Windsor 1105, extended by Nicholas de Carew in C13, damaged by Parliamentary forces in 1645.
Carisbrooke	Isle of Wight	Norman castle founded by William Fitz Osbern c1070, extended by Baldwin de Redvers in 1130s gatehouse erected c1335, now owned by English Heritage.
Carlisle	Cumbria	Norman castle built by William Rufus in 1192, improved by David I of Scotland, rebuilt 1541 for Henry VIII by Stefan von Hashenperg, now owned by English Heritage.
Carmarthen	Dyfed	Norman Motte & Bailey castle founded early C12, captured by Llywelyn the Great 1215, rebuilt and extended by English during C13, held by Glyndwr 1403–9.
Carreg Cennen	Dyfed	Courtyard castle built in C13 on site of Roman fort, demolished by Yorkists 1462.
Castell y Bere	Gwynedd	Enclosure castle founded c1221 by Llywelyn the Great, captured by Edward I 1283, restored 1286–90, abandoned by 1300.
Castle Acre, priory	Norfolk	Norman castle founded by William de Warenne C11, stone keep rebuilt C1140, now owned by English Heritage.
Castle Bytham	Lincolnshire	Norman castle founded c1169, besieged and demolished 1221, rebuilt by William de Colville 1220s.

Name	Location	General Information
Castle Drogo	Devon	Granite castle designed by Edwin Lutyens 1910–30.
Castle Hedingham	Essex	Tower keep built by Aubrey de Vere III 1141 on site of late C11 timber castle, now owned by English Heritage.
Castle Rising	Norfolk	Tower keep built by William II d'Albini c1140, now owned by English Heritage.
Castle Rushen	Castletown, I.O.M.	Probably the best-preserved medieval castle in the British Isles. Built c1200; partly destroyed in a siege by Robert the Bruce in 1313; but rebuilt by Sir William Montacute in c1344. The castle chapel houses a clock presented by Queen Elizabeth I in 1597.
Cause	Shropshire	Norman Motte & Bailey castle founded by Roger Fitz Corbet, fortified in stone C12, demolished 1645.
Cawdor	Inverness	Built 1454, seat of Earls of Cawdor.
Chepstow	Gwent	Norman castle with stone keep founded by William Fitz Osbern 1070, extended C13, disused from 1690, now owned by Welsh Historic Monuments.
Chester	Cheshire	Norman Motte & Bailey castle built on site of Roman fortress, improved C13, now lost.
Chilham	Kent	Norman castle founded by Fulbert of Dover, octagonal keep built for Henry II 1171–5.
Chirk	Clwyd	Motte & Bailey castle founded mid-C12, new castle founded nearby by Roger Mortimer 1274–1310.
Christchurch	Dorset	Norman Motte & Bailey castle founded by Richard de Redvers c1100, ruins now owned by English Heritage.
Cilgerran	Dyfed	Norman enclosure castle founded by Gerald of Windsor c1110, rebuilt and extended c1233.
Clare	Suffolk	Norman Motte & Bailey castle founded by Richard Fitzgilbert, improved by Gilbert de Clare.
Clavering	Essex	Norman castle founded by Robert Fitz Wimarc c1050.
Claypotts	Tayside	Built C16.
Clifford's Tower	York	Quatrefoil keep on motte founded by Henry III 1245 on site of Norman castle of 1069, burnt down 1190 whilst housing Jewish refugees, rebuilt and blown down 1228, now owned by English Heritage.
Clitheroe	Lancashire	Norman castle founded by Roger de Poitou.
Clun	Shropshire	Norman castle founded by Roger de Say, tower keep built in motte C12 by William Fitz Alan.
Cockermouth	Cumbria	Built C13 by William de Fortibus, rebuilt by Anthony de Lucy in 1360, slighted in Civil War.
Coity	Mid Glamorgan	Norman castle founded by Payn de Turberville, extended late C12, altered C14.
Colchester	Essex	Norman castle founded by William the Conqueror 1076–80; largest Norman tower keep, partly demolished 1683.
Conisborough	Yorkshire	Norman castle founded by William de Warenne, rebuilt with cylindrical tower keep by Hamelin, Earl of Surrey c1180, now owned by English Heritage.
Conwy	Gwynedd	Edwardian castle erected by Master James of St George 1283–7.
Cooling	Kent	Double quadrangular castle founded in 1380s, erected by Henry Yevele.
Corfe	Dorset	Norman castle founded by William I c1080, great tower erected by Henry I, gloriette erected by John, dismantled in Civil War (1646), now owned by National Trust.
Coulthalley	Strathclyde	Founded C12, rebuilt c1375, altered c1415 and c1520, rebuilt after siege 1557.
Craignethan	Strathclyde	Built in C16 by Sir James Hamilton, fortified courtyards with provision for artillery surrounding tower house, slighted 1579.
Criccieth	Gwynedd	Enclosure castle founded early C13, probably by Llywelyn the Great, Edwardian additions to site 1290, ruined by Glyndwr 1404.
Crichton	Lothian	Castle founded by John de Crichton late C14, extended C15.
Croft	Herefordshire	Medieval quadrangular castle of C14, named after family who built it, now owned by National Trust.
Cruggleton	Dumfries & Galloway	Motte & Bailey castle founded C12, reinforced in stone C13.
Dartmouth	Devon	Artillery fort built 1481 by Dartmouth corporation to protect town, now owned by English Heritage.
Deal	Kent	Henrician artillery fort built in 1539–40, besieged 1648, now owned by English Heritage.
Deganwy	Gwynedd	Double Motte & Bailey castle founded c1090, taken by Henry III 1241 and rebuilt/extended, destroyed by Llywelyn 1257.
Denbigh	Clwyd	Edwardian castle built by Henry de Lacy, designed by Master James of St George, 1282–1311, destroyed in 1650s.
Devizes	Wiltshire	Norman castle founded late C11, used as prison by Henry II and Henry III, demolished in Civil War.

Name	Location	General Information
Dinefwr	Dyfed	Castle founded C12, rebuilt with cylindrical donjon C13, damaged by fire C18, modern castle constructed 1856.
Dirleton	Lothian	Founded by de Vaux family C12, stone buildings built C13, extended C14/C15.
Dolbadarn	Gwynedd	Castle with cylindrical donjon erected by Llywelyn the Great early C13, partially dismantled by Edward I in 1284.
Dolwyddelan	Gwynedd	Castle founded by Iorwerth Trwyndwn c1170, captured by English 1282 and repaired.
Donnington	Berkshire	Enclosure castle founded late C14 by Richard de Adderbury, destroyed in 1646, now owned by English Heritage.
Doune	Perth & Kinrosshire	Enclosure castle founded by Duke of Albany late 14th Century.
Dover	Kent	Norman castle founded 1066 by William I, rebuilt with tower keep designed by Maurice the Engineer for Henry II in 1180–9, concentric fortifications built at same time, besieged 1216, extra fortifications added C19.
Dudley	West Midlands	Norman Motte & Bailey castle founded by William Fitzansculf, destroyed by Henry II 1175, rebuilt c1270 by John de Somery, extended early C14 by John de Somery, slighted 1647.
Duffus	Grampian	Motte & Bailey castle founded by Freskin de Moravia C12, rebuilt c1300 in stone, north-west corner of Donjon slid down motte late C14.
Dumbarton	Strathclyde	Built upon Dumbarton Rock.
Dundonald	Strathclyde	Founded by Walter Stewart c1250, expanded by Robert II, 1371–90.
Dunstaffnage	Strathclyde	Enclosure castle built by MacDougall in the 13th century.
Dunstanburgh	Northumberland	Enclosure castle founded by Thomas, 2nd Earl of Lancaster 1313–16, altered by John of Gaunt, now owned by English Heritage.
Dunster	Somerset	Norman castle founded by William de Mohun, fortified manor built on site C14, owned by Luttrells from 1376, remodelled by Salvin C19, now owned by National Trust.
Dunvegan	Skye	Home of the Chiefs of Clan Macleod since foundation in C13.
Durham	County Durham	Norman castle founded by William I c1072, rebuilt C12 in stone, keep C14, rebuilt 1840, now used by University of Durham.
Edinburgh	Lothian	Wooden fortress erected by Malcolm III C11, rebuilt C12/13, taken by Edward I 1296, taken by Earl of Moray and destroyed 1313, rebuilt C14.
Edlingham	Northumberland	Castle founded by Sir William Felton late C12, triangular enclosure with separate great tower.
Egremont	Cumbria	Norman castle built by William de Meschines in 1130.
Eilean Donan	Western Ross	Built in C13, probably by Alexander II, rebuilt in C20.
Etal	Northumberland	Castle with donjon and gatehouse tower at opposing corners, founded 1342 by Manners family, captured 1513 by James IV.
Ewloe	Clwyd	Castle founded 1146 by Owain Gwynedd, rebuilt in stone c1200 by Llywelyn the Great.
Ewyas Harold	Herefordshire	Norman castle built c1050, refortified by William FitzOsbern.
Exeter	Devon	Norman castle founded by William I in 1067 in corner of Roman walls, largely demolished in 1744, stone gatehouse c1068 still extant.
Eynsford	Kent	Norman enclosure castle fortified in stone c1088, extended C12.
Farleigh Hungerford	Somerset	Castle erected c1370–83 by Sir Thomas Hungerford, enlarged C15 by Walter Hungerford, now owned by English Heritage.
Farnham	Surrey	Norman Motte & Bailey castle founded by Henry de Blois C12, slighted by Henry II 1155, rebuilt late C12 with stone encasing motte, slighted 1648, now owned by English Heritage.
Flint	Clwyd	Edwardian castle erected by Master James of St George 1277–80, donjon separate from rest of castle, slighted 1646.
Ford	Northumberland	Quadrangular castle founded 1338 by William Heron, attacked by Scots 1385, 1513, 1549, rebuilt 1861 by Marchioness of Waterford.
Fotheringhay	Northants	Norman Motte & Bailey castle, famous as the site of Mary Queen of Scots' beheading.
Framlingham	Suffolk	Norman castle founded c1100 by Roger Bigod, destroyed by Henry II 1175, rebuilt as enclosure castle by Roger II Bigod c1189–1200.
Gloucester	Gloucestershire	Norman Motte & Bailey castle founded by William I, Great Tower built by Henry I c1112.
Goodrich	Hereford and Worcester	Keep built mid-C12, converted into quadrangular castle by de Valence family late C13. Barbican erected C14, slighted 1646, now owned by English Heritage.
Grosmont	Gwent	Castle founded late C11, rebuilt in stone c1210, extended by Hubert de Burgh 1220–40.

Name	Location	General Information
Guildford	Surrey	Norman Motte & Bailey castle, keep erected on side of motte mid-C12.
Hadleigh	Essex	Enclosure castle founded by Hubert de Burgh C13, extended by Edward III 1361–70, now owned by English Heritage.
Hailes	Lothian	Founded C13, owned from C14 by Hepburns, who extended castle, besieged by Percys c1400.
Hallaton	Leicestershire	Norman Motte & Bailey castle, motte almost as large as bailey.
Harbottle	Northumberland	Motte & Bailey castle with shell keep erected 1159–60 by Robert d'Umfraville.
Harlech	Gwynedd	Edwardian concentric castle erected 1283–9 by Master James of St George, besieged 1294, 1401–5, 1408–9, 1468, 1647, now owned by Welsh Historic Monuments.
Hastings	East Sussex	Norman Motte & Bailey castle founded by William I 1066, appears in Bayeux Tapestry, later converted to stone, only C13 ruins extant.
Haughley	Suffolk	Norman Motte & Bailey castle, one of largest in Britain, dismantled by Henry II c1173.
Haverfordwest	Dyfed	Norman castle founded c1120 by Gilbert de Clare, strengthened by William de Valence C13, besieged by Glyndwr 1405.
Hawarden	Clwyd	Norman Motte & Bailey castle, fortified in stone early C13, destroyed by Llywelyn 1265, rebuilt 1277, slighted 1647/8.
Hay-on-Wye	Powys	Norman Motte & Bailey castle founded early C12 by William Revell, destroyed by King John, C13 replacement built on different site, destroyed by Glyndwr.
Helmsley	North Yorkshire	Norman castle founded by Robert de Mortain, held by Walter l'Espec and de Roos family, who constructed current structure 1186–1227. Enclosure castle with keep, keep heightened early C14, slighted 1644/5.
Hereford	Hereford and Worcester	Norman Motte & Bailey castle possibly founded c1050, held by William Fitz Osbern 1066–71, stoneworks C13 with tower on motte, now destroyed.
Hermitage	Borders	Founded early C14, captured by Scots 1338, owned by the Douglases, who extended it C14/15.
Herstmonceux	East Sussex	Brick quadrangular castle founded 1441 by Sir Roger Fiennes, restored C20.
Hertford	Herts	Norman Motte & Bailey castle founded c1067 by William I, major works on castle C15, demolished C17.
Hever	Kent	Manor house founded 1270s, fortified 1340 by William de Hever and in 1384 by Sir John Cobham, bought by Boleyn family 1462 and modified, restored by Viscount Astor 1903–7.
Holt	Clwyd	Edwardian enclosure castle founded by John de Warenne 1280s, demolished late C17.
Hopton	Shropshire	Norman Motte & Bailey castle founded C12, donjon built on motte by Walter de Hopton c1300.
Huntingdon	Cambridgeshire	Norman Motte & Bailey castle founded 1069 by William I, 2nd motte added C12, demolished 1174 by Henry II.
Huntly	Grampian	Motte & Bailey castle founded C12, rebuilt in stone and extended by 1st Earl of Huntly C15, blown up by James VI 1594, rebuilt by 1st Marquis of Huntly c1600–06.
Inverlochy	Highland	Enclosure castle founded c1270–80.
Inverness	Highland	Founded C12, later reclad in stone. Destroyed by Young Pretender 1746.
Jedburgh	Borders	Motte & Bailey castle founded C12 by David I, destroyed c1410 by Regent Albany.
Kenilworth	Warwickshire	Enclosure castle with motte & donjon founded c1120 by William de Clinton, donjon rebuilt later C12, water defences added C13, besieged for 6 months 1266, remodelled by John of Gaunt 1370s, slighted 1649, now owned by English Heritage.
Kidwelly	Dyfed	Norman castle founded by Roger, Bishop of Salisbury c1106, burnt by Welsh 1215, enclosure castle built 1270s, concentric curtain added C14.
Kiessimut	Barra, Western Isles	Enclosure castle of late C12/early C13, restored by MacNeils.
Kildrummy	Grampian	Enclosure castle of C13 on site of C12 Motte & Bailey castle.
Kirby Muxloe	Leicestershire	Unfinished quadrangular castle built by Lord Hastings c1480–3, now owned by English Heritage.
Knaresborough	North Yorkshire	Norman castle built C12 by Eustace Fitzjohn, improved by Edward II and III 1307–50, slighted 1648.
Lancaster	Lancashire	Norman castle built early C12 by Roger de Poitou, extended by King John, improved by Henry IV, partially demolished 1649.
Laugharne	Dyfed	Castle founded C12, rebuilt in C13 and 14 including cylindrical keep.
Launceston	Cornwall	Norman Motte & Bailey castle of Dunheved, built by Robert of

BRITAIN

Name	Location	General Information
		Mortain, rebuilt with shell keep C13 by Richard of Cornwall. George Fox imprisoned in gatehouse 1656, owned by English Heritage.
Leeds	Kent	Norman castle founded by the de Crevecoeur family, rebuilt by Edward I after 1278, restored C19.
Leicester	Leicestershire	Norman Motte & Bailey castle founded c1068, fortified in stone by 2nd Earl of Leicester mid-C12, improved by Henry IV and V.
Lewes	East Sussex	Norman double Motte & Bailey castle built by William de Warenne c1069–70, shell keep added C13, barbican added C14.
Lincoln	Lincolnshire	Norman Double Motte & Bailey castle founded by William 1 1068, shell keep (Lucy Tower) added C12.
Llandovery	Dyfed	Norman Motte & Bailey castle founded early C12 by Robert Fitzpons, captured by Welsh 1116, recovered c1158, stonework added late C12, slighted by Cromwell.
Llanstephan	Dyfed	Enclosure castle founded C12, captured by Welsh 1146, retaken by Henry II, given to William de Camville, strengthened c1192, extended C13, captured by Glyndwr 1403.
Loch Doon	Strathclyde	Enclosure castle of late C13 erected on an island; moved to western shore of loch 1934–5.
Longtown	Hereford & Worcester	Norman Motte & Bailey castle founded late C11, cylindrical donjon added on motte early C14.
Ludgershall	Wiltshire	Norman Motte & Bailey castle founded late C11, unfinished donjon added mid-C12, replacement tower added c1200, now owned by English Heritage.
Ludlow	Shropshire	Norman enclosure castle with flanking towers erected c1086 by Roger de Lacy.
Lydford	Devon	Norman castle founded C11, donjon added C12 and extended with motte built around base C13.
Lympne	Kent	Norman castle founded 1080s, reconstructed C14.
Manorbier	Dyfed	Norman enclosure castle founded by Otto de Barri late C11, strengthened C12, birthplace of Giraldus Cambrensis 1146.
Marlborough	Wiltshire	Norman Motte & Bailey castle, extended by Henry II, shell keep added by King John and added to by Henry III.
Middleham	North Yorkshire	Norman Motte & Bailey castle founded c1086, tower keep built on nearby site by Robert Fitzranulph c1170, quadrangular curtain added C13, slighted in Civil War, now owned by English Heritage.
Monmouth	Gwent	Norman Motte & Bailey castle founded by William FitzOsbern c1070, keep added on motte c1120–30, birthplace of Henry V 1387, slighted during Civil War.
Montacute	Somerset	Norman Motte & Bailey castle founded by Robert of Mortain 1069/70, dismantled C12 by Cluniac monks of Montacute Priory.
Montfichet	London	Norman Motte & Bailey castle founded by William I 1066/7, dismantled C13.
Montgomery (I) (Hen Domen)	Powys	Norman Motte & Bailey castle built by Roger de Montgomery c1071, dismantled C12.
Montgomery (II)	Powys	Enclosure castle founded 1223 by Baldwin de Boller, slighted 1649.
Morpeth	Northumberland	Norman Motte & Bailey castle founded late C11, destroyed by King John 1215, castle rebuilt in bailey mid-C13.
Mountsorrell	Leicestershire	Norman Motte & Bailey castle, dismantled 1217.
Neroche	Somerset	Norman enclosure castle founded C11 by Robert of Mortain, motte added early C12, shell keep added mid-C12.
Nether Stowey	Somerset	Norman Motte & 2 Bailey castle, tower keep added on motte mid-C12.
Newark	Nottinghamshire	Norman enclosure castle built by Bishop of Lincoln 1130s, major reconstruction early C13, slighted 1646.
New Buckenham	Norfolk	Built by William II d'Albini c1140, cylindrical tower keep (first in Britain), demolished by Sir Philip Knyvey 1649.
Newcastle	Tyne & Wear	Norman Motte & Bailey castle founded c1080, rebuilt with keep designed by Maurice the Engineer 1068–77.
Newport	Gwent	Norman castle founded C12, rebuilt C13, sacked by Glyndwr and rebuilt C15.
Norham	Northumberland	Norman Motte & Bailey castle founded c1120 by Ranulf Flambard, destroyed by Scots 1140s, rebuilt by Bishop Hugh of Durham 1158–74, taken by Scots 1513, now owned by English Heritage.
Northampton	Northants	Norman Motte & Bailey castle founded c1080, enlarged by Henry I. tower keep added c1170.
Norwich	Norfolk	Norman Motte & Bailey castle founded by William FitzOsbern for William I 1067, tower keep added on motte 1125–35, stone curtain added 1268–70, keep restored by Salvin 1834–9, now serving as museum (since 1894).

Name	Location	General Information
Nottingham	Nottinghamshire	Norman Motte & Bailey castle founded 1068 by William I, modified by Henry II. Keep built 1213, demolished 1651 by Colonel Hutchinson, renovated 1878 by the Corporation and now a museum.
Nunney	Somerset	Rectangular moated Great Tower with cylindrical towers at corners built 1373 by Sir John de la Mare, slighted 1645, now owned by English Heritage.
Oakham	Rutland	Norman Motte & Bailey castle, stone added C12, Great Hall built by Wakelin de Ferrers c1180 still extant.
Odiham	Hampshire	Octagonal keep built by King John 1207–12.
Ogmore	Mid–Glamorgan	Norman castle founded c1110, stone donjon built late C12, fortified in stone C13.
Okehampton	Devon	Norman Motte & Bailey castle founded by Baldwin Fitzgilbert c1070, extended and tower built on motte early C14.
Ongar	Essex	Norman Motte & Bailey castle founded early C12 by de Lucy family, stone tower built on motte 1150s.
Orford	Suffolk	Castle with polygonal keep founded by Henry II 1165–72, now owned by English Heritage.
Oswestry	Shropshire	Norman Motte & Bailey castle founded late C11 by Rainald de Bailleul, shell keep built C12.
Oxford	Oxfordshire	Norman Motte & Bailey castle founded c1071 by Robert d'Oilly, St George's Tower built on motte late C11, shell keep built on motte C12.
Oystermouth	West Glamorgan	Norman castle built c1100, destroyed 1215, rebuilt C13 by William de Braose.
Peel Castle	Peel, I.O.M.	Situated on St Patrick's Isle near Peel harbour and built by William Le Scrope in 1392. The castle houses the ruins of St German's Cathedral, named from Germanus a disciple of Patrick who is thought to have brought Christianity to the island.
Peel of Lumphanan	Grampian	Motte & Bailey castle founded C12, shell keep erected early C13.
Pembridge	Hereford & Worcester	Castle founded C13 by Ralph de Pembridge, includes moat and cylindrical donjon, ruined in Civil War.
Pembroke	Dyfed	Norman enclosure castle founded c1090 by Arnulf de Montgomery, extended and cylindrical donjon built by William Marshal early C13, slighted by Cromwell 1648/9.
Pendennis	Cornwall	Henrician artillery fort built to protect Falmouth, now owned by English Heritage.
Penhow	Gwent	Enclosure castle founded early C13 by Sir William St Maur.
Penrice	West Glamorgan	Norman enclosure castle founded c1100, stone castle raised on nearby site mid-C13, cylindrical donjon.
Penrith	Cumbria	Tower built C14, quadrangular castle erected on site c1397–9 by William Strickland, Bishop of Carlisle.
Pevensey	East Sussex	Norman castle built within the site of old Roman fort, founded C11 by Robert of Mortain, donjon added c1100 by William of Mortain, strengthened early C13, now owned by English Heritage.
Peveril	Derbyshire	Norman castle founded by William Peverel, also known as Peak Castle, improved by Henry II, tower keep erected 1176, now owned by English Heritage.
Pickering	North Yorkshire	Norman Motte & Bailey castle founded c1100, shell keep built c1218–36, improved early C14.
Picton	Dyfed	Norman Motte & Bailey castle founded c1090 by William de Picton, enclosure castle built on nearby site mid-C13.
Pleshey	Essex	Norman Motte & Bailey castle founded early C12, destroyed 1157, refortified 1167–80, donjon on motte.
Pontefract	West Yorkshire	Norman Motte & Bailey castle founded 1069 by Ilbert de Lacy, improved by Thomas, Earl of Lancaster, and John of Gaunt C14, destroyed 1649.
Portchester	Hampshire	Norman castle founded by Henry I c1120 in corner of old Roman fort, keep raised by Henry II, palace constructed for Richard II 1396–9, now owned by English Heritage.
Powis	Powys	Castle founded C13 by Gruffydd, Baron de la Pole, destroyed in 1270s by Llywelyn the Last and rebuilt, modified by the Herberts after purchase in 1587, now owned by the National Trust.
Raglan	Gwent	Norman Motte & Bailey castle founded c1070 by the Bloet family, major reconstruction C15, hexagonal Yellow Tower of Gwent constructed by Sir William ap Thomas, other works 1450–69 by Sir William Herbert, slighted 1646, now owned by Welsh Historic Monuments.
Ravenscraig	Fife	Coastal artillery fortress founded 1460 by James II, erected 1460–3.
Restormel	Cornwall	Norman castle founded C11 by Baldwin FitzUrstin, C12 shell

B
R
I
T
A
I
N

Name	Location	General Information
		keep built by Robert of Cardinham, now owned by English Heritage.
Rhuddlan	Clwyd	Norman Motte & Bailey castle founded c1070, Edwardian concentric castle erected nearby by Master James of St George 1282, slighted 1648.
Richards Castle	Hereford & Worcester	Norman Motte & Bailey castle founded by Richard Fitzscrub pre-Conquest, stone tower built on motte c1175.
Richborough	Kent	Roman fort situated near Sandwich and thought to be the landing point of the Roman invasion armies in AD 43.
Richmond	North Yorkshire	Norman enclosure castle founded by Count of Penhievre 1071, late C11 stone hall (Scolland's Hall) built by Alan the Red, great tower added by Conan, Duke of Brittany, c1150–70, now owned by English Heritage.
Ripley	Harrogate, North Yorks	C19 castle owned by Sir Thomas Ingilby, a baronet, who inherited the stately home on his 18th birthday.
Rochester	Kent	Norman Motte & Bailey castle founded c1080 and built by Bishop Gundulf, stone curtain added c1088, stone keep built c1126–40 by William de Corbeuil, besieged and taken by John 1215, recaptured by Louis of France 1216, keep repaired c1225 with cylindrical corner added, besieged by de Montfort 1264, captured by Wat Tyler 1381, now owned by English Heritage.
Rockingham	Northants	Norman Motte & Bailey castle founded by William I, improved by Henry II, gatehouse built by Edward I c1280, damaged in Civil War, alterations by Salvin C19.
Rothesay	Isle of Bute, Strathclyde	Motte & Bailey castle founded C12, shell keep erected C13.
Roxburgh	Borders	Motte & Bailey castle founded early C12, captured 1314 by Scots and demolished, rebuilt by Edward III 1335–7, extended by Richard II, taken by Scots 1460 with loss of James II and destroyed.
Ruthin	Clwyd	Edwardian castle founded 1277, held by Prince Dafydd to 1282 when taken by Reginald de Grey, slighted 1647, converted into a hotel C19.
Saffron Walden	Essex	Norman Motte & Bailey castle founded C11 by Geoffrey de Mandeville, flint tower added C12.
St Andrews	Fife	Castle founded late C12, slighted by Andrew Moray 1337, rebuilt late C14, extended early C16, besieged and damaged 1546–7, John Knox amongst besieged.
St Briavels	Gloucestershire	Norman enclosure castle founded C12 by Milo Fitzwalter, tower added mid-C12, gatehouse built by Edward I c1292–3, keep collapsed 1752.
St Donats	South Glamorgan	Double enclosure castle founded by the Stradlings c1300.
St Mawes	Cornwall	Henrician artillery fort built 1540 to protect Falmouth, now owned by English Heritage.
Saltwood	Kent	Norman enclosure castle founded by Henry of Essex c1150–60, improved by Archbishop Courtenay of Canterbury 1380s, designed by Henry Yevele, rendered uninhabitable by an earthquake 1580, formerly owned by Alan Clark MP.
Sandal	West Yorkshire	Norman Motte & Bailey castle founded c1157, converted to stone c1200–80, besieged 1645 and slighted 1646.
Sauvey	Leicestershire	Motte & Bailey castle founded by King John early C13, disused from 1260s.
Scarborough	North Yorkshire	Norman castle founded c1136 by William of Aumale, keep built by Henry II, barbican added c1240, Piers Gaveston besieged 1312, now owned by English Heritage.
Scotney	Kent	Moated castle founded late C14 by Roger Ashburnham, only cylindrical turret remaining, now owned by National Trust.
Sherborne	Dorset	Norman enclosure castle founded by Roger, Bishop of Salisbury, c1107–35, I-shaped donjon added mid-C12, besieged and ruined 1645, now owned by English Heritage.
Shrewsbury	Shropshire	Norman Motte & Bailey castle founded by Roger de Montgomery c1067–9, converted to stone by Henry II, tower on motte collapsed c1270, altered by Thomas Telford C18 for Sir William Pulteney.
Skenfrith	Gwent	Norman Motte & Bailey castle founded late C11, cylindrical donjon and stone curtain walls built c1220–40 by Hubert de Burgh.
Skipsea	East Yorkshire	Norman Motte & Bailey castle founded c1086, motte separated from bailey by a marsh, destroyed by Henry III.
Skipton	North Yorkshire	Norman D-shaped enclosure castle founded c1080, extended with six round towers added by Robert Clifford c1310–14, besieged and severely damaged 1645, renovated by Lady Anne Clifford C17.
Southampton	Hampshire	Norman Motte & Bailey castle founded early C12, refortified C14 by Richard II with tower built by Henry Yevele.

Name	Location	General Information
South Mimms	Hertfordshire	Norman Motte & Bailey castle founded c1140–2 by Geoffrey de Mandeville, motte built around base of tower.
Stafford	Staffordshire	Norman Motte & Bailey castle founded c1070, destroyed by 1086, restored late C11, tower built on motte 1348 by Ralph, 1st Earl of Stafford, decayed C16.
Stamford	Lincolnshire	Norman Motte & Bailey castle founded late C11, shell enclosure built on motte C12, extended late C12.
Stirling	Stirling	Timber castle founded C12, taken 1296, 1297, 1298, 1299, 1304, 1314 (whence dismantled), rebuilt under the Stewarts C15.
Stogursey	Somerset	Norman enclosure castle founded late C11, improved by de Courcys C12, demolished c1216.
Stokesay	Shropshire	Fortified manor house crenellated by Lawrence de Ludlow 1291.
Sulgrave	Northants	Norman triangular enclosure castle founded late C11, stone tower added early C12.
Sutton Valence	Kent	Castle founded mid-C12 with great tower, altered by William de Valence C13.
Swansea	West Glamorgan	Norman Motte & Bailey castle founded by Henry Beaumont, burned 1115/6, C12 enclosure castle constructed nearby, rebuilt early C14, damaged by Glyndwr.
Sween	Strathclyde	Castle founded by McSwine family early C12, earliest stone castle in Scotland. Remodelled by Earls of Menteith C13 and extended by Lords of the Isles C14.
Tamworth	Staffordshire	Norman castle with shell enclosure founded early C12 by the Marmions.
Tantallon	Lothian	Founded by the 1st Earl of Douglas c1360, besieged by Stewarts 1492 and 1526, damaged by General Monck 1651.
Tattershall	Lincolnshire	Castle with Great Tower built in brick by Ralph, Lord Cromwell 1433–43, rescued by Lord Curzon 1911, now owned by National Trust.
Taunton	Somerset	Norman enclosure castle founded c1110 by William Gifford, tower and other buildings raised by Henry de Blois mid-C12, improved 1207.
Tenby	Dyfed	Norman castle founded after 1153, sacked by Welsh 1187 and 1260.
Thetford	Norfolk	Norman Motte & Bailey castle founded C11, destroyed by Henry II 1174.
Thornbury	Avon	Last military castle built in England c1511 by Edward Stafford, Duke of Buckingham, never completed.
Threave	Dumfries and Galloway	Founded by Archibald, 3rd Earl of Douglas, c1370, extended c1454, taken by James II 1455.
Tickhill	South Yorkshire	Norman Motte & Bailey castle founded late C11 by Robert de Belleme, 11-sided tower built on motte c1178–80 by Henry II.
Tintagel	Cornwall	Norman castle built c1145 by Reginald, Earl of Cornwall, modified by Richard, Earl of Cornwall, C13, now owned by English Heritage.
Tonbridge	Kent	Norman Motte & Bailey castle founded 1080s by Richard Fitzgilbert, shell enclosure added C12, gatehouse built by Gilbert de Clare C13.
Totnes	Devon	Norman Motte & Bailey castle founded C11 by the Nonants, shell keep added C13.
Tower of London	London	Norman enclosure castle founded by William I 1067, White Tower built by Gundulf of Rochester 1078–c1100, concentric fortifications added C13 by Henry III & Edward I.
Trematon	Cornwall	Norman Motte & Bailey castle founded C11, shell keep added C12.
Tretower	Powys	Norman Motte & Bailey castle founded by Sir Miles Picard c1100, shell keep added by Simon Picard mid-C12, cylindrical donjon added by Roger Picard c1220.
Turnberry	Strathclyde	Cylindrical Tower castle of C13, childhood home of Robert Bruce.
Tutbury	Staffordshire	Norman Motte & Bailey castle founded by Henry de Ferrers, improved by John of Gaunt from 1350, added to C15, slighted 1646.
Tynemouth	Tyne and Wear	Enclosure castle crenellated by Robert de Mowbray 1296, gatehouse added 1390s.
Urquhart	Highland	Motte & Bailey castle founded c1150, taken by Edward I, in 1313 passed to Randolph, Earl of Moray, extended C14.
Usk	Gwent	Norman earthwork castle founded by de Clares c1138, rebuilt C14, slighted in Civil War.
Wakefield	West Yorkshire	Motte & 2 Bailey castle erected c1140–50, possibly by William de Warenne.
Wallingford	Oxfordshire	Norman Motte & Bailey castle erected c1071, stonework added C12, demolished 1652.

Name	Location	General Information
Wardour	Wiltshire	Old Wardour castle – hexagonal construction founded by John, 5th Lord Lovell, 1393, damaged after siege 1644. New Wardour 'Castle' built 1769–76.
Wareham	Dorset	Norman castle with keep founded by Henry I, destroyed in Civil War.
Wark	Northumberland	Norman Motte & Bailey castle dismantled by David I of Scotland 1138, rebuilt by Henry II 1158, decayed C14.
Warkworth	Northumberland	Norman Motte & Bailey castle founded by Henry, Earl of Northumberland, c1140, taken by William the Lion 1173, rebuilt by Clavering family C13, multiangular tower added by Henry Percy mid-C14, owned by Percys 1332–1922, now owned by English Heritage.
Warwick	Warwickshire	Norman Motte & Bailey castle founded by William I 1068, shell keep added C12, rebuilt C14 by Thomas Beauchamp, unfinished additions by Richard III C15, repaired by Fulke Greville C17.
West Malling	Kent	Stone tower built c1100 by Bishop Gundulf of Rochester, now ruined.
White Castle	Gwent	Norman castle founded by Pain Fitzjohn, stone fortifications built c1184–6 by William de Braose, refortified by Edward I 1260s.
Whittington	Shropshire	Norman Motte & Bailey castle, improved by Fulke de Warenne from 1219 with tower built on motte.
Wigmore	Hereford & Worcester	Norman Motte & Bailey castle founded c1067 by William FitzOsbern, shell keep built C12, reconstructed C14.
Winchester	Hampshire	Norman Motte & Bailey castle founded 1067 by William I, Domesday Book originally housed in castle, site destroyed 1141, rebuilt shortly after, donjon added by Henry II, cylindrical tower on motte and Great Hall added by Henry III, only the Great Hall presently remains.
Windsor	Berkshire	Norman Motte & 2 Bailey castle founded 1067 by William I, shell keep added by Henry I, site rebuilt in stone and keep improved by Henry II, major rebuilding by Edward III c1350–77 with keep raised, alterations by Wyatville for George IV C19, damaged by fire 1992.
Wolvesey	Hampshire	Ecclesiastical castle-palace founded c1100, rebuilt in quadrangular form with great tower by Henry of Blois c1135–70.
Worcester	Hereford & Worcester	Norman Motte & Bailey castle founded c1069, burned down 1113, rebuilt C12, motte levelled 1830.
Wressle	East Yorkshire	Quadrangular enclosure castle founded c1380 by Sir Thomas Percy, damaged in Civil War.
Yester	Lothian	Motte & Bailey castle founded C12, C13 tower erected on motte, extended C15.
York	North Yorkshire	Norman Motte & Bailey castle on Baile Hill founded by William I 1068–9, destroyed 1069 and rebuilt, now lost.

Castles: General Information

Adulterine Castles	Unlicensed private castles built by barons primarily during the Anarchy (1135–54) of King Stephen's reign
Berkeley Castle	Edward II murdered in south tower
Bolingbroke Castle	Henry IV born Apr 1366
Caernarfon Castle	Edward II born 25 Apr 1284
Cardiff Castle	Built on the site of a Roman fort. Robert Curthose imprisoned for 28 years
Carisbrooke Castle	Prison of Charles I 1647–8
Carlisle Castle	Prison of Mary Queen of Scots when she first entered England
Castle: Terms	
allure	Wall-walk along the top of the battlements: the basic fighting platform for archers and crossbowmen
bailey	A courtyard in a castle
barbican	An outer fortification in front of the gate of a castle
bartizan	Turret projecting from a tower or wall
bastion	Tower projecting from a wall length or junction of two walls, designed to cover dead ground
battlement	Parapet or wall with indentures or embrasures, originally for shooting through
berm	Space between curtain wall and moat
buttery	One of the 2 service rooms (the other is the kitchen), used for dispensing drinks
caponier	A covered gallery running across a ditch, housing guns to fire along the ditch
casemate	Armoured compartment in which guns are mounted
concentric	Possessing more than one curtain wall
counterscarp	Outer side of the moat

crenel	Openings formed in top of a wall or parapet between the merlons, having slanting sides as in a battlement
curtain wall	Wall around the perimeter of a castle or one of its courtyards
drawbridge	Bridge that may be raised to prevent access
embrasure	The opening in a wall behind a window or an arrow loop
forebuilding	Structure protecting the entrance to a tower
garderobe	Latrine
gatehouse	Guarded building above or beside an entrance gate
great tower	Most important tower also called the donjon and, since the 16th century, the keep
hourd	(also hoarding) Timber gallery carried on beams outside the battlements. Stones could be dropped on attackers via holes in the floor
keep	see great tower
loop	Slit in wall for firing arrows
machicolation	Permanent stone version of a hourd
mangonel	Stone-throwing siege machine
merlon	Length of protective parapet between the openings of a battlement
mews	Building or yard where the hawks are kept
moat	Wide, often water-filled ditch surrounding a castle preventing land access
motte	Large, usually round flat-topped mound which supported a tower
murder hole	Opening over an entrance passage
oubliette	Dungeon or pit under the floor, usually below ground level, reached by a trap-door
palisade	Strong wooden fence
portcullis	Iron or wooden grating hanging vertically in gateway of castle, set in grooves and able to be raised and lowered
postern	Subsidiary gate in the outer wall
rampart	Surrounding embankment of a castle
revetment	Facing of stones or sandbags to protect a wall or embankment
scarp	Side of a moat surrounding a castle cut nearest to and immediately below a rampart
trebuchet	Stone-throwing siege engine powered by counterpoise weights; successor to the mangonel, and far more powerful
turret	Small tower that projects from the wall of a castle
ward	Courtyard in a castle
Dover Castle	Known as the 'Key of England'
First Castles	Imported by the Normans after 1066, although four possible sites c1050 built by Norman friends of Edward the Confessor
Flint Castle	Richard II formally surrendered his crown to Henry Bolingbroke
Fotheringhay Castle	Richard III born 2 Oct 1452; Mary Queen of Scots executed 8 Feb 1587
Framlingham Castle	Mary Tudor proclaimed Queen while staying there
Henry VIII's reign: built	Calshot, Camber, Deal, Hurst, Pendennis, St Mawes, Sandgate, Southsea, Walmer
Keep: largest	Colchester castle
Largest Castle : England	Windsor
Scotland	Doune
Wales	Caerphilly
Leaning Keep	Bridgnorth, Shropshire
Lewes Castle	Two mottes
Ludlow Castle	King Edward IV made Royal property when he ascended the throne
Marlborough Castle	John Lackland was married in the castle chapel and Henry III was married in the chapel
Newark Castle	King John died of dysentery 19 Oct 1216
Oldest inhabited, UK	Berkeley, Gloucestershire
Pembroke Castle	Birthplace of Henry VII
Pontefract Castle	Richard II died c14 Feb 1400
Powys Castle	Clive of India Museum
Roman forts: built in	Pevensey and Portchester Castles built within old Roman forts
Sherborne Castle	Once owned by Sir Walter Raleigh
Stone-built: first	Chepstow, Gwent
Stone keep: first	Tower of London (White Tower) 1078; Colchester built c1087
Thornbury Castle	Last built for military purposes
Tintagel Castle	Linked with Arthurian legend
Towers of similar design :	Colchester and White Tower, London
	Castle Rising, Norwich and Falaise (Normandy)
	Castle Hedingham and Rochester
	Dover and Newcastle
Walmer Castle	Lord Warden of the Cinque Ports resides there; it houses a Madame Tussaud's Waxworks
Windsor Castle	Queen Mary's dolls' house, St George's Chapel, Royal Mausoleum Frogmore. Oldest royal residence still in regular use. Edward III born 13 Nov 1312. George III, George IV, William IV all died there

BRITAIN

British Cathedrals

Name	Location	General Information
Aberdeen	Grampian	Dedicated to St Andrew. Seat of Episcopal diocese of Aberdeen and Orkney.
Aberdeen	Grampian	Dedicated to St Machar. Presbyterian cathedral founded 1424.
Aberdeen	Grampian	Dedicated to St Mary. RC Gothic revival Victorian cathedral.
Arundel	West Sussex	Dedicated to Our Lady and St Philip Howard. RC since 1965 for see of Arundel and Brighton, designed by J.A. Hansom.
Ayr	Ayrshire	RC cathedral, seat of Bishop of Galloway.
Bangor	Gwynedd	Founded by and dedicated to St Deiniol and extensively restored in 1866.
Beverley Minster	Humberside	Destroyed by Danes, refounded by King Athelstan c935.
Birmingham	West Midlands	Dedicated to St Philip. Built by Thomas Archer 1715, became a cathedral 1905.
Birmingham	West Midlands	Dedicated to St Chad. RC cathedral from 1850, designed by Augustus Pugin 1841.
Blackburn	Lancashire	Dedicated to St Mary, became Anglican cathedral 1927.
Bradford	West Yorkshire	Dedicated to St Peter, designed by Sir Edward Maufe, became Anglican cathedral 1914.
Brecon	Powys	Benedictine priory of St John the Evangelist became cathedral 1923 for the see of Swansea and Brecon.
Brentwood	Essex	Dedicated to St Mary and St Helen, RC cathedral from 1917.
Bristol	Avon	Dedicated to the Holy Trinity, Anglican cathedral founded 1142 but rebuilt by G.E. Street.
Bristol	Avon	Dedicated to SS. Peter and Paul, RC cathedral, seat of Bishop of Clifton since 1850.
Bury St Edmunds	Suffolk	Dedicated to St James, Anglican cathedral designed by John Wastell / Gilbert Scott 1914, seat of Bishop of St Edmonsbury and Ipswich.
Canterbury	Kent	Dedicated to Christ, rebuilt 1174 by William of Sens.
Cardiff	Glamorgan	Dedicated to St David, RC cathedral from 1920, replacing Belmont, designed by Edward Pugin.
Carlisle	Cumbria	Dedicated to the Holy Trinity, original site of Church of the Augustinian priory, founded 1093.
Chelmsford	Essex	Dedicated to SS. Mary, Peter and Cedd, refurbished by Charles Nicholson 1913, became cathedral 1914.
Chester	Cheshire	Dedicated to Christ and Blessed Virgin Mary, Henry VIII gave cathedral status in 1541.
Chichester	West Sussex	Dedicated to the Holy Trinity, founded by Bishop Ralph de Luffa 1108.
Coventry	West Midlands	Dedicated to St Michael, designed by Basil Spence, dedicated 1962.
Derby	Derbyshire	Dedicated to All Saints, became Anglican cathedral 1927, designed by James Gibbs.
Dundee	Central	Dedicated to St Paul. Seat of Episcopal Bishop of Brechin.
Dundee	Central	RC cathedral, seat of Bishop of Dunkeld.
Durham	Durham	Dedicated to Christ and Blessed Mary the Virgin c1093.
Edinburgh	Lothian	Dedicated to St Giles. High Kirk & National Church of Scotland.
Edinburgh	Lothian	Dedicated to St Mary. Episcopal cathedral.
Edinburgh	Lothian	RC cathedral, seat of Bishop of St Andrews and Edinburgh.
Elgin	Moray	Founded in 1224, rebuilt in form of Jerusalem cross, now ruined.
Ely	Cambridgeshire	Dedicated to the Holy Trinity, founded by Simeon, Abbot of Ely, became cathedral 1109.
Exeter	Devon	Dedicated to St Peter, consecrated 1133 and rebuilt c1275.
Glasgow	Strathclyde	Dedicated to St Mary. Seat of Episcopal Bishop of Glasgow and Galloway.
Glasgow	Strathclyde	Dedicated to St Mungo (St Kentigern). Built in C12.
Gloucester	Gloucestershire	Dedicated to St Peter and Holy Trinity, founded 681, became cathedral 1541.
Guildford	Surrey	Dedicated to the Holy Spirit, Anglican cathedral designed by Sir Edward Maufe, completed 1968.
Hereford	Hereford and Worcester	Dedicated to the Blessed Virgin Mary and St Ethelbert, founded 676 by Bishop Putta, restored 1908.
Inverness	Highland	Dedicated to St Andrew. Seat of Episcopal Bishop of Moray, Ross and Caithness. Part of the worldwide Anglican Communion.
Kirkwall	Orkney	Dedicated to St Magnus. Founded in 1137 by St Rognvald, a Viking ruler, in honour of his martyred uncle.
Lancaster	Lancashire	Dedicated to St Peter, built 1859, became RC cathedral 1924.
Leeds	West Yorkshire	Dedicated to St Anne, RC cathedral from 1878.

Name	Location	General Information
Leicester	Leicestershire	Dedicated to St Martin, redesigned by Sir Charles Nicholson 1927.
Lichfield	Staffordshire	Dedicated to the Blessed Virgin Mary and St Chad. Built in C13/14.
Lincoln	Lincolnshire	Dedicated to the Blessed Virgin Mary. Norman cathedral built by Geoffrey de Noiers.
Liverpool	Merseyside	Dedicated to Christ. Neo-Gothic Anglican cathedral founded 1904 but completed 1978.
Liverpool	Merseyside	Dedicated to Christ the King. Roman Catholic Metropolitan cathedral completed 1967. Nicknamed 'Paddy's Wigwam'. Original design by Lutyens rejected on grounds of cost.
Llandaff	Cardiff	Dedicated to St Peter and St Paul. Founded by St Teilo, rebuilt by Bishop Urban C12.
London	London	Dedicated to St Paul. Designed by Sir Christopher Wren, built 1675–1710.
Manchester	Greater Manchester	Dedicated to St Mary, St Denys and St George. Cathedral founded 1847.
Middlesbrough	Cleveland	Dedicated to St Mary. RC cathedral completed 1986.
Millport	Great Cumbrae Island, Ayrshire	Collegiate Church of the Holy Spirit. Anglican church known as the Cathedral of the Isles.
Motherwell	Strathclyde	Roman Catholic cathedral designed by Edward Pugin.
Newcastle	Tyne & Wear	Dedicated to St Nicholas. C14 cathedral rebuilt by R.J. Johnson.
Newcastle	Tyne & Wear	Dedicated to St Mary. RC cathedral from 1850, seat of Bishop of Hexham and Newcastle.
Newport	Newport	Dedicated to St Woolos. Seat of Bishop of Monmouth.
Northampton	Northamptonshire	Dedicated to Our Lady and St Thomas. RC cathedral completed in 1864.
Norwich	Norfolk	Dedicated to the Holy Trinity. Norman cathedral founded by William I in 1068.
Norwich	Norfolk	Dedicated to St John the Baptist. RC cathedral from 1976, seat of Bishop of East Anglia.
Nottingham	Nottinghamshire	Dedicated to St Barnabas. RC cathedral from 1850, designed by Augustus Pugin 1842.
Oban	Strathclyde	Dedicated to St John. Seat of Episcopal Bishop of Argyll and the Isles.
Oban	Strathclyde	Roman Catholic cathedral, seat of Bishop of Argyll and the Isles.
Oxford	Oxfordshire	Dedicated to St Frideswide. Smallest cathedral in England, also known as Christ Church.
Paisley	Glasgow	Roman Catholic cathedral built in the 1930s.
Perth	Perthshire	Dedicated to St Ninian. Seat of Episcopal Bishop of St Andrews, Dunkeld & Dunblane. Built between 1850 and 1890.
Peterborough	Cambs	Dedicated to St Peter, St Paul and St Andrew. Consecrated 1238 and became cathedral 1541.
Plymouth	Devon	Dedicated to St Mary and St Boniface. RC cathedral completed 1858.
Portsmouth	Hampshire	Dedicated to St Thomas of Canterbury. Founded in C12, became a cathedral in 1927.
Portsmouth	Hampshire	Dedicated to St John the Evangelist. RC cathedral from 1882.
Ripon	North Yorkshire	Dedicated to St Peter and St Wilfred. Built in the C15.
Rochester	Kent	Dedicated to Christ and the Blessed Virgin Mary. Medieval church renovated by Bishop Gundulf 1125–30.
Salford	Greater Manchester	Dedicated to St John the Evangelist. RC cathedral from 1850, designed by Matthew Hadfield.
Salisbury	Wiltshire	Dedicated to the Blessed Virgin Mary. Founded 1220 by Richard Poore replacing prior foundation at Old Sarum.
Sheffield	South Yorkshire	Dedicated to St Peter and St Paul. Built by Charles Nicholson.
Sheffield	South Yorkshire	Dedicated to Saint Marie. RC cathedral from 1980, designed by Matthew Hadfield. Seat of the Bishop of Hallam.
Shrewsbury	Shropshire	Dedicated to Our Lady Help of Christians and St Peter of Alcontara. RC cathedral built by Edward Pugin, completed 1856.
Southwark	London	Dedicated to St Saviour and St Mary Overie. Sir Arthur Blomfield rebuilt 1890s.
Southwark	London	Dedicated to St George. RC cathedral from 1850, rebuilt 1858.
Southwell	Nottinghamshire	Dedicated to the Blessed Virgin Mary.
St Albans	Hertfordshire	Dedicated to St Alban. Built in 1077 and designated a cathedral in 1877.
St Andrews	Fife	Medieval cathedral completed in 1144, now ruined.
St Asaph	Clwyd	Dedicated to St Asaph. Restored C19 by Gilbert Scott.
St Davids	Dyfed	Dedicated to St David & St Andrew. Norman cathedral restored in C19.
Swansea	Swansea	Dedicated to St Joseph. RC cathedral 1875, seat of Bishop of Menevia.

BRITAIN

Name	Location	General Information
Truro	Cornwall	Dedicated to St Mary. Designed by J.L. Pearson 1879–1910.
Wakefield	West Yorkshire	Dedicated to All Saints. Designed by J.L. Pearson.
Wells	Somerset	Dedicated to St Andrew. Built C12 by Reginald de Bohun.
Westminster	London	Dedicated to the Most Precious Blood. RC cathedral designed by James Bentley 1895.
Winchester	Hampshire	Dedicated to Holy Trinity, St Peter, St Paul and St Swithin. Restored by Bishop Walkelin c1090.
Worcester	Hereford and Worcester	Dedicated to Christ and Blessed Virgin Mary. Wulfstan restored Worcester cathedral 1084, improved C19.
Wrexham	Clwyd	Dedicated to Our Lady of Sorrows. RC cathedral built by Edward Pugin.
York Minster	North Yorkshire	Dedicated to St Peter. Thomas of Bayeux built St Peter's church c1070; restored C13.

NB: Although St Giles is known as Edinburgh Cathedral it does not have a cathedra so is technically a church. However, it is included in the listing because it has the same standing in Scotland as Westminster Abbey in England.

British Cathedrals: General Information

Arundel Screen   Part of Chichester cathedral.

Bell Harry Tower   Tower of Canterbury cathedral erected 1490.

Bell-tower: detached   Chichester.

Birmingham Cathedral   Edward Burne-Jones designed four windows in 1880 and William Morris made them.

Bishop's eye window   Lincoln cathedral.

Black stone fonts   Lincoln and Winchester both have black stone fonts from Belgium.

Canterbury Cathedral   Tombs for Henry IV and Edward the Black Prince and Trinity Chapel Shrine of Thomas Becket. William of Sens fell from scaffolding and work completed by William the Englishman. T.S. Eliot's play Murder in the Cathedral first performed in the Chapter House in 1935. Destroyed by fire in 1174, rebuilt by William of Sens with stone from Caen. Based on the Monastic Church of St Etienne in Caen where Lanfranc had been Abbot.

Carlisle Cathedral   Sir Walter Scott was married there.

Cathedral: definition   Church that contains a cathedra, or throne of the bishop of the diocese.

Cathedral: longest   Winchester 556 ft.

Cathedral: widest in England   Manchester at 114 ft.

Cathedrals: shape   Cruciform, traditionally.

Chichester Cathedral   Houses tomb for Bishop Robert Sherburne, who died in 1536. Houses monument for Walter Huskisson, Chichester MP (dressed as Roman).

Chichester: windows   Designed by Marc Chagall.

Christ Church Gateway   Canterbury cathedral.

Clock with no face   Salisbury cathedral.

Coventry Cathedral   Tapestry of the Risen Christ by Graham Sutherland 1952. Statue of Christ being doomed (behold the man) by Jacob Epstein. Windows by John Piper. Benjamin Britten's War Requiem first performed.

Coventry Cathedral: Old   Destroyed by bombing 1940.

Durham Cathedral   Completed by Ranulf Flambard and houses tomb of St Cuthbert.

Gloucester Cathedral   Contains tomb of Edward II, murdered in Berkeley castle; also tomb of Robert Curthose, Duke of Normandy.

Great Paul   17-ton bell in St Paul's.

Hedda Stone: Sculpture   Peterborough Cathedral.

Hereford Cathedral   Map of the World (Mappa Mundi) by Richard of Haldingham and Lafford C13, based on C5 work of Orosius. Africa is labelled as Europe, and vice versa. Jerusalem is centre of the world. Largest chained library (1,450 books) includes Anglo-Saxon Chronicle. Restored by Lewis Cottingham and Sir George Gilbert Scott. Houses shrine of St Thomas Cantilupe. Highpoint of Hereford is a tower, not a spire.

Highest Spire   Salisbury cathedral 404 ft; 2nd highest spire is Norwich at 315 ft.

Inverted Arches   Wells cathedral.

Largest Gothic Church   York Minster, in England.

Lichfield Cathedral   Houses the Sleeping Children statue. Three spires named The Ladies of the Vale. Name means Field of the Dead (Emperor Diocletian martyred 1,000 Christians). Previous name – Bishopric called the diocese of 'Lichfield and Coventry' until 1836.

Lincoln   Highest spire 524 ft until it was blown down in 1584.

Liverpool Anglican   Designed by Sir Giles Gilbert Scott after winning competition.

Llandaff Cathedral   Houses Christ in His Majesty by Jacob Epstein.

Longest Nave   St Albans has England's longest nave at 275½ feet.

Magna Carta: copies   Lincoln and Salisbury cathedrals; the other two are in the British Library.

Mostyn Christ   Bangor cathedral.

Nelson's Column   Hereford cathedral had a Nelson's Column long before the London monument.

New Cathedrals of 1927   Isle of Wight and South Hampshire became Anglican Diocese, creating many new cathedrals.

Norwich Cathedral   Edith Cavell buried. It also has the largest cloisters in England.

Old St Paul's   The Norman cathedral was 600 ft long; its spire was 490 ft high.

Oldest clock (1380)   Salisbury cathedral (no dial).

Peterborough Cathedral   Catherine of Aragon buried there 1536 and Mary Queen of Scots 1587 (moved to Westminster Abbey).

Priest and people: face   East, traditionally.

Ribbed Vault 1st   Durham cathedral.

Ripon Cathedral   Crypt by St Wilfred and Reredos by Ninian Comper.

Scott, Sir George Gilbert   Restored Westminster Abbey, Ely, Lichfield and Salisbury cathedrals.

Smallest Cathedral   St Asaph's, Clwyd.

Southwark Cathedral   John Harvard, founder of Harvard University, baptised 1607. Bunyan and Chaucer windows.

St Albans: dedicatee   St Alban, Britain's first Christian martyr (executed circa 209).

St Augustine's Chair   Canterbury cathedral.

St David's Cathedral   Based on the Spanish Santiago de Compostela.

St Giles Cathedral   Jenny Geddes flung stool at preacher for reading an Anglican text. John Knox, the religious reformer, was buried there in 1572. White stork's nest was recorded on roof in 1416, the only British breeding occurrence.

St Lucy's Chapel   Oxford cathedral.

St Paul's Cathedral   Henry Moore's statue *Mother and Child*. Bombed in December 1940. Statue of Queen Anne outside. St Paul's destroyed by fire in 1666. All Souls Chapel is memorial to Kitchener and other casualties of World War I. Whispering Gallery is famous for its acoustics. Frescoes on the inside of the dome by Sir James Thornhill. Houses Wellington's monument by Alfred Stevens and Nelson's statue by John Flaxman.

Three Spires   Lichfield, Truro and St Mary's Edinburgh.

Triforium 1st   Canterbury cathedral.

Twenty-four-hour clock   Wells cathedral.

Wastell's Tower   Canterbury cathedral.

Westminster Abbey   Not a cathedral as such, as it lacks a Bishop's Throne. Official name is the Collegiate Church of St Peter. George II was last Sovereign to be buried in the Abbey, as Windsor Castle was subsequently used. Tombs include Henry III, Edward I, Edward III, Henry V, Elizabeth I, Mary Queen of Scots and the Unknown Warrior.

Westminster Cathedral   Houses Eric Gill's *14 Stations of the Cross*.

Whispering Gallery   St Paul's cathedral.

Winchester Cathedral   Canute and other Danish kings are buried here. So are Jane Austen and Izaak Walton. When St Swithin's remains were transferred in 971 it rained for 40 days. Nave was built C14 by William of Wykeham and William of Edington.

Worcester Cathedral   Houses the tomb of King John.

Wren's tomb inscription   Lector, si monumentum requiris, circumspice – 'Reader, if you seek his monument, look around you.'

York Minster   Great East window by John Thornton 1405–8; St Cuthbert's (bishop in 685) window 1440.

Top 100 Greatest Britons of all time, as voted by internet and BBC viewers

1	Winston Churchill	41	Charles Dickens
2	Isambard Kingdom Brunel	42	Frank Whittle
3	Diana, Princess of Wales	43	John Peel
4	Charles Darwin	44	John Logie Baird
5	William Shakespeare	45	Aneurin Bevan
6	Isaac Newton	46	Boy George
7	Elizabeth I	47	Douglas Bader
8	John Lennon	48	William Wallace
9	Horatio Nelson	49	Francis Drake
10	Oliver Cromwell	50	John Wesley
11	Ernest Shackleton	51	King Arthur (mythical king)
12	James Cook	52	Florence Nightingale
13	Robert Baden Powell	53	TE Lawrence
14	Alfred the Great	54	Robert Falcon Scott
15	1st Duke of Wellington	55	Enoch Powell
16	Margaret Thatcher	56	Cliff Richard
17	Michael Crawford	57	Alexander Graham Bell
18	Queen Victoria	58	Freddie Mercury
19	Paul McCartney	59	Julie Andrews
20	Alexander Fleming	60	Edward Elgar
21	Alan Turing	61	Queen Elizabeth, the Queen Mother
22	Michael Faraday	62	George Harrison
23	Owain Glyndwr	63	David Attenborough
24	Elizabeth II	64	James Connoly
25	Stephen Hawking	65	George Stephenson
26	William Tyndale	66	Charlie Chaplin
27	Emmeline Pankhurst	67	Tony Blair
28	William Wilberforce	68	William Caxton
29	David Bowie	69	Bobby Moore
30	Guy Fawkes	70	Jane Austen
31	Leonard Cheshire	71	William Booth
32	Eric Morecambe	72	Henry V
33	David Beckham	73	Aleister Crowley (occult leader)
34	Thomas Paine	74	Robert the Bruce
35	Boudicca	75	Bob Geldof
36	Steve Redgrave	76	The Unknown Soldier
37	Thomas More	77	Robbie Williams
38	William Blake	78	Edward Jenner
39	John Harrison	79	David Lloyd George
40	Henry VIII	80	Charles Babbage

B
R
I
T
A
I
N

81 Geoffrey Chaucer
82 Richard III
83 JK Rowling
84 James Watt
85 Richard Branson
86 Bono
87 John Lydon
88 Montgomery of Alamein
89 Donald Campbell
90 Henry II

91 James Clerk Maxwell
92 JRR Tolkien
93 Walter Raleigh
94 Edward I
95 Barnes Wallis
96 Richard Burton (actor)
97 Tony Benn
98 David Livingstone
99 Tim Berners Lee (WWW inventor)
100 Marie Stopes

Wedding Anniversaries

1	Cotton / Paper	8	Bronze / Pottery	15	Crystal	50	Golden
2	Paper / Cotton	9	Pottery / Willow	20	China	55	Emerald
3	Leather	10	Tin	25	Silver	60	Diamond
4	Fruit / Flowers	11	Steel	30	Pearl	65	Blue Sapphire
5	Wood	12	Silk / Linen	35	Coral	70	Platinum
6	Sugar	13	Lace	40	Ruby	75	Gold or Diamond
7	Wool / Copper	14	Ivory	45	Sapphire		

NB: Wedding anniversaries are an area of frustration for quiz players because there are slight variations to many of the gifts that are traditionally given on wedding anniversaries, and to complicate matters even more, some of the gifts have changed over the years: e.g. diamonds were traditionally given on a 75th wedding anniversary but after Queen Victoria celebrated her 'Diamond' Jubilee in 1897, this became the established gift for a 60th anniversary, and the 75th which was previously Diamond then became Gold, as opposed to 'Golden' for a 50th. A more common cause of frustration is the gift for a first anniversary. Cotton was traditionally given, as the 'binding' of two people who have tied the knot, but as in the case of so many infrequently used customs it has become traditional to think of a first anniversary as a paper one, after the certificate of marriage. Neither is right or wrong, as they have never been observed for any reason other than a convenient question to ask in a quiz. In fairness, it would be better for quiz-setters to avoid the more controversial anniversaries – e.g. 1st, 2nd, 75th – or if insisting on using them, it would be advisable to phrase the question in the form 'If paper is a first anniversary, what is a second?'

Months of the French Revolutionary Calendar

Vendémiaire	(Grape harvest)	23 Sep –22 Oct	Germinal	(Buds)	22 Mar –20 Apr	
Brumaire	(Mist)	23 Oct –21 Nov	Floréal	(Flowers)	21 Apr –20 May	
Frimaire	(Frost)	22 Nov –21 Dec	Prairial	(Meadows)	21 May –19 Jun	
Nivôse	(Snow)	22 Dec –20 Jan	Messidor	(Harvest)	20 Jun –19 Jul	
Pluviôse	(Rain)	21 Jan –19 Feb	Thermidor	(Heat)	20 Jul –18 Aug	
Ventôse	(Wind)	20 Feb –21 Mar	Fructidor	(Fruit)	19 Aug –22 Sep	

Months of the Jewish Calendar

Tishri	30 days	Adar*	29 days	Tammuz	29 days
Marheshvan	29 / 30 days	Ve-Adar†	30 days	Av	30 days
Kislev	29 / 30 days	Nisan	30 days	Elul	29 days
Tevet	29 / 30 days	Iyyar	29 days		
Shevat	30 days	Sivan	30 days		

*30 days in a leap year
†13th month every 3rd, 6th, 8th, 11th, 14th, 17th, & 19th year of a 19-year cycle
NB: The Jewish calendar places the creation at 3761 BCE.

Months of the Muslim Calendar

1	Muharram	30 days	5	Jumâda I	30 days	9	Ramadan	30 days
2	Safar	29 days	6	Jumâda II	29 days	10	Shawwal	29 days
3	Rabia I	30 days	7	Rajab	30 days	11	Dhâl-Qa'da	30 days
4	Rabia II	29 days	8	Shaaban	29 days	12	Dhâl-Hijja	29 days*

*30 days in a leap year
NB: The Muslim calendar starts in 622 CE. 1 Muharram of the year I was 16 July 622; it marks the Prophet's move from Mecca to Medina.

Other Calendars

Indian		
	Vikrama Era	Dates from 23 Feb 57 BC
	Saka Era	Dates from 3 Mar AD 78
	Buddhist Era	Dates from 543 BC
	Jain Era	Dates from 527 BC
		(death of Vardhamana)
	Parsee Era	Dates from 16 Jun AD 632

Coptic Egypt and Ethiopia; dates from 29 Aug AD 284

Japanese Days (months are numbered)		
Nichiyobi	Sun-day
Getsuyobi	Moon-day
Kayobi	Fire-day
Suiyobi	Water-day
Mokuyobi	Wood-day
Kinyobi	Metal-day
Doyobi	Earth-day

Commemorative Days

Advent Sunday	Sunday nearest to 30 Nov
All Saints' Day	1 Nov
All Souls' Day	2 Nov
Andrew's Day, St	30 Nov
Ascensiontide	Ascension day to Whitsun Eve (10 days)
Ash Wednesday	The 1st day of Lent
Assumption	15 Aug
Australia Day	26 Jan
Barnabas's Day, St	11 Jun
Bartholomew's Day, St	24 Aug
Bastille Day	14 Jul
Burns Night	25 Jan
Calends / Kalends	First day of each month in ancient Roman Calendar
Cecilia's Day, St	22 Nov
Commonwealth Day	2nd Monday in March
Corpus Christi	Thursday after Trinity Sunday
Crispin's Day, St	25 Oct
David's Day, St	1 Mar
Easter Sunday	The 1st Sunday after the full moon following the vernal equinox
Epiphany	6 Jan
First day of year pre-1752	25 Mar
Francis of Assisi's Day, St	4 Oct
George Washington Day (USA)	17 Feb
George's Day, St	23 Apr
Giles' Day, St	1 Sept
Good Friday	Day before Easter Saturday
Holy Saturday	Last day of Lent
Immaculate Conception Day	8 Dec
Independence Day (USA)	4 Jul
John the Baptist's Day, St	24 Jun
John the Evangelist's, St	27 Dec
Labor Day (USA)	Equivalent to our May Day, First Monday of September
Lady Day	25 Mar
Lent	The 40 days between Ash Wednesday and Easter Saturday

	excluding Sundays
Low Sunday	The 1st after Easter
Luke's Day, St	18 Oct
Maggie Thatcher Day	10 Jan on Falkland Islands
Mark's Day, St	25 Apr
Martin Luther King Day (USA)	15 Jan
Martin's Day, St	11 Nov
Matthew's Day, St	21 Sept
Maundy Thursday	Day before Good Friday
May Day	Became public holiday in 1978
Michael's Day, St	29 Sept
Mothering Sunday	4th in Lent and 3rd before Easter
New Year's Day	Became public holiday in 1974
Nicholas' Day, St	6 Dec
Nones (Roman Calendar)	The 9th day before the ides of each month i.e. 7th of March, May, July and October and 5th of other months
Orangeman's Day	Celebrated by Irish protestants on 12 July
Palm Sunday	Sunday before Easter Sunday
Passion Sunday	Sunday before Palm Sunday
Patrick's Day, St	17 Mar
Paul's Day, St	29 Jun
Pentecost (Whit Sunday)	7th Sunday after Easter Sunday
Peter's Day, St	29 Jun
Shrove Tuesday	Day before Ash Wednesday
Stephen's Day, St	26 Dec
Swithin's Day, St	15 Jul
Sylvester's Day, St	31 Dec
Thomas' Day, St	21 Dec
Trafalgar Day	21 Oct
Trinity Sunday	1st Sunday after Whitsun
Twelfth Night	5 Jan
United Nations Day	24 Oct
Valentine's Day, St	14 Feb

English Quarter Days

Lady Day	25 March
Midsummer Day	24 June
Michaelmas	29 September
Christmas Day	25 December

NB: A useful mnemonic for remembering English Quarter Days is that three of the days end with the same number as letters in the month e.g. March has five letters so Lady Day is the 25th, June has four letters so Midsummer Day is 24th, September has nine letters so Michaelmas is 29th. Christmas Day should never be forgotten.

Scottish Quarter Days

Candlemas	28 February
Whitsuntide	28 May
Lammas	28 August
Martinmas	28 November

NB: Although the names of the four Scottish Quarter Days have remained the same, the dates changed in 1991. Candlemas used to be on 2 Feb, Lammas was 1 Aug and Martinmas was on 11 Nov. The date of Whitsuntide varied.

Birthstones

January	Garnet
February	Amethyst
March	Bloodstone or Aquamarine
April	Diamond
May	Emerald
June	Pearl, Agate Moonstone, or Alexandrite
July	Ruby or Cornelian
August	Sardonyx or Peridot
September	Sapphire or Chrysolite
October	Opal or Tourmaline
November	Topaz
December	Turquoise or Zircon

NB: Birthstones are also controversial, as once again some months have more than one stone. Attempts to introduce birthstones for each sign of the Zodiac have fallen largely out of use.

Chinese Years

Snake (serpent)	2001
Horse	2002
Sheep (ram)	2003
Monkey	2004
Rooster (cock)	2005
Dog	2006
Pig	2007
Rat	2008
Ox	2009
Tiger	2010
Rabbit	2011
Dragon	2012

NB: The calendar goes in 12-year cycles, so it continues Snake, 2013; Horse, 2014; and so on.

Watches at Sea

First Watch	8pm–midnight
Middle Watch	midnight–4am
Morning Watch	4am–8am
Forenoon Watch	8am–midday
Afternoon Watch	midday–4pm
First Dog Watch	4pm–6pm
Last Dog Watch	6pm–8pm

NB: A bell is rung every half-hour during a watch, which therefore ends on eight bells or four for a dog watch. The New Year is brought in with 16 bells. Incidentally 'Dog' is thought to be a corruption of 'dodge', which was introduced to enable easier rostering.

Zodiac

Aries	21 Mar–19 Apr
Taurus	20 Apr–20 May
Gemini	21 May–21 Jun
Cancer	22 Jun–22 Jul
Leo	23 Jul–22 Aug
Virgo	23 Aug–22 Sep
Libra	23 Sep–23 Oct
Scorpio	24 Oct–21 Nov
Sagittarius	22 Nov–21 Dec
Capricorn	22 Dec–19 Jan
Aquarius	20 Jan–18 Feb
Pisces	19 Feb–20 Mar

CALENDAR

CINEMA

A–Z of Films

A.I. Artificial Intelligence (2001) Haley Joel Osment (David), Jude Law (Gigolo Joe), William Hurt, Brendan Gleeson, Frances O'Connor. Child robot searches for the mother who abandoned him. *Dir.* Steven Spielberg.

À Nous la Liberté (1931) Raymond Cordy, Henri Marchand. Factory owner is blackmailed about his past and is helped by an old prison friend. US title: *Freedom for Us. Dir.* René Clair.

Abbott & Costello Go to Mars (1953) Bud Abbott, Lou Costello, Mari Blanchard, Martha Hyer, Robert Paige. Despite the title, they land first in Louisiana and then on Venus! *Dir.* Charles Lamont.

Abbott & Costello Meet Captain Kidd (1952) Bud Abbott, Lou Costello, Charles Laughton, Leif Erickson. *Dir.* Charles Lamont.

Abbott & Costello Meet Dr Jekyll & Mr Hyde (1953) Bud Abbott, Lou Costello, Boris Karloff, Craig Stevens. This film starring Boris Karloff was given an 'X' certificate in its day. *Dir.* Charles Lamont.

Abbott & Costello Meet Frankenstein (1948) Bud Abbott, Lou Costello, Bela Lugosi, Lon Chaney Jnr. Dracula and the Wolf Man also feature. GB title: *Abbott & Costello Meet the Ghosts. Dir.* Charles Barton.

Abbott & Costello Meet the Killer, Boris Karloff (1948) Bud Abbott, Lou Costello, Boris Karloff, Gary Moore. Boris Karloff is not the killer and appears very little. *Dir.* Charles Barton.

Abe Lincoln in Illinois (1940) Raymond Massey (Abraham Lincoln), Ruth Gordon. GB title: *Spirit of the People. Dir.* John Cromwell.

Abominable Dr Phibes, The (1971) Vincent Price, Joseph Cotten, Terry-Thomas. Dr Phibes, a disfigured musical genius, avenges his wife's death at the hands of surgeons. Sequel: *Dr Phibes Rises Again* (1972), starred Price, Terry-Thomas, Beryl Reid, John Thaw. *Dir.* Robert Fuest.

Abominable Snowman, The (1957) Peter Cushing, Forrest Tucker, Richard Wattis. US title: *The Abominable Snowman of the Himalayas. Dir.* Val Guest.

About a Boy (2002) Hugh Grant, Nicholas Hoult, Sharon Small, Madison Cook, Jordan Cook, Toni Collette, Rachel Weisz. Layabout philanderer exploits single mothers but has responsibility, in the form of a 12-year-old boy, thrust upon him. Based on a Nick Hornby novel. *Dir.* Chris and Paul Weitz.

About Schmidt (2002) Jack Nicholson (Warren Schmidt), Hope Davis (Jeannie), Dermot Mulroney (Randall Hertzel), Kathy Bates (Roberta Hertzel), Len Cariou (Ray), Howard Hesseman (Larry), June Squibb (Helen Schmidt). A retired actuary has to deal with life as an aged widower. *Dir.* Alexander Payne.

Above and Beyond (1952) Robert Taylor (Colonel Paul Tibbets, who dropped the first atomic bomb on Japan). *Dir.* Melvin Frank and Norman Panama.

Absence of Malice (1981) Paul Newman, Sally Field. *Dir.* Sydney Pollack.

Absent-Minded Professor, The (1961) Fred MacMurray, Tommy Kirk, Keenan Wynn, Ed Wynn. Lighter than air substance called 'Flubber' allows the Professor's Model-T Ford to fly. Sequel *Son of Flubber. Dir.* Robert Stevenson.

Absolute Beginners (1986) Eddie O'Connell, Patsy Kensit, David Bowie (Vendice Partners), Ray Davies, James Fox, Steven Berkoff, Mandy Rice Davies, Robbie Coltrane, Irene Handl, Eric Sykes, Lionel Blair. Teen life in 1958 London. *Dir.* Julien Temple.

Absolute Power (1997) Clint Eastwood, Gene Hackman (President Richmond), Ed Harris, EG Marshall, Laura Linney, Judy Davis. *Dir.* Clint Eastwood.

Accident (1967) Dirk Bogarde, Stanley Baker, Vivien Merchant, Michael York. Screenplay by Harold Pinter. *Dir.* Joseph Losey.

Accidental Hero (1992) Dustin Hoffman (Bernie Laplante), Geena Davis (Gale Gayley), Andy Garcia (John Bubber). Screenplay by David Webb Peoples, the writer of *Unforgiven* and *Blade Runner. Dir.* Stephen Frears.

Accidental Tourist, The (1988) William Hurt, Kathleen Turner, Geena Davis. Geena Davis won Academy Award for Best Supporting Actress. *Dir.* Lawrence Kasdan.

Accused, The (1988) Kelly McGillis (Kathryn Murphy), Jodie Foster (Sarah Tobias), Bernie Coulson. Jodie Foster won Academy Award for Best Actress. *Dir.* Jonathan Kaplan.

Ace in the Hole (1951) Kirk Douglas (Chuck Tatum), Jan Sterling (Lorraine), Porter Hall (Boot), Ray Teal (Sheriff). In order to boost newspaper sales a journalist delays the rescue of a man trapped in a cave. Aka: *The Big Carnival. Dir.* Billy Wilder.

Ace Ventura, Pet Detective (1994) Jim Carrey, Courteney Cox, Sean Young, Tone Loc. Ace is hired to recover the Miami Dolphins' dolphin mascot. *Dir.* Tom Shadyac.

Ace Ventura, When Nature Calls (1995) Jim Carrey, Ian McNeice, Simon Callow, Adewalé. Ace goes to Africa to find a sacred white bat. *Dir.* Steve Oedekerk.

Across the Pacific (1942) Humphrey Bogart (Rick Leland), Mary Astor (Alberta Marlow), Sydney Greenstreet (Dr Lorenz). Huston was called up mid-film and it was eventually completed by Vincent Sherman. *Dir.* John Huston.

Actress, The (1928) Norma Shearer, Ralph Forbes. This film was the opening attraction at London's Empire Theatre, Leicester Square. GB title: *Trelawney of the Wells. Dir.* Sidney Franklin.

Adam's Rib (1949) Spencer Tracy, Katharine Hepburn, Judy Holliday. *Dir.* George Cukor.

Adaptation (2002) Nicolas Cage (Charlie Kaufman/Donald Kaufman), Meryl Streep (Susan Orlean), Chris Cooper (John Laroche), Tilda Swinton (Valerie), Cara Seymour (Amelia), Brian Cox (Robert McKee), Judy Greer (Alice the Waitress), Maggie Gyllenhaal (Caroline). Cage plays twin brothers, a neurotic screenwriter with writer's block struggling to adapt a book about a Florida orchid-breeder and a happier individual who writes a script about a serial killer. *Dir.* Spike Jonze.

Addams Family, The (1991) Anjelica Huston (Morticia), Raul Julia (Gomez), Christopher Lloyd (Uncle Fester). Impostor arrives at the Addams family home purporting to be a long-lost elder brother. *Dir.* Barry Sonnenfeld.

Addams Family Values (1993) Anjelica Huston (Morticia), Raul Julia (Gomez), Christopher Lloyd (Uncle Fester). Sequel in which the Addams children try, unsuccessfully, to kill the new baby. *Dir.* Barry Sonnenfeld.

Addicted To Love (1997) Meg Ryan (Maggie), Matthew Broderick (Sam), Kelly Preston (Linda), Tcheky Karyo (Anton) *Dir.* Griffin Dunne.

Addiction, The (1996) Christopher Walken, Lili Taylor. *Dir.* Abel Ferrara.

Admirable Crichton, The (1957) Kenneth More, Cecil Parker, Sally Ann Howes, Diane Cilento, Peter Graves, Gerald Harper. US title: *Paradise Lagoon*. *Dir.* Lewis Gilbert.

Adolf Hitler – My Part In His Downfall (1972) Jim Dale (Spike Milligan), Spike Milligan (Milligan's father), Arthur Lowe, Bill Maynard. Notable for appearance of Spike Milligan playing the part of his father. *Dir.* Norman Cohen.

Adventure of Sherlock Holmes' Smarter Brother, The (1975) Gene Wilder, Marty Feldman, Madeline Kahn, Thorley Walters. *Dir.* Gene Wilder.

Adventures of Arsène Lupin, The (1956) Robert Lamoureux, Liselotte Pulver, Otto Hasse. Based on the Jewel Thief character created by Maurice Leblanc. *Dir.* Jacques Becker.

Adventures of Baron Munchausen (1989) John Neville, Eric Idle, Sarah Polley, Oliver Reed, Uma Thurman. *Dir.* Terry Gilliam.

Adventures of Barry Mackenzie, The (1972) Barry Crocker, Barry Humphries (Edna Everage), Peter Cook, Spike Milligan, Dennis Price. *Private Eye* comic strip fantasy. (The 1974 sequel was called *Barry Mackenzie Holds His Own*.) *Dir.* Bruce Beresford.

Adventures of Captain Marvel (1941) Tom Tyler (Billy Batson alias Captain Marvel). Assistant radio operator on scientific trip to Siam is endowed with superpowers by the mysterious 'Shazam' and battles against the evil 'Scorpion'. *Dir.* John English & William Witney.

Adventures of Mark Twain (1944) Fredric March (Twain), Alexis Smith, Alan Hale. *Dir.* Irving Rapper.

Adventures of Milo and Otis (1986) Narrated by Dudley Moore, the tale of a puppy in search of his friend, a kitten. This film was the second most popular film ever made in Japan. *Dir.* Masanori Hata.

Adventures of Pinocchio, The (1996) Martin Landau, Jonathan Taylor Thomas, Geneviève Bujold, Griff Rhys Jones, Dawn French. *Dir.* Steve Barron.

Adventures of Priscilla Queen of the Desert (1994) Terence Stamp, Hugo Weaving, Bill Hunter, Guy Pearce. Two transvestites and a transsexual drive a bus from Sydney to Alice Springs for a cabaret gig. *Dir.* Stephan Elliott.

Adventures of Robin Hood, The (1938) Errol Flynn (Robin), Basil Rathbone (Guy of Gisbourne), Claude Rains (Prince John), Olivia de Havilland (Marian), Alan Hale (Little John), Ian Hunter (King Richard), Melville Cooper (Sheriff of Nottingham). Won Academy Awards for Music and Editing. *Dir.* William Keighley and Michael Curtiz.

Adventures of Robinson Crusoe, The (1953) Dan O'Herlihy (Crusoe), Jaime Fernandez (Friday). *Dir.* Luis Buñuel.

Adventures of Sherlock Holmes, The (1939) Basil Rathbone, Nigel Bruce, George Zucco (Moriarty), Mary Gordon (Mrs Hudson). GB title: *Sherlock Holmes*. *Dir.* Alfred Werker.

Adventures of Tom Sawyer, The (1938) Tommy Kelly (Tom), Jackie Moran (Huck), Ann Gillis (Becky Thatcher). *Dir.* Norman Taurog.

Advise and Consent (1962) Charles Laughton, Henry Fonda, Walter Pidgeon, Don Murray. *Dir.* Otto Preminger.

African Queen, The (1951) Humphrey Bogart (Charlie Allnutt), Katharine Hepburn (Rose Sayer), Robert Morley. Based on the CS Forester novel. Humphrey Bogart awarded the Best Actor Oscar. *Dir.* John Huston.

Agatha (1979) Vanessa Redgrave (Agatha Christie), Dustin Hoffman, Timothy Dalton. Tells the story of Agatha Christie's disappearance in 1926. *Dir.* Michael Apted.

Age of Innocence, The (1993) Daniel Day-Lewis, Michelle Pfeiffer, Winona Ryder, Richard E Grant. Wealthy lawyer falls in love with his wife's cousin. *Dir.* Martin Scorsese.

Agony and the Ecstasy, The (1965) Charlton Heston (Michelangelo), Rex Harrison (Pope Julius II). Based on the Irving Stone novel. *Dir.* Carol Reed.

Aida (1953) Sophia Loren, Lois Maxwell. Based on Verdi's opera. *Dir.* Clemente Fracassi.

Airborne (1993) Shane McDermott, Seth Green, Brittney Powell. Surfer moves to Cincinnati and becomes a rollerblade champion. *Dir.* Rob Bowman.

Airforce One (1997) Harrison Ford (President James Marshall), Jurgen Prochnow (General Radek), Gary Oldman (Korshunov) *Dir.* Wolfgang Petersen.

Airplane! (1980) Robert Stack, Lloyd Bridges, Leslie Nielsen, Peter Graves, Kareem Abdul-Jabbar, Julie Hagerty. (The 1982 sequel, *Airplane II*, was directed by Ken Finkleman.) *Dir.* J. Abrahams, David and Jerry Zucker.

Airport (1970) Burt Lancaster, Dean Martin, Jean Seberg, Helen Hayes (Best Supporting Actress Oscar). Based on the Arthur Hailey novel. *Dir.* George Seaton.

Al Capone (1959) Rod Steiger (Capone), Fay Spain, Nehemiah Persoff, Martin Balsam. *Dir.* Richard Wilson.

Aladdin (1992) Voices of Robin Williams (Genie), Linda Larkin (Jasmine), Scott Weinger (Aladdin). 'Whole New World' won Best Song Oscar (music by Alan Menken, lyrics by Tim Rice) *Dir.* John Musker and Ron Clements.

Alamo, The (1960) John Wayne (Davy Crockett), Richard Widmark (Jim Bowie), Laurence Harvey (Travis), Frankie Avalon (Smitty), Richard Boone (Houston) *Dir.* John Wayne.

Alamo, The (2004) Dennis Quaid (Sam Houston), Billy Bob Thornton (Davy Crockett), Jason Patric (Jim Bowie), Patrick Wilson (William Travis), Emilio Echevarria (Antonio Lopez de Santa Ana). Based on the 1836 battle. *Dir.* John Lee Hancock.

Albert RN (1953) Jack Warner, Anthony Steel, Robert Beatty, Anton Diffring. POWs build a life-like dummy to cover the absence of escapers. US title: *Break to Freedom*. *Dir.* Lewis Gilbert.

Albino Alligator (1997) Faye Dunaway, Matt Dillon. Villains hold a group of New Yorkers hostage in a bar. *Dir.* Kevin Spacey.

Alexander the Great (1956) Richard Burton (Alexander), Fredric March, Claire Bloom. *Dir.* Robert Rossen.

Alexander's Ragtime Band (1938) Tyrone Power, Alice Faye, Don Ameche, Ethel Merman. *Dir.* Henry King.

Alf Garnett Saga, The (1972) Warren Mitchell, Dandy Nichols. The Una Stubbs and Tony Booth parts were played by Adrienne Posta and Mike Angelis. *Dir.* Bob Kellett.

Alfie (1966) Michael Caine (Alfie), Vivien Merchant, Shirley Anne Field, Julia Asher, Millicent Martin, Shelley Winters. Theme song sung by Cher. *Dir.* Lewis Gilbert.

Alfie (2004) Jude Law (Alfie), Marisa Tomei (Julie),

Omar Epps (Marlon), Nia Long (Lonette), Jane Krakowski (Dorie), Sienna Miller (Nikki), Tara Summers (Carol), Susan Sarandon (Liz). Not so much a remake of the 1960s film, more a reinvention of it. *Dir.* Charles Shyer.

Alfie Darling (1975)   Alan Price, Jill Townsend, Joan Collins, Annie Ross, Hannah Gordon, Rula Lenska. Alan Price takes over the Michael Caine role as well as contributing the music. *Dir.* Ken Hughes.

Algiers (1938)   Charles Boyer, Hedy Lamarr, Alan Hale. The famous line 'Come with me to the Casbah' was never actually said in this film. *Dir.* John Cromwell.

Ali (2001)   Will Smith (Ali), Jamie Foxx (Drew 'Bundini' Brown), Jon Voight (Howard Cosell), Mario Van Peebles (Malcolm X), Ron Silver (Angelo Dundee), Mykelti Williamson (Don King), LeVar Burton (Martin Luther King Jr), Albert Hall (Elijah Muhammad), Giancarlo Esposito (Ali's father), Michael Michele (Veronica), Nona Gaye (Belinda). *Dir.* Michael Mann.

Ali G Indahouse (2002)   Sacha Baron Cohen, Michael Gambon, Charles Dance, Kellie Bright (Me Julie), Martin Freeman. Black rapper becomes a national hero after becoming an MP. *Dir.* Mark Mylod.

Alice (1990)   Mia Farrow, Joe Mantegna, Alec Baldwin, William Hurt. *Dir.* Woody Allen.

Alice Doesn't Live Here Any More (1974)   Ellen Burstyn, Kris Kristofferson, Jodie Foster, Diane Ladd, Alfred Lutter. Ellen Burstyn won Academy Award for Best Actress. *Dir.* Martin Scorsese.

Alice in Wonderland (1933)   Charlotte Henry (Alice), WC Fields (Humpty Dumpty), Cary Grant (Mock Turtle), Gary Cooper (White Knight). Ida Lupino was brought from the UK for the title role but ultimately not used. *Dir.* Norman Z McLeod.

Alice's Adventures in Wonderland (1972)   Fiona Fullerton (Alice), Michael Crawford (White Rabbit), Robert Helpmann (Mad Hatter), Dudley Moore (Dormouse), Spike Milligan (Gryphon), Peter Sellers (March Hare), Michael Hordern (Mock Turtle), Ralph Richardson (Caterpillar) *Dir.* William Sterling.

Alice's Restaurant (1969)   Arlo Guthrie, Pat Quinn, James Broderick. *Dir.* Arthur Penn.

Alien (1979)   Tom Skerritt, Sigourney Weaver, John Hurt, Ian Holm, Harry Dean Stanton. *Dir.* Ridley Scott.

Alien Resurrection (1997) Sigourney Weaver, Winona Ryder, Dominique Pinou, Ron Perlman. *Dir.* Jean-Pierre Jeunet.

Aliens (1986)   Sigourney Weaver, Carrie Henn, Michael Biehn, Bill Paxton. Sequel to *Alien* which won Academy Award for Special Visual Effects. *Dir.* James Cameron.

Alien 3 (1992) Sigourney Weaver, Charles S Dutton, Charles Dance, Paul McGann. *Dir.* David Fincher.

All about Eve (1950)   Bette Davis (Margo Channing), George Sanders (Addison de Witt; Best Supporting Actor, Anne Baxter (Eve), Marilyn Monroe (Miss Caswell). Won Best Film Oscar. As well as Oscars above, Joseph L Mankiewicz won Academy Awards for Writing & Directing. *Dir.* Joseph L Mankiewicz.

All Creatures Great and Small (1974)   Anthony Hopkins, Simon Ward, TP McKenna. Sponsored by *Reader's Digest. Dir.* Claude Whatham.

All of Me (1984)   Steve Martin (Roger Cobb), Lily Tomlin (Edwina Cutwater), Victoria Tennant (Terry Hoskins) *Dir.* Carl Reiner.

All or Nothing (2002)   Timothy Spall, Lesley Manville, Alison Garland, James Cordon, Ruth Sheen, Marion Bailey. *Dir.* Mike Leigh.

All Quiet on the Western Front (1930)   Lew Ayres

(Paul Baumer), Louis Wolheim (Katczinsky). Based on novel by Erich Maria Remarque. *Dir.* Lewis Milestone.

All That Jazz (1979)   Roy Scheider, Jessica Lange, Ann Reinking, Leland Palmer, Ben Vereen. Semi-autobiographical musical of Fosse's life which won Oscars for Editing, Art Direction, Musical Adaptation & Costume Design. *Dir.* Bob Fosse.

All That Money Can Buy (1941)   Walter Huston (Mr Scratch), Edward Arnold (Daniel Webster). Bernard Herrmann won Oscar for his music for this Faustian version of Stephen Vincent Benet's *The Devil and Daniel Webster. Dir.* William Dieterle.

All the Fine Young Cannibals (1960)   Robert Wagner, Natalie Wood, Pearl Bailey. A fine young pop group took their name from the title of this film. *Dir.* Michael Anderson.

All the King's Men (1949)   Broderick Crawford, Joanne Dru, John Ireland, Mercedes McCambridge (Best Film Oscar). Academy Awards for Broderick Crawford (Best Actor) and Mercedes McCambridge (Best Supporting Actress). *Dir.* Robert Rossen.

All the President's Men (1976)   Robert Redford, Dustin Hoffman, Jason Robards Jnr. Reconstruction of the White House link with the Watergate affair by the *Washington Post. Dir.* Alan J Pakula.

Almost an Angel (1990)   Paul Hogan (Terry Dean), Elias Koteas (Steve), Linda Kozlowski (Rose Garner) *Dir.* John Cornell.

Alphabet Murders, The (1965)   Tony Randall, Robert Morley, Anita Ekberg, Margaret Rutherford (cameo role as Miss Marple). Based on *The ABC Murders* by Agatha Christie. This film is notable for the fact that Tony Randall plays several characters as well as Poirot. *Dir.* Frank Tashlin.

Always (1989)   Richard Dreyfuss, Holly Hunter, Audrey Hepburn. Remake of the 1944 film *A Guy Named Joe* about a dead pilot's ghostly return to matchmake his girlfriend. *Dir.* Steven Spielberg.

Amadeus (1984)   F Murray Abraham (Salieri), Tom Hulce (Mozart), Elizabeth Berridge (Constance Mozart). Filmed mainly in Prague. The part of Constance was originally Meg Tilly's but she was injured in a soccer match the day before shooting began. *Dir.* Milos Forman.

Amélie (2001)   Audrey Tautou (Amélie), Mathieu Kassovitz (Nino Quincampoix), Rufus (Raphael Poulain). A young woman full of joie de vivre has a rejuvenating effect on the people of a French town. French title: *Le Fabuleux Destin d'Amélie Poulain. Dir.* Jean-Pierre Jeunet.

American Beauty (1999) Kevin Spacey (Lester Burnham), Annette Bening, Thora Birch, Wes Bentley. *Dir.* Sam Mendes.

American Gigolo (1980)   Richard Gere, Lauren Hutton. Music by Giorgio Moroder. Christopher Reeve allegedly refused $1 million to play the lead. *Dir.* Paul Schrader.

American Graffiti (1973)   Richard Dreyfuss, Ron Howard, Candy Clark. Film was set in 1962 California. *Dir.* George Lucas.

American in Paris, An (1951)   Gene Kelly, Oscar Levant, Leslie Caron. *Dir.* Vincente Minnelli.

America's Sweethearts (2001)   Julia Roberts, Billy Crystal, Catherine Zeta-Jones, John Cusack, Christopher Walken. *Dir.* Joe Roth.

Amityville Horror, The (1979)   James Brolin, Margot Kidder, Rod Steiger, Don Stroud. (The 1982 film *Amityville II: The Possession* was in fact a prequel.) *Dir.* Stuart Rosenberg.

Anaconda (1997)   Jennifer Lopez, Ice Cube, Jon Voight, Eric Stoltz. *Dir.* Luis Llosa.

Anastasia (1956)   Ingrid Bergman, Yul Brynner, Helen Hayes. Bergman's award-winning performance was all the more noteworthy as this was her comeback after being ostracised for 'immoral behaviour'. *Dir.* Anatole Litvak.

Anchors Aweigh (1945)   Frank Sinatra, Gene Kelly, Katherine Grayson. Notable for the homophonic spelling of the title and a memorable dance scene between Gene Kelly and Jerry Mouse. *Dir.* George Sidney.

And God Created Woman (1988)   Rebecca DeMornay (Robin Shay), Frank Langella (Jim Tiernan), Donovan Leitch (Pete Moran). Remake of the 1957 classic starring Brigitte Bardot. *Dir.* Roger Vadim.

And Soon The Darkness (1970)   Michele Dotrice, Pamela Franklin, Sandor Eles, John Nettleton. Cult film about 2 young nurses on a cycling holiday in France. *Dir.* Robert Fuest.

And Then There Were None (1945)   Walter Huston, Barry Fitzgerald, Richard Haydn, Queenie Leonard. GB title: *Ten Little Niggers* (after the novel it was based on by Agatha Christie) *Dir.* René Clair.

And Then There Were None (1974)   Oliver Reed, Richard Attenborough, Elke Sommer, Charles Aznavour, Herbert Lom. US title: *Ten Little Indians*. The writer Peter Welbeck is in fact Harry Alan Towers, a curious character who has made a living out of remaking this film. *Dir.* Peter Collinson.

Angela's Ashes (1999)   Emily Watson (Angela), Robert Carlyle, Joe Breen (Young Frank), Ciaran Owen (Adolescent Frank), Michael Legge (Grown-up Frank). Based on Frank McCourt bestseller about the life of a Roman Catholic writer brought up in poverty-stricken Limerick. Ultimately fails to capture the spirit and sense of identity of the Irish people but a touching story of triumph over adversity. *Dir.* Alan Parker.

Angels With Dirty Faces (1938)   James Cagney, Pat O'Brien, Dead End Kids, Ann Sheridan, Humphrey Bogart. Memorable final scenes when the gangster goes to the electric chair. *Dir.* Michael Curtiz.

Animal Crackers (1930)   Groucho Marx (Captain Spaulding), Chico, Harpo, Zeppo, and Margaret Dumont. Thieves covet a valuable oil painting unveiled at a swank party. *Dir.* Victor Heerman.

Anna and the King of Siam (1946)   Irene Dunne, Rex Harrison, Linda Darnell. In 1862 an English governess arrives in Bangkok to teach the 67 children of the King. *Dir.* John Cromwell.

Anna Christie (1930)   Greta Garbo, Charles Bickford, Marie Dressler. Prostitute falls in love with a seaman. This was the film in which Garbo first talked. *Dir.* Clarence Brown.

Anna Karenina (1935)   Greta Garbo (Anna), Fredric March (Count Vronsky). Based on the Tolstoy novel. A 1948 British version starring Vivien Leigh was less successful. *Dir.* Clarence Brown.

Anne of Green Gables (1934)   Anne Shirley (Anne), Tom Brown. Based on the LM Montgomery novel set on Prince Edward Island and notable for the fact that its star changed her name from Dawn O'Day to Anne Shirley to play the part. *Dir.* George Nicholls Jnr.

Anne of the Thousand Days (1969)   Richard Burton (Henry VIII), Geneviève Bujold (Boleyn) John Colicos (Thomas Cromwell). Highly acclaimed film with many Oscar nominations but no awards. *Dir.* Charles Jarrott.

Annie Get Your Gun (1950)   Betty Hutton (Annie Oakley), Howard Keel, Edward Arnold. Judy Garland was originally cast but was fired after her displays of temperament. *Dir.* George Sidney.

Annie Hall (1977)   Woody Allen, Diane Keaton, Paul Simon, Shelley Duvall. Oscars for Best Picture, Script, Direction Actress. Classic line by Woody Allen: 'Hey, don't knock masturbation. It's sex with someone I love'. *Dir.* Woody Allen.

Another Woman (1988)   Gena Rowlands, Mia Farrow, Ian Holm, Gene Hackman. *Dir.* Woody Allen.

Anthony Adverse (1936)   Fredric March, Olivia de Havilland, Claude Rains, Akim Tamiroff. Based on the novel by Hervey Allen, this film won minor Academy Awards. *Dir.* Mervyn Le Roy.

Antonia's Line (1995)   Willeke van Ammelrooy, Els Dottemans, Jan Decleir. *Dir.* Marleen Gorris.

Antony and Cleopatra (1972)   Charlton Heston, Hildegarde Neil, Fernando Rey, John Castle (Octavius). Based on Shakespeare's play. Both Olivier and Orson Welles were sought for the lead. *Dir.* Charlton Heston.

Antz (1998) Voices of Woody Allen, Dan Aykroyd, Anne Bancroft, Sharon Stone, Sylvester Stallone. *Dir.* Eric Darnell and Tim Johnson.

Anything Goes (1936)   Bing Crosby, Ethel Merman, Charles Ruggles, Ida Lupino. PG Wodehouse adapted much of the script from the successful Broadway show but only 3 of Cole Porter's songs were retained. *Dir.* Lewis Milestone.

Anything Goes (1956)   Bing Crosby, Donald O'Connor, Zizi Jeanmaire, Mitzi Gaynor. Same story of the stars of a musical comedy each signing a different female lead. *Dir.* Robert Lewis.

Apartment, The (1960)   Jack Lemmon (CC Baxter), Shirley Maclaine (Fran Kubelik), Fred MacMurray (Jeff D Sheldrake). Insurance co. name: Consolidated Life. Last line of film by Miss Kubelik: 'Shut up and deal'. *Dir.* Billy Wilder.

Apocalypse Now (1979)   Martin Sheen, Robert Duvall, Marlon Brando, Harrison Ford. Vittorio Storaro won Oscar for Photography. Harvey Keitel originally played Willard but was replaced by Martin Sheen. *Dir.* Francis Coppola.

Apollo 13 (1995)   Tom Hanks, Bill Paxton, Kevin Bacon, Ed Harris, Emile Ann Lloyd. Won Oscar for Sound Effects. *Dir.* Ron Howard.

Aria (1987)   Theresa Russell, Nicola Swain, Jack Kyle, Marion Peters, Beverley D'Angelo, Elizabeth Hurley, John Hurt, Bridget Fonda. Ten episodes each based on a different opera. *Ten Directors*: Nicolas Roeg, Jean-Luc Godard, Charles Sturridge, Julien Temple, Bruce Beresford, Robert Altman, Franc Roddam, Ken Russell, Derek Jarman, Bill Bryden.

Around the World in Eighty Days (1956)   David Niven, Cantinflas, Robert Newton, Shirley Maclaine. Although, winning a Best Film Oscar, this film is more notable for the galaxy of stars that had cameos., e.g. Sinatra, George Raft, John Mills, Noël Coward, Buster Keaton, Marlene Dietrich. *Dir.* Mike Anderson and Kevin McClory.

Arsenic and Old Lace (1942) released 1944. Cary Grant (Mortimer Brewster), Josephine Hull (Abby), Jean Adair (Martha), Raymond Massey (Jonathan), John Alexander (Teddy), Peter Lorre (Dr Einstein), Grant Mitchell (Rev Harper). Two old ladies poison unsuspecting visitors with elderberry wine and have their mad brother, who believes they are yellow fever victims, bury them in the cellar. Raymond Massey was imitating Boris Karloff. *Dir.* Frank Capra.

Arthur (1981)   Dudley Moore (Arthur Bach), John Gielgud (Hobson), Liza Minnelli (Linda Marolla). Gielgud won Oscar as Best Supporting Actor and 'Best That You Can Do' won Best Song Oscar. *Dir.* Steve Gordon.

Arthur 2: On the Rocks (1988)   Dudley Moore (Arthur Bach), John Gielgud (Hobson), Liza Minnelli

C
I
N
E
M
A

(Linda Marolla Bach). Brogan Lane, the ex-Mrs Moore, appears briefly as 'Cindy'. *Dir.* Bud Yorkin.

As Good As It Gets (1997)   Jack Nicholson (Best Actor Oscar), Helen Hunt (Best Actor Oscar), Greg Kinnear. *Dir.* James L Brooks.

Ashanti (1979)   Michael Caine, Omar Sharif, Peter Ustinov, Rex Harrison, William Holden. Wife of a member of the World Health Organisation is seized by slave traders in West Africa. *Dir.* Richard Fleischer.

Ask a Policeman (1938)   Will Hay, Graham Moffatt, Moore Marriott. Classic written by Val Guest and remade by him in 1983 as the somewhat less popular *The Boys in Blue* starring Cannon and Ball. *Dir.* Marcel Varnel.

Asphalt Jungle, The (1950)   Sterling Hayden (Dix Handley), Louis Calhern (Alonzo D Emmerich), Marilyn Monroe (Angela Phinlay) *Dir.* John Huston.

Assassination Bureau, The (1968)   Oliver Reed, Diana Rigg, Telly Savalas, Curt Jurgens. In 1906, a woman journalist breaks up an international gang of professional killers by falling in love with their leader. *Dir.* Basil Dearden.

Assassins (1995)   Sylvester Stallone, Antonio Banderas, Julianne Moore. Hitman decides to quit but is menaced by a younger rival. *Dir.* Richard Donner.

Associate, The (1996)   Whoopi Goldberg (Laurel Ayres and 'male' alter ego Robert S Cutty), Dianne Wiest (Sally), Tim Daly, Eli Wallach. *Dir.* Donald Petrie.

Asterix and the Big Fight (1989)   Voices of Bill Oddie, Bernard Bresslaw, Ron Moody, Sheila Hancock, Brian Blessed, Peter Hawkins. Asterix attempts to restore the village soothsayer's memory in order to make a potion to defeat the invading Romans. *Dir.* Philippe Grimond.

Atlantis: The Lost Empire (2001)   Voices of Michael J Fox (Milo Thatch), Claudia Christian (Helga Sinclair), James Garner (Commander Rourke), John Mahoney (Preston B Whitmore), Corey Burton (Mole), Cree Summer (Princess Kida). Animated film in which a polyglot leads an expedition to discover Atlantis in 1914. *Dir.* Gary Trousdale and Kirk Wise.

Attila the Hun (1954)   Anthony Quinn, Sophia Loren. *Dir.* Pietro Francisci.

August (1995)   Anthony Hopkins, Leslie Phillips, Kate Burton. *Dir.* Anthony Hopkins.

Austin Powers in Goldmember (2002)   Mike Myers (Austin Powers/Goldmember/Fat Bastard/Dr Evil), Beyoncé Knowles (Foxxy Cleopatra), Michael Caine (Nigel Powers), Seth Green (Scott Evil), Verne Troyer (Mini-Me), Michael York (Basil Exposition), Robert Wagner (No. 2), Mindy Sterling (Frau Farbissina). *Dir.* Jay Roach.

Austin Powers: International Man of Mystery (1997) Mike Myers, Elizabeth Hurley, Michael York, Mimi Rogers, Robert Wagner, Seth Green. *Dir.* Jay Roach.

Austin Powers: The Spy Who Shagged Me (1999) Mike Myers (Austin Danger Powers/Dr Evil/Fat Bastard), Robert Wagner (No 2), Elizabeth Hurley (Vanessa Kensington Powers), Heather Graham (Felicity Shagwell), Michael York (Basil Exposition), Rob Lowe (Young No. 2), Seth Green (Scott Evil). *Dir.* Jay Roach.

Autumn Leaves (1956)   Joan Crawford, Cliff Robertson, Lorne Greene, Vera Miles. Spinster marries a young man who turns out to be a pathological liar and tries to murder her. *Dir.* Robert Aldrich.

Aviator, The (2004)   Leonardo DiCaprio (Howard Hughes), Cate Blanchett (Katharine Hepburn), Kate Beckinsale (Ava Gardner), John C Reilly (Noah Dietrich), Alec Baldwin (Juan Trippe), Alan Alda (Senator Ralph Owen Brewster), Ian Holm (Professor Fitz), Kelli Garner (Faith Domergue), Brent Spiner (Robert Gross), Jude Law (Errol Flynn), Matt Ross (Glenn Odekirk), Adam Scott (Johnny Meyer), Gwen Stefani (Jean Harlow), Willem Dafoe (Roland Sweet), Danny Huston (Jack Frye). Biopic of a 20-year period in the life of Howard Hughes. *Dir.* Martin Scorsese.

Awakening, The (1980)   Charlton Heston, Susannah York, Jill Townsend, Stephanie Zimbalist. Based on the Bram Stoker novel *Jewel of the Seven Stars* about an archaeologist who believes the spirit of an Egyptian queen has entered the soul of his daughter. *Dir.* Mike Newell.

Awakenings (1990)   Robert De Niro (Leonard Lowe) Robin Williams (Dr Sayer) Max Von Sydow (Dr Ingham). Based on factual development in treatment of mental illness. Robin Williams broke De Niro's nose accidentally. *Dir.* Penny Marshall.

Awfully Big Adventure, An (1994)   Georgina Cates, Hugh Grant, Alan Rickman, Peter Firth, Prunella Scales, Nicola Pagett. Romance in a Liverpool repertory theatre in 1947. *Dir.* Mike Newell.

Babe (1995)   James Cromwell, Magda Szubanski, Roscoe Lee Browne (Narrator). Orphaned piglet is adopted by a sheepdog. Based on a book by Dick King-Smith. *Dir.* Chris Noonan.

Babe, The (1992)   John Goodman, Kelly McGillis, Bruce Boxleitner. *Dir.* Arthur Hiller.

Babette's Feast (1987)   Stéphane Audran, Jean-Philippe Lafont, Jarl Kulle, Birgitte Federspiel. Best Foreign Language Oscar for this Danish film about a Lottery winner laying on an enormous banquet. The original story on which the film was based was written by Karen Blixen. *Dir.* Gabriel Axel.

Baby Doll (1956)   Karl Malden, Eli Wallach, Carroll Baker. *Dir.* Elia Kazan.

Back to the Future (1985)   Michael J Fox (Marty McFly), Christopher Lloyd (Dr Emmett Brown), Crispin Glover (George McFly). Notable for cameo roles by Billy Zane as Match, and Huey Lewis, who sings 'Power of Love'. *Dir.* Robert Zemeckis.

Back to the Future II (1989)   Michael J Fox (Marty McFly), Christopher Lloyd (Dr Emmett Brown), Lea Thompson (Lorraine Baines). Crispin Glover refused to take part for less than $1 million so lookalikes were used. *Dir.* Robert Zemeckis.

Back to the Future III (1990)   Michael J Fox (Marty / Seamus McFly), Christopher Lloyd (Dr Emmett Brown), Lea Thompson (Lorraine Baines / Maggie McFly). Set in the Wild West of the 1880s. *Dir.* Robert Zemeckis.

Backdraft (1991)   Kurt Russell (Stephen McCaffrey), William Baldwin (Brian McCaffrey), Rebecca DeMornay (Helen McCaffrey) Robert De Niro (Donald Rimgale) Donald Sutherland (Ronald Bartel). Two brothers track down an arsonist and expose corruption in the fire department. *Dir.* Ron Howard.

Bad and the Beautiful, The (1952)   Kirk Douglas (Jonathan Shields), Lana Turner (Georgia Lorrison), Walter Pidgeon (Harry Pebbel), Dick Powell (James Lee Bartlow). A director, a star, a screenwriter and an executive recall their experiences at the hands of a go-getting Hollywood producer. *Dir.* Vincente Minnelli.

Bad Day at Black Rock (1955)   Spencer Tracy, Robert Ryan, Lee Marvin, Walter Brennan. Action takes place within 24 hours and concerns a one-armed stranger greeted with hostility by a town with something to hide. *Dir.* John Sturges.

Bad Education (2004)   Fele Martinez (Enrique Goded), Gael Garcia Bernal (School Friend/Zahara), Daniel Giménez Cacho (Father Manolo), Lluis Homar (Sir Berenguer), Javier Camara (Paca), Petra Martinez (Mother), Raul Garcia Forneiro (Young Enrique). A director, inspired by meeting an actor who claims to be his childhood lover, makes a film based on his schooldays; its story concerns a transsexual who, as a boy, was abused by a priest and later attempted to blackmail him. *Dir.* Pedro Almodóvar.

Bad Influence (1990)   Rob Lowe (Alex), James Spader (Michael Ball). Notable scene where Lowe tries to blow up a car by connecting a broken tail-light with a petrol tank is apparently a terrorist trick from which one important step was omitted. *Dir.* Curtis Hanson.

Badlands (1973)   Martin Sheen, Sissy Spacek, Warren Oates. Teenage girl and garbage collector wander across America leaving a trail of murder. *Dir.* Terrence Malick.

Ballad of the Sad Café, The (1991)   Vanessa Redgrave (Miss Amelia Evans), Keith Carradine (Marvin Macy), Rod Steiger (Reverend Willin). Tale of a Southern town run by the despotic Redgrave, based on the novella by Carson McCullers. The film was shot at Willie Nelson's farm. *Dir.* Simon Callow.

Bananas (1971)   Woody Allen, Louise Lasser, Carlos Montalban, Sylvester Stallone (walk-on as mugger). When asked why he called the film *Bananas*, Allen replied, 'Because there are no bananas in it.' *Dir.* Woody Allen.

Bandit Queen (1994)   Seema Biswas, Nirmal Pandey, Manjoj Baipal. Story of Phoolan Devi, a real-life Indian bandit and rape victim. *Dir.* Sheka Kapur.

Bandits (2001)   Bruce Willis, Billy Bob Thornton, Cate Blanchett, Troy Garity. *Dir.* Barry Levinson.

Bank Dick, The (1940)   WC Fields, Franklin Pangborn, Shemp Howard, Jack Norton. Fields wrote the script using his nom de plume of Mahatma Kane Jeeves, which derived from characters in old English plays. They would say 'M'Hat, M'cane, Jeeves'. GB title: *The Bank Detective. Dir.* Eddie Cline.

Barabbas (1962)   Anthony Quinn, Silvano Mangano, Ernest Borgnine, Jack Palance. The eclipse of the Sun at the beginning was a real one filmed in Nice. *Dir.* Richard Fleischer.

Barb Wire (1996)   Pamela Anderson Lee, Temuera Morrison, Victoria Rowell. Set in civil-war-ravaged USA in the year 2017. *Dir.* David Hogan.

Barbarella (1967)   Jane Fonda, John Phillip Law, Milo O'Shea, David Hemmings, Marcel Marceau. Beautiful 40th-century astronaut prevents positronic ray from getting into the wrong hands. *Dir.* Roger Vadim.

Barbarian Invasions, The (2003)   Rémy Girard (Rémy), Stéphane Rousseau (Sebastien), Marie-Josée Croze (Nathalie), Marina Hands (Gaelle), Dorothée Berryman (Louise), Johanne Marie Tremblay (Sister Constance), Dominique Michel (Dominique), Louise Portal (Diane). French-Canadian film set in Montreal. A dying philandering academic is gradually reconciled with his son, a wealthy city trader. *Dir.* Denys Arcand.

Barbarosa (1981)   Willie Nelson (Barbarosa), Gary Busey (Karl), Isela Vega (Josephina). Old-style Western that was well received by critics. *Dir.* Fred Schepisi.

Barbary Coast (1935)   Edward G Robinson, Miriam Hopkins, Joel McCrea, Walter Brennan. Set during the San Francisco gold rush. *Dir.* Howard Hawks.

Barefoot Contessa, The (1954)   Humphrey Bogart (Harry Dawes), Ava Gardner (Maria Vargas), Edmond O'Brien (Muldoon). O'Brien won Best Supporting Actor Oscar. *Dir.* Joseph L Mankiewicz.

Barefoot in the Park (1967)   Robert Redford (Paul Bratter), Jane Fonda (Corie Bratter), Charles Boyer (Victor Velasco), Mildred Natwick (Ethel Banks). Based on Neil Simon's play. *Dir.* Gene Saks.

Barkleys of Broadway, The (1949)   Fred Astaire, Ginger Rogers, Oscar Levant. Judy Garland was originally cast but withdrew through illness. *Dir.* Charles Walters.

Barretts of Wimpole Street, The (1934)   Norma Shearer (Elizabeth Barrett), Fredric March (Robert Browning), Charles Laughton (Edward Moulton-Barrett), Maureen O'Sullivan (Henrietta). The 1956 remake starred Jennifer Jones and Bill Travers. *Dir.* Sidney Franklin.

Basic Instinct (1992)   Michael Douglas (Nick Curran), Sharon Stone (Catherine Tramell), George Dzundza (Gus), Jeanne Tripplehorn (Dr Beth Garner), Leilani Sarelle (Roxy). Famous for a scene where the knickerless Stone crosses her legs. *Dir.* Paul Verhoeven.

Basket Case (1982)   Kevin Van Hentenryck, Terri Susan Smith, Beverly Bonner. First of 3 (to date) cult films – followed by *Basket Case II* (1990) and *Basket Case 3: The Progeny* (1992) – depicting Siamese twins with attitude. *Dir.* Frank Henenlotter.

Batman (1989)   Michael Keaton (Batman), Jack Nicholson (Joker), Kim Basinger (Vicki Vale), Jerry Hall (Alicia) Jack Palance (Grissom). *Batman Returns* (1992) starred Danny De Vito as Penguin (Oswald Cobblepot). *Dir.* Tim Burton.

Batman and Robin (1997)   George Clooney (Batman), Chris O'Donnell (Robin), Alicia Silverstone (Batgirl), Arnold Schwarzenegger (Mr Freeze), Uma Thurman (Poison Ivy). Schwarzenegger line: 'Revenge is a dish best served cold' originally heard in *Star Trek: The Wrath of Khan. Dir.* Joel Schumacher.

Batman Forever (1995)   Val Kilmer (Batman), Tommy Lee Jones (Harvey Two-Face), Jim Carrey (Riddler), Chris O'Donnell (Robin), Nicole Kidman, Drew Barrymore. *Dir.* Joel Schumacher.

Battle of Britain (1969)   Laurence Olivier (Dowding), Robert Shaw, Michael Caine, Christopher Plummer, Kenneth More, Susannah York, Trevor Howard, Ralph Richardson, Michael Redgrave, Edward Fox. *Dir.* Guy Hamilton.

Battle of the Bulge (1965)   Henry Fonda, Robert Shaw, Robert Ryan, Telly Savalas, Ty Hardin. Story of the German counter-attack in the Ardennes in December 1944. *Dir.* Ken Annakin.

Battle of the River Plate (1956)   John Gregson, Anthony Quayle, Peter Finch. US title: *Pursuit of the Graf Spee. Dir.* Emeric Pressburger & Michael Powell.

Beach, The (2000)   Leonardo DiCaprio (Richard), Tilda Swinton (Sal), Virginie Ledoyen (Françoise), Guillaume Canet (Etienne), Robert Carlyle (Duffy), Peter Youngblood Hills (Zeph). American traveller discovers a hippy community living by a perfect beach on a remote island in Thailand. *Dir.* Danny Boyle.

Beaches (1988)   Bette Midler (CC Bloom), Barbara Hershey (Hillary Whitney Essex). Singer visits her dying friend, a lawyer, and recalls their long and volatile friendship. *Dir.* Garry Marshall.

Bean (1997)   Rowan Atkinson, Peter MacNicol, Pamela Reed, Burt Reynolds, John Mills, Peter Egan, Harris Yulin, Richard Gant, Tricia Vessey, Peter Capaldi, Andrew Lawrence. *Dir.* Mel Smith.

Beau Brummell (1954)   Stewart Granger, Elizabeth Taylor, Robert Morley (George III), Peter Ustinov (Prince of Wales). Remake of the 1924 film starring John Barrymore and Mary Astor. *Dir.* Curtis Bernhardt.

Beau Geste (1939)   Gary Cooper, Ray Milland, Brian Donlevy, Susan Hayward. Remake of the 1926 film starring Ronald Colman and based on PC Wren's novel. *Dir.* William Wellman.

Beautiful Mind, A (2001)   Russell Crowe (John Nash), Jennifer Connelly, Ed Harris, Christopher Plummer, Paul Bettany. Biopic of Nobel Prize-winning mathematician John Nash's struggle against mental illness. Multiple Oscar-winning film. *Dir.* Ron Howard.

Beauty and the Beast (1991)   Voices of Robby Benson (Beast), Paige O'Hara (Belle), Angela Lansbury (Mrs Potts). Disney classic which became the best-selling video of all time in the USA. *Dir.* Gary Trousdale & Kirk Wise.

Beavis and Butthead Do America (1996)   Created by animator Mike Judge. Voices include Robert Stack and Bruce Willis. *Dir.* Mike Judge.

Becket (1964)   Richard Burton (Becket), Peter O'Toole (Henry II), John Gielgud, Sian Phillips. Based on Jean Anouilh's bitter stage play. *Dir.* Peter Glenville.

Bed Sitting Room, The (1969)   Ralph Richardson, Rita Tushingham, Michael Hordern, Arthur Lowe, Spike Milligan, Harry Secombe, Peter Cook, Dudley Moore. After a nuclear war, motley survivors turn into bed sitting rooms, cupboards and parakeets. *Dir.* Richard Lester.

Bedazzled (1967)   Peter Cook, Dudley Moore, Michael Bates, Raquel Welch, Eleanor Bron. *Dir.* Stanley Donen. Short-order cook is saved from suicide by Mr Spiggott, who offers him seven wishes in exchange for his soul.

Bedknobs and Broomsticks (1971)   Angela Lansbury, David Tomlinson, Bruce Forsyth, Tessie O'Shea. *Dir.* Robert Stevenson.

Beetlejuice (1988)   Alec Baldwin (Adam), Geena Davis (Barbara), Michael Keaton (Betelgeuse), Winona Ryder (Lydia Deetz). *Dir.* Tim Burton.

Before Sunset (2004)   Ethan Hawke (Jesse), Julie Delpy (Celine). Nine years after Jesse and Celine first meet they encounter one another on the French leg of Jesse's book tour. *Dir.* Richard Linklater.

Beguiled, The (1971)   Clint Eastwood, Geraldine Page, Elizabeth Hartman, Darleen Carr. Wounded Union soldier hides out in a Confederate girls' school. *Dir.* Don Siegel.

Behind Enemy Lines (2001)   Owen Wilson, Gene Hackman, Gabriel Macht, Charles Malik Whitfield, David Keith, Joaquim de Almeida. US naval pilot is shot down over Bosnia and hunted by Serbian troops. *Dir.* John Moore.

Beijing Bastards (1993)   Cui Jian, Li Wei, Wu Gang, Bian Tianshuo. Original title: *Beijing Zazhong*. Story of disillusionment by the young Chinese. *Dir.* Zhang Yuan.

Being Human (1994)   Robin Williams, John Turturro, Anna Galiena, Theresa Russell (as narrator). Box office flop about a father who fails to provide for his family in five historic eras. *Dir.* Bill Forsyth.

Being John Malkovich (1999)   John Cusack, Cameron Diaz, Catherine Keener, John Malkovich. *Dir.* Spike Jonze.

Being There (1979)   Peter Sellers, Shirley MacLaine, Melvyn Douglas. Melvyn Douglas won Best Supporting Actor Oscar for this film about a simple gardener who becomes philosopher and sage to the American people. *Dir.* Hal Ashby.

Bell, Book and Candle (1958)   James Stewart, Kim Novak, Jack Lemmon, Hermione Gingold. Publisher slowly realises that his girlfriend is a witch. *Dir.* Richard Quine.

Belles of St Trinian's, The (1954)   Alastair Sim, George Cole (Flash Harry), Joyce Grenfell, Beryl Reid, Irene Handl. Based on Ronald Searle's cartoons. *Dir.* Frank Launder.

Bells of St Mary's, The (1945)   Bing Crosby (Father O'Malley), Ingrid Bergman (Sister Benedict). Sequel to *Going My Way. Dir.* Leo McCarey.

Belstone Fox, The (1973)   Eric Porter, Rachel Roberts, Dennis Waterman, Jeremy Kemp, Bill Travers. Based on the novel *The Ballad of the Belstone Fox* by David Rook. *Dir.* James Hill.

Ben Hur (1925)   Ramon Novarro, Francis X Bushman, Carmel Myers. Based on the Lew Wallace novel. Originally, Charles Brabin was director and George Walsh the star; both were replaced when Louis Mayer saw the first rushes. *Dir.* Fred Niblo.

Ben Hur (1959)   Charlton Heston, Haya Harareet, Jack Hawkins, Stephen Boyd, Hugh Griffith. Multi-award-winning film but critics generally regard the 1925 silent epic as definitive. *Dir.* William Wyler.

Bend it Like Beckham (2002)   Parminder K Nagra, Keira Knightley, Jonathan Rhys-Meyers, Anupam Kher, Shaznay Lewis. Teenage London girl wants to become a professional footballer but is thwarted by her Punjabi Sikh parents, who want her to study law. *Dir.* Gurinder Chadha.

Beneath the Planet of the Apes (1970)   James Franciscus, Charlton Heston, Linda Harrison, Kim Hunter. Sequel to *Planet of the Apes. Dir.* Ted Post.

Benji (1974)   Peter Breck, Edgar Buchanan, Christopher Connelly. Popular film about a stray mongrel dog who saves two kidnapped children. *Dir.* Joe Camp.

Benny Goodman Story (1955)   Steve Allen (Goodman), Donna Reed, Berta Gersten, Harry James, Gene Krupa, Sammy Davis Snr. Steve Allen went on to host one of America's leading variety shows on television. *Dir.* Valentine Davies.

Bequest to the Nation (1973)   Peter Finch, Glenda Jackson, Michael Jayston, Margaret Leighton, Anthony Quayle. US title: *The Nelson Affair*. Story of Nelson's long affair with the tempestuous Lady Hamilton. *Dir.* James Cellan Jones.

Bespoke Overcoat, The (1956)   Alfie Bass, David Kossoff. Won Academy Award for Best Short Film and launched its stars as successful TV actors. *Dir.* Jack Clayton.

Best Years of Our Lives, The (1946)   Fredric March, Myrna Loy, Teresa Wright, Dana Andrews, Virginia Mayo, Hoagy Carmichael. Multi-award-winning film notable for the performance of Harold Russell, a veteran who had lost his hands; he had no previous acting experience. *Dir.* William Wyler.

Beverly Hillbillies, The (1993)   Diedrich Bader, Dabney Coleman, Erika Eleniak, Cloris Leachman, Buddy Ebsen, Zsa Zsa Gabor, Dolly Parton. *Dir.* Penelope Spheeris.

Beverly Hills Cop (1984)   Eddie Murphy (Axel Foley), Judge Reinhold (Det Billy Rosewood), Steven Berkoff (Victor Maitland). Detroit cop races to Los Angeles to track down the killers of his best friend. *Dir.* Martin Brest.

Beverly Hills Cop 2 (1987)   Eddie Murphy (Axel Foley), Judge Reinhold (Det Billy Rosewood), Brigitte Nielsen (Karla Fry). Ironically Sylvester Stallone was to play Axel Foley in the original film and his ex Brigitte Nielsen appears in this sequel. *Dir.* Tony Scott.

Beverly Hills Cop 3 (1994)   Eddie Murphy (Axel Foley), Judge Reinhold (Det Billy Rosewood), John Saxon. Cop discovers that the head of security at a Los Angeles theme park is a murderer. *Dir.* Tony Scott.

Beyond Bedlam (1994)   Craig Fairbrass, Elizabeth Hurley, Keith Allen, Anita Dobson, Georgina Hale. *Dir.* Vadim Jean.

Beyond the Poseidon Adventure (1979)   Michael Caine, Telly Savalas, Karl Malden, Sally Field. Not so much a sequel, more an alternative ending to the original. *Dir.* Irwin Allen.

Bible, The (1966)   Michael Parks (Adam), Ulla Bergryd (Eve), Richard Harris (Cain), John Huston (Noah), George C Scott (Abraham), Peter O'Toole (the 3 Angels). Remembered for Huston's whispered commentary and the eye-catching photography as well as Toshiro Mayuzumi's musical interpretation. *Dir.* John Huston.

Big (1988)   Tom Hanks (Josh Baskin), Elizabeth Perkins (Susan), Robert Loggia (MacMillan). Story of 12-yr-old who wishes he were 'Big' and wakes up 20 yrs older. Steven Spielberg was originally going to direct and Harrison Ford to star. *Dir.* Penny Marshall.

Big Business (1929)   Oliver Hardy, Stan Laurel, James Finlayson. Laurel & Hardy classic about their failure to sell a Christmas tree to a belligerent householder. Memorable for the scene of mutual destruction. *Dir.* James W Horne.

Big Business (1988)   Bette Midler (Sadie Shelton / Ratcliff), Lily Tomlin (Rose Shelton / Ratcliff). Story of twins mixed up at birth. *Dir.* Jim Abrahams.

Big Chill, The (1983)   Tom Berenger (Sam), Glenn Close (Sarah), William Hurt (Nick), Jeff Goldblum (Michael), Kevin Kline (Harold), Meg Tilly (Chloe). Story of a students' reunion after the suicide of one of them. Kevin Costner plays the corpse, Alex, although only his hands, torso and legs are seen in the final version. *Dir.* Lawrence Kasdan.

Big Country, The (1958)   Gregory Peck, Jean Simmons, Charlton Heston, Burl Ives, Carol Baker, Charles Bickford, Chuck Connors. Story of the Terrills' and the Hannesseys' feud over water rights. Burl Ives won Best Supporting Actor Oscar. *Dir.* William Wyler.

Big Fat Liar (2002)   Frankie Muniz, Paul Giamatti, Amanda Bynes, Amanda Detmer, Lee Majors. *Dir.* Shawn Levy.

Big Fish (2003)   Ewan McGregor (Ed Bloom (young)), Albert Finney (Ed Bloom (senior)), Billy Crudup (Will Bloom), Jessica Lange (Sandra Bloom (senior)), Helena Bonham Carter (Jenny (young and senior) and The Witch), Alison Lohman (Sandra Bloom (young)), Robert Guillaume (Dr Bennett (senior)), Matthew McGrory (Karl the Giant), Loudon Wainwright (Beamen), Steve Buscemi (Norther Winslow), Danny DeVito (Amos Calloway). A salesman, prone to telling fantastic tales, reconciles with his son. *Dir.* Tim Burton.

Big Hand for the Little Lady, A (1966)   Henry Fonda, Joanne Woodward, Jason Robards, Kevin McCarthy, Charles Bickford, Burgess Meredith. GB title: *Big Deal at Dodge City* (though the action, in fact, takes place in Laredo). *Dir.* Fielder Cook.

Big Man, The (1990)   Liam Neeson, Joanne Whalley-Kilmer, Billy Connolly, Ian Bannen. Unemployed miner becomes a bare-knuckle fighter. *Dir.* David Leland.

Big Sleep, The (1946)   Humphrey Bogart (Philip Marlowe), Lauren Bacall (Vivian Sherwood Rutledge), John Ridgely (Eddie Mars), Martha Vickers (Carmen Sternwood). Based on Raymond Chandler's Novel but adapted by William Faulkner, Leigh Brackett and Jules Furthman. (Alternative version with 18 minutes of different footage exists.) *Dir.* Howard Hawks.

Big Sleep, The (1978)   Robert Mitchum (Philip Marlowe), Sarah Miles, Richard Boone, Candy Clark, James Stewart, Edward Fox, Oliver Reed, Richard Todd. Remake of the 1946 film but set in London. *Dir.* Michael Winner.

Big Trouble in Little China (1986)   Kurt Russell (Jack Burton), Kim Cattrall (Gracie Law). *Dir.* John Carpenter.

Bill and Ted's Excellent Adventure (1989)   Keanu Reeves (Ted 'Theodore' Logan), Alex Winter (Bill S Preston). Napoleon, Billy the Kid, Socrates, Freud, Genghis Khan, Joan of Arc and Abe Lincoln are some of the famous people met on their journey. *Dir.* Stephen Herek.

Billy Bathgate (1991)   Dustin Hoffman, Nicole Kidman, Bruce Willis. Based on EL Doctorow's novel. Teenager becomes an assistant to top gangster Dutch Schultz. *Dir.* Robert Benton.

Billy Budd (1962)   Peter Ustinov, Robert Ryan, Terence Stamp, Melvyn Douglas, David McCallum. Based on Herman Melville's novel about the young Billy Budd, who kills the sadistic master-at-arms of a British warship in 1797. *Dir.* Peter Ustinov.

Billy Elliot (2000)   Julie Walters (Mrs Wilkinson), Jamie Bell (Billy Elliot), Gary Lewis (Billy's Dad), Jamie Draven (Tony). Young son of a working-class miner has aspirations to become a ballet dancer. *Dir.* Stephen Daldry.

Billy Liar (1963)   Tom Courtenay, Julie Christie, Wilfred Pickles, Leonard Rossiter. Written by Keith Waterhouse and inspired by *The Secret Life of Walter Mitty. Dir.* John Schlesinger.

Birdcage, The (1996)   Robin Williams, Nathan Lane, Gene Hackman, Dianne Wiest. Remake of French film, *La Cage aux Folles.* Son of a homosexual club-owner persuades his father to act the heterosexual with his future very conservative in-laws. *Dir.* Mike Nichols.

Birdman of Alcatraz (1962)   Burt Lancaster (Robert Stroud), Karl Malden, Thelma Ritter, Edmond O'Brien, Neville Brand, Telly Savalas. True story of Robert Stroud, who spent nearly 60 years in prison and made a name for himself as an ornithologist. *Dir.* John Frankenheimer.

Birds, The (1963)   Rod Taylor, Tippi Hedren, Jessica Tandy, Suzanne Pleshette. Birds turn against humans. Action takes place at Bodega Bay, California. *Dir.* Alfred Hitchcock.

Birdy (1984)   Matthew Modine (Birdy), Nicolas Cage (Al Columbato). *Dir.* Alan Parker.

Birth of a Nation (1915)   Lillian Gish, Henry B Walthall, Mae Marsh, Donald Crisp. Originally *The Clansman*, this story of US Civil War strife was the first big screen epic. *Dir.* DW Griffith.

Black Beauty (1994)   Alan Cummings (voice), Sean Bean, David Thewlis, Jim Carter, Peter Davison, Eleanor Bron, Peter Cook. Story is told by the horse itself. *Dir.* Caroline Thompson.

Black Hawk Down (2001)   Josh Hartnett, Eric Bana, Tom Sizemore, Ewan McGregor, Sam Shepard, William Fichtner. Graphic war film set in 1993 troubled Mogadishu. Won Oscars for sound and editing. *Dir.* Ridley Scott.

Black Narcissus (1946)   Deborah Kerr, Sabu, Jean Simmons, Flora Robson. Anglo-Catholic nuns in the Himalayas have trouble with climate and morale. *Dir.* Michael Powell & Emeric Pressburger.

Black Robe (1991)   Lothaire Bluteau, Aden Young, Sandrine Holt. Jesuit priest travels through Quebec

C
I
N
E
M
A

to convert the Indians in the 17th century. *Dir.* Bruce Beresford.

Blackboard Jungle, The (1955)   Glenn Ford, Anne Francis, Louis Calhern, Sidney Poitier, Vic Morrow. Notable for the music of Bill Haley and the Comets. *Dir.* Richard Brooks.

Blackmail (1929)   Anny Ondra, Sara Allgood, Charles Paton. Hitchcock's first talkie involves a Scotland Yard inspector who finds his girl is involved in a murder but conceals the fact and is blackmailed. *Dir.* Alfred Hitchcock.

Blade Runner (1982)   Harrison Ford (Deckard), Rutger Hauer (Roy Batty), Sean Young (Rachel), Daryl Hannah (Pris). Set in LA in 2019. Ridley Scott released his 'Director's Cut' in 1992 which had a more satisfactory conclusion. Based on the novel *Do Androids Dream of Electric Sheep?* by Philip K Dick. *Dir.* Ridley Scott.

Blair Witch Project, The (1999)   Heather Donahue, Michael C Williams, Joshua Leonard. *Dir.* Daniel Myrick and Eduardo Sanchez.

Blair Witch 2: Book of Shadows (2000)   Tristen Skyler, Stephen B Turner, Jeffery Donovan. *Dir.* Joe Berlinger.

Blazing Saddles (1974)   Cleavon Little, Gene Wilder, Slim Pickens, Mel Brooks, Madeline Kahn. Black railroad worker and an alcoholic ex-gunfighter foil a crooked attorney. Famous for its beans scene. *Dir.* Mel Brooks.

Blind Shaft (2003)   Li Yixiang (Song Jinming), Wang Shuangbao (Tang Zhaoyang). Set in northern China. Two workmen blackmail mine owners into paying them compensation for the deaths of their fellow workers due to deficiencies in their working environment. *Dir.* Li Yang.

Blob, The (1958)   Steve McQueen, Aneta Corseaut, Earl Rowe. *Dir.* Irwin S Yeaworth.

Blockheads (1938)   Oliver Hardy, Stan Laurel, Billy Gilbert. Twenty years after WW1, Stan is still guarding a trench because nobody told him to stop. *Dir.* John G Blystone.

Blondie (1938)   Arthur Lake, Penny Singleton, Daisy the Dog, Jonathan Hale. Mr & Mrs Small Town America, Dagwood Bumstead and wife Blondie, spawned many sequels. *Dir.* Frank R Strayer.

Blow (2001)   Johnny Depp (George Jung), Penelope Cruz, Franka Potente, Rachel Griffiths, Jordi Molla. True-life story of a Boston boy who grows up in the 1970s to become the biggest smuggler of cocaine into the United States from Colombia. *Dir.* Ted Demme.

Blow Up (1966)   David Hemmings, Sarah Miles, Vanessa Redgrave. London fashion photographer thinks he sees a murder, but the evidence disappears. *Dir.* Michelangelo Antonioni.

Blue Angel, The (1930)   Emil Jannings, Marlene Dietrich (Lola). Story of a professor's infatuation with a nightclub singer. *Dir.* Josef von Sternberg.

Blue Bird, The (1940)   Shirley Temple, Johnny Russell, Gale Sondergaard (the cat), Eddie Collins (the dog). Two children of a poor woodcutter seek the bluebird of happiness. *Dir.* Walter Lang.

Blue Bird, The (1976)   Elizabeth Taylor (Mother, Maternal Love, Light & The Witch), Ava Gardner, Jane Fonda, George Cole. Remake of the 1940 classic. *Dir.* George Cukor.

Blue Dahlia (1946)   Alan Ladd, Veronica Lake, William Bendix, Howard de Silva. Raymond Chandler story of a returning war veteran who finds his faithless wife murdered and himself suspected. *Dir.* George Marshall.

Blue Lagoon (1949)   Jean Simmons, Donald Houston, Cyril Cusack. Shipwrecked boy and girl grow up on a desert island. *Dir.* Frank Launder.

Blue Lagoon (1980)   Brooke Shields, Christopher Atkins, Leo McKern. Remake of the 1949 film. *Dir.* Randal Kleiser.

Blue Lamp, The (1949)   Jack Warner, Jimmy Hanley, Dirk Bogarde, Dora Bryan. Famous for its opening shooting scene and the subsequent reincarnation of George Dixon for *Dixon of Dock Green*, which ran for 20 years on Television. *Dir.* Basil Dearden.

Blue Max, The (1966)   George Peppard, James Mason, Ursula Andress, Jeremy Kemp. *Dir.* John Guillermin.

Blues Brothers, The (1980)   John Belushi (Jake), Dan Aykroyd (Elwood), Carrie Fisher, Cab Calloway. *Dir.* John Landis.

Bob and Carol and Ted and Alice (1969)   Robert Culp, Natalie Wood, Elliott Gould, Dyan Cannon. *Dir.* Paul Mazursky.

Body Heat (1981)   William Hurt, Kathleen Turner, Richard Crenna, Ted Danson. Florida lawyer becomes involved with a married woman and they plot to kill her husband. *Dir.* Lawrence Kasdan.

Bodyguard, The (1992)   Kevin Costner (Frank Farmer), Whitney Houston (Rachel Marron), Gary Kemp (Sy Spector). *Dir.* Mick Jackson.

Bonfire of the Vanities (1990)   Tom Hanks (Sherman McCoy), Bruce Willis (Peter Fallow), Melanie Griffith (Maria Ruskin). Based on Tom Wolfe's novel of the same name. *Dir.* Brian de Palma.

Bonnie and Clyde (1967)   Warren Beatty (Clyde Barrow), Faye Dunaway (Bonnie Parker), Gene Hackman (Buck), Estelle Parsons, Michael J Pollard, Gene Wilder. Estelle Parsons won Academy Award for Best Supporting Actress. *Dir.* Arthur Penn.

Boom! (1968)   Elizabeth Taylor, Richard Burton, Noël Coward. Based on Tennessee Williams's play *The Milk Train Doesn't Stop Here Anymore*. *Dir.* Joseph Losey.

Born on the Fourth of July (1989)   Tom Cruise (Ron Kovic), Kyra Sedgwick (Donna), Willem Dafoe, Tom Berenger. *Dir.* Oliver Stone.

Bourne Identity, The (2002)   Matt Damon, Franka Potente, Chris Cooper, Clive Owen, Brian Cox. Story of a secret agent trying to piece together the threads of his life whilst suffering total amnesia. *Dir.* Doug Liman.

Bowling for Columbine (2002)   Documentary examining America's attitude towards guns, beginning with the shooting rampage by students at Columbine High School. Cleverly edited film to ensure the point is made effectively. *Dir.* Michael Moore.

Box of Moonlight (1996)   John Turturro (Al Fountain), Sam Rockwell (The Kid). *Dir.* Tom DiCillo.

Boxing Helena (1993)   Julian Sands, Sherilyn Fenn, Bill Paxton, Art Garfunkel. Most memorable for Kim Basinger being sued for changing her mind over starring in it. Court ordered her to pay $8 million but studio settled for $3 million. *Dir.* Jennifer Chambers Lynch.

Boys Don't Cry (1999)   Peter Sarsgaard (John), Brendan Sexton III (Tom), Alison Folland (Kate). *Dir.* Kimberly Peirce.

Boys from Brazil, The (1978)   Gregory Peck (Josef Mengele), Laurence Olivier, James Mason, Lilli Palmer. Based on the Ira Levin novel. *Dir.* Franklin Schaffner.

Brassed Off (1996)   Peter Postlethwaite (Danny), Tara Fitzgerald (Gloria), Ewan McGregor. *Dir.* Mark Herman.

Braveheart (1995)   Mel Gibson, Sophie Marceau, Patrick McGoohan, Ian Bannen. *Dir.* Mel Gibson.

Brazil (1985)   Jonathan Pryce, Robert De Niro, Michael Palin, Peter Vaughan, Bob Hoskins. *Dir.* Terry Gilliam.

Breaking the Waves (1996)   Emily Watson, Stellan Skarsgard, Katrin Cartlidge, Jean-Marc Barr. Award-winning film set in Scotland, it concerns a woman who humiliates herself in the hope of saving the life of her husband, paralysed in an oil rig accident. *Dir.* Lars von Trier.

Bridge on the River Kwai (1957)   Alec Guinness (Colonel Nicholson), Sessue Hayakawa (Colonel Saito), William Holden (Shears), Jack Hawkins (Major Warden). Based on the novel by Pierre Boulle. *Dir.* David Lean.

Bridges of Madison County (1995)   Clint Eastwood, Meryl Streep, Annie Corley. Written by Richard LaGravenese. *Dir.* Clint Eastwood.

Bridget Jones's Diary (2001)   Renée Zellweger, Hugh Grant, Colin Firth, Gemma Jones, Jim Broadbent. Cameo performances by Jeffrey Archer and Salman Rushdie. *Dir.* Sharon Maguire.

Brief Encounter (1945)   Celia Johnson (Laura Jesson), Trevor Howard (Alec Harvey), Stanley Holloway, Joyce Carey. Based on a Noël Coward play, *Still Life*. The theme music was Rachmaninov's Piano Concerto No 2 and the railway station was Carnforth. *Dir.* David Lean.

Brigadoon (1954)   Gene Kelly, Cyd Charisse, Van Johnson. Scottish village awakens only once every hundred years. *Dir.* Vincente Minnelli.

Bringing Up Baby (1938)   Katharine Hepburn (Susan), Cary Grant (David Huxley), May Robson. The baby of the title was, in fact, a leopard. *Dir.* Howard Hawks.

Broken Arrow (1996)   John Travolta, Christian Slater, Samantha Mathis. *Dir.* John Woo.

Browning Version, The (1951)   Michael Redgrave, Jean Kent, Nigel Patrick, Wilfrid Hyde-White, Bill Travers. Based on Terence Rattigan's one-act play. *Dir.* Anthony Asquith.

Browning Version, The (1994)   Albert Finney, Greta Scacchi, Matthew Modine, Julian Sands, Michael Gambon. Ronald Howard's adaptation of Terence Rattigan play. *Dir.* Mike Figgis.

Brubaker (1980)   Robert Redford, Yaphet Kotto, Jane Alexander, Morgan Freeman, Murray Hamilton. Setting: Wakefield Prison Farm. *Dir.* Stuart Rosenberg.

Bugsy Malone (1976)   Scott Baio, Jodie Foster, Florrie Dugger. All the parts are played by children and the guns fire ice cream. *Dir.* Alan Parker.

Bullitt (1968)   Steve McQueen, Jacqueline Bisset, Robert Vaughn, Robert Duvall. Based on the novel *Mute Witness* by Robert L Pike. *Dir.* Peter Yates.

Burbs, The (1989)   Tom Hanks, Bruce Dern, Carrie Fisher, Corey Feldman. *Dir.* Joe Dante.

Buster (1988)   Phil Collins, Julie Walters (June Edwards), Larry Lamb, Stephanie Lawrence, Martin Jarvis. *Dir.* David Green.

Butch Cassidy and the Sundance Kid (1969)   Paul Newman, Robert Redford, Katharine Ross. 'Raindrops Keep Falling on My Head' won Oscar for Best Song. *Dir.* George Roy Hill.

Butterfield 8 (1960)   Elizabeth Taylor, Laurence Harvey, Eddie Fisher. Taylor won Best Actress Oscar for her role as a society call girl. The title *Butterfield 8* was her telephone number. *Dir.* Daniel Mann.

Cabaret (1972)   Liza Minnelli, Joel Grey, Michael York. Based on the novel *Goodbye to Berlin* by Christopher Isherwood and John Van Druten's play *I Am a Camera*. *Dir.* Bob Fosse.

Cabin in the Sky (1943)   Eddie 'Rochester' Anderson (Little Joe), Lena Horne (Georgia Brown), Ethel Waters (Petunia), Louis Armstrong. All black cast. *Dir.* Vincente Minnelli.

Cable Guy, The (1996)   Jim Carrey, Matthew Broderick, George Segal. *Dir.* Ben Stiller.

Cactus Jack (1979)   Kirk Douglas, Arnold Schwarzenegger, Ann-Margret. US title: *The Villain*. *Dir.* Hal Needham.

Caesar and Cleopatra (1945)   Claude Rains, Vivien Leigh, Stewart Granger, Flora Robson. Britain's most expensive film to this date was based on George Bernard Shaw's comedy. *Dir.* Gabriel Pascal.

Caine Mutiny, The (1954)   Humphrey Bogart (Capt Queeg), José Ferrer (Lt Barney Greenwald), Van Johnson (Lt Steve Maryk), Fred MacMurray (Lt Tom Keefer), Lee Marvin (Meatball), Claude Akins (Horrible). Based on Herman Wouk's novel. *Dir.* Edward Dmytryk.

Calamity Jane (1953)   Doris Day, Howard Keel. Memorable for its opening rendition of 'The Deadwood Stage' and the Oscar-winning song 'Secret Love'. *Dir.* David Butler.

California Suite (1978)   Michael Caine, Maggie Smith, Walter Matthau, Alan Alda, Jane Fonda, Bill Cosby, Richard Pryor. Misadventures of 4 groups of guests at the Beverly Hills Hotel. *Dir.* Herbert Ross.

Caligula (1979)   Malcolm McDowell, John Gielgud, Peter O'Toole, Helen Mirren. *Dir.* Tinto Brass.

Callan (1974)   Edward Woodward, Eric Porter, Carl Mohner, Catherine Schell, Peter Egan, Russell Hunter. Aka: *The Neutralizer*. *Dir.* Don Sharp.

Camille (1936)   Greta Garbo (Marguerite Gautier), Robert Taylor (Armand Duval), Lionel Barrymore, Henry Daniell. Based on Alexandre Dumas' novel. *Dir.* George Cukor.

Candyman (1992)   Virginia Madsen, Tony Todd, Xander Berkeley, Vanessa Williams. Story of a mythical hook-handed serial killer which had an unsuccessful 1995 sequel *Candyman: Farewell to the Flesh*. *Dir.* Bernard Rose.

Cape Fear (1991)   Robert De Niro (Max Cady), Nick Nolte (Sam Bowden), Jessica Lange (Leigh Bowden), Robert Mitchum (Lt Elgart), Gregory Peck (Lee Heller). Notable for cameo roles of Mitchum, Peck and Martin Balsam, who were all in original 1962 film. *Dir.* Martin Scorsese.

Captain America (1944)   Dick Purcell, Lionel Atwill, Lorna Gray. District Attorney in guise of Capt America battles The Scarab (in guise of a museum curator). *Dir.* John English.

Captain America (1989)   Matt Salinger, Ronny Cox, Ned Beatty, Bill Mumy. Captain America is freed from his deep-ice captivity to battle arch-enemy The Red Skull. *Dir.* Albert Pyun.

Captain Corelli's Mandolin (2001)   Nicholas Cage (Corelli), Penelope Cruz, John Hurt, Christian Bale, David Morrissey. *Dir.* John Madden.

Captains Courageous (1937)   Spencer Tracy, Lionel Barrymore, Freddie Bartholomew, Mickey Rooney. Spoiled rich boy falls off a cruise liner and lives for a while among fisherfolk. *Dir.* Victor Fleming.

Caravaggio (1986)   Nigel Terry, Sean Bean, Tilda Swinton, Robbie Coltrane. *Dir.* Derek Jarman.

Caretaker, The (1964)   Alan Bates, Robert Shaw, Donald Pleasence. Based on Pinter's play about 2 men who invite a tramp to share their attic. US title: *The Guest*. *Dir.* Clive Donner.

Carnal Knowledge (1971)   Jack Nicholson, Art Garfunkel, Candice Bergen, Ann-Margret, Rita Moreno. *Dir.* Mike Nichols.

Carousel (1956)   Gordon Macrae, Shirley Jones, Cameron Mitchell. *Dir.* Henry King.

Carpetbaggers, The (1964)   George Peppard, Alan

CINEMA

Ladd, Carroll Baker, Martin Balsam, Elizabeth
Ashley, Lew Ayres, Archie Moore, Leif Erickson.
Dir. Edward Dmytryk.

Carrie (1952)   Laurence Olivier, Jennifer Jones,
Eddie Albert. Based on Theodore Dreiser's novel
Sister Carrie. *Dir.* William Wyler.

Carrie (1976)   Sissy Spacek, Piper Laurie, Amy
Irving, John Travolta. Based on the Stephen King
novel. *Dir.* Brian De Palma.

Carrington (1995)   Emma Thompson (Carrington),
Jonathan Pryce (Strachey), Janet McTeer (Vanessa
Bell). Based on Lytton Strachey's book. *Dir.*
Christopher Hampton.

Carry On Columbus (1992)   Jim Dale (Chris
Columbus), Bernard Cribbins (Mort), Maureen
Lipman (Countess Esmerelda), Alexei Sayle, Julian
Clary, Rik Mayall. Last of the series of Carry Ons.
Dir. Gerald Thomas.

Carry On Sergeant (1958)   Bob Monkhouse, William
Hartnell, Kenneth Williams, Charles Hawtrey, Shirley
Eaton, Kenneth Connor. First of the series of 30
Carry Ons. *Dir.* Gerald Thomas.

Carve Her Name With Pride (1958)   Virginia
McKenna (Violette Szabo), Paul Scofield, Jack
Warner, Sydney Tafler. Based on RJ Minney's book
about young British WW2 spy shot by a German
firing squad. *Dir.* Lewis Gilbert.

Casablanca (1942)   Humphrey Bogart (Rick Blaine),
Ingrid Bergman (Ilse Lund), Paul Henreid (Victor
Laszlo), Claude Rains (Captain Louis Renault),
Sydney Greenstreet (Ferrari), Peter Lorre (Ugarte),
Conrad Veidt (Major Strasser), Dooley Wilson (Sam).
Closing line, 'Louis, I think this is the beginning of a
beautiful friendship.' Ronald Reagan and Ann
Sheridan were originally cast as the leads.
Dir. Michael Curtiz.

Casanova (1976)   Donald Sutherland, Tina Aumont,
Cicely Browne. Aka *Fellini's Casanova*. *Dir.* Federico
Fellini.

Casino (1995)   Sharon Stone, Robert De Niro, Joe
Pesci, James Woods. *Dir.* Martin Scorsese.

Casino Royale (1967)   David Niven, Deborah Kerr,
Orson Welles, Peter Sellers, Ursula Andress, Woody
Allen, William Holden, Charles Boyer, Jean-Paul
Belmondo, Peter O'Toole, John Huston, George
Raft. Sir James Bond is called out of retirement to
tackle the power of 'SMERSH'. Joe McGrath was
originally the sole director but was fired after Sellers
walked out and Huston, Ken Hughes, Robert
Parrish, Val Guest and Richard Talmadge finished
the film. This was the first James Bond book but
clearly not the first film. *Dir.* John Huston & others.

Cassandra Crossing, The (1976)   Sophia Loren,
Richard Harris, Ava Gardner, Burt Lancaster, Martin
Sheen, OJ Simpson. *Dir.* George Pan Cosmatos.

Cast a Dark Shadow (1955)   Dirk Bogarde, Margaret
Lockwood. Wife-murderer marries an ex-barmaid
and tries again. *Dir.* Lewis Gilbert.

Cast a Giant Shadow (1966)   Kirk Douglas, Angie
Dickinson, Chaim Topol, John Wayne, Frank Sinatra,
Yul Brynner, Gordon Jackson, Jeremy Kemp,
Michael Hordern. Biopic of Colonel David Marcus's
fight against the Arabs in the Israel of 1947. *Dir.*
Melville Shavelson.

Castaway (1987)   Oliver Reed (Gerald Kingsland),
Amanda Donohue, Georgina Hale, John Sessions.
Based on Lucy Irvine's autobiographical book.
Dir. Nicolas Roeg.

Casualties of War (1989)   Michael J Fox (Eriksson),
Sean Penn (Sgt Meserve). Story of the gang rape of
a Vietnamese girl. *Dir.* Brian De Palma.

Cat and the Canary, The (1939)   Bob Hope (Wally

Campbell), Paulette Goddard (Joyce Norman), Gale
Sondergaard (Miss Lu). *Dir.* Elliott Nugent.

Cat Ballou (1965)   Jane Fonda, Lee Marvin, Nat King
Cole, Stubby Kaye. Oscar-winning performances by
Lee Marvin as twin brothers. *Dir.* Elliot Silverstein.

Cat on a Hot Tin Roof (1958)   Paul Newman (Brick),
Burl Ives (Big Daddy), Elizabeth Taylor (Maggie).
Based on the play by Tennessee Williams. *Dir.*
Richard Brooks.

Cat People (1942)   Simone Simon, Tom Conway,
Kent Smith. Yugoslavian girl believes she can turn
into a panther and deaths follow, although the
monster is never seen. *Dir.* Jacques Tourneur.

Cat People (1982)   Nastassja Kinski, Malcolm
McDowell. Kinky version of the 1942 classic.
Dir. Paul Schrader.

Catch Me If You Can (2002)   Leonardo DiCaprio
(Frank Abagnale Jnr), Tom Hanks (Carl Hanratty),
Christopher Walken (Frank Abagnale Snr), Martin
Sheen (Roger Strong), James Brolin (Jack Barnes),
Nathalie Baye (Paula Abagnale), Amy Adams
(Brenda Strong). True-life story of a con-man and his
attempts to remain one step ahead of an FBI agent.
Dir. Steven Spielberg.

Catch My Soul (1973)   Richie Havens, Lance
LeGault, Season Hubley, Tony Joe White. Rock and
country musical version of *Othello*. *Dir.* Patrick
McGoohan.

Catch 22 (1970)   Alan Arkin (Yossarian), Martin
Balsam, Richard Benjamin, Art Garfunkel, Bob
Newhart, Orson Welles, Martin Sheen, Jon Voight,
Anthony Perkins. Based on Joseph Heller's novel.
Dir. Mike Nichols.

Catholic Boys (1985)   Donald Sutherland (Brother
Thadeus), John Heard (Brother Timothy). Originally
called *Heaven Help Us*. *Dir.* Michael Dinner.

Cats & Dogs (2001)   Jeff Goldblum (Professor
Brody), Elizabeth Perkins (Mrs Brody), Alexander
Pollock (Scott Brody), Miriam Margolyes (Sophie).
Story of a Persian cat's attempt to conquer the
world, mixing actors and animation. Voices of Tobey
Maguire (Lou), Alec Baldwin (Butch), Susan
Sarandon (Ivy), Charlton Heston (The Mastiff), Sean
Hayes (Mr Tinkles), Joe Pantoliano (Peek), Jon
Lovitz (Calico). *Dir.* Lawrence Guterman.

Catwoman (2004)   Halle Berry (Patience
Phillips/Catwoman), Benjamin Bratt (Tom Lone),
Sharon Stone (Laurel Hedare), Lambert Wilson
(George Hedare), Frances Conroy (Ophelia). *Dir.* Pitof.

Celebrity (1998)   Kenneth Branagh, Hank Azaria,
Judy Davis, Leonardo DiCaprio, Melanie Griffith,
Winona Ryder. *Dir.* Woody Allen.

Celia (1989)   Rebecca Smart (Celia), Nicholas Eadie
(Ray). *Dir.* Ann Turner.

Cemetery Man (1994)   Rupert Everett, François
Hadji-Lazaro, Anna Falci. *Dir.* Michele Soavi.

Central Station (1998)   Fernanda Montenegro,
Marilia Pera, Vinicius de Oliveira, Soia Lira, Othon
Bastos. *Dir.* Walter Salles.

Chain Reaction (1996). Keanu Reeves, Morgan
Freeman, Rachel Weisz. *Dir.* Andrew Davis.

Chamber, The (1996)   Gene Hackman (Sam
Cayhall), Chris O'Donnell (Adam Hall), Faye
Dunaway. *Dir.* James Foley.

Champ, The (1931)   Wallace Beery, Jackie Cooper.
Frances Marion won Oscar for Best Original Story.
Dir. King Vidor.

Champ, The (1979)   Jon Voight, Faye Dunaway, Ricky
Schroeder. Remake of the 1931 classic. *Dir.* Franco
Zeffirelli.

Champions (1983)   John Hurt (Bob Champion),
Edward Woodward (Josh Gifford). Story of a jockey's

fight against cancer and his subsequent Grand
National success in 1981. *Dir.* John Irvin.

Chance of a Lifetime (1950)   Bernard Miles,
Kenneth More, Hattie Jacques. *Dir.* Bernard Miles.

Changing Lanes (2002)   Ben Affleck, Samuel L
Jackson, Kim Staunton, Toni Collette, Sydney
Pollack, William Hurt, Amanda Peet. *Dir.* Roger
Michell.

Chaplin (1992)   Robert Downey Jnr, Dan Aykroyd
(Mack Sennett), Geraldine Chaplin (Hannah
Chaplin), Kevin Dunn (J Edgar Hoover), Kevin Kline
(Douglas Fairbanks), John Thaw (Fred Karno),
Marisa Tomei (Mabel Normand). *Dir.* Richard
Attenborough.

Chariots of Fire (1981)   Ben Cross (Harold
Abrahams), Ian Charleson (Eric Liddell), Nigel
Havers. Oscars include: Best Film, Costume Design,
Music and Script (Colin Welland). *Dir.* Hugh Hudson.

Charley Varrick (1973)   Walter Matthau, Joe Don
Baker. Story of a bank robber who discovers he has
stolen mafia money. *Dir.* Don Siegel.

Charley's Aunt (1941)   Jack Benny, Kay Francis,
Anne Baxter, Laird Cregar. Based on play by
Brandon Thomas. *Dir.* Archie Mayo.

Charlie Chan (Series)   Warner Oland (1931–37),
Sidney Toler (1938–47), Roland Winters (1947–49).
Based on Earl Derr Biggers's character. *Dir.* Various.

Charlotte Gray (2001)   Cate Blanchett (Charlotte),
Billy Crudup, Michael Gambon, James Fleet, Jack
Shepherd. Based on a Sebastian Faulks bestseller
about a young Scotswoman who becomes a spy in
France during the Second World War. *Dir.* Gillian
Armstrong.

Che! (1969)   Omar Sharif (Che Guevara), Jack
Palance (Castro). *Dir.* Richard Fleischer.

Cheech and Chong's Next Movie (1980)   Cheech
Marin, Thomas Chong, Evelyn Guerrero. GB title: *High
Encounters of the Ultimate Kind. Dir.* Thomas Chong.

Cheyenne Autumn (1964)   Richard Widmark, Carroll
Baker, Karl Malden, Dolores del Rio, Sal Mineo,
Edward G Robinson, James Stewart (Wyatt Earp).
Dir. John Ford.

Chicago (2002)   Richard Gere (Billy Flynn), Renée
Zellweger (Roxie Hart), Catherine Zeta-Jones
(Velma Kelley), Queen Latifah, Taye Diggs.
Adaptation of Bob Fosse's 1975 Broadway musical
about two dreamers Velma Kelley and Roxie Hart.
Velma is the Windy City's top nightclub star until the
night she guns down her cheating husband, after
which she becomes an even bigger celebrity, thanks
to smooth lawyer Billy Flynn. Roxie also desperately
wants fame, so decides to shoot her abusive lover
dead. After Roxie replaces her, an outraged Velma
plots Roxie's demise. *Dir.* Rob Marshall.

Chicago Joe and the Showgirl (1990)   Kiefer
Sutherland (Ricky Allen), Emily Lloyd (Georgina
Grayson), Patsy Kensit (Joyce Cook). *Dir.* Bernard
Rose.

Children of a Lesser God (1986)   William Hurt
(James), Marlee Matlin (Sarah), Piper Laurie (Mrs
Norman). Deaf woman falls in love with her speech
therapist. *Dir.* Randa Haines.

Child's Play (1988)   Catherine Hicks (Karen Barclay),
Chris Sarandon (Mike Norris). Dying killer Brad
Dourif's soul passes into a Chucky Doll. *Dir.* Tom
Holland.

China Syndrome, The (1979)   Jane Fonda, Jack
Lemmon, Michael Douglas. *Dir.* James Bridges.

Chinatown (1974)   Jack Nicholson, Faye Dunaway,
John Huston, Roman Polanski, Diane Ladd.
Dir. Roman Polanski.

Chitty Chitty Bang Bang (1968)   Dick Van Dyke,
Sally Ann Howes (Truly Scrumptious), Lionel
Jeffries, Benny Hill, Robert Helpmann, Gert Frobe,
James Robertson Justice. Roald Dahl adapted the
original Ian Fleming story. *Dir.* Ken Hughes.

Chocolat (2000)   Juliette Binoche (Vianne Rocher),
Alfred Molina (Comte de Reynaud), Carrie-Anne
Moss (Caroline Clairmont), Johnny Depp (Roux),
Judi Dench (Armande Voizin), Lena Olin (Josephine
Muscat). Based on Joanne Harris bestseller. *Dir.*
Lasse Hallstrom.

Chorus Line, A (1985)   Michael Douglas (Zach),
Alyson Reed (Cassie), Terrence Mann (Larry).
Dir. Richard Attenborough.

Chorus of Disapproval (1989)   Anthony Hopkins
(Dafydd Ap Llewellyn), Jeremy Irons (Guy Jones),
Prunella Scales (Hannah), Jenny Seagrove (Fay
Hubbard). *Dir.* Michael Winner.

Christmas Carol: The Movie (2001)   Simon Callow
(Charles Dickens), voices of Kate Winslet (Belle),
Nicolas Cage (Jacob Marley), Jane Horrocks (Ghost
of Christmas Past), Simon Callow (Scrooge),
Michael Gambon (Ghost of Christmas Present),
Rhys Ifans (Cratchit), Juliet Stevenson (Mrs
Cratchit/Mother Gimlet). Animated version – other
than Callow's Dickens. *Dir.* Jimmy T Murakami.

Christopher Columbus: The Discovery (1992)
Marlon Brando (Torquemada), Tom Selleck (King
Ferdinand), Georges Corraface (Columbus), Rachel
Ward (Queen Isabella), Catherine Zeta Jones
(Beatriz). *Dir.* John Glen.

Cincinnati Kid, The (1965)   Steve McQueen, Edward
G Robinson, Karl Malden, Ann-Margret, Tuesday
Weld. Based on Richard Jessup's novel concerning
battle for supremacy among stud poker experts.
Dir. Norman Jewison.

Citadel, The (1938)   Robert Donat, Rosalind Russell,
Ralph Richardson, Rex Harrison. Based on AJ
Cronin's novel, which also spawned the TV series *Dr
Finlay's Casebook. Dir.* King Vidor.

Citizen Kane (1941)   Orson Welles (Kane), Joseph
Cotten (Jedediah Leland), Agnes Moorehead (Kane's
mother). Based loosely on the newspaper magnate
William Randolph Hearst. Welles also co-wrote the
script with Herman J Mankiewicz. *Dir.* Orson Welles.

City Hall (1996)   Al Pacino, John Cusack, Bridget
Fonda, Danny Aiello. *Dir.* Harold Becker.

City Heat (1984)   Clint Eastwood (Lt Speer), Burt
Reynolds (Mike Murphy), Madeline Kahn (Caroline
Howley). Reynolds broke his jaw when a prop chair
turned out to be a real one!. *Dir.* Richard Benjamin.

City of God (2003)   Matheus Nachtergaele (Sandro
Cenoura), Seu Jorge (Mane Galinha), Buscape
(Alexandre Rodrigues). Set in the slums of Rio de
Janeiro; a poor wretch, eager to improve himself,
watches his contemporaries turn to drugs and crime.
Dir. Fernando Meirelles.

City of Industry (1997)   Harvey Keitel, Stephen
Dorff, Timothy Hutton. *Dir.* John Irvin.

City Slickers (1991)   Billy Crystal (Mitch Robbins),
Daniel Stern (Phil Berquist), Jack Palance (Curly).
Oscar for Jack Palance as Best Supporting Actor.
Dir. Ron Underwood.

Class Act (1992)   Christopher Reid, Christopher
Martin, Karyn Parsons. Two students swap identities.
Dir. Randall Miller.

Class Action (1991)   Gene Hackman, Mary
Elizabeth Mastrantonio, Colin Friels. Father and
daughter, both lawyers, find themselves on opposing
sides in the courtroom. *Dir.* Michael Apted.

Cleopatra (1934)   Claudette Colbert, Henry Wilcoxon
(Antony), Warren William (Caesar). *Dir.* Cecil B de
Mille.

CINEMA

Cleopatra (1963)   Elizabeth Taylor, Richard Burton, Rex Harrison. *Dir.* Joseph L Mankiewicz.

Clockers (1995)   Harvey Keitel, John Turturro, Delroy Lindo, Mekhi Phifer, Pee Wee Love, Sticky Fingaz. A clocker is a small-time crack dealer working on the streets. *Dir.* Spike Lee.

Clockwise (1986)   John Cleese (Timpson), Alison Steadman (Gwenda), Penelope Wilton (Pat Garden). *Dir.* Christopher Morahan.

Clockwork Orange, A (1971)   Malcolm McDowell, Adrienne Corri, Patrick Magee, Michael Bates, Warren Clarke. Based on Anthony Burgess's novel. *Dir.* Stanley Kubrick.

Close Encounters of the Third Kind (1977)   Richard Dreyfuss, François Truffaut, Teri Garr. *Dir.* Steven Spielberg.

Closer (2004)   Natalie Portman (Alice), Jude Law (Dan), Julia Roberts (Anna), Clive Owen (Larry), Nick Hobbs, Colin Stinton. Set in London, the story of four strangers and their chance meetings, instant attractions and subsequent betrayals. Based on the play by Patrick Marber. *Dir.* Mike Nichols.

Coal Miner's Daughter (1980)   Sissy Spacek (Loretta Lynn), Tommy Lee Jones. *Dir.* Michael Apted.

Cocktail (1988)   Tom Cruise (Brian Flanagan), Bryan Brown (Doug Coughlin), Elizabeth Shue (Jordan Mooney). *Dir.* Roger Donaldson.

Cocoanuts, The (1929)   Four Marx Brothers, Margaret Dumont. First of the Marx Brothers films. *Dir.* Robert Florey and Joseph Santley.

Cocoon (1985)   Don Ameche (Art Selwyn), Steve Guttenberg (Jack Bonner), Jessica Tandy (Alma Finley), Tahnee Welch, (Kitty). There was a 1988 sequel *Cocoon: The Return. Dir.* Ron Howard.

Cold Comfort Farm (1995)   Kate Beckinsale (Flora Poste), Joanna Lumley, Stephen Fry, Eileen Atkins, Ian McKellen. *Dir.* John Schlesinger.

Cold Mountain (2002)   Jude Law (Inman), Nicole Kidman (Ada Monroe), Renée Zellweger (Ruby Thewes), Donald Sutherland (Reverend Monroe), Ray Winstone (Teague), Brendan Gleason (Stobrod), Philip Seymour Hoffman (Veasey), Natalie Portman (Sara), Kathy Baker (Sally Swanger), Giovanni Ribisi (Junior), Eileen Atkins (Maddy), Charlie Hunnam (Bosie). Set in 1864 during the American Civil War, a Confederate soldier deserts to make his way back to the woman he fleetingly loved. *Dir.* Anthony Minghella.

Color of Money, The (1986)   Paul Newman (Eddie Felson), Tom Cruise (Vincent), Mary Elizabeth Mastrantonio (Carmen). Sequel to *The Hustler. Dir.* Martin Scorsese.

Color of Night (1994)   Bruce Willis, Jane March, Ruben Blades, Lesley Ann Warren, Scott Bakula. Psychiatrist takes over a group that includes the person who murdered a colleague. *Dir.* Richard Rush.

Color Purple, The (1985)   Whoopi Goldberg (Celie), Danny Glover (Albert Johnson) Oprah Winfrey (Sofia), Willard Pugh (Harpo). Based on the novel by Alice Walker. *Dir.* Steven Spielberg.

Comfort and Joy (1984)   Bill Paterson (Alan), Eleanor David (Maddy), CP Grogan (Charlotte). Ice cream empires are called 'Mr McCool' and 'Mr Bunny' and the music is by Mark Knopfler. *Dir.* Bill Forsyth.

Coming Home (1978)   Jane Fonda, Jon Voight, Bruce Dern. *Dir.* Hal Ashby.

Commitments, The (1991)   Robert Arkins (Jimmy Rabbitte), Andrew Strong (Deco Cuffe), Michael Aherne (Steve Clifford). Story of a Dublin soul band. *Dir.* Alan Parker.

Con Air (1997)   Nicolas Cage, John Cusack, John Malkovich. *Dir.* Simon West.

Conspiracy Theory (1997)   Mel Gibson (Jerry Fletcher), Julia Roberts (Alice Sutton). *Dir.* Richard Donner.

Contact (1997)   Jodie Foster (Ellie). Based on Carl Sagan's book. *Dir.* Robert Zemeckis.

Control Room (2004)   Documentary on perception of the United States' war with Iraq, with an emphasis on Al Jazeera's coverage. *Dir.* Jehane Noujaim.

Cook, the Thief, His Wife and Her Lover, The (1989)   Richard Bohringer (Richard the Cook), Michael Gambon (Albert the Thief), Helen Mirren (Georgina, His Wife), Alan Howard (Michael, Her Lover). *Dir.* Peter Greenaway.

Cool Hand Luke (1967)   Paul Newman (Lucas Jackson), George Kennedy, Jo Van Fleet. Luke was imprisoned for sawing off a parking meter. Famous scene where Luke swallows 50 eggs in an hour. *Dir.* Stuart Rosenberg.

Cotton Club, The (1984)   Richard Gere (Dixie Dwyer), Gregory Hines (Sandman Williams), Bob Hoskins (Owney Madden), Nicolas Cage (Vincent Dwyer). *Dir.* Francis Ford Coppola.

Courage under Fire (1996)   Denzel Washington (Colonel Serling), Meg Ryan (Captain Karen Walden). *Dir.* Edward Zwick.

Courtneys of Curzon Street, The (1947)   Anna Neagle, Michael Wilding, Michael Medwin. *Dir.* Herbert Wilcox.

Cousins (1989)   Ted Danson (Larry Kozinski), Isabella Rossellini (Maria Hardy), Sean Young (Tish Kozinski), Lloyd Bridges (Uncle Vince). *Dir.* Joel Schumacher.

Cowboy Way, The (1994)   Woody Harrelson, Kiefer Sutherland, Ernie Hudson. *Dir.* Gregg Champion.

Craft, The (1996)   Robin Tunney, Fairuza Balk. *Dir.* Andrew Fleming.

Crash (1996)   James Spader (James), Deborah Unger (Catherine), Holly Hunter (Helen). *Dir.* David Cronenberg.

Crimes and Misdemeanors (1989)   Caroline Aaron (Barbara), Alan Alda (Lester), Woody Allen (Cliff Stern), Claire Bloom (Miriam Rosenthal), Mia Farrow (Halley Reed), Anjelica Huston (Dolores Paley). *Dir.* Woody Allen.

Crimes of the Heart (1986)   Diane Keaton (Lenny Magrath), Jessica Lange (Meg), Sissy Spacek (Babe). Three kooky sisters argue about which one of them is going to go completely mad, first. *Dir.* Bruce Beresford.

Critters (1986)   Dee Wallace Stone, M Emmet Walsh, Billy Green Bush. Hair-ball creatures arrive from an asteroid and devastate Kansas. *Dir.* Stephen Herek.

Crocodile Dundee (1986)   Paul Hogan (Mick Dundee), Linda Kozlowski (Sue Charlton), John Meillon (Wally Reilly). As so often the case with sequels, *Crocodile Dundee II* was not as big a hit. *Dir.* Peter Faiman.

Crocodile Dundee in Los Angeles (2001)   Paul Hogan, Linda Kozlowski, Jere Burns, Jonathan Banks, Mike Tyson (as himself). Second sequel made 13 years after the previous one but similar plot. *Dir.* Simon Wincer.

Cromwell (1970)   Richard Harris, Alec Guinness, Frank Finlay, Robert Morley. *Dir.* Ken Hughes.

Crossing Guard, The (1995)   Jack Nicholson, David Morse, Anjelica Huston, Piper Laurie. Alcoholic jeweller plans to kill the man who killed his daughter in a drink driving incident. *Dir.* Sean Penn.

Crossroads (2002)   Britney Spears (Lucy), Zoe Saldana (Kit), Justin Long, Dan Aykroyd, Anson

Mount, Kim Cattrall, Taryn Manning (Mimi). Three girls go to Los Angeles following their graduation. *Dir.* Tamara Davis.

Crouching Tiger, Hidden Dragon (1999)   Michelle Yeoh, Chang Chen, Zhang Ziyi, Chow Yun-Fat. *Dir.* Ang Lee.

Crow, The (1994)   Brandon Lee, Ernie Hudson, Michael Wincott. Brandon Lee died in a shooting accident during filming. *Dir.* Alex Proyas.

Cruel Sea, The (1953)   Jack Hawkins, Donald Sinden, Stanley Baker. Eric Ambler adapted the novel of Nicholas Monsarrat. *Dir.* Charles Frend.

Crumb (1994)   Robert Crumb, Charles Crumb, Maxon Crumb, Dana Crumb, Beatrice Crumb, Aline Kominsky. Documentary about the creator of Fritz the Cat and Mr Natural. *Dir.* Terry Zwigoff.

Cry Freedom (1987)   Kevin Kline (Donald Woods), Denzel Washington (Steve Biko). *Dir.* Richard Attenborough.

Cry in the Dark, A (1988)   Meryl Streep (Lindy Chamberlain), Sam Neill (Michael). True story of a mother, convicted of killing her baby, who maintained a dingo had run off with it. *Dir.* Fred Schepisi.

Crying Freeman (1995)   Mark Dacascos, Julie Condra (Emu O'Hara). *Dir.* Christophe Gans.

Crying Game, The (1992)   Stephen Rea (Fergus), Miranda Richardson (Jude), Forest Whitaker (Jody). *Dir.* Neil Jordan.

Curse of the Pink Panther, The (1983)   David Niven (Sir Charles Litton), Robert Wagner (George Litton), Herbert Lom (Dreyfus), Joanna Lumley (Chandra), Capucine (Lady Litton). David Niven's voice was dubbed by Rich Little. *Dir.* Blake Edwards.

Cutthroat Island (1995)   Geena Davis (Morgan), Matthew Modine (William Shaw), Frank Langella. *Dir.* Renny Harlin.

Cyrano de Bergerac (1990)   Gérard Depardieu, Anne Brochet, Vincent Perez. *Dir.* Jean-Paul Rappeneau.

Daddy Longlegs (1931)   Janet Gaynor, Warner Baxter. Orphan girl grows up to fall in love with a mysterious benefactor. *Dir.* Alfred Santell.

Daddy Longlegs (1955)   Fred Astaire, Leslie Caron, Fred Clark. Musical remake of the 1931 film. *Dir.* Jean Negulesco.

Daleks: Invasion Earth 2150 AD (1966)   Peter Cushing, Bernard Cribbins. *Dir.* Gordon Flemyng.

Dam Busters, The (1954)   Michael Redgrave (Barnes Wallis), Richard Todd (Guy Gibson). *Dir.* Michael Anderson.

Damien: Omen Two (1978)   William Holden, Lee Grant, Jonathan Scott-Taylor, Sylvia Sidney. *Dir.* Don Taylor.

Dance with a Stranger (1985)   Miranda Richardson (Ruth Ellis), Rupert Everett (David Blakely), Ian Holm, Stratford Johns. *Dir.* Mike Newell.

Dances with Wolves (1990)   Kevin Costner (Lt John J Dunbar), Mary McDonnell (Stands With a Fist), Graham Greene (Kicking Bird). *Dir.* Kevin Costner.

Dangerous Ground (1997)   Elizabeth Hurley, Ice Cube. *Dir.* Darrell James Roodt.

Dangerous Liaisons (1988)   Glenn Close (Marquise de Merteuil), John Malkovich (Vicomte de Valmont), Michelle Pfeiffer (Madame de Tourvel), Keanu Reeves (Chevalier Danceny), Uma Thurman (Cecile de Volanges). *Dir.* Stephen Frears.

Danny the Champion of the World (1989)   Jeremy Irons (William Smith), Samuel Irons (Danny), Robbie Coltrane (Victor Hazell). Based on a Roald Dahl book. *Dir.* Gavin Millar.

Dante's Peak (1997)   Pierce Brosnan, Linda Hamilton. *Dir.* Roger Donaldson.

Darkman (1990)   Liam Neeson (Peyton Westlake / Darkman). Scientist left for dead by thugs re-emerges as Darkman. *Dir.* Sam Raimi.

Darling (1965)   Julie Christie, Dirk Bogarde, Laurence Harvey. *Dir.* John Schlesinger.

Dave (1993)   Kevin Kline, Sigourney Weaver, Frank Langella, Ben Kingsley. US President suffers a stroke and a Baltimore businessman is hired to impersonate him. *Dir.* Ivan Reitman.

David Copperfield (1934)   Freddie Bartholomew (young David), Frank Lawton (David as a man), WC Fields (Micawber). Charles Laughton was original choice for Micawber but resigned after 2 days. *Dir.* George Cukor.

Day at the Races, A (1937)   First of the high-budget Marx Brothers films. *Dir.* Sam Wood.

Day of the Beast (1995)   Alex Angulo, Armando de Razza, Santiago Segura. Priest attempts to track down the Anti-Christ who is to be born in Madrid. *Dir.* Alex de la Iglesia.

Day of the Jackal, The (1973)   Edward Fox, Michael Lonsdale, Alan Badel, Eric Porter. *Dir.* Fred Zinnemann.

Day of the Triffids, The (1962)   Howard Keel, Kieron Moore, Janette Scott, Nicole Maurey. *Dir.* Steve Sekely.

Daylight (1996)   Sylvester Stallone, Amy Brenneman, Viggo Mortensen, Karen Young, Claire Bloom. Diverse group of people are trapped in Manhattan's Holland Tunnel. *Dir.* Rob Cohen.

Days of Thunder (1990)   Tom Cruise (Cole Trickle), Robert Duvall (Harry Hogge), Nicole Kidman (Dr Claire Lewicki). *Dir.* Tony Scott.

Dead Again (1991)   Kenneth Branagh (Roman Strauss / Mike), Andy Garcia (Gray Baker), Derek Jacobi (Franklyn Madson), Emma Thompson (Margaret Strauss / Grace). *Dir.* Kenneth Branagh.

Dead Calm (1989)   Sam Neill (John Ingram), Nicole Kidman (Rae Ingram), Billy Zane (Hughie Warriner). *Dir.* Phillip Noyce.

Dead Man Walking (1995)   Susan Sarandon (Sister Helen Prejean), Sean Penn (Matthew Poncelet). *Dir.* Tim Robbins.

Dead Men Don't Wear Plaid (1982)   Steve Martin, Rachel Ward, Carl Reiner, Reni Santoni. Bogart, Ladd, Bacall, Stanwyck also appear in film-clip editing. *Dir.* Carl Reiner.

Dead Poets Society (1989)   Robin Williams (John Keating), Robert Sean Leonard, Ethan Hawke, Josh Charles. Keating's motto: 'Carpe Diem (Seize the Day)'. *Dir.* Peter Weir.

Dead Pool, The (1988)   Clint Eastwood (Harry Callahan), Patricia Clarkson, Liam Neeson, Evan C Kim. Famous scene of a car chase involving a toy car. Jim Carrey has small part as a murder victim. *Dir.* Buddy van Horn.

Dead Ringers (1988)   Jeremy Irons (Beverly / Elliot Mantle), Geneviève Bujold (Claire Niveau). Concerns identical twins, gynaecologists. *Dir.* David Cronenberg.

Dealers (1989)   Paul McGann (Daniel Pasco), Rebecca DeMornay (Anna Schuman), Derrick O'Connor (Robby Barrell). TV series *Capital City* was a spin-off. *Dir.* Colin Bucksey.

Dear Diary (1994)   Jennifer Beals, Nanni Moretti, Alexandre Rockwell. *Dir.* Nanni Moretti.

Death in Venice (1971)   Dirk Bogarde, Bjorn Andresen, Silvana Mangano Gustav Mahler's music is memorable. *Dir.* Luchino Visconti.

Death of a Salesman (1985)   Dustin Hoffman (Willy Loman), Charles Durning (Charley), Kate Reid (Linda), Stephen Lang (Happy), John Malkovich

C
I
N
E
M
A

Screenplay: Arthur Miller. Film was made for cable TV. *Dir*. Volker Schlondorff.

Death on the Nile (1978)   Peter Ustinov, Bette Davis, Mia Farrow, David Niven, Maggie Smith. Agatha Christie novel with Hercule Poirot. *Dir*. John Guillermin.

Death Race 2000 (1975)   David Carradine, Simone Griffeth, Sylvester Stallone. *Dir*. Paul Bartel.

Death Wish (1974)   Charles Bronson, Hope Lange, Vincent Gardenia. Four follow-on films – 1981, 1985, 1987, 1993 – similar plots. *Dir*. Michael Winner.

Deathtrap (1982)   Michael Caine, Christopher Reeve, Dyan Cannon. From the play by Ira Levin. *Dir*. Sidney Lumet.

Deepstar Six (1989)   Taurean Blacque, Nancy Everhard, Greg Evigan. Underwater thriller. *Dir*. Sean Cunningham.

Deer Hunter, The (1978)   Robert De Niro, John Savage, Christopher Walken, Meryl Streep. Vietnam thriller that won 3 Oscars. *Dir*. Michael Cimino.

Defence of the Realm (1985)   Gabriel Byrne (Nick Mullen), Greta Scacchi (Nina Beckman), Denholm Elliott (Vernon Bayliss), Robbie Coltrane (Leo McAskey). *Dir*. David Drury.

Defiant Ones, The (1958)   Tony Curtis, Sidney Poitier, Theodore Bikel, Lon Chaney Jnr. Prison escape drama, with black and white prisoners chained together, that won 3 Oscars. *Dir*. Stanley Kramer.

Delinquents, The (1989)   Notable only for being Kylie Minogue's debut feature. *Dir*. Chris Thomson.

Deliverance (1972)   Burt Reynolds, Jon Voight, Ned Beatty. From James Dickey's novel. *Dir*. John Boorman.

Demolition Man (1993)   Sylvester Stallone (John Spartan), Wesley Snipes (Simon Phoenix), Lori Petty, Nigel Hawthorne, Melinda Dillon. Futuristic thriller with Stallone as former cop released from suspended animation. *Dir*. Marco Brambilla.

Dennis the Menace (1993)   Walter Matthau, Mason Gamble, Joan Plowright, Christopher Lloyd, Lea Thompson. Story of the 6-yr-old menace. *Dir*. Nick Castle.

Desert Fox, The (1951)   James Mason, Jessica Tandy, Cedric Hardwicke. Biography of Erwin Rommel. *Dir*. Henry Hathaway.

Desert Rats, The (1953)   James Mason (Rommel), Richard Burton, Robert Newton. *Dir*. Robert Wise.

Desperado (1995)   Antonio Banderas, Salma Hayek, Joaquin de Almeida, Cheech Marin, Quentin Tarantino. Man with guitar case full of weapons walks into a Mexican town and starts shooting. *Dir*. Robert Rodriguez.

Desperate Hours (1990)   Mickey Rourke (Michael Bosworth), Anthony Hopkins (Tim Cornell), Mimi Rogers (Nora). *Dir*. Michael Cimino.

Desperate Measures (1998)   Michael Keaton, Andy Garcia. Detective Frank Connor is forced to choose between his badge and his son. *Dir*. Barbet Schroeder.

Desperately Seeking Susan (1985)   Madonna, Aidan Quinn, Rosanna Arquette. Madonna's first starring role. *Dir*. Susan Seidelman.

Destiny Turns on the Radio (1995)   James LeGros, Dylan McDermott, Quentin Tarantino, James Belushi, Nancy Travis. Bank robber gets out of jail and travels to Las Vegas to reclaim his loot. *Dir*. Jack Baran.

Devil Rides Out, The (1968)   Christopher Lee, Charles Gray, Patrick Mower. From Dennis Wheatley's novel. *Dir*. Terence Fisher.

Devils, The (1970)   Vanessa Redgrave, Oliver Reed, Dudley Sutton, Gemma Jones. *Dir*. Ken Russell.

Devil's Own, The (1997)   Harrison Ford (Tom O'Meara), Brad Pitt (Frankie McGuire). *Dir*. Alan J Pakula.

Diabolique (1996)   Sharon Stone, Isabelle Adjani, Kathy Bates. Wife and mistress of unpleasant schoolmaster conspire to murder him. *Dir*. Jeremiah Chechnik.

Dial M for Murder (1954)   Ray Milland, Grace Kelly, Robert Cummings. Shot in 3D but never released in 3D form. *Dir*. Alfred Hitchcock.

Diamonds Are Forever (1971)   Sean Connery, Charles Gray (Blofeld), Jill St John (Tiffany Case), Lana Wood (Plenty O'Toole). Theme song sung by Shirley Bassey. *Dir*. Guy Hamilton.

Dick Tracy (1990)   Warren Beatty, Madonna (Breathless Mahoney), Dick Van Dyke, Al Pacino (Big Boy Caprice), Dustin Hoffman (Mumbles), Charlie Korsmo (Kid), Kathy Bates (Mrs Green), James Caan (Spaldini). Won 3 Oscars. *Dir*. Warren Beatty.

Die Another Day (2002)   Pierce Brosnan (James Bond), Halle Berry (Jinx), Rick Yune (Zao), Madonna (Verity), Judi Dench (M), John Cleese (Q), Rosamund Pike (Miranda Frost), Michael Madsen (Damian Falco), Toby Stephens (Gustav Graves), Samantha Bond (Moneypenny). Theme song sung by Madonna. *Dir*. Lee Tamahori.

Die Hard (1988)   Bruce Willis (John McClane), Bonnie Bedelia (Holly Gennaro McClane), Alan Rickman (Hans Gruber). 3 sequels followed. *Dir*. John McTiernan.

Diner (1982)   Steve Guttenberg (Eddie), Daniel Stern (Shrevie), Mickey Rourke (Boogie), Kevin Bacon (Fenwick), Ellen Barkin (Beth), Timothy Daly (Billy). Five men on verge of manhood hang out at Fells Point Diner. *Dir*. Barry Levinson.

Dirty Dancing (1987)   Patrick Swayze (Johnny Castle), Jennifer Grey (Baby Houseman). Variant on *Saturday Night Fever*. *Dir*. Emile Ardolino.

Dirty Dingus Magee (1970)   Frank Sinatra, George Kennedy. Western comedy. *Dir*. Burt Kennedy.

Dirty Dozen, The (1967)   Lee Marvin, Robert Ryan, Charles Bronson, Telly Savalas, Ernest Borgnine, Jim Brown, John Cassavetes, George Kennedy, Richard Jaeckel, Trini Lopez, Ralph Meeker, Clint Walker, Donald Sutherland. *Dir*. Robert Aldrich.

Dirty Mary, Crazy Larry (1974)   Peter Fonda, Susan George, Roddy McDowall (uncredited). *Dir*. John Hough.

Dirty Rotten Scoundrels (1988)   Steve Martin (Freddie Benson), Michael Caine (Lawrence Jamieson). Remake of *Bedtime Story* (1964). *Dir*. Frank Oz.

Distinguished Gentleman, The (1992)   Eddie Murphy (Thomas Jefferson Johnson), Lane Smith (Dick Dodge), James Garner. *Dir*. Jonathan Lynn.

DOA (1950)   Edmond O'Brien, Pamela Britton, Neville Brand, Luther Adler. Title stands for 'Dead on Arrival' and concerns a professor, who has been poisoned by a slow-acting drug, in a race against time to track down his murderer. *Dir*. Rudolph Maté.

DOA (1988)   Dennis Quaid (Dexter Cornell), Meg Ryan (Sydney Fuller), Charlotte Rampling (Mrs Fitzwaring). Remake of the 1950 classic. *Dir*. Rocky Morton and Annabel Jankel.

Doc Hollywood (1991)   Michael J Fox (Dr Benjamin Stone), Julie Warner (Lou), Bridget Fonda (Nancy Lee), George Hamilton (Dr Halberstrom). Famous scene of Warner urinating to throw hunters off their prey's scent. *Dir*. Michael Caton-Jones.

Doctor and the Devils (1986)   Timothy Dalton (Dr Thomas Rock), Jonathan Pryce (Robert Fallon), Twiggy (Jenny Bailey), Beryl Reid, TP McKenna, Patrick Stewart. Screenplay by Dylan Thomas. *Dir.* Freddie Francis.

Dr Dolittle (1967)   Rex Harrison, Anthony Newley, Samantha Eggar, Richard Attenborough. Oscars for Best Song ('Talk to the Animals') and Special Effects. LB Abbott. *Dir.* Richard Fleischer.

Dr Dolittle (1998)   Eddie Murphy (Dr Dolittle), Ossie Davis, Oliver Platt, Peter Boyle. *Dir.* Betty Thomas.

Dr Dolittle 2 (2001)   Sequel to the 1998 film with similar cast. *Dir.* Steve Carr.

Doctor in the House (1954)   Dirk Bogarde, Kenneth More, Kay Kendall, Donald Sinden. First of many *Doctor* stories, followed by TV series. *Dir.* Ralph Thomas.

Doctor No (1962)   Sean Connery, Ursula Andress (Honeychile Rider), Joseph Wiseman (Dr No), Jack Lord. First of the James Bond stories to be filmed (James Bond theme by Monty Norman). *Dir.* Terence Young.

Dr Strangelove (1963)   Peter Sellers, George C Scott. Black comedy Peter Sellers plays 3 parts. *Dir.* Stanley Kubrick.

Dr Who and the Daleks (1965)   Peter Cushing, Roy Castle, Roberta Tovey, Jennie Linden. First *Dr Who* film; sequel in 1966. *Dir.* Gordon Flemyng.

Doctor Zhivago (1965)   Omar Sharif, Julie Christie, Rod Steiger, Alec Guinness, Rita Tushingham, Geraldine Chaplin, Tom Courtenay, Adrienne Corri. Oscars for Maurice Jarre (Music), Freddie Young (Photography), and Robert Bolt (Screenplay). *Dir.* David Lean.

Dog Day Afternoon (1975)   Al Pacino, John Cazale, Charles Durning, Chris Sarandon, Sully Boyar. *Dir.* Sidney Lumet.

Dog Soldiers (2002)   Sean Pertwee (Sgt Harry Wells), Kevin McKidd, Emma Cleasby. Story of an army patrol in the Highlands of Scotland besieged by werewolves. *Dir.* Neil Marshall.

Dogville (2003)   Nicole Kidman (Grace), Harriet Anderson (Gloria), Lauren Bacall (Ma Ginger), Jean-Marc Barr (The Man with the Big Hat), Paul Bettany (Tom Edison), Blair Brown (Mrs Henson), James Caan (The Big Man), Patricia Clarkson (Vera), Jeremy Davies (Bill Henson), Ben Gazzara (Jack McKay), Philip Baker Hall (Tom Edison Snr), Udo Kier (The Man in the Coat), Chloe Sevigny (Liz Henson), Stellan Skarsgard (Chuck), John Hurt (Narrator). Set in the 1930s. A woman flees from gangsters and is protected by the residents of a small town until they realise the risks involved. Innovative film methods are used including lines of white paint to depict streets and buildings in order to distinguish public and private behaviour. *Dir.* Lars von Trier.

Dolores Claiborne (1995)   Kathy Bates, Jennifer Jason Leigh, Judy Parfitt, Christopher Plummer. Housekeeper acquitted of murder is then arrested for killing her boss. *Dir.* Taylor Hackford.

Donnie Brasco (1997)   Al Pacino (Ben 'Lefty' Ruggiero), Johnny Depp (Donnie Brasco / Joe Pistone), Michael Madsen (Sonny). *Dir.* Mike Newell.

Don't Look Now (1973)   Donald Sutherland, Julie Christie. Daphne du Maurier story, set in Venice. *Dir.* Nicolas Roeg.

Doors, The (1991)   Val Kilmer (Jim Morrison), Meg Ryan (Pamela Courson), Billy Idol (Cat). *Dir.* Oliver Stone.

Double Indemnity (1944)   Fred MacMurray, Barbara Stanwyck, Edward G Robinson, Tom Powers, Porter Hall, Jean Heather, Byron Barr. An insurance agent connives with the wife of a client to kill her husband and claim on the policy. Screenplay by Billy Wilder and Raymond Chandler based on the novel by James M Cain. *Dir.* Billy Wilder.

Down and Out in Beverly Hills (1986)   Nick Nolte (Jerry Baskin), Richard Dreyfuss (Davie Whiteman), Bette Midler (Barbara Whiteman), Little Richard (Orvis Goodnight). *Dir.* Paul Mazursky.

Downhill Racer (1969)   Robert Redford, Gene Hackman, Camilla Sparv. Plotless film about a skier. *Dir.* Michael Ritchie.

Dracula (1931)   Bela Lugosi, Helen Chandler, David Manners. Numerous follow-on films from this Bram Stoker novel. *Dir.* Tod Browning.

Dracula 2001 (2000)   Christopher Plummer (Van Helsing), Jonny Lee Miller, Justine Waddell, Gerard Butler (Dracula). US title: *Dracula 2000. Dir.* Patrick Lussier.

Dragnet (1987)   Dan Aykroyd (Joe Friday), Tom Hanks (Streebek), Christopher Plummer (Whirley), Harry Morgan (Bill Gannon). *Dir.* Tom Mankiewicz.

Dragon: The Bruce Lee Story (1993)   Jason Scott Lee, Robert Wagner, Michael Learned, Lauren Holly, Nancy Kwan. *Dir.* Rob Cohen.

Dragonheart (1996)   Dennis Quaid, David Thewlis, Pete Postlethwaite, voice of Sean Connery. *Dir.* Rob Cohen.

Dream Team, The (1989)   Michael Keaton (Billy Caulfield), Christopher Lloyd (Henry Sikorsky), Peter Boyle (Jack McDermott), Stephen Furst (Albert Ianuzzi). Four mental patients have to fend for themselves in Manhattan. *Dir.* Howard Zieff.

Dreamscape (1984)   Dennis Quaid (Alex), Max Von Sydow (Paul), Christopher Plummer (Bob), Kate Capshaw (Jane), George Wendt (Charlie). *Dir.* Joseph Ruben.

Dressed to Kill (1980)   Michael Caine, Angie Dickinson, Nancy Allen. Michael Caine plays a transvestite killer. *Dir.* Brian De Palma.

Dresser, The (1983)   Albert Finney (Sir), Tom Courtenay (Norman), Edward Fox (Oxenby). *Dir.* Peter Yates.

Driven (2001)   Sylvester Stallone (Joe Tanto), Burt Reynolds (Carl Henry), Kip Pardue (Jimmy Bly), Gina Gershon (Cathy Moreno), Stacy Edwards (Lucretia Clans). *Dir.* Renny Harlin.

Driving Miss Daisy (1989)   Jessica Tandy (Daisy Werthan), Morgan Freeman (Hoke Colburn), Dan Aykroyd (Boolie). Won 4 Oscars. *Dir.* Bruce Beresford.

Drugstore Cowboy (1989)   Matt Dillon (Bob Hughes), Kelly Lynch (Dianne Hughes), Heather Graham (Nadine), William S Burroughs (Tom the Priest). *Dir.* Gus Van Sant.

Dry White Season, A (1989)   Donald Sutherland (Ben Du Toit), Janet Suzman (Susan), Susan Sarandon (Melanie Bruwer), Marlon Brando (Ian McKenzie). Set in apartheid South Africa. *Dir.* Euzhan Palcy.

Duck Soup (1933)   The Marx Brothers, Margaret Dumont. According to *Time Out* the best Marx Bros film. *Dir.* Leo McCarey.

Duet for One (1986)   Julie Andrews (Stephanie Anderson), Alan Bates (David Cornwallis), Max Von Sydow (Dr Louis Feldman), Liam Neeson (Totter). Famous violinist develops multiple sclerosis. *Dir.* Andrei Konchalovsky.

CINEMA

Duke Wore Jeans, The (1958) Tommy Steele, June Laverick, Michael Medwin. *Dir.* Gerald Thomas.

Dune (1984) Kyle MacLachlan (Paul Atreides), Francesca Annis (Lady Jessica), Sting (Feyd Rautha), Kenneth McMillan (Baron Harkonnen). Based on Frank Herbert's epic SF novel. *Dir.* David Lynch.

Dunkirk (1958) John Mills, Richard Attenborough, Bernard Lee. Directed by Barry Norman's father. Factual story. *Dir.* Leslie Norman.

Eagle Has Landed, The (1976) Michael Caine, Donald Sutherland, Jenny Agutter, Robert Duvall, Donald Pleasence (Himmler). Involves a Nazi plot to kill Churchill. *Dir.* John Sturges.

Earth Girls Are Easy (1988) Geena Davis (Valerie Dale), Jeff Goldblum (Mac), Jim Carrey (Wiploc), Julie Brown (Candy Pink). *Dir.* Julien Temple.

Earthquake (1974) Charlton Heston, Ava Gardner, Lorne Greene, George Kennedy. First film to use 'Sensurround'. Big box-office hit. *Dir.* Mark Robson.

East of Sudan (1964) Anthony Quayle, Sylvia Syms, Jenny Agutter. *Dir.* Nathan Juran.

Easter Parade (1948) Fred Astaire, Judy Garland, Ann Miller. Music by Irving Berlin. *Dir.* Charles Walters.

Easy Street (1917) Charles Chaplin, Edna Purviance, Albert Austin. Tramp is reformed by missionary and becomes a policeman. *Dir.* Charles Chaplin.

Eddie (1996) Whoopi Goldberg (Eddie), Frank Langella (Wild Bill Burgess), Dennis Farina (John Bailey). *Dir.* Steve Rash.

Educating Rita (1983) Michael Caine (Dr Frank Bryant), Julie Walters (Rita), Maureen Lipman (Trish), Michael Williams (Brian). From the play by Willie Russell; shot in Ireland for tax reasons. *Dir.* Lewis Gilbert.

Edward Scissorhands (1990) Johnny Depp, Winona Ryder (Kim Boggs), Dianne Wiest (Peg), Alan Arkin (Bill), Vincent Price (Inventor). *Dir.* Tim Burton.

Eiger Sanction, The (1975) Clint Eastwood, George Kennedy, Vonetta McGee. Art teacher returns to CIA post as an exterminator. *Dir.* Clint Eastwood.

8 Mile (2002) Eminem, Kim Basinger, Brittany Murphy, Mekhi Phifer. *Dir.* Curtis Hanson.

Eight and a Half (1963) Marcello Mastroianni, Claudia Cardinale, Anouk Aimée. Fellini self portrait. Best Foreign Film Oscar. (The 8 1/2 refers to the number of films Fellini had then made.) *Dir.* Federico Fellini.

18 Again! (1988) George Burns (Jack Watson), Charlie Schlatter (David Watson), Tony Roberts (Arnold). *Dir.* Paul Flaherty.

84 Charing Cross Road (1987) Anne Bancroft (Helene), Anthony Hopkins (Frank Doel), Judi Dench (Nora Doel). Based on a true story of the late Helene Hanff. *Dir.* David Jones.

Elephant (2003) Alex Frost (Alex), Eric Deulen (Eric), John Robinson (John McFarland), Elias McConnell (Elias), Jordan Taylor (Jordan), Timothy Bottoms (John McFarland's father), Matt Molloy (Mr Luce). Drama depicting real high school students and adult actors. Based on the Columbine High School killings of 1999 where two Colorado students killed 12 other students and a teacher. The action is set in Portland, Oregon. Executive producer was Diane Keaton. *Dir.* Gus Van Sant.

Elephant Boy (1937) Sabu, Wilfrid Hyde-White. Based on a Kipling novel, made a star of Sabu. *Dir.* Robert Flaherty.

Elephant Man, The (1980) Anthony Hopkins, John Hurt (John Merrick), Anne Bancroft, John Gielgud. *Dir.* David Lynch.

Elmer Gantry (1960) Burt Lancaster, Jean Simmons, Arthur Kennedy, Shirley Jones. Oscars for Lancaster, Jones and Brooks (writer). *Dir.* Richard Brooks.

Emma (1996) Gwyneth Paltrow, Toni Collette, Ewan McGregor, Greta Scacchi, Sophie Thompson, Phyllida Law. Rachel Portman won Oscar for Music. *Dir.* Douglas McGrath.

Emmanuelle (1974) Sylvia Kristel, Marika Green, Daniel Sarky. Big soft-porn cinema hit, spawned 6 sequels. *Dir.* Just Jaeckin.

Empire of the Sun (1987) Christian Bale (Jim), John Malkovich (Basie), Miranda Richardson (Mrs Victor), Screenplay by Tom Stoppard, from JG Ballard's autobiographical novel. *Dir.* Steven Spielberg.

Empire Strikes Back, The (1980) Mark Hamill, Harrison Ford, Carrie Fisher. Second of the *Star Wars* films. *Dir.* Irvin Kershner.

Enchanted April (1991) Miranda Richardson (Rose Arbuthnot), Joan Plowright (Mrs Fisher), Alfred Molina (Mellersh Wilkins), Josie Lawrence (Lottie Wilkins). A quartet of Edwardian ladies go on holiday in an Italian villa. *Dir.* Mike Newell.

Endless Summer, The (1966) Study of surfing round the world. Documentary which has become a cult among surfers. *Dir.* Bruce Brown.

Enemy at the Gates (2001) Joseph Fiennes (Danilov), Jude Law (Vassili Zaitsev), Rachel Weisz, Bob Hoskins, Ed Harris. Setting of the Siege of Stalingrad. *Dir.* Jean-Jacques Annaud.

Enforcer, The (1976) Clint Eastwood, Tyne Daly, Bradford Dillman. Third of the *Dirty Harry* films. *Dir.* James Fargo.

English Patient (1996) Ralph Fiennes (Count Almasy), Kristin Scott-Thomas, Juliette Binoche, Willem Dafoe, Colin Firth. Dying Hungarian count recalls his doomed affair with the English wife of a colleague. Based on Michael Ondaatje's book. Won 9 Academy Awards. *Dir.* Anthony Minghella.

Entertainer, The (1960) Laurence Olivier, Joan Plowright, Alan Bates, Albert Finney. *Dir.* Tony Richardson.

Equinox (1992) Matthew Modine, Lara Flynn Boyle, Marisa Tomei, Fred Ward, Lori Singer. Timid garage mechanic discovers he has a killer brother. *Dir.* Alan Rudolph.

Eraser (1996) Arnold Schwarzenegger, James Caan, James Coburn, Vanessa Williams. Agent for the Federal Witness Protection Program discovers he can trust no one. *Dir.* Charles Russell.

Erik the Viking (1989) Tim Robbins (Erik), Mickey Rooney (Erik's grandfather), Eartha Kitt (Freya), Terry Jones (King Arnulf), John Cleese. *Dir.* Terry Jones.

Erin Brockovich (1999) Julia Roberts, Aaron Eckhart, Albert Finney, Marg Helgenberger, Cherry Jones, Peter Coyote, Veanne Cox. *Dir.* Steven Soderbergh. (The film was made in late 1999, too late for the 2000 Oscars.) True story of a twice-divorced single parent lawyer who took on the might of the Pacific Gas and Electric, accusing them of contaminating a town's water supply.

Escape from Alcatraz (1979) Clint Eastwood, Patrick McGoohan, Jack Thibeau. *Dir.* Don Siegel.

Escape from LA (1996) Kurt Russell (Snake Plissken), Steve Buscemi. Set in year 2013. *Dir.* John Carpenter.

ET – The Extra Terrestrial (1982)   Dee Wallace (Mary), Henry Thomas (Elliott), Drew Barrymore (Gertie). ET was 3 million light years from home. *Dir.* Steven Spielberg.

Eternal Sunshine of the Spotless Mind (2004)   Jim Carrey (Joel Barish), Kate Winslet (Clementine Kruczynski), Kirsten Dunst (Mary), Mark Ruffalo (Stan), Elijah Wood (Patrick), Tom Wilkinson (Dr Howard Mierzwiak), Jane Adams (Carrie), David Cross (Rob). A man discovers that his former lover has had all memory of their romance erased from her mind and decides to do the same. *Dir.* Michel Gondry.

Ethan Frome (1993)   Liam Neeson, Patricia Arquette, Joan Allen. Massachusetts community is setting for story of minister and his crippled driver. *Dir.* John Madden.

Etre et Avoir (2002)   Georges Lopez (the teacher), Alizé (female student), Axel (male student), Guillaume (male student). English title: *To Be and to Have*. Documentary portrait of a one-room school in rural France. *Dir.* Nicolas Philibert.

Eureka (1983)   Gene Hackman, Theresa Russell, Rutger Hauer, Jane Lapotaire, Mickey Rourke, Joe Pesci. Gold prospector strikes it rich, but at a price. *Dir.* Nicolas Roeg.

Every Which Way But Loose (1978)   Clint Eastwood, Sondra Locke, Ruth Gordon. The 1980 sequel *Any Which Way You Can* is the same story. *Dir.* James Fargo.

Everyone Says I Love You (1996)   Woody Allen, Julia Roberts, Drew Barrymore, Alan Alda, Goldie Hawn. *Dir.* Woody Allen.

Evil That Men Do, The (1984)   Charles Bronson (Holland), Theresa Saldana, José Ferrer. *Dir.* J Lee Thompson.

Evil under the Sun (1982)   Peter Ustinov, James Mason, Diana Rigg, Maggie Smith, Roddy McDowall. Agatha Christie novel starring Hercule Poirot. *Dir.* Guy Hamilton.

Evita (1996)   Madonna, Antonio Banderas, Jonathan Pryce, Jimmy Nail. Best Song Oscar: 'You Must Love Me' (Andrew Lloyd-Webber & Tim Rice). *Dir.* Alan Parker.

Evolution (2001)   David Duchovny, Julianne Moore, Orlando Jones, Seann William Scott, Ted Levine. *Dir.* Ivan Reitman.

Executive Suite (1954)   Fredric March, William Holden, June Allyson, Barbara Stanwyck, Walter Pidgeon, Shelley Winters. Boardroom battle. *Dir.* Robert Wise.

Exorcist, The (1973)   Ellen Burstyn, Max Von Sydow, Linda Blair, Lee J Cobb. *Dir.* William Friedkin.

Expresso Bongo (1959)   Cliff Richard, Laurence Harvey, Sylvia Syms, Gilbert Harding. *Dir.* Val Guest.

Eyes Wide Shut (1999)   Tom Cruise (Dr Bill Hayard), Nicole Kidman, Madison Eginton, Marie Richardson. *Dir.* Stanley Kubrick.

Fabulous Baker Boys, The (1989)   Jeff Bridges (Jack Baker), Beau Bridges (Frank), Michelle Pfeiffer (Susie Diamond). Pianist brothers ginger up their act by taking on a singer. *Dir.* Steve Kloves.

Face (1997)   Robert Carlyle, Ray Winstone, Damon Albarn. Five criminals undertake a robbery, one of them is a traitor. *Dir.* Antonia Bird.

Face Off (1997)   John Travolta, Nicolas Cage. *Dir.* John Woo.

Fahrenheit 9/11 (2004)   Michael Moore's view on what happened to the United States after September 11; and how the Bush administration allegedly used the tragic event to push forward its agenda for unjust wars in Afghanistan and Iraq. *Dir.* Michael Moore.

Faithful (1996)   Cher, Chazz Palminteri, Ryan O'Neal, Paul Mazursky, Amber Smith. Hitman chats to his victim whilst waiting for the signal to kill. *Dir.* Paul Mazursky.

Falling Down (1993)   Michael Douglas (D-Fens), Robert Duvall (Prendergast), Barbara Hershey (Beth), Tuesday Weld (Mrs Prendergast). *Dir.* Joel Schumacher.

Fan, The (1996)   Robert De Niro (Gil Renard), Wesley Snipes (Bobby Rayburn), Ellen Barkin. Baseball fan kidnaps the son of a star player. *Dir.* Tony Scott.

Fantasia (1940)   Cartoon characters to music of Bach, Tchaikovsky, Dukas, Stravinsky, Beethoven, Ponchielli, Schubert and Mussorgsky. *Dir.* Ben Sharpsteen.

Fantastic Voyage (1966)   Stephen Boyd, Raquel Welch, Edmond O'Brien, Donald Pleasence, Arthur O'Connell, Arthur Kennedy. *Dir.* Richard Fleizcher.

Far From Heaven (2002)   Julianne Moore (Cathy Whitaker), Dennis Quaid (Frank Whitaker), Dennis Haysbert (Raymond Deagan), Patricia Clarkson (Eleonor Fine). In a wealthy suburb during 1957 a wife discovers her marriage is a sham and develops a love for her black gardener. *Dir.* Todd Haynes.

Far from the Madding Crowd (1967)   Julie Christie, Peter Finch, Alan Bates, Terence Stamp (Sgt Troy). Set in Victorian Wessex. *Dir.* John Schlesinger.

Farewell My Lovely (1944)   Dick Powell, Claire Trevor, Anne Shirley, Mike Mazurki, Otto Kruger. Aka: *Murder My Sweet*. *Dir.* Edward Dmytryk.

Farewell My Lovely (1975)   Robert Mitchum, Charlotte Rampling, John Ireland, Sylvia Miles. Remake of the Raymond Chandler classic. *Dir.* Dick Richards.

Fargo (1996)   Frances McDormand, William H Macy, Steve Buscemi, Harve Presnell, Peter Stormare. Car salesman with money troubles hires criminals to kidnap his wife for ransom. Nothing goes to plan. *Dir.* Joel Coen.

Fast and the Furious, The (2001)   Paul Walker, Vin Diesel, Michelle Rodriguez, Rick Yune, Jordana Brewster. *Dir.* Rob Cohen.

Fatal Attraction (1987)   Michael Douglas (Dan Gallagher), Glenn Close (Alex Forrest), Anne Archer (Beth Gallagher), Fred Gwynne (Arthur). *Dir.* Adrian Lyne.

Father of the Bride (1950)   Spencer Tracy, Elizabeth Taylor, Leo G Carroll. *Dir.* Vincente Minnelli.

Father of the Bride (1991)   Steve Martin (George Banks), Diane Keaton (Nina Banks), Kimberly Williams (Annie Banks). Remake of the Spencer Tracy classic. *Dir.* Charles Shyer.

Father's Day (1997)   Robin Williams (Dale), Billy Crystal (Jack), Nastassja Kinski (Colette), Charlie Hofheimer (Scott), Mel Gibson. *Dir.* Ivan Reitman.

Fear (1996)   Reese Witherspoon, Mark Wahlberg. *Dir.* James Foley.

Ferris Bueller's Day Off (1986)   Matthew Broderick (Ferris Bueller), Alan Ruck (Cameron Frye), Mia Sara (Sloane Peterson). *Dir.* John Hughes.

Fever Pitch (1996)   Colin Firth, Ruth Gemmell, Neil Pearson. Obsession with Arsenal FC creates romantic problems for teacher. *Dir.* David Evans.

Few Good Men, A (1992)   Tom Cruise (Lt JG Kaffee), Jack Nicholson (Colonel Jessep), Demi Moore (Lt Cdr Galloway), Kevin Bacon (Capt Ross), Kiefer Sutherland (Lt Kendrick). *Dir.* Rob Reiner.

C
I
N
E
M
A

Fiddler on the Roof (1971)   Topol, Norma Crane, Molly Picon. Topol recreates his classic stage role. *Dir.* Norman Jewison.

Field, The (1990)   Richard Harris (Bull McCabe), Sean Bean (Tadgh McCabe), Frances Tomelty (Widow), Brenda Fricker (Maggie McCabe), John Hurt (Bird O'Donnell), Tom Berenger (The American). *Dir.* Jim Sheridan.

Field of Dreams (1989)   Kevin Costner (Ray Kinsella), Amy Madigan (Annie), James Earl Jones (Terence Mann), Burt Lancaster (Dr Moonlight Graham), Ray Liotta (Shoeless Joe Jackson). Famous line: 'If you build it, he will come'. *Dir.* Phil Alden Robinson.

Fierce Creatures (1997)   John Cleese, Jamie Lee Curtis, Kevin Kline, Michael Palin, Ronnie Corbett, Robert Lindsay. Unsuccessful follow-up to *A Fish Called Wanda*. Fred Schepisi replaced Young as director for three weeks whilst refilming the final scenes. *Dir.* Robert Young.

Fifth Element, The (1997)   Gary Oldman (Zorg), Bruce Willis (Will Dallas), Milla Jovovich (Leeloo), Ian Holm (Cornelius). Costumes by Jean-Paul Gaultier. *Dir.* Luc Besson.

51st State, The (2001)   Samuel L Jackson (Elmo McElroy), Meatloaf (The Lizard), Robert Carlyle (Felix DeSouza), Sean Pertwee (Detective Virgil Kane), Ricky Tomlinson (Leopold Durant), Emily Mortimer (Dakota Phillips), Steven Walters (Blowfish). American inventor of a new drug goes to Liverpool to sell the formula for $20 million to a local drug baron. *Dir.* Ronny Yu.

Fight Club (1999)   Brad Pitt, Edward Norton, Helena Bonham Carter, Meatloaf. *Dir.* David Fincher.

Final Fantasy: The Spirits Within (2001)   Voices of Ming-Na, Alec Baldwin, Ving Rhames, Steve Buscemi, Peri Gilpin, Donald Sutherland, James Woods, Jean Simmons. Animation film about a female scientist in 2065 and her battle to rid the world of powerful aliens known as phantoms. *Dir.* Hironobu Sakaguchi and Moto Sakakibara.

Finding Nemo (2003)   Voices of Albert Brooks (Marlin), Ellen DeGeneres (Dory), Alexander Gould (Nemo), Willem Dafoe (Gill), Brad Garrett (Bloat), Allison Janney (Peach), Austin Pendleton (Gurgle), Geoffrey Rush (Nigel), Barry Humphries (Bruce), Eric Bana (Anchor), Bruce Spence (Chum), Bill Hunter (Dentist). A neurotic clownfish goes in search of his adventurous son, who has been captured and placed on display in an aquarium. *Dir.* Andrew Stanton.

Finding Neverland (2004)   Johnny Depp (JM Barrie), Kate Winslet (Sylvia Llewelyn Davies), Julie Christie (Mrs Emma du Maurier), Radha Mitchell (Mary Ansell Barrie), Dustin Hoffman (Charles Frohman), Kelly Macdonald (Peter Pan). The story of JM Barrie's friendship with a family who inspired him to create Peter Pan. *Dir.* Marc Forster.

Finian's Rainbow (1968)   Fred Astaire, Petula Clark, Tommy Steele. Tommy Steele plays a leprechaun. *Dir.* Francis Ford Coppola.

Firm, The (1993)   Tom Cruise (Mitch Deere), Gene Hackman, Jeanne Tripplehorn. Cruise is the new boy at a Memphis law firm run, unknown to him, by the Mafia. Based on bestseller by John Grisham. *Dir.* Sydney Pollack.

First Blood (1982)   Sylvester Stallone (John Rambo), Richard Crenna (Trautman), Brian Dennehy (Teasle). Q Moonblood on the writing credits is Stallone. *Dir.* Ted Kotcheff.

First Great Train Robbery, The (1978)   Sean Connery, Donald Sutherland, Lesley-Anne Down. Wayne Sleep makes his first movie appearance. *Dir.* Michael Crichton.

First Knight (1995)   Sean Connery, Richard Gere, Julia Ormond, Ben Cross, John Gielgud. King Arthur story that lost money at the box office. *Dir.* Jerry Zucker.

Fish Called Wanda, A (1988)   John Cleese (Archie Leach), Jamie Lee Curtis (Wanda), Kevin Kline (Otto), Michael Palin (Ken). Big box office hit, Oscar for Kevin Kline. *Dir.* Charles Crichton.

Fisher King, The (1991)   Robin Williams (Parry), Jeff Bridges (Jack Lucas), Amanda Plummer (Lydia), Ted Ross (Limo Bum), Tom Waits. *Dir.* Terry Gilliam.

Five Easy Pieces (1970)   Jack Nicholson, Karen Black, Fannie Flagg. Jack Nicholson plays a pianist. *Dir.* Bob Rafelson.

Flash Gordon (1980)   Topol, Max Von Sydow, Brian Blessed, Timothy Dalton. Music by Queen. *Dir.* Michael Hodges.

Flashdance (1983)   Jennifer Beals (Alex Owens), Michael Nouri (Nick Hurley), Lilia Skala (Hanna Long). *Dir.* Adrian Lyne.

Flatliners (1990)   Kiefer Sutherland (Nelson Wright), Julia Roberts (Rachel Mannus), Kevin Bacon (David Labraccio), William Baldwin (Joe Hurley). *Dir.* Joel Schumacher.

Fletch (1985)   Chevy Chase (Fletch), Joe Don Baker (Chief Karlin). Sequel: *Fletch Lives* (1989). *Dir.* Michael Ritchie.

Flintstones, The (1994)   John Goodman, Elisabeth Perkins, Rick Moranis, Rosie O'Donnell, Elizabeth Taylor. *Dir.* Brian Levant.

Fly, The (1958)   David Hedison, Patricia Owens, Vincent Price, Herbert Marshall. Classic horror film. *Dir.* Kurt Neumann.

Fly, The (1986)   Jeff Goldblum (Seth Brundle), Geena Davis (Veronica Quaife). David Cronenberg makes a cameo performance as the gynaecologist. *Dir.* David Cronenberg.

Fools Rush In (1997)   Matthew Perry, Salma Hayek, Jon Tenney, Jill Clayburgh. *Dir.* Andy Tennant.

Footloose (1984)   Kevin Bacon (Ren), Lori Singer (Ariel), John Lithgow (Reverend Shaw Moore). *Dir.* Herbert Ross.

For Me and My Gal (1942)   Judy Garland, Gene Kelly, George Murphy. *Dir.* Busby Berkeley.

For the Boys (1991)   Bette Midler (Dixie Leonard), James Caan (Eddie Sparks), George Segal (Art Silver). *Dir.* Mark Rydell.

For Your Eyes Only (1981)   Roger Moore, Topol, Carole Bouquet (Melina), Julian Glover (Kristatos). Ian Fleming does not get credit of any kind for this film. (Theme song: Sheena Easton.) *Dir.* John Glen.

Forbidden Planet (1956)   Walter Pidgeon, Anne Francis, Leslie Nielsen, Warren Stevens, Jack Kelly. Set in AD 2200 and follows the plot of Shakespeare's *The Tempest*. *Dir.* Fred M Wilcox.

Forever Amber (1947)   Linda Darnell, Cornel Wilde, George Sanders (Charles II), Richard Greene, Jessica Tandy. Costume drama set in the reign of Charles II. *Dir.* Otto Preminger.

Forever Young (1992)   Mel Gibson (Daniel), Jamie Lee Curtis (Claire), Elijah Wood (Nat), George Wendt (Harry). *Dir.* Steve Miner.

Forrest Gump (1994)   Tom Hanks, Robin Wright, Gary Sinise, Sally Field, Hanna R Hall. Won 6 Oscars. *Dir.* Robert Zemeckis.

Fort Apache (1948) Henry Fonda, John Wayne, Shirley Temple, Victor McLaglen, Ward Bond. *Dir*. John Ford.

Fort Apache, the Bronx (1980) Paul Newman, Ed Asner, Ken Wahl, Danny Aiello. *Dir*. Daniel Petrie.

Fortune Cookie, The (1966) Walter Matthau, Jack Lemmon. GB title: *Meet Whiplash Willie*. *Dir*. Billy Wilder.

40 Days and 40 Nights (2002) Josh Hartnett (Matt), Shannyn Sossamon (Erica Sutton), Paulo Costanzo (Ryan), Adam Trese (John), Emmanuelle Vaugier, Vinessa Shaw. Computer whizz-kid gives up sex for Lent. *Dir*. Michael Lehmann.

48 Hrs (1982) Nick Nolte (Jack Cates), Eddie Murphy (Reggie Hammond), Annette O'Toole (Elaine). Sequel: *Another 48 Hrs* (1990). *Dir*. Walter Hill.

49th Parallel (1941) Eric Portman, Laurence Olivier, Leslie Howard, Raymond Massey, Glynis Johns. US title: *The Invaders*. *Dir*. Michael Powell.

Foul Play (1978) Goldie Hawn, Chevy Chase, Burgess Meredith, Rachel Roberts, Dudley Moore. Two innocents in San Francisco get involved in plot to assassinate the Pope. *Dir*. Colin Higgins.

Four for Texas (1963) Dean Martin, Frank Sinatra, Anita Ekberg, Ursula Andress, Charles Bronson, Victor Buono, 3 Stooges. *Dir*. Robert Aldrich.

Four Horsemen of the Apocalypse, The (1921) Rudolph Valentino, Alice Terry, Alan Hale, Wallace Beery. Young Argentinian fights for his father's country, France, in WWI. 1961 remake starred Glenn Ford. *Dir*. Rex Ingram.

Four Musketeers, The (Revenge of Milady), (1974) Michael York, Oliver Reed, Frank Finlay, Richard Chamberlain, Raquel Welch, Faye Dunaway, Charlton Heston. *Dir*. Richard Lester.

Four Weddings and a Funeral (1994) Hugh Grant, Andie MacDowell, Kristin Scott Thomas, Simon Callow. *Dir*. Mike Newell.

1492: Conquest of Paradise (1992) Gérard Depardieu (Columbus), Armand Assante (Sanchez), Sigourney Weaver (Queen Isabel). *Dir*. Ridley Scott.

Fourth Protocol, The (1987) Michael Caine (John Preston), Pierce Brosnan (Petrofsky), Joanna Cassidy (Vassileva). Thriller by Frederick Forsyth. *Dir*. John Mackenzie.

Fox, The (1968) Anne Heywood, Sandy Dennis, Keir Dullea. Based on DH Lawrence's novella. *Dir*. Mark Rydell.

Francis (1949) Donald O'Connor, Patricia Medina, Chill Wills (as voice of Francis the Mule). Series of sequels followed. *Dir*. Arthur Lubin.

Frankenstein (1931) Boris Karloff, Colin Clive, Mae Clarke, Edward Van Sloan. Series of sequels followed. *Dir*. James Whale.

Frankie and Johnny (1966) Elvis Presley, Donna Douglas, Nancy Kovack. *Dir*. Frederick De Cordova.

Frankie and Johnny (1991) Al Pacino (Johnny), Michelle Pfeiffer (Frankie). *Dir*. Garry Marshall.

Frantic (1988) Harrison Ford (Richard Walker), Betty Buckley (Sondra Walker), Emmanuelle Seigner. American cardiologist searching for his kidnapped wife in Paris becomes embroiled with Arabs. *Dir*. Roman Polanski.

Freebie and the Bean (1974) Alan Arkin, James Caan, Loretta Swit. *Dir*. Richard Rush.

French Connection, The (1971) Gene Hackman (Popeye Doyle), Roy Scheider, Fernando Rey. Oscars for Best Picture, Best Director, Best Actor (Hackman) and Ernest Tidyman took Oscar for Best

Adapted Screenplay. *Dir*. William Friedkin.

French Lieutenant's Woman (1981) Meryl Streep, Jeremy Irons, Leo McKern, Peter Vaughan. Harold Pinter adaption of John Fowles's novel. *Dir*. Karel Reisz.

Frenzy (1972) Barry Foster, Jon Finch, Alec McCowen, Vivien Merchant, Anna Massey, Billie Whitelaw. Anthony Shaffer adapted *Goodbye Piccadilly, Farewell Leicester Square* by Arthur La Bern. *Dir*. Alfred Hitchcock.

Freshman, The (1990) Marlon Brando (Carmine Sabatini), Matthew Broderick (Clark Kellogg), Maximilian Schell (Larry London). *Dir*. Andrew Bergman.

Freud (1962) Montgomery Clift, Larry Parks, Susannah York, David McCallum. *Dir*. John Huston.

Friday the 13th (1980) Betsy Palmer, Adrienne King, Jeannine Taylor, Robbi Morgan. Others in series include part 4 *The Final Chapter* and the last (part 8), *Jason Takes Manhattan*. *Dir*. Sean S. Cunningham.

Fried Green Tomatoes at the Whistle Stop Cafe (1992) Kathy Bates (Evelyn Couch), Jessica Tandy (Ninny Threadgoode). *Dir*. Jon Avnet.

Friendly Persuasion (1956) Gary Cooper, Dorothy McGuire, Anthony Perkins. No script credit (the writer, Michael Wilson, was blacklisted). *Dir*. William Wyler.

Fright Night (1985) Chris Sarandon (Jerry Dandridge), Roddy McDowall (Peter Vincent). William Ragsdale (Charley Brewster). Present-day vampires. McDowall's character named as tribute to Peter Cushing and Vincent Price. *Dir*. Tom Holland.

Fright Night Part 2 (1988) Roddy McDowall, William Ragsdale. *Dir*. Tommy Lee Wallace.

Frisco Kid, The (1979) Gene Wilder, Harrison Ford, Leo Fuchs. *Dir*. Robert Aldrich.

Fritz the Cat (1971) First 'X'-rated cartoon, about the adventures of an alleycat in New York. *Dir*. Ralph Bakshi.

From Hell (2001) Johnny Depp (Inspector Fred Abberline), Heather Graham (Mary Kelly), Ian Holm, Robbie Coltrane. Twist on the Jack the Ripper story. *Dir*. Albert Hughes and Allen Hughes.

From Here to Eternity (1953) Burt Lancaster, Deborah Kerr, Frank Sinatra, Montgomery Clift. *Dir*. Fred Zinnemann.

From Russia with Love (1963) Sean Connery, Robert Shaw (Red Grant), Daniela Bianchi (Tatiana Romanova), Lotte Lenya (Rosa Kleb), Bernard Lee, Lois Maxwell, Pedro Armendariz. Theme song sung by Matt Monro. *Dir*. Terence Young.

Front Page, The (1931) Adolph Merjon, Pat O'Brien, Mary Brian, Walter Catlett, Edward Everett Horton. *Dir*. Lewis Milestone.

Front Page, The (1974) Walter Matthau, Jack Lemmon, Susan Sarandon, David Wayne, Vincent Gardenia. *Dir*. Billy Wilder.

Fugitive, The (1993) Harrison Ford (Dr Richard Kimble), Tommy Lee Jones (Lt Gerard). *Dir*. Andrew Davis.

Full Metal Jacket (1987) Matthew Modine (Private Joker), Adam Baldwin (Animal Mother), Dorian Harewood (Eightball), Vincent D'Onofrio (Private Pyle). *Dir*. Stanley Kubrick.

Full Monty, The (1997) Robert Carlyle (Gaz), Mark Addy (Dave), Tom Wilkinson (Gerald), Hugo Speer (Guy), Paul Barber (Horse), Steve Huison (Lomper). Unemployed Sheffield welders decide to become male strippers. *Dir*. Peter Cattaneo.

CINEMA

Funeral, The (1996)   Christopher Walken, Isabelle Adjani, Chris Penn, Annabella Sciorra. *Dir*. Abel Ferrara.

Funeral in Berlin (1967)   Michael Caine (Harry Palmer), Oscar Homolka, Eva Renzi, Hugh Burden. *Dir*. Guy Hamilton.

Funny Girl (1968)   Barbra Streisand (Fanny Brice), Omar Sharif, Walter Pidgeon, Kay Medford. *Dir*. William Wyler.

Funny Lady (1975)   Barbra Streisand, James Caan, Ben Vereen, Omar Sharif, Roddy McDowall. *Dir*. Herbert Ross.

Funny Thing Happened on the Way to the Forum, A (1966)   Zero Mostel, Phil Silvers, Michael Crawford, Michael Hordern, Buster Keaton. *Dir*. Richard Lester.

Futureworld (1976)   Peter Fonda, Blythe Danner, Yul Brynner, Arthur Hill, Stuart Margolin. *Dir*. Richard T Heffron.

Game, The (1997)   Michael Douglas (Nicholas Van Orton), Sean Penn (Conrad Van Orton). *Dir*. David Fincher.

Games, The (1970)   Stanley Baker, Michael Crawford, Ryan O'Neal, Charles Aznavour. Four men take part in the Rome Olympics marathon. *Dir*. Michael Winner.

Gandhi (1982)   Ben Kingsley (Gandhi), Candice Bergen (Margaret Bourke-White), Edward Fox (General Dyer), Daniel Day Lewis (Colin). *Dir*. Richard Attenborough.

Gangs of New York (2002)   Leonardo DiCaprio (Amsterdam Vallon), Daniel Day-Lewis (William 'Bill the Butcher' Cutting), Cameron Diaz (Jenny Everdeane), Jim Broadbent (William 'Boss' Tweed), Henry Thomas (Johnny Sirocco), Liam Neeson (Priest Vallon, Amsterdam's father), Brendan Gleeson (Walter 'Monk' McGinn), John C Reilly ('Happy' Jack Mulraney), David Hemmings (Mr Schermerhorn). In 1863, Amsterdam Vallon returns to the Five Points area of New York City seeking revenge against Bill the Butcher, his father's killer. *Dir*. Martin Scorsese.

Garden State (2004)   Zach Braff (Andrew Largeman), Kenneth Graymez (Busboy), George C Wolfe (Restaurant Manager), Austin Lysy (Waiter), Gary Gilbert (Young Hollywood Guy), Jill Flint (Obnoxious Girl), Ian Holm (Gideon Largeman). A young man returns home for his mother's funeral after being estranged from his family for a decade. *Dir*. Zach Braff.

Gardens of Stone (1987)   James Caan (Clell Hazard), Anjelica Huston (Samantha Davis), James Earl Jones (Goody Nelson). Vietnam War from the perspective of soldiers guarding Arlington National Cemetery. *Dir*. Francis Ford Coppola.

Gaslight (1940)   Anton Walbrook, Diana Wynyard, Frank Pettingell, Robert Newton, Jimmy Hanley. Victorian schizophrenic tries to drive his wife insane because of his guilty past. *Dir*. Thorold Dickinson.

Gaslight (1944)   Charles Boyer, Ingrid Bergman, Joseph Cotten, Angela Lansbury. Remake of the 1940 film. *Dir*. George Cukor.

Genevieve (1953)   Dinah Sheridan, John Gregson, Kay Kendall, Kenneth More, Joyce Grenfell. Genevieve was a classic car (Darracq). *Dir*. Henry Cornelius.

Genghis Khan (1964)   Omar Sharif, Stephen Boyd, James Mason, Telly Savalas, Françoise Dorléac. *Dir*. Henry Levin.

Gentleman Jim (1942)   Errol Flynn, Alan Hale, Ward Bond. Based on the life of world heavyweight boxing champion Jim Corbett. *Dir*. Raoul Walsh.

Gentlemen Marry Brunettes (1955)   Jane Russell, Jeanne Crain, Alan Young, Rudy Vallee. Sequel to *Gentlemen Prefer Blondes*. *Dir*. Richard Sale.

Gentlemen Prefer Blondes (1953)   Jane Russell, Marilyn Monroe, Charles Coburn. Based on Anita Loos's novel. *Dir*. Howard Hawks.

Geordie (1955)   Bill Travers, Alastair Sim, Norah Gorsen, Stanley Baxter. Sickly Scottish boy becomes Olympic hammer thrower. *Dir*. Frank Launder.

George Raft Story, The (1961)   Ray Danton, Julie London, Jayne Mansfield, Frank Gorshin, Neville Brand (Al Capone). GB title: *Spin of a Coin*. *Dir*. Joseph M Newman.

Georgy Girl (1966)   James Mason, Lynn Redgrave, Charlotte Rampling, Alan Bates, Rachel Kempson. *Dir*. Silvio Narizzano.

Gerald McBoing Boing (1951)   Cartoon written by Dr Seuss (Theodore Geisel), which won an Oscar. *Dir*. Robert Cannon.

Gerry (2003)   Matt Damon, Casey Affleck, Gus Van Sant. Drama of two friends (Damon and Affleck) each called 'Gerry', who go hiking in a remote area and lose their way in the forbiddingly beautiful terrain. *Dir*. Gus Van Sant.

Get Carter (1971)   Michael Caine, John Osborne, Ian Hendry, Britt Ekland. Based on Ted Lewis's novel *Jack's Return Home*. *Dir*. Mike Hodges.

Get Shorty (1995)   John Travolta, Gene Hackman, Rene Russo, Danny De Vito. Miami debt collector for the Mob goes to Las Vegas and discovers a talent for film production. *Dir*. Barry Sonnenfeld.

Getaway, The (1972)   Steve McQueen, Ali MacGraw, Ben Johnson, Sally Struthers, Slim Pickens. *Dir*. Sam Peckinpah.

Getaway, The (1994)   Alec Baldwin, Kim Basinger, Michael Madsen, James Woods. *Dir*. Roger Donaldson.

Ghost (1990)   Patrick Swayze (Sam Wheat), Demi Moore (Molly Jensen), Whoopi Goldberg (Oda Mae Brown). *Dir*. Jerry Zucker.

Ghost in the Machine (1993)   Karen Allen, Chris Mulkey, Ted Marcoux, Nancy Fish. *Dir*. Rachel Talalay.

Ghost World (2001)   Thora Birch (Enid), Scarlett Johansson (Rebecca), Steve Buscemi (Seymour), Teri Garr (Maxine). Two teenagers leave high school and feel inadequate in the adult world. *Dir*. Terry Zwigoff.

Ghostbusters (1984)   Bill Murray (Dr Peter Venkman), Dan Aykroyd (Dr Raymond Stantz), Harold Ramis (Dr Egon Spengler), Sigourney Weaver (Dana Barrett), Rick Moranis (Louis Tully). *Ghostbusters II* (1989), was sequel. Ramis and Aykroyd also wrote the screenplay. *Dir*. Ivan Reitman.

Ghosts from the Past (1997)   Alec Baldwin (DeLaughter), Whoopi Goldberg (Myrlie), James Woods (Byron De La Beckwith). Original title: *Ghosts of Mississippi*. *Dir*. Rob Reiner.

GI Jane (1997)   Demi Moore (Lt Jordan O'Neill), Anne Bancroft (Senator Lillian DeHaven). *Dir*. Ridley Scott.

Giant (1956)   Rock Hudson, Elizabeth Taylor, James Dean, Mercedes McCambridge, Carroll Baker, Chill Wills, Rod Taylor, Earl Holliman. *Dir*. George Stevens.

Gigi (1958)   Leslie Caron, Louis Jourdan, Maurice Chevalier, Hermione Gingold, Eva Gabor. *Dir*. Vincente Minnelli.

Gilda (1946)   Rita Hayworth, Glenn Ford, George

Macready. *Dir*. Charles Vidor.

Girl 6 (1996)   Theresa Randle, Isaiah Washington, Spike Lee. Unsuccessful actress is employed as a sex chat operator. *Dir*. Spike Lee.

Girls Girls Girls (1962)   Elvis Presley, Stella Stevens, Laurel Goodwin. *Dir*. Norman Taurog.

Give My Regards to Broad Street (1984)   Paul McCartney, Bryan Brown, Ringo Starr, Barbara Bach, Tracey Ullman, Ralph Richardson. *Dir*. Peter Webb.

Gladiator (2000)   Russel Crowe (Maximus), Joaquin Phoenix (Commodus), Connie Nielson, Derek Jacobi, Richard Harris (Emperor Marcus Aurelius), Oliver Reed (Proximo). *Dir*. Ridley Scott.

Glass Menagerie, The (1950)   Gertrude Lawrence, Jane Wyman, Kirk Douglas, Arthur Kennedy. Shy, crippled girl seeks escape from her shabby life in St Louis. *Dir*. Irving Rapper.

Glass Menagerie, The (1987)   Joanne Woodward, John Malkovich, Karen Allen. Remake of earlier version of Tennessee Williams' play. *Dir*. Paul Newman.

Glass Mountain, The (1949)   Michael Denison, Dulcie Gray, Tito Gobbi. Nino Rota's music score is memorable and haunting. *Dir*. Henry Cass.

Gleaming the Cube (1988)   Christian Slater, Steven Bauer, Richard Herd. Skateboarding film. *Dir*. Graeme Clifford.

Glenn Miller Story, The (1954)   James Stewart, June Allyson, Harry Morgan, Charles Drake, Louis Armstrong, Gene Krupa. *Dir*. Anthony Mann.

Gloria (1980)   Gena Rowlands, John Adames, Buck Henry. *Dir*. John Cassavetes.

Glory (1989)   Matthew Broderick (Col Robert G Shaw), Denzel Washington (Private Trip), Cary Elwes (Maj Cabot Forbes), Morgan Freeman (Sgt Maj John Rawlins). *Dir*. Edward Zwick.

Go-Between, The (1970)   Alan Bates, Julie Christie, Michael Redgrave, Dominic Guard, Michael Gough, Margaret Leighton, Edward Fox. Harold Pinter adaptation of LP Hartley's novel. *Dir*. Joseph Losey.

Godfather, The (1972).   Marlon Brando, Al Pacino, James Caan, Robert Duvall, Diane Keaton, Richard Conte. *Dir*. Francis Ford Coppola.

Godfather Part II, The (1974)   Al Pacino, Robert De Niro, Diane Keaton, Robert Duvall, Lee Strasberg, Troy Donahue. The first sequel to win a Best Picture Oscar (and 5 others). *Dir*. Francis Ford Coppola.

Godfather Part III, The (1990)   Al Pacino, Diane Keaton, Talia Shire, Andy Garcia, Eli Wallach, Sofia Coppola. *Dir*. Francis Ford Coppola.

Godzilla (1955)   Raymond Burr, Takashi Shimura, Momoko Kochi. *Dir*. Inoshiro Honda.

Godzilla (1998)   Matthew Broderick, Jean Reno, Maria Pitillo, Hank Azaria, Kevin Dunn, Michael Lerner, Harry Shearer. As a result of French nuclear tests in the Pacific, a giant lizard invades Manhattan. Remake of the Japanese classic. *Dir*. Roland Emmerich.

Goin' South (1978)   Jack Nicholson, Mary Steenburgen, Christopher Lloyd, John Belushi. *Dir*. Jack Nicholson.

Going My Way (1944)   Bing Crosby (Father O'Malley), Barry Fitzgerald, Rise Stevens, Gene Lockhart. *Dir*. Leo McCarey.

Goldeneye (1995)   Pierce Brosnan, Sean Bean (Alec Trevelyan), Izabella Scorupco (Natalaya Simonova), Famke Janssen (Xenia Onatopp), Judi Dench (M), Desmond Llewelyn (Q), Samantha Bond (Miss Moneypenny), Joe Don Baker (Jack Wade), Robbie Coltrane (Valentin). Title song written by Bono and The Edge and performed by Tina Turner. *Dir*. Martin Campbell.

Goldfinger (1964)   Sean Connery, Honor Blackman (Pussy Galore), Gert Fröbe (Auric Goldfinger), Harold Sakatá (Oddjob), Bernard Lee, Lois Maxwell, Desmond Llewellyn, Shirley Eaton. Theme song sung by Shirley Bassey. *Dir*. Guy Hamilton.

Gone with the Wind (1939)   Clark Gable, Vivien Leigh, Olivia de Havilland, Leslie Howard, Thomas Mitchell, Hattie McDaniel, Butterfly McQueen. *Dir*. Victor Fleming (with George Cukor, Sam Wood, B Reeves Eason).

Good Earth, The (1937)   Paul Muni, Luise Rainer, Keye Luke. Chinese peasant grows rich but loses his wife. *Dir*. Sidney Franklin.

Good Morning, Vietnam (1987)   Robin Williams (Adrian Cronauer), Forest Whitaker (Edward Garlick). *Dir*. Barry Levinson.

Good Mother, The (1988)   Diane Keaton (Anna), Liam Neeson (Leo). *Dir*. Leonard Nimoy.

Good Son, The (1993)   Macaulay Culkin, Elijah Wood, Wendy Crewson, Quinn Culkin. Ten-year-old boy is a sadistic killer. *Dir*. Joseph Ruben.

Good, the Bad and the Ugly, The (1966)   Clint Eastwood, Eli Wallach, Lee Van Cleef. *Dir*. Sergio Leone.

Good Will Hunting (1997)   Robin Williams, Matt Damon (Will Hunting), Ben Affleck, Minnie Driver, Stellan Skarsgard. Janitor is spotted as a mathematical genius. *Dir*. Gus Van Sant.

Goodbye, Columbus (1969)   Richard Benjamin, Ali MacGraw, Jack Klugman. Jewish librarian has an affair with daughter of a nouveau riche family. *Dir*. Larry Peerce.

Goodbye Girl, The (1977)   Richard Dreyfuss, Marsha Mason, Quinn Cummings. Neil Simon story. *Dir*. Herbert Ross.

Goodbye, Mr Chips (1939)   Robert Donat, Greer Garson, Paul Henreid, John Mills. James Hilton's novel adapted by RC Sherriff, Claudine West & Eric Maschwitz. *Dir*. Sam Wood.

Goodbye, Mr Chips (1969)   Peter O'Toole, Petula Clark, Michael Redgrave, Sian Phillips. Musical remake of the 1939 classic. *Dir*. Herbert Ross.

Goodfellas (1990)   Robert De Niro (James Conway), Ray Liotta (Henry Hill), Joe Pesci (Tommy De Vito), Lorraine Bracco (Karen Hill), Catherine Scorsese (Tommy's mother). *Dir*. Martin Scorsese.

Goonies, The (1985)   Sean Astin (Mickey), Josh Brolin (Brand), Jeff Cohen (Chunk), Corey Feldman (Mouth). Screenplay by Chris Columbus, based on a Steven Spielberg story. *Dir*. Richard Donner.

Gorillas in the Mist (1988)   Sigourney Weaver (Diane Fossey), Bryan Brown (Bob Campbell). *Dir*. Michael Apted.

Gorky Park (1983)   William Hurt (Arkady Renko), Lee Marvin (Jack Osborne). Filmed mainly in Helsinki. *Dir*. Michael Apted.

Gosford Park (2001)   Maggie Smith (Constance, Countess of Trentham), Michael Gambon (Sir William McCordle), Kristin Scott Thomas (Lady Sylvia McCordle), Camilla Rutherford (Isobel McCordle), Eileen Atkins (Mrs Croft), Jeremy Northam (Ivor Novello), Clive Owen (Robert Parks), Alan Bates (Jennings), Helen Mirren (Mrs Wilson), Stephen Fry (Inspector Thompson), Sophie Thompson (Dorothy), Derek Jacobi (Probert), Richard E Grant (George). Set in a country house in the 1930s, the weekend guests fall under suspicion when the host is killed twice! Julian Fellowes won an Oscar for his script. *Dir*. Robert Altman.

Grace of My Heart (1996)   Illeana Douglas, John Turturro, Eric Stoltz, Patsy Kensit, Bridget Fonda, Matt Dillon. Based loosely on Carole King, with Illeana Douglas's voice dubbed by Kristen Vigard. *Dir*. Allison Anders.

Graduate, The (1967)   Dustin Hoffman (Benjamin Braddock), Anne Bancroft (Mrs Robinson), Katharine Ross, William Daniels. *Dir*. Mike Nichols.

Grand Canyon (1991)   Danny Glover, Kevin Kline, Steve Martin. Black truck driver and white lawyer form an unlikely friendship. *Dir*. Lawrence Kasdan.

Grand Hotel (1932)   Greta Garbo (Grusinskaya), John Barrymore, Lionel Barrymore, Joan Crawford. Famous Garbo line: 'I want to be alone'. *Dir*. Edmund Goulding.

Grand Prix (1966)   James Garner, Eva Marie Saint, Yves Montand. *Dir*. John Frankenheimer.

Grande Illusion, La (1937)   Pierre Fresnay, Erich Von Stroheim, Jean Gabin. Three captured French WWI pilots have uneasy relationship with their German commandant. *Dir*. Jean Renoir.

Grapes of Wrath, The (1940)   Henry Fonda, Jane Darwell, John Carradine, Grant Mitchell. From the John Steinbeck novel. Oklahoma farmers trek to California after dust bowl disaster of the Thirties. *Dir*. John Ford.

Grease (1978)   John Travolta, Olivia Newton-John, Stockard Channing, Frankie Avalon, Jeff Conaway, Sha Na Na, Eve Arden, Sid Caesar. School: Rydell High. *Dir*. Randal Kleiser.

Grease 2 (1982)   Maxwell Caulfield, Michelle Pfeiffer, Lorna Luft, Eve Arden, Sid Caesar. *Dir*. Patricia Birch.

Great Balls of Fire (1989)   Dennis Quaid (Jerry Lee Lewis), Winona Ryder (Myra Gale Lewis), John Doe (JW Brown). Peter Cook is 'First English Reporter'. *Dir*. Jim McBride.

Great Caruso, The (1951)   Mario Lanza, Ann Blyth, Jarmila Novotna, Alan Napier. *Dir*. Richard Thorpe.

Great Escape, The (1963)   James Garner, Steve McQueen, Richard Attenborough, Charles Bronson, Donald Pleasence, James Coburn, David McCallum, Gordon Jackson, John Leyton. *Dir*. John Sturges.

Great Expectations (1934)   Phillip Holmes (Pip), Jane Wyatt (Estella), Henry Hull (Magwitch), Alan Hale (Joe Gargery), Francis L Sullivan (Jaggers), Florence Reed (Miss Havisham). *Dir*. Stuart Walker.

Great Expectations (1946)   John Mills, Bernard Miles, Finlay Currie, Martita Hunt, Valerie Hobson, Jean Simmons, Alec Guinness, Francis L Sullivan. *Dir*. David Lean.

Great Gatsby, The (1949)   Alan Ladd, Macdonald Carey, Barry Sullivan. Based on novel by F Scott Fitzgerald. *Dir*. Elliott Nugent.

Great Gatsby, The (1974)   Robert Redford, Mia Farrow, Karen Black, Sam Waterston, Lois Chiles. Screenplay by Francis Ford Coppola. Nelson Riddle gained Oscar for music. *Dir*. Jack Clayton.

Great Muppet Caper, The (1981)   Diana Rigg, Charles Grodin, John Cleese, Peter Ustinov, Robert Morley, Trevor Howard. Peter Falk has cameo as a tramp. *Dir*. Jim Henson.

Great St Trinian's Train Robbery, The (1966)   Frankie Howerd, Dora Bryan, Reg Varney, George Cole. *Dir*. Frank Launder.

Great Santini, The (1979)   Robert Duvall, Michael O'Keefe, Blythe Danner, Julie Anne Haddock. *Dir*. Lewis John Carlino.

Great Scout and Cathouse Thursday, The (1976)   Lee Marvin, Oliver Reed, Kay Lenz, Robert Culp, Elizabeth Ashley, Sylvia Miles, Strother Martin. *Dir*. Don Taylor.

Great Waldo Pepper, The (1975)   Robert Redford, Bo Svenson, Bo Brundin, Susan Sarandon. *Dir*. George Roy Hill.

Great Waltz, The (1938)   Fernand Gravet, Luise Rainer, Miliza Korjus. Biopic of Johann Strauss the Younger. *Dir*. Julien Duvivier.

Great White Hope, The (1970)   James Earl Jones, Jane Alexander, Lou Gilbert, Hal Holbrook. Jack Johnson story (he's called Jefferson in the film). *Dir*. Martin Ritt.

Great White Hype, The (1996)   Samuel L Jackson, Jeff Goldblum, John Rhys-Davies. *Dir*. Reginald Hudlin.

Great Ziegfeld, The (1936)   William Powell, Luise Rainer (Anna Held), Myrna Loy (Billie Burke), Frank Morgan, Ray Bolger, Fanny Brice. Biopic of impresario Florenz Ziegfeld. *Dir*. Robert Z Leonard.

Greatest, The (1977)   Muhammad Ali, Ernest Borgnine, Robert Duvall, Ben Johnson, James Earl Jones. *Dir*. Tom Gries.

Greatest Show on Earth, The (1952)   Betty Hutton, Cornel Wilde, Charlton Heston, James Stewart, Dorothy Lamour, John Ringling North. *Dir*. Cecil B de Mille.

Greatest Story Ever Told, The (1965)   Max Von Sydow, Dorothy McGuire, Claude Rains, José Ferrer, David McCallum, Charlton Heston, Sidney Poitier, John Wayne, Pat Boone, Telly Savalas, Angela Lansbury. Famous John Wayne line: 'Truly this man was the Son of God'. *Dir*. George Stevens.

Greed (1925)   Gibson Gowland, Zasu Pitts, Jean Hersholt. Ex-miner dentist kills his wife and later in Death Valley kills her lover but is bound to him by handcuffs. Re-edited by June Mathis, this film is memorable for its original length of nearly 9 hours. *Dir*. Erich Von Stroheim.

Green Berets, The (1968)   John Wayne, David Janssen, Jim Hutton, Aldo Ray, Patrick Wayne. Vietnam War film. *Dir*. John Wayne.

Gremlins (1984)   Zach Galligan (Billy), Hoyt Axton (Rand Peltzer), Phoebe Cates (Kate), Keye Luke (Grandfather), Judge Reinhold (Gerald). Don't get them wet and never feed them after midnight. Sequel: *Gremlins II (The New Batch)*. *Dir*. Joe Dante.

Greystoke: The Legend of Tarzan, Lord of the Apes (1984)   Christopher Lambert (John Clayton / Tarzan), Ralph Richardson (Lord Greystoke), Andie MacDowell (Jane Porter). *Dir*. Hugh Hudson.

Gridlock'd (1997)   Tim Roth (Stretch), Tupac Shakur (Spoon), Thandie Newton (Cookie). *Dir*. Vondie Curtis-Hall.

Grifters, The (1990)   Anjelica Huston (Lily Dillon), John Cusack (Roy Dillon), Annette Bening (Myra Langtry). *Dir*. Stephen Frears.

Groundhog Day (1993)   Bill Murray (Phil), Andie MacDowell (Rita). Weatherman Murray is cursed to live the same day over and over. *Dir*. Harold Ramis.

Groundstar Conspiracy, The (1972)   George Peppard, Michael Sarrazin, James Olson. *Dir*. Lamont Johnson.

Group, The (1966)   Joanna Pettet, Candice Bergen, Jessica Walter, Joan Hackett, Elizabeth Hartman, Kathleen Widdoes, Larry Hagman, Hal Holbrook, Robert Emhardt. *Dir.* Sidney Lumet.

Guarding Tess (1994)   Shirley MacLaine, Nicolas Cage, Austin Pendleton, Richard Griffiths. Secret Service agent engages in battle of wills with a former First Lady. *Dir.* Hugh Wilson.

Guess Who's Coming to Dinner (1967)   Spencer Tracy, Katherine Hepburn, Sidney Poitier, Katharine Houghton. Katherine Houghton is the niece of Katharine Hepburn. *Dir.* Stanley Kramer.

Gunfight at the OK Corral (1957)   Burt Lancaster, Kirk Douglas, Jo Van Fleet, Rhonda Fleming, John Ireland. *Dir.* John Sturges.

Gunfighter, The (1950)   Gregory Peck, Helen Westcott, Karl Malden. *Dir.* Henry King.

Guns of Navarone (1961)   Gregory Peck, David Niven, Stanley Baker, Anthony Quinn, Anthony Quayle, James Darren, James Robertson Justice, Richard Harris. *Dir.* J Lee Thompson.

Guys and Dolls (1955)   Frank Sinatra, Marlon Brando, Jean Simmons, Vivian Blaine, Stubby Kaye. *Dir.* Joseph L Mankiewicz.

Gypsy (1962)   Rosalind Russell, Natalie Wood, Karl Malden. *Dir.* Mervyn Le Roy.

Hairspray (1988)   Sonny Bono (Franklin Von Tussle), Ruth Brown (Motormouth Maybell), Divine (Edna Turnblad / Arvin Hodgepile), Deborah Harry (Velma Von Tussle), Ricki Lake (Tracy Turnblad), Pia Zadora (Beatnik chick). *Dir.* John Waters.

Half Moon Street (1986)   Sigourney Weaver (Lauren Slaughter), Michael Caine (Lord Bullbeck). *Dir.* Bob Swaim.

Halloween (1978)   Jamie Lee Curtis, Donald Pleasence (Dr Loomis). *Dir.* John Carpenter.

Halloween 2 (1981)   Jamie Lee Curtis, Donald Pleasence (Dr Loomis). *Dir.* Rick Rosenthal.

Halloween 3: Season of the Witch (1983)   Tom Atkins, Stacey Nelkin, Dan O'Herlihy. *Dir.* Tommy Lee Wallace.

Halloween 4: The Return of Michael Myers (1988)   Donald Pleasence, Ellie Cornell, Danielle Harris. *Dir.* Dwight H Little.

Halloween 5: The Revenge of Michael Myers (1989)   Donald Pleasence, Danielle Harris, Wendy Kaplan, Ellie Cornell, Donald L Shanks, Jeffrey Landman, Beau Starr. *Dir.* Dominique Othenin-Girard.

Halloween H2O (1998)   Jamie Lee Curtis, Adam Arkin, Josh Harnett, Michelle Williams, Adam Hann-Byrd. *Dir.* Steve Miner.

Halloween: Resurrection (2002)   Jamie Lee Curtis, Brad Loree, Busta Rhymes, Tyra Banks, Luke Kirby. When a group of teenagers win a contest to spend a night in Michael Myers's childhood home to be broadcast live on the internet, they believe they are in for a little fun and some free publicity. But it all goes frightfully wrong and the game turns into a battle for survival. *Dir.* Rick Rosenthal.

Hamlet (1948)   Laurence Olivier, Eileen Herlie, Jean Simmons, Peter Cushing, Patrick Troughton. *Dir.* Laurence Olivier.

Hamlet (1990)   Mel Gibson, Glenn Close, Alan Bates, Paul Scofield, Helena Bonham Carter, Ian Holm. *Dir.* Franco Zeffirelli.

Hand that Rocks the Cradle, The (1992)   Rebecca DeMornay (Peyton Flanders), Annabella Sciorra (Claire Bartel), Matt McCoy (Michael Bartel). *Dir.* Curtis Hanson.

Handful of Dust (1988)   James Wilby (Tony Last), Kristin Scott Thomas (Brenda Last), Anjelica Huston (Mrs Rattery), Stephen Fry (Reggie), Alec Guinness (Mr Todd), Judi Dench (Mrs Beaver). *Dir.* Charles Sturridge.

Hang 'em High (1967)   Clint Eastwood, Inger Stevens, Pat Hingle. *Dir.* Ted Post.

Hannah and Her Sisters (1986)   Woody Allen (Micky), Michael Caine (Elliot), Mia Farrow (Hannah), Carrie Fisher (April), Barbara Hershey (Lee), Maureen O'Sullivan (Hannah's mother). *Dir.* Woody Allen.

Hannibal Brooks (1968)   Oliver Reed, Michael J Pollard. *Dir.* Michael Winner.

Hanover Street (1979)   Harrison Ford, Lesley-Anne Down, Christopher Plummer, Alec McCowen, Max Wall. *Dir.* Peter Hyams.

Hans Christian Andersen (1952)   Danny Kaye, Zizi Jeanmaire, Farley Granger. *Dir.* Charles Vidor.

Happiest Days of Your Life, The (1950)   Alastair Sim, Margaret Rutherford, Joyce Grenfell, Richard Wattis. *Dir.* Frank Launder.

Happy Hooker, The (1975)   Lynn Redgrave (Xaviera Hollander). *Dir.* Nicholas Sgarro.

Hard Day's Night, A (1964)   Beatles, Wilfrid Brambell, John Junkin, Norman Rossington, Victor Spinetti, Brian Epstein. *Dir.* Richard Lester.

Hard Way, The (1991)   Michael J Fox (Nick Lang), James Woods (John Moss), Annabella Sciorra (Susan). *Dir.* John Badham.

Harder They Fall, The (1956)   Humphrey Bogart, Rod Steiger, Max Baer, Jan Sterling. Bogart's last film. *Dir.* Mark Robson.

Hardy Family (1936–58)   Mickey Rooney, Lewis Stone, Fay Holden, Cecilia Parker, Sara Haden, Spring Byington, Lionel Barrymore. Howard Koch directed the last of the series: *Andy Hardy Comes Home. Dir.* George B Seitz.

Harry and Tonto (1974)   Art Carney, Ellen Burstyn, Chief Dan George, Larry Hagman. Tonto was a cat. *Dir.* Paul Mazursky.

Harry Potter and the Chamber of Secrets (2002)   Largely the same cast and characters as in *Philosopher's Stone* although new characters include Kenneth Branagh (Gilderoy Lockhart). *Dir.* Chris Columbus.

Harry Potter and the Philosopher's Stone (2001)   Daniel Radcliffe (Harry Potter), Rupert Grint (Ron Weasley), Emma Watson (Hermione Granger), Robbie Coltrane (Hagrid), Richard Griffiths (Uncle Vernon Dursley), Richard Harris (Albus Dumbledore), Ian Hart (Professor Quirrell / Voldemort), John Hurt (Mr Ollivander), Alan Rickman (Professor Snape), Fiona Shaw (Aunt Petunia Dursley), Maggie Smith (Professor McGonagall), Julie Walters (Mrs Weasley), John Cleese (Nearly Headless Nick), Richard Bremner (He Who Must Not Be Named), Tom Felton (Draco Malfoy). US title: *Harry Potter and the Sorcerer's Stone. Dir.* Chris Columbus.

Harry Potter and the Prisoner of Azkaban (2004)   Daniel Radcliffe (Harry Potter), Rupert Grint (Ron Weasley), Emma Watson (Hermione Granger), Gary Oldman (Sirius Black), David Thewlis (Professor Lupin), Michael Gambon (Albus Dumbledore), Alan Rickman (Professor Severus Snape), Maggie Smith (Professor Minerva McGonagall), Robbie Coltrane (Rubeus Hagrid), Tom Felton (Draco Malfoy), Emma Thompson (Professor Sybil Trelawney), Julie Walters (Mrs Weasley), Timothy Spall (Peter Pettigrew), Julie Christie (Madame Rosmerta). Sirius Black, the wizard imprisoned for killing Harry's father, escapes and heads for Hogwarts School in search of Harry. *Dir.* Alfonso Cuarón.

CINEMA

Harvey (1950)   James Stewart (Elwood P Dowd), Josephine Hull (Veta Louise), Victoria Horne. *Dir.* Henry Koster.

Hawk the Slayer (1980)   Jack Palance, John Terry, Bernard Bresslaw. *Dir.* Terry Marcel.

Head (1968)   Monkees, Victor Mature. Written by Jack Nicholson & Bob Rafelson. *Dir.* Bob Rafelson.

Hear My Song (1992)   Ned Beatty (Josef Locke: voice of Vernon Midgley), Adrian Dunbar (Mickey O'Neill), Shirley Anne Field (Cathleen Doyle), David McCallum (Jim Abbott). *Dir.* Peter Chelsom.

Heart Is a Lonely Hunter, The (1968)   Alan Arkin, Sondra Locke, Stacy Keach. Based on Carson McCullers's story of a deaf mute. *Dir.* Robert Ellis Miller.

Heartbreak Ridge (1986)   Clint Eastwood (Highway), Marsha Mason (Aggie). *Dir.* Clint Eastwood.

Heartburn (1986)   Meryl Streep (Rachel), Jack Nicholson (Mark), Jeff Daniels (Richard), Stockard Channing (Julie). *Dir.* Mike Nichols.

Heat (1995)   Al Pacino, Robert De Niro, Val Kilmer, Jon Voight. Based on TV movie: *L.A. Takedown.* First film in which the 2 stars actually filmed scenes together. *Dir.* Michael Mann.

Heathers (1989)   Winona Ryder (Veronica Sawyer), Christian Slater (JD), Shannen Doherty (Heather Duke), Lisanne Falk (Heather McNamara), Kim Walker (Heather Chandler). *Dir.* Michael Lehmann.

Heaven and Earth (1993)   Tommy Lee Jones, Joan Chen, Haing S Ngor, Debbie Reynolds. Vietnamese woman endures hardships and torments from both sides during the war. *Dir.* Oliver Stone.

Heaven Can Wait (1943)   Don Ameche, Gene Tierney, Laird Cregar, Charles Coburn. *Dir.* Ernst Lubitsch.

Heaven Can Wait (1978)   Warren Beatty, Julie Christie, James Mason (Mr Jordan), Dyan Cannon, Vincent Gardenia. Remake of *Here Comes Mr Jordan* (1941). *Dir.* Warren Beatty.

Heaven Knows, Mr Allison (1957)   Robert Mitchum, Deborah Kerr. Marine and nun marooned on Pacific island during WW2. *Dir.* John Huston.

Heavenly Creatures (1994)   Melanie Lynskey, Kate Winslet, Diane Kent. *Dir.* Peter Jackson.

Heavens Above (1963)   Peter Sellers, Isabel Jeans, Ian Carmichael, Irene Handl, Eric Sykes, Bernard Miles. *Dir.* John Boulting.

Heaven's Gate (1980)   Kris Kristofferson, Christopher Walken, John Hurt, Jeff Bridges. Famous Western, remembered as a box office disaster. *Dir.* Michael Cimino.

Hedda (1975)   Glenda Jackson, Peter Eyre, Jennie Linden, Patrick Stewart, Timothy West. *Dir.* Trevor Nunn.

Heidi (1937)   Shirley Temple, Jean Hersholt, Arthur Treacher. Based on Johanna Spyri's novel. *Dir.* Allan Dwan.

Heiress, The (1949)   Olivia de Havilland, Ralph Richardson, Montgomery Clift, Miriam Hopkins, Ray Collins. Based on Henry James's novel *Washington Square* and the play of the same name by Ruth and Augustus Goetz. *Dir.* William Wyler.

Helen Morgan Story, The (1957)   Ann Blyth, Paul Newman, Walter Woolf King (Ziegfeld). GB title: *Both Ends of the Candle. Dir.* Michael Curtiz.

Hellfire Club, The (1960)   Keith Michell, Peter Arne, Adrienne Corri, Peter Cushing, David Lodge. *Dir.* Robert S Baker and Monty Berman.

Hello Dolly (1969)   Barbra Streisand, Walter Matthau, Michael Crawford, Marianne McAndrew, Tommy Tune. Based on Thornton Wilder's play *The Matchmaker. Dir.* Gene Kelly.

Hell's Angels (1930)   Ben Lyon, James Hall, Jean Harlow. *Dir.* Howard Hughes.

Hellzapoppin (1942)   Ole Olsen, Chic Johnson, Hugh Herbert, Martha Raye, Mischa Auer. Montage of Mirth and Madness. *Dir.* HC Potter.

Help! (1965)   Beatles, Leo McKern, Eleanor Bron, Victor Spinetti. *Dir.* Dick Lester.

Henry and June (1990)   Fred Ward (Henry Miller), Uma Thurman (June Miller), Maria De Medeiros (Anaïs Nin). Censors created a new 'NC-17' rating to cover rude but artistically worthwhile films. *Dir.* Philip Kaufman.

Henry V (1944)   Laurence Olivier, Robert Newton, Leslie Banks, Esmond Knight, Renée Asherson. *Dir.* Laurence Olivier.

Henry V (1989)   Kenneth Branagh, Derek Jacobi, Brian Blessed, Ian Holm, Alec McCowen, Robbie Coltrane (Falstaff), Emma Thompson (Katherine). *Dir.* Kenneth Branagh.

Henry VIII and His Six Wives (1972)   Keith Michell, Frances Cuka (Aragon), Charlotte Rampling (Boleyn), Jane Asher (Seymour), Jenny Bos (Cleves), Lynne Frederick (Howard), Barbara Leigh-Hunt (Parr). *Dir.* Waris Hussein.

Hercules (1997)   Voices of: Tate Donovan (Hercules), Rip Torn (Zeus), James Woods (Hades), Danny De Vito (Philoctetes), Susan Egan (Meg). Cartoons by Gerald Scarfe. *Dir.* John Musker & Ron Clements.

Here Come the Huggetts (1948)   Jack Warner, Kathleen Harrison, Susan Shaw, Petula Clark, Jimmy Hanley, Diana Dors. Britain's answer to the Hardys. *Dir.* Ken Annakin.

Here Comes Mr Jordan (1941)   Robert Montgomery, Evelyn Keyes, Claude Rains. Much-copied plot about a prizefighter cum saxophonist arriving in heaven too early. *Dir.* Alexander Hall.

Hero (2004)   Jet Li, Tony Leung Chiu-Wai, Maggie Cheung Man-Yuk. The Kingdom of Qin is the most ruthless and ambitious of China's seven warring states. Its king is the target of numerous assassins, including Broken Sword, Flying Snow and Sky. When Nameless kills all three he is offered an audience with the king and explains how he used the personal relationships of the assassins to expose their weaknesses. The king tells a different version of the same story. *Dir.* Yimou Zhang.

Heroes of Telemark, The (1965)   Kirk Douglas, Richard Harris, Ulla Jacobsson, Roy Dotrice, Michael Redgrave. *Dir.* Anthony Mann.

High Anxiety (1977)   Mel Brooks, Madeline Kahn, Cloris Leachman. Psychologist suspects his predecessor was murdered. *Dir.* Mel Brooks.

High Noon (1952)   Gary Cooper (Will Kane), Grace Kelly, Thomas Mitchell, Lloyd Bridges, Lon Chaney. Tex Ritter sang Dimitri Tiomkin's theme tune. Action takes place during the 85 minutes of running time. *Dir.* Fred Zinnemann.

High School High (1996)   Jon Lovitz (Mr Clark), Tia Carrere (Victoria). School is Marion Berry High. *Dir.* Hart Bochner.

Highlander (1986)   Christopher Lambert (Connor MacLeod), Roxanne Hart (Brenda Wyatt), Sean Connery (Ramirez). *Highlander II: The Quickening* was the 1990 sequel. *Dir.* Russell Mulcahy.

His Girl Friday (1940)   Cary Grant, Rosalind Russell, Ralph Bellamy, Gene Lockhart. Remake of *The Front Page* (1931). *Dir.* Howard Hawks.

History of Mr Polly, The (1949)   John Mills, Sally Ann Howes, Megs Jenkins, Finlay Currie. Based on HG Wells's novel. *Dir.* Anthony Pelissier.

Hit, The (1984)   John Hurt, Terence Stamp, Tim Roth, Laura Del Sol, Fernando Rey. *Dir.* Stephen Frears.

Hitler – The Last Ten Days (1973)   Alec Guinness, Simon Ward, Doris Kunstmann, Diane Cilento, Eric Porter, Joss Ackland. *Dir.* Ennio de Concini.

Hobson's Choice (1953)   Charles Laughton, Brenda de Banzie, John Mills, Helen Haye, Prunella Scales. Based on Harold Brighouse's play. *Dir.* David Lean.

Hoffa (1992)   Jack Nicholson, Danny De Vito, Armand Assante. *Dir.* Danny De Vito.

Holiday Inn (1942)   Bing Crosby, Fred Astaire, Walter Abel, Marjorie Reynolds. Won Oscar for the song 'White Christmas'. *Dir.* Mark Sandrich.

Hollywood or Bust (1956)   Dean Martin, Jerry Lewis, Pat Crowley, Anita Ekberg. Last of the Martin & Lewis films. *Dir.* Frank Tashlin.

Home Alone (1990)   Macaulay Culkin (Kevin McCallister), Joe Pesci (Harry), Daniel Stern (Marv), John Candy (Gus). *Dir.* Chris Columbus.

Home Alone 2: Lost in New York (1992)   Macaulay Culkin (Kevin McCallister), Joe Pesci (Harry), Daniel Stern (Marv), Brenda Fricker (Pigeon Lady). *Dir.* Chris Columbus.

Homeboy (1988)   Mickey Rourke (Johnny Walker), Christopher Walken (Wesley), Kevin Conway (Grazziano). *Dir.* Michael Seresin.

Honey, I Blew up the Kid (1992)   Rick Moranis (Wayne Szalinski), Lloyd Bridges (Clifford Sterling), Marcia Strassman (Diane). 'Blew up' in as much as the baby grows to 100 feet tall. *Dir.* Randal Kleiser.

Honey, I Shrunk the Kids (1989)   Rick Moranis (Wayne Szalinski), Matt Frewer (Big Russ Thompson), Marcia Strassman (Diane), Kristine Sutherland (Mae Thompson). *Dir.* Joe Johnston.

Honkytonk Man (1982)   Clint Eastwood (Red Stovall), Kyle Eastwood (Whit), John McIntire (Grandpa). *Dir.* Clint Eastwood.

Honorary Consul, The (1983)   Michael Caine (Charley Fortnum), Richard Gere (Dr Plarr), Bob Hoskins (Col Perez). US title: *Beyond the Limit*. *Dir.* John MacKenzie.

Hook (1991)   Dustin Hoffman (Capt Hook), Robin Williams (Peter Banning / Pan), Julia Roberts (Tinkerbell), Bob Hoskins (Smee). *Dir.* Steven Spielberg.

Hoop Dreams (1994)   William Gates, Arthur Agee, Emma Gates. *Dir.* Steve James.

Hooper (1978)   Burt Reynolds, Sally Field, Brian Keith, Jan Michael Vincent, Adam West. Ageing stuntman decides on one last sensational stunt. *Dir.* Hal Needham.

Hoosiers (1986)   Gene Hackman, Barbara Hershey, Dennis Hopper, Sheb Wooley. Triumphs of an Indiana high school basketball team. *Dir.* David Anspaugh.

Horse Feathers (1932)   Groucho (Wagstaff), Chico, Zeppo, Harpo Marx, Thelma Todd. College football team needs to win. *Dir.* Norman Z McLeod.

Hotel Rwanda (2004)   Don Cheadle (Paul Rusesabagina), Sophie Okonedo (Tatiana Rusesabagina), Nick Nolte (Colonel Oliver), Joaquin Phoenix (Jack). True story of hotel manager Paul Rusesabagina, who sheltered over a thousand Tutsis refugees during their struggle against the Hutu militia in Rwanda. *Dir.* Terry George.

Hound of the Baskervilles (1939)   Basil Rathbone, Nigel Bruce, Richard Greene, John Carradine. *Dir.* Sidney Lanfield.

Hound of the Baskervilles (1959)   Peter Cushing, André Morell, Christopher Lee, John Le Mesurier. *Dir.* Terence Fisher.

Hound of the Baskervilles (1977)   Peter Cook (Sherlock Holmes), Dudley Moore (Watson), Denholm Elliott (Stapleton), Terry-Thomas (Mortimer), Max Wall, Spike Milligan, Penelope Keith. *Dir.* Paul Morrissey.

Hours, The (2002)   Meryl Streep (Clarissa Vaughan), Julianne Moore (Laura Brown), Nicole Kidman (Virginia Woolf), Ed Harris (Richard Brown), Toni Collette (Kitty Barlowe), Claire Danes (Julia Vaughan), Jeff Daniels (Louis Waters), Stephen Dillane (Leonard Woolf). Explores how Woolf's novel *Mrs Dalloway* affects three generations of women, all of whom have dealt with suicides in their lives. *Dir.* Stephen Daldry.

House of Flying Daggers (2004) Takeshi Kaneshiro (Jin), Andy Lau (Leo), Ziyi Zhang (Mei), Dandan Song (Yee). Beautifully filmed martial arts film of undercover espionage and romance. *Dir.* Yimou Zhang.

Houseboat (1958)   Cary Grant, Sophia Loren, Martha Hyer, Harry Guardino. *Dir.* Melville Shavelson.

Housesitter (1992)   Steve Martin (Davis), Goldie Hawn (Gwen). One-night stand turns into a comic fatal attraction. *Dir.* Frank Oz.

How Green Was My Valley (1941)   Walter Pidgeon, Maureen O'Hara, Roddy McDowall. Based on Richard Llewellyn's novel. *Dir.* John Ford.

How I Won the War (1967)   Michael Crawford, John Lennon, Roy Kinnear, Lee Montague, Michael Hordern. *Dir.* Richard Lester.

How the West Was Won (1962)   Debbie Reynolds, Carroll Baker, Lee J Cobb, Henry Fonda, James Stewart, Gregory Peck. Spencer Tracy was the narrator. *Dir.* Henry Hathaway, John Ford, George Marshall.

How to Marry a Millionaire (1953)   Lauren Bacall, Marilyn Monroe, Betty Grable, William Powell, Cameron Mitchell. *Dir.* Jean Negulesco.

Howard's End (1992)   Anthony Hopkins (Henry Wilcox), Vanessa Redgrave (Ruth), Helena Bonham Carter (Helen), Emma Thompson (Margaret Schlegel). The Howard's End of the title is a house. *Dir.* James Ivory.

Howling, The (1980)   Dee Wallace, Patrick Macnee, Kevin McCarthy. *Dir.* Joe Dante.

Howling II: Your Sister Is a Werewolf (1985)   Christopher Lee, Annie McEnroe, Reb Brown. Filmed in Czechoslavakia and not a sequel to *The Howling*. *Dir.* Philippe Mora.

Hud (1963)   Paul Newman, Patricia Neal, Melvyn Douglas, Brandon De Wilde. *Dir.* Martin Ritt.

Hue and Cry (1946)   Alastair Sim, Jack Warner, Harry Fowler. First of the Ealing comedies concerns crooks passing information in a boys' paper. *Dir.* Charles Crichton.

Hunchback of Notre Dame, The (1939)   Charles Laughton, Cedric Hardwicke, Maureen O'Hara, Edmond O'Brien, Thomas Mitchell. Remake of the Lon Chaney 1923 film. *Dir.* William Dieterle.

Hunchback of Notre Dame, The (1956)   Anthony Quinn, Gina Lollobrigida. French / Italian production of the classic story. *Dir.* Jean Delannoy.

C
I
N
E
M
A

Hunger, The (1983)   Catherine Deneuve (Miriam), David Bowie (John), Susan Sarandon (Sarah Roberts). *Dir.* Tony Scott.

Hunt for Red October, The (1990)   Sean Connery (Capt Marko Ramius), Alec Baldwin (Jack Ryan), Sam Neill (Capt Borodin). *Dir.* John McTiernan.

Hunter, The (1980)   Steve McQueen, Eli Wallach, Ben Johnson. McQueen's last film. *Dir.* Buzz Kulik.

Hurlyburly (1998)   Sean Penn (Eddie), Kevin Spacey (Mickey), Robin Wright Penn, Garry Shandling, Meg Ryan, Chazz Pálminteri, Anna Paquin. *Dir.* Anthony Drazan.

Husbands and Wives (1992)   Woody Allen (Gabe Roth), Judith Lewis (Rain), Blythe Danner (Rain's mother), Mia Farrow (Judy Roth), Judy Davis (Sally). *Dir.* Woody Allen.

Hustler, The (1961)   Paul Newman, Jackie Gleason, George C Scott, Piper Laurie. *Dir.* Robert Rossen.

Hustler White (1996)   Tony Ward, Bruce LaBruce, Kevin Kramer. *Dir.* Bruce LaBruce.

I Accuse (1958)   José Ferrer (Dreyfus), Anton Walbrook (Esterhazy), Emlyn Williams (Zola). Written by Gore Vidal. *Dir.* José Ferrer.

I Am a Camera (1955)   Julie Harris, Laurence Harvey, Shelley Winters, Anton Diffring. John Collier adaptation of Isherwood stories and the stage play by John Van Druten. *Dir.* Henry Cornelius.

I Am a Fugitive from a Chain Gang (1932)   Paul Muni, Glenda Farrell, Helen Vinson, Preston Foster. *Dir.* Mervyn Le Roy.

I Confess (1953)   Montgomery Clift, Anne Baxter, Brian Aherne, Karl Malden. Priest hears confession of a murderer and has a dilemma. *Dir.* Alfred Hitchcock.

I Married a Witch (1942)   Fredric March, Veronica Lake, Cecil Kellaway, Susan Hayward, Elizabeth Patterson. *Dir.* René Clair.

I Wanna Hold Your Hand (1978)   Nancy Allen, Bobby diCicco, Marc McClure. *Dir.* Robert Zemeckis.

I Want to Live (1958)   Susan Hayward, Simon Oakland, Virginia Vincent, Theodore Bikel. Based on the Barbara Graham story of a prostitute executed despite doubts as to her guilt. *Dir.* Robert Wise.

I Was a Male War Bride (1949)   Cary Grant, Ann Sheridan, Marion Marshall. *Dir.* Howard Hawks.

I Was Monty's Double (1958)   John Mills, Cecil Parker, ME Clifton-James. US title: *Hell, Heaven and Hoboken*. *Dir.* John Guillermin.

Ice-Age (2002)   Voices of Ray Romano (Manfred), John Leguizamo (Sid), Denis Leary (Diego), Goran Visnjic (Soto), Jack Black (Zeke), Tara Strong (Roshan). Animated sloth, mammoth and sabre-toothed tiger combine to return a lost child to his tribe during the ice-age. *Dir.* Carlos Saldanha and Chris Wedge.

Ice Cold in Alex (1958)   John Mills, Sylvia Syms, Anthony Quayle, Harry Andrews. *Dir.* J Lee Thompson.

Ice Station Zebra (1968)   Rock Hudson, Patrick McGoohan, Ernest Borgnine, Jim Brown. Based on the Alistair MacLean story. *Dir.* John Sturges.

Ideal Husband, An (1999)   Cate Blanchett, Minnie Driver, Rupert Everett, Peter Vaughan, Julianne Moore. *Dir.* Oliver Parker.

If (1968)   Malcolm McDowell, David Wood, Richard Warwick, Arthur Lowe. *Dir.* Lindsay Anderson.

If These Walls Could Talk (1996)   Demi Moore, Cher. TV movie. *Dir.* Nancy Savoka and Cher.

I'm All Right Jack (1959)   Ian Carmichael, Peter Sellers, Irene Handl, Richard Attenborough, Terry-Thomas, Dennis Price, Margaret Rutherford. *Dir.* John Boulting.

Importance of Being Earnest, The (1952)   Michael Redgrave, Michael Denison, Edith Evans, Margaret Rutherford, Dorothy Tutin. *Dir.* Anthony Asquith.

Importance of Being Earnest, The (2002)   Rupert Everett, Colin Firth, Frances O'Connor, Reese Witherspoon, Judi Dench. *Dir.* Oliver Parker.

In Good Company (2004)   Dennis Quaid (Dan Foreman), Topher Grace (Carter Duryea), Scarlett Johansson (Alex Foreman). A middle-aged advertising executive is faced with a new boss nearly half his age who is sleeping with his daughter. *Dir.* Paul Weitz.

In Search of the Castaways (1961)   Maurice Chevalier, Hayley Mills, George Sanders, Wilfrid Hyde-White, Wilfrid Brambell. *Dir.* Robert Stevenson.

In the Bleak Midwinter (1995)   Michael Maloney, Richard Briers, Julia Sawalha, Joan Collins, Jennifer Saunders. Story of a production of *Hamlet* in a village church. *Dir.* Kenneth Branagh.

In the Heat of the Night (1967)   Sidney Poitier, Rod Steiger, Warren Oates. *Dir.* Norman Jewison.

In Which We Serve (1942)   Noël Coward, Bernard Miles, John Mills, Richard Attenborough, Celia Johnson, Michael Wilding. Viewed as one of the best propaganda wartime films. *Dir.* Noël Coward and David Lean.

Inchon (1981)   Laurence Olivier (General MacArthur), Jacqueline Bisset, David Janssen, Ben Gazzara, Richard Roundtree. *Dir.* Terence Young.

Incredible Journey, The (1963)   Disney cartoon about 2 dogs and a cat and their 250-mile journey home after being separated from their owners. *Dir.* Fletcher Markle.

Incredible Shrinking Man, The (1957)   Grant Williams, Randy Stuart, April Kent. Radioactive mist is the cause of the shrinking. *Dir.* Jack Arnold.

Incredible Shrinking Woman, The (1981)   Lily Tomlin, Charles Grodin, Ned Beatty, Henry Gibson. A new perfume causes the diminution in this case. *Dir.* Joel Schumacher.

Incredibles, The (2004)   Voices of Craig T Nelson (Mr Incredible/Bob Parr), Holly Hunter (Elastigirl/Helen Parr), Samuel L Jackson (Frozone/Lucius Best), Jason Lee (Syndrome/Buddy Pine), Dominique Louis (Bomb Voyage), Teddy Newton (Newsreel Narrator), Jean Sincere (Mrs Hogenson), Eli Fucile and Maeve Andrews (Jack Jack Parr), Wallace Shawn (Gilbert Huph), Spencer Fox (Dashiell 'Dash' Parr), Lou Romano (Bernie Kropp), Sarah Vowell (Violet Parr), Michael Bird (Tony Rydinger). Animation in which insurance man Bob Parr and his family try to live a quiet suburban life but are forced to adopt their former superhero guises in order to save the world. *Dir.* Brad Bird.

Indecent Proposal (1993)   Robert Redford (John Gage), Demi Moore (Diana Murphy), Woody Harrelson (David Murphy), Billy Connolly (Auction MC). *Dir.* Adrian Lyne.

Independence Day (1996)   Will Smith (Capt Steve Hiller), Bill Pullman (President Whitmore), Jeff Goldblum, Judd Hirsch, Harry Connick Jnr, Brent Spiner. Pilot and computer expert battle an alien force. *Dir.* Roland Emmerich.

Indiana Jones and the Last Crusade (1989)   Harrison Ford, Sean Connery (Professor Henry Jones), Denholm Elliott (Marcus Brody), John Rhys-Davies (Sallah), Julian Glover (Walter Donovan). *Dir.* Steven Spielberg.

Indiana Jones and the Temple of Doom (1984)   Harrison Ford, Kate Capshaw (Willie Scott), Ke Huy Quan (Short Round). Prequel to *Raiders of the Lost*

Ark (action takes place in 1935). *Dir.* Steven Spielberg.

Indiscreet (1958) Cary Grant, Ingrid Bergman, Phyllis Calvert, Cecil Parker, David Kossoff, Megs Jenkins. Not very indiscreet as it happens, as the loving couple are both single. *Dir.* Stanley Donen.

Informer, The (1935) Victor McLaglen, Heather Angel, Margot Grahame, Una O'Connor. Story of IRA allegiances. *Dir.* John Ford.

Inherit the Wind (1960) Spencer Tracy, Fredric March, Dick York, Florence Eldridge, Gene Kelly. Fictionalised account of the Scopes Monkey Trial of 1925 when a teacher was accused of teaching Darwin's Theory of Evolution and, consequently, blasphemy. *Dir.* Stanley Kramer.

Inn of the Sixth Happiness, The (1958) Ingrid Bergman, Curt Jurgens, Robert Donat. Biopic of the missionary Gladys Aylward and her work in China. *Dir.* Mark Robson.

Inner Circle, The (1991) Tom Hulce (Ivan Sanshin), Lolita Davidovich (Anastasia), Bob Hoskins (Beria), Alexandre Zbruev (Stalin). Cinema projectionist goes to work for Stalin. *Dir.* Andrei Konchalovsky.

Innerspace (1987) Dennis Quaid (Lt Tuck Pendleton), Martin Short (Jack Putter), Meg Ryan (Lydia Maxwell), Kevin McCarthy (Victor Scrimshaw). Version of *The Fantastic Voyage*. *Dir.* Joe Dante.

Insider, The (1999) Al Pacino (Lowell Bergman), Russell Crowe (Jeffrey Wigand), Rip Torn (John Scanlon), Christopher Plummer (Mike Wallace), Diane Venora (Liare Wigand) Michael Gambon (Thomas Sandefor). *Dir.* Michael Mann.

Insignificance (1985) Gary Busey (The Ballplayer), Tony Curtis (The Senator), Michael Emil (The Professor), Theresa Russell (The Actress), Will Sampson (The Elevator Attendant). Four people resembling Monroe, Einstein, McCarthy & Di Maggio meet in New York hotel. *Dir.* Nicolas Roeg.

Insomnia (2002) Al Pacino, Martin Donovan, Hilary Swank, Paul Dooley. Not to be confused with the 1997 Norwegian film of the same name. *Dir.* Christopher Nolan.

Inspector Calls, An (1954) Alastair Sim, Jane Wenham, Bryan Forbes, Arthur Young. *Dir.* Guy Hamilton.

International Velvet (1978) Nanette Newman, Tatum O'Neal, Anthony Hopkins, Christopher Plummer. *Dir.* Bryan Forbes.

Intersection (1994) Sharon Stone, Richard Gere, Martin Landau. *Dir.* Mark Rydell.

Intermezzo (1939) Leslie Howard, Ingrid Bergman, John Halliday, Edna Best, Cecil Kellaway. A virtuoso violinist has an affair with his musical protégée. *Dir.* Gregory Ratoff (William Wyler is thought to have assisted).

Intolerance (1916) Mae Marsh, Lillian Gish, Constance Talmadge. Four stories depicting intolerance and persecution through the ages. *Dir.* DW Griffith.

Invasion of the Body Snatchers (1956) Kevin McCarthy, Dana Wynter, Larry Gates, King Donovan, Carolyn Jones, Sam Peckinpah. Small American town is taken over by aliens. *Dir.* Don Siegel.

Invasion of the Body Snatchers (1978) Donald Sutherland, Brooke Adams, Leonard Nimoy, Jeff Goldblum, Kevin McCarthy, Don Siegel. San Francisco becomes the venue for the remake of the 1956 classic. *Dir.* Philip Kaufman.

Invisible Man, The (1933) Claude Rains (Dr Griffin), Gloria Stuart, Una O'Connor. *Dir.* James Whale.

Ipcress File, The (1965) Michael Caine (Harry Palmer), Nigel Green, Sue Lloyd, Gordon Jackson. The Michael Caine character was never named in the novel by Len Deighton. *Dir.* Sidney J Furie.

IQ (1994) Tim Robbins, Meg Ryan, Walter Matthau (Einstein), Stephen Fry, Keene Curtis (Eisenhower). *Dir.* Fred Schepisi.

Iris (2001) Judi Dench (Iris Murdoch), Jim Broadbent (John Bayley), Kate Winslet (Young Iris), Hugh Bonneville (Young John), Penelope Wilton (Janet Stone), Juliet Aubrey (Young Janet), Eleanor Bron, Joan Bakewell. Jim Broadbent won Oscar as Best Supporting Actor. *Dir.* Richard Eyre.

Irma La Douce (1963) Shirley MacLaine, Jack Lemmon, Lou Jacobi. Paris policeman falls for a prostitute and becomes her pimp. *Dir.* Billy Wilder.

Ishtar (1987) Warren Beatty (Lyle Rogers), Dustin Hoffman (Chuck Clarke), Isabelle Adjani (Shirra Assel). Second biggest flop of all time. *Dir.* Elaine May.

Island of Dr Moreau (1977) Burt Lancaster, Michael York, Nigel Davenport, Barbara Carrera. Story of shipwrecked sailors on a Pacific Island in 1911. *Dir.* Don Taylor.

It Happened One Night (1934) Clark Gable, Claudette Colbert, Walter Connolly, Alan Hale, Ward Bond. Earned Oscars for both its stars. *Dir.* Frank Capra.

It Takes Two (1995) Kirstie Alley, Steve Guttenberg, Mary-Kate and Ashley Olsen. *Dir.* Andy Tennant.

Italian Job, The (1969) Michael Caine, Noël Coward, Benny Hill, Rossano Brazzi, Irene Handl, Fred Emney, John Le Mesurier, Simon Dee, Robert Powell. Crooks stage a traffic jam in Turin to pull off a robbery. *Dir.* Peter Collinson.

It's a Mad Mad Mad Mad World (1963) Spencer Tracy, Jimmy Durante, Mickey Rooney, Phil Silvers, Terry-Thomas, Peter Falk, Buster Keaton, The 3 Stooges. Buried loot is the instigator of mayhem. *Dir.* Stanley Kramer.

It's a Wonderful Life (1946) James Stewart, Henry Travers (Clarence), Donna Reed, Lionel Barrymore, Thomas Mitchell. James Stewart's favourite film and many believe Frank Capra's finest. *Dir.* Frank Capra.

It's a Wonderful World (1939) James Stewart, Claudette Colbert, Frances Drake, Guy Kibbee. *Dir.* WS Van Dyke II.

Jack (1996) Robin Williams, Diane Lane, Jennifer Lopez, Bill Cosby. *Dir.* Francis Ford Coppola.

Jack the Bear (1993) Danny De Vito, Robert J Steinmiller Jnr, Miko Hughes. *Dir.* Marshall Herskovitz.

Jackal, The (1997) Bruce Willis (The Jackal), Richard Gere (Declan Mulqueen), Sidney Poitier (Preston), Diane Venora (Valentina Koslova), Mathilda May (Isabella). *Dir.* Michael Caton-Jones.

Jackie Brown (1998) Pam Grier (Jackie Brown), Samuel L Jackson (Ordell Robbie), Robert Forster (Max Cherry), Michael Keaton, Michael Bowen, Robert De Niro (Louis Gara). Air stewardess smuggles cash into America for a gun-runner. *Dir.* Quentin Tarantino.

Jagged Edge (1985) Jeff Bridges (Jack Forrester), Glenn Close (Teddy Barnes), Robert Loggia (Sam Ransom). *Dir.* Richard Marquand.

Jailhouse Rock (1957) Elvis Presley (Vince Everett), Judy Tyler (Peggy Van Alden), Mickey Shaughnessy, Vaughn Taylor, Jennifer Holden. After serving a stretch for manslaughter, young tearaway Vince Everett becomes a rock star. *Dir.* Richard Thorpe.

James and the Giant Peach (1996) Paul Terry, Joanna Lumley, Pete Postlethwaite. *Dir.* Henry Selick.

CINEMA

Jason X (2002)   Kane Hodder (Jason), Lexa Doig (Rowan), Chuck Campbell (Tsunaron), Lisa Ryder (KAY-EM 14), Peter Mensah (Sgt Brodski), David Cronenberg (Dr Wimmer). Science fiction story set in the 25th century concerning students aboard a spaceship who revive a frozen serial killer. *Dir.* Jim Isaac.

Jaws (1975)   Robert Shaw, Roy Scheider, Richard Dreyfuss, Lorraine Gary. Long Island resort: Amity. *Dir.* Steven Spielberg.

Jaws 2 (1978)   Roy Scheider, Lorraine Gary. *Dir.* Jeannot Szwarc.

Jaws 3-D (1983)   Dennis Quaid (Mike), Bess Armstrong (Kathryn), Simon MacCorkindale (Philip), Louis Gossett Jr (Calvin). *Dir.* Joe Alves.

Jaws: the Revenge (1987)   Lorraine Gary (Ellen Brody), Lance Guest (Michael), Mario Van Peebles (Jake), Karen Young (Carla), Michael Caine (Hoagie). *Dir.* Joseph Sargent.

Jazz Singer, The (1927)   Al Jolson, May McAvoy, Warner Oland. Notable for being the first talkie. *Dir.* Alan Crosland.

Jean de Florette (1987)   Yves Montand (Cesar Soubeyran), Gérard Depardieu (Jean de Florette), Daniel Auteuil (Ugolin), Elisabeth Depardieu (Aimée), Ernestine Mazurowna (Manon). Sequel: *Manon des Sources*. *Dir.* Claude Berri.

Jennifer 8 (1992)   Andy Garcia (John Berlin), Uma Thurman (Helena Robertson). Serial killer preys on blind women. *Dir.* Bruce Robinson.

Jerry Maguire (1996)   Tom Cruise, Cuba Gooding Jnr. *Dir.* Phillip Noyce.

Jesus Christ Superstar (1973)   Ted Neeley, Carl Anderson, Yvonne Elliman. Melvyn Bragg wrote the screenplay with Jewison. *Dir.* Norman Jewison.

Jewel of the Nile (1985)   Michael Douglas (Jack), Kathleen Turner (Joan), Danny De Vito (Ralph). Film is dedicated to Diane Thomas, the writer of *Romancing the Stone*. *Dir.* Lewis Teague.

Jezebel (1938)   Bette Davis, Henry Fonda. US Civil War epic. *Dir.* William Wyler.

JFK (1991)   Kevin Costner (Jim Garrison), Sissy Spacek (Liz Garrison), Tommy Lee Jones (Clay Shaw), Joe Pesci (David Ferrie), Gary Oldman (Lee Harvey Oswald), Brian Doyle-Murray (Jack Ruby). *Dir.* Oliver Stone.

Jim Thorpe, All-American (1951)   Burt Lancaster (Thorpe), Charles Bickford, Phyllis Thaxter.Truish story of the Native American who became a star footballer. *Dir.* Michael Curtiz.

Jingle All the Way (1996)   Arnold Schwarzenegger (Howard Langston), Rita Wilson (Liz Langston), Jake Lloyd (Jamie Langston), Sinbad, James Belushi. *Dir.* Brian Levant.

Joan of Arc (1948)   Ingrid Bergman, José Ferrer, Francis L Sullivan. *Dir.* Victor Fleming.

John Paul Jones (1959)   Robert Stack, Charles Coburn (Benjamin Franklin), Bette Davis (Catherine the Great). Notable for its unending list of star cameos. *Dir.* John Farrow.

Johnny Belinda (1948)   Jane Wyman, Lew Ayres, Charles Bickford, Agnes Moorehead. Deaf mute is raped and the local doctor is suspected of being the father of the baby. *Dir.* Jean Negulesco.

Joker Is Wild, The (1957)   Frank Sinatra, Mitzi Gaynor, Eddie Albert, Jeanne Crain. The song 'All the Way' won an Academy Award. *Dir.* Charles Vidor.

Jokers, The (1967)   Michael Crawford, Oliver Reed, Harry Andrews, James Donald, Daniel Massey, Michael Hordern, Frank Finlay, Rachel Kempson. Two brothers decide to 'borrow' and replace the crown jewels. *Dir.* Michael Winner.

Jolson Story, The (1946)   Larry Parks (voice of Jolson), Evelyn Keyes. *Dir.* Alfred E Green.

Journey into Fear (1942)   Joseph Cotten, Dolores del Rio, Orson Welles. Munitions expert finds himself in danger from assassins in Istanbul. *Dir.* Norman Foster.

Journey to Shiloh (1967)   James Caan, Michael Sarrazin, Brenda Scott, Paul Petersen, Don Stroud, Harrison Ford. Seven young Texans leave home to fight in the Civil War. *Dir.* William Hale.

Journey to the Center of the Earth (1959)   James Mason, Arlene Dahl, Pat Boone, Diane Baker. Film ends with the team being catapulted out of Stromboli. *Dir.* Henry Levin.

Judge Dredd (1995)   Sylvester Stallone, Armand Assante, Diane Lane, Ian Dury, Max Von Sydow. Set in Mega City One in AD 2139. *Dir.* Danny Cannon.

Judgment at Nuremberg (1961)   Spencer Tracy, Marlene Dietrich, Burt Lancaster, Richard Widmark, Maximilian Schell, Judy Garland, Montgomery Clift, William Shatner. *Dir.* Stanley Kramer.

Judgment in Berlin (1988)   Martin Sheen (Herbert J Stern), Sam Wanamaker (Bernard Hellring). Director is Sean Penn's father. *Dir.* Leo Penn.

Juggernaut (1974)   Richard Harris, David Hemmings, Omar Sharif, Anthony Hopkins. Transatlantic liner is threatened by a mad bomber. *Dir.* Richard Lester.

Julia (1977)   Jane Fonda, Vanessa Redgrave, Jason Robards Jnr, Maximilian Schell, Hal Holbrook. Based on Lillian Hellman's book *Pentimento*. *Dir.* Fred Zinnemann.

Julius Caesar (1953)   John Gielgud, Marlon Brando, James Mason, Greer Garson, Deborah Kerr. *Dir.* Joseph L Mankiewicz.

Jumanji (1995)   Robin Williams, Bonnie Hunt, Kirsten Dunst. Two children play a mysterious board game that releases, after 25 years, a child and some ferocious animals. *Dir.* Joe Johnston.

Jumpin' Jack Flash (1986)   Whoopi Goldberg (Terry Doolittle), Tracey Ullman, James Belushi, Jonathan Pryce. *Dir.* Penny Marshall.

Jungle Fever (1991)   Wesley Snipes (Flipper Purify), Annabella Sciorra (Angela Tucci), Spike Lee (Cyrus), Anthony Quinn (Lou Carbone), Samuel L Jackson (Gator Purify). *Dir.* Spike Lee.

Jurassic Park (1993)   Richard Attenborough, Jeff Goldblum, Sam Neill, Laura Dern, Samuel L Jackson, Bob Peck. *Dir.* Steven Spielberg.

Jurassic Park III (2001)   Sam Neill (Dr Alan Grant), William H Macy, Tea Leoni, Laura Dern. *Dir.* Joe Johnston.

Just a Gigolo (1978)   David Bowie, Sydne Rome, Kim Novak, Marlene Dietrich, David Hemmings, Curt Jurgens. *Dir.* David Hemmings.

K-9 (1989)   James Belushi (Thomas Dooley), Mel Harris (Tracy), Kevin Tighe (Lyman). Not the same K-9 as in *Dr Who*. *Dir.* Rod Daniel.

K-19: The Widowmaker (2002)   Harrison Ford (Captain Alexi Vostrikov), Sam Spruell, Liam Neeson (Mikhail Polenin), Peter Sarsgaard (Vadim Ratchenko), George Anton (Konstantin Poliansky), Steve Cumyn, Steve Nicholson, Chris Redman, Tygh Runyan. Based on a true-life story which follows the fate of Captain Alexi Vostrikov who, at the height of the Cold War, is ordered to take over command of nuclear missile submarine K-19, pride of the Soviet Navy. His assignment: prepare the K-19 for sea and take her out on patrol – no matter what the cost. But problems with the K-19 arise that may lead to a core meltdown and explosion that will certainly kill all aboard, and possibly trigger nuclear war. In a daring act of heroism, Vostrikov must choose between his orders from the Kremlin and the lives of his men and his country. *Dir*. Kathryn Bigelow.

Kaleidoscope (1966)   Warren Beatty, Susannah York, Clive Revill, Eric Porter. Playboy breaks into card factory to mark the cards and so enable him to clean up. *Dir*. Jack Smight.

Kansas City (1996)   Jennifer Jason Leigh, Miranda Richardson, Harry Belafonte. Woman kidnaps a politician's drug addicted wife in a bid to get her husband released by the gangsters holding him. *Dir*. Robert Altman.

Karate Kid, The (1984)   Ralph Macchio (Daniel), Pat Morita (Miyagi), Elisabeth Shue (Ali), Martin Kove (Kreese), William Zabka (Johnny). *Dir*. John G Avildsen.

Karate Kid Part II, The (1986)   Ralph Macchio, Pat Morita, Nobu McCarthy (Yukie), Danny Kamekona (Sato). *Dir*. John G. Avildsen.

Karate Kid III, The (1989)   Ralph Macchio, Pat Morita (Miyagi), Robyn Lively (Jessica Andrews). *Dir*. John G Avildsen.

Kate and Leopold (2001)   Meg Ryan (Kate McKay), Hugh Jackman (Leopold), Liev Schreiber, Natasha Lyonne, Breckin Meyer. An English duke is transported from 1876 to the present day and falls in love. *Dir*. James Mangold.

Kelly's Heroes (1970)   Clint Eastwood, Telly Savalas, Don Rickles, Donald Sutherland. *Dir*. Brian G Hutton.

Kentuckian, The (1955)   Burt Lancaster, Dianne Foster, Walter Matthau, John McIntire. *Dir*. Burt Lancaster.

Kes (1969)   David Bradley, Lynne Perrie, Colin Welland, Brian Glover. *Dir*. Ken Loach.

Key Largo (1948)   Humphrey Bogart, Lauren Bacall, Claire Trevor, Edward G Robinson, Lionel Barrymore. *Dir*. John Huston.

Kickboxer (1989)   Jean Claude Van Damme, Dennis Alexio, Tong Po (Michel Qissi). *Dir*. Mark DiSalle and David Worth.

Kid, The (1921)   Charles Chaplin, Jackie Coogan, Edna Purviance. *Dir*. Charles Chaplin.

Kid for Two Farthings, A (1955)   Celia Johnson, Diana Dors, David Kossoff, Primo Carnera, Sydney Tafler. *Dir*. Carol Reed.

Kid from Brooklyn, The (1946)   Danny Kaye, Virginia Mayo, Eve Arden, Walter Abel. Timid milkman becomes a prizefighter. *Dir*. Norman Z McLeod.

Kid Galahad (1937)   Edward G Robinson, Bette Davis, Humphrey Bogart, Harry Carey. *Dir*. Michael Curtiz.

Kid Galahad (1962)   Elvis Presley, Lola Albright, Gig Young, Charles Bronson. *Dir*. Phil Karlson.

Kidnapped (1971)   Michael Caine, Lawrence Douglas, Trevor Howard, Jack Hawkins, Donald Pleasence, Gordon Jackson. Other versions starred Warner Baxter and Freddie Bartholomew (1938), and Peter Finch and James MacArthur (1959). *Dir*. Delbert Mann.

Kids (1995)   Lee Fitzpatrick, Sarah Henderson, Justin Pearce. Day in the life of teenagers includes sex and skateboarding. *Dir*. Larry Clark.

Kill Bill Vol. 1 (2003)   Uma Thurman (The Bride/Black Mamba), Lucy Liu (O-Ren Ishii/Cottonmouth), Vivica A Fox (Vernita Green/Copperhead), Daryl Hannah (Elle Driver/California Mountain Snake), Michael Madsen (Budd/Sidewinder), David Carradine (Bill), Michael Parks (Sheriff), Sonny Chiba (Hattori Hanzo), Chiaki Kuriyama (Go Go Yubari), Gordon Liu Chia-hui (Johnny Mo). An assassin, left for dead by her former colleagues, awakens from four years in a coma to exact her revenge. *Dir*. Quentin Tarantino.

Kill Bill Vol. 2 (2004)   Uma Thurman (The Bride/Black Mamba), Daryl Hannah (Elle Driver/California Mountain Snake), Michael Madsen (Budd/Sidewinder), David Carradine (Bill), Gordon Liu (Pai-Mei), Michael Parks (Esteban Vihaio), Perla Haney-Jardine (BB), Samuel L Jackson (Rufus), Bo Svenson (Reverend Harmony). An assassin continues seeking her revenge for the murder of her friends. *Dir*. Quentin Tarantino.

Killer: A Journal of Murder (1996)   James Woods (Carl Panzram), Robert Sean Leonard (Henry Lesser). True story set in Leavenworth Prison, Kansas. *Dir*. Tim Metcalfe.

Killers, The (1946)   Burt Lancaster, Edmond O'Brien, Ava Gardner. *Dir*. Robert Siodmak.

Killers, The (1964)   John Cassavetes, Lee Marvin, Clu Gulager, Angie Dickinson, Ronald Reagan. Ronald Reagan's last film and the first in which he played a bad guy. *Dir*. Don Siegel.

Killing Fields, The (1984)   Sam Waterston (Sydney Schanberg), Haing S Ngor (Dith Pran), John Malkovich (Al Rockoff). *Dir*. Roland Joffé.

Killing of Sister George, The (1969)   Beryl Reid, Susannah York, Coral Browne, Patricia Medina, Roland Fraser. *Dir*. Robert Aldrich.

Kind Hearts and Coronets (1949)   Dennis Price, Alec Guinness, Valerie Hobson, Joan Greenwood, Arthur Lowe. Alec Guinness plays the 8 members of the D'Ascoyne family. *Dir*. Robert Hamer.

Kind of Loving, A (1962)   Alan Bates, June Ritchie, Thora Hird, Bert Palmer. Keith Waterhouse & Willis Hall adapted Stan Barstow's story. *Dir*. John Schlesinger.

Kindergarten Cop (1990)   Arnold Schwarzenegger (John Kimble), Penelope Ann Miller (Joyce Paulmarie), Pamela Reed (Phoebe O'Hara), Linda Hunt (Miss Schlowski). *Dir*. Ivan Reitman.

King and I, The (1956)   Yul Brynner, Deborah Kerr, Rita Moreno. *Dir*. Walter Lang.

King and I, The (1999)   Voices of Miranda Richardson, Ian Richardson, Martin Vidnovic, Darrell Hammond. *Dir*. Richard Rich.

King David (1985)   Richard Gere (David), Edward Woodward (Saul), Alice Krige (Bathsheba), Dennis Quilley (Samuel). *Dir*. Bruce Beresford.

King Kong (1933)   Fay Wray, Robert Armstrong (Carl Denham), Bruce Cabot. *Dir*. Merian C Cooper & Ernest B Schoedsnack.

King Kong (1976)   Jeff Bridges, Charles Grodin, Jessica Lange. This Dino de Laurentiis production was something of a spoof. *Dir*. John Guillermin.

King of Comedy, The (1983)   Robert De Niro (Rupert Pupkin), Jerry Lewis (Jerry Langford), Diahnne Abbott (Rita). *Dir*. Martin Scorsese.

King of Kings (1961)   Jeffrey Hunter, Robert Ryan, Siobhan McKenna. *Dir*. Nicholas Ray.

King Ralph (1991)   John Goodman (Ralph Jones), Peter O'Toole (Sir Cedric Willingham), John Hurt (Lord Graves), Joely Richardson (Princess Anna), Leslie Phillips (Gordon), Julian Glover (King Gustav), Judy Parfitt (Queen Katherine). The whole of the Royal Family are wiped out, leaving a lounge pianist as King. *Dir*. David S Ward.

King Rat (1965)   George Segal, Tom Courtenay, John Mills, James Fox, Leonard Rossiter. Based on James Clavell novel about collaboration in Changi POW camp during WW2. *Dir*. Bryan Forbes.

King Solomon's Mines (1950)   Stewart Granger, Deborah Kerr, Richard Carlson. *Dir*. Compton Bennett.

CINEMA

King Solomon's Mines (1985)　Richard Chamberlain, Sharon Stone, Herbert Lom, John Rhys-Davies. *Dir.* J Lee Thompson.

King's Row (1941)　Ann Sheridan, Robert Cummings, Ronald Reagan (Drake), Claude Rains. Reagan took the name of his autobiography from a line in this film. *Dir.* Sam Wood.

Kinsey (2004)　Liam Neeson (Alfred Kinsey), Laura Linney (Clara McMillen), Chris O'Donnell (Wardell Pomeroy), Peter Sarsgaard (Clyde Martin), Timothy Hutton (Paul Gebhard), John Lithgow (Alfred Seguine Kinsey), Tim Curry (Thurman Rice). Biopic of Alfred Kinsey, a pioneer in the area of human sexuality research. *Dir.* Bill Condon.

Kipps (1941)　Michael Redgrave, Phyllis Calvert, Diana Wynyard, Michael Wilding. Later turned into a musical as *Half a Sixpence*. *Dir.* Carol Reed.

Kismet (1955)　Howard Keel, Ann Blyth, Vic Damone, Sebastian Cabot. Musical based on Borodin. *Dir.* Vincente Minnelli.

Kiss Me Kate (1953)　Howard Keel, Kathryn Grayson, Ann Miller, Keenan Wynn. Musical version of *The Taming of the Shrew*. *Dir.* George Sidney.

Kiss of the Spider Woman (1985)　William Hurt (Molina), Raul Julia (Valentin), Sonia Braga (Leni Lamaison / Marta). Flamboyant gay shares South American prison cell with a radical activist. *Dir.* Hector Babenco.

Kissin' Cousins (1963)　Elvis Presley, Arthur O'Connell, Glenda Farrell, Jack Albertson. Presley plays 2 parts. *Dir.* Gene Nelson.

Kitty Foyle (1940)　Ginger Rogers, Dennis Morgan, James Craig, Eduardo Ciannelli. *Dir.* Sam Wood.

Klansman, The (1974)　Lee Marvin, Richard Burton, Cameron Mitchell, OJ Simpson, Linda Evans. *Dir.* Terence Young.

Klute (1971)　Jane Fonda, Donald Sutherland, Roy Scheider. *Dir.* Alan J Pakula.

Knack, The (1965)　Michael Crawford, Ray Brooks, Rita Tushingham. *Dir.* Richard Lester.

Knight's Tale, A (2001)　Heath Ledger, Rufus Sewell, Paul Bettany (Chaucer), Laura Fraser, Mark Addy. *Dir.* Brian Helgeland.

Kotch (1971)　Walter Matthau, Deborah Winter. *Dir.* Jack Lemmon.

Krakatoa, East of Java (1968)　Maximilian Schell, Diane Baker, Brian Keith, Rossano Brazzi, Sal Mineo. Krakatoa is actually west of Java. *Dir.* Bernard Kowalski.

Kramer versus Kramer (1979)　Dustin Hoffman, Justin Henry, Meryl Streep, Jane Alexander, Howard Duff. Based on an Avery Corman novel. *Dir.* Robert Benton.

Krays, The (1990)　Gary Kemp (Ronnie), Martin Kemp (Reggie), Billie Whitelaw (Violet), Susan Fleetwood (Rose), Jimmy Jewell (Cannonball Lee), Tom Bell (Jack 'The Hat' McVitie). *Dir.* Peter Medak.

L-Shaped Room, The (1962)　Leslie Caron, Tom Bell, Brock Peters, Cicely Courtneidge, Bernard Lee, Avis Bunnage, Pat Phoenix, Emlyn Williams. *Dir.* Bryan Forbes.

La Bamba (1987)　Lou Diamond Phillips (Ritchie Valens), Esai Morales (Bob Morales), Rosana De Soto (Connie Valenzuela). *Dir.* Luis Valdez.

LA Confidential (1997)　Danny De Vito (Sid Hudgens), Kim Basinger (Lynn Bracken), Kevin Spacey (Jack Vincennes), Russell Crowe (Bud White), Guy Pearce (Ed Exley). Hooker with a facial similarity to Veronica Lake gets mixed up in murder investigation. *Dir.* Curtis Hanson.

LA Story (1991)　Steve Martin (Harris K Telemacher), Victoria Tennant (Sara McDowel), Iman (Cynthia), Richard E Grant (Roland), Marilu Henner (Trudi), Patrick Stewart (Maître d' at L'Idiot). *Dir.* Mick Jackson.

Labyrinth (1986)　David Bowie (Jareth), Jennifer Connelly (Sarah), Toby Froud (Toby), Shelley Thompson (Stepmother). *Dir.* Jim Henson.

Lady Caroline Lamb (1972)　Sarah Miles, Jon Finch, Richard Chamberlain (Byron), Margaret Leighton, John Mills (Canning), Ralph Richardson (George III), Laurence Olivier (Wellington). *Dir.* Robert Bolt.

Lady Sings the Blues (1972)　Diana Ross (Billie Holliday), Billy Dee Williams, Richard Pryor. *Dir.* Sidney J Furie.

Lady Vanishes, The (1938)　Margaret Lockwood, Michael Redgrave, Dame May Whitty, Googie Withers. A 1979 remake starring Cybill Shepherd and Elliott Gould flopped. *Dir.* Alfred Hitchcock.

Lady with the Lamp, The (1951)　Anna Neagle, Michael Wilding. *Dir.* Herbert Wilcox.

Ladykillers, The (1955)　Alec Guinness, Katie Johnson, Peter Sellers, Herbert Lom, Frankie Howerd. *Dir.* Alexander Mackendrick.

Lamerica (1994)　Enrico Lo Verso, Michele Placido. *Dir.* Gianni Amelio.

Land and Freedom (1995)　Ian Hart, Rosana Pastor, Iciar Bollain. *Dir.* Ken Loach.

Lantana (2001)　Anthony LaPaglia, Geoffrey Rush, Barbara Hershey, Kerry Armstrong. *Dir.* Ray Lawrence.

Lara Croft: Tomb Raider (2001)　Angelina Jolie (Lara), Iain Glen, Noah Taylor, Leslie Philips, Chris Barrie, Daniel Craig. *Dir.* Simon West. Angelina Jolie's father Jon Voight is cast as her on-screen father in this film.

Lassie Come Home (1943)　Roddy McDowall, Elizabeth Taylor, Donald Crisp. Based on an Eric Knight story. *Dir.* Fred M Wilcox.

Last Action Hero, The (1993)　Arnold Schwarzenegger, Mercedes Ruehl, F Murray Abraham, Art Carney, Anthony Quinn. *Dir.* John McTiernan.

Last Boy Scout, The (1992)　Bruce Willis (Joe Hallenbeck), Damon Wayans (Jimmy Dix), Chelsea Field (Sarah Hallenbeck). *Dir.* Tony Scott.

Last Dance (1996)　Sharon Stone (Cindy Liggett), Rob Morrow (Rick Hayes). *Dir.* Bruce Beresford.

Last Detail, The (1973)　Jack Nicholson, Otis Young, Randy Quaid, Clifton James. *Dir.* Hal Ashby.

Last Emperor, The (1987)　John Lone (Pu Yi), Peter O'Toole (RJ), Joan Chen (Wan Jung). *Dir.* Bernardo Bertolucci.

Last Exit to Brooklyn (1990)　Stephen Lang (Harry Black), Jennifer Jason Leigh (Tralala), Burt Young (Big Joe), Peter Dobson (Vinnie). *Dir.* Uli Edel.

Last Hard Men, The (1976)　Charlton Heston, James Coburn, Barbara Hershey, Christopher Mitchum. *Dir.* Andrew V McLaglen.

Last Man Standing (1996)　Bruce Willis, Christopher Walken, Bruce Dern, Alexandra Powers. Set in Texas during the Depression of the 1930s, it concerns a gunman on the run and rival bootleggers. *Dir.* Walter Hill.

Last of the Dogmen (1995)　Tom Berenger, Barbara Hershey, Kurtwood Smith, Steve Reevis. Bounty hunter discovers a group of Cheyenne in Montana. *Dir.* Tab Murphy.

Last of the Mohicans, The (1992)　Daniel Day-Lewis (Hawkeye), Madeleine Stowe (Cora), Russell Means (Chingachgook), Eric Schweig (Uncas). *Dir.* Michael Mann.

Last Orders (2001)　Michael Caine (Jack), Bob Hoskins (Ray), Tom Courtenay (Vic), David Hemmings (Lenny), Ray Winstone (Vince), Helen

Mirren (Amy). Three elderly Londoners reminisce on past lives and loves as they gather for a trip to the seaside to scatter the ashes of a mutual friend. Based on a novel by Graham Swift. *Dir.* Fred Schepisi.

Last Picture Show, The (1971) Timothy Bottoms, Jeff Bridges, Cybill Shepherd, Ben Johnson, Cloris Leachman, Ellen Burstyn. *Dir.* Peter Bogdanovich.

Last Seduction, The (1994) Linda Fiorentino, Peter Berg, Bill Nunn, Bill Pullman. Woman leaves her husband taking with her a million dollars he made from a drug deal. *Dir.* John Dahl.

Last Summer (1969) Barbara Hershey, Richard Thomas, Bruce Davison, Cathy Burns, Ralph Waite. *Dir.* Frank Perry.

Last Tango in Paris (1972) Marlon Brando, Maria Schneider. *Dir.* Bernardo Bertolucci.

Last Temptation of Christ, The (1988) Willem Dafoe (Jesus), Harvey Keitel (Judas), Barbara Hershey (Mary Magdalene), David Bowie (Pontius Pilate). *Dir.* Martin Scorsese.

Last Tycoon, The (1976) Robert De Niro, Robert Mitchum, Tony Curtis, Jeanne Moreau, Jack Nicholson, Donald Pleasence. *Dir.* Elia Kazan.

Lavender Hill Mob, The (1951) Alec Guinness, Stanley Holloway, Sid James, Alfie Bass, Audrey Hepburn. Bank clerk masterminds bullion robbery by moulding Eiffel Towers in gold to be smuggled to France. *Dir.* Charles Crichton.

Lawrence of Arabia (1962) Peter O'Toole, Omar Sharif, Arthur Kennedy, Jack Hawkins, Alec Guinness. Screenplay by Robert Bolt. *Dir.* David Lean.

Le Fils (2002) Olivier Gourmet (Olivier), Morgan Marinne (Francis), Isabella Soupart (Magali). A carpentry teacher working with delinquent boys takes on a youth who killed his son. *Dir.* Jean-Pierre Dardenne.

League of Gentlemen, The (1960) Jack Hawkins, Richard Attenborough, Roger Livesey, Bryan Forbes, Nigel Patrick, Nanette Newman. *Dir.* Basil Dearden.

Leaving Las Vegas (1995) Nicolas Cage, Elisabeth Shue, Julian Sands, Richard Lewis. Alcoholic writer goes to Las Vegas to drink himself to death. *Dir.* Mike Figgis.

Left-Handed Gun, The (1958) Paul Newman (Billy the Kid), John Dehner (Pat Garrett). *Dir.* Arthur Penn.

Legally Blonde (2001) Reese Witherspoon, Luke Wilson, Selma Blair, Matthew Davis, Victor Garber. *Dir.* Robert Luketic.

Legend of the Lone Ranger, The (1981) Klinton Spilsbury, Michael Horse, Christopher Lloyd, Matt Clark. *Dir.* William A Fraker.

Lemon Drop Kid, The (1951) Bob Hope, Marilyn Maxwell, Lloyd Nolan. Based on a Damon Runyon story. *Dir.* Sidney Lanfield.

Lemony Snicket: A Series of Unfortunate Events (2004) Jim Carrey (Count Olaf), Meryl Streep (Aunt Josephine), Jude Law (Lemony Snicket (voice)), Emily Browning (Violet Baudelaire), Lia Aiken (Klaus Baudelaire), Timothy Spall (Mr Poe), Billy Connolly (Uncle Monty). Three wealthy children's parents are killed in a fire. When they are sent to a distant relative, they find out that he is plotting to kill them and seize their fortune. Based on the books of Daniel Handler. *Dir.* Brad Silberling.

Lenny (1974) Dustin Hoffman (Lennie Bruce), Valerie Perrine. *Dir.* Bob Fosse.

Les Misérables (1995) Jean-Paul Belmondo, Michel Boujenah, Rufus. *Dir.* Claude Lelouch.

Lethal Weapon (1987) Mel Gibson (Martin Riggs), Danny Glover (Roger Murtaugh), Gary Busey (Joshua). Vietnam veteran turned cop is unhinged by his wife's death and has a death wish. *Dir.* Richard Donner.

Lethal Weapon 2 (1989) Mel Gibson, Danny Glover, Joe Pesci (Leo Getz), Patsy Kensit (Rika Van Den Haas), Joss Ackland. South African drug runners unfortunately meet Martin Riggs. *Dir.* Richard Donner.

Lethal Weapon 3 (1992) Mel Gibson, Danny Glover, Joe Pesci, Rene Russo (Lorna Cole). *Dir.* Richard Donner.

Let's Make Love (1960) Yves Montand, Marilyn Monroe, Tony Randall, Wilfrid Hyde-White, Frankie Vaughan, Bing Crosby, Gene Kelly. Multi-millionaire learns he is to be burlesqued, so joins the cast. *Dir.* George Cukor.

Letter to Brezhnev (1985) Alfred Molina (Sergei), Peter Firth (Peter), Margi Clarke (Teresa), Tracy Lea (Tracy). Liverpool lass falls in love with a Russian sailor. *Dir.* Chris Bernard.

Liar Liar (1997) Jim Carrey (Fletcher Reede), Amanda Donohoe, Justin Cooper, Jennifer Tilly. (Out-takes shown as end credits roll.) *Dir.* Tom Shadyac.

Licence to Kill (1989) Timothy Dalton, Carey Lowell (Pam Bouvier), Anthony Zerbe (Milton Krest), Robert Davi (Frank Sanchez), Caroline Bliss (Moneypenny), Robert Brown (M), Talisa Soto (Lupe Lamora). Book title: *Licence Revoked.* Title song by Gladys Knight. *Dir.* John Glen.

Licensed to Kill (1965) Tom Adams, Veronica Hurst, Karel Stepanek. US title: *The Second Best Secret Agent in the Whole Wide World. Dir.* Lindsay Shonteff.

Life Aquatic With Steve Zissou, The (2004) Bill Murray (Steve Zissou), Owen Wilson (Ned Plimpton), Cate Blanchett (Jane Winslett-Richardson), Anjelica Huston (Eleanor Zissou), Willem Dafoe (Klaus Daimler), Jeff Goldblum (Alistair Hennessey), Michael Gambon (Oseary Drakoulias). Seeking revenge on the mythical shark that killed his partner, oceanographer Zissou assembles a crew including his estranged wife (Huston), a journalist (Blanchett), and a man who may or may not be his son (Wilson). *Dir.* Wes Anderson.

Life at the Top (1965) Laurence Harvey (Joe Lampton), Jean Simmons, Honor Blackman, Michael Craig, Margaret Johnston. *Dir.* Ted Kotcheff.

Life Is Beautiful (1997) Roberto Benigni, Nicoletta Braschi, Giustino Durano, Horst Buchholz. *Dir.* Roberto Benigni.

Lilo & Stitch (2002) Voices of Daveigh Chase (Lilo), Chris Sanders (Stitch), Tia Carrere, Zoe Caldwell, Ving Rhames. Lilo is a young Hawaiian girl who adopts a 'dog' named Stitch who is actually an alien genetic experiment gone horribly awry. Stitch has crash-landed on Earth, where he immediately begins wreaking havoc. Through her generosity, Lilo teaches Stitch the one thing he wasn't designed to do: to care about others. *Dir.* Dean DeBlois and Chris Sanders.

Limelight (1952) Charlie Chaplin, Claire Bloom, Buster Keaton, Sydney Chaplin. *Dir.* Charlie Chaplin.

Lion in Winter, The (1968) Katharine Hepburn (Eleanor of Aquitaine), Peter O'Toole (Henry II), Anthony Hopkins. *Dir.* Anthony Harvey.

Lion King, The (1994) Voices of Matthew Broderick, Rowan Atkinson, Whoopi Goldberg, Jeremy Irons, Robert Guillaume, James Earl Jones. Songs include: 'Can You Feel the Love Tonight', 'Circle of Life' & 'Hakuna Matata'. (Music by Elton John, lyrics by Tim Rice.) *Dir.* Roger Allers.

Liquidator, The (1965) Rod Taylor, Trevor Howard, David Tomlinson, Wilfrid Hyde-White, Derek Nimmo. *Dir.* Jack Cardiff.

CINEMA

List of Adrian Messenger, The (1963)   George C
Scott, Kirk Douglas, Clive Brook, Dana Wynter, Robert
Mitchum, Frank Sinatra, Tony Curtis, Burt Lancaster.
The cameos by the last 4 listed stars are debatable as
they are unrecognisable. *Dir.* John Huston.

Lisztomania (1975)   Roger Daltrey, Sara Kestelman,
Paul Nicholas, Fiona Lewis, Ringo Starr. *Dir.* Ken
Russell.

Little Big Man (1970)   Dustin Hoffman, Martin
Balsam, Faye Dunaway, Chief Dan George. *Dir.*
Arthur Penn.

Little Caesar (1931)   Edward G Robinson, Douglas
Fairbanks Jnr, Glenda Farrell. *Dir.* Mervyn Le Roy.

Little Dorrit (1987)   Derek Jacobi (Arthur Clennam),
Alec Guinness (William Dorrit), Max Wall
(Flintwinch). There are 211 people named on the
cast list, which is a record for a British film. *Dir.*
Christine Edzard.

Little Foxes, The (1941)   Bette Davis, Herbert
Marshall, Teresa Wright, Dan Duryea. Based on a
Lillian Hellman story. *Dir.* William Wyler.

Little Giants (1994)   Rick Moranis, Ed O'Neil, John
Madden. Wimp decides to create a young football
team full of misfits. *Dir.* Duwayne Dunham.

Little Shop of Horrors (1986)   Rick Moranis
(Seymour Krelborn), Ellen Greene (Audrey), Vincent
Gardenia (Mushnik), Steve Martin (Orin Scrivello,
DDS). Voice of the plant (Audrey II): Levi Stubbs of
the Four Tops. *Dir.* Frank Oz.

Little Women (1933)   Katharine Hepburn, Paul
Lukas, Joan Bennett, Frances Dee, Spring Byington.
Dir. George Cukor.

Little Women (1949)   June Allyson, Elizabeth Taylor,
Peter Lawford, Margaret O'Brien, Janet Leigh, Mary
Astor. *Dir.* Mervyn Le Roy.

Little Women (1994)   Winona Ryder, Gabriel Byrne,
Trini Alvarado, Samantha Mathis, Susan Sarandon.
Dir. Gillian Armstrong.

Live and Let Die (1973)   Roger Moore, Yaphet Kotto
(Dr Kananga), Jane Seymour (Solitaire). Paul
McCartney wrote and performed theme song.
Dir. Guy Hamilton.

Living Daylights (1987)   Timothy Dalton, Maryam
d'Abo (Kara Milovy), Jeroen Krabbe (Gen Georgi
Koskov), Joe Don Baker (Brad Whitaker), John
Rhys-Davies (Gen Leonid Pushkin), Robert Brown
(M), Desmond Llewellyn (Q), Caroline Bliss
(Moneypenny), John Terry (Felix Leiter). Theme
Song by A-Ha. *Dir.* John Glen.

Local Hero (1983)   Burt Lancaster (Happer), Peter
Riegert (Mac), John Gordon Sinclair (Ricky). TV
series *Northern Exposure* was strongly influenced by
this film. *Dir.* Bill Forsyth.

Loch Ness (1995)   Ted Danson, Joely Richardson,
Ian Holm, John Savident. US scientist tries to
debunk the monster myth. *Dir.* John Henderson.

Lock Up (1989)   Sylvester Stallone (Frank Leone),
Donald Sutherland (Warden Drumgoole). *Dir.* John
Flynn.

Logan's Run (1976)   Michael York, Richard Jordan,
Jenny Agutter, Farrah Fawcett-Majors, Peter Ustinov.
Based on SF novel by William F Nolan. *Dir.* Michael
Anderson.

Lolita (1962)   James Mason, Shelley Winters, Sue
Lyon, Peter Sellers. Lolita is 14 years old.
Dir. Stanley Kubrick.

London Kills Me (1991)   Justin Chadwick, Steven
Mackintosh, Emer McCourt, Roshan Seth, Fiona
Shaw. Down on his luck drug pusher is told he can
have a job as a waiter if he can acquire a decent pair
of shoes. *Dir.* Hanif Kureishi.

Loneliness of the Long Distance Runner, The
(1962)   Tom Courtenay, Michael Redgrave, James
Bolam, Avis Bunnage. *Dir.* Tony Richardson.

Lonely Are the Brave (1962)   Kirk Douglas, Walter
Matthau, Gena Rowlands, Carroll O'Connor. Modern
technology is pitted against a last rebel cowboy.
Dir. David Miller.

Long and the Short and the Tall, The (1960)
Laurence Harvey, Richard Todd, David McCallum,
Richard Harris. US title: *Jungle Fighters*. *Dir.* Leslie
Norman.

Long Good Friday, The (1980)   Bob Hoskins, Helen
Mirren, Dave King, Bryan Marshall, Eddie
Constantine, Stephen Davis. *Dir.* John Mackenzie.

Long Goodbye, The (1973)   Elliott Gould, Nina Van
Pallandt, Sterling Hayden, Mark Rydell, Henry
Gibson. *Dir.* Robert Altman.

Long Kiss Goodnight, The (1996)   Geena Davis,
Samuel L Jackson, Patrick Malahide. *Dir.* Renny
Harlin.

Long Riders, The (1980)   Stacy Keach, James
Keach, David Carradine, Keith Carradine, Robert
Carradine, Dennis Quaid, Randy Quaid. Story of
the Younger, Miller and James boys. *Dir.* Walter
Hill.

Longest Day, The (1962)   John Wayne, Robert
Mitchum, Henry Fonda, Robert Ryan, Roddy
McDowall, Robert Wagner, Paul Anka, Fabian,
Jeffrey Hunter, Rod Steiger, Red Buttons, Richard
Burton, Sean Connery. *Dir.* Andrew Marton.

Look Back in Anger (1959)   Richard Burton, Mary
Ure, Claire Bloom, Edith Evans, Donald Pleasence.
Dir. Tony Richardson.

Look Who's Talking (1989)   John Travolta (James),
Kirstie Alley (Mollie), Olympia Dukakis (Rosie),
George Segal (Albert). Bruce Willis was the voice of
Mikey. *Dir.* Amy Heckerling.

Look Who's Talking Too (1990)   John Travolta,
Kirstie Alley, Olympia Dukakis, Roseanne Arnold
(voice of Julie), Mel Brooks (voice of Mr Toilet
Man), Bruce Willis (voice of Mikey). *Dir.* Amy
Heckerling.

Loot (1970)   Richard Attenborough, Lee Remick,
Hywel Bennett, Milo O'Shea, Dick Emery. *Dir.* Silvio
Narizzano.

Lord of the Flies (1963)   James Aubrey, Tom Chapin,
Hugh Edwards. Remake in 1990 was directed by
Harry Hook. *Dir.* Peter Brook.

Lord of the Rings (1978)   Cartoon version of
Tolkien's book with voices of Christopher Guard and
John Hurt. *Dir.* Ralph Bakshi.

Lord of the Rings: The Fellowship of the Ring, The
(2001)   Ian McKellen (Gandalf), Elijah Wood (Frodo
Baggins), Viggo Mortensen (Aragorn), Sean Astin
(Sam), Cate Blanchett (Galadriel), Sean Bean
(Boromir), John Rhys-Davies (Gimli), Liv Tyler
(Arwen), Billy Boyd (Pippin), Christopher Lee
(Saruman), Ian Holm (Bilbo Baggins), Andy Serkis
(Gollum), Dominic Monaghan (Merry), Orlando
Bloom (Legolas). Multiple Oscar winner concerning
a hobbit who inherits a magic ring that could
enslave all the people of Middle Earth unless it is
destroyed. *Dir.* Peter Jackson.

Lord of the Rings: The Return of the King, The
(2003)   The third chapter in Tolkien's trilogy is the
longest and most spectacular of them all. The former
Fellowship of the Ring prepare for the final battle for
Middle Earth, while the hobbits Frodo and Sam
approach Mount Doom to destroy the cursed ring.
The usual cast is reprised without Sean Bean, Brad
Dourif, Christopher Lee, Karl Urban and David
Wenham. *Dir.* Peter Jackson.

Lord of the Rings: The Two Towers, The (2002) The second chapter in the JRR Tolkien saga. The hobbits Frodo and Sam brave terrible dangers in an attempt to have the evil ring destroyed, while Aragorn, Legolas and their allies strive to rescue the abducted hobbits Pippin and Merry from the clutches of evil. The great wizard Gandalf also makes his miraculous return to aid in the struggle against the united towers of Saruman and Sauron (Sala Baker). *The Two Towers* has the same cast as *The Fellowship of the Ring* but new characters include Bernard Hill's Théoden, David Wenham's Faramir, Karl Urban's Éomer, and Brad Dourif as Grima Wormtongue. *Dir.* Peter Jackson.

Lost Highway (1997) Bill Pullman, Patricia Arquette, Balthazar Getty. *Dir.* David Lynch.

Lost Horizon (1937) Ronald Colman, HB Warner, Thomas Mitchell, Sam Jaffe. Remade in 1972 with Peter Finch in Colman role. *Dir.* Frank Capra.

Lost in Translation (2003) Bill Murray (Bob Harris), Scarlett Johansson (Charlotte), Giovanni Ribisi (John), Anna Faris (Kelly), Fumihiro Hayashi (Charlie), Catherine Lambert (Jazz Singer). A tired actor, making a whisky advert in Tokyo, meets a young married woman and they imagine how their lives could have been different. *Dir.* Sofia Coppola.

Lost Weekend, The (1945) Ray Milland (Don Birnam), Jane Wyman, Howard da Silva. *Dir.* Billy Wilder.

Lost World, The: Jurassic Park (1997) Jeff Goldblum (Dr Ian Malcolm), Julianne Moore, Pete Postlethwaite, Richard Attenborough (John Hammond). *Dir.* Steven Spielberg.

Love Is a Many-Splendored Thing (1955) Jennifer Jones, William Holden, Torin Thatcher. Sammy Fain & Paul Francis Webster won an Academy Award for the title song. *Dir.* Henry King.

Love Me Tender (1956) Richard Egan, Debra Paget, Elvis Presley, Neville Brand, James Drury. *Dir.* Robert D Webb.

Love Me Tonight (1932) Maurice Chevalier, Jeanette MacDonald, Charles Butterworth, Myrna Loy. *Dir.* Rouben Mamoulian.

Love on the Dole (1941) Deborah Kerr, Clifford Evans, George Carney. Based on Walter Greenwood's novel. *Dir.* John Baxter.

Love Story (1970) Ali MacGraw, Ryan O'Neal (Oliver Barrett IV), Ray Milland. 1978 sequel: *Oliver's Story.* *Dir.* Arthur Hiller.

Lust for Life (1956) Kirk Douglas (Vincent Van Gogh), Anthony Quinn (Paul Gauguin). *Dir.* Vincente Minnelli.

Mad Dog and Glory (1992) Robert De Niro, Uma Thurman, Bill Murray. Timid cop is given a present of a beautiful girl for a week by a gangster. *Dir.* John McNaughton.

Mad Max (1979) Mel Gibson, Joanne Samuel. *Dir.* George Miller.

Mad Max 2 (1981) Mel Gibson, Bruce Spence, Vernon Wells. *Dir.* George Miller.

Mad Max beyond Thunderdome (1985) Mel Gibson, Tina Turner, Angelo Rossitto, Helen Buday. *Dir.* George Miller.

Madame Bovary (1949) Jennifer Jones, Van Heflin, James Mason, Louis Jourdan. A 1991 remake starring Isabelle Huppert kept to the original plot a little better. *Dir.* Vincente Minnelli.

Made in America (1993) Whoopi Goldberg, Ted Danson, Will Smith. Black teenager, born by artificial insemination, discovers her father is a white car salesman. *Dir.* Richard Benjamin.

Madness of King George, The (1994) Nigel Hawthorne, Helen Mirren, Ian Holm, Amanda Donohoe, Rupert Everett, Rupert Graves. *Dir.* Nicholas Hytner.

Magic Christian (1969) Peter Sellers, Ringo Starr, Richard Attenborough, Laurence Harvey, Spike Milligan, Raquel Welch, John Cleese. Yul Brynner cameo as a transvestite nightclub singer. *Dir.* Joseph McGrath.

Magnificent Seven, The (1960) Yul Brynner, Steve McQueen, Robert Vaughn, James Coburn, Charles Bronson, Brad Dexter, Horst Buchholz. *Dir.* John Sturges.

Malcolm X (1992) Denzil Washington, Angela Bassett, Albert Hall, Al Freeman Jnr, Spike Lee. Based on the book *Autobiography of Malcolm X as told to Alex Haley. Dir.* Spike Lee.

Mame (1974) Lucille Ball, Beatrice Arthur, Robert Preston, Bruce Davison. *Dir.* Gene Saks.

Man and a Woman, A (1966) Anouk Aimée, Jean-Louis Trintignant. Best Foreign Film Oscar. Concerns a racing driver and a script girl who fall in love. *Dir.* Claude Lelouch.

Man Called Horse, A (1970) Richard Harris, Judith Anderson, Jean Gascon, Manu Tupou. Sequels: *Return of a Man Called Horse* (1976), & *Triumphs of a Man Called Horse* (1984). *Dir.* Elliot Silverstein.

Man for All Seasons, A (1966) Paul Scofield, Wendy Hiller, Susannah York, Robert Shaw, Orson Welles, John Hurt, Corin Redgrave. Events leading to the execution of Sir Thomas More. *Dir.* Fred Zinnemann.

Man in the Iron Mask, The (1939) Louis Hayward, Warren William (D'Artagnan), Alan Hale, Bert Roach, Joseph Schildkraut. King Louis XIV keeps his twin brother prisoner. *Dir.* James Whale.

Man of the Year (1995) Dirk Shafer, Vivian Paxton, Deidra Shafer. Documentary about events surrounding the homosexual Dirk Shafer's awarding of the 1992 *Playgirl* magazine's Man of the Year. *Dir.* Dirk Shafer.

Man Who Came to Dinner, The (1941) Bette Davis, Monty Woolley, Ann Sheridan, Jimmy Durante (spoofing Harpo Marx). *Dir.* William Keighley.

Man Who Could Work Miracles, The (1936) Roland Young, Ralph Richardson, Ernest Thesiger, George Sanders. Based on the HG Wells story. *Dir.* Lothar Mendes.

Man Who Fell to Earth, The (1976) David Bowie, Rip Torn, Candy Clark. *Dir.* Nicolas Roeg.

Man Who Knew too Much, The (1934) Leslie Banks, Edna Best, Peter Lorre. *Dir.* Alfred Hitchcock.

Man Who Knew too Much, The (1956) James Stewart, Doris Day, Bernard Miles. Remake of the 1934 film. *Dir.* Alfred Hitchcock.

Man Who Shot Liberty Valance, The (1962) John Wayne, James Stewart, Lee Marvin, Vera Miles. John Wayne shot Liberty Valance. *Dir.* John Ford.

Man Who Wasn't There, The (2001) Billy Bob Thornton (Ed Crane), Frances McDormand (Doris Crane), Michael Badalucco, James Gandolfini. Set in the 1940s. *Dir.* Joel Coen.

Man Who Would Be King, The (1975) Sean Connery, Michael Caine, Christopher Plummer (Kipling), Shakira Caine, Saeed Jaffrey. Based on a Rudyard Kipling story. *Dir.* John Huston.

Man with the Golden Arm (1956) Frank Sinatra, Kim Novak, Eleanor Parker, Arnold Stang. Golden Arm refers to the card-dealing expertise of the lead character. *Dir.* Otto Preminger.

Man with the Golden Gun (1974) Roger Moore, Christopher Lee (Scaramanga), Britt Ekland (Mary Goodnight), Maud Adams (Andrea Anders), Hervé Villechaize, Clifton James, Richard Loo. Title song performed by Lulu. *Dir.* Guy Hamilton.

CINEMA

Man without a Face, The (1993)   Mel Gibson, Margaret Whitton, Fay Masterson, Viva. Boy remembers how he was helped to enter a military academy by a disfigured former teacher. *Dir*. Mel Gibson.

Manchurian Candidate, The (1962)   Frank Sinatra (Capt./Maj. Bennett Marco), Laurence Harvey (Sgt Raymond Shaw), Janet Leigh (Eugenie Rose Chaney), Angela Lansbury (Mrs Iselin), Henry Silva (Chunjin). A former Korean War veteran is brainwashed by Communists into becoming a political assassin. *Dir*. John Frankenheimer.

Manchurian Candidate, The (2004)   Denzel Washington (Ben Marco), Meryl Streep (Eleanor Shaw), Liev Schreiber (Raymond Shaw), Jon Voight (Senator Thomas Jordan). In the midst of the Gulf War, soldiers are kidnapped and brainwashed for sinister purposes. *Dir*. Jonathan Demme.

Mandy (1952)   Jack Hawkins, Terence Morgan, Phyllis Calvert, Mandy Miller. Little deaf girl is sent to a special school. *Dir*. Alexander Mackendrick.

Manhattan (1979)   Woody Allen, Diane Keaton, Meryl Streep, Mariel Hemingway. *Dir*. Woody Allen.

Manhattan Murder Mystery (1993)   Woody Allen, Alan Alda, Anjelica Huston, Diane Keaton. *Dir*. Woody Allen.

Marathon Man (1976)   Dustin Hoffman, Laurence Olivier, Roy Scheider, William Devane. *Dir*. John Schlesinger.

Maria Full of Grace (2004)   Catalina Sandino Moreno (Maria Alvarez), Yenny Paola Vega (Blanca). A young Colombian girl accepts a risky offer in order to seek her country for the United States. *Dir*. Joshua Marston.

Marnie (1964)   Tippi Hedren, Sean Connery, Martin Gabel, Diane Baker. Rich man marries a kleptomaniac who sees red when she sees red! *Dir*. Alfred Hitchcock.

Mars Attacks! (1996)   Jack Nicholson, Glenn Close, Annette Bening, Michael J Fox, Pierce Brosnan, Rod Steiger, Danny De Vito, Tom Jones. *Dir*. Tim Burton.

Marty (1955)   Ernest Borgnine, Betsy Blair, Jerry Paris. *Dir*. Delbert Mann.

Mary of Scotland (1936)   Katharine Hepburn, Fredric March, Donald Crisp. *Dir*. John Ford.

Mary Poppins (1964)   Julie Andrews, Dick Van Dyke, Glynis Johns, David Tomlinson, Elsa Lanchester, Arthur Treacher. Among many other awards, the song 'Chim Chim Cheree' won the Oscar for Best Song. *Dir*. Robert Stevenson.

Mary Queen of Scots (1971)   Vanessa Redgrave, Glenda Jackson, Trevor Howard, Patrick McGoohan, Nigel Davenport. *Dir*. Charles Jarrott.

M*A*S*H (1970)   Donald Sutherland, Elliott Gould, Sally Kellerman, Robert Duvall, Gary Burghoff. *Dir*. Robert Altman.

Mask, The (1994)   Jim Carrey, Amy Yasbeck, Peter Riegert. *Dir*. Charles Russell.

Master and Commander: The Far Side of the World (2003)   Russell Crowe (Captain Jack Aubrey), Paul Bettany (Dr Stephen Maturin), Billy Boyd (Barrett Bonden), James D'Arcy (First Lt Thomas Pullings), Lee Ingleby (Hollom), George Innes (Joe Plaice), Mark Lewis Jones (Mr Hogg), Chris Larkin (Captain Howard, Royal Marines), David Threlfall (Killick), Max Pirkis (Lord Blakeney). Based on the Patrick O'Brian novels. Although his ship is almost destroyed in an attack, a British sea captain chases a superior French warship across the oceans. *Dir*. Peter Weir.

Matilda (1997)   Danny De Vito, Mara Wilson (Matilda), Rhea Perlman, Pam Ferris. Based on Roald Dahl's bestseller. *Dir*. Danny De Vito.

Matter of Life and Death, A (1946)   David Niven, Roger Livesey, Kim Hunter, Marius Goring, Raymond Massey, Abraham Sofaer. US title: *Stairway to Heaven*. *Dir*. Michael Powell.

Maverick (1994)   Mel Gibson, Jodie Foster, James Garner, Graham Greene, James Coburn, Alfred Molina. *Dir*. Richard Donner.

Mean Creek (2004)   Rory Culkin (Sam), Ryan Kelley (Clyde), Scott Mechlowicz (Marty 'Martini' Blank), Trevor Morgan (Rocky). When a teenager is bullied, his brother and friends lure the bully into the woods to seek revenge. *Dir*. Jacob Aaron Estes.

Mean Streets (1973)   Robert De Niro, Harvey Keitel, Amy Robinson. *Dir*. Martin Scorsese.

Meet Me in St Louis (1944)   Judy Garland, Margaret O'Brien, Tom Drake, Mary Astor. *Dir*. Vincente Minnelli.

Men, The (1950)   Marlon Brando, Teresa Wright, Everett Sloane, Jack Webb. Reissue title: *Battle Stripe*. *Dir*. Fred Zinnemann.

Men in Black II (2002)   Tommy Lee Jones, Will Smith, Rip Torn. Sequel to *MIB (Men In Black)*. *Dir*. Barry Sonnenfeld.

Men of Respect (1990)   John Turturro, Katherine Borowitz, Dennis Farina, Peter Boyle, Rod Steiger. Gangster setting for Shakespeare's *Macbeth*. *Dir*. William Reilly.

Mercury Rising (1998)   Bruce Willis, Alec Baldwin, Miko Hughes, Chi McBride, Kim Dickens, Robert Stanton, Carrie Preston, Bodhi Pine Elfman, LL Ginter, John Carroll Lynch, Peter Stormare. *Dir*. Harold Becker.

Mermaids (1990)   Cher, Bob Hoskins, Winona Ryder. Daughter, torn between becoming a nun and her feelings for a handsome boy, resolves her difficulties with her flirtatious mother. *Dir*. Richard Benjamin.

Merry Christmas, Mr Lawrence (1982)   David Bowie, Tom Conti, Ryuichi Sakamoto, Takeshi. *Dir*. Nagisa Oshima.

Metro (1997)   Eddie Murphy (Scott Roper), Michael Rapaport, Kim Miyori. *Dir*. Thomas Carter.

Mexican, The (2001)   Brad Pitt (Jerry Welbach), Julia Roberts (Samantha), James Gandolfini (Leroy). Incompetent crook is sent to Mexico to bring back a priceless pistol for his boss whilst his girlfriend is held as ransom. Gene Hackman as Arnold Margolese is uncredited. *Dir*. Gore Verbinski.

Miami Rhapsody (1995)   Sarah Jessica Parker, Gil Bellows, Antonio Banderas, Mia Farrow, Paul Mazursky, Naomi Campbell. Woman contemplating marriage observes the marital errors being committed by her siblings and friends. *Dir*. David Frankel.

MIB (Men in Black), (1997)   Tommy Lee Jones (K), Will Smith (J), Linda Fiorentino (Dr Weaver), Rip Torn (Zed). SF film in which Will Smith performs title track & Snoop Doggy Dogg the soundtrack album. *Dir*. Barry Sonnenfeld.

Michael Collins (1996)   Liam Neeson (Michael Collins), Aidan Quinn (Harry Boland), Julia Roberts (Kitty Kiernan). *Dir*. Neil Jordan.

Microcosmos (1996)   French documentary film revolving around stag beetles' attempts to gain control of a twig. *Dir*. Marie Perennau & Claude Nuridsany.

Midnight Cowboy (1969)   Dustin Hoffman, Jon Voight, Brenda Vaccaro, Sylvia Miles. *Dir*. John Schlesinger.

Midnight Express (1978)   John Hurt, Brad Davis, Randy Quaid, Bo Hopkins. *Dir*. Alan Parker.

Midsummer Night's Dream, A (1935)   James Cagney, Dick Powell, Jean Muir, Mickey Rooney, Olivia de Havilland. *Dir*. Max Reinhardt.

Midsummer Night's Dream, A (1996) Lindsay Duncan, Alex Jennings, Alfred Burke. *Dir.* Adrian Noble.

Mighty, The (1998) Sharon Stone, Gena Rowlands Harry Dean Stanton, Gillian Anderson, Meatloaf. *Dir.* Peter Chelsom.

Mighty Aphrodite (1995) Woody Allen, Helena Bonham Carter, Mira Sorvino, F Murray Abraham, Olympia Dukakis, Peter Weller, Claire Bloom, Michael Rapaport. Sportswriter's attempt to rescue the mother of his adopted son from life as a prostitute. *Dir.* Woody Allen.

Mighty Ducks, The (1992) Emilio Estevez, Joss Ackland, Lane Smith, Heidi King. Lawyer on community service for drink-driving adopts a hockey team. GB title: *Champions*. *Dir.* Stephen Herek.

Mighty Quinn, The (1989) Denzel Washington, James Fox, Mimi Rogers, M Emmet Walsh, Norman Beaton. Caribbean police investigate the murder of an American. *Dir.* Carl Shenkel.

Mike Bassett: England Manager (2001) Ricky Tomlinson (Mike Bassett), Amanda Redman, Bradley Walsh, Philip Jackson, Phil Jupitus, Pele (as himself). *Dir.* Steve Barron.

Million Dollar Baby (2004) Clint Eastwood (Frankie Dunn), Hilary Swank (Maggie Fitzgerald), Morgan Freeman (Eddie 'Scrap-Iron' Dupris). Moving story set around a boxing gym, and in particular the relationship between a wannabe female fighter in her early 30s and her reluctant trainer. *Dir.* Clint Eastwood.

Million Pound Note, The (1953) Gregory Peck, Jane Griffiths, Ronald Squire, Joyce Grenfell, Wilfrid Hyde-White. Based on a Mark Twain story. *Dir.* Ronald Neame.

Minority Report (2002) Tom Cruise, Colin Farrell, Samantha Morton, Max von Sydow, Lois Smith. *Dir.* Steven Spielberg.

Miracle (2004) Kurt Russell (Herb Brooks), Patricia Clarkson (Patty Brooks), Noah Emmerich (Craig Patrick). True story of player-turned-coach Herb Brooks, who led the 1980 US Olympic hockey team to victory over the previously invincible Russian squad. *Dir.* Gavin O'Connor.

Miracle on 34th Street (1994) Richard Attenborough, Elizabeth Perkins, Robert Prosky. Remake of the 1947 film starring Edmund Gwenn & Maureen O'Hara. *Dir.* Les Mayfield.

Miracle Worker, The (1962) Anne Bancroft, Patty Duke, Victor Jory. *Dir.* Arthur Penn.

Miranda (1947) Glynis Johns, Griffith Jones, Googie Withers, Margaret Rutherford, David Tomlinson. Sequel to this mermaid movie was *Mad About Men*, starring Johns and Donald Sinden. *Dir.* Ken Annakin.

Misery (1990) James Caan, Kathy Bates, Richard Farnsworth, Lauren Bacall. Disturbed fan kidnaps an injured novelist and forces him to write a novel. *Dir.* Rob Reiner.

Misfits, The (1961) Clark Gable, Marilyn Monroe, Montgomery Clift, Eli Wallach, Kevin McCarthy. Film about cowboys in the Nevada desert roping mustangs but more famous for its co-stars' imminent deaths. *Dir.* John Huston.

Mission, The (1986) Robert De Niro, Jeremy Irons, Ray McAnally, Liam Neeson, Cherie Lunghi. Music by Ennio Morricone. *Dir.* Roland Joffe.

Mission Impossible (1996) Tom Cruise, Jon Voight, Kristin Scott-Thomas, Vanessa Redgrave. *Dir.* Brian De Palma.

Missionary, The (1983) Michael Palin, Maggie Smith, Trevor Howard, Michael Hordern, Denholm Elliott. *Dir.* Richard Loncraine.

Mississippi Burning (1988) Gene Hackman, Willem Dafoe, Frances McDormand. *Dir.* Alan Parker.

Missouri Breaks (1976) Marlon Brando, Jack Nicholson, Randy Quaid, Kathleen Lloyd. *Dir.* Arthur Penn.

Moby Dick (1956) Gregory Peck, Richard Basehart, Orson Welles, James Robertson Justice. Based on Herman Melville's novel. *Dir.* John Huston.

Mommie Dearest (1981) Faye Dunaway, Diana Scarwid, Steve Forrest, Howard da Silva (Louis B Mayer). Joan Crawford life story. *Dir.* Frank Perry.

Mona Lisa (1986) Bob Hoskins, Cathy Tyson, Michael Caine, Robbie Coltrane. *Dir.* Neil Jordan.

Money Train (1995) Wesley Snipes, Woody Harrelson, Jennifer Lopez. *Dir.* Joseph Ruben.

Monster (2003) Charlize Theron (Aileen Wuornos), Christina Ricci (Selby Wall), Bruce Dern (Thomas), Scott Wilson (Horton), Pruitt Taylor Vince (Gene), Lee Tergesen (Vincent Corey), Annie Corley (Donna Tentler). True-life crime story of Aileen Wuornos, a prostitute who shot at least six men. *Dir.* Patty Jenkins.

Monster's Ball (2001) Billy Bob Thornton (Hank Grotowski), Halle Berry (Leticia Musgrove), Heath Ledger (Sonny Grotowski), Peter Boyle, Sean Combs, Mos Def, Amber Rules. After a family tragedy, a racist prison guard re-examines his attitudes while falling in love with the African-American wife of the last prisoner he executed. *Dir.* Marc Forster.

Monty Python and the Holy Grail (1975) John Cleese, Graham Chapman, Terry Gilliam, Eric Idle, Michael Palin, Terry Jones. *Dir.* Terry Gilliam and Terry Jones.

Monty Python's Life of Brian (1979) John Cleese, Graham Chapman, Terry Gilliam, Eric Idle, Michael Palin, Terry Jones. *Dir.* Terry Jones.

Monty Python's The Meaning of Life (1983) John Cleese, Graham Chapman, Terry Gilliam, Eric Idle, Michael Palin, Terry Jones. *Dir.* Terry Jones.

Moolaadé (2004) Fatoumata Coulibaly (Collé Gallo Ardo Sy), Maimouna Hélène Diarra (Hadjatou). Set in Burkina Faso, an examination of the subject of female circumcision. *Dir.* Ousmane Sembene.

Moon is Blue, The (1953) Maggie McNamara, David Niven, William Holden, Tom Tully, Dawn Addams. *Dir.* Otto Preminger.

Moonlighting (1982) Jeremy Irons, Eugene Lipinski, Jiri Stanislaw. Four Polish building workers arrive in London to renovate a house and hear of social unrest at home. *Dir.* Jerzy Skolimowski.

Moonraker (1979) Roger Moore, Lois Chiles (Holly Goodhead), Michael Lonsdale (Hugo Drax). Title song performed by Shirley Bassey. *Dir.* Lewis Gilbert.

Moonstruck (1987) Cher, Nicolas Cage, Vincent Gardenia, Olympia Dukakis, Danny Aiello. Young widow falls for the estranged brother of her husband-to-be. *Dir.* Norman Jewison.

Moonwalker (1988) Michael Jackson, Joe Pesci, Sean Lennon. *Dir.* Colin Chilvers.

Motorcycle Diaries, The (2004) Gael Garcia Bernal (Che Guevara), Rodrigo de la Serna (Alberto Granado). True story of a 23-year-old medical student from Argentina, Che Guevara, who travelled across South America on a motorcycle with his friend Alberto Granado in 1951–2, in a personal odyssey which would ultimately inspire him to become a revolutionary. *Dir.* Walter Salles.

Moulin Rouge (2001) Nicole Kidman, Ewan McGregor, Jim Broadbent, John Leguizamo (Toulouse-Lautrec), Matthew Whittet (Satie), Kylie Minogue (Green Fairy), Garry McDonald (The Doctor). *Dir.* Baz Luhrmann.

C
I
N
E
M
A

Mouse on the Moon, The (1963) Margaret Rutherford, Ron Moody, Bernard Cribbins, David Kossoff, Terry-Thomas, Michael Crawford. Sequel to *The Mouse That Roared*; concerning home-made wine making excellent rocket-fuel. *Dir*. Richard Lester.

Mouse That Roared, The (1959) Peter Sellers (three roles), Jean Seberg, David Kossoff, William Hartnell, Leo McKern. Tiny Duchy of Grand Fenwick is bankrupt, so decides to declare war on USA, be defeated, and then accept aid. *Dir*. Jack Arnold.

Move over Darling (1963) Doris Day, James Garner, Polly Bergen, Chuck Connors. Wife returns home after shipwreck to find her husband remarried. *Dir*. Michael Gordon.

Mr and Mrs Bridge (1990) Paul Newman, Joanne Woodward, Robert Sean Leonard, Blythe Danner, Simon Callow. Inhibited lawyer gradually erodes his wife's personality. *Dir*. James Ivory.

Mr Deeds Goes to Town (1936) Gary Cooper, Jean Arthur, Raymond Walburn, Margaret Seddon. Small-town poet inherits fortune and sets New York on its heels with his honesty. *Dir*. Frank Capra.

Mr Jones (1993) Richard Gere, Lena Olin, Anne Bancroft. Manic depressive begins an affair with his psychiatrist. *Dir*. Mike Figgis.

Mr Smith Goes to Washington (1939) James Stewart, Claude Rains, Jean Arthur, Thomas Mitchell, Edward Arnold. Senator exposes corruption in high places. *Dir*. Frank Capra.

Mrs Brown (1997) Billy Connolly (John Brown), Dame Judi Dench (Queen Victoria). *Dir*. John Madden.

Mrs Dalloway (1998) Vanessa Redgrave, Rupert Graves, Natascha McElhone, Michael Kitchen. *Dir*. Marleen Gorris.

Mrs Doubtfire (1993) Robin Williams, Sally Field, Pierce Brosnan, Robert Prosky. *Dir*. Chris Columbus.

Mrs Miniver (1942) Greer Garson, Walter Pidgeon, Teresa Wright. Multi-award winning film. *Dir*. William Wyler.

Mrs Pollifax – Spy (1970) Rosalind Russell, Darren McGavin. Written by CA McKnight, who was, in fact, Rosalind Russell. *Dir*. Leslie Martinson.

Much Ado about Nothing (1993) Kenneth Branagh, Emma Thompson, Richard Briers, Michael Keaton, Denzel Washington. *Dir*. Kenneth Branagh.

Mudlark, The (1950) Alec Guinness, Irene Dunne, Andrew Ray, Anthony Steel, Finlay Currie. Scruffy boy from the docks breaks into Windsor Castle to visit Queen Victoria. *Dir*. Jean Negulesco.

Mulholland Falls (1996) Nick Nolte, Melanie Griffith, Treat Williams, John Malkovich, Bruce Dern. *Dir*. Lee Tamahori.

Multiplicity (1996) Michael Keaton, Andie MacDowell, Ann Cusack. *Dir*. Harold Ramis.

Mummy, The (1932) Boris Karloff, Zita Johann, David Manners, Arthur Byron, Edward Van Sloan. Boris Karloff was billed as 'Karloff the Uncanny'. *Dir*. Karl Freund.

Mummy Returns, The (2001) Brendan Fraser, Rachel Weisz, John Hannah, Arnold Vosloo (The Mummy), Kevin O'Conner. *Dir*. Stephen Sommers. Acting debut of wrestling superstar 'The Rock' as The Scorpion King.

Mummy, The (1959) Peter Cushing, Christopher Lee, Yvonne Furneaux, Eddie Byrne, Felix Aylmer, Raymond Huntley, John Stuart. *Dir*. Terence Fisher.

Mummy, The (1999) Brendan Fraser, Rachel Weisz, John Hannah, Arnold Vosloo, Kevin O'Connor. *Dir*. Stephen Sommers.

Muppet Movie, The (1979) Charles Durning, Edgar Bergen, Bob Hope, Milton Berle, Mel Brooks, James Coburn, Dom DeLuise, Elliott Gould, Cloris Leachman, Telly Savalas, Orson Welles. *Dir*. James Frawley.

Muppets Take Manhattan, The (1984) Dabney Coleman, Art Carney, James Coco, Joan Rivers, Gregory Hines, Linda Lavin. *Dir*. Frank Oz.

Murder by Decree (1978) Christopher Plummer, James Mason, Anthony Quayle, David Hemmings, Susan Clark, John Gielgud, Donald Sutherland, Frank Finlay, Geneviève Bujold. Sherlock Holmes investigates the murders of 'Jack the Ripper'. *Dir*. Bob Clark.

Murder Most Foul (1964) Margaret Rutherford, Ron Moody, Charles Tingwell, Andrew Cruickshank, Megs Jenkins, Ralph Michael, James Bolam, Stringer Davis, Francesca Annis, Dennis Price, Terry Scott. Based on the Agatha Christie novel *Mrs McGinty's Dead*. *Dir*. George Pollock.

Murder on the Orient Express (1974) Albert Finney, Ingrid Bergman, Lauren Bacall, Wendy Hiller, Sean Connery, Vanessa Redgrave, Michael York, Martin Balsam, Richard Widmark, Jacqueline Bisset, Jean-Pierre Cassel, Rachel Roberts, George Coulouris, John Gielgud, Anthony Perkins, Colin Blakely, Jeremy Lloyd, Denis Quilley. Hercule Poirot solves this Agatha Christie story. *Dir*. Sidney Lumet.

Murders in the Rue Morgue (1932) Bela Lugosi, Sidney Fox, Leon Ames, Bert Roach, Brandon Hurst. *Dir*. Robert Florey.

Murders in the Rue Morgue (1971) Jason Robards Jnr, Herbert Lom, Lilli Palmer, Adolfo Celi, Michael Dunn, Christine Kaufmann. *Dir*. Gordon Hessler.

Muriel's Wedding (1994) Toni Collette, Bill Hunter, Rachel Griffiths, Jeanie Drynan. *Dir*. PJ Hogan.

Murphy's Law (1986) Charles Bronson, Carrie Snodgress, Kathleen Wilhoite, Robert F Lyons, Richard Romanus. *Dir*. J Lee Thompson.

Murphy's War (1971) Peter O'Toole, Sian Phillips, Philippe Noiret, Horst Janson. *Dir*. Peter Yates.

Music Lovers, The (1970) Richard Chamberlain, Glenda Jackson, Christopher Gable, Max Adrian, Isabelle Telezynska, Maureen Pryor, Andrew Faulds. Screenplay written by Melvyn Bragg. *Dir*. Ken Russell.

Music Man, The (1962) Robert Preston, Shirley Jones, Buddy Hackett, Hermione Gingold, Pert Kelton, Paul Ford. *Dir*. Morton da Costa.

Mutiny on the Bounty (1935) Charles Laughton, Clark Gable, Franchot Tone, Movita, Dudley Digges. *Dir*. Frank Lloyd.

Mutiny on the Bounty (1962) Trevor Howard, Marlon Brando, Richard Harris, Hugh Griffith, Tarita, Richard Haydn, Gordon Jackson. *Dir*. Lewis Milestone.

My Beautiful Laundrette (1985) Saeed Jaffrey, Roshan Seth, Daniel Day-Lewis, Shirley Anne Field. Based on the Hanif Kureishi work. *Dir*. Stephen Frears.

My Big Fat Greek Wedding (2002) Nia Vardalos, John Corbett, Michael Constantine, Andrea Martin. Low-budget, unlikely smash hit of the year. Apparently the wedding dress featured in the film was bought by a viewer for a pittance and sold following the film's success for an amount approaching the budget of the film!! *Dir*. Joel Zwick.

My Favourite Martian (1999) Christopher Lloyd, Jeff Daniels, Elizabeth Hurley, Daryl Hannah, Ray Walston. *Dir*. Donald Petrie. Based on the TV series starring Ray Walston and Bill Bixby.

Mysterious Dr Fu Manchu, The (1929) Warner Oland played the Sax Rohmer character in early films in the series. *Dir*. Various.

Mystic River (2003)   Sean Penn (Jimmy Markum), Tim Robbins (Dave Boyle), Kevin Bacon (Sean Devine), Laurence Fishburne (Whitney Powers), Marcia Gay Harden (Celeste Boyle), Laura Linney (Annabeth Markum), Kevin Chapman (Val Savage), Thomas Guiry (Brendan Harris), Emmy Rossum (Katie Markum). Situated in Boston, concerns the murder of the daughter of an ex-con and the interaction of three old friends whose lives were devastated by a previous tragedy. *Dir.* Clint Eastwood.

Naked (1993)   David Thewlis, Lesley Sharp, Katrin Cartlidge, Greg Cruttwell. *Dir.* Mike Leigh.

Naked Edge, The (1961)   Gary Cooper, Deborah Kerr, Peter Cushing, Michael Wilding, Diane Cilento. *Dir.* Michael Anderson.

Naked Gun, The: From the Files of Police Squad (1988)   Leslie Nielsen, Priscilla Presley, Ricardo Montalban, OJ Simpson, George Kennedy. *Dir.* David Zucker.

Naked Gun 2 1/2, The: The Smell of Fear (1991)   Leslie Nielsen, Priscilla Presley, Robert Goulet, OJ Simpson, George Kennedy. *Dir.* David Zucker.

Naked Gun 33 1/3, The: The Final Insult (1994)   Leslie Nielsen, Priscilla Presley, Fred Ward, OJ Simpson, George Kennedy, Anna Nicole Smith. *Dir.* Peter Segal.

Naked in New York (1993)   Eric Stoltz, Mary-Louise Parker, Ralph Macchio, Jill Clayburgh, Tony Curtis, Kathleen Turner, Timothy Dalton, Whoopi Goldberg, Quentin Crisp. *Dir.* Dan Algrant.

Naked Lunch (1991)   Peter Weller, Judy Davis, Ian Holm, Roy Scheider, Julian Sands. Drug-addicted writer emulates William Tell with fatal results. *Dir.* David Cronenberg.

Name of the Rose, The (1986)   Sean Connery (William of Baskerville), F Murray Abraham (Bernardo Gui), Christian Slater (Adso of Melk), Feodor Chaliapin (Jorge de Burgos), William Hickey (Ubertino de Casale). Based on Umberto Eco novel. *Dir.* Jean-Jacques Annaud.

Narrow Margin (1952)   Charles McGraw, Marie Windsor, Jacqueline White, Queenie Leonard. Police try to guard a witness on a train from Chicago to LA. The 1990 remake starred Gene Hackman and Anne Archer. *Dir.* Richard Fleischer.

National Lampoon's Animal House (1978)   John Belushi, Tim Matheson, Donald Sutherland, John Vernon. First of the series which continued with *Movie Madness* (1981), *Class Reunion* (1982), *Vacation* (1983), *European Vacation* (1985), *Christmas Vacation* (1989), *Loaded Weapon* (1993), and *Senior Trip* (1995). The Chevy Chase character in 3 of the films was Clark Griswold. *Dir.* John Landis.

National Velvet (1945)   Mickey Rooney, Elizabeth Taylor, Anne Revere, Donald Crisp, Angela Lansbury. *Dir.* Clarence Brown.

Natural, The (1984)   Robert Redford (Roy Hobbs), Robert Duvall (Max Mercy), Glenn Close (Iris), Kim Basinger (Memo Paris), Barbara Hershey (Harriet Bird), Robert Prosky (Judge), Joe Don Baker (The Whammer). Ups and downs of a baseball star. *Dir.* Barry Levinson.

Natural Born Killers (1994)   Woody Harrelson, Juliette Lewis, Robert Downey Jnr, Tommy Lee Jones. Young couple become mass murderers while winning the affection of the media. *Dir.* Oliver Stone.

Ned Kelly (1970)   Mick Jagger, Allen Bickford, Geoff Gilmour, Mark McManus. Story of the 19th-century Australian outlaw. *Dir.* Tony Richardson.

Nell (1994)   Jodie Foster, Liam Neeson, Natasha Richardson. Two doctors endeavour to talk to a young woman who speaks a solitary language. *Dir.* Michael Apted.

Net, The (1995)   Sandra Bullock, Jeremy Northam, Dennis Miller, Diane Baker. *Dir.* Irwin Winkler.

Network (1976)   Peter Finch (Howard Beale), William Holden (Max Schumacher), Faye Dunaway, Robert Duvall, Ned Beatty. Peter Finch was awarded a posthumous Academy Award. *Dir.* Sidney Lumet.

Nevada Smith (1966)   Steve McQueen, Karl Malden, Brian Keith, Suzanne Pleshette. Scenes from the early life of the *Carpetbaggers* character. *Dir.* Henry Hathaway.

Never Been Kissed (1998)   Drew Barrymore, David Arquette, Michael Vartan, Leelee Sobieski, Jeremy Jordan. *Dir.* Raja Gosnell.

Never on Sunday (1959)   Melina Mercouri, Jules Dassin. Original title: *Pote tin Kyriaki*. *Dir.* Jules Dassin.

Never Say Never Again (1983)   Sean Connery, Klaus Maria Brandauer (Largo), Max Von Sydow (Blofeld), Alec McCowen (Q), Kim Basinger (Domino), Edward Fox, Rowan Atkinson, Barbara Carrera (Fatima). Remake of *Thunderball*, so titled because Connery vowed he would never make another Bond movie after *Diamonds Are Forever*. *Dir.* Irvin Kershner.

New York, New York (1977)   Liza Minnelli, Robert De Niro, Lionel Stander, Barry Primus. *Dir.* Martin Scorsese.

New York Stories (1989)   *Life Lessons*: Nick Nolte, Patrick O'Neal, Rosanna Arquette, Steve Buscemi, Debbie Harry, Peter Gabriel. *Dir.* Martin Scorsese. *Life without Zoe*: Talia Shire, Giancarlo Giannini, Heather McComb, Carmine Coppola. *Dir.* Francis Ford Coppola. *Oedipus Wrecks*: Woody Allen, Mia Farrow, Julie Kavner, Mae Questel, Mayor Ed Koch. *Dir.* Woody Allen.   Teacher sets the 3 top boys an essay – topic: 'My Story about New York' and the 3 separately directed stories follow.

Next of Kin (1989)   Patrick Swayze (Truman Gates), Liam Neeson (Briar Gates), Adam Baldwin (Joey Rosselini). *Dir.* John Irvin.

Niagara (1952)   Joseph Cotten, Jean Peters, Marilyn Monroe. *Dir.* Henry Hathaway.

Nicholas and Alexandra (1971)   Michael Jayston, Janet Suzman, Laurence Olivier, Jack Hawkins, Tom Baker, Michael Redgrave. Life of Tsar Nicholas II from 1904 until the execution of his family in 1918. *Dir.* Franklin Schaffner.

Nickelodeon (1976)   Ryan O'Neal, Burt Reynolds, Tatum O'Neal, Brian Keith, Stella Stevens. Events leading up to the premiere of *The Birth of a Nation*. *Dir.* Peter Bogdanovich.

Night and Day (1946)   Cary Grant (Cole Porter), Alexis Smith, Monty Woolley, Mary Martin, Jane Wyman, Eve Arden. *Dir.* Michael Curtiz.

Night and the City (1992)   Robert De Niro (Harry Fabian), Jessica Lange (Helen Nasseros), Alan King (Boom Boom Grossman). Remake of the 1950 classic starring Richard Widmark and Gene Tierney. *Dir.* Irwin Winkler.

Night at the Opera, A (1935)   Groucho Marx, Chico Marx, Harpo Marx, Margaret Dumont. *Dir.* Sam Wood.

Night Crossing (1982)   John Hurt, Jane Alexander, Beau Bridges, Ian Bannen. East Germans escape to the West via air balloon. *Dir.* Delbert Mann.

Night Falls on Manhattan (1997)   Andy Garcia (Sean Casey), Ian Holm. *Dir.* Sidney Lumet.

Night in Casablanca, A (1946)   Groucho Marx (Kornblow), Chico Marx, Harpo Marx, Lisette Verea (Beatrice). *Dir.* Archie Mayo.

CINEMA

Night of the Hunter (1955)   Robert Mitchum, Shelley Winters, Lillian Gish, Peter Graves. Psychopathic preacher on the trail of hidden loot. *Dir*. Charles Laughton.

Night of the Iguana (1964)   Richard Burton, Deborah Kerr, Ava Gardner, Sue Lyon. Disbarred clergyman becomes a courier in Mexico and is chased by teenage nymphomaniac. *Dir*. John Huston.

Night on Earth (1992)   Winona Ryder (Corky), Gena Rowlands (Victoria Snelling), Giancarlo Esposito (Yo Yo). Five people take simultaneous taxi rides in 5 cities, i.e. LA, New York, Paris, Rome & Helsinki. *Dir*. Jim Jarmusch.

Night Porter, The (1973)   Dirk Bogarde, Charlotte Rampling. Wife of opera conductor recognises porter as a former SS officer. *Dir*. Liliana Cavani.

Night Shift (1982)   Henry Winkler, Michael Keaton, Shelley Long, Gina Hecht, Kevin Costner (Frat Boy). *Dir*. Ron Howard.

Night They Raided Minsky's, The (1968)   Jason Robards, Britt Ekland, Norman Wisdom, Bert Lahr. *Dir*. William Friedkin.

Night to Remember, A (1958)   Kenneth More, Honor Blackman, David McCallum. *Dir*. Roy Baker.

Nightmare Before Christmas, The (1993)   Voices of Danny Elfman, Chris Sarandon, William Hickey, Catherine O'Hara. Based on a Tim Burton story. *Dir*. Henry Selick.

Nightmare on Elm Street, A (1984)   John Saxon, Ronee Blakley, Robert Englund (Freddie). *Dir*. Wes Craven.

Nightmare on Elm Street, A, 2: Freddy's Revenge (1985)   Mark Patton, Clu Gulager, Hope Lange, Kim Myers, Robert Englund (Freddie). *Dir*. Jack Sholder.

Nightmare on Elm Street, A, 3: Dream Warriors (1987)   Heather Langenkamp, Patricia Arquette, Robert Englund (Freddie). *Dir*. Chuck Russell.

Nightmare on Elm Street, A, 4: The Dream Master (1988)   Rodney Eastman, Danny Hassel, Robert Englund (Freddie). *Dir*. Renny Harlin.

Nightmare on Elm Street, A: The Dream Child (1989)   Lisa Wilcox, Kelly Jo Minter, Danny Hassel, Robert Englund (Freddie). Last of the series called *Freddy's Dead: The Final Nightmare* (1991). *Dir*. Stephen Hopkins.

Nil by Mouth (1997)   Ray Winstone (Ray), Kathy Burke (Valerie). *Dir*. Gary Oldman.

Nine and a Half Weeks (1986)   Mickey Rourke, Kim Basinger. *Dir*. Adrian Lyne.

976–EVIL (1988)   Stephen Geoffreys (Hoax), Sandy Dennis (Aunt Lucy). The title refers to the Devil's freephone number. *Dir*. Robert Englund.

9/30/55 (1977)   Richard Thomas, Susan Tyrrell, Dennis Quaid. Title refers to the death of James Dean and the effect on an Arkansas student. *Dir*. James Bridges.

Nine to Five (1980)   Jane Fonda, Dolly Parton, Lily Tomlin, Dabney Coleman, Sterling Hayden. Three office women plot to get rid of their boss. *Dir*. Colin Higgins.

1984 (1984)   John Hurt (Winston Smith), Richard Burton (O'Brien), Suzanna Hamilton (Julia), Cyril Cusack (Carrington). A 1955 version starred Michael Redgrave and Edmond O'Brien. *Dir*. Michael Radford.

1941 (1979)   Dan Aykroyd, Ned Beatty, John Belushi, Christopher Lee, Robert Stack, Lorraine Gary. Farce concerning a stray Japanese submarine terrorising Hollywood after Pearl Harbor. *Dir*. Steven Spielberg.

Ninotchka (1939)   Greta Garbo, Melvyn Douglas, Bela Lugosi. *Dir*. Ernst Lubitsch.

Nixon (1995)   Anthony Hopkins (Nixon), Joan Allen (Pat Nixon), Powers Boothe (Alexander Haig), Ed Harris (E Howard Hunt), Paul Sorvino (Henry Kissinger). *Dir*. Oliver Stone.

Nobody's Fool (1994)   Paul Newman, Jessica Tandy, Bruce Willis, Melanie Griffith. A 60-yr-old handyman has a chance to make up for a disappointing life. *Dir*. Robert Benton.

Noises Off (1992)   Carol Burnett (Dotty Otley / Mrs Clackett), Michael Caine (Lloyd Fellowes), Denholm Elliott, Julie Hagerty, Marilu Henner, Christopher Reeve. Adaptation of Michael Frayn's farce about a second-rate touring company. *Dir*. Peter Bogdanovich.

No Place To Go (*Die Unberührbare*) (2001)   Hannelore Elsner (Hanna), Vadim Glowna, Tonio Arango, Michael Gwisdek, Bernd Stempel. *Dir*. Oskar Röhler.

North by Northwest (1959)   Cary Grant, Eva Marie Saint, James Mason. *Dir*. Alfred Hitchcock.

North Dallas Forty (1979)   Nick Nolte, Mac Davis, Charles Durning, Bo Svenson. Gruelling life of an American football player. *Dir*. Ted Kotcheff.

Notorious (1946)   Cary Grant, Ingrid Bergman, Claude Rains, Louis Calhern. Lady marries a Nazi in Rio to help the American government. *Dir*. Alfred Hitchcock.

Notre Musique (2004)   Sarah Adler (Judith Lerner), Nade Dieu (Olga Brodsky), Rony Kramer (Ramos Garcia). Divided into three 'kingdoms' – Enfer (Hell), Purgatoire (Purgatory) and Paradis (Paradise) – the film serves as an insight into war and memory. *Dir*. Jean-Luc Godard.

Notting Hill (1999)   Julia Roberts, Hugh Grant, Hugh Bonneville, Emma Chambers, Alec Baldwin. *Dir*. Roger Michell.

Nuns on the Run (1990)   Eric Idle, Robbie Coltrane, Janet Suzman, Doris Hare. *Dir*. Jonathan Lynn.

Nun's Story, The (1959)   Audrey Hepburn, Peter Finch, Edith Evans, Peggy Ashcroft. Belgian girl joins a strict order of nuns. *Dir*. Fred Zinnemann.

Nurse Edith Cavell (1939)   Anna Neagle, George Sanders. Based on Reginald Berkeley's novel *Dawn*. *Dir*. Herbert Wilcox.

Nutty Professor, The (1996)   Eddie Murphy (plays 7 roles), James Coburn, Jada Pinkett. *Dir*. Tom Shadyac.

Object of Beauty, The (1991)   John Malkovich, Andie MacDowell, Joss Ackland, Bill Paterson, Jack Shepherd. *Dir*. Michael Lindsay-Hogg.

Objective Burma! (1945)   Errol Flynn, James Brown, William Prince. Exploits of a US platoon during the Burma campaign. The film caused a furore among the Burma Star Organisation and nearly created a diplomatic fallout by failing to mention the British contribution. *Dir*. Raoul Walsh.

Obsession (1976)   Cliff Robertson, Geneviève Bujold, John Lithgow. Widower meets the double of his dead wife. *Dir*. Brian De Palma.

Ocean's Eleven (1960)   Frank Sinatra, Peter Lawford, Sammy Davis Jnr, Dean Martin, Richard Conte, Ilka Chase, Cesar Romero, Joey Bishop, Patrick Wymore, Akim Tamiroff, Henry Silva, Angie Dickinson. *Dir*. Lewis Milestone.

Ocean's Eleven (2001)   George Clooney (Danny Ocean), Julia Roberts (Tess Ocean), Brad Pitt (Rusty Ryan), Matt Damon (Linus), Andy Garcia (Terry Benedict), Casey Affleck (Virgil Malloy), Scott Caan (Turk Malloy), Don Cheadle (Basher Tarr), Elliott Gould (Reuben Tishkoff), Carl Reiner (Saul Bloom). Remake of the 1960 film of the same name. *Dir*. Steven Soderbergh.

Octopussy (1983)   Roger Moore, Maud Adams (Octopussy), Louis Jourdan (Prince Kamel Khan), Steven Berkoff (Orlov), Robert Brown (M), Desmond Llewelyn (Q). Tennis player Vijay Amritraj appeared in a cameo role. Title song performed by Rita Coolidge. *Dir.* John Glen.

Odd Couple, The (1968)   Jack Lemmon (Felix Unger), Walter Matthau (Oscar Goldman). Written by Neil Simon. *Dir.* Gene Saks.

Odessa File, The (1974)   Jon Voigt, Maria Schell, Maximilian Schell, Derek Jacobi. *Dir.* Ronald Neame.

Of Mice and Men (1939)   Burgess Meredith, Lon Chaney Jnr, Betty Field, Charles Bickford. Itinerant worker looks after his immensely strong but mentally retarded cousin. The 1992 remake starred John Malkovich and Gary Sinise. *Dir.* Lewis Milestone.

Officer and a Gentleman, An (1982)   Richard Gere (Zack Mayo), Debra Winger, Lou Gossett Jnr, David Keith, Lisa Blount. Oscars for Lou Gossett Jnr (Best Supporting), and song ('Up Where We Belong'). *Dir.* Taylor Hackford.

Oh What a Lovely War (1969)   Ralph Richardson, Meriel Forbes, John Gielgud, Kenneth More, John Clements, Joe Melia, Paul Daneman, Jack Hawkins, Maggie Smith, John Mills, Michael Redgrave, Laurence Olivier, Susannah York, Dirk Bogarde, Phyllis Calvert, Vanessa Redgrave. Musical fantasia of World War I. *Dir.* Richard Attenborough.

O.H.M.S. (1936)   John Mills, Wallace Ford, Anna Lee. British forces in China are joined by an American gangster on the run, who dies a hero. US title: *You're in the Army Now*. *Dir.* Raoul Walsh.

Oklahoma (1955)   Gordon Macrae, Shirley Jones, Rod Steiger, Eddie Albert. *Dir.* Fred Zinnemann.

Oklahoma Kid, The (1939)   James Cagney, Humphrey Bogart, Rosemary Lane, Donald Crisp, Ward Bond. *Dir.* Lloyd Bacon.

Old Gringo (1989)   Jane Fonda (Harriet Winslow), Gregory Peck (Ambrose Bierce), Jimmy Smits (Tomas Arroyo). *Dir.* Luis Puenzo.

Old Man and the Sea, The (1958)   Spencer Tracy, Felipe Pazos, Harry Bellaver. *Dir.* John Sturges.

Old Mother Riley (1935–52)   Arthur Lucan (Old Mother Riley), Kitty McShane (his daughter). Series of films with Lucan and his real-life wife playing mother and daughter. *Stars on Parade* was the first of the series and *Mother Riley Meets the Vampire* the last. *Dir.* Maclean Rogers.

Oliver! (1968)   Ron Moody, Oliver Reed, Harry Secombe, Mark Lester, Shani Wallis, Jack Wild. *Dir.* Carol Reed.

Oliver Twist (1948)   Alec Guinness, Robert Newton, Francis L Sullivan, John Howard Davies, Anthony Newley, Diana Dors, Mary Clare, Kay Walsh. *Dir.* David Lean.

Oliver's Story (1978)   Ryan O'Neal, Candice Bergen, Nicola Pagett, Ray Milland. *Dir.* John Korty.

Omega Man, The (1971)   Charlton Heston, Rosalind Cash, Anthony Zerbe. Based on the novel *I am Legend* by Richard Matheson. Set in 1977 Los Angeles after a germ warfare plague has decimated the world's population. *Dir.* Boris Sagal.

Omen, The (1976)   Gregory Peck, Lee Remick, David Warner, Billie Whitelaw, Leo McKern, Patrick Troughton. Three inferior sequels were made. *Dir.* Richard Donner.

On Deadly Ground (1994)   Steven Seagal, Michael Caine, Joan Chen, Chief Irvin Brink. *Dir.* Steven Seagal.

On Golden Pond (1981)   Henry Fonda, Katharine Hepburn, Jane Fonda, Dabney Coleman, Doug McKeon. *Dir.* Mark Rydell.

On Her Majesty's Secret Service (1969)   George Lazenby, Diana Rigg (Tracy Vicenzo née Draco), Telly Savalas (Blofeld). *Avengers* fans note: not only does Diana Rigg become Mrs Bond but Joanna Lumley is one of the lovelies in the Swiss Alps and Honor Blackman is visible in a clip from *Goldfinger* in the opening titles. *Dir.* Peter Hunt. Theme song: 'We have all the time in the world' performed by Louis Armstrong.

On the Beach (1959)   Gregory Peck, Ava Gardner, Fred Astaire, Anthony Perkins, Donna Anderson. Crew of serving American submarine wait for the devastation of atomic war to catch up with them in Australia. *Dir.* Stanley Kramer.

On the Buses (1971)   Reg Varney, Doris Hare, Anna Karen, Michael Robbins, Stephen Lewis. Sequels: *Mutiny on the Buses* (1972), and *Holiday on the Buses* (1973). *Dir.* Harry Booth.

On the Double (1961)   Danny Kaye, Dana Wynter, Wilfrid Hyde-White, Diana Dors, Margaret Rutherford, Allan Cuthbertson, Jesse White. American private is asked to impersonate a British Intelligence officer. *Dir.* Melville Shavelson.

On the Fiddle (1961)   Alfred Lynch, Sean Connery, Wilfrid Hyde-White, Kathleen Harrison, Cecil Parker, Alan King, Eleanor Summerfield, Eric Barker, John Le Mesurier, Terence Longdon. US title: *Operation Snafu*. Wide boy and slow-witted gypsy's adventures in the RAF. *Dir.* Cyril Frankel.

On the Town (1949)   Frank Sinatra, Gene Kelly, Jules Munshin, Ann Miller, Vera-Ellen, Betty Garrett. Gene Kelly directed the dance scenes. *Dir.* Stanley Donen.

On the Waterfront (1954)   Marlon Brando, Eva Marie Saint, Rod Steiger, Lee J Cobb, Karl Malden. *Dir.* Elia Kazan.

Once a Jolly Swagman (1948)   Dirk Bogarde, Renée Asherson, Bonar Colleano, Bill Owen. US title: *Maniacs on Wheels*. Factory worker becomes a speedway rider. *Dir.* Jack Lee.

Once Around (1991)   Richard Dreyfuss, Holly Hunter, Danny Aiello, Gena Rowlands, Laura San Giacomo. *Dir.* Lasse Hallstrom.

Once Bitten (1985)   Lauren Hutton, Jim Carrey, Karen Kopins, Cleavon Little. Teenage sex problems are complicated by a visiting vampiress. *Dir.* Howard Storm.

Once More with Feeling (1960)   Yul Brynner, Kay Kendall, Geoffrey Toone, Maxwell Shaw, Mervyn Johns. Volatile private life of an orchestral conductor. *Dir.* Stanley Donen.

Once Upon a Crime (1992)   John Candy, James Belushi, Cybill Shepherd, Sean Young, Joss Ackland. *Dir.* Eugene Levy.

Once Upon a Horse (1958)   Dan Rowan, Dick Martin, Martha Hyer, Leif Erickson, Nita Talbot, James Gleason. Two cowboys steal a herd of cattle but can't afford to feed them. The two stars later went on to revolutionise TV comedy with their *Laugh-in* shows. *Dir.* Hal Kanter.

Once Upon a Time in America (1984)   Robert De Niro (Noodles), James Woods (Max), Elizabeth McGovern (Deborah), Treat Williams (Jimmy O'Donnell), Tuesday Weld (Carol), Joe Pesci (Frankie), Danny Aiello (Police Chief Aiello), William Forsythe (Cockeye). Story of four Jewish gangsters known as the 'Kosher Nostra', from 1922 to 1968. It is a 228-minute film which has a 147-minute version. *Dir.* Sergio Leone.

Once Upon a Time in the West (1969)   Henry Fonda, Claudia Cardinale, Jason Robards, Charles Bronson. Notable for its opening credits which last for the first 12 minutes of film time. *Dir.* Sergio Leone.

C
I
N
E
M
A

Once Were Warriors (1994)   Rena Owen, Temuera Morrison. This film is the top NZ film as regards box office takings. *Dir.* Lee Tamahori.

One-Eyed Jacks (1961)   Marlon Brando, Karl Malden, Pina Pellicer, Katy Jurado, Slim Pickens, Ben Johnson. Based on the novel *The Authentic Death of Hendry Jones* by Charles Neider. *Dir.* Marlon Brando.

One False Move (1992)   Bill Paxton (Dale 'Hurricane' Dixon), Cynda Williams (Fantasia / Lila), Michael Beach (Pluto), Billy Bob Thornton (Ray Malcolm), Jim Metzler (Dud Cole). Two killers on the run with their black girlfriend go to Alabama where the sheriff is waiting. Cynda Williams and Billy Bob Thornton fell in love on set and married soon after. *Dir.* Carl Franklin.

One Fine Day (1996)   Michelle Pfeiffer, George Clooney, Charles Durning, Mae Whitman. Two busy single parents fall in love. *Dir.* Michael Hoffman.

One from the Heart (1982)   Frederic Forrest (Hank), Teri Garr (Frannie), Raul Julia (Ray), Nastassja Kinski (Leila). Rebecca DeMornay's screen debut in the restaurant scene with the line: 'Excuse me, I think those are my waffles'. First film for Coppola's Zoetrope studios. *Dir.* Francis Ford Coppola.

187 (1997)   Samuel L Jackson (Trevor Garfield), Tony Plana. Title refers to the Californian penal code for murder. School: John Quincy Adams High. *Dir.* Kevin Reynolds.

101 Dalmatians (1996)   Glenn Close, Jeff Daniels, Joan Plowright, Joely Richardson, Hugh Laurie. Live-action remake of the 1961 animated film. *Dir.* Stephen Herek. The sequel *102 Dalmatians* was released in 2000.

One Hundred Men and a Girl (1937)   Deanna Durbin was the girl and the men were an orchestra. *Dir.* Henry Koster.

One Million Years BC (1966)   John Richardson, Raquel Welch, Robert Brown. *Dir.* Don Chaffey.

One Woman or Two (1985)   Gérard Depardieu (Julien Chayssac), Sigourney Weaver (Jessica Fitzgerald), Dr Ruth Westheimer (Mrs Heffner). Advertising woman uses an archaeologist as basis for a new campaign and falls in love. *Dir.* Daniel Vigne.

Onibaba (1964)   Nobuko Otowa, Jitsuko Yoshimura, Kei Sato. Mother and daughter live by preying on stray soldiers. Aka: *The Hole. Dir.* Kaneto Shindo.

Operation Crossbow (1965)   George Peppard, Tom Courtenay, John Mills, Sophia Loren, Lilli Palmer, Trevor Howard. *Dir.* Michael Anderson.

Ordinary People (1980)   Donald Sutherland, Mary Tyler Moore, Timothy Hutton, Judd Hirsch. Oscars for Hutton, Redford and Alvin Sargent (screenplay). *Dir.* Robert Redford.

Othello (1965)   Laurence Olivier, Frank Finlay, Maggie Smith, Derek Jacobi. The 1995 Oliver Parker film starred Laurence Fishburne and Ken Branagh (Iago). *Dir.* Stuart Burge.

Others, The (2001)   Nicole Kidman (Grace), Christopher Eccleston (Charles), Fionnula Flanagan (Mrs Mills), James Bentley (Nicholas), Eric Sykes (Mr Tuttle), Elaine Cassidy (Lydia). Set in the 1940s. *Dir.* Alejandro Amenabar.

Our Man Flint (1965)   James Coburn, Lee J Cobb. *Dir.* Daniel Mann.

Our Man in Havana (1965)   Alec Guinness, Noël Coward, Burl Ives, Maureen O'Hara, Ralph Richardson. *Dir.* Carol Reed.

Out of Africa (1985)   Robert Redford (Denys), Meryl Streep (Karen Blixen), Klaus Maria Brandauer, Michael Gough. *Dir.* Sydney Pollack.

Outbreak (1995)   Dustin Hoffman, Rene Russo, Morgan Freeman, Donald Sutherland, Kevin Spacey. *Dir.* Wolfgang Petersen.

Outland (1981)   Sean Connery, Peter Boyle, Kika Markham. *Dir.* Peter Hyams.

Outlaw Josey Wales, The (1976)   Clint Eastwood, Chief Dan George, Sondra Locke. *Dir.* Clint Eastwood.

Outrageous Fortune (1987)   Bette Midler (Sandy), Shelley Long (Lauren), Robert Prosky, Peter Coyote. *Dir.* Arthur Hiller.

Outsiders, The (1983)   Matt Dillon (Dallas Winston), Ralph Macchio (Johnny Cade), Patrick Swayze (Darrel Curtis), Robb Lowe (Sodapop Curtis), Emilio Estevez (Two-Bit Matthews), Tom Cruise (Steve Randle). *Dir.* Francis Ford Coppola.

Over the Top (1987)   Sylvester Stallone (Lincoln Hawk), Robert Loggia (Jason Cutler), Susan Blakely (Chris Hawk). *Dir.* Menahem Golan.

Overboard (1987)   Goldie Hawn (Joanna / Annie), Kurt Russell (Dean Proffitt), Roddy McDowall (Andrew). *Dir.* Garry Marshall.

Owl and the Pussycat, The (1970)   Barbra Streisand, George Segal, Robert Klein, Allen Garfield. *Dir.* Herbert Ross.

Paint Your Wagon (1969)   Lee Marvin, Clint Eastwood (Pardner), Jean Seberg, Harve Presnell, Ray Walston. *Dir.* Joshua Logan.

Pal Joey (1957)   Frank Sinatra, Rita Hayworth, Kim Novak. *Dir.* George Sidney.

Pale Rider (1985)   Clint Eastwood (Preacher), Michael Moriarty, Carrie Snodgrass, Chris Penn, Richard Kiel. *Dir.* Clint Eastwood.

Paleface, The (1948)   Bob Hope, Jane Russell, Robert Armstrong. Song 'Buttons and Bows' (music by J Livingston, lyrics by Ray Evans) won Oscar. Sequel was *Son of Paleface* and 1968 remake was *The Shakiest Gun in the West. Dir.* Norman Z Mcleod.

Pallbearer (1996)   David Schwimmer, Gwyneth Paltrow, Michael Rapaport, Barbara Hershey. *Dir.* Matt Reeves.

Palm Beach Story, The (1942)   Claudette Colbert, Joel McCrea, Rudy Vallee (Hackensacker), Robert Dudley (Weenie King). Engineer's wife travels to Florida with her sights set on a millionaire. *Dir.* Preston Sturges.

Palookaville (1996)   Adam Trese (Jerry), William Forsythe (Sid), Vincent Gallo (Russ), Frances McDormand. Story of 3 bungling would-be criminals. *Dir.* Alan Taylor.

Panic Room (2002)   Jodie Foster, Kristen Stewart, Forest Whitaker, Jared Leto, Dwight Yoakam. *Dir.* David Fincher.

Panther (1995)   Kadeem Hardison, Bokeem Woodbine, Joe Don Baker, Nefertiti. Black Vietnam vet recalls his role in the Black Panther movement. *Dir.* Mario Van Peebles.

Paper, The (1994)   Michael Keaton, Glenn Close, Marisa Tomei, Robert Duvall, Randy Quaid. *Dir.* Ron Howard.

Paper Chase, The (1973)   Timothy Bottoms, Lindsay Wagner, John Houseman, Graham Bickel. Based on John Jay Osborn Jnr novel. Houseman won Oscar and film spawned a successful TV series of the same name. *Dir.* James Bridges.

Paper Moon (1973)   Ryan O'Neal, Tatum O'Neal, Madeline Kahn, John Hillerman. Tatum O'Neal won an Oscar. *Dir.* Peter Bogdanovich.

Paper Tiger (1975)   David Niven, Toshiro Mifune, Hardy Kruger, Ando, Ronald Fraser, Ivan Desny. Englishman becomes tutor to the son of a Japanese ambassador. *Dir.* Ken Annakin.

Papillon (1973)   Dustin Hoffman, Steve McQueen. *Dir.* Franklin Schaffner.

Paradise (1991)   Melanie Griffith (Lily Reed), Don Johnson (Ben Reed), Elijah Wood, Louise Latham. The first film that Griffith and Johnson starred in together. Remake of *Le Grand Chemin* directed in 1987 by Jean-Loup Hubert. *Dir.* Mary Agnes Donoghue.

Parallax View, The (1974)   Warren Beatty, Paula Prentiss, William Daniels. Witnesses to political assassination are systematically killed. *Dir.* Alan J Pakula.

Parenthood (1989)   Steve Martin (Gil), Mary Steenburgen (Karen), Dianne Wiest (Helen), Jason Robards (Frank), Rick Moranis (Nathan), Tom Hulce (Larry), Keanu Reeves (Tod), Leaf Phoenix (Gary). Four generations of a large family have different approaches to parenthood. *Dir.* Ron Howard.

Parole Officer, The (2001)   Steve Coogan (Simon Garden), Lena Headey, Om Puri, Steven Waddington, Ben Miller, Stephen Dillane, Jenny Agutter, Omar Sharif (Victor Bondarenko). *Dir.* John Duigan.

Passage to India, A (1984)   Judy Davis (Adela Quested), Victor Banerjee (Dr Aziz), Peggy Ashcroft (Mrs Moore), James Fox (Richard Fielding), Alec Guinness (Godbole), Nigel Havers, Art Malik Richard Wilson (Turton), Saeed Jaffrey, Clive Swift, Roshan Seth. David Lean's first film for 14 years. It was also his last. *Dir.* David Lean.

Passion of the Christ, The (2004)   Jim Caviezel (Jesus), Monica Bellucci (Mary Magdalen), Hristo Naumov Shopov (Pontius Pilate), Maia Morgenstern (Mary), Francesco De Vito (Peter), Luca Lionello (Judas), Mattia Sbragia (Caiaphas), Rosalinda Celentano (Satan). This truly graphic and disturbing film based on the last hours of Jesus Christ serves as both a *memento mori* and *memento vivere* to all who watch it. Dialogue in Aramaic, Latin and Hebrew with English subtitles. *Dir.* Mel Gibson.

Passport to Pimlico (1949)   Stanley Holloway, Margaret Rutherford, Basil Radford, Sydney Tafler, Hermione Baddeley. Part of postwar London is discovered to belong to Burgundy and the residents find themselves free of rationing restrictions. Based on a real-life story whereby the Canadian government presented to Holland the room where Princess Juliana was to bear a child. *Dir.* Henry Cornelius.

Pat and Mike (1952)   Spencer Tracy, Katharine Hepburn, Aldo Ray. Small-time sports promoter takes on a female intellectual multi-champion. *Dir.* George Cukor.

Patriot Games (1992)   Harrison Ford (Jack Ryan), Anne Archer, Patrick Bergin, Sean Bean, Samuel L Jackson James Fox, Richard Harris, James Earl Jones, Thora Birch. *Dir.* Philip Noyce.

Patton (1969)   George C Scott, Karl Malden, Michael Bates. Famous for Scott's refusal to collect his Oscar. *Dir.* Franklin Schaffner.

Patty Hearst (1988)   Natasha Richardson, William Forsythe, Ving Rhames, Frances Fisher. *Dir.* Paul Schrader.

Peacemaker, The (1997)   Nicole Kidman (Dr Julia Kelly), George Clooney (Lt Col Thomas Devoe). First film from Steven Spielberg's Dreamworks Studio. *Dir.* Mimi Leder.

Pearl Harbor (2001)   Ben Affleck, Josh Hartnett, Kate Beckinsale, Cuba Gooding, Jon Voight, Dan Aykroyd, Alec Baldwin, James King, Tom Sizemore, *Dir.* Michael Bay.

Pearl of Death, The (1944)   Basil Rathbone (Holmes), Nigel Bruce (Watson), Dennis Hoey, Miles Mander, Rondo Hatton. Based on Conan Doyle's 'The Six Napoleons'. *Dir.* Roy William Neill.

Peggy Sue Got Married (1986)   Kathleen Turner (Peggy Sue), Nicolas Cage (Charlie Bodell), Jim Carrey (Walter Getz), Barry Miller, Catherine Hicks, Joan Allen, Helen Hunt (Beth Bodell). *Dir.* Francis Ford Coppola.

Pelican Brief, The (1993)   Julia Roberts, Denzel Washington, Sam Shepard, John Heard, Robert Culp. Law student is stalked by hitmen after she suspects their involvement in murder of 2 judges. *Dir.* Alan J Pakula.

People vs Larry Flint, The (1996)   Woody Harrelson (Larry Flynt, the self-styled King of Sleaze), Courteney Love, Edward Norton. Biopic of the publisher of soft porn mag *Hustler. Dir.* Milos Forman.

Perez Family, The (1995)   Marisa Tomei, Alfred Molina, Anjelica Huston. *Dir.* Mira Nair.

Perfect (1985)   John Travolta (Adam), Jamie Lee Curtis (Jessie), Anne De Salvo (Frankie). Journalist falls in love with aerobics teacher he is investigating. *Dir.* James Bridges.

Perfect Storm, The (1999)   George Clooney, Mark Wahlberg, Diane Lane, Mary Elizabeth Mastrantonio, Michael Ironside. Six Massachusetts fishermen encounter a raging storm in their boat 'Andrea Gail'. *Dir.* Wolfgang Peterson.

Perfect World, A (1993)   Clint Eastwood, Kevin Costner, Laura Dern. *Dir.* Clint Eastwood.

Performance (1970)   James Fox, Mick Jagger, Anita Pallenberg, Allan Cuthbertson. *Dir.* Nicolas Roeg & Donald Cammell.

Perils of Pauline, The (1934)   Betty Hutton, John Lund, Billy de Wolfe. The career of silent serial queen Pearl White. *Dir.* George Marshall.

Personal Services (1987)   Julie Walters (Christine Painter), Alec McCowen (Wing Commander Morton), Shirley Stellfox. Read 'Cynthia Payne' for Christine Painter. *Dir.* Terry Jones.

Peter's Friends (1992)   Kenneth Branagh (Andrew), Alphonsia Emmanuel (Sarah), Stephen Fry (Peter), Hugh Laurie (Roger), Phyllida Law (Vera), Rita Rudner (Carol), Emma Thompson (Maggie). *Dir.* Kenneth Branagh.

Phantom of the Opera (1925)   Lon Chaney, Mary Philbin, Norman Kerry. Remakes include 1943 version with Claude Rains, 1962 film with Herbert Lom and 1989 version with Robert Englund. *Dir.* Rupert Julian.

Phenomenon (1996)   John Travolta, Kyra Sedgwick, Robert Duvall, Forest Whitaker, Brent Spiner. Simpleton is struck by a strange light which raises his IQ and his sensitivity. *Dir.* James Cameron.

Philadelphia (1993)   Tom Hanks, Denzel Washington, Jason Robards, Mary Steenburgen, Antonio Banderas, Joanne Woodward, Robert Ridgely. Homosexual lawyer with AIDS sues his firm for unfair dismissal. *Dir.* Jonathan Demme.

Philadelphia Story, The (1940)   Katharine Hepburn, Cary Grant, James Stewart, Ruth Hussey. *Dir.* George Cukor.

Pianist, The (2002)   Adrien Brody (Wladyslaw Szpilman), Thomas Kretschmann (Captain Wilm Hosenfeld), Frank Finlay (the father), Maureen Lipman (the mother), Emilia Fox (Dorota), Ed Stoppard (Henryk), Julia Rayner (Regina), Jessica Kate Meyer (Halina), Ruth Platt (Janina). Based on the autobiography of Wladyslaw Szpilman, a Polish Jew who survived the Nazi occupation of World War II. A composer and pianist, he plays the last live music

C
I
N
E
M
A

heard over Polish radio before the invasion. Eluding deportation, he remains in the devastated Warsaw ghetto and struggles to stay alive. *Dir.* Roman Polanski.

Piano, The (1993)   Holly Hunter, Harvey Keitel, Sam Neill, Genevieve Lemon. *Dir.* Jane Campion.

Picnic (1955)   William Holden, Kim Novak, Rosalind Russell, Susan Strasberg. *Dir.* Joshua Logan.

Picnic at Hanging Rock (1975)   Rachel Roberts, Dominic Guard, Helen Morse, Vivian Gray. *Dir.* Peter Weir.

Picture of Dorian Gray, The (1945)   Hurd Hatfield (Gray), George Sanders (Sir Henry), Donna Reed, Angela Lansbury. *Dir.* Albert Lewin.

Pillow Talk (1959)   Doris Day, Rock Hudson, Tony Randall, Thelma Ritter. First of the partnership films of Day and Hudson, this one concerning a party line love affair. *Dir.* Michael Gordon.

Pink Panther, The (1963)   David Niven, Peter Sellers, Capucine, Claudia Cardinale, Robert Wagner. The seven sequels were *A Shot in the Dark, Inspector Clouseau, Return of the Pink Panther, The Pink Panther Strikes Again, The Revenge of the Pink Panther, Trail of the Pink Panther* and *Son of the Pink Panther. Dir.* Blake Edwards.

Pirates of the Caribbean: The Curse of the Black Pearl (2003)   Johnny Depp (Jack Sparrow), Geoffrey Rush (Barbossa), Orlando Bloom (Will Turner), Keira Knightley (Elizabeth Swann), Jack Davenport (Norrington), Kevin R McNally (Joshamee Gibbs), Zoe Saldana (Anamaria), Jonathan Pryce (Governor Weatherby Swann). *Dir.* Gore Verbinski.

Pit and the Pendulum, The (1961)   Vincent Price, Barbara Steele, John Kerr. *Dir.* Roger Corman.

Place in the Sun, A (1951)   Montgomery Clift, Elizabeth Taylor, Shelley Winters, Raymond Burr. Man is offered the chance of a rich wife, but allows himself to be convicted and executed for the accidental death of his former fiancée. *Dir.* George Stevens.

Planes, Trains and Automobiles (1987)   Steve Martin (Neal Page), John Candy (Del Griffith), Laila Robbins, Kevin Bacon. Yuppie attempts to get home to his family for a snowy Thanksgiving. *Dir.* John Hughes.

Planet of the Apes (1968)   Charlton Heston, Roddy McDowall, Kim Hunter, James Whitmore. John Chambers won Oscar for Make-up. Sequels included *Beneath the Planet of the Apes* (1969), *Escape from the Planet of the Apes* (1970), *Conquest of the Planet of the Apes* (1972), and *Battle for the Planet of the Apes* (1973). *Dir.* Franklin Schaffner.

Platoon (1986)   Tom Berenger (Sgt Barnes), Willem Dafoe (Sgt Elias), Charlie Sheen (Chris), Johnny Depp (Lerner), Forest Whitaker (Big Harold). *Dir.* Oliver Stone.

Play Misty for Me (1971)   Clint Eastwood, Jessica Walter, Donna Mills, John Larch. *Dir.* Clint Eastwood.

Player, The (1992)   Tim Robbins (Griffin Mill), Greta Scacchi (June Gudmundsdottir), Fred Ward (Walter Stuckel), Whoopi Goldberg (Det. Avery), Richard E Grant (Tom Oakley), Sydney Pollack (Dick Mellen). This satire on Hollywood also starred 65 other stars who accepted nominal fees, including, Steve Allen, Cher, James Coburn, Peter Falk, Teri Garr, Jeff Goldblum, Elliott Gould, Joel Grey, Anjelica Huston, Sally Kellerman, Jack Lemmon, Marlee Matlin, Nick Nolte, Malcolm McDowell, Burt Reynolds, Julia Roberts, Mimi Rogers, Annie Ross, Jill St John, Susan Sarandon, Rod Steiger, Lily Tomlin, Robert Wagner, Bruce Willis. *Dir.* Robert Altman.

Ploughman's Lunch, The (1983)   Jonathan Pryce (James Penfield), Tim Curry (Jeremy Hancock),

Charlie Dore (Sue Barrington). British journalist furthers his career by rewriting history. *Dir.* Richard Eyre.

Pocahontas (1995)   Voices of Mel Gibson, Irene Bedard, David Ogden Stiers, Judy Kuhn, Billy Connolly. *Dir.* Mike Gabriel and Eric Goldberg.

Point Blank (1967)   Lee Marvin, Angie Dickinson, Keenan Wynn, Carroll O'Connor. Based on the novel *The Hunter* by Richard Stark. *Dir.* John Boorman.

Point Break (1991)   Patrick Swayze (Bodhi), Keanu Reeves (Johnny Utah), Gary Busey, Lori Petty. FBI man Reeves infiltrates a gang of surfers to investigate bank robberies. *Dir.* Kathryn Bigelow.

Pokemon: The First Movie (1999)   Animation based on the popular Japanese characters. To date two subsequent sequels have arisen – *Pokemon 2: The Power of One; Pokemon 3 the Movie: Spell of the Unknown. Dir.* Kunihiko Yuyama.

Polar Express, The (2004)   Tom Hanks (Hero Boy/Father/Conductor/Hobo/Scrooge/Santa Claus), Leslie Harter Zemeckis (Sister Sarah/Mother (as Leslie Zemeckis), Eddie Dezeen (Know-it-All). Santa Claus does not exist. Or does he? For one doubting boy (voice of Daryl Sabara and Tom Hanks), an astonishing event occurs. *Dir.* Robert Zemeckis.

Police Academy (1984)   Steve Guttenberg (Carey), Kim Cattrall (Karen), Bubba Smith (Moses), GW Bailey (Lt. Harris), David Graf (Tackleberry), Donovan Scott (Leslie). Sequels include *2: Their First Assignment; 3: Back in Training; 4: Citizens on Patrol; 5: Assignment Miami Beach; 6: City under Siege. Dir.* Hugh Wilson.

Poltergeist (1982)   JoBeth Williams, Craig T Nelson, Beatrice Straight, Oliver Robbins, Dominique Dunne. Two inferior sequels were made. *Dir.* Tobe Hooper.

Pope Joan (1972)   Liv Ullmann, Trevor Howard, Olivia de Havilland, Franco Nero, Maximilian Schell. *Dir.* Michael Anderson.

Pope Must Die, The (1991)   Robbie Coltrane, Beverly D'Angelo, Herbert Lom, Alex Rocco, Annette Crosbie. *Dir.* Peter Richardson.

Popeye (1980)   Robin Williams, Shelley Duvall, Ray Walston. *Dir.* Robert Altman.

Postcards From the Edge (1990)   Meryl Streep, Shirley MacLaine, Dennis Quaid, Gene Hackman, Richard Dreyfuss, Annette Bening. *Dir.* Mike Nichols.

Postman Always Rings Twice, The (1981)   Jack Nicholson, Jessica Lange, Anjelica Huston. Remake of the 1946 film starring Lana Turner & John Garfield. *Dir.* Bob Rafelson.

Predator (1987)   Arnold Schwarzenegger (Dutch), Carl Weathers (Dillon), Kevin Peter Hall (The Predator). *Predator 2* starred Danny Glover and Gary Busey. *Dir.* John McTiernan.

Prêt-à-Porter (1994)   Anouk Aimée, Lauren Bacall, Kim Basinger, Sophia Loren, Marcello Mastroianni, Julia Roberts, Teri Garr, Tracey Ullman, Richard E Grant. Aka *Ready to Wear. Dir.* Robert Altman.

Pretty Woman (1990)   Richard Gere (Edward Lewis), Julia Roberts (Vivian Ward), Ralph Bellamy (James Morse). *Dir.* Garry Marshall.

Prick up Your Ears (1987)   Gary Oldman (Joe Orton), Alfred Molina (Kenneth Halliwell), Vanessa Redgrave (Peggy), Julie Walters (Elsie Orton), Lindsay Duncan (Anthea Lahr). *Dir.* Stephen Frears.

Prime of Miss Jean Brodie, The (1969)   Maggie Smith, Robert Stephens, Pamela Franklin, Celia Johnson, Gordon Jackson. *Dir.* Ronald Neame.

Prince and the Pauper (1937)   Errol Flynn, Claude Rains, Billy and Bobby Mauch, Montagu Love (Henry VIII). Edward VI changes place with a street urchin. *Dir.* William Keighley. The 1977 remake starred Mark

Lester, Oliver Reed and Raquel Welch (*Dir*. Richard Fleischer).

Prince and the Showgirl (1957)   Laurence Olivier, Marilyn Monroe, Sybil Thorndike. *Dir*. Laurence Olivier.

Prince of Tides, The (1991)   Nick Nolte (Tom Wingo), Barbra Streisand (Susan Lowenstein), Blythe Danner, Kate Nelligan. *Dir*. Barbra Streisand.

Prisoner of Zenda (1952)   Stewart Granger, James Mason, Deborah Kerr, Louis Calhern. *Dir*. Richard Thorpe. Remake of the 1937 classic starring Ronald Colman and Douglas Fairbanks Jr (*Dir*. John Cromwell). A further remake of 1979 starred Peter Sellers and Lynne Frederick (*Dir*. Richard Thorpe).

Private Function, A (1984)   Michael Palin, Maggie Smith, Denholm Elliott, Richard Griffiths, Betty the Pig. *Dir*. Malcolm Mowbray.

Private Life of Henry VIII, The (1933)   Charles Laughton, Elsa Lanchester, Robert Donat, Merle Oberon. *Dir*. Alexander Korda.

Private Parts (1996)   Howard Stern (as himself), Mary McCormack (Alison). Screen biography of top US disc jockey. *Dir*. Betty Thomas.

Prizzi's Honor (1985)   Jack Nicholson, Kathleen Turner, Robert Loggia, Anjelica Huston. *Dir*. John Huston.

Producers, The (1968)   Zero Mostel, Gene Wilder, Kenneth Mars. The play within the film is *Springtime for Hitler*. *Dir*. Mel Brooks.

Prospero's Books (1991)   John Gielgud, Michael Clark, Tom Bell, Mark Rylance. *Dir*. Peter Greenaway.

Psycho (1960)   Anthony Perkins, Vera Miles, Janet Leigh, John Gavin, Martin Balsam. Shower stabbing scene was directed by Saul Bass. Two sequels also starring Perkins in 1983 and 1986. *Dir*. Alfred Hitchcock.

Pulp Fiction (1994)   John Travolta, Samuel L Jackson, Uma Thurman, Harvey Keitel, Tim Roth, Bruce Willis, Rosanna Arquette. *Dir*. Quentin Tarantino.

Punchline (1988)   Sally Field (Lilah Krytsick), Tom Hanks (Steven Gold), John Goodman (John Krytsick), Mark Rydell (Romeo), Kim Greist (Madeline Urie). As the title suggests the film examines the world of a stand-up comedian. *Dir*. David Seltzer.

Quadrophenia (1979)   Phil Daniels, Mark Wingett, Philip Davis, Sting, Leslie Ash, Toyah Willcox. *Dir*. Frank Roddam.

Queen Christina (1933)   Greta Garbo, John Gilbert, Ian Keith, Lewis Stone, Reginald Owen. Queen of Sweden roams the country to escape a political marriage. *Dir*. Rouben Mamoulian.

Quick and the Dead, The (1995)   Sharon Stone, Gene Hackman, Leonard DiCaprio. *Dir*. Sam Raimi.

Quiet American, The (2002)   Michael Caine, Brendan Fraser, Do Thi Hai Yen, Rade Sherbedgia. Set in Vietnam in 1952 during the Vietnamese liberation war against French rule, this is the story of a romantic triangle that develops between a young CIA agent (Fraser), a beautiful young Vietnamese woman (Do Hai Yen) and a British reporter (Caine). Based on the Graham Greene novel. *Dir*. Phillip Noyce.

Quiet Man, The (1952)   John Wayne, Maureen O'Hara, Barry Fitzgerald, Victor McLaglen, Ward Bond. *Dir*. John Ford.

Quigley Down Under (1990)   Tom Selleck, Laura San Giacomo, Alan Rickman, Chris Haywood. In 1860s Australia, an American hired gun is outlawed. *Dir*. Simon Wincer.

Quiller Memorandum, The (1966)   George Segal, Max Von Sydow, Alec Guinness, Senta Berger, George Sanders. *Dir*. Michael Anderson.

Quiz Show (1994)   John Turturro, Ralph Fiennes, Rob Morrow, Paul Scofield, Martin Scorsese. *Dir*. Robert Redford.

Quo Vadis (1951)   Robert Taylor, Deborah Kerr, Peter Ustinov, Leo Genn. *Dir*. Mervyn Le Roy.

Rabbit-Proof Fence (2002)   Everlyn Sampi (Molly Craig), Tianna Sansbury (Daisy Craig), Laura Monaghan (Gracie Fields), David Gulpilil (Moodoo), Kenneth Branagh (AO Neville), Deborah Mailman (Mavis), Jason Clarke (Constable Riggs), Ningali Lawford (Molly's Mother). True story based on the book *Follow the Rabbit-Proof Fence* by Molly's daughter Doris Pilkington Garimara, concerning three young aborigine girls who are taken away from their mother to be integrated into white society in 1930s Australia. *Dir*. Phillip Noyce.

Radio Days (1987)   Woody Allen (Narrator), Mia Farrow (Sally White), Seth Green (Little Joe), Julie Kavner (Mother), Michael Tucker (Father), Diane Keaton (New Year's singer). *Dir*. Woody Allen.

Rage, The: Carrie 2 (1999)   Emily Bergl, Jason London, Dylan Bruno, Amy Irving, John Doe, Zachery Ty Bryan. *Dir*. Katt Shea.

Rage in Harlem, A (1991)   Forest Whitaker, Gregory Hines, Robin Givens, Danny Glover. *Dir*. Bill Duke.

Raging Bull (1980)   Robert De Niro, Cathy Moriarty, Joe Pesci. *Dir*. Martin Scorsese.

Raiders of the Lost Ark (1981)   Harrison Ford, Karen Allen, John Rhys-Davies, Denholm Elliott. *Dir*. Steven Spielberg.

Railway Children, The (1970)   Dinah Sheridan, William Mervyn, Jenny Agutter, Sally Thomsett, Bernard Cribbins. *Dir*. Lionel Jeffries.

Rain Man (1988)   Dustin Hoffman (Raymond Babbitt), Tom Cruise (Charles Babbitt), Valerie Golino (Susanna). *Dir*. Barry Levinson.

Raising Arizona (1987)   Nicolas Cage (HI), Holly Hunter (Ed), Trey Wilson (Nathan Arizona Sr), John Goodman (Gale). *Dir*. Joel Coen.

Raising Victor Vargas (2002)   Victor Rasuk (Victor Vargas), Judy Marte (Judy Ramirez), Melonie Diaz (Melonie), Altagracia Guzman (Grandma), Silvestre Rasuk (Nino Vargas), Krystal Rodriguez (Vicki Vargas), Kevin Rivera (Harold), Wilfree Vasquez (Carlos). A 16-year-old in New York's Lower East Side struggles to come to terms with growing up. *Dir*. Peter Sollett.

Rambo: First Blood Part II (1985)   Sylvester Stallone, Richard Crenna, Steven Berkoff. Written by Sylvester Stallone & James Cameron. *Dir*. George Pan Cosmatos.

Rambo III (1988)   Sylvester Stallone, Richard Crenna, Marc de Jonge. Written by Sylvester Stallone and Sheldon Lettich. *Dir*. Peter MacDonald.

Ran (1985)   Tatsuya Nakadai, Satoshi Terao. Japanese version of *King Lear*. *Dir*. Akira Kurosawa.

Ray (2004)   Jamie Foxx (Ray Charles), CJ Sanders (young Ray Robinson), Regina King (Margie Hendricks), Kerry Washington (Della Bea Robinson), Clifton Powell (Jeff Brown), Aunjanue Ellis (Mary Ann Fisher), Harry Lennix, Terrence Dashon Howard, Larenz Tate (Quincy Jones), Sharon Warren. The life story of legendary singer Ray Charles, who went blind, aged seven, after witnessing his younger brother's accidental death. *Dir*. Taylor Hackford.

Reach for the Sky (1956)   Kenneth More (Douglas Bader), Muriel Pavlow. *Dir*. Lewis Gilbert.

Rear Window (1954)   James Stewart, Grace Kelly, Raymond Burr. *Dir*. Alfred Hitchcock.

Rebecca (1940)   Laurence Olivier, Joan Fontaine, George Sanders. *Dir*. Alfred Hitchcock.

C
I
N
E
M
A

Rebel without a Cause (1955)   James Dean, Natalie Wood, Jim Backus, Sal Mineo, Dennis Hopper. *Dir.* Nicholas Ray.

Red Heat (1988)   Arnold Schwarzenegger (Ivan Danko), James Belushi (Art Ridzik), Peter Boyle (Lou Donnelly). *Dir.* Walter Hill.

Red Sonja (1985)   Arnold Schwarzenegger (Kalifor), Brigitte Nielsen (Red Sonja). *Dir.* Richard Fleischer.

Reds (1981)   Warren Beatty (John Reed), Diane Keaton, Edward Herrmann, Jerzy Kosinski, Jack Nicholson. *Dir.* Warren Beatty.

Relic, The (1997)   Tom Sizemore (D'Agosta), Penelope Ann Miller (Dr Margo Green). *Dir.* Peter Hyams.

Remains of the Day, The (1993)   Anthony Hopkins, Emma Thompson, James Fox, Christopher Reeve, Peter Vaughan, Hugh Grant. *Dir.* James Ivory.

Repulsion (1965)   Catherine Deneuve, Ian Hendry, John Fraser, Patrick Wymark. *Dir.* Roman Polanski.

Reservoir Dogs (1991)   Lawrence Tierney, Harvey Keitel (Mr White), Tim Roth (Mr Orange), Eddie Bunker (Mr Blue), Michael Madsen (Mr Blonde), Steve Buscemi (Mr Pink), Quentin Tarantino (Mr Brown). *Dir.* Quentin Tarantino.

Resident Evil (2002)   Milla Jovovich (Alice), Michelle Rodriguez (Rain), Eric Mabius (Matt), Michaela Dicker (Red Queen). Virus turns workers into flesh-eating zombies. *Dir.* Paul WS Anderson.

Return of the Swamp Thing (1989)   Louis Jourdan (Dr Anton Arcane), Heather Locklear (Abby Arcane), Dick Durock (Swamp Thing). *Dir.* Jim Wynorski.

Return of the Jedi (1983)   Mark Hamill, Harrison Ford, Carrie Fisher, Billy Dee Williams. *Dir.* Richard Marquand.

Revenge (1990)   Kevin Costner (Jay Cochran), Anthony Quinn (Tiburon), Madeleine Stowe (Miryea). *Dir.* Tony Scott.

Revenge of the Pink Panther (1978)   Peter Sellers, Herbert Lom, Dyan Cannon. *Dir.* Blake Edwards.

Reversal of Fortune (1990)   Jeremy Irons (Claus Von Bulow), Glenn Close (Sunny Von Bulow), Julie Hagerty (Alexandra). *Dir.* Barbet Schroeder.

Revolution (1985)   Al Pacino (Tom Dobb), Donald Sutherland (Sgt Major Peasy), Nastassja Kinski (Daisy). Notable for being the biggest flop of all time. *Dir.* Hugh Hudson.

Rhapsody in Blue (1945)   Robert Alda (George Gershwin), Joan Leslie, Alexis Smith. *Dir.* Irving Rapper.

Richard III (1995)   Ian McKellen, Annette Bening, Jim Broadbent, Robert Downey Jnr, Kristin Scott-Thomas, Maggie Smith, Nigel Hawthorne. Ian McKellen wrote the screenplay. *Dir.* Richard Loncraine.

Rififi (1955)   Jean Servais, Carl Mohner, Jules Dassin. Famous for its 25 minutes of silence whilst robbery is taking place. *Dir.* Jules Dassin.

Right Stuff, The (1983)   Sam Shepard (Chuck Yeager), Barbara Hershey (Glennis), Scott Glenn (Alan Shepard), Ed Harris (John Glenn), Fred Ward (Gus Grissom), Dennis Quaid (Gordon Cooper). *Dir.* Philip Kaufman.

Rising Sun (1993)   Sean Connery, Harvey Keitel, Wesley Snipes, Mako. *Dir.* Philip Kaufman.

Road House (1989)   Patrick Swayze, Kelly Lynch, Sam Elliott, Ben Gazzara, Marshall Teague. *Dir.* Rowdy Herrington.

Road to Hong Kong (1962)   Bob Hope, Bing Crosby, Dorothy Lamour, Joan Collins, Peter Sellers, Frank Sinatra, Dean Martin, David Niven. Last of the seven *Road* films. *Dir.* Norman Panama.

Road to Perdition (2002)   Tom Hanks (Michael Sullivan), Paul Newman (John Rooney), Jude Law (Maguire), Jennifer Jason Leigh (Annie Sullivan), Tyler Hoechlin (Michael Sullivan Jr) *Dir.* Sam Mendes.

Road to Singapore (1940)   Bob Hope, Bing Crosby, Dorothy Lamour, Anthony Quinn. First of the seven *Road* films, destination followed by Zanzibar, Moscow, Utopia, Rio, Bali and Hong Kong. *Dir.* Victor Schertzinger.

Rob Roy (1995)   Liam Neeson, Jessica Lange, John Hurt, Tim Roth. *Dir.* Michael Caton-Jones.

Robe, The (1953)   Richard Burton, Jean Simmons, Michael Rennie, Victor Mature, Richard Boone. *Dir.* Henry Koster.

Robin Hood (1991)   Patrick Bergin, Uma Thurman, Edward Fox. *Dir.* John Irvin.

Robin Hood: Men in Tights (1993)   Cary Elwes, Richard Lewis, Roger Rees, Tracey Ullman, Mel Brooks, Isaac Hayes, Patrick Stewart. *Dir.* Mel Brooks.

Robin Hood: Prince of Thieves (1991)   Kevin Costner, Morgan Freeman, Christian Slater, Alan Rickman, Sean Connery (uncredited). Title song: 'Everything I Do I Do for You' by Bryan Adams. *Dir.* Kevin Reynolds.

Robocop (1987)   Peter Weller, Nancy Allen, Ronny Cox. *Dir.* Paul Verhoeven.

Rock, The (1996)   Sean Connery, Nicolas Cage, Ed Harris. *Dir.* Michael Bay.

Rocking Horse Winner, The (1949)   John Mills, Valerie Hobson, John Howard Davies, Cyril Smith. Based on a DH Lawrence short story. *Dir.* Anthony Pelissier.

Rocky (1976)   Sylvester Stallone, Burgess Meredith, Talia Shire, Carl Weathers. Written by Sylvester Stallone. *Dir.* John G Avildsen.

Rocky II (1979)   Stallone, Meredith, Shire, Weathers. Written and directed by Stallone.

Rocky III (1982)   Stallone, Meredith, Shire, Weathers, Mr T, Hulk Hogan. Written and directed by Stallone.

Rocky IV (1985)   Stallone, Dolph Lundgren, T Shire, Weathers, Brigitte Nielsen. Written and directed by Stallone.

Rocky V (1990)   Stallone, Meredith, Shire, Burt Young, Sage Stallone. Written by Stallone. *Dir.* John G Avildsen.

Rocky Horror Picture Show, The (1975)   Tim Curry, Susan Sarandon, Meat Loaf, Little Nell. *Dir.* Jim Sharman.

Roman Holiday (1953)   Gregory Peck, Audrey Hepburn, Eddie Albert, Hartley Power. *Dir.* William Wyler.

Roman Scandals (1933)   Eddie Cantor, Gloria Stuart, Ruth Etting, Edward Arnold. *Dir.* Frank Tuttle.

Romancing the Stone (1984)   Michael Douglas, Kathleen Turner, Danny De Vito, Zack Norman. *Dir.* Robert Zemeckis.

Rookie, The (1990)   Clint Eastwood (Nick Pulovski), Charlie Sheen (David Ackerman), Raul Julia (Strom). *Dir.* Clint Eastwood.

Rookie of the Year (1993)   Gary Busey, Thomas Ian Nicholas, Albert Hall, John Candy (uncredited). Young boy becomes pitcher for the Chicago Cubs after his arm is injured in an accident. *Dir.* Daniel Stern.

Room at the Top (1959)   Laurence Harvey, Simone Signoret, Heather Sears, Donald Wolfit. Based on John Braine's novel. *Dir.* Jack Clayton.

Room with a View, A (1986)   Maggie Smith (Charlotte Bartlett), Helena Bonham Carter (Lucy Honeychurch). Opens in Italy in 1907. *Dir.* James Ivory.

Rope (1948)   James Stewart, John Dall, Farley Granger, Joan Chandler. Two homosexuals murder a friend for the thrill of it and hide his body in a trunk from which they serve cocktails to a party. *Dir*. Alfred Hitchcock.

Rose, The (1979)   Bette Midler, Alan Bates, Frederic Forrest, Harry Dean Stanton. *Dir*. Mark Rydell.

Rosencrantz and Guildenstern Are Dead (1990)   Gary Oldman (Rosencrantz), Tim Roth (Guildenstern), Iain Glen (Prince Hamlet). *Dir*. Tom Stoppard.

Running Man, The (1987)   Arnold Schwarzenegger (Ben Richards), Maria Conchita Alonso (Amber Mendez), Yaphet Kotto (Laughlin), Jim Brown (Fireball). *Dir*. Paul Michael Glaser.

Rush Hour (1998)   Jackie Chan (Lee), Chris Tucker (Carter), Tom Wilkinson, Elizabeth Pena, Mark Rolston, Tzi Ma, Philip Baker Hall. Chinese detective joins a disgraced LA cop in bringing a master criminal to justice. *Dir*. Brett Ratner.

Rush Hour 2 (2001)   Jackie Chan (Lee), Chris Tucker (Carter), John Lone (Ricky Tan), Zhang Ziyi (Hui Li). Sequel set in Hong Kong. *Dir*. Brett Ratner.

Russia House, The (1990)   Sean Connery, Michelle Pfeiffer, Roy Scheider, James Fox. *Dir*. Fred Schepisi.

Ruthless People (1986)   Bette Midler, Danny De Vito, Judge Reinhold, Helen Slater. *Dir*. Jim Abrahams.

Ryan's Daughter (1970)   Robert Mitchum, Sarah Miles, John Mills, Trevor Howard. *Dir*. David Lean.

Saint, The (1997)   Val Kilmer (Simon Templar), Elisabeth Shue (Emma Russell). Roger Moore's voice heard on car radio. *Dir*. Phillip Noyce.

Santa Claus: The Movie (1985)   Dudley Moore (Patch), John Lithgow (BZ), David Huddleston (Claus), Burgess Meredith (Elf). *Dir*. Jeannot Szwarc.

Saturday Night and Sunday Morning (1960)   Albert Finney, Shirley Anne Field, Rachel Roberts. Nottingham factory worker is dissatisfied with his lot. *Dir*. Karel Reisz.

Saturday Night Fever (1977)   John Travolta, Karen Lynn Gorney, Barry Miller. *Dir*. John Badham.

Save the Last Dance (2001)   Julia Stiles (Sara), Sean Patrick Thomas (Derek), Kerry Washington (Chenille), Fredro Starr (Malakai). Young white ballerina moves to Chicago and falls in love with a black youth. *Dir*. Thomas Carter.

Saving Private Ryan (1998)   Tom Hanks, Edward Burns, Tom Sizemore, Matt Damon, Ted Danson, Harve Presnell. *Dir*. Steven Spielberg. (Author's Note: I believe this is the first work to be published which highlights a subtle continuity error. After losing one of the eight original platoon members all eight can be seen marching across a field, but fortunately become seven again on arrival at a radar station!)

Scandal (1989)   John Hurt (Stephen Ward), Joanne Whalley-Kilmer (Christine Keeler), Bridget Fonda (Mandy Rice-Davies), Ian McKellen (John Profumo), Leslie Phillips, Britt Ekland, Jean Alexander, Jeroen Krabb, Michael Ironside. *Dir*. Michael Caton-Jones.

Scanners (1981)   Stephen Lock, Jennifer O'Neill, Patrick McGoohan, Michael Ironside. *Dir*. David Cronenberg.

Scanners II: The New Order (1991)   David Hewlett, Yvan Ponton, Raoul Trujillo. *Dir*. Christian Duguay.

Scanners III: The Takeover (1992)   Liliana Komorowska, Valerie Valcis, Steve Parrish, Harry Hill. *Dir*. Christian Duguay.

Scarface (1983)   Al Pacino (Tony Montana), Steven Bauer (Manny Ray), Michelle Pfeiffer (Elvira), Mary Elizabeth Mastrantonio (Gina), Robert Loggia (Frank Lopez), F Murray Abraham (Omar). *Dir*. Brian De Palma.

Scarlet Letter, The (1995)   Demi Moore, Gary Oldman, Robert Duvall, Robert Prosky, Joan Plowright. Set in C17 Massachusetts; a settler's wife gives birth to an illegitimate daughter. Based on the Nathaniel Hawthorne novel, the scarlet letter is 'A' for adultery. *Dir*. Roland Joffé.

Scary Movie (2000)   Marlon Wayans (Shorty), Shawn Wayans (Ray), Anna Faris (Cindy), Shannon Elizabeth (Buffy), Cheri Oteri (Gail Hailstorm). A killer murders high-school children in this horror-movie spoof. *Dir*. Keenen Ivory Wayans.

Scary Movie 2 (2001)   Marlon Wayans (Shorty), Shawn Wayans (Ray), Anna Faris (Cindy), Regina Hall (Brenda), Chris Masterson (Buddy), Tim Curry (The Professor), Kathleen Robertson (Theo), James Woods (Father McFeely). Sequel concerning psychology professor who invites students to spend a weekend in a haunted house. *Dir*. Keenen Ivory Wayans.

Scenes from a Mall (1991)   Bette Midler, Woody Allen, Paul Mazursky. *Dir*. Paul Mazursky.

Scent of a Woman (1992)   Al Pacino, Chris O'Donnell, Gabrielle Anwar. Blind ex-officer takes young man under his wing. *Dir*. Martin Brest.

Schindler's List (1993)   Liam Neeson, Ben Kingsley, Ralph Fiennes. *Dir*. Steven Spielberg.

School of Rock, The (2003)   Jack Black (Dewey Finn), Joan Cusack (Rosalie Mullins), Mike White (Ned Schneebly), Sarah Silverman (Patty Di Marco), Joey Gaydos Jnr (Zack), Robert Tsai (Lawrence), Maryam Hassan (Tomika), Kevin Clark (Freddy Jones). A wannabe rock musician impersonates a teacher at an upmarket school and turns a class of ten-year-olds into a successful band. *Dir*. Richard Linklater.

Scooby-Doo (2002)   Freddie Prinze Jr (Fred), Sarah Michelle Gellar (Daphne), Matthew Lillard (Shaggy), Linda Cardellini (Velma). Real-life version of the Hanna-Barbera cartoon. *Dir*. Raja Gosnell.

Scorpion King, The (2002)   Dwayne Johnson, Steven Brand, Michael Clarke Duncan, The Rock (Mathayus/The Scorpion King), Kelly Hu, Bernard Hill. Spin-off from *The Mummy Returns*. *Dir*. Chuck Russell.

Scream (1996)   David Arquette, Neve Campbell (Sidney), Courteney Cox (Gale Weathers), Drew Barrymore. *Dir*. Wes Craven.

Screamers (1996)   Peter Weller, Roy Dupuis, Jennifer Rubin, Ron White. Set in 2078 on the planet Sirius 6B where killer robots run amok. *Dir*. Christian Duguay.

Sea of Love (1989)   Al Pacino (Frank Keller), Ellen Barkin (Helen Cruger), John Goodman (Sherman Touhy). Cop investigating murders of lonely hearts advertisers places an ad himself. *Dir*. Harold Becker.

Seabiscuit (2003) Tobey Maguire (Red Pollard), Jeff Bridges (Charles Howard), Chris Cooper (Tom Smith), Elizabeth Banks (Marcela Howard), Gary Stevens (George Woolf), William H Macy (Tick-Tock McGlaughlin), Kingston DuCoeur (Sam), Eddie Jones (Samuel Riddle). Based on Laura Hillenbrand's book about the true story of champion racehorse Seabiscuit. *Dir*. Gary Ross.

Searchers, The (1956)   John Wayne (Ethan Edwards), Jeffrey Hunter (Martin Pawley), Vera Miles (Laurie Jorgenson), Natalie Wood (Debbie Edwards), Ward Bond (Rev. Capt. Samuel Johnston Clayton), Henry Brandon (Chief Cicatrice, aka Scar), Lana Wood (Debbie Edwards (child)). A civil war veteran spends years searching for his young niece, captured by Indians. *Dir*. John Ford.

C
I
N
E
M
A

Sebastiane (1976)   Leonardo Treviglio, Barney James, Neil Kennedy, Ken Hicks. Title character is banished by Emperor Diocletian and suffers further tragedy. Dialogue is in Latin with English subtitles. *Dir.* Derek Jarman and Paul Humfress.

Secret Garden, The (1949)   Margaret O'Brien, Herbert Marshall, Gladys Cooper, Elsa Lanchester, Dean Stockwell, Brian Roper. Adaptation of the novel by Frances Hodgson Burnett which was shot in black and white but the scenes in the garden were filmed in Technicolor. A 1993 remake starred Maggie Smith. *Dir.* Fred M Wilcox.

Secrets and Lies (1995)   Timothy Spall, Phyllis Logan, Brenda Blethyn, Claire Rushbrook, Marianne Jean-Baptiste. *Dir.* Mike Leigh.

See No Evil, Hear No Evil (1989)   Gene Wilder (Dave Lyons), Richard Pryor (Wally Karew). Pryor is blind and Wilder is deaf. *Dir.* Arthur Hiller.

Seize the Day (1986)   Robin Williams, Joseph Wiseman. Based on a Saul Bellow novel. *Dir.* Fielder Cook.

Sense and Sensibility (1995)   Emma Thompson, Alan Rickman, Kate Winslet, Hugh Grant, Hugh Laurie, Gemma Jones. Emma Thompson wrote the screenplay. *Dir.* Ang Lee.

September (1987)   Denholm Elliott (Howard), Dianne Wiest (Stephanie), Mia Farrow (Lane), Elaine Stritch. *Dir.* Woody Allen.

Serendipity (2001)   John Cusack, Kate Beckinsale, Jeremy Piven, Molly Shannon. *Dir.* Peter Chelsom.

Sgt Bilko (1996)   Steve Martin, Dan Aykroyd. *Dir.* Jonathan Lynn.

Sgt Pepper's Lonely Hearts Club Band (1978) Peter Frampton, Bee Gees, George Burns, Frankie Howerd, Donald Pleasence, Paul Nicholas, Alice Cooper, Steve Martin, Earth Wind & Fire, Sandy Farina. *Dir.* Michael Schultz.

Seven (1995)   Brad Pitt, Morgan Freeman, Richard Roundtree, Kevin Spacey. *Dir.* David Fincher.

Seven Brides for Seven Brothers (1954)   Howard Keel, Jane Powell, Jeff Richards, Russ Tamblyn. *Dir.* Stanley Donen.

Seven Year Itch, The (1955)   Tom Ewell, Marilyn Monroe, Sonny Tufts, Evelyn Keyes. *Dir.* Billy Wilder.

Seven Years in Tibet (1997)   Brad Pitt, David Thewlis, BD Wong. *Dir.* Jean-Jacques Annaud.

Shadow, The (1994)   Alec Baldwin, Penelope Ann Miller, Tim Curry. In the 1930s a former criminal battles against a descendant of Genghis Khan. *Dir.* Russell Mulcahy.

Shakespeare in Love (1998)   Gwyneth Paltrow, Joseph Fiennes, Geoffrey Rush, Colin Firth, Ben Affleck, Judi Dench, Rupert Everett, Simon Callow, Martin Clunes, Antony Sher, Imelda Staunton. *Dir.* John Madden. Judi Dench won Best Supporting Actor Oscar although only on screen for eight minutes. Daniel Day-Lewis and Julia Roberts turned down the lead roles.

Shadowlands (1993)   Anthony Hopkins, Debra Winger, John Wood. Biopic of CS Lewis and his love for an American woman. *Dir.* Richard Attenborough.

Shallow Hal (2001)   Gwyneth Paltrow, Jack Black (Hal), Jason Alexander, René Kirby. Man who judges women on superficial looks is hypnotised to see only their inner beauty and falls for a 300lb woman. *Dir.* Bobby Farrelly and Peter Farrelly.

Shaun of the Dead (2004)   Simon Pegg (Shaun), Kate Ashfield (Liz), Lucy Davis (Di), Nick Frost (Ed), Dylan Moran (David), Bill Nighy (Philip), Penelope Wilton (Barbara), Jessica Stevenson (Yvonne). Spoof horror movie concerning flesh-eating zombies which arrive in North London but are thwarted by a shop assistant and his dishevelled friend. Written by Simon Pegg and Edgar Wright. *Dir.* Edgar Wright.

Shawshank Redemption, The (1994)   Tim Robbins, Morgan Freeman, Bob Gunton, James Whitmore. *Dir.* Frank Darabont.

Sheena, Queen of the Jungle (1984)   Tanya Roberts, Ted Wass, Donovan Scott. *Dir.* John Guillermin.

Sheik, The (1921)   Rudolph Valentino, Agnes Ayres. English heiress falls for a desert chieftain. Notable for two reasons: it was the film that made a star of Valentino; and it was based on the novel by EM Hull, often considered the first novel of the Romantic Fiction genre. *Dir.* George Melford.

Shine (1996)   Armin Mueller-Stahl, Geoffrey Rush, Noah Taylor, Lynn Redgrave, Googie Withers, John Gielgud. Based on the life of pianist David Helfgott. *Dir.* Scott Hicks.

Ship of Fools (1965)   Vivien Leigh, Simone Signoret, Oskar Werner, Lee Marvin. German line *Vera Cruz* leaves for Bremerhaven with a mixed bag of passengers. *Dir.* Stanley Kramer.

Shirley Valentine (1989)   Pauline Collins, Tom Conti, Julia McKenzie, Alison Steadman, Joanna Lumley, Bernard Hill. *Dir.* Lewis Gilbert.

Shooting Fish (1997)   Dan Futterman, Stuart Townsend, Kate Beckinsale, Annette Crosbie, Jane Lapotaire, Phyllis Logan. *Dir.* Stefan Schwartz.

Shooting Party, The (1984)   James Mason (Ralph Nettleby), Dorothy Tutin, Edward Fox, Cheryl Campbell, John Gielgud. *Dir.* Alan Bridges.

Shootist, The (1976)   John Wayne, Lauren Bacall, James Stewart, Ron Howard, Hugh O'Brian. *Dir.* Don Siegel.

Short Cuts (1993)   Andie MacDowell, Bruce Davison, Jack Lemmon, Robert Downey Jnr. Lives of 9 dysfunctional suburban couples intertwine. *Dir.* Robert Altman.

Shrek (2001)   Voices of Mike Myers (Shrek), Eddie Murphy (Donkey), Cameron Diaz (Princess Fiona), John Lithgow (Lord Farquaad), Vincent Cassel (Monsieur Hood). Animation in which an ugly green ogre agrees to rescue a princess in return for having his swamp vacated but falls in love with her. *Dir.* Andrew Adamson and Vicky Jenson.

Shrek 2 (2004)   Voices of Mike Myers (Shrek), Eddie Murphy (Donkey), Cameron Diaz (Princess Fiona), Julie Andrews (Queen), Antonio Banderas (Puss in Boots), John Cleese (King), Rupert Everett (Prince Charming), Jennifer Saunders (Fairy Godmother), Aron Warner (Wolf), Cody Cameron (Pinocchio/Three Pigs), Conrad Vernon (Gingerbread Man/Cedric/Announcer/Muffin Man/Mongo), Christopher Knights (Blind Mouse), David P Smith (Herald/Man with Box), Kelly Asbury (Page/Elf/Nobleman/Nobleman's Son), Mark Moseley (Mirror/Dresser). Princess Fiona's parents invite her and Shrek to dinner to celebrate her marriage, unaware the newlyweds are both ogres. *Dir.* Andrew Adamson, Kelly Asbury, Conrad Vernon.

Sideways (2004)   Paul Giamatti, Thomas Haden Church, Patrick Gallagher, Alex Kalognomos, Virginia Madsen, Joe Marinelli, Sandra Oh, Alysia Reiner. Comedy concerning Miles Faymond, a failed writer teaching junior high school English, and his best friend, Jack, an actor whose popularity is diminishing, who take a week-long drive up to 'wine country' in California to explore the nature of their failures. *Dir.* Alexander Payne.

Signs (2002)   Mel Gibson (Graham Hess), Joaquin Phoenix (Merrill Hess), Cherry Jones (Officer

Caroline Paski), Rory Culkin (Morgan Hess). A lapsed priest regains his faith after a supernatural experience. *Dir.* M Night Shyamalan.

Silence of the Lambs (1991) Jodie Foster (Clarice Starling), Anthony Hopkins (Dr Hannibal Lecter), Scott Glen. *Dir.* Jonathan Demme.

Silkwood (1983) Meryl Streep, Cher, Kurt Russell. Female worker in nuclear processing plant mysteriously dies before she denounces safety aspects of the plant. *Dir.* Mike Nichols.

Silverado (1985) Scott Glen, Kevin Costner, John Cleese, Kevin Kline, Rosanna Arquette, Danny Glover. *Dir.* Lawrence Kasdan.

Single White Female (1992) Bridget Fonda (Allison Jones), Jennifer Jason Leigh (Hedra Carlson), Steven Weber. *Dir.* Barbet Schroeder.

Sirens (1994) Hugh Grant, Tara FitzGerald, Sam Neill, Elle MacPherson. *Dir.* John Duigen.

Sister Act (1992) Whoopi Goldberg, Maggie Smith, Harvey Keitel. *Dir.* Emile Ardolino.

Sister Act 2: Back in the Habit (1993) Whoopi Goldberg, Maggie Smith, James Coburn. *Dir.* Bill Duke.

Sixth Sense, The (1999) Bruce Willis (Malcolm Crowe), Toni Collette, Haley Joel Osment (Cole). *Dir.* M. Night Shyamalan.

Sleeper (1973) Woody Allen, Diane Keaton, John Beck. *Dir.* Woody Allen.

Sleeping with the Enemy (1990) Julia Roberts, Patrick Bergin. *Dir.* Joseph Ruben.

Sleepless in Seattle (1993) Tom Hanks, Meg Ryan, Ross Malinger. *Dir.* Nora Ephron.

Sleepy Hollow (1999) Johny Depp (Ichabod Crane), Christina Ricci (Katrina Van Tassel), Michael Gambon (Bactus Van Tassel), Christopher Lee (Burgomaster), Christopher Walken (Hessian Horseman). *Dir.* Tim Burton.

Sliding Doors (1998) Gwyneth Paltrow, John Hannah, John Lynch, Jeanne Tripplehorn, Virginia McKenna. *Dir.* Peter Howitt.

Sliver (1993) Sharon Stone, William Baldwin, Tom Berenger, Martin Landau. Based on an Ira Levin novel. *Dir.* Philip Noyce.

Smilla's Feeling for Snow (1997) Julia Ormond (Smilla), Gabriel Byrne, Richard Harris (Tork), Vanessa Redgrave, Bob Peck, Jim Broadbent, Robert Loggia. *Dir.* Bille August.

Sneakers (1992) Robert Redford, Dan Aykroyd, Ben Kingsley, River Phoenix, Sidney Poitier. Experts hired to recover electronic device that can penetrate the government's most secure computer systems. *Dir.* Phil Alden Robinson.

Snow Dogs (2002) Cuba Gooding Jr (Ted Brooks), James Coburn (Thunder Jack), Sisqo, Graham Greene, Michael Bolton (as himself). Dentist goes to Alaska to search for his roots. *Dir.* Brian Levant.

Snow White: A Tale of Terror (1997) Monica Keena (Lilli), Sam Neill (Baron Hoffman), Sigourney Weaver (Claudia).

Some Like It Hot (1939) Bob Hope, Shirley Ross, Una Merkel, Gene Krupa. Sideshow owner runs out of money. *Dir.* George Archainbaud.

Some Like It Hot (1959) Tony Curtis, Jack Lemmon, Marilyn Monroe, Joe E Brown, George Raft. *Dir.* Billy Wilder.

Somebody up There Likes Me (1956) Paul Newman (Rocky Graziano), Pier Angeli, Sal Mineo, Steve McQueen. *Dir.* Robert Wise.

Something's Gotta Give (2003) Jack Nicholson (Harry Sanborn), Diane Keaton (Erica Barry), Keanu Reeves (Julian Mercer), Frances McDormand (Zoe), Amanda Peet (Martin), Jon Favreau (Leo), Paul

Michael Glaser (Dave), Rachel Ticotin (Dr Martinez). While convalescing, a middle-aged playboy begins to develop feelings for his girlfriend's mother. *Dir.* Nancy Meyers.

Sommersby (1993) Richard Gere, Jodie Foster. Remake of *The Return of Martin Guerre*. *Dir.* Jon Amiel.

Son of Lassie (1945) Peter Lawford, Donald Crisp, Nigel Bruce. The first sequel to *Lassie Come Home*; many more followed. *Dir.* S Sylvan Simon.

Son of the Pink Panther (1993) Robert Benigni, Herbert Lom, Claudia Cardinale, Burt Kwouk. *Dir.* Blake Edwards.

Song of Bernadette, The (1943) Jennifer Jones, Charles Bickford, William Eythe. *Dir.* Henry King.

Song to Remember, A (1944) Cornel Wilde, Merle Oberon, Paul Muni. Life and death of Chopin. *Dir.* Charles Vidor.

Sophie's Choice (1982) Meryl Streep, Kevin Kline, Josh Mostel. *Dir.* Alan J Pakula.

Sound of Music, The (1965) Julie Andrews, Christopher Plummer, Richard Haydn, Marni Nixon. *Dir.* Robert Wise.

Soylent Green (1973) Charlton Heston, Edward G Robinson, Leigh Taylor-Young. Set in 2022, the Soylent Green of the title is synthetic food. *Dir.* Richard Fleischer.

Space Jam (1996) Michael Jordan, Bugs Bunny, voice of Danny De Vito. *Dir.* Joe Pytka.

Space Truckers (1997) Dennis Hopper, Stephen Dorff, Debi Mazar, Charles Dance. Set in 2196; BMW's Bio-Mechanical Warriors. *Dir.* Stuart Gordon.

Specialist, The (1994) Sharon Stone, Sylvester Stallone, Rod Steiger, James Woods. *Dir.* Luis Llosa.

Speed (1994) Sandra Bullock, Keanu Reeves, Dennis Hopper, Jeff Daniels. *Dir.* Jan de Bont.

Spellbound (2002) Documentary following eight children taking part in the final of the United States National Spelling Bee. *Dir.* Jeffrey Blitz.

Spiceworld (1997) Spice Girls, Richard E Grant. Originally called: *Five*. *Dir.* Bob Spiers.

Spider-Man (2002) Tobey Maguire (Peter Parker / Spider-Man), Willem Dafoe (Norman Osborn / The Green Goblin), Kirsten Dunst (Mary Jane Watson), James Franco (Harry Osborn), Cliff Robertson (Ben Parker), Rosemary Harris (May Parker). *Dir.* Sam Raimi.

Spider-Man 2 (2004) Tobey Maguire (Peter Parker/Spider-Man), Willem Dafoe (Norman Osborn/The Green Goblin), Kirsten Dunst (Mary Jane Watson), James Franco (Harry Osborn), Alfred Molina (Doc Ock/Dr Otto Octavius), Rosemary Harris (May Parker), Cliff Robertson (Ben Parker), JK Simmons (J Jonah Jameson), Donna Murphy (Rosalie Octavius), Daniel Gillies (John Jameson), Ted Raimi (Hoffman). While Peter Parker is beset with personal problems, his alter-ego confronts the brilliant Dr Octavius who has been transformed into 'Doctor Octopus' (aka Doc Ock), a multi-tentacled super-villain. *Dir.* Sam Raimi.

Spitfire Grill, The (1996) Ellen Burstyn, Marcia Gay Harden, Alison Elliott. *Dir.* Lee David Zlotoff.

Splash! (1984) Tom Hanks (Allen Bauer), Daryl Hannah (Madison), John Candy, Eugene Levy. *Dir.* Ron Howard.

Splitting Heirs (1993) Rick Moranis (Henry), Eric Idle (Tommy Patel), Barbara Hershey, Catherine Zeta Jones, John Cleese (Raoul P Shadgrind), Stratford Johns, Eric Sykes. *Dir.* Robert Young.

Spy Hard (1996) Leslie Nielsen (Agent WD-40), Andy Griffith, Nicollette Sheridan. *Dir.* Rick Friedberg.

C
I
N
E
M
A

Spy Who Loved Me, The (1977)   Roger Moore, Barbara Bach (Major Anya Amasova), Curt Jurgens (Stromberg). Theme song 'Nobody Does it Better' performed by Carly Simon. *Dir.* Lewis Gilbert.

Stagecoach (1939)   John Wayne, Claire Trevor, Thomas Mitchell, Andy Devine. The 1966 remake starred Ann-Margret & Bing Crosby. *Dir.* John Ford.

Stalag 17 (1953)   William Holden, Don Taylor, Otto Preminger, Peter Graves, Neville Brand. *Dir.* Billy Wilder.

Stanley and Iris (1990)   Jane Fonda, Robert De Niro. *Dir.* Martin Ritt.

Stanza del Figlio, La (2001)   Nanni Moretti (Giovanni), Laura Morante (Paola). Apparent family bliss falls apart when the young son dies in an accident. *Dir.* Nanni Moretti.

Star! (1968)   Julie Andrews, Richard Crenna, Daniel Massey (Noël Coward), Bruce Forsyth, Beryl Reid. Biopic of Gertrude Lawrence. *Dir.* Robert Wise.

Star Is Born, A (1937)   Janet Gaynor, Fredric March, Adolphe Menjou, Andy Devine. *Dir.* William A Wellman.

Star Is Born, A (1954)   Judy Garland, James Mason, Charles Bickford. *Dir.* George Cukor.

Star Is Born, A (1976)   Barbra Streisand, Kris Kristofferson, Gary Busey, Paul Mazursky. *Dir.* Frank Pierson.

Star Trek: First Contact (1996)   Patrick Stewart, Jonathan Frakes, Brent Spiner, Michael Dorn, LeVar Burton. *Dir.* Jonathan Frakes.

Star Trek: Generations (1994)   Patrick Stewart, William Shatner, Malcolm McDowell, Jonathan Frakes, Brent Spiner, Whoopi Goldberg. *Dir.* David Carson.

Star Trek: The Motion Picture (1979)   William Shatner, Leonard Nimoy, DeForest Kelley, Persis Khambatta. *Dir.* Robert Wise.

Star Trek II: The Wrath of Khan (1982)   William Shatner, Leonard Nimoy, DeForest Kelley, Ricardo Montalban. Sequel to TV episode 'Space Seed'. *Dir.* Nicholas Meyer.

Star Trek III: The Search for Spock (1984)   William Shatner, Leonard Nimoy, DeForest Kelley, Robert Hooks. *Dir.* Leonard Nimoy.

Star Trek IV: The Voyage Home (1986)   William Shatner, Leonard Nimoy, DeForest Kelley, Catherine Hicks, Jane Wyatt. *Dir.* Leonard Nimoy.

Star Trek V: The Final Frontier (1989)   William Shatner, Leonard Nimoy, DeForest Kelley, David Warner. *Dir.* William Shatner.

Star Trek VI: The Undiscovered Country (1991)   William Shatner, Leonard Nimoy, DeForest Kelley, David Warner, Christian Slater, Christopher Plummer. *Dir.* Nicholas Meyer.

Star Wars (1977)   Mark Hamill, Harrison Ford, Alec Guinness, Carrie Fisher, Anthony Daniels (C3PO), Kenny Baker (R2D2), Dave Prowse. *Dir.* George Lucas.

Star Wars: Episode I – The Phantom Menace (1999)   Liam Neeson, Ewan McGregor, Natalie Portman, Jake Lloyd, Frank Oz, Ray Park, Ian McDiarmid, Samuel L Jackson, Brian Blessed, Sofia Coppola, Pernilla August. *Dir.* George Lucas.

Star Wars: Episode II – Attack of the Clones (2002)   Ewan McGregor (Obi-Wan Kenobi), Natalie Portman (Padme), Christopher Lee (Count Dooku), Hayden Christensen (Anakin Skywalker), Samuel L. Jackson (Mace Windu), Yoda (voice of Frank Oz), Kenny Baker (R2-D2), Anthony Daniels (C-3PO). *Dir.* George Lucas.

Starman (1984)   Jeff Bridges, Karen Allen. Alien arrives in Wisconsin. *Dir.* John Carpenter.

Starship Troopers (1997)   Casper van Dien, Dina Meyer, Denise Richards, Jake Busey, Michael Ironside. *Dir.* Paul Verhoeven.

Stay Hungry (1976)   Jeff Bridges, Sally Field, Arnold Schwarzenegger, Robert Englund. *Dir.* Bob Rafelson.

Staying Alive (1983)   John Travolta, Cynthia Rhodes, Finola Hughes, Steve Inwood. Sequel to *Saturday Night Fever*, Tony Manero becomes a Broadway dancer. *Dir.* Sylvester Stallone.

Steaming (1985)   Vanessa Redgrave (Nancy), Sarah Miles (Sarah), Diana Dors (Violet), Patti Love, Brenda Bruce. *Dir.* Joseph Losey.

Steel Magnolias (1989)   Sally Field, Dolly Parton, Shirley MacLaine, Daryl Hannah, Olympia Dukakis, Julia Roberts, Tom Skerritt. *Dir.* Herbert Ross.

Stepford Wives, The (1974)   Katharine Ross, Paula Prentiss, Nanette Newman, Patrick O'Neal. *Dir.* Bryan Forbes.

Stepford Wives, The (2004)   Nicole Kidman (Joanna), Glenn Close, Christopher Walken, John Cusack, Joan Cusack, Matthew Broderick, Bette Midler. Inferior remake of the 1974 film based on Ira Levin's novel. *Dir.* Frank Oz.

Sting, The (1973)   Paul Newman, Robert Redford, Robert Shaw. *Dir.* George Roy Hill.

Stormy Monday (1988)   Melanie Griffith (Kate), Tommy Lee Jones (Cosmo), Sting (Finney), Sean Bean (Brendan). *Dir.* Mike Figgis.

Strange Days (1995)   Ralph Fiennes (Lenny Nero), Angela Bassett, Juliette Lewis, Tom Sizemore, Michael Wincott. *Dir.* Kathryn Bigelow.

Strangers on a Train (1951)   Farley Granger, Robert Walker, Ruth Roman, Patricia Hitchcock. *Dir.* Alfred Hitchcock.

Straw Dogs (1971)   Dustin Hoffman, Susan George, Peter Vaughan, David Warner, TP McKenna. Based on Gordon M Williams novel *The Siege of Trencher's Farm*. *Dir.* Sam Peckinpah.

Striptease (1996)   Demi Moore (Erin Grant), Burt Reynolds (David Dilbeck). Strip club name: The Eager Beaver. *Dir.* Andrew Bergman.

Stuart Little (1999)   Geena Davis (Mrs Little), Hugh Laurie (Mr Little), Jonathan Lipnicki (George Little), Dabney Coleman (Dr Beechwood), voices of Michael J Fox (Stuart Little), Nathan Lane. *Dir.* Rob Minkoff.

Stuart Little 2 (2002)   Geena Davis (Mrs Little), Hugh Laurie (Mr Little), voice of Michael J Fox (Stuart Little). *Dir.* Rob Minkoff

Substitute, The (1996)   Tom Berenger, Ernie Hudson, Diane Venora. Commando-trained man takes over teaching position when his girlfriend is beaten up. *Dir.* Robert Mandel.

Sudden Impact (1983)   Clint Eastwood (Callahan), Sondra Locke (Jennifer Spencer), Pat Hingle. *Dir.* Clint Eastwood.

Suddenly Last Summer (1959)   Katharine Hepburn, Elizabeth Taylor, Mongomery Clift. *Dir.* Joseph L Mankiewicz.

Summer Holiday (1962)   Cliff Richard, Lauri Peters, Melvyn Hayes, Una Stubbs. *Dir.* Peter Yates.

Summer of '42 (1971)   Jennifer O'Neill, Gary Grimes, Jerry Houser. *Dir.* Robert Mulligan.

Sunday, Bloody Sunday (1971)   Glenda Jackson, Peter Finch, Murray Head. *Dir.* John Schlesinger.

Sundowners, The (1960)   Robert Mitchum, Deborah Kerr, Glynis Johns, Peter Ustinov. *Dir.* Fred Zinnemann.

Sunset (1988)   Bruce Willis (Tom Mix), James Garner (Wyatt Earp), Malcolm McDowell. *Dir.* Blake Edwards.

Sunset Boulevard (1950)   William Holden, Gloria Swanson, Erich Von Stroheim, Cecil B de Mille, Buster Keaton, Hedda Hopper. *Dir.* Billy Wilder.

Sunshine State (2002)   Edie Falco (Marly Temple), Angela Bassett (Desiree Perry), Jane Alexander (Delia Temple), Ralph Waite (Furman Temple), James McDaniel (Reggie), Timothy Hutton (Jack Meadows), Mary Alice (Eunice Stokes), Bill Cobbs (Dr Lloyd), Mary Steenburgen (Francine Pickney), Miguel Ferrer (Lester). Attempts by property companies to redevelop a small Florida coastal town meet resistance by local residents. *Dir.* John Sayles.

Super Mario Brothers (1993)   Bob Hoskins, Dennis Hopper, John Leguizamo. *Dir.* Rocky Morton and Annabel Jankel.

Supergirl (1984)   Faye Dunaway (Selena), Helen Slater (Supergirl / Linda Lee), Peter O'Toole (Zeitar), Peter Cook, Simon Ward, Brenda Vaccaro, Mia Farrow. *Dir.* Jeannot Szwarc.

Superman (1978)   Christopher Reeve, Marlon Brando, Susannah York, Margot Kidder, Glenn Ford, Gene Hackman, Trevor Howard. *Dir.* Richard Donner.

Superman 2 (1980)   Christopher Reeve, Susannah York, Margot Kidder, Gene Hackman, Ned Beatty, Terence Stamp. *Dir.* Richard Lester.

Superman 3 (1983)   Christopher Reeve, Richard Pryor, Jackie Cooper, Margot Kidder, Pamela Stephenson, Robert Vaughn. *Dir.* Richard Lester.

Superman 4: The Quest for Peace (1987)   Christopher Reeve, Gene Hackman, Jackie Cooper, Margot Kidder. *Dir.* Sidney J Furie.

Surviving Picasso (1996)   Anthony Hopkins (Picasso), Natascha McElhone (Françoise). *Dir.* James Ivory.

Swallows and Amazons (1974)   Virginia McKenna, Ronald Fraser, Simon West, Sophie Neville. *Dir.* Claude Whatham.

Sweet Charity (1969)   Shirley MacLaine, Ricardo Montalban, Chita Rivera, Stubby Kaye, Sammy Davis Jnr. *Dir.* Bob Fosse.

Sweet Liberty (1986)   Alan Alda, Michael Caine, Michelle Pfeiffer, Lilian Gish, Bob Hoskins. College professor is alarmed as he watches the Hollywood filming of his historical novel. *Dir.* Alan Alda.

Swing Shift (1984)   Goldie Hawn, Kurt Russell, Fred Ward, Christine Lahti. *Dir.* Jonathan Demme.

Swiss Family Robinson, The (1960)   John Mills, Dorothy McGuire, James MacArthur, Janet Munro. *Dir.* Ken Annakin.

Sword of Sherwood Forest (1960)   Richard Greene, Peter Cushing, Richard Pasco, Niall MacGinnis, Oliver Reed. *Dir.* Terence Fisher.

Swordfish (2001)   John Travolta (Gabriel Shear), Hugh Jackman, Halle Berry (Ginger), Don Cheadle, Vinnie Jones (Marco). Computer hacker is hired by a secret agent and thief to steal government funds. *Dir.* Dominic Sena.

Taking of Pelham 123, The (1974)   Walter Matthau, Robert Shaw, Martin Balsam, Hector Elizondo. Four gunmen hold a New York subway train to ransom. *Dir.* Joseph Sargent.

Tale of Two Cities, A (1958)   Dirk Bogarde, Dorothy Tutin, Christopher Lee, Donald Pleasence, Alfie Bass. Remake of 1935 classic. *Dir.* Ralph Thomas.

Talented Mr Ripley, The (1999)   Matt Damon (Tom Ripley), Jude Law (Dickie Greenleaf), Gwyneth Paltrow (Marge Sherwood), Cate Blanchett (Meredith Logue), Philip Seymour Hoffman (Freddie Miles). *Dir.* Anthony Minghella. Anthony Minghella wrote the screen play based on Patricia Highsmith's novel.

Tales from the Darkside: The Movie (1991)   Debbie Harry is a cannibal waiting to eat a young boy once he has told her 3 stories. *The Wraparound Story*: Deborah Harry (Betty), Matthew Lawrence (Timmy). *Lot 249*: Christian Slater, Steve Buscemi, Robert Sedgwick, Julianne Moore. *Cat from Hell*: David Johansen, William Hickey. *Lover's Vow*: James Remar, Rae Dawn Chong, Robert Klein. *Dir.* John Harrison.

Talk Radio (1988)   Eric Bogosian (Barry Champlain), Ellen Greene, Leslie Hope, Alec Baldwin. *Dir.* Oliver Stone.

Tall Guy, The (1989)   Jeff Goldblum (Dexter King), Emma Thompson (Kate Lemon), Rowan Atkinson (Ron Anderson). *Dir.* Mel Smith.

Tango and Cash (1989)   Kurt Russell, Sylvester Stallone, Jack Palance, Teri Hatcher, Michael J Pollard. *Dir.* Andrei Konchalovsky.

Tank Girl (1994)   Lon Petty, Ice T, Naomi Watts, Malcolm McDowell. *Dir.* Rachel Talalay.

Tank Malling (1988)   Ray Winstone, Jason Connery, Amanda Donohoe, John Conteh, Terry Marsh, Nick Berry. *Dir.* James Marcus.

Tap (1989)   Gregory Hines, Suzanne Douglas, Sammy Davis Jnr (Little Mo). *Dir.* Nick Castle.

Taps (1981)   Timothy Hutton, George C Scott, Sean Penn, Tom Cruise. *Dir.* Harold Becker.

Taras Bulba (1962)   Yul Brynner, Tony Curtis, Christine Kaufmann, Sam Wanamaker. *Dir.* J Lee Thompson.

Tarnation (2004)   Having documented his life since the age of 11, Jonathan Caouette weaves a psychedelic whirlwind of snapshots, Super-8 movies, answering machine messages, video diaries, early short films, snippets of '80s pop culture and dramatic re-enactments to create an epic portrait of an American family torn apart by dysfunction and reunited through the power of love. *Dir.* Jonathan Caouette.

Tarzan the Apeman (1981)   Bo Derek, Miles O'Keeffe (Tarzan), Richard Harris, John Phillip Law, Wilfrid Hyde-White. *Dir.* John Derek.

Taste of Honey, A (1961)   Rita Tushingham, Dora Bryan, Murray Melvin. Based on Shelagh Delaney play. *Dir.* Tony Richardson.

Taxi Driver (1976)   Robert De Niro (Travis Bickle), Jodie Foster, Cybill Shepherd, Harvey Keitel. *Dir.* Martin Scorsese.

Teenage Mutant Ninja Turtles (1990)   Judith Hoag (April O'Neil), Elias Koteas (Casey Jones), Josh Pais (Raphael), Michelan Sisti (Michelangelo), Leif Tilden (Donatello), David Forman (Leonardo). Michael Pressman's 1991 sequel: *Teenage Mutant Ninja Turtles II: The Secret of the Ooze. Dir.* Steve Barron.

10 (2002)   Mania Akbari (Driver), Amin Maher (Amin), Roya Arabshahi, Katayoun Taleidzadeh, Mandana Sharbaf, Amerie Moradi. Thought-provoking film about 10 conversations between a woman driver and the people to whom she gives lifts over a period of two days in Tehran. *Dir.* Abbas Kiarostami.

Ten Commandments, The (1956)   Charlton Heston (Moses), Yul Brynner, Edward G Robinson, Anne Baxter, Yvonne De Carlo. *Dir.* Cecil B de Mille.

Ten Little Indians (1965)   Wilfrid Hyde-White, Dennis Price, Stanley Holloway, Shirley Eaton, Hugh O'Brian, Daliah Lavi, Fabian, Mario Adorf. Based on Agatha Christie's novel. *Dir.* George Pollock.

Ten Rillington Place (1971)   Richard Attenborough, John Hurt, Judy Geeson. Account of the Christie murders of the 1940s. *Dir.* Richard Fleischer.

10 Things I Hate About You (1999)   Heath Ledger, Julia Stiles, Joseph-Gordon Levitt, Andrew Keegan, Susan May Pratt. *Dir.* Gil Junger. Teenage comedy loosely based on Shakespeare's *The Taming of the Shrew*.

10 to Midnight (1983)   Charles Bronson (Leo Kessler), Lisa Eilbacher (Laurie), Andrew Stevens, Gene Davis. *Dir.* J Lee Thompson.

C
I
N
E
M
A

Tender Mercies (1982)   Robert Duvall, Tess Harper, Betty Buckley. Robert Duvall sang the songs himself. *Dir*. Bruce Beresford.

Tequila Sunrise (1988)   Mel Gibson (McKussic), Michele Pfeiffer, Kurt Russell, Raul Julia. *Dir*. Robert Towne.

Terminator, The (1984)   Arnold Schwarzenegger, Linda Hamilton, Michael Biehn. *Dir*. James Cameron.

Terminator 2: Judgment Day (1991)   Arnold Schwarzenegger, Linda Hamilton, Edward Furlong. *Dir*. James Cameron.

Terms of Endearment (1983)   Shirley MacLaine, Jack Nicholson, Debra Winger, Danny De Vito. *Dir*. James L Brooks.

Texas Chainsaw Massacre, The (1974)   Marilyn Burns, Allen Danziger, Paul A Partain. *Dir*. Tobe Hooper.

Thelma and Louise (1991)   Susan Sarandon (Louise Sawyer), Geena Davis (Thelma Dickinson), Harvey Keitel, Brad Pitt. *Dir*. Ridley Scott.

There's No Business Like Show Business (1954) Ethel Merman, Dan Dailey, Marilyn Monroe, Donald O'Connor, Johnny Ray, Mitzi Gaynor, Hugh O'Brian. *Dir*. Walter Lang.

They Died with Their Boots On (1941)   Errol Flynn, Olivia de Havilland, Arthur Kennedy, Anthony Quinn, Sidney Greenstreet. Biopic of General Custer. *Dir*. Raoul Walsh.

They Shoot Horses, Don't They? (1969)   Gig Young, Jane Fonda, Susannah York, Red Buttons. Tragedy during a six-day marathon dance contest in the 1930s. *Dir*. Sydney Pollack.

Thief of Baghdad (1940)   Conrad Veidt, John Justin (died in 2002), Sabu, June Duprez. The visual effects make this the best version of this oft-filmed story. The 1924 film starred Douglas Fairbanks, the 1960 film Steve Reeves, and the 1978 film Roddy McDowall, Frank Finlay, Terence Stamp and Peter Ustinov. The 1924 film won Oscars for photography and art direction. *Dir*. Michael Powell, Ludwig Berger and Tim Whelan.

Thin Man, The (1934)   William Powell, Myrna Loy, Maureen O'Sullivan. *Dir*. WS Van Dyke.

Thing, The (1951)   Robert Cornthwaite, Kenneth Tobey, James Arness (the Thing). GB title: *The Thing from Another World*. *Dir*. Christian Nyby.

Thing, The (1982)   Kurt Russell, A Wilford Brimley, TK Carter. Remake of the 1951 film, although this 'Thing' is a metamorphic creature that can now enter and take over the protagonists. *Dir*. John Carpenter.

Things To Do in Denver When You're Dead (1995) Andy Garcia (Jimmy the Saint), Christopher Walken, Christopher Lloyd. *Dir*. Gary Fleder.

Thinner (1987)   Robert John Burke (William Halleck). Stephen King wrote the novel under the pseudonym Richard Bachman. *Dir*. Tom Holland.

Third Man, The (1949)   Orson Welles (Harry Lime), Joseph Cotten, Trevor Howard, Alida Valli, Bernard Lee, Wilfrid Hyde-White. *Dir*. Carol Reed.

Thirteen (2003)   Holly Hunter (Melanie), Evan Rachel Wood (Tracy), Nikki Reed (Evie Zamora), Jeremy Sisto (Brady), Brady Corbett (Mason), Deborah Kara Unger (Brooke), Kip Pardue (Luke), Sarah Clarke (Birdie), DW Moffett (Travis). A young teenager becomes a drug-taking delinquent under the influence of her new best friend. *Dir*. Catherine Hardwicke.

Thirty-Nine Steps, The (1935)   Robert Donat, Madeleine Carroll, Peggy Ashcroft. *Dir*. Alfred Hitchcock.

Thirty-Nine Steps, The (1959)   Kenneth More, Taina Elg, Barry Jones. *Dir*. Ralph Thomas.

Thirty-Nine Steps, The (1978)   Robert Powell, Karen Dotrice, John Mills. *Dir*. Don Sharp.

This Is Spinal Tap (1984)   Michael McKean (David St Hubbins), Christopher Guest (Nigel Tufnel), Harry Shearer (Derek Smalls), RJ Parnell (Mick Shrimpton), Rob Reiner (Marti DiBerti). Cameos by Anjelica Huston, Patrick Macnee and Billy Crystal. *Dir*. Rob Reiner.

This Sporting Life (1963)   Richard Harris, Rachel Roberts, Alan Badel, William Hartnell, Arthur Lowe, Colin Blakely. *Dir*. Lindsay Anderson.

Thomas Crown Affair, The (1968)   Steve McQueen, Faye Dunaway, Yaphet Kotto. *Dir*. Norman Jewison.

Thoroughly Modern Millie (1967)   Julie Andrews, Mary Tyler Moore, James Fox. *Dir*. George Roy Hill.

Three Amigos! (1986)   Chevy Chase (Dusty Bottoms), Steve Martin (Lucky Day), Martin Short (Ned Nederlander). *Dir*. John Landis.

Three Colours: Blue (1993)   Juliette Binoche, Benoît Régent, Florence Pernel. First part of trilogy based on the colours of the French tricolour. *Dir*. Krzysztof Kieslowski.

Three Colours: Red (1994)   Juliette Binoche, Irene Jacob, Jean-Louis Trintignant, Julie Delpy. Third part of trilogy based on the colours of the French tricolour. *Dir*. Krzysztof Kieslowski.

Three Colours: White (1993)   Zbigniew Zamachowski, Julie Delpy, Juliette Binoche, Florence Pernel. Second part of trilogy based on the colours of the French tricolour. *Dir*. Krzysztof Kieslowski.

Three Days of the Condor (1975)   Robert Redford, Faye Dunaway, Cliff Robertson, Max Von Sydow. *Dir*. Sydney Pollack.

Three Faces of Eve, The (1957)   Joanne Woodward, Lee J Cobb. Introduced by Alistair Cooke. *Dir*. Nunnally Johnson.

Three Fugitives (1989)   Nick Nolte (Dan Lucas), Martin Short (Ned Perry), Sarah Rowland Doroff, James Earl Jones. *Dir*. Francis Veber.

Three Kings (1999)   George Clooney (Major Archie Gates), Ice Cube (Chief Elgin), Mark Wahlberg (Sgt Barlow). *Dir*. David O. Russell.

Three Men and a Baby (1987)   Tom Selleck (Peter), Steve Guttenberg (Michael), Ted Danson (Jack), Nancy Travis. *Dir*. Leonard Nimoy.

Three Men and a Little Lady (1990)   Tom Selleck, Steve Guttenberg, Ted Danson, Nancy Travis, Sheila Hancock. *Dir*. Emilio Ardelino.

Three Men in a Boat (1956)   David Tomlinson, Jimmy Edwards, Laurence Harvey, Shirley Eaton, Jill Ireland. *Dir*. Ken Annakin.

Three Musketeers, The (1993)   Charlie Sheen, Kiefer Sutherland, Chris O'Donnell, Rebecca DeMornay. *Dir*. Stephen Herek.

Three Musketeers, The (The Queen's Diamonds), (1973)   Michael York, Oliver Reed, Richard Chamberlain, Frank Finlay, Raquel Welch, Geraldine Chaplin, Spike Milligan, Faye Dunaway, Charlton Heston, Christopher Lee. *Dir*. Richard Lester.

Throw Momma from the Train (1987)   Danny De Vito (Owen), Billy Crystal (Larry), Kim Greist (Beth), Anne Ramsey (Momma), Kate Mulgrew, Rob Reiner, Annie Ross, Oprah Winfrey (as herself). *Dir*. Danny De Vito.

Thunderball (1965)   Sean Connery, Adolfo Celi (Emilio Largo), Claudine Auger (Domino). Title song performed by Tom Jones. *Dir*. Terence Young.

Thunderbolt and Lightfoot (1974)   Clint Eastwood, Jeff Bridges, George Kennedy, Catherine Bach. *Dir*. Michael Cimino.

THX 1138 (1970)   Robert Duvall, Donald Pleasence. *Dir*. George Lucas.

Tiger Bay (1959)   Hayley Mills, John Mills, Horst Buchholz, Megs Jenkins. *Dir.* J Lee Thompson.

Tightrope (1984)   Clint Eastwood (Wes Block), Geneviève Bujold (Beryl Thibodeax), Alison Eastwood (Amanda). *Dir.* Richard Tuggle.

Time after Time (1980)   Malcolm McDowell, David Warner, Mary Steenburgen. Jack the Ripper in modern San Francisco via HG Wells's time machine. *Dir.* Nicholas Meyer.

Time Bandits (1981)   John Cleese (Robin Hood), Sean Connery (Agamemnon), Ian Holm (Napoleon), Ralph Richardson (God), David Warner (Satan). *Dir.* Terry Gilliam.

Time Machine, The (1960)   Rod Taylor, Yvette Mimieux, Alan Young, Sebastian Cabot. Victorian scientist builds a machine which transports him to the year 802701. *Dir.* George Pal.

Time of Your Life (1948)   James Cagney, William Bendix, Jeanne Cagney, Wayne Morris, Broderick Crawford, Ward Bond. Group of eccentrics meet in a San Francisco bar. *Dir.* HC Potter.

Time to Kill, A (1996)   Sandra Bullock, Matthew McConaughey, Samuel L Jackson, Donald & Kiefer Sutherland. Ku Klux Klan still has power in small Mississippi town. *Dir.* Joel Schumacher.

Tin Cup (1996)   Kevin Costner, Rene Russo, Don Johnson. *Dir.* Ron Shelton.

Tin Men (1987)   Richard Dreyfuss (Bill 'BB' Babowsky), Danny De Vito (Ernie Tilley), Barbara Hershey (Nora). *Dir.* Barry Levinson.

Titanic (1997)   Kate Winslet, Leonardo DiCaprio. Equalled the record of Ben Hur by gaining 11 Oscars (14 nominations). *Dir.* James Cameron.

To Be or Not to Be (1983)   Mel Brooks (Frederick Bronski), Anne Bancroft (Anna), Tim Matheson (Lt Andre Sobinski), Charles Durning (Col Erhardt), José Ferrer (Prof Siletski), Christopher Lloyd (Capt Schultz). *Dir.* Alan Johnson.

To Catch a Thief (1955)   Cary Grant, Grace Kelly. *Dir.* Alfred Hitchcock.

To Die For (1995)   Nicole Kidman, Matt Dillon, Joaquin Phoenix, David Cronenberg, George Segal (uncredited). Fame-obsessed weather woman on local TV station describes how she murdered her husband. *Dir.* Gus Van Sant.

To Have and Have Not (1945)   Humphrey Bogart, Lauren Bacall, Walter Brennan, Hoagy Carmichael. US charter boat captain in Martinique gets involved with Nazis. *Dir.* Howard Hawks.

To Kill A Mockingbird (1962)   Gregory Peck (Atticus Finch), Mary Badham (Jean Louise 'Scout' Finch), Philip Alford (Jem Finch), John Megna (Dill Harris), Frank Overton (Sheriff Heck Tate), Brock Peters (Tom Robinson), Rosemary Murphy (Miss Maudie Atkinson), Robert Duvall (Arthur 'Boo' Radley). Kim Stanley was the narrator as the older Scout Finch. Screenplay by Horton Foote and based on Harper Lee novel about a black man, Tom Robinson, being falsely accused of rape and the attempt to defend him by Atticus Finch, the whole struggle seen through the eyes of his young daughter, Scout. Music by Elmer Bernstein. Won Oscars for Best Screenplay and Best Actor. *Dir.* Robert Mulligan.

To Sir with Love (1967)   Sidney Poitier, Judy Geeson, Suzy Kendall, Lulu. *Dir.* James Clavell.

Tokyo Godfathers (2003)   Voices of Toru Emari (Gin), Yoshiaki Umegaki (Hana), Ava Okamoto (Miyuki), Shozo Iizuka (Oota), Seizo Kato (Mother), Hiroya Ishimaru (Yasuo). Animated story concerning three motley vagrants, an alcoholic, a teenage runaway and a former drag queen, who discover an abandoned baby and wander the streets of Tokyo in search of its mother. *Dir.* Satoshi Kon.

Tom Brown's Schooldays (1940)   Freddie Bartholomew, Jimmy Lydon, Cedric Hardwicke, Billy Halop, Gale Storm. The 1951 remake starred Robert Newton and John Howard Davies (Tom). *Dir.* Robert Stevenson.

Tom Horn (1979)   Steve McQueen, Linda Evans, Slim Pickens. *Dir.* William Wiard.

Tombstone (1993)   Kurt Russell, Val Kilmer, Sam Elliott, Charlton Heston. Narrated by Robert Mitchum. *Dir.* George P Cosmatos.

Tomorrow Never Dies (1997)   Pierce Brosnan (James Bond), Michelle Yeoh (Wai Lin), Teri Hatcher (Paris Carver), Jonathan Pryce (Elliot Carver). Theme song sung by Sheryl Crow. *Dir.* Roger Spottiswoode.

Too Hot to Handle (1991)   Kim Basinger (Vicki Rosemary Anderson), Alec Baldwin (Charley Raymond Pearl), Robert Loggia, Elisabeth Shue, Armand Assante. *Dir.* Jerry Rees.

Tootsie (1982)   Dustin Hoffman (Michael Dorsey / Dorothy), Teri Garr, Dabney Coleman, Jessica Lange, Charles Durning, Bill Murray, Sydney Pollack, Geena Davis. *Dir.* Sydney Pollack.

Top Gun (1986)   Tom Cruise (Maverick), Kelly McGillis (Charlie), Val Kilmer (Ice), Tom Skerritt (Viper), Anthony Edwards (Goose), Michael Ironside (Jester), John Stockwell (Cougar), Meg Ryan (Carole), Tim Robbins (Merlin), Barry Tubb (Wolfman), Clarence Gilyard (Sundown). *Dir.* Tony Scott.

Top Hat (1935)   Fred Astaire, Ginger Rogers. *Dir.* Mark Sandrich.

Tora! Tora! Tora! (1970)   Martin Balsam, Joseph Cotten, Jason Robards. Events leading up to Pearl Harbor. *Dir.* Richard Fleischer.

Torn Curtain (1966)   Paul Newman, Julie Andrews. *Dir.* Alfred Hitchcock.

Total Eclipse (1995)   Leonardo DiCaprio (Arthur Rimbaud, the 19th-century poet), David Thewlis (Verlaine). *Dir.* Agnieszka Holand.

Total Recall (1990)   Sharon Stone, Arnold Schwarzenegger (Doug Quaid), Rachel Ticotin, Michael Ironside. *Dir.* Paul Verhoeven.

Touching the Void (2003)   Brendan Mackey (Joe Simpson), Nicholas Aaron (Simon Yates), Ollie Ryall (Richard Hawking), Joe Simpson (as himself), Simon Yates (as himself), Richard Hawking (as himself). Based on Joe Simpson's book. Two mountaineers recall an accident during a climb in Peru that left one of them for dead. *Dir.* Kevin Macdonald.

Tough Guys (1986)   Burt Lancaster (Harry Doyle), Kirk Douglas (Archie Long), Charles Durning, Eli Wallach. *Dir.* Jeff Kanew.

Towering Inferno, The (1974)   Paul Newman, Steve McQueen, William Holden, Faye Dunaway, Fred Astaire, OJ Simpson, Robert Wagner, Jennifer Jones, Robert Vaughn, Richard Chamberlain. *Dir.* John Guillermin.

A Town Like Alice (1956)   Virginia McKenna, Peter Finch, Takagi, Marie Lohr, Maureen Swanson, Jean Anderson. Life among women prisoners of the Japanese in Malaya. Based on Nevil Shute's novel. *Dir.* Jack Lee.

Toxic Avenger, The (1985)   Andree Maranda, Mitchell Cohen, Pat Ryan Jnr. Archetypal Troma trash-fest. Ron Fazio took over the role of the supercharged weakling in the sequels. *Dir.* Michael Herz.

Toy Story (1995)   Voices of Tom Hanks, Don Rickles, Jim Varney, Tim Allen. First full-length computer-

C
I
N
E
M
A

animated feature film. Song: 'You've Got a Friend in Me' (music and lyrics by Randy Newman). *Dir.* John Lasseter.

Toy Story 2 (1999)　Voice of Woody (Tom Hanks), Tim Allen, Joan Cusack. *Dir.* Ash Brannan and John Lasseter.

Toys (1992)　Robin Williams, Michael Gambon, LL Cool J, Joan Cusack, Donald O'Connor. *Dir.* Barry Levinson.

Trading Places (1983)　Dan Aykroyd, Eddie Murphy, Ralph Bellamy, Don Ameche, Jamie Lee Curtis, Denholm Elliott. *Dir.* John Landis.

Trail of the Pink Panther (1982)　Peter Sellers, Joanna Lumley, Herbert Lom, David Niven. *Dir.* Blake Edwards.

Trainspotting (1996)　Ewan McGregor, Ewen Bremner, Jonny Lee Miller, Robert Carlyle, Kelly MacDonald. *Dir.* Danny Boyle.

Trapeze (1956)　Burt Lancaster, Tony Curtis, Gina Lollobrigida, Sid James. *Dir.* Carol Reed.

Treasure Island (1990)　Charlton Heston, Oliver Reed, Christian Bale, Christopher Lee, Richard Johnson. *Dir.* Raúl Ruiz. Earlier versions 1934 (*Dir.* Victor Fleming); 1950 (*Dir.* Byron Haskin).

Treasure of the Sierra Madre, The (1948) Humphrey Bogart, Walter Huston, Tim Holt, John Huston. *Dir.* John Huston.

Trial, The (1962)　Orson Welles, Jeanne Moreau, Anthony Perkins. Joseph K is tried and condemned for an unspecified crime. *Dir.* Orson Welles. 1992 remake (*Dir.* David Jones) starred Anthony Hopkins & Kyle MacLachlan.

Trials of Oscar Wilde, The (1960)　Peter Finch, Yvonne Mitchell, John Fraser, James Mason. US title: *The Man with the Green Carnation. Dir.* Ken Hughes.

Trilogy: On the Run, An Amazing Couple, After Life (2002) Francois Morel (Alain Costes), Dominique Blanc (Agnes Manise), Gilbert Melki (Pascal Manise), Lucas Belvaux (Bruno Le Roux), Catherine Frot (Jeanne), Valerie Mairesse (Claire), Raphaele Godin (Louise). The lives of a left-wing revolutionary, who is now a school teacher, a policeman and his drug-addicted wife, and a lawyer and his suspicious wife become intertwined. Three films that total 5½ hours viewing but stand alone although featuring the same characters. *Dir.* Lucas Belvaux.

Triplettes de Belleville, Les (2002)　Voices of Jean-Claude Donda, Michel Robin, Monica Viegas. A club-footed old lady, an overweight dog and a trio of aged singers help rescue a cyclist who is kidnapped during the Tour De France. GB title: *Belleville Rendezvous. Dir.* Sylvain Chomet.

Trouble with Girls, The (1969)　Elvis Presley, Marlyn Mason, Vincent Price. Manager of an educational medicine show (a chautauqua) gets involved in a murder. *Dir.* Peter Tewksbury.

True Grit (1969)　John Wayne, Kim Darby, Glen Campbell, Robery Duvall, Dennis Hopper. *Dir.* Henry Hathaway.

True Lies (1994)　Arnold Schwarzenegger, Jamie Lee Curtis, Tom Arnold, Charlton Heston. US secret agent pretends to be a computer salesman to his wife. *Dir.* James Cameron.

True Romance (1993)　Christian Slater, Patricia Arquette, Dennis Hopper, Val Kilmer, Brad Pitt, Gary Oldman, Christopher Walken. Quentin Tarantino story about a shop assistant and a callgirl who go on the run with a case full of cocaine. *Dir.* Tony Scott.

True Stories (1986)　David Byrne (Narrator), John Goodman (Louis Fyne), Annie McEnroe (Kay Culver). Famous for the club scene where a multitude of characters mime to Byrne's voice. *Dir.* David Byrne.

Truly, Madly, Deeply (1990)　Juliet Stevenson (Nina), Alan Rickman (Jamie), Bill Paterson, Michael Maloney. *Dir.* Anthony Minghella.

Truman Show, The (1998)　Jim Carrey, Laura Linney, Noah Emmerich, Ed Harris, Natascha McElhone. *Dir.* Peter Weir.

Tunes of Glory (1960)　Alec Guinness, John Mills, Susannah York, Dennis Price, Kay Walsh, Duncan Macrae. *Dir.* Ronald Neame.

Tupac: Resurrection (2003)　Home movies, photographs and recited poetry illuminate the life of Tupac Shakur, the godfather of gangsta rap. *Dir.* Lauren Lazin.

Turbulence (1997)　Lauren Holly (Teri Halloran), Ray Liotta (Ryan Weaver), Brenda Gleeson (Stubbs). *Dir.* Robert Butler.

Turner & Hooch (1989)　Tom Hanks, Mare Winningham, John McIntire. Cop teams up with a dog to solve a murder. *Dir.* Roger Spottiswoode.

Turning Point, The (1977)　Anne Bancroft, Shirley MacLaine, Mikhail Baryshnikov, Tom Skerritt. *Dir.* Herbert Ross.

Twelfth Night (1996)　Helena Bonham Carter, Richard E Grant, Nigel Hawthorne, Mel Smith, Imogen Stubbs. *Dir.* Trevor Nunn.

Twelve Angry Men (1957)　Henry Fonda, Lee J Cobb, EG Marshall, Jack Warden, Ed Begley, George Voskovec, Jack Klugman, John Fiedler, Martin Balsam, Robert Webber, Edward Binns, Joseph Sweeney. *Dir.* Sidney Lumet.

Twelve Monkeys (1995)　Bruce Willis, Brad Pitt, Madeleine Stowe, Christopher Plummer. Set in 2035; a convict is sent back to 1996 to discover cause of pandemic disease. *Dir.* Terry Gilliam.

Twelve O'Clock High (1949)　Gregory Peck, Hugh Marlowe, Gary Merrill, Dean Jagger. *Dir.* Henry King.

28 Days (2000)　Sandra Bullock (Gwen Cummings), Viggo Mortensen (Eddie Boone), Dominic West (Jasper), Diane Ladd (Bobbie Jean), Elizabeth Perkins (Lily), Steve Buscemi (Cornell). An alcoholic woman is sent to a rehabilitation centre to dry out, hence the title. *Dir.* Betty Thomas.

28 Days Later ... (2002)　Cillian Murphy, Naomie Harris, Megan Burns, Brendan Gleeson, Noah Huntley. Not a sequel to *28 Days* but a science fiction drama concerning a deadly virus unleashed on the British public following a raid on a primate research centre. The virus causes a deadly rage. *Dir.* Danny Boyle.

21 Grams (2003)　Sean Penn (Paul), Benicio Del Toro (Jack), Naomi Watts (Cristina), Charlotte Gainsbourg (Mary), Melissa Leo (Marianne), Clea DuVall (Claudia), Danny Huston (Michael), Paul Calderon (Brown). After her family are killed in a traffic accident, a middle-class housewife's life becomes intertwined with those of an academic and an ex-convict in ways that involve drug-taking, adultery and murder. *Dir.* Alejandro Gonzalez.

Twenty Thousand Leagues under the Sea (1954) Kirk Douglas, James Mason, Paul Lukas, Peter Lorre. *Dir.* Richard Fleischer.

Twilight Zone: The Movie (1983)　Dan Aykroyd, Vic Morrow, Scatman Crothers, Kevin McCarthy. Four supernatural stories. *Dir.* John Landis, Steven Spielberg, Joe Dante, George Miller.

Twin Town (1997)　Rhys Ifans, Llyr Evans, Keith Allen. *Dir.* Kevin Allen.

Twinky (1969)　Charles Bronson, Susan George, Trevor Howard. 16-yr-old schoolgirl marries a dissolute 40-yr-old American author. *Dir.* Richard Donner.

Twins (1988)　Arnold Schwarzenegger (Julius

Benedict), Danny De Vito (Vincent Benedict). *Dir*. Ivan Reitman.

Twister (1996) Helen Hunt, Bill Paxton, Lois Smith. *Dir*. Jan de Bont.

Two Days in the Valley (1996) Danny Aiello, James Spader, Jeff Daniels, Teri Hatcher, Louise Fletcher, Keith Carradine. *Dir*. John Herzfeld.

Two Much (1996) Antonio Banderas, Melanie Griffith, Danny Aiello, Daryl Hannah. Art dealer, engaged to wealthy woman, invents a twin brother so that he can marry her sister. *Dir*. Fernando Trueba.

Two Mules for Sister Sara (1969) Clint Eastwood, Shirley MacLaine. *Dir*. Don Siegel.

2001: A Space Odyssey (1968) Keir Dullea, Gary Lockwood, Leonard Rossiter, Robert Beatty, Douglas Rain (voice of Hal). Film based on Arthur C Clarke story 'The Sentinel'. Computer: Hal 9000 stands for Holistic Algorithmic. Journeyed to moon of Jupiter, although it was to the rings of Saturn in the book. *Dir*. Stanley Kubrick.

2010 (1984) Roy Scheider, Helen Mirren, John Lithgow, Keir Dullea. *Dir*. Peter Hyams.

Two-Way Stretch (1960) Peter Sellers, Wilfrid Hyde-White, Lionel Jeffries, Bernard Cribbins, David Lodge, Beryl Reid, Irene Handl. Three convicts break out of jail to do a robbery. *Dir*. Robert Day.

Ultimate Warrior, The (1975) Yul Brynner, Max Von Sydow, Joanna Miles. Set in New York AD 2012. *Dir*. Robert Clouse.

Unforgiven (1992) Clint Eastwood, Gene Hackman, Morgan Freeman, Richard Harris. *Dir*. Clint Eastwood.

Unforgiven, The (1960) Burt Lancaster, Audrey Hepburn, Audie Murphy. *Dir*. John Huston.

Universal Soldier (1992) Jean-Claude Van Damme, Dolph Lundgren. *Dir*. Roland Emmerich.

Unsinkable Molly Brown, The (1964) Debbie Reynolds, Harve Presnell, Ed Begley. *Dir*. Charles Walters.

Untouchables, The (1987) Kevin Costner, Sean Connery (Jim Malone), Robert De Niro (Al Capone), Andy Garcia. *Dir*. Brian De Palma.

Uptown Saturday Night (1974) Sidney Poitier, Bill Cosby, Harry Belafonte, Flip Wilson, Richard Pryor. Friends pursue crooks who have stolen a winning lottery ticket. *Dir*. Sidney Poitier.

Urban Cowboy (1980) John Travolta, Debra Winger. *Dir*. James Bridges.

Used Cars (1980) Kurt Russell, Gerrit Graham, Jack Russell. *Dir*. Robert Zemeckis.

Usual Suspects, The (1995) Gabriel Byrne, Stephen Baldwin, Kevin Spacey, Pete Postlethwaite. *Dir*. Bryan Singer.

Valentino (1977) Rudolf Nureyev, Leslie Caron, Michelle Phillips. *Dir*. Ken Russell.

Valley of the Dolls (1967) Barbara Parkins, Patty Duke, Susan Hayward, Sharon Tate, Martin Milner. *Dir*. Mark Robson.

Vanilla Sky (2001) Tom Cruise (David Aames), Penelope Cruz, Cameron Diaz, Kurt Russell, Jason Lee, Noah Taylor, Timothy Spall, Tilda Swinton. Accused of murder, a publishing tycoon explains to a prison psychiatrist how his life fell apart. *Dir*. Cameron Crowe.

Vera Drake (2004) Imelda Staunton (Vera Drake), Richard Graham (George), Eddie Marsan (Reg), Anna Keaveney (Nellie), Sam Troughton (David), Alex Kelly (Ethel). Abortionist Vera Drake finds her beliefs and practices clash with the morals of 1950s Britain, a conflict that leads to tragedy for her family. Extraordinary film veiled in secrecy throughout its unscripted filming which gives a dramatic heightening of its content. *Dir*. Mike Leigh.

Verdict, The (1982) Paul Newman, James Mason, Charlotte Rampling. *Dir*. Sidney Lumet.

Vertigo (1958) James Stewart (Detective John 'Scottie' Ferguson), Kim Novak (Madeleine Elster / Judy Barton), Barbara Bel Geddes (Marjorie 'Midge' Wood), Tom Helmore (Gavin Elster), Henry Jones (Coroner). A detective with a fear of heights is hired by old schoolfriend Gavin Elster to follow his wife Madeleine. Ferguson falls in love with her but she apparently falls to her death. Then he meets her double. *Dir*. Alfred Hitchcock.

Very Important Person (1961) James Robertson Justice, Stanley Baxter, Leslie Phillips. *Dir*. Ken Annakin.

Vice Versa (1988) Judge Reinhold, Fred Savage, Corinne Bohrer. *Dir*. Brian Gilbert.

Victor / Victoria (1982) James Garner, Julie Andrews, Robert Preston, John Rhys-Davies. *Dir*. Blake Edwards.

View to a Kill, A (1985) Roger Moore, Christopher Walken (Max Zorin), Grace Jones (May Day), Tanya Roberts (Stacey Sutton), Patrick MacNee, Fiona Fullerton, David Yip. Title song performed by Duran Duran. *Dir*. John Glen.

Vikings, The (1958) Kirk Douglas, Tony Curtis, Janet Leigh, Ernest Borgnine. Orson Welles was the narrator. *Dir*. Richard Fleischer.

Village of the Damned (1960) George Sanders, Barbara Shelley, Laurence Naismith. Village women simultaneously give birth to fair-haired, genius level, telepathic children with eerie results. *Dir*. Wolf Rilla.

Village of the Damned (1995) Christopher Reeve, Kirstie Alley, Linda Kozlowski, Mark Hamill. *Dir*. John Carpenter.

Villain (1971) Richard Burton, Ian McShane, Nigel Davenport, TP McKenna. *Dir*. Michael Tuchner.

VIPs, The (1963) Richard Burton, Elizabeth Taylor, Rod Taylor, Maggie Smith, Orson Welles, Louis Jourdan, Lance Percival. *Dir*. Anthony Asquith.

Virginian, The (1929) Gary Cooper, Walter Huston. 1946 remake starred Joel McCrea & Brian Donlevy. *Dir*. Victor Fleming.

Viva Las Vegas (1964) Elvis Presley, Ann-Margret. Presley plays a sports car racer. *Dir*. George Sidney.

Viva Zapata (1952) Marlon Brando, Anthony Quinn, Jean Peters, Joseph Wiseman. *Dir*. Elia Kazan.

Volcano (1997) Tommy Lee Jones (Mike Roark), Gaby Hoffmann, Don Cheadle, Anne Heche (Dr Amy Barnes). *Dir*. Mick Jackson.

Von Ryan's Express (1965) Frank Sinatra, Trevor Howard, Sergio Fantoni. *Dir*. Mark Robson.

Voyage to the Bottom of the Sea (1961) Walter Pidgeon, Robert Sterling, Joan Fontaine, Peter Lorre, Barbara Eden. Spawned a long-running TV series. *Dir*. Irwin Allen.

Wag the Dog (1998) Dustin Hoffman, Robert De Niro. *Dir*. Barry Levinson.

Wages of Fear, The (1953) Yves Montand, Folco Lulli, Peter Van Eyck, Charles Vanel. Nitro-glycerine is the substance transported over dangerous roads to put out oil well fire. *Dir*. Henri-Georges Clouzot.

Wait until Dark (1967) Audrey Hepburn, Alan Arkin, Richard Crenna, Efrem Zimbalist Jnr. *Dir*. Terence Young.

Walkabout (1970) Jenny Agutter, Lucien John, David Gulpilil. *Dir*. Nicolas Roeg.

War, The (1994) Kevin Costner, Elijah Wood, LaToya Chisholm. *Dir*. Jon Avnet.

War Games (1983) Matthew Broderick, Dabney Coleman, John Wood. *Dir*. John Badham.

C
I
N
E
M
A

War of the Roses, The (1989)   Michael Douglas, Kathleen Turner, Danny De Vito. *Dir*. Danny De Vito.

Waterworld (1995)   Kevin Costner, Dennis Hopper, Jeanne Tripplehorn. *Dir*. Kevin Reynolds.

Way We Were, The (1973)   Robert Redford, Barbra Streisand, Patrick O'Neal. *Dir*. Sydney Pollack.

Wedding Banquet, The (1993)   Mitchell Lichtenstein, Winston Chao, May Chin. *Dir*. Ang Lee.

Welcome II The Terrordome (1994)   Suzette Llewellyn, Saffron Burrows. *Dir*. Ngozi Onwurah.

Welcome to the Dollhouse (1995)   Heather Matarazzo, Victoria Davis. *Dir*. Todd Solondz.

We're No Angels (1954)   Humphrey Bogart, Peter Ustinov, Aldo Ray, Basil Rathbone. *Dir*. Michael Curtiz.

We're No Angels (1989)   Robert De Niro, Sean Penn, Demi Moore. Remake of the 1954 film. *Dir*. Neil Jordan.

West Side Story (1961)   Natalie Wood, Richard Beymer, Russ Tamblyn, George Chakiris, Rita Moreno. *Dir*. Robert Wise.

Westerner, The (1940)   Gary Cooper, Walter Brennan, Charlton Heston. *Dir*. William Wyler.

Westworld (1973)   Yul Brynner, Richard Benjamin, James Brolin. *Dir*. Michael Crichton.

Whatever Happened to Baby Jane? (1962)   Bette Davis, Joan Crawford, Victor Buono. *Dir*. Robert Aldrich.

What's New Pussycat? (1965)   Peter O'Toole, Peter Sellers, Woody Allen, Ursula Andress, Capucine. *Dir*. Woody Allen.

What's Up Doc? (1972)   Barbra Streisand, Ryan O'Neal. *Dir*. Peter Bogdanovich.

When Saturday Comes (1996)   Sean Bean (Jimmy Muir), Emile Lloyd (Annie Doherty), Pete Postlethwaite. *Dir*. Maria Giese.

When We Were Kings (1996)   Documentary of Muhammad Ali's defeat of George Foreman in Zaïre. *Dir*. Leon Gast.

Where Eagles Dare (1969)   Richard Burton, Clint Eastwood, Mary Ure. Seven Allied agents land in Bavarian Alps to rescue officer from impregnable castle during World War II. *Dir*. Brian G Hutton.

Whistle down the Wind (1961)   Hayley Mills, Bernard Lee, Alan Bates, Norman Bird. Three children think a murderer on the run is Jesus. *Dir*. Bryan Forbes.

White Christmas (1954)   Bing Crosby, Danny Kaye, Rosemary Clooney, Dean Jagger. *Dir*. Michael Curtiz.

White Heat (1949)   James Cagney, Edmond O'Brien, Margaret Wycherly, Virginia Mayo. *Dir*. Raoul Walsh.

White Hunter, Black Heart (1990)   Clint Eastwood (John Wilson), Jeff Fahey (Pete Verrill), Marisa Berenson (Kay Gibson), Timothy Spall (Hodkins). Fictionalised account of John Huston during the shooting of *The African Queen*. *Dir*. Clint Eastwood.

White Men Can't Jump (1992)   Wesley Snipes, Woody Harrelson, Rosie Perez. *Dir*. Ron Shelton.

White Mischief (1987)   Charles Dance, Greta Scacchi, John Hurt, Sarah Miles, Trevor Howard. *Dir*. Michael Radford.

White Nights (1985)   Mikhail Baryshnikov, Gregory Hines, Helen Mirren, Isabella Rossellini. Best Song Oscar for 'Say You, Say Me' by Lionel Richie. *Dir*. Taylor Hackford.

White Squall (1996)   Jeff Bridges (Christopher 'Skipper' Sheldon). Boat: *The Albatross*. *Dir*. Ridley Scott.

Who Framed Roger Rabbit? (1988)   Bob Hoskins (Eddie Valiant). Animation synchronised with live action. Christopher Lloyd (Judge Doom). Jessica Rabbit's speaking voice was Kathleen Turner and

singing voice was Amy Irving. *Dir*. Robert Zemeckis.

Whoops Apocalypse (1986)   Loretta Swit (President Adams), Peter Cook (Sir Mortimer Chris). *Dir*. Tom Bussmann.

Who's Afraid of Virginia Woolf? (1966)   Richard Burton, Elizabeth Taylor, George Segal, Sandy Dennis. Based on Edward Albee's play. *Dir*. Mike Nichols.

Wicked Lady, The (1945)   Margaret Lockwood, James Mason, Michael Rennie. The 1983 remake starred Faye Dunaway in the Lockwood role. *Dir*. Leslie Arliss.

Wild Bunch, The (1969)   William Holden, Ernest Borgnine, Robert Ryan, Warren Oates, Edmond O'Brien. *Dir*. Sam Peckinpah.

Wild One, The (1954)   Marlon Brando, Lee Marvin, Mary Murphy. The Garutso lens created the sharpness of photography. *Dir*. Laslo Benedek.

Willard (1971)   Bruce Davison, Elsa Lanchester, Ernest Borgnine, Sondra Locke. Shy, introverted man breeds and trains rats to kill his enemies. *Dir*. Daniel Mann.

William Shakespeare's Romeo and Juliet (1996) Leonardo DiCaprio, Claire Danes, Brian Dennehy, Pete Postlethwaite. *Dir*. Baz Luhrmann.

Wind in the Willows, The (1996)   Steve Coogan (Mole), Eric Idle (Rat), Terry Jones (Toad), Stephen Fry, Julia Sawalha. *Dir*. Terry Jones.

Winslow Boy, The (1948)   Robert Donat, Cedric Hardwicke, Margaret Leighton, Wilfrid Hyde-White, Kathleen Harrison. Father endeavours to prove the innocence of naval cadet son, expelled for stealing postal order. *Dir*. Anthony Asquith.

Wish You Were Here (1987)   Emily Lloyd, Tom Bell, Clare Clifford. *Dir*. David Leland.

Witches of Eastwick, The (1987)   Jack Nicholson, Cher, Susan Sarandon, Michelle Pfeiffer. *Dir*. George Miller.

Witness (1985)   Harrison Ford, Kelly McGillis, Lukas Haas, Alexander Godunov. *Dir*. Peter Weir.

Witness for the Prosecution (1957)   Charles Laughton, Tyrone Power, Marlene Dietrich, Elsa Lanchester. *Dir*. Billy Wilder.

Wiz, The (1978)   Diana Ross, Michael Jackson, Lena Horne, Richard Pryor. *Dir*. Sidney Lumet.

Wizard of Oz, The (1939)   Judy Garland, Frank Morgan, Bert Lahr (Lion), Jack Haley (Tin Man), Ray Bolger (Scarecrow). *Dir*. Victor Fleming.

Wolf (1994)   Jack Nicholson, Michelle Pfeiffer, James Spader, Kate Nelligan, Christopher Plummer. *Dir*. Mike Nichols.

Woman in a Dressing Gown (1957)   Yvonne Mitchell, Anthony Quayle, Sylvia Syms, Andrew Ray. *Dir*. J Lee Thompson.

Women in love (1969)   Glenda Jackson, Jennie Linden, Alan Bates, Oliver Reed. Famous for its nude wrestling scene between Bates and Reed. *Dir*. Ken Russell.

Working Girl (1988)   Harrison Ford, Sigourney Weaver, Melanie Griffith, Alec Baldwin, Olympia Dukakis. *Dir*. Mike Nichols.

Working Girls (1986)   Louise Smith, Ellen McElduff, Amanda Goodwin. *Dir*. Lizzie Borden.

World Is Not Enough, The (1999)   Pierce Brosnan, Robert Carlyle (Renard), Sophie Marceau (Elektra), Denise Richards (Christmas Jones), Judi Dench (M), Robbie Coltrane, John Cleese (R). Theme song performed by Shirley Manson of Garbage. *Dir*. Michael Apted.

World of Suzie Wong, The (1960)   William Holden, Nancy Kwan, Sylvia Syms, Michael Wilding, Jackie Chan. *Dir*. Richard Quine.

Wrong Box, The (1966)   Ralph Richardson, John Mills, Michael Caine, Peter Cook, Dudley Moore, Peter Sellers, Tony Hancock, Nanette Newman. Two Victorian brothers are last survivors of a tontine agreement and try to kill each other. *Dir*. Bryan Forbes.

Wrong Man, The (1957)   Henry Fonda, Vera Miles, Anthony Quayle. *Dir*. Alfred Hitchcock.

Wuthering Heights (1939)   Laurence Olivier, Merle Oberon, David Niven, Flora Robson. *Dir*. William Wyler.

Wuthering Heights (1970)   Timothy Dalton, Anna Calder-Marshall, Ian Ogilvy. *Dir*. Robert Fuest.

Wyatt Earp (1994)   Kevin Costner, Dennis Quaid, Gene Hackman, Mark Harmon, Isabella Rossellini. *Dir*. Lawrence Kasdan.

Xanadu (1980)   Olivia Newton-John, Gene Kelly, Michael Beck. *Dir*. Robert Greenwald.

xXx (2002)   Samuel L Jackson (Agent Gibbons), Vin Diesel (Xander Cage / Triple X), Marton Csokas (Yorgi), Asia Argento (Yelena). Spy thriller in which agents infiltrate a cult group, Anarchy 99, who have made a biological weapon named Silent Night. *Dir*. Rob Cohen.

Y Tu Mama También (2001)   Maribel Verdu (Luisa Cortes), Gael Garcia Bernal (Julio Zapata). Two Mexican youths learn about life and love from an older woman while travelling to find the perfect beach. *Dir*. Alfonso Cuaron.

Yankee Doodle Dandy (1942)   James Cagney, Walter Huston, Eddie Foy Jnr. Life story of dancer George M Cohan. *Dir*. Michael Curtiz.

Yanks (1979)   Vanessa Redgrave, Richard Gere, Rachel Roberts. *Dir*. John Schlesinger.

Year of the Dragon, The (1985)   Mickey Rourke, John Lone, Ariane. *Dir*. Michael Cimino.

Yearling, The (1946)   Gregory Peck, Jane Wyman. *Dir*. Clarence Brown.

Yellow Rolls Royce, The (1964)   Rex Harrison, Jeanne Moreau, Omar Sharif, Ingrid Bergman, Shirley MacLaine. Aristocrat, gangster and millionairess in turn own an expensive car. *Dir*. Anthony Asquith.

Yellowbeard (1983)   Graham Chapman, Peter Cook, Marty Feldman, Eric Idle, John Cleese, Spike Milligan, Beryl Reid, Susannah York. *Dir*. Mel Damski.

Yentl (1983)   Barbra Streisand, Mandy Patinkin, Amy Irving, Nehemiah Persoff. Barbra Streisand also co-wrote with Jack Rosenthal. *Dir*. Barbra Streisand.

You Only Live Twice (1967)   Sean Connery, Akiko Wakabayashi (Aki), Tetsuro Tamba, Charles Gray, Donald Pleasence (Blofeld), Bernard Lee, Mie Hama (Kissy Suzuki). Theme song sung by Nancy Sinatra. *Dir*. Lewis Gilbert.

Young Adam (2003)   Ewan McGregor (Joe Taylor), Tilda Swinton (Ella Gault), Peter Mullan (Les Gault), Emily Mortimer (Cathie Dimly). Set in the 1950s, concerning a Scottish drifter who brings death and mayhem to those who cross his path. Based on a novel by Alexander Trocchi. *Dir*. David Mackenzie.

Young Bess (1953)   Jean Simmons, Stewart Granger, Charles Laughton (Henry VIII), Kay Walsh, Deborah Kerr. *Dir*. George Sidney.

Young Frankenstein (1974)   Gene Wilder, Marty Feldman, Madeline Kahn, Gene Hackman. *Dir*. Mel Brooks.

Young Guns (1988)   Emilio Estevez, Kiefer Sutherland, Charlie Sheen, Terence Stamp, Jack Palance, Patrick Wayne. *Dir*. Christopher Cain.

Young Guns II (1990)   Emilio Estevez, Kiefer Sutherland, Lou Diamond Phillips, Christian Slater, James Coburn. *Dir*. Geoff Murphy.

Zardoz (1974)   Sean Connery, Charlotte Rampling, John Alderton. Set in the year 2293. *Dir*. John Boorman.

Ziegfeld Follies (1946)   Fred Astaire, Lucille Ball, Jimmy Durante, Fanny Brice, Lena Horne, Esther Williams, Judy Garland, Red Skelton, Gene Kelly. *Dir*. Vincente Minnelli.

Zorba the Greek (1964)   Anthony Quinn, Alan Bates, Lila Kedrova. *Dir*. Michael Cacoyannis.

Zorro the Gay Blade (1981)   George Hamilton, Lauren Hutton, Brenda Vaccaro, Ron Leibman, James Booth. *Dir*. Peter Medak.

Zulu (1964)   Stanley Baker, Jack Hawkins, Michael Caine, James Booth, Ivor Emmanuel. *Dir*. Cy Endfield.

Zulu Dawn (1979)   Burt Lancaster, Denholm Elliott, Peter O'Toole, John Mills. *Dir*. Douglas Hickox. Famous for being the last listed film in *Halliwell's Film Guide*.

NB: It is hoped that this is a fairly representative catalogue of cinematic history, but it is inevitable that some films of quality will not be listed.

C
I
N
E
M
A

Films: General Information

Abba hits featured   *Muriel's Wedding*.

Acromegaly: sufferer   Rondo Hatton (d.1946), often billed as 'The Brute Man' or 'The Creeper', suffered from this enlargement of the bones.

Aramaic dialogue   *Passion of the Christ* (2004).

Archers: nickname   Film makers Michael Powell and Emeric Pressburger (and name of their film company).

Bafta President   Princess Anne, The Princess Royal.

Barons   Richard Attenborough (Richmond on Thames), Laurence Olivier (Brighton).

Benchley shorts   Popular one-reel shorts delivered by Robert Benchley, sitting behind a desk, pontificating on aspects of modern living.

Bond Cars   All four-wheeled transport driven by the six Bonds. *Dr No* (Sunbeam Alpine), *From Russia with Love* (Bentley Mark IV), *Goldfinger* (Aston Martin DB5), *Thunderball* (Aston Martin DB5), *Casino Royale* (black Bentley), *On Her Majesty's Secret Service* (Aston Martin DBS), *Diamonds Are Forever* (moon buggy and Ford Mustang Mach 1), *Live and Let Die* (double-decker bus and white Coronado), *The Man with the Golden Gun* (red AMC Hornet), *The Spy Who Loved Me* (white Lotus Esprit), *Moonraker* (MP Roadster), *For Your Eyes Only* (Lotus Esprit Turbo and Citroen 2CV), *Octopussy* (Mercedes 250SE), *Never Say Never Again* (black Bentley), *A View to a Kill* (Renault 11), *The Living Daylights* (Aston Martin DBS V8 Vantage as a coupé and as a soft-top Volante version, also drove an Audi 200 Quattro), *Licence to Kill* (Kenworth W900B Truck), *Goldeneye* (BMW Z3 Roadster and Aston Martin DB5), *Tomorrow Never Dies* (BMW 750iL and Aston Martin DB5), *The World Is Not Enough* (silver BMW Z8), *Die Another Day* (Aston Martin V12 Vanquish).

Bowery Boys   Leo Gorcey, Huntz Hall, Bob Jordan, Gabriel Dell, Bernard Gorcey, David Gorcey, Billy Benedict, Bennie Bartlett.

Carry On Cleo: US video title   *Caligula's Funniest Home Videos.*

Carry On films   *Carry On Sergeant* (1958), *Carry On Nurse* (1959), *Carry On Teacher*, (1959), *Carry On Constable* (1960), *Carry On Regardless* (1961), *Carry On Cruising* (1962), *Carry On Cabby* (1963), *Carry On Cleo* (1964), *Carry On Spying* (1964), *Carry On Jack* (US title: *Carry On Venus*) (1964), *Carry On Cowboy* (1965), *Carry On – Don't Lose Your Head* (1966), *Carry On – Follow that Camel* (1966), *Carry On Screaming* (1966), *Carry On Doctor* (1968), *Carry On Up the Khyber* (1968), *Carry On Again Doctor* (1969), *Carry On Camping* (1969), *Carry On Up the Jungle* (1970), *Carry On Loving* (1970), *Carry On Henry* (1971), *Carry On at Your Convenience* (1971), *Carry On Abroad* (1972), *Carry On Matron* (1972), *Carry On Girls* (1973), *Carry On Dick* (1974), *Carry On Behind* (1975), *Carry On England* (1976), *Carry On Emmanuelle* (1978), *Carry On Columbus* (1992).

Celluloid film: innovator   William Friese-Greene (1888).

Cinéma vérité   Film technique that utilises raw, natural sound, hand-held cameras and little rehearsal.

Cinemascope: first film   *The Robe* (1953).

Cinematic projections: early examples   Stroboscope, zoetrope, thaumatrope and praxinoscope.

Cinerama: invented   New York 1952.

Directors: film with 10   *Aria* (1988).

Documentary: term coined by John Grierson (8 February 1926) while reviewing Robert Flaherty's ethnographic film *Moana* for the *New York Sun.*

Dolby Stereo: invented   1980.

Film à clef   Film that appears to be a fictional work, but is in fact based on a true story.

Film festival: first   Venice, 1932.

Film: first British feature   *Oliver Twist* (Aug 1912).

Film: first before paying audience   *Young Griffo v Battling Charles Barnett* (New York, 20 May 1895).

Film: first over one hour long   *The Story of the Kelly Gang* (Melbourne, 24 Dec 1906).

Film: most expensive shot in Britain   *The Fifth Element* (1997).

Gulf War story   *Courage under Fire.*

Hitchcock cameos   *The Lodger* (1926) Seen seated at desk in a newsroom, and later he's one of the onlookers watching arrest of Ivor Novello. *Blackmail* (1929) Bothered by a young boy on the Underground as he is trying to read a book. *Murder!* (1930) He is a passer-by on the street. *The Thirty-Nine Steps* (1935) Again, he is a passer-by on the street. *Young and Innocent* (1937) Appears as a clumsy press photographer. *The Lady Vanishes* (1938) Appears in a London railway station. *Rebecca* (1940) Appears standing outside a telephone booth while George Sanders is making a call. *Foreign Correspondent* (1940) Reading newspaper on the street, before Joel McCrea meets Van Meer (Albert Basserman). *Mr & Mrs Smith* (1941) On the street, unaware of Robert Montgomery. *Saboteur* (1942) At the news-stand. *Shadow of a Doubt* (1943) Holding a full house whilst playing poker on a train. *Lifeboat* (1944) Pictured in a before-and-after weight reduction advertisement in paper read by William Bendix. *Spellbound* (1945) Getting out of a crowded hotel lift. *Notorious* (1946) Drinking champagne at a party. *The Paradine Case* (1948) Carrying a cello case. *Rope* (1948) Crossing the street during the opening credits. *Under Capricorn* (1949) Seen first at Governor's house and then on steps of Government House. *Stage Fright* (1950) Turning round in the street to look at Jane Wyman, who's talking to herself. *Strangers on a Train* (1951) Boarding a train carrying a bass violin. *I Confess* (1953) Crossing the screen at the top of a long staircase. *Dial M for Murder* (1954) In a class reunion photo. *Rear Window* (1954) Winding a clock in the musician's apartment. *To Catch a Thief* (1955) On a bus, next to Cary Grant. *The Trouble with Harry* (1955) At an outdoor exhibition. *The Man Who Knew Too Much* (1956) Watching Arab acrobats in Marrakesh marketplace. *Vertigo* (1958) Crossing the street. *North by Northwest* (1959) Running to catch a bus, with the door slamming in his face. *Psycho* (1960) Standing outside the real-estate office, wearing a ten gallon hat. *The Birds* (1963) Exiting a pet shop, with 2 Scottie dogs. *Marnie* (1964) Coming out of a hotel room. *Torn Curtain* (1966) In hotel lobby with baby on his lap (his theme tune playing softly). *Topaz* (1969) Wheelchair-bound being attended by a nurse (in an airport). *Frenzy* (1972) Spectator in a crowd scene. *Family Plot* (1976) In silhouette behind the door of the Office of Vital Statistics.

Hollywood studio: first   Centaur Film Company (Horsley).

Latin dialogue   *Sebastiane* (directed by Derek Jarman), *Passion of the Christ* (directed by Mel Gibson).

Marilyn Monroe: film shooting when died   *Something's Gotta Give.*

Miss Ohio winner   Halle Berry (also Miss Teen All-American, and in 1986 was first runner-up in the Miss USA pageant, becoming the first African-American to represent the USA in Miss World).

Monarch acted in film   Edward VIII (whilst Prince of Wales), *The Power of Right* & *The Warrior Strain* (1919). Prince Charles was the first member of the Royal Family to speak in a fiction film: *Grime Goes Green* (1990).

Movie camera: first patent   William Friese-Greene (1888).

Nicolas Cage: famous relation   Nephew of Francis Ford Coppola.

Oscar: first British   Charles Laughton for *Private Life of Henry VIII* in 1934.

Oscar nominations: most without winning   *The Color Purple* and *The Turning Point* each had 11 Oscar nominations but failed to win a single award.

Oscar nominations: records   Meryl Streep was nominated for a record 13th time in 2003 while Jack Nicholson was nominated for a record 12th time in 2003, in the acting categories.

Oscar statuettes   Designed by Cedric Gibbons and sculpted by George Stanley.

Oscars: film with most awards   *Ben Hur* (1959) and *Titanic* (1997): 11.

Oscars: films with most nominations   *All About Eve* (1950) and *Titanic* (1998), each nominated in 14 categories.

Pamela Stephenson: film sued for £3.5m   *Hello, She Lied* (renamed *Miami Hustle*); replaced by Kathy Ireland.

Pearl and Dean: music called   Asteroid.

Picasso painting in lieu of cash   Robin Williams received a $7 million Picasso in lieu of earnings for *Aladdin.*

Road films: first in colour   *Road to Bali* (1952).

Road films: order   Singapore, Zanzibar, Morocco, Utopia, Rio, Bali, Hong Kong.

Ronald Reagan films: include   *Accidents Will Happen* (1938), *Angels Wash their Faces* (1939), *Bedtime for Bonzo* (1951), *Hellcats of the Navy* (1957), *Cattle Queen of Montana* (1954), *The Killers* (1964).

Smell-O-Vision: first film   *The Scent of Mystery* (1959).

Sound film: first   *Jazz Singer* (1927).

Tarzan: actors played   Johnny Weissmuller 1932–48, Lex Barker 1949–53, Gordon Scott 1955–60, Jock Mahoney 1962–3, Mike Henry 1966–8. Also Miles O'Keeffe, Buster Crabbe, Frank Merrill, Christopher Lambert.

Third Man: famous quote   'In Italy for 30 years under the Borgias they had warfare, terror, murder and bloodshed, but they produced Michelangelo, Leonardo da Vinci and the Renaissance. In Switzerland, they had brotherly love, they had 500 years of democracy and peace – and what did they produce? The cuckoo clock.'

Triangle Film Corporation   Formed in 1915 by DW Griffiths, Thomas Ince and Mack Sennett.

United Artists   Formed in 1919 by Mary Pickford, Douglas Fairbanks, Charlie Chaplin and DW Griffiths.

Videodrome: presenters   Alex Cox, Mark Cousins.

Western film: first in USA   *The Great Train Robbery* (directed by Edwin Porter, 1903).

First Films

Actor	Film
Danny Aiello	*Bang the Drum Slowly* (1973)
Claude Akins	*A Place in the Sun* (1951)
Alan Alda	*Gone Are the Days* (1963)
Woody Allen	*What's New Pussycat* (1965)
Kirstie Alley	*One More Chance* (1981)
June Allyson	*All Girl Revue* (1937)
Mädchen Amick	*The Borrower* (1989)
Dana Andrews	*Lucky Cisco Kid* (1938)
Harry Andrews	*Red Beret, The* (1952)
Julie Andrews	*Mary Poppins* (1964) As extra: *The Reluctant Debutante* (1958) Voice only: *Rose of Baghdad* (1952)
Gabrielle Anwar	*Manifesto* (1988)
Anne Archer	*The All-American Boy* (1970; released 1973)
Eve Arden	*Song of Love* (1929)
Alan Arkin	*Calypso Heat Wave* (1957)
George Arliss	*Devil, The* (1921)
Edward Arnold	*The Heart of Virginia Keep* (1916) Short: *When the Man Speaks* (1916)
Rosanna Arquette	*More American Graffiti* (1979) TV film: *Having Babies II* (1977)
Jean Arthur	*Cameo Kirby* (1923) Short: *Somebody Lied* (1923)
Armand Assante	*The Lords of Flatbush* (1974)
Fred Astaire	*Dancing Lady* (1933) Short: *Municipal Bandwagon* (1932)
Mary Astor	*Hope* (1922) Short: *The Beggar Maid* (1921)
Rowan Atkinson	*The Secret Policeman's Ball* (1979)
Richard Attenborough	*In Which We Serve* (1942)
Gene Autry	*In Old Santa Fe* (1934)
Dan Aykroyd	*Love at First Sight* (1976) Short and voice only: *The Gift of Winter* (1974)
Lew Ayres	*The Sophomore* (1929)
Charles Aznavour	*Les Disparus de Saint-Agil* (1938) US title: *Boys' School*
Lauren Bacall	*To Have and Have Not* (1944)
Kevin Bacon	*National Lampoon's Animal House* (1978)
Carroll Baker	*Easy to Love* (1953)

Actor	Film
Joe Don Baker	*Cool Hand Luke* (1967)
Stanley Baker	*Undercover* (1943)
Alec Baldwin	*Forever Lulu* (1987) TV film: *Sweet Revenge* (1984)
William Baldwin	*Born on the Fourth of July* (1989)
Martin Balsam	*On the Waterfront* (1954)
Anne Bancroft	*Don't Bother to Knock* (1952)
Theda Bara	*A Fool There Was* (1914)
Brigitte Bardot	*Le Trou Normand* (1952)
Ellen Barkin	*The Diner* (1982)
Drew Barrymore	*Altered States* (1980)
Ethel Barrymore	*The Nightingale* (1914)
John Barrymore	*An American Citizen* (1913)
Lionel Barrymore	*Men and Women* (1914) Short: *Friends* (1969)
Kim Basinger	*Hard Country* (1981)
Alan Bates	*It's Never Too Late* (1956)
Kathy Bates	*Taking Off* (1971)
Anne Baxter	*Twenty Mule Team* (1940)
Sean Bean	*Caravaggio* (1986) TV film: *Winter Flight* (1984)
Warren Beatty	*Splendor in the Grass* (1961)
Bonny Bedelia	*The Gypsy Moths* (1969)
Harry Belafonte	*Bright Road* (1953)
Ralph Bellamy	*The Secret Six* (1931)
William Bendix	*Woman of the Year* (1942)
Tom Berenger	*The Sentinel* (1976)
Candice Bergen	*The Group* (1966)
Ingrid Bergman	*Munkbrogreven* (1934)
Halle Berry	*Jungle Fever* (1991)
Juliette Binoche	*Liberty Belle* (1981)
Jacqueline Bisset	*The Knack* (1964)
Honor Blackman	*Daughter of Darkness* (1947)
Cate Blanchett	*Paradise Road* (1997) Australia-only release: *Police Rescue* (1994)
Claire Bloom	*The Blind Goddess* (1948)
Dirk Bogarde	*Dancing With Crime* (1947) As extra: *Come on George* (1939)
Humphrey Bogart	*A Devil with Women* (1930). As extra: *The Dancing Team* (1928)
Ernest Borgnine	*China Corsair* (1951)
Clara Bow	*Beyond the Rainbow* (1921)
Stephen Boyd	*Lilacs in the Spring* (1954) US title: *Let's Make Up*
Charles Boyer	*L'Homme du Large* (1920)

CINEMA

Actor	Film	Actor	Film
Kenneth Branagh	*High Season* (1986)	Ronald Colman	*The Toilers* (1919)
Marlon Brando	*The Men* (1950)		Short: *The Live Wire* (1917)
Walter Brennan	*Watch Your Wife* (1926)	Sean Connery	*Lilacs in the Spring* (1954)
Beau Bridges	*No Minor Vices* (1948)	Tom Conti	*Flame* (1974)
Jeff Bridges	*The Company She Keeps* (1950) (as baby)	Jackie Coogan	*Skinner's Baby* (1916)
Lloyd Bridges	*They Dare Not Love* (1941)	Gary Cooper	*Blind Justice* (1923)
Adrien Brody	*New York Stories* (1989) ('Life Without Zoe' segment)	Harry H Corbett	*Never Look Back* (1952)
		Kevin Costner	*Night Shift* (1982) (*Sizzle Beach, USA* made in late 70s but not shown till 1986)
Charles Bronson	*You're in the Navy Now* (1951) Aka *USS Teakettle* (as Charles Buchinski)	Joseph Cotten	*Citizen Kane* (1941)
Mel Brooks	*Putney Swope* (1969)		Unreleased: *Too Much Johnson* (1938)
	As narrator: *The Critic* (1963)	Tom Courtenay	*Loneliness of the Long Distance Runner* (1962)
Pierce Brosnan	*The Long Good Friday* (1980)	Noël Coward	*Hearts of the World* (1918)
	Short: *Resting Rough* (1979)	Broderick Crawford	*Woman Chases Man* (1937)
Yul Brynner	*Port of New York* (1949)	Joan Crawford	*Lady of the Night* (1925)
Sandra Bullock	*A Fool and His Money* (1988)		Short: *Miss MGM* (1925)
George Burns	*Lamb Chops* (1929)	Michael Crawford	*Soap Box Derby* (1957)
Raymond Burr	*San Quentin* (1946)	Bing Crosby	*King of Jazz* (1930)
Richard Burton	*The Last Days of Dolwyn* (1948)		Short: *Ripstitch the Tailor* (1930)
Max Bygraves	*Bless 'em All* (1949)	Russell Crowe	*Blood Oath* (1990)
Gabriel Byrne	*The Outsider* (1979)	Tom Cruise	*My Bodyguard* (1980)
	BFI 'Art' film: *On a Paving Stone Mounted* (1978)	Billy Crystal	*Rabbit Test* (1978)
			TV film: *Death Flight* (1977)
James Caan	*Irma La Douce* (1963)	Macaulay Culkin	*Rocket Gibraltar* (1988)
Nicolas Cage	*Fast Times at Ridgemont High* (1982).	Rory Culkin	*You Can Count On Me* (2000)
	TV film: *The Best of Times* (1981) as Nicolas Coppola (both)	Robert Culp	*PT 109* (1963)
		Jamie Lee Curtis	*Halloween* (1978)
			TV film: *Operation Petticoat* (1977)
James Cagney	*Sinner's Holiday* (1930)	Tony Curtis	*Criss Cross* (1948)
Michael Caine	*A Hill in Korea* (1956)	John Curtis	*Class* (1983)
Simon Callow	*Amadeus* (1984)	Peter Cushing	*The Man in the Iron Mask* (1939)
John Candy	*Class of '44* (1973)		
Claudia Cardinale	*Goha* (1957)	Willem Dafoe	*Heaven's Gate* (1980)
	Short: *Chaines d'Or* (1956)	Jim Dale	*6.5 Special* (1958)
Ian Carmichael	*Bond Street* (1948)	Timothy Dalton	*The Lion in Winter* (1968)
Leslie Caron	*An American in Paris* (1951)	Matt Damon	*Mystic Pizza* (1988)
David Carradine	*Taggart* (1965)	Charles Dance	*The Spy Who Loved Me* (1977)
Keith Carradine	*A Gunfight* (1970)		
Jim Carrey	*Introducing Janet* (1982)	Jeff Daniels	*Ragtime* (1981)
	TV film: *Rubberface* (1981)	Ted Danson	*The Onion Field* (1979)
Richard Chamberlain	*The Secret of the Purple Reef* (1960)	Kim Darby	*The Restless Ones* (1965)
			As extra: *Bye Bye Birdie* (1963)
Lon Chaney	*Storm and Sunshine* (1910)	Sammy Davis Jnr	*The Benny Goodman Story* (1956)
Charlie Chaplin	*Charlie as a Piano Mover* (1910)		
			Short: *Rufus Jones for President* (1933)
Cyd Charisse	*Something to Shout About* (1942).	Bette Davis	*Bad Sister* (1931)
	Short: *Rhumba Serenade* (1941)	Geena Davis	*Tootsie* (1982)
Cher	*Wild on the Beach* (1965)	Nancy Davis	*Shadow on the Wall* (1950)
Maurice Chevalier	*Le Mauvais Garçon* (1921)	Daniel Day-Lewis	*Sunday, Bloody Sunday* (1971)
	Short: *Trop Crédule* (1908)	Doris Day	*Romance on the High Seas* (1948) GB title: *It's Magic*
Julie Christie	*Crooks Anonymous* (1962)		Short: *My Lost Horizon* (1941)
John Cleese	*Interlude* (1968)	Yvonne De Carlo	*Harvard Here I Come* (1941) GB title: *Here I Come*
Montgomery Clift	*The Search* (1948)		
George Clooney	*Grizzly II – The Predator* (1982)		Short: *I Look at You* (1941)
Glenn Close	*The World According to Garp* (1982)	Olivia De Havilland	*A Midsummer Night's Dream* (1935)
	TV film: *Orphan Train* (1979)	Rebecca DeMornay	*One From the Heart* (1982)
James Coburn	*Ride Lonesome* (1959)	Robert De Niro	*Trois Chambres à Manhattan* (1966)
Claudette Colbert	*For the Love of Mike* (1927)	Danny De Vito	*Dreams of Glass* (1969)
George Cole	*Cottage to Let* (1941)	James Dean	*Sailor Beware* (1951)
Joan Collins	*Lady Godiva Rides Again* (1951)	Judi Dench	*The Third Secret* (1964)
		Catherine Deneuve	*Les Collégiennes* (1956)

Actor	Film
Gérard Depardieu	Le Beatnik et le Minet (1965)
Johnny Depp	A Nightmare on Elm Street (1984)
Bruce Dern	Wild River (1960)
Laura Dern	Teachers (1984)
	As child actress: White Lightning (1973)
Brad Dexter	The Asphalt Jungle (1950)
Leonardo DiCaprio	Critters 3 (1991)
Marlene Dietrich	So Sind die Männer (1922) Aka Der Kleine Napoleon
Matt Dillon	Over the Edge (1979)
Robert Donat	Men of Tomorrow (1932)
Amanda Donohoe	Foreign Body (1986)
	Castaway (1986) released at the same time
Diana Dors	The Shop at Sly Corner (1946)
Kirk Douglas	The Strange Love of Martha Ivers (1946)
Michael Douglas	Hail, Hero (1969)
	TV film: The Experiment (1968)
Richard Dreyfuss	The Graduate (1967)
Faye Dunaway	The Happening (1967)
Deanna Durbin	Three Smart Girls (1936)
	Short: Every Sunday (1936)
Robert Duvall	To Kill a Mockingbird (1962)
	TV film: John Brown's Raid (1960)
Clint Eastwood	Revenge of the Creature (1955)
	Short: A Day in a Hollywood Star Factory (1955)
Michael Elphick	Fraulein Doktor (1968)
Eminem	Da Hip Hop Witch (2000)
Edith Evans	A Honeymoon for Three (1915)
Douglas Fairbanks	The Lamb (1915)
Douglas Fairbanks Jr	Stephen Steps Out (1923)
Peter Falk	Wind across the Everglades (1958)
Mia Farrow	John Paul Jones (1959)
Marty Feldman	The Bed Sitting Room (1969)
Sally Field	Moon Pilot (1962)
Gracie Fields	Sally in Our Alley (1931)
WC Fields	Janice Meredith (1924) GB title: The Beautiful Rebel
	Short: Pool Sharks (1915)
Ralph Fiennes	Emily Brontë's Wuthering Heights (1992)
	A Dangerous Man – Lawrence after Arabia (1991) was a TV film never released in cinemas
Peter Finch	Dad and Dave Come to Town (1938)
	Unreleased: Magic Shoes (1935)
Albert Finney	The Entertainer (1960)
Errol Flynn	Dr H. Erben's New Guinea Expedition (1932)
Henry Fonda	The Farmer Takes a Wife (1935)
Jane Fonda	Tall Story (1960)
Joan Fontaine	No More Ladies (1935) (as Joan Burfield)
Glenn Ford	Heaven With a Barbed Wire Fence (1939)
	Short: Night in Manhattan (1937)
Harrison Ford	Dead Heat on a Merry-Go-Round (1966)
George Formby	By the Shortest of Heads (1915)
Jodie Foster	Napoleon and Samantha (1972)

Actor	Film
Edward Fox	The Mind Benders (1962)
James Fox	The Miniver Story (1950) (as William Fox)
Michael J Fox	Letters From Frank (1979)
Jamie Foxx	Toys (1992)
Tony Franciosa	A Face in the Crowd (1957)
Clark Gable	Forbidden Paradise (1924)
Greta Garbo	Fortune Hunter (1921)
	Short: How Not to Dress (1921)
Andy Garcia	Blue Skies Again (1983)
	TV film: Hill Street Blues (1980) Pilot for series
Ava Gardner	HM Pulham Esq (1941)
	Short: Fancy Answers (1941)
Judy Garland	Pigskin Parade (1936)
	GB title: Harmony Parade.
	Short: The Meglin Kiddie Revue (1929) (billed as a Gumm sister)
James Garner	Toward the Unknown (1956)
	GB title: Brink of Hell
Greer Garson	Goodbye Mr Chips (1939)
	As extra: 21 Days (1937) US title: 21 Days Together
Richard Gere	Report to the Commissioner (1974). GB title: Operation Undercover
Mel Gibson	Summer City (1977)
John Gielgud	Who is the Man? (1924)
Lillian Gish	Judith of Bethulia (1914)
	Short: Oil and Water (1912)
Whoopi Goldberg	Citizen (1982) (released 1983)
Jeff Goldblum	Death Wish (1974)
Elliott Gould	The Confession (1964) GB title: Quick, Let's Get Married!
Betty Grable	Happy Days (1929)
Stewart Granger	A Southern Maid (1933)
	As stand-in: I Spy (1933)
Cary Grant	This Is the Night (1932)
Hugh Grant	Privileged (1982)
Richard E Grant	Withnail and I (1986)
	TV film: Honest, Decent and True (1985)
Richard Greene	Four Men and a Prayer (1938)
Sydney Greenstreet	The Maltese Falcon (1941)
John Gregson	Saraband for Dead Lovers (1948)
Melanie Griffith	Smith! (1969)
Charles Grodin	Rosemary's Baby (1968)
	TV film: The Meanest Men in the West (1962)
Alec Guinness	Great Expectations (1946)
	As extra: Evensong (1934)
Gene Hackman	Mad Dog Coll (1961)
Larry Hagman	Ensign Pulver (1964)
	TV film: The Member of the Wedding (1958)
Susan Hampshire	The Woman in the Hall (1947)
Tony Hancock	Orders Are Orders (1954)
Tom Hanks	He Knows You're Alone (1980)
Daryl Hannah	The Fury (1978)
Oliver Hardy	Outwitting Dad (1913)
Jean Harlow	Moran of the Marines (1928)
Woody Harrelson	Harper Valley PTA (1978)
Ed Harris	Coma (1977)
	TV film: The Amazing Howard Hughes (1977)
Richard Harris	Alive and Kicking (1958)

Actor	Film	Actor	Film
Rex Harrison	*The Great Game* (1930)		Short: *April Showers* (1926)
Laurence Harvey	*House of Darkness* (1948)	Tommy Lee Jones	*Love Story* (1970)
Rutger Hauer	*Repelstweltje* (1973)	Louis Jourdan	*Le Corsaire* (1939)
Ethan Hawke	*Explorers* (1985)	Boris Karloff	*The Dumb Girl of Portici* (1916)
Jack Hawkins	*Birds of Prey* (1930)	Danny Kaye	*Up in Arms* (1944)
Goldie Hawn	*The One and Only Genuine Original Family Band* (1968)		Short: *Dime a Dance* (1937)
Will Hay	*Those Were the Days* (1934)	Stacy Keach	*The Heart Is a Lonely Hunter* (1968)
	Short: *Know Your Apples* (1933)	Buster Keaton	*The Saphead* (1920)
Susan Hayward	*Hollywood Hotel* (1937)		Short: *A Reckless Romeo* (1917)
Rita Hayworth	*Cruz Diablo* (1934)	Diane Keaton	*Lovers and Other Strangers* (1970)
	Short: *La Fiesta* (1926) (as Rita Cansino)	Michael Keaton	*Night Shift* (1982)
Van Heflin	*A Woman Rebels* (1936)	Howard Keel	*The Small Voice* (1948) (as Harold Keel)
David Hemmings	*Night and the City* (1950)	Harvey Keitel	*Who's That Knocking at My Door* (1968)
Ian Hendry	*Simon and Laura* (1955)		Unreleased: *Bring on the Dancing Girls* (1965)
Audrey Hepburn	*Nederlan in 7 Lessen* (1948)	Gene Kelly	*For Me and My Gal* (1942)
Katharine Hepburn	*A Bill of Divorcement* (1932)		GB title: *For Me and My Girl*
Barbara Hershey	*With Six You Get Egg Roll* (1968)	Grace Kelly	*Fourteen Hours* (1951)
Charlton Heston	*Peer Gynt* (1941)	George Kennedy	*The Little Shepherd of Kingdom Come* (1961)
Wendy Hiller	*Lancashire Luck* (1937)	Patsy Kensit	*For the Love of Ada* (1972)
Dustin Hoffman	*The Tiger Makes Out* (1967)	Deborah Kerr	*Major Barbara* (1941)
Paul Hogan	*Fatty Finn* (1980)		*Contraband* (1940) first film but scene was cut
William Holden	*Prison Farm* (1938)	Nicole Kidman	*Bush Christmas* (1982)
Judy Holliday	*Greenwich Village* (1944)	Val Kilmer	*Top Secret!* (1984)
	Unreleased: *Too Much Johnson* (1938)	Ben Kingsley	*Fear Is the Key* (1972)
Stanley Holloway	*The Rotters* (1921)	Nastassja Kinski	*Falsche Bewegung* (1975)
Ian Holm	*Girls at Sea* (1958)		GB title: *Wrong Movement*
Bob Hope	*The Big Broadcast of 1938* (1938)	Eartha Kitt	*Casbah* (1948)
	Short: *Paree, Paree* (1934)	Kevin Kline	*Sophie's Choice* (1982)
Anthony Hopkins	*The Lion in Winter* (1968)	Kris Kristofferson	*The Last Movie* (1971)
	Short: *Changes* (1963)	Alan Ladd	*Once in a Lifetime* (1932)
Dennis Hopper	*Johnny Guitar* (1954)	Veronica Lake	*All Women Have Secrets* (1939) (as Constance Keane)
Bob Hoskins	*Up the Front* (1972)	Hedy Lamarr	*Geld auf der Strasse* (1930) (as Hedy Kiesler)
Leslie Howard	*The Happy Warrior* (1917)	Christopher Lambert	*Le Bar du Téléphone* (1981)
	Short: *The Heroine of Mons* (1914)	Dorothy Lamour	*The Jungle Princess* (1936)
Trevor Howard	*Volga-Volga* (1944) (dubbed voice)		Short: *The Stars Can't Be Wrong* (1936)
Frankie Howerd	*The Runaway Bus* (1954)	Burt Lancaster	*The Killers* (1946)
Rock Hudson	*Fighter Squadron* (1948)	Michael Landon	*I Was A Teenage Werewolf* (1957)
Holly Hunter	*The Burning* (1981)	Jessica Lange	*King Kong* (1976)
Jeffrey Hunter	*A Date with Judy* (1948)		Short: *Home Is Where the Heart Is* (1970)
Isabelle Huppert	*Faustine et le Bel Été* (1971) GB title: *Faustine*	Angela Lansbury	*Gaslight* (1944). GB title: *The Murder in Thornton Square*
John Hurt	*The Wild and the Willing* (1962)	Mario Lanza	*Winged Victory* (1944)
William Hurt	*Altered States* (1980)	Charles Laughton	*Piccadilly* (1929)
	TV film: *Verna the USO Girl* (1978)		Short: *Bluebottles* (1928)
Anjelica Huston	*Sinful Davey* (1969)	Stan Laurel	*Lucky Dog* (1917)
John Huston	*The Shakedown* (1928)	Jude Law	*Shopping* (1994)
Jeremy Irons	*Nijinsky* (1980)	Peter Lawford	*Poor Old Bill* (1930)
Burl Ives	*Smoky* (1946)	Bruce Lee	*Golden Gate Girl / Tears of S. Francisco* (1941, aged 3 months)
Glenda Jackson	*The Extra Day* (1956)		*The Birth of Mankind* (1946, first professional role)
Gordon Jackson	*The Foreman Went to France* (1942)	Christopher Lee	*Corridor of Mirrors* (1948)
Derek Jacobi	*Othello* (1965)	Gypsy Rose Lee	*You Can't Have Everything* (1937) (as Louise Hovick)
Sid James	*Black Memory* (1947)	Janet Leigh	*The Romance of Rosy Ridge* (1947)
Martin Jarvis	*Secrets of a Windmill Girl* (1965)		
Lionel Jeffries	*Stage Fright* (1950)		
Scarlett Johansson	*North* (1994)		
Celia Johnson	*Dirty Work* (1934)		
Don Johnson	*Good Morning ... and Goodbye!* (1967) GB title: *The Lust Seekers* (Russ Meyer epic!)		
Al Jolson	*The Jazz Singer* (1927)		

Actor	Film
Jennifer Jason Leigh	*Eyes of a Stranger* (1981)
Vivien Leigh	*Things Are Looking Up* (1934)
Jack Lemmon	*It Should Happen to You* (1953)
Jerry Lewis	*My Friend Irma* (1949)
Juliette Lewis	*Any Which Way You Can* (1980)
Jet Li	*Shaolin Temple* (1982)
Emily Lloyd	*Wish You Were Here* (1987)
Harold Lloyd	*Samson and Delilah* (1913)
Margaret Lockwood	*Lorna Doone* (1934)
Gina Lollobrigida	*L'Aguila Nera* (1946)
Herbert Lom	*Zena Pod Krizem* (1937)
Carole Lombard	*A Perfect Crime* (1921) (as Jane Peters)
Sophia Loren	*Cuori Sul Mare* (1950) (as Sofia Scicolone)
Peter Lorre	*Bomben auf Monte Carlo* (1931)
Rob Lowe	*The Outsiders* (1983) TV film: *Thursday's Child* (1982)
Myrna Loy	*Pretty Ladies* (1925)
Bela Lugosi	*Alarscobal* (1917)
Dolph Lundgren	*For Your Eyes Only* (1981)
Ida Lupino	*The Love Race* (1932)
David McCallum	*Ill Met By Moonlight* (1956)
Jeanette MacDonald	*The Love Parade* (1929)
Roddy McDowall	*Grime Doesn't Pay* (1935)
Andie MacDowell	*Greystoke: The Legend of Tarzan Lord of Apes* (1984)
Malcolm McDowell	*If* (1968). *Poor Cow* (1967) first film but scene was cut
Kelly McGillis	*Reuben, Reuben* (1983)
Patrick McGoohan	*The Dam Busters* (1954)
Ali MacGraw	*A Lovely Way to Die* (1968) GB title: *A Lovely Way to Go*
Ewan McGregor	*Being Human* (1993) TV film: *Lipstick On Your Collar* (1993)
Virginia McKenna	*Father's Doing Fine* (1952)
Leo McKern	*Murder in the Cathedral* (1952)
Kyle MacLachlan	*Dune* (1984)
Victor McLaglen	*The Call of the Road* (1920)
Shirley MacLaine	*The Trouble with Harry* (1955)
Fred MacMurray	*Girls Gone Wild* (1929)
Patrick MacNee	*Sailors Three* (1940)
Steve McQueen	*Somebody up There Likes Me* (1956)
Ian McShane	*The Wild and the Willing* (1962)
Madonna	*A Certain Sacrifice* (1978)
Anna Magnani	*Scampolo* (1927)
Tobey Maguire	*This Boy's Life* (1993)
Lee Majors	*Strait-Jacket* (1964) (as Lee Yeary)
Karl Malden	*They Knew What They Wanted* (1940)
John Malkovich	*Places in the Heat* (1984) TV film: *Word of Honor* (1981)
Jayne Mansfield	*Prehistoric Women* (1950)
Fredric March	*The Devil* (1920)
Dean Martin	*My Friend Irma* (1949)
Steve Martin	*Sgt Pepper's Lonely Heart's Club Band* (1978) Short: *The Absent-Minded Waiter* (1977)
Lee Marvin	*Teresa* (1950)
Marx Brothers	*The Cocoanuts* (1929) Limited release: *Humorist* (1926)
Harpo Marx	*Too Many Kisses* (1925)
James Mason	*Late Extra* (1935) (The name of his fan club's news letter)
Raymond Massey	*The Crooked Billet* (1929) Aka *International Spy*

Actor	Film
Marcello Mastroianni	*I Miserabili* (1947) As extra: *Marionette* (1938)
Walter Matthau	*The Kentuckian* (1955)
Jessie Matthews	*The Beloved Vagabond* (1923)
Victor Mature	*The Housekeeper's Daughter* (1939)
Virginia Mayo	*Stand by for Action* (1942) GB title: *Cargo of Innocents*
Melina Mercouri	*Stella* (1954)
Ethel Merman	*Follow the Leader* (1930)
Bette Midler	*Hawaii* (1966)
Toshiro Mifune	*Shin Baka Jidai* (1946)
Sarah Miles	*Term of Trial* (1962)
Ray Milland	*The Plaything* (1929) (as Spike Milland)
Max Miller	*The Good Companions* (1933)
Spike Milligan	*Penny Points to Paradise* (1951)
Hayley Mills	*Tiger Bay* (1959)
John Mills	*The Midshipmaid* (1932) Limited release: *Words and Music* (1932)
Juliet Mills	*In Which We Serve* (1942) (as baby)
Liza Minnelli	*Easter Parade* (1948) (as baby)
Kylie Minogue	*The Delinquents* (1989)
Carmen Miranda	*A Voz do Carnaval* (1933)
Helen Mirren	*Herostratus* (1967)
Robert Mitchum	*Hoppy Serves a Writ* (1943)
Tom Mix	*The Heart of Texas Ryan* (1917). Short: *On the Little Big Horn* (1909)
Marilyn Monroe	*The Shocking Miss Pilgrim* (1946)
Yves Montand	*Etoile sans Lumière* (1945)
Demi Moore	*Choices* (1981)
Dudley Moore	*The Wrong Box* (1966) As narrator: *The Hat* (1964)
Julianne Moore	*Tales From the Darkside* (1990) TV film: *Money, Power, Murder* (1989) Limited release: *Slaughterhouse II* (1988)
Roger Moore	*Caesar and Cleopatra* (1945)
Jeanne Moreau	*Dernier Amour* (1948)
Kenneth More	*Look up and Laugh* (1935)
Robert Morley	*Marie Antoinette* (1938)
Zero Mostel	*DuBarry Was a Lady* (1943)
Paul Muni	*The Valiant* (1929)
Eddie Murphy	*48 Hrs* (1982)
Audie Murphy	*Beyond Glory* (1948)
Bill Murray	*Meatballs* (1979) Short: *The Hat Act* (1976) Voice only: *Jungle Burger* (1975)
Anna Neagle	*Those Who Love* (1929) (as Marjorie Robertson)
Liam Neeson	*Excalibur* (1981)
Sam Neill	*Ashes* (1975)
Anthony Newley	*The Little Ballerina* (1947) Short: *Dusty Bates* (1947)
Paul Newman	*The Silver Chalice* (1954)
Jack Nicholson	*The Cry Baby Killer* (1958)
Leslie Nielsen	*The Vagabond King* (1956)
David Niven	*There Goes the Bride* (1932)
Nick Nolte	*The Feather Farm* (1965)
Chuck Norris	*The Wrecking Crew* (1968)
Kim Novak	*The Veils of Baghdad* (1953)
Ivor Novello	*Call of the Blood* (1919)
Warren Oates	*Up Periscope!* (1958)

CINEMA

Actor	Film
Merle Oberon	*The Three Passions* (1929)
Edmond O'Brien	*Prison Break* (1938)
Pat O'Brien	*Compliments of the Season* (1930)
Donald O'Connor	*Melody for Two* (1937)
Maureen O'Hara	*Kicking the Moon Around* (1938) as Maureen Fitzsimmons
Gary Oldman	*Remembrance* (1982)
Laurence Olivier	*Too Many Crooks* (1930)
Ryan O'Neal	*The Big Bounce* (1969) TV film: *This Rugged Land* (1962)
Tatum O'Neal	*Paper Moon* (1973)
Maureen O'Sullivan	*Song o' My Heart* (1930)
Richard O'Sullivan	*Dance Little Lady* (1954)
Peter O'Toole	*The Savage Innocents* (1959)
Al Pacino	*Me Natalie* (1969)
Jack Palance	*Panic in the Streets* (1950) (as Walter Palance)
Lilli Palmer	*Crime Unlimited* (1935)
Gwyneth Paltrow	*Shout* (1991)
Vanessa Paradis	*Noce Blanche* (1990)
Dolly Parton	*The Nashville Sound* (1970)
Gregory Peck	*Days of Glory* (1944)
Sean Penn	*Taps* (1981) TV film: *The Killing of Randy Webster* (1980)
George Peppard	*The Strange One* (1957) GB title: *End as a Man*
Anthony Perkins	*The Actress* (1953)
Joe Pesci	*Hey, Let's Twist* (1961) (as Joe Ritchie)
Michelle Pfeiffer	*Falling in Love Again* (1979)
Leslie Phillips	*A Lassie from Lancashire* (1935)
River Phoenix	*Explorers* (1985) TV film: *Surviving* (1985)
Mary Pickford	*Through the Breakers* (1909)
Walter Pidgeon	*Mannequin* (1925)
Brad Pitt	*Cutting Class* (1989) TV film: *A Stoning in Fulham County* (1988)
Donald Pleasence	*The Beachcomber* (1954)
Christopher Plummer	*Wind Across the Everglades* (1958)
Sidney Poitier	*From Whence Cometh My Help* (1949)
Eric Portman	*The Girl from Maxim's* (1933)
Dick Powell	*Street Scene* (1931)
Robert Powell	*Robbery* (1967)
William Powell	*When Knighthood Was In Flower* (1922)
Tyrone Power	*Tom Brown of Culver* (1932)
Stefanie Powers	*Tammy Tell Me True* (1961)
Elvis Presley	*Love Me Tender* (1956)
Robert Preston	*King of Alcatraz* (1938)
Dennis Price	*A Canterbury Tale* (1944) As extra: *No Parking* (1938)
Vincent Price	*Service de Luxe* (1938)
Richard Pryor	*The Busy Body* (1966)
Bill Pullman	*Ruthless People* (1986)
Dennis Quaid	*Crazy Mama* (1975)
Anthony Quayle	*Moscow Nights* (1935)
Aidan Quinn	*Reckless* (1984)
Anthony Quinn	*The Milky Way* (1936)
George Raft	*Queen of the Night Clubs* (1929)
Luise Rainer	*Ja, der Himmel über Wien* (1930)
Claude Rains	*Build Thy House* (1920)
Charlotte Rampling	*The Knack and How to Get it* (1965)
Basil Rathbone	*Innocent* (1921)
Ronald Reagan	*Love Is on the Air* (1937) GB title: *The Radio Murder Mystery*
Robert Redford	*War Hunt* (1962). TV film: *In the Presence of Mine Enemies* (1960). (Charles Laughton played a rabbi in this film!)
Lynn Redgrave	*Tom Jones* (1963)
Michael Redgrave	*Secret Agent* (1936)
Vanessa Redgrave	*Behind the Mask* (1958)
Oliver Reed	*Value for Money* (1955)
Christopher Reeve	*Gray Lady Down* (1977)
Keanu Reeves	*The Prodigal* (1984). Video only: *Act of Vengeance* (1984)
Lee Remick	*A Face in the Crowd* (1957)
Burt Reynolds	*Angel Baby* (1961)
Debbie Reynolds	*June Bride* (1948)
Cliff Richard	*Serious Charge* (1959)
Joely Richardson	*The Charge of the Light Brigade* (1968)
Miranda Richardson	*Dance with a Stranger* (1984)
Natasha Richardson	*The Charge of the Light Brigade* (1968)
Ralph Richardson	*The Ghoul* (1933)
Brian Rix	*Reluctant Heroes* (1951)
Jason Robards Jnr	*The Journey* (1958)
Tim Robbins	*No Small Affair* (1984)
Julia Roberts	*Blood Red* (1988 but released 1990) *Baja Oklahoma* (shown in selected cinemas) 1988
Rachel Roberts	*Valley of Song* (1953)
Cliff Robertson	*Corvette K-225* (1943) GB title: *The Nelson Touch*
Dale Robertson	*The Boy with Green Hair* (1948)
Paul Robeson	*Body and Soul* (1924)
Edward G Robinson	*Arms and the Woman* (1916)
Flora Robson	*Gentleman of Paris* (1931)
Ginger Rogers	*Queen High* (1930) Short: *Campus Sweethearts* (1929)
Roy Rogers	*Way Up Thar* (1935) (as Dick Weston) Short: *Slightly Static* (1935) (as Leonard Slye)
Will Rogers	*Laughing Bill Hyde* (1918)
Gilbert Roland	*The Lady Who Lied* (1925)
Cesar Romero	*The Shadow Laughs* (1933)
Mickey Rooney	*Orchids and Ermine* (1927) Short: *Not to Be Trusted* (1926)
Katharine Ross	*Shenandoah* (1965)
Isabella Rossellini	*A Matter of Time* (1976)
Leonard Rossiter	*The Two-Headed Spy* (1958)
Tim Roth	*Meantime* (1983) TV film: *Made in Britain* (1983)
Richard Roundtree	*What Do You Say to a Naked Lady* (1969)
Mickey Rourke	*1941* (1979). TV film: *Panic on Page One* (1979) Aka *City in Fear*
Gena Rowlands	*The High Cost of Loving* (1958)
Jane Russell	*The Outlaw* (1943)

Actor	Film
Kurt Russell	The Absent-Minded Professor (1961)
Rosalind Russell	Forsaking All Others (1934)
Theresa Russell	The Last Tycoon (1976)
Rene Russo	Major League (1989)
Margaret Rutherford	Talk of the Devil (1936)
Meg Ryan	Rich and Famous (1981)
Robert Ryan	The Ghost Breakers (1940)
Winona Ryder	Lucas (1986)
George Sanders	Love, Life and Laughter (1934)
Susan Sarandon	Joe (1970)
Telly Savalas	The Young Savages (1961)
John Saxon	It Should Happen to You (1953)
Greta Scacchi	Das Zweite Gesicht (1982) Short: Dead on Time (1981)
Roy Scheider	The Curse of the Living Corpse (1963) as Roy R Scheider
Maximilian Schell	Die Letzte Brücke (1954)
Romy Schneider	Wenn der Weisse Flieder Wieder Blüht (1953)
Arnie Schwarzenegger	Hercules Goes Bananas (1969) (as Arnold Strong)
Paul Scofield	That Lady (1955)
Kristin Scott-Thomas	Under the Cherry Moon (1986)
Randolph Scott	Sharp Shooters (1928)
George C Scott	The Hanging Tree (1959)
Steven Seagal	Above the Law (1988) GB title: Nico
Jean Seberg	Saint Joan (1957)
Harry Secombe	Hocus Pocus (1948)
George Segal	The Young Doctors (1961)
Tom Selleck	Myra Breckinridge (1970) Judd for the Defense: The Holy Ground (1969) was a made-for-TV film series
Peter Sellers	Penny Points to Paradise (1951) As extra: Oliver Twist (1948) Voice only: The Black Rose (1950)
Jane Seymour	Oh What a Lovely War (1969)
Omar Sharif	The Blazing Sun (1954) (as Omar el Cherif)
William Shatner	The Brothers Karamazov (1958) TV film: The Defenders (1957)
Robert Shaw	The Lavender Hill Mob (1951)
Norma Shearer	Way Down East (1920)
Charlie Sheen	Grizzly II: The Predator (1982) TV film: The Execution of Private Slovik (1974)
Martin Sheen	The Incident (1967)
Sam Shepard	Renaldo and Clara (1977) Voice only: Easy Rider (1969)
Cybill Shepherd	The Last Picture Show (1971)
Ann Sheridan	Search for Beauty (1934) (as Clara Lou Sheridan)
Dinah Sheridan	I Give My Heart (1934)
Brooke Shields	Communion / Alice Sweet Alice (1977)
Dinah Shore	Thank Your Lucky Stars (1943)
Simone Signoret	Le Prince Charmant (1942)
Phil Silvers	Hit Parade of 1941 (1940) Short: Here's Your Hat (1937)
Alicia Silverstone	The Crush (1993) TV film: Scattered Dreams (1992)
Alastair Sim	Riverside Murder (1935)
Jean Simmons	Give Us the Moon (1944)
Frank Sinatra	Las Vegas Nights (1941) GB title: The Gray City

Actor	Film
	Short: Major Bowes' Amateur Theatre of the Air (1935)
Donald Sinden	Portrait from Life (1948)
Christian Slater	The Legend of Billie Jean (1985). TV film. Living Proof: The Hank Williams Jr Story (1983)
Maggie Smith	Child in the House (1956)
Jimmy Smits	Running Scared (1986) TV film: Rockabye (1986)
Wesley Snipes	Wildcats (1986)
Elke Sommer	Das Totenschiff (1958)
Ann Sothern	Broadway Nights (1927)
Sissy Spacek	Prime Cut (1972) As extra: Trash (1970)
James Spader	Team-Mates (1978)
Robert Stack	First Love (1939)
Sylvester Stallone	Party at Kitty and Studs (1970) Re-released as: The Italian Stallion
Terence Stamp	Billy Budd (1962)
Barbara Stanwyck	Broadway Nights (1927)
Imelda Staunton	Comrades (1987)
Anthony Steel	Quartet (1948)
Tommy Steele	Kill Me Tomorrow (1957)
Mary Steenburgen	Goin' South (1978)
Rod Steiger	Teresa (1951)
Inger Stevens	Man on Fire (1957)
Stella Stevens	Say One for Me (1959)
James Stewart	The Murder Man (1935) Short: Important News (1935)
Sting	Quadrophenia (1979)
Eric Stoltz	Fast Times at Ridgemont High (1982) TV film: The Grass Is Always Greener over the Septic Tank (1978)
Sharon Stone	Stardust Memories (1980)
The 3 Stooges	Hollywood on Parade (1930)
Meryl Streep	Julia (1977) Voice only: Everybody Rides a Carousel (1976)
Barbra Streisand	Funny Girl (1968)
Donald Sutherland	The World Ten Times Over (1963)
Kiefer Sutherland	Max Dugan Returns (1983)
Hilary Swank	Buffy the Vampire Slayer (1992)
Gloria Swanson	Her Decision (1918) Short: The Romance of an American Duchess (1915)
Patrick Swayze	Skatetown USA (1979)
Tilda Swinton	Caravaggio (1986) Uncredited: Monty Python's Meaning of Life (1983)
Eric Sykes	Orders Are Orders (1954)
Sylvia Syms	My Teenage Daughter (1955)
Russ Tamblyn	Boy with Green Hair (1948) (as Rusty Tamblyn)
Jacques Tati	Retour à la Terre (1938) Short: Oscar, Champion de Tennis (1932)
Elizabeth Taylor	One Born Every Minute (1942) Short: Man or Mouse (1942)
Robert Taylor	Handy Andy (1934)
Rod Taylor	The Sturt Expedition (1951) (as Rodney Taylor)
Shirley Temple	The Red-Haired Alibi (1932) Short: War Babies (1932)

CINEMA

Actor	Film
Charlize Theron	2 Days in the Valley (1996)
	As extra: Children of the Corn III: Urban Harvest (1995)
Terry Thomas	It's Love Again (1936)
Emma Thompson	The Tall Guy (1989)
Sybil Thorndike	Moth and Rust (1921)
Uma Thurman	Kiss Daddy Good Night (1987)
Gene Tierney	The Return of Frank James (1940)
Richard Todd	For Them That Trespass (1948)
Marisa Tomei	The Flamingo Kid (1984)
Lily Tomlin	Nashville (1975)
David Tomlinson	Garrison Follies (1940)
	Short: Name, Rank and Number (1940)
Spencer Tracy	Up the River (1930)
	Short: Taxi Talks (1930)
Bill Travers	Conspirator (1950)
John Travolta	The Devil's Rain (1975)
Claire Trevor	Life in the Raw (1933)
Tommy Trinder	Almost a Honeymoon (1938)
Jean-Louis Trintignant	Si Tous les Gars du Monde (1955) GB title: Race for Life
	Short: Pechinef (1955)
Forrest Tucker	The Westerner (1940)
Kathleen Turner	Body Heat (1981)
Lana Turner	A Star Is Born (1937)
Rita Tushingham	A Taste of Honey (1961)
Twiggy	The Boy Friend (1971)
Liv Ullman	Fjol til Fjells (1957)
Robert Urich	Magnum Force (1973)
Peter Ustinov	Hullo Fame! (1940)
Rudolph Valentino	My Official Wife (1914)
Rudy Vallee	Vagabond Lover (1929)
	Short: Radio Rhythm (1929)
Lee Van Cleef	The Showdown (1950)
Jean-Claude Van Damme	Rue Barbar (1983) US title: Street of the Damned
Dick Van Dyke	Bye Bye Birdie (1963)
Frankie Vaughan	Ramsbottom Rides Again (1957)
	Singing commentary: Escape in the Sun (1956)
Robert Vaughn	The Ten Commandments (1956)
Conrad Veidt	Der Spion (1916)
Monica Vitti	Ridere, Ridere, Ridere (1955)
Jon Voight	The Hour of the Gun (1967)
Erich Von Stroheim	Captain McLean (1914)
Max Von Sydow	Bara en Mor (1949)
Robert Wagner	The Happy Years (1950)
Christopher Walken	Me and My Brother (1968)
Clint Walker	Mighty Joe Young (1949) (as Norman Walker)
Eli Wallach	Baby Doll (1956)
	TV film: Danger (1952)
Julie Walters	Educating Rita (1983)
	Short: Occupy! (1976)
Rachel Ward	Night School (1980) GB title: Terror Eyes
Simon Ward	If (1968)
David Warner	Loneliness of the Long Distance Runner (1962)
Jack Warner	The Dummy Talks (1943)
Denzel Washington	Carbon Copy (1981)
	TV film: Wilma (1977)
Dennis Waterman	Night Train for Inverness (1959)
John Wayne	Brown of Harvard (1926)
Dennis Weaver	Riders of Vengeance (1952)
Sigourney Weaver	Annie Hall (1977)

Actor	Film
Clifton Webb	Polly with a Past (1920)
Johnny Weissmuller	Glorifying the American Girl (1929)
Raquel Welch	Roustabout (1964)
Tuesday Weld	The Wrong Man (1956)
Orson Welles	Citizen Kane (1941)
	Short: The Hearts of Age (1934) (Home-made)
	Unreleased: Too Much Johnson (1938).
	As narrator: Swiss Family Robinson (1940)
Mae West	Night after Night (1932)
	Short: unidentified 'Screen Snapshot' (1930)
Joanne Whalley-Kilmer	The Wall (1982)
Billie Whitelaw	The Fake (1953)
Pearl White	The Life of Buffalo Bill (1910)
Richard Widmark	Kiss of Death (1947)
Gene Wilder	Bonnie and Clyde (1967)
Cornel Wilde	The Lady With Red Hair (1940)
Michael Wilding	Heads We Go (1933)
	As extra: Bitter Sweet (1933)
Nicol Williamson	Inadmissible Evidence (1968)
	Short: The Six-Sided Triangle (1963)
Emlyn Williams	The Frightened Lady (1932)
Esther Williams	Andy Hardy's Double Life (1942)
Kenneth Williams	Trent's Last Case (1952)
Robin Williams	Can I Do It 'til I Need Glasses (1977)
Bruce Willis	The First Deadly Sin (1980)
	TV film: Ziegfeld – The Man & His Women (1978)
Barbara Windsor	Belles of St Trinian's (1954)
Oprah Winfrey	The Color Purple (1985)
Debra Winger	Slumber Party '57 (1976)
Kate Winslet	Heavenly Creatures (1994)
Shelley Winters	What a Woman! (1943) GB title: The Beautiful Cheat
Norman Wisdom	A Date with a Dream (1948)
Googie Withers	The Girl in the Crowd (1934)
Sir Donald Wolfit	Down River (1931)
Natalie Wood	Happy Land (1943) (as Natasha Gurdin)
James Woods	The Visitors (1971)
Edward Woodward	Where There's a Will (1955)
Joanne Woodward	Count Three and Pray (1955)
Fay Wray	What Price Goofy (1925)
	Short: Gasoline Love (1923)
Teresa Wright	The Little Foxes (1941)
Jane Wyman	The Kid from Spain (1932) (as Sarah Jane Fulks)
Michael York	The Mind Benders (1962)
Susannah York	Tunes of Glory (1960)
Gig Young	Misbehaving Husbands (1940) (as Byron Barr)
Loretta Young	The Only Way (1917) (as Gretchen Young)
Robert Young	The Black Camel (1931)
Sean Young	Stripes (1981).
	TV film: Jane Austen in Manhattan (1980)
Pia Zadora	Santa Claus Conquers the Martians (1964)
Catherine Zeta-Jones	Les Mille et Une Nuits (1001 Nights) (1989)
Mai Zetterling	Lasse-Maja (1941)

NB: This is an area where many fine sources of information will inevitably differ, depending on the definition given of 'first film'. To give an example of the inherent dangers in answering questions on screen debuts, we can look at the early career of Orson Welles.

The 1941 classic, *Citizen Kane*, is often considered to be Welles's first film performance; but whilst it was certainly his first feature film, he did in fact do various film work before this. His potential was first spotted in his home-made film of 1934, *The Hearts of Age*, a film short that never went on general release. The unreleased film *Too Much Johnson* (1938) was shown to private audiences, although it was eventually lost to the world in a fire at Welles's Spanish home.

If narration is considered a film role, then the 1940 film *Swiss Family Robinson*, starring Thomas Mitchell and Freddie Bartholomew, could also be regarded as his big screen debut.

The approach taken in listing these is to cite an actor's debut in a film on general release and to mention prior work underneath. Many jobbing screen actors start their careers making 'film shorts', often shown before a main feature, but these films are rarely listed in cinema catalogues and are only included here if they predate a debut in a full-length feature. 'Made for television' films are treated in a similar vein.

Last Films

Actor	Film
Fred Astaire	*Ghost Story* (1981)
Mary Astor	*Hush, Hush, Sweet Charlotte* (1964)
Gene Autry	*It's Showtime* (1976)
Lew Ayres	*Letters from Frank* (1979)
	TV film: *Cast the First Stone* (1989)
Ingrid Bergman	*Autumn Sonata* (1978)
	TV film: *A Woman Called Golda* (1982)
Humphrey Bogart	*The Harder They Fall* (1956)
Stephen Boyd	*The Squeeze* (1977)
Charles Boyer	*A Matter of Time* (1976)
Charles Bronson	*Death Wish V: The Face of Death* (1994)
	TV film: *Family of Cops III* (1998)
Yul Brynner	*Futureworld* (1976)
Horst Buchholz	*The Enemy* (2000)
George Burns	*Radioland Murders* (1994)
Raymond Burr	*Delirious* (1991)
	TV film: *Perry Mason: The Case of the Killer Kiss* (1993)
Richard Burton	*1984* (1984)
	TV film: *Ellis Island* (1984)
James Cagney	*Ragtime* (1981)
	TV film: *Terrible Joe Moran* (1984)
John Candy	*Canadian Bacon* (1995)
Lon Chaney	*The Unholy Three* (1930)
Charlie Chaplin	*A Countess from Hong Kong* (1966)
Maurice Chevalier	*Monkeys Go Home* (1967)
	Voice only: *The Aristocats* (1970)
Montgomery Clift	*The Defector* (1966)
James Coburn	*Snow Dogs* (2002)
Claudette Colbert	*Parrish* (1961)
	TV film: *The Two Mrs Grenvilles* (1987)
Ronald Colman	*The Story of Mankind* (1957)
Jackie Coogan	*The Prey* (1983)
Gary Cooper	*The Naked Edge* (1961)
Harry H Corbett	*Silver Dream Racer* (1980)
Joseph Cotten	*Rambo Sfida la Citta* (1982)
Noël Coward	*The Italian Job* (1969)
Broderick Crawford	*Liar's Moon* (1981)
Joan Crawford	*Trog* (1970)
	TV film: *We're Going to Scare You to Death* (1975)
Richard Crenna	*Wrongfully Accused* (1998)

Actor	Film
	TV film: *Out of the Ashes* (2003)
Bing Crosby	*That's Entertainment* (1974)
Peter Cushing	*Biggles* (1986)
Bette Davis	*Wicked Stepmother* (1989)
	Short: *Hairway to the Stars* (1989)
Sammy Davis Jnr	*Tap* (1988)
	TV film: *The Kid Who Loved Christmas* (1990)
James Dean	*Giant* (1956)
Brad Dexter	*Secret Ingredient* (1990)
Marlene Dietrich	*Marlene* (1984)
Robert Donat	*The Inn of the Sixth Happiness* (1958)
Diana Dors	*Steaming* (1985)
Michael Elphick	TV film: *Ken Russell's Treasure Island* (1995)
Edith Evans	*Nasty Habits* (1976)
Douglas Fairbanks	*The Private Life of Don Juan* (1934)
Marty Feldman	*Yellowbeard* (1983)
Gracie Fields	*Madame Pimpernel* (1945)
WC Fields	*Sensations of 1945* (1944)
Peter Finch	*Network* (1976)
	TV film: *Raid on Entebbe* (1977)
Errol Flynn	*Cuban Rebel Girls* (1959)
Henry Fonda	*On Golden Pond* (1981)
	TV film: *Summer Solstice* (1981)
George Formby	*George in Civvy Street* (1946)
Clark Gable	*The Misfits* (1961)
Greta Garbo	*Two-Faced Woman* (1941)
Ava Gardner	*Roma Regina* (1982)
Judy Garland	*I Could Go on Singing* (1963)
Greer Garson	*Directed by William Wyler* (1986)
Lillian Gish	*The Whales of August* (1987)
Betty Grable	*How to Be Very Very Popular* (1955)
Stewart Granger	*Oro Fina (Fine Gold)* (1988)
	TV film: *Chameleons* (1989)
Cary Grant	*Elvis – That's the Way It Is* (1970)
Sydney Greenstreet	*Malaya* (1949)
	GB title: *East of the Rising Sun*
John Gregson	*The Tiger Lily* (1975)
Tony Hancock	*The Wrong Box* (1966)
Oliver Hardy	*Meet Bela Lugosi and Oliver Hardy* (1952)

C
I
N
E
M
A

Actor	Film
Jean Harlow	*Saratoga* (1937)
Richard Harris	*Harry Potter and the Chamber of Secrets* (2002)
Rex Harrison	*A Time to Die* (1983). Aka *Seven Graves for Rogan*
Jack Hawkins	*The Last Lion* (1973) TV film: *QB VII* (1974)
Susan Hayward	*The Revengers* (1972) TV film: *Say Goodbye, Maggie Cole* (1972)
Rita Hayworth	*Circle* (1976)
Will Hay	*My Learned Friend* (1943)
Van Heflin	*The Big Bounce* (1969) TV film: *The Last Child* (1971)
David Hemmings	*The League of Extraordinary Gentlemen* (2003)
Audrey Hepburn	*Always* (1989)
Katharine Hepburn	*Love Affair* (1994)
Thora Hird	*Julie and the Cadillacs* (1999)
William Holden	*S.O.B.* (1981) TV film: *Mysteries of the Sea* (1981) (as narrator)
Judy Holliday	*Bells Are Ringing* (1960)
Stanley Holloway	*Journey into Fear* (1976)
Leslie Howard	*The First of the Few* (1942)
Trevor Howard	*The Dawning* (1988) Died whilst filming *Stille Nacht,* about the author of the carol 'Silent Night'
Frankie Howerd	*Sgt Pepper's Lonely Hearts Club Band* (1978)
Rock Hudson	*The Ambassador* (1984) TV film: *The Vegas Strip Wars* (1985)
Jeffrey Hunter	*Mafia Mob* (1969)
John Huston	*John Huston and the Dubliners* (1987)
Burl Ives	*Two Moon Junction* (1988)
Gordon Jackson	*The Whistle Blower* (1986) TV film: *The Lady and the Highwayman* (1989)
Sid James	*Carry On Dick* (1974)
Celia Johnson	*The Prime of Miss Jean Brodie* (1968) TV film: *The Hostage Tower* (1980)
Al Jolson	*Rhapsody in Blue* (1945) Voice only: *Jolson Sings Again* (1949)
Boris Karloff	*The Incredible Invasion* (1969). Limited release: *House of Evil* (1972) Unseen footage: *Transylvania Twist* (1989)
Danny Kaye	*The Madwoman of Chaillot* (1969) Short: *Pied Piper* (1972) TV film: *Once They Marched through a Thousand Towns* (1981) US title: *Skokie*
Buster Keaton	*A Funny Thing Happened on the Way to the Forum* (1966) Short: *The Scribe* (1966)
Howard Keel	*My Father's House* (2002)
Gene Kelly	*That's Entertainment III* (1994)
Grace Kelly	*Invitation to Monte Carlo* (1959) As narrator: *The Children of Theatre Street* (1978)
Alan Ladd	*The Carpetbaggers* (1964)
Veronica Lake	*Flesh Feast* (1970)

Actor	Film
Dorothy Lamour	*Creepshow 2* (1987)
Burt Lancaster	*Field of Dreams* (1989) TV film: *Separate but Equal* (1991)
Dinsdale Landen	*The Steal* (1994)
Mario Lanza	*For the First Time* (1959)
Charles Laughton	*Advise and Consent* (1962)
Stan Laurel	*Atoll K* (1951). GB title: *Robinson Crusoeland*
Peter Lawford	*Where Is Parsifal?* (1984)
Bruce Lee	*Game of Death* (1978, posthumously)
Gypsy Rose Lee	*The Trouble with Angels* (1966) TV film: *The Over the Hill Gang* (1969)
Vivien Leigh	*Ship of Fools* (1965)
Harold Lloyd	*The Sins of Harold Diddlebock* (1947) GB title: *Mad Wednesday*
Margaret Lockwood	*The Slipper and the Rose* (1976)
Carole Lombard	*To Be or Not to Be* (1942)
Peter Lorre	*Muscle Beach Party* (1964)
Myrna Loy	*Just Tell Me What You Want* (1980). TV film: *Summer Solstice* (1981)
Bela Lugosi	*Plan 9 from Outer Space* (1957)
Ida Lupino,	*Deadhead Miles* (1982)
Jeanette MacDonald	*The Sun Comes Up* (1948) TV film: *Charley's Aunt* (1957)
Leo McKern	*Molokai – The Story of Father Damien* (1999)
Victor McLaglen	*The Italians Are Crazy* (1958)
Fred MacMurray	*The Swarm* (1978)
Anna Magnani	*Fellini's Roma* (1972)
Jayne Mansfield	*Mondo Hollywood* (1967)
Fredric March	*The Iceman Cometh* (1973)
Dean Martin	*Cannonball Run II* (1983) TV film: *Half Nelson* (1985)
Lee Marvin	*The Delta Force* (1986)
Marx Brothers	*Love Happy* (1950) Guest appearances in separate episodes of *The Story of Mankind* (1957) TV film: *The Incredible Jewel Robbery* (1960) Later films did not include all 3 main brothers
James Mason	*The Assisi Underground* (1984)
Raymond Massey	*MacKenna's Gold* (1969) TV film: *The President's Plane Is Missing* (1973)
Marcello Mastroianni	*Journey to the Beginning of the World* (1996)
Jessie Matthews	*Never Never Land* (1980)
Victor Mature	*Firepower* (1979) TV film: *Samson and Delilah* (1984)
Steve McQueen	*The Hunter* (1980)
Melina Mercouri	*Keine Zufallige Geschichte* (1983) US title: *Not by Coincidence*
Ethel Merman	*Airplane!* (1980)
Ray Milland	*The Sea Serpent* (1985)
Max Miller	*Asking for Trouble* (1943)
Carmen Miranda	*Scared Stiff* (1953)
Robert Mitchum	*Waiting for Sunset* (1997)
Tom Mix	*Rustlers' Roundup* (1933) Short film Series: *The Miracle Rider* (1935)

Actor	Film	Actor	Film
Marilyn Monroe	The Misfits (1961) (uncompleted) Something's Got to Give	George Raft	The Man with Bogart's Face (1979)
Yves Montand	IP5: L'Ile aux Pachydermes (1992)	Claude Rains	The Greatest Story Ever Told (1965)
Kenneth More	The Spaceman and King Arthur (1979) TV film: A Tale of Two Cities (1981)	Basil Rathbone	Hillbillies in a Haunted House (1968)
		Ronald Reagan	The Killers (1964)
		Michael Redgrave	Nicholas and Alexandra (1971) As narrator: Roosevelt: The Power behind the Smile (1975)
Robert Morley	Istanbul (1989) TV film: The Lady and the Highwayman (1989)		
Zero Mostel	Best Boy (1979)	Christopher Reeve	Village of the Damned (1995) TV film: Rear Window (1998)
Paul Muni	The Last Angry Man (1959)	Lee Remick	The Vision (1987)
Audie Murphy	A Time for Dying (1969)	Ralph Richardson	Directed by William Wyler (1986) (posthumously)
Anna Neagle	The Lady Is a Square (1959)		
David Niven	Curse of the Pink Panther (1983)	Rachel Roberts	Charlie Chan and the Curse of the Dragon Queen (1980) TV film: The Hostage Tower (1980)
Ivor Novello	Autumn Crocus (1934)		
Warren Oates	Blue Thunder (1983)		
Merle Oberon	Interval (1973)	Paul Robeson	Paul Robeson: Tales of Manhattan (1979)
Edmond O'Brien	Dream No Evil (1976)		
Pat O'Brien	Ragtime (1981)	Edward G Robinson	Soylent Green (1973)
Laurence Olivier	War Requiem (1988)	Flora Robson	Clash of the Titans (1981)
Lili Palmer	The Holcroft Covenant (1985) TV film: Peter the Great (1986)	Ginger Rogers	The Confession (1964) GB title: Let's Get Married TV film: Harlow (1964)
Gregory Peck	Cape Fear (1991) TV film: Moby Dick (1998)	Will Rogers	In Old Kentucky (1935)
George Peppard	The Tigress (1992)	Gilbert Roland	Barbarosa (1982)
Anthony Perkins	The Mummy Lives (1992) TV film: In the Deep Woods (1992)	Cesar Romero	The Player (1992)
		Rosalind Russell	Mrs Pollifax – Spy (1970) TV film: The Crooked Hearts (1972)
River Phoenix	The Thing Called Love (1993) Uncompleted: Dark Blood (1994)	Margaret Rutherford	Arabella (1969)
		Robert Ryan	The Outfit (1973)
		George Sanders	Psychomania (1972)
Mary Pickford	Star Night at the Cocoanut Grove (1935)	Telly Savalas	Backfire (1994)
Walter Pidgeon	Sextette (1977)	Romy Schneider	La Passante du Sans-Souci (1981)
Donald Pleasence	Halloween 6: The Curse of Michael Myers (1995) Uncompleted: Fotogrammi Mortal (1996) (aka Fatal Frames). After he died his role was played by an actor in his face mask (as was Rossano Brazzi's, who also died). David Warbeck (the 'Milk Tray' man) died soon after the release of the film	Randolph Scott	Ride the High Country (1962). GB title: Guns in the Afternoon
		Jean Seberg	The Wild Duck (1976)
		Peter Sellers	Trail of the Pink Panther (1982) (posthumous)
		Robert Shaw	Avalanche Express (1979) (posthumous)
		Norma Shearer	Her Cardboard Lover (1942)
		Ann Sheridan	Triangle on Safari (1957) TV film: Without Incident (1957)
Eric Portman	Deadfall (1968)	Dinah Shore	Health (1979) TV film: Death Car on the Freeway (1979)
Dick Powell	Susan Slept Here (1954)		
William Powell	Mister Roberts (1955)		
Tyrone Power	Witness for the Prosecution (1957)	Simone Signoret	L'Etoile du Nord (1982): As narrator: Des 'Terroristes' à la Retraite (1983)
Elvis Presley	That's the Way It Is (1970) TV film: Elvis on Tour (1972)	Phil Silvers	Hollywood Blue (1980) aka The Happy Hooker Goes to Hollywood
Robert Preston	The Last Starfighter (1984) TV film: Outrage (1986)		
Dennis Price	Theatre of Blood (1973) Unreleased: Son of Dracula (1974) Aka Count Downe (also starred Ringo Starr)	Alastair Sim	Escape from the Dark (1976)
		Barbara Stanwyck	The Night Walker (1965) TV film: The Thorn Birds (1983)
		Anthony Steel	The Monster Club (1981)
		Rod Steiger	Poolhall Junkies (2002)
Vincent Price	Edward Scissorhands (1990) TV film: The Heart of Justice (1992) Voice only: The Thief and the Cobbler (1995) Aka Arabian Knight	James Stewart	A Tale of Africa (1981) TV film: North and South II (1986) Voice only: An American Tail 2: Fievel Goes West (1991)
Anthony Quayle	King of the Wind (1989)	The 3 Stooges	Dr Death – Seeker of Souls (1973)

C
I
N
E
M
A

Actor	Film
Gloria Swanson	*Airport 1975* (1974)
Jacques Tati	*Traffic* (1971)
	Limited release: *Parade* (1974)
Robert Taylor	*The Glass Sphinx* (1968)
Shirley Temple	*A Kiss for Corliss* (1949)
John Thaw	*Chaplin* (1992)
	TV film: *Buried Treasure* (2001)
Terry Thomas	*Happy Birthday Harry!* (1981)
Sybil Thorndike	*Uncle Vanya* (1963)
Gene Tierney	*The Pleasure Seekers* (1964)
	TV film: *Daughter of the Mind* (1969)
Spencer Tracy	*Guess Who's Coming to Dinner* (1967)
Bill Travers	*Christian the Lion* (1973)
	TV film: *Bloody Ivory* (1979)
Tommy Trinder	*Barry McKenzie Holds His Own* (1974)
Lana Turner	*Witches' Brew* (1978; released 1985)
Robert Urich	*Jock – A True Tale of Friendship* (2001)
Peter Ustinov	*Luther* (2003)
Rudolph Valentino	*Son of the Sheik* (1926)
Rudy Vallee	*The Perfect Woman* (1978)
Lee Van Cleef	*Speed Zone* (1989)
Conrad Veidt	*Above Suspicion* (1943)
Erich Von Stroheim	*L'Homme Aux Cent Visages* (1956).

Actor	Film
	GB title: *Man of a Thousand Faces*
Jack Warner	*Dominique* (1978)
John Wayne	*The Shootist* (1976)
Clifton Webb	*Satan Never Sleeps* (1962)
Johnny Weissmuller	*Devil Goddess* (1955)
	Guest appearance: *That's Entertainment II* (1976)
Orson Welles	*Someone to Love* (1987) (posthumous)
Mae West	*Sextette* (1977)
Pearl White	*Perils of Paris* (1925)
Cornel Wilde	*Vultures in Paradise / Flesh and Bullets* (1983)
Michael Wilding	*Lady Caroline Lamb* (1972)
	TV film: *Frankenstein: The True Story* (1973)
Emlyn Williams	*The Walking Stick* (1970)
	TV film: *Past Caring* (1985)
Kenneth Williams	*Carry On Emmanuelle* (1978)
Sir Donald Wolfit	*The Charge of the Light Brigade* (1968)
Natalie Wood	*Brainstorm* (1981; released posthumously, 1983)
Fay Wray	*Summer Love* (1957).
	TV film: *Gideon's Trumpet* (1980)
Gig Young	*Game of Death* (1978)
Mai Zetterling	*Morfars Resa* (1993)

Oscars (Academy Awards)

*Year	Best Film	Best Actor	Best Actress	Best Director
1929	Wings (1927)	Emil Jannings (The Way of All Flesh)	Janet Gaynor (Seventh Heaven)	Frank Borzage (Seventh Heaven), Lewis Milestone (Two Arabian Knights)†
1930	The Broadway Melody	Warner Baxter (In Old Arizona)	Mary Pickford (Coquette)	Frank Lloyd (The Divine Lady)
1931	All Quiet on the Western Front	George Arliss (Disraeli)	Norma Shearer (The Divorcee)	Lewis Milestone (All Quiet on the Western Front)
1932	Cimarron (1930)	Lionel Barrymore (A Free Soul)	Marie Dressler (Min and Bill)	Norman Taurog (Skippy)
1933	Grand Hotel	Fredric March (Dr Jekyll and Mr Hyde), Wallace Beery (The Champ)	Helen Hayes (The Sin of Madelon Claudet)	Frank Borzage (Bad Girl)
1934	Cavalcade (1932)	Charles Laughton (Private Life of Henry VIII)	Katharine Hepburn (Morning Glory)	Frank Lloyd (Cavalcade)
1935	It Happened One Night	Clark Gable (It Happened One Night)	Claudette Colbert (It Happened One Night)	Frank Capra (It Happened One Night)
1936	Mutiny on the Bounty	Victor McLaglen (The Informer)	Bette Davis (Dangerous)	John Ford (The Informer)
1937	The Great Ziegfeld	Paul Muni (The Story of Louis Pasteur)	Luise Rainer (The Great Ziegfeld)	Frank Capra (Mr Deeds Goes to Town)
1938	The Life of Emile Zola	Spencer Tracy (Captains Courageous)	Luise Rainer (The Good Earth)	Leo McCarey (The Awful Truth)
1939	You Can't Take It with You	Spencer Tracy (Boys Town)	Bette Davis (Jezebel)	Frank Capra (You Can't Take It With You)
1940	Gone with the Wind	Robert Donat (Goodbye Mr Chips)	Vivien Leigh (Gone with the Wind)	Victor Fleming (Gone with the Wind)
1941	Rebecca	James Stewart (The Philadelphia Story)	Ginger Rogers (Kitty Foyle)	John Ford (The Grapes of Wrath)
1942	How Green Was My Valley	Gary Cooper (Sergeant York)	Joan Fontaine (Suspicion)	John Ford (How Green Was My Valley)
1943	Mrs Miniver	James Cagney (Yankee Doodle Dandy)	Greer Garson (Mrs Miniver)	William Wyler (Mrs Miniver)
1944	Casablanca (1942)	Paul Lukas (Watch on the Rhine)	Jennifer Jones (The Song of Bernadette)	Michael Curtiz (Casablanca)
1945	Going My Way	Bing Crosby (Going My Way)	Ingrid Bergman (Gaslight)	Leo McCarey (Going My Way)
1946	The Lost Weekend	Ray Milland (The Lost Weekend)	Joan Crawford (Mildred Pearce)	Billy Wilder (The Lost Weekend)
1947	The Best Years of Our Lives	Fredric March (The Best Years of Our Lives)	Olivia de Havilland (To Each His Own)	William Wyler (The Best Years of Our Lives)
1948	Gentleman's Agreement	Ronald Colman (A Double Life)	Loretta Young (The Farmer's Daughter)	Elia Kazan (Gentleman's Agreement)
1949	Hamlet	Laurence Olivier (Hamlet)	Jane Wyman (Johnny Belinda)	John Huston (The Treasure of the Sierra Madre)
1950	All the King's Men	Broderick Crawford (All the King's Men)	Olivia De Havilland (The Heiress)	Joseph L Mankiewicz (A Letter To Three Wives)
1951	All about Eve	José Ferrer (Cyrano de Bergerac)	Judy Holliday (Born Yesterday)	Joseph L Mankiewicz (All about Eve)
1952	An American In Paris	Humphrey Bogart (The African Queen)	Vivien Leigh (A Streetcar Named Desire)	George Stevens (A Place in the Sun)
1953	The Greatest Show on Earth	Gary Cooper (High Noon)	Shirley Booth (Come Back Little Sheba)	John Ford (The Quiet Man)
1954	From Here to Eternity	William Holden (Stalag 17)	Audrey Hepburn (Roman Holiday)	Fred Zinnemann (From Here to Eternity)
1955	On the Waterfront	Marlon Brando (On the Waterfront)	Grace Kelly (The Country Girl)	Elia Kazan (On the Waterfront)
1956	Marty	Ernest Borgnine (Marty)	Anna Magnani (The Rose Tattoo)	Delbert Mann (Marty)
1957	Around the World in Eighty Days	Yul Brynner (The King and I)	Ingrid Bergman (Anastasia)	George Stevens (Giant)
1958	The Bridge on the River Kwai	Alec Guinness (The Bridge on The River Kwai)	Joanne Woodward (The Three Faces of Eve)	David Lean (The Bridge on the River Kwai)
1959	Gigi	David Niven (Separate Tables)	Susan Hayward (I Want To Live)	Vincente Minnelli (Gigi)
1960	Ben Hur	Charlton Heston (Ben Hur)	Simone Signoret (Room at the Top)	William Wyler (Ben Hur)
1961	The Apartment	Burt Lancaster (Elmer Gantry)	Elizabeth Taylor (Butterfield 8)	Billy Wilder (The Apartment)
1962	West Side Story	Maximilian Schell (Judgment at Nuremberg)	Sophia Loren (Two Women)	Jerome Robbins & Robert Wise (West Side Story)

CINEMA

*Year	Best Film	Best Actor	Best Actress	Director
1963	Lawrence of Arabia	Gregory Peck (To Kill a Mockingbird)	Anne Bancroft (The Miracle Worker)	David Lean (Lawrence of Arabia)
1964	Tom Jones	Sidney Poitier (Lilies of the Field)	Patricia Neal (Hud)	Tony Richardson (Tom Jones)
1965	My Fair Lady	Rex Harrison (My Fair Lady)	Julie Andrews (Mary Poppins)	George Cukor (My Fair Lady)
1966	The Sound of Music	Lee Marvin (Cat Ballou)	Julie Christie (Darling)	Robert Wise (The Sound of Music)
1967	A Man for All Seasons	Paul Scofield (A Man for All Seasons)	Elizabeth Taylor (Who's Afraid of Virginia Woolf)	Fred Zinnemann (A Man for All Seasons)
1968	In the Heat of the Night	Rod Steiger (In the Heat of the Night)	Katharine Hepburn (Guess Who's Coming To Dinner)	Mike Nichols (The Graduate)
1969	Oliver!	Cliff Robertson (Charly)	Katharine Hepburn (The Lion in Winter) Barbra Streisand (Funny Girl)†	Carol Reed (Oliver!)
1970	Midnight Cowboy	John Wayne (True Grit)	Maggie Smith (The Prime of Miss Jean Brodie)	John Schlesinger (Midnight Cowboy)
1971	Patton	George C Scott (Patton) refused Oscar	Glenda Jackson (Women in Love)	Franklin Schaffner (Patton)
1972	The French Connection	Gene Hackman (The French Connection)	Jane Fonda (Klute)	William Friedkin (The French Connection)
1973	The Godfather	Marlon Brando (The Godfather, refused Oscar)	Liza Minnelli (Cabaret)	Bob Fosse (Cabaret)
1974	The Sting	Jack Lemmon (Save the Tiger)	Glenda Jackson (A Touch of Class)	George Roy Hill (The Sting)
1975	The Godfather Part II	Art Carney (Harry and Tonto)	Ellen Burstyn (Alice Doesn't Live Here Any More)	Francis Ford Coppola (The Godfather Part II)
1976	One Flew over the Cuckoo's Nest	Jack Nicholson (One Flew over the Cuckoo's Nest)	Louise Fletcher (One Flew Over the Cuckoo's Nest)	Milos Forman (One Flew over the Cuckoo's Nest)
1977	Rocky	Peter Finch (Network: posthumously awarded)	Faye Dunaway (Network)	John G Avildsen (Rocky)
1978	Annie Hall	Richard Dreyfuss (The Goodbye Girl)	Diane Keaton (Annie Hall)	Woody Allen (Annie Hall)
1979	The Deer Hunter	Jon Voight (Coming Home)	Jane Fonda (Coming Home)	Michael Cimino (The Deer Hunter)
1980	Kramer versus Kramer	Dustin Hoffman (Kramer versus Kramer)	Sally Field (Norma Rae)	Robert Benton (Kramer versus Kramer)
1981	Ordinary People	Robert De Niro (Raging Bull)	Sissy Spacek (Coal Miner's Daughter)	Robert Redford (Ordinary People)
1982	Chariots of Fire	Henry Fonda (On Golden Pond)	Katharine Hepburn (On Golden Pond)	Warren Beatty (Reds)
1983	Gandhi	Ben Kingsley (Gandhi)	Meryl Streep (Sophie's Choice)	Richard Attenborough (Gandhi)
1984	Terms of Endearment	Robert Duvall (Tender Mercies)	Shirley MacLaine (Terms of Endearment)	James L Brooks (Terms of Endearment)
1985	Amadeus	F Murray Abraham (Amadeus)	Sally Field (Places in the Heart)	Milos Forman (Amadeus)
1986	Out of Africa	William Hurt (Kiss of the Spider Woman)	Geraldine Page (The Trip to Bountiful)	Sydney Pollack (Out of Africa)
1987	Platoon	Paul Newman (The Color of Money)	Marlee Matlin (Children of a Lesser God)	Oliver Stone (Platoon)
1988	The Last Emperor	Michael Douglas (Wall Street)	Cher (Moonstruck)	Bernardo Bertolucci (The Last Emperor)
1989	Rain Man	Dustin Hoffman (Rain Man)	Jodie Foster (The Accused)	Barry Levinson (Rain Man)
1990	Driving Miss Daisy	Daniel Day Lewis (My Left Foot)	Jessica Tandy (Driving Miss Daisy)	Oliver Stone (Born on the Fourth of July)
1991	Dances with Wolves	Jeremy Irons (Reversal of Fortune)	Kathy Bates (Misery)	Kevin Costner (Dances with Wolves)
1992	Silence of the Lambs	Anthony Hopkins (Silence of the Lambs)	Jodie Foster (Silence of the Lambs)	Jonathan Demme (Silence of the Lambs)
1993	Unforgiven	Al Pacino (Scent of a Woman)	Emma Thompson (Howard's End)	Clint Eastwood (Unforgiven)
1994	Schindler's List	Tom Hanks (Philadelphia)	Holly Hunter (The Piano)	Steven Spielberg (Schindler's List)
1995	Forrest Gump	Tom Hanks (Forrest Gump)	Jessica Lange (Blue Sky)	Robert Zemeckis (Forrest Gump)
1996	Braveheart	Nicolas Cage (Leaving Las Vegas)	Susan Sarandon (Dead Man Walking)	Mel Gibson (Braveheart)
1997	The English Patient	Geoffrey Rush (Shine)	Frances McDormand (Fargo)	Anthony Minghella (The English Patient)
1998	Titanic	Jack Nicholson (As Good As it Gets)	Helen Hunt (As Good As it Gets)	James Cameron (Titanic)
1999	Shakespeare in Love	Roberto Benigni (Life is Beautiful)	Gwyneth Paltrow (Shakespeare in Love)	Steven Spielberg (Saving Private Ryan)

*Year	Best Film	Best Actor	Best Actress	Director
2000	American Beauty	Kevin Spacey (American Beauty)	Hilary Swank (Boys Don't Cry)	Sam Mendes (American Beauty)
2001	Gladiator	Russell Crowe (Gladiator)	Julia Roberts (Erin Brockovich)	Steven Soderbergh (Traffic)
2002	A Beautiful Mind	Denzel Washington (Training Day)	Halle Berry (Monster's Ball)	Ron Howard (A Beautiful Mind)
2003	Chicago	Adrien Brody (The Pianist)	Nicole Kidman (The Hours)	Roman Polanski (The Pianist)
2004	The Lord of the Rings: Return of the King	Sean Penn (Mystic River)	Charlize Theron (Monster)	Peter Jackson (The Lord of the Rings: Return of the King)
2005	Million Dollar Baby	Jamie Foxx (Ray)	Hilary Swank (Million Dollar Baby)	Clint Eastwood (Million Dollar Baby)

* Probably the most frustrating question for any quiz player is in determining what a question setter means when asking a question about the Oscars. The confusion arises because the Oscars are awarded for films made the previous year, which means the question must be qualified – e.g. the 1997 Best Film Oscar was awarded to The English Patient, which was a 1996 film release. It must be said that the real confusion lies in the fact that, even when the question is qualified, bad research will cause a wrongly given answer by an unaware question setter. The suggested phraseology to use in such a question would be: 'At the 1996 Oscar ceremony, which film was awarded the Best Film Oscar?'. The answer is Braveheart. However, if the question was: 'Which 1996 film won the Oscar for Best Film?' then the answer would clearly be The English Patient. The problem with the question 'Which film won the Best Film Oscar in 1996?' is that although seemingly unambiguous, as clearly only one Oscar ceremony took place in 1996, many sources refer to the film release date, quite wrongly. I can only suggest that question setters take more care with such questions or that an appropriately qualified answer must be accepted. All of the above films were premiered in the year prior to the award unless the date is specifically given, since as on rare occasions a film has been released too late for consideration for a nomination, as in the case of Casablanca.

† Separate award for Comedy Director.

CINEMA

Oscars (Academy Awards) continued

Best Supporting Actor

Year	Actor	Film
1937	Walter Brennan	Come and Get It
1938	Joseph Schildkraut	The Life of Emile Zola
1939	Walter Brennan	Kentucky
1940	Thomas Mitchell	Stagecoach
1941	Walter Brennan	The Westerner
1942	Donald Crisp	How Green Was My Valley
1943	Van Heflin	Johnny Eager
1944	Charles Coburn	The More the Merrier
1945	Barry Fitzgerald	Going My Way
1946	James Dunn	A Tree Grows in Brooklyn
1947	Harold Russell	The Best Years of Our Lives
1948	Edmund Gwenn	Miracle on 34th Street
1949	Walter Huston	The Treasure of the Sierra Madre
1950	Dean Jagger	Twelve O'Clock High
1951	George Sanders	All about Eve
1952	Karl Malden	A Streetcar Named Desire
1953	Anthony Quinn	Viva Zapata!
1954	Frank Sinatra	From Here to Eternity
1955	Edmond O'Brien	The Barefoot Contessa
1956	Anthony Quinn	Lust for Life
1957	Red Buttons	Sayonara
1958	Burl Ives	The Big Country
1959	Hugh Griffith	Ben-Hur
1960	Peter Ustinov	Spartacus
1961	George Chakiris	West Side Story
1962	Ed Begley	Sweet Bird of Youth
1963	Melvyn Douglas	Hud
1964	Peter Ustinov	Topkapi
1965	Martin Balsam	A Thousand Clowns
1966	Walter Matthau	The Fortune Cookie
1968	George Kennedy	Cool Hand Luke
1969	Jack Albertson	The Subject Was Roses
1970	Gig Young	They Shoot Horses Don't They?
1971	John Mills	Ryan's Daughter
1972	Ben Johnson	The Last Picture Show
1973	Joel Grey	Cabaret
1974	John Houseman	The Paper Chase
1975	Robert De Niro	The Godfather Part II
1976	George Burns	The Sunshine Boys
1977	Jason Robards	All the President's Men
1978	Jason Robards	Julia
1979	Christopher Walken	The Deer Hunter
1980	Melvyn Douglas	Being There
1981	Timothy Hutton	Ordinary People
1982	John Gielgud	Arthur
1983	Louis Gossett Jr	An Officer and a Gentleman
1984	Jack Nicholson	Terms of Endearment
1985	Haing S Ngor	The Killing Fields
1986	Don Ameche	Cocoon
1987	Michael Caine	Hannah and Her Sisters
1988	Sean Connery	The Untouchables
1989	Kevin Kline	A Fish Called Wanda
1990	Denzel Washington	Glory
1991	Joe Pesci	Goodfellas
1992	Jack Palance	City Slickers
1993	Gene Hackman	Unforgiven
1994	Tommy Lee Jones	The Fugitive
1995	Martin Landau	Ed Wood

Best Supporting Actress

Year	Actress	Film
1937	Gale Sondergaard	Anthony Adverse
1938	Alice Brady	In Old Chicago
1939	Fay Bainter	Jezebel
1940	Hattie McDaniel	Gone with the Wind
1941	Jane Darwell	The Grapes of Wrath
1942	Mary Astor	The Great Lie
1943	Teresa Wright	Mrs Miniver
1944	Katina Paxinou	For Whom the Bell Tolls
1945	Ethel Barrymore	None but the Lonely Heart
1946	Anne Revere	National Velvet
1947	Anne Baxter	The Razor's Edge
1948	Celeste Holm	Gentleman's Agreement
1949	Claire Trevor	Key Largo
1950	Mercedes McCambridge	All the King's Men
1951	Josephine Hull	Harvey
1952	Kim Hunter	A Streetcar Named Desire
1953	Gloria Grahame	The Bad and the Beautiful
1954	Donna Reed	From Here to Eternity
1955	Eva Marie Saint	On the Waterfront
1956	Jo Van Fleet	East of Eden
1957	Dorothy Malone	Written on the Wind
1958	Miyoshi Umeki	Sayonara
1959	Wendy Hiller	Separate Tables
1960	Shelley Winters	The Diary of Anne Frank
1961	Shirley Jones	Elmer Gantry
1962	Rita Moreno	West Side Story
1963	Patty Duke	The Miracle Worker
1964	Margaret Rutherford	The V.I.P.s
1965	Lila Kedrova	Zorba the Greek
1966	Shelley Winters	A Patch of Blue
1967	Sandy Dennis	Who's Afraid of Virginia Woolf?
1968	Estelle Parsons	Bonnie and Clyde
1969	Ruth Gordon	Rosemary's Baby
1970	Goldie Hawn	Cactus Flower
1971	Helen Hayes	Airport
1972	Cloris Leachman	The Last Picture Show
1973	Eileen Heckart	Butterflies Are Free
1974	Tatum O'Neal	Paper Moon
1975	Ingrid Bergman	Murder on the Orient Express
1976	Lee Grant	Shampoo
1977	Beatrice Straight	Network
1978	Vanessa Redgrave	Julia
1979	Maggie Smith	California Suite
1980	Meryl Streep	Kramer vs. Kramer
1981	Mary Steenburgen	Melvin and Howard
1982	Maureen Stapleton	Reds
1983	Jessica Lange	Tootsie
1984	Linda Hunt	The Year of Living Dangerously
1985	Peggy Ashcroft	A Passage to India
1986	Anjelica Huston	Prizzi's Honor
1987	Dianne Wiest	Hannah and Her Sisters
1988	Olympia Dukakis	Moonstruck
1989	Geena Davis	The Accidental Tourist
1990	Brenda Fricker	My Left Foot
1991	Whoopi Goldberg	Ghost
1992	Mercedes Ruehl	The Fisher King
1993	Marisa Tomei	My Cousin Vinny
1994	Anna Paquin	The Piano
1995	Dianne Wiest	Bullets over Broadway

Year	Actor	Film	Actress	Film
1996	Kevin Spacey	The Usual Suspects	Mira Sorvino	Mighty Aphrodite
1997	Cuba Gooding Jr	Jerry Maguire	Julliette Binoche	The English Patient
1998	Robin Williams	Good Will Hunting	Kim Basinger	L.A. Confidential
1999	James Coburn	Affliction	Judi Dench	Shakespeare in Love
2000	Michael Caine	The Cider House Rules	Angelina Jolie	Girl Interrupted
2001	Benicio Del Toro	Traffic	Marcia Gay Harden	Pollock
2002	Jim Broadbent	Iris	Jennifer Connelly	A Beautiful Mind
2003	Chris Cooper	Adaptation	Catherine Zeta-Jones	Chicago
2004	Tim Robbins	Mystic River	Renée Zellweger	Cold Mountain
2005	Morgan Freeman	Million Dollar Baby	Cate Blanchett	The Aviator

Best Original Song

Year	Film	Artist	Song
1935	The Gay Divorcee	Con Conrad (composer), Herb Magidson (lyricist)	The Continental
1936	Gold Diggers	Harry Warren (composer), Al Dunin (lyricist)	Lullaby of Broadway
1937	Swing Time	Jerome Kern (composer), Dorothy Fields (lyricist)	The Way You Look Tonight
1938	Waikiki Wedding	Harry Owens	Sweet Leilani
1939	The Big Broadcast	Ralph Rainger (composer), Leo Robin (lyricist)	Thanks for the Memory
1940	The Wizard of Oz	Harold Arlen (composer), EY Harburg (lyricist)	Over the Rainbow
1941	Pinocchio	Leigh Harline (composer), Ned Washington (lyricist)	When You Wish upon a Star
1942	Lady Be Good	Jerome Kern (composer), Oscar Hammerstein II (lyricist)	The Last Time I Saw Paris
1943	Holiday Inn	Irving Berlin	White Christmas
1944	Hello, Frisco, Hello	Harry Warren (composer), Mack Gordon (lyricist)	You'll Never Know
1945	Going My Way	James Van Heusen (composer), Johnny Burke (lyricist)	Swinging on a Star
1946	State Fair	Richard Rodgers (composer), Oscar Hammerstein II (lyricist)	It Might As Well Be Spring
1947	The Harvey Girls	Harry Warren (composer), Johnny Mercer (lyricist)	On the Atchison, Topeka and the Santa Fe
1948	Song of the South	Allie Wrubel (composer), Ray Gilbert (lyricist)	Zip-A-Dee-Doo-Dah
1949	The Paleface	Jay Livingston (composer), Ray Evans (lyricist)	Buttons and Bows
1950	Neptune's Daughter	Frank Loesser	Baby, It's Cold Outside
1951	Captain Carey U.S.A.	Jay Livingston (composer), Ray Evans (lyricist)	Mona Lisa
1952	Here Comes the Groom	Hoagy Carmichael (composer), Johnny Mercer (lyricist)	In the Cool, Cool, Cool of the Evening
1953	High Noon	Dimitri Tiomkin (composer), Ned Washington (lyricist)	High Noon (Do Not Forsake Me, Oh My Darlin')
1954	Calamity Jane	Sammy Fain (composer), Paul Francis Webster (lyricist)	Secret Love
1955	Three Coins in the Fountain	Jule Styne (composer), Sammy Cahn (lyricist)	Three Coins in the Fountain
1956	Love is a Many-Splendored Thing	Sammy Fain (composer), Paul Francis Webster (lyricist)	Love is a Many-Splendored Thing
1957	The Man Who Knew Too Much	Jay Livingston (composer), Ray Evans (lyricist)	Whatever Will Be, Will Be (Que Sera, Sera)
1958	The Joker Is Wild	James Van Heusen (composer), Sammy Cahn (lyricist)	All The Way
1959	Gigi	Frederick Loewe (composer), Allan Jay Lerner (lyricist)	Gigi
1960	A Hole in the Head	James Van Heusen (composer), Sammy Cahn (lyricist)	High Hopes
1961	Never on Sunday	Manos Hadjidakis	Never On Sunday
1962	Breakfast at Tiffany's	Henry Mancini (composer), Johnny Mercer (lyricist)	Moon River
1963	Days of Wine and Roses	Henry Mancini (composer), Johnny Mercer (lyricist)	Days of Wine and Roses

CINEMA

Year	Film	Artist	Song
1964	*Papa's Delicate Condition*	James Van Heusen (composer), Sammy Cahn (lyricist)	Call Me Irresponsible
1965	*Mary Poppins*	Richard M Sherman (composer), Robert B Sherman (lyricist)	Chim Chim Cher-ee
1966	*The Sandpiper*	Johnny Mandel (composer), Paul Francis Webster (lyricist)	The Shadow of Your Smile
1967	*Born Free*	John Barry (composer), Don Black (lyricist)	Born Free
1968	*Doctor Dolittle*	Leslie Bricusse	Talk to the Animals
1969	*The Thomas Crown Affair*	Michel Legrand, Alan Bergman, Marilyn Bergman	The Windmills of Your Mind
1970	*Butch Cassidy and the Sundance Kid*	Burt Bacharach (composer), Hal David (lyricist)	Raindrops Keep Fallin' On My Head
1971	*Lovers and Other Strangers*	Fred Karlin, Robb Royer [aka Robb Wilson] James Griffin [aka Arthur James]	For All We Know
1972	*Shaft*	Isaac Hayes	Theme from Shaft
1973	*The Poseidon Adventure*	Al Kasha (composer), Joel Hirschhorn (lyricist)	The Morning After
1974	*The Way We Were*	Marvin Hamlisch, Alan Bergman, Marilyn Bergman	The Way We Were
1975	*The Towering Inferno*	Al Kasha (composer), Joel Hirschhorn (lyricist)	We May Never Love Like This Again
1976	*Nashville*	Keith Carradine	I'm Easy
1977	*A Star is Born*	Barbara Streisand (composer), Paul Williams (lyricist)	Evergreen (Love Theme from A Star is Born)
1978	*You Light Up My Life*	Joseph Brooks	You Light Up My Life
1979	*Thank God It's Friday*	Paul Jabara	Last Dance
1980	*Norma Rae*	David Shire (composer), Norman Gimbel (lyricist)	It Goes Like It Goes
1981	*Fame*	Michael Gore (composer), Dean Pitchford (lyricist)	Fame
1982	*Arthur*	Burt Bacharach, Carole Bayer Sager, Christopher Cross, Peter Allen	Arthur's Theme (Best That You Can Do)
1983	*An Officer and a Gentleman*	Jack Nitzsche, Buffy Saint-Marie, Will Jennings	Up Where We Belong
1984	*Flashdance*	Giorgio Moroder, Keith Forsey, Irene Cara	Flashdance . . . What a Feeling
1985	*The Woman in Red*	Stevie Wonder	I Just Called to Say I Love You
1986	*White Nights*	Lionel Richie	Say You, Say Me
1987	*Top Gun*	Giorgio Moroder (composer), Tom Whitlock (lyricist)	Take My Breath Away
1988	*Dirty Dancing*	Franke Previte, John DeNicola, Donald Markowitz	(I've Had) The Time of My Life
1989	*Working Girl*	Carly Simon	Let the River Run
1990	*The Little Mermaid*	Alan Menken (composer), Howard Ashman (lyricist)	Under the Sea
1991	*Dick Tracy*	Stephen Sondheim	Sooner Or Later (I Always Get My Man)
1992	*Beauty and the Beast*	Alan Menken (composer), Howard Ashman (lyricist)	Beauty and the Beast
1993	*Aladdin*	Alan Menken (composer), Tim Rice (lyricist)	A Whole New World
1994	*Philadelphia*	Bruce Springsteen	Streets of Philadelphia
1995	*The Lion King*	Elton John (composer), Tim Rice (lyricist)	Can You Feel the Love Tonight
1996	*Pocahontas*	Alan Menken (composer), Stephen Schwartz (lyricist)	Colors of the Wind
1997	*Evita*	Andrew Lloyd Webber (composer), Tim Rice (lyricist)	You Must Love Me
1998	*Titanic (1997)*	James Horner (composer), Will Jennings (lyricist)	My Heart Will Go On
1999	*The Prince of Egypt*	Stephen Schwartz	When You Believe
2000	*Tarzan*	Phil Collins	You'll Be In My Heart
2001	*Wonderboys*	Bob Dylan	Things Have Changed
2002	*Monsters Inc*	Randy Newman	If I Didn't Have You
2003	*8 Mile*	Eminem	Lose Yourself
2004	*The Lord of the Rings: Return of the King*	Frances Walsh, Howard Shore, Annie Lennox	Into the West
2005	*The Motorcycle Diaries*	Jorge Drexler	Al Otro Lado Del Rio (To the other side of the river)

COMPUTERS

Common Terms

Artificial Intelligence A word coined in the USA in 1956 as the ultimate aim for electronic processing ability. Although great strides have been made towards a device that would stimulate human thought processes, as yet, no such device exists and the term is used to describe advanced programs such as PROLOG which allows empirical evidence to guide future decisions.

ASCII American Standard Code for Information Interchange (computer code for representing alphanumeric characters.

bit (binary digit) Smallest unit of data manageable by a computer.

bootstrap Technique for loading the first few program instructions into a computer main store to enable the rest of the program to be introduced from an input device.

busbar Group of electrical conductors maintained at low voltage, used for carrying data in binary form between the various parts of a computer or its peripherals.

byte Equivalent of eight bits (generally makes up a character of information). It is possible to have a six-bit byte.

computer: definition A machine that carries out a programmed sequence of instructions by translation of coded data. Digital computers use binary code which is represented by eletrical current being turned off and on. Analogue computers use continuous variables as opposed to the discreet data of digital machines. A simple example of an analogue computer would be a set of scales.

computer generations The developement of computers is sometimes viewed as falling into several phases or generations. First generation began with the ENIAC (electronic numerical integrator and calculator) modern computers designed by J. Presper Eckert and John W Mauchly, both of the University of Pennsylvania. Completed in 1946, this was first all-purpose, all-electronic digital computer. A special-purpose, all-electronic computing machine called Colossus had earlier been developed at Bletchley Park, in England, and was in operation by December 1943. The Colossus was designed (by the computer genius Alan Turing) to decipher codes generated by the German electromechanical enciphering devices known as Enigma machines. The successor to ENIAC was EDVAC (Electronic Discrete Variable Automatic Computer).

The 'second generation' of modern computers began in 1959, when machines employing semiconductor devices known as transistors became commercially available.

The 'third generation' of modern computers began in the late 1960s, when integrated circuits were imprinted on silicon chips. This permitted the construction of large 'mainframe' computers with much higher operating speeds.

The 'fourth generation' of modern computers began in the 1980s. This and subsequent generations have continued to develop very large-scale integration (VLSI) and have promoted the advancement of virtual reality (VR) and computer aided design (CAD).

The 'fifth generation' of modern computers is an ongoing general development of recent technological advances. Using recent engineering advances for example, computers are able to accept spoken word instructions (voice recognition) and imitate human reasoning. The ability to translate a foreign language is now commonplace.

Computer Programming languages (high-level)

ADA Designed for dealing with real-time processing problems and used for military and other systems. It was named after Augusta Ada Byron, Lady Lovelace (assistant to Charles Babbage), and developed in the late 1970s by the US Defense Department.

AED Algol Extended for Design.

ALGOL ALGorithmic Orientated Language, principally used for scientific and mathematical problems (types: ALGOL 60 and ALGOL 68).

APL A Programming Language.

APT Automatically Programmed Tools.

BASIC Beginners All-purpose Symbolic Instruction Code.

BCPL Basic Computer Programming Language.

C Introduced at Bell Laboratories in 1974 and originally developed for use in the UNIX operating system.

COBOL COmmon Business-Oriented Language (developed in 1959).

COGO CO-ordinate GeOmetry.

COMAL COMmon Algorithmic Language.

CORAL Computer On-line ReAL time.

FORTH Name derives from an intention to provide a language for fourth-generation computers. It uses a notation called reverse polish, in which an operator is always preceded by its arguments. FORTH is popularly used for writing video game programs.

FORTRAN FORmula TRANslation (Invented in 1956).

GPSS General Purpose Systems Simulation.

LISP LISt Processor (introduced in 1960). Its basic entity is an s-expression (symbolic expression) which is either an atomic symbol or a list structure.

LOGO A simple, interactive language which is compact enough to run on most microcomputers but also embodies powerful programming facilities. It is used extensively for teaching programming to children.

ML Meta Language.

PASCAL ALGOL-related language named after the scientist-philosopher Blaise Pascal (1623–62). Pascal is a teaching language developed in the late 1960s.

PERL Practical Extraction and Report Language.

PL/1 Programming Language 1, a multipurpose programming language designed for solving both business and scientific problems.

PL/M Programming Language for Micro Computers.

PROLOG PROgramming in LOGic. There the emphasis is on description rather than on action, eg to find the greater of two input numbers, one would describe what 'greater of' meant and then query it with the given numbers as data.

SAIL   Stanford Artificial Intelligence Language.

SIMULA   SIMUlation LAnguage.

SNOBOL   StriNg-Oriented symBOlic Language, provides facilities for the manipulation of strings of characters by pattern-matching expressions. SNOBOL is particularly applicable for text editing, linguistics and the compiling and symbolic manipulation of algebraic expressions.

SQL   Structured Query Language.

computer: makes and models: Commodore: Amiga and PET; Apple: Macintosh; Sinclair: Spectrum and ZX80 / 1; Packard Bell: Legend; DEC: Vax; IBM: PS/2; Acorn: BBC Micro; Digital: Equipment Corporation-PDP Series.

computer: mechanical pioneers   Charles Babbage (1791–1871) designed computing machines that he called the 'Difference Engine' and 'Analytical Engine' in the 1820s and 30s. They were never built but the first practical programmed computer built by Georg Scheutz of Stockholm and exhibited at the Paris Exposition of 1855 was based on Babbage's Difference Engine. The mechanical adding machine developed by Blaise Pascal in 1642 which used a 10:1 gearing ratio to represent decimal columns, can be regarded as the ancestor of the computer.

computer programmer: first   Ada Byron, Countess Lovelace, assistant to Charles Babbage (see computer mechanical pioneers), is generally recognised as the first 'computer programmer'.The first proposal for a computer language, however, was by German philosopher Gottfried Leibniz (1646–1716), who devised a system allowing logic statements to be dealt with mathematically, using the digit 0 for false and 1 for true.)

computer: types   Micro, mini, mainframe (computers can also be categorised as digital and analog).

CPU   Central Processing Unit; the electronic decision making device within a computer.

DTP   Desktop Publishing; the production of high-quality printed matter using a desktop computer and a laser printer. Some examples of packages are Pagemaker and QuarkXpress, Adobe Illustrator, Microsoft Publisher, Corel Draw, GST and Serif.

exabyte   one billion billion characters of information.

gigabyte   one billion characters of information.

GIGO   Garbage In, Garbage Out. Computer user's proverb meaning if you use unreliable data you will get unreliable results.

Hardware   The electronic and mechanical components of a computer are called the hardware; this includes the processing unit.

high-level language   Computer programming language that is closer to human language or mathematical notation than to machine language.

home computer: first   Apple-1; created by Steve Wozniak and Steve Jobs in 1977.

k   Kilobyte (1,024 bytes).

Internet   An international computer network linking computers from educational institutions, government agencies, and industry.

Lara Croft   Heroine of the video game 'Tomb Raider'.

Laptops: first   Became prevalent in 1987, although the first laptop machine with a full colour screen was developed in 1990.

Laser printer   developed in 1987 using the principle of the Xerox copier.

LCD   Liquid Crystal Display.

low-level language   Computer-programming. language that is closer to machine language than to human language.

m   Megabyte (1,024 kilobytes).

microprocessor: first   Intel 4004.

modem   Acronym for MOdulator DEModulator, a device used to enable computers to communicate with one another via telephone lines.

motherboard   Printed circuit board through which all hardware and software devise send electronic to talk to each other.

MS-DOS   MicroSoft Disc Operating System.

network   Group of computers connected in order to share and exchange information.

nibble   Equivalent of four bits.

OS   Operating System: a program that controls the overall operation of a computer system, typically by performing such tasks as memory allocation, job scheduling and input/output control.

pixel   Picture element: one of the number of very small dots that make up the picture on a visual display unit.

port   Socket used to connect a computer to other devices.

punched card: inventor   The American Dr Herman Hollerith (1860–1929) invented the punched-card system in 1890; his company, the Tabulating Machine Co. became IBM in 1924. Hollerith's device enabled a census to be taken in six weeks rather than the six years required by manual analysis. Mechanical punched cards had been suggested earlier by Charles Babbage; and the 'Jacquard Loom' of 1801 is an even earlier example of punched card principles but Hollerith patented the system and was the first to use electrical contacts.

RAM   Random Access Memory; temporary storage space that is lost when the computer is switched off.

ROM   Read-Only Memory; permanent storage device that holds data that cannot be altered by the user.

software   the programs and operating information used by a computer.

spreadsheets: first   The first spreadsheet program Visicalc was developed on the Apple-2 in 1979.

terabyte   Approximately a thousand billion characters of information.

Turing Test   Test for successful artificial intelligence that depends on a human not being able to tell that he or she is communicating with a computer. No computer has ever passed the Turing Test.

VGA   Video Graphics Array (Super VGA is the advanced array).

video games: 1st   Pong (established in Italy in the early 1970s).

Video games: famous   Super Mario Brothers by Nintendo, Sonic the Hedgehog by Sega, Donkey Kong by Atari, Tomb Raider by Eios, Duke Nukem by 3D Realms, and Doom by Idoh.

Windows   User-friendly operating system created by Microsoft.

NB: Many computer acronyms (eg AI, DOS, WYSIWYG, VDU, and MIPS) can be found listed in the Abbreviations section

Internet Chat Abbreviations

Abbreviation	Meaning		Abbreviation	Meaning
AAMOF	as a matter of fact		ITA	I totally agree
AFAIK	as far as I know		ITFA	in the final analysis
AFK	away from keyboard		IWALU	I will always love you
AIM	AOL instant messenger		IWALY	I will always love you
ASAP	as soon as possible		J/K	just kidding
ASL?	age, sex, location?		JK	joke
ATK	at the keyboard		JMO	just my opinion
B4	before		K	okay
BBIAB	be back in a bit		KISS	keep it simple, stupid
BB4N	bye bye for now		KOL	kiss on lips
BBFN	bye bye for now		L8R	later
BBL	be back later		L8R G8R	later 'gator
BBS	be back soon		LJBF	let's just be friends
BEG	big evil grin		LMAO	laughing my arse off
BF	boyfriend		LOL	laughing out loud
BFN	bye for now		LOLOL	laughing out loud online
BION	believe it or not		LTNS	long time no see
BOT	back on topic		LTNT	long time no type
BRB	be right back		LUVYA	love ya (you)
BRB NC	be right back, nature calls		LY4E	love you for ever
BRS	big red switch		M/F	male or female?
BTW	by the way		MOTD	message of the day
BWL	bursting with laughter		MSG	message
CID	crying in disgrace		MYOB	mind your own business
CRBT	crying real big tears		NBD	no big deal
CSG	chuckle, snigger, grin		N1	nice one
C U L8ER	see you later		NM	never mind
C U L8TER	see you later		NP	no problem
C YA	see ya (you)		NQA	no questions asked
DC'D	disconnected		NRN	no reply necessary
DIKU	do I know you		OAUS	on an unrelated subject
EG	evil grin		OMG	oh my god
FAQ	frequently asked questions		OIC	oh I see
FCOL	for crying out loud		OTOH	on the other hand
FFS	for fuck sake		12345	talk about school
FOAF	friend of a friend		PDS	please don't shout
FTF	face to face		PM	private message
F2F	face to face		PMBI	pardon my butting in
FUBAR	fucked up beyond all recognition		PML	pissing myself laughing
FUD	fear, uncertainty and doubt		POV	point of view
FWIW	for what it's worth		PTMM	please tell me more
FYI	for your information		RHIP	rank has its privileges
GF	girlfriend		ROFL	rolling on floor laughing
GG	good game		ROTF	rolling on the floor
GMTA	great minds think alike		ROTFL	rolling on the floor laughing
GR8	great		ROTFLMAO	rolling on the floor laughing my arse off
GL	good luck		RTBM	read the bloody manual
GTG	got to go		RTFM	read the fucking manual
H&K	hugs and kisses		RTM	read the manual
HAGN	have a good night		RTSM	read the stupid manual
HAND	have a nice day		RYS	read your screen
HB	hurry back		SICS	sitting in chair sniggering
HLOL	hysterically laughing out loud		SLM	see last mail
HTH	hope that helps		SO	significant other
IAAA	I am an accountant		SS	so sorry
IAAL	I am a lawyer		SUAKM	shut up and kiss me
IANALB	I am not a lawyer . . . but		SWIM	see what I mean
IC	I see		SWL	screaming with laughter
IJWTS	I just want to say		SYT	sweet young thing
ILU	I love you		TANJ	there ain't no justice
ILY	I love you		TCOB	taking care of business
IMHO	in my humble opinion		TOBAL	there oughta be a law
IMY	I miss you		TPTB	the powers that be
INPO	in no particular order		TSR	totally stupid rules
IOW	in other words		TTFN	ta ta for now
IRL	in real life		TTYL	talk to you later
ISRN	I'll stop rambling now		TY	thank you

C
O
M
P
U
T
E
R
S

TYCLO	turn your caps lock off	:-)	smiling
TYVM	thank you very much	:-0	shock
VG	very good	:'-(	crying
VN	very nice	X=	fingers crossed
WAEF	when all else fails	:-w	a liar – speaks with forked tongue
WB	welcome back	:=)	little Hitler
WG	wicked grin	:*	kissing
WTF	what the fuck	:-X	kissing
WTG	way to go	$-)	greedy
WTGP	want to go private?	:-L~~	drooling
WTH	what/who the hell	}:	devil
YGLT	you're gonna love this	<:-)	idiot
YMMV	your mileage may vary	:-S	confused
YW	you're welcome	:-(	sad

CURRENT AFFAIRS

Daily Record 2003

January

1   The *Vicky*, a Turkish tanker carrying 70,000 tonnes of diesel oil, struck the wreck of the Norwegian car-carrier *Tricolor* in the English Channel. The *Tricolor* sank on 14 December 2002 after colliding with a cargo vessel near Ramsgate.

2   Police investigating the murder of two women whose body parts were found in bin-bags in North London arrested a man near Great Ormond Street Hospital.

5   Tony Hardy, 52, was charged with the murder of three women; the body of the first, prostitute Sally Rose White, 31, was found in a locked room in his flat in January 2002, the remains of the other two were found in bin-bags in North London in December.

8   Harriet Harman, QC, the Government's Solicitor-General, was caught speeding at 99mph on the M4 between junctions 16 and 17.

9   Britain's longest-running siege ended after 15 days when the body of Eli Hall, a gunman holed up since Boxing Day, was found in a flat in Hackney, East London.

11   Controversy surrounded rock musician Pete Townshend following his revelations that he paid to enter a child pornography website in order to carry out research for a book he is writing.

12   Seb Clover, 15, became the youngest person to cross the Atlantic single-handed. He arrived in Antigua in his 32ft yacht, *Reflection*, 24 days and 2,700 miles after setting out from Tenerife in the Canary Islands.

14   Detective Constable Stephen Oake, 40, was stabbed to death while taking part in a raid on terrorist suspects in Crumpsall, Manchester.

15   Two of Britain's greatest living artists, David Hockney and Lucian Freud, unveiled portraits of one another.

20   At the annual Golden Globe awards in Hollywood a British-made film, *The Hours*, won Best Film while Nicole Kidman won Best Actress for the same film. Jack Nicholson won Best Actor for his performance in *About Schmidt*.

21   Detailed analysis of the chromosomes of mammals showed that the closest relative to man is the aardvark!

23   The Tupperware party, a British institution for over 30 years, was committed to history when the Florida-based manufacturer announced that it was to close its British direct-selling business.

29   Athina Roussel, the granddaughter and sole surviving heir of Aristotle Onassis, celebrated her 18th birthday by inheriting half of the shipping tycoon's £5 billion fortune, making her one of the richest women in the world.

30   Richard Reid, the British so-called 'shoe bomber' who attempted to blow up a transatlantic jet with hidden explosives, was sentenced to life imprisonment by a court in Boston, Massachusetts.

February

1   *Columbia*, the oldest and heaviest of Nasa's four space shuttles, disintegrated 39 miles above the plains of Texas as it re-entered the Earth's atmosphere for a landing in Florida, killing all seven astronauts on board.

3   Kevin Spacey, the double Oscar-winning actor, became the new artistic director of the Old Vic Theatre in London, joining other luminaries Sir Elton John, the theatre's chairman, and Lord Attenborough, the chairman of Old Vic Productions.

4   Martin Narey, the Director-General of the Prison Service, claimed that Ashfield jail, a privately run prison near Bristol, was the worst-run prison in England and Wales 'by some measure'.

6   Artist Dan Shelton, 23, sealed himself in a wooden crate and posted himself, via the Securicor freight company, from his home in Brighton to Tate Britain, London. The living-art project was funded by Charles Webb and his female partner, Fred. Mr Webb is best known for giving away the film rights for his book *The Graduate* for £14,000 in 1963.

7   The world's first hospital dedicated solely to vultures was opened in India. The white-back vulture is now almost extinct in India and the population of the long-billed vulture has fallen by 92 per cent in the last ten years.

9   BBC3 was launched by comedian and presenter Johnny Vaughan.

17   The £5 congestion charge for driving into Central London was implemented.

20   At the annual Brit Awards Ms Dynamite won Best British Female Solo Artist and Best British Urban Act. Other winners included Robbie Williams (Best British Male Solo Artist), Coldplay (Best British Group and Album – *A Rush of Blood to the Head*), Liberty X (Best British Single – 'Just a Little'), Sugababes (Best British Dance Act), Will Young (Best British Breakthrough Act), Blue (Best British Pop Act), Eminem (Best International Male solo artist and International Album – *The Eminem Show*), Red Hot Chili Peppers (Best International Group), Pink (Best International Female solo artist), Nora Jones (Best International Breakthrough Act) and a special Outstanding Contribution award to Tom Jones.

23   At the annual Bafta Awards ceremony the two leading actor awards were won by Daniel Day-Lewis for *Gangs of New York* and Nicole Kidman for her performance as Virginia Woolf in *The Hours*. Other awards included Catherine Zeta-Jones for her supporting role in *Chicago*, and Christopher Walken for his supporting role in *Catch Me If You Can*. Roman Polanski won the David Lean Award for achievement in direction (*The Pianist*).

24   Michael Moore's satire on American politics, *Stupid White Men*, was voted Book of the Year at the British Book Awards.

25   *Pioneer 10*, the first man-made object to leave the solar system, lost contact with Mission Control more than 30 years after setting out on its epic journey. The probe was the first to photograph Mars and Jupiter at close quarters and to venture through the asteroid belt. A Nasa spokesman reported that it had simply run

out of fuel but will continue its journey through space unheralded and unrecorded, and is expected to reach the red star Aldebaran, 68 light years away, in two million years.

26 Derek Bond, 72, was finally released from a South African police cell where he had been held since being arrested on an international warrant issued by FBI agents in Houston, Texas, 21 days previously, while on a wine-tasting holiday in the province of KwaZulu-Natal. Mr Bond, a retired civil engineer from Bristol, was the victim of identity theft and the real fugitive was arrested in Las Vegas.

Stephen Hearn, 41, was cleared of a drink-driving offence at Warwick Crown Court after the judge accepted the defence that he was sleepwalking when he crashed his car under the influence last November.

27 Dr Rowan Williams was enthroned as the 104th Archbishop of Canterbury at Canterbury Cathedral.

Rachel Lomax, the Permanent Secretary at the Department of Transport, was announced as the successor to Mervyn King as Deputy Governor of the Bank of England when Mr King becomes Bank Governor in July.

28 Claire Tomalin's biography of Samuel Pepys beat her husband Michael Frayn's novel *Spies* to the Whitbread Book of the Year award.

March

5 The *Who Wants to Be a Millionaire?* cheating case began at Southwark Crown Court. Major Charles Ingram won the jackpot in September 2001 but stood accused of conspiring to dishonestly procure the cheque with his wife, Diana, and a lecturer, Tecwen Whittock. The prosecution claimed a series of coughs from Mr Whittock guided Ingram into making several correct decisions. Major Ingram's wife won £32,000 on *Millionaire* in April 2001 and her brother Adrian Pollock won the same amount the previous year.

7 Ulrika Jonsson, Ruby Wax, Fearne Cotton, Jo Brand, John Thomson, Paul Ross, Will Mellor and Kwame Kwei-Armah entered BBC's *Fame Academy* on behalf of Comic Relief. The ninth member, David Ginola, pulled out and was replaced by *Smack the Pony* star Doon Mackichan. The first person voted out by the inmates was Paul Ross who sang 'That's Life'.

10 Danny, a Pekinese (kennel name Yakee A Dangerous Liaison), became Supreme Champion at Crufts after winning his Toy class for the third year running. Danny was victorious over 120,000 others across the seven classes at the NEC, Birmingham.

12 Zoran Djindjic, the Prime Minister of Serbia, was assassinated in Belgrade. Dr Djindjic was shot twice and died instantly.

13 Elizabeth Smart, a 15-year-old Mormon girl abducted at knifepoint from her bedroom nine months ago, was found, seemingly unharmed, 12 miles from her home in Salt Lake City, Utah.

14 Actor Will Mellor won the viewers' vote over Ruby Wax to win the *Comic Relief Does Fame Academy* show. Red Nose Day raised more than £35m for Comic Relief, an increase of 50 per cent over the amount raised in 2001.

15 An outbreak of Severe Acute Respiratory Syndrome (SARS), thought to be spread via air travel, warranted the issue of an emergency travel advisory by the World Health Organisation. The deadly type of pneumonia has so far claimed at least nine lives.

18 Qusay Hussein, the second son of Saddam Hussein, was reported to have removed $1 billion (£620 million) from Iraq's Central Bank in Baghdad.

20 The invasion of Iraq by British and US troops began in the early hours of the morning in an attempt to overthrow the country's dictator Saddam Hussein and liberate the Iraqi people. Initial bombing targets were artillery posts but protection of oil fields was also carried out to try and prevent the wide-scale burning of wells that took place by Iraqi soldiers during the 1991 conflict.

21 Eight British Royal Marines and four US air crew were killed in a helicopter crash in Kuwait. The marines, from 3 Commando Brigade, died when the aircraft came down nine miles from the Iraqi border. The Sea Knight, used to move troops from ships or camps, apparently had problems with visibility due to smoke from burning oil wells.

22 ITN reporter Terry Lloyd was killed in Iraq when caught in crossfire while in a convoy of two Land Rovers on a road driving towards the southern port city of Basra. He was the brother of actor Kevin Lloyd, who died in May 1998.

23 Welsh actress Catherine Zeta-Jones won the Best Supporting Actress Oscar for the musical *Chicago*. The film was also named Best Picture, one of six awards it collected. Nicole Kidman won the Best Actress Oscar for *The Hours* and 29-year-old Adrien Brody, star of *The Pianist*, became the youngest man to win the Best Actor award. Best Documentary winner Michael Moore was cheered but mainly booed for criticising President Bush over the Iraq war in his acceptance speech.

26 A native wooden spear, reputedly used to kill Captain James Cook in February 1779, was sold at Lyon and Turnbull auction house in Edinburgh for £135,000 to an anonymous buyer from London. The spear, fashioned from Kavila wood, was recovered from an Hawaiian beach by Cook's navigation officer Captain Bligh, later of the famously mutinous *Bounty*.

April

1 Two illegal immigrants, who raised money for Osama bin Laden's al-Qa'ida terrorist network through credit-card fraud, were each jailed for 11 years at Leicester Crown Court. Algerians Baghdad Meziane and Brahim Benmerzouga became the first terrorists to be convicted in the battle against global terrorism that followed the 11 September attacks.

2 US Private Jessica Lynch was rescued from al-Nasiriyah general hospital by US troops in tanks and helicopters. Private Lynch was part of a 15-member US Army maintenance company convoy that was ambushed after taking a wrong turn near the city on 23 March. She sustained a head injury, a broken arm and leg, a pulmonary oedema and a bullet wound to her leg.

3 British forces inched their way into Basra while American troops took control of Saddam International Airport near Baghdad.

5   The outbreak of Severe Acute Respiratory Syndrome (SARS) around the world was identified as possibly having its source in Hong Kong, where almost a thousand people have so far contracted the virus resulting in 16 deaths on the island.

6   David Hempleman-Adams became the first person to walk solo and unaided to the geographic North Pole.

7   Three people who tried to defraud the television quiz show *Who Wants to Be a Millionaire?* out of its £1 million top prize were found guilty of deception at Southwark Crown Court. Major Charles Ingram and his wife, Diana, were sentenced to 18 months in prison, suspended for two years. Each was fined £15,000 and ordered to pay £10,000 costs. Their accomplice, Tecwen Whittock, whose 19 strategic coughs steered the Royal Engineers major to the jackpot win, was sentenced to 12 months in prison, also suspended for two years, fined £10,000 and ordered to pay £7,500 costs.

9   As the city of Baghdad fell under the control of coalition troops it was reported that the Iraqi information minister Mohammed Saeed al-Sahhaf had given himself up to coalition forces.

11   Catherine Zeta-Jones and Michael Douglas won a High Court case against *Hello!* magazine for publishing photographs of their wedding and reception at the Plaza Hotel, New York, in November 2002. The official pictures of the wedding were sold to *OK!* magazine for £1 million.

12   A 12-year-old Iraqi boy, Ali Ismaeel Abbas, became the symbol of the devastation of war in Iraq. Ali lost his father, pregnant mother, brother, aunt, three cousins and three more distant relatives in a missile strike during a firefight as US forces swept into Baghdad. Ali himself received 35 per cent burns and lost both his arms in the crossfire.

13   Dana Blake, 32, a New York bouncer, was stabbed to death after ordering two men to put out their cigarettes at Manhattan's trendy Guernica club. The incident occurred as a result of a ban on smoking in all workplaces, including bars and restaurants, by Mayor Bloomberg on 1 April.

15   Volkert van der Graaf, 33, an animal rights activist, was sentenced to 18 years in prison for the murder of the populist right-wing leader Pim Fortuyn, the first political assassination in the Netherlands since the 18th century.

17   The Queen distributed the Maundy money to 77 men and 77 women, each receiving 77 pence in specially minted Maundy coins, the only silver currency still made in Britain. The number of recipients, and the amount, is determined by the Queen's age; she celebrates her 77th birthday on 21 April.

23   A virus that kills the deadly strain of the food-poisoning bacterium *E. coli* was discovered at Evergreen State College in Washington State. The new virus, named CVI, is still undergoing tests.

24   Tariq Aziz, the former Deputy Prime Minister of Iraq, no. 43 – the eight of spades – in a pack of cards issued by the US to its military personnel and depicting the coalition's list of Iraq's most wanted fugitives, surrendered to coalition forces in Baghdad.

    Britain's oldest known bird, a 52-year-old black and white Manx shearwater, was found on Bardsey Island off the Lleyn peninsula, North Wales.

25   Winnie Madikizela-Mandela, the former wife of Nelson Mandela, was sentenced to five years' imprisonment for fraud and theft.

28   Daniella Westbrook, Catalina Guirado, Sian Lloyd, Toyah Willcox, Linda Barker, Phil Tufnell, John Fashanu, Chris Bisson, Wayne Sleep and Antony Worrall-Thompson began their two-week stint in a Queensland jungle for the ITV television series *I'm a Celebrity Get Me Out of Here!*

May

4   Huda Salih Mahdi Ammash, better known as Chemical Sally or Mrs Anthrax, one of Saddam Hussein's senior biological weapons scientists, was held in Baghdad. She was no. 53 on the coalition's most wanted list and depicted on the five of hearts in the deck of cards issued by the US to its military personnel. She is the only woman on the list and her detention brings to 19 the number in custody, of the 55 wanted.

6   Buckingham Palace confirmed that the Countess of Wessex is expecting a baby in December.

7   Rock musician Pete Townshend was placed on the Sex Offenders Register for five years after receiving a police caution for viewing a website containing child pornography which he had paid to download.

12   Phil Tufnell was crowned King of the Jungle in the ITV series *I'm a Celebrity Get Me Out of Here!*, following a closely run viewers' vote in which John Fashanu, the former Wimbledon footballer, emerged as runner-up and designer Linda Barker placed third.

    Clare Short resigned her Cabinet position of International Development Secretary and was replaced by Baroness Amos.

    Michael Morpurgo became the third Children's Laureate since the position was established in 1998. His two-year appointment follows those of writers Quentin Blake and Anne Fine.

13   Boris, a 15-month-old male badger weighing in at 15kg and measuring 2½ft long, caused havoc in the Greenhill area of Evesham, Worcestershire, when he attacked several passers-by and viciously savaged Michael Fitzgerald, 67, a retired BBC producer. Before being caught and put down, Boris went for two policemen who were forced to take refuge on the bonnet of their patrol car.

15   Car dealer Jason McAllister, 28, was sentenced to five months' imprisonment and banned for four years after being caught speeding while disqualified in his BMW M3 on the A90 between Aberdeen and Dundee. His top speed during his journey was 156.7mph, the fastest ever recorded by Scottish police.

    Antony Gormley, the creator of the *Angel of the North*, unveiled his latest sculpture at the Baltic Arts Centre in Gateshead. *Domain Field* is a room full of life-size depictions of the human form made out of stainless steel rods.

    The Gulbenkian Prize, at £100,000 Britain's largest arts award, was won by The National Centre for Citizenship and the Law. Bamber Gascoigne, the chairman of the judges, praised the Nottingham-based museum for its dedication and inventiveness.

19   Old Harrovian Pen Hadow, 41, became the first man to walk solo and unaided to the geographic North Pole from the Canadian side, on his own, without airdrops of food, equipment or fuel. The trek began on 17 March and took 64 days.

CURRENT AFFAIRS

20	Scotland's First Minister, Jack McConnell, unveiled his Cabinet with a promise to restore public confidence in devolution. Jim Wallace, the Lib Dem leader and Deputy First Minister, moved from Justice to Enterprise and Lifelong Learning. He was joined by two other Lib Dem Cabinet ministers, Nicol Stephen at Transport and Ross Finnie at Environment. The former Education Minister, Cathy Jamieson, became Justice Minister, responsible for overseeing the Labour youth crime initiative, which would penalise the parents of persistent young offenders.
21	David Blakey, a Home Office watchdog, condemned Nottinghamshire Police as the worst force in the country. In his report, Mr Blakey warned Steve Green, the Chief Constable, that the force could become the first to be taken over and run by Home Office appointees.
22	Sir David Attenborough was awarded the Michael Faraday Prize by the Royal Society in recognition of his 'unparalleled contribution' to the public communication of science in his series *The Life of Mammals*.
23	The 12 housemates taking part in *Big Brother* 4 were named as Ray Shah, Federico Martone, Nush Nowak, Scott Turner, Steph Smith, Tania Do-Nascimento, Cameron Stout, Anouska Golebiewski, Justine Seliman, Joanne 'Sissy' Rooney, Herjender 'Gos' Gosal, and Jon Tickle.
24	The Eurovision Song Contest was won by Sertab Erener representing Turkey. Her song 'Every Way That I Can' narrowly beat the Belgian entry and the Russian superstar duo, Tatu. The United Kingdom song 'Cry Baby', performed by Jemini, placed 26th and last, receiving no points at all.
25	At the Cannes Film Festival, the Palme d'Or for best film was won by *Elephant*, directed by Gus Van Sant.
30	Britain's biggest personal injury claims company, The Accident Group, made 2,500 of its staff redundant when The Amulet Group, the parent company, called in administrators.
31	Anouska Golebiewski became the first person evicted from the latest series of Channel 4's *Big Brother*.

June

2	The *Beagle 2* space probe began its journey to Mars aboard a Russian *Soyuz* rocket. The British machine, the size of a roulette wheel, will parachute from its mother ship on Christmas Day and once landed will play a tune by pop group Blur before opening up like a pocket watch, unfolding cameras and instruments to search for evidence of life.
3	Valerie Martin, 54, from New Orleans, won the Orange Prize for Fiction with her 200-page novel *Property*.
4	President George Bush, Mahmoud Abbas, the Palestinian Prime Minister, and Ariel Sharon, the Israeli leader, met at the King of Jordan's summer palace in Aqaba to give hope of an end to the half a century of relentless conflict in the Middle East.
6	Justine Seliman became the second person evicted from the *Big Brother* house.
8	Martin Hill, in his 10,000hp jet-propelled car *Fireforce 2*, covered a quarter of a mile in 7.8 seconds to break his own Scottish land speed record at Crail airfield in Fife.
	Poland voted to join the European Union following a referendum with 78.2 per cent in favour.
11	Trupti Patel, the mother accused of suffocating her three babies and disguising the killings as cot deaths, was cleared of all three counts of murder at Reading Crown Court.
	In a survey of 200,000 pet owners the most popular name for a dog was Ben, while the top feline name was Charlie.
12	Alan Milburn resigned his position of Health Secretary and was replaced by Dr John Reid. Other Cabinet changes included Lord Falconer of Thoroton being brought into the Cabinet in the new post of Secretary of State for Constitutional Affairs. The new department will incorporate the existing Scotland and Wales offices and take over most of the roles of the Lord Chancellor's Department, including the administration of the courts. Lord Irvine of Lairg is to retire as Lord Chancellor and Lord Falconer will be sworn in as replacement while the new department is developed. Helen Liddell, the Scottish Secretary, is also to leave the Cabinet as part of the reconstruction.
13	A High Court judge, Mr Justice Sumner, ruled that the standard childhood vaccinations, including MMR, were in the best interests of a child and ordered that two girls should undergo the programme despite the opposition of their mothers.
	In the Queen's Birthday Honours List there was a knighthood for actor Roger Moore for his tireless work for Unicef. Other award winners included actress Helen Mirren and Body Shop founder Anita Roddick, who both become Dames.
	Sissy Rooney became the third person evicted from the *Big Brother* house.
18	Lord Falconer of Thoroton was duly sworn in as Lord Chancellor. The ceremony was attended by senior Law Lords including Lord Woolf, the Lord Chief Justice, and Lord Phillips of Worth Matravers, Master of the Rolls.
19	Jason Joab Phillips, 24, better known as G-Man, the executive producer of garage music collective So Solid Crew, was jailed for four years after being found guilty of taking a loaded gun to a West End premiere.
20	The Royal Mint produced a gold £1,000 coin to mark Prince William's 21st birthday. The 21 Prince William Alderney coins, which have the highest face value of any coin minted in the United Kingdom, will be on sale at £14,500 apiece.
	Federico Martone and Jon Tickle became the fourth and fifth *Big Brother* evictees.
21	JK Rowling's fifth book in the Harry Potter series, *Harry Potter and the Order of the Phoenix*, went on sale.
22	Aaron Barschak, disguised as Osama bin Laden, gatecrashed Prince William's 21st birthday party at Windsor Castle, causing concern over the lack of security controls.
23	In a twist to the *Big Brother* experience British inmate Cameron Stout was transferred to the South African house and Gaetano Kagwa was flown over to enter the British house for a four-day exchange.
24	It was reported that six military policemen had been killed by an angry terrorist mob 100 miles north of Basra. The six Red Caps were named as Sgt Simon Hamilton-Jewell, Cpl Russell Aston, Cpl Paul Long, Cpl Simon Miller, L/Cpl Ben Hyde and L/Cpl Tom Keys.
25	The latest edition of the *Collins English Dictionary* went on sale with a host of controversial new entries including *bootylicious* – sexually attractive, especially with curvaceous buttocks; *booty calls* – a meeting arranged for the purpose of having sex; *bifter* – a cannabis cigarette; *bodypacker* – a person smuggling

drugs within their body; *mixologists* – people who work behind bars; *dad rock* – disparaging term for music that appeals to, and is often played by, more mature people; and *yummy mummy* – an attractive woman who has had children.

26   Chris Evans, the former television presenter, was branded a 'petulant prima donna' by Mr Justice Lightman. Evans' damages claim against Virgin Radio for non-payment of shares cash was thrown out.

27   Tania Do-Nascimento became the sixth member of the *Big Brother* house to be evicted.

28   Lisa Jeynes entered the *Big Brother* house as an unexpected new contestant.

July

1   Banking giant HSBC announced it was to axe 1,400 jobs over the next six months due to tax increases. Mervyn King took over from Eddie George as Governor of the Bank of England. Rachel Lomax became the new Deputy Governor.

2   Silvio Berlusconi, the Italian Prime Minister, caused a major diplomatic furore at the launch of his country's six-month EU presidency term. In reply to heckling by German MEP Martin Schulz he countered, 'Mr Schulz. I know there is a producer in Italy making a film on the Nazi concentration camps. I'll suggest you for the role of Kapo. You'd be perfect.' Kapos were petty criminals, sometimes Jewish, used by German death camp commandants to keep their fellow prisoners in line.

3   Film director Ken Loach and painter Bridget Riley were among the five winners of the Japanese Praemium Imperiale awards, worth £85,000 to each recipient, the first time two Britons have won one of the world's richest arts awards in the same year.
Lady Archer won a High Court gagging order against her former personal assistant, Jane Williams. Damages of £2,500 were awarded although Ms Williams is also liable for the six-figure legal costs. The action was taken after details of a face-lift operation were leaked to publicist Max Clifford.

5   Herjender 'Gos' Gosal left the *Big Brother* house, but only after a security scare delayed the evictions for 24 hours.

6   Dr Jeffrey John withdrew his acceptance of the post of Bishop of Reading amid pressure from the conservative element in the Anglican Church over his homosexuality.

8   Ladan and Laleh Bijani, Iranian twins born joined at the head in 1974, lost their lives during an operation to separate them.

9   Railtrack employees Alistair Cook, Sean Fugill, Keith Lea and Charles Pollard were charged with manslaughter at St Albans Magistrates' Court for their part in the Hatfield train crash three years ago in which four people died and more than 100 were injured. Similar charges were laid against Nicholas Jeffries and Anthony Walker, former employees of the maintenance contractor Balfour Beatty. Network Rail, the successor to Railtrack, and Balfour Beatty were also charged with manslaughter. Vernon Bullen, Kenneth Hedley, Keith Hughes, Stephen Huxley, Christopher Leah and the former chief executive of Railtrack Gerald Corbett (now chairman of Woolworths) were charged with lesser breaches of the Health and Safety at Work Act.

10   The Bank of England cut the interest rate by a quarter-point to 3.5 per cent, the lowest since January 1955.

11   Lisa Jeynes was evicted from the *Big Brother* house without making a nomination and an unexpected new contestant, in the guise of former inmate Jon Tickle, re-entered the house after winning a viewers' vote.

13   Twenty-five Iraqis representing a cross-section of the country's ethnically diverse population came together for the first meeting of the nation's new interim Governing Council.

18   Dr David Kelly, the former Iraq weapons inspector, was found dead in an Oxfordshire wood close to his home. The Ministry of Defence adviser was said to be under considerable stress after being named as a possible source for BBC claims that Alastair Campbell had 'sexed up' an intelligence dossier on Iraq to strengthen the case for war. Dr Kelly had an unauthorised lunch with Andrew Gilligan, the *Today* defence correspondent, and within days found himself appearing before a televised session of the Commons Foreign Affairs Select Committee. Dr Kelly is thought to have taken a packet of painkillers and cut his wrists while in a disturbed frame of mind.
Chinese pianist Lang Lang played Tchaikovsky's Piano Concerto No. 1 with the BBC Symphony Orchestra conducted by Leonard Slatkin to open the First Night of the Proms at the Royal Albert Hall. This year's theme is Greek Mythology.
Nush Nowak became the final evacuee from the *Big Brother* house before the final week commences.

19   Dr Christian Kermer carried out the world's first successful tongue transplant in the Vienna General Hospital.

21   Prisoner FF8282, Lord Archer of Weston-super-Mare, was released from Hollesley Bay Colony open prison after serving two years and two days of a four-year sentence for perjury.

22   Saddam Hussein's sons Uday and Qusay were killed by US troops after a six-hour gunbattle in the northern Iraqi city of Mosul.

25   Cameron Stout emerged victorious from the Channel 4 series of *Big Brother*. Runner-up was Ray Shah with Scott Turner and Steph Smith placing third and fourth.

30   A Eurostar train reached 208mph, on a stretch of track between Ashford and Dartford in Kent, to beat the UK speed record. The world record is 322mph by a French TGV in 1990.

31   Felix Baumgartner, a 34-year-old Austrian, became the first man to fly unassisted across the Channel. The bizarre Icarus 2 mission was completed when Felix jumped from a plane at 30,000ft above Dover and, using a 6ft carbon fibre wing strapped to his back, glided to earth at Cap Blanc Nez, six minutes and 22 seconds later. (By contrast, Louis Blériot first flew the Channel in 1909 in a fragile monoplane, taking 36 minutes to fly the 22 miles from Calais to Dover.)

August

1   The BBC Symphony Orchestra announced they are to abandon white tie and tails in favour of black suits and black open-necked shirts from the autumn. Women will continue to wear all-black outfits but they will be free to be more casual.

CURRENT AFFAIRS

6   Dr Cesare Galli of the Laboratory of Reproductive Technology in Cremona, Italy, announced his team had cloned a horse. DNA tests proved that the filly, Prometea, was genetically identical to her surrogate mother Comet Star, which means she is her mum's twin sister!

7   Amrozi bin Nurhasyim was sentenced to death by firing squad for his role in the Bali bombings that killed 202 people last October. The 40-year-old Javanese garage mechanic punched the air in delight after sentencing in the Denpasar court.
     Royal Navy chiefs announced a change to the motto of the Special Boat Service. 'Not By Strength, By Guile' is to become 'By Strength and Guile'. The motto will accompany a logo depicting a dagger facing upwards, with two blue lines through it portraying ocean waves. The logo contrasts with the downward winged dagger of the SAS. (The Special Boat Section was formed in 1940 and became the Special Boat Squadron after the Second World War and the Special Boat Service in the 1980s.)

8   Sanderson Wallpapers, for a century and a half the epitome of countrified British style, called in the receivers.

9   Sophie Pritchard and Lee Davey, contestants in last year's Big Brother series, were married at Marlow, Buckinghamshire.

10   Joni Rimm paid $50,000 for a 45-second snog from actress Sharon Stone. The money went towards Project Angel Foods – a Los Angeles-based charity providing free meals for people with HIV and Aids.
     Britain endured its hottest day on record, the thermometer reaching 38.1C (100.6F) in Gravesend, Kent.
     Ukrainian cosmonaut Yuri Malenchenko, 41, and 27-year-old Russian emigrée Ekaterina Dmitriev made history by getting married by proxy while the bride was at the Johnson Space Center in Houston and the commander of the International Space Station was orbiting at 17,500mph. Mr Malenchenko will return to Earth in October for the honeymoon.

11   Charles Taylor stood down as President of Liberia in the hope that the bloody civil war will be ended. His vice-president, Moses Blah, took over as Taylor left the country to begin his exile in Nigeria.

12   A Leeds University professor researching the relative muscle strengths of animals concluded that, ounce for ounce, the pheasant has the most powerful muscles of any creature relative to its size.

14   A power cut crippled the cities of New York, Detroit, Cleveland, Toronto and Ottawa, creating havoc as all transport systems were shut down and many people were trapped in lifts and subways.

16   Leruo Molotlegi was crowned as King of the Bafokeng people, one of the richest tribes in Africa.
     The world's richest shipwreck, thought to contain gold coins worth £112 million, was discovered at a depth of 1,700ft about 100 miles south-east of Savannah, Georgia. The steamer SS Republic sank in 1865 in a hurricane off the US coast of Georgia.

17   The European Space Agency announced it is to launch its first mission to the Moon next month. The unmanned Smart 1 probe will be propelled by an ion drive, similar to the concept used in science fiction series such as Star Trek. The launch will be effected from the European space port in French Guiana on an Ariane 5 rocket on 4 September.

18   Three masked intruders burgled the Buckinghamshire home of television personality Cilla Black and assaulted her 22-year-old son Jack. The thieves were estimated to have got away with £1 million in jewellery, cash and gold.

21   Ali Hasan al-Majid, better known as Chemical Ali, was arrested by coalition forces, four months after Saddam Hussein's most brutal general was believed to have been killed in a bombing raid. Ali was no. 5 and king of spades in the US 'wanted' list.
     Princess Alice, the Duchess of Gloucester, became the longest-living member of the Royal Family in history at 101 years and 239 days. Queen Elizabeth the Queen Mother held the previous record.

24   The Directory Enquiries number 192 passed into history as several six-digit numbers beginning 118 replaced it.

27   A Leonardo da Vinci painting, Madonna with the Yarnwinder, worth at least £25 million, was stolen from Drumlanrig Castle, one of the stately homes of the Duke of Buccleuch, by two men who posed as tourists before overpowering a woman guide.
     The 60th Venice Film Festival opened with the world premiere of Woody Allen's 'serious comedy' Anything Else.
     Mars made its closest pass to the Earth for 60,000 years. A mere 34,646,418 miles separated the planets.
     The world's biggest battery was plugged in to provide emergency power for Fairbanks, Alaska, in case of a blackout. The rechargeable battery is bigger than a football pitch at 2,000 square metres and weighs 1,300 tonnes.

28   In excess of 250,000 commuters were evacuated from the London Underground system after a power failure hit South London.

29   Alastair Campbell, the Prime Minister's closest political confidant, announced his retirement as director of communications and strategy.

30   Fashion designer Stella McCartney, daughter of former Beatle Paul McCartney, married publisher Alasdhair Willis at Mount Stuart House, the home of former racing driver Johnny Dumfries, the Marquis of Bute.

September

2   Radio 4 announcers Brian Perkins and Peter Donaldson announced they are to step down from their duties after more than 70 years of experience between them. Perkins will remain a freelance with the BBC while Donaldson, although quitting as chief announcer, will continue to read the news.

3   The Aquada, a two-wheel drive, 175hp vehicle, which uses unleaded petrol, was launched on the Thames. Made by Gibbs Technologies, the amphibious vehicle is designed to travel at 100mph on land and more than 30mph on water.

8   Leni Riefenstahl, the controversial German director of Triumph of the Will (1935), a propaganda film of the Nuremberg rallies, and the 1936 film Olympia featuring the Berlin Olympics, died aged 101.

10   Princess Stephanie of Monaco married Portuguese circus acrobat Adans Lopez Peres in Geneva, Switzerland.

11   Anna Lindh, the Swedish foreign minister, died after being stabbed in a Stockholm shopping centre yesterday.
     Former Spice Girl Mel C was rushed to hospital for a knee operation following a judo practice session with Miss World Azra Akin, the 21-year-old beauty queen from Turkey, for a Channel 4 television show, *The Games*.

13   Winds of up to 135mph battered South Korea. Typhoon Maemi devastated the port of Pusan, killing 87 people.

14   Sweden voted not to adopt the European single currency by 56 per cent to 42 per cent.

16   Hurricane Isabel devastated the east coast of America with winds of up to 105mph leaving a trail of destruction.

17   Francisco Costa, a 34-year-old Brazilian fashion designer, took over as design director for Calvin Klein to bring an end to Klein's 30-year reign as head of his fashion empire.
     Gossip columnist Nigel Dempster announced he is to step down as diary editor of the *Daily Mail* next month after 30 years.

22   Tate Britain acknowledged that two paintings by JMW Turner were not views of the city of Venice as previously thought, but were more likely to be views of Portsmouth. The painting *Festive Lagoon Scene, Venice* has been renamed *The Arrival of Louis-Philippe at Portsmouth*, and the painting *Procession of Boats with Distant Smoke, Venice* has been renamed *Disembarkation of Louis-Philippe at Portsmouth*.
     At the Emmy Awards in Los Angeles, the Best Dramatic Series award was won by *The West Wing*. Best Dramatic Actor was won by James Gandolfini and Best Dramatic Actress by Edie Falco, both awards for *The Sopranos*.

25   A black standard poodle called Shadow entered the history books by becoming the first dog to have its DNA deciphered.
     The controversial rapper 50 Cent won three Mobo (Music of Black Origin) awards at London's Albert Hall. Other winners included Justin Timberlake for Best R&B Act and Christina Aguilera for Best Video.

26   The BBC announced it is to reprise the pioneering science fiction series *Doctor Who* in 2005. The series will be written by Russell T Davies, creator of the Channel 4 *Queer as Folk* gay drama.

27   Mike Fuller, 44, currently Deputy Assistant Commissioner at Scotland Yard, was announced as the successor to Bob Ayling as Chief Constable of Kent. Mr Fuller will become the first black Chief Constable.

28   The Pope created 31 new cardinals in an apparent move to prepare the way for the election of his successor as his health deteriorates.

29   David Hempleman-Adams, the 46-year-old adventurer, became the first person to fly solo across the Atlantic in an open wicker-basket balloon. He landed at Hambleton, Lancashire, at 6pm, 83 hours, 14 minutes and 35 seconds after taking off from Sussex, New Brunswick, Canada.

October

2   South African writer JM Coetzee won the 2003 Nobel Prize for Literature, worth £900,000.

4   The Archbishop of Canterbury, Dr Rowan Williams, accompanied by Cardinal Cormac Murphy-O'Connor, the head of the Catholic Church in England and Wales, met the Pope in the Vatican.
     Alex Parks, 19, won the BBC1 *Fame Academy* series and with it a £1 million record deal and use of a London luxury flat.

6   Professor Sir Peter Mansfield, of the University of Nottingham, shared the Nobel Prize for Medicine with Paul Lauterbur, of the University of Illinois. Each receive £400,000. The award was granted for their pioneering work on magnetic resonance imaging (MRI) body scanners.
     Hilary Benn, son of veteran Labour left-winger Tony Benn, was promoted to the Cabinet as International Development Secretary. Benn succeeds Lady Amos, who becomes the Leader of the House of Lords.

7   Professor Anthony Leggett, 65, was awarded the 2003 Nobel Prize for Physics for his work on quantum physics. The British physicist shares the prize with the Russian scientists Alexei Abrikosov and Vitaly Ginzburg.
     The £4.5 billion merger of Granada and Carlton Television was waved through by the Government, effectively creating a single ITV company for the first time in its 48-year history.

8   Actor Arnold Schwarzenegger, the Republican candidate, became governor of California.

10   Shirin Ebadi, a former Iranian judge, became the first Muslim woman to win the Nobel Peace Prize. The human rights campaigner was a controversial choice as it was expected that the Pope would win the award in his 25th anniversary year.
     Lesley Douglas was appointed as the new Controller of Radio 2 as replacement for the outgoing James Moir.

11   Former Fide world chess champion Ruslan Ponomariov became the first player to be disqualified at a major event for allowing his mobile phone to ring during a game.

12   The Reverend Jamie Allen, star of the BBC2 series *A Country Parish*, resigned his parish due to pressure of the overwhelming response to his performance in the series. The tattooed former disc jockey was the vicar of three Wiltshire villages, Seend, Bulkington and Poulshot, but the sheer volume of requests on his time have 'irrevocably compromised' his ability to minister.

13   Alicia Roland, 12, became the voice of the Speaking Clock. Alicia won a competition to become the famous voice for a week and raise money for ChildLine. It is only the fifth time the voice of the Speaking Clock has changed.

14   DBC Pierre won the £50,000 Man Booker Prize with his debut novel, *Vernon God Little*. Pierre, whose real name is Peter Finley, made an extraordinary reception speech when he declared he could now pay off debts he ran up during a nine-year period as a cocaine addict and heavy gambler.
     A Georgian armchair became the world's most expensive chair when it was bought by an American collector for £386,400 at Sotheby's.

15   At least 10 people were killed and 34 badly injured when a Staten Island ferry crashed into a wooden pier

as it was docking in the New York harbour. The side of the *Andrew J Barberi* was torn away after high winds caused the collision.

16 Television presenter Evelyne Thomas, 39, was chosen as the next Marianne, the embodiment of France and equivalent of the British Britannia.

19 Kirk Jones became the first man to plunge over Niagara Falls without a protective device and live. Mr Jones, 40, slid down an embankment to the rocks below, stepped into the water and was swept over the 167ft drop.

The Pope beatified Mother Teresa of Calcutta in a special Mass in St Peter's Square. The service came six years after Mother Teresa's death, making it the fastest beatification in church history.

Magician David Blaine, who had been suspended over the River Thames for 44 days while taking on no solid foods, left his Perspex prison having successfully completed his publicity stunt.

20 Cheryl Tweedy, the 20-year-old pop singer with Girls Aloud, was ordered to undertake 120 hours of community service and pay £500 compensation to her victim, Sophie Amogbokpa. Tweedy was convicted of an assault which took place at The Drink nightclub in Guildford.

21 Michael Green, the chairman of the television group Carlton Communications, agreed to stand down as chairman designate of the proposed new ITV group to be formed by merging with Granada.

23 George Galloway, MP for Glasgow, was expelled from the Labour Party for his extreme criticism of the Iraq war made during a television interview in Abu Dhabi on 28 March.

24 Concorde ended its 34 years of passenger flight when three of the supersonic jets landed at Heathrow for the final time.

28 Sir Paul McCartney and his wife Heather Mills became parents of a daughter, Beatrice Milly, born at St John and St Elizabeth hospital in North London.

29 Iain Duncan Smith lost a confidence vote by 75 votes to 90 and was forced to resign as leader of the Conservative Party.

November

1 A pilot scheme to set up a national blood bank for dogs was successful after blood was taken from 20 former racing greyhounds. The uniqueness of greyhounds is that their blood type can be matched to all breeds.

2 The Worldwide Anglican Church found itself facing criticism following the consecration of Canon Gene Robinson as Bishop of New Hampshire, the first openly active homosexual bishop.

4 Gucci, the Italian designer goods group, announced the departure of its chief designer Tom Ford and its chief executive Domenico De Sole.

5 Michael Howard was announced as the new leader of the Conservative Party.

10 Michael Howard's Conservative Party Shadow Cabinet included Michael Ancram (Foreign Secretary and Deputy Leader), David Curry (Local and Devolved Government Affairs), David Davis (Home, Constitutional and Legal Affairs), Dr Liam Fox and Lord Saatchi (Party Chairmen), Oliver Letwin (Chancellor of the Exchequer), Theresa May (Environment and Transport), David Maclean (Chief Whip), Lord Strathclyde (Leader of the Opposition in the Lords), David Willetts (Head of Policy Co-Ordination) and Tim Yeo (Health and Education).

12 Dennis the Menace, the *Beano*'s world's wildest boy, appeared in *Heebie Jeebie Holiday* and *Monster Surprise*, two novels published today by DC Thomson.

14 James Murdoch, the 30-year-old son of chairman Rupert Murdoch, became chief executive of BSkyB.

Michael Howard capped his first week as leader of the Conservative Party by being named as Parliamentarian of the Year. The annual award was presented by *The Spectator* magazine for Mr Howard's mastery at the dispatch box.

16 The world bridge title was decided on the last card played after a two-week contest in Monte Carlo. The US beat Italy 304–303.

18 The latest riverside attraction was opened in London. The Shell Electric Storm harnesses wind power to drive a display of mist, music and light. Speakers, water jets and powerful lamps have been installed in trees along the south bank of the Thames near the London Eye. The whole effect is linked to a control panel that responds to wind, sunlight and pressure.

19 Phil Spector, the American music producer, was charged with shooting dead actress Lana Clarkson at his Californian home.

20 The British Consulate and the HSBC Bank in Istanbul were victims of suspected al-Qa'ida suicide bombers. A senior British diplomat was killed during the attack, as were at least two dozen Turks.

Hari Kunzru, winner of the Llewellyn Rhys Prize for his first book *The Impressionist*, turned down the £5,000 prize in protest at the immigration policy of the sponsoring newspaper, the *Mail on Sunday*.

Martha Lane Fox announced her retirement from her successful business venture Lastminute.com.

Pop star Michael Jackson was arrested and charged in Los Angeles with multiple counts of child molestation.

22 The world's first genetically engineered pet, a tropical zebra fish, will be on sale in American pet shops in the new year. Under normal light the fish will glow red and under ultraviolet light they will be fluorescent.

23 Eduard Shevardnadze, the last of Europe's ruling Communist strongmen, was forced to resign as President of Georgia after furious protesters reached the gates of his hill-top residence. The uprising, which began on 2 November, when voting for a new party was held, was led by Mikhail Saakashvili, leader of the opposition forces.

24 Aaron Barschak, the self-styled comedy terrorist who gatecrashed Prince William's 21st birthday party at Windsor Castle, was jailed for 28 days after admitting throwing paint over Jake Chapman, an artist nominated for the Turner Prize, at the Museum of Modern Art in Oxford.

26 The Earl and Countess of Wessex named their three-week-old daughter Louise Alice Elizabeth Mary Mountbatten-Windsor.

Concorde touched down for the very last time after a special flight from Heathrow to Filton airfield in Bristol, the site where the supersonic jet was made in 1979. The Duke of York was present to welcome the flight on behalf of the Bristol community.

The superyacht *Mirabella V* became the last to be launched from the Vosper Thornycroft yard in Southampton before the yard moves to Portsmouth. The *Mirabella*, which is powered by sail, will be the largest single-masted yacht in the world. The vital statistics are: length 247ft, beam 48ft, mast height 290ft, speed 16 to 20 knots, crew 12, sail area 30,042 sq ft, full load displacement 765 tonnes, maximum draught centre-board down 33ft, maximum draught centre-board up 13ft.

29   Akhmed Zakayev, the leader of the Chechen rebels, was granted political asylum in Britain.
30   New legislation was brought in to make it illegal to use hand-held mobile phones while driving. A fixed penalty of £30 will be payable although a maximum fine of £1,000 will be payable if the case goes to court. Scotland Yard appointed its first woman commander of the Special Branch. Janet Williams has joined Eliza Manningham-Buller, the head of MI5, in the front line of anti-terrorism.

December
1   On International Aids Day Nelson Mandela made an appeal to the world to help South Africa fight his country's epidemic.
6   Rosanna Davison, the daughter of singer Chris de Burgh, won the Miss World title in Beijing, China.
7   The Tate Gallery's jury maintained its recent reputation for controversy by awarding the £20,000 Turner Prize to Grayson Perry, a transvestite who scratches explicit phallic imagery and disturbing scenes of child abuse on to the surfaces of ceramic vases.
      President Robert Mugabe announced that Zimbabwe had withdrawn its membership of the Commonwealth.
9   Alistair Darling, the Transport Secretary, opened Britain's first private motorway toll road on a 27-mile stretch of the M6 north of Birmingham.
10   Angela Cannings, who spent 20 months in prison after being convicted of smothering her two baby sons, was freed by the Court of Appeal who held that her conviction should be quashed as unsafe.
13   Former Iraqi dictator Saddam Hussein was captured by American forces in an 8ft deep hole under the floor of a mud hut on the outskirts of his home town, Tikrit. In the hut, a suitcase with $750,000 in cash was found. The first words Saddam uttered were 'Don't shoot, I am Saddam Hussein, the president of the Republic of Iraq.' Saddam was the ace of spades in the US most-wanted pack of cards.
17   Ian Huntley was jailed for life for the murder last August of the Soham schoolgirls Holly Wells and Jessica Chapman.
19   In an historic move, Colonel Muammar Gaddafi, the Libyan dictator, announced he was to dismantle all his country's chemical, biological and nuclear weapons programmes in order to end its diplomatic isolation and secure the lifting of US sanctions.
20   Michelle McManus, 23, the 15-stone Glaswegian songster, won the ITV talent show *Pop Idol*.
      The surprise Christmas Number One pop record was 'Mad World' by Gary Jules.
22   One of the Queen's corgis, Pharos, was savaged and killed by Princess Anne's English bull terrier, Dotty. The Princess was fined £500 and ordered to keep the same dog on a lead in public places after it attacked two children last year.
23   Lenny Bruce, the American 'beat' comedian, was granted a posthumous pardon by the New York governor almost 40 years after his conviction on obscenity charges. (Bruce was sentenced to four months in the workhouse in 1964 for a routine that blended profanity with musings on politics, religion, sex and race. He died 18 months later of a morphine overdose while free on bail.)
26   More than 25,000 people were killed at dawn when an earthquake virtually destroyed the ancient Iranian city of Bam.
      The largest ocean-going liner afloat, the 150,000-ton Cunard liner *Queen Mary 2*, arrived in her home port of Southampton on her maiden voyage.
27   The most popular names for children in 2003 were Jack, for baby boys, and Chloe, for baby girls.

Obituaries 2003

January
1   Cyril Shaps, actor, born 13 October 1923
2   Peter Harris, footballer, born 19 December 1925
      Alastair Wood, athlete, born 13 January 1933
      Sydney Omarr, astrologer, born 5 August 1926
3   Monique Wittig, writer, born 13 July 1935
      José Maria Gironella, novelist, born 31 December 1917
      Sid Gillman, American football coach, born 26 October 1911
4   Conrad Hall, cinematographer, born in Papeete, Tahiti, 21 June 1926
      Yfrah Neaman, violinist, born 13 February 1923
5   Jean Kerr, writer, born 10 July 1923
      Lord (Roy) Jenkins of Hillhead, politician, born 11 November 1920
7   David Harries, composer and pianist, born 24 March 1933
8   Ron Goodwin, popular music composer, born 17 February 1925
9   Peter Tinniswood, comedy writer, born 21 December 1936
      BC Sanyal, artist, born 22 April 1901
      Penny Valentine, journalist, born 13 February 1943
10   Pat McCarthy, draughts player, born 31 December 1943
11   Sir Anthony Havelock-Allan, film producer, born 28 February 1904

	Mickey Finn, percussionist with T. Rex, born 3 June 1947
	Maurice Pialat, film director, born 31 August 1925
	Margaret Birkinshaw, writer, born 3 August 1907
	William Russo, jazz composer and bandleader, born 25 June 1928
12	Paul Pender, boxer, born 20 June 1930
	Maurice Gibb, musician, born 22 December 1949
	General Leopoldo Galtieri, President of Argentina 1981–2, born 15 July 1926
	Terence Gorman, economist, born 17 June 1923
13	Elisabeth Croft, actress, born 22 September 1907
14	Monica Furlong, author and campaigner for the ordination of women, born 17 January 1930
	Suma Lamonte, variety artiste, born 9 November 1927
	Bob Williams, journalist and broadcaster, born 11 April 1934
16	Jeannette Campbell, swimmer, born 8 March 1916
17	Alan Edwards, actor and drama teacher, born 17 January 1925
	Richard Crenna, actor, born 30 November 1926
18	Gavin Lyall, thriller writer and journalist, born 9 May 1932
	Harivansh Rai Bachchan, writer, born 27 November 1907
	Audrey Laski, novelist and teacher, born 12 March 1931
19	Françoise Giroud, journalist and politician, born 21 September 1916
20	Tony O'Malley, painter, born 25 September 1913
	Bill Werbeniuk, snooker player, born 14 January 1947
	David Battley, actor, born 5 November 1935
21	Lionel Hamilton-Renwick, equestrian artist, born 15 August 1917
22	Bill Maudlin, cartoonist, born 29 October 1921
	Peter Russell, poet, born 16 September 1921
	Mary Chubb, archaeologist and writer, born 22 March 1903
24	Giovanni Agnelli, chairman of Fiat, 1966–96, born 12 March 1921
25	Lady (Diana) Menuhin, ballerina, born 12 November 1912
26	Viscount (George) Younger of Leckie, politician, born 22 September 1931
	Valeriy Brumel, high jumper, born April 14th 1942
	John Browning, pianist, born May 23rd 1933
28	Commander Edward Young, wartime submarine captain, author and publisher (designed the Penguin logo), born 17 November 1913
	Arthur Jackson, artist and architect, born 1 August 1911
29	Edna Iles, pianist, born 18 May 1905
	Natalia Dudinskaya, ballerina, born 21 August 1912
	Peter Falconer, architect, born 7 March 1916
	Anthony Eisley, actor, born 19 January 1925
	Leslie Fiedler, critic and novelist, born 8 March 1917
30	Mary Ellis, actress, born 15 June 1897
31	Louis Fitzgibbon, author, born 6 January 1925
	Julie Alexander, model and actress, born 9 May 1938

February

1	Mongo Santamaria, Cuban percussionist and composer, born 7 April 1922
	Richard Nelson, radio operator on the *Enola Gay*, born 26 April 1927
	Norma Skemp, founder of Listening Books, born 9 June 1915
	Peter Deakin, rugby administrator, born 18 October 1953
2	Lou Harrison, composer, born 14 May 1917
3	William Kelley, scriptwriter and novelist, born in 1929
4	Marvin Rosenberg, author and Shakespeare scholar, born 6 November 1912
	Robert Arnold, actor, born 26 June 1931
5	Peter Steiner, cellist, born 19 August 1928
	Georgina Boosey, managing editor of *Vogue* 1978–93, born 3 January 1936
	Alec Stokes, scientist, born 27 June 1919
	Manfred von Brauchitsch, racing driver, born 15 August 1905
6	Sir Peter Saunders, theatre manager and producer, born 23 November 1911
	Will Hastie, musician (The Laird Himself), born 25 December 1926
	Eric Ashby, naturalist, born 19 January 1918
	Malcolm Roberts, singer, born 31 March 1944
8	Augusto Monterroso, author, born 21 December 1921
	Dorothy Clewes, children's writer, born 6 July 1907
9	Ted Perry, founder of Hyperion Records, born 15 May 1931
	Vera Ralston, actress, born 12 July 1923
	Ruby Braff, jazz cornettist and trumpeter, born 16 March 1927
	Ron Ziegler, press secretary to US President Nixon, born 12 May 1939
11	Arndt Bause, German songwriter, born 30 November 1936
12	Kemmons Wilson, founder of Holiday Inn, born 5 January 1913
13	Kid Gavilan (Gerardo González), boxer (inventer of the bolo punch), born 6 January 1926
	John Trench, mystery writer, born 17 October 1920
14	Nick Duncombe, rugby player, born 21 January 1982
	Dolly the Scottish black-faced sheep, first animal to be cloned, born 5 July 1996

15	Alexander Bennett, ballet dancer and teacher, born 27 July 1929
17	Aleksandar Tisma, writer, born 16 January 1924
18	Isser Harel, head of Mossad 1952–63, born in 1912
	Jack Brodsky, film producer, born in 1932
	Johnny Paycheck, country music performer, born 31 May 1938
19	Tanya Moiseiwitsch, stage and theatre designer, born 3 December 1914
	Nadine, Countess of Shrewsbury, founder of Opera at Ingestre, born 24 January 1913
20	Maurice Blanchot, writer and critic, born 27 September 1907
21	Harry Matthews, boxer, born 9 December 1922
	Barry Bucknell, television DIY expert, born 26 January 1912
22	Daniel Taradash, film writer, born 29 January 1913
23	Marcel Prawy, opera producer, born 29 December 1911
24	Christopher Hill, historian, born 6 February 1912
	John Shaw, baritone, born 12 October 1924
	Alberto Sordi, actor, born 15 June 1919
26	Richard Worcester, pilot and aviation writer, born 11 March 1917
27	Charles Knott, cricketer and sports promoter, born 26 November 1914
28	Chris Brasher, athlete and founder of the London Marathon, born 21 August 1928
	Roger Needham, computer scientist, born 9 February 1935

March

1	Ian Connell, racing driver and engineer, born 15 October 1913
2	Malcolm Williamson, Master of the Queen's Music, born 21 November 1931
	William Blezard, pianist and composer, born 10 March 1921
	Hank Ballard, singer and songwriter, born 18 November 1936
	Goffredo Petrassi, composer, born 16 July 1904
3	Horst Buchholz, actor, born 14 December 1933
	Peter Smithson, architect, born 18 September 1923
4	Fedora Barbieri, mezzo-soprano, born 4 June 1920
	Sébastien Japrisot (Jean-Baptiste Rossi), born 4 July 1931
5	Sir Hardy Amies, fashion designer, born 17 July 1909
	Lloyd Shirley, television producer and director, born 28 December 1931
6	Ludek Pachman, chess grandmaster, born 11 May 1924
	Sam Scorer, architect, born 2 March 1923
	Linton Garner, jazz pianist, born 25 March 1915
8	Adam Faith, singer, actor and businessman, born 23 June 1940
	Marina Ladynina, actress, born 24 June 1908
	Karen Morley, actress, born 12 December 1909
	Professor Lim Kok Ann, chess player and bacteriologist, born 27 January 1920
10	Barry Sheene, motorcycle racer, born 11 September 1950
	Lord (Thomas) Boardman, politician and businessman, born 12 January 1919
11	Kevin Laffan, scriptwriter, born 24 May 1922
12	Zoran Djindjic, Prime Minister of the Republic of Serbia since January 2001, born 1 August 1952
	Andrei Kivilev, cyclist, born 21 September 1973
	Howard Fast, author, born 11 November 1914
13	Ian Samwell, songwriter (notably Cliff Richard's 'Move It') and record producer, born 19 January 1937
15	Dame Thora Hird, actress, born 28 May 1911
16	Major Ronald Ferguson, former polo manager to the Duke of Edinburgh and the Prince of Wales, born 10 October 1931
17	Lewis Bernard Cannell, rugby player and radiologist, born 10 June 1926
	Frank Rowley, civil engineer, born 4 May 1940
18	Alan Keith, broadcaster, born 19 October 1908
	Adam Osborne, manufacturer of the first portable computer, born 6 March 1939
	Karl Kling, racing driver, born 16 September 1910
20	John Cotton, poet and headmaster, born 7 March 1925
22	Terry Lloyd, ITN reporter, born 21 November 1952
23	Fritz Spiegl, musician, writer and broadcaster, born 27 January 1926
24	John Cavanagh, couturier, born 28 September 1914
	Philip Yordan, film writer and producer, born 1 April 1914
25	Michael Kidron, economist and author, born 20 September 1930
26	Daniel Patrick Moynihan, American politician, born 16 March 1927
27	Edwin Carr, composer, born 10 August 1926
	Leigh Jackson, scriptwriter, born 5 July 1950
28	Bill Jolly, biographer and science writer, born 2 December 1922
29	Kerim Kerimov, rocket scientist, born 17 November 1917
	Owen Wood, illustrator, born 22 October 1929
30	Valentin Pavlov, former Prime Minister of the Soviet Union, born 26 September 1937
	Nick Enright, playwright, born 22 December 1950

April

1	Leslie Cheung, pop singer and actor, born 12 September 1956
	John East, author and actor, born 10 September 1932

CURRENT AFFAIRS

Richard Caddel, poet and editor, born 13 July 1949
2   Edwin Starr, singer, born 21 January 1942
     Michael Wayne, film producer, born 23 November 1934
3   Homer Banks, singer and songwriter, born 2 August 1941
4   Anthony Caruso, actor, born 7 April 1916
     Jean-Yves Escoffier, cinematographer, born 12 July 1950
     Michael Kelly, journalist, born 17 March 1957
7   Elsie Duncan-Jones, literary critic, born 2 July 1908
     Cecile De Brunhoff, pianist and teacher, born 16 October 1903
8   Maki Ishii, composer, born 28 May 1936
     Pamela Bowden, contralto, born 17 April 1925
9   Vera Zorina, dancer, born 2 January 1917
     Jorge Oteiza, sculptor, born 21 October 1908
10   Eva Boyd (Little Eva), singer, born 29 June 1943
12   Jim Mathieson, sculptor, born 21 June 1931
14   John Kent, cartoonist and illustrator, born 21 June 1937
     Professor Robert Stanton, botanist, born 24 February 1923
15   Regina Fong (Reginald Bundy), female impersonator, born in 1946
     Maurice Rapf, screenwriter, born 19 May 1914
16   Jasper Derby Smith, traditional singer, born 25 June 1921
17   Sir Paul Getty, philanthropist, born 7 September 1932
     John Latsis, shipowner, born 14 September 1910
     Dr Robert Atkins, nutritionist and author, born 17 October 1930
     Earl King, singer, songwriter, guitarist and producer, born 7 February 1934
19   Cholly Atkins, dancer and choreographer, born 13 September 1913
     Conrad Leonard, musician, born 24 October 1898
     Max Bozzoni, ballet dancer and choreographer, born 30 May 1917
20   Teddy Edwards, jazz tenor saxophonist, born 26 April 1924
     Nina Simone, singer and pianist, born 21 February 1933
     Johnny Douglas, composer and musical arranger, born 19 June 1920
     Bertram Ross, dancer and singer, born 13 November 1920
     Walter Fuller, jazz trumpeter, born 15 February 1910
22   Andrea King, actress, born 1 February 1919
     Felice Bryant, songwriter, born 7 August 1925
     Louis Shenkin, bridge player and administrator, born 17 January 1917
24   Vernon Pugh, rugby union administrator and barrister, born 5 July 1945
25   Lynn Chadwick, sculptor, born 24 November 1914
     Ted Joans, poet and artist, born 4 July 1928
27   Piet Roozenburg, draughts player, born 24 October 1924
29   Sue Sally Hale, polo player, born 23 August 1937
     John Hurst, archaeologist, born 15 August 1927
30   Wim Van Est, cyclist, born 25 March 1923

May
2   Peter Jackson, illustrator and authority on London, born 4 March 1922
     Mohammed Dib, Algerian writer, born 21 July 1920
3   Suzy Parker, model and actress, born 28 October 1933
     Patrick Gwynne, architect, born 24 March 1913
4   Sister Mary Barbara (Barbara Vernon Bailey), original artist of the Bunnykins china range, born 28 June
     1910
     Michaela Denis, writer and wildlife film-maker, born 28 August 1914
     Sesto Bruscantini, opera singer, born 10 December 1919
5   Walter Sisulu, South African politician, born 18 May 1912
     Roger Pilkington, author, born 17 January 1915
6   Jocelyn Herbert, stage designer, born 22 February 1917
7   Alan Green, artist, born 22 December 1932
8   Desmond O'Neill, photographer, born 14 February 1923
9   Sir George Grenfell-Baines, architect and town planner, born 30 April 1908
     David Hofman, actor, writer and television announcer, born 26 September 1908
     John Cogger, president of the National Union of Rail, Maritime and Transport Workers, born 8 April 1941
     Bernard Spear, actor, born 11 September 1919
10   Milan Vukcevich, chemist and chess problem-setter, born 11 March 1937
     Leonard Michaels, writer, born 2 January 1933
11   Ernie Toshack, Australian cricketer, born 8 December 1914
     Geoffrey Buckley, pianist, born 3 April 1930
12   Jeremy Sandford, writer of *Cathy Come Home*, born 5 December 1930
     Noel Redding, rock guitarist, born 25 December 1945
13   Theo Aronson, writer, born 13 November 1929
14   Dame Wendy Hiller, actress, born 15 August 1912
     Robert Stack, actor and US national skeet-shooting champion, born 13 January 1919
     Otto Edelmann, bass-baritone, born 5 February 1917
     Max Nasatyr, architect, born 12 November 1934

15	June Carter Cash, country singer, born 23 June 1929
	Rick Van Steenbergen, Belgian cyclist, born 9 October 1924
16	Mark McCormack, sports promoter and writer, born 6 November 1930
18	Evelyn Rose, cookery writer, born 2 December 1925
	Albert Sendrey, composer and arranger, born 26 December 1911
19	Ivo Zidek, operatic tenor, born 4 June 1926
20	Joe 'Guitar' Hughes, blues guitarist and vocalist, born 29 September 1937
21	Alejandro de Tomaso, car racer and manufacturer, born 10 July 1928
23	Rachel Kempson, actress, born 28 May 1910
	Jean Yanne, actor, director and writer, born 18 July 1933
25	Sloan Wilson, writer, born 8 May 1920
	Gerald Hawkins, astronomer, born 20 April 1928
26	Kathleen Winsor, novelist, born 16 October 1919
27	Luciano Berio, composer, born 24 October 1925
	Geoffrey Bawa, architect, born 23 July 1919
28	Oleg Makarov, cosmonaut, born 6 January 1933
	Janet Collins, prima ballerina and choreographer, born 7 March 1917
	Hans Schwarz, artist, born 29 December 1922
	James Plunkett, writer, born 21 May 1920
	Martha Scott, actress, born 22 September 1912
29	Basil Langton, actor and theatre manager, born J9 anuary 1912
	Trevor Ford, footballer, born 1 October 1923
30	Mickie Most, record producer, born 20 June 1938

June

1	Sir Peter Yarranton, rugby player and administrator, born 30 September 1924
	Christina Fanto, charity fundraiser, born 1 January 1944
2	Dick Cusack, writer and actor, born 29 August 1925
	Frank Lynton Giles, artist, born 21 October 1910
	Makoto Kozuru, Japanese baseball player, born 17 December 1922
3	Peter Bromley, racing commentator, born 30 April 1929
6	Dave Rowberry, musician with The Animals, born 4 July 1940
7	Olav Ulland, ski jumper, born 23 November 1910
	Belle Chrystall, actress, born 25 April 1910
8	Leighton Rees, darts player, born 17 January 1940
9	Art Cooper, editor of *GQ* (Gentleman's Quarterly), born 15 October 1937
10	Donald Regan, Chief of Staff in the Reagan White House 1985–7, and Sec of US Treasury 1981–5, born 21 December 1918
11	Dennis Wicks, bass singer, born 6 October 1928
12	Gregory Peck, actor, born 5 April 1916
13	Henry Robin Ian Russell, 14th Duke of Bedford, born 21 January 1940
14	Alec Dakin, cryptographer, born 3 April 1912
	Jimmy Knepper, jazz trombonist, born 22 November 1927
15	Hume Cronyn, actor, born 18 July 1911
	Rollie McKenna (born Rosalie Thorne), photographer, born 15 November 1918
	Philip Stone, actor, born 14 April 1924
	Evgeni Kolobov, conductor, born 19 January 1946
	Enrico Baj, artist, born 31 October 1924
16	Peter Redgrove, poet, born 2 January 1932
	Professor GH von Wright, philosopher, born 14 June 1916
18	Larry Doby, baseball player and manager, born 13 December 1923
19	Laura Sadler (Staff Nurse Sandy Harper), *Holby City* actress, born 25 December 1980
	Peanuts Hucko, jazz clarinettist, born 7 April 1918
	Neville Conder, architect, born 30 April 1922
21	Leon Uris, novelist, born 3 August 1924
	Burt Rhodes, musical director and composer, born 17 April 1923
23	Doug Ring, Australian cricketer, born 14 October 1918
24	Lady Ayer (Dee Wells), journalist and author, born 19 March 1925
	Richard Pough, ornithologist, author and conservationist, born 19 April 1904
25	Terence Parkes, the cartoonist Larry, born 19 November 1927
	Lester Maddox, Governor of Georgia 1966–70, born 30 September 1915
26	Sir Denis Thatcher, businessman, born 10 May 1915
	Marc-Vivien Foe, footballer, born 1 May 1975
	Strom Thurmond, Senator for South Carolina 1954–2003, born 5 December 1902
27	Ken Smith, poet, born 4 December 1938
	David Newman, scriptwriter, born 4 February 1937
	Sir John Stokes, politician, born 23 July 1917
28	Russell Endean, South African cricketer, born 31 May 1924
	George Baxt, novelist and screenwriter, born 11 June 1923
29	Katharine Hepburn, actress, born 12 May 1907
	Cliff Harrison, rugby union player, born 10 May 1911
30	Buddy Hackett, comedian and actor, born 31 August 1924

CURRENT AFFAIRS

July
1 Khieu Ponnary, first wife of Pol Pot, teacher and president of the Democratic Kampuchea Women's Association, born in 1920
   George Roper, comedian, born 15 May 1934
   Herbie Mann, flautist, born 16 April 1930
2 Barbara Weeks (born Sue Kingsley), actress, born 4 July 1913
   Briggs Cunningham. racing driver and yachtsman, born 19 January 1907
   N!xau, Bushman and film star, born c. 1944
3 Harold Creighton, former owner and editor of *The Spectator*, born 11 September 1927
4 Barry White, singer, born 12 September 1944
6 Buddy Ebsen, actor, born 2 April 1908
   Kathleen Raine, poet, born 14 June 1908
   Charles Kindleberger II, economist, born 10 October 1910
9 Polly Bide, television producer, born 25 August 1949
10 Winston Graham, author, born 30 June 1910
   Alvin Alcorn, jazz trumpeter, born 7 September 1912
11 The 6th Marquess of Salisbury, landowner and former MP, born 24 October 1916
   Kenneth Whyld, chess historian, born 6 March 1926
   Mickey Deans, singer and pianist (5th husband of Judy Garland), born in 1934
12 Benny Carter, jazz saxophonist, trumpeter, bandleader and composer, born 8 August 1907
15 Alexander Walker, film critic and biographer, born 22 March 1930
   Elisabeth Welch, singer, born 27 February 1904
16 Celia Cruz, singer, born 21 October 1924
   Carol Shields, writer, born 2 June 1935
17 Rosalyn Tureck, pianist, born 14 December 1914
   Kaouding Cissokho, kora player, born 2 November 1964
18 Dr David Kelly, scientist and UN arms inspector, born 17 May 1944
19 Pierre Graber, President of Switzerland 1975, born 6 December 1908
20 Nicolas Freeling, writer, born 3 March 1927
   Carol Matthau, actress, born 11 September 1925
22 Norman Lewis, writer, born 28 June 1908
   Serge Silberman, film producer, born 1 May 1917
   Noel Picarda-Kemp, satirist and broadcaster, born 14 December 1937
   Uday Saddam Hussein, son of Saddam Hussein, born 18 July 1964
   Qusay Saddam Hussein, son of Saddam Hussein, born 17 May 1966
24 Kurt Pahlen, composer and conductor, born 26 May 1907
25 John Schlesinger, film, television, theatre and opera director, born 16 February 1926
26 Sir William Dargie, artist, born 4 June 1912
27 Bob Hope, comedian and actor, born 29 May 1903
28 Valerie, Lady Goulding, Irish senator, born 12 September 1918
   Aaron Bell, jazz double bass player, born 24 April 1922
   Professor Michael Brawne, architect, born 5 May 1925
30 Sam Phillips, founder of Sun Records, born 5 January 1923
   Steve Hislop, motorcycle racer, born 11 January 1962

August
1 Marie Trintignant, actress, born 21 January 1962
2 Don Estelle, actor and singer, born 22 May 1933
   Alonzo Pettie, rodeo champion, born 18 June 1910
3 Monica Poole, wood engraver, born 20 May 1921
   Raymond Inskeep, archaeologist, born 18 November 1926
4 True Boardman, child actor, born 25 October 1909
6 Grover Mitchell, trombonist and band leader, born 17 March 1930
   Adrian Seligman, master mariner and writer, born 26 November 1909
7 Frank Templeton (FT) Prince, poet, born in Kimberley, South Africa, 13 September 1912
8 Sir Edward Pickering, journalist, born 4 May 1912
   Jack Noreiga, West Indian cricketer, born 15 April 1936
   Antonis Samarakis, Greek novelist, born 16 August 1919
9 Gregory Hines, dancer and actor, born 14 February 1946
   Trevor Smith, footballer, born 13 April 1936
10 Constance Chapman, actress, born 29 March 1912
   John Banks, bookmaker and racehorse owner, born 19 August 1934
11 Herb Brooks, ice hockey coach, born 5 August 1937
13 Ed Townsend, songwriter, born 16 April 1929
14 Helmut Rahn, German footballer, born 16 August 1929
   Lothar Emmerich, German footballer, born 29 November 1941
   James Hale, publisher and literary agent, born 8 January 1946
16 Idi Amin, President of Uganda 1971–9, born c.1924
18 Tony Jackson, bass player and vocalist with The Searchers, born 16 July 1940
19 Robin Hodgkin, mountaineer, born 12 February 1916
20 Andrew Ray, actor, born 31 May 1939
21 Betty Vacani (Betty Hankinson, born Elizabeth Burch), choreographer, born 2 July 1908

22	Tony Rudd, car designer and engineer, born 8 March 1923
24	Sir Wilfred Thesiger, explorer, born 3 June 1910
	Kent Walton, television commentator, born in Cairo, 22 August 1917
	Zena Walker, actress, born 7 March 1934
29	Ayatollah Mohammed Baqer Al-Hakim, Shi'ite Muslim cleric, born in 1939
	Patrick Procktor, artist, born 12 March 1936
30	Charles Bronson, actor, born 3 November 1921
31	Anne, Duchess of Westminster, owner of Arkle, born 13 April 1915

September

1	Rand Brooks, actor and businessman, born 21 September 1918
	Sir Terry Frost, abstract painter, born 13 October 1915
2	Peter West, television presenter, born 12 August 1920
4	Susan Chilcott, soprano, born 8 July 1963
	Tibor Varga, violinist, born 4 July 1921
5	CH (Charles Hubert) Sisson, poet, born 22 April 1914
7	Anton Barichievich, Canadian strongman, born in Zagreb, Yugoslavia, 10 October 1925
8	Hélène Bertha Amelie (Leni) Riefenstahl, film director, born 22 August 1902
	Gulubhai Ramchand, Indian cricketer, born 26 July 1927
9	Edward Teller, scientist (father of the hydrogen bomb), born in Budapest, 15 January 1908
11	John Ritter, actor, born 17 September 1948
	Anna Lindh, Swedish Foreign Secretary, born 19 June 1957
12	Johnny Cash, singer, born 26 February 1932
15	Jack Brymer, clarinettist, born 27 January 1915
18	Richard Charles 'Bob' Mitchell, politician, born 22 August 1927
19	Slim Dusty (born David Gordon Kirkpatrick), country singer, born 13 June 1927
20	Lord Williams of Mostyn, Lord Privy Seal and Leader of the House of Lords, born 5 February 1941
	Gordon Mitchell (born Charles Pendleton), bodybuilder and actor, 29 July 1923
22	Tony Shryane, producer of *The Archers* 1951–79, born 20 January 1919
	Norman Hoffman, pioneer of freefall skydiving, born 24 February 1924
	Ernie Fossey, boxing promoter, born 2 September 1930
24	Lyle Bettger, actor, born 13 February 1915
25	George Plimpton, journalist and writer, born 18 March 1927
	Alastair Borthwick, broadcaster and writer, born 17 February 1913
26	Robert Palmer, pop musician, born 19 January 1949
27	Donald O'Connor, dancer and actor, born 28 August 1925
	Harold Fielding, theatrical impresario, born in 1917
28	Althea Gibson, tennis player, born 25 August 1927
	Elia Kazan (born Elia Kazanjoglou), stage and film director, born 7 September 1909
	Edward Bishop, author and writer of obituaries, born 24 May 1924
30	Johnny Hawkesworth, television producer, born 7 December 1920

October

1	George Perry-Smith, cook (proprietor of the Hole in the Wall restaurant 1952–72), born 10 October 1922
	Chubby Jackson, double-bass player, born 25 October 1918
2	Ian Davies, flamenco guitarist, born 9 May 1954
	Denis Moore, cricketer, born 26 September 1910
3	William Steig, cartoonist and children's author (*Shrek!*), born 14 November 1907
4	Dame Mary Donaldson, first woman Lord Mayor of London, born 29 August 1921
5	Denis Quilley, actor, born 26 December 1927
6	Joe Baker, footballer, born 17 July 1940
7	Eleanor Lambert, founder of the International Best-Dressed List, born 10 August 1903
	John Herring, athlete, born 10 April 1935
10	Eugene Istomin, pianist, born 26 November 1925
	Julia Trevelyan Oman (wife of writer Sir Roy Strong), theatre and opera designer, born 11 July 1930
12	Bill Shoemaker, jockey, born 19 August 1931
	Ram Gopal, dancer, born 20 November 1917
	Vivien Alcock, author, born 23 September 1924
13	Bertram Brockhouse, physicist and Nobel Laureate, born 15 July 1918
14	Milos Sadlo, cellist, born 13 April 1912
15	Anne Ziegler, singer, born 22 June 1910
16	Laszlo Papp, boxer, born 25 March 1926
17	Janice Rule, actress, born 15 August 1931
	Clare Venables, theatre director, born 17 March 1943
18	David Lodge, actor, born 19 August 1921
20	Jack Elam, actor, born 13 November 1918
23	Madame Chiang Kai-Shek, widow of the Chinese Nationalist leader, born 5 March 1897
	Tony Capstick, folk singer and comedian, born 27 July 1944
26	Elem Klimov, film director, born 9 July 1933
27	Elisabeth Lambert Ortiz, writer, born 17 June 1915
29	Franco Corelli, tenor, born 8 April 1921
	Hal Clement, science fiction writer, born 30 May 1922

CURRENT AFFAIRS

30   Steve O'Rourke, former manager of rock band Pink Floyd, born 1 October 1940
        Franco Bonisolli, tenor, born 25 April 1937
31   Professor Richard Neustadt (husband of Lady Williams of Crosby), political scholar, born 26 June 1919

November
2   Christabel Bielenberg, writer, born 18 June 1909
        Cecilia Green, dancer and model, born 29 August 1931
4   Charles Causley, poet, born 24 August 1917
        Lotte Berk (Lieselotte Heymansohn), dancer and fitness guru, born 17 January 1913
        Margaret Green, painter, born 7 March 1925
5   Dorothy Fay Ritter (wife of Tex Ritter), actress, born 4 April 1915
        Bobby Hatfield, singer with the Righteous Brothers, born 10 August 1940
7   Michael John, singer and musician, born 16 November 1927
8   Bob Grant, actor (Jack Harper of *On the Buses* fame), born 21 April 1932
        Gordon Onslow Ford, artist, born 26 December 1912
9   Art Carney, actor and comedy stooge, born 4 November 1918
        Mario Merz, artist, born 1 January 1925
        Stephen Benton, inventor of the rainbow hologram, born 1 December 1941
10   Canaan Banana, former President of Zimbabwe, born 5 March 1936
11   Lord Walker of Doncaster, Labour politician, born 12 July 1927
        Kathryn Sergava, dancer, born 30 July 1909
12   Tony Thompson, drummer with pop group Chic, born 15 November 1954
13   Joanna Carrington, artist, born 6 November 1931
14   Gene Anthony Ray, dancer and actor, born 24 May 1962
17   Don Gibson, country singer and songwriter, born 3 April 1928
18   Michael Kamen, composer, born 15 April 1948
19   Gillian Barge, actress, born 27 May 1940
20   David Dacko, former President of the Central African Republic, born 24 March 1930
        Robert Addie, actor, born 10 February 1960
23   Patricia Burke, actress, born 23 March 1917
        Paul Grant, Mr Universe 1973, born 26 June 1943
24   Teddy Wilburn, country musician, born 30 November 1931
25   Jacques Francois, actor, born 16 May 1920
26   Charles Chenevix Trench, writer, born 29 June 1914
        Gordon Reid, actor, born 8 June 1939
27   Will Quadflieg, actor, born 15 September 1914
        Dai Francis, singer with the Black and White Minstrels, born in Swansea in 1930
28   Antonia Forest, children's author, born May 26th 1915
30   Gertrude Ederle, first woman to swim the English Channel, born 23 October 1906

December
3   David Hemmings, actor, born 18 November 1941
        Ellen Drew, actress, born 23 November 1914
5   Antony Rowe, submariner, Olympic rower, and book printer, born 4 August 1924
6   Jose Maria Jimenez, racing cyclist, born 6 February 1971
        Hans Hotter, bass-baritone, born 19 January 1909
8   Sir Stephen Tumim, lawyer and prison reformer, born 15 August 1930
9   Ruben Gonzalez, pianist, born in April 1919
10   Lt-General Sir John Watts, former director of the SAS, born 27 August 1930
12   Heydar Aliyev, President of Azerbaijan, born 10 May 1923
        Alfred Kitchin, concert pianist, born 23 January 1910
14   Jeanne Crain, actress, born 25 May 1925
15   Johnny Cunningham, fiddler, born 27 August 1957
16   Glynn Boyd Harte, artist and illustrator, born 1 May 1948
18   Susan Travers, first female member of the French Foreign Legion, born 23 September 1909
19   Hope Lange, actress, born 28 November 1933
21   Hans Koller, saxophonist, born 12 February 1921
26   Hugh Bean, violinist, born 22 September 1929
27   Sir Alan Bates, actor, born 17 February 1934
29   Bob Monkhouse, comedian and writer, born 1 June 1928
        Dinsdale Landen, actor, born 4 September 1932
        Richard Davis, cricketer, born 18 March 1966
30   Patricia Roc (Felicia Miriam Ursula Herold), actress, born 7 June 1915
        Anita Mui, singer and actress, born 10 October 1963

Daily Record 2004

January

1   Kurt Nilsen, 24, winner of the Norwegian version of the ITV series *Pop Idol*, was crowned as World Idol in a programme where the winners from around the world competed for the ultimate accolade. Kelly Clarkson of the USA was second and Britain's Will Young was fifth.

5   Ray Davies, the lead singer of the Kinks, was shot in the leg by a mugger in New Orleans.

6   Tony Blair welcomed Ken Livingstone back into the Labour Party so he could be its official candidate for the London mayoral election in June.

9   The BBC banned the daytime *Kilroy* show with immediate effect following remarks made in presenter Robert Kilroy-Silk's newspaper column which could be construed as attacking Arabs.

10 British explorer Fiona Thornewill, 37, completed the fastest solo trek to the South Pole. The 700-mile journey from Hercules Inlet on the edge of the Antarctic took 41½ days.

13 Harold Shipman, Britain's most prolific serial killer, was found hanging from the bars of his cell at Wakefield Prison.

15 The Ghan, a freight train almost a mile long, left Adelaide on its 1,865 mile journey across Australia to Darwin via Alice Springs. The train was named after the Afghan camel handlers who explored Australia in the 19th century.
    Scarlett Johansson won the Best Actress award at the Bafta Awards in London for her role in *Lost in Translation*. Bill Murray won Best Actor for the same film. The Best Film award went to *Lord of the Rings: The Return of the King*.

19 The £10,000 TS Eliot Prize for poetry was won by Don Paterson for his collection called *Landing Light*. He became the first person to win the award twice, having previously won in 1997 with his collection *God's Gift to Women*.

22 The Chinese New Year began. 2004 will be the year of the monkey, following the year of the ram.
    After 847 miles, 15 arrests and almost five months in jail, the so-called naked rambler finally completed his trek from Land's End to John O'Groats. Steve Gough, 44, set out from Cornwall on 16 June 2003.

26 The BBC comedy series *The Office* won two Golden Globe awards. Ricky Gervais won Best Actor in a Comedy and the show also won Best Comedy Series.

27 Former athlete David Bedford was successful in his submission that his trademark droopy moustache and red socks were used without his permission by The Number, operators of the 118 118 directory enquiry service. Ofcom, the media regulator, ruled that it was clearly and unequivocally a caricature of the former 10,000 metres champion.

28 Gavyn Davies, Chairman of Governors of the BBC, resigned in the wake of Lord Hutton's report on David Kelly's suicide. The report cleared the Government of bad behaviour and malpractice but was scathing in its criticism of the BBC.
    Charlotte Atkinson, 32, made history by becoming the first woman to command an operational British warship. The Royal Navy lieutenant took charge of *Brecon*, a 200ft, 750-ton Hunt class mine counter-measures vessel.

February

5   John Lydon, aka Johnny Rotten of The Sex Pistols, walked out of the Australian jungle in the latest ITV series of *I'm a Celebrity Get Me Out of Here!*

6   German Chancellor Gerhard Schröder was forced to resign as leader of his Social Democratic party amid strong criticism of his government's reform programme.

9   Kerry McFadden returned victorious from the Australian jungle as the winner of the ITV series *I'm a Celebrity Get Me Out of Here!*
    Pop singer Diana Ross was ordered to spend two days in jail after admitting a charge of drink-driving dating back to 30 December 2002.
    At the annual Grammy Awards, Record of the Year was awarded to Coldplay for 'Clocks'.

10 In an internet poll instigated by London mayor Ken Livingstone, Mary Seacole, a Jamaican nurse working during the Crimean War, was voted the Greatest Black Briton of all time.

12 Dame Catherine Cookson's 17-year reign as the author most borrowed in public libraries was brought to an end by Jacqueline Wilson. Public Lending Right announced that Wilson clocked up more than two million loans in 2003.
    A team of South Korean scientists created 30 cloned embryos using tissue and eggs donated by women. The scientific breakthrough is expected to revolutionise medicine.

21 In a landmark legal case in Austria, the nation's Appeal Court ruled that Christian Hainz should be reimbursed 499,729 euros (£336,709) by the operator of two casinos where he claimed that he lost up to 2.5 million euros over the last three years.

22 At the annual Laurence Olivier Awards the Best Actor award was won by Matthew Kelly for his portrayal of Lennie in *Of Mice and Men*. The Best New Musical award was won by *Jerry Springer – The Opera*.

24 Sir Peter Burt was appointed chairman of ITV and will take up his post on 15 March.

25 Christopher Finney became the youngest recipient of the George Cross. The 19-year-old trooper received his honour for risking his life to save a colleague during a 'friendly fire' attack in Iraq.

26 Former Cabinet minister Clare Short was accused by Prime Minister Tony Blair of endangering national security after standing by her allegations that British intelligence agents spied on Kofi Annan, the United Nations Secretary-General, before the Iraq war.

CURRENT AFFAIRS

March

1   Peter Maxwell Davies became Master of the Queen's Music following the death of Malcolm Williamson last March.

2   The Government announced plans to drop the word 'Crown' from the Crown Prosecution Service. The new name will be the Public Prosecution Service. Her Majesty's Prison Service was recently renamed the National Offender Management Service.
    Alistair Cooke announced his retirement from broadcasting his *Letter from America*, at the age of 95. Since his debut in 1946 he has presented 2,869 *Letters*.

7   A whippet called Deedee (kennel name Cobyco Call the Tune) was named Best in Show at Crufts, at the NEC, Birmingham.

11 A series of simultaneous bomb explosions tore through four packed commuter trains in Madrid, killing 201 people. Al-Qa'ida admitted responsibility for the atrocity.

17 Chancellor of the Exchequer Gordon Brown's Budget for 2004/5 included marginal changes to the tax bands. The starting rate of 10 per cent was extended from £0–£2,020, the basic rate of 22 per cent from £2,021–£31,400, and the higher rate of 40 per cent over £31,400. Personal Allowances increased by £130 to £4,745 for a single person. The other main feature was the Government promise to refurbish or rebuild with 'world-class technology' every secondary modern school by 2015.

19 Coca-Cola recalled every bottle of their new brand of water, Dasani, after admitting it had originally come from a mains tap in Sidcup, Kent, and had become contaminated with illegally high levels of bromate, a cancer-causing chemical.

20 The BBC announced that actor Christopher Eccleston will become the latest Doctor when the series *Doctor Who* returns to the screen.
    Student Rosie Reid admitted selling her virginity to a 44-year-old man for £8,400 via an internet auction.

22 Sheikh Ahmed Yassin, the spiritual leader of Hamas, the militant Islamic group, was killed in a dawn missile raid by Israeli helicopters outside his local mosque in Gaza City.

25 The world's most prestigious prize for mathematics, equivalent to the Nobel Prize, was awarded jointly to Sir Michael Atiyah, the former president of the Royal Society, and Professor Isadore Singer. The £475,000 Abel Prize was awarded to the eminent mathematicians for their pioneering work in aiding physicists to understand the fundamental structure of matter through their 'Atiyah–Singer index theorem'.

27 In a poll commissioned by the BBC, *Only Fools and Horses*, Britain's longest-running comedy, was voted the nation's favourite sitcom.

28 Smoking was banned in all pubs and other places of work in Ireland from midnight.

April

1   Beverley Hughes resigned as immigration minister because she had given a 'misleading impression – albeit unwittingly' that she had not known that British diplomats had expressed concern about forged and bogus visa applications from Bulgaria and Romania. She was replaced by Des Browne, the former minister of state responsible for work.

2   Michael Grade, the former chief executive of Channel 4, was named as the new Chairman of the BBC.

3   Guadalupe Lopez, mother of film star Jennifer Lopez, won $2.4 million from a slot machine in an Atlantic City casino.

5   Thames Trains was fined £2 million for its part in the Paddington rail disaster of 1999 in which 31 people died.

6   President Paksas of Lithuania became the first European leader to be impeached when parliament removed him from office over his relationship with a businessman linked with the Russian mafia. The impeachment comes a week after the Baltic state joined Nato and less than a month before its accession to the European Union.

7   Timothy the tortoise, former ship's mascot during the Crimean War, died at the home of the Earl of Devon, aged 160.

18 At the annual Bafta Awards, Best Actor was won by Bill Nighy for *State of Play*, Best Actress by Julie Walters for *The Wife of Bath*, and Best Comedy Performance by Ricky Gervais for *The Office Christmas Special*.

23 The world's tallest man was discovered to be living in Podoliantsi in the Ukraine. Leonid Stadnyk stands 8ft 4ins tall.

30 US military police were condemned for their inhumane treatment of Iraqi prisoners at the Abu Ghraib prison in Baghdad.

May

1   The Czech Republic, Estonia, Hungary, Latvia, Lithuania, Poland, Slovakia, Slovenia, Cyprus and Malta joined the European Union to increase its membership from 15 to 25 nations.

3   Violinist Nicola Benedetti, 16, won the BBC's *Young Musician of the Year* competition.

6   John Scarlett, the chairman of the Joint Intelligence Committee, was announced by the Government as the next chief of MI6 and is to take up the post in July on the retirement of Sir Richard Dearlove.
    A mystery buyer paid a world record $104.1m for Pablo Picasso's *Boy with a Pipe*.

7   A small landmark in radio history was reached when listeners to *The Archers* heard a door open with a slow creak, and then a muffled cry. Brian Aldridge had just discovered his gamekeeper, Greg Turner, lying on the floor of a hut with a bullet in his brain. It was the first suicide in the radio drama's 53-year history.

10 Akhmad Kadyrov, President of the republic of Chechnya, was among several fatalities when a bomb exploded at a Victory Day parade in a stadium in the capital, Grozny. Islamic militants were thought to be the perpetrators.

11 Britain's richest arts prize, the £100,000 Gulbenkian Museum of the Year Award, was won by the Scottish National Gallery of Modern Art.

12 Radio 4 was named Station of the Year for the second year running and won six other Sony Radio Academy Awards.

13 Sonia Gandhi, the 57-year-old Italian-born widow of the assassinated Indian Prime Minister Rajiv Gandhi, became the new Indian Prime Minister after the Congress party won 145 seats in the election.

14 Piers Morgan was sacked as the editor of the *Daily Mirror* and its board made an unreserved apology for publishing fake pictures of British troops torturing Iraqi prisoners.
Mary Donaldson, 32, an estate agent from Tasmania, married Denmark's Crown Prince Frederik and was thus the first Australian to become a European queen.

17 Izzedin Salim, the leader of Iraq's Governing Council, was killed by a suicide car bomber in Baghdad. His death is the second murder of a council member following the death of Aquila al-Hashimi, one of three women members, last September.

23 Five people were killed when part of the roof of a new Air France terminal at Charles de Gaulle airport, Paris, collapsed.

26 The Sudanese civil war which has been ongoing since the country's independence in 1956 was halted and a peace deal agreed.

27 Abu Hamza, the Muslim cleric, was arrested in London on an American extradition warrant listing 11 terrorist charges.
A new bridge was opened at Gatwick airport enabling passengers to board their aircraft via a live taxiway instead of making the journey by bus. The 650ft enclosed glass bridge is the longest and highest at any airport in the world and will allow planes to taxi beneath its span. The bridge, designed by the British architects Wilkinson Eyre, weighs 2,400 tonnes and will be fully operational by next spring.

June

8 Andrea Levy won the £30,000 Orange Prize for her fourth novel, *Small Island*, detailing the circumstances of Britain's first wave of immigrants from Jamaica.

11 Labour lost more than 450 councillors across England and Wales. The party's 26 per cent share of the vote in the local elections put it in third place behind the Tories on 38 per cent and the Lib Dems on 29 per cent.
Former West Ham and England football star Trevor Brooking was awarded a knighthood in the Queen's Birthday Honours.

14 Spaniard Francisco Arce Montes, 54, was sentenced to 30 years' imprisonment in Rennes, France, for the rape and murder of 13-year-old Caroline Dickinson.
Joyti De-Laurey, 35, a Goldman Sachs secretary who stole £4.5 million from her employers, was jailed for seven years at Southwark Crown Court.
Conservative Party leader Michael Howard restructured his Shadow Cabinet. Andrew Lansley and Tim Collins became Health and Education spokesmen respectively. Theresa May was moved from Transport and Environment and given a new post of Shadow Secretary for the Family, a position with no corresponding Cabinet minister for her to shadow. Tim Yeo became spokesman for Transport and the Environment.
Former Labour MP Robert Kilroy-Silk became a Euro MP representing the United Kingdom Independence Party (UKIP). The party quadrupled its MEPs to 12 and announced its intention to contest Westminster seats next year.

26 The Czech Prime Minister, Vladimir Spidla, resigned following a dismal showing in the European Parliament elections by his Social Democratic Party.

28 Sovereignty was handed over to Iraq two days before the agreed deadline, thereby ending the 15-month occupation. The new government is led by Iyad Allawi, the Prime Minister, while the new President is Sheikh Ghazi Yawer.

July

5 Senator John Kerry, the Democratic presidential candidate, chose Senator John Edwards as his vice-presidential running mate.

6 The Queen gave a speech in praise of Diana, Princess of Wales, at the official opening of her memorial fountain in Hyde Park.

7 Karen Parlour, the former wife of the Arsenal and England footballer Ray Parlour, won a High Court claim for a third of his future income. The landmark judgement took into account the severe reduction in earnings after a footballer's playing days.

9 Jennifer Donnelly, a little-known American author, won the Carnegie Medal for children's literature for *A Gathering Light*, a book inspired by the murder of an unmarried pregnant 19-year-old in rural upstate New York in the early 1900s.

16 Martha Stewart, the American domestic style guru, was sentenced in a Manhattan court house to five months in prison for insider trading. Stewart was also sentenced to five months' house arrest for conspiracy and obstruction of justice.

19 Former *Blue Peter* presenter Peter Duncan became Britain's ninth Chief Scout since the tradition began under Robert Baden-Powell in 1921.

29 Actors Ewan McGregor, 33, and Charley Boorman, 37, arrived in New York after completing a motorbike journey around the world. The 20,000-mile journey started in London three months ago.

August

1 The Archbishop of York, Dr David Hope, announced he will retire at the end of February 2005 to become vicar of St Margaret's in Ilkley, Yorkshire.

2 Three years later than planned and vastly over budget, the new Scottish Parliament building in Edinburgh became a working office.
John Scarlett was appointed as the new head of MI6.

6 Nadia Almada emerged the winner of the Channel 4 television series *Big Brother* 5.

10 Goh Chok Tong resigned as Prime Minister of Singapore and was replaced by Lee Hsien Loong, the son of Singapore's founding father and first Prime Minister Lee Kuan Yew.

CURRENT AFFAIRS

| 12 | Former Cabinet minister Peter Mandelson was appointed Brussels commissioner in charge of trade. |

12   Former Cabinet minister Peter Mandelson was appointed Brussels commissioner in charge of trade.

14   At least 50 people were feared dead in Florida as Hurricane Charley devastated the American state.

16   Flash floods in the Cornish village of Boscastle created havoc with more than 50 cars being swept into the sea, while 60 people needed airlifting to safety from cars and trees.

22   Armed robbers held up the Munch Museum in Oslo and stole two of the Norwegian master's most famous paintings, *Madonna* and *The Scream*. A better-known version of *The Scream* was stolen from the Norwegian National Gallery in February 1994 on the opening day of the Winter Olympics in Lillehammer. A third version of the masterpiece is held in private hands.

25   Police in Cape Town arrested Sir Mark Thatcher, son of former Prime Minister Margaret Thatcher, on suspicion of involvement in a plot to overthrow the government of Equatorial Guinea.

31   Westlife grabbed their place in pop history by heading the first official digital music top 10. The Irish band's 1999 single 'Flying Without Wings' beat Blazin' Squad, Maroon 5 and Shapeshifters to lead the inaugural UK Download Chart. The new chart is based on a compilation of figures from Napster, Apple iStore, OD2 and other legal download sites.

September

1   Up to 40 Islamic terrorists, believed to be Chechen extremists, took over a school in Beslan, North Ossetia, close to the border with Chechnya. More than 1,200 children were taken hostage in the siege.

3   The Beslan siege ended in a bloodbath when Russian security forces, backed by local people carrying assorted weapons, stormed the school after terrorists opened fire while others blew themselves up. The death toll may be as high as 600.

4   President Bill Clinton entered hospital to have a quadruple bypass operation after complaining of chest pains.
Alan Milbanke, 32, became the first person in Britain to be charged with causing death by dangerous driving while talking on a mobile phone. Milbanke was jailed for three years at Newcastle Crown Court.
Andrew Smith resigned his Cabinet position as Work and Pensions Secretary.

7   129 MSPs sat in the newly opened Scottish Parliament building in Edinburgh.
Franz Ferdinand, a four-piece rock band from Glasgow, won the £20,000 Mercury Music Prize.

8   Alan Johnson, the higher education minister, was promoted to the Cabinet to replace Andrew Smith as Work and Pensions Secretary. Alan Milburn, who quit the Cabinet last year, returns as Chancellor of the Duchy of Lancaster, a non-departmental post that will give him a wide-ranging campaigning role as policy supremo for the next election.
Michael Howard increased his Shadow Cabinet to 17 by promoting David Cameron to Head of Policy Co-ordination, John Redwood to Deregulation Spokesman and Nicholas Soames to Defence Spokesman.

15   Pro-hunting demonstrators descended on Westminster, storming the Commons chamber and causing chaotic scenes inside and outside Parliament. The demonstrators included Luke Tomlinson, a friend of Prince William and Prince Harry, and Otis Ferry, son of rock singer Bryan Ferry. Despite the disruption, the Government succeeded in pushing the Hunting Bill through all its stages in one sitting and it was sent to the Lords.

20   Terrorists beheaded an American hostage in Iraq and threatened to murder two others unless their demands were met. Eugene Armstrong, a construction contractor, was kidnapped in Baghdad four days ago and his decapitation was shown via video to a shocked world.
A Virgin Pendolino tilting train set a non-stop record for the journey between London and Manchester. The 184 miles were covered in 1 hour 54 minutes, almost a quarter of an hour faster than the previous best achieved 12 years ago.

21   A second US hostage, Jack Hensley, suffered the same fate as Eugene Armstrong while the third hostage, Briton Kenneth Bigley, made an emotional plea to British Prime Minister Tony Blair to intercede if possible.
Cat Stevens, who changed his name to Yusuf Islam after becoming a Muslim, was mysteriously refused entry to the United States and his Washington-bound flight was rerouted to Bangor in Maine. The former pop idol was then interrogated by the FBI and flown back to the UK.

23   The *Dandy*, the world's longest-running comic, introduced new characters including Dreadlock Holmes and his Afro-Caribbean family, and Jak, a modern-day Dennis the Menace.

October

6   The British Army announced that a Scottish super-regiment made up of five battalions is to be created from Scotland's six infantry regiments. The Royal Scots and the King's Own Scottish Borderers are to form a single battalion while the remaining four are the Black Watch, the Argyll and Sutherland Highlanders, the Royal Highland Fusiliers and the Highlanders.

7   Elfriede Jelinek, the 57-year-old Austrian feminist writer, was awarded the Nobel Prize for Literature.

8   It was confirmed that Kenneth Bigley, the 62-year-old British engineer held hostage by terrorists in Iraq since 16 September, was beheaded in the same way as the two American hostages who were murdered last month.
Wangari Maathai, a Kenyan environmentalist and human rights campaigner, was awarded the Nobel Peace Prize, becoming the first African woman to win the prestigious award.

13   A huge seam of gold deposits was discovered in the Curraghinalt mine in the Sperrin Mountains, near Gortin, Co. Tyrone.

18   The fixtures and fittings from Damien Hirst's failed restaurant Pharmacy sold for £11.1 million at Sotheby's in London. *Fragile Truth*, an 8ft high stainless steel sectionalised medicine cabinet, sold for £1,237,600.

19   The £50,000 Man Booker Prize was won by Alan Hollinghurst for *The Line of Beauty*, a homosexually explicit book about an ambitious Tory MP during the Thatcher years. The chairman of the judging panel at the Royal Horticultural Halls in Westminster, London, was former Cabinet minister Chris Smith.
Former DJ Mike Read's musical *Oscar Wilde* broke the record for the shortest run in British musical history when it opened at the Shaw Theatre in Euston and closed after one day.

22   American actor Nathan Lane made his debut in the West End production of *The Producers*, after Oscar-winning actor Richard Dreyfuss mysteriously pulled out of the London run of the record-breaking Broadway show before its opening.

27   Former Labour MP and television presenter Robert Kilroy-Silk quit the UK Independence Party following his public condemnation of Roger Knapman, the party's leader.

28   In a unique collaboration between the Dana Centre at the Science Museum in London and the Liberty Science Center in New Jersey, a 140-strong audience watched the British public's first televised brain surgery operation, beamed live to West London from an American operating table. Dr Richard Hodosh removed a two-inch brain tumour from a 71-year-old American man.

29   Dame Helen Mirren was named as Naturist of the Year by the British Naturism organisation.

November

2   Theo van Gogh, 47, a Dutch film-maker, was shot and stabbed to death by a pro-Islamic terrorist while cycling through the heart of Amsterdam. The murder is thought to be linked to his latest film, *Submission*, which highlights the repression of women in some Islamic cultures.

3   President George W Bush won a second term of office after John Kerry, the Democratic challenger, conceded defeat in a close but decisive battle for the presidency. Dick Cheney also gained a second term as Vice-President.

4   Three soldiers from the Black Watch regiment, recently seconded to Iraq, were killed during a suicide bomb attack.

6   At least seven people were killed and up to 150 injured when a high-speed passenger train derailed after striking a vehicle at a level crossing at Ufton Nervet, near the village of Theale, Berkshire. The 5.35 Paddington to Plymouth collided with the car soon after 6pm in what is thought to have been a suicide attempt by the car driver, who was one of the dead.

11   Palestinian leader Yasser Arafat died and was replaced by Mahmoud Abbas for the interim.

13   Boris Johnson, MP for Henley and editor of *The Spectator*, was relieved of his duties as shadow arts minister and Conservative Party vice-chairman amid allegations about his private life.

15   Colin Powell stepped down as American Secretary of State after four years in office.

16   Margaret Hassan, a senior aid agency official taken hostage in Iraq in October, was reported to have been shot in the head and killed by her captives.
     Jim Speechley, 67, the former Conservative leader of Lincolnshire County Council, who was imprisoned for 18 months in March, had the dubious distinction of becoming the first person to have his appeal hearing filmed by television cameras.

23   A protest by 200,000 anti-government demonstrators outside the presidential palace in Kiev, lent support to Viktor Yushchenko, the recently defeated pro-Western Ukrainian presidential candidate, who lost amid allegations of voting fraud and an attempt to poison him.

29   Home Secretary David Blunkett called for an independent inquiry into accusations that he fast-tracked a visa application for the nanny of his former lover, Kimberly Quinn.

December

5   Miss Peru, Maria Garcia, won the Miss World title in Sanya, China.
     Shaun Wallace, a 44-year-old barrister, became the first black winner of the BBC quiz *Mastermind*.

6   Comedian Joe Pasquale won the latest series of the ITV programme *I'm a Celebrity Get Me Out of Here!*
     Gayathri Kumar, 13, won the BBC's *Hard Spell* quiz show to gain the title of best young speller in Britain.
     The Turner Prize was won by Jeremy Deller, a 38-year-old who admits he can neither draw or paint. His submitted work included *The History of the World 1997–2004*, a wall painting of words and phrases, a wall of photographs of strange memorials he has erected around the country, and a bench he installed near the home of the late Brian Epstein.

8   The Ukrainian parliament voted 402–21 for a deal whereby a presidential run-off will take place on 26 December following the 'Orange Revolution' over rigged election results. Under the compromise, the president will be able to veto parliament's choice of prime minister, foreign minister and defence minister but will have no voice in other appointments.

11   *EastEnders* actress Jill Halfpenny and her professional partner Darren Bennet won the BBC's *Strictly Come Dancing* series with a faultless final display, scoring full marks from all four judges.
     Steve Brookstein won the ITV series *The X Factor*, beating a cappella singing group G4 in the final.
     A sheep who strayed on to a Swindon highway was shot dead by police for causing an obstruction to traffic.

15   David Blunkett resigned as Home Secretary after an inquiry found that his office had been involved in fast-tracking a visa application for the nanny of his former lover. Charles Clarke, the Education Secretary, was promoted to Home Secretary and Ruth Kelly, the Cabinet Office minister, took over at Education.

16   Geoff Hoon, the Defence Secretary, announced a major reorganisation of the British Army. Five English regiments will disband: the Queen's Lancashire Regiment, the King's Regiment, the King's Own Royal Border Regiment, the Devon and Dorset Regiment, and the Royal Gloucestershire, Berkshire and Wiltshire. Fourteen others will amalgamate, reducing 26 line infantry regiments to 12 and introducing five new names: the Royal Regiment of Scotland, the Mercian Regiment, the King's Lancashire and Border Regiment, the Yorkshire Regiment, and the Royal Welsh Regiment. All six of the Scottish line infantry regiments were amalgamated to form a single Scottish regiment.

17   Desmond Shawe-Taylor, the director of Dulwich Picture Gallery, was appointed the next Surveyor of the Queen's Pictures from July 2005.

18   Religious activists smashed windows and tried to storm the stage of Birmingham Repertory Theatre in protest at the depiction in a play of rape and murder in a Sikh temple. *Behzti* (Punjabi for dishonour) by Gurpreet Kaur Bhatti was cancelled indefinitely.

23 Little Nicky, the first commercially cloned cat, was created at a cost of £26,000 for a Texas airline worker, using the DNA of her much-loved pet Nicky who died aged 17.
26 More than 150,000 people were feared dead in southern Asia after an underwater earthquake registering 9.0 on the Richter scale devastated the Indian Ocean. The tsunami crashed into the coasts of Sri Lanka, southern India, Indonesia, Thailand and Malaysia, with its epicentre west of Sumatra.
28 Viktor Yushchenko won the Ukrainian presidential election by more than 2 million votes over Viktor Yanukovich, although the defeated candidate threatened to stop prime minister Yushchenko going to work in the government buildings.

Obituaries 2004

January
2   Geoff Edrich, cricketer, born 13 July 1918
4   Joan Aiken, author, born 4 September 1924
    Jeff Nuttall, painter, poet, author and performance artist, born 8 July 1933
    Michael Straight, writer and publisher, born 1 September 1916
    Brian Gibson, television and film director, born 22 September 1944
    Jake Hess, gospel singer, born 24 December 1927
5   Vivian Jenkins, rugby player and journalist, born 2 November 1911
    Charles Dumas, first man to clear 7ft in the high jump, born 12 February 1937
6   Reg Smith, footballer and manager, born 20 January 1912
    Pierre Charles, prime minister of Dominica (2000–04), born 30 June 1954
    Thomas Stockham, digital audio and video pioneer, born 22 December 1933
7   Ingrid Thulin, actress, born 27 January 1926
    Lyndon Brook, actor, born 10 April 1926
10 Alexandra Ripley, author, born 8 January 1934
13 Arne Naess, shipping magnate and former husband of Diana Ross, born 8 December 1937
14 Uta Hagen, actress, born 12 June 1919
    Eric Sturgess, tennis player, born 10 May 1920
15 Olivia Goldsmith, novelist, born in 1949
17 Ray Stark, film producer, born 3 October 1915
    Elsa Buchanan, actress, born 22 December 1908
19 David Hookes, Australian cricketer, born 3 May 1955
    Stewart Steven, journalist and newspaper editor, born 30 September 1935
21 Yordan Radichkov, Bulgarian writer, born 29 October 1929
22 Billy May, jazz and big band arranger, born 10 November 1916
    Ann Miller (Lucille Ann Collier), tap dancer and actress, born 12 April 1923
    Milt Bernhart, trombonist, born 25 May 1926
23 Helmut Newton, photographer, born 31 October 1920
24 Leonidas da Silva, Brazilian footballer, born 6 September 1913
    Gordon Brook-Shepherd, author, born 24 March 1918
25 Fanny Blankers-Koen, athlete, born 26 April 1918
    Perry Jones, television producer, born 18 August 1922
26 Lord (Hugh) Jenkins of Putney, politician, born 27 July 1908
    Wilhelmina Barns-Graham, painter, born 8 June 1912
27 Lord (Hugh) Scanlon, president of the Amalgamated Union of Engineering Workers 1968–78, born 26 October 1913
28 Rikki Fulton, comedian and actor, born 15 April 1924
    Midge Mackenzie, documentary film-maker, born 6 March 1938
29 Janet Frame, novelist, born 28 August 1924
31 Eleanor Holm, swimmer, born 6 December 1913

February
1   Ally MacLeod, former Scotland football manager, born 26 February 1931
    Bob Stokoe, footballer and manager, born 21 September 1930
    John Stephen, fashion designer, born 28 August 1934
2   Owen Prosser, founder of the Railway Development Association, born in 1922
3   Sam Fullbrook, artist, born 14 April 1922
5   Frances Partridge, last survivor of the Bloomsbury set, born 15 March 1900
6   Dr Humphry Osmond, psychiatrist who coined the term 'psychedelic', born 1 July 1917
    Sir David Meyrick, 4th Bt, Olympic oarsman, born 2 December 1926
7   Norman Thelwell, artist, born 3 May 1923
11 Jozef Lenart, former prime minister of Czechoslovakia, born 3 April 1923
12 Martin Booth, author, born 7 September 1944
    Stephen Cartwright, children's book illustrator, born 28 December 1947
13 Peter Gellhorn, conductor and pianist, born 24 October 1912
14 Marco Pantani, cyclist, born 13 January 1970
16 Doris Troy, soul singer, born 6 January 1937
17 José López Portillo, President of Mexico 1976–82, born 16 June 1920
18 Jean Rouch, documentarist, born 31 May 1917

21	John Charles, footballer, born 27 December 1931
	Irina Press, athlete, born 10 March 1939
	Les Gray, pop singer with Mud, born 9 April 1946
22	Roque Maspoli, Uruguayan goalkeeper, born 12 October 1917
23	Don Cornell (born Luigi Francisco Varlarlo), singer, born 21 April 1919
	Neil Ardley, composer and author, born 26 May 1937
	Bob Mayo, rock musician, born 25 August 1951
	Stan Cohen, politician, born 31 July 1927
24	Albert Axelrod, foil fencer, born 21 February 1921
	Estelle Axton, co-founder of the Stax record label, born 11 September 1918
25	Jack Flavell, cricketer, born 15 May 1929
	AC Read, blues saxophonist, born 9 May 1926
26	Boris Trajkovski, President of Macedonia, born 25 June 1956
28	Daniel Boorstin, historian, born 1 October 1914
	Carmen Laforet, author, born 6 September 1921
	Gene Allison, rhythm and blues singer, born 29 August 1934
29	Jerome Lawrence, playwright, born 14 July 1915

March

2	Mercedes McCambridge, actress, born 17 March 1916
3	Alec Zino, ornithologist, born 9 February 1916
4	John McGeoch, guitarist, born 28 May 1955
7	Spalding Gray, writer and performer of autobiographical monologues, born 5 June 1941
	Paul Winfield, actor, born 22 May 1941
	Ted Johns, declarer of UDI for the Isle of Dogs, born 19 September 1932
9	Alf Bicknell, chauffeur to the Beatles, born 28 October 1928
	John Mayer, composer, born 28 October 1930
12	Milton Resnick, artist, born 8 January 1917
13	Sydney Carter, poet and songwriter, born 6 May 1915
14	IA Shapiro, literary scholar, born 7 November 1904
	Vic Roberts, rugby player, born 6 August 1924
18	Richard Marner, actor, born 27 March 1921
19	Henry Swanzy, broadcaster, born 14 June 1915
20	Princess Juliana, former Queen of the Netherlands, born 30 April 1909
	Doug Keller, rugby player, born 18 June 1922
21	Ludmila Tchèrina, actress, born Monique Tchemerzine in Paris, 10 October 1924
22	Sheikh Ahmed Yassin, leader of Hamas, born in 1937
	David Oates, archaeologist, born 25 February 1927
24	Richard Leech (Richard Leeper McClelland), actor, born 24 November 1922
25	Fred Hoyles, Wimbledon tennis referee-in-chief 1976–82, born 1 October 1923
26	Tony Traversi, member of Sid Millward's band The Nitwits, born 12 February 1915
	Jan Berry, pop star (half of Jan and Dean), born 3 April 1941
28	Sir Peter Ustinov, actor, director and writer, born 16 April 1921
29	Bob Copper, folk singer, born 6 January 1915
	Hubert Gregg, composer, actor and broadcaster, born 19 July 1914
	Alistair Cooke, broadcaster and journalist, born 20 November 1908
30	Salvatore Burruni, world champion boxer, born 11 April 1933
	Babs Atkins, last inhabitant of the 22-acre St George's Island, Looe, Cornwall, born 3 June 1917

April

1	Paul Atkinson, lead guitarist of the pop group The Zombies, born 19 March 1946
	Denis Stevens, musician, born 2 March 1922
	Carrie Snodgress, actress, born 27 October 1946
4	Alberic Schotte, Belgian cyclist, born 7 September 1919
5	Fred Winter, racehorse trainer and champion jockey, born 20 September 1926
	Leonard Reed, tap dancer, born 7 January 1907
7	Ursula Bentley, writer, born 18 September 1945
	Robert Sangster, racehorse owner and breeder, born 23 May 1936
	Maureen Potter, comedian and actress, born in 1925
9	Aelred Bartlett, artist and church restorer, born 6 April 1918
11	Paul Hamburger, pianist, born 3 September 1920
12	Ronnie Adams, winner of the 1956 Monte Carlo Rally, born 8 March 1916
	Juanito Valderrama, flamenco singer, born 24 May 1916
	Herbert Barnes, first torchbearer for the Wembley Olympics of 1948, born 2 December 1910
13	Caron Keating, television presenter, born 5 October 1962
	Maria Denis, actress, born 22 November 1916
17	Bob Law, artist, born 22 January 1934
	Lord Geraint (Wyn Howells), politician, born 15 April 1925
18	Ratu Sir Kamisese Mara, former President of Fiji, born 13 May 1920
19	George Hardwick, footballer, born 2 February 1920
	Philip Locke, actor, born 19 March 1928
	Norris McWhirter, co-founder of the *Guinness Book of Records*, born 12 August 1925

20	Ronnie Simpson, footballer, born 11 October 1930
24	Estée Lauder (Josephine Ester Mentzer), founder of cosmetics empire, born 1 July 1906
	Willie Watson, cricketer and footballer, born 7 March 1920
25	Thom Gunn, poet, born 29 August 1929
	Jacques Rouxel, cartoonist, born 26 February 1931
	Nick Gordon, wildlife film-maker, born 9 May 1952
	Claude Williams, jazz violinist, born 22 February 1908
	Eddie Hopkinson, goalkeeper, born 29 October 1935
26	Hubert Selby Jr, writer, born 23 July 1928
	Adam Shand Kydd, writer, born 5 September 1954
	Denis Hills, writer and adventurer, born 8 November 1913
30	Jeff Butterfield, rugby player, born 9 August 1929
	Boris Pergamenschikov, Russian cellist, born 29 August 1948

May

2	Duncan Carse, polar explorer, radio broadcaster and actor (played Dick Barton, Special Agent, on the radio), born 28 July 1913
3	The 11th Duke of Devonshire, born 2 January 1920
	Anthony Ainley, actor (The Master in *Doctor Who*), born 30 August 1932
4	Erik Smith, record producer, born 25 March 1931
	Clement 'Sir Coxsone' Dodd, record producer, born 26 January 1932
6	Barney Kessel, jazz guitarist, born 17 October 1923
7	Robert Fulton, adventurer and inventor, born 15 April 1909
9	Akhmad Kadyrov, President of Chechnya, born 23 August 1950
	Percy Young, musicologist, born 17 May 1912
	Alan King (Irwin Alan Kniberg), comedian, born 26 December 1927
	Brenda Fassie, South African singer, born 3 November 1964
10	Portland Mason, actress (daughter of James Mason), born 26 November 1948
	Cora Goffin (aka Lady Littler), principal boy, born 26 April 1902
11	Alf Valentine, West Indian cricketer, born 28 April 1930
	John Whitehead, pop singer, born 2 July 1948
14	Shaun Sutton, television producer, born 14 October 1919
	Anna Lee (Joan Boniface Winnifrith), actress, born 2 January 1913
15	Colonel Bob Morgan, pilot of the B-17 Flying Fortress *Memphis Belle* during the Second World War, born 31 July 1918
16	Admiral of the Fleet Lord Hill-Norton, born 8 February 1915
18	Elvin Jones, jazz drummer, born 9 September 1927
	Raglan Squire, architect, born 30 January 1912
19	Robert David MacDonald, playwright, born 27 August 1929
	Arnold Dwight 'Gateman' Moore, blues singer, born 8 November 1913
20	Lord (Lionel, aka Len) Murray, former General Secretary of the Trades Union Congress, born 2 August 1922
21	Milton Shulman, drama critic, born 30 August 1913
	Andrew Green, writer and parapsychologist, born 28 July 1927
23	Sally Gilmour, ballerina, born 2 November 1921
	Adèle Leigh, soprano, born 15 June 1928
	Sheila Wickham, born Sheila Macneal (with her sister, known as the 'Belles of Biggin Hill'), born 1 July 1916
25	Nicholas Luard, writer and co-owner of *Private Eye* and the Establishment Club, born 26 June 1937
	John RT Davies, jazz musician, born 20 March 1927
27	Umberto Agnelli, chairman of Fiat motor company, born 1 November 1934
	Ronald Smith, concert pianist, born 3 January 1922
28	Michael Alison, Conservative politician, born 27 June 1926
	Irene Manning (Inez Harvuot), actress, born 12 July 1912
29	Jack Rosenthal, dramatist, born 8 September 1931
31	Robert Quine, tax lawyer and rock guitarist, born 30 December 1942

June

2	Dom Moraes, Indian poet, born 19 July 1938
	Nicolai Ghiaurov, operatic bass, born 13 September 1929
3	Frances Shand Kydd (born Frances Ruth Burke Roche) mother of Diana, Princess of Wales, born 20 January 1936
4	Joe Carr (born Joseph Benedict Waters), Irish amateur golfer, born 18 February 1922
	Steve Lacy (born Steven Lackritz), jazz soprano saxophonist, born 23 July 1934
5	Ronald Reagan, 40th President of the United States, born 6 February 1911
	Iona Brown, violinist and conductor, born 7 January 1941
	Fiore de Henriquez, sculptress, born 20 June 1921
6	Judy Campbell, actress, born 31 May 1916
	Jock West, motorcycle racing champion, born 28 February 1909
7	Mary Holland, journalist, born 19 June 1936
8	Fosco Maraini, anthropologist, photographer and mountaineer, born 11 November 1912
10	Ray Charles (Ray Charles Robinson), singer and songwriter, born 23 September 1930
12	Geoffrey Thompson, showman, born 16 November 1936
13	Professor Sir Stuart Hampshire, philosopher, born 1 October 1914

14	Max Rosenberg, film producer, born 13 September 1914
15	Lennie Bush, double bass player, born 6 June 1927
17	Paul Neagu, artist, born 22 February 1938
18	Doris Dowling, actress, born 15 May 1923
23	Doris Thompson (Queen Mother of Blackpool), former chairman of Blackpool Pleasure Beach, born 12 January 1903
24	Polly Havers (Polly Williams), actress and model, born 5 January 1950
25	Imanol Larzabal, folk singer, born 11 November 1947
27	Agnes 'Sis' Cunningham, accordionist, born 19 February 1909
28	Anthony Buckeridge, author, born 20 June 1912
30	Jules Cartwright, mountaineer, born 13 December 1974

July

1	Marlon Brando, actor, born 3 April 1924
	Jasper Ridley, writer, born 25 May 1920
	Peter Barnes, playwright, born 10 January 1931
3	Andrian Nikolayev, cosmonaut, born 5 September 1929
	John Barron, actor, born 24 December 1920
6	Syreeta Wright, singer, born 28 February 1946
	Thomas Klestil, President of Austria, born 4 November 1932
	Eric Douglas, actor, born 21 June 1958
9	The 4th Viscount Esher (Lionel Gordon Baliol Brett), architect, born 18 July 1913
	Carlo Di Palma, cinematographer, born 17 April 1925
11	Joe Gold, bodybuilder and stuntman, born 10 March 1922
	Walter Wager, author, born 4 September 1924
	Dorothy Hart, actress, born 4 April 1923
12	Betty Oliphant, dance teacher, born 5 August 1918
13	Arthur 'Killer' Kane, bass player with the New York Dolls, born in 1949
	Carlos Kleiber, conductor, born 3 July 1930
15	Ena Baga, organist, born 5 January 1906
16	Carl Mydans, photographer, born 20 May 1907
17	Queen Susan of the Albanians, born Susan Cullen-Ward in Australia, 28 January 1941
	Pat Roach, professional wrestler and actor, born 19 May 1937
18	Paul Foot, journalist, born 8 November 1937
	Sebastian Graham-Jones, actor and director, born 1 August 1947
	Georgine Darcy, dancer, model and actress, born 14 January 1936
20	Antonio Gades, flamenco dancer and choreographer, born 14 November 1936
	James Williams, pianist, composer, bandleader and teacher, born 8 March 1951
21	Jerry Goldsmith, composer, born 10 February 1929
	Edward Lewis, Nobel Laureate for Medicine, born 20 May 1918
22	Sacha Distel, singer, born 29 January 1933
	Serge Reggiani, actor, born 2 May 1922
	Joan Morgan, actress, born 2 February 1905
23	Illinois Jacquet, tenor sax player, born 31 October 1922
	Nick Rossiter, television documentary maker, born 17 July 1961
25	John Passmore, philosopher, born 9 September 1914
26	Muriel Angelus, actress, born 10 March 1909
28	Bob Tisdall, athlete, born 16 May 1907
	Francis Crick, biologist, born 8 June 1916
31	Laura Betti, actress, born 1 May 1934
	Virginia Grey, actress, born 22 March 1917

August

1	Madeleine Robinson, actress, born 5 November 1916
2	Henri Cartier-Bresson, photographer, born 22 August 1908
4	Alec Stewart, racehorse trainer, born 21 June 1955
6	Rick James, rock musician, born 1 February 1948
	Gordon Smith, footballer, born 5 May 1924
	Donald Justice, poet and teacher, born 12 August 1925
7	Paul 'Red' Adair, oil well firefighter, born 18 June 1915
	Bernard Levin, broadcaster and journalist, born 19 August 1928
	Colin Bibby, ornithologist, born 20 November 1948
8	Leon Golub, artist, born 23 January 1922
9	David Raskin, film music composer, born 4 August 1912
11	Brian Bagnall, cartoonist, born 22 April 1921
	Giovanna Fontana, couturier, born 27 November 1915
12	Sir Godfrey Hounsfield, Nobel Laureate for Medicine, born 28 August 1919
13	Peter Woodthorpe, actor, born 25 September 1931
	Rodney Wilkinson, painter and soldier, born 9 March 1924
	Julia Child, television chef, born 15 August 1912
14	Czeslaw Milosz, Nobel Laureate for Literature, born 30 June 1911
16	Melvin Endsley, composer of 'Singin' the Blues', born 30 January 1934

CURRENT AFFAIRS

Acquanetta (Burnu Acquanetta, lit. burning fire, deep water), actress, born 17 July 1921
17   Thea Astley, novelist, born 25 August 1925
      Gérard Souzay, baritone, born 8 December 1918
18   Elmer Bernstein, composer, born 4 April 1922
      Hugh Manning, actor, born 19 August 1920
19   Jill Lowe, writer, born 31 July 1937
22   Captain Norman Todd, pilot of Concorde on its first commercial flight on 21 January 1976, born 14 June 1924
25   Don Ashton, art director and production designer, born 26 June 1919
26   Laura Branigan, singer, born 3 July 1957
30   Fred Whipple, astronomer, born 5 November 1906
      Derek Johnson, athlete, born 5 January 1933
31   Carl Wayne, singer and actor, born 18 August 1943

September
1   Dick Everitt, television producer, born 28 July 1933
      Patricia Flower, aviatrix and archer, born 4 February 1915
      Lady Victoria Waymouth, interior designer, born 22 February 1947
5   Fritha Goodey, actress, born 23 October 1972
6   Elly Ann Schneider (aka Tiny Doll), actress, born 23 July 1914
8   Frank Thomas, Disney animator, born 5 September 1912
      Michael Theakston, brewer, born 15 August 1925
10   Glyn Owen, actor, born 6 March 1928
      Dennie Mancini, boxing cutsman, born 22 August 1933
11   Fred Ebb, lyricist, born 8 April 1933
      Margaret Kelly, founder of the Bluebell Girls dancing troupe, born 24 June 1910
13   Geoffrey Rees-Jones, rugby player and founder member of 5 Commando, born 8 July 1914
15   Johnny Ramone, punk guitarist, born 8 October 1948
16   Michael Donaghy, poet, born 24 May 1954
17   Sir Robert Hunt, businessman, born 11 May 1918
18   Russ Meyer, film director, born 21 March 1922
      Finlay Best, rowing coach, born 12 July 1912
19   Skeeter Davis, country singer, born 30 December 1931
      Kenneth Sandford, baritone, born 28 June 1924
20   Brian Clough, football manager, born 21 March 1935
22   Harold Zinkin, bodybuilder, born in 1922
23   Nigel Nicolson, writer, editor and publisher, born 19 January 1917
24   Françoise Sagan, writer, born 21 June 1935
28   Mulk Raj Anand, writer, born 12 December 1905
      Geoffrey Beene, fashion designer, born 30 August 1927
29   Patrick Wormald, historian, born 9 July 1947
30   Michael Relph, scenic designer and film producer, born 16 February 1915

October
1   Richard Avedon, fashion photographer, born 15 May 1923
3   Janet Leigh, actress, born 6 July 1927
5   Maurice Wilkins, molecular biologist and Nobel Laureate, born 15 December 1916
6   Pete McCarthy, writer and broadcaster, born 9 November 1951
8   Dame Rosemary Murray, scientist and founder of New Hall College, Cambridge, born 28 July 1913
9   Jacques Derrida, philosopher, born 15 July 1930
10   Christopher Reeve, actor, born 25 September 1952
      Maurice Shadbolt, New Zealand short-story writer, born 4 June 1932
      The Right Reverend Denis Wakeling, Bishop of Southwell 1970–85, born 12 December 1918
11   Keith Miller, cricketer, born 28 November 1919
12   Nerina Shute, writer, born 17 July 1908
13   Bernice Rubens, novelist, born 26 July 1928
      Michal Hambourg, pianist, born 9 June 1919
      Major Michael Pope, racehorse trainer, born 11 July 1917
      Ivor Wood, animator, born 4 May 1932
14   Professor Conrad Russell, the 5th Earl Russell, historian, born 15 April 1937
      Sheila Keith, actress, born 9 June 1920
15   Bill Eyden, drummer, born 4 May 1930
      Dave Godin, music writer who coined the term 'northern soul', born 21 June 1936
16   Vincent Brome, writer, born 14 July 1910
18   Nancy Carline, painter, born 30 November 1909
19   Lord Francis Joseph Chapple, born 8 August 1921
20   Lynda Lee-Potter, newspaper columnist, born 2 May 1935
      Anthony Hecht, poet, born 16 January 1923
23   Bill Nicholson, football manager, born 26 January 1919
      Robert Merrill, baritone, born 14 June 1917
25   John Peel, disc jockey, born 30 August 1939
28   Graham Roberts, actor, born in 1929
      Rosalind Hicks, daughter of crime-novelist Agatha Christie, born 5 August 1919

Jimmy 'Babyface' McLarnin, boxer, born 19 December 1907
29   Princess Alice, Duchess of Gloucester, born 25 December 1901
Peter Twinn, first Briton to break an Enigma cipher at Bletchley Park, born 9 January 1916

November
1   Lord Hanson, politician and businessman, born 20 January 1922
Mae Madison, actress, born 14 September 1914
3   Joe Bushkin, jazz pianist, born 7 November 1916
6   Fred Dibnah, steeplejack and broadcaster, born 28 April 1938
Robert Lang, actor, born 24 September 1934
7   Howard Keel (born Harold Clifford Leek), actor, born 13 April 1919
Bill Bennett, pioneer of hang-gliding, born 26 September 1931
Eddie Charlton, snooker player, born 31 October 1929
8   Frank Shelley, actor/manager, born 6 February 1912
9   Emlyn Hughes, footballer, born 28 August 1947
11   Yasser Arafat, Palestinian leader, born in Cairo, 24 August 1929
12   Frederik Prausnitz, conductor, born 26 August 1920
Bill 'Uke' Scott, music hall artist, born 12 March 1923
13   Keith Weller, footballer, born 11 June 1946
Russell Jones (Ol' Dirty Bastard), rap singer, born 15 November 1968
18   Cy Coleman, composer and pianist, born 14 June 1929
19   Terry Melcher, singer/songwriter (son of Doris Day), born 8 February 1942
24   Arthur Hailey, writer, born 5 April 1920
26   Bill Alley, cricketer, born 3 February 1919
27   Philippe de Broca, film director, born 15 March 1933
John Dunn, disc jockey, born 4 March 1934
Maude Lloyd, dancer, born 16 August 1908
28   Molly Weir, actress, born 2 February 1910
29   John D Barrymore, actor, born 4 June 1932
Arthur Howes, documentary film-maker, born 15 July 1950
30   Bill Brown, goalkeeper, born 8 October 1931

December
1   HRH Prince Bernhard of the Netherlands, born 29 June 1911
Norman Newell, lyricist and producer, born 25 January 1919
2   Dame Alicia Markova (born Lilian Alicia Marks), prima ballerina, born 1 December 1910
Larry Buchanan, film director, born 31 January 1923
4   Elena Souliotis, soprano, born 28 May 1943
5   Ivan Marks, angler, born in 1936
Tania Alexander, author and translator, born 15 January 1915
8   Lord (Leslie George) Scarman, law reformer, born 29 July 1911
'Dimebag' Darrell Abbott, rock guitarist, born 20 August 1966
13   Fernando Poe Jr, actor and politician, born in 1939
15   Sidonie Goossens, harpist, born 19 October 1899
16   Agnes Martin, abstract expressionist painter, born 22 March 1912
Peter Coker, realist painter, born 27 July 1926
17   Dick Heckstall-Smith, jazz saxophonist, born 26 September 1934
18   Vijay Hazare, cricketer, born 11 March 1915
Anthony Sampson, writer and broadcaster, born 3 August 1926
19   Renata Tebaldi, soprano, born 1 February 1922
23   PV (Pamulaparti Venkata) Narasimha Rao, prime minister of India 1991–6, born 28 June 1921
24   Sir Anthony Meyer, Conservative politician, born 27 October 1920
25   Gennady Strekalov, cosmonaut and engineer, born 29 October 1940
26   Sir Angus Ogilvy, husband of Princess Alexandra, born 14 September 1928
Professor Frank Pantridge, inventor of the portable defibrillator, born 3 October 1916
27   Hank Garland, guitarist, born 11 November 1930
28   Susan Sontag, writer, born 16 January 1933
Jerry Orbach, actor, born 20 October 1935
29   Julius Axelrod, pharmacologist and Nobel Prize winner, born 30 May 1912
30   Artie Shaw (born Arthur Jacob Arshawsky), bandleader, born 23 May 1910
31   Gerard Debreu, Nobel Prize-winning economist, born 4 July 1921

Birthdays 2004

January
1   JD Salinger, author, 85, John Fuller, poet, 67, Baroness Miller of Chilthorne Domer, 50
2   David Bailey, photographer, 66, Sir Richard Bayliss, physician to the Queen 1970–85, 87, Tia Carrere, actress, 37
3   Michael Schumacher, racing driver, 35, Mel Gibson, actor, 48, Sir George Martin, record producer, 78
4   Grace Bumbry, opera singer, 67, Iain Cuthbertson, actor, 74, Margaret Marshall, opera singer, 55, David
Millar, cyclist, 27, Michael Stipe, vocalist with REM, 44

5 Diane Keaton, actress, 58, General Sir Michael Rose, soldier, 64, Maurizio Pollini, pianist, 62, Marilyn Manson, singer, 35, Robert Duvall, actor, 73
6 Rowan Atkinson, comedian, 49, Kapil Dev, cricketer, 45, Angus Deayton, broadcaster and writer, 48, Terry Venables, football manager and writer, 61, Barry John, rugby player, 59
7 Ian La Frenais, screenwriter, 67, Nicolas Cage, actor, 40, Ross Norman, squash player, 45
8 David Bowie, singer, 57, Shirley Bassey, singer, 67, Stephen Hawking, physicist, 62, Ron Moody, actor, 80
9 Joan Baez, singer, 63, Joely Richardson, actress, 39, Clive Dunn, actor, 82, Susannah York, actress, 62
10 Rod Stewart, singer, 59, Derek Hammond-Stroud, operatic baritone, 78, Pat Benatar, singer, 51
11 Henry Cecil, racehorse trainer, 61, Bryan Robson, football manager, 47, Arthur Scargill, trade unionist, 66
12 Michael Aspel, broadcaster, 71, PW Botha, former President of South Africa, 88, Kirstie Alley, actress, 49, Joe Frazier, heavyweight boxer, 60, Des O'Connor, entertainer, 72, Brendan Foster, athlete, 56, Howard Stern, radio broadcaster, 50
13 Stephen Hendry, snooker player, 35, Michael Bond, author, 78, Ronan Rafferty, golfer, 40
14 Faye Dunaway, actress, 63, Trevor Nunn, theatre director, 64, Warren Mitchell, actor, 78, Peter Barkworth, actor, 75, Richard Briers, actor, 70, Maina Gielgud, ballerina, 59, LL Cool J, rap artist, 36
15 Princess Michael of Kent, 59, Margaret Beckett, politician, 61, Frank Bough, broadcaster, 71
16 Christine Janes (Truman), tennis player, 63, Cliff Thorburn, snooker player, 56, Kate Moss, model, 30, Roy Jones Jr, boxer, 35, Aaliyah, singer and actress, 25
17 Muhammad Ali, heavyweight boxer, 57, Vidal Sassoon, hair stylist, 76, Jim Carrey, actor, 42, Moira Shearer, ballerina, 78, Kip Keino, athlete, 64
18 Kevin Costner, actor, 49, Paul Keating, former Australian Prime Minister, 60, John Boorman, film director, 71, Chief Emeka Anyaoku, Commonwealth Secretary-General 1999–2000, 71, Raymond Briggs, illustrator, 70, David Bellamy, botanist and broadcaster, 71, Peter Beardsley, footballer, 43, Mark Rylance, theatre director, 44
19 Stefan Edberg, tennis player, 38, Dolly Parton, singer, 58, Simon Rattle, conductor, 49, Richard Dunwoody, jockey, 40, Michael Crawford, actor, 62, Richard Lester, film director, 72, Phil Everly, singer, 65
20 Buzz Aldrin, astronaut, 74, Tom Baker, actor, 70, Liza Goddard, actress, 54, David Lynch, film director, 58
21 Placido Domingo, operatic tenor, 63, Jack Nicklaus, golfer, 64, Paul Scofield, actor, 82, John Kentish, tenor, 94, Geena Davis, actress, 47, Billy Ocean, singer, 54
22 Nigel Benn, boxer, 40, George Foreman, boxer and actor, 56, John Hurt, actor, 64, Claire Rayner, agony aunt, 73, Mary Hayley Bell, playwright, 93
23 Jeanne Moreau, actress, 76, Lord Strathcarron, 80, Lord Sutherland, 72, Princess Caroline of Monaco, 47, Rutger Hauer, actor, 60
24 Neil Diamond, singer, 63, Bamber Gascoigne, author, 69, Desmond Morris, zoologist, 76, Nastassja Kinski, actress, 43
25 Cory Aquino, former President of the Philippines, 71, Raymond Baxter, broadcaster, 82, Angela Thorne, actress, 65, David Ginola, footballer, 37, Emma Freud, broadcaster, 42
26 Paul Newman, actor, 79, Ronald Allison, author, 72, Christopher Hampton, playwright, 58, Eddie Van Halen, guitarist, 49, Ellen DeGeneres, actress and comedienne, 46
27 Lord Rix, actor and president of Mencap, 80, Nina Milkina, pianist, 85, Bridget Fonda, actress, 40
28 Mikhail Baryshnikov, ballet dancer, 56, Alan Alda, actor, 68, Sir John Tavener, composer, 60
29 Germaine Greer, writer and broadcaster, 65, Tom Selleck, actor, 59, John Junkin, actor and writer, 74, Leslie Bricusse, composer and lyricist, 73, Peter Byrne, actor, 76, Andy Roberts, cricketer, 53, Raman Subba Row, cricketer, 72, Oprah Winfrey, actress and talk show host, 50
30 Phil Collins, rock singer, 53, Gene Hackman, actor, 74, Vanessa Redgrave, actress, 67, John Profumo, politician, 89
31 Queen Beatrix of the Netherlands, 66, Minnie Driver, actress, 33, Norman Mailer, author, 81, Jean Simmons, actress, 75

February
1 Boris Yeltsin, Russian President 1991–9, 73, Josceline Dimbleby, cookery writer, 61, Don Everly, vocalist, 67, Peter Sallis, actor, 83, Dame Muriel Spark, writer, 86
2 Andrew Davis, conductor, 60, David Jason, actor, 64, Valery Giscard d'Estaing, President of France 1974–81, 78, Elaine Stritch, actress, 79, Carolina Kluft, athlete, 21
3 Val Doonican, singer, 75, Gillian Ayres, painter, 74, Kirsty Wark, television presenter, 49, Blythe Danner, actress, 61, Morgan Fairchild, actress, 54, Nathan Lane, actor, 48
4 Norman Wisdom, actor and comedian, 89, Russell Hoban, writer, 79, Matthew Yates, athlete, 35, Natalie Imbruglia, singer, 29, Alice Cooper, rock star, 56
5 Douglas Hogg, politician, 59, Charlotte Rampling, actress, 58, Susan Hill, playwright and novelist, 62, Jennifer Jason Leigh, actress, 42, Barbara Hershey, actress, 56
6 Patrick MacNee, actor, 82, Keith Waterhouse, writer, 75, Kevin Whately, actor, 53, Jimmy Tarbuck, comedian, 64, Fred Trueman, cricketer, 73, Denis Norden, broadcaster, 82, Gayle Hunnicutt, actress, 61
7 Peter Jay, broadcaster, 67, Dora Bryan, actress, 80, Eddie Izzard, comedian, 42, David Park, author, 51
8 John Williams, composer, 72, John Grisham, author, 49, Osian Ellis, harpist, 76, Rachel Cusk, author, 37
9 Mia Farrow, actress, 59, Sandy Lyle, golfer, 46, Ben E King, singer, 66, Janet Suzman, actress, 65, Brian Bennett, drummer, 64, Dr Garret Fitzgerald, Prime Minister of the Republic of Ireland 1981–2 and 1982–7, 78, Joe Pesci, actor, 61
10 Greg Norman, golfer, 49, Mark Spitz, swimmer, 54, Michael Apted, film director, 63, Nicholas Owen, broadcaster, 57, Laura Dern, actress, 37
11 Dennis Skinner, politician, 72, Leslie Nielsen, actor, 78, John Surtees, motor racing champion, 70, Jennifer Aniston, actress, 35
12 Steve Backley, javelin thrower, 35, Franco Zeffirelli, film director, 81, Simon MacCorkindale, actor, 52

13	Liam Brady, footballer, 48, Kim Novak, actress, 71, Robbie Williams, singer, 30, George Segal, actor, 70, Peter Gabriel, rock singer, 54
14	Kevin Keegan, football manager, 53, Alan Parker, film director, 60, Michael Rudman, theatre producer, 65
15	Claire Bloom, actress, 73, Jane Seymour, actress, 53, Clare Short, politician, 58, John Adams, composer, 54
16	Anthony Dowell, ballet dancer, 61, John McEnroe, tennis player, 45, Iain Banks, author, 50, Paul Bailey, novelist, 67, FGR Cuming, painter, 74, David Griffiths, portrait painter, 65
17	Barry Humphries, entertainer and writer, 70, Baroness Rendell of Babergh, author, 74, Patricia Routledge, actress, 70, Julia McKenzie, actress and singer, 63, Norman Pace, comedian, 51, Michael Jordan, basketball player, 41
18	Bobby Robson, football manager, 71, Prue Leith, cookery writer, 64, Milos Forman, film director, 72, Gary Neville, footballer, 29, Len Deighton, author, 75, Graeme Garden, actor, 61, Colin Jackson, athlete, 37, Ned Sherrin, writer and broadcaster, 73, John Travolta, actor, 50, Yoko Ono, artist and writer, 71
19	HRH The Duke of York, 44, Hana Mandlikova, tennis player, 42, Smokey Robinson, singer, 64, Gwen Taylor, actress, 65
20	Robert Altman, film director, 79, Jimmy Greaves, footballer, 64, Mike Leigh, dramatist, 61, Sidney Poitier, actor, 77, Cindy Crawford, model, 38
21	Harald V, King of Norway, 67, Jilly Cooper, author, 67, Alan Rickman, actor, 58, Peter McEnery, actor, 64, Kelsey Grammer, actor, 49, Tyne Daly, actress, 58
22	Bruce Forsyth, entertainer, 76, Sir John Mills, actor, 96, Nigel Planer, actor, 51, Sheila Hancock, actress, 71, Julie Walters, actress, 54, Niki Lauda, racing driver, 55, Drew Barrymore, actress, 29
23	Helena Sukova, tennis player, 39, Sylvie Guillem, ballet dancer, 39, Anton Mosimann, chef, 57, Joe Calzaghe, boxer, 31
24	Brian Close, cricketer, 73, Denis Law, footballer, 64, Richard Hamilton, painter, 82, Paul Jones, singer and actor, 62, Dennis Waterman, actor, 56, Peter Terson, dramatist, 72, Derek Randall, cricketer, 53, Billy Zane, actor, 38
25	Elkie Brooks, singer, 59, Sir Tom Courtenay, actor, 67, Lord Puttnam, film producer, 63
26	Sir Everton Weekes, cricketer, 79, Emma Kirkby, soprano, 55, Tony Selby, actor, 66, Colin Bell, footballer, 58, Michael Bolton, singer, 51
27	Paddy Ashdown, Leader of Liberal Democrats 1988–99, 63, Elizabeth Taylor, actress, 72, Timothy Spall, actor, 47, Dame Antoinette Sibley, prima ballerina, 65, Rabbi Julia Neuberger, 54, Ralph Nader, consumer protection pioneer, 70
28	Peter Alliss, golfer, 73, Barry McGuigan, boxer, 43, Stephanie Beacham, actress, 55, Alfred Burke, actor, 86
29	Joss Ackland, actor, 76, Mario Andretti, racing driver, 64

March

1	Harry Belafonte, singer, 77, David Broome, show jumper, 64, Roger Daltrey, singer and actor, 60
2	John Gardner, composer, 87, Mikhail Gorbachev, Russian politician, 73, Ian Woosnam, golfer, 46, Dame Naomi James, yachtswoman and author, 55, Lou Reed, rock singer, 60, JPR Williams, rugby player, 55, Jon Bon Jovi, rock singer, 42
3	Miranda Richardson, actress, 46, Fatima Whitbread, athlete, 43, Ronald Searle, artist and cartoonist, 84, Jackie Joyner-Kersee, athlete, 42
4	Kenny Dalglish, footballer, 53, Patrick Moore, astronomer and presenter, 81, Bernard Haitink, conductor, 75, Alan Sillitoe, writer, 76, Peter Skellern, composer and singer, 57, Ralph Kirshbaum, cellist, 58, Patsy Kensit, actress, 42
5	Elaine Page, singer, 56, Richard Hickox, conductor, 56, Barry Tuckwell, horn player and conductor, 73
6	Valentina Tereshkova, first woman in space, 67, Dame Kiri Te Kanawa, opera singer, 60, Dick Fosbury, athlete, 57
7	Viv Richards, cricketer, 52, Sir Ranulph Fiennes, explorer and author, 60, Ivan Lendl, tennis player, 44, Earl of Snowdon, photographer, 74, Piers Paul Read, author, 63, Sir Eduardo Paolozzi, sculptor, 80
8	Lynn Redgrave, actress, 61, Phil Edmonds, cricketer, 53, Gyles Brandreth, broadcaster and author, 56, Lord Hurd of Westwell, 74, Sir Anthony Caro, sculptor, 80, Lynn Seymour, ballerina, 65, David Wilkie, swimmer, 50
9	Bill Beaumont, rugby player, 52, Juliette Binoche, actress, 40, Bobby Fischer, chess player, 61, Raul Julia, actor, 64
10	Prince Edward, The Earl of Wessex, 40, Fou Ts'ong, concert pianist, 70, Andrew Parrott, conductor, 57, Sharon Stone, actress, 46, Chuck Norris, martial artist and actor, 64
11	Lord Lawson of Blaby, 72, Rupert Murdoch, chairman of News Corporation, 73, Louis Brough, tennis player, 81
12	Liza Minnelli, actress and singer, 58, David Mellor, broadcaster, 55, Edward Albee, dramatist, 76, Norbert Brainin, violinist, 81, Anish Kapoor, artist and sculptor, 50, Googie Withers, actress, 87, James Taylor, singer, 56
13	Neil Sedaka, singer and composer, 65, Sir Robert Mark, former police commissioner, 87, David Nobbs, writer, 69, Joe Bugner, boxer, 54
14	Michael Caine, actor, 71, Pam Ayres, poet, 57, Sir Colin St John Wilson, architect, 82, Jasper Carrott, comedian, 59, Tessa Sanderson, athlete, 48, Rita Tushingham, actress, 62, Billy Crystal, actor and comedian, 57
15	Ben Okri, author, 45, Mike Love, singer with the Beach Boys, 60, Robert Nye, author and poet, 65
16	Bernardo Bertolucci, film director, 63, Teresa Berganza, singer, 69, Kate Nelligan, actress, 53
17	Sir Robin Knox-Johnston, yachtsman, 65, Kurt Russell, actor, 53, Penelope Lively, writer, 71, Galina Samsova, ballerina, 67, Michael Whitaker, show jumper, 44, Alexander McQueen, fashion designer, 35, Rob Lowe, actor, 40
18	Ron Atkinson, football manager, 65, Alex Higgins, snooker player, 55, Pat Eddery, jockey, 52, Courtney Pine, saxophonist, 40, John Updike, author, 72, Queen Latifah, singer, 34

CURRENT AFFAIRS

19   Glenn Close, actress, 57, Patrick McGoohan, actor, 76, Bruce Willis, actor, 49, Philip Roth, author, 71, Ursula Andress, actress, 68

20   William Hurt, actor, 54, Dame Vera Lynn, singer, 87, Brian Mulroney, politician, 65, Spike Lee, actor and director, 47, Holly Hunter, actress, 46

21   Timothy Dalton, actor, 58, Ann Mackay, soprano, 48, Ieuan Evans, rugby player, 40, Lord Oaksey, jockey and racing pundit, 75, Lord Heseltine, politician, 71, Michael Foreman, writer and illustrator, 66, Matthew Broderick, actor, 42, Gary Oldman, actor, 46

22   George Benson, jazz guitarist and singer, 61, Lord Lloyd Webber, composer, 56, Marcel Marceau, mime artist, 81, Stephen Sondheim, composer, 74, William Shatner, actor, 73, Leslie Thomas, author, 73, Reese Witherspoon, actress, 28

23   Princess Eugenie of York, 14, Mike Atherton, cricketer, 36, Norman Bailey, baritone, 71, Wasim Bari, cricketer, 56, Roger Bannister, athlete, 75, Sir Steven Redgrave, rower, 42, Sir David McNee, policeman, 79, Chaka Khan, singer, 51

24   Sir Alan Sugar, Amstrad chairman, 57, Benjamin Luxon, baritone, 67, Dario Fo, playwright and actor, 78

25   Aretha Franklin, singer, 62, Richard O'Brien, actor and writer, 62, Sir Elton John, composer and singer, 57, Sarah Jessica Parker, actress, 39

26   Pierre Boulez, composer and conductor, 79, Leonard Nimoy, actor and producer, 73, Diana Ross, singer, 60, Kyung-Wha Chung, violinist, 56, William Hague, politician, 43, Elizabeth Jane Howard, novelist, 81

27   Mstislav Rostropovich, conductor and cellist, 77, Michael York, actor, 62, Quentin Tarantino, film director, 41, Julian Glover, actor, 69, Maria Ewing, opera singer, 54, Mariah Carey, singer, 34

28   Richard Eyre, theatre director, 61, Neil Kinnock, politician, 62, Michael Parkinson, broadcaster, 69, Richard Stilgoe, lyricist and entertainer, 61, Rosemary Ashe, soprano, 51, Nasser Hussain, cricketer, 36

29   Lord Tebbit, politician, 73, Eric Idle, comedic actor, 61, Sir Richard Rodney Bennett, composer, 68, John Major, politician, 61, Jennifer Capriati, tennis player, 28, John Suchet, television journalist, 60, Lucy Lawless, actress, 36, Elle Macpherson, model, 40

30   Warren Beatty, actor, 67, Eric Clapton, rock musician, 59, Tom Sharpe, novelist, 76, Rolf Harris, singer and artist, 74, Sue Cook, broadcaster, 55, Lord MacLaurin of Knebworth, 67, Celine Dion, singer, 36, MC Hammer, singer, 42

31   Richard Chamberlain, actor, 70, Robbie Coltrane, actor and comedian, 54, Al Gore, US Vice-President, 56, John Fowles, writer, 78, Lord Steel of Aikwood, politician, 66, Roger Black, athlete, 38, Ewan McGregor, actor, 33

April

1   David Gower, cricketer, 47, Steve Race, musician, 83, Stephen Fleming, New Zealand cricketer, 31

2   Linford Christie, athlete, 44, Penelope Keith, actress, 64, Sue Townsend, writer, 58, Jack Brabham, racing driver, 78, Catherine Gaskin, author, 75, Dermot Reeve, cricketer, 41, Barry Hills, racehorse trainer, 67

3   Alec Baldwin, actor, 46, Tony Benn, politician, 79, Doris Day, actress and singer, 80, Jonathan Lynn, director, 61, Eddie Murphy, actor, 43, John Virgo, snooker player and presenter, 58

4   Margaret Dupont, tennis player, 86, Maya Angelou, author, 76, Trevor Griffiths, playwright, 69

5   Jane Asher, actress, 58, General Colin Powell, US Secretary of State, 67

6   Felicity Palmer, opera singer, 60, Roger Cook, broadcaster, 61, Paul Daniels, magician, 66, André Previn, musician, 75, Rory Bremner, impressionist, 43, Joan Carlyle, soprano, 73, Lord Frederick Windsor, 25

7   Francis Ford Coppola, film director, 65, Sir David Frost, broadcaster, 65, Ian Richardson, actor, 70, Russell Crowe, actor, 40, James Garner, actor, 76, Gerry Cottle, circus proprietor, 59, Ravi Shankar, sitar player, 84, Cliff Morgan, broadcaster, 74, Jackie Chan, actor, 50

8   Ian Smith, Rhodesian politician, 85, Alec Stewart, cricketer, 41, Tony Banks, politician, 61, Hywel Bennett, actor, 60, Kofi Annan, Secretary-General of the UN, 66, Julian Lennon, musician, 41, Vivienne Westwood, fashion designer, 63, Patricia Arquette, actress, 36

9   Seve Ballesteros, golfer, 47, Hannah Gordon, actress, 63, Alan Knott, cricketer, 58, Valerie Singleton, broadcaster, 67, Vincent O'Brien, racehorse trainer, 87, Iain Duncan Smith, politician, 50, Jacques Villeneuve, racing driver, 33, Hugh Hefner, businessman, 78

10   Gloria Hunniford, broadcaster, 64, Omar Sharif, actor, 72, Dave Moorcroft, athlete, 51, Paul Theroux, writer, 63, Lesley Garrett, soprano, 49, Stan Mellor, jockey and racehorse trainer, 67, Steven Seagal, actor, 52

11   Gervase de Peyer, clarinettist, 78, Clive Exton, scriptwriter and playwright, 74, Lisa Stansfield, singer, 38

12   Sir Alan Ayckbourn, playwright, 65, Montserrat Caballe, opera and concert singer, 71, Bryan Magee, writer, 74, Jeremy Beadle, television presenter and charity fundraiser, 56, Shannen Doherty, actress, 33, Andy Garcia, actor, 48, Tom Clancy, author, 57, Herbie Hancock, musician, 64

13   Davis Love III, golfer, 40, Edward Fox, actor, 67, Seamus Heaney, poet, 65, Jonjo O'Neill, jockey and trainer, 52, Garry Kasparov, chess player, 41, Peter Davison, actor, 53

14   Julie Christie, actress, 63, Rod Steiger, actor, 79, Julian Lloyd Webber, cellist, 53, Paddy Hopkirk, rally driver, 71, David Hope, Archbishop of York and former Archbishop of London, 64, Sarah Michelle Gellar, actress, 27, Ritchie Blackmore, guitarist, 59

15   Lord Archer of Weston-super-Mare, author and politician, 64, Claudia Cardinale, actress and photographer, 66, Sir Neville Marriner, conductor, 80, Emma Thompson, actress, 45, Alan Plater, scriptwriter, 69, Samantha Fox, model and singer, 38

16   Joan Bakewell, broadcaster, writer and chairman of the British Film Institute, 71, Conchita Martinez, tennis player, 32, Merce Cunningham, choreographer, 85, Lynne Franks, writer, 56

17   Dr Michael Stroud, explorer, 49, Clare Francis, yachtswoman and writer, 58, Chris Barber, jazz trombonist, 74, Bella Freud, fashion designer, 43, Nick Hornby, writer, 47, Riccardo Patrese, racing driver, 50, Victoria Beckham, singer, 30, Sean Bean, actor, 45, Olivia Hussey, actress, 53, James Last, bandleader, 75, Henry Kelly, broadcaster, 58

18   Hayley Mills, actress, 58, Teddy Taylor, politician, 67, Nick Farr-Jones, Australian rugby player, 42, Conan O'Brien, television presenter, 41, James Woods, actor, 57

19   Sue Barker, television presenter and former tennis player, 48, Ruby Wax, comedian and actress, 51, Michel Roux, chef, 63, Dickie Bird, cricket umpire, 71, Trevor Francis, footballer, 50, Murray Perahia, pianist, 57, Kelly Holmes, athlete, 34, Tim Curry, actor, 58

20   Nicholas Lyndhurst, actor, 43, Ray Brooks, actor, 65, Jessica Lange, actress, 55, Sebastian Faulks, author, 51, Gro Harlem Brundtland, Director-General of the World Health Organisation, 65, Ryan O'Neal, actor, 63, Rachel Whiteread, sculptor, 41, Luther Vandross, singer, 53, Peter Snow, broadcaster, 66, Leslie Phillips, actor, 80, Carmen Electra, actress and singer, 32

21   Her Majesty Queen Elizabeth II, 78, John Mortimer, QC, barrister, playwright and author, 81, Angela Barrett, tennis player, 72, Andie MacDowell, actress, 46, Iggy Pop, singer, 57

22   George Cole, actor, 79, Jack Nicholson, actor, 67, Glen Campbell, singer, 66

23   Lady Gabriella Windsor, daughter of Prince and Princess Michael of Kent, 23, Shirley Temple Black, actress, 76, JP Donleavy, author, 78, Professor George Steiner, author, 75, Lady Victoria Glendinning, author, 67, Lee Majors, actor, 64

24   Jean Paul Gaultier, fashion designer, 52, Barbra Streisand, actress and singer, 62, Bridget Riley, artist, 73, Shirley Maclaine, actress, 70, Clement Freud, writer, 80, Johan Cruyff, footballer, 57, John Williams, guitarist, 63

25   Al Pacino, actor, 64, Earl of Lichfield, photographer, 65, Eric Bristow, darts player, 47, David Shepherd, artist, 73

26   David Coleman, sports commentator, 78, Peter Schaufuss, ballet dancer, 54, Marquess of Bute, racing driver, 46

27   Darcey Bussell, ballerina, 35, Igor Oistrakh, violinist, 73, Michael Fish, meteorologist, 60, John Daly, golfer, 38, Lady Helen Taylor, daughter of the Duke and Duchess of Kent, 40, Dr Jeffrey Tate, conductor, 61, Sheena Easton, singer, 45

28   Kenneth Kaunda, Zambian politician, 80, Nicola LeFanu, composer, 57, Mike Brearley, cricketer, 62, Ian Rankin, author, 44, Bradley Wiggins, cyclist, 24, Jay Leno, television presenter, 54, Saddam Hussein, dictator, 77

29   André Agassi, tennis player, 34, Zubin Mehta, conductor, 68, Zizi Jeanmaire, dancer, 80, Michelle Pfeiffer, actress, 47, Daniel Day-Lewis, actor, 47, Johnny Miller, golfer, 57, Jonah Barrington, squash player, 63, Jeremy Thorpe, politician, 75, Uma Thurman, actress, 34

30   Leslie Grantham, actor, 58, Dickie Davies, sports commentator, 71, Bobby Vee, singer, 61, Jill Clayburgh, actress, 60, Willie Nelson, singer and actor, 73, Tony Harrison, poet, 67, Percy Heath, jazz musician, 81, Cloris Leachman, actress, 78

May

1   Lady Sarah Chatto, 40, Steve Cauthen, jockey, 44, Joanna Lumley, actress, 58, Gordon Greenidge, cricketer, 53, Rita Coolidge, singer, 59

2   Brian Lara, cricketer, 35, Jimmy White, snooker player, 42, David Beckham, footballer, 29, David Suchet, actor, 58, John Neville, actor, 79, Alan Titchmarsh, horticulturalist, writer and broadcaster, 55, Engelbert Humperdinck, singer, 68

3   James Brown, soul singer, 71, Henry Cooper, boxer, 70, Allan Wells, athlete, 52, Sandi Toksvig, writer and comedienne, 46, Ben Elton, writer and comedian, 45

4   Michael Barrymore, comedian and actor, 52, Eric Sykes, writer and comedian, 81, Marisa Robles, harpist, 67

5   Michael Palin, actor and television presenter, 61

6   7th Marquess of Bath, 72, Tony Blair, politician, 51, Graham Souness, football manager, 51, George Clooney, actor, 43

7   Scobie Breasley, jockey, 89, Peter Carey, novelist, 61, Richard O'Sullivan, actor, 60, Elisabeth Soderstrom, soprano, 77

8   David Attenborough, broadcaster and naturalist, 78, Jack Charlton, footballer, 69, Lord Lamont of Lerwick, 62, Viviana Durante, ballerina, 37, Heather Harper, soprano, 74, Dame Felicity Lott, soprano, 57

9   Richard Adams, author, 84, Alan Bennett, dramatist, 70, Candice Bergen, actress, 58, Terry Downes, boxer, 68, Albert Finney, actor, 68, Glenda Jackson, actress and politician, 68, Billy Joel, singer, 55, Geraldine McEwan, actress, 72

10   Maureen Lipman, actress, 58, Michael Shea, former press secretary to the Queen, 66, Bono, lead singer with U2, 43, Barbara Taylor Bradford, writer, 71

11   John Parrott, snooker player and television personality, 40, Jeremy Paxman, broadcaster, 54, Judith Weir, composer, 50, Sir Rhodes Boyson, politician, 79, Lady Rachel Billington, writer, 62, Natasha Richardson, actress, 41, Jason Queally, cyclist, 34

12   Burt Bacharach, composer, 75, Alan Ball, footballer, 59, Michael Ignatieff, writer, 57, Jenni Murray, broadcaster, 54, Susan Hampshire, actress, 62, Steve Winwood, rock musician, 56, Dr Miriam Stoppard, writer and broadcaster, 67, Emilio Estevez, actor, 42

13   Peter Gabriel, musician, 54, Richard Madeley, broadcaster, 48, Stevie Wonder, musician, 54, Bea Arthur, actress, 79, Zoë Wanamaker, actress, 55, Helen Sharman, astronaut, 41, Selina Scott, broadcaster, 53, Tim Pigott-Smith, actor, 58, Harvey Keitel, actor, 65

14   George Lucas, film director, 60, Francesca Annis, actress, 59, Sir Chay Blyth, yachtsman, 64, Sian Phillips, actress, 70, Cate Blanchett, actress, 35

15   Zara Phillips, 23, Ted Dexter, cricketer, 69, Peter Shaffer, playwright, 78, Mike Oldfield, composer, 51

16   Judy Finnegan, broadcaster, 56, Roy Hudd, comedian and actor, 68, Gabriella Sabatini, tennis player, 34, Janet Jackson, singer, 38

17   Sir Michael Beetham, Marshal of the RAF, 81, Sugar Ray Leonard, boxer, 48, Birgit Nilsson, soprano, 86, Enya, singer, 43

CURRENT AFFAIRS

18   Pope John Paul II, 84, Toyah Willcox, singer and actress, 46, Nobby Stiles, footballer, 62, John Bruton, politician, 57

19   David Jacobs, broadcaster, 78, Edward de Bono, lateral thinker, 71, James Fox, actor, 65, Victoria Wood, comedian, 51, Sandy Wilson, composer, 80, Stephen Varcoe, baritone, 55, Pete Townshend, guitarist, 59, Grace Jones, singer and actress, 52

20   Lynn Davies, athlete, 62, Cher, singer and actress, 58, Earl Spencer, 40, Keith Fletcher, cricketer, 60, Joe Cocker, singer, 60

21   Mary Robinson, President of Ireland 1990–7 and United Nations High Commissioner for Human Rights, 60, Malcolm Fraser, Prime Minister of Australia 1975–83, 74, Rosalind Plowright, soprano, 55, Mr T, actor, 52

22   Cheryl Campbell, actress, 55, Kenny Ball, trumpeter, 73, George Best, footballer, 58, Anthony Holden, writer, 57, Katie Price (aka Jordan), model, 26

23   Anatoly Karpov, chess player, 53, Nigel Davenport, actor, 76, Humphrey Lyttelton, broadcaster and jazz writer, 83, Joan Collins, actress, 71, Graeme Hick, cricketer, 38, John Newcombe, tennis player, 60, Jewel, singer, 30

24   Liz McColgan, athlete, 40, Bob Dylan, songwriter, 63, Arnold Wesker, playwright, 72, Stanley Baxter, comedian, 78, Adrian Moorhouse, swimmer, 40, William Trevor, writer, 76, Eric Cantona, footballer, 38, Sean Kelly, cyclist, 48, Patti LaBelle, singer, 60

25   Julian Clary, comedian, 45, Sir Ian McKellen, actor, 65, Beverly Sills, soprano, 75, David Wynne, sculptor, 78, Mike Myers, actor, 41

26   Helena Bonham-Carter, actress, 38, Zola Budd, athlete, 38, Roy Dotrice, actor, 79, Philip Treacy, fashion designer, 37, Lenny Kravitz, singer, 40, Stevie Nicks, singer, 56, Pam Grier, actress, 55

27   Pat Cash, tennis player, 39, Henry Kissinger, US Secretary of State 1973–77, 81, Paul Gascoigne, footballer, 37, Thea Musgrave, composer, 76, Christopher Lee, actor, 82, Duncan Goodhew, swimmer, 47, Lewis Collins, actor, 58, Paul Bettany, actor, 33, Lou Gossett Jr, actor, 68

28   Faith Brown, impressionist, 57, Rachel Kempson, actress, 94, Julian Slade, composer, 74, Kylie Minogue, singer and actress, 36

29   Nanette Newman, actress, 65, Martin Pipe, racehorse trainer, 59, Francis Rossi, musician, 55, Annette Bening, actress, 46

30   Harry Enfield, comedian, 43, Bob Willis, cricketer, 55, Ray Cooney, theatre producer, 72, Andrew Farrell, rugby player, 29

31   John Prescott, politician, 66, Terry Waite, former special envoy for the Archbishop of Canterbury, 65, Clint Eastwood, actor, 74, Lynda Bellingham, actress, 56, Ben de Lisi, fashion designer, 49, Peter Winterbottom, rugby player, 44, Brooke Shields, actress, 39, Sharon Gless, actress, 61

June
1   Lord Foster of Thames Bank, architect, 69, Robert Powell, actor, 60, Gerald Scarfe, artist, 68, Edward Woodward, actor, 74, Lord Deedes, editor of the *Daily Telegraph* 1974–86, 91, Paco Peña, guitarist, 62, Alanis Morissette, singer, 30

2   King Constantine of the Hellenes, 64, Charlie Watts, drummer, 63, Marvin Hamlisch, composer, 60, Robin Orr, composer, 95, Steve Waugh, cricketer, 39, Mark Waugh, cricketer, 39

3   Penelope Wilton, actress, 58, Tony Curtis, actor, 79, Alain Resnais, film director, 82, Suzy Quatro, singer, 54

4   Geoffrey Palmer, actor, 77, Bob Champion, jockey and trainer, 56, Andrea Jaeger, tennis player, 39

5   Moira Anderson, singer, 64, Sheila Sim, actress, 82, Margaret Drabble, author, 65, David Hare, playwright, 57, Kenny G, singer, 48

6   David Blunkett, politician, 57, Bjorn Borg, tennis player, 48, Mike Gatting, cricketer, 47, Frank Tyson, cricketer, 74, Giacomo Aragall, tenor, 66, Sara Banerji, writer, 72, Paul Esswood, counter-tenor, 62, Willie-John McBride, rugby player, 64

7   Virginia McKenna, actress, 73, Curtis Robb, athlete, 32, James Ivory, film director, 76, Ronald Pickup, actor, 64, Liam Neeson, actor, 52, Michael Pennington, actor, 61, Tom Jones, singer, 64, Neal Radford, cricketer, 47, Anna Kournikova, tennis player and model, 23, Prince, singer and songwriter, 46

8   Norma Shaw, bowler, 67, Ray Illingworth, cricketer, 72, Derek Underwood, cricketer, 59

9   Tony Britton, actor, 80, Charles Saatchi, advertising executive, 61, Michael J Fox, actor, 43, Lady Anita Burgh, novelist, 67, Johnny Depp, actor, 41

10   HRH Prince Philip, Duke of Edinburgh, 83, Gordon Burns, television presenter, 62, David Platt, footballer, 38, Anthony Rooley, lutenist, 60, Saul Bellow, writer, 89, Elizabeth Hurley, actress, 39, Lionel Jeffries, actor, 78

11   Gene Wilder, actor, 69, Jackie Stewart, racing driver, 65, Jean Alesi, racing driver, 40, Tony Allcock, bowler, 49, Diana Armfield, painter, 84, Michael Cacoyannis, film director, 82, Gemma Craven, actress, 54, Hugh Laurie, actor, 45

12   Vic Damone, singer, 76, George Bush, US President, 80, Pat Jennings, footballer, 59, Oliver Knussen, composer, 52

13   Peter Scudamore, National Hunt jockey, 46, Gwynne Howell, opera singer, 66, Malcolm McDowell, actor, 61

14   Anthony Sher, actor and writer, 55, Paul Boateng, politician, 53, Steffi Graf, tennis player, 35, Mike Yarwood, entertainer, 63, Boy George, pop singer, 43, Donald Trump, businessman, 58

15   Johnny Herbert, racing driver, 40, Richard Baker, broadcaster, 79, Simon Callow, actor, 55, Courtney Cox, actress, 40

16   Dame Eileen Atkins, actress, 70, Professor Erich Segal, writer, 67, James Bolam, actor, 66, Simon Williams, actor, 58, Jan Zelezny, athlete, 38

17   Professor Sir Alan Walters, economist, 78, Ken Livingstone, Mayor of London, 59, Ken Loach, television and film director, 68, Barry Manilow, singer and composer, 58, Sir Edward Downes, conductor, 80, Venus Williams, tennis player, 24

18   Isabella Rossellini, actress, 52, Michael Blakemore, film and theatre director, 76, Sir Paul McCartney, musician, 62, Ian Carmichael, actor, 84, Peter Donohoe, pianist, 51, Delia Smith, cookery writer and broadcaster, 63

19 Aung San Suu Kyi, Nobel Laureate, 59, The Earl of Minto, 76, Charlie Drake, comedian, 79, Salman Rushdie, writer, 57, Kathleen Turner, actress, 50, Rory Underwood, rugby player, 41, Barry Hearn, businessman, 56, Paula Abdul, singer, 42

20 Wendy Craig, actress, 70, Stafford Dean, opera singer, 67, Allan Lamb, cricketer, 50, Stephen Frears, film director, 63, Duchess of Gloucester, 58, Nicole Kidman, actress, 37, Vikram Seth, novelist, 52, Lionel Richie, singer and songwriter, 55, Brian Wilson, singer and songwriter, 62, John Goodman, actor, 52

21 Prince William of Wales, 22, Ray Davies, singer and songwriter, 60, Don Black, lyricist, 66, John Edrich, cricketer, 67, Benazir Bhutto, Prime Minister of Pakistan 1988–90 and 1993–96, 51, Ian McEwan, author, 56, Jane Russell, actress, 83

22 RJ Montague, founder of Tiphook, 56, Dame Cicely Saunders, founder of St Christopher's Hospice, Sydenham, 86, Prunella Scales, actress, 72, Esther Rantzen, broadcaster, 64, Alastair Stewart, broadcaster, 52, Meryl Streep, actress, 55, Kris Kristofferson, actor, 68

23 Lord Irvine of Lairg, former Lord Chancellor, 64, Kim Begley, tenor, 52, Julian Hipwood, polo player, 58, Miriam Karlin, actress, 79

24 Anita Desai, novelist, 67, Betty Jackson, fashion designer, 55, Jeff Beck, guitarist, 60, Mick Fleetwood, drummer, 62, Ian Christie, clarinettist and film critic, 77

25 George Michael, singer, 41, Peter Blake, artist, 72, Sidney Lumet, film director, 80, Vladimir Kramnik, world chess champion, 29, Carly Simon, singer, 59

26 Claudio Abbado, conductor, 71, Colin Wilson, author, 73, Georgie Fame, singer and songwriter, 61, Greg LeMond, cyclist, 43, Chris O'Donnell, actor, 34

27 Hugh Wood, composer, 72, Alan Coren, writer and broadcaster, 66, Mary McAleese, Irish politician, 53

28 Kathy Bates, actress, 56, Harold Evans, former editor of *The Times* and *Sunday Times*, 76, Stan Barstow, writer, 76, Howard Barker, playwright and poet, 58, Correlli Barnett, author, 77, Mel Brooks, actor and film director, 78

29 Charlotte Bingham, playwright, 62, Sir Rex Hunt, Governor and Commander-in-Chief, Falkland Islands, 1980–2, 78, Amanda Donohoe, actress, 42

30 Lena Horne, singer, 87, John Fortune, actor and scriptwriter, 65, Christopher Lloyd, Surveyor of the Queen's Pictures, 54, Ralf Schumacher, racing driver, 29, MJK Smith, cricketer, 71, Mike Tyson, boxer, 38

July

1 Leslie Caron, actress, 73, Garry Schofield, rugby league player, 39, Carl Lewis, athlete, 43, Dan Aykroyd, actor, 52, Olivia de Havilland, actress, 88, Hans Werner Henze, composer, 78, Trevor Eve, actor, 53, Pamela Anderson, actress, 37, Debbie Harry, singer, 59

2 John Timpson, broadcaster, 76, Eva Lambert, artist, 69, Mary Craig, writer and broadcaster, 76, Jerry Hall, model, 48

3 Tom Stoppard, playwright, 67, Julie Burchill, writer, 45, Tom Cruise, actor, 42, Brigitte Fassbaender, mezzo-soprano, 65, Sir Richard Hadlee, cricketer, 53, Carlos Kleiber, conductor, 74, Ken Russell, film director, 77, Susan Penhaligon, actress, 55

4 Alec and Eric Bedser, cricketers, 86, Colin Welland, actor and playwright, 70, René Arnoux, racing driver, 56, Henri Leconte, tennis player, 41, Gina Lollobrigida, actress, 77, Neil Simon, playwright, 77, Bill Withers, singer, 66

5 Gianfranco Zola, footballer, 38, John Wright, cricketer, 50, Elizabeth Emanuel, fashion designer, 51, Mark Cox, tennis coach, 61

6 George W Bush, US President, 58, Geraldine James, actress, 54, The Dalai Lama, 69, Vladimir Ashkenazy, pianist and conductor, 67, Dame Mary Peters, athlete, 65, Jonathon Porritt, environmentalist, 54, Geoffrey Rush, actor, 53, Jennifer Saunders, comedienne, 46, Tony Lewis, cricketer, 66, Sylvester Stallone, actor, 58

7 Gian Carlo Menotti, composer, 93, Pierre Cardin, fashion designer, 82, Ringo Starr, drummer, 64, Bill Oddie, actor, 63, Tony Jacklin, golfer, 60, Michael Howard, politician, 63, Michael Ancram, politician, 59, Jeremy Guscott, rugby player, 39

8 Keith Fielding, rugby league player, 55, Mal Meninga, rugby league player, 44, Pauline Quirke, actress, 45, Brian Walden, broadcaster and Labour MP for Birmingham, All Saints, 1964–74, 72, Kevin Bacon, actor, 48, Anjelica Huston, actress, 53

9 Richard Wilson, actor, 68, Tom Hanks, actor, 48, David Hockney, artist, 67, Professor Richard Demarco, watercolourist, 74, Courtney Love, actress and singer, 40, Kelly McGillis, actress, 47, OJ Simpson, American football player and actor, 57

10 Ian Wallace, actor and broadcaster, 85, Sunil Gavaskar, cricketer, 55, Virginia Wade, tennis player, 59, John Dunlop, racehorse trainer, 65, Josephine Veasey, opera singer, 74, James Aldridge, author, 86

11 Gough Whitlam, former Australian PM, 88, Richard Chartres, Bishop of London, 57, Giorgio Armani, fashion designer, 70, Suzanne Vega, singer, 45

12 Gareth Edwards, rugby player, 57, Sir Alastair Burnet, newsreader, 76, Bill Cosby, actor and comedian, 67

13 Ian Hislop, editor of *Private Eye*, 44, Patrick Stewart, actor, 64, Harrison Ford, actor, 62, David Storey, playwright, 71

14 Bruce Oldfield, designer, 54, Gerald Ford, US President, 91, Sue Lawley, broadcaster, 58, Ingmar Bergman, director, 86

15 Julian Bream, guitarist and lutenist, 71, Carmen Callil, founder of Virago publishing house, 66, Linda Ronstadt, singer, 58, Sir Harrison Birtwistle, composer, 70, Robert Conquest, writer, 87, Ann Jellicoe, playwright and theatre director, 77, Professor Jocelyn Bell Burnell, astronomer, 61, Geoffrey Burgon, composer, 63, Juliet Pannett, portrait painter, 93, Jan-Michel Vincent, actor, 60, Jesse Ventura, wrestler, actor and politician, 53

16 Pinchas Zukerman, violinist, 56, Margaret Court, tennis player, 62, Dr Anita Brookner, author and art historian, 76, Shirley Hughes, author and illustrator, 77, Joanna MacGregor, pianist, 45, James Macmillan, composer, 45, Shaun Pollock, cricketer, 31

17	Marques de Samaranch, President of International Olympic Committee 1980–2001, 84, Wayne Sleep, dancer and choreographer, 56, Donald Sutherland, actor, 69, Tim Brooke-Taylor, actor, 64, David Hasselhoff, actor, 52
18	Richard Branson, founder and chairman of the Virgin Group, 54, Nick Faldo, golfer, 47, Senator John Glenn, astronaut, 83, Nelson Mandela, statesman, 86, Yevgeny Yevtushenko, poet, 71, Jim Watt, boxer, 56, Dennis Lillee, cricketer, 56, David Hemery, athlete, 60, Richard Pasco, actor, 78, Paul Verhoeven, film director, 66
19	Brian May, guitarist, 57, Ilie Nastase, tennis player, 58, Evelyn Glennie, percussionist, 39, Adrian Noble, theatre director, 54
20	Diana Rigg, actress, 66, Charlie Magri, boxer, 48, Jacques Delors, former President of Commission of the EEC, 79, Sir Edmund Hillary, first man to reach the summit of Mount Everest, 85, Carlos Santana, guitarist, 57
21	Norman Jewison, film director, 78, Karel Reisz, film director, 78, Sir Jonathan Miller, opera and theatre director, 70, Bill Pertwee, actor, 78, Julian Pettifer, broadcaster, 69, Robin Williams, actor and comedian, 52, Cat Stevens (Yusuf Islam), singer, 56
22	Bryan Forbes, film producer, 78, Jimmy Hill, broadcaster, 76, Danny Glover, actor, 57, Helen Lawrence, mezzo-soprano, 62, Willem Dafoe, actor, 49, Bonnie Langford, actress, 40, Terence Stamp, actor, 66
23	David Essex, singer and actor, 57, Danny La Rue, entertainer, 77, Lord Rogers of Riverside, architect, 71, Graham Gooch, cricketer, 51, Clive Rice, South African and Notts cricketer, 55, Michael Foot, politician, 91, Woody Harrelson, actor, 43
24	Peter Yates, film director and producer, 75, Quinlan Terry, architect, 67, Martin Keown, footballer, 38, Jennifer Lopez, singer and actress, 34, Linda Carter, actress, 53
25	Lord Nicholas Windsor, 34, Right Revd Barry Rogerson, Bishop of Bristol, 68, Iman, supermodel, 49, James Butler, sculptor, 73, Matt LeBlanc, actor, 37
26	Mick Jagger, singer, 61, Blake Edwards, film maker, 82, Helen Mirren, actress, 59, Lance Percival, actor and singer, 71, Pauline Clare, Chief Constable of Lancashire, 57, Sir Brian Mawhinney, politician, 64, Barbara Jefford, actress, 74, Kevin Spacey, actor, 45
27	Michael Ball, singer, 42, Allan Border, cricketer, 49, Jack Higgins, novelist, 75, Baroness Williams of Crosby, politician, 74, Christopher Dean, ice skater, 46, Joe Durie, tennis player, 44, Bobbie Gentry, singer, 60, Don Galloway, actor, 67
28	Ian McCaskill, meteorologist, 66, Sir Garfield Sobers, cricketer, 68, Riccardo Muti, conductor, 63
29	Sally Gunnell, athlete, 38, Joe Johnson, snooker player, 52, Max Faulkner, golfer, 88
30	Peter Bogdanovich, film director, 66, Kate Bush, singer, 46, Arnold Schwarzenegger, actor and politician, 57, Stan Stennett, actor, 77, Teresa Cahill, opera singer, 60, Richard Johnson, actor, 77, Daley Thompson, athlete, 46, Sir Clive Sinclair, inventor, 64, Lisa Kudrow, actress, 41
31	Evonne Cawley, tennis player, 53, Jonathan Dimbleby, broadcaster, 60, Peter Nichols, playwright, 77, Milton Friedman, economist, 92, JK Rowling, author, 39, Dean Cain, actor, 38, Wesley Snipes, actor, 42

August

1	Yves St Laurent, fashion designer, 68, Sam Mendes, film and theatre director, 39, Frank Hauser, theatre director, 82, Coolio, singer, 41
2	Peter O'Toole, actor, 72, Alan Whicker, broadcaster, 83, Rose Tremain, novelist and playwright, 61, Karl Miller, writer, 73
3	Terry Wogan, broadcaster, 66, Tony Bennett, singer, 78, Jack Straw, politician, 58, Martin Sheen, actor, 64, Steven Berkoff, actor, director and writer, 67, Baroness James of Holland Park, writer, 84
4	William Cooper, novelist, 94, Georgina Hale, actress, 61, Martin Jarvis, actor, 63, Dr Jack Cunningham, politician, 62, Mary Decker-Slaney, athlete, 46
5	Neil Armstrong, astronaut, 74, John Whittaker, show jumper, 49, Barbara Flynn, actress, 56, Alan Howard, actor, 67, Carla Lane, writer, 67, Jimmy Webb, songwriter, 58, Oleg Luzhny, footballer, 36, Billy Bingham, football manager, 73
6	Dom Mintoff, Prime Minister of Malta 1971–84, 88, Chris Bonington, mountaineer, 70, Jack Parnell, drummer, 81, Frank Finlay, actor, 78, Freddie Laker, entrepreneur, 82, Barbara Windsor, actress, 67, Charles Wood, writer, 72, Billy Boston, rugby union player, 70, Michael Deeley, film producer, 72, Sir Howard Hodgkin, painter, 72, Geri Halliwell, singer, 32
7	Greg Chappell, cricketer, 56, Alexei Sayle, comedian, 52, Walter Swinburn, jockey, 43, Nick Ross, broadcaster, 57, Kenneth Kendall, broadcaster, 80, Philip Snow, author, 89, Dominic Cork, cricketer, 33, David Duchovny, actor, 44
8	Princess Beatrice of York, 16, Nigel Mansell, racing driver 51, Dustin Hoffman, actor, 67, Keith Barron, actor, 70, Chris Eubank, boxer, 38
9	Melanie Griffith, actress, 47, Whitney Houston, singer, 41, Rod Laver, tennis player, 66, Posy Simmonds, cartoonist, 59, James Naughtie, broadcaster and journalist, 53
10	Roy Keane, footballer, 33, Kate O'Mara, actress, 65, Rosanna Arquette, actress, 45, John Alldis, conductor, 75, Barry Unsworth, author, 74, Lawrence Dallaglio, rugby union player, 32, Paul Newlove, rugby league player, 33
11	Anna Massey, actress, 67, Tamàs Vasary, pianist and conductor, 71, Raymond Leppard, conductor, 77, Don Boyd, film director, 56, Professor Alun Hoddinott, composer, 75, Steve Wozniak, founder of Apple Computers, 54
12	Mark Knopfler, guitarist, 55, Pete Sampras, tennis player, 33, Les Ferdinand, footballer, 38, Suzanne Vega, singer, 45
13	Fidel Castro, President of Cuba, 78, Alan Shearer, footballer, 34, Marie Helvin, model, 52, Tony Jarrett, athlete, 36, Sheila Armstrong, soprano, 62, George Shearing, jazz pianist, 85
14	Sarah Brightman, singer, 43, Buddy Greco, singer, 78, Steve Martin, actor, 59, Frederic Raphael, author, 73, Halle Berry, actress, 36

15   The Princess Royal, 54, Oscar Peterson, jazz pianist, 79, Lord Waldegrave of North Hill, politician, 58, Tony Robinson, actor and writer, 58, Ben Affleck, actor, 32

16   Helen Storey, fashion designer, 45, Trevor McDonald, broadcaster, 65, Madonna, singer, 46, Jeff Thomson, cricketer, 54, Sean Brady, Archbishop of Armagh and Primate of All Ireland, 65, Katherine Hamnett, fashion designer, 57, James Cameron, film director, 50

17   Robert de Niro, actor, 61, Nelson Piquet, racing driver, 52, Sir Vidia (VS) Naipaul, author and Nobel Laureate, 72, George Melly, jazz singer, 78, Alan Minter, boxer, 53, Robin Cousins, ice-skater, 47, Guillermo Vilas, tennis player, 52, Thierry Henry, footballer, 27, Sean Penn, actor, 44

18   Brian Aldiss, writer, 79, Caspar Weinberger, US Secretary of Defense 1981–7, 87, Patrick Swayze, actor, 52, Robert Redford, actor and director, 67, Roman Polanski, film director, 71

19   Bill Clinton, US President, 58, Richard Ingrams, editor of *The Oldie*, 67

20   Finlay Calder, rugby player, 47, John Emburey, cricketer, 52, Robert Plant, rock singer, 56, Dame Anne Evans, soprano, 63

21   Barry Norman, broadcaster and journalist, 71, Kenny Rogers, country music singer, 66, Dame Janet Baker, mezzo-soprano, 71, Kim Cattrall, actress, 48

22   Ray Bradbury, author, 84, Steve Davis, snooker player, 47, Mats Wilander, tennis player, 40, Honor Blackman, actress, 78, Boris Schapiro, bridge player, 95, General Norman Schwarzkopf, Commander US Central Command 1988–91, 70, Karlheinz Stockhausen, composer, 76

23   Geoff Capes, shot-putter and strongman, 55, Peter Lilley, politician, 61, Willy Russell, author and dramatist, 57, Shelley Long, actress, 55

24   Stephen Fry, actor and writer, 47, Sam Torrance, golfer, 51, Dame Antonia Byatt, writer, 68, Paul Barker, writer and broadcaster, 69, Carlo Curley, organist, 52, Tommy Docherty, football manager, 76, Jean-Michel Jarre, musician, 56, Cardinal Cormac Murphy-O'Connor, Archbishop of Westminster, 72, Steve Guttenberg, actor, 46

25   Sean Connery, actor, 74, Martin Amis, writer, 55, Frederick Forsyth, author, 66, Anne Archer, actress, 57, Claudia Schiffer, model, 34, Elvis Costello, musician, 50

26   The Duke of Gloucester, 60, Alison Steadman, actress, 58, Chris Boardman, cyclist, 36, Macaulay Culkin, actor, 24

27   Lady Antonia Fraser, writer, 72, Gerhard Berger, racing driver, 45, Bernard Langer, golfer, 47, Derek Warwick, racing driver, 50, John Lloyd, tennis player, 50, Michael Holroyd, author, 69, Jeanette Winterson, writer, 45, Paul Reubens (Peewee Herman), actor, 52, Barbara Bach, actress, 57

28   Imogen Cooper, concert pianist, 55, David Soul, actor and singer, 61, Shania Twain, pop singer, 39

29   William Friedkin, film director, 65, Elliot Gould, actor, 66, Michael Jackson, singer, 46, Lenny Henry, comedian, 46, Lord (Richard) Attenborough, actor, 81, Lord (Marmaduke) Hussey, former chairman of the BBC, 81, Rebecca De Mornay, actress, 42, Bob Beamon, athlete, 58

30   Lord Healey, politician, 87, Countess of Longford, writer, 98, Cameron Diaz, actress, 32

31   Richard Gere, actor, 55, Van Morrison, singer, 59, Clive Lloyd, cricketer, 60, Liz Forgan, writer and broadcaster, 60, Ed Moses, athlete, 49, Itzhak Perlman, violinist, 59, Professor Sir Bernard Lovell, founder of Jodrell Bank, 91, Debbie Gibson, singer, 34

September

1   Gloria Estefan, singer, 47, Ruud Gullit, footballer, 42, Barry Gibb, singer, 61, Lord Parkinson, politician, 73, Margaret Ewing, politician, 59, Marquess of Exeter, writer, 69

2   Jimmy Connors, tennis player, 52, Victor Spinetti, actor, 71, Michael Hastings, playwright, 66, Lennox Lewis, boxer, 39, Aimee Osbourne, singer, 31, Salma Hayek, actress, 36, Keanu Reeves, actor, 40

3   Pauline Collins, actress, 64, Geoff Arnold, cricketer, 60, Al Jardine, singer, 62, Charlie Sheen, actor, 39, Susan Milan, flautist, 57, Gareth Southgate, footballer, 34

4   Tom Watson, golfer, 55, Air Marshal Sir John Cheshire, 62, Bill Kenwright, actor and theatrical impresario, 59, Ione Skye, actress, 34

5   Tracy Edwards, yachtswoman, 42, Dick Clement, scriptwriter, 67, GW Tremlett, author and broadcaster, 65, Raquel Welch, actress, 64

6   Roger Knight, Secretary of the MCC, 58, Greg Rusedski, tennis player, 31, Tim Henman, tennis player, 30, John Young, rugby player and chairman of Lloyd's Regulatory Board, 67, Roger Law, puppeteer and satirist, 63

7   Kevin Curran, cricketer, 45, George Ellis, athlete, 72, Peter Gill, stage director, 65, Chrissie Hynde, singer, 53, Gloria Gaynor, singer, 55

8   Anne Diamond, presenter, 50, Jeannette Altwegg, ice skater, 74, Michael Frayn, novelist and playwright, 71, Geoff Miller, cricketer, 52, Sir Peter Maxwell Davies, composer and conductor, 70

9   Michael Keaton, actor, 53, Chaim Topol, actor, 69, Dave Stewart, musician, 52, Raine, Countess Spencer, 75, Hugh Grant, actor, 44, Neil Holmes, powerboat racer, 45, Julia Sawalha, actress, 36, Margaret Tyzack, actress, 73

10   Arnold Palmer, golfer, 75, Beryl Cook, painter, 78, Sir Thomas Allen, opera singer, 60, Colin Firth, actor, 44, Bill Rogers, golfer, 53, Norman Morrice, choreographer, 73, Michael Barry, food journalist and broadcaster, 63, Amy Irving, actress, 51

11   Franz Beckenbauer, footballer, 59, Anthony Browne, book illustrator, 58, Eddie George, former Governor of the Bank of England, 66, Herbert Lom, actor, 87, Judith Howarth, soprano, 42, Brian de Palma, film director, 60, Harry Connick Jr, singer and actor, 37

12   Sir Ian Holm, actor, 73, Maria Aitken, actress, 59, Bertie Ahern, Prime Minister of the Republic of Ireland, 53

13   Jacqueline Bisset, actress, 60, Goran Ivanisevic, tennis player, 33, Lord (Colin) Moynihan, 49, Shane Warne, cricketer, 35, Michael Johnson, athlete, 37, Robert Millar, cyclist, 46

14   Ray Wilkins, footballer, 48, Nicol Williamson, actor, 66, Sandra Blow, painter, 79, Martyn Hill, tenor, 60, Hicham El Guerrouj, athlete, 30

15 Prince Henry of Wales, 20, Oliver Stone, film director, 58, Richard Gordon, author, 83, Tommy Lee Jones, actor, 58, Graham Taylor, football manager, 60, Jessye Norman, soprano, 59

16 Lauren Bacall, actress, 80, BB King, guitarist and singer, 79, Charles Haughey, former Irish Prime Minister, 79, Lee Kuan Yew, former Prime Minister of Singapore, 81, Loyd Grossman, broadcaster, 54, Andy Irvine, rugby player, 53, David Copperfield, magician, 48, Mickey Rourke, actor, 48

17 Damon Hill, racing driver, 44, Sir Stirling Moss, racing driver, 75, Des Lynam, broadcaster, 62, Mary Stewart, novelist, 88, Tessa Jowell, politician, 57, Karen Straker-Dixon, show jumper, 40, Anne Bancroft, actress, 73

18 Peter Shilton, goalkeeper, 55, Marjorie Mowlam, politician, 55, Jack Cardiff, film director, 90, Russ Abbot, entertainer, 57, Ray Alan, ventriloquist, 74, Sol Campbell, footballer, 30, Darren Gough, cricketer, 34, Siobhan Davies, choreographer, 54

19 Kate Adie, broadcaster, 59, Jeremy Irons, actor, 56, Zandra Rhodes, fashion designer, 64, Captain Jim Fox, athlete, 63, Twiggy, actress, 55, Pete Murray, broadcaster, 76, Rosemary Harris, actress, 74, Ray Cooper, percussionist, 62, David Seaman, goalkeeper, 41, Arthur Willis, composer, 78, Kurt Sanderling, conductor, 92, David McCallum, actor, 71

20 John Dankworth, jazz musician, 77, Sophia Loren, actress, 70, Jane Manning, soprano, 66

21 Larry Hagman, actor, 73, Jimmy Young, broadcaster, 81, Shirley Conran, writer, 72, Leonard Cohen, singer and poet, 70, Curtly Ambrose, cricketer, 41, Simon Mayo, broadcaster, 46, Bill Murray, actor, 54, Ricky Lake, actress and television presenter, 36, Stephen King, author, 57

22 Captain Mark Phillips, equestrian, 56, Fay Weldon, writer, 73, Gina Fratini, fashion designer, 73, Dannie Abse, writer, 81, Ronaldo Luiz Nazario de Lima, Brazilian footballer, 28, Maria Charles, actress, 75, Nick Cave, singer, 47

23 Mickey Rooney, actor, 84, Bruce Springsteen, rock singer, 55, Cherie Booth, QC, 50, Julio Iglesias, singer, 61, Norma Winstone, singer, 63, Nicholas Witchell, broadcaster, 51, Frank Foster, saxophonist, 76

24 John Rutter, composer and conductor, 59, Jack Dee, comedian, 43, Brian Glanville, author and journalist, 73

25 Felicity Kendal, actress, 58, Lord (Leon) Brittan of Spennithorne, politician, 65, Catherine Zeta-Jones, actress, 35, Ronnie Barker, actor, 75, Colin Davis, conductor, 77, Michael Douglas, actor, 60, Will Smith, actor and singer, 36, Timothy Severin, author and explorer, 64, Barbara Walters, US television presenter, 73, Heather Locklear, actress, 43, Mark Hamill, actor, 53

26 Ian Chappell, cricketer, 61, Bryan Ferry, singer, 59, Lucette Aldous, ballerina, 66, Anne Robinson, broadcaster, 60, Serena Williams, tennis player, 23, Olivia Newton-John, singer, 56

27 Diane Abbott, politician, 51, Josephine Barstow, opera singer, 64, Barbara Dickson, singer and actress, 56, Meatloaf, rock singer, 57, Denis Lawson, actor, 57, Gordon Honeycombe, author and broadcaster, 68

28 Brigitte Bardot, actress, 70, Jon Snow, television journalist, 57, Mika Hakkinen, racing driver, 36, Peter Egan, actor, 58, Gwyneth Paltrow, actress, 32, John Scott, former England rugby captain, 50, Mira Sorvino, actress, 37

29 Lord (Sebastian) Coe, athlete and politician, 48, Lech Walesa, former President of Poland and Nobel Laureate, 61, Michelangelo Antonioni, film director, 92, Richard Bonynge, opera conductor, 74, Colin Dexter, author, 74, Patricia Hodge, actress, 58, Gareth Davies, former rugby captain of Wales, 48, Jennifer Rush, singer, 44, Ian McShane, actor, 62

30 Viscount Cranborne, politician, 58, Deborah Kerr, actress, 83, Angie Dickinson, actress, 73, Anthony Green, painter, 65, Johnny Mathis, singer, 69, Ian Ogilvy, actor, 62, Victoria Tennant, actress, 54, Rula Lenska, actress, 57

October

1 Julie Andrews, actress, 69, Phil de Glanville, rugby player, 36, Sandy Gall, broadcaster, 77, Jimmy Carter, US President, 80, Cardinal Cahal Daly, former Primate of All Ireland, 87, Harry Hill, comedian, 40

2 Trevor Brooking, footballer, 56, Sting (Gordon Sumner), singer, 53, Jan Morris, writer, 78, Wade Dooley, rugby player, 47, Jana Novotna, tennis player, 36, Jon Speelman, chess player, 48, Anna Ford, broadcaster, 61, Peter Frankl, pianist, 69

3 Shridath (Sonny) Ramphal, former Secretary-General of the Commonwealth, 76, Kevin Richardson, vocalist, 32, Gore Vidal, author, 79, Zeinab Badawi, broadcaster, 45, Christopher Bruce, dancer, 59, Chubby Checker, singer, 63, Lindsey Buckingham, rock guitarist, 57, Fred Couples, golfer, 45, Ruggero Raimondi, operatic bass, 63, Neve Campbell, actress, 31, Tommy Lee, drummer, 42

4 Jackie Collins, novelist, 67, Basil D'Oliveira, cricketer, 73, Charlton Heston, actor, 80, Ray Floyd, golfer, 62, Susan Sarandon, actress, 58, Sir Terence Conran, restaurateur and designer, 73, Anneka Rice, broadcaster, 46, Alicia Silverstone, actress, 28

5 Bob Geldof, singer and founder of Band Aid, 50, Vaclav Havel, President of Czech Republic, 68, Glynis Johns, actress, 81, Laura Davies, golfer, 41, Ray Clemence, footballer, 56, Robert Kee, author and broadcaster, 85, Kate Winslet, actress, 29

6 Lord (Melvyn) Bragg, broadcaster, 65, Tony Greig, cricketer, 58, Richie Benaud, cricketer, 74, Britt Ekland, actress, 62

7 Jayne Torvill, ice skater, 47, Desmond Tutu, former Archbishop of Cape Town, 73, Clive James, broadcaster, 65, Yo Yo Ma, cellist, 49, Thomas Keneally, author, 69, Sir Timothy Ackroyd, actor, 46, June Allyson, actress, 87, Christopher Booker, journalist and author, 67, Professor Harold Dexter, organist, 84, Vladimir Putin, Russian politician, 52

8 Betty Boothroyd, politician, 75, Chevy Chase, actor, 61, Sigourney Weaver, actress, 55, Maurice Cockrill, artist, 68, Bel Mooney, writer and broadcaster, 58, Albert Roux, chef and restaurateur, 69, Ray Reardon, snooker player, 72

9 The Duke of Kent, 69, Joe Ashton, politician, 71, Steve Ovett, athlete, 49, John Doubleday, sculptor, 57, Bill Tidy, cartoonist, 71, Donald Sinden, actor, 81, Brian Blessed, actor, 68, Sir Nicholas Grimshaw, architect, 65, Annika Sorenstam, golfer, 34, Andy Platt, rugby league player, 41, Sally Burgess, singer, 51, Peter Elliott, athlete, 42

10 Charles Dance, actor, 58, Harold Pinter, playwright, 74, Chris Tarrant, broadcaster, 58, Tony Adams, footballer, 38, Nicholas Parsons, broadcaster, 76, Midge Ure, singer, 51, Ben Vereen, actor, 58, Willard White, singer and actor, 58, Matthew Pinsent, rower, 34, David Hempleman-Adams, explorer, 48, Lance Cairns, cricketer, 55, Sharon Osbourne, television personality, 52, David Lee Roth, singer, 49

11 Sir Bobby Charlton, footballer, 67, Dawn French, actress, 47, Maria Bueno, tennis player, 65, David Rendall, tenor, 56, Luke Perry, actor, 38

12 Magnus Magnusson, broadcaster, 75, Luciano Pavarotti, tenor, 69, Rick Parfitt, guitarist, 56, David Threlfall, actor, 51, Angela Rippon, broadcaster and chairman of English National Ballet, 60, Kenneth Griffith, actor and writer, 83, Marion Jones, athlete, 29

13 Baroness Thatcher, politician, 79, Edwina Currie, politician, 58, John Snow, cricketer, 63, John Regis, athlete, 38, Paul Simon, musician, 63, Michael Heath, cartoonist, 69, Javier Sotomayor, athlete, 37, Marie Osmond, singer, 45

14 Steve Cram, athlete, 44, Roger Moore, actor, 77, Sir Cliff Richard, vocalist, 64, Roger Taylor, tennis player, 63, Christopher Timothy, actor, 64, Justin Hayward, singer, 58, Ralph Lauren, fashion designer, 65

15 The Duchess of York, 45, David Trimble, Northern Ireland's First Minister, 60, Chris De Burgh, singer, 56, Professor JK Galbraith, economist, 96, Craig Chalmers, rugby player, 36, Andy Cole, footballer, 33

16 Max Bygraves, entertainer, 82, Terry Griffiths, snooker player, 57, Baroness Nicholson of Winterbourne, politician, 63, Peter Bowles, actor, 68, Dr Stefan Buczacki, biologist, 59, Gunter Grass, writer, 77, Angela Lansbury, actress, 79

17 Harry Carpenter, broadcaster, 79, Margot Kidder, actress, 56, Ann Jones, tennis player, 66, Stephen Kovacevich, pianist, 64, Graeme Le Saux, footballer, 36, Sir Cameron Mackintosh, musical producer, 58, Ernie Els, golfer, 35

18 Michael Stich, tennis player, 36, Martina Navratilova, tennis player, 48, Mary Symes, the first woman coroner, 92, Chuck Berry, rock 'n' roll singer, 78, Jean-Claude Van Damme, actor, 44, Paul Palmer, swimmer, 30

19 John Le Carre, author, 73, Admiral of the Fleet Sir Michael Pollock, 88, Sir Michael Gambon, actor, 64, Evander Holyfield, boxer, 42, Phil Davies, rugby player, 41, Bernard Hepton, actor, 79, John Lithgow, actor, 59

20 Chris Cowdrey, cricketer, 47, Lord Montagu of Beaulieu, 78, Eddie Macken, show jumper, 55, Allan Donald, cricketer, 38, Emma Tennant, writer, 67, Ian Rush, footballer, 43, Timothy West, actor, 70, Snoop Dogg, singer, 32, Tom Petty, singer, 54

21 Sir Malcolm Arnold, composer, 83, Geoff Boycott, cricketer, 64, Peter Mandelson, politician, 51, Simon Gray, playwright, 68, David Campese, rugby player, 42, Paul Ince, footballer, 37, Manfred Mann, musician, 64, Sir William Whitfield, architect, 84, Nadia Nerina, ballerina, 77, Carrie Fisher, actress, 48, Benjamin Netanyahu, Israeli politician, 55

22 Derek Jacobi, actor, 66, Joan Fontaine, actress, 87, Catherine Deneuve, actress, 61, Sir Michael Stoute, racehorse trainer, 59, Jeff Goldblum, actor, 52, Doris Lessing, author, 85, Christopher Lloyd, actor, 66, John Blashford-Snell, explorer, 68

23 Pele, footballer, 64, Anita Roddick, businesswoman, 62, Maggi Hambling, artist, 59, George Cohen, footballer, 65, Michael Crichton, author, 62, 'Weird' Al Yankovic, entertainer, 45

24 Jonathan Davies, rugby player, 42, Bill Wyman, bass guitarist, 68, Sir Mark Tully, journalist and broadcaster, 69, Kevin Kline, actor, 57, Marquess of Salisbury, 88, Frank Delaney, writer, 62

25 Galina Vishnevskaya, soprano, 78, Joe Mercer, jockey, 70, Imran Khan, cricketer, 52, Michael Lynagh, rugby player, 41

26 Bob Hoskins, actor, 62, Gyorgy Pauk, violinist, 68, John Arden, playwright, 74, Adam Mars-Jones, writer, 50, Hillary Clinton, New York senator, 57, Andrew Motion, Poet Laureate, 52, Audley Harrison, boxer, 33

27 David Bryant, bowler, 73, John Cleese, actor, 65, Leonard Rosoman, painter, 91, Mark Taylor, cricketer, 40, Glenn Hoddle, footballer and manager, 47, AN Wilson, author, 54, Roberto Benigni, actor, 52, Simon Le Bon, singer, 46, Kelly Osbourne, singer, 20

28 Carl Davis, composer and conductor, 68, Julia Roberts, actress, 37, Bill Gates, chairman of Microsoft, 49, David Dimbleby, broadcaster, 66, Dame Cleo Laine, singer, 77, Hank Marvin, guitarist, 63, Michael Noakes, painter, 71, Joan Plowright (Lady Olivier), actress, 75, Geoff Reeve, film producer, 72, Miyako Yoshida, ballerina, 39

29 Richard Dreyfuss, actor, 57, Robert Hardy, actor, 79, Jack Shepherd, actor, 64, Jon Vickers, tenor, 78, Frank Sedgman, tennis player, 77, Michael Jayston, actor, 69, Michael Vaughan, cricketer, 30, Winona Ryder, actress, 33

30 Michael Winner, film director, 69, Juliet Stevenson, actress, 48, Richard Alston, choreographer, 56, Diego Maradona, footballer, 44, Harry Hamlin, actor, 53, Grace Slick, singer, 65

31 Sir James Savile, broadcaster, 78, Dick Francis, author, 84, Michael Collins, astronaut, 74, Barrie Keeffe, dramatist, 59, Barbara Bel Geddes, actress, 82, Charles Moore, former editor of the *Daily Telegraph*, 48

November

1 Gary Player, golfer, 69, Victoria de los Angeles, singer, 81, Nick Owen, broadcaster, 57, Gerald Ratner, businessman, 55, Jenny McCarthy, actress and presenter, 32

2 Ken Rosewall, tennis player, 70, Alan Jones, racing driver, 58, Bruce Welch, guitarist, 63, Paul Johnson, writer, 76, Stefanie Powers, actress, 62

3 Viscount Linley, designer, 43, Roseanne Arnold, actress, 52, Roy Emerson, tennis player, 68, Lulu, singer, 56, Ian Wright, footballer, 41, Albert Reynolds, former Prime Minister of the Republic of Ireland, 72, Ludovic Kennedy, broadcaster, 85, Violetta Elvin, ballerina, 79, Larry Holmes, boxer, 55, Vanni Treves, former chairman of Channel 4 Television, 64, Dolph Lundgren, actor, 45, Adam Ant, singer, 50

4 Walter Cronkite, broadcaster, 88, Michael Meacher, politician, 65, Malandra Burrows, actress, 39, Sean 'P Diddy' Combs, rap artist, 34, Rodney Marsh, cricketer, 57, Loretta Swit, actress, 67, Joan Rodgers, soprano, 48, Laura Welch Bush, First Lady of USA, 58

5   Bryan Adams, singer, 45, Art Garfunkel, musician, 63, Lester Piggott, jockey, 69, Dennis Andries, boxer, 53, Sam Shepard, playwright and actor, 61, Jim Moir, former Controller, BBC Radio 2, 63, Tatum O'Neal, actress, 41, Elke Sommer, actress, 64

6   Sally Field, actress, 58, Frank Carson, comedian, 78, Mike Nichols, film director, 73, Nigel Havers, actor, 53, PJ Proby, vocalist, 66, Bernat Klein, designer, 82, Daniele Gatti, conductor, 43, Ethan Hawke, actor, 36

7   John Barnes, footballer, 41, Dame Gwyneth Jones, soprano, 68, Billy Graham, evangelist, 86, Helen Suzman, politician, 87, Jonathan Palmer, racing driver, 48, Su Pollard, actress, 55, Dame Joan Sutherland, soprano, 78

8   Ken Dodd, entertainer, 73, Rifat Ozbek, fashion designer, 51, Martin Peters, footballer, 61, Rupert Allason, author, 53, Alain Delon, actor, 69, Kazuo Ishiguro, author, 50, Gordon Ramsay, restaurateur, 38, Richard Stoker, composer, 66, Jack Osbourne, drummer and music scout, 19

9   Tom Weiskopf, golfer, 62, Ronald Harwood, writer, 70, Alistair Horne, author, 79, Hugh Leonard, playwright, 78, Tony Slattery, writer and actor, 45, Marina Warner, writer and critic, 58, David Duval, golfer, 33, Roger McGough, poet, 67

10 Tim Rice, lyricist and broadcaster, 60, Robert Carrier, cookery writer, 81, Roy Scheider, actor, 69

11 Ron Greenwood, football manager, 84, Demi Moore, actress, 42, June Whitfield, actress, 79, Rodney Marsh, cricketer, 57, Leonardo DiCaprio, actor, 30

12 Chad Varah, founder of the Samaritans, 93, Nadia Comaneci, gymnast, 43, Dame Peggy Fenner, politician, 82, David Schwimmer, actor, 38, Neil Young, singer, 59

13 Rt Revd Lord (George) Carey of Clifton, former Archbishop of Canterbury, 69, Alexandra Shulman, editor of *Vogue*, 47, Whoopi Goldberg, actress, 49, Lord Jacobs, chairman of the British School of Motoring 1973–90, 73

14 Prince of Wales, 56, Steffano Gabbana, fashion designer, 42, Mark Le Fanu, general secretary of the Society of Authors, 58, Dr Boutros Boutros-Ghali, former Secretary-General of the United Nations, 82, Koji Tatsuno, fashion designer, 42

15 Peter Phillips, son of the Princess Royal, 27, JG Ballard, writer, 74, Daniel Barenboim, musician, 62, Petula Clark, singer, 72

16 Frank Bruno, boxer, 43, Willie Carson, jockey, 62, Griff Rhys Jones, actor and writer, 51, Waqar Younis, cricketer, 33, Sir Magdi Yacoub, cardiothoracic surgeon, 69, Lorraine Heggessey, former Controller, BBC1, 48, Paul Scholes, footballer, 30, Lisa Bonet, actress, 37

17 Martin Scorsese, film director, 62, Danny De Vito, actor and film director, 60, Jonathan Ross, broadcaster, 44, Michael Adams, chess player, 33, Sir Charles Mackerras, conductor, 79, Fenella Fielding, actress, 70

18 Admiral of the Fleet Sir Henry Leach, 81, Baroness Jay of Paddington, politician, 65, Linda Evans, actress, 62

19 Jodie Foster, actress, 42, Lady Davina Windsor, 27, Meg Ryan, actress, 43, David Lloyd-Jones, conductor, 70, Calvin Klein, fashion designer, 62, Gail Devers, athlete, 38

20 Dulcie Gray, actress, 84, Gareth Chilcott, rugby player, 48, Nadine Gordimer, author, 81, Bo Derek, actress, 48

21 Goldie Hawn, actress, 59, Natalia Makarova, ballerina, 64, Dame Beryl Bainbridge, writer, 70, Georgina Battiscombe, author, 99, Alberto Juantorena, athlete, 54, Bjork, singer, 39

22 Boris Becker, tennis player, 37, Jamie Lee Curtis (Lady Haden-Guest), actress, 46, Billie Jean King, tennis player, 61, Tom Conti, actor, 62, Terry Gilliam, film animator, 64, Sir Peter Hall, drama director, 74, John Bird, actor and writer, 68, Robert Vaughn, actor, 72

23 Most Revd Patrick Kelly, Archbishop of Liverpool, 66, Alan Mullery, footballer, 63, Michael Gough, actor, 88, Krzysztof Penderecki, composer, 71, Diana Quick, actress, 58, Christopher Logue, poet, 78

24 Ian Botham, cricketer, 49, Billy Connolly, comedian, 62, Paul Thorburn, rugby player, 42, David Kossoff, actor and author, 85, Charles Osborne, author, 77, Vivien Saunders, golfer, 58

25 Imran Khan, cricketer, 52, Charles Kennedy, politician, 45, Yvonne Kenny, opera singer, 54, Christina Applegate, actress, 33

26 John Gummer, politician, 65, Tina Turner, singer, 65, Charles Forte, businessman, 96

27 John Alderton, actor, 64, Rodney Bewes, actor, 69, Sir John Maddox, writer and broadcaster, 79, Viktoria Mullova, violinist, 45, Verity Lambert, film and television producer, 67, Alan Simpson, writer, 75, Robin Givens, actress, 40

28 Kriss Akabusi, athlete, 46, Dervla Murphy, author, 73, Stephen Roche, cyclist, 45, Manolo Blahnik, fashion-shoe designer, 62, Fiona Armstrong, broadcaster, 48, Sonia O'Sullivan, athlete, 35, Anna Nicole Smith, actress, 37, Ed Harris, actor, 54

29 Jacques Chirac, French President, 72, Ryan Giggs, footballer, 31, Derek Jameson, journalist and broadcaster, 75, John Mayall, blues musician, 71, Louise Winter, mezzo-soprano, 45, Geoffrey Moorhouse, writer, 73, Garry Shandling, actor and comedian, 55, Jeff Fahey, actor, 48

30 Gary Lineker, footballer, 44, Marguerite Porter, ballerina, 56, David Mamet, writer, stage and film director, 57, George Graham, footballer, 60, Radu Lupu, pianist, 59, Laurent Jalabert, cyclist, 36, Ridley Scott, film director, 67, Billy Idol, singer, 49

December

1   Woody Allen, actor and director, 69, Bette Midler, actor and singer, 59, Andy Ripley, rugby player and rower, 57, Stephen Poliakoff, playwright, 52, Lee Trevino, golfer, 65, Keith Michell, actor, 76, Arjuna Ranatunga, Sri Lankan cricketer, 41, Sarfraz Nawaz, Pakistani cricketer, 56, Mike Denness, England cricketer, 64, Richard Pryor, actor and comedian, 64

2   Alexander Haig, former US Secretary of State, 80, Peter Harding, Marshal of the RAF, 71, Monica Seles, tennis player, 31, Britney Spears, singer, 23

3   Trevor Bailey, cricketer, 81, Jean-Luc Godard, film director, 74, Mel Smith, comedian, 52, Daryl Hannah, actress, 44, Franz Klammer, skier, 51, Andy Williams, singer, 74, Paul Nicholas, actor, 54, Craig Raine, poet, 60, Ozzy Osbourne, rock singer, 56

4   Jeff Bridges, actor, 55, Ronnie Corbett, comedian, 74, Pamela Stephenson, actress and writer, 54, Yvonne Minton, mezzo-soprano, 66, Gemma Jones, actress, 62, Costantino Rocca, golfer, 48, Deanna Durbin, actress and singer, 83, Anke Huber, tennis player, 30, Marisa Tomei, actress, 40

5   Lord Chalfont, chairman of the Radio Authority 1991–4, 85, Little Richard, entertainer, 69, Jose Carreras, tenor, 58, Hanif Kureishi, author, 50, Sheridan Morley, author and broadcaster, 63, Ronnie O'Sullivan, snooker player, 29, Lanny Wadkins, golfer, 55, Paddy McMahon, show jumper, 71

6   Dave Brubeck, jazz musician, 84, Gerry Francis, footballer, 53, Eric Newby, writer, 85, Peter Willey, cricketer, 55, Charles Vance, actor and producer, 75, Keke Rosberg, racing driver, 56, Nick Park, animator, 45, Richard Krajicek, tennis player, 33, Per-Ulrik Johansson, golfer, 38, Helen Liddell, politician, 54, Geoff Hoon, politician, 51

7   Sir Sidney Samuelson, British Film Commissioner 1991–7, 79, Eli Wallach, actor, 89, Helen Watts, opera singer, 77, Nicole Appleton, singer, 30, Sue Johnston, actress, 61, Chris Joynt, rugby league player, 33

8   Kim Basinger, actress, 51, Lucien Freud, artist, 82, Sir James Galway, flautist, 65, Sir Geoff Hurst, footballer, 63, Les Ferdinand, footballer, 38, Sir David Hay, cardiologist and twin brother of Sir Hamish Hay, New Zealand politician, 77, Sinead O'Connor, singer, 38, Teri Hatcher, actress, 40, David Carradine, actor, 68

9   Kirk Douglas, actor, 88, Bob Hawke, Australian politician, 75, Joan Armatrading, singer, 54, John Malkovich, actor, 51, Dame Elisabeth Legge-Schwarzkopf, opera singer, 89, Dame Judi Dench, actress, 70, Joanna Trollope, writer, 61, Susan Bullock, soprano, 46, Mervyn Davies, rugby player, 58, Ian McIntyre, writer and broadcaster, 73, Donny Osmond, singer, 47, Beau Bridges, actor, 63

10   Lord (John) Birt, Director-General of the BBC 1992–2000, 60, Kenneth Branagh, actor, 44, Nicolas Kynaston, organist, 63, Raphael Maklouf, sculptor, 67, Jahangir Khan, squash player, 41

11   Carlo Ponti, film director, 91, Alexander Solzhenitsyn, author, 86, Cliff Michelmore, broadcaster, 85, Anna Carteret, actress, 62, Vishy Anand, chess player, 35, Teri Garr, actress, 55, Donna Mills, actress, 62

12   Will Carling, rugby union player, 39, Dionne Warwick, singer, 63, Emerson Fittipaldi, racing driver, 58, Lionel Blair, dancer, 73, Jasper Conran, fashion designer, 45, Connie Francis, singer, 66, Cliff Holden, painter, 85, Denise Coffey, actress, 68, Tracy Austin, tennis player, 44, Anne Coates, film producer and editor, 79

13   The Aga Khan, 68, John Francome, jump jockey, 52, George Shultz, US politician, 84, Dick Van Dyke, actor, 79, Anouska Hempel (Lady Weinberg), hotelier and designer, 63, Robert Lindsay, actor, 55, Christopher Plummer, actor, 75

14   Stan Smith, tennis player, 58, Michael Owen, footballer, 25, Barbara Leigh-Hunt, actress, 69

15   Lanfranco (Frankie) Dettori, jockey, 34, Edna O'Brien, author, 68, Ida Haendel, violinist, 80, Michael Bogdanov, theatre director, 66, Don Johnson, actor, 55, Joe Jordan, footballer, 53, Oscar Niemeyer, architect, 97, Henrietta Knight, racehorse trainer, 58

16   Arthur C Clarke, science fiction writer, 87, Liv Ullmann, actress, 66, Joel Garner, cricketer, 52, Peter Dickinson, author, 77, Richard Cockerill, rugby union player, 34, Trevor Pinnock, harpsichordist and conductor, 58, Donovan Bailey, athlete, 37

17   Kerry Packer, businessman, 67, Robert Robinson, broadcaster, 77, Tommy Steele, entertainer, 68, Bernard Hill, actor, 60, Christopher Cazenove, actor, 59, Dominic Lawson, editor of the *Sunday Telegraph*, 48, Paula Radcliffe, athlete, 31

18   Keith Richards, guitarist, 61, Steven Spielberg, film director, 57, Arantxa Sanchez Vicario, tennis player, 33, Christina Aguilera, singer, 34, Brad Pitt, actor, 41

19   Marquess of Queensbury, 75, Upamanyu Chatterjee, novelist, 45, Tim Parks, novelist, 50, Steven Isserlis, cellist, 46, Alyssa Milano, actress, 32

20   Jenny Agutter, actress, 52, Uri Geller, showman and spoon-bender, 58, Michael Beaumont, Seigneur of Sark, 77

21   Jane Fonda, actress, 67, Chris Evert, tennis player, 50, Kurt Waldheim, Austrian politician, 86, Greville Starkey, jockey, 65, Michael Tilson Thomas, conductor, 60, Geoff Lewis, jockey and trainer, 69, Phil Donahue, television presenter, 69

22   Robin Gibb, pop singer, 55, Duke of Westminster, 53, James Burke, broadcaster, 68, Ken Whitmore, playwright, 65

23   Helmut Schmidt, former German Chancellor, 86, Emperor Akihito of Japan, 71, Christopher Lawrence, goldsmith, 68, Belinda Lang, actress, 51, Graham Kelly, former chief executive of the Football Association, 59

24   Carol Vorderman, television presenter, 44, Professor Anthony Clare, psychiatrist, 62, Philip Ziegler, author, 75, Ricky Martin, singer, 33

25   Annie Lennox, singer, 50, Princess Alexandra, 68, Jim Bolger, racehorse trainer, 63, Nigel Starmer-Smith, sports commentator, 60, Dido, singer, 33, Sissy Spacek, actress, 55

26   Jane Lapotaire, actress, 60, Dame Thea King, clarinettist, 79, Harry Christophers, conductor, 51, Dermot Murnaghan, broadcaster, 47, Anna Scher, founder of the Anna Scher Theatre, 60

27   Gérard Depardieu, actor, 56, Janet Street-Porter, journalist and broadcaster, 58, Polly Toynbee, journalist, 58, Pat Moss, rally driver, 70

28   Nigel Kennedy, violinist, 48, Dame Maggie Smith, actress, 70, Denzel Washington, actor, 50, Sir Max Hastings, former editor of the *Daily Telegraph* and *Evening Standard*, 59, Lord Hattersley, politician, 72

29   Ted Danson, actor, 57, Martin Offiah, rugby league player, 38, Harvey Smith, show jumper, 66, Jon Voight, actor, 66, Bernard Cribbins, actor, 76, Mary Tyler Moore, actress and television executive, 68, Alan Rusbridger, journalist, 51, Jude Law, actor, 32

30   Gordon Banks, goalkeeper, 67, Bo Diddley, guitarist and singer, 76, Timothy Mo, writer, 54, Ben Johnson, athlete, 43, Tiger Woods, golfer, 29, Tracey Ullman, actress and comedienne, 45, Davy Jones, singer and actor, 59

31   Anthony Hopkins, actor, 67, Ben Kingsley, actor, 61, Alex Salmond, politician, 50, Sir Alex Ferguson, football manager, 63, Michael Bonallack, golfer, 70, Stephen Cleobury, conductor, 56, Tess Jaray, artist, 67, Jean-Pierre Rives, rugby player, 52, Val Kilmer, actor, 45

CURRENT AFFAIRS

EDUCATION

Public Schools	Founded
King's School, Canterbury, Kent	600
King's School, Rochester, Kent	604
St Peter's School, York	627
Sherborne School, Dorset*	705
St Alban's	948
King's School, Ely	973
Winchester	1382
Eton	1440
City of London	1442
Loughborough	1495
St Paul's	1509
Giggleswick School, N. Yorks	1512
Manchester Grammar	1515
Sedbergh School, Cumbria	1525
Bristol Grammar	1532
Berkhamsted, Herts	1541
Christ College, Brecon	1541
King's Worcester	1541
Bristol Cathedral	1542
Bradford Grammar School, West Yorkshire	1548
Bedford	1552
Leeds Grammar School	1552
Christ's Hospital, Horsham	1553
Tonbridge	1553
Shrewsbury	1552
Gresham's School, Holt, Norfolk	1555
Oundle, Northants	1556
Repton, Derby	1557
Merchant Taylors', Northwood	1560
Westminster	1560
Kingston	1561
Felsted, Dunmow, Essex	1564
Highgate	1565
Rugby	1567
Harrow	1571
Uppingham, Oakham	1584
Stonyhurst, RC, Clitheroe	1593
Wellingborough, Northants	1595
Trinity School, Croydon	1596
Whitgift School, Croydon	1596
Blundell's, Tiverton	1604
Downside, RC, Somerset	1607
Charterhouse, Godalming	1611
Douai, RC	1615
Dulwich College	1619
Merchant Taylors', Liverpool	1620
Haberdashers' Aske's, Herts	1690

Public Schools	Founded
Dame Allan's Boys', Newcastle upon Tyne	1705
Churcher's College, Petersfield	1722
Robert Gordon, Aberdeen	1729
James Allen's Girls' School	1741
Ampleforth, RC, North Yorkshire	1802
Wellington School, Somerset	1837
Cheltenham	1841
Marlborough College, Wiltshire	1843
Brighton College	1845
Radley College, Abingdon	1847
Lancing	1848
Hurstpierpoint, West Sussex	1849
Bradfield, Reading	1850
City of London Freemen's, Ashtead	1854
Cheadle Hulme, Cheshire	1855
Ardingly, West Sussex	1858
Oratory School, RC, Woodcote, Berks	1859
Wellington College, Crowthorne, Berks	1856
King's, Tynemouth	1860
Clifton, Bristol	1862
Haileybury, Hertford	1862
Cranleigh	1863
Fettes, Edinburgh	1870
Leys, Cambridge	1875
John Lyon, Harrow, Middlesex	1876
Alleyn's School	1882
Roedean	1885
Merchant Taylors' Girls, Liverpool	1888
Bedales, Petersfield	1893
Benenden, Cranbrook, Kent	1923
Cranford, Wimbourne	1923
Stowe, Buckinghamshire	1923
Gordonstoun, Elgin	1934
Millfield, Street, Somerset	1935

British Universities	Founded
Oxford	1249
Cambridge	1284
St Andrew's	1411
Glasgow	1451
Aberdeen	1495
Edinburgh	1583

British Universities	Founded
UMIST	1824
Durham	1832
London	1836
Manchester	1851
Newcastle Upon Tyne	1852
Wales, Cardiff	1893
Birmingham	1900
Liverpool	1903
Leeds	1904
Sheffield	1905
Queen's, Belfast	1908
Bristol	1909
Reading	1926
Nottingham	1948
Southampton	1952
Hull	1954
Exeter	1955
Leicester	1957
Sussex	1961
Keele	1962
East Anglia	1963
York	1963
Lancaster	1964
Essex	1964
Strathclyde, Glasgow	1964
Warwick, Coventry	1965
Kent	1965
Ulster	1965
Loughborough	1966
Heriot-Watt, Edinburgh	1966
Surrey, Guildford	1966
Bradford	1966
Bath	1966
Brunel, Uxbridge	1966
City	1966
Aston, Birmingham	1966
Stirling	1967
Dundee	1967
Salford	1967
Open	1969
Cranfield	1969
Buckingham	1976

British Universities: Former Polytechnics	Founded
Leeds Metropolitan	1992
Kingston	1992
Huddersfield	1992
Hertfordshire	1992
Greenwich	1992
North London	1992

NB: There are currently over 1,000 Independent Schools (Public Schools). The list here is not comprehensive, rather it is a cross-section of the better-known ones.

*Education at Sherborne was started by St Aldhelm when he became the first bishop of Sherborne in 705. However the school was linked with the Benedictine Abbey. The earliest known Master was Thomas Copeland in 1437. Edward VI refounded the school in 1550 on its present site.

British Universities: Former Polytechnics	Founded
Wolverhampton	1992
Glamorgan	1992
Westminster	1992
West of England (Bristol)	1992
Paisley	1992
Plymouth	1992
Portsmouth	1992
Robert Gordon (Aberdeen)	1992
Sheffield Hallam	1992
South Bank	1992
Staffordshire	1992
Sunderland	1992
Teesside	1992
Thames Valley	1992
Northumbria at Newcastle	1992
Nottingham Trent	1992
Liverpool John Moores	1992
Manchester Metropolitan	1992
Middlesex	1992
Napier (Edinburgh)	1992
De Montfort (Leicester)	1992
Anglia Polytechnic (Chelmsford)	1992
Bournemouth	1992
Brighton	1992
Coventry	1992
Central England (Perry Barr)	1992
Central Lancashire (Preston)	1992
Luton	1993
Oxford Brookes	1993
Derby	1993
Glasgow Caledonian	1993
East London	1993
Abertay Dundee	1994
Lincoln and Humberside	1996
Gloucestershire	2001
London Metropolitan	2002

University of Cambridge

College	Founded
Peterhouse	1284
Clare	1326
Pembroke	1347
Gonville and Caius	1348
Trinity Hall	1350
Corpus Christi	1352
King's	1441
Queens'	1448
St Catharine's	1473
Jesus	1496
Christ's	1505
St John's	1511
Magdalene	1542
Trinity	1546
Emmanuel	1584
Sidney Sussex	1596
Downing	1800
Homerton	1824
Girton	1869
Newnham	1871
Selwyn	1882
Hughes Hall	1885
St Edmund's	1896
New Hall	1954
Churchill	1960
Darwin	1964
Lucy Cavendish	1965
Wolfson	1965
Clare Hall	1966
Fitzwilliam	1966
Robinson	1977

University of Oxford

College	Founded
University	1249
Balliol	1263
Merton	1264
St Edmund Hall	1278
Exeter	1314
Oriel	1326
The Queen's	1340
New College	1379
Lincoln	1427
All Souls	1438
Magdalen	1458
Brasenose	1509
Corpus Christi	1517
Christ Church	1546
Trinity	1554
St John's	1555
Jesus	1571
Wadham	1612
Pembroke	1624
Worcester	1714
Harris Manchester	1786
Regent's Park*	1810
Keble	1868
Hertford	1874
Wycliffe Hall*	1877
Lady Margaret Hall	1878
Somerville	1879
St Hugh's	1886
Mansfield	1886
Campion Hall*	1896
St Benet's Hall*	1897
Greyfriars*	1910
Blackfriars*	1921
St Peter's	1929
Nuffield	1937
St Hilda's	1938
St Antony's	1950
St Anne's	1952
Linacre	1962
St Catherine's	1962
St Cross	1965
Templeton	1965
Wolfson	1966
Green	1979
Kellogg**	1990

*classified as Permanent Private Halls
**from 1990 to 1994 called Rewley House

University of London
College
Birkbeck College
British Institute in Paris
Charing Cross and Westminster Medical
Courtauld Institute of Art
Goldsmith's College
Heythrop College
Imperial College of Science
King's College London
London Business School
London Hospital Medical College
London School of Economics and Political Science
London School of Hygiene and Tropical Medicine
London School of Jewish Studies
Queen Mary and Westfeld College
Royal Free Hospital School of Medicine
Royal Holloway
Royal Postgraduate Medical School
Royal Veterinary College
School of Oriental and African Studies
School of Pharmacy
St Bartholomew's and the Royal London School
    of Medicine and Dentistry
St George's Hospital Medical School
United Medical and Dental Schools of Guy's and
    St Thomas' Hospitals
University College London
Wye College

University of Durham
College
Collingwood
George Stephenson
Grey
Hatfield
Neville's Cross
St Aidan's
St Chad's
St Cuthbert's Society
St Hild & St Bede
St John's
St Mary's
Trevelyan
University
Ushaw
Ustinov
Van Mildert

Miscellaneous Information

A-Level	Consists of six units of assessment (three AS and three A2).
Baker Days	Part of the controversial education reform bill, during Kenneth Baker's tenancy as Education Minister 1986–89. His legislation on the in-service training days for teachers came to be known as Baker Days.
City Technology Colleges	Set up in the 1980s in an attempt to widen the choices of secondary education in disadvantaged urban areas. There are seven CTCs at present and they are state-aided.
Dulwich College	Founded by the English actor Edward Alleyn in 1619 but a distinct school from Alleyn's School, founded in 1882. Old Boys of Dulwich College are however known as Old Alleynians.
GCSE	General Certificate of Secondary Education.
GNVQ	General National Vocation Qualification (Further Education).
Gordonstoun	Founded by Kurt Hahn in 1934.
Grant-Maintained Schools	Came into being as a result of the 1988 Education Act which permits schools with more than 300 pupils to opt out of local authority control if the majority of parents wish to do so. These schools are funded by central government.
Independent Schools	Receive no grants from Public Funds and are funded by fees and contributions, and run by trusts.
Lyceum school	Founded by Aristotle.
Mottoes	Eton – Floreat Etona (May Eton Flourish), Rugby – Orando Laborando (By Praying and by Working), Winchester – Manners Makyth Man, Ampleforth College – Dieu le Ward (God Protect Him), The Ridings, Calderdale – Together We Make the Difference.
National Curriculum	Under the 1988 Education Act the National Curriculum was set out in four Key Stages of a child's development. Key Stage 1 and 2 concerned 5–11-year-olds and stated that Core Subjects would include English, (Welsh in Welsh-speaking schools) Maths and Science; and the Foundation Subjects would be Design & Technology, Information Technology, History, Geography, Art, Music and PE. Key Stage 3 caters for 11–14-year-olds and states that a Modern Foreign Language must be included. Key Stage 4 concerns 14–16-year-olds. The Act states that the child must be tested at the end of each Key Stage i.e. 7, 11, and 14-years-old. 16-year-olds only require testing if staying in education.
Newnham College: 1st Male Fellow	Dr Rachel Padman (who had a sex change operation in 1982).
Parents Charter	Booklet informing parents about the education system.

Public Schools: Famous Founders	John Lyon (Harrow), Elizabeth I (Westminster), William of Wykeham (Winchester), Henry VI (Eton), Thomas Sutton (Charterhouse), Edward Alleyne (Dulwich College), Lawrence Sheriff (Rugby), John Colet (St Paul's), Edward VI (Shrewsbury).
Public Schools: Meaning	In recent years the term 'Public School' applies to those Independent Schools in membership of the Headmasters' and Headmistresses' Conference, the Governing Bodies Association or the Governing Bodies of Girl's Schools Association. Historically Public Schools were fee-paying private boarding schools, for pupils aged 13 years and above, which gained sufficient reputation to attract pupils from backgrounds of social worthiness.
	Public schools were contrasted with 'Private Schools' which were run for the profit of their proprietors.
	In Scotland, the term Public School refers to a free state school, open to all.
School Age Limits	In Great Britain schooling is compulsory between the ages of 5 and 16 (4 and 16 in Northern Ireland).
Scotvec	Scottish Vocational Education Council (Further Education).
St Andrews: Colleges	United College of St Salvator & St Leonard, College of St Mary.
Subfusc	Formal academic dress, especially at Oxford University.
UCAS	The Universities and Colleges Admissions Service acts as a clearing-house for those applying for admission to full-time first degree and first diploma courses at universities and other higher education institutions in the UK. UCAS was established in 1993 from the merger of the former Universities Central Council on Admissions (UCCA), the Polytechnics Central Admissions System (PCAS) and the Standing Conference on University Entrance (SCUE).
University: Most Students	Open University has the most registered students although London University has most on campus.

E
D
U
C
A
T
I
O
N

FAMOUS PEOPLE

Occupations: Former and Alternative

Joseph Addison (essayist)   MP for Malmesbury (1708–19)

Aesop (fable writer)   Phrygian slave

Prince Albert (husband of Queen Victoria)   musician

Woody Allen (comic actor and director)   jazz clarinet player

Idi Amin (Ugandan politician)   British army sergeant

Kingsley Amis (writer)   English lecturer at Swansea University

Clive Anderson (comedian and broadcaster)   barrister

Andrew, St (Apostle)   fisherman

John Arlott (cricket commentator)   policeman

Henry Armstrong (American boxer)   Baptist minister

Paddy Ashdown (politician)   Royal Marine

Isaac Asimov (science fiction writer)   biochemist

Clement Attlee (British prime minister)   lawyer and social worker

WH Auden (poet and essayist)   stretcher bearer (Spanish Civil War)

Alfred Austin (poet)   lawyer

Alan Ayckbourn (playwright)   BBC Radio drama producer

Francis Bacon (philosopher)   Lord Chancellor

Mily Balakirev (composer)   railway official

Hastings Banda (Malawian politician)   physician

Roger Bannister (athlete)   doctor

Brendan Behan (author)   painter & decorator and IRA member

Alexander Graham Bell (inventor)   speech therapist to the deaf

Hilaire Belloc (poet and writer)   Liberal MP

Arnold Bennett (novelist)   solicitor's clerk

Cilla Black (entertainer)   coat checker-In (Cavern Club, Liverpool)

RD Blackmore (novelist)   lawyer

Alexander Borodin (composer)   professor of chemistry

Jim Bowen (comedian)   teacher

John Buchan (novelist)   lawyer, publisher and MP for Scottish Universities (1927–35)

Robert Burns (poet)   excise officer and farmer

Michael Caine (actor)   Billingsgate fish porter

James Callaghan (British prime minister)   civil servant (tax officer)

Geoff Capes (athlete)   policeman

Lewis Carroll (writer)   mathematics lecturer

Jimmy Carter (US president)   peanut farmer

Joyce Cary (novelist)   civil servant in Nigeria

Giacomo Casanova (Italian adventurer)   librarian, spy and lottery director

Fidel Castro (Cuban President)   film extra

Miguel Cervantes (novelist)   professional soldier

Geoffrey Chaucer (poet)   customs officer, MP and soldier

Claude Lorraine (artist)   pastry cook

William Cobbett (writer)   soldier and MP for Oldham (1832–5)

Edward Coke (lawyer)   MP for Aldeburgh (1589)

Perry Como (singer)   barber

Sean Connery (actor)   coffin polisher and Royal Navy sailor

Billy Connolly (comedian and actor)   shipyard worker

Gary Cooper (actor)   photographer and stuntman

Tommy Cooper (comic magician)   guardsman

Andres Courrèges (fashion designer)   civil engineer

AJ Cronin (novelist)   inspector of mines

César Cui (Russian composer)   military engineer

Dante Alighieri (Italian poet)   embassy official

Walter De La Mare (poet and novelist)   oil company worker

Christopher Dean (figure skater)   policeman

Dave Dee (pop singer)   policeman

Daniel Defoe (writer)   brickmaker and shopkeeper

Charles Dickens (writer)   court stenographer and factory shoe black

Bruce Dickinson (rock singer)   commercial airline pilot

Benjamin Disraeli (British prime minister)   novelist

John Donne (poet)   dean of St Paul's Cathedral (1621–31)

Sir Arthur Conan Doyle (writer)   doctor (ophthalmologist)

John Boyd Dunlop (inventor)   veterinary surgeon

Albrecht Dürer (painter and engraver)   draughtsman

John Dyer (poet and painter)   lawyer

Clint Eastwood (actor)   swimming instructor

Thomas Alva Edison (inventor)   telegraph operator and newsboy

Albert Einstein (physicist)   Patent Office clerk

TS Eliot (poet and dramatist)   clerk with Lloyd's Bank

Juan Fangio (racing driver)   bus driver

Michael Faraday (physicist)   bookseller and laboratory technician

William Faulkner (novelist)   postmaster

Kathleen Ferrier (contralto)   telephone operator

Frank Finlay (actor)   butcher

F Scott Fitzgerald (novelist)   Hollywood scriptwriter

Ian Fleming (novelist)   intelligence officer and journalist

Errol Flynn (actor)   policeman (Tasmania)

Gerald Ford (US President)   male model

George Foreman (boxer)   minister

George Formby (entertainer)   jockey

Benjamin Franklin (US statesman)   printer and scientist

Frederick II, the Great (king of Prussia)   musician

Billy Fury (singer)   tugboat worker

Clark Gable (actor)   lumberjack

Galileo Galilei (astronomer)   doctor, mathematician and natural philosopher

Greta Garbo (actress)   milliner's model

Graeme Garden (comic actor)   doctor

Giuseppe Garibaldi (Italian patriot)   candlemaker and privateer

James Garner (actor)   swimsuit model

David Garrick (actor)   wine merchant

Richard Gatling (US inventor)   doctor

Paul Gauguin (artist)   stockbroker and labourer on Panama Canal

Jean Genet (author)   professional criminal and male prostitute

Edward Gibbon (historian)   MP for Liskeard (1774–80)

William S Gilbert (librettist)   barrister and cartoonist

Joseph Goebbels   newspaper editor

Johann Goethe (poet and dramatist)   fire chief, newspaper critic and Court Official

Sam Goldwyn (film producer)   glove salesman

WG Grace (cricketer)   doctor

Kenneth Grahame (writer)   secretary to Bank of England

Cary Grant (actor)   acrobat

Robert Graves (poet and novelist)   professor of English (Cairo University)

Fulke Greville (poet)   MP for Warwickshire

Zane Grey (writer)   dentist

Terry Griffiths (snooker player)   postman

Che Guevara (revolutionary leader)   doctor

Gareth Hale (comedian)   PE teacher

Thomas Hardy (writer)   architect

Bob Harris (broadcaster)   policeman

Russell Harty (broadcaster)   teacher

Alex Harvey (musician)   lion tamer

Nathaniel Hawthorne (writer)   American consul in Liverpool (1853–7)

AP Herbert (writer)   MP for Oxford University (1935–50)

William Herschel (astronomer)   music teacher

Benny Hill (comedian)   milkman

Harry Hill (comedian)   doctor

Adolf Hitler (dictator)   painter of postcards

Ho Chi Minh (Vietnamese politician)   hotel worker and pastry cook

Bob Hope (comedian)   boxer

Gerard Manley Hopkins (poet)   classics professor (University College Dublin)

Bob Hoskins (actor)   market porter, fire-eater, steeplejack and seaman

AE Housman (poet)   classics teacher

Rod Hull (comedian)   electrician

Gareth Hunt (actor)   merchant seaman

Henryk Ibsen (dramatist)   pharmacist

Julio Iglesias (vocalist)   goalkeeper

Charles Ives (composer)   insurance executive

David Jason (actor)   electrician

Andrew Johnson (US president)   tailor

James Prescott Joule (physicist)   brewer

James Robertson Justice (actor)   naturalist

Wassily Kandinsky (artist)   lawyer

Harvey Keitel (actor)   US marine

Charles Kingsley (author)   Cambridge history professor

Alphonse de Lamartine (poet and historian)   French foreign minister (1848)

Burt Lancaster (actor)   circus acrobat

Eddie Large (comedian)   electrician

Philip Larkin (poet)   librarian (of Hull University)

Antoine Lavoisier (chemist)   tax collector

Lee Kuan Yew (Singapore politician)   barrister

Vladimir Lenin (Russian revolutionary)   lawyer

Leopold I of Habsburg (Holy Roman Emperor)   musician

Franz Liszt (musician)   priest

Little Richard (musician)   minister

Syd Little (comedian)   decorator

Henry Wadsworth Longfellow (poet)   Harvard lecturer

St Luke (New Testament evangelist)   painter and physician

John Lydgate (poet)   monk

Thomas Macaulay (author)   lawyer and MP for Calne, Leeds, and Edinburgh

Harold MacMillan (British prime minister)   publisher

Norman Mailer (writer)   candidate for NY mayor (4th of 5)

André Malraux (writer)   archaeologist and pilot in the Spanish civil war

Thomas Malthus (economist)   clergyman

Nelson Mandela (South African statesman)   lawyer

Walter de la Mare (poet and novelist)   Standard Oil Company employee

John Marston (dramatic poet)   lawyer

Andrew Marvell (poet)   MP for Hull (1659–78)

Karl Marx (political and economic theorist)   journalist and editor

Marcello Mastroianni (actor)   draughtsman and cashier

Quentin Matsys (Massys) (Flemish painter)   blacksmith

St Matthew (apostle)   tax collector

William Somerset Maugham (writer)   surgeon and wartime secret agent

Herman Melville (writer)   customs officer, bank clerk and adventurer

Gregor Mendel (biologist and botanist)   monk

Jonathan Miller (stage director and author)   doctor

John Mills (actor)   toilet paper salesman

Robert Mitchum (actor)   miner and professional boxer

Matt Monro (singer)   bus driver

Roger Moore (actor)   male model

Samuel Morse (inventor)   artist

Arthur Mullard (actor)   professional boxer

Modest Mussorgsky (composer)   civil servant

Dame Anna Neagle (actress)   dance instructor

Jawaharlal Nehru (Indian statesman)   lawyer

Thomas Newcomen (inventor)   blacksmith

Bob Newhart (comedian)   accountant

Paul Newman (actor)   motor racing driver

Isaac Newton (scientist)   warden of the Mint and MP

Harold Nicolson (author and critic)   MP for West Leicester (1935-45)

David Niven (actor)   army officer

Julius Nyerere (Tanzanian politician)   teacher

Milton Obote (Ugandan politician)   labourer, clerk and salesman

Sean O'Casey (playwright)   building labourer

Tom O'Connor (comedian)   teacher

Bruce Oldfield (musician)   art teacher

George Orwell (novelist)   policeman (Burma)

David Owen (politician)   doctor

Norman Pace (comedian)   PE teacher

Thomas Love Peacock (novelist and poet)   chief examiner of East India Company

Peter I, the Great (Russian tsar)   shipwright

St Peter (apostle)   fisherman

François André Philidor (composer)   chess master

Enoch Powell (politician)   professor of Greek

Magnus Pyke (science broadcaster)   nutritionist

Salvatore Quasimodo (poet)   engineer

FAMOUS PEOPLE

Edgar Quinet (writer)   politician

François Rabelais (satirist)   doctor and monk

Sir Walter Raleigh (explorer and navigator)   MP for Devon (1585)

Charles Reade (writer)   lawyer

Ray Reardon (snooker player)   policeman and miner

Paul Revere (American patriot)   silversmith

Arthur Rimbaud (poet)   gun runner and merchant

Joan Rivers (comedian)   fashion co-ordinator for Bond Stores

Auguste Rodin (sculptor)   ornamental mason

Peter Roget (thesaurus writer)   doctor

Leonard Rossiter (actor)   insurance agent

Henri Rousseau (painter)   customs officer

Salman Rushdie (writer)   actor and advertising copywriter

Willie Rushton (satirist)   cartoonist

Sir Walter Scott (novelist and poet)   lawyer

William Shakespeare (writer)   actor

Richard Brinsley Sheridan (dramatist)   MP for Stafford and Ilchester

Nevil Shute (writer)   engineer (worked on RI00)

Sir Philip Sidney (poet)   professional soldier

Norodom Sihanouk (Cambodian politician)   musician

Delia Smith (cookery writer)   hairdresser and Norwich City FC director

CP Snow (novelist)   parliamentary sec (Ministry of technology) and physicist

Benjamin Spock (paediatrician)   Naval officer and olympic oarsman

Jerry Springer (talk-show host)   lawyer

Joseph Stalin (Soviet leader)   trainee monk

Freddie Starr (comedian)   bricklayer

Sir Richard Steele (essayist)   MP for Stockbridge (1713)

Tommy Steele (entertainer)   merchant seaman

Laurence Sterne (novelist)   clergyman

Wallace Stevens (poet)   insurance company executive

Rod Stewart (singer)   footballer (Brentford) and gravedigger

David Storey (writer)   Rugby League professional

Jonathan Swift (writer)   clergyman

Charles Talleyrand-Périgord (statesman)   abbot

Jimmy Tarbuck (comedian)   milkman

Pyotr Tchaikovsky (composer)   civil servant

Shirley Temple (actress)   US ambassador to Ghana

Valentina Tereshkova (astronaut)   cotton mill worker

Margaret Thatcher (British prime minister)   research chemist and barrister

John Thaw (actor)   market porter

JRR Tolkien (writer)   Oxford English professor

Leo Tolstoy (writer)   army officer

Anthony Trollope (writer)   Post Office worker

Harry S Truman (US president)   haberdasher

Desmond Tutu (archbishop of Cape Town)   schoolteacher

Liv Ullmann (actress)   UNICEF ambassador

John Vanbrugh (playwright)   architect

Vincent Van Gogh (artist)   trainee priest

Jules Verne (writer)   librettist

King Vidor (film director)   cinema projectionist and cameraman

Kurt Vonnegut (writer)   soldier

Lech Walesa (Polish politician)   electrician

Lew Wallace (author)   soldier

Bradley Walsh (comedian)   footballer (Brentford)

George Washington (US president)   British army colonel

Noah Webster (lexicographer)   lawyer and teacher

Chaim Weizmann (Israeli statesman)   biochemist

Orson Welles (actor and director)   picador

HG Wells (writer)   draper's assistant and teacher

Walt Whitman (poet)   teacher and printer

William Wilberforce (philanthropist)   MP for Hull and Yorkshire

Billy Wilder (film director)   journalist and crime reporter

Tennessee Williams (playwright)   poet-waiter and cinema usher

Ludwig Wittgenstein (philosopher)   teacher, porter, gardener and engineer

Terry Wogan (broadcaster)   bank clerk

Ermanno Wolf-Ferrari (composer)   artist

William Wordsworth (poet)   stamp distributor

Harry Worth (comic actor)   miner

Sir Christopher Wren (architect)   professor of astronomy

Tammy Wynette (singer)   beautician

JR Wyss (writer and philosopher)   Swiss national anthem writer

Yohji Yamamoto (fashion designer)   lawyer

Boris Yeltsin (Russian president)   construction company director

Andrew John Young (poet)   clergyman

Brigham Young (Mormon leader)   carpenter, painter and glazier

Lazarus Zamenhof (language inventor)   oculist and philologist

Franco Zeffirelli (film director)   actor and costume designer

Count Von Zeppelin (airship inventor)   US Civil War soldier

Emile Zola (novelist)   clerk in publishing house

Assassinations

681BC	*Sennacherib of Assyria*	Murdered by his two sons.
514BC	*Hipparchus of Athens*	Killed by Harmodius and Aristogeiton, two Athenians.
465BC	*Xerxes I of Persia*	Killed by members of his court, led by Artabanus.
336BC	*Philip II of Macedon*	Killed by Pausanias, a Spartan regent and general.
330BC	*Darius III (Codomannus) of Persia*	Slain by a satrap, Arterxes (Ardashir), whilst fleeing Alexander the Great.
44BC	*Julius Caesar (Roman dictator)*	Stabbed by Brutus, Cassius and others in the Senate.
41	*Caligula (Roman emperor)*	Murdered by Cassius Chaerea, an officer of his guard.
54	*Claudius I (Roman Emperor)*	Ate poisoned mushrooms served by his wife, Agrippina the Younger.
96	*Domitian (Roman dictator)*	Stabbed in his bedroom by Stephanus, a freed slave.
192	*Commodus (Roman Emperor)*	Strangled by wrestler Narcissus, at the behest of his mistress, Marcia.
978	*Edward the Martyr (King of England)*	Murdered at Corfe Castle by his younger half-brother Ethelred's household, led by Elfthryth.
1057	*Macbeth (King of Scotland)*	Killed by Malcolm III, Canmore, at Lumphanan (15 August).
1170	*Thomas à Becket*	Killed by four knights, Fitzurse, Tracy, De Merville and Le Breton in Canterbury Cathedral.
1192	*Conrad, King of Jerusalem*	Killed by members of the militant Islamic sect, the Assassins, who gave assassination their name.
1327	*Edward II of England*	Murdered in Berkeley Castle possibly with a red-hot poker at the instigation of his wife, Isabella, and her lover Roger de Mortimer; possible perpetrators were De Gournay and Maltravers.
1437	*James I of Scotland*	Murdered in court residence, a Dominican monastery, by assassins led by Sir Robert Graham.
1471	*Henry VI of England*	Murdered in the Tower of London, possibly by Richard of Gloucester, the future Richard III.
1488	*James III of Scotland*	Murdered following defeat of royal army at Sauchieburn by unknown.
1533	*Atahualpa (Last Inca ruler)*	Strangled by Spanish forces under Francisco Pizarro.
1541	*Francisco Pizarro*	Murdered at his home in Lima, possibly by Juan de Rada at the instigation of Diego de Almagro.
1567	*Henry, Lord Darnley (husband of Mary, Queen of Scots)*	Strangled by Scottish nobles after explosion at Kirk O' Field.
1584	*William the Silent (aka William of Orange)*	Shot at Delft by Balthasar Gerard.
1589	*Henry III of France*	Stabbed by Jacques Clément, a fanatical Dominican.
1610	*Henry IV of France*	Murdered by François Ravaillac, a Catholic fanatic.
1628	*Duke of Buckingham*	Stabbed at Portsmouth en route for La Rochelle by John Felton, a discontented subaltern.
1634	*Prince Wallenstein (German general)*	Killed by Devereux.
1762	*Peter III, Tsar of Russia*	Strangled in captivity by Count Aleksei Orlov, the lover of his wife and future empress, Catherine.
1793	*Jean Paul Marat (French Revolutionary)*	Stabbed in his bath by Charlotte Corday.
1801	*Paul I of Russia*	Strangled by army officers who had conspired to force his abdication.
1812	*Spencer Perceval (PM)*	Shot while entering lobby of the House of Commons by John Bellingham, a bankrupt Liverpool broker.
1865	*Abraham Lincoln*	Shot by actor John Wilkes Booth in Ford's Theater, Washington, while watching *Our American Cousin*.
1872	*Richard Burke, Earl of Mayo*	Stabbed to death by Shere Ali, a convict, while inspecting the settlement at Port Blair on the Andaman Islands.
1881	*James A Garfield (US President)*	Shot in a station by Charles Guiteau, a disappointed office-seeker.
	Alexander II of Russia	Died from injuries after a bomb was thrown near his palace by Nihilists, led by Sophia Perovskaya.
1882	*Lord Frederick Cavendish (Chief Secretary for Ireland)*	Murdered by 'Irish invincibles' in Phoenix Park, Dublin.
1894	*Marie François Carnot (French President)*	Stabbed by anarchist Cesare Giovanni Santo Caserio.
1897	*Antonio Cánovas del Castillo (Spanish Premier)*	Shot by Italian anarchist Angiolillo at the bath of Santa Agueda, Vitoria.
1900	*Umberto I of Italy*	Murdered by anarchist G Bresci in Monza.
1901	*William McKinley (US President)*	Shot by anarchist Leon Czolgosz in Buffalo, NY.
1903	*Alexander Obrenovich (King of Serbia)*	Murdered by military conspirators, along with his wife, Draga.
1913	*George I of Greece*	Murdered by a Greek, Schinas, in Salonika.
1914	*Archduke Franz Ferdinand*	Shot in a car by Gavrilo Princip in Sarajevo (28 June); the assassination helped to precipitate World War I.
	Jean Jaurès (French Socialist)	Shot by nationalist Raoul Villain in café.
1916	*Rasputin (Russian monk)*	Killed and dumped in River Neva by group of nobles led by Prince Feliks Yusupov and Grand Duke Dimitry Pavlovich, revenging his influence over Tsarina Alexandra.
1922	*Michael Collins (Sinn Fein leader)*	Killed in an ambush between Bandon and Macroom in the Irish Free State.
1923	*Pancho Villa (Mexican Revolutionary)*	Assassinated on his ranch at Parral, Mexico (20 June).

FAMOUS PEOPLE

1934   Dr Engelbert Dollfuss   (Austrian Chancellor)   Shot by Nazis in the Chancellery.

Sergey Mironovich Kirov   (Russian Communist)   Shot by Leonid Nikolayev at the Communist Party HQ (1 December); Stalin subsequently purged Leningrad of all suspected anti-Stalinists.

Alexander I of Yugoslavia   (King of the Serbs, Croats and Slovenes)   Murdered in Marseilles by a Macedonian terrorist.

1935   Huey Long   (US politician)   Murdered by Dr Carl Austin Weiss.

1940   Leon Trotsky   (exiled Russian leader)   Killed with an ice pick in Mexico by Ramón Mercader.

1942   Reinhard Heydrich   (second-in-command in the Nazi Secret Police)   Murdered by Czech resistance fighters.

1943   Isoruku Yamamoto (Japanese Admiral)   Plane intercepted and shot down by US P-38 fighter squad after Japanese naval code was broken.

1948   Mohandas Gandhi   (Indian leader)   Shot by Hindu fanatic Nathuran Godse at Birla House, New Delhi.

Count Folke Bernadotte   (Swedish diplomat)   Murdered by Jewish extremists in ambush in Jerusalem.

1951   Abdullah I of Jordan   Murdered by member of Jihad faction.

Liaquat Ali Khan   (Pakistani PM)   Murdered in Rawalpindi by fanatics advocating war with India.

1958   Faisal II of Iraq   Murdered with his entire household during a military coup.

1959   Solomon Bandaranaike   (Sri Lankan statesman)   Murdered by Buddhist monk Talduwe Somarama.

Rafael Trujillo Molina   (Dominican Republic dictator)   Machine-gunned in car by assassins including General JT Diaz.

1963   John F Kennedy   (US President)   Shot while riding in open Lincoln Continental in Dallas, Texas, by rifleman Lee Harvey Oswald (22 Nov).

1965   Malcolm X   (Black Muslim leader)   Shot at political rally.

1966   Hendrik Verwoerd   (South African Premier)   Stabbed by parliamentary messenger Dimitri Tsafendas.

1968   Martin Luther King   (civil rights leader)   Shot on hotel balcony by James Earl Ray in Memphis, Tennessee.

Robert F Kennedy   (US Senator)   Shot by Jordanian Arab immigrant Sirhan Bishara Sirhan in the Hotel Ambassador, Los Angeles.

1975   King Faisal of Saudi Arabia   Murdered by his nephew, Prince Faisal.

1976   Christopher Ewart-Biggs   (British Ambassador to Eire)   Car blown up by IRA landmine.

Georgi Markov (Bulgarian dissident)   Infected with poisoned pellet on Westminster Bridge by Bulgarian agent.

1978   Aldo Moro, former Italian PM   Kidnapped by Red Brigade and later found dead.

Wafizulah Amin (President of Afghanistan)   Killed with his mistress in the presidential palace, Kabul, by KGB commandos.

1979   Airey Neave, MP   Killed by IRA bomb in House of Commons car park.

Lord Mountbatten   Killed by IRA bomb in sailing boat while fishing off County Sligo, Ireland.

Park Chung Hee   (South Korean President)   Shot in restaurant by chief of Korean Central Intelligence Agency.

1980   John Lennon   (former Beatle)   Shot by Mark Chapman outside his apartment in New York.

Oscar Romero   (Salvadorean RC Prelate)   Murdered by government troops.

1981   Anwar Sadat   (Egyptian President)   Shot by rebel soldier Khalid Ahmed Shawki and others while reviewing military parade.

Zia ur-Rahman   (Bangladeshi President)   Shot by military and replaced as President by Abdus Sattar.

1983   Benigno Aquino   (Filipino politician)   Shot in the head at Manila airport by a government-backed assassin.

1984   Indira Gandhi   (Indian PM)   Murdered by members of her Sikh bodyguard (Satwant and Beant Singh).

1986   Olof Palme   (Swedish PM)   Shot in Stockholm as he walked home from cinema by unknown hand.

1988   General Zia ul-Haq   (Pakistani leader)   Killed in air crash owing to sabotage.

1991   Rajiv Gandhi   (Former Indian PM)   Blown up during an election campaign by Thanu.

1992   Muhammad Boudiaf   (President of Algeria's High State Council)   Murdered during a speech.

1995   Yitzhak Rabin   (Israeli PM)   Murdered by Yigal Amir.

2002   Pim Fortuyn (Dutch politician)   Shot six times whilst walking to his car in Hilversum. Six months after the shooting Volkert Van de Graaf confessed to the murder.

Attempted Assassinations

Count Otto von Bismarck   Attempts by Kulimann (1874) and Blind (1866).

Cassius Marcellus Clay (US Emancipationist and Senator)   Shot point-blank during a speech in 1843 and used a Bowie knife to cut off the attacker's ear and nose and also cut out one of his eyes! Not to be confused with his illustrious namesake, who presumably would have dispatched the assailant with a swift left hook.

Queen Elizabeth I   Numerous plots to replace Elizabeth on the throne by Mary Queen of Scots, notably the Ridolfi and Babington plots, but the only person to be put to death for an alleged direct attempt was Dr Lopez, her physician, in 1594.

Gerald Ford   Assassination attempt by Lynette 'Squeaky' Fromme, member of Charles Manson's 'family' (1975).

Henry Frick   Steel magnate who was shot and stabbed by anarchist Alexander Berkman (1892).

George III   James Hadfield attempted assassination in 1800 but was acquitted due to insanity.

Hitler Bomb planted by Colonel Von Stauffenberg at his Wolf's Lair HQ in E Prussia in 1944 exploded but failed to kill him.

John Paul II Shot by Mehmet Ali Agca in 1981.

Lenin Assassination attempt by Fanny Kaplan in 1918 caused his health to go into steady decline.

Leopold II Gennaro Rubino made an attempt on the life of the Belgian king in 1902.

Napoleon III Felice Orsini attempted his assassination, but Napoleon eventually died of a gall bladder infection.

Prince of Wales Jean Baptiste Sipido made an attempt on the life of the future King Edward VII (1900).

Ronald Reagan Shot by John Hinckley in 1981.

Franklin Delano Roosevelt In 1933 he and Chicago mayor Anton Cermak were shot at by Giuseppe Zangara. Cermak was mortally wounded, whilst Roosevelt became President.

Theodore Roosevelt Attempt on life by John F Schrank, 14 October 1912. Despite being shot in the chest at a political rally managed to continue his speech for 90 minutes before seeking medical assistance.

William Henry Seward (US Senator) Survived an assassination attempt on 14 April 1865 (the same night Abraham Lincoln was shot) when Lewis Payne, an associate of John Wilkes Booth, broke into his bedroom and stabbed him repeatedly.

Shah of Persia Francois Salsou made an attempt on the life of the Shah in 1900.

Margaret Thatcher The IRA Grand Hotel bombing in Brighton (Oct 1984) was an attempt on her life.

Queen Victoria Attempts by Edward Oxford (1840), John William Bean (1842), John Francis (1842), William Hamilton (1849), Robert Pate (1850), Arthur O'Connor (1872) and Roderick Maclean (1882).

George Wallace Left paralysed after being shot by Arthur Bremer in 1972.

Andy Warhol Shot by Valerie Solanis, one of his starlets, in 1968.

Catchphrases and Slogans

NB: The list below shows a phrase and the most identifiable body to that phrase. In most cases the details are self-explanatory and where the phrase has actually been coined by a person then his information is given. Many phrases will be of doubtful origin and no attempt has been made to authenticate entries as original spoutings. To give Robert Walpole as an example from my list: the phrase 'every man has his price' is identified with the prime minister but the phrase was almost certainly used as a maxim centuries earlier, although impossible to research. Many more catchphrases associated with household products will be found in the TV Advert section.

a good idea . . . son Max Bygraves (as Archie Andrew's tutor in *Educating Archie*)

all human life is there News of the World (advertising slogan from a Henry James novel)

all done in the best possible taste Kenny Everett (in the guise of the leggy Miss Cupid Stunt)

a man of my cal-aye-ber Tony Hancock (originally coined in *Hancock's Half-Hour*)

and now for something completely different John Cleese (in *Monty Python*)

and that's the way it is Walter Cronkite (in concluding his CBS TV *Evening News* programme)

and the next Tonight will be tomorrow night Cliff Michelmore (at the end of the nightly BBC magazine programme)

are you looking for a punch up the bracket? Tony Hancock (originally coined in *Hancock's Half-Hour*)

are you sitting comfortably ? Julia Lang (on BBC radio's *Listen with Mother*)

as it happens Jimmy Savile

ask the audience Chris Tarrant (in *Who Wants to be a Millionaire*)

as the art mistress said to the gardener Monica (Beryl Reid) as Archie Andrew's posh friend in *Educating Archie*

aw don't embarrass me Lenny the Lion (ventriloquist Terry Hall's creation)

awight at the back (sic) Michael Barrymore (at the start of many of his shows)

beam me up, Scotty Attributed to Captain Kirk (William Shatner) in *Star Trek*

because it is there George Leigh Mallory (on being asked why he wanted to climb Mt Everest)

before you can say Jack Robinson Richard Brinsley Sheridan (in the Commons to avoid using a fellow MP's name)

before your very eyes Arthur Askey (from the name of his first television series as a proof of live TV)

be like dad, keep mum 1941 propaganda slogan advising civilians to not talk about war-related issues)

be prepared Pears' Soap usurped the slogan from the motto of the Boy Scout movement

Bernie, the bolt Bob Monkhouse (in the *Golden Shot*). Bernie's real name was Derek Young

better red than dead Bertrand Russell (in a 1958 article stating Communism was preferable over death)

bet you can't eat three Ian Botham (used in an advertising campaign for Shredded Wheat)

Beulah, peel me a grape Mae West (first said by the actress to a black maid in the film *I'm No Angel*)

Big Bang, the Nickname for the London Stock Exchange deregulation of 27 October 1986

Big Brother is watching you George Orwell in his novel *Nineteen Eighty-Four* first coined this cry for democracy

big-hearted Arthur, that's me Arthur Askey (introducing himself on radio's *Band Wagon*)

black is beautiful Stokely Carmichael (at a civil rights rally in Memphis in 1966)

black power Usually attributed to Stokely Carmichael after shooting of James Meredith in 1966

blonde bombshell Jean Harlow (not so much a catchphrase more a description and nickname)

book 'em Danno Steve McGarrett (Jack Lord) to Detective 'Danno' Williams in *Hawaii Five O*

boom, boom Billy Bennett (the comedian coined the phrase to underline the punchline of a gag). Basil Brush and Eric Morecambe usurped Billy Bennett's catchphrase in their acts

booyakasha! Sacha Baron Cohen in the guise of rapper Ali G.

born 1820, still going strong   Johnnie Walker whisky slogan first used in 1908

British are coming, the   Colin Welland (after collecting an Oscar for the film *Chariots of Fire*)

buck stops here, the   Harry S Truman (from a sign on his desk in the Oval Office)

bumper bundle   Coined by Jean Metcalfe whilst introducing *Two-Way Family Favourites*. The phrase denotes a large number of requests for the same record

can I do you now sir?   Mrs Mopp (Dorothy Summers) in *ITMA* i.e. *It's That Man Again*

can we talk?   Joan Rivers (interjection used by the comedienne to link her jokes)

can you hear me, mother ?   Sandy Powell (coined in 1932, probably the first radio catchphrase that caught on)

carry on London   Freddie Grisewood (at the end of BBC radio's *In Town Tonight*)

clap hands, here comes Charley   Charlie Kunz (became the signature tune of the *American pianist*)

clunk, click, every trip   Jimmy Savile (from a seat-belt campaign launched in 1971)

come on down   The Price is Right (originated in America when the popular show began in 1957)

come up and see me sometime   Mae West (originally said as 'Why don't you come up sometime and see me)

come with me to the Casbah   Charles Boyer (attributed to the 1938 film *Algiers* although not in the final cut)

customer is always right, the   H Gordon Selfridge (the American pioneer of the large department store)

daft as a brush   Ken Platt (comedian who corrupted the northern phrase 'soft as a brush')

day war broke out, the   Robb Wilton (after WWII the comedian substituted 'peace' for 'war')

dead as a door-nail   From Langland's *Piers Plowman* (door-nail was a knob on which a knocker struck)

did you spot this week's deliberate mistake?   Lionel Gamlin (from his BBC radio series *Monday Night at Seven*)

didn't he do well?   Bruce Forsyth (at the end of the conveyor belt finale of the *Generation Game*)

dig for victory   Sir Reginald Dorman Smith (slogan asking people to grow food during WWII)

disgusted . . . Tunbridge Wells   Stock phrase used when the writer does not want to give their name

dodgy   Norman Vaughan (the phrase was accompanied by a thumbs-down gesture)

doesn't it make you want to spit?   Arthur Askey (from the radio show *Band Wagon*)

don't forget the fruit gums mum   Roger Musgrave (the copywriter coined the phrase for Rowntree's Fruit Gums)

don't spit, remember the Johnstown flood   US admonition against spitting (citing the 1889 flood caused by a dam bursting)

don't touch me   Julian Clary (said by the comedian when any contact is made on his person)

don't worry, be happy   George Bush (unofficial campaign slogan used in the 1988 presidential election)

do you know the Bishop of Norwich?   An allusion to a port drinker who is holding on to the bottle and not passing it round

Drinka Pinta Milka Day   Bertrand Whitehead (the Executive Officer of the National Milk Publicity Council)

eat my shorts   Bart Simpson in the cartoon series *The Simpsons*

economical with the truth   Sir Robert Armstrong (whilst being cross-examined in 1986 regarding MI5 secrets)

elementary, my dear Watson   Sherlock Holmes (attributed to him but not to be seen in Conan Doyle's writings)

eleventh commandment, the   George Whyte-Melville (cites 'thou shalt not be found out' in his book *Holmby House*)

'er indoors   Arthur Daley (George Cole) in the ITV series *Minder*

evening all   George Dixon (Jack Warner) in *Dixon of Dock Green*

ever-open door, the   Dr Barnardo's Homes (slogan used to describe the homes in the 1950s)

everybody out   Paddy (Miriam Karlin) as the shop steward in the BBC's *The Rag Trade*

everybody wants to get into the act   Jimmy Durante (subsequently changed to everybody wants to get in on the act)

every man has his price   Often attributed to Robert Walpole

every picture tells a story   Appears to originate in 1904 as a slogan for Doan's Backache and Kidney Pills. The slogan was accompanied by a picture of a person bent over with back pain

everything in the garden's lovely   Marie Lloyd (from the title of one of her popular songs)

expletive deleted   Made famous by the Watergate transcripts but a general US term in documents

exterminate . . . exterminate   Daleks (in the BBC television series *Dr Who*)

eyes and ears of the world, the   Slogan promoting the cinema newsreel, *Paramount News* 1927–57

fifty fifty   Chris Tarrant (in *Who Wants to be a Millionaire*)

fleet's lit up, the   Cdr Tommy Woodrooffe (the BBC radio commentator coined the phrase in 1937)

flippin' kids   Tony Hancock (as Archie Andrew's tutor in *Educating Archie*)

Flying Fickle Finger of Fate Award, the   Prize in a mock talent contest in Rowan and Martin's *Laugh In*

F. T. A. (Fuck The Army)   Popular American graffiti used since 1960 among US Army recruits to express a dislike for orders especially in the Vietnam conflict. Protestants use F. T. P. to express their dislike for the Pope and N. Irish patriots use F. T. Q. for the Queen

fully paid-up member of the human race   Kenneth Clarke (described as such by the *Observer* on 31 July 1988)

get out of that   Eric Morecambe (whilst pressing his down-turned palm under Ernie Wise's chin)

gis a job   Yosser Hughes (Bernard Hill) in *Boys from the Blackstuff*

give 'em the money Barney   Wilfred Pickles (*Have a Go*) to Barney Colehan

give 'em the money Mabel   Wilfred Pickles (to his wife Mabel in radio's *Have a Go*)

go ahead, make my day   Harry Callahan (Clint Eastwood) originally in the 1983 film *Sudden Impact*. Ronald Reagan (in an address to the 1985 American Business Conference)

Godfrey Daniel   WC Fields (used in place of 'God, damn you' to comply with the strict Hay's Code

gone for a Burton   RAF expression of WWII denoting a presumed dead person had gone for a drink *good game, good game* Bruce Forsyth (at the end of each round of the *Generation Game*)

good morning sir; was there something? Sam Costa (in the radio programme *Much Binding in the Marsh*)

goodnight children everywhere Uncle Mac (Derek McCulloch) in BBC radio's *Children's Hour*

goodnight, Mrs Calabash . . . wherever you are Jimmy Durante (when ending his radio and television appearances)

goody, goody gumdrops Humphrey Lestocq (presenter of BBC television's *Whirligig* in the 1950s)

greatest show on earth, the PT Barnum (describing the merger of his circus with Bailey's in 1881)

happy as a sandboy The phrase alludes to the happiness of the door-to-door sellers of sand during the nineteenth century. Sand was bought as an absorber of liquids and scourer

happy as Larry An Australian expression of delight referring to the boxer Larry Foley 1847–1917

hat-trick Originating in cricket parlance when the taker of 3 successive wickets would be awarded a new hat for his feat. The term is now used for any triple success

have a gorilla Neddie Seagoon (Harry Secombe) offering a cigarette in the *Goon Show*

haves and the have-nots Sancho Panza (in Miguel Cervantes' *Don Quixote*)

he can't fart and chew gum at the same time President Lyndon Johnson's insulting description of President Gerald Ford

he can't walk and chew gum at the same time Revision of Lyndon Johnson's words when Ford became President in 1974

Heinz the Bolt Jackie Rae (in television's the *Golden Shot*). Heinz later became Bernie the Bolt

hello folks Tommy Handley (eponymous hero of *It's That Man Again*)

hello folks and world Neddie Seagoon (Harry Secombe) in the *Goon Show*

hello, good evening, and welcome David Frost (coined in the *Frost Programme* but has become his stock greeting)

hello, it's me, Twinkletoes Bernard Bresslaw (as Archie Andrews' tutor in *Educating Archie*)

hello my darlings Charlie Drake (usual opening greeting of the diminutive funny man)

hello peeps Stavros (Harry Enfield)

hello playmates Arthur Askey (introducing himself on radio's *Band Waggon*)

hello possums Dame Edna Everage (Barry Humphries)

hello sailor Minnie Bannister (Spike Milligan) in the classic Goon's script *Tales of Men's Shirts*. The phrase has entered the language as a camp double-entendre

here and now, before your very eyes Arthur Askey (original catchphrase from the series *Before Your Very Eyes*)

here's another fine mess you've gotten me into Oliver Hardy (invariably to his long-suffering partner Stan Laurel)

here's a pretty kettle of fish Queen Mary (to Stanley Baldwin referring to the abdication crisis of 1936)

here's Johnny Ed McMahon (introduction to Johnny Carson on NBC's *Tonight show*)

here's looking at you kid Rick Blaine (Humphrey Bogart) in *Casablanca*. The phrase is used four times

here we are again Joey the Clown (Joseph Grimaldi) one of the oldest attributable catchphrases

he's fallen in the water Little Jim (Spike Milligan) in the *Goon Show*

he's loo-vely, Mrs Hoskins . . . . he's loo-oo-vely Ivy (Ted Ray) in the comedian's hit radio programme *Ray's a Laugh*

hi there pop pickers Alan Freeman (Australian disc-jockey) whilst presenting *Pick of the Pops*

how's about that then, guys and gals Jimmy Savile (phrase used by the disc-jockey after a particularly good record)

how tickled I am Ken Dodd (whilst usually shoving a tickling stick between his legs from behind)

I am the greatest Muhammad Ali (Cassius Clay) usurped the phrase from wrestler Gorgeous George

I could do that Yosser Hughes (Bernard Hill) in *Boys from the Blackstuff*

I didn't get where I am today . . . CJ (John Barron) in *The Fall and Rise of Reginald Perrin*

I do not like this game Bluebottle (Peter Sellers) in the *Goon Show*

I don't mind if I do Colonel Chinstrap (Jack Train) in *ITMA* whenever a drink was offered him

if it ain't broke, why fix it? Bert Lance (President Carter's Director of the Office of Management and Budget) speaking on the subject of governmental reorganisation

If it's up there I'll give you the money myself Les Dennis (in *Family Fortunes*)

If you can't stand the heat, get out of the kitchen Harry S Truman (when he gave his reason for not standing in the 1952 elections). Truman himself was quoting Major-General Harry Vaughan

I got a horse Ras Prince Monolulu (Peter Carl McKay) racing pundit of the 1930s to the 1950s

I'll be leaving you now, sir Claud Snudge (Bill Fraser) in Granada Television's *Bootsie and Snudge*

illegitimi non carborundum General 'Vinegar Joe' Stilwell used this motto during WWII under the pretence that it meant 'don't let the bastards grind you down'

I'll give it foive Janice Nicholls; a member of the public who took part in *Thank Your Lucky Stars* Spin-a-Disc panel and became famous when she gave a maximum five

I'll give you the results in reverse order Eric Morley (giving *Miss World* results)

I'm a laydee Emily Howard (David Walliams) in the BBC television comedy, *Little Britain*

I'm a little worried about Jim Mrs Dale (in *Mrs Dale's Diary*)

I mean that most sincerely, friends Hughie Green (phrase usually accompanied by a clenched fist gesture)

I'm afraid that I was very, very drunk Rowley Birkin QC (Paul Whitehouse) in the BBC television comedy, *The Fast Show*

I'm a little bit werrrr, a little bit weyyyy! Chris Jackson (the geezer who'd nick anything) as played by Paul Whitehouse in the BBC comedy *The Fast Show*

I'm in charge Bruce Forsyth (whilst introducing the Beat the Clock section at the Palladium)

I'm not a number, I'm a free man The Prisoner (Patrick McGoohan) spoken in defiance of his number 6 nomenclature

I'm smarter than the average bear Yogi Bear (whilst constantly outwitting ranger John Smith in Jellystone Park)

I'm the only gay in the village Daffyd (Matt Lucas) in the BBC television comedy, *Little Britain*

in like Flynn   Errol Flynn (alluding to his legendary bedroom prowess)

I only arsked (sic)   Popeye Popplewell (Bernard Bresslaw) in *The Army Game*

I say, I say, I say   Murray and Mooney; a famous double act of the 1930s in which Harry Mooney would utter the immortal words and Harry Murray would invariably reply with 'I don't wish to know that, kindly leave the stage'

I say, what a smasher   Charlie Chester (from the BBC radio programme *Stand Easy*)

is she a friend of Dorothy?   An allusion to a homosexual (from Judy Garland's character in *The Wizard of Oz*). The phrase arose from Judy Garland's friendships within male homosexual circles

I thang you (sic)   Arthur Askey (from the radio show *Band Waggon*)

I think the answer lies in the soil   Arthur Fallowfield (Kenneth Williams) in *Beyond Our Ken*

I think we should be told   Attributed to John Junor by *Private Eye* in a parody of his opinion column in the *Sunday Express*. Although the column invariably used the phrase it is doubtful whether Junor ever actually used the phrase himself

it'll play in Peoria   Coined by John Ehrlichman during the Nixon election campaign of 1969. The phrase was an allusion to whether policies would appeal to 'Middle America'. Peoria is in Illinois and was chosen as it had four syllables and scanned well

it never rains, but it pours   John Arbuthnot (the inventor of 'John Bull' coined this phrase in 1726)

it's goodnight from me . . . and it's goodnight from him   Ronnie Barker and Ronnie Corbett (*The Two Ronnies*)

it's only a bloody game   Magnus Magnusson would invariably say this to settle the nerves of contenders of *Mastermind*; of course, this ice-breaker was only for the ears of the audience and participants

it's the way I tell 'em   Frank Carson (full phrase is 'you've heard them all before but it's the way I tell 'em')

it's turned out nice again   George Formby (invariably opened his act with this phrase)

I've arrived, and to prove it, I'm here   Max Bygraves (as Archie Andrews' tutor in *Educating Archie*)

I've found it, I've found the lost chord   Jimmy Durante (whilst playing the piano he would feign this new discovery)

I've got a million of 'em   Jimmy Durante (after telling a joke) Max Miller later used this phrase

I've got his pecker in my pocket   Lyndon B Johnson (dates from his time as Senate Majority leader in Washington)

I've started so I'll finish   Magnus Magnusson would say this if he had started asking a question on the BBC's *Mastermind* programme but the time had elapsed and the hooter sounded

I wanna tell you a story   Max Bygraves (as Archie Andrew's tutor in *Educating Archie*)

I want me tea   Grandma Grove (Nancy Roberts) who often made this demand in the *Grove Family*

I want to be alone   Greta Garbo never actually spoke these words off-set although she was very reclusive. The most often quoted origin of these words on screen is in the 1932 film *Grand Hotel*, however she utters the immortal words in the earlier 1929 film *The Single Standard* but as it was a silent film it was subtitled

I won't take me coat off; I'm not stopping   Ken Platt, the northern comedian's catchphrase was coined by

Ronnie Taylor, producer of radio's *Variety Fanfare*, in 1951

jolly hockey sticks   Monica (Beryl Reid) as Archie Andrews' posh friend in *Educating Archie*

just give me the facts, ma'am   Joe Friday (Jack Webb) in *Dragnet*

just like that   Tommy Cooper (sometimes the master comedian would say 'not like that, like that')

K-E-Y-N-S-H-A-M   Horace Batchelor, the football pools export on Radio Luxembourg would always end his advert by spelling out his address in Bristol

Kilroy was here   Phrase used in WWII to allude to the US Air Transport Command. The phrase is of doubtful origin but it is beloved of graffiti writers

kiss of death, the   Stock phrase deriving from the kiss of betrayal given by Judas to Christ

lady bountiful   George Farquhar coined the phrase from the name of a character in his 1707 work *The Beaux Stratagem* but phrase is now applied to a woman who is conspicuously generous to others less fortunate than herself

laugh and the world laughs with you   From Ella Wheeler Wilcox poem 'Solitude', it continues 'weep and you weep alone'

left hand down a bit   Leslie Phillips (in *The Navy Lark*) Jon Pertwee would reply 'left hand down it is, sir'

let's get outta here   In a survey of stock film phrases this is the most often said in film history

life begins at forty   William B Pitkin (Professor of Journalism at Columbia University in a 1932 book)

listening bank, the   Midland Bank (advertising slogan used from 1980 onwards)

little of what you fancy does you good, a   Marie Lloyd popularised the phrase in a song written by Fred W Leigh and George Arthurs. The phrase was invariably accompanied by a suggestive wink

Lloyd George knew my father   Tommy Rhys Roberts, whose father did indeed know Lloyd George, popularised the phrase, which became a Welsh standard song, sung to the tune of 'Onward Christian Soldiers'

loadsamoney   Harry Enfield character (first seen in *Friday Night Live*) who was a plasterer by trade

loook   Alf Garnett (Warren Mitchell) in *Till Death Us Do Part*

love me, love my dog   St Bernard of Clairvaux first espoused this philosophical metaphor, which meant in effect, you must love me warts and all. Incidentally St Bernard of Clairvaux is not the St Bernard (of Menthon) after whom the breed of Alpine dog is named

love you madly   Duke Ellington often said 'We'd like you to know that the boys in the band all . . .'

man for all seasons, a   Robert Bolt's title for his 1960 play about Sir Thomas More has entered the language to describe an adaptable, all-round accomplished person

man on the Clapham omnibus, the   Lord Bowen first coined this phrase in 1903 when summing up a case. The phrase has entered the modern idiom to represent the ordinary man in the street

man they couldn't gag, the   Peter Wilson (nickname of the *Daily Mirror* sports columnist)

man you love to hate, the   Erich von Stroheim (epithet rather than catchphrase)

Martini . . . shaken not stirred   James Bond (The line is first spoken in *Goldfinger* but does not appear in the books)

mean! moody! magnificent   Jane Russell (epithet

rather than catchphrase) first used as slogan for *The Outlaw*

mind how you go George Dixon (Jack Warner) in *Dixon of Dock Green*

mind my bike Jack Warner popularised this unlikely hit phrase on radio

moment of truth, the The phrase derives from a Spanish bullfighting term 'El momento de la verdad' in which the final sword thrust kills the animal

Mounties always get their man, the Unofficial motto of the Royal Canadian Mounted Police first coined by John J Healy, although the official motto since 1873 is 'Maintain the Right'

Mr Big Ian Fleming coined the phrase in his second novel *Live and Let Die* (1954). The character's name was Buonaparte Ignace Gallia, hence Mr Big. The phrase has come to mean any top man in an organisation

Mr Clean James Baker the American Secretary of State was given this epithet

Much Binding in the Marsh Not so much a catchphrase but this popular radio programme, that grew out of an edition of *Merry-Go-Round* and starred Kenneth Horne and Richard Murdoch, became the instigator of many catchphrases and a song of the same title

mum, mum, they're laughing at me Arthur English (whilst playing his cockney spiv character and unfurling his kipper tie)

my flabber has never been so gasted Frankie Howerd coined this ridiculous phrase that became an essential part of his act. He would say 'I'm flabbergasted, in fact my flabber has never been so gasted'

my name's Monica Beryl Reid (as Archie Andrew's posh friend in *Educating Archie*)

nah . . . Luton airport Lorraine Chase (in a famous advert for Campari)

never change / swap horses in midstream Abraham Lincoln is identified with the phrase in a citation of 1864

never knowingly undersold John Lewis Partnership (slogan) devised by John Spedan Lewis in 1920

nice 'ere innit Lorraine Chase (in a famous advert for Campari)

nice to see you, to see you nice Bruce Forsyth (originally from the *Generation Game* but often used in other shows)

night of the long knives, the Originally referred to the night of 2 July 1934 when Hitler, aided by Himmler's black-shirted SS, liquidated the leadership of the brown-shirted SA. The phrase has entered modern vernacular to mean a surprise bloodless purge, for example Harold Macmillan's wholesale reorganisation of his cabinet in 1962

nine days' wonder Possibly traced back to Geoffrey Chaucer and more recently alluding to the fact that a puppy is blind for the first nine days of its life. The phrase has come to mean anything of short-lived appeal

no such thing as a free lunch The Nobel Prize-winning economist Milton Friedman is identified with the saying and he wrote a book of this name, but the phrase dates back to the 19th century

not a lot Paul Daniels (usually before doing a trick he would say 'you're going to like this . . .')

not 'arf Alan Freeman would say this phrase out of context, which perhaps gave it appeal

not tonight, Josephine Napoleon I (attributed but never actually said)

now that's magic Paul Daniels (after successfully performing a slick trick)

nudge nudge, wink wink, say no more squire Eric Idle (in *Monty Python*) showing suspect pictures to Terry Jones

often a bridesmaid, but never a bride Milton Feasley wrote this slogan for Listerine mouthwash in 1923

oh hello, I'm Julian, and this is my friend Sandy Hugh Paddick (referring to Kenneth Williams in *Round the Horne*)

old soldiers never die, they simply fade away General Douglas MacArthur whilst addressing congress on 19 April 1951 after being dismissed by President Truman. The phrase originated much earlier

one foot in the grave Jonathan Swift in *Gulliver's Travels* (1726) made the phrase popular in connection with the Struldbruggs of Laputa

one small step for man Neil Armstrong's exact words when walking on the moon were 'That's one small step for a man, one giant leap for mankind'

only the names have been changed Narrator of the detective series *Dragnet* would continue . . . .'to protect the innocent'

on with the motley (vesti la giubba) From Leoncavallo's opera *I Pagliacci* relating to the fact that the clown must carry on despite a broken heart

on your bike Norman Tebbit, addressing the Conservative Party conference on 15 Oct 1981. He related how his father was brought up with unemployment but instead of rioting got on his bike and looked for work

ooh Betty Frank Spencer (Michael Crawford) in *Some Mothers do 'ave 'em*

ooh you are awful, but I like you Mandy (Dick Emery) accompanied by a slap on the interviewer's shoulder

oooo arr, me ol' pal, me ol' beauty Walter Gabriel (Chris Gittins) in the *Archers*

orft we jolly well go Jimmy Young (after finishing the link with Terry Wogan would utter these words)

pass The stock reply of contenders on the BBC's *Mastermind* programme to save time if the answer did not immediately spring to mind

pass the sick-bag, Alice John Junor (used in his *Sunday Express* column and parodied by *Private Eye*)

phone a friend Chris Tarrant (in *Who Wants to Be a Millionaire*)

pile it high, sell it cheap Sir John Cohen, founder of Tesco supermarkets, coined this phrase

play it again Sam attributed to Humphrey Bogart as Rick Blaine in *Casablanca*, although he never actually said these words

pop goes the weasel W R Mandale wrote the rhyme 'Up and down the City Road, In and out the Eagle, That's the way the money goes, Pop goes the weasel'. The meaning of the rhyme is uncertain but 'Pop' means to pawn

probably the best lager in the world Carlsberg (1973 advertising slogan voiced by Orson Welles)

public enemy No. 1 John Dillinger (Attorney General Homer Cummings gave this name to the murderer)

Queen Anne's dead Phrase of uncertain origin but used to put down someone who delights in telling you some very old news or what you knew already

quick and the dead, the from the New Testament 2

F
A
M
O
U
S

P
E
O
P
L
E

Timothy 4:1. The quick in this context meant the living

read my lips George Bush popularised this phrase in his acceptance speech for the Republican nomination on 19 August 1988. The rest of the line was 'no new taxes'

real thing, it's the Coca-Cola (advertising slogan dating from 1942)

refreshes the parts other beers cannot reach Heineken (advertising slogan for the lager)

respec' Sacha Baron Cohen in the guise of rapper Ali G

right monkey Al Read (the popular northern comedian also used 'cheeky monkey' in his act)

rock on, Tommy Bobby Ball (the comedian would often tug his braces at the same time)

Rodney, you plonker Del Boy (David Jason) to his younger brother in *Only Fools and Horses*

roses grow on you Norman Vaughan (advertising campaign for Roses Chocolates)

say goodnight Dick Dan Rowan (in *Rowan and Martin's Laugh In*) to his co-star Dick Martin

say goodnight Gracie George Burns (to his wife and co-star Gracie Allen)

say it with flowers Patrick O' Keefe, an advertising agent, coined the phrase in 1917

shame, shame Bruce Forsyth (usually accompanied by a cuddle from him)

she who must be obeyed Horace Rumpole (Leo McKern) referring to his wife in John Mortimer's *Rumpole of the Bailey*. The original expression came from Henry Rider Haggard's novel *She* and referred to the all-powerful Ayesha

short, fat, hairy legs Eric Morecambe (referring to Ernie Wise)

shut that door Larry Grayson (turning towards the wings and intimating a draught)

silly old moo Alf Garnett (Warren Mitchell) referring to Elsie, his wife, in *Till Death Us Do Part*

sit (sssit) Barbara Woodhouse (whilst demonstrating her methods of training dogs)

slow, slow, quick, quick, slow Victor Sylvester popularised this quickstep tempo in his radio and television series

smile, you're on . . . Candid Camera (first coined by Allen Funt in the original American version)

sock it to me Judy Carne (in *Rowan and Martin's Laugh In*)

somebody up there likes me Rocky Graziano (world champion boxer had a film and book about him with this title)

some mothers do 'ave 'em Jimmy Clitheroe (corruption of the phrase 'don't some mothers have 'em')

somewhere to the right of Genghis Khan Arthur Scargill relating a political standpoint to John Mortimer

speak as you find, that's my motto Nola Purvis (Pat Coombs) in the radio series *Hello Playmates*

spend, spend, spend, I'm going to Viv Nicholson (after winning £152,000 on Littlewoods football pools in 1961)

stone me Tony Hancock (originally coined in *Hancock's Half-Hour*)

stop me and buy one Lionel and Charles Rodd came up with this slogan for Wall's ice-cream in 1923 although in those days it was for ice-cream tricycles rather than vans

stop messin' abaht (sic) Kenneth Williams (originally coined by Williams in *Hancock's Half-Hour*)

suck it and see Charlie Naughton of the Crazy Gang coined this phrase, which meant 'try it'

suit you sir! Ken and Kenneth the tailors in the BBC comedy series *The Fast Show*

sweet Fanny Adams The phrase originates from the murder of an eight-year-old child in 1867. Fanny Adams was the victim of Frederick Booth, a solicitor's clerk, who grotesquely mutilated her body. As these things tend to go, at around the same time, the Royal Navy issued tinned meat which sailors flippantly said probably contained the remains of the little girl. Fanny Adams became slang for mutton or stew and later any worthless item. In modern day vernacular 'Sweet F. A.' can also mean sweet fuck-all

swinging Norman Vaughan (the phrase was accompanied by a thumbs-up gesture)

ten, four Dan Matthews (Broderick Crawford) in the American detective series *Highway Patrol*. The phrase signified agreement and was always being bellowed into the radio

thank you music lovers Spike Jones, the American musician, would murder a classic piece of music along the same lines as Les Dawson or Eric Morecambe and then proceed to say . . .

that'll do nicely, sir American Express (advertising slogan originating in the late 1970s)

that's all folks Merry Melodies (Warner Brothers cartoons) written at the end of their cartoons

that's magic Paul Daniels (after completion of a successful trick or illusion)

the ranger ain't gonna like it Yogi Booboo bear (when Yogi bear had inventive ideas for stealing picker-nick baskets)

there's more Jimmy Cricket (whilst telling a joke in his act)

there's no answer to that Eric Morecambe (cleverly used if the quick-witted comedian was stuck for words)

thinking man's crumpet, the Frank Muir coined this phrase about television presenter Joan Bakewell

this is Funf speaking Funf the spy (in *ITMA*, i.e. *It's That Man Again*)

today is the first day of the rest of your life Charles Dederich (founder of anti-heroin centres in the USA)

too little, too late Professor Allan Nevins wrote this in an article in *Current History* (1935), referring to the Nazi menace in Germany and the lack of remedial action

T. T. F. N. (ta-ta for now) Mrs Mopp (Dorothy Summers) in *ITMA*. Jimmy Young adopted this phrase in his popular Radio Two morning show

turn on, tune in, drop out Dr Timothy Leary coined this pro drug phrase in 1967, although he himself suggests that he stole the phrase from Marshall McLuhan

unacceptable face of capitalism Edward Heath coined this phrase in 1973 when replying to a question from Jo Grimond in the House of Commons

up and under Eddie Waring (the much imitated rugby commentator was synonymous with the phrase)

very interesting, but stupid Arte Johnson (in *Rowan and Martin's Laugh In*) dressed as a German soldier and smoking a cigarette in a holder

wakey, wakey Billy Cotton (a fanfare of *Somebody Stole My Gal* would follow this cry) *walkies* Barbara Woodhouse (whilst demonstrating her methods of training dogs)

weekend starts here, the Ready Steady Go (the Friday night pop show was always preceded by these words)

week is a long time in politics, a Harold Wilson (also deliberated that 48 hours was a long time in politics)

well, he would, wouldn't he? Mandy Rice-Davies (referring to Lord Astor's denial of involvement with her)

were you truly wafted here from paradise? Terry Howard wrote this Campari advert, which made Lorraine Chase a star

what do you think of it so far? Eric Morecambe would rhetorically ask this question whilst either performing one of Ernie's plays or during a lull between sketches. The stock reply by Eric himself was 'rubbish', which was often said through an inanimate object by way of him throwing his voice or saying it between clenched teeth

what's new pussycat? Warren Beatty (coined the phrase and had the film originally written for him)

what's on the table Mabel? Wilfred Pickles (to his wife Mabel in radio's Have a Go)

what's up, doc? Bugs Bunny originally said these words to his adversary Elmer J Fudd, a doctor, but eventually would say this as a form of greeting to almost everyone. The full phrase was 'er, what's up doc?' followed by a crunch on a carrot

when the going gets tough, the tough get going Joseph P Kennedy, the father of John F Kennedy, used this phrase in the bringing up of his sons, in an effort to help them through adversity

who dares wins, Rodney Del Boy (David Jason) in Only Fools and Horses

who loves ya, baby? Theo Kojak (Telly Savalas) in the popular American detective series, Kojak

wind of change, the Harold Macmillan used this phrase, written by Sir David Hunt, in describing the change of political standing in Africa in 1960

winter of discontent, the The phrase originates in the opening line of the eponymous Richard of Gloucester in Shakespeare's Richard III, however the term is now used as a description of the winter of 1978/79 when industrial action became rife due to the Labour Government's endeavours to curb pay rises

without hesitation, deviation or repetition Just a Minute (the popular radio panel game meant guests had to speak for a minute)

world's favourite airline, the British Airways slogan

wot, no Chad The phrase was very common in Britain during WWII and was accompanied by a depiction of a bald-headed man appearing over a wall and inquiring 'wot, no . . .' the blank being filled in by any commodity in short supply. Its origin is uncertain

yaroooo Billy Bunter (created by Frank Richards)

yeah, but no, but yeah, but Vicky Pollard (Matt Lucas) in the BBC television comedy, Little Britain

you ain't heard nothin' yet Al Jolson (the most often misquoted catchphrase of all. The line is from The Jazz Singer)

you ain't seen nothin' yet President Ronald Reagan used this phrase as a slogan during his 1984 re-election bid

you bet your sweet bippy Dick Martin (in Rowan and Martin's Laugh In) popular 1960s US comedy show

you cannot be serious John McEnroe (much caricatured phrase that the tennis player often said on court)

you can run but you can't hide Joe Louis (said of Billy Conn, a nifty heavyweight of the day who Louis knocked out)

you can't see the join Eric Morecambe (talking about Ernie Wise's fictitious wig)

you dirty old man Harold Steptoe (Harry H Corbett) addressing his father in Steptoe and Son

you dirty rat Cagney, James (dirty double-crossing rat were actual words in Blonde Crazy 1931)

you dirty rotten swine, you Bluebottle (Peter Sellers) in the Goon Show

you lucky people Tommy Trinder used this phrase whilst compering the Sunday Night at the London Palladium shows and it became his stock phrase identified with him

your starter for ten Bamber Gascoigne (an on the buzzer question to teams in University Challenge)

you too can have a body like mine Charles Atlas (slogan used for his mail-order body-building lessons)

you've never had it so good Harold MacMillan (actually said 'most of our people have never had it so good')

FAMOUS PEOPLE

Causes of Death

Ace, Johnny Rhythm and blues act, died playing Russian roulette (1954).

Alexander the Great Died aged 32 after a prolonged banquet and drinking bout (323 BC).

Alkan, Charles-Henri Valentin French pianist and composer who died when bookshelf collapsed on him whilst reaching for the Talmud (1888).

Antony, Mark Roman triumvir, committed suicide by running onto his sword in 31 BC (misled by a false report of Cleopatra's death).

Archer, Fred English champion jockey, shot himself during an attack of typhoid (1886).

Astor, John Jacob American financier, went down in the Titanic in 1912.

Bach, Johann Sebastian German composer, suffered stroke following unsuccessful eye operation (1750).

Ballard, Florence Supremes vocalist, died of a heart attack aged 32 yrs 7 mths.

Barnett, Lady Isobel Committed suicide in her bathroom on 20 October 1980, one week after being found guilty of shoplifting.

Bartók, Bela Hungarian composer, died of leukaemia (1945).

Beethoven, Ludwig van German compuser, died of cirrhosis of the liver (lupus erythematosus is sometimes considered an alternative cause) (1827).

Belushi, John American actor, died of drug-related illness, aged 33 yrs 1 mth (1982).

Berg, Alban Austrian composer, died from infection from a septic insect bite (1935).

Berlioz, Hector French composer, died following brain haemorrhage (1869).

Billy the Kid   Pseudonym of Henry McCarty, aka William H Bonney, American bandit, shot by sheriff Pat Garrett in 1881.

Bizet, Georges   French composer, died of angina pectoris complicated by rheumatoid arthritis (1875).

Bolan, Marc   T Rex singer, died in car crash aged 30 yrs 2 mths (1977).

Bonham, John   Led Zeppelin member, died of alcohol poisoning, aged 32 yrs 3 mths (1980).

Brahms, Johannes   German composer, died of liver cancer (1897).

Brooke, Rupert   English poet, died of septicaemia, aged 27 yrs (1915).

Brown, Grace   Murdered by Chester Gillett in 1906; formed basis for Theodore Dreiser's book *An American Tragedy*.

Calmette, Gaston   Editor of *Le Figaro*, shot by Madame Caillaux, wife of the French Finance Minister, accusing her husband of fraud; she was later acquitted (1914).

Calvi, Roberto   Italian banker, found hanging from scaffolding under Blackfriars Bridge (18 June 1982).

Carpenter, Karen   American vocalist and drummer, died aged 32 yrs 11 mths from heart attack caused by anorexia nervosa (1983).

Castlereagh, Viscount   British statesman, stabbed himself with a penknife (1822).

Chausson, Ernest   French composer, died in a bicycle accident (1899).

Childers, Erskine   Irish nationalist, was executed in 1922 by the Irish Free State authorities.

Chopin, Fryderyk   Polish composer, died of pulmonary tuberculosis (1849).

Clarke, Ossie   Fashion designer, murdered by his flatmate Diego Cogolato (7 August 1996).

Cleopatra   Queen of Egypt, allegedly committed suicide by allowing an asp to bite her breast (30 BC).

Cline, Patsy   Top American country singer, died in a plane crash aged 30 yrs 5 mths (1963).

Clive, Robert (of Plassey)   English soldier, committed suicide (after several attempts) by shooting himself (1774).

Cobain, Kurt   Lead singer of Nirvana, shot himself dead aged 27 yrs 1 mth (1994).

Cogan, Alma   English singer, died of cancer aged 34 yrs 5 mths (1966).

Cooke, Sam   American soul singer, shot dead aged 33 yrs 9 mths (1964).

Crane, Harold Hart   American poet, committed suicide by leaping from a steamboat into the Caribbean (1932).

Davison, Emily   Suffragette, threw herself under the King's horse in the 1913 Epsom Derby.

Dean, James   American actor, died in a car crash in 1955, aged 24.

Debussy, Claude   French composer, died of cancer of the rectum (1918).

Delius, Frederick   English composer, died of syphilis in 1934.

Diana, Princess of Wales   Died in Paris car crash (31 Aug 1997).

Dvořák, Antonín   Czech composer, died of a brain haemorrhage (1904).

Eastman, George   American inventor of the Kodak camera, shot himself in 1932.

Elgar, Edward   English composer, died of a brain tumour in 1934.

Elliot, 'Mama' Cass   American singer, died of a heart attack, aged 32 yrs 10 mths (1974).

Epstein, Brian   Manager of the Beatles, died of a drugs overdose in 1967.

Fayed, Dodi   Son of Harrods director, died in Paris car crash (31 Aug 1997).

Freud, Sigmund   Austrian neurologist and founder of psychoanalysis, died of cancer in 1939.

Garland, Judy   American entertainer, died of a drugs overdose in 1969.

Genovese, Kitty   Famous New York murder; nobody answered her calls for help.

Gershwin, George   American composer, died of a brain tumour (1937).

Gibb, Andy   Brother of the Bee Gees, died aged 30 of drug-related illness (1988).

Gibb, Maurice   Member of the Bee Gees, died of a heart attack following an operation to clear an intestinal blockage. Maurice was born 22 December 1949 and died 12 January 2003.

Granados, Enrique   Spanish composer, died when his ship SS *Sussex* was torpedoed by a German sub in the English Channel (1916).

Grieg, Edvard   Norwegian composer, died from coronary artery disease with angina pectoris (1907).

Ham, Pete   Badfinger member and co-writer of 'Without You', committed suicide after depression brought on possibly by royalty problems (1975).

Hancock, Tony   Birmingham-born comedian, took a drug overdose in a Sydney hotel room in 1968.

Hannibal   Carthaginian soldier, committed suicide by poison when the Romans demanded his surrender (182 BC).

Haydn, Franz Joseph   Austrian composer, died of arteriosclerosis (1809).

Hemingway, Ernest   American novelist, shot himself in the mouth in Ketchum, Idaho (1961).

Hendrix, Jimi   American guitarist, suffocated in his own vomit after mixing drugs and alcohol aged 27 yrs 9 mths (1970).

Hickok, Wild Bill   American gunfighter, shot from behind by Jack McCall whilst playing poker in 1876. Hickok's hand was a queen and 2 pair aces over eights (Dead man's hand).

Himmler, Heinrich   German Nazi leader committed suicide with a cyanide phial concealed in his mouth (1945).

Holly, Buddy   Rock and roll pioneer, died aged 22 yrs 5 months in a plane crash (with Ritchie Valens, 17 yrs 9 mths, and the Big Bopper, 29 yrs 4 mths) in 1959.

Hutchence, Michael   Lead singer with INXS, found hanging in a Sydney hotel room (21 Nov 1997).

Iliffe, Marc   (Britain's Strongest Man 2002) Hanged himself in his gym in February 2003.

Ingram, Herbert   English journalist, founder of the *Illustrated London News* and MP for Boston from 1856, drowned in a boat collision on Lake Michigan in 1860.

Ireton, Henry   English Parliamentarian soldier, died of the plague in 1651.

Irving, Laurence   Novelist son of actor Sir Henry Irving, drowned in the *Empress of Ireland* disaster in 1914.

James, Jesse   Wild West robber, shot in the back of the head by Bob Ford (1882).

Jones, Brian   Member of the Rolling Stones, drowned in a swimming pool (aged 27 yrs 4 mths) soon after leaving the group in 1969.

Joplin, Janis American folk singer, died aged 27 yrs 8 mths of heroin overdose (1970).

Klee, Paul Swiss artist, died of a heart attack (1940).

Koestler, Arthur and Cynthia Hungarian-born British author and his wife, committed suicide together in 1983 when he became terminally ill.

Leclair, Jean Marie French composer, stabbed in his own home, possibly by his wife (1764).

Liszt, Franz Hungarian composer, died of pneumonia (1886).

London, Jack American novelist, committed suicide by taking poison in 1916.

Lully, Jean-Baptiste French composer, died of gangrene and blood poisoning after he struck himself in the foot whilst conducting with a pointed cane (1687).

Lynott, Phil Thin Lizzy vocalist and guitarist, died of drug-related illness aged 34 yrs 4 mths (1986).

Markov, Georgi Bulgarian defector, famously murdered by the poison 'ricin' dispensed from the tip of an umbrella (1978).

Marten, Maria Mole-catcher's daughter, murdered by William Corder in May 1827 at the Red Barn at Polstead nr Ipswich.

Mendelssohn, Felix German composer, died of brain haemorrage (1847).

Milk, Harvey US gay rights activist and politician, killed alongside San Francisco Mayor, George Moscone, by ex-city employee Dan White (1978).

Mishima, Yukio Japanese writer, born Hiraoka Kimitake, committed Seppuku in 1970.

Monroe, Marilyn American model and actress, died from an overdose of sleeping pills in 1962.

Moon, Keith Who drummer, died of alcoholic poisoning aged 32 (in the same flat that Mama Cass died, owned by Harry Nilsson) in 1978.

Morrison, Jim Doors vocalist, died of drug related illness in 1971 (aged 27 yrs 6 mths); buried in Paris.

Mozart, Wolfgang Austrian composer died of heated military fever (nowadays usually considered to be Bright's Disease) (1791).

Murrell, Hilda Famous botanist (rose grower) and peace campaigner, found stabbed in a wood (1984) in suspicious circumstances as she was linked with documents about the sinking of the *General Belgrano*.

Niven, David English actor, died of motor neurone disease (1983).

Orton, Joe English dramatist, struck by hammer wielded by lover Kenneth Halliwell (1967), who subsequently committed suicide.

Owen, Wilfred English poet, killed on the bank of the Oise-Sambre Canal, nr Ors, one week before the armistice was signed in 1918.

Palach, Jan Czech philosophy student, set fire to himself in Jan 1969 in protest at the Russian invasion of Czechoslovakia the previous year.

Pasolini, Pier Paolo Italian writer and director, murdered, possibly as a result of a homosexual encounter, by Giuseppe Pelosi (1975).

Plath, Sylvia Poet wife of Ted Hughes, committed suicide by gassing herself (1963).

Pliny the Elder Roman writer, died in Stabiae (Castellamare) in AD 79 overcome by fumes from Vesuvius.

Presley, Elvis American singer, died of drug-related illnesses in 1977.

Prokofiev, Sergei Russian composer, died of brain haemorrage (1953).

Puccini, Giacomo Italian composer, died of throat cancer (1924).

Quisling, Vidkun Norwegian Fascist leader and puppet PM in occupied Norway, executed in May 1945.

Rachmaninov, Sergei Russian composer and pianist, died of malignant melanoma (1943).

Ravel, Maurice French composer, died of brain tumour (1937).

Redding, Otis Soul singer, died aged 26 yrs 3 mths in a plane crash (1967).

Relf, Keith Yardbirds musician, electrocuted himself, aged 33 yrs 1 mth (1976).

Rimsky-Korsakov, Nikolai Russian composer, died of coronary artery disease with angina pectoris (1908).

Riperton, Minnie American singer, died of cancer aged 31 yrs 8 mths (1979).

Rivett, Sandra Children's nanny, probably murdered by Lord Lucan in 1974 (convicted in absentia 19 June 1975).

Rizzio, David Italian courtier to Mary Queen of Scots, murdered by Scottish noblemen including the Earls of Morton and Lindsay, at the instigation of Lord Darnley (1566).

Robsart, Amy Wife of the Earl of Leicester (favourite of Elizabeth I), found dead at the bottom of a flight of stairs at Cumnor Place, Berkshire (1560).

Rossini, Gioacchino Italian composer, died of cancer of the rectum (1868).

Rothko, Mark Latvian-born American painter, committed suicide by slashing his wrists (1970).

Schubert, Franz Austrian composer, died of typhoid fever (1828).

Scriabin, Alexander Russian composer, died of an infection of a facial carbuncle (1915).

Shannon, Del American pop singer, shot himself whilst depressed (1990).

Siddall, Elizabeth Wife of Dante Gabriel Rossetti, took overdose of laudanum (1862).

Silkwood, Karen US nuclear activist, died in a car crash; her car was suspected to have been forced off the road (1973).

Stradella, Alessandro Italian composer, murdered by persons unknown (1682).

Tchaikovsky, Piotr Russian composer, died of cholera in 1893.

Tone, Wolfe Irish nationalist, cut his throat with a penknife whilst awaiting hanging in Dublin (1798).

Tyler, Wat Leader of the Peasants' Revolt of 1381, wounded by William Walworth, Mayor of London and subsequently dragged from his hospital bed (St Bartholomew's) and beheaded.

Van Gogh, Vincent Dutch painter, shot himself whilst depressed (1890).

Versace, Gianni Murdered outside his Miami home (15 July 1997) by serial killer Andrew Cunanan, who committed suicide shortly afterwards.

Wagner, Richard German composer, died of coronary artery disease with angina pectoris (1883).

Wallace, William Scottish patriot, famously depicted in the film *Braveheart*. After being hanged, drawn and quartered by the British, his quarters were sent to Newcastle, Berwick, Stirling and Perth, as a reminder of his insurrection (1305).

Weber, Carl German composer, died of pulmonary tuberculosis and ulcerated larynx (1826).

FAMOUS PEOPLE

Webern, Anton von   Austrian composer, shot and killed by an American military policeman whilst out after curfew (1945).

Westbrook, Harriet   First wife of the poet PB Shelley, committed suicide by drowning herself in the Serpentine, Hyde Park (1816).

Woolf, Virginia   English novelist, drowned herself in the River Ouse, near her home at Rodmell in Sussex (1941).

Yamamoto, Isoruku   Japanese admiral who directed the attack on Pearl Harbor; his plane was shot down over the Solomon Islands in 1943.

Zweig, Stefan   Austrian-born British writer, committed suicide with his second wife in 1942.

NB: This section gives only a selective list; further death details may be found in other sections, eg Assassinations and Monarchs.

Countries of Birth

John Dalberg, 1st Baron Acton   (Italy)   English Historian

Joy Adamson   (Austria)   British Naturalist

Shmuel Yosef Agnon   (Poland)   Israeli Writer

Viscount Alanbrooke   (France)   British Soldier

Josef Albers   (Germany)   American Painter

Alexander Alekhine   (Russia)   French Chess master

Gubby Allen   (Australia)   English Cricketer

Peter Alliss   (Germany)   British Golfer

Lawrence Alma-Tadema   (Holland)   British Painter

Jeanette Altwegg   (India)   British Skating Gold Medallist

Leopold Amery   (India)   English Tory Politician

Lindsay Anderson   (India)   British Film Director

Mario Andretti   (Italy)   US Racing Driver

Edward Ardizzone   (Vietnam)   British Illustrator

Michael Arlen   (Bulgaria)   British Novelist

Pamela Armstrong   (Borneo)   British Newscaster

Paddy Ashdown   (India)   English Politician

Vladimir Ashkenazy   (Russia)   Icelandic Pianist

Frederick Ashton   (Ecuador)   English Choreographer

John Jacob Astor   (Germany)   American Financier

Nancy Astor   (USA)   British Politician

WH Auden   (England)   American Writer

John Audubon   (Haiti)   American Ornithologist

Frank Auerbach   (Germany)   British Artist

Charles Aznavour   (Armenia)   French Singer

Leo Baekland   (Belgium)   American Chemist

Bruce Bairnsfather   (India)   British Cartoonist

George Baker   (Bulgaria)   British Actor

JG Ballard   (China)   British Writer

Daniel Barenboim   (Argentina)   Israeli Pianist

Victor Barna   (Hungary)   British Table-Tennis Champion

John Barnes   (Jamaica)   English Footballer

Raymond Barre   (Réunion)   French Politician

Lord Beaverbrook   (Canada)   British Newspaper Magnate

Bee Gees   (Isle of Man)   Australian Pop Group

Menachem Begin   (Poland [now Russia])   Israeli Statesman

Georg von Bekesy   (Hungary)   US Physiologist

Hilaire Belloc   (France)   British Writer

Saul Bellow   (Canada)   US Writer

Baruj Benacerraf   (Venezuela)   US Immunologist

Floella Benjamin   (Trinidad)   British TV Presenter

Jill Bennett   (Straits Settlement, now Malaysia)   British Actress

Irving Berlin   (Russia)   US Composer

Isaiah Berlin   (Latvia)   British Philosopher

Pete Best   (India)   British Musician

Hans A Bethe   (Germany [Strasbourg, now France])   US Physicist

Lord Beveridge   (India)   British Economist

Zulfikar Ali Bhutto   (India)   Pakistani Statesman

Isla Blair   (India)   British Actress

George Blake   (Netherlands)   British Spy (for Soviet Union)

Nicolas Bloembergen   (Netherlands)   US Physicist

Paul Boateng   (Ghana)   British Politician

Andrew Bonar Law   (Canada)   English Prime Minister

Alan Bond   (England)   Australian Businessman

Daniel Bovet   (Switzerland)   Italian Pharmacologist

Anne Bradstreet   (England)   US Poet

Gyles Brandreth   (West Germany)   British Author and Politician

Frank Brangwyn   (Belgium)   Welsh Painter

Chris Brasher   (British Guiana)   British Athlete

Walter Houser Brattain   (China)   US Physicist

Fenner Brockway   (India)   English Politician

Joseph Brodsky   (Russia)   US Poet

Ford Madox Brown   (France)   English Painter

Herbert C Brown   (England)   US Chemist

Yul Brynner   (Russia)   US Actor

Frances Hodgson Burnett   (England)   US Novelist

Terry Butcher   (Singapore)   English Footballer

Andrew Caddick   (New Zealand)   English Cricketer

Maria Callas   (United States)   Greek Soprano

Albert Camus   (Algeria)   French Writer

Jacques Canetti   (Bulgaria)   French Record Producer

Frank Capra   (Sicily)   US Film Director

Claudia Cardinale   (Tunisia)   Italian Actress

Barbara Carrera   (Nicaragua)   US Actress

Anna Carteret   (India)   British Actress

Gian Domenico Cassini   (Genoa)   French Astronomer

Marc Chagall   (Russia)   French Artist

Ernst Boris Chain   (Germany)   British Biochemist

William Chambers   (Sweden)   Scottish Architect

Philippe de Champaigne   (Belgium)   French Painter

Subrahmanyan Chandrasekhar   (India [Lahore, now Pakistan])   US Astrophysicist

Louis Chevrolet   (Switzerland)   US Automobile Engineer

Erskine Childers   (England)   Irish Writer and Nationalist

Glynn Christian   (New Zealand)   British TV Broadcaster

Julie Christie (India) English Actress
Linford Christie (Jamaica) British Olympic Gold Medallist
Christo (Bulgaria) American Artist
Elizabeth Connell (South Africa) Irish Soprano
Joseph Conrad (Poland) English Novelist
Alistair Cooke (UK) American Journalist and Broadcaster
Harry H Corbett (Burma) English Actor
Carl Ferdinand Cori (Czechoslovakia) US Biochemist
Allan Cormack (South Africa) US Physicist
John Cornforth (Australia) British Chemist
Sir Michael Costa (Italy) British Conductor
André Frédéric Cournand (France) US Physicist
Cicely Courtneidge (Australia) English Actress
Colin Cowdrey (India) English Cricketer
Frederic Cowen (Jamaica) English Composer
Kid Creole (Canada) US Singer
Cyril Cusack (South Africa) Irish Actor
György Cziffra (Hungary) French Pianist
Frank Damrosch (Germany) US Conductor
Walter Damrosch (Germany) US Conductor
Dana (Rosemary Scallon) (England) Irish Singer
Edward Dannreuther (Alsace) English Pianist
Edward De Bono (Malta) British Psychologist
Chris De Burgh (Argentina) British Singer
Christian R De Duve (England) Belgian Biochemist
Hans Dehmelt (Germany) US Physicist
Max Delbruck (Germany) US Biophysicist
Eamon De Valera (USA) Irish Politician
Ted Dexter (Italy) English Cricketer
Thomas Dolby (Egypt) British Musician
Gabrielle Drake (Pakistan) British Actress
Marcel Duchamp (France) American artist
Renato Dulbecco (Italy) American Biologist
George Du Maurier (France) English Writer
Lawrence and Gerald Durrell (India) English Writers
Sophie-Carmen Eckhardt-Gramatté (Russia) Canadian Composer
Glynn Edwards (Malaya) British Actor
Albert Einstein (Germany) Swiss physicist
Brian Elias (India) English Composer
Iso Elinson (Russia) British Pianist
TS Eliot (USA) British Poet
Mary Ellis (USA) English Soprano
Gloria Estefan (Cuba) American Singer
Eusebio (Mozambique) Portuguese Footballer
Enrico Fermi (Italy) US Nuclear Physicist
Edmond H Fischer (China) US Chemist
Bob Fitzsimmons (England) American Boxer
Errol Flynn (Tasmania) American Actor
CS Forester (Egypt) British Writer
Malcolm Forsyth (South Africa) Canadian Composer
Harry Freedman (Poland) Canadian Composer
Lucien Freud (Germany) British Artist
Marya Freund (Poland) French Soprano
Géza Frid (Hungary) Dutch Composer
Oskar Fried (Germany) Russian Conductor
Fiona Fullerton (Nigeria) British Actress

Henry Fuseli (Switzerland) British Painter
Dennis Gabor (Hungary) British Physicist
Ivan Galamian (Iran) US Violinist
Sandy Gall (Malaya) British Newsreader
Lamberto Gardelli (Italy) Swedish Conductor
Baron Francois Gérard (Italy) French Painter
Ivar Giaever (Norway) US Physicist
Mel Gibson (USA) Australian Actor
Werner Wolf Glaser (Germany) Swedish Composer
Vinko Globokar (France) Yugoslav Trombonist
Alma Gluck (Romania) American Soprano
Maria Goeppert-Mayer (Germany [Katowice, now Poland]) US Physicist
James Goldsmith (France) British Tycoon
Adam Lindsay Gordon (Azores) Australian Poet
Arshile Gorky (Armenia) US Painter
Bryan Gould (New Zealand) British Politician
Ragnar Granit (Finland) Swedish Physiologist
Bernie Grant (British Guiana) English Politician
Cary Grant (England) US Actor
El Greco (Crete (Candia)) Spanish Painter
Silvia Greenberg (Romania) Israeli Soprano
Tony Greig (South Africa) English Cricketer
André Grétry (Belgium) French Composer
Dulcie Grey (Malaya) British Actress
Frederick Grinke (Canada) British Violinist
Walter Gropius (Germany) US Architect
Georg Grosz (Germany) US Painter
Giovanni Guardi (Austria) Venetian Painter
Roger Guillemin (France) US Physiologist
Richard Hageman (Holland) US Composer
Thomas Duffus Hardy (Jamaica) English Archivist
Friedrich von Hayek (Austria) British Economist
Jascha Heifetz (Lithuania) US Violinist
László Heltay (Hungary) British Conductor
Victor Hely-Hutchinson (South Africa) English Composer
Audrey Hepburn (Belgium) American Actress
William Herschel (Germany) British Astronomer
Gerhard Herzberg (Germany) Canadian Physical Chemist
Rudolf Hess (Egypt) German Politician
Victor Hess (Austria) US Physicist
Hermann Hesse (Germany) Swiss Novelist
Dorothy Hodgkin (Egypt) English Chemist
Roald Hoffmann (Poland) US Chemist
Adam Hollioake (Australia) English Cricketer
Ben Hollioake (Australia) England Cricketer
Bob Holness (South Africa) British Presenter
Gordon Honeycombe (India [now Pakistan]) British TV Presenter
Bob Hope (England) US Comedian
Harry Houdini (Hungary) US Escapologist
John Houseman (Hungary) US Actor / Director
Charles B Huggins (Canada) American Surgeon
William Morris Hughes (Wales) Australian Statesman
Olivia Hussey (Argentina) British Actress
Anjelica Huston (Ireland) American Actress
Alec Issigonis (Turkey) British Automobile Designer
Eddie Izzard (Yemen) English Comedian
Sid James (South Africa) British Actor

FAMOUS PEOPLE

Karl Jaspers (Germany) Swiss Philosopher
Niels K Jerne (England) Danish Immunologist
Ruth Prawer Jhabvala (Germany) British Novelist
Alexander Johnson (England) American
  Philosopher
Dom Joly (Lebanon) British Comedian
Vasily Kandinsky (Russia) French Painter
Anna Karen (South Africa) British Actress
Boris Karloff (England) US Actor
Yousef Karsh (Turkey) Canadian Photographer
Kenneth Kendall (India) British TV Presenter
Har Gobind Khorana (India [Raipur, now Pakistan])
  US Molecular Chemist
Nicole Kidman (Honolulu, Hawaii, USA)
  Australian Actress
Wilson Kipketer (Kenya) Danish Athlete
Rudyard Kipling (India) English Writer
Henry Kissinger (Germany) US Politician
Aaron Klug (Lithuania) British Biophysicist
Godfrey Kneller (Germany) British Artist
Arthur Koestler (Hungary) British Author
Oskar Kokoschka (Austria) British Artist
Tjalling Koopmans (Netherlands) US Economist
Alexander Korda (Hungary) British Film Producer
Alexis Korner (France) British Musician
Hans Adolf Krebs (Germany) British Biochemist
Polykarp Kusch (Germany) US Physicist
Simon Kuznets (Russia) US Economist
John Lang (Scotland) Australian Clergyman
Angela Lansbury (England) US Actress
Danny La Rue (Ireland) British Entertainer
Charles Laughton (England) US Actor
Stan Laurel (England) US Actor / Comedian
Sir Austen Layard (France) English Archaeologist
Bernard Leach (Hong Kong) English Potter
Vivien Leigh (India) British Actress
Peter Lely (Netherlands) British Painter
Philipp EA Lenard (Hungary) German Physicist
Wassily Leontief (Russia) US Economist
Doris Lessing (Persia [now Iran]) British Writer
W Arthur Lewis (St Lucia) British Economist
Wyndham Lewis (Canada) English Novelist /
  Painter
Eric Liddell (China) Scottish Athlete
Basil Liddell Hart (France) English Historian
Fritz A Lipmann (Germany) US Biochemist
David Lloyd George (England) Welsh Politician
Margaret Lockwood (India) British Actress
Frederick Loewe (Austria) US Composer
Peter Lorre (Hungary) US Actor
David Low (New Zealand) British Political Cartoonist
Henry Luce (China) US Magazine Publisher
Bela Lugosi (Lugos Hungary [Lugos, now
  Romania]) US Actor
Jean-Baptiste Lully (Italy) French Composer
Joanna Lumley (Kashmir) British Actress
Salvador Luria (Italy) US Biologist
Rosa Luxemburg (Poland) German Revolutionary
Roddy McDowall (England) US Actor
John McEnroe (West Germany) US Tennis Player
Thomas McGee (Ireland) Canadian Writer
Patrick McGoohan (USA) British Actor
Shane MacGowan (England) Irish Musician
Donald McIntyre (New Zealand) English Bass-
  Baritone

Leo McKern (Australia) British Actor
Jean-Paul Marat (Switzerland) French
  Revolutionary
Ann-Margret (Sweden) US Actress
Raymond Massey (Canada) US Actor
William Somerset Maugham (France) British Writer
Robert Maxwell (Czechoslovakia) British
  Businesman
Jules Mazarin (Italy) French Prelate
Peter B Medawar (Brazil) British Zoologist
Golda Meir (Ukraine) Israeli Politician
Gian-Carlo Menotti (Italy) US Composer
Freddie Mercury (Zanzibar) British Singer
William Mervyn (Kenya) British Actor
Albert Michelson (Germany) US Physicist
Bette Midler (Hawaii [now US State]) US Singer
Ludwig Mies Van Der Rohe (Germany) USA
  Architect
Spike Milligan (India) British Comedian
Guy Mitchell (Yugoslavia) US Singer
Franco Modigliani (Italy) US Economist
Yves Montand (Italy) French Actor and Singer
Lola Montez (Eire) US Dancer
Benjamin Mottelson (USA) Danish Physicist
Vladimir Nabokov (Russia) US Novelist
Sam Neill (New Zealand) Australian Actor
Olivia Newton-John (UK) Australian Actress
Mike Nichols (Germany) US Film Director
Harold Nicolson (Persia [now Iran]) British
  Diplomat
Merle Oberon (India) British Actress
Severo Ochoa (Spain) US Biochemist
Jacques Offenbach (Germany) French Composer
Claes Oldenburg (Sweden) US Sculptor
Isaac Oliver (France) English Painter
Charles Chadwick Oman (India) English Historian
Lars Onsager (Norway) US Physical Chemist
Eugene Ormandy (Hungary) US Conductor
George Orwell (India) British Novelist
Thomas Paine (England) US Writer and
  Revolutionary
George Palade (Romania) US Biologist
Lili Palmer (Austria) French Actress
Adelina Patti (Spain) Italian Soprano
IM Pei (China) US Architect
Susan Penhaligon (Philippines) British Actress
Arno Penzias (Germany) US Astrophysicist
Max F Perutz (Austria) British Biochemist
Antoine Pevsner (Russia) French Painter
Harry Philby (Ceylon [Sri Lanka]) English Arabist
  and Explorer
Kim Philby (India) British Spy (for Soviet Union)
HRH Prince Philip (Greece) British Duke and
  Consort to the Queen
Camille Pissarro (West Indies [St Thomas])
  French Painter
Sidney Poitier (Bahamas) US Actor
Roman Polanski (France) Polish Film Maker
Nyree Dawn Porter (New Zealand) British Actress
Vladimir Prelog (Bosnia) Swiss Chemist
Emeric Pressburger (Hungary) British Film Writer
Ilya Prigogine (Russia) Belgian Chemist
Victoria Principal (Japan) US Actress
Juliet Prowse (South Africa) US Dancer
Anthony Quinn (Mexico) US Actor

Peter Rachman (Poland) British Property Developer
Stamford Raffles (Jamaica [at sea]) English Colonial Administrator
Basil Rathbone (South Africa) British Actor
Cyril Regis (French Guiana) English Footballer
Elisabeth Rethberg (Germany) US Soprano
Cliff Richard (India) British Vocalist
Frederick Sleigh Roberts (India) English Soldier
Edward G Robinson (Romania) US Actor
Richard Rogers (Italy) English Architect
Ronald Ross (India) British Physician
Mark Rothko (Latvia) US Painter
Eero Saarinen (Finland) US Architect
Albert Sabin (Poland) American Physician
Andrew Sachs (Germany) British Actor
Nelly Leonie Sachs (Germany) Swedish Poet and Playwright
Yves Saint Laurent (Algeria) French Fashion Designer
Pamela Salem (India) British Actress
George Sanders (Russia) British Actor
Tessa Sanderson (Jamaica) British Olympic Gold Medallist
John Singer Sargent (Italy) US Painter
Andrew Schally (Poland) US Biochemist
Elsa Schiaparelli (Italy) French Fashion Designer
Shaun Scott (Canada) British Actor
Emilio Segre (Italy) US Physicist
Harry Selfridge (USA) British Merchant
Aloys Senefelder (Czechoslovakia) German Printer and Inventor
Robert Service (England) Canadian Poet
Yitzhak Shamir (Poland) Israeli Politician
William Bradford Shockley (England) US Physicist
Walter Sickert (Germany) English Artist
Claude Simon (Madagascar) French Novelist
Isaac Bashevis Singer (Poland) US Writer
Israel Singer (Poland) US Writer
Elaine Smith (Scotland) Australian Actress
Sydney Smith (New Zealand) British Poet
George Solti (Hungary) British Conductor
Basil Spence (India) Scottish Architect

Sheila Steafel (South Africa) British Actress
Brian Stein (South Africa) English Footballer
Max Steiner (Austria) US Composer
Edward Stourton (Nigeria) UK TV Presenter
Robert Swinhoe (India) English Naturalist
Yves Tanguy (France) US Painter
Mother Teresa (Yugoslavia) Indian Roman Catholic Nun
WM Thackeray (India) British Author
Roy Thomson (Canada) British Newspaper Magnate
Angela Thorne (India [now Pakistan]) British Actress
Debbie Thrower (Kenya) British TV Presenter
Dmitri Tiomkin (Russia) US Composer
Richard Todd (Ireland) English Actor
JRR Tolkien (South Africa) English Novelist
Walter Trog (Canada) British Cartoonist
Liv Ullmann (Japan) Norwegian Actress
Rudolph Valentino (Italy) American Actor
Victor Vasarely (Hungary) French Painter
Hendrik Verwoerd (Holland) South African Politician
Colin Viljoen (South Africa) English Footballer
Selman A Waksman (Russia) US Biochemist
Hugh Walpole (New Zealand) British Novelist
Max Weber (Russia) US Painter
Vanessa-Mae (Singapore) British Violinist
Victor Weisz (Germany) British Political Cartoonist
Benjamin West (USA) English Painter
Alan Whicker (Egypt) British Broadcaster
Joseph Blanco White (Spain) English Poet
Patrick White (England) Australian Author
Terence Hanbury White (India) British Novelist
Roger Whittaker (Kenya) South African Singer
Eugene Paul Wigner (Hungary) US Physicist
Billy Wilder (Austria) US Film Maker
David Wilkie (Sri Lanka) Scottish Swimmer
John Williams (Australia) British Guitarist
Malcolm Williamson (Australia) British Composer
Bruce Willis (Germany) US Actor
Orde Wingate (India) British Soldier
William Wyler (Germany [Mulhausen, now France]) US Film Maker

Dying Words

Independence for ever **John Adams** *US President*
It is the last of Earth, I am content **John Quincy Adams** *US President*
See in what peace a Christian can die **Joseph Addison** *Essayist*
Kurt **Alfred Adler** *Psychologist*
If I feel in good form I shall take the difficult way up. If I do not, I shall take the easy one. I shall join you in an hour **Albert I** *King of Belgium*
I have had wealth, rank and power, but if these were all I had, how wretched I would be **Prince Albert** *Queen Victoria's Consort*
I have such sweet thoughts **Prince Albert** *Queen Victoria's Consort*
Is it not meningitis? **Louisa M Alcott** *American writer*
I am sweeping through the gates, washed in the blood of the lamb **Alexander II** *Russian Tsar*

Clasp my hand dear friend, I am dying **Vittorio Alfieri** *Italian Poet*
Haircut! **Albert Anastasia** *US gangster*
Give the boys a holiday **Anaxagoras** *Philosopher*
Monsieur, I beg your pardon. I did not do it on purpose **Marie Antoinette** *French Queen*
I see my God He calls me to Him **Antony of Padua** *Monk*
Wait till I have finished my problem **Archimedes** *Greek Mathematician*
May God forgive me for putting on any other **Benedict Arnold** *American Traitor*
I desire to die and be with Christ **Roger Ascham** *Elizabeth I's tutor*
Am I dying, or is this my birthday? **Nancy Astor** *British Politician*
Do you think I have played my part pretty well through the farce of life? **Augustus** *Roman Emperor*

The murder of the Queen has been represented to me as a deed; lawful and meritorious, I die a firm Catholic **Anthony Babington** *Plotter against Elizabeth I*

My name and memory I leave to men's charitable speeches, to foreign nations and to the next age **Francis Bacon** *Statesman and philosopher*

Oh God, here I go ... **Max Baer** *Heavyweight Boxer*

Let me have my own fidgets **Walter Bagehot** *Economist*

I can't sleep **JM Barrie** *Scottish Author*

I am a priest, fie, fie! All is gone **Cardinal Beaton** *Scottish prelate*

I am prepared to die for Christ and his Church **Thomas à Becket** *Archbishop of Canterbury*

Gloria Patri et Filio et Spiritu Sancto **Venerable St Bede** *Theologian and historian*

It is well, you have said the truth, it is indeed **Venerable St Bede** *Theologian and historian*

Now comes the mystery **Henry Ward Beecher** *US Clergyman*

Too bad, too bad! It's too late **Ludwig Van Beethoven** *Composer*

I shall hear in heaven **Ludwig van Beethoven** *Composer*

I thank God for having enabled me to meet my fate with so much fortitude and resignation **John Bellingham** *Assassin of Spencer Perceval*

One thousand greetings to Balakirev **Hector Berlioz** *Composer*

I want to live because there are a few things I want to do **Aneurin Bevan** *British Politician*

Who's there? **Billy the Kid** *American Outlaw*

I do not fear death **Thomas Blood** *Irish Adventurer*

My belief is rooted in hope **Léon Blum** *French Prime Minister*

I should never have switched from scotch to Martinis **Humphrey Bogart** *Film Actor*

It is a great consolation to a poet on the point of death that he has never written a line injurious to good morals **Nicolas Boileau** *French Poet*

The executioner is, I believe, very expert; and my neck is very slender **Anne Boleyn** *Queen Consort*

Take my baggage on board the frigate **Simon Bolivar** *Venezuelan Revolutionary*

Goodbye and God bless you, I'll see you again, tomorrow **Horatio Bottomley** *British Politician*

At least one knows that death will be easy **Bertold Brecht** *German Playwright*

puddle it, puddle it and puddle it again **James Brindley** *Engineer*

'tis enough – I shall need no more **James Brindley** *Engineer* (according to Josiah Wedgwood)

Take courage Charlotte, take courage **Anne Brontë** *Author*

If you will send for the doctor I will see him now **Emily Brontë** *Author*

Decay is inherent in all component things **Buddha (Prince Gautama Siddhartha)** *Founder of Buddhism*

I wish Johnny would come **Buffalo Bill** *American Frontiersman*

Well I think it is about time to go to bed now **Sir Redvers Buller** *Colonial Administrator*

World without end **John Bunyan** *Religious Writer*

With the best that was in me I have tried to write more happiness into the world **Frances Hodgson Burnett** *American Novelist*

Don't let the awkward squad fire over my grave **Robert Burns** *Scottish Poet*

I must sleep now **Lord George Byron** *English Poet*

Now I shall go to sleep **Lord George Byron** *English Poet*

Et tu, Brute **Julius Caesar** *Roman Statesman*

I am still alive! **Caligula** *Roman Emperor*

Spain and Portugal **George Canning** *British Prime Minister*

So this is death, well ... **Thomas Carlyle** *Historian and essayist*

Take away those pillows, I shall need them no more **Lewis Carroll** *Author*

Bankhead, let me fall into your arms. It is all over **Viscount Robert Castlereagh** *British statesman*

Stand by me, Tom, and we will die together **Robert Catesby** *Gunpowder Plotter*

Lord, into thy hands I commend my spirit **Catherine of Aragon** *Henry VIII's first wife*

Now I am master of myself **Marcus Porcius Cato (The Younger)** *Roman statesman*

Patriotism is not enough. I must have no hatred or bitterness towards anyone **Edith Cavell** *Nurse*

Italy is made – all is safe **Camillo Cavour** *Italian Patriot*

Pontier! Pontier! **Paul Cézanne** *French artist*

Approaching dissolution brings relief **Neville Chamberlain** *British Prime Minister*

Lord, into thy hands I commend my spirit **Charlemagne** *King of the Franks*

Remember **Charles I** *British King*

I have been a most unconscionable time a-dying, but I hope you will excuse it **Charles II** *English King*

Do not, do not let poor Nelly starve **Charles II** *English King*

Nurse, Nurse, what murder, what blood! Oh! I have done wrong, God pardon me **Charles IX** *French King*

I hope never again to commit a mortal sin, nor even a venial one, if I can help it **Charles VIII** *French King*

Give Dayrolles a chair **Philip Dormer Chesterfield** *English Statesman*

The issue now is clear, it is between light and darkness and everyone must choose his side **GK Chesterton** *British Essayist*

Glory to God for all things **St John Chrysostom** *Syrian Churchman*

Oh I'm so bored with it all **Winston Churchill** *British Prime Minister*

Strike **Marcus Tullius Cicero** *Roman Statesman*

Doctor, do you think it could have been the sausage? **Paul Claudel** *French writer*

I wish to be buried standing – facing Germany **Georges Clemenceau** *French Premier*

Thy kingdom come, thy will be done **Edward Coke** *English Jurist*

Honour these grey hairs young man **Admiral Gaspard Coligny** *French Huguenot Leader*

I am signing my death warrant **Michael Collins** *Irish Patriot*

Lord, into thy hands I commend my spirit **Christopher Columbus** *Italian Explorer*

What an irreparable loss **Auguste Comte** *French Philosopher*

My time has come to die **Confucius** *Chinese Philosopher*

You, Jess, I am better this morning. I can always get a rise out of you **Joseph Conrad** *British Author*

Now, O Lord, set thy servant free **Nicolas Copernicus** *Polish Astronomer*

That was the best ice-cream soda I ever tasted **Lou Costello** *American Comedian*

Goodnight my darlings, I'll see you tomorrow **Noël Coward** *British Playwright*

That unworthy hand! **Thomas Cranmer** *Archbishop of Canterbury*

My design is to make what haste I can to be gone **Oliver Cromwell** *Lord Protector of England*

That was a great game of golf, fellers **Bing Crosby** *American Singer*

Benteen – come on – big village – be quick – bring packs **George Custer** *US soldier*

Nurse, it was I that discovered that leeches had red blood **Georges Cuvier** *French naturalist*

Be sure you show the mob my head, it will be a long time before they see its like **Georges Danton** *French Revolutionary Leader*

I am not in the least afraid to die **Charles Darwin** *English Naturalist*

My fun days are over **James Dean** *American Film Star*

Lord, into thy hands I commend my spirit **Robert Devereux** *Earl of Essex*

The bullet hasn't been made that can kill me **Legs Diamond** *Gangster*

On the ground! **Charles Dickens** *Author*

The first step towards philosophy is incredulity **Denis Diderot** *French man of letters*

Dammit! put them back on. This is funny **Doc Holliday** *Gambler and gunfighter*

I have deserved a thousand deaths **John Dudley** *Duke of Northumberland*

Adieu my friends, I go on to glory **Isadora Duncan** *Dancer*

It is very beautiful over there **Thomas Alva Edison** *American Inventor*

Carry my bones before you on your march, for the rebels will not be able to endure the sight of me **Edward I** *King of England*

Trust in God and you need not fear **Jonathan Edwards** *American Philosopher*

All my possessions for a moment of time **Elizabeth I** *Queen of England*

I die for my king and for France **Louis Duke of Enghien** *French soldier*

Dear God! **Desiderius Erasmus** *Dutch Humanist*

Channel 5 is shit! **Adam Faith** *Singer and Actor*

Now I'll have eine kleine pause **Kathleen Ferrier** *Opera Singer*

On the whole, I'd rather be in Philadelphia **WC Fields** *American Comedian*

The nourishment is palatable **Millard Fillmore** *US President*

I've had a hell of a lot of fun and I've enjoyed every minute of it **Errol Flynn** *Actor*

I am a dead man, Lord have mercy upon me **Gaston de Foix** *French Soldier*

I suffer nothing, but I feel a sort of difficulty in living longer **Bernard Fontenelle** *French Author*

It don't signify, my dearest, dearest Liz **Charles James Fox** *English Statesman*

Never heed! The Lord's power is over all weakness and death **George Fox** *English Religious Leader*

We are all going to Heaven and Van Dyke is of the company **Thomas Gainsborough** *English landscape painter*

Yet it still moves **Galileo Galilei** *Astronomer*

Feed them when I am gone **Giuseppe Garibaldi** *Italian Patriot*

Wally, what is this? It is death, my boy. They have deceived me **George IV** *British King*

Bugger Bognor **George V** *British King*

How is the Empire? **George V** *British King*

Put your hands on my shoulders and don't struggle **WS Gilbert** *Librettist*

Let's do it **Gary Gilmore** *American Murderer*

Light, more light **Johann Wolfgang Goethe** *German poet and dramatist*

Where is the Mahdi? **Charles Gordon** *British general*

I want nobody distressed on my account **Ulysses S Grant** *American Soldier and Statesman*

It is done **Horace Greeley** *American Politician*

Lord, into thy hands I commend my spirit **Lady Jane Grey** *English Queen*

Well if it must be so **Edvard Grieg** *Composer*

I hope to see you on Tuesday at 10.30 am **Earl Douglas Haig** *British General*

I regret that I have but one life to give for my country **Nathan Hale** *American Soldier*

Remember, my Eliza, you are a Christian **Alexander Hamilton** *American Politician*

The rest is silence **Hamlet** *Shakespearean Character*

Let us now relieve the Romans of their fears by the death of a feeble old man **Hannibal** *Carthaginian Soldier*

That's good. Go on, read some more **Warren Harding** *US President*

Four sixes to beat **John Wesley Hardin** *American Outlaw*

I am about the extent of a tenth of a gnat's eyebrow better **Joel Chandler Harris** *American Author*

Cheer up, children, I'm all right **Franz Joseph Haydn** *Composer*

I know I'm going where Lucy is **Rutherford B Hayes** *US President*

Monks! Monks! Monks! **Henry VIII** *King of England*

One more summer and another winter **Hermann Hesse** *German Novelist*

Moderately, I am continuing to orbit **Richard Hillary** *English fighter pilot and writer*

And I wish myself the joy of your fellowship at Whitsuntide **Gustav Holst** *Composer*

I am tired of fighting. I guess this thing is going to get me **Harry Houdini** *Escapologist*

I'll tell that story on the golden floor **AE Housman** *Poet*

Texas, Texas, Margaret **Sam Houston** *Texan patriot*

I die a Queen, but I would rather die the wife of Culpepper. **Catherine Howard** *Henry VIII's Fifth Wife*

God have mercy on my soul. Good people, I beg you pray for me. I see the black light **Victor Hugo** *French Poet*

Truth, truth **Anne Hyde** *Duchess of York*

Let us cross over the river and sit in the shade of the trees **Thomas Jackson** *US Civil War General*

It came with a lass and it will go with a lass **James V** *King of Scotland*

Do not hack me as you did my Lord Russell **James, Duke of Monmouth** *Charles II's illegitimate son*

That picture is crooked **Jesse James** *Train Robber*

Jesus Jesus Jesus, blessed be God **Joan of Arc** *French Patriot*

I commit my soul to God and my body to Saint Alstane **John** *King of England*

This is it, I'm going, I'm going **Al Jolson** *Singer*

Napoleon! Elba! Marie Louise! **Josephine** *French Empress*

Give me another horse, Howard! **Edmund Kean** *British Actor*

Such is life **Ned Kelly** *Australian Outlaw*

I wish to God you had heard them as I have heard them, and I praise God of that heavenly sound **John Knox** *Scottish Church Reformer*

Ah well, it is not the first time an innocent man has been condemned **Henri Landru** *French Murderer*

We shall this day light such a candle, by God's grace, in England, as I trust shall never be put out **Hugh Latimer** *Protestant Martyr*

I think it is time for morphine **DH Lawrence** *British Author*

Strike the tent **Robert E Lee** *Confederate General*

Now I have finished with all earthly business, and high time too **Franz Lehar** *Hungarian Composer*

Yes, yes, my dear child, now comes death. They won't think anything about it **Abraham Lincoln** *US President*

Tristan! **Franz Liszt** *Composer*

Jerusalem, Jerusalem **Louis IX** *French King*

Why weep you? Did you think I would live for ever? I thought dying was harder **Louis XIV** *French King*

Repeat those words, Monsieur Almoner, repeat them **Louis XV** *French King*

Frenchmen I Die guiltless of the crimes imputed to me. Pray God my blood falls not on France **Louis XVI** *French King*

I shall drink the cup to the last dregs **Louis XVI** *French King*

A king should die standing up **Louis XVIII** *French King*

Marty **Lucky Luciano** *US gangster*

Keep Paddy behind the big mixer **Alfred MacAlpine** *British building tycoon*

Lay on Macduff, and damned be him that first cries 'hold enough' **Macbeth** *Shakespearean Character*

Now all is over, let the piper play 'Return no More' **Rob Roy MacGregor** *Scottish Outlaw*

I love my country more than my soul **Niccolo Machiavelli** *Italian Statesman*

We are all going, we are all going ... oh dear! **William McKinley** *US President*

Mozart! **Gustav Mahler** *Composer*

Let's cool it, brothers **Malcolm X** *Black Muslim Leader*

I love the rain, I want the feeling of it on my face **Katherine Mansfield** *Writer*

Act in accordance with past principles **Mao Zedong** *Chinese Ruler*

Last words are for fools who haven't said enough **Karl Marx** *Philosopher*

My Lord, why do you not go on? I am not afraid to die **Mary II** *English Queen*

When I am dead and opened, you shall find Calais lying in my heart **Mary Tudor** *English Queen*

Thank you, Monsieur **Mata Hari** *Dutch Spy*

Dying is a very dull, dreary affair. My advice to you is to have nothing whatever to do with it **William Somerset Maugham** *British Writer*

Lotte! **Ferdinand-Joseph Maximilian** *Mexican Emperor*

I am crossing a beautiful wide river and the opposite shore is coming nearer and nearer **George Meade** *US Civil War General*

Ah, my God, I am dead **Catherine de Medici** *Florentine Ruler*

God bless Captain Vere **Herman Melville** *US Author*

Forgive some sinner and wink your eye at some homely girl **HL Mencken** *American Essayist*

Weary, very weary **Felix Mendelssohn** *Composer*

My soul I resign to God, my body to the Earth, My worldly goods to my next of kin **Michelangelo** *Italian sculptor and painter*

O Allah! Pardon my sins. Yes I come **Muhammad** *Founder of Islam*

For all my misfortunes, Malinche, I bear you no ill will **Montezuma II** *Aztec Emperor*

Commend your souls to God, for our bodies are the foe's **Simon de Montfort** *British Aristocrat*

See me safe up; for my coming down let me shift for myself **Thomas More** *English Statesman*

Did I not tell you I was writing this for myself **Wolfgang Amadeus Mozart** *Composer*

Put that bloody cigarette out **HH Munro** *British Author*

But, but, Mr Colonel ... **Benito Mussolini** *Italian Dictator*

France! Army! Head of the army! Josephine! **Napoleon I** *French Emperor*

I don't need anything more ... Poultices **Napoleon II** *Duke of Reichstadt*

Were you at Sedan? **Napoleon III** *French Emperor*

Thank God I have done my duty, kiss me, Hardy **Horatio Nelson** *British Naval commander*

What an artist the world is losing in me **Nero** *Roman Emperor*

I seem to have been only a boy playing on the seashore and diverting myself in now and then finding a smoother pebble or prettier shell than the ordinary whilst the great ocean of truth lay all undiscovered before me **Isaac Newton** *Scientist*

I am just going outside and I may be some time **Captain Lawrence Oates** *Explorer*

Die, my dear doctor, that's the last thing I shall do **Viscount Palmerston** *British Prime Minister*

Get my swan costume ready **Anna Pavlova** *Ballerina*

What is the scaffold? A short cut to Heaven **Charles Peace** *Murderer*

To be like Christ is to be a Christian **William Penn** *English Quaker*

Murder! **Spencer Perceval** *British Prime Minister*

Do not weep, do not grieve **Henri Pétain** *French Soldier*

Drink to me **Pablo Picasso** *Spanish Artist*

The hearse, the horse, the driver and – enough **Luigi Pirandello** *Italian Dramatist*

I think I could eat one of Bellamy's veal pies **William Pitt (the younger)** *British Prime Minister*

Oh my country, how I leave thee **William Pitt (the younger)** *British Prime Minister*

Lord help my soul **Edgar Allan Poe** *Writer*

I am dying, sir, of a hundred good symptoms **Alexander Pope** *Poet*

Turn up the lights, I don't want to go home in the dark **William Porter (O'Henry)** *US Short Story Writer*

I am going to sleep like you, but we shall all awake together and, I trust to everlasting happiness **Joseph Priestley** *Chemist*

My poor Elvira, my poor wife **Giacomo Puccini** *Composer*

Sister, sister, sister **Thomas de Quincey** *British Writer*

I could wish this tragic scene were over, but I hope to go through it with becoming dignity **James Quin** *Irish Actor*

Let down the curtain, the farce is over **François Rabelais** *French writer*

I am going to seek the great, perhaps **François Rabelais** *French writer*

It matters little how the head lies, so the heart be right **Walter Raleigh** *English Explorer and Statesman*

I look like a Moor **Maurice Ravel** *French Composer*

I know that all things on earth must have an end, and now I am come to mine **Joshua Reynolds** *English Artist*

Turn me over, Jack **Cecil Rhodes** *South African Statesman*

So little done, so much to do **Cecil Rhodes** *South African Statesman*

Take off his chains, give him a hundred shillings, and let him go **Richard I** *King of England*

Treason, treason! **Richard III** *King of England*

I have no enemies save those of the state **Cardinal Richelieu** *French Statesman*

Don't you think I'll be back? **Manfred von Richthofen** *German Air Ace*

O Liberty! What crimes are committed in thy name **Madame Marie Roland** *French Revolutionary*

I have a terrific headache **FD Roosevelt** *US President*

We are the first victims of American fascism **Ethel Rosenberg** *Alleged Atom Spy*

There is God! Yes, God Himself, who is opening his arms and inviting me to taste at last that eternal and unchanging joy that I had so long desired **Jean-Jacques Rousseau** *French Political Theorist*

You can keep the things of bronze and stone and give me one man to remember me just once a year **Damon Runyon** *American Writer*

The bitterness of death is now past **Lord William Russell** *English Whig Statesman*

Of all his victories, realms and riches, nothing remains to him but this **Saladin** *Sultan of Egypt and Syria*

I am leaving you with your worries, good luck **George Sanders** *British Film Star*

Ah, my children, you cannot cry for me so much as I have made you laugh **Paul Scarron** *French Writer*

Many things are growing plain and clear to my understanding. One look at the sun **Johann Von Schiller** *German Dramatist*

Here, here is my end **Franz Schubert** *Composer*

French Canadian bean soup. I want to pay. Let them leave me alone **Dutch Schultz** *New York Gangster*

God bless you all, I feel myself again **Sir Walter Scott** *British Novelist*

I can't live any longer with my nerves **Jean Seberg** *US Film Star*

They couldn't hit an elephant at this dist ... **John Sedgwick** *US General*

I am absolutely undone **Richard Brinsley Sheridan** *Irish Writer and Statesman*

I believe we must adjourn the meeting to some other place **Adam Smith** *Economist*

Let me go **Capt EJ Smith** *Captain of SS Titanic*

That's right Brother Taylor, parry them off as well as you can **Joseph Smith** *Mormon Martyr*

Crito, we owe a cock to Aesculapius; pay it and do not let it pass **Socrates** *Greek Philosopher*

Beautifully done **(Sir) Stanley Spencer** *British Artist*

Four o'clock. How strange, so that is time. Strange, enough! **Sir Henry Stanley** *Explorer*

I feel faint **Adlai Stevenson** *American Politician*

If this is dying, I don't think much of it **Lytton Strachey** *Biographer*

Put not your trust in princes **Thomas Strafford** *English Statesman*

Thy necessity is yet greater than mine **Philip Sydney** *British Soldier and Poet*

Lord, into thy hands I commend my spirit **Torquato Tasso** *Italian Poet*

How sweet it is to rest **John Taylor** *English Poet*

I have tried to do my duty, and am not afraid to die. I am ready **Zachary Taylor** *US President*

Brother warriors, we are about to enter an engagement from which I will not return. My body will remain on the field of battle **Tecumseh** *Indian Chief*

I have opened it **Lord Alfred Tennyson** *Poet*

Gentlemen of the jury, you may retire **Charles Tenterden** *Lord Chief Justice*

And my heart throbbed with an exquisite bliss **William Thackeray** *British Novelist*

To the health of the fair Critias **Theramenes** *Athenian Statesman*

I shall soon know the grand secret **Arthur Thistlewood** *English Conspirator*

I've had 18 straight whiskies, I think that's a record ... after 39 yrs this is all I've done **Dylan Thomas** *Poet*

I leave this world without a regret **Henry Thoreau** *American Essayist*

God bless ... God damn **James Thurber** *American humorist*

I'll be shot if I don't believe I'm dying **Edward Thurlow** *English Politician*

Oh look, see how the cherry blossoms fall mutely **Hideki Tojo** *Japanese Politician and Soldier*

The enemy have demanded a surrender and I have answered the summons with a cannon shot and our flag still waves proudly from the walls **W Barrett Travis** *Commander of the Alamo*

Now I stretch out my hand, and from the further shore I bid adieu to all who have cared to read any among the many words I have written **Anthony Trollope** *British Novelist*

I feel here that this time they have succeeded **Leon Trotsky** *Russian Leader*

The sun is God **JMW Turner** *British Artist*

Death, the only immortal, who treats us all alike, whose peace and whose refuge are for all, the soiled and the pure, the rich and the poor, the loved and unloved **Mark Twain** *American Novelist*

Lord forgive my sins. Especially my sins of omission   **James Ussher**   *Archbishop of Armagh*

I want the sunlight to greet me   **Rudolph Valentino**   *Film star*

I shall never get rid of this depression   **Vincent Van Gogh**   *Artist*

I suppose I am now becoming a God   **Vespasian**   *Roman Emperor*

Oh that peace may come   **Victoria**   *British Queen*

Do let me die in peace   **Voltaire**   *French Author and Philosopher*

I am fond of them, of the inferior beings of the abyss, of those who are full of longing   **Richard Wagner**   *Composer*

It is well, I die hard, but am not afraid to go   **George Washington**   *US President*

A last interview ...   **Ethel Waters**   *US Blues Singer*

Life, life, death, death, how curious it is   **Daniel Webster**   *American Statesman*

Go away, I'm all right   **HG Wells**   *Author*

I shall be satisfied with thy likeness – satisfied   **Charles Wesley**   *English Hymn Writer*

I am dying as I have lived: beyond my means   **Oscar Wilde**   *Dramatist*

Either this wallpaper goes or I do   **Oscar Wilde**   *Dramatist*

O my God, have mercy upon this poor people   **William the Silent**   *Stadholder of the Netherlands*

Edith   **Woodrow Wilson**   *US President*

I fear not this fire   **George Wishart**   *Scottish Reformer*

Give me back my youth   **John Wolcot**   *English Satirist*

What! do they run already? Then I die happy   **James Wolfe**   *English General*

Had I but served God as diligently as I have served the King, He would not have given me over in my grey hairs   **Thomas Wolsey**   *English Prelate*

Is that you Dora?   **William Wordsworth**   *Poet*

Mind your own business   **Percy Wyndham-Lewis**   *British artist*

Better fighting death than a slave's life   **Emiliano Zapata**   *Mexican Revolutionary*

Make my skin into drumheads for the Bohemian cause   **John Ziska**   *Bohemian Hussite Leader*

NB: This is an area of uncertainty and vagueness and cannot be said to be a true and exact glossary of last words. That is because quite often there would be some controversy over the reported words uttered before death by a solitary witness, and even when witnessed by many people there would often be a conflict of opinion, hence the need for double entries for various persons. It is thought, perhaps, that some of the more witty sayings were possibly the sort of thing that a particular person would have said and it is in the way of a tribute to a person that not too many questions would be asked. The point to remember about these last utterances is not so much the truth of the speech *per se*, but rather the fact that the words are universally identifiable with these people. Several persons have more than one entry for the reasons stated above.

First Names
(of people better known by other names)

Alvar Aalto – Hugo   *Finnish Architect*

Patrick Abercrombie – Leslie   *English Architect*

Pepper Anderson – Suzanne   *TV character (Police Woman)*

Antonioni – Michelangelo   *Film Director*

Corazon Aquino – Maria   *Filipino President*

Yasser Arafat – Mohammed   *Palestinian Resistance Leader*

Louis Armstrong – Daniel   *Jazz Musician*

Cash Asmussen – Brian Keith   *US Jockey*

Avon – Kerr   *Blake 7 character*

Balakirev – Mily   *Russian Composer*

Balzac – Honoré de   *French Writer*

Banacek – Thomas   *TV Character*

Batista – Fulgencio   *Cuban President*

Max Beerbohm – Henry   *English Writer and Caricaturist*

Bix Beidebecke – Leon   *Jazz Cornet Player*

Hilaire Belloc – Joseph   *French-born Writer*

Arnold Bennett – Enoch   *English Novelist*

Ingmar Bergman – Ernst   *Film Director*

Busby Berkeley – William   *Choreographer and Director*

Hector Berlioz – Louis   *French Composer*

Ali Bhutto – Zulfikar   *Pakistani Statesman*

John Biffen – William   *English Politician*

Laurence Binyon – Robert   *Poet*

Bizet – Georges Alexandre Césare Léopold   *French Composer*

Blake – Roj   *'Blake's 7' Character*

Boccaccio – Giovanni   *Italian Writer*

Bodie and Doyle – William and Ray   *TV Characters ('The Professionals')*

Bootsie (Pte 'excused boots' Bisley) – Montague   *TV Character ('The Army Game')*

Lord Byron – George   *English Poet*

Calamity Jane – Martha   *Wild West Heroine*

James Callaghan – Leonard   *British Politician*

Callan – David   *TV Character*

Hoss Cartwright – Eric   *TV Western Hero ('Bonanza')*

Casanova – Giovanni Jacopo   *Poet and Libertine*

Casey Jones – John Luther   *TV Character based on Ballad*

Emmanuel Chabrier – Alexis   *French Composer*

Paddy Chayevsky – Sidney   *Playwright*

Chekov – Pavel   *Star Trek Character*

Erskine Childers – Robert   *Anglo-Irish Writer*

Colette – Sidonie   *French Novelist*

Colin Cowdrey – Michael   *English Cricketer*

Crane – Richard   *TV Character*

Sonny Crockett – James   *Miami Vice Character*

Cui – César   *Russian Composer*

Robert Cummings – Charles   *US Actor*

Bette Davis – Ruth   *US Actress*

Debussy – Achille-Claude   *French Composer*

Edgar Degas – Hilaire-Germain   *French Artist*

Paul Delaroche – Hippolyte   *French Painter*

Delibes – Léo   *French Composer*

Delius – Frederick   *English Composer*

Legs Diamond – Jack   *Gangster*
Fats Domino – Antoine   *US Vocalist*
Lonnie Donegan – Anthony   *Skiffle Musician*
Donizetti – Gaetano   *Italian Composer*
Faye Dunaway – Dorothy   *US Actress*
Dvorak – Antonin   *Czech Composer*
Eddie 'the eagle' Edwards – Michael   *British Skijumper*
Samantha Eggar – Victoria   *US Actress*
Erasmus – Desiderius   *Dutch Humanist*
Escoffier – Auguste   *French Chef*
Max Faulkner – Herbert   *English Golfer*
Private Fender – Sam   *TV Character ('Bilko')*
Figgis – Roy   *TV Character ('Only When I Laugh')*
Finlay, Dr – Alan (Bill Simpson)   *TV Character*
Finlay, Dr – John (David Rintoul)   *TV Character*
Private Fraser – James   *'Dad's Army' Character*
Paul Gauguin – Eugène   *French Post-Impressionist*
Gigli – Beniamino   *Italian Tenor*
Gill, Eric – Arthur   *English Sculptor*
Glinka – Mikhail   *Russian Composer*
Glover – Archie   *TV Character ('Only When I Laugh')*
Gluck – Christoph   *German Composer*
Private Godfrey – Charles   *'Dad's Army' Character*
Joseph Goebbels – Paul   *Nazi Leader*
Pancho Gonzales – Richard   *US Tennis Player*
Gounod – Charles   *French Composer*
Goya – Francisco   *Spanish Painter*
Ulysses S Grant – Hiram   *US President*
Graham Greene – Henry   *British Novelist*
Florence Griffith-Joyner – Delorez   *US Athlete*
Brothers Grimm – Jacob and Wilhelm   *Folktale collectors*
Che Guevara – Ernesto   *Argentinian Revolutionary Leader*
Colonel Hall – John   *TV Character ('Bilko')*
Mrs Hall – Nell   *TV Character ('Bilko')*
Dashiell Hammett – Samuel   *US Novelist*
Learned Hand – Billings   *American Jurist*
Patsy Hendren – Elias   *England Cricketer*
Barbara Hepworth – Jocelyn   *English Sculptor*
William Herschel – Frederick   *British Astronomer*
Rudolf Hess – Richard   *Nazi Leader*
Patricia Highsmith – Mary   *US Novelist*
Hinge and Bracket – Dr Evadne and Dame Hilda   *comic duo*
Doc Holliday – John   *Western gunfighter*
Holman Hunt – William   *English Painter*
Honegger – Arthur   *Swiss Composer*
Ron L Hubbard – Lafayette   *SF Writer and Scientology Founder*
John Humphreys – Desmond   *TV and Radio Presenter*
Lauren Hutton – Mary   *US Actress*
Ivanhoe – Wilfred   *Literary Character*
Jacuzzi – Candido   *Inventor of luxury bath*
Storm Jameson – Margaret   *British Novelist*
Janáček – Leoš   *Czech Composer*
Jeeves – Reginald   *PG Wodehouse character (named after Warwickshire Cricketer)*
Corporal Jones – Jack   *'Dad's Army' Character*
Miss Jones – Ruth   *TV Character ('Rising Damp')*
Khachaturian – Aram   *Armenian Composer*
Kookie – Gerald (Lloyd Kookson III)   *TV Character ('77 Sunset Strip')*

Lucky Luciano – Charles   *Gangster*
Lugg – Magersfontein   *Literary Character: Campion's Manservant*
Lytton Strachey – Giles   *Biographer*
Harold Macmillan – Maurice   *British Prime Minister*
Magnificent Evans – Plantagenet   *TV Character*
Mr Magoo – Quincy   *Cartoon Character*
Captain Mainwaring – George   *Dad's Army Character*
Paul McCartney – James   *Beatle*
Campbell Menzies – Walter   *MP and Former Athlete*
Mrs Merton – Dorothy   *TV Character*
Mies Van Der Rohe – Ludwig   *Architect*
Milhaud – Darius   *French Composer*
Glen Miller – Alton   *Bandleader*
Monteverdi – Claudio   *Italian Composer*
Morse – Endeavour   *Fictional detective*
Angela Mortimer – Florence   *British Wimbledon Champion*
Mulder and Scully – Fox and Dana   *TV Characters ('X Files')*
Brian Mulroney – Martin   *Canadian Politician*
Murillo – Bartolomé   *Spanish Painter*
Mussorgsky – Modest   *Russian Composer*
Ogden Nash – Frederic   *American Poet*
Birgit Nilsson – Märta   *Swedish Soprano*
Captain Oates – Lawrence   *Explorer*
Milton Obote – Apollo   *Ugandan Politician*
Offenbach – Jacques   *French Composer*
King Oliver – Joseph   *American Cornet-player*
Ozzy Osbourne – John   *British Rock Singer*
Palestrina – Giovanni   *Italian Composer*
Captain Peacock – Stephen   *TV Character*
Petrocelli – Tony   *TV Character*
Brad Pitt – William   *US Actor*
Graeme Pollock – Robert   *South African Cricketer*
Jackson Pollock – Paul   *American Action Painter*
Ponchielli – Amilcare   *Italian Composer*
Potsie Weber – Warren   *TV Character (Happy Days)*
Beatrix Potter – Helen   *English Children's Writer*
Enoch Powell – John   *British Politician*
Pressburger and Powell – Emeric and Michael   *Film Makers*
Princip – Gavrilo   *Assassin*
Prokofiev – Sergey   *Russian Composer*
Puccini – Giacomo   *Italian Composer*
Captain Pugwash – Horatio   *TV Character*
Professor Quatermass – Bernard   *TV Character*
Dan Quayle – James   *US Vice-President*
Rachmaninoff – Sergey   *Russian Composer*
Sonny Ramphal – Shridath   *Secretary-General of the Commonwealth*
Ravel – Maurice   *French Composer*
Django Reinhardt – Jean Baptiste   *Belgian Guitarist*
Viv Richards – Isaac   *West Indian Cricketer*
Cardinal Richelieu – Armand   *French politician-prelate*
Rigsby – Rupert   *TV Character ('Rising Damp')*
Rimsky-Korsakov – Nikolay   *Russian Composer*
Sergeant Ritzik – Rupert   *TV Character ('Bilko')*
Auguste Rodin – René-François   *French Sculptor*
Rossini – Gioachino   *Italian Composer*
Rostropovich – Mstislav   *Russian Musician*
Mr Rumbold – Cuthbert   *TV Character*
Salman Rushdie – Ahmed   *British Novelist*
Anwar Sadat – Mohamed   *Egyptian President*

Saint-Saens – Charles Camille   *French Composer*
Vicario Sanchez – Arantxa   *Tennis Player*
Savonarola – Girolamo   *Italian Religious Reformer*
Schubert – Franz Peter   *Austrian Composer*
Schumann – Robert   *German Composer*
Paul Scofield – David   *English Actor*
Scottie – Montgomery   *'Star Trek' Character*
Norman Shaw – Richard   *English Architect*
Shelley – James   *TV Character*
Phones (Sheridan) – George   *TV Character ('Stingray')*
Shostakovich – Dmitry   *Russian Composer*
Sibelius – Jean   *Finnish Composer*
Mrs Slocombe – Betty   *TV Character*
Smetana – Bedrich   *Czech Composer*
Colonel Hannibal Smith – John   *TV Character*
Snudge – Claude   *TV Character ('Army Game')*
Leland Stanford – Amasa   *US Railway Magnate*
Starsky and Hutch – David and Ken   *TV policemen*
Nobby Stiles – Norbert   *Footballer*
Stockhausen – Karlheinz   *German Composer*
August Strindberg – Johann   *Swedish Playwright*
Sulu – Hikaru   *'Star Trek' character*
Booth Tarkington – Newton   *US Author*

Tchaikovsky – Pyotr   *Russian Composer*
Tinker – Edward Sexton   *Blake's Assistant*
Daley Thompson – Francis   *Athlete*
Wolfe Tone – Theobald   *Irish Nationalist*
Topol – Chaim   *Israeli Actor*
Uccello – Paolo   *Florentine Painter*
Verdi – Giuseppe   *Italian Composer*
Vivaldi – Antonio   *Italian Composer*
Richard Wagner – Wilhelm   *German Composer*
Private Walker – James   *'Dad's Army' Character*
Dionne Warwick – Marie   *US Singer*
Dr Watson – John   *Literary Character*
Weber – Carl   *German Composer*
Webern – Anton   *Austrian Composer*
Orson Welles – George   *Film Maker and Actor*
Andy Williams – Howard   *US Singer*
Harold Wilson – James   *British Prime Minister*
Debra Winger – Marie   *US Actress*
Terry Wogan – Michael   *Broadcaster*
Wolf-Ferrari – Ermanno   *Italian Composer*
Roy Wood – Ulysses   *Pop Musician*
Tiger Woods – Eldrick   *US Golfer*
Virginia Woolf – Adeline   *English Novelist*

Firsts

Air hostess Ellen Church	1930
Airmail (GB) 9 Sept	1911
Airmail stickers 17 Aug	1918
Appendix operation	
George Thomas Morton	1887
Athlete to use crouch start	
Charles Sherrill	1888
Atom bomb	
Alamogordo Air Base, New Mexico (16 July)	1945
Atom bomb (UK)	
Monte Bello Islands off West Australia	1952
Atomic power station (large-scale)	
Calder Hall, Cumbria	1956
Atomic research centre (UK)	
Harwell in Berkshire	1946
Baronet Nicholas Bacon of Redgrove	1611
Bikini 24 June	1950
Blood transfusion	
Montpellier University, France	1667
Boy Scout movement	
Brownsea Island, Poole, Dorset	1907
Breakfast cereal (ready to eat)	
Shredded Wheat	1893
Bus conductress Kate Barton	1909
Bus service (scheduled) Shillibeer's	
Marylebone to Euston Rd Service	1829
Capital Gains Tax 6 April	1965
Car tax discs	
On windowscreen from 1 Jan	1921
Casino (UK) Metropole in Brighton	1962
Catamaran	
Experiment, built for Sir William Petty:	
adaptation from traditional Polynesian	
design	1662
Channel swim: both ways (UK)	
Kevin Murphy (non-stop) in 35 hrs 10 mins	1970
Chelsea Flower Show	
20–22 May by Royal Horticultural Society	1913

Christmas card John Calcott Horsley	
designed for Henry Cole	1843
Christmas speech of sovereign	
Elizabeth II	1957
Christmas tree From German idea	1605
Circumnavigation of Earth	
Juan Sebastian Del Cano in *Victoria*	
(Magellan killed en route)	1522
Circumnavigation of Earth: non-stop solo	
Robin Knox-Johnston in *Suhaili*	1969
Club colours	
Black, Red, Gold of I Zingari Cricket Club	1845
Coeducational school	
Henry Morley opened Marine Terrace,	
Cheshire	1849
Comic *Comic Cuts* an 8-page weekly	1890
Comic strip in newspaper	
Richard Outcault's 'Yellow Kid'	1897
Credit card Diners Club, New York	1950
Cremation (UK)	
Honoretta Pratt	1769
Cub Scouts	
Robertsbridge, Sussex (2 Feb)	1914
Daylight Saving (UK) Clocks put forward	
I hour	1916
Detective story Edgar Allan Poe's	
The Murders in the Rue Morgue	1841
Diet (scientifically planned)	
Dr Harvey for undertaker William Banting	1862
Dinner jacket	
Worn by G Lorillard, Tuxedo Park Country	
Club, NY	1886
Dresswear hire firm (UK)	
Moss Bros of Covent Garden	1860
Driving tests (UK) Leslie Hore-Belisha	
instigated voluntary tests	1935
Duke (UK)	
Edward, Duke of Cornwall	1337

Electric lamp   J Lindsay developed
but did not patent lamp   1835

Electric oven   Installed Hotel Bernina,
Samaden, Switzerland   1889

Electric power station
Central Power Station, Godalming, Surrey   1881

Escalator (UK)
Harrods Department Store   1898

Family allowance   15 June (5s per child)   1945

Film festival   Hotel Excelsior Venice, Italy   1932

Fire brigade (UK)
Nicholas Barbon established in London   1684

Fixed penalty parking ticket (UK)
19 Sept   1961

Football: televised live (UK)
Wembley Cup Final   1938

Four-minute mile
Roger Bannister in 3: 59.4 (Oxford)   1954

Fruit machine
Liberty Bell designed by Charles Frey   1889

GCE 'O' and 'A' Levels
Introduced to replace School Certificate   1950

GCSE   Introduced to replace CGE 'O' Level   1988

Girl Guide   Allison Cargill   1908

Gold disc
Glen Miller's 'Chattanooga Choo Choo'   1941

Greetings card   Designer W Harvey
engraved by J Thompson   1829

Heart transplant
Christiaan Barnard, Groote Schuur Hospital   1967

Helicopter (free flight)   Twin-rotor machine
designed by Paul Cornu   1907

Hydrofoil (UK)
'Miranda III' by John Thornycroft   1909

Hydrogen bomb   Detonated by USA
at Eniwetok, Marshall Isles   1952

Indianapolis 500   Won by Ray Harroun
(30 May)   1911

In-flight movie   Conan Doyle's
The Lost World   1925

Isle of Man TT Races
Won by Charles Collier on a Matchless   1907

Jazz band   Led by Buddy Bolden,
New Orleans   1900

Jukebox   Installed at Palais Royal Saloon,
San Francisco   1889

Life insurance policy   Taken out by London
Alderman Richard Martin   1583

Lighthouse (UK)   Spurn Point, Yorkshire   1427

Lord Mayor's Show   Instigated by
Sir John Norman   1453

Loudspeaker
Auxetophone by Horace Short   1900

Luncheon Vouchers (UK)   1 Jan   1955

Meteorological satellite   Tiros I   1960

Miss World Contest   19 April   1951

Monarch to Abdicate: English   Richard II   1399

MOT test   12 Sept   1960

Motorway   Avus Autobahn, Germany   1921

Moving staircase (UK)   Earls Court Station   1911

National park   Yellowstone, Wyoming   1872

National park: GB   Peak District   1950

National Savings stamps
On sale from 8 July   1918

Newspaper colour supplement (UK)
Sunday Times   1962

North Sea gas   Piped ashore by BP   1967

Nuclear merchant vessel
Savannah (launched in New Jersey)   1962

Old age pensions
Bismarck introduced in Germany   1889

Old age pensions (UK)
Introduced on 1 Jan   1909

Old school tie   Old Etonian, of narrow
blue and broad black stripes   1900

Opera
Jacopo Peri's *Dafne*, libretto by Rinuccini   1597

Oral contraceptive (UK)
Marketed on 18 Aug (invented 1954)   1960

Parachute jump (aeroplane)
Albert Berry from a height of 1,500 feet   1912

Parachute jump (balloon)   André-Jacques
Garnerin from a height of 2,230 feet   1797

Parcel post   Introduced on 1 Aug   1883

Parking meter (UK)
(America had them from 1935)   1958

Parking ticket (UK)
Dr Thomas Creighton was first victim   1960

Pedestrian crossing (UK)
Parliament Square, London   1926

Photo finish: horse race
Introduced by Ernest Marks, New Jersey   1888

Photographic process
Louis Daguerre first commercial success   1839

Pneumatic motor car tyres
Michelin fitted first tyre to a 4hp Daimler   1895

Policewoman
Mrs Alice Stebbins Wells of the LAPD   1910

Policewoman (UK)   27 Nov   1914

Postage stamp (adhesive)
James Chalmers of Dundee printed first   1834

Postage stamp (perforations)
Penny Red, issued in Feb   1854

Postal orders (UK)
Introduced on 1 Jan   1881

Postcard (UK)   Introduced on 1 Oct   1870

Premium Bonds   On sale from 1 Nov   1956

Prince of Wales: English
Edward of Caernarvon, later Edward II   1301

Prisoner of War camp
Norman X Depot, Stilton, for French PoWs   1797

Public library (UK)
Jerrom Goodwyn Library, Norwich   1608

Recorded delivery   1 Feb   1961

Registered letters
Introduced by GPO on 1 Jan   1878

Row across the Atlantic
Capt John Ridgway and Sgt Chay Blyth   1966

Row across the Atlantic (solo)
Tom McLean in 20 ft dory *Super Silver*   1969

Sex change operation   George/Christine
Jorgensen by Dr K Hamburger   1952

Space flight (manned)
Vostok I, piloted by Yuri Gagarin   1961

Space flight (by woman)
Vostok VI, piloted by Valentina Tereshkova   1963

Space walk
Aleksey Leonov, from *Voshkod II*   1965

Spacecraft on the Moon   *Luna II*   1959

Spiritualist mediums
Margaretta and Kate Fox from New York   1848

FAMOUS PEOPLE

Starting stalls: horse race (UK)
Newmarket on 8 July   1965

Tape recorder
Telagraphone by Valdemar Poulsen   1898

Telegrams (UK)
I shilling for 20 words (1st worldwide in 1843)   1870

Telephone directory (UK)
Published by London Telephone Co   1880

Telephone speaking clock (UK)
Aka TIM was voice of Ethel Cain for 20 yrs   1936

Television announcer (UK)   Leslie Mitchell   1936

Television commercial, black and white (UK)
Gibbs SR Toothpaste   1955

Television commercial, colour (UK)
Birds Eye Peas   1969

Television licence (UK)   Cost of £2   1946

Television communications satellite
Bell Telephone 'Telstar'   1962

Traffic lights   Parliament Square, London   1868

Traffic lights: electric (UK)   July   1926

Traffic lights: automatic (UK) 5 Nov   1927

Traffic wardens (UK)
15 Sept in London   1960

Train accident fatality
William Huskisson MP, run down by *Rocket*   1830

Traveller's cheques
Introduced on 1 Jan   1772

Underground railway (UK)
Metropolitan Line Paddington to Farringdon   1863

Underground railway (electric)
City branch of the Northern line   1890

Underground map
Albert Stanley, Lord Ashfield instigated   1908

Underground (Tube) train (automatic)
Central Line Woodford to Hainault   1964

Vending machine
So-called 'Honesty' tobacco boxes, 1d a go   1615

Vending machine (automatic)
Patented by Carl Ade in Germany   1867

Victoria Cross   Mate Charles Lucas, for
action aboard HMS *Hecla*   1854

Voting rights for women
New Zealand was 1st country to allow   1893
Finland 1st in Europe 1906

Windscreen wipers (mechanical)
Introduced in the USA   1916

Windscreen wipers (electrical)
The 'Berkshire', produced in the USA   1923

Woman cabinet minister (UK)
Margaret Bondfield, Minister of Labour   1929

Woman doctor (US)   Elizabeth Blackwell   1849

Woman doctor (UK)
Elizabeth Garrett Anderson   1859

Woman MP (UK)   Constance, Countess
Markievicz, Sinn Fein MP   1918

Woman MP (to take seat)
Nancy Astor for Plymouth Sutton   1919

Woman novelist   Lady Murasaki, Japan   c1004

Woman novelist (UK)   Aphra Behn   1687

Woman pilot   Baronne Elise de la Roche   1909

Woman prime minister
Mrs Sirimavo Bandaranaike of Ceylon   1960

Women's Institute
Stoneycreek, Ontario, Canada   1897

Yellow lines restricting parking   Laid in
Slough   1956

Zebra crossing   31 Oct   1951

NB: Although this topic of 'firsts' has been listed in the Famous People section, many of the entries relate to inanimate objects. This is purely a matter of expediency and is not an oversight on the part of the author.

Initials: Known by

WH Auden   Wystan Hugh
British poet

AJ Ayer   Alfred Jules
English philosopher

CPE Bach   Carl Philipp Emanuel
German composer

JC Bach   Johann Christian
German composer

JS Bach   Johann Sebastian
German composer

RM Ballantyne,   Robert Michael
Scottish author

JG Ballard   James Graham
British writer

JC Bamford   Joseph Cyril
Founder of JCB Company

BA Baracus   Bad Attitude
Fictional TV character ('A Team')

PT Barnum   Phineas Taylor
US showman

JM Barrie   James Matthew
Scottish novelist

HE Bates   Herbert Ernest
English novelist

CC Beck   Clarence
US graphic artist

AC Benson   Arthur Christopher
English author and poet

EF Benson   Edward Frederic
English author

EC Bentley   Edmund Clerihew
English journalist and novelist

RD Blackmore   Richard
Doddridge   *English novelist*

PW Botha   Pieter Willem
South African politician

RA Butler   Richard Austen
British politician

AS Byatt   Antonia Susan
English novelist and critic

GK Chesterton   Gilbert Keith
English novelist

JM Coetzee   John Michael
South African novelist

GDH Cole   George Douglas
Howard   *British economist*

AE Coppard   Alfred Edgar
English poet and writer

AJ Cronin   Archibald Joseph
Scottish novelist

ee cummings   Edward Estlin
American writer and painter

WH Davies   William Henry
British poet

JW De Forest   John William   *US
novelist and historian*

FW De Klerk,   Frederik Willem
South African politician

RF Delderfield   Ronald Frederick
English playwright

EL Doctorow   Edgar Lawrence
US novelist

JP Donleavy   James Patrick
Irish novelist

TS Eliot   Thomas Stearns
poet and dramatist

JK Ewers   John Keith   *Australian
writer*

JR Ewing   John Ross
Fictional TV character ('Dallas')

UA Fanthorpe   Ursula Askham
British poet

JG Farrell   James Gordon
English novelist

EH Fellowes   Edmund Horace
English musicologist

WC Fields   William Claude
American comedy actor

CS Forester Cecil Scott
British writer

EM Forster Edward Morgan
English novelist

AJ Foyt Anthony Joseph
US racing driver

EA Freeman Edward Augustus
British historian

CB Fry Charles Burgess
English sportsman

JK Galbraith John Kenneth
economist

TS Garp Technical Sergeant
John Irving character

WS Gilbert William Schwenck
English operetta librettist

KC Gillette King Camp
American inventor

WE Gladstone William Ewart
British politician

EW Godwin Edward William
English architect and designer

HL Gold Horace Leonard
science fiction writer

WG Grace William Gilbert
English cricketer

DW Griffith David Wark
American film director

AB Guthrie Alfred Bertram
US writer

MC Hammer Master of
Ceremonies *US rap artist*

WC Handy William Christopher
US Blues composer

LP Hartley Leslie Poles
English author

HJ Heinz Henry John
US food manufacturer

WE Henley William Ernest
English poet and critic

GA Henty George Alfred
English novelist

AP Herbert Alan Patrick
English writer

AD Hope Alec Derwent
Australian poet

EW Hornung Ernest William
English writer

AE Housman Alfred Edward
English poet

EM Hull Edith Maude *British
writer*

TE Hulme Thomas Ernest
British essayist and poet

CLR James Cyril Lionel Robert
Trinidadian writer

MR James Montague Rhodes
ghost story writer

PD James Phyllis Dorothy
English writer

WE Johns William Earl
English writer and aviator

MM Kaye Mary Margaret
British writer

HRF Keating Henry Raymond
Fitzwalter *UK detective
story writer*

AL Kennedy Alison Louise
British writer

BB King Blues Boy
singer/guitarist

WP Kinsella William Patrick
Canadian writer

RB Kitaj Ronald Brooks
American painter

LC Knight Lionel Charles
British critic and author

RD Laing Ronald David
Scottish psychiatrist

CJ Lamb Cara Jean
fictional TV character (LA Law)

kd lang Kathryn Dawn
Canadian singer

DH Lawrence David Herbert
English novelist

TE Lawrence Thomas Edward
British soldier and writer

FR Leavis Frank Raymond
English literary critic

GH Lewes George Henry
British writer

CS Lewis Clive Staples *Irish writer*

HP Lovecraft Howard Phillips
US science fiction writer

LS Lowry Laurence Stephen
English artist

HL Mencken Henry Louis
US journalist

AA Michelson Albert Abraham
US physicist

AA Milne Alan Alexander
children's writer

LM Montgomery Lucy Maud
Canadian novelist

CL Moore Catherine Lucille *US
science fiction writer*

JP Morgan John Pierpoint
US financier

JB Morton John Bingham
British journalist (Beachcomber)

HH Munro Hector Hugh
English writer (Saki)

VS Naipaul Vidiadhar
Surajprasad *Trinidadian novelist*

RK Narayan Rasipuram
Kirshnaswamy *Indian novelist*

PH Newby Percy Howard
British novelist

TV Olsen Theodore Victor
US Westerns writer

PJ O'Rourke Patrick John
US journalist

CJ Parker Casey Jean
*Fictional TV character
('Baywatch')*

SJ Perelman Sydney Joseph
US writer

TF Powys Theodore Francis
British writer

JB Priestley John Boynton
English novelist

VS Pritchett Victor Sawdon
English writer

JD Rockefeller John Davison
US businessman

AV Roe Alliot Verdon
English aviation pioneer

JK Rowling Joanne Kathleen
English children's writer

JD Salinger Jerome David
US novelist

EH Shepard Ernest Howard
English illustrator

RC Sherriff Robert Cedric
English novelist

NF Simpson Norman Frederick
British playwright

OJ Simpson Orenthal James
US sportsman

VP Singh Vishwanath Pratap
Indian politician

CH Sisson Charles Hubert
British poet

BF Skinner Burrhus Fredric
US psychologist

EE 'Doc' Smith Edward Elmer
US science fiction writer

WH Smith William Henry
English newsagent

CP Snow Charles Percy
English novelist

HM Stanley Henry Morton
journalist and explorer

JIM Stewart John Innes
Mackintosh *English writer*

JEB Stuart James Ewell Brown
Confederate general

JM Synge John Millington *Irish
dramatist*

AJP Taylor Alan John Percivale
English historian

DM Thomas Donald Michael
English writer

EP Thompson Edward Palmer
British historian

EMW Tillyard Eustace Mandeville
Wetenhall *British scholar and
critic*

JRR Tolkien John Ronald Reuel
philologist and author

PL Travers Pamela Lyndon
author of Mary Poppins

AE Van Vogt Alfred Elton
science fiction writer

HG Wells Herbert George
English novelist

EB White Elwyn Brooks
US essayist and novelist

TH White Terence Hanbury
English novelist

JPR Williams John Peter Rhys
Welsh rugby player

WD and HO Wills William Day
and Henry Overton
tobacco manufacturers

PG Wodehouse Pelham Grenville
English novelist

FW Woolworth Frank Winfield
US businessman

PC Wren Percy Christopher
English novelist

WB Yeats William Butler
Irish poet

Inventions and Discoveries

Adding machine *Blaise Pascal*	1642
Aeroplane (steam powered) *Clement Ader*	1886
Aeroplane *Wright Brothers*	1903
Aerosol *Erik Rotheim*	1926
Air pump *Otto Von Guericke*	1654
Airship (non-rigid) *Henri Giffard*	1852
Airship (rigid) *Ferdinand Von Zeppelin*	1900
Ambulance *Baron Dominique Jean Larrey*	1792
Anaesthesia *William Morton*	1846
Antiseptic surgery *Joseph Lister*	1867
Aqualung *Cousteau and Gagnan*	1943
Aspirin (synthesization) *Kolbe, Heinrich*	1859
Aspirin (intro into medicine) *H Dresser of Bayer AG*	1899
Assembly line *Samuel Colt*	1855
Atom bomb *Frisch, Bohr, Peierls*	1939
Baby incubator *Dr Alexandre Lion*	1891
Bakelite *Leo H Baekeland*	1907
Balloon *Montgolfier Brothers*	1783
Balloons: rubber *Michael Faraday*	1824
Balloons: toy *JG Ingram*	1847
Ball-point pen *John T Loud*	1888
Ball-point pen (mass-produced) *László Biro*	1938
Barbed wire (manufacture) *Joseph Glidden*	1874
Barbed wire (patent) *Lucien B Smith*	1867
Barometer *Evangelista Torricelli*	1643
Battery (electric) *Alessandro Volta*	1800
Bell (electric) *Joseph Henry*	1831
Betatron *Donald Kerst*	1940
Bicycle *Kirkpatrick MacMillan*	1839
Bicycle (spoked wheels) *James Starley*	1870
Bifocal Lens *Benjamin Franklin*	1780
Bikini *Louis Reard*	1946
Boy Scout movement *Sir Robert Baden-Powell*	1907
Bra (cantilevered) *Robard Howard Hughes*	1943
Breakfast cereal (ready to eat) *Henry D Perky*	1893
Bunsen burner *Robert Wilhelm Bunsen*	1855
Burglar alarm *Edwin T Holmes*	1858
Cable-car *W Ritter*	1866
Calculating clock *Wilhelm Schickard*	1623
Calculus *Leibniz and Newton*	1684
Canning *Nicholas Appert*	1795
Car (3 process wheel steam tractor) *Nicolas Cugnot*	1769
Car (petrol) *Karl Benz*	1888
Car speedometer *Thorpe and Salter*	1902
Carbon fibres *Courtaulds*	1964
Carbon paper *Ralph Wedgewood*	1806
Carburettor *Gottlieb Daimler*	1876
Carpet sweeper *Melville R Bissell*	1876
Cash register *James Ritty*	1879
Cats' eyes *Percy Shaw*	1933
Cellophane *Dr Jacques Brandenberger*	1908
Celluloid *Alexander Parkes*	1861
Cement (Portland) *Joseph Aspdin*	1824
Centigrade thermometer *Anders Celsius*	1742
Chewing gum (commercial) *John Curtis*	1848
Chocolate (solid) *François-Louis Cailler*	1819
Christmas card *Sir Henry Cole*	1843
Chronometer *John Harrison*	1735
Cinematography *Lumière brothers*	1895
Circulation of the blood *William Harvey*	1628
Clock (mechanical) *I-Hsing and Liang-Tsan*	725
Clock (quartz) *Warren Alvin Marrison*	1929
Cloud chamber *Charles Thomson Rees Wilson*	1927
Cluedo *Anthony Pratt*	1948
Coca-Cola *Dr John Pemberton*	1886
Coffee (instant) *Nestles*	1937
Compact disc *Philips and Sony*	1979
Computer *Charles Babbage*	1835
Computer (electronic) *Eckert and Mauchly*	1946
Concrete (reinforced) *François Hennebique*	1892
Condensed milk *Gail Borden*	1858
Condom *Gabriel Fallopius*	1560
Contact lens *Adolph E Fick*	1887
Contraceptive pill *Dr Gregory Pincus*	1950
Cordite *Dewar and Abel*	1905
Corrugated iron *Pierre Carpentier*	1853
Credit card *Ralph Scheider*	1950
Crossword puzzle *Arthur Wynne*	1913
Cyclotron *James Chadwick*	1935
DDT *Paul Muller*	1939
Decompression chamber *Robert H Davis*	1929
Disc brake *Dr F Lanchester*	1902
Diving suit *Andrew Becker*	1715
DNA structure *Francis Crick and James Watson*	1953
Dome (geodesic) *Richard Buckminster Fuller*	1945
Double-entry bookkeeping *Lucas Paciolus*	1495
Doughnut (with hole) *Hanson Gregory*	1847
Drill (electric) *Wilhelm Fein*	1895
Drill (pneumatic) *Germain Sommelier*	1861
Dry-cleaning *M Jolly-Bellin*	1849
Dynamite *Alfred Nobel*	1863
Dynamo *Hippolyte Pixii*	1832
Elastic bands *Stephen Perry*	1845
Electric chair *Harold Brown and EA Kenneally*	1890
Electric fan *Dr Schuyler Skaats*	1882
Electric flat iron *HW Seeley*	1882
Electric generator *Michael Faraday*	1831
Electric guitar *Rickenbacker, Barth and Beauchamp*	1931
Electric heating system *Dr W Leigh Burton*	1887
Electric lamp *Independently invented by Joseph, Swan and Thomas Alva Edison*	1879
Electric motor (AC) *Nikola Tesla*	1888
Electric motor (DC) *Zenobe Gramme*	1873
Electrocardiography *Willem Einthoven*	1903
Electromagnet *William Sturgeon*	1824
Electron *JJ Thomas*	1897
Electronic computer (dedicated) *Alan Turing*	1943
Electronic computer (general purpose) *Eckert and John Mauchly*	1946
Electronic computer (commercially available) *Eckert and Mauchly*	1951
Endoscope *Pierre Segalas*	1827
Equals sign (mathematics) *Robert Record*	1557

Escalator *Jesse W Reno*	1892	
Esperanto *Dr Ludovic Zamenhof*	1887	
Exclamation mark *J Day*	1553	
Facsimile machine (Fax) *Arthur Korn*	1907	
Ferrofluids *Ronald Rosensweig*	1968	
Film (Moving outlines) *Louis Le Prince*	1885	
Film (Musical sound) *Lee De Forest*	1923	
Film (Talking) *Engl, Mussolle and Vogt*	1922	
Fingerprint classification *Francis Galton*	1891	
Fire extinguisher *M Fuches*	1734	
Flying doctor service *KH Vincent Welsh*	1928	
Foam rubber *John Boyd Dunlop*	1929	
Food processor *Kenneth Wood*	1947	
Fountain pen *Lewis Edson Waterman*	1884	
Frozen food *Clarence Birdseye*	1930	
Galvanometer *André-Marie Ampère*	1834	
Gas fire *Philippe Lebon*	1799	
Gas lighting *William Murdock*	1792	
Gas meter *William Clegg*	1815	
Gearbox (automatic) *Hermann Fottinger*	1910	
Genetics *Gregor Mendel*	1865	
Geodesic dome *Richard Buckminster Fuller*	1945	
Gift coupons *Benjamin Talbert Babbit*	1865	
Girl Guides *Robert and Agnes Baden-Powell*	1910	
Glider *Sir George Cayley*	1853	
Golliwog *Florence K Upton*	1895	
Gramophone *Thomas Alva Edison*	1878	
Gravitation, laws of *Isaac Newton*	1684	
Gun cotton *Christian Friedrich Schønbein*	1845	
Gyro-compass *Elmer Sperry*	1911	
Gyroscope *Leon Foucault*	1852	
Half-tone process *Carl Gustaf Wilhelm Carleman*	1871	
Hearing aid (electric) *Miller Reese Hutchinson*	1901	
Heart (artificial) *Vladimir Demikhov*	1937	
Helicopter *Louis and Jacques Breguet*	1907	
Holography *Dennis Gabor*	1947	
Hovercraft *Christopher Cockerell*	1955	
Hydrofoil *Comte de Lambert*	1897	
Ice-cream cones *Italo Marcioni*	1896	
Identikit *Hugh McDonald*	1959	
Insulin *Frederick Grant Banting and Charles Herbert Best*	1921	
Intelligence test (IQ) *Alfred Binet*	1896	
Iron Lung *Philip Drinker*	1927	
Jeans *Levi Strauss*	1850	
Jet engine *Sir Frank Whittle*	1937	
Jigsaw puzzle *John Spilsbury*	1767	
Jukebox (pre-selective) *John C Dunton*	1905	
Kaleidoscope *Sir David Brewster*	1816	
Knitting machine *William Lee*	1589	
Laser *Theodore Maiman*	1960	
Lathe, screw-cutting *Henry Maudslay*	1800	
Launderette *JF Cantrell*	1934	
Lawn mower *Edwin Budding and John Ferrabee*	1830	
Lie detector *John Larson*	1928	
Lift (mechanical) *Elisha G Otis*	1852	
Lightning conductor *Benjamin Franklin*	1752	
Linoleum *Frederick Walton*	1860	
Lithography *Aloys Senefelder*	1796	
Locomotive *Richard Trevithick*	1804	
Logarithms *John Napier*	1614	
Loom, power *Edmund Cartwright*	1785	
Loudspeaker *Horace Short*	1898	

Loudspeaker (electric) *Miller Reece Hutchinson*	1906	
Machine gun *James Puckle*	1718	
Margarine *Hippolyte Mège-Mouriés*	1869	
Maser *Charles H Townes*	1953	
Match *Robert Boyle*	1680	
Match (friction) *John Walker*	1826	
Match (safety) *JE Lundstrom*	1855	
Metronome *Dietrich Nikolaus Winkel*	c1800	
Microchip *Jack Saint Clair Kilby*	1958	
Microphone *Alexander Graham Bell*	1876	
Micro-processor *Moore and Hoff Noyce*	1971	
Microscope *Zacharias Janssen*	1590	
Microscope (electron) *EAF Ruska*	1933	
Microwave oven *Percy Spencer*	1945	
Miner's safety lamp *Sir Humphry Davy*	1816	
Missile (air-to-air) *Herbert Wagner*	1943	
Monopoly *Charles Darrow*	1931	
Motor cycle *Gottlieb Daimler*	1885	
Neon lamp *Georges Claude*	1910	
Neptune (planet) *Johann Gottfried Galle*	1846	
Neutron *James Chadwick*	1935	
Non-stick pan *Marc Gregoir*	1954	
Nylon *Wallace Carothers*	1937	
Optical fibres *Navinder Kapany*	1955	
Oven (electric) *Bernina Hotel, Switzerland*	1889	
Ozone *Christian Friedrich Schönbein*	1840	
Pacemaker (implantable) *Wilson Greatbach*	1956	
Paint (acrylic) *Reeves Ltd*	1964	
Paint (fluorescent) *Joe and Bob Switzer*	1933	
Paper *Tsai Lun*	105	
Paper (from wood pulp) *Gottlob Keller*	1844	
Paper clip *Johann Vaaler*	1900	
Parachute *Jean-Pierre Blanchard*	1785	
Parachute (patent) *André-Jacques Garnerin*	1802	
Parking meter *Carlton Magee*	1935	
Pasteurisation *Louis Pasteur*	1863	
Pen (ball-point) *Laszlo Biro*	1938	
Pen (fountain) *Lewis Waterman*	1884	
Pencil (using pulverised graphite lead) *Nicolas Jacques Conté*	1795	
Pendulum clock *Christiaan Huygens*	1656	
Penicillin *Sir Alexander Fleming*	1928	
Periodic table *Dmitri Mendelev*	1866	
Photoelectric cell *Johann Phillip Elster and Hans F Geitel*	1896	
Photographic lens *William H Wollaston*	1812	
Photography (on pewter plate) *Joseph Nicéphore Niepce*	1826	
Photography (on paper) *William Henry Fox Talbot*	1835	
Photography (colour) *James Clerk Maxwell*	1861	
Photography (on film) *John Carbutt*	1888	
Pianoforte *Bartolomeo Cristofori*	1709	
Pillar box (UK) *Anthony Trollope*	1851	
Plastics *Alexander Parkes*	1852	
Pluto (planet) *Clyde Tombaugh*	1930	
Plutonium *GT Seaborg, JW Kennedy and AC Wahl*	1940	
Pneumatic bicycle tyres *John Boyd Dunlop*	1887	
Pneumatic tyres *RW Thompson.*	1845	
Pocket calculator *Kilby, Tassell and Merryman*	1972	
Polio vaccine (injection) *Jonas Salk*	1952	
Polio vaccine (oral) *Albert Sabin*	1957	
Polythene *RO Gibson*	1933	

FAMOUS PEOPLE

Potato crisps *George Crum*	1853	
Pressure cooker *Denis Papin*	1679	
Printing press (wooden) *Johann Gutenberg*	1455	
Printing (rotary) *Richard Hoe*	1846	
Propeller (boat, hand-operated) *David Bushnell*	1775	
Propeller (ship) *Francis Smith*	1837	
Propeller (ship), patent *Isambard Kingdom Brunel*	1844	
Proton *Ernest Rutherford*	1920	
Pyramid *Imhotep*	2650BC	
Radar (application) *Taylor and Young*	1930	
Radar (theory) *Nikola Tesla*	1900	
Radar (UK) *Robert Watson-Watt*	1935	
Radio telegraphy *Mahlon Loomis*	1864	
Radio telegraphy (transatlantic) *Guglielmo Marconi*	1901	
Radioactivity *Henri Becquerel*	1896	
Rails (iron) *Abraham Darby*	1738	
Railway airbrake *George Westinghouse*	1863	
Railway (electric) *Ernst Siemens*	1878	
Railway (underground) *Charles Pearson*	1843	
Rayon *Joseph Swan*	1883	
Razor (safety) *King Camp Gillette*	1895	
Razor (electric) *Jacob Schick*	1931	
Record (flat disc) *Emil Berliner*	1888	
Record (LP) *Peter Goldmark*	1948	
Refrigerator *James Harrison and Alexander Catlin Twinning*	1850	
Revolver *Samuel Colt*	1835	
Rickshaw *Jonathan Scobie*	1869	
Roller skates *Joseph Merlin*	1760	
Roulette wheel *Blaise Pascal*	1647	
Rubber (latex foam) *Dunlop Rubber Co*	1928	
Rubber (tyres) *Thomas Hancock*	1846	
Rubber (vulcanised) *Charles Goodyear*	1841	
Rubber (waterproof) *Charles Macintosh*	1823	
Rubik cube *Erno Rubik*	1975	
Safety pin *Walter Hunt*	1849	
Scooter *Walter Lines*	1897	
Scotch tape *Richard Drew*	1930	
Scrabble *James Brunot*	1950	
Sealing wax *Gerard Hermann*	1554	
Seismographic scale *Charles Francis Richter*	1935	
Self-starter motor (UK) *Charles F Kettering*	1911	
Sewing machine *Thomas Saint*	1790	
Shorthand *Marcus Tullius Tiro*	63BC	
Shorthand (modern world) *Timothy Bright*	1588	
Skyscraper *William Le Baron Jenny*	1882	
Slide rule *William Oughtred*	1621	
Snooker *Sir Neville Chamberlain*	1875	
Spectacles *Salvino degli Armati and Alessandro delle Spina*	c1280	
Spinning frame *Richard Arkwright*	1769	
Spinning jenny *James Hargreaves*	1764	
Spinning mule *Samuel Crompton*	1779	
Spirit level *JM Thévenot*	1666	
Stamp (perforations) *Henry Archer*	1854	
Stapler *Charles Henry Gould*	1868	
Steam engine *Thomas Savery*	1698	
Steam engine (condenser) *James Watt*	1765	
Steam engine (piston) *Thomas Newcomen*	1712	
Steamship *JC Perier*	1775	
Steamturbine (ship's) *Charles Parsons*	1894	
Steel production *Henry Bessemer*	1855	
Steel (stainless) *Harry Brearley*	1913	
Stereotype *William Ged*	1725	

Stethoscope *René Laennec*	1816	
Stopwatch *Jean Moyse*	1776	
Submarine *Cornelius Jacobszoon Drebbel*	1624	
Sun-tan cream *Eugene Schueller*	1936	
Syringe (hypodermic) *Charles Gabriel Pravaz*	1835	
Table tennis *James Gibb*	1890	
Tampon *Earl Hass*	1830	
Tank *Ernest Swinton*	1914	
Tape recorder *Louis Blattner*	1929	
Telegraph (electric) *George Louis Lesage*	1774	
Telegraph *M Lammond*	1787	
Telegraph code *Samuel Morse*	1837	
Telephone *Antonio Meucci*	1849	
Telephone (patent) *Alexander Graham Bell*	1876	
Telephone switchboard *Almon B Strowger*	1889	
Telescope (refractor) *Hans Lippershey*	1608	
Television (mechanical) *John Logie Baird*	1926	
Tennis *Walter G Wingfield*	1873	
Terylene *JR Whinfield and JT Dickson*	1941	
Thermometer *Galileo Galilei*	1593	
Thermometer (mercury) *Gabriel Fahrenheit*	1714	
Thimble *Nicolas Van Benschoten*	1684	
Toothbrush *William Addis*	1649	
Top hat *John Hetherington*	1797	
Torpedo (UK) *Robert Whitehead*	1866	
Traffic lights *JP Knight*	1868	
Traffic lights (automatic) *Alfred Benesch*	1914	
Transformer *Michael Faraday*	1831	
Transistor *John Bardeen, William Bradley Shockley and Walter Brattain*	1948	
Travel agency *Thomas Cook*	1841	
Travellers cheques *Robert Herries*	1772	
Travellers cheques (commercial) *American Express*	1891	
Tubercle bacillus *Robert Koch*	1882	
Tuning fork *John Shore*	1711	
Turbojet *Frank Whittle*	1928	
Typewriter *Pellegrine Tarri*	1808	
Typewriter (patent) *William Burt*	1829	
Typewriter (mass production) *Christopher Sholes*	1874	
Ultrasonography (obstetric) *Ian Donald*	1979	
Uranus *William Herschel*	1781	
Vaccination *Edward Jenner*	1770	
Vacuum cleaner (electric) *Hubert Cecil Booth*	1901	
Vacuum cleaner (steam) *Ives McGaffrey*	1871	
Vacuum flask *James Dewar*	1892	
Vending machine *Percival Everitt*	1883	
Ventilator *Théophile Guibal*	1858	
Video recorder *Ampex Co*	1956	
Videophone *American Telegraph and Telephone Co*	1927	
Vulcanised rubber *Charles Goodyear*	1839	
Washing machine (electric) *Hurley Machine Co*	1907	
Watch *Bartholomew Manfredi*	1462	
Watch (waterproof) *Rolex*	1927	
Water closet *Sir John Harington*	1589	
Welder (electric) *Elisha Thomson*	1877	
Wheel *Mesopotamians*	c3500BC	
White road markings *Edward Norris Hines*	1911	
Wire recorder (mechanical) *Valdemar Poulsen*	1898	
Xerox copier *Chester Carlson*	1938	
X-ray *Wilhelm Konrad Röntgen*	1895	
Zip fastener *Whitcomb L Judson*	1891	

Marriages: By Female Spouse

Diahnne Abbott	Actress	Robert De Niro	Actor
Paula Abdul (2)	Singer	Emilio Estevez	Actor
Victoria Adams	Spice girl	David Beckham	Footballer
Princess Adelaide of Saxe-Coburg Meiningen	German noblewoman	William IV	British king
Agrippina	Roman noblewomen	Claudius	Roman emperor
Pauline de Ahna	Soprano	Richard Strauss	Composer
Anouk Aimée (2)	Actress	Albert Finney (5)	Actor
Aisha	Muhammad's favourite wife	Muhammad	Founder of Islam
Maria Aitken	Actress	Nigel Davenport	Actor
Nadiya Aja (2)	Saudi tycoon's daughter	Omar Sharif	Actor and bridge player
Kitty Aldridge	Actress	Mark Knopfler	Musician
Princess Alexandra of Schlesung-Holstein-Sorderburg	Danish princess	Edward VII	British king
Princess Alexandra	British princess	Angus Ogilvy	Businessman
Alison Allen	TV producer	Keith Allen	Actor
Catherine Allen	Secretary	Frankie Dettori	Jockey
Gracie Allen	Comedienne	George Burns	Comedian and actor
Lorraine Allen (2)	Singer	Xavier Cugat	Band leader
June Allyson (2)	Actress	Dick Powell	Actor
Amphitrite	Greek mythical sea nymph	Poseidon	Greek god of the Sea
Debra Anderson (1)	Childhood sweetheart	Sean Bean	Actor
Loni Anderson (2)	Actress	Burt Reynolds (3)	Actor
Pamela Anderson (3)	Actress	Tommy Lee	Singer
Nina Andreevskaya	Moscow socialite	Wassily Kandinsky	Russian artist
Ursula Andress (1)	Actress	John Derek	Actor and director
Julie Andrews	Actress/singer	Blake Edwards (2)	Film director
Marie Angel	Australian soprano	David Freeman	Opera director
Jennifer Aniston	Actress	Brad Pitt	Actor
Princess Anne	British princess	Mark Phillips (1)	Equestrian rider
		Tim Laurence (2)	Naval Officer
Princess Anne	Danish princess	James I	British king
Anne of Bohemia (1)	Emperor Charles IV's daughter	Richard II	English king
Queen Anne	British queen	George of Denmark	Danish Prince
Marie Antoinette	French princess	Louis XVI	King of France
Aphrodite	Greek goddess of Love	Hephaestus	Greek god of fire
Frances Appleton	Socialite	Henry W Longfellow	US poet
Natalie Appleton	Pop singer	Liam Howlett	Musician
Ariadne	Mythical daughter of King Minos of Crete	Dionysus	Greek god of wine
Jean Armour	Socialite	Robert Burns	Poet
Patricia Arquette	Actress	Nicholas Cage	Actor
Debbie Ash (1)	Actress	Eddie Kidd	Stunt motorcyclist
Leslie Ash	Actress	Lee Chapman	Footballer
Jane Asher	Cook	Gerald Scarfe	Cartoonist
Edwina Ashley	Heiress and charity worker	Louis Mountbatten	Naval commander
Elizabeth Ashley	Actress	James Farentino (1)	Actor
		George Peppard (2)	Actor
Atalanta	Mythical Greek huntress	Milanion	Mythical Greek athlete
Rosalind Ayres	Actress	Martin Jarvis	Actor
Lauren Bacall	Actress	Humphrey Bogart (1)	Actor
		Jason Robards (2)	Actor
Barbara Bach (2)	Actress	Ringo Starr	Musician
Maria Barbara Bach (1)	Cousin of JS Bach	JS Bach	Composer
Enid Bagnold	Author	Sir G Roderick Jones	MD of Reuters
Lilian Bailey	American soprano	George Henschel	Baritone
Barbara Bain	Actress	Martin Landau	Actor
Shakira Baksh (2)	Actress and model	Sir Michael Caine	Actor
Jill Balcon	Actress	Cecil Day-Lewis	Poet
Caroline Balestier	Publishing heiress	Rudyard Kipling	Novelist and poet
Lucille Ball	Comedienne and actress	Desi Arnaz	Musician and actor
Zoe Ball	TV presenter	Norman Cook	Musician
Rose Bampton	Soprano	Wilfred Pelletier	Conductor
Anne Bancroft	Actress	Mel Brooks	Actor/producer
Glynis Barber	Actress	Michael Brandon (2)	Actor
Emma Bardac (2)	Socialite	Claude Debussy	Composer

Brigitte Bardot (1)	Actress	Roger Vadim	Film director
Margherita Barezzi (1)	Daughter of Verdi's sponsor	Giuseppe Verdi	Composer
Ellen Barkin	Actress	Gabriel Byrne	Actor
Nora Barnacle	Socialite	James Joyce	Irish writer
Pinkie Barnes	Table tennis international	Sam Kydd	Actor
Roseanne Barr	Actress	Tom Arnold (2)	Actor
	Actress	Ben Thomas (3)	Actor
Elizabeth Barrett	Poet	Robert Browning	Poet
Kim Basinger	Actress	Alec Baldwin (2)	Actor
Elizabeth Batts	Captain's wife	James Cook	Seaman and explorer
Stephanie Beacham	Actress	John McEnery	Actor
Priscilla Beaulieu	Actress	Elvis Presley	Singer
Mary Hayley Bell	Playwright	John Mills	Actor
Annette Bening	Actress	Warren Beatty	Actor
Jill Bennett	Actress	John Osborne (1)	Playwright
		Willis Hall (2)	
Veronica Bennett	Singer	Phil Spector	Record producer
Berengaria	Princess of Navarre	Richard 1	English king
Candice Bergen (3)	Actress	Louis Malle	Director
Ingrid Bergman (2)	Actress	Roberto Rossellini (2)	Director
Joy Beverley	Singer	Billy Wright	Footballer
Anne Birley (3)	Lady Annabel Vane-Tempest Stewart	James Goldsmith	Tycoon
Blanche of Lancaster (1)	English noblewoman	John of Gaunt	English prince
Melanie Blatt	Pop singer	Stuart Zender	Musician
Renate Blauel	Actress	Elton John	Vocalist and composer
Joan Blondell	Actress	Dick Powell (1)	Actor
		Mike Todd (2)	Showman and film producer
Claire Bloom	Actress	Rod Steiger (1)	Actor
		Philip Roth (3)	Novelist
Maureen Blott (2)	Actress	Harry H Corbett	Actor
Jean Boht	Actress	Carl Davis	Composer
Cherie Booth	Barrister	Tony Blair	Politician
Connie Booth	Actress	John Cleese	Actor
Catherine Boucher	Illiterate pauper	William Blake	Poet and painter
Boudicca	Queen of Iceni	Prasutagus	King of Iceni
Margaret Bourke-White	Photo-journalist	Erskine Caldwell	US author
Jacqueline Bouvier	Socialite	John F Kennedy (1)	US president
Elizabeth Bowen	Irish novelist	Alan Charles Cameron	Businessman
Marjory Bowes (1)	John Knox's 1st wife	John Knox	Religious reformer
Patti Boyd	Model	George Harrison (1)	Musician
		Eric Clapton (2)	Musician
Elizabeth Boyle	Socialite	Edmund Spenser	English poet
Philippa Braithewaite (2)	TV Producer	Martin Clunes	Actor
Sarah Brightman (2)	Singer	Andrew Lloyd Webber (2)	Composer
Cosima Von Bülow	Franz Liszt's daughter	Hans von Bülow (1)	Conductor
Christie Brinkley (2)	Model	Billy Joel (2)	Singer
May Britt	Actress	Sammy Davis Jnr	Entertainer
Vera May Brittain	Writer	George Catlin	Professor of politics
Charlotte Brontë	Writer	Arthur Bell Nicholls	Curate
Janet Brown	Impressionist	Peter Butterworth	Actor
Melanie Brown	Spice girl	Jimmy Gulzar	Musician
Coral Browne	Actress	Vincent Price	Actor
Jill Browne	Actress	John Alderton (1)	Actor
		Brian Wolfe (2)	Theatre producer
Anna Brueghel	Daughter of Jan Brueghel	David Teniers the Younger	Flemish painter
Sheila Buckley	Secretary	John Stonehouse	Politician
Cosima von Bülow (2)	Franz Liszt's daughter	Richard Wagner	Composer
Fanny Burney	English novelist	General D'Arblay	French émigré
Margaret Burr	Daughter of 4th Duke of Beaufort	Thomas Gainsborough	English painter
Irene Busch	Musician	Rudolf Serkin	Pianist
Penny Calvert	Dancer	Bruce Forsyth (1)	Entertainer
		Peter Murray Hill (2)	Actor and bookseller
Dyan Cannon (4)	Actress	Cary Grant	Actor
Sarah Caplin	TV executive	Nick Ross	Broadcaster
Kate Capshaw (2)	Actress	Steven Spielberg (2)	Director
Mariah Carey	Singer	Tommy Mottola	President of Sony Music
Judy Carne	Actress	Burt Reynolds	Actor
Caroline of Ansbach	German noblewoman	George II	British king
Caroline of Brunswick	German noblewoman	George IV	British king

Caroline of Monaco	Princess	Pierre Junot (1)	Businessman
		Stefano Casiraghi (2)	Businessman
		Prince Ernst August (3)	Hanoverian Prince
Leslie Caron	Actress	Peter Hall	Theatre director
Theresa Carreño (1)	Pianist	Eugène D'Albert	Composer and pianist
June Carter	Singer	Johnny Cash	Singer
Martita Casals	Pablo Casals' widow	Eugene Istomin	Pianist
Carmen Castillo (1)	Singer	Xavier Cugat	Bandleader
Phoebe Cates	Actress	Kevin Kline	Actor
Princess Catherine	Valois princess	Owen Tudor (1)	Grandfather of Henry V11
Catherine I	Russian empress	Peter the Great (2)	Russian Tsar
Catherine II (the Great)	Russian empress	Peter III	Russian Tsar
Catherine de-Medici	Queen of France	Henry II	French king
Catherine of Braganza	Portuguese princess	Charles II	English king
Catherine of Valois	French princess	Henry V (2)	English king
Anna Cermakova	Socialite	Antonin Dvorák	Composer
Alice Charigot	Socialite	Pierre-Auguste Renoir	French painter
Charlotte Sophia	German noblewoman	George III	British king
Charlotte Charpentier	Daughter of French émigré	Walter Scott	Scottish novelist
Cher	Actress/Singer	Sonny Bono (1)	Actor and politician
		Greg Allmann (2)	Musician
Helen Cherry	Actress	Trevor Howard	Actor
Chiang Ching (3)	Actress	Mao Zedong	Chinese leader
Agatha Christie	Writer	Max Mallowan	Archaeologist
Diane Cilento (1)	Actress	Sean Connery	Actor
Cleopatra VII	Queen of Egypt	Ptolemy XIII (1)	Egyptian Ruler
		Mark Antony (2)?	Roman General
Rosemary Clooney	Singer	José Ferrer	Actor
Clotilda	Queen of the Franks	Clovis I	King of the Franks
Clytemnestra	Mythical Queen of Mycenae	Agamemnon	Mythical King of Mycenae
Isabella Colbran (1)	Spanish soprano	Gioacchino Rossini	Composer
Venetia Collett-Barrett (1)	Actress	Edward Woodward	Actor
Joan Collins (1)	Actress	Anthony Newley (1)	Actor and singer
Pauline Collins (2)	Actress	John Alderton	Actor
Jane Colt (1)	Farmer's daughter	Thomas More	Chancellor of England
Shirley Conran	Authoress	Terence Conran	Businessman
Constance of Castile (2)	Castilian princess	John of Gaunt	English prince
Sarah Cook	Schoolgirl (13 when married)	Musa Komeagac	Turkish waiter
Rita Coolidge (2)	Singer	Kris Kristofferson	Actor
Dolores Costello	Actress	John Barrymore	Actor
Cicely Courtneidge	Actress	Jack Hulbert	Actor
Courtney Cox	Actress	David Arquette	Actor
Maureen Cox (1)	Childhood sweetheart	Ringo Starr	Musician
Charlotte Mary Craddock (1)	Socialite	Henry Fielding	English novelist
Jill Craigie	TV scriptwriter and author	Michael Foot	Politician
Gemma Craven (1)	Actress	Frazer Hines	Actor
Cindy Crawford	Supermodel	Richard Gere	Actor
Joan Crawford	Actress	Douglas Fairbanks Jnr (2)	Actor
Creusa	Mythical Roman character	Aeneas	Mythical Trojan prince
Cristina	Spanish Infanta	Inaki Vrdangarin	Handball player
Abigail Cruttenden (3)	Actress	Sean Bean	Actor
Cynthia Curzon (1)	English noblewoman	Oswald Mosley	Politician
Sinead Cusack	Actress	Jeremy Irons	Actor
Martha Custis	Socialite	George Washington	President of USA
Sasha Czack (1)	Theatre usher	Sylvester Stallone	Actor
Lili Damita (1)	Socialite	Errol Flynn	Actor
Mary Daniel (2)	Maid	Henry Fielding	English novelist
Bebe Daniels	Radio comedienne	Ben Lyon	Radio comedian
Blythe Danner	Actress	Bruce Paltrow	Director
Joy Davidman	Poet	CS Lewis	Author
Geena Davis	Actress	Renny Harlin (1)	Film director
		Jeff Goldblum (2)	Actor
Nancy Davis (2)	Actress	Ronald Reagan	US president
Sharron Davis	Swimmer	Derek Redmond	Athlete
Isabel Dean	Actress	William Fairchild	Playwright
Sandra Dee	Actress	Bobby Darin	Singer
Judi Dench	Actress	Michael Williams	Actor
Catherine Deneuve (2)	Actress	David Bailey	Photographer
Bo Derek (3)	Actress	John Derek	Actor and director
Donna D'Errico	'Baywatch' actress	Nikki Sixx	Motley Crue guitarist
Félicité Desmousseaux	Actress	César Franck	Composer

FAMOUS PEOPLE

Colleen Dewhurst	Socialite	*George C Scott*	*Actor*
Angie Dickinson (2)	Actress	*Burt Bacharach (2)*	*Composer*
Sandra Dickinson	Actress	*Peter Davison*	*Actor*
Marlene Dietrich	Actress	*Rudolf Seiber (1)*	*Production assistant*
Kitty Dobbs	Niece of Beatrice Webb	*Malcolm Muggeridge*	*Journalist*
Hilda Doolittle	US poet	*Richard Aldington*	*Poet and novelist*
Diana Dors	Actress	*Alan Lake (3)*	*Actor*
		Dickie Dawson (2)	*US comedian*
Michele Dotrice (2)	Actress	*Edward Woodward*	*Actor*
Angela Douglas	Irish actress	*Kenneth More*	*Actor*
Lesley-Anne Down (2)	Actress	*William Friedkin (1)*	*Film director*
Margaret Drabble	Novelist	*Clive Swift (1)*	*Author*
		Michael Holroyd (2)	*Biographer*
Isadora Duncan (1)	Dancer	*Sergei Yessenin*	*Poet*
Jacqueline Du Pré	Cellist	*Daniel Barenboim*	*Pianist*
Otilie Dvorák	Daughter of Antonin Dvorák	*Josef Suk*	*Violinist*
Linda Eastman	Photographer	*Paul McCartney (2)*	*Musician*
Nora Eddington (3)	Actress	*Errol Flynn*	*Actor*
Martha Eggerth	Soprano	*Jan Kiepura*	*Tenor*
Anita Ekberg	Actress	*Anthony Steele*	*Actor*
Britt Ekland	Actress	*Peter Sellers (1)*	*Actor*
		Slim Jim Phantom McDonnell (2)	*Musician*
Eleanor of Aquitaine	French noblewoman	*Louis VII (1)*	*French king*
		Henry II	*English king*
Eleanor of Castile	Castilian princess	*Edward I*	*English king*
Eleanor of Provence	French noblewoman	*Henry III*	*English king*
George Eliot	Authoress	*John Walter Cross*	*Banker*
Elizabeth Bowes-Lyon	Earl of Strathmore's daughter	*George VI*	*British king*
Elizabeth of York	English princess	*Henry VII*	*English King*
Elizabeth Woodville	English noblewoman	*Edward IV*	*English King*
Jill Esmond (1)	Actress	*Laurence Olivier*	*Actor*
Eudoxia	Russian noblewoman	*Peter the Great (1)*	*Russian Tsar*
Dale Evans	Actress and singer	*Roy Rogers*	*Actor and singer*
Linda Evans (2)	Actress	*John Derek*	*Actor and director*
Chris Evert	Tennis player	*John Lloyd (1)*	*Tennis player*
Siobhan Fahey	Singer	*Dave Stewart*	*Musician*
Mia Farrow	Actress	*Frank Sinatra (1)*	*Singer*
		André Previn (2)	*Conductor*
Farrah Fawcett (2)	Actress	*Lee Majors (1)*	*Actor*
		Ryan O'Neal (2)	*Actor*
Gracie Fields	Singer	*Monty Banks*	*Film director*
Judy Finnegan	TV presenter	*Richard Madeley*	*TV presenter*
Carina Fitzalan-Howard (2)	Noblewoman	*David Frost*	*Broadcaster*
Carrie Fisher (2)	Actress	*Paul Simon*	*Singer and composer*
Jennifer Flavin (3)	Model	*Sylvester Stallone*	*Actor*
Jane Fonda	Actress	*Roger Vadim (1)*	*Film director*
		Tom Hayden (2)	*Politician*
	Politician	*Ted Turner (3)*	*Media Mogul*
Anna Ford	Broadcaster	*Mark Boxer*	*Cartoonist and journalist*
Margaret Forster	Author	*Hunter Davies*	*Author*
Helen Frankenthaler	US artist	*Robert Motherwell*	*US artist*
Lady Antonia Fraser (2)	Authoress	*Harold Pinter*	*Playwright*
Lynne Frederick	Actress	*Peter Sellers (1)*	*Actor*
		David Frost (2)	*Broadcaster*
Dido Freire (2)	Brazilian film-maker's daughter	*Jean Renoir*	*Film director*
Dawn French	Comedienne	*Lenny Henry*	*Comedian*
Valerie French	Actress	*Michael Pertwee*	*Actor*
Agnes Frey	Merchant's daughter	*Albrecht Dürer*	*German painter*
Edith Fricker	Socialite	*Robert Southey*	*Poet*
Sarah Fricker	Socialite	*Samuel Taylor Coleridge*	*Poet*
Sadie Frost	Actress	*Gary Kemp (1)*	*Actor and musician*
		Jude Law (2)	*Actor*
Fiona Fullerton (1)	Actress	*Simon MacCorkindale*	*Actor*
Magda Gabor (4)	Actress	*George Sanders (3)*	*Actor*
Zsa Zsa Gabor	Actress	*Conrad Hilton (2)*	*Businessman*
		George Sanders (3)	*Actor*
Myte Garcia	Belly dancer	*Prince (Symbol)*	*Singer*
Ava Gardner (2)	Actress	*Mickey Rooney (1)*	*Actor*
		Artie Shaw (2)	*Bandleader*
		Frank Sinatra (3)	*Singer*

Judy Garland	Actress	*Vincente Minnelli (2)*	*Film director*
		Sid Luft (3)	*Entertainer*
Jill Gascoigne (1)	Actress	*Alfred Molina (2)*	*Actor*
Sarah Michelle Gellar	Actress	*Freddie Prinze Jnr*	*Actor*
Elvira Gemignani	Socialite	*Giacomo Puccini*	*Composer*
Susan George (2)	Actress	*Simon MacCorkindale*	*Actor*
Robin Givens (1)	Actress	*Mike Tyson (2)*	*Boxer*
Alma Gluck	Soprano	*Efrem Zimbalist*	*Violinist*
Liza Goddard	Actress	*Colin Baker (1)*	*Actor*
		Alvin Stardust (3)	*Pop singer*
Paulette Goddard (3)	Actress	*Charlie Chaplin (2)*	*Actor*
		Burgess Meredith (3)	*Actor*
		Erich Maria Remarque (4)	*Author*
Lady Godiva	Countess of Mercia	*Leofric*	*Earl of Mercia*
Beatrix Godwin	Widow of EW Godwin (architect)	*James McNeill Whistler*	*Artist*
Mary Godwin	Writer	*Percy Bysshe Shelley*	*Poet*
Jane Goldman	Writer	*Jonathan Ross*	*TV presenter*
Stephanie Goldner	Harpist	*Eugene Ormandy*	*Conductor*
Jemima Goldsmith	Heiress	*Imran Khan*	*Cricketer*
Betty Grable	Actress	*Jackie Coogan (1)*	*Actor*
		Harry James (2)	*Musician*
Dulcie Gray	Actress	*Michael Denison*	*Actor*
Effie Gray	Artist	*John Ruskin (1)*	*Art Critic*
		John Everett Millais (2)	*Artist*
Elspet Gray	Actress	*Brian Rix*	*Actor*
Alex Greaves	Jockey	*David Nicholls*	*Horseracing trainer*
Sarah Greene	TV presenter	*Mike Smith*	*TV presenter*
Debbie Greenwood	TV presenter (former Miss UK)	*Paul Coia*	*TV presenter*
Lady Jane Grey	English noblewoman	*Lord Guildford Dudley*	*English nobleman*
Lita Grey (2)	Actress	*Charlie Chaplin*	*Actor*
Melanie Griffith	Actress	*Don Johnson (1) + (3)*	*Actor*
		Antonio Banderas (4)	*Actor*
Tammie Grimes	Actress	*Christopher Plummer*	*Actor*
Diana Guinness (2)	Nancy Mitford's sister	*Oswald Mosley*	*Politician*
Nina Hagerup	Singer (Grieg's Cousin)	*Edvard Grieg*	*Composer*
Geneviève Halévy	Composer's daughter	*Georges Bizet*	*Composer*
Faten Hamama (1)	Actress	*Omar Sharif*	*Actor and bridge player*
Alana Hamilton (1)	Model	*Rod Stewart (2)*	*Singer*
Sheila Hancock	Actress	*John Thaw (2)*	*Actor*
Sue Hanson	Actress	*Carl Wayne*	*Actor and Singer*
Harriet Harman	British politician	*Jack Dromey*	*Trade unionist*
Harmonia	Mythical daughter of Ares and Aphrodite	*Cadmus*	*Mythical founder of Thebes*
Mildred Harris (1)	Actress	*Charlie Chaplin*	*Actor*
Deborah Harry (common law)	Singer	*Chris Stein* (common law)	*Guitarist*
Teri Hatcher	Actress	*Jon Tenney*	*Actor*
Ann Hathaway	Farmer's daughter	*William Shakespeare*	*Playwright*
June Haver	Actress	*Fred MacMurray*	*Actor*
Jacquetta Hawkes	Archaeologist	*JB Priestley*	*Author*
Goldie Hawn	Actress	*Kurt Russell*	*Actor*
Anne Hayes (1)	Housewife	*Peter Sellers*	*Actor*
Rita Hayworth	Actress	*Orson Welles (2)*	*Actor and director*
		Aly Khan (3)	*Middle Eastern prince*
Patty Hearst	Heiress	*Bernard Shaw*	*Bodyguard*
Lillian Hellman	Playwright	*Dashiell Hammett*	*Author*
Heloise	Abelard's wife	*Peter Abelard*	*French philosopher*
Marie Helvin (3)	Model	*David Bailey*	*Photographer*
Anouska Hempel	Actress	*Mark Weinberg*	*Businessman*
Henrietta Maria	French princess	*Charles I*	*British king*
Audrey Hepburn	Actress	*Mel Ferrer*	*Actor*
Barbara Hepworth	Sculptor	*John Skeaping (1)*	*Sculptor*
		Ben Nicholson (2)	*Artist*
Hera (3)	Sister of Zeus	*Zeus*	*Greek supreme god*
Lady Herries	Racehorse trainer	*Colin Cowdrey*	*Cricketer*
Irene Hervey	Actress	*Allan Jones*	*Singer and actor*
Eva Herzigova	Model	*Tico Torres*	*Pop musician (Bon Jovi)*
Andrée Heurschling (1)	Artist's model	*Jean Renoir*	*Film director*
Hildegarde	Queen of the Franks	*Charlemagne*	*King of the Franks*
Faith Hill	Country singer	*Tim McGraw*	*Country singer*

Melanie Hill (2)	Actress ('Bread')	Sean Bean	Actor
Tracy Hilton	Housewife	Jim Davidson	Comedian
Gill Hinchcliffe	TV Production assistant	David Jason	Actor
Liz Hobbs (2)	Waterskier	Frazer Hines	Actor
Valerie Hobson	Actress and dancer	John Profumo (2)	Politician
Chaatal Hochuli (1)	Swiss Heiress	Ernst August	Prince of Hanover
Catherine Hogarth	Newspaper magnate's daughter	Charles Dickens	Author
Alison Holloway	Presenter	Jim Davidson	Comedian
Lauren Holly	Actress	Jim Carrey	Actor
Marilyn Horne	Mezzo-soprano	Henry Lewis	Conductor
Whitney Houston	Singer	Bobby Brown	Singer
Elizabeth Jane Howard	Novelist	Kingsley Amis	Novelist and poet
Clementine Hozier	Charity worker	Winston Churchill	Politician
Mabel Hubbard	Deaf student	Alexander Graham Bell	Inventor
Benita Hume	Actress	Ronald Culman (1)	Actor
		George Sanders (2)	Actor
Kirsty Hume	Model	Donovan Leitch	Actor
Gayle Hunnicutt	Actress	David Hemmings	Actor
Rachel Hunter (2)	Model	Rod Stewart	Singer
Anjelica Huston	Actress and director	Robert Graham	Sculptor
Mary Hutchinson	Socialite	William Wordsworth	Poet
Barbara Hutton (2)	Actress	Cary Grant	Actor
Judy Huxtable (2)	Actress	Peter Cook	Comedian and writer
Anne Hyde (1)	Daughter of Earl of Clarendon	James II	English King
Georgie Hyde-Lees	Socialite	WB Yeats	Poet
Ildico	Consort of Attila	Attila the Hun	Hunnish ruler
Iman	Model	David Bowie (2)	Singer/composer
Jill Ireland	Actress	David McCallum (1)	Actor
		Charles Bronson (2)	Actor
Isabella	Daughter of Philip IV of France	Edward II	English king
Isabella of Angoulême (2)	French noblewoman	John	King of England
Isabelle (2)	Daughter of Charles VI of France	Richard II	English king
Hattie Jacques	Actress	John Le Mesurier	Actor
Storm Jameson	Novelist	Guy Chapman (2)	Historian
Susan Jameson	Actress	James Bolam	Actor
Samantha Janus	Actress	Mauro Mantovani	Actor
Aino Järnefelt	General's daughter	Jean Sibelius	Composer
Zizi Jeanmaire	Dancer	Roland Petit	Choreographer
Cécile Jeanrenaud	Clergyman's daughter	Felix Mendelssohn	Composer
Ffion Jenkins	Ex-civil servant	William Hague	Politician
Jenny Jerome	Daughter of NY businessman	Lord Randolph Churchill	Politician
Jezebel	Queen of Israel	Ahab	King of Israel
Amy Johnson	Aviator	Jim Mollison	Aviator
Angelina Jolie	Actress	Johnny Lee Miller (1)	Actor
		Billy Bob Thornton (2)	Actor
Jennifer Jones	Actress	Robert Walker (1)	Actor
		David O'Selznick (2)	Director
Joséphine de Beauharnais	French noblewoman	Napoleon I	French emperor
Yootha Joyce	Actress	Glyn Edwards	Actor
Angelica Kauffmann	Swiss painter	Antonio Zucchi	Venetian painter
Ruby Keeler	Actress	Al Jolson	Entertainer
Maria Anna Keller	Hairdresser's daughter	Franz Joseph Haydn	Composer
Barbara Kelly	Actress and presenter	Bernard Braden	Actor and presenter
Margaret Kempson (1)	Housewife	Denis Thatcher	Businessman
Rachel Kempson	Actress	Michael Redgrave	Actor
Kay Kendall (3)	Actress	Rex Harrison	Actor
Suzy Kendall (1)	Actress	Dudley Moore	Entertainer
Cherly Kennedy	Actress	Tom Courtenay	Actor
Jacqueline Kennedy	Socialite	Aristotle Onassis (2)	Businessman
Patsy Kensit	Actress	Jim Kerr (2)	Musician
		Liam Gallagher (3)	Pop musician
Nicole Kidman (2)	Actress	Tom Cruise	Actor
Carole King	Singer/composer	Gerry Goffin	Composer
Henrietta Knight	Racehorse trainer	Terry Biddlecombe	Jockey
Vivienne Knight (3)	Scriptwriter	Patrick Campbell	Irish writer and wit
Gertrud Kolisch (2)	Musician	Arnold Schoenberg	Composer
Cleo Laine	Jazz singer	John Dankworth (2)	Jazz musician

Elsa Lanchester	Actress	Charles Laughton	Actor
Abbe Lane (3)	Singer	Xavier Cugat	Bandleader
Brogan Lane (3)	Actress	Dudley Moore	Entertainer
Hope Lange	Actress	Alan J Pakula (2)	Film director
Louise Lasser (2)	Actress	Woody Allen	Actor/director
Sue Lawley	Broadcaster	Hugh Williams	TV magnate
Evelyn Lear	Soprano	Thomas Stewart	Baritone
Kelly Le Brock	Actress	Steven Seagal (2)	Actor
Michelle Lee (2)	Actress and singer	James Farentino	Actor
Jane Leeves	Actress	Marshall Coben	US television executive
Janet Leigh	Actress	Tony Curtis (3)	Actor
Vivien Leigh (2)	Actress	Laurence Olivier (2)	Actor
Margaret Leighton	Actress	Laurence Harvey (2)	Actor
		Michael Wilding (3)	Actor
Rula Lenska (3)	Actress	Dennis Waterman (2)	Actor
Lotte Lenya	Actress/singer	Kurt Weill (1)	Composer
Kay Lenz	Actress	David Cassidy	singer
Tea Leoni	Actress	David Duchovny (2)	Actor
Lyubov Leonidovna (2)	Russian ballerina	Marius Petipa	French choreographer
Ginette Lery (2)	Secretary	JamesGoldsmith	Tycoon
Astriel Lindstrom (2)	Model	Bill Wyman	Musician
Muriel Ling (1)	Model	Harold Robbins	Writer
Elizabeth Linley	Composer's daughter	Richard Brinsley Sheridan	Irish dramatist
Maureen Lipman	Actress	Jack Rosenthal	Playwright
Constance Lloyd	Socialite	Oscar Wilde	Playwright/novelist
Sue Lloyd	Actress	Ronald Allen	Actor
Lina Llubera	Spanish singer	Sergei Prokofiev	Composer
Heather Locklear (2)	Actress	Tommy Lee	Singer
Victoria Lockwood	Model	Earl Charles Spencer	English nobleman
Carole Lombard (1)	Actress	William Powell (1)	Actor
		Clark Gable (2)	Actor
Claudine Longet	Actress	Andy Williams	Singer
Anita Lonsborough	Swimmer	Hugh Porter	Cyclist
Lydia Lopokova	Ballerina	John Maynard Keynes	Economist
Sophia Loren	Actress	Carlo Ponti	Film producer
Courtney Love	Actress/singer	Kurt Cobain (2)	Musician (Nirvana)
Sarah Lowndes	Poet	Bob Dylan	Musician
Lorna Luft	Singer	Colin Freeman	Musical director
Linda Lusardi	Actress and model	Sam Kane	Actor
Emma Lyon	Blacksmith's daughter	William Hamilton	Scottish diplomat
Lulu	Singer	Maurice Gibb	Singer
Carol McGiffin	Radio DJ	Chris Evans	Television presenter
Cathy McGowan	Broadcaster	Hywel Bennett	Actor
Ali MacGraw	Actress	Steve McQueen (2)	Actor
Heather McIntyre	Actress and playwright	William Hartnell	Actor
Virginia McKenna	Actress	Denholm Elliott (1)	Actor
		Bill Travers (2)	Actor
Alison McNair	Doctor's daughter	Donald Dewar (1)	British politician
		Alexander AM Irvine (2)	Lord Chancellor
Kitty McShane	Music-hall artist	Arthur Lucan	Music-hall artist
Madonna	Singer and actress	Sean Penn (1)	Actor
		Guy Ritchie (2)	Film director
Justine Mahler	Sister of Gustav Mahler	Arnold Rosé	Austrian violinist
Madame de Maintenon	Louis XIV's 2nd wife	Louis XIV	King of France
Maria Malibran	Contralto	Charles de Bériot	Violinist and composer
Erika Mann	Writer	WH Auden	Poet and essayist
Jayne Mansfield	Actress	Mickey Hargitay	Body-builder
Katherine Mansfield	NZ writer	George Bowden (1)	Businessman
		John Middleton Murry	Writer and critic
Leslie Manville (1)	Actress	Gary Oldman	Actor
Margaret of Anjou	French noblewoman	Henry VI	English king
Princess Margaret	Elizabeth II's sister	Anthony Armstrong Jones	Photographer
Maria Theresa	Spanish princess	Louis XIV	King of France
Marie Louise	Austrian archduchess	Napoleon I	French emperor
Jean Marsh (1)	Actress	Jon Pertwee	Actor
Marion Marshall (2)	Actress	Robert Wagner	Actor
Barbara Marx (4)	Actress	Frank Sinatra	Singer
Mary II	British queen	William III	British king
Mary of Guise	French noblewoman	James V	King of Scotland
Mary of Modena (2)	Italian noblewoman	James II	British king

FAMOUS PEOPLE

Mary of Teck	German noblewoman	*George V*	*British king*
Mary Stewart	Queen of Scots	*Francis II (1)*	*French Dauphin then king*
		Henry Darnley (2)	*English nobleman*
		Earl of Bothwell (3)	*Scottish nobleman*
Anna Massey	Actress	*Jeremy Brett*	*Actor*
Meg Matthews	Record company secretary	*Noel Gallagher*	*Pop musician*
Luisa Mattioli (2)	Housewife	*Roger Moore*	*Actor*
Sharon Maughan	Actress	*Trevor Eve*	*Actor*
Patricia Maynard (2)	Actress	*Dennis Waterman*	*Actor*
Patricia Medina	Actress	*Richard Greene*	*Actor*
Wilnelia Merced (3)	Beauty queen	*Bruce Forsyth*	*Entertainer*
Vivien Merchant (1)	Actress	*Harold Pinter*	*Playwright*
Melina Mercouri	Actress	*Jules Dassin*	*Film director*
Ethel Merman	Singer	*Ernest Borgnine (3)*	*Actor*
Messalina (3)	Roman noblewoman	*Nero*	*Roman emperor*
Jean Metcalfe	Broadcaster	*Cliff Michelmore*	*Broadcaster*
Metis (1)	Greek sea nymph	*Zeus*	*Greek supreme god*
Alice Middleton (2)	Widow of London mercer	*Thomas More*	*Chancellor of England*
Annabella Milbanke	Heiress	*Lord Byron*	*Poet*
Sarah Miles	Actress	*Robert Bolt*	*Playwright*
Antonina Miliukova	Pupil of Tchaikovsky	*Pyotr Tchaikovsky*	*Composer*
Rebecca Miller	Actress (Arthur Miller's daughter)	*Daniel Day-Lewis*	*Actor*
Elizabeth Minshull (3)	Milton's 3rd wife	*John Milton*	*Poet*
Marilyn Monroe	Actress	*Jim Dougherty (1)*	*Policeman*
		Joe Di Maggio (2)	*Baseball player*
		Arthur Miller (3)	*Playwright*
Margaret Montgomerie	Socialite	*James Boswell*	*Biographer*
Elizabeth Montgomery (3)	Actress	*Gig Young*	*Actor*
LM Montgomery	Canadian novelist	*Ewan Macdonald*	*Presbyterian minister*
Fanny Moody	English soprano	*Charles Manners*	*Irish bass and impresario*
Bel Mooney	Writer and broadcaster	*Jonathan Dimbleby*	*Broadcaster*
Demi Moore	Actress	*Bruce Willis*	*Actor*
Jeanne Moreau (1)	Actress	*William Friedkin (3)*	*Film director*
Anne Morrow	Writer	*Charles Lindbergh*	*Aviator*
Angela Mortimer	British Wimbledon champion	*John Barrett*	*Tennis commentator*
Iris Murdoch	Writer	*John Bayley*	*Professor of literature*
Patricia Neal	Actress	*Roald Dahl*	*Writer*
Nefertiti	Egyptian queen	*Akhenaton*	*Egyptian king*
Hildegarde Neil (2)	Actress	*Brian Blessed*	*Actor*
Wendy Neuss	Producer ('Star Trek')	*Patrick Stewart*	*Actor (StarTrek)*
Anne Nevill	English Noblewoman	*Richard III*	*English king*
Nanette Newman	Actress	*Bryan Forbes*	*Actor and director*
Sue Nicholls	Actress	*Mark Eden*	*Actor*
Mary Ellen Nicolls (1)	Daughter of Thomas Love Peacock	*George Meredith*	*English novelist*
Brigitte Nielsen (2)	Actress	*Sylvester Stallone*	*Actor*
Frances Nisbet	Doctor's widow	*Horatio Nelson*	*English naval hero*
Catherine Nossenko (1)	Stravinsky's cousin	*Igor Stravinsky*	*Composer*
Kim Novak	Actress	*Richard Johnson (1)*	*Actor*
Jane Nugent	Secretary	*Edmund Burke*	*British statesman*
Louise Nurding	Pop singer	*Jamie Redknapp*	*Footballer*
Merle Oberon (2)	Actress	*Alexander Korda*	*Film director*
Octavia (1)	Roman noblewoman	*Nero*	*Roman emperor*
Octavia (1)	Emperor Augustus' sister	*Marc Antony*	*Roman general*
Georgia O'Keefe	US painter	*Alfred Stieglitz*	*US photographer*
Tamsin Olivier	Pub owner	*Simon Dutton*	*Actor*
Julia Trevelyan Oman	Designer	*Roy Strong*	*Writer and historian*
Tatum O'Neal	Actress	*John McEnroe*	*Tennis player*
Oona O'Neill (4)	Playwright's daughter	*Charlie Chaplin*	*Actor*
Yoko Ono (2)	Artist	*John Lennon (2)*	*Musician*
Dorothy Osborne	Daughter of governor of Guernsey	*William Temple*	*Diplomat and essayist*
Fanny Osbourne	Actress	*Robert Louis Stevenson*	*Author*
Ann Packer	Athlete	*Robbie Brightwell*	*Athlete*
Wendy Padbury	Actress	*Melvyn Hayes*	*Actor*
Geraldine Page	Actress	*Rip Torn*	*Actor*
Grace Palermo (5)	Socialite	*Harold Robbins*	*Writer*
Lilli Palmer (2)	Actress	*Rex Harrison (1)*	*Actor*
Pandora	First woman of Greek myth	*Epimetheus*	*Titan*

May Pang	Authoress	Tony Visconti	Record producer
Vanessa Paradis	Singer	Johnny Depp	Actor
Euphrosyne Parepa	Soprano	Karl Rosa	German conductor
Mary Parker	Actress	Harold French	Actor and theatre director
Sarah Jessica Parker	Actress	Matthew Broderick	Actor
Isabel Patiño (1)	Bolivian tin magnate's daughter	James Goldsmith	Tycoon
Charlotte Payne-Townshend	Heiress	George Bernard Shaw	Dramatist
Olympie Pélissier (2)	Parisian hostess	Gioacchino Rossini	Composer
Penelope	Daughter of King Icarius of Sparta	Odysseus	Mythical king of Ithaca
Christine Perfect	Singer	John McVie	Musician
Rhea Perlman	Actress	Danny DeVito	Actor
Jean Peters	Actress	Howard Hughes	Businessman
Sandy Pflueger (2)	Equestrian rider	Mark Phillips	Equestrian rider
Maggie Philbin	TV presenter	Keith Chegwin	TV presenter
Philippa Hainault	Dutch noblewoman	Edward III	English king
Fiona Phillips	GMTV presenter	Martin Frizell	GMTV presenter
Michelle Phillips	Actress and singer	Dennis Hopper	Actor
Siân Phillips	Actress	Peter O'Toole (2)	Actor
Pat Phoenix (2)	Actress	Anthony Booth (3)	Actor
Paloma Picasso	Beautician and businesswoman	Rafael Lopez-Cambil	Argentinian playwright
Evelyn Pickering	Pre-Raphaelite artist	William Frend De Morgan	Pre-Raphaelite artist
Mary Pickford (2)	Actress	Douglas Fairbanks Snr	Actor
Billie Piper	Pop singer	Chris Evans	Disc Jockey
Valerie Pitts	TV presenter	Georg Solti	Conductor
Minna Planer (1)	Opera singer and actress	Richard Wagner (1)	Composer
Sylvia Plath	Poet	Ted Hughes	Poet
Suzanne Pleshette	Actress	Troy Donahue	Actor
Joan Plowright (3)	Actress	Laurence Olivier	Actor
Pocahontas	Princess	John Rolfe	English colonist
Lily Pons	Soprano	André Kostelanetz	Conductor
Poppaea (2)	Roman noblewoman	Nero	Roman emperor
Elizabeth Porter	Schoolteacher	Samuel Johnson	Writer and lexicographer
Beatrix Potter	Author and illustrator	William Heelis	Solicitor
Eleanor Powell (3)	Actress	Glenn Ford	Actor
Mary Powell (1)	Royalist sympathiser	John Milton	Poet
Stefanie Powers	Actress	Gary Lockwood	Actor
Lisa-Marie Presley	Actress	Danny Keough (1)	Rock musician
		Michael Jackson (2)	Entertainer
		Nicolas Cage (3)	Actor
Iris Pressagh (1)	Interior designer	Billy Connolly (1)	Scottish comedian
Kelly Preston	Actress	John Travolta	Actor
Soon-Yi Previn (3)	Personal assistant	Woody Allen	Actor/director
Libby Purves	Broadcaster	Paul Heiney	Broadcaster
Pyrrha	Daughter of Epimetheus and Pandora	Deucalion	Son of Prometheus
Miranda Quarry (3)	Actress	Peter Sellers	Actor
Gilda Radner	Psychotherapist	Gene Wilder	Actor
Anna Raeburn	Agony Aunt	Nick Lilley	Businessman
Gillian Raine (2)	Actress	Leonard Rossiter	Actor
Charlotte Rampling	Actress	Jean-Michel Jarre	Musician
Esther Rantzen	Broadcaster	Desmond Wilcox	Producer
Anthea Redfern (2)	Presenter	Bruce Forsyth	Entertainer
Vanessa Redgrave	Actress	Franco Nero (1)	Actor
		Tony Richardson (2)	Film producer
Alma Reville	Actress	Alfred Hitchcock	Film director
Debbie Reynolds (2)	Actress	Eddie Fisher	Singer
Ingeborg Rhosea (2)	Novelist	Jon Pertwee	Actor
Anneka Rice	TV presenter	Nick Allott	Theatre producer
Frieda von Richthofen	Socialite	DH Lawrence	Writer
Rachel Robards	Colonel's daughter	Andrew Jackson	US president
Amy Robbins	Student	HG Wells	Author
Margaret Roberts (2)	Politician	Dennis Thatcher	Businessman
Rachel Roberts (4)	Actress	Rex Harrison	Actor
Amy Robsart	Socialite	Robert Dudley	Earl of Leicester
Julie Rogers	Singer	Michael Black	Theatrical agent
Mimi Rogers (1)	Actress	Tom Cruise	Actor
Wenda Rogerson	Fashion model	Norman Parkinson	Photographer

FAMOUS PEOPLE

Primula Rollo	Cipher clerk	*David Niven*	*Actor*
Micheline Roquebrune (2)	Artist	*Sean Connery*	*Actor*
Isabella Rossellini (4)	Actress	*David Lynch (1)*	*Actor*
		Martin Scorsese (2)	*Director*
Jelka Rosen	Singer	*Frederick Delius*	*Composer*
Hannah Rothschild	Heiress	*Lord Rosebery*	*Scottish statesman*
Nicole Rothschild (4th)	Actress	*Dudley Moore*	*Entertainer*
Debbie Rowe (2)	Nurse	*Michael Jackson*	*Entertainer*
Gena Rowlands	Actress	*John Cassavetes*	*Actor*
Roxana	Queen of Macedon	*Alexander the Great*	*King of Macedon*
Meg Ryan (2)	Actress	*Dennis Quaid*	*Actor*
Sue Ryder	Philanthropist	*Leonard Cheshire*	*Philanthropist*
Vita Sackville-West	Poet and novelist	*Harold Nicolson*	*Diplomat*
Carol Bayer Sager (3)	Singer	*Burt Bacharach*	*Composer*
Jill St John	Actress	*Jack Jones (1)*	*Singer*
		Robert Wagner (2)	*Actor*
Beatrice Salkeld	Illustrator	*Brendan Behan*	*Irish writer*
Olga Samaroff (1)	Pianist	*Leopold Stokowski*	*Conductor*
Susan Sarandon	Actress	*Tim Robbins*	*Actor*
(common law)		(common law)	
Maria Elena Santiago	Secretary	*Buddy Holly*	*Musician*
Jennifer Saunders	Comedienne	*Ade Edmondson*	*Comedian*
Zelda Sayre	Socialite	*Francis Scott Fitzgerald*	*Novelist*
Prunella Scales	Actress	*Timothy West*	*Actor*
Alma Maria Schindler	Artist and musician	*Gustav Mahler (1)*	*Composer*
		Walter Gropius (2)	*Architect*
		Franz Werfel (3)	*Writer*
Elizabeth Schumann	German soprano	*Carl Alwin*	*German pianist/*
			conductor
Coretta Scott	Music graduate	*Martin Luther King*	*Civil rights leader*
Janette Scott (3)	Actress	*Mel Tormé (1)*	*Singer*
		Jackie Rae (3)	*TV presenter*
Kyra Sedgwick	Actress	*Kevin Bacon*	*Actor*
Phyllis Sellick	Pianist	*Cyril Smith*	*Pianist*
Sandie Shaw	Singer	*Jeff Banks*	*Fashion designer*
Moira Shearer	Ballet dancer	*Ludovic Kennedy*	*Broadcaster*
Evgenia Shelepin (2)	Trotsky's secretary	*Arthur Ransome*	*Writer*
Dinah Sheridan	Actress	*Jimmy Hanley (2)*	*Entertainer*
		Sir John Davis (2)	*Rank chairman*
Brooke Shields	Actress	*André Agassi*	*Tennis player*
Elizabeth Siddal	Model	*Dante Gabriel Rossetti*	*Poet and painter*
Simone Signoret	Actress	*Yves Montand (2)*	*Actor*
Sheila Sim	Actress	*Richard Attenborough*	*Actor*
Jean Simmons	Actress	*Stewart Granger*	*Actor*
Carly Simon	Singer	*James Taylor*	*Composer*
Wallis Simpson	American socialite	*Edward VIII*	*British king*
Carole Smillie	TV presenter	*Alex Knight*	*Restaurateur*
Anna Nicole Smith	Actress	*J Howard Marshall II*	*Oil Tycoon*
Delia Smith	Cookery writer	*Michael Wynn Jones*	*Publisher*
Maggie Smith	Actress	*Robert Stephens*	*Actor*
Mandy Smith (3)	Model	*Bill Wyman*	*Rolling Stone*
Michelle Smith	Irish swimmer	*Erik De Bruin*	*Dutch discus thrower*
Harriet Smithson	Irish actress	*Hector Berlioz*	*Composer*
Wendy Snowden	Actress	*Peter Cook*	*Comedian and writer*
Sophia Dorothea	German noblewoman	*George I*	*British king*
Britney Spears (1)	Singer	*Kevin Federline (2)*	*Dancer*
Dorothy Squires (1)	Singer	*Roger Moore (2)*	*Actor*
Barbara Stanwick	Actress	*Robert Taylor*	*Actor*
Jann Stapp (6)	Businesswoman	*Harold Robbins*	*Writer*
Alison Steadman	Actress	*Mike Leigh*	*Dramatist*
Sheila Steafel (1)	Actress	*Harry H Corbett*	*Actor*
Marion Stein	Musician	*7th Earl of*	*English nobleman*
		Harewood (1)	
		Jeremy Thorpe (2)	*Politician*
Virginia Stephen	Novelist	*Leonard Woolf*	*Publisher and writer*
Pamela Stephenson	Actress and comedienne	*Nicholas Ball (1)*	*Actor*
		Billy Connolly (2)	*Scottish comedian*
Margaret Stewart (2)	Lord Ochiltree's daughter	*John Knox*	*Religious reformer*
Miriam Stoppard	TV presenter and journalist	*Christopher Hogg (2)*	*Industrialist*
Susan Stranks	Presenter	*Robin Ray*	*Broadcaster*
Barbra Streisand	Singer and actress	*Elliot Gould (1)*	*Actor*
		James Brolin (2)	*Actor*

Giuseppina Strepponi (2)	Soprano	Giuseppe Verdi	Composer
Imogen Stubbs (3)	Actress	Trevor Nunn	Artistic director
Una Stubbs	Actress	Peter Gilmore (1)	Actor
		Nicky Henson (2)	Entertainer
Trudie Styler (2)	Actress	Sting	Singer
Vera de Bosset Sudekeine (2)	Ballet dancer	Igor Stravinsky	Composer
Margaret Sullavan	Actress	William Wyler	Film director
Anna Beth Sully (1)	Actress	Douglas Fairbanks Snr	Actor
Mariya Surovshchikova (1)	Russian ballerina	Marius Petipa	French choreographer
Joan Sutherland	Soprano	Richard Bonynge	Conductor
Janet Suzman (1)	Actress	Trevor Nunn	Artistic director
Gloria Swanson	Actress	Wallace Beery	Actor
Catherine Swynford (3)	Former mistress	John of Gaunt	English Prince
Jessica Tandy	Actress	Jack Hawkins (1)	Actor
		Hume Cronyn (2)	Actor
Sharon Tate (2)	Actress	Roman Polanski	Director
Christine Taylor	Actress	Ben Stiller	Actor
Elizabeth Taylor	Actress	Nicky Hilton (1)	Hotelier
		Michael Wilding (2)	Actor
		Mike Todd (3)	Film producer
		Eddie Fisher (4)	Singer
		Richard Burton (5 and 6)	Actor
		John Warner (7)	Senator
		Larry Fortensky (8)	Builder
Kiri Te Kanawa	Opera singer	Desmond Park	Mining engineer
Victoria Tennant	English actress	Steve Martin	US actor
Ellen Terry	English actress	George Frederick Watts (1)	English painter
		James Carew (2)	US actor
		Charlie Kelly (3)	Actor
Josephine Tewson (1)	Actress	Leonard Rossiter	Actor
Rosalie Texier (1)	Dressmaker	Claude Debussy	Composer
Themis (2)	Daughter of Gaia and Uranus	Zeus	Greek supreme god
Theodora	Actress	Justinian	East Roman emperor
Thetis	Mythical sea nymph (Nereid)	Peleus	Mythical King of Phthia
Emma Thompson	Actress	Kenneth Branagh	Actor
Elspeth Thomson	Socialite	Kenneth Grahame	Children's writer
Sybil Thorndike	Actress	Lewis Casson	Actor and manager
Hester Thrale	Writer	Gabriel Piozzi	Musician
Julia Thuillier	Socialite	Walter Savage Landor	Writer
Uma Thurman	Actress	Gary Oldman (1)	Actor
		Ethan Hawke (2)	Actor
Pauline Tiltson	Businesswoman	John Prescott	British politician
Ann Todd	Actress	David Lean	Film director
Mary Todd	Socialite	Abraham Lincoln	US president
Frances Tomelty (1)	Actress	Sting	Singer
Wanda Toscanini	Musician	Vladimir Horowitz	Pianist
Ludmilla Tourischeva	Gymnast	Valeri Borzov	Athlete
Marie Truffot	Socialite	Camille Saint-Saëns	Composer
Ivana Trump	Former wife of Donald Trump	Ricardo Mazzucchelli (2)	Italian businessman
Anthea Turner	TV presenter	Peter Powell (1)	Disc jockey and producer
		Grant Bovey (2)	Businessman
Cora Turner	Opera singer	Hawley Crippen	Murderer
Lana Turner	Actress	Lex Barker (5)	Actor
		Artie Shaw (1)	Bandleader
Martha Turner	Farmer's daughter	John Clare	Poet
Monica Turner (2)	Actress	Mike Tyson (1)	Boxer
Twiggy	Model and actress	Leigh Lawson (2)	Actor
Cathy Tyson	Actress	Craig Charles	Actor
Mary Ure	Actress	John Osborne (1)	Playwright
		Robert Shaw (2)	Actor
Saskia Uylenburgh	Burgomaster's daughter	Rembrandt Van Rijn	Dutch painter
Joanna Van Gyseghem (1)	Actress	Ralph Bates	Actor
Eva Marie Violetti	Viennese dancer	David Garrick	Actor
Galina Vishnevskaya	Soprano	Mstislav Rostropovich	Cellist and conductor
Carol Vorderman	TV presenter	Paddy King	Businessman
Marie Vulliamy (2)	Socialite	George Meredith	English novelist

Lindsay Wagner	Actress	*Alan Rider (1)*	*Music publisher*
		Michael Brandon (2)	*Actor*
		Henry Kingi (3)	*Stuntman*
		Lawrence Mortoff (4)	*Producer*
Lillias Walker (2)	Actress	*Peter Vaughan*	*Actor*
Lalla Ward (2)	Actress	*Tom Baker*	*Actor*
Rachel Ward	Actress	*Bryan Brown*	*Australian actor*
Sophie Ward	Actress	*Paul Hobson*	*Vet*
Sandra Warfield	Soprano	*James McCracken*	*Tenor*
Lavinia Warren	Circus performer	*Tom Thumb*	*Circus performer*
Jan Waters (2)	Actress	*Peter Gilmore (1)*	*Actor*
Ruby Wax	Comedienne	*Edward Bye*	*Producer*
Constance Weber	Singer	*Wolfgang Amadeus Mozart*	*Composer*
Denise Welch	Actress	*Tim Healy*	*Actor*
Tuesday Weld (2)	Actress	*Dudley Moore (2)*	*Entertainer*
Jane Baillie Welsh	Doctor's daughter	*Thomas Carlyle*	*Essayist*
Joanne Whalley	Actress	*Val Kilmer*	*Actor*
Billie Whitelaw (1)	Actress	*Peter Vaughan*	*Actor*
Clara Wieck	Pianist	*Robert Schumann*	*Composer*
Cynda Williams	Actress	*Billy Bob Thornton*	*Actor*
Esther Williams (4)	Actress	*Fernando Lamas (4)*	*Actor*
Penelope Wilton (4)	Actress	*Ian Holm*	*Actor*
Shelley Winters	Actress	*Tony Franciosa (2)*	*Actor*
Reese Witherspoon	Actress	*Ryan Phillippe*	*Actor*
Natalie Wood	Actress	*Robert Wagner*	*Actor*
Victoria Wood	Comedienne	*Geoffrey Durham*	*Comedian*
Catherine Woodcock (2)	Commoner	*John Milton*	*Poet*
Catherine Woodville	Sister-in-law of Edward IV	*Henry Stafford*	*2nd Duke of Buckingham*
Joanne Woodward	Actress	*Paul Newman*	*Actor*
Helen Worth	Actress	*Michael Angelis*	*Actor*
Syreeta Wright	Singer	*Stevie Wonder*	*Musician*
Anna Magdalena Wülken (2)	Soprano	*JS Bach*	*Composer*
Tessa Wyatt	Actress	*Tony Blackburn*	*Disc jockey*
Jane Wyman (1)	Actress	*Ronald Reagan (3)*	*US president*
Patrice Wymore (2)	Actress	*Errol Flynn*	*Actor*
Xanthippe	Athenian	*Socrates*	*Philosopher*
Paula Yates	Broadcaster	*Bob Geldof*	*Singer*
Cecilia Young	Singer	*Thomas Arne*	*Composer*
Mathilde von Zemlinsky (1)	Musician	*Arnold Schoenberg*	*Composer*
Catherine Zeta Jones (2)	Actress	*Michael Douglas*	*Actor*
Marta Ziegler	Socialite	*Béla Bartók*	*Composer*
Anna Zimmerman	Housewife	*Charles Gounod*	*Composer*

Marriages: By Male Spouse

Peter Abelard	French philosopher	*Héloïse*	*Abelard's Roman wife*
Aeneas	Mythical Trojan prince	*Creusa*	*Mythical character*
Agamemnon	Mythical king of Mycenae	*Clytemnestra*	*Mythical queen of Mycenae*
André Agassi	Tennis player	*Brooke Shields*	*Actress*
Ahab	King of Israel	*Jezebel*	*Queen of Israel*
Akhenaton	Egyptian king	*Nefertiti*	*Egyptian queen*
John Alderton	Actor	*Jill Browne (1)*	*Actress*
		Pauline Collins (2)	*Actress*
Richard Aldington	Poet/novelist	*Hilda Doolittle*	*US poet*
Alexander the Great	King of Macedon	*Roxana*	*Queen of Macedon*
Keith Allen	Actor	*Alison Allen*	*Television producer*
Ronald Allen	Actor	*Sue Lloyd*	*Actress*
Woody Allen	Actor and director	*Louise Lasser (2)*	*Actress*
		Soon-Yi Previn (3)	*Personal assistant*
Greg Allmann (2)	Musician	*Cher*	*Actress and singer*
Nick Allott	Theatre producer	*Anneka Rice*	*TV presenter*
Carl Alwin	German pianist and conductor	*Elizabeth Schumann*	*German soprano*
Kingsley Amis	Novelist and poet	*Elizabeth Jane Howard*	*Novelist*
Michael Angelis	Actor	*Helen Worth*	*Actress*
Mark Antony	Roman general	*Octavia (1)*	*Emperor Augustus' sister*
		Cleopatra VII	*Queen of Egypt*

Thomas Arne	Composer	*Cecilia Young*	*Singer*
Desi Arnaz	Musician and actor	*Lucille Ball*	*Comedienne and actress*
Tom Arnold (2)	Actor	*Roseanne Barr*	*Actress*
David Arquette	Actor	*Courtney Cox*	*Actress*
Richard Attenborough	Actor	*Sheila Sim*	*Actress*
Attila the Hun	Hunnish ruler	*Ildico*	*Consort of Attila*
WH Auden	Poet and essayist	*Erika Mann*	*Writer*
JS Bach	Composer	*Maria Barbara Bach (1)*	*Cousin of JS Bach*
		Anna Magdalena Wülken (2)	*Soprano*
Burt Bacharach	Composer	*Angie Dickinson*	*Actress*
		Carol Bayer Sager (3)	*Singer*
Kevin Bacon	Actor	*Kyra Sedgwick*	*Actress*
David Bailey	Photographer	*Marie Helvin (3)*	*Model*
		Catherine Deneuve (2)	*Actress*
Colin Baker (1)	Actor	*Liza Goddard (1)*	*Actress*
Tom Baker	Actor	*Lalla Ward (2)*	*Actress*
Alec Baldwin (2)	Actor	*Kim Basinger*	*Actress*
Nicholas Ball (1)	Actor	*Pamela Stephenson*	*Actress and comedienne*
Antonio Banderas (4)	Actor	*Melanie Griffith (2)*	*Actress*
Jeff Banks	Fashion designer	*Sandie Shaw*	*Singer*
Monty Banks	Film director	*Gracie Fields*	*Singer*
Daniel Barenboim	Pianist	*Jacqueline Du Pré*	*Cellist*
Lex Barker (5)	Actor	*Lana Turner (3)*	*Actress*
John Barrett	Tennis commentator	*Angela Mortimer*	*British Wimbledon champion*
John Barrymore	Actor	*Dolores Costello*	*Actress*
Béla Bartók	Composer	*Marta Ziegler*	*Socialite*
Ralph Bates	Actor	*Joanna Van Gyseghem (1)*	*Actress*
John Bayley	Professor of literature	*Iris Murdoch*	*Writer*
Sean Bean	Actor	*Debra Anderson (1)*	*Childhood sweetheart*
		Melanie Hill (2)	*Actress ('Bread')*
		Abigail Cruttenden (3)	*Actress ('Sharpe')*
Warren Beatty	Actor	*Annette Bening*	*Actress*
David Beckham	Footballer	*Victoria Adams*	*Spice Girl*
Wallace Beery	Actor	*Gloria Swanson*	*Actress*
Brendan Behan	Irish writer	*Beatrice Salkeld*	*Illustrator*
Alexander Graham Bell	Inventor	*Mabel Hubbard*	*Deaf student*
Hywel Bennett	Actor	*Cathy McGowan*	*Broadcaster*
Charles de Beriot	Violinist	*Maria Malibran*	*Contralto*
Hector Berlioz	Composer	*Harriet Smithson*	*Irish actress*
Terry Biddlecombe	Jockey	*Henrietta Knight*	*Racehorse trainer*
Georges Bizet	Composer	*Geneviève Halévy*	*Composer's daughter*
Michael Black	Theatrical agent	*Julie Rogers*	*Singer*
Tony Blackburn	Disc jockey	*Tessa Wyatt*	*Actress*
Tony Blair	Politician	*Cherie Booth*	*Barrister*
William Blake	English poet and painter	*Catherine Boucher*	*Illiterate pauper*
Brian Blessed	Actor	*Hildegarde Neil (2)*	*Actress*
Humphrey Bogart (1)	Actor	*Lauren Bacall (4)*	*Actress*
James Bolam	Actor	*Susan Jameson*	*Actress*
Robert Bolt	Playwright	*Sarah Miles*	*Actress*
Sonny Bono (1)	Actor and politician	*Cher (2)*	*Actress and singer*
Richard Bonynge	Conductor	*Joan Sutherland*	*Soprano*
Anthony Booth (3)	Actor	*Pat Phoenix (2)*	*Actress*
Ernst Borgnine (3)	Actor	*Ethel Merman (3)*	*Singer*
Valeri Borzov	Athlete	*Ludmilla Tourischeva*	*Gymnast*
James Boswell	Biographer	*Margaret Montgomerie*	*Socialite*
Earl of Bothwell (3)	Scottish nobleman	*Mary Stewart*	*Queen of Scots*
Grant Bovey (2)	Businessman	*Anthea Turner*	*TV presenter*
George Bowden (1)	Businessman	*Katherine Mansfield*	*NZ writer*
David Bowie (2)	Singer and composer	*Iman*	*Model*
Mark Boxer	Cartoonist	*Anna Ford*	*Broadcaster*
Bernard Braden	Actor and presenter	*Barbara Kelly*	*Actress and presenter*
Kenneth Branagh	Actor	*Emma Thompson*	*Actress*
Michael Brandon (2)	Actor	*Glynis Barber*	*Actress*
		Lindsay Wagner	*Actress*
Jeremy Brett	Actor	*Anna Massey*	*Actress*
Robbie Brightwell	Athlete	*Ann Packer*	*Athlete*
Matthew Broderick	Actor	*Sarah Jessica Parker*	*Actress*
James Brolin (2)	Actor	*Barbara Streisand (3)*	*Singer and actress*
Charles Bronson (2)	Actor	*Jill Ireland (2)*	*Actress*

Mel Brooks	Actor and producer	*Anne Bancroft*	*Actress*
Bobby Brown	Singer	*Whitney Houston*	*Singer*
Bryan Brown	Australian actor	*Rachel Ward*	*Actress*
Robert Browning	Poet	*Elizabeth Barrett*	*Poet*
Hans von Bülow (1)	Conductor	*Cosima von Bülow*	*Franz Liszt's daughter*
Edmund Burke	British statesman	*Jane Nugent*	*Secretary*
George Burns	Comedian and actor	*Gracie Allen*	*Comedienne*
Robert Burns	Poet	*Jean Armour*	*Socialite*
Richard Burton (5 and 6)	Actor	*Elizabeth Taylor*	*Actress*
Peter Butterworth	Actor	*Janet Brown*	*Impressionist*
Edward Bye	Producer	*Ruby Wax*	*Comedienne*
Gabriel Byrne	Actor	*Ellen Barkin*	*Actress*
Lord Byron	Poet	*Annabella Milbanke*	*Heiress*
Cadmus	Mythical founder of Thebes	*Harmonia*	*Daughter of Ares and Aphrodite*
Nicolas Cage	Actor	*Patricia Arquette (1)*	*Actress*
		Lisa-Marie Presley (2)	*Singer and actress*
Michael Caine	Actor	*Shakira Baksh (2)*	*Actress and model*
Erskine Caldwell	American author	*Margaret Bourke-White*	*Photo-journalist*
Alan Charles Cameron	Businessman	*Elizabeth Bowen*	*Irish novelist*
Patrick Campbell	Irish writer and wit	*Vivienne Knight (3)*	*Scriptwriter*
James Carew (2)	US actor	*Ellen Terry*	*English actress*
Thomas Carlyle	Essayist	*Jane Baillie Welsh*	*Doctor's daughter*
Jim Carrey	Actor	*Lauren Holly*	*Actress*
Johnny Cash	Singer	*June Carter*	*Singer*
Stefano Casiraghi (2)	Businessman	*Caroline of Monaco*	*Princess*
John Cassavetes	Actor	*Gena Rowlands*	*Actress*
David Cassidy	Singer	*Kay Lenz*	*Actress*
Lewis Casson	Actor and manager	*Sybil Thorndike*	*Actress*
George Catlin	Professor of politics	*Vera May Brittain*	*Writer*
Charlie Chaplin	Actor	*Mildred Harris (1)*	*Actress*
		Lita Grey (2)	*Actress*
		Paulette Goddard (3)	*Actress*
		Oona O'Neil (4)	*Playwright's daughter*
Guy Chapman (2)	Historian	*Storm Jameson*	*Novelist*
Lee Chapman	Footballer	*Leslie Ash*	*Actress*
Charlemagne	King of the Franks	*Hildegarde*	*Queen of the Franks*
Charles I	British king	*Henrietta Maria*	*French princess*
Charles II	British king	*Catherine of Braganza*	*Portuguese princess*
Craig Charles	Actor	*Cathy Tyson*	*Actress*
Keith Chegwin	TV presenter	*Maggie Philbin*	*TV presenter*
Leonard Cheshire	Philanthropist	*Baroness Sue Ryder*	*Philanthropist*
Lord Randolph Churchill	Politician	*Jenny Jerome*	*Daughter of NY businessman*
Winston Churchill	Politician	*Clementine Hozier*	*Charity worker*
Eric Clapton (2)	Musician	*Patti Boyd (1)*	*Model*
John Clare	Poet	*Martha Turner*	*Farmer's daughter*
Claudius	Roman emperor	*Agrippina*	*Roman noblewomen*
John Cleese	Actor	*Connie Booth*	*Actress*
Clovis I	King of the Franks	*Clotilda*	*Queen of the Franks*
Martin Clunes	Actor	*Philippa Braithewaite (2)*	*TV producer*
Kurt Cobain (2)	Musician (Nirvana)	*Courtney Love*	*Actress and singer*
Marshall Coben	US television executive	*Jane Leeves*	*Actress*
Paul Coia	TV presenter	*Debbie Greenwood*	*TV presenter (former Miss UK)*
Samuel Taylor Coleridge	Poet	*Sarah Fricker*	*Socialite*
Ronald Colman	Actor	*Benita Hume (2)*	*Actress*
Sean Connery	Actor	*Diane Cilento (1)*	*Actress*
		Micheline Roquebrune (2)	*Artist*
Billy Connolly (2)	Scottish comedian	*Iris Pressagh (1)*	*Interior designer*
		Pamela Stephenson (2)	*Actress and comedienne*
Terence Conran	Businessman	*Shirley Conran*	*Authoress*
Jackie Coogan (1)	Actor	*Betty Grable*	*Actress*
James Cook	British seaman and explorer	*Elizabeth Batts*	*Captain's wife*
Norman Cook	Musician	*Zoe Ball*	*TV presenter*
Peter Cook	Comedian and writer	*Wendy Snowden (1)*	*Actress*
		Judy Huxtable (2)	*Actress*
Harry H Corbett	Actor	*Sheila Steafel (1)*	*Actress*
		Maureen Blott (2)	*Actress*
Tom Courtenay	Actor	*Cheryl Kennedy*	*Actress*
Colin Cowdrey	Cricketer	*Lady Herries*	*Racehorse trainer*
Hawley Crippen	Murderer	*Cora Turner*	*Opera singer*

Hume Cronyn (2)	Actor	*Jessica Tandy* — *Actress*
John Walter Cross	Banker	*George Eliot* — *Authoress*
Tom Cruise	Actor	*Mimi Rogers (1)* — *Actress*
		Nicole Kidman (2) — *Actress*
Xavier Cugat	Bandleader	*Carmen Castillo (1)* — *Singer*
		Lorraine Allen (2) — *Singer*
		Abbe Lane (3) — *Singer*
Tony Curtis (3)	Actor	*Janet Leigh* — *Actress*
Roald Dahl	Writer	*Patricia Neal* — *Actress*
Eugène D'Albert	Composer and pianist	*Theresa Carreño (1)* — *Pianist*
John Dankworth (2)	Jazz musician	*Cleo Laine* — *Jazz singer*
General D'Arblay	French émigré	*Fanny Burney* — *English novelist*
Bobby Darin	Singer	*Sandra Dee* — *Actress*
Henry Darnley (2)	English nobleman	*Mary Stewart* — *Queen of Scots*
Jules Dassin	Film director	*Melina Mercouri* — *Actress*
Nigel Davenport	Actor	*Maria Aitken* — *Actress*
Jim Davidson	Comedian	*Tracy Hilton* — *Housewife*
		Alison Holloway — *TV presenter*
Hunter Davies	Author	*Margaret Forster* — *Author*
Carl Davis	Composer	*Jean Boht* — *Actress*
Sir John Davis (2)	Rank chairman	*Dinah Sheridan* — *Actress*
Sammy Davis Jnr	Entertainer	*May Britt* — *Actress*
Peter Davison	Actor	*Sandra Dickinson* — *Actress*
Dickie Dawson (2)	US comedian	*Diana Dors* — *Actress*
Cecil Day-Lewis	Poet	*Jill Balcon* — *Actress*
Daniel Day-Lewis	Actor	*Rebecca Miller* — *Actress (Arthur Miller's daughter)*
Erik De Bruin	Dutch discus thrower	*Michelle Smith* — *Irish swimmer*
William Frend De Morgan	Pre-Raphaelite artist	*Evelyn Pickering* — *Pre-Raphaelite artist*
Robert De Niro	Actor	*Diahnne Abbott* — *Actress*
Claude Debussy	Composer	*Rosalie Texier (1)* — *Dressmaker*
		Emma Bardac (2) — *Socialite*
Frederick Delius	Composer	*Jelka Rosen* — *Singer*
Michael Denison	Actor	*Dulcie Gray* — *Actress*
Johnny Depp	Actor	*Vanessa Paradis* — *Singer*
John Derek	Actor and director	*Ursula Andress (1)* — *Actress*
		Linda Evans (2) — *Actress*
		Bo Derek (3) — *Actress*
Frankie Dettori	Jockey	*Catherine Allen* — *Secretary*
Deucalion	Son of Prometheus	*Pyrrha* — *Daughter of Epimetheus and Pandora*
Danny DeVito	Actor	*Rhea Perlman* — *Actress*
Donald Dewar (1)	British politician	*Alison McNair* — *Doctor's daughter*
Joe Di Maggio (2)	Baseball player	*Marilyn Monroe (2)* — *Actress*
Charles Dickens	Author	*Catherine Hogarth* — *Newspaper magnate's daughter*
Jonathan Dimbleby	Broadcaster	*Bel Mooney* — *Writer and broadcaster*
Dionysus	Greek god of wine	*Ariadne* — *Mythical daughter of King Minos of Crete*
Troy Donahue	Actor	*Suzanne Pleshette* — *Actress*
Jim Dougherty (1)	Policeman	*Marilyn Monroe* — *Actress*
Michael Douglas	Actor	*Catherine Zeta Jones (2)* — *Actress*
Jack Dromey	Trade unionist	*Harriet Harman* — *British politician*
David Duchovny (2)	Actor	*Tea Leoni* — *Actress*
Lord Guilford Dudley	English nobleman	*Lady Jane Grey* — *English noblewoman*
Robert Dudley	Earl of Leicester	*Amy Robsart* — *Socialite*
Albrecht Dürer	German painter	*Agnes Frey* — *Merchant's daughter*
Geoffrey Durham	Comedian	*Victoria Wood* — *Comedienne*
Simon Dutton	Actor	*Tamsin Olivier* — *Pub owner*
Antonin Dvorák	Composer	*Anna Cermakova* — *Socialite*
Bob Dylan	Musician	*Sarah Lowndes* — *Poet*
Mark Eden	Actor	*Sue Nicholls* — *Actress*
Ade Edmondson	Comedian	*Jennifer Saunders* — *Comedienne*
Edward I	English king	*Eleanor* — *Castilian princess*
Edward II	English king	*Isabella* — *Daughter of Philip IV of France*
Edward III	English king	*Philippa Hainault* — *Dutch noblewoman*
Edward IV	English king	*Elizabeth Woodville* — *English noblewoman*
Edward VII	British king	*Alexandra* — *Danish princess*
Edward VIII	British king	*Wallis Simpson* — *American socialite*
Blake Edwards (2)	Film director	*Julie Andrews* — *Actress and singer*
Glyn Edwards	Actor	*Yootha Joyce* — *Actress*

Denholm Elliott (1)	Actor	*Virginia McKenna*	*Actress*
Epimetheus	Greek Titan	*Pandora*	*First woman of Greek myth*
Ernst August of Hanover (3)	Hanoverian prince	*Chantal Hochuli (1)*	*Swiss Heiress*
		Caroline of Monaco (2)	*Princess*
Emilio Estevez	Actor	*Paula Abdul (2)*	*Singer*
Chris Evans	Disc jockey	*Carol McGiffin (1)*	*Radio DJ*
		Billie Piper (2)	*Pop singer*
Trevor Eve	Actor	*Sharon Maughan*	*Actress*
Douglas Fairbanks Jnr (2)	Actor	*Joan Crawford*	*Actress*
Douglas Fairbanks Snr	Actor	*Anna Beth Sully (1)*	*Actress*
Douglas Fairbanks Snr (2)	Actor	*Mary Pickford (2)*	*Actress*
William Fairchild	Playwright	*Isabel Dean*	*Actress*
James Farentino	Actor	*Elizabeth Ashley (1)*	*Actress*
		Michele Lee (2)	*Actress and singer*
Kevin Federline (2)	Dancer	*Britney Spears (1)*	*Singer*
José Ferrer	Actor	*Rosemary Clooney*	*Singer*
Mel Ferrer	Actor	*Audrey Hepburn*	*Actress*
Henry Fielding	English novelist	*Charlotte Mary Craddock (1)*	*Socialite*
		Mary Daniel (2)	*Maid*
Albert Finney (5)	Actor	*Anouk Aimée (2)*	*Actress*
Eddie Fisher (1)	Singer	*Debbie Reynolds (2)*	*Actress*
		Elizabeth Taylor (3)	*Actress*
		Connie Stevens (4)	*Actress*
Francis Scott Fitzgerald	Novelist	*Zelda Sayre*	*Socialite*
Errol Flynn	Actor	*Patrice Wymore (2)*	*Actress*
		Lili Damita (1)	*Socialite*
Michael Foot	Politician	*Jill Craigie*	*TV scriptwriter and author*
Bryan Forbes	Actor and director	*Nanette Newman*	*Actress*
Glenn Ford	Actor	*Eleanor Powell (3)*	*Actress*
Bruce Forsyth	Entertainer	*Wilnelia Merced (3)*	*Beauty queen*
		Penny Calvert (1)	*Dancer*
		Anthea Redfern (2)	*Presenter*
Larry Fortensky (8)	Builder	*Elizabeth Taylor*	*Actress*
Tony Franciosa (2)	Actor	*Shelley Winters*	*Actress*
Francis II (1)	French Dauphin then king	*Mary Stewart*	*Queen of Scots*
César Franck	Composer	*Félicité Desmousseaux*	*Actress*
Colin Freeman	Musical director	*Lorna Luft*	*Singer*
David Freeman	Operatic director	*Marie Angel*	*Australian soprano*
Harold French	Actor and theatre director	*Mary Parker*	*Actress*
William Friedkin	Film director	*Lesley-Anne Down (2)*	*Actress*
		Jeanne Moreau (1)	*Actress*
Martin Frizell	GMTV presenter	*Fiona Phillips*	*GMTV presenter*
David Frost	Broadcaster	*Lynne Frederick (1)*	*Actress*
		Carina Fitzalan Howard (2)	*Noblewoman*
Clark Gable (2)	Actor	*Carole Lombard (3)*	*Actress*
Thomas Gainsborough	English painter	*Margaret Burr*	*Daughter of 4th Duke of Beaufort*
Liam Gallagher (3)	Pop musician	*Patsy Kensit*	*Actress and singer*
Noel Gallagher	Pop artist	*Meg Matthews*	*Record company secretary (Creation)*
David Garrick	Actor	*Eva Marie Violetti*	*Viennese dancer*
Bob Geldof	Singer	*Paula Yates*	*Broadcaster*
George I	British king	*Dorothea Sophia*	*German noblewoman*
George II	British king	*Caroline of Ansbach*	*German noblewoman*
George III	British king	*Charlotte Sophia*	*German noblewoman*
George IV	British king	*Caroline of Brunswick*	*German noblewoman*
George V	British king	*Mary of Teck*	*German noblewoman*
George VI	British king	*Elizabeth Bowes-Lyon*	*Earl of Strathmore's daughter*
George of Denmark	Danish Prince	*Queen Anne*	*British queen*
Richard Gere	Actor	*Cindy Crawford*	*Supermodel*
Maurice Gibb	Musician	*Lulu*	*Singer*
Peter Gilmore (1)	Actor	*Jan Waters (2)*	*Actress*
		Una Stubbs (1)	*Actress*
Gerry Goffin	Composer	*Carole King*	*Singer and composer*
Jeff Goldblum (2)	Actor	*Geena Davis*	*Actress*
James Goldsmith	Tycoon	*Ginette Lery (2)*	*Secretary*
		Isabel Patiño (1)	*Bolivian tin magnate's daughter*

Male Spouse	Occupation	Female Spouse	Occupation
		Anne Birley (3)	Lady Annabel Vane-Tempest Stewart
Elliot Gould (1)	Actor	Barbra Streisand	Singer and actress
Charles Gounod	Composer	Anna Zimmerman	Housewife
Robert Graham	Sculptor	Anjelica Huston	Actress and director
Kenneth Grahame	Children's writer	Elspeth Thomson	Socialite
Stewart Granger	Actor	Jean Simmons	Actress
Cary Grant	Actor	Barbara Hutton (2)	Actress
		Dyan Cannon (4)	Actress
Richard Greene	Actor	Patricia Medina	Actress
Edvard Grieg	Composer	Nina Hagerup	Singer (Grieg's cousin)
Walter Gropius (2)	Architect	Alma Maria Schindler (1)	Musician
Jimmy Gulzar	Musician	Melanie Brown	Spice Girl
William Hague	Politician	Ffion Jenkins	Ex Civil Servant
Peter Hall	Theatre director	Leslie Caron	Actress
Willis Hall	Writer	Jill Bennett (2)	Actress
William Hamilton	Scottish diplomat	Emma Lyon	Blacksmith's daughter
Dashiell Hammett	Author	Lillian Hellman	Playwright
Jimmy Hanley	Entertainer	Dinah Sheridan (1)	Actress
7th Earl of Harewood (1)	English nobleman	Marion Stein	Musician
Hargitay (2)	Body-builder	Jayne Mansfield	Actress
Renny Harlin (1)	Film director	Gena Davis	Actress
George Harrison (1)	Musician	Patti Boyd (1)	Model
Rex Harrison	Actor	Lilli Palmer (2)	Actress
		Kay Kendall (3)	Actress
		Rachel Roberts (4)	Actress
William Hartnell	Actor	Heather McIntyre	Actress and playwright
Laurence Harvey (2)	Actor	Margaret Leighton	Actress
Ethan Hawke (2)	Actor	Uma Thurman	Actress
Jack Hawkins (1)	Actor	Jessica Tandy	Actress
Tom Hayden (2)	Politician	Jane Fonda	Actress
Franz Joseph Haydn	Composer	Maria Anna Keller	Hairdresser's daughter
Melvyn Hayes	Actor	Wendy Padbury	Actress
Tim Healy	Actor	Denise Welch	Actress
William Heelis	Solicitor	Beatrix Potter	Author and illustrator
Paul Heiney	Broadcaster	Libby Purves	Broadcaster
David Hemmings	Actor	Gayle Hunnicutt	Actress
Henry II	French king	Catherine de Medici	Queen of France
Henry II (2)	English king	Eleanor of Aquitaine	French noblewoman
Henry III	English king	Eleanor of Provence	French noblewoman
Henry V (2)	English king	Catherine of Valois	French princess
Henry VI	English king	Margaret of Anjou	French noblewoman
Henry VII	English king	Elizabeth of York	English princess
Lenny Henry	Comedian	Dawn French	Comedienne
George Henschel	Baritone	Lilian Bailey	American soprano
Nicky Henson (2)	Entertainer	Una Stubbs	Actress
Hephaestus	Greek god of fire	Aphrodite	Greek goddess of Love
Peter Murray Hill	Actor and bookseller	Phyllis Calvert	Actress
Conrad Hilton (2)	Hotelier	Zsa Zsa Gabor	Actress
Nicky Hilton Jnr	Hotelier	Elizabeth Taylor	Actress
Frazer Hines	Actor	Gemma Craven (1)	Actress
		Liz Hobbs (2)	Waterskier
Alfred Hitchcock	Film director	Alma Reville	Actress
Paul Hobson	Vet	Sophie Ward	Actress
Christopher Hogg (2)	Industrialist	Miriam Stoppard	TV presenter and journalist
Buddy Holly	Musician	Maria Elena Santiago	Secretary
Ian Holm	Actor	Penelope Wilton (4)	Actress
Michael Holroyd (2)	Biographer	Margaret Drabble	Novelist
Dennis Hopper	Actor	Michelle Phillips	Actress and singer
Vladimir Horowitz	Pianist	Wanda Toscanini	Musician
Trevor Howard	Actor	Helen Cherry	Actress
Liam Howlett	Musician	Natalie Appleton	Pop singer
Howard Hughes	Businessman	Jean Peters	Actress
Ted Hughes	Poet	Sylvia Plath	Poet
Jack Hulbert	Actor	Cicely Courtneidge	Actress
Timothy Hutton	Actor	Debra Winger	Actress
Jeremy Irons	Actor	Sinead Cusack	Actress
Alexander Irvine (2)	Irvine of Lairg	Alison McNair	Doctor's daughter
Eugene Istomin	Pianist	Martita Casals	Pablo Casals' widow
Andrew Jackson	US president	Rachel Robards	Colonel's daughter
Michael Jackson	Entertainer	Lisa-Marie Presley (1)	Singer and actress
		Debbie Rowe (2)	Nurse

FAMOUS PEOPLE

James I	English king		Anne	Danish princess
James II	English king		Anne Hyde (1)	Daughter of the Earl of Clarendon
			Mary of Modena (2)	Italian noblewoman
James V	King of Scotland		Mary of Guise	French noblewoman
Harry James	Musician		Betty Grable	Actress
Jean-Michel Jarre	Musician		Charlotte Rampling	Actress
Martin Jarvis	Actor		Rosalind Ayres	Actress
David Jason	Actor		Gill Hinchcliffe	TV production assistant
Billy Joel (2)	Singer		Christie Brinkley (2)	Model
John	King of England		Isabella of Angoulême (2)	French noblewoman
John of Gaunt	English prince		Blanche of Lancaster (1)	English noblewoman
			Constance of Castile (2)	Castilian princess
			Catherine Swynford (3)	Former mistress
Elton John	Vocalist and composer		Renate Blauel	Actress
Don Johnson (1) & (3)	Actor		Melanie Griffith	Actress
Richard Johnson (1)	Actor		Kim Novak	Actress
Samuel Johnson	Writer and lexicographer		Elizabeth Porter	Schoolteacher
Al Jolson	Entertainer		Ruby Keeler	Actress
Allan Jones	Singer and actor		Irene Hervey	Actress
Anthony Armstrong Jones	Photographer		Princess Margaret	Elizabeth II's sister
Sir G Roderick Jones	MD of Reuters		Enid Bagnold	Authoress
Jack Jones (2)	Singer		Jill St John (2)	Actress
James Joyce	Irish writer		Nora Barnacle	Socialite
Pierre Junot	Businessman		Caroline of Monaco	Princess
Justinian	East Roman emperor		Theodora	Actress
Wassily Kandinsky	Russian artist		Nina Andreevskaya	Moscow socialite
Sam Kane	Actor		Linda Lusardi	Actress and model
Charles Kelly (2)	Actor		Ellen Terry	Actress
Gary Kemp (1)	Actor and musician		Sadie Frost	Actress
John F Kennedy (1)	US president		Jacqueline Bouvier	Socialite
Ludovic Kennedy	Broadcaster		Moira Shearer	Ballet dancer
Danny Keough (1)	Rock musician		Lisa-Marie Presley	Singer and actress
Jim Kerr (2)	Musician		Patsy Kensit	Actress
John Maynard Keynes	Economist		Lydia Lopokova	Ballerina
Aly Khan (3)	Middle Eastern prince		Rita Hayworth (1)	Actress
Imran Khan	Cricketer		Jemima Goldsmith	Heiress
Eddie Kidd	Stunt motorcyclist		Debbie Ash (1)	Actress
Jan Kiepura	Tenor		Martha Eggerth	Soprano
Val Kilmer	Actor		Joanne Whalley	Actress
Martin Luther King	Civil rights leader		Coretta Scott	Music graduate
Paddy King	Businessman		Carol Vorderman	TV presenter
Henry Kingi (3)	Stuntman		Lindsay Wagner	Actress
Rudyard Kipling	Novelist and poet		Caroline Balestier	Publishing heiress
Kevin Kline	Actor		Phoebe Cates	Actress
Alex Knight	Restaurateur		Carole Smillie	TV presenter
Mark Knopfler	Musician		Kitty Aldridge	Actress
John Knox	Religious reformer		Marjory Bowes (1)	John Knox's 1st wife
			Margaret Stewart (2)	Lord Ochiltree's daughter
Musa Komeagac	Turkish waiter		Sarah Cook	Schoolgirl (13 when married)
Alexander Korda	Film director		Merle Oberon (2)	Actress
André Kostelanetz	Conductor		Lily Pons	Soprano
Kris Kristofferson	Actor		Rita Coolidge (2)	Singer
Sam Kydd	Actor		Pinkie Barnes	Table tennis international
Alan Lake (3)	Actor		Diana Dors	Actress
Fernando Lamas (4)	Actor		Esther Williams (4)	Actress
Martin Landau	Actor		Barbara Bain	Actress
Walter Savage Landor	Writer		Julia Thuillier	Socialite
Charles Laughton	Actor		Elsa Lanchester	Actress
Tim Laurence (2)	Naval officer		Princess Anne	British princess
Jude Law (2)	Actor		Sadie Frost	Actress
DH Lawrence	Writer		Frieda von Richthofen	Socialite
Leigh Lawson (2)	Actor		Twiggy	Model and actress
David Lean	Film director		Ann Todd	Actress
John Le Mesurier	Actor		Hattie Jacques	Actress
Tommy Lee	Singer		Heather Locklear (2)	Actress
			Pamela Anderson (3)	Actress
Mike Leigh	Dramatist		Alison Steadman	Actress
Donovan Leitch	Actor		Kirsty Hume	Model
John Lennon (2)	Musician		Yoko Ono (2)	Artist

Leofric	Earl of Mercia	*Lady Godiva*	*Countess of Mercia*
CS Lewis	Author	*Joy Davidman*	*Poet*
Henry Lewis	Conductor	*Marilyn Horne*	*Mezzo-soprano*
Nick Lilley	Businessman	*Anna Raeburn*	*Agony aunt*
Abraham Lincoln	US president	*Mary Todd*	*Socialite*
Charles Lindbergh	Aviator	*Anne Morrow*	*Writer*
John Lloyd (1)	Tennis player	*Chris Evert*	*Tennis player*
Andrew Lloyd Webber (2)	Composer	*Sarah Brightman (2)*	*Singer*
Gary Lockwood	Actor	*Stefanie Powers*	*Actress*
Henry W Longfellow	US poet	*Frances Appleton*	*Socialite*
Rafael Lopez-Cambil	Argentinian playwright	*Paloma Picasso*	*Beautician and businesswoman*
Louis VII (1)	King of France	*Eleanor of Aquitaine*	*French noblewoman*
Louis XIV	King of France	*Maria Theresa (1)*	*Spanish princess*
		Madame de Maintenon (2)	*Louis X1V's 2nd wife*
Louis XVI	King of France	*Marie Antoinette*	*French princess*
Arthur Lucan	Music-hall artist	*Kitty McShane*	*Music-hall artist*
Sid Luft (3)	Entertainer	*Judy Garland*	*Actress*
David Lynch	Director	*Isabella Rossellini (3)*	*Actress*
Ben Lyon	Radio comedian	*Bebe Daniels*	*Radio comedienne*
Simon MacCorkindale	Actor	*Fiona Fullerton (1)*	*Actress*
		Susan George (2)	*Actress*
Ewan Macdonald	Presbyterian minister	*LM Montgomery*	*Canadian novelist*
Fred MacMurray	Actor	*June Haver*	*Actress*
Richard Madeley	TV presenter	*Judy Finnegan*	*TV presenter*
Gustav Mahler	Composer	*Alma Maria Schindler (1)*	*Musician*
Lee Majors	Actor	*Farrah Fawcett (2)*	*Actress*
Louis Malle	Director	*Candice Bergen (3)*	*Actress*
Max Mallowan	Archaeologist	*Agatha Christie*	*Writer*
Charles Manners	Irish bass and impresario	*Fanny Moody*	*English soprano*
Mauro Mantovani	Actor	*Samantha Janus*	*Actress*
Mao Zedong	Chinese leader	*Chiang Ching*	*Actress*
J Howard Marshall II	Oil tycoon	*Anna Nicole Smith*	*Actress*
Steve Martin	Actor	*Victoria Tennant*	*Actress*
Ricardo Mazzucchelli (2)	Italian businessman	*Ivana Trump*	*Former wife of Donald Trump*
David McCallum (1)	Actor	*Jill Ireland*	*Actress*
Paul McCartney (2)	Musician	*Linda Eastman*	*Photographer*
James McCracken	Tenor	*Sandra Warfield*	*Soprano*
Slim Jim Phantom McDonnell	Musician	*Britt Ekland (1)*	*Actress*
John McEnery	Actor	*Stephanie Beacham*	*Actress*
John McEnroe	Tennis player	*Tatum O'Neal*	*Actress*
Tim McGraw	Country singer	*Faith Hill*	*Country singer*
Steve McQueen (2)	Actor	*Ali MacGraw*	*Actress*
John McVie	Musician	*Christine Perfect*	*Singer*
Felix Mendelssohn	Composer	*Cécile Jeanrenaud*	*Clergyman's daughter*
Burgess Meredith (3)	Actor	*Paulette Goddard*	*Actress*
George Meredith	English novelist	*Mary Ellen Nicolls (1)*	*Daughter of Thomas Love Peacock*
		Marie Vulliamy (2)	*Socialite*
Cliff Michelmore	Broadcaster	*Jean Metcalfe*	*Broadcaster*
Milanion	Mythical Greek athlete	*Atalanta*	*Mythical Greek huntress*
John Everett Millais (2)	Artist	*Effie Gray*	*Artist*
Arthur Miller (3)	Playwright	*Marilyn Monroe*	*Actress*
Johnny Lee Miller (1)	Actor	*Angelina Jolie*	*Actress*
John Mills	Actor	*Mary Hayley Bell*	*Playwright*
John Milton	Poet	*Mary Powell (1)*	*Royalist sympathiser*
		Catherine Woodcock (2)	*Second wife*
		Elizabeth Minshull (3)	*Third wife*
Vincente Minnelli (2)	Film director	*Judy Garland*	*Actress*
Alfred Molina (2)	Actor	*Jill Gascoigne (1)*	*Actress*
Jim Mollison	Aviator	*Amy Johnson*	*Aviator*
Yves Montand (2)	Actor	*Simone Signoret*	*Actress*
Dudley Moore	Entertainer	*Suzy Kendall (1)*	*Actress*
		Tuesday Weld (2)	*Actress*
		Brogan Lane (3)	*Actress*
		Nicole Rothschild (4th)	*Actress*
Roger Moore	Actor	*Dorothy Squires (1)*	*Singer*
		Luisa Mattioli (2)	*Housewife*
Kenneth More	Actor	*Angela Douglas*	*Irish actress*

Thomas More	Chancellor of England	Jane Colt (1)	Farmer's daughter
		Alice Middleton (2)	Widow of London mercer
Lawrence Mortoff (4)	Producer	Lindsay Wagner	Actress
Oswald Mosley	Politician	Cynthia Curzon (1)	English noblewoman
		Diana Guinness (2)	(Nancy Mitford's sister)
Robert Motherwell	US artist	Helen Frankenthaler	US artist
Tommy Mottola	President of Sony Music	Mariah Carey	Singer
Louis Mountbatten	Naval commander	Edwina Ashley	Heiress and charity worker
Wolfgang Amadeus Mozart	Composer	Constance Weber	Singer
Malcolm Muggeridge	Journalist	Kitty Dobbs	Niece of Beatrice Webb
Muhammad	Founder of Islam	Aisha	Muhammad's favourite wife
John Middleton Murry (2)	Writer and critic	Katherine Mansfield	NZ short story writer
Napoleon I	French emperor	Josephine de Beauharnais (1)	French empress
		Marie Louise (2)	Austrian archduchess
Liam Neeson (2)	Actor	Natasha Richardson	
Horatio Nelson	English naval hero	Frances Nisbet	Doctor's widow
Nero	Roman emperor	Octavia (1)	Roman noblewoman
		Poppaea (2)	Roman noblewoman
		Messalina (3)	Roman noblewoman
Franco Nero (1)	Actor	Vanessa Redgrave	Actress
Anthony Newley (1)	Actor and singer	Joan Collins (1)	Actress
Paul Newman	Actor	Joanne Woodward	Actress
Arthur Bell Nicholls	Curate	Charlotte Brontë	Writer
David Nicholls	Horseracing trainer	Alex Greaves	Jockey
Ben Nicholson (2)	Artist	Barbara Hepworth	Sculptor
Harold Nicolson	Diplomat	Vita Sackville-West	Poet and novelist
David Niven	Actor	Primula Rollo	Cipher Clerk
Trevor Nunn	Artistic director	Janet Suzman (1)	Actress
		Imogen Stubbs (3)	Actress
Odysseus	Mythical king of Ithaca	Penelope	Daughter of King Icarius of Sparta
Angus Ogilvy	Businessman	Princess Alexandra	British princess
Gary Oldman	Actor	Leslie Manville (1)	Actress
		Uma Thurman (2)	Actress
Laurence Olivier	Actor	Jill Esmond (1)	Actress
		Vivien Leigh (2)	Actress
		Joan Plowright (3)	Actress
Aristotle Onassis (2)	Businessman	Jacqueline Kennedy	Socialite
Ryan O'Neal (2)	Actor	Farrah Fawcett	Actress
Eugene Ormandy	Conductor	Stephanie Goldner	Harpist
John Osborne	Playwright	Mary Ure (2)	Actress
		Jill Bennett (4)	Actress
Peter O'Toole (2)	Actor	Sian Phillips	Actress
Alan J Pakula (2)	Film director	Hope Lange	Actress
Bruce Paltrow	Television director	Blythe Danner	Actress
Desmond Park	Mining engineer	Kiri Te Kanawa	Opera singer
Norman Parkinson	Photographer	Wenda Rogerson	Model
Peleus	Mythical king of Phthia	Thetis	Mythical sea nymph (Nereid)
Wilfred Pelletier	Conductor	Rose Bampton	Soprano
Sean Penn (1)	Actor	Madonna	Singer and actress
George Peppard (2)	Actor	Elizabeth Ashley	Actress
Jon Pertwee	Actor	Jean Marsh (1)	Actress
	Actor	Ingeborg Rhosea (2)	Novelist
Michael Pertwee	Actor	Valerie French	Actress
Peter the Great (1)	Russian tsar	Catherine I	Russian empress
		Eudoxia	Russian noblewoman
Peter III	Russian tsar	Catherine II (the Great)	Russian empress
Marius Petipa	French choreographer	Mariya Surovshchikova (1)	Russian ballerina
		Lyubov Leonidovna (2)	Russian ballerina
Roland Petit	Choreographer	Zizi Jeanmaire	Dancer
Ryan Phillippe	Actor	Reese Witherspoon	Actress
Mark Phillips	Equestrian rider	Sandy Pflueger (2)	Equestrian rider
		Princess Anne (1)	British princess
Harold Pinter	Playwright	Vivien Merchant (1)	Actress
		Lady Antonia Fraser (2)	Authoress
Gabriel Piozzi	Musician	Hester Thrale	Writer
Brad Pitt	Actor	Jennifer Aniston	Actress
Christopher Plummer	Actor	Tammie Grimes	Actress

Roman Polanski	Director	*Sharon Tate (2)*	*Actress*
Carlo Ponti	Film producer	*Sophia Loren*	*Actress*
Hugh Porter	Cyclist	*Anita Lonsborough*	*Swimmer*
Poseidon	Greek god of the sea	*Amphitrite*	*Mythical Greek sea nymph*
Dick Powell	Actor	*Joan Blondell (1)*	*Actress*
		June Allyson (2)	*Actress*
Peter Powell (1)	Disc jockey and producer	*Anthea Turner*	*TV presenter*
William Powell	Actor	*Carole Lombard*	*Actress*
Prasutagus	King of Iceni	*Boudicca*	*Queen of Iceni*
John Prescott	British politician	*Pauline Tiltson*	*Businesswoman*
Elvis Presley	Singer	*Priscilla Beaulieu*	*Actress*
André Previn (2)	Conductor	*Mia Farrow (3)*	*Actress*
Vincent Price	Actor	*Coral Browne*	*Actress*
JB Priestley	Author	*Jacquetta Hawkes*	*Archaeologist*
Prince (Symbol)	Singer	*Myte Garcia*	*Belly dancer*
Freddie Prinze Jnr	Actor	*Sarah Michelle Gellar*	*Actress*
John Profumo	Politician	*Valerie Hobson*	*Actress and dancer*
Sergei Prokofiev	Composer	*Lina Llubera*	*Spanish singer*
Ptolemy XII	Egyptian ruler	*Cleopatra III*	*Queen of Egypt*
Ptolemy XIII (1)	Egyptian Ruler	*Cleopatra VII*	*Queen of Egypt*
Giacomo Puccini	Composer	*Elvira Gemignani*	*Socialite*
Dennis Quaid	Actor	*Meg Ryan (2)*	*Actress*
Jackie Rae (3)	TV presenter	*Janette Scott*	*Actress*
Arthur Ransome	Writer	*Evgenia Shelepin (2)*	*Trotsky's secretary*
Robin Ray	Broadcaster	*Susan Stranks*	*TV presenter*
Ronald Reagan	US president	*Jane Wyman (1)*	*Actress*
		Nancy Davis (2)	*Actress*
Michael Redgrave	Actor	*Rachel Kempson*	*Actress*
Jamie Redknapp	Footballer	*Louise Nurding*	*Pop singer*
Derek Redmond	Athlete	*Sharron Davis*	*Swimmer*
Erich Maria Remarque (4)	Author	*Paulette Goddard*	*Actress*
Rembrandt Van Rijn	Dutch painter	*Saskia Uylenburgh*	*Burgomaster's daughter*
Jean Renoir	Film director	*Andrée Heurschling (1)*	*Artist's model*
		Dido Freire (2)	*Brazilian film-maker's daughter*
Pierre-Auguste Renoir	French painter	*Alice Charigot*	*Socialite*
Burt Reynolds	Actor	*Judy Carne (1)*	*Actress*
		Loni Anderson (2)	*Actress*
Richard I	English king	*Berengaria*	*Princess of Navarre*
Richard II	English king	*Anne of Bohemia (1)*	*Emperor Charles IV's daughter*
		Isabelle (2)	*Daughter of Charles VI of France*
Richard III	English king	*Anne Nevill*	*English noblewoman*
Tony Richardson (2)	Film producer	*Vanessa Redgrave*	*Actress*
Shane Richie	Comedian	*Coleen Nulan*	*Singer*
Guy Ritchie (2)	Film director	*Madonna*	*Singer and Actress*
Allan Rider (1)	Music publisher	*Lindsay Wagner*	*Actress*
Brian Rix	Actor	*Elspet Gray*	*Actress*
Jason Robards (2)	Actor	*Lauren Bacall (3)*	*Actress*
Harold Robbins	Writer	*Muriel Ling (1)*	*Model*
		Grace Palermo (5)	*Socialite*
		Jann Stapp (6)	*Businesswoman*
Tim Robbins (common law)	Actor (common law)	*Susan Sarandon (common law)*	*Actress*
Roy Rogers	Actor and singer	*Dale Evans*	*Actress and singer*
John Rolfe	English Colonist	*Pocahontas*	*Indian princess*
Mickey Rooney	Actor	*Ava Gardner*	*Actress*
Karl Rosa	German conductor	*Euphrosyne Parepa*	*Soprano*
Arnold Rosé	Violinist	*Justine Mahler*	*Sister of Gustav Mahler*
Lord (Primrose) Rosebery	Scottish statesman	*Hannah Rothschild*	*Heiress*
Jack Rosenthal	Playwright	*Maureen Lipman*	*Actress*
Jonathan Ross	TV presenter	*Jane Goldman*	*Writer*
Nick Ross	Presenter	*Sarah Caplin*	*TV executive*
Roberto Rossellini (2)	Director	*Ingrid Bergman (2)*	*Actress*
Dante Gabriel Rossetti	Poet and painter	*Elizabeth Siddal*	*Model*
Gioacchino Rossini	Composer	*Isabella Colbran (1)*	*Spanish soprano*
		Olympie Pélissier (2)	*Parisian hostess*
Leonard Rossiter	Actor	*Josephine Tewson (1)*	*Actress*
		Gillian Raine (2)	*Actress*
Mstislav Rostropovich	Cellist and conductor	*Galina Vishnevskaya*	*Soprano*

FAMOUS PEOPLE

Philip Roth	Novelist	Claire Bloom	Actress
John Ruskin (1)	Art Critic	Effie Gray	Artist
Kurt Russell	Actor	Goldie Hawn	Actress
Camille Saint-Saëns	Composer	Marie Truffot	Socialite
George Sanders	Actor	Zsa Zsa Gabor (2)	Actress
		Benita Hume (3)	Actress
		Magda Gabor (4)	Actress
Gerald Scarfe	Cartoonist	Jane Asher	Actress and cook
Arnold Schoenberg	Composer	Mathilde	Musician
		von Zemlinsky (1)	
		Gertrud Kolisch (2)	Musician
Robert Schumann	Composer	Clara Wieck	Pianist
Martin Scorsese	Director	Isabella Rossellini (4)	Actress
George C Scott	Actor	Colleen Dewhurst	Socialite
Walter Scott	Scottish novelist	Charlotte Charpentier	Daughter of French émigré
Steven Seagal (2)	Actor	Kelly Le Brock	Actress
Rudolf Seiber (1)	Production assistant	Marlene Dietrich	Actress
Peter Sellers	Actor	Anne Hayes (1)	Housewife
		Britt Ekland (2)	Actress
		Miranda Quarry (3)	Actress
		Lynne Frederick (4)	Actress
David O Selznick (2)	Director	Jennifer Jones (2)	Actress
Rudolf Serkin	Pianist	Irene Busch	Musician
William Shakespeare	Playwright	Ann Hathaway	Farmer's daughter
Omar Sharif	Actor and bridge player	Faten Hamama (1)	Actress
		Nadiya Aja (2)	Saudi tycoon's daughter
Artie Shaw	Bandleader	Lana Turner (1)	Actress
		Ava Gardner (2)	Actress
Bernard Shaw	Bodyguard	Patty Hearst	Heiress
George Bernard Shaw	Dramatist	Charlotte	Heiress
		Payne-Townshend	
Robert Shaw (2)	Actor	Mary Ure	Actress
Percy Bysshe Shelley	Poet	Mary Godwin	Writer
Richard Brinsley Sheridan	Irish dramatist	Elizabeth Linley	Composer's daughter
Jean Sibelius	Composer	Aino Järnefelt	General's daughter
Paul Simon	Singer and composer	Carrie Fisher (2)	Actress
Frank Sinatra	Singer	Ava Gardner (2)	Actress
		Mia Farrow (3)	Actress
		Barbara Marx (4)	Actress
Nikki Sixx	Motley Crue guitarist	Donna D'Errico	'Baywatch' actress
John Skeaping (1)	Sculptor	Barbara Hepworth	Sculptor
Cyril Smith	Pianist	Phyllis Sellick	Pianist
Mike Smith	TV presenter	Sarah Greene	TV presenter
Socrates	Philosopher	Xanthippe	Athenian
David Solkin	Businessman	Janet Street-Porter	TV presenter
Georg Solti	Conductor	Valerie Pitts	TV presenter
Robert Southey	Poet	Edith Fricker	Socialite
Phil Spector	Record producer	Veronica Bennett	Singer
Earl Charles Spencer	English nobleman	Victoria Lockwood	Model
Edmund Spenser	English poet	Elizabeth Boyle	Socialite
Steven Spielberg (2)	Director	Kate Capshaw (2)	Actress
		Amy Irving (1)	Actress
Henry Stafford	2nd Duke of Buckingham	Catherine Woodville	Sister-In-law of Edward IV
Sylvester Stallone	Actor	Sasha Czatv (1)	Theatre usher
		Brigitte Nielsen (2)	Actress
		Jennifer Flavin (3)	Model
Alvin Stardust (3)	Pop singer	Liza Goddard	Actress
Ringo Starr	Musician	Maureen Cox (1)	Childhood sweetheart
		Barbara Bach (2)	Actress
Anthony Steele	Actor	Anita Ekberg	Actress
Rod Steiger (1)	Actor	Claire Bloom	Actress
Chris Stein	Guitarist	Deborah Harry	Singer
(common law)		(common law)	
Robert Stephens	Actor	Maggie Smith	Actress
Robert Louis Stevenson	Author	Fanny Osbourne	Actress
Dave Stewart	Musician	Siobhan Fahey	Singer
Patrick Stewart	Actor ('Startrek')	Wendy Neuss	Producer ('Startrek')
Rod Stewart	Singer	Alana Hamilton (1)	Model
		Rachel Hunter (2)	Model
Thomas Stewart	Baritone	Evelyn Lear	Soprano
Alfred Stieglitz	US photographer	Georgia O' Keeffe	US painter
Ben Stiller	Actor	Christine Taylor	Actress

Sting	Singer	Frances Tomelty (1)	Actress
		Trudi Styler (2)	Actress
Leopold Stokowski	Conductor	Olga Samaroff (1)	Pianist
John Stonehouse	Politician	Sheila Buckley	Secretary
Richard Strauss	Composer	Pauline de Ahna	Soprano
Igor Stravinsky	Composer	Catherine Nossenko (1)	Stravinsky's cousin
		Vera de Bosset Sudekeine (2)	Ballet dancer
Roy Strong	Writer and historian	Julia Trevelyan Oman	Designer
Josef Suk	Violinist	Otilie Dvořák	Daughter of Antonin Dvořák
Clive Swift (1)	Author	Margaret Drabble	Novelist
James Taylor	Composer	Carly Simon	Singer
Robert Taylor	Actor	Barbara Stanwyck	Actress
Pyotr Tchaikovsky	Composer	Antonina Miliukova	Pupil of Tchaikovsky
William Temple	Diplomat and essayist	Dorothy Osborne	Daughter of governor of Guernsey
David Teniers the Younger	Flemish painter	Anna Brueghel	Daughter of Jan Brueghel
Jon Tenney	Actor	Teri Hatcher	Actress
Denis Thatcher	Businessman	Margaret Kempson (1)	Housewife
		Margaret Roberts (2)	Politician
John Thaw (2)	Actor	Sheila Hancock	Actress
Ben Thomas (2)	Actor	Roseanne Barr	Actress
Billy Bob Thornton	Actor	Cynda Williams (1)	Actress
		Angelina Jolie (2)	Actress
Jeremy Thorpe (2)	Politician	Marion Stein	Musician
Tom Thumb	Circus performer	Lavinia Warren	Circus performer
Mike Todd	Showman	Elizabeth Taylor (3)	Actress
		Joan Blondell (2)	Actress
Mel Tormé (1)	Singer	Janette Scott (3)	
Rip Torn	Actor	Geraldine Page	Actress
Tico Torres	Pop musician (Bon Jovi)	Eva Herzigova	Model
Bill Travers	Actor	Virginia McKenna (2)	Actress
John Travolta	Actor	Kelly Preston	Actress
Owen Tudor (1)	Grandfather of Henry VII	Catherine	Valois princess
Ted Turner (3)	Media mogul	Jane Fonda	Actress
Mike Tyson	Boxer	Robin Givens (1)	Actress
		Monica Turner (2)	Actress
Inaki Urdangarin	Handball player	Christina	Spanish Infanta
Roger Vadim	Film director	Brigitte Bardot (1)	Actress
		Jane Fonda (2)	Actress
Peter Vaughan	Actor	Billie Whitelaw (1)	Actress
		Lillias Walker (2)	Actress
Giuseppe Verdi	Composer	Margherita Barezzi (1)	Daughter of Verdi's sponsor
		Giuseppina Strepponi (2)	Soprano
Tony Visconti	Record producer	May Pang	Author
Richard Wagner	Composer	Minna Planer (1)	Opera singer and actress
		Cosima Von Bülow (2)	Franz Liszt's daughter
Robert Wagner	Actor	Natalie Wood (1) and (3)	Actress
		Marion Marshall (2)	Actress
		Jill St John (4)	Actress
Robert Walker (1)	Actor	Jennifer Jones	Actress
John Warner (7)	Senator	Elizabeth Taylor	Actress
George Washington	US president	Martha Custis	Socialite
Dennis Waterman	Actor	Patricia Maynard (2)	Actress
		Rula Lenska (3)	Actress
George Frederick Watts (1)	English painter	Ellen Terry	English actress
Carl Wayne	Actor and singer	Sue Hanson	Actress
Kurt Weill	Composer	Lotte Lenya	Actress and singer
Mark Weinberg	Businessman	Anouska Hempel	Actress
Orson Welles (2)	Actor and director	Rita Hayworth (2)	Actress
HG Wells	Author	Amy Robbins	Student
Franz Werfel (3)	Writer	Alma Maria Schindler	Musician
Timothy West	Actor	Prunella Scales	Actress
James McNeill Whistler	Artist	Beatrix Godwin	Widow of EW Godwin (architect)
Desmond Wilcox	Producer	Esther Rantzen	Broadcaster
Herbert Wilcox	Film director	Anna Neagle	Actress
Oscar Wilde	Playwright and novelist	Constance Lloyd	Socialite
Gene Wilder	Actor	Gilda Radner	Psychotherapist
Michael Wilding	Actor	Elizabeth Taylor (2)	Actress
		Margaret Leighton (4)	Actress

FAMOUS PEOPLE

William III	British king	*Mary II*	*British queen*
William IV	British king	*Adelaide*	*German noblewoman*
Andy Williams	Singer	*Claudine Longet*	*Actress*
Hugh Williams	TV magnate	*Sue Lawley*	*Broadcaster*
Michael Williams	Actor	*Judi Dench*	*Actress*
Bruce Willis	Actor	*Demi Moore*	*Actress*
Brian Wolfe (2)	Theatre producer	*Jill Browne*	*Actress*
Stevie Wonder	Musician	*Syreeta Wright*	*Singer*
Edward Woodward	Actor	*Venetia Barrett (1)*	*Actress*
		Michelle Dotrice (2)	*Actress*
Leonard Woolf	Publisher and writer	*Virginia Stephen*	*Novelist*
William Wordsworth	Poet	*Mary Hutchinson*	*Socialite*
Billy Wright	Footballer	*Joy Beverley*	*Singer*
William Wyler	Film director	*Margaret Sullavan*	*Actress*
Bill Wyman	Rolling Stone	*Astrid Lundstrom (2)*	*Model*
		Mandy Smith (3)	*Model*
Michael Wynn Jones	Publisher	*Delia Smith*	*Cookery writer*
WB Yeats	Poet	*Georgie Hyde-Lees*	*Socialite*
Sergei Yessenin	Poet	*Isadora Duncan (1)*	*Dancer*
Gig Young	Actor	*Elizabeth Montgomery (3)*	*Actress*
Stuart Zender	Musician	*Melanie Blatt*	*Pop singer*
Zeus	Greek supreme god	*Metis (1)*	*Greek sea nymph*
		Themis (2)	*Daughter of Gaia and Uranus*
		Hera (3)	*Sister of Zeus*
Efrem Zimbalist	Violinist	*Alma Gluck*	*Soprano*
Antonio Zucchi	Venetian painter	*Angelica Kaufmann*	*Swiss painter*

Middle Names: Ordered by Middle Name

First Name	Middle Name(s)	Surname	
Søren	**Aabye**	KIERKEGAARD	Danish philosopher
Herbert	**Aaron**	HAUPTMAN	US physicist
Elvis	**Aaron**	PRESLEY	US singer
Selman	**Abraham**	WAKSMAN	US biochemist
James	**Abram**	GARFIELD	US president
Claude	**Achille**	DEBUSSY	Composer
John	**Addington**	SYMONDS	Author
Hans	**Adolph**	KREBS	British biochemist
Walter	**Adolf**	GROPIUS	Architect
Henry	**Agard**	WALLACE	US vice-president
Robin	**Airling**	HANBURY-TENISON	Explorer
Chester	**Alan**	ARTHUR	US president
Bob	**Alan**	DYLAN	Singer and composer
Graham	**Alan**	GOOCH	Cricketer
James	**Albert**	MICHENER	Author
Francis (Frank)	**Albert**	SINATRA	Singer
Hans	**Albrecht**	BETHE	US physicist
John	**Alden**	CARPENTER	Musician and businessman
Gene	**Alden**	HACKMAN	Actor
Nelson	**Aldrich**	ROCKEFELLER	US vice-president
Nicholas	**Alexander**	FALDO	Golfer
Alan	**Alexander**	MILNE	Author
Robert	**Alexander**	RUNCIE	Archbishop of Canterbury
Peter	**Alexander**	USTINOV	Actor and writer
Henry	**Alfred**	KISSINGER	US statesman
Marcus	**Algernon**	ADAMS	Photographer
Enid	**Algerine**	BAGNOLD	Author
Ellen	**Alice**	TERRY	Actress
Charles	**Allston**	COLLINS	Artist
Tony	**Aloysius**	HANCOCK	TV character
James	**Aloysius**	HANSOM	Designer
Thomas	**Alva**	EDISON	Inventor
Pedro	**Alvarez**	CABRAL	Navigator
Elmer	**Ambrose**	SPERRY	US inventor
Billy	**Ambrose**	WRIGHT	Footballer
Meyer	**Amschel**	ROTHSCHILD	German financier
Nikolai	**Andreievich**	RIMSKY-KORSAKOV	Composer
Michael J	**Andrew**	FOX	Actor

First Name	Middle Name(s)	Surname	
Miguel	**Angel**	ASTURIAS	Guatemalan poet
George	**Anthony**	NEWLEY	Actor and singer
Giacomo	**Antonio**	PUCCINI	Composer
Hendrik	**Antoon**	LORENTZ	Dutch physicist
Benjamin	**Apthorp**	GOULD	US astronomer
Spangler	**Arlington**	BROUGH	Actor
Enoch	**Arnold**	BENNETT	Author
Philip	**Arnold**	HESELTINE	Composer
Eric	**Arthur**	BLAIR	Author
Kenneth	**Arthur**	DODD	Comedian
Cliff	**Arthur**	MICHELMORE	Broadcaster
Robert	**Arthur Talbot**	CECIL	British prime minister
Arthur	**Asher**	MILLER	US playwright
Pierre	**Athanase**	LAROUSSE	French publisher
George	**Augustus**	ARLISS	Actor
Charles	**Augustus**	LINDBERGH	US aviator
Francis	**Aungier**	LONGFORD	Prison reformer
Richard	**Austen**	BUTLER	Politician
Henry	**Austin**	DOBSON	Poet
Erik	**Axel**	KARLFELDT	Swedish poet
Julia	**Babette Sarah**	NEUBERGER	Rabbi
Thomas	**Babington**	MACAULAY	Author
Brian	**Baden**	MOORE	Football commentator
Thomas	**Bailey**	ALDRICH	Author
Jane	**Baillie**	CARLYLE	Wife of Thomas Carlyle
Lyndon	**Baines**	JOHNSON	US president
Ronnie	**Balfour**	CORBETT	Comedian
Robert	**Banks**	JENKINSON	British prime minister
Robert	**Bannatyne**	FINLAY	Politician
Jocelyn	**Barbara**	HEPWORTH	Sculptor
Ruth	**Barbara**	RENDELL	Crime novelist
Peter	**Barker Howard**	MAY	Cricketer
John	**Barry**	HUMPHRIES	Comedian and writer
Isaac	**Bashevis**	SINGER	Writer
George	**Basil**	HUME	Cardinal
Upton	**Beall**	SINCLAIR	US novelist
Claire	**Berenice**	RAYNER	Broadcaster
Alan	**Beresford**	B' STARD	TV character ('New Statesman')
Norman	**Beresford**	TEBBIT	Politician
Colin	**Berkeley**	MOYNIHAN	Politician
Henry	**Bernard**	LEVIN	Journalist and author
Desmond	**Bernard**	O'CONNOR	Entertainer
George	**Bernard**	SHAW	Author
John (Jack)	**Berry**	HOBBS	English cricketer
George	**Biddell**	AIRY	Astronomer
Rutherford	**Birchard**	HAYES	US president
John	**Bird**	SUMNER	Archbishop of Canterbury
John ('Dizzy')	**Birks**	GILLESPIE	Jazz trumpeter
Bill	**Blackledge**	BEAUMONT	Rugby union player
Joseph	**Blanco**	WHITE	English poet
Cecil	**Blount**	DE MILLE	Film director
John	**Bodkin**	ADAMS	Doctor and murder suspect
Christian	**Boehmer**	ANFINSEN	US biochemist
Wilson	**Boit**	KIPKETER	Kenyan s/chase WR 13/8/97
Ulrich	**Bonnell**	PHILLIPS	US historian
Ernst	**Boris**	CHAIN	German biochemist
Arthur	**Bowden**	ASKEY	Comedian
Richard	**Bowdler**	SHARPE	Ornithologist
Lester	**Bowles**	PEARSON	Canadian politician
Leslie	**Bowyer**	CHARTERIS	Author
John	**Boyd**	DUNLOP	Inventor
John	**Boynton**	PRIESTLEY	Author
William	**Bradford**	SHOCKLEY	American physicist
James	**Branch**	CABELL	Novelist
Charles	**Brenton**	HUGGINS	American surgeon
William	**Bridges**	ADAMS	Engineer
George	**Brinton**	McCLELLAN	US soldier
Roy	**Broadbent**	FULLER	Poet
Amos	**Bronson**	ALCOTT	Transcendentalist
Susan	**Brownell**	ANTHONY	Suffragette

First Name	Middle Name(s)	Surname	
Marshall	**Bruce**	MATHERS III	Rap artist (aka Eminem)
Lawrence	**Bruno Nero**	DALLAGLIO	Rugby player
Lee	**Buck**	TREVINO	American golfer
Matthew	**Bunker**	RIDGWAY	US soldier
Charles	**Burgess**	FRY	Sportsman
Walter	**Burley**	GRIFFIN	US architect
Lawrence	**Burnett**	GOWING	Painter
Robert	**Burns**	WOODWARD	American chemist
Stephen	**Burton**	LANCASTER	Actor
Paul	**Bustill Le Roy**	ROBESON	Actor
William	**Butler**	YEATS	Author
James	**Byron**	DEAN	Actor
Percy	**Bysshe**	SHELLEY	Poet
John	**Cabell**	BRECKINRIDGE	US vice-president
Henry	**Cabot**	LODGE	US senator
Ben	**Caine**	HOLLIOAKE	English cricketer
John	**Caldwell**	CALHOUN	US vice-president
Hugh	**Callum**	LAURIE	Actor and comedian
John	**Calvin**	COOLIDGE	US president
Edward	**Calvin**	KENDALL	American chemist
John	**Cameron**	MORTON	Journalist
King	**Camp**	GILLETTE	Inventor
Donald	**Campbell**	DEWAR	British politician
Patricia	**Campbell**	HEARST	Heiress
Archibald	**Campbell**	TAIT	Archbishop of Canterbury
Christopher	**Carandini**	LEE	Actor
John	**Carew**	ECCLES	Australian neurophysiologist
Peter	**Carl**	FABERGÉ	Russian goldsmith
Peter	**Carl**	GOLDMARK	Inventor
Wilhelm	**Carl**	GRIMM	Folklorist
Linus	**Carl**	PAULING	Scientist
Daniel	**Carleton**	GAJDUSEK	US virologist
Hugh	**Carleton**	GREENE	Journalist and broadcaster
Percy	**Carlyle**	GILCHRIST	Metallurgist
Gertrude	**Caroline**	EDERLE	US swimmer
Hugh	**Caswell Tremenheere**	DOWDING	RAF chief
Maureen	**Catherine**	CONNOLLY	Tennis pro
George	**Catlett**	MARSHALL	US soldier and statesman
Lawrence (Larry)	**Cecil**	ADLER	Musician
James	**Cellan**	JONES	Film director
Thomas	**Chandler**	HALIBURTON	Canadian writer
Joel	**Chandler**	HARRIS	Author
Samuel	**Chao Chung**	TING	US physicist
Frederick	**Chapman**	ROBBINS	US physiologist
Kenneth	**Charles**	BRANAGH	Actor
Tjalling	**Charles**	KOOPMANS	US economist
Anthony	**Charles Lynton**	BLAIR	Politician
Richard	**Charles Nicholas**	BRANSON	Entrepreneur
Denis	**Charles Scott**	COMPTON	Cricketer
Rodney	**Charlton**	TROTTER	'Fools and Horses' character
Walter	**Chauncy**	CAMP	American footballer
Rupert	**Chawner**	BROOKE	Poet
Johann	**Christian**	BACH	Composer
Patrick	**Christopher**	STEPTOE	Gynaecologist
Dennis	**Christopher George**	POTTER	Playwright
Chris	**Clairmonte**	LEWIS	Cricketer
Herbert	**Clark**	HOOVER	US president
William	**Claude**	FIELDS	Comedian and actor
Roy	**Claxton**	ACUFF	Country musician
Harold	**Clayton**	LLOYD	US film comedian
Thomas	**Clayton**	WOLFE	Novelist
Elizabeth	**Cleghorn**	GASKELL	Writer
Edmund	**Clerihew**	BENTLEY	Writer
Marcus	**Cocceius**	NERVA	Roman emperor
John	**Cody Fiddler**	SIMPSON	News reporter
Michael	**Colin**	COWDREY	Cricketer
Norman	**Colin**	DEXTER	Author
Stephen	**Collins**	FOSTER	US songwriter
Mel	**Columcille**	GIBSON	Actor
Louis	**Comfort**	TIFFANY	Glassmaker

First Name	Middle Name(s)	Surname	
Milner	**Connorton**	GRAY	Graphic designer
George	**Corley**	WALLACE	Governor of Alabama
Gianfranco	**Corsi**	ZEFFIRELLI	Film director
Alfred	**Cort**	HADDON	Anthropologist
Ingvar	**Costa**	CARLSSON	Swedish politician
Reginald	**Cotterell**	BUTLER	Sculptor
John	**Couch**	ADAMS	Astronomer
Ludovic	**Coverley**	KENNEDY	Broadcaster
John	**Cowdery**	KENDREW	English biochemist
Cornelius	**Crane**	CHASE	Actor
Elzie	**Crisler**	SEGAR	US strip cartoonist
Betsy	**Cromer**	BYARS	Novelist
John	**Crowe**	RANSOM	US poet and critic
Dorothy	**Crowfoot**	HODGKIN	Scientist
William	**Cullen**	BRYANT	Poet
Gene	**Curran**	KELLY	Dancer
Gordon	**Cuthbert**	GREENIDGE	Cricketer
Len	**Cyril**	DEIGHTON	Novelist
Herman	**Cyril**	McNEILE	Author
Austin	**Danger**	POWERS	Film character
Gabriel	**Daniel**	FAHRENHEIT	Physicist
Arnold	**Daniel**	PALMER	Golfer
Dwight	**David**	EISENHOWER	US president
Benny	**David**	GOODMAN	US jazz clarinetist
Jerome	**David**	SALINGER	Author
Joan	**Dawson**	BAKEWELL	Broadcaster
Alfred	**Day**	HERSHEY	US biologist
Humphrey	**De Forest**	BOGART	Actor
Everton	**Decourcey**	WEEKES	West Indian cricketer
Franklin	**Delano**	ROOSEVELT	US president
William	**Denby**	HANNA	US animated cartoonist
Danny	**Dennio**	BLANCHFLOWER	Footballer
Michael	**Denzil Xavier**	PORTILLO	Politician
Earl	**Derr**	BIGGERS	US novelist
Henri	**Desire**	LANDRU	French murderer
Andrew	**Dewar**	GIBB	Scottish jurist
Miles	**Dewey**	DAVIS	Jazz musician
James	**Dewey**	WATSON	US biologist
Maureen	**Diane**	LIPMAN	Actress
Michael	**Dibdin**	HESELTINE	Politician
John	**Dickson**	CARR	US detective writer
Richard	**Doddridge**	BLACKMORE	Author
Juan	**Domingo**	PERÓN	Argentinian president
Frederick	**Donald**	COGGAN	Archbishop of Canterbury
Harry	**Donald**	SECOMBE	Comedian and singer
Alan	**Donald**	WHICKER	Broadcaster
Stella	**Dorothea**	GIBBONS	Writer
Phyllis	**Dorothy**	JAMES	Authoress
Heber	**Doust**	CURTIS	US astronomer
Henry	**Drysdale**	DAKIN	Chemist
Donald	**Duart**	MACLEAN	English traitor
Thomas	**Duffus**	HARDY	Archivist
Charlie	**Dunbar**	BROAD	Philosopher
John	**Dunmore**	LANG	Clergyman
Bob	**Dylan**	WILLIS	Cricketer
Anthony	**Dymoke**	POWELL	English novelist
James	**Earl**	CARTER	US president
Alfred	**Edgar**	COPPARD	Writer
John	**Edgar**	HOOVER	FBI director
Billy	**Edmund**	BUTLIN	Businessman
Ferdinand	**Edralin**	MARCOS	Filipino president
Lewis	**Edson**	WATERMAN	Inventor
Alfred	**Edward**	HOUSMAN	Author
Thomas	**Edward**	LAWRENCE	Author and soldier
Jonas	**Edward**	SALK	Biologist
Joseph	**Eggleston**	JOHNSTON	US soldier
Michael	**Elias**	BALCON	Film producer
Walt	**Elias**	DISNEY	Film producer
Gottlieb	**Eliel**	SAARINEN	Finnish/US architect
Mary	**Elizabeth**	PETERS	Pentathlete

First Name	Middle Name(s)	Surname	
Mai	**Elizabeth**	ZETTERLING	Actress and director
James	**Elroy**	FLECKER	Poet
Douglas	**Elton**	FAIRBANKS (Snr)	Actor
Charles	**Elwood**	YEAGER	US test pilot
George	**Emil**	PALADE	US biologist
Angelina	**Emily**	GRIMKE	US feminist
Barry	**Emmanuel**	TUCKWELL	Australian musician
John	**Enoch**	POWELL	British politician
George	**Eric**	NEWBY	Author
Oswald	**Ernald**	MOSLEY	British politician
Herbert	**Ernest**	BATES	Author
John	**Ernest**	STEINBECK	US novelist
Nigel	**Ernest James**	MANSELL	Racing driver
Robert	**Erskine**	CHILDERS	Writer
Richard	**Erskine Frere**	LEAKEY	Palaeontologist and naturalist
Bartolomé	**Estebàn**	MURILLO	Spanish painter
Maria	**Esther**	BUENO	Tennis player
Linda	**Esther**	GRAY	Scottish soprano
Willis	**Eugene**	LAMB	American physicist
Richard	**Evelyn**	BYRD	Explorer
Norman	**Everard**	BROOKES	Tennis player
William	**Ewart**	GLADSTONE	British prime minister
Adlai	**Ewing**	STEVENSON	US politician
Charles	**Farrar**	BROWNE	Humorist and writer
Pearl	**Fay**	WHITE	US actress
Igor	**Fedorovich**	STRAVINSKY	Composer
Isidor	**Feinstein**	STONE	US journalist
David	**Feodorovich**	OISTRAKH	Violinist
Carl	**Ferdinand**	CORI	American biochemist
Max	**Ferdinand**	PERUTZ	British biochemist
Ana	**Fidelia**	QUIROT	Cuban athlete
Dwight	**Filley**	DAVIS	Founder of Davis Cup
Oscar	**Fingal O'Flahertie Wills**	WILDE	Writer
Robin	**Finlayson**	COOK	Politician
Samuel	**Finley Breese**	MORSE	US inventor
Harlan	**Fiske**	STONE	US judge
John	**Fitzgerald**	KENNEDY	US president
Harry	**Flood**	BYRD	Politician
Lillian	**Florence**	HELLMAN	US playwright
Sarah	**Flower**	ADAMS	English poet
Chester	**Floyd**	CARLSON	US inventor
Sade	**Folasade**	ADU	Singer
Leopoldo	**Fortunato**	GALTIERI	Argentinian politician
Norman	**Foster**	RAMSEY	US physicist
Geoffrey	**Francis**	FISHER	Archbishop of Canterbury
Robert	**Francis**	KENNEDY	US politician
Donald	**Francis**	TOVEY	Pianist and composer
Daley	**Francis Morgan**	THOMPSON	Athlete
James	**Franciscus**	DURANTE	Entertainer
Charles	**François**	GOUNOD	Composer
Anatole	**François**	THIBAULT	Author
John	**Franklin**	CANDY	Actor
Samuel	**Franklin**	CODY	Aviator
John	**Franklin**	ENDERS	US bacteriologist
Billy	**Franklin**	GRAHAM	US evangelist
Robert	**Franklin**	STROUD	Birdman of Alcatraz
William	**Frederick**	CODY	Showman
Ronald	**Frederick**	DELDERFIELD	Author
Alexander	**Frederick**	DOUGLAS-HOME	British prime minister
Spencer	**Frederick**	GORE	Painter
George	**Frederick**	HANDEL	Composer
Walter	**Frederick (Fritz)**	MONDALE	US vice-president
Thomas	**Frognall**	DIBDIN	Librarian
Robert	**Gabriel**	MUGABE	Zimbabwean president
Mario	**Gabriele**	ANDRETTI	Racing driver
Sidonie	**Gabrielle**	COLETTE	Author
Matthew	**Galbraith**	PERRY	US naval officer
Warren	**Gamaliel**	HARDING	US president
Gabriel	**Garcia**	MARQUEZ	Columbian author
Jan	**Garrigue**	MASARYK	Czech statesman

First Name	Middle Name(s)	Surname	
Charles	**Gates**	DAWES	US vice-president
Johannes	**Gensfleisch**	GUTENBERG	German printer
Billy	**George**	BUNTER	Fictional character
Lawrence	**George**	DURRELL	Novelist
Rodney	**George**	LAVER	Tennis player
Roger	**George**	MOORE	Actor
Andre	**George**	PREVIN	Conductor
William	**Gerald**	GOLDING	Novelist
John	**Gerard**	BRAINE	Novelist
William	**Gershom**	COLLINGWOOD	Artist
Roger	**Gilbert**	BANNISTER	Athlete
William	**Gilbert**	GRACE	Cricketer
Ian	**Gillett**	CARMICHAEL	Actor
Eugene	**Gladstone**	O'NEILL	US playwright
William	**Gladstone**	STEWART	TV broadcaster/producer
Alton	**Glenn**	MILLER	Band leader
Charles	**Glover**	BARKLA	English physicist
Robson	**Golightly**	GREEN	Actor
Dean	**Gooderham**	ACHESON	US statesman
Sydney	**Goodsir**	SMITH	Poet
James	**Gordon**	BROWN	Politician
George	**Gordon**	BYRON	Poet
Neil	**Gordon**	KINNOCK	Politician
Harry	**Gordon**	SELFRIDGE	British merchant
Robert	**Graeme**	POLLOCK	Cricketer
Norman	**Graham**	HILL	Racing driver
James	**Graham**	BALLARD	Author
Frederick	**Grant**	BANTING	Physiologist
Lewis	**Grassic**	GIBBON	Novelist
Elisha	**Graves**	OTIS	Inventor
Charles	**Greely**	ABBOT	Astrophysicist
Emily	**Greene**	BALCH	US social reformer
Eldred	**Gregory**	PECK	Actor
Pelham	**Grenville**	WODEHOUSE	Author
Jack	**Griffith**	LONDON	US novelist
Thomas	**Griffiths**	WAINEWRIGHT	Art critic and murderer
Samuel	**Griswold**	GOODRICH	US publisher
Stephen	**Grover**	CLEVELAND	US president
James	**Grover**	THURBER	Humorist
Carl	**Gustav**	JUNG	Swiss psychiatrist
Magdi	**Habib**	YACOUB	Surgeon
Edvard	**Hagerup**	GRIEG	Norwegian composer
William	**Hale**	WHITE	Writer
Barbara	**Hamilton**	CARTLAND	Writer
George	**Hamilton**	GORDON	British prime minister
Charles	**Hamilton**	SORLEY	Poet
Glen	**Hammond**	CURTISS	US air pioneer
Terence	**Hanbury**	WHITE	Novelist
Fred	**Handel**	ELLIOTT	'Coronation Street' character
John	**Hanning**	SPEKE	Explorer
Martin	**Harcourt**	CHIVERS	Footballer
Charles	**Hard**	TOWNES	American physicist
Terence (Terry)	**Hardy**	WAITE	Religious adviser
Maurice	**Harold**	MACMILLAN	British prime minister
James	**Harold**	WILSON	British prime minister
Emma	**Harriet**	NICHOLSON	Politician
Roy	**Harris**	JENKINS	Politician
Kenneth	**Harry**	CLARKE	Politician
Francis	**Harry Compton**	CRICK	Biologist
Hawley	**Harvey**	CRIPPEN	Murderer
John	**Harvey**	KELLOGG	Inventor
Willis	**Haviland**	CARRIER	US inventor
Alfred	**Hawthorne**	HILL	Comedian
Mary	**Hayley**	BELL	Playwright
David	**Hayward**	BOWIE	Musician
Oliver	**Hazard**	PERRY	US naval officer
Publius	**Helvius**	PERTINAX	Roman emperor
Joan	**Henrietta**	COLLINS	Actress
Herbert	**Henry**	ASQUITH	British prime minister
William	**Henry**	CAVENDISH-BENTINCK	British prime minister

FAMOUS PEOPLE

First Name	Middle Name(s)	Surname	
Augustus	**Henry**	FITZROY	British prime minister
William	**Henry**	HARRISON	US president
Fiorello	**Henry**	LA GUARDIA	US politician
Richard	**Henry Simpson**	STILGOE	Songwriter and broadcaster
Robert	**Hepler**	LOWE	Actor
Horatio	**Herbert**	KITCHENER	Irish soldier and statesman
David	**Herbert**	LAWRENCE	Author
George	**Herbert Walker**	BUSH	US president
Elton	**Hercules**	JOHN	Singer and composer
John	**Herschel**	GLENN	US astronaut and politician
Cyrus	**Herzl**	GORDON	US Hebrew scholar
Margaret	**Hilda**	THATCHER	British prime minister
Virginia	**Hilda Brunette Maxwell**	BOTTOMLEY	Politician
Henry	**Hinchcliffe**	AINLEY	Actor
Dag	**Hjalmar Agne Carl**	HAMMARSKJÖLD	Swedish statesman
Arthur	**Holly**	COMPTON	Physicist
Eric	**Honeywood**	PARTRIDGE	Lexicographer
James	**Hopwood**	JEANS	Physicist and astronomer
Hubert	**Horatio**	HUMPHREY	US vice-president
Katharine	**Houghton**	HEPBURN	US actress
Walter	**Houser**	BRATTAIN	American physicist
Jeffrey	**Howard**	ARCHER	Author
Tasker	**Howard**	BLISS	Soldier and statesman
William	**Howard**	STEIN	US biochemist
William	**Howard**	TAFT	US president
Bernard	**Howell**	LEACH	English potter
William	**Howson**	TAYLOR	Potter
George	**Hoy**	FORMBY	Singer and musician
John	**Hoyer**	UPDIKE	Author
Elinor	**Hoyt**	WYLIE	US author
Thomas	**Huckle**	WELLER	US physiologist
Wystan	**Hugh**	AUDEN	Poet
Michael	**Hugh**	MEACHER	Politician
Hector	**Hugh**	MUNRO	Author
Mark	**Hume**	McCORMACK	Promoter
David	**Hunter**	HUBEL	US neurophysiologist
William	**Hunter Fisher**	CARSON	Jockey
Robert	**Hutchings**	GODDARD	US rocket pioneer
Leonid	**Ilich**	BREZHNEV	USSR president
Vladimir	**Ilyich**	LENIN	Russian revolutionary
Pyotr	**Ilyich**	TCHAIKOVSKY	Composer
Reginald	**Iolanthe**	PERRIN	TV character
Alexander	**Isaevich**	SOLZHENITSYN	Author
Jeremy	**Israel**	ISAACS	Arts mogul
George	**Ivan**	MORRISON	Singer and composer
James	**Jackson**	JEFFRIES	Boxing champion
Paul	**Jackson**	POLLOCK	US artist
Samuel	**Jackson**	SNEAD	Golfer
Lucinda	**Jane**	GREEN	Three-day eventer
Kiri	**Janette**	TE KANAWA	Opera singer
Abel	**Janszoon**	TASMAN	Navigator
Stanley	**Jasspon**	KUNITZ	US poet
William	**Jefferson**	HAGUE	Politician
William	**Jefferson Blyth**	CLINTON	US president
Michael	**Jeffrey**	JORDAN	US basketball player
Ada	**Jemima**	CROSSLEY	Australian contralto
John	**Jeremy**	THORPE	Politician
Gary	**Jim**	PLAYER	Golfer
Barbra	**Joan**	STREISAND	Singer
Liv	**Johanne**	ULLMANN	Norwegian actress
Stephen	**John**	FRY	Actor and author
Tony	**John**	HANCOCK	Comedy actor
Arthur	**John**	GIELGUD	Actor
Frederick	**John**	ROBINSON	British prime minister
Henry	**John**	TEMPLE	British prime minister
Jeremy	**John Durham**	ASHDOWN	Politician
Charles	**John Huffam**	DICKENS	Author
Ralph	**Johnson**	BUNCHE	American economist
Angelina	**Jolie**	VOIGHT	Actress
Irene	**Joliot**	CURIE	Nuclear physicist

First Name	Middle Name(s)	Surname	
Anders	**Jonas**	ANGSTROM	Physicist
Samuel	**Jones**	TILDEN	US politician
Richard	**Jordan**	GATLING	Inventor
Michael	**Joseph**	CAINE	Actor
Archibald	**Joseph**	CRONIN	Author
Bruce	**Joseph**	FORSYTH	Entertainer
Israel	**Joshua**	SINGER	Writer
Stephen	**Joshua**	SONDHEIM	Composer and lyricist
River	**Jude**	PHOENIX	Actor
Diane	**Julie**	ABBOTT	Politician
Ferdinand	**Julius**	COHN	Botanist
Annie	**Jump**	CANNON	US astronomer
Seamus	**Justin**	HEANEY	Poet
Aimo	**Kaarlo**	CAJANDER	Finnish politician
Niels	**Kai**	JERNE	Danish immunologist
Julius	**Kambarage**	NYERERE	Tanzanian president
Hastings	**Kamuzu**	BANDA	Malawi politician
Mohandas	**Karamchand**	GANDHI	Indian leader
Uma	**Karuna**	THURMAN	Actress
Haldan	**Keffer**	HARTLINE	US physiologist
Gilbert	**Keith**	CHESTERTON	Author
Will	**Keith**	KELLOGG	Inventor
Dennis	**Keith**	LILLEE	Australian cricketer
Lester	**Keith**	PIGGOTT	Jockey
Michael	**Kemp**	TIPPETT	Composer
Edward ('Duke')	**Kennedy**	ELLINGTON	Composer and pianist
Tom	**Kennerley**	WOLFE	Novelist
Edith	**Kermit**	ROOSEVELT	US First Lady
Laurence	**Kerr**	OLIVIER	Actor
Philip	**Kindred**	DICK	US writer
Henry	**Kirke**	BROWN	Sculptor
Ragnar	**Kittil**	FRISCH	Norwegian economist
Jerome	**Klapka**	JEROME	Author
Hablot	**Knight**	BROWNE	Illustrator
James	**Knox**	POLK	US president
Sally	**Kristen**	RIDE	US astronaut
Ian	**Lancaster**	FLEMING	English novelist
Raymond	**Landry**	POINCARÉ	French statesman
Edwin	**Landseer**	LUTYENS	English architect
Samuel	**Langhorne**	CLEMENS	Author
Mervyn	**Laurence**	PEAKE	Author and artist
Bernard	**Law**	MONTGOMERY	Field marshal
Edward	**Lawrie**	TATUM	US biochemist
James	**Leathes**	PRIOR	Politician
George	**Ledyard**	STEBBINS	US botanist
Sheldon	**Lee**	GLASHOW	US physicist
Dustin	**Lee**	HOFFMAN	Actor
Arthur	**Lehman**	GOODHART	US jurist
Walter	**Leland**	CRONKITE	US broadcaster
James	**Leonard**	CALLAGHAN	British prime minister
George	**Leonard**	CAREY	Archbishop
Geoffrey	**Leonard**	CHESHIRE	Philanthropist
Aldous	**Leonard**	HUXLEY	Novelist
Winston	**Leonard Spencer**	CHURCHILL	British prime minister
Nelly	**Leonie**	SACHS	Swedish poet and playwright
Mstislav	**Leopoldovich**	ROSTROPOVICH	Cellist
John	**Leslie**	PRESCOTT	Politician
Bob	**Leslie Townes**	HOPE	Comedian
Basil	**Lewis**	D'OLIVEIRA	Cricketer
David	**Lewis**	JACOBS	Broadcaster
Harry (Bing)	**Lillis**	CROSBY	Vocalist and actor
Adam	**Lindsay**	GORDON	Australian poet
John	**Liptrot**	HATTON	Composer
Chris	**Livingstone**	EUBANK	Boxer
Adam	**Llewellyn De Vere**	ADAMANT	Fictional TV character
James	**Logie**	ROBERTSON	Poet
Val	**Logsdon**	FITCH	US physicist
Hugh	**Longbourne**	CALLENDAR	Physicist
Ezra	**Loomis**	POUND	Poet
Siegfried	**Lorraine**	SASSOON	Poet

First Name	Middle Name(s)	Surname	
Carl	Lotus	BECKER	US historian
John	Loughborough	PEARSON	Architect
Esther	Louise	RANTZEN	TV presenter
Thomas	Love	PEACOCK	Novelist and poet
Thomas	Lovell	BEDDOES	Poet and physiologist
Verney	Lovett	CAMERON	Explorer
Anita	Lucia	RODDICK	Businesswoman
Jacques	Lucien Jean	DELORS	European politician
Caroline	Lucretia	HERSCHEL	Astronomer
Lazarus	Ludwig	ZAMENHOF	Inventor of Esperanto
Jacob	Ludwig Carl	GRIMM	Folklorist
Maria	Lurdes	MUTOLA	Mozambican athlete
Jean	Lyndsey Torren	MARSH	Actress
Kenneth	Mackenzie	CLARK	Art historian
Michael	Mackintosh	FOOT	Politician
Bruce	MacLeish	DERN	US actor
William	Maddock	BAYLISS	Physiologist
Eartha	Mae	KITT	Singer
William	Makepeace	THACKERAY	Author
onald	Malcolm	CAMPBELL	Car and boat racer
Gerald	Malcolm	DURRELL	Writer and naturalist
James	Mallahan	CAIN	Writer
Alice	Malsenior	WALKER	US novelist
Gerard	Manley	HOPKINS	Poet
Vosdanig	Manoog	ADOIAN	Painter
Cassius	Marcellus	CLAY	Boxer
Leon	Marcus	URIS	US author
William	Marcy	TWEED	US politician and criminal
Penelope	Margaret	LIVELY	Writer
Erich	Maria	REMARQUE	Author
Victor	Marie	HUGO	French writer
Dylan	Marlais	THOMAS	Poet
John	Marlan	POINDEXTER	US naval officer
David	Martin Scott	STEEL	Politician
John	Marwood	CLEESE	Actor
Meryl	Mary Louise	STREEP	Actress
Thomas	Massa	ALSAGER	Newspaper manager
Thomas	Masterman	HARDY	Naval officer
Kenneth	Mathieson	DALGLISH	Footballer
Alan	Mathison	TURING	Mathematician
James	Matthew	BARRIE	Author
Gerald	Maurice	EDELMAN	US biochemist
Hugh	Maxwell	CASSON	Architect
Liza	May	MINNELLI	Singer
Quintin	McGarel	HOGG	Politician
James	McGill	BUCHANAN	American economist
Edwin	McMasters	STANTON	US statesman
Frank	Meadow	SUTCLIFFE	Photographer
Alexander	Meigs	HAIG	US soldier
Friedrich	Melchior	GRIMM	Journalist
Maria	Meneghini	CALLAS	Operatic soprano
Richard	Mentor	JOHNSON	US vice-president
Iain	Menzies	BANKS	Author
Isaac	Merritt	SINGER	US inventor
Robert	Merton	SOLOW	American economist
William	Mervyn	PICKWOAD	Actor
Ian	Michael	CHAPPELL	Cricketer
Arthur	Michael	RAMSEY	Archbishop of Canterbury
Arthur	Michell	RANSOME	Author
Frank	Michler	CHAPMAN	Ornithologist
John	Middleton	MURRY	Writer and critic
George	Mifflin	DALLAS	US vice-president
Richard	Milhous	NIXON	US president
Ernest	Millar	HEMINGWAY	American novelist
Dorothy	Miller	RICHARDSON	English novelist
John	Millington	SYNGE	Author
Thomas	Milner	GIBSON	Politician
Philip	Milton	ROTH	Novelist
Samora	Moises	MACHEL	Mozambique president
Charles	Monroe	SCHULZ	US cartoonist

First Name	Middle Name(s)	Surname	
Augustus	**Montague**	TOPLADY	Clergyman and hymnist
Edward	**Montgomery**	CLIFF	Actor
Sarah	**Moore**	GRIMKE	US feminist
Edward	**Moore**	KENNEDY	US politician
Edward	**Morgan**	FORSTER	Author
Barry	**Morris**	GOLDWATER	US politician
Bill	**Morris**	LAWRY	Australian cricketer
Jack	**Morris**	ROSENTHAL	Playwright
Frank	**Mortimer Magilinne**	WORRELL	Cricketer
Henry	**Morton**	STANLEY	Explorer and journalist
John	**Moses**	BROWNING	Gunsmith and inventor
Stephen	**Moulton**	BABCOCK	US agricultural chemist
Kenesaw	**Mountain**	LANDIS	Baseball commissioner
Desmond	**Mpilo**	TUTU	South African prelate
Joshua	**Mqabuko Nyongolo**	NKOMO	Zimbabwean politician
Nicholas	**Murray**	BUTLER	US educationist
Christopher	**Murray**	GRIEVE	Poet
Michael	**Murray**	HORDERN	Actor
John	**Nance**	GARNER	US vice-president
Maggie	**Natalie**	SMITH	Actress
Christian	**Neethling**	BARNARD	Surgeon
Pablo	**Neftali Reyes**	NERUDA	Poet
Leon	**Neil**	COOPER	US physicist
Omar	**Nelson**	BRADLEY	US soldier
Johann	**Nepomuk**	HUMMEL	Austrian pianist
Johann	**Nepomuk**	MAELZEL	German inventor
Bob	**Nesta**	MARLEY	Musician
Arthur	**Neville**	CHAMBERLAIN	Politician
Sebastian	**Newbold**	COE	Athlete and politician
Godfrey	**Newbold**	HOUNSFIELD	English electrical engineer
Edith	**Newbold**	WHARTON	Author
Joseph	**Nicéphore**	NIEPCE	Inventor
Conrad	**Nicholson**	HILTON	Businessman
Louis	**Nicolas**	VAUQUELIN	Chemist
Herbert	**Nigel**	GRESLEY	Locomotive engineer
Florence	**Nightingale**	GRAHAM	Beautician
Boris	**Nikolayevich**	YELTSIN	Russian president
Dirk	**Niven**	BOGARDE	Actor
Alfred	**North**	WHITEHEAD	Philosopher and mathematician
Cyril	**Northcote**	PARKINSON	Political scientist
Oliver	**Norville**	HARDY	Actor
William	**Nunn**	LIPSCOMB	US chemist
Thomas	**Octave Murdoch**	SOPWITH	Aircraft designer
Frederick	**Ogden**	NASH	Poet
Donald	**Olding**	HEBB	Canadian psychologist
Robert	**Oliver**	REED	British actor
David	**Oliver**	SELZNICK	US cinema mogul
Donald	**Oliver**	SOPER	Methodist minister
Judi	**Olivia**	DENCH	Actress
Henri	**Omer**	PÉTAIN	French statesman
James	**Orchard**	HALLIWELL-PHILLIPPS	Shakespearean scholar
Ronald	**Ossary**	DUNLOP	Irish painter
Hamilton	**Othanel**	SMITH	US molecular biologist
Selma	**Ottiliana Lovisa**	LAGERLOF	Swedish novelist
Robert	**Oxton**	BOLT	Playwright
George	**Paget**	THOMSON	English physicist
Richard	**Palethorpe**	TODD	Actor
Publius	**Papinius**	STATIUS	Roman poet
David	**Paradine**	FROST	Interviewer and presenter
Clifton	**Parmelee**	WEBB	Actor
Levi	**Parsons**	MORTON	US vice-president
James	**Patrick**	DONLEAVY	Author
Nigel	**Paul**	KENNEDY	Violinist
James	**Paul**	MCCARTNEY	Musician and composer
Anton	**Pavlovich**	CHEKHOV	Russian author
George	**Peabody**	GOOCH	Politician
Walter	**Percy**	CHRYSLER	Automobile manufacturer
Charles	**Percy**	SNOW	Author
Vladimir	**Petrovich**	KUTS	Russian athlete
Francis	**Peyton**	ROUS	American pathologist

First Name	Middle Name(s)	Surname	
Anthony	**Philip**	HOPKINS	Actor
Archibald	**Philip**	PRIMROSE	British prime minister
Georg	**Philipp**	TELEMANN	Composer
Harry	**Philmore**	LANGDON	US comedian
Noël	**Pierce**	COWARD	Actor and dramatist
Samuel	**Pierpont**	LANGLEY	US aeronautic pioneer
Hilaire	**Pierre**	BELLOC	Writer
Lionel	**Pigot**	JOHNSON	Poet
Leslie	**Poles**	HARTLEY	Author
Klas	**Pontus**	ARNOLDSON	Swedish politician
James	**Prescott**	JOULE	Physicist
John	**Presper**	ECKERT	American inventor
Bob	**Primrose**	WILSON	Goalkeeper and broadcaster
Bob	**Prometheus**	FITZSIMMONS	Boxer
Arthur	**Quiller**	COUCH	Man of letters
John	**Quincy**	ADAMS	US president
Edward (Ted)	**Ralph**	DEXTER	Cricketer
James	**Ramsay**	MACDONALD	British prime minister
William	**Randal**	CREMER	Nobel laureate
Leroy	**Randle**	GRUMMAN	US aircraft pioneer
Joseph	**Randolf**	ACKERLEY	Author
Philip	**Ranulph**	DE GLANVILLE	Rugby Union player
Clement	**Raphael**	FREUD	Liberal politician
Michael	**Ray Dibdin**	HESELTINE	Politician
Tyrus	**Raymond**	COBB	Baseball player
Anna	**Raymond**	MASSEY	Actress
Daniel	**Raymond**	MASSEY	Actor
Brian	**Rayner**	COOK	English baritone
Miller	**Reece**	HUTCHINSON	Inventor
Edward	**Regan**	MURPHY	US comedian
Georges	**Remi**	HERGÉ	Belgian cartoonist
Jaques	**René**	CHIRAC	Prime minister
Christian	**René**	DE DUVE	Belgian biochemist
John	**Richard**	SCHLESINGER	Film director
Humphrey	**Richard Adeane**	LYTTELTON	Musician
Nigel	**Richard Patton**	DEMPSTER	Gossip columnist
Henry	**Rider**	HAGGARD	Novelist
Howard	**Robard**	HUGHES	Businessman
Ian	**Robert**	MAXWELL	Businessman
Sheridan	**Robert**	MORLEY	Author and broadcaster
Trevor	**Robert**	NUNN	Theatre director
Christopher	**Robert**	SMITH	British politician
Henry	**Robinson**	LUCE	US magazine publisher
Joseph	**Roland**	BARBERA	US animated cartoonist
Nelson	**Rolihlahla**	MANDELA	South African president
Kenneth	**Ronald**	ROSEWALL	Tennis player
John	**Ronald Reuel**	TOLKIEN	Author
Elizabeth	**Rosemond**	TAYLOR	Actress
Henry	**Rowley**	BISHOP	Composer
John	**Roy**	MAJOR	British prime minister
Benjamin	**Roy**	MOTTELSON	Danish physicist
Johann	**Rudolf**	WYSS	Swiss writer
Gerald	**Rudolph**	FORD	US president
William	**Rufus de Vane**	KING	US vice-president
Keith	**Rupert**	MURDOCH	Businessman
John	**Rushworth**	JELLICOE	Naval commander
David	**Russell**	LANGE	New Zealand politician
Steve	**Russell**	RACE	Broadcaster
Carlos	**Saavedra**	LAMAS	Argentinian jurist
Garfield	**St Aubrun**	SOBERS	Cricketer
Ahmed	**Salman**	RUSHDIE	Author
Richard	**Samuel**	ATTENBOROUGH	Actor
Baruch	**Samuel**	BLUMBERG	US biochemist
Robert	**Sanderson**	MULLIKEN	American chemist
Cherilyn (Cher)	**Sarkisian**	LAPIERRE	Singer
Arthur	**Sarsfield**	WARD	Author
Carlos	**Saul**	MENEM	Argentinian politician
Walter	**Savage**	LANDOR	Writer
Victor	**Sawdon**	PRITCHETT	Writer and critic
Wilfrid	**Scawen**	BLUNT	Poet

First Name	Middle Name(s)	Surname	
James	**Schoolcraft**	SHERMAN	US vice-president
William	**Schwenck**	GILBERT	Librettist
Jimmy	**Scott**	CONNORS	Tennis player
Cecil	**Scott**	FORESTER	Author
Michael	**Scudamore**	REDGRAVE	Actor
Peter	**Seamus**	O'TOOLE	Irish actor
Johann	**Sebastian**	BACH	Composer
John	**Selwyn**	GUMMER	Politician
Tiberius	**Sempronius**	GRACCHUS	Roman statesman
Sergei	**Sergeyevich**	PROKOFIEV	Composer
William	**Seward**	BURROUGHS	Author
Clarence	**Seward**	DARROW	US lawyer
Frederick (Freddy)	**Sewards**	TRUEMAN	Cricketer
Robert	**Seymour**	BRIDGES	Poet
Jane	**Seymour**	FONDA	Actress
Arthur	**Seymour**	SULLIVAN	Composer
Hugh	**Seymour**	WALPOLE	Novelist
Edward	**Sheriff**	CURTIS	US photographer
Charles	**Sherwood**	STRATTON	Circus performer
Philip	**Showalter**	HENCH	American physician
Ulysses	**Simpson**	GRANT	US president
Harry	**Sinclair**	LEWIS	US novelist
Frederick	**Sleigh**	ROBERTS	British soldier
Simon	**Smith**	KUZNETS	US economist
Aristotle	**Socrates**	ONASSIS	Shipping magnate
Canaan	**Sodindo**	BANANA	Zimbabwe president
William	**Somerset**	MAUGHAM	Author
Richard	**Southwell**	BOURKE	Earl of Mayo
John	**Spedan**	LEWIS	Businessman
Charlie	**Spencer**	CHAPLIN	Comedy actor
Herbert	**Spencer**	GASSER	US physiologist
Henry	**Spencer**	MOORE	Sculptor
Elizabeth	**Sprague**	COOLIDGE	American pianist
Stavros	**Spyros**	NIARCHOS	Greek ship owner
Richard	**Stafford**	CRIPPS	Politician
Thomas	**Stamford**	RAFFLES	Colonial administrator
Clive	**Staples**	LEWIS	Author
Thomas	**Stearns**	ELIOT	Poet
Gavin	**Steel**	STRANG	Politician
Greg	**Stephen**	CHAPPELL	Cricketer
Laurence	**Stephen**	LOWRY	Artist
Hunter	**Stockton**	THOMPSON	US writer
Robert	**Strange**	McNAMARA	Businessman
John	**Stuart**	BLACKIE	Scholar
Jenny	**Susan**	PITMAN	Racehorse trainer
Henrietta	**Swan**	LEAVITT	US astronomer
Pearl	**Sydenstricker**	BUCK	Author
William	**Sydney**	PORTER	Author
John	**Taliaferro**	THOMPSON	US soldier and inventor
Booker	**Taliaferro**	WASHINGTON	US educationalist
William	**Tatem**	TILDEN	US tennis player
Phineas	**Taylor**	BARNUM	Showman
Barbara	**Taylor**	BRADFORD	Novelist
Samuel	**Taylor**	COLERIDGE	Poet
Charles	**Taze**	RUSSELL	Religious leader
William	**Tecumseh**	SHERMAN	General
Joseph	**Teodor**	CONRAD	Author
Ernesto	**Teodoro**	MONETA	Italian journalist
Michael	**Terence**	ASPEL	Broadcaster
Ian	**Terence**	BOTHAM	Cricketer
Michael	**Terence**	WOGAN	Broadcaster
Spiro	**Theodore**	AGNEW	US vice-president
René	**Théophile Hyacinthe**	LAENNEC	French physician
Randall	**Thomas**	DAVIDSON	Archbishop of Canterbury
Alfred	**Thompson**	DENNING	Law lord
Wednesday	**Thursday**	ADDAMS	'Addams Family' character
James	**Tiberius**	KIRK	Starship captain ('Star Trek')
Hugh	**Todd Naylor**	GAITSKELL	Politician
Rex	**Todhunter**	STOUT	US detective writer
Roger	**Tory**	PETERSON	US ornithologist

FAMOUS PEOPLE

First Name	Middle Name(s)	Surname	
Marcus	Tullius	TIRO	Inventor
William	Turner	WALTON	Composer
Ranulph	Twistleton-Wykeham	FIENNES	Explorer
Bobby	Tyre	JONES	US golfer
Gabriel	Urbain	FAURE	Composer
Basil	Urwin	SPENCE	Architect
Comer	Vann	WOODWARD	US historian
Sergey	Vasilyevich	RACHMANINOV	Composer
Ralph	Vaughan	WILLIAMS	Composer
Nicholas	Verity	KNIGHT	Cricketer
Eddie	Vernon	RICKENBACKER	Fighter pilot
Eugene	Victor	DEBS	US politician
Mia	Villiers	FARROW	Actress
Michael	Vincent	O'BRIEN	Racehorse trainer
Sarah	Virginia	WADE	Tennis player
Adeline	Virginia	WOOLF	Novelist
Henry	Wager	HALLECK	US soldier
Ralph	Waldo	EMERSON	US poet
King	Wallis	VIDOR	Film director
Luis	Walter	ALVAREZ	US physicist
John	Warcup	CORNFORTH	British chemist
David	Wark	GRIFFITH	Film director
Henry	Warren	BEATY	Actor
Dave	Warren	BRUBECK	Jazz musician
Charles	Warren	FAIRBANKS	US vice-president
Marshall	Warren	NIRENBERG	US biochemist
Jimmy	Warren	WHITE	Snooker player
George	Washington	CABLE	Novelist
Norman	Washington	MANLEY	Jamaican politician
James	Watson	CRONIN	US physicist
Charles	Watson	WENTWORTH	British prime minister
Richard	Wayne	PENNIMAN	Musician
George	Wells	BEADLE	US biochemical geneticist
Rainer	Werner	FASSBINDER	Film director
Marthinus	Wessels	PRETORIUS	South African general
William	Wetmore	STORY	Poet and sculptor
Edward	Wheewall	HOLDEN	Motor pioneer
Alan	Whipper	WELLS	Athlete
Jack	Whitaker	STRAW	Politician
Edward	White	BENSON	Archbishop of Canterbury
Arnold	Whittaker	WOLFENDALE	Astronomer
Caryl	Whittier	CHESSMAN	Convict and author
Bertie	Wilberforce	WOOSTER	Fictional character
Robert	Wilhelm	BUNSEN	Physicist
William	Wilkie	COLLINS	Novelist
Caspar	Willard	WEINBERGER	US politician
Johnnie	William	CARSON	US TV personality
Emile	William Ivanhoe	HESKEY	Footballer
Jack	William	NICKLAUS	Golfer
Brian	Wilson	ALDISS	Science fiction writer
Woodrow (Woodie)	Wilson	GUTHRIE	US folk singer
Ronald	Wilson	REAGAN	US president
Joseph	Wilson	SWAN	Physicist
James (Jimmy)	Wilson Vincent	SAVILE	Broadcaster
Frank	Winfield	WOOLWORTH	US businessman
Arthur	Wing	PINERO	Playwright
Gary	Winston	LINEKER	Footballer
John	Winston (then Ono)	LENNON	Musician and composer
Wells	Wintemute	COATES	Architect
John	Winthrop	HACKETT	Soldier and academic
Victor	Witter	TURNER	Anthropologist
Roger	Wolcott	SPERRY	US neuroscientist
Jonathan	Wolfe	MILLER	Broadcaster
Theobald	Wolfe	TONE	Irish nationalist
Robert	Woodrow	WILSON	US physicist
Thomas	Woodrow	WILSON	US president
Dickinson	Woodruff	RICHARDS	American physician
Ronald	Wreyford	NORRISH	English chemist
William	Wymark	JACOBS	Short story writer
William	Wyndham	GRENVILLE	British prime minister

First Name	Middle Name(s)	Surname	
Franz	**Xaver**	HABERL	German musicologist
Denis	**Yates**	WHEATLEY	Novelist
Paul	**Yaw**	BOATENG	Politician
Susannah	**Yolande**	YORK	Actress
Shmuel	**Yosef**	AGNON	Israeli novelist
Konrad	**Zacharias**	LORENZ	Austrian zoologist

Middle Names: Ordered by Surname

First Name	Middle Name(s)	Surname	
Charles	**Greely**	ABBOT	Astrophysicist
Diane	**Julie**	ABBOTT	Politician
Dean	**Gooderham**	ACHESON	American statesman
Joseph	**Randolf**	ACKERLEY	Author
Roy	**Claxton**	ACUFF	Country musician
Adam	**Llewellyn De Vere**	ADAMANT	Fictional TV character
John	**Bodkin**	ADAMS	Doctor and murder suspect
John	**Couch**	ADAMS	Astronomer
John	**Quincy**	ADAMS	US president
Marcus	**Algernon**	ADAMS	Photographer
Sarah	**Flower**	ADAMS	English poet
William	**Bridges**	ADAMS	Engineer
Wednesday	**Thursday**	ADDAMS	'Addams Family' character
Lawrence (Larry)	**Cecil**	ADLER	Musician
Vosdanig	**Manoog**	ADOIAN	Painter
Sade	**Folasade**	ADU	Singer
Spiro	**Theodore**	AGNEW	US vice-president
Shmuel	**Yosef**	AGNON	Israeli novelist
Henry	**Hinchcliffe**	AINLEY	Actor
George	**Biddell**	AIRY	Astronomer
Amos	**Bronson**	ALCOTT	Transcendentalist
Brian	**Wilson**	ALDISS	Science fiction writer
Thomas	**Bailey**	ALDRICH	Author
Thomas	**Massa**	ALSAGER	Newspaper manager
Luis	**Walter**	ALVAREZ	US physicist
Mario	**Gabriele**	ANDRETTI	Racing driver
Christian	**Boehmer**	ANFINSEN	US biochemist
Anders	**Jonas**	ANGSTROM	Physicist
Susan	**Brownell**	ANTHONY	Suffragette
Jeffrey	**Howard**	ARCHER	Author
George	**Augustus**	ARLISS	Actor
Klas	**Pontus**	ARNOLDSON	Swedish politician
Chester	**Alan**	ARTHUR	US president
Jeremy	**John Durham**	ASHDOWN	Politician
Arthur	**Bowden**	ASKEY	Comedian
Michael	**Terence**	ASPEL	Broadcaster
Herbert	**Henry**	ASQUITH	British prime minister
Miguel	**Angel**	ASTURIAS	Guatemalan poet
Richard	**Samuel**	ATTENBOROUGH	Actor
Wystan	**Hugh**	AUDEN	Poet
Alan	**Beresford**	B'STARD	TV character ('New Statesman')
Stephen	**Moulton**	BABCOCK	US agricultural chemist
Johann	**Christian**	BACH	Composer
Johann	**Sebastian**	BACH	Composer
Enid	**Algerine**	BAGNOLD	Author
Joan	**Dawson**	BAKEWELL	Broadcaster
Emily	**Greene**	BALCH	US social reformer
Michael	**Elias**	BALCON	Film producer
James	**Graham**	BALLARD	Author
Canaan	**Sodindo**	BANANA	Zimbabwean president
Hastings	**Kamuzu**	BANDA	Malawi politician
Iain	**Menzies**	BANKS	Author
Roger	**Gilbert**	BANNISTER	Athlete
Frederick	**Grant**	BANTING	Physiologist
Joseph	**Roland**	BARBERA	US animated cartoonist
Charles	**Glover**	BARKLA	English physicist
Christian	**Neethling**	BARNARD	Surgeon
Phineas	**Taylor**	BARNUM	Showman

First Name	Middle Name(s)	Surname	
James	**Matthew**	BARRIE	Author
Herbert	**Ernest**	BATES	Author
William	**Maddock**	BAYLISS	Physiologist
George	**Wells**	BEADLE	US biochemical geneticist
Henry	**Warren**	BEATY	Actor
Bill	**Blackledge**	BEAUMONT	Rugby Union player
Carl	**Lotus**	BECKER	US historian
Thomas	**Lovell**	BEDDOES	Poet and physiologist
Mary	**Hayley**	BELL	Playwright
Hilaire	**Pierre**	BELLOC	Writer
Enoch	**Arnold**	BENNETT	Author
Edward	**White**	BENSON	Archbishop of Canterbury
Edmund	**Clerihew**	BENTLEY	Writer
Ernst	**Ingmar**	BERGMAN	Film producer
Hans	**Albrecht**	BETHE	US physicist
Earl	**Derr**	BIGGERS	US novelist
Henry	**Rowley**	BISHOP	Composer
John	**Stuart**	BLACKIE	Scholar
Richard	**Doddridge**	BLACKMORE	Author
Anthony	**Charles Lynton**	BLAIR	Politician
Eric	**Arthur**	BLAIR	Author
Danny	**Dennio**	BLANCHFLOWER	Footballer
Tasker	**Howard**	BLISS	Soldier and statesman
Baruch	**Samuel**	BLUMBERG	US biochemist
Wilfrid	**Scawen**	BLUNT	Poet
Paul	**Yaw**	BOATENG	Politician
Dirk	**Niven**	BOGARDE	Actor
Humphrey	**De Forest**	BOGART	Actor
Robert	**Oxton**	BOLT	Playwright
Ian	**Terence**	BOTHAM	Cricketer
Virginia	**Hilda Brunette Maxwell**	BOTTOMLEY	Politician
Richard	**Southwell**	BOURKE	Earl of Mayo
David	**Hayward**	BOWIE	Musician and singer
Barbara	**Taylor**	BRADFORD	Novelist
Omar	**Nelson**	BRADLEY	US soldier
John	**Gerard**	BRAINE	Novelist
Kenneth	**Charles**	BRANAGH	Actor
Richard	**Charles Nicholas**	BRANSON	Entrepreneur
Walter	**Houser**	BRATTAIN	US physicist
John	**Cabell**	BRECKINRIDGE	US vice-president
Leonid	**Ilich**	BREZHNEV	USSR president
Robert	**Seymour**	BRIDGES	Poet
Charlie	**Dunbar**	BROAD	Philosopher
Rupert	**Chawner**	BROOKE	Poet
Norman	**Everard**	BROOKES	Tennis player
Spangler	**Arlington**	BROUGH	Actor
Henry	**Kirke**	BROWN	Sculptor
James	**Gordon**	BROWN	Politician
Charles	**Farrar**	BROWNE	Humorist and writer
Hablot	**Knight**	BROWNE	Illustrator
John	**Moses**	BROWNING	Gunsmith and inventor
Dave	**Warren**	BRUBECK	Jazz musician
William	**Cullen**	BRYANT	Poet
James	**McGill**	BUCHANAN	American economist
Pearl	**Sydenstricker**	BUCK	Author
Maria	**Esther**	BUENO	Tennis player
Ralph	**Johnson**	BUNCHE	American economist
Robert	**Wilhelm**	BUNSEN	Physicist
Billy	**George**	BUNTER	Fictional character
William	**Seward**	BURROUGHS	Author
George	**Herbert Walker**	BUSH	US president
Nicholas	**Murray**	BUTLER	US educationist
Reginald	**Cotterell**	BUTLER	Sculptor
Richard	**Austen**	BUTLER	Politician
Billy	**Edmund**	BUTLIN	Businessman
Betsy	**Cromer**	BYARS	Novelist
Richard	**Evelyn**	BYRD	Explorer
Harry	**Flood**	BYRD	Politician
George	**Gordon**	BYRON	Poet
James	**Branch**	CABELL	Novelist

First Name	Middle Name(s)	Surname	
George	**Washington**	CABLE	Novelist
Pedro	**Alvarez**	CABRAL	Navigator
James	**Mallahan**	CAIN	Writer
Michael	**Joseph**	CAINE	Actor
Aimo	**Kaarlo**	CAJANDER	Finnish politician
John	**Caldwell**	CALHOUN	US vice-president
James	**Leonard**	CALLAGHAN	British prime minister
Maria	**Meneghini**	CALLAS	Operatic soprano
Hugh	**Longbourne**	CALLENDAR	Physicist
Verney	**Lovett**	CAMERON	Explorer
Walter	**Chauncy**	CAMP	American footballer
Donald	**Malcolm**	CAMPBELL	Car and boat racer
John	**Franklin**	CANDY	Actor
Annie	**Jump**	CANNON	US astronomer
George	**Leonard**	CAREY	Archbishop
Chester	**Floyd**	CARLSON	US inventor
Ingvar	**Costa**	CARLSSON	Swedish politician
Jane	**Baillie**	CARLYLE	Wife of Thomas Carlyle
Ian	**Gillett**	CARMICHAEL	Actor
John	**Alden**	CARPENTER	Musician and businessman
John	**Dickson**	CARR	US detective writer
Willis	**Haviland**	CARRIER	US inventor
Johnnie	**William**	CARSON	US TV personality
William	**Hunter Fisher**	CARSON	Jockey
James	**Earl**	CARTER	US president
Barbara	**Hamilton**	CARTLAND	Writer
Hugh	**Maxwell**	CASSON	Architect
William	**Henry**	CAVENDISH-BENTINCK	British prime minister
Robert	**Arthur Talbot**	CECIL	British prime minister
Ernst	**Boris**	CHAIN	German biochemist
Arthur	**Neville**	CHAMBERLAIN	Politician
Charlie	**Spencer**	CHAPLIN	Comedy actor
Frank	**Michler**	CHAPMAN	Ornithologist
Greg	**Stephen**	CHAPPELL	Cricketer
Ian	**Michael**	CHAPPELL	Cricketer
Leslie	**Bowyer**	CHARTERIS	Author
Cornelius	**Crane**	CHASE	Actor
Anton	**Pavlovich**	CHEKHOV	Russian author
Geoffrey	**Leonard**	CHESHIRE	Philanthropist
Caryl	**Whittier**	CHESSMAN	Convict and author
Gilbert	**Keith**	CHESTERTON	Author
Robert	**Erskine**	CHILDERS	Writer
Jaques	**René**	CHIRAC	French prime minister
Martin	**Harcourt**	CHIVERS	Footballer
Walter	**Percy**	CHRYSLER	Automobile manufacturer
Winston	**Leonard Spencer**	CHURCHILL	British prime minister
Kenneth	**Mackenzie**	CLARK	Art historian
Kenneth	**Harry**	CLARKE	Politician
Cassius	**Marcellus**	CLAY	Boxer
John	**Marwood**	CLEESE	Actor
Samuel	**Langhorne**	CLEMENS	Author
Stephen	**Grover**	CLEVELAND	US president
Edward	**Montgomery**	CLIFT	Actor
William	**Jefferson Blyth**	CLINTON	US president
Wells	**Wintemute**	COATES	Architect
Tyrus	**Raymond**	COBB	Baseball player
Samuel	**Franklin**	CODY	Aviator
William	**Frederick**	CODY	Showman
Sebastian	**Newbold**	COE	Athlete and politician
Frederick	**Donald**	COGGAN	Archbishop of Canterbury
Ferdinand	**Julius**	COHN	Botanist
Samuel	**Taylor**	COLERIDGE	Poet
Sidonie	**Gabrielle**	COLETTE	Author
William	**Gershom**	COLLINGWOOD	Artist
Charles	**Allston**	COLLINS	Artist
Joan	**Henrietta**	COLLINS	Actress
William	**Wilkie**	COLLINS	Novelist
Arthur	**Holly**	COMPTON	Physicist
Denis	**Charles Scott**	COMPTON	Cricketer
Maureen	**Catherine**	CONNOLLY	Tennis player

First Name	Middle Name(s)	Surname	
Jimmy	Scott	CONNORS	Tennis player
Joseph	Teodor	CONRAD	Author
Brian	Rayner	COOK	English baritone
Robin	Finlayson	COOK	Politician
Elizabeth	Sprague	COOLIDGE	American pianist
John	Calvin	COOLIDGE	US president
Leon	Neil	COOPER	US physicist
Alfred	Edgar	COPPARD	Writer
Ronnie	Balfour	CORBETT	Comedian
Carl	Ferdinand	CORI	American biochemist
John	Warcup	CORNFORTH	British chemist
Arthur	Quiller	COUCH	Man of letters
Noel	Pierce	COWARD	Actor and dramatist
Michael	Colin	COWDREY	Cricketer
William	Randal	CREMER	Nobel Laureate
Francis	Harry Compton	CRICK	Biologist
Hawley	Harvey	CRIPPEN	Murderer
Richard	Stafford	CRIPPS	Politician
Archibald	Joseph	CRONIN	Author
James	Watson	CRONIN	US physicist
Walter	Leland	CRONKITE	US broadcaster
Harry (Bing)	Lillis	CROSBY	Singer and actor
Ada	Jemima	CROSSLEY	Australian contralto
Irene	Joliot	CURIE	Nuclear physicist
Heber	Doust	CURTIS	US astronomer
Edward	Sheriff	CURTIS	US photographer
Glen	Hammond	CURTISS	US air pioneer
Henry	Drysdale	DAKIN	Chemist
Kenneth	Mathieson	DALGLISH	Footballer
Lawrence	Bruno Nero	DALLAGLIO	Rugby player
George	Mifflin	DALLAS	US vice-president
Clarence	Seward	DARROW	US Lawyer
Randall	Thomas	DAVIDSON	Archbishop of Canterbury
Dwight	Filley	DAVIS	Founder of Davis Cup
Miles	Dewey	DAVIS	Jazz musician
Charles	Gates	DAWES	US vice-president
Christian	René	DE DUVE	Belgian biochemist
Philip	Ranulph	DE GLANVILLE	Rugby Union player
Cecil	Blount	DE MILLE	Film director
James	Byron	DEAN	Actor
Eugene	Victor	DEBS	US politician
Claude	Achille	DEBUSSY	Composer
Len	Cyril	DEIGHTON	Novelist
Ronald	Frederick	DELDERFIELD	Author
Jacques	Lucien Jean	DELORS	European politician
Nigel	Richard Patton	DEMPSTER	Gossip columnist
Judi	Olivia	DENCH	Actress
Alfred	Thompson	DENNING	Law lord
Bruce	MacLeish	DERN	US actor
Donald	Campbell	DEWAR	British politician
Norman	Colin	DEXTER	Author
Edward (Ted)	Ralph	DEXTER	Cricketer
Thomas	Frognall	DIBDIN	Librarian
Philip	Kindred	DICK	US writer
Philip	Kindred	DICK	US science fiction writer
Charles	John Huffam	DICKENS	Author
Walt	Elias	DISNEY	Film producer
Henry	Austin	DOBSON	Poet
Kenneth	Arthur	DODD	Comedian
Basil	Lewis	D'OLIVEIRA	Cricketer
James	Patrick	DONLEAVY	Author
Alexander	Frederick	DOUGLAS-HOME	British prime minister
Hugh	Caswell Tremenheere	DOWDING	RAF chief
John	Boyd	DUNLOP	Inventor
Ronald	Ossary	DUNLOP	Irish painter
James	Franciscus	DURANTE	Entertainer
Gerald	Malcolm	DURRELL	Writer and naturalist
Lawrence	George	DURRELL	Novelist
Bob	Alan	DYLAN	Singer and composer
John	Carew	ECCLES	Australian neurophysiologist

First Name	Middle Name(s)	Surname	
John	**Presper**	ECKERT	American inventor
Gerald	**Maurice**	EDELMAN	US biochemist
Gertrude	**Caroline**	EDERLE	US swimmer
Thomas	**Alva**	EDISON	Inventor
Dwight	**David**	EISENHOWER	US president
Thomas	**Stearns**	ELIOT	Author
Edward ('Duke')	**Kennedy**	ELLINGTON	Pianist
Fred	**Handel**	ELLIOTT	'Coronation Street' character
Ralph	**Waldo**	EMERSON	US poet
John	**Franklin**	ENDERS	US bacteriologist
Chris	**Livingstone**	EUBANK	Boxer
Peter	**Carl**	FABERGÉ	Russian goldsmith
Gabriel	**Daniel**	FAHRENHEIT	Physicist
Charles	**Warren**	FAIRBANKS	US vice-president
Douglas	**Elton**	FAIRBANKS (Snr)	Actor
Nicholas	**Alexander**	FALDO	Golfer
Mia	**Villiers**	FARROW	Actress
Rainer	**Werner**	FASSBINDER	Film director
Gabriel	**Urbain**	FAURÉ	Composer
William	**Claude**	FIELDS	Comedian and actor
Ranulph	**Twistleton-Wykeham**	FIENNES	Explorer
Robert	**Bannatyne**	FINLAY	Politician
Geoffrey	**Francis**	FISHER	Archbishop of Canterbury
Val	**Logsdon**	FITCH	US physicist
Augustus	**Henry**	FITZROY	British prime minister
Bob	**Prometheus**	FITZSIMMONS	Boxer
James	**Elroy**	FLECKER	Poet
Ian	**Lancaster**	FLEMING	English novelist
Jane	**Seymour**	FONDA	Actress
Michael	**Mackintosh**	FOOT	Politician
Gerald	**Rudolph**	FORD	US president
Cecil	**Scott**	FORESTER	Author
George	**Hoy**	FORMBY	Vocalist and musician
Edward	**Morgan**	FORSTER	Author
Bruce	**Joseph**	FORSYTH	Entertainer
Stephen	**Collins**	FOSTER	US songwriter
Michael J	**Andrew**	FOX	Actor
Clement	**Raphael**	FREUD	Liberal politician
Ragnar	**Kittil**	FRISCH	Norwegian economist
Kermit	**The**	FROG	Muppet
David	**Paradine**	FROST	Interviewer and presenter
Charles	**Burgess**	FRY	Sportsman
Stephen	**John**	FRY	Actor and author
Roy	**Broadbent**	FULLER	Poet
Hugh	**Todd Naylor**	GAITSKELL	Politician
Daniel	**Carleton**	GAJDUSEK	US virologist
Leopoldo	**Fortunato**	GALTIERI	Argentinian politician
Mohandas	**Karamchand**	GANDHI	Indian leader
James	**Abram**	GARFIELD	US president
John	**Nance**	GARNER	US vice-president
Elizabeth	**Cleghorn**	GASKELL	Writer
Herbert	**Spencer**	GASSER	US physiologist
Richard	**Jordan**	GATLING	Inventor
Andrew	**Dewar**	GIBB	Scottish jurist
Lewis	**Grassic**	GIBBON	Novelist
Stella	**Dorothea**	GIBBONS	Writer
Mel	**Columcille**	GIBSON	Actor
Thomas	**Milner**	GIBSON	Politician
Arthur	**John**	GIELGUD	Actor
William	**Schwenck**	GILBERT	Librettist
Percy	**Carlyle**	GILCHRIST	Metallurgist
John	**Birks**	GILLESPIE	Jazz trumpeter
King	**Camp**	GILLETTE	Inventor
William	**Ewart**	GLADSTONE	British prime minister
Sheldon	**Lee**	GLASHOW	US physicist
John	**Herschel**	GLENN	US astronaut and politician
Robert	**Hutchings**	GODDARD	US rocket pioneer
William	**Gerald**	GOLDING	Novelist
Peter	**Carl**	GOLDMARK	Inventor
Barry	**Morris**	GOLDWATER	US politician

First Name	Middle Name(s)	Surname	
George	**Peabody**	GOOCH	Politician
Graham	**Alan**	GOOCH	Cricketer
Arthur	**Lehman**	GOODHART	US jurist
Benny	**David**	GOODMAN	US jazz clarinetist
Samuel	**Griswold**	GOODRICH	US publisher
Adam	**Lindsay**	GORDON	Australian poet
Cyrus	**Herzl**	GORDON	US Hebrew scholar
George	**Hamilton**	GORDON	British prime minister
Spencer	**Frederick**	GORE	Painter
Benjamin	**Apthorp**	GOULD	US astronomer
Charles	**François**	GOUNOD	Composer
Lawrence	**Burnett**	GOWING	Painter
Tiberius	**Sempronius**	GRACCHUS	Roman statesman
William	**Gilbert**	GRACE	Cricketer
Billy	**Franklin**	GRAHAM	US evangelist
Florence	**Nightingale**	GRAHAM	Beautician
Ulysses	**Simpson**	GRANT	US president
Milner	**Connorton**	GRAY	Graphic designer
Linda	**Esther**	GRAY	Scottish soprano
Lucinda	**Jane**	GREEN	Three-day eventer
Robson	**Golightly**	GREEN	Actor
Hugh	**Carleton**	GREENE	Journalist and broadcaster
Gordon	**Cuthbert**	GREENIDGE	Cricketer
William	**Wyndham**	GRENVILLE	British prime minister
Herbert	**Nigel**	GRESLEY	Locomotive engineer
Edvard	**Hagerup**	GRIEG	Norwegian composer
Christopher	**Murray**	GRIEVE	Poet
Walter	**Burley**	GRIFFIN	US architect
David	**Wark**	GRIFFITH	Film director
Angelina	**Emily**	GRIMKE	US feminist
Sarah	**Moore**	GRIMKE	US feminist
Friedrich	**Melchior**	GRIMM	Journalist
Jacob	**Ludwig Carl**	GRIMM	Folklorist
Wilhelm	**Carl**	GRIMM	Folklorist
Walter	**Adolph**	GROPIUS	Architect
Leroy	**Randle**	GRUMMAN	US aircraft pioneer
John	**Selwyn**	GUMMER	Politician
Johannes	**Gensfleisch**	GUTENBERG	German printer
Woodrow	**Wilson**	GUTHRIE	US folk singer
Franz	**Xaver**	HABERL	German musicologist
John	**Winthrop**	HACKETT	Soldier and academic
Gene	**Alden**	HACKMAN	Actor
Alfred	**Cort**	HADDON	Anthropologist
Henry	**Rider**	HAGGARD	Novelist
William	**Jefferson**	HAGUE	Politician
Alexander	**Meigs**	HAIG	US soldier
Thomas	**Chandler**	HALIBURTON	Canadian writer
Henry	**Wager**	HALLECK	US soldier
James	**Orchard**	HALLIWELL-PHILLIPPS	Shakespearean scholar
Dag	**Hjalmar Agne Carl**	HAMMARSKJÖLD	Swedish statesman
Robin	**Airling**	HANBURY-TENISON	Explorer
Tony	**Aloysius**	HANCOCK	TV character
Tony	**John**	HANCOCK	Comedy actor
George	**Frederick**	HANDEL	Composer
William	**Denby**	HANNA	US animated cartoonist
James	**Aloysius**	HANSOM	Designer
Warren	**Gamaliel**	HARDING	US president
Oliver	**Norville**	HARDY	Comedy actor
Thomas	**Duffus**	HARDY	Archivist
Thomas	**Masterman**	HARDY	Naval officer
Joel	**Chandler**	HARRIS	Author
William	**Henry**	HARRISON	US president
Leslie	**Poles**	HARTLEY	Author
Haldan	**Keffer**	HARTLINE	US physiologist
John	**Liptrot**	HATTON	Composer
Herbert	**Aaron**	HAUPTMAN	US physicist
Rutherford	**Birchard**	HAYES	US president
Seamus	**Justin**	HEANEY	Poet
Patricia	**Campbell**	HEARST	Heiress
Donald	**Olding**	HEBB	Canadian psychologist

First Name	Middle Name(s)	Surname	
Lillian	**Florence**	HELLMAN	US playwright
Ernest	**Millar**	HEMINGWAY	US novelist
Philip	**Showalter**	HENCH	US physician
Katharine	**Houghton**	HEPBURN	US actress
Jocelyn	**Barbara**	HEPWORTH	Sculptor
Georges	**Remi**	HERGÉ	Belgian cartoonist
Caroline	**Lucretia**	HERSCHEL	Astronomer
Alfred	**Day**	HERSHEY	US biologist
Michael	**Ray Dibdin**	HESELTINE	Politician
Philip	**Arnold**	HESELTINE	Composer
Emile	**William Ivanhoe**	HESKEY	Footballer
Alfred	**Hawthorne**	HILL	Comedian
Norman	**Graham**	HILL	Racing driver
Conrad	**Nicholson**	HILTON	Businessman
John (Jack)	**Berry**	HOBBS	English cricketer
Dorothy	**Crowfoot**	HODGKIN	Scientist
Dustin	**Lee**	HOFFMAN	Actor
Quintin	**McGarel**	HOGG	Politician
Edward	**Wheewall**	HOLDEN	Motor pioneer
Ben	**Caine**	HOLLIOAKE	English cricketer
Herbert	**Clark**	HOOVER	US president
John	**Edgar**	HOOVER	FBI director
Bob	**Leslie Townes**	HOPE	Comedian
Gerard	**Manley**	HOPKINS	Poet
Anthony	**Philip**	HOPKINS	Actor
Michael	**Murray**	HORDERN	Actor
Godfrey	**Newbold**	HOUNSFIELD	English electrical engineer
Alfred	**Edward**	HOUSMAN	Author
David	**Hunter**	HUBEL	US neurophysiologist
Charles	**Brenton**	HUGGINS	US surgeon
Howard	**Robard**	HUGHES	Businessman
Victor	**Marie**	HUGO	French writer
George	**Basil**	HUME	Cardinal
Johann	**Nepomuk**	HUMMEL	Austrian pianist
Hubert	**Horatio**	HUMPHREY	US vice-president
John	**Barry**	HUMPHRIES	Comedian and writer
Miller	**Reece**	HUTCHINSON	Inventor
Aldous	**Leonard**	HUXLEY	Novelist
Jeremy	**Israel**	ISAACS	Arts mogul
David	**Lewis**	JACOBS	Broadcaster
William	**Wymark**	JACOBS	Short story writer
Phyllis	**Dorothy**	JAMES	Authoress
James	**Hopwood**	JEANS	Physicist and astronomer
James	**Jackson**	JEFFRIES	Boxing champion
John	**Rushworth**	JELLICOE	Naval commander
Roy	**Harris**	JENKINS	Politician
Robert	**Banks**	JENKINSON	British prime minister
Niels	**Kai**	JERNE	Danish immunologist
Jerome	**Klapka**	JEROME	Author
Elton	**Hercules**	JOHN	Vocalist and composer
Lyndon	**Baines**	JOHNSON	US president
Lionel	**Pigot**	JOHNSON	Poet
Richard	**Mentor**	JOHNSON	US vice-president
Joseph	**Eggleston**	JOHNSTON	US soldier
James	**Cellan**	JONES	Film director
Bobby	**Tyre**	JONES	US golfer
Michael	**Jeffrey**	JORDAN	US basketball player
James	**Prescott**	JOULE	Physicist
Carl	**Gustav**	JUNG	Swiss psychiatrist
Erik	**Axel**	KARLFELDT	Swedish poet
John	**Harvey**	KELLOGG	Inventor
Will	**Keith**	KELLOGG	Inventor
Gene	**Curran**	KELLY	Dancer
Edward	**Calvin**	KENDALL	US chemist
John	**Cowdery**	KENDREW	English biochemist
Edward	**Moore**	KENNEDY	US politician
John	**Fitzgerald**	KENNEDY	US president
Ludovic	**Coverley**	KENNEDY	Broadcaster
Nigel	**Paul**	KENNEDY	Violinist
Robert	**Francis**	KENNEDY	US politician

First Name	Middle Name(s)	Surname	
Søren	Aabye	KIERKEGAARD	Danish philosopher
William	Rufus de Vane	KING	US vice-president
Neil	Gordon	KINNOCK	Politician
Wilson	Boit	KIPKETER	Athlete
James	Tiberius	KIRK	Starship captain ('Star Trek')
Henry	Alfred	KISSINGER	USA statesman
Horatio	Herbert	KITCHENER	Irish soldier and statesman
Eartha	Mae	KITT	Singer
Nicholas	Verity	KNIGHT	Cricketer
Tjalling	Charles	KOOPMANS	US economist
Hans	Adolf	KREBS	British biochemist
Stanley	Jasspon	KUNITZ	US poet
Vladimir	Petrovich	KUTS	Russian athlete
Simon	Smith	KUZNETS	US economist
Fiorello	Henry	LA GUARDIA	US politician
René	Théophile Hyacinthe	LAENNEC	French physician
Selma	Ottiliana Lovisa	LAGERLOF	Swedish novelist
Carlos	Saavedra	LAMAS	Argentinian jurist
Willis	Eugene	LAMB	US physicist
Stephen	Burton	LANCASTER	Actor
Kenesaw	Mountain	LANDIS	Baseball commissioner
Walter	Savage	LANDOR	Writer
Henri	Désiré	LANDRU	French murderer
John	Dunmore	LANG	Clergyman
Harry	Philmore	LANGDON	US comedian
David	Russell	LANGE	New Zealand politician
Samuel	Pierpont	LANGLEY	US aeronautic pioneer
Cherilyn (Cher)	Sarkisian	LAPIERRE	Singer
Pierre	Athanase	LAROUSSE	French publisher
Hugh	Callum	LAURIE	Actor and comedian
Rodney	George	LAVER	Tennis player
Thomas	Edward	LAWRENCE	Author and soldier
David	Herbert	LAWRENCE	Author
Bill	Morris	LAWRY	Australian cricketer
Bernard	Howell	LEACH	English potter
Richard	Erskine Frere	LEAKEY	Palaeontologist and naturalist
Henrietta	Swan	LEAVITT	US astronomer
Christopher	Carandini	LEE	Actor
Vladimir	Ilyich	LENIN	Russian revolutionary
John	Winston (then Ono)	LENNON	Musician and composer
Henry	Bernard	LEVIN	Journalist and author
Harry	Sinclair	LEWIS	US novelist
Chris	Clairmonte	LEWIS	Cricketer
Clive	Staples	LEWIS	Author
John	Spedan	LEWIS	Businessman
Dennis	Keith	LILLEE	Australian cricketer
Charles	Augustus	LINDBERGH	US aviator
Gary	Winston	LINEKER	Footballer
Maureen	Diane	LIPMAN	Actress
William	Nunn	LIPSCOMB	US chemist
Penelope	Margaret	LIVELY	Writer
Harold	Clayton	LLOYD	US film comedian
Henry	Cabot	LODGE	US senator
Jack	Griffith	LONDON	US novelist
Francis	Aungier	LONGFORD	Prison reformer
Hendrik	Antoon	LORENTZ	Dutch physicist
Konrad	Zacharias	LORENZ	Austrian zoologist
Robert	Hepler	LOWE	Actor
Laurence	Stephen	LOWRY	Artist
Henry	Robinson	LUCE	US magazine publisher
Edwin	Landseer	LUTYENS	English architect
Humphrey	Richard Adeane	LYTTELTON	Musician
Thomas	Babington	MACAULAY	Author
George	Brinton	McCLELLAN	US soldier
Mark	Hume	McCORMACK	Promoter
James	Ramsay	MACDONALD	British prime minister
Samora	Moises	MACHEL	Mozambican president
Donald	Duart	MACLEAN	English traitor
Jarnes	Paul	McCARTNEY	Musician and composer
Maurice	Harold	MACMILLAN	British prime minister

First Name	Middle Name(s)	Surname	
Robert	Strange	McNAMARA	Businessman and politician
Herman	Cyril	McNEILE	Author
Johann	Nepomuk	MAELZEL	German inventor
John	Roy	MAJOR	British prime minister
Nelson	Rolihlahla	MANDELA	South African president
Norman	Washington	MANLEY	Jamaican prime minister
Nigel	Ernest James	MANSELL	Racing driver
Ferdinand	Edralin	MARCOS	Filipino president
Bob	Nesta	MARLEY	Musician
Gabriel	Garcia	MARQUEZ	Columbian author
Jean	Lyndsey Torren	MARSH	Actress
George	Catlett	MARSHALL	American soldier and statesman
Jan	Garrigue	MASARYK	Czech statesman
Anna	Raymond	MASSEY	Actress
Daniel	Raymond	MASSEY	Actor
Marshall	Bruce	MATHERS III	Rap artist (aka Eminem)
William	Somerset	MAUGHAM	Author
Ian	Robert	MAXWELL	Businessman
Peter	Barker Howard	MAY	Cricketer
Michael	Hugh	MEACHER	Politician
Carlos	Saul	MENEM	Argentinian politician
Cliff	Arthur	MICHELMORE	Broadcaster
James	Albert	MICHENER	Author
Arthur	Asher	MILLER	US playwright
Alton	Glenn	MILLER	Bandleader
Jonathan	Wolfe	MILLER	Broadcaster
Alan	Alexander	MILNE	Author
Liza	May	MINNELLI	Singer
Walter	Frederick (Fritz)	MONDALE	US vice-president
Ernesto	Teodoro	MONETA	Italian journalist
Bernard	Law	MONTGOMERY	Field marshal
Brian	Baden	MOORE	Football commentator
Henry	Spencer	MOORE	Sculptor
Roger	George	MOORE	Actor
Sheridan	Robert	MORLEY	Author and broadcaster
George	Ivan (Van)	MORRISON	Singer and composer
Samuel	Finley Breese	MORSE	US inventor
John	Cameron	MORTON	Journalist
Levi	Parsons	MORTON	US vice-president
Oswald	Ernald	MOSLEY	British politician
Benjamin	Roy	MOTTELSON	Danish physicist
Colin	Berkeley	MOYNIHAN	Politician
Robert	Gabriel	MUGABE	Zimbabwean president
Robert	Sanderson	MULLIKEN	American chemist
Hector	Hugh	MUNRO	Author
Keith	Rupert	MURDOCH	Businessman
Bartolomé	Estebán	MURILLO	Spanish painter
Edward	Regan	MURPHY	US comedian
John	Middleton	MURRY	Writer and critic
Maria	Lurdes	MUTOLA	Mozambique athlete
Frederic	Ogden	NASH	Poet
Pablo	Neftali Reyes	NERUDA	Poet
Marcus	Cocceius	NERVA	Roman emperor
Julia	Babette Sarah	NEUBERGER	Rabbi
George	Eric	NEWBY	Author
George	Anthony	NEWLEY	Actor and singer
Stavros	Spyros	NIARCHOS	Greek shipowner
Emma	Harriet	NICHOLSON	Politician
Jack	William	NICKLAUS	Golfer
Joseph	Nicéphore	NIEPCE	Inventor
Marshall	Warren	NIRENBERG	US biochemist
Richard	Milhous	NIXON	US president
Joshua	Mqabuko Nyongolo	NKOMO	Zimbabwean politician
Ronald	Wreyford	NORRISH	English chemist
Trevor	Robert	NUNN	Theatre director
Julius	Kambarage	NYERERE	Tanzanian president
Michael	Vincent	O'BRIEN	Racehorse trainer
Desmond	Bernard	O'CONNOR	Entertainer
David	Feodorovich	OISTRAKH	Violinist
Laurence	Kerr	OLIVIER	Actor

First Name	Middle Name(s)	Surname	
Aristotle	**Socrates**	ONASSIS	Shipping magnate
Eugene	**Gladstone**	O'NEILL	US playwright
Elisha	**Graves**	OTIS	Inventor
Peter	**Seamus**	O'TOOLE	Irish actor
George	**Emil**	PALADE	US biologist
Arnold	**Daniel**	PALMER	Golfer
Cyril	**Northcote**	PARKINSON	Political scientist
Eric	**Honeywood**	PARTRIDGE	Lexicographer
Linus	**Carl**	PAULING	Scientist
Thomas	**Love**	PEACOCK	Novelist and poet
Mervyn	**Laurence**	PEAKE	Author and artist
John	**Loughborough**	PEARSON	Architect
Lester	**Bowles**	PEARSON	Canadian politician
Eldred	**Gregory**	PECK	Actor
Richard	**Wayne**	PENNIMAN	Musician
Juan	**Domingo**	PERÓN	Argentinian president
Reginald	**Iolanthe**	PERRIN	TV character
Matthew	**Galbraith**	PERRY	US naval officer
Oliver	**Hazard**	PERRY	US naval officer
Publius	**Helvius**	PERTINAX	Roman emperor
Max	**Ferdinand**	PERUTZ	British biochemist
Henri	**Omer**	PÉTAIN	French statesman
Mary	**Elizabeth**	PETERS	Pentathlete
Roger	**Tory**	PETERSON	US ornithologist
Ulrich	**Bonnell**	PHILLIPS	US historian
River	**Jude**	PHOENIX	Actor
William	**Mervyn**	PICKWOAD	Actor
Lester	**Keith**	PIGGOTT	Jockey
Arthur	**Wing**	PINERO	Playwright
Jenny	**Susan**	PITMAN	Racehorse trainer
Gary	**Jim**	PLAYER	Golfer
Raymond	**Landry**	POINCARÉ	French statesman
John	**Marlan**	POINDEXTER	US naval officer
James	**Knox**	POLK	US president
Robert	**Graeme**	POLLOCK	Cricketer
Paul	**Jackson**	POLLOCK	US artist
William	**Sydney**	PORTER	Author
Michael	**Denzil Xavier**	PORTILLO	Politician
Dennis	**Christopher George**	POTTER	Playwright
Ezra	**Loomis**	POUND	Poet
Anthony	**Dymoke**	POWELL	English novelist
John	**Enoch**	POWELL	British politician
Austin	**Danger**	POWERS	Film character
John	**Leslie**	PRESCOTT	Politician
Elvis	**Aaron**	PRESLEY	American singer
Marthinus	**Wessels**	PRETORIUS	South African general
André	**George**	PREVIN	Conductor
John	**Boynton**	PRIESTLEY	Author
Archibald	**Philip**	PRIMROSE	British prime minister
James	**Leathes**	PRIOR	Politician
Victor	**Sawdon**	PRITCHETT	Writer and critic
Sergei	**Sergeyevich**	PROKOFIEV	Composer
Giacomo	**Antonio**	PUCCINI	Composer
Ana	**Fidelia**	QUIROT	Cuban athlete
Steve	**Russell**	RACE	Broadcaster
Sergey	**Vasilyevich**	RACHMANINOV	Composer
Thomas	**Stamford**	RAFFLES	Colonial administrator
Arthur	**Michael**	RAMSEY	Archbishop of Canterbury
Norman	**Foster**	RAMSEY	US physicist
John	**Crowe**	RANSOM	US poet and critic
Arthur	**Michell**	RANSOME	Author
Esther	**Louise**	RANTZEN	TV presenter
Claire	**Berenice**	RAYNER	Broadcaster
Ronald	**Wilson**	REAGAN	US president
Michael	**Scudamore**	REDGRAVE	Actor
Robert	**Oliver**	REED	British actor
Erich	**Maria**	REMARQUE	Author
Ruth	**Barbara**	RENDELL	Crime novelist
Dickinson	**Woodruff**	RICHARDS	US physician
Dorothy	**Miller**	RICHARDSON	English novelist

First Name	Middle Name(s)	Surname	
Eddie	Vernon	RICKENBACKER	Fighter pilot
Sally	Kristen	RIDE	US astronaut
Matthew	Bunker	RIDGWAY	US soldier
Nikolai	Andreievich	RIMSKY-KORSAKOV	Composer
Frederick	Chapman	ROBBINS	US physiologist
Frederick	Sleigh	ROBERTS	British soldier
James	Logie	ROBERTSON	Poet
Paul	Bustill Le Roy	ROBESON	Actor
Frederick	John	ROBINSON	British prime minister
Nelson	Aldrich	ROCKEFELLER	US vice-president
Anita	Lucia	RODDICK	Businesswoman
Edith	Kermit	ROOSEVELT	US First Lady
Franklin	Delano	ROOSEVELT	US president
Jack	Morris	ROSENTHAL	Playwright
Kenneth	Ronald	ROSEWALL	Tennis player
Mstislav	Leopoldovich	ROSTROPOVICH	Cellist
Philip	Milton	ROTH	Novelist
Meyer	Amschel	ROTHSCHILD	German financier
Francis	Peyton	ROUS	American pathologist
Robert	Alexander	RUNCIE	Archbishop of Canterbury
Ahmed	Salman	RUSHDIE	Author
Charles	Taze	RUSSELL	Religious leader
Gottlieb	Eliel	SAARINEN	Finnish–US architect
Nelly	Leonie	SACHS	Swedish poet and playwright
Jerome	David	SALINGER	Author
Jonas	Edward	SALK	Biologist
Seigfried	Lorraine	SASSOON	Poet
James	Wilson Vincent	SAVILE	Broadcaster
John	Richard	SCHLESINGER	Film director
Charles	Monroe	SCHULZ	US strip cartoonist
Harry	Donald	SECOMBE	Comedian and singer
Elzie	Crisler	SEGAR	US strip cartoonist
Harry	Gordon	SELFRIDGE	British merchant
David	Oliver	SELZNICK	US cinema mogul
Richard	Bowdler	SHARPE	Ornithologist
George	Bernard	SHAW	Author
Percy	Bysshe	SHELLEY	Poet
James	Schoolcraft	SHERMAN	US vice-president
William	Tecumseh	SHERMAN	General
William	Bradford	SHOCKLEY	US physicist
John	Cody Fiddler	SIMPSON	News reporter
Francis (Frank)	Albert	SINATRA	Singer
Upton	Beall	SINCLAIR	US novelist
Isaac	Bashevis	SINGER	Writer
Israel	Joshua	SINGER	Writer
Isaac	Merritt	SINGER	US inventor
Christopher	Robert	SMITH	British politician
Hamilton	Othanel	SMITH	US molecular biologist
Maggie	Natalie	SMITH	Actress
Sydney	Goodsir	SMITH	Poet
Samuel	Jackson	SNEAD	Golfer
Charles	Percy	SNOW	Author
Garfield	St Auburn	SOBERS	Cricketer
Robert	Merton	SOLOW	American economist
Aleksandr	Isaevich	SOLZHENITSYN	Author
Stephen	Joshua	SONDHEIM	Composer and lyricist
Donald	Oliver	SOPER	Methodist minister
Thomas	Octave Murdoch	SOPWITH	Aircraft designer
Charles	Hamilton	SORLEY	Poet
John	Hanning	SPEKE	Explorer
Basil	Urwin	SPENCE	Architect
Elmer	Ambrose	SPERRY	US inventor
Roger	Wolcott	SPERRY	US neuroscientist
Henry	Morton	STANLEY	Explorer and journalist
Edwin	McMasters	STANTON	US statesman
Publius	Papinius	STATIUS	Roman poet
George	Ledyard	STEBBINS	US botanist
David	Martin Scott	STEEL	Politician
William	Howard	STEIN	US biochemist
John	Ernest	STEINBECK	US novelist

First Name	Middle Name(s)	Surname	
Patrick	Christopher	STEPTOE	Gynaecologist
Adlai	Ewing	STEVENSON	US politician
William	Gladstone	STEWART	TV broadcaster and producer
Richard	Henry Simpson	STILGOE	Songwriter and broadcaster
Isidor	Feinstein	STONE	US journalist
Harlan	Fiske	STONE	US judge
William	Wetmore	STORY	Poet and sculptor
Rex	Todhunter	STOUT	US detective writer
Gavin	Steel	STRANG	Politician
Charles	Sherwood	STRATTON	Circus performer
Igor	Fedorovich	STRAVINSKY	Composer
Jack	Whitaker	STRAW	Politician
Meryl	Mary Louise	STREEP	Actress
Barbra	Joan	STREISAND	Singer
Arthur	Seymour	SULLIVAN	Composer
John	Bird	SUMNER	Archbishop of Canterbury
Frank	Meadow	SUTCLIFFE	Photographer
Joseph	Wilson	SWAN	Physicist
John	Addington	SYMONDS	Author
John	Millington	SYNGE	Author
William	Howard	TAFT	US president
Archibald	Campbell	TAIT	Archbishop of Canterbury
Abel	Janszoon	TASMAN	Navigator
Elizabeth	Rosemond	TAYLOR	Actress
Edward	Lawrie	TATUM	US biochemist
William	Howson	TAYLOR	Potter
Pyotr	Ilyich	TCHAIKOVSKY	Composer
Kiri	Janette	TE KANAWA	Opera Singer
Norman	Beresford	TEBBIT	Politician
George	Philipp	TELEMANN	Composer
Henry	John	TEMPLE	British prime minister
Ellen	Alice	TERRY	Actress
William	Makepeace	THACKERAY	Author
Margaret	Hilda	THATCHER	British prime minister
Anatole	François	THIBAULT	Author
Dylan	Marlais	THOMAS	Poet
Daley	Francis Morgan	THOMPSON	Athlete
John	Taliaferro	THOMPSON	US soldier and inventor
Hunter	Stockton	THOMPSON	US writer
George	Paget	THOMSON	English physicist
John	Jeremy	THORPE	Politician
James	Grover	THURBER	Humorist
Uma	Karuna	THURMAN	Actress
Louis	Comfort	TIFFANY	Glassmaker
Samuel	Jones	TILDEN	US politician
William	Tatem	TILDEN	US tennis player
Samuel	Chao Chung	TING	US physicist
Michael	Kemp	TIPPETT	Composer
Marcus	Tullius	TIRO	Inventor
Richard	Palethorpe	TODD	Actor
John	Ronald Reuel	TOLKIEN	Author
Theobald	Wolfe	TONE	Irish nationalist
Augustus	Montague	TOPLADY	Clergyman and hymnist
Donald	Francis	TOVEY	Pianist and composer
Charles	Hard	TOWNES	American physicist
Lee	Buck	TREVINO	American golfer
Rodney	Charlton	TROTTER	'Fools and Horses' character
Frederick (Freddy)	Sewards	TRUEMAN	Cricketer
Barry	Emmanuel	TUCKWELL	Australian musician
Alan	Mathison	TURING	Mathematician
Victor	Witter	TURNER	Anthropologist
Desmond	Mpilo	TUTU	South African prelate
William	Marcy	TWEED	US politician and criminal
Liv	Johanne	ULLMANN	Norwegian actress
John	Hoyer	UPDIKE	Author
Leon	Marcus	URIS	US author
Peter	Alexander	USTINOV	Actor and writer
Louis	Nicolas	VAUQUELIN	Chemist
King	Wallis	VIDOR	Film director
Angelina	Jolie	VOIGHT	Actress

First Name	Middle Name(s)	Surname	
Sarah	Virginia	WADE	Tennis player
Thomas	Griffiths	WAINEWRIGHT	Art critic and murderer
Terence (Terry)	Hardy	WAITE	Religious adviser
Selman	Abraham	WAKSMAN	US biochemist
Alice	Malsenior	WALKER	US novelist
George	Corley	WALLACE	Governor of Alabama
Henry	Agard	WALLACE	US vice-president
Hugh	Seymour	WALPOLE	Novelist
William	Turner	WALTON	Composer
Arthur	Sarsfield	WARD	Author
Booker	Taliaferro	WASHINGTON	US educationist
Lewis	Edson	WATERMAN	Inventor
James	Dewey	WATSON	US biologist
Clifton	Parmelee	WEBB	Actor
Everton	Decourcey	WEEKES	West Indian cricketer
Caspar	Willard	WEINBERGER	US politician
Thomas	Huckle	WELLER	US physiologist
Alan	Whipper	WELLS	Athlete
Charles	Watson	WENTWORTH	British prime minister
Edith	Newbold	WHARTON	Author
Denis	Yates	WHEATLEY	Novelist
Alan	Donald	WHICKER	Broadcaster
Jimmy	Warren	WHITE	Snooker player
Joseph	Blanco	WHITE	English poet
Pearl	Fay	WHITE	US actress
Terence	Hanbury	WHITE	Novelist
William	Hale	WHITE	Writer
Alfred	North	WHITEHEAD	Philosopher and mathematician
Oscar	Fingal O'Flahertie Wills	WILDE	Playwright and novelist
Ralph	Vaughan	WILLIAMS	Composer
Bob	Dylan	WILLIS	Cricketer
Bob	Primrose	WILSON	Goalkeeper and broadcaster
James	Harold	WILSON	British prime minister
Robert	Woodrow	WILSON	US physicist
Thomas	Woodrow	WILSON	US president
Pelham	Grenville	WODEHOUSE	Author
Michael	Terence	WOGAN	Broadcaster
Thomas	Clayton	WOLFE	Novelist
Tom	Kennerley	WOLFE	Novelist
Arnold	Whittaker	WOLFENDALE	Astronomer
Comer	Vann	WOODWARD	US historian
Robert	Burns	WOODWARD	American chemist
Adeline	Virginia	WOOLF	Novelist
Frank	Winfield	WOOLWORTH	US businessman
Bertie	Wilberforce	WOOSTER	Fictional character
Frank	Mortimer Magilinne	WORRELL	Cricketer
Billy	Ambrose	WRIGHT	Footballer
Elinor	Hoyt	WYLIE	US author
Johann	Rudolf	WYSS	Swiss writer
Magdi	Habib	YACOUB	Surgeon
Charles	Elwood	YEAGER	US test pilot
William	Butler	YEATS	Author
Boris	Nikolayevich	YELTSIN	Russian president
Susannah	Yolande	YORK	Actress
Lazarus	Ludwig	ZAMENHOF	Inventor of Esperanto
Gianfranco	Corsi	ZEFFIRELLI	Film director
Mai	Elizabeth	ZETTERLING	Actress and director

F
A
M
O
U
S

P
E
O
P
L
E

Nicknames

Joseph Addison **Atticus**
Aeschylus **Father of Greek Tragedy**
Muhammed Ali **Louisville Lip**
Queen Anne **Brandy Nan**
Anne of Cleves **Flanders Mare**
Lord George Anson **Father of the Royal Navy**
Thomas Aquinas **Angelic Doctor**

Aristophanes **Father of Comedy**
Richard Arkwright **Father of the Factory System**
Henry Armstrong **Homicide Hank**
Louis Armstrong **Satchmo (Satchel Mouth)**
Charles Atlas **World's Most Perfectly Developed Man**
Attila the Hun **Scourge of God**

Aurelian (Roman emperor)   **Restorer of the World**
Stephen Babcock   **Father of Scientific Dairying**
Francis Bacon   **Father of Inductive Philosophy**
Roger Bacon   **Father of Philosophy, Admirable Doctor (Doctor Mirabilis)**
John Logie Baird   **Father of Television**
Joan Bakewell   **Thinking Man's Crumpet** (by Frank Muir)
Theda Bara   **Vamp**
John Barbour   **Father of Scottish Poetry**
Sir John Barnard   **Father of London**
John Barrymore   **Great Profile**
Sir Edmund Barton   **Father of Australia**
Elyesa Bazna (spy)   **Cicero**
Bill Beaumont   **Amiable Geronimo**
Aphra Behn   **Divine Astraea**
Alexander Graham Bell   **Father of the Telephone**
John Bell   **Father of Sunday Newspapers**
Jeremy Bentham   **Father of Utilitarianism**
Lavrenti Beria   **Himmler of Russia**
David Berkowitz   **Son of Sam**
Irving Berlin   **Father of Published Ragtime**
Tim Berners-Lee   **Father of the Web**
Sarah Bernhard   **Divine Sarah**
John Biddle   **Father of English Unitarianism**
Clarence Birdseye   **Father of Frozen Food**
Bismarck   **Iron Chancellor**
Dr Greene Valadiman Black   **Father of Modern Dentistry**
Simon Bolivar   **Liberator**
Peter Bonetti   **Cat**
Bononcini and Handel   **Tweedle Dee and Tweedle Dum**
Jean Borotra   **Bounding Basque**
James Boswell   **Will O' the Wisp**
Clara Bow   **It Girl**
Robert Boyle   **Father of Chemistry**
Bessie Braddock   **Workers' Champion**
William Bradford   **Father of American History**
James Brindley   **Father of Britain's Canals**
William Hill Brown   **Father of the American Novel**
William Cullen Bryant   **Father of American Poetry**
Martha Jane Burke   **Calamity Jane**
Robert Burns   **Bard of Ayrshire**
Richard Burton   **The Voice**
George Bush   **Wimp**
Francis X Bushman   **Handsomest Man in the World**
David Bushnell   **Father of the Submarine**
Caedmon   **Father of English Song**
Cab Calloway   **King of Hi de Ho**
Walter Chauncey Camp   **Father of American Football**
Martha Jane Canary (Burke)   **Calamity Jane**
Thomas Carlyle   **Sage of Chelsea**
Primo Carnera   **Ambling Alp**
Judy Carne   **Sock-it-to-me-girl**
Georges Carpentier   **Orchid Kid**
Jacques Cartier   **Father of Canada**
John Cartwright   **Father of Reform**
Johnny Cash   **Man in Black**
Nicholas Catinat   **Father Thoughtful**
William Caxton   **Father of English Printing**
Sir George Cayley   **Father of Aviation**
Craig Chalmers   **Sponge**
Wilton Chamberlain   **Wilt the Stilt**
Lon Chaney Snr   **Man of a thousand Faces**

Charles I   **Martyr King, Ahab of the Nation, Britain's Josiah, White King**
Charles II   **Blackbird, Old Rowley, Merry Monarch**
Eddie Charlton   **Steady Eddie**
Henri Charrière   **Papillon**
Chris Chataway   **Red Fox**
Geoffrey Chaucer   **Father of English Poetry**
Cicero   **Father of his Country**
Cassius Clay   **Louisville Lip**
Georges Clemenceau   **Tiger**
Daniel Cohn-Bendit   **Danny the Red**
Mary Collier   **The Washer-woman (Poet)**
Peter Cook   **Cambridge Rapist**
John Calvin Coolidge   **Silent Cal**
Jim Corbett   **Gentleman Jim**
Paul Cotton   **Poco**
Noël Coward   **The Master**
Colin Cowdrey   **Kipper**
Alexander Cozens   **Father of English Watercolour**
Brigadier-General Alfred Critchley   **Father of Greyhound Racing**
Oliver Cromwell   **Old Noll, Nose Almighty, Old Ironsides**
Richard Cromwell   **Tumbledown Dick**
Aleister Crowley   **Wickedest Man in the World**
Duke of Cumberland   **Butcher**
Laurie Cunningham   **Black Pearl**
Edwina Currie   **Vindaloo**
Clarence Darrow   **Attorney for the Damned**
Freddie Davies (comedian)   **Parrot Face**
William Henry Davies   **Supertramp**
Steve Davis   **Interesting**
William Morris Davis   **Father of Geomorphology**
Eamon De Valera   **Father of the Irish Republic**
Rodrigo de Vivar   **El Cid**
Daniel Defoe   **Father of Modern Prose Fiction**
Jack Dempsey (heavyweight)   **Manassa Mauler, Nonpareil**
Joe Di Maggio   **Yankee Clipper**
Mildred Didrikson   **Babe**
Graham Dilley (cricketer)   **Picca**
Tommy Docherty   **Doc**
Antoine Domino   **Fats**
General Abner Doubleday   **Father of Baseball**
Antony Dowell and Antoinette Sibley   **Golden Pair**
Jimmy Durante   **Schnozzle**
Valentine Dyall   **Man in Black**
Nelson Eddy and Jeanette MacDonald   **America's Sweethearts**
Thomas Alva Edison   **Wizard of Menlo Park**
Edmund II   **Ironside**
Edward I   **Longshanks**
Edward III   **Father of English Commerce**
Edward V and brother Richard   **Princes in the Tower**
Edward (son of Edward III)   **Black Prince**
Eddie Edwards   **Eagle**
George Edwards   **Father of Ornithologists**
Elizabeth I   **Virgin Queen**
Elizabeth II   **Brenda** (by *Private Eye*)
Elizabeth Stuart (of Bohemia)   **Winter Queen**
Eminem   **The Real Slim Shady**
Empress Tzu Hsi   **Old Buddha**
Arthur English   **Prince of the Wide Boys**
Ethelred II   **Unready**
Eusebio   **Black Panther**

Eusebius of Caesarea **Father of Ecclesiastical History**
Derrick Evans **Mr Motivator**
Henry Fielding **Father of the English Novel**
Tom Finney **White Ghost**
Bob Fitzsimmons **Cornishman, Antipodean**
George Formby Snr **Wigan Nightingale**
Tregonwell Frampton **Father of the English Turf**
Francis I of France **Father of Letters**
John Francome **Greatest Jockey** (by John McCririck)
Frederick I **Barbarossa**
Frederick II **Wonder of the World**
William Frederick **Great Elector (of Brandenburg)**
Alan Freeman **Fluff**
Tony Galento **Two Ton**
Gandhi **Mahatma ('Great Soul')**
Joel Garner **Big Bird**
George III **Farmer George**
George IV **Adonis of Fifty**
Cass Gilbert **Father of the Skyscraper**
Ian Gillis **Mycroft**
Bernard Gilpin **Father of the Poor**
Giotto Di Bondone **Father of Modern Art**
Thomas Girtin **Father of Modern Watercolour**
William Gladstone **Grand Old Man (GOM)**
Captain Sir John Hawley Glover **Father of the Hausas**
Major General Sir John Bagot Glubb **Father of the Chin, Glubb Pasha**
Sir James Goldsmith **Goldenballs** (by *Private Eye*)
Barry Goldwater **AuH2O**
Graham Gooch **Zap**
Benny Goodman **King of Swing**
Charles Goodnight **Father of the Cowboys**
Betty Grable **Million Dollar Legs**
Ulysses Simpson Grant **Uncle Sam**
Zachary Grey **Father of Modern Commentators**
Florence Griffith-Joyner **Flo Jo**
Grock **King of Clowns**
Marvin Hagler **Marvellous (later became first name)**
Archie Hahn **Milwaukee Meteor**
John George Haigh **Acid Bath Murderer, Vampire Killer**
Handel and Bononcini **Tweedle Dum and Tweedle Dee**
WC Handy **Father of the Blues**
Harold I **Harefoot**
Russell Harty **Sooty**
Mark Hateley (footballer) **Attila**
Sir Christopher Hatton **Mutton, the Dancing Chancellor**
Franz Josef Haydn **Father of the Symphony**
Edward Heath **Grocer**
Henry I of England **Beauclerc**
Henry IV of France **Father of the People**
Henry V **Bluff Prince Hal**
Herodotus **Father of History**
Michael Heseltine **Tarzan, Veronica Lake, Action Man, Goldilocks**
Alex Higgins **Hurricane**
Jimmy Hill **Rabbi**
Bernard Hinault (cyclist) **Badger**
Hippocrates **Father of Medicine**
Bob Hite (Canned Heat) **Bear**

James Hogg **Ettrick Shepherd**
John Philip Holland **Father of the Military Submarine**
Billie Holliday **Lady Day**
Homer **Father of Epic Poetry**
Thomas Hooker **Father of American Democracy**
Matthew Hopkins **Witchfinder General**
Lesley Hornby **Twiggy**
Geoffrey Howe **Mogadon Man**
Edmond Hoyle **Father of the Game of Whist**
George Hudson **Railway King**
Cordell Hull **Father of the United Nations**
Barbara Hutton **Poor Little Rich Girl**
Hypatia **Divine Pagan**
Thomas Ince **Father of Westerns**
Andrew Jackson **Old Hickory**
General Thomas Jackson **Stonewall (Battle of Bull Run)**
Joseph Holson Jagger **Man Who Broke the Bank at Monte Carlo**
James I **Wisest Fool in Christendom** (by Henry IV of France)
James II **King over the Water**
Thomas Jefferson **Moonshine Philosopher**
James J Jeffries **Boilermaker**
Edward Jenner **Father of Immunology**
William Le Baron Jenney **Father of the Skyscraper**
Gilbert Jessop (cricketer) **The Croucher**
Joan of Arc **Maid of Orleans**
Samuel Johnson **Great Cham**
Sir John Harvey Jones **Admiral**
Ben Jonson **Father of Poets**
Janis Joplin **Pearl**
Scott Joplin **Father of Ragtime**
William Joyce **Lord Haw Haw**
Alberto Juantorena **White Lightning**
Helen Kane **Boop a Doop Girl**
Nora Kaye **Duse of the Dance**
Buster Keaton **The Great Stone Face**
Joseph Keaton **Buster** (coined by Houdini)
Fanny Kemble **Anne of Swansea**
Rev Geoffrey Kennedy **Woodbine Willie**
Ludovic Kennedy **Uckers**
Admiral Sir Henry Keppel **Father of the Fleet**
Graham Kerr **Galloping Gourmet**
King John **Lackland**
Peter Kurten **Monster of Düsseldorf**
Henri Landru **Bluebeard**
Allen Lane **Father of Penguin Paperbacks**
Niki Lauda **Clockwork Mouse**
Rod Laver **Rockhampton Rocket**
Antoine Lavoisier **Father of Modern Chemistry**
Florence Lawrence **Biograph Girl**
Frances Lawrence (novelist) **Gidget**
John Lawrence **Noble Lord** (by John McCririck)
Major General Stringer Lawrence **Father of the Indian Army**
TE Lawrence **Lawrence of Arabia**
Jean-Baptiste Le Moyne **Father of Louisiana**
Jerry Lee Lewis **Killer**
Eric Liddell **Flying Scotsman**
Fred Lillywhite (cricketer) **Nonpareil Bowler**
Jenny Lind **Swedish Nightingale**
Charles Lindbergh **Lone Eagle**
David Lloyd George **Welsh Wizard**

Harry Longbaugh **Sundance Kid**
Lord Longford **Lord Porn**
Konrad Lorenz **Father of Ethology**
Lorenzo de' Medici **Father of Letters,
The Magnificent**
Louis XII **Father of the People**
Louis XIV **Sun King**
Joe Louis **Brown Bomber**
Lord Lucan **Lucky**
Vera Lynn **Forces Sweetheart**
Ma Rainey **Mother of the Blues**
Mary McCauley **Molly Pitcher**
Derek McCulloch **Uncle Mac**
John McEnroe **Superbrat**
Barry McGuigan **Clones Cyclone**
Harold Macmillan **Supermac**
McPartlin and Donnelly **Ant and Dec**
James Madison **Father of the Constitution**
Mary Mallon **Typhoid Mary**
Rocky Marciano **Brockton Blockbuster**
Frances Marion **Swamp Fox**
Duchess of Marlborough **Mrs Freeman**
Duke of Marlborough (1st) **Anne's Great Captain**
Major William Martin (WW2 decoy) **Man Who
Never Was**
Mary I **Bloody Mary**
Matilda **Empress Maud**
Stanley Matthews **Wizard of Dribble**
Colin Meads **Pine Tree**
Bette Midler **Divine Miss M**
Henry Miller **Father of the Four Letter Word**
Joseph Miller **Father of Jests**
Max Miller **Cheekie Chappie**
Carmen Miranda **Brazilian Bombshell**
Thelonius Monk **High Priest of Bop**
Duke of Monmouth (James Scott) **Absalom**
Jean Monnet **Father of the Common Market**
Lady Mary Wortley Montague **Sappho**
Helen Wills Moody **Little Miss Poker Face**
Lewis Henry Morgan **Father of American
Anthropology**
Jedediah Morse **Father of American Geography**
Charles Morton **Father of Variety, Champagne,
Father of the Halls**
Lord Louis Mountbatten **Dickie**
Richard Murdoch **Stinker**
Lindley Murray **Father of English Grammar**
James Naismith **Father of Basketball**
Renaldo Nehemiah (athlete) **Skeets**
Jawaharlal Nehru **Pandit ('Wise Man')**
Donald Neilson (Nappey) **Black Panther**
Richard Neville (Earl of Warwick) **Kingmaker**
Marshal Ney **Bravest of the Brave**
Jack Nicklaus **Golden Bear**
Florence Nightingale **Lady with the Lamp**
Richard Nixon **Tricky Dicky**
Kwame Nkrumah **Showboy**
Greg Norman **Great White Shark**
Senator George Norris **Father of the
20th Amendment**
Paavo Nurmi **Flying Finn**
Lord John Oaksey **Noble Lord** (by John McCririck)
Ronald O'Bryan **Candy Man Killer**
Chris Old (cricketer) **Chilly**
Sir Henry Oliver **Father of Modern Navigation**

Christina Onassis **Thunderthighs**
Dr Robert Oppenheimer **Father of the Atom Bomb**
Count D'Orsay **Last of the Dandies**
Tessie O'Shea **Two-Ton Tessie**
Richard Fellow Outcault **Father of the Comic Strip**
Robert Owen **Father of British Socialism**
Jesse Owens **Ebony Antelope**
Lord Palmerston **Pam**
Bonnie Parker **Suicide Sal**
Charlie Parker **Bird**
Archbishop Matthew Parker **Nosey Parker**
General George Patton **Old Blood and Guts**
Cynthia Payne **Madame Sin**
Pele **Black Pearl**
Vladimir Peniakoff (Belgian soldier) **Popski**
Sir Henry Percy **Hotspur**
Joseph Père **Grey Eminence**
William Perry **Refrigerator**
John Joseph Pershing **Black Jack**
Marius Petipa **Father of Classical Ballet**
Louis Philippe **Citizen King**
Edith Piaf **Little Sparrow**
Mary Pickford **America's Sweetheart**
William Pitt **Aeolus**
William Pitt the Elder **Great Commoner**
Gary Player **Man in Black**
John Playford **Father of British Music Publishing**
Edgar Allan Poe **Father of the Detective Story**
Alexander Pope **Wasp of Twickenham**
Elvis Presley **The Pelvis, The King**
Princess Michael of Kent **Princess Pushy**
Ferenc Puskas **Galloping Major**
Rufus Putnam **Father of Ohio**
Max Quartermann **Superhod**
Fabius Quintus **Cunctator (Delayer)**
Rabelais **Father of Ridicule**
Luise Rainer **Viennese Teardrop**
Sonny Ramadhin **Spin King**
Derek Randall (cricketer) **Arkle**
Maharajah Ranjit Singh **Lion of the Punjab**
Ranulf de Glanvill **Father of Jurisprudence**
John Ray **Father of English Natural History**
Johnny Ray **Prince of Wails**
Nancy Reagan **Smiling Mamba**
Ronald Reagan **Teflon President**
Ray Reardon **Dracula**
John Redwood **Vulcan**
John Reid **Father of American Golf**
John Rich **Father of Harlequins, Father of English
Pantomime**
Richard I **Lionheart, Yea and Nay**
Richard de Beauchamp **Father of Courtesy**
Richard de Clare (2nd Earl of Pembroke)
Strongbow
Richard Duke of York and Edward V **Princes in the
Tower**
Samuel Richardson **Father of the English Novel**
Cardinal Richelieu **Red Eminence**
Manfred von Richthofen **Red Baron**
Eddie Rickenbacker **Ace of Aces**
Robespierre **Sea-Green Incorruptible**
George Robey **Prime Minister of Mirth**
Derek Robinson **Red Robbo**
Jimmie Charles Rodgers **Father of Country Music**

Steve Rogers **Captain America**
Erwin Rommel **Desert Fox**
Ken Rosewall **Muscles**
Stanley Rous **Father of English Football**
William Hepburn Russell **Father of the Pony Express**
Babe Ruth **Sultan of Swat**
Ernest Rutherford **Father of Nuclear Physics**
William Sacheverell **First Whig**
St Anthony **Father of Christian Monasticism**
St Ethelwold **Father of Monks**
St Thomas Aquinas **Father of Moral Philosophy**
Albert de Salvo **Boston Strangler**
Sir Malcolm Sargent **Flash Harry**
Sir Walter Scott **Wizard of the North, Great Unknown, Ariosto of the North, Old Peveril**
William Shakespeare **Swan of Avon, Bard of Avon**
Percy Bysshe Shelley **Ariel**
Ann Sheridan **Oomph Girl**
Manny Shinwell **Sinbad the Tailor**
Willie Shoemaker (jockey) **Shoe**
Antoinette Sibley and Anthony Dowell **Golden Pair**
Igor Sikorsky **Father of the Helicopter**
OJ Simpson **The Juice**
Frank Sinatra **The Voice**
Dennis Skinner **Beast of Bolsover**
Adam Smith **Father of Economics**
Bob Smith **Wolfman Jack**
William Smith **Father of English Geology**
Soeur Sourire **Singing Nun**
John Philip Sousa **March King**
Ursula Southiel **Old Mother Shipton**
Countess Spencer **Acid Raine**
John Spencer **Sniffer**
Bruce Springsteen **The Boss**
Craig Stadler (golfer) **Walrus**
Sylvester Stallone **Italian Stallion**
George Stephenson **Father of Railways**
Sir Rowland Stephenson **Father of Indian Railways**
Robert Franklin Stroud **Birdman of Alcatraz**
Charles Edward Stuart **Bonnie Prince Charlie, Young Pretender, Young Chevalier**
James Edward Stuart **Old Pretender, Old Chevalier**
Louis Sullivan (architect) **Father of Modernism**
Peter Sutcliffe **Yorkshire Ripper**
Thomas Tallis **Father of English Church Music**
James T Tanner **Father of Musical Comedy**
David Taylor (snooker player) **Silver Fox**
John Taylor **Water Poet**
Edward Teach **Blackbeard**
Norman Tebbit **Chingford Skinhead**
Temujin **Genghis Khan**
Alfred Lord Tennyson **Merlin**

Margaret Thatcher **Iron Lady, The Milk Snatcher, Attila the Hen**
Cliff Thorburn (snooker player) **Grinder**
William Tilden **Big Bill**
Timon (Athenian nobleman) **Misanthrope of Athens**
Thomas Tompion **Father of English Clockmaking**
Mel Tormé **Velvet Fog**
Charles Townshend **Turnip**
Hugh Montague Trenchard **Father of the RAF**
Lee Trevino **Super-Mex**
Richard Trevilthick **Father of the Locomotive**
Freddie Trueman **Fiery Fred**
Lyman Trumbell **Father of the 13th Amendment**
Sophie Tucker **Last of the Red Hot Mamas**
JMW Turner **Admiral Pugsy Booth, Blackbirdy**
Lana Turner **Sweater Girl**
William Turner (Dean of Wells) **Father of English Botany**
Christopher Tye **Father of the Anthem**
Frank Tyson (cricketer) **Typhoon**
Mike Tyson **Catskill Thunder**
Uganda **Pearl of Africa**
US Defense Dept **Foggy Bottom**
Rudolph Valentino **Pink Powder Puff**
Rudy Vallee **Vagabond Lover**
Venerable Bede **Father of English History**
Queen Victoria **Widow of Windsor**
Horace Walpole **Autocrat of Strawberry Hill**
Rosalind P Walter **Rosie the Riveter**
Izaak Walton **Father of Angling**
George Washington **Father of his Country**
Isaac Watts **Father of English Hymnody**
James Watt **Father of Steam**
John Wayne **Duke**
Josiah Wedgwood **Father of English Pottery**
Duke of Wellington **Iron Duke, Old Nosey, Achilles of England**
Jimmy White **Whirlwind**
William White (US writer) **Sage of Emporia**
Ann Widdecombe **Doris Karloff**
Bishop Samuel Wilberforce **Soapy Sam**
William Willett **Father of Daylight Saving**
William I **Conqueror**
William I of Orange **Silent**
William II **Rufus**
William IV **Silly Billy**
Esther Williams **Hollywood's Mermaid**
Walter Winchell **Father of the Gossip Column**
Orde Wingate **Robin Hood**
Sir Henry Wood **Old Timber**
Harry Wragg (jockey) **The Head Waiter**
Philemon Wright **Father of Ottawa**
Francis Xavier **Apostle of the Indies**

FAMOUS

PEOPLE

Traditional Occupations and Hobbies

This list of definitions includes some now-defunct traditional occupations alongside hobbies, pastimes, and colloquial names for certain types of worker. It also lists some lesser-known meanings for familiar professions.

Actuary Person employed to assess risks for insurance companies, a statistician

Alderman Senior member of a local council (until 1974)

Ale conner Inspector of beer and bread

Almoner Hospital social worker

Amanuensis Secretary employed to take dictation or copy manuscripts

Artificer Serviceman trained in mechanics

Bhishti (bheesty) Formerly a water carrier, in India

Bibliophile Collector of books

Bibliopole Dealer in rare books

Boatswain/bosun Petty officer on a merchant ship or warrant officer on a warship, responsible for maintenance

Bowyer Person who makes or sells archery bows

Broderer Person who embroiders

Bumbailiff Formerly, an officer employed to collect debts and arrest non-payers

Bursar Official in charge of finance in educational institutions

Campanologist Bell ringer

Cartographer Person who draws maps

Cartomancer Person who tells fortunes by use of playing cards

Cartophilist Collector of cigarette cards

Cartwright Maker of carts

Chandler Maker or seller of candles; grocer

Charcutier Pork butcher

Cobbler Shoemaker

Colporteur Hawker of books, especially bibles

Conchologist Collector of shells

Cooper Maker of barrels

Cordwainer Shoemaker, leather worker

Costermonger Fruit and vegetable salesman (formerly an apple vendor)

Couturier Person who designs, makes and sells fashion clothes for women

Coxswain Helmsman of a boat

Curator Person in charge of a collection, e.g. in a museum or library

Currier Person who grooms horses or curries leather

Deltiologist Picture-postcard collector

Didactics The art or science of teaching

Draper Person who sells cloth and cloth goods

Ecdysiast Striptease artist

Equerry Formerly, an officer in the royal household responsible for the horses

Farrier Person who shoes horses

Fletcher Maker of arrows

Founder Maker of bells and castings

Franklin Substantial landowner of free but not noble birth (Middle Ages)

Fromologist Person who collects cheese labels

Funambulist Tightrope walker

Gatherer Glass blower, and formerly a bookbinder

Glazier Person who fits windows, doors etc, with glass

Goliard Wandering scholar of 12th and 13th centuries, famed for riotous behaviour

Gombeen man An Irish moneylender

Gricer Person who seeks out and photographs unusual trains

Groom Person employed to clean and generally look after horses

Haberdasher Seller of sewing articles, e.g. buttons, needles, zips and ribbons

Haberdasher (USA) Men's clothes outfitter

Hack Run of the mill journalist

Hard hat Construction worker

Horner Person who made objects such as spoons and combs out of horn

Hosier Person who sells stockings

Houseman Junior doctor who is a member of the medical staff attached to a hospital

Ikebanist Practitioner of the Japanese decorative art of flower arranging

Intern North American equivalent to a houseman; it is also a US term for a student teacher

Ironmonger Dealer in hardware, eg nuts, bolts and locks, etc

Jobber Dealer in stocks and shares

Joiner Person skilled in making finished woodwork, eg windows, doors and stairs

Kamikaze Japanese pilot who performed suicide missions in World War II

Lepidopterist Butterfly and moth collector

Locum tenens Person who deputises for another in the same profession

Longshoreman American equivalent of a docker or stevedore

Lorimer/loriner Person who makes bits, spurs and other small metal objects

Matador Principal bullfighter

Mercer Textile dealer

Milliner Person who makes or sells women's hats

Millwright Engineer who designs, builds or repairs grain mills or mill machinery

Modiste Fashionable dressmaker or milliner

Navvy Labourer on a building site

Notary public Solicitor licensed to prepare legal documents

Numismatist Collector of coins and medals

Obstetrician Physician who specialises in childbirth

Ocularist Person who makes artificial eyes

Optometrist Person qualified to examine the eyes and prescribe lenses; also called optician or ophthalmologist

Origamist Person who folds paper into ornate figures and decorations

Paediatrician Physician who specialises in children and their diseases

Paramedic Person such as a laboratory technician who supplements the work of the medical profession

Pedagogue A teacher or educator

Pedant Archaic term for a teacher

Philatelist Stamp collector

Phillumenist Person who collects matchbox labels

Picador   In bullfighting or horseman who lances the bull in early stages in order to weaken it

Pilot   Person qualified to steer or guide a ship into or out of port

Potholer   Cave and underground passage explorer

Prestidigitator   Magician, especially one skilled in close sleight of hand

Publican   In Roman times, a tax collector

Purser   On a ship or plane, officer who keeps the accounts and attends to passenger welfare

Quantity surveyor   Person who estimates the cost of the materials and labour necessary for a construction job

Radiographer/radiologist   Person who takes X-rays

Recorder   Barrister or solicitor of at least ten years, standing appointed to sit as a judge in the Crown Court

Registrar   Hospital doctor, senior to a houseman but junior to a consultant

Roughneck   Worker in an oil-drilling operation

Saddler   Person who makes saddles, harnesses and other leather equipment for horses

Sandhog   North American term for person who works in underground or underwater construction projects

Scrivener   Formerly, a person who wrote out legal documents, a notary

Sempstress/seamstress   Woman who sews and makes clothes

Sensei   Japanese teacher of martial and other arts

Sexton   Church helper responsible for church upkeep

Shaman   Medicine man or witch doctor

Shipwright   Artisan skilled in shipbuilding

Spelunker   Cave explorer

Spodomancer   Person who makes prophecies by divination of ashes

Stationer   Person who sells stationery; formerly a publisher or bookseller

Steeplejack   Person skilled in construction and felling of steeples, spires, chimneys and towers

Stenographer   North American name for a shorthand typist

Stevedore   Person employed to load or unload a ship

Stoker   Person employed to tend a furnace, as on a steamship

Subaltern   Army officer below the rank of captain, usually a second lieutenant

Tanner   Person who tans skins and hides into leather

Timbrologist   Stamp collector

Topiarist   Person who shapes hedges into ornate shapes

Toreador   Rank-and-file bullfighter

Turner   Lathe operator

Upholsterer   Person who upholsters furniture

Vexillologist   Person who studies and collects information about flags

Vintner   Wine merchant

Vulcanologist   Person who studies volcanoes

Wainwright   Maker of wagons, wains and carts

Wheelwright/wheeler   Maker of wheels

Philosophers and Political Thinkers

Thales (c624–c545 BC)   Greek natural philosopher and astronomer, born in Miletus, traditionally seen as the founder of European philosophy. Thales identified water as the basis of the universe and also predicted the solar eclipse that took place in 585 BC. He was included in the traditional canon of 'Seven Wise Men' and was the original 'absent-minded professor', having allegedly fallen into a well whilst looking at the stars.

Anaximander (c611–546 BC)   Greek natural philosopher and astronomer, born in Miletus, and possibly a pupil of Thales. Anaximander is credited with producing the first maps. He was the second of the three great Milesian thinkers (the third was Anaximenes).

Pythagoras (c580– c500 BC)   Greek philosopher and mathematician, born in Samos, Ionia. He established his ethico-political academy at Croton (now Crotona) in southern Italy. Famous for his theorem concerning properties of right-angled triangles.

Heraclitus (554–483 BC)   Greek philosopher, born in Ephesus and nicknamed at various times 'the obscure' and 'the riddler'. Most famous doctrine is that everything is in a state of flux and that fire is the ultimate constituent of the world.

Confucius (551–479 BC)   Chinese philosopher, born in what is now Shantung province. His birthday is celebrated on 28 September and is an official holiday in Taiwan ('Teacher's Day'). Although Confucius was not greatly revered in his lifetime, Confucianism, as expressed in his *Analects*,

subsequently dominated Chinese life as both a religious and philosophical way of life.

Parmenides of Elea (510–483 BC)   Greek philosopher from southern Italy and founder of the Eleatic school, which included his pupils Zeno and Melissus. His great work *On Nature* was written in hexameter verse.

Empedocles (c490–c430 BC)   Greek philosopher, poet, statesman, religious teacher and physiologist, born in Acragas in Sicily. Empedocles held that the world is composed of four elements – air, fire, earth and water – which are governed by the opposing forces of love and discord. Heralded by his followers as a god, he allegedly died by leaping into the volcanic crater of Mount Etna whilst attempting to prove his divinity.

Socrates (469–399 BC)   Athenian philosopher, held in such esteem that all earlier Greek philosophy is known as pre-Socratic. Little is known about him other than that he had an apparently shrewish wife, Xanthippe, and took part in military campaigns at Potidaea, Delium and Amphipolis. Socrates wrote nothing but was eulogised in the 'Dialogues' of his pupil, Plato. Socrates' approach was to question everything. He chose to pick holes in the deliberations of others and asked people to think for themselves. He was eventually charged with 'Impiety' and 'Corrupting the youth of Athens' and forced to die by drinking hemlock.

Democritus (c460–c370 BC)   Greek philosopher, born in Abdera in Thrace and known as the 'laughing philosopher' because of his wry amusement at human foibles. A prolific writer, he is best known for the atomistic theory he developed from Leucippus.

Plato (c428–348 BC) Athenian philosopher who related the story of Socrates' trial in three of his *Dialogues*: the *Apology*, the *Crito* and the *Phaedo*. In c387 BC he founded the Academy, which became a famous establishment for philosophical, mathematical and scientific research. His writings comprise around 30 dialogues and a series of letters (only the seventh and eighth are likely to be genuine). The dialogue *Symposium* is an allegory of the search for love, and the *Republic* is an allegory of the search for justice. Plato was the teacher of Aristotle.

Aristotle (384–322 BC) Greek philosopher and scientist, born in Stagira, son of the court physician to the King of Macedon. Aristotle is one of the two most important philosophers of the ancient world, and one of the four or five most important of any time or place. For twenty years he was a member of Plato's Academy. When Plato died, Speusippus became head of the academy and Aristotle left Athens and became tutor to Alexander the Great (then aged 13). He returned to Athens in 335 BC and founded his 'Lyceum', so called from its proximity to the temple of Apollo Lyceius. The 'Aristotelian corpus' (1,462 pages of Greek text, including some spurious works) is probably derived from the lectures he gave in the Lyceum. Aristotle's followers became known as peripatetics (from his habit of walking around whilst lecturing). There is no doubt that many of the sub-categories of modern philosophy were formulated by Aristotle. He argued that although philosophy encompassed all areas of intellectual enquiry, there were distinct disciplines within this structure. Some areas in which Aristotle made a fundamental contribution in the expansion of philosophy as a science include logic, the study of nature, metaphysics, philosophy of mind, ethics and politics, and literary criticism and rhetorical theory. His works include the *Nicomachean Ethics*, *De Anima*, *Politics*, *Poetics*, *Metaphysics*, and the *Organon* (treatises on logic).

Epicurus (341–270 BC) Greek philosopher, born in Samos. His ethical philosophy was based on simple pleasures, friendship, and reflection. When Epicurus came to Athens in 306 BC he bought a house and established a school in the garden which became known as Ho Kepos (The Garden), where men and women of any background could attend. Like many of his predecessors he wrote treatises 'On Nature' but his best works were his ethical and theological dialogues, which made him a revered figure long after his death.

Lucretius (c99–55 BC) Roman philosopher and poet whose great works are his hexameter poem *De rerum natura* and his treatises attempting to separate philosophy from religion, which he denounced as the one great source of man's wickedness and misery. He was said to have died mad from the effects of a love potion administered by his wife, Lucilia.

Plotinus (c205–70) Born in Egypt of Roman parentage. His prolific writings were posthumously edited and arranged by his pupil, Porphyry, into six 'groups of nine books' or *Enneads*. These established the foundations of Neoplatonism, which combined Platonic with Pythagorean, Aristotelian and Stoic doctrines.

St Augustine of Hippo (354–430) Born in Tagaste in Numidia (modern Tunisia) of Roman descent, he was converted to Christianity in 386 and described his conversion in his most famous work *Confessions*. His other masterpiece was *The City of God*.

Roger Bacon (c1214–92) English philosopher and scientist, probably born near Ilchester, Somerset. His soubriquet 'Doctor Mirabilis' was gained because of his learning in magic and alchemy and he was the first European to describe the process for making gunpowder. Bacon held radical philosophical views and was imprisoned by the Franciscans for some time because of his suspected heretical teachings.

St Thomas Aquinas (c1225–74) Italian Dominican philosopher and theologian, born in the castle of Roccasecca, near Aquino, Sicily. His early education was at the monastery of Monte Cassino and then the University of Naples. He was a pupil of the Dominican scholar, Albertus Magnus, at the University of Paris and from 1256 began teaching there himself. In 1259 he was appointed theological adviser to the papal Curia. His two major works are *Summa theologica* and *Summa contra gentiles*. Thomas was known as 'Doctor Angelicus' and canonised a saint in 1323 by Pope John XXII. Thomism was the standard teaching of the Dominican order and has recently had a revival.

John Duns Scotus (c1265–1308) Scottish scholastic philosopher who became a Franciscan and was ordained a priest in St Andrew's Church, Northampton in 1291. He taught at Cologne, where he died and was buried. Duns Scotus was known by contemporaries as 'Doctor Subtilis' because of his extremely nuanced and technical resoning, but in the Renaissance the Scotists were dubbed 'Dunses' (hence the word 'dunce'). His important works include the *Opus Pariense* (Parisian Lectures), *Opus Oxiense* (Oxford Lectures, also known as the *Ordinatio*), *Tractatus de Primo Principio* and *Quaestiones Quodlibetales*.

William of Ockham (c1285–c1349) English philosopher, theologian and political writer, born in Ockham, Surrey. William entered the Franciscan order after studying theology at Oxford, although he failed to graduate hence his nickname, 'the Venerable Inceptor'. He was excommunicated by John XXII and fled to Bavaria where he died of the Black Death. His works greatly upset the papacy and included *Summa Logicae*, *Quodlibeta Septem* and commentaries on the sentences of Peter Lombard and Aristotle His greatest philosophical contribution is 'Ockham's razor' or the 'Law of Parsimony', which states that entities are not to be multiplied beyond necessity. The principle was invoked previously by Durand de Saint-Pourçain but Ockham's frequent and sharp employment of the doctrine ensured that his name would be identified with the principle.

Nicholas of Cusa (1401–64) German philosopher, scientist and churchman, born in Cues, Trier. He studied at Heidelberg and Padua, was ordained in 1430 and subsequently became a papal diplomat and Cardinal. Nicholas stressed the incomplete nature of man's knowledge of God and the universe. His main philosophical work is *De Docta Ignorantia* (1440) but he was the precursor of Copernicus as regards his non-geocentric theories.

Niccolò Machiavelli (1469–1527) Italian political philosopher, statesman and writer, born in Florence. He rose to prominence after the demise of Savonarola's regime in 1498. He had a controversial career and was in and out of favour dependent on the political climate. His masterpiece, *The Prince*, was dedicated to Lorenzo de Medici and published 1532. This work epitomised his ethic of evil sometimes being necessary in order for good to prevail. Other works include *The Art of War*, and *Mandragola*, a comic play about seduction, as well as a discourse on Livy. He is buried in Santa Croce, Florence.

Giordano Bruno (1548–1600) Italian philosopher, born in Nola, near Naples. He became a Dominican but came into conflict with the Inquisition due to his championing of Copernicus' heliocentricity theory, and his pantheistic views. He was eventually burned at the stake in Rome.

Sir Francis Bacon (1561–1626) English philosopher and statesman who became Viscount St Albans. He was a leading proponent of Empiricism and rejected Aristotelian deductive logic. His works include *The Advancement of Learning*, *Novum Organum* and *The New Atlantis*. Bacon was also a leading parliamentarian and his methodical and logical approach was not trusted by his uncle, Lord Burghley. An example of his political expediency was to try to convict his former friend, the Earl of Essex. He apparently died from hypothermia caused while carrying out food preservation experiments on chickens.

Thomas Hobbes (1588–1679) English political philosopher, born in Malmesbury (apparently prematurely, after his mother heard news of the approaching Spanish Armada). His first published work was a translation of Thucydides' *History* (1629); other works include *Elements of Law Natural and Politic* and his masterpiece 'Leviathan' (1651), in which he argues that absolutist government is needed to ensure law and order. His later works were published in Holland, the most famous being *Behemoth: a History of the causes of the Civil Wars of England*.

René Descartes (1596–1650) French philosopher and mathematician, born near Tours in a town now called La-Haye, later renamed Descartes in his honour. He is often called the father of modern philosophy. Descartes was in Germany with the army of the Duke of Bavaria in 1619 when, on November 10th, he had a visionary dream in a stove-heated room, which revealed a scientific postulate that would link all possible human knowledge together into an all-embracing wisdom. Most of his major works were published shortly after the death of his illegitimate daughter, Francine, in 1640, the most famous being the *Discourse on Method* which framed the basis for Cartesian philosophy, the phrase '*Cogito ergo sum*' (I think therefore I am) encapsulating his rational methodology. He died of pneumonia and his last words were supposedly 'So my soul a time for parting'. He was buried in Stockholm but was later moved to Saint-Germain-des-Prés, Paris.

Baruch Spinoza (1632–77) Dutch philosopher, born in Amsterdam. He was expelled from his Jewish community for heresy in 1656 and made a living grinding and polishing lenses (the glass dust was to cause his untimely death from consumption). His *Principia Philosophiae* was the only book published in his lifetime with his name on it. His main work, *Ethics*, was published posthumously. Spinoza is also known for his contributions to the development of an historical approach to the Bible.

John Locke (1632–74) English empiricist philosopher, born in Wrington, Somerset. Locke's *Essay Concerning Human Understanding* was the basis for the resurgence of Empiricism as an alternative to Cartesianism. He believed the mind at birth was a *tabula rasa*, as opposed to the Cartesian view that knowledge is derived from first principles.

Gottfried Wilhelm von Leibniz (1646–1716) German philosopher and mathematician, born in Leipzig. His optimism and faith in enlightenment and reason was satirised by Voltaire in *Candide* ('all is for the best in the best of all possible worlds'). His most famous work is the *Monadology*, in which he argues that the world is made up of an infinite number of units (monads), the highest of which is God. Apart from his philosophical essays, Leibniz also invented differential calculus, although the Royal Society formally declared Newton as its inventor in 1711 (nowadays both are credited).

Giovanni Vico (1668–1744) Italian philosopher, born in Naples. His major work, *Scienza Nuova* (The New Science), is concerned with the differences between scientific and historical explanation.

George Berkeley (1685–1753) Irish Anglican bishop and philosopher, born at Dysert Castle, Kilkenny. Bishop Berkeley was Dean of Derry and then Bishop of Cloyne; in between he tried to establish a college in the Bermudas but only got as far as Rhode Island. His celebrated claim that 'to be is to be perceived', whereby the contents of the material world are 'ideas' that only exist when they are perceived by a mind, is set out in his *Essay Towards a New Theory of Vision* and *A Treatise Concerning the Principles of Human Knowledge*. His other major work is *Three Dialogues Between Hylas and Philanous*.

David Hume (1711–76) Scottish philosopher and historian, born in Edinburgh. Hume's life was dogged in its early stages with fits of depression which he came to terms with whilst tutoring the insane nobleman, the Marquis of Annandale. His major works, *A Treatise of Human Nature* and *Dialogues Concerning Natural Religion* had a profound effect on Immanuel Kant and provoked the Idealists to counter Hume's scepticism. Hume was a friend of Rousseau but became embroiled in a famously bitter quarrel with him.

Jean-Jacques Rousseau (1712–78) French political philosopher, born in Geneva (his mother died in childbirth). He worked as a secretary and music copier in his early life. After a brief affair with Mme Louise de Warens he formed a lifelong liaison with Thérèse le Vasseur, with whom he had five children and eventually married in 1768. In 1762 he published his masterpiece *The Social Contract* which begins, 'Man is born free; and everywhere he is in chains.' His text, with its slogan 'Liberty, Equality, Fraternity', became the Bible of the French Revolution. At the invitation of David Hume, he lived at Wootton Hall near Ashbourne in Derbyshire. Here he began his *Confessions* but became increasingly paranoiac and returned to Paris where he completed the work. He became seriously insane and died in Ermenonville. His remains were placed alongside Voltaire's in the Panthéon in Paris.

Denis Diderot (1713–84) French philosopher and man of letters, born in Langres in Champagne, the son of a master cutler. He was a precursor of the Romanticists and was patronised by Catherine II, (the Great) of Russia. In 1743 he married Antoinette Champion, daughter of a linendraper, although his father disapproved. Diderot set out a philosophy of the arts and sciences which took the progress of civilisation to be a measure of mankind's moral improvement and perceived the Christian religion as morally harmful. From 1745 to 1772 Diderot served as chief editor of the *Encyclopédie*, one of the principal works of the Age of Enlightenment.

Immanuel Kant (1724–1804) German philosopher, born in Königsberg in Prussia (now Kaliningrad), the son of a saddler. He taught at the university and was known for his ordered way of life (locals allegedly set their watches by the time of his daily walks). Kant was a keen astronomer who predicted the existence of the planet Uranus before Herschel's discovery in 1781. Kant's most famous works, such as *Critique of Pure Reason* (1781), *Critique of Practical Reason* (1788) and *Critique of Judgement* (1790) were all pubished late in his life. Kant described his philosophy as 'transcendental' or 'critical' idealism.

Edmund Burke (1729–97) Irish philosopher and statesman, born in Dublin, and educated at a Quaker school and Trinity College. Burke's *Thoughts on the Present Discontents* and *Reflections on the French Revolution* were his masterpieces. Although a Whig all his life, Burke's political thought became, with Disraeli's, the philosophy of modern Conservatism.

Thomas Paine (1737–1809) English-born, American revolutionary philosopher and writer, born in Thetford, Norfolk, the son of a Quaker. He followed his father's trade as a corset maker before becoming, firstly a sailor, then a schoolmaster and ultimately an exciseman. It was during this period that he first showed his tendency to speak out against what he felt were injustices and was dismissed for disturbing the status quo by deriding the lack of pay increases. Benjamin Franklin helped him emigrate to America, where he settled in Philadelphia and became a radical journalist. He published a pamphlet *Common Sense* following the outbreak of the American Revolutionary War urging an immediate declaration of independence. He returned to England, after visiting France, and published *The Rights of Man* (1792) a reply to Burke's *Reflections on the French Revolution*. He was indicted for treason but fled to France whereupon he fell foul of Robespierre and was imprisoned but later freed on the grounds of his American citizenship (1795). His book *The Age of Reason* (1796) mostly written in prison, upset many of his American friends, including George Washington. He died alone and in poverty on his farm in New Rochelle, New York.

Jeremy Bentham (1748–1832) English philosopher, jurist and social reformer, born in London. Bentham is best known as a proponent of Utilitarianism, as seen in his pioneering works *A Fragment on Government* (1776) and *Introduction to the Principles of Morals and Legislation* (1789), in which he argued that the proper objective of all conduct and legislation is 'the greatest happiness of the greatest number'. He developed 'hedonic calculus' to estimate the effects of different actions. Bentham became an honorary French citizen in 1792 and published treatises on social and penal reform. He also planned a special prison (Panopticon) and school (Chrestomathia), helped start the *Westminster Review* (1823) and founded University College, where his clothed skeleton is preserved.

Johann Fichte (1762–1814) German philosopher, born in Rammenau, Saxony, the son of a ribbon weaver. In 1793 Fichte married Johanna Maria Rahn and in the same year published two anonymous works, the most important being *Contribution to the Correction of the Public's Judgments Regarding the French Revolution*. He developed Kant's critical philosophy into a system of his own, which he named 'Theory of Science' (*Wissenschaftslehre*).

Georg Hegel (1770–1831) German Idealist philosopher, born in Stuttgart. After studying theology he became a lecturer at Jena but Napoleon's victory there in 1806 interrupted his career. Hegel worked temporarily as a newspaper editor at Bamberg and then headmaster of the gymnasium at Nuremberg. Hegel's first great work was *The Phenomenology of Mind* (1807), which describes the human mind's progression from mere consciousness through self-consciousness, reason, spirit and religion, to absolute knowledge. His second great work was *The Science of Logic* which gained him the chair at Heidelberg in 1816. Hegel's dialectic method of reasoning involved a sequence of thesis, antithesis and synthesis, and his doctrines influenced Karl Marx and contributed to the development of 'Modern Totalitarianism'. In 1818 he succeeded Fichte as professor in Berlin and remained there until his death from cholera.

Charles Fourier (1772–1837) French philosopher and social theorist, born in Besançon. He published a number of utopian socialist works including *The Social Destiny of Man; or, Theory of the Four Movements* (1857). Fourier argued for the existence of a natural social order corresponding to Newton's ordering of the physical universe, claiming that both evolved in eight ascending periods. In Harmony, the highest stage, human emotions would be freely expressed. Fournier declared that this stage could be attained by dividing society into phalanges, each comprising a commune approximately 1,800 people within which all property would be collectively owned. His other works include *Treatise on Domestic Agricultural Association* and *The New Industrial World*.

Friedrich Schelling (1775–1854) German idealist philosopher, born in Leonberg in Württemberg. His early work was influenced by Kant and Fichte, and included *On the Possibility and Form of Philosophy in General* and *Of the Ego as Principle of Philosophy* in which he discusses the theological concept of the 'Absolute'. Schelling's major work *System of Transcendental Idealism* was an attempt to unite his concept of nature having a spiritual separateness from man, with Fichte's philosophy that nature is merely a tool of man. Schelling spent time in Jena, where he replaced Fichte in his teaching post, and in 1803, married Caroline Schlegel, a leading German Romanticist. A disagreement with Hegel concerning the dispute with Fichte caused him to retreat to Munich. After the death of Caroline, he married her friend, Pauline Gotter.

Arthur Schopenhauer (1788–1860) German philosopher, born in Danzig, and whose metaphysical doctrines of the will were in contrast to Hegelian idealism. He was strongly influenced firstly by Plato, and then by Immanuel Kant, and also became friendly with the playwright and poet Goethe, who invited his assistance with some problems concerning his 'Farbenlehre' (theory of colours). After finishing *On Vision and Colours*, Schopenhauer began his masterpiece, *The World as Will and Idea*, which expounds his pessimismistic and atheistic views. The premise being that man's nature as willing beings inevitably leads to suffering and such a life is worse than non-existence.

Auguste Comte (1798–1857) French philosopher and social theorist, born in Montpellier, and usually considered the founder of modern sociology and Positivism. Comte was nicknamed the 'Thinker' and was rebellious by nature. He was the first thinker to advocate the use of scientific procedures in the study of economics and politics. In a typical non conformist act he married a prostitute, Caroline Massin, in 1821. He then became increasingly depressed and mentally disturbed culminating in a suicide attempt in the Seine which seemed to bring him to his senses. His wife, however, resorted to her previous occupation and Comte formed an alliance with Clotilde de Vaux which lasted for two years until her death in 1846. Comte's major work was *The Positive Philosophy of Auguste Comte*, which became the bible for students of Positivism.

John Stuart Mill (1806–73) English philosopher and social reformer, born in London, the son of Scottish philosopher James Mill. He began publishing in *The Traveller* in 1822 and helped form the Utilitarian Society, which met in Jeremy Bentham's house, and he ultimately modified some of Bentham's doctrines. As with many philosophers, both before and after, Mill endured a phase of severe depression but in 1830 met and eventually married the bluestocking, Harriet Taylor, who influenced his future works. Mill's works include *System of Logic, On Liberty, Principles of Political Economy, Utilitarianism*, as well as a celebrated autobiography.

Søren Kierkegaard (1813–55) Danish philosopher, born in Copenhagen, the son of a Jewish merchant. Kierkegaard is considered the founder of Existentialism. His most famous work is probably *Either-Or*, in which he opposes Hegel by arguing the importance of individual choice. He was a convert to Christianity, although he fought against the formal structure of religion and believed that God and some special disciples were above moral laws as we know them. His other works include *The Concept of Irony, Christian Discourses, Fear of Trembling*, and *The Sickness Unto Death*.

Karl Marx (1818–1883) German social, political and economic theorist, born in Trier. His Jewish parents converted to Protestantism out of political expediency. Marx became the inspiration for international Communism. He studied at Bonn and then Berlin University, where he met the 'young Hegelians' who were chiefly concerned with the critique of religion. His doctoral dissertation was on 'The Difference between the Philosophies of Nature in Democritus and Epicurus'. Marx worked firstly as a journalist and then editor of the liberal Cologne paper *Rheinische Zeitung* but after the paper was suppressed by the government, Marx emigrated to Paris and became a communist. It was here that he first stated his belief that the proletariat must itself be the agent of revolutionary change in society, and wrote his first critique of capitalism, 'Economic and Philosophical Manuscripts of 1844' (not published until 1932). Marx had by now become friendly with Friedrich Engels and under political pressure they moved to Brussels, where they wrote *German Ideology* and the famous *Communist Manifesto* (1848) which ends with the Communist rallying cry: 'The workers have nothing to lose but their chains. They have a world to win. Workers of all lands, unite!' Marx moved to London in 1849 and wrote the first volume of his most famous work, *Das Kapital*, in 1867 (future volumes followed in 1884 and 1894) where he forecast the classless society. Marx is buried in Highgate cemetery, London.

Wilhelm Dilthey (1833–1911) German philosopher, born in Biebrich, Hesse. His central theme was the radical distinction between the natural sciences (*Naturwissenshaften*) and human sciences (*Geisteswissenschaften*). He also developed a theory of hermeneutics for the interpretation of historical texts and wrote biographies of Hegel, Lessing, Schleiermacher, and Goethe.

Friedrich Wilhelm Nietzsche (1844–1900) German philosopher, scholar and writer, born in Röcken, Saxony, son of a Lutheran pastor. He was seen by Nazi ideologists as a precursor of Nazism due to his doctrine of the superman (*Übermensch*) expounded in *Thus Spake Zarathustra* and *Beyond Good and Evil*. Nietzsche rejected Christianity by arguing that 'God is Dead'. His first work was *The Birth of Tragedy*, which compared Dionysian and Apollonian values, and was dedicated to Richard Wagner, whose operas he regarded as the true successors to Greek tragedy. Other works include *On the Genealogy of Morals, Beyond Good and Evil, Untimely Meditations* and his autobiography *Ecce Homo* (published posthumously in 1908).

Henri Bergson (1859–1941) French philosopher, born in Paris, son of a Polish Jewish musician and an English mother. Bergson claimed that time (which he calls duration), cannot be analysed as a set of moments, but is unitary. He claimed the same distribution between movement and the trajectory it covers. This became known as 'process philosophy'. He won the Nobel Prize for Literature in 1927. His major works include *Time and Freewill, Matter and Memory* and *Creative Evolution*.

Edmund Husserl (1859–1938) German philosopher, born in Prossnitz in the Austrian empire, of Jewish parentage. He studied mathematics at Berlin and psychology at Vienna, under Franz Brentano, a leading Aristotelian scholar. Husserl taught at Halle, Göttingen and Freiburg. He was the founder of the philosophical school of phenomenology which gave rise to Gestalt psychology. Works include *On the Goals and Problems of Metaphysics, Logical Investigations* (in which Husserl employed his Phenomenological methods) and *Ideas: General Introduction to Pure Phenomenology*.

Nishida Kitarō (1870–1945) Japanese philosopher, born near Kanazawa, Ishikawa, son of a school teacher. Nishida is considered Japan's first original modern philosopher and his work typifies Japanese attempts to absorb Western philosophy into the oriental spiritual tradition. His memoirs, entitled *A Certain Professor's Statement upon Retirement from Kyoto Imperial University, December 1928*, became a Japanese best-seller.

Bertrand Russell (1872–1970) Welsh philosopher, mathematician and author, born in Trelleck, Gwent, and brought up by his grandmother (the widow of the Liberal PM) following the death of both his parents in his youth. Russell was educated at Trinity College, Cambridge and became British Embassy attaché in Paris. He married Alys Pearsall Smith in 1895 and wrote his first book, *German Social Democracy*, soon after. Russell's first major philosophical work was *The Problems of Philosophy* (1912), which is often heralded as the perfect introduction for students of the subject. His pacifism caused the loss of his Trinity fellowship in 1916 and his imprisonment in 1918, after which he visited the Soviet Union and met Lenin, Trotsky and Gorky. He subsequently wrote *Theory and Practice of*

Bolshevism. Russell's philosophy was now based on the premise that scientific knowledge was the only factual knowledge. His other major philosophical work was *A History of Western Philosophy*. Russell was also the co-author (with AN Whitehead) of *Principia Mathematica*.

Otto Neurath (1882–1945)   Austrian socialist philosopher, economist and historian. Neurath was famous for creating the Isotype language for visual education. He was a founder member of the Vienna Circle.

György Lukács (1885–1971)   Hungarian Marxist philosopher and critic, born in Budapest, of a wealthy Jewish family. Early works include *Soul and Form*, and *Theory of the Novel*. He joined the Hungarian Communist Party in 1918 but after the defeat of the uprising in 1919 travelled to Vienna and then Moscow. His major work on Marxism, *History and Class Consciousness* (1923), was condemned by the Russian Communist party as heretical.

Ludwig Wittgenstein (1889–1951)   Austrian-born British philosopher, born in Vienna, son of an industrialist. Wittgenstein studied mechanical engineering at Berlin but became increasingly interested in mathematics and went to Cambridge to study under Bertrand Russell. He served in the Austrian army in WWI and was captured and held as a POW near Monte Cassino. Here he wrote *Tractatus Logico Philosophicus*, which expounded his 'picture theory' and the nature and limits of language whereby the deep truths of the nature of reality and representation cannot properly be said but can only be shown. Wittgenstein became a naturalised British citizen in 1938 and spent much of his time in Cambridge, although he worked as a porter in Guy's Hospital during World War II. Wittgenstein is undoubtedly one of the pre-eminent philosophers of the twentieth century.

Martin Heidegger (1889–1976)   German philosopher, born in Messkirch in Baden, son of a Catholic sexton. Heidegger was appointed rector at Freiburg in 1933 and pledged support for Hitler in his inaugural address. His writings concern the nature and predicament of human existence, the search for 'authenticity' and the distractions of Angst (anxiety). His major work, *Being and Time* (1927), although considered a masterpiece, is often misunderstood in philosophical circles due to its complexity. The essence of the work as a description of a fundamental ontology where he names the human entity 'Dasein' (the being) and argues that Dasein's own being is intrinsically temporal in as existential sense.

Rudolf Carnap (1891–1970)   German-born American philosopher of Logical Positivism. He was a prominent member of the Vienna Circle and made significant contributions to logic, the philosophy of science, model theory and probability. He was viewed as an 'enfant terrible' in his early career but became one of the most respected philosophers of the twentieth century. Carnap was a great advocate of international languages (e.g. Esperanto).

Hans-Georg Gadamer (1900–2002)   German philosopher, born in Marburg, Hesse. A pupil of Heidegger, his major work, *Truth and Method*, expounds his hermeneutic beliefs.

Karl Raimund Popper (1902–1994)   Austrian-born British philosopher. Popper's greatest contributions are in philosophy of sciences and in political and social philosophy. His 'falsificationism' reverses the usual view that accumulated experience leads to scientific hypotheses. He was a member of the Vienna Circle.

Jean-Paul Sartre (1905–80)   French philosopher, dramatist and novelist, born in Paris. He studied at the Sorbonne with Simone de Beauvoir, with whom he had a lifelong relationship. He taught philosophy at Le Havre, Paris and Berlin but joined the French army in 1939 and became a POW in 1941. On his release he became a key member of the French Resistance. In 1946, Sartre and De Beauvoir founded the avant-garde monthly *Les Temps Modernes* and Sartre began to develop his Existentialist doctrines. He declined the 1964 Nobel Prize for Literature and campaigned against American involvement in Vietnam. Sartre's major works were *Being and Nothingness* and his semi-autobiographical work *Nausea*, and a later more detailed autobiography, *Words (Les Mots)*.

Maurice Merleau-Ponty (1908–61)   French philosopher, born in Rochefort-sur-Mer, Charente-Maritime. Although, he was closely associated with Sartre and helped him and De Beauvoir found *Les Temps Modernes* in 1945 his philosophy was more akin to that of the German phenomenonologists Husserl and Heidegger. His major work was *The Phenomenology of Perception*.

Willard Quine (1908–2000)   American philosopher, born in Akron, Ohio. He was professor of philosophy at Harvard from 1948 to 1978 and was much influenced by Carnap, the Vienna Circle and Empiricism. His major works include *Two Dogmas of Empiricism*, *Word and Object* and *The Roots of Reference*.

Sir Alfred Jules Ayer (1910–89)   English philosopher, born in London. Ayer was educated at Eton and Oxford and served in the Welsh Guards in World War II before becoming a professor at University College London in 1947 and professor at Oxford in 1947. His major work, which was also his first, was *Language, Truth & Logic* (1936), which reflected the views of the Vienna Circle and established him a the leading English representative of logical positivism. It was dubbed 'The Young Man's book'. Ayer was knighted in 1970. His other major work was *The Problem of Knowledge*.

Albert Camus (1913–60)   French writer, born in Mondovi, Algeria, son of a farm labourer. After studying philosophy at Algiers, Camus became an actor, schoolmaster, playwright and journalist before World War II, and subsequently became a French Resistance activist. He then became co-editor of the left-wing newspaper *Combat* and wrote his Existentialist novel *The Stranger,* after which he became identified with 'the absurd'. His other great work was *The Plague*, in which a plague-stricken city, Oran, symbolises man's isolation. He was awarded the 1957 Nobel Prize for Literature for having 'illuminated the problems of the human conscience in our times.' He died in a car accident.

Michel Foucault (1926–84)   French philosopher, born in Poitiers. Foucault argued that social attitudes are manipulated by those in power, so that areas such as criminality, illness, sexuality and insanity have changing levels of acceptability dependent on the aims of government and others in positions of influence. His major works are *Madness and Civilization*, *The Order of Things*, and *The History of Sexuality*.

NB: The list above does not contain religious reformers such as John Calvin, or writers such as Voltaire. The people cited above have all made some contribution to the furtherance of philosophical theory. Although some writers are known for their philosophical utterances – e.g. Proudhon's 'property is theft' or Voltaire's 'if God did not exist it would be necessary to invent him' – this alone is not enough to warrant inclusion in this section. Karl Marx is a notable exception to this rule of thumb. It is true that he was not a philosopher by design but his words and deeds enhanced and expanded political and philosophical thought to such an extent that it would be crass to omit him. It should also be noted that many of the works listed above are English translations of foreign titles and as such are open to slight variations in interpretations.

An Explanation of Some Philosophical Terms

Dialectics	The philosophy of metaphysical contradictions and their solutions.
Empiricism	The belief that all knowledge derives from experience and that the mind cannot postulate in advance.
Existentialism	Modern philosophical movement that stresses the importance of personal experience and responsibility and the demands that they make on the individual, who is seen as a free agent in a deterministic and seemingly meaningless universe. Although Jean-Paul Sartre is often accredited as being the first person to name himself an existentialist, the works of Søren Kiekegaard have retrospectively been attributed as existential.
Hermeneutics	The art of interpretation of human behaviour and social institutions. Hermeneutics was originally the theory and method of interpreting the Bible and other theological texts but Wilhelm Dilthey extended it to the interpretation of all human acts and products.
Marxism	Marxism is a broad term that covers many different philosophical doctrines but ultimately relates to the various schools of thought that have flourished since the death of Karl Marx in 1883. Western Marxism usually includes those thinkers that were influenced by the Hegelian idea of dialectics and who focused their attention on the cultural as opposed to the economic aspects of capitalism.
Metaphysics	The branch of philosophy concerning first principles, especially of being and knowing. It is the study of the nature of reality and deals with such questions as the existence of God and the external world.
Nihilism	Philosophy of negation, rejection, or denial of some or all aspects of thought or life. An example would be moral nihilism, whereby any possibility of justifying or criticising moral judgements is rejected because morality is a cloak for egoistic self-seeking and therefore a sham. Nihilism is an extreme form of scepticism.
Ontology	The branch of metaphysics that deals with the nature of being.
Pascal's Wager	The postulate that it is better to wager that God does exist rather than on his non-existence.
Phenomenology	Movement founded by Husserl that concentrates on the detailed description of conscious experience without recourse to explanation, metaphysical assumptions or traditional philosophical questions.
Positivism	Extreme form of empiricism that rejects metaphysics and theology as seeking knowledge beyond the scope of experience and holds that experimental investigation and observation are the only sources of knowledge.
Scepticism	The view that we fail to know anything and the rejection of the postulate that some term of positive epistemic appraisal applies to our beliefs.
Solipsism	The extreme form of scepticism which denies the possibility of any knowledge other than of one's own existence.
Sophist	Pre-Socratic itinerant teacher of oratory and argument who was prepared to debate any matter however specious.
Stoicism	Greek philosophical system founded by Zeno of Citium (334–262 BC) in Athens c3000 BC. It views the world as permeated by rationality and divinely planned as the best possible organisation of matter. Moral goodness and happiness are achieved by replicating a perfect rationality in oneself, and by enacting one's own assigned role in the cosmic scheme of things.
Thomism	The name derives from Thomas Aquinas and relates to a body of philosophical and theological ideas that seek to articulate the intellectual content of Catholic Christianity.
Totalitarianism	Term adopted in the 1920s by the Italian Giovanni Gentile to describe the ideal fascist state. Totalitarianism has attracted the attention of philosophers because a number of classical philosophical systems have been suspected of harbouring totalitarian aspirations.
Vienna Circle	Group of about thirty to forty thinkers drawn from the social and natural sciences, logic and mathematics who met regularly in Vienna between the two world wars to discuss philosophy. Its manifesto was published in 1929 *The Scientific Conception of the World: The Vienna Circle* by Carnap, Hahn and Neurath. The inner sanctum of the group called the 'Schlick Circle', organised by the physics professor Moritz Schlick in 1924. Its members included Carnap, Neurath, Philip Frank, Kurt Gödel, and Edgar Zilsel. Other eminent philosophers such as Ludwig Wittgenstein and Karl Popper often joined discussion groups. The public profile of the circle was provided by the Ernst Mach Society, but in 1934 the society was suspended for political reasons, and in 1936 Moritz Schlick was murdered. The circle gradually disintegrated when many of its members were forced to leave Austria for racial and political reasons.

FAMOUS PEOPLE

Real Names: By Original Name

NB: This is not intended to be a comprehensive listing of pseudonyms but a selection of some of the best-known and most intriguing examples. It is an area that is surrounded with much uncertainty and potential for error. Generally the 'Assumed Name' is the more familiar, but not always (for instance when authors adopt a pen-name for a particular kind of writing). For people who have acquired titles, the title is given as the 'Assumed Name', although in such cases the 'Original Name' is of course equally valid. There is necessarily some overlap between this section and that on Nicknames.

Original Name		Assumed Name		
Abbott	Janet	*Baker*	Janet	Mezzo-Soprano
Abelsohn	Frank	*Vaughan*	Frankie	Vocalist
Abruza	Sophie	*Tucker*	Sophie	Music Hall Singer
Adair	William Penn	*Rogers*	Will	US Actor
Adams	Nathaniel	*Cole*	Nat King	Vocalist
Aday	Marvin Lee	*Meatloaf*		Vocalist
Addington	Henry	*Sidmouth*	Viscount	Prime Minister of Great Britain
Addison	Joseph	*Atticus*	(satirised by Pope)	Essayist and Politician
Adoian	Vosdanig Manoog	*Gorky*	Arshile	US Painter
Adu	Helen Folasade	*Sade*		Vocalist
Agopsowicz	Adolphus	*Vernon*	John	US Actor
Ahenobarbus	Lucius Domitius	*Nero*		Roman Emperor
Aherne	Michael	*Warrior*		Gladiator
Aken	Jerome van	*Bosch*	Hieronymus	Dutch Painter
Albert	Harold	*Cathcart*	Helen	Royal Biographer
Alepoudelis	Odysseus	*Elytis*	Odysseus	Greek Poet
Alexeyev	Konstantin Sergeivitch	*Stanislavsky*		Actor
Allason	Rupert	*West*	Nigel	MP and Author
Allegri	Antonio	*Correggio*		Artist
Amey	Ian	*Tich*		Guitarist
Amis	Kingsley	*Markham*	Robert	Novelist
Anderson	Roberta Joan	*Mitchell*	Joni	Vocalist/Composer
Andrews	Augustus George	*Arliss*	George	Actor
Andrews	William Forrest	*Forrest*	Steve	US Actor
Anson	Thomas Patrick John	*Lichfield*	Lord	Photographer
Arango	Dovoteo	*Villa*	Pancho	Mexican Patriot
Arbuckle	Penelope	*Dripping*	Lizzie	Literary Character
Arbuckle	Roscoe (Fatty)	*Goodrich*	William B	Actor
Arcelos	Raul Rafael Y	*Julia*	Raul	Actor
Arenson	Max	*Anderson*	Bronco Billy	Entertainer
Armstrong née Mitchell	Helen Porter	*Melba*	Dame Nellie	Opera Singer
Armstrong-Jones	David Albert Charles	*Linley*	Viscount	Furniture Maker
Arouet	François Marie	*Voltaire*		Philosopher
Ashdown	Jeremy	*Ashdown*	Paddy	Politician
Ashton	Winifred	*Dane*	Clemence	English Dramatist
Ashurst	Anne	*Craven*	Sara	Novelist and 'Mastermind' Winner
Asquith	Herbert	*Oxford*	Earl of	Prime Minister of Great Britain
Aurness	James	*Arness*	James	US Actor
Austerlitz	Frederick	*Astaire*	Fred	Dancer and Actor
Aznavurjal	Shahnovr	*Aznavour*	Charles	Singer and Actor
Bailey	William	*Rose*	Axl	Pop Singer
Baker	George	*Divine*	Father	Religious Leader
Baker	Norma Jean	*Monroe*	Marilyn	Actress
Baker	Tammy Marie	*Fox*		TV Gladiator
Balanchivadze	Georgi Melitonivich	*Balanchine*	George	Choreographer
Baldwin	Stanley	*Bewdley*	Earl of	Prime Minister of Great Britain
Baline	Israel	*Berlin*	Irving	Composer
Balsame	Guiseppe	*Cagliostro*	'Count'	Italian Adventurer
Barbarelli	Giorgio	*Giorgione*		Artist
Barbella	Rocco	*Graziano*	Rocky	Boxer
Barbieri	Gian-Francesco	*Guercino*		Italian Painter
Barker	Ronnie	*Wylie*	Gerald	Writer
Barr	Byron	*Young*	Gig	Actor
Barratt	Michael	*Stevens*	Shaking	Vocalist

Original Name		Assumed Name		
Barrow	Joseph	Louis	Joe	Boxer
Bartholomew	John Eric	Morecambe	Eric	Comedian
Basie	William	Basie	Count	Musician
Bates	Ellas	Diddley	Bo	Vocalist
Batson	Billy	Marvel	Captain	Comic Book Hero
Baumgartner	James	Garner	James	Actor
Bean	Frederick	Avery	Tex	Cartoonist
Beaty	Shirley	Maclaine	Shirley	Actress
Beaty	Warren	Beatty	Warren	Actor
Beauchamp	Katherine	Mansfield	Katherine	NZ Writer
Beedle	William	Holden	William	Actor
Begleiter	Lionel	Bart	Lionel	Composer
Benevetto	Anthony Dominic	Bennett	Tony	Vocalist
Bernardone	Giovanni de	Francis of Assisi	Saint	Religious Leader
Bernstein	Morris	Louis	Morris	US Painter
Berra	Lawrence Peter	Berra	Yogi	Baseball Player
Berry	Mike	Bennett	Lennie	Comedian
Beyle	Marie-Henri	Stendhal		Author
Bickel	Frederick	March	Fredric	Actor
Biden	Edmund	Sturges	Preston	Writer and Director
Bingham	Richard John	Lucan	Lord	Suspected Murderer
Bingzhi	Jiang	Ding Ling		Chinese Novelist
Birkinshaw	Franklin	Weldon	Fay	Writer
Birnbaum	Nathan	Burns	George	Comedian
Blair	Eric Arthur	Orwell	George	Author
Blamauer	Karoline Wilhelmine	Lenya	Lotte	Austrian Actress
Blau	Jenö	Ormandy	Eugene	Musician
Blixen	Karen	Dinesen	Isak	Authoress
Blythe	Ethel	Barrymore	Ethel	Actress
Blythe	John	Barrymore	John	Actor
Blythe	Lionel	Barrymore	Lionel	Actor
Bogaerde	Derek van den	Bogarde	Dirk	Actor
Bojaxhiu	Agnes Gonxha	Theresa	Mother	Roman Catholic Nun
Bollea	Terry	Hogan	Hulk	Professional Wrestler and Actor
Bookbinder	Elaine	Brooks	Elkie	Vocalist
Booth	George Hoy	Formby Jnr	George	Music Hall Entertainer
Booth	James	Formby Snr	George	Music Hall Entertainer
Bottom	Charles	Bart	Black	Outlaw
Bourgeois	Jeanne Marie	Mistinguett		French Dancer
Breitenberger	Edward	Byrnes	Edd	Actor
Bright	Gerald	Geraldo		Musician
Broadbent	Dora	Bryan	Dora	Actress and Comedienne
Broadbent	Shirley Ann	Barrie	Amanda	Actress
Broadus	Calvin	Snoop Dogg		Rapper
Brodribb	John Henry	Irving	Henry	Actor
Bronstein	Lev Davidovitch	Trotsky	Leon	Russian Revolutionary
Bronte	Anne	Bell	Acton	Author
Bronte	Charlotte	Bell	Currer	Author
Bronte	Emily	Bell	Ellis	Author
Brophy	Brigid Antonia	Levey	Lady	Author and Playwright
Brough	Spangler	Taylor	Robert	Actor
Brown	Angeline	Dickinson	Angie	Actress
Brown	Rosemary	Dana		Singer and Politician
Browne	Charles Farrar	Ward	Artemus	Humorist and Writer
Browne	Hablot Knight	Phiz		Illustrator
Broz	Josip	Tito	Marshal	Yugoslav Leader
Buchinski	Charles	Bronson	Charles	Actor
Bukht	Michael	Barry	Michael	Food Journalist
Bullock	Annie Mae	Turner	Tina	Vocalist
Bulsara	Frederick	Mercury	Freddie	Vocalist
Burgess	George	Meredith	Burgess	Actor
Burke	Martha Jane	Jane	Calamity	Frontierswoman
Burnett	Chester Arthur	Wolf	Howling	Vocalist and Composer
Burns	Ray	Sensible	Captain	Vocalist
Burrell	Orville Richard	Shaggy		Pop Singer
Burrell	Stanley Kirk	Hammer	MC	Rapper
Butterfield	Sylvia	Dawn	Elizabeth	Actress
Bygraves	Walter	Bygraves	Max	Entertainer
Byron	James	Dean	James	Actor

FAMOUS PEOPLE

Original Name		Assumed Name		
Caliari	Paolo	Veronese	Paolo	Venetian Painter
Calloway	Mark	Undertaker		Wrestler
Calvin	George	Leno	Dan	English Comedian
Campbell	Patrick	Glenavy	Baron	Irish Writer and Wit
Canale	Giovanni Antonio	Canaletto		Artist
Cansino	Marguerita	Hayworth	Rita	Actress
Caplin	Alfred Gerald	Capp	Al	Cartoonist
Carpentier	Harlean	Harlow	Jean	Actress
Carr	John Dickson	Dickson	Carter	US Detective Writer
Carroll	Daniel	La Rue	Danny	Female Impersonator
Carter	Charlton	Heston	Charlton	Actor
Cassavitis	Michael	Orlando	Tony	Vocalist
Cassotto	Robert Walden	Darin	Bobby	Vocalist
Castellucio	Frank	Valli	Frankie	Vocalist
Cavendish	William	Devonshire	Duke of	Prime Minister of Great Britain
Cavendish-Bentinck	William Henry	Portland	Duke of	Prime Minister of Great Britain
Cecil	Robert Arthur Talbot	Salisbury	Marquis of	Prime Minister of Great Britain
Cernick	Al	Mitchell	Guy	Vocalist
Chalupek	Appolonia	Negri	Pola	Actress
Chambers	James	Cliff	Jimmy	Vocalist
Chapman	John	Appleseed	Johnny	Missionary and Nurseryman
Chauchoin	Lily	Colbert	Claudette	Actress
Chauvin/Cauvin	Jean	Calvin	Jean	French Theologian
Chavarri	Emperatriz	Sumac	Yma	Musician
Cheeseman	Patrick	Wymark	Patrick	Actor
Chomette	Rene Lucien	Clair	Rene	Film Director
Christie	Agatha	Westmacott	Mary	Authoress
Ciccone	Madonna Louise	Madonna		Vocalist and Actress
Clapp	Eric	Clapton	Eric	Guitarist/Singer
Clary	Julian	Joan Collins' Fan Club		Entertainer
Clay	Cassius Marcellus	Ali	Muhammed	Boxer
Clemens	Samuel Langhorne	Twain	Mark	Author
Cobbett	William	Porcupine	Peter	Writer
Cobblepot	Oswald	Penguin		Batman Character
Cochrane	Elizabeth	Bly	Nellie	Aviatrix
Cocozza	Alfredo	Lanza	Mario	Opera Singer
Cody	William	Bill	Buffalo	Showman
Cohen	Sacha Baron	Ali G		Comedian
Cole	Maurice	Everett	Kenny	Disc Jockey and Comedian
Coles	Elizabeth	Taylor	Elizabeth	Novelist
Collins	Cathleen	Derek	Bo	Actress
Collins	Chris	Skinner	Frank	Comedian
Colon	Cristobel	Columbus	Christopher	Explorer
Compton	Spencer	Wilmington	Earl of	Prime Minister of Great Britain
Connery	Thomas	Connery	Sean	Actor
Connor	William	Cassandra	(Daily Mirror column)	Journalist
Cook	David	Essex	David	Vocalist and Actor
Cooper	Francis	Cooper	Gary	Actor
Coppola	Nicholas	Cage	Nicolas	US Actor
Cornwell	David	Le Carré	John	Author
Crabtree	Shirley	Daddy	Big	Wrestler
Craddock	Eugene Vincent	Vincent	Gene	Vocalist
Crane	Randolph	Scott	Randolph	Actor
Cripps	Bruce	Welch	Bruce	Guitarist
Cristillo	Louis	Costello	Lou	Comedian
Crocetti	Dino	Martin	Dean	Actor
Cromwell	Richard	Clark	John	Lord Protector of England
Crosby	Harry Lillis	Crosby	Bing	Vocalist and Actor
Crossley	James	Hunter		Gladiator
Crummey	Chris	Curtis	Chris	Pop Musician
Culkin	Bonnie	Bedelia	Bonnie	TV Actress
Czaczkes	Shmuel Josef	Agnon	Shmuel Yosef	Israeli Novelist

Original Name		Assumed Name		
Da Ponte	Giacomo	*Bassano*	Jacopo	*Italian Painter*
D'Abruzzo	Alfonso	*Alda*	Alan	*Actor*
Dallion	Susan	*Sioux*	Siouxsie	*Vocalist*
Daly	Sandra	*Khashoggi*	Soraya	*Millionairess*
Dannay	Frederick	*Queen*	Ellery	*Author*
		Ross	Barnaby	*Author*
D'Antonguolla	Rudolpho	*Valentino*	Rudolph	*Actor*
Darnell Browder	Thomas August	*Creole*	Kid	*Vocalist*
Davies	David Ivor	*Novello*	Ivor	*Composer*
Davies	Nigel	*Villeneuve*	Justin de	*Hair Stylist*
Davies	Robert	*Carrott*	Jasper	*Comedian*
Davies	Sharron	*Amazon*		*TV Gladiator and Swimmer*
Davies	Trevor	*Dozy*		*Bass Player*
De Havilland	Joan	*Fontaine*	Joan	*Actress*
Deeks	Barbara	*Windsor*	Barbara	*Actress*
Demsky	Issar Danielovitch	*Douglas*	Kirk	*Actor*
Dénes	Gábor	*Gabor*	Dennis	*Physicist*
Denning	Alfred Thompson	*Whitchurch*	Baron of	*Law Lord*
Derbyshire	Tommy	*Cannon*	Tommy	*Comedy Straight Man*
Deutschendorf Jnr	Henry John	*Denver*	John	*Vocalist and Composer*
Dibley	Dwayne	*Cat*		*TV Character 'Red Dwarf'*
Dick	Derek	*Fish*		*Vocalist*
Dickens	Charles	*Boz*	(Monthly Magazine)	*Author*
Dinh Khai	Phan	*Le Duc Tho*		*Vietnamese Politician*
Disraeli	Benjamin	*Beaconsfield*	Earl of	*Prime Minister of Great Britain*
Dodgson	Charles Lutwidge	*Carroll*	Lewis	*Author*
Donaghue	Patrick	*Magenta*	Captain	*TV Fictional Character*
Doolittle	Hilda	*HD*		*Author*
Dorléac	Catherine	*Deneuve*	Catherine	*Actress*
Dorsey	Arnold	*Dorsey*	Gerry	*Vocalist*
		Humperdinck	Englebert	*Vocalist*
Douglas	Michael	*Keaton*	Michael	*Actor*
Douglas-Home	Alec	*Hirsel*	Lord Home of the	*Prime Minister of Great Britain*
Dudevant	Amandine Lucie Dupin	*Sand*	George	*Author*
Dukenfield	William Claude	*Fields*	WC	*Comedian and Actor*
		Kane Jeeves	Mahatma	*Comedian and Actor*
Dumble-Smith	Michael	*Crawford*	Michael	*Actor and Singer*
Dutt	Narendranath	*Vivekananda*	Swami	*Hindu Missionary*
Dwight	Reginald Kenneth	*John*	Elton Hercules	*Vocalist and Composer*
Dymond	John	*Beaky*		*Guitarist*
Dzhugashvili	Iosif Vissarionovich	*Stalin*	Joseph	*Russian Leader*
Eberst	Jakob	*Offenbach*	Jacques	*Composer*
Eden	Anthony	*Avon*	Earl of	*Prime Minister of Great Britain*
Edwards	Eileen Regina	*Twain*	Shania	*Pop Singer*
Egstrom	Norma	*Lee*	Peggy	*Vocalist*
Eichelbaum	Jack Leonard	*Warner*	Jack Leonard	*Film Mogul*
Einstein	Albert	*Brooks*	Albert	*Actor*
Elizabeth	of Romania	*Sylva*	Carmen	*Queen of Romania*
Elliot	Marion	*Styrene*	Poly	*Punk-Rock Singer*
Enos	William	*Berkeley*	Busby	*Choreographer*
Ercolani	James	*Darren*	James	*US Actor*
Estevez	Ramon	*Sheen*	Martin	*Actor*
Evans	Dave	*Edge*	The	*Musician*
Evans	Ernest	*Checker*	Chubby	*Vocalist*
Evans	Mary Ann	*Eliot*	George	*Author*
Fagan	Eleanora	*Holiday*	Billie	*Vocalist*
Fairfield	Cicely Isabel	*West*	Rebecca	*Author*
Fawkes	Ernest	*Trog*	Walter	*Cartoonist*
Federkiewicz	Stefania	*Powers*	Stefanie	*Actress*
Feld	Marc	*Bolan*	Marc	*Vocalist and Musician*
Fellows	Graham	*John*	Jilted	*Pop Singer Creation*
		Shuttleworth	John	
Fiersohn	Reba	*Gluck*	Alma	*American Soprano*
Filipepi	Alessandro	*Botticelli*	Sandro	*Artist*
Finklea	Tula Ellice	*Charisse*	Cyd	*Dancer*
Firbank	Louis	*Reed*	Lou	*Vocalist and Composer*

Original Name		Assumed Name		
Fischman	Harve	**Bennett**	Harve	US TV Producer
Fitzroy	Augustus Henry	**Grafton**	Duke of	Prime Minister of Great Britain
Fitzsimmons	Maureen	**O'Hara**	Maureen	Actress
Flaccus	Quintus Horatius	**Horace**		Poet
Flegenheimer	Arthur	**Schultz**	Dutch	Gangster
Fletcher	Susannah	**York**	Susannah	Actress
Foe	Daniel	**Defoe**	Daniel	Author
Forte	Fabiano	**Fabian**		Vocalist
Fowles	Gloria	**Gaynor**	Gloria	Vocalist
Frahm	Karl Herbert	**Brandt**	Willy	German Chancellor
Francabilla	Marchesa Caterina de	**Boyle**	Katie	TV Presenter
Francis	Leigh	**Merrion**	Avid	Comedian
Franconers	Concetta	**Francis**	Connie	Vocalist
Frankel	Bernice	**Arthur**	Beatrice	US Actress
Frankenberg	Joyce	**Seymour**	Jane	Actress
Frazier	Richard	**Ochre**	Captain	TV Fictional Character
Frece	Lady De	**Tilley**	Vesta	Comedian
Frewer	Matt	**Headroom**	Max	TV Fictional Character
Fries	Victor	**Freeze**	Mr	Fictional Super-Villain
Frith	Mary	**Cutpurse**	Moll	Pick Pocket and Robber
Fucini	Renato	**Tanfucio**	Neri	Italian Writer
Fuertes	Dolores Adios	**Menken**	Adah Isaacs	US Actress & Poet
Fuhrhop	Roland	**Rowland**	Tiny	Businessman
Fulks	Sarah Jane	**Wyman**	Jane	Actress
Furnier	Vincent	**Cooper**	Alice	Vocalist
Fyffe	Patrick	**Bracket**	Hilda	TV Transvestite
Gadd	Paul	**Glitter**	Gary	Vocalist
Gaines	Donna Andrea	**Summers**	Donna	Vocalist
Garfunkel	Art	**Graph**	Tom	Half of 'Tom & Jerry' Duo
Gassion	Edith	**Piaf**	Edith	Vocalist
Gazzimos	Brenda Gail	**Gayle**	Crystal	Vocalist
Geisel	Theodore Seuss	**Seuss**	Dr	Author
Gelee	Claude	**Lorrain**	Claude	Landscape Painter
Gellen	Arthur	**Hunter**	Tab	Singer and Actor
Gendre	Louis	**Jordan**	Louis	Actor
George III	(in gardening periodicals)	**Robinson**	Ralph	British King
Georgiou	Stephen	**Stevens**	Cat	Vocalist
Gheraerd	Gheraerd	**Erasmus**	Desiderius	Scholar
Gilbert	Maria Eliza (Délores)	**Montez**	Lola	American Dancer
Gilhooly	Brenda	**Tuesday**	Gayle	Comedienne
Gillis	Ian	**Mycroft**		Brain of Britain
Gillis	Lester	**Nelson**	Baby Face	Gangster
Gillorly	Edna	**Burstyn**	Ellen	Actress
Glover	Brian	**Arras**	Leon	Professional Wrestler
Goddard	Stuart	**Ant**	Adam	Vocalist
Godfree	Edward	**Aldington**	Richard	English Poet
Goffage	John	**Rafferty**	Chips	Entertainer
Gold	Jacqueline	**Summers**	Ann	Businesswoman
Goldbert	Cyril Louis	**Wyngarde**	Peter	Actor
Goldenberg	Emmanuel	**Robinson**	Edward G	Actor
Goldenburger	Avron	**Todd**	Mike	Producer
Goldfish	Sam	**Goldwyn**	Sam	Film Producer
Goldstein	Elliott	**Gould**	Elliot	Actor
Gonne	Maud	**MacBride**	Maud	Irish Nationalist
Gonzalez	José Victoriano	**Gris**	Juan	Spanish Cubist Painter
Goodman	Theodosia	**Bara**	Theda	Vamp Actress
Goodrich	Samuel	**Parley**	Peter	US Publisher
Goodrich	Sandra	**Shaw**	Sandie	Vocalist
Gordon	George Hamilton	**Aberdeen**	Earl of	Prime Minister of Great Britain
Gorowicz	Vladimir	**Horowitz**	Vladimir	Russian Pianist
Gossart	Jan	**Mabuse**	Jan	Flemish Painter
Gothardt	Mathis	**Grünewald**	Mathias	German Painter
Gough	Damon	**Badly Drawn Boy**		Singer and Songwriter
Goyathlay		**Geronimo**		Apache Indian Chief
Graham	Florence Nightingale	**Arden**	Elizabeth	Beautician

Original Name		Assumed Name		
Grasemann	Ruth	*Rendell*	Ruth	Crime Novelist
Gravelet	Jean François	*Blondin*	Charles	French Acrobat
Gray	Charles	*White*	Colonel	TV Fictional Character
Grayson	Dick	*Robin*		Fictional Super Hero
Green	David	*Ben-Gurion*	David	Israeli Statesman
Greenbaum	Peter	*Green*	Peter	Musician
Greene	Gladys	*Arthur*	Jean	Actress
Gregson	Michael	*Craig*	Michael	Actor
Gretzky	Wayne	*Great One*	The	Ice Hockey Player
Grieve	Christopher Murray	*MacDiarmid*	Hugh	Poet
Griffith	John	*London*	Jack	Author
Griffiths	Seymour	*Green*	LT	TV Fictional Character
Grossell	Ira	*Chandler*	Jeff	Actor
Gudjonsson	Halldór	*Laxness*	Halldor	Icelandic Novelist
Guiche	Lilian	*Gish*	Lilian	Actress
Guidi, Di Simone	Tommaso Di Giovanni	*Masaccio*		Florentine Painter
Guillerm	Nelly	*Verdy*	Violette	French Dancer
Gumm	Frances	*Garland*	Judy	Actress and Singer
Gurdin	Natasha	*Wood*	Natalie	Actress
Gustaffson	Greta	*Garbo*	Greta	Actress
Gutteridge	John	*Pallo*	Jackie	Wrestler
Guttoveggio	Joseph	*Creston*	Paul	Musician
Guynes	Demi	*Moore*	Demi	Actress
Hackenbacker	Hiram J	*Brains*	(Thunderbirds)	Scientist
Hall	Diane	*Keaton*	Diane	Actress
Halliley	John Elton	*Le Mesurier*	John	Actor
Hamill	Christopher	*Limahl*	(Kajagoogoo)	Vocalist
Hamilton	Charles	*Conquest*	Owen	Author
		Richards	Frank	Author
Hansen	Emil	*Nolde*	Emil	German Painter
Hardin	Charles	*Holly*	Buddy	Vocalist
Haris	Derek	*Derek*	John	Actor
Harmon	David	*Dee*	Dave	Vocalist
Harmsworth	Harold Sydney	*Rothermere*	Viscount	Newspaper Magnate
Harper	Robert	*Ball*	Bobby	Comedian
Harris	Joel Chandler	*Remus*	Uncle	Author
Harrison	Gerald	*Gee*	Dustin	Impressionist
Hartley	Vivien	*Leigh*	Vivien	Actress
Hartree	George	*Hawtrey*	Charles	Actor
Hatcher	Charles	*Starr*	Edwin	Vocalist
Haussman	Jacques	*Houseman*	John	Actor
Hawkins	Anthony	*Hope*	Anthony	Author
Hawkins	Christian	*Slater*	Christian	Actor
Hawkins	Jack	*Hedley*	Jack	Actor
Haynes	Brian	*Laine*	Denny	Guitarist
Haynes Jr	Cornell	*Nelly*		Rapper
Healey-Kay	Patrick	*Dolin*	Anton	Choreographer
Hearne	Richard	*Pastry*	Mr	Actor
Heemstra	Edda Hepburn Van	*Hepburn*	Audrey	Actress
Heimberger	Eddie	*Albert*	Eddie	US Actor
Hellwig	James	*Ultimate Warrior*		Professional Wrestler
Hensley	Virginia	*Kline*	Patsy	Vocalist
Herzstein	Barbara	*Hershey*	Barbara	Actress
Heseltine	Les	*Dennis*	Les	Comedian
Heseltine	Philip Arnold	*Warlock*	Peter	Composer
Hesketh-Harvey	Kit	*Kit*		Musical act 'Kit and the Widow'
Heurschling	Andrée	*Hessling*	Catherine	Jean Renoir's Wife (actress)
Hewson	Paul	*Bono*		Vocalist
Hickenlooper	Lucie	*Samaroff*	Olga	Musician
Hicks	Thomas	*Steele*	Tommy	Entertainer
Hieronymus	Eusebius Sophronius	*Jerome*	St	Italian Scholar
Higginbottom	Minnie	*Staff*	Kathy	Actress
Hill	Alfred Hawthorne	*Hill*	Benny	Comedian
Hinault	Bernard	*Badger (Le Blaireau)*		Cyclist
Hoch	Jan Ludvik	*Maxwell*	Robert	Businessman
Hogg	James	*Ettrick Shepherd*		Poet

Original Name		Assumed Name		
Hogg	Quintin	Hailsham of Marylebone	Baron	Politician
Holden	Bradley	Grey	Captain	TV Fictional Character
Hollenbeck	Webb Parmelee	Webb	Clifton	Actor
Hook/Aherne	Caroline	Merton	Mrs	Comedian
Hookham	Margaret	Fonteyn	Margot	Ballerina
Hopkins	Gaynor	Tyler	Bonnie	Vocalist
Hornby	Leslie	Twiggy		Actress
Horowitz	Winona	Ryder	Winona	Actress
Hovick	Rose Louise	Rose Lee	Gypsy	Entertainer
Howell	Vernon	Koresh	David	Branch Davidian cult Leader
Huffman	Barbara	Eden	Barbara	US Actress
Huggins	Peter Jeremy	Brett	Jeremy	Actor
Humphries	Barry	Everage	Dame Edna	Comedian
Humphries	Barry	Patterson	Sir Les	Comedian
Hunter	Evan	McBain	Ed	Writer
Hyde	Edward	Clarendon	Earl of	Statesman
Illingworth	Harry	Worth	Harry	Comedian
Ingolia	Concetta	Stevens	Connie	Actress
Irving	Washington	Knickerbocker	Diedrich	Author
Iskowitz	Edward	Cantor	Eddie	Comedian
Isley	Pamela	Ivy	Poison	Fictional Super-Villain
Italiano	Anna Maria	Bancroft	Anne	Actress
Ivanhoe	Burl	Ives	Burl	Actor and Singer
Iyotake	Tatanka	Sitting Bull		Sioux Indian Chief
Jackson	Curtis	50 Cent		Rapper
Jackson	O'Shea	Ice Cube		Rapper and Actor
Jacob	Lee	Cobb	Lee J	Actor
Jacobs	Glen	Kane		Professional Wrestler
Jacobs	Rosetta	Laurie	Piper	US Actress
James	Michael	Jayston	Michael	Actor
Javal	Camille	Bardot	Brigitte	Actress
Jeanneret	Charles Edouard	Corbusier	Le	Architect
Jefferson	Arthur Stanley	Laurel	Stan	Comedy Actor
Jeffries	James Jackson	Boilermaker		Boxing Champion
Jenkins	Harold Lloyd	Twitty	Conway	Vocalist
Jenkins	Richard	Burton	Richard	Actor
Jenkinson	Robert Banks	Liverpool	Earl of	Prime Minister of Great Britain
Jensen	Anita	Genée	Adeline	Ballerina
Jewry	Bernard	Fenton	Shane	Vocalist
		Stardust	Alvin	Vocalist
Johnson	Bruce	Forsyth	Bruce	Entertainer
Johnson	Carol Diahann	Carroll	Diahann	Actress
Johnson	Caryn	Goldberg	Whoopi	US Actress
Johnson	Dwayne	Rock		Actor and Wrestler
Johnson	Hewlett	Red Dean		English Prelate
Johnson	Lawrence	Naismith	Laurence	Actor
Johnson	Mike	York	Michael	Actor
Johnson	William Eugene	Pussyfoot		US Reformer
Jones	David	Bowie	David	Vocalist and Composer
Jones	Edith	Wharton	Edith	Author
Jones	Edward	German	Edward	English Composer
Jones	Magnolia	Angel	Melody	'Captain Scarlet' Character
Judkins	Steveland	Wonder	Stevie	Vocalist and Composer
Judson	Edward Zane	Buntline	Ned	Inventor
Kalageropoulos	Cecilia	Callas	Maria	Operatic Soprano
Kam	Lee Yuen	Lee	Bruce	Actor and Martial Artist
Kaminker	Henriette Charlotte	Signoret	Simone	Actress
Kaminsky	David Daniel	Kaye	Danny	Entertainer
Kaminsky	Melvin	Brooks	Mel	Actor
Kaminsky	Noah	Diamond	Neil	Vocalist and Composer
Kappelhoff	Doris Von	Day	Doris	Actress and Singer
Katz	Phoebe	Cates	Phoebe	Actress
Kaumeyer	Dorothy Mary	Lamour	Dorothy	Actress
Kaye	Paul	Pennis	Dennis	Actor and Comedian
Kazanjoglou	Elia	Kazan	Elia	Film Director
Keane	Molly	Farrell	MJ	Irish Novelist
Kemal	Mustafa	Ataturk	Kemal	Turkish Statesman

Original Name		Assumed Name			
Khan Jnr	Taidje	*Brynner*	Yul	*Actor*	
Khaury	Herbert	*Tim*	Tiny	*Vocalist*	
Kiesler	Hedwig	*Lamarr*	Hedy	*Actress*	
Kilmister	Ian	*Lemmy*	(Motorhead)	*Vocalist*	
King	Leslie	*Ford*	Gerald	*President USA*	
King	Jefferson	*Shadow*		*TV Gladiator*	
Kingsley	Charles	*Lot*	Parson	*Author*	
Klass	Eugene	*Barry*	Gene	*US Actor*	
Klein	Carole	*King*	Carol	*Vocalist*	
Konigsberg	Allen	*Allen*	Woody	*Actor*	
Koreff	Nora	*Kaye*	Nora	*American Ballerina*	
Korzeniowski	Jozef Teodor Konrad	*Conrad*	Joseph	*Author*	
Kostrowitzky	Apollinaris	*Apollinaire*	Guillaume	*French Poet*	
Kouyoumdjian	Dikran	*Arlen*	Michael	*British Novelist*	
Kramer	Erich Maria	*Remarque*	Erich Maria	*Author*	
Krampke	Hugh	*O'Brien*	Hugh	*Actor*	
Kubelsky	Benjamin	*Benny*	Jack	*Comedian*	
Kwan	Chan	*Angel*	Harmony	*'Captain Scarlet' Character*	
Lake	Margaret	*Meg*	Mystic	*TV Personality*	
Lamb	Charles	*Elia*		*Essayist*	
Lamb	William	*Melbourne*	Viscount	*Prime Minister of Great Britain*	
Lamburn	Richmal	*Crompton*	Richmal	*Author*	
Landru	Henri	*Bluebeard*		*French Murderer*	
Lange	Cedric	*Hawk*	Jeremy	*Actor and TV Presenter*	
Langemanke	Lucille	*Astor*	Mary	*Actress*	
Lawrence	Thomas Edward	*Ross*	Aircraftsman John Hume	*Soldier and Author*	
		Shaw	T E (Royal Tank Corps)	*Soldier and Author*	
Lawrie	Marie McLaughlin	*Lulu*		*Vocalist*	
Lawson	Nigel	*Blaby*	Lord Lawson of	*Politician*	
Leach	Archibald	*Grant*	Cary	*Actor*	
Lee	Manfred B	*Queen*	Ellery	*Author*	
		Ross	Barnaby	*Author*	
Léger	Alexis Saint-Léger	*Saint-John Perse*		*French Poet*	
Leitch	Donovan	*Donovan*		*Vocalist*	
Letz	George	*Montgomery*	George	*Actor*	
Levesque	Paul Michael	*HHH*		*Wrestler*	
Levitch	Joseph	*Lewis*	Jerry	*Actor and Comedian*	
Levy	Ivo	*Montand*	Yves	*Actor*	
Levy	Marion	*Goddard*	Paulette	*Actress*	
Lewis	Cecil Day	*Blake*	Nicholas	*Detective Writer*	
Lewis	CS	*Hamilton*	Clive	*Irish Writer*	
Lewis	Mike	*Saracen*		*TV Gladiator*	
Liddell	Eric	*Flying Scotsman*		*Athlete*	
Little	Malcolm	*X*	Malcolm	*Civil Rights Leader*	
Lloyd George	David	*Gwynedd of Dwyfor*	Viscount	*Prime Minister of Great Britain*	
Loewenstein	Laszlo	*Lorre*	Peter	*Actor*	
Logan	George	*Hinge*	Dr Evadne	*TV Transvestite*	
Longbaugh	Henry	*Sundance Kid*		*Outlaw*	
Lorimer	Maxwell George	*Wall*	Max	*Actor and Comedian*	
Loughran	Angus	*Statto*		*TV Soccer Pundit*	
Louis	Joe	*Brown Bomber*		*Boxer*	
Louis	Marilyn	*Fleming*	Rhonda	*Actress*	
Lubbertszoon	Meyndert	*Hobbema*	Meindert	*Dutch Painter*	
Lubowitz	Michael	*Mann*	Manfred	*Musician*	
Lucas	Matt	*Dawes (He's a baby)*	George	*Comedian*	
Luta	Mahpiua	*Red Cloud*	Oglala Teton Dakota	*(Sioux) Chief*	
Lydon	John	*Rotten*	Johnny	*Vocalist*	
Lyon	Emma (Amy)	*Hamilton*	Emma	*Lady*	
Lytle	Donald Eugene	*Paycheck*	Johnny	*Country Singer*	
Mabovitch	Golda	*Meir*	Golda	*Israeli PM*	
McDaniel	Ellas	*Diddley*	Bo	*Vocalist*	
McCarthy	Henry	*Bonney*	William	*Billy the Kid*	
McGillicuddy	Cornelius	*Mack*	Connie	*Baseball Player*	
McGregor	Robert	*Roy*	Rob	*Scottish Freebooter*	
McGuinness	Eddie	*Large*	Eddie	*Comedian*	

Original Name		Assumed Name		
McGurran	Aidan	Lottery	Lenny	National Lottery Expert
Mackay	Mary	Corelli	Marie	English Novelist
McLoughlin	Mark	Pellow	Marti	Vocalist
McManus	Declan	Costello	Elvis	Vocalist and Composer
McMasters	Luke	Haystacks	Giant	Wrestler
McMath	Virginia	Rogers	Ginger	Actress and Dancer
Macmillan	Harold	Stockton	Earl of	Prime Minister of Great Britain
McMillan	Anthony Robert	Coltrane	Robbie	Actor and Comedian
McMurray	Barbara	Flynn	Barbara	Actress
McNeile	HC	Sapper		Author
McPherson	Graham	Suggs		Vocalist
Maddox	No-Name	Manson	Charles	Cult Leader
Mainwaring	Edward Stewart	Stewart	Ed	Disc Jockey
Makonnen	Ras Tafari	Selassie	Hailie	Ethiopian Emperor
Mapother	Tom Cruise	Cruise	Tom	Actor
Mariano	Agnolo di Cosimo	Bronzino	Il	Painter
Marks	Lilian Alice	Markova	Alicia	Ballerina
Maro	Publius Vergilius	Virgil		Poet
Marrow	Tracy	Ice-T		Rapper and Actor
Martin	Paul	Merton	Paul	Comedian
Marx	Adolph	Marx	Harpo	Actor
Marx	Herbert	Marx	Zeppo	Actor
Marx	Julius	Marx	Groucho	Actor
Marx	Leonard	Marx	Chico	Actor
Marx	Milton	Marx	Gummo	Actor
Massaccesi	Aristide	D'Amato	Joe	Film Director
Mathers III	Marshall	Eminem		Rapper and Actor
Mathieu	Henri Donat	Saint-Laurent	Yves	French Designer
Matthews	Pauline	Dee	Kiki	Vocalist
Matuschanskavasky	Walter	Matthau	Walter	Actor
Mavor	Osborne Henry	Bridie	James	Dramatist
		Henderson	Mary	Dramatist
Mayer	David	Janssen	David	Actor
Mayson	Isabella	Beeton	Mrs Isabella	Cookery Writer
Mazzola	Girolamo Francesco M	Parmigiano		Italian Painter
Mead	Cyril	Little	Syd	Comedian
Mellencamp	John	Cougar	John	Vocalist
Mellor	John	Strummer	Joe	Rock Star
Mendelssohn-Bartholdy	Felix	Mendelssohn	Felix	Composer
Menendez	Andres Arturo Garcia	Garcia	Andy	Actor
Mennini	Peter	Mennin	Peter	Musician
Mercer	Cecil William	Yates	Dornford	Novelist
Merisi	Michelangelo	Caravaggio		Artist
Merowitz	Rena	Sable		Professional Wrestler
Meservey	Robert	Preston	Robert	Actor
Metcalfe	Paul	Scarlet	Captain	TV Animation Character
Micklewhite	Maurice	Caine	Michael	Actor
Middleton	Peggy	De Carlo	Yvonne	Actress
Middleton	Roger	Colbourne	Maurice	Actor
Mikhailovich	Sergius	Stepnyak		Russian Revolutionary
Millar	William	Boyd	Stephen	Actor
Miller	James	MacColl	Ewan	Folk Singer
Millet	Jean-François	Francisque		Belgian Painter
Milligan	Terence Alan	Milligan	Spike	Comedian and Writer
Mitchell	Ian	Finch	Peter	Actor
Mitchell	James Leslie	Gibbon	Lewis	Novelist
Mizell	George	Mitchell	Cameron	Actor
Modini	Robert	Stack	Robert	Actor
Moir	Jim	Reeves	Vic	Comedian
Molinsky	Joan	Rivers	Joan	Comedienne
Monro	Hector Hugh	Saki		Author
Montagu	John	Sandwich	Earl of	Inventor of Sandwich
Montgomery	Edward	Clift	Montgomery	Actor
Moodnick	Ronald	Moody	Ron	Actor
Moore	Alicia	Pink		Actress and Singer
Morganfield	McKinley	Waters	Muddy	Vocalist
Morhange	Charles-Valentin	Alkan	Charles-Valentin	French Musician

Original Name		Assumed Name		
Morrison	George Ivan	*Morrison*	Van	*Vocalist and Composer*
Morrison	Jeanette	*Leigh*	Janet	*Actress*
Morrison	Marion	*Wayne*	John	*Actor*
Morrow	Jennifer Lee	*Leigh*	Jennifer Jason	*Actress*
Morton	John Cameron	*Beachcomber*	(*Daily Express* column)	*Journalist*
Mostel	Samuel Joel	*Mostel*	Zero	*Actor*
Mozee	Phoebe	*Oakley*	Annie	*Frontierswoman*
Mulgrew	Jimmy	*Cricket*	Jimmy	*Comedian*
Müller	Lucas	*Cranach*	Lucas	*German Painter*
Müller	Johannes	*Regiomontanus*		*German Mathematician*
Munker	Ariane	*Foster*	Jodie	*US Actress*
Nakszynski	Nastassja	*Kinski*	Nastassia	*Actress*
Nankeville	Robert	*Davro*	Bobby	*Comic Impressionist*
Nascimento	Edson Arantes Do	*Pele*		*Footballer*
Needham	Yootha	*Joyce*	Yootha	*Actress*
Nelhams	Terry	*Faith*	Adam	*Vocalist*
Nelson	Benjamin	*King*	Ben E	*Vocalist*
Nelson	Prince Rogers	*Prince (formerly)*		*Vocalist and Composer*
Nice	Stephen	*Harley*	Steve	*Pop Singer*
Niewoehner	Dirk	*Benedict*	Dirk	*US Actor*
Norway	Neville	*Shute*	Neville	*Author*
Oaxaca	Rudolph	*Quinn*	Anthony	*US Actor*
O'Brien	Mary	*Springfield*	Dusty	*Vocalist*
O'Day	Dawn	*Shirley*	Anne	*Actress*
O'Donovan	Michael	*O'Connor*	Frank	*Irish Writer*
O'Dowd	George	*George*	Boy	*Vocalist*
O'Fearna	Sean	*Ford*	John	*Film Director*
O'Flaherty	Katherine	*Chopin*	Kate	*Author and Feminist*
O'Grady	Paul	*Savage*	Lily	*Female Impersonator*
Ohm	Peter	*Vaughan*	Peter	*Actor*
Olden	Charles	*Ray*	Ted	*Comedian*
Olsson	Ann-Margret	*Margret*	Ann	*Actress*
O'Mahoney	Tynian	*Allen*	Dave	*Comedian*
O'Nolan	Brian	*O'Brien*	Flann	*Irish Writer*
Ord	Irene	*Larrigan*	Tex	*Author of Westerns*
Orowitz	Eugene Maurice	*Landon*	Michael	*US Actor*
Orrico	Carmen	*Saxon*	John	*Actor*
Orton	Joe	*Wellthorpe*	Edna	*Fictional Letter Writer*
Osterberg	James Jewel	*Pop*	Iggy	*Vocalist*
Ostlere	Gordon	*Gordon*	Richard	*Doctor and Author*
O'Sullivan	Raymond	*O'Sullivan*	Gilbert	*Vocalist*
Pakenham	Francis Aungier	*Longford*	Lord	*Prison Reformer*
Pal (Female)		*Lassie (Male)*		*Dog*
Palaniuk	Walter	*Palance*	Jack	*Actor*
Palmer	Keith	*Reality*	Maxim	*MC*
Palmer	Vera Jane	*Mansfield*	Jayne	*Actress*
Panayiotou	Georgios	*Michael*	George	*Vocalist and Composer*
Papaceo	Anthony	*Franciosa*	Tony	*Actor*
Parker	Peter	*Spiderman*		*Fictional Hero*
Parker	Robert LeRoy	*Cassidy*	Butch	*Outlaw Leader*
Paton	Alison	*Siren*		*TV Gladiator*
Patterson	Henry	*Higgins*	Jack	*Author*
Paul	Maury	*Knickerbocker*	Cholly	*NY Gossip Columnist*
Paup	Theresa	*Russell*	Theresa	*Actress*
Peiser	Lilli	*Palmer*	Lilli	*Actress*
Pelham-Holles	Thomas	*Newcastle*	Duke of	*Prime Minister of Great Britain*
Penniman	Richard Wayne	*Richard*	Little	*Vocalist and Musician*
Pennington	Michael	*Vegas*	Johnny	*Comedian*
Penrose	Elizabeth	*Markham*	Elizabeth	*Writer for Children*
Perelmuth	Jacob Pincus	*Peerce*	Jan	*Musician*
Perez	Manuel Benitez	*Cordobes*	El	*Matador*
Perido	Nick	*Como*	Perry	*Vocalist*
Perks	William	*Wyman*	Bill	*Musician*
Perry	William	*Refrigerator*		*American Footballer*
Perske	Betty Joan	*Bacall*	Lauren	*Actress*
Peschkowsky	Michael	*Nichols*	Mike	*US Film Director*
Peshkov	Max	*Gorky*	Maxim	*Author*
Peters	Jane	*Lombard*	Carole	*Actress*

FAMOUS PEOPLE

Original Name		Assumed Name		
Petty-Fitzmaurice	William	Shelburne	Earl of	Prime Minister of Great Britain
Pickwoad	William	Mervyn	William	Actor
Pierre	Cherilyn Sarkisian La	Cher		Vocalist and Actress
Pietro/Fiesoli	Guido di	Angelico	Fra	Artist
Pisperikos	Elizabeth	Perkins	Elizabeth	Actress
Plemiannkov	Roger	Vadim	Roger	Film Director
Pointon	Juliette	Angel	Destiny	'Captain Scarlet' Character
Poire	Emmanuel	D'Ache	Caran	French Illustrator
Poliakov	Nikolai	Coco		Clown
Popley	Bernard	Youens	Bernard	Actor
Poquelin	Jean-Baptiste	Molière		Playwright
Porter	William Sydney	O'Henry		Author
Pound	Ezra Loomis	Atheling	William	Poet
Powell	Clive	Fame	Georgie	Vocalist and Musician
Powles	Matilda Alice	Tilley	Vesta	Comedian
Pratt	Denis	Crisp	Quentin	Writer
Pratt	William Henry	Karloff	Boris	Actor
Prendergast	John Barry	Barry	John	Musician
Price	Ellen	Wood	Mrs Henry	English Novelist
Price	Katie	Jordan		Model
Priestley	John Boynton	Goldsmith	Peter	Author
Primrose-Pechey	Phyllis	Craddock	Fanny	Television Cook
Prior-Palmer	Lucinda	Green	Lucinda	Three-Day Eventer
Pugh	Wynette	Wynette	Tammy	Vocalist
Quedens	Eunice	Arden	Eve	Actress
Quiller-Couch	Arthur	Q		Author
Quincey	Thomas	De Quincey	Thomas	Essayist
Quoirez	Françoise	Sagan	Françoise	Author
Rajan	John	Lord	Jack	Actor
Ramée, de la	Marie Louise	Ouida		English Novelist
Ranft	George	Raft	George	Actor
Rankin	Brian	Marvin	Hank	Guitarist
Ravenscroft	John	Peel	John	Disc Jockey
Reibnitz	Marie von	Michael of Kent	Princess	Austrian Princess
Relph	Harry	Tich	Little	Comedian
Relyea	Walter	Hayden	Sterling	Actor
Rendell	Ruth	Vine	Barbara	Crime Novelist
Richards	Pauline	Rocket		TV Gladiator
Richardson	Jiles Perry (JP)	Bopper	The Big	Vocalist
Riddle	James	Hoffa	Jimmy	US Union Leader
Riley	Helena	Panther		TV Gladiator
Ritchie	John	Vicious	Sid	Vocalist
Ritchie	Robert	Kid Rock		Rock Star
Robbins	Anne Frances	Davis	Nancy	Actress
Roberts	Russ	Abbot	Russ	Comedian
Robertson	Anna Mary	Moses	Grandma	Artist
Robertson	James Logie	Haliburton	Hugh	Poet
Robertson	Marjorie	Neagle	Anna	Actress
Robinson	Frederick John	Goderich	Viscount	Prime Minister of Great Britain
Robinson	Ray Charles	Charles	Ray	Vocalist
Robusti	Jacopo	Tintoretto		Artist
Rolfe	Frederick William	Corvo	Baron	Novelist
Rosenbaum	Borge	Borge	Victor	Comic Musician
Rosenberg	Leonard	Randall	Tony	Actor
Rose-Price	Dennistoun Franklyn	Price	Dennis	Actor
Rothschild	Dorothy	Parker	Dorothy	Author
Rowlands	John	Stanley	Henry Morton	Explorer
Ruane	Martin	McMasters	Luke	Wrestler
Rubin	Harold	Robbins	Harold	Author
Rubin	Lynsey	De Paul	Lynsey	Vocalist
Ruiz	Pablo	Picasso	Pablo	Artist
Russell	George William	AE		Irish Poet
Ruston	Audrey	Hepburn	Audrey	Actress
Saillot	Félicité	Desmousseaux	Félicité	Actress
Samaniegos	Ramon	Novarra	Ramon	Actor
Samuel	Henry	Seal		Vocalist
Samuels	Miriam	Karlin	Miriam	Actress

Original Name		Assumed Name		
Sánchez	Illich Ramirez	**Carlos the Jackal**		Guerrilla
Sandeman	Mary	**Aneka**		Pop Singer
Santi/Sanzio	Raffaello	**Raphael**		Artist
Sarstedt	Richard	**Kane**	Eden	Vocalist
Sättler	Elisabeth	**Rethberg**	Elisabeth	Musician
Scallon (née Brown)	Rosemary	**Dana**		Singer and Politician
Scherer Jnr	Roy	**Hudson**	Rock	Actor
Schicklgrüber	Adolf	**Hitler**	Adolf	Dictator
Schipani	Pia	**Zadora**	Pia	Actress
Schneider	Guenther	**Arnold**	Edward	Actor
Schrift	Shirley	**Winters**	Shelley	Actress
Schwabe	Cecil	**Parker**	Cecil	Actor
Schwartz	Bernard	**Curtis**	Tony	Actor
Schwatt	Aaron	**Buttons**	Red	Actor
Schweider	Alfred	**Bruce**	Lenny	Comedian
Scicolone	Sofia	**Loren**	Sophia	Actress
Scudéry	Madeleine de	**Sappho**		French Novelist
Seagull	Barbara	**Hershey**	Barbara	US Actress
Sekolovich	Mladen	**Malden**	Karl	Actor
Shalhoub	Michael	**Sharif**	Omar	Actor
Sharpe	Alexander John	**Ellis**	Alexander John	English Philologist
Shaw	George Bernard	**Corno Di Bassetto**	(Music critic for *Star*)	Author
Siciliano	Angelo	**Atlas**	Charles	Athlete
Siddhartha	Gautama	**Buddha**		Buddhism Founder
Sieffert	Ernst	**Tauber**	Richard	Austrian Tenor
Sigursteinnson	Magnus	**Magnusson**	Magnus	Broadcaster
Silberman	Jerome	**Wilder**	Gene	Actor
Silverman	Belle	**Sills**	Beverly	Musician
Simon	Paul	**Landis**	Jerry	Half of 'Tom & Jerry' Duo
Sims	Diane	**Angel**	Rhapsody	'Captain Scarlet' Character
Sinnott	Michael	**Sennett**	Mack	Film Producer
Sisson	Richard	**Widow**		Musical act 'Kit and the Widow'
Skikne	Larushka Mischa	**Harvey**	Laurence	Actor
Sklodowska	Manya	**Curie**	Marie	Physicist
Skryabin	Vyacheslav Mikhaylovich	**Molotov**	Vyacheslav Mikhaylovich	Russian Statesman
Skurnick	Estelle	**Nicole**		Renault Clio Advert
Slye	Leonard	**Rogers**	Roy	Actor
Smith	Gladys Mary	**Pickford**	Mary	Actress
Smith	Harold J	**Silverheels**	Jay	Actor
Smith	James Marcus	**Proby**	PJ	Vocalist
Smith	James Todd	**Cool James**	Ladies Love (LL Cool J)	Rapper
Smith	Julie Anne	**Moore**	Julianne	US Actress
Smith	Kim	**Wilde**	Kim	Vocalist
Smith	Reginald	**Wilde**	Marty	Vocalist
Smith	Robert	**Jack**	Wolfman	Disc Jockey
Smith	Walker	**Robinson**	Sugar Ray	Boxer
Solberg	David	**Soul**	David	Actor
Sorya	Françoise	**Aimée**	Anouk	Actress
Southill	Ursula	**Mother Shipton**		Witch and Prophet
Spartanero	Franco	**Nero**	Franco	Actor
Springall	Charles	**Drake**	Charlie	Comedian
Stainer	Leslie	**Howard**	Leslie	Actor
Stanley	Edward	**Derby**	Earl of	Prime Minister of Great Britain
Stanley	Henry Morton	**Rowlands**	John	Explorer and Journalist
Stansfield	Grace	**Fields**	Gracie	Actress and Singer
Starkey	Richard	**Starr**	Ringo	Drummer and Composer
Steele	Richard	**Bickerstaffe**	Isaac	Author
Stengland	Inger	**Stevens**	Inger	Actress
Stephens	Yvette Marie	**Khan**	Chaka	Vocalist
Stern	Miriam	**Stoppard**	Miriam	Broadcaster
Stevens	Cat	**Islam**	Yusuf	Vocalist and Composer
Stevens	Ruby	**Stanwyck**	Barbara	Actress
Stevens	Shaking	**Kent**	Clark	Vocalist
Stevens	Terry	**Thomas**	Terry	Comedy Actor
Stevenson	Elizabeth	**Gaskell**	Elizabeth	Writer
Stewart	Charles Edward	**Burke**	Betty	Scottish Pretender

FAMOUS PEOPLE

Original Name		Assumed Name		
Stewart	James	*Granger*	Stewart	Actor
Stewart	John	*Innes*	Michael	Author
Stoppelmoor	Cheryl	*Ladd*	Cheryl	Actress
Stoute	Jenny	*Rebel*		TV Gladiator
Stovenour	June	*Haver*	June	Actress
Strataki	Anastasia	*Stratas*	Teresa	Soprano
Stratemeyer	Edward	*Dixon*	Franklin W	Author
Stratemeyer	Edward	*Hope*	Laura Lee	Author
Stratemeyer	Edward	*Keene*	Carolyn	Author
Stratton	Charles	*Thumb*	Tom	Circus Performer
Straussler	Thomas	*Stoppard*	Tom	Dramatist
Stringer	Lynne	*Caine*	Marti	Comedienne and Singer
Stuart	Charles Edward	*Burke*	Betty	Bonnie Prince Charlie
Stuart	John	*Bute*	Earl of	Prime Minister of Great Britain
Sueur	Lucille le	*Crawford*	Joan	Actress
Sullivan (née Hopkins)	Gaynor	*Tyler*	Bonnie	Vocalist
Sumner	Gordon	*Sting*		Vocalist and Musician
Svenson	Adam	*Blue*	Captain	TV Fictional Character
Svenson	Beryl	*Grey*	Beryl	Ballerina
Svensson	Gloria	*Swanson*	Gloria	Actress
Swift	Jonathan	*Bickerstaffe*	Isaac	Author
Sykes	Norma	*Sabrina*		Model
Tarpley	Brenda	*Lee*	Brenda	Vocalist
Tatischeff	Jacques	*Tati*	Jacques	Actor
Teach	Edward	*Blackbeard*		Pirate
Tejada	Raquel	*Welch*	Raquel	Actress
Temple	Henry John	*Palmerston*	Viscount	Prime Minister of Great Britain
Tennenbaum	Irving	*Stone*	Irving	US Novelist
Tennyson	Alfred Lord	*Merlin*		Poet
Terzi	Orhan	*DJ Quicksilver*		Turkish Pop Star
Thackeray	William Makepeace	*Titmarsh*	Michael Angelo	Author
Thann	Nguyen Van	*Chi-Minh*	Ho	Vietnamese Politician
Thatcher	Margaret	*Kesteven*	Baroness Thatcher of	Prime Minister of Great Britain
Theotocopoulos	Domenico	*Greco*	El	Artist
Thibault	Anatole François	*France*	Anatole	Author
Thomas	George	*Tonypandy*	Viscount	Speaker of Commons
Thompson	Estelle	*Oberon*	Merle	Actress
Thornburg	Betty June	*Hutton*	Betty	US Comedy Actress
Thornley	Peter	*Nagasaki*	Kendo	Professional Wrestler
Ticker	Reuben	*Tucker*	Richard	Singer
Tidbury	Eldred	*Gray*	Donald	South African Actor
Titta	Ruffo	*Ruffo*	Titta	Baritone
Tomaling	Susan	*Sarandon*	Susan	Actress
Touchinsky	Alfred	*Marks*	Alfred	Actor/Comedian
Trendle	Doug	*Bloodvessel*	Buster	Vocalist
Trevorrow	Mark	*Downe*	Bob	Australian Comedian
Trimmler	Deborah	*Kerr*	Deborah	Actress
Truscott-Jones	Reginald	*Milland*	Ray	Actor
Tsering	Lhamo Thondup	*Tenzin Gyatso*		14th Dalai Lama
Tullius	Marcus	*Cicero (from wart on nose)*		Roman Statesman
Tureaud	Lawrence	*T*	Mr	Actor
Turner	Conrad	*Black*	Captain	'Captain Scarlet' Character
Ullman	Douglas	*Fairbanks*	Douglas	Actor
Ulyanov	Vladimir Ilyich	*Lenin*	Vladimir Ilyich	Russian revolutionary
Upchurch	Lou	*Phillips*	Lou Diamond	Actor
Uttini	Giuseppe	*Verdi*		Vocalist
Valentino	Wladziu	*Liberace*		Pianist
Valenzuela	Ritchie	*Valens*	Ritchie	Vocalist
Van Aken	Jerome	*Bosch*	Hieronymus	Dutch Painter
Van Den Bogaerde	Derek Niven	*Bogarde*	Dirk	Actor
Van der Faes	Pieter	*Lely*	Peter	British Painter
Van Varenberg	Jean-Claude	*Van Damme*	Jean-Claude	Actor
Vander Walt	Lize	*Gold*		TV Gladiator
Vecchio	Frank Lo	*Laine*	Frankie	Vocalist
Vecellio	Tiziano	*Titian*		Artist
Velline	Robert Thomas	*Vee*	Bobby	Vocalist

Original Name		Assumed Name		
Vincent	Mark	*Diesel*	Vin	*Actor*
Vivar	Rodrigo diaz de	*Cid*	El	*Spanish Warrior*
Vliet	Don Van	*Beefheart*	Captain	*Vocalist*
Wainewright	Thomas Griffiths	*Weathercock*	Janus	*Art Critic and Murderer*
Wainwright	Karen	*Angel*	Symphony	*'Captain Scarlet' Character*
Walker	Edmund	*Kemp*	Jeremy	*Actor*
Wallace	Christopher	*B.I.G.*	Notorious	*Pop Singer*
Waller	Thomas Wright	*Waller*	Fats	*Jazz Pianist*
Walpole	Robert	*Orford*	Earl of	*Prime Minister of Great Britain*
Walters	Mrs Daryl	*Blyton*	Enid	*Author*
Ward	Arthur Sarsfield	*Rohmer*	Sax	*Author*
Warner	Brian	*Manson*	Marilyn	*Pop Star*
Waters	Jack	*Warner*	Jack	*Actor*
Watkins	Ian	*H*		*Pop Singer*
Wayman	Eunice	*Simone*	Nina	*Vocalist*
Wayne	Bruce	*Batman*		*Fictional Super Hero*
Webb	Gary	*Numan*	Gary	*Vocalist and Composer*
Webb	Harold	*Richard*	Cliff	*Singer*
Weinstein	Bernie	*Winters*	Bernie	*Comedian*
Weiss	Ehrich	*Houdini*	Harry	*Illusionist*
Welch	Vera	*Lynn*	Vera	*Singer*
Wellesley	Arthur	*Wellington*	Duke of	*Prime Minister of Great Britain*
Wells	Julia	*Andrews*	Julie	*Actress and Singer*
Wentworth	Charles Watson	*Rockingham*	Marquis of	*Prime Minister of Great Britain*
Wesley	Arthur	*Wellesley*	Arthur	*Prime Minister of Great Britain*
Westcott	Fred	*Karno*	Fred	*Impresario*
Westover	Charles	*Shannon*	Del	*Singer*
Wettach	Adrien	*Grock*		*Clown*
White	David	*Jason*	David	*Actor*
White	PD	*James*	PD	*Author*
White	Priscilla	*Black*	Cilla	*Vocalist and Presenter*
White	William	*Grayson*	Larry	*Comedian*
		Breen	Billy	
White	William Hale	*Rutherford*	Mark	*Writer*
Whittaker	James	*Bowen*	Jim	*Comedian*
Wight	James	*Herriot*	James	*Vet and Author*
Wight	Paul	*Big Show*		*Professional Wrestler*
Wilde	Oscar	*Melmoth*	Sebastian	*Author*
Wilfred	Sir	*Ivanhoe*		*Literary Character*
Wilkens	Maybritt	*Britt*	May	*Actress*
Wilkie	Edward	*Fawn*	Doctor	*'Captain Scarlet' Character*
William	Walter	*Maynard*	Bill	*Actor*
Williams	Kim	*Lightning*		*Gladiator*
Wilson	Anthony	*Burgess*	Anthony	*Writer*
Wilson	Barbara	*Batgirl*		*Fictional Film Hero*
Wilson	Harold	*Rievaulx*	Lord	*Prime Minister of Great Britain*
Windsor	Albert	*George VI*	King	*Sovereign*
Winkle	Robert Van	*Vanilla Ice*		*Rapper and Actor*
Winogradsky	Boris	*Delfont*	Bernard	*Impresario*
Winogradsky	Louis	*Grade*	Lew	*Impresario*
Winter	Richard	*Warwick*	Richard	*Actor*
Wiseman	Ernest	*Wise*	Ernie	*Comedian*
Witko	Tasunko	*Crazy Horse*		*Sioux Indian Chief*
Witz	Chaim	*Simmons*	Gene	*Rock Singer*
Wojtyla	Karol	*John Paul II*	Pope	*Bishop of Rome*
Wolcot	John	*Pindar*	Peter	*Satirist*
Wood	Henry	*Klenovsky*	Paul	*English Conductor*
Wood	Mathilda	*LLoyd*	Marie	*Actress*
Woodward	Thomas	*Jones*	Tom	*Vocalist*
Worrell	Charles	*I Spy*	Big Chief	*Author*
Wright	Archibald	*Moore*	Archibald	*Boxer*
Wunderman	Leslie	*Carlisle*	Belinda	*Vocalist*
Wupperman	Frank	*Morgan*	Frank	*Actor*
Wycherly	Ronald	*Fury*	Billy	*Vocalist*
Yanks	Byron	*Janis*	Byron	*Musician*
Yeary	Harvey Lee	*Majors*	Lee	*Actor*

Original Name		Assumed Name		
Yin	Leslie Charles Bowyer	**Charteris**	Leslie	Author
Youdale	Diane	**Jet**		TV Gladiator
Young	Leslie Ronald	**Young**	Jimmy	Broadcaster
Young	Sandy	**Phoenix**		Gladiator
Young	Sarah	**Carr**	Sally	Vocalist
Yule Jnr	Joseph	**Rooney**	Mickey	Actor
Ze Schluderpacheru	Herbert	**Lom**	Herbert	Actor
Zerby	Deborah	**Darby**	Kim	Actress
Zimmerman	Ethel	**Merman**	Ethell	Singer
Zimmerman	Robert Alan	**Dylan**	Bob	Vocalist and Composer
Zogu	Ahmed Bey	**Zog**	King	Albanian King
Zoine	Vincento	**Edwards**	Vince	US Actor
Zuck	Alexandra	**Dee**	Sandra	Actress
Zwinge	James Randall	**Randi**	Amazing	Magician

Real Names: By Assumed Name

Assumed Name		Original Name		
Abbot	Russ	**Roberts**	Russ	Comedian
Aberdeen	Earl of	**Gordon**	George Hamilton	British Prime Minister
AE		**Russell**	George William	Irish Poet
Agnon	Shmuel Yosef	**Czaczkes**	Shmuel Josef	Israeli Novelist
Aimée	Anouk	**Sorya**	Françoise	Actress
Albert	Eddie	**Heimberger**	Eddie	US Actor
Alda	Alan	**D'Abruzzo**	Alfonso	Actor
Aldington	Richard	**Godfree**	Edward	English Poet
Ali	Muhammad	**Clay**	Cassius Marcellus	Boxer
Ali G	–	**Cohen**	Sacha Baron	Comedian
Alkan	Charles-Valentin	**Morhange**	Charles-Valentin	French Musician
Allen	Dave	**O'Mahoney**	Tynian	Comedian
Allen	Woody	**Konigsberg**	Allen	Actor and Director
Amazon		**Davies**	Sharron	Swimmer and TV Gladiator
Anderson	Bronco Billy	**Arenson**	Max	Entertainer
Andrews	Julie	**Wells**	Julia	Actress and Singer
Aneka		**Sandeman**	Mary	Pop singer
Angel	Destiny	**Pointon**	Juliette	'Captain Scarlet' Character
Angel	Harmony	**Kwan**	Chan	'Captain Scarlet' Character
Angel	Melody	**Jones**	Magnolia	'Captain Scarlet' Character
Angel	Rhapsody	**Sims**	Diane	'Captain Scarlet' Character
Angel	Symphony	**Wainwright**	Karen	'Captain Scarlet' Character
Angelico	Fra	**di Pietro**	Guido di	Artist
Ant	Adam	**Goddard**	Stuart	Singer
Apollinaire	Guillaume	**de Kostrowitzky**	Wilhelm Apollinaris	French Poet
Appleseed	Johnny	**Chapman**	John	Missionary Nurseryman
Arden	Elizabeth	**Graham**	Florence Nightingale	Beautician
Arden	Eve	**Quedens**	Eunice	Actress
Arlen	Michael	**Kouyoumdjian**	Dikran	British Novelist
Arliss	George	**Andrews**	Augustus George	Actor
Arness	James	**Aurness**	James	US Actor
Arnold	Edward	**Schneider**	Guenther	Actor
Arras	Leon	**Glover**	Brian	Professional Wrestler
Arthur	Beatrice	**Frankel**	Bernice	US Actress
Arthur	Jean	**Greene**	Gladys	Actress
Astaire	Fred	**Austerlitz**	Frederick	Dancer and Actor
Astor	Mary	**Langemanke**	Lucille	Actress
Ataturk	Kemal	**Kemal**	Mustafa	Turkish Statesman
Atheling	William	**Pound**	Ezra Loomis	Poet
Atlas	Charles	**Siciliano**	Angelo	Athlete
Atticus		**Addison**	Joseph	Essayist and Politician
Avery	Tex	**Bean**	Frederick	Cartoonist

Assumed Name		Original Name		
Aznavour	Charles	Aznavurjal	Shahnovr	Singer and Actor
Bacall	Lauren	Perske	Betty Joan	Actress
Badger (Le Blaireau)		Hinault	Bernard	Cyclist
Badly Drawn Boy	–	Gough	Damon	Singer and Songwriter
Baker	Janet	Abbott	Janet	Mezzo-soprano
Balanchine	George	Balanchivadze	Georgi Melitonivich	Choreographer
Bancroft	Anne	Italiano	Anna Maria	Actress
Bara	Theda	Goodman	Theodosia	Actress
Bardot	Brigitte	Javal	Camille	Actress
Barrie	Amanda	Broadbent	Shirley Ann	Actress
Barry	Gene	Klass	Eugene	US Actor
Barry	John	Prendergast	John Barry	Musician
Barry	Michael	Bukht	Michael	Food Journalist
Barrymore	Ethel	Blythe	Ethel	Actress
Barrymore	John	Blythe	John	Actor
Barrymore	Lionel	Blythe	Lionel	Actor
Bart	Black	Bottom	Charles	Outlaw
Bart	Lionel	Begleiter	Lionel	Composer
Basie	Count	Basie	William	Musician
Bassano	Jacopo	Da Ponte	Giacomo	Italian Painter
Batgirl		Wilson	Barbara	Comic and Film Heroine
Batman		Wayne	Bruce	Comic and Film Hero
Beachcomber	John	Morton	Cameron	Newspaper Columnist
Beaky		Dymond	John	Guitarist
Beatty	Warren	Beaty	Warren	Actor
Bedelia	Bonnie	Culkin	Bonnie	Actress
Beefheart	Captain	Van Vliet	Don	Musician
Beeton	Mrs	Mayson	Isabella	Cookery Writer
Bell	Acton	Brontë	Anne	Novelist
Bell	Currer	Brontë	Charlotte	Novelist
Bell	Ellis	Brontë	Emily	Novelist
Benedict	Dirk	Niewoehner	Dirk	US Actor
Ben-Gurion	David	Green	David	Israeli Statesman
Bennett	Harve	Fischman	Harve	US TV Producer
Bennett	Lennie	Berry	Mike	Comedian
Bennett	Tony	Benevetto	Anthony Dominic	Vocalist
Benny	Jack	Kubelsky	Benjamin	Comedian
Berkeley	Busby	Enos	William	Choreographer
Berlin	Irving	Baline	Israel	Composer
Bernhardt	Sarah	Bernard	Rosine	Actress
Berra	Yogi	Berra	Lawrence Peter	Baseball Player
Bickerstaffe	Isaac	Steele	Richard	Author (shared pen-name)
Bickerstaffe	Isaac	Swift	Jonathan	Author (shared pen-name)
B.I.G.	Notorious	Wallace	Christopher	Pop Singer
Big Show		Wight	Paul	Professional Wrestler
Bill	Buffalo	Cody	William	Showman
Billy the kid		McCarty	Henry	Outlaw
Blaby	Lord Lawson of	Lawson	Nigel	Politician
Captain Black		Turner	Conrad	'Captain Scarlet' Character
Black	Cilla	White	Priscilla	Singer and TV Presenter
Blackbeard		Teach	Edward	Pirate
Blake	Nicholas	Day-Lewis	Cecil	Detective Writer
Blondin	Charles	Gravelet	Jean François	French Acrobat
Bloodvessel	Buster	Trendle	Doug	Singer
Blue	Captain	Svenson	Adam	TV Fictional Character
Bluebeard		Landru	Henri	French Murderer
Bly	Nellie	Cochrane	Elizabeth	Aviator
Blyton	Enid	Walters	Mrs Daryl	Author
Bogarde	Dirk	Van Den Bogaerde	Derek	Actor
Boilermaker		Jeffries	James Jackson	Boxing Champion
Bolan	Marc	Feld	Marc	Musician
Bono		Hewson	Paul	Musician
Big Bopper		Richardson	Jiles Perry (JP)	Musician
Bonney	William	McCarthy	Henry	Outlaw Billy the Kid
Borge	Victor	Rosenbaum	Borge	Comic and Musician
Bosch	Hieronymus	Van Aken	Jerome	Dutch Painter
Botticelli	Sandro	Filepepi	Alessandro	Artist
Bowen	Jim	Whittaker	James	Comedian
Bowie	David	Jones	David	Musician

FAMOUS PEOPLE

Assumed Name		Original Name		
Boyd	Stephen	*Millar*	William	*Actor*
Boyle	Katie	*Francabilla*	Marchesa Caterina de	*TV Presenter*
Boz		*Dickens*	Charles	*Author (occasional pen-name)*
Bracket	Hilda	*Fyffe*	Patrick	*Entertainer*
Brains		*Hackenbacker*	Hiram J	*'Thunderbirds' Character*
Brandt	Willy	*Frahm*	Karl Herbert	*German Chancellor*
Breen	Billy	*White*	William	*Comedian*
Brett	Jeremy	*Huggins*	Peter Jeremy	*Actor*
Bridie	James	*Mavor*	Osborne Henry	*Dramatist*
Britt	May	*Wilkens*	Maybritt	*Actress*
Bronson	Charles	*Buchinski*	Charles	*Actor*
Bronzino	il	*Mariano*	Agnolo di Cosimo	*Painter*
Brooks	Albert	*Einstein*	Albert	*Actor*
Brooks	Elkie	*Bookbinder*	Elaine	*Singer*
Brooks	Mel	*Kaminsky*	Melvin	*Actor and Director*
Brown Bomber		*Louis*	Joe	*Boxer*
Bruce	Lenny	*Schweider*	Alfred	*Comedian*
Bryan	Dora	*Broadbent*	Dora	*Actress and Comedienne*
Brynner	Yul	*Khan Jnr*	Taidje	*Actor*
Buddha		*Siddhartha*	Gautama	*Founder of Buddhism*
Buntline	Ned	*Judson*	Edward Zane	*Inventor*
Burgess	Anthony	*Wilson*	Anthony	*Writer*
Burke	Betty	*Stuart*	Charles Edward	*Bonnie Prince Charlie*
Burns	George	*Birnbaum*	Nathan	*Comedian*
Burstyn	Ellen	*Gillorly*	Edna	*Actress*
Burton	Richard	*Jenkins*	Richard	*Actor*
Buttons	Red	*Schwatt*	Aaron	*Actor*
Bygraves	Max	*Bygraves*	Walter	*Entertainer*
Byrnes	Edd	*Breitenberger*	Edward	*Actor*
Cage	Nicolas	*Coppola*	Nicholas	*US Actor*
Cagliostro	Count	*Balsame*	Giuseppe	*Italian Adventurer*
Caine	Marti	*Stringer*	Lynne	*Comedienne and Singer*
Caine	Michael	*Micklewhite*	Maurice	*Actor*
Callas	Maria	*Kalageropoulos*	Cecilia	*Operatic Soprano*
Calvin	Jean	*Chauvin/Cauvin*	Jean	*French Theologian*
Canaletto		*Canale*	Giovanni Antonio	*Artist*
Cannon	Tommy	*Derbyshire*	Tommy	*Comedy Straight Man*
Cantor	Eddie	*Iskowitz*	Edward	*Comedian*
Capp	Al	*Caplin*	Alfred Gerald	*Cartoonist*
Caravaggio		*Merisi*	Michelangelo	*Artist*
Carlisle	Belinda	*Wunderman*	Leslie	*Vocalist*
Carlos 'the Jackal'		*Sánchez*	Illich Ramirez	*Revolutionary and Assassin*
Carr	Sally	*Young*	Sara	*Vocalist*
Carroll	Diahann	*Johnson*	Carol Diahann	*Actress*
Carroll	Lewis	*Dodgson*	Charles Lutwidge	*Author*
Carrott	Jasper	*Davies*	Robert	*Comedian*
Cassandra		*Connor*	William	*Journalist*
Cassidy	Butch	*Parker*	Robert LeRoy	*Outlaw Leader*
Cat		*Dibley*	Dwayne	*TV Character ('Red Dwarf')*
Cates	Phoebe	*Katz*	Phoebe	*Actress*
Cathcart	Helen	*Albert*	Harold	*Royal Biographer*
Chandler	Jeff	*Grossell*	Ira	*Actor*
Charisse	Cyd	*Finklea*	Tula Ellice	*Dancer*
Charles	Ray	*Robinson*	Ray Charles	*Singer*
Charteris	Leslie	*Yin*	Leslie Charles Bowyer	*Author*
Checker	Chubby	*Evans*	Ernest	*Singer*
Cher		*La Pierre*	Cherilyn Sarkisian	*Singer and Actress*
Chi-Minh	Ho	*Thann*	Nguyen Van	*Vietnamese Politician*
Chopin	Kate	*O'Flaherty*	Katherine	*Author*
Cicero		*Tullius*	Marcus	*Roman Statesman*
Cid	El	*Vivár*	Rodrigo Díaz de	*Spanish Warrior*
Clair	René	*Chomette*	René Lucien	*Film Director*
Clapton	Eric	*Clapp*	Eric	*Guitarist and Singer*
Clarke	John	*Cromwell*	Richard	*Son of Oliver Cromwell*
Cliff	Jimmy	*Chambers*	James	*Singer*

Assumed Name		Original Name		
Clift	Montgomery	*Montgomery*	Edward	*Actor*
Cobb	Lee J	*Jacob*	Lee	*Actor*
Coco		*Poliakov*	Nikolai	*Clown*
Colbert	Claudette	*Chauchoin*	Lily	*Actress*
Colbourne	Maurice	*Middleton*	Roger	*Actor*
Cole	Nat King	*Adams*	Nathaniel	*Singer*
Coltrane	Robbie	*McMillan*	Anthony Robert	*Actor and Comedian*
Como	Perry	*Perido*	Nick	*Singer*
Connery	Sean	*Connery*	Thomas	*Actor*
Conquest	Owen	*Hamilton*	Charles	*Author*
Conrad	Joseph	*Korzeniowski*	Jozef Teodor Konrad	*Author*
Cool James	Ladies Love	*Smith*	James Todd	*Rap Singer*
Cooper	Alice	*Furnier*	Vincent	*Singer*
Cooper	Gary	*Cooper*	Francis	*Actor*
Le Corbusier		*Jeanneret*	Charles Edouard	*Architect*
El Cordobes		*Perez*	Manuel Benitez	*Matador*
Corelli	Marie	*Mackay*	Mary	*English Novelist*
Corno di Bassetto		*Shaw*	George Bernard	*Author (as music critic)*
Correggio		*Allegri*	Antonio	*Artist*
Corvo	Baron	*Rolfe*	Frederick William	*Novelist*
Costello	Elvis	*McManus*	Declan	*Singer and Composer*
Costello	Lou	*Cristillo*	Louis	*Comedian*
Cougar	John	*Mellencamp*	John	*Vocalist*
Craddock	Fanny	*Primrose-Pechey*	Phyllis	*Television Cook*
Craig	Michael	*Gregson*	Michael	*Actor*
Cranach	Lucas	*Müller*	Lucas	*German Painter*
Craven	Sara	*Ashurst*	Anne	*Novelist*
Crawford	Joan	*Le Sueur*	Lucille	*Actress*
Crawford	Michael	*Dumble-Smith*	Michael	*Actor and Singer*
Crazy Horse		*Witko*	Tasunko	*Sioux Indian Chief*
Creole	Kid	*Darnell Browder*	Thomas August	*Singer*
Creston	Paul	*Guttoveggio*	Joseph	*Musician*
Cricket	Jimmy	*Mulgrew*	James	*Comedian*
Crisp	Quentin	*Pratt*	Denis	*Writer*
Crompton	Richmal	*Lamburn*	Richmal	*Author*
Crosby	Bing	*Crosby*	Harry Lillis	*Singer and Actor*
Cruise	Tom	*Mapother*	Tom Cruise	*Actor*
Curie	Marie	*Sklodowska*	Manya	*Physicist*
Curtis	Chris	*Crummey*	Chris	*Pop Musician*
Curtis	Tony	*Schwartz*	Bernard	*Actor*
Cutpurse	Moll	*Frith*	Mary	*Pickpocket and Robber*
D'Ache	Caran	*Poire*	Emmanuel	*French Illustrator*
Daddy	Big	*Crabtree*	Shirley	*Wrestler*
D'Amato	Joe	*Massaccesi*	Aristide	*Film Director*
Dana		*Scallon (née Brown)*	Rosemary	*Singer and Politician*
Dane	Clemence	*Ashton*	Winifred	*English Dramatist*
Darby	Kim	*Zerby*	Deborah	*Actress*
Darin	Bobby	*Cassotto*	Robert Walden	*Singer*
Darren	James	*Ercolani*	James	*US Actor*
Davis	Nancy	*Robbins*	Anne Frances	*Actress*
Davro	Bobby	*Nankeville*	Robert	*Comic Impressionist*
Dawes (He's a baby)	George	*Lucas*	Matt	*Comedian*
Dawn	Elizabeth	*Butterfield*	Sylvia	*Actress*
Day	Doris	*Kappelhoff*	Doris Von	*Actress and Singer*
De Carlo	Yvonne	*Middleton*	Peggy	*Actress*
De Paul	Lynsey	*Rubin*	Lynsey	*Singer*
De Quincey	Thomas	*Quincey*	Thomas	*Essayist*
Dean	James	*Byron*	James	*Actor*
Dee	Dave	*Harman*	David	*Vocalist*
Dee	Kiki	*Matthews*	Pauline	*Singer*
Dee	Sandra	*Zuck*	Alexandra	*Actress*
Defoe	Daniel	*Foe*	Daniel	*Author*
Delfont	Bernard	*Winogradsky*	Boris	*Impresario*
Deneuve	Catherine	*Dorléac*	Catherine	*Actress*
Dennis	Les	*Heseltine*	Les	*Comedian*
Denver	John	*Deutschendorf Jnr*	Henry John	*Singer and Composer*
Derek	Bo	*Collins*	Cathleen	*Actress*
Derek	John	*Harris*	Derek	*Actor*
Desmousseaux	Félicité	*Saillot*	Félicité	*Actress*

F
A
M
O
U
S

P
E
O
P
L
E

Assumed Name		Original Name		
Diamond	Neil	Kaminsky	Noah	Singer and Composer
Dickinson	Angie	Brown	Angeline	Actress
Dickson	Carter	Carr	John Dickson	US Detective Writer
Diddley	Bo	Bates	Otha Ellas	Singer
Diesel	Vin	Vincent	Mark	Actor
Dinesen	Isak	Blixen	Karen	Writer
Ding Ling		Bingzhi	Jiang	Chinese Novelist
Divine	Father	Baker	George	Religious Leader
Dixon	Franklin W	Stratemeyer	Edward	Author
DJ Quicksilver		Terzi	Orhan	Turkish Pop Star
Dolin	Anton	Healey-Kay	Patrick	Choreographer
Donovan		Leitch	Donovan	Singer
Dorsey	Gerry	Dorsey	Arnold	Singer
Douglas	Kirk	Demsky	Issur Danielovitch	Actor
Downe	Bob	Trevorrow	Mark	Australian Comedian
Dozy		Davies	Trevor	Bass Player
Drake	Charlie	Springall	Charles	Comedian
Dylan	Bob	Zimmerman	Robert Alan	Singer and Composer
Eden	Barbara	Huffman	Barbara	US Actress
Edge	The	Evans	Dave	Musician
Edwards	Vince	Zoine	Vincento	US Actor
Elia		Lamb	Charles	Essayist
Eliot	George	Evans	Mary Ann	Novelist
Ellis	Alexander John	Sharpe	Alexander John	English Philologist
Elytis	Odysseus	Alepoudelis	Odysseus	Greek Poet
Eminem		Mathers III	Marshall	Rapper and Actor
Erasmus	Desiderius	Gheraerd	Gheraerd	Scholar
Essex	David	Cook	David	Singer and Actor
Everage	Dame Edna	Humphries	Barry	Comedian
Everett	Kenny	Cole	Maurice	Disc Jockey and Comedian
Fabian		Forte	Fabiano	Singer
Fairbanks	Douglas	Ullman	Douglas	Actor
Faith	Adam	Nelhams	Terry	Singer
Fame	Georgie	Powell	Clive	Musician
Farrell	MJ	Keane	Molly	Irish Novelist
Fawn	Doctor	Wilkie	Edward	'Captain Scarlet' Character
Fenton	Shane	Jewry	Bernard	Singer
Fields	Gracie	Stansfield	Grace	Actress and Singer
Fields	WC	Dukenfield	William Claude	Comedian and Actor
50 Cent		Jackson	Curtis	Rapper
Finch	Peter	Mitchell	Ian	Actor
Fish		Dick	Derek	Vocalist
Fleming	Rhonda	Louis	Marilyn	Actress
Flying Scotsman		Liddell	Eric	Athlete
Flynn	Barbara	McMurray	Barbara	Actress
Fontaine	Joan	De Havilland	Joan	Actress
Fonteyn	Margot	Hookham	Margaret	Ballerina
Ford	Gerald	King	Leslie	US President
Ford	John	O'Fearna	Sean	Film Director
Formby Jnr	George	Booth	George Hoy	Music Hall Entertainer
Formby Snr	George	Booth	James	Music Hall Entertainer
Forrest	Steve	Andrews	William Forrest	US Actor
Forsyth	Bruce	Johnson	Bruce	Entertainer
Foster	Jodie	Munker	Ariane	US Actress
Fox		Baker	Tammy Marie	TV Gladiator
France	Anatole	Thibault	Anatole François	Author
Franciosa	Tony	Papaceo	Anthony	Actor
Francis	Connie	Franconers	Concetta	Singer
Francis of Assisi	Saint	de Bernardone	Giovanni	Religious Leader
Francisque		Millet	Jean-François	Belgian Painter
Freeze	Mr	Fries	Victor	Fictional Super-Villain
Fury	Billy	Wycherly	Ronald	Vocalist
Gabor	Dennis	Dénes	Gábor	Physicist
Garbo	Greta	Gustaffsson	Greta Louisa	Actress
Garcia	Andy	Menendez	Andres Arturo Garcia	Actor
Garfunkel	Art	Graph	Tom	Half of 50s Singing Duo 'Tom & Jerry'
Garland	Judy	Gumm	Frances	Actress and Singer
Garner	James	Baumgartner	James	Actor
Gaskell	Elizabeth	Stevenson	Elizabeth	Writer

Assumed Name		Original Name		
Gayle	Crystal	Gazzimos	Brenda Gail	Singer
Gaynor	Gloria	Fowles	Gloria	Singer
Gee	Dustin	Harrison	Gerald	Impressionist
Genée	Adeline	Jensen	Anita	Ballerina
George	Boy	O'Dowd	George	Singer
Geraldo		Bright	Gerald	Musician
German	Edward	Jones	Edward	English Composer
Geronimo		Goyathlay		Apache Indian Chief
Giant Haystacks		McMasters	Luke	Wrestler
Gibbon	Lewis	Mitchell	James Leslie	Novelist
Giorgione		Barbarelli	Giorgio	Artist
Gish	Lillian	Guiche	Lilian	Actress
Glitter	Gary	Gadd	Paul	Singer
Gluck	Alma	Fiersohn	Reba	American Soprano
Goddard	Paulette	Levy	Marion	Actress
Gold		Vander Walt	Lize	TV Gladiator
Goldberg	Whoopi	Johnson	Caryn	US Actress
Goldsmith	Peter	Priestley	John Boynton	Author
Goldwyn	Sam	Gelbfisz	Samuel	Film Producer
Goodrich	William B	Arbuckle	Roscoe Conkling (Fatty)	Actor
Gordon	Richard	Ostlere	Gordon	Doctor and Author
Gorky	Arshile	Adoian	Vosdanig Manoog	US Painter
Gorky	Maxim	Peshkov	Max	Author
Gould	Elliott	Goldstein	Elliott	Actor
Grade	Lew	Winogradsky	Louis	Impresario
Granger	Stewart	Stewart	James	Actor
Grant	Cary	Leach	Archibald	Actor
Gray	Donald	Tidbury	Eldred	South African Actor
Grayson	Larry	White	William	Comedian
Graziano	Rocky	Barbella	Rocco	Boxer
El Greco		Theotocopoulos	Domenico	Artist
L T Green		Griffiths	Seymour	TV Fictional Character
Green	Lucinda	Prior-Palmer	Lucinda	Three-Day Eventer
Green	Peter	Greenbaum	Peter	Musician
Grey	Beryl	Svenson	Beryl	Ballerina
Grey	Captain	Holden	Bradley	TV Fictional Character
Gris	Juan	González	Juan Victoriano	Cubist Painter
Grock		Wettach	Adrien	Clown
Grünewald	Matthias	Gothardt	Mathis	German Painter
Guercino		Barbieri	Gian-Francesco	Italian Painter
H		Watkins	Ian	Pop Singer
Haliburton	Hugh	Robertson	James Logie	Poet
Hamilton	Clive	Lewis	CS	British Writer
Hamilton	Emma	Lyon	Emma	Lord Nelson's Mistress
Hammer	MC	Burrell	Stanley Kirk	Rapper
Harley	Steve	Nice	Stephen	Pop Singer
Harlow	Jean	Carpentier	Harlean	Actress
Hart	Emma	Lyon	Emma (Amy)	Blacksmith's Daughter
Harvey	Laurence	Skikne	Larushka Mischa	Actor
Haver	June	Stovenour	June	Actress
Hawk	Jeremy	Lange	Cedric	Actor and TV Presenter
Hawtrey	Charles	Hartree	George	Actor
Hayden	Sterling	Relyea	Walter	Actor
Hayworth	Rita	Cansino	Marguerita	Actress
HD		Doolittle	Hilda	Writer
Headroom	Max	Frewer	Matt	Fictional TV Character
Hedley	Jack	Hawkins	Jack	Actor
Henderson	Mary	Mavor	Osborne Henry	Dramatist
Hepburn	Audrey	Van Heemstra	Edda Hepburn	Actress
Hepburn	Audrey	Ruston	Audrey	Actress
Herriot	James	Wight	James	Vet and Author
Hershey	Barbara	Herzstein	Barbara	Actress
Hershey	Barbara	Seagull	Barbara	US Actress
Hessling	Catherine	Heurschling	Andrée	Jean Renoir's Wife (Actress)
Heston	Charlton	Carter	Charlton	Actor
HHH (Triple H)	(Hunter Hearst Helmsley)	Levesque	Paul Michael	Wrestler
Higgins	Jack	Patterson	Henry	Author
Hill	Benny	Hill	Alfred Hawthorne	Comedian

Assumed Name		Original Name		
Hinge	Evadne	Logan	George	Entertainer
Hirsel	Lord Home of the	Douglas-Home	Alec	Prime Minister of Great Britain
Hitler	Adolf	Schicklgrüber	Adolf	Dictator
Hobbema	Meindert	Lubbertszoon	Meyndert	Dutch Painter
Hoffa	Jimmy	Riddle	James	US Union Leader
Hogan	Hulk	Bollea	Terry	Professional Wrestler and Actor
Holden	William	Beedle	William	Actor
Holiday	Billie	Fagan	Eleanora	Singer
Holly	Buddy	Hardin	Charles	Singer
Hope	Anthony	Hawkins	Anthony	Author
Hope	Laura Lee	Stratemeyer	Edward	Author
Horowitz	Vladimir	Gorowicz	Vladimir	Russian Pianist
Houdini	Harry	Weiss	Ehrich	Illusionist
Houseman	John	Haussman	Jacques	Actor
Howard	Leslie	Stainer	Leslie	Actor
Hudson	Rock	Scherer Jnr	Roy	Actor
Humperdinck	Engelbert	Dorsey	Arnold	Singer
Hunter		Crossley	James	Gladiator
Hunter	Tab	Gellen	Arthur	Singer and Actor
Hutton	Betty	Thornburg	Betty June	US Comedy Actress
I Spy	Big Chief	Worrell	Charles	Author
Ice Cube		Jackson	O'Shea	Rapper and Actor
Ice-T		Marrow	Tracy	Rapper and Actor
Innes	Michael	Stewart	John	Author
Irving	Henry	Brodribb	John Henry	Actor
Islam	Yusuf	Stevens	Cat	Singer and Composer
Ives	Burl	Ivanhoe	Burl	Actor and Singer
Ivy	Poison	Isley	Pamela	Fictional Super-Villain
Jack	Wolfman	Smith	Robert	Disc Jockey
James	PD	White	PD	Writer
Jane	Calamity	Canary	Martha Jane	Frontierswoman
Janis	Byron	Yanks	Byron	Musician
Janssen	David	Mayer	David	Actor
Jason	David	White	David	Actor
Jayston	Michael	James	Michael	Actor
Jet		Youdale	Diane	TV Gladiator
Joan Collins' Fan Club		Clary	Julian	Entertainer
John	Elton Hercules	Dwight	Reginald Kenneth	Singer and Composer
John	Jilted	Fellows	Graham	Pop Singer
John Paul II	Pope	Wojtyla	Karol	Pope
Jolie	Angelina	Voight	Angelina	Actress
Jones	Tom	Woodward	Thomas	Singer
Jordan	Price	Katie		Model
Jordan	Louis	Gendre	Louis	Actor
Joyce	Yootha	Needham	Yootha	Actress
Julia	Raul	Rafael Y Arcelos	Raul	Actor
Kane		Jacobs	Glen	Professional Wrestler
Kane	Eden	Sarstedt	Richard	Singer
Kane Jeeves	Mahatma	Dukenfield	William Claude	Comedian and Actor
Karlin	Miriam	Samuels	Miriam	Actress
Karloff	Boris	Pratt	William Henry	Actor
Karno	Fred	Westcott	Fred	Impresario
Kaye	Danny	Kaminsky	David Daniel	Entertainer
Kaye	Nora	Koreff	Nora	Ballerina
Kazan	Elia	Kazanjoglou	Elia	Film Director
Keaton	Diane	Hall	Diane	Actress
Keaton	Michael	Douglas	Michael	Actor (Batman Actor)
Keene	Carolyn	Stratemeyer	Edward	Author
Kemp	Jeremy	Walker	Edmund	Actor
Kerr	Deborah	Trimmler	Deborah	Actress
Kesteven	Baroness Thatcher of	Thatcher	Margaret	Prime Minister of Great Britain
Khan	Chaka	Stephens	Yvette Marie	Singer
Khashoggi	Soraya	Daly	Sandra	Millionairess
Kid Rock		Ritchie	Robert	Rock Star
King	Ben E	Nelson	Benjamin	Singer
King	Carol	Klein	Carole	Singer

Assumed Name		Original Name		
Kinski	Nastassia	*Nakszynski*	Nastassja	*Actress*
Kit		*Hesketh-Harvey*	Kit	*Musical act 'Kit and the Widow'*
Klenovsky	Paul	*Wood*	Henry	*English Conductor*
Kline	Patsy	*Hensley*	Virginia	*Singer*
Knickerbocker	Cholly	*Paul*	Maury	*NY Gossip Columnist*
Knickerbocker	Diedrich	*Irving*	Washington	*Author*
Koresh	David	*Howell*	Vernon	*Branch Davidian Cult Leader*
La Rue	Danny	*Carroll*	Daniel	*Female Impersonator*
Ladd	Cheryl	*Stoppelmoor*	Cheryl	*Actress*
Laine	Denny	*Haynes*	Brian	*Guitarist*
Laine	Frankie	*Vecchio*	Frank Lo	*Vocalist*
Lamarr	Hedy	*Kiesler*	Hedwig	*Actress*
Lamour	Dorothy	*Kaumeyer*	Dorothy Mary	*Actress*
Landis	Jerry	*Simon*	Paul	*Half of 50s Singing Duo 'Tom & Jerry'*
Landon	Michael	*Orowitz*	Eugene Maurice	*US Actor*
Lanza	Mario	*Cocozza*	Alfredo	*Opera Singer*
Large	Eddie	*McGuinness*	Eddie	*Comedian*
Larrigan	Tex	*Ord*	Irene	*Author of Westerns*
Lassie (male)		*Pal (female)*		*Film Dog*
Laurel	Stan	*Jefferson*	Arthur Stanley	*Comedy Actor*
Laurie	Piper	*Jacobs*	Rosetta	*US Actress*
Laxness	Halldór	*Gudjonsson*	Halldór	*Icelandic Novelist*
Le Carré	John	*Cornwell*	David	*Author*
Le Duc Tho		*Dinh Khai*	Phan	*Vietnamese Politician*
Le Mesurier	John	*Halliley*	John Elton	*Actor*
Lee	Brenda	*Tarpley*	Brenda	*Vocalist*
Lee	Bruce	*Kam*	Lee Yuen	*Actor and Martial Artist*
Lee	Peggy	*Egstrom*	Norma	*Vocalist*
Leigh	Janet	*Morrison*	Jeanette	*Actress*
Leigh	Jennifer Jason	*Morrow*	Jennifer Lee	*Actress*
Leigh	Vivien	*Hartley*	Vivien	*Actress*
Lely	Peter	*Van der Faes*	Pieter	*Artist*
Lemmy		*Kilmister*	Ian	*Singer (Motorhead)*
Lenin	Vladimir Ilich	*Ulyanov*	Vladimir Ilich	*Russian Revolutionary*
Leno	Dan	*Calvin*	George	*English Comedian*
Lenya	Lotte	*Blamauer*	Karoline Wilhelmine	*Austrian Actress*
Lewis	Jerry	*Levitch*	Joseph	*Actor and Comedian*
Liberace		*Valentino*	Wladziu	*Pianist and Entertainer*
Lightning		*Williams*	Kim	*TV Gladiator*
Limahl		*Hamill*	Christopher	*Singer (Kajagoogoo)*
Little	Syd	*Mead*	Cyril	*Comedian*
Lloyd	Marie	*Wood*	Mathilda	*Actress*
Lom	Herbert	*Ze Schluderpacheru*	Herbert	*Actor*
Lombard	Carole	*Peters*	Jane	*Actress*
London	Jack	*Griffith*	John	*Author*
Lord	Jack	*Ryan*	John Joseph	*Actor*
Loren	Sophia	*Scicolone*	Sofia	*Actress*
Lorraine	Claude	*Gelée*	Claude	*Landscape Painter*
Lorre	Peter	*Loewenstein*	Laszlo	*Actor*
Lot	Parson	*Kingsley*	Charles	*Author*
Lottery	Lenny	*McGurran*	Aidan	*National Lottery Expert*
Louis	Joe	*Barrow*	Joseph	*Boxer*
Louis	Morris	*Bernstein*	Morris	*US Painter*
Lulu		*Lawrie*	Marie McLaughlin	*Singer*
Lynn	Vera	*Welch*	Vera	*Singer*
Mabuse	Jan	*Gossart*	Jan	*Flemish Painter*
MacBride	Maud	*Gonne*	Maud	*Irish Nationalist*
MacColl	Ewan	*Miller*	James	*Folk Singer*
MacDiarmid	Hugh	*Grieve*	Christopher Murray	*Poet*
Mack	Connie	*McGillicuddy*	Cornelius	*Baseball Player*
Maclaine	Shirley	*Beaty*	Shirley	*Actress*
Madonna		*Ciccone*	Madonna Louise	*Singer*
Magenta	Captain	*Donaghue*	Patrick	*Fictional TV Character*
Magnusson	Magnus	*Sigursteinnson*	Magnus	*Broadcaster*
Majors	Lee	*Yeary*	Harvey Lee	*Actor*
Malden	Karl	*Sekolovich*	Mladen	*Actor*
Mann	Manfred	*Lubowitz*	Michael	*Musician*

Assumed Name		Original Name		
Mansfield	Jayne	Palmer	Vera Jane	Actress
Mansfield	Katherine	Beauchamp	Kathleen	NZ Writer
Manson	Charles	Maddox	No-Name	Cult Leader
Manson	Marilyn	Warner	Brian	Pop Star
March	Fredric	Bickel	Frederick	Actor
Margret	Ann	Olsson	Ann-Margret	Actress
Markham	Elizabeth	Penrose	Elizabeth	Writer for Children
Markham	Robert	Amis	Kingsley	Novelist
Markova	Alicia	Marks	Lilian Alice	Ballerina
Marks	Alfred	Touchinsky	Alfred	Actor and Comedian
Martin	Dean	Crocetti	Dino	Actor
Marvel	Captain	Batson	Billy	Comics Hero
Marvin	Hank	Rankin	Brian	Guitarist
Marx	Chico	Marx	Leonard	Actor
Marx	Groucho	Marx	Julius	Actor
Marx	Gummo	Marx	Milton	Actor
Marx	Harpo	Marx	Adolph	Actor
Marx	Zeppo	Marx	Herbert	Actor
Masaccio	di Simone Guidi	de Giovanni	Tommaso	Florentine Painter
Matthau	Walter	Matuschanskavasky	Walter	Actor
Maxwell	Robert	Hoch	Jan Ludvik	Businessman
Maynard	Bill	William	Walter	Actor
McBain	Ed	Hunter	Evan	Writer
McMasters	Luke	Ruane	Martin	Wrestler
Meatloaf		Aday	Marvin Lee	Singer
Meg	Mystic	Lake	Margaret	TV Personality
Meir	Golda	Mabovitch	Golda	Israeli PM
Melba	Dame Nellie	Armstrong, née Mitchell	Helen Porter	Opera Singer
Melbourne	Viscount	Lamb	William	British Prime Minister
Melmoth	Sebastian	Wilde	Oscar	Author
Mendelssohn	Felix	Mendelssohn-Bartholdy	Felix	Composer
Menken	Adah Isaacs	Fuertes	Dolores Adios	American Actress and Poet
Mennin	Peter	Mennini	Peter	Musician
Mercury	Freddie	Bulsara	Frederick	Singer
Meredith	Burgess	Burgess	George	Actor
Merlin		Tennyson	Alfred Lord	Poet
Merman	Ethel	Zimmerman	Ethel	Singer
Merrion		Francis	Leigh	Comedian
Merton	Mrs	Hook/Aherne	Caroline	Comedienne
Merton	Paul	Martin	Paul	Comedian
Mervyn	William	Pickwoad	William	Actor
Michael	George	Panayiotou	Georgios	Vocalist and Composer
Michael of Kent	Princess	von Reibnitz	Marie	Princess
Milland	Ray	Truscott-Jones	Reginald	Actor
Milligan	Spike	Milligan	Terence Alan	Comedian and Writer
Mistinguett		Bourgeois	Jeanne Marie	French Dancer
Mitchell	Cameron	Mizell	George	Actor
Mitchell	Guy	Cernick	Al	Singer
Mitchell	Joni	Anderson	Roberta Joan	Singer and Composer
Molière		Poquelin	Jean-Baptiste	Playwright
Molotov	Vyacheslav Mikhaylovich	Skryabin	Vyacheslav Mikhaylovich	Russian Statesman
Monroe	Marilyn	Baker	Norma Jean	Actress
Montand	Yves	Levy	Ivo	Actor
Montez	Lola	Gilbert	Maria Eliza (Délores)	American Dancer
Montgomery	George	Letz	George	Actor
Moody	Ron	Moodnick	Ronald	Actor
Moore	Archibald	Wright	Archibald	Boxer
Moore	Demi	Guynes	Demi	Actress
Moore	Julianne	Smith	Julie Anne	US Actress
Morecambe	Eric	Bartholomew	John Eric	Comedian
Morgan	Frank	Wupperman	Frank	Actor
Morrison	Van	Morrison	George Ivan	Singer and Composer
Moses	Grandma	Robertson	Anna Mary	Artist
Mostel	Zero	Mostel	Samuel Joel	Actor
Mycroft		Gillis	Ian	'Brain of Britain'
Nagasaki	Kendo	Thornley	Peter	Professional Wrestler
Naismith	Laurence	Johnson	Lawrence	Actor
Neagle	Anna	Robertson	Marjorie	Actress

Assumed Name		Original Name		
Negri	Pola	Chalupek	Appolonia	Actress
Nelly	Haynes Jr	Cornell	Rapper
Nelson	Baby Face	Gillis	Lester	Gangster
Nero	Ahenobarbus	Lucius Domitius	Roman Emperor
Nero	Franco	Spartanero	Franco	Actor
Newcastle	Duke of	Pelham-Holles	Thomas	British Prime Minister
Nichols	Mike	Peschkowsky	Michael	American Film Director
Nicole	Skurnick	Estelle	'Renault Clio' Star of Advert
Nolde	Emil	Hansen	Emil	German Painter
Novarra	Ramon	Samaniegos	Ramon	Actor
Novello	Ivor	Davies	David Ivor	Composer
Numan	Gary	Webb	Gary	Vocalist and Composer
Oakley	Annie	Mozee	Phoebe	Frontierswoman
Oberon	Merle	Thompson	Estelle	Actress
O'Brien	Flann	O'Nolan	Brian	Irish Writer
O'Brien	Hugh	Krampke	Hugh	Actor
Ochre	Captain	Frazier	Richard	Fictional TV Character
O'Connor	Frank	O'Donovan	Michael	Irish Writer
Offenbach	Jacques	Eberst	Jakob	Composer
O'Hara	Maureen	Fitzsimmons	Maureen	Actress
O'Henry	Porter	William Sydney	Author
Orlando	Tony	Cassavitis	Michael	Vocalist
Ormandy	Eugene	Blau	Jenö	Musician
Orwell	George	Blair	Eric Arthur	Author
O'Sullivan	Gilbert	O'Sullivan	Raymond	Singer
Ouida	Ramée, de la	Marie Louise	English Author
Palance	Jack	Palaniuk	Walter	Actor
Pallo	Jackie	Gutteridge	John	Wrestler
Palmer	Lilli	Peiser	Lilli	Actress
Panther	Riley	Helena	TV Gladiator
Parker	Cecil	Schwabe	Cecil	Actor
Parker	Dorothy	Rothschild	Dorothy	Author
Parley	Peter	Goodrich	Samuel	US Publisher
Parmigianino	Il	Mazzola	Girolamo Francesco Maria	Italian Painter
Pastry	Mr	Hearne	Richard	Actor
Patterson	Sir Les	Humphries	Barry	Comedian
Paycheck	Johnny	Lytle	Donald Eugene	Country Singer
Peel	John	Ravenscroft	John	Disc Jockey
Peerce	Jan	Perelmuth	Jacob Pincus	Musician
Pele	do Nascimento	Edson Arantes Do	Footballer
Pellow	Marti	McLoughlin	Mark	Singer
Penguin	Cobblepot	Oswald	Batman Character
Pennis	Dennis	Kaye	Paul	Actor and Comedian
Perkins	Elizabeth	Pisperikos	Elizabeth	Actress
Phillips	Lou Diamond	Upchurch	Lou	Actor
Phiz	Browne	Hablot Knight	Illustrator
Phoenix	Young	Sandy	Gladiator
Piaf	Edith	Gassion	Edith	Singer
Pickford	Mary	Smith	Gladys Mary	Actress
Pindar	Peter	Wolcot	John	Satirist
Pink	Moore	Alicia	Actress and Singer
Pop	Iggy	Osterberg	James Jewel	Singer
Porcupine	Peter	Cobbett	William	Writer
Powers	Stefanie	Federkiewicz	Stefania	Actress
Preston	Robert	Meservey	Robert	Actor
Price	Dennis	Rose-Price	Dennistoun Franklyn	Actor
Prince	Nelson	Prince Rogers	Singer and Composer
Proby	PJ	Smith	James Marcus	Singer
Pussyfoot	Johnson	William Eugene	US Reformer
Q	Quiller-Couch	Arthur	Author and Anthologist
Queen	Ellery	Dannay	Frederick	Joint Authors
		Lee	Manfred B	
Quinn	Anthony	Oaxaca	Rudolph	US Actor
Rafferty	Chips	Goffage	John	Entertainer
Raft	George	Ranft	George	Actor
Randall	Tony	Rosenberg	Leonard	Actor
Randi	Amazing	Zwinge	James Randall	Magician
Raven	Paul	Gadd	Paul	Vocalist
Ray	Ted	Olden	Charles	Comedian

FAMOUS PEOPLE

Assumed Name		Original Name		
Reality	Maxim	*Palmer*	Keith	*MC*
Rebel		*Stoute*	Jenny	*TV Gladiator*
Red Cloud		*Iuta*	Mahpiua	*(Sioux) Chief*
Reed	Lou	*Firbank*	Louis	*Singer and Composer*
Reeves	Vic	*Moir*	Jim	*Comedian*
Regiomontanus		*Müller*	Johannes	*German Mathematician*
Remarque	Erich Maria	*Kramer*	Erich Maria	*Author*
Rendell	Ruth	*Grasemann*	Ruth	*Crime Novelist*
Rethberg	Elisabeth	*Sättler*	Elisabeth	*Musician*
Richard	Cliff	*Webb*	Harold	*Singer*
Richard	Little	*Penniman*	Richard Wayne	*Singer*
Richards	Frank	*Hamilton*	Charles	*Author*
Rivers	Joan	*Molinsky*	Joan	*Comedienne*
Robbins	Harold	*Rubin*	Harold	*Author*
Robin		*Grayson*	Dick	*Comics Character*
Robinson	Edward G	*Goldenberg*	Emmanuel	*Actor*
Robinson	Ralph	*George III*		*British King (in Garden Periodicals)*
Robinson	Sugar Ray	*Smith*	Walker	*Boxer*
Rock		*Johnson*	Dwayne	*Actor and Wrestler*
Rocket		*Richards*	Pauline	*TV Gladiator*
Rogers	Ginger	*McMath*	Virginia	*Actress and Dancer*
Rogers	Roy	*Slye*	Leonard	*Actor*
Rogers	Will	*Adair*	William Penn	*US Actor*
Rohmer	Sax	*Ward*	Arthur Sarsfield	*Author*
Rooney	Mickey	*Yule Jnr*	Joseph	*Actor*
Rose	Axl	*Bailey*	William	*Singer*
Rose Lee	Gypsy	*Hovick*	Rose Louise	*Entertainer*
Ross	Aircraftsman John Hume	*Lawrence*	Thomas Edward	*Soldier and Author*
Ross	Barnaby	*Dannay*	Frederick	*Joint Authors*
		Lee	Manfred B	
Rotten	Johnny	*Lydon*	John	*Singer*
Rowland	Tiny	*Fuhrhop*	Roland	*Businessman*
Rowlands	John	*Stanley*	Henry Morton	*Explorer/Journalist*
Roy	Rob	*McGregor*	Robert	*Scottish Outlaw*
Ruffo	Titta	*Titta*	Ruffo	*Baritone*
Russell	Theresa	*Paup*	Theresa	*Actress*
Rutherford	Mark	*White*	William Hale	*Writer*
Ryder	Winona	*Horowitz*	Winona	*Actress*
Sable		*Merowitz*	Rena	*Professional Wrestler*
Sabrina		*Sykes*	Norma	*Model*
Sade		*Adu*	Helen Folasade	*Singer*
Sagan	Françoise	*Quoirez*	Françoise	*Novelist*
Saint-John Perse		*Léger*	Alexis Saint-Léger	*French Poet*
Saint-Laurent	Yves	*Mathieu*	Henri Donat	*French Designer*
Saki		*Monro*	Hector Hugh	*Writer*
Samaroff	Olga	*Hickenlooper*	Lucie	*Musician*
Sand	George	*Dudevant*	Amondine Lucie Dupin	*Writer*
Sapper		*McNeile*	Herman Cyril	*Author*
Sappho		*de Scudéry*	Madeleine	*French Novelist*
Saracen		*Lewis*	Mike	*TV Gladiator*
Sarandon	Susan	*Tomaling*	Susan	*Actress*
Savage	Lily	*O'Grady*	Paul	*Entertainer*
Saxon	John	*Orrico*	Carmen	*Actor*
Scarlet	Captain	*Metcalfe*	Paul	*Animated TV Character*
Schultz	Dutch	*Flegenheimer*	Arthur	*Gangster*
Scott	Randolph	*Crane*	Randolph	*Actor*
Seal		*Samuel*	Henry	*Singer*
Selassie	Hailie	*Makonnen*	Ras Tafari	*Ethiopian Emperor*
Sennett	Mack	*Sinnott*	Michael	*Film Producer*
Sensible	Captain	*Burns*	Ray	*Singer*
Dr Seuss		*Geisel*	Theodore Seuss	*Author*
Seymour	Jane	*Frankenberg*	Joyce	*Actress*
Shadow		*King*	Jefferson	*TV Gladiator*
Shaggy		*Burrell*	Orville Richard	*Pop Singer*
Shannon	Del	*Westover*	Charles	*Singer*
Sharif	Omar	*Shalhoub*	Michael	*Actor*
Shaw	Sandie	*Goodrich*	Sandra	*Singer*

Assumed Name		Original Name		
Shaw	TE	**Lawrence**	Thomas Edward	Soldier and Author (in Royal Tank Corps)
Sheen	Martin	**Estevez**	Ramon	Actor
Shipton	Mother	**Southill/Southiel**	Ursula	Prophetess
Shirley	Anne	**O'Day**	Dawn	Actress
Shute	Neville	**Norway**	Neville	Author
Shuttleworth	John	**Fellows**	Graham	Singer and Songwriter
Signoret	Simone	**Kaminker**	Henriette Charlotte	Actress
Sills	Beverly	**Silverman**	Belle	Musician
Silverheels	Jay	**Smith**	Harold J	Actor
Simmons	Gene	**Witz**	Chaim	Rock Singer
Simone	Nina	**Wayman**	Eunice	Singer
Sioux	Siouxsie	**Dallion**	Susan	Singer
Siren		**Paton**	Alison	TV Gladiator
Sitting Bull		**Iyotanka**	Tatanka	Sioux Hunkpapa Chief
Skinner	Frank	**Collins**	Chris	Comedian
Slater	Christian	**Hawkins**	Christian	Actor
Snoop Dogg		**Broadus**	Calvin	Rapper
Soul	David	**Solberg**	David	Actor
Spiderman		**Parker**	Peter	Fictional Superhero
Springfield	Dusty	**O'Brien**	Mary	Singer
Stack	Robert	**Modini**	Robert	Actor
Staff	Kathy	**Higginbottom**	Minnie	Actress
Stalin	Joseph	**Dzhugashvili**	Iosif Vissarionovich	Russian Leader
Stanislavsky		**Alexeyev Sergeivitch**	Konstantin	Actor
Stanley	Henry Morton	**Rowlands**	John	Explorer
Stanwyck	Barbara	**Stevens**	Ruby	Actress
Stardust	Alvin	**Jewry**	Bernard	Singer
Starr	Edwin	**Hatcher**	Charles	Singer
Starr	Ringo	**Starkey**	Richard	Drummer and Composer
Statto		**Loughran**	Angus	TV Soccer Pundit
Steele	Tommy	**Hicks**	Thomas	Entertainer
Stendhal		**Beyle**	Marie-Henri	Author
Stepniak		**Kravchinski**	Sergei Mikhailovich	Russian Revolutionary
Stevens	Cat	**Georgiou**	Stephen	Singer
Stevens	Connie	**Ingolia**	Concetta	Actress
Stevens	Inger	**Stengland**	Inger	Actress
Stevens	Shakin'	**Barrett**	Michael	Singer
Stewart	Ed	**Mainwaring**	Edward Stewart	Disc Jockey
Sting		**Sumner**	Gordon	Vocalist and Musician
Stone	Irving	**Tennenbaum**	Irving	US Novelist
Stoppard	Miriam	**Stern**	Miriam	Broadcaster
Stoppard	Tom	**Straussler**	Thomas	Dramatist
Stratas	Teresa	**Strataki**	Anastasia	Soprano
Strummer	Joe	**Mellor**	John	Rock Star
Sturges	Preston	**Biden**	Edmund Preston	Writer and Director
Styrene	Poly	**Elliot**	Marion	Punk-Rock Singer
Suggs		**McPherson**	Graham	Singer (Madness)
Sumac	Yma	**Chavarri**	Emperatriz	Musician
Summer	Donna	**Gaines**	Donna Andrea	Singer
Summers	Ann	**Gold**	Jacqueline	Businesswoman
Sundance Kid		**Longabaugh**	Henry	Outlaw
Swanson	Gloria	**Svensson**	Gloria	Actress
Sylva	Carmen	**Elizabeth**	of Romania	Queen of Romania
T	T	**Tureaud**	Lawrence	Actor
Tanfucio	Neri	**Fucini**	Renato	Italian Writer
Tati	Jacques	**Tatischeff**	Jacques	Actor
Tauber	Richard	**Seiffert**	Ernst	Austrian Tenor
Taylor	Elizabeth	**Coles**	Elizabeth	Novelist
Taylor	Robert	**Brough**	Spangler	Actor
Tenzin Gyatso		**Tsering**	Lhamo Thondup	14th Dalai Lama
Theresa	Mother	**Bojaxhiu**	Agnes Gonxha	Roman Catholic Nun
Thomas	Terry	**Stevens**	Terry	Comedy Actor
Thumb	Tom	**Stratton**	Charles	Circus Performer
Tich		**Amey**	Ian	Guitarist
Tich	Little	**Relph**	Harry	Comedian
Tilley	Vesta	**Powles**	Matilda Alice	Male Impersonator
Tim	Tiny	**Khaury**	Herbert	Singer
Tintoretto		**Robusti**	Jacopo	Artist

FAMOUS PEOPLE

Assumed Name		*Original Name*		
Titmarsh	Michael Angelo	**Thackeray**	William Makepeace	*Author*
Tito		**Broz**	Josip	*Yugoslav Leader*
Todd	Mike	**Goldenburger**	Avron	*Producer*
Trog		**Fawkes**	Walter Ernest	*Cartoonist and Clarinettist*
Trotsky	Leon	**Bronstein**	Lev Davidovitch	*Russian Revolutionary*
Tucker	Richard	**Ticker**	Reuben	*Singer*
Tucker	Sophie	**Abruza**	Sophie	*Music Hall Singer*
Tuesday	Gayle	**Gilhooly**	Brenda	*Comedienne*
Turner	Tina	**Bullock**	Annie Mae	*Singer*
Twain	Mark	**Clemens**	Samuel Langhorne	*Author*
Twain	Shania	**Edwards**	Eileen Regina	*Pop Singer*
Twiggy		**Hornby**	Leslie	*Model and Actress*
Twitty	Conway	**Jenkins**	Harold Lloyd	*Singer*
Tyler	Bonnie	**Sullivan (née Hopkins)**	Gaynor	*Singer*
Ultimate Warrior		**Hellwig**	James	*Professional Wrestler*
Uncle Remus		**Harris**	Joel Chandler	*Author*
Undertaker		**Calloway**	Mark	*Wrestler*
Vadim	Roger	**Plemiannikov**	Roger Vadim	*Film Director*
Valens	Ritchie	**Valenzuela**	Ritchie	*Singer*
Valentino	Rudolph	**D'Antonguolla**	Rudolpho	*Actor*
Valli	Frankie	**Castellucio**	Frank	*Singer*
Van Damme	Jean-Claude	**Van Varenberg**	Jean-Claude	*Actor*
Vanilla Ice		**Winkle**	Robert van	*Rapper and Actor*
Vaughan	Frankie	**Abelsohn**	Frank	*Singer*
Vaughan	Peter	**Ohm**	Peter	*Actor*
Vee	Bobby	**Velline**	Robert Thomas	*Singer*
Vegas	Johnny	**Pennington**	Michael	*Comedian*
Verdy	Violette	**Guillerm**	Nelly	*French Dancer*
Vernon	John	**Agopsowicz**	Adolphus	*US Actor*
Veronese	Paolo	**Caliari**	Paolo	*Venetian Painter*
Vicious	Sid	**Ritchie**	John	*Singer*
Villa	Pancho	**Arango**	Doroteo	*Mexican Patriot*
Villeneuve	Justin	**Davies**	Nigel	*Hair Stylist*
Vincent	Gene	**Craddock**	Eugene Vincent	*Singer*
Vine	Barbara	**Rendell**	Ruth	*Novelist*
Vivekananda	Swami	**Dutt**	Narendranath	*Hindu Missionary*
Voltaire		**Arouet**	François-Marie	*Philosopher*
Wall	Max	**Lorimer**	Maxwell George	*Actor and Comedian*
Ward	Artemus	**Browne**	Charles Farrar	*Writer and Humorist*
Warlock	Peter	**Heseltine**	Philip Arnold	*Composer*
Warner	Jack	**Waters**	Jack	*Actor*
Warner	Jack Leonard	**Eichelbaum**	Jack Leonard	*Film Mogul*
Warrior		**Aherne**	Michael	*TV Gladiator*
Warwick	Richard	**Winter**	Richard	*Actor*
Waters	Muddy	**Morganfield**	McKinley	*Singer*
Wayne	John	**Morrison**	Marion	*Actor*
Weathercock	Janus	**Wainewright**	Thomas Griffiths	*Art Critic and Murderer*
Webb	Clifton	**Hollenbeck**	Webb Parmalee	*Actor*
Welch	Bruce	**Cripps**	Bruce	*Guitarist*
Welch	Raquel	**Tejada**	Raquel	*Actress*
Weldon	Fay	**Birkinshaw**	Franklin	*Writer*
Wellthorpe	Edna	**Orton**	Joe	*Dramatist (as Fictional Letter Writer)*
West	Nigel	**Allason**	Rupert	*MP and Author*
West	Rebecca	**Fairfield**	Cicely Isabel	*Author*
Westmacott	Mary	**Christie**	Agatha	*Author (as Romantic Novelist)*
Wharton	Edith	**Jones**	Edith	*Author*
White	Colonel	**Gray**	Charles	*Fictional TV Character*
Widow		**Sisson**	Richard	*Musical act 'Kit and the Widow'*
Wilde	Kim	**Smith**	Kim	*Singer*
Wilde	Marty	**Smith**	Reginald	*Singer*
Wilder	Gene	**Silberman**	Jerome	*Actor*
Windsor	Barbara	**Deeks**	Barbara	*Actress*
Winters	Bernie	**Weinstein**	Bernie	*Comedian*
Winters	Shelley	**Schrift**	Shirley	*Actress*
Wise	Ernie	**Wiseman**	Ernest	*Comedian*
Wolf	Howling	**Burnett**	Chester Arthur	*Singer and Composer*
Wonder	Stevie	**Judkins**	Steveland	*Singer and Composer*

Assumed Name		Original Name		
Wood	Mrs Henry	*Price*	Ellen	*English Novelist*
Wood	Natalie	*Gurdin*	Natasha	*Actress*
Worth	Harry	*Illingworth*	Harry	*Comedian*
Wylie	Gerald	*Barker*	Ronnie	*Writer*
Wyman	Bill	*Perks*	William	*Musician*
Wyman	Jane	*Faulks*	Sarah Jane	*Actress*
Wymark	Patrick	*Cheeseman*	Patrick	*Actor*
Wynette	Tammy	*Pugh*	Wynette	*Singer*
Wyngarde	Peter	*Goldbert*	Cyril Louis	*Actor*
X	Malcolm	*Little*	Malcolm	*Civil Rights Leader*
Yates	Dornford	*Mercer*	Cecil William	*Novelist*
York	Michael	*Johnson*	Mike	*Actor*
York	Susannah	*Fletcher*	Susannah	*Actress*
Youens	Bernard	*Popley*	Bernard	*Actor*
Young	Gig	*Barr*	Byron	*Actor*
Young	Jimmy	*Young*	Leslie Ronald	*Broadcaster*
Zadora	Pia	*Schipani*	Pia	*Actress*

NB: The area of pseudonyms is a veritable minefield for misinformation and errors, and although an attempt has been made to verify as many entries as possible it is inevitable that there will be doubt relating to some entries. To give an example of the intricacies that make an infallible list almost impossible to compile, many sources refer to Marlene Dietrich's original name as Von Losch, this is only partly true, as in fact her original name was Dietrich and changed to von Losch only when her mother remarried after the death of her father.

Where a person has more than one pseudonym an attempt has been made to place them in order of usage, for example, the wrestler Giant Haystacks was born Martin Ruane but initially fought under the name Luke McMasters and indeed is credited in the 1984 film, *Give My Regards to Broad Street*, under that name.

In format the tables are basically surnames followed by Christian names, but where the person is titled or is known by just a single name, then the familiar name is in the left-hand box. This is not meant to be a fully comprehensive listing, as it would be possible to fill this whole book with pseudonyms and pen-names, but it is hoped that all the more common ones and a few less known but interesting ones are present. There is a small overlap between this section and the nicknames section as some of the entries warrant inclusion in both, because a nickname is sometimes adopted as the most famous title of a person.

Relationships

NB: Relations appear in alphabetical order within each category.
The relationship given is that of the second column to the first.

Arthur Conan Doyle	EW Hornung	*Brother-in-law*
Stanley Baldwin	Rudyard Kipling	*Cousin*
Richard Briers	Terry-Thomas	*Cousin*
George Clooney	Miguel Ferrer	*Cousin*
Elizabeth I	Mary Queen of Scots	*Cousin*
King George V	Kaiser Wilhelm II	*Cousin*
Christopher Lee	Ian Fleming	*Cousin*
Patrick McNee	David Niven	*Cousin*
Kate Robbins	Paul McCartney	*Cousin*
Ginger Rogers	Rita Hayworth	*Cousin*
Franklin D Roosevelt	Theodore Roosevelt	*5th cousin*
Herbert H Asquith	Violet Bonham-Carter	*Daughter*
Ingrid Bergman	Isabella Rossellini	*Daughter*
Tony Booth (actor)	Cherie Blair	*Daughter*
Vera Brittain	Shirley Williams	*Daughter*
William Jennings Bryan	Ruth Rohde	*Daughter*
Blythe Danner	Gwyneth Paltrow	*Daughter*
Chris De Burgh	Rosanna Davidson (Miss World)	*Daughter*
Debbie Reynolds and Eddie Fisher	Carrie Fisher	*Daughter*
Judy Garland	Lorna Luft	*Daughter*
	Liza Minnelli	*Daughter*
Jeremy Hawk	Belinda Lang	*Daughter*
Tippi Hedren	Melanie Griffith	*Daughter*
Helios & Perse	Circe	*Daughter*
Roger Kemble	Sarah Siddons	*Daughter*
King Agenor and Queen Telephassa	Europa	*Daughter*
King Cepheus and Queen Cassiopeia	Andromeda	*Daughter*
King Priam and Queen Hecuba	Cassandra	*Daughter*

Phyllida Law	Sophie Thompson	*Daughter*
	Emma Thompson	*Daughter*
Lord Longford	Lady Antonia Fraser	*Daughter*
Mary of Guise and James V	Mary Queen of Scots	*Daughter*
Arthur Miller	Rebecca Miller	*Daughter*
Thomas Moore	Margaret Roper	*Daughter*
Muhammad	Fatima	*Daughter*
Jawaharlal Nehru	Indira Gandhi	*Daughter*
Nanette Newman	Emma Forbes	*Daughter*
Tsar Nicholas II	Anastasia	*Daughter*
Oedipus and Jocasta	Antigone	*Daughter*
Christina Onassis	Athina Roussel	*Daughter*
Ravi Shankar	Norah Jones	*Daughter*
Maureen O'Sullivan	Mia Farrow	*Daughter*
Jon Voight	Angelina Jolie	*Daughter*
Zeus and Leda	Helen and Clytemnestra	*Daughters*
Zeus and Metis	Athene	*Daughter*
Zeus and Themis	Clotho (one of the 3 Fates)	*Daughter*
Emmeline Pankhurst	Christabel and Sylvia	*Daughters*
Aristotle Onassis	Athina Roussel	*Granddaughter*
Sigmund Freud	Clement and Lucian	*Grandsons*
Genghis Khan	Kublai Khan	*Grandson*
Herbert Beerbohm Tree	Oliver Reed	*Grandson*
Josiah Wedgwood	Charles Darwin	*Grandson*
Sigmund Freud	Emma (journalist) and Bella (fashion designer)	*Great-granddaughters*
Queen Victoria	Queen Elizabeth II	*Great-great-grand-daughter*
Queen Victoria	Duke of Edinburgh	*Great-great-grandson*
Bonnie Bedelia	Macaulay Culkin	*Nephew*
Rosemary Clooney	George Clooney	*Nephew*
Francis Ford Coppola	Nicolas Cage	*Nephew*
Lucian Freud	Matthew (PR guru)	*Nephew*
Lord Salisbury	Arthur Balfour	*Nephew*
Carol Reed	Oliver Reed	*Nephew*
Ellen Terry	John Gielgud	*Nephew*
Circe	Medea	*Niece*
Sarah Siddons	Fanny Kemble	*Niece*
Echidna and Typhon	Cerberus, Chimaera, Hydra	*Offspring*
Poseidon and Medusa	Pegasus	*Offspring*
Dana Andrews	Steve Forrest	*Sibling*
Thomas Arne	Susanna Cibber	*Sibling*
Balarama	Krishna	*Sibling*
Warren Beatty	Shirley Maclaine	*Sibling*
David Broome	Liz Edgar	*Sibling*
Duggie Brown	Lynn Perrie	*Sibling*
Keith Chegwin	Janice Long	*Sibling*
Catherine Deneuve	Françoise Dorléac	*Sibling*
Margaret Drabble	AS Byatt	*Sibling*
Adila Fachiri (violinist)	Jelly Arányi (violinist)	*Sibling*
Marty Feldman	Fenella Fielding	*Sibling*
Joan Fontaine	Olivia de Havilland	*Sibling*
Lady Antonia Fraser	Rachel Billington	*Sibling*
Lucian Freud	Clement	*Sibling*
Crystal Gayle	Loretta Lynn	*Sibling*
Graham Greene	Hugh Carleton Greene	*Sibling*
Michael Hamburger (poet)	Paul Hamlyn (publisher)	*Sibling*
Hannibal	Hasdrubal	*Sibling*
Eden Kane	Peter and Robin Sarstedt	*Siblings*
John Kemble	Sarah Siddons	*Sibling*
Jimmy Logan	Annie Ross	*Sibling*
Lord Rothermere	Lord Northcliffe	*Sibling*
Paul McCartney	Mike McGear	*Sibling*
John Mills	Annette Mills	*Sibling*
Liza Minnelli	Lorna Luft	*Sibling*
Gary Oldman	Laila Morse	*Sibling*
River Phoenix	Leaf, Rainbow, Summer, Liberty	*Siblings*
Brian Rix	Sheila Mercier	*Sibling*
Kate Robbins	Ted Robbins	*Sibling*

Eric Roberts	Julia Roberts	*Sibling*
Georhe Sanders	Tom Conway	*Sibling*
Julia Sawalha	Nadia Sawalha	*Sibling*
Talia Shire	Francis Ford Coppola	*Sibling*
Tanita Tikaram	Ramon Tikaram	*Sibling*
Jack Warner	Elsie and Doris Waters	*Siblings*
Virginia Woolf	Vanessa Bell	*Sibling*
Aeacus and Endeis	Peleus	*Son*
Anu and Ki	Enki and Enlil	*Sons*
Ares and Aphrodite	Eros	*Son*
Atreus and Aerope	Agamemnon	*Son*
David Carradine and Barbara Hershey	Free (changed to Tom)	*Son*
Charles Martel	Pepin the Short	*Son*
Cleopatra and Julius Caesar	Caesarion (Ptolemy XV)	*Son*
Cecil Day-Lewis and Jill Balcon	Daniel Day-Lewis	*Son*
Elizabeth and Zacharias	John the Baptist	*Son*
Erebos and Nyx	Charon	*Son*
Eric the Red	Leif Eriksson	*Son*
Clement Freud	Matthew (PR guru)	*Son*
Indira Gandhi	Rajiv Gandhi	*Son*
Hamilcar	Hannibal	*Son*
Helios and Clymene	Phaethon	*Son*
Iapetus and Clymene	Prometheus, Atlas, Epimetheus, Menoetius	*Sons*
Jenny Jerome	Winston Churchill	*Son*
Jupiter and Latona	Apollo	*Son*
Rosa Kaufman (pianist)	Boris Pasternak	*Son*
King Agenor and Queen Telephassa	Cadmus	*Son*
King Glaucus and Queen Eurynome	Bellerophon	*Son*
King Laius and Queen Jocasta	Oedipus	*Son*
Mary Martin	Larry Hagman	*Son*
Mary Queen of Scots	James VI (Scotland) I (England)	*Son*
Osiris and Nephthys	Anubis	*Son*
Norrie Paramour	John Paramour (golf director)	*Son*
Peleus and Thetis	Achilles	*Son*
Pepin the Short	Charlemagne	*Son*
Priam and Hecuba of Troy	Paris	*Son*
Martin Sheen	Emilio Estevez and Charlie Sheen	*Sons*
Ellen Terry and EW Godwin	Edward Gordon Craig	*Son*
Suzanne Valadon	Maurice Utrillo	*Son*
Zebedee	St John	*Son*
Zeus and Danaë	Perseus	*Son*
Zeus and Leda	Castor, Polydeuces	*Sons*
Zeus and Leto	Apollo	*Son*
De Mille, Cecil B	Anthony Quinn	*Son-in-law*
Franz Liszt	Richard Wagner	*Son-in-law*
Thomas Mann	WH Auden	*Son-in-law*
Arthur Miller	Daniel Day Lewis	*Son-in-law*
Rupert Murdoch	Matthew Freud (PR guru)	*Son-in-law*
Eugene O'Neill	Charlie Chaplin	*Son-in-law*
Peter Vaughan	Gregor Fisher	*Son-in-law*

FAMOUS PEOPLE

Crime and Punishment

Dr John Bodkin Adams (1899–1983) Physician who was tried in 1957 after one of his patients, Edith Morrell, died suspiciously. Like other elderly patients before her, Edith had made Adams a beneficiary of her will before dying by morphine overdose. On acquittal Adams was struck off but continued to treat private patients and was in fact reinstated by the General Medical Council in 1961. Whether he merely practised euthanasia or killed for personal gain will never be proven and the secret died with him.

Susan Barber (1956–) In May 1981 Susan Barber placed half a teaspoonful of weedkiller in her husband Michael's steak-and-kidney pie after he caught her in bed with her lover and threw him out

of the window. Michael Barber was diagnosed with Goodpasture's syndrome, a rare nervous condition, but died shortly after. The cause of death was recorded as pneumonia and kidney failure. His wife gained £15,000 from her husband's pension fund and set up home with her defenestrated lover, Richard Collins. David Evans, the pathologist who conducted the post mortem, began to have a few doubts and sent organs from Barber's body to ICI, the manufacturers of the weedkiller Gramoxone, and sure enough, traces of the poison were detected. Barber and Collins were arrested in April 1982 and he was sentenced to two years imprisonment for conspiracy while Susan Barber was jailed for life.

Anne Bonny (1692–?) Irish pirate who lived in the early 18th century. Anne showed her fiery temper at an early age and is thought to have killed a servant girl with a case-knife. She was disinherited by her lawyer father and sailed to the Bahamas with her husband, the cause of the disinheritance. Bonny fell in with Captain John Rackham, the notorious Calico Jack, and sailed with him disguised as a man. Bizarrely enough another member of Jack's crew was Mary Read, who was also sailing under the guise of a man, and an amusing incident whereby Read tried to seduce Bonny proved to be the unveiling of both. In October 1720 Calico Jack's ship, *The Revenge*, was captured by a sloop on the orders of the governor of Jamaica and Jack was hung and Read and Bonny imprisoned. Mary Read died of a fever but Bonny managed to escape and her whereabouts remained a mystery.

Charles Bronson (1952–) Born Michael Gordon Peterson and first imprisoned in 1974 for robbing a jeweller of £35, but his aggressive behaviour has added an extra 25 years to his sentences and he has experienced only a total of 69 days of freedom since then. Bronson has shown some ability as a cartoonist and poet. He married Miss Saira Rehman in June 2001 at Woodhill Prison and Lord Longford was best man.

Burke and Hare William Burke (1792–1829) and William Hare (1790–c1860) met at Logue's lodging house, Edinburgh, in 1818. Sharing the same building was an army pensioner known as Old Donald, who died in 1827 owing Hare £4. Burke and Hare opened his coffin and substituted a sack of bark for his body and sold it for £7 10/- to Dr Robert Knox of Edinburgh's Anatomy School. Over the next 10 months Dr Knox became a regular customer of the pair, who at first produced a legitimate supply of corpses, but then began to create their own by foul means. Burke's common-law wife, Helen McDougal, or Hare's, Maggie Laird, would lure a victim back to the lodgings and then ply them with drink, Burke would then kneel on their chest, while stopping their breathing by placing his hands over their nose and mouth. This method became known as 'burking'. Victims included Mary Paterson, a local prostitute, and a local idiot called Daft Jamie, both of whose murders were suspected by Knox, who remained quiet. Eventually they slipped up by leaving the body of Margaret Docherty where other lodgers could find it. Hare and Laird escaped prosecution by turning King's evidence and the case against McDougal was unproven, but Burke was publicly hanged on 28 January 1829.

Capital punishment Relevant dates in the history of capital punishment in Britain are as follows: In 1868 public execution was abolished, Michael Barrett (26 May) being the last victim. On 13 July 1955 Ruth Ellis was the last woman to be hanged in Britain. On 13 August 1964 Peter Anthony Allen and Gwynne Owen Evans were the last victims of a British hanging. On 9 November 1965 the death penalty was suspended for a trial period of five years, but in December 1969 Parliament confirmed the permanent abolition.

Mary Ann Cotton (1832–73) District nurse from West Auckland, County Durham, who killed at least five people including her second husband Frederick, his two stepsons, and two lovers, a local excise officer named Quick-Manning and her lodger Joseph Natrass. She was suspected of killing many more, possibly 30. Her motive was invariably either to collect insurance money or to pave the way for a new liaison. Her chosen method of disposal was arsenic. She was eventually tried and sentenced to death in 1873. The hangman bungled the execution, causing her to take three and a half minutes to stop convulsing before dying at the rope's end.

Dr Hawley Harvey Crippen (1862–1910) Crippen, a patent medicine salesman and physician, poisoned his second wife, Cora Turner, a would-be music-hall artiste working under the name of Belle Elmore, after becoming infatuated with his young secretary Ethel Le Neve. After the murder at their home at 39 Hilltop Crescent, Islington, North London, Ethel, who was privy to the murder, became anxious of its detection so the couple fled to Canada aboard the SS *Montrose* under the names of Mr Robinson and his son (Ethel). The ship's captain became suspicious and contacted Scotland Yard by radio telegraphy and the couple were arrested. The case was famous for being the first example of a successful conviction by use of radio. Crippen was tried for murder at the Old Bailey on 18 October 1910, found guilty and hanged at Pentonville on 23 November. Neve was tried separately but ably defended by FE Smith and acquitted. She lived till 1967.

DNA DNA provides the building blocks of life – the unique gene code that makes us what we are. In 1985, Sir Alec Jeffreys developed the system, first discovered by Crick and Watson in 1953, so that police could take an individual's genetic 'fingerprint' to establish guilt. Colin Pitchfork was the first person to be convicted using DNA evidence when he was jailed for life in 1988 for murdering two schoolgirls. Pitchfork murdered 15-year-old Lynda Mann in 1983 in Narborough, Leicestershire. Three years later he killed Dawn Ashworth, also 15. A 17-year-old confessed to killing Dawn, but a DNA test proved his innocence, and the screening of 5,000 locals showed Pitchfork to be the culprit. DNA has also been used retrospectively, and James Hanratty, hanged for murdering civil servant Michael Gregston and raping and maiming his mistress, is the most famous example. Hanratty hijacked the couple in their car off the A6 in Berkshire, then attacked them near Bedford. He denied the crime, and family members battled for 40 years to prove his innocence, but his body was exhumed in 2001 and DNA tests proved his guilt.

Ruth Ellis (1927–55) Model and nightclub manageress, Ellis shot and killed her lover, racing driver David Blakely, outside the Magdala public house in Hampstead on Good Friday 1955. She was tried and convicted at the Old Bailey in June and hanged at Holloway prison on 13 July 1955, the last woman to be hanged in England.

John George Haigh (1910–49) Whilst living in a small hotel in Kensington, Haigh became friendly with Olive Durand-Deacon, a wealthy 69-year-old widow, who told him of her ideas for the marketing of cosmetics. Haigh invited her to his factory in Crawley, West Sussex, where she was shot and her body disposed of in a vat of sulphuric acid. On 20 February 1949 he then presented himself at Chelsea police station and reported her missing. Police became suspicious and checked his factory where they found the murder weapon and Mrs Durand-Dickson's plastic dentures. Haigh made a statement admitting to eight other murders, including three members of a family called McSwann, a Dr and Mrs Henderson and three other people whose identities he had never established. He was tried at Lewes Crown Court in July 1949 and was executed at Wandsworth Prison on 10 August 1949.

Hangmen   The most famous British public executioner was probably Albert Pierrepoint, who notched up 700 victims before his retirement. Albert died in 1982, leaving Syd Dernley as the last hangman to die since hanging was abolished. Dernley aided in the execution of 20 criminals between 1949 and 1953 but was removed from the register in 1954. He died in 1994. William Calcraft (1800–79) was the last to perform in public as hangings were held in prisons after 1868. James Berry (1852–1913) is probably the second most famous hangman after Albert Pierrepoint, although John Ellis became a celebrity after becoming the executioner of Dr Crippen and Sir Roger Casement. Ellis (1874–1926) was haunted by the aftermath of his career and eventually cut his own throat with a barber's razor. Other famous hangmen include Richard Arnett (1674–1728), Edward Dennis (1717–86), Jack Ketch, byname of John Ketch (d.1686), the Billington family, James (1847–1901), Thomas (1872–1902), William (1873–1934) and John (1880–1905), William Marwood (1820–83), George Smith (1805–74), Henry Pierrepoint (1874–1922) and Thomas Pierrepoint (1870–1954).

Jack the Ripper   Unknown murderer of five prostitutes between August and November 1888 in Whitechapel, London. The five unfortunate victims were Mary Ann 'Polly' Nichols (42), Dark Annie Chapman (47), Elizabeth 'Long Liz' Stride (45), Catharine 'Kate Kelly' Eddowes (43) and Mary Jane Kelly (25). The inspector who initially investigated the murders was George Frederick Abberline (1843–1929).

William Kidd (1645–1701)   Originally a respected sea captain in New York when hired by a Whig syndicate in 1695 as a government- commissioned privateer authorised to seize pirates, freebooters and sea-rovers in the name of the British government, Kidd decided to turn pirate himself. During an angry exchange with a crew member in 1697 he shot and killed his gunner, William Moore. On 9 May 1701 Kidd was found guilty of the murder of Moore and on five indictments of piracy. He was hanged immediately at Execution Dock, Wapping. Unfortunately for Kidd the rope broke the first time, he fell to the ground in his drunken state, and had to be strung up a a second time.

Kray Twins   Reggie Kray (1933–2000) and his twin brother Ronnie (1933–95) established a grip on the criminal underworld in the 1960s through their protection rackets and frauds. They opened a club, the Double R, in Bow Road, east London, which soon became popular with a showbiz clientele. Ronnie, a closet homosexual, was the dominant twin, and earned the nickname 'The Colonel', Reggie had more of a business brain. In 1965 Reggie married Frances Shea, but she committed suicide in 1967. The Firm, as they became known, became increasingly involved in hostilities with Charlie Richardson's south London gang, and they arranged the escape from Dartmoor of Frank Mitchell, the so-called Mad Axeman, whose murder they subsequently ordered. On 8 March 1966 Ronnie Kray shot dead George Cornell, a Richardson henchman, in the Blind Beggar public house on the Mile End Road. Cornell's offence had been to call Ronnie 'a fat poof'. In October 1966 Reggie Kray fatally stabbed a small-time thief called Jack 'the Hat' McVitie in a borrowed flat in Stoke Newington. Jack's crime had apparently been to show disrespect to the boys by wearing Bermuda shorts in one of their clubs. Detective Superintendent Leonard 'Nipper' Read eventually established a case against the twins and they were brought to trial at the Old Bailey in January 1969, after a member of the 'Firm', Albert Donaghue, had turned Queen's evidence. They were acquitted of the Mitchell murder but were convicted of murdering Cornell and McVitie.

Lord Lucan (1934–?)   John Bingham, the 7th Earl of Lucan, an inveterate gambler and merchant banker, inherited a quarter of a million pounds on the death of his father. By 1974 he was almost bankrupt. On the night of 7 November 1974 he killed Sandra Rivett, the nanny of his two children, in his house in Lower Belgrave Street, London, in mistake for his wife Veronica. After attacking his wife too, but failing to kill her, he drove to the house of his friend, Susan Maxwell-Scott, at Uckfield in Sussex. His car was discovered at Newhaven but he was never seen again.

Donald Merrett (1910–54)   At the age of 17 Merrett murdered his mother for the price of a motor bicycle. Twenty-five years later, and now calling himself Ronald Chesney, he murdered his wife and her mother. The first murder was in 1927, and although he claimed she shot herself in the neck, it became apparent over the course of her surviving 15 days that he murdered her for money, as he repeatedly forged her cheques during this period. He was charged with murder and forgery after her death, but due to the defence testimony of the eminent pathologist Bernard Spilsbury, who was appearing for the only time as a defence witness, was acquitted and served only twelve months on the forgery charge. On his release Merrett changed his name to Ronald Chesney and lived a life of petty crime until in 1954 he called on his wife, whom he had married when first released from prison, and knocked her out with drink before drowning her in the bath. He also killed her mother, who had intercepted him on leaving the house. He flew back to Germany but had been seen at the scene of the crime, an old people's home in Ealing, and before Interpol could arrest him he shot himself in the head in a wood near Cologne. Before he died he confessed to his German girlfriend that his real name was Donald Merrett and that when he was 17 he had killed his mother.

Moors Murderers   On 28 October 1965, Ian Brady, a 27-year-old stock-clerk, and Myra Hindley, a 23-year-old typist, were charged with the murder of ten-year-old Lesley Ann Downey at Chester Assizes. Lesley's body was found on Saddleworth Moor 13 days earlier. Police were subsequently alerted by a call from Hindley's brother-in-law, David Smith, who had witnessed the killing of 17-year-old Edward Evans with an axe. Police searched Brady's house and found Evans's body in a blanket. The police subsequently found a left-luggage ticket in Hindley's prayer book which led them to a suitcase containing tapes and pornographic photographs, one of which showed Hindley posing with a dog at what turned out to be the grave of a third murdered child, John Kilbride, aged 12. On 6 May, 1966, Brady was sentenced to three concurrent terms of life imprisonment for the murders of all three children while Hindley received two concurrent life sentences for the murders of Edward Evans and Lesley Ann Downey. Hindley died of lung cancer on 15 November 2002.

Charles Peace (1832–79)   Born in Manchester, the son of an animal trainer, Peace suffered an accident in childhood that left him crippled. To hide the loss of one finger he wore a false arm made of gutta-percha with a steel plate and a hook at the end of it. In 1876 he shot and killed a policeman whilst burgling a house. Two brothers were arrested for the murder and Peace attended the trial at which one of them, William Habron, was sentenced to death. Peace's next victim was a Mr Dyson, whose wife had formed a loose liaison with Peace, although it was to soon become a stalking situation. As a result of this murder, Peace became a wanted man and moved to London, where he rented a villa in Peckham. He now changed his name to John Ward and lived with his wife and his mistress, Susan Thompson, maintaining his lifestyle by a series of burglaries that he would attend in his pony and trap, carrying his tools in a violin case. He was eventually caught after wounding a policeman in Blackheath. He was sentenced to life imprisonment for wounding the policeman and then taken to Sheffield to stand trial for the murder of Arthur Dyson. On the way to Sheffield he managed to escape from the train, but was injured in the fall and was soon recaptured. He was tried for murder at Leeds assizes, found guilty and hanged by William Marwood after being refused a last drink. William Habron was released with a full pardon and awarded £1,000 compensation.

Peter Reyn-Bardt (1919–93)   In May 1983 two peat-cutters working at Lindow Moss, near Wilmslow, Cheshire, dug up the skull of a middle-aged woman. Police reported the find to Peter Reyn-Bardt, a former executive with BOAC, whose wife Malika had disappeared in 1960, and under interrogation he confessed to her murder. He had strangled his wife, chopped up her body and buried the remains in the peat bog. He was tried and found guilty at Chester Crown Court and sentenced to life imprisonment. Subsequently the skull was sent to Oxford University for radiocarbon dating and was found to be dated *circa* 410 AD. The following year another skeleton was found in the bog with more obvious evidence of a violent death. However, this one turned out to be the remains of a man who had been killed in a ritualistic death circa 300 BC. The whereabouts of Mrs Reyn-Bardt's body remain a mystery.

Harold Shipman   Harold Frederick Shipman studied at Leeds University medical school and eventually achieved a mediocre degree. His mother had died of lung cancer in June 1963 and it is believed it was seeing her daily morphine administered by the local GP that led to his compulsion to set himself up as an angel of mercy, albeit in some cases for personal gain. Shipman married his fiancée Primrose and took up his first practice in 1974 at the age of 28 in the small Yorkshire town of Todmorden. In 1975 a suspicious receptionist, Marjorie Walker, noticed some peculiar entries in the controlled substances ledger of a local pharmacist whereby large quantities of pethidine, a morphine-based painkiller had been ordered by Dr Shipman. His explanation was that he was injecting the drug himself and he was fined £600 and booked into a drug rehabilitation centre without being struck off. In 1977 Shipman began working at the Donneybrook Medical Centre

in Hyde, Manchester, and proceeded to rebuild his career. Despite doubts by several people over the years it was not until the death of Mrs Grundy, an 81-year-old former mayor of Hyde, on 24 June 1998, that questions were asked by Mrs Grundy's daughter Angela Woodruff, a solicitor by profession. Mrs Grundy had made a will in 1986 and lodged it with her daughter's law firm but now she was asked to believe that her mother had made another one without her knowledge and left £386,000 to Dr Shipman. Detective Superintendent Bernard Postles investigated and on reviewing the will came to the conclusion that Kathleen Grundy's signature had been forged and began to build a solid case against Shipman with the help of several interested parties who now came forward and expressed their own doubts about him. His trial began in October 1999 at Preston Crown Court and on 31 January 2000 Shipman was found guilty of 15 counts of murder. The Department of Health estimates that Shipman may have killed 236 patients between 1974 and 1998.

George Joseph Smith (1872–1915)   Perpetrator of the Brides in the Bath Murders. In 1898 Smith married 19-year-old Beatrice Thornhill, his only legal wife. In 1910 he met and bigamously married Bessie Mundy in Weymouth calling himself Henry Williams. He eventually murdered Bessie by drowning her in a tin bath and attesting that she had a fit and drowned by misadventure. Smith subsequently gained from a trust fund set up in Bessie's name. He then bigamously married Alice Burnham in Southsea in November 1913 and then 'married' Margaret Lofty, a clergyman's daughter at Bath in 1914. In both cases he took his wives to the doctors before dispatching them, to show that they suffered from fits. A newspaper report of Margaret Lofty's death was seen by Alice Burnham's father, who alerted the police. The police soon realised that Smith was a murderer, and with the help of Bernard Spilsbury he was tried and found guilty, sentenced to death and hanged at Maidstone Prison on Friday 13 August 1915.

Peter Sutcliffe   Between 1975 and 1980 Sutcliffe murdered 13 women in the north of England. Many of his victims were prostitutes and were invariably banged over the head with a ball-pein hammer before being stabbed and mutilated. He was eventually caught during a routine check when he was found in a car with a prostitute. He asked the police if he could relieve himself and unknown to them at the time he hid his murder weapons behind an oil storage tank. The police ran a routine check on his car and found it had false plates. Sutcliffe was arrested and while in custody was found to be on the list of possible suspects. Sutcliffe, now nicknamed the Yorkshire Ripper, made a full confession and on 22 May 1981 was sentenced to life imprisonment. He began his sentence at Parkhurst but after being attacked was transferred to Broadmoor High Security Mental Institution, where he resides today.

FASHION AND DRESS

General Information

aba   Loose gown worn in the Muslim world.

agal   fillet of two or three cords used to fasten a keffiyeh on the head.

Agnès B   Born Agnès Troublé in Versailles, France, 1941, she worked as a junior editor on *Elle* magazine before opening her first boutique. Her style is characterised by precise tailoring, simple subdued colours, usually black, natural materials and casual looks. In 1987 she launched her 'Le B' perfume range and a maternity collection.

aigrette   Spray of gems worn on the head.

Alaia, Azzedine   Tunisian designer who was a leading light throughout the 1980s but is experiencing a revival with his merger with Prada.

alb   Long, white linen vestment with sleeves, usually worn by priests.

alpargata   Light canvas shoe with a plaited fibre sole; an espadrille.

amice   Rectangular piece of white linen worn by priests around the neck and shoulders under the alb, or formerly, on the head. Also a furred hood with long ends hanging down in front.

Amies, Sir Hardy (1909–2003)   Queen's dressmaker for 50 years. Amies showed his first collection in 1946 and remained at the top of his profession until his death.

Armani, Giorgio   Italian fashion designer based in Milan and New York. Armani opened his first fashion house in 1974 and, although well respected within his industry, rose to fame after dressing Richard Gere in the 1980 film *American Gigolo*.

Ashley, Laura   Born in Merthyr Tydfil, South Wales (1925–85) as Laura Mountney. Married Bernard Ashley in 1949 and started a business manufacturing furnishing materials and wallpaper with patterns based upon document sources mainly from the 19th century. After giving up work to start a family she experimented with designing and making clothes, and this transformed the business into an international chain of boutiques, selling clothes, furnishing fabrics and wallpapers.

astrakhan wool   Obtained from the Karakul breed of sheep.

babouche   Turkish or oriental heelless slipper.

babushka   Headscarf tied under the chin and worn by Russian peasant women.

Badgley Mischka   American designers Mark Badgley and James Mischka. The duo are best known for their stellar beaded creations and 'aged look'. Their material is made in Italy and embroidered in Bombay, India.

balbriggan   Knitted, unbleached cotton fabric, from which underwear is often made.

baldric   Wide silk sash or leather belt worn over the opposite shoulder to the hip, for carrying a sword.

Balenciaga, Cristobal   Spanish fashion designer (1895–1972) opened the House of Balenciaga in Paris, 1937, and retired in 1968.

Balmain, Pierre   French fashion designer (1914–82) famous for his elegant simplicity. Immortalised by Peter Sarstedt in 'Where do you go to my lovely'.

Balmoral   Can be a laced walking shoe, a woollen petticoat, a Scottish brimless hat, traditionally made of dark blue wool with a cockade and plume, a cloak, a jacket or mantle – all these styles set by Queen Victoria and Prince Albert in the 1850s and 60s.

bandanna   Square of silk or cotton with spotted pattern, tied round the head or neck.

Banks, Jeff   Born in Wales, 1943, became widely known in the mid 70s when he launched the 'Warehouse' chain. Presenter of the first dedicated television fashion programme, *The Clothes Show*.

banyan   Loose-fitting shirt or jacket originally worn in India.

batiste   Fine plain-weave cotton or linen fabric, used for shirts and dresses.

batwing sleeve   Sleeve of a garment with a deep armhole and tight wrist.

bauchle   General term for an old, worn shoe.

Bebe   Top international brand name for designer shoes as in the name of their stores.

Belle and Bunty   Label formed by Alice-Louise Shreeve and Hannah Coniam (née Roff). Their first collection, Go Wild, was launched at the National Army Museum and made a huge impact. The label's name derives from the childhood nicknames of its founders.

Benetton   Fashion empire based in Treviso, Italy and identified with its sponsorship of rugby, basketball and volleyball but especially Formula One racing team.

Biba founder   Barbara Hulanicki.

biggin   Plain, close-fitting cap, often tied under the chin, popular in 16th and 17th centuries based on coif-like caps worn by the Béguines lay sisters.

bijouterie   Costume jewellery or trinkets, particularly finger-rings, from which the name derives.

bikini designer   Louis Réard.

Bikkembergs, Dirk   Born in Cologne, Germany, 1959, of Belgian extraction, first came to prominence as a shoe designer before establishing himself as a top ready-to-wear designer. Along with Ann Demeulemeester, Dirk Van Saene, Walter Van Beirendonck, Dries Van Noten, and Martin Margiela, one of the so-called Anvers 'Group of Six'.

billycock   Any of several round-crowned brimmed hats of felt, named after William Coke, for whom it was first made in the 19th century.

biretta   Stiff clerical cap with either three or four upright pieces projecting outwards from the centre to the edge, coloured black for priests, purple for bishops, red for cardinals and white for certain members of religious orders.

Blahnik, Manolo   Born in the Canary Islands of a Spanish mother and Czech father, Blahnik is a British-based designer of fashion shoes.

Bloomers   Named after, and designed by Amelia Jenks Bloomer (1818–94), a New York campaigner for temperance and women's rights. Bloomers were originally the full-length Turkish trousers worn under a skirt in the 1850s, but evolved firstly into a knickerbock style, and made popular by lady cyclists in the 1890s, and subsequently into any loose-fitting ladies baggy undergarments.

boa   Woman's long round scarf, usually of feathers or fur.

bodkin   Blunt, large-eyed needle used for drawing tape through openwork, also a pin used in ancient times to fasten women's hair.

Body Shop founder   Anita Roddick.

bolero   Short jacket, just reaching the waist, as worn by men in Spain; also a woman's short, open jacket, with or without sleeves.

bonnet rouge   Red cap worn by ardent supporters of the French Revolution.

Boudicca   London-based label founded by Zowie Broach and Brian Kirkby. Named after the Queen of the Iceni who rebelled against the Romans in 61 AD.

bowler   Hard felt hat with a rounded crown and a narrow curled brim, named after William Bowler in the US who designed it in 1850; in the US, a derby.

breeks   Scottish name for breeches.

British warm   Army officer's full-length, thick overcoat.

brogue (1)   Rough shoe of untanned hide, formerly worn in Ireland but now having ornamental perforated bands and worn throughout the world.

brogue (2)   Waterproof leggings with feet, used by anglers.

buckram   Originally a fine cotton or linen fabric stiffened with size, later used in lining or stiffening clothes as well as bookbinding.

Bui, Barbara   French fashion designer best known for her clean lines and offbeat femininity that combines various cultural and ethnic influences. Daughter of a French mother and Vietnamese father, Bui first came to prominence when opening her 'Kabuki' boutique in the 1980s with her actor husband William Halimi. In 1998 she started her 'BB Initials' line and more recently has started a line in designer shoes.

buibui   Piece of black cloth worn as a shawl by Muslim women, especially on the North African coast.

bumfreezer   Short jacket ; also a slang name for an Eton jacket.

Burberry   Drapery business opened in Basingstoke, Hampshire, England, in 1865 by 21-year old Thomas Burberry, producing waterproof garbardine raincoats. Since 1988 has enjoyed success with its youthful collections although appearing keen to distance itself from the so-called 'chav' culture.

burlap   Coarse fabric woven from jute or hemp.

burnous   Arab or Moorish hooded cloak, now worn as a fashion accessory in the Western world.

busby   Tall, fur helmet with a bag hanging from the top to the right side as worn by certain soldiers, usually hussars; it is also another name for a bearskin.

buskin   Originally, a thick-soled boot worn by tragic actors in ancient Athenian theatre; now a half-boot.

bustle   Pad or frame worn to puff out the top of a woman's skirt at the back.

Busuuti   Long garment with short sleeves and square neckline, as worn by Ugandan women.

cagoule   Thin-hooded outer jacket, especially one that is windproof and waterproof, and worn by mountaineers and others following outdoor pursuits.

calash (also calèche)   Woman's folding, hooped hood, worn in 18th century.

calico   White or unbleached cotton fabric with no printed design (originally from 'Calicut, on the Malabar coast,' a town in India).

calotte   Skullcap worn by Roman Catholic clergy.

cambric   Originally a fine white linen fabric of the late Tudor and early Stuart period and imported from the French town of Cambrai. The lightness of the material made it popular as a decorative accompaniment to dress as ruffs, cuffs, bands and handkerchiefs. Modern cambric is made from high-quality American or Egyptian cotton and is identified with good-quality underwear.

camisole   Woman's under-bodice with shoulder straps, originally designed as a cover for a corset.

capote   Long cloak or soldier's coat, usually with a hood; also a kind of 19th-century bonnet.

capuchin   Woman's cloak and hood resembling the dress of a Capuchin friar.

casque   Piece of armour to cover the head; a helmet.

castor   Hat made of beaver fur.

Cerruti   Founded in 1881 in Biella, Milan, by Antonio Cerruti as a fabric mill company, Cerruti became fashionable when Nino Cerruti, grandson of the founder developed the business into a ready-to-wear fashion house in 1957 when he opened 'Hitman' in Milan. In 1967 Nino opened 'Cerruti 1881', a men's couture house in the centre of Paris and soon established an international reputation. In 1976 Cerruti developed a women's ready-to-wear market and is now established in all aspects of haute couture.

cestus (1)   Pugilist's gauntlet of bull's hide loaded or studded with metal.

cestus (2)   Girdle, named after the girdle of Aphrodite.

chador/chuddar   Large shawl or veil worn by Muslim or Hindu women that covers them from head to foot.

Chanel, Coco   French fashion designer (1883–1971), worked as a milliner until 1912 and following service as a nurse during World War I, opened a couture house in Paris. She revolutionised women's fashions during the 1920s, her designs including the 'chemise' dress, the collarless cardigan jacket, and the 'little black dress'. Her designer perfume Chanel No. 5 became the ultimate status symbol. Chanel retired in 1938 but made a successful comeback in 1954 and her innovations such as the vogue for costume jewellery and the evening scarf have maintained their popularity.

Ch'ao-fu   Pre-modern Chinese man's robe with kimono-style upper body with long, close-fitting sleeves that terminated in the horse-hoof cuff introduced by the Manchus, and a closely-fitted neckband over which was worn a detached collar with wing-like tips that extended over the shoulders. The lower body consisted of a full, pleated skirt with a banded waist. Colours were dependent on rank.

chaplet   Ornamental wreath of flowers or beads worn on the head. Also a precious metal circlet, possibly set with gems.

chaps   protective leather trousers worn by American cowboys. The name comes from the Mexican 'chaparejos'.

chasuble   Long, sleeveless outer vestment worn by a priest when celebrating Mass.

chemise   Woman's loose-fitting undergarment or dress hanging straight from the shoulders.

cheongsam   Woman's garment with high neck and slit skirt, worn in China.

chiffon (1)   Light, diaphanous, plain-woven fabric of silk or nylon.

chiffon (2)   Trimmings or other adornments on a woman's dress.

chi-fu   Straight, kimono-sleeved robe, alternatively

called lung-p'ao 'dragon robes', worn formally by both sexes in China under the Manchu empire.

chignon Arrangement of long hair in a roll or knot at the back of the head.

ch'ima Korean pleated skirt, as worn by women from the 15th century onward.

chintz Brightly patterned cotton fabric with glazed finish (from a Hindi word that indicates a spatter or stain).

chiton Long tunic worn in ancient Greece made of wool, linen or cotton.

chlamys Short woollen cloak worn mostly by men in Ancient Greece.

choga Loose Afghan garment with long sleeves.

chōgori Traditional Korean jacket.

choli Short-sleeved blouse worn under a sari.

clinquant Imitation gold leaf worn as a fashion accessory.

cloche Woman's close-fitting bell-shaped hat.

Clothes Show BBC television programme that ran from 1985–8. Its presenters included Jeff Banks, Brenda Emmanus, Caryn Franklin, Tim Vincent and Margherita Taylor.

Coach Leading brand name in the field of luxury customised handbags for all occasions.

codpiece Bagged appendage to the fork of a man's breeches or close-fitting hose.

coif Close-fitting cap, worn under a veil in the Middle Ages or under a chainmail hood and tied under the chin with strings, now worn only by nuns.

coiffeur Professional hair-stylist.

coli Short-sleeved breast-length jacket, usually worn by Muslim women over a ghaghra.

Cook, Emma British designer who graduated in St Martins and like her classmates Stella McCartney and Alexander McQueen has become a leading light of the fashion industry. Formerly a consultant with Ghost, she is now freelance.

combinations One-piece woollen undergarment with long sleeves and legs; known in the USA as a union suit.

cote hardie Medieval close-fitting sleeved tunic, when worn by men long enough to cover the buttocks and belted around the hips; when worn by women, full-length and often unbelted..

cowl A cap or hood especially on a monk's habit.

Cox, Patrick Born in Canada, 1963, as a student he designed shoes for Vivian Westwood, Body Map and later for John Galliano. Cox introduced his own label 1987 and his fleurs-de-lys-logo is a sign of elegant fashion and quirky design.

cracowe Long pointed shoe named after the Polish city of Cracow (Kraków). It is thought that the marriage of Richard II of England to Anne of Bohemia in 1382 was responsible for the fashion in England.

cravat A scarf of silk or fine wool, worn round the neck, especially by men. Cravats were popularised by Croats in the French army during the Thirty Years' War and the name is a corruption of Croat.

crinoline In the 1830s a stiff fabric made of horsehair and cotton or linen thread, used for linings, hats and skirts. Later a petticoat with steel hoops worn under a skirt to make it stand out from the body in a bell-shape.

cuisse Piece of armour for the front of the thigh.

culottes Woman's breeches that hang like a skirt but have separate legs.

cymar (also simar, cimarra) Woman's loose gown, popular in the 17th and 18th centuries.

dalmatica Wide-sleeved, tunic-like vestment, open at the sides, worn by deacons and bishops. Originally worn by Roman noblemen from the 2nd century on and made of white Dalmatian wool.

damask Richly figured woven material, originally of silk, with a pattern visible on either side. It originated in Damascus in Syria.

dashiki Loose brightly coloured shirt worn in West Africa and also in the USA.

décolleté Low-cut neckline.

deerstalker Cloth cap, peaked in front and behind, with earflaps that are usually tied up on the top.

De La Renta, Oscar Born in the Dominican Republic, 1932, but became a naturalised American in the 1960s. He started his own company in 1965 with a reputation for opulent, ornately trimmed clothes, particularly evening dresses. In 1993 he became the first American to design for a French couture house, Pierre Balmain.

denim Originally serge de Nîmes (named from Nîmes, in France), now a twilled, hard-wearing, cotton fabric used for jeans.

dernier cri Latest fashion ('last cry').

dhoti Loincloth worn by male Hindus. The ends are passed between the legs and tucked in at the waist.

Dinnigan, Collette Born in South Africa to an Irish father and South African mother, she was brought up in New Zealand and after completing her education, emigrated to Australia. She started her own label in 1990 and in 1995 became the first Australian to have a full-scale ready-to-wear parade in Paris.

Dior, Christian French fashion designer (1905–57). Founded his fashion house in 1945 and achieved worldwide fame with his long-skirted 'New Look' of 1947. His later designs included the 'H' line and the 'A' line.

dirndl Dress in the style of an Alpine female peasant costume, with close-fitting bodice and full skirt.

Dolce & Gabbana Founded in Milan in 1982 by Domenico Dolce, a shy bearded Sicilian, and the Venetian Stefano Gabbana. Throughout the 1990s they expanded their operations into menswear and a popular youth line. A further division of their operations created a White Line for day-to-day basics, and a Black Line for fantasy goods. In February 2005 they announced the end of their 19-year romantic liaison, although making clear the label is in no danger.

Dolly Varden Woman's large hat, named after a Dickens' character in *Barnaby Rudge*; also a flowered dress.

dolman (1) Long Turkish robe, open in the front and with narrow sleeves.

dolman (2) Hussar's jacket worn with the sleeves hanging loose.

dolman (3) Woman's mantle with dolman sleeves.

dolman sleeve Loose sleeve made in one piece with the body of a coat; it has a wide armhole but a tight wrist.

domino (1) Large, hooded cloak, worn with an eye mask at a masquerade.

domino (2) The eye mask worn at masquerades.

Donna Karan Born in New York as Donna Faske in 1948, she began her career as a designer for Anne Klein and subsequently took control on her death in 1974. Karan eventually began her own company with second husband Stephen Weis.

FASHION AND DRESS

doublet Close-fitting body garment with or without sleeves and a short skir, worn by men from the medieval times to the 17th century.

duchesse Soft, heavy kind of satin; also a type of chaise longue.

dundreary Long sidewhiskers worn without a beard, named after Lord Dundreary, a character in Tom Taylor's comedy (1858).

dungaree Coarse cotton fabric used chiefly for work clothes from a Hindi word.

durzi An Indian tailor.

Emanuels David, born 1952, and Elizabeth, born 1953, launched their label in 1975 but split up in the 1990s. Their most famous creation was the wedding dress of Diana, Princess of Wales. Co-authors of *Style for all Seasons*.

Erotokritos Cyprus-born, Paris-based fashion designer who launched his own label in 1994 and since his first Paris show in 1996 has built a reputation for chic yet casual clothing.

Eton jacket Waist-length jacket with a V-shaped back, open in the front, formerly worn by pupils of Eton College.

Etro Italian company that specialises in selling extraordinary crafted, brightly coloured paisley (Etro's hallmark), foulard and brocade ties and vests, as well as finely tailored suits. Gimno Etro is the head of the empire and his three sons, Ippolito, Jacopo and Kean, are directors.

Farhi, Nicole French-born Algerian designer known for her luxurious and sensual woman's collections. She opened her first store in 1983 as part of a Harvey Nichols and in 1984 opened a boutique in New York. Farhi's home shop is in Clifford Street London.

farjī Long, gown-like coat with short sleeves, made of wool or cotton (silk is forbidden to men by the Koran), as worn by Muslim priests or high officials.

farthingale Framework of hoops, or a hooped petticoat, used the 15th to 17th century to extend the skirts of a woman's dress.

Fendi Established in Rome, 1918, as a leather and fur workshop by Adele Casagrande (d. 1978). The named changed in 1925 when Adele married Edoardo Fendi. Since the death of Edoardo in 1954 the company has being run by his five daughters, Alda, Anna, Carla, Franca and Paola, although a controlling interest is now shared by Prada and Louis Vuitton. Karl Lagerfeld has designed the Fendi fur collection since 1962.

Ferré, Gianfranco Born in Legnano, Italy, 1944, he formed the Gianfranco Ferré company in 1978 with business partner Franco Mattioli. Unusually, Ferré has maintained a popularity in all aspects of the fashion industry, having had successful women's, men's and children's clothing lines and fragrances.

fez rimless felt or woollen cap, cylindrical in shape, usually red and with a tassel, usually worn by men in Muslim coutries and formerly the national head-dress of Turkey.

fichu Woman's small triangular shawl of lace for the shoulders and neck. Late 18th to late 19th century.

filibeg / philibeg Kilt worn by Scottish Highlanders.

finnesko Boot of reindeer skin with the hair on the outside.

forage cap Soldier's undress cap.

Ford, Tom Born in Texas 1962, he rose to prominence when taken on as Creative Director of Gucci and made an immediate impact. Ford is sometimes known as the 'It' Boy of the fashion world, or more recently the 'King of Cool'. He has often been targeted by animal rights activists for his refusal to stop using fur in his designs. His former womenswear director, Alessandra Facchinetti, took over his position at Gucci in 2004 before herself being replaced by Frida Giannini in 2005.

Franz Josef Long sidewhiskers, merging into a moustache, named in honour of the emperor of Austria.

frippery Originally old or second-hand clothes or tawdry adornment in dress; now means showy.

frog Decorative braided coat-fastening, originally forming part of military dress, consisting of a spindle-shaped button and a loop and a braided loop that retains it.

furisode Long-sleeved outer kimono traditionally worn by young, unmarried Japanese girls (married women wearing the short-sleeved kimono known as a kosode).

gabardine Raincoat made from a smooth, durable, twill-woven cloth of worsted or cotton; also a long loose cloak.

gaberdine Twill-weave worsted, cotton, or spun-rayon fabric.

Galliano, John British fashion designer currently head of the Dior fashion empire.

galligaskins Loose, wide breeches or hose, especially as worn by men in the 16th and 17th centuries; also the leather leggings worn in the 19th century.

gallus Trouser braces of a type worn in the USA, where braces are called suspenders.

galosh Originally a clog, or wooden sole attached to a shoe, but now an overshoe, usually made of rubber or plastic.

Garroudi, Pierre Born in Tehran, Iran, 1959, and educated in Paris. He moved to New York in 1986 and opened his own fashion house in 1993. His designs are daring and innovative and his shows are erotic, witty and provocative.

georgette Thin silk or crêpe dress material, named after Georgette de la Plante, a French dressmaker.

gewgaw Worthless piece of frippery worn to be showy.

ghāghrā Open-fronted pleated skirt, as worn by Muslim women.

Ghost Tanya Sarne's 'Ghost' is well know for its trademark garment-dyed vintage-look viscose and ultra feminine garments. Its clothes are created by women for women.

Gibbs, Bill Scottish fashion designer (1943–88), launched his own label in 1971 in partnership with Kate Franklin. Inspired by the vast diversity and volume of ethnic costume as well as Scottish Highland dress. His signature motif was the bee (B for Bill).

Gibson girl Young woman typifying the fashionable ideal of around 1900, as represented in the work of Charles Dana Gibson (1867–1944) US artist.

gilet Waist-length, sleeveless garment, usually quilted and fastened up the front, designed to be worn over a blouse and often worn as part of a ballet dancer's costume. Gilet literally means waistcoat in French.

gingham Plain-woven cotton cloth, especially striped or checked (literally means 'striped' in Malay).

gipon   Close-fitting padded tunic, buttoned down the front, the sleeves long enough to cover the knuckles, the neck round and low. Originally worn under medieval body armour.

Givenchy, Hubert   Born in Beauvais, France, 1927, Hubert Givenchy opened his own house in 1952, producing ready-to-wear clothes under his Nouvelle Boutique label.

Gladstone bag   A light portmanteau opening into two equal compartments and named after the British Prime Minister who carried such a bag.

Glengarry   Brimless Scottish hat with a cleft down the centre and two ribbons hanging down the back, chiefly worn as part of Highland dress.

gorget (1)   Collar-like piece of armour worn to protect the throat.

gorget (2)   Part of a wimple worn by women to cover the neck and shoulders, especially in the late Middle Ages.

greave   Piece of armour protecting the leg below the knee.

Gucci, Guccio   Italian fashion designer (1881–1953) born in Florence. He opened his first shop in Florence, 1920, and became known for his leather craftsmanship and accessories. His four sons joined the firm and in 1953 the first overseas shop opened in New York. The empire has had several corporate identities and after Gucci's grandson Maurizio's (1949–95) presidency from 1989 to 1993, the company was sold to the multinational Investcorp.

habergeon   Sleeveless coat of mail.

haik   Large cloak, usually white, worn by both sexes in North Africa.

hakama   Very full men's trousers, as worn in Japan from the 7th century onwards.

Hartnell, Sir Norman (1901–78)   Born in London and educated at Magdalene College, Cambridge. Started his own couturier business in 1923 and received the Royal Warrant in 1940. He was president of the Incorporated Society of London Fashion Designers (1946–56) and became famous for designing costumes for leading actresses of the day and Princess Elizabeth's Wedding and Coronation gowns.

hauberk   Piece of defensive armour, for neck and shoulders at first, but soon developed into a long mail shirt or military tunic.

haute couture   High fashion, literally 'high dressmaking'; collectively the leading dressmakers and fashion houses or their products.

Hermès   Founded in 1837 by Thierry Hermès, the world-famous fashion house began life as a manufacturer of equestrian accessories such as saddles, riding boots and bridles. The present regime is headed by Jean-Louis Dumas, the fifth family successor to the Hermès empire. The current head designer is Martin Margiela, who has expanded the repertoire into his trademark camel coats and grunge apparel but the reputation of Hermès is built upon the success of their silk scarf and handbag market. The 'Kelly' bag, as popularised by Grace Kelly, is still a bestseller.

himation   Outer garment worn over the left shoulder, and under the right, in ancient Greece.

hitatare   The formal court dress of a Samurai.

hobble skirt   Skirt so narrow at the hem as to impede walking; introduced before World War I

Holland   Smooth hard-wearing linen fabric.

Homburg   Man's felt hat with a narrow curled brim and a lengthwise dent in the crown.

houppelande   Medieval tunic or gown worn by both sexes, with full sleeves and long train, belted at the waist. The collar was high, often with a dagged edge.

imperial   Pointed tuft of whiskers on the chin, named in honour of Napoleon III (Emperor of France 1852–70).

isar   Wide trousers, usually worn by Muslim men under the jāmah.

Jacobs, Marc   Artistic director at Louis Vuitton since 1987 and now known as a leading designer in his own right. His colourful mat finishes in a 1960s style have become popular with celebrities and actress Winona Ryder was accused of shoplifting for Marc Jacob's designs.

Jacquard   Method of weaving a design directly into the fabric instead of being printed or dyed on. The piece of apparatus used for this type of weave is called a Jacquard loom, after its French inventor Joseph M Jacquard (1752–1834).

jāmah   Long-sleeved coat that reaches to, or below, the knees and has a belted waist; as worn by Muslim men.

jeans inventor   Levi Strauss.

Jimmy Choo   Born in 1961, his label was founded in 1996 in partnership with Tamara Yeardye and Sandra Choi, who is the Creative Director and designer of their popular fashion shoes which are affectionately known as 'Jimmys'.

Joseph   Founded by Joseph Ettedgui, born 1935, a highly influential retailer who provides a showcase for top designers

Jon, Anand   Indian fashion designer whose 'functional luxury' style is currently en vogue.

Juliet cap   Small net ornamental cap worn by brides etc.

Jungle Jap shops   Opened by Kenzo Takada in 1970.

juni hitoe   Japanese noblewoman's full court costume meaning 'twelve layer' but possibly with more.

karaginu   Outermost garment of the juni hitoe, consisting of a wide-sleeved jacket reaching only to the waist.

keffiyeh   Bedouin Arab's kerchief or larger square of wool cotton or linen worn as a headdress and held in place by an agal.

kebaya (1)   Light loose tunic of a type worn in SE Asia by both sexes.

kebaya (2)   Short tight-fitting long-sleeved jacket, together with a sarong the traditional dress of Malay and Indonesian women.

Kenzo   Popular name of Kenzo Takada, Japanese fashion designer, born in Kyoto. He had small success in his home country before moving to Paris and producing freelance collections in 1964. His Jungle Jap shop built his reputation as an innovator and his creations blend Oriental and Western influences with traditional designs. Kenzo is also a trendsetter in the field of knitwear.

képi   French military cap with a circular top and a horizontal peak.

kimono   A Japanese loose sashed ankle-length garment with wide sleeves. Literally means wear thing.

kirtle   Old English name for a woman's skirt or dress; also the name of a man's tunic or coat, usually reaching to the knees.

F
A
S
H
I
O
N

A
N
D

D
R
E
S
S

Klein, Anne   Native New Yorker Anne Klein made her name when setting up her company in 1968 and introducing a sporty element into US fashion. Following her death in 1974, Donna Karan and Louis Dell'Olio continued as co-designers and Dell'Olio remains the head designer and the overseer of the company's latest manifestation, Anne Klein II.

Klein, Calvin   Born in New York, USA, in 1942. Opened his first store in 1968 in partnership with long-time friend and businessman Barry Schwartz. The simple but sophisticated style of his clothes soon gained him recognition and this became universal when actress Brooke Shields modelled his designer jeans in the late 1970s. Klein popularised designer men's underwear in 1982 and following the success of his fragrances, Obsession, Eternity and Escape, his CK One became the first of the unisex fragrances. In September 2003 Francisco Costa, a 34-year-old Brazilian fashion designer, took over as design director to bring an end to Klein's 30-year reign as head of his fashion empire.

knickerbockers   Short, loose-fitting trousers gathered in at the knee or calf. Named after Diedrich Knickerbocker, fictitious author of a *History of New York* actually written by Washington Irving (1783–1859).

Lacroix, Christian   Born in 1951, the French fashion designer opened the House of Lacroix in Paris, 1987, and specialises in ornate and frivolous designs.

Lagerfeld, Karl   Born in 1939, Lagerfeld has been head of Chanel since 1983 and was previously chief designer of Chloe from 1963–84.

Lang, Helmut   Born in Vienna, Austria, 1956, Lang has become a pioneer in many areas of the fashion industry. He is known for his use of techno fabrics, minimalism and deconstructionism. He sold his label to the Prada Group in November 2003 and resigned as creative director of his own brand in January 2005.

La Perla   Founded by Ada Masotti in Italy, 1954, and known for high-quality and luxurious, intimate apparel. Pioneered the wearing of bodysuits as outerwear, and sleepwear as casual clothes.

Laroche, Guy   French fashion designer (1923–89), born in La Rochelle. He worked in millinery, first in Paris, then New York, before returning to Paris to start his own company. By 1961 he was producing both couture and ready-to-wear clothes. From 1966 his designs included menswear.

leghorn   Hat made of fine plaited straw.

leg-of-mutton sleeve   Sleeve which is full and loose on the upper arm but close-fitting on the forearm.

lei   Polynesian garland made of flowers, feathers or shells; often given as a symbol of affection.

leotard   Close-fitting one-piece garment named after Jules Léotard, a French trapeze artist (1830–70).

Levi's   Proprietary name for a type of blue denim jeans, produced by Levi Strauss as working clothes in the 1860s.

Liripipe / Liripoop   In medieval times, the extended tail of a hood which could be as much as five or six feet long; also a medieval slang name for a shoelace.

Louis Vuitton   Founded in 1854 by luggage manufacturer Louis Vuitton Malletier, the label has become the most imitated of all top fashion houses. The reputation was founded on their luxurious leather bags, often using exotic leathers such as alligator, ostrich and lizard. In March 1987 Marc Jacobs became the artistic director.

mantelet / mantlet   Women's short, loose, sleeveless cloak.

mantilla   Light scarf, often made from black lace, worn over the head and shoulders, especially by Spanish women.

mantua   Woman's loose gown of the 17th and 18th centuries. So spelled after an Italian city but originally from French manteau.

Marocain   Dress fabric of ribbed crêpe.

McCartney, Stella   Born in 1971, the daughter of Sir Paul McCartney, Stella was chief designer of the Chloe fashion house (1997–2001) before taking up an appointment with Gucci. She marrked Alasdhair Willis, the publisher of *Wallpaper* magazine, in August 2003.

McQueen, Alexander   Chief designer of the Givenchy fashion house and a contemporary of Emma Cook and Stella McCartney.

mignonette   Light, fine, narrow lace used for trimming.

miniskirt   Created by André Courrèges and popularised by Mary Quant.

Missoni   Founded in Gallarate, Varese, Italy, 1953, by Ottavio Missoni and his wife Rosita (née Jelmeni). The Missoni label, created in 1958, is known for its fluidity and colour of its creations, which have an affinity to art.

mitra / mitre (1)   Headband worn by women in ancient Greece.

mitra / mitre (2)   Tall Asian head-dress, regarded by the Romans as effeminate when worn by men; the ceremonial turban of a high priest. Also the deeply-cleft head-dress worn in the Christian Church by a bishop or abbot, especially as a symbol of episcopal office, forming in outline the shape of a pointed arch, and often made of embroidered white linen or satin.

Miyake, Issey   Japanese fashion designer born in Hiroshima in 1938. His distinctive style combines Eastern and Western influences in his loose-fitting garments which have a theatrical quality to them by the use of dramatic asymmetric outline and varied textures.

mo   Women's pleated train, part of the formal court costume established in Japan by the time of the 8th century.

mob cap   Large indoor cap covering all the hair, worn by women in 18th and 19th centuries.

moccasin   Soft leather shoe, originally worn by Native Americans.

Monmouth   Flat, round cap formerly worn by soldiers and sailors.

Montana, Claude   Began his career in London with the Carnaby Street movement, where he designed jewellery made from large coloured stones embedded in papier mâché. On his return to Paris he became popular for his designer leather outfits and his 1976 show at the Angelina tea rooms in Paris caught the imagination of the fashion industry.

Montera / montero   Spanish peaked travelling cap with a spherical crown and flaps for lowering over the ears;also the black hat worn by bullfighters.

muff   Soft insulated covering, cylindrical, into which both hands may be thrusted at opposite ends to keep warm.

mutch   Woman's or child's linen cap.

mutton chops   Sidewhiskers narrow at the top and broad and rounded at the bottom.

muu-muu   Woman's loose, brightly coloured dress from Hawaii.

Naga-Bakama Japanese formal undergarment made of a stiff red cloth and fastened high up under the breast and covering the feet at the front but extending out to a train at the back.

napery Household linen, especially table linen.

New Look Christian Dior's 1947 creation of women's dress with narrow shoulders and long, full skirts.

Norfolk jacket Man's loose belted sporting jacket with box pleats.

Nutter, Tommy Welsh fashion designer (1943–92), revolutionised menswear by introducing high fashion to Savile Row in 1969, funded by pop singer Cilla Black.

nylons Stockings or tights made from a synthetic polymeric amid. The process was invented by Wallace Carothers in the 1930s and named after New York and London.

Oldfield, Bruce Born in 1950, launched his own label in 1975. Famous for his pretty and glamorous evening wear.

Oxfords Can be a type of shoe, shirt, or trousers (Oxford bags).

Ozbek, Rifat Turkish-born, 1953, British fashion designer who bizarrely first came to prominence for his extraordinary resemblance to Diana Vreeland. His transposing of ethnically inspired clothes into a modern context such as Indonesian Ikat patterns printed on slinky lycra tube skirts, and his opulent Oriental brocades woven into the English gentleman's tailcoats are trademark Ozbek creations.

Paddington Designer handbag produced by Chloé for their 2005 spring season. The soft, washed leather bag comes in chocolate brown, cream or tan and is distinguished by its brass padlock.

paji Traditional Korean trousers.

palisado During the reign of Elizabeth, women wore their hair turned back from the forehead over a pad or a wire known as a palisado.

palla Loose outer garment or outdoor wrap, usually worn by women in ancient Rome and Byzantium.

pallium (1) Man's large rectangular outdoor cloak worn in ancient Rome.

pallium (2) Woollen vestment conferred by the Pope on an archbishop, consisting of a narrow circular band worn round the shoulders with a short flap hanging from front and back.

Panama Hat made originally from the plaited leaves of the jipijapa plant of Ecuador.

pannier Framework, used to extend and support the skirt of a woman's dress in the late 17th and 18th centuries, and usually made from osier reeds or whalebone.

parure Matching set of jewels designed to be worn together.

pashmina A cashmere shawl made from pashm, the underfur of various Tibetan animals, but especially the goat.

patten Shoe or clog with a raised sole, or set on an iron ring, for walking over mud or on uneven ground.

pauldron Piece of shoulder armour.

pea-jacket Sailor's short, double-breasted overcoat of coarse dark blue cloth, also pilot or reefer jacket.

pelerine Woman's narrow cape with long, pointed ends in front (literally means 'pilgrim'); 18th and 19th century.

peplos Half- or full-length loose outer robe often two lengths of fabric pinned at the shoulders worn by women in ancient Greece.

perizoma Short pants worn by athletes in ancient Greece.

Perrin, Christina New York-based designer of Swedish extraction. Popular in the late 1990s for her silhouettes in distinctive fabrications, avant-garde use of leather and fur, and her unusual tailoring and richness of colour.

Persian lamb Silky, tightly curled fur of a breed of lamb called a Karakul, used in clothing.

peruke Kind of wig worn in Europe from 1660 to 1800. A skullcap covered with hair at first imitating the natural hair of the head, later often much more elaborate and imposing (also periwig, perruque).

petasos Low-crowned, wide-brimmed hat of ancient Greece, often with a cord which allowed it to be slung over the wearer's back when the weather permitted.

Petersham (1) Thick, corded, silk ribbon used for stiffening in dressmaking.

Petersham (2) A heavy overcoat or the rough cloth (usually dark blue) from which it was made.

petticoat Woman's undergarment, but also, in Elizabethan times, a small coat worn by men under the doublet.

Piccadilly Weepers Long sidewhiskers, worn without a beard.

pickelhaube German soldier's spiked helmet.

pileus Brimless, close-fitting felt cap, worn in ancient Greece; a similar cap was called a pilos.

pillbox A small cylindrical hat worn at the back of the head and popularised by Jacqueline Kennedy in the 1960s.

pinking shears Dressmaker's serrated shears for cutting a zigzag edge.

pith helmet Light sun-helmet made of the dried pith of the sola plant.

plus-fours Men's baggy knickerbockers reaching below the knee, now only worn for hunting or golf.

Poiret, Paul French couturier (1879–1944), the most fashionable dress designer of pre-war Paris, and designer of the hobble skirt.

poleyn Piece of armour for the knee.

poor boy Type of pullover.

Prada Since the mid 1990s there have been few status symbols as potent as the Prada-embossed silver triangle. Prada began life as a family-run leather goods business in Milan but enjoyed the patronage of a growing number of celebrities. The Prada empire has been run since 1978 by Patrizio Bertelli and his wife Miuccia Prada, the grand-daughter of the founder. In 1992 a youth-targeted 'Miu Miu' line was introduced as well as a 'Granello' and 'Prada Sport' range. Miuccia Prada has won critical praise for her innovative experiments in both fabric design and use of colour and her businessman husband equal praise for his shrewd purchasing of large share-holdings of rival operations such as Gucci, Lang, Alaia and Sander.

praetexta Toga with purple edge, worn by some Roman magistrates and pre-adult boys.

Proenza Schouler The label of the young New York duo Lazaro Hernandez and Jack McCollough. Their signature ideas encompass proportion (shrunken pea coats, pencil skirts), colour (army greens, browns, battleship greys), and silhouette (sleek, minimal). The label derives its name from the maiden names of the mothers of the founders.

p'u-fu Three-quarter-length coat worn by men and women in China over their ch'ao-fu or chi-fu.

F
A
S
H
I
O
N

A
N
D

D
R
E
S
S

puggaree (also pagari)   Indian word for a full turban; also a pleated scarf around the crown of some hats, especially sun hats.

puttee (1)   A strip of cloth wound round the leg from ankle to knee as a legging.

puttee (2)   Leather-legging.

Quant, Mary   Born in London, 1934, opened her first boutique in Chelsea in 1955, and married one of her partners, Alexander Plunket Greene. She was the inventor of the mini skirt in the 1960s and hot pants in the early 1970s.

Rabanne, Paco   Born in the Basque area of Spain in 1934, Rabanne's first collection in 1966 entitled 'Twelve Unwearable Dresses' set the scene for his unconventional career. He has designed in plastic, chain metal, fluorescent leather, ostrich feathers, aluminium, paper, laser discs, fibre optic wire, socks and doorknobs.

Ralph Lauren   Born in the Bronx, NY in 1939 as Ralph Lifshitz, Lauren introduced the Polo label in 1967 and became popular following the 1974 film *The Great Gatsby* after many of his designs were worn.

reefer   An overcoat, as worn in North America, often called a gaitor or reefer jacket.

rerebrace   Piece of armour developed to cover the upper arm but later protecting to the shoulder and elbow.

Rhinegraves   Late 17th-century breeches, loose at the knee and wide like shorts, often with frilly embellishments.

Rhodes, Zandra   Born in 1940, first came to prominence when she opened the Fulham Road Clothes Shop in 1967. She is noted for her distinctive exotic designs in floating chiffons and silks.

roquelaure   Man's knee-length cloak with a cape collar, fashionable in the 18th century.

ruff   Decorative frill encircling the neck developed in mid-16th-century Spain and fashionable in Europe, in Jacobean and Elizabethan times. Also a frill around the sleeve of a garment.

sabaton   Piece of armour for the foot.

sabot   Shoe made from a single block of wood; a clog or, in Holland, a klomp.

Saint-Laurent, Yves   Born in Oran, Algeria, 1936, he studied in Paris and joined the House of Dior in 1955 after winning a Wool Secretariat design competition. On Dior's death in 1957 he took over the house. In 1962 he opened his own house and launched the first of his 160 Rive Gauche boutiques in 1966, selling ready-to-wear clothes, a trend that was soon copied by other fashion houses. Saint-Laurent also creates costumes for theatre, ballet, and films, and in 1985 was awarded a Best Fashion Design Oscar.

Sander, Jill   Born in Wesselburen, Germany, 1943, Sander is best known for her long, lean silhouettes. She has brought minimalism in fashion to an art form and superfluous buttons and zips have been banished. The Prada corporation presently own a large shareholding in the Sander fashion empire.

sand-shoe   Light canvas shoe with a rubber sole; a plimsoll.

sari   Traditional garment of Indian women, worn over a choli and an underskirt, consisting of a length of cotton, silk, or other cloth wrapped around the waist and draped over one shoulder.

sarong   Traditional skirtlike garment of the Malay archipelago, Java, and some Pacific islands, consisting of a long strip of cloth worn tucked round the waist or under the armpits by both sexes. Popularised by actress Dorothy Lamour in the 'Road' series of films.

sarong kebaya   Traditional dress of Malay and Indonesian women, consisting of a sarong and a kebaya.

Schiaparelli, Elsa   Italian fashion designer (1896–1973) born in Rome. After studying philosophy she worked as a film scriptwriter in America before venturing to Paris in 1920 and receiving her first order for a black sweater knitted with a white bow, ironically from an American store. Her following designs were innovative and sensational, and she was noted for her use of colour, including 'shocking pink', and also for her outrageous hats and use of zippers and buttons.

seersucker   Material of linen or cotton with a puckered surface.

semmit   An undervest, as worn in Scotland.

serge   Durable woollen or worsted fabric.

shako   Tall, cylindrical, military peaked cap worn with a plume or pompom.

Shilling, David   Born in 1953, from the age of 12 he designed the extravagant headwear made famous by his mother Gertrude at Royal Ascot. Launched his own label in 1975. Author of *Thinking Rich – A Personal Guide to Luxury Living.*

shitagasane   Kimono of white damask, worn under the ho, with an elongated train of up to 12 feet long.

sideburns   Short sidewhiskers, originally called Burnsides, after US Union General Ambrose Everett Burnside (1824–81) who wore them.

Siemens, Crystal   Canadian fashion designer who uses combinations of materials and colour to give an effect of light playing off the fabric.

Simons, Raf   Born in Belgium, 1968, his first show was in Milan in 1995. Subsequent shows in Paris and New York have highlighted his influence by pop culture, particularly David Bowie, and are described by himself as fashion, youth culture, music and performance parades.

skinny rib   Type of pullover.

smock-frock   Loose protective garment of coarse homepin linen or cotton reaching below the knees, traditionally worn by farm labourers before the machine age.

snood (1)   Pouchlike hat, often of net, loosely holding a woman's hair at the back.

snood (2)   Headband, formerly worn by young unmarried women in Scotland.

sokutai   Japanese court costume, exclusively worn by the emperor, with a yellow outer robe (ho) patterned with hō-ō birds and kilin, and baggy white damask trousers (ue-no-hakama).

soup and fish   Men's evening dress.

sou'wester   Waterproof hat with a very broad rim behind, worn especially by seamen.

spat   A short gaiter worn over the instep and reaching a little way above the ankle, worn to keep trousers or stockings clean, especially when riding. Spat is an abbreviation for Spatterdash, although nowadays a distinction is drawn between the fashion accessories.

spatterdash   Long gaiter or legging of leather or cloth, worn to keep trousers or stockings clean.

Stetson   Man's felt slouch hat with a broad brim and high crown, named after John Stetson (1830–1906), the hatter who designed it.

stock   Long white scarf worn with formal riding dress.

stomacher Originally an ornamental 'V' or 'U' shaped piece of stiff material worn under a man's doublet to cover the chest and stomach. Later, an ornamental triangular panel filling the open front of a woman's dress, covering the breast and stomach, and often jewelled or embroidered.

suberakashi The elaborate coiffure worn as part of the juni-hitoe, consisting of a lacquered, gold-sprinkled comb surmounted by a gold-lacquered chrysanthemum crest.

Sui, Anna Born in Detroit, Michigan, USA, 1955, of Chinese extraction. Her baby-doll dresses of the early 1990s became in vogue with the inception of the grunge movement. Her designs are popular with pop musicians and models.

surplice Loose, white linen vestment with wide sleeves, reaching to the knees or feet and worn over a cassock by clergy and choristers at church services.

surtout Can be either a man's overcoat or a woman's hooded mantle.

tabard (1) Coarse outer garment formerly worn by the peasantry or by monks and foot-soldiers.

tabard (2) Short, open surcoat worn by a knight over his armour and emblazoned with armorial bearings.

taffeta Fine, lustrous silk with a crisp texture, used for making formal dresses.

tallith A shawl with fringed corners, traditionally worn by male jews whilst at prayer.

tam-o'-Shanter Scottish, brimless woollen cap, with a bobble in the centre, usually worn pulled down at one side.

tammy Glazed woollen or mixed fabric, used for linings or undergarments.

tarboosh Cap, similar to a fez, usually of red felt with a tassel at the top, worn by Muslim men either alone or as part of a turban.

tasset Piece of armour for the upper thigh.

tebenna Forerunner of the Roman toga, as worn in ancient Greece.

tika dot Mark on the forehead of Hindu women, indicating caste, or worn by both sexes as an ornament.

tiki An amulet or figurine in the form of a carved representation of an ancestor, worn in some Polynesian cultures.

tippet (1) In Elizabethan times, a long streamer-like part to a sleeve or hood. Also a woman's fur cape for the shoulders, often consisting of the whole fur of a fox or marten.

tippet (2) The long stole worn by Anglican clergy during a service.

toga Loose, flowing outer garment worn by Roman citizens and made of a single piece of cloth covering the whole body except the right arm.

toga virilis White toga donned as a sign of manhood at the age of 14.

topi Hat, originally Indian but now a type of pith helmet.

toque (1) Woman's small, round, brimless hat, popular in Edwardian times.

top 10 fashion items In a poll of 3,500 shoppers carried out in February 2005 by Harvey Nichols, the miniskirt was voted Britain's favourite fashion item ever. The full top 10 were 1) Miniskirt 2) Jeans 3) Little black dress 4) Flares 5) Cowboy boots 6) Platform shoes 7) Poncho 8) Trainers 9) Combats 10) Trench coat.

toque (2) Hat with a small brim and pouched crown, popular in the 16th century.

toque (3) Canadian, close-fitting knitted hat, often with a tassel or pompom.

torchon Coarse bobbin lace with geometrical designs.

toreador pants Women's close-fitting, calf-length trousers.

trabea Roman toga ornamented with horizontal purple stripes, worn as a state robe by kings, consuls and other men of rank in ancient Rome.

tricorn Hat with the brim turned up on three sides.

trilby Soft felt hat with a narrow brim and indented crown, resembling that worn in the stage version of *Trilby* by the eponymous heroine of George Du Maurier's novel of 1894.

trousseau Clothes collected by a bride in preparation for her marriage.

turumagi Traditional Korean overcoat.

Tuscan straw Fine yellow wheat straw used for hats.

tutu Ballet dancer's skirt made up of layers of stiffened frills, very short and standing out from the legs.

tutulus Head-dress formed by plaiting the hair in a cone above the forehead, worn especially by a flamen and his wife.

tuxedo Dinner jacket, named after Tuxedo Park in New York, site of a country club where the garment was first worn.

tweed Rough-surfaced woollen cloth of varying texture, usually of mixed flecked colours, originally made in Scotland.

uchikake Outer kimono, fashionable in the Muromachi period (14th–16th centuries), sometimes with a short-sleeved kimono (kosode), but later (18th century) with a coloured sash (obi) around the waist and bunched at the back.

uwagi Outer kimono, of rich brocade, under which it is usual to wear a plain purple kimono and generally a third kimono-type robe known as itsutsu-ginu (usually having five bands of coloured silks attached at the sleeves, neckline and hem).

Valentino Popular name of Valentino Garavani, Italian fashion designer, born in Rome, 1933. He opened his first house in 1959 and achieved universal recognition following his Florence show in 1962.

vambrace Piece of armour for the arm, especially the forearm.

Van Dyke Broad, lace or linen collar or neckerchief, with an edge deeply cut into large points, and fashionable after the life of the painter (d. 1641) until the mid 18th century.

veldskoen Strong suede or leather shoe or boot of South African origin.

vent Opening or slit in a garment, especially in the lower edge of the back of a coat or skirt.

Versace, Donatella Took over as head of the Versace empire following the murder of her brother in 1997. Under the terms of Gianni Versace's will Donatella was left a 20% shareholding, her brother Santo having a 35% shareholding and her daughter Allegra a 45% holding.

Versace, Gianni Designer shot dead outside his Miami mansion by Andrew Cunanan (15 July 1997).

viyella Fabric made from a twilled mixture of cotton and wool, named from Via Gellia, a valley in Derbyshire where it was first made.

Vreeland, Diana Legendary fashion editor (1903–1989) of *Harper's Bazaar* and editor-in-chief of *Vogue*. Much parodied as the epitome of a fashion icon.

Watteau gown Loose gown, worn over a tight bodice, with long, vertical pleats falling from the

F
A
S
H
I
O
N

A
N
D

D
R
E
S
S

shoulders to the ground, popular in the early 18th
century and named after costumes depicted by the
French artist.

Westwood, Vivienne   Born in 1941, and first came
to prominence in 1971 when she began a 13-year
collaboration with Malcolm McLaren. She became
the first British designer to show in Paris since Mary
Quant when her 'Bufalo Collection', based on
Peruvian women's fashion, caught the imagination
in 1982. She was active in the punk rock fashion of
the 1970s and the pioneer of the 'New Romantic'
style of the early 1980s. Her designs have included
leather bondage gear, latex lounge dresses, flesh-
coloured body suits, slashed t-shirts and mink g-
strings.

wide-awake   Soft felt hat with a low crown and wide
brim.

Williamson, Matthew   Born and educated in London
and known for his unique colour sense and
exquisite embroidery and beading. His debut
collection was in 1997 and his name is synonymous
with 'The Karma Kit', a white leather clutch bag
complete with leather flower, jasmine flower mist, a
peppermint pulse-point balm, incense perfume and
a pink travel candle.

wimple   Piece of cloth draped around the head to
frame the face, worn by women in the Middle Ages
and still a part of the habit of some nuns.

winceyette   Lightweight napped flannelette used for
nightclothes.

windcheater   Warm jacket, usually with a close-
fitting knitted neck, cuffs and waistband.

Wong, Farida   Dress designer who has carved a
niche as a high-quality designer of ballroom gowns
for both amateurs and professionals.

Wrap dress inventor   Diane von Furstenberg.

Xuly Bët   Popular name of Kouyaté Lamine
Badian, born in Bamako, Mali, 1962. His Xuly Bët
(name means voyeur in his native Wolof dialect)
label is identified with cheap and cheerful but
quality goods, often recycled but always with an
aesthetic quality. Very popular with the French
youth culture.

Yamamoto, Yohji   Born in Tokyo, 1943, he is the
only Japanese fashion designer to be awarded
the French Chevalier de l'Ordre des Arts et
Lettres. Apart from his very successful clothing
creations he also designs opera costumes and
ballet sets.

yarmulka   Skullcap worn by Jewish men.

yashmak   Veil concealing the face, except the eyes,
worn by some Muslim women when in public.

yukata   Cotton kimono, worn by both men and
women, formerly after bathing but now as outdoor
wear on hot summer evenings.

Zoller, Amy   Chicago-based fashion designer
originally known for her minimalist silhouettes. Her
reputation increased throughout the 1990s and she
now has two shows a year in Chicago, Houston,
New York and Los Angeles.

zucchetto   Skullcap worn by Roman Catholic
ecclesiastics: black for priests, purple for bishops,
red for cardinals, and white for the Pope.

NB: This section is simply an A–Z of historical costume and dress, plus a few interesting snippets of additional
information relating to designers and materials.

Other Fashion Designers

Christopher Bailey	Peter Jensen	Todd Oldham
Luella Bartley	Betsey Johnson	Zac Posen
Bill Blass	Michael Kors	Agatha Ruiz Deha Prada
Robert Cary-Williams	Victoria Lesser	Emilio Pucci
Jasper Conran	Julien MacDonald	Ghulam Sakina
Giles Deacon	Jane MacMillan	Sir Paul Smith
Ebru Ercon	Marese	Rebecca Taylor
Rudi Gernreich	Martin Margiela	Philip Treacy
Ashish Gupta	Carlos Miele	Amand Wakeley
Caroline Herrera	Roland Mouret	Karen Walker
Margaret Howell	Jean Muir	
Betty Jackson	Jessica Ogden	

Miss World Winners

1951	Kiki Haakonson, Sweden	1977	Mary Stavin, Sweden
1952	May Louise Flodin, Sweden	1978	Silvana Suarez, Argentina
1953	Denise Perrier, France	1979	Gina Swainson, Bermuda
1954	Antigone Costanda, Egypt	1980	Kimberly Santos, Guam
1955	Carmen Zubillaga, Venezuela	1981	Pilin Leon, Venezuela
1956	Petra Schurmann, Germany	1982	Mariasela Lebron, Dominican Republic
1957	Marita Lindahl, Finland	1983	Sarah Jane Hutt, United Kingdom
1958	Penelope Coelen, South Africa	1984	Astrid Herrera, Venezuela
1959	Corine Rottschafer, Holland	1985	Hofi Karlsdottir, Iceland
1960	Norma Cappagli, Argentina	1986	Giselle Laronde, Trinidad
1961	Rosemarie Frankland, United Kingdom	1987	Ulla Weigerstorfer, Austria
1962	Catharine Lodders, Holland	1988	Linda Petursdottir, Iceland
1963	Carole Crawford, Jamaica	1989	Andeta Kreglicka, Poland
1964	Ann Sidney, United Kingdom	1990	Gina Marie Tolleson, USA
1965	Lesley Langley, United Kingdom	1991	Ninebeth Jiminez, Venezuela
1966	Reita Faria, India	1992	Julia Kourotchkina, Russia
1967	Madeiline Hartog Bel, Peru	1993	Lisa Hanna, Jamaica
1968	Penelope Plummer, Australia	1994	Aishwariya Rai, India
1969	Eva Reuber Staier, Austria	1995	Jacqueline Aquilera, Venezuela
1970	Jennifer Hosten, Grenada	1996	Irene Skliva, Greece
1971	Lucia Petterle, Brazil	1997	Diana Hayden, India
1972	Belinda Green, Australia	1998	Linor Abargil, Israel
1973	Marjorie Wallace, USA	1999	Yukta Mookhey, India
1974	Anneline Kriel, South Africa (Helen Morgan the original winner was disqualified for being a wife and having an illegitimate child.)	2000	Priyanka Chopra, India
		2001	Agbani Darego, Nigeria
		2002	Azra Akin, Turkey
1975	Winelia Merced, Puerto Rico	2003	Rosanna Davidson, Ireland
1976	Cindy Breakspeare, Jamaica	2004	Maria Garcia, Peru

British Hairdressers of the Year

1985	Trevor Sorbie	1995	Anthony Mascolo
1986	Trevor Sorbie	1996	Charles Worthington
1987	Irvine & Rita Rusk	1997	Andrew Collinge
1988	Anthony Mascolo	1998	Charles Worthington
1989	John Frieda	1999	Umberto Giannini
1990	Anthony Mascolo	2000	Mark Hill
1991	Trevor Sorbie	2001	Beverly Cobella
1992	Trevor Sorbie	2002	Beverly Cobella
1993	Andrew Collinge	2003	Mark Hill
1994	Nicky Clarke	2004	Antoinette Beenders

FASHION AND DRESS

FOOD AND DRINK
Dishes, Ingredients and Terms

Aemono   Japanese term for a salad; 'dressed things'. A dress aemono may include fish, shellfish and seaweeds, poultry and cooked vegetables or may be made of only one ingredient

Agemono   Japanese culinary term for something deep-fried

Aïoli   Provençal sauce, mayonnaise, seasoned with garlic

Alboni sauce   brown sauce with pine kernels and redcurrants, served with venison

Allumettes   French, vegetables cut into matchstick-sized strips

Armoricaine   in the Breton fashion, with wine, brandy and tomato sauce

Angels on horseback   oysters wrapped in bacon

Antipasto   Italian term meaning 'before the meal', comparable to the French hors d'oeuvres

Artsoppa   Swedish, dried pea soup with ham

Avgolemono   Greek, sauce made with egg and lemon

Babka   Polish bread similar to a fruit cake

Bagna cauda   Italian sauce of garlic, anchovy and olive oil

Baklava   Turkish/Greek filo (Phyllo) pastry filled with nuts (usually walnuts and almonds), honey flavoured

Balti   (lit. bucket) Round-bottomed metal dish like a wok with two handles. Balti food is freshly prepared and healthy because the rapid stir-fry process retains the goodness of the food. Balti cooking is popular in Indian restaurants and particularly in the Midlands, Birmingham often being referred to as the Balti capital of Britain. Balti cooking originates from the Himalayan mountain region of Pakistani Kashmir, in Baltistan province

Bannock   Scottish dish of oatmeal, soda and salt usually served with butter, honey or jam

Barquettes   boat-shaped pastry moulds served with assorted fillings (lit. little boats)

Béarnaise   French, egg yolk and butter sauce

Béchamel   French, white sauce flavoured with onion

Bel Paese   Creamy Italian cheese with a mild sweet flavour

Beurre, au   French, cooked in butter

Bifteki   Greek, hamburger patties

Bigarade   French, orange-flavoured sauce served with duck

Biltong   South African, dried meat

Bird's nest soup   Chinese soup, contains saliva of swiftlet

Biryani   Indian dish of pilau rice and meat or fish in spiced gravy

Bisque   creamy soup usually made with sea food and enriched with cream or egg yolks

Black pudding   sausage made of pig's blood and fat with oatmeal and seasoning

Blanquette   French, meat stew made with white sauce

Blini   Russian, stuffed pancake made with buckwheat flour and classically topped with sour cream and caviar

Blintz   Jewish, pancakes stuffed with various sweet or savoury fillings, then fried

Bloater   herring or sometimes a mackerel, that has been salted, smoked and cured (kipper is slit open, a bloater is not)

Blutwurst   German, blood sausage

Boeuf bourguignon   French beef dish in red wine sauce

Bombe   spherical dessert dish consisting of an outer layer of ice cream or sherbet and a softer, inner layer of custard or mousse

Bonne femme   French, in country style, or housewife style, homely, also sole poached in fish stock

Bordelaise   Sauce of red wine, artichokes or shallots and marrow fat

Börek   Turkish savoury pastry filled with spinach, eggs, pumpkin, cheese, meat or fruit

Borsch (1) borsht   Russian, beetroot soup served with a sour cream garnish

Bouillabaisse   French fish stew cooked in a highly flavoured stock with oil, spices and herbs

Bouillon   French broth made by simmering meat, chicken, fish or vegetables in water (derives from 'to boil')

Bourride   Provençal fish stew with aïoli sauce

Bratwurst   German, fried sausage, usually pork

Bretonne, à la   French, garnished with beans

Brochette, en   French, on a skewer

Brouillé   French, scrambled

Bruxelloise   garnish for meat, composed of Brussel sprouts and pommes château, i.e. barrel-shaped potatoes, cooked in butter to a golden brown colour

Bubble and squeak   Originally meat, cabbage and potatoes fried up as leftovers

Calamares   Spanish fried squid or cuttlefish

Cannelloni   Italian pasta stuffed with meat or cheese in cheese sauce

Carpetbag steak   Australian, thick cut of steak stuffed with oysters

Cassata   Italian, ice cream dish of two types, cassata gelata and cassata siciliana. The siciliana is filled with ricotta cheese, the gelate with chopped nuts or candied fruit

Cassoulet   French casserole with haricot beans, meat and vegetables

Ceviche   South American dish of marinated raw fish

Chapatti   Indian, bread pancake

Charlotte russe   cold dessert made in a mould with sponge fingers enclosing a mash of whipped cream, lemon jelly and glacé cherries (literal meaning 'Russian Charlotte)

Charlotte: apple   hot dessert of bread pudding with an apple filling

Charlotte: strawberry   cold dessert similar to a Charlotte Russe but with a strawberry base

Chasseur   French sauce of white wine, mushrooms and onions

Châteaubriand   thick fillet steak

Chawan-mushi   the most popular example of mushimono. Small pieces of poultry, fish or vegetables mixed with beaten eggs and dashi are steamed in a cup. Chawan-mushi literally means 'teacup steamed' and is the only Japanese dish to be eaten with a spoon

Chicken Kiev boned and flattened chicken breast wrapped around chilled butter lightly flavoured with chives, dipped in egg and breadcrumbs and fried

Chicken Marengo Italian fried chicken in a sauce of garlic, tomatoes and white wine supposedly named after Napoleonic battle when the owner of an inn was forced to use any food available to make a dish

Chicken Maryland Fried chicken served cold, iced or chilled

Chilli con carne Mexican minced beef with chilli and beans

Chop suey Originally a Cantonese dish that literally means 'bits and pieces' a way of dealing with leftovers by stir-frying; widely adopted in the USA under this Americanised name

Chorizo Spanish, spiced pork sausage

Chow mein Chinese-American fried noodles served with diced chicken, pork or seafood

Chowder fish or seafood thick soup or stew

Churro Spanish choux pastry fritter usually, served with a mug of chocolate

Ciabatta moist aerated Italian bread made from olive oil. Ciabatta literally means slipper (from the shape of the loaf)

Cocido Spanish, meat and vegetable stew

Cock-a-leekie Scottish, leek served onions and sometimes with prunes and chicken stew

Colbert French with lemon sauce, parsley and madeira

Colcannon Irish, potato and cabbage dish

Coleslaw Dutch and then American, shredded cabbage salad

Compôte dish of fruit cooked in a light sugar syrup and served hot or cold

Conchiglie Italian, pasta shaped like conch shells

Consommé French, clear soup

Coppa Italian, salted dried sausage made from neck or shoulder of pork

Coquilles Saint-Jacques French scallops

Coulibiac Russian, fish pie with buckwheat and chopped up hard-boiled eggs

Coulis French term meaning 'to strain' and often referring to a thin vegetable or fuit pureé

Couscous North African, steamed wheat mixed with semolina to form pasta-like pellets

Crécy, a la French, garnished with carrots

Crêpe suzette French, pancake with orange syrup and liqueur (Curacao)

Croque-monsieur French, toasted cheese sandwich with ham

Croûte, en French, in pastry

Cullen skink Scottish, traditional soup made from finnan haddock and potatoes. Cullen is the village on the coast of the Moray Firth where the recipe originated and skink refers to the stock or broth, usually fish stock, but water or milk is occasionally used. An onion is often added for enhancement of flavour and the soup is garnished with parsley

Cumberland sauce redcurrant-based sauce

Dashi the basic Japanese soup stock consisting of dried bonito (Katsuobushi) and giant kelp (Kombu)

Daube, en French, braised with vegetables in red wine and stock

Déglacer French, deglaze, to add wine, cream or stock to juices in a pan, thereby making a gravy

Dente al Italian, firm to the teeth

Devils on horseback stuffed prunes wrapped in bacon

Dhall general name for a variety of beans, peas and lentils used a staple in Indian cookery

Diablé French, devilled

Dolmades Greek/Turkish, vine leaves stuffed with meat and rice

Doner kebab Middle Eastern, a block of seasoned, sliced lamb roasted on a spit

Doré French, brushed with egg yolk

Dosa rice-based bread of southern India

Duchesse potatoes mashed in butter and egg shaped and then baked

Enchiladas Mexican, fried, stuffed pancakes cooked with chilli-flavoured sauce

Entrecôte steak cut from between two ribs

Espagnole French, brown sauce (fat and flour cooked in oven to light brown colour with stock added)

Falafel Middle Eastern, chickpea patties

Farci French, stuffed

Farfalle Italian, butterfly-shaped pasta

Fettucine Italian, ribbon-shaped pasta

Filet mignon Henri IV French, steak dish served with potatoes, artichoke hearts and Béarnaise sauce

Financière French sauce made with Madeira and truffles

Florentine French, with spinach

Focaccia a flat savoury Italian bread made with and usually seasoned with herbs

Fondue Swiss, melted cheese in white wine eaten with bread dips

Forestière French, with bacon, mushrooms and potatoes

Forno, à la from the oven

Fricassée French meat stew in white sauce

Frikadelle Swedish boiled meat ball

Fritto misto Italian, seafood fried in batter

Fusilli Italian, corkscrew-shaped pasta

Gado gado Indonesian, dish of vegetables in white sauce

Galantine chopped meat in calves-head jelly

Garni French, garnished

Gaspacho Spanish, cold vegetable soup

Glaze French, glossy finish produced by brushing food with beaten egg, milk, jelly or sugar syrup

Gnocchi Italian, savoury dumplings

Goulash Hungarian, paprika-flavoured meat stew

Granita Italian, water ice

Gratin, au French, browned with cheese and breadcrumbs

Gravlax Scandinavian, raw pickled salmon with mustard and dill sauce

Grecque, à la French, means ('Greek style'), cooked in oil and lemon juice (also an hors d'oeuvre with rice)

Guacamole Mexican, avocado dip

Gumbo stew with okra and rice

Haggis Scottish, sheep's stomach filled with offal, oatmeal, suet and seasoning

Halva Middle Eastern sesame seed, honey and almond sweet

Hoisin sauce sauce made from soya beans

Hollandaise French, sauce with egg yolk, vinegar, lemon juice and butter

Hot dog   Frankfurter in bun

Hummus   chickpea, garlic and sesame purée

Indienne, à la   French, curried

Jardinière   French, with garnish of fresh vegetables cut in julienne method

Julienne   French, vegetables cut in fine strips

Kebab   Turkish, lamb or mutton cooked on skewers (lit. on skewers)

Kedgeree   Originally Indian, rice and bean dish adapted as breakfast dish by the British with flaked fish and hard-boiled eggs

Korma   An Indian cooking instruction meaning 'to braise'

Kulfi   Indian ice cream made with reduced milk and nuts

Larding   threading strips of lard through lean meat to prevent dryness during roasting

Lasagne   flat pasta dish with minced meat, tomatoes and white cheese sauce

Laulau   Hawaiian, steamed pork and fish cooked in leaves

Liaison   French, binding agent such as egg yolk or cream

Lobscouse   fisherman's stew associated with Liverpool but similar dishes with similar names come from Denmark, Germany and Norway

Lumaconi   Italian, pasta shaped like giant snails

Lyonnaise   sauce with white wine and onions fried in butter

Macédoine   French, mixture of fruit or vegetables cut into small pieces

Madeleine   small sponge cake

Maître d'hotel   French, sauce with butter, parsley, lemon and cayenne pepper (lit. headwaiter)

Marrons glacés   French candied chestnuts

Melba sauce   sauce made with fresh raspberries and served with peach melba

Melba toast   thin toast named after opera singer Dame Nellie Melba by French chef Auguste Escoffier

Meringue   baked pudding made with egg white and sugar

Meunière   French, floured and cooked in butter with salt, pepper and lemon juice and garnished with parsley

Mez(z)e   Selection of hot and cold dishes served as an hors d'oeuvres in Eastern Mediterranean regions

Miso   a paste made from fermented soya beans and barley or rice malt, used in Japanese cookery

Mocha   Arabian, a kind of coffee flavouring, often with chocolate

Mornay   French, béchamel sauce with grated Parmesan cheese

Mortadella   Italian, sausage from Bologna

Moussaka   Greek, minced lamb, aubergine and tomato dish topped with cheese

Mulligatawny   Indian, curried soup (means 'pepper water')

Mushimono   Japanese culinary term for steamed dishes such as chicken, fish or vegetables, often treated with saké

Nabemono   Japanese culinary term for one-pot dishes usually cooked at the table by the diners. Sukiyaki is a typical example of nabemono

Naan   Wheatflour leavened bread, with yoghurt base, cooked in a clay tandoor

Nasi goreng   Indonesian, meat and fried rice dish

Neige, à la   French, white of egg beaten stiffly (literally means 'snow')

Nimono   Japanese culinary term meaning 'to simmer'

Nougat   French, sweet made from almonds and honey

Okashi   Japanese culinary term for accompaniments to tea. Okashi can be made from various ingredients but usually based on sweet bean paste made with azuki bean

Orecchiette   Italian, pasta from Puglia (literally means 'little ears')

Osso bucco   Italian, braised knuckle of veal dish cooked with wine and tomatoes

Paella   Spanish, baked saffron rice with chicken, seafood and vegetables

Pancetta   Italian cured belly of pork often used in pasta dressings. The name pancetta derives from the Italian for 'belly'

Panettone   Italian, tall fat egg-rich cake studded with candied fruit and traditionally eaten at Christmas and Easter

Pappardelle   Italian, ribbon-shaped pasta about an inch wide

Papillote, en   French, cooked in a greased paper bag

Parata   Indian flaky unleavened bread smeared with ghee and rolled and stuffed before frying

Parisienne   French, with round, ball artichoke hearts or other vegetables, shaped potatoes and leeks

Parmentier   potato, diced and fried in butter (named from Baron Parmentier, who first introduced potatoes into France)

Pâté de foie gras   French goose liver pâté

Paupiette   French, thin slice of meat, or fillet of fish, rolled around a savoury filling

Pavlova   fruit, cream and meringue dessert (named after ballerina Anna Pavlova)

Paysanne, à la   French, in peasant style

Peach melba   dessert made of halved peaches and vanilla ice cream and topped with raspberry purée – named after opera singer Dame Nellie Melba by French chef Auguste Escoffier

Pecorino   Italian, general name given to fresh, medium aged or matured cheeses made from sheep's milk. Fresh (*fresco*) Pecorino cheeses are soft and white with a mild, lemony flavour, such as Ricotta Salata. Their texture ranges from soft and moist to crumbly and granular

Penne   Italian, quill-shaped pasta

Peperoni   Italian, sweet peppers, also called capsicums

Périgueux   sauce made with Madeira and truffles

Pesto   Italian, sauce of basil, garlic, pine nuts and cheese.

Petit four   French small cakes or crystallised fruit or sweets (literally means 'little oven').

Pilau/pilaf   The cleaning of surface starch by means of simmering and steaming of rice to ensure separate grains

Piperade   Basque tomatoes and peppers with egg beaten to a fluffy consistency

Pirozhki   Russian, small pies with filling

Pissaladière   French, pastry flan with onion, anchovy and black olives

Pizza   Italian, flat-baked dough with various coverings (lit. pie)

Plat du jour   French, dish of the day

Polenta   Italian dish of maize, flour and water

Poivre, au   French, with pepper

Pollo   Italian, chicken

Polpetta   Italian, meatball

Pomodori   Italian, tomatoes

Profiteroles   choux pastry puffs, covered with chocolate, usually with cream filling

Prosciutto   Italian, smoked ham

Provençale   French, prepared with garlic, oil and often, tomatoes

Pumpernickel   German, malted rye bread

Quiche lorraine   French, savoury flan with egg, bacon and cheese filling

Radiatori   Italian, pasta shaped like radiator grilles

Ragoût   meat and vegetable stew

Raita   Indian yoghurt-based cucumber salad

Ratatouille   French, dish of aubergine, courgette, onions, peppers and tomatoes stewed in oil

Ravioli   Italian, small pasta casings with stuffing

Red cooked   braised in soy sauce and wine

Rijstafel   Indonesian, a selection of dishes served with rice

Risotto   Italian, rice dish cooked with stock

Rissole   fried minced meat ball

Rogan josh   Kashmiri, lamb curry with yoghurt

Rollmop   German, raw herring with onion or gherkin pickled

Roti   Indian, unleavened unsalted bread

Roux   butter and flour cooked and constantly stirred until blended

Rum baba   small sponge cake soaked in rum and syrup (invented by a Polish king: Stanislaus)

Ruote   Italian, pasta shaped like wagon wheels

Sachertorte   Austrian, chocolate sponge cake named after Sacher Hotel in Vienna

Salade niçoise   tuna and anchovies

Saignant   French, rare or underdone

Salmagundi   English dish popular in 18th century and consisting of mixed salad items possibly with meat, eggs anchovies and onions

Salsa   A spicy sauce especially served with Mexican food

Saltimbocca   Italian, veal and ham dish

Sambal   Indonesian spiced pickle

Samosa   In Indian cuisine, small, crisp, flaky pastries, usually fried but may be baked. Samosas are stuffed with a variety of fillings such as cheese, egg, spiced minced meat, vegetables or sweets

Sashimi   Japanese, raw fish

Satay   Malaysian, grilled skewers of meat

Sauerkraut   German, pickled cabbage

Scotch broth: cereal used   barley

Scotch woodcock   anchovies and eggs on toast

Searing   browning meat rapidly with fierce heat to seal in the juices

Shiromono   Generic Japanese culinary term describing all soups but thick soups in particular

Shish kebab   Turkish, skewered meat pieces

Smörgasbord   Swedish buffet including herring, seafood, cheese and crispbread

Smørrebrød   Danish, open sandwich

Solyanka   Russian, cucumber soup

Sorbet   water ice, used to cleanse palate between courses

Soubise   white sauce with onion or purée of onions and rice to accompany some cuts of meat

Soufflé   French, dish of eggs whisked and baked

Soufflé cheese   Parmesan and Gruyère are the two cheeses used traditionally

Steak à la tartare   raw minced beef bound with egg into rissoles

Stollen   German, fruit loaf

Stroganoff   Russian, dish of thin strips of fillet of beef cooked in butter with sour cream and shallots

Strudel   German, thin sheet of filled dough rolled up and baked (literally meaning 'eddy' or 'whirlpool')

Suimono   Generic Japanese culinary term describing all clear soups

Sukiyaki   Japanese dish of beef and vegetables in soy sauce

Sunomono   Japanese culinary term meaning 'vinegared things' and referring to salad items given a vinegar dressing

Sushi   Japanese, vinegared rice with fresh fish or other seafood

Syllabub   dish dates from Elizabethan times. One definition claims that a favourite white wine in those days came from 'Sillery' in the Champagne region of France; the slang term for a bubbly drink was 'bub'; therefore the mixture of still wine and frothy cream became known as a 'syllabub'

Tabouli   cracked wheat with lemon, parsley, tomato and mint

Taco   Mexican, stuffed fried pancake

Tagliatelle   Italian, ribbon-shaped pasta

Tandoori   dish in a clay oven

Tapas   Spanish small appetisers served in bars and varied according to season and locality

Taramasalata   Greek, grey mullet smoked cod roe dip.

Tartare   mayonnaise sauce mixed with hard-boiled egg yolks, onions or chives or herbs, capers and gherkins

Tempura   Japanese, fish or vegetables deep-fried in butter

Teriyaki   Japanese culinary term referring to a special glaze of soy sauce, saké, and mirin, applied to fish, meat or poultry when partly grilled

Terrine, en   French, potted

Tikka   Indian term referring to meat or poultry cooked on skewers

Tiramisu   Italian dessert consisting of layers of sponge cake soaked in coffee and brandy or liqueur with powdered chocolate and mascarpone cheese. Tiramisu literally means 'pick-me-up'

Toad in the hole   English sausage in batter

Tortillas   Mexican, pancakes cooked on a griddle

Tournedos Rossini   named after the composer by French chef Auguste Escoffier; thick round slices of fillet steak garnished with sliced sautéed truffles and foie gras

Tourtière   Pie dish, for small pies

Tsukemono   Japanese culinary term referring to various pickled vegetables and also for pickled umeboshi, a plum-like fruit

Tzatziki   Greek, cucumber in yoghurt

Veal escalope   veal fried in breadcrumbs

Velouté   French, smooth white sauce with added white meat or fish stock

Vermicelli   Italian, thin spaghetti (literally means 'little worms')

Vichyssoise   potato and leek soup, usually cold

Vindaloo   Indian, hot vinegary pork curry

Vol au vent   puff pastry shell with a variety of filling

Waffle   crisp golden brown pancake with deep indentations caused by the waffle-iron it is cooked in, often served with maple syrup

FOOD AND DRINK

Wai-Wai popular snack in Nepal, Sikkim and parts of West Bengal; a kind of noodle eaten raw or in soup. Unlike ordinary noodles, wai-wai is pre-cooked, flavoured, seasoned and fried before packaging

Waldorf salad American, celery, apples, mayonnaise and walnuts named after the Waldorf Astoria Hotel in New York City

Wellington English or Irish beef (or often any meat or fish) cooked in pastry

Welsh rarebit cheese on toast sometimes melted with mustard and with beer added

White sauce a roux with added milk used as a base for numerous sauces

Wiener schnitzel Austrian, breaded veal cutlet

Wonton Chinese, meat-filled dumplings

Yakimono Japanese culinary term for something grilled

Zensai Japanese culinary term for appetisers comparable to the French hors d'oeuvres

Zabaglione Italian dessert made from egg yolks with marsala and sugar

Zampone Italian, speciality sausage made from pig's leg stuffed with minced pork

Fruit and Vegetable Varieties

Apple Allington pippin, Api, Blanche d'hiver, Blenheim, Bramley, Braeburn Calville, Cortland, Costard, Cox's Orange Pippin, Discovery, Ellison's Orange, Faro, Flower of Kent, Fuji, Gala, Gillyflower, Gladstone, Golden Delicious, Granny Smith, Gravenstein, Idared, James Grieve, Jonathans, Laxton's Superb, McIntosh, Macoun, Mutsu, Newtown Pippin, Northern Spy, Pearmain Pippin, Reinette, Ribston Pippin, Rome Beauty, Russet, Star Kings, Wealthy, White Joaneting, White Transparent, Winesnap, Worcester, York Imperial.

Beetroot Cheltenham Green Top, Crimson Globe, Nutting's Red Globe.

Broad bean Bonny Lad, Bunyard's Exhibition, Express, Green Windsor, Red Epicure, Sutton, White Windsor.

Brussels sprout Bedford-Fillbasket, Bedford Winter Harvest, Cambridge No 5, Early Half Tall, Fortress, Huizer's Late, Peer Gynt, Predora, Welland, Wellington, Widgen.

Cabbage April, Christmas Drumhead, Derby Day, Durham Early, Golden Acre, Greyhound, Hargenger, Hispy, January King, June Star, Ormskirk, Quickstep, Rear Guard, Spivoy, Spring Hero, Velocity, Winnigstadt, Wivoy.

Carrot Autumn King, Early Giant, Favourite, Figaro, Regulus Imperial, St Valery.

Cauliflower Alpha, Canberra, Dominant, Nevada, Snow Cap, Snow Crown.

Cherry Amarelle, Bigarreau, Bing, Black Tartarian, Bradbourne Black, Cherokee, Coe's Transparent, Early Rivers, Griotte, Guigne, May Duke, Montmorency, Morello, Napoleon, Rainier, Stella, Van.

Cucumber Bushcrop, Conqueror, King of the Ridge, Pacer, Pepita, Stockwood Ridge, Telegraph, Tokyo Slicer.

Dates Asharasi, Barhi, Deglet Noor, Fardh, Gundila, Halawi, Hilali, Khadrawi, Khalas, Khustawi, Khidri, Medjool, Mactoum, Naghal, Yatimeh, Zahidi.

French bean Cordon, Loch Ness, Long Bow, Masterpiece, Remus, Sprite, Tendergreen.

Gooseberry Admiral Beattie, Alma, Aston Red, Australia, Bellona, Blucher, Broom Girl, Careless, Clayton, Cousin's Seedling, Criterion, Crown Bob, Dan's Mistake, Early Sulphur, Firbob, Freedom, Green Gem, Green Ocean, Guido, Gunner, Heart of Oak, Hero of the Nile, Howard's Lancer, Ironmonger, Jubilee, Keepsake, King of Trumps, Lancashire Lad, Leveller, London, Lord Derby, Lord Kitchener, Macherauch's Seedling, Marigold, Matchless, May Duke, Peru, Plunder, Queen of Hearts, Queen of Trumps, Sir George Brown, Speedwell, Sultan Juror, Surprise, Suter Johnny, Talford, Trumpeter, Whinham's Industry, White Eagle, White Lion, Whitesmith, Woodpecker, Yellow Champagne.

Grape Alicante, Almeria, Barbera, Baresana, Barlinka, Cabernet Franc, Cabernet Sauvignon, Cardinal, Cassidy, Catawba, Chasselas, Cinsaut, Chardonnay, Concord, Delaware, Emporer, Gamay, Hermitage, Gewürztraminer, Grenache, Hanepoot, Irikara, Italia, Kishmishi, Madeleine Royale, Malaga, Malvasia, Merlot, Montefiascone, Muscat, Nebbiolo, Niagara, Palamino, Perlette, Pinot Blanc, Pinot Gris, Pinot Noir, Portugieser, Red Emporer, Regina, Ribier, Riesling, Sangiovese, Sémillon, Shiraz, Simone, Sultanina, Syrah, Thompson's Seedless, Tokay, Ugni Blanc, Viognier, Waltham Cross, Zinfandel.

Grapefruit Duncan, Marsh.

Leek Catalina, Early Market, Giant Winter-Wila, Lyon Prizetaker, Musselburgh, Royal Favourite, Walton Mammoth.

Lettuce Arctic King, Cos, Density, Fortune, Iceberg, Lakeland, Little Gem, Lobjoit's Green, Sabin, Saladin, Sigmaball, Stanstead Park, Paris White, Tom Thumb, Unrivalled, Webb's Wonder White.

Nut Acorn, Almond, Beech, Brazil, Breadnut, Calumpang, Candlenut, Chestnut, Cobnut, Coco de Mer, Coconut, Dika, Filbert, Gabon, Gingko, Gnetum, Groundnut, Hazelnut, Hickory, Illipe, Java Olive, Jojoba, Karaka, Kedrouvie, Kepayang, Kubuli, Macadamia, Madia, Manketti, Naras, Ngapi, Niger Seed, Okari, Olive, Oyster, Palm, Pecan, Pignut, Pili, Pine, Pistachio, Safflower, Sandalwood, Sapucaya, Sesame, Shea Butter, Souari, Sunflower, Walnut, Yeheb.

Onion Ailsa Craig, Autumn Queen, Bedfordshire Champion, Blood Red, Brunswick, Dobies Allrounder, Lancastrian, Marshall's Giant Fenglobe, North Holland Blood Red, Pearl Pickler, Ricardo, Southport Red Globe, Stuttgarter Giant, Sturon, Turbo.

Parsnip Improved Hollow Crown, The Student, Tender and True, White Gem.

Pea Feltham First, Histon Mini, Hurst Beagle, Hurst Green, Kelvedon Wonder, Little Marvel, Meteor, Onward, Semitar, Shaft.

Pear Abbé, Anjou, Bartlett, Beurré, Clapp Favourite, Conference, Doyenne du Comice, Glou Morceau, Jargonelle, Josephine de Malines, Kaiser, Louise Bonne der Jersey, Olivier de Serres, Passe Crasanne, Seckel, Wardens, Williams Bon Chrétien, Winter Nelis.

Plum Ambarella, Bokhara, Brazil, Burbank, Chrétien, Chickasaw, Czar, Davidson's, Denniston's Superb, Early Rivers, El Dorado, Greengage, Hog, Imperial Gage, Jew, Laxton's Cropper, Pershore, President, Prince's Gage, Red Gage, Santa Rosa, Victoria, Warwickshire Drooper, Washington.

Potato Arran Pilot, Arran Victory, Blue, Catriona, Craig's Royal, Desiree, Edgecote Purple, Esteema, King Edward, Majestic, Maris Piper, May Queen, Pink Fir Apple, Romano, Vanessa, Whites, Wilja.

Raspberry Lloyd George, Newburgh, Norfolk Giant.

Rhubarb Brandy Carr Scarlet, Cawood Delight, Royal Albert, Stock Bridge Arrow.

Runner bean Butler, Kelvedon Marvel, Mergoles.

Strawberry Baron Solemacher, Cambridge Vigour, Florence, Grandee, Hapil, Pegasus, Red Gauntlet.

Tomato Ailsa Craig, Alfresco, Alicante, Big Boy, Dombito, Early Girl, Eurocross, Golden Boy, Herald, Marmande, Minibel, Moneymaker, Piranto, Red Alert, Shirley, Tiny Tim, Supersonic.

Turnip Golden Ball, Green Globe, Model White, Veitch's Red Globe.

Fruit: Latin Names and Origin

English Name	Species	Origin
Apple	*Malus sylvestris*	Temperate regions
Apricot	*Prunus armeniaca*	Asia
Avocado	*Persea americana*	Central America
Banana	*Musa various species*	India/Asia
Bilberry	*Vaccinium myrtillus*	Europe/Asia
Blackberry	*Rubus fruticosus and other species*	Europe/Asia
Blackcurrant	*Ribes nigrum*	Europe/Asia/Africa
Blueberry	*Vaccinium various species*	Europe/USA
Breadfruit	*Artocarpus atilis*	Malaysia
Carambola	*Averrhoa carambola*	Asia
Cherry (sour)	*Prunus cerasus*	Temperate regions
Cherry (sweet)	*Prunus avium*	Temperate regions
Clementine	*Citrus reticulata*	Mediterranean
Coconut	*Cocos nucifera*	Pacific
Cranberry	*Oxycoccus macrocarpus*	North America
Damson	*Prunus institia*	Temperate regions
Date	*Phoenix dactylifera*	Persian Gulf
Fig	*Ficus carica*	Asia
Gooseberry	*Ribes grossularia*	Europe
Grape	*Vitis vinifera*	Asia
Grapefruit	*Citrus paradisi*	West Indies
Greengage	*Prunus domestica*	Temperate regions
Kiwi fruit	*Actinidia deliciosa*	China
Kumquat	*Fortunella margarita*	China
Lemon	*Citrus limon*	Asia
Lime	*Citrus aurantifolia*	Asia
Loganberry	*Rubus loganobaccus*	America
Loquat	*Eriobotrya japorica*	China/Japan
Mandarin	*Citrus reticulata*	China
Mango	*Mangifera indica*	Asia
Medlar	*Mespilus germanica*	Europe/Asia
Mulberry	*Morus nigra*	Asia
Nectarine	*Prunus persica*	China
Olive	*Olea europaea*	East Mediterranean
Orange	*Citrus sinensis*	China
Passion fruit	*Passiflora edulis*	South America
Peach	*Prunus persica*	China
Pear	*Pyrus cummunis*	Middle East/Europe
Persimmon	*Diospyros kaki*	Far East
Pineapple	*Ananas comosus*	South America
Plum	*Prunus domestica*	Temperate regions
Pomegranate	*Punica granatum*	Persia
Pomelo	*Citrus grandis*	Asia
Quince	*Cydonia oblonga*	Persia
Raspberry	*Rubus idaeus*	Northern hemisphere
Redcurrant	*Ribes rubrum*	Worldwide
Rhubarb	*Rheum rharbararum*	Asia
Satsuma	*Citrus nobilis*	Japan
Strawberry	*Fragaria x ananassa*	Europe/Asia
Ugli fruit	*Citrus reticulata*	Jamaica
Watermelon	*Citrullus lanatus*	Africa
Whitecurrant	*Ribes rubrum*	Europe

FOOD AND DRINK

Vegetables: Latin Names and Origin

English Name	Species	Origin
Artichoke, Chinese	Stachys affinis	China
Artichoke, globe	Cynara scolymus	Mediterranean
Artichoke, Jerusalem	Helianthus tuberosus	North America
Aubergine	Solanum melongena	Asia/Africa
Avocado	Persea americana	Central America
Bean sprout	Vigna radiata Glycirve maximus	China
Broad bean	Vicia faba	Africa/Europe
Kidney bean	Phaseolus vulgaris	America
Runner bean	Phaseolus coccineus	America
Soya bean	Glycine soja	East Asia
Beetroot	Beta vulgaris	Mediterranean
Broccoli	Brassica oleracea	Europe
Brussels sprout	Brassica oleracea	North Europe
Cabbage	Brassica oleracea	Europe/Asia
Celery	Apium graveolens	Europe/Africa/USA
Chick-pea	Cicer arietinum	West Asia
Chives	Allium schoenoprasum	Europe/USA
Courgette	Cucurbita pepo	Africa/S. America
Cucumber	Cucumis sativus	Uncertain
Fennel	Foeniculum vulgare	Italy
Garlic	Allium sativum	Uncertain
Gherkin	Cucumis anguria	Northern India
Kale	Brassica oleracea acephala	East Mediterranean
Kohlrabi	Brassica oleracea caulorapa	Asia
Leek	Allium porrum	Africa/Europe
Lettuce	Lactuca sativa	Middle East
Lettuce: lamb's tongue	Valerianella locusta	Europe
Mange-tout	Pisum sativum saccharatum	Near East
Mushroom	Agaricus campestris	Worldwide
Okra	Hibiscus esculentus	Africa
Onion	Allium cepa	Central Asia
Parsley	Petroselinum crispum	East Mediterranean
Parsnip	Pastinaca sativa	Europe
Pea	Pisum sativum	Asia/Europe
Pepper	Capsicum annuum	South America
Potato	Solanum tuberosum	South America
Pumpkin	Cucurbita pepo	South America
Radish	Raphanus sativus	China/Japan
Salsify	Tragopogon porrifolius	Europe
Sorrel	Rumex acetosa	Europe
Spinach	Spinacia oleracea	Persia
Squash, summer	Cucurbita pepo	America
Squash, winter	Cucurbita maxima	America
Swede	Brassica napus	Europe
Sweetcorn	Zea mays	Central & South America
Sweet potato	Ipomaea batatas	Central America
Tomato	Lycopersicon esculentum	South America
Turnip	Brassica rapa	Middle East
Water chestnut, Chinese	Eleocharis dulcis	China
Watercress	Nasturtium officinale	Europe/Asia
White cabbage	Brassica oleracea capitata	East Mediterranean
Yam	Dioscorea various species	Tropics

Spices: Latin names and Origin

English Name	Species	Origin
Acitrón	Echinocactus grandis	Mexico
Agar wood	Aquillaria agallocha	Asia
Ajmud	Trachyspermum roxburghianum	Asia
Ajowan	Trachyspermum ammi	Asia
Alexanders	Smyrnium olusatrum	Mediterranean
Allspice	Pimenta dioica	West Indies
Angelica	Angelica archangelica	Europe

English Name	Species	Origin
Anise	Pimpinella anisum	Mediterranean
Annatto	Bixa orellana	West Indies
Asafoetida	Ferula assafoetida	Asia
Ashanti pepper	Piper guineense	West Africa
Balm	Melissa officinalis	Mediterranean
Balsam	Myroxylon balsamum	Asia
Basil	Ocimum basilicum	Asia
Bay	Laurus nobilis	Mediterranean
Bergamot	Monarda fistulosa	Mexico
Bistort	Polygonum bistorta	Europe
Bitter berries	Solanum aethiopicum	North Africa
Black cumin	Nigella sativa	Asia
Borage	Borago officinalis	Mediterranean
Burnet	Sanguisorba officinalis	Europe
Calamint	Calamintha sylvatica	Europe
Caper	Capparis spinosa	Mediterranean
Caraway	Carum carvi	Europe/Asia
Cardamom	Ellataria cardamomum	Asia
Cassia	Cinnamonum cassia	Asia
Cayenne	Capsicum frutescens	America/Africa
Cherry laurel	Laurocerasus officinalis	Mediterranean
Chervil	Anthriscus cerefolium	Asia
Chinese keys	Boesenbergia pandurata	Asia
Cinnamon	Cinnamomum zeylanicum	Asia
Clary	Salvia sclarea	Europe
Cleavers	Galium aparine	Europe
Chilli pepper	Capsicum annuum	America
Cloves	Syzygium aromaticum	Moluccas
Coltsfoot (common)	Tussilago farfara	Europe
Coltsfoot (sweet)	Petasites japonicus	Japan
Comfrey	Symphytum officinalis	Europe
Coriander	Coriandrum sativum	Mediterranean
Corkwing	Glehnia littoralis	Asia
Costmary	Tanacetum balsamita	Asia
Costus	Saussurea lappa	Asia
Cowslip	Primula veris	Eurasia
Cubeb	Piper cubeba	Indonesia
Cumin seed	Cuminum cyminum	Mediterranean
Curry leaf	Murraya koenigii	India
Daun salam	Syzygium polyanthum	Indonesia
Dill	Anethum graveolens	Asia
Elecampane	Inula helenium	Europe
Epazote	Chenopodium ambrosioides	Mexico
Fennel	Foeniculum vulgare	Europe
Fenugreek	Trigonella foenum-graecum	India/Europe
Galingale/Galangal	Alpinia galanga	Asia
Garden mace	Archillea decolorans	Europe
Ginger	Zingiber officinale	Asia
Golden needles	Hemerocallis fulva	Asia
Grains of selim	Xylopia aethiopica	Africa
Ground Elder	Aegopodium podagraria	Europe
Guascas/huascas	Galinsoga parviflora	South America
Hedge garlic	Alliaria petiolata	Europe
Hogweed	Heracleum sphondylium	Eurasia
Horehound	Marrubium vulgare	Eurasia
Horseradish	Armoracia rusticana	Europe
Khus khus	Vetiveria zizanioides	Asia
Lemon grass	Cymbopogon citratus	Asia
Lemon verbena	Lippia triphyllos	Europe
Lime flowers	Tilia platyphyllos	Europe
Lovage	Levisticum officinalis	Europe
Mace	Myristica fragrans	Moluccas
Marjoram (sweet)	Origanum majorana	Mediterranean
Marjoram (wild)	Origanum vulgare	Europe
Mastic	Pistacia lentiscus	Mediterranean
Meadowsweet	Filipendula ulmaria	Northern Hemisphere
Melegueta pepper	Aframomum melegueta	Africa
Mint (water)	Mentha aquatica	Worldwide
Mint (wild)	Mentha arvensis	Asia
Mitsuba	Cryptotaenia japonica	Japan

F
O
O
D

A
N
D

D
R
I
N
K

English Name	Species	Origin
Mugwort	*Artemisa vulgaris*	Northern Hemisphere
Mustard, black	*Brassica nigrar*	Worldwide
Mustard, white	*Sinapis aba*	Europe/Asia
Nasturtium	*Tropaeolum majus*	South America
Nutmeg	*Myristica fragrans*	Moluccas
Palilo	*Escobedia scabrifolio*	Peru
Paprika	*Capsicum annuum*	South America
Parsley	*Petroselenum crispum*	Mediterranean
Pennyroyal	*Mentha pulegium*	Asia
Pepper	*Piper nigrum*	India
Rau ram	*Polygonum odoratum*	Brazil
Rosemary	*Rosmarinus officinalis*	Mediterranean
Rue	*Ruta graveolens*	Mediterranean
Saffron	*Crocus sativus*	Eurasia
Sage	*Salvia officinalis*	Eurasia
Samphire (marsh)	*Salicornia europaea*	Europe
Samphire (rock)	*Crithmum maritmum*	Mediterranean
Sandalwood	*Santalum album*	India/Australia
Sansho	*Zanthoxylum piperitum*	Asia
Sarsaparilla	*Smilax officinalis*	America
Savory (summer)	*Satureja hortensis*	Mediterranean
Savory (winter)	*Satureja montana*	Mediterranean
Shado béni	*Eryngium foetidum*	Caribbean
Shiso	*Perilla frutescens*	Japan
Sichuan pepper	*Zanthoxylum silulans*	China
Smartweed	*Persicaria hydropiper*	Eurasia
Southernwood	*Artemisia abrotanum*	Europe
Spanish needles	*Bidens pilosa*	Worldwide
Spanish thyme	*Plectranthus amboinicus*	Uncertain
Spearmint	*Mentha spicata*	Mediterranean
Star anise	*Illicium verum*	China
Sweet cicely	*Myrrhis odorata*	Europe
Tansy	*Tanacetum vulgare*	Northern Hemisphere
Tarragon	*Artemisia dracunculus*	Eurasia
Thyme	*Thymus vulgaris*	Mediterranean
Turmeric	*Curcuma longa*	Asia
Vanilla	*Vanilla planifolia*	Central America
Vervain	*Verbena officinalis*	Europe
Wasabi	*Eutrema wasabi*	Japan
Water dropwort	*Oenanthe javanica*	Asia
Wintergreen	*Gaultheria procumbens*	North America
Woodruff	*Galium odoratum*	Eurasia
Wormwood (common)	*Artemisia absinthium*	Eurasia
Wormwood (Roman)	*Artemisia pontica*	Eurasia
Ylang-ylang	*Cananga odorata*	Asia
Zedoary	*Curcuma zedoaria*	Asia

Miscellaneous information

Abalone	shellfish
Aga: stoves from	Sweden (full name: Aktienbolagetgasackumalator)
Agurketid (Danish silly season)	literally means 'cucumber time': the season when they are served
Allspice: other name	pimento, Jamaican pepper
Associated with a place:	
Aberdeen	rowies (rolls) sausage
Arbroath	smokies
Bakewell	tart
Banbury	cake
Bath	bun, Oliver (biscuits)
Battenberg	cake
Berwick	cockles
Black Forest	gateau
Bologna	Bolognese sauce
Boston	baked beans, brown bread
Brussels	sprouts
Cayenne	pepper

Chelsea	bun
Cornish	pasty
Coventry	Godcakes
Cumberland	sausage, sauce
Denmark	pastries
Dublin	prawn
Dundee	cake
Eccles	cake
Frankfurt	sausage
Geneva	pudding
Genoa	fruit cake
Hamburg	hamburger
Hungary	goulash
Ireland	stew
Kendal	mint cake
Kiev	chicken
Lancashire	hot-pot
Lima	bean
Lorraine	quiche
Madeira	cake
Manchester	pudding
Maryland	chicken
Melton Mowbray	pork pie
Norway	lobster
Pontefract	liquorice cake
Seville	orange
Siena	cake
Switzerland (Swiss)	roll
Tabasco	sauce
Vichy	Vichyssoise soup
Vienna	loaf
Wales (Welsh)	(rabbit) rarebit
Whitstable	oysters
Windsor	bean
Worcester	sauce
Yorkshire	pudding
Bagel	doughnut-shaped roll cooked in water, then baked
Bain-Marie	large pan of boiling water in which a smaller pan is placed to help the cooking process
Baking powder	bicarbonate of soda, cream of tartar and starch
Banana: cooking variety	plantain
Bombay duck	fish
Bouquet garni	parsley, thyme, bay leaf, used as flavouring in stews etc.
Brawn	pig's head (occasionally sheep or cow's head)
Brisling	small herring-like fish
Caboc cheese	soft, Scottish cheese rolled in toasted oatmeal
Caviar	roe of sturgeon
Cendrés cheeses	coated with ashes originally from vine roots, later from industrial charcoal
Champignon	French name for mushrooms, but usually refers to button mushrooms
Charcuterie	French name for pork products (and for a shop that sells these)
Chayote	Mexican vegetable related to the gourd family also called choko, christifine, custard marrow, militon
Cheeses: blue veined	Gorgonzola, bleu d' Auvergnes, bleu de Bresse, Roquefort, Stilton
Cheese: holes formed by	carbon dioxide gas produced by bacteria in the milk sugar
Cheese: agent used to curdle milk for	rennet (from calf's stomach)
Cheese: largest producer	USA
Cheese: unusual types	
Emmental	Swiss, cheese with bigger holes than Gruyère
Feta	Greek, salted, based on sheep or goat's milk.
Gorgonzola	made from ewe's milk with blue veins (named after village near Milan)
Mozzarella	originally made from buffalo milk
Parmesan	made from skimmed milk
Ricotta	sweet cottage cheese
Roquefort	made from ewe's milk
Stilton	adds cream of one day to milk of next
Chef: 'Architect of French Cuisine'	Antonin Carême
Chewing gum: original base	chicle, the latex of the sapodilla tree
Cinnamon: from	bark of tree
Clementine: cross between	orange and tangerine

Coffee: source	pips of fruit (not beans)
Condensed milk: inventor	Gail Borden, US patent granted in 1856
Consumption: beer, most	Germany
Consumption: tea, most	Ireland
Consumption: wine, most	France consumes most wine overall but Portugal most per capita
Crab: how to tell if fresh	it should feel heavy but have no sound of water in it
Croissant	French, crescent-shaped roll
Croutons	toast pieces, fried in butter
Cuisses de grenouilles	frog's legs
Cuts of meat: beef neck	aka clod or sticking, it is usually used for stewing
beef sirloin	behind the neck (best beef for roasting)
beef topside	top of hind quarters of steer
Dariole (mould)	small and narrow with sloping sides used for setting creams and jellies or for steaming puddings
Denby Dale pie: created for	George III's recovery from an illness in 1788
Devon Garland cheese	layer of herbs pressed into the middle
Dredging	sprinkling with flour or icing sugar
E (European) numbers	code numbers used on food packaging which represent substances deemed safe by the EU
Edible grain crops: 9	wheat, barley, maize, oats, buckwheat, millet, rye, sorghum and rice
Eggs: brown or white more nutritious	no difference
Endive: English word for	chicory
Escargots	French, snails
Filbert: fruit of	hazel tree
Fines herbes	French, fresh chopped chives, chervil, parsley and tarragon but other fresh herbs may be added
Five-spice powder	Chinese, anise, pepper, cinnamon, cloves, fennel
Flageolet	a kind of haricot bean
Foodstuff: most extensively grown and eaten most generally by people	wheat (also used as animal fodder), rice
Fruit: nutrition	avocado is the most nutritious and cucumber the least
Gammon: part of pig from	thigh of legs (when salted and cured, this is ham)
Garam masala	mixed spices used in curry
Gas marks	Mark 1 – 250°F, Mark 2 – 275°F, Mark 3 – 300°F, Mark 4 – 325°F, Mark 5 – 350°F
Ghee	Indian clarified butter
Gohan	steamed rice
Grenadilla: aka	passion fruit
Grilling: Americans call	Broiling
Guinea pig: where eaten	Peru
Honey: nectar for 1 lb	from 2 million flowers
Huitres	oysters
Indian bread	poori, chapati, naan
Indian cinnamon tea	masala chai
Indian prawn dish	jhinga
Indian rice: most often used	Basmati (grown in the Himalayan foothills)
Indian-style chicken	murghi
Insect: most eaten	grasshopper
Instant potato: invented	Edward Asselberg (1941)
Kipper	split smoked herring
Langouste	crayfish
Larousse Gastronomique:	
original author	Prosper Montagné
Licence: chefs require to prepare	fugu (puffer fish) in Japan, lethal if toxic parts are not completely removed
Loganberry	cross between a raspberry and a blackberry
Loquat: aka	Japanese medlar
Margarine: 1st ingredients	chopped sheep intestine, cow's udder, beef suet
Meat: cholesterol-free	kangaroo, possum
Milk: most protein	reindeer's milk contains three times as much protein as cow's milk
Milk: UHT; stands for	Ultra High Temperature
Miso	Japanese fermented soya bean paste
Mooli	long, parsnip-shaped vegetable, which tastes like radish
MSG	monosodium glutamate (used to intensify flavour)
Naan	Indian flat bread

Noisette	hazelnut (French)
Okra: called in Indian supermarkets	bhindi (aka ladies' fingers)
Omelette and a glass of wine, An	Elizabeth David book of the 1960s which challenged British eating habits
Onion family: smallest plant in	chive
Oranges: best for marmalade	Seville
Oysters: when to eat; saying	When there is an 'r' in the month
Palm trees: two fruits that grow on	coconuts and dates
Parboil	derived from old French for 'boiling thoroughly'; now means 'boiling preliminary to further cooking'
Pasteurisation: temperature	approx 63° C
Petits pois	small French green peas
Pitta	Middle Eastern flat bread
Potato: poisonous parts	leaves and fruit (tubers eaten)
Prosciutto	Italian smoked ham
Prunes: made from	dried plums
Quargel cheese: from	Austria (sharp cheese, caraway-flavoured)
Quotations:	
Clement Attlee	The House of Lords is like a glass of champagne that has stood for 5 days.
James Beard	A gourmet who thinks of calories is like a tart who looks at her watch.
Paul Bocuse	Cuisine is like fireworks display, nothing remains. It is *une fête*, rapid, ephemeral.
Michel Bourdin	Cooking is a way of giving and making yourself desirable.
Mel Brooks	Where you eat is sacred.
George Burns	Actually, it only takes one drink to get me loaded. Trouble is, I can't remember if it's the thirteenth or the fourteenth.
Robert Byrne	Anybody who believes that the way to man's heart is through his stomach flunked geography.
Lord Byron	Let us have wine and women, mirth and laughter, Sermons and soda water the day after.
Titus Lucretius Carus	What is food to one man is bitter poison to others.
Malcolm de Chazal	Women eat when they talk, men talk when they eat.
Winston Churchill	[of champagne] In victory you deserve it, in defeat you need it.
Shirley Conran	Life is too short to stuff a mushroom.
Alexandre Dumas (Père)	Le Montrachet [a top Burgundy] should be drunk on the knees with head bared.
Edward VII	One not only drinks wine, one smells it, observes it, tastes it, sips it and – one talks about it.
William M Evarts	It was a brilliant affair – water flowed like champagne. (Description of a dinner given by teetotal President Rutherford B Hayes.)
Clifton Fadiman	Cheese – milk's leap towards immortality.
Sir Alexander Fleming	If penicillin can cure those who are ill, Spanish sherry can bring the dead back to life.
Clement Freud	If a bird says, 'Cluk bik bik bik bik' and 'Caw' you may kill it, eat it or ask Fortnums to pickle it in Napoleon brandy with wild strawberries. If it says, 'tweet' it is a dear and precious friend and you'd better lay off it if you want to remain a member of the Boodles.
Gail Greene	Great food is like great sex, the more you have the more you want.
Galileo	Wine is sunlight, held together by water.
Nubar Gulbenkian	The best number for a dinner party is two – myself and a damn good head waiter.
Philip W Haberman Jr	A gourmet is just a glutton with brains.
Ernest Hemingway	Wine is the most civilised thing in the world.
Horace	Wine is Life.
Jerome K Jerome	We drink one another's health and spoil our own.
Dr Johnson	Claret is the liquor for boys; port for men; but he who aspires to be a hero must drink brandy.
John Keats	Wine is only sweet to happy men.
Prue Leith	When you get to fifty-two food becomes more important than sex.
Joe E Lewis	A man is never drunk if he can lie on the floor without holding on.
Arnold Lobel	All's well that ends with a good meal.
Martin Luther	Who loves not women, wine and song, remains a fool his whole life long.
W Somerset Maugham	At a dinner party one should eat wisely but not too well, and talk well, but not too wisely.
George Mikes	On the Continent people have good food, in England people have good table manners.
Robert Morley	No man is lonely while eating spaghetti.
Napoleon	Champagne banishes etiquette.
Ogden Nash	Celery raw, develops the jaw; But celery stewed, Is more easily chewed.
Louis Pasteur	Wine is the most healthful and most hygienic of beverages. A meal without wine is like a day without sunshine.

FOOD AND DRINK

St Paul	Use a little wine for thy stomach's sake.
Madame de Pompadour	Champagne is the only wine that leaves a woman beautiful after drinking it.
Anthony Powell	Dinner at Huntercombes' possessed only two dramatic features – the wine was a farce and the food a tragedy.
William Shakespeare	The food that to him now is as luscious as locusts, shall be to him shortly as bitter as coloquintida.
Robert Louis Stevenson	Wine is bottled poetry.
Jonathan Swift	I have been assured by a very knowing American of my acquaintance in London, that a young healthy child well nursed is at a year old a most delicious, nourishing and wholesome food, whether stewed, roasted, baked or boiled and I make no doubt that it will equally serve in a fricassee, or a ragout.
Raclette	Swiss mild cheese; also a dish made from it with potatoes, pickled onions and gherkins
Raisins: made from	dried grapes
Rambutan: aka	hairy lychee
Ramekin	small casserole dish
Ratafia	1. type of macaroon, small biscuit, 2. liqueur made from fruit juice and brandy, or essence of bitter almond
Restaurant guide: first European	Michelin 1900
Restaurant: first	Boulanger's, Paris (1765)
Sago	starch from the pith of a palm
Salami	Italian sausage flavoured with garlic (Latin for salted)
Sally Lunn: cake named after	legendary lady from Bath
Singin' hinny	Northumberland fruit loaf; it gets its name from the sound it makes as it cooks
Spam: name from	spiced ham
Spice: from same plant	nutmeg, mace
Spice: most expensive by weight	saffron
Stilton cheese	made in Leicester but became famous in the early 18th century, when it was sold in the Bell Inn, a coaching house on the Great North Road, at Stilton, Cambridgeshire
Sweetbread from	pancreas
Tabasco: name from	Mexican state
Tapioca: source	root of cassava (manioc)
Tartrazine	azo dye that produces a yellow colour (E102)
Tava	concave cast-iron plate used for cooking bread
Tea: the Champagne of Tea	Darjeeling
Tea: country that produces most	India produces 30% of the world's tea crop annually
Tea: originally dried over burning ropes	lapsang souchong
Tea: spoon used for extracting floating tea leaves	mote spoon
Tea: weekly ration during WW2	2 oz per week
Terrine	pot used for pâté or savoury mixtures
Tofu	Japanese soya bean curd
Tripe	cow's, sheep's or other animal's stomach lining
Truffles: how found	detected by trained pigs in France; by dogs in N/W Italy
Turmeric: obtained from	rhizomes of curcuma plant
Ugli: fruit cross between	grapefruit, tangerine and orange
Vegetable: oldest known	broad bean (also called fava)
Wok	hemispherical pan used in Chinese stir-fry cookery
Worcester Sauce: origin	India
Yarg	Cornish cheese that is wrapped in nettles

Cocktails

Adonis dry sherry (2 parts), red vermouth (1 part), dash of orange bitters, twist of orange peel

Affinity scotch whisky (2 parts), dry vermouth (1 part), 2 dashes Angostura bitters

Afrodizzy white rum, banana liqueur, passion fruit juice, lemonade

Alaska gin (3 parts), yellow Chartreuse (1 part)

Alexander cognac (3 parts), crème de caçao (1 part) & cream (1 part)

Ambassador tequila (2 parts), sugar syrup (1 part), orange juice, slice of orange

American Beauty brandy, dry vermouth, white crème de menthe, port, orange juice, grenadine

Americano Campari, sweet vermouth, soda water, slice of orange

Angel Face dry gin (1/3), apricot brandy (1/3), calvados (1/3)

Angel's Kiss sloe gin, dark crème de caçao, prunelle liqueur, whipping cream

Atta Boy gin, dry vermouth, grenadine

Bacardi white rum (2 parts), lemon juice (1 part), a dash of grenadine

Bamboo dry sherry (1/2), dry vermouth (1/2), a dash of orange bitters

Bellini champagne, peach juice

Bentley calvados (1/2), Dubonnet (1/2)

Between the Sheets Cointreau, brandy, rum, lemon juice

Black Russian vodka, Kahlúa, cola

Black Velvet champagne, stout (equal measures)

Black Widow white rum, Kahlúa

Blarney Stone Irish whiskey, dry vermouth, green curaçao, orange bitters

Block and Fall cognac (2 parts), Cointreau (2 parts), calvados (1 part), anisette (1 part)

Bloody Mary vodka, tomato juice, lemon juice, Worcester sauce, salt and pepper

Blue Heaven white rum, blue curaçao, amaretto, lime juice, pineapple juice, sugar syrup

Blue Star gin, dry vermouth, blue curaçao, orange juice

Bobby Burns whisky, sweet vermouth, Benedictine

Bombay brandy (2 parts), dry vermouth (1 part), red vermouth (1 part), dash of pastis, 2 dashes curaçao

Boomerang Canadian Club whiskey, Swedish punch, dry vermouth, lemon, Angostura

Bosom Caresser brandy, orange curaçao, grenadine, egg yolk

Bronx gin, sweet vermouth, dry vermouth, orange juice

Brooklyn rye whiskey (2 parts), red vermouth (1 part), 1 dash of maraschino, 1 dash of Amer Picon

Bucks Fizz champagne, orange juice, grenadine (optional)

Butt Wobbler gin, calvados, dry vermouth, Pernod, lemonade

Buttock Clencher tequila, gin, melon liqueur, pineapple juice, lemonade

Caruso gin, dry vermouth, green crème de menthe

Casino dry gin (9 parts), maraschino (1 part), lemon juice (1 part), orange bitters (1)

Champagne Cocktail champagne, brandy

Champs-Elysées brandy, Chartreuse, lemon juice, Angostura

Cinderella pineapple juice, orange juice, lemon juice, soda water, sugar

Claridge dry gin (2 parts), dry vermouth (2 parts), apricot brandy (1 part), Cointreau (1)

Clover Club gin, grenadine, lime juice, egg white

Corcovado tequila, Drambuie, blue curaçao, Lemonade

Corpse Reviver brandy, sweet vermouth, calvados

Crème Puff crème de menthe, milk, soda water

Cuba Libre rum, lime juice, cola.

Czarina vodka (2 parts), dry vermouth (1 part), apricot brandy (1 part), dash of Angostura bitters

Daiquiri rum (4 parts), lemon juice (1 part), or lime juice, sugar

Dempsey calvados, gin, Pernod, grenadine

Depth Charge brandy, calvados, grenadine, lemon juice

Derby dry gin (55ml, 2oz), 2 dashes of peach bitters, 2 sprigs of fresh mint

Diki-Diki calvados (4 parts), Swedish punch (1 part), grapefruit juice (1 part)

Double or Drop tequila, brandy, lime juice, honey

Dry Martini gin (4 parts), vermouth (1 part)

Duchess red vermouth (1 part), dry vermouth (1 part), pastis (1 part)

Earthquake whisky, gin, and Pernod

East-India brandy (6 parts), curaçao (1 part), orange juice (1 part)

Eclipse sloe gin, grenadine, gin, a cherry

El Presidente white rum (3 parts), curaçao (1 part), dry vermouth (1 part), dash of grenadine

Eve cognac, curaçao, caster sugar, Pernod, pink champagne

Fair and Warmer white rum, sweet vermouth, orange curaçao

Fallen Angel gin, lime juice, white crème de menthe, Angostura, lemonade

Floppy Dick brandy, dry vermouth, sweet vermouth, triple sec, vermouth

Flu Canadian Club whiskey, lemon juice, rock candy syrup, ginger brandy, Jamaican ginger

Fluffy Navel brandy, dry vermouth, sweet vermouth, triple sec, Pernod

Fourth Degree gin, sweet vermouth, dry vermouth, Pernod

Gibson gin (4 parts), vermouth (1 part), served with a cocktail onion

Gimlet gin, lime juice

Gin Fizz gin (4parts), lemon juice (2parts), sugar, soda water

Gin Sling gin, lemon juice, sugar (aka Pimm's No 1)

Gin Swizzle gin, soda water, lime juice, sugar syrup, Angostura

Glad Eye Pernod, crème de menthe

Grand Slam Swedish punch, sweet vermouth, dry vermouth

Grasshopper green crème de menthe, white crème de caçao, whipping cream

Green Dragon champagne, Midori

Harvey Wallbanger vodka (1 part), orange juice (2 parts), 2 teaspoons of Galliano (named after surfer, Tom Harvey)

Highball whisky, Angostura bitters, ginger ale

Hoopla brandy, Cointreau, dry vermouth, lemon juice

Hoots Mon whisky, sweet vermouth, dry vermouth

Horse's Neck brandy, Angostura, dry ginger ale

Hula Hula gin, orange juice, Cointreau

Hurricane rum, lime juice, passion fruit juice, orange juice, pineapple juice

Jelly Bean ouzo, blue curaçao, grenadine, lemonade, jelly beans

John Collins gin, lemon juice, spoonful of sugar, soda water

Jungle Juice Pisang Ambon, Mandarine Napoléon, gin, orange juice, sugar

Kicker Bacardi rum, calvados, sweet vermouth

Kir glass of white wine with a teaspoon of crème de cassis stirred in

Kir Royale glass of champagne with a teaspoon of crème de cassis stirred in

Knickerbocker gin, dry vermouth, sweet vermouth

Knock Out Punch gin, cider, Bénédictine, brandy, peach brandy, lemonade

Leap Year gin, Grand Marnier, sweet vermouth, lemon juice

Macaroni Pernod, sweet vermouth

Manhattan rye whiskey (2 parts), sweet vermouth (1 part), bitters, maraschino cherry
Named after a NY club and invented by Jenny Jerome (Winston Churchill's mother)

Margarita tequila (2 parts), lemon juice (1 part), curaçao (1 part), glass is salted

Mary Pickford white rum (1/2), natural pineapple juice (1/2), teaspoon grenadine, 6 dashes maraschino

Merry Widow gin, dry vermouth, Bénédictine, Pernod, Angostura

Mikado brandy (40 ml, 1 1/2oz), 2 drops curaçao, 2 drops crème de noyaux, 2 drops orange curaçao, 2 drops Orgeat, 2 drops Angostura bitters

Mint Julep bourbon, sugar syrup, sprigs of mint

Monkey Gland gin, orange juice, grenadine, 2 dashes of pastis

Monkey Wrench white rum, grapefruit juice, lemon juice

Morning Glory whisky, lemon juice, soda water, Angostura, sugar, egg white

Moscow Mule Smirnoff vodka, lime juice, dry ginger ale

Negroni red vermouth (1/3), Campari (1/3), dry gin (1/3)

Oh! Henry! whisky, Bénédictine, ginger ale

Old Fashioned bourbon, sugar cube, Angostura, 1/2 slice lemon, 1/2 slice orange, dash of soda water

Old Pal rye whiskey (1/3), dry vermouth (1/3), Campari (1/3)

Orange Blossom gin, orange juice, grenadine, orange bitters

Oriental rye whiskey (1/2), red vermouth (1/4), white curaçao (1/4), 2 teaspoons fresh lemon juice

Paradise gin, apricot brandy, orange juice

Parisian dry gin (2 parts), dry vermouth (2 parts), créme de cassis (1 part)

Parisian Blonde dark rum, triple sec, double cream, sugar syrup

Pimms 1–6 long drink with spirit base and fruit flavouring, bases as follows:

(1) gin (2) whisky (3) brandy (4) rum (5) rye whisky (6) vodka

Pina Colada rum, pineapple juice, coconut milk, whipping cream, sugar

Pink Elephant bourbon, lemon juice, grenadine, egg white

Pink Lady gin, grenadine, egg white

Planter's Punch lime juice (1 part), sugar syrup (2 parts), rum (3 parts), Ice (4 parts), 2 dashes Angostura

Planter's Punch Rhyme one of sour, two of sweet, three of strong, four of weak

Presto brandy, sweet vermouth, orange juice, Pernod

Princeton dry gin (2 parts), port (1 part), dash orange bitters, twist lemon peel

Prohibition dry vermouth, gin, apricot brandy, orange juice

Purple Cactus tequila, passion fruit juice, sweet sherry, grenadine

Rob Roy Scotch whisky, vermouth, Angostura bitters

Rolls Royce brandy, Cointreau, orange juice, egg white

Rose dry vermouth (2 parts), Kirsch (1 part), dash strawberry syrup

Rusty Nail whisky, Drambuie

Screwdriver vodka orange juice

Sensation gin, lemon juice, Maraschino, sprigs of mint

Sidecar brandy, Cointreau, lemon juice

Singapore Sling gin, Angostura bitters, lemon juice

Slow Comfortable Screw vodka, Southern Comfort, sloe gin, orange juice

Snowball Advocaat, lime juice, lemonade

Sporran Free Drambuie, whisky, lemon juice, Angostura, soda water

Starboard Light crème de menthe (9 parts), brandy (1 part)

Stinger brandy, white crème de menthe

Tackety Boot whisky, Drambuie, sweet vermouth, dry vermouth, lemonade

Tequila Sunrise tequila, orange juice, grenadine

Third Degree gin, dry vermouth, Pernod

Third Rail white rum, brandy, calvados, Pernod

TNT tequila, Tia Maria, Mandarine Napoléon

Tom and Jerry rum, eggs, cinammon, sugar, cloves, allspice, soda, brandy, milk, nutmeg

Tom Collins gin (1 part), lemon juice (1 part), sugar syrup (1 teaspoon), soda water

Tonsil Teaser Grand Marnier, crème de banane, coffee liqueur, cream

Torpedo brandy, coffee liqueur, egg white

Triple Testosterone dark rum, white rum, triple sec, lime juice, Grenadine

Trouser Rouser whisky, mango juice, pineapple, lime juice, crème de banane, egg white

Wembley whiskey, dry vermouth, pineapple juice

Whisky Mac whisky, green ginger wine

White Lady gin, Cointreau, lemon juice

Whizz Bang whisky, dry vermouth, orange bitters, Absinthe, Grenadine

Za-Za Dubonnet (1/2), dry gin (1/2), dash Angostura bitters

Zombie white rum, dark rum, pineapple juice, sugar

Flavouring

Absinthe green alcoholic drink, technically a gin, originally having high wormwood content

Aki plum-flavoured alcoholic drink

Akvavit Scandinavian spirit made from potatoes and flavoured with caraway

Amaretto almond-flavoured alcoholic drink

Angostura bitters bitter aromatic tonic made from gentian and various spices, the true angostura bitters being obtained from the angostura bark

Arrack rice-based spirit with a coconut flavour from Eastern countries

Aurum orange-flavoured alcoholic drink (literal meaning 'gold'), based on Italian brandy

Ava Polynesian drink made from peppers

B & B Brandy and Bénédictine based liqueur

Beer barley, flavoured with hops and fermented with yeast

Brandy spirit distilled from the grape (literal meaning 'burnt wine'), Dutch 'brandewijn'

Calvados spirit distilled from apples grown in the Basse-Normandie region

Cassis blackcurrant-flavoured spirit

Chartreuse either of two liqueurs, green or yellow, with an orange flavour

Cider alcoholic drink made from the fermented juice of apples

Cointreau colourless liqueur with orange flavouring

Curaçao orange-flavoured liqueur originally made on the Caribbean island of that name

Drambuie Scottish liqueur made from whisky and heather honey (secret recipe given by Bonnie Prince Charlie to MacKinnon family in 1746)

Gin distilled grain flavoured with juniper berries

Grand Marnier French cognac-based liqueur with an orange flavour

Izarra Basque herb liqueur on an armagnac base that may be green or yellow (basque word for 'star')

Kahlúa Mexican coffee-flavoured liqueur

Kirsch brandy distilled from cherries, made principally in the Black Forest

Kriek-Lambic cherry-flavoured Belgian beer

Kumiss/Koumiss fermented mare's milk

Kümmel Dutch grain liqueur flavoured with cumin and aniseed

Kvass barley-flavoured East European drink distilled from stale bread

Lassi yoghurt-based drink served with either salt or sugar

Maraschino liqueur-flavoured with kernels of the marasca cherry and tasting of bitter almonds

Mastic aniseed-flavoured liquor which has additional flavour from mastic gum resin

Mead wine made by fermenting a solution of honey

Mirabelle plum-flavoured alcoholic drink

Ouzo Greek spirit with a strong aniseed flavour

Pastis aniseed-flavoured apéritif from France

Pernod aniseed-flavoured apéritif from France

Perry alcoholic drink made from the fermented juice of pears

Port sweet fortified dessert wine distilled from grapes

Pulque Mexican drink made from the juice of the maguey, a kind of agave plant, literal meaning 'decomposed', since it will only keep for a day

Raki/Rakee strong spirit distilled in Turkey and Yugoslavia and flavoured with aniseed

Retsina Greek wine flavoured with pine wood resin

Ricard aniseed-flavoured alcoholic drink

Rum spirit made from sugar cane and flavoured with molasses

Sake/Saki Japanese alcoholic drink made from fermented rice

Samshu Chinese alcoholic drink made from fermented rice

Sangria orange-flavoured Spanish red wine with cinnamon and cloves (literal meaning 'a bleeding')

Sherry fortified wine made from grapes, originally only made in Jerez and San Lucar, Spain

Shochu alcoholic drink flavoured by sweet potatoes

Slivovitz plum brandy from Eastern Europe, particularly Southern Slav regions

Southern Comfort peach and orange-flavoured liqueur with Bourbon base

Tequila Mexican drink made from the juice of the agave plant

Tia Maria coffee-flavoured liqueur from the West Indies

Tisane herbal infusion commonly with mint vervair or camomile. Literal meaning 'barley water'

Van der Hum South African Cape brandy liqueur with tangerine and a touch of rum. Literal meaning 'What's his name' or 'So and So'

Vodka alcoholic drink originating in Russia and distilled from either potato or grain

Whiskey Irish whiskey (spelt with an 'e' in Ireland); the same spelling is always used in the USA

Whisky (grain) spirit made by distilling various kinds of grain. Literal meaning 'water of life'

Whisky (malt) spirit made by distilling barley. Literal meaning 'water of life'

Wine alcoholic drink produced by fermenting grapes

FOOD AND DRINK

General Information

Alcohol: coffee effect on	makes worse
Alcohol content of beers and wines	on average, beers contain between 3 and 7% alcohol, whilst wines contain between 8 and 15%
Anjou rosé wine: from	Loire Valley
Asti Spumante: grape used	Muscat
Barbed wire	Australian term for lager, especially Castlemaine XXXX
Beer: highest alcohol content	barley wine
Bénédictine liqueur: distilled	Fécamp in Normandy (it is also distilled in the UK, where the most popular distillery is in Blackburn because a Lancashire regiment was stationed at Fécamp during the First World War)
Bottle sizes: Bordeaux	Magnum (2 bottles)
	Marie-Jeanne (3)
	Double Magnum (4)
	Jéroboam (6)
	Impériale (8)
Bottle sizes: other wines	Magnum (2)
	Jeroboam (4)
	Rehoboam (6)
	Methuselah (8)
	Salmanazar (12)
	Balthazar (16)
	Nebuchadnezzar (20)
Breweries, British: headquarters	Adnams – Suffolk; Badger – Dorset; Belhaven – Dunbar; Burtonwood – Warrington; Felinfoel – Llanelli; Greene King – Bury St Edmunds; Jennings – Cockermouth; King & Barnes – Horsham in Sussex; Marston's – Burton on Trent; Moorhouse's – Burnley; Morland – Abingdon; Rectory – Sussex; Wyre Piddle – Evesham, Worcs
Brewery: oldest in the world	Weihenstephan Brewery in Freising near Munich (founded 1040)
Cap Bon wine: from	Tunisia
Champagne: designations	brut (very dry), demi-sec (sweet), extra-sec (medium dry), Sec (medium sweet)
Champagne making: remuage	process of tilting the bottle and tapping it to help the sediment fall to the cork for subsequent removal, previously a manual process but now mechanical
Coca-Cola: original constituent	cocaine (until 1903)
Coffee: types	Blue Mountain, Bourbon, Caturra, Maragogype, Mocha, Mysore and Teaberry
Cru: French wine term	refers to the product of a growth from a single vineyard
Drink: drinking once could cause excommunication	chocolate (Central America in the 18th century)
Firkin of beer	9 gallons
French wine: only region to name its wines after the grape used	Alsace, eg. Riesling, Gewürztraminer and Muscat
Gin: former names	geneva (From French for juniper); Hollands (because the Dutch were the first to distil it)
Halbtrocken	any medium-dry German wine
Huckle-my-buff	Sussex drink of beer, eggs and brandy
Iced tea: inventor	Richard Blechynden (St Louis World Fair, 1904)
Iskra sparkling wine: from	Bulgaria (Iskra, meaning 'spark', is also from Russia)
Johnnie Walker Red Label: malt whisky used in blending of	Talisker, a single malt whisky from the Isle of Skye
Kvass	traditional Russian drink similar to beer made from rye flour mixed with a little sprouted barley
Monbazillac wine: from	Bergerac region of France
Port: aka	'the Englishman's Wine', because it was originally produced by British traders settled there
Port: maturity	it can take 40 years for a vintage port to reach maturity
Port: name from	Oporto, Portugal
Prohibition in USA	Between 1920 and 1933
Pub name: most popular in England	King's Head
Pub name: most popular in UK	Red Lion
Real ales: names (examples)	Brewer's Droop, Double Dragon, How's Your Father, Nessie's Monster Mash, Old Horny, Old Speckled Hen, Piddle in the Snow,

	Rector's Revenge, St Andrew's Witches' Brew, Snecklifter, Spingo, Workie Ticket
Red Stripe lager: from	Jamaica
Rioja	Northern Spanish wine-producing region divided into Alta, Alavesa and Baja
Scotch whisky: matured in	oak casks (formerly in sherry butts, now in casks sprayed with sherry concentrate)
Sheeps dip: aka	single malt Scotch whisky
Sherry: name from	Jerez, Spain
Sherry: standard cask	butt (contains 108 gallons)
Sherry: standard glass	copita (Tulip shaped)
Sherry: types	fino (dry, pale, young wine); oloroso (darker, heavier and fuller); amontillado (fuller both in colour and body and made by ageing finos); Manzanilla (palest and driest of finos)
Solera system	tiered system of blending wines in the making of sherry
Sparkling wine: invented by	Dom Pérignon (1639–1715), a Benedictine monk from Hautvillers Abbey
Spätlese	German term for 'late picked' wine; the riper grapes make the wine sweeter
Spingo beer: from	Helston in Cornwall
Spirit: best selling in the world	Bacardi
Stirrup cup	sloe gin is the traditional drink to take before hunting
Strega: liqueur from	Italy (literal meaning 'witch')
Table wine: Americans call	jug wine
Tea: bergamot-flavoured	Earl Grey
categories	black (fermented); green (unfermented); oolong (semi-fermented)
Chinese word for	cha
grades	orange pekoe (highest), pekoe, pekoe souchong, congou, pekoe dust, dust
Japanese ceremony	chanoyu
Original use	medicine
Used as currency	Siberia
Tiger beer: from	Singapore and Malaysia
Trocken	drier style of German wine
Tulip : glasses	best glass for serving cognac as balloon glass loses bouquet
Ullage	air gap between the cork and the wine, often found in very old wine; also refers to the space created in a wine barrel by evaporation
Vermouth: types	French has come to mean 'dry white', whilst Italian is 'sweet red'
VSOP	Very Special/Superior Old Pale: not more than 5 years old
Whisky: bourbon and rye contrast	bourbon comes from Kentucky, whilst rye comes from the USA and Canada; bourbon is aged in cold warehouses whilst rye is aged in heated rooms
Whisky: Johnnie Walker Black Label matured for	twelve years
Whisky: largest malt whisky distillery in the world	Suntory distillery at Hakushu, Japan
Whisky: meaning	water of life
Whisky: world's best-selling single-malt Scottish whisky	Glenfiddich
White Horse whisky: malt whisky used in blending of	Lagavulin
Wine: some famous Bordeaux districts	Entre-Deux-Mers, Graves, Margaux, Sauternes, St Emilion, Médoc, Pomerol
Wine: difference between English and British	English wine is made from grapes grown in England, British wine is made in Britain from concentrated grape juice imported from abroad and reconstituted with British water
Wine: difference between sweet & dry	sweet wine is taken from the vat before all the sugar is converted to alcohol by fermentation
Wine: grape colours	red and rosé wines are made with red grapes, but white wine may be made with red or white grapes
Wine labels: AC, control designation	Appellation Contrôlée (French quality-control designation)
Wine labels: Cava	found on best sparkling wines from Spain (not quite as good as champagne), mostly from Catalonia
Wine labels: DOC, control designation	Denominazione di Origine Controllata (Italian quality-control designation)
Wine: Lacrima Christi	made on the south slopes of Mt Vesuvius, near Naples

FOOD AND DRINK

Wine: length of cork denotes	the longer the cork, the longer period of time the wine is intended to be laid down for
Wine: louse that attacks vine roots of Vitis vinifera	*Phylloxera vastatrix* accidentally imported into Europe from the USA in the 1860s
Wine making: chapeau (hat)	term that refers to the layer of grape skins which rise to the surface during red wine fermentation
Wine making terms: must	unfermented grape juice seeds and skins; first stage in wine-making process or crushed grapes
Wine making: difference between red and white	skins of red grapes must be left in contact with the crushed grapes during fermentation, whilst the skins are removed before fermentation in production of white wine
Wine: marc	spirit distilled from grape skins and stalks
Wine: minimum alcohol content under EC laws	7%
Wine: off licence scale of sweetness	from 1 to 9: sweetest is 9 and driest is 1
Wine: origins	somewhere between the Black and Caspian seas, around 4000 BC
Wine producer: world's largest	Italy, in 8 years out of every 10, on average; otherwise France
Wine: rosé	basically white wine made from red grapes that causes it to be given a little colour and flavour by being left a short time with the skins
Wine: Sauternes, most expensive	Château Yquem
Wine: sparkling	sparkling wine is a wine which undergoes a second fermentation effervesces when poured
Wine: sparkling: production methods	méthode champenoise (bottle fermentation – method for best wines); cuve close; transfer system; transversage
Wine stored horizontally: reason	to keep cork in contact with the wine so that it does not shrink and admit air to the bottle
Wine: study of	oenology
Wine: some tasting terms:	
beefy	red wines high in alcohol, big, solid and chunky
buttery	refers to the soft, rich vanilla flavour imparted by new oak barrels
chewy	plenty of of tannin and a strong flavour
clean	no chemical or bacterial faults, and a straightforward, simple flavour
fat	heavy, perhaps clumsy
grapy	most common with Muscat, Gewürztraminer, and Müller-Thurgau, it denotes the flavour of the grape itself
green	unripe or tart
hard	red wines that have too much tannin
length	length of time and the way the flavour of wine continues to develop in the mouth after swallowing
prickly	refers to a wine with some residual gas left in it
stony	rather dull, empty dryness in either a red or white
tough	too much tannin
Wines: types:	
Amontillado	sherry
Amoroso	sherry
Asti Spumante	sparkling Italian wine from Muscat grape
Bull's Blood	Hungarian wine from Eger region
Chianti	Italian red wine from Tuscany
Claret	red Bordeaux wine (traditional English name for)
Fino	dry, light sherry
Hock	German Rhine wine (from the village called Hochheim)
Liebfraumilch	type of hock (blended wine from Rhine area)
Manzanilla	sherry (dry)
Marsala	Sicilian fortified wine
Moselle	German white wine
Oloroso	dark sherry
Retsina	Greek wine
Soave	white Italian wine
Tokay	Hungarian wine
Vinho Verde	white wine from the north of Portugal
Wine: vintage & non-vintage	vintage wine comes from a single harvest, whilst non-vintage is a blend of wines of more than one year
Wine: what it is	fermented juice of the grape; fermentation being a bio-chemical reaction in which sugar in grape juice is converted into ethyl alcohol and carbon dioxide gas
Wine: world's best seller	Lambrusco (especially popular in USA)
Zymurgy	the art or practice of fermentation in wine-making, brewing and distilling

Geography

British Dependent Territories

Anguilla
Bermuda (Somers Islands)
British Antarctic Territory
British Indian Ocean Territory
British Virgin Islands
Cayman Islands
Falkland Islands

Gibraltar
Montserrat
Pitcairn Islands
St Helena and Dependencies
 (Ascension and Tristan Da Cunha)
South Georgia and South Sandwich Islands
Turks and Caicos Islands

Capitals: by country

Country, State, County or Area	Capital or Admin Centre	Country, State, County or Area	Capital or Admin Centre
A'āli an-Nil (Upper Nile) (Sudan)	Malakāi	Al-Wādi al-Jadid (Egypt)	Al-Kharijah
Aargau (Swiss canton)	Aarau	Amambay (Paraguay)	Pedro Juan
Abaco and Mores Island (Bahamas)	Marsh Harbour		Caballero
Abalang (Kiribati)	Tuarabu	Amapá (Brazil)	Macapá
Abemama (Kiribati)	Kariatebike	Amazonas (Brazil)	Manaus
Abkhaziya (CIS)	Sukhumi	Amazonas (Colombia)	Leticia
Abruzzi (Italy)	L'Aquila	Amazonas (Peru)	Chachapoyas
Abyān (Yemen)	Zinjibār	Ambae/Maéwo (Vanuatu)	Longana
Acklins Island (Bahamas)	Pompey Bay	Ambrym (Vanuatu)	Eas
Acre (Brazil)	Rio Branco	**American Samoa**	Pago Pago
Adamous (Cameroon)	Ngaoundéré	Amou (Togo)	Amiamé
Ad-Dagahliyah (Egypt)	Al-Mansurah	An Giang (Vietnam)	Long Xuyen
Adrar (Mauritania)	Atar	Anambra (Nigeria)	Enugu
Adygeya (Russia)	Maikop	Ancash (Peru)	Huaraz
Afghanistan	Kabul	Andalucia (Spain)	Seville
Agin-Buryat (Russia)	Aginskoe	Andaman and Nicobar Islands	Port Blair
Aichi (Japan)	Nagoya	Andhra Pradesh (India)	Hyderabad
Ain (France)	Bourg-en-Bresse	**Andorra**	Andorra La Vella
Aisén del Gen Carlos Ibáñez del Campo (Chile)	Coihaique	Andros Island (Bahamas)	Kemps Bay
		Angola	Luanda
Aisne (France)	Laon	**Anguilla**	The Valley
Akwa Ibom (Nigeria)	Uyo	Anhui (aka Anhwei) (China)	Hefei (aka Ho-fei)
Alabama (USA)	Montgomery	An-Nil al-Azraq (Blue Nile) (Sudan)	Ad-Damazin
Alagoas (Brazil)	Maceió	**Antigua and Barbuda**	St John's
Al-Anbār (Iraq)	Ar-Ramādi	Antioquia (Colombia)	Medellín
Alania (Russia) / North Ossetia	Vladikavkaz	Antofagasta (Chile)	Antofagasta
Alaska (USA)	Juneau	Antrim (NI)	Belfast
Al-Bahr al-Ahmar (Egypt)	Al-Ghurdaqah	Anzoátegui (Venezuela)	Barcelona
Albania	Tirana	Aorangi (NZ)	Timaru
Alberta (Canada)	Edmonton	Appenzell Ausser-Rhoden (Swiss canton)	Herisau
Al-Biqa (Lebanon)	Zahlah		
Al-Buhayrah (Egypt)	Damanhur	Appenzell Inner-Rhoden (Swiss canton)	Appenzell
Alderney	St Annes		
Algeria	Algiers	Apulia (Italy)	Bari
Al-Gharbiyah (Egypt)	Tanjā	Apure (Venezuela)	San Fernando de Apure
Alifu (Maldives)	Mahibadhoo		
Al-Janub (Lebanon)	Sidon/Saydā	Apurimac (Peru)	Abancay
Al-Lādhiqiyah (Syria)	Latakia	Aqua Grande (São Tomé and Principe)	São Tomé
Allier (France)	Moulins		
Al-Mahrah (Yemen)	Al-Ghaydah	Aquitaine (France)	Bordeaux
Al-Minufiyah (Egypt)	Shibin al-Kawm	Aragón (Spain)	Zaragoza
Alonissos (Sporades)	Patitiri	Aragua (Venezuela)	Maracay
Alpes-de-Haute-Provence (France)	Digne	Arakan/Rakhine (Burma)	Sittwe (aka Akyab)
Alpes-Maritimes (France)	Nice	Aranuka (Kiribati)	Takaeang
Al-Qalyubiyah (Egypt)	Banhā	Araucanía (Chile)	Temuco
Alsace (France)	Strasbourg	Ardèche (France)	Privas
Altai (Russia)	Gorno	Ardennes (France)	Charleville-Mézières
Alta Verapaz (Guatemala)	Cobán		
Alto Paraguay (Paraguay)	Fuerte Olimpio	**Argentina**	Buenos Aires
Alto Paraná (Paraguay)	Ciudad del Este	Arges (Romania)	Pitesti
Älvsborg (Sweden)	Vänersborg	Arhangay (Mongolia)	Tsetserieg

Country, State, County or Area	Capital or Admin Centre	Country, State, County or Area	Capital or Admin Centre
Ariège (France)	Foix	Basilicata (Italy)	Potenza
Arizona (USA)	Phoenix	Basque Country (Spain)	Vitoria
Arkansas (USA)	Little Rock	Bas-Rhin (France)	Strasbourg
Armagh (NI)	Armagh	Basse-Kotto (Cape Verde)	Mobaye
Armenia	Yerevan	Basse-Normandie (France)	Caen
Arorae (Kiribati)	Roreti	Bas-Zaïre (Dem Rep of Congo)	Matadi
Arsi (Ethiopia)	Asela	Batha (Chad)	Ati
Artibonite (Haiti)	Gonaives	Bavaria (Germany)	Munich
Arua (Uganda)	Olaki	Bay (Somalia)	Baidoa
Aruba	Oranjestad		(Baydhabo)
Arunāchal Pradesh (India)	Itānagar	Bay of Plenty (NZ)	Tauranga
Ascension	Georgetown	Bazéga (Burkina Faso)	Kombissiri
Ashanti (Ghana)	Kumasi	Bedfordshire (Eng)	Bedford
Ash-Shamāl (Lebanon)	Tripoli/Tarābulus	Belait (Brunei)	Kuala Belait
Ash-Sharqiyah (Egypt)	Az-Zaqāziq	**Belarus**	Minsk
Assam (India)	Dispur	**Belgium**	Brussels
Assoli (Togo)	Bafilo	**Belize**	Belmopan
Asturias (Spain)	Oviedo	Bendel (Nigeria)	Benin City
Atacama (Chile)	Copiapó	Bengo (Angola)	Caxito
Atacora (Benin)	Natitingou	Beni (Bolivia)	Trinidad
Atlántico (Colombia)	Barranquilla	**Benin**	Porto Novo (*de*
Atlántida (Honduras)	La Ceiba		*facto* Cotonou)
Atlantique (Benin)	Cotonou	Benue (Nigeria)	Makurdi
Aube (France)	Troyes	Berea (Lesotho)	Teyateyaneng
Aude (France)	Carcassonne	Berkshire (Eng)	Reading
Aust-Agder (Norway)	Arendal	**Bermuda**	Hamilton
Australia	Canberra	Berry Island (Bahamas)	Nicolls Town
Australian Capital Territory	Canberra	Beru (Kiribati)	Taubukinberu
Austria	Vienna	**Bhutan (aka Druk-Yul)**	Thimphu
Austurland (Iceland)	Egilsstadhir	Bié (Angola)	Kuito
Auvergne (France)	Clermont-Ferrand	Bihar (India)	Patna
Aveyron (France)	Rodez	Bihor (Romania)	Oradea
Avon (Eng)	Bristol	Bimini Islands (Bahamas)	Alice Town
Azerbaijan	Baku	Binah (Togo)	Pagouda
Azores (Portugal)	Ponta Delgada	Binh Dinh (Vietnam)	Quy Nhon
Azuay (Ecuador)	Cuenca	Binh Duong (Vietnam)	Thu Dau Mot
Ba Ria (Vietnam)	Vung Tau	Binh Phuoc (Vietnam)	Dung Xoai
Baa (Maldives)	Eydhafushi	Binh Thuan (Vietnam)	Phan Thiet
Bābil (Iraq)	Al-Hillah	Bíobío (Chile)	Concepción
Bács-Kiskun (Hungary)	Kecskemét	Bioko (Equatorial Guinea)	Malabo
Baden-Württemberg (Germany)	Stuttgart	Biombo (Guinea-Bissau)	Bissau
Bahamas	Nassau	Blekinge (Sweden)	Karlskrona
Bahia (Brazil)	Salvador	Boavista (Cape Verde)	Sal Rei
Bahoruco (Dominican Republic)	Neiba	Bokeo (Laos)	Houayxay
Bahr al-Ghazāl (Sudan)	Wāu	Bolikhamxay (Laos)	Pakxan
Bahrain	Manama	Bolivar (Colombia)	Cartagena
Baja California Norte (Mexico)	Mexicali	Bolivar (Ecuador)	Guaranda
Baja California Sur (Mexico)	La Paz	Bolivar (Venezuela)	Ciudad Bolivar
Baja Verapaz (Guatemala)	Salamá	**Bolivia**	Sucre – judicial
Bakool (Somalia)	Oddur (Xuddur)		La Paz –
Bale (Ethiopia)	Goba		administrative
Balearic Islands (Spain)	Palma de	Bombali (Sierra Leone)	Makeni
	Mallorca	Bomi (Liberia)	Tubmanburg
Bali (Indonesia)	Denpassar	Bonaire (Netherland Antilles)	Kralendijk
Baluchistān (Pakistan)	Quetta	Bong (Liberia)	Gbarnga
Bam (Burkina Faso)	Kongoussi	Bophuthatswana (South Africa)	Mmabatho
Bamingui-Bangoran (Cape Verde)	Ndélé	Boquerón (Paraguay)	Dr Pedro P. Peña
Banaadir (Somalia)	Mogadishu	Bora-Bora (French Polynesia)	Vaitape
	(Muqdisho)	Borders (Scotland)	Newtown St
Banaba (Kiribati)	Anteeren		Boswells
Bangladesh	Dhaka	Borgou (Benin)	Parakou
Banks/Torres (Vanuatu)	Sola	Borkou-Ennedi-Tibesti (Chad)	Faya
Baranya (Hungary)	Pécs	Bornholm (Denmark)	Renne
Barbados	Bridgetown	Borno (Nigeria)	Malduguri
Bari (Somalia)	Bender Cassim	Borsod-Abaúj-Zemplén (Hungary)	Miskolc
	(Boosaaso)	**Bosnia and Hercegovina**	Sarajevo
Barima/Waini (Guyana)	Mabaruma	**Botswana**	Gaborone
Basel-Landschaft (Swiss canton)	Liestal	Botswana (Central)	Serowe
Basel-Stadt (Swiss canton)	Basel	Botswana (North East)	Masunga
Bashkir (Russia)	Ufa	Botswana (South East)	Ramotswa

Country, State, County or Area	Capital or Admin Centre	Country, State, County or Area	Capital or Admin Centre
Bouches-du-Rhône (France)	Marseille	Cayo (Belize)	San Ignacio
Bouenza (Congo)	Madingou	Ceará (Brazil)	Fortaleza
Bougouriba (Burkina Faso)	Diébougou	Central (Scotland)	Stirling
Boulgou (Burkina Faso)	Tenkodogo	**Central African Republic**	Bangui
Boulkiemde (Burkina Faso)	Koudougou	Central District (Israel)	Ramla
Bourgogne/Burgundy (France)	Dijon	Central Islands (Solomon Isles)	Tulagi
Boyacá (Colombia)	Tunja	Central Nepal	Kāthmāndu
Brabant (Flemish)	Louvain (Leuven)	Central Province (Fiji)	Suva
Brabant (Walloon)	Wavre	Central Province (Kenya)	Nyeri
Brakna (Mauritania)	Aleg	Central Province (Zambia)	Kabwe
Brandenburg (Germany)	Potsdam	Central Region (Ghana)	Cape Coast
Brava (Cape Verde)	Nova Sintra	Central Region (Paraguay)	Asunción
Brazil	Brasilia	Centrale Region (Togo)	Sokodé
Bretagne/Brittany (France)	Rennes	Centre Département (Haiti)	Hinche
British Columbia (Canada)	Victoria	Centre Province (Cameroon)	Yaoundé
British Indian Ocean Territory	Diego Garcia	Cerro Largo (Uruguay)	Melo
Brong-Ahafo (Ghana)	Sunyani	Cesar (Colombia)	Valledupar
Brunei	Bandar Seri Begawan	Chaco (Argentina)	Resistencia
		Chaco (Paraguay)	Mayor Pablo Lagerenza
Buckinghamshire (Eng)	Aylesbury		
Buenos Aires (Argentina)	La Plata	**Chad**	N'Djamena
Bulgaria (aka Narodna Republic)	Sofia	Chagang-do (North Korea)	Kanggye
		Champagne-Ardenne (France)	Châlons-sur-Marne
Bumthang (Bhutan)	Jakar		
Bundibugyo (Uganda)	Busaru	Champasak (Laos)	Pakxé
Burgenland (Austria)	Eisenstadt	Charente (France)	Angoulême
Burkina Faso	Ouagadougou	Charente-Maritime (France)	La Rochelle
Burundi	Bujumbura	Chari-Baguirmi (Chad)	N'Djaména
Buryat (Russia)	Ulan-Ude	**Chechnya**	Grozny (aka Djohar)
Bushenyi (Uganda)	Bumbaire		
Buskerud (Norway)	Drammen	Cher (France)	Bourges
Caaguazú (Paraguay)	Coronel Oviedo	Cheshire (Eng)	Chester
Cabañas (El Salvador)	Sensuntepeque	Chiapas (Mexico)	Tuxtla Gutiérrez
Cabo Delgado (Mozambique)	Pemba	**Chile**	Santiago
Calabria (Italy)	Catanzaro	Chimborazo (Ecuador)	Riobamba
Caldas (Colombia)	Manizales	Chimbu (Papua New Guinea)	Kundiawa
California (USA)	Sacramento	Chin (Myanmar)	Hakha
Calvados (France)	Caen	**China**	Beijing (aka Peking)
Cambodia	Phnom Penh		
Cambridgeshire (Eng)	Cambridge	Chirang (Bhutan)	Damphu
Cameroon	Yaoundé	Chiriqui (Panama)	David
Campania (Italy)	Naples	Chobe (Botswana)	Kasane
Canada	Ottawa	Chocó (Colombia)	Quibdó
Cañar (Ecuador)	Azoques	Chŏlla-namdo (South Korea)	Kwangju
Canary Islands (Spain)	Santa Cruz de Tenerife	Chŏlla-pukto (South Korea)	Ch'ŏnju
		Christmas Island (Aus)	Flying Fish Cove
Canendiyú (Paraguay)	Salto del Guairá	Christmas Island/Kiritimati Atoll (Kiribati)	London
Cantabria (Spain)	Santander		
Cantagaio (São Tomé and Principe)	Santana	Chubut (Argentina)	Rawson
Cantal (France)	Aurillac	Chukut (Russia)	Anadyr
Canterbury (NZ)	Christchurch	Chuquisaca (Bolivia)	Sucre
Cape Verde	Praia	Chuvashia (Russia)	Cheboksary
Caprivi (Namibia)	Katima Mulilo	Ciskei (South Africa)	Bisho
Caquetá (Colombia)	Florencia	Citta (San Marino)	San Marino
Carabobo (Venezuela)	Valencia	Clare (Rep of Ireland)	Ennis
Caras-Severin (Romania)	Resita	Clarendon (Jamaica)	May Pen
Carchi (Ecuador)	Tulcan	Cleveland (Eng)	Middlesbrough
Carlow (Rep of Ireland)	Carlow	Clwyd (Wales)	Mold
Caroni (Trinidad and Tobago)	Chaguanas	Coahuila (Mexico)	Saltillo
Casanare (Colombia)	Yopal	Coast Province (Kenya)	Mombasa
Castilla-La Mancha (Spain)	Toledo	Coclé (Panama)	Penonomé
Castilla-León (Spain)	Valladolid	Cocos (aka Keeling Islands) (Aus)	West Island
Cat Island (Bahamas)	Arthur's Town	Cojedes (Venezuela)	San Carlos
Catalonia (Spain)	Barcelona	**Colombia**	Bogotá
Catamarca (Argentina)	San Fernando	Colón (Honduras)	Trujillo
Cauca (Colombia)	Popoyán	Colorado (USA)	Denver
Caué (São Tomé and Principe)	São João Angolares	Commewijne (Suriname)	Nieuw Amsterdam
Cavan (Rep of Ireland)	Cavan	Comoé (Burkina Faso)	Banfora
Cayman Islands	George Town	**Comoros Islands**	Moroni

GEOGRAPHY

Country, State, County or Area	Capital or Admin Centre	Country, State, County or Area	Capital or Admin Centre
Congo: Democratic Republic	Kinshasa	Drôme (France)	Valence
Congo: People's Republic	Brazzaville	Duarte (Dominican Republic)	San Francisco de
Connecticut (USA)	Hartford		Macoris
Cook Islands (New Zealand)	Ararua	Dublin (Rep of Ireland)	Dublin
Copperbelt (Zambia)	Ndola	Dumfries and Galloway (Scotland)	Dumfries
Coquimbo (Chile)	La Serena	Dundgovi (Mongolia)	Mandalgov
Cordillera (Paraguay)	Caacupé	Durham (Eng)	Durham
Córdoba (Colombia)	Montería	Dyfed (Wales)	Carmarthen
Corfu	Kerkira	Dzavhan (Mongolia)	Uliastay
Cork (Rep of Ireland)	Cork	East Berbice/Corentyne (Guyana)	New Amsterdam
Cornwall (Eng)	Truro	East Cape (NZ)	Gisborne
Coronie (Suriname)	Totness	East Flanders (Belgium)	Ghent
Corrèze (France)	Tulle	East New Britain (Papua	
Corse-du-Sud (France)	Ajaccio	New Guinea)	Rabaul
Corsica (France)	Ajaccio	East Sepik (Papua New Guinea)	Wewak
Cortés (Honduras)	San Pedro Sula	East Sussex (Eng)	Lewes
Costa Rica	San José	**East Timor**	Dili
Côte-d'Or (France)	Dijon	Easter Island	Hanga Roa
Côtes-du-Nord (France)	Saint-Brieuc	Eastern Equatoria (Sudan)	Jubã
Cotopaxi (Ecuador)	Latacunga	Eastern Highlands (Papua	
Covasna (Romania)	Sfintu Gheorghe	New Guinea)	Goroka
Crete	Khania	Eastern Nepal	Dhankutã
Creuse (France)	Guéret	Eastern Province (Fiji)	Levuka
Croatia	Zagreb	Eastern Province (Kenya)	Embu
Crooked Island (Bahamas)	Colonel Hill	Eastern Province (Sierra Leone)	Kenema
Cross River (Nigeria)	Calabar	Eastern Province (Zambia)	Chipata
Csongrád (Hungary)	Szeged	Eastern Region (Ghana)	Koforidua
Cuba	Havana	Eastern Timor (Pacific)	Dili
Cumbria (Eng)	Carlisle	**Ecuador**	Quito
Cundinamarca (Colombia)	Bogotá	Efaté (Vanuatu)	Vila
Cunene (Angola)	N'Giva	**Egypt**	Cairo
Curaçao (Netherland Antilles)	Willemstad	Ehime (Japan)	Matsuyama
Cuscatlán (El Salvador)	Cojutepeque	El Oro (Ecuador)	Machala
Cuvette (Congo)	Owando	El Paraiso (Honduras)	Yuscarán
Cuzco (Peru)	Cuzco	**El Salvador**	San Salvador
Cyprus	Nicosia	El-Acâba (Mauritania)	Kiffa
Czech Republic	Prague	Elba	Portoferraio
Dac Lac (Vietnam)	Buon Ma Thuot	Emilia-Romagna (Italy)	Bologna
Dadra and Nagar Haveli (India)	Silvassa	Enga (Papua New Guinea)	Wabag
Dagestan (Russia)	Makhachkala	**England**	London
Dãrfur (Sudan)	Al-Fâshir	Entre Rios (Argentina)	Paraná
Darién (Panama)	La Palma	Epi (Vanuatu)	Ringdove
Delaware (USA)	Dover	Equateur (Dem Rep of Congo)	Mbandaka
Demerara/Mahaica (Guyana)	Paradise	**Equatorial Guinea**	Malabo
Denmark	Copenhagen	**Eritrea**	Asmara
Derbyshire (Eng)	Matlock	Erongo (Namibia)	Swakopmund
Des Plateaux (Togo)	Atakpamé	Espaillat (Dom Republic)	Moca
Des Savanes (Togo)	Dapaong	Espirito Santo (Brazil)	Vitória
Deux-Sèvres (France)	Niort	Essequibo Islands (Guyana)	Vreed-en-Hoop
Devon (Eng)	Exeter	Essex (Eng)	Chelmsford
Dhaalu (Maldives)	Kudahuvadhoo	Essonne (France)	Évry
Dhi Qãr (Iraq)	An-Nãsiriyah	Est (Cameroon)	Bertoua
Dibër (Albania)	Peshkopi	**Estonia**	Tallinn
Dimashq (Syria)	Damascus	Estuaire (Gabon)	Libreville
Dimbovita (Romania)	Tirgoviste	**Ethiopia**	Addis Ababa
Djibouti	Djibouti	Eua (Tonga)	Ohonua
Dolj (Romania)	Craiova	Eure (France)	Évreux
Dominica	Roseau	Eure-et-Loire (France)	Chartres
Dominican Republic	Santo Domingo	Evenki (Russia)	Tura
Donegal (Rep of Ireland)	Lifford	Extremadura (Spain)	Mérida
Dong Nai (Vietnam)	Bien Hoa	Extrême-Nord (Cameroon)	Maroua
Dong Thap (Vietnam)	Sa Dec	Faafu (Maldives)	Magoodhoo
Dordogne (France)	Périgueux	**Faeroe Islands**	Thorshavn
Dornod (Mongolia)	Choybaisan	Falcón (Venezuela)	Coro
Dornogovi (Mongolia)	Saynshand	**Falkland Islands**	Stanley
Dorset (Eng)	Dorchester	Fanning/Tabuaeran (Kiribati)	Paelau
Doubs (France)	Besançon	Fãrs (Iran)	Shirãz
Doufelgou (Togo)	Niamtougou	Far-Western Nepal	Dipãyal
Down (NI)	Downpatrick	Fejér (Hungary)	Székesfehérvár
Drenthe (Netherlands)	Assen	Fermanagh (NI)	Enniskillen

Country, State, County or Area	Capital or Admin Centre	Country, State, County or Area	Capital or Admin Centre
Fife (Scotland)	Glenrothes	Granma (Cuba)	Bayamo
Fiji	Suva	Graubunden (Swiss canton)	Chur
Finistère (France)	Quimper	Greater Accra (Ghana)	Accra
Finland	Helsinki	Greater London (Eng)	London
Finnmark (Norway)	Vardø	Greater Manchester (Eng)	Manchester
Flevoland (Netherlands)	Lelystad	**Greece**	Athens
Flores (Uruguay)	Trinidad	**Greenland** (aka Kalaallit Nunaat)	Godthaab
Florida (USA)	Tallahassee		(aka Nuuk)
Fogo (Cape Verde)	São Filipe	**Grenada**	St George's
France	Paris	Gribingui-Economique (CA Rep)	Kaga-Bandoro
Francisco Morazán (Honduras)	Tegucigalpa	Guadalcanal (Solomon Isles)	Honiara
Frederiksborg (Denmark)	Hillerod	**Guadeloupe**	Basse-Terre
French Guiana	Cayenne	Guainia (Colombia)	Puerto Inirida
French Polynesia	Papeete	Guairá (Paraguay)	Villarica
Friesland (Netherlands)	Leeuwarden	**Guam**	Agana
Friuli-Venezia Giulia (Italy)	Trieste	Guanacaste (Costa Rica)	Liberia
Fujian (aka Fukien) (China)	Fuzhou (aka Foochow)	Guangdong (aka Kwangtung) (China)	Guangzhou (aka Canton)
Fyn (Denmark)	Odense	Guangxi Zhuang (aka Kwangsi Chuang) (China)	Nanning
Gaafu-Alifu (Maldives)	Vilgili		
Gaafu-Dhaalu (Maldives)	Thinadhoo	Guárico (Venezuela)	San Juan de Los Morros
Gabon	Libreville		
Galguduud (Somalia)	Dusa Marreb (Dhuusamarreeb)	**Guatemala**	Guatemala City
		Guayas (Ecuador)	Guayaquil
Galicia (Spain)	Santiago de Compostela	Guéra (Chad)	Mongo
		Guernsey	St Peter Port
Galway (Rep of Ireland)	Galway	Guerrero (Mexico)	Chilpancingo
Gambia	Banjul	Guidimaka (Mauritania)	Sélibaby
Gambier Islands (French Polynesia)	Rikitea	**Guinea**	Conakry
		Guinea-Bissau	Bissau
Gansu (aka Kansu) (China)	Lanzhou (aka Lan-chou)	Guizhou (aka Kweichow) (China)	Guiyang (aka Kuei-yang)
Ganzourgou (Burkina Faso)	Zorgho	Gujarāt (India)	Gāndhinagar
Gard (France)	Nîmes	Gulf (Papua New Guinea)	Kerema
Gaza (Mozambique)	Xai-Xai	Gulu (Uganda)	Bungatira
Gazankulu (South Africa)	Giyani	Gumma (Japan)	Maebashi
Gedo (Somalia)	Garbahaarrey	**Guyana**	Georgetown
Gelderland (Netherlands)	Arnhem	Gwent (Wales)	Cwmbran
Gemu Gofa (Ethiopia)	Arba Minch	Gwynedd (Wales)	Caernarfon
Georgia	Tbilisi	Ha Nan (Vietnam)	Phu Ly
Georgia (USA)	Atlanta	Ha Tay (Vietnam)	Ha Dong
Germany	Berlin	Haa-Alifu (Maldives)	Dhidhdhoo
Gers (France)	Auch	Haa-Dhaalu (Maldives)	Nolhivaranfaru
Ghana	Accra	Ha'apai (Tonga)	Pangai
Gia Lai (Vietnam)	Plei Ku	Hadramawt (Yemen)	Al-Mukallā
Gilān (Iran)	Rasht	Haho (Togo)	Notsé
Gilbert Isles (Kiribati)	Bairiki	Hainan (China)	Haikou
Gironde (Aquitaine, France)	Bordeaux	Hainaut (Belgium)	Mons
Gloucestershire (Eng)	Gloucester	**Haiti**	Port-au-Prince
Gnagna (Burkina Faso)	Bogandé	Hajdú-Bihar (Hungary)	Debrecen
Gnyaviyani (Maldives)	Foah Mulah	Halab (Syria)	Aleppo
Goa (India)	Panaji	Halland (Sweden)	Halmstad
Goiás (Brazil)	Goiânia	Häme (Finland)	Hämeenlinna
Gojam (Ethiopia)	Debre Markos	Hamgyong-namdo (North Korea)	Hamhung
Golfe (Togo)	Lomé	Hamgyong-pukto (North Korea)	Ch'ŏngjin
Gongola (Nigeria)	Yola	Hampshire (Eng)	Winchester
Gorgol (Mauritania)	Kaédi	Hanover (Jamaica)	Lucea
Gorj (Romania)	Tirgu Jiu	Hararge (Ethiopia)	Harer
Gotland (Sweden)	Visby	Hardap (Namibia)	Mariental
Gourma (Burkina Faso)	Fada N'Gourma	Harghita (Romania)	Miercurea-Ciuc
Gozo (Malta)	Victoria	Haryana (India)	Chandigarh
Gracias a Dios (Honduras)	Puerto Lempira	Hau Giang (Vietnam)	Can Tho
Grampian (Scotland)	Aberdeen	Haute-Corse (France)	Bastia
Gran Canaria	Las Palmas	Haute-Garonne (France)	Toulouse
Grand Bahama	Freeport	Haute-Kotto (CA Rep)	Bria
Grand Bassa (Liberia)	Buchanan	Haute-Loire (France)	Le Puy
Grand Cape Mount (Liberia)	Robertsport	Haute-Marne (France)	Chaumont
Grand Gedeh (Liberia)	Zwedru	Haute-Normandie (France)	Rouen
Grand Kru (Liberia)	Barclayville	Hautes-Alpes (France)	Gap
Grande Anse (Haiti)	Jérémie	Haute-Sangha (CA Rep)	Berbérati

GEOGRAPHY

Country, State, County or Area	Capital or Admin Centre	Country, State, County or Area	Capital or Admin Centre
Haute-Saône (France)	Vesoul	Independencia (Dominican Republic)	Jimani
Haute-Savoie (France)	Annecy	**India (aka Bharat)**	New Delhi
Hautes-Pyrénées (France)	Tarbes	**Indonesia**	Jakarta
Haute-Vienne (France)	Limoges	Indre (France)	Châteauroux
Haute-Zaïre (Dem Rep of Congo)	Kisangani	Indre-et-Loire (France)	Tours
Haut-Mbomou (CA Rep)	Obo	Ingushetia (Russia)	Nazran
Haut-Ogooué (Gabon)	Masuku	Inner Mongolia (aka Nei Monggol)	Hu-ho-hao-t'e (aka Hohhot)
Haut-Rhin (France)	Colmar		
Hauts-de-Seine (France)	Nanterre		
Hawaii (USA)	Honolulu	Intibucá (Honduras)	La Esperanza
Hawke's Bay (NZ)	Napier	Iowa (USA)	Des Moines
Hebei (China)	Shijazhuang	**Iran**	Tehran
Hedmark (Norway)	Hamar	**Iraq**	Baghdad
Heilongjiang (China)	Harbin	**Ireland, Republic of**	Dublin
Henan (China)	Zhengzhou	Irian Jaya (Indonesia)	Jayapura
Hentiy (Mongolia)	Öndörhaan	Isabel (Solomon Isles)	Buala
Hérault (France)	Montpellier	Isère (France)	Grenoble
Hercegovina	Mostar	Ishikawa (Japan)	Kanazawa
Hereford and Worcester (Eng)	Worcester	Islas de la Bahia (Honduras)	Roatán
Herrera (Panama)	Chitré	Isle of Man	Douglas
Hertfordshire (Eng)	Hertford	Isle of Wight	Newport
Hessen (Germany)	Wiesbaden	**Israel**	Jerusalem
Heves (Hungary)	Eger	**Italy**	Rome
Hhohho (Swaziland)	Mbabane	Itapúa (Paraguay)	Encarnación
Hidalgo (Mexico)	Pachuca	**Ivory Coast**	Yamoussoukro – admin
Highland (Scotland)	Inverness		
Hiiraan (Somalia)	Beledweyne		Abidjan – legislative
Himāchal Pradesh (India)	Shimla		
Hims (Syria)	Homs	Iwate (Japan)	Morioka
Hodh-ech-Chargui (Mauritania)	Néma	Izabal (Guatemala)	Puerto Barrios
Hodh-el-Gharbi (Mauritania)	Ayoûn el-Atroûs	Jakarta Raya (Indonesia)	Jakarta
Höfudhborgarsvaedhi (Iceland)	Reykjavik	Jalisco (Mexico)	Guadalajara
Hokkaidō (Japan)	Sapporo	**Jamaica**	Kingston
Honduras	Tegucigalpa	Jammu and Kashmir (India)	Srinagar (in summer)
Hong Kong (aka Hsiang Kang)	Victoria (on Hong Kong Isle)		
			Jammu (in winter)
Hordaland (Norway)	Bergen		
Horowhenua (NZ)	Levin	Jämtland (Sweden)	Östersund
Houaphan (Laos)	Xam Nua	**Japan**	Tokyo
Houet (Burkina Faso)	Bobo-Dioulasso	Jawar Barat (Indonesia)	Bandung
Hövsgöl (Mongolia)	Mörön	Jawar Tengah (Indonesia)	Semarang
Hubei (China)	Wuhan	Jawar Timur (Indonesia)	Surabaya
Huila (Colombia)	Neiva	Jersey	St Helier
Huita (Angola)	Lubango	Jiangsu (aka Kiangsu) (China)	Nanjing (aka Nanking)
Humberside (Eng)	Beverley		
Hunan (China)	Changsha	Jiangxi (aka Kiangsi) (China)	Nanchang
Hunedoara (Romania)	Deva	Jilin (aka Kirin) (China)	Changchun
Hungary	Budapest	Johor (Malaysia)	Johor Baharu
Hwanghae-namdo (North Korea)	Haeju	**Jordan**	Amman
Hwanghae-pukto (North Korea)	Sariwön	Jubbada Dhexe (Somalia)	Bu'aale
Hyōgo (Japan)	Kōbe	Jubbada Hoose (Somalia)	Chisimayu (Kismaayo)
Ialomita (Romania)	Siobozia		
Ibaraki (Japan)	Mito	Jujuy (Argentina)	San Salvador
Iceland	Reykjavik	Junin (Peru)	Huancayo
Idaho (USA)	Boise	Junquli (Jongley) (Sudan)	Bor
Iganga (Uganda)	Bulamogi	Jura (France)	Lons-le-Saunier
Île-de-France (France)	Paris	Jura (Swiss canton)	Delémont
Îles Australes (French Polynesia)	Mataura	Kaafu (Maldives)	Male
Îles du Vent (French Polynesia)	Papeete	Kabale (Uganda)	Rubale
Îles Marquises (French Polynesia)	Taiohae	Kabardino-Balkaria (Russia)	Nalchik
Îles sous le Vent (French Polynesia)	Uturoa	Kabarole (Uganda)	Karambe
Îles Tuamotu et Gambier (French Polynesia)	Papeete	Kachin (Myanmar)	Myitkyinā
		Kadiogo (Burkina Faso)	Ouagadougou
Ille-et-Vilaine (France)	Rennes	Kagawa (Japan)	Takamatsu
Illinois (USA)	Springfield	Kalimantan Barat (Indonesia)	Pontianak
Ilubabor (Ethiopia)	Metu	Kalimantan Selatan (Indonesia)	Banjarmasin
Imbabura (Ecuador)	Ibarra	Kalimantan Tengah (Indonesia)	Palangkaraya
Imo (Nigeria)	Owerri	Kalmuck (Russia)	Elista
Inagua, Great and Little	Matthew Town	Kamuli (Uganda)	Namendwa
Inchiri (Mauritania)	Akjoujt	Kanagawa (Japan)	Yokohama

Country, State, County or Area	Capital or Admin Centre	Country, State, County or Area	Capital or Admin Centre
Kanem (Chad)	Mao	KwaZulu (South Africa)	Ulundi
KaNgwane (South Africa)	Louieville	Kweneng (Botswana)	Molepolole
Kangwŏn-do (North Korea)	Wŏnson	Kymi (Finland)	Kouvola
Kangwŏn-do (South Korea)	Ch'unch'ŏn	Kyŏnggi-do (South Korea)	Suwŏn
Kansas (USA)	Topeka	Kyŏngsang-namdo (South Korea)	Masan
Kao-hsiung (Taiwan)	Feng-shan	Kyŏngsang-pukto (South Korea)	Taegu
Kapchorwa (Uganda)	Rukoki	**Kyrgyzstan**	Bishkek
Karachai-Cherkessia (Russia)	Cherkesst	La Altagracia (Dominican Republic)	Higüey
Kara-Kalpak (Russia)	Nukus	La Estrelleta (Dominican Republic)	Elias Piña
Karas (Namibia)	Keetmanshoop	La Guajira (Colombia)	Riohacha
Karelian (Russia)	Petrozavodsk	La Habana (Cuba)	Havana
Karen (Myanmar)	Pa-an	La Libertad (El Salvador)	Nueva San
Karnataka (India)	Bangalore		Salvador
Kärnten (Austria)	Klagenfurt	La Libertad (Peru)	Trujillo
Kasai-Occidental (Dem Rep of Congo)	Kananga	La Pampa (Argentina)	Santa Rosa
		La Paz (El Salvador)	Zacatecoluca
Kasai-Oriental (Dem Rep of Congo)	Mbuji-Mayi	La Rioja (Spain)	Logrono
		Laamu (Maldives)	Hithadhoo
Kayah (Myanmar)	Loi-kaw	Lac (Chad)	Bol
Kazakhstan	Astana	Lacs (Togo)	Aného
Kedah (Malaysia)	Alor Setar	Lagos (Nigeria)	Lkeja
Kefa (Ethiopia)	Jima	Lai Chau (Vietnam)	Dien Bien
Kelantan (Malaysia)	Kota Bharu	Lakshadweep Islands (India)	Kavaratti Island
Kemo-Gribingui (CA Rep)	Sibut	Lam Dong (Vietnam)	Da Lat
Kénédougou (Burkina Faso)	Orodara	Lambayeque (Peru)	Chiclayo
Kent (Eng)	Maidstone	Lampung (Indonesia)	Tanjung Karang
Kentucky (USA)	Frankfort	Lancashire (Eng)	Preston
Kenya	Nairobi	Landes (France)	Mont-de-Marsan
Kerala (India)	Trivandrum	Languedoc-Roussillon (France)	Montpellier
Kéran (Togo)	Kandé	Laois/Leix (Rep of Ireland)	Portlaoise
Kerry (Rep of Ireland)	Tralee	**Laos**	Vientiane
Keski-Suomi (Finland)	Jyväskylä	Lappi (Finland)	Rovaniemi
Kgalagadi (Botswana)	Tsabong	Lara (Venezuela)	Barquisimeto
Kgatleng (Botswana)	Mochudi	**Latvia**	Riga
Khakassia (Russia)	Abakan	Lavalleja (Uruguay)	Minas
Khammouan (Laos)	Thakhek	Lazio (Italy)	Rome
Khanh Hoa (Vietnam)	Nha Trang	**Lebanon**	Beirut
Khanty-Mansi (Russia)	Khanty-Mansüsk	Lebowa (South Africa)	Lebowakgomo
Khomas (Namibia)	Windhoek	Leicestershire (Eng)	Leicester
Kien Giang (Vietnam)	Rach Gia	Leitrim (Rep of Ireland)	Carrick-on-
Kildare (Rep of Ireland)	Naas		Shannon
Kilimanjaro (Tanzania)	Moshi	Lékoumou (Congo)	Sibiti
Kilkenny (Rep of Ireland)	Kilkenny	Lemba (São Tomé and Principe)	Neves
Kiribati	Bairiki on Tarawa Island	Lempira (Honduras)	Gracias
		Leribe (Lesotho)	Hiotse
Kitgum (Uganda)	Labongo	**Lesotho**	Maseru
Kloto (Togo)	Kpalimé	Lhaviyani (Maldives)	Naifaru
Koinaduga (Sierra Leone)	Kabala	Liaoning (China)	Shenyang
Kolonjë (Albania)	Ersekë	**Liberia**	Monrovia
Komárom (Hungary)	Tatabánya	Libertador Gen Bernardo O'Higgins (Chile)	Rancagua
Kombo St Mary (Gambia)	Kanifing		
Komi (Russia)	Syktyv-Kar	**Libya**	Tripoli
Komy Permyak (Russia)	Kudymkar	**Liechtenstein**	Vaduz
Kono (Sierra Leone)	Sefadu	Liguria (Italy)	Genoa
Kopparberg (Sweden)	Falun	Likouala (Congo)	Impfondo
Koryak (Russia)	Palana	Limburg (Belgium)	Hasselt
Kosovo (Yugoslavia)	Pristina	Limburg (Netherlands)	Maastricht
Kossi (Burkina Fasso)	Nouna	Limerick (Rep of Ireland)	Limerick
Kouilou (Congo)	Pointe-Noire	Limousin (France)	Limoges
Kouritenga (Burkina Faso)	Koupéla	Lincolnshire (Eng)	Lincoln
Kozah (Togo)	Kara	Line Isles (Kiribati)	Kiritimati
Kronoberg (Sweden)	Växjö	**Lithuania**	Vilnius
Kuando Kubango (Angola)	Menongue	Littoral (Cameroon)	Douala
Kuanza Norte (Angola)	N'Dalatando	Lobata (São Tomé and Principe)	Guadalupe
Kuanza Sul (Angola)	Sumbe	Lobaye (CA Rep)	Mbaiki
Kunene (Namibia)	Opuwo	Lofa (Liberia)	Voinjama
Kuria (Kiribati)	Tabontebike	Logone Occidental (Chad)	Moundou
Kuwait	Kuwait	Logone Oriental (Chad)	Doba
KwaNdebele (South Africa)	Siyabuswa	Loire (France)	Saint-Etienne
Kwara (Nigeria)	Llorin	Loire-Atlantique (France)	Nantes

GEOGRAPHY

Country, State, County or Area	Capital or Admin Centre	Country, State, County or Area	Capital or Admin Centre
Loiret (France)	Orléans	Margibi (Liberia)	Kakata
Loir-et-Cher (France)	Blois	Maria Trinidad Sánchez	
Lombardy (Italy)	Milan	(Dominican Republic)	Nagua
Londonderry (NI)	Londonderry	Mari-El (Russia)	Yoshkar-Ola
Long An (Vietnam)	Tan An	Maritime Region (Togo)	Lomé
Long Island (Bahamas)	Clarence Town	Markazi (Iran)	Arāk
Longford (Rep of Ireland)	Longford	Marlborough (NZ)	Blenheim
Loreto (Peru)	Iquitos	Marne (France)	Châlons-sur-
Lorraine (France)	Metz		Marne
Los Lagos (Chile)	Puerto Montt	Marowijne (Suriname)	Albina
Los Rios (Ecuador)	Babahoyo	**Marshall Islands**	Dalap-Uliga-Darrit
Los Santos (Panama)	Las Tablas	Martinique (France)	Fort-de-France
Lot (France)	Cahors	Maryland (Liberia)	Harper
Lot-et-Garonne (France)	Agen	Maryland (USA)	Annapolis
Lothian (Scotland)	Edinburgh	Masaka (Uganda)	Kaswa Bukoto
Louisiana (USA)	Baton Rouge	Mashonaland Central (Zimbabwe)	Bindura
Louth (Rep of Ireland)	Dundalk	Mashonaland East (Zimbabwe)	Marondera
Lower River (Gambia)	Mansakonko	Mashonaland West (Zimbabwe)	Chinhoyi
Lower Saxony (Germany)	Hanover	Masindi (Uganda)	Nyangeya
Lozère (France)	Mende	Massachusetts (USA)	Boston
Luapula (Zambia)	Mansa	Mat (Albania)	Burrel
Lubombo (Swaziland)	Siteki	Matabeleland North (Zimbabwe)	Bulawayo
Lunda Norte (Angola)	Lucapa	Matabeleland South (Zimbabwe)	Gwanda
Lunda Sol (Angola)	Saurimo	Mato Grosso (Brazil)	Cuiabá
Luxembourg	Luxembourg	Mato Grosso do Sul (Brazil)	Campo Grande
Luxembourg (Belgium)	Arlon	Matruh (Egypt)	Marsā Matruh
Macao (Portugal)	Macao	Maule (Chile)	Talca
MacCarthy Island (Gambia)	Kuntaur/	**Mauritania**	Nouakchott
	Georgetown	**Mauritius**	Port Louis
Macedonia	Skopje	Mayaguana (Bahamas)	Abraham's Bay
Macedonia (Greece)	Thessaloniki	Mayenne (France)	Laval
Madagascar	Antananarivo	Mayo (Rep of Ireland)	Castlebar
Madeira (Portugal)	Funchal	Mayo-Kebbi (Chad)	Bongor
Madhya Pradesh (India)	Bhopal	Mayotte (France)	Mamoudzou
Madre de Dios (Peru)	Puerto	Maysān (Iraq)	Al-Amārah
	Maldonado	Māzandarān (Iran)	Sari
Magallanes y de la Antártica	Punta Arenas	Mbale (Uganda)	Bunkoko
Chilena (Chile)		Mbarara (Uganda)	Kakika
Magdalena (Colombia)	Santander	Mbomou (CA Rep)	Bangassou
Mahaica/Berbice (Guyana)	Fort Wellington	Meath (Rep of Ireland)	Trim
Maharashtra (India)	Bombay	Mecklenburg-West Pomerania	Schwerin
Mahé (Seychelles)	Victoria	(Germany)	
Maiana (Kiribati)	Tebangetua	Meemu (Maldives)	Muli
Maine (USA)	Augusta	Meghālaya (India)	Shillong
Maine-et Loire (France)	Angers	Mehedinti (Romania)	Drobeta-Turnu-
Maio (Cape Verde)	Porto Inglês		Severin
Makira (Solomon Isles)	Kira Kira	Melaka (Malaysia)	Melaka
Malaita (Solomon Isles)	Auki	Merseyside (Eng)	Liverpool
Malawi	Lilongwe	Meta (Colombia)	Villavicencio
Malaysia	Kuala Lumpur	Metropolitan (Chile)	Santiago
Maldives	Malé	Meurthe-et-Moselle (France)	Nancy
Malekula (Vanuatu)	Lakatoro	Meuse (France)	Bar-le-Duc
Mali	Bamako	**Mexico**	Mexico City
Malta	Valletta	México (Mexican state)	Toluca
Maluku (Indonesia)	Ambon	Mé-zóchi (São Tomé	
Manabi (Ecuador)	Portoviejo	and Principe)	Trinidade
Manawatu (NZ)	Palmerston North	Michigan (USA)	Lansing
Manche (France)	Saint-Lô	Michoacán (Mexico)	Morelia
Manchester (Jamaica)	Mandeville	**Micronesia**	Kolonia/Palikir
Manica (Mozambique)	Chimolo	Mid-Glamorgan (Wales)	Cardiff
Manicaland (Zimbabwe)	Mutare	Midi-Pyrénées (France)	Toulouse
Maniema (Dem Rep of Congo)	Kindu	Midland Province (Zimbabwe)	Gweru
Manipur (India)	Imphāl	Mid-Western Nepal	Surkhet
Manitoba (Canada)	Winnipeg	Mie (Japan)	Tsu
Manus (Papua New Guinea)	Lorengau	Milne Bay (Papua New Guinea)	Samarai
Mara (Tanzania)	Musoma	Minas Gerais (Brazil)	Belo Horizonte
Marakei (Kiribati)	Rawannawi	Minnesota (USA)	St Paul
Maramures (Romania)	Baia Mare	Minorca (Spain)	Mahon
Maranhão (Brazil)	São Luis	Miranda (Venezuela)	Los Teques
Marche (Italy)	Ancona	Mirditë (Albania)	Rrëshen

Country, State, County or Area	Capital or Admin Centre	Country, State, County or Area	Capital or Admin Centre
Misiones (Argentina)	Posadas	Nevada (USA)	Carson City
Misiones (Paraguay)	San Juan Bautista	Nevis (St Kitts and Nevis)	Charlestown
		New Brunswick (Canada)	Fredericton
Mississippi (USA)	Jackson	New Caledonia (France)	Nouméa
Missouri (USA)	Jefferson City	New Hampshire (USA)	Concorde
Miyagi (Japan)	Sendai	New Ireland (Papua New Guinea)	Kavieng
Mizorãm (India)	Āïzawi	New Jersey (USA)	Trenton
Moili (Comoros)	Fomboni	New Mexico (USA)	Santa Fe
Moldova	Chisinau	New Providence (Bahamas)	Nassau
Moluccas (Indonesia)	Amboina	New South Wales	Sydney
Mon (Myanmar)	Moulmein	New York (USA)	Albany
Monaco	Monaco-Ville	**New Zealand**	Wellington
Monagas (Venezuela)	Maturin	Newfoundland (Canada)	St Johns
Monaghan (Rep of Ireland)	Monaghan	Ngamiland (Botswana)	Maun
Mongolia	Ulan Bator	Ngazidja (Comoros)	Moroni
Mono (Benin)	Lokossa	Nghe Tinh (Vietnam)	Vinh
Monseñor Nouel (Dominican Republic)	Bonao	Ngounié (Gabon)	Mouila
		Ngwaketse (Botswana)	Kanye
Montana (USA)	Helena	Niari (Congo)	Loubomo
Montenegro	Podgorica	Niassa (Mozambique)	Lichinga
Montserrado (Liberia)	Bensonville	**Nicaragua**	Managua
Montserrat	Plymouth	Nickerie (Suriname)	Nieuw Nickerie
Morazán (El Salvador)	San Francisco (Gotera)	Nicobar Islands (India)	Car Nicobar
		Nidwalden (Swiss canton)	Stans
Morbihan (France)	Vannes	Niederösterreich (Austria)	Sankt Pölten
Mordovia (Russia)	Saransk	Nièvre (France)	Nevers
Møre og Romsdal (Norway)	Molde	**Niger**	Niamey
Morelos (Mexico)	Cuernavaca	Niger (Nigeria)	Minna
Morobe (Papua New Guinea)	Lae	**Nigeria**	Abuja
Morocco	Rabat	Nikunau (Kiribati)	Rungata
Morona-Santiago (Ecuador)	Macas	Nimba (Liberia)	Sanniquellie
Moroto (Uganda)	Katikekile	Ninawã (Iraq)	Mosul
Moselle (France)	Metz	Ningxia Hui (China)	Yinchuan
Mouhoun (Burkina Faso)	Dédougou	Ninh Thuan (Vietnam)	Phan Rang
Moxico (Angola)	Lwena	Niuas (Tonga)	Hihifo
Moyen-Chari (Chad)	Sarh	Niue (New Zealand)	Alofi
Moyen-Ogooué (Gabon)	Lambaréné	Nógrád (Hungary)	Salgótarján
Mozambique	Maputo	Nonouti (Kiribati)	Teuabu
Mubende (Uganda)	Bageza	Noonu (Maldives)	Manadhoo
Mudug (Somalia)	Galcaio (Gaalkacyo)	Noord-Brabant (Netherlands)	s-Hertogenbosch
		Noord-Holland (Netherlands)	Haarlem
Mures (Romania)	Tirgu Mures	Nord (Cameroon)	Garoua
Musandam (Oman)	Khasab	Nord (France)	Lille
Myanmar (formerly Burma)	Yangon (Rangoon)	Nord (Haiti)	Cap-Haitien
		Nord-Est (Haiti)	Fort-Liberté
Nãgãland (India)	Kohima	Nordhurland eystra (Iceland)	Akureyri
Nahouri (Burkina Faso)	Pô	Nordhurland vestra (Iceland)	Saudhárkrókur
Namentenga (Burkina Faso)	Boulsa	Nordjylland (Denmark)	Alborg
Namibia	Windhoek	Nord-Kivu (Dem Rep of Congo)	Goma
Nana-Mambere (CA Rep)	Bouar	Nordland (Norway)	Bode
Napo (Ecuador)	Tena	Nord-Ouest (Cameroon)	Bamenda
Nariño (Colombia)	Pasto	Nord-Ouest (Haiti)	Port-de-Paix
Nariva/Mayaro (Trinidad and Tobago)	Rio Claro	Nord-Pas-de-Calais (France)	Lille
		Nord-Trønelag (Norway)	Steinkjer
Natal (South Africa)	Pietermaritsburg	Norfolk (Eng)	Norwich
National Capital District (Papua New Guinea)	Port Moresby	Norfolk Island (Aus)	Kingston
		Norrbotten (Sweden)	Luleá
Nauru	Yaren	Norte de Santander (Colombia)	Cúcuta
Navarre (Spain)	Pamplona	North Bank (Gambia)	Kerewan
Nayarit (Mexico)	Tepic	North Carolina (USA)	Raleigh
Ndzouani (Comoros)	Mutsamudu	North Dakota (USA)	Bismarck
Neamt (Romania)	Piatra Neamt	North Eastern Province (Kenya)	Garissa
Nebraska (USA)	Lincoln	**North Korea (aka Choson)**	Pyongyang
Ñeembucu (Paraguay)	Pilar	North Otago (NZ)	Dunedin
Negeri Sembilan (Malaysia)	Seremban	North Rhine–Westphalia (Germany)	Düsseldorf
Nelson Bays (NZ)	Nelson		
Nenets (Russia)	Naryan-Mar	North Solomons (Papua New Guinea)	Buka
Nepal	Kãthmãndu	North West Frontier (Pakistan)	Peshãwar
Netherlands Antilles	Willemstad	North Yorkshire (Eng)	Northallerton
Netherlands	Amsterdam		

Country, State, County or Area	Capital or Admin Centre	Country, State, County or Area	Capital or Admin Centre
Northamptonshire (Eng)	Northampton	Oudomxay (Laos)	Xay
Northern District (Israel)	Tiberias	Ouémé (Benin)	Porto-Novo
Northern Ireland	Belfast	Ouest (Cameroon)	Bafoussam
Northern Mariana Islands (USA)	Chalan Kanoa	Ouest (Haiti)	Port-au-Prince
Northern Province (Fiji)	Labasa	Ouham (CA Rep)	Bossangoa
Northern Province (Papua New Guinea)	Popondetta	Ouham-Pendé (CA Rep)	Bozoum
		Overijssel (Netherlands)	Zwolle
Northern Province (Sierra Leone)	Makeni	Övörhangay (Mongolia)	Arvayheer
Northern Province (Zambia)	Kasama	Oxfordshire (Eng)	Oxford
Northern Region (Ghana)	Tamale	Oyo (Nigeria)	Ibadan
Northern Territory (Aus)	Darwin	Paama (Vanuatu)	Liro
Northland (NZ)	Whangarei	Paguê (São Tomé and Principe)	Principe
Northumberland (Eng)	Morpeth	**Pakistan**	Islamabad
Northwest Territories (Canada)	Yellowknife	**Palau**	Koror Island
North-Western Province (Zambia)	Solwezi	**Panama**	Panama City
Norway	Oslo	Panama Canal Zone	Balboa Heights
Nottinghamshire (Eng)	Nottingham	Pando (Bolivia)	Cobija
Nova Scotia (Canada)	Halifax	**Papua New Guinea**	Port Moresby
Nueva Asunción (Paraguay)	General Eugenio A. Garay	Pará (Brazil)	Belém
		Para (Suriname)	Onverwacht
Nueva Esparta (Venezuela)	La Asunción	**Paraguay**	Asunción
Nuevo León (Mexico)	Monterrey	Paraíba (Brazil)	João Pessoa
Nugaal (Somalia)	Garoowe	Paraná (Brazil)	Curitiba
Nunavut (Canada)	Iqaluit	Pas-de-Calais (France)	Arras
Nusa Tenggara Barat (Indonesia)	Mataram	Passoré (Burkina Faso)	Yako
Nusa Tenggara Timur (Indonesia)	Kupang	Pastaza (Ecuador)	Puyo
Nyanga (Gabon)	Tchibanga	Paúl (Cape Verde)	Pombas
Nyanza (Kenya)	Kisumu	Pays de la Loire (France)	Nantes
Oberösterreich (Austria)	Linz	Pemba North (Tanzania)	Wete
Obwalden (Swiss canton)	Sarnen	Pemba South (Tanzania)	Chake Chake
Offaly (Rep of Ireland)	Tullamore	Penang/Pinang (Malaysia)	George Town
Ogooué-Ivindo (Gabon)	Makokou	P'eng-hu (Taiwan)	Ma-kung
Ogooué-Lolo (Gabon)	Koulamoutou	Pennsylvania (USA)	Harrisburg
Ogooué-Maritime (Gabon)	Port-Gentil	Pentecost (Vanuatu)	Loltong
Ogou (Togo)	Atakpamé	Peravia (Dominican Republic)	Bani
Ogun (Nigeria)	Abeokuta	Pernambuco (Brazil)	Recife
Ohangwena (Namibia)	Oshikango	**Peru**	Lima
Ohio (USA)	Columbus	Pest (Hungary)	Budapest
Oio (Guinea-Bissau)	Farim	Petén (Guatemala)	Ciudad Flores
Oise (France)	Beauvais	**Philippines**	Manila
Okavango (Namibia)	Rundu	Phoenix Isles (Kiribati)	Kanton
Okinawa (Japan)	Naha City	Phu Khanh (Vietnam)	Nha Trang
Oklahoma (USA)	Oklahoma City	Phu Tho (Vietnam)	Viet Tri
Olancho (Honduras)	Juticalpa	Phu Yen (Vietnam)	Tuy Hoa
Olt (Romania)	Slatina	Piauí (Brazil)	Teresina
Omaheke (Namibia)	Gobabis	Picardie (France)	Amiens
Oman	Muscat	Pichincha (Ecuador)	Quito
Ombella-Mpoko (CA Rep)	Bimbo	Piedmont (Italy)	Turin
Ömnögovi (Mongolia)	Dalandzadgad	Pitcairn Islands	Adamstown
Omusati (Namibia)	Outapi	Plateau (Nigeria)	Jos
Ondo (Nigeria)	Akure	Plateaux (Congo)	Djambala
Onotoa (Kiribati)	Buariki	Pohjois-Karjala (Finland)	Joensuu
Ontario (Canada)	Toronto	Poitou-Charentes (France)	Poitiers
Oppland (Norway)	Lillehammer	**Poland**	Warsaw
Orange Free State (South Africa)	Bloemfontein	Pomeroon/Supenaam (Guyana)	Anna Regina
Oregon (USA)	Salem	Poni (Burkina Faso)	Gaoua
Orissa (India)	Bhubaneswar	Pool (Congo)	Kinkala
Orkney Islands	Kirkwall	Portland (Jamaica)	Port Antonio
Orne (France)	Alen	**Portugal**	Lisbon
Oshana (Namibia)	Oshakati	Portuguesa (Venezuela)	Guanare
Oshikoto (Namibia)	Tsumeb	Powys (Wales)	Llandrindod Wells
Ossetia	Vladikavkaz	Prahova (Romania)	Ploiesti
Östergötland (Sweden)	Linköping	President Hayes (Paraguay)	Pozo Colorado
Østfold (Norway)	Moss	Prince Edward Island (Canada)	Charlottetown
Oti (Togo)	Sansanné-Mango	Principe (São Tomé and Principe)	São António
Otjozondjupa (Namibia)	Grootfontein	Provence-Alpes-Côte d'Azur	Marseille
Ouaddai (Chad)	Abéché	**Puerto Rico (USA)**	San Juan
Ouaka (CA Rep)	Bambari	Puglia (Italy)	Bari
Oubritenga (Burkina Faso)	Ziniaré	Punjab (India)	Chandigarh
Oudalan (Burkina Faso)	Gorom Gorom	Punjab (Pakistan)	Lahore

Country, State, County or Area	Capital or Admin Centre
Putumayo (Colombia)	Mocoa
Puy-de-Dôme (France)	Clermont-Ferrand
Pwani (Tanzania)	Dar es Salaam
P'yongan-namdo (North Korea)	P'yŏngsan
P'yongan-pukto (North Korea)	Sinujiu
Pyrénées-Atlantiques (France)	Pau
Pyrénées-Orientales (France)	Perpignan
Qatar	Doha
Qinghai (aka Tsinghai) (China)	Xining (aka Hsi-ning)
Quang Binh (Vietnam)	Dong Hoi
Quang Nam (Vietnam)	Hoi An
Quang Nam-Hoi An (Vietnam)	Ha Long City
Quang Ninh (Vietnam)	Ha Long City
Quang Tri (Vietnam)	Dong Ha
Quebec (Canada)	Quebec
Queensland (Aus)	Brisbane
Quiché (Guatemala)	Santa Cruz
Quinara (Guinea-Bissau)	Fulacunda
Quindio (Colombia)	Armenia
Quintana Roo (Mexico)	Chetumal
Qwaqwa (South Africa)	Phuthaditjhaba
Raa (Maldives)	Ugoofaaru
Ragged Island (Bahamas)	Duncan Town
Raiatea (French Polynesia)	Uturoa
Rajasthan (India)	Jaipur
Rakai (Uganda)	Byakabanda
Región Autónoma del Atlántico Norte (Nicaragua)	Rosita
Región Autónoma del Atlántico Sur (Nicaragua)	Bluefields
Región I (Nicaragua)	Esteli
Región II (Nicaragua)	León
Región III (Nicaragua)	Managua
Región IV (Nicaragua)	Jinotepe
Región V (Nicaragua)	Juigalpa
Región VI (Nicaragua)	Matagalpa
Réunion (France)	Saint-Denis
Rhineland Palatinate (Germany)	Mainz
Rhode Island (USA)	Providence
Rhodes (Greece)	Rhodes
Rhône (France)	Lyon
Rhône-Alpes (France)	Lyon
Riau (Indonesia)	Pakanbaru
Ribeira Grande (Cape Verde)	Ponta do Sol
Rift Valley (Kenya)	Nakuru
Rio Grande do Norte (Brazil)	Natal
Rio Grande do Sul (Brazil)	Pôrto Alegre
Rio Muni (Equatorial Guinea)	Bata
Rio Negro (Argentina)	Viedma
Rio Negro (Uruguay)	Fray Bentos
Risaraldo (Colombia)	Pereira
Rivercess (Liberia)	Rivercess City
Rivers (Nigeria)	Port-Harcourt
Rogaland (Norway)	Stavanger
Romania	Bucharest
Rondônia (Brazil)	Pôrto Velho
Roraima (Brazil)	Boa Vista
Roscommon (Rep of Ireland)	Roscommon
Rukungiri (Uganda)	Kagunga
Rukwa (Tanzania)	Sumbawanga
Russia	Moscow
Ruvuma (Tanzania)	Songea
Rwanda	Kigali
Ryukyu Islands (Japan)	Naha City (on Okinawa)
Saarland (Germany)	Saarbrücken
Saba (Netherland Antilles)	The Bottom
Sabah (Malaysia)	Kota Kinabalu

Country, State, County or Area	Capital or Admin Centre
Sacatepéquez (Guatemala)	Antigua Guatemala
St Andrew and St David (Trinidad and Tobago)	Sangre Grande
St Catherine (Jamaica)	Spanish Town
St Croix (US Virgins)	Christiansted
St Elizabeth (Jamaica)	Black River
St Eustatius (Netherland Antilles)	Oranjestad
St Helena	Jamestown
St James (Jamaica)	Montego Bay
St Kitts (St Kitts and Nevis)	Basseterre
St Kitts and Nevis	Basseterre
St Lucia	Castries
St Maarten (Netherland Antilles)	Philipsburg
St Martin and St Barthélemy (Guadeloupe)	Marigot
St Mary (Jamaica)	Port Maria
St Patrick (Trinidad and Tobago)	Siparia
St Thomas (Jamaica)	Morant Bay
St Thomas and St John (US Virgins)	Charlotte Amalie
St Vincent and Grenadines	Kingstown
St-Pierre and Miquelon (France)	St-Pierre
Saipan	Chalan Kanoa
Saitama (Japan)	Urawa
Sakha (Russia)	Yakutsk
Sakhalin Island	Yuzhno-Sakhalinsk
Sal (Cape Verde)	Santa Maria
Salaj (Romania)	Zalău
Salamat (Chad)	Am Timan
San Andrés y Providencia	San Andrés
San Marino (Most Serene Republic)	San Marino
San Martín (Peru)	Moyobamba
San Salvador and Rum Cay (Bahamas)	Cockburn Town
Sanaag (Somalia)	Erigavo (Ceerigaabo)
Sánchez Ramirez (Dominican Republic)	Cotui
Sangha (Congo)	Ouesso
Sangha-Économique (CA Rep)	Nola
Sanguie (Burkina Faso)	Réo
Sanmatenga (Burkina Faso)	Kaya
Santa Catarina (Brazil)	Florianópolis
Santa Catarina (Cape Verde)	Assomada
Santa Cruz (Argentina)	Rio Gallegos
Santa Cruz (Cape Verde)	Pedra Badejo
Santa Rosa (Guatemala)	Cuilapa
Santander (Colombia)	Bucaramanga
Santiago (Dominican Republic)	Santiago de los Caballeros
Santo/Maio (Vanuatu)	Luganville
São Nicolau (Cape Verde)	Ribeira Brava
São Tomé and Príncipe	São Tomé
São Vicente (Cape Verde)	Mindelo
Saône-et-Loire (France)	Mâcon
Saramacca (Suriname)	Groningen
Sarawak (Malaysia)	Kuching
Sardinia (Italy)	Cagliari
Sarthe (France)	Le Mans
Saskatchewan (Canada)	Regina
Saudi Arabia	Riyadh
Savoie (France)	Chambéry
Saxony (Germany)	Dresden
Saxony-Anhalt (Germany)	Magdeburg
Schleswig-Holstein (Germany)	Kiel
Scilly Isles	Hugh Town
Scotland	Edinburgh

GEOGRAPHY

Country, State, County or Area	Capital or Admin Centre	Country, State, County or Area	Capital or Admin Centre
Seenu (Maldives)	Hithadoo	South Georgia and the South Sandwich Islands	King Edward Point
Seine-et-Marne (France)	Melun		
Seine-Maritime (France)	Rouen	South Glamorgan (Wales)	Cardiff
Seine-Saint-Denis (France)	Bobigny	**South Korea**	Seoul
Selenge (Mongolia)	Sühbaatar	South Ossetia	Tskhinvali
Senegal	Dakar	South Yorkshire (Eng)	Barnsley
Sèno (Burkina Faso)	Dori	Southern District (Israel)	Beersheba
Serbia	Belgrade	Southern Highlands (Papua New Guinea)	Mende
Sergipe (Brazil)	Aracaju		
Seychelles	Victoria	Southern Province (Sierra Leone)	Bo
Shaanxi (aka Shensi)	Xi'an (aka Sian)	Southern Province (Zambia)	Livingstone
Shaba (Dem Rep of Congo)	Lubumbashi	Southland (NZ)	Invercargill
Shabeellaha Dhexe (Somalia)	Giohar (Jawhar)	**Spain**	Madrid
Shabeellaha Hoose (Somalia)	Merca (Marka)	**Sri Lanka**	Colombo
Shabwah (Yemen)	Atãq	Staffordshire (Eng)	Stafford
Shan (Myanmar)	Taunggyi	Stann Creek (Belize)	Dangriga
Shandong (aka Shantung) (China)	Jinan (aka Tsinan)	Steiermark (Austria)	Graz
Shanxi (China)	Taiyuan	Storstrom (Denmark)	Nykebing
Shaviyani (Maldives)	Farukolhu	Strathclyde (Scotland)	Glasgow
	Funadhoo	Suchitepéquez (Guatemala)	Mazatenango
Shepherd (Vanuatu)	Morua	Sucre (Colombia)	Sincelejo
Shetland Islands	Lerwick	Sucre (Venezuela)	Cumaná
Shewa (Ethiopia)	Addis Ababa	Sud (Cameroon)	Ebolowa
Shiga (Japan)	Ōtsu	Sud (Haiti)	Les Cayes
Shimane (Japan)	Matsue	**Sudan**	Khartoum
Shiselweni (Swaziland)	Nhlangano	Sud-Est (Haiti)	Jacmel
Shropshire (Eng)	Shrewsbury	Sudhurland (Iceland)	Selfoss
Sichuan (China)	Chengdu	Sudhurnes (Iceland)	Keflavik
Sicily (Italy)	Palermo	Sud-Kivu (Dem Rep of Congo)	Bukavu
Sidamo (Ethiopia)	Awasa	Sud-Ouest (Cameroon)	Buea
Sierra Leone	Freetown	Suffolk (Eng)	Ipswich
Sikkim (India)	Gangtok	Sühbaatar (Mongolia)	Baruun-urt
Sinā' al-Janubiyah (Egypt)	At-Tur	Sulawesi Selatan (Indonesia)	Ujung Pandang
Sinā' ash-Shamãliyah (Egypt)	Al-'Arish	Sulawesi Tengah (Indonesia)	Palu
Sinaloa (Mexico)	Culiacán	Sulawesi Tenggara (Indonesia)	Kendari
Sind (Pakistan)	Karãchi	Sulawesi Utara (Indonesia)	Menado
Singapore	Singapore	Sumatera Barat (Indonesia)	Padang
Sinoe (Liberia)	Greenville	Sumatera Utara (Indonesia)	Medan
Sissilli (Burkina Faso)	Léo	**Suriname**	Paramaribo
Sistãn va Baluchestãn (Iran)	Zãhedãn	Surrey (Eng)	Kingston-upon-Thames
Skaraborg (Sweden)	Mariestad		
Skrapar (Albania)	Corovoda	**Swaziland**	Mbabane
Sligo (Rep of Ireland)	Sligo	**Sweden**	Stockholm
Slovakia	Bratislava	**Switzerland**	Berne
Slovenia	Llubljana	**Syria**	Damascus
Society Islands	Papeete	Szabics-Szatmár (Hungary)	Nyiregyháza
Socotra (Yemen)	Tamrida	Tabasco (Mexico)	Villahermosa
Södermanland (Sweden)	Nyköping	Tabiteuea North (Kiribati)	Utiroa
Sofala (Mozambique)	Beira	Tabiteuea South (Kiribati)	Buariki
Sogn og Fjordane (Norway)	Leikanger	Táchira (Venezuela)	San Cristóbal
Solomon Islands	Honiara	Taféa (Vanuatu)	Isangei
Somalia	Mogadishu	Tagant (Mauritania)	Tidjikdja
Somaliland	Berbera	**Tahiti (France)**	Papeete
Somerset (Eng)	Taunton	T'ai-chung (Taiwan)	Feng-yuan
Somme (France)	Amiens	Taimyr (Russia)	Dudinka
Somogy (Hungary)	Kaposvár	Tai-nan (Taiwan)	Hsin-ying
Sonderjylland (Denmark)	Abenra	Tai-pei (Taiwan)	Pan-ch'iao
Sonora (Mexico)	Hermosillo	**Taiwan**	Taipei
Soriano (Uruguay)	Mercedes	**Tajikistan**	Dushanbe
Sor-Trøndelag (Norway)	Trondheim	Tamana (Kiribati)	Bakaka
Soum (Burkina Faso)	Djibo	Tamaulipas (Mexico)	Ciudad Victoria
Sourou (Burkina Faso)	Tougan	Tamil Nadu (India)	Madras
South Africa	Pretoria–admin Capetown–legislative Bloemfontein–judicial	Tandjilé (Chad)	Lai
		Tanzania	Dodoma
		Tapoa (Burkina Faso)	Diapaga
		Taranaki (NZ)	New Plymouth
South Australia	Adelaide	Tarapacá (Chile)	Iquique
South Carolina (USA)	Columbia	Tarawa North (Kiribati)	Abaokoro
South Dakota (USA)	Pierre	Tarawa South (Kiribati)	Bairiki
		Tarn (France)	Albi

Country, State, County or Area	Capital or Admin Centre	Country, State, County or Area	Capital or Admin Centre
Tarn-et-Garonne (France)	Montauban	Udmurtia (Russia)	Izhevsk
Tasmania (Aus)	Hobart	**Uganda**	Kampala
Tatarstan (Russia)	Kazan	**Ukraine**	Kiev
Tayside (Scotland)	Dundee	Umbria (Italy)	Perugia
Tchaoudjo (Togo)	Sokodé	**United Arab Emirates**	Abu Dhabi
Telemark (Norway)	Skien	**United Kingdom**	London
Teleorman (Romania)	Alexandria	**United States of America**	Washington DC
Temburong (Brunei)	Bangar	Upper Demerara/Berbice (Guyana)	Linden
Temotu (Solomon Isles)	Santa Cruz	Upper East (Ghana)	Bolgatanga
Tennessee (USA)	Nashville	Upper River (Gambia)	Basse
Territoire de Belfort (France)	Belfort	Upper West (Ghana)	Wa
Texas (USA)	Austin	Uri (Swiss canton)	Altdorf
Thaa (Maldives)	Veymandhoo	**Uruguay**	Montevideo
Thailand	Bangkok	Ust-Ordyn-Buryat (Russia)	Ust-Ordynsk
Thames Valley (NZ)	Thames-Coromandel	Utah (USA)	Salt Lake City
		Uttar Pradesh (India)	Lucknow
Thua Thien (Vietnam)	Hue	Uusimaa (Finland)	Helsinki
Thurgau (Swiss canton)	Frauenfeld	Uvs (Mongolia)	Ulaangom
Thuringia (Germany)	Erfurt	**Uzbekistan**	Tashkent
Tibet (aka Xizang) (China)	Lhasa	Vaavu (Maldives)	Felidhoo
Ticino (Swiss canton)	Bellinzona	Vakaga (CA Rep)	Birao
Tien Giang (Vietnam)	My Tho	Valais (Swiss canton)	Sion
Tierra Del Fuego (Argentina)	Ushuaia	Val-de-Marne (France)	Créteil
Tigray (Ethiopia)	Mekele	Val-d'Oise (France)	Pontoise
Timis (Romania)	Timisoara	Valle (Honduras)	Nacaome
Timor Timur (Indonesia)	Dili	Valparaíso (Chile)	Valparaiso
Tipperary (Rep of Ireland)	Clonmel	Valverde (Dominican Republic)	Mao
Tiris Zemmour (Mauritania)	Fdérik	**Vanuatu**	Vila
Tirol (Austria)	Innsbruck	Var (France)	Toulon
Tobago (Trinidad and Tobago)	Scarborough	Värmland (Sweden)	Karlstad
Tocantins (Brazil)	Miracema do Tocantins	Vas (Hungary)	Szombathely
		Västerbotten (Sweden)	Umea
Tochigi (Japan)	Utsunomiya	Västernorrland (Sweden)	Härnösand
Togdheer (Somalia)	Burao (Burco)	Västmanland (Sweden)	Västerås
Togo	Lome	Vaucluse (France)	Avignon
Toledo (Belize)	Punta Gorda	Vaud (Swiss canton)	Lausanne
Tolima (Colombia)	Cali	Vaupés (Colombia)	Mitú
Tolna (Hungary)	Szekszárd	Vava'u (Tonga)	Neiafu
Tombali (Guinea-Bissau)	Catió	Venda (South Africa)	Thohoyandou
Tône (Togo)	Dapaong	Vendée (France)	La Roche-sur-Yon
Tonga	Nuku'alofa	**Venezuela**	Caracas
Tongariro (NZ)	Taupo	Veracruz (Mexico)	Jalapa
Tongatapu (Tonga)	Nuku'alofa	Veraguas (Panama)	Santiago
Tonkolili (Sierra Leone)	Magburaka	Vermont (USA)	Montpelier
Tororo (Uganda)	Sukulu	Vest-Agder (Norway)	Kristiansand
Töv (Mongolia)	Dzuunmod	Vestfirdhir (Iceland)	Isafjördhur
Transkei (South Africa)	Umtata	Vestfold (Norway)	Tønsberg
Transvaal (South Africa)	Pretoria	Vestjaelland (Denmark)	Sore
Trarza (Mauritania)	Rosso	Vesturland (Iceland)	Borgarnes
Trelawny (Jamaica)	Falmouth	Vichada (Colombia)	Puerto Carreño
Trinidad and Tobago	Port of Spain	Victoria (Aus)	Melbourne
Tripura (India)	Agartala	Victoria (Trinidad and Tobago)	Princes Town
Tristan da Cunha	Edinburgh	Vienne (France)	Poitiers
Tropojë (Albania)	Bajram	**Vietnam**	Hanoi
Trujillo (Venezuela)	Trujillo	Villa Clara (Cuba)	Santa Clara
Tucumán (Argentina)	San Miguel	Vinh Phuc (Vietnam)	Vinh Yen
Tungurahua (Ecuador)	Ambato	**Virgin Islands (British)**	Road Town
Tunisia	Tunis	**Virgin Islands (USA)**	Charlotte Amalie
Turkey	Ankara	Virginia (USA)	Richmond
Turkmenistan	Ashkhabad	Vo (Togo)	Vogan
Turks and Caicos Islands	Grand Turk	Vojvodina (Yugoslavia)	Novi Sad
Turku ja Pori (Finland)	Turku	Volta (Ghana)	Ho
Tuscany (Italy)	Florence	Vorarlberg (Austria)	Bregenz
Tuva (Russia)	Kyzyl	Vosges (France)	Épinal
Tuvalu	Fongafale (on Funafuti Isle)	Vrancea (Romania)	Focsani
		Waikato (NZ)	Hamilton
Tyne and Wear (Eng)	Newcastle-upon-Tyne	Wairarapa (NZ)	Masterton
		Wales	Cardiff
Tyrone (NI)	Omagh	Wallis and Futuna Islands (France)	Mata-Utu
Ucayali (Peru)	Pucallpa	Warwickshire (Eng)	Warwick

GEOGRAPHY

Country, State, County or Area	Capital or Admin Centre	Country, State, County or Area	Capital or Admin Centre
Washington (USA)	Olympia	Wisconsin (USA)	Madison
Wasit (Iraq)	Al-Kut	Woleu-Ntem (Gabon)	Oyem
Waterford (Rep of Ireland)	Waterford	Woqooyi Galbeed (Somalia)	Hargeysa
Wawa (Togo)	Badou	Wyoming (USA)	Cheyenne
Welega (Ethiopia)	Nekemte	Xékong (Laos)	Thong
Welo (Ethiopia)	Dese	Xianghoang (Laos)	Phônsavan
West Bengal (India)	Calcutta	Xinjiang Uighur (China)	Urumqi
West Coast (NZ)	Greymouth	Yamalo-Nenets (Russia)	Salekhard
West Flanders (Belgium)	Bruges	Yamanashi (Japan)	Kōfu
West Glamorgan (Wales)	Swansea	Yanggang-do (North Korea)	Hyesan
West Midlands (Eng)	Birmingham	Yaracuy (Venezuela)	San Felipe
West New Britain (Papua New Guinea)	Kimbe	Yatenga (Burkina Faso)	Ouahigouya
		Yemen	Sana'a
West Sepik (Papua New Guinea)	Vanimo	Yogyakarta (Indonesia)	Yogyakarta
West Sussex (Eng)	Chichester	Yonne (France)	Auxerre
West Virginia (USA)	Charleston	Yoto (Togo)	Tabligbo
West Yorkshire (Eng)	Wakefield	Yucatán (Mexico)	Mérida
Western Area (Sierra Leone)	Freetown	**Yugoslavia**	Belgrade
Western Australia	Perth	Yukon Territory (Canada)	Whitehorse
Western Division (Gambia)	Brikama	Yün-lin (Taiwan)	Tou-liu
Western Equatoria (Sudan)	Yambio	Yunnan (China)	Kunming
Western Highlands (Papua New Guinea)	Mount Hagen	Yvelines (France)	Versailles
		Zaïre (Angola)	M'Banza Kongo
Western Isles (Scotland)	Stornoway (Lewis)	Zambézia (Mozambique)	Quelimane
Western Nepal	Pokharã	**Zambia**	Lusaka
Western Province (Fiji)	Lautoka	Zamora-Chinchipe (Ecuador)	Zamora
Western Province (Kenya)	Kakamega	Zanzibar North (Tanzania)	Mkokotoni
Western Province (Papua New Guinea)	Daru	Zanzibar South and Central (Tanzania)	Koani
Western Province (Solomon Isles)	Gizo	Zanzibar West (Tanzania)	Zanzibar
Western Province (Zambia)	Mongu	Zeeland (Netherlands)	Middleburg
Western Region (Ghana)	Sekondi-Takoradi	Zhejiang (aka Chekiang) (China)	Hangzhou (aka Hangchow)
Western Sahara	Laâyoune (El Aaiún)		
		Zimbabwe	Harare
Western Samoa	Apia	Zio (Togo)	Tsévié
Westmeath (Rep of Ireland)	Mullingar	Zona Especial III (Nicaragua)	San Carlos
Westmoreland (Jamaica)	Savanna-la-Mar	Zou (Benin)	Abomey
Wexford (Rep of Ireland)	Wexford	Zoundwéogo (Burkina Faso)	Manga
Wicklow (Rep of Ireland)	Wicklow	Zuid-Holland (Netherlands)	Hague
Wiltshire (Eng)	Trowbridge	Zulia (Venezuela)	Maracaibo

Capitals: by capital

Capital or Admin Centre	Country, State, County or Area	Capital or Admin Centre	Country, State, County or Area
Aarau	Aargau (Swiss Canton)	Agen	Lot-et-Garonne (France)
Abancay	Apurimac (Peru)	Aginskoe	Agin-Buryat (Russia)
Abaokoro	Tarawa North (Kiribati)	**Ajaccio**	**Corsica (France)**
Abéché	Ouaddai (Chad)		Corse-du-Sud (France)
Abenra	Sonderjylland (Denmark)	Akjoujt	Inchiri (Mauritania)
Abeokuta	Ogun (Nigeria)	**Akmola**	**Kazakhstan**
Aberdeen	Grampian (Scotland)	Akure	Ondo (Nigeria)
Abidjan-legislative	**Ivory Coast**	Akureyri	Nordhurland eystra (Iceland)
Abomey	Zou (Benin)		
Abraham's Bay	Mayaguana (Bahamas)	Al-Amãrah	Maysãn (Iraq)
Abu Dhabi	United Arab Emirates	Al-'Arish	Sinã' ash-Shamãliyah (Egypt)
Abuja	**Nigeria**		
Accra	**Ghana**	Albany	New York (USA)
	Greater Accra (Ghana)	Albi	Tarn (France)
Adamstown	Pitcairn Islands	Albina	Marowijne (Suriname)
Ad-Damazin	An-Nil al-Azraq (Blue Nile) (Sudan)	Alborg	Nordjylland (Denmark)
		Aleg	Brakna (Mauritania)
Addis Ababa	**Ethiopia**	Alen	Orne (France)
	Shewa (Ethiopia)	Aleppo	Halab (Syria)
Adelaide	South Australia	Alexandria	Teleorman (Romania)
Agana	**Guam**	Al-Fãshir	Dãrfur (Sudan)
Agartala	Tripura (India)	Al-Ghaydah	Al-Mahrah (Yemen)

Capital or Admin Centre	Country, State, County or Area	Capital or Admin Centre	Country, State, County or Area
Al-Ghurdaqah	Al-Bahr al-Ahmar (Egypt)	Atlanta	Georgia (USA)
Algiers	**Algeria**	At-Tur	Sinā' al-Janubiyah (Egypt)
Al-Hillah	Bābil (Iraq)	Auch	Gers (France)
Alice Town	Bimini Islands (Bahamas)	Augusta	Maine (USA)
Al-Kharijah	Al-Wādi al-Jadid (Egypt)	Auki	Malaita (Solomon Isles)
Al-Kut	Wasit (Iraq)	Aurillac	Cantal (France)
Al-Mansurah	Ad-Dagahliyah (Egypt)	Austin	Texas (USA)
Al-Mukallā	Hadramawt (Yemen)	Auxerre	Yonne (France)
Alofi	Niue (Pacific)	Avignon	Vaucluse (France)
Alor Setar	Kedah (Malaysia)	Awasa	Sidamo (Ethiopia)
Altdorf	Uri (Swiss Canton)	Aylesbury	Buckinghamshire (Eng)
Āizawi	Mizorām (India)	Ayoûn el-Atroûs	Hodh-el-Gharbi
Am Timan	Salamat (Chad)		(Mauritania)
Ambato	Tungurahua (Ecuador)	Azoques	Cañar (Ecuador)
Amboina	Moluccas (Indonesia)	Az-Zaqāziq	Ash-Sharqiyah (Egypt)
Ambon	Maluku (Indonesia)	Babahoyo	Los Rios (Ecuador)
Amiamé	Amou (Togo)	Bac Giang	Ha Bac (Vietnam)
Amiens	Picardie (French Region)	Bac Lieu	Minh Hai (Vietnam)
	Somme (French	Badou	Wawa (Togo)
	Department)	Bafilo	Assoli (Togo)
Amman	**Jordan**	Bafoussam	Ouest (Cameroon)
Amsterdam	**Netherlands**	Bageza	Mubende (Uganda)
Anadyr	Chukut (Russia)	**Baghdad**	**Iraq**
Ancona	Marche (Italy)	Baia Mare	Maramures (Romania)
Andalucia	Seville (Spain)	Baidoa (Baydhabo)	Bay (Somalia)
Andorra La Vella	Andorra	**Bairiki on Tarawa Island**	**Kiribati**
Aného	Lacs (Togo)		Tarawa South (Kiribati)
Angers	Maine-et Loire (France)	Bairiki Islet	Gilbert Isles (Kiribati)
Angoulême	Charente (France)	Bajram	Tropojë (Albania)
Ankara	**Turkey**	Bakaka	Tamana (Kiribati)
Anna Regina	Pomeroon/Supenaam	**Baku**	**Azerbaijan**
	(Guyana)	Balboa Heights	Panama Canal Zone
Annapolis	Maryland (USA)	**Bamako**	**Mali**
An-Nāsiriyah	Dhi Qār (Iraq)	Bambari	Ouaka (C. A. Rep)
Annecy	Haute-Savoie (France)	Bamenda	Nord-Ouest (Cameroon)
Antananarivo	**Madagascar**	**Bandar Seri Begawan**	**Brunei**
Anteeren	Banaba (Kiribati)	Bandung	Jawar Barat (Indonesia)
Antigua Guatemala	Sacatepéquez (Guatemala)	Banfora	Comoé (Burkina Faso)
Apia	**Samoa**	Bangalore	Karnataka (India)
Appenzell	Appenzell Inner-Rhoden	Bangar	Temburong (Brunei)
	(Swiss Canton)	Bangassou	Mbomou (C. A. Rep)
Aracaju	Sergipe (Brazil)	**Bangkok**	**Thailand**
Arāk	Markazi (Iran)	**Bangui**	**Central African Republic**
Ararua	Cook Islands	Banhā	Al-Qalyubiyah (Egypt)
	(New Zealand)	Bani	Peravia (Dom Republic)
Arba Minch	Gemu Gofa (Ethiopia)	Banjarmasin	Kalimantan Selatan
Arendal	Aust-Agder (Norway)		(Indonesia)
Arlon	Luxembourg (Belgium)	**Banjul**	**Gambia**
Armagh	Armagh (N.I.)	Barcelona	Anzoátegui (Venezuela)
Armenia	Quindio (Colombia)	Barcelona	Catalonia (Spain)
Arnhem	Gelderland (Netherlands)	Barclayville	Grand Kru (Liberia)
Ar-Ramādi	Al-Anbār (Iraq)	Bari	Apulia a.k.a. Puglia (Italy)
Arras	Pas-de-Calais (France)	Bar-le-Duc	Meuse (France)
Arthur's Town	Cat Island (Bahamas)	Barnsley	South Yorkshire (Eng)
Arvayheer	Övörhangay (Mongolia)	Barquisimeto	Lara (Venezuela)
Asela	Arsi (Ethiopia)	Barranquilla	Atlántico (Colombia)
Ashkhabad	Turkmenistan	Baruun-urt	Sühbaatar (Mongolia)
Asmara	Eritrea	Basel	Basel-Stadt (Swiss Canton)
Assen	Drenthe (Netherlands)	Basse	Upper River (Gambia)
Assomada	Santa Catarina	**Basse-Terre**	**Guadeloupe**
	(Cape Verde)	Basseterre	St Kitts and Nevis
Asunción	**Paraguay**		St Kitts (St Kitts and
	Central Region (Paraguay)		Nevis)
Atakpamé	Des Plateaux (Togolese	Bastia	Haute-Corse (France)
	Region)	Bata	Rio Muni (Equatorial
	Ogou (Togolese Prefecture)		Guinea)
Atāq	Shabwah (Yemen)	Baton Rouge	Louisiana (USA)
Atar	Adrar (Mauritania)	Bayamo	Granma (Cuba)
Athens	**Greece**	Beauvais	Oise (France)
Ati	Batha (Chad)	Bedford	Bedfordshire (Eng)

Capital or Admin Centre	Country, State, County or Area	Capital or Admin Centre	Country, State, County or Area
Beersheba	Southern District (Israel)	Borgarnes	Vesturland (Iceland)
Beijing (aka Peking)	**China**	Bossangoa	Ouham (C. A. Rep)
Beira	Sofala (Mozambique)	Boston	Massachusetts (USA)
Beirut	**Lebanon**	Bouar	Nana-Mambere (C. A. Rep)
Beledweyne	Hiiraan (Somalia)	Boulsa	Namentenga
Belém	Pará (Brazil)		(Burkina Faso)
Belfast	**Northern Ireland**	Bourg-en-Bresse	Ain (France)
	Antrim (N.I.)	Bourges	Cher (France)
Belfort	Territoire de Belfort	Bozoum	Ouham-Pendé (CA Rep)
	(France)	**Brasilia**	**Brazil**
Belgrade	**Yugoslavia**	**Bratislava**	**Slovakia**
	Serbia	**Brazzaville**	**Congo: People's Republic**
Bellinzona	Ticino (Swiss Canton)	Bregenz	Vorarlberg (Austria)
Belmopan	**Belize**	Bria	Haute-Kotto (CA Rep)
Belo Horizonte	Minas Gerais (Brazil)	Bridgetown	**Barbados**
Bender Cassim		Brikama	Western Division (Gambia)
(Boosaaso)	Bari (Somalia)	Brisbane	Queensland (Aus)
Benin City	Bendel (Nigeria)	Bristol	Avon (Eng)
Bensonville	Montserrado (Liberia)	Bruge	West Flanders (Belgium)
Berbera	Somaliland	**Brussels**	**Belgium**
Berbérati	Haute-Sangha (C. A. Rep)		Brabant (Belgium)
Bergen	Hordaland (Norway)	Bu'aale	Jubbada Dhexe (Somalia)
Berlin	**Germany**	Buala	Isabel (Solomon Isles)
Berne	**Switzerland**	Buariki	Onotoa (Kiribati)
Bertoua	Est (Cameroon)		Tabiteuea South (Kiribati)
Besancon	Doubs (France)	Bucaramanga	Santander (Colombia)
Beverley	Humberside (Eng)	Buchanan	Grand Bassa (Liberia)
Bhopal	Madhya Pradesh (India)	**Bucharest**	**Romania**
Bhubaneswar	Orissa (India)	**Budapest**	**Hungary**
Bien Hoa	Dong Nai (Vietnam)		Pest (Hungary)
Bimbo	Ombella-Mpoko (C. A. Rep)	Buea	Sud-Ouest (Cameroon)
Bindura	Mashonaland Central	**Buenos Aires**	**Argentina**
	(Zimbabwe)	**Bujumbura**	**Burundi**
Birao	Vakaga (C. A. Rep)	Buka	North Solomons
Birmingham	West Midlands (Eng)		(Papua New Guinea)
Bishkek	**Kyrgyzstan**	Bukavu	Sud-Kivu (Dem Rep of
Bisho	Ciskei (South Africa)		Congo)
Bismarck	North Dakota (USA)	Bulamogi	Iganga (Uganda)
Bissau	**Guinea-Bissau**	Bulawayo	Matabeleland North
	Biombo (Guinea-Bissau)		(Zimbabwe)
Black River	St Elizabeth (Jamaica)	Bumbaire	Bushenyi (Uganda)
Blenheim	Marlborough (NZ)	Bungatira	Gulu (Uganda)
Bloemfontein – judicial	**South Africa**	Bunkoko	Mbale (Uganda)
	Orange Free State	Buon Me Thoat	Dac Lac (Vietnam)
	(South Africa)	Burao (Burco)	Togdheer (Somalia)
Blois	Loir-et-Cher (France)	Burrel	Mat (Albania)
Bluefields	Región Autónoma del	Busaru	Bundibugyo (Uganda)
	Atlántico Sur (Nic)	Byakabanda	Rakai (Uganda)
Bo	Southern Province	Caacupé	Cordillera (Paraguay)
	(Sierra Leone)	Caen	Basse Normandie
Boa Vista	Roraima (Brazil)		(French Region)
Bobigny	Seine-Saint-Denis (France)		Calvados (French
Bobo-Dioulasso	Houet (Burkina Faso)		Department)
Bode	Nordland (Norway)	Caernarfon	Gwynedd (Wales)
Bogandé	Gnagna (Burkina Faso)	**Cagliari**	**Sardinia (Italy)**
Bogotá	**Colombia**	Cahors	Lot (France)
	Cundinamarca	**Cairo**	**Egypt**
	(Colombia)	Calabar	Cross River (Nigeria)
Boise	Idaho (USA)	Calcutta	West Bengal (India)
Bol	Lac (Chad)	Cali	Tolima (Colombia)
Bolgatanga	Upper East (Ghana)	Cambridge	Cambridgeshire (Eng)
Bologna	Emilia-Romagna (Italy)	Campo Grande	Mato Grosso do Sul
Bombay (Mumbai)	Maharashtra (India)		(Brazil)
Bonao	Monseñor Nouel	Can Tho	Hau Giang (Vietnam)
	(Dom Republic)	**Canberra**	**Australia**
Bongor	Mayo-Kebbi (Chad)		Australian Capital
Bor	Junquli (Jongley) (Sudan)		Territory
Bordeaux	Aquitaine (French Region)	Cape Coast	Central Region (Ghana)
	Gironde (French	**Capetown – legislative**	**South Africa**
	Department)	Cap-Haitien	Nord (Haiti)

Capital or Admin Centre	Country, State, County or Area
Car Nicobar	Nicobar Islands
Caracas	**Venezuela**
Carcassonne	Aude (France)
Cardiff	**Wales**
	Mid-Glamorgan (Wales)
	South Glamorgan (Wales)
Carlisle	Cumbria (Eng)
Carlow	Carlow (Eire)
Carmarthen	Dyfed (Wales)
Carrick-on-Shannon	Leitrim (Eire)
Carson City	Nevada (USA)
Cartagena	Bolivar (Colombia)
Castlebar	Mayo (Eire)
Castries	**Saint Lucia**
Catanzaro	Calabria (Italy)
Catió	Tombali (Guinea-Bissau)
Cavan	Cavan (Eire)
Caxito	Bengo (Angola)
Cayenne	**French Guiana**
Chachapoyas	Amazonas (Peru)
Chaguanas	Caroni (Trinidad & Tobago)
Chake Chake	Pemba South (Tanzania)
Chalan Kanoa	Northern Mariana Islands (Pacific)
Chalan Kanoa	Saipan
Châlons-sur-Marne	Champagne-Ardenne (French Region)
	Marne (French Department)
Chambéry	Savoie (France)
Chandigar	Haryana (India)
Chandigar	Punjab (India)
Changchun	Jilin (aka Kirin)
Changsha	Hunan (China)
Charleston	West Virginia (USA)
Charlestown	Nevis (St Kitts and Nevis)
Charleville-Mézières	Ardennes (France)
Charlotte Amalie	**Virgin Islands (USA)**
	St Thomas & St John (US Virgins)
Charlottetown	Prince Edward Island (Canada)
Chartres	Eure-et-Loire (France)
Châteauroux	Indre (France)
Chaumont	Haute-Marne (France)
Cheboksary	Chuvasia (Russia)
Chelmsford	Essex (Eng)
Chengdu	Sichuan (China)
Cherkesst	Karachai-Cherkessia (Russia)
Chester	Cheshire (Eng)
Chetumal	Quintana Roo (Mexico)
Cheyenne	Wyoming (USA)
Chichester	West Sussex (Eng)
Chiclayo	Lambayeque (Peru)
Chilpancingo	Guerrero (Mexico)
Chimolo	Manica (Mozambique)
Chinhoyi	Mashonaland West (Zimbabwe)
Chipata	Eastern Province (Zambia)
Chisimayu (Kismaayo)	Jubbada Hoose (Somalia)
Chisinau	**Moldova**
Chitré	Herrera (Panama)
Ch'ŏngjin	Hamgyong-pukto (North Korea)
Ch'ŏnju	Chŏlla-pukto (South Korea)
Choybaisan	Dornod (Mongolia)
Christchurch	Canterbury (NZ)
Christiansted	St Croix (US Virgins)
Ch'unch'ŏn	Kangwŏn-do (South Korea)

Capital or Admin Centre	Country, State, County or Area
Chur	Graubunden (Swiss Canton)
Ciudad Bolivar	Bolivar (Venezuela)
Ciudad del Este	Alto Paraná (Paraguay)
Ciudad Flores	Petén (Guatemala)
Ciudad Victoria	Tamaulipas (Mexico)
Clarence Town	Long Island (Bahamas)
Clermont-Ferrand	Auvergne (Frech Region)
Puy-de-Dôme	(French Department)
Clonmel	Tipperary (Eire)
Cobán	Alta Verapaz (Guatemala)
Cobija	Pando (Bolivia)
Cockburn Town	San Salvador & Rum Cay
Cojutepeque	Cuscatián (El Salvador)
Colhaique (Chile)	Aisén del Gen Carlos Ibáñez del Campo
Colmar	Haut-Rhin (France)
Colombo	**Sri Lanka**
Colonel Hill	Crooked Island (Bahamas)
Columbia	South Carolina (USA)
Columbus	Ohio (USA)
Conakry	**Guinea**
Conception	Bio-Bio (Chile)
Concorde	New Hampshire (USA)
Copenhagen	**Denmark**
Copiapó	Atacama (Chile)
Cork	Cork (Eire)
Coro	Falcón (Venezuela)
Coronel Oviedo	Caaguazú (Paraguay)
Corovoda	Skrapar (Albania)
Cotonou	Atlantique (Benin)
Cotui	Sánchez Ramirez (Dom Republic)
Craiova	Dolj (Romania)
Créteil	Val-de-Marne (France)
Cúcuta	Norte de Santander (Colombia)
Cuenca	Azuay (Ecuador)
Cuernavaca	Morelos (Mexico)
Cuiabá	Mato Grosso (Brazil)
Cuilapa	Santa Rosa (Guatemala)
Culiacán	Sinaloa (Mexico)
Cumaná	Sucre (Venezuela)
Curitiba	Paraná (Brazil)
Cuzco	Cuzco (Peru)
Cwmbran	Gwent (Wales)
Da Lat	Lam Dong (Vietnam)
Dakar	**Senegal**
Dalandzadgad	Ömnögovi (Mongolia)
Damanhur	Al-Buhayrah (Egypt)
Damascus	**Syria**
	Dimashq (Syria)
Damphu (Bhutan)	Chirang
Dangriga	Stann Creek (Belize)
Dapaong	Des Savanes (Togolese Region)
	Tône (Togolese Prefecture)
Dar es Salaam	Pwani (Tanzania)
Darrit-Uliga-Dalap (on Majuro isle)	Marshall Islands
Daru	Western Province (Papua New Guinea)
Darwin	Northern Territory (Aus)
David	Chiriqui (Panama)
Debre Markos	Gojam (Ethiopia)
Debrecen	Hajdú-Bihar (Hungary)
Dédougou	Mouhoun (Burkina Faso)
Delémont	Jura (Swiss Canton)

GEOGRAPHY

Capital or Admin Centre	Country, State, County or Area	Capital or Admin Centre	Country, State, County or Area
Denpassar	**Bali (Indonesia)**	Elista	Kalmuck (CIS)
Denver	Colorado (USA)	Embu	Eastern Province (Kenya)
Des Moines	Iowa (USA)	Encarnación	Itapúa (Paraguay)
Dese	Welo (Ethiopia)	Ennis	Clare (Eire)
Deva	Hunedoara (Romania)	Enniskillen	Fermanagh (N.I.)
Dhaka	**Bangladesh**	Enugu	Anambra (Nigeria)
Dhankutã	Eastern Nepal	Épinal	Vosges (France)
Dhidhdhoo	Haa-Alifu (Maldives)	Erfurt	Thuringia (Germany)
Diapaga	Tapoa (Burkina Faso)	Erigavo (Ceerigaabo)	Sanaag (Somalia)
Diébougou	Bougouriba (Burkina Faso)	Ersekë	Kolonjë (Albania)
Diego Garcia	British Indian Ocean Territory	Esteli	Región 1 (Nicaragua)
Dien Bien	Lai Chau (Vietnam)	Évreux	Eure (France)
Digne	Alpes-de-Haute-Provence (France)	Évry	Essonne (France)
		Exeter	Devon (Eng)
Dijon	Bourgogne/Burgundy (French Region) Cote-d'Or (French Department)	Eydhafushi	Baa (Maldives)
		Fada N'Gourma	Gourma (Burkina Faso)
		Falmouth	Trelawny (Jamaica)
		Falun	Kopparberg (Sweden)
		Farim	Oio (Guinea-Bissau)
Dili	**Eastern Timor (Pacific)**	Farukolhu Funadhoo	Shaviyani (Maldives)
Dili	Timor Timur (Indonesia)	Faya	Borkou-Ennedi-Tibesti (Chad)
Dipãyal	Far-Western Nepal		
Dispur	Assam (India)	Fdérik	Tiris Zemmour (Mauritania)
Djambala	Plateaux (Congo)	Felidhoo	Vaavu (Maldives)
Djibo	Soum (Burkina Faso)	Feng-shan	Kao-hsiung (Taiwan)
Djibouti	**Djibouti**	Feng-yuan	T'ai-chung (Taiwan)
Doba	Logone Oriental (Chad)	Florence	Tuscany (Italy)
Dodoma	**Tanzania**	Florencia	Caquetá (Colombia)
Doha	**Qatar**	Florianópolis	Santa Catarina (Brazil)
Dong Ha	Quang Tri (Vietnam)	Flying Fish Cove	Christmas Island (Aus)
Dong Hoi	Quang Binh (Vietnam)	Foah Mulah	Gnyaviyani (Maldives)
Dorchester	Dorset (Eng)	Focsani	Vrancea (Romania)
Dori	Sèno (Burkina Faso)	Foix	Ariège (France)
Douala	Littoral (Cameroon)	Fomboni	Moili (Comoros)
Douglas	Isle of Man	**Fongafale (on Funafuti atoll)**	**Tuvalu**
Dover	Delaware (USA)	Fort Wellington	Mahaica/Berbice (Guyana)
Downpatrick	Down (N.I.)	Fortaleza	Ceará (Brazil)
Dr Pedro P. Peña	Boquerón (Paraguay)	**Fort-de-France**	**Martinique (France)**
Drammen	Buskerud (Norway)	Fort-Liberté	Nord-Est (Haiti)
Dresden	Saxony (Germany)	Franceville	Haut-Ogooué (Gabon)
Drobeta-Turnu-Severin	Mehedinti (Romania)	Frankfort	Kentucky (USA)
Dublin	**Republic of Ireland** Dublin (rep of Ireland)	Frauenfeld	Thurgau (Swiss Canton)
		Fray Bentos	Rio Negro (Uruguay)
Dudinka	Taimyr (Russia)	Fredericton	New Brunswick (Canada)
Dumfries	Dumfries and Galloway (Scotland)	Freeport	Grand Bahama
		Freetown	**Sierra Leone** Western Area (Sierra Leone)
Duncan Town	Ragged Island (Bahamas)		
Dundalk	Louth (Eire)	Fuerte Olimpio	Alto Paraguay (Paraguay)
Dundee	Tayside (Scotland)	Fulacunda	Quinara (Guinea-Bissau)
Dunedin	North Otago (NZ)	**Funchal**	**Madeira**
Dungxoai	Binh Phuoc (Vietnam)	Fuzhou (aka Foochow)	Fujian (aka Fukien)
Durham	Durham (Eng)	**Gabarone**	**Botswana**
Dusa Marreb (Dhuusamarreeb)	Galguduud (Somalia)	Galcaio (Gaalkacyo)	Mudug (Somalia)
Dushanbe	**Tadzhikstan**	Galway	Galway (Eire)
Düsseldorf	Nordrhein-Westfalen (Germany)	Gãndhinagar	Gujarãt (India)
		Gangtok	**Sikkim (India)**
Dzuunmod	Töv (Mongolia)	Gaoua	Poni (Burkina Faso)
Eas	Ambrym (Vanuatu)	Gap	Haute-Alpes (France)
Ebolowa	Sud (Cameroon)	Garbahaarrey	Gedo (Somalia)
Edinburgh	**Scotland** Lothian (Scotland)	Garissa	North Eastern Province (Kenya)
Edinburgh	Tristan da Cunha	Garoowe	Nugaal (Somalia)
Edmonton	Alberta (Canada)	Garoua	Nord (Cameroon)
Eger	Heves (Hungary)	Gbarnga	Bong (Liberia)
Egilsstadhir	Austurland (Iceland)	General Eugenio A. Garay	Nueva Asunción (Paraguay)
Eisenstadt	Burgenland (Austria)	Genoa	Liguria (Italy)
Elias Piña	La Estrelleta (Dom Republic)	George Town	Penang/Pinang (Malaysia)
		Georgetown	Ascension

Capital or Admin Centre	Country, State, County or Area	Capital or Admin Centre	Country, State, County or Area
Georgetown	**Cayman Islands**	**Hamilton**	**Bermuda**
Georgetown	**Guyana**	Hamilton	Waikato (NZ)
Ghent	East Flanders (Belgium)	Hanga Roa	Easter Island
Gibeon	Namaland (Namibia)	Hangzhou	
Giohar Jawhar	Shabeellaha Dhexe (Somalia)	(aka Hangchow)	Zhejiang (aka Chekiang)
Gibeon	Namaland (Namibia)	**Hanoi**	**Vietnam**
Giohar (Jawhar)	Shabeellaha Dhexe (Somalia)	Hanover	Niedersachsen (Germany)
		Harare	**Zimbabwe**
Gisborne	East Cape (NZ)	Harbin	Heilongjiang (China)
Giyani	Gazankulu (South Africa)	Harer	Hararge (Ethiopia)
Gizo	Western Province (Solomon Isles)	Hargeysa	Woqooyi Galbeed (Somalia)
Glasgow	Strathclyde (Scotland)	Härnösand	Västernorrland (Sweden)
Glenrothes	Fife (Scotland)	Harper	Maryland (Liberia)
Gloucester	Gloucestershire (Eng)	Harrisburg	Pennsylvania (USA)
Goba	Bale (Ethiopia)	Hartford	Connecticut (USA)
Gobabis	Omaheke (Namibia)	Hasselt	Limburg (Belgium)
Godthaab (aka Nuuk)	**Greenland (aka Kalaallit Nunaat)**	**Havana**	**Cuba** La Habana (Cuba)
Goiânia	Goiás (Brazil)	Hefei (aka Ho-fei)	Anhui (aka Anhwei)
Goma	Nord-Kivu (Dem Rep of Congo)	Helena	Montana (USA)
		Helsinki	**Finland** Uusimaa (Finland)
Gonaives	Artibonite (Haiti)	Herisau	Appenzell Ausser-Rhoden (Swiss Canton)
Goroka	Eastern Highlands (Papua New Guinea)	Hermosillo	Sonora (Mexico)
Gorom Gorom	Oudalan (Burkina Faso)	Hertford	Hertfordshire (Eng)
Gracias	Lempira (Honduras)	Higüey	La Altagracia (Dom Republic)
Grand Turk	**Turks and Caicos Islands**	Hihifo	Niuas (Tonga)
Graz	Steiermark (Austria)	Hillerod	Frederiksborg (Denmark)
Greenville	Sinoe (Liberia)	Hinche	Centre Departement (Haiti)
Grenoble	Isère (France)	Hiotse	Leribe (Lesotho)
Greymouth	West Coast (NZ)	Hithadhoo	Laamu (Maldives)
Groningen	Saramacca (Suriname)	Hithadoo	Seenu (Maldives)
Grootfontein	Otjozondjupa (Namibia)	Ho	Volta (Ghana)
Grozny (aka Djohar)	**Chechnya**	Hobart	Tasmania
Guadalajara	Jalisco (Mexico)	Hoi An	Quang Nam (Vietnam)
Guadalupe	Lobata (São Tomé & Principe)	Homs	Hims (Syria)
Guanare	Portuguesa (Venezuela)	**Honiara**	**Solomon Islands** Guadalcanal (Solomon Isles)
Guangzhou (aka Canton)	Guangdong (aka Kwangtung)	Honolulu	Hawaii (USA)
Guaranda	Bolivar (Ecuador)	Houayxay	Bokeo (Laos)
Guatemala City	**Guatemala**	Hsin-ying	Tai-nan (Taiwan)
Guayaquil	Guayas (Ecuador)	Huancayo	Junin (Peru)
Guéret	Creuse (France)	Huaraz	Ancash (Peru)
Guiyang (aka Kuei-yang)	Guizhou (aka Kweichow)	Hue	Bin Tri Thien (Vietnam)
Gwanda	Matabeleland South (Zimbabwe)	Hugh Town	Scilly Isles
Gweru	Midland Province (Zimbabwe)	Hu-ho-hao-t'e (aka Hohhot)	Inner Mongolia (aka Nei Monggol)
Ha Dong	Ha Tay (Vietnam)	Hyderabad	Andhra Pradesh (India)
Ha Giang	Ha Tuyen (Vietnam)	Hyesan	Yanggang-do (North Korea)
Ha Long City	Quang Nam-Hoi An (Vietman)	Ibadan	Oyo (Nigeria)
Ha Long City	Quang Ninh (Vietman)	Ibarra	Imbabura (Ecuador)
Haarlem	Noord-Holland (Netherlands)	Impfondo	Likouala (Congo)
		Imphāl	Manipur (India)
Haeju	Hwanghae-namdo (North Korea)	Innsbruck	Tirol (Austria)
		Invercargill	Southland (NZ)
Hague	Zuid-Holland (Netherlands)	Inverness	Highland (Scotland)
		Ipswich	Suffolk (Eng)
Haikou	Hainan (China)	Iqaluit	Nunavut (Canada)
Hakha	Chin (Myanmar)	Iquique	Tarapacá (Chile)
Halifax	Nova Scotia (Canada)	Iquitos	Loreto (Peru)
Halmstad	Halland (Sweden)	Isafjördhur	Vestfirdhir (Iceland)
Hamar	Hedmark (Norway)	Isangei	Taféa (Vanuatu)
Hämeenlinna	Häme (Finland)	**Islamabad**	**Pakistan**
Hamhung	Hamgyong-namdo (North Korea)	Itānagar	Arunāchal Pradesh (India)
		Izhevsk	Udmurtia (Russia)
		Jackson	Mississippi (USA)

GEOGRAPHY

Capital or Admin Centre	Country, State, County or Area	Capital or Admin Centre	Country, State, County or Area
Jacmel	Sud-Est (Haiti)	Kenema	Eastern Province (Sierra Leone)
Jaipur	Rajasthan (India)		
Jakar	Bumthang (Bhutan)	Kerema	Gulf (Papua New Guinea)
Jakarta	**Indonesia**	Kerewan	North Bank (Gambia)
	Jakarta Raya (Indonesia)	**Kerkira**	**Corfu**
Jalapa	Veracruz (Mexico)	**Khania**	**Crete**
Jamestown	St Helena	**Khartoum**	**Sudan**
Jayapura	**Irian Jaya (Indonesia)**	Khanty-Mansüsk	Kharty-Mansi (Russia)
Jefferson City	Missouri (USA)	Khasab	Musandam (Oman)
Jérémie	Grande Anse (Haiti)	Khorixas	Damaraland (Namibia)
Jerusalem	**Israel**	Kiel	Schleswig-Holstein (Germany)
Jima	Kefa (Ethiopia)		
Jimani	Independencia (Dom Republic)	**Kiev**	**Ukraine**
		Kiffa	El-Acâba (Mauritania)
Jinan (aka Tsinan)	Shandong (aka Shantung)	**Kigali**	**Rwanda**
Jinotepe	Región IV (Nicaragua)	Kilkenny	Kilkenny (Eire)
João Pessoa	Paraíba (Brazil)	Kimbe	West New Britain (Papua New Guinea)
Joensuu	Pohjois-Karjala (Finland)		
Johor Baharu	Johor (Malaysia)	Kindu	Maniema (Dem Rep of Congo)
Jos	Plateau (Nigeria)		
Jubã	Eastern Equatoria (Sudan)	King Edward Point	South Georgia and the South Sandwich Islands
Juigalpa	Región V (Nicaragua)		
Juneau	Alaska (USA)	**Kingston**	**Jamaica**
Juticalpa	Olancho (Honduras)	Kingston	Norfolk Island
Jyväskylä	Keski-Suomi (Finland)	Kingston-upon-Thames	Surrey (Eng)
Kabala	Koinaduga (Sierra Leone)	Kingstown	St Vincent and Grenadines
Kabul	**Afghanistan**	Kinkala	Pool (Congo)
Kabwe	Central Province (Zambia)	**Kinshasa**	**Congo: Democratic Republic**
Kaédi	Gorgol (Mauritania)		
Kaga-Bandoro	Gribingui-Economique (CA Rep)	Kira Kira	Makira (Solomon Isles)
		Kiritimati	Line Isles (Kiribati)
Kagunga	Rukungiri (Uganda)	Kirkwall	Orkney Islands
Kakamega	Western Province (Kenya)	Kisangani	Haute-Zaïre (Dem Rep of Congo)
Kakata	Margibi (Liberia)		
Kakika	Mbarara (Uganda)	**Kishinev**	**Moldavia**
Kampala	**Uganda**	Kisumu	Nyanza (Kenya)
Kananga	Kasai-Occidental (Dem Rep of Congo)	Kizyl	Tuva (CIS)
		Klagenfurt	Karnten (Austria)
Kanazawa	Ishikawa (Japan)	Koani	Zanzibar South & Central (Tanzania)
Kandé	Kéran (Togo)		
Kanggye	Chagang-do (North Korea)	Kōbe	Hyōgo (Japan)
Kanifing	Kombo St. Mary (Gambia)	Koforidua	Eastern Region (Ghana)
Kanton	Phoenix Isles (Kiribati)	Kōfu	Yamanashi (Japan)
Kanye	Ngwaketse (Botswana)	Kohima	Nāgālaland (India)
Kaposvár	Somogy (Hungary)	Kolonia/Palikir	Micronesia (Pacific)
Kara	Kozah (Togo)	Kombissiri	Bazéga (Burkina Faso)
Karãchi	Sind (Pakistan)	Kongoussi	Bam (Burkina Faso)
Karambe	Kabarole (Uganda)	Koror Island	Palau (Pacific)
Kariatebike	Abemama (Kiribati)	Kota Bharu	Kelantan (Malaysia)
Karlskrona	Blekinge (Sweden)	Kota Kinabalu	Sabah (Malaysia)
Karlstad	Värmland (Sweden)	Koudougou	Boulkiemde (Burkina Faso)
Kasama	Northern Province (Zambia)		
Kasane	Chobe (Botswana)	Koulamoutou	Ogooué-Lolo (Gabon)
Kaswa Bukoto	Masaka (Uganda)	Koupéla	Kouritenga (Burkina Faso)
Kãthmãndu	**Nepal**	Kouvola	Kymi (Finland)
	Central Nepal	Kpalimé	Kloto (Togo)
Katikekile	Moroto (Uganda)	Kralendijk	Bonaire (Netherland Antilles)
Katima Mulilo	Caprivi Oos (Namibia)		
Kavaratti Island	Lakshadweep Islands (India)	Kristiansand	Vest-Agder (Norway)
		Kuala Belait	Belait (Brunei)
Kavieng	New Ireland (Papua New Guinea)	**Kuala Lumpur**	**Malaysia**
		Kuching	**Sarawak (Malaysia)**
Kaya	Sanmatenga (Burkina Faso)	Kudahuvadhoo	Dhaalu (Maldives)
Kazan	Tatarstan	Kudymkar	Komy Permyak (Russia)
Kecskemét	Bács-Kiskun (Hungary)	Kuito	Bié (Angola)
Keetmanshoop	Karas (Namibia)	Kumasi	Ashanti (Ghana)
Keflavik	Sudhurnes (Iceland)	Kundiawa	Chimbu (Papua New Guinea)
Kemps Bay	Andros Island (Bahamas)		
Kendari	Sulawesi Tenggara (Indonesia)	Kunming	Yunnan (China)
		Kuntaur/Georgetown	MacCarthy Island (Gambia)

Capital or Admin Centre	Country, State, County or Area	Capital or Admin Centre	Country, State, County or Area
Kupang	Nusa Tenggara Timur (Indonesia)	Lincoln	Nebraska (USA)
		Linden	Upper Demerara/Berbice (Guyana)
Kuwait	**Kuwait**		
Kwangju	Chŏlla-namdo (South Korea)	Linköping	Östergötland (Sweden)
		Linz	Oberosterreich (Austria)
La Asunción	Nueva Esparta (Venezuela)	Liro	Paama (Vanuatu)
La Ceiba	Atlántida (Honduras)	**Lisbon**	**Portugal**
La Esperanza	Intibucá (Honduras)	Little Rock	Arkansas (USA)
La Palma	Darién (Panama)	Liverpool	Merseyside (Eng)
La Paz	Baja California Sur (Mexico)	Livingstone	Southern Province (Zambia)
La Paz – admin	**Bolivia**		
La Plata	Buenos Aires	**Ljubljana**	**Slovenia**
La Rochelle	Charente-Maritime (France)	Lkeja	Lagos (Nigeria)
		Llandrindod Wells	Powys (Wales)
La Roche-sur-Yon	Vendée (France)	Llorin	Kwara (Nigeria)
La Serena	Coquimbo (Chile)	Logrono	La Rioja (Spain)
Laâyone (El Aaiún)	Western Sahara	Loi-kaw	Kayah (Myanmar)
Labasa	Northern Province (Fiji)	Lokossa	Mono (Benin)
Labongo	Kitgum (Uganda)	Loltong	Pentecost (Vanuatu)
Lae	Morobe (Papua New Guinea)	**Lomé**	**Togo**
			Golfe (Togolese Prefecture)
Lahore	Punjab (Pakistan)		Maritime Region (Togo)
Lai	Tandjilé (Chad)	London	Christmas Island/Kiritimati Atoll (Kiribati)
Lakatoro	Malekula (Vanuatu)		
Lambaréné	Moyen-Ogooué (Gabon)	**London**	**England**
Lansing	Michigan (USA)		Greater London (Eng)
Lanzhou (aka Lan-chou)	Gansui (aka Kansu)		United Kingdom
Laon	Aisne (France)	Londonderry	Londonderry (N.I.)
L'Aquila	Abruzzi (Italy)	Long Xuyen	An Giang (Vietnam)
Las Palmas	Gran Canaria	Longana	Ambae/Maéwo (Vanuatu)
Las Tablas	Los Santos (Panama)	Longford	Longford (Eire)
Latacunga	Cotopaxi (Ecuador)	Lons-le-Saunier	Jura (France)
Latakia	Al-Lādhiqiyah (Syria)	Lorengau	Manus (Papua New Guinea)
Lausanne	Vaud (Swiss Canton)		
Lautoka	Western Province (Fiji)	Los Teques	Miranda (Venezuela)
Laval	Mayenne (France)	Loubomo	Niari (Congo)
Le Mans	Sarthe (France)	Louieville	KaNgwane (South Africa)
Le Puy	Haute-Loire (France)	Louvain (Leuven)	Brabant (Flemish)
Lebowakgomo	Lebowa (South Africa)	**Luanda**	**Angola**
Leeuwarden	Friesland (Netherlands)	Lubango	Huíta (Angola)
Leicester	Leicestershire (Eng)	Lubumbashi	Shaba (Dem Rep of Congo)
Leikanger	Sogn og Fjordane (Norway)	Lucapa	Lunda Norte (Angola)
		Lucea	Hanover (Jamaica)
Lelystad	Flevoland (Netherlands)	Lucknow	Uttar Pradesh (India)
Léo	Sissilli (Burkina Faso)	Luganville	Santo/Maio (Vanuatu)
León	Región II (Nicaragua)	Luleá	Norrbotten (Sweden)
Lerwick	Shetland Islands	**Lusaka**	**Zambia**
Les Cayes	Sud (Haiti)	**Luxembourg**	**Luxembourg**
Leticia	Amazonas (Colombia)	Lwena	Moxico (Angola)
Levin	Horowhenua (NZ)	Lyon	Rhône (France)
Levuka	Eastern Province (Fiji)	Lyon	Rhône-Alpes (France)
Lewes	East Sussex (Eng)	Maastricht	Limburg (Netherlands)
Lhasa (China)	**Tibet (aka Xizang)**	Mabaruma	Barima/Waini (Guyana)
Liberia	Guanacaste (Costa Rica)	Macao	Macao (Portugal)
Libreville	**Gabon**	Macapá	Amapá (Brazil)
	Estuaire (Gabon)	Macas	Morona-Santiago (Ecuador)
Lichinga	Niassa (Mozambique)	Maceió	Alagoas (Brazil)
Liestal	Basel-Landschaft (Swiss Canton)	Machala	El Oro (Ecuador)
		Mâcon	Saône-et-Loire (France)
Lifford	Donegal (Eire)	Madingou	Bouenza (Congo)
Lille	Nord (France)	Madison	Wisconsin (USA)
Lille	Nord-Pas-de-Calais (France)	Madras	Tamil Nadu (India)
Lillehammer	Oppland (Norway)	**Madrid**	**Spain**
Lilongwe	**Malawi**	Maebashi	Gumma (Japan)
Lima	**Peru**	Magburaka	Tonkolili (Sierra Leone)
Limerick	Limerick (Eire)	Magdeburg	Saxony-Anhalt (Germany)
Limoges	Haute-Vienne (French Department)	Magoodhoo	Faafu (Maldives)
	Limousin (French Region)	Mahibadhoo	Alifu (Maldives)
Lincoln	Lincolnshire (Eng)	Mahon	Minorca

GEOGRAPHY

Capital or Admin Centre	Country, State, County or Area
Maidstone	Kent (Eng)
Mainz	Rheinland-Pfalz (Germany)
Makeni	Bombali (Sierra Leone) Northern Province (Sierra Leone)
Makhachkala	Dagestan (CIS)
Makokou	Ogooué-Ivindo (Gabon)
Ma-kung	P'eng-hu (Taiwan)
Makurdi	Benue (Nigeria)
Malabo	**Equatorial Guinea** Bioko (Equatorial Guinea)
Malakãi	A'äli an-Nil (Upper Nile) (Sudan)
Malduguri	Borno (Nigeria)
Male	**Maldives** Kaafu (Maldives)
Mamoudzou	**Mayotte**
Manadhoo	Noonu (Maldives)
Managua	**Nicaragua**
Managua	Región III (Nicaragua)
Manama	**Bahrain**
Manaus	Amazonas (Brazil)
Manchester	Greater Manchester (Eng)
Mandalgov	Dundgovi (Mongolia)
Mandeville	Manchester (Jamaica)
Manga	Zoundwéogo (Burkina Faso)
Manila	**Philippines**
Manizales	Caldas (Colombia)
Mansa	Luapula (Zambia)
Mansakonko	Lower River (Gambia)
Mao	Kanem (Chad)
Mao	Valverde (Dom Republic)
Maputo	**Mozambique**
Maracaibo	Zulia (Venezuela)
Maracay	Aragua (Venezuela)
Mariestad	Skaraborg (Sweden)
Marigot	St-Martin & St Barthelemy (Guadeloupe)
Marondera	Mashonaland East (Zimbabwe)
Maroua	Extrême-Nord (Cameroon)
Marsã Matruh	Matruh (Egypt)
Marseille	Bouches-du-Rhône (French Department) Provence-Alpes-Côte d'Azur (Region)
Marsh Harbour	Abaco & Mores Island
Masan	Kyõngsang-namdo (South Korea)
Maseru	**Lesotho**
Masterton	Wairarapa (NZ)
Masunga	Botswana (North East)
Matadi	Bas-Zaïre (Dem Rep of Congo)
Matagalpa	Región VI (Nicaragua)
Mataram	Nusa Tenggara Barat (Indonesia)
Mataura	Îles Australes (French Polynesia)
Mata-Utu	Wallis and Futuna Islands
Matlock	Derbyshire (Eng)
Matsue	Shimane (Japan)
Matsuyama	Ehime (Japan)
Matthew Town	Inagua, Great & Little
Maturin	Monagas (Venezuela)
Maun	Ngamiland (Botswana)
May Pen	Clarendon (Jamaica)
Mayor Pablo Lagerenza	Chaco (Paraguay)

Capital or Admin Centre	Country, State, County or Area
Mazatenango	Suchitepéquez (Guatemala)
Mbabane	**Swaziland** Hhohho (Swaziland)
Mbaiki	Lobaye (CA Rep)
Mbandaka	Equateur (Dem Rep of Congo)
M'Banza Kongo	Zaïre (Angola)
Mbuji-Mayi	Kasai-Oriental (Dem Rep of Congo)
Medan	Sumatera Utara (Indonesia)
Medelin	Antioquia (Colombia)
Mekele	Tigray (Ethiopia)
Melaka	Melaka (Malaysia)
Melbourne	Victoria (Aus)
Melo	Cerro Largo (Uruguay)
Melun	Seine-et-Marne (France)
Menado	Sulawesi Utara (Indonesia)
Mende	Lozère (France)
Mende	Southern Highlands (Papua New Guinea)
Menongue	Kuando Kubango (Angola)
Merca (Marka)	Shabeellaha Hoose (Somalia)
Mercedes	Soriano (Uruguay)
Merida	Extremadura (Spain)
Mérida	Yucatán (Mexico)
Metu	Ilubabor (Ethiopia)
Metz	Lorraine (French Region)
Metz	Moselle (French Department)
Mexicali	Baja California Norte (Mexico)
Mexico City	**Mexico**
Middleburg	Zeeland (Netherlands)
Middlesbrough	Cleveland (Eng)
Miercurea-Ciuc	Harghita (Romania)
Milan	Lombardy (Italy)
Minas	Lavalleja (Uruguay)
Mindelo	São Vicente (Cape Verde)
Minna	Niger (Nigeria)
Minsk	**Belarus**
Miracema do Tocantins	Tocantins (Brazil)
Miskolc	Borsod-Abaúj-Zemplén (Hungary)
Mito	Ibaraki (Japan)
Mitú	Vaupés (Colombia)
Mkokotoni	Zanzibar North (Tanzania)
Mmabatho	Bophuthatswana (South Africa)
Mobaye	Basse-Kotto (Cape Verde)
Moca	Espaillat (Dom Republic)
Mochudi	Kgatleng (Botswana)
Mocoa	Putumayo (Colombia)
Mogadishu (Muqdisho)	**Somalia** Banaadir (Somalia)
Mold	Clwyd (Wales)
Molde	Møre og Romsdal (Norway)
Molepolole	Kweneng (Botswana)
Mombasa	Coast Province (Kenya)
Monaco-Ville (aka Monaco)	**Monaco**
Monaghan	Monaghan (Eire)
Mongo	Guéra (Chad)
Mongu	Western Province (Zambia)
Monrovia	**Liberia**
Mons	Hainaut (Belgium)
Montauban	Tarn-et-Garonne (France)
Mont-de-Marsan	Landes (France)
Montego Bay	St James (Jamaica)
Montería	Córdoba (Colombia)

Capital or Admin Centre	Country, State, County or Area	Capital or Admin Centre	Country, State, County or Area
Monterrey	Nuevo León (Mexico)	N'Dalatando	Kuanza Norte (Angola)
Montevideo	**Uruguay**	Ndélé	Bamingui-Bangoran (Cape Verde)
Montgomery	Alabama (USA)		
Montpelier	Vermont (USA)	**N'Djamena**	**Chad**
Montpellier	Hérault (French Department)		Chari-Baguirmi (Chad Prefecture)
	Languedoc-Roussillon (French Region)	Ndola	Copperbelt (Zambia)
		Neiafu	Vava'u (Tonga)
Morant Bay	St Thomas (Jamaica)	Neiba	Bahoruco (Dom Repuplic)
Morelia	Michoacán (Mexico)	Neiva	Huila (Colombia)
Morioka	Iwate (Japan)	Nekemte	Welega (Ethiopia)
Mörön	Hövsgöl (Mongolia)	Nelson	Nelson Bays (NZ)
Moroni	**Comoros Island**	Néma	Hodh-ech-Chargui (Mauritania)
	Ngazidja (Comoros)		
Morpeth	Northumberland (Eng)	Nevers	Nièvre (France)
Morua	Shepherd (Vanuatu)	Neves	Lemba (São Tomé & Principe)
Moscow	**Russia**		
Moshi	Kilimanjaro (Tanzania)	New Amsterdam	East Berbice/Corentyne (Guyana)
Moss	Østfold (Norway)		
Mostar	**Hercegovina**	**New Delhi**	**India (aka Bharat)**
Mosul	Ninawā (Iraq)	New Plymouth	Taranaki (NZ)
Mouila	Ngounié (Gabon)	Newcastle-upon-Tyne	Tyne and Wear (Eng)
Moulins	Allier (France)	Newport	Isle of Wight
Moulmein	Mon (Myanmar)	Newtown St Boswells	Borders (Scotland)
Moundou	Logone Occidental (Chad)	Ngaoundéré	Adamous (Cameroon)
Mount Hagen	Western Highlands (Papua New Guinea)	N'Giva	Cunene (Angola)
		Nha Trang	Khanh Hoa (Vietnam)
Moyobamba	San Martin (Peru)	Nha Trang	Phu Khanh (Vietnam)
Muli	Meemu (Maldives)	Nhlangano	Shiselweni (Swaziland)
Mullingar	Westmeath (Eire)	**Niamey**	**Niger**
Munich	Bavaria (Germany)	Niamtougou	Doufelgou (Togo)
Muscat	**Oman**	Nice	Alpes-Maritimes (France)
Musoma	Mara (Tanzania)	Nicolls Town	Berry Island (Bahamas)
Mutare	Manicaland (Zimbabwe)	**Nicosia**	**Cyprus**
Mutsamudu	Ndzouani (Comoros)	Nieuw Amsterdam	Commewijne (Suriname)
My Tho	Tien Giang (Vietnam)	Nieuw Nickerie	Nickerie (Suriname)
Myitkyinā	Kachin (Myanmar)	Nîmes	Gard (France)
Naas	Kildare (Eire)	Niort	Deux-Sèvres (France)
Nacaome	Valle (Honduras)	Nola	Sangha-Économique (CA Rep)
Nagoya	Aichi (Japan)		
Nagua	Maria Trinidad Sánchez (Dom Republic)	Nolhivaranfaru	Haa-Dhaalu (Maldives)
		Northallerton	North Yorkshire (Eng)
Naha City	Okinawa (Japan)	Northampton	Northamptonshire (Eng)
	Ryukyu Islands (Japan)	Norwich	Norfolk (Eng)
Naifaru	Lhaviyani (Maldives)	Notsé	Haho (Togo)
Nairobi	**Kenya**	Nottingham	Nottinghamshire (Eng)
Nakuru	Rift Valley (Kenya)	**Nouakchott**	**Mauritania**
Nalchik	Kabardino-Balkar (CIS)	Nouméa	New Caledonia (France)
Namendwa	Kamuli (Uganda)	Nouna	Kossi (Burkina Fasso)
Nanchang	Jiangxi (aka Kiangsi)	Nova Sintra	Brava (Cape Verde)
Nancy	Meurthe-et-Moselle (France)	Novi Sad	Vojvodina (Yugoslavia)
		Nueva San Salvador	La Libertad (El Salvador)
Nanjing (aka Nanking)	Jiangsu (aka Kiangsu)	**Nuku'alofa**	**Tonga**
Nanning (China)	Kwangsi Chuang (aka Guangxi Zhuang)		Tongatapu (Tonga)
		Nukus	Kara-Kalpak (CIS)
Nanterre	Hauts-de-Seine (France)	Nyangeya	Masindi (Uganda)
Nantes	Loire-Atlantique (French Department)	Nyeri	Central Province (Kenya)
		Nyiregyháza	Szabics-Szatmár (Hungary)
	Pays de la Loire (French Region)	Nykebing	Storstrom (Denmark)
		Nyköping	Södermanland (Sweden)
Napier	Hawke's Bay (NZ)	Obo	Haut-Mbomou (CA Rep)
Naples	Campania (Italy)	Oddur (Xuddur)	Bakool (Somalia)
Naryan-Mar	Nennets (Russia)	Odense	Fyn (Denmark)
Nashville	Tennessee (USA)	Ohonua	Eua (Tonga)
Nassau	**Bahamas**	Okakarara	Hereroland-Wes (Namibia)
	New Providence (Bahamas)	Oklahoma City	Oklahoma (USA)
		Olaki	Arua (Uganda)
Natal	Rio Grande do Norte (Brazil)	Olympia	Washington (USA)
		Omagh	Tyrone (N.I.)
Natitingou	Atacora (Benin)	Öndörhaan	Hentiy (Mongolia)

GEOGRAPHY

Capital or Admin Centre	Country, State, County or Area	Capital or Admin Centre	Country, State, County or Area
Onverwacht	Para (Suriname)	Penonomé	Coclé (Panama)
Opuwo	Kaokoland (Namibia)	Pereira	Risaraldo (Colombia)
Oradea	Bihor (Romania)	Périgueux	Dordogne (France)
Oranjestad	**Aruba**	Perpignan	Pyrénées-Orientales
Oranjestad	St Eustatius (Netherland Antilles)		(France)
Orléans	Loiret (France)	Perth	Western Australia
Orodara	Kénédougou (Burkina Faso)	Perugia	Umbria (Italy)
Oshakati	Oshana (Nambia)	Peshãwar	North West Frontier (Pakistan)
Oshikango	Ohangwena (Nambia)	Peshkopi	Dibër (Albania)
Oslo	**Norway**	Petrozavodsk	Karelian (CIS)
Östersund	Jämtland (Sweden)	Phan Rang	Ninh Thuan (Vietnam)
Ōtsu	Shiga (Japan)	Phan Thiet	Thuan Hai (Vietnam)
Ottawa	**Canada**	Philipsburg	St Maarten (Netherland Antilles)
Ouagadougou	**Burkina Faso**		
Ouagadougou	Kadiogo (Burkina Faso)	**Phnom Penh**	**Cambodia**
Ouahigouya	Yatenga (Burkina Faso)	Phoenix	Arizona (USA)
Ouesso	Sangha (Congo)	Phônsavan	Xianghoang (Laos)
Outapi	Omusati (Namibia)	Phu Ly	Ha Nan (Vietnam)
Oviedo	Asturias (Spain)	Phuthaditjhaba	Qwaqwa (South Africa)
Owando	Cuvette (Congo)	Piatra Neamt	Neamt (Romania)
Owerri	Imo (Nigeria)	Pierre	South Dakota (USA)
Oxford	Oxfordshire (Eng)	Pietermaritsburg	Natal (South Africa)
Oyem	Woleu-Ntem (Gabon)	Pilar	Ñeembucu (Paraguay)
Pa-an	Karen (Myanmar)	Pitesti	Arges (Romania)
Pachuca	Hidalgo (Mexico)	Plei Ku	Gia Lai (Vietnam)
Padang	Sumatera Barat (Indonesia)	Ploiesti	Prahova (Romania)
Paelau	Fanning/Tabuaeran (Kiribati)	**Plymouth**	**Montserrat**
Pago Pago	American Samoa	Pô	Nahouri (Burkina Faso)
Pagouda	Binah (Togo)	Pointe-Noire	Kouilou (Congo)
Pakanbaru	Riau (Indonesia)	Poitiers	Poitou-Charentes
Pakxan	Bolikhamxay (Laos)	Poitiers	Vienne (France)
Pakxé	Champasak (Laos)	Pokharã	Western Nepal
Palana	Koryak (Russia)	Pombas	Paúl (Cape Verde)
Palangkaraya	Kalimantan Tengah (Indonesia)	Pompey Bay	Acklins Island (Bahamas)
		Ponta Delgada	Azores
Palermo	**Sicily (Italy)**	Ponta do Sol	Ribeira Grande (Cape Verde)
Palma de Mallorca	Balearic Islands (Spain)		
Palmerston North	Manawatu (NZ)	Pontianak	Kalimantan Barat (Indonesia)
Palu	Sulawesi Tengah (Indonesia)	Pontoise	Val-d'Oise (France)
Pamplona	Navarre (Spain)	Popondetta	Northern Province (Papua New Guinea)
Panaji	Goa (India)		
Panama City	**Panama**	Popoyán	Cauca (Colombia)
Pan-ch'iao	Tai-pei (Taiwan)	Port Antonio	Portland (Jamaica)
Pangai	Ha'apai (Tonga)	Port Blair	Andaman and Nicobar Islands
Papeete	**French Polynesia**		
	Society Islands	**Port Louis**	**Mauritius**
	Tahiti	Port Maria	St Mary (Jamaica)
	Îles Tuamotu et Gambier (French Polynesia)	**Port Moresby**	**Papua New Guinea**
	Îles du Vent (French Polynesia)		National Capital District (PNG)
Paradise	Demerara/Mahaica (Guyana)	**Port of Spain**	**Trinidad and Tobago**
		Port-au-Prince	**Haiti**
Parakou	Borgou (Benin)		Ouest (Haiti)
Paramaribo	**Suriname**	Port-de-Paix	Nord-Ouest (Haiti)
Paraná	Entre Rios (Argentina)	Port-Genttil	Ogooué-Maritime (Gabon)
Paris	**France**	Port-Harcourt	Rivers (Nigeria)
	Île-de-France (France)	Portlaoise	Laois/Leix (Eire)
Pasto	Nariño (Colombia)	Pôrto Alegre	Rio Grande do Sul (Brazil)
Patitiri	Alonissos (Sporades)	Porto Inglês	Maio (Cape Verde)
Patna	Bihar (India)	**Porto Novo**	
Pau	Pyrénées-Atlantiques (France)	(*de facto* Cotonou)	**Benin**
		Pôrto Velho	Rondônia (Brazil)
Pécs	Baranya (Hungary)	Porto-Novo	Ouémé (Benin)
Pedra Badejo	Santa Cruz (Cape Verde)	Portoferraio	Elba
Pedro Juan Caballero	Amambay (Paraguay)	Portoviejo	Manabi (Ecuador)
Pemba	Cabo Delgado (Mozambique)	Posadas	Misiones (Argentina)
		Potenza	Basilicata (Italy)
		Potsdam	Brandenburg (Germany)

Capital or Admin Centre	Country, State, County or Area	Capital or Admin Centre	Country, State, County or Area
Pozo Colorado	President Hayes (Paraguay)	Rio Claro	Nariva/Mayaro (Trinidad & Tobago)
Prague	**Czech Republic**	Rio Gallegos	Santa Cruz (Argentina)
Praia	**Cape Verde**	Riobamba	Chimborazo (Ecuador)
Preston	Lancashire (Eng)	Riohacha	La Guajira (Colombia)
Pretoria	Transvaal (South Africa)	Rivercess City	Rivercess (Liberia)
Pretoria-admin	**South Africa**	**Riyadh**	**Saudi Arabia**
Princes Town	Victoria (Trinidad & Tobago)	**Road Town**	**Virgin Islands (British)**
Principe	Paguê (São Tomé & Principe)	Roatán	Islas de la Bahia (Honduras)
Pristina	Kosovo (Yugoslavia)	Robertsport	Grand Cape Mount (Liberia)
Privas	Ardèche (France)	Rodez	Aveyron (France)
Providence	Rhode Island (USA)	**Rome**	**Italy**
Pucallpa	Ucayali (Peru)		Lazio (Italy)
Puerto Barrios	Izabal (Guatemala)	Roreti	Arorae (Kiribati)
Puerto Carreño	Vichada (Colombia)	Roscommon	Roscommon (Eire)
Puerto Inirida	Guainia (Colombia)	**Roseau**	**Dominica**
Puerto Lempira	Gracias a Dios (Honduras)	Rosita	Región Autónoma del Atlántico Norte (Nic)
Puerto Maldonado	Madre de Dios (Peru)		
Puerto Montt	Los Lagos (Chile)	Rosso	Trarza (Mauritania)
Punta Arenas (Chile)	Magallanes y de la Antártica Chilena	Rouen	Haute-Normandie (French Region)
Punta Gorda	Toledo (Belize)		Seine-Maritime (French Department)
Puyo	Pastaza (Ecuador)		
P'yŏngsan	P'yongan-namdo (North Korea)	Rovaniemi	Lappi (Finland)
		Rrëshen	Mirditë (Albania)
Pyongyang	**North Korea (aka Choson)**	Rubale	Kabale (Uganda)
Quebec	Quebec (Canada)	Rukoki	Kapchorwa (Uganda)
Quelimane	Zambézia (Mozambique)	Rundu	Kavango (Namibia)
Quetta	Baluchistãn (Pakistan)	Rungata	Nikunau (Kiribati)
Qui Nhon	Nghia Binh (Vietnam)	Saarbrücken	Saarland (Germany)
Quibdó	Chocó (Colombia)	Sacramento	California (USA)
Quimper	Finistère (France)	Sa Dec	Dong Thap (Vietnam)
Quito	**Ecuador**	St Annes	Alderney
	Pichincha (Ecuador)	Saint-Brieuc	Côtes-du-Nord (France)
Quy Nhon	Binh Dinh (Vietnam)	**Saint-Denis**	**Réunion**
Rabat	**Morocco**	Saint-Etienne	Loire (France)
Rabaul	East New Britain (Papua New Guinea)	**St George's**	**Grenada**
		St Helier	Jersey
Rach Gia	Kien Giang (Vietnam)	**St Johns**	**Antigua and Barbuda**
Raleigh	North Carolina (USA)	Saint-Lô	Manche (France)
Ramla	Central District (Israel)	St Paul	Minnesota (USA)
Ramotswa	Botswana (South East)	St Peter Port	Guernsey
Rancagua (Chile)	Libertador Gen Bernardo O'Higgins	Sal Rei	Boavista (Cape Verde)
		Salamá	Baja Verapaz (Guatemala)
Rangoon (Yangon)	**Burma (now Myanmar)**	Salem	Oregon (USA)
Rasht	Gilãn (Iran)	Salgótarján	Nógrád (Hungary)
Rawannawi	Marakei (Kiribati)	Salt Lake City	Utah (USA)
Rawson	Chubut (Argentina)	Saltillo	Coahuila (Mexico)
Reading	Berkshire (Eng)	Salto del Guairá	Canendiyú (Paraguay)
Recife	Pernambuco (Brazil)	Salvador	Bahia (Brazil)
Regina	Saskatchewan (Canada)	Samarai	Milne Bay (Papua New Guinea)
Renne	Bornholm (Denmark)		
Rennes	Bretagne/Brittany (French Region)	San Andrés	San Andrés y Providencia
	Ille-et-Vilaine (French Department)	San Carlos	Cojedes (Venezuela)
		San Carlos	Zona Especial III (Nicaragua)
Réo	Sanguie (Burkina Faso)		
Resistencia	Chaco (Argentina)	San Cristóbal	Táchira (Venezuela)
Resita	Caras-Severin (Romania)	San Felipe	Yaracuy (Venezuela)
Reykavik	**Iceland**	San Fernando	Catamarca (Argentina)
	Höfudhborgarsvaedhi (Iceland)	San Fernando de Apure	Apure (Venezuela)
		San Francisco de Macoris	Duarte (Dom Republic)
Rhodes	**Rhodes**	San Francisco (Gotera)	Morazán (El Salvador)
Ribeira Brava	São Nicolau (Cape Verde)	San Ignacio	Cayo (Belize)
Richmond	Virginia (USA)	**San José**	**Costa Rica**
Riga	**Latvia**	**San Juan**	**Puerto Rico**
Rikitea	Gambier Islands	San Juan Bautista	Misiones (Paraguay)
Ringdove	Epi (Vanuatu)	San Juan de Los Morros	Guárico (Venezuela)
Rio Branco	Acre (Brazil)		

GEOGRAPHY

Capital or Admin Centre	Country, State, County or Area	Capital or Admin Centre	Country, State, County or Area
San Marino	San Marino (Most Serene Republic)	Shijazhuang	Hebei (China)
	Citta (San Marino)	Shillong	Meghālaya (India)
San Miguel	Tucumán (Argentina)	Shimla	Himāchal Pradesh (India)
San Pedro Sula	Cortés (Honduras)	Shirāz	Fārs (Iran)
San Salvador	El Salvador	Shrewsbury	Shropshire (Eng)
San Salvador	Jujuy (Argentina)	Sibiti	Lékoumou (Congo)
Sana	Yemen Republic	Sibut	Kemo-Gribingui (CA Rep)
Sangre Grande	St Andrew & St David (Trinidad & Tobago)	Sidon/Saydā	Al-Janub (Lebanon)
		Silvassa	Dadra and Nagar Haveli (India)
Sankt Pölten	Niederösterreich (Austria)	Sincelejo	Sucre (Colombia)
Sanniquellie	Nimba (Liberia)	Singapore	Singapore
Sansanné-Mango	Oti (Togo)	Sinujiu	P'yongan-pukto (North Korea)
Santa Clara	Villa Clara (Cuba)		
Santa Cruz	Quiché (Guatemala)	Siobozia	Ialomita (Romania)
Santa Cruz	Temotu (Solomon Isles)	Sion	Valais (Swiss Canton)
Santa Cruz de Tenerife	Canary Islands (Spain)	Siparia	St Patrick (Trinidad & Tobago)
Santa Fe	New Mexico (USA)		
Santa Maria	Sal (Cape Verde)	Siteki	Lubombo (Swaziland)
Santa Rosa	La Pampa (Argentina)	Sittwe (aka Akyab)	Arakan/Rakhine (Burma)
Santana	Cantagaio (São Tomé & Principe)	Siyabuswa	KwaNdebele (South Africa)
		Skien	Telemark (Norway)
Santander	Cantabria (Spain)	Skopje	Macedonia (Yugoslavia)
Santander	Magdalena (Colombia)	Slatina	Olt (Romania)
Santiago	Chile	Sligo	Sligo (Eire)
Santiago	Metropolitan (Chile)	Sofia	Bulgaria (aka Narodna Republic)
Santiago	Veraguas (Panama)		
Santiago de Compostela	Galicia (Spain)	Sokodé	Centrale Region (Togo)
Santiago de los Caballeros	Santiago (Dom Republic)		Tchaoudjo (Togolese Prefecture)
Santo Domingo	Dominican Republic	Sola	Banks/Torres (Vanuatu)
São António	Principe (São Tomé & Principe)	Solwezi	North-Western Province (Zambia)
São Filipe	Fogo (Cape Verde)	Songea	Ruvuma (Tanzania)
São João Angolares	Caué (São Tomé & Principe)	Sore	Vestjaelland (Denmark)
		Spanish Town	St Catherine (Jamaica)
São Luis	Maranhão (Brazil)	Springfield	Illinois (USA)
São Tomé	São Tomé and Príncipe	Srinigar	Jammu and Kashmir (India)
	Aqua Grande (São Tomé & Principe)	Stafford	Staffordshire (Eng)
		Stanley	Falkland Islands
Sapporo	Hokkaidō (Japan)	Stans	Nidwalden (Swiss Canton)
Saransk	Mordovia (Russia)	Stavanger	Rogaland (Norway)
Sarajevo	Bosnia and Hercegovina	Steinkjer	Nord-Trønelag (Norway)
Sarh	Moyen-Chari (Chad)	Stirling	Central (Scotland)
Sari	Māzandarān (Iran)	Stockholm	Sweden
Sariwŏn	Hwanghae-pukto (North Korea)	Stornoway (Lewis)	Western Isles (Scotland)
		St-Pierre	St-Pierre and Miquelon
Sarnen	Obwalden (Swiss Canton)	Strasbourg	Alsace (French Region)
Saudhárkrókur	Nordhurland vestra (Iceland)		Bas-Rhin (French Department)
Saurimo	Lunda Sol (Angola)	Stuttgart	Baden-Württemberg (Germany)
Savanna-la-Mar	Westmoreland (Jamaica)		
Saynshand	Dornogovi (Mongolia)	St Johns	Newfoundland (Canada)
Scarborough	Tobago	Sucre-judicial	Bolivia
Sefadu	Kono (Sierra Leone)		Chuquisaca (Bolivia)
Sekondi-Takoradi	Western Region (Ghana)	Sühbaatar	Selenge (Mongolia)
Selfoss	Sudhurland (Iceland)	Sukhumi	Abkhaziya (CIS)
Sélibaby	Guidimaka (Mauritania)	Sukulu	Tororo (Uganda)
Semarang	Jawar Tengah (Indonesia)	Sumbawanga	Rukwa (Tanzania)
Sendai	Miyagi (Japan)	Sumbe	Kuanza Sul (Angola)
Sensuntepeque	Cabañas (El Salvador)	Sunyani	Brong-Ahafo (Ghana)
Seoul	South Korea	Surabaya	Jawar Timur (Indonesia)
Seremban	Negeri Sembilan (Malaysia)	Surkhet	Mid-Western Nepal
Serowe	Botswana (Central)	Suva	Central Province (Fiji)
Seville	Andalucia (Spain)	Suva	Fiji
Sfintu Gheorghe	Covasna (Romania)	Suwŏn	Kyŏnggi-do (South Korea)
Shenyang	Liaoning (China)	Swakopmund	Erongo (Namibia)
s-Hertogenbosch	Noord-Brabant (Netherlands)	Swansea	West Glamorgan (Wales)
		Sydney	New South Wales
Shibin al-Kawm	Al-Minufiyah (Egypt)	Syktyv-Kar	Komi (CIS)

Capital or Admin Centre	Country, State, County or Area
Szeged	Csongrád (Hungary)
Székesfehérvár	Fejér (Hungary)
Szekszárd	Tolna (Hungary)
Szombathely	Vas (Hungary)
Tabligbo	Yoto (Togo)
Tabontebike	Kuria (Kiribati)
Taegu	Kyŏngsang-pukto (South Korea)
Taiohae	Îles Marquises (French Polynesia)
Taipei	**Taiwan**
Taiyuan	Shanxi (China)
Takaeang	Aranuka (Kiribati)
Takamatsu	Kagawa (Japan)
Talca	Maule (Chile)
Tallahassee	Florida (USA)
Tallinn	**Estonia**
Tamale	Northern Region (Ghana)
Tamrida	Socotra (Yemen)
Tan An	Long An (Vietnam)
Tanjã	Al-Gharbiyah (Egypt)
Tanjung Karang	Lampung (Indonesia)
Tarbes	Haute-Pyrénées (France)
Tashkent	**Uzbekistan**
Tatabánya	Komárom (Hungary)
Taubukinberu	Beru (Kiribati)
Taunggyi	Shan (Myanmar)
Taunton	Somerset (Eng)
Taupo	Tongariro (NZ)
Tauranga	Bay of Plenty (NZ)
Tbilisi	**Georgia (CIS)**
Tchibanga	Nyanga (Gabon)
Tebangetua	Maiana (Kiribati)
Tegucigalpa	**Honduras**
	Francisco Morazán (Honduras)
Tehran	**Iran**
Temuco	Araucania (Chile)
Tena	Napo (Ecuador)
Tenkodogo	Boulgou (Burkina Faso)
Tepic	Nayarit (Mexico)
Teresina	Piauí (Brazil)
Teuabu	Nonouti (Kiribati)
Teyateyaneng	Berea (Lesotho)
Thakhek	Khammouan (Laos)
Thames-Coromandel	Thames Valley (NZ)
The Bottom	Saba (Netherland Antilles)
Thessalonika	**Macedonia (Greece)**
Thimphu	**Bhutan (aka Druk-Yul)**
Thinadhoo	Gaafu-Dhaalu (Maldives)
Thohoyandou	Venda (South Africa)
Thong	Xékong (Laos)
Thorshavn	**Faeroe Islands**
Thu Dau Mot	Binh Duong (Vietnam)
Tiberias	Northern District (Israel)
Tidjikdja	Tagant (Mauritania)
Timaru	Aorangi (NZ)
Timisoara	Timis (Romania)
Tirana	**Albania**
Tirgoviste	Dimbovita (Romania)
Tirgu Jiu	Gorj (Romania)
Tirgu Mures	Mures (Romania)
Titograd	**Montenegro**
Tokyo	**Japan**
Toledo	Castilla-La-Mancha (Spain)
Toluca	México (Mexican State)
Tønsberg	Vestfold (Norway)
Topeka	Kansas (USA)
Toronto	Ontario (Canada)
Totness	Coronie (Suriname)

Capital or Admin Centre	Country, State, County or Area
Tougan	Sourou (Burkina Faso)
Tou-liu	Yün-lin (Taiwan)
Toulon	Var (France)
Toulouse	Haute-Garonne (French Department)
	Midi-Pyrénées (French Region)
Tours	Indre-et-Loire (France)
Tralee	Kerry (Eire)
Trenton	New Jersey (USA)
Trieste	Friuli-Venezia Giulia (Italy)
Trim	Meath (Eire)
Trinidad	Flores (Uruguay)
Trinidad	Beni (Bolivia)
Trinidade	Mé-zóchi (São Tomé & Principe)
Tripoli	**Libya**
Tripoli/Tarābulus	Ash-Shamāl (Lebanon)
Trivandrum	Kerala (India)
Trondheim	Sor-Trøndelag (Norway)
Trowbridge	Wiltshire (Eng)
Troyes	Aube (France)
Trujillo	Colón (Honduras)
Trujillo	La Libertad (Peru)
Trujillo	Trujillo (Venezuela)
Truro	Cornwall (Eng)
Tsabong	Kgalagadi (Botswana)
Tsetserieg	Arhangay (Mongolia)
Tsévié	Zio (Togo)
Tskhinvali	South Ossetia
Tsu	Mie (Japan)
Tsumeb	Oshikoto (Namibia)
Tsumkwe	Boesmanland (Namibia)
Tuarabu	Abalang (Kiribati)
Tubmanburg	Bomi (Liberia)
Tulagi	Central Islands (Solomon Isles)
Tulcan	Carchi (Ecuador)
Tullamore	Offaly (Eire)
Tulle	Corrèze (France)
Tunis	**Tunisia**
Tunja	Boyacá (Colombia)
Tura	Evenki (Russia)
Turin	Piedmont (Italy)
Turku	Turku ja Pori (Finland)
Tuxtla Gutiérrez	Chiapas (Mexico)
Tuy Hoa	Phu Yen (Vietnam)
Ufa	Bashkir (CIS)
Ugoofaaru	Raa (Maldives)
Ujung Pandang	Sulawesi Selatan (Indonesia)
Ulaangom	Uvs (Mongolia)
Ulan Bator	**Mongolia**
Ulan-Ude	Buryat (CIS)
Uliastay	Dzavhan (Mongolia)
Ulundi	KwaZulu (South Africa)
Umea	Västerbotten (Sweden)
Umtata	Transkei (South Africa)
Urawa	Saitama (Japan)
Urumchi (aka Urumqi)	Sinkiang Uighur (aka Xinjiang Uygur)
Ushuaia	Tierra Del Fuego (Argentina)
Ust-Ordynsk	Ust-Ordyn-Buryat (Russia)
Utiroa	Tabiteuea North (Kiribati)
Utsunomiya	Tochigi (Japan)
Uturoa	Îles sous le Vent (French Polynesia)
	Raiatea (French Polynesia)

GEOGRAPHY

Capital or Admin Centre	Country, State, County or Area	Capital or Admin Centre	Country, State, County or Area
Uyo	Akwa Ibom (Nigeria)	Wete	Pemba North (Tanzania)
Vaduz	**Liechtenstein**	Wewak	East Sepik (Papua New Guinea)
Vaitape	Bora-Bora		
Valence	Drôme (France)	Wexford	Wexford (Eire)
Valencia	Carabobo (Venezuela)	Whangarei	Northland (NZ)
Valladolid	Castilla-León (Spain)	Whitehorse	Yukon Territory (Canada)
Valledupar	Cesar (Colombia)	Wicklow	Wicklow (Eire)
Valletta	**Malta**	Wiesbaden	Hessen (Germany)
Valley, The	**Anguilla**	**Willemstad**	**Netherland Antilles**
Valparaiso	Valparaiso (Chile)		Curaçao (Netherland Antilles)
Vänersborg	Älvsborg (Sweden)		
Vanimo	West Sepik (Papua New Guinea)	Winchester	Hampshire (Eng)
		Windhoek	**Namibia**
Vannes	Morbihan (France)	Windhoek	Khomas (Namibia)
Vardø	Finnmark (Norway)	Winnipeg	Manitoba (Canada)
Västerás	Västmanland (Sweden)	Wŏnson	Kangwŏn-do (North Korea)
Växjö	Kronoberg (Sweden)	Worcester	Hereford and Worcester (Eng)
Versailles	Yvelines (France)		
Vesoul	Haute-Saône (France)	Wuhan	Hubei (China)
Veymandhoo	Thaa (Maldives)	Xai-Xai	Gaza (Mozambique)
Victoria	British Columbia (Canada)	Xam Nua	Houaphan (Laos)
		Xay	Oudomxay (Laos)
Victoria	**Seychelles**	Xi'an (aka Sian)	Shaanxi (aka Shensi)
	Mahé (Seychelles)	Xining (aka Hsi-ning)	Qinghai (aka Tsinghai)
Victoria (Guzo)	Malta	Yako	Passoré (Burkina Faso)
Victoria (on Hong Kong Island)	**Hong Kong (aka Hsiang Kang)**	Yakutsk	Yakut (CIS)
		Yambio	Western Equatoria (Sudan)
Viedma	Rio Negro (Argentina)	**Yamoussoukro-admin**	**Ivory Coast**
Vienna	**Austria**	Yangon	Myanmar
Vientiane	**Laos**	Yaoundé	Cameroon
Viet Tri	Phu Tho (Vietnam)		Centre Province (Cameroon)
Vila	**Vanuatu**		
	Efaté (Vanuatu)	**Yaren**	**Nauru**
Vilgili	Gaafu-Alifu (Maldives)	Yellowknife	Northwest Territories (Canada)
Villahermosa	Tabasco (Mexico)		
Villarica	Guairá (Paraguay)	**Yerevan**	**Armenia**
Villavicencio	Meta (Colombia)	Yinchuan	Ningxia Hui (China)
Vilnius	**Lithuania**	Yogyakarta	Yogyakarta (Indonesia)
Vinh	Nghe Tinh (Vietnam)	Yokohama	Kanagawa (Japan)
Vinh Yen	Vinh Phuc (Vietnam)	Yola	Gongola (Nigeria)
Visby	Gotland (Sweden)	Yopal	Casanare (Colombia)
Vitoria	Basque Country (Spain)	Yushkar-Ola	Mari-El (Russia)
Vitória	Espirito Santo (Brazil)	Yuscarán	El Paraiso (Honduras)
Vladikavkaz	Alania (Russia) / North Ossetia	Yuzhno-Sakhalinsk	Sakhalin Island
		Zacatecoluca	La Paz (El Salvador)
Vogan	Vo (Togo)	**Zagreb**	**Croatia**
Voinjama	Lofa (Liberia)	Zähedän	Sistän va Baluchestän (Iran)
Vreed-en-Hoop	Essequibo Islands (Guyana)	Zahlah	Al-Biqa (Lebanon)
Wa	Upper West (Ghana)	Zalău	Salaj (Romania)
Wabag	Enga (Papua New Guinea)	Zamora	Zamora-Chinchipe (Ecuador)
Wakefield	West Yorkshire (Eng)		
Warsaw	**Poland**	Zanzibar	Zanzibar West (Tanzania)
Warwick	Warwickshire (Eng)	Zaragosa	Aragón (Spain)
Washington DC	**United States of America**	Zhengzhou	Henan (China)
Waterford	Waterford (Eire)	Ziniaré	Oubritenga (Burkina Faso)
Wãu	Bahr al-Ghazãl (Sudan)	Zinjibãr	Abyãn (Yemen)
Wavre	Brabant (Walloon)	Zorgho	Ganzourgou (Burkina Faso)
Wellington	**New Zealand**	Zwedru	Grand Gedeh (Liberia)
West Island	Cocos (aka Keeling Islands) (Aus)	Zwolle	Overijssel (Netherlands)

NB: This section is a fully comprehensive listing of all the world's capital cities, chief towns, and administrative centres. It can be assumed that where a capital is not included in this section it is because the State, County or Area has a capital with the same name. To simplify the process of researching the more obscure capitals, when the continent or country is perhaps unknown, all areas, be it Country, State, Island or City, which have a capital, admin centre or chief town, have been sorted alphabetically. Similarly, any area which is the capital, chief town, or administrative centre, of a larger area, has also been sorted alphabetically. This methodology ensures that, as long as you know one half of the equation, the other half can be found very quickly. All countries, and some of the more significant islands and states, have been printed in bold type.

Capitals: former

Aachen Holy Roman Empire
Aarau (Switzerland) Helvetic Republic
Abeokuta (Nigeria) Egba State
Aden South Yemen
Agra India
Akmola Kazakhstan
Alexandria Egypt
Amarapura Burma
Angkor Thom Cambodia
Antigua Guatemala Guatemala
Antioch Ancient Syria
Anuradhapura Ceylon
Arras Artois Province
Ashur (Assur) Assyria
Auch Gascony
Auckland New Zealand
Augusta Georgia, USA
Ava Burma
Ayutthaya (Ayuthia) Thailand
Babylon Babylonia
Baeza (Spain) Moorish Kingdom
Bakhchisarai Crimean Khans
Bamburgh Northumbria
Bastia Corsica
Belize Belize
Bingerville Ivory Coast
Bucharest Wallachia
Calcutta India
Chan Chan Chimú Empire
Ctesiphon Parthia
Cuzco Inca Empire
Danzig West Prussia
Dar Es Salaam Tanzania
Dawson Yukon
Entebbe Uganda
Fillmore Utah
Gondar Ethiopia
Gordium Phrygia
Grytviken South Georgia and South Sandwich Islands
Guthrie Oklahoma (USA)
Hague, The Netherlands
Hattusa Hittite Empire
Hué Annam
Jerusalem Palestine
Karachi Pakistan
Kaunas Lithuania
Kracow Poland
Kyoto Japan
Kzyl-Orda Kazakhstan
Lagos Nigeria
Levuka Fiji

Livingstone Northern Rhodesia
Mandalay Burma
Maribo Lolland (Denmark)
Marrakesh Morocco
Melbourne Australia
Memphis Ancient Egypt
Mocha Yemen
M(o)ukden Manchuria
Nafplio Greece
Nanking China
Nara (Heijo-Kyo) Japan
New Haven Connecticut
New Orleans Louisiana (USA)
New York USA (1785–90)
Nineveh Assyria
Olomouc Moravia
Omaha Nebraska
Palio Horio (aka Chora) Alonissos (Greece)
Persepolis Persia
Perth Scotland
Philadelphia USA (1790–1800)
Quezon City Philippines
Rawalpindi Pakistan
Rio de Janeiro Brazil
Rovigno Istria
Saigon South Vietnam
St George Bermuda
St Mary's City Maryland (USA)
St Petersburg Russia
Sardis Lydia
Scodra Illyra
Sitka Alaska
Stettin Pomerania
Susa Elam (Persian Empire)
Sydney Australia
Tenochtitlán Aztec Empire
Thebes Ancient Egypt
Toledo Spain
Toulouse Languedoc
Trenton USA (1784–5)
Trondheim Norway
Trujillo Honduras
Turku Finland
Tyre Phoenicia
Vathy Ithaca
Wheeling West Virginia
Winchester England
Yankton South Dakota
Yasodharapura Cambodia
Zanzibar Oman
Zomba Malawi

GEOGRAPHY

Continents

Continents	Area (Sq Miles)	% of Earth's Land	Lowest Point	Estimated population mid-1990
Asia	16,988,000	29.9	Dead Sea (-400 m)	3,317,800,000
Africa	11,506,000	20.3	Lake Assal (-156 m)	654,600,000
North America	9,365,000	16.5	Death Valley (-86 m)	435,800,000
South America	6,820,000	12.0	Valdés Peninsula (-40 m)	299,900,000
Antarctica	5,400,000	9.5	ice-covered (-2538 m)	No indigenous population
Europe	3,745,000	6.6	Caspian Sea (-28 m)	684,400,000
Australia	2,941,526	5.2	Lake Eyre (-16 m)	17,800,000

Deserts: World's Largest

		Area (Sq Miles)				Area (Sq Miles)
1	Sahara	3,500,000	9	Thar		100,000
2	Arabian	900,000	10	Somali		100,000
3	Australian	600,000	11	Kyzyl Kum		100,000
4	Gobi	500,000	12	Atacama		70,000
5	Kalahari	225,000	13	Dasht-e Lut		20,000
6	Sonoran	120,000	14	Mojave		13,500
7	Kara Kum	120,000	15	Desierto de Sechura		10,000
8	Namib	110,000				

NB: The Gobi Desert includes the Takla Makan area, comprising 125,000 sq miles. The Kara Kum and the Kyzyl Kum are often considered as one large desert, the Turkestan. The Australian Desert comprises the Great Sandy, Simpson, Gibson and Great Victoria Deserts. The Arabian Desert comprises the Eastern Desert and the Western Desert (sometimes called the Libyan Desert) and most of the Saudi Arabian peninsula, including the Rub al Khali (empty quarter) which is the size of the Kalahari.

Earth's Extremes

coldest place	Plateau Station, Antarctica: annual average temperature -56.7 deg C
deepest canyon	Colca River Canyon, Peru: 3,625 m
driest place	Atacama Desert, Chile: rainfall negligible
greatest tides	Bay of Fundy, Nova Scotia: 16 m
highest waterfall	Angel, Venezuela: 3,212′ (979 m)
hottest place	Dalol, Danakil Depression, Ethiopia: annual average temperature 35 deg C
largest canyon	Grand Canyon, Colorado River, Arizona: 466 km long and 183 m to 29 km wide, about 1.6 km deep
longest reef	Great Barrier Reef, Australia: 2,012 km
most predictable geyser	Old Faithful, Wyoming: annual average interval 69 to 78 minutes
wettest place	Mount Waialeale, Hawaii: annual average rainfall 16,800 mm

Major Earthquakes

	Richter scale	Estimated deaths	Year
Antioch, Turkey		250,000	526
Corinth, Greece		45,000	856
Shensi Province, China		830,000	1556
Catania, Italy		60,000	1693
Calcutta, India		300,000	1737
Lisbon, Portugal		60,000	1755
Calabria, Italy		50,000	1783
San Francisco	8.3	452	1906
Messina	7.5	83,000	1908
Avezzano, Italy	7.5	29,980	1915
Gansu, China	8.6	100,000	1920
Tokyo	8.3	140,000	1923
Nan-Shan, China	8.3	200,000	1927
Gansu, China	7.6	70,000	1932

	Richter scale	Estimated deaths	Year
Quetta, India	7.5	30,000	1935
Erzincan, Turkey	7.9	30,000	1939
Chillán, Chile	8.3	28,000	1939
Assam, India	8.7	1,526	1950
USSR	7.3	110,000	1948
Agadir, Morocco	5.8	12,000	1960
Anchorage, Alaska	9.2	131	1964
Northern Peru	7.7	66,794	1970
Managua, Nicaragua	6.5	7,000	1971
Guatemala City	7.5	23,000	1976
Tangshan, China	8.2	242,000	1976
NE Iran	7.7	25,000	1978
El Asnam, Algeria	7.3	20,000	1980
Mexico	8.1	25,000	1985
Armenia, USSR	6.9	25,000	1988
San Francisco	7.1	300	1989
Roudhon, NW Iran	7.7	50,000	1990
Latur, India	6.5	9,748	1993
Kobe, Japan	7.2	5,500	1995
Neftegursk, Russia	7.5	1,989	1995
Qayen, NE Iran	7.1	4,000	1997
Ismit, Turkey	7.8	2,000+	1999
Gujarat, India	7.7	20,023	2001
Indian Ocean	9.0	283,106	2004

NB: The estimated deaths caused by these earthquakes are listed purely to indicate the devastation. It is very hard to draw accurate conclusions, as government statistics are in some instances based on bodies recovered. To give Tokyo 1923 as an example, the official death toll was 99,330, but that figure does not take into account the deaths caused by fire, famine, pestilence, and shock in the aftermath or the persons missing presumed dead.

European Cities of Culture

1985	Athens
1986	Florence
1987	Amsterdam
1988	Berlin
1989	Paris
1990	Glasgow
1991	Dublin
1992	Madrid
1993	Antwerp
1994	Lisbon
1995	Luxemburg
1996	Copenhagen
1997	Thessaloniki
1998	Stockholm
1999	Weimar
2000	Avignon, Bergen, Bologna, Brussels, Helsinki, Krakow, Prague, Reykjavik, Santiago de Compostela (Spain)
2001	Rotterdam and Porto
2002	Bruges and Salamanca
2003	Graz
2004	Genoa and Lille
2005	Cork
2006	Patras

NB: In 1999 the European Cities of Culture were renamed European Capitals of Culture.

GEOGRAPHY

General Information

anabranch   Stream that leaves a river and re-enters it lower down, especially in Australia.

Appalachian trail   Public footpath that runs for over 2,000 miles between Mount Springer in Georgia and Mount Katahdin in Maine.

arroyo   Dry channel in a semi-arid area that may be subject to flash flooding during seasonal downpours.

atmospheric layers   Troposphere is the lowest layer, 11 miles thick at the equator. Stratosphere lies above the troposphere, contains most of the ozone layer. Mesosphere lies above the stratosphere and is often considered part of it. Thermosphere lies between the mesosphere and the exosphere reaching altitudes of 250 miles. Ionosphere is the area charged by the Sun's radiation, between 40 and 600 miles, and has 4 main layers: the D-layer (40–60 miles), E-layer (60–95 miles), F1 and F2-layers (95–250 miles). Exosphere is the outermost layer of the Earth's atmosphere.

berg   Hot, dry north wind of Cape Province and Natal.

Bermuda: nine counties   Devonshire, Hamilton, Paget, Pembroke, Sandys, Smith's, Southampton, Warwick, St George's

bise   Cold, dry north wind prevalent in Switzerland and southern France.

bora   Strong northerly wind that blows in the northern Adriatic.

brickfielder   Hot, dry north wind of Australia.

bridge: longest by span   Akashi-Kaikyo, Shikoku, Japan (6,528′).

building: tallest inhabited   Taipei 101, Taiwan (1,667′). The 2nd tallest is the Petronas Towers, Kuala Lumpur (1,482′). The Sears Tower, Chicago, is the 3rd tallest (1,454′) but with the television mast is 1,707′. Canary Wharf Tower, designed by Cesar Pelli, is currently the tallest British building (800′).

building: tallest uninhabited   Warszawa Radio Mast, Konstantynow, Poland (2,120′), although under repair after collapsing in 1991. 2nd tallest structure is KTHI-TV Mast, N. Dakota (2,063′). 3rd is the CN Tower, Toronto (1,822′).

buran   Snowstorm accompanied by high winds, chiefly prevalent in the Russian Steppes.

Cape Doctor   Strong south-east wind which blows on the South African coast.

cataract   A large, rushing waterfall, usually over a precipice.

Caver   A gentle Hebridean breeze. Also spelt Kaver.

chinook   Warm dry wind that blows in the Rocky Mountain region of North America.

clouds: classification   *High cloud:* Cirrus – detached clouds resembling feathers, named from the Latin for 'lock of hair'. Cirrocumulus – rounded small clouds appearing in the form of grains or ripples. Cirrostratus – white veil of smooth fibrous ice crystals, often forming a halo of light. *Middle cloud:* Altocumulus – grey or white clouds having rounded shapes, sometimes touching. Altostratus – flat, grey sheet cloud, often obscuring the Sun and often bringing drizzle. Nimbostratus – flat, shapeless clouds which are the main source of rain and snow. *Low Cloud:* Cumulus – detached clouds that vary from small fleeces to large cauliflower shapes. Cumulonimbus – often anvil-shaped and noted for its accompaniment of thunder. Stratus – shapeless thin, grey cloud, often starting as fog. Stratocumulus – round-shaped patchy cloud

often formed as Cumulus but thinning out.

coastline: longest   Canada (152,100 miles).

coastline: shortest   Monaco (3.5 miles).

continental extremities   west–east–north–south *Africa* – Cape Vert, Senegal; Ras Hafun, Somalia; Cape Blanc, Tunisia; Cape Agulhas, South Africa. *Asia* – Cape Baba, Turkey; Cape Dezneva, Russia; Cape Celjuskin, Russia; Cape Piai, Malaysia. *Australia* – Steep Point; Cape Byron; Cape York; South East Point, Tasmania. *Europe* – Cape Roca, Portugal; Kara River; North Cape, Norway; Point Tarifa, Spain. *North America* – Cape Prince of Wales, Alaska; Cape Charles, Newfd; Boothia peninsula, NWT; SW Panama. *South America* – Punta Pariña, Peru; Cape Branco, Brazil; Punta Gallinas, Colombia; Cape Horn. It should be noted that some countries are included in different continents from the country that administers them, e.g. Greenland is administered by Denmark, although part of North America.

cordillera   System or group of parallel mountain ranges together with intervening plateaux, especially of the Andes and in Central America and Mexico.

dams: tallest   Rogun Dam in Tajikistan (1,098′) is the tallest, followed by Nurek Dam in Tajikistan (984′). The 3rd tallest dam is the Grande Dixence in Switzerland (935′).

depression: deepest   Dead Sea (1,296′ below sea level), Turfan Depression, China (505′), Qattara Depression, Egypt (436′).

desert: meaning   From the Latin word *desertus* meaning 'abandoned'.

Diablo   Northern Californian wind, sometimes gusting in excess of 60mph, due to high pressure over Nevada and lower pressure along the central Californian coast.

dictionary of places   Gazetteer.

driest place on Earth   Calama in the Atacama Desert, Chile, has no recorded rainfall.

Earth: composition   The most abundant elements of the Earth's composition are iron (35.9%), oxygen (28.5%), magnesium and silicon (each about 15%). The most abundant elements of the Earth's crust are oxygen, silicon, and aluminium.

Earth: dimensions
Mass 5,974,000,000,000,000,000,000 metric tons.
Area 510,066,000 square Kilometres.
Land 148,429,000 square Kilometres (29.1%).
Water 361,637,000 square Kilometres (70.9%).
Population 5,420,391,000 approximately.

Earth's layers   crust, mantle, core.

El Niño   Destructive climatic phenomenon involving a periodic change of direction in the prevailing trade winds and ocean currents flowing from the Americas to Asia across the southern Pacific.

Elephanta   Strong southerly or south-easterly wind which blows on the Malabar coast of India during September and October, marking the end of the monsoon season.

Etesian   Dry north wind blowing over the Aegean and eastern Mediterranean during the summer months (aka Meltemi).

Euros   Greek name for the rainy, stormy south-east wind.

Fö(e)hn   Hot southerly wind on the northern slopes of the Alps.

footpaths Dales Way – runs for 81 miles from Ilkley in West Yorkshire to Bowness-on-Windermere. Icknield Way – most ancient road in Britain, 105 miles from Ridgeway to Peddars Way. Mid Shires Way – opened in 1994 covering 225 miles from Buckinghamshire to Greater Manchester. North Downs Way – stretches 141 miles from south-west of London (Farnham) to the Dover coast. Offa's Dyke – follows the English/Welsh border for 168 miles via the Wye Valley. Peddars Way – 94-mile stretch from Thetford to Cromer. Pembrokeshire Coastal Path – 186-mile stretch from Amroth on Carmarten Bay to west of Cardigan. Pennine Way – follows course of the Pennines from Edale in Derbyshire to Kirk Yetholm in the Borders. Ridgeway – runs 85 miles from Avebury to Ivinghoe Beacon. South Downs Way – 106-mile walk from Beachy Head to Winchester. South-west Coastal Path – runs 600 miles from Minehead in Somerset to Poole Harbour. West Highland Way – 95-mile route from Milngavie, near Glasgow to north of Fort William.

Fremantle Doctor Cooling sea breeze prevalent during the Western Australian summer.

fumarole Opening in or near a volcano through which hot vapours emerge.

ghibli Hot, dry southerly wind of Libya.

glacier types continental, mountain, piedmont.

grasslands Africa – savannah; Argentina/Paraguay – pampas; North America – prairies; Russia – Steppes. In other South American countries the general term for a grassland is llanos. The Sahel of West Africa is a semi-arid transitional area between grassland and desert.

Great Lakes: mnemonic HOMES Huron, Ontario, Michigan, Erie, Superior

Green Line Boundary dividing Cyprus between Greek south and Turkish north since the 1974 Turkish invasion.

gregale Strong north-east wind blowing in the Mediterranean.

Gutenberg discontinuity The core–mantle boundary of the Earth.

haboob Violent and oppressive seasonal wind blowing in Sudan and causing fierce sand storms.

harmattan Parching dusty land-wind of the W African coast, blowing from the Sahara Desert.

helm Violent wind of the Lake District of England which often culminates in the formation of a cloud hanging over the mountain tops.

hypsography Description or mapping of the contours of the earth's surface.

isocheim Line on a map connecting places having the same average temperature in winter.

isohyet Line on a map connecting places having the same amount of rainfall in a given period.

Itaipu dam Joint project by Brazil and Paraguay on the River Parana. Largest hydro-electric dam in the world.

jungle: meaning From the Hindi *Jangal* meaning 'wilderness'.

Kanaks Native Melanesian population of the French overseas territory of New Caledonia.

Kashmir Territory in the north-west of the Indian subcontinent which has been the subject of rival claims by India and Pakistan and the cause of 2 wars between them in 1948 and 1965.

Kentish man West of the Medway.

khamsin Hot south or south-easterly wind occurring in Egypt for about 50 days in March, April and May.

Levant Area of the Mediterranean bordering Syria and the Lebanon.

lithosphere Rigid outer part of the earth consisting of the crust and upper mantle.

Maghreb Region of North Africa bordering the Mediterranean and comprising Morocco, Algeria, Tunisia and Libya.

man of Kent East of the Medway.

Mashriq Geographical region including Egypt, Sudan, Saudi Arabia, Yemen, Oman, Kuwait, UAE, Jordan, Lebanon, Syria and Iraq.

Medway towns Chatham, Gillingham, Rochester, Strood.

mistral Cold northerly wind that blows down the Rhône valley and southern France into the Mediterranean.

mofette Exhalation of vapour from a volcano. Sometimes used as an alternative name for the fumarole itself.

Moho Abbreviation for the Mohorovicic discontinuity, the boundary separating the earth's crust and mantle.

monsoon Seasonal wind of SW Asia and the Indian Ocean which brings heavy summer rain.

pampero Strong cold SW wind in S. America blowing from the Andes towards the Atlantic.

peninsulas Arabian is the largest (1,250,000 sq miles); second largest is the Southern Indian (800,000 sq miles).

permafrost General term for ground that is permanently frozen (see tundra).

Pig Island Australian and NZ slang word for New Zealand.

puna Cold, dry wind of the Andes in Peru.

rock: types Igneous, sedimentary, metamorphic.

Sargasso Sea Area of the North Atlantic, named after the 'Sargassum' seaweed that floats on the surface. The Sargasso lies south of Bermuda and is noted for having no land borders.

simoom Hot, suffocating wind of North Africa.

sirocco Hot, dusty wind blowing from North Africa across southern Europe via the Mediterranean. Called a léveche in Spain.

solano Hot, dusty south-easterly wind of mainland Spain.

Sumatra Violent wind in the Strait of Malacca and the Malay peninsula blowing from the direction of Sumatra.

taiga (cold forest) Coniferous forests of sub-Arctic North America and Eurasia bordered by tundra and steppes.

tectonic plates Regions of the Earth's crust that may be oceanic or continental, and relate to the activity within the Earth, creating new surface material, moving the plates against or underneath each other, changing their location over time, forming mountain ranges and causing earthquakes and volcanic activity.

temperature: highest recorded Al' Aziziyah, Libya, at 136 degrees Fahrenheit (58°C).

temperature: lowest recorded Vostock Station, Antarctica, at -129 degrees Fahrenheit (-89°C).

tombolo Narrow sand or shingle bar linking a small island with mainland.

tramontana Cold north wind in the Adriatic.

tundra Area south of the North Pole where the layers of soil are permanently frozen.

tunnels: longest vehicular Seikan Rail Tunnel, Japan (33.49 miles); Channel Tunnel, Cheriton, Kent – Sangatte, Calais (31.03 miles).

tunnels: longest non-vehicular Delaware Aqueduct, NY State (105 miles).

GEOGRAPHY

twilight: types   Civil, nautical, astronomical (6, 12 and 18 degrees angle of the sun below the horizon).

typhoon   Tropical storm in the western Pacific.

volcanic eruptions: famous   Krakatoa (1883); Mont Pelée, Martinique (1902); Mount St Helens, Washington State (1980).

volcano: classifications   active, dormant, extinct.

volcano: highest   Cotopaxi in Ecuador is the highest continuously active volcano (19,347′), although Guallatiri in Chile at 19,882′ is the highest dormant and Aconcagua at 22,834′, and also in the Andes, is the highest extinct volcano (excluding underwater volcanoes).

Volcano Islands   Three small volcanic islands, San Alexander (Kita-Iō) Iwo Jima (Iō) San Augustino (Minami-Iō), of the West Pacific between the Bonin Islands and the Mariana Islands. Japan has claimed the islands since 1891, apart from a brief USA administration from 1951 to 1968.

volcano: types   Fissure and central.

williwaw   Sudden, strong cold wind originally describing the squall through the Strait of Magellan but now describing any sudden strong wind of Alaska and Canada.

Willy-willy   Tropical Australian cyclone, known by this name particularly in the south-west.

Zanzibar   Principal islands are Zanzibar and Pemba islands. Joined with Tanganyika in 1964 to become Tanzania. Zanzibar's African population call themselves 'Shirazi' after the ancient Persian principality of Shîrāz, as traders from the Persian Gulf began to settle there after the 7th century.

zonda   Hot dusty north wind of Argentina.

Geological Ages

Era	Period	Epoch	Years ago (m)	Life forms
Cenozoic		Holocene	0.01	
	Quaternary	Pleistocene	1.64	humans appeared
		Pliocene	5.2	
		Miocene	23.5	
	Tertiary	Oligocene	35.5	
		Eocene	56.5	
		Palaeocene	65	mammals flourished
Mesozoic	Cretaceous		146	heyday of dinosaurs
	Jurassic		208	first birds
	Triassic		245	first mammals and dinosaurs
Palaeozoic	Permian		290	reptiles expanded
	Carboniferous		363	first reptiles
	Devonian		409	first amphibians
	Silurian		439	first land plants
	Ordovician		510	first fish
	Cambrian		570	first fossils
Precambrian	Proterozoic		3500	earliest living things
	Archaean		4600	

Ice Ages: years before present

Pleistocene	1.64m–10,000
Permo-Carboniferous	330–250m
Ordovician	440–430m
Varangian	615–570m
Sturtian	820–770m
Gnejsö	940–880m
Huronian	2700–1800m

Island Groups

Group	Administered by	Sea Area	Main Islands
Admiralty	Papua New Guinea	Pacific Ocean	Manus, Los Reyes, Rambutyo, Tong, Pak, Baluan. Lou Purdy Islands are a sub division of the Admiralty Islands.
Aeolian (aka Eolie)	Italy	Tyrrhenian Sea	Stromboli, Lipari, Vulcano, Salina, Filicudi, Panarea.
Åland	Finland	Gulf of Bothnia	Åland, Ahvenanmaa, Eckero, Lemland, Lumparland, Vardo.
Aleutian	Alaska, USA	Pacific Ocean	Andreanof, Adak, Amchitka, Atka, Attu, Fox, Kiska, Near, Rat, Seguam, Umnak, Unalaska, Unimak, Yunaska.

Group	Administered by	Sea Area	Main Islands
Alexander Archipelago	Alaska, USA	Gulf of Alaska	Baranof (chief city Sitka), Prince of Wales, Chichagof, Admiralty, Mitkof, Wrangell, Revillagigedo (chief city Ketchikan), Kupreanof, Zaremba, Kuiu, Kosciusko, Yakobi, Heceta.
Andaman (204 islands)	India	Bay of Bengal	North, Middle and South Andaman Islands (collectively known as Great Andaman).
Andreanof	Alaska, USA	Pacific Ocean	Kanaga, Great Sitkin, Amlia, Atka, Adak, Tanaga, Delarof. Andreanof Islands are a sub-division of the Aleutians.
Antilles, Greater	Various	Caribbean Sea	Cuba, Jamaica, Hispaniola, Puerto Rico.
Antilles, Lesser	Various	Caribbean Sea	Windward, Leeward, Netherlands Antilles.
Azores	Portugal	Atlantic Ocean	Flores, Corvo, Terceira, Graciosa, São Jorge, Faial, Pico, Santa Maria, Formigar, São Miguel.
Bahamas (700)	UK	Atlantic Ocean	Great Abaco, Acklins, Andros, Berry, Cay, New Providence, Grand Bahama, Inagua, Long, Mayaguana, Bimini, Cat, Exuma, Ragged, Crooked, Eleuthera. Nassau, the capital, is on New Providence and it was here that Columbus made his first landfall in the New World, 12 Oct 1492. Highest point: Mt Alvernia (formerly Como Hill), 206', on Cat Island.
Balearic	Spain	Mediterranean	Ibiza, Majorca, Minorca, Formentera, Cabrera.
Banks	Vanuatu	Pacific Ocean	Vanua Lava, Santa Maria (Gaua), Mota, Mota Lava (Saddle).
Bay Islands	Honduras	Caribbean Sea	Utila, Roatan, Guanja.
Bermuda (138) (aka Somers' Isles)	UK	Atlantic Ocean	Great Bermuda (aka Main), Boaz, Ireland, St David's, St George's, Somerset. All these inhabited islands are now joined by bridges.
Bismarck Archipelago	Papua New Guinea	Pacific Ocean	New Britain, New Ireland, Admiralty, Lavonga, New Hanover.
Bissagos	Guinea-Bissau	Atlantic Ocean	Orango, Formosa, Caravela, Roxa.
Canadian Arctic	Canada	Arctic Ocean	Baffin, Victoria, Queen Elizabeth, Banks.
Canaries	Spain	Atlantic Ocean	Tenerife, Gomera, Las Palmas, Lanzarote, Hierro, Fuerteventura, Gran Canaria.
Cape Verde Islands (10)	Cape Verde	Atlantic Ocean	Windward Islands: Barlavento, Santo Antão, São Vicente, São Nicolau, Boa Vista, Sal Sotavento, Santa Luzia. Leeward Islands: São Tiago, Maio Fogo, Brava.
Caroline (680)	USA	Pacific Ocean	Yap, Ponape (Ascension or Pohnpei), Truk, Kusac, Belau.
Chagos	UK	Indian Ocean	Diego Garcia, Peros, Banhos, Salomon.
Channel	UK	English Channel	Jersey, Guernsey, Alderney, Sark, Herm.
Channel (Santa Barbara)	USA	Pacific Ocean	San Miguel, Santa Rosa, Santa Cruz, Anacapa, Santa Barbara, San Nicolas, Santa Catalina, San Clemente.
Chonos Archipelago	Chile	Pacific Ocean	Chaffers, Benjamin, James, Melchior, Victoria, Luz.
Commander	Russia	Bering Sea	Bering, Medny.
Comoros	Comoros	Mozambique Channel	Grande Comore, Anjouan, Mohéli, Mayotte.
Cook	New Zealand	Pacific Ocean	Rarotonga, Palmerston, Mangaia, Aitutaki.
Crozet	France	Indian Ocean	Île de la Possession, Îles des Pingouins, Îles des Apôtres.
Cyclades (220)	Greece	Aegean Sea	Andros, Mikonos, Milos, Naxos, Paros, Kithnos, Serifos, Siros, Tinos.
Denmark	Denmark	Baltic Sea	Zealand, Fyn, Lolland, Falster, Sjael/Langeland, Bornholm.
Desolation	France	Indian Ocean	Kerguelen, Grande Terre.
Dodecanese	Greece	Aegean Sea	Kasos, Karpathos, Rhodes, Samos, Khalki, Tilos, Simi, Astipalaia, Kalimnos, Leros, Patmos, Kos.
Egadi (Aegadi)	Italy	Mediterranean	Favignana, Levanzo, Marettimo.
Ellice	Tuvalu	Pacific Ocean	Funafuti, Nukefetau, Nukulailai, Nanumea.
Falkland (200)	UK	Atlantic Ocean	West Falkland, East Falkland, South Georgia, South Sandwich.
Farne (Staple)	UK	North Sea	House, Long Stone (lighthouse was the home of Grace Darling). St Cuthbert died on House (Inner Farne) in 687. Nowadays the group is a bird sanctuary and home for grey seals.
Faroe (17 inhabited)	Denmark	Atlantic Ocean	Stromo (Streymoy), Ostero (Eysturoy), Vågø (Vágar), Sando (Sandoy), Bordo (Bordhoy), Sudero (Sudhuroy).

GEOGRAPHY

Group	Administered by	Sea Area	Main Islands
Fiji	Fiji	Pacific Ocean	Viti Levu, Vanua Levu.
Frisian, East	Germany	North Sea	Borkum, Juist, Norderney, Langeoog, Spiekeroog, Wangerooge.
Frisian, North	Germany and Denmark	North Sea	Sylt, Fohr, Nordstrand, Pellworm, Amrum (German); Romo, Fano, Mando (Danish).
Frisian, West	Netherlands	North Sea	Texel, Vlieland, Terschelling, Ameland, Schiermonnikoog.
Galapagos (19)	Ecuador	Pacific Ocean	San Cristobal, Santa Cruz, Isabela, Floreana, Santiago, San Salvador, Rabida, Darwin, Wolf, Pinta, Marchena, Genovesa, Española, Santa Maria, Santa Fe, Pinzon, Fernandina, Baltra. Isabela (Albemarle) is largest, Santa Cruz (Indefatigable) is 2nd. Highest point is Mt Azul.
Gilbert	Kiribati	Pacific Ocean	Tarawa, Makin, Abaiang, Abemama, Tabiteuea, Nonouti, Beru.
Gotland	Sweden	Baltic Sea	Gotland, Faro, Karlso.
Great Britain	United Kingdom	Atlantic Ocean	Isle of Wight, Orkneys, Shetlands, Hebrides, Scillies, Skomer, Ramsey, Skokholm, Caldey, Holy, Lundy, Brownsea, Rat, Sully, Flat Holm, Horsey, Osea, Skerries, Bardsey, Hilbre, Little Eye, Read's, Calf of Man, Ailsa Crag, Craigleith, Fidra, Bass Rock, May, St Serfs (in Loch Leven).
Greater Sunda	Indonesia	South China Sea	Sumatra, Java, Borneo, Celebes (Sulawesi), Belitung. North-west Borneo is not under Indonesian administration.
Greenland	Denmark	Atlantic/Arctic	Greenland, Disko.
Hawaiian	USA	Pacific Ocean	Hawaii, Oahu, Maui, Lanai, Kauai, Molokai, Kahoolawe, Niihau.
Heard and McDonald	Australia	Indian Ocean	Heard, McDonald, Shag.
Hebrides, Inner	UK	Atlantic Ocean	Skye (chief town is Portree; home of the Cuillin Hills; also famous as the refuge of the Young Pretender in 1746), Raasay, Mull (chief town is Tobermory; contains Ben More at 3,171'); Eigg, Coll, Tiree, Iona, Staffa, Jura, Islay, Rum, Muck, Arran (containing Goat Fell at 2,868'), Colonsay and Oronsay.
Hebrides, Outer	UK	Atlantic Ocean	Lewis with Harris, North and South Uist, Benbecula, Baleshare, Barra, Bernera, Berneray, Eriskay, Grimsay, Scalpay, Vatersay.
Indonesia (13,677)	Indonesia	Pacific Ocean	Java, Sumatra, Kalimantan, Celebes, Lesser Sundas, Moluccas, Rian-Lingga Archipelago, Irian Jaya.
Ionian	Greece	Aegean Sea	Kerkira, Kefallinia, Zakinthos, Levkas.
Japan	Japan	Pacific Ocean	Hokkaido, Honshu, Shikoku, Kyushu, Ryuku.
Juan Fernandez	Chile	Pacific Ocean	Mas a Tierra (Nearer Land Island, aka Robinson Crusoe Island), Mas Afuera (Farther Out Island, aka Alexander Selkirk Island).
Kermadec	New Zealand	South Pacific	Raoul (Sunday), Macauley, Curtis. Highest point is Mt Mumukai at 1723' on Raoul Island.
Kuril (56)	Russia	Pacific Ocean	Shumsu, Iturup, Urup, Paramushir, Onekotan, Shiaskhotan, Kunashir, Shimushir, Shikotanto.
Lakshadweep	India	Arabian Sea	Amindivi, Laccadive, Minikoy (Maliku), Androth, Kavaratti.
Leeward Islands	Lesser Antilles	Caribbean Sea	Virgin Islands, Anguilla, Saint-Martin, St Christopher and Nevis, Antigua and Barbuda, Montserrat, Guadeloupe. Highest point is Mt Soufrière (on Guadeloupe) at 4813'.
Lesser Sunda	Indonesia/Timor	Indian Ocean	Bali, Lombok, Sumbawa, Sumba, Flores, Timor, Alor.
Line	Kiribati	Pacific Ocean	Christmas, Fanning, Washington.
Lipari	Italy	Tyrrhenian Sea	see Aeolian Islands.
Lofoten	Norway	Norwegian Sea	Hinney, Austvagey, Vestvagey, Moskenes.
Madeira	Portugal	Atlantic Ocean	Madeira, Ilha do Porto Santo, Ilhas Desertas, Ilhas Selvagens.
Malay Archipelago	Malaysia	Pacific/Indian	Borneo, Celebes, Java, Luzon, Mindanao, New Guinea, Sumatra.
Maldives (200 inhabited)	Maldives	Indian Ocean	The atolls of the Maldives are listed in the

Group	Administered by	Sea Area	Main Islands
			'capitals'. The word 'atoll' is, in fact, a Maldive word.
Malta	Malta	Mediterranean	Malta, Gozo, Comino.
Mariana (14)	USA	Pacific Ocean	Saipan, Tinian, Rota, Pagan, Guguan.
Marquesas	France	Pacific Ocean	Nuku Hiva, Ua Pu, Ua Huka, Hiva Oa, Tahuata, Fatu Hiva, Eiao Hatutu.
Marshall	Marshall	Pacific Ocean	Bikini, Wotha, Kwajalein, Eniwetok, Maiura, Jalut, Rogelap.
Mascarenes	France/Mauritius	Indian Ocean	Réunion, Mauritius, Rodrigues.
Melanesia	Various	Pacific Ocean	Solomon Islands, Bismarck Archipelago, New Caledonia, Papua New Guinea, Fiji, Vanuatu.
Mentawai	Indonesia	Indian Ocean	Siberut, Sipura, Pagai, Utara (North Pagai), Pagai Selatan Utara and Pagai Selatan (South Pagai), aka Nassau Islands.
Micronesia	Various	Pacific Ocean	Caroline, Gilberts, Marianas, Marshalls, Guam, Kiribati, Nauru.
Moluccas (Maluku)	Indonesia	Pacific Ocean	Halmahera, Bacan, Sula, Obi, Moratai, Ternate.
Mussau	Papua New Guinea	Pacific Ocean	Mussau, Emira, Tench, Emira, Emananus, Tabalo.
Near	Alaska, USA	Pacific Ocean	Agattu, Semichi, Attu, Alaid, Nizki, Shemya. Near Islands are a sub division of the Aleutians.
New Hebrides	Vanuatu	Pacific Ocean	Espiritu Santo, Malekula, Efate, Ambrim, Eromanga, Tanna, Epi, Pentecost, Aurora.
New Siberian	Russia	Arctic Ocean	Kotelny, Faddeyevski.
Newfoundland	Canada	Atlantic Ocean	Prince Edward, Anticosti.
Nicobar (12)	India	Bay of Bengal	Great Nicobar, Camorta with Nancowry, Car Nicobar, Teressa, Little Nicobar. Usually considered with the Andamans as a joint group.
Ninigo Islands	Papua New Guinea	Pacific Ocean	Manu, Aua, Wuvulu, Heina, Kaniet Islands, Hermit Islands.
Northeastern Aegean	Greece	Aegean Sea	Samos, Chios, Ikaria, Lesbos, Limnos, Samothraki, Thassos.
Northern Land	Russia	Arctic Ocean	Komsomolets, Bolshevik, October Revolution.
Norway	Vietnam	Gulf of Tonkin	aka Xuy Nong Chao.
Novaya Zemlya	Russia	Arctic Ocean	North and South Novaya Zemlya.
Orkney	UK	North Sea	Mainland, North and South Ronaldsay, Stronsay, Papa Westray, Hoy, Shapinsay, Rousay, Sanday, Burray, Eday, Flotta and Fara, Westray.
Parry	NWT Canada	Arctic Ocean	Bathurst, Melville, Cornwallis, Devon.
Pelagian	Italy	Mediterranean	Lampedusa, Linosa, Lampione.
Philippines (7100)	Philippines	Pacific Ocean	Luzon, Mindanao, Samar, Palawan, Mindoro, Panay, Negros, Leyte, Masbate, Bohol, Cebu.
Phoenix	Kiribati	Pacific Ocean	Canton, Gardner, Phoenix, Sydney, Hull.
Polynesia	Various	Pacific Ocean	New Zealand, French Polynesia, Phoenix Islands, Hawaii, Line, Pitcairn, Tokelau, Tonga, Society, Easter, Samoa, Kiribati, Ellice, Cook.
Pribilof (Fur Seal)	Alaska, USA	Bering Sea	St Paul, St George, Walrus, Otter.
Prince Edward	South Africa	Indian Ocean	Prince Edward, Marion.
Queen Charlotte (150)	Canada	Pacific Ocean	Prince Rupert, Graham, Moresby, Louise, Lyell, Kunghit.
Queen Elizabeth	NWT Canada	Arctic Ocean	Ellesmere, Mackenzie King, Parry Islands, Zverdrup Islands.
Rat	Alaska, USA	Pacific Ocean	Kiska, Amchitka, Semisopochnoi, Little Sitkin, Little Kiska. Rat Islands are a subdivision of the Aleutians.
Safety (Iles du Salut)	French Guiana	Atlantic Ocean	Devil's Island (Ile du Diable), Royale, Saint-Joseph.
Santa Barbara	USA	Pacific Ocean	see Channel Islands.
São Tomé and Principe	São Tomé	Atlantic Ocean	São Tomé, Principe.
Saronic Gulf	Greece	Saronic Gulf	Aegina, Angistri, Hydra, Poros, Salamis, Spetses.
Scilly (150)	UK	English Channel	St Mary's, St Martin's, Tresco, St Agnes, Bryher.
Seychelles (115)	Seychelles	Indian Ocean	Praslin, La Digue, Silhouette, Mahé, Bird.
Shetland (100)	UK	North Sea	Mainland, Unst, Yell, Fetlar, Whalsay, Bressay, Muckle Roe, Trondra, West Burra, Housay, Fair Isle, East Burra.
Society	France	Pacific Ocean	Windward and Leeward, Tahiti.

GEOGRAPHY

Group	Administered by	Sea Area	Main Islands
Solomon	Solomon	Pacific Ocean	Choiseul, Guadalcanal, Malaita, New Georgia, San Cristobal, Santa Isabel, Vella Lavella, Kolombangara. Highest point is Mt Makarakomburu.
South Orkney	UK	Atlantic Ocean	Coronation, Signy, Laurie, Inaccessible.
South Shetland	UK	Atlantic Ocean	King George, Elephant, Clarence, Gibbs, Nelson, Livingstone, Greenwich, Snow.
Sporades (11)	Greece	Aegean Sea	Skiathos, Skopelos, Skyros, Alonissos (the four inhabited islands).
Sri Lanka	Sri Lanka	Indian Ocean	Mannar, Sri Lanka.
Taiwan	China	China Sea/Pacific	Taiwan, Lan Hsu, Lu Tao, Quemoy, Pescadores.
Tasmania	Australia	Tasman Sea	Tasmania, King, Flinders, Bruny.
Tierra Del Fuego	Arg/Chile	Pacific Ocean	Tierra Del Fuego, Isla de los Estados, Hoste, Navarino, Wollaston, Desolación, Santa Ines, Clarence, Dawson, Diego Ramirez.
Tres Marias	Mexico	Pacific Ocean	Maria Madre, Maria Magdalena, Maria Cleofas, San Juanito.
Tristan da Cunha	UK	Atlantic Ocean	Tristan da Cunha, Gough, Inaccessible, Nightingale.
Tuamotu Archipelago	France	Pacific Ocean	Makatea, Fakarava, Rangiroa, Anaa, Hao, Reao, Gambier, Duke of Gloucester.
Vesterålen	Norway	Norwegian Sea	Hinnoy, Langoya, Andoya, Hadseloy.
Virgin	USA	Caribbean Sea	St Croix, St Thomas, St John.
Virgin	UK	Caribbean Sea	Tortola, Virgin Gorda, Anegada, Jost Van Dyke.
Visayas (Bisayas)	Philippines	Philippine/Sulu Sea	Bohol, Cebu, Leyte, Masbate, Negros, Panay, Samar.
Windward Islands	Lesser Antilles	Caribbean Sea	Dominica, Martinique, St Lucia, St Vincent, Grenada, Grenadines.
Zanzibar	Tanzania	Indian Ocean	Zanzibar, Tumbatu, Kwale.
Zemlya Frantsa-Iosifa	Russia	Arctic Ocean	Graham Bell, Wilczekland, Georgeland, Hooker, Zemlya Alexsandry, Ostrov Rudol'fa.

Islands

Island	Area	Administered by	Sq Miles
Adelaide	British Antarctic Territory	Great Britain	1,400
Admiralty	Alexander Archipelago	Alaska, USA	1,709
Alderney	English Channel Nearest of the Channel Islands to France	Great Britain	3
Alexander I	British Antarctic Territory Largest island in Antarctica	Great Britain	16,700
Andros	Atlantic Ocean	Bahamas	2,300
Andros	Aegean Sea The 2nd largest island of the Cyclades	Greece	145
Anticosti	Gulf of St Lawrence	Quebec, Canada	3,066
Ascension (Pohnpei)	Pacific Ocean Highest peak is Mt Totolom at 2,595'	Micronesia	129
Ascension	Atlantic Ocean	Great Britain	34
Bali	Indian Ocean	Indonesia	2,147
Bananal	Goiás State World's largest inland island	Brazil	7,720
Banks	Beaufort Sea	NWT, Canada	27,038
Bathurst	Timor Sea	NT Australia	1,000
Bathurst	Arctic Ocean	NWT Canada	6,194
Bioko	Gulf of Guinea	Equatorial Guinea	779
Bolshevik	Arctic Ocean	Russia	4,368
Bougainville	Solomon Sea Highest peaks Mt Balbi 9,000', Mt Bagana 6,560', Mt Takuan 7,358'	Papua New Guinea	3,880
Bouvet	South Atlantic	Norway	23
Cape Breton	Nova Scotia	Canada	3,981
Cebu	Bohol Sea	Philippines	1,703
Chatham Island	South Pacific Chief town is Waitangi	New Zealand	348
Chiloé	Pacific Ocean Chief town is Castro	Chile	3,241
Christmas	Indian Ocean Highest point is Murry Hill at 1,184'	Australia	52

Island	Area	Administered by	Sq Miles
Christmas (Kiritimati)	Pacific Ocean Largest island of purely coral formation in the world	Kiribati	150
Clipperton	Pacific Ocean	France	2
Coats	Northwest Territories	Canada	2,123
Cocos	Pacific Ocean	Costa Rica	9
Cornwallis	Northwest Territories	Canada	2,701
Corsica	Mediterranean Highest peak is Mont Cinto 8,890'	France	3,352
Crete	Mediterranean Highest peak is Mt Ida 8,058'	Greece	3,190
Cyprus	Mediterranean	Cyprus	3,572
Desolation Island	Indian Ocean aka Kerguélen Island	French Antarctica	2,239
Devon	Northwest Territories	Canada	21,331
Disko	Davis Strait	Greenland	3,312
East Falkland	South Atlantic Highest peak is Mt Usborne, 2,312'	Great Britain	2,550
Easter (Rapa Nui)	Pacific Ocean Famous for rongorongo hieroglyphs and stone statues in human form	Chile	63
Éfaté	Pacific Ocean aka Vaté or Sandwich; highest peak is Mt Macdonald, 2,123'	Vanuatu	353
Ellesmere	Northwest Territories	Canada	75,767
Euboea	Aegean Sea The 2nd largest island in Greece after Crete	Greece	1,412
Flores	Indian Ocean	Indonesia	5,500
Flores	Azores Highest peak is Morro Grande, 3,087'	Portugal	55
Fyn	Baltic Sea	Denmark	1,152
Gotland	Baltic	Sweden	1,212
Graham	British Columbia	Canada	2,456
Guernsey	English Channel The 2nd largest of the Channel Islands	Great Britain	24
Hai-nan	Kwangtung	China	12,962
Halmahera	Moluccas	Indonesia	6,865
Heard	Indian Ocean Highest peak is Mt Mawson on Big Ben Mountain at 9,005'	Australia	351
Hispaniola	Caribbean Offshore islands include Gonâve and Tortuga Island	Haiti/Dominican Republic	29,418
Holy Island (Lindisfarne)	North Sea St Aidan established church and monastery in 635 and the 7th-century Lindisfarne Gospels are now housed in the British Museum. Of the other Holy Islands, the most notable is the one off the coast of Anglesey	Great Britain	2
Hoste	Pacific Ocean	Chile	1,590
Ibiza	Mediterranean Highest point is La Atalaya at 1,558'	Spain	221
Iturup	Sea of Okhotsk	Russia	2,596
Iwo Jima	West Pacific Famous photo of marines raising the US flag over Mt Suribachi in Feb 1945	Japan	8
Jan Mayen	Greenland Sea Home of the Beerenberg volcano, 7,470'	Norway	144
Jersey	English Channel Largest and southernmost of the Channel Islands	Great Britain	44
Kangaroo	South Australia	Australia	1,680
Kerguélen	Indian Ocean aka Desolation Island	French Antarctica	2,239
Kiritimati	Pacific Ocean	Kiribati	see Christmas Islands
Kodiak	Gulf of Alaska	Alaska, USA	3,588
Kyushu	Pacific Kyushu means 'the nine provinces'	Japan	16,274
Lanzarote	Atlantic Ocean Easternmost of the Canary Islands	Spain	307
Leyte	Philippine Sea	Philippines	2,785

Island	Area	Administered by	Sq Miles
Lindisfarne	North Sea	Great Britain	see Holy Island
Long Island	New York	USA	1,723
Lundy	Bristol Channel	Great Britain	1
Mackenzie King	Northwest Territories	Canada	1,949
Mactan	Bohol Strait	Philippines	24
	Ferdinand Magellan was killed here by Chief Lapulapu on 27 Apr 1521		
Majorca	Mediterranean	Spain	1,405
Man	Irish Sea	Great Britain	221
Mansel	Northwest Territories	Canada	1,228
Marajó	Atlantic Ocean	Brazil	15,500
Martinique	Caribbean	France	417
	Site of the Carbet Mountains: highest peaks Lacroix, 3,924′, Piquet, 3,806′; Dumauzé, 3,638′; Alma, 3,625′; Boucher, 3,510′		
Melville	Timor Sea	NT Australia	2,240
Milne Land	Arctic Ocean	Greenland	1,400
Minorca	Mediterranean	Spain	258
	The 2nd largest of the Balearics		
Náxos	Aegean Sea	Greece	165
	Largest island of the Cyclades, highest peak Mt Zeus at 3,377′		
Negros	Philippine Sea	Philippines	4,905
New Britain	Bismarck Archipelago	Papua New Guinea	14,100
New Caledonia	Coral Sea	France	6,467
New Ireland	Bismarck Archipelago	Papua New Guinea	3,340
Norway	Beaufort Sea	NWT, Canada	13
Palawan	South China Sea	Philippines	4,550
Panay	Sulu Sea	Philippines	4,446
Pitcairn	Pacific Ocean	Great Britain	2
Pohnpei	Pacific Ocean	Micronesia	see Ascension
Prince Charles	Foxe Basin	NWT, Canada	3,676
Prince Edward	Gulf of St Lawrence	Canada	2,184
Prince of Wales	Alexander Archipelago	Alaska, USA	2,731
	Islands of the same name in Canada and Australia		
Puerto Rico	Caribbean	USA	3,435
Réunion	Indian Ocean	France	970
Riesco	Pacific Ocean	Chile	1,973
Roosevelt	East River	NY City, USA	1
Roosevelt	Ross Sea	NZ Antarctica	2,900
St Helena	South Atlantic	Great Britain	47
	Peaks include Mt Actaeon at 2,685′ and Diana Peak at 2,700′		
St Lawrence	Bering Sea	Alaska, USA	1,780
Samar	Philippine Sea	Philippines	5,050
Santa Catalina	Pacific Ocean	USA	74
	One of the Channel Islands, highest peak Mt Orizaba at 2,130′		
Sardinia	Mediterranean	Italy	9,194
Sark	English Channel	Great Britain	2
	Sark's area includes Brechou		
Seram (Ceram)	West Pacific	Indonesia	6,621
	Highest point is Mt Binaiyi 9,905′		
Shikoku	Pacific Ocean	Japan	7,261
Sicily	Mediterranean	Italy	9,830
Socotra	Indian Ocean	Yemen	1,400
Somerset	Northwest Territories	Canada	9,570
South Georgia	Falklands Islands	Great Britain	1,450
Southampton	Hudson Bay	NWT, Canada	15,913
Spitsbergen	Barents Sea	Norway	15,075
Stewart Island	Pacific Ocean	New Zealand	674
	Third largest NZ island after North and South		
Sumbawa	Indian Ocean	Indonesia	5,965
Taiwan (Formosa)	Pacific Ocean	Taiwan (Formosa)	13,851
Tasmania	Indian Ocean	Australia	24,868
	Other islands in the Tasmanian state include Bruny, King, Flinders and Macquarie		
Tenerife	Atlantic Ocean	Spain	795
	Largest of the Canary Islands		
Timor	Indian Ocean	Indonesia/Timor	11,883

Island	Area	Administered by	Sq Miles
Traill	Greenland Sea	Greenland	1,300
Vancouver	Pacific Ocean	BC, Canada	12,079
Vanua Levu	Pacific Ocean	Fiji	2,137
Viti Levu	Pacific Ocean	Fiji	4,011
Wellington	Pacific Ocean	Chile	2,549
West Falkland	South Atlantic	Great Britain	1,750
Wight	English Channel	Great Britain	147
	Largest British island outside the mainland		
Wrangel	Chukchi Sea	Russia	2,800
Yap	Pacific Ocean	USA Micronesia	21
	Highest peak is Mt Tabiwol at 568′		
Zealand (Sjaelland)	Baltic Sea	Denmark	2,713
Zemlya Aleksandry	Franz Josef Land	Russia	1,080
Zemlya Georga	Franz Josef Land	Russia	1,120

Islands: world's largest

		Area (Sq Miles)	Location
1	Greenland	840,000	Arctic Ocean
2	New Guinea	306,000	Western Pacific
3	Borneo	280,100	Western Pacific
4	Madagascar	226,658	Indian Ocean
5	Baffin Island	195,928	Arctic Ocean
6	Sumatra	165,000	Indian Ocean
7	Honshu	87,805	North Pacific
8	Great Britain	84,186	North Atlantic
9	Victoria Island	83,897	Arctic Ocean
10	Ellesmere Island	75,767	Arctic Ocean
11	Celebes (Sulawesi)	69,000	Indian Ocean
12	South Island (NZ)	58,305	South Pacific
13	Java	48,900	Indian Ocean
14	Cuba	44,218	North Atlantic
15	North Island (NZ)	44,035	South Pacific
16	Newfoundland	42,030	North Atlantic
17	Luzon	40,880	West Pacific
18	Iceland	39,770	North Atlantic
19	Mindanao	36,775	West Pacific
20	Ireland	31,839	North Atlantic
21	Hokkaido	30,077	North Pacific
22	Hispaniola	29,418	North Atlantic
23	Sakhalin	28,597	North Pacific
24	Tasmania	26,383	South Pacific
25	Sri Lanka	25,332	Indian Ocean

NB: What is the largest island in the world? This is the subject of constant frustration to the more enlightened quiz player. In fact, the answer is very simple when one understands that the dictionary defines an island as a body of land, smaller than a continent, that is wholly surrounded by water. The dictionary defines Australia as the smallest continent and consequently, although it is surrounded by water, it clearly should not be included in geographical listings of islands. If an island was to be considered any area of land wholly surrounded by water then the whole of mainland Eurasia would in fact be far larger than Australia!

Lakes: world's largest

		Location	Area Sq Miles	Details
1	Caspian Sea	Russia, Kazakhstan, Turkmenistan, Azerbaijan, Iran	143,552	classed as a brackish lake; although salinity rises to 32% in the Kara-Bogaz-Gol Gulf, it is negligible around the Volga area
2	Superior	Canada, USA	31,795	often considered the largest freshwater lake in the world, although the Caspian Sea is freshwater in parts; the largest of the Great Lakes of North America
3	Victoria	Uganda, Tanzania, Kenya	26,834	aka Victoria Nyanza, the chief reservoir of the Nile
4	Huron	Canada, USA	23,011	one of the Great Lakes, often considered as a single entity with Lake Michigan

GEOGRAPHY

		Location	Area Sq Miles	Details
5	Michigan	USA	22,394	one of the Great Lakes, often considered as a single entity with Lake Huron
6	Aral Sea	Uzbekistan, Kazakhstan	15,444	the largest true salt lake in the world, although its area has been severely diminished
7	Tanganyika	Dem Rep of Congo, Tanzania, Zambia, Burundi	12,703	at 410 miles it is the longest true freshwater lake in the world, and at 4,710' the second deepest in the world
8	Great Bear	Northwest Territories (Canada)	12,279	lying astride the Arctic Circle, it is the largest lake wholly in Canada
9	Baikal	Russia	11,776	world's deepest lake at 5,314'
10	Malawi (Nyasa)	Malawi, Tanzania, Mozambique	11,429	aka Lake Nyasa (which means 'lake')
11	Great Slave	Northwest Territories (Canada)	11,031	links the Mackenzie River to the Slave River
12	Erie	Canada, USA	9,910	one of the 5 Great Lakes of North America
13	Winnipeg	Manitoba (Canada)	9,417	named from the Cree Indian words for 'muddy water'
14	Ontario	Canada, USA	7,550	smallest of the Great Lakes of North America
15	Balkhash	Kazakhstan	7,115	shallow salt lake whose area has varied considerably over the years
16	Chad	Cameroon, Chad, Niger, Nigeria	6,875	freshwater lake whose area varies from about 4,000 to 10,000 sq miles
17	Ladoga (Ladozhskoye)	Russia	6,835	largest lake in Europe, situated near the Gulf of Finland; there is also a small lake in Indiana, USA, of the same name
18	Maracaibo	Venezuela	5,150	large brackish inlet of the Caribbean Sea, lying in the Maracaibo Basin
19	Bangweulu	Zambia	3,800	Bangweulu is Bantu for 'large water'
20	Onega	Russia	3,753	second-largest lake in Europe, situated between Lake Ladoga and the White Sea
21	Eyre	South Australia	3,600	dry for most of the year
22	Volta	Ghana	3,283	artificial lake
23	Titicaca	Peru, Bolivia	3,200	highest navigable lake in the world at 12,500' above sea level
24	Nicaragua	Nicaragua	3,190	freshwater lake, the largest lake of Central America
25	Athabasca	Saskatchewan, Alberta (Canada)	3,064	explored by Samuel Hearne in 1771, who named it 'Lake of the Hills'
26	Reindeer	Saskatchewan, Manitoba (Canada)	2,568	the Reindeer River links the lake to the Churchill River
27	Tonle Sap	Cambodia	2,525	linked to the Mekong by the Tonle Sap River
28	Rudolf	Ethiopia, Kenya	2,473	known as Lake Turkana in Kenya
29	Issyk Kul	Kyrgyzstan	2,408	salt lake
30	Torrens	South Australia	2,230	dry for most of the year
31	Albert	Uganda, Dem Rep of Congo	2,160	aka Albert Nyanza and since 1973 Lake Mobuto Sese Seko
32	Vänern	Sweden	2,156	largest lake in Sweden and a major source of hydroelectric power
33	Urmia	Iran	2,150	salt lake
34	Netilling	Northwest Territories (Canada)	2,140	situated in Baffin Island
35	Winnipegosis	Manitoba (Canada)	2,075	situated north of Lake Manitoba and west of Lake Winnipeg
36	Kariba	Zambia, Zimbabwe	2,000	artificial lake formed by the damming of the Zambesi River
37	Mweru	Zambia, Dem Rep of Congo	1,900	Mweru is the Bantu word for 'lake'
38	Nipigon	Ontario (Canada)	1,872	Nipigon is the Indian word for 'deep, clear water'
39	Gairdner	South Australia	1,845	dry for most of the year
40	Manitoba	Manitoba (Canada)	1,799	lies south of lakes Winnipeg and Winnipegosis
41	Koko Nor	Tsinghai (China)	1,770	salt lake, aka Ch'ing Hai or Tsing Hai
42	Taymyr	Russia	1,760	freshwater lake
43	Kyoga	Uganda	1,710	freshwater lake
44	Great Salt	Utah (USA)	1,700	salt lake that has varied from about 2,400 sq miles in 1873 to 950 sq miles in 1963 depending on the level of evaporation and the flow of the surrounding rivers; largest salt lake in the Western Hemisphere
	Iso Saimaa	Finland	1,700	largest lake in Finland
46	Kharka (Hsing-K'ai)	Russia, China	1,690	freshwater lake
47	Lake of the Woods	Canada, USA	1,679	situated where the provinces of Ontario and Manitoba and the US State of Minnesota meet
48	Dubawnt	Northwest Territories (Canada)	1,480	freshwater lake
49	Van	Turkey	1,434	salt lake

		Location	Area Sq Miles	Details
50	Tana	Ethiopia	1,418	freshwater lake
51	Peipus	Estonia, Russia	1,400	freshwater lake
52	P'o-yang	Kiangsi (China)	1,383	freshwater lake
53	Uvs	Mongolia	1,300	salt lake
54	Amadjuak	Northwest Territories (Canada)	1,203	freshwater lake
55	Tung-t-'ing	Hunan (China)	1,089	freshwater lake
56	Kivu	Rwanda, Dem Rep of Congo	1,040	freshwater lake
57	Wollaston	Saskatchewan (Canada)	1,035	freshwater lake
58	Alakol	Kazakhstan	1,025	salt lake
59	Hövsgöl	Mongolia	1,012	freshwater lake
60	Illamna	Alaska (USA)	1,000	freshwater lake
	Poopó	Bolivia	1,000	salt lake
	Rukwa	Tanzania	1,000	salt lake
	Chilwa	Malawi, Mozambique	1,000	salt lake
64	Edward (Idi Amin Dada)	Uganda, Dem Rep of Congo	970	freshwater lake
65	Chany	Russia	960	salt lake
66	Tangra (T'ang-ku-la-yu-mu)	Tibet, China	950	salt lake
67	T'ai	Chekiang, Kiangsu (China)	936	freshwater lake
68	Mistassini	Quebec (Canada)	902	freshwater lake
69	Frome	South Australia	900	dry for most of the year
70	Hu-lun	Inner Mongolia	894	freshwater lake
71	Leopold II (Mai-Ndombe)	Dem Rep of Congo	890	freshwater lake
72	Nueltin	Northwest Territories, Manitoba (Canada)	880	freshwater lake
73	Southern Indian	Manitoba (Canada)	868	freshwater lake
74	Buenos Aires	Chile, Argentina	865	freshwater lake
75	Michikamau	Newfoundland (Canada)	784	freshwater lake
76	Lama	Russia	772	freshwater lake
77	Lop Nor (Lo-pu)	Sinkiang (China)	770	dry for most of the year
78	Hung-tse	Anhwei, Kiangsu (China)	757	freshwater lake
79	Hamar	Iraq	750	freshwater lake
80	Na-mu (Nam)	Tibet, China	741	salt lake
81	Vättern	Finland	738	freshwater lake
82	Baker	Northwest Territories (Canada)	729	freshwater lake
83	Ch'i-lin (Zilling)	Tibet, China	720	salt lake
84	Chiquita	Argentina	714	salt lake
85	Okeechobee	Florida (USA)	700	freshwater lake
86	Martre	Northwest Territories (Canada)	686	freshwater lake
87	Har Us	Mongolia	680	freshwater lake
88	Williston	British Columbia (Canada)	641	freshwater lake
89	Seul	Ontario (Canada)	640	freshwater lake
90	Pontchartrain	Louisiana (USA)	625	usually considered a tidal lagoon, as it is connected to the Gulf of Mexico by the Rigolets
91	Tengiz	Kazakhstan	614	salt lake
92	Tuz	Turkey	580	salt lake
	Po-ssu-t'eng (Baghrash)	Sinkiang (China)	580	freshwater lake
94	Yathkyed	Northwest Territories (Canada)	559	freshwater lake
95	Claire	Alberta (Canada)	555	freshwater lake
96	Cree	Saskatchewan (Canada)	554	freshwater lake
97	Argentino	Argentina	546	freshwater lake
	Ronge	Saskatchewan (Canada)	546	freshwater lake
99	Hyargas	Mongolia	543	salt lake
100	Eau Claire	Quebec (Canada)	534	freshwater lake
101	Moose	Manitoba (Canada)	528	freshwater lake
102	Sevan	Armenia	525	freshwater lake
103	Cedar	Manitoba (Canada)	522	freshwater lake
104	Kasba	Northwest Territories (Canada)	518	freshwater lake
105	Bienville	Quebec (Canada)	482	freshwater lake
106	Island	Manitoba (Canada)	472	freshwater lake
107	St Clair	Canada, USA	460	freshwater lake
108	Becharof	Alaska (USA)	458	freshwater lake
109	Lesser Slave	Alberta (Canada)	451	freshwater lake
	Red	Minnesota (USA)	451	freshwater lake

G
E
O
G
R
A
P
H
Y

		Location	Area Sq Miles	Details
111	Abaya	Ethiopia	448	freshwater lake
112	Gods	Manitoba (Canada)	444	freshwater lake
113	Toba	Sumatra (Indonesia)	440	freshwater lake
	Mälaren	Sweden	440	freshwater lake
115	Champlain	Canada, USA	435	freshwater lake
116	Aberdeen	Northwest Territories (Canada)	425	freshwater lake
	Stefanie	Ethiopia	425	salt lake
118	Päyänne	Finland	421	freshwater lake
119	Viedma	Argentina	420	freshwater lake
120	Chapala	Mexico	417	freshwater lake
	Napaktulik	Northwest Territories (Canada)	417	freshwater lake
122	Mackay	Northwest Territories (Canada)	410	freshwater lake
123	Managua	Nicaragua	402	freshwater lake
124	Eyasi	Tanzania	400	salt lake
125	Dead Sea	Israel, Jordan	394	salt lake; the lowest body of water on Earth at 1,312′ below sea level
126	San Martin (O'Higgins)	Argentina, Chile	391	freshwater lake
127	Saint-Jean	Quebec (Canada)	387	freshwater lake
128	Wei-shan	Kiangsu, Shantung (China)	386	freshwater lake
	Ebi	Sinkiang (China)	386	salt lake
	Inari	Finland	386	freshwater lake
131	Limen	Russia	379	freshwater lake
132	Pipmuacan	Quebec (Canada)	378	freshwater lake
133	Garry	Northwest Territories (Canada)	377	freshwater lake
134	Contwoyto	Northwest Territories (Canada)	370	freshwater lake
135	Abitibi	Ontario (Canada)	360	freshwater lake
	Rainy	Canada, USA	360	freshwater lake
137	Bay	Luzon (Philippines)	356	salt lake
138	Hottah	Northwest Territories (Canada)	354	freshwater lake
139	Natron	Tanzania	350	salt lake
140	Oulu	Finland	348	freshwater lake
141	Salton Sea	California (USA)	340	salt lake
	P'u-mo (Pomo)	Tibet, China	340	freshwater lake
	Amadeus	Northern Territories (Australia)	340	dry for most of the year
144	Llanquihue	Chile	330	freshwater lake
145	Pielinen	Finland	328	freshwater lake
146	Aylmer	Northwest Territories (Canada)	327	freshwater lake
147	Eskimo North	Northwest Territories (Canada)	324	freshwater lake
148	Nipissing	Ontario (Canada)	321	freshwater lake
149	Teshekpuk	Alaska (USA)	315	freshwater lake
150	Imandra	Russia	314	freshwater lake
151	Terinam (Cha-jih-nan-mu)	Tibet, China	313	freshwater lake
152	Colhué Huapi	Argentina	310	freshwater lake
153	Yamdrok (Yang-cho-yung)	Tibet, China	309	freshwater lake
	Ch'ao	Anhwei (China)	309	freshwater lake
155	Nonacho	Northwest Territories (Canada)	303	freshwater lake
156	Abe	Djibouti, Ethiopia	300	salt lake
	Peter Pond	Saskatchewan (Canada)	300	freshwater lake
	Seletyteniz	Kazakhstan	300	freshwater lake
159	Atlin	British Columbia, Yukon (Canada)	299	freshwater lake
160	Minto	Quebec (Canada)	294	freshwater lake
161	Cross	Manitoba (Canada)	292	freshwater lake

Other Notable Lakes	Location	Area Sq Miles	Details
Bala (Llyn Tegid)	Gwynedd, Wales	1.69	deepest lake in Wales (125′)
Balaton	Hungary	230.96	largest lake of central Europe
Bassenthwaite Water	Cumbria, England	2.06	Lake District lake
Bitter Lakes	Suez Canal	219.86	named for its high concentrations of sodium sulphate, as opposed to alkali lakes which contain sodium carbonate
Coniston	Cumbria, England	1.89	famous for the water speed exploits of both Malcolm and his son Donald Campbell
Constance (Bodensee)	Switzerland, Germany, Austria	209.69	forms part of the River Rhine; first flight of the Zeppelin (2 July 1900) was from a floating hangar on Lake Constance

	Location	Area Sq Miles	Details
Crater	Oregon (USA)	28.14	deepest lake in USA (1,932')
Derwent Water	Cumbria, England	2.06	Lake District lake
Ellesmere	South Island (New Zealand)	69.76	brackish lake
Geneva (Lac Léman)	Switzerland, France	225.19	lake is formed by the Rhône River
Lomond	Strathclyde Region, Scotland	27.46	largest lake of mainland Britain
Mead	Arizona, Nevada	229.84	reservoir of Hoover Dam formed by the damming of the Colorado River, it forms, with Lake Powell, the extremities of the Grand Canyon National Park
Menteith	Central Region, Scotland	1.48	the only true Scottish lake, as all the others are lochs. The lake contains 3 islands including Inchmahome, the temporary hideaway of the young Mary, Queen of Scots after the Battle of Pinkie in 1547
Mono	California	87.62	devoid of any life due to its high alkalinity
Morar	Highlands, Scotland	10.33	deepest lake in Great Britain (1,017')
Neagh	Northern Ireland	147.39	largest lake in the British Isles; it borders all the 6 counties bar Co Fermanagh
Ness	Highlands, Scotland	21.87	famous for its monster legend
Ohrid	Albania, Former Yugoslav Rep of Macedonia	134.49	deepest lake in the Balkans (938')
Seneca	New York (USA)	67.44	largest and deepest (618') of the Finger Lakes
Tahoe	California, Nevada (USA)	193.79	freshwater lake
Tiberias (Sea of Galilee)	Israel	64.34	Old Testament name 'Kinneret', later 'Gennesaret'
Ullswater	Cumbria, England	3.44	the 2nd largest lake in England
Vyrnwy	Powys, Wales	1.75	largest lake in Wales
Wastwater	Cumbria, England	1.12	deepest lake in England (260')
Windermere	Cumbria, England	5.69	largest lake in England. Henry Segrave died on this lake in 1930 while attempting a water speed record
Zurich	Zurich (Switzerland)	34.11	freshwater lake

Mountains

10 Highest	Height (ft)	Height (m)	Range	First Climbed	By	Country
Everest	29,035	8,850	Himalaya	29 May 1953	Hillary (NZ) and Tenzing Norgay	Nepal/Tibet
K2 (Chogori)	28,250	8,610	Karakorum	31 July 1954	Compagnoni and Lacedelli (Italian)	Pakistan
Kanchenjunga	28,208	8,597	Himalaya	25 May 1955	Charles Evans (British)	Nepal/Sikkim
Lhotse	27,923	8,511	Himalaya	18 May 1956	Luchsinger and Reiss (Swiss)	Nepal/Tibet
Makalu 1	27,824	8,481	Himalaya	15 May 1955	Couzy and Terray (French)	Nepal/Tibet
Dhaulagiri 1	26,795	8,167	Himalaya	13 May 1960	Max Eiselin (Swiss)	Nepal
Manaslu 1 (Kutang)	26,760	8,156	Himalaya	9 May 1956	Japanese expeditions	Nepal
Cho Oyu	26,750	8,153	Himalaya	19 Oct 1954	Tichy and Jochler (Austrian)	Nepal/Tibet
Nanga Parbat (Diamir)	26,660	8,124	Himalaya	3 Jul 1953	Hermann Buhl (Austrian)	Pakistan
Annapurna 1	26,546	8,091	Himalaya	3 Jun 1950	Herzog and Lachenal (French)	Nepal

Highest subsidiary peaks	Height (ft)	Height (m)	Range	First Climbed
Everest South Summit	28,707	8,750	Himalaya	26 May 1953
Lhotse (Zemu gap peak)	27,591	8,410	Himalaya	unclimbed
Kanchenjunga West	27,894	8,502	Himalaya	14 May 1973
Kanchenjunga South Peak	27,848	8,488	Himalaya	19 May 1978
Kanchenjunga Middle Peak	27,806	8,475	Himalaya	22 May 1978
Lhotse Shar	27,504	8,383	Himalaya	12 May 1970

Highest Continental Peaks	Height (ft)	Height (m)	Range	General Info
Africa – Kilimanjaro (Kibo peak)	19,340	5,895	Monarch	dormant Tanzanian volcano 1st climbed by Meyer and Purtscheller 1889

GEOGRAPHY

Highest Continental Peaks	Height (ft)	Height (m)	Range	General Info
Antarctica – Vinson Massif	16,864	5,140	Ellsworth	first climbed in 1966
Asia – Everest	29,035	8,856	Himalaya	29 May 1953 Hillary (NZ) and Tenzing Norgay
Europe, East – Elbrus	18,510	5,642	Caucasus	extinct volcano, first climbed in 1874
Europe, West – Mt Blanc	15,771	4,807	Alps	first climbed by Jacques Balmat in 1786
North America – Mt McKinley	20,320	6,194	Alaska Range	known to local Indians as Denali and 1st climbed on 7 June 1913 by Stuck and Karstens, although smaller North Peak was climbed by Taylor and Anderson in 1910
Mainland North America – Whitney	14,494	4,418	Sierra Nevada	first climbed by AH Johnson, CD Begole, J Lucas in 1873
South America – Aconcagua	22,834	6,960	Andes	first climbed by Matthias Zurbriggen in 1897
Australia – Kosciusko	7,316	2,228	Great Dividing Range	named by Paul Strzelecki in 1840 in honour of Polish patriot

Mountain Ranges: longest

	Miles	Kilometres	High Point	Height (ft)
Andes	4,500	7,240	Aconcagua (Arg)	22,834
Rockies (Western America)	3,000	4,827	Mt Elbert (US)	14,433
Himalaya–Karakorum–Hindu Kush	2,400	3,861	Everest (China/Nepal)	29,035
Great Dividing Range (Aus)	2,250	3,620	Kosciusko	7,316
Trans-Antarctic Mts	2,200	3,540	Vinson	16,863
Brazilian Atlantic Coast Range	1,900	3,057	Bandeira	9,482
West Sumatran–Javan Range	1,800	2,896	Kerintji	12,484
Aleutian Range (Alaska)	1,600	2,574	Shishaldin	9,387
Tien Shan (Kyrgyzstan/China)	1,400	2,252	Pik Pobeda	24,406
Central New Guinea Range	1,250	2,011	Jayakusumu (Ngga Pulu)	16,503
Altai Mountains (Russia/Mongolia)	1,250	2,011	Gora Belukha	14,783
Urals (Russia)	1,250	2,011	Gora Narodnaya	6,214
Kamchatka (Russia)	1,200	1,930	Klyuchevskaya Sopka	15,910
Atlas (North Africa)	1,200	1,930	Jebel Toubkal (Morocco)	13,665
Verkhoyansk (Russia)	1,000	1,609	Gora Mas Khaya	9,708
Western Ghats (India)	1,000	1,609	Anai Madi	8,841
Sierra Madre Oriental (Mexico)	950	1,528	Orizaba (Citlaltépetl)	18,406
Zagros (Iran)	950	1,528	Zard Kuh	14,921
Scandinavian Range (Nor/Swed)	950	1,528	Galdhopiggen (Nor)	8,098
Semien Mountains (Ethiopia)	900	1,448	Ras Dashen	15,158
Sierra Madre Occidental (Mexico)	900	1,448	Nevado de Colima	13,993
Malagasy Range (Madagascar)	850	1,367	Tsaratanana	9,465
Drakensberg (S Africa)	800	1,287	Thabana Ntlenyana	11,425
Chersky Range (Russia)	800	1,287	Gora Pobeda (Mt Victory)	10,325
Caucasus (Geor/Rus/Azer)	750	1,206	Elbrus, West Peak	18,510
Alaska Range	700	1,126	McKinley, South Peak	20,320
Assam–Burma Range	700	1,126	Hkakabo Razi	19,296
Cascades (USA/Canada)	700	1,126	Rainier (US)	14,410
Crocker Range (Borneo)	700	1,126	Kinabalu (Mal)	13,455
Apennines (Italy)	700	1,126	Corno Grande	9,617
Appalachians (Eastern USA)	700	1,126	Mt Mitchell	6,684
Alps	650	1,045	Mt Blanc (Fr)	15,771
Elburz Mountains (Iran)	560	900	Mt Damavand	18,386
Allegheny Mountains (USA)	500	800	Spruce Knob	4,862
Pyrenees (France/Spain)	270	434	Mt Aneto (Spa)	11,178
Jura (France/Switzerland)	225	360	Crêt de la Neige (Fr)	5,636

NB: A definition of a mountain is an upward projection of the Earth's surface with an altitude of at least 600 m (about 1,968′), often having a rocky surface.

Mountains that are not part of a designated range, e.g. Kilimanjaro, are known as monarchs.

The list of mountains and ranges that follows is a fair representation of the major peaks and systems in the world, but more information can be found in the World Geographical Gazetteer (see below).

The list also contains details of the major volcanic mountains. A few general terms are listed below.

Mountain Ranges: general

Name	Area	Details
Absaroka Range	USA	Situated in north-western Wyoming and southern Montana, highest point is Francs Peak
Adirondacks	USA	Situated in north-eastern New York state, highest peak being Mt Marcy
Aleutian Range	USA	Stretching across southern Alaska and north Pacific islands, highest peak being Shishaldin
Allegheny Mountains	USA	Part of the Appalachians extending south-southwestward for more than 500 miles from north-central Pennsylvania to south-western Virginia
Alps	Central Europe	Extending about 650 miles from the Gulf of Genoa in the south-west to Vienna in the north-east. Highest peak is Mont Blanc
Altai Mountains	Central Asia	Running in a southeast–northwest direction from the Gobi desert to the West Siberian Plain, through Chinese, Mongolian and Soviet territory. Highest peak is Belukha
Amambai Mountains	Brazil–Paraguay	Situated in western Mato Grosso do Sul state of Brazil, and eastern Paraguay
Andes	South America	Stretching the length of the South American continent from Lake Maracaibo in the north to the Tierra del Fuego archipelago in the south
Apennine Range	Italy	The backbone of peninsular Italy extending from the Colle di Cadibona, close to the maritime Alps in the north-west, as far as the Egadi Islands to the west of Sicily
Appalachians	USA	Extending from the Gaspé Peninsula in Quebec through eastern United States southward to central Alabama
Apuseni Range	Romania	Subgroup of the Western Carpathians, lying north of the Mures River in north-western Romania
Arãvalli Range	India	Situated in northern India and running north-easterly for 350 miles through Rãjasthãn state. Highest point is Guru Sikhar on Mount Abu
Armorican Massif	France	Flattened erosional upland encompassing the western French départements of Finistère, Côtes-du-Nord, Morbihan, and Ille-et-Vilaine and parts of Manche, Orne, Mayenne, Maine-et-Loire, Loire-Atlantique, and Vendée. Highest mountain in the Massif is Avaloirs, in Orne at 1,368′
Atherton Tableland	Australia	Also called the Atherton Plateau, part of the Great Dividing Range
Athos Range	Antarctica	Located in West Antarctica, joining the Lambert Glacier
Atlas	North Africa	Running north-east to south-west through the three countries of the Maghrib i.e. Morocco, Algeria, and Tunisia, the highest point Jebel Toubkal being in Morocco
Australian Alps	Australia	Part of the Great Dividing Range, occupying the south-easternmost corner of Australia, in eastern Victoria and south-eastern New South Wales
Balkan Mountains	Bulgaria	Extending from the Timok Valley near the Yugoslav border and stretching eastward towards the Black Sea, highest point is Botev Peak
Baranya Mountains	Hungary	See Mecsek Mountains
Beartooth Range	USA	North-eastern spur of the Absarokas, highest point is Granite Peak
Berkshire Hills	USA	Segment of the Appalachians in western Massachusetts, Mt Greylock being the highest point in the state
Black Mountain Range	Bhutan	Southern spur of the Assam Himalayas
Black Mountains	Wales	Situated in east Dyfed and west Powys, highest peak being Carmarthen Van
Black Mountains	Wales	Situated in east Gwent, highest peak being Waun Fach
Black Mountains	USA	Situated in Yancey County in western North Carolina, extending from the Blue Ridge Mountains
Blue Ridge Mountains	USA	Part of the Appalachians extending south-west from Carlisle, Pennsylvania, through Maryland, Virginia, N. Carolina, South Carolina, to Mt Oglethorpe in Georgia
Brecon Beacons	Wales	Red sandstone mountains
Cader Idris	Wales	Situated in Gwynedd, highest point is Pen-y-Gader (Cader Idris means 'chair of Idris')
Caribou Mountains	Canada	Major subdivision of the Columbia Mountains in British Columbia, highest peak is Mt Sir Wilfrid Laurier
Carpathians	East Europe	Crescent-shaped continuation of the Alps running through parts of The Czech Republic, Poland, Hungary, Romania, and the Ukraine, highest peak being Mt Gerlach (Gerlachovsky Stit)
Cascades	USA–Canada	Extending 700 miles from Lassen Peak in northern California, through Oregon and Washington to the Fraser River in southern British Columbia
Catskills	USA	Dissected segment of the Allegheny Plateau, and part of the

GEOGRAPHY

Name	Area	Details
		Appalachians, lying mainly in Greene and Ulster counties of south-eastern New York. Highest point is Slide Mountain
Caucasus	East Europe	Situated between the Black Sea and the Caspian Sea on the border of Russia, Georgia and Azerbaijan, highest point being Mt Elbrus
Cheviots	England	Range of rounded hills, mainly in Northumberland, forming the border between England and Scotland, highest point is Cheviot Peak
Chilterns	England	Range of chalk hills stretching 40 miles north-east from the Thames near Reading, highest point is Coombe Hill
Columbia Mountains	Canada – USA	Major mountain group of British Columbia that includes the Selkirk, Monashee, Cariboo, and Purcell ranges.
Dângrêk Mountains	Asia	Situated between Thailand and Cambodia
Darling Range	Australia	Situated on the south-west coast of Western Australia, highest peaks are Mt Cooke, Mt Solus and Mt Dale
Dartmoor	England	Area of high moorland in Devon, highest peak being High Willhays
Dauphiné Alps	France	Western spur of the Cottian Alps in south-eastern France
Dolomites	Italy	Eastern section of the northern Italian Alps, named after the 18th-century French geologist, Dieudonné Dolomieu, highest peak being Marmolada
Dome Rock Mountains	USA	Situated in western Arizona in the Sonoran Desert region near the California border
Drakensberg	South Africa	Extends from north-eastern Transvaal, through Lesotho, to south-eastern Cape Province, highest peak being Mt Thabana Ntlenyana
Durack Range	Australia	Situated in northern Western Australia, forming the eastern edge of the Kimberley Plateau
Elburz Mountains	Iran	Situated in northern Iran, highest point Mt Damāvand
Exmoor	England	Area of high moorland on the border of Somerset and Devon, highest point being Dunkery Beacon
Fan Si Pan Mountains	Vietnam	Situated in northern Vietnam, the highest peak is Mt Fan Si Pan
Flinders Range	Australia	Situated in eastern South Australia between Lake Torrens and Lake Frome, highest peak is St Mary
Gawler Ranges	Australia	Situated in South Australia, the eastern sector is known as the Middleback Ranges; the highest peak is Mount Bluff
Ghāts	India	Two ranges, East and West, forming the eastern and western edges of the Deccan Plateau of peninsular India. Ghāts means 'river landing stairs'
Golan Heights	Middle East	Situated in south-western Syria, overlooking the upper Jordan Valley, occupied by Israel since 1967 and unilaterally annexed in 1981
Grampians	Scotland	Dividing the Highlands and Lowlands, and including Ben Nevis, highest peak in the UK, the Cairngorms & Schiehallion
Great Dividing Range	Australia	Parallels the coasts of Queensland, New South Wales, and Victoria
Great Smoky Mountains	USA	Western segment of the Appalachian Mountains between Asheville, North Carolina and Knoxville, Tennessee; they are sometimes considered part of the Unaka Mountains
Great Western Mountains	Australia	Situated in central Tasmania, highest peak is Ironstone Mountain
Hamersley Range	Australia	Situated in the Pilbara region, north-western Western Australia, highest peak Mt Bruce
Himalayas	Central Asia	Extends in a south-easterly arc from Nanga Parbat peak in Jammu and Kashmir, to Namcha Barwa peak in Tibet, it contains 9 of the 14 highest peaks in the world and touches India, China, Nepal, Sikkim, and Bhutan
Hindu Kush	Central Asia	Stretches 1000 miles from the Pakistan/Chinese border in the east to a south-westerly point in Afghanistan; highest point is Tirich Mir
Jura Mountains	Central Europe	Situated on the Franco-Swiss border from the Rhône River to the Rhine
Karakoram Range	Central Asia	Northern extension of the Himalayas stretching from easternmost Afghanistan south-eastward into Jammu and Kashmir, highest peak being K2
Kibara Mountains	Zaïre	Reaching heights of 6,070' and situated in the Upemba National Park
King Leopold Ranges	Australia	Situated in northern Western Australia, forming the south-western edge of the Kimberley Plateau, highest peak is Mt Ord at just over 3,000'
Kipengere Range	Tanzania	Situated north of Lake Malawi
Kunlun Mountains	China	Extends from the Pamirs due east along the coast of Sinkiang to the Sino-Tibetan range of Tsinghai
Kwanto Range	Japan	Aka Kantō-sammyaku, situated on Honshu, the northern range is known as the Chichibu Mts
Kyrenia Mountains	Cyprus	Extending 100 miles east to west from Cape St Andreas to Cape Kormakiti, highest point being Mt Kyparissovouno
Lofty Range	Australia	Situated on the Tropic of Capricorn in Western Australia

Name	Area	Details
MacDonnell Ranges	Australia	Situated in south central Northern Territory, west of Alice Springs; Mt Ziel being the highest peak
Malverns	England	Granite ridge of Hereford and Worcester, high point being Worcester Beacon
Mealy Mountains	Canada	Situated south of Lake Melville in the Labrador peninsula of Newfoundland
Mecsek Mountains	Hungary	Aka Baranya Mts, situated in Baranya (Megye) county, southern Hungary. Highest peak is at Zengö
Monashee	Canada	Major subdivision of the Columbia Mountains in British Columbia
Mount Lofty Ranges	Australia	Situated in South Australia as a continuation of the Flinders range, highest point is Mt Byron
North Yolla Bolly Mountains	USA	California mountain range
Ore Mountains	East Europe	Situated on the border of Czech Republic and Eastern Germany highest peak is Klinovec at 4080′
Ozark Mountains	USA	Extends south-westward from St Louis, Missouri to the Arkansas River, highest point being Taum Sauk Mountain
Pamirs	Tajikistan	Often called 'The Roof of the World', highest point Communism Peak
Pare Range	Tanzania	Situated near the border with Kenya
Parecis Range	Brazil	Situated near the border with Bolivia
Peak District	England	Hill area in Derbyshire, forming the southern end of the Pennines, highest peak being Kinder Scout
Pennines	England	Range of limestone hills with a footpath stretching from Edale in Derbyshire to Kirk Yetholm in the Borders, highest point is Cross Fell
Pisgah Range	Jordan	Situated north-east of the Dead Sea, the ridge includes Mt Nebo
Przhevalsky Range (Arkatag)	Central Asia	Extension of the Kunlun Mountains, highest peak being Wu-Lu-k'o-mu-shih Ling
Purcell Range	Canada – USA	Major subdivision of the Columbia Mountains extending from British Columbia into northern Idaho
Queen Alexandra Range	Antarctica	Situated in the Ross Dependency (NZ admin), highest point Mt Kirkpatrick
Queen Elizabeth Range	Antarctica	Situated in the Ross Dependency (NZ admin), highest point Mt Miller
Queen Maud Range	Antarctica	Situated in the Ross Dependency (NZ admin), the range is a subdivision of the Transarctic Mountains
Rhodope Mountains	Balkan Peninsula	Situated mainly in Bulgaria, but extends into Macedonia, Greece, and Turkey, highest point being Golyam Perelik
Ring of Fire	Pacific	Not a mountain range but a colloquial name for the band of volcanoes that circle the Pacific and erupt frequently
Rockies	USA – Canada	Extending from British Columbia to New Mexico, highest peak is Mt Elbert
Ruwenzori Range	Zaire – Uganda	Highest mountain in the range is Mt Stanley, the highest peak being Margherita
Salt Range	Pakistan	Situated between the valleys of the Indus and Jhelum rivers of the northern Punjab, highest point being Mt Sakesar
San Bernardino Mountains	USA	Segment of the Pacific coast Ranges of southern California extending from Cajon Pass to Gorgonio Pass, highest point being San Gorgonio
San Francisco Peaks	USA	Three summits, Humphreys, Agassiz, and Fremont, on the ridge of an eroded volcano, 10 miles north of Flagstaff in north central Arizona
San Gabriel Mountains	USA	Segment of the Pacific coast Ranges of southern California extending from Newhall Pass to Cajon Pass, highest point being Mt San Antonio
San Jacinto Mountains	USA	Segment of the Pacific Coast Ranges of southern California extending from Gorgonio Pass to Santa Rosa Mountains
Sangre de Cristo Mountains	USA	Segment of the southern Rockies, extending south-eastward for about 250 miles, from Poncha Pass in south Colorado to north central New Mexico, highest point being Blanca Peak
Santa Marta Mountains	Colombia	Part of the Andes of northern Colombia, highest point Pico Cristóbal Colón is also the highest peak in Colombia
Sarykol Range	Central Asia	Borders Tajikistan and China, highest point being Mt Lyavirdyr
Sawatch Range	USA	Segment of the southern Rocky Mountains in central Colorado stretching from the Eagle River to Saguache, highest point being Mt Elbert
Selkirk Mountains	Canada – USA	Major subdivision of the Columbia Mountains extending for 200 miles from British Columbia into northern Idaho and Montana, highest peak is Mt Sir Stanford
Sentinel Range	Antarctica	Located in West Antarctica, joining the Heritage Range, making up the Ellsworth Mountain Range, contains the Continent's highest peak, Vinson Massif
Sierra Madre	Mexico	Includes the 3 ranges, Sierra Madre Occidental, Sierra Madre Oriental, and Sierra Madre del Sur (to the south)

GEOGRAPHY

Name	Area	Details
Sierra Madre de Chiapas	Mexico	Aka Sierra de Soconusco, and extending to the south-east along the Pacific Coast from the Isthmus of Tehuantepec to the Guatemalan border
Sierra Nevada	Spain	Highest division of the Penibético Mountain System of south-eastern Spain, highest point being Cerro de Mulhacén
Sierra Nevada Range	USA	Extending for more than 250 miles along the eastern edge of California, from the Mojave Desert in the south to the Cascades in the north, highest peak is Mt Whitney
Southern Alps	New Zealand	Situated on South Island and extending from Haast Pass, north-eastwards to Arthur's Pass, highest point being Mt Cook
Sperrin Mountains	N. Ireland	Situated 20 miles south-east of Londonderry, major peaks include, Mullaclogher, Sawel, and Mullaghaneany
St Elias Range	Canada	Situated in south-western Yukon Territory near the Pacific coast, highest peak is Mt Logan
Tatras	East Europe	Situated along the Slovak – Polish border, it is the highest range of the Central Carpathians, high point being Mt Gerlach
Transylvanian Alps	Romania	Aka Southern Carpathians, the section of the Carpathians between the Prahova River Valley and the gap between the Timis and Cerna rivers, highest point Mt Moldoveanu
Uinta Mountains	USA	Mountain range in N.E. Utah, part of the Rocky Mountains, the highest point being Kings Peak
Unaka Mountains	USA	Extending from south-west Virginia, along the Tennessee-North Carolina border, into northern Georgia. Unaka means 'white' in Cherokee
Urals	Russia	Extending from the Arctic Ocean to northern Kazakhstan, forming part of the boundary between Europe and Asia, highest peak Mt Narodnaya
Velikonda Range	India	Situated in Andhra Pradesh state of southern India
Virunga Range	Central Africa	Also spelled Birunga, and also called M'Fumbiro Mountains. The range straddles Zaire, Rwanda and Uganda, although, the highest peak, Karisimbi, borders Zaire & Rwanda
Vosges Mountains	France	Extending west of the Rhine River Valley in the Haut-Rhin, Bas-Rhin, and Vosges départements of eastern France; highest point Ballon de Guebwiller
White Mountains	USA	Segment of the Appalachians extending across New Hampshire and into western Maine, highest point is Mt Washington
Wilhelmina Gebergte	Suriname	Forming part of South America's granitic Precambrian Guiana Shield, highest point being Juliana Top
Wilson's Promontory	Australia	Not a range of mountains as such but the southernmost point of the Australian mainland, in Victoria; it is a mountainous area, highest point being Mt Latrobe
Wind River Range	USA	Situated in the central Rocky Mountains, west central Wyoming, the highest peak being Gannett Peak
Wrangell Mountains	USA	Segment of the Pacific Coast Range, extending southward in south-eastern Alaska for about 100 miles from the Copper River to the St Elias Mountains near the Yukon border; the highest point is Mt Blackburn
Yablonovy Range	Russia	Situated in the Transbaikalia region of Chita and Buryat, highest point being Mt Kusotuy
Zagros Mountains	Iran	Situated in south-west Iran, extending north-west to south-east from the Sirvān (Diyala) river to Shiráz, the highest peak being Zard Kuh
Zambales Mountains	Philippines	Situated in the south-western part of northern Luzon, from Lingayen Gulf in the north to the entrance to Manila Bay in the south, highest point being High Peak
Zeravshan Range	Tadzhik – Uzbek	Extends 230 miles as an east-west parallel to the Turkistan Range, highest point being Chimtorga

Mountain Passes, Valleys and Gorges

Arthur's the lowest pass (3,038′) of the Southern Alps, west-central South Island, New Zealand, the Otira Tunnel crosses the Alps at this point

Berthoud situated in the Front Range of the central Rocky Mountains at an altitude of 11,315′

Bran situated to the west of Predeal Pass and linking Brasov to Cimpulung between the Bucegi Massif and the Fagaras Mountains, Romania

Brenner lying on the Italian–Austrian border and at 4,498′ one of the lowest Alpine passes

Cameron situated in the extreme southerly end of the Medicine Bow Mountains in Colorado at an altitude of 10,285′

Great Saint Bernard lying on the Italian–Swiss border and at 8,100′ one of the highest Alpine passes

Gumal	situated between the Khyber pass and Bolãn pass and connects Ghazni in eastern Afghanistan with Tãnk and Dera Ismãil Khãn in Pakistan
Iron Gate	last gorge of the Djerdap gorge system on the Danube River, dividing the Carpathian and Balkan mountains and forming part of the boundary between Yugoslavia and Romania. The gorge is two miles long and 530′ wide
Katára (Métsovo in Albania)	situated in the Pindus Mountains of northern Greece and southern Albania at an altitude of 5,593′
Khyber	Connecting Kãbul, Afghanistan, with Peshãwar, Pakistan. The pass is extremely undulating and reaches 3,518′ at its highest point
Kicking Horse	situated on the Alberta–British Columbia border, the highest point on the Canadian Pacific Railway at 5,338′
Little Saint Bernard	at 7,178′ one of the highest passes of the French Alps. The road across the pass links France and Italy
Lolo	situated in the Bitterroot Range along the Idaho–Montana border at an altitude of 5,236′
Loveland	situated in the Front Range of the central Rocky Mountains at an altitude of 11,990 feet.
Marias	situated in the Lewis Range of the northern Rockies at an elevation of 5,216′
Métsovo (Katára in Greece)	situated in the Pindus Mountains of northern Greece and southern Albania at an altitude of 5,593′
Pajares	railway pass through the Cantabrian Mountains of northern Spain linking Oviedo and León at an altitude of 4,524′
Pele	cuts through the Black Mountain Range of the Assam Himalayas at an altitude of 11,055′
Plöcken (Passo di Monte Croce) Predeal	situated at an elevation of 4,462′ in the Carnic Alps on the Austrian–Italian border links the city of Brasov and the Birsei Depression to the north with the city of Ploiesti and the Danube Plain to the south, across the Transylvanian Alps (Southern Carpathians)
Predel	separates the Julian Alps at the Italian–Slovenian border at an altitude of 3,793′
Radstädter Tauern	situated in the Niedere Tauern Range at an elevation of 5,705′
Saint Gothard	a 16-mile-long pass situated in the Lepontine Alps of southern Switzerland. The pass has an altitude of 6,916′; the nine-mile-long St Gothard railway tunnel underneath the pass links Italy and Switzerland via Milan and Luzern; the ten-mile long St Gothard road tunnel links Göschenen and Airolo
Simplon	situated in the southern Swiss Alps at an altitude of 6,581′; the Simplon railway tunnel cuts through beneath the pass and connects Brig, Switzerland and Iselle, Italy
Uspallata	situated in the Andes, at 12,500′, connecting Mendoza, Argentina and Santiago, Chile

Mountains (General)

Name	Area	Height (ft)	Details
Abu (Guru Sikhar)	India	5,650	highest mountain in the Arãvalli range of northern India
Aconcagua	Argentina	22,834	highest peak in the Andes and in the Western Hemisphere, first climbed in 1897
Adam's Peak	Sri Lanka	7,360	situated in south-western Sri Lanka, 11 miles north-east of Ratnapura; famous for its footprint (5′4″ x 2′6″) revered as the Buddha's, Adam's or Siva's, dependent on faith
Alverstone	North America	14,565	situated in the St Elias Mountains, on the Yukon/Alaska border, and first climbed in 1951
Ampato	Peru	20,702	situated in the Andes, first climbed in 1972
Anai Mudi	India	8,842	situated in Kottayam district, eastern Kerala state, SW India, in the Western Ghãts, highest point of peninsular India
Annapurna	Nepal	26,546	first peak above 26,000′ to be climbed to the summit, on 3 June 1950, by Maurice Herzog and Louis Lachenal
Apo	Philippines	9,690	volcanic mountain, the highest point of the Philippines, part of the Cordillera Central
Aragats	Armenia	13,418	highest point in both Armenia, and the Little Caucasus range
Ararat (Agri Dagi)	Turkey	17,011	extinct volcano, highest peak in Turkey. Little Ararat (Kucuk Agri Dagi) rises to 12,782′
Aspiring	New Zealand	9,932	situated in the Southern Alps of west central South Island, first climbed in 1909 by Major Bernard Head
Athos	Greece	6,670	situated in northern Greece, it is also the site of a semi-autonomous republic of Greek Orthodox monks
Backbone	USA	3,360	highest point in Maryland
Baden-Powell	USA	9,389	twin peak, with North Baldy, and situated in the San Gabriel Mountains
Baker	USA	10,778	volcano situated in the Cascade range in Washington
Ballon de Guebwiller	France	4,672	highest peak of the Vosges Mountains
Bandeira	Brazil	9,482	situated on the border of Espirito Santo and Minas Gerais states, eastern Brazil; until Neblina peak was discovered in 1962 Bandeira was the highest known peak in Brazil
Batu	Ethiopia	14,130	situated in the Eastern Highlands between the Genale and Shebele rivers

GEOGRAPHY

Name	Area	Height (ft)	Details
Bear	USA	14,831	situated in the Wrangell Mountains, first climbed in 1951
Belukha	Russia	14,783	highest peak in the Altai Mountain range
Ben Macdui	Scotland	4,296	highest peak of the Cairngorm Mountains and the second highest mountain in the British Isles
Ben Nevis	Scotland	4,406	highest mountain of the British Isles
Betling Sib	India	3,280	highest peak of the Tripura Hills of north-eastern India
Big Black Mountain	USA	4,150	highest peak of Kentucky
Blackburn	USA	16,523	highest point in Alaska's Wrangell Mountains, first climbed in 1912
Blanc	France/Italy	15,771	highest peak in the Alps
Blanca Peak	USA	14,345	highest peak in the Sangre de Cristo Mountains of Colorado/New Mexico
Blue Mountain Peak	Jamaica	7,402	highest peak of the Blue Mountains in eastern Jamaica
Bluff	Australia	1,550	highest peak of the Gawler ranges of South Australia
Bolivar	Venezuela	16,427	situated in the Sierra Nevada National Park of Mérida and Barinas states, north-western Venezuela; Pico Bolivar (Columna) is marginally higher than Humboldt and Bonpland and is the highest peak in Venezuela: the cable-car running from Mérida to nearby Pico Espejo (Mirror Peak), 15,600', is thought to be the highest in the world
Bona	USA	16,421	situated in the Wrangell Mountains, first climbed in 1930
Botev Peak	Bulgaria	7,795	highest point in the Balkan Mountain range
Boundary Peak	USA	13,140	highest point in Nevada
Brasstown Bald	USA	4,784	highest point in Georgia, part of the Unaka range of the Blue Ridge
Brown	USA	14,530	situated in the Alaska range
Bruce	Australia	4,056	highest peak in the Hamersley range, and the highest in Western Australia
Bukit Maxwell	Malaysia	3,399	situated in Taiping, West Malaysia, and formerly called Mazwells Hill
Byron	Australia	3,058	highest point of the Mount Lofty ranges of South Australia
Carmarthen Van	Wales	2,632	highest peak of the Black Mountains of east Dyfed
Carn Mairg	Scotland	3,087	highest peak of the Monadhliath Mountains in the Highlands between Loch Ness and the River Spey; aka Grey Hills
Carrantuohill	Ireland	3,414	highest point of Macgillicuddy's Reeks in County Kerry and highest mountain in Ireland
Chances Peak	Montserrat	3,002	situated east of the capital Plymouth in the Soufrière Hills
Cheaha	USA	2,407	highest point in Alabama
Cheviot Peak	England	2,676	highest point of the Cheviots of northern England
Chimborazo	Ecuador	20,561	extinct volcano in the Andes of central Ecuador
Chimtorga	Tajik/Uzbek	18,009	highest point of the Zeravshan range
Churchill	USA	15,638	situated in the Wrangell Mountains
Cleveland	USA–Canada	10,479	highest peak of the Lewis range in the northern Rockies
Clingman's Dome	USA	6,643	highest point in Tennessee, situated in the Great Smoky Mountains National Park
Cloud Peak	USA	13,165	highest peak of the Bighorn Mountains in the northern Rocky Mountains, southern Montana
Communism Peak	Tajikistan	24,590	highest point of the Pamirs, and highest point of Tajikistan
Cook	New Zealand	12,349	situated in the Southern Alps, the highest peak of New Zealand
Cooke	Australia	1,910	highest peak in the Darling range of Western Australia
Coombe Hill	England	825	highest peak of the Chilterns
Corn Ddu	Wales	2,863	twin peak, with Pen-y-Fan, of the Brecon Beacons
Cotopaxi	Ecuador	19,347	active volcano situated in the Andes, last eruption in 1975
Crêt de la Neige	France	5,636	situated in the French segment of the Jura Mountains
Cristóbal Colón	Colombia	18,947	situated in the Santa Marta Mountains and is the highest peak in Colombia
Cross Fell	England	2,930	highest peak in the Pennines
Curcubăta Marc	Romania	6,063	highest peak of the Bihor Massif in the Apuneni Mountains
Dandenong	Australia	2,077	highest peak in the Dandenong range of southern Victoria
Davis	USA	3,213	highest point in Pennsylvania, part of the Allegheny Mountains
Dhaulagiri	Nepal	26,795	Himalayan mountain; name means 'White Mountain' in Sanskrit
Djebel Chélia	Algeria	7,638	situated in the Aurès range of Northern Algeria
Doda Betta	India	8,652	highest peak in Tamil Nādu state, south-eastern India, and 2nd highest peak in the Western Ghāts
Dom Mountain	Indonesia	4,396	situated on the island of New Guinea, there is also a Dom Peak in the Apennines
Dome Fuji Peak	Antarctica	12,487	situated on Queen Maud Land
Dome Mountain	Canada	896	situated south of Lake Melville in Newfoundland
Dufourspitze	Switzerland	15,203	highest peak in Switzerland, in the Monte Rosa Massif

Name	Area	Height (ft)	Details
Dunkery Beacon	England	1,750	highest peak of Exmoor, on the border of Somerset and Devon
Eagle	USA	2,300	highest peak in Minnesota
Ebal	Palestine	3,084	situated in the West Bank just north of Mt Gerizim
Edith	USA	9,504	highest peak of the Big Belt Mountains, a segment of the northern Rocky Mountains
Egmont	New Zealand	8,260	extinct volcano on the Taranaki peninsula of North Island
Eiger	Switzerland	13,026	first climbed in 1858 by Charles Barrington and Christian Almer. The 6,000′ North Face was first climbed in July 1938 by Heinrich Harrer, Fritz Kasparek, Anderl Heckmair and Ludwig Vorg; the difficulty of this climb earned the Eiger Nordwand many nicknames, including 'The White Spider', 'The White Cobra' and 'Murder Wall'
El Capitan	USA	3,604	highest peak in Yosemite National Park, central California. El Capitan is a granite buttress, part of Sierra Nevada range
El Misti	Ecuador	19,233	volcano situated in the Ecuadorean Andes; last eruption in 1878
Elbert	USA	14,433	situated in the Sawatch range of the Rockies in central Colorado, the highest point in Colorado and the Rockies
Elbright Road	USA	442	situated in New Castle County, the highest point in Delaware
Elbrus	Russia	18,510	highest peak in the Caucasus and highest in Russia, just north of the Georgia border
Elgon	Kenya/Uganda	14,140	extinct volcano on the Kenya/Uganda border, first climbed by Sir Frederick Jackson and Ernest Gedge in 1890, highest peak is Wagagai
Encuolo	Ethiopia	14,144	situated in the Eastern Highlands north of the Shebele river
Erebus	Antarctica	12,448	volcano situated on Ross Island, discovered by Sir James Ross in 1841 and named after his ship
Etna	Italy	10,855	situated on the island of Sicily, this volcano, the highest in Europe, had a major eruption in 1669 when 20,000 people were killed and the city of Catania was devastated
Evans	USA	14,264	highest peak of the Front range in the central Rocky Mountains
Everest	Nepal/Tibet	29,035	highest point on Earth, named after George Everest, Surveyor General of India (1830–43), and called Peak XV until 1865; Dalai Lama 1st gave permission to climb in 1920 and Sir John Hunt led the 1953 successful expedition; Dougal Haston and Doug Scott in 1976 became the first British climbers; Reinhold Messner was the first to make a successful climb without oxygen; Junko Tabei of Japan became the first woman to climb Everest on 16 May 1975; Alison Hargreaves became first woman to climb Everest without oxygen but died soon after on K2; Everest is also called Goddess Mother of the World (Chomolungma in the Tibetan language); previously believed to be 29,028′; remeasured on 5 May 1999 with GPS equipment
Fairweather	North America	15,299	situated in the St. Elias Mountains, on the British Columbia/Alaska border, and first climbed in 1931
Fan Si Pan	Vietnam	10,308	highest peak in Vietnam
Fanthams Peak	New Zealand	6,438	extinct volcano on the Taranaki peninsula of North Island
Fichtelberg	Germany	3,983	highest peak on the German side of the Ore Mountains
Finsteraarhorn	Switzerland	14,022	highest peak of the Bernese Alps
Foraker	USA	17,400	situated in the Alaska range, and first climbed in 1934
Francs Peak	USA	13,140	highest peak of the Absaroka range of the northern Rocky Mountains in northwestern Wyoming and southern Montana
Fremont Peak	USA	13,730	situated in the Wind River range of Wyoming
Galtymore	Ireland	3,018	highest peak of the Galty Mountains of Western Ireland
Gannett Peak	USA	13,763	highest peak in the Wind River range and also the highest peak in Wyoming
Gerizim (Jabal At-Tur)	Palestine	2,890	Since 1967 has been part of the West Bank of Judaea and Samaria, under Israeli administration, it is twinned with Mt Ebal, which is just north of Gerizim
Gerlach	Slovakia	8,711	situated in the Tatra segment of the Carpathian Mountains and is the highest peak of the Carpathians
Glittertinden	Norway	8,110	situated in the Jotunheimen (Giant's Home) Mountain and although twelve feet higher than Galdhopiggen the peak is a 65 ft thick permanent, glacial ice cap
Golyam (Great) Perelik	Balkans	7,188	highest peak in the Rhodope Mountains
Goodsir	Canada	11,683	situated in the Yoho National Park of eastern British Columbia
Grandfather	USA	5,964	situated in North Carolina, part of the Blue Ridge Mountains
Granite Peak	USA	12,799	highest peak in Montana, part of the Beartooth range
Greylock	USA	3,491	situated in the Berkshire Hills, the highest point in Massachusetts

Name	Area	Height (ft)	Details
Guadalupe Peak	USA	8,749	highest point in Texas
Guge	Ethiopia	13,790	situated west of Lake Abaya
Guru Sikhar	India	5,650	See Mt Abu
Hagen	New Guinea	12,392	situated in the Central Highlands of New Guinea Island, Papua New Guinea
Harney Peak	USA	7,242	highest peak in South Dakota situated in the Black Hills
Hartz Mountain	Australia	4,111	highest peak of the Hartz Mountain range in Southern Tasmania
Harvard	USA	14,420	situated in the Sawatch Mountains, a segment of the Rockies running through Colorado
Hermon	Syria/Lebanon	9,232	aka Jabal ash-Shaikh, and situated west of Damascus, Hermon means 'Forbidden Place'
High Peak	Philippines	6,683	highest peak of the Zambales Mountains
High Point	USA	1,803	highest peak in New Jersey
High Willhays	England	2,039	highest peak in the Dartmoor National Park of Devon
Hochgolling	Austria	9,393	highest peak of the Niedere Tauern range of the Eastern Alps
Hood	USA	11,235	situated in the Cascade range, highest peak in Oregon
Huascarán	Peru	22,205	extinct volcano in west Peru, in the Peruvian Andes, highest peak in Peru
Hubbard	North America	15,015	situated in the St Elias Mountains, on the Yukon/Alaska border, and first climbed in 1951
Humphrey's Peak	USA	12,633	one of the three San Francisco Peaks, the highest peak in Arizona
Hunter	USA	14,573	situated in the Alaska range
Ida	Crete	8,058	highest peak on the island at 2,456m, it is just three metres higher than Mt Pachnes, the second highest peak
Ingleborough	England	2,376	one of the so called Three Peaks of the Yorkshire Dales National Park
Ironstone	Australia	4,736	highest peak of the Great Western Mountains in Tasmania
Isto	USA	9,058	highest peak of the Brooks range in the northern Rocky Mountains near the Canadian border
Iztaccíhuatl	Mexico	17,159	dormant volcano which last erupted in 1868, situated on the México-Puebla state line in central Mexico, 10 miles north of its twin, Popocatépetl
Jerimoth Hill	USA	812	highest peak in Rhode Island, less than a mile from the Connecticut border
Juliana Top	Suriname	4,199	highest peak of the Wilhelmina Gebergte range of central Suriname
Jungfrau	Switzerland	13,642	situated in the Bernese Alps 11 miles south-east of Interlaken; first climbed by two Swiss brothers, Rudolf and Hieronymus Meyer, in 1811
K2	Pakistan	28,250	situated in the Karakorum range in the Himalayas, on the western side of the Indian/Pakistani line of control in Jammu and Kashmir, first climbed by Compagnoni and Lacedelli in 1954 K2 is also known as Mt Godwin Austen, Dapsang, and Chogori
Kanchenjunga	Nepal/India	28,208	on the border of Nepal and Sikkim, the 3rd highest mountain in the world was first climbed in 1955, although Charles Evans stopped short of the summit in deference to Sikkimese religious beliefs; Kanchenjunga means 'Five Treasuries of the Great Snow' (Sikkim)
Karisimbi	Dem Rep Congo/ Rwanda	14,787	highest peak of the Virunga range
Katahdin	USA	5,268	highest peak in Maine
Kellerwand	Austria	9,121	highest peak of the Carnic Alps
Kennedy Peak	Myanmar	2,704	situated on the Tropic of Cancer near the Indian border
Kennesaw	USA	551	situated in Atlanta, Georgia
Kenya (Batian Peak)	Kenya	17,057	extinct volcano, first climbed in 1899 by Halford and Mackinder of Great Britain
Kerintji	Indonesia	12,484	highest peak in the West Sumatran/Java range
Kilimanjaro	Tanzania	19,340	Volcanic mountain near the Kenyan border, the Kibo peak being the highest point in Tanzania and probably the only snow-covered point on the equator; the other main peak is Mawenzi
Kimpō	Japan	8,514	situated in the Chichibu Mountains, the northern extension of the Kwanto range
Kinabalu	Malaysia	13,455	highest peak in the Malay Archipelago, situated on the island of Borneo, it was formerly known as St Peter's Mount
Kinder Scout	England	2,088	highest point in the Peak District
King	Canada	16,972	situated in the St Elias Mountains, Yukon Territory, and first climbed in 1952
Kings Peak	USA	13,528	highest point in Utah, situated in the Uintas range
Kirkpatrick	Antarctica	14,856	highest point of the Queen Alexandra range
Klinovec	Czech Republic	4,080	highest peak in the Ore Mountains

Name	Area	Height (ft)	Details
Klyuchevskaya Sopka	Russia	15,584	highest active volcano in Asia, situated in Kamchatka Peninsula
Kompasberg	South Africa	8,215	highest peak of the Sneeuberg (Snow Mountain) range in central Cape Province
Kosciusko	Australia	7,316	situated in the Snowy Mountains of New South Wales, the highest peak in Australia
Krakatoa	Indonesia	2,667	famous for the eruption of 1883 when 163 villages were destroyed and 36,417 people were killed. Despite the title of the 1968 film, Krakatoa is actually west of Java
Kriván	East Europe	8,182	one of the highest peaks of the High Tatras on the Poland/Slovakia border
Kusotuy	Russia	5,512	highest point of the Yablonovy range
Kyparissovouno	Cyprus	3,360	highest point of the Kyrenia Mountains
La Dôle	Switzerland	5,545	situated in the Swiss segment of the Jura Mountains
Lascar	Chile	18,508	Volcano situated in the Chilean Andes, last eruption in 1969
Lassen	USA	10,457	Volcano situated in the Cascade range in California
Latrobe	Australia	2,475	highest point of Wilson's Promontory in southern Victoria
Le Reculet	France	5,633	situated in the French segment of the Jura Mountains
Les Écrins	France	13,461	highest peak of the Dauphiné Alps
Lhotse (E)	Nepal/Tibet	27,923	situated just south of Everest, to which it is joined by a 25,000' ridge; The 'E' of its original name stands for Everest
Llullaillaco	S America	22,058	Dormant volcano situated in the Andes on the Argentina/Chile border, last eruption in 1877
Logan	Yukon	19,550	2nd highest peak in North America, first climbed in 1925 by MacCarthy and Lambert; mountains with the same name in Quebec, Arizona and Washington
Lomnicky	East Europe	8,635	one of the highest peaks of the High Tatras on the Poland/Slovakia border
Lozère	France	5,584	highest peak of the Cévennes range of southern France
Lucania	Canada	17,146	situated in the St Elias Mountains, Yukon Territory, and first climbed in 1937
Lugnaquilla	Ireland	3,039	highest peak of the Wicklow Mountains
Lyavirdyr	Tajikistan	20,837	highest point of the Sarykol range
Magazine	USA	2,753	highest peak in Arkansas
Mansfield	USA	4,393	highest point in Vermont
Marcy	USA	5,344	highest peak of the Adirondacks, and the highest peak of New York state
Mariveles	Philippines	4,659	Most southerly peak of the Zambales Mountains, lying opposite Manila Bay
Markham	Antarctica	14,272	highest point of the Queen Elizabeth range
Marmolada	Italy	10,964	highest peak in the Dolomites
Mary's Peak	USA	4,097	South-west of Corvallis, the highest point of the Oregon Coastal range
Massive	USA	14,421	situated in the Sawatch Mountains, a segment of the Rockies running through Colorado
Matterhorn	Switzerland/Italy	14,691	First climbed 14 Jul 1865 by British explorer Edward Whymper, although the Italian ridge was scaled 3 days later by Giovanni Carrel; Matterhorn was named after the Swiss city of Zermatt; Italian name is Monte Cervino
Mauna Kea	USA	13,796	Dormant volcano situated on Hawaii Island, the highest point in Hawaii state, in fact, its 32,000' height from the seafloor makes it the world's highest peak from base to tip
Mauna Loa	USA	13,678	situated on Hawaii Island, the actual height of the volcano from its base on the seafloor is second only to Mauna Kea; last erupted in 1988
McIntyre	USA	5,114	situated in the Adirondack range of New York state; highest peak is Algonquin
McKinley	USA	20,320	situated in the Alaska range, and first climbed in 1913, the highest peak of North America
Mercedario	Argentina	22,211	situated in the Andes, first climbed in 1934
Meru	Tanzania	14,980	located near the Kenyan border, south-west of Kilimanjaro
Mikeno	Dem Rep Congo/ Rwanda	14,557	situated in the Virunga Mountains
Miller	Antarctica	13,646	situated in the Queen Elizabeth range
Mitchell	USA	6,684	highest point in North Carolina, situated in the Black Mountains, part of the Blue Ridge Mountains; highest peak east of the Mississippi
Moldoveanu	Romania	8,346	situated in the Transylvanian Alps, the highest peak in Romania
Mönch	Switzerland	13,448	flanked by the Eiger and Jungfrau in the Bernese Alps
Mount Darwin	Zimbabwe	4,951	situated in northern Zimbabwe, locals call it Pfura, meaning 'rhinoceros'

GEOGRAPHY

Name	Area	Height (ft)	Details
Mulhacén	Spain	11,421	situated in the Sierra Nevadas of southern Spain, the highest mountain of the Iberian Peninsula
Nanda Devi	India	25,643	situated in the Uttar Pradesh segment of the Himalayas
Nanga (Naked) Parbat	Kashmir	26,660	often regarded as the first major peak of the western Himalayas; the local name is Diamir (King of the Mountains)
Neblina	Brazil	9,889	situated in the Serra Tapirapeó, Amazonas state, highest peak in Brazil
Nebo	Jordan	2,631	highest point of the Pisgah Ridge, from which Moses viewed the Promised Land
North Baldy	USA	9,131	Twin peak, with Mt Baden-Powell, and situated in the San Gabriel Mountains of southern California
Ojos del Salado	S America	22,588	Although the mountain straddles the Chile/Argentina border, the highest peak is totally in Chile and is the highest point, first climbed in 1937. Ojos del Salado is also the highest active volcano in the world. It was previously designated as dormant but it started to 'steam' in 1981 and has recently produced vents
Olga	Australia	3,507	situated in Uluru National Park, Mt Olga is the most westerly of Australia's 3 giant tors, the others being Ayers Rock at 2,845′ and Mt Conner
Orizaba (Citlaltépetl)	Mexico	18,406	dormant volcano situated in Altiplano de Mexico, last erupted in 1687, the highest point in Mexico
Pelée	Martinique	4,582	In 1902 the town of St Pierre was destroyed by this volcano's eruption, which killed all 26,000 inhabitants, except for a prisoner who survived in the thick-walled prison
Pen-y-Fan	Wales	2,906	highest point of the Brecon Beacons
Pen-y-Gader	Wales	2,927	highest point of the Cader Idris range
Pen-y-Ghent	England	2,278	one of the so called Three Peaks of the Yorkshire Dales National Park
Pinátubo	Philippines	5,723	situated in Luzon, this volcano last erupted in 1991, when 847 people were killed – the most lethal eruption of the 20th century
Pissis	Argentina	22,241	situated in the Andes, first climbed in 1937
Popocatépetl	Mexico	17,930	volcano which last erupted in 1997, the first eruption since 1802, although it does emit large clouds of smoke periodically; known locally as Nahuatl (smoking mountain)
Poroshiri	Japan	6,732	highest peak of the Hidaka–Sammyaku range on Hokkaido
Profitis	Greece	1,857	volcanic mountain on the island of Thera in the Cyclades, the highest point on the island
Punta Pora	Paraguay	2,296	second-highest peak in Paraguay
Puy de Sancy	France	6,184	highest peak of the Massif Central
Rainier	USA	14,410	dormant volcano, highest peak of the Cascade range and also the highest peak in Washington state, first climbed in 1870
Ramlo	Ethiopia	6,988	situated inland of the Red Sea coast, north of Djibouti
Revelstoke	Canada	6,375	situated in the Selkirk Mountains of south-eastern British Columbia
Rock Creek Butte	USA	9,105	highest peak of the Blue Mountains, situated on the Elkhorn Ridge on the Oregon/Washington border
Rogers	USA	5,729	highest point in Virginia, part of the Blue Ridge Mountains
Rosa	Switzerland/Italy	15,203	situated SE of Zermatt, often identified with Dufourspitze, although Monte Rosa has many other named peaks
Round	Australia	5,300	highest peak of the New England range, NSW
Ruapehu	New Zealand	9,177	active volcano and highest point on North Island
Rushmore	South Dakota	6,040	situated in the Black Hills, and famous for its carved faces (60′ high) of Washington, Lincoln, Jefferson and Roosevelt, executed by Gutzon Borglum between 1927 and 1941
St Helens	USA	8,360	volcano situated in Washington state (Cascades); it erupted in 1980 after lying dormant from 1857
St Mary	Australia	3,825	highest peak in the Flinders ranges
Sajama	Bolivia	21,391	situated in the Andes, first climbed in 1939, the highest peak of Bolivia
Sakesar	Pakistan	4,992	highest peak of the Salt range in the northern Punjab
San Antonio	USA	10,080	Nicknamed 'Old Baldy' and the highest peak of the San Gabriel Mountains of southern California
San Bernardino	USA	10,630	situated in the San Bernardino Mountains of southern California
San Gorgonio	USA	11,502	situated in the San Bernardino Mountains, highest point in southern California
San Jacinto Peak	USA	10,804	highest point of the San Jacinto Mountains of southern California
San Pedro	Chile	20,339	volcano situated in the Chilean Andes, last eruption in 1960
Sanford	USA	16,237	situated in the Wrangell Mountains of south-eastern Alaska, first climbed in 1938

Name	Area	Height (ft)	Details
Santorini	Greece	1,960	see Thera
Sassafras	USA	3,560	highest point in South Carolina, part of the Blue Ridge Mountains
Scafell	England	3,162	south-west of Scafell Pike, the 2nd-highest peak in England
Scafell Pike	England	3,210	situated in the Lake District of Cumbria, highest point in England
Scott Peak	USA	11,394	highest peak of the Bitterroot range in the northern Rocky Mountains, Idaho
Shasta	USA	14,162	extinct volcano situated in the Cascade range of northern California
Shirane	Japan	10,472	highest mountain of the Japanese Alps, on Honshu island; the peak of the mountain is named Ontake
Shishaldin	USA	9,387	volcanic mountain in the Unimak Islands, the highest point in the Aleutian range of Alaska
Sierra Blanca	USA	12,003	highest peak of the Sacramento Mountains in the southern Rockies
Sinai	Egypt	7,497	situated on the Sinai Peninsula, under Israeli administration from the Six-Day War of 1967 until 1979, when it was returned to Egypt; God is purported to have given Moses the Ten Commandments here
Sir James McBrien	Canada	9,061	highest peak of the Mackenzie Mountains in the Yukon Territory
Sir Sanford	Canada	11,590	highest peak of the Selkirk Mountains
Sir Wilfrid Laurier	Canada	11,299	highest peak of the Cariboo range of British Columbia
Slide	USA	4,204	highest point of the Catskill Mountains
Slieve Donard	N Ireland	2,796	highest peak of the Mourne Mountains
Snaefell	Isle of Man	2,034	highest peak of the Isle of Man
Snowdon	Wales	3,560	situated in Snowdonia National Park, Clwyd and Gwynedd, highest peak in Wales
Solomon's Throne	Pakistan	18,481	situated in the Sulaimân range of central Pakistan
Spruce Knob	USA	4,862	highest point in West Virginia, part of the Allegheny Mountains
Stanley	Dem Rep Congo/ Uganda	16,795	highest mountain in the Ruwenzori range (highest peak named after Queen Margherita of Italy), first climbed in 1906 by Luigi Abruzzi
Steele	Canada	16,644	situated in the St Elias Mountains, Yukon Territory, and first climbed in 1935
Sugar Loaf	Brazil	1,325	overlooking the entrance of Guanabara Bay, south-eastern Brazil
Sunflower	USA	4,039	highest point in Kansas, situated south-east near the Colorado border
Table (Tafelberg)	South Africa	3,563	Flat-topped mountain overlooking Cape Town and Table Bay; the highest peak is Maclear's Beacon, subsidiary peaks include Lion's Head (2,195') and Devil's Peak (3,281')
Tahan	Malaysia	7,175	situated in Taman Negara National Park, West Malaysia
Tahat	Algeria	9,852	situated in the Hoggar Massif of the southern Saharan Atlas mountains
Talo	Ethiopia	14,478	situated in central Ethiopia in the Gojam Massif
Tambora	Indonesia	9,350	situated on Sumbawa and famous for its eruption of 1815 when over 90,000 people perished
Tapuaenuku	New Zealand	9,465	highest peak of the Kaikoura range on South Island
Taum Sauk	USA	1,772	highest peak of the Ozark Mountains, and highest point in Missouri
Teide	Spain	12,190	volcanic mountain situated on the island of Tenerife in the Canaries, last erupted in 1909
Tendre	Switzerland	5,550	situated in the Swiss segment of the Jura Mountains
Thabana Ntlenyana	Lesotho	11,425	highest peak in the Drakensberg Mountains
Thera	Greece	1,960	southernmost island of the Cyclades group, aka Santorini, and famous for its volcanic eruption c1550 BC which possibly gave rise to the legend of the lost city of Atlantis
Timpanogos	USA	12,008	highest peak of the Wasatch range in the south central Rocky Mountains
Tirich Mir	Pakistan	25,230	highest peak in the Hindu Kush range, lying 155 miles north of Peshawar
Titano	San Marino	2,424	highest peak and dominant feature of San Marino
Toluca	Mexico	4,577	volcano situated in Mexico state, central Mexico near Toluca, the crater partly filled by a lake
Triglav	Slovenia	9,396	highest peak of the Julian Alps of Slovenia, first climbed in 1778
Tsiafajavona	Madagascar	8,671	situated in the Ankaratra Mountain region, 2nd-highest peak of Madagascar
Tupungato	S. America	22,310	situated in the Andes, on the Argentina/Chile border, first climbed in 1897
Tyree	Antarctica	16,289	situated in the Sentinel range of the Ellsworth Mountains, first climbed in 1967

GEOGRAPHY

Name	Area	Height (ft)	Details
Vancouver	North America	15,700	situated in the St Elias Mountains, on the Yukon/Alaska border, and first climbed in 1949
Veleta	Spain	11,128	situated in the Sierra Nevadas of southern Spain, the 2nd highest mountain of mainland Spain
Vesuvius	Italy	4,198	volcano situated in the Bay of Naples, first major eruption in AD 79 and the last in 1944
Victoria	Myanmar	10,150	highest peak of the Arakan Yoma range separating Myanmar from the Indian subcontinent
Vikhren	Bulgaria	9,564	situated in the Rhodope Mountains; second-highest peak in Bulgaria
Vinson Massif	Antarctica	16,864	situated in the Sentinel range of the Ellsworth Mountains, first climbed in 1966
Waddington	Canada	13,104	highest peak of the Coast Mountains of British Columbia
Walsh	Canada	14,780	situated in the St Elias Mountains, Yukon Territory, and first climbed in 1941
Warren	USA	13,720	situated in the Wind River range of Wyoming
Washington	USA	6,288	highest peak in the Presidential range of the White Mountains, and the highest peak in New Hampshire
Waun Fach	Wales	2,660	highest peak of the Black Mountains of east Gwent
Wheeler Peak	USA	13,161	situated in the Sangre de Cristo Mountains, the highest point in New Mexico
Whernside	England	2,416	one of the so-called Three Peaks of the Yorkshire Dales National Park
White Butte	USA	3,506	highest peak in North Dakota
Whiteface	USA	4,865	situated in the Adirondacks of New York
Whitney	USA	14,494	highest peak of Sierra Nevada range in California and the highest peak of the 48 coterminous United States of America
Wilson	USA	5,710	situated in the San Gabriel Mountains of southern California
Wood	Canada	15,886	situated in the St Elias Mountains, Yukon Territory, and first climbed in 1941
Woodroffe	Australia	4,724	highest peak of South Australia situated in the Musgrave ranges
Worcester Beacon	England	1,395	highest peak of the Malverns
Wrangell	USA	14,163	situated in the Wrangell Mountains of south-eastern Alaska
Wu-t'ai	China	10,033	situated in north-east Shansi Province, the name meaning 'five terraces'
Yes Tor	England	2,028	situated in the Dartmoor National Park of Devon, and twinned with High Willhays
Zengö	Hungary	2,237	highest peak of the Mecsek Mountains of southern Hungary
Ziel	Australia	4,954	highest peak of the MacDonnell ranges of Australia
Zomba	Malawi	6,846	highest point of the Zomba Massif in southern Malawi
Zugspitze	Germany	9,721	part of the Wettersteingebirge in the Bavarian Alps, lying on the Austrian border, the highest point in Germany

Oceans

	Area (Sq Miles)	% of Earth's Water	Deepest Point
Pacific	64,186,300	46.0	Challenger Deep
Atlantic	33,420,000	23.9	Milwaukee Deep
Indian	28,350,500	20.3	Planet Deep
Arctic	5,105,700	3.6	Eurasia Basin

British Place Names:
meanings of suffixes and prefixes

Name	Meaning	Name	Meaning	Name	Meaning
aber	river mouth	dal	field	kyle	strait
ac	oak or acorn	dar	water	lade	river mouth
agh	field	dean	wooded vale	law	rising ground
aig	nook or creek	dearg	red	lea	meadow
aird	height	del	dale	leck	field of corpses
ald	old	den	wooded vale	lee	meadow
alt	brook	dene	wooded vale	leigh	woodland glade or
alt	steep place	der	water		meadow
an	terminal diminutive	dhu	black	ley	woodland glade or
ard	height	don	hill or water		meadow
ath	ford	dor	water	linn	waterfall
auch	field	dour	water	lis	enclosure
auchter	summit	drom	ridge	litch	field of corpses
avon	river	drum	ridge	llan	church
ax	water	dum	fortress	llech	smooth cliff
ay	island	dun	hill (England)	llwyd	grey or hoary
bal	village or town	dun	fortress (Scotland +	llwyn	wood
balloch	pass		Ireland)	llyn	lake
bally	village or town	dur	water	loch	lake
ban	white or fair	dwfr	water	lough	lake
bar	point or projecting	dyke	ditch	low	rising ground or mound
	height	ea	island	lynn	waterfall
beath	birch tree	eccles	church	madah	wolf
beck	brook	egles	church	madan	fair
bedd	grave	ennis	island	maen	stone
beg	little	esk	water	magh	plain
ben	mountain	ex	water	mawr	great
bere	barley	ey	island	mere	lake or marsh
blair	plain	fell	mountain	mickle	great or much
borough	fortified place	field	clearing	minster	monastic
bourne	stream	fin	white or fair		establishment
brae	promontory	fleet	river	moor	lake or marsh
bre	promontory	force	waterfall	mor	great
brogh	fortified place	ford	shallow river crossing	moss	bog
bruach	slope or brae	gair	short	mull	headland
bryn	ridge	garth	enclosure	nant	brook or valley
burg	fortified place	gate	passage	ness	promontory
burn	brook	ghyll	ravine	ock	water
bury	fortified place	gill	ravine	oke	water
by	village	glen	narrow valley	or	river or sea shore
caer	camp or fortified place	ham	home or enclosure	pen	hill or headland
cairn	pile of stones	hampton	home farm or village	pike	mountain summit
cambus	crooked	hanger	wood on hillside	pont	bridge
carn	pile of stones	haugh	meadow between hills	port	harbour
carrick	cliff	hause	pass or col	pwil	pool
caster	walled camp	hay	hedge	rath	round earthwork
cefn	ridge	head	headland or hill	rhos	moor
cester	walled camp	hithe	haven	rhyd	ford
cheap	market	holme	river island	rigg	ridge
chester	walled camp	holt	small wood	ross	promontory
chipping	market place	hoo	heel of land	royd	ridded of trees
clach	stone	hurst	thick wood on a hill	scar	cliff
clere	hill	inch	island	seat	cultivated place or
clon	meadow	ing	meadow		dwelling
coe	narrow	ing	son of	set	settlement
coln	colony	ing	people of	sex	Saxon
combe	grassy hollow	innis	island	shan	mountain
cote	mud cottage	inver	river mouth	shaw	shady place
craig	rock or cliff	keld	spring	shot	protruding land
crick	cliff	ken	head	shott	protruding land
croe	sheepfold	kil	church	slievh	mountain
croft	enclosure	kirk	church	staple	store or market
cwm	grassy valley	knock	knoll	stead	place or holding
dal	dale	knoll	hill top	stock	palisaded place

Name	Meaning	Name	Meaning	Name	Meaning
stoke	palisaded place	ton	farm or town	walt	wood
stow	holy place or enclosure	tor	rocky hill	weald	wood
strat	roman road	tre	dwelling or small town	wich	marshy meadow
strath	broad valley	tree	post, cross or crucifix	wick	village or farm
tam	wide	try	dwelling	win	plain
thorpe	farm or village	twistle	boundary	wold	wood
thwaite	clearing	ty	house	worth	protected enclosure
tober	well	ux	water	ystrad	vale
toft	enclosure	wald	wood		

British Place Names: meanings

Name	Meaning	Name	Meaning
Accrington	Acorn Farm	Oundle	Non-sharing Ones
Crawley	Crows Wood	Pontypridd	Bridge by the Earthen House
Croydon	Saffron Valley		
Cumbernauld	Meeting of the Streams	Powys	Provincial
Cumbria	Fellow Countrymen	Prestatyn	Priest's Village
Derby	Deer Village	Preston	Priest's Village
Derwent	Oak River	Prestwick	Priest's Outlying Farm
Devizes	Boundaries	Purbeck	Bittern's Beak
Diss	Ditch	Purley	Pear-Tree Wood
Ely	Eel	Ramsey	Land of Wild Garlic
Epping	Look-out Place	Ramsgate	Raven's Gap
Falkirk	Speckled Church	Redhill	Red Slope
Gateshead	Goat's Head	Reigate	Doe Gate
Gatwick	Goat Farm	Renfrew	Current Point
Harlow	Army Mound	Rhondda	Noisy One
Harrogate	Heap of Stones Road	Ribble	Tearing One
Harwich	Military Settlement	Rievaulx	Rye Valley
Hendon	High Hill	Salford	Willow-Tree Ford
Hythe	Landing Place	Selby	Village by the Willows
Kesteven	Wood Meeting Place	Sherborne	Bright Stream
Lampeter	St Peter's Church	Skye	Wing
Leatherhead	Grey Ford	Snaefell	Snow Mountains
Lerwick	Mud Bay	Soho	Hunting Cry (named after)
Lichfield	Open Land by the Grey Forest	Solihull	Muddy Hill
		Staines	Stone
Llanfair-Pwllgwyngyllgogerych wyrndrobwillantysiliogog-ogoch	St Mary's Church in the hollow of the White Hazel	Stevenage	Place at the firm Oak
		Stranraer	Fat Peninsula
		Streatham	Home by a Roman Road
		Surrey	Southern District
Lundy	Puffin (Norse meaning)	Sussex	South Saxons
Malpas	Bad Step	Sutton	Southern Farm
March	Boundary	Swindon	Pig Hill
Margate	Sea Gate	Tay	Silent One
Matlock	Assembly Oak	Tees	Seething One
Melrose	Bare Moor	Tenby	Little Fort
Menai	Carrying	Tintagel	Throat Fort
Merton	Farm by a Pool	Tobermory	St Mary's Well
Morecambe	Curved Sea	Tranmere	Cranes
Morpeth	Murder Path	Tresco	Elder-Tree Farm
Moulton	Mule's Settlement	Tring	Tree-covered Hillside
Neasden	Nose-shaped Hill	Trossachs	Transverse Hills
Neath	Shining One	Unst	Abode of Eagles
Nottingham	Home of Snot's People		

World Place Names: meanings

Name	Meaning	Name	Meaning
Aachen	Water Springs	Bruges	Bridge
Acapulco	Place where the Reeds Grow	Brussels	Marsh Room
Accra	Ant	Bulawayo	Place of the Massacre
Aceldama	Field of Blood	Bulgaria	Mixed Race
Acropolis	Citadel	Burkina Faso	Land of the Worthy Men
Addis Ababa	New Flower	Cairo	The Fort
Africa	People of the Dusty Land	Calvary	Skull
Agadir	Wall	Cambrai	Crayfish
Agulhas, Cape	Needle	Canada	Camp
Ajaccio	Resting Place	Canberra	Meeting Place
Alamo	Cottonwood	Carlow	Four Lakes
Alaska	Great Land	Carmel	Garden
Amritsar	Immortal Lake	Carthage	New Town
Anatolia	Sunrise East	Casablanca	White House
Angostura	Strait Narrows	Cayman Islands	Alligator
Anguilla	Eel	Ceylon	Lion
Annapurna	Abundant Food	Chattanooga	Rock Rising to a Point
Antananarivo	City of a Thousand	Chicago	Garlic Place
Antofagasta	Hidden Copper	Chittagong	White Village
Antrim	One House	Clonmel	Meadow of Honey
Antwerp	Wharfside	Comoros	Moon
Appenzell	Abbot's Cell	Conakry	Over the Water
Aquitaine	Water Land	Coney Island	Rabbit Island
Arabia	Tent Dweller	Copenhagen	Merchant's Port
Aral Sea	Island Sea	Cork	Marsh
Aran Islands	Kidney Islands	Costa Dorada	Gold Coast
Ararat	Mountain of Sorrow	Costa Rica	Rich Coast
Ardennes	Land of Forests	Cotonou	Dead Person Lagoon
Argentina	Land of Silver	Cotopaxi	Shining Mountain
Arizona	Dry Region	Cyprus	Copper
Arnhem	Sand Homestead	Dahomey	On the Stomach of Dan
Asturias	Rock Water	Dalmatia	Young Animal
Atacama	Black Duck	Danube	River of Sheep
Australia	Southern Land	Dar es Salaam	House of Peace
Austria	Eastern Borderland	Darjeeling	Diamond Island (literal) aka Place of the Thunderbolt
Azores	Goshawks		
Babylon	Gate of the Gods		
Baden	Baths	Davos	Behind
Baghdad	Gift of God	Deauville	Damp Plain
Bahrain	Two Seas	Dijon	Divine
Baku	Windward	Djibouti	Plate
Bangkok	Region of Olive Trees	Dnieper	Far River
(see Krung Thep)		Dodecanese	Twelve Islands
Bangui	Rapids	Dominica	Lord's Day
Banjui	Rope Matting	Donegal	Fort of Foreigners
Barbados	Bearded	Drakensberg	Dragon Mountain
Basse-Terre	Low Land	Druk Yul (see Bhutan)	Land of the Dragon
Baton Rouge	Red Stick	Dublin	Black Pool
Beijing	Northern Capital	Dubrovnik	Oak Forest
Beirut	The Wells	Dumbarton	Fort of the Britons
Belfast	Mouth of the Sandbank	Dunkirk	Dune Church
Belgrade	White City	Dunsinane	Hill of the Teat
Belorussia	White Russia	Dushanbe	Monday
Bern	Bear	Egypt	Temple of Soul Ptah
Bethany	House of Poverty	Eindhoven	End Property
Bethlehem	House of Bread	Ephesus	Overseer
Bethphage	House of Figs	Eritrea	Red
Betws-y-Coed	Chapel in the Woods	Ethiopia	Burnt Appearance
Bhutan (see Druk Yul)	End of Tibet	Faeroes	Islands of Sheep
Bihar	Monastery	Fair Isle	Islands of Sheep
Bikini	Surface Coconut	Formosa	Beautiful
Bizerta	Stable Flowing Through	Franche-Comté	Free County
Bloemfontein	Fountain of Flowers	Fray Bentos	Brother Benedict
Boise	Wooded	Galapagos	Giant Tortoise
Bosporus	Oxford	Gallipoli	Beautiful Town
Brindisi	Deer	Galway	Stony
Brno	Clay	Gangtok	Hill Summit

GEOGRAPHY

Name	Meaning	Name	Meaning
Geelong	Marshy Place	Lesbos	Wooded
Gelderland	Yellow Mountain	Levant	Rising
Georgia	Fertile Earth/Tilled Land	Lhasa	City of the Gods
Ghent	Confluence	Liepaja	Lime Tree
Gibraltar	Mountain of Tariq	Limburg	Lime-Tree Fortress
Grasse	Fat	Limerick	Bare Area of Ground
Graubunden	Grey League	Limoges	Elm-Tree Village
Graz	Small Fort	Limpopo	Crocodile River
Greece	Venerable	Linkoping	Flax Market
Gretna	Gravel Hill	Linz	Lime Tree
Groningen	Green	Lisburn	Fort of the Gamblers
Grozny	Awesome	Lodz	Boat
Guadalajara	River of Stones	Lofoten	Fox Foot
Guadalupe	River Wolf	Lombardy	Long Beards/Axes
Guatemala	Land of the Eagle	Longjumeau	New Market
Haarlem	Height Silt	Los Angeles	City of Angels
Haiphong	Sea Room	Luanda	Tax
Haiti	Mountain Land/Nest	Luxembourg	Little Fort
Hanoi	Inside the River	Machu Picchu	Old Man Peak
Hanover	High Bank	Malaga	Queen
Harbin	Place Where Fish is Dried	Malmo	Mineral Island
Harfleur	High Estuary	Managua	Rain Spirit
Harlech	Beautiful Rock	Manama	Place of Rest/Dreams
Harz	Forest	Mandalay	Circle
Hawaii	Place of the Gods	Marathan	Fennel
Hebron	To Unite	Marianske Lazne	Mary's Springs
Hekla	Cloak	Marmara	Marble
Hokkaido	North Sea Province	Marrakesh	Fortified
Holm	Island	Massachusetts	People of the Big Hill
Honshu	Main District	Mato Grosso	Dense Forest
Huang Hai	Yellow Sea	Matsuyama	Pine Mountain
Huang Ho	Yellow River	Mayo	Plain of the Yew Tree
Hunan	South of the Lake	Meath	Middle
Hyderabad	Lion Town	Mecca	Ruined/Sanctuary
Ibadan	Worship	Mechelen	Meeting Place
Ibiza	Island of Perfumes	Medina	The City
Inchon	Virtue River	Melanesia	Black Islands
Iona	Yew Tree	Memphis	His Beauty
Irian Jaya	Cloud-Covered Victory	Mesopotamia	Between the Rivers
Jaffa	Beautiful	Monaghan	Little Thickets
Japan	Sun Origin	Monte Carlo	Charles's Mountain
Jericho	Moon Month	Montenegro	Black Mountain
Johore	To Tie	Montreal	Royal Mountain
Kanchenjunga	Five Treasures of the Snow	Morocco	Far West
Kara Kum	Black Sands	Munich	Monk
Katmandu	Wooden Temples	Munster	Monastery
Kattegat	Boat Way	Muscat	Hidden
Kawasaki	River Cape	Myanmar	The Strong
Kazan	Cauldron	Nairobi	Marsh
Khartoum	End of Elephant's Trunk	Nanking	Southern Capital
Kildare	Church of the Oak	Narvik	Narrow Bay
Kilimanjaro	Mountain of the God of Cold	Natal	Christmas
Killarney	Church of the Sloes	N'Djamena	Resting Place
Kobe	House of God	Negev	South
Koblenz	Confluence	Nepal	Fly Down
Kosovo	Blackbird	Netherlands	Lower Land
Kronstadt	Crown City	Neuchâtel	New Castle
Krung Thep (see Bangkok)	City of Angels	Neustria	New Western Kingdom
		Nevada	Snowy
Kuala Lumpur	Mouth of the Muddy River	New York (named after)	Future James II
Kyushu	Nine Provinces	Newry	Yew Tree
Kyzyl Kum	Red Sand	Nicosia	Victory
Labrador	Labourer	Nijmegen	New Market
Lagos	Lakes	Nîmes	Sanctuary
Las Vegas	Meadows	Norrkoping	Northern Trading Place
Latakia	People Ruler	Nova Scotia	New Scotland
Lebanon	White	Nullarbor	No Trees
Leipzig	Lime Tree	Oahu	Place of Assembly
Leitrim	Grey Ridge	Omaha	Those Who Live Upstream on the River

Name	Meaning	Name	Meaning
Omsk	Calm	Saskatoon	Fruit of Tree of Many Branches
Orinoco	Place of Paddling		
Oruro	Black and White	Schaffhausen	Sheep House
Osnabrück	Current Bridge	Shaba	Copper
Pacific	Calm	Shikoku	Four Provinces
Padua	Pine	Shiraz	Good Grape
Pagalu	Father Cockerel	Sichuan	Four Rivers
Pakistan	Land of the Pure	Sierra Leone	Lion Mountains
Palermo	Safe Anchorage	Sierra Madre	Mother Range
Palestine	Land of the Philistines	Sierra Nevada	Snowy Mountains
Pamplona	Pompey's City	Sikkim	Summit
Panmunjom	Floor Gate Shop	Singapore	Lion House
Papeete	Water Basket	Smolensk	Tar
Pemba	Green Island	Society Islands (after)	Royal Society
Peshawar	Frontier Town	Solferino	Sulphur
Petra	Rock	Soweto (acronym)	South Western Townships
Philadelphia	Brotherly Love	Sporades	Disseminated
Philippines (named after)	Philip II of Spain	Sri Lanka	Island of the Blessed
Phnom Penh	Mountain of Plenty	Srinagar	City of Happiness
Picardy	Pike	Stromboli	Round
Piedmont	Foot of the Mountain	Stuttgart	Mares Garden
Plovdiv	Philip's Town	Sudan	Land of the Blacks
Po	Pines	Sulawesi	Spear Iron
Pomerania	By the Sea	Surabaya	Hero Danger
Pompeii	Five	Tabor	Navel
Pont-L'Évêque	Bishop's Bridge	Taipei	Northern Taiwan
Popocatepetl	Smoking Mountain	Taiwan	Terrace Bay
Port Louis (named after)	Louis XV of France	Tegucigalpa	Silver Mountain
Portugal	Warm Harbour	Tehran	Level
Potomac	Where Goods are Brought in	Tel Aviv	Hill Spring
Potsdam (Germany)	Under the Oaks	Temirtau	Mountain of Iron
Prague	Threshold	Teplice	Warm
Praia	Beach	Texas	Friends
Prince Edward Isle (named after)	Father of Queen Victoria	Thailand	Free People
		Tigris	Arrow
Puerto Rico	Rich Harbour	Timor	East
Punta Arenas	Sandy Point	Tiruchchirappalli	Town of the Sacred Rock
Pusan	Pot Mountain	Tokyo	Eastern Capital
Pyongyang	Flat Land	Topeka	A Good Place to Dig Potatoes
Quebec	Place Where Waters Narrow		
		Transylvania	Beyond the Forest
Quemoy	Golden Gate	Trieste	Trade Market
Rajasthan	Land of Kings	Trinidad	Trinity
Reykjavik	Bay of Smoke	Tripoli	Three Towns
Rio de Janeiro	River of January	Tsushima	Pair of Horses
Rio Muni	Silent River	Turku	Market Place
Riyadh	Gardens	Tuscany (named after)	Etruscans
Robben Island	Seal Island	Tuvalu	Eight Standing Together
Roncesvalles	Bramble Valley	Tyre	Stone
Roquefort	Strong Rock	Ukraine	Border Country
Roscoff	Hill of the Blacksmith	Ulan Bator	Town of the Red Hero
Roubaix	Horse Stream	Ulm	Marsh
Rub-al-Khali	Empty Quarter	Utah	Mountain Men
Ryukyu	Ball of Precious Stones	Uttar Pradesh	North State
'sHertogenbosch	Duke's Wood	Xinjiang	New Frontier
Sahara	Desert	Yucatan	Massacre
Sakhalin	Black River	Zagreb	Beyond the Bank
Samos	Dune	Zamora	Emerald
Santo Domingo	Holy Sunday	Zanzibar	Black Coast
Sapporo	Pavillion of Banknotes	Zermatt	At the Pasture
Saratov	Yellow Mountain	Zhengzhou	Solemn Region
Sarayevo	Palace	Zimbabwe	House of Stones
Saskatchewan	Rapid Flowing River		

GEOGRAPHY

Places: alternative names

Aachen	Aix-La-Chapelle	Lake Constance	Bodensee
Almaty	Alma-Ata	Lake Geneva	Lac Léman
Banaba	Ocean Island	Lake Gennesaret	Sea of Galilee
Bangkok	Krung Thep	Lake Tiberias	Sea of Galilee
Bavaria	Bayern	Le Havre	Newhaven
Belarus	Belorussia	Lhasa	Forbidden City
Belfast	Athens of Ireland	Liberec	Reichenburg
Bermuda	Somers Islands	Lindisfarne	Holy Island
Bhutan	Druk Yul	Livorno	Leghorn
Bioko	Fernando Po	London	The Smoke
Bogotá	Santa Fé de Bogotá	Lushun	Port Arthur
Boston	Athens of the New World	Macao	Aomin
Bulgaria	Narodna Republic	Munich	München
Burma	Myanmar	New Orleans	The Big Easy
Cairo	Al-Qāhirah	New York	The Big Apple
China	Cathay	New Zealand	Pig Island
Christiansted	Bassin	Niue	Savage Island
Cordoba	Athens of the West	Osaka	Venice of Japan
Croagh Patrick, Mt	Reek	Peking	Beijing – Celestial City
Edinburgh	Athens of the North	Persian Gulf	Arabian Gulf
Egypt	Misr	Regensburg	Ratisbon
Florence	Firenze	Rio Grande	Rio Bravo
Gambier Islands	Mangareva Islands	Rome	Eternal City
Godthaab	Nuuk	Sousse	Susa
Golgotha	Calvary	Sweden	Sverige
Gravelly Hill Interchange	Spaghetti Junction	Switzerland	Confederation of Helvetia
Grenada	Isle of Spice		
Istanbul	Stamboul	Sydney	The Big Smoke
Japan	Nihon – Nippon	Thessaloníki	Salonika
K2	Godwin Austen	Turin	Torino
Korea	Choson	Victoria (Mt)	Tomaniivi (Fiji)

Places: former names

Albany (NY)	Fort Orange
Almaty	Zailiyskoye (1854–55), Verny (1855–1921)
Alvernia (Mt)	Como Hill (Bahamas)
Annapolis	Providence, Town of Proctor's, Town at the Severn, Anne Arundel Town
Astana	Akmola
Bangladesh	East Bengal (until 1947), East Pakistan (1947–70)
Belize	British Honduras (until 1973)
Benin	Dahomey (until 1975)
Bermuda	Somers Islands
Bioko	Macias Nguema Biyogo (1973–79)
Black Sea	The Euxine
Bodrum	Halicarnassus
Bolivia	Upper Peru
Botswana	Bechuanaland (until 1966)
Bujumbura	Usumbura
Burkina Faso	Upper Volta (until 1984)
Burundi	Urundi
Cambodia	Kampuchea, Khmer Empire
Canada	New France
Cape Horn	Elizabetha
Central African Republic	Ubanghi Shari
Congo, Dem	Zaïre, Belgian Congo, Congo
Dardanelles	Hellespont
Djakarta	Sunda Kelapa
Djibouti	French Somaliland
Donetsk	Stalino

Duarte (Mt)	Trujillo (Dominican Republic)
Dunaujváros	Sztalinvaros (Hungary)
Dushanbe	Stalinabad
East Timor	Portuguese Timor
Edirne	Adrianople
Equatorial Guinea	Spanish Guinea
Ethiopia	Abyssinia
Frunze	Pishpek
Ghana	Gold Coast
Grenada	Conception
Guinea	French Guinea
Guinea-Bissau	Portuguese Guinea
Guyana	British Guiana
Harare	Salisbury
Hawaii	Sandwich Islands
Ho Chi Minh City	Saigon
Indonesia	Dutch East Indies
Iran	Persia
Iraq	Mesopotamia
Istanbul	Constantinople, Byzantium
Izmir	Smyrna
Iznik	Niacaea
Jordan	Transjordan
Kathmandu	Manju-Patan
Katowice	Stalinogrod
Kinshasa	Léopoldville (until 1966)
Kiribati	Gilbert Islands
Klagenfurt	Chlagenvurt
Klondyke	River of Fish
Kota Kinabalu	Jesselton
Kyrgyzstan	Khirgizia

Ladoga	Neva
Ladysmith	Windsor
Lahore	Lava
Lahti	Bay (Finland)
Le Mans	Cenomannis
Le Puy	Podium
Leningrad	St Petersburg (1703–1914 and 1991 to present), Petrograd (1914–24)
Lesotho	Basutoland
Malawi	Nyasaland
Mali	French Sudan
Maputo	Lourenço Marques
Marianske Lazne	Marienbad
Mariupol	Zhdanov
Marseille	Ville-sans-Nom
Mauritius	Île de France
Micronesia	Caroline Islands
Moldova	Moldavia, Bessarabia
Mongolian People's Republic	Outer Mongolia
Montreal	Ville Marie
Myanmar	Burma
Namibia	South West Africa
N'Djamena	Fort-Lamy
New Britain	Neu-Pommern
New York	New Amsterdam (1625–64)
Novokuznetsk	Stalinsk
Novomoskovsk	Stalinogorsk
Nuuk	Godthaab
Olympia	Smithfield
Oman	Muscat and Oman
Oslo	Kristiania
Ottawa	Bytown
Palm Beach	Palm City
Palm Springs	Agua Caliente
Palmyra	Tadmor
Pittsburgh	Fort Duquesne
Prince Edward Island	Île Saint-Jean
Princeton	Stony Brook
Puerto Rico	San Juan (Puerto Rico was then capital)

Réunion	Île Bonaparte
	Île Bourbon
	Île Mascareigne
Richmond (Eng)	Sheen
Seychelles	Seven Sisters
Shaba	Katanga
Shenyang	Mukden
Sofia	Serdica
Sousse	Hadrumetum
Sparta	Lacedaemonia
Sri Lanka	Ceylon, Serendip
Stepanakert	Khankendy
Suriname	Dutch Guiana
Tahiti	King George III Island, Nouvelle-Cythère
Taiwan	Formosa
Tanzania	Tanganyika
Tasmania	Van Diemen's Land
Thailand	Siam
Tiruchchirappalli	Trichinopoly
Toronto	York
Troy	Ilium
Tuvalu	Ellice Islands
Ubangi-Shari	French Equatorial Africa
Ulyanovsk	Simbirsk
Uskudar	Scutari
United Arab Emirates	Trucial States
Vanuatu	New Hebrides
Volgograd	Tsaritsyn (1589–1925) Stalingrad (1925–61)
Western Sahara	Spanish Sahara
Yangon	Rangoon
Yemen	Aden
Zambia	Northern Rhodesia
Zanzibar	Shirazi
Zimbabwe	Southern Rhodesia (1911–64) Rhodesia (1964–79) Zimbabwe Rhodesia (1979–80)

GEOGRAPHY

World's Longest Rivers

		Source	Length (miles)	Course and Outflow
1	Nile	Kagera River, Burundi	4,145	Tanzania/Uganda/Sudan/Egypt to eastern Mediterranean.
2	Amazon	Apurimac River, Peru	4,007	Colombia to Brazil to South Atlantic (Canal do Sul).
3	Mississippi-Missouri	Jefferson (Red Rock) River, Montana	3,710	N and S Dakota/Nebraska/Iowa/Missouri/Kansas/Illinois/Kentucky/Tennessee/Arkansas/Mississippi/Louisiana to Gulf of Mexico. Although the Missouri is a tributary of the Mississippi, it is also an extension via Lake Itasca (see individual entries), so the system is made up of the total length of the Missouri and 1,395 miles of the Mississippi.
4	Yenisey	Selenga River, Mongolia	3,442	Flows due north through central Russia to the Kara Sea.
5	Yangtze (Chang-Jiang)	Kunlun Mts, China	3,436	Flows in an easterly course across China to the East China Sea near Shanghai.
6	Yellow River (Huang Ho)	Qinghai, China	3,395	Flows north of the Yangtze in an easterly course to the Yellow Sea.
7	Ob'-Irtysh	Altai Mts, Russia	3,361	Northern course touching Kazakhstan and through Russia to Kara Sea.

	Source	Length (miles)	Course and Outflow
8 Paraná	Paranáiba and Grande confluence, Brazil	3,032	Flows south via Paraguay border and Argentina into confluence with River Uruguay to the Rio de la Plata (River Plate) estuary in the South Atlantic near Buenos Aires. The system is aka Rio de la Plata-Paraná.
9 Zaïre (Congo)	Chambeshi River, Zambia	2,920	Called Lualaba in Dem Rep of Congo. Runs along Congo border into Atlantic at Angola.
10 Amur-Argun	China	2,782	See individual entries of the 2 rivers.
11 Lena	Kirenga River, Siberia	2,734	Russia and northward to Laptev Sea in the Arctic Ocean.
12 Mackenzie-Peace	Finlay/Parsnip confluence, BC	2,635	Flows eastwards to Alberta and then north via NWT to Beaufort Sea. The system is linked by the Slave River between Lake Athabasca and the Great Slave Lake.
13 Mekong	Lants'ang, Tibet	2,600	China/Burma/Laos/Thailand/Cambodia/Vietnam to South China Sea.
14 Niger	Loma Mts, Guinea	2,590	Flows through Mali, Niger and along Benin border into Nigeria before discharging into the Gulf of Guinea in the Atlantic.
15 Murray-Darling	New England Plateau, NSW/Queensland	2,330	See individual entries of the 2 rivers.
16 Zambesi	Kalene Hill, Zambia	2,200	Flows south across Angola and western Zambia, then north-eastward forming the border between Zambia and Zimbabwe, and finally south-eastward across Mozambique to its delta on the Indian Ocean.
17 Volga	Valdai Hills, nr Moscow	2,193	Flows generally south-eastward to discharge into the Caspian Sea in Russia. The Volga is considered the longest river in Europe as the longer Russian rivers flow east of the Urals which are considered the boundary into Asia.
18 Madeira	Mamoré and Beni Rivers, Bolivia	2,082	Joins the Amazon 90 miles east of Manaus, it is the 2nd longest tributary in the world.
19 Jurua	Puerto Portillo, Peru	2,040	Flows east and north into Brazil before joining the Amazon south of Fonte Boa.
20 Purus	Loreto Department, Peru	1,995	Flows north and east into Brazil to join the Amazon upstream from Manaus (Solimões River).

NB: A usual definition of a river might be 'a freshwater channelled body of water that flows from its source into another river, a lake, the sea, or an inland desert', in which case the Missouri and Mississippi Rivers would make the above listing as separate entries. However, the table above includes the system as a whole and both the rivers are dealt with individually below. The alphabetic listing is for ease of reference, as in many of the sections, but is in no way an attempt to be fully comprehensive; it is merely a useful gazetteer of some interesting rivers.

Other Notable Rivers

	Source	Length (miles)	Course and Outflow
Achelous (Akhelóös)	Pindus Mountains	140	Divides Aetolia from Acarnania and discharges into the Ionian Sea.
Amu Darya (Oxus)	Eastern Pamirs	1,578	Follows the Afghanistan/Tajikistan border and then the Turkmenistan/Uzbekistan border before discharging into the Aral Sea. The source of the Amu Darya is often thought to be the confluence of the Vakhsh and Pyandzh rivers but in fact its longest headstream is the Daryā-ye Vākhjir in the Eastern Pamirs.
Amur	Russia/China	1,755	Tatar Strait of the Pacific Ocean.
Argun	Khingan range, China	1,007	Joins Amur at the confluence of the Shilka.
Arkansas	Sawatch range of Rocky Mountains	1,459	Flows east-southeastward to the Mississippi at Arkansas City via Kansas and Oklahoma.
Arno	Monte Falterona, Tuscan Apennines	150	Flows westwards via Florence and Pisa to the Ligurian Sea area of the Mediterranean.
Athabasca	Columbia Icefield, Canadian Rockies	765	Forms the southernmost part of the Mackenzie River system in northern Alberta and discharges into Lake Athabasca.

	Source	Length (miles)	Course and Outflow
Avon	Devizes, Wiltshire	48	Aka Hampshire Avon or East Avon, flows generally south via Salisbury to the English Channel at Christchurch Harbour.
Avon (Lower)	Cotswolds	75	Aka Bristol Avon, flows through Gloucester, Wiltshire, and Avon before entering the Bristol Channel via the Severn estuary, at Avonmouth, the ocean port of Bristol.
Avon (Upper)	Naseby, Leicester/Northants border	96	Aka Warwickshire Avon, flows generally south-westward through Northants, Leicestershire, Warwickshire, and Hereford and Worcester before joining the Severn at Tewkesbury, Gloucs.
Axe	Beaminster, Dorset	24	Flows westward to form the boundary between Dorset and Somerset before reaching Axminster in Devon and entering the English Channel south of Axmouth.
Bann	Co Down, NI	76	Longest river of Northern Ireland; flows into the Atlantic Ocean.
Black	Yunnan Province, China	498	Flows south-east into northern Vietnam parallel to the Red River, which it joins near Hanoi.
Black	Ozark Mountains, Missouri	280	Flows south-eastward to Poplar Bluff, Missouri, and then flows south-west before entering the White River near Newport, Arkansas.
Black Volta (Mouhoun)	Bobo Dioulasso, Burkina Faso	720	Flows along the border of Burkina Faso and Côte D'Ivoire with Ghana before discharging into Lake Volta in northern Ghana.
Boyne	Bog of Allen, Co Kildare	70	Flows north-east to enter the Irish Sea just south of Drogheda.
Brahmaputra	Tibetan Himalayas	1,800	Confluence with the Ganges as the Jamuna and into the Bay of Bengal in Bangladesh.
Bug	Western Ukraine	516	Flows into Poland via Brest in Belarus and discharges into the Vistula just south of Warsaw.
Camel	Davidstow, Cornwall	30	Generally flows northward into the Celtic Sea at Padstow.
Cher	North-west Massif Central, France	217	Flows north across the Combrailles Plateau, eventually reaching the Loire at Cinq-Mars-la-Pile.
Cimarron	Capulin Mt Monument, New Mexico	698	Flows eastwards past the Black Mesa peak in Oklahoma and into Kansas via Colorado before re-entering Oklahoma and discharging into the Arkansas River near Tulsa.
Clyde	Lowther Hills, Strathclyde	98	Flows north-westerly into the Firth of Clyde.
Colorado	Rockies, Colorado	1,450	Flows south-west to the Gulf of California.
Colorado	Grande and Barrancas confluence	530	Flows south-eastward across Patagonia and into the Atlantic Ocean south of Bahia Blanca.
Columbia	Rockies, British Columbia	1,243	Flows south through central Washington to the Oregon border and then due west before discharging into the Pacific Ocean.
Danube	Black Forest, Germany	1,775	Flows through Germany, Austria, Czech Republic, Hungary, Croatia, Yugoslavia, Bulgaria, Romania, Moldova, and into the Black Sea in the Ukraine.
Darling	New England Plateau, NSW Queensland	1,702	Follows the NSW/Queensland border into NSW to join the Murray at Wentworth, on the Victoria border. Longest river of Australia.
Dee	Cairngorms	87	Famous for its salmon, the Dee flows easterly to the North Sea at Aberdeen. The 17-mile stretch of the Dee between Braemar and Ballater has become known as 'Royal Deeside' because Balmoral Castle is a popular holiday retreat of the Royal Family.
Dee	Snowdonia National Park	70	Flows via Lake Bala and then north-east to Corwen and eastward past Llangollen before travelling northward to Chester and out to the Irish Sea at Flint.
Dee	Dumfries and Galloway	50	Flows south and enters the Solway Firth at Kircudbright.
Delaware	Schoharie County, New York	405	Flows along the border between New York and Pennsylvania, New Jersey and Pennsylvania, and Delaware and New Jersey before discharging into the Atlantic Ocean at Delaware Bay.
Demerara	Central Guyana	215	Flows northward to the Atlantic Ocean at Georgetown.

GEOGRAPHY

	Source	Length (miles)	Course and Outflow
Derwent	Tasmania	107	Flows south-east to the Tasman Sea.
Derwent	Peak District	60	Flows south-east through Derby to the River Trent.
Derwent	Fylingdales Moor	57	Flows south joining the Ouse just west of the Humber estuary.
Derwent	Borrowdale Fells, Cumbria	34	Flows north and west to the Irish Sea.
Dnestr	Carpathian Mountains	877	Flows south from Ukraine into Moldova before emptying into the Black Sea.
Dnieper (Dnepr)	Valdai Hills, Smolensk	1,367	Flows through Russia, Belarus and the Ukraine into the Black Sea.
Don	Novomoskovsk, Russia	1,224	Flows south and discharges into the Gulf of Taganrog in the Sea of Azov.
Don	Grampians	78	Flows south-eastward into the North Sea at the Bridge of Don.
Douro	Sierra de Urbión, Spain	556	Flows across Spain and northern Portugal to the Atlantic Ocean at Foz do Douro.
Dunajec	Tatra Mountains, Czech/Polish border	156	Flows north-east across Poland into the Vistula.
Ebro	Fontibre, Cantabrian Mts	565	Longest river in Spain. Flows in a south-easterly direction via Zaragosa and into the Balearic Sea area of the Mediterranean.
Eden	Lake District Fells	90	Flows north-westward to the Irish Sea at the Solway Firth inlet.
Elbe	Czech/Polish border	724	Flows westward through Czech Republic (where it is known as the Labe) until it starts a north-westerly run east of Prague through Germany to discharge into the North Sea.
Euphrates	South-west Turkey	1,700	Flows in south-easterly direction through northern Syria and Iraq to the Persian Gulf.
Exe	The Chains, Somerset	60	Flows south across Devon and into the English Channel at Exmouth.
Forth	Ben Lomond	65	Flows eastward into the Firth of Forth, near Kincardine.
Frome	Evershot, Dorset	40	Flows eastward into Poole Harbour at Wareham.
Gambia	Guinea Republic	700	Flows westwards via the Gambia into the Atlantic Ocean.
Ganges	Indian Himalayas	1,553	Confluence with the Brahmaputra as the Jamuna and into the Bay of Bengal in Bangladesh.
Garonne	Spanish Pyrenees	357	Flows north-east to Toulouse then north-west to the Bay of Biscay via the Gironde estuary.
Great Ouse	Brackley, Northants	150	Flows through Buckinghamshire, Bedfordshire and Cambridgeshire before discharging into the North Sea at the Wash.
Hudson	Lake Tear of Clouds, New York State	315	Flows south-eastward to Corinth in Saratoga County and then north-eastwards to Hudson Falls before travelling south to New York Bay.
Hunter	Mt Royal Range, New South Wales	287	Flows south-west through Glenbawn Reservoir before entering the Tasman Sea at Newcastle.
Iguaçu	Serra do Mar, Brazil	808	Flows westward before joining the Paraná at border of Argentina, Brazil and Paraguay.
Indus	Tibet	1,790	Runs through Pakistan from north to south and discharges into the Arabian Sea.
Irrawaddy	Northern Myanmar	1,337	Flows south through Mandalay and eventually west of Yangon into the Andaman Sea.
Isar	Karwendelgebirge, Innsbruck, Austria	183	Flows into Germany at Scharnitz Pass then after travelling through Munich enters the Danube.
James	Jackson and Cowpasture confluence, Virginia	340	Flows in an easterly direction, crossing the Blue Ridge Mountains near Lynchburg and continuing past Richmond into the southern end of Chesapeake Bay at the Hampton Roads.
Jordan	Mount Hermon, Syria	223	Lowest river in the world, flows south across Israel and into Jordan before draining into the Dead Sea. The distance between the Sea of Galilee and the Dead Sea is approximately 100 miles and yet the Jordan's length is double that distance due to its meandering course. The Jordan became the cease-fire line during the Israeli–Jordanian hostilities.
Jumna (Yamuna)	Jamnotri, Himalayas	855	Flows from Uttar Pradesh along the border with Haryāna and then via Delhi to the Agra Canal before joining the Ganges at its most sacred point.

	Source	Length (miles)	Course and Outflow
Liffey	Wicklow Mountains	50	Flows through Co Wicklow, Kildare and Dublin before entering the Irish Sea at Dublin Bay.
Limpopo	Witwatersrand, South Africa	1,100	Rises as the Crocodile River and flows in an arc first north-east and then east, forming the border between Transvaal and Botswana and then Transvaal and Zimbabwe before veering south-east into Mozambique and into the Indian Ocean north of Maputo. It becomes the Limpopo at the Crocodile's confluence with the Marico on the Transvaal/Botswana border.
Loire	Southern Massif Central	634	Longest river in France. Flows north and west towards the Brittany peninsula, where it discharges into the Bay of Biscay in the Atlantic Ocean.
Mackenzie	Great Slave Lake, NWT, Canada	1,060	Beaufort Sea in Arctic Ocean.
Magdalena	Colombian Andes	930	Flows northward to the Caribbean Sea.
Manzanares	El Pardo Reservoir, Madrid	42	Minor river that discharges into a canal system south of Madrid, it is notable only for being the river on which Madrid stands (at over 2,100' the highest capital of Europe).
Marañón	Peruvian Andes	879	Flows northwest from northeast Peru before receiving the Huallaga River and combining with the Ucayali River, to form the Amazon.
Marne	Langres, Plateau de Langres, France	326	Flows north-northwest past Chaumont and Saint-Dizier, then turns west-northwest to Epernay before veering south of Paris and discharging into the Seine at Charenton.
Medina	St Catherine's Downs	13	Flows from the south of the Isle of Wight to its northern outflow into the Solent.
Medway	East Grinstead, West Sussex	70	Follows the Sussex/Kent boundary to Ashurst before turning north-east to the Thames at the Sheerness delta. Traditionally those born in Kent west of the Medway are called Kentish Men, and those born east of the Medway, Men of Kent.
Merrimack	White Mts, New Hampshire	110	Flows southward into Massachusetts before veering north-east to empty into the Atlantic.
Mersey	Confluence of Goyt, Etherow, Tame	70	Flows eastward to the Irwell and the Manchester Ship Canal.
Meuse	Pouilly, Plateau de Langres, France	590	Flowing north through Belgium and the Netherlands to the North Sea.
Mississippi	Lake Itasca, Minnesota	2,348	Gulf of Mexico.
Missouri (Big Muddy)	Beaverhead Co, Montana	2,315	Joins Mississippi 10 miles north of St Louis; it is the longest tributary in the world.
Motagua	Chichicastenango	250	Longest river in Guatemala, flowing east-north-east into the Gulf of Honduras.
Murray	Snowy Mts, NSW	1,609	Flows along the boundary of NSW and Victoria, bends south at Morgan, South Australia, and discharges into the Indian Ocean at Encounter Bay in the Great Australian Bight.
Negro	Eastern Colombia	1,400	Major tributary of the Amazon that follows the Colombian/Venezuelan border and into Brazil to join the Amazon at the Solimões confluence.
Negro	Bagé, Brazil	500	Flows south-westward into Uruguay before joining the Uruguay River at Soriano.
Negro	Chilean Andes	400	Flows south-eastward across northern Patagonia and discharges into the Atlantic Ocean south-east of Viedma and Carmen de Patagones.
Neisse (Nysa)	Sudeten Mountains	157	Forms part of the German/Polish frontier before joining the Oder River. There is another Neisse which also rises in the Sudeten Mountains but lies totally in Poland.
Nene	Northants/Leics	102	Flows north-easterly via Peterborough to the North Sea in the Wash.
Oder	Oder Mountains, Czechoslovakia	531	Flows north-east then north when it picks up the Neisse and flows into the Baltic Sea.
Ohio	Allegheny and Monongahela, Pittsburgh	981	Flows north-west out of Pennsylvania then south-westward, forming boundaries between Ohio/Kentucky, Indiana/Kentucky, and Illinois/Kentucky before joining the Mississippi at Cairo, Illinois.

GEOGRAPHY

	Source	Length (miles)	Course and Outflow
Omo	Ethiopian Highlands	290	Flows south across Ethiopia before emptying into Lake Rudolf on the Ethiopia/Sudan border.
Orange	Sinqu River, Lesotho	1,300	Flows west along the Orange Free State/Cape Province border through Upington and along the southern border of Namibia before discharging into the Atlantic Ocean at Alexander Bay.
Orinoco	Venezuela–Brazil border	1,700	Flows in a northern arc forming the boundary between Venezuela and Colombia before veering north-eastward across Venezuela and into the Atlantic Ocean near Trinidad.
Ouse	Swale and Ure Confluence	57	Flows south-east to the Humber estuary.
Parramatta	Sydney	15	Meaning 'plenty of eels'. Flows through Sydney and into Port Jackson on the Tasman Sea.
Patuca	Guayape and Guayambre confluence	200	Flows from north-eastern Honduras and crosses the Mosquito Coast before discharging into the Caribbean at Patuca Point.
Peace	Finlay River, BC, Canada	1,195	Slave River in Wood Buffalo National Park.
Pechora	Northern Urals	1,124	Flows south and then west and north across Russia before emptying into the Barents Sea.
Pecos	Mora County, New Mexico	735	Flows into Texas and empties into the Rio Grande at the Amistad National Recreation Area.
Piddle	Alton Pancras, Dorset	21	Aka the Trent, and flowing south-eastward to Poole Harbour.
Po	Monte Viso Mts, Cottian Alps	405	Longest river in Italy. Flows eastwards in its upper course then northward through Turin and finally eastward to its delta on the Gulf of Venice in the Adriatic area of the Mediterranean.
Potomac	Appalachian Mts, West Virginia	383	Forms boundary between Maryland and Virginia via Washington DC and into Chesapeake Bay.
Red River	New Mexican Plains	1,270	Flows south-eastward through Texas, Oklahoma and Louisiana and into the Gulf of Mexico via the Mississippi River near Baton Rouge.
Red River (Hong)	Yunnan Province, SW China	750	Principal river of northern Vietnam, flowing south-east across the Tonkin region through Hanoi before discharging into the Gulf of Tonkin.
Red Volta	NW of Ouagadougou, Burkina Faso	200	Flows south-south-east to join the White Volta near the Gambaga scarp, northern Ghana.
Rhine	Swiss Alps	865	Forms the boundary between Switzerland, Liechtenstein and Germany and then runs north, bordering France and Germany and finally north-westward towards the North Sea via the Netherlands.
Rhône	Swiss Alps	505	Flows into Lake Geneva and then through France, merging with the Saône at Lyons, before entering the Mediterranean west of Marseille in the Golfe du Lion.
Ribble	Gayle and Cam confluence, Yorkshire	75	Flows south into Lancashire after rounding Whernside, at 2,419′ the highest peak in the Yorkshire Dales National Park; on entering Preston it flows due west towards the Irish Sea near Lytham St Annes.
Rio Grande	Rockies, Colorado	1,885	Forms the boundary between Texas and Mexico before discharging into the Gulf of Mexico. The Rio Grande is known in Mexico as the Rio Bravo.
Salween	Eastern Tibet	1,500	Flows east and south through China and forms the border between Myanmar and Thailand before emptying into the Gulf of Martaban
São Francisco	Serra da Canastra, Minais Gerais, Brazil	1,811	The longest river totally in Brazil flows in a north-easterly direction to the Atlantic.
Sava	Triglav Mts, Slovenia	584	Flows south-east through Slovenia and Croatia and follows border of Bosnia and Herzegovina into northern Yugoslavia to discharge into the Danube at Belgrade.
Scheldt	Northern France	270	Flows north and north-east through western Belgium to Antwerp, then north-west to the North Sea in the Netherlands.
Seine	Langres Plateau, nr Dijon	485	Flows north-westerly through Paris before emptying into the English Channel near Le Havre.
Severn	Finger Lakes, Ontario	610	Flows north-east through Severn Lake to Hudson Bay.

	Source	Length (miles)	Course and Outflow
Severn (Hafren)	Plynlimon, Northern Powys	220	Flows south via Shropshire, Worcestershire, Gloucestershire, and into Bristol Channel in the Atlantic Ocean. It is the longest river in Britain.
Shannon	Tiltinbane Mts, Co Cavan	240	Flows through Leitrim and boundaries of Roscommon, Longford, Westmeath, Offaly, Galway, Tipperary, Clare, Limerick, and discharges into the Atlantic Ocean at Loop Head, Co Clare.
Shenandoah	Virginia	370	Flows north to meet the Potomac at Harper's Ferry.
Spey	Corrieyairack Forest	107	Flows north-east across the Highlands into the North Sea, east of the Moray Firth.
Spree	Lusatian Mts, Germany	250	Rising near the Czech/Polish border, the Spree flows north through Berlin and into the Havel River, a tributary of the Elbe, at Spandau.
St Lawrence	St Louis River, Minnesota	1,945	Gulf of St Lawrence in Quebec. (The St Lawrence proper is 760 miles in length, as the remainder runs from its source via the Great Lakes, except Lake Michigan.)
Stour	East Cambridgeshire	47	Flows eastward through East Anglia, forming most of the Suffolk/Essex boundary, and discharges into the North Sea at Harwich.
Stour (Dorset)	Stourhead, Wiltshire	51	Flows south-eastward through Blandford Forum and into the English Channel at Christchurch Harbour.
Stour (Great)	South of Ashford	40	Aka Kentish Stour, flows through the Weald, past Ashford to Canterbury and Sandwich and into the English Channel.
Suir	Devil's Bit Mountains	114	Flows south across Co Tipperary through Thurles before discharging into Waterford Harbour.
Susquehanna	Otsego Lake, New York State	444	Flows south through western Pennsylvania and into Chesapeake Bay in Maryland.
Sutlej (Zaradros)	Lan-ka Ts'o, SW Tibet	900	Longest of the Punjab's 'Five Rivers', flowing into India and Pakistan, where it joins the Chenāb River, west of Bahāwalpur.
Swan	Corrigin, Western Australia	224	Rises as the Avon and flows through Perth to the Indian Ocean at Fremantle.
Syr Darya	Naryn and Karadarya confluence	1,374	The Syr Darya is 1,876 miles long including the 500 miles of the Naryn. On leaving the Fergana Valley the river flows north-west via Kyrgyzstan and into the Aral Sea at Kazakhstan.
Taff	Brecon Beacons	38	Flows southwards through Merthyr Tydfil, Pontypridd and finally Cardiff.
Tagus	Sierra de Albarracin, Spain	626	Flows westward into Portugal before discharging into the Atlantic Ocean near Lisbon.
Tamar	Woolley, Morwenstow	61	Flows south along the border between Devon and Cornwall and into the English Channel at Plymouth Sound.
Tay	Ben Lui, southern Grampians	117	Longest river in Scotland flows out to the Firth of Tay in the North Sea.
Tees	Cross Fell, Pennines	70	Flows eastwards defining the boundary of Cumbria and Durham then into Cleveland, passing through Stockton and Middlesbrough and into the North Sea.
Teifi	Strata Florida, Cambrian Mts	56	Famous for the many castle ruins along its banks, the Teifi flows generally south-westward through Lampeter and Cenarth Falls, where salmon can be seen climbing the artificial ladder up the falls, before discharging into the bay at Cardigan.
Test	Overton, nr Basingstoke, Hants	45	Famous trout river that flows southward via Winchester into Southampton Water, the last 16 miles between Romsey and Southampton Water are famous for their salmon.
Thames	Cotswolds, Gloucs	215	Flows easterly into the North Sea at Tilbury. Tributaries include the Churn, Coln, Windrush, Evenlode, Cherwell, Ock, Thame, Kennett, Loddon, Colne, Wey and Mole.
Tiber (Tevere)	Monte Fumaiolo, Apennines	252	Flows in a southerly direction through the city of Rome and into the Tyrrhenian Sea area of the Mediterranean near Ostia Antica.

GEOGRAPHY

	Source	Length (miles)	Course and Outflow
Tigris	South-west Turkey	1,180	Flows south into Iraq, through Baghdad and joins Euphrates before discharging into the Persian Gulf between Iraq and Iran.
Towy (Tywi)	Rhandirmwyn, Cambrian Mts	65	The longest river wholly in Wales, although since the damming of its main headwater in 1972 to form Llyn Brianne Reservoir it is slightly shorter than before.
Trent	Pennines, Staffordshire	170	Historically the boundary between north and south England, running south-east through the Potteries and Stoke-on-Trent, then north-east via Burton-on-Trent and Nottingham before entering the North Sea by the Humber estuary.
Tweed	Peebles	96	Flows easterly into the North Sea.
Tyne	Peel Fell, near Kielder, Northumberland	62	Flows eastward along the Northumberland/Co Durham border before discharging into the North Sea at the Tyne estuary in Tynemouth, near Newcastle.
Urubamba	Peruvian Andes	450	Flows northward to meet the Apurimac to become the Ucayali.
Uruguay	Southern Brazil	990	Flows west through Brazil and then south-westward forming the Argentina/Brazil border before veering southward to form the Argentina/Uruguay border and discharging into the Rio de la Plata estuary at its confluence with the Paraná.
Usk	Black Mountain, Brecon Beacons	57	Flows generally south via Abergavenny and into the Bristol Channel at Newport.
Vistula (Wisła)	Beskidy Mts, Poland	664	Longest river of Poland, flows northwards via Kracow and Warsaw before entering the Baltic Sea on the Gulf of Gdansk; it is the longest river that empties into the Baltic Sea.
Vltava (Moldau)	South-west Bohemia	270	Longest river of the Czech Republic, flows north through Prague before discharging into the Elbe (Labe) at Melnik, just north of Prague.
Volta	Black and White Voltas	1,000	The extension of the Black and White Voltas through Lake Volta, discharging into the Gulf of Guinea in Ghana, near the Togo border.
Wear	Waskerley Beck, Co Durham	65	Flows south-east towards Bishop Auckland then north-east to Durham before discharging into the North Sea at Sunderland.
White Volta (Nakambe)	Ouagadougou, Burkina Faso	400	Flows generally southward into Lake Volta in northern Ghana.
Witham	Leicestershire	80	Flows through Lincoln and then south-east into the North Sea at the Wash.
Wye	Plynlimon, Northern Powys	130	Rises within 2 miles of the Severn and flows south-west into England at Hay before travelling through Hereford and back into Wales just south of Monmouth and finally through Tintern and Chepstow to discharge into the Bristol Channel at the Severn estuary.
Yare	Norfolk Broads	55	Flows through the middle of Broadland into Yarmouth and the North Sea; its tributary the Wensum flows through Norwich City.
Yarqon	Rosh ha-'Ayin	16	Flows westward north of Tel Aviv via the Plain of Sharon to the Mediterranean.
Yarra	Mt Matlock, Victoria	153	Flows west to Melbourne and discharges into Hobson's Bay, at the head of Port Phillip Bay.
Yellowstone	Yount Peak, Wyoming	671	Flows northeasterly via the Yellowstone National Park into Montana before joining the Missouri River on the border of Montana and North Dakota.
Yukon	Tagish Lake, Yukon-BC	1,875	Flows north-west into Alaska and discharges into the Bering Sea at Norton Sound.
Zaradros (Sutlej)	Lan-ka Ts'o, SW Tibet	900	Longest of the Punjab's 'Five Rivers', flowing into India and Pakistan where it joins the Chenāb River, west of Bahāwalpur.
Zeravshan	Eastern Turkestan Range	545	Flows west through Tajikistan and south-eastern Uzbekistan to Chardzhou.

Seas of the World

	Details	Sq Miles	Ocean
Adriatic	arm of the Mediterranean between Italy, Slovenia, Croatia and Yugoslavia	50,590	inland
Aegean	arm of the Mediterranean between Greece and Turkey; Crete is its southern boundary	83,000	inland
Andaman	bounded by Myanmar, Thailand, Malay Peninsula, Sumatra and the Andaman and Nicobar Islands	218,100	Indian
Arabian	bounded to the east by India, to the north by Pakistan and Iran and to the west by the Arabian Peninsula and the Horn of Africa	1,490,000	Indian
Arafura	situated between the north coast of Australia, the Gulf of Carpentaria and the south coast of New Guinea, it lies east of the Timor Sea, from which it is separated by the Torres Strait	250,000	Pacific
Azov	inland sea north of the Black Sea between Ukraine and Russia	15,000	inland
Baltic	bordered by Norway, Sweden, Denmark, Germany, Poland, Lithuania, Latvia, Estonia, Russia and Finland	147,500	Atlantic
Banda	bounded by the Moluccas and Lesser Sunda Islands	180,000	Pacific
Barents	formerly known as the Murmean Sea, bounded by the Russian and Norwegian mainlands to the south, Franz Josef Land to the north, the Norwegian and Greenland seas to the west, Spitsbergen to the north-west and the Novaya Zemlya archipelago to the east	542,000	Arctic
Beaufort	situated north of Alaska and Canada	184,000	Arctic
Bering	separates the Asian and North American continents and contains St Lawrence Island, St Matthew Island, Nunivak Island and the Pribilof Islands and the northern border of the Aleutians	875,750	Pacific
Bismarck	lies north of the Solomon Sea off the north-east coast of Papua New Guinea	15,000	Pacific
Black	inland sea lying between Turkey, Bulgaria, Romania, Moldova, Ukraine, Russia and Georgia	196,100	inland
Caribbean	deepest sea in the world, average depth about 8,000′ and maximum depth 30,249′	971,400	Atlantic
Celebes (Sulawesi)	bounded to the north by the Sulu Sea, to the east by the Sangi Islands, to the south by Celebes and to the west by Borneo	110,000	Pacific
Chukchi	situated north of the Bering Sea separating Alaska and Russia	225,000	Arctic
Coral	lies off the east coast of Australia north of the Tasman Sea	1,886,000	Pacific
East China	bounded by South Korea, Japan, Taiwan and China	256,600	Pacific
East Siberian	lying between the Laptev Sea and the Chukchi Sea	361,000	Arctic
English Channel	separates the southern coast of England from the northern coast of France; the French call the Channel 'La Manche' (the sleeve) and its minimum width of 21 miles lies between Dover and Calais	34,700	Atlantic
Flores	situated between the Lesser Sunda Islands to the south and Sulawesi (Celebes) Island to the north	93,000	Pacific
Greenland	borders Greenland to the west, Iceland and the Norwegian Sea to the south and the Arctic Ocean to the north	465,000	Arctic
Ionian	arm of the Mediterranean between Greece to the east, Sicily to the south-west and the Italian mainland to the west	49,500	inland
Irish	bounded by Scotland on the north, England on the east, Wales on the south and Ireland on the west	34,200	Atlantic
Japan	northern extension of the East China Sea, bounded by Japan and Sakhalin Island to the east and by Korea and Russia to the west	391,100	Pacific
Java	bounded by Borneo to the north and Java to the south	167,000	Pacific
Kara	situated off the northern coast of Russia between the Barents Sea and the Laptev Sea	340,000	Arctic
Laccadive	bordering the south-west coast of mainland India, Lakshadweep Islands and the Maldives	209,000	Indian
Laptev	until 1935 known as the Siberian Sea, lying between the Kara Sea and East Siberian Sea	276,000	Arctic
Ligurian	arm of the Mediterranean between the north-west coast of Italy and Corsica to the south	9,800	inland
Mediterranean	largest inland sea in the world, linked to the Atlantic in the west by the Strait of Gibraltar; it encompasses many named sea areas	966,500	inland
Molucca	merges with the Ceram Sea to the south-east and the Banda Sea to the south	77,000	Pacific
North	extends southward from the Norwegian Sea between Norway and the UK, connecting the Skagerrak with the English Channel	164,900	Atlantic
Norwegian	bordered by the Greenland and Barents seas, Norwegian mainland, Shetland and Faeroe islands, Icelandic mainland, Jan Mayen Island, North Sea and Atlantic Ocean	712,000	Atlantic

GEOGRAPHY

	Details	Sq Miles	Ocean
Okhotsk	bounded by the east Russian mainland, Japan and the Kuril Islands	537,500	Pacific
Philippine	lying east of the Philippines and Japan, its southern boundary includes the Caroline Islands, its western boundary includes Guam, and the northern boundary by the Volcano Islands to the north-east and Honshu to the north-west	400,000	Pacific
Red	inland sea extending from Suez in Egypt to the Strait of Bāb el-Mandeb in the south, it washes the shores of Egypt, Sudan, Eritrea, Ethiopia, Djibouti, Saudi Arabia and Yemen	174,900	inland
Savu	situated in the Lesser Sunda Islands between Timor and Sumba Islands	41,000	Pacific
Sea of Marmara (Propontis)	inland sea separating parts of Asian Turkey from European Turkey	4,429	inland
Solomon	lies north of the Coral Sea off the east coast of New Guinea	280,000	Pacific
South China	bounded by the Malay Peninsula, Taiwan, Philippines, Borneo, China and Vietnam	1,148,500	Pacific
Sulu	situated in the Philippine Islands north of the Celebes Sea	100,000	Pacific
Tasman	situated between the south-east coast of Australia and New Zealand	900,000	Pacific
Timor	lies south-west of the Arafura Sea off the north-west coast of Australia	235,000	Indian
Tyrrhenian	bounded by Sicily and the Italian mainland to the east and Corsica and Sardinia to the west	51,000	inland
White	lying south of the Barents Sea off the north-west coast of Russia	35,000	Arctic
Yellow	lying between the People's Republic of China to the north and west, and Korea to the east	113,500	Pacific
Zuiderzee (Southern Sea)	inlet of the North Sea washing the shores of the Netherlands	2,000	Atlantic

NB: The areas given for the above seas, as well as the following gulfs, straits and bays, are as produced by the latest world statistics, which are open to interpretation because it is not always clear at what point the waters merge. Most lists of seas only include those recognised by the International Hydrographic Bureau, and this is a controversial area as, although the reasoning is that seas not recognised are either parts of larger seas or oceans, in fact many of the seas that are recognised – e.g. the Caribbean – are also part of larger sea areas. Surely the Panama Canal links the Atlantic to the Pacific and not merely the Caribbean to the Pacific! The criterion used by the Bureau appears to be that a sea must be surrounded by large areas of land to enable it to be separately identifiable from the oceans but, apart from the inland seas noted above, all other seas are purely geographical markings. In order not to be too controversial I have given the best judgements possible of the areas usually considered as seas by cartographers in the list above, but have remained true to tradition when listing the seas by size elsewhere in this section. This will mean that although the South China Sea will be listed as the world's largest sea in the relevant section, this is inconsistent with the above table which shows the Coral Sea as the largest. If the question is asked, 'What is the largest sea in the world?' then the safe answer would be the South China Sea, which is part of the much larger Malay Sea, no longer recognised by the Bureau, but one has to be aware that large sea areas such as the Coral Sea and Arafura Sea are, rather ambiguously, classed as parts of oceans.

Seas: world's largest

		Area (Sq Miles)
1	South China	1,148,500
2	Caribbean	971,400
3	Mediterranean	966,500
4	Bering	875,750
5	Gulf of Mexico	582,100
6	Okhotsk	537,500
7	Sea of Japan	391,100
8	Hudson Bay	281,900
9	East China	256,600
10	Andaman	218,100
11	Black	196,100
12	Red	174,900

NB: The Malay Sea, which embraced the South China Sea and the Strait of Malacca, is no longer recognised by the International Hydrographic Bureau. Similarly, many other large seas (e.g. the Coral and the Arafura) would normally be included in the list but are also not recognised by the Bureau.

Straits of the World

Bass	Named by English navigator Matthew Flinders after the surgeon-explorer George Bass, the strait is 180 miles in length with an area of 28,950 sq mi; it separates the Tasman Sea area of the Pacific from the Indian Ocean. Technically it is the Tasman Sea that separates Victoria from Tasmania, but the whole of the northern coast of Tasmania borders the waters of the Bass Strait.
Belle Isle Strait	Links the Atlantic to the Gulf of St Lawrence between Newfoundland and Labrador; it is 90 miles long.
Bosporus (Bosphorus)	Links the Black Sea and the Sea of Marmara, and separates part of Asian Turkey from European Turkey. The strait is 19 miles in length.
Cabot	A 60-mile-long channel linking the Gulf of St Lawrence to the Atlantic between Newfoundland and Nova Scotia.
Cook	Links the Tasman Sea to the South Pacific between North Island and South Island, New Zealand. The Cook Strait is 14 miles wide at its narrowest point.
Dardanelles (Hellespont)	Formerly called the Hellespont, they are 38 miles long and link the Aegean Sea with the Sea of Marmara.
Davis	Links Baffin Bay and the Labrador Sea between Greenland and Baffin Island, part of the Northwest Passage linking the Atlantic to the Pacific, it is approximately 400 miles long and wide.
Denmark	Links the Greenland Sea to the North Atlantic between Greenland and Iceland. The British battleship *Hood* was sunk by the German battleship *Bismarck* in the strait on 24 May 1941.
Dover	Links the English Channel (Fr. La Manche) to the North Sea. Its width is approximately 20 miles. The French refer to this stretch of water as the Pas-de-Calais.
Florida	Links the Gulf of Mexico and the Atlantic between Florida and Cuba; it is 110 miles in length. The Spanish explorer Ponce de León was the first European to navigate the strait, in 1513.
Foveaux	Links the Tasman Sea to the South Pacific between South Island and Stewart Island, New Zealand.
Gibraltar	Links the Mediterranean Sea to the Atlantic Ocean. The western extreme is 27 miles wide between the capes of Trafalgar and Spartel and the eastern extreme is 14 miles wide between the Rock of Gibraltar (Pillars of Hercules) and Mount Hacho. The length of the strait is 36 miles and it is also known as Fretum Herculeum.
Hormuz	Links the Persian Gulf to the Gulf of Oman between Iran and the Arabian Peninsula.
Hudson	Links Hudson Bay and the Labrador Sea between Baffin Island and Quebec and is approximately 500 miles in length.
Johore	The northern arm of the Singapore Strait between Singapore Island and Johor State, Malaysia, it is 30 miles in length.
Kattegat	Links the Baltic to the North Sea (Skagerrak inlet) and separates Denmark and Sweden; it is 137 miles in length.
Magellan	Links the Atlantic and Pacific Oceans, between the mainland southern tip of South America and Tierra del Fuego. It is 350 miles in length.
Makassar	Links the Celebes Sea to the Java Sea between Borneo and Celebes; it stretches for approximately 500 miles.
Malacca	Links the Andaman Sea to the South China Sea between Sumatra and the Malay Peninsula; it is 500 miles in length and has an area of 25,000 sq miles.
Messina	Links the Tyrrhenian Sea and the Ionian Sea between Sicily and mainland Italy; it is 20 miles in length and ranges from 2 to 10 miles in width.
North Channel	Links the Irish Sea and the North Atlantic Ocean and washes the shores of Northern Ireland and Scotland. The minimum width of 13 miles lies between the Mull of Kintyre and Torr Head; it is 52 miles long.
Otranto	Links the Adriatic Sea and the Ionian Sea between Albania and Italy. Capo d'Otranto is the most easterly point in Italy and from that point the width of the strait is 40 miles.
St George's Channel	Links the Irish Sea to the Celtic Sea in the North Atlantic, its minimum width of 47 miles lies between Carnsore Point, near Rosslare, Ireland and St David's Head in Dyfed, Wales. It is 100 miles in length.
Singapore	Links the Strait of Malacca and the South China Sea between Singapore Island and the Riau Islands of Indonesia; it is 65 miles in length and 10 miles in width.
Taiwan (Formosa)	Links the South China Sea and the East China Sea between Fukien Province of China and Taiwan; its former name of Formosa means 'beautiful' in Portuguese.
Torres	Links the Coral Sea and the Arafura Sea between New Guinea to the north and Cape York Peninsula, Queensland, Australia, to the south. It is about 80 miles wide between these points. The many islands in the Torres Strait may be remnants of a land bridge that once linked Asia and Australia.
Yucatán Channel	Although not actually called a strait, it links the Gulf of Mexico and the Caribbean Sea between Cuba and Mexico, and is 135 miles in length.

GEOGRAPHY

Towns and Cities on Rivers

Aberdeen	Dee and Don
Adelaide	Torrens
Albuquerque	Rio Grande
Alexandria	Nile
Alloa	Forth
Amsterdam	Amstel
Anstruther	Forth
Antwerp	Scheldt
Astrakhan	Caspian Sea
Augusta	Savannah
Aviemore	Spey
Avignon	Rhône
Babylon	Euphrates
Baghdad	Tigris
Baku	Caspian Sea
Balmoral	Dee
Bamako, Mali	Niger
Bangkok	Chao Phraya
Bangui	Ubangi
Basel	Rhine
Basra	Shatt al Arab
Bath	Bristol Avon
Baton Rouge	Mississippi
Bedford	Great Ouse
Belfast	Lagan
Belgrade	Danube, Sava
Benares	Ganges
Berlin	Spree
Berne	Aare
Berwick	Tweed
Birkenhead	Mersey
Blandford Forum	Dorset Stour
Bonn	Rhine and Seig
Bootle	Mersey
Bordeaux	Garonne
Bowness	Forth
Bratislava	Danube
Brecon	Usk
Bremen	Weser
Brest, Belarus	Bug
Brighouse	Calder
Bristol	Bristol Avon
Brussels	Senne
Bucharest	Danube tributary: Dimbovita
Buckhaven	Forth
Buckingham	Ouse
Budapest	Danube
Buenos Aires	Rio de la Plata
Buffalo	Lake Erie
Cairo	Nile (Rosetta and Damietta)
Calcutta	Hoogly
Cambridge	Cam (aka Granta)
Canterbury	Stour
Cardiff	Taff
Carlisle	Eden
Carmarthen	Towy
Chester	Dee
Chicago	Lake Michigan
Chichester	Lavant
Chongqing	Yangzi
Cincinnati	Ohio
Cockermouth	Derwent and Cocker
Colchester	Colne

Coldstream	Tweed
Coleraine	Bann
Cologne	Rhine
Concord, NH	Merrimack
Cork	Lee
Cowes	Medina
Delft	Schie
Derby	Derwent
Derry	Foyle
Detroit	Lake St Clair
Dewsbury	Calder
Doncaster	Don
Dorchester	Frome
Dorking	Mole
Dresden	Elbe
Dublin	Liffey
Dumbarton	Clyde
Dumfries	Nith
Dundee	Tay
Dunoon	Clyde
Durham	Wear
Düsseldorf	Rhine
Edinburgh	Forth, Firth of
Ennis	Fergus
Enniskillen	Erne
Evesham	Warwickshire Avon
Exeter	Exe
Falmouth	Fa
Florence	Arno
Frankfurt am Main	Main
Frankfurt an der Oder	Oder
Fremantle	Swan
Geneva	Rhône
Geneva	Lake Geneva
Gillingham	Medway
Glasgow	Clyde
Gloucester	Severn
Godalming	Wey
Grantchester	Granta
Grantham	Witham
Gravesend	Thames
Greenock	Clyde
Grenoble	Isère
Grimsby	Humber
Guangzhou	Zhujiang
Guildford	Wey
Hamburg	Elbe
Hanoi	Song-Koi (Red)
Harrogate	Nidd
Harwich	Stour
Haverfordwest	Cleddau
Hawick	Teviot and Slitrig
Heidelberg	Neckar
Helensburgh	Clyde
Hereford	Wye
Hertford	Lea
Ho Chi-Minh City	Saigon
Hull	Humber
Huntingdon	Ouse
Hyderabad	Indus
Ilkley	Wharfe
Indianapolis	White
Inverness	Ness
Ipswich	Orwell
Jarrow	Tyne

Kathmandu	Vishnumati
Kelso	Tweed and Teviot
Khartoum	White Nile and Blue Nile
Kidderminster	Stour
Kiev	Dnieper
Kilkenny	Nore
Kilmarnock	Irvine
King's Lynn	Great Ouse
Lahore	Ravi
Lancaster	Lune
Langholm	Esk
Le Havre	Seine
Leamington Spa	Warwickshire Avon
Leeds	Aire
Leicester	Soar
Leipzig	Pleisse, Parthe, Elster
Lima	Rimac
Limerick	Shannon
Limoges	Vienne
Lincoln	Witham
Linz	Danube
Lisbon	Tagus
Lisburn	Lagan
Littlehampton	Arun
Liverpool	Mersey
London	Thames
Loughborough	Soar
Louisville	Ohio
Luton	Lea
Lyons	Rhône and Saône
Madrid	Manzanares
Maidstone	Medway
Maldon	Blackwater
Mallow	Blackwater
Manchester	Irwell
Manchester, NH	Merrimack
Mandalay	Irrawaddy
Maputo	Delagoa Bay
Marlow	Thames
Melbourne	Yarra
Melrose	Tweed
Middlesbrough	Tees
Midhurst	Rother
Milan	Olono
Mold	Alyn
Montreal	St Lawrence and Ottawa
Morpeth	Wansbeck
Moscow	Moskva
Munich	Isar
Nantes	Loire
Nantwich	Weaver
Nashville	Cumberland
New Delhi	Jumna
New Orleans	Mississippi Gulf of Mexico
New York	Hudson
Newbury	Kennet
Newcastle	Tyne
Newport (Gwent)	Usk
Newport (I of W)	Medina
Niamey, Niger	Niger
Northampton	Nene

Norwich	Wensum	Rome	Tiber	Swansea	Tawe
Nottingham	Trent	Rotterdam	Rhine, Maas,	Taunton	Tone
Nuneaton	Anker		Scheldt	Tewkesbury	Severn,
Omdurman	Nile	Rugby	Warwickshire		Warwickshire
Oporto	Douro		Avon		Avon
Orléans	Loire	Rye	Rother	Thebes (Egypt)	Nile
Oxford	Thames	Salisbury	Hampshire Avon	Tidmarsh	Pang
	(Isis and		and Wily	Tintern Abbey	Wye
	Cherwell)	São Paulo	Tiete	Tipperary	Ara
Pangbourne	Thames	Seoul	Han	Tiverton	Exe
Paris	Seine	Shanghai	Hwangpu	Tonbridge	Medway
Patna	Ganges	Sheffield	Don, and Sheaf	Totnes	Dart
Peebles	Tweed	Shoreham-	Adur	Turin	Po
Perth, Australia	Swan	by-Sea		Vienna	Danube
Perth, Scotland	Tay	Shrewsbury	Severn	Wakefield	Calder
Peterborough	Nene	Sligo	Garavogue	Wareham	Frome
Philadelphia	Delaware	Southampton	Test, and Itchen	Warsaw	Vistula
Phnom Penh	Mekong	Southend-	Thames	Warwick	Warwickshire
Pisa	Arno	on-Sea			Avon
Pittsburgh	Ohio	Spalding	Welland	Washington DC	Potomac
Plock	Vistula	St Albans	Ver	Waterford	Suir
Prague	Vltava	St Ives (Cambs)	Ouse	Whalley	Calder
Preston	Ribble	St Louis	Mississippi	Whitby	Esk
Quebec	St Lawrence,	St Petersburg	Neva	Wimborne	Stour and Allen
	St Charles	Stafford	Sow	Winchester	Itchen
Reading	Thames and	Stoke	Trent	Windsor	Thames
	Kennet	Strabane	Mourne	Worcester	Severn
Richmond	Swale	Strasbourg	Ill	Wuhan	Han and Yangzi
(Yorks)		Stratford	Warwickshire	Yonkers	Hudson
Richmond (Va)	James		Avon	York	Ouse
Ripon	Ure	Stuttgart	Neckar	Zagreb	Sava
Rochester	Medway	Sunderland	Wear	Zurich	Limmat

Trenches: deepest

Trench	Deepest Point
Marianas Trench (Pacific)	Challenger Deep 35,840'
Puerto Rico Trench (Atlantic)	Milwaukee Deep 28,232'
Java Trench (Indian)	Planet Deep 23,376'
Eurasia Basin (Arctic)	Eurasia Basin 17,880'

Waterways

Aden Links the Red Sea to the Arabian Sea and borders Yemen to the north and Somalia to the south. The gulf is 920 miles in length and has an area of 205,000 sq miles.

Alaska Inlet of the North Pacific on the south coast of Alaska, and bordered by Kodiak Island to the west and Cape Spencer to the east, it has an area of 592,000 sq miles.

Alphonse XIII Canal Opened in 1926 and runs for 53 miles, linking Seville to the Atlantic via the Gulf of Cadiz.

Angel Falls Situated in the Guiana Highlands in Bolivar state, south-eastern Venezuela, on the Rio Churún, a tributary of the Caroni. At 3,212' the falls are the highest in the world.

Aqaba North-eastern arm of the Red Sea between Saudi Arabia and the Sinai Peninsula. The gulf is 100 miles in length.

Baffin Bay Inlet of the North Atlantic with an area of 266,000 sq miles, situated between Greenland and Baffin Island.

Bengal, Bay of Inlet of the Indian Ocean bordering India, Myanmar, Sri Lanka, and the Andaman and Nicobar Islands; it occupies an area of 839,000 sq miles.

Biscay, Bay of Inlet of the North Atlantic bordering northern Spain and south-west France; it has an area of 86,000 sq miles.

Biscayne Bay Inlet of the Atlantic in south-eastern Florida; it is 40 miles in length and between 2 and 10 miles in width.

Bothnia Northern arm of the Baltic between Sweden on the west and Finland on the east.

Boyoma Falls Formerly called the Stanley Falls; situated on the Lualaba River in the Democratic Republic of Congo, it has a drop of 200' and is the world's greatest waterfall by volume of water.

Bridgewater Canal Opened in 1761 and named after Francis Egerton, 3rd Duke of Bridgewater. The canal was built by James Brindley and originally ran for 10 miles, carrying barges over the Irwell at Barton; it was extended to Liverpool in 1776, joining the Mersey at Runcorn.

Bristol Channel Inlet of the Atlantic between South Wales and the English counties of Somerset, Devon and Cornwall.

GEOGRAPHY

Caledonian Canal   Built by Thomas Telford in 1803–21 and opened in 1822, it has 29 locks and links the east and west coasts of Scotland via the lakes of the Great Glen.

California   Aka Sea of Cortés and situated in northwestern Mexico, it is 750 miles in length and has an area of 62,000 sq miles.

Carpentaria   Inlet of the Arafura Sea indenting the north-eastern coast of Australia. The gulf has an area of 120,000 sq miles.

Cauldron Snout   Situated on the River Tees, Cumbria/Durham border, the highest waterfall in England (200′).

Churchill Falls   Discovered in 1839 by John McLean and known as the Grand Falls until 1965, when they were renamed in honour of Winston Churchill. Situated on the Churchill River, in west Labrador, Newfoundland, the falls have a drop of 245′.

Corinth   Inlet of the Ionian Sea separating the Peloponnese from mainland Greece.

Delagoa Bay   Situated on the south-east coast of Mozambique, it is 19 miles in length and 16 miles wide.

Eas a' Chuàl Aluinn   Situated in Sutherland in the Scottish Highlands in Glas Bheinn, the highest waterfall in the British Isles (658′).

False Bay   Inlet of the Atlantic, south of Cape Town, South Africa.

Finland   Eastern arm of the Baltic between Finland to the north, Estonia to the south, and Russia to the east.

Florida Bay   Triangular-shaped body of water at the southern tip of mainland Florida stretching from Cape Sable in the west, Key Largo in the east and Long Key in the south.

Fundy, Bay of   Inlet of the Atlantic between New Brunswick and Nova Scotia; it stretches for 94 miles.

Genoa   Inlet of the Ligurian Sea stretching eastwards for 90 miles around the north-west coast of Italy from Imperia to La Spezia.

Grand Canal   Waterway that splits the city of Venice from St Mark's Cathedral to Sta Chiara church; it is 2.1 miles in length.

Grand Canal (China)   Often considered a river system rather than a canal system, but much of its 1,107 miles is artificial waterway made by damming rivers and lakes. Nowadays it is treated in the same fashion as the St Lawrence Seaway and not included in lists of canals. It runs from Beijing to Hangzhou, was opened in AD 610 and has been regularly reconstructed ever since.

Grand Union Canal   Before 1929 was known as the Grand Junction Canal but was enlarged by amalgamating several canals and is now a main line between London and Birmingham and has several forks, the largest connecting to Leicester. The main sideshoots of the system are the Regent's Canal (Little Venice), the Paddington Arm to Brentford, the Aylesbury Arm, the Northampton Arm, and the Erewash Canal, which extends to the Leicester branch.

Great Australian Bight   Inlet of the Indian Ocean extending eastwards from West Cape, Western Australia, to South-West Cape, Tasmania.

Guinea   Inlet of the Atlantic washing the coasts of Liberia (Grain Coast), Côte D'Ivoire (Ivory), Ghana (Gold), Togo (Slave), Benin (Slave), Nigeria (Slave), Equatorial Guinea, Gabon, and Cameroon (Bight of Bonny).

Hauraki (North Wind)   Inlet of the South Pacific indenting eastern North Island, New Zealand, covering an area of 884 sq miles.

Houston Canal   Shipping channel running through Houston, Texas, into Galveston Bay and ultimately the Gulf of Mexico after a journey of 56.7 miles. The Houston Canal has no locks.

Hudson Bay   Inland sea bordering Manitoba, Ontario, Quebec, and Northwest Territories; it has an area of 281,900 sq miles and contains Belcher Islands, Mansel Island, Coats Island and Southampton Island. The southern section has an inlet between Ontario and Quebec (James Bay).

Islands, Bay of   Situated in the north of North Island, New Zealand, it has a shoreline of 500 miles.

James Bay   Southern extension of the larger Hudson Bay; it is 275 miles in length and 135 miles in width and contains many islands the largest being, Akimiski.

Khone Falls   Situated on the Mekong River, Laos, on the border with Cambodia, it has a drop of 45′ and is the world's second greatest waterfall by volume.

Kiel Canal (North Sea)   Stretches for 60.9 miles and links the North Sea (at the mouth of the Elbe) to Kiel Harbour on the Baltic.

Love Canal   Not a canal at all nowadays but an area of Niagara Falls, New York, which, in 1978, was the scene of the worst environmental disaster involving chemical wastes in US history. The area, which had become a dumping ground for nuclear waste, has become a byword for similar areas.

Manchester Ship Canal   Opened in 1894 and runs for 39.7 miles linking Manchester to the Irish Sea.

Mexico, Gulf of   Large body of water occupying an area of 582,000 square miles situated on the southeast coast of North America and connected to the Atlantic Ocean by the Straits of Florida and to the Caribbean Sea by the Yucatan Channel.

Mozambique Channel   Channel of the Indian Ocean between Madagascar and Mozambique which stretches for about 1,000 miles.

Niagara Falls   Situated on the Niagara River, the falls are divided into two cataracts divided by Goat Island. The larger cataract is called the Horseshoe Falls with its drop of 162′ and crest line of 2,600′; the smaller is called the American Falls with its drop of 167′ but much smaller crest line of 1,000′ across. Niagara Falls is the world's third greatest waterfall by volume of water.

Oman   Northwestern arm of the Arabian Sea between Oman and Iran, it is 350 miles in length and is linked to the Persian Gulf via the Strait of Hormuz.

Panama Canal   Connecting the Atlantic and Pacific oceans and stretching for 50.71 miles, the canal was begun by Ferdinand de Lesseps in 1879, but numerous difficulties caused its cancellation until the Hay-Bunau-Varilla Treaty of 1903 between Panama and the USA granted the United States the building rights. The engineer, John F Stevens, drafted the final plan in 1906 but was succeeded as chief engineer by George Washington Goethals in 1907. The canal opened on 15 August 1914, and under the Carter-Torrijos Treaty of 1977 was officially handed back to Panama on 31 December 1999 by US President Bill Clinton. The 6 locks are the Gatún Locks (a set of three), Pedro Miguel Lock and Miraflores Locks (a set of two) . The Caribbean entrance is at Limón Bay and its southern entrance is in the Bay of Panama. Vessels cannot navigate the waters under their own power.

Persian Gulf   Shallow body of water between the Arabian Peninsula and Iran. The surface area of this inlet of the Indian Ocean is approximately 88,800 square miles.

Pistyll-y-Llyn Situated on the Powys/Dyfed border, at 240′ the highest waterfall in Wales.

Port Phillip Bay Inlet of Bass Strait on the south central coast of Victoria, Australia. Its entrance is known as 'the Rip'.

Powerscourt Falls Situated in the River Dargle, Co Wicklow, the highest waterfall in Ireland (350′).

Prince William Sound Inlet of the Gulf of Alaska with Hinchinbrook and Montague islands at its entrance.

Princess Charlotte Bay Inlet of the Coral Sea off the coast of Queensland; named after the daughter of George IV, it is bounded by Cape Melville to the east and Claremont Point to the west.

Ribbon Falls Situated in the Yosemite National Park, California.

Riga Inlet of the Baltic bounded by the northern coast of Latvia and the western coast of Estonia, it has an area of 7,000 sq miles.

Saint Lawrence Truly, a sea area of 91,800 sq miles with borders on Quebec, Newfoundland, Nova Scotia and New Brunswick; and containing Prince Edward Island.

Saint Lawrence Seaway Stretching from the Atlantic Ocean to the western end of the Great Lakes, the seaway was begun in August 1954, completed in April 1959 and measures 2,342 miles in length. It is a series of nearly 60 canals, of which the Welland is the longest.

Saint Vincent Inlet of the Indian Ocean on the south-east coast of South Australia, it is 90 miles in length.

Saronic (Aegina) Inlet of the Aegean Sea lying east of the Gulf of Corinth from which it is separated by the Corinth Canal.

Skagerrak Arm of the North Sea between Norway and the Jutland peninsula of Denmark on the south.

Spencer Inlet of the Great Australian Bight between the Eyre and Yorke peninsulas of South Australia, it contains many small islands including Gambier, Thistle, Sir Joseph Banks, and Neptune.

Suez North-western arm of the Red Sea between Africa and the Sinai Peninsula, it is 195 miles in length and its most northerly point at Suez marks the beginning of the Suez Canal.

Suez Canal The first fact to determine about the Suez Canal is its length, a subject that is one of the most frequently asked quiz questions. It is officially 100.6 miles long, but many reputable sources will have it listed anywhere between 100 and 105 miles; this difference is mainly due to alterations to accommodate larger vessels. The canal was built by Ferdinand de Lesseps (1805–94) and opened in 1869; its extremities are Port Said at the northern

end and Suez to the south; it links two broad areas of sea, the Mediterranean and the Red Sea (via the Gulf of Suez), and is therefore technically, like many canals, a strait. It has no locks.

Sutherland Falls Situated in the Arthur River near Milford Sound, Otago, South Island, New Zealand; at 1,904′ the fifth-highest waterfall in the world.

Tadjoura Situated at the western end of the Gulf of Aden around the port of Djibouti. The gulf is 50 miles in length.

Taranto Arm of the Ionian Sea in southern Italy between Cape Santa Maria di Leuca and Cape Colonne, forming the hollow in front of the 'boot' of Italy.

Thailand (Siam) Bordering Thailand, Cambodia, and South Vietnam, the gulf is 350 miles wide and 450 miles in length.

Thérmai Inlet of the Aegean Sea in north eastern Greece between Macedonia, Thessaly, and the Chalcidice Peninsula.

Tonkin Inlet of the South China Sea bounded by China, Hainan Island, and North Vietnam. The gulf is 300 miles in length and 150 miles in width.

Tugela Falls Situated in the Tugela River, Natal, South Africa; at 3,110′ the second highest cataract in the world.

Utigård Falls Situated in the Jostedal Glacier, Nesdale, Norway, the highest of the many great waterfalls of Norway and with a total drop of 2,625′ the third highest in the world.

Victoria Falls Truly breathtaking waterfall on the Zambesi River on the border between Zambia and Zimbabwe, its drop is 355′ and it is known locally as 'The Smoke That Thunders'.

Volga–Don Shipping Canal Runs from Kalach on the Tsimlyansk Reservoir on the Don 62.2 miles to Krasnoarmeysk on the Volga; it was completed in 1952 and joins the Black Sea to the Caspian Sea.

Welland Canal Completed in 1932 and now part of the St Lawrence Seaway, it is 27.6 miles in length and is situated in southern Ontario between Lake Erie to the south and Lake Ontario to the north; it was built as an alternative route through the River Niagara because of the impassable falls.

White Sea–Baltic Canal Longest ship canal in the world (141 miles), between Povenets and Belomorsk in Russia; it has 19 locks and was opened in 1933 as the Stalin Canal.

Yosemite Falls Situated in Yosemite National Park, central California, USA. The Upper Yosemite Fall drops 1,430′ and the Lower Falls 320′ with the cascades between making a total drop of 2,425′.

G
E
O
G
R
A
P
H
Y

Definitions of Waterways

bay a wide semicircular indentation of a shoreline, especially between two headlands or peninsulas.

canal an artificial waterway constructed for navigational aid, irrigation, or hydro-electric power.

lake a body of water, either freshwater or salt, completely surrounded by land.

ocean very large stretch of sea, especially one of the 4 main oceans of the world, i.e. Pacific, Atlantic, Indian, Arctic. The Antarctic Ocean is made up of the southern extremities of the Atlantic, Pacific and Indian Oceans.

river see definition in relevant section.

sea a mass of salt water that may be part of one of the Earth's oceans or part of a larger sea area.

strait a narrow channel of the sea, bordered by land and linking two larger sea areas. It is often confusing to think of a strait as connecting waters, as opposed to land, because it is usually the land boundaries of the strait that are better known. To give a typical example, most people realise that the Bass Strait lies between mainland Australia and Tasmania, but few will know that the strait links the Tasman Sea area of the Pacific and the Indian Ocean.

Sea Areas

Weather forecasts are broadcast on a regular basis for the Shipping Forecast Areas around the British coast and neighbouring countries. It should be noted that the areas listed below are the boundaries set by Britain and are not universally accepted by other countries who have their own boundary limits and names.

The areas will be described firstly by clockwise coastal areas around Great Britain, starting with the northernmost point of Scotland, and then the coastal regions of Ireland, starting with the northernmost point, before describing other areas and their locations relative to one another.

German Bight was previously called Heligoland until 1956 and FitzRoy (named after the Met office founder and HMS *Beagle* captain, Admiral Robert Fitzroy) was called Finisterre until 2002.

Around Great Britain
Fair Isle: southeast of Faeroes, west of Viking, northeast of Hebrides, northwest of Forties
Cromarty: west of Forties
Forth: west of Forties
Tyne: west of Dogger
Humber: west of German Bight and touching the coast of the Netherlands
Thames: bordering the Netherlands and touching the coast of Belgium
Dover: bordering France and Belgium
Wight: bordering France
Portland: bordering France
Plymouth: east of Sole and bordering France
Lundy: east of Fastnet and touching the coast of Ireland
Irish Sea: surround Anglesey and the Isle of Man
Hebrides: east of Bailey, northeast of Rockall and containing the Outer Hebrides
Malin: east of Rockall and containing the Inner Hebrides

Around Ireland
Malin: east of Rockall and containing the Inner Hebrides
Irish Sea: surround Anglesey and the Isle of Man
Lundy: east of Fastnet and touching the coast of Ireland
Fastnet: north of Sole and bordering the southern coast of Ireland
Shannon: north of Sole
Rockall: south of Bailey and touching the western coast of Ireland

South-East Iceland: most northerly sea area; north of Bailey and northwest of Faeroes and bordering Iceland
Faeroes: southeast of SE Iceland, northwest of Fair Isle, northeast of Bailey, north of Hebrides
Viking: east of Fair Isle, west of North Utsire, north of Forties, northwest of South Utsire
North Utsire: east of Viking, north of South Utsire, and bordering the coast of Norway
South Utsire: southeast of Viking, south of North Utsire, north of Fisher and bordering the coast of Norway
Fisher: south of South Utsire, north of German Bight, east of Forties, and bordering the Skaggerak
Forties: bordered by Fair Isle, Viking, South Utsire, Fisher, Dogger, Forth, and Cromarty
German Bight: south of Fisher, east of Dogger, east of Humber, and bordering Denmark and Germany
Dogger: south of Forties, west of German Bight, north of Humber, east of Tyne
Biscay: south of Plymouth, east of FitzRoy, and bordering France and Spain
FitzRoy: west of Biscay, south of Sole, north of Trafalgar and bordering Spain
Trafalgar: south of FitzRoy and bordering Spain and Portugal
Sole: west of Plymouth and south of Shannon and Fastnet
Bailey: south of SE Iceland, southwest of Faeroes, west of Hebrides, north of Rockall

Beaufort Scale
0	Calm
1	Light air
2	Light breeze
3	Gentle breeze
4	Moderate breeze
5	Fresh breeze
6	Strong breeze
7	Moderate gale
8	Fresh gale
9	Strong gale
10	Whole gale
11	Storm
12	Hurricane

(Devised in 1805 by Francis Beaufort. Force 13 to 17 were added in 1955 by the US Weather Bureau but are seldom used.)

Roman Place Names of Britain

Roman Name	British Name	Roman Name	British Name
Abone	Sea Mills, Avon	Crococalana	Brough, Nottinghamshire
Aballava	Burgh by Sands, Cumbria	Cunetio	Mildenhall, Wiltshire
Ad Ansam	Higham, Suffolk	Danum	Doncaster, South Yorkshire
Ad Pontem	East Stoke, Nottinghamshire	Delgovicia	Millington, East Yorkshire
Aesica	Great Chesters, Northumberland	Derventio	Malton, North Yorkshire
			Littlechester, Derbyshire
Ageloco	Littleborough, Lancashire		Papcastle, Cumbria
Alabum	Llandovery, Dyfed	Deva	Chester, Cheshire
Alauna	Maryport, Cumbria	Dubris	Dover, Kent
	Ardoch, Tayside	Dunum	Hod Hill, Dorset
	Watercrook, Cumbria	Durnovaria	Dorchester, Dorset
Albion	England	Durobrivae	Rochester, Kent
Anderitum	Pevensey, East Sussex		Water Newton, Cambridgeshire
Aquae Arnemetiae	Buxton, Derbyshire	Durocobrivis	Dunstable, Bedfordshire
Aquae Sulis	Bath, Avon	Durocornovium	Wanborough, Wilts
Arbeia	South Shields, Tyne & Wear	Duroliponte	Cambridge, Cambs
Ardotalia	Melandra Castle, Derbyshire	Durovernum	Canterbury, Kent
Ariconium	Weston-under-Penyard, Hereford &Worcestershire	Cantiacorum	
		Durovigutum	Godmanchester, Cambridgeshire
Banna	Birdoswald, Cumbria		
Bannaventa	Whilton Lodge, Northamptonshire	Eboracum	York, North Yorkshire
		Epiacum	Whitley Castle, Northumberland
Bannovalum	Horncastle, Lincolnshire	Esmeduna	Liverpool
Bibra	Beckfoot, Cumbria	Fanumcocium	Bewcastle, Cumbria
Blatobulgium	Birrens, Dumfries and Galloway	Gabrosentum	Moresby, Cumbria
Bovio	Holt, Cheshire	Galava	Ambleside, Cumbria
Bovivum	Tilston, Cheshire	Gariannum	Burgh Castle, Norfolk
Branodunum	Brancaster, Norfolk	Gernemuta magna	Great Yarmouth
Bravoniacum	Kirkby Thore, Cumbria	Glanibanta	Ambleside, Cumbria
Bravonium	Leintwardine, Hereford & Worcestershire	Glevum	Gloucester, Gloucestershire
		Gobanneum	Abergavenny, Gwent
Bremenium	High Rochester, Northumberland	Granta	Cambridge
		Habitancum	Risingham, Northumberland
Bremetenacum Veteranorum	Ribchester, Lancashire	Hibernia	Ireland
		Isca	Caerleon, Gwent
Bremia	Llanio, Dyfed	Isca Dumnoniorum	Exeter, Devon
Brocavum	Brougham, Cumbria	Isurium Brigantum	Aldborough, North Yorkshire
Brocolitia	Carrawburgh, Northumberland	Itunocelum	Ravenglass, Cumbria
Burrium	Usk, Gwent	Lactodurum	Towcester, Northamptonshire
Caesaria	Sark	Lagentium	Castleford, West Yorkshire
	Jersey	Launa	Learchild, Northumberland
Caesaromagus	Chelmsford, Essex	Lavatris	Bowes, Durham
Calacum	Burrow in Lonsdale, Lancashire	(Portus) Lemanis	Lympne, Kent
Calcaria	Tadcaster, North Yorkshire	Letocetum	Wall, Staffordshire
Caledonia	Scotland	Leucarum	Loughor, West Glamorgan
Calleva Atrebatum	Silchester, Hampshire	Leucomagus	East Anton, Hampshire
Camboglanna	Castlefields, Cumbria	Levobrinta	Forden Gear, Powys
Camboritum	Lackford, Suffolk	Lindinis	Ilchester, Somerset
Cambria	Wales	Lindum	Lincoln, Lincolnshire
Camulodunum	Colchester, Essex	Londinium	London, Greater London
	Slack, West Yorkshire	Longovicium	Lanchester, Durham
Canonium	Kelvedon, Essex	Luentinum	Pumsaint, Dyfed
Canovium	Caerhun, Gwynedd	Luguvalium	Carlisle, Cumbria
Castra Exploratorum	Netherby, Cumbria	Lunecastrum	Lancaster
Cataractonium	Catterick, North Yorkshire	Magiovinium	Dropshort, Buckinghamshire
Causennis	Saltersford, Lincolnshire	Magis	Burrow Walls, Cumbria
Cecucmum	Y Gaer, Powys	Maglona	Old Carlisle, Cumbria
Cilurnum	Chesters, Northumberland	Magna	Carvoran, Northumberland
Clausentum	Bitterne, Hampshire	Magnis	Kenchester, Herefordshire
Combretovium	Baylham House, Suffolk	Maia	Bowness-on-Solway, Cumbria
Concangis	Chester-le-Street, Durham	Mamucium/	Manchester, Greater
Concavata	Drumburgh, Cumbria	Mancunium	Manchester
Condate	Northwich, Cheshire	Manavia	Isle of Man
Condercum	Benwell, Tyne & Wear	Manduessedum	Mancetter, Warwickshire
Coria	Corbridge, Northumberland	Margidunum	Castle Hill, Nottinghamshire
Corinium Dobunnorum	Cirencester, Gloucestershire	Mediobogdum	Hardknott, Cumbria
		Mediolanum	Whitchurch, Shropshire

GEOGRAPHY

Roman Name	British Name	Roman Name	British Name
Mona	Isle of Anglesey	Segelocum	Littleborough, Nottinghamshire
Morbium	Piercebridge, Co. Durham	Segontium	Caernarfon, Gwynedd
Moridunum	Carmarthen, Dyfed	Sorviodunum	Old Sarum, Wiltshire
	Seaton, Devon	Sullon Iacis	Brockley Hill, Greater London
Navio	Brough, Derbyshire	Trimontium	Newstead, Borders
Nemeto Statio	North Tawton, Devon	Tripontium	Cave's Inn, Warwickshire
Nidum	Neath, West Glamorgan	Uxacona	Redhill, Shropshire
Noviomagus	Crayford, Greater London	Uxelodunum	Stanwix, Cumbria
Noviomagus	Chichester, West Sussex	Vagniacis	Springhead, Kent
Regnorum		Varis	St Asaph, Clwyd
Olenacum	Elslack, North Yorkshire	Vectis	Isle of Wight
Onnum	Halton, Northumberland	Veluniate	Carriden, Falkirkshire
Orcades Insulae	Orkney Islands	Venonis	High Cross, Leicestershire
Othona	Bradwell-on-Sea, Essex	Venta Belgarum	Winchester, Hampshire
Pennocrucium	Water Eaton, Staffordshire	Venta Icenorum	Caistor St Edmund, Norfolk
Petuarea	Brough on Humber,	Venta Silurum	Caerwent, Gwent
	Humberside	Verbeia	Ilkley, West Yorkshire
Pons Aelius	Newcastle, Tyne & Wear	Vercovicium	Housesteads, Northumberland
Pontes	Staines, Surrey	Verlucio	Sandy Lane, Wiltshire
Portus Ardaoni	Portchester, Hants (also	Vernemetum	Willoughby, Nottinghamshire
	Portus Ardurni)	Verteris	Brough, Cumbria
Portus Dubris	Dover, Kent	Verulamium	St Albans, Hertfordshire
Ranatis/Tanatus	Thanet	Vigornia	Worcester
Ratae Corieltavorum	Leicester, Leicestershire	Vindobala	Rudchester, Northumberland
Regodunum	Castleshaw, Greater	Vindocladia	Badbury, Dorset
	Manchester	Vindolanda	Chesterholm, Northumberland
Regulbium	Reculver, Kent	Vindomora	Ebchester, Durham
Riduna	Alderney, Channel Islands	Vinovia	Binchester, Durham
Rutupiae	Richborough, Kent	Viroconium	Wroxeter, Shropshire
Salinae	Droitwich, Worcestershire	Cornoviorum	
	Middlewich, Cheshire	Virosidum	Brough-by-Bainbridge,
Sarnia	Guernsey		North Yorkshire
Segedunum	Wallsend, Tyne & Wear	Voreda	Old Penrith, Cumbria

NB The above are sites of Roman cities during their occupation in the first four centuries AD.
A few of the situations are doubtful and alternatives are given in areas of uncertainty.

Roman Place Names of the World

Roman Name	British Name	Roman Name	British Name
Abbatis Cella (Abbot's Cell)	Appenzell	Italia	Italy
Aegyptus	Egypt	Langobardus	Lombardy
Africa	Libya / Tunisia	Lausodunum	Lausanne
Aquincum	Budapest	Limonum	Poitiers
Arabia Felix	Arabia	Lugdunum	Lyon
Arabona	Gyor	Lusitania	Portugal
Arenacum	Arnhem	Lutetia	Paris
Ariminum	Rimini	Massilia	Marseilles
Augusta Taurinorum	Turin	Matisco	Macon
Aurelianum	Orléans	Mauretania	Morocco
Caesarea Augusta	Zaragoza	Mediolanum	Milan
Caesaria	Jersey	Noviomagus	Longjumeau
Caesaria Maritima	Palestine	Noviomagus	Nijmegen
Candia	Crete	Olisipo	Lisbon
Cibinium	Sibiu	Patavium	Padua
Crassus	Grasse	Pinciacum	Poissy
Curicum	Krk	Portus Cale	Oporto
Dacia	Romania	Portus Veneris	Port-Vendres
Fiscamnum	Fécamp	Praenestum	Palestrina
Fretum Herculaneum	Gibraltar (Strait of)	Puteoli	Pozzuoli
Gades	Cadiz	Sexantaprista	Ruse
Gallia	France	Sparnacum	Epernay
Germania	Germany	Trajectum Castrum	Utrecht
Graecia	Greece	Turicum	Zurich
Helvetia	Switzerland	Vapincum	Gap
Hibernia	Ireland	Vasconia	Gascony
Hispania	Spain	Vindobona	Vienna

World Table: Geographical Gazetteer

Country	GMT	Currency	Split into 100	UN Member	Common-wealth	Europe	Official Languages	Highest Point	Area Sq Km	Area Sq Miles	Population
Afghanistan	+4	afghani	puls	1946			Pashto, Dari Persian	Noshaq (24,581')	647,497	249,999	28,513,677
Albania	+1	Lek	qindarka	1955			Albanian	Korabi (9,026')	28,748	11,100	3,544,808
Algeria	+1	dinar	centimes	1962			Arabic, Berber, French	Tahat (9,852')	2,381,741	919,591	32,129,324
Andorra	+1	euro	cents	1993			Catalan, French, Spanish	Pla del'Estany (9,678')	468	181	69,865
Angola	+1	kwanza	lweis	1976			Portuguese	Serra Moco (8,563')	1,246,700	481,351	10,978,552
Antigua and Barbuda	-4	East Caribbean dollar	cents	1981	1981		English	Boggy Peak (1,319')	442	171	68,320
Argentina	-3	peso	austral	1945			Spanish	Aconcagua (22,834')	2,766,889	1,068,297	39,144,753
Armenia	+4	dram	louma	1992			Armenian	Aragats (13,418')	29271	11,302	2,991,360
Australia	+8-+11	dollar	cents	1945	1931		English	Kosciusko (7,316')	7,686,848	2,967,895	19,913,144
Austria	+1	euro	cents	1955		1995	German	Grossglockner (12,462')	83,849	32,374	8,174,762
Azerbaijan	+4	manat	gopik	1992			Azeri	Bazar-dyuzi (15,156')	86,600	33,436	7,868,385
Bahamas	-5	dollar	cents	1973	1973		English	Alvernia (on Cat Island) (206')	13,935	5,380	299,697
Bahrain	+3	dinar	fils (1,000)	1971			Arabic	Jabal ad-Dukhan (440')	622	240	677,886
Bangladesh	+6	taka	poisha	1974	1972		Bengali	Keokradong (4,034')	143,998	55,598	141,340,476
Barbados	-4	dollar	cents	1966	1966		English	Hillaby (1,115')	430	166	278,289
Belarus	+2	rouble	kopeks	1945			Belarussian	Dzerzhinsky (1,135')	207,600	80,154	10,310,520
Belgium	+1	euro	cents	1945		1958	Dutch, French, German	Botrange (2,277')	30,513	11,781	10,348,276
Belize	-6	dollar	cents	1981	1981		English	Victoria Peak (3,681')	22,965	8,867	272,945
Benin	+1	franc	centimes	1960			French, Fon, Adja, Yoruba	Atacora Massif (2,103')	122,622	47,344	7,250,033
Bermuda	-4	dollar	cents				English	Gibb's Hill (245')	53	20	64,935
Bhutan	+6	ngultrum	chetrum	1971			Dzongkha, Bumthangka	Khula Kangri (24,784')	47,000	18,147	2,185,569
Bolivia	-4	boliviano	centavos	1945			Spanish, Quechua, Amyara	Nevado Sajama (21,391')	1,098,581	424,163	8,724,156
Bosnia-Hercegovina	+1	marka	fening	1992			Bosnian	Bobotov Kuk (8,274')	51,129	19,741	4,007,608
Botswana	+2	pula	thebes	1966	1966		Setswana, English	Otse (4,886')	581,730	224,606	1,561,973
Brazil	-2--5	real	centavos	1945			Portuguese	Pico da Bandeira (9,482')	8,511,965	3,286,473	184,101,109
Brunei	+8	dollar	sen	1984	1984		Malay, English	Bukit Belalong (3,098')	5,765	2,226	365,251
Bulgaria	+2	lev	stotinki	1955			Bulgarian	Musala (9,596')	110,912	42,823	7,517,973
Burkina Faso	0	franc	centimes	1960			French, Mossi	Tema (2,457')	274,200	105,869	13,574,820
Burundi	+2	franc	centimes	1962			Rundi, French, Swahili	Muramvya (8,809')	27,834	10,747	6,231,221
Cambodia	+7	riel	sen	1955			Khmer, French	Ka-Kup (5,722')	181,035	69,898	13,363,421
Cameroon	+1	franc	centimes	1960	1995		French, English	Cameroon (13,350')	475,442	183,568	16,063,678
Canada	-4--8	dollar	cents	1945	1931		English, French	Logan (19,550')	9,976,185	3,851,809	32,507,874
Cape Verde	-1	escudo	centavos	1975			Portuguese, Crioulo	Pico do Cano (9,285')	4,033	1,557	415,294
Central African Rep	+1	franc	centimes	1960			French, Sangho	Gaou (4,659')	622,984	240,534	3,742,482

GEOGRAPHY

Country	GMT	Currency	Split into 100	UN Member	Common-wealth	Europe	Official Languages	Highest Point	Area Sq Km	Area Sq Miles	Population
Chad	+1	franc	centimes	1960			French, Arabic	Emi Koussi (11,204')	1,284,000	495,753	9,538,544
Chile	-3--5	peso	centavos	1945			Spanish	Ojos del Salado (22,588')	756,945	292,257	15,823,957
China	+8	yuan	fen	1945			Mandarin Chinese	Everest (29,035')	9,596,961	3,705,390	1,298,847,624
Colombia	-5	peso	centavos	1945			Spanish	Pico Cristobal Colon (18,947')	1,141,748	440,829	42,310,775
Comoros	+3	franc	centimes	1975			French, Arabic, Comoran	Kartala (7,746')	2,171	838	651,901
Congo, Dem Rep of	+1--2	franc	centimes	1960			French, Lingala, Kiswahili	Stanley (Ngaliema) (16,795')	2,345,409	905,563	58,317,930
Congo, Rep of	+1	franc	centimes	1960			French	Foungouti (3,412')	342,000	132,046	2,998,040
Costa Rica	-6	colon	centimos	1945			Spanish	Chirripo (12,533')	50,700	19,575	3,956,507
Croatia	+1	kuna	lipas	1993			Croatian	Velika Peak (7,200')	56,538	21,829	4,496,869
Cuba	-5	peso	centavos	1945			Spanish	Pico Turquino (6,467')	110,861	42,803	11,308,764
Cyprus	+2	pound	cents	1960	1961	2004	Greek, Turkish	Olympus (6,401')	9,251	3,572	775,927
Czech Republic	+1	koruna	haléru	1993		2004	Czech, Slovak	Snezka (5,256')	78,644	30,364	10,246,178
Denmark	+1	krone	ore	1945		1973	Danish	Yding Skovhoj (568')	43,069	16,629	5,413,392
Djibouti	+3	franc	centimes	1977			French, Arabic, Afar, Somali	Mousa (6,769')	22,000	8,494	466,900
Dominica	-4	East Caribbean $	cents	1978	1978		English	Imray's View (4,747')	748	289	69,278
Dominican Republic	-4	peso	centavos	1945			Spanish	Pico Duarte (10,417')	48,734	18,816	8,833,634
East Timor	+9	US dollar	cents				Portuguese	Tata Mailau (9,679')	14,874	5,743	1,019,252
Ecuador	-5	US dollar	cents	1945			Spanish	Chimborazo (20,561')	283,561	109,483	13,212,742
Egypt	+2	pound	piastres	1945			Arabic	Jebel Katherina (8,651')	1,001,449	386,660	76,117,421
El Salvador	-6	colon	centavos	1945			Spanish	Santa Ana (7,812')	21,041	8,124	6,587,541
Equatorial Guinea	+1	franc (was epkwele)	centimos	1968			Spanish	Moka (9,350')	28,051	10,831	523,051
Eritrea	+3	nafka	cents	1993			English, Arabic	Ramlo (7,235')	121,320	46,842	4,447,307
Estonia	+2	kroon	sent	1991		2004	Estonian	Munamagi (1,042')	45,125	17,423	1,341,664
Ethiopia	+3	birr	cents	1945			Amharic, Galla, Somali	Ras Dashen (15,158')	1,128,221	435,607	67,851,281
Fiji	+13	dollar	cents	1970 left 1987	1970		English, Fijian	Victoria (Tomaniivi) 4,341'	18,274	7,056	880,874
Finland	+2	euro	cents	1955		1995	Finnish, Swedish	Haltiatunturi (4,344')	338,000	130,502	5,214,512
France	+1	euro	cents	1945		1958	French	Blanc (15,771')	547,026	211,207	60,424,213
Gabon	+1	franc	centimes	1960			French, Fang, Eshira, Mbete	Iboundji (5,185')	267,667	103,346	1,355,246
Gambia	0	dalasi	butut	1965	1965		English	No land above 66'	11,295	4,361	1,546,848
Georgia	+4	lari	tetri	1992			Georgian, Russian, Armenian	Shkhara (16,627')	69,700	26,911	4,693,892
Germany	+1	euro	cents	1973		1958	German	Zugspitze (9,721')	357,050	137,857	82,424,609
Ghana	0	cedi	pesewas	1957	1957		English, Asante, Ewe, Fante	Afadjato (2,860')	238,537	92,099	20,757,032
Greece	+2	euro	cents	1945		1981	Greek	Olympus (9,550')	131,944	50,944	10,647,529
Greenland	-3	krone	ore				Greenlandic, Danish	Gunnbjorns Field (12,139)	2,175,600	840,000	56,384

Country	GMT	Currency	Split into 100	UN Member	Common-wealth	Europe	Official Languages	Highest Point	Area Sq Km	Area Sq Miles	Population
Grenada	-4	East Caribbean $	cents	1974	1974		English	St Catherine (2,756')	344	133	89,357
Guatemala	-6	quetzal	centavos	1945			Spanish	Tajumulco (13,881')	108,889	42,042	14,280,596
Guinea	0	franc	centimes	1958			French	Nimba (5,748')	245,857	94,925	9,246,462
Guinea-Bissau	0	franc	centimes	1974			Portuguese, Creole, Fulani	Fouta Djallon (600')	36,125	13,948	1,388,363
Guyana	-4	dollar	cents	1966	1966		English, Hindu, Urdu	Roraima (9,094')	214,969	83,000	705,803
Haiti	-5	gourde	centimes	1945			French, Creole	Pic La Selle (8,793')	27,750	10,714	7,656,166
Honduras	-6	lempira	centavos	1945			Spanish	Cerro Las Minas (9,400')	112,088	43,277	6,823,568
Hong Kong	+8	dollar	cents				Chinese, English	no named mountains	1,071	414	6,855,125
Hungary	+1	forint	filler	1955		2004	Magyar	Kekes (3,330')	93,030	35,919	10,032,375
Iceland	0	krona	aurar	1946			Icelandic	Hvannadalshnukur (6,952')	103,000	39,768	293,966
India	+5.5	rupee	paisa	1945	1947		Hindi, English	Nanda Devi (25,645')	3,287,590	1,269,340	1,065,070,607
Indonesia	+7-+9	rupiah	sen	1950			Bahasa Indonesia	Puncak Jaya (16,020')	1,904,569	735,355	238,452,952
Iran	+3.5	rial	dinars	1945			Farsi	Qolleh-ye Damavand (18,386')	1,648,000	636,293	69,018,924
Iraq	+3	dinar	fils-1000	1945			Arabic	Kurdistan Range (12,000')	434,924	167,924	25,374,691
Ireland	0	euro	cents	1955	left 1949	1973	Irish, English	Carrantuohill (3,414')	70,283	27,136	3,969,558
Israel	+2	Shekel	Agorot	1949			Hebrew, Arabic	Atzmon (Har Meron) 3,963'	20,770	8,019	6,199,008
Italy	+1	euro	cents	1955		1958	Italian	Blanc (15,616')	301,225	116,303	58,057,477
Ivory Coast	0	franc	centimes	1960			French	Toukui (6,900')	322,463	124,503	17,327,724
Jamaica	-5	dollar	cents	1962	1962		English	Blue Mountain Peak (7,402')	10,991	4,244	2,713,130
Japan	+9	yen	sen	1956			Japanese	Fuji (12,388')	369,792	142,777	127,333,002
Jordan	+2	dinar	fils-1,000	1955			Arabic	Jabal Ramm (5755')	97,740	37,737	5,611,202
Kazakhstan	+4-+6	tenge	tiyn	1992			Kazakh, Russian	Khan-Tengri Peak (5,000')	2,717,300	1,049,151	15,143,704
Kenya	+3	shilling	cents	1963	1963		Swahili, English, Kikuyu	Kenya (17,057')	582,646	224,960	32,021,856
Kiribati	+12-+13	Australian $	cents	1979	1979		English, Kiribati (Gilbertese)	Banaba Peak (265')	728	281	100,798
Korea, North (Chosun)	+9	won	chon	1991			Korean	Pektu San (9,003')	120,538	46,540	22,697,553
Korea, South	+9	won	jeon	1991			Korean	Halla-san (6,398')	98,477	38,022	48,598,175
Kuwait	+3	dinar	fils-1000	1963			Arabic	Ash-Shaqaya (951')	17,818	6,880	2,257,549
Kyrgyzstan	+5	som	tyiyn	1992			Kirghiz, Russian	Victory Peak (24,406') (Pik Pobedy)	198,500	76,641	5,081,429
Laos	+7	kip	at	1955			Lao, French	Phou Bia (9252')	231,800	89,498	6,068,117
Latvia	+2	lat	santims	1991		2004	Latvian	Vidzeme (Livonia) 1020'	63,935	24,685	2,306,306
Lebanon	+2	pound	piastres	1945			Arabic	Qurnat as-Sawda (10131')	10,400	4,015	3,777,218
Lesotho	+2	loti	lisente	1966	1966		Sesotho, English	Thabana Ntlenyana (11425')	30,355	11,720	1,865,040
Liberia	0	dollar	cents	1945			English	Peak of Mt Nimba (4500')	111,369	43,000	3,390,635
Libya	+1	dinar	dirhams-1000	1955			Arabic	Pico Bette (7500')	1,759,540	679,359	5,631,585
Liechtenstein	+1	Swiss franc	rappen/centimes	1990			German	Grauspitze (8526')	158	61	33,436
Lithuania	+2	litas	centas	1991		2004	Lithuanian	Juozapine (964')	65,200	25,174	3,607,899

GEOGRAPHY

Country	GMT	Currency	Split into 100	UN Member	Common-wealth	Europe	Official Languages	Highest Point	Area Sq Km	Area Sq Miles	Population
Luxembourg	+1	euro	cents	1945		1958	French, German, Letzeburgesch	Bourgplatz (1833')	2,586	998	462,690
Macedonia	+1	denar	denis	1993			Macedonian, Albanian	Kajmakcalan (8271')	25,713	9,928	2,071,210
Madagascar	+3	franc	centimes	1960			Malagasy, French	Maromokotro (9436')	587,041	226,657	17,501,871
Malawi	+2	kwacha	tambala	1964	1964		English, Chichewa	Mlanje Sapitwa (9843')	118,484	45,747	11,906,855
Malaysia	+8	ringgit	sen	1957	1957		Malay, Chinese, English	Kinabalu (13455')	329,749	127,316	23,522,482
Maldives	+5	rufiyaa	laaris	1965	1982		Divehi	no land above 8'	298	115	339,330
Mali	0	franc	centimes	1960			French, Bambara, Fulani	Hombori Tondo (3789')	1,240,000	478,764	11,956,788
Malta	+1	lira	cents	1964	1964	2004	Maltese, English, Italian	Sceberras (816')	246	95	396,851
Marshall Islands	+12	US dollar	cents	1991			Marshallese, English	no land above 20'	181	70	57,738
Mauritania	0	ouguiya	khoums—5	1961			Arabic, French, Hassaniya	Kediet Ijill (3,002')	1,030,700	397,954	2,998,563
Mauritius	+4	rupee	cents	1968	1968		English	Black River Mountain (2,711')	2,045	790	1,220,481
Mexico	-6/-8	peso	centavos	1945			Spanish	Orizaba (18,406')	1,972,547	761,601	104,959,594
Moldova	+2	leu	bani	1992			Moldovan, Russian	Balaneshty (1,409')	33,700	13,012	4,446,455
Monaco	+1	euro	cents	1992			French	On Chemin de Revoires (533')	1.9	0.73	32,270
Mongolia	+8	tugrik	möngö	1961			Khalkha Mongolian	Monh Hayrhan Uul (14,311')	1,565,000	604,247	2,751,314
Morocco	0	dirham	centimes	1956			Arabic, French, Berber	Jebel Toubkal (13,655')	446,550	172,413	33,209,101
Mozambique	+2	metical	centavos	1975	1995		Portuguese	Monte Binga (7,992')	801,590	309,494	18,811,731
Myanmar (Burma)	+6	kyat	pyas	1948			Burmese, English	Hkakado Razi (19,296')	676,552	261,217	42,720,196
Namibia	+2	Namibian $	cents	1990	1990		Afrikaans, English	Brandberg (8,461')	824,292	318,259	1,954,033
Nauru	+12	Australian $	cents	1968	1968		English	Nauru Peak (225')	21	8	12,809
Nepal	+5.75	rupee	paisa	1955			Nepali	Everest (29,035')	140,747	54,342	27,070,666
Netherlands	+1	euro	cents	1945		1958	Dutch	Vaalserberg (1,053')	40,844	15,770	16,318,199
New Zealand	+13	dollar	cents	1945	1931		English, Maori	Cook (12,349')	268,867	103,810	3,993,817
Nicaragua	-6	cordoba	centavos	1945			Spanish	Pico Mogoton (6,913')	130,000	50,193	5,359,759
Niger	+1	franc	centimes	1960			French, Hausa, Tuareg	Greboun (6,562')	1,267,000	489,189	11,360,538
Nigeria	+1	naira	kobo	1960	1960		English, Hausa, Ibo, Yoruba	Dimlang (6,700')	923,768	356,667	137,253,133
Norway	+1	krone	ore	1945			Norwegian	Galdhopiggen (8,098')	386,958	149,405	4,574,560
Oman	+4	rial omani	baizas—1000	1971			Arabic	Jabal ash Sham (10,400')	212,457	82,030	2,903,165
Pakistan	+5	rupee	paisa	1947	1947		Urdu	K2 (Godwin Austen) 28,250'	883,254	341,025	159,196,336
Panama	-5	balboa	centesimos	1945			Spanish	Chiriqui (11,467')	77,082	29,761	3,000,463
Papua New Guinea	+10	kina	toea	1975	1975		English, Pidgin, Moru	Wilhelm (15,400')	461,691	178,259	5,420,280
Paraguay	-3	guarani	céntimos	1945			Spanish, Guarani	Cerro Tatug (2,297')	406,752	157,047	6,191,368
Peru	-5	new sol	cents	1945			Spanish, Quechua	Huascaran (22,205')	1,285,216	496,222	27,544,305
Philippines	+8	peso	centavos	1945			Filipino, English	Apo (9,690')	300,000	115,830	86,241,697
Poland	+1	zloty	groszy	1945		2004	Polish	Rysy (8,199')	312,677	120,725	38,626,349
Portugal	0	euro	cents	1955		1986	Portuguese	Estrela (6,539')	88,880	34,317	10,524,145
Qatar	+3	riyal	dirhams	1971			Arabic	no named mountains	11,000	4,247	840,290

Country	GMT	Currency	Split into 100	UN Member	Common-wealth	Europe	Official Languages	Highest Point	Area Sq Km's	Area Sq Miles	Population
Romania	+2	leu	bani	1955			Romanian	Moldoveanu (8,346')	237,500	91,699	22,355,551
Russia	+2→+12	rouble	kopeks	1991			Russian	Elbrus (18,510')	17,075,400	6,592,819	143,782,338
Rwanda	+2	franc	centimes	1962			French, Kinyarwanda	Karisimbi (14,787')	26,338	10,169	7,954,013
St Kitts and Nevis	-4	East Caribbean $	cents	1983	1983		English	Liamuiga Nevis (3,792')	269	104	38,836
St Lucia	-4	East Caribbean $	cents	1979	1979		English	Gimie (3,145)	616	238	164,213
St Vincent	-4	East Caribbean $	cents	1980	1979		English	Soufrière (4,048')	388	150	117,193
Samoa	-11	tala	sene	1976	1970		Samoan, English	Mauga Silisili (6,094')	1,714	662	177,714
San Marino	+1	euro	cents	1992			Italian	Titano (2,424')	61	24	28,503
São Tomé	0	dobra	centavos	1975			Portuguese	Pico Gago Coutinho (6,640')	964	372	181,565
Saudi Arabia	+3	riyal	halalah	1945			Arabic	Jebel Razikh (12,002')	2,149,640	829,977	25,795,938
Senegal	0	franc	centimes	1960			French,Wolof, Fulani	Gounou (4,970')	196,192	75,750	10,852,147
Serbia and Montenegro	+1	dinar	paras	1945			Serbo Croat, Macedonian, Slovenic	Daravica (8,714')	102,350	39,517	10,825,900
Seychelles	+4	rupee	cents	1976	1976		Creole, English, French	Seychellois (2,992')	456	176	80,832
Sierra Leone	0	leone	cents	1961	1961		English, Krio, Mende	Bintimani (6,390')	71,740	27,699	5,883,889
Singapore	+8	dollar	cents	1965	1965		Malay, Chinese, Tamil, English	Bukit Timah (581')	639	247	4,353,893
Slovakia	+1	koruna	hallers	1993		2004	Slovak, Hungarian, Czech	Gerlachovsky (8,711')	49,035	18,932	5,423,567
Slovenia	+1	tolar	stotin	1993		2004	Slovene, Hungarian	Triglav (9,396')	20,251	7,819	2,011,473
Solomon Islands	+11	dollar	cents	1978	1978		English, Pidgin	Makarakombou (8,028')	28,446	10,983	523,617
Somalia	+3	shilling	cents	1960			Somali, Arabic, English	Surud Ad (7,894')	637,657	246,200	8,304,601
South Africa	+2	rand	cents	1945	1931		Afrikaans, English, Xhosa, Zulu	Injasuti (11,182')	1,221,031	471,441	42,718,530
Spain	+1	euro	cents	1955		1986	Spanish	Teide (12,190') Canaries	504,782	194,897	40,280,780
Sri Lanka	+6	rupee	cents	1955	1948		Sinhalese, Tamil	Pidurutalagala (8,292')	65,610	25,332	19,905,165
Sudan	+3	dinar	pounds-10	1956			Arabic	Kinyeti (10,456')	2,505,813	967,495	39,148,162
Suriname	-3	guilder/florin	cents	1975			Dutch, Hindustani, Sranang Tongo	Julianatop (4,218')	163265	63,037	436,935
Swaziland	+2	lilangeni	cents	1968	1968		English, Swazi	Emlembe (6,113')	17,363	6,704	1,169,241
Sweden	+1	krona	ore	1946		1995	Swedish, Finnish	Kebnekaise (6,965')	449,964	173,731	8,986,400
Switzerland	+1	Swiss franc	centimes/ rappen				German, French, Italian, Romansch	Dufourspitze (15,203')	41,293	15,943	7,450,867
Syria	+2	pound	piastres	1945			Arabic, Kurdish, Armenian	Jabal ash–Shaikh (Hermon) (9,232')	185,180	71,498	18,016,874
Taiwan	+8	dollar	cents				Mandarin Chinese	Yu Shan (Morrison) (13,113')	35,742	13,800	22,749,838
Tajikistan	+5	somoni	dirams	1992			Tajik, Uzbek, Russian	Communism Peak (24,590')	143,100	55,251	7,011,556
Tanzania	+3	shilling	cents	1964	1961		English, Kiswahili	Kilimanjaro (19,340')	945,087	364,898	36,588,225
Thailand	+7	baht	satang	1946			Thai	Doi Inthanon (8,452')	514,000	198,456	64,865,523

GEOGRAPHY

Country	GMT	Currency	Split into 100	UN Member	Common-wealth	Europe	Official Languages	Highest Point	Area Sq Km's	Area Sq Miles	Population
Togo	0	franc	centimes	1960			French, Ewe, Kabiye	Baumann (3,235') aka Agou	56,785	21,925	5,556,812
Tonga	+14	pa'anga	seniti	1970	1970		Tongan, English	Kao (3,380')	699	270	110,237
Trinidad and Tobago	-4	dollar	cents	1962	1962		English, Hindi, French, Spanish	Cerro Aripo (3,085')	4,828	1864	1,096,585
Tunisia	+1	dinar	millemes—1,000	1956			Arabic, French	Djebel Chambi (5,066')	164,150	63,378	9,974,722
Turkey	+2	lira	kurus	1945			Turkish	Buyuk Agridagi (Ararat) (17,011')	814,578	314,509	68,893,918
Turkmenistan	+5	manat	tenge	1992			Turkmenian, Russian, Uzbek	Koitendag Peak (11,293')	488,100	188,456	4,863,169
Tuvalu	+12	dollar	cents	1978	1978		Tuvaluan, English	no land above 15'	16	6	11,468
Uganda	+3	shilling	cents	1962	1962		English, Swahili, Luganda	Stanley (16,795')	236,036	91,134	26,404,543
Ukraine	+2	hryvna	kopiykas	1945			Ukrainian, Russian	Kamul (1,549')	603,700	233,089	47,732,079
United Arab Emirates	+4	dirham	fils	1971			Arabic	Western Al-Hajar (3,900')	83,600	32,278	2,523,915
United Kingdom	0	pound	pence	1945	1931	1973	English	Ben Nevis (4,406')	240,883	93,005	60,270,708
USA	-5/-10	dollar	cents	1945			English	McKinley (20,320')	9,158,960	3,536,278	293,027,571
Uruguay	-3	peso	centesimos	1945			Spanish	Cerro de Las Animas (1,643')	176,215	68,037	3,399,237
Uzbekistan	+5	sum	tiyin	1992			Uzbek, Russian, Tajik	Beshtor (14,104')	447,400	172,741	26,410,416
Vanuatu	11	vatu	centimes	1981	1980		Bislama, French, English	Tabwebesana (6,195')	12,190	4,707	202,609
Vatican City	+1	euro	cents				Italian, Latin, Polish	none	0.44	0.17	921
Venezuela	-4	bolivar	centimos	1945			Spanish	La Pico Columna (Bolivar) (16,427')	912,050	352,143	25,017,387
Vietnam	+7	dong (=10 Hao)	xu	1977			Vietnamese	Fan si Pan (10,308')	329,556	127,242	82,689,518
Yemen	+3	riyal	fils	1947			Arabic	Jabalan Nabi Shu'ayb (12,336')	527,969	203,849	20,024,867
Zambia	+2	kwacha	ngwee	1964	1964		English, Bemba, Nyanja	Muchinga (7,350')	752,614	290,585	10,462,436
Zimbabwe	+2	dollar	cents	1980	1980		English, Sindebele, Chishona	Inyangani (8,503')	390,580	150,803	12,671,860

NB: Of the 54 Commonwealth members, 16 have Queen Elizabeth II as head of state, 33 are republics and five have their own monarchies. Pakistan left the Commonwealth in 1972 but rejoined in 1989, but was suspended on 18 October 1999. Zimbabwe was suspended on 20 March 2002.

Country	International Car Registration	Drives	International Civil Aircraft Markings	Type of Government	Religion	National Day	IDD Codes from UK	IDD Codes to UK
Afghanistan	AFG	right	YA	democratic republic	Islam	19 Aug	0093	operator
Albania	AL	right	ZA	socialist republic	Islam	11 Jan	00355	0044
Algeria	DZ	right	7T	democratic republic	Islam	1 Nov	00213	0044
Andorra	AND	right	C3	unicameral co-principality	RC	8 Sept	00376	0044
Angola	ANG	right	D2	people's republic	none	11 Nov	00244	0044
Antigua and Barbuda			V2	constitutional monarchy	RC	1 Nov	001268	01144
Argentina	RA	right	LQ, and LV	federal republic	RC	25 May	0054	0044
Armenia	ARM	right	EK	federal state	none	21 Sept	00374	81044
Australia	AUS	left	VH	federal parliamentary state	none	26 Jan	0061	001144
Austria	A	right	OE	federal republic	none	26 Oct	0043	0044
Azerbaijan	AZ	right	4K	constitutional monarchy	Shia Muslim	28 May	00994	81044
Bahamas	BS	left	C6	constitutional monarchy	none	10 July	001242	01144
Bahrain	BRN	right	A9C	monarchy	Islam	16 Dec	00973	044
Bangladesh	BD	left	S2	people's republic	Islam	26 Mar	00880	0044
Barbados	BDS	left	8P	constitutional monarchy	none	30 Nov	001246	01144
Belarus	BY	right	EW	federal republic	RC	27 July	00375	81044
Belgium	B	right	OO	constitutional monarchy	RC	21 July	0032	0044
Belize	BH	right	V3	constitutional monarchy	none	21 Sept	00501	01144
Benin	DY	right	TY	people's republic	none	30 Nov	00229	01144
Bermuda			VP-B	British colony	none		001441	01144
Bhutan		left	A5	constitutional monarchy	Buddhism	17 Dec	00975	0044
Bolivia	BOL	right	CP	republic	RC	6 Aug	00591	0044
Bosnia-Hercegovina	BIH	right	T9	federal republic	Islam	1 Mar	00396	9944
Botswana	RB	left	A2	republic	none	30 Sept	00267	9944
Brazil	BR	right	PP, and PT	federal republic	RC	7 Sept	0055	0044
Brunei	BRU	left	V8	monarchy (sultanate)	Islam	23 Feb	00673	0144
Bulgaria	BG	right	LZ	socialist republic	none	3 Mar	00359	0044
Burkina Faso	XT	right	XT	military regime	none	11 Dec	00226	0044
Burundi	RU	right	9U	military regime	none	1 July	00257	9044
Cambodia	K	right	XU	people's republic	Buddhism	9 Nov	00855	0044
Cameroon	CAM	right	TJ	republic	none	20 May	00237	0044
Canada	CDN	right	C	federal parliamentary state	none	1 July	001	01144
Cape Verde	D4	right	D4	republic	RC	5 July	00238	044
Central African Rep	RCA	right	TL	republic	none	1 Dec	00236	0044
Chad	TCH		TT	republic	none	13 Apr	00235	0044
Chile	RCH	right	CC	military regime	RC	18 Sept	0056	0044
China	RC		B	republic	none	1 Oct	0086	0044
Colombia	CO	right	HK	republic	RC	20 July	0057	9044
Comoros	D6	right	D6	republic	Islam	6 July	00269	1044
Congo, Dem Rep of	CD	right	9Q	federal republic	RC	24 Nov	00243	0044
Congo, Rep of	RCB	right	TN	people's republic	RC	15 Aug	00242	0044

GEOGRAPHY

Country	International Car Registrations	Drives	International Civil A/C Markings	Type of government	Religion	National Day	IDD Codes from UK	IDD Codes to UK
Costa Rica	CR	right	TI	republic	RC	15 Sept	00506	0044
Croatia	HR	right	9A	republic	RC	30 May	00385	9944
Cuba	C	right	CU	socialist republic	none	1 Jan	0053	11944
Cyprus	CY	left	5B	republic (unicameral parliament)	Greek Orthodox	1 Oct	00357	0044
Czech Republic	CZ	right	OK	federal republic	RC	28 Oct	00420	0044
Denmark	DK	right	OY	constitutional monarchy	Evangelical Lutheran	5 June	0045	0044
Djibouti			J2	republic	none	27 June	00253	0044
Dominica	WD	left	J7	republic	none	3 Nov	001809	01144
Dominican Republic	DOM	right	HI	republic	none	27 Feb	001809	01144
East Timor		left	PK	republic	RC	20 May	0062	00144
Ecuador	RI	right	HC	republic	none	10 Aug	00593	0144
Egypt	EC	right	SU	republic	Islam	23 July	0020	0044
El Salvador	ET	right	YS	republic	none	15 Sept	00503	0044
Equatorial Guinea	ES	right	3C	republic	none	12 Oct	00240	1944
Eritrea	ER	right	E3	unicameral republic	Lutheran	24 May	00291	operator
Estonia	EST	right	ES	people's republic	none	24 Feb	00372	80044
Ethiopia	ETH	right	ET		none	28 May	00251	0044
Falkland Islands		left	VP-F		none		00500	0144
Fiji	FJI	left	DQ	republic	none	10 Oct	00679	0544
Finland	FIN	right	OH	republic	none	6 Dec	00358	99044
France	F	right	F	republic	none	14 July	0033	0044
Gabon	GAB	right	TR	republic	none	17 Aug	00241	0044
Gambia	WAG	right	C5	republic	none	18 Feb	00220	81044
Georgia	GE	right	4L	republic	none	26 May	00995	0044
Germany	D	right	D	republic	none	3 Oct	0049	0044
Ghana	GH	right	9G	republic	none	6 Mar	00233	0044
Gibraltar	GBZ	right	VR-G		none		00350	0044
Greece	GR	right	SX	republic	Eastern Orthodox	25 Mar	0030	0044
Greenland		right		constitutional monarchy (Denmark)	Evangelical Lutheran		00299	00944
Grenada	WG	left	J3	constitutional monarchy	none	7 Feb	001809	01144
Guatemala	GCA	right	TG	republic	none	15 Sept	00502	0044
Guinea	RG	right	3X	republic	none	2 Oct	00224	0044
Guinea-Bissau		right	J5	republic	none	24 Sept	00245	operator
Guyana	GUY	left	8R	republic	none	26 May	00592	00144
Haiti	RH	right	HH	republic	none	1 Jan	00509	operator
Honduras	HN	right	HR	republic	none	15 Sept	00504	0044
Hong Kong	HK	left	B-H	territory of China	none		00852	00144
Hungary	H	right	HA	people's republic	none	15 Mar, 20 Aug, 23 Oct	0036	0044
Iceland	IS	right	TF	republic	Evangelical Lutheran	17 June	00354	0044
India	IND	left	VT	republic	none	26 Jan	0091	0044

Country	International Car Registrations	Drives	International Civil A/C Markings	Type of government	Religion	National Day	IDD Codes from UK	IDD Codes to UK
Indonesia	RI	left	PK	republic	Monotheism	17 Aug	0062	00144
Iran	IR	right	EP	republic	Islam	11 Feb	0098	0044
Iraq	IRQ	right	YI	republic	Islam	17 July	00964	0044
Ireland	IRL	left	EI, and EJ	republic	none	17 Mar	00353	0044
Israel	IL	right	4X	republic	none		00972	0044
Italy	I	right	I	republic	none	2 June	0039	0044
Ivory Coast	CI	right	TU	republic	none	7 Dec	00225	0044
Jamaica	JA	left	6Y	constitutional monarchy	none	Aug 1st Mon	001879	01144
Japan	J	left	JA	constitutional monarchy	none	23 Dec	0081	00144
Jordan	HKJ	right	JY	Hashemite kingdom	Islam	25 May	00962	0044
Kazakhstan	KZ	right	UN	republic	Islam	16 Dec	007	81044
Kenya	EAK	left	5Y	republic	none	12 Dec	00254	00044
Kiribati			T3	republic	none	12 July	00686	0044
Korea, North	P	right	P	democratic people's republic	none	8 Sept	00850	01044
Korea, South	ROK	right	HL	republic	none	15 Aug	0082	00144
Kuwait	KWT	right	9K	constitutional monarchy	Islam	25 Feb	00965	0044
Kyrgyzstan	KS	right	EX	republic	Islam	31 Aug	00996	81044
Laos	LAO	right	RDPL	democratic people's republic	Islam	2 Dec	00856	operator
Latvia	LV	right	YL	republic	Lutheran	18 Nov	00371	81044
Lebanon	RL	right	OD	republic	none	22 Nov	00961	0044
Lesotho	LS	left	7P	constitutional monarchy	none	4 Oct	00266	0044
Liberia	LB	right	A8	republic	none	26 July	00231	0044
Libya	LAR	right	5A	socialist republic	Islam	1 Sept	00218	0044
Liechtenstein	FL	right	HB	principality	RC	15 Aug	0041	0044
Lithuania	LT	right	LY	republic	RC	16 Feb	00370	81044
Luxembourg	L	right	LX	grand duchy	none	23 June	00352	0044
Macedonia	MK	right	Z3	republic	none	18 Sept	00389	9944
Madagascar	RM	right	5R	democratic republic	none	26 June	00261	0044
Malawi	MW	left	7Q	republic	none	6 July	00265	10144
Malaysia	MAL	left	9M	constitutional monarchy	Islam	31 Aug	0060	0044
Maldives			8Q	republic	Islam	26 July	00960	0044
Mali	RMM	right	TZ	republic	none	22 Sept	00223	0044
Malta	M	left	9H	republic	RC	31 Mar	00356	0044
Marshall Islands			V7		none	21 Oct	00692	01244
Mauritania	RIM	right	5T	Islamic republic	Islam	28 Nov	00222	0044
Mauritius	MS	left	3B	constitutional monarchy	none	12 Mar	00230	0044
Mexico	MEX	right	XA, XB, XC	federal republic	none	16 Sept	0052	9844
Micronesia			V6	federal states	none		00691	01144
Moldova	MD	right	ER	republic	none	27 Aug	00373	81044
Monaco	MC	right	3A	principality	none	19 Nov	0037793	0044
Mongolia	MGL	right	JU	people's republic	none	11 July	00976	operator

GEOGRAPHY

Country	International Car Registrations	Drives	International Civil A/C Markings	Type of government	Religion	National Day	IDD Codes from UK	IDD Codes to UK
Morocco	MA	right	CN	kingdom	Islam	3 Mar	00212	0044
Mozambique	MOC	left	C9	people's republic	none	25 June	00258	0044
Myanmar (Burma)	BUR	right	XY, XZ	military regime	none	4 Jan	0095	044
Namibia	NAM	left	V5	federal state	none	21 Mar	00264	0944
Nauru	NAU	left	C2	republic	none	31 Jan	00674	0044
Nepal	NEP	left	9N	kingdom	Hinduism	18 Feb	00977	0044
Netherlands	NL	right	PH	kingdom	none	30 April	0031	0044
New Zealand	NZ	left	ZK	constitutional monarchy	none	6 Feb	0064	0044
Nicaragua	NIC	right	YN	republic	none	15 Sept	00505	0044
Niger	RN	right	5U	republic	none	18 Dec	00227	0044
Nigeria	WAN	right	5N	federal republic	none	1 Oct	00234	00944
Norway	N	right	LN	constitutional monarchy	Evangelical Lutheran	17 May	0047	09544
Oman	OM	right	A40	Sultanate	Islam	18 Nov	00968	0044
Pakistan	PK	left	AP	republic	Islam	23 Mar & 14 Aug	0092	0044
Panama	PA	right	HP	republic	none	3 Nov	00507	0044
Papua New Guinea	PNG	left	P2	constitutional monarchy	none	16 Sept	00675	0544
Paraguay	PY	right	ZP	republic	RC	15 May	00595	00244
Peru	PE	right	OB	republic	RC	28 July	0051	0044
Philippines	RP	right	RP	republic	RC	12 June	0063	0044
Poland	PL	right	SP	republic	none	3 May	0048	0044
Portugal	P	right	CS	republic	RC	10 June	00351	0044
Qatar	QA	right	A7	constitutional monarchy	Islam	3 Sept	00974	O44
Romania	RO	right	YR	republic	none	1 Dec	0040	0044
Russia	RUS	right	RA	federal republic	none	12 June	007	81044
Rwanda	RWA	right	9XR	republic	none	1 July	00250	0044
Samoa	WS	right	5W	constitutional monarchy	none	1 June	00685	144
San Marino	RSM	right	T7	serene republic	RC	3 Sept	00378	0044
São Tomé	STP	right	S9	republic	RC	12 July	00239	0044
Saudi Arabia	SA	right	HZ	kingdom	Islam	23 Sept	00966	0044
Senegal	SN	right	6V	republic	none	4 Apr	00221	0044
Serbia and Montenegro	YU	right	YU	socialist federal republic	none	27 Apr	00381	9944
Seychelles	SY	left	S7	republic	RC	5 June	00248	044
Sierra Leone	WAL	right	9L	republic	none	27 Apr	00232	044
Singapore	SGP	left	9V	republic	none	9 Aug	0065	00544
Slovakia	SK	right	OM	republic	RC	1 Jan	0042	0044
Slovenia	SLO	right	S5	republic	RC	25 June	00386	0044
Solomon Islands			H4	constitutional monarchy	RC	7 July	00677	0044
Somalia	SO	right	6O	democratic republic	Islam	tba	00252	operator
South Africa	ZA	left	ZS	republic	none	27 April	0027	0944
Spain	E	right	EC	kingdom	none	12 Oct	0034	0744

Country	International Car Registrations	Drives	International Civil A/C Markings	Type of government	Religion	National Day	IDD Codes from UK	IDD Codes to UK
Sri Lanka	CL	left	4R	democratic socialist republic	none	4 Feb	0094	0044
St Kitts and Nevis	SCN		V4	constitutional monarchy	none	19 Sept	001869	operator
St Lucia	WL	left	J6	constitutional monarchy	none	22 Feb	001758	044
St Vincent	WV	left	J8	constitutional monarchy	none	27 Oct	001809	0044
Sudan	SUD	right	ST	republic	none	1 Jan	00249	0044
Surinam	SME	left	PZ	republic	none	25 Nov	00597	00144
Swaziland	SD	left	3D	kingdom	none	6 Sept	00268	0044
Sweden	S	right	SE	constitutional monarchy	Lutheran	6 June	0046	00744
Switzerland	CH	right	HB	federal republic	none	1 Aug	0041	0044
Syria	SYR	right	YK	republic	none	17 Apr	00963	0044
Taiwan	RC	right	B	republic	none	10 Oct	00886	00244
Tajikistan	TJ		EY	republic	Islam	9 Sept	007	81044
Tanzania	EAT/EAZ	left	5H	republic	none	26 Apr	00255	0044
Thailand	T	left	HS	constitutional monarchy	Buddhism	5 Dec	0066	00144
Togo	TG	right	5V	republic	none	13 Jan	00228	0044
Tonga			A3	constitutional monarchy	none	4 June	00676	0044
Trinidad and Tobago	TT	left	9Y	republic	none	31 Aug	001868	01144
Tunisia	TN	right	TS	republic	Islam	20 Mar	00216	0044
Turkey	TR	right	TC	republic	none	29 Oct	0090	0044
Turkmenistan	TM	right	EZ	republic	Islam	27 Oct	00993	81044
Tuvalu		left	T2	constitutional monarchy	Protestant	1 Oct	00688	0044
Uganda	EAU	left	5X	republic	none	9 Oct	00256	0044
UK	GB	left	G	constitutional monarchy	None			
Ukraine	VA	right	UR	republic	RC	24 Aug	00380	81044
UAE	UAE	right	A6	federal monarchy	Islam	2 Dec	00971	0044
Uruguay	ROU	right	CX	republic	RC	25 Aug	00598	0044
USA	USA	right	N	federal republic	none	4 July	001	01144
Uzbekistan	UZ	right	UK	republic	Islam	1 Sept	007	81044
Vanuatu			YJ	republic	none	30 July	00678	0044
Vatican City	V	right	HV	state	RC	22 Oct	003966982	0044
Venezuela	YV	right	YV	republic	none	5 July	0058	0044
Vietnam	VN	right	VN	socialist republic	none	2 Sept	0084	0044
Yemen	YAR	right	7O	people's democratic republic	Islam	22 May	00967	0044
Zambia	Z	left	9J	republic	none	24 Oct	00260	0044
Zimbabwe	ZW	left	Z	republic	none	18 Apr	00263	11044

NB: Any gaps in the World Geographical Gazetteer or table above indicate information that has not been verifiable.

GEOGRAPHY

National Anthems

Country	National Anthem	Country	National Anthem
Afghanistan	Soroud-e-Melli First line: As long as the earth and heavens exist	**Gambia, The**	For The Gambia, Our Homeland
		Germany	Unity and Right and Freedom
Albania	The Flag that in Battle United Us	**Ghana**	God bless our Homeland, Ghana
Algeria	Qassaman First line: We swear by the lightning that destroys	**Greece**	Hymn to Freedom
		Guatemala	Happy Guatemala
		Guinea	People of Africa
Andorra	Great Charlemagne, My Father	**Guyana**	Dear land of Guyana
Angola	Angola Avante	**Haiti**	La Dessalinienne
Antigua and	Fair Antigua and Barbuda	**Honduras**	Your Flag is a Heavenly Light
Barbuda		**Hungary**	God Bless the Hungarians
Argentina	Hear, Oh Mortals, the Sacred Cry of Liberty	**Iceland**	O God of Our Country
		India	Jana-gana-mana
Australia	Advance Australia Fair	**Indonesia**	Indonesia, Our Native Land
Austria	Land of Mountains, Land on the River (from Mozart's 'Little Masonic Cantata')	**Iran**	Soorod-e Jomhoori-e Eslami
		Iraq	Salute of the Republic
		Ireland	The Soldier's Song
		Israel	The Hope (Hatikvah)
Bahamas	March on, Bahamaland	**Italy**	Inno di Mameli
Bangladesh	Amar Sonar Bangla First line: My golden Bengal, I love you	**Ivory Coast**	L'Abidjanaise
		Jamaica	First line: Jamaica, Land We Love
		Japan	Kimi ga yo Wa (May Your Peaceful Reign Last Long) First line: The reign of our emperor
Barbados	In Plenty and in Time of Need		
Belarus	Soviet anthem with words omitted		
Belgium	La Brabançonne	**Jordan**	Long Live the King
Belize	O Land of the Free	**Kenya**	Ee Mungu nguvu yetu (Oh God of all creation)
Benin	The New Dawn		
Bolivia	Oh Bolivia, Our Long-Felt Desires First line: Bolivians, propitious fate has crowned our hopes	**Kiribati**	Stand up, Kiribati
		Korea, North	Shine Bright O Dawn on This Land So Fair
Botswana	Fatshe Leno La Rona First line: Blessed be this noble land	**Korea, South**	Aegukka
		Laos	Xatlao tangtae dayma Lao First line: thook thuana nentxoo soo tehay (for the whole of time the Lao people glorified their Fatherland)
Brazil	From Peaceful Ypiranga's Banks		
Brunei	O God, Long Live Our Majesty the Sultan		
Bulgaria	Stara Planina's Peaks Proudly Rise	**Latvia**	God Bless Latvia
Burkina Faso	Against the Humiliating Bars, a Thousand Years Ago	**Lebanon**	We All Belong to the Homeland
		Lesotho	Lesotho fatsela bontat'a rona (Lesotho, land of our fathers)
Burundi	Dear Burundi, O Pleasant Land		
Cambodia	Nokoreach	**Liberia**	All Hail, Liberia, Hail
Cameroon	O Cameroon Thou Cradle of Our Forefathers	**Liechtenstein**	High on the Rhine
		Lithuania	Lietuva tevyne musu (Lithuania, Our land)
Canada	O Canada, Our Home and Native Land		
		Luxembourg	Our Homeland
Chile	Dulce Patria, Recibe Los Votos	**Macedonia**	Today over Macedonia
China	March of the Volunteers	**Madagascar**	Ry tanindrazanay Malala o (O beloved Fatherland)
Colombia	Oh Gloria Inmarcesible		
Croatia	Our Beautiful Homeland	**Malawi**	O God Bless our Land of Malawi
Cuba	To Battle, Men of Bayamo	**Malaysia**	Negara-Ku (My Country)
Cyprus	Ode to Freedom	**Maldives**	Qawmee Salaam
Czech	Where is my Motherland	**Mali**	A ton appel, Mali (at your call Mali)
Republic		**Malta**	L-Innu Malti
Denmark	King Christian Stood by the Lofty Mast	**Mauritius**	Glory to Thee, Motherland
		Mexico	Mexicans, the War Cry
Dominica	Isle of Beauty	**Monaco**	Hymne Monégasque
Dominican	Brave men of Quisqueya, Let Us Raise Our Song	**Morocco**	Hymn of the Sharif
Rep		**Mozambique**	Long Live Frelimo
East Timor	Patria Patria (Fatherland, fatherland)	**Myanmar**	We Shall Love Burma Evermore
Egypt	Biladi	**(Burma)**	
El Salvador	Let Us Proudly Hail the Fatherland	**Nepal**	May Glory Crown Our Illustrious Sovereign
Estonia	My Fatherland		
Ethiopia	Ityopya, Ityopya Kidemi	**Netherlands**	Wilhelmus van Nassaue
Fiji	God bless Fiji	**New Zealand**	God Defend New Zealand/God Save the Queen
Finland	Oi aamme Suomi (Our Land, Finland)		
		Nicaragua	Hail, Nicaragua
France	La Marseillaise	**Nigeria**	Arise, O Compatriots
Gabon	Uni dans la Concorde	**Norway**	Yes, We Love This Country

Country	National Anthem
Oman	God Save Our Sultan Said
Pakistan	Quami Tarana
Panama	Victory Is Ours at Last
Papua New Guinea	Arise, All You Sons of This Land
Paraguay	Paraguayans, Republic or Death
Peru	We Are Free, Let Us Remain So Forever
Philippines	Bayang Magiliw First line: Beloved land, pearl of the Orient
Poland	Poland Has Not Yet Been Destroyed
Portugal	A Portuguesa
Romania	Desteaptate, Romane, din somnul cel de moarte (wake up Romanians, from your deadly slumber)
Russia	Slavsya (Be Great)
Samoa	The Banner of Freedom
Saudi Arabia	Long Live Our Beloved King
Serbia and Montenegro	Oh Slavs, Our Ancestors' Words Still Live
Seychelles	Koste Seselwa (Seychelles Unite)
Sierra Leone	High We Exalt Thee, Realm of the Free
Singapore	Majulah Singapura
Slovak Republic	Storm over the Tatras
Slovenia	A Toast
Solomon Islands	God Bless our Solomon Islands
South Africa	The Call of South Africa, and God Bless South Africa
Spain	Marcha Real Española
Sri Lanka	Sri Lanka Matha, Apa Sri Lanka (Mother Sri Lanka, thy Sri Lanka)
St Kitts and Nevis	O Land of Beauty
St Lucia	Sons and Daughters of Saint Lucia

Country	National Anthem
St Vincent	St Vincent, Land So Beautiful
Sudan	We Are the Army of God
Swaziland	Ingoma Yesive
Sweden	Thou Ancient, Thou Freeborn
Switzerland	Step into the Rosy Dawn
Syria	Defenders of the Homeland, Greetings
Tanzania	God Bless Africa
Thailand	Pleng Chart
Togo	Terre de nos aieux (Land of our forefathers)
Tonga	Oh Almighty God Above
Trinidad and Tobago	Forged from the Love of Liberty
Tunisia	Humata Al Hima First line: Immortal and precious the blood we have shed
Turkey	The Independence March First line: Korkma Sünmez bu safaklarda yüzen al sancak (Be not afraid! Our flag will never fade)
Tuvalu	Tuvalu for the Almighty
Uganda	Oh, Uganda First line: Pearl of Africa
UK	God Save the Queen
Uruguay	Easterners, the Fatherland or Death
USA	The Star-Spangled Banner
Vanuatu	First line: Yumi, yumi, yumi i glat blong tale se, yumi, yumi, yumi i man blong Vanuatu (We, we, we are glad to tell, we, we we are the people of Vanuatu)
Venezuela	Glory to the Brave People
Vietnam	Soldiers of Vietnam, We Are Advancing
Zambia	Stand and Sing of Zambia, Proud and Free
Zimbabwe	Blessed be the Country of Zimbabwe

HISTORY

Chronicles of World History

AD 1   The accepted year of Jesus' birth as calculated by Dionysius Exiguus in AD 525. (The more probable date is now considered to be 4 or possibly 6 BC.)
The King of the Trinovantes tribe, in Southern England, Addedomarus, dies and is succeeded by Dubnovellaunus.

2   Lucius Caesar (the 1st grandson of Augustus) dies.

3   The future Roman Emperor Galba is born.

4   Gaius Caesar (2nd grandson of Augustus) dies leaving Tiberius, the Emperor's newly adopted grandson, as heir.

5   Romans defeat the Lombard tribes on the lower Elbe.

6   Chinese initiate 'Civil Service' examinations for prospective politicians.

7   Ovid works on his masterpiece, *Metamorphoses*.

8   Ovid is exiled to Tomis (now Constanta, in present-day Romania) by the Emperor Augustus for reasons unknown.

9   Germans under Arminius wipe out 3 Roman legions in the Teutoburg Forest. Titus Livius (Livy), from Padua, completes his 142-volume *History of Rome*.

10   Cunobelinus (Cymbeline) rules over most of southern England from his HQ at Camulodunum (Colchester).

12   Gaius Caesar (later nicknamed Caligula, meaning 'little boots') is born.

13   Tiberius is appointed his successor by Augustus.

14   Death of Augustus. His adopted son Agrippa Postumus is immediately executed, and Tiberius becomes emperor.

15   The law of 'Maiestas', making it a crime to harm the interests of Rome, and therefore of the Emperor, is brought back by Tiberius to ensure that his sovereign power is not undermined.

16   An attempt to overthrow Tiberius is thwarted when a slave of Agrippa Postumus, named Clemens, is killed.

17   The poet Ovid dies in exile. Livy dies in Patavium (Padua).

18   In China, the usurper Emperor Wang Mang's forces fail to subdue the rebel band known as the Red Eyebrows at Shandong.

19   Tiberius' nephew Germanicus is poisoned in Syria, possibly by Gnaeus Calpurnius Piso, the governor of Syria.

20   Piso commits suicide during his trial.

21   A revolt by the Gallic tribes, the Treveri and the Aedui, is put down by Gaius Silius.

22   Wang Mang is defeated and killed, during a revolt by followers of the Han regime.

23   Drusus, the son of Tiberius, is poisoned by Lucius Aelius Sejanus, commander of the Praetorian Guard.

24   Tacfarinas, king of the Numidians, is killed by the Romans after a 7-year revolt.

25   Tiberius retires to Capri on the advice of the increasingly dominating Sejanus. Buddha is represented in human form for the first time at Gandhara.

26   Pontius Pilate becomes the 5th Roman procurator of Judaea and Samaria.

27   Tiberius leaves Rome and settles on Capri.

29   Agrippina, widow of Germanicus, is arrested on the orders of Tiberius.

30   Jesus of Nazareth is crucified at Golgotha. Dionysius Exiguus, the inventor of the Christian calendar, wrongly dated the birth of Jesus according to the Roman system, i.e. 754 years after the founding of Rome.

31   Sejanus is executed by Tiberius when the extent of his plotting emerges.

32   In Rome, interest rates rocket as a result of a currency shortage. The Emperor Otho is born.

35   Tiberius makes Caligula and Tiberius Gemellus heirs to his private estate.

36   The future Emperor Nerva is born.

37   Tiberius dies at Misenum and is succeeded by Gaius Caesar (Caligula). The Emperor Nero is born.

38   Drusilla, beloved sister and consort of Caligula, dies, and is deified.

39   Caligula puts down a conspiracy by the governor of higher Germany, Gaetulicus.

40   King Ptolemy of Mauretania is assassinated by order of Caligula.

41   Caligula declares himself a god and is assassinated shortly afterwards. Claudius succeeds him.

42   Cunobelinus, ruler of most of Southern England, dies.

43   The Romans, on the orders of Claudius, invade Britain.

44   James becomes the first Christian apostle to be martyred.

45   The philosopher Philo dies.

46   The kingdom of Thrace becomes a province of Rome.

47   Messalina, wife of the Emperor Claudius, is acquiring a reputation as a sexual profligate.

48   Emperor Guang Wudi re-establishes Chinese domination of the people of inner Mongolia. Claudius has Messalina executed for infidelity.

49   Claudius expels Jewish Christians from Rome.

50   Claudius adopts his stepson Nero.

51   Caractacus, son of Cunobelinus, is captured by the Romans at Ludlow.

52   The future Emperor Domitian is born.

53   Nero marries his stepsister Octavia.

54   Claudius dies after eating poisoned mushrooms administered by the Empress Agrippina. Nero succeeds him.

55   Britannicus, son of Claudius, dies, possibly poisoned by Nero.

57	Paul is arrested at Caesarea and held for trial.
58	Paul writes an epistle to the Romans.
59	Nero has his mother, Agrippina, killed.
60	Mark, a disciple of Jesus, chronicles the life of his master, from baptism by his cousin, John, to his eventual death.
61	During a rebellion led by Queen Boudicca of the Iceni, the Trinovantes and Iceni tribes sack Roman Colchester, St Albans and London. Boudicca commits suicide after defeat by Suetonius Paulinus.
62	Paul is put under 'house arrest' in Rome.
63	The Armenian throne is returned to Tiridates after the peace of Rhandeia.
64	Paul of Tarsus is executed, as is Peter the apostle. Fire destroys over half of the city of Rome.
65	Nero's pregnant wife dies after being kicked by him.
66	The courtier Gaius Petronius is accused of treason and has to commit suicide.
67	The Jews rise up against the Romans.
68	Nero commits suicide to end the Julio-Claudian line of Roman Emperors. He is succeeded by Servius Sulpicius Galba.
69	The year of 4 Roman emperors, Galba, Vitellius, Otho and Vespasian.
70	Vespasian's son, Titus, sacks Jerusalem, destroying most of the 3rd Temple; only the 'Wailing Wall' is left standing.
71	The 'Arch of Titus', in celebration of the sacking of Jerusalem, is erected in Rome.
73	Chinese forces under General Ban Chao gain control over the 'Oasis' states. After a two-year siege, the fortress of Masada in Judea falls to the Romans.
74	Vespasian institutes 'Latin Rights' which give inhabitants of towns identical civil rights to 'Citizens' except for holding public office.
75	Vespasian completes his Temple of Peace in Rome.
76	Johanan Ben Zakkai re-establishes the Sanhedrin, the Jewish religious court.
77	Gnaeus Julius Agricola arrives in Britain to complete the conquest.
78	Vima Kadphises, the Kushan king, who rules India from Benares, sends a delegation to Rome to arrange a surprise attack on the Parthians.
79	Vesuvius erupts, destroying Pompeii and the neighbouring towns of Herculaneum and Stabiae. Pliny the Elder is one of the victims. Vespasian dies, and his son Titus succeeds him.
80	The apostle Luke begins to write his gospel. The Colosseum is opened in Rome.
81	Titus dies of the plague and is succeeded by his brother, Titus Flavius Domitianus (Domitian). Domitian consecrates the triumphal arch to celebrate Titus's victory over the Jews.
82	Spanish poet Marcus Valerius Martialis (Martial) begins his *Epigrams*.
83	Agricola defeats the Caledonians at Mount Graupius.
84	Agricola is called back to Rome.
85	Domitian appoints himself censor for life, thereby giving himself complete control of the composition of the Senate.
86	The future Emperor Antoninus is born.
87	The Romans suffer a serious setback in the Dacian War.
88	The revolt of Saturninus, governor of Upper Germany, leads to Domitian declaring that only one legion is to be quartered in each Roman camp, to prevent any local commander from gaining excessive influence over troops.
89	Domitian is forced to sign a peace treaty with the Dacian king, Decebalus.
90	Domitian begins the persecution and execution of opponents.
91	Chinese general Ban Chao defeats the Indian Kushans.
92	The Iazyges, a nomadic tribe, invade Dacia. Domitian leads his soldiers in person and succeeds in repelling them.
94	General Ban Chao completes his conquest of the Tarim basin.
95	Malaria appears in rural areas around Rome.
96	Emperor Domitian is stabbed to death by plotters led by his wife, Domitia. Senator Marcus Cocceius Nerva succeeds him.
97	Emperor Nerva recalls General Marcus Ulpius Trajanus (Trajan) from Upper Germany and adopts him.
98	Emperor Nerva dies, and is succeeded by Trajan.
99	Julius Frontinus, a former governor of Britain, surveys and describes the aqueducts of Rome in his capacity as superintendent of Rome's water supply.
100	The Sun and Moon pyramids are begun at Teotihuacán in Mexico.
101	Trajan invades Dacia (in present-day Romania), fearing the increasing dominance of Decebalus.
102	Sarmizegethusa, capital of Dacia, is taken by Trajan; Decebalus agrees to become a Roman ally.
104	Martial dies at Bibilis, in Spain.
105	Tsai Lun, a Chinese eunuch, invents a kind of paper made from tree bark, hemp and rags.
106	Dacia becomes a Roman province after King Decebalus and his chiefs commit suicide.
110	Pliny the Younger is appointed governor of Bithynia. Juvenal publishes his first book of *Satires* in Rome, highlighting corruption, vice and the unjust treatment of the poor.
114	Trajan's Column and Basilica are built. Armenia is annexed to the Roman Empire.
115	Mesopotamia is occupied by the Romans.
116	Assyria is annexed to the Roman Empire.
117	Trajan dies and is succeeded by Publius Aelius Hadrianus (Hadrian). Cornelius Tacitus, the celebrated historian, dies.
120	Construction of the Pantheon in Rome is begun.
122	Construction of Hadrian's Wall is begun.
123	Emperor Hadrian meets the king of Parthia, thus averting war.

125	Plague and famine in North Africa.
128	The Greek physician Galen is born.
132	The Jewish population of Jerusalem revolts over the construction of a shrine to Jupiter on the site of the Temple.
135	The Romans retake and demolish Jerusalem; Jewish leader Simon Bar-Kokhba killed near Caesarea; diaspora begins.
138	Hadrian dies and is succeeded by his recently adopted son Antonius Pius.
139	The Romans advance northwards under governor Quintus Lollius Urbicus from Hadrian's Wall to the Clyde–Forth line.
142	Construction of the Antonine Wall is begun.
154	Brigantian revolt in Pennines put down by governor Julius Verus, but troops withdrawn from Caledonia as a result.
155	Partial destruction by indigenous Picts of the Antonine Wall.
161	Antonius dies and is succeeded by his adopted son Marcus Annius Verus (Marcus Aurelius).
163	Antonine Wall abandoned.
167	Barbarians attack Rome, but are repelled by Marcus Aurelius. The Marcomanni and Quadi cross the Danube into Roman territory.
168	The Marcomanni, who have occupied North-western Italy, are conquered by Marcus Aurelius.
169	The Marcomanni revolt, but the revolt is crushed.
174	The Germanic Quadi tribe defeated by Marcus Aurelius.
175	Avidius Cassius encourages the legions in Asia to revolt, but is assassinated and his head sent to Marcus Aurelius.
177	Persecution of Christians recommences in Rome; they adopt the fish symbol as an emblem of their faith.
180	Marcus Aurelius dies and is succeeded by his son Commodus.
185	Mass mutiny of the Roman army in Britain eventually quelled by newly appointed governor Publius Helvius Pertinax.
192	Commodus murdered by his mistress and chamberlain, who found their names on an execution list.
193	Pertinax is chosen as emperor by the senate, but his strict rule leads to his assassination. Didius Julianus becomes emperor after an auction but has already been deposed and killed by the time that Septimius Severus, the Pannonian legate, invades Rome and is declared emperor.
197	Clodius Albinus, the British legate, revolts, but is defeated and killed by Severus at Lyons.
200	Japanese empress, Jingu, sends a fleet to invade Korea, which surrenders on sight of it.
205	Plotinus, founder of Neoplatonism, is born.
209	Roman legions under Severus and Caracalla march against the Caledonii, advancing as far as Aberdeen; forts built on Firths of Forth and Tay.
211	Septimus Severus dies at York; he is succeeded by his sons Caracalla and Geta.
212	Caracalla murders Geta and slaughters thousands of his brother's supporters. He extends Roman citizenship to all free inhabitants of the Empire by the Edict of Caracalla.
215	Manes, who develops the dualist philosophy known as Manichaeism, is born in southern Mesopotamia.
216	Britannia is divided into two provinces – Upper Britain (south and west) and Lower Britain (north).
217	Caracalla is murdered by his officers, and is succeeded by Macrinus.
218	Macrinus is defeated in battle near Antioch and executed. He is succeeded by Varius Avitus Bassianus, who takes the name Heliogabalus.
220	Fall of the Han Dynasty in China, which splits into a number of smaller states.
222	Heliogabalus is murdered by the Praetorian Guard. His cousin and adopted son Bassianus succeeds him, taking the name Severus Alexander.
225	Southern India breaks up into several kingdoms with the end of the Andgra dynasty.
226	The rebel prince Ardashir takes control of Persia, founding the Sassanid dynasty.
234	Severus Alexander decrees that bread, rather than grain, be given to Rome's poor.
235	The Alemanni invade Gaul, but are bought off by Severus Alexander. As a result, he is murdered by his army, who proclaim Maximinus as Emperor.
238	The African provinces set up Gordianus I, a descendant of Trajan, as Emperor. Gordianus commits suicide when his son is killed by supporters of Maximinus, but when Maximinus is assassinated by the Praetorian Guard, Gordianus' grandson, Gordianus III, becomes emperor.
244	Gordianus III defeats the Persians at Resaena, but soon after is murdered during a mutiny by Marcus Philippus, who replaces him and makes peace with the Persians.
248	Games are held to celebrate Rome's millennium.
249	Decius usurps the throne from Philippus, who is killed. The Goths cross the River Danube and lay waste several Roman provinces.
250	Decius initiates further persecution of Christians.
251	Decius dies in battle against the Goths; his successor Gallus bribes the Goths to return from whence they came.
253	Aemilian revolts against Gallus, who dies by the hand of his own troops. Aemilian dies and Valerianus becomes Emperor.
254	Origen, one of the leading Christian scholars, dies.
255	Plague sweeps across Europe.
257	The Goths move into the Black Sea area.
258	The Alemanni and Suevi invade Northern Italy, but are repulsed at Milan.
260	Valerianus seized by the Persians and dies in captivity; his son Gallienus succeeds him.
267	Prince Odenathus of Palmyra assassinated with Gallienus' complicity.
268	Gallienus murdered by his own troops at Milan. Claudius II becomes emperor.
269	The Goths invade the Balkans, sacking Athens, Sparta and Corinth, but are defeated in battle by Claudius II.

270	Claudius II dies. His brother Quintillus succeeds him, but commits suicide when his troops desert him. Aurelian becomes emperor.
271	Aurelian ejects the Alemanni from Italy, and rebuilds the walls of Rome.
272	Aurelian conquers the kingdom of Palmyra.
274	A rebellion at Châlons is put down by Aurelian, who returns to Rome in triumph.
275	The Romans pull back to the Danube and Rhine, which are established as the Empire's frontier. Aurelian is assassinated by his officers, and Tacitus succeeds him as emperor.
276	Tacitus killed by his own troops after defeating the Goths in Asia Minor. His brother Florianus succeeds, only to be killed also. Marcus Aurelius Probus becomes Emperor. Mani is crucified on the grounds of heresy.
282	The Franks and Alemanni invade Gaul, but are repulsed by Probus, who is killed by his troops in Egypt. Marcus Aurelius Carus replaces him.
283	Marcus Aurelius Carus dies, to be succeeded by his son Numerianus.
284	Numerianus is assassinated, to be replaced by Diocletian.
285	Diocletian partitions the Empire – he rules in the East, to counter the barbarian threat there, while Maximian is appointed to run the Western portion.
286	Carausius, commander of the Channel fleet, revolts and seizes Britain, where construction begins on a series of forts to guard the south-eastern coast (the Saxon Shore forts).
290	Construction begins on the amphitheatre in Verona.
291	Persian King Vahram II kills the Manichaean Sisih.
293	Carausius murdered by Allectus, his finance minister, who seizes power in Britain.
296	Allectus defeated and killed by Constantius Chlorus in battle near Silchester.
300	Diocletian builds a palace at Ragusa (later Dubrovnik).
301	Christianity proclaimed the state religion in Armenia.
303	The notary Genesius is martyred. Diocletian begins a general persecution of Christians.
304	The Kingdom of Cheng Han is founded in Sichuan.
305	Diocletian and his co-ruler Maximian abdicate and are succeeded by Galerius and Constantius Chlorus respectively.
306	Constantius Chlorus dies near York. His son Constantine is proclaimed Emperor, but Galerius raises Severus instead.
307	Severus dies; Galerius raises Licinius to co-Emperor.
308	Maxentius, son of Maximian, becomes despot in Rome.
311	Galerius attempts to expel Maxentius, but is defeated and dies soon after.
312	Constantine defeats Maxentius, his rival Western emperor, at the Milvian Bridge.
313	Christianity tolerated in the Roman Empire by the Edict of Milan.
316	The Xiongnu, later identified with the Huns, invade China.
323	Constantine and Licinius at war; Constantine victorious.
324	Licinius executed; Constantine becomes sole ruler. Christianity declared the official religion of the Roman Empire.
325	Council of Nicaea declares Christ and God are of the same substance – 'consubstantial'.
330	Constantinople (formerly Byzantium; known today as Istanbul) is dedicated as the new capital of the Roman Empire.
335	Church of the Holy Sepulchre consecrated in Jerusalem.
337	Constantine I dies, not long after taking Christian baptism; he is succeeded by his three sons, Constantine II, Constantius II and Constans.
338	Jewish calendar reformed by establishing variable year lengths.
340	Constantine II killed at Aquileia fighting Constans; Empire splits into East under Constantius II and West under Constans.
350	Constans murdered by General Magnentius in a coup.
352	Magnentius is defeated by Constantius II at Mursa in Mesopotamia.
353	Magnentius commits suicide. Constantius II reunites Empire.
356	All pagan temples in the Roman Empire ordered closed by Constantius II.
360	Lo-tsun founds the Caves of the Thousand Buddhas in Gansu, China. The Huns invade Europe for the first time.
361	Constantius II dies, and is succeeded by his pagan cousin Julian.
363	Julian dies in battle against the Persians; Jovian, captain of the Imperial Bodyguard, succeeds to the throne.
364	Jovian cedes Armenia to Shah Shapur II of Persia, and dies on his return. Valentinian I becomes emperor, and appoints his brother Valens to rule in the Eastern half.
367	Picts, Scots, Angles and Saxons invade Britain in a joint attack.
369	Theodosius, a Roman general, re-establishes order in Britain.
372	Buddhism reaches Korea from China.
375	Valentinian I dies. His 4-year-old son Valentinian II nominally succeeds him in the West but his older half-brother Gratian has effective control.
376	The Huns invade Russia and defeat the Visigoths. From now on, tribes pushed westward by the Huns press harder into the Roman Empire.
378	Visigoths defeat and kill the Emperor Valens at the battle of Adrianople.
379	Gratian's general, Theodosius becomes Emperor in the East.
382	Visigoths settled as Foederati (military allies) in the Balkans by Theodosius.
383	Magnus Maximus mutinies against Gratian, who is assassinated. Magnus rules in Britain, Gaul and Spain.
386	Hymn singing introduced by St Ambrose, Bishop of Milan.
388	Magnus Maximus invades Italy, to be defeated by Theodosius and murdered. Valentinian II established in power in the West.

391	The library at Alexandria is destroyed in a fire started by a Christian mob seeking to eradicate non-Christian works.
392	The Frankish general Arbogast organises the assassination of Valentinian II and replaces him with a puppet emperor, Eugenius.
394	Eugenius defeated and killed by Theodosius, who reunites the Empire. Arbogast commits suicide.
395	Theodosius dies, and the Roman Empire splits in two for good. His son Arcadius rules in the East, Honorius in the West.
396	Alaric the Visigoth invades Greece.
397	Stilicho, regent to Honorius, ejects the Visigoths from Greece and crushes a rebellion in North Africa.
401	The Visigoths invade Northern Italy.
402	Visigoths halted by Stilicho at the battle of Pollentia.
405	The Colosseum closed by Honorius.
406	Stilicho halts barbarian invasion of Italy. Vandals under Gunderic invade Gaul.
407	Roman troops depart Britain under the pretender Constantine III; Britain left to fend for itself.
408	Stilicho is murdered on Honorius' orders. Arcadius dies. His son Theodosius II becomes emperor in Constantinople.
409	The Vandals cross the Pyrenees and enter Spain.
410	Visigoths under Alaric sack Rome. Alaric dies shortly afterwards; his brother Ataulf takes command.
411	Constantine III defeated and executed by troops loyal to Honorius. Pelagius calls on St Augustine at Hippo but Augustine refuses to see him.
412	The Visigoths enter Gaul from Italy and establish a kingdom there.
415	Neoplatonist philosopher Hypatia is killed in Alexandria by a Christian mob who scraped her to death with oyster shells.
416	Vandal kingdom of Spain falls to the Visigoths.
418	Franks enter Gaul and settle.
420	Nanjing becomes the capital of northern China once more. Eastern Qin state in China is overthrown by its general Liu Yu, who founds the Liu Song state. St Jerome dies.
422	Theodosius II makes peace with Shah Varahran of Persia, and agrees an annual tribute with the Huns.
423	Death of Honorius, emperor of the West.
425	Constantinople University founded.
426	Yash Kukhmol arrives from Teotihuacán in Copán, founding a Mayan dynasty.
427	Korean capital moved to Pyongyang by King Changsu.
429	Vandals invade Africa, led by King Gaiseric. The British, led by Bishop Germanus, defeat barbarian invaders (the 'Alleluia Victory').
430	Cunedda, chief of the Gododdin, moves at the Welsh King Vortigern's behest from Scotland to Gwynedd, whose royal house he thereby founds.
431	Council of Ephesus deposes Patriarch Nestorius of Constantinople for his belief that Jesus had two natures, one human and one divine.
432	Saint Patrick sent as a missionary to Ireland.
433	Attila becomes co-ruler of the Huns.
439	Carthage taken by Gaiseric's Vandals, who make it their capital.
440	The town of Ys in Armorica (later Brittany) is submerged in a great flood. The Vandals invade Sicily.
441	Britain invaded by Angles, Saxons and Jutes.
443	The Alemanni settle in Alsace.
444	The wheelbarrow developed in China.
446	Britain told to fend for itself when it appeals to Rome for help against barbarian invaders.
450	Theodosius II dies, to be succeeded by Marcian, who refuses to continue paying tribute to the Huns to prevent them from attacking.
451	Huns defeated at battle of Châlons by Romans and Visigoths under Flavius Aetius.
452	Venice founded by refugees from the Huns.
453	Death of Attila on his wedding night.
455	The Vandals sack Rome.
457	Marcian dies, to be succeeded by Leo I.
460	Roman fleet destroyed by the Vandals off Cartagena.
461	Severus III becomes Western emperor.
466	Theodoric II of the Visigoths killed by his brother Euric, who succeeds him.
467	Anthemius elected Western emperor at Leo I's behest; they mount a joint expedition against the Vandals in North Africa.
468	The Vandals successfully repulse the Roman invasion.
471	Goths and Eastern Romans clash due to a feud caused by the failure of the expedition against the Vandals.
472	Ricimer the Visigoth captures Anthemius, and appoints Olybrius in his stead. Both Ricimer and Olybrius subsequently die; Gundobad the Burgundian takes control.
473	Gundobad names Glycerinus Western emperor, but he is deposed by Julius Nepos, a protégé of Leo I.
474	Leo I dies, to be succeeded by his son-in-law Zeno.
475	Orestes deposes Julius Nepos and makes his son Romulus Augustulus Western emperor.
476	Romulus Augustulus deposed by Odoacer at Ravenna; Western Roman Empire ends.
477	Sussex founded by Aelle, who lands with his sons at Selsey.
478	Shinto shrines appear in Japan.
481	At the age of 15, Clovis I succeeds his father Childeric I as king of the Franks.
484	Armenia revolts successfully against the Persians led by Vahan Mamikonian. Freedom of religious worship was restored to them by the Treaty of Nvarsag.

486	Clovis defeats governor Syragius at Soissons and takes control of Northern Gaul.
488	The Ostrogoths, led by Theodoric and prompted by Zeno, invade Italy, now ruled by Odoacer.
491	Zeno dies, to be succeeded by Anastasius, who marries his widow. The South Saxons under Aelle capture Pevensey Castle.
493	Odoacer surrenders to Theodoric at Ravenna after a siege, and is murdered by him. Theodoric founds the Ostrogoth kingdom of Italy.
495	Cerdic, founder of Wessex, lands near Southampton.
496	Clovis defeats the Alemanni near Strasbourg, and converts to Christianity, being baptised by Bishop Remigius of Rheims.
500	The Marcomanni invade Bavaria from Bohemia, which is settled by the Czechs. Incense is added to Christian services to cover the smell of unwashed worshippers.
502	King Gundobad of Burgundy issues a legal code that establishes equality before the law for Burgundians and Romans.
507	Clovis defeats the Visigoths, killing King Alaric II at Vouillé, near Poitiers, and goes on to conquer Southern Gaul.
508	The Ostrogoths under Theodoric conquer Provence and Septimania.
511	Death of Clovis. His kingdom of Francia is divided into four to provide kingdoms for his four sons.
516	The British comprehensively defeat the Saxons at Mons Badonicus.
517	Emperor Wudi introduces Buddhism to central China.
518	Emperor Anastasius I dies, to be succeeded by Justin I, chief of the imperial guard, who entrusts much imperial policy to his nephew Justinian.
519	Eastern and Western Churches reconciled.
520	Priscian codifies Latin grammar with his long treatise, the *Institutiones Grammaticae*.
522	The philosopher and statesman Boethius arrested on a charge of conspiring against Theodoric.
523	King Thrasamund of the Vandals dies and is succeeded by Hilderic.
524	Boethius writes *The Consolation of Philosophy* and is executed shortly after.
525	Yemen invaded by Abyssinians under Caleb. Dionysius Exiguus wrongly sets the date of Christ's birth as 25 December in the 753rd year of Rome.
526	Theodoric the Ostrogoth dies, and is succeeded by his 10-year-old grandson Athalaric.
527	Death of Justin I; his nephew Justinian succeeds him.
528	Hun King Grod converted to Christianity and was killed. The Korean state of Silla officially recognised Buddhism.
529	Benedict of Nursia founds the monastery of Monte Cassino. Justinian closes the non-Christian Academy at Athens.
530	The great Byzantine general Belisarius defeats the Persians at Dara. King Hilderic of the Vandals dies, to be succeeded by Gelimer.
531	Chosroes I becomes Shah of Persia. The Franks conquer Thuringia.
532	Burgundy invaded by the Franks.
533	Belisarius conquers the Vandal kingdom of North Africa, reclaiming it for Byzantium.
534	Toledo made capital of the Visigoth kingdom of Spain. Malta captured by the Byzantine army.
535	Belisarius invades and captures Sicily, and moves into Southern Italy.
536	Belisarius takes Rome from the Ostrogoths.
537	Arthur and Medrault fall at the battle of Camlann.
539	Witigis, leader of the Ostrogoths, is captured by Belisarius at Ravenna. Belisarius recalled to Constantinople.
540	Totila, an Ostrogoth leader, expels the Byzantines from Italy. The Roman statesman and author Cassiodorus founds the monastery at Vivarium in Calabria and retires there.
541	Totila succeeds to the Ostrogothic throne on the death of his uncle Hildebad. The bubonic 'Plague of Justinian' pandemic starts in Constantinople.
542	The Welsh monk Gildas writes *De Excidio et Conquestu Britanniae*, a history of the Roman conquest and Anglo-Saxon invasion of Britain.
543	Justinian condemns the writings of Origen.
546	Totila captures Rome. Audoin establishes a new Lombard kingdom in Austria.
547	The Plague of Justinian reaches Britain. The Angle king Ida accedes to the throne of Bernicia, in north-east England.
549	The last games are held in Rome.
550	The Toltecs overrun Teotihuacán. St David converts the Welsh.
551	The Byzantines defeat an Ostrogothic fleet in a naval battle.
552	Totila killed at Taginae fighting the Byzantines under Narses. Justinian sends missionaries to China to smuggle silkworms out. Buddhism arrives in Japan from Korea.
553	Rome and Naples annexed by Narses for Byzantium.
554	Narses appointed Exarch of Italy.
558	Reunification of Francia by Chlothar I after the death of his brother Childebert I.
559	The Bulgars attack Constantinople, but are repelled by Belisarius.
560	Aethelbert I becomes king of Kent. Ceawlin becomes king of Wessex.
561	Death of Chlothar I – Francia again split in four by his sons.
563	Foundation of monastery on Iona by Columcille (Saint Columba).
565	St Columba subdues a monster on Loch Ness. Belisarius dies. Justinian I dies, and is succeeded by his nephew Justin II.
567	With the death of Charibert, Francia reorganised into Austrasia in the east, Neustria in the west and Burgundy in the south.
568	Alboin founds a Lombard kingdom in Northern and Central Italy.

570	Muhammad born in Mecca. The Persians take the Yemen from the Abyssinians.
571	Foundation of the kingdom of East Anglia.
572	War breaks out between Persia and Byzantium.
573	Sigebert of Austrasia attacks Chilperic of Neustria over the murder of Galswintha, sister of Sigebert's wife Brunhilda.
574	Aidan ordained king of the Argyll Scots by St Columba.
575	King Sigebert assassinated on the orders of Chilperic's wife and former mistress Fredegunde; Brunhilda seeks revenge.
577	Celtic kings Coinmail, Condidan and Farinmail killed at the battle of Dyrham by West Saxons under Cuthwine and Ceawlin.
578	Death of Justin II, to be succeeded by Tiberius II.
579	Death of Shah Chosroes of Persia.
581	China's Sui dynasty founded by Emperor Wendi (Yang Jian).
582	Death of Tiberius II, to be succeeded by his son-in-law Maurice.
583	Wendi moves into the new city of Chang'an, soon to become the world's largest city.
584	Death of Chilperic of Neustria, who is succeeded by his son Chlothar II.
585	King Leovigild of the Visigoths puts down a revolt by his son Hermenegild, whom he kills, and proceeds to conquer the rest of the Iberian peninsula.
586	King Leovigild dies, leaving the Visigothic throne to his son Recared. Disputes in Japan between Shinto and Buddhist adherents.
587	The Visigoths convert from Arianism to Catholicism. The first Buddhist monastery is built in Japan.
588	Shah Hormizd of Persia deposed and murdered after defeats by Byzantines; replaced by his son Chosroes II.
589	Wendi defeats the Chen at Jian-Kang and reunites China. Chosroes II deposed in Persia, fleeing to Constantinople.
590	Gregory I the Great becomes Pope and undertakes reforms in Rome, as well as helping to expel the plague from the city.
591	Maurice helps restore Chosroes II to the Persian throne in return for territorial concessions.
592	Ceawlin of Wessex deposed by Ceol. The Bretwaldaship (overlordship) of the English peoples south of the Humber passes to Aethelbert of Kent.
593	The newly crowned Aethelfrith unites Bernicia and Deira to create the kingdom of Northumbria.
594	The 'Plague of Justinian' pandemic comes to an end. Gregory of Tours dies.
596	St Augustine dispatched by Pope Gregory to convert Britain.
597	Saint Augustine arrives in Kent, converts King Aethelbert and founds the archdiocese of Canterbury.
600	Tibet begins to develop into a unitary state.
602	Emperor Maurice killed and replaced by Phocas.
603	Battle of Catraeth (Catterick): Aethelfrith of Northumbria defeats a coalition of British from Lothian, North Wales and North West England.
604	The Japanese code of Prince Shotoku Taishi demands the veneration of Buddha, his priests and his laws.
606	Harsha of Thanesar founds an empire in Northern India, the last indigenous ruler to do so for several centuries.
607	Horyuji temple and hospital, the oldest surviving wooden building in the world, constructed in Japan.
609	Consecration of the Pantheon in Rome.
610	Emperor Phocas deposed and killed by Heraclius. Muhammad has a vision of the angel Gabriel on Mount Hira.
611	Death of Ceolwulf of Wessex, succeeded by Cynegils.
612	Harsha of Thanesar takes the title of Emperor of the Five Indies. St Gall founds the hermitage, later a monastery of St Gallen in Switzerland.
613	Francia reunited under Chlothar II after his conquest of Austrasia.
614	Chlothar II issues the *Edictum Chlotacharii*, which defines the rights of kings, nobles and Church within Francia.
615	Jerusalem sacked by the Persians, who take the 'True Cross' as booty.
616	Aethelbert of Kent dies; Raedwald of East Anglia becomes Bretwalda; he kills Aethelfrith of Northumbria at the River Idle, replacing him by the exiled Edwin.
618	Sui dynasty replaced by the Tang.
619	Publication of the *Suan-Ching*, textbooks for use in public examinations in China.
620	Chosroes II takes Rhodes, thus restoring the Persian Empire to the extent it reached under Darius I.
622	In July Muhammad flees from Mecca to Medina (the hegira, from which the Islamic calendar year 1 is dated).
623	Samo, a Frankish merchant, frees Slav tribes in Carinthia from Avar overlordship and becomes their ruler.
625	Death of Raedwald; Edwin of Northumbria becomes Bretwalda.
626	Chinese Emperor Gaozu abdicates in favour of his son Taizong.
627	The Byzantines decisively defeat the Persians at Nineveh.
628	Chosroes II murdered by his son Kavadh II, who succeeds him.
629	Chlothar II dies, to be succeeded by his son Dagobert I. Emperor Heraclius recovers Jerusalem from the Persians.
630	Mecca falls to Muhammad who writes letters on the principles of Islam to various rulers.
632	Death of Muhammad; Abu Bakr chosen as Caliph.
633	Edwin of Northumbria killed by Mercian/Welsh forces at Hatfield. They proceed to ravage the kingdom, which splits back in two.
634	Abu Bakr dies; Umar becomes Caliph. Oswald re-establishes the kingdom of Northumbria and becomes Bretwalda.

635	Islamic forces take Damascus, which becomes the capital of the Caliphate. Harsha invades the land of the Chalukyas, but is repulsed.
638	Jerusalem falls to Islamic forces under Umar.
639	Dagobert I of Francia dies; the kingdom is split again.
641	Great Library at Alexandria destroyed in a fire.
642	Oswald of Northumbria dies in battle at Maserfelth (near Oswestry) fighting King Penda of Mercia; he is succeeded in Bernicia by Oswy. Persia is conquered and made subject to the Caliphate.
644	Byzantine forces capture Alexandria, which revolted against Islamic rule, but the Arabs retake it. Caliph Umar dies, to be succeeded by Uthman.
646	The Taikwa reform in Japan establishes centralised government under Imperial control.
647	Harsha of Thanesar dies, and his Northern Indian empire fragments as a result.
649	Cyprus falls to Islamic forces.
650	The Bulgarian Empire, then in Southern Russia, conquered by the Khazars.
652	Arabs come to an agreement with the Nubians, establishing Aswan as the southern limit of the Caliphate in Egypt.
653	The Visigothic king Recesswinth of Spain draws up a legal code for his domains, the *Liber ludicorium*.
654	Penda of Mercia, Aethelhere of East Anglia and various other royals are killed in the battle of the River Winwaed by Oswy of Bernicia, who re-establishes Northumbria.
655	A Byzantine fleet led by Constans II defeated at Lycia by an Arab fleet.
656	Caliph Uthman is murdered in Medina. Muhammad's son-in-law Ali replaces him. Grimoald attempts to usurp the throne of Austrasia after the death of Clovis II.
657	Mercia released from Northumbrian rulership; Wulfhere son of Penda becomes king.
661	Ali deposed and murdered; the Umayyad dynasty, founded by Muawiya, assumes the Caliphate at Damascus.
664	The English Church adopts the Roman liturgy in preference to the Irish at the Synod of Whitby.
668	Emperor Constans II dies mysteriously in his bath at Syracuse.
669	Theodore of Tarsus ordained Archbishop of Canterbury, and proceeds to reform the English Church.
670	Death of Oswy of Northumbria, the last Bretwalda; his son Ecgfrith succeeds him.
671	The weapon Greek fire – an inflammable liquid that could be propelled through bronze tubes – invented by Kallinikos of Byzantium.
672	The see of Canterbury given authority over the church in England by the Synod of Hertford.
674	The Arabs penetrate as far as the Indus.
678	After several years' siege, the Arabs fail to take Constantinople and establish a 30-year peace with the Byzantine Empire.
680	Caliph Yaezid puts down a revolt by Hussain, son of Ali, who is killed.
682	Islamic forces overrun Tripoli, Carthage and Tangiers, expelling the Byzantines from North Africa.
685	Ecgfrith of Northumbria falls in battle against the Picts at Nechtanesmere; he is succeeded by Aldfrith.
687	Pepin II of Hérstal defeats his foes at Tertry and gains effective control of all of Francia. He and his successors rule as 'mayors of the palace', holding real power under figurehead Merovingian kings.
688	Caedwalla of Wessex resigns the kingship and goes on pilgrimage to Rome, succeeded by Ine.
689	Justinian II defeats Slavic forces in Thrace, and deports many of them to Anatolia.
690	Wihtred becomes King of Kent.
692	Brihtwold becomes the first native Archbishop of Canterbury; the Irish church accepts the authority of Rome at the Synod of Tara.
694	King Ine codifies the laws of Wessex.
695	Emperor Justinian II deposed by his officers, who cut off his nose and exile him; he is replaced by Leontius.
696	Paoluccio Anafesto is appointed the first doge of Venice.
697	Carthage destroyed by the Arabs.
698	Emperor Leontius deposed and replaced by Tiberius III.
700	The Agilofings, dukes of Bavaria, make Ratisbon their capital.
701	The Japanese emperor passes a law making him the sole proprietor of land in the country.
705	Justinian II restored as emperor.
709	Deaths of bishops Aldhelm of Sherborne, who converted Wessex, and St Wilfrid of Hexham.
710	Nara established as the capital of Japan.
711	Fall of the Visigothic kingdom in Spain to the invading Arab and Moorish forces after the defeat and death of King Roderick; only Asturias remains a Christian kingdom. Justinian II murdered by Philip Bardanes, who takes the throne as Philippicus.
712	The Arabs take Samarkand, where they discover the art of making paper, and Sind.
713	Emperor Philippicus deposed and replaced by Anastasius II.
714	Death of Pepin II in Francia. His son, Charles Martel, begins to unify the Frankish kingdom.
715	Winfrith, the future St Boniface, begins his missionary work among the Germans.
716	Emperor Anastasius II deposed; he is replaced by Theodosius III. Aethelbald becomes king of Mercia, succeeding Ceolred.
717	Theodosius III deposed by Leo III. The Arabs besiege Constantinople. Omar II becomes caliph and grants a tax exemption to true believers.
718	Constantinople fights off the Arab siege; Greek fire is spectacularly used to decimate the Arab fleet.
720	The Arabs conquer Sardinia and cross the Pyrenees, taking Narbonne.
722	St Boniface made the first bishop among the Germans.
725	The heathen Oak of Thor felled by St Boniface.
726	Ine of Wessex dies on pilgrimage in Rome; succeeded by Aethelheard.
730	Emperor Leo III excommunicated by Pope Gregory II over his iconoclastic policies, which forbid making images of Christ, the Virgin Mary or the saints.
731	Bede completes his *Ecclesiastical History of the English People*.

732	Charles Martel defeats the Arabs at the battle of Tours (or Poitiers), their furthest incursion into Europe.
735	Burgundy conquered by Charles Martel. The Venerable Bede dies.
737	Death of King Theuderic IV of Francia.
739	Bishoprics at Passau, Ratisbon and Salzburg founded by St Boniface. Charles Martel and his Lombard allies expel the Moors and Arabs from Provence.
741	Death of Charles Martel, who divides his mayoralty between his sons Carloman in Neustria and Pepin in Austrasia.
743	Childeric III becomes king of Francia after a six-year interregnum.
744	Swabia added to territory of Francia.
746	Constantine V retakes Cyprus from the Arabs. Carloman retires to a monastery, leaving Pepin as mayor of all of Francia.
748	The first printed newspaper published in what is now Beijing.
749	The Neighing Stallion sculpted out of fire-clay in China. As-saffah establishes Abbasid rule in Baghdad.
750	Umayyad Caliph Marwan II deposed and killed by the Abbasids, descended from the Prophet's uncle.
751	Childeric III, last Merovingian monarch, replaced as king by Pepin III the Short, who founds the Carolingian dynasty.
754	Pepin III assists Pope Stephen III against the Lombards.
756	Abd-al-Rahman establishes the Umayyad Emirate of Cordoba.
757	Offa succeeds Aethelbald as king of Mercia after the latter's murder.
758	King Edbriht of Northumbria abdicates to become a monk, succeeded by his son Osulf.
759	Narbonne retaken from the Moors by Frankish troops.
760	Turkish empire founded by a Tartar tribe in Armenia.
762	Caliph Mansur founds Baghdad as capital of the Abbasid Caliphate.
765	China invaded by a Tibetan army.
768	Pepin III dies; Francia is split between his sons Charles (later Charlemagne) and Carloman.
770	Death of the poet Tu Fu.
771	Carloman dies; kingdom reunited under Charlemagne.
772	Charlemagne invades and subdues Saxony.
773	Charlemagne invades and subdues Lombardy.
774	Charlemagne confims the Donation of Pepin, a grant of lands made by his father to Pope Stephen II in 757, which creates the Papal States.
775	Tibet and China confirm a boundary agreement.
776	Kent gains temporary independence from Mercia as a result of winning the battle of Otford.
778	Roland, Lord of the Breton Marches, killed by Basques at Roncesvalles as Charlemagne's army withdraws from a venture in Spain.
779	Offa defeats Cynewulf of Wessex near Benson and becomes de facto ruler of England.
780	On the death of her husband, Leo IV, the Empress Irene becomes Regent of the Byzantine Empire and restores Image Worship.
781	Nestorian Christians in China develop monasteries.
782	Charlemagne executes 4,500 Saxon hostages at Verdun and annexes Saxony.
783	Widukind leads a Saxon revolt against Frankish rule.
784	Work commences on Offa's Dyke.
785	Widukind submits to Charlemagne and is baptised.
786	Harun al-Rashid becomes Caliph, succeeding his brother al-Hadi.
787	First Viking raid on England, near Wareham.
788	Charlemagne annexes Bavaria, deposing Duke Tassilo.
789	Frankish ports closed to English merchants due to a dispute between Charlemagne and Offa.
790	Irish monks sail to Iceland in skin-frame vessels.
792	Offa has King Aethelbert of East Anglia beheaded, and annexes his kingdom.
793	Lindisfarne and Jarrow sacked by the Vikings.
794	The Japanese capital moves from Nara to Heian (later known as Kyoto).
795	First Viking attacks on Ireland.
796	Death of Offa brings his son Ecgfrith to the throne. He dies soon after, and Cenwulf succeeds him.
797	Empress Irene of Byzantium deposes and blinds her son Constantine VI.
798	Revolt in Kent against Mercian rule subdued by King Cenwulf, who blinds the Kentish royal leader Eadbert and cuts off his hands.
799	Charlemagne captures and destroys Fiume.
800	Charlemagne crowned Holy Roman Emperor on Christmas Day.
802	Empress Irene deposed by her finance minister Nicephorus; Egbert succeds Brihtric as king of Wessex.
803	The Bulgarians free themselves from Tartar overlordship.
804	Charlemagne finally defeats the Saxons.
805	The Japanese Buddhist priest Saicho brings tea to Japan.
807	Monastery founded by Cellach of Iona at Kells.
808	Foundation of Fez, in Morocco, as a tent colony.
809	Death of Harun al-Rashid, succeeded by his son al-Amin.
810	Musa al-Khwarazmi writes a book on equations, introducing the Hindu numerals now known as Arabic.
812	Byzantine Empire recognises Charlemagne as emperor in the West.
813	Al-Mamun murders and succeeds his brother Caliph al-Amin.
814	Death of Charlemagne. His son Louis the Pious succeeds him.
815	Cornwall conquered by Egbert of Wessex.
817	Louis the Pious partitions the Holy Roman Empire amongst his sons and makes Lothair, his eldest son, co-emperor.

821	Tibetan independence from China ratified by treaty at Chang'an.
825	Egbert of Wessex defeats Beornred of Mercia at Ellandun, near Swindon, and briefly controls all England.
826	Islamic pirates capture Crete and use it as a base for raids in the Aegean. Nominoë becomes Count of Brittany.
827	Sicily invaded by Arab forces.
829	Louis the Pious invests his son Charles the Bald with the dukedom of Swabia, upsetting the status quo.
830	The Great Moravian Empire founded by Prince Moimir.
831	Anskar is created bishop of Hamburg, with responsibility for converting Scandinavia.
832	Emperor Theophilus issues an edict banning the worship of images.
833	Louis the Pious defeated by his elder sons at Colmar and imprisoned.
834	Louis the Pious restored to his throne by loyalists; his eldest son Lothair retires to his Italian sub-kingdom.
838	The Arabs sack Marseilles and also cross to Southern Italy.
839	Egbert of Wessex dies, and is succeeded by his son Aethelwulf.
840	Death of Louis the Pious. The Holy Roman Empire splits into three, but the new emperor, Lothair, seeks to conquer his brothers' portions.
841	Lothair defeated by his brothers Louis the German and Charles the Bald at Fontenoy, thus frustrating his imperial plans. The Vikings found the city of Dublin in Ireland.
842	Emperor Theophilus dies, and is succeeded by his son Michael III. Under the regency of his mother, Theodora, image worship is restored.
843	Treaty of Verdun establishes the territories of the three remaining sons of Louis the Pious, thus dividing for good the lands of the Holy Roman Empire. Kenneth MacAlpin, king of Dalriada since 840, unites the Picts and Scots into a single kingdom (Alba), the forerunner of Scotland.
845	Buddhism suppressed in China by Emperor Wu Tsung.
846	Rome is attacked and badly damaged by Arab forces.
847	Al-Mutawakkil succeeds his brother al-Wathiq as caliph.
849	Birth of Alfred the Great of Wessex, at Wantage.
850	Rurik the Norseman becomes the ruler of Kiev.
851	The Vikings sack London and Canterbury, but are halted in their depredations by Aethelwulf of Wessex and his son Aethelbald at Aclea.
852	Muhammad I succeeds to the Emirate of Cordoba on the death of his father Abdul-Rahman II.
853	Kudawara Kudanari, the first major Japanese painter, dies.
855	Holy Roman Emperor Lothair I dies; his portion of the empire is divided amongst his three sons; Louis II succeeds his father as Emperor.
856	Aethelbald replaces Aethelwulf as king in Wessex, Kent, Surrey and Sussex. Vikings burn Paris.
857	Ergotism epidemics, caused by poisoned grain, begin to appear in Europe.
858	Death of Aethelwulf of Wessex. Aethelbald becomes sole king of Wessex but grants his brother Aethelbert an under-kingship.
859	Norse marauders enter the Mediterranean and cause havoc.
860	Aethelbald of Wessex dies, to be succeeded by his brother Aethelbert.
861	Cologne, Paris, Aix-la-Chapelle, Toulouse and Worms sacked by Viking raiders.
862	Novgorod, capital of Kiev Rus, founded by Rurik.
863	The Cyrillic alphabet is developed by Cyril and his brother Methodius in Moravia.
864	King Boris I of Bulgaria converts to Christianity.
865	Ivar the Boneless and his brother Halfdan arrive in England in an attempt to conquer the country. Aethelbert of Wessex dies; his brother Aethelred I succeeds him.
867	Basil I, the Macedonian, murders Michael III and becomes Byzantine emperor.
868	Ahmad ibn Tulun establishes the Tulunid dynasty in Egypt.
869	Malta captured by Islamic forces.
870	Martyrdom of King (later St) Edmund of East Anglia at the hands of the Vikings.
871	Vikings defeated by Wessex at Ashdown but victorious at Reading, Basing, Merton and Wilton. Alfred succeeds Aethelred I as king of Wessex.
874	The Vikings begin to colonise Iceland. Burgred, last independent English king of Mercia, forced to abdicate by the Vikings, who replace him with their puppet Ceolwulf II.
875	Holy Roman Emperor Louis II dies; his uncle Charles the Bald establishes himself as his successor.
876	Louis the German dies; his portion of the Holy Roman Empire is divided amongst his three sons.
877	Charles the Bald dies; he is succeeded as French king by his son Louis II the Stammerer. The imperial throne is left unfilled.
878	Alfred, after a period in hiding at Athelney, decisively defeats the Vikings at Edington, Wiltshire, and preserves Wessex as an English kingdom.
879	The treaty of Wedmore establishes the Danelaw in parts of England: Danish laws and customs will prevail there. Louis II dies; his sons Louis III and Carloman jointly succeed him.
880	Southern Italy reconquered from the Arabs by the Byzantine Emperor Basil.
881	Charles III, king of Swabia, crowned Holy Roman Emperor.
882	Louis III of France dies; his brother Carloman reigns alone. Kiev replaces Novgorod as capital of Kiev Rus under Oleg.
883	The Zenj rebellion of African slaves in Chaldea, which has lasted fourteen years, finally suppressed by al-Muwaffiq, brother of Caliph al-Mu'tamid.
884	Carloman of France dies while hunting. Emperor Charles III the Fat takes control, temporarily reuniting most of the Holy Roman Empire.
885	Ashot IV, Prince of Armenia, assumes the title King Ashot I.
886	Paris besieged by Vikings, who are paid off by Charles the Fat. London retaken by Alfred, who gives it and English Mercia to his son-in-law Aethelred.

887	Charles III deposed as emperor at Tribur; the Carolingian Empire falls apart.
888	Odo Count of Paris elected king of France; Berengar I of Friuli, grandson of Louis the Pious, becomes king of Italy. Rudolf I becomes king of a reformed Burgundy.
889	Donald II succeeds his cousin Eochaid as king of Scotland. Guido of Spoleto replaces Berengar I as king of Italy.
890	Alfred the Great establishes an English navy and militia. Harald I Finehair defeats his opponents at Hafursfjord and claims the sovereignty of Norway.
891	Guido of Spoleto crowned first non-Carolingian Holy Roman Emperor. Arnulf of Germany drives the Vikings from his country.
892	Caliph al-Mu'tamid dies; he is succeeded by his nephew al-Mu'tadid. The Vikings launch another invasion attempt on England.
893	The Vikings are decisively defeated by Alfred's son, Edward the Elder, at Farnham. Asser writes his life of Alfred.
894	Guido of Spoleto dies; his son Lambert succeeds him in Italy and as Emperor. Svatopluk I of Moravia, who has created the greater Moravian kingdom dies; his sons Moimir I and Svatopluk II jointly succeed him.
895	The Magyars, expelled from southern Russia, move under Arpad into Hungary.
896	By request of Pope Formosus, Arnulf of Germany replaces Lambert of Spoleto as Holy Roman Emperor, re-establishing Carolingian rule. Alfred defeats the Vikings at sea and ends their threat.
897	Pope Formosus' body is exhumed, dressed in papal vestments and tried for perjury; found guilty, it has three fingers cut off and is thrown into the Tiber.
898	Odo of France dies. The Carolingian pretender Charles III the Simple replaces him. Lambert of Spoleto dies and Berengar I reclaims the Italian crown.
899	Alfred the Great dies, and his son Edward succeeds him. Emperor Arnulf dies, and is succeeded in Germany by his son Louis III the Child.
900	Gunbjorn discovers Greenland. The Arab physician al-Razi identifies measles, smallpox, plague, consumption and rabies.
901	Louis III of Provence, grandson of Emperor Louis II, crowned Holy Roman Emperor. Edward the Elder takes the title 'King of the Angles and Saxons'.
902	With the fall of Taormina to the Arabs, Sicily is lost to Byzantium.
903	Pope Leo V is deposed after one month as Pontiff by Christopher, who lasts a year.
904	Leo of Tripoli commands an Arab fleet that sacks Thessalonica. The election of Pope Sergius III leads to a period of pornocracy in the Vatican.
905	Emperor Louis III surprised and blinded by insurgents, leading to his deposition from the imperial throne. Sancho I of Navarre succeeds his brother Fortun Garces and makes the county a kingdom. Shaiban succeeds his nephew Harun as king of Egypt, but is deposed shortly after; the Tulunid dynasty falls as a result.
906	Annam gains independence from China.
907	Fall of the Tang dynasty following conquest by Khitan Mongols. The Later Liang Dynasty under Taizu replaces it. The Magyars invade and destroy the Moravian empire of Moimir I, who perishes in the invasion.
909	The Fatimid dynasty is founded in Tunisia when al-Mahdi claims the caliphate.
910	The Byzantine Emperor Leo VI is forced to pay tribute to the Magyars. The kingdom of Asturias is renamed the kingdom of León its new capital. The Abbey of Cluny is founded.
911	Normandy established as a Norse province by the treaty of Saint-Clair-sur-Epte; Hrolf (Rollo) becomes duke. Louis III of Germany dies, the Carolingians die out and Conrad I of Franconia is elected king in his place.
912	Abdul-Rahman III succeeds his grandfather Abdullah as emir of Cordoba. The Byzantine Emperor Leo VI dies; his brother Alexander II succeeds him.
913	Emperor Alexander II dies; his nephew Constantine VII, still a child, succeeds him. Byzantium refuses to pay its tribute to Symeon of Bulgaria, who calls himself Emperor of the Romans but fails to take Constantinople.
914	With the death of Pope Lando, no Pope until John Paul I in 1978 will take a name that has not been used by a Pope before, starting with Lando's successor, John X.
915	Berengar I of Italy is crowned Holy Roman Emperor, the last Carolingian to hold the title.
916	Essex taken from the Vikings by king Edward the Elder.
917	Symeon of Bulgaria overruns Thrace and now controls the Balkans.
918	Deaths of Conrad I of Germany and Lady Aethelflaed of the Mercians. The latter acknowledge Edward the Elder as their king; he now controls all England south of the Humber.
919	Henry the Fowler, duke of Saxony, elected king of Germany. Ragnald the Viking seizes York, and makes himself king.
920	Edward the Elder acknowledged as overlord by the kings of Scotland, York and Strathclyde.
921	Sitric Caoch of Dublin succeeds Ragnald as king of York.
922	Charles III of France deposed by his barons, who elect Robert Capet, duke of Francia, king in his place; Charles raises an army to contest this.
923	Robert of France killed at the battle of Soissons, but Charles III is defeated and imprisoned; Duke Rudolf of Burgundy, Robert's son-in-law, is elected by the barons as king. Fall of the Later Liang dynasty in China, Li Cunxu of the Later Tang replacing Modi as emperor, taking the name Zhuengzong.
924	Edward the Elder of Wessex and England dies; his son Athelstan is hailed king in Mercia but Wessex disputes the succession. Symeon of Bulgaria unsuccessfully attacks Constantinople. Emperor Berengar, king of Italy, dies; the Imperial crown falls into abeyance.
925	Athelstan crowned king of England, having finally been accepted by Wessex. Henry the Fowler conquers Lorraine.
926	Symeon of Bulgaria defeated by Croat allies of the Byzantine Empire. Hugh of Arles becomes king of Italy after Rudolf II of Burgundy resigns the throne.

927	Symeon of Bulgaria dies. His son Peter succeeds him and signs a peace treaty with the Byzantines. Sitric of York dies. He is succeeded by his brother Guthfrith who is forced to flee when Athelstan conquers York and Southern Northumbria. The kings of Scotland and Strathclyde acknowledge Athelstan as their overlord.
928	Cornwall subdued by Athelstan, who sets the River Tamar as its boundary.
929	Duke Wenceslas of Bohemia murdered by non-Christians led by his brother Boleslav I, who succeeds him. Charles III of France dies, leaving Rudolf II as sole king. Emir Abdul-Rahman III of Corboba proclaims himself caliph.
930	The Black Stone stolen from the Kaaba in Mecca by the Carmathians, a Muslim sect.
931	Rameiro II succeeds his brother Alfonso IV as king of León.
932	William Longsword succeeds his father Rollo as duke of Normandy.
933	Henry the Fowler defeats Magyar raiders at the battle of Merseburg.
934	Scotland invaded by Athelstan, whose fleet ravages the coast as far as Caithness.
936	Louis IV (d'Outremer) returns from exile in England to be king of France after the death of Duke Rudolf of Burgundy. Henry the Fowler dies, and is succeeded by his son Otto I. The Tang dynasty falls in China; Shi Jing-tang of the Later Jin replaces Feidi as emperor, taking the name Gaozu.
937	Athelstan defeats a coalition of his foes at Brunanburh (whereabouts unknown), cementing his power in Britain. King Rudolf of Burgundy dies, his son Conrad succeeding him.
938	Yenching (later Peking and Beijing) founded as a Khitan capital.
939	Athelstan dies, and is succeeded by his half-brother Edmund (the Elder). Olaf Guthricson retakes York for the Vikings. Otto I defeats Eberhard of Franconia and his ducal allies at Andernach, confirming his monarchical authority in Germany.
940	Olaf of York invades the Midlands. By the treaty of Leicester much of the old Danelaw is ceded to him.
941	Igor of Kiev attacks Constantinople by way of the River Dnieper and the Black Sea, but his fleet is destroyed by Greek fire. Olaf of York dies; his cousin Olaf Sitricsson succeeds him.
942	Richard the Old succeeds his father William Longsword as duke of Normandy after the latter's murder by Arnold I of Flanders. The Five Boroughs of Derby, Leicester, Lincoln, Nottingham and Stamford are recovered by Edmund the Elder. Erik Bloodaxe succeeds his father Harald I Finehair as king of Norway on the latter's abdication at the age of 80.
943	Constantine I of Scotland abdicates and retires to a monastery, his son Malcolm I succeeds him. Byzantine troops recover the Mandylion.
944	Edmund the Elder recovers York, expelling Ragnald Guthricson, who had usurped the throne from his cousin Olaf the previous year.
945	Igor of Kiev dies; he is succeeded by his wife Olga. Mozambique attacked by Indonesians. Imad ibn-Buwayhid conquers Baghdad, keeping Caliph al-Mustaqfi as a figurehead. Louis IV taken prisoner by Hugh the Great, duke of France.
946	Caliph al-Mustaqfi deposed and blinded by the Buwayhids; his cousin al-Muti replaces him. Edmund the Elder and Otto I act in support of Louis IV, who is freed. Edmund the Elder assassinated at Pucklechurch; his brother Eadred succeeds him.
947	Eric Bloodaxe deposed as king of Norway by his brother Haakon I due to his violence. He flees to England where Wulfstan of York makes him king of that city. Hugh of Arles dies; his son Lothair of Arles succeeds him as king of Italy. The Later Jin dynasty falls in China, Emperor Chudi being replaced by Gaozu of the Later Han.
948	Eadred ravages Northumbria in response to their crowning of Eric Bloodaxe, who is forced to flee.
949	Olaf Sitricsson is invited to return as king of York.
950	Hywel Dda, prince of Deheubarth and Gwynedd and creator of a Welsh law code, dies; Gwynedd and Deheubarth separate. Mixcoatl, Toltec emperor, is assassinated and deified as a result; Lothair of Arles dies; Italy ruled jointly by Berengar II of Ivrea and his son Adalbert.
951	The Later Han dynasty falls in China; Emperor Yindi is replaced by Guo Wei of the Later Zhou, who takes the name Taizu.
952	Eric Bloodaxe returns to York and resumes the kingship.
954	Louis IV of France dies; his son Lothair succeeds him. Eric Bloodaxe forced to flee from York and is killed soon after; Eadred now rules all England.
955	Otto I decisively defeats the Magyars at the battle of Lechfeld. Eadred of England dies; his nephew Eadwig succeeds him.
956	St Dunstan, abbot of Glastonbury, exiled from England after a quarrel with King Eadwig.
957	Mercia and Northumbria rebel against Eadwig and choose his younger brother Edgar as their king.
959	Eadwig of Wessex dies; his brother Edgar the Peaceable succeeds him and reunites the kingdom of England. Emperor Constantine VII dies, his son Romanus II succeeds him.
960	Northern Song dynasty established by Zhao Kuangyin, who takes the name Taizu, replacing Gongdi of the Later Zhou. The kingdom of Poland created by King Mieszko I, who founds the Piast dynasty.
961	A Byzantine fleet commanded by Nicephorus Phocas recaptures Crete from the Arabs. Caliph Abdul-Rahman III of Corboba dies; his son al-Hakam II succeeds him.
962	Otto I of Germany is crowned Holy Roman Emperor, re-establishing that title.
963	The Byzantine Emperor Romanus II is poisoned by his wife Theophano, who marries Nicephorus Phocas, elevating him to the imperial crown.
965	Cyprus recaptured from the Arabs by Byzantine forces. Al-Mutannabi, the Arab poet, is murdered by bandits.
966	Sancho I of León dies; he is succeeded by his son Ramiro III. King Dub of Scotland dies; he is succeeded by his third cousin Culen.
967	Duke Boleslav I of Bohemia dies; he is succeeded by his son Boleslav II.
968	Dinh Tien-Hoang De becomes king of North Vietnam, founding the Dinh dynasty.

969   Byzantine Emperor Nicephorus II Phocas murdered by his wife's lover, John Tzimisces, who rules in his stead. Cairo founded by the Fatimids, who have conquered Egypt.

970   Garcia II of Navarre dies, and is succeeded by his son Sancho II.

971   Culen of Scotland dies; he is succeeded by his third cousin Kenneth II. St Swithin reinterred inside Winchester Cathedral; 40 days of rain follow.

972   Boris II of Bulgaria forced to abdicate by the invading Byzantines, ending the Krum dynasty's reign in that country.

973   Holy Roman Emperor Otto I dies; he is succeeded by his son Otto II. Edgar of England crowned king at Bath.

975   Edgar dies, and is succeeded by his son Edward. Modern arithmetical notation introduced into Europe by the Arabs.

976   Byzantine Emperor John I Tzimisces dies; succeeded by Basil II, son of Romanus II. Leopold I of the house of Babenberg made Margrave of Austria. Caliph al-Hakam II of Cordoba dies; his son Hisham II succeeds him. Samuel makes himself Tsar of Bulgaria. Duke Henry the Quarrelsome of Bavaria deposed by Otto II.

978   Edward (the Martyr) assassinated at Corfe and succeeded by his half-brother Aethelred II (Unraed). Mohammad ibn abi-Amir al-Mansur, regent of Cordoba, takes effective control of the Caliphate there.

979   Dinh Tien-Hoang De of Dai Vet (Vietnam) dies; succeeded by his son Dinh De-Toan.

980   Le Dai-Hanh Hoang-De usurps the Dai Vet throne from Dinh De-Toan, establishing the Earlier Le Dynasty. Vladimir of Novgorod seizes Kiev from his brother Yaropolk I.

981   León made tributary to the Caliphate of Cordoba. Italy invaded by Arabs; Otto II marches against them but the Byzantines offer them support.

982   Otto II defeated by a combination of Byzantine and Arab forces at Basientello. Eric the Red settles in Greenland.

983   Emperor Otto II dies, his three-year-old son Otto III succeeds him.

984   Henry the Quarrelsome seizes Otto III in an attempt to make himself regent, but is thwarted by Otto II's widow Theophano of Byzantium.

985   Henry the Quarrelsome returned to the dukedom of Bavaria. Harald I Bluetooth of Denmark dies, and is succeeded by his son Sweyn I Forkbeard. Otto-William, a Carolingian prince, establishes the county of Burgundy.

986   Lothair of France dies, he is succeeded by his son Louis V. Sultan Sabuk-Tigan of Ghazni invades India. Bjarni Herjolfsson sights the coast of Labrador.

987   Louis V dies; the Carolingians are replaced as kings of France by the Capetians, when Hugh I is crowned King.

988   Vladimir of Kiev converts to Christianity, marries Anne, sister of Emperor Basil II, and sets about converting his subjects.

989   Emperor Basil II, with the aid of Russian troops, defeats Anatolian insurgents led by Bardas Phocas.

990   William IV of Aquitaine dies; succeeded by his son William V. Ghanaian forces take Awdaghost and establish the king of Ghana as the most powerful ruler in non-Islamic Africa.

991   Norsemen raid England led by Olaf Tryggvesson, defeating English forces under Ealdorman Byrhtnoth at Maldon; they are paid to leave by Danegeld.

992   Mieszko I of Poland dies, and is succeeded by his son Boleslav I the Brave, who invades Pomerania to gain access to the Baltic.

993   Khitan Mongols annex Korea .

994   Sweyn of Denmark, assisted by Olaf Tryggvesson, raids England, unsuccessfully besieges London and is paid off by Aethelred II. Olaf Tryggvesson converts to Christianity.

995   Syria retaken by the Byzantine Empire. Olaf Tryggvesson succeeds to the throne of Norway, and forcibly attempts to convert his subjects to Christianity.

996   Otto III crowned Holy Roman Emperor by his cousin Pope Gregory V. Hugh I of France dies, and is succeeded by his son Robert II. Richard I the Old, Duke of Normandy dies; succeeded by his son Richard II the Good. Emperor Basil II defeats the Bulgarians and recovers Greece.

997   Duke Geza of Hungary dies; succeeded by his son Stephen I. Sultan Sabuk-Tagin of Ghazni, in modern Afghanistan, dies; succeeded by his son Ismail.

998   Sultan Ismail of Ghazni dies; succeeded by his brother Mahmud.

999   Boleslav I of Poland conquers Silesia. Gerbert of Aurillac becomes Pope, taking the name Sylvester II; he is the first French Pope. Brian Boru conquers Dublin from the Norse settlers.

1000   Ceylon conquered by King Rajaraja of the Cholas. Stephen I of Hungary becomes king with Papal approval. Olaf Tryggvesson commits suicide after his defeat by the kings of Denmark and Sweden at the naval battle of Svolder; Erik Jarl of Lade replaces him as king of Norway.

1002   Emperor Otto III dies of malaria; succeeded by his cousin Henry II. Al-Mansur, chief minister of Cordoba dies, the Caliphate begins to decline. Aethelred II marries Emma, sister of Richard II of Normandy, and orders the massacre of Danish settlers in southern England.

1003   King Sweyn of Denmark raids England in revenge for the massacre of his countrymen, exacting tribute from Aethelred.

1004   China pays tribute to the Khitan Mongols as the result of a peace treaty. Emperor Henry II defeats Ardoin of Lombardy and is crowned king of that country.

1005   Kenneth III of Scotland is killed in battle against his cousin Malcolm II, who succeeds him.

1006   Islamic settlers arrive in north-western India. Mount Metrop erupts in Java, killing King Dharmawangs.

1007   Danegeld of £36,000 paid by Aethelred II to protect England from raids for two years.

1008   Sultan Mahmud of Ghazni defeats Hindu forces at Peshawar and expands his realms.

1009   Caliph al-Hakim of Egypt sacks the Church of the Holy Sepulchre in Jerusalem. Caliph Hisham II of Cordoba deposed by his cousin Muhammad II, who is deposed in his turn by his cousin Suleiman.

1010   The 'Peace of God' established in France by Robert II. Danish forces under Thorkell the Tall defeat the East

Anglians at Ringmere. Muhammad II regains the caliphate of Cordoba from Suleiman, but is ousted again, this time by a returning Hisham II.

1011	Canterbury taken by the Danes, who capture Archbishop Alphege.
1012	Danegeld of £48,000 paid to the Danes, who nevertheless kill Alphege before they leave. Thorkell the Tall defects to the English. Persecution of heretics in Germany commences.
1013	Sweyn Forkbeard conquers England, helped by Thorkell, who redefects. Aethelred II flees to Normandy. Hisham II of Cordoba dies, and is succeeded by Suleiman.
1014	Sweyn dies, and Aethelred returns from exile. Brian Boru wins the battle of Clontarf but is killed. Emperor Basil II seizes Western Bulgaria and blinds the resisting native army.
1015	Olaf II succeeds Eric as king of Norway and establishes its independence from Denmark. Cnut invades England and Wessex submits to him.
1016	Aethelred II dies, succession disputed between his son Edmund Ironside and Cnut. Cnut wins the battle of Ashingdon; Edmund allowed to reign in Wessex but dies shortly afterwards.
1017	Cnut divides England into four earldoms, Wessex, East Anglia, Mercia and Northumbria, for administrative purposes.
1018	The treaty of Bautzen ends the war between Germany and Poland. Macedonia regained by the Byzantines after the submission of the Bulgarians.
1019	Yaroslav I the Wise succeeds his brother Sviatopolk I as prince of Kiev. Cnut becomes king of Denmark on the death of his brother Harald II.
1020	Corsica annexed by Pisa. Faroes, Shetlands and Orkneys recognise Olaf II of Norway as king. Godwin becomes earl of Wessex.
1021	Emperor Basil II invades Armenia. An epidemic of St Vitus' Dance sweeps Europe.
1022	Emperor Henry II defeats a Byzantine army in Southern Italy. The Synod of Pavia decrees celibacy for higher clergy.
1023	Abdul-Rahman V becomes caliph of Cordoba, replacing the Hammudid al-Qasim of Malaga.
1024	Emperor Henry II dies. He is succeeded by his second cousin twice removed, Conrad II of Franconia. Boleslav I of Poland is crowned king of that country.
1025	Emperor Basil II dies, and is succeeded by his brother Constantine VIII. Boleslav I of Poland dies and is succeeded by his son Mieszko II and reverts to the title of prince.
1026	Cnut thwarts a combined Norwegian and Swedish attack at the sea battle of the Holy River. Guido d'Arezzo introduces solmisation in music.
1027	Robert I the Devil becomes duke of Normandy on the death of his brother Richard III.
1028	Cnut conquers Norway and sends his son Sweyn to rule it. Emperor Constantine VIII dies, succeeded by his daughter Zoë. Romanus III becomes co-emperor upon marrying her. Sancho III of Navarre conquers Castile.
1030	Olaf II of Norway attempts to win back his throne, but is defeated and killed by Cnut's forces at Stiklestad. Sultan Mahmud of Ghazni dies, and is succeeded by his son Muhammad.
1031	Muhammad of Ghazni deposed and blinded by his brother Masud I. Caliph Hisham III deposed, ending the Umayyad Caliphate of Cordoba, which fragments. Robert II the Pious of France dies; succeeded by his son Henry I.
1032	Rudolf III of Burgundy dies without an heir, and Conrad II unites the kingdom with the Empire.
1033	Mieszko II of Poland defeated by combined German and Russian forces and his realm forced to become a fief of the Empire. Castile granted independence from Navarre.
1034	Empress Zoe murders Romanus III and marries Michael IV, who becomes co-Emperor. Mieszko of Poland dies; his son Kasimir I succeeds him but the country plunges into civil war. Malcolm II of Scotland dies, and is succeeded by his grandson Duncan I.
1035	Duke Robert the Magnificent of Normandy dies on pilgrimage to Jerusalem. His illegitimate son William (the future 'Conqueror') succeeds, sparking a succession dispute. Sancho III of Navarre dies, and is succeeded in Navarre by his son Garcia IV and in Castile by his son Ferdinand I. Cnut dies. Harthacnut succeeds him in Denmark and England, but his brother Harold seizes England for himself. Magnus I the Good, son of Olaf II, regains Norwegian independence, defeating Sweyn.
1036	Alfred, son of Aethelred II, returns to England but is murdered by Godwin of Wessex. Harold I (Harefoot) proclaimed Regent of England.
1037	Harold I proclaimed king of England. Ferdinand I of Castile conquers León, deposing Vermudo III. The Islamic philosopher and physician Avicenna dies.
1038	King Stephen of Hungary dies, and is succeeded by his nephew by marriage Peter Orseolo.
1039	Emperor Conrad II dies, succeeded by his son Henry III. Gruffydd ap Llywelyn, prince of Gwynedd, defeats an English invading force on the River Severn.
1040	Macbeth defeats and kills King Duncan of Scotland and assumes the crown. Harold I dies; Harthacnut successfully claims the English crown by right of succession.
1041	Samuel Aba usurps the Hungarian throne from Peter Orseolo. Co-Emperor Michael IV dies; his nephew Michael V fills the breach.
1042	Harthacnut dies; his half-brother Edward the Confessor is elected king whilst Magnus of Norway takes Denmark. Michael V imprisons the Empress Zoë, but a rebellion blinds him, locks him in a monastery and frees Zoë, who marries Constantine IX and makes him co-Emperor.
1043	Samuel Aba of Hungary invades Bavaria, where he is countered by Emperor Henry III. Coventry Abbey founded by Leofric of Mercia.
1044	Emperor Henry III defeats Samuel Aba's Hungarians and restores Peter Orseolo to his throne. Anawrata founds the Pagan dynasty in Burma.
1045	The deposed Pope Benedict IX retakes the throne from Sylvester III by force, and then sells it to Gregory VI.
1046	Peter Orseolo of Hungary deposed by his second cousin Andras I. Emperor Henry III forces Gregory VI to

HISTORY

abdicate on grounds of simony, ratifies the depositions of his two predecessors and installs Clement II at the Synod of Rome.

1047 Norman rebels defeated at Val-ès-Dunes by Duke William, who thus lies secure in his rule. King Magnus dies. Sweyn II, a nephew of Cnut, succeeds him in Denmark, whilst Harald III Hardrada, Magnus' uncle, succeeds him in Norway.

1048 Last Viking raid on south-east England, the raiders flee to Flanders, which is attacked by Edward the Confessor and Emperor Henry III.

1049 Leo IX elected Pope after the death of Damasus II.

1050 Empress Zoë dies, her older sister Theodora succeeding her. Robert of Jumièges becomes Archbishop of Canterbury.

1051 Earl Godwin of Wessex rebels unsuccessfully against Edward the Confessor, he and his family flee to Flanders.

1052 Earl Godwin and his family return to power in England. Stigand uncanonically becomes Archbishop of Canterbury as Archbishop Robert is forced to flee. Pisa takes Sardinia from the Arabs.

1053 Robert Guiscard defeats Papal forces at Civitate, capturing Leo IX, before taking Benevento from the Byzantines and founding a Norman state in Southern Italy. Godwin of Wessex dies, his son Harold succeeding him as earl.

1054 Final schism between Roman Catholic and Orthodox churches. Henry I of France invades Normandy and is defeated at Mortemer. Macbeth defeated by Malcolm Canmore and Earl Siward of Northumbria at Dunsinane.

1055 Seljuk Turks led by Togril-Beg enter Baghdad to liberate the Abbasid Caliphate from Shiite control; Togril-Beg makes himself the Caliph's temporal master. Co-Emperor Constantine IX dies, Theodora reigns alone. Earl Siward of Northumbria dies, and is succeeded six-year-old by Tostig Godwinson.

1056 Emperor Henry III dies, succeeded by his son Henry IV. Empress Theodora dies, ending the reign of the Macedonian dynasty in Byzantium. Michael VI succeeds her.

1057 Macbeth killed by Malcolm III Canmore at Lumphanan, but is succeeded by his stepson Lulach. Isaac Comnenus overthrows Emperor Michael VI.

1058 Lulach killed by Malcolm III Canmore, who becomes king of Scotland. Prince Kasimir I of Poland dies; succeeded by his son Boleslav II.

1059 By the treaty of Melfi Robert Guiscard becomes Duke of Apulia and Sicily and swears fealty to the Papacy. Emperor Isaac Comnenus abdicates in favour of Constantine X.

1060 Andras I of Hungary deposed by his brother Bela I. Henry I of France dies; succeeded by his son Philip I.

1061 Northumbria raided by Malcolm III of Scotland. Duke Spitihnev II of Bohemia dies, succeeded by his brother Vratislav II.

1062 By the Coup d'Etat of Kaiserswerth, Emperor Henry IV seized by Archbishop Anno of Cologne, who takes power in Germany alongside Archbishop Adalbert of Bremen.

1063 Gwynedd conquered by Earls Harold and Tostig; Prince Gruffydd killed by his own men. Bela I of Hungary dies, succeeded by his nephew Salomon, son of deposed king Andras. Alp Arslan succeeds his uncle Togril-Beg as sultan of the Seljuk Turks.

1064 Belgrade seized by the Hungarians from Byzantium. Armenia conquered by Alp Arslan.

1065 Ferdinand I of Castile and León dies; succeeded by his sons Sancho II in Castile and Alfonso VI in León. Westminster Abbey is consecrated.

1066 Death of Edward the Confessor causes succession dispute in England. Harold II Godwinson chosen king, defeats and kills Harald Hardrada at Stamford Bridge but is defeated and killed at Hastings by William of Normandy, who becomes king.

1067 Emperor Constantine X dies; his widow marries Romanus IV Diogenes, who becomes Emperor. Boleslav II of Poland captures Kiev. El Cid founds the world's first leper hospital in Castile.

1068 Earls Edwin and Morcar rebel against William I, but are defeated in York.

1069 Northumbrians and Mercians rebel, with Danish help, against William I, but the risings are put down and William devastates Northumbria ('the harrying of the North').

1070 The Order of the Knights of St John founded in Jerusalem by Amalfian merchants. Sweyn II of Denmark attacks England, but is bought off by William I, who puts down the revolt of Hereward the Wake.

1071 Robert Guiscard captures Bari, thus expelling the Byzantines from Italy. Byzantine forces heavily defeated at Manzikert under Alp Arslan, by Seljuk Turks who capture Emperor Romanus. When released he is blinded by the Byzantines, who select Michael VII as Emperor, and dies soon after. The Seljuqs now control Asia Minor.

1072 Sancho II of Castile murdered at the siege of Zamora whilst fighting Navarrese forces. He is succeeded by his brother Alfonso VI of León. Palermo taken by Robert and Roger Guiscard. Alp Arslan murdered by a captive while campaigning in Transoxiana; his son Malik Shah becomes sultan.

1073 Hildebrand of Soana elected Pope, taking the title Gregory VII.

1074 Salomon of Hungary deposed by his cousin Geza I. Robert Guiscard excommunicated by Gregory VII, who also excommunicates all married priests.

1075 Malik Shah subdues Syria and Palestine. Gregory VII bans simony and declares the Pope to be absolute sovereign of the Church.

1076 German bishops at the Synod of Worms declare Gregory VII deposed and Henry IV demands Gregory's abdication. Gregory excommunicates the bishops and Henry, whom he declares deposed. Thus the 'Investiture Contest' begins between Emperor and Pope, over the right of the Emperor to appoint bishops, who hold secular as well as spiritual power.

1077 When Henry IV does penance at Canossa to Gregory VII, the Germans declare him deposed and elect Rudolf of Swabia as anti-king. Geza I of Hungary dies, and is succeeded by his brother Ladislas I.

1078 Emperor Michael VII abdicates; Nicephorus III elected in his place.

1079 King Boleslav II of Poland excommunicated by Bishop (later Saint) Stanislas of Cracow, who is assassinated on Boleslav's orders. Gregory VII excommunicates Boleslav, who is deposed by a revolt by his nobles and succeeded by his brother Vladislav I Herman, who reverts to the title Prince.

1080   Anti-king Rudolf of Swabia defeated and killed by Henry IV's forces. Gregory VII again excommunicates and deposes Henry IV, who then seeks to depose Gregory, replacing him with the Archbishop of Ravenna as Clement III.

1081   Emperor Nicephorus III abdicates in favour of Alexius I Comnenus. Emperor Henry IV invades Italy seeking to establish Clement III as Pope.

1082   Bishop Odo, Earl of Kent, revolts against his half-brother William I, but is stripped of his earldom and imprisoned.

1083   The Kiyowara family revolt in northern Japan; Yoshiiye Minamoto sent to quell the rebellion.

1084   The Synod of Rome deposes Gregory VII and recognises Clement III, but Henry IV and Clement III are forced to withdraw when Robert Guiscard advances in support of Gregory from Southern Italy.

1085   Toledo taken from the Arabs by Alfonso VI of Castile. Pope Gregory VII dies at Salerno. Robert Guiscard dies, and is succeeded as duke of Apulia by his son Roger Borsa. William I commissions the Domesday Book.

1086   Islamic rule in Southern Spain rejuvenated by the Almoravids of Morocco, who defeat Alfonso VI of Castile at Zallaka. The Domesday Book is compiled. Cnut IV of Denmark dies, ending an invasion threat to England. His brother Olaf IV succeeds him.

1087   William I dies of an injury sustained at the siege of Mantes, and is succeeded by his sons Robert in Normandy and William II Rufus in England.

1088   Urban II elected Pope, but only partially recognised. Bishop Odo and various Norman barons in England rebel against William II, but the revolt is crushed.

1089   Archbishop Lanfranc of Canterbury dies, but no successor is chosen, so William II can enjoy the revenues of the see.

1090   Count Roger Guiscard of Sicily captures Malta from the Arabs.

1091   William II of England and Robert of Normandy make their peace by the treaty of Caen. Malcolm III of Scotland invades Northumbria, but is repulsed by William and Robert and acknowledges William as his overlord.

1092   The Seljuk vizier Nizam al-Malik assassinated by the Ismailite sect, the Hashishin (Assassins). King Vratislav of Bohemia dies. He is succeeded for a short while by his brother Conrad and then his son Bretislav II, who reverts to the title Duke. William II takes Cumberland from the Scots and refounds Carlisle as his north-western outpost.

1093   William II falls gravely ill and appoints St Anselm to the see of Canterbury, recovering soon after. Malcolm III invades Northumbria again but is killed near Alnwick; his wife Margaret dies 4 days later. He is succeeded by his brother Donald III Bane.

1094   Rodrigo Diaz de Vivar, El Cid, takes Valencia from the Moors. Donald Bane is deposed from the Scottish throne by his nephew Duncan II, who dies after six months. Donald Bane returns to the throne.

1095   Ladislas I of Hungary conquers Croatia and Dalmatia but dies soon after, and is succeeded by his nephew Koloman. Olaf IV of Denmark dies, and is succeeded by his brother Erik I. First Crusade launched by Pope Urban II at the council of Clermont, aiming to take Jerusalem and the Holy Land from the Seljuk Turks.

1096   Peter the Hermit preaches the crusade in France and Germany, assembling a rag-tag force which goes East. Germans such as Ermich of Leiningen take advantage of crusade hysteria to persecute Jews in the Holy Roman Empire. Robert of Normandy leases his duchy to William II in order to go on crusade.

1097   Peter the Hermit's crusaders massacred near Nicaea in Asia Minor by Seljuk Turks, but the main crusading force wins major victories both there and at Dorylaeum. Donald Bane of Scotland deposed with William II's help, and replaced by his nephew Edgar.

1098   Robert de Molesme founds the monastery of Cîteaux, and thereby the Cistercian order. Magnus III of Norway seizes the Orkneys, Hebrides and Isle of Man. Crusaders take Antioch after a lengthy siege.

1099   Jerusalem captured by the crusaders; Godfrey of Bouillon becomes Advocate of the Holy Sepulchre. El Cid dies at Cuenca after defeat by the Almoravids.

1100   Godfrey of Bouillon dies, and his brother Baldwin succeeds him and founds the Kingdom of Jerusalem. William II of England dies whilst hunting, and is succeeded by his brother Henry I.

1101   Robert of Normandy invades England to take the throne from brother Henry, but is bought off by the treaty of Alton. Roger d'Hauteville, count of Sicily, dies; succeeded by his son Simon.

1102   Vladislav I of Poland abdicates, and is succeeded after a power struggle by his son Boleslav III. Alfonso VI of Castile raises the year-long siege of Valencia.

1103   Magnus III of Norway invades Ireland, but is killed in battle; his son Eysten I succeeds him. Bohemund of Otranto ransomed from captivity by the Danishmend Emir.

1104   Acre taken by crusaders under Baldwin I of Jerusalem. Mount Hekla in Iceland erupts violently.

1105   Emperor Henry IV is captured by his son Henry and is forced to abdicate in favour of him; when he breaks the terms of his abdication he is imprisoned.

1106   Henry IV escapes from prison but dies whilst raising an army against his son, who succeeds him. Henry of England defeats Robert of Normandy at Tinchebrai, dispossessing Robert of his duchy and imprisoning him.

1107   King Edgar of Scotland dies, and is succeeded by his brother Alexander I.

1108   Philip I of France dies, and is succeeded by his son Louis VI. Bohemund of Otranto defeated by the Emperor Alexius at Durazzo.

1109   Boleslav III of Poland defeats Emperor Henry V at Hundsfeld. Crusaders led by Raymond of St Gilles take Tripoli and Beirut; Raymond founds the County of Tripoli.

1110   The earliest known miracle play performed at Dunstable.

1111   Henry V crowned emperor under duress by Pope Paschal II. Bohemund of Otranto dies, and is

HISTORY

succeeded as prince of Antioch by his nephew Tancred. Count Roger of Apulia dies; his son William II succeeds him.

1112 Emperor Henry V excommunicated. Tancred of Antioch dies, and is succeeded by his nephew Roger of Salerno. Henry of Burgundy, count of Portugal, dies, and is succeeded by his son Alfonso I.

1113 Pisa conquers the Balearic Islands. Sviatopolk of Kiev dies, and is succeeded by his cousin Vladimir II Monomach. The Knights Hospitaller resolve to defend the Holy Land.

1114 Pipe rolls introduced by Bishop Roger of Salisbury as a means of recording Exchequer accounts.

1115 St Bernard founds a monastery at Clairvaux and becomes its first abbot. The Juchens create the Chinese state of Jin under their chieftain Aguda.

1116 Coloman of Hungary dies; succeeded by his son Stephen II.

1117 St Magnus, earl of Orkney, murdered on the island of Egilsay on the orders of his cousin Earl Haakon.

1118 The Knights Templar founded in Jerusalem by Hugh de Payens. Emperor Alexius I dies, and is succeeded by his son John II. Baldwin I of Jerusalem dies, and is succeeded by his great-nephew Baldwin II. Alfonso I of Aragon takes Zaragoza from the Almoravids and makes it his capital.

1119 Count Baldwin VII of Flanders dies; succeeded by his cousin Charles the Good. Crusading armies are heavily defeated at the Field of Blood in Syria. Roger of Antioch is killed.

1120 Prince William, heir and only legitimate son of Henry I, drowns in the wreck of the *White Ship*.

1121 Peter Abelard's teachings on the Trinity condemned at the Synod of Soissons.

1122 Emperor John II wipes out the Pecheneg Turks in the Balkans. The Investiture Question is finally settled with the Concordat of Worms; Emperor Henry V renounces the right of investiture.

1123 Emperor John II defeats the Serbs in the Balkans. Marriage of priests banned by the First Lateran Council. The Augustinian canon Rahere founds St Bartholomew's Hospital in London.

1124 Emperor John II defeats the Hungarians. Alexander I of Scotland dies; succeeded by his brother David I.

1125 Emperor Henry V dies, leaving no successor; Lothair of Saxony is elected to succeed him. Morocco conquered by the Almohads.

1126 Emperor Lothair III makes his son-in-law, Henry X the Proud, duke of Bavaria, succeeding Henry's father, Henry IX. Chinese Emperor Huizong dies after being captured by the Jin; his son Qinzong succeeds him.

1127 The Jin overrun Northern China and Emperor Qinzong perishes; his brother Gaozong flees south and establishes the Southern Song dynasty. Count William III of Apulia dies, Roger of Sicily claims overlordship, but the inhabitants appeal to the Pope for protection. Roger is excommunicated.

1128 Count Charles the Good of Flanders is murdered; Louis VI attempts to impose Robert of Normandy on the county but the inhabitants install Thierry of Alsace, a cousin of Charles. The Templars gain papal recognition; St Bernard draws up their rule. Alfonso I of Portugal defeats Alfonso VII of Castile at São Mamede and shakes off Castilian overlordship. Pope Honorius accepts Roger of Sicily's claim to Apulia and invests him as count.

1129 First Cistercian abbey founded in England, at Waverley. Henry of Blois becomes Bishop of Winchester. Count Fulk V of Anjou resigns the county to his son Geoffrey and goes to Jerusalem to marry Melisande, heiress to King Baldwin II.

1130 Pope Honorius II dies. Innocent II is elected to succeed him but the election is disputed and an antipope, Anacletus II, is also elected. Innocent II flees to France, where he is championed by St Bernard, while Anacletus is backed by Roger II of Sicily, whom he crowns king of that country.

1131 Baldwin II of Jerusalem dies, and is succeeded by his son-in-law Fulk V. Rievaulx Abbey founded.

1132 Fountains Abbey founded.

1133 Lothair III crowned Emperor by Innocent II in the Lateran while the antipope Anacletus II is established in St Peter's. St Bartholomew's Fair founded in London.

1134 Emperor Lothair makes Albert the Bear margrave of Brandenburg and head of the North March.

1135 Henry I of England dies of a surfeit of lampreys; although he made his barons swear that his daughter Matilda would succeed him, his nephew Stephen of Blois engineers his own coronation as king.

1136 Emperor Lothair takes Apulia from Roger II of Sicily. Peter Abelard writes his *Historia calamitatum mearum*.

1137 Louis VI of France dies, and is succeeded by his son Louis VII. Gruffydd ap Cynan, prince of Gwynedd, dies, and is succeeded by his son Owain Gwynedd. Emperor Lothair III dies.

1138 Conrad III of Hohenstaufen elected emperor to succeed Lothair III. When Boleslav III of Poland dies, his country is divided amongst his four sons. David I of Scotland invades England in support of Matilda but is defeated at the battle of the Standard.

1139 The Second Lateran Council ends the schism in the Church. Innocent II is now universally recognised as Pope. Alfonso I crowned king of Portugal. Matilda lands at Arundel, staking her claim to the English throne; anarchy breaks out in the country.

1140 Prince Sobeslav I of Bohemia dies, and is succeeded by his son Vladislav II. Peter Abelard is condemned for heresy at the council of Sens, on a motion railroaded through by St Bernard.

1141 Stephen of England taken prisoner after defeat at Lincoln. Matilda proclaimed queen, but her high-handed behaviour alienates many, in particular London. Stephen is released in exchange for Robert, earl of Gloucester, and Matilda is forced back on the defensive.

1142 The duchy of Bavaria is conferred by Conrad III on Margrave Henry II of Austria. Peter Abelard dies, worn out by the Church's ill-treatment.

1143 Emperor John II of Byzantium dies, and is succeeded by his son Manuel I. Fulk V of Jerusalem dies; his son Baldwin III succeeds him.

1144 Geoffrey of Anjou subdues Normandy and is proclaimed duke. Imad-ud-Din Zangi, sultan of Mosul, captures Edessa, in eastern Turkey, causing alarm in Outremer and in Western Europe.

1145 Arnold of Brescia establishes a republic in Rome; the newly-crowned Pope Eugenius III is forced to flee. St Bernard takes the lead in proclaiming the Second Crusade, to avenge the fall of Edessa.

1146 Zangi of Mosul is murdered, and succeeded by his formidable son Nur-ud-Din, who consolidates the conquest of Edessa.

1147	The Second Crusade collapses in chaos as the crusaders attack Damascus, an ally of Jerusalem, thus alienating it. Lisbon however is taken from the Moors by King Alfonso of Portugal. Matilda leaves England; her son Henry is left to carry on the fight, though only fourteen.
1148	Sugar brought back from the Middle East by returning crusaders.
1149	Raymond of Poitiers, prince of Antioch, killed by Nur-ud-Din.
1150	The University of Paris is founded. *The Black Book of Carmarthen*, an anthology of ancient Welsh poetry, is compiled.
1151	Geoffrey of Anjou dies, and is succeeded in Anjou, Normandy and associated domains by his son Henry. Fire and plague insurance policies are developed in Iceland.
1152	Emperor Conrad III dies and is succeeded by his nephew Frederick I Barbarossa. Louis VII divorces Eleanor of Aquitaine, who promptly marries Henry of Anjou.
1153	David I of Scotland dies; succeeded by his grandson Malcolm IV. Ascalon falls to Baldwin III of Jerusalem. St Bernard of Clairvaux dies. The Treaty of Wallingford brings the English anarchy to an end by recognising Henry of Anjou as Stephen's heir.
1154	Roger II of Sicily dies; succeeded by his son William I. Damascus surrenders to Nur-ud-Din, who now controls most of Syria. Stephen of England dies and is succeeded by Henry, who now rules half of France as well as England. On the death of Anastasius IV, Nicholas Breakspear is elected Pope, taking the name Adrian IV.
1155	Ireland bestowed on Henry II by Pope Adrian IV. Adrian IV restores papal authority in Rome. Arnold of Brescia is hanged as a heretic by Emperor Frederick. St Berthold founds the Carmelite order of monks.
1156	Austria made a duchy with special status by Emperor Frederick. William I of Sicily recovers Bari from the Greeks and makes his peace with Rome.
1157	Erik IX of Sweden conquers and forcibly converts Finland. Alfonso VII of Castile dies; he is succeeded by his sons Sancho III in Castile and Ferdinand II in León.
1158	Prince Vladislav of Bohemia elevated to king by Emperor Frederick. Sancho III of Castile dies, and is succeeded by his infant son Alfonso VIII.
1159	Pope Adrian IV dies, and is succeeded by Alexander III. John of Salisbury writes the *Policraticus*, a treatise on government.
1160	Emperor Frederick, incensed by witnessing the inhabitants of Crema dismembering their prisoners during his siege, hurls his own prisoners over the walls before entering and destroying the city.
1161	Edward the Confessor is canonised.
1162	Emperor Frederick destroys Milan. Thomas Becket is chosen as Archbishop of Canterbury. Danegeld – by now just a general tax – is collected in England for the final time.
1163	The Welsh rebel against Henry II, but the revolt is suppressed and Prince Rhys ap Gruffydd is imprisoned. Henry II and Thomas Becket quarrel over the Church's status vis-à-vis the monarch.
1164	Legal rights of Church and State codified by Henry II at the council of Clarendon; Becket rejects the code and is forced to flee after he is condemned at the council of Northampton. Héloïse dies and is buried next to Abelard.
1165	Emperor Manuel allies with Venice against Emperor Frederick. Malcolm IV of Scotland dies, and is succeeded by his brother William the Lion. Charlemagne is canonised.
1166	*The Song of Cnut* written down by a monk of Ely. The erection of jails in all English counties ordered by the Assize of Clarendon. William I of Sicily dies, and is succeeded by his son William II.
1167	Oxford University is created when English students are barred from attending Paris.
1168	Milan is rebuilt. Prince Andrei I Bogoliubsky of Vladimir-Suzdal sacks Kiev and assumes the title Grand Prince.
1169	Saladin becomes vizier to the Fatimid caliph al-'Adid of Cairo, effectively controlling Egypt. Norman-Welsh barons land at Wexford supporting King Dermot of Leinster's efforts to regain his throne.
1170	Henry II has his son Henry crowned joint-king (the 'Young King'). Richard Strongbow, earl of Pembroke, takes Waterford and marries Dermot of Leinster's daughter. Thomas Becket returns to Canterbury, but is murdered four weeks later.
1171	Dermot of Leinster dies, and is succeeded by his son-in-law Richard Strongbow, who is forced to accept Henry II as his overlord when Henry crosses to Ireland. Saladin abolishes the Fatimid caliphate and rules Egypt himself.
1172	Henry II receives homage from the Irish at Cashel, but his wife Eleanor raises Aquitaine against him, forcing him to seek a reconciliation with Pope Alexander at Avranches.
1173	Henry II's wife and sons revolt against him, supported by William the Lion of Scotland and Louis VII of France. Eleanor of Aquitaine is captured and imprisoned. Thomas Becket is canonised.
1174	Henry II does public penance for Becket's murder and subdues the revolt against him. Nur-ud-Din dies and a fight for power in the Arab world ensues. Saladin takes Damascus. Amalric I of Jerusalem dies, and is succeeded by his leper son Baldwin IV.
1175	By the treaty of Windsor Rory O'Connor recognised as High King of Ireland under Henry II's overlordship.
1176	The Lombard League defeats Emperor Frederick at Legnano. The first eisteddfod is held at Cardigan Castle. Construction starts at London Bridge.
1177	Baldwin IV of Jerusalem defeats Saladin at Ramleh. Angkor Wat, capital of the Khmer empire, falls to Champa invaders.
1178	Construction starts on the bridge at Avignon.
1179	The Waldensians, Roman Catholic reformers are forbidden to preach by the Pope without the permission of bishops. The Third Lateran Council rules that popes will henceforth be elected by a two-thirds majority of the College of Cardinals.
1180	Louis VII of France dies, and is succeeded by his son Philip Augustus. Emperor Manuel I dies, and is succeeded by his son Alexius II. Henry II reforms the English coinage.
1181	Pope Alexander III dies; Lucius III succeeds him.

1182	Valdemar I of Denmark dies, and is succeeded by his son Cnut VI. Revolts in Byzantium force Emperor Alexius II to make his father's cousin Andronicus co-Emperor.
1183	Emperor Alexius II murdered, and replaced by his co-emperor, Andronicus I. Emperor Frederick, the Pope and the Lombard League make the Peace of Constance. Saladin takes Aleppo. Henry the 'Young King', rebellious son of Henry II of England, dies.
1184	Cyprus gains freedom from Byzantium. Giorgi III of Georgia dies, and is succeeded by his daughter Thamar. Glastonbury Abbey burns down.
1185	Emperor Andronicus I killed by rioters and succeeded by Isaac II Angelus. Bulgarians under Peter and Ivan Asen revolt against Byzantium. Saladin takes Mosul. Prince John sent to govern Ireland, antagonises the local lords and is recalled.
1186	Emperor Frederick marries his son Henry to Constance, heiress of Sicily, and has him crowned Caesar. Baldwin V of Jerusalem dies. The crown passes to Guy of Lusignan.
1187	Saladin defeats a crusader army at Hattin and takes Jerusalem. The Punjab conquered by the Ghaznavid Mohammad of Ghur. Bulgaria becomes independent under Ivan Asen.
1188	The Third Crusade is proclaimed; to this end the first general tax, the Saladin Tithe, is levied in France. Henry II quarrels with his son Richard and Philip II of France over his French lands and the succession.
1189	Henry II dies, and is succeeded by his son Richard, whose coronation is accompanied by a massacre of Jews. William II of Sicily dies; his bastard cousin Tancred takes the throne.
1190	Emperor Frederick I Barbarossa drowns in Cilicia whilst on crusade, he is succeeded by his son Henry VI. The Jews in York are massacred, but the city is fined.
1191	Richard I conquers Cyprus from the Byzantines and sells it to the Templars, before capturing Acre. Philip II returns to France after falling ill. Richard defeats Saladin at Arsuf. The Order of Germanic Hospitallers is founded at Acre. Zen Buddhism is introduced to Japan.
1192	Richard I, realizing he cannot win in Palestine, makes a truce with Saladin, ending the Third Crusade. On his return home, he is captured and imprisoned by Leopold, duke of Austria. Sultan Muhammad of Ghur captures Delhi, which becomes the Muslim capital in India. Yoritomo Minamoto becomes the first shogun (warlord) of Japan, effectively ruling under a figurehead emperor.
1193	Richard I is handed over to Emperor Henry VI, who demands ransom for his release. Prince John takes the opportunity to foment rebellion whilst Hubert Walter, archbishop of Canterbury, raises the sum. Saladin dies, and is succeeded in Cairo by his son Imad-ud-Din, whilst his relatives rule elsewhere in Arabia.
1194	The Yellow River changes course. Spitsbergen discovered by Norsemen. Richard I is freed after the ransom is paid, returns to England briefly to put down John's rebellion and leaves the country permanently for France. Emperor Henry VI conquers Sicily, deposing William III, son of Tancred. Prince Dafydd of Gwynedd dies, and is succeeded by his nephew Llywelyn ap Iorwerth the Great.
1195	Emperor Isaac II deposed, blinded and imprisoned by his brother Alexius III.
1196	Alfonso II of Aragon dies, and is succeeded by his son Pedro II. Bela III of Hungary dies; his son Imre succeeds him.
1197	Emperor Henry VI dies, sparking a succession dispute. Peter Asen of Bulgaria is murdered, and succeeded by his brother Kalojan. Prince Rhys of Deheubarth dies, and is succeeded by his son Gruffydd.
1198	Pope Celestine III dies. He is succeeded by Innocent III, who excommunicates Philip II of France for repudiating his wife Ingeborg of Denmark. Two rival emperors are established: Philip of Swabia, brother of Henry VI, and Otto, Duke of Saxony.
1199	Richard I dies after an injury at the siege of Chalus. He is succeeded by his brother John, although Philip II goes to war in France in support of John's nephew Arthur of Brittany. The Declaration of Speyer gives the German princes the right to elect their king.
1200	John of England and Philip II of France make peace at Le Goulet, with John confirmed in the Angevin lands in France under Philip's overlordship. Llywelyn the Great seizes Anglesey.
1201	The St Gotthard Pass is opened in Switzerland.
1202	The Fourth Crusade is proclaimed by Innocent III, with leadership given to Count Boniface III of Montferrat. The crusaders get into debt with Venice, whose doge, Enrico Dandolo, persuades them to take Zara for Venice. For this the crusaders are excommunicated by Innocent III.
1203	John murders his nephew, Arthur of Brittany, causing his French possessions to revolt. Crusaders and Venetians agree to help Isaac II regain the Byzantine throne from Alexius III, and are successful.
1204	Emperor Isaac II and his son Alexius IV deposed by Alexius V Ducas. The crusaders conquer Constantinople, and Alexius V flees to Morea, where he is captured and executed. Baldwin of Flanders is elected emperor, but the Byzantine empire disintegrates as relatives of the former ruling families set up independent states. Eleanor of Aquitaine dies. Normandy is captured by Philip Augustus.
1205	The Duchy of Athens is founded by Othon de la Roche. William of Champlitte founds the Principate of Achaea. Emperor Baldwin is defeated and executed by Kalojan of Bulgaria at Adrianople; he is succeeded by his brother Henry. Ladislas III of Hungary deposed by his uncle Andras II.
1206	The Mongol leader Temujin is proclaimed Genghis Khan at Karakorum. Qutb-ud-Din Aibak kills Sultan Muhammad and founds the Sultanate of Delhi. Theodore I Lascaris elected Legitimist Emperor at Nicaea.
1207	Marco I Sanudo founds the duchy of Naxos. Boniface of Montferrat, king of Thessalonica dies, and is succeeded by his son Demetrius.
1208	Philip of Swabia, pretender to the Holy Roman Empire, murdered by Otto of Wittelsbach, who is elected to succeed him and betrothed to his daughter. England placed under interdict by Innocent III. The Albigensian Crusade is proclaimed by Innocent III against Cathar heretics in Languedoc.
1209	The Albigensian fortress of Carcassonne is brutally taken by crusaders under Simon de Montfort. Otto of Wittelsbach crowned Emperor Otto IV in Rome. King John is excommunicated by Innocent III. Cambridge University founded by students leaving Oxford due to town and gown clashes.
1210	The order of the Friars Minor, founded by Francis of Assisi, approved by Innocent III. *Tristan und Isolde* written by Gottfried von Strassburg.

1211	Genghis Khan invades China. Sancho I of Portugal dies, and is succeeded by his son Alfonso II. Emperor Otto deposed by the German princes.
1212	Frederick II elected king by the German princes. Alfonso VIII of Castile decisively defeats the Moors at Las Navas de Tolosa. Stephen of Cloyes leads the Children's Crusade to its doom: many of the children who sail from Marseilles for the Holy Land end up in slavery.
1213	King John submits to the Papacy. Simon de Montfort invades Aragon, defeating the Aragonese at Muret and killing Pedro II, whose infant son James I is put into the care of the Templars.
1214	King John, Otto IV and other lords form alliance against Philip Augustus, who defeats the allied troops at Bouvines, Flanders. William the Lion of Scotland dies, and is succeeded by his son Alexander II.
1215	A revolt by barons in England leads to the signing under duress by King John of Magna Carta; rebel barons later capture Rochester Castle but John retakes it. Frederick II crowned emperor at Aachen. St Dominic founds the Dominican Order.
1216	Baronial revolts against King John gather force and the Dauphin Louis is invited to become king of England. John loses his baggage in the Wash and dies at Newark; he is succeeded by his son Henry III, with William Marshal, earl of Pembroke, proclaimed Regent. Pope Innocent III dies, and is succeeded by Honorius III.
1217	William Marshal defeats baronial rebels at Lincoln; the French fleet is later defeated off Sandwich and Prince Louis sues for peace. Henry III established as unchallenged king of England. The Fifth Crusade is launched under the leadership of John de Brienne.
1218	Persia overrun by Genghis Khan's Mongols. Deposed Emperor Otto IV dies, leaving Frederick II unchallenged. The Dannebrog is adopted as the flag of Denmark.
1219	Sultan Ka'us I of Rum dies, and is succeeded by his brother Kubadh I. Robert succeeds his mother Yolande as emperor in Constantinople. William Marshal dies.
1220	The Dresden Boys' choir founded. Building commences on Salisbury and Amiens cathedrals.
1221	Samarkand sacked by Genghis Khan. The Fifth Crusade ends in failure.
1222	University of Oxford establishes St George's Day, 23 April, as national holiday of England.
1223	Philip Augustus of France dies, and is succeeded by his son Louis VIII. Russians defeated by the Mongols at Kalka River. Alfonso II of Portugal dies, and is succeeded by his son Sancho II.
1224	The Jodo Shin (True Pure Land) sect founded in Japan by Shinran Shonin. Poitou and Gascony, possessions of Henry III of England, invaded by Louis VIII of France.
1225	Magna Carta is reissued in definitive form.
1226	Louis VIII of France dies, and is succeeded by his son Louis IX. St Francis of Assisi dies. The Teutonic Knights are commissioned to conquer and convert Prussia.
1227	Genghis Khan dies; his empire is divided among his three sons. Pope Honorius III dies, and is succeeded by Gregory IX. Frederick II embarks upon crusade, but is forced back by illness and excommunicated by Gregory IX for temporizing.
1228	Frederick II embarks upon crusade whilst Pope Gregory IX invades his realm. Francis of Assisi canonised.
1229	Frederick II reaches an agreement with Sultan Malik-al-Kamil, gaining Jerusalem, Bethlehem, Nazareth and an access corridor from Acre with a 15-year truce, and has himself crowned king of Jerusalem in Jerusalem. Returning from Palestine, Frederick defeats his enemies in Italy. The Balearic Islands conquered by Aragon.
1230	Frederick II and Pope Gregory IX reach an agreement at San Germano and Frederick's excommunication is lifted. Alfonso IX of León; dies his son Ferdinand III of Castile unites the two kingdoms.
1231	The Japanese shogun Fujiwara Yoritsune forbids the selling of children into slavery. Frederick II founds a medical school at Salerno.
1232	Muhammad I al-Ghalib comes to power in Granada, founding the Nasrid dynasty. Anthony of Padua canonised a year after his death.
1233	Pope Gregory IX founds the Papal Inquisition for the suppression of heresy and entrusts it to the Dominicans. The earl of Pembroke, aided by Llywelyn of Wales, leads a baronial revolt against Henry III.
1234	The earl of Pembroke is murdered in Ireland defending his Leinster estates against royalist attacks. Henry III and Llywelyn of Wales make peace.
1235	The Jin state in China falls to the Great Khan Ogedei's Mongols. Andras II of Hungary dies, and is succeeded by his son Bela IV.
1236	Alexander Nevsky succeeds to the Grand Duchy of Novgorod.
1237	The Mongols, led by Subutai and Ogedei, invade Russia, capture Moscow and devastate Poland.
1238	Moorish Valencia surrenders to James I of Aragon.
1239	Emperor Frederick II excommunicated again by Gregory IX.
1240	Prince Llywelyn of Gwynedd dies, and is succeeded by his son Dafydd. Richard of Cornwall and his brother-in-law Simon de Montfort lead a crusade to the Holy Land. The Mongol leader Batu, a grandson of Genghis Khan, takes and destroys Kiev.
1241	The Mongols advance into Eastern Europe, routing the Germans at Liegnitz in Silesia, but the death of Khan Ogedei saves Europe from invasion. Pope Gregory IX dies, and is succeeded by Celestine IV, who dies after seventeen days as Pontiff.
1242	Batu establishes the Golden Horde Mongols at Sarai on the Volga. Alexander Nevsky defeats the Teutonic Knights on the frozen Lake Peipus.
1243	Innocent IV elected Pope after an eighteen-month delay due to quarrels with Emperor Frederick II.
1244	Pasha Khwarazmi of Egypt recaptures Jerusalem for the Arabs. The Cathar stronghold of Montségur falls to Catholic besiegers and a mass execution of the defenders takes place outside.
1245	The Council of Lyon declares Frederick II deposed, causing civil war in Germany. Sancho II of Portugal deposed by Pope Innocent IV, who offers the throne to Sancho's brother Alfonso III.
1246	Landgrave Henry Raspe of Thuringia is elected German king. He defeats Frederick II's son Conrad at Nidda but is driven out of Thuringia by Conrad and Duke Otto II of Bavaria. Duke Frederick II of Austria dies; Emperor Frederick II seizes his duchy.

HISTORY

1247	Buda founded by Bela IV of Hungary to replace Pest, destroyed by the Mongols. With the demise of Henry of Thuringia, William II of Holland is elected anti-king in Germany.
1248	Louis IX of France sets off on the Seventh Crusade. Rhodes taken from the Byzantines by the Genoese. Moorish Seville falls after a two-year siege to Ferdinand III of Castile.
1249	The crusaders land in Egypt and take Damietta. Alexander II of Scotland dies, and is succeeded by his son Alexander III.
1250	Louis IX of France captured by Caliph Turan Shah of Egypt at the battle of Fariskur but released after paying ransom. The Mamluks depose and kill Turan Shah; Musa, a cousin of Turan Shah, becomes Caliph but rules in name only. Emperor Frederick II dies, and is succeeded by his son Conrad IV.
1251	Ottokar, margrave of Moravia, elected duke of Austria.
1252	Ferdinand III of Castile dies; his son Alfonso X succeeds him. Duke Andrei II of Vladimir deposed by the Great Khan Mongka in favour of his younger brother Alexander Nevsky.
1253	Wenceslas I of Bohemia dies, and is succeeded by his son Ottokar II, duke of Austria. The Buddhist monk Nichiren founds his own sect in Japan.
1254	Pope Innocent IV offers the Sicilian throne to Edmund, son of Henry III, who accepts on his behalf. Louis IX of France returns from crusade. Emperor Conrad IV dies. The succession of his infant son Conradin is blocked by opponents of the Hohenstaufens.
1255	Prince Llywelyn of Gwynedd ousts his brother Owen from joint rulership of the Principality.
1256	Venice and Genoa go to war. The order of Augustinian Hermits is founded. Hulagu, a grandson of Genghis Khan, conquers Persia.
1257	Richard, earl of Cornwall, is elected Holy Roman Emperor, but his election is disputed by Alfonso X of Castile.
1258	Hulagu Khan conquers Baghdad, killing Caliph al-Musta'sim and bringing the Abbasid Caliphate to an end. The Provisions of Oxford establish a form of parliamentary government in England. Manfred, regent of Sicily, crowns himself king, deposing his nephew Conradin, and is excommunicated by Pope Alexander IV.
1259	By the treaty of Paris Henry III gives up his claim to Normandy, Anjou and Poitou, and does homage for Gascony and Aquitaine to Louis IX.
1260	The Mamluk Baibars I becomes sultan in Egypt and defeats the Mongols at Ain Jalut in Palestine, saving Egypt from invasion and turning the tide of Mongol attacks. Kublai Khan comes to power in China.
1261	The Greeks reconquer Constantinople, driving the Latin Emperor Baldwin II from the city. The Nicaean Emperor Michael VIII Palaeologus succeeds him.
1262	Haakon IV of Norway unites Greenland and Iceland with his kingdom. Cadiz taken from the Moors.
1263	Alexander III of Scotland defeats Haakon IV of Norway at Largs and takes the Hebrides. Haakon dies on his way home and is succeeded by his son Magnus VI.
1264	Civil war erupts in England between Henry III and a baronial alliance led by Simon de Montfort; de Montfort defeats and captures Henry at Lewes, becoming de facto ruler of England.
1265	Charles of Anjou granted crusading privileges to conquer Sicily by Pope Clement IV. Simon de Montfort summons parliament, but is defeated and killed at Evesham by Prince Edward, who has escaped from imprisonment.
1266	Charles of Anjou defeats and kills Manfred of Sicily at Benevento and becomes king of Sicily. The Hebrides and the Isle of Man granted to Scotland by Norway under the terms of the Treaty of Perth.
1267	Llewelyn of Gwynedd, recognised as Prince of Wales by the treaty of Montgomery, pays homage to Henry III.
1268	Sultan Baibars captures Jaffa and Antioch. Conradin attempts to reclaim Sicily from Charles of Anjou, but is captured and executed. Pope Clement IV dies; the Papacy is left vacant.
1269	Louis IX of France orders Jews in his country to wear a purple wheel on their clothing.
1270	Louis IX of France dies in Tunisia whilst leading the Eighth Crusade; he is succeeded by his son Philip III. The poet Tannhäuser dies.
1271	Pope Gregory X elected to the three-years-vacant papal throne. Marco Polo accompanies his father and uncle to the Far East.
1272	Richard of Cornwall, king of the Romans, dies. Henry III of England dies, and is succeeded by his son Edward I, who is on crusade.
1273	Rudolf, count of Habsburg, elected German king and Holy Roman Emperor.
1274	Thomas Aquinas dies, leaving unfinished his *Summa Theologiae*. Kublai Khan sends an invasion fleet to Japan, but it is destroyed by a typhoon.
1275	Moses de León completes the Jewish mystical text the *Zohar*. Prince Llywelyn of Wales refuses homage to Edward I.
1276	Pope Gregory dies, followed by his successors Innocent V and Hadrian V; John XXI becomes 4th Pope of the year. Ottokar of Bohemia outlawed by Rudolf of Habsburg, but submits to him and is allowed to keep Bohemia and Moravia.
1277	Roger Bacon imprisoned for heresy. Sultan Baibars I of Egypt dies, and is succeeded by his son Baraka Khan. Llywelyn of Gwynedd forced to submit to Edward I by the treaty of Conway.
1278	Ottokar of Bohemia defeated and killed by Rudolf of Habsburg at Dürnkrut. He is succeeded by his son Wenceslas II. The glass mirror is invented.
1279	Alfonso III of Portugal dies near Macao, and is succeeded by his son Diniz. Kublai Khan defeats the Southern Song dynasty in a sea battle and reunites China under the rule of his Yuan dynasty.
1280	Magnus VI of Norway dies; his son Erik II succeeds him.
1281	When Kublai Khan sends a second invasion fleet to Japan it is again decimated by a typhoon, which the Japanese call *kamikaze*, divine wind.
1282	When his younger brother David starts a rebellion against Edward I, Llywelyn of Gwynedd is forced to take part, but is killed near Builth. His brother succeeds him. In the Sicilian Vespers, Sicilian nobles revolt

against Charles of Anjou, who flees whilst his countrymen are massacred. Pedro III of Aragon is offered the Sicilian crown and arrives to accept it.

1283   Prussia subdued by the Teutonic Knights. Edward I conquers Wales. Prince David of Gwynedd is surrendered by his men and executed by Edward.

1284   Kublai Khan invades Vietnam, but his army is destroyed by local guerrillas. Edward I settles Welsh affairs by the Statute of Rhuddlan and arranges for his son Edward to be born in Caernarfon castle.

1285   Charles of Anjou, king of Naples, dies whilst preparing to invade Sicily, succeeded by his son Charles II. Philip III of France dies, and is succeeded by his son Philip IV the Fair. Pedro III of Aragon and Sicily dies, to be succeeded in Aragon by his son Alfonso III and in Sicily by his son James.

1286   Alexander III of Scotland dies on a night ride; his heir is his granddaughter Margaret, the Maid of Norway.

1287   Kublai Khan invades Burma.

1288   Charles II of Naples is released from custody in Aragon on the condition that he accepts Aragonese rule in Sicily.

1289   Tripoli falls to Egyptian forces. Block printing is introduced to Europe at Ravenna.

1290   Edward I expels the Jews from England. Richard of Haldingham draws the *Mappa Mundi*. Margaret of Norway dies whilst on board ship to Scotland; the throne is vacant.

1291   Acre falls to Egyptian forces, ending crusader interest in Outremer. The Knights Hospitallers settle in Cyprus. Rudolf of Habsburg dies. The cantons of Uri, Schwyz and Unterwalden form the Everlasting League, the beginnings of Switzerland.

1292   Adolf, count of Nassau, elected German king. Edward I grants the Scottish throne to John de Balliol.

1293   Kublai Khan sends an expedition to take Java, but it fails.

1294   Philip IV of France confiscates Gascony; Edward I declares war but preparations are disrupted by revolt in Wales. Kublai Khan dies, and is succeeded by his grandson Temür.

1295   A Welsh revolt collapses after defeat at Maes Moydog. Scotland, resentful of a summons to help Edward I, forms the Auld Alliance with France. The Model Parliament convenes at Westminster.

1296   The Genoese defeat the Venetian fleet at Curzola; Marco Polo is amongst those captured. Edward I invades Scotland, forces John de Balliol to abdicate and takes the Stone of Scone, where Scottish kings are crowned, to Westminster.

1297   William Wallace leads a Scottish revolt against Edward I, defeating the English at Stirling Bridge and invading Northumberland and Cumberland. Giant moas become extinct on New Zealand's North Island.

1298   Adolf of Nassau is dethroned by his electors and killed at the battle of Göllheim; Albrecht of Austria, son of Rudolf of Habsburg, replaces him as German king. Edward I invades Scotland, defeating the Scots at Falkirk; Wallace flees abroad.

1299   Osman I, first of the Ottomans, becomes sultan of Turkey.

1300   Arnaud de Villeneuve distils brandy at Montpellier. Edward I invades Scotland again, but makes a truce after a Papal appeal to withdraw. Henry of Great Poland is deposed; Wenceslas II of Bohemia is elected to succeed him.

1301   Andras III of Hungary dies, ending the rule of the Arpad dynasty. Wenceslas II of Bohemia becomes king in his stead, but civil war breaks out. Edward I makes his son Edward Prince of Wales.

1302   The Black faction drive the Whites from Florence; Dante is exiled as a result. The Estates-General of France meet for the first time. Flemish burghers defeat the French at the battle of the Spurs.

1303   Philip IV of France sends Guillaume de Nogaret to capture Pope Boniface VIII and bring him to face trial in France. De Nogaret is thwarted by the Roman citizens, but Boniface dies a virtual prisoner and a broken man in the Vatican shortly after.

1304   The Scottish barons submit to Edward I at St Andrews whilst Stirling Castle only submits after a siege.

1305   Bertrand de Got, Archbishop of Bordeaux, elected Pope as Clement V. Wenceslas II of Bohemia, Poland and Hungary dies. He is succeeded in Bohemia and Poland by his son Wenceslas III, but in Hungary by Otto III of Bavaria. William Wallace is captured, tried and executed by the English.

1306   Wenceslas III of Bohemia and Poland is murdered. Albrecht of Austria invests his son Rudolf with Bohemia whilst Ladislas IV of Kujavia succeeds in Poland. Jews expelled from France. Rhodes purchased by the Knights Hospitallers. Robert Bruce murders John Comyn and is subsequently crowned king of Scots at Scone. The English invade Scotland and force Bruce to flee.

1307   Edward I of England dies, and is succeeded by his son Edward II, who creates Piers Gaveston earl of Cornwall. Philip IV seizes the property of the Knights Templar in France so as to replenish his treasury, but some of the Templar treasure is hidden away.

1308   The Templars are suppressed in England. Parliament forces Edward II to banish Piers Gaveston, who is created Lieutenant in Ireland. Albrecht of Austria is murdered on orders of his nephew John; Henry IV of Luxembourg is elected his successor.

1309   Clement V moves the Papacy to Avignon, thus beginning The 'Babylonian Captivity'.

1310   Parliament forces Edward II to appoint 21 Lords Ordainers to reform the government. A Council of Ten is appointed to rule Venice.

1311   The English Parliament orders baronial consent to appointments by Edward II. Robert Bruce raids Northumberland.

1312   The Knights Templar are abolished in France. Lyons is incorporated into France by the treaty of Vienne. Piers Gaveston is captured by barons and executed.

1313   Perth, Roxburgh, Edinburgh and the Isle of Man taken by the Scots, who besiege Stirling Castle. Emperor Henry VII dies.

1314   Jacques de Molay, Grand Master of the Knights Templar, is burned as a heretic; he curses Philip IV and Pope Clement V at the stake, both of whom die before the year is out. Edward II invades Scotland, but is routed at Bannockburn. Louis X succeeds his father Philip. Louis of Bavaria is elected German king, but a faction elects his rival Frederick of Austria as anti-king; civil war breaks out in Germany.

1315   Edward Bruce, Robert's brother, is offered the High Kingship of Ireland; he sails to Ireland and defeats the
        Earl of Ulster near Connor.
1316   Edward Bruce, is crowned high king of Ireland. Louis X of France dies. He is briefly succeeded by his son
        Jean I, who dies soon after his father, and then by his brother Philip V. John XXII elected Pope after a two
        year hiatus.
1317   The Salic Law is adopted by the French royal family: from now on females and descendants of the female
        line may not inherit the crown or other titles.
1318   Edward Bruce is killed in the battle of Faughart.
1319   Scots raid into England, defeating an army at the battle of Myton-in-Swaledale; a truce is subsequently
        made between the English and Scots.
1320   Vladislav IV is crowned king of Poland. The Declaration of Arbroath asserts Scots independence and
        loyalty to Robert Bruce. Tughluq Shah I founds the Tughluq dynasty as rulers of the sultanate of Delhi,
        overthrowing Khusraw Shah of the Khalji dynasty.
1321   Parliament forces Edward II to banish his close supporters Hugh Despenser and his son, but he recalls
        them and raises an army. Dante Alighieri dies.
1322   Philip V of France dies, and is succeeded by his brother Charles IV. Edward II defeats his cousin Thomas,
        earl of Lancaster, at Boroughbridge; Lancaster is executed and Edward's opponents punished. Frederick of
        Austria defeated and taken prisoner by Louis of Bavaria at the battle of Mühldorf.
1323   Thomas Aquinas is canonised.
1324   Marco Polo dies. Charles IV of France invades Gascony.
1325   Tughluq Shah I of Delhi is murdered by his son Muhammad Shah I, who replaces him as Sultan. Louis of
        Bavaria accepts Frederick of Austria as co-regent of Germany, but the move is unsuccessful.
1326   Osman I of Turkey dies; his son Orkhan succeeds him. Queen Isabella of England and her lover Roger
        Mortimer invade England; Edward II is captured and the Despensers executed.
1327   Edward II is forced to abdicate in favour of his son Edward III, and is murdered 8 months later in Berkeley
        Castle. Munich is devastated by fire.
1328   Charles IV of France dies, and is succeeded by his cousin Philip VI, first of the Valois dynasty. Robert
        Bruce is recognised as king of the Scots by the treaty of Northampton; Pope John XXII also recognises
        him.
1329   Robert Bruce dies of leprosy; he is succeeded by his son David II.
1330   Frederick of Austria dies; by the treaty of Hagenau Louis of Bavaria is recognised as emperor by the
        Habsburg faction. Edward III takes control of government in England, capturing and executing Roger
        Mortimer.
1331   Stephen Urosh III of Serbia overthrown and murdered by his son Stephen Urosh IV Dushan, who
        replaces him as king.
1332   Lucerne joins the Swiss League. Edward Balliol invades Scotland, defeating loyalist forces at Dupplin Moor,
        and is crowned king, but is then defeated by loyalists and flees to England.
1333   Vladislav IV of Poland dies, and is succeeded by his son Casimir III the Great. Edward III and Edward
        Balliol besiege Berwick and defeat a relieving force at Halidon Hill. The Isle of Man is seized by
        England.The Black Death pandemic – a combination of bubonic and pneumonic plague passed on by fleas
        from infected rats – emerges in China.
1334   Casimir III of Poland encourages Jewish immigration. David II of Scotland flees to France and loyalist
        revolts break out. Berwick ceded to England by Edward Balliol. Pope John XXII dies, and is succeeded by
        Benedict XII.
1335   Emperor Andronicus III conquers Thessaly.
1336   Alfonso IV of Aragon dies, and is succeeded by his son Pedro IV. The Vijayanagar Empire is founded in
        southern India by Harihara I of the Yadava dynasty.
1337   Edward III claims the throne of France, thus precipitating the Hundred Years War.
1338   The French initiate hostilities against England, burning Portsmouth and Southampton. Edward III and
        Emperor Louis IV enter into an alliance. The university of Pisa is founded. Ashikaga Takaufi founds the
        Ashikaga shogunate.
1339   Venice conquers Treviso, thus gaining its first mainland possession.
1340   Waldemar IV, youngest son of the deposed Christopher II, ascends the Danish throne, ending eight years
        of anarchy. The English win a decisive naval victory over the French at Sluys.
1341   David II returns to Scotland, forcing the withdrawal of Edward Balliol. Emperor Andronicus III dies, and is
        succeeded by his 9-year-old son John V. When John's guardian, John Cantacuzene, attempts to set
        himself up as emperor, civil war erupts.
1342   Edward III conquers most of Brittany. Charles Robert, king of Hungary dies, and is succeeded by his son
        Louis I the Great.
1343   The Peruzzi banking house of Florence collapses as Edward III defaults on his loan repayments. The Black
        Death spreads amongst the Tartars in the Crimea.
1344   The Bardi banking house in Florence collapses. The Yellow River floods 16,000 square km of China and
        changes its course. Alfonso XI of Castile conquers Algeciras from the Moors.
1345   Stephen Urosh IV Dushan proclaims himself emperor of the Serbs and prepares to attack Byzantium.
1346   The French annihilated at Crécy by English bowmen. John of Luxembourg perishes in the battle, and is
        succeeded by his son Charles I, who is subsequently crowned German king. Scottish forces under David II
        invade England but are routed at Neville's Cross with David II taken prisoner.
1347   John Cantacuzene is victorious in the Byzantine civil war and reigns, nominally as co-emperor with John V,
        as John VI. Cola di Rienzi overthrows the Roman plutocracy, but attracts the enmity of Pope Clement VI
        and is forced to abdicate. Calais surrenders to Edward III after an 11-month siege. Emperor Louis IV dies
        during a bear hunt, and is succeeded by his rival Charles I of Luxembourg. The Black Death reaches the
        Black Sea, Sicily and Marseilles.

1348	The Black Death sweeps across Europe and has entered England by summer. Despite Pope Clement VI absolving them of blame, Jews are blamed in areas of France, Germany and Switzerland for the plague pandemic and are persecuted. Many leave for Poland and Russia which are more tolerant. Edward III founds the Order of the Garter.
1349	The Black Death reaches Scotland, Ireland and Poland. A flagellant movement appears as a response to the plague pandemic, but it is denounced and suppressed by Clement VI.
1350	Philip VI of France dies, and is succeeded by his son Jean II. Alfonso XI of Castile dies of the plague whilst besieging Gibraltar, and is succeeded by his son Pedro I the Cruel. Cola di Rienzi appears in Prague, where he is imprisoned by Charles of Luxembourg.
1351	Zurich joins the Swiss League. Florence and Milan go to war over Tuscany. The Statute of Labourers fixes wage rates and restricts movement of labourers in England, as a result of Black Death depopulation and the economic strain of war.
1352	Glarus and Zug join the Swiss League. The Black Death penetrates Russia. Cola di Rienzi is sentenced to death at Avignon, but is saved when Clement VI dies and his successor Innocent VI pardons him.
1353	Bern joins the Swiss League. Giovanni Boccaccio completes *The Decameron*.
1354	The Ottoman Turks take Gallipoli. Innocent VI grants Cola di Rienzi the title Senator and sends him to Rome, but he is killed in a riot within two months. The Genoese defeat a Venetian fleet at Sapienza.
1355	Stephen Urosh IV Dushan of Serbia dies, and is succeeded by his son Stephen Urosh V. The St Scholastica's Day riots in Oxford last three days, with many students killed in 'town and gown' clashes.
1356	Jean II of France captured by the English at the battle of Poitiers, where the Black Prince Edward Prince of Wales, gains a crushing victory.
1357	Parisian merchants, led by Etienne Marcel and Robert le Coq, revolt against the dauphin's administration. David II of Scotland ransomed by the treaty of Berwick.
1358	French peasants revolt in the Jacquerie uprising in the Beauvais but it is suppressed with English assistance. Etienne Marcel is assassinated in Paris by a supporter of the dauphin.
1359	Revolutionaries in red hats storm Bruges in an unsuccessful attempt to overthrow the patrician government. Ivan II of Muscovy dies, and is succeeded by his son Dimitri Donskoy.
1360	England and France sign the treaty of Brétigny, which gives England territorial gains and stipulates the payment of a ransom for Jean II. When the ransom cannot be raised Jean II voluntarily goes back into captivity. Sultan Orkhan of Turkey dies, and is succeeded by Murad I.
1361	Murad I takes Adrianople and makes it the Ottoman capital. The Black Death reappears in England and France.
1362	The Black Prince is appointed ruler of Aquitaine.
1363	Tughlug Timur, shah in Turkestan, dies; he is succeeded by his son Ilyas Khoja, establishing Zungarian Chaghatai rule.
1364	Jean II of France dies in captivity in England, and is succeeded by his son Charles V.
1365	By the Statute of Praemunire the English parliament repudiates Papal overlordship of the country and forbids appeals to the Papal court.
1366	Amadeus of Savoy takes Gallipoli as part of his crusade against the Turks. Pedro the Cruel of Castile is deposed in favour of his half-brother Henry of Trastamara.
1367	Pedro I of Portugal dies and is succeeded by his son Ferdinand. The Black Prince invades Castile in support of Pedro the Cruel, defeating Castilian and French forces at Najera and restoring Pedro's crown.
1368	Chinese Yuan Emperor Shundi is deposed by the Ming Zhu Yuanzhang, who takes the throne with the name Hongwu.
1369	Pedro the Cruel of Castile offends the Black Prince, who abandons him. Besieged by Henry of Trastamara at Montiel, Pedro is defeated and killed by Henry who replaces him as king. France declares war on England.
1370	The Mongol ruler Timur the Lame (Tamburlaine) takes the throne of Samarkand. The Black Prince sacks Limoges. Casimir III of Poland dies in a hunting accident; the last Piast king, he is succeeded by his nephew Louis of Anjou, the king of Hungary.
1371	David II of Scotland dies; he is succeeded by his nephew Robert II, the first of the Stuarts. Sultan Murad I wins the battle of Chernomen – Macedonia, Bulgaria and the Byzantines are forced to admit his suzerainty.
1372	The English defeated by Castilian forces at sea off La Rochelle, which falls, along with Poitou, to the French.
1373	Brandenburg annexed by Emperor Charles IV from Otto V of Bavaria, and is given to his son Wenceslas to rule.
1374	A mysterious dancing craze affects Aix-La-Chapelle, when the inhabitants inexplicably dance themselves to exhaustion.
1375	England and France sign the truce of Bruges – English possessions in France much reduced as a result. The Mamluks take Sis from the Armenian King León V, ending Armenian independence.
1376	Edward, the Black Prince, dies. The Good Parliament is convened; Sir Peter de la Mare is chosen Speaker for the House of Commons.
1377	Pope Gregory XI returns the Papacy to Rome. Edward III dies, and is succeeded by his grandson Richard II; John of Gaunt becomes Regent. The French raid Sussex and Kent, burning Rye and Hastings.
1378	Pope Gregory XI dies. Urban VI is elected his successor but tries to reform the College of Cardinals, leading the French Cardinals to create Robert of Geneva Pope Clement VII at Anagni. He moves his Curia to Avignon and the Great Schism begins. Emperor Charles IV dies, and is succeeded by his son Wenceslas.
1379	Henry II of Castile dies, and is succeeded by his son Juan I.
1380	St Catherine of Siena dies. Charles V of France dies, and is succeeded by his son Charles VI the Mad. Dmitri III Donskoi, prince of Moscow, defeats the Mongols at Kulikovo.
1381	Wat Tyler and John Ball lead the Peasants' Revolt in England. Archbishop Sudbury is murdered outside the Tower by a mob but Tyler is stabbed to death by William Walworth, mayor of London, on meeting Richard II at Smithfield. Ball is executed and the rising is suppressed. Venice defeats Genoa in the war of Chioggia.

HISTORY

1382	The religious reformer John Wycliffe is condemned by Archbishop William Courtenay and barred from teaching at Oxford. Louis of Anjou, king of Hungary and Poland, dies, and is succeeded by his daughters Mary in Hungary and Jadwiga in Poland.
1383	The Bishop of Norwich leads the 'Norwich Crusade' to Flanders in support of Pope Urban VI, but is repulsed and impeached at home by Chancellor Michael de la Pole. Ferdinand of Portugal dies, and is succeeded by his daughter Beatrix.
1384	Juan I of Castile marries Beatrix of Portugal, but the Portuguese resist his claim to their throne. John Wycliffe dies.
1385	Scottish forces, aided by the French, raid Northumbria. Portuguese forces defeat Juan of Castile at the battle of Aljubarrota; João of Aviz, an illegitimate son of Pedro I, takes the kingship.
1386	England and Portugal sign the treaty of Windsor, sealed by the marriage of João I with John of Gaunt's daughter Philippa. Jadwiga of Poland marries Jagiello of Lithuania, who takes the name Vladislav V. Leopold III of Styria and Tyrol defeated and killed by the Swiss at the battle of Sempach; his 4 sons jointly succeed him.
1387	Olaf V of Denmark and Norway dies, and is succeeded by his mother Margaret I. Sigismund of Luxembourg, margrave of Brandenburg, marries Mary of Hungary, becoming king. Geoffrey Chaucer begins *The Canterbury Tales*.
1388	At the battle of Otterburn (Chevy Chase) the Scots under the earl of Douglas defeat and capture Henry 'Hotspur' Percy, though Douglas himself is killed.
1389	Margaret I of Denmark and Norway is offered the Swedish throne, invades and defeats King Albert II of Mecklenburg at Falköping, and thereby unites the Scandinavian thrones. Sultan Murad I defeats a Serb-led coalition at Kosovo and conquers Serbia. Murad is subsequently assassinated by the Serb noble Lazar, who is captured and put to death by Murad's son and successor Bayazid I.
1390	Byzantine Emperor John V is deposed by his grandson John VII, but his son Manuel restores him to the throne. Robert II of Scotland dies, and is succeeded by his son Robert III. Juan I of Castile dies, and is succeeded by his son Henry III.
1391	Emperor John V dies, and is succeeded by his son Manuel II. Jews persecuted in Andalusia and Barcelona, as scapegoats for plague. Gedun Truppa is the first Dalai Lama in Tibet.
1392	Charles VI of France suffers his first fit of madness. Yi Songgye founds the Yi Dynasty in Korea, supplanting the Koryo Dynasty and making Kyongsong (later known as Seoul) the capital.
1393	Bulgaria subdued by Sultan Bayazid I. Timur the Lame takes Baghdad. Emperor Wenceslas IV tortures and murders St John of Nepomuk in Prague.
1394	Emperor Wenceslas taken prisoner by his cousin Jobst of Moravia. Anti-Pope Clement VII dies, and is replaced by Benedict XXIII. Richard II goes to Ireland and sets the limit of the territory later known as 'The Pale'.
1395	Richard II receives the submission of 80 Irish chiefs and returns to England. Albert of Mecklenburg renounces the Swedish throne, confirming Margaret of Denmark as queen.
1396	England and France agree a 28-year truce. Sigismund of Hungary leads a Crusade to Nicopolis, where his army is routed by the Ottoman Turks. Gian Galeazzo Visconti buys the title Duke of Milan from Emperor Wenceslas.
1397	Scandinavian nobles assembled in the Union of Kalmar officially recognise the union of Denmark, Norway and Sweden under Queen Margaret. Sultan Bayazid besieges Constantinople but withdraws when Timur the Lame appears in his lands.
1398	Richard II orders a duel to settle the dispute between John of Gaunt's son Henry Bolingbroke and the duke of Norfolk; he then intercedes and banishes the pair. Timur the Lame conquers and sacks Delhi.
1399	John of Gaunt dies. Richard II confiscates the Lancastrian inheritance of Gaunt. Bolingbroke returns from exile, engineers the deposition of Richard II, and is crowned Henry IV in his stead.
1400	Richard II murdered in Pontefract Castle. Emperor Wenceslas is deposed for drunkenness and incompetence; Rupert III of the Palatinate elected to replace him. Owain Glyndwr attacks Lord Grey of Ruthin, proclaims himself prince of Wales and engineers a revolt in the Principality.
1401	Baghdad and Damascus fall to Timur the Lame.
1402	Sultan Bayazid defeated and captured by Timur the Lame at the battle of Ankara; Bayazid is forced to become Timur's footstool while his favourite wife Despina is made a naked waitress. Duke Gian Galeazzo Visconti of Milan dies whilst besieging Florence, and is succeeded by his son Giovanni Maria. The earl of Northumberland and his son Hotspur capture the earl of Douglas at the battle of Homildon Hill.
1403	Sultan Bayazid dies in captivity at Timur's camp; his sons Suleiman and Muhammad dispute the succession. The Doge of Venice imposes quarantine as an attempt to ward off the Black Death. The earl of Northumberland rebels against Henry IV but is defeated at Shrewsbury, where his son Hotspur perishes.
1404	Owain Glyndwr holds a Welsh parliament at Dolgellau.
1405	Timur the Lame dies, and is succeeded by his sons Miran Shah and Shah Rukh and by Miran Shah's son Khalil Sultan in his domains. Owain Glyndwr is defeated at Grosmont by John Talbot and at Usk by Henry, Prince of Wales. Richard Scrope, Archbishop of York, leads a revolt against Henry IV, but the rebellion collapses and Scrope is executed.
1406	Robert III of Scotland sends his son James to France for safety, fearing his brother Albany, but James is captured by the English at sea and imprisoned. Robert III dies and Albany becomes regent as James is kept captive.
1407	Louis, duke of Orléans, is assassinated on the orders of John the Fearless, duke of Burgundy, causing a feud between Burgundian and Armagnac followers in France.
1408	The last threat to Henry IV in England is extinguished by the Sheriff of Yorkshire's victory at Bramham Moor; the earl of Northumberland dies in the battle.
1409	Henry, prince of Wales, captures Harlech castle, kills Edmund Mortimer and subdues the Welsh revolt. In

an attempt to end the Great Schism a conclave of cardinals announces that both Gregory XII and Benedict XIII are deposed, and elects Alexander V in their stead. Both Gregory and Benedict refuse to accept this election, and there are now three contending popes. Dalmatia recovered by Venice.

1410 Anti-Pope Alexander V dies and John XXIII replaces him as the third pope. Emperor Rupert dies. Sigismund of Hungary, brother of the deposed Wenceslas, is elected to succeed him. The Teutonic Knights are decisively defeated by a Polish-Lithuanian force at Tannenberg.

1411 Portugal and Castile make peace. Poland and the Teutonic Knights make the Peace of Thorn.

1412 Duke Giovanni Visconti of Milan is assassinated, and succeeded by his brother Filippo Maria of Pavia. Margaret of Denmark, Sweden and Norway dies, and is succeeded by her great-nephew Erik of Pomerania.

1413 Henry IV of England dies; his son Henry V succeeds him. Civil war amongst the Ottomans ends when Muhammad I defeats and kills his brother Musa outside Constantinople.

1414 The Lollards, radical religious reformers, under Sir John Oldcastle, revolt against Henry V, but are suppressed. The Council of Constance is convened by John XXIII at the instigation of Sigismund of Hungary, in an attempt to end the Great Schism.

1415 The Council of Constance deposes John XXIII and accepts the abdication of Gregory XII, but Benedict XIII refuses to abdicate. Jan Hus is burnt for heresy, causing outrage in Bohemia. Henry V goes to war with France after the failure of negotiations to marry Catherine of Valois, and gains a crushing victory at Agincourt.

1416 Jerome of Prague, a follower of Hus, is burned for heresy. The Venetians defeat the Ottomans in the Dardanelles.

1417 Caen falls to Henry V. Oddo, Colonna is elected Pope, taking the name Martin V, and the Great Schism comes to an end, although Benedict XIII and a small number of clerics hold out.

1418 Madeira discovered by Portuguese explorers under the aegis of Henry the Navigator. John the Fearless of Burgundy takes control of the French government, but the Dauphin Charles sets up a rival administration at Bourges.

1419 Rouen, and subsequently Normandy fall to Henry V. Hussites rebel in Bohemia, defenestrating Catholic councillors in Prague. John the Fearless of Burgundy is assassinated by Armagnacs supporting Dauphin Charles, driving his successor Philip the Good to an alliance with England.

1420 The Anglo-Burgundian alliance makes the treaty of Troyes with Charles VI of France; Henry is made Charles' heir and marries his daughter Catherine. Chinese Emperor Yongle moves his capital to Dadu and renames it Beijing ('northern capital').

1421 Sultan Muhammad I dies, and is succeeded by his son Murad II. Florence buys the city of Livorno. The Zuider Zee is formed by an irruption of the North Sea; 100,000 perish in the process.

1422 Henry V dies, and is succeeded by his nine month-old son Henry VI. Charles VI of France dies and his son Charles VII declares himself king, but Henry VI is proclaimed king by Protector Bedford in the Anglo-Burgundian areas in accordance with the treaty of Troyes.

1423 Thessalonica is purchased from the Byzantines by Venice in an attempt to prevent the Ottomans taking it. James I of Scotland is freed from captivity by the treaty of London on payment of a ransom.

1424 Chinese Emperor Yongle dies and is succeeded by his son Hongxi. James I returns to Scotland and takes up government from his uncle Albany. The English defeat Charles VII at Verneuil.

1425 James I of Scotland executes his uncle Albany and his family. Emperor Manuel II dies, and is succeeded by his son John VIII. Le Mans falls to the English. Henry the Navigator takes the Canary Islands from Castile.

1426 Venice and Milan go to war.

1427 Yeshak of Ethiopia attempts to form an anti-Islamic alliance with Aragon and France.

1428 By the terms of the Treaty of Delft, Duke Phillip of Burgundy is made governor of Hainault, Holland and Zeeland and heir to Jacqueline of Bavaria, Countess of these lands.

1429 French lose to the English at Rouvray (battle of the Herrings) but under the leadership of Jeanne d'Arc relieve Orleans and are victorious at Patay, where Talbot is captured. Charles VII is crowned at Rheims.

1430 Thessalonica falls to the Ottomans of Murad II. Jeanne d'Arc is captured by the Burgundians at Compiègne and sold to the English, who imprison her at Rouen.

1431 A Lollard conspiracy led by 'Jack Sharp' is crushed by the duke of Gloucester. Jeanne d'Arc is burned as a witch at Rouen.

1432 The Azores are discovered by the Portuguese sailor Gonzalo Cabral. Sultan Murad II takes Albania.

1433 Lucca defeats Florence. Timbuktu falls to the Tuaregs. João I of Portugal dies, and is succeeded by his son Duarte. Duke Phillip of Burgundy forces Jacqueline of Bavaria to abdicate in Hainault, Holland and Zeeland after she had incited a failed revolt against him.

1434 The Khmer move their capital from Angkor to Phnom Penh. Cosimo de Medici is recalled from exile to rule Florence. Vladislav V of Poland dies, and is succeeded by his son Vladislav VI. Jan Van Eyck paints Giovanni Arnolfini and his wife.

1435 The Riksdag of Sweden meets for the first time and makes Engelbrecht Engelbrechtson regent for the ineffectual King Erik. Alfonso V of Aragon attempts to capture Naples, thus reuniting Naples and Sicily under one crown but is captured and later released. France and Burgundy are reconciled by the peace of Arras.

1436 The Compact of Iglau ends the Hussite wars in Bohemia and Emperor Sigismund is acknowledged king. Paris falls to the French. The Scots fail to capture Roxburgh Castle.

1437 James I of Scotland is murdered at Perth by Sir Robert Graham, who is executed for the deed. James II succeeds his father. Emperor Sigismund dies, and is succeeded by his son-in-law Albrecht II of Habsburg.

1438 Pahacutec founds the Inca dynasty in Peru. Erik of Denmark, Norway and Sweden flees from rebellions to Gotland, where he takes up piracy.

1439 Serbia falls to Sultan Murad II. The Council of Florence ratifies the union of Roman and Byzantine churches under Rome's primacy. German King Albrecht II dies, leaving his wife pregnant.

1440	Frederick III of Styria is elected German king. Ladislas Posthumus is born and succeeds his late father Albrecht in Austria and Bohemia; in Hungary Vladislav VI of Poland is invited to be king. Eton College is founded by Henry VI.
1441	The Churches of Rome and Ethiopia sign an act of union. The Portuguese sell Africans as slaves in Lisbon: from this the slave trade will develop.
1442	Eleanor Cobham, duchess of Gloucester, is divorced and imprisoned on charge of attempting to kill Henry VI by sorcery.
1443	The Ottomans defeated by the Hungarian hero Janos Hunyadi at Nish; George Castriota, governor of Albania, takes advantage of this defeat by declaring his province independent.
1444	Christians and Ottomans declare a truce at Adrianople and George Brankovich is restored to his principality of Serbia; Hungarians break the truce but are defeated at Varna; Vladislav VI of Poland perishes there and Ladislas Posthumus succeeds to the Hungarian throne.
1445	Cape Verde discovered by Diniz Diaz of Portugal. Copenhagen becomes the capital of Denmark.
1446	Corinth falls to the Ottomans. Janos Hunyadi is elected regent of Hungary for Ladislas.
1447	Casimir of Lithuania, a brother of the late Vladislav VI, is elected king of Poland. Milan becomes a republic on the death of Filippo Maria Visconti. Shah Rukh, Lord of Turkestan dies, and is succeeded by his son Ulugh Beg.
1448	With the death of Christopher of Bavaria, king of Sweden, Denmark and Norway, the Union of Kalmar dissolves. Christian of Oldenburg reigns in Denmark and Norway whilst Karl Knutsen is elected king of Sweden. Sultan Murad defeats the Hungarians under Janos Hunyadi at the second battle of Kosovo. Emperor John VIII dies, and is succeeded by his brother Constantine XI.
1449	Ulugh Beg, Lord of Turkestan, is executed by his son Abd al-Latif, who also puts his brother Abd al-Aziz to death. The Timurid provinces in Turkestan fragment as a result, and Babur ibn Baisonqur, a nephew of Ulugh Beg, takes power in Khurasan.
1450	Abd al-Latif dies; his cousin Abdullah Mirza succeeds him as Lord of Turkestan. Francesco Sforza overthrows the republic in Milan and makes himself duke. Normandy reconquered by France. Jack Cade leads a revolt in Kent and Sussex; it fails and Cade is killed, but Henry VI is forced to flee for safety to Kenilworth for a while.
1451	Gascony reconquered by the French. Sultan Murad II dies, and is succeeded by his son Muhammad II.
1452	Borso of Este is created duke of Modena by Emperor Frederick III. James II of Scotland murders the earl of Douglas at Stirling. John Talbot leads an expedition to Gascony and reconquers much of it.
1453	Constantinople falls to the Ottoman Sultan Muhammad II; Emperor Constantine XI perishes in the fighting and the Byzantine Empire is no more. The French win a decisive victory over the English at Castillon, where Talbot dies. Gascony is reconquered and the English hold only Calais in France. The Hundred Years War is thus brought to an end. Henry VI has a bout of insanity.
1454	The duke of York is appointed protector during Henry VI's incapacity. The Peace of Lodi is reached between Venice and Milan and their allies. Venice signs a treaty with Sultan Muhammad II.
1455	Henry VI recovers his sanity and dismisses the duke of York from the post of Protector. The Wars of the Roses begin when York and the earl of Warwick raise an army and defeat and capture Henry VI at St Albans. York is made Constable of England but pro-Lancastrian riots break out. Johannes Gutenberg produces the first printed Bible, using the movable metal type that he started to perfect in the 1450s.
1456	The Ottomans capture Athens but are repulsed from Belgrade by Janos Hunyadi, who dies soon after from plague. Vlad III the Impaler retakes the Wallachian throne from Vladislav II.
1457	Karl VIII of Sweden is driven out and replaced by Christian I of Denmark. Laszlo Hunyadi, son of Janos, is arrested and beheaded in Buda, sparking outrage in Hungary; Ladislas Posthumus is forced to flee to Prague, where he dies suddenly. Emperor Frederick III succeeds in Austria; George Podiebrad, leader of the Hussites, is elected king in Bohemia.
1458	Matthias Corvinus, second son of Janos Hunyadi, is elected king of Hungary. Alfonso V of Aragon dies, and is succeeded in Aragon and Sicily by his brother Juan II and in Naples by his bastard son Ferdinand.
1459	Civil war is renewed in England. The Yorkists are victorious at Blore Heath but defeated at Ludford Bridge. The Irish come out in support of the Yorkists.
1460	Henry VI defeated and captured by the Yorkists at Northampton; the duke of York is named heir to Henry but dies at the battle of Wakefield, where the Lancastrians are victorious. James II of Scotland dies when a cannon misfires at Roxburgh, and is succeeded by his son James III. Henry the Navigator dies.
1461	Yorkists victorious at Mortimer's Cross, where Owen Tudor is captured and executed, but defeated at St Albans. Henry VI is rescued by the Lancastrians. Edward of York deposes Henry VI and crushes the Lancastrians at Towton; Henry VI and his family flee to Scotland. Charles VII of France dies, and is succeeded by his son Louis XI. Trebizond falls to the Ottomans.
1462	Vlad III the Impaler of Wallachia is deposed and replaced by his pro-Turkish brother Radu III. Prince Vasili of Moscow dies, and is succeeded by his son Ivan III the Great.
1463	Bosnia conquered by the Ottomans, who go to war with the Venetians. England, France and Burgundy sign the Truce of Hesdin, the latter two recognizing Edward IV of York as king of England.
1464	Yorkists victorious at Hedgeley Moor and Hexham, and gain control of Northern England. Louis XI of France founds the *Poste Royale*. Cosimo de Medici dies, and is succeeded by his son Piero I.
1465	Henry VI captured in Ribblesdale and imprisoned in the Tower. Louis XI of France defeated by a coalition of royal dukes at Montlhéry and is forced to sign the treaty of Conflans.
1466	The Medicis form an alliance with the Vatican to finance alum mining in the Papal States. George Podiebrad, king of Bohemia, excommunicated by Pope Paul II.
1467	Philip the Good of Burgundy dies, and is succeeded by his son Charles the Bold.
1468	Zara Ya'kob Constantine of Ethiopia dies, and is succeeded by his son Ba'eda Maryam I. James III of Scotland contracts to marry Margaret, daughter of Christian I of Denmark; the Orkneys and Shetlands are pledged as security for her dowry.

1469   Rebellion develops in England against Edward IV and the power of his wife's family. Edward is imprisoned after his army deserts him at Olney, and is released with a promise to appease the rebels. Piero de Medici dies; his sons Lorenzo the Magnificent and Giuliano succeed him. Ferdinand, heir to the throne of Aragon, marries Isabella, heiress of Castile.

1470   Portuguese seafarers reach the Gold Coast. Edward IV defeats a rebel army at Empingham, but Warwick and the Lancastrians reach an accord and invade, forcing Edward to flee to Burgundy. Henry VI is restored to the throne.

1471   Edward IV returns to England, defeats and kills Warwick at Barnet and then decisively defeats the Lancastrians at Tewkesbury, where Edward Prince of Wales perishes. Henry VI is murdered in the Tower. Louis XI of France and Charles the Bold of Burgundy go to war.

1472   Lopo Gonçalves is the first European to cross the Equator. Ivan III of Moscow marries Zoe, niece of Emperor Constantine XI, thus attempting to transfer imperial lustre to himself.

1473   Charles the Bold of Burgundy occupies Lorraine and Alsace. Cyprus falls under Venetian rule.

1474   The Union of Constance is formed against Charles the Bold of Burgundy, who makes an anti-French alliance, via the treaty of London, with Edward IV. Henry IV of Castile dies, and is succeeded by his half-sister Isabella and her husband Ferdinand, son of Juan II of Aragon.

1475   Edward IV invades France but is let down by his absent ally Charles the Bold and goes on to sign a 7-year truce with Louis XI via the treaty of Picquigny.

1476   Charles the Bold makes war on the Swiss, but is defeated at Granson, and later at Morat. Duke Galeazzo Sforza of Milan is assassinated by republicans, but is succeeded by his son Gian Galeazzo. William Caxton establishes the first English printing press.

1477   Edward IV bans early forms of skittles and cricket due to their interference with archery practice. Charles the Bold of Burgundy dies fighting the Swiss at the battle of Nancy; his state implodes and is effectively shared between Louis XI and Charles' son-in-law Maximilian, son of Emperor Frederick III.

1478   The duke of Clarence is drowned in a butt of Malmsey while imprisoned in the Tower of London. Novgorod subdued by Ivan the Great of Muscovy. Isabella of Castile unleashes the Inquisition on Jewish converts. Pope Sixtus VI and the Pazzi family plot to assassinate the Medicis; Giuliano is killed but Lorenzo escapes and decimates the Pazzis in revenge.

1479   Juan II of Aragon dies. His son Ferdinand succeeds him and the thrones of Castile and Aragon are thus united. The treaty of Constantinople ends the war between Venice and the Ottoman Empire.

1480   Ivan III frees Muscovy from Tartar domination. Duke René of Anjou dies; his domains, including Provence, are annexed by Louis XI. Otranto is taken by the Ottomans.

1481   Sultan Muhammad II dies, and is succeeded by his son Bayazid II. Alfonso V of Portugal dies, and is succeeded by his son João II.

1482   Venice goes to war with Ferrara. Louis XI and the Habsburgs make the Peace of Arras, partitioning the Burgundian domains.

1483   Edward IV dies, and is succeeded by his son Edward V, who disappears along with his brother Richard in the Tower. Their uncle Richard assumes the kingship. Louis XI of France dies, and is succeeded by his son Charles VIII. The Dominican Tomás de Torquemada takes control of the Spanish Inquisition.

1484   Diogo Cão discovers the mouth of the River Congo. Pope Innocent VIII issues the bull *Summis Desiderantes* against witchcraft.

1485   Emperor Frederick III expelled from Vienna by Matthias Corvinus of Hungary. Henry Tudor invades England against Richard III, defeats and kills him at Bosworth Field, and takes the throne. Caxton publishes Malory's *Morte d'Arthur*.

1486   Matthias Corvinus devises a law code for Hungary. Henry VII marries Elizabeth of York and unites the houses of Lancaster and York. Krämer and Spränger publish the *Malleus Maleficarum* attacking witches and witchcraft.

1487   Lambert Simnel leads revolt against Henry VII, claiming to be Edward IV's nephew, but is defeated at Stoke and sent to work in the royal kitchens. Bartholomew Diaz sails around the Cape of Good Hope, which he names the Cape of Storms.

1488   James III of Scotland is murdered; his son James IV succeeds him. Duke Francis of Brittany dies, and is succeeded by his daughter Anne. Johann Widmann develops the use of the symbols (+), (&), and (-). Bartholomew Diaz returns to Lisbon, where João II gives the Cape of Good Hope its name.

1489   Typhus is brought to Aragon by soldiers returning from Cyprus. Catherine Cornaro of Cyprus is forced to sell her kingdom to Venice. Henry VII signs the anti-French treaty of Redon with Brittany.

1490   Matthias Corvinus of Hungary dies without an heir, and is succeeded by Ladislas of Bohemia.

1491   Perkin Warbeck claims to be Richard, duke of York, and rallies support for his cause in France and Ireland. Charles VIII of France annexes Brittany by forcing Anne of Brittany to marry him.

1492   Granada, the last Moorish city, conquered by Ferdinand and Isabella; Spain effectively one country. Lorenzo the Magnificent of Florence dies, and is succeeded by his son Piero II. Casimir IV of Poland and Lithuania dies, and is succeeded by his sons John Albert in Poland and Alexander in Lithuania. Rodrigo Borgia elected Pope as Alexander VI. Henry VII invades France and is bought off by Charles VIII under the treaty of Étaples, with compensation for Brittany's annexation and the expulsion of Warbeck. Jews in Spain are ordered to convert or quit the country. Christopher Columbus discovers Cuba and Hispaniola.

1493   Columbus returns home from the Indies, and is sent back as governor of the new lands by Isabella of Castile, discovering Dominica. Pope Alexander VI publishes the bull *Inter Cetera Divina* dividing the New World between Spain and Portugal. Emperor Frederick III dies, and is succeeded by his son Maximilian I.

1494   Emperor Maximilian I recognises Warbeck as king of England. Spain and Portugal divide the New World by the treaty of Tordesillas. Charles VIII of France invades Italy, deposes Piero de Medici in Florence and takes Rome. Duke Gian Galeazzo of Milan dies, probably poisoned by his uncle Lodovico, who succeeds him.

1495   Charles VIII of France expels Alfonso II of Naples and is crowned king of the state, but is forced to retreat by Alfonso's son Ferdinand II, who assumes the kingship. Syphilis strikes the state and the French soldiers are badly affected by it. The Diet of Worms is established to modernise the Holy Roman Empire. João II of Portugal dies, and is succeeded by his cousin Manuel the Fortunate. Warbeck received by James IV of Scotland. A dry-dock is built in Portsmouth, establishing the dockyard there.

1496	Henry VII commissions John Cabot to search for new lands. The Canary Islands conquered by Spain. Ferdinand II of Naples dies, and is succeeded by his uncle Frederick IV. James IV invades Northumberland in support of Warbeck. Manuel I of Portugal expels the Jews from his country.
1497	John and Sebastian Cabot reach Labrador and Newfoundland. The Cornish rebel against taxation but are defeated at Blackheath; Warbeck lands in Cornwall but is captured. John of Denmark defeats the Swedish at Brunkeberg and revives the Union of Kalmar. Savonarola stages a bonfire of vanities in Florence. Vasco da Gama rounds the Cape of Good Hope and gives Natal its name as he discovers it on Christmas Day.
1498	Charles VIII of France dies, and is succeeded by his second cousin once removed Louis XII, duke of Orléans. Savonarola burned at the stake for heresy. Vasco da Gama reaches Malindi in East Africa and then Calicut in India. Columbus embarks on a third voyage, discovering Trinidad and the Orinoco River.
1499	Louis XII of France divorces his wife Jeanne and marries Anne of Brittany to keep the duchy in French hands. Emperor Maximilian and the Swiss go to war; by the Peace of Basel, Swiss independence is granted. Venice and the Ottomans go to war; the Venetian fleet is defeated at Sapienza. Montenegro falls to the Ottomans. Louis XII takes Milan, forcing Ludovico Sforza to flee to the Tyrol. Perkin Warbeck is executed.
1500	Ludovico Sforza recaptures Milan, but the French return and capture Sforza on retaking the city. Pedro Cabral discovers Brazil when blown off course en route for India.
1501	Lithuania invaded by Ivan III of Moscow. Basel and Schaffhausen admitted to the Swiss Confederation. Frederick IV of Naples dies; Pope Alexander VI declares Louis XII Frederick's successor. Ismail I, sheikh of Ardabil, defeats Shah Alwand of Persia at Shurur and establishes Safavid rule in the country. Emperor Maximilian I recognises the French conquests in Italy by the Peace of Trent.
1502	St Helena discovered by João de Nova. Arthur, prince of Wales, dies at Ludlow.
1503	Louis XII of France abandons his claim to the Neapolitan throne after his alliance with Ferdinand of Aragon collapses. Gonzalo de Cordoba defeats a French army and enters Naples. James IV of Scotland marries Margaret Tudor, daughter of Henry VII. Pope Alexander VI dies, and is succeeded briefly by Pius III, and then by Julius II.
1504	Albert of Bavaria defeats Rupert, son of the Elector Palatine in the Bavarian War, during which at Landshut the Frankonian knight Götz von Berlichingen loses his right hand and has it replaced by one of iron. Michelangelo's statue of *David* is put on display in Florence.
1505	Ivan III of Muscovy dies, and is succeeded by his son Vasili III.
1506	Niccolò Machiavelli forms a Florentine militia, the first national army established in Italy. Christopher Columbus dies. 4,000 Jews perish in a riot in Lisbon. Philip the Handsome, son of the Emperor Maximilian and husband of the de jure Castilian Queen Juana (Joanna) dies, sending his wife mad.
1507	Cesare Borgia dies whilst besieging Viana, in Spain.
1508	Juan Ponce de León colonises Puerto Rico. Pope Julius II confirms that the German King will automatically become Holy Roman Emperor. Michelangelo starts painting the ceiling of the Sistine Chapel.
1509	Francisco de Almeida destroys a Muslim fleet at the battle of Diu, guaranteeing Portuguese control of the spice trade. Pope Julius II excommunicates the Venetian Republic, which is defeated by the French at Agnadello. Henry VII dies, and is succeeded by his son Henry VIII.
1510	Afonso de Albuquerque seizes Goa for Portugal. Sir Richard Empson and Edmund Dudley beheaded by Henry VIII for their unpopular fiscal policies under his father.
1511	Portuguese forces under Albuquerque seize Malacca, the centre of the spice trade. Julius II forms the Holy League with Venice to drive the French from Italy and enlists the support of Ferdinand of Aragon and Henry VIII.
1512	Forces of the Holy League are defeated by the French at Ravenna, but the French are then driven from Milan; Massimiliano Sforza, son of the deposed Duke Ludovico, becomes duke. Sultan Bayazid dies mysteriously after being deposed by his Janissaries; his son Selim I the Grim succeeds him.
1513	Juan Ponce de León discovers Florida. John of Denmark dies, and is succeeded by his son Christian II, who is rejected by the Swedes. Pope Julius II dies, and is succeeded by Leo X. Henry VIII invades France, where he and Emperor Maximilian are successful in the battle of Guinegatte (the Spurs). James IV of Scotland takes advantage of the English in France to invade, but his army is routed at Flodden and James is killed, to be succeeded by his infant son James V.
1514	The *Henry Grace a Dieu*, the largest warship in the world, is launched in England. Thomas Wolsey becomes Archbishop of York. The Ottoman Sultan Selim invades Persia and routs the Persian army at Chaldiran.
1515	Louis XII of France dies, and is succeeded by his son-in-law François I, who defeats the Swiss and Venetians at Marignano and takes Milan.
1516	Ferdinand of Aragon dies, and is succeeded on the Spanish throne by his grandson Charles I. Pope Leo X and François I of France sign the Concordat of Bologna, giving France freedom in ecclesiastical appointments. Sultan Selim I defeats the Mamluks at Marjdabik and takes Syria. Thomas More publishes *Utopia*.
1517	Egypt falls to the Ottoman Turks, to whom the Sharif of Mecca submits, leaving Arabia under Ottoman control. Martin Luther nails 95 theses to the door of Wittenberg Cathedral attacking the sale of indulgences.
1518	Huldrych Zwingli forces the expulsion from Zurich of Barnardin Samson, a Franciscan seller of indulgences. Wolsey negotiates the Peace of London between England, France, the Holy Roman Empire, Spain and the Papacy; they agree to crusade against the Turks.
1519	Emperor Maximilian dies, and is succeeded by his grandson Charles V (I of Spain). Vasco de Balboa is beheaded in Panama as he loses the power struggle amongst the Spanish in Central America. Hernán

Cortés enters Tenochtitlán, the Aztec capital, and is received by Emperor Montezuma, whom he takes prisoner.

1520   Christian II of Denmark invades Sweden and is successful at Tiveden and Uppsala before taking Stockholm; despite proclaiming an amnesty he executes numerous leading Swedes. Henry VIII and François I meet at the Field of the Cloth of Gold near Calais. Cortés driven from Tenochtitlán by Cuauhtemoc. Sultan Selim I dies, and is succeeded by his son Suleiman I the Magnificent. Ferdinand Magellan sails through the Strait of Magellan and names the Pacific.

1521   Martin Luther is interrogated by the Diet of Worms; refusing to recant he is put in the castle of Wartburg for his own protection by Frederick of Saxony and begins a German translation of the Bible. Ferdinand Magellan dies in a skirmish in the Philippines. Cortés overthrows the Aztec empire; Montezuma II dies in the fighting. Sultan Suleiman I takes Belgrade. Henry VIII is awarded the title 'Defender of the Faith' by Leo X for an anti-Lutheran work.

1522   Luther returns to Wittenberg and initiates church services in German. Sultan Suleiman takes Rhodes from the Knights of St John. Juan Sebastiano del Cano returns home after finishing Magellan's circumnavigation of the world.

1523   Christian II of Denmark deposed by his nobles for cruelty and replaced by his uncle Frederick I. Gustavus Vasa takes advantage of the situation to be crowned king of Sweden. Sir Thomas More elected Speaker of the House of Commons. Zwingli publishes his 67 Articles in Zurich.

1524   Giovanni da Verrazano discovers New York Bay, naming Manhattan Angoulême. Denmark confirms Swedish independence by the treaty of Malmö. Shah Ismail I of Persia dies, and is succeeded by his son Tahmasp I.

1525   Emperor Charles V defeats François I of France at Pavia, imprisons him and establishes control over Italy. Albert von Brandenburg, Grand Master of the Teutonic Knights, makes himself duke of Prussia. A peasants' revolt in Germany is suppressed, and its leader Thomas Müntzer executed. Cardinal Wolsey gives Hampton Court to Henry VIII.

1526   François I of France signs the treaty of Madrid, ceding various lands to Charles V, but renounces it because the terms were extorted from him, and allies himself with Sultan Suleiman, who defeats and kills Louis II of Hungary at the battle of Mohacs. Ferdinand, brother of Emperor Charles V is chosen to succeed Louis II in Hungary and Bohemia, but the Hungarians elect John Zapolya as king. Zahir-ud-Din Babur defeats Sultan Ibrahim Lodi of Delhi at Panipat, takes Agra and founds the Mughal Empire.

1527   The Mughal Emperor Babur defeats Rajput forces at Kanvaha. England and France ally via the treaty of Westminster. Imperial troops sack Rome; Pope Clement VII is imprisoned in the Castel Sant' Angelo. Holbein paints Thomas More and his family.

1528   The physician and alchemist Paracelsus is forced from Basel due to his unorthodox medical opinions and treatments.

1529   François I of France and Emperor Charles V make peace via the treaty of Cambrai. Suleiman the Magnificent takes Buda and besieges Vienna but fails to take it. Cardinal Wolsey falls from power due to his inability to secure a divorce for Henry VIII from Catherine of Aragon. Sir Thomas More replaces him as Lord Chancellor, the first layman to hold the post.

1530   The Knights of St John are settled in Malta by Emperor Charles V. Melanchthon prepares the Confession of Augsburg as a statement of faith for the German Protestant princes, who form the Schmalkaldic League against Emperor Charles V. Cardinal Wolsey is arrested for treason, but dies whilst on his way to trial. The Mughal Emperor Babur dies, and is succeeded by his son Humayun.

1531   Lisbon is destroyed by an earthquake. The Catholic Swiss Cantons attack and defeat Zurich in the battle of Kappel; Zwingli dies in the fighting.

1532   The English clergy recognise Henry VIII as Supreme Head of the Church. Sultan Suleiman invades Hungary. The Inca chief Atahualpa seized by Pizarro, who reintroduces horses to South America. François Rabelais publishes Pantagruel.

1533   Henry VIII divorces Catherine of Aragon and marries Anne Boleyn with the sanction of Thomas Cranmer, newly appointed archbishop of Canterbury; this leads to Henry's excommunication. Pizarro executes Atahualpa by strangling and causes the downfall of the Incas. Holbein paints The Ambassadors. Vasili III of Moscow dies, and is succeeded by his son Ivan IV the Terrible.

1534   John of Leiden sets up the radical Protestant Anabaptist kingdom of Zion at Münster. Jacques Cartier sails for the New World by command of François I and reaches the Gulf of St Lawrence. Ignatius Loyola founds the Society of Jesus (Jesuits). The Act of Supremacy marks the final break between England and Rome, comfirming Henry VIII as Supreme Head of the Church of England.

1535   Jacques Cartier sails up the St Lawrence to Montreal. Thomas Cromwell is appointed Vicar-General to investigate religious houses in England. Francis of Waldeck retakes Münster from the Anabaptists. John Fisher, Bishop of Rochester, and Sir Thomas More executed for refusing to take an oath supporting Henry VIII's acts. Emperor Charles V conquers Tunis, defeating the pirate leader Khair ad-Din. Duke Francesco Sforza of Milan dies; the duchy reverts to Emperor Charles V.

1536   John of Leiden is executed in Münster. The Anabaptist Jacob Hutter is burned at the stake. Dissolution of the monasteries commences in England, leading to a rising under Robert Aske (the Pilgrimage of Grace). Henry VIII executes Anne Boleyn on the grounds of adultery and marries Jane Seymour. Wales is formally united with England. William Tyndale is executed for heresy.

1537   Pope Paul III prohibits enslavement of New World natives and excommunicates Catholic slave traders. Robert Aske is received by Henry VIII and Cromwell, but is later executed for treason. Jane Seymour dies after bearing the future Edward VI.

1538   Pope Paul III allies with Charles V and the Venetians in a Holy League against the Ottoman Empire, but the combined Venetian, Genoese and papal fleet is defeated at Prevesa by the Ottomans.

1539   Charles V and François I make peace with the treaty of Toledo. The Six Articles are passed in England, enforcing Catholic orthodoxy. Dissolution of the monasteries ends; the abbots of Reading, Colchester and Glastonbury are executed in the process.

1540	Henry VIII marries Anne of Cleves but quickly repudiates her. The marriage is annulled and he marries Catherine Howard. Thomas Cromwell falls from grace over the Cleves marriage and is executed. The Jesuits are recognised by Pope Paul III. The Norse colony of Greenland comes to an end, with the last colonist discovered dead outside his hut with a dagger in his hand.
1541	John Calvin sets up a theocratic government in Geneva. Henry VIII is accepted by the Irish Parliament as king of Ireland and head of the Irish Church.
1542	Henry VIII executes Catherine Howard for adultery. Pope Paul III establishes the Universal Inquisition to repress the Reformation. James V of Scotland raids Cumberland, but is defeated badly at Solway Moss. He dies soon after and is succeeded by his six-day-old daughter, Mary.
1543	Pope Paul III establishes an index of prohibited books. The Spanish Inquisition commences burning Protestants at the stake. Henry VIII marries Catherine Parr. Copernicus publishes his *De revolutionibus orbium coelestrium*, stating his belief that the planets orbit a stationary Sun.
1544	Henry VIII captures Boulogne, but subsequently retires from France when his ally Charles V and François I make peace with the treaty of Crépy-en-Valois.
1545	The *Mary Rose* capsizes off Portsmouth. Charles V and Suleiman the Magnificent make a truce with the treaty of Adrianople. The Council of Trent meets, in an attempt by the Catholic church to establish a Counter-Reformation.
1546	England and France make peace with the treaty of Ardres, by which England holds Boulogne for eight years before returning it to France. The Paris printer Etienne Dolet is executed for heresy and blasphemy as a result of publishing humanist works by the likes of Erasmus.
1547	Ivan IV the Terrible of Moscow crowned Tsar of Russia. Henry VIII dies, and is succeeded by his nine-year-old son Edward VI. François I laughs on receiving news of Henry's death, develops a fever and dies, to be succeeded by his son Henri II. John Knox is captured at St Andrews and sent to work on a French galley. Protector Somerset, ruling on behalf of his nephew Edward, invades Scotland and defeats the Scots at Pinkie.
1548	Francis Xavier founds a Jesuit mission in Japan. Sigismund I of Poland dies, and is succeeded by his son Sigismund II Augustus.
1549	Ivan IV summons the first Russian national assembly. The Protestant Book of Common Prayer is imposed in England, leading to risings in Devon and Cornwall. Robert Kett leads a revolt in Norfolk against land enclosures, but is defeated at Dussindale.
1550	England makes peace with France and Scotland by the treaty of Boulogne; Boulogne is returned to France and John Knox released from galley labour. Cricket is first referred to.
1551	Henri II of France disavows the Council of Trent and renews the war against Charles V. The Ottomans attack Malta, but are repulsed and take Tripoli instead.
1552	The duke of Somerset is executed. Tsar Ivan IV takes Kazan and attacks Astrakhan. The second Book of Common Prayer is introduced.
1553	Richard Chancellor opens a trade route to Moscow via the White Sea and Archangel. Edward VI dies, and is succeeded by his Catholic half-sister Mary, despite the duke of Northumberland's efforts to install Lady Jane Grey, his daughter-in-law, as a Protestant queen. Northumberland is later executed.
1554	Sir Thomas Wyatt leads revolt from Kent over Mary I's proposed marriage to Philip of Spain, but is defeated and executed. Lady Jane Grey is also executed, whilst Mary's half-sister Elizabeth is imprisoned in the Tower.
1555	Pope Julius III dies, his successor Marcellus II dies after a month, and Paul IV succeeds. Paul walls in Rome's Jewish quarter, creating a ghetto. John Knox returns to Scotland. Tobacco is brought to Europe from America. Mary I persecutes Protestants; Latimer and Ridley are burned at the stake in Oxford. Charles V hands sovereignty of the Netherlands to his son Philip.
1556	Thomas Cranmer is dismissed as Archbishop of Canterbury and burned at the stake. Emperor Charles V abdicates; his brother Ferdinand succeeds him as Emperor whilst his son Philip II succeeds in Spain. Indian Mughal emperor Humayun dies after falling from his library roof, and is succeeded by his son Jalal-ud-Din Akbar I.
1557	Tsar Ivan IV invades Poland. Macao founded by the Portuguese, whose King João III dies, and is succeeded by his grandson Sebastian. The Spanish drive the French from Italy after victory at the battle of St Quentin.
1558	Calais, England's last continental possession, falls to the French. Mary I dies, and is succeeded by her half-sister Elizabeth. William Cecil becomes Secretary of State. John Knox writes his *First Blast of the Trumpet Against the Monstrous Regiment of Women*.
1559	Christian III of Denmark dies, and is succeeded by his son Frederick II; Christian's imprisoned predecessor Christian II also dies. The Act of Supremacy restores the Church of England. The war between England, Spain and France is ended by the treaty of Cateau-Cambrésis. Henri II of France dies after a jousting accident, and is succeeded by his son François II.
1560	The treaty of Berwick is made between England and the Protestant Scottish lords against the French, whose troops are forced to return home; the Scots Parliament approves Knox's Calvinistic Confession of Faith. Louis de Bourbon organises the Huguenot Conspiracy of Amboise against the Catholic Guises, but is thwarted by the Dowager Queen Catherine de Medici. François II of France dies, and is succeeded by his brother Charles IX.
1561	Philip II declares Madrid the capital of Spain. Persecution of French Huguenots suspended by the Edict of Orléans. Flemish Calvinist refugees settle in England. St Paul's Cathedral damaged by fire after a lightning strike.
1562	The duc de Guise orders the massacre of Huguenots at Vassy, thus precipitating the Wars of Religion in France. The English establish the 39 Articles of Religion.
1563	The duc de Guise is murdered by a Huguenot; Catherine de Medici is left in charge of the Catholic faction and grants limited toleration to the Huguenots by the Peace of Amboise, ending the First War of Religion. John Foxe's *Book of Martyrs* is published. The Council of Trent comes to an end.

1564   England and France make peace by the treaty of Troyes: in return for 220,000 crowns Elizabeth renounces claim to Calais. Emperor Ferdinand I dies, and is succeeded by his son Maximilian II.

1565   The Ottomans besiege Malta, but 700 Knights of St John under Jean de La Valette hold them off for 4 months before Spanish troops relieve them and force the Ottomans to withdraw. Mary Queen of Scots marries her cousin Henry, Lord Darnley.

1566   Mary Queen of Scots' secretary, David Rizzio, is murdered at Holyrood. Calvinists riot in the Netherlands and petition the Regent, Margaret of Palma, to abolish the Inquisition. Suleiman the Magnificent dies, and is succeeded by his son Selim II.

1567   Lord Darnley is murdered at Kirk o'Field; the earl of Bothwell, who is believed to have ordered the assassination, marries Mary Queen of Scots. The earl of Morton discovers the possibly fabricated Casket Letters incriminating Bothwell and Mary; the Scots Lords rebel against Mary, imprison her in Lochleven Castle and force her abdication in favour of her son James VI, with Moray as Regent. Philip II sends the duke of Alba to eliminate Protestant resistance in the Netherlands, where he begins a reign of terror. Regent Margaret resigns.

1568   The Second War of Religion in France is ended by the treaty of Longjumeau. Mary Queen of Scots escapes Lochleven, raises an army, but is defeated by Moray at Langside and flees to England. Alba beheads Counts Egmont and Hoorn in Brussels for opposing the Inquisition and confiscates the estates of those who failed to attend the Council of Blood. Erik XIV of Sweden is deposed due to mental illness and replaced by his brother John III. The first modern Eisteddfod is held at Caerwys.

1569   Elizabeth orders Mary of Scots' detention in Tutbury Castle and imprisons the duke of Norfolk, who seeks to marry Mary. Catholics under the duc d'Anjou defeat Huguenot forces at Jarnac. Mercator publishes his map of the world and establishes his projection. The Union of Lublin unites Poland and Lithuania. Catholic earls of Northumberland and Westmorland revolt, seize Durham, but are forced to flee by Baron Hunsdon. Cosimo de Medici is made the Grand duke of Tuscany by Pope Pius V.

1570   Regent Moray is assassinated; the earl of Lennox takes over the regency. Elizabeth I is excommunicated. The third War of Religion is ended by the Peace of St Germain-en-Laye. Tsar Ivan IV establishes a reign of terror in Great Novgorod and violently purges his government in Moscow. Denmark recognises Swedish independence by the Peace of Stettin.

1571   Pope Pius V establishes the anti-Turkish Maritime League with Spain, Venice, Malta and Genoa; its fleet gains a decisive victory over the Turks at Lepanto. Roberto di Ridolfi plots to free Mary Queen of Scots and depose Elizabeth I, but the plots are exposed and fail. Sir Thomas Gresham's bourse is chartered as the Royal Exchange. Regent Lennox is murdered at Stirling; the earl of Mar replaces him.

1572   The duke of Norfolk is executed for treason in assisting the Ridolfi plot. Sigismund II of Poland dies without an heir; the Polish estates declare the crown elective. Catherine de Medici organises the Massacre of St Bartholomew's Day against the Huguenots; Admiral Gaspard de Coligny is disembowelled and defenestrated while still living. 3,000 Protestants die; Pope Gregory XIII congratulates Catherine. The fourth War of Religion commences. Regent Mar dies, replaced by the earl of Morton.

1573   The Peace of Constantinople ends the war between Venice and the Turks. Poland elects Henri, duc d'Anjou as king. The Edict of Boulogne ends the fourth War of Religion. Francis Walsingham is appointed Elizabeth's Secretary of State.

1574   The fifth War of Religion breaks out. Charles IX of France dies, and is succeeded by his brother Henri III, who abandons the Polish throne. Juan Fernandez discovers the Juan Fernandez Islands. Sultan Selim II dies after a fall in his bath, succeeded by his son Murad III.

1575   Dutch rebels fail to reach agreement with the Spanish Governor-General Requesens at Breda. The duc de Guise defeats the Huguenots at Dormans. Stephen Bathory of Transylvania is elected king of Poland.

1576   The Peace of Chastenoy ends the fifth War of Religion, but grants so many concessions to the Huguenots that the French Catholics ally with Philip II; Henri III outlaws Protestantism to appease them. Spanish troops rampage in the Netherlands, sacking Antwerp; the Pacification of Ghent allies the Lowland provinces in a pact for independence as a result. Emperor Maximilian II dies, and is succeeded by his son Rudolf II. Shah Tahmasp is murdered, and succeeded by his son Ismail II. The Theatre, England's first playhouse, is opened by Richard Burbage in Shoreditch.

1577   The sixth War of Religion breaks out; Catholic forces are victorious but to curb the power of the Holy League Henri III grants the Huguenots terms via the Peace of Bergerac. Don John of Austria arrives to take up the Governorship of the Netherlands, but his Perpetual Edict is rejected by William the Silent, who enters Brussels in triumph.

1578   Alessandro Farnese, duke of Parma, sent with an army to the Netherlands, where he defeats the Dutch at Gemblours and succeeds as governor on the death of Don John. Shah Isma'il II dies, and is succeeded by his brother Muhammad Kundabanda. King Sebastian of Portugal invades Morocco, but perishes along with most of his army at Al Kasr al Kebir, although the king of Fez is also killed. A cult develops around the dead king and four pretenders appear, who are all executed. Sebastian's great-uncle Henry succeeds him.

1579   The Union of Arras unites the Walloons of the Netherlands whilst the Dutch provinces unite under the Union of Utrecht and sign a military alliance with England. Francis Drake lands in California and claims English sovereignty over the area he calls 'New Albion'.

1580   The seventh War of Religion breaks out in France, but is ended by the treaty of Fleix. The Spanish invade Portugal led by the duke of Alva, defeat the Portuguese at Alcantara and conquer the country. Francis Drake completes a circumnavigation of the world.

1581   Stephen Bathory of Poland invades Russia. William the Silent appoints François, duc d'Alençon, king of the Netherlands. Tsar Ivan the Terrible kills his heir with his own hands. The Jesuit Edmund Campion is arrested, tortured, tried and executed.

1582   Tsar Ivan the Terrible makes peace with Poland and Sweden with the Peace of Jam-Zapolski and abandons Livonia and Estonia to Poland. James VI of Scotland kidnapped by pro-English nobles at Ruthven. Pope Gregory XIII introduces the Gregorian calendar, devised by Aloysius Lilius.

1583   James VI of Scotland escapes from his captors after 10 months. Humphrey Gilbert founds a colonial settlement in Newfoundland at St John's, but drowns on the return journey. Plots against Elizabeth I by John Somerville and Francis Throckmorton are foiled.

1584   Walter Raleigh founds a colony on Roanoke Island, Virginia. Tsar Ivan the Terrible dies, and is succeeded by his son Feodor I. François, duc d'Alencon dies, leaving Henri III with no direct heir; Henri of Navarre becomes nearest male heir. William the Silent is assassinated at Delft by Balthazar Gérard, but his son Maurice of Nassau continues the struggle against Spain.

1585   The Eighth War of Religion (the War of the Three Henris) breaks out in France as the Holy League under Henri, duc de Guise, attempt to stop Henri of Navarre from succeeding to the throne. The Netherlands are taken under English protection by the treaty of Nonsuch and a force under the earl of Leicester is sent to assist them.

1586   Kashmir annexed by the Emperor Akbar. Francis Drake raids Spanish New World colonies and rescues the survivors from the failed Roanoke settlement. Anglo-Dutch forces defeat the Spanish at Zutphen but Sir Philip Sidney dies as a result of a wound sustained there. Sir Anthony Babington plots against Elizabeth I, but Walsingham uncovers the plot and Babington is executed. Mary Queen of Scots is tried for her involvement and sentenced to death. Stephen Bathory of Poland dies.

1587   Mary Queen of Scots executed at Fotheringhay Castle. Sir Francis Drake raids Cadiz, 'singeing the king of Spain's beard' and disrupting preparations for the Armada. Sir Christopher Hatton is appointed Lord Chancellor. Poland elects Sigismund, son of John of Sweden, as king. Henri of Navarre defeats the Catholic League at Coutras.

1588   Frederick II of Denmark dies, and is succeeded by his son Christian IV. Henri, duc de Guise, enters Paris and forces Henri III to flee. The Spanish Armada sails for England under the duke of Medina Sidonia, but is defeated by the English and the weather. Although the tonnage of the 2 fleets was similar the Spanish lost nearly half of their 130 ships and the English none. Henri III arranges for Guise's assassination.

1589   The Russian Orthodox Church makes itself independent of Constantinople. Henri III of France is assassinated at St Cloud by Jacques Clément, a Dominican monk; he nominates Henri of Navarre as his successor, who founds the Bourbon line and defeats the Catholic League at Arques. The Rev. William Lee invents the first knitting machine, whilst Sir John Harington invents the Ajax, a flushing toilet.

1590   Shah Akbar conquers Orissa. Shah Abbas of Persia and Sultan Murad make peace, with Georgia, Azerbaijan and other provinces passing to the Turks. The Catholic League proclaim the cardinal Charles de Bourbon king of France; he dies soon after whilst Henri IV defeats them at Ivry. Edmund Spenser writes the first three books of The Faerie Queene. Shakespeare writes the Henry VI trilogy.

1591   The Tsarevich Dmitri is murdered, probably on order of the Regent Boris Godunov. Sir Richard Grenville dies after his ship, Revenge, battles a Spanish squadron single-handed for 15 hours.

1592   Galileo Galilei is forced to move from Pisa to Padua after publishing his results on falling weights. The Japanese warlord Hideyoshi invades Korea and takes Seoul and Pyongyang. John III of Sweden dies, and is succeeded by his son Sigismund, king of Poland.

1593   The Chinese enter Korea and force Hideyoshi to retreat to the south coast. Christopher Marlowe is stabbed to death in Deptford by Ingram Frizer during a tavern brawl. Henri IV converts to Catholicism to win over his subjects (saying 'Paris is well worth a mass'). Salisbury Cathedral's organist strikes the Dean in a fit of rage and is dismissed from his post.

1594   Henri IV enters Paris and grants Huguenots freedom of worship by the Edict of St Germain-en-Laye. John Lancaster returns to Britain after sailing to the East Indies and establishes a spice trade. The philosopher Giordano Bruno is seized by the Vatican for espousing the Copernican theory of the Solar System.

1595   Sultan Murad III dies, and is succeeded by his son Muhammad III. Henri IV drives the Spanish from Burgundy after victory at Fontaine-Française. Spanish forces attack Cornwall, burning Penzance and Mousehole. Francis Drake and John Hawkins leave Plymouth to raid Panama; Hawkins dies en route near Puerto Rico.

1596   Francis Drake dies of dysentery off Panama. The tomato is introduced to England. The Catholic League submit to Henri IV, ending the Wars of Religion. Willem Barents discovers Spitsbergen. The English sack Cadiz whilst Spain captures Calais. The Ottomans defeat the Hungarians at Erlau and Keresztes.

1597   Philip II sends a second Armada to England, but it is scattered by storms and fails. Transylvania ceded to Emperor Rudolf II by Sigmund Bathory.

1598   Tsar Feodor I dies; his brother-in-law Boris Godunov seizes the throne and forces the national assembly to accept him. Henri IV of France grants rights to Huguenots by the Edict of Nantes. France and Spain make peace by the treaty of Vervins. Philip II of Spain dies, and is succeeded by his son Philip III.

1599   The Globe Theatre is built in London. The earl of Essex is made Lord Lieutenant of Ireland, but after signing an unauthorised truce with the earl of Tyrone returns to England and is arrested by Elizabeth I. The Swedish Diet deposes Sigismund III and makes Karl of Sodermanlund, uncle of Sigismund, regent for Sigismund's younger brother John.

1600   The East India Company is founded. Giordano Bruno is burned at the stake for heresy in Rome due to his support for the Copernican system. Ieyasu Tokugawa defeats his rivals at Sekigahara and takes control of Japan, moving the capital from Kyoto to Edo (Tokyo); the shipwrecked English mariner Will Adams becomes an adviser to him. Will Kemp morris-dances from London to Norwich.

1601   The earl of Essex leads a revolt against Elizabeth I, which fails and Essex is executed for treason. Moghul Emperor Akbar the Great annexes Berar, Ahmadnagar and Khandesh. A Spanish army lands in Ireland to support Tyrone's revolt.

1602   The Spaniards in Ireland surrender to Mountjoy at Kinsale. The Dutch East India Company is founded. Emperor Rudolf II suppresses the Moravian Brethren.

1603   Elizabeth I dies, her cousin twice removed; James VI of Scotland, succeeds her. Tyrone submits to Mountjoy in Ireland, where James proclaims an amnesty. Walter Raleigh attempts to put Arabella Stuart on the throne rather than James, and is imprisoned for treason. Ieyasu founds the Tokugawa Shogunate in Japan. Sultan Muhammad III dies, and is succeeded by his son Ahmed I.

1604 The Hampton Court Conference convenes to discuss religious matters, and commissions an English translation of the Bible. Regent Karl becomes king of Sweden after his nephew John renounces the throne. England and Spain make peace. Ostend falls to the Spanish after a three-year siege.

1605 Tsar Boris Godunov dies; his son Feodor II succeeds him but is assassinated. A pretender, Dmitri, who claims to be a son of Ivan the Terrible, enters Moscow and is crowned Tsar. Akbar the Great dies, and is succeeded by his son Jahangir. Shogun Ieyasu retires in favour of his son Hidetada. Robert Catesby leads a plot to assassinate James I, but the plot fails and Guy Fawkes is caught red-handed under the House of Lords. Miguel de Cervantes publishes part one of *Don Quixote*.

1606 Tsar Dmitri is assassinated by the boyar (noble) Vasili Shuisky, who is elected Tsar. The Virginia Company is set up and 120 colonists leave London, led by Captain Christopher Newport. Shakespeare's *Macbeth* and *King Lear* are first performed.

1607 The English Parliament rejects the union of England and Scotland. Jamestown, Virginia is founded by Christopher Newport, who returns to England leaving Captain James Smith in charge; captured by the Algonquin, Smith's life is saved by the chief's daughter Pocahontas.

1608 Tsar Vasili Shuisky is defeated by a second 'False Dmitri', who advances on Moscow. Frederick IV of the Palatinate organises a Protestant Union in Germany. Emperor Rudolf II is forced to cede Hungary, Austria and Moravia to his brother Matthias. The Jesuit state of Paraguay is established.

1609 Philip III of Spain signs a 12-year truce with the Dutch, effectively recognising their independence. Duke Maximilian of Bavaria organises a Catholic League to oppose the Protestant Union in Germany. John-William of Jülich-Cleves dies without an heir; Brandenburg and Neuburg quarrel over the territory. James I begins settling Protestants in Ulster.

1610 Galileo observes four moons orbiting Jupiter. Henri IV of France is assassinated by François Ravaillac; he is succeeded by his son Louis XIII. The Jamestown colonists abandon their settlement, but on meeting a ship of new settlers return and try again. Tsar Vasili Shuisky is deposed by Sigismund III of Poland and abducted to Warsaw; Vladislav, Sigismund's son, is offered the throne. Frederick IV of the Palatinate dies, and is succeeded by his son Frederick V.

1611 Henry Hudson is marooned by mutineers whilst searching for the North-west Passage and is never heard of again. Denmark declares war on Sweden. Emperor Rudolf II is forced to resign the Bohemian crown in favour of his brother Matthias. Karl IX of Sweden dies, and is succeeded by his son Gustavus II Adolphus.

1612 Emperor Rudolf II dies, and is succeeded as Holy Roman Emperor by his brother Matthias. Prince Dmitri Pojarsky forces the Polish in Moscow to surrender, thwarting Vladislav of Poland's claim for the throne. Henry, prince of Wales, dies of typhoid.

1613 Sweden and Denmark make the Peace of Knärod; Sweden gives up Finland. Mikhail Romanov, son of the Patriarch of Moscow, is elected Tsar by the boyars. The Globe Theatre burns down during a performance of Shakespeare's *Henry VIII*.

1614 Pocahontas marries John Rolfe, a settler. The 'Addled Parliament' meets, but is dissolved after clashes with James I over finance. The French parliament, the Estates-General convene, but is dismissed by the duc de Richelieu. The Virginian colonists resist French colonial attempts in Maine and Nova Scotia. Jülich-Cleves is divided between Brandenburg and Neuburg by the treaty of Xanten. John Napier publishes a book of logarithms.

1615 The Moluccas seized from the Portuguese by the Dutch, whilst the English defeat a Portuguese fleet off Bombay. Osaka falls to the Tokugawa shogunate. Lady Arabella Stuart starves herself to death in the Tower of London.

1616 Baffin Bay discovered by William Baffin. Francis Beaumont and Miguel de Cervantes die. William Shakespeare dies on his 52nd birthday. Manchurian Tartars invade China. Walter Raleigh is released from the Tower to search for El Dorado. James I sells peerages to raise funds. Maximilian of Tyrol and Archduke Albert renounce their claims to the Imperial throne in favour of Ferdinand of Styria. Galileo is arrested for heresy.

1617 Russia and Sweden make the Peace of Stolbovo; Novgorod is returned to Russia but Karelia is ceded to Sweden. Pocahontas is received by James I at court, but dies of smallpox soon after. Sultan Ahmad I dies, and is succeeded by his brother Mustafa I.

1618 Richelieu is exiled to Avignon after conspiring with the Queen Mother. Bohemian rebels throw the regents, Jaroslav von Martinitz and William Slawata, out of the Hradcany Palace in the Defenestration of Prague, an act which precipitates the Thirty Years War, as rebels led by Heinrich von Thurn advance on Austria and an Imperial army is raised to face them. Duke Albert Frederick of Prussia dies, his duchy passes to John Sigismund of Brandenburg. Francis Bacon is made Lord Chancellor. Walter Raleigh returns from his fruitless expedition to South America, and is executed by James I for treason to appease the Spaniards. Sultan Mustafa I is declared unfit to rule and is replaced by his nephew Osman II.

1619 Emperor Matthias dies. His cousin Ferdinand II of Styria succeeds him, but is deposed by the Bohemian Diet in favour of Frederick V of the Palatinate. A Bohemian army under Count von Thurn besieges Vienna, but is forced to withdraw. Louis XIII recalls Richelieu to subdue a revolt by Marie de Medici; the treaty of Angoulême ends the conflict. William Harvey establishes the circulation of the blood.

1620 Gustavus Adolphus of Sweden occupies Livonia after declaring war on Poland. The Pilgrim Fathers depart from Plymouth to America; the *Speedwell* is forced to turn back but the *Mayflower* arrives at Cape Cod; the settlement is called New Plymouth. Count Von Tilly leads a Catholic Union army to victory in the battle of the White Mountain against Frederick of Bohemia, who is deposed; the Bohemian revolt is suppressed by Emperor Frederick. Oliver Cromwell is denounced for playing cricket.

1621 Frederick V of the Palatinate is placed under Imperial Ban and his electorate invaded. The Huguenots rebel against Louis XIII. Philip III of Spain dies, and is succeeded by his son Philip IV, who resumes the war with the Netherlands. Count Olivares becomes chief minister of Spain. The Dutch West India Company is founded. Francis Bacon is impeached by Parliament for corruption, but is pardoned by James I.

HISTORY

1622	Richelieu is created a cardinal by Louis XIII, who makes peace with the Huguenots by reaffirming the Edict of Nantes. Count von Tilly is defeated at Wiesloch, but defeats Baden at Wimpfen and Brunswick at Höchst. Sultan Osman II is murdered by his Janissaries after planning to reform them and Mustafa I is restored to the throne.
1623	Abbas I of Persia takes Baghdad and Mosul from the Ottomans. Sultan Mustafa I is removed again from the throne and replaced by his nephew Murad IV. Count von Tilly defeats Brunswick at Stadtlohn and advances on Westphalia. Shogun Hidetada abdicates in favour of his son Iemitsu. Velázquez is appointed Court Painter to Philip IV of Spain. The First Folio of Shakespeare's plays is published.
1624	Cardinal Richelieu is made the chief minister of Louis XIII of France.
1625	James I dies, and is succeeded by his son Charles I. Sir William Courteen establishes a settlement on Barbados. Henri duc de Rohan leads a Huguenot rebellion against Louis XIII. Emperor Ferdinand II makes Wallenstein general of the Imperial forces and duke of Friedland. Breda falls to the Spanish after an eleven-month siege. Count von Tilly invades Saxony.
1626	Peter Minuit buys Manhattan from the Wappinger Confederacy for 60 guilders, founding New Amsterdam. The French colonise Madagascar. Louis XIII and the Huguenots make the Peace of La Rochelle. Wallenstein defeats a Protestant army at the Bridge of Dessau. The Duchy of Urbino is bequeathed to the Pope.
1627	Pirates attack Reykjavik. The Huguenots rise again; Richelieu besieges La Rochelle, which the duke of Buckingham tries but fails to relieve. Imperial forces conquer Silesia, Brunswick, Mecklenburg, Schleswig, Holstein and Jutland, forcing Christian IV of Denmark to retire from the war. Shah Jahangir dies, and is succeeded by his grandson Dawar Bakhsh.
1628	Wallenstein obtains the Duchy of Mecklenburg, assumes the title Admiral of the Baltic, but fails to take Stralsund. Shah Dawar Bahsh is removed from the throne by his uncle Shah Jahan I. Gustavus Adolphus enters the Thirty Years War. The duke of Buckingham is assassinated by John Felton at Portsmouth. La Rochelle capitulates to Louis XIII. Ignatius Loyola is canonised.
1629	Shah Abbas of Persia dies, and is succeeded by his grandson Safi I. Charles I dissolves Parliament and assumes direct rule. Emperor Ferdinand II issues the Edict of Restitution, restoring Church estates and permitting freedom of worship only to adherents of the Confession of Augsburg, which the Catholic League ruthlessly enforces. Christian IV of Denmark regains his lands by the Peace of Lübeck, on condition he refrains from intervening in Imperial affairs. Sweden and Poland make the Peace of Altmark. Bethlen Gabor of Transylvania dies, and is succeeded by his wife Catherine of Brandenburg.
1630	Gustavus Adolphus invades Germany whilst Emperor Ferdinand II dismisses Wallenstein and replaces him with Tilly. Boston founded by John Winthrop. Sultan Murad IV defeats the Persians and captures Hamadan. Anglo-French hostilities are ended by the treaty of Madrid. George Rakoczy I is elected prince of Transylvania on the death of Stephen Bethlen.
1631	Richelieu and the German Protestant princes ally with Gustavus Adolphus against Emperor Ferdinand II. Urbino is annexed by the Papacy. Tilly brutally sacks Magdeburg, burns Halle and invades Saxony, but is defeated by Gustavus Adolphus at the battle of Breitenfeld. Gustavus Adolphus takes Frankfurt-am-Oder, Würzburg and Mainz. Wallenstein is reappointed by Emperor Ferdinand II.
1632	Gustavus Adolphus defeats Tilly, who is mortally wounded, at the Lech and takes Munich. At the battle of Lützen he defeats Walenstein but is killed in action. His daughter Christina succeeds him on the Swedish throne. Shah Jehan orders the destruction of Hindu temples. Charles I issues a charter for the colony of Maryland under the governorship of Lord Baltimore. The first coffee shop opens in London. Sigismund III of Poland dies, and is succeeded by his son Vladislav VII.
1633	Wallenstein defeats Bernard of Saxe-Weimar and a Swedish army at Steinau and occupies Bohemia. Galileo is forced by the Inquisition to abjure the theories of Copernicus.
1634	The Oberammergau Passion Play is enacted for the first time. Russia and Poland make peace via the treaty of Polianovska; Vladislav VII renounces his claim to Russia. Emperor Ferdinand II relieves Wallenstein of command, replacing him with Matthias Gallas. Wallenstein is assassinated soon after, whilst Imperial troops defeat the Swedes at Nördlingen and conquer Württemberg and Franconia.
1635	Cardinal Richelieu founds the Académie Française. Emperor Ferdinand II settles differences with Elector John George of Saxony via the Peace of Prague, after France and Sweden formally ally against him, formally bringing France into the Thirty Years War. Sweden and Poland agree a 20-year truce via the treaty of Stuhmsdorf. France and Saxe-Weimar ally by the treaty of St Germain-en-Laye. The first General Post Office in England opens in Bishopsgate, London.
1636	Persia and the Ottoman Empire make peace. Olivares invades Picardy. Swedish troops defeat the Saxons at the battle of Wittstock. Harvard College is founded in Cambridge, Massachusetts.
1637	Emperor Ferdinand II dies, and is succeeded by his son Ferdinand III. Bogislav XIV of Pomerania dies without an heir; his lands are divided between Sweden and Prussia. The Dutch under Frederick Henry of Orange recapture Breda.
1638	The Scottish Covenant is drawn up and signed, forcing Charles I to withdraw Laud's liturgy in Scotland. Bernhard of Saxe-Weimar takes Freiburg and Breisach. Sultan Murad IV retakes Baghdad from the Persians. Torture is abolished in England.
1639	The First Bishops' War erupts in Scotland between the Covenanters and Charles I. Peace comes by the Pacification of Berwick, and Charles I grants the Scots a General Assembly and Parliament, which he dissolves at the end of the year. Dutch admiral Maarten Tromp destroys a Spanish fleet in the decisive battle of the Downs.
1640	Catalonia revolts against Spanish taxes and control. Sultan Murad IV dies, and is succeeded by his brother Ibrahim. Charles I is forced to reconvene Parliament but the 'Short Parliament' refuses to authorise any taxes and is dissolved. The Scots revolt in the Second Bishops' War, defeating the English at Newburn. Thomas Wentworth is created earl of Strafford. The Great Council of Peers summoned by Charles I concludes the treaty of Ripon, paying off the Scots, and insists on the election of Parliament. The 'Long

Parliament', is duly elected. João of Braganza is elected king of Portugal, which breaks free from Spain, but Spain refuses to recognise this. Elector George William of Brandenburg dies, and is succeeded by his son Frederick William, the 'Great Elector'. Strafford and Laud are impeached.

1641   Tsar Michael I forbids the sale and use of tobacco, yet makes the substance a State monopoly. Strafford is executed. Parliament abolishes the Star Chamber. Parliament sends the Grand Remonstrance to Charles I, who is infuriated. The comte de Soissons plots against Louis XIII, but Jean d'Orléans, the king's brother, exposes him. The Irish Catholics revolt.

1642   Charles I enters the House of Commons to arrest Hampden, Pym, Holles, Haselrig and Strode for treason, but the quintet have been warned and take refuge in the City of London. Charles I flees London, rejects Parliament's 19 Propositions and raises his standard in Nottingham, triggering the Civil War. Rupert of the Rhine defeats the Parliamentarians at Powick Bridge and Edgehill. Blaise Pascal invents an adding machine. Cardinal Richelieu dies; Cardinal Mazarin replaces him as first minister of France. Abel Tasman discovers Van Diemen's Land (Tasmania) and New Zealand.

1643   Evangelista Torricelli develops the barometer. Parliamentarians under Fairfax take Leeds. Cromwell is victorious at Grantham, but Hampden is defeated and killed at Chalgrove Field. Louis XIII of France dies, and is succeeded by his son Louis XIV. French troops defeat a combined Spanish, Italian, Dutch and Flemish army at the battle of Rocroi. Royalists are victorious at Roundway Down and take Bristol, but are defeated at Gloucester, Newbury and Winceby. John Pym dies of cancer. Olivares falls from power in Spain.

1644   Ming Emperor Chongzhen commits suicide as Peking falls to the bandit Li Zicheng, thus ending his dynasty's rule. Li proclaims himself emperor, but is driven out by the Manchus, who found the Qing dynasty with Shunzhi as Emperor. John Milton writes his pamphlet the *Areopagitica*, on press freedom. The Scottish Covenanters join the Civil War on the Parliamentarian side. After a Royalist victory at Cropredy Bridge, Cromwell heavily defeats Prince Rupert at Marston Moor and takes York. Scottish royalists under Montrose defeat the Covenanters at Tippermuir, Charles captures Fowey, whilst the second battle of Newbury is indecisive.

1645   Archbishop Laud is executed. Montrose defeats the Covenanters at Inverlochy. The Ottomans and Venice war over Crete. Armistice talks between Charles I and Parliament fail at Uxbridge. John Lilburne publicizes Leveller ideas. Swedish troops defeat the Imperial army at Jankau and take Moravia. The Dutch occupy St Helena. Parliament creates the New Model Army under Fairfax and Cromwell which decisively defeats the royalists at Naseby. Tsar Michael I dies, and is succeeded by his son Alexei. The French defeat the Bavarians at Nördlingen. Prince Rupert surrenders Bristol, incurring his uncle's wrath. Covenanters rout Montrose at Philiphaugh.

1646   The Swedes take Prague, and in concert with the French invade Bavaria. Royalist armies in Exeter and Oxford capitulate to Parliamentarians; Charles surrenders to the Covenanters at Southwell. Held in Newcastle, Charles fails to reach agreement with Parliament and tries, but fails, to escape.

1647   George Fox founds the 'Friends of the Truth', later to become the Quakers. Matthew Hopkins, the 'Witchfinder General', is found guilty of witchcraft himself and hanged. Bear baiting and folk dancing are banned in England. The Scots hand over Charles I to Parliament in return for £400,000. Stadtholder Frederick Henry of Holland dies, and is succeeded by his son William II. Naples revolts against Spanish rule. Bavaria and Cologne state their neutrality in the Thirty Years War by the treaty of Ulm, but Emperor Ferdinand III gains their support. Mainz and Hesse withdraw from the fray.

1648   Parliament loses patience with Charles I after he makes a secret treaty with the Scots, who rebel along with the Welsh. Spain reasserts its rule over Naples. Ukrainians under Bogdan Chmielnicki lead a pogrom of Jews in a bid to establish independence from Poland. Sultan Ibrahim is deposed and killed by his Janissaries for lifting the siege of Heraklion, and is succeeded by his son Muhammad IV. The Second Civil War is short-lived, Cromwell defeating the Scots at Preston, and Colonel Thomas Pride purges Parliament to ensure Charles I is put on trial. The Fronde riots break out in Paris asserting the rights of the Paris Parlement (Parliament). The Peace of Westphalia ends the Thirty Years War, but is condemned by Pope Innocent X.

1649   Charles I is tried by Parliament and executed; Parliament abolishes the monarchy and the House of Lords, proclaiming a 'Commonwealth'. The War of the Fronde is ended by the treaty of Rueil; however, a second Fronde uprising breaks out. The Levellers and Diggers are suppressed. Royalists rebel in Ireland; Cromwell sacks Drogheda and Wexford.

1650   Mazarin allies himself with the leaders of the first Fronde, and imprisons the leaders of the second. René Descartes dies whilst in the service of Queen Christina. Montrose leads a Scottish uprising against Parliament but is defeated at Carbisdale, betrayed by Neil McLeod and hanged. Archbishop James Ussher calculates that the Earth was created in 4004 BC. Charles II arrives in Scotland. Cromwell invades Scotland and is victorious at Dunbar. Stadtholder William II dies of smallpox, leaving a posthumously born heir, William III. The Holy Roman Empire and Sweden reach an accord with the treaty of Nuremberg.

1651   Charles II is crowned at Scone and invades England but is defeated by Cromwell at Worcester, evades capture and flees to France. Thomas Hobbes publishes *Leviathan*, and John Playford *The English Dancing Master*. Paris Parlement votes for the release of the Great Condér, leader of the Fronde, forcing Mazarin from the country, but he returns with an army to suppress the rebellion. Shogun Iemitsu dies, and is succeeded by his son Ietsuna, who quickly suppresses two rebellions.

1652   Jan Van Riebeck founds Cape Town. The Great Condé defeats a royalist army at Bléneau and is welcomed in Paris, where a rebel government is formed; however, the government quarrels with the Parisian middle class, which lets Louis XIV into the city. Parliament publishes the reconciliatory Act of Pardon and Oblivion. Admiral Robert Blake defeats Maarten Tromp off Dover, and England and Holland go to war, but Blake is defeated off Dungeness.

1653   The pirate Zheng Chenkong ravages the Chinese coast in his war with the Manchus. Mazarin returns to Paris and suppresses the Fronde. Lorenzo Tonti devises the Tontine system of life insurance. The English fleet defeats the Dutch off Portland, North Foreland and Texel. Cromwell dissolves the Long Parliament, and after the unsuccessful Barebones Parliament is made Lord Protector. Izaak Walton publishes *The Compleat Angler.*

1654   The treaty of Westminster ends the Anglo-Dutch War. Queen Christina of Sweden abdicates, and is succeeded by her cousin Karl X. Bogdan Chmielnicki swears allegiance to Russia, which goes to war with Poland, taking Smolensk.

1655   Colonel Penruddock leads a rising against Cromwell in Wiltshire, which is suppressed. The English under Vice-Admiral Penn take Jamaica from the Spanish. Karl X of Sweden invades Poland, precipitating the first Northern War. Elector Frederick William of Brandenburg invades Prussia. Cromwell divides England into 11 districts, each governed by a major-general. Cromwell readmits Jews into England.

1656   Sweden and Prussia ally by the treaty of Königsberg, whilst Denmark, Russia and the Holy Roman Empire declare war on Sweden. Spain declares war on Britain. Sweden defeats Poland at the battle of Warsaw. Baruch Spinoza is excommunicated for heresy. João IV of Portugal dies, and is succeeded by his son Alfonso VI.

1657   Christiaan Huygens develops the pendulum clock. Cromwell rejects an offer of the crown and establishes a nominated House of Lords. Emperor Ferdinand dies, and is succeeded by his son Leopold I. Admiral Blake destroys a Spanish treasure fleet at Santa Cruz. Brandenburg allies with Poland against Sweden by the treaty of Bromberg.

1658   The stage coach service is established in England. Jan Swammerdam observes red blood cells for the first time. The treaty of Roskilde ends the first Northern War, but Charles X of Sweden starts a second by unsuccessfully attacking Copenhagen. An Anglo-French force defeats the Spanish at the battle of the Dunes and England acquires Dunkirk. Shah Jahan I is imprisoned by his son Aurangzeb Alamgir I, who replaces him as Mughal emperor. Oliver Cromwell dies; his son Richard becomes Lord Protector.

1659   Elector Frederick William of Brandenburg drives the Swedes from Prussia. Richard Cromwell resigns as Lord Protector; conflict between army and Parliament leads to a state of near-anarchy. France and Spain make the Peace of the Pyrenees.

1660   General Monck, commanding general in Scotland, leads his troops to London to call for a new Parliament, which meets and votes for the restoration of the monarchy under Charles II. Karl X of Sweden dies, and is succeeded by his son Karl XI. Charles II makes the Declaration of Breda promising religious toleration and returns to England. The Peace of Oliva ends the hostilities between Sweden, Poland, Brandenburg and the Holy Roman Empire. Denmark reaches peace with and cedes Skania to Sweden by the treaty of Copenhagen. The Royal Society for the Promotion of Natural Knowledge is founded. George Racoczy II of Transylvania dies in battle against the Turks.

1661   Michael Apafi I is elected to replace the deceased George Racoczy III as Prince of Transylvania. Chinese living within 10 miles of the coast are ordered to move inland in an attempt to deter pirate Zheng Chenkong. Cardinal Mazarin dies, letting Louis XIV begin personal rule. The Cavalier Parliament meets in England. The Peace of Kardis between Sweden and Russia finally ends the second Northern War. Tangier and Bombay are ceded to England by Portugal in a treaty of alliance.

1662   France and Holland ally against England. The revised Prayer Book is imposed on Anglicans. The Royal Society is granted a Royal Charter by Charles II. Dunkirk is sold to France by Charles II for £400,000.

1663   The Theatre Royal, Drury Lane, opens with a performance of John Fletcher's *The Humorous Lieutenant.* Colbert founds the Académie des Inscriptions et Belles Lettres in Paris. The Ottomans declare war on the Holy Roman Empire and invade Hungary. Colbert makes New France into a colony with Quebec as the capital.

1664   France and Saxony make an alliance. The Conventicle Act bans unauthorised religious meetings of more than 5 people in England, in an attempt to suppress nonconformism. Austrian troops defeat the Turks at St Gotthard on the Raab River and make the Truce of Vasvar. New Amsterdam under Peter Stuyvesant surrenders to the English, who rename it New York.

1665   The Great Plague hits London. The second Anglo-Dutch War opens; the Dutch are defeated off Lowestoft. Anglo-Portuguese forces defeat the Spanish at Villaviciosa and Montes Claros, securing Portuguese independence. Philip IV of Spain dies, and is succeeded by his son Charles II.

1666   Louis XIV founds a French Academy of Sciences. Holland allies with Brandenburg, Brunswick and Denmark to secure its safety, whilst France declares war on England. The English and Dutch fleets meet in the inconclusive Four Days Battle before an English victory at Orford Ness. London is ravaged by a Great Fire starting in Pudding Lane.

1667   Russia and Poland make peace with the treaty of Andrusovo, ending their 13-year war; Kiev, Smolensk and the Eastern Ukraine are ceded to Russia. John Milton's *Paradise Lost* is published. French troops invade Flanders and Hainault, starting the War of Devolution. The Dutch sail up the Medway to Chatham, sinking several ships and taking the English flagship back to Holland. England, Holland and France make peace by the treaty of Breda. The Medway débâcle leads to the fall of Clarendon, and the Cabal administration under Clifford, Arlington, Buckingham, Ashley and Lauderdale is formed. (Cabal is a mnemonic for its members but the word does not derive from them.) The Regent Pedro banishes Alfonso VI of Portugal to the Azores.

1668   England, Holland and Sweden ally by the treaty of the Hague. John Dryden is appointed the first Poet Laureate. Spain recognises Portuguese independence by the treaty of Lisbon. The War of Devolution is ended by the Peace of Aix-La-Chapelle, whilst Louis XIV and Emperor Leopold I reach an agreement over future partition of Spanish realms. John Kasimir of Poland abdicates.

1669   The Lithuanian Michael Wisniowecki is elected king of Poland. The Mughal Aurangzeb bans Hinduism in India and destroys Hindu temples, leading to widespread revolts. Crete falls to the Ottomans. The Hanseatic League holds its last meeting. Antonio Stradivari makes his first violin. Samuel Pepys ceases writing his diary.

1670   Frederick III of Denmark dies, and is succeeded by his son Christian V. The Ukrainian Cossacks rebel against Polish rule, but are suppressed by Jan Sobieski. Gabriel Mouton, a French clergyman, proposes the establishment of decimal measurements. France and Bavaria make a defensive alliance, whilst Charles II makes the secret treaty of Dover with Louis XIV, pledging anti-Dutch collaboration and conversion to Roman Catholicism at an appropriate moment.

1671   The buccaneer Henry Morgan captures Panama City, is tried for piracy but pardoned and knighted by Charles II and later becomes Deputy Governor of Jamaica. The Ottomans declare war on Poland. The Don Cossacks under Stenka Razin revolt, but their rising is quelled and Razin executed. Milton publishes *Paradise Regained* and Aphra Behn *The Forced Marriage*.

1672   The Russian serfs rebel. Charles II issues the Declaration of Indulgence. Louis XIV declares war on the Dutch and sends his troops in; an English fleet defeats the Dutch at Southwold Bay. The Dutch Grand Pensionary Jan de Witt and his brother Cornelius are murdered by a mob, after William III of Orange has been appointed to the revived office of Stadtholder and put in charge of the Dutch army.

1673   Parliament forces Charles II to revoke the Declaration of Indulgence and instead passes the Test Act. Brandenburg pledges to refuse assistance to enemies of France by the treaty of Vossen, whilst Leopold I declares war on France. Michael Wisniowecki of Poland dies; the next day Jan Sobieski defeats the Ottomans at Khorzim.

1674   France devastates the Palatinate whilst Spain deters the anti-French coalition. Jan Sobieski is elected king of Poland. England and Holland make peace by the the treaty of Westminster. The bandit Sivaji Bhonsala founds a Marãthã state as independent from the Mughal Empire.

1675   France recovers Alsace after victory at Turkheim. Sweden goes to war with Denmark and Brandenburg, but is defeated by the latter at Fehrbellin. The Royal Greenwich Observatory is founded, with John Flamsteed as first Astronomer Royal.

1676   Tsar Alexis dies, and is succeeded by his son Feodor III. Jan Sobieski of Poland makes peace with the Ottomans under the treaty of Zuravno, ceding the Polish Ukraine. The Swedes defeat the Danes at Lunden.

1677   The Dutch are defeated by the French at Cassel, but with the Danes defeat a Swedish fleet at Öland. Jean Racine's tragedy *Phèdre* is first performed. Edmund Halley returns from St Helena, having catalogued the Southern Night Sky.

1678   France captures Ghent and Ypres. Russia joins the war against Sweden. France, Spain and Holland make the peace of Nijmegen; Holland regains its lost territories. False allegations made by Titus Oates and others of a 'Popish Plot' to kill Charles II lead to severe anti-Catholic measures. Hungarians under Emeric Tokolyi rebel against Imperial rule. Brandenburg takes Stralsund from the Swedes. The factional terms Whig and Tory enter use in Parliament.

1679   The Cavalier Parliament is dissolved. Archbishop Sharp of St Andrews murdered by Covenanters, whose rising is defeated by Monmouth at Bothwell Brig. Louis XIV forces the Peace of St Germain-en-Laye on Sweden and Brandenburg; the latter relinquishes its conquests. Sweden and Denmark make peace by the treaty of Lund. Henry Purcell is appointed organist of Westminster Abbey.

1680   Sivaji Bhonsala dies, and is succeeded by his son Sambhaji I, but Emperor Aurangzeb attempts to reconquer the Marathas. Shogun Ietsuna dies, and is succeeded by his brother Tsunayoshi.

1681   Charles II grants Pennsylvania as a nonconformist colony to William Penn. Emperor Kangxi suppresses the Rebellion of the Three Feudatories. France annexes Strasbourg. Bank cheques are issued for the first tiime in England.

1682   Louis XIV moves his court to Versailles. The Chelsea Hospital is founded. La Salle reaches the mouth of the Mississippi, names the surrounding area 'Louisiana' claiming it for France. Tsar Feodor III of Russia dies. His sister Sophia becomes regent for her younger brothers, Ivan V, who is mentally defective, and her half-brother Peter I, and seeks to kill Peter's supporters as a threat to her position.

1683   By the League of The Hague, Spain and the Holy Roman Empire join Holland and Sweden in an anti-French coalition. The Rye House Plot against Charles II and James, duke of York is unmasked; Lord William Russell and Algernon Sidney are executed for their roles in the plot and the earl of Essex commits suicide. Alfonso VI of Portugal dies, and is succeeded by his brother Pedro II. Ottomans besiege Vienna, but are forced to withdraw by Jan Sobieski of Poland and Charles, duke of Lorraine. China captures Formosa (Taiwan).

1684   The Japanese poet Saikaku composes 23,500 verses in 24 hours. The Holy Roman Empire, Poland and Venice form the Holy League of Linz against the Turks. Jews are expelled from Bordeaux.

1685   Charles II dies, and is succeeded by his brother James II, but his illegitimate son the duke of Monmouth leads an uprising which ends in defeat at Sedgemoor. Monmouth is beheaded and Judge Jeffreys conducts the 'Bloody Assizes' against Monmouth's followers. Louis XIV revokes the Edict of Nantes, forcing Huguenots to flee abroad and damaging the French economy.

1686   The Institut de Saint Louis is founded by Madame de Maintenon to educate the daughters of poor gentlefolk; the curriculum includes cookery; graduates are given a blue ribbon – the *cordon bleu*. The League of Augsburg is formed against Louis XIV by the Holy Roman Empire, Spain, Sweden, Saxony, Bavaria and the Palatinate. Buda is liberated from the Ottomans, whilst Russia declares war on them.

1687   Shogun Sunayoshi forbids the killing of animals in Japan. James II proclaims freedom of worship and receives the Papal Nuncio. Ottomans defeated by Charles of Lorraine at Mohács who expell them from Hungary, they lose the Greek Peloponnese and Athens to the Venetians. Sultan Muhammad IV is deposed by his Janissaries and replaced by his brother Suleiman III. Newton's *Principia* is published.

1688   Elector Frederick William of Brandenburg dies, and is succeeded by his son Frederick III. An heir to James II is born. To forestall a Catholic succession William of Orange is invited to replace James, which he does in the 'Glorious Revolution'. James II flees to exile in France. The Ottomans surrender Belgrade to the Austrians. France invades the Palatinate. A marine insurance society is founded in Edward Lloyd's Coffee House in London.

1689   Natal becomes a Dutch colony. Louis XIV declares war on Britain whilst James II arrives in Ireland and besieges Londonderry. A Jacobite rising in Scotland defeats a Covenanter army at Killiecrankie before being defeated at Dunkeld. Regent Sophia is deposed in Russia after conspiring to abduct Peter I, who is established as tsar. The Declaration of Rights is proclaimed in England.

1690   Marlborough captures Cork and Kinsale from Jacobite supporters. Spain and Savoy join the League of Augsburg, which is defeated at Fleurus. The French defeat an Anglo-Dutch fleet off Beachy Head and burn Teignmouth. William III defeats James II at the battle of the Boyne, forcing James back to France. Calcutta is founded by the East India Company. The Ottomans retake Transylvania, Serbia, Belgrade and Bulgaria.

1691   The first directory of addresses is published in Paris. Sultan Suleiman III dies, and is succeeded by his brother Ahmad II, whose reign starts poorly with defeat at Slankamen and expulsion from Hungary. The Irish Jacobites are defeated at Aughrim and pacified by the treaty of Limerick.

1692   The Campbells massacre the MacDonalds at Glencoe. Marlborough is briefly imprisoned for suspected treasonable contact with James II. The Salem witch trials commence. The English defeat a French invasion fleet at La Hogue, but an Anglo-Dutch army is defeated at Steenkirk. Ernst Augustus of Brunswick is made Elector of Hanover.

1693   William III borrows £1 million, instigating the National Debt. French fleet defeats an Anglo-Dutch one at Cape St Vincent and Lagos; French armies are also successful at Neerwinden and Marsaglia.

1694   William Paterson leads the founding of the Bank of England, with Sir John Houblon as its first Governor. Shah Suleiman I of Persia dies, and is succeeded by his son Husain I. Mary II of England dies.

1695   Princess Anne returns to court to act as hostess for her brother-in-law William III. Sultan Ahmad II dies, and is succeeded by his nephew Mustafa II. William Paterson helps found the Bank of Scotland. Peter the Great besieges Azov, but is forced to withdraw by the Turks with heavy losses. William III takes Namur.

1696   Jan Sobieski of Poland dies. Peter the Great takes Azov and conquers Kamchatka. The Window Tax is introduced in England, whilst John Locke and Isaac Newton reform the coinage.

1697   Peter the Great travels incognito from Russia to study European ways of life. Karl XI of Sweden dies, and is succeeded by his son Karl XII. Elector Frederick-Augustus I of Saxony is elected king of Poland, taking the title Augustus II. France, Britain, Spain and the Holy Roman Empire make peace by the treaty of Ryswick. Eugene of Savoy heavily defeats the Turks at Zenta.

1698   Elector Ernst Augustus of Hanover dies, and is succeeded by his son George. Leopold of Anhalt-Dessau introduces goose-stepping to the Prussian army. Whitehall Palace is largely destroyed by fire. The Streltzy, elite musketeer regiments, revolt in Moscow, but the rising is quelled.

1699   Turkey signs the Peace of Karlowitz with Austria, to which it cedes Hungary, Croatia and Transylvania. Turkey also cedes its portion of the Ukraine to Poland, and Morea and Dalmatia to Venice. Christian V of Denmark dies, and is succeeded by his son Frederick IV. Denmark, Russia, Poland and Saxony sign the treaty of Preobrazhenskoe to carve up the Swedish Empire. William Dampier explores the western Australian coast. Henry Winstanley builds the first Eddystone Lighthouse.

1700   The German Protestant states adopt the Gregorian calendar. The Great Northern War opens with concerted attacks on Sweden; Saxony invades Livonia and Denmark invades Schleswig, but Sweden invades Zeeland, forces the Danes from the war by the treaty of Travendal, and defeats Russia at Narva. The duke of Gloucester dies, leaving no direct Stuart heir after Princess Anne (James Stuart being unacceptable). Charles II of Spain dies, the Habsburg line ends with him and the throne goes to Philip V, grandson of Louis XIV.

1701   Elector Frederick of Brandenburg makes himself king of Prussia; Emperor Leopold acquiesces in return for military aid. The War of the Spanish Succession opens; England, Holland and Savoy join the Holy Roman Empire in the Grand Alliance. Karl XII of Sweden invades Poland. Eugene of Savoy defeats the French at Carpi and Chiara. Antoine Cadillac founds Detroit. The Act of Settlement provides for the succession in England to pass to Electress Sophia of Hanover after Princess Anne. Jethro Tull develops the seed drill.

1702   William III dies, and is succeeded in England by his sister-in-law Anne, whilst in Holland the Stadtholdership is put into abeyance. The *Daily Courant* becomes London's first daily newspaper. Karl XII of Sweden takes Warsaw and Cracow. Marlborough captures Venlo, Roermond and Liège, and is raised from an earl to a Duke. Protestant peasants, the Camisards, revolt in the Cévennes.

1703   The Swedish defeat the Russians at Pulutsk. Marlborough takes Cologne and Bonn. Peter the Great founds St Petersburg. The Grand Alliance proclaims Archduke Charles of Austria king of Spain. Portugal joins the Grand Alliance and signs the Methuen treaty with England. The Eddystone Lighthouse is destroyed as a great storm hits Southern England.

1704   Sweden secures the deposition of Augustus II of Poland in favour of Stanislas Leszczynski. Gibraltar is captured by the English, who defeat a relieving force at Velez Malaga. Marlborough and Eugene of Savoy heavily defeat the French at Blenheim. Beau Nash becomes Master of Ceremonies at Bath.

1705   Edmund Halley predicts the return in 1758 of the comet that will bear his name. Emperor Leopold dies, and is succeeded by his son Joseph I. Peter the Great's westernization provokes revolts in Astrakhan. Barcelona falls to the Grand Alliance.

1706   Karl XII of Sweden defeats a Russo-Saxon army at Fraustadt. Marlborough defeats the French at Ramillies; Brussels, Antwerp, Ghent and Ostend quickly capitulate to him. Archduke Charles is installed in Madrid, but is driven out after 3 months by Philip V of Spain. Eugene of Savoy defeats the French at Turin and drives them from Lombardy. Augustus II of Poland abdicates, recognizing his usurper Stanislas I.

1707   Emperor Aurangzeb dies, and is succeeded by his son A'zam Shah, whose death soon after puts his brother Bahadur Shah I on the throne. A French army under the duke of Berwick defeats an Anglo-Portuguese force at Almanza. England and Scotland formally unite with the Act of Union. Prussia and Sweden sign a Perpetual Alliance. Admiral Sir Cloudesley Shovell's squadron runs aground in the Scillies, only one man survives. Fortnum & Mason's opens in Piccadilly.

1708   Marlborough and Eugene of Savoy defeat the French at Oudenarde; Marlborough subsequently captures Lille. Minorca captured by the British. The East India Company and the New East India Company merge. The Sikh guru Govind Singh is assassinated by order of the Mughal Bahadur Shah. Karl XII of Sweden invades the Ukraine.

1709   The *Tatler* is launched by Richard Steele and Joseph Addison. Tsar Peter defeats Karl XII of Sweden at Poltava, forcing Karl to take refuge in Anatolia and breaking Sweden's power. Augustus II takes advantage of this by driving Stanislas I from Poland and regaining the throne. Marlborough and Eugene of Savoy take Tournai and Mons and defeat the French at Malplaquet. Abraham Darby develops coke-fuelled iron smelting at Coalbrookdale.

1710   Stanhope is victorious at Almenara and Saragossa but is defeated and captured at Brihuega. Handel is appointed Kapellmeister to Elector George of Hanover. Christopher Wren completes St Paul's Cathedral.

1711   Addison and Steele launch the *Spectator*. Queen Anne establishes Ascot racecourse. Emperor Joseph I dies, and is succeeded by his brother Charles VI, who guarantees a Hungarian constitution by the Peace of Szathmar. Russia and Turkey sign the treaty of Pruth; Tsar Peter is forced to return Azov to the Turks. Rio de Janeiro is captured by the French. The South Sea Company is established. Marlborough is dismissed from command and replaced by Ormonde.

1712   Civil war breaks out in Switzerland; the Protestant cantons are victorious at Villmergen and peace is re-established by the treaty of Aarau. The Mughal Emperor Bahadur Shah I dies; his sons quarrel over the succession.

1713   Farrukhsiyar, grandson of Bahadur Shah, establishes himself as Mughal emperor. Karl XII of Sweden is taken prisoner by the Ottomans at Bender in Moravia. Frederick I of Prussia dies and is succeeded by his son Frederick William I. The treaties of Utrecht end the War of the Spanish Succession, with Philip V allowed to keep the throne, establishing the Bourbon dynasty in the country; the thrones of France and Spain are never to be united. Emperor Charles VI does not sign. Charles VI issues the Pragmatic Sanction, allowing female succession in Habsburg domains. Shogun Ienobu dies, and is succeeded by his infant son Ietsugu.

1714   The Board of Longitude promises a £20,000 reward for anybody who can discover a method of divining longitude. Russia gains control of Finland after victory at the battle of Storkyro. Charles VI makes peace with France at Rastatt and Baden. Queen Anne dies, and is succeeded by her second cousin George I, as his mother Sophia had died shortly before. Karl XII of Sweden is released by the Turks.

1715   Louis XIV dies, and is succeeded by his great-grandson Louis XV. Mir Vais, chief of Kandahar, dies; his son Mir Maahmoud succeeds him, but is assassinated by his uncle Mir Abdullah who takes power. The earl of Mar leads a Jacobite rising in Scotland; the Old Pretender James lands at Peterhead to support the rising, but his supporters are defeated at Sheriffmuir and Preston.

1716   The Old Pretender returns to France as the '15 rebellion fizzles out. Shogun Ietsugu dies aged seven and is succeeded by Yoshimune, a distant relation. Eugene of Savoy defeats the Ottomans at Peterwardein; Emperor Charles VI joins the war and Temesvar, the last Ottoman possession in Hungary, falls. The Tsarevich Alexei flees Russia and places himself under the protection of Charles VI.

1717   The Grand Lodge of the Freemasons is established at the Goose and Gridiron Tavern, Covent Garden. School attendance is made compulsory in Prussia. Lhasa is occupied by Mongols. Eugene of Savoy defeats the Ottomans at Belgrade.

1718   Edward Teach, Blackbeard, is killed in a fight in North Carolina. The first English banknotes are issued. Philip V of Spain sends troops into Sicily; the Quadruple Alliance of the Empire, France, England and Holland is formed to counter him. Tsarevich Alexei is killed by order of Peter the Great and his friends executed. Karl XII is killed at Fredriksten during an expedition into Norway, and is succeeded by his sister Ulrika.

1719   Liechtenstein becomes an independent principality under Count Hans von Liechtenstein, who has bought the territory. Herat rebels against Shah Hussein, and defeats an army sent to subdue the area. Sweden and Hanover make the Peace of Stockholm. The Mughal emperor Farrukhsiyar dies, creating a succession dispute which is eventually resolved when his cousin Muhammad ascends the throne.

1720   The Great Northern War is brought to an end as Sweden makes peace with her neighbours. Ulrika of Sweden abdicates in favour of her husband Frederick of Hesse. A plague outbreak in Marseille is the final time the Black Death pandemic strikes. The South Sea Company collapses (South Sea Bubble), as does John Law's Mississippi Company, bringing ruin to many. China makes Tibet a protectorate.

1721   A revolt in Formosa is suppressed by China. A regular postal service is established between London and New England. John Aislabie, Chancellor of the Exchequer, is dismissed and imprisoned for fraud. Robert Walpole is appointed First Lord of the Treasury by George I, becoming the first prime minister. Sweden and Russia sign the treaty of Nystadt; Russia gains Estonia. Peter the Great is proclaimed Emperor of All the Russias.

1722   Mir Mahmoud of Kandahar conquers Afghanistan, defeats the Persians at Gulnabad, and takes Isfahan. Shah Hussein abdicates in favour of his son Tahmasp, but Mahmoud proclaims himself Shah. Russia and the Ottoman Empire exploit the situation and invade; the Russians withdraw after an outbreak of ergotism. Hungary rejects Emperor Charles' Pragmatic Sanction. Jacob Roggeveen discovers Rapa Nui, naming it Easter Island.

1723   Louis XV of France attains his majority, ending the Regency period. Britain and Prussia sign the treaty of Charlottenburg, arranging marriages between the two royal houses.

1724   Philip V of Spain abdicates in favour of his son Luis, who dies some months after, and Philip returns to the throne. Russia and the Ottoman Empire make a treaty for the dismemberment of Persia, where Mir Mahmoud goes insane.

1725   Tsar Peter the Great dies, and is succeeded by his widow Catherine I. The Pragmatic Sanction is guaranteed by the treaty of Vienna. Tabriz falls to the Ottomans. Mir Mahmoud kills 39 Persian princes; the surviving nobles elect his cousin Ashraf to replace the insane Shah, who is murdered on order of Ashraf. The treaty of Hanover allies Britain, Prussia and France against Austria and Spain.

1726   Voltaire is exiled in England. General George Wade commences a programme of road-building in Scotland. Montevideo is founded. Cardinal Fleury becomes chief minister to Louis XV.

1727   Spain besieges Gibraltar, but does not formally declare war on Britain. Shah Ashraf defeats an Ottoman army and the two powers make peace. Catherine I of Russia dies, and is succeeded by Peter II, a grandson of Peter I. George I dies of apoplexy, and is succeeded by his son George II.

H
I
S
T
O
R
Y

1728   The Kiakhta treaty sets the border and terms of trade between China and Russia. Spain abandons its siege of Gibraltar when the Convention of the Prado settles a truce with Britain. Roman Catholics are disenfranchised in Ireland. Vitus Bering discovers the Bering Strait. The Empire and Prussia make the treaty of Berlin. A Freemasons' Lodge is founded in Madrid, but is quickly suppressed by the Inquisition.

1729   Emperor Yongzheng bans opium smoking in China. Corsica temporarily becomes independent of Genoa. France, Britain and Spain end hostilities with the treaty of Seville. Charles Wesley founds the Holy Club at Oxford with his brother John and George Whitehead.

1730   Peter II of Russia dies of smallpox; his cousin Anne takes power in a coup. Shah Ashraf is murdered after defeat near Shiraz; Tahmasp II returns to power. Viscount Townshend improves crop husbandry with the use of turnips after leaving Walpole's government. Crown Prince Frederick of Prussia is imprisoned at Küstrin after attempting to flee to England. Sultan Ahmad III is deposed, and replaced by his nephew Mahmud I. Frederick IV of Denmark dies, and is succeeded by his son Christian VI.

1731   John Hadley invents the reflecting quadrant. Shah Tahmasp is defeated by the Ottomans at Arijan and sues for peace, ceding large tracts of land to the Ottomans. Tahmasp is imprisoned by his brother-in-law Nadir Kuli and his infant son Abbas III set up as Shah. The Holy Roman Empire makes the treaty of Vienna with Britain, Holland and Spain, securing support for the Pragmatic Sanction.

1732   Genoa regains control of Corsica.

1733   James Oglethorpe establishes a colony at Savannah, founding the state of Georgia. John Kay invents a flying shuttle loom. Augustus II of Poland dies; France persuades Polish nobles to restore Stanislas I but Austria and Russia demand that Augustus' son, Frederick Augustus of Saxony, succeed his father. In the War of the Polish Succession, they invade Poland.

1734   Persia and the Ottoman Empire go to war. France and Spain defeat Austrian armies in Naples and Parma. Danzig falls to the invading Russian army, but Stanislas I escapes to Prussia.

1735   William Pitt is elected MP for Old Sarum. The treaty of Vienna ends the War of the Polish Succession, and Augustus III is established on the Polish throne. Russia allies with the Persian Nadir Kuli against the Ottoman Empire; Nadir defeats the Ottomans at Baghavand and takes Tiflis. John Harrison develops his chronometer. Linnaeus publishes *Systema naturae*, the origin of modern classification of plants and animals.

1736   Shah Abbas III dies, and Nadir Kuli succeeds him. Claudius Aymond performs the first successful appendectomy. Freemasonry is condemned by Pope Clement XII. Statutes against witchcraft are repealed in England. Emperor Yongzheng dies, and is succeeded by his son Qianlong.

1737   Benjamin Franklin creates the Philadelphia police force, the first of its kind. The Licensing Act orders all plays to submit to the Lord Chamberlain's censorship. Gian Gastone di Medici dies, last of his line. The Grand Duchy of Tuscany passes to Francis of Lorraine, whilst Lorraine passes to Stanislas I of Poland as a reward for renouncing his claim to the Polish throne.

1738   Orsova falls to the Ottomans, who drive the Imperial troops back to Belgrade. Jean H.L. Orry imposes the corvée, compulsory labour, to construct roads in France. John and Charles Wesley form the Methodist Society.

1739   Dick Turpin is hanged at York. Shah Nadir of Persia sacks Delhi, drastically diminishing Mughal power in India. Nadir seizes the Koh-i-Noor diamond. Emperor Charles VI makes peace with the Ottomans by the treaty of Belgrade, ceding the city to the Ottomans. England and Spain go to war (the War of Jenkins' Ear) over alleged Spanish transgressions. Porto Bello in Panama is seized by Admiral Vernon.

1740   Frederick William I of Prussia dies, and is succeeded by his son Frederick II the Great, who invades Silesia. Emperor Charles VI dies; he is succeeded in his kingdoms by his daughter Maria Theresa, but Saxony, Bavaria and Spain dispute her right to succeed and the War of the Austrian Succession begins. Tsarina Anna dies, and is succeeded by her infant great-nephew Ivan VI.

1741   Frederick the Great defeats the Austrians at Mollwitz and captures Brieg, Neisse, Glatz and Olmütz before the British mediate. Prague is occupied by a French, Bavarian and Saxon army. Elizabeth, daughter of Peter the Great, deposes Tsar Ivan VI and rules herself.

1742   Anders Celsius develops the centigrade thermometer system. Elector Charles Albert of Bavaria is elected to the vacant title of Holy Roman Emperor. Robert Walpole resigns as Prime Minister, replaced by the earl of Wilmington. Prussia defeats the Austrians at Chotusitz, before signing treaty of Berlin with Austria, gaining upper and lower Silesia. Britain and Prussia sign the treaty of Westminster, safeguarding Hanover.

1743   George II leads a multinational Pragmatic Army to victory over the French at Dettingen. Pogroms of Jews occur in Russia. Persia and the Ottoman Empire go to war. Austria and Saxony ally, whilst Bavaria is conquered by Austria.

1744   Frederick the Great invades Saxony and Bohemia, taking Prague before being driven back to Saxony. Maria Theresa launches a series of pogroms in Moravia and Bohemia against the Jews.

1745   Emperor Charles VII dies. Francis of Lorraine, grand duke of Tuscany and husband of Maria Theresa, is elected the new Emperor. The French defeat an army led by the duke of Cumberland at Fontenoy and advance into the Austrian Netherlands. The Prussians defeat the Austrians and Saxons at Hohenfriedberg and the Austrians at Soor. Charles Edward Stuart lands on Eriskay, proclaiming his father king. He gains support from various Scottish clans, takes Edinburgh and is victorious at Prestonpans, but loses his nerve on reaching Derby and withdraws.

1746   The retreating Jacobites are victorious at Falkirk but are routed by Cumberland at Culloden. The Young Pretender escapes, and helped by Flora MacDonald reaches Skye, from where he returns to France. Cumberland severely represses the Scots, and the wearing of tartan is outlawed. Canaletto moves to England. Philip V of Spain dies, and is succeeded by his son Ferdinand VI. France defeats Austria at Raucoux and takes the Austrian Netherlands.

1747   The Republic of the United Provinces is overthrown by the French and William IV of Orange-Nassau resumes the post of Stadtholder. Prussia and Sweden form a defensive alliance. The French defeat an Anglo-Dutch army at Laufeld. Shah Nadir is murdered in Afghanistan; his nephew Adil succeeds him whilst

Ahmed Shah Durrani takes advantage of the situation to establish an independent Afghanistan. Lord Lovat is beheaded for Jacobitism on Tower Hill, the last man to be executed there.

1748 The treaty of Aix-la-Chapelle ends the War of the Austrian Succession with a stalemate peace. This gives general recognition to the Pragmatic Sanction and the Prussian conquest of Silesia.

1749 Thomas Chippendale opens a workshop. Admiral Anson reforms the Royal Navy. Henry Fielding publishes *Tom Jones*.

1750 Henry Fielding and his brother John found the Bow Street Runners. Thomas Gray's 'Elegy Written in a Country Churchyard' is written in Stoke Poges. The Jockey Club is founded in the Star and Garter Coffee House, Pall Mall. JS Bach dies. João V of Portugal dies, and is succeeded by his son Jose I, who appoints the marquis of Pombal as his chief minister. Pombal strips the Inquisition of its power.

1751 China invades Tibet. Robert Clive seizes Arcot from the French. Stadtholder William IV dies, and is succeeded by his infant son William V. Britain adopts January 1 as the beginning of the New Year, instead of 25 March.

1752 Britain adopts the Gregorian calendar system; 11 days disappear from September. Benjamin Franklin invents the lightning conductor. Ahmed Shah of Afghanistan takes Lahore. Spain and the Holy Roman Empire sign the treaty of Aranjuez.

1753 Sir Hans Sloane dies; his legacy of books and collections are used to found the British Museum and British Library. The Marriage Act forbids unlicensed weddings in Britain. The Jewish Naturalisation Act seeks to remove disabilities for Jews in Britain, but the hostility it engenders leads to its repeal.

1754 The Royal and Ancient Golf Club is founded at St Andrews, and codifies the rules of the sport. William Cookworthy pioneers English porcelain production. The first iron-rolling mill is built, in Fareham, Hampshire. In North America the Albany Convention is convened by several colonies and the Iroquois to form a joint defence against the French, who defeat two expeditions led by George Washington. The Convention agrees to Franklin's proposal for the union of the 13 colonies. Sultan Mahmud I dies while dismounting from his horse, and is succeeded by his brother Osman III.

1755 Casanova is imprisoned in Venice for spying. Pasquale de Paoli is elected general in Corsica, and leads a revolt against Genoa. In North America, General Braddock is killed in the battle of the Wilderness, as the French rout a British expedition, but the French are subsequently defeated at Lake George. Lisbon is devastated by an earthquake and tidal wave; 30,000 die.

1756 A porcelain factory is founded at Sèvres. John Smeaton builds a new Eddystone Lighthouse. England and Prussia ally by the treaty of Westminster. Minorca surrenders to Franco-Spanish forces after Admiral Byng breaks off a naval action. Britain declares war on France, but Montcalm drives the British from the Great Lakes. Siraj-ud-Daula, a French ally, seizes Calcutta, imprisoning 146 Britons in a small guardroom (Black Hole of Calcutta); according to English propaganda, only 23 emerge alive the next morning. Seven Years War erupts as Prussia invades Saxony, which has allied with France, Austria, Russia and Sweden against it.

1757 John Campbell invents the sextant. Ahmed Shah of Afghanistan takes Delhi and the Punjab. Robert Clive recovers Calcutta and defeats Siraj-ud-Daula at Plassey. For his role in losing Minorca, Admiral Byng is shot 'pour encourager les autres' at Portsmouth. Frederick the Great defeats the Austrians at Prague, but is defeated at Kolin before further victories at Rossback and Leuthen. Cumberland is routed by the French at Hastenbeck and is forced by the Convention of Klosterzeven to surrender Hanover to them. Sultan Osman III dies, and is succeeded by his cousin Mustafa III.

1758 Britain promises assistance to Prussia by the treaty of London. Samuel Johnson founds *The Idler*. Clive becomes governor of Bengal. An English army fighting for Frederick II of Prussia defeats the French at Krefeld, and Frederick crushes the Russians at Zorndorf but is defeated by the Austrians at Hochkirch. Fort Duquesne is captured from the French by George Washington and John Forbes and renamed Pittsburgh.

1759 Handel dies. Guadeloupe is captured by the British. Samuel Johnson publishes *Rasselas*. The French defeat Brunswick at Brunswick, but are defeated by an Anglo-Prussian army at Minden. Ferdinand VI of Spain dies, and is succeeded by his half-brother Charles III. Frederick the Great is defeated by an Austro-Russian army at Kunersdorf. General Wolfe defeats Montcalm on the Plains of Abraham outside Quebec; both generals die in battle. Quebec falls to the British. Admiral Hawke destroys a French squadron off Quiberon.

1760 Earl Ferrers is hanged at Tyburn, the last peer to be executed in Britain. Austria defeats Prussia at Landshut, but is defeated at Liegnitz. Amherst captures Montreal. Russian troops capture and burn Berlin. George II dies, and is succeeded by his grandson George III. Prussia defeats the Austrians at Torgau. John Harrison develops his H-4 chronometer.

1761 Ahmed Shah of Afghanistan defeats the Marathas at Panipat. Pondicherry, the French base in southern India, falls to Sir Eyre Coote. France and Spain invade Portugal; Portugal asks for British help. Spain and the Bourbon Italian states ally with France against Britain.

1762 Tsarina Elizabeth dies, and is succeeded by her nephew Peter III who withdraws from the Seven Years War and returns Pomerania to Prussia. St Vincent, Martinique Grenada and St Lucia seized by the British under Rodney. Jean-Jacques Rousseau writes the *Social Contract*. Sweden and Prussia ally by the treaty of Hamburg. Peter is assassinated on behalf of his wife, who succeeds him as Catherine II.

1763 The treaty of Paris ends the Seven Years War. Spain cedes Florida to Britain. The *Almanach de Gotha* is first published. Augustus III of Poland and Saxony dies; he is succeeded in Saxony only by his son Frederick-Christian, who also dies, and is succeeded by his son Frederick-Augustus III.

1764 James Hargreaves invents the spinning jenny. Stanislas Poniatowski is elected to the vacant Polish throne. Hyder Ali takes Mysore. Sir Hector Monro defeats the Nawab of Oudh at Buxar, and takes control of Bengal. Ex-Tsar Ivan VI is murdered in prison.

1765 Frederick the Great founds the Bank of Prussia. The Stamp Act imposes taxation on the American colonists, much to their disgust. Emperor Francis I dies, and is succeeded by his son Joseph II. The auto-da-fé is abolished in Lisbon.

HISTORY

1766	On the death of ex-king Stanislas, duke of Lorraine, the duchy reverts to France. The Stamp Act is repealed, but the Declaratory Act affirms the right of Parliament to tax the American colonists. Frederick V of Denmark dies, and is succeeded by his son Christian VII.
1767	Siam is invaded by the Burmese. Nevil Maskelyne, the Astronomer Royal, issues the first Nautical Almanac. Clive leaves India.
1768	The Royal Academy of Arts is founded, with Joshua Reynolds as the first president. The first edition of the *Encyclopaedia Britannica* is published. The Gurkha king Prithvi Naryan Shah makes Nepal a unitary kingdom. Corsica is bought by the French from Genoa. Austria renounces all claims to Silesia.
1769	Austria occupies the Lvov and Zips regions of Poland. Frederick the Great and Emperor Joseph II meet at Neisse to discuss the partition of Poland. Richard Arkwright develops the spinning frame. James Watt patents a steam engine. Josiah Wedgwood opens his pottery works at Etruria. Wellington, Napoleon, Ney and Soult are born.
1770	Joseph Cugnot constructs a steam-powered road vehicle in France. Lord North replaces Grafton as prime minister. The 'Boston Massacre', a brawl between civilians and troops, leaves 3 dead. All taxes, bar that on tea, on the American colonists are repealed. An Anglo-Spanish dispute over the Falklands is resolved by French mediation. Captain James Cook lands at Botany Bay, Australia. A Russian fleet defeats the Ottomans at the battle of Chesme.
1771	The Crimea is conquered by Russian Cossacks. Duke Charles-Emmanuel III of Savoy abolishes serfdom. Adolphus Frederick of Sweden dies, and is succeeded by his son Gustav III. The Marathas drive the Afghans from Delhi.
1772	The Danish nobility rebel against Count Johann von Struensee, who has held absolute power for a year, torturing and beheading him. George III secures the passage of the Royal Marriages Act to control whom the royal family may marry. Russia, Prussia and Austria perform the first partition of Poland. Gustav III of Sweden re-establishes absolute monarchy. Carl Wilhelm Scheele discovers oxygen (Priestley discovers it independently in 1774); Daniel Rutherford, Joseph Priestley, Henry Cavendish and Carl Wilhelm Scheele independently discover nitrogen.
1773	Emperor Joseph II expels the Jesuits, prompting Pope Clement XIV to dissolve the order. Tea is thrown into the sea in the protest known as the Boston Tea Party as a protest against the tea duty. The first Stock Exchange opens in London. Captain Cook enters the Antarctic Circle. Denmark cedes Oldenburg to Russia. Thomas Pritchard constructs the Ironbridge at Coalbrookdale.
1774	The Coercive Acts against Massachusetts include closing the port of Boston. Lord North is robbed by a highwayman at Chiswick. Louis XV of France dies, and is succeeded by his grandson Louis XVI. Sultan Mustafa III dies, and is succeeded by his brother Abdul-Hamid I. Russia acquires the northern Black Sea coast by the treaty of Kuchuk-Kainardji with Turkey. Joseph Priestley discovers oxygen. Austria occupies Bukovina. The Continental Congress, comprising all the America colonies bar Georgia, convenes, deciding to ban imports from and exports to Britain.
1775	Paul Revere rides to Lexington to warn of British troop movements. The American War of Independence opens. The colonists win victories at Concord, Fort Ticonderoga and Crown Point. The Second Continental Congress convenes and John Hancock is elected its president. The British defeat the rebels at Bunker Hill.
1776	Adam Smith publishes *The Wealth of Nations*. The St Leger is first run (founded by Colonel Barry St Leger). Grigori Potemkin organises a Russian Black Sea Fleet. Russia and Denmark sign the treaty of Copenhagen. The American colonists issue the Declaration of Independence. After defeat at Long Island and on Lake Champlain they score a major victory at Trenton.
1777	Spain and Portugal settle their differences over their South American colonies. The Americans are victorious at Princeton, Ridgefield and Bennington, but lose at the Brandywine and Germantown before victory at Bemis Heights provokes Burgoyne to surrender at Saratoga. Elector Maximilian III of Bavaria dies; with no direct heir, the Electorship passes to Count Karl Theodor of the Palatine.
1778	Joseph Bramah patents an improved water closet. Captain Cook discovers and names the Sandwich Islands. France signs treaties of alliance with the United States. Frederick the Great opens the War of the Bavarian Succession by invading Bohemia. The British take Savannah.
1779	Samuel Crompton develops the spinning mule. Captain Cook is killed by natives in Hawaii. The Oaks is first run (named after the house at Epsom leased by the 12th earl of Derby). Warren Hastings sends British troops against the Marathas. The Peace of Teschen settles the War of the Bavarian Succession. British troops are defeated at Baton Rouge by an augmented American army. Spain declares war on Britain.
1780	Admiral Rodney defeats the Spanish off Cape St Vincent. Lord George Gordon whips up anti-Catholic hysteria in London into the Gordon riots. The Americans are defeated at Camden, but are victorious at Kings Mountain. Emperor Joseph II abolishes serfdom in Bohemia and Hungary. Maria Theresa dies, and is succeeded in Habsburg territories by her son Emperor Joseph. The Derby is first run. Peruvian Indians rebel against Spanish rule, led by the Inca descendant Tupac Amaru, who is executed next year as the revolt is suppressed.
1781	William Herschel discovers Uranus. Warren Hastings plunders the treasure of the Nabob of Oudh. Emperor Joseph II grants religious tolerance in the Holy Roman Empire and abolishes serfdom in Austria. General Cornwallis surrenders to the Americans at Yorktown, ending British military operations in America.
1782	Spain captures Minorca from Britain, and completes the conquest of Florida. Lord North resigns as prime minister, and is succeeded by Rockingham; on his death Shelburne replaces him, and Pitt the Younger becomes chancellor of the exchequer. Admiral Rodney defeats the French at the battle of the Saints. Rama I founds the Chakri dynasty as kings of Siam, ruling from Bangkok. The *Royal George* sinks off Portsmouth, with the loss of 800 men.
1783	Shelburne resigns as prime minister, succeeded by Portland, whose government falls; Pitt the Younger becomes prime minister at the age of 24. Henry Cort develops a method of puddling iron. The treaty of Versailles recognises American Independence and cedes Florida to Spain. The Montgolfier brothers make the first balloon flight at Annonay. Potemkin annexes the Crimea for Russia.

1784   Turkey is forced to accept the Russian annexation of the Crimea by the treaty of Constantinople. John
        Wesley draws up his 'Deed of Declaration', providing for the continuance of the Methodist movement. A
        revolt in Transylvania persuades Emperor Joseph II to suspend the Hungarian constitution. The East India
        Company is put under government control.

1785   Jean Blanchard and John Jefferies cross the English Channel by balloon. *The Daily Universal Register*, later
        renamed *The Times*, is founded. The prince of Wales secretly weds Maria Fitzherbert. Warren Hastings
        resigns as governor-general of India. The Diamond Necklace affair discredits Marie Antoinette and leads to the
        arrest of Cardinal de Rohan. Austria and Holland settle their differences by the treaty of Fontainebleau.

1786   Jacques Balmat and Michel-Gabriel Paccard make the first ascent of Mont Blanc. Penang is ceded by the
        Rajah of Kedah to Britain. Frederick the Great of Prussia dies, and is succeeded by his nephew Frederick
        William II.

1787   The Marylebone Cricket Club is founded, and Thomas Lord opens his first cricket ground. Warren Hastings
        is impeached by Edmund Burke. George Washington chairs a Constitutional Convention in America which
        draws up the constitution. Russia and Turkey go to war. Delaware, Pennsylvania and New Jersey are the
        first states to join the union of the United States.

1788   William Symington develops a workable steamboat. The First Fleet lands convicts at Botany Bay and
        Sydney is founded to house them. The trial for corruption of Warren Hastings begins. Gustavus III of
        Sweden invades Russian Finland. Louis XVI is persuaded to summon the Estates-General in France.
        George III suffers a bout of mental illness.

1789   Sultan Abdul Hamid I is poisoned and succeeded by his nephew Selim III. George Washington is elected
        the first president of the United States. A mutiny takes place, led by Fletcher Christian, on HMS *Bounty*;
        Christian and the mutineers settle on Pitcairn Island; Captain Bligh, set adrift, navigates across 3,600 miles
        of ocean to Timor. George III recovers from his illness The Estates-General meet at Versailles; the Third
        Estate declares itself a National Assembly and swears not to dissolve until a constitution is granted. The
        Paris mob storm the Bastille, starting a revolution. Feudalism is abolished in France. The National
        Assembly issues the Declaration of the Rights of Man. Louis XVI and his family are forced to go to Paris as
        the mob attacks Versailles. Belgrade and Bucharest are taken by Austria.

1790   Emperor Joseph II dies, and is succeeded by his brother Leopold II. Louis XVI accepts a revolutionary
        constitution. Philadelphia becomes the American capital. Alexander Hamilton founds Washington DC.

1791   Marie Harel develops Camembert cheese. The *Observer* begins publication. Boswell's *Life of Johnson* and
        Tom Paine's *Rights of Man* are published. John Wesley dies. The Canada Constitutional Act splits Canada
        into Upper and Lower Canada, with legislatures in Ontario and Quebec. Louis XVI flees Paris, but is
        captured at Varennes and forced to return. Mozart's *The Magic Flute* is 1st performed. The Bill of Rights,
        consisting of the first ten amendments to the American constitution, is codified.

1792   Denmark abjures slavery. The Democratic Republican and Federalist parties are founded in America.
        Russia and Turkey make the Peace of Jassy. Cornwallis defeats Tipu Sultan of Mysore at Seringapatam
        and takes half of Mysore. Emperor Leopold II dies, and is succeeded by his son Francis II. Gustavus III of
        Sweden is assassinated in Stockholm Opera House, and is succeeded by his son Gustavus IV. Prussia
        and Austria ally against France, which declares war on them and Sardinia. Prussia takes Verdun but the
        French are victorious at Valmy and conquer the Austrian Netherlands. The Paris mob storms the Tuileries;
        the Swiss Guard fire on them. Louis XVI is imprisoned in the Temple and the National Convention
        abolishes the monarchy. The Jacobins seize power and the guillotine is put into use.

1793   Louis XVI is executed, as are his cousin Philippe Égalité, duke of Orléans, and Queen Marie Antoinette.
        France declares war on Britain, Holland and Spain, which join the First Coalition against France. The
        Vendée rises against republican excesses, but a rebel army is routed at Savenay. America declares its
        neutrality, unable to decide which side to back. The Committee of Public Safety take power; Robespierre
        heads a government which embarks on the Reign of Terror. Prussia and Russia perform the Second
        Partition of Poland, seizing half of Poland's territory. Marat is murdered by Charlotte Corday. Toulon is
        occupied by the British, but recaptured by a force including Napoleon.

1794   King Kamehameha of Polynesia cedes Hawaii to George III, but the cession is not ratified. Shah Lutf Ali of
        Persia is defeated and killed by Agha Muhammad, who founds the Qajar dynasty. Kosciusko leads a rising
        of Polish patriots, which is suppressed by the Russians. The Reign of Terror reaches a height as Danton
        and Desmoulins are executed. Habeas Corpus is suspended in Britain. Admiral Howe defeats the French
        fleet on the 'Glorious First of June', but the French have revenge at Charleroi and Fleurus. Robespierre
        holds the Festival of the Supreme Being; Thermidorean moderates stage a coup – Robespierre and St Just
        are executed and the Jacobin Club closed.

1795   The French capture the Dutch fleet in the River Texel; Stadtholder William V is forced to flee to England and
        the French form the Batavian republic in the Netherlands. Prussia makes peace with France by the treaty of
        Basel. The Speenhamland magistrates devise a new form of poor relief. Warren Hastings is acquitted. The
        Chouan uprising occurs in Brittany. Cape Town and Trincomalee are taken by the British. The Directory, led
        by Barras, comes to power in France. Austria, Prussia, and Russia perform the Third Partition of Poland;
        Stanislas II is forced to abdicate as his country ceases to exist.

1796   Colombo is taken by the British, establishing British control over Ceylon. Emperor Qianlong abdicates, and
        is succeeded by his son Jiaqing. Napoleon leads an army into Italy; it defeats the Austrians at Millesimo,
        Lodi and Arcol and establishes the Lombard Republic. François Babeuf leads a conspiracy to overthrow
        the Directory, but it fails. Edward Jenner discovers a vaccine against smallpox. Elba is captured by Britain.
        Robert Burns dies aged 37. Spain and Britain go to war. Tsarina Catherine the Great dies, and is
        succeeded by her son Paul I.

1797   Napoleon defeats the Austrians at Rivoli, seizes Mantua, and founds the Ligurian republic in Genoa and
        the Cisalpine Republic. Trinidad and St Lucia are taken by the British from the French. Admiral Jervis
        defeats the Spanish at Cape St Vincent. French troops are landed at Fishguard, but are quickly captured.
        The first £1 banknotes are issued. John Adams succeeds George Washington as American President. The

Royal Navy suffers mutinies at the Nore and Spithead, but defeats a Franco-Dutch fleet at Camperdown. Barras thwarts a royalist reaction by the coup d'état of Fructidor. By the Peace of Campo Formio, the Austrian Netherlands are annexed by France whilst Venice and its territories are passed to Austria; Venice thus loses its independence. Frederick William II of Prussia dies, and is succeeded by his son Frederick William III.

1798   Thomas Malthus produces his *Essay on the Principles of Population*. Coleridge and Wordsworth publish *Lyrical Ballads*. Napoleon captures Rome, proclaiming the Roman Republic and forcing Pope Pius VI into custody at Valence. The Helvetic Republic, encouraged by the French, is proclaimed in Bern. Napoleon then captures Malta en route to Egypt, where he defeats the Mamluks at the battle of the Pyramids, but Nelson destroys his fleet at the battle of the Nile. Irish rebels are defeated at Vinegar Hill, whilst French troops landing in support are forced to surrender at Ballinamuck. The Irish nationalist Wolfe Tone is captured, condemned, but commits suicide. Ferdinand IV of Naples enters Rome, but is driven out by the French and Naples overrun. Income Tax is introduced in Britain.

1799   Napoleon invades Syria, but is repulsed by Sir Sidney Smith at Acre. The Rosetta Stone is discovered. Britain and Hyderabad share Mysore after Tipu Sultan is killed at Seringapatam. The Second Coalition against France is organised by Pitt. Russian troops defeat the French at Zurich, but are eventually driven out; after victory at Cassano they overthrow the Cisalpine Republic. Napoleon defeats an Anglo-Turkish army at Aboukir. On 18 Brumaire Napoleon overthrows the Directory and becomes First Consul.

1800   The American capital is transferred from Philadelphia to Washington DC. The French defeat the Turks at Heliopolis. Austrian troops starve Genoa into submission, but are defeated at Marengo, giving Napoleon control of Italy. Malta is captured by the British.

1801   Great Britain and Ireland unite. France adopts a metric system of weights and measures. The Bank of France is founded. Austria and France make the peace of Lunéville, which destroys the viability of the Holy Roman Empire. Thomas Jefferson becomes American president. Pitt the Younger resigns as prime minister over Catholic Emancipation, and is replaced by Addington. Tsar Paul I is assassinated, succeeded by his son Alexander I. Nelson defeats the Danish fleet at Copenhagen (after the famous incident of him turning a blind eye to Parker's orders). The French troops in Egypt surrender to the English.

1802   William Cobbett founds the *Political Register*. The *Charlotte Dundas*, the world's first steamship, is built by William Symington. Madame Tussaud mounts her first waxworks exhibition in London. Napoleon becomes president of the Italian Republic, which has superseded the Cisalpine Republic. Britain and France make peace by the treaty of Amiens. Napoleon creates the Légion d'Honneur, is made First Consul for life and annexes Piedmont, Parma and Piacenza.

1803   The Swiss cantons regain their independence by the Act of Mediation. Henry Shrapnel develops an explosive shell. The United States purchase the Louisiana territory – over 800,000 sq. miles of land west of the Mississippi – from France. Thomas Telford commences building the Caledonian Canal. France and Britain resume hostilities; France occupies Hanover. Arthur Wellesley (the future duke of Wellington) leads British troops to victory against Sindhia of Gwalior in the Second Maratha War.

1804   Richard Trevithick develops a steam locomotive. The duc d'Enghien is executed for plotting a Bourbon restoration. The Code Napoleon comes into force. Addington is forced to resign by Pitt the Younger, who replaces him. Napoleon is proclaimed Emperor of the French, crowning himself in the presence of Pope Pius VII. A revolt forces the French to withdraw from Haiti. Former US treasury secretary Alexander Hamilton is killed in a duel with Vice-President Aaron Burr.

1805   Francis Beaufort devises the Beaufort Scale. Mungo Park explores the Upper Niger. Muhammad Ali is proclaimed Pasha of Egypt. Napoleon crowns himself king of Italy in Milan wih the old Lombard crown. Austria, Russia, Sweden and Britain form the Third Coalition against France. The British fleet is victorious at Trafalgar over a Franco-Spanish fleet, but Nelson is mortally wounded. On the same day Napoleon defeats an Austro-Russian army at Ulm, and is subsequently victorious at Austerlitz. France and Austria make peace by the treaty of Pressburg; Austria is forced to yield the Tyrol and her Italian possessions whilst Bavaria and Württemberg become kingdoms and Baden a grand duchy.

1806   Britain occupies the Cape of Good Hope. Pitt the Younger dies; Grenville forms a coalition, the 'Ministry of All the Talents', to replace him. Britain establishes a blockade of the European coastline; Napoleon retaliates by the Berlin Decree establishing the Continental System to bar European ports to British ships. Napoleon makes his brothers Joseph and Louis kings of Naples and Holland respectively. France organises the Confederation of the Rhine; the Holy Roman Empire thus ceases to exist and Francis II is merely Emperor of Austria. Prussia joins the Third Coalition. Napoleon defeats the Prussians at Jena and Auerstadt and enters Berlin. Saxony becomes a kingdom by the Peace of Posen.

1807   Charles and Mary Lamb's *Tales from Shakespeare* is published; Charles is guardian to his sister, who stabbed their mother during a bout of insanity. Slavery is prohibited in Britain. Sultan Selim III is deposed by his Janissaries and succeeded by his cousin Mustapha IV. HMS *Leopard* takes deserters from USS *Chesapeake*, enraging the Americans. Napoleon meets Tsar Alexander at Tilsit and makes the peace by the treaty of Tilsit. Napoleon makes his brother Jerome king of Westphalia. Copenhagen is bombarded by the British. Baron von Stein becomes Prussian prime minister and emancipates the serfs there. France invades Portugal, which has refused to join the Continental System; the Portuguese royal family flees to Brazil.

1808   French troops under Murat invade Spain. Charles IV of Spain abdicates in favour of his son Ferdinand VII, but Napoleon orders Murat to force Joseph Bonaparte upon them. Spanish resistance puts Joseph to flight, but Napoleon takes Madrid and restores him. Grand Vizier Bairakdar attempts to restore Sultan Selim III, who is strangled by the janissaries. Bairakdar deposes and murders Sultan Mustafa IV, replacing him with his brother Mahmud II. Murat replaces Joseph as king of Naples.

1809   Sir John Moore is mortally wounded as British troops evacuate Corunna. Gustavus IV of Sweden is captured in a coup; the Duke of Sudermania forms a government and Gustavus is forced to abdicate. Gustavus IV's uncle Karl XIII eventually succeeds him. Britain and the Sikhs make a pact of friendship by the treaty of Amritsar. Napoleon annexes the Papal States, taking Pope Pius VII prisoner, and to further his dynastic ambitions, divorces Josephine. Wellington defeats Soult at Oporto and Jourdan at Talavera. Napoleon is defeated by the Austrians at Aspern, but is victorious at Wagram and makes peace with Austria by the treaty of Schönbrunn. Canning, British foreign secretary, and Castlereagh, war minister, fight a duel on Putney Heath and resign from office. Metternich becomes Austrian minister of foreign affairs. Austria joins the Continental System.

1810   Napoleon marries Marie Louise of Austria. Andreas Hofer leads an Austrian rebellion, but is executed at Mantua. Napoleon annexes Holland when his brother Louis abdicates, and later annexes Hanover and various German ports. Jean Bernadotte is invited to become heir to the Swedish throne as Karl XIII has no children. The Krupp steel works open in Essen.

1811   George III descends into madness and the prince of Wales is declared Regent. Belgrade is seized by the Russians. Pasha Muhammad Ali massacres the Mamluks at Cairo. Luddism erupts in the Midlands. Wellington defeats the French at Fuentes de Onoro and Albuera. Francisco de Miranda declares Venezuelan independence; Paraguay follows suit. William Harrison defeats the Shawnee at Tippecanoe.

1812   In Spain, Wellington takes Ciudad Rodrigo and Badajoz, defeats Marmont at Salamanca and enters Madrid. Prime minister Spencer Perceval is assassinated by John Bellingham, and is succeeded by the earl of Liverpool. America declares war on Britain. Napoleon leads his Grand Army into Russia. Britain, Russia and Sweden ally via the treaty of Örebro. De Miranda is made dictator of Venezuela after an earthquake, but is captured by the Spanish. After victory at Smolensk and an inconclusive outcome at Borodino Napoleon takes an evacuated Moscow, which is then burned down by Russian saboteurs. He orders a retreat, and has to suffer terrible losses in crossing the River Berezina. General Claude Malet attempts to depose Napoleon in his absence, but is executed as the conspiracy fails.

1813   The locomotive 'Puffing Billy' is developed by William Hedley. Prussia declares war on France, but is defeated, along with Russia, by Napoleon at Lützen, Bautzen and Wurschen. Wellington defeats Jourdan at Vittoria and crosses into France. Simon Bolívar becomes dictator of Venezuela. Austria declares war on France. Prusso-Russian troops defeat Napoleon at Grossbeeren and Wahlstatt, but are defeated at Dresden before further victory at Dennewitz. An Austro-Prusso-Russian army defeats Napoleon at Leipzig, and drives him back across Germany. Mexico declares independence from Spain. The French are expelled from Holland.

1814   Denmark cedes Heligoland to Britain by the treaty of Kiel. Murat deserts Napoleon and joins the Allies, who inflict defeats on Napoleon at La Rothière, Laon, Arcis and Fère-Champenoise before entering Paris. Wellington defeats the French at Toulouse. Napoleon abdicates, is banished to Elba, and is granted its sovereignty. Louis XVIII returns from exile. Ferdinand VII returns to the Spanish throne. The Austrian Netherlands and Holland unite to form the kingdom of the Netherlands. The White House is burned down by British troops. The Cape of Good Hope becomes a British colony. The Congress of Vienna opens. The treaty of Ghent ends hostilities between Britain and America.

1815   Napoleon returns from Elba, forcing Louis XVIII to flee to Ghent. His forces under Ney are victorious at Quatre Bras, but Wellington defeats him at Waterloo. After surrendering to the British, he is exiled to St Helena. Louis XVIII returns, Ney is executed and Murat deposed from Naples; he is executed when trying to regain his throne. Spanish troops reconquer Venezuela, forcing Bolívar to flee. To protect domestic growers against cheaper imports, the Corn Laws are passed in Britain. The treaty of Vienna draws up a new political map of Europe: Norway is passed to Denmark, the Rhineland to Prussia, Poland to Russia and various monarchs restored to their thrones.

1816   Argentina declares itself independent, as does Brazil under the Portuguese prince João, who succeeds to the Portuguese throne on the death of his mother Maria I, but remains in Brazil. The first Diet of the German Confederation opens in Frankfurt. Cobbett's *Political Register* increases its radical influence after a price cut to 2d.

1817   José de San Martín and Bernardo O'Higgins defeat the Spanish at Chacabuco and establish an independent Chile. The last major Luddite attack takes place in Loughborough. The 'Blanketeers' march from Manchester to protest against the suspension of the Habeas Corpus Act, but are halted at Stockport; there are similar riots elsewhere. Bolivar reestablishes an independent Venezuela. The Ottomans grant partial autonomy to the Serbs.

1818   The Rajput states and Indore come under British control by the treaty of Mundosir. Karl XIII of Sweden dies, and is succeeded by Bernadotte, who takes the name Karl XIV. The American-Canadian border is defined along the 49th parallel. James Blundell performs the first successful blood transfusion. At the Congress of Aix-la-Chapelle, the victorious allies agree to withdraw their troops from France, which has paid the war indemnity imposed in 1815.

1819   Stamford Raffles founds the city of Singapore. The United States take over Florida from Spain. The reactionary Karlsbad Decrees are promulgated in Germany. The Peterloo Massacre kills 11 people in Manchester, when yeomen attack a reformist crowd. The reactionary Six Acts are passed in England. Simon Bolivar becomes president of the newly independent Colombia.

1820   Liberia is founded for the repatriation of American Negroes. There are revolts in Spain, where Ferdinand VII is forced to restore the constitution of 1812, and in Portugal, demanding a constitution. George III dies, and is succeeded by his son George IV. The duc de Berry, heir to the French throne, is assassinated; a son, the comte de Chambord, is born posthumously. At the Congress of Troppau, Prussia, Austria and Russia discuss concerted action against revolutionary movements with Britain and France. The Cato Street Conspiracy to murder British cabinet ministers is discovered and its leaders executed. Keats publishes *Lamia, Isabella, The Eve of St Agnes and other Poems*.

1821   A Carbonarist uprising in Naples is put down by the Austrians, sanctioned by the Congress of Laibach. Bolívar defeats the Spanish at Carabobo, ensuring Venezuelan independence. Peru declares independence under José de San Martín. El Salvador, Honduras, Costa Rica, Guatemala and Panama follow suit. Greeks start an insurgence against the Ottomans in an attempt to gain independence. Victor

Emmanuel of Piedmont is forced to abdicate in favour of his more liberal brother Charles Felix. The Austrians intervene, defeating the Piedmontese at Novara and reasserting control over the country.

1822   Viceroy Wellesley is attacked by Orangemen in Dublin in the 'Bottle Riots'. The Ottomans capture Chios and massacre its inhabitants. Agostín de Itúrbide is declared emperor of Mexico. A Greek flotilla burns an Ottoman fleet, bringing further reprisals. British foreign secretary Castlereagh commits suicide. Regent Pedro, son of João VI of Portugal, declares Brazil independent.

1823   Michael Faraday succeeds in liquefying chlorine. Emperor Agostín de Itúrbide is forced to abdicate as Mexico declares itself a republic. *The Lancet* is first published. A revolt in Spain is quelled with French assistance. President Monroe issues the Monroe Doctrine, closing the Americas to European colonialism.

1824   The RNLI is founded. The First Burmese War between Britain and Burma commences; Rangoon is taken by the British. Lord Byron dies at Missolonghi whilst assisting the Greeks. Beethoven's 9th Symphony is first performed. Louis XVIII of France dies, and is succeeded by his brother Charles X.

1825   Ferdinand I of the Two Sicilies dies, and is succeeded by his son Francis I. John Quincy Adams is elected American president by the House of Representatives after none of the four candidates gains a majority in the election. Bolivia under Jose de Sucre declares independence from Peru, and Uruguay, with Argentine support, from Brazil. The Stockton–Darlington railway opens, the first passenger-carrying line. The Erie Canal links the Hudson River to the Great Lakes and the American Midwest. Tsar Alexander I dies, and is succeeded by his brother Nicholas I, who is confronted by the Decembrist revolt of officers, which he puts down.

1826   The First Burmese War is ended by the treaty of Yandabo. João VI of Portugal dies, and is succeeded by his son Pedro IV, who abdicates in favour of his daughter Maria II and remains in Brazil. Persia and Russia go to war; the Russians are victorious at Ganja. Stamford Raffles founds the Royal Zoological Society in London.

1827   Peru secedes from Colombia. Count Kapodistrias is elected president of Greece as Britain, France and Russia sign the treaty of London pledging support for the Greeks; an allied fleet crushes an Ottoman and Egyptian fleet at Navarino. Russia defeats Persia and takes Yerevan.

1828   Wellington becomes prime minister. Russia makes peace with Persia by the treaty of Turkmanchai, and subsequently declares war on the Ottomans. Maria II of Portugal is deposed by her uncle, the Regent Dom Miguel, and flees to England as civil war breaks out. The treaty of Rio de Janeiro confirms Uruguayan independence. Thomas Arnold becomes headmaster of Rugby School.

1829   The Catholic Emancipation Act is passed in Britain. Wellington fights a duel with the earl of Winchelsea. The Metropolitan Police is founded by Robert Peel. The first Boat Race takes place at Henley. The London Protocol establishes Greek independence; the treaty of Adrianople ends Russo-Turkish hostilities. Stephenson's *Rocket* wins the Rainhill Trials. Slavery is abolished in Mexico.

1830   Joseph Smith founds the Church of Jesus Christ of Latter-Day Saints. The Swing riots, caused by the introduction of threshing machines and rural unemployment, start in Kent and spread west and north. George IV dies, and is succeeded by his brother William IV. Algeria is conquered by France, but an uprising in Paris forces Charles X to abdicate in favour of his grandson, however Louis-Philippe, duc d'Orléans, usurps the throne. Belgium secedes from the Kingdom of the Netherlands. Wellington is ousted as prime minister after a general election, and replaced by earl Grey.

1831   Independence agitations in Italy are quelled by Austrian troops. Pedro I of Brazil abdicates, and is succeeded by his son Pedro II. A Polish revolt is put down after Russian troops are victorious at Ostroleka. Leopold of Saxe-Coburg is elected king of the Belgians. Charles Felix of Piedmont dies, and is succeeded by his distant relation Charles Albert. The Greek President Kapodistrias is assassinated. Faraday invents the dynamo. The defeat of Grey's Reform Bill in the Lords causes anti-clerical agitation. Mazzini founds Young Italy.

1832   The First Reform Act is passed, doubling the franchise. Otto of Bavaria is elected king of Greece.

1833   Britain annexes the Falkland Islands. The Convention of Kutahya passes control of Syria to Muhammad Ali of Egypt. Slavery is abolished in the British Empire. Ferdinand VII of Spain dies, and is succeeded by his infant daughter Isabella II. Santa Anna becomes President of Mexico whilst civil war looms in the country.

1834   The Zollverein customs union comes into operation in Germany. The Spanish Inquisition is abolished. To protect their constitutions, Portugal and Spain form a Quadruple Alliance with France and Britain. Don Carlos attempts to usurp the Spanish throne from his niece Isabella II, plunging the country into civil war, whilst in Portugal Dom Miguel is forced to flee as troops led by his brother Pedro restore Maria II to her throne. For forming a trade union, the Tolpuddle Martyrs are arrested and transported to Australia. Fire destroys the Houses of Parliament.

1835   Francis II of Austria dies, and is succeeded by his son Ferdinand I. Juan de Rosas becomes dictator of Argentina. The Boers begin the 'Great Trek'. Texas attempts to secede from Mexico.

1836   Santa Anna takes the Alamo at San Antonio; Davy Crockett and Jim Bowie are killed. Sam Houston defeats and captures Santa Anna at San Jacinto; Texas gains independence with Houston as president. Louis Napoleon Bonaparte attempts a revolt at Strasbourg, and is banished to America.

1837   William IV dies, and is succeeded in England by his niece Victoria and in Hanover by his brother Ernst Augustus, duke of Cumberland, who promptly cancels the constitution of 1833 there. Brunel launches the *Great Western*. Births, marriages and deaths are officially registered in England and Wales. Isaac Pitman develops shorthand. French Canadians revolt against British rule.

1838   Chopin begins his liaison with George Sand. Richard Cobden establishes the Anti-Corn Law League. The 'People's Charter' is published. Grace Darling assists in the rescue from the wreck of the *Forfarshire*. The First Afghan War begins; the British capture Kabul and imprison the Emir Dost Muhammad. The Boers defeat the Zulus at Blood River.

1839   The Rebecca Riots against the Poor Law Amendment Act take place in Wales (rioters disguise themselves as women). Goodyear discovers how to vulcanise rubber. Argentina and Uruguay go to war. The Ottomans invade Syria but are defeated by Ibrahim Pasha at Nezib. The treaty of London guarantees Belgian independence and neutrality. Sultan Mahmud II is poisoned, and succeeded by his son Abdul Mejid. Chinese attempts to stop the importation of opium lead to the Opium War with Britain. Frederick VI of Denmark dies, and is succeeded by his nephew, Christian VIII. Bradshaw's provides first railway timetables.

1840   The Maoris cede sovereignty of New Zealand to England by the treaty of Waitangi. Rowland Hill introduces the Penny Post. Frederick William III of Prussia dies, and is succeeded by his son Frederick William IV. Britain, Austria, Prussia and Russia ally against Muhammad Ali of Egypt by the treaty of London; after Beirut and Acre are captured, Muhammad agrees to return Syria to Ottoman rule. Lower and Upper Canada are united under a single legislature. Rafael Carrera becomes dictator of Guatemala. Louis Napoleon Bonaparte is imprisoned at Ham after another attempt to foment revolt fails. William I of Holland abdicates, and is succeeded by his son William II.

1841   Hong Kong is taken by the British. William Harrison dies after catching cold giving his inaugural address as US president, and is succeeded by John Tyler. Thomas Cook arranges his first excursion, to a temperance meeting. The Straits Convention closes the Bosporus to warships. Carlos Lopez becomes President of Paraguay. The first issue of *Punch* is published.

1842   Crawford W Long performs the first operation under anaesthesia. British troops in Afghanistan are massacred. The second Chartist petition is rejected. Civil war erupts in Uruguay. The Webster-Ashburton treaty defines the US–Canadian border. The treaty of Nanking ends the Opium War; Hong Kong is ceded to Britain. Alexander Karageorgevich deposes Michael Obrenovich as prince of Serbia. Marx meets Engels. Britain withdraws from Afghanistan.

1843   The Thames Tunnel opens, first underwater tunnel in the world. Brunel launches the *Great Britain*. Sind is conquered by General Charles Napier. Hawaii becomes independent, with recognition from France and Britain.

1844   George Williams founds the YMCA. Karl XIV of Sweden dies, and is succeeded by his son Oscar I. The Factory Act fixes maximum workdays of 6½ hours for children, 12 hours for women. Samuel Morse transmits his first telegraph message. The Dominican Republic gains independence from Haiti. The Co-operative movement is founded in Rochdale.

1845   The Irish famine begins as the potato crop fails. Henry Newman converts to Catholicism. Sir John Franklin sets out with the *Erebus* and *Terror* to find the North-West Passage. British incursions in the Punjab and Kashmir cause the Anglo-Sikh War. The Sonderbund is formed when 7 Catholic cantons secede from the Confederation in Switzerland.

1846   The Anglo-Sikh War is ended by the treaty of Lahore. Cracow is annexed by Austria. Louis Napoleon Bonaparte escapes from prison and moves to London. The treaty of Washington settles the Oregon–Canada border along the 49th Parallel. America goes to war with Mexico after failing to purchase New Mexico; after victories at Palo Alto and Resaca de la Palma New Mexico is annexed by the United States. Peel repeals the Corn Laws, fatally splitting his party and forcing him to resign as prime minister; Lord John Russell replaces him. Charles Dickens founds the *Daily News*.

1847   Mexican troops under Santa Anna are defeated by the Americans at Buena Vista and Cerro Gordo. Liberia is proclaimed an independent republic. The Catholic cantons refuse to dissolve the Sonderbund, precipitating war in Switzerland.

1848   Christian VIII of Denmark dies, and is succeeded by his son Frederick III. Gold is discovered in California. The treaty of Guadalupe Hidalgo ends the conflict between America and Mexico, which is forced to yield its lands north of the Rio Grande. Marx and Engels publish the *Communist Manifesto*. Paris erupts in revolt, forcing Louis Philippe to abdicate. The Second French Republic is formed; a workers' revolt is put down (the June Days) and Louis Napoleon Bonaparte is elected President. The revolution in France inspires a wave of revolts across Europe: Metternich falls in Austria; Milan, Parma, Venice, Hungary and the Czechs revolt against Austrian dominion; liberals rise across Germany, creating a National Assembly; Rome rises against Papal war, forcing Pope Pius IX to flee to Gaeta. Piedmont declares war on Austria, but after victories at Goito and Pastrengo is defeated by Radetzky at Custozza. Windischgrätz suppresses the Czech rising; nevertheless, Emperor Ferdinand I is forced to abdicate in favour of his nephew Franz Josef. The Second Anglo-Sikh war breaks out. The third Chartist petition is presented amid a meeting which collapses in farce, and is rejected. Switzerland becomes a federal union. The Pre-Raphaelite Brotherhood is founded.

1849   The Sikhs are defeated by the British at Chillianwalla and forced to surrender at Rawalpindi; the Punjab is annexed by Britain. A Roman republic under Mazzini is formed, but French, Austrian, Spanish, Neapolitan and Tuscan troops capture Rome and restore Pope Pius IX. Radetzky defeats the Piedmontese at Novara. Charles Albert of Piedmont abdicates in favour of his son Victor Emmanuel II and the Peace of Milan ends hostilities. The German National Assembly elects Frederick William IV 'Emperor of the Germans', but he refuses the title and the Assembly collapses in chaos. Hungary proclaims independence under Kossuth, but Russian troops invade and are victorious at Temesvar; Kossuth flees and Hungary returns to Austrian rule. Venice submits to the Austrians.

1850   Palmerston blockades Piraeus over the Don Pacifico Affair, forcing the Greeks to comply with his wishes, but is censured in parliament. Prussia and Denmark reach an accord on Schleswig-Holstein by the treaty of Berlin. Hong Xiuquan leads the Taiping rebellion in China. Count Camillo Cavour becomes chief minister of Piedmont.

1851   Danilo II succeeds Peter II in Montenegro and makes the state a principality. The Great Exhibition is held in Hyde Park. The Americas Cup yacht race is first held around the Isle of Wight. The Australian Gold Rush begins. Louis Napoleon Bonaparte stages a coup d'état in France.

1852   Juan Manuel de Rosas, Argentine dictator, is forced to flee after defeat by insurgents with Uruguayan and Brazilian help at Caseros. The Second Burmese War breaks out between Britain and Burma. Louis Napoleon Bonaparte proclaims the Second Empire, crowning himself Napoleon III.

1853   Pegu is taken by Britain as the Second Burmese War ends. Shogun Ieyoshi dies, and is succeeded by his son Iesada, who opens two Japanese ports to foreign trade. Russia invades the Ottoman Danubian principalities and destroys the Turkish fleet at Sinope. Maria II of Portugal dies, and is succeeded by her son Pedro V.

1854   The Convention of Bloemfontein leaves the Orange Free State free for the Boers and withdraws the British south of the Orange River. America makes the treaty of Kanagawa with Japan over trade and the Elgin treaty with Britain over Canadian trade. Britain and France declare war on Russia in support of Turkey and are victorious at the Alma, Balaklava (where the Charge of the Light Brigade takes place), and Inkerman, before besieging Sebastopol.

1855   Piedmont joins the anti-Russian alliance in the Crimean War by the treaty of Turin. Aberdeen resigns as prime minister over the conduct of the war, and is replaced by Palmerston.Tsar Nicholas I dies, and is succeeded by his son Alexander II. Britain and Afghanistan sign the anti-Persian treaty of Peshawar. The *Daily Telegraph* is first published. Sebastopol falls to the allied armies.

1856   The Victoria Cross is instituted. Britain annexes Oudh and establishes Natal as a Crown Colony. The Crimean War is ended by the treaty of Paris; the integrity of the Ottoman Empire is recognised and the Black Sea demiltitarised. The Chinese board the *Arrow* off Canton over suspected piracy; British ships bombard Canton in response. Marthinius Pretorius establishes the Transvaal republic. Henry Bessemer introduces his steel-making converter.

1857   Britain forces Afghani independence on the Persians by the treaty of Paris. The Sepoys in Meerut revolt, sparking a general Indian Mutiny; the inhabitants of Cawnpore are massacred and Lucknow besieged for six months. Garibaldi forms the Italian National Association. British and French forces occupy Canton.

1858   Felice Orsini attempts to assassinate Napoleon III, causing Anglo-French tension and turning Napoleon's mind towards Italy; he has secret meetings at Plombières with Cavour. Anglo-Chinese hostilities are ended by the treaty of Tianjin. The Indian Mutiny is suppressed; the East India Company is wound up and its powers transferred to the British crown. Frederick William IV is declared insane; his brother William is made Regent. Alexander Karageorgevich is deposed by the Serbian Diet and replaced by Milos Obrenovich. France launches *La Gloire*, a naval vessel partially clad in iron.

1859   Piedmont traps Austria into war, and backed by Napoleon III is victorious at Magenta and Solferino. Ferdinand of the Two Sicilies dies, and is succeeded by his son Francis II. Napoleon III and Franz Josef of Austria make the Peace of Villafranca; Lombardy is passed to Piedmont. John Brown raids Harpers Ferry. Darwin publishes the *Origin of Species*. Queensland is established as a separate colony with Brisbane as its capital.

1860   Piedmont cedes Nice and Savoy to France by the treaty of Turin. Plebiscites in the Italian duchies favour union with Piedmont. Garibaldi and his 1,000 redshirts sail from Genoa to Sicily, take the island and then progress to Naples, where he proclaims Victor Emmanuel II of Piedmont king of Italy. Piedmontese troops invade the Papal States en route to the Two Sicilies, which Garibaldi hands to Victor Emmanuel II; Garibaldi retires to Caprera. South Carolina secedes from the Union in protest at the election of Abraham Lincoln as president. The Second Maori War breaks out in New Zealand. Richard Cobden negotiates an Anglo-French trade treaty. Anglo-French forces bombard Sinho, occupy the Tagu forts, defeat the Chinese army at Ba Lizhao and burn the Summer Palace in Peking in retaliation for Chinese treaty breaches and cruelty to captives; the treaty of Peking forces further concessions on the Chinese.

1861   Frederick William IV of Prussia dies and is succeeded by his brother Wilhelm I. Tsar Alexander II emancipates the Russian serfs. The kingdom of Italy is proclaimed, with its capital at Florence, as Rome refuses to join. The Confederate States of America are proclaimed at the Congress of Montgomery and go to war with the Union by bombarding Fort Sumter: the Civil War begins. The Confederates are victorious at Bull Run. Prince Albert dies. With the commissioning into the Royal Navy of the iron-hulled HMS *Warrior*, all other naval vessels are rendered effectively obsolete.

1862   In America the ironclad USS *Monitor* launches, which fights the Confederate ironclad *Merrimack* to a draw in Hampton Roads.The battle of Shiloh is a bloody draw, whilst the Confederates are subsequently victorious at the second battle of Bull Run and Fredericksburg. Napoleon III sends French troops to establish a Catholic empire in Mexico, forcing the withdrawal of British and Spanish troops; the French are heavily defeated at Puebla. Bismarck is appointed prime minister of Prussia. A military revolt forces Otto I of Greece to abdicate and return to Bavaria.

1863   The first underground railway, from Farringdon Street to Paddington, is opened. The Greeks elect Prince Alfred of Britain as their new king, but he is forced to reject the position; William of Denmark is elected instead, taking the title George I. The Confederates are victorious at Chancellorsville, but are routed at Gettysburg, which proves a turning point. The Union has further victories at Vicksburg and Chattanooga but is defeated at Chickamauga. Lincoln gives the Gettysburg Address at the dedication of the cemetery there. Mexico City falls to the French, who invite Archduke Maximilian of Austria to become emperor of the country. Japan closes its ports and expels foreign traders, prompting Britain to bombard Kagoshima. Frederick VII of Denmark dies, and is succeeded by his nephew Christian IX, who incorporates Schleswig into the country after German pressure on the area. The English Football Association is founded.

1864   Austrian and Prussian troops invade Schleswig-Holstein, defeating the Danes at Düppel. A conference in London fails to settle the dispute, and Prussia and Austria force Denmark to cede the area by the treaty of Vienna. Archduke Maximilian accepts the Mexican crown. Brazil invades Uruguay after a dispute with Paraguay. The Taiping Rebellion is suppressed, with help from General Gordon's troops; Hong Xiuquan commits suicide. Ulysses S Grant takes command of the Union army. In the Wilderness campaign in Virginia, the Union loses 60,000 of an army of over 100,000, the Confederacy 20,000 of its 60,000 men. Sherman takes Atlanta and Savannah as his Union army marches through Georgia. General George Thomas wipes out a Confederate army under JB Hood at Nashville.

1865   The Confederate states surrender to the Unionists at Appomattox; five days later Abraham Lincoln is assassinated by John Wilkes Booth. William Booth founds the Christian Revival Association (later the Salvation Army). Edward Whymper climbs the Matterhorn. Edward Lister's use of carbolic acid founds modern antiseptic surgery. Lord Palmerston dies in office, and is succeeded as prime minister by Lord

John Russell. Leopold I of Belgium dies, and is succeeded by his son Leopold II. The Thirteenth Amendment abolishes slavery in the US.

1866   Prince Alexander of Romania is dethroned and replaced by Carol I of Hohenzollern. Bismarck, with Italian assistance, engineers war against Austria and allied German states, defeating the Austrians at Sadowa, although the Italians are defeated at Custozza and the naval battle of Lissa. The Peace of Prague gives Prussia Hanover, Hesse, Nassau, Frankfurt and Holstein. Shogun Iemochi dies, and is succeeded by his kinsman Yoshinobu. The treaty of Vienna cedes Venetia to Italy.

1867   The Ausgleich creates the Dual Monarchy of Austria-Hungary. Alaska is sold by Russia to America. The Dominion of Canada is created. Emperor Maximilian of Mexico surrenders to insurgents after the French abandon him and is executed. Prussia forms the North German Confederation. The Second Reform Act doubles the British electorate. Garibaldi marches on Rome, but is defeated by a Franco-Papal army at Mentana and taken prisoner. The Queensberry Rules on boxing are drawn up.

1868   The Shogunate is abolished in Japan; by the Meiji Restoration power passes to Emperor Matsuhito. Disraeli becomes prime minister, but is defeated in a general election by Gladstone, who replaces him. Prince Michael of Serbia is assassinated, succeeded by his kinsman Milan II Isabella II of Spain is deposed after a revolution in Spain. The first Trades Union Congress meets in Manchester. The last public hangings in England take place.

1869   The first Nihilist Congress meets in Basel. The *Cutty Sark* is launched. Napoleon III reintroduces a parliamentary system into France. The Suez Canal is opened.

1870   Papal infallibility is proclaimed. Isabella II of Spain abdicates in favour of her son Alfonso XII but the throne is offered to Leopold of Hohenzollern, who is forced to decline it after French protests. These protests are edited by Bismarck into the 'Ems telegram' and used to foment war between France and Prussia. After a French victory at Saarbrücken, Prussia is victorious at Weissenberg, Wörth, Mars-la-Tour, Gravelotte and Sedan. Napoleon III surrenders and abdicates as Paris revolts and proclaims the Third Republic. Paris is besieged by the Prussians. Italian troops enter Rome and absorb it into the kingdom; it is made the capital. Amadeus of Savoy accepts the Spanish throne.

1871   Wilhelm I of Prussia is proclaimed emperor of a federal Germany at Versailles. Paris surrenders to the Prussians. The leftist Commune takes power there, and is repressed with the loss of 20,000 lives. The Convention of London abolishes the demilitarization of the Black Sea. Britain and America settle differences by the treaty of Washington. France and Germany make the Peace of Frankfurt; Alsace-Lorraine is ceded to Germany and an indemnity paid by France. Stanley meets Livingstone at Ujiji (now in Tanzania). Bank holidays are introduced.

1872   Wanderers win the first FA Cup final. Don Carlos invades Spain, but is routed at Oroquista and forced to withdraw. The secret ballot is introduced in Britain. Germany, Austria-Hungary and Russia form the Three Emperors League. The *Marie Celeste* is found deserted.

1873   A Spanish republic is proclaimed and Amadeus I forced to abdicate. Sultan Bargash Sayyid closes the slave markets in Zanzibar. The cities of Buda and Pest are united to form the Hungarian capital. WC Wingfield invents Sphairistike (lawn tennis).

1874   Disraeli defeats Gladstone in the General Election. Japan invades Formosa, and withdraws on payment of compensation by China. Fiji is annexed by Britain. Alfonso XII of Spain proclaims his reign at Sandhurst.

1875   Bismarck foments tension between Germany and France ('Is War in Sight?' article in the *Berlin Post*). Bosnia-Herzegovina revolts against Turkish rule. Matthew Webb swims the English Channel. Disraeli arranges the purchase of shares in the Suez Canal. Sir Joseph Bazalgette completes the London sewerage system. The MCC codifies the rules of lawn tennis.

1876   Korea becomes independent from China. Alexander Graham Bell patents the telephone. Bulgaria rises against Turkey, but is savagely repressed, drawing Gladstone out of retirement. Queen Victoria is proclaimed Empress of India and is officially inaugurated in January 1877. Sultan Abdul Aziz is deposed in favour of his nephew Murad V and commits suicide; Murad is himself deposed in favour of his brother Abdul Hamid II. General Custer is defeated and killed by the Sioux at the battle of Little Big Horn. Serbia and Montenegro declare war on Turkey, but the Serbs are routed at Alexinatz. Wild Bill Hickok is shot dead.

1877   Rutherford B Hayes is elected American president after an electoral commission decides in his favour. Russia declares war on Turkey and takes Kars and Plevna. Britain warns Russia off taking Constantinople. Serbia also declares war on Turkey. Australia beats England in the first cricket Test match. The first Lawn Tennis Championships are held at Wimbledon.

1878   Victor Emmanuel II of Italy dies, and is succeeded by his son Umberto I. Russia takes Adrianople; the Turks capitulate and sign the treaty of San Stefano, in which Bulgarian, Romanian and Serbian independence is fully established. The provisions are unacceptable to other European powers; differences are resolved at the Congress of Berlin, where the San Stefano provisons are reduced in scale.

1879   The Irish Land League is founded. Britain goes to war with the Zulus, who massacre the British at Isandhlwana but are held at Rorke's Drift and defeated at Ulundi. Their king Cetewayo is captured and deported and the Zulu wars end; the Prince Imperial, heir of Napoleon III, is a casualty. Britain occupies the Khyber Pass by the treaty of Gandamak with Afghanistan and invades when the legation in Kabul is massacred, taking the city and deposing Emir Yakub. Khedive Ismail of Egypt is deposed in favour of his son Tewfik. The Tay Bridge collapses in a storm; 78 lives are lost as a train crossing the bridge falls into the river.

1880   Andrew Carnegie presents Dunfermline with a free library. Gladstone defeats Disraeli in the General Election. Tahiti is annexed by France. Morocco gains independence. Captain Boycott is ostracised by his tenants in County Mayo. Paul Kruger declares the Transvaal an independent republic.

1881   Boers repulse the British at Laing's Neck and defeat them at Majuba Hill; peace is made by the treaty of Pretoria, which recognises an independent Transvaal as the South African Republic. James Garfield is inaugurated as American president but is shot and fatally wounded soon after. Tsar Alexander II is assassinated; he is succeeded by his son Alexander III, who responds by introducing repressive measures. Tunisia is made a French protectorate.

1882   Prince Milan II of Serbia declares himself king. The Hague Convention establishes a three-mile limit for territorial waters. The Fenians assassinate two British ministers in Phoenix Park, Dublin. Nationalist riots in Egypt led by Arabi Pasha lead to the British fleet bombarding Alexandria; Sir Garnet Wolseley defeats Arabi at Tel-el-Kebir and occupies Cairo.

1883   Paul Kruger becomes president of the South African Republic. Krakatoa erupts in spectacular fashion. Khedive Tewfik appoints a British agent to assist his government; Sir Evelyn Baring takes up the post. The Orient Express makes its first run. The Mahdi stirs up a revolt in Sudan and defeats an Anglo-Egyptian army at El Obeid.

1884   The Fabian Society is established. General Gordon reaches Khartoum intent on evacuating the city but decides to stay. China declares war on France after the latter bombards Formosa as a reprisal for China's refusal to acknowledge a French protectorate over Indo-China. The Third Reform Act is passed in Britain.

1885   Wolseley defeats the Mahdi's followers at Abu Klea but reaches Khartoum two days after its fall and Gordon's death. Wolseley is forced to withdraw and the news helps contribute to the fall of Gladstone's government. The Congo becomes the personal possession of Leopold II of Belgium. Germany annexes Tanganyika and Zanzibar. The Mahdi dies, but his successor Abdullah el Tasshi gains control over Sudan. Alfonso XII of Spain dies; his pregnant widow Maria Christina becomes regent.

1886   General Boulanger becomes French war minister. Gladstone's conversion to Irish Home Rule splits the Liberals; Joseph Chamberlain leads the Liberal Unionists into partnership with the Conservatives. Alfonso XIII of Spain is born king. France banishes the Bonaparte and Orléans families. Prince Alexander of Bulgaria abdicates after a coup. Randolph Churchill resigns as chancellor in a fit of pique and destroys his political career in the process. The discovery of gold in Transvaal transforms the politics of southern Africa.

1887   The First Colonial Conference opens in London. Germany and Russia make the secret Reinsurance Treaty. Zululand is annexed by Britain. Ferdinand of Saxe-Coburg is elected prince of Bulgaria. Italy and Abyssinia go to war; the Italians are routed at Dogali. Macao is ceded to Portugal.

1888   Kaiser Wilhelm I dies; his son Frederick III succeeds him, but dies soon after and is succeeded by his son Wilhelm II. Brazil frees its slaves. The Jack the Ripper murders take place in London. The first beauty contest is held in Spa, Belgium. The Suez Canal Convention, guaranteeing freedom of access to the canal, is signed in Constantinople.

1889   Urged by his supporters to stage a coup d'état, Boulanger refuses and flees abroad. Crown Prince Rudolf of Austria shoots his mistress and commits suicide at Mayerling. Milan II of Serbia abdicates in favour of his son Alexander II. Gustave Eiffel completes the Eiffel Tower for the Paris Exhibition. The first Pan-American Conference meets in Washington. The Brazilian army deposes King Pedro II and installs General Manuel de Fonseca as president.

1890   The Forth Railway Bridge opens. Kaiser Wilhelm forces Bismarck's resignation as Chancellor. Social insurance is introduced in Switzerland. Heligoland is exchanged for the German colonies of Zanzibar and Pemba by Britain. The first Japanese elections are held. William III of Holland dies, and is succeeded by his daughter Wilhelmina. Luxembourg separates from the Netherlands under Duke Adolf of Nassau. Sitting Bull is captured and killed; American troops massacre 200 Sioux at Wounded Knee.

1891   WL Judson invents the zip. President Fonseca of Brazil is ousted in favour of Vice-President Floriano Peixoto.

1892   Khedive Tewfik of Egypt dies, and is succeeded by his son Abbas II. Lizzie Borden murders her parents. Gladstone forms his fourth administration at the age of 82 after victory in the general election.

1893   The Independent Labour Party is founded in Bradford. Natal is granted self-government. The Matabele rise against the British South Africa Company, but Jameson crushes the revolt and takes Bulawayo, forcing King Lobengula into exile. Gladstone's Irish Home Rule Bill is defeated in the House of Lords. Transvaal annexes Swaziland.

1894   The Manchester Ship Canal is opened. Gladstone resigns from office, and is replaced as prime minister by Lord Rosebery. Uganda becomes a British protectorate. The Ottomans massacre thousands of Armenians in suppressing a revolt. President Carnot of France is assassinated by an Italian anarchist at Lyon. Korea and Japan declare war on China. Albert Dreyfus is arrested on a treason charge; convicted, he is imprisoned on Devil's Island.

1895   The treaty of Shimonoseki ends the Sino-Japanese War after the Japanese crush the Chinese at Wei hai wei; Formosa and Port Arthur are ceded to Japan but returned in exchange for an indemnity. Italy invades Abyssinia, but is defeated at Amba Alagi. The British South Africa Company's land south of the Zambezi is renamed Rhodesia. Premier Stamboulov of Bulgaria is assassinated. The Kiel Canal is opened. Wilhelm Röntgen discovers X-rays. The first public film show takes place. Jameson raids Transvaal, but fails to foment a rebellion against its Boer rulers.

1896   Jameson is captured by the Boers at Doorn Kop. Kaiser Wilhelm sends the Kruger Telegram, inflaming Anglo-German relations. Becquerel discovers radioactivity in uranium. Italy is defeated by the Abyssinians at Adowa and withdraws by the treaty of Addis Ababa. The first modern Olympic Games are held in Athens. Shah Nasir-ud-Din of Persia is assassinated; he is succeeded by his son Muzaffir-ud-Din. Marconi patents wireless telegraphy. Kitchener leads an Anglo-Egyptian force into the Sudan. Over 50,000 Armenians are massacred by the Turks.

1897   Crete proclaims union with Greece, prompting a war between Greece and Turkey; the Turks are victorious and the island stays under Turkish hands by the treaty of Constantinople. Hawaii is annexed by the United States. The first Zionist Congress meets in Basel.

1898   Zola publishes 'J'accuse' over the Dreyfus affair, proved to have been fabricated by anti-Semitic army officers. The USS *Maine* explodes in Havana harbour, Spanish involvement is suspected, and war breaks out between America and Spain; the Spanish fleet in Manila Bay is destroyed and the Americans are successful at San Juan and Santiago Bay; peace is made by the treaty of Paris, by which Spain cedes

Cuba, Puerto Rico, Guam and the Philippines in return for $20m. Empress Elizabeth of Austria is murdered by an Italian anarchist. Kitchener defeats the Sudanese at Omdurman, retakes Khartoum and advances to Fashoda, where he discovers a French force which is ordered to withdraw after the British government protests to the French.

1899   The First Hague Peace Conference meets. Dreyfus is pardoned by presidential decree after being found guilty again in a second trial prompted by public opinion. Transvaal declares war on Britain; the Orange Free State allies with Transvaal. The Boers besiege Kimberley, Mafeking and Ladysmith and are victorious at Stormberg, Magersfontein and Colenso.

1900   The Boers are victorious at Spion Kop, but Kimberley, Ladysmith and Mafeking are relieved and Bloemfontein, Johannesburg and Pretoria are taken by the British, who annex the Orange Free State and Transvaal. Kruger flees to Germany but is refused an audience by Kaiser Wilhelm II. The Labour Representation Committee is established, with Ramsay MacDonald as secretary. The Boxer Rebellion against foreign influence in China breaks out; the German ambassador is murdered and the foreign legations in Beijing besieged, but are subsequently relieved. The first Zeppelin airship takes to the air. Umberto I of Italy is assassinated by an anarchist; his son Victor Emmanuel III succeeds him.

1901   The Commonwealth of Australia is created. The Boers begin guerrilla warfare against the British. The first British submarine, *Holland I*, is launched. Queen Victoria dies, and is succeeded by her son Edward VII. US President William McKinley is assassinated by an anarchist; Vice-President Theodore Roosevelt succeeds him. The Boxer Rebellion is ended by the Peace of Beijing. The first Nobel Prizes are awarded. Marconi, who is in Newfoundland receives a wireless message from Cornwall.

1902   Britain allies with Japan. St Pierre, Martinique, is destroyed by the eruption of Mount Pelée. The treaty of Vereeniging ends the Boer War with British sovereignty imposed. Trotsky escapes from prison in Siberia and flees to London, where he meets Lenin. The Order of Merit is established.

1903   King Alexander I and Queen Draga of Serbia are assassinated by supporters of the rival Karageorgevich dynasty, whose heir Peter I ascends the throne in their place. The first Tour de France takes place. The Russian Social Democratic Party splits into Mensheviks and Bolsheviks at its London conference. The Wright Brothers perform the first successful powered flight.

1904   The wireless distress signal CQD is adopted. The Japanese attack the Russians in Port Arthur, setting off war between the two countries; the Japanese are subsequently victorious at Liaoyang. Britain and France ally by the 'Entente Cordiale'. The Rolls-Royce motor company is founded. Vycheslav Plehve, Russian minister of the interior, is assassinated. The British enter Tibet by imposing the treaty of Lhasa; they aim to safeguard it from Russian penetration. The Russian fleet attacks Hull trawlers off the Dogger Bank, mistaking them for Japanese warships; the French mediate between Britain and Russia and the matter is resolved.

1905   Port Arthur surrenders to the Japanese; the resulting protests in St Petersburg are brutally crushed (Bloody Sunday); revolts flare up in Russia as a result, exacerbated by defeats at Mukden and the Tsushima Strait, where the navy is annihilated; the battleship *Potemkin* mutinies; the Russo-Japanese war is ended by the treaty of Portsmouth, a Soviet is established in St Petersburg and Tsar Nicholas II issues a liberal policy (the October Manifesto). Crete revolts against Turkish rule. Kaiser Wilhelm II visits Tangier, where he emphasizes German interests, to the alarm of other countries. Norway separates from Sweden; Prince Charles of Denmark is elected king, taking the name Haakon VII. The Conservative Party splits over tariff reform; Balfour resigns as PM as a result and Campbell-Bannerman replaces him. Albert Einstein publishes his special theory of relativity.

1906   The Liberals gain a landslide victory in the General Election. HMS *Dreadnought* is launched in Britain, making all other warships outdated and precipitating a naval arms race. The Algeciras Conference settles the Moroccan question and defuses European tension. San Francisco is hit by a severe earthquake. The Duma meets in Russia, but it is too liberal for the Tsar's liking and is dissolved. As the Tsar's control is re-established over the country, he backtracks on his liberal reforms. Dreyfus is rehabilitated in France and awarded the Légion d'Honneur. South Sinai is ceded to Egypt by the Turks under British pressure. Transvaal and the Orange River colonies are granted self-government.

1907   Sinn Fein ('We ourselves') is established. France and Japan reach agreement on an 'open door' policy in China. The Second Hague Peace Conference meets. Emperor Ko-jong of Korea is forced to abdicate by the Japanese, who establish a protectorate over the country with his son Sun-jong as a figurehead emperor. Britain and Russia reach an entente, forming the Triple Entente with France as a counterweight to the Triple Alliance of Germany, Italy and Austria-Hungary. New Zealand becomes a dominion.

1908   Carlos I of Portugal and his heir are assassinated; his younger son Manuel II succeeds him. The Young Turks revolt at Resina before gaining a majority in the new Ottoman parliament and introducing reforms. The first Ford Model T is sold. Bulgaria declares independence; Prince Ferdinand assumes the title of Tsar. Austria annexes Bosnia-Herzegovina, to international consternation. Crete declares union with Greece again.

1909   Turkey and Serbia are forced to accept the Austrian annexation of Bosnia-Herzegovina. Sultan Abdul Hamid II is deposed by the Young Turks in favour of his brother Muhammad V. Shah Muhammad Ali of Persia is deposed in favour of his son Ahmad by Ali Kuli Khan. Louis Blériot crosses the English Channel by aeroplane. The House of Lords rejects Lloyd-George's 'People's Budget', causing a constitutional crisis; Asquith calls a general election .

1910   Liberals and Tories tie in a General Election; Asquith's government depends on Labour and Irish Nationalist votes. Premier Boutros Ghali of Egypt is assassinated by a nationalist fanatic, whilst Islamic agitation increases. Edward VII dies, and is succeeded by his son George V, who inherits a constitutional crisis. South Africa becomes a dominion. Japan annexes Korea. Montenegro declares itself a kingdom under Nicholas I. Manuel II of Portugal is deposed by a revolution which declares Portugal a republic headed by Teofilo Braga. A second election produces another hung parliament.

1911   Electric escalators are installed for the first time at Earl's Court Station. Germany sends the gunboat *Panther* to Agadir, creating another international crisis. The Parliament Bill is passed by the Lords, under duress, settling the constitutional crisis. Italy declares war on Turkey as it attempts to invade Tripolitania (Libya). Sun Yat-sen leads a revolution overthrowing the Manchu monarchy in China and establishing a republic, with himself as its first president. The Mexican Civil War is ended by the establishment in power of the revolutionary, Francisco Madero. Roald Amundsen becomes the first man to reach the South Pole.

1912   The *Titanic* sinks on its maiden voyage, with the loss of over 1,500 lives. It becomes the first ship to use the newly adopted SOS distress signal. Emperor Meiji (Mutsuhito) of Japan dies, and is succeeded by his son Yoshihito. The treaty of Lausanne makes peace between Italy and Turkey, and accepts Italy's conquest of Tripolitania. The first Balkan War takes place when Serbia, Montenegro and Bulgaria declare war on Turkey, whose remaining European possessions are overrun.

1913   Greece joins the anti-Turkish alliance in the Balkans. George I of Greece is assassinated; his son Constantine I succeeds him. The great powers force the treaty of London on the combatants, which leaves none of them satisfied. Suffragette Emily Davison throws herself under the king's horse at the Derby. A Second Balkan War, precipitated by Bulgaria, erupts, with Serbia, Greece, Russia and Turkey against the country; this war is resolved by the treaty of Bucharest but tensions still simmer.

1914   Archduke Franz Ferdinand of Austria is assassinated by a Serb extremist in Sarajevo. Austria seeks to punish Serbia, but merely succeeds in dragging most of Europe into World War I. The British Expeditionary Force lands to support the French. Russia invades Germany, but is repulsed at Tannenberg and defeated at the Masurian Lakes. Germany invades Belgium and France, but is held at the Marne. The First battle of Ypres is a bloody draw and the trench system of warfare emerges on the Western Front. The British fleet is defeated by the Germans at Coronel but victorious at the Falkland Islands. Ireland is pushed to the brink of civil war over Home Rule, but the onset of war diverts attention away from the crisis. The Panama Canal opens.

1915   Germany uses poison gas for the first time at the Second battle of Ypres. The British attempt to surprise Turkey at Gallipoli, but are repulsed. German U-boat sinks the *Lusitania*, causing international outrage. Italy is enticed on to the Entente side in the war by the secret treaty of London and attacks Austria, but fails to advance. Edith Cavell is shot after accusations that she helped Allied soldiers escape from Brussels.

1916   The Mexican revolutionary Pancho Villa raids New Mexico. Germany and France fight a bloody draw over Verdun, which remains in French hands. Irish republicans stage the Easter Rising in Dublin, but the coup fails and the leaders are executed. American troops act as peacekeepers in the Dominican Republic. The British and German fleets fight the battle of Jutland, which proves indecisive but the German fleet withdraws to Kiel and remains there. Allied troops mount a major offensive on the Somme, which gains them some ground after 5 months of bloody battle. Emperor Franz Joseph of Austria dies, and is succeeded by his great-nephew Charles I. The Russian monk Rasputin is assassinated by a group of nobles concerned about his influence at court. Einstein publishes his general theory of relativity.

1917   The Orders of the Companions of Honour and of the British Empire are established. America, Cuba and China enter the war on the Allied side. The Allies are victorious at Arras and Passchendaele, although with much loss of life at the latter. Constantine I of Greece abdicates in favour of his son Alexander I. Mata Hari is executed as a spy. The Balfour Declaration over a Jewish homeland in Palestine is issued. Tanks are used for the first time with any effect at Cambrai. Troops mutiny in Russia; the worsening situation prompts Tsar Nicholas II to abdicate in favour of his brother Grand Duke Michael, who refuses the throne and the Tsardom collapses. A provisional government is set up, but fails to manage the war any better. Revolts against it in July are suppressed, as is Brusilov's coup attempt. However, the Bolsheviks succeed in a coup in November, forcing prime minister Kerensky to flee. Lenin is established in power.

1918   In Britain, a Representation of the People Act gives the vote to all men over 21 and all women over 30. Russia withdraws from the war by making the treaty of Brest-Litovsk with Germany; Finland, Poland and the Baltic States are given independence. A coalition of Bolshevik opponents declare war on them, starting civil war in Russia. The Bolsheviks murder the Tsar and his family. A German offensive is successful on the Western Front, but the Allies regroup and push them back, being victorious at the marne and Amiens. Ferdinand I of Bulgaria abdicates in favour of his son Boris III. The Austro-Hungarian Empire collapses; Emperor Charles I abdicates and the Empire becomes several republics. Allied forces remove the Turks from the Middle East. The Czechs declare independence under Tomas Masaryk. The German navy mutinies. Kaiser Wilhelm II abdicates; Germany becomes a republic. An armistice is signed ending action in World War I. The kingdom of Yugoslavia, under Peter I of Serbia, is proclaimed. A Spanish Influenza pandemic begins.

1919   The Eighteenth Amendment is passed, establishing Prohibition in America. The Allies convene in Paris to settle the world map after World War I; the treaties of Versailles with Germany, Saint-Germain with Austria and Neuilly with Bulgaria are imposed. The Bolsheviks establish the Third International. The League of Nations is founded. Alcock and Brown become the first men to fly the Atlantic. The German fleet is scuttled in Scapa Flow. In India, British troops kill 379 demonstrators in the Amritsar Massacre. Austria exiles the Habsburgs.

1920   Irish republicans begin guerrilla war against continued British rule. President Venustiano Carranza of Mexico is assassinated; he is succeeded by Adolfo de la Huerta. The treaties of Trianon with Hungary and Sèvres with Turkey are imposed. The International Court of Justice is established at The Hague. The Little Entente of Czechoslovakia and Yugoslavia (joined next year by Romania) is formed. King Alexander I of Greece dies; his father Constantine I resumes the throne.

1921   The first All-India parliament is opened in Delhi. Reza Khan Pahlevi organises a coup d'etat in Persia. Ex-Emperor Charles fails to regain the Hungarian throne. The Bolsheviks are victors in the Russian Civil War, but the economy is ruined, forcing Lenin to adopt the New Economic Policy. The Allied Reparations Commission levies compensation of £6,650m on Germany. Britain and Irish republicans reach an accord; Northern Ireland is granted its own parliament with Sir James Craig as prime minister. Spanish troops in Morocco are annihilated by Berber rebels, at Anual. Faisal I is elected king of Iraq after a plebiscite. Eduardo Iradier, prime minister of Spain is assassinated by an anarchist. Takashi Hara, prime minister of Japan, is assassinated.

1922   The treaties of Washington establish a Pacific status quo. The Irish Free State is established, but the IRA declares civil war against the government in Dublin and assassinates Prime Minister Michael Collins. The kingdom of Egypt is established under Fuad I. Mustafa Kemal evicts the Greeks from Smyrna. The Arabs in Palestine reject the British mandate. Constantine I of Greece abdicates again, in favour of his son George II. The Conservatives withdraw from the coalition government, bringing down Lloyd George. Bonar Law becomes prime minister. Mussolini leads the Fascists in a March on Rome and succeeds in forming a government. Mustafa Kemal proclaims Turkey a republic; Sultan Muhammad VI is deposed; his cousin Abdul-Majid II maintains the title Caliph. Howard Carter opens Tutankhamun's tomb. The BBC begins its radio broadcasts. The Union of Soviet Socialist Republics (USSR) is formed.

1923   The French occupy the Ruhr after the Germans default on reparations. Prime minister Stamboliski of Bulgaria is removed from office by a coup and shot while trying to escape. The treaty of Lausanne resolves the war between Greece and Turkey. President Warren Harding of America dies in office, and is succeeded by his laconic Vice-President Calvin Coolidge. Germany is hit by hyper-inflation. Primo de Rivera establishes a dictatorship in Spain with the approval of Alfonso XIII. Mustafa Kemal moves the Turkish capital to Ankara. Hitler mounts the 'Beer Hall Putsch'; it fails and he is imprisoned. The Greek army deposes George II.

1924   Venizelos becomes prime minister of Greece. Lenin dies; a triumvirate of Stalin, Kamenev and Zinoviev replaces him in power. After a general election produces a hung parliament, Ramsay MacDonald forms the first Labour government in Britain; he is defeated in a subsequent election, in which the Conservatives are helped by the forged Zinoviev Letter. Kemal abolishes the Caliphate and exiles the Ottomans from Turkey.

1925   Norway renames its capital Oslo and annexes Spitsbergen. Sun Yat-sen dies; Chiang Kai-shek is appointed his replacement by the Guomindang (Chinese Nationalist Party). Hindenburg is elected president of Germany. Hitler sets up the SS (Schutzstaffel) as his personal bodyguard. Reza Khan Pahlavi deposes Shah Ahmad of Persia and ascends the throne himself. The Locarno treaties are signed, guaranteeing the common borders of Belgium, France and Germany, and demilitarizing the Rhineland.

1926   Abdul-Aziz II Ibn Saud of Najd becomes king of the Hijaz. The General Strike is called in Britain, but fails to achieve much. Pilsudski stages a coup d'état in Poland. Lebanon is proclaimed a republic. Stalin forces the banishment of Trotsky and Zinoviev from Moscow as he assumes control of Russia. Emperor Yoshihito of Japan dies, and is succeeded by his son Hirohito. John Logie Baird develops television.

1927   Charles Lindbergh makes the first solo flight across the Atlantic. Trotsky is expelled from the Communist Party. Ferdinand I of Romania dies, and is succeeded by his infant nephew Michael.

1928   In Britain, all women receive the vote. The anti-war Kellogg-Briand Pact is signed. Albania becomes a kingdom under Ahmed Bey Zogu, who takes the title Zog I. The first Five Year Plan is outlined by Stalin. Chiang Kai-shek is formally elected president of China.

1929   Alexander I of Yugoslavia suppresses the constitution and proclaims a dictatorship. Italy and the Vatican make the Lateran Treaties, establishing an independent Vatican City. The St Valentine's Day Massacre of gangsters occurs in Chicago. Labour wins a general election for the first time and Ramsay MacDonald returns to office as prime minister. The Wall Street Crash leads to a collapse of share prices and the onset of severe economic depression in America.

1930   France starts work on the Maginot Line of defences. Primo de Rivera resigns office through ill health and dies soon after. Brüning forms a right-wing coalition government in Germany. Haile Selassie becomes king of Abyssinia. Carol II of Romania replaces his young son Michael as King. President Leguia of Peru is forced from office by a military coup. José Uriburu leads a military coup in Argentina. The R101 airship crashes and burns. Getulio Vargas leads a revolution in Brazil and is named President. The Youth Hostels Association is founded.

1931   Oswald Mosley leaves the Labour Party and forms the short-lived New Party. Alfonso XIII of Spain abdicates and leaves the country. The Credit-Anstalt bank of Austria collapses, creating a financial crisis in central Europe. The Invergordon mutiny over pay cuts occurs. Japan occupies Manchuria. MacDonald forms a National Government to deal with the deteriorating economic situation, but the Labour Party mostly splits from him. The Statute of Westminster defines dominion statutes and creates the Commonwealth.

1932   Gandhi is arrested after the Indian National Congress is declared illegal. President Doumer of France is assassinated by a Russian émigré. The Nazis win the German general election, but refuse to serve under President Hindenburg's nominee as Chancellor, Von Papen, who is later forced to resign. Iraq ceases to be a British mandate. Mosley founds the British Union of Fascists. Franklin D Roosevelt defeats President Hoover in a landslide victory in the American presidential elections.

1933   Hitler is appointed German Chancellor. Prohibition is abolished in America. The Reichstag, Germany's parliament, building burns down; Communists are blamed. Chancellor Dollfuss of Austria rules by decree, provoking riots from Austrian Nazis. The first German concentration camps are opened. Hitler takes dictatorial powers; systematic persecution of Jews begins; the Gestapo is founded. Nadir Shah of Afghanistan is assassinated, succeeded by his son Muhammad Zahir Shah.

1934   Hitler purges the Nazi party in the 'Night of the Long Knives'. Austrian Nazis assassinate Dollfuss in a failed putsch; Schuschnigg becomes chancellor. Hitler becomes German president on the death of Hindenburg. The USSR joins the League of Nations. King Alexander of Yugoslavia is assassinated together with the French foreign minister, Louis Barthou, at Marseille by a Croat revolutionary based in Hungary; he is succeeded by his son Peter II. Mao Zedong leads the Chinese Communists on the Long March. Sergei Kirov is assassinated in Leningrad, giving Stalin a pretext to purge the Russian Communists of his opponents.

1935   The Saar is returned to Germany after a plebiscite; Hitler repudiates the Versailles treaty and passes the Nuremberg decrees against Jews. Persia is renamed Iran by order of the Shah. Alcoholics Anonymous is established. Japan withdraws from the League of Nations. Italy invades Abyssinia; the League of Nations imposes sanctions against Italy but the Anglo-French Hoare–Laval plan proposes partial acquiescence in the conquest. George II of Greece returns to his throne. The US creates the Commonwealth of the Philippines, a step towards Filipino independence.

1936   George V dies, his son Edward VIII succeeds him but abdicates in favour of his brother George VI after
        falling in love with Wallis Simpson. The Japanese army attempts a coup, but fails. Germany reoccupies the
        Rhineland. King Fuad of Egypt dies, and is succeeded by his son Farouk. Italy completes its conquest of
        Abyssinia. Spanish generals, led by Franco, revolt against the Republican government; this leads to civil
        war. Television broadcasts start in Britain.

1937   Guernica is destroyed by aircraft of the German Condor Legion assisting Franco's rebels. The Peel
        Commission on Palestine proposes partition into Arab and Jewish states with a British mandate for
        Jerusalem and Bethlehem. Amelia Earhart disappears on a Pacific flight. Japan invades China, surprising
        the Chinese at the Marco Polo Bridge and capturing Beijing, Nanjing, Tianjin and Shanghai; the Chinese
        government moves to Chongqing. The legitimate Spanish government moves to Barcelona. Italy withdraws
        from the League of Nations.

1938   Austria is forced to unite with Germany (the Anschluss). Continuing his Great Purge of all potential
        opposition, Stalin tries and executes former colleagues including Buthasin, Rykor and Yagoda. The
        Sudeten Germans demand secession from Czechoslovakia; Britain and France appease Hitler at Munich
        and allow this, to much public disgust. Britain drops the Peel proposals on Palestine, prompting terrorist
        attacks in the area. Hungary annexes southern Slovakia. The anti-Jewish Kristallnacht takes place in
        Germany. Kemal Ataturk dies, and is succeeded as Turkish president by Ismet Inonu.

1939   Germany occupies the rump Czech lands and places Slovakia under protection. Franco's insurgents
        capture Madrid and are victorious in the Spanish Civil War. Italy invades Albania. Hungary and Spain quit
        the League of Nations. Germany and Russia conclude a non-aggression pact and carve up Poland
        between them. Poland is invaded by the two countries; Britain and France, who have pledged to
        guarantee Poland, declare war on Germany as a result. A German u-Boat sinks HMS *Royal Oak* in Scapa
        Flow. Russia invades Finland and the Baltic States and is expelled from the League of Nations. The *Graf
        Spee* is scuttled after losing the battle of the River Plate.

1940   Finland and Russia make peace. Germany invades Norway, Denmark, Benelux and France. Churchill
        replaces Chamberlain as prime minister. Allied troops are evacuated at Dunkirk. Italy declares war on
        Britain and France. The puppet Vichy France is established. The British destroy the French fleet at Mers-el-
        Kebir to prevent it falling into Vichy hands. The Home Guard is founded. A German aerial assault on Britain
        is repulsed (the Battle of Britain). Trotsky is assassinated in Mexico, possibly on Stalin's orders. Germany,
        Italy and Japan form the 'Axis'.

1941   British troops help the Abyssinians expel the Italians; Haile Selassie is restored to his throne. The pro-Nazi
        Regent Paul of Yugoslavia is deposed; Germany invades the country. Germany invades Russia. Reich
        Marshal Hermann Göring instructs Reinhard Heydrich, deputy chief of the SS, 'to carry out the final
        solution of the Jewish question'. Iran is invaded by Britain and Russia; Reza Shah abdicates in favour of his
        pro-Allied son Muhammad Reza. Mass deportations begin to death camps such as Auschwitz, Chelmno
        and Treblinka. Japan bombs Pearl Harbor and invades the Philippines; America thereby enters the war.
        Hong Kong falls to the Japanese.

1942   The Japanese take the Philippines, Dutch East Indies, Singapore and Burma, but lose the naval battles of
        the Coral Sea and Midway to the Americans. Two Czech resistance men sent from Britain assassinate
        Reinhard Heydrich; the Nazis burn Lidice as revenge. Rommel, after taking Tobruk, is defeated at El
        Alamein and forced to retreat across North Africa. The battle of Stalingrad begins.

1943   Churchill, Roosevelt and De Gaulle meet at Casablanca. The Germans surrender at Stalingrad and are
        driven back West. Guadalcanal falls to the US. Allied aircraft destroy a Japanese convoy at the Bismarck
        Sea. The Warsaw Ghetto is attacked by the Germans, falls after a siege, and survivors are deported to
        concentration camps. The Allies drive the Germans from North Africa and cross into Sicily and Italy. The
        Soviets score a major victory at Kursk in the largest-ever tank battle. Mussolini is forced to resign and
        Badoglio replaces him. Italy signs an armistice with the Allies, but the Germans keep up the fight in the
        country. Churchill, Stalin and Roosevelt meet at Tehran.

1944   The Allies land at Anzio and take Rome. Leningrad is relieved by the Russians. The Solomon and Marshall
        Islands fall to the Americans, who defeat the Japanese at the Philippine Sea. The D-Day landings provide
        the springboard for the reconquest of France. Iceland gains independence from Denmark. Warsaw rises
        against the Germans. Guam falls to the Americans. The Russians enter Romania, Czechoslovakia,
        Bulgaria and Hungary. Stauffenberg leads a failed attempt on Hitler's life; Rommel is implicated and forced
        to commit suicide. The Germans fight back at the battle of the Bulge. North Burma is retaken by the British.

1945   The Allies enter Germany. The Americans take the Philippines and Okinawa. The League of Arab States is
        founded. FD Roosevelt dies, and is succeeded as American president by Truman. Mussolini is killed by
        partisans. Hitler commits suicide. Burma is recaptured by the British. Germany surrenders to the Allies.
        Churchill, Truman and Stalin meet at Potsdam to consider the future. Attlee replaces Churchill after a
        Labour landslide at the general election. America drops atomic bombs on Hiroshima and Nagasaki and
        Japan surrenders. Ho Chi Minh declares Vietnam an independent republic. The United Nations is founded.
        The Nuremberg trials commence. Peter II of Yugoslavia is deposed by the Communists.

1946   The United Nations convenes in London, as the League of Nations is formally wound up. Jewish terrorism
        recommences in Palestine. Juan Perón becomes president of Argentina. Mao Zedong proclaims war
        against the Guomindang regime in China. Victor Emmanuel III of Italy abdicates in favour of his son
        Umberto II, who is exiled when a referendum votes to abolish the monarchy. Transjordan becomes an
        independent state under King Abdullah. Bulgaria votes to abolish its monarchy and becomes a communist
        state. The Fourth Republic is established in France.

1947   The Dead Sea Scrolls are discovered. Mount Hekla erupts in Iceland. The Palestine question is passed to
        the United Nations for resolution after British partition proposals are rejected there. United Nations partition
        proposals are rejected by the Arabs. George II of Greece dies, and is succeeded by his brother Paul I.
        India, Pakistan and Burma become independent states. Michael of Romania is forced to abdicate by the
        communists.

1948   Gandhi is assassinated by a Hindu fundamentalist. The communists mount a coup in Czechoslovakia. The British leave Palestine once their mandate expires; Ben Gurion proclaims the state of Israel, which is immediately attacked by its Arab neighbours but fights them off. The Russians blockade West Berlin; the Allies respond by an airlift. Apartheid laws are passed in South Africa. Wilhelmina of Holland abdicates in favour of her daughter Juliana. Nehru sends Indian troops to force Hyderabad to join India, and the Nizam gives way under force.

1949   NATO is created. The Republic of Ireland is proclaimed. The Council of Europe is created. West and East Germany are created. Transjordan is renamed Jordan. The Chinese communists drive the Guomindang from China; it takes refuge on Formosa. Mao Zedong becomes the head of state of China. Indonesia is granted independence; Sukarno is elected president.

1950   North Korea invades South Korea, but the United Nations sends troops to defend it; when North Korea is forced to withdraw, China sends troops to assist it. Leopold III of Belgium returns from exile, but decides to abdicate after protests against him. China invades Tibet.

1951   MacArthur is replaced as UN commander in Korea, as the war develops into stalemate. The spies Burgess and Maclean flee to Moscow. King Abdullah of Jordan is assassinated, and is succeeded by his son Talal. Japan is granted independence after military occupation. A general election makes Churchill prime minister again.

1952   George VI dies, and is succeeded by his daughter Elizabeth II. Kenyatta heads the Mau Mau resistance to drive the British from Kenya. General Naguib leads a coup in Egypt; King Farouk is forced to abdicate in favour of his infant son Fa'ad II. King Talal of Jordan is deposed after being declared unfit to rule and is succeeded by his son Hussein. Britain produces an atomic bomb. America develops the H-bomb.

1953   Stalin dies; Malenkov succeeds to his posts; Khrushchev is appointed First Secretary. Hillary and Tensing achieve the first successful ascent of Mount Everest. A republic is proclaimed in Egypt and Naguib is granted dictatorial powers. The combatants in the Korean War sign an armistice at Panmunjon, ending the active war. The Federation of Rhodesia and Nyasaland is established.

1954   The Vietnamese communists defeat the French at Dien Bien Phu and occupy Hanoi. Alfredo Stroessner is elected president of Paraguay on the death of President Lopez. Vietnam is split into two at a conference in Geneva. SEATO is established. Rebellion breaks out in French Algeria. Colonel Nasser seizes power in Egypt from General Naguib. Laos gains independence from France.

1955   Malenkov resigns in Russia, and is replaced by Bulganin. Churchill resigns as prime minister, and is replaced by Eden. The Warsaw Pact is established as a communist counterweight to NATO. Austrian independence is restored by the Vienna Treaty. Juan Perón is ousted by a military coup in Argentina.

1956   The first Eurovision Song Contest is won by Switzerland. Sudan and Tunisia become independent republics. Morocco becomes an independent kingdom. Archbishop Makarios and Cypriot Enosis (union with Greece) agitators are deported to the Seychelles. Nasser nationalizes the Suez Canal. Imre Nagy is returned to power in Hungary after demonstrations, but proves too independent for Russia. Israel invades the Sinai, encouraged by Britain and France, who send troops to the Suez Canal to 'protect' it. Under international pressure, they withdraw when UN forces arrive. Russian troops are sent to Hungary; Nagy is seized and executed.

1957   Eden resigns as prime minister after the Suez fiasco, and is succeeded by Harold Macmillan. Ghana is granted independence. The European Economic Community is established by the treaty of Rome. Russia launches Sputnik I, the first space satellite. Mao Zedong decrees the disastrous Great Leap Forward in Chinese agriculture and rural industry.

1958   Egypt and Sudan unite as the United Arab Republic under Nasser. Khrushchev ousts Bulganin as Chairman of the Council of Ministers in Russia and has effective control of the government. The Fourth Republic in France collapses through the ramifications of the Algerian crisis; De Gaulle forms a government, establishes the Fifth Republic and is elected president. General Kassem stages a coup in Iraq, assassinating King Faisal, his son and the premier and taking power.

1959   Fidel Castro ousts President Batista from Cuba and creates a communist state there. The Dalai Lama is forced to flee Tibet as China represses the indigenous population. Mao Zedong resigns as China's head of state in favour of Liu Shaoqi, but remains in power as chairman of the communists. Singapore gains independence under prime minister Lee Kuan Yew. Cyprus is granted independence; Archbishop Makarios is elected president.

1960   The South African police fire on a protest in Sharpeville, killing 69. Gary Powers is shot down over Russia, causing US/Russian tension. Belgium grants independence to the Congo. Mrs Bandaranaike becomes prime minister in Ceylon, the first woman anywhere to hold such a post.

1961   Yuri Gagarin is launched into space in *Vostok 1*. Cuban rebels, assisted by America, land at the Bay of Pigs, but are repulsed by the Cuban army. South Africa leaves the Commonwealth. The Berlin Wall is constructed. UN Secretary-General Dag Hammarskjöld is killed in a plane crash in the Congo; U Thant is elected as his successor.

1962   Algeria is granted independence by France. Former SS administrator Adolf Eichmann is hanged by Israel for war crimes. Russia attempts to send arms to Cuba and establish a missile base there; President Kennedy blockades the island and forces Khrushchev to withdraw; for a few days the spectre of nuclear war looms large.

1963   Kim Philby flees to Moscow after his espionage activities are uncovered. The Profumo crisis develops in Britain, weakening Macmillan's government. Doctor Beeching's report initiates harsh cuts in the British railway system. The nuclear submarine USS *Thresher* sinks. A nuclear test ban treaty is signed by the US, USSR and Britain. Martin Luther King makes his 'I have a dream' speech. Macmillan resigns through ill health, and is replaced by Alec Douglas-Home. A military coup succeeds in South Vietnam. President Kennedy is assassinated; his assumed killer Lee Harvey Oswald is shot dead days later by Jack Ruby.

1964   Fighting breaks out in Cyprus between the Greek and Turkish communities; Greece refuses direct talks while the UN sends peacekeeping troops. King Paul of Greece dies, and is succeeded by his son Constantine II. Ian Smith becomes prime minister of Southern Rhodesia. Nelson Mandela, found guilty in the Rivonia treason trial, is sentenced to life imprisonment. Nyasaland gains independence as Malawi.

HISTORY

America escalates operations against North Vietnam. Malta gains independence. Khrushchev is ousted from power in the USSR; Brezhnev and Kosygin take over. Northern Rhodesia becomes independent as Zambia.

1965   Nicolae Ceausescu becomes premier of Romania. In reprisals after a failed communist coup, the Indonesian army kills half a million people. Rhodesia declares independence from Britain; sanctions are imposed on it as an illegal state. General Mobutu takes power in the Belgian Congo in a coup.

1966   Mrs Gandhi becomes prime minister of India. France withdraws from NATO. England win the football World Cup, defeating West Germany 4–2. South African prime minister Hendrik Verwoerd is assassinated, replaced by Vorster. Harold Wilson and Ian Smith discuss the Rhodesia affair on HMS *Tiger*, but the talks come to nothing.

1967   A military coup in Greece removes Constantine II from the throne; he is forced to flee as a counter-coup fails. Arab nations invade Israel, but Israel forces them back and captures Sinai, the West Bank and the Golan Heights in the Six Days War. Colour television begins in Britain. Jerusalem is proclaimed a united city under Israeli rule. General de Gaulle encourages the secession of Quebec whilst on a visit there, causing a diplomatic storm. Che Guevara is captured and shot in Bolivia. South Yemen gains independence.

1968   The communists begin the Tet Offensive in Vietnam. America commits the My Lai Massacre. Martin Luther King and Robert Kennedy are assassinated. Alexander Dubcek comes to power in Czechoslovakia, but his liberalization policies are unpopular in Russia, which sends in troops to re-establish a government more to its liking. Dubcek is arrested. Student riots in Paris destabilise the government, but de Gaulle uses his personal authority to reestablish effective government.

1969   Yasser Arafat is elected chairman of the PLO. General de Gaulle resigns as President of France, and is replaced by Georges Pompidou. America begins to withdraw troops from Vietnam. America lands men on the moon. Civil unrest in Northern Ireland spills over into fighting and terrorism; troops are sent to maintain order. Colonel Gaddafi deposes King Idris of Libya and assumes power.

1970   The Nigerian civil war ends with the capitulation of Biafra. Brazil win the football World Cup with the best team ever according to the popular press. The Portuguese dictator Salazar dies, and is succeeded as premier by Marcello Caetano. King Hussein of Jordan and Pope Paul VI survive assassination attempts. Salvador Allende is elected President of Chile. President Nasser of Egypt dies, and is succeeded by Anwar Sadat. The Japanese novelist Yukio Mishima commits suicide after failing to launch a military coup to purge the disgrace of defeat in 1945.

1971   Idi Amin seizes power in Uganda. The Vietnam war spreads into Laos and Cambodia. Decimal coinage is introduced in Britain. President François Duvalier of Haiti dies, and is succeeded by his son Jean-Claude (Baby Doc). Internment is introduced in Northern Ireland. The Congo is renamed Zaïre by President Mobutu. East Pakistan gains independence as Bangladesh.

1972   The Bloody Sunday shootings take place in Londonderry. President Nixon's visit to China initiates US-Chinese détente. Direct rule is imposed in Northern Ireland. Ceylon becomes the republic of Sri Lanka. The Democratic headquarters in the Watergate building, Washington are burgled; President Nixon is implicated, but is re-elected for a 2nd term. Palestinian terrorists seize and kill Israeli athletes at the Munich Olympics. Idi Amin expels Asians from Uganda.

1973   Britain, Ireland and Denmark join the EEC. A ceasefire is proclaimed in the Vietnam War, but fighting still continues in the area. The Cod War between Britain and Iceland develops. General Pinochet ousts President Allende of Chile in a violent coup, in which Allende perishes. Egypt and Syria attack Israel in the Yom Kippur War, but Israel repulses them. Vice-President Spiro Agnew of America resigns over income tax evasion; Gerald Ford replaces him. Arab oil producers embargo shipments to the West, which supports Israel in the war, causing an energy crisis. A coal strike in Britain forces the government to declare a three-day working week.

1974   After a coup in Portugal, Portuguese Guinea gains independence as Guinea-Bissau. Chancellor Willy Brandt of West Germany resigns when one of his aides is unmasked as an East German spy. Cypriot rebels overthrow Archbishop Makarios; Turkish forces invade Cyprus and occupy much of the north. The military junta in Greece resigns and a civilian government under Karamanlis is restored. President Nixon is forced to resign as a result of the Watergate affair; Gerald Ford replaces him and grants a pardon.

1975   North Vietnam overruns South Vietnam; America withdraws and Vietnam is reunited under a communist leadership. Portugal grants independence to Angola and Mozambique. Eritrean secessionists begin a guerrilla war in Ethiopia. King Faisal of Saudi Arabia is assassinated by his nephew Prince Faisal, who is beheaded for murder; the King's brother Khalid succeeds him. Chiang Kai-Shek dies, and is succeeded as President of Taiwan by Yan Jiangan. The Khmer Rouge declare Year Zero in Cambodia and embark on a programme of mass executions. General Franco dies; the country reverts to a monarchy under Juan Carlos I, grandson of Alfonso XIII.

1976   Chou En-lai and Mao Zedong die in China; the 'Gang of Four' attempt to take over but are arrested. Spain withdraws from Spanish Sahara, which is promptly seized by Morocco; Mauritania also takes a portion. Concorde enters regular passenger service. Harold Wilson resigns as prime minister and is succeeded by James Callaghan. Palestinian terrorists hijack an Air France plance, but Israeli commandos storm it at Entebbe.

1977   President Bante of Ethiopia and 10 aides are killed in a gun battle in a council meeting in Addis Ababa; Colonel Mengistu fills the void. Two Boeing 747s collide on the runway at Tenerife; 577 die. Deng Xiaoping assumes power in China. President Sadat of Egypt visits Israel. Jean Bedel Bokassa crowns himself Emperor of the Central African Empire (Republic) in an extravagant ceremony.

1978   Secessionist rebels, backed by Angola, Cuba and Russia, invade Katanga in Zaïre, but are repulsed with American help. Red Brigade terrorists abduct and kill former Italian premier Aldo Moro. Communists seize control in South Yemen, and assassinate the President of North Yemen. Pope Paul VI dies, as does his successor John Paul I after 33 days; Karol Wojtyla is elected the first non-Italian Pope for 455 years and takes the name John Paul II. The first transatlantic balloon crossing is made. In Nicaragua the Sandinista guerrillas begin a campaign of violence against President Somoza. Israel and Egypt sign the Camp David accords. The Shah of Iran imposes martial law to curb dissent.

1979   The Khmer Rouge are overthrown in Cambodia. The Shah of Iran flees to Egypt and an Islamic fundamentalist regime under Ayatollah Khomeini is established; when the seriously ill Shah is allowed into America, extremists seize the American embassy in Tehran. Former prime minister Bhutto of Pakistan is hanged by the regime of General Zia. Margaret Thatcher comes to power in Britain. Saddam Hussein comes to power in Iraq, replacing Hassan al-Bakr. The Sandinistas overthrow Somoza and establish a junta in Nicaragua. Lord Mountbatten is assassinated by the IRA. Emperor Bokassa is deposed and the Central African Republic restored. Soviet troops enter Afghanistan, supposedly at the request of the government there, igniting civil war.

1980   Zimbabwe gains independence; Robert Mugabe comes to power. Queen Juliana of Holland abdicates in favour of her daughter Beatrix. President Tito of Yugoslavia dies, leaving a power vacuum. The SAS retake the Iranian Embassy, which had been taken by opponents of the Islamic regime. Mount St Helens erupts. The Moscow Olympic Games are boycotted by America and other countries in protest over Afghanistan. Solidarity is formed by shipyard workers in Gdansk. Iran and Iraq go to war.

1981   Ronald Reagan becomes US president. Iran releases the American Embassy hostages. The Space Shuttle makes its maiden space flight. Pope John Paul II is wounded in an assassination attempt in Rome by an extremist Turk. Several attacks on Iranian government officials leave many of the government dead, but it survives. President Sadat of Egypt is assassinated by extremists; Hosni Mubarak replaces him. Jerry Rawlings takes power in Ghana after a coup.

1982   Argentina invades the Falklands, but Britain sends a task force and retakes them; the military junta in Argentina falls as a result of this defeat. Israel withdraws from Sinai, but becomes enmeshed in Lebanon by trying to subdue the PLO's activities there. The Lebanese President Bashir Gemayel is assassinated; his brother Amin succeeds him. Leonid Brezhnev dies; Yuri Andropov replaces him as Soviet leader.

1983   Benigno Aquino is killed on returning to the Philippines in a government conspiracy to muzzle opposition. The Soviets shoot down a Boeing 747 that had strayed into Soviet airspace off Sakhalin. A coup in Grenada leaves prime minister Maurice Bishop and most of his cabinet dead; America sends troops in to restore order, to some anger in Britain.

1984   Yuri Andropov dies; Konstantin Chernenko replaces him as Soviet leader. Sikh extremists occupy the Golden Temple at Amritsar; over 200 die when Mrs Gandhi sends troops in to clear them. York Minster catches fire shortly after the modernist David Jenkins is enthroned as bishop of Durham. Britain agrees to hand Hong Kong back to China in 1997 on the expiration of the lease on the New Territories. Sikhs in revenge organise the assassination of Mrs Gandhi; her son Rajiv succeeds her as prime minister.

1985   Uruguay returns to civilian rule under President Sanguinetti. Chernenko dies; Mikhail Gorbachev succeeds him as Soviet leader and undertakes policies of openness (Glasnost) and reform (Perestroika). Brazil returns to civilian rule under President José Sarney. Enver Hoxha dies, and is succeeded by Ramiz Alia as President of Albania. A military coup removes Milton Obote from power in Uganda. The army, under General Babangida, takes power in Nigeria. The cruise liner *Achille Lauro* is hijacked by Palestinian guerrillas.

1986   All 7 crew die when the space shuttle *Challenger* explodes shortly after take-off. President Jean-Claude Duvalier of Haiti resigns and flees to Paris after revolts against his regime. The government of President Marcos of the Philippines falls; Cory Aquino is elected his successor. Prime minister Olof Palme of Sweden is mysteriously assassinated. America bombs Libya in reprisal for Libyan-sponsored terrorist actions. The nuclear power station in Chernobyl, Ukraine, suffers meltdown and explodes. The London Stock Exchange is computerised in the 'big bang'.

1987   Terry Waite is taken hostage in Lebanon whilst seeking to free others. *The Herald of Free Enterprise* capsizes outside Zeebrugge. A great storm crosses southern England, causing much damage. Boris Yeltsin is dismissed in Moscow for complaining at the slow pace of reform. An escalator catches fire at King's Cross; 31 die in the ensuing conflagration. America and Russia sign a nuclear weapons reduction treaty.

1988   The USSR begins withdrawal from Afghanistan. Iran and Iraq end their 8-year war. Iraq gasses dissident Kurds. General Zia of Pakistan is killed in a plane crash. Benazir Bhutto is subsequently elected prime minister of Pakistan. A terrorist bomb brings down a Pan-Am 747 over Lockerbie. USS *Vincennes* mistakenly shoots down an Iranian Airbus.

1989   Emperor Hirohito of Japan dies, and is succeeded by his son, Akihito. Alfredo Stroessner, dictator of Paraguay, is overthrown. General Noriega is defeated in the Panama general elections but ignores the result, causing the Americans to send in troops to remove him. Ayatollah Khomeini dies and Hojatolislam Rafsanjani becomes president of Iran. Communist governments collapse in Poland, Hungary, Czechoslovakia and Romania. The Berlin Wall comes down. President Ceausescu is executed in Romania.

1990   Nelson Mandela is released from prison. Lithuania secedes from the USSR, which sends troops in an attempt to bring it to heel. East and West Germany are reunited. Iraq invades and annexes Kuwait. Sanctions are imposed by the UN, which sends troops to expel Iraq. The premiership of Mrs Thatcher collapses; John Major is elected to replace her.

1991   Somali rebels overthrow President Barre. The UN force expels Iraq from Kuwait, but leaves Saddam Hussein in power in Iraq. Rajiv Gandhi is assassinated by Tamil extremists while campaigning in the Indian general election. Croatia and Slovenia declare independence from Yugoslavia; Serbs and Croats begin a series of ethnic wars. Hard-line Communists attempt to overthrow President Gorbachev, but fail, and communism in Russia collapses. The Baltic states are granted independence. Gorbachev resigns as Russian president and Boris Yeltsin is elected his successor. The USSR dissolves into its constituent parts.

1992   Algerian general elections are declared void when Islamic fundamentalists win; the latter begin a terrorist campaign. The sovereignty of Bosnia-Herzegovina is recognised by the EC and US, but Bosnian Serbs declare independence under Radovan Karadzic, and a vicious civil war develops; 'ethnic cleansing' kills thousands of Albanians and displaces hundreds of thousands. Hindu militants destroy the mosque at Ayodhya.

1993   Czechoslovakia splits into the Czech Republic and Slovakia. Israel and the PLO sign a peace accord. Cultists led by David Koresh kill American government officials at Waco and commit suicide after being besieged. President Premadasa of Sri Lanka is killed by a Tamil terrorist. The Russian communists rebel against President Yeltsin, but the revolt is quelled.

1994   Nelson Mandela is elected President of South Africa. The US invades Haiti. Jordan and Israel sign a peace treaty. Russia invades Chechnya.

1995   The World Trade Organization is founded. The Russians take the Chechen capital, Grozny; resistance continues elsewhere, but peace is agreed. Prime minister Yitzhak Rabin of Israel is assassinated by a Jewish fanatic; Shimon Peres succeeds him.

1996   Yasser Arafat is elected first president of Palestine. Benjamin Netanyahu defeats Shimon Peres in the Israeli general election; his hardline policies set back the peace process.

1997   Deng Xiaoping dies; Jiang Zemin takes power in China. Hong Kong is passed to China. Diana, Princess of Wales, is killed in a car crash. Labour wins a landslide victory in the general election; Tony Blair becomes prime minister. President Mobutu is overthrown in Zaïre, which the new government renames the Democratic Republic of Congo. The treaty of Amsterdam, providing for further European integration, is signed. Mother Teresa of Calcutta dies in her adopted city, aged 87. Jenny Shipley is sworn in as New Zealand's first woman prime minister.

1998   Frank Sinatra dies following a long illness. Frenchman Benoit Lecomte becomes the first man to swim the Atlantic; his 3,716-mile swim from Cape Cod to Quiberon, takes 72 days. Gerhard Schröder, the Social Democrat leader, replaces Christian Democrat leader Helmut Kohl as German Chancellor.

1999   Bill Clinton is impeached but cleared of high crimes and misdemeanours. The Australian people vote to 're-elect' the Queen as their Head of State. Cardinal Basil Hume, Archbishop of Westminster dies.

2000   General Augusto Pinochet, who was to stand trial in Britain for human rights violations, is allowed home to Santiago, Chile, following medical opinion that he is not fit enough to face the ordeal. Pope John Paul II makes an historic visit to the Holy Land and begins it by standing on Mount Nebo in Jordan, the peak from where Moses is said to have seen the Promised Land. The Right Reverend Lord (Donald) Coggan, Archbishop of Canterbury, 1974–80, dies.

2001   North America is subjected to a devastating series of terrorist attacks. American Airlines flight AA11, a Boeing 767 from Boston, is hijacked en route to Los Angeles and crashes into the World Trade Center North Tower at 8.58am (1.58pm BST), killing all 92 on board. United Airlines flight UA175, a Boeing 767 from Boston, is also hijacked en route to Los Angeles and crashes into the World Trade Center South Tower at 9.16am (2.16pm BST), killing all 65 on board. American Airlines flight AA77, a Boeing 757, is hijacked en route from Washington to Los Angeles and crashes into the Pentagon at 9.43am (2.43pm BST), killing 64 on board. United Airlines flight UA93, a Boeing 757 from Newark to San Francisco, targeted on Camp David, crashes at 10.30am (3.30pm BST), 80 miles south-east of Pittsburgh, killing 45 on board. Thousands more are killed in the buildings and on the streets below. The terrorist group al-Qa'ida and its leader Osama bin Laden are thought to be responsible for the atrocities.

2002   Her Majesty Queen Elizabeth the Queen Mother dies, aged 101. Switzerland joins the United Nations. HRH Princess Margaret dies.

NB. The chronology above is a brief cross-section of British and world events of the last two thousand years. Some of the data will inevitably be duplicated in other sections but it is useful to be reminded of the order of events relative to other happenings of the day.

In a book that endeavours to seek the truth it seems incongruous to chronicle prehistorical events which by definition must be open to some doubt, even with all the latest DNA and radiocarbon dating techniques. The approach adopted is to give a brief overview of the order of events that are likely to be of interest to the reader and to chronicle other events, although still open to interpretation, of a more definite nature.

Every schoolchild learns to classify prehistory into Stone Age, Bronze Age and Iron Age but it is very difficult to be pedantic and say when one age started and another ended. In fact, of course the Stone and Bronze ages never really ended anyway. The Paleolithic Period or Old Stone Age is deemed to have commenced over two million years ago with evidence of the use of rudimentary chipped stone tools, probably by a distant relative of modern man. Fossil remains of this precursor of *Homo sapiens* were found at Olduvai Gorge, Tanzania, in 1964 and variously assigned the names *Homo habilis*, *Australopithecus africanus*, or *Australopithecus robustus*, although the latter two names are often applied to an even older relative of modern man thought to have existed millions of years earlier. Fossil remains of Peking Man and Java Man suggested another forerunner of modern man, *Homo erectus*, dated from over a million years ago until 300,000 years ago. From about 300,000 BC other species of early man evolved and were given the general name of *Homo sapiens*. In 1856 the remains of a species of *Homo sapiens* was discovered in the Neander Valley in Germany and dated between 200,000 BC and 30,000 BC. The species of *Homo sapiens* that archaeologists and prehistorians call 'Modern Man' appears to date from circa 38,000 BC. The period from the identification of 'Modern Man' to the end of the Old Stone Age was characterised by the production of Paleolithic cave drawings, the oldest of which, the Chauvet paintings of southeast France, were discovered in 1994 and dated circa 29,000 BC, making them circa 15,000 years older than the Lascaux paintings, Dordogne. This period also saw the beginning of organised tool-making industries beginning with the Aurignacian Culture and developing via the Gravettian (Périgordian), Solutrean, and Magdalenian Culures to the Azilian industry which specialised in microlith tools for catching fish, birds and small mammals as the big game of the last ice age disappeared.

The next classification of prehistory is the Neolithic Period or New Stone Age, characterised by stone tools shaped by polishing or grinding. This period of our history corresponds to the geological Holocene Epoch circa 8,000 BC, the most recent interval of the Earth's geological history. This period also corresponds to the end of the last ice age. In circa 10,400 BC a major climatic warming occurred, the Bolling interstadial, which lasted for approximately 400 years and this was followed by the Allerod interstadial between circa 9,800 BC and circa 9,000 BC. This intermittent global warming became constant in circa 8,000 BC and can be classified as the end of the last ice age, which began around the same time as the emergence of 'Modern Man', and the beginning of the New Stone Age. The first free-standing stone buildings were built during the Neolithic Period, the oldest of which is Cgantija, a temple on the edge of the Xaghra plateau in the middle of the Maltese island of Gozo, circa 3,600 BC. The most recent archaeological find attributed to the Neolithic Period was the ice-man 'Otzi', discovered in the Otzal Alps on the Austrian–Italian border at an altitude of 3,210 metres, in 1991. Modern technology has established 'Otzi's size, looks, apparel and enabled a reconstruction in the Museum of Archaeology in Bolzano, Italy, the country that claimed him. The consensus opinion is that 'Otzi' lived circa 3,300 BC. It is very difficult to approximate the beginning of the Bronze Age as there was a long period of quasi-copper-based tools being produced. This period is referred to as the Chalcolithic (Copper-Stone) Age and even this period was precursed by the use of pure copper in Anatolia by 6,500 BC. The speculative classification of a Bronze Age perhaps can be dated to circa 3,000 BC, when it is established that the Greeks first added tin to copper, although this practice only became widespread a thousand years later. The last technological and cultural period in our classification is the Iron Age, which once again is very difficult to give a definite date of identification as there was a long period of overlapping with the Bronze Age. There is evidence of sparse use of iron in the Middle East as early as 3,000 BC, but it did not replace bronze as a superior metal until circa 1,200 BC.

5508	The year of creation as adopted in Constantinople in 7th century and used by the Eastern Orthodox Church for 1,000 years.
5490	The year of creation as calculated by early Christians in Syria.
4004	James Ussher's 17th-century postulate as being the date of the creation of the universe.
3150	Egypt is united under Menes, the first king of the First Dynasty, and the first prehistoric human whose name we know. Sumerians invent a primitive writing system.
3100	Stonehenge is laid out.
3000	Egyptians pioneer the use of hieroglyphs.
2650	Pyramid of Zoser at Saqqara is built by Imhotep.
2566	The Great Pyramid of Khufu (aka Cheops), at Giza, is built and stands 480 feet high.
2500	A mysterious cult of 'Beaker folk' spreads throughout Europe, warriors being buried with their ornate cups.
2100	In Mesopotamia the first code of law is devised by Ur-Nammu and his son, Shulgi.
1700	Abraham, a prince of Ur, moves to Canaan and founds a religion.
1650	Jewish religion is developed by Abraham's grandson, Jacob.
1349	The young Pharaoh, Tutankhamun, is buried at Thebes.
1237	Ramesses II of Egypt dies and is succeeded by his son Merneptah.
1198	Ramesses III rallies the Egyptians against Mediterranean invaders known as 'Sea Peoples'.
1193	King Priam's city of Troy falls to the Greeks under Agamemnon.
1025	Samuel anoints Saul as king of Israel.
1012	Saul and his son, Jonathan, are killed at the battle of Mount Gilboa, and succeeded by David.
1005	Jerusalem falls to King David who is anointed King of Judea by Samuel.
1000	The Rig Veda (Hindu hymns) are written.
990	Absalom, 3rd son of King David, kills Amnon in revenge for the rape of his sister, Tamar, and is banished by David.
978	Absalom leads a rebellion but is killed by David's nephew, Joab.
961	David dies and is succeeded by his son, Solomon, who executes Joab for killing Absalom.
922	Solomon is succeeded by his son, Rehoboam, but 10 northern tribes establish Israel, with Jeroboam as king.
850	In Babylon an epic poem 'When on High' is dedicated to the great god, Marduk.
800	The Vedas are written.
776	The first Olympic Games are held in Olympia, Greece.
753	Rome is founded by Romulus and Remus.
750	*Iliad* and *Odyssey* become popular in Greece. Etruscans settle in Tuscany from the Middle East.
722	Israel's capital since 879 BC, the Hill of Samaria, falls to Assyrian forces.
721	The 27,000 Israelites are taken off by the Assyrians and become known as 'The Lost Tribes of Israel'.
658	Byzantium is founded by Greek colonists from Megara.
630	*The Shi Jing (Book of Songs)*, an early book of Chinese poems is written.
629	King Ashurbanipal of Assyria dies, leaving a library of over 25,000 books.
621	The Athenian lawgiver Draco issues a code of laws that makes almost every offence punishable by death.
597	Jerusalem falls to Nebuchadnezzar II, who exiles Jews in what becomes known as 'The Babylonian Captivity'.
586	The transportation of Judaeans to Babylon, known as the Babylon Exile or Captivity.
582	The first Pythian games are held.
563	Siddhartha Gautama (Buddha) is born.
550	The Temple of Artemis is built at Ephesus in Turkey.
551	Kung Fu-tse (Confucius) is born.
538	Cyrus allows the Jews to return to Jerusalem, thus ending the Babylonian Exile.
528	Buddhism is founded in India.
509	Tarquinius Superbus, King of Rome, is overthrown and Rome becomes a republic.
490	Battle of Marathon gives Athens victory over the Persians.
483	Siddhartha Gavtama (Budda) dies.
480	Battle of Thermopylae gives the Persians, under Xerxes, victory over the Spartans and Thespians, under Leonidas. Battle of Salamis gives the Greeks (400 ships) victory over the Persians (1,000 ships).

HISTORY

456	Aeschylus dies after writing 90 plays, of which only 7 are to survive.
356	The Temple of Artemis, built by Croesus, king of Lydia, is burned by a madman, Herostratus.
354	Mausoleum at Halicarnassus is built.
336	Alexander the Great succeeds his father on the Macedonian throne.
323	Alexander the Great dies, aged 32, in Babylon.
276	First Syrian War begins.
265	Archimedes invents his 'Archimedean Screw' for raising irrigation water.
264	The First Punic War between Rome and Carthage begins.
237	Hamilcar Barca leads a Carthaginian army in an invasion of Spain.
228	Hamilcar Barca is killed and his command in Spain passes to his son-in-law Hasdrubal.
221	Hasdrubal is assassinated and his command passes to Hannibal, the 26-year-old son of Hamilcar Barca.
220	The Flaminian Way between Rome and Rimini is completed.
218	The second Punic War begins.
217	Battle of Lake Trasimene in Umbria gives Hannibal victory over Gaius Flaminius and 16,000 Romans.
216	Battle of Cannae gives Hannibal a resounding victory over the Romans.
190	Battle of Magenta, near Smyrna, gives Rome a victory over Antiochus III of Syria.
183	Hannibal poisons himself.
160	Judas Maccabaeus is killed, his brother, Jonathan is destined to make Judaea a largely independent state.
149	Romans invade North Africa and besiege Carthage.
135	Rome's first Slave War begins.
102	Julius Caesar is born. (It is possible he was born up to 2 years later.)
83	Mark Antony is born.
73	Third Slave War breaks out under the leadership of Spartacus, a Thracian slave. Herod the Great is born.
63	Cicero, a Roman Consul, unmasks a conspiracy led by Catiline, the former governor of Africa.
60	The first Roman Triumvirate is formed by Julius Caesar, Pompey, and Crassus.
55	Julius Caesar's first invasion of Britain.
54	Julius Caesar's second invasion of Britain; Cassivellaunus agrees to pay tribute.
52	Gang warfare in Rome between supporters of Clodius and Milo results in the death of Clodius in a brawl.
49	Julius Caesar leads his legions across the Rubicon into Italy to begin the civil war.
47	Julius Caesar leads his legions across Asia Minor where he defeats Pharnaces III, King of Pontus, near Zela. announcing his victory in the dispatch 'Veni, Vidi, Vici' (I came, I saw, I conquered).
45	Julian calendar introduced by Sosigenes.
44	Julius Caesar is assassinated on the Ides of March.
43	The second Roman Triumvirate is formed by Octavian, Mark Antony, and Marcus Lepidus. Cicero is beheaded on the orders of Mark Antony.
42	Brutus and Cassius are defeated at Philippi in Macedonia; Cassius orders his shield-bearer to cut his throat, while Brutus runs on to the sword of his friend, Strato.
41	Mark Antony meets Cleopatra at Tarsus and as Julius Caesar had before him, he forms an alliance.
37	Herod the Great becomes King of Judea.
31	Battle of Actium gives victory to Octavian but Cleopatra escapes to Egypt.
30	Mark Antony commits suicide and Cleopatra follows soon after; her son, Caesarion is murdered. Egypt becomes a Roman province.
27	Augustus becomes the first Roman Emperor after changing his name from Octavian.

Modern History

Agent Orange Notorious herbicide used by the US military machine in Vietnam in the 1960s and 1970s; its active ingredient 245-T was also used in weedkillers and caused devastation.

A6 Murder Michael Gregsten and Valerie Storie were shot in their car in a lay-by off the A6 between Luton and Bedford in August 1961. Storie, who survived the shooting, picked out James Hanratty at an identity parade, which led to his hanging in April 1962. Journalist Paul Foot has campaigned on behalf of Hanratty pointing out that Peter Alphon confessed to the murder.

Balfour Declaration A milestone on the way to establishing the state of Israel. Arthur Balfour the former Conservative PM, served as foreign secretary in 1916–19, and in November 1917 wrote to Lord Rothschild, leader of the British Jewish community, to the effect that Britain favoured a national home for the Jewish people provided that it did not prejudice the civil and religious rights of existing non-Jewish communities in Palestine.

Barlow Clowes Fraudulent investment company, details of which came to light in 1988. Elizabeth Barlow disappeared but Peter Clowes was

sentenced to 10 years imprisonment in 1992. The government at first refused to pay compensation, but the Ombudsman found maladministration by the Department of Trade and Industry so £150 m was provided.

Beveridge Report Report laying down the framework for the development of the Welfare State. Published in 1942 and accepted by the coalition government in 1944, it became operational in 1948.

Big Bang Transformation of the London Stock Exchange in October 1986 which reflected the advent of global stock and bond trading networks and of round-the-clock trading. It also abolished the different categories of stockbrokers and jobbers.

Birmingham Six Patrick Hill, Richard McIlkenny, John Walker, William Power, Gerard Hunter and Hugh Callaghan wrongly imprisoned for IRA activities following the bombing of 2 public houses in Birmingham in November 1974. Their convictions were quashed in the Appeal Court in March 1991.

Bloody Sunday A day of serious conflict in the Bogside area of Londonderry on 30 January 1972 when the security forces opened fire on a civil rights march, killing 13 civilians.

Blue Streak British rocket which in the 1950s was expected to provide a nuclear delivery capability independent of US technological expertise; abandoned in 1960 in favour of the US Skybolt missile.

Bridgewater Four Michael and Vincent Hickey, James Robinson and Patrick Molloy were convicted of killing newspaper delivery boy Carl Bridgewater at Yew Tree Farm in Staffordshire, largely because of a confession made by Molloy, who died in prison in 1981. The remaining 3 were released on 20 February 1997 after evidence of police corruption.

Chiltern Hundreds British MPs cannot resign directly, but they may not hold an office of profit under the crown. The solution is to apply for the stewardship of various crown sinecures, of which the Chiltern Hundreds is the best-known.

Citizens' Charter Government charter instigated by John Major in 1991 with the intention of improving standards of public services in the UK.

Cod War A series of disputes between UK and Iceland in the 1960s over fishing rights.

Cuban Missile Crisis US hostility towards the Cuban revolution, together with Castro's open espousal of communism, had brought Cuba into a close relationship with USSR. Following the US-sponsored Bay of Pigs invasion, Castro requested Soviet atomic weaponry to improve their defences. When US reconnaissance spotted missile sites being built, President Kennedy declared a blockade, on 22 October 1961. For several days a confrontation of superpowers appeared likely, but the Russians backed off, and the blockade ended on 20 November.

Dikko Affair UK customs found the exiled Nigerian politician Umari Dikko drugged in a crate at Stansted airport in July 1984. Three Israelis and a Nigerian diplomat concealed in another crate were charged with kidnapping and administering drugs.

Doomsday Clock Picture of a clock, the hands of which indicate the time estimated to remain before nuclear war (midnight), which has been printed in every issue of the *Bulletin of Atomic Scientists* since its founding in 1945. It stood at 11.58 during the cold war but was put back to 11.50 in 1989.

Echo 1 First US communications satellite; a large aluminium-coated balloon that reflected radio signals. Launched on 12 August 1960 by NASA as part of the US effort to close the satellite telecommunications lead achieved by the USSR with the Sputnik.

Elgin Marbles Sculptures from the Parthenon obtained cheaply from the occupying Turks by the British Ambassador Lord Elgin in 1801 and later sold to the British Museum. The continuing Greek campaign for their return was spearheaded by Melina Mercouri as Minister for Culture and the injustice is often highlighted by the well-known television producer and quiz show host, William G Stewart.

Fourth Estate Term used in modern times to describe the power of the press. The Middle Ages divided society into 3 estates: nobility, church and commons.

Fourth Man Anthony Blunt was given this epithet when revealed as a spy in 1979 following the defections to the USSR of the spies Burgess and Maclean in 1951 and Kim Philby in 1963.

Gaza Strip A 146-sq-mile area of land bordered by the Mediterranean, Israel and Egypt, captured by Israel from Egypt during the Six-Day War of 1967 and inhabited by 700,000 people, mostly stateless Palestinians living in refugee camps.

General Strike Staged by the TUC from 3 to 13 May 1926 in an unsuccessful attempt to support coalminers. The strike provoked retaliatory legislation against trade unions.

Geneva Summit 1985 First of a series of bilateral superpower summit meetings held in the later 1980s involving Mikhail Gorbachev and Ronald Reagan (followed by George Bush).

Golan Heights Range of strategic hills in south-west Syria overlooking northern Israel, captured by Israel from Syria in the Six-Day War of 1967.

Gold Standard Economic system in which a country's paper currency is supported by gold, anyone having the right to demand from the national bank the same amount of gold as the face value of a banknote. Britain was on the gold standard from 1821 to 1914, partly returned to it in 1925 as a result of Churchill's wishes, but finally abandoned it in 1931 under the chancellorship of Philip Snowden.

Great Leap Forward Campaign undertaken by Mao Zedong between 1957 and 1960 to organise China's vast population into large-scale rural communes and local manufacturing units, to meet the country's economic problems.

Guildford Four Patrick Armstrong, Gerard Conlon, Carole Richardson and Paul Hill were sentenced to life imprisonment in 1975 for the murder of 7 people in 1974 after the bombing of 2 public houses in Guildford and 1 in Woolwich. They were released on appeal in 1989 after police evidence was found to be misleading.

Herald of Free Enterprise British car ferry owned by Townsend Thoresen which overturned and sank off the Belgian port of Zeebrugge on 6 March 1987 with the loss of 193 lives after the bow doors were left open.

Heysel Stadium Disaster Death of 39 Belgian and Italian spectators on 29 May 1985 at the final of the European Cup football competition between Liverpool and Juventus in Belgium's Heysel Stadium when visiting British fans caused a wall and safety barriers to collapse.

Hiroshima Southern Japanese city destroyed on 6 August 1945 by the first atomic bomb, nicknamed Little Boy and dropped from the US B-29 bomber *Enola Gay*.

Hiss Case Legal case which typified US anti-communist paranoia. On 29 January 1950 Alger Hiss, accused by Whittaker Chambers of being a communist during the 1930s while working for the US State Department, was given a 5-year prison term.

Ho Chi Minh Trail Network of concealed tracks through eastern Laos developed during the early stages of the Vietnam War as a supply route for North Vietnamese and Viet Cong forces in South Vietnam.

Holt Drowning Disappearance and presumed death of Australian PM and Liberal Party leader Harold Holt while swimming at Portsea near Melbourne on 17 December 1967.

Human Shield After Iraq's occupation of Kuwait in August 1990 Saddam Hussein used Western nationals captured there as a defence against possible action by the opposing coalition forces during operation Desert Shield.

100 Flowers Bloom Political slogan adopted by Mao

HISTORY

Zedong (Mao Tse-tung) in 1956 and launched as a movement in February 1957 to allow more free speech in Communist China. The high level of strikes that followed caused Mao to retract his original statement and suggested that the campaign was a means of identifying reactionary elements.

Hungarian Uprising   Popular uprising against Soviet domination in 1956 when after 4 days of demonstrations in Budapest, on 24 October the former communist PM, Imre Nagy, formed a revolutionary multi-party government and proclaimed Hungary's withdrawal from the Warsaw Pact. The Soviet Union crushed the uprising and Janos Kadar took over as head of a pro-Soviet regime and supervised the normalisation policy. Nagy was executed by the new government in 1958.

Hutton Report   In September 2002 the Government published a dossier about alleged Iraqi weapons of mass destruction, including claims they could be deployed within 45 minutes. In May 2003 the BBC *Today* programme's Andrew Gilligan claimed Downing Street 'sexed up' the dossier. On 17 July 2003 Dr David Kelly, the Government scientist at the centre of the controversy, was found dead in an Oxfordshire wood. In August 2003 Lord Hutton began six weeks of hearings about the circumstances around Dr Kelly's death. In January 2004 the Hutton Report found that Dr Kelly had killed himself. It fully exonerated the Government but was scathing in its criticism of the BBC. Gavyn Davies, Chairman of Governors of the BBC, resigned in the wake of Lord Hutton's report.

In Place of Strife   Document published by the Labour government of the UK on 17 January 1969 setting out its policy for controlling industrial relations through legal sanctions.

Intifada   (Arabic: 'shaking off') Palestinian mass popular uprising in the Gaza Strip and West Bank which started in December 1987 with demonstrations, strikes and violent confrontation between Palestinian youths and Israeli occupying forces. Israel responded with an iron-fist approach which included beatings and deportations.

Iranian Embassy Siege   Storming of the Iranian embassy in London by the SAS after it was seized on 30 April 1980 by Iranian dissidents seeking to draw attention to the plight of the Arab minority in Iran and demanding the release of 91 of their comrades imprisoned in Khuzestan.

Iron Curtain   Frontier dividing the Eastern Europe of the communist bloc from the capitalist West. Winston Churchill popularised the phrase, using it in a 1946 speech at Westminster College, Fulton, Missouri when he said: 'From Stettin in the Baltic to Trieste in the Adriatic, an iron curtain has descended across the continent'. Joseph Goebbels has been credited with inventing the term.

ITT Scandal   Scandal involving the activities of International Telephone and Telegraph in the USA and overseas. The scandal broke in 1972 when a plan to nationalise the Chilean Telephone Company (Chitelco) was sabotaged; ITT's collusion with the CIA culminated in the 1973 coup which overthrew the Allende government.

JAL Air Disaster   World's worst air crash involving a single aircraft: a Boeing 747 on a Japan Airlines flight from Tokyo to Osaka crashed in mountainous terrain near Tokyo on 12 August 1985 and killed 520 of the 524 passengers and crew.

Jamahiriya   Term coined by Colonel Gaddafi, who in 1977 changed the name of Libya to 'Socialist

People's Libyan Arab Jamahiriya'. The word means 'State of the masses'.

Jonestown Massacre   Mass death of 913 children, men and women at Jonestown, in the Guyana jungle, on 29 November 1978. The Rev. Jim Jones, founder of the People's Temple in Indianapolis in 1957, had set up a commune in Guyana in 1977. After murdering investigators, he led and apparently enforced a mass suicide using cyanide.

Khaki Election   General election of October 1900, called by Salisbury's Conservative-Unionist government, and named after the new khaki uniform worn by the British army in the Boer war.

Korean War   War in 1950–3 between communist North Korea (supported by the USSR and China) and South Korea (supported by the USA and UN).

Lame-Duck President   Term used to describe an outgoing US president between the elections in November and the beginning of the new president's term on 20 January the following year.

Lancaster House Agreement   UK Foreign and Commonwealth Secretary Lord Carrington brokered this agreement which ended UDI and heralded the independence of Zimbabwe. It was signed on 21 December 1979 by former Rhodesian leader Ian Smith, PM Bishop Abel Muzorewa, Robert Mugabe and Joshua Nkomo, as well as by Carrington and Sir Ian Gilmour representing the British delegation. Lord Soames became governor during the transitional period.

LDC   Least Developed Country, a category used by the UN to describe many of its poorer member states. According to UN estimates, over 500 million people lived in LDCs in 1990.

Limehouse Declaration   Political statement issued on 25 January 1981 by four senior members of the British Labour Party, Roy Jenkins, David Owen, William Rodgers and Shirley Williams, who became popularly known as the gang of four, effectively launching the Social Democratic Party (SDP).

Lockerbie   Scottish town on which a Pan Am airliner PA103 en route from London to New York crashed after a mid-air explosion on 21 December 1988, killing all 259 passengers and crew as well as 11 townspeople. Two Libyans went on trial in Holland in 2000, accused of organising the bombing. Abdelbaset Ali Mohamed Al Megrahi was found guilty and sentenced to life but Al Amin Khalifa Fhimah was freed due to lack of evidence.

Lockheed Scandal   Political scandal which emerged in Japan in 1976, involving the acceptance of bribes by Kakuei Tanaka, PM 1972–4, from the Lockheed Aircraft Corporation.

Long March   The 6,000-mile journey undertaken in 1934–5 by forces of the Chinese Communist Party from Jiangxi province to Yan'an in north Shaanxi to avoid encirclement by the forces of the nationalist Guomindang.

Los Angeles Riots   Major disturbances which occurred in LA between 29 April and 4 May 1992 involving widespread destruction and ethnic violence that brought 58 deaths. The riots were sparked off when an all-white jury acquitted 4 white police officers who had been filmed beating black motorist Rodney King in March 1991.

Maastricht   Netherlands town where the 12 EU member states met in December 1991 for the summit that concluded the treaty on European Union. They returned on 7 Feb 1992 for the formal signing of what became the Maastricht Treaty, which was an accord on European political union and on EMU (European Monetary Union).

MAD Mutually Assured Destruction, which would result from a full-scale nuclear war between the superpowers according to the theorists of deterrence by the 'balance of terror'.

Markov Affair Controversy associated with the death in London on 15 September 1978 of Georgi Markov, a Bulgarian journalist employed by the BBC World Service, who was injected with the poison ricin from a specially adapted umbrella by an agent of the Bulgarian security service.

Marshall Plan Plan to assist the economic recovery of post-war Europe, proposed by US Secretary of State George Marshall in June 1947. The scheme offered US funding to European countries (eventually over $12 billion) if they co-operated with each other in drafting recovery programmes.

Mason-Dixon Line Boundary between the US states of Maryland and Pennsylvania which marks the border between former slave states of the south and northern states where slavery was illegal.

McCarthyism Anti-communist hysteria endemic in the USA in the early 1950s, built upon a foundation established by the House Committee on Un-American Activities. Senator Joseph McCarthy of Wisconsin made a speech in Wheeling, West Virginia, in February 1952 which began the series of anti-communist witch hunts.

Messina Conference June 1955 meeting between the foreign ministers of Belgium, France, Italy, Luxemburg, Netherlands and West Germany which led to the Rome Treaty of March 1957.

Mildenhall Treasure Hoard of Roman silver of the 4th century AD, discovered during ploughing in Suffolk in 1942. The main item of value is the 'Great Dish'.

Montgomery Bus Boycott Year-long boycott of the public transport system in Montgomery, Alabama, which provided a key early victory for the US civil rights movement. It began on 5 December 1955, after a black woman, Rosa Parks, was arrested for refusing to give up her seat on a bus to a white passenger.

Montreal Protocol Agreement signed in September 1987 by 24 countries which undertook to halve their CFC production by 1999. The protocol aims to reduce damage to the ozone layer.

Moro Affair Circumstances surrounding the kidnapping on 16 March 1978 of Aldo Moro, president of the Italian Christian Democratic Party, by the left-wing Brigate Rosse, and his assassination on 9 May after the government refused to meet the kidnappers' demands.

Nagasaki Target city on 9 August 1945 of the second atomic bomb which caused the Japanese surrender in World War II.

Normalisation Sinister name for the programme aimed at stabilising communist rule in Czechoslovakia after the suppression of the 1968 Prague Spring. Under Gustav Husak, Normalisation featured a purge of tens of thousands of politically unreliable professionals and communist party members as well as an end to freedom of speech.

Pairing Convention whereby pairs of MPs, one each from the government and opposition sides, agree that if one is unable to be present to vote, the other will abstain.

Peacock Throne Metaphor for the pre-1979 Iranian monarchy and a reference to the throne used by the two Pahlavi shahs at their coronations. The original Peacock Throne was stolen by the Iranian conqueror

Nadir Shah during a raid on the Mughal bastion, the Red Fort, in Delhi in 1793.

Perestroika Restructuring, slogan adopted by Soviet leader Mikhail Gorbachev in late 1986 to denote his policies of pragmatic reform.

***Pieds Noirs* (Black Feet)** Term used to describe white French settlers resident in France's North African colonies, especially Algeria, and who returned to France after decolonisation in the 1960s.

Ponting Affair Trial and acquittal of Clive Ponting in the UK in 1985 under the 1911 Official Secrets Act. Ponting, a high-flying civil servant in the MOD, was accused of leaking classified information to Labour MP Tam Dalyell, relating to the sinking of the Argentinian cruiser *Belgrano* during the 1982 Falklands War.

Potsdam Conference held from 17 July to 2 August 1945 between the USSR, UK and USA, the Big Three allied powers of World War II, to decide the treatment of defeated Germany.

Poulson Affair The events leading to the resignation on 18 July 1972 of Reginald Maudling as home secretary in the UK Conservative Cabinet. John Poulson was an architect who built up a major international practice in the 1960s and increased his standing through contacts with influential politicians. By the early 1970s he faced bankruptcy and was subsequently charged with corruption relating to bribes given to national and local politicians aimed at winning contracts. Poulson was sentenced to 7 years whilst Maudling, who had been chairman of the Poulson company, resigned.

Profumo Affair Scandal leading to the resignation in 1963 of John Profumo as secretary of state for war in the UK Conservative Cabinet. Profumo had formed a liaison with Christine Keeler, who simultaneously was having a relationship with a Soviet military attaché in London, Eugene Ivanov.

Rivers of Blood Controversial speech made by UK Conservative MP Enoch Powell on 20 April 1968 in which he warned of what he saw as the social and economic consequences of continued immigration into the UK of black people from the Commonwealth. Powell compared himself to a Roman in Virgil's Aeneid who had a vision of the River Tiber foaming with blood.

Roe v Wade The landmark 1973 Supreme Court decision which made abortion legal in the USA.

Rosenbergs US couple, Julius and Ethel, who were executed in Sing Sing prison in 1953 for having allegedly supplied the Soviet Union with atomic bomb secrets.

San Francisco Conference International conference held April–June 1945 after which participants signed the UN charter. The conference was attended by 47 fully independent states as well as Byelorussia and Ukraine, which were Soviet constituents, and India and the Philippines, which had not at that stage achieved full independence.

Scarman Report Serious racial disturbances in South-East London in April 1981 led to Lord Scarman carrying out a thorough public inquiry, whose findings were published in November.

Schuman Plan Proposal advanced by French foreign minister Robert Schuman on 9 May 1950 which formed the European Coal and Steel Community.

Seles stabbing Tennis player Monica Seles was stabbed by a crazed fan of her rival, Steffi Graf, during a match in Hamburg on 30 April 1993.

Sellafield Site on the west coast of England, in Cumbria, run by British Nuclear Fuels. The first

HISTORY

nuclear power station opened here, at Calder Hall, in 1956. At that time the area was known as Windscale, but on 10 October 1957 an atomic pile overheated, causing a near-catastrophe and some long-term fatalities. To protect the image of the industry the name of the site was changed.

Sharpeville Massacre   In this South African township 50 miles from Johannesburg on 21 March 1960 the police killed 69 peaceful demonstrators protesting against the Pass Laws. The UN subsequently called for the abandonment of apartheid.

Six-Day War   Threatened by a build-up of hostile Arab forces, between 5 and 10 July 1967 Israel attacked Egypt, Jordan and Syria and occupied the Sinai peninsula, the Gaza Strip, East Jerusalem, the West Bank and the Golan Heights, before declaring a ceasefire.

Social Contract   Informal agreement between the UK Labour government and the TUC in the mid-1970s aiming to balance wage restraint against a loosening of legal restrictions on trade unions.

Spin Doctor   In politics, a public relations expert working behind the scenes to have the media interpret events from the viewpoint favoured by a particular individual, faction of party.

Stockholm Syndrome   Psychological condition in which hostages grow to empathise with their captors' political or personal convictions. The term derives from a bank robbery in Stockholm in 1973 when several people taken as hostages lent their support to the robbers.

Suez Crisis   Middle East crisis precipitated by the nationalisation of the mainly British and French-owned Suez Canal by Egyptian President Gamal Abdel Nasser on 26 July 1956. Nasser acted after the USA had reneged on a commitment to help finance the construction of the Aswan High Dam. Israel invaded on 29 October; acting in collusion, French and British forces intervened a week later, under guise of keeping the peace. By March 1957, all 3 had withdrawn under strong UN pressure.

Sutton Hoo Ship Burial   Anglo-Saxon treasure unearthed in 1939 at Sutton Hoo in Suffolk and believed to have been the tomb of an Anglo-Saxon king buried about 625, possibly Raedwald. Mrs Pretty, who owned the land and hence the treasure, kindly donated the find to the British Museum.

TD   Gaelic for Teachta Dála, a member of the Irish Dáil or lower house of parliament.

Territorial Waters   The offshore area in which a coastal state claims sovereign jurisdiction, save for the customary rights of freedom of navigation for merchant shipping. At present 12 miles is the accepted boundary of territorial waters, with a few exceptions, mostly in Africa and Central and South America.

Third Man   Kim Philby, a UK journalist and former intelligence officer who defected to the Soviet Union in January 1963, was given this epithet after the earlier defections of Guy Burgess and Donald Maclean in 1951.

***Tiger*Talks**   Negotiations held aboard HMS *Tiger* off Gibraltar on 2–4 December 1966 between Harold Wilson and Ian Smith, which failed to end Rhodesian UDI.

Trident   Multiple-warhead submarine-launched nuclear missile with a range of 4,500 miles, introduced in 1979 by the US Navy in refitted Poseidon submarines, and in larger *Ohio*-class submarines first delivered in 1981. A more powerful Trident 2 missile was introduced in 1990.

Union Carbide Disaster   In December 1984 a leak of toxic gas from Union Carbide pesticide plant near Bhopal, India, killed 2,500 and injured 200,000.

Vatican II   The 2nd Vatican Council (the first was in 1869-70), which met in 4 sessions between 11 October 1962 and 8 December 1965. Launched by Pope John XXIII, it was concluded by his successor Pope Paul VI. Vatican II was the 21st Ecumenical Council in the history of the Roman Catholic Church and brought a reformist, liberalising outlook to existing dogma.

Vietnam War   The 1954–75 war between North and South Vietnam, the latter assisted from 1961 by the USA. The war resulted in victory for the North and the union of the two Vietnams in 1976.

Vincennes   On 3 July 1988 the US warship *Vincennes*, serving in the Persian Gulf, mistook an Iran Air A3000 Airbus for an attacking bomber and shot it down, costing 290 civilian lives.

Waco Siege   A 51-day siege of the HQ of the Branch Davidian religious cult near Waco, Texas, began on 28 February 1993 and ended on 19 April when the FBI stormed the compound and fire broke out, killing its leader David Koresh and 70 of its members.

Warnock Report   UK report published in July 1984 on bio-ethics as well as the social and legal implications of recent and potential developments in the field of human-assisted reproduction. Chaired by Dame Mary Warnock, the committee recommended that certain forms of infertility treatment should be viewed as ethically acceptable.

Warren Commission   Chaired by the head of the US Supreme Court, Chief Justice Earl Warren, the Commission investigated circumstances surrounding the assassination of President JF Kennedy in Dallas on 22 November 1963. The Commission's report concluded on 22 September 1964 that Lee Harvey Oswald had been solely responsible for the killing.

West Bank   Territory of Palestine west of the River Jordan, claimed from 1949 to 1988 as part of Jordan, but occupied by Israel since the Six-Day War of 1967. The territory, excluding East Jerusalem, is widely referred to within Israel by its biblical names, Judea and Samaria, and is considered part of Eretz Israel. In September 1993 Israeli forces withdrew from the West Bank but the territory is still disputed by many Israelis.

Winter of Discontent   Time of industrial unrest in the UK over the severe winter of 1978–9.

Wolfenden Report   Report of the UK Committee on Homosexual Offences and Prostitution, chaired by Sir John Wolfenden, which recommended in particular the decriminalisation of homosexual acts between consenting adult males and an increase in penalties for soliciting by prostitutes. The landmark report published on 4 September 1957 led to the Street Offences Act of 1959 and to the Sexual Offences Act of 1967.

Year Zero   Slogan adopted by the Khmer Rouge to denote the start of their 4-year period of rule in Cambodia in April 1975.

Yom Kippur War   On 6 October 1973 Syria and Egypt mounted a surprise attack on Israel as it observed Yom Kippur (the Jewish Day of Atonement), aiming to regain territory lost during the Six-Day War of 1967. Although Israel was caught off guard initially, by 24 October the Israelis were advancing on Cairo and Damascus and a ceasefire was declared, restoring the status quo.

Zeebrugge Disaster   see *Herald of Free Enterprise*.

LANGUAGE

Derivation of Popular Phrases

Phrase	Meaning	Derivation
A1	the highest quality	Lloyd's Register of Shipping use an alphanumeric code in classifying ships for insurance purposes. The state of a ship's hull is designated by letters and that of the anchors, cables and other moveable parts by figures. A1 therefore denotes vessels of the highest quality.
above board	honest and open	Phrase which originated in the gaming community. If card players kept their hands above the table (board) they could be seen to be playing fairly.
according to Hoyle	according to the highest authority in a particular field	English writer Edmond Hoyle (1672–1769) wrote books on the rules and customs of backgammon (1743) and chess (1761), but was best known for his definitive treatise on whist (1742) and it is from this that the phrase derives.
Aga saga	a type of popular novel set in middle England, populated by the middle classes	Phrase coined in the 1990s, referring to novels about the lives of people who have a high standard of living and live in the English countryside; the type indeed that might own Aga cookers. The works of Joanna Trollope are often spoken of as Aga sagas. Contrast **kitchen sink**.
argy-bargy	wrangle or verbal dispute	Corruption of a Scottish dialect phrase *argle-bargle*, first recorded in 1887. It is itself a composite word deriving from 'argue' and 'haggle'.
back to square one	back to the beginning	Phrase thought to have derived from early BBC radio broadcasts of football. Lance Sieveking, the producer of the first broadcast on 22 January 1927, used a grid system of eight numbered squares to explain to listeners where the action was taking place on the pitch. The squares were designated square one and two, defence, square three, four, five and six, midfield, square seven and eight, attack. A thwarted attack and punt downfield may well have been referred to as 'back to square one' during these commentaries.
baker's dozen	thirteen	In the Middle Ages in England there were severe penalties for anyone who gave short weight. Bakers were often uneducated and unable to count. To guard against miscounting 12 as 11 they habitually gave 13 loaves when selling a dozen. The 13th loaf was known as the 'vantage loaf'.
balaclava	close-fitting woollen hood that covers the ears, neck and head	Named after Balaclava, the Black Sea port on the Crimea made famous by the battle that took place there (25 October 1854).
bandy words	to argue fervently	Bandy is a ferocious Irish game in which the ball is played to and fro with sticks. In John Webster's The White Devil (1612), the term was applied to tennis, at that date probably real tennis: 'He had been bandying at tennis'.
barmy army	a raucous and undisciplined group	Coined in the UK and most often used as an ironic nickname for the travelling supporters of the English cricket team. Barmy, or balmy, means crazy; barm is the froth made by fermenting yeast. Barmy people are those that froth at the mouth, like rabid dogs.
battle royal	a fierce contest	Phrase derived from cockfighting contests, where 16 birds were often engaged in fights to the death, the surviving eight then contesting the quarter-finals and so on until only one bird remained.
bed of roses, a	a situation of ease and pleasure	First mention of this phrase was in the third verse of Christopher Marlowe's poem 'The Passionate Shepherd To His Love' (1599): 'There will I make thee beds of roses And a thousand fragrant posies'.
bee in your bonnet, to have a	to be preoccupied or obsessed with an idea	Phrase became popular after a verse in Robert Herrick's poem 'Mad Maid's Song' (1648): 'For pity, sir, find out that bee Which bore my love away. I'll seek him in your bonnet brave'.
bee's knees. the	excellent – the highest quality	Phrase first coined in America in 1922 and which is merely a catchy sounding rhyme, often corrupted to 'the business'. Another similar expression of the day was 'the mutt's nuts', which itself was corrupted to 'the dog's bollocks'.
below the belt	unfair or cowardly	The Marquis of Queensberry formulated rules for boxing in 1867 which disallowed hitting below the belt.

Phrase	Meaning	Derivation
below the salt	common or lowly	In medieval England, nobility sat at a high table and commoners at lower trestle tables. Salt was expensive and only the nobs were provided with it. Hence the peasantry were below the salt.
belt and braces	careful – not taking any chances	Using both belt and braces is a double insurance against having your trousers fall down.
berk	a stupid person	Rhyming slang derivation: Berkshire Hunt – cunt.
beware of Greeks bearing gifts	be on your guard against trickery	An allusion to the incident in Virgil's *Aeneid* where the Greeks tricked their way into Troy by hiding in a huge wooden horse, apparently offered as a gift, before springing out at night and taking the city.
beyond the pale	unacceptable; outside agreed standards of decency	The 'pale' derives from paling, meaning fence. In the United Kingdom the Pale was the region of Dublin under English rule; areas outside this zone were considered unsafe and uncivilised.
bigwig	an important person	From the large, imposing wigs worn by the aristocracy from the 17th century.
blacklist	to exclude a person from an activity due to unsuitability	Errant students in early British universities had their names placed in black books as a form of disgrace. As a noun the phrase refers to the list itself.
blinking idiot	a stupid person	Mild expletive first coined in Shakespeare's *The Merchant of Venice* (1596–7), Act 2 Scene 9. After the Prince of Aragon decides to open the silver casket in an attempt to win the hand of Portia, within is but a portrait of a 'blinking idiot'.
blot on the landscape	something that spoils the view or ruins a previously comfortable situation	TE Lawrence first coined the phrase in a letter of 1912. The phrase was further popularised by Tom Sharpe's 1975 novel of that name, where Blott was the name of the leading character.
bluestocking	formerly, a learned woman who dispensed with traditional feminism	This phrase originally described a group of intellectuals under the patronage of Elizabeth Montagu in London around 1750. Benjamin Stillingfleet, a prominent member, was in the habit of wearing blue stockings and James Boswell further popularised the group by describing Stillingfleet in his *Life of Johnson* (1791).
Bob's your uncle	used to imply that an intended task or mission is as good as completed	Piers Brendon, in *Eminent Edwardians* (1979), suggests the origin as being the unexpected promotion of Arthur Balfour as Chief Secretary for Ireland by his uncle Robert Arthur Talbot Gascoyne-Cecil, 3rd Marquis of Salisbury, the Prime Minister.
booby prize	a consolation prize given to the loser (the booby) in a contest or game	Booby has been in use meaning dunce since at least the late 15th century.
booby trap	a concealed trap for the unaware	See **booby prize** above. This form of trap would quite easily catch a person of low intelligence.
Boxing Day	public holiday on the day after Christmas Day	St Stephen's Day became known as Boxing Day via the tradition whereby casual offerings left in the church-box were counted on Christmas Day and distributed to the poor the next day. A similar practice of giving tradesmen a gratuity or 'Christmas Box' is still followed.
boycott, to	to ostracise	Captain Boycott (1832–97) was an unforgiving and harsh English land agent for the Earl of Erse in County Mayo in the late 19th century. He would dispossess tenants for the slightest arrears and was reviled and hated by all. Charles Parnell of the Irish Land League advised tenants to treat Boycott and his type as lepers; hence the phrase.
brown goods	large electrical goods usually found in the lounge	Marketing term for consumer goods such as televisions, radios and videos, traditionally finished in brown colours.
bunny boiler	an obsessive and dangerous female, in pursuit of a lover who has spurned her	From the 1987 film *Fatal Attraction*. The plot concerns a woman scorned (played by Glenn Close) who obsessively pursues her ex-lover (played by Michael Douglas). The phrase comes from the plot device where the woman boils the man's daughter's pet rabbit.
by hook or by crook	by any means possible	Derives from Cromwell's attempt to capture the city of Waterford. He is reported as saying he would take the city 'by hook or by crook'. Hook is the headland on the Wexford side and Crook is the name of the Waterford side.
cardigan	woollen sweater with buttons down the front	Named after James Thomas Brudenell, 7th Earl of Cardigan (1797–1868) who wore such a garment during his service in the Crimean War to ward off the severe cold.
caviare to the general	of no interest to the average man	Derives from Shakespeare's *Hamlet* (1601), Act 2 Scene 2; the 'general' cited is the general public and the phrase refers

Phrase	Meaning	Derivation
		to the notion that such a novel delicacy was not for the edification of the common man.
chav	streetwise youngster who loves designer labels	Expression which became fashionable in southern England in 2004 and is thought to be a corruption of 'chavi', the Romany word for a child. The chav society have their own sign language of derogatory terms and are usually seen sporting hooded tops and baseball caps. (Other terms associated with youth culture and fashion, but deriving from the USA, include bling or bling-bling, breakbeat and phat.)
cold enough to freeze the balls off a brass monkey	extremely cold	A brass monkey was the name given to the tray on which cannon balls were stacked aboard Royal Navy warships of the early 19th century. In severe cold weather the brass would contract and the balls would topple off the top of the pile.
disgusted, Tunbridge Wells	reference to a critical correspondent without specifying name	The reference to Tunbridge Wells has no significance other than that it was originally the name of a character played by Wallas Eaton in the radio comedy series *Take it From Here* from 1953.
doolally	out of one's mind	Named after Deolali, a town near Bombay with a sanatorium where many British soldiers were detained before being shipped home. The term became military slang for a crazy person circa 1925.
dressed up like a dog's dinner	describes something that is messy	Derives from the description in 2 Kings where Jezebel adorned herself before being defenestrated and eaten by dogs. This phrase often has the word 'breakfast' substituted for 'dinner'.
eat crow	to be forced to do something humiliating	Term dates back to the War of 1812 where a New England soldier entered British lines and shot a crow. An unarmed British officer feigned interest in the American's firearm and, when allowed to examine it, turned the gun on the soldier and forced him to take a bite of the crow.
eat humble pie	to be humiliated	Expression derives from the tradition of offering the less appealing parts of a hunted deer, the numbles (entrails, later corrupted to umbles) to those of inferior rank or standing.
feather in one's cap	an achievement to be proud of	Dates from the Battle of Crécy (1346) when Edward, the Black Prince, was awarded the crest of three ostrich feathers of King John of Bohemia; these became the symbol of every subsequent Prince of Wales.
fifth column	an organised body working for the enemy within a country at war	Originally coined by Emilio Mola Vidal, a Nationalist general during the Spanish Civil War (1936–9). As four of his army columns moved on Madrid, the general referred to his militant supporters within the capital as his 'fifth column', intent on undermining the loyalist government from within.
flash in the pan	short-lived success before ultimate failure	Derives from the propensity of the old flintlock pistols to misfire. A hammer strikes a flint, producing a spark which explodes the charge. The powder in the chamber, named the pan, often flashed but failed to ignite the charge.
fourth estate	the press	The general usage of the term dates back to 1828 when Thomas Macaulay wrote of the House of Commons, 'The gallery in which the reporters sit has become the fourth estate of the realm'. The established three estates were the House of Lords, divided into the Lords Spiritual and the Lords Temporal, and the House of Commons.
full monty, the	the whole thing	There have been suggestions that the expression derives from the somewhat large breakfasts enjoyed by Field Marshal Montgomery, but it is more likely to be a reference to the famous men's tailor Montague Burton whose standard outfit was a two-piece suit, but who offered as an optional extra a waistcoat and a second pair of trousers. Paying the extra was going for the full Monty. The feature film of the 1990s gave the word a very different meaning, making an allusion to the fact that a group of male strippers would 'go all the way' if the price were right.
gamp	an umbrella	Nickname derives from Dickens' character Sarah Gamp in *Martin Chuzzlewit*, who always carried a large umbrella.
get out of the wrong side of bed	to start the day in a foul mood	An early 16th-century phrase arising from the tradition that it was unlucky to place the left foot on the ground before the right when getting out of bed.
get the sack	to be dismissed from a job	Dates from circa 1825, in the days when tradesmen owned their tools and gave the sack or bag in which they carried them to the employer to mind for them. When dismissed from

LANGUAGE

Phrase	Meaning	Derivation
		his job, the employee's sack would be returned to him by the employer.
gone for a Burton	person or object that is missing	The most probable source is from RAF slang where to go for a Burton meant to have 'bought it', an allusion to buying a beer from the famous Burton-on-Trent brewery. Another possible derivation, also RAF slang, is from the fact that a Blackpool billiard hall over a Montague Burton tailor shop was used as a Morse code instruction centre. The phrase was used to describe failure on the course.
Gordon Bennett!	an exclamation of surprise – one of the many euphemisms that avoid the use of the word God	James Gordon Bennett II (1841–1918), editor-in-chief of the *New York Herald*, was the man who sent Henry Morton Stanley in search of David Livingstone in Africa. He was also an adventurer and one of his many reported exploits was an incident where he flew an aeroplane through an open barn. The surprised onlookers were supposed to have said 'That was Gordon Bennett!'
grockle	a tourist	This supposedly Devonshire dialect word for a tourist, particularly one from north of the Watford Gap, was popularised in the 1962 film *The System*, which was set in the Devon resort of Torquay, although its exact origin is disputed. One idea is that it derives from the resemblance between the famous clown named 'Grock' and a red-faced tourist with a knotted handkerchief on his head. The other, more probable derivation is simply from a cartoon strip of the time in the *Dandy* comic entitled 'Danny and his Grockle', the grockle being a dragon-like creature.
gung ho	over-eager and undisciplined	From the Chinese *kung* and *ho*, meaning 'work together'.
hat-trick	in a sporting context, to score three times or take three wickets	In early cricket, a bowler taking three wickets with three successive balls was entitled to a new hat at the expense of the club.
Hobson's choice	no choice at all	Thomas Hobson (1544–1631) was a coachman and hirer of horses in Cambridge. The phrase derives from Hobson's insistence that the customer could hire any horse they liked, as long as it was the one nearest the door!
hoist with one's own petard	ruined by one's own devices against others	Derives from Shakespeare's *Hamlet* (1601), Act 3 Scene 3. A petard was an explosive device used to break through walls.
Hooray Henry	loud, upper-class man with extravagant manners	Phrase coined by Jim Godbolt in 1951 in reference to the upper-class contingent attracted to a jazz club at 100 Oxford Street, London, where Humphrey Lyttelton played trumpet. The term itself derives from a character in Damon Runyon's 'Tight Shoes' (1936).
hwyl	to put body and soul into something	Welsh word that has various meanings but in the patriotic sense has come to mean to approach a task with vigour and energy: 'Put some hwyl into it'.
jam tomorrow	a promise which is never likely to be kept	From Lewis Carroll's *Through the Looking Glass and What Alice Found There* (1871), in which The White Queen offers Alice 'Jam to-morrow and jam yesterday – but never jam today'. Socialist circles often used it to ridicule the capitalist system as offering the same empty promise.
kiss the Blarney Stone	to have a way with words	In 1602 it is said that Cormac Macarthy was to surrender Blarney Castle, near Cork, as a declaration of his loyalty to Elizabeth I, but his prevarication gave cause for the Queen to exclaim 'Odds bodikins, more Blarney talk.'
kitchen sink	descriptive of dramas that reflect ordinary life	Phrase coined in the 1950s to describe dramas centred on the unsatisfactory nature of the UK's class system and working-class life. John Osborne was a leading exponent of such plays and when Shelagh Delaney's novel *A Taste of Honey* was made into a feature film in 1961, the term became a stock phrase to describe any drama form dealing with domestic reality. Contrast **Aga saga**.
knuckle down	to apply oneself to an exacting task	Phrase derives from about 1740, when a game of marbles commenced with the knuckle being placed on the ground in order to shoot.
lager lout	alliterative name for a person with a propensity for drunken violence	Phrase coined by Simon Walters, the political correspondent of *The Sun*, in 1988, and used to describe football hooligans and other drunken, unruly young males.
lame duck	person or thing that is disabled or ineffectual	Phrase used from about 1761 and deriving from defaulters on the London Stock Exchange who were seen to waddle out of Exchange Alley like the proverbial lame duck.
left-footer	a Roman Catholic	Irish phrase referring to an agricultural labourer's tendency to use his left foot when making the initial thrust of his spade

Phrase	Meaning	Derivation
		into the ground, the assumption being that most Irish labourers are Catholics.
let the cat out of the bag	disclose a secret	Phrase derives from the mid-18th century when a crowd would be shown a pig at a country fair and the vendor would then place the animal in a bag before sale, only for the unsuspecting purchaser to find it had been substituted by a less valuable cat!
living dog is better than a dead lion, a	even a wretched existence is better than no existence while hope remains	Ecclesiastes 9:4 expresses this philosophical idiom and the sentiment is fairly evident. While a person lives they have hope of salvation and can know death but when dead they know nothing.
mad as a hatter	completely and utterly crazy	Phrase deriving from the character in Lewis Carroll's *Alice's Adventures in Wonderland* (1865), who was decidedly eccentric in his mannerisms. The related phrase 'mad as a March hare' dates from the early 16th century; Carroll based his character of the March Hare on this phrase.
man on the Clapham omnibus	the ordinary person in the street	Legal term first used by Lord Bowen in 1903 when summing-up in a case of negligence, his exact words being: 'We must ask ourselves what the man on the Clapham omnibus would think.'
mind your ps and qs	be cautious and careful	The ps and qs in question relate to pints and quarts and refer to an innkeeper's custom of chalking up a customer's tally on the slate.
Mrs Grundy	a censorious person	The name derives from Thomas Morton's play *Speed the Plough* (1798) in which a character would often show disapproval by saying 'What will Mrs Grundy say?' In the 19th century Mrs Ormiston Chant was an actual campaigner against vulgarity in the music hall and in the 20th century her equivalent was Mrs Mary Whitehouse.
Morton's Fork	the dictate that no man is spared taxes on the premise that the rich have obvious wealth while the ostensibly poor must therefore have savings	John Morton (1420–1500) was Archbishop of Canterbury (1486–1500) but it was in his position as Lord Chancellor from 1487 that the phrase derives. In order to raise revenue during the reign of Henry VII, Morton propounded the theory that became known as Morton's Fork in order to ensure that no man was excluded from paying taxes.
namby-pamby	weak and insipid	The phrase derives from the nickname of Ambrose Phillips (died 1749) whose pastoral verse was criticised for its insipidity. Fellow poet Henry Carey is thought to have first used this derogatory name in 1726.
nine days' wonder	something with short-lived appeal	Phrase deriving from the proverb 'A wonder lasts nine days, and then the puppy's eyes are open', an allusion to the fact that a puppy is born blind and innocent but then its eyes are opened to the world.
no room to swing a cat	a small confined space	The 'cat' referred to was not a feline at all, but a flail-like whip used to punish sailors in the British Navy from the 17th century.
Old Bill	policeman	Term deriving from the cartoon character of the same name invented by British Army Captain Bruce Bairnsfather (1888–1959) during his convalescence from shell-shock during World War I. The name was used as a nickname for policemen from the outbreak of World War II.
on tenterhooks	in a state of anxious suspense	Phrase derived from the process of cleaning woollen cloth after weaving. To prevent shrinkage the cloth was placed in a wooden frame called a tenter and was stretched by fixing hooks. The word tenter in this sense comes from the Latin *tendere* (to stretch). The first usage of the phrase was in Tobias Smollett's *Roderick Random* (1748).
page three girl	a topless photographic model	Phrase derived from a feature that began in *The Sun* newspaper on 17 November 1970 when the then editor Larry Lamb introduced topless pin-ups to page three. The term is now used generically for any such nude model or for describing any overtly beautiful woman.
pass the buck	to shift responsibility to another	Phrase derived from the game of poker where a marker, known as a buck, is placed in front of the dealer as a reminder of who the dealer is.
pathetic fallacy	attribution of human feelings to inanimate objects in nature	Literary term coined by John Ruskin in *Modern Painters*, vol. 3 part 4 (1856) where he gives examples of the attribution of emotions to inanimate objects in poetry, e.g.: 'The spendthrift crocus bursting through the mould, naked and shivering, with his cup of gold'.
Peeping Tom	a voyeur	Derived from the name of Tom the Tailor, who was struck blind

L
A
N
G
U
A
G
E

Phrase	Meaning	Derivation
		when he peeped at Lady Godiva (wife of Leofric, Earl of Mercia and Lord of Coventry) as she rode naked through the streets of Coventry to excuse her husband's tenants from his exactions. The legend was recorded by Roger of Wendover (died 1236) in his *Flores Historiarum*, although the addition of Tom to the legend was made much later, during the reign of Charles II.
pommy	Australian slang term for British immigrants	Term first coined in Sydney, Australia, in 1912. DH Lawrence described its derivation in his novel *Kangaroo* (1923) as corrupted rhyming slang: pomegranate – immigrant. Other more popular derivations such as Prisoner of Mother England (POME) bear no semblance of truth.
quiz	set of questions to test knowledge	Came into use in 1782 when Mr Daly, a Dublin theatre manager, made a wager that he could introduce a new word into the language within 24 hours. This he achieved by scrawling the word 'quiz' all over the walls of Dublin. Its meaning was given as 'an odd, or eccentric person' – as many quiz players are, of course! The present sense of the word came into common usage in the 1860s.
real McCoy	the genuine article	Phrase derived from the name of middleweight boxing champion Charles 'Kid' McCoy who had two ways of fighting; occasionally lacklustre, on his day he was unbeatable in the middleweight division, taking the world title on the retirement of Bob Fitzsimmons in 1897.
red letter day	a special day	High days and holidays used to be marked in red on church calendars. Dates from the Reformation.
red tape	bureaucratic rules and paperwork	Legal documents were traditionally bound with red tape.
rob Peter to pay Paul	use money allocated to one project to complete another without any overall benefit	Westminster Abbey is dedicated to St Peter. In 1540 Henry VIII had designated the Abbey a cathedral with its own bishop and diocese. However, when the bishopric was dissolved in 1550 and the church made a second cathedral in the diocese of London, some lands belonging to the church were exchanged or sold off. Some of this money was used for the repair of (old) St Paul's cathedral, hence robbing St Peter's church to pay for St Paul's cathedral.
sandwich	two slices of bread filled with any foodstuff	Coined by John Montagu, 4th Earl of Sandwich (1718–92), an avid gambler who disliked leaving the gaming tables and so sent out for snacks to be brought to him while playing. To this day sandwiches are supplied at the tables of many gaming clubs.
scot free	get away with something without penalty	Phrase deriving from a medieval tax called 'scot and lot'. The scot is a Scandinavian word for a contribution and the lot was a shortened version of allotment. A person able to circumvent the rules for payment was said to have got off scot free. The 1832 Reform Act dispensed with the tax.
snob	person who behaves condescendingly to those perceived as of lower class	Term first used in the late 18th century as slang for a cobbler. Although cobblers were perceived as being from humble origins, the term later became attached to those who looked down on such honest craftsmen.
splice the mainbrace	to have an alcoholic drink	The mainbrace is the rope which controls the movement of sails aboard ship and the phrase compares the degree of difficulty in gaining an extra rum ration from the Royal Navy with that of controlling the mainbrace.
spoonerism	the transposition of parts of words	The Reverend William Spooner (1844–1930), warden of New College, Oxford, was famous for muddling his words and the phrase entered common usage by 1885. The classic example of a spoonerism is 'Sir, you have tasted two whole worms, you have hissed all my mystery lectures and have been caught fighting a liar in the quad; you will leave Oxford by the next town drain', although this is thought to be apocryphal. If the good reverend had been a film fan, perhaps he would have liked *Shaving Ryan's Privates*!
spud	colloquial name for a potato	Name given to the implement used to dig a potato out of the ground, first coined in the diary of Samuel Pepys in 1667. The Irish people immediately used this expression for the humble potato, although Murphy remains another popular term. People with the surname Murphy are invariably nicknamed Spud.
square meal	a hearty meal	In the Royal Navy it was traditional for sailors to receive their substantial meals on a square plate.

Phrase	Meaning	Derivation
stool pigeon	a police informer	Hunters traditionally used decoy pigeons fixed to posts (stools) to lure their quarry. The term was later adopted to describe people who helped the police by luring criminals into police traps. It later came to mean anyone who helped the police by informing on others.
tell it to the Marines	exclamation of disbelief	The phrase derives from the fact that marines were perceived as being neither one thing or the other as they operated on land and sea; hence they were classed as second-rate and stupid, and open to believe a tall story. In fact, of course, marines are among the brightest and toughest of servicemen.
thin blue line	defensive barrier of policemen	A line of policemen, particularly those holding back a surging crowd. More recent adaptation of the **thin red line**.
thin red line	defensive barrier formed by soldiers	According to jingoistic folklore in the UK, a small group of British soldiers (who wore red jackets) were enough to hold back a mob of warlike foreigners.
third degree, the	close interrogation	In a masonic lodge there are three ranks or degrees: the first is called Entered Apprentice, the second Fellowcraft, and the third is Master Mason. When a candidate receives the third degree in a Masonic lodge, he is subjected to activities that include an interrogation and are more physically challenging than those entailed in the first two degrees.
throw one's hat into the ring	show an intention to join an enterprise	Phrase derived from early 18th century prize-fights when it was traditional to throw one's hat into the ring when making a challenge to the resident fighter.
Tin Pan Alley	centre of musical creativity	The area around Denmark Street, off Charing Cross Road, was known as Tin Pan Alley by 1934, although the name itself was used as early as 1908 to refer to a similar area of musical activity in Manhattan, New York, where the noise of countless pianos being tinkled sounded like the crashing of tin pans.
turn the tables	achieve a reversal of fortune	Phrase derived from the quick reversal of fortunes experienced while playing backgammon. The gameboard is divided into four quarters, two being designated the inner table and two the outer table. An errant throw of the dice can quickly change a position from a favourable to a precarious one.
Walter Plinge	an actor's alternative name	Mr Plinge was said to be a stage-struck pub landlord working near the Theatre Royal, Drury Lane, in the 19th century and in homage to his enthusiasm actors would use his name in programmes when playing two parts. Sometimes the name was used for a fictional character to boost the cast list and at other times because of uncertainty of final casting. The American equivalent is George Spelvin.
whipping boy	a scapegoat punished for the inadequacies of others	It used to be the practice in some cultures that the nobility could not be touched. When they committed a crime that warranted physical punishment it was therefore delegated to an unfortunate victim – the whipping boy. Barnaby Fitzpatrick stood as whipping boy for Edward VI and Mungo Murray for Charles I before they were crowned. This seemingly outlandish practice was in reality a means to instil a sense of justice and righteousness in future monarchs; it was hoped they would behave appropriately in the knowledge that an innocent bystander might be punished on their behalf.
white bread	pertaining to white middle classes in the USA. Something that is more trouble than it is worth	Derogatory term that refers to the supposed bland and uninteresting nature of white middle-class culture in the USA, brown wholemeal bread being more exciting and generally beneficial.
white elephant	Something that is more trouble than its worth	White (albino) elephants were regarded as holy in ancient times in Thailand and other Asian countries. To keep a white elephant was a very expensive task, since you had to provide the elephant with special food, and provide access for people who wanted to come and worship it. If a king became dissatisfied with a subordinate, he would sometimes give him a white elephant in order to ruin him.
white goods	large electrical kitchen goods	Marketing term used to describe large household appliances such as refrigerators, microwaves and cookers which are often finished in white enamel. The term is also used to describe household linen such as sheets, towels and tablecloths.

LANGUAGE

Phrase	Meaning	Derivation
white knight	an organisation that comes to the aid of another during a hostile takeover	Making an analogy to the bygone age of chivalry, the phrase became common at the Stock Exchange by 1981. The knight would rescue a targeted company by offering to acquire it far above the pursuer's value and generally under better terms.
wooden spoon, receive the	to finish last in a competition	In the University of Cambridge, England, the scholar whose name stood last of all on the printed list of honours, at the Bachelors' Commencement in January, was scoffingly said to gain the wooden spoon. Eventually an actual wooden spoon was presented to the person placed last in the mathematical tripos.

Foreign Words and Phrases

ab initio (L.) from the beginning

à bon marché (Fr.) a good bargain, cheap (lit. at a good market)

a cappella (It.) without instrumental accompaniment (lit. in chapel style)

à cheval (Fr.) on horseback (also denotes two roulette numbers)

achtung (Ger.) look out, beware, take heed (lit. attention)

ad astra (L.) to the stars

ad hoc (L.) for this special purpose (lit. to this)

ad libitum (L.) at pleasure

ad rem (L.) to the purpose, to the point (lit. to the matter)

Agnus Dei (L.) lamb of God

à la carte (Fr.) each dish priced separately (lit. according to the menu)

à la mode (Fr.) according to custom or fashion

al dente (It.) firm when bitten (lit. to the teeth)

al fresco (It.) in the open air (lit. in the fresh)

alloi kamon, alloi onanto (Gr.) some toil, others reap the advantage

Alma Mater (L.) applied to former school, university, or college, (lit. fostering or bounteous mother)

alter ego (L.) other self

amor vincit omnia (L.) love conquers all

Angst (Ger.) anxiety

annus mirabilis (L.) a remarkable year (lit. year of wonder)

Anschauung (Ger.) point of view (lit. looking around)

Anschluss (Ger.) joining together

ante bellum (L.) before the war

a priori (L.) from cause to effect (lit. from the previous)

à propos (Fr.) to the purpose

auberge (Fr.) inn, tavern

au courant (Fr.) fully acquainted with (lit. in the current)

Aufklärung (Ger.) clarification, enlightenment

auf Wiedersehen (Ger.) till we meet again

au pair (Fr.) home-help from a foreign country (lit. on an equal basis)

au revoir (Fr.) till we meet again

auto-da-fé (Port.) act of faith

avant-garde (Fr.) progressive or radical artists and thinkers (lit. vanguard)

bain-marie (Fr.) a double saucepan (lit. bath of Maria)

baksheesh (Pers.) gratuity or tip (lit. a present)

banzai (Jap.) a Japanese battle-cry (lit. 10,000 years)

barrio (Sp.) district, suburb (lit. open country)

bas bleu (Fr.) literary woman, blue-stocking worker (lit. under blue)

batik (Malay) cloth dyeing method using wax, the cloth itself, (lit. painted)

bête noire (Fr.) a bugbear, pet aversion (lit. black beast)

bibelot (Fr.) trinket, curio, knick-knack (lit. small book)

bidet (Fr.) bestridable bath (lit. small horse)

Bildungsroman (Ger.) novel concerning early development of its central figure, (lit. education novel)

billet-doux (Fr.) love letter (lit. sweet note)

Blitzkrieg (Ger.) intense military attack (lit. lightning war)

Boche (Fr.) French slang for a German soldier (lit. rascal)

bois brûlé (Fr.) French-Canadian Indian (lit. burnt wood)

bona fide (L.) with good faith

bona-roba (It.) prostitute, wench (lit. good dress)

bona vacantia (L.) goods without any apparent owner and to which the Crown has the rights (lit. ownerless goods)

bonheur du jour (Fr.) small writing-table (lit. happiness of the day)

bonhomie (Fr.) good-nature (lit. good man)

bon mot (Fr.) witty remark (lit. good word)

bonsai (Jap.) miniature tree in a pot (lit. bowl growing)

bourgeois (Fr.) middle-class person (lit. town dweller)

cacoethes (Gr) bad habit, mania (lit. evil habit)

carabiniere (It.) member of Italian police force

carpe diem (L.) seize the day

carte blanche (Fr.) freedom of action, card hand with no court cards (lit. blank card)

caveat emptor (L.) let the buyer beware

cave canem (L.) beware of the dog

cela va sans dire (Fr.) needless to say, that goes without saying

c'est la vie (Fr.) that's life

ceteris paribus (L.) other things being equal

cinquecento (Fr.) classical style of art of the 16th century (lit. five hundred)

cire perdue (Fr.) bronze casting using wax technique (lit. lost wax)

cogito, ergo sum (L.) I think, therefore I am

compos mentis (L.) sound of mind

corpus delicti (L.) body or substance of a crime

corregidor (Sp.) chief magistrate of a Spanish town (lit. to correct)

corrida (Sp.) a bullfight (lit. corral)

corrigenda (L.) things to be corrected

coup de foudre (Fr.) love at first sight, sudden event (lit. flash of lightning)

coup de grâce (Fr.) action that puts an end to something, (lit. stroke of mercy)

coup d'état (Fr.) sudden and violent change of government, (lit. stroke of state)

cri de coeur (Fr.) heartfelt appeal or protest (lit. cry from the heart)

cru (Fr.) French vineyard (lit. growth)

cucullus non facit monachum (L.) the cowl does not make the monk

cui bono (L.) to whose benefit

cul-de-sac (Fr.) road with one end blocked off, dead end (lit. bottom of the bag)

cum grano salis (L.) with a grain of salt

curriculum vitae (L.) course of life

dacha (Rus.) Russian country villa (lit. gift)

de facto (L.) in fact

déjà vu (Fr.) already seen

de jure (L.) by right (lit. from the law)

de profundis (L.) out of the depths

de rigueur (Fr.) required by etiquette (lit. of strictness)

Dei gratia (L.) by God's grace

Deo volente (L.) God willing

dernier cri (Fr.) latest fashion, last word (lit. last cry)

de trop (Fr.) superfluous, not wanted (lit. too much)

die dulci fruere (L.) have a nice day

Doppelgänger (Ger.) wraith, look-a-like (lit. double goer)

dos-à-dos (Fr.) a seat on which the users sit back to back, (lit. back to back)

dramatis personae (L.) cast of a play

duce (It.) leader

duende (Sp.) Imp, goblin, ghost

Dummkopf (Ger.) dumb-head

e pluribus unum (L.) one out of many

Ecce Homo (L.) artistic representation of Christ crowned with thorns. From the words of Pontius Pilate to his accusers, (lit. behold the man)

echt (Ger.) real, genuine, authentic

effendi (Turk.) mister (lit. master)

emeritus (L.) honourably retired (lit. meritorious)

ersatz (Ger.) replacement, substitute, imitation

esprit de corps (Fr.) pride in belonging to a group (lit. spirit of a body)

eureka (Gr.) I have found it

ex cathedra (L.) with authority

ex officio (L.) by virtue of his office (lit. out of duty)

fabricati diem (L.) make my day

fac ut gaudeam (L.) make my day

fait accompli (Fr.) thing already done (lit. accomplished fact)

fartlek (Swed.) interval athletics training (lit. speed play)

fatwa (Arab.) a legal decision

faux pas (Fr.) social blunder, indiscretion (lit. false step)

Fidei Defensor (L.) defender of the faith

flagrante delicto (L.) in the act of a crime

floreat (L.) let it flourish

force de frappe (Fr.) French nuclear deterrent (lit. striking force)

Führer (Ger.) leader

Gastarbeiter (Ger) person with temporary permission to work, in a foreign country (lit. guest-worker)

Gauleiter (Ger.) district leader

gestalt (Ger.) organised whole in which each part affects every other part (lit. shape)

Gesundheit (Ger.) your health (lit. healthy sound)

glasnost (Rus.) openness

Götterdämmerung (Ger.) In German mythology the final destruction of the world (lit. twilight of the gods)

goût (Fr.) taste, artistic discernment

gravitas (L.) solemn demeanour

gringo (Sp.) term used by Latin-Americans for foreigners, (lit. foreigner)

gulag (Rus.) labour camp

habeas corpus (L.) a writ to produce a prisoner before a court, (lit. you should have the body)

haiku (Jap.) amusement verse

hajj (Arab.) pilgrimage

Hakenkreuz (Ger.) swastika (lit. hooked cross)

halal (Arab.) cooked according to Muslim law (lit. lawful)

haute couture (Fr.) high fashion (lit. high dressmaking)

haute cuisine (Fr.) high-class cooking

haute école (Fr.) classic style of riding (lit. high school)

hic et nunc (L.) here and now

hic et ubique (L.) here and everywhere

hic jacet (L.) here lies

hic sepultus (L.) here buried

hoi polloi (Gr.) common people or rabble (lit. the many)

hominis est errare (L.) to err is human

homme d'affaires (Fr.) businessman

homme d'esprit (Fr.) man of wit or genius

honi soit qui mal y pense (Fr.) shamed be he who thinks evil

honores mutant mores (L.) honours change manners

hors de combat (Fr.) disabled or injured (lit. out of the fight)

hors d'oeuvre (Fr.) savoury appetiser (lit. out of the course)

hwyl (W.) fervour

Ibidem (L.) in the same place

Ich dien (Ger.) I serve

id est (L.) that is

ignorantia juris neminem excusat (L.) ignorance of the law excuses no one

illegitimi non carborundum (L.) don't let the bastards grind you down

in camera (L.) in secret (Lit. in the chamber)

incunabulum (L.) book printed before 1501 (lit. from cradle), original Latin meaning was 'swaddling clothes'

in extremis (L.) at the point of death (lit. in the last)

in flagrante delicto (L.) in the act of a crime or red-handed, (lit. with the crime still ablaze), sometimes written 'flagrante delicto'

infra dig(nitatem) (L.) beneath one's dignity

in loco parentis (L.) in place of a parent

in petto (It.) when a cardinal is selected by the pope but not yet anounced (lit. in the breast)

inshallah (Arab.) equivalent to the term 'touch wood' (lit. if Allah wills)

inter alia (L.) among other things

intra vires (L.) within the powers of

in utero (L.) before birth (lit. in the womb)

in vino veritas (L.) drunken people often speak the truth, (lit. in wine, truth)

in vitro (L.) in a test tube (lit. in glass)

ipso facto (L.) by the fact itself

jacquerie (Fr.) a peasants' revolt as in France in 1358 (lit. peasant)

j'adoube (Fr.) I adjust (chess term)

je ne sais quoi (Fr.) indefinable quality (lit. I know not what)

jeune premier (fem. -ière) (Fr.) juvenile lead in musical play or theatrical production (lit. first youth)

jeunesse dorée (Fr.) rich and fashionable young people (lit. gilded youth)

jihad (Arab.) a Muslim holy war (lit. conflict)

joie de vivre (Fr.) joy of living

Jugendstil (Ger.) art nouveau (lit. youth style)

Junker (Ger.) class of Prussian land-owning aristocracy (lit. young lord)

juste milieu (Fr.) happy medium or golden mean (lit. the right mean or the right course)

kamikaze (Jap.) Japanese suicide pilots in WWII (lit. divine wind)

Kapellmeister (Ger.) person in charge of an orchestra (lit. chapel master)

karaoke (Jap.) Japanese entertainment of singing to backing tapes, (lit. empty orchestra)

Katzenjammer (Ger.) colloquial term for a hangover (lit. cat's wailing)

kia ora (Maori) good luck (lit. be well)

kibbutz (Heb.) Jewish community in Israel (lit. gathering)

kibitzer (Yid.) person who gives unwanted advice especially at a card game, (lit. lapwing or plover)

kitsch (Ger.) worthless art

kolkhoz (Rus.) Russian collective farm

kulak (Rus.) land-owning peasant (lit. fist)

Kulturkampf (Ger.) culture struggle

la dolce vita (It.) the sweet life

laissez-faire (Fr.) unrestricted commerce (lit. allow to do)

Langlauf (Ger.) cross-country skiing (lit. long run)

lapsus calami (L.) slip of the pen

lapsus linguae (L.) slip of the tongue

lares et penates (L.) household goods

l'chaim (Heb.) a Jewish toast (lit. to life)

Lebensraum (Ger.) territory needed by a state for its natural development, (lit. living space)

Lederhosen (Ger.) leather trousers

lèse-majesté (Fr.) high treason (lit. injured majesty)

lex scripta (L.) written law

lex talionis (L.) law of retaliation (lit. such law)

litterae humaniores (L.) name given to study of classics at Oxford University (lit. more humane letters)

locum tenens (L.) a deputy (lit. place held)

locus classicus (L.) authoritive and oft-quoted passage from a standard text (lit. classical place)

lycée (Fr.) in France, a state secondary school (lit. pupil)

magnum opus (L.) a great work of art or literature

maharishi (Hin.) Hindu teacher of religious doctrine (lit. great sage)

mahatma (Sans.) Brahman sage (lit. great soul)

maillot (Fr.) tights worn for balet or gymnastics (lit. swaddling clothes)

mal de mer (Fr.) seasickness

mañana (Sp.) tomorrow

manqué (Fr.) unfulfilled potential (lit. having missed)

maven (Yid.) a connoisseur (lit. understanding)

mazel tov (Heb.) congratulations or good luck (lit. good star)

mea culpa (L.) by my own fault

memento mori (L.) reminder of death

mene, mene, tekel, upharsin (Aram.) words that appeared on the wall during Belshazzar's Feast (lit. numbered, numbered, weighed, divided)

mens rea (L.) criminal intent (lit. guilty mind)

modus operandi (L.) method of working

mot juste (Fr.) appropriate word

multum in parvo (L.) much in little

mutatis mutandis (L.) with required changes

né(e) (Fr.) born

ne plus ultra (L.) extreme perfection (lit. not more beyond)

nil desperandum (L.) never despair (lit. nothing to be despaired)

nisi (L.) coming into effect unless otherwise stated (lit. unless)

noblesse oblige (Fr.) obligation of nobility or privileged to be honourable (lit. nobility obliges)

nom de guerre (Fr.) an assumed name (lit. name of war)

nom de plume (Fr.) pen-name

non sequitur (L.) statement that has no relevance to what went before (lit. it does not follow)

nota bene (L.) note well

nuit blanche (Fr.) sleepless night (lit. white night)

Nunc Dimittis (L.) the Canticle of Simeon (Luke 2:29–32), (lit. now depart)

obiter dictum (L.) said in passing

objet d'art (Fr.) small object of artistic worth (lit. object of art)

objet trouvé (Fr.) ordinary object seen from an artistic viewpoint, (lit. found object)

oeuvre (Fr.) total output of an artist or writer

om mani padme hum (Sans.) Tibetan Buddhists' meditational chant. Aka Shadakshari mantra (lit. hail, jewel in the lotus)

omnia vincit amor (L.) love conquers all

panem et circenses (L.) bread and circuses (written by Juvenal of the loves of the typical Roman citizen)

parador (Sp.) Inn or tavern

par avion (Fr.) by airmail (lit. by air)

parvenu (Fr.) an upstart or social climber (lit. to attain)

paterfamilias (L.) male head of a household (lit. father of the family)

patois (Fr.) dialect

pax vobiscum (L.) peace be with you

per ardua ad astra (L.) through adversity to the stars

perestroika (Rus.) reconstruction

per se (L.) In itself

persona non grata (L.) unacceptable person

petit bourgeois (Fr.) lower middle-class

petit four (Fr.) small rich, sweet cakes, usually with icing (lit. little oven)

petit mal (Fr.) mild form of epilepsy with short bouts of unconsciousness (lit. little illness)

pied à terre (Fr.) temporary lodging (lit. foot to the ground)

pince-nez (Fr.) spectacles without ear-pieces (lit. pinch nose)

pinxit (L.) an inscription found after an artist's name on a painting (lit. painted)

pis aller (Fr.) a compromise or last resort (lit. the worst going)

plongeur (Fr.) washer-up (lit. plunger)

poco a poco (It.) little by little

poilu (Fr.) French equivalent of 'Tommy', an infantryman (lit. hairy)

posada (Sp.) an inn in a Spanish-speaking country (lit. place for stopping)

pose plastique (Fr.) theatrical presentation of the motionless nude female form (lit. flexible pose)

post meridiem (L.) after midday

pousse-café (Fr.) small glass of spirits especially brandy or a liqueur (lit. push-coffee)

prêt-à-porter (Fr.) ready to wear or off the peg

prima donna (It.) leading female operatic star (lit. first lady)

prima facie (L.) at first sight (lit. first face)

primus inter pares (L.) first among equals

pro tempore (L.) for the time being

quattrocento (It.) the 15th century especially in relation to Italian arts (lit. four hundred) short for milquattrocento '1400'

que será será (Sp.) whatever will be will be

quidnunc (L.) person eager to learn news or scandal, a gossipmonger, (lit. what now)

quid pro quo (L.) one thing for another

qui tacet consentit (L.) silence implies consent

quod erat demonstrandum (L.) which was to be demonstrated

quod vide (L.) usually seen as qv after a word treated more fully elsewhere (lit. which see) raison d'être (Fr.)   reason for being

rapporteur (Fr.)   person appointed by a committee to prepare reports of meetings, (lit. reporter)

Realpolitik (Ger.)   ruthlessly realistic and opportunist approach to statesmanship

repéchage (Fr.)   heat of a contest in which eliminated contestants compete again (lit. fishing out again)

requiescat in pace (L.)   rest in peace

res ipsa loquitur (L.)   the thing speaks for itself

rien ne va plus (Fr.)   roulette term meaning no more bets are to be placed (lit. nothing further goes)

Risorgimento (It.)   the 19th century movement for the political unification of Italy (lit. to rise again)

roman à clef (Fr.)   novel in which real people are depicted under disguised names (lit. novel with a key)

sang-froid (Fr.)   composure in the face of danger (lit. cold blood)

sanpaku (Jap.)   visibility of the white of the eye below the iris and on both sides (lit. three white)

sansculotte (Fr.)   low-class Republican during the French Revolution (lit. without knee breeches)

sans souci (Fr.)   without cares

sasquatch   America's equivalent of the abominable snowman, aka big foot

satyagraha (Sans.)   a policy of non-violent resistance to British rule in India, (lit. truth pertinacity)

savoir-faire (Fr.)   knowing how to act

sayonara (Jap.)   goodbye

Schadenfreude (Ger.)   delighting in another's misfortune (lit. harm joy)

schlock (Yid.)   cheap or shoddy (lit. damaged merchandise)

schmaltz (Yid.)   sentimentality (lit. melted fat)

schmuck (Yid.)   contemptible person (lit. penis)

schweinhund (Ger.)   term of abuse (lit. pig dog)

seicento (It.)   the 17th century especially in relation to Italian arts (lit. six hundred) short for milseicento '1600'

semper eadem (L.)   always the same (motto of Elizabeth I and Anne Boleyn)

semper fidelis (L.)   always faithful

semper ubi sub ubi (L.)   always wear underwear (Latin scholar's joke)

seppuku (Jap.)   the correct term in Japan for hara-kiri, which is a colloquialism (lit. cut open the stomach)

shiatsu (Jap.)   acupuncture using fingers instead of needles (lit. finger pressure)

shmatte (Yid.)   shabbiness especially of clothes (lit. rag)

sic (L.)   bracketed insert in a text to indicate questionable word is correct (lit. thus or so)

sic transit gloria mundi (L.)   thus passes the glory of the world

Sieg Heil (Ger.)   Nazi salute accompanied by the raising of the right arm (lit. hail to victory)

sine die (L.)   without a fixed date (lit. without a day)

sine prole (L.)   without offspring

sine qua non (L.)   an essential condition or requirement (lit. without which not)

son et lumière (Fr.)   entertainment staged at night to set off a building artistically (lit. sound and light)

sotto voce (It.)   musical term 'In an undertone' (lit. under voice)

soupçon (Fr.)   trace, hint, small amount (lit. suspicion)

sputnik (Rus.)   unmanned artificial Earth satellite (lit. travelling companion)

stet (L.)   literary mark in proofing meaning correction should be ignored (lit. let it stand)

Sturm und Drang (Ger.)   late 18th century German literary style (lit. storm and stress)

subbotnik (Rus.)   voluntary Saturday work to assist economy (lit. Saturday)

sub judice (L.)   under consideration of a judge

sub poena (L.)   writ compelling a court attendance (lit. under a penalty)

sub rosa (L.)   in secret (lit. under the rose)

summa cum laude (L.)   with the highest praise

table d'hôte (Fr.)   fixed-price meal with set courses (lit. host's table)

tabula rasa (L.)   clean slate (lit. scraped table)

tai chi (Chin.)   Chinese system of callisthenics (lit. great fist)

tempus fugit (L.)   time flies

terra firma (L.)   firm ground

tête-bêche (Fr.)   double-headed stamp (lit. head to double-head)

tot homines, quot sententiae (L.)   so many men, so many minds

tour de force (Fr.)   masterly accomplishment (lit. show of strength)

trecento (It.)   the 14th century especially in relation to Italian arts (lit. three hundred) short for miltrecento '1300'

tricoteuse (Fr.)   woman who knitted at executions during French Revolution (lit. knitter)

trompe l'oeil (Fr.)   appearance of reality in art (lit. deceives the eye)

ultra vires (L.)   beyond the powers of

urbi et orbi (L.)   to the city and the world

veni, vidi, vici (L.)   I came, I saw, I conquered

verbum sat sapienti (L.)   a word is enough for a wise man

victor ludorum (L.)   overall winner of a competition (lit. winner of the games)

videlicet (L.)   namely

vis-à-vis (Fr.)   in relation to (lit. face to face)

viva voce (L.)   orally (lit. with the living voice)

vox populi (L.)   voice of the people

Wanderjahr (Ger.)   wonder year

Wehrmacht (Ger.)   German forces 1921–45 (lit. defence force)

Wunderkind (Ger.)   a highly talented child (lit. wonder child)

yordim (Heb.)   emigrants from the state of Israel

Zaibatsu (Jap.)   family business conglomerate (lit. wealthy clique)

Zeitgeist (Ger.)   spirit of the times

Cockney Rhyming Slang

Cockney–Standard

Abergavenny	penny	alligator	later
Adam and Eve	believe	almond rocks	socks
airs and graces	faces	Alphonse	ponce
	braces	Andy Cain	rain
	Epsom Races	Anna Maria	fire
alderman's nail	tail	'apenny dip	ship

Term	Meaning
apple fritter	bitter (beer)
apples and pears	stairs
April fools	stools
	tools
	football pools
April showers	flowers
Aristotle	bottle
army and navy	gravy
artful dodger	lodger
Auntie Ella	umbrella
Auntie Nellie	belly
babbling brook	cook
	crook
bacon and eggs	legs
ball of chalk	walk
balloon car	saloon bar
band in the box	pox
band of hope	soap
Barnaby Rudge	judge
Barnet Fair	hair
bat and wicket	ticket
Bath bun	son
	sun
battle-cruiser	boozer
bazaar	bar (pub)
bear's paw	saw
Beecham's Pill	bill
	still (photo)
bees and honey	money
beggar my neighbour	on the labour (dole)
bird lime	time
biscuits and cheese	knees
bladder of lard	card
boat race	face
Bob Squash	wash
Bo-Peep	sleep
boracic lint	skint
bottle and glass	arse
bow and arrow	sparrow
bread and butter	gutter
bread and cheese	sneeze
Bristol Cities	titties
Brussels sprouts	scouts
bubble and squeak	beak (magistrate)
	Greek
bucket and pail	jail
bull and cow	row
burnt cinder	window
Burton-on-Trent	rent
bushel and peck	neck
Bushey Park	lark
butcher's hook	look
Cain and Abel	table
canal boat	tote
Cape of Good Hope	soap
Captain Cook	book
carving knife	wife
cash and carried	married
cat and mouse	house
Chalk Farm	arm
cheerful giver	liver
Cherry Hogg	dog
Chevy Chase	face
china plate	mate
chop sticks	six
clickety click	sixty-six
cobbler's awls	balls
cock linnet	minute
cockroach	coach
cock sparrow	barrow
cocoa	say so
Conan Doyle	boil
country cousin	dozen
crust of bread	head
cuddle and kiss	miss
currant bun	son
	sun
custard and jelly	telly
cuts and scratches	matches
daffydown dilly	silly
Daily Mail	tale
daisy roots	boots
dickory dock	clock
dicky bird	word
Dicky Dirt	shirt
dig in the grave	shave
ding dong	song
ding dong bell	hell
dinky doo	twenty-two
Doctor Crippen	dripping
dog and bone	phone
do me goods	Woods (Woodbines)
Duchess of Fife	wife
Duke of York	chalk
	cork
	fork
dustbin lids	kids
early hours	flowers
earwig	twig (understand)
eighteen pence	sense
elephant's trunk	drunk
field of wheat	street
fife and drum	bum
fine and dandy	brandy
fisherman's daughter	water
flowery dell	cell
four by two	Jew
frog and toad	road
front wheel skid	yid
garden gate	magistrate
gay and frisky	whisky
German bands	hands
ginger beer	queer
	engineer
Glasgow Rangers	strangers
God forbids	kids
goose's neck	cheque
Gordon and Gotch	watch
grasshopper	copper
greengages	wages
Hampstead Heath	teeth
Hampton Wick	prick
Harry Randall	candle
Harvey Nichols	pickles
hearts of oak	broke
hit and miss	kiss
holy friar	liar
iron hoof	pouf
iron tank	bank
Isle of Wight	right
I suppose	nose
Jack and Jill	hill
	bill
	till
jackdaw	jaw
Jack Jones	alone
Jack Tar	bar
Jack the Ripper	kipper
jam jar	car
Jerry O'Gorman	Mormon
Jimmy Riddle	piddle
Jim Skinner	dinner
Joanna	piano

Johnnie Horner	corner	pen and ink	stink
Kate and Sydney	steak and kidney	piccolo and flute	suit
Kate Karney	army	pig's ear	beer
Khyber Pass	arse	pimple and blotch	scotch
kidney punch	lunch	pitch and toss	boss
la-di-dah	car	plates of meat	feet
Lilian Gish	fish	pleasure and pain	rain
Lilley and Skinner	dinner	potatoes in the mould	cold
	beginner	rabbit and pork	talk
linen draper	paper	read and write	fight
lion's lair	chair	Richard the Third	bird
loaf of bread	head	Rory O'More	door
loop the loop	soup	Rosy Lee	tea
Lord Lovell	shovel	round the houses	trousers
Lord Mayor	swear	rub-a-dub-dub	pub
lousy brown	Rose and Crown	Salford Docks	rocks
Lucy Locket	pocket	salmon and trout	stout
macaroni	pony	sausage and mash	cash
Marie Corelli	telly		crash
Mickey Mouse	house	Scapa Flow	go
mince pies	eyes	Scotch pegs	legs
Molly Malone	phone	Sexton Blake	cake
monkeys' tails	nails		fake
Mother Hubbard	cupboard	skin and blister	sister
mother's ruin	gin	sky rocket	pocket
Mrs Chant	aunt	sorry and sad	bad
Mutt and Jeff	deaf	stammer and stutter	butter
nanny goat	boat	stand at ease	cheese
	tote	tea leaf	thief
	coat	tea pot lid	yid
near and far	bar		quid
	car		kid
needle and pin	gin	tiddly wink	drink
Nervo and Knox	pox	tit for tat	hat
	goggle box	Tod Sloan	(on one's) own
Newington Butts	guts	Tom and Dick	sick
Noah's ark	park	Tommy Tucker	supper
	nark	Tom Thumb	rum
north and south	mouth	trouble and strife	wife
oily rag	fag	two and eight	state
old pot and pan	old man	Uncle Bert	shirt
Oliver Twist	fist	Uncle Fred	bread
on the floor	poor	Uncle Ned	bed
orchestra stalls	balls	weasel and stoat	coat
Owen Nares	chairs	weeping willow	pillow
Oxford scholar	dollar	whistle and flute	suit
peas in the pot	hot	you and me	tea

L
A
N
G
U
A
G
E

Greek Alphabet

A	α	alpha	N	ν	nu		
B	β	beta	Ξ	ξ	xi		
Γ	γ	gamma	O	o	omicron		
Δ	δ	delta	Π	π	pi		
E	ε	epsilon	P	ρ	rho		
Z	ζ	zeta	Σ	σ	sigma		
H	η	eta	T	τ	tau		
Θ	θ	theta	Y	υ	upsilon		
I	ι	iota	Φ	φ	phi		
K	κ	kappa	X	χ	chi		
Λ	λ	lambda	Ψ	ψ	psi		
M	μ	mu	Ω	ω	omega		

Hebrew Alphabet

Tet (T)   Chet (Ch)   Zayin (Z)   Vav (V/O/U)   He (H)   Dalet (D)   Gimel (G)   Bet (B/V)   Alef (Silent)

Samech (S)   Nun (N)   Mem (M)   Lamed (L)   Kaf (K/Kh)   Yod (Y)

Tav (T/S)   Shin (Sh/S)   Resh (R)   Qof (Q)   Tzade (Tz)   Pe (P/F)   Ayin (Silent)

NB There are 22 letters in the alef-bet and Hebrew script is written from right to left, alef being the first letter and tav the last. Kaf, mem, nun, pe and tzade have different characters when used at the end of a word.

Americanisms

English word	American equivalent	English word	American equivalent
A (film rating)	M (Mature film rating)	caravan site	trailer park
AA (film rating)	R (Restricted film rating)	caretaker	janitor
accumulator bet	parlay	cashier	teller
Akela	Den Mother	casserole	pot roast
Alf Garnett	Archie Bunker	catapult	slingshot
Alsatian	German Shepherd	cattle grid	Texas gate
aluminium	aluminum	chat	confab
anorak	parka	cheat	gyp
approved school	reform school	chemist's shop	drug store
Armistice Day	Veteran's Day	cheque	check
articulated lorry	trailer truck	chest of drawers	bureau
aubergine	eggplant	chick-pea	garbanzo bean
autumn	fall	chimney	smokestack
avocado	alligator pear	chips	french fries
baby's liquid feed	formula	chiropodist	podiatrist
baby's dummy	pacifier	cigar box	humidor
bag	sack	city centre	down town
baking tray	cookie sheet	class/form	grade
bank account	checking account	commis waiter	bus boy
bank holiday	legal holiday	complimentary ticket	Annie Oakley
bank note	bill	condom	rubber
bed (folding)	murphy bed	convict	yardbird
beggar	pan handler	coriander	cilantro
big wheel	ferris wheel	cos lettuce	romaine lettuce
biscuit	cookie	courgette	zucchini
Black Maria	patrol wagon	cravat	Ascot
blue-eyed boy (pet)	fair-haired boy (pet)	cream cracker	soda cracker
bottom drawer	hope chest	crisps	chips
bowler hat	derby	cupboard	closet
box room	lumber room	current account	checking account
braces	suspenders	curriculum vitae	résumé
broad bean	Lima bean	curtains	drapes
budgerigar	parakeet	curtains (net)	sheers/underdrapes
bullseye	zinger	death duties	estate tax
bum	fanny	dinner jacket	tuxedo
bum-bag	fanny pack	directory inquiries	information
by-law	ordinance	district	precinct
camp bed	cot	docker	longshoreman
candy floss	cotton candy	double cream	whipping cream
car bonnet	hood	drainpipe	downspout
car boot	trunk	draughts	checkers
car park	parking lot	drawing pin	thumb tack

English word	American equivalent	English word	American equivalent
dress circle	mezzanine/loge	lame	gimpy
dressing gown	bathrobe	lantern	jacklight
dual carriageway	divided highway	lay-by	pull-off
dustbin	garbage pail	level crossing	grade crossing
earth wire	ground wire	lift	elevator
eiderdown	comforter	limited (company)	incorporated (inc)
elastic band	rubber band	lodger	roomer
estate agent	realtor	long jump	broad jump
estate car	station wagon	lorry	truck
Europe	yarrup	lovebite	hickey
evening classes	night school	lucky dip	grab bag
fan light	transom	maize	corn
fill in (a form)	fill out (a form)	megaphone	bullhorn
fire hydrant	fire plug	men's outfitter	haberdasher
firework	firecracker	merry-go-round	carousel
flannel	wash cloth	minced meat	hamburger meat
flat (leased or owned)	apartment		ground meat
flat (owned)	condominium	money paid illicitly	kickback
flatterer	apple polisher	motorway	throughway
flautist	flutist		freeway
flex	wire		expressway
flick knife	switchblade		superhighway
floor	deck	mudguard (car)	fender
flyover	overpass	music-hall	vaudeville
foot and mouth	hoof and mouth	muslin	cheesecloth
foyer	lobby	Naafi	PX (Post Exchange)
frying pan	skillet	nappy	diaper
full stop	period	non-alcoholic drink	root beer
funny bone	crazy bone	notepad	scratchpad
garage	bodyshop	noughts & crosses	tic tac toe
garden	yard	offal	variety meat
gardening	yard work	okra	gumbo
gear lever	gearshift	open air stands	bleachers
girl guide	girl scout	oven	range
glow worm	lightning bug	oven gloves	pot holders
goods van (train)	box car	packed lunch	sack lunch
goods wagon (train)	freight car	pageboy (hotel)	bellhop
gossip	scuttle butt	paraffin	kerosene
got	gotten	patience (card game)	solitaire
greaseproof paper	wax paper	paunch (spare tyre)	bay window
green fingers	green thumb	pavement	sidewalk
grill	broil	pedestrian crossing	crosswalk
gundog	birddog	pelmet	valance
guttering	eavestrough	Perspex (trade name)	Plexiglas
haberdashery	notions	persuade	buffalo
handbag	pocketbook	petrol	gas
	purse	petrol station	filling station
hat (woollen)	toque	pharmacist	druggist
Heath Robinson	Rube Goldberg	phone-in	call-in
hire purchase	instalment plan	pimple	zit
hob	burner	plaster (medical dressing)	Band-Aid
homeless woman	bag lady	plus fours	knickers
hot dog	weenie	police patrol car	prowl car
housewife	homemaker	policeman (uniformed)	patrolman
housing estate	sub-division	porter	bellhop
hymen	cherry	post code	zip code
ice lolly	popsicle	pouffe	hassock
icing sugar	confectionery sugar	primary school	grade school
	powdered sugar	public convenience	comfort station
ignorant person	redneck	public school	private school
illegal immigrant	wet-back	pushchair	stroller
income support	relief	queue	line
influenza	grippe	quilt	comforter
jam	jelly	railway porter	redcap
jelly	jello	receptionist	desk clerk
jemmy	jimmy	reef knot	square knot
jug	pitcher	refrigerator	icebox
jumble sale	rummage sale	reserve price	upset price
knacker's yard	glue factory	residential area	uptown
ladder (in stockings)	run (in tights)	revision (for exams)	review
ladybird	ladybug	riding whip	quirt

English word	American equivalent	English word	American equivalent
ring doughnut	cruller	sweets	candy
road	pavement	Swiss roll	jelly roll
rosé wines	blush wines	tallboy	highboy
rota	roster	tap	faucet
roundabout	traffic circle	telephone box	phone booth
rubbish	garbage	television	boot tube
sack	fire	tennis shoes	sneakers
sailor (US navy)	bluey jacket	ticket (free)	Annie Oakley
saloon car	sedan	tie-pin	stick-pin
salt beef	corned beef	tobacconist's shop	cigar store
sandpit	sand box	toilet (domestic)	restroom
sausages	links	toilet (outdoor)	out-house
scarf	neckerchief	torch	flashlight
season ticket	commuter ticket	tornado	twister
second-hand	pre-owned	training camp (military)	boot camp
self-catering	cook-in	tram	streetcar
semi-detached	duplex	trilby	fedora
short-hand typist	stenographer	trousers	pants
short trousers	knee pants	truncheon	nightstick
sideboards	sideburns	turn-ups (trousers)	cuffs
skipping rope	jumping rope	U (Universal film rating)	G (General film rating)
skirting board	base board	underground (tube)	subway
	mopboard	underpants	shorts
smoked salmon	lox	undertaker	mortician
smoking jacket	lounge jacket	up to you	down to you
sofa	davenport	US marine	leatherneck
solicitor	attorney	use hindsight after the event	second-guess
sorbet	sherbet		
spanner	wrench	verruca	plantar wart
spare room	glory hole	vest	undershirt
stalls	orchestra seats	VIP address book	blue book
state school	public school	waistcoat	vest
states on Gulf of Mexico	Gulf States	waiter (apprentice)	bus boy
stiletto heels	spike heels	walk with style	sashay
stock	inventory	wallet	billfold
streaming (in schools)	tracking	washing up bowl	dishpan
string	cord	wedding ring	wedding band
striptease artist	peeler	wet paint	fresh paint
suitcase	valise	wheelbarrow	pushcart
surgical spirit	rubbing alcohol	wholemeal biscuit	graham cracker
swede	rutabaga	windscreen	windshield
sweet potato	yam	zed (z)	zee

Forenames: Meanings

Aaron high mountain/bright
Abdullah servant of God
Abel breath
Abelard resolute
Abigail father rejoices
Abner father of light
Abraham father on high/father of a multitude
Absalom father of peace
Ada noble/happy/prosperous
Adam red earth
Adolph noble wolf
Adrian dark one of the Adriatic
Aesop burnt faced
Agatha good
Agnes lamb/chaste
Ahab uncle
Ajax eagle
Akram excellent
Alan harmony/handsome
Alaric ruler of all

Alastair form of Alexander
Albert nobly bright
Alexander defender of men
Alfred elf/wise counsellor
Algernon bearded
Ali protected by God/the greatest
Alison of noble kind
Alma apple/norishing/loving
Amadeus lover of God
Amanda fit to be loved
Ambrose immortal
Amelia hard-working
Amos burden
Amy beloved
Andrea female form of Andrew
Andrew manly
Angela messenger/angel
Anita grace, mercy
Anne English form of Hannah
Anthea flowery
Anthony inestimable

April name of a month
Arnold eagle power
Arthur bear/stone/valorous
Audrey noble strength
Aziz famous
Barbara strange/foreign land
Barry fair-headed/spear
Baruch blessed
Basil royal/kingly
Beatrice bringer of joy
Belinda beautiful and pretty
Benjamin son of my right hand
Berenice one who brings victory
Bernard brave bear
Bertram glorious raven
Beth pet form of Elizabeth
Betty pet form of Elizabeth
Bill pet form of William
Bipin forest
Bjorn bear
Bob pet form of Robert

Boris fighter
Brandon broom-covered hill
Brenda burning/a flame
Brian hill/strength
Bronwyn white breasted
Bud brother
Byron from the cottage
Carl man/husbandman
Cameron crooked nose/awesome
Carmen garden/song
Carol female form of Charles
Casper treasure
Catherine pure
Cecilia blind
Charles man/husbandman
Cher beloved
Christine anointed
Christopher carrier of Christ
Claire bright/shining
Colette victorious
Colin form of Nicholas
Cordelia jewel of the sea
Craig rock
Cressida golden
Cyril lord
Damian to tame
Daniel God is my judge
Danielle female form of Daniel
Darius wealthy
Darren beloved
David beloved/friend
Dean valley/leader
Deborah bee/eloquent
Declan man of prayer
Dennis of Dionysus (Greek God of wine)
Derek gifted ruler (form of Theodonic)
Dermot free man
Derry red-haired
Diane divine
Donald world ruler
Donna lady
Donovan dark warrior
Doris gift of the sea
Dorothy gift of God
Douglas from the dark water
Dudley of the people's meadows
Eamon rich protector
Ebenezer stone of help
Edward prosperous guardian
Eileen Irish form of Helen
Eldridge wise ruler
Elijah Jehovah is my God
Elizabeth my God is bountiful
Elvis all wise
Emily industrious
Emma all-embracing
Emmanuel God with us
Enoch dedicated
Eric ruler of all
Erasmus lovable
Esther star

Ethan firm/strong
Eugenie well born
Evelyn pleasant
Ezekiel God will strengthen
Ezra helper
Felipe lover of horses
Felix fortunate
Ferdinand adventuresome
Fidel faithful
Finlay fair hero
Floyd grey-haired
Frank Frenchman/freeman
Franklin freeholder
Frederick peaceful ruler
Gabriel God is my strength
Gail pet form of Abigail
Gareth gentle/firm spear
Garth protector
Gary spear/form of Gareth
Gavin hawk
Gemma gem
Geoffrey peaceful ruler/God's peace
George husbandman/farmer
Gerard bold spear
Graham warlike person
Gregory on the watch
Griselda grey battle maid
Gudrun God secret
Gulliver glutton
Guy lovely
Habib beloved
Hamish (variant of Jacob)
Hanif believer
Hannah grace/favour
Hans (variant of John)
Harold leader of armies
Harry pet form of Henry
Hayley hay-meadow
Hector steadfast
Helen bright/shining one
Henry household ruler
Hermione well-born lady
Hilary joyful
Hilda battle maid
Hiram most noble
Homer pledge
Horace keeper of the hours
Hortense gardener
Howard guardian
Hubert bright minded
Hugh heart/mind
Humphrey warrior peace
Ian Scottish form of John
Ichabod departed glory
Ida work
Imran strong
Ira watchful
Irene peace
Iris rainbow
Irvin handsome/fair
Isaac he will laugh
Isaiah God is salvation
Ishmael God will hear

Ivan his favour
Jacqueline female form of James
James one who takes by the heel
Jane female form of John
Jared descending
Jason to heal
Javier owner of a new horse
Jed hard
Jemima dove
Jennifer fair
Jeremy Jehovah exalts/appointed by God
Jess wealthy
Jessica God beholds
Jethro superabundance
Jezebel domination
Joab God is the father
Joachim God will judge
Joan helper
John Jehovah has been gracious
Jonathan Jehovah's gift
Joseph Jehovah adds
Joyce joyful
Julie descended from Jove/youthful
Julian descended from Jove/youthful
Karen from Katarina/pure
Katarina (form of Catherine)
Keir dark skinned
Keith of the forest
Kelly warlike one
Kenneth handsome; fair one or fire sprung
Kevin handsome at birth
Lakisha woman
Latoya Antonia
Laura bay/laurel
Leah gazelle
Lee of the meadow
Leila night
Leonard strong lion
Leslie of the grey, fortress
Letitia joy
Lilith of the night
Linda pretty
Lindsay pool on the island
Lloyd grey
Loretta pure
Lucille light
Lyn cascade
Madhur sweet
Madison warrior's son
Magnus great
Malcolm dove
Mandy much loved
Marcus war-like
Margaret pearl
Mario war-like
Mark Mars (god of war)
Martin Mars (god of war)
Marvin sea friend
Mary 'bitterness' or wished-for child

LANGUAGE

Matilda   battle maiden
Matthew   gift of the Lord
Maureen   little Mary
Maurice   dark-skinned
Melissa   bee/honey
Merill   famous
Michael   like the Lord
Miranda   fit to be wondered at
Moses   saved
Nadia   hope
Nancy   pet form of Anne
Natalie   birthday of the Lord
Neil   champion
Nicholas   victory of the people
Noah   rest/comfort
Omar   first son
Pamela   all honey
Patricia   noble
Paul   small
Peter   stone/rock
Philip   lover of horses
Quentin   fifth born child
Rachel   ewe
Randolph   edge wolf/house wolf
Raphael   God has healed
Raymond   counsel for the

defence/wise protection
Rebecca   noose/one who brings peace
Rhoda   rose
Richard   strong ruler
Robert   bright fame
Roger   famous spear
Rolf   swift wolf
Ronald   counsel/power
Ronan   little seal
Rowan   red
Roxane   dawn
Ruth   vision of beauty
Samuel   heard/name of God
Sarah   princess
Saskia   protector of the universe
Sean   (form of John)
Sebastian   revered
Sharon   the plain
Shirley   bright clearing
Simon   listening attentively
Stacey   resurrection
Stephen   crown
Stuart   steward
Susan   lily
Sylvia   forest

Teresa   woman of Theresia/reaper
Theodoric   gifted ruler
Thomas   twin
Tiffany   manifestation of God
Timothy   honouring God
Tracy   pet form of Teresa
Trevor   big village/prudent
Tristan   the noisy one
Ursula   she bear
Vera   faith/truth
Victoria   victory
Vincent   conquer
Virgil   flourishing
Virginia   maiden
Vladimir   possess peace
Walter   ruling people
Wayne   wagon maker
William   helmet of resolution
Xavier   bright
Yuri   farmer
Yusuf   one chosen by God
Zachariah   God's remembrance
Zadok   just
Zia   enlightened
Zoe   life

LITERATURE

Autobiographies in Title Order

Title	Author
Absolutely Mahvelous	Billy Crystal
Absolutely Now	Lynn Franks
Accidental MP, An	Martin Bell
Actor and His Time, An	John Gielgud
Acts of Defiance	Jack Ashley
Acts of Faith	Adam Faith
Against Goliath	David Steel
Against the Grain	Boris Yeltsin
Alderman's Tale, The	Don Mosey
All Above Board	Wilfrid Brambell
All Creatures Great and Small	James Herriott
Alliss in Wonderland	Peter Alliss
All My Yesterdays	Edward G Robinson
All Those Tomorrows	Mai Zetterling
Almost a Gentleman (1991)	John Osborne
Along My Line	Gilbert Harding
Also Known as Shirley (1987)	Shelley Winters
Always Playing	Nigel Kennedy
An Actor's Life for Me	Lilian Gish
An American Comedy	Harold Lloyd
Animal Days	Desmond Morris
Another Part of the Wood (1974)	Kenneth Clark
Anything for a Quiet Life	Jack Hawkins
Apple Sauce	Michael Wilding
Arias and Raspberries	Sir Harry Secombe
As I Remember Them (1962)	Eddie Cantor
As I Walked Out One Midsummer's Morning	Laurie Lee (1929)
As It Happened (1954)	Clement, Attlee
As It Happens (1975)	Jimmy Savile
As It Seemed to Me	John Cole
Astronomer by Chance	Bernard Lovell
Backward Glance, A	Edith Wharton
Banjaxed	Terry Wogan
Bardot, Deneuve, and Fonda	Roger Vadim
Battling for Peace	Shimon Peres
Beam Ends (1934)	Errol Flynn
Beating Time	Antony Hopkins (conductor)
Before I Forget	James Mason
Before the Dawn	Gerry Adams
Beginning	Kenneth Branagh
Being Myself	Martina Navratilova
Beneath the Underdog	Charlie Mingus
Best of Times, Worst of Times	Shelley Winters
Better Class of Person, A (1981)	John Osborne
Blessings in Disguise (1985)	Alec Guinness
Bonus of Laughter, The	Leslie Crowther
Born Lucky	John Francome
Born to Believe (1953)	Lord Longford
Bound for Glory	Woody Guthrie
Boy	Roald Dahl
Bring on the Empty Horses	David Niven
British Picture, A (1985)	Ken Russell
Buried Day, The	Cecil Day Lewis
By Myself	Lauren Bacall
Can You Have It All	Nicola Horlick
Caught in the Act (1986)	Richard Todd
Change Lobsters and Dance	Lili Palmer
Changing	Liv Ullmann
Child of My Love	Sue Ryder
Choices	Liv Ullmann
Chronicles of Wasted Time	Malcolm Muggeridge
Cider With Rosie (1959)	Laurie Lee
Citizen Jane	Jane Fonda
Cleared for Take Off (1996)	Dirk Bogarde
Clear Water Stream, A (1958)	Henry Williamson
Closing Ranks (1997)	Dirk Bogarde
Coal Miner's Daughter, The	Loretta Lynn
Coming Attraction (1988)	Terence Stamp
Confessions	Jean-Jacques Rousseau
Confessions of an Actor	John Barrymore
Confessions of an Actor	Laurence Olivier
Confessions of an English Opium-Eater	Thomas De Quincey
Courting Triumph	Virginia Wade
Crying with Laughter	Bob Monkhouse
Cuban Rebel Girls (1959)	Errol Flynn
Dancing in the Light (1985)	Shirley MacLaine
Dancing in the Moonlight	Ronnie Barker
Dear Me	Peter Ustinov
Diet for Life	Lynn Redgrave
Don't Fall off the Mountain (1970)	Shirley MacLaine
Don't Laugh at Me	Norman Wisdom
Door Marked Summer, The	Michael Bentine
Double Feature (1989)	Terence Stamp
Drums under the Window (1945)	Sean O' Casey
Duke, The	David Nicholson
Ecstasy and Me	Hedy Lamarr
Ed Wynn's Son	Keenan Wynn
80 Not Out	Patrick Moore
Eternal Male, The	Omar Sharif
Evening All	Ted Willis
Every Other Inch a Lady	Beatrice Lilley
Every Shot I Take	Davis Love III
Eye of the Tiger	Frank Bruno
Facing the Music	Jane Torvill & Christopher Dean
Falling towards England	Clive James
Farce about Face	Brian Rix
Final Dress (1983)	John Houseman
Fire over England (1994)	Ken Russell
First Interval	Donald Wolfit
Five Lives (1964)	Lord Longford
For Dogs and Angels	Chili Boucher
Free House, A	Walter Sickert
From a Bundle of Rags	Jim Bowen
Front and Center (1980)	John Houseman
Full Monty, The	Jim Davidson
Fun in a Chinese Laundry	Josef von Sternberg
Future Indefinite (1954)	Noel Coward
Gay Illiterate, The (1944)	Louella Parsons
Gift of Joy, A (1965)	Helen Hayes
Girl Power	Spice Girls
Glorious Uncertainty	Jenny Pitman
Good Vibrations	Jacqueline Gold (Ann Summers)
Good Vibrations	Evelyn Glennie
Goodbye to All That	Robert Graves
Goodness Had Nothing to Do with It	Mae West (1959)
Good, the Bad and the Bubbly, The	George Best
Grace Abounding	John Bunyan
Grain of Wheat (1974)	Lord Longford
Grand Inquisitor	Robin Day

Title	Author
Greatest Game of All, The (1969)	Jack Nicklaus
Great Meadow (1992)	Dirk Bogarde
Great Morning (1947)	Osbert Sitwell
Halfway Through the Door	Alan Arkin
Happy Go Lucky (1959)	Kenneth More
Happy Hooker, The	Xavier Hollander
Haunted Life, A	Anthony Perkins
Have Tux Will Travel (1958)	Bob Hope
Here Lies	Eric Ambler
His Eye Is on the Sparrow	Ethel Waters
Hitting across the Line	Viv Richards
Hollywood in a Suitcase (1980)	Sammy Davis Jnr
Hons and Rebels	Jessica Mitford
Hundred Different Lives, A	Raymond Massey
I Can't Stay Long (1975)	Laurie Lee
I.E. (1965)	Mickey Rooney
I Knock at the Door (1939)	Sean O' Casey
I Like What I Know	Vincent Price
I'm Still Here	Yvonne De Carlo
I'm Still Here (1989)	Eartha Kitt
In and Out of Character	Basil Rathbone
In Camera (1989)	Richard Todd
In Darkness and Light	Anthony Hopkins
Inishfallen Fare Thee Well (1949)	Sean O' Casey
In My Father's Court	Isaac Bashevis Singer
In My Mind's Eye (1983)	Michael Redgrave
In Search of History: A Personal Adventure	Theodore H White
Inside the Third Reich	Albert Speer
Intermission	Anne Baxter
I Owe Russia $2000 (1963)	Bob Hope
I Paid Hitler	Baron Von Thyssen
I Reach for the Stars	Barbara Cartland
I Search for Rainbows (1967)	Barbara Cartland
I Seek the Miraculous (1978)	Barbara Cartland
I Was Born Greek	Melina Mercouri
Is It Me	Terry Wogan
Isthmus Years, The (1943)	Barbara Cartland
It Doesn't Take a Hero	Norman Schwarzkopf
It's All in the Playing (1987)	Shirley MacLaine
It's Been Fun (1949)	Anna Neagle
It's Me, O Lord! (1957)	AE Coppard
Jack of All Trades	Jack Warner
Jacob's Ladder	David Jacob
Jump Jockeys Don't Cry	Sharron Murgatroyd
Just Resting	Leo McKern
Just Williams	Kenneth Williams
Kentish Lad, A	Frank Muir
King's Story, A (1951)	Duke of Windsor
Kink	Dave Davies
Knock Wood	Candice Bergen
Last Christmas Show, The (1976)	Bob Hope
Laugh Is on Me, The	Phil Silvers
Laughter in the Next Room (1948)	Osbert Sitwell
Leaving a Doll's House	Claire Bloom
Left Hand: Right Hand (1944)	Osbert Sitwell
Let's Get through Wednesday	Reginald Bosanquet
Let the Chips Fall	Rudy Vallee
Life for Life's Sake	Richard Aldington
Life in Movies, A	Michael Powell
Life in Movies, A	Fred Zinneman
Life Is a Banquet	Rosalind Russell
Life Is Too Short (1991)	Mickey Rooney
Life Lines (1989)	Jill Ireland

Title	Author
Life of an American Workman, The	Walter Percy Chrysler
Life on Film (1971)	Mary Astor
Life, Sex and ESP (1975)	Mae West
Life Wish (1987)	Jill Ireland
Limelight and After	Claire Bloom
Little Clown, The	Reg Varney
Little Girl Lost	Drew Barrymore
Little Wilson and Big God (1987)	Anthony Burgess
Lonely Life, The (1962)	Bette Davis
Long Banana Skin, The	Michael Bentine
Long Walk to Freedom	Nelson Mandela
Lorenzo Goes to Hollywood	Edward Arnold
Love Is a Many-Splendoured Thing	Han Suyin
Love Is an Uphill Thing (1975)	Jimmy Savile
Man Who Listens to Horses, The	Monty Roberts
Martha, Jane and Me	Mavis Nicholson
Mask or Face (1958)	Michael Redgrave
Master of None	Gilbert Harding
Me	Katherine Hepburn
Mein Kampf	Adolf Hitler
Memoirs of an Unfit Mother	Anne Robinson
Memoirs of a Professional Cad	George Sanders
Memories	Ethel Barrymore
Middle of My Century, The (1989)	Shelley Winters
Mingled Chime, A	Thomas Beecham
Minnie the Moocher and Me	Cab Calloway
Mirror in My House (1956)	Sean O' Casey
Moab Is My Washpot	Stephen Fry
Moment of War, A	Laurie Lee
Moon's a Balloon, The	David Niven
More or Less (1978)	Kenneth More
Mother Goddam (1975)	Bette Davis
Movies, Mr Griffith and Me, The	Lilian Gish
Mr Nice	Howard Marks
Musician at Large	Steve Race
My American Journey	Colin Powell
My Days and Dreams	Edward Carpenter
My Double Life	Sarah Bernhardt
My Early Life (1981)	Ronald Reagan
My Life	Richard Wagner
My Life Line	Lady Isobel Barnett
My Lucky Stars: A Hollywood Memory (1989)	Shirley Maclaine
My Many Lives	Lotte Lehmann
My Name Escapes Me (1996)	Alec Guinness
My Story (1959)	Mary Astor
My Ten Years in the Studios (1940)	George Arliss
My Turn	Nancy Reagan
My Wicked Wicked Ways (1955)	Errol Flynn
Naked Civil Servant, The	Quentin Crisp
Nice One Cyril	Cyril Fletcher
Noa-Noa	Paul Gauguin
No Bed of Roses	Joan De Havilland
No Bells on Sunday	Rachel Roberts
Noble Essences (1950)	Osbert Sitwell
No Minor Chords	André Previn
Nostalgia Isn't What It Used to Be	Simone Signoret
Nothing's Impossible	Brian Blessed
Not the Whole Truth	Patrick Lichfield
Now and Then	Roy Castle
Oak and the Calf, The	Alexander Solzhenitsyn
Odd Man Out	Ronnie Biggs

Title	Author	Title	Author
Odd Woman Out	Muriel Box	Straight Man, The	Nicholas Parsons
On and Off the Fairway (1979)	Jack Nicklaus	Straight Shooting	Robert Stack
On and Off the Lee	Dorothy Hamill	Suite in Four Movements	Eric Coates
One Day at a Time	Bernie Winters	Summoned by Bells	John Betjeman
One Hump or Two	Frank Worthington	Sunday Night at Seven	Jack Benny
One Man Tango	Anthony Quinn	Sunset and Evening Star (1955)	Sean O'Casey
One Small Footprint (1980)	Molly Weir	Surprised by Joy	CS Lewis
On My Way to the Club	Ludovic Kennedy	Take It Like a Man	Boy George
On Reflection (1969)	Helen Hayes	Take My Life (1957)	Eddie Cantor
On the Other Hand	Fay Wray	Taken on Trust	Terry Waite
On the Stage (1926)	George Arliss	Tall, Dark and Gruesome	Christopher Lee
Open Book, An	John Huston	Tell It to Louella (1962)	Louella Parsons
Opening Up	Mike Atherton	Testament of Youth	Vera Brittain
Ordeal	Linda Lovelace	Testing Times	Graham Gooch
Orderly Man, An (1983)	Dirk Bogarde	There's Always Tomorrow (1974)	Anna Neagle
Original Sin, The	Anthony Quinn	There's Lovely	Johnny Morris
Other Half, The (1977)	Kenneth Clark	Things I Had to Learn, The	Loretta Young
Other Side of the Street, The	Jean Alexander	Those Twentieth Century	Michael Tippett
Outline	Paul Nash	Blues	
Out of Africa	Isak Dinesen / Karen Blixen	Thursday's Child	Eartha Kitt
		Time and Chance	James Callaghan
Out on a Limb	Heather Mills	Time to Declare	David Owen
Out on a Limb (1983)	Shirley MacLaine	To Hell and Back	Niki Lauda
Peacework (1991)	Spike Milligan	To Hell and Back	Audie Murphy
People	Edgar Wallace	To Keep the Ball Rolling	Anthony Powell
Pictures in the Hallway (1942)	Sean O' Casey	Travelling Player	Michael York
Please Don't Hate Me	Dmitri Tiomkin	Tree Is a Tree, A	King Vidor
Poet in the Family, A	Dannie Abse	Twenty Questions	Norman Hackforth
Point of View, A	Barry Took	Twice Over Lightly (1981)	Helen Hayes
Polly Wants a Zebra	Michael Aspel	Two-Way Story	Cliff Michelmore & Jean Metcalfe
Postillion Struck by Lightning, A (1977)	Dirk Bogarde	Unreliable Memoirs	Clive James
Precious Little Sleep	Wayne Sleep	Up from Slavery	Booker T Washington
Present Indicative (1937)	Noël Coward	Up in the Clouds, Gentlemen Please	John Mills
Prick up Your Ears	Joe Orton		
Prima Donna's Progress, A	Joan Sutherland	Up the Ladder to Obscurity	David Lodge
Quite Contrary	Mary Whitehouse	Up the Years from Bloomsbury (1927)	George Arliss
Ragman's Son, The	Kirk Douglas		
Rebel with a Cause	Hans Eysenck	Vanished World, The (1969)	HE Bates
Reluctant Jester, The	Michael Bentine	Vie d'Henri Brulard, La	Stendhal
Road to Hollywood (1977)	Bob Hope	Voyage (1978)	Sterling Hayden
Roamin' in the Gloaming	Sir Harry Lauder	Walking in the Shade	Doris Lessing
Roar of the Crowd	Gentleman Jim Corbett	Walking Tall	Simon Weston
		Wanderer (1963)	Sterling Hayden
Runthrough (1972)	John Houseman	Way I See It, The (1959)	Eddie Cantor
Scarlet Tree, The (1946)	Osbert Sitwell	Wet Flanders Plain, The (1929)	Henry Williamson
Screening History	Gore Vidal	What Falls Away	Mia Farrow
Second Act	Joan Collins	What's It All About	Michael Caine
Self Consciousness	John Updike	When I Was Young	Raymond Massey
Self Portrait	Gene Tierney	Where Have All the Bullets Gone (1985)	Spike Milligan
Shelley (1980)	Shelley Winters		
Shoes Were for Sunday (1970)	Molly Weir	Where's Harry	Harry Carpenter
Shooting the Actor	Simon Callow	Where's the Rest of Me	Ronald Reagan
Short Walk from Harrods, A (1994)	Dirk Bogarde	Why Me (1989)	Sammy Davis Jnr
		Will This Do	Auberon Waugh
Silver and Gold	Norman Hartnell	With Nails	Richard E Grant
Snakes and Ladders (1978)	Dirk Bogarde	Words	Jean-Paul Sartre
Some Other Rainbow	John McCarthy and Jill Morrell	World Elsewhere, A	Michael Hordern
		World of Yesterday, The	Stefan Zweig
Spend Spend Spend	Vivian Nicholson	World Within World	Stephen Spender
Stamp Album (1987)	Terence Stamp	Years of Opportunity, The (1947)	Barbara Cartland
Stand By Your Man	Tammy Wynette	Yes I Can (1966)	Sammy Davis Jnr
Stare Back and Smile	Joanna Lumley	Yo Yo Man, The	Bill Maynard
Steps in Time	Fred Astaire	You Can Get There from Here (1975)	Shirley MacLaine
Still Dancing	Lew Grade		
Still on My Way to Hollywood	Ernie Wise	Yours Indubitably	Robertson Hare
Story of a Bad Man	Thomas Aldrich	You've Had Your Time (1990)	Anthony Burgess
Story of a Soul, The	Thérèse of Lisieux	Zero to Hero	Frank Bruno

LITERATURE

NB: Dates are only provided when authors listed have more than one volume of autobiography or in instances where an author's identity may need clarification.

First Lines of Books and Poems

Adams, Richard *Shardik* Even in the dry heat of summer's end, the great forest was never silent.

Agee, James *A Death in the Family* We are talking now of summer evenings in Knoxville, Tennessee in the time that I lived there so successfully disguised to myself as a child.

Albom, Mitch *The Five People You Meet in Heaven* This is a story about a man named Eddie and it begins at the end, with Eddie dying in the sun.

Alcott, Louisa May *Good Wives* In order that we may start afresh and go to Meg's wedding with free minds, it will be well to begin with a little gossip about the Marches.

Alcott, Louisa May *Little Men* Please, sir, is this Plumfield? asked a ragged boy of the man who opened the great gate at which the omnibus left him.

Alcott, Louisa May *Little Women* Christmas won't be Christmas without any presents, grumbled Jo, lying on the rug.

Angelou, Maya *I Know Why the Caged Bird Sings* When I was three and Bailey was four, we had arrived in the musty little town.

Arnold, Matthew 'Dover Beach' The sea is calm tonight. The tide is full, the moon lies fair.

Ashford, Daisy *The Young Visiters* Mr Salteena was an elderly man of 42 and was fond of asking peaple (sic) to stay with him.

Asimov, Isaac *Foundation* His name was Gaal Dornick and he was just a country boy who had never seen Trantor before.

Asimov, Isaac *I, Robot* I looked at my notes and I didn't like them. I'd spent three days at U.S. Robots and might as well have spent them at home with the Encyclopedia Tellurica.

Atwater, Richard & Florence *Mr. Popper's Penguins* It was an afternoon in late September. In the pleasant city of Stillwater, Mr. Popper, the house painter, was going home from work.

Atwood, Margaret *Cat's Eye* Time is not a line but a dimension, like the dimensions of space.

Auden, WH *Night Mail* This is the Night Mail crossing the border, bringing the cheque and the postal order.

Austen, Jane *Emma* Emma Woodhouse, handsome, clever, and rich, with a comfortable home and happy disposition, seemed to unite some of the best blessings of existence.

Austen, Jane *Mansfield Park* About thirty years ago, Miss Maria Ward of Huntingdon with only seven thousand pounds had the good luck to captivate Sir Thomas Bertram.

Austen, Jane *Northanger Abbey* No one who had ever seen Catherine Morland in her infancy would have supposed her born to be a heroine.

Austen, Jane *Persuasion* Sir Walter Elliot, of Kellynch Hall, in Somersetshire, was a man who, for his own amusement, never took up any book but the Baronetage . . .

Austen, Jane *Pride and Prejudice* It is a truth universally acknowledged, that a single man in possession of a good fortune, must be in want of a wife.

Austen, Jane *Sense and Sensibility* The family of Dashwood has long been settled in Sussex.

Baldwin, James *Go Tell It on the Mountain* Everyone had always said that John would be a preacher when he grew up, just like his father.

Banks, Lynne Reid *The Indian in the Cupboard* It was not that Omri didn't appreciate Patrick's birthday present to him.

Barrie, JM *Peter Pan* All children, except one, grow up.

Barth, John *Giles Goat-Boy* George is my name; my deeds have been heard of in Tower Hall, and my childhood has been chronicled in the *Journal of Experimental Psychology*.

Barth, John *The Sot-Weed Factor* In the last years of the seventeenth century there was to be found among the fops & fools of the London coffee-houses one rangy, gangling flitch called Ebenezer Cooke, more ambitious than talented, and yet more talented than prudent.

Baum, Frank *The Wonderful Wizard of Oz* Dorothy lived in the midst of the great Kansas prairies, with Uncle Henry, who was a farmer, and Aunt Em, who was the farmer's wife.

Bellow, Saul *Herzog* If I am out of my mind, it's all right with me thought Moses Herzog.

Bellow, Saul *Humboldt's Gift* The book of ballads published by Von Humboldt Fleisher in the Thirties was an immediate hit.

Bemelmans, Ludwig *Madeline* In an old house in Paris that was covered with vines lived 12 little girls in two straight lines.

Benchley, Peter *Jaws* The great fish moved silently through the night water, propelled by short sweeps of its crescent tail.

Berryman, John *Homage to Mistress Bradstreet* The Governor your husband lived so long.

Bester, Alfred *The Stars My Destination* This was a Golden Age, a time of high adventure, rich living, and hard dying . . . but nobody thought so.

Betjeman, John 'A Subaltern's Love-Song' Miss J. Hunter Dunn, Miss J. Hunter Dunn, Furnish'd and burnish'd by Aldershot sun.

Blake, William 'Tyger!' Tyger! Tyger! burning bright In the forests of the night, What immortal hand or eye Could frame thy fearful symmetry?

Blatty, William Peter *The Exorcist* Like the brief doomed flare of exploding suns that registers dimly on blind men's eyes, the beginning of the horror passed almost unnoticed.

Böll, Heinrich *The Clown* It was dark by the time I reached Bonn, and I forced myself not to succumb to the series of mechanical actions which had taken hold of me in five years of travelling back and forth.

Boyle, T Coraghessan *The Road to Wellville* Dr. John Harvey Kellogg, inventor of the cornflake and peanut butter, not to mention caramel-cereal coffee, Bromose, Nuttolene and some seventy-five other gastronomically correct foods, paused to level his gaze on the heavyset women in front of him.

Bradbury, Ray *Fahrenheit 451* It was a pleasure to burn.

Bradley, Marion Zimmer *Mists of Avalon* Even in high summer, Tintagel was a haunted place; Igraine, Lady of Duke Gorlois, looked out over the sea from the headland.

Braine, John *Life at the Top* She woke me up by lifting my eyelids; then she slipped under the bed clothes beside me and lay there smiling.

Brautigan, Richard   *A Confederate General from Big Sur*   When I first heard about Big Sur I didn't know that it was a member of the Confederate States of America.

Brontë, Anne   *Agnes Grey*   All true histories contain instruction, though in some, the treasure may be hard to find, and when found, so trivial in quantity that the dry shrivelled kernel scarcely compensates for the trouble of cracking the nut.

Brontë, Anne   *The Tenant of Wildfell Hall*   You must go back with me to the autumn of 1827.

Brontë, Charlotte   *Jane Eyre*   There was no possibility of taking a walk that day.

Brontë, Charlotte   *The Professor*   The other day, in looking over my papers, I found in my desk the following copy of a letter.

Brontë, Charlotte   *Villette*   My Godmother lived in a handsome house in the clean and ancient town of Bretton.

Brontë, Emily   *Wuthering Heights*   1801 – I have just returned from a visit to my landlord.

Brooke, Rupert   'The Soldier'   If I should die, think only this of me: That there's some corner of a foreign field That is forever England.

Brown, Dan   *Angels & Demons*   High atop the steps of the Pyramid of Giza a young woman laughed and called down to him.

Brown, Dan   *The Da Vinci Code*   Robert Langdon awoke slowly.

Brown, Dan   *Deception Point*   Toulos Restaurant, adjacent to Capitol Hill, boasts a politically incorrect menu of baby veal and horse carpaccio . . .

Brown, Dan   *Digital Fortress*   They were in the Smoky Mountains at their favorite bed-and-breakfast.

Brown, Margaret Wise   *Goodnight Moon*   In the great green room, there was a telephone and a red balloon.

Brown, Rita Mae   *Rubyfruit Jungle*   No one remembers her beginnings.

Brown, Rita Mae   *Venus Envy*   Dying's not so bad. At least I won't have to answer the telephone.

Browning, Elizabeth Barrett   'How Do I Love Thee'   How do I love thee? Let me count the ways. .

Browning, Robert   'Childe Roland to the Dark Tower Came'   My first thought was, he lied in every word.

Browning, Robert   'Home-Thoughts: from Abroad'   Oh, to be in England now that April's there . . .

Buchan, John   *The Thirty-Nine Steps*   I returned from the city about three o'clock on that May afternoon, pretty well disgusted with life.

Buck, Pearl   *The Good Earth*   It was Wang Lung's marriage day.

Bulwer-Lytton, Edward   *Paul Clifford*   It was a dark and stormy night and the rain fell in torrents – except at occasional intervals, when it was checked by a violent gust of wind which swept up the streets (for it is in London that our scene lies), rattling along the housetops, and fiercely agitating the scanty flame of the lamps that struggled against the darkness.

Bunyan, John   *The Pilgrim's Progress*   As I walked through the wilderness of this world, I lighted on a certain place where was a Den, and I laid me down in that place to sleep: and, as I slept, I dreamed a dream.

Burgess, Anthony   *A Clockwork Orange*   What's it going to be then, eh?

Burgess, Anthony   *Earthly Powers*   It was the afternoon of my eighty-first birthday and I was in bed with my catamite when Ali announced that the Archbishop had come to see me.

Burnett, Frances Hodgson   *A Little Princess*   Once on a dark winter's day, when the yellow fog hung so thick and heavy in the streets of London that the lamps were lighted and the shop windows blazed with gas as they do at night, an odd-looking little girl sat in a cab with her father and was driven rather slowly through the big thoroughfares.

Burnett, Frances Hodgson   *The Secret Garden*   When Mary Lennox was sent to Misselthwaite Manor to live with her uncle everybody said she was the most disagreeable-looking child ever seen.

Burns, Robert   'A Red Red Rose'   O my luve's like a red, red rose, That's newly sprung in June.

Burns, Robert   'To a Field Mouse'   Wee, sleekit, cow'rin', tim'rous beastie, O what a panic's in thy breastie.

Butler, Samuel   *The Way of All Flesh*   When I was a small boy at the beginning of the century I remember an old man who wore knee-breeches and worsted stockings, and used to hobble about the street of our village with the help of a stick.

Byron, Lord   'She Walks in Beauty'   She walks in beauty, like the night Of cloudless climes and starry skies.

Caldwell, Taylor   *Great Lion of God*   He is very ugly, said his mother.

Camus, Albert   *The Stranger*   Mother died today. Or perhaps it was yesterday, I don't know.

Capote, Truman   *Breakfast at Tiffany's*   I am always drawn back to the places where I have lived, the houses & their neighborhoods.

Capote, Truman   *In Cold Blood*   The village of Holcomb stands on the high wheat plains of western Kansas, a lonesome area that other Kansans call 'out there'.

Carey, Peter   *Jack Maggs*   It was a Saturday night when the man with the red waistcoat arrived in London.

Carroll, Lewis   *Alice's Adventures in Wonderland*   Alice was beginning to get very tired of sitting by her sister on the bank, and of having nothing to do: once or twice she had peeped into the book her sister was reading, but it had no pictures or conversations in it, 'and what is the use of a book, thought Alice 'without pictures or conversation?'

Carroll, Lewis   *Through the Looking Glass and What Alice Found There;*   One thing was certain, that the *white* kitten had had nothing to do with it – it was the black kitten's fault entirely.

Castaneda, Carlos   *The Teachings of Don Juan*   My notes on my first session with don Juan are dated June 23,1961.

Cather, Willa   *My Ántonia*   I first heard of Ántonia on what seemed to me an interminable journey across the great midland plains of North America.

Cervantes, Miguel de   *Don Quixote*   At a village of La Mancha, whose name I do not wish to remember, there lived a little while ago one of those gentlemen who are wont to keep a lance in the rack, an old buckler, a lean horse and a swift greyhound.

Chandler, Raymond   *The Big Sleep*   It was about eleven o'clock in the morning, mid-October, with the sun not shining and a look of hard wet rain in the clearness of the foothills.

Chang, Jung   *Wild Swans*   At the age of fifteen my grandmother became the concubine of a warlord general.

Chaucer, Geoffrey *The Canterbury Tales* Whan that Aprill with his shoures soote The droghte of March hath perced to the roote.

Chesterton, GK *The Man Who Was Thursday* The suburb of Saffron Park lay on the sunset side of London, as red and ragged as a cloud of sunset.

Chesterton, GK *The Donkey* When fishes flew and forests walked and figs grew upon thorn.

Chopin, Kate *The Awakening* A green and yellow parrot, which hung in a cage outside the door, kept repeating over and over: 'Allez vous-en! Allez vous-en ! Sapristi ! That's all right !'

Christie, Agatha *The Mirror Crack'd* Miss Jane Marple was sitting by her window.

Clarke, Arthur C *Childhood's End* The Volcano that had reared Taratua up from the Pacific depths had been sleeping now for half a million years. Yet in a little while, thought Reinhold, the island would be bathed in fires fiercer than any that had attended its birth.

Clarke, Arthur C *The City and the Stars* Like a glowing jewel, the city lay upon the breast of the desert. Once it had known change and alteration, but now time passed it by. Night and day fled across the desert's face, but in Diaspar it was always afternoon, and darkness never came.

Clarke, Arthur C *2001: A Space Odyssey* The drought had lasted now for ten million years, and the reign of the terrible lizards had long since ended.

Cleland, John *Fanny Hill* Madam, I sit down to give you an undeniable proof of my considering your desires as indispensable orders.

Coelho, Paulo *The Alchemist* The boy's name was Santiago.

Collins, Wilkie *The Moonstone* In the first part of Robinson Crusoe, at page one hundred and twenty-nine, you will find it thus written: 'Now I saw, though too late, the Folly of beginning a Work before we count the Cost, and before we judge rightly of our own strength to go through with it.'

Collins, Wilkie *The Woman in White* This is the story of what a Woman's patience can endure, and what a Man's resolution can achieve.

Condon, Richard *Prizzi's Honor* Corrado Prizzi's granddaughter was being married before the baroque altar of Santa Grazia de Traghetto, the lucky church of the Prizzi family.

Conrad, Joseph *Heart of Darkness* Nellie, a cruising yawl, swung to her anchor without a flutter of sails, and was at rest.

Conrad, Joseph *Lord Jim* He was an inch, perhaps two, under six feet, powerfully built, and he advanced straight at you with a slight stoop of the shoulders, head forward, and a fixed from-under stare which made you think of a charging bull.

Conrad, Joseph *Nostromo* In the time of Spanish rule, and for many years afterwards, the town of Sulaco – the luxuriant beauty of the orange gardens bears witness to its antiquity – had never been commercially anything more important than a coasting port with a fairly large local trade in ox-hides and indigo.

Conrad, Joseph *An Outcast of the Islands* When he stepped off the straight and narrow path of his peculiar honesty, it was with an inward assertion of unflinching resolve.

Conrad, Joseph *The Secret Agent* Mr Verloc, going out in the morning, left his shop nominally in charge of his brother-in-law.

Coolidge, Susan *What Katy Did Next* The September sun was glinting cheerfully into a pretty bedroom furnished with blue.

Cooper, James Fenimore *The Last of the Mohicans* It was a feature peculiar to the colonial wars of North America, that the toils and dangers of the wilderness were to be encountered before the adverse hosts could meet.

Crane, Stephen *The Red Badge of Courage* The cold passed reluctantly from the earth, and the retiring fogs revealed an army stretched out on the hills, resting.

Dahl, Roald *Charlie and the Chocolate Factory* These two very old people are the father and mother of Mr. Bucket.

Dante, Alighieri *Divine Comedy* Midway along the path of life.

Davies, Robertson *The Cunning Man* Should I have taken the false teeth?

Davies, WH 'Leisure' What is this life if, full of care, We have no time to stand and stare?

Defoe, Daniel *Robinson Crusoe* I was born in the year 1632, in the city of York, of a good family, though not of that country, my father being a foreigner of Bremen, who settled first at Hull. He got a good estate by merchandise, and leaving off his trade lived afterward at York, from whence he had married my mother, whose relations were named Robinson, a good family in that country, and from whom I was called Robinson Kreutznear.

Deighton, Len *Catch a Falling Spy* Smell that air, said Major Mann.

Deighton, Len *The Ipcress File* They came through on the hot line at about half past two in the afternoon.

De La Mare, Walter 'The Listeners' 'Is there anybody there?' said the Traveller, Knocking on the moonlit door.

Dick, Philip K *Do Androids Dream of Electric Sheep?* A merry little surge of electricity piped by automatic alarm from the mood organ beside his bed awakened Rick Deckard.

Dickens, Charles *Barnaby Rudge* In the year 1775, there stood upon the borders of Epping Forest, at a distance of about twelve miles from London – measuring the Standard in Cornhill, or rather from the spot on or near to which the Standard used to be in days of yore – a house of public entertainment called the Maypole; which fact was demonstrated to all such travellers as could neither read nor write (and at that time a vast number both of travellers and stay-at-homes were in this condition) by the emblem reared on the roadside over and against the house, which, if not of those goodly proportions that Maypoles were wont to present in olden times, was a fair young ash, thirty feet in height, and straight as any arrow that ever English yeoman drew.

Dickens, Charles *Bleak House* London. Michaelmas term lately over, and the Lord Chancellor sitting in Lincoln's Inn Hall.

Dickens, Charles *A Christmas Carol* Marley was dead, to begin with. There is no doubt whatever about that.

Dickens, Charles *David Copperfield* Whether I shall turn out to be the hero of my own life, or whether that station will be held by anybody else, these pages must show.

Dickens, Charles *Dombey and Son* Dombey sat in the corner of the darkened room in the great armchair by the bedside, and Son lay tucked up in a warm little basket bedstead, carefully disposed on a low settee immediately in front of the fire and close to it, as if his constitution were analogous to that of a muffin, and it was essential to toast him brown while he was very new.

Dickens, Charles *Great Expectations* My father's family name being Pirrip, and my christian name Philip, my infant tongue could make of both names nothing longer or more explicit than Pip.

Dickens, Charles *Hard Times* Now, what I want is Facts.

Dickens, Charles *Little Dorrit* Thirty years ago, Marseilles lay burning in the sun, one day.

Dickens, Charles *Martin Chuzzlewit* As no lady or gentleman, with any claims to polite breeding, can possibly sympathise with the Chuzzlewit Family without being first assured of the extreme antiquity of the race, it is a great satisfaction to know that it undoubtedly descended in a direct line from Adam and Eve; and was, in the very earliest times, closely connected with the agricultural interest.

Dickens, Charles *The Mystery of Edwin Drood* An ancient English Cathedral Tower?

Dickens, Charles *Nicholas Nickleby* There once lived, in a sequestered part of the county of Devonshire, one Mr Godfrey Nickleby: a worthy gentleman, who, taking it into his head rather late in life that he must get married, and not being young enough or rich enough to aspire to the hand of a lady of fortune, had wedded an old flame out of mere attachment, who in her turn had taken him for the same reason.

Dickens, Charles *The Old Curiosity Shop* Night is generally my time for walking.

Dickens, Charles *Oliver Twist* Among other public buildings in a certain town, which for many reasons it will be prudent to refrain from mentioning, and to which I will assign no fictitious name, there is one anciently common to most towns, great or small – to wit, a workhouse; and in this workhouse was born, on a day and date which I need not trouble myself to repeat, inasmuch as it can be of no possible consequence to the reader, in this stage of the business at all events, the item of mortality whose name is prefixed to the head of this chapter.

Dickens, Charles *Our Mutual Friend* In these times of ours, though concerning the exact year there is no need to be precise, a boat of dirty and disreputable appearance, with two figures in it, floated on the Thames, between Southwark Bridge which is of iron, and London Bridge which is of stone, as an autumn evening was closing in.

Dickens, Charles *Pickwick Papers* The first ray of light which illumines the gloom, and converts into a dazzling brilliancy that obscurity in which the earlier history of the public career of the immortal Pickwick would appear to be involved, is derived from the perusal of the following entry in the transactions of the Pickwick Club, which the editor of these papers feels the highest pleasure in laying before his readers as a proof of the careful attention, indefatigable assiduity, and nice discrimination, with which his search among the multifarious documents confided to him has been conducted.

Dickens, Charles *A Tale of Two Cities* It was the best of times, it was the worst of times, it was the age of wisdom, it was the age of foolishness, it was the epoch of belief, it was the epoch of incredulity, it was the season of Light, it was the season of Darkness, it was the spring of hope, it was the winter

of despair, we had everything before us, we had nothing before us, we were all going direct to Heaven, we were all going direct the other way – in short, the period was so.

Dickinson, Emily untitled poem I heard a Fly buzz – when I died . . .

Doctorow, EL *Ragtime* In 1902 Father built a house at the crest of the Broadview Avenue hill in New Rochelle, New York.

Dos Passos, John *1919* Oh the infantree the infantree With the dirt behind their ears

ARMIES CLASH AT VERDUN IN GLOBE'S GREATEST BATTLE 150,000 MEN AND WOMEN PARADE

but another question and a very important one is raised.

Dostoevsky, Fyodor *The Brothers Karamazov* Alexey Fyodorovitch Karamazov was the third son of Fyodor Pavlovitch Karamazov, a landowner well known in our district in his own day, and still remembered among us owing to his gloomy and tragic death, which happened thirteen years ago, and which I shall describe in its proper place.

Dostoevsky, Fyodor *Crime and Punishment* On an exceptionally hot evening early in July a young man came out of the garret in which he lodged in S. Place and walked slowly, as though in hesitation, towards K. bridge.

Doyle, Sir Arthur Conan *The Hound of the Baskervilles* Mr. Sherlock Holmes, who was usually very late in the mornings, save upon those not infrequent occasions when he was up all night, was seated at the breakfast table.

Dryden, John *Absalom and Achitophel* In pious times, ere priestcraft did begin . . .

Du Maurier, Daphne *The King's General* September 1653. The last of summer. The first chill winds of autumn.

Du Maurier, Daphne *Rebecca* Last night I dreamt I went to Manderley again.

Dumas, Alexandre *The Count of Monte Cristo* On the 24th of February, 1815, the lookout of Notre Dame de la Garde signalled the three-master, the *Pharaon*, from Smyrna, Trieste, and Naples. As usual, a pilot put off immediately, and rounding the Chateau d'If, got on board the vessel between Cape Morgion and the Isle of Rion.

Dumas, Alexandre *The Three Musketeers* On the first Monday of the month of April, 1625, the town of Meung, in which the author of The Romance of the Rose was born, appeared to be in a perfect state of revolution as if the Huguenots had just made a second Rochelle of it.

Eliot, George *Middlemarch* Miss Brooke had that kind of beauty which seems to be thrown into relief by poor dress.

Eliot, George *The Mill on the Floss* A wide plain, where the broadening Floss hurries on between its green banks to the sea, and the loving tide, rushing to meet it, checks its passage with an impetuous embrace.

Eliot, George *Silas Marner* In the days when the spinning-wheels hummed busily in the farmhouses – and even great ladies, clothed in silk and thread-lace, had their toy spinning-wheels of polished oak – there might be seen in districts far away among the lanes, or deep in the bosom of the hills, certain pallid undersized men, who, by the side of the brawny country-folk, looked like the remnants of a disinherited race.

Eliot, TS *East Coker* In my beginning is my end.

Eliot, TS *'The Love Song of J. Alfred Prufrock'* Let us go then, you and I . . .

Ellison, Ralph *Invisible Man* I am an invisible man.

Farmer, Philip Jose *To Your Scattered Bodies Go* His wife had held him in her arms as if she could keep death away from him. He had cried out, 'My God, I am a dead man!'

Faulkner, William *Go Down, Moses* Isaac McCaslin, 'Uncle Ike', past seventy and nearer eighty than he ever corroborated any more, a widower now and uncle to half a country and father to one.

Faulkner, William *Sanctuary* From behind the screen of bushes which surrounded the spring, Popeye watched the man drinking.

Faulkner, William *The Sound and the Fury* Through the fence, between the curling flower spaces, I could see them hitting.

Fielding, Henry *Tom Jones* An author ought to consider himself not as a gentleman who gives a private or eleemosynary treat.

Fitzgerald, F Scott *The Great Gatsby* In my younger and more vulnerable years my father gave me some advice that I've been turning over in my mind ever since.

Flaubert, Gustave *Madame Bovary* We were in the study-hall when the headmaster entered, followed by a new boy not yet in school uniform and by the handyman carrying a large desk.

Fleming, Ian *Chitty-Chitty-Bang-Bang* Most motorcars are conglomerations (this is a long word for bundles) of steel and wire and rubber and plastic, and electricity and oil and gasoline and water, and the toffee papers you pushed down the crack in the back seat last Sunday.

Fleming, Ian *Goldfinger* James Bond, with two double bourbons inside him, sat back in the final departure lounge of Miami Airport and thought about life and death.

Ford, Ford Madox *The Good Soldier* This is the saddest story I have ever heard.

Forster, EM *A Passage to India* Except for the Marabar Caves – and they are twenty miles off – the city of Chandrapore presents nothing extraordinary.

Forsyth, Frederick *The Odessa File* Everybody seems to remember what they were doing on November 22nd 1963, when Kennedy was shot.

Fowles, John *The French Lieutenant's Woman* An easterly is the most disagreeable wind in Lyme Bay – Lyme Bay being that largest byte from the underside of England's outstretched southwestern leg – and a person of curiousity could at once have deduced several strong probabilities about the pair who began to walk down the quay at Lyme Regis, the small but ancient eponym of the inbite, one incisively sharp and blustery morning in the late March of 1867.

Gallico, Paul *The Poseidon Adventure* At seven o'clock, the morning of the 26th of December, the S.S. *Poseidon*, 81,000 tons, homeward bound for Lisbon after a month-long Christmas cruise to African and South American ports, suddenly found herself in the midst of an unaccountable swell, 400 miles south-west of the Azores, and began to roll like a pig.

Galsworthy, John *The Man of Property* Those privileged to be present at a family festival of the Forsythes have seen that charming and instructive sight – an upper middle class family in full plumage.

Gardner, John *Grendel* The old ram stands looking down over rockslides, stupidly triumphant.

Gibson, William *Neuromancer* The sky above the port was the color of television, tuned to a dead channel.

Gide, André *The Fruits of the Earth* Do not hope, Nathaniel, to find God here or there – but everywhere.

Gipson, Fred *Old Yeller* We called him Old Yeller.

Golding, William *Lord of the Flies* The boy with fair hair lowered himself down the last few feet of rock and began to pick his way towards the lagoon.

Golding, William *The Princess Bride* This is my favorite book in all the world, though I have never read it.

Goldman, William *Marathon Man* Everytime he drove through Yorkville, Rosenbaum got angry, just on general principles.

Goldsmith, Oliver *'Elegy on the Death of a Mad Dog'* Good people all, of every sort, Give ear unto my song.

Grahame, Kenneth *The Wind in the Willows* The Mole had been working very hard all the morning, spring-cleaning his little home.

Grass, Günter *The Tin Drum* Granted: I am an inmate of a mental hospital; my keeper is watching me, he never lets me out of his sight; there's a peephole in the door, and my keeper's eye is the shade of brown that can never see through a blue-eyed type like me.

Graves, Robert *I, Claudius* I, Tiberius Claudius Drusus Nero Germanicus This-that-and-the-other (for I shall not trouble you yet with all my titles) who was once, and not so long ago either, known to my friends and relatives and associates as 'Claudius the Idiot', or 'That Claudius', or 'Claudius the Stammerer', or 'Clau-Clau-Claudius' or at best as 'Poor Uncle Claudius', am now about to write this strange history of my life; starting from my earliest childhood and continuing year by year until I reach the fateful point of change where, some eight years ago, at the age of fifty-one, I suddenly found myself caught in what I may call the 'golden predicament' from which I have never since become disentangled.

Gray, Thomas *'Elegy Written in a Country Churchyard'* The curfew tolls the knell of parting day . . .

Gray, Thomas *'The Progress of Poesy'* Awake, Aeolian lyre, awake

Greene, Graham *The Power and the Glory* Mr Tench went out to look for his ether cylinder, into the blazing Mexican sun.

Greene, Graham *The Quiet American* After dinner I sat and waited for Pyle in my room over the rue Catinat: he had said, 'I'll be with you at latest by ten,' and when midnight had struck I couldn't stay quiet any longer and went down into the street.

Guterson, David *Snow Falling on Cedars* The accused man, Kabuo Miyamoto, sat proudly upright with a rigid grace.

Høeg, Peter *Miss Smilla's Feeling for Snow* It's freezing – an extraordinary 0° fahrenheit – and it's snowing, and in the language that is no longer mine the snow is qanik –

Haggard, H Rider *King Solomon's Mines* It is a curious thing that at my age, fifty-five last birthday, I should find myself taking up a pen to try and write a history.

Haggard, H Rider *She* There are some events of which each circumstance and surrounding detail seem to be graven on the memory in such a fashion that we cannot forget them.

Hailey, Arthur *Airport* At half-past six on a Friday

evening in January, Lincoln International Airport, Illinois, was functioning, though with difficulty.

Haley, Alex *Roots* Early in the spring of 1750, in the village of Juffure, four days upriver from the coast of Gambia, West Africa, a manchild was born to Omoro and Binta Kinte.

Hammett, Dashiell *The Maltese Falcon* Samuel Spade's jaw was long and bony, his chin a jutting 'V' under the more flexible 'V' of his mouth.

Hammett, Dashiell *The Thin Man* I was leaning against a bar in a speak-easy on Fifty-second Street, waiting for Nora to finish her Christmas shopping, when a girl got up from the table where she had been sitting.

Hardy, Thomas *Far from the Madding Crowd* When Farmer Oak smiled, the corners of his mouth spread till they were within an unimportant distance of his ears, his eyes were reduced to chinks, and diverging wrinkles appeared round them, extending upon his countenance like the rays in a rudimentary sketch of the rising sun.

Hardy, Thomas *Jude the Obscure* The schoolmaster was leaving the village, and everybody seemed sorry.

Hardy, Thomas *The Mayor of Casterbridge* One evening of late summer, before the nineteenth century had reached one-third of its span, a young man and woman, the latter carrying a child, were approaching the large village of Weydon-Priors, in Upper Wessex, on foot.

Hardy, Thomas *Tess of the D'Urbervilles* On an evening in the latter part of May a middle-aged man was walking homeward from Shaston to the village of Marlott, in the adjoining Vale of Blakemore or Blackmoor.

Harris, Robert *Fatherland* Thick cloud had pressed down on Berlin all night and now it was lingering into what passed for morning.

Hartley, LP *The Go-Between* The past is a foreign country, they do things differently there.

Hawthorne, Nathaniel *The House of the Seven Gables* Halfway down a bystreet of one of our New England towns stands a rusty wooden house, with seven acutely peaked gables, facing towards various points of the compass, and a huge, clustered chimney in the midst.

Hawthorne, Nathaniel *The Scarlet Letter* A throng of bearded men, in sad-colored garments and gray, steeple-crowned hats, intermixed with women, some wearing hoods, and others bareheaded, was assembled in front of a wooden edifice, the door of which was heavily timbered with oak, and studded with iron spikes.

Heinlein, Robert *The Moon Is a Harsh Mistress* I see in *Lunaya Pravda* that Luna City Council has passed on first reading a bill to examine, license, inspect – and tax – public food vendors operating inside municipal pressure.

Heinlein, Robert *Stranger in a Strange Land* Once upon a time there was a Martian named Valentine Michael Smith.

Heller, Joseph *Catch-22* It was love at first sight.

Heller, Joseph *Something Happened* I get the willies when I see closed doors.

Hemans, Felicia 'Casabianca' The boy stood on the burning deck, Whence all but he had fled.

Hemingway, Ernest *The Old Man and the Sea* He was an old man who fished alone in a skiff in the Gulf stream and he had gone 84 days now without taking a fish.

Herrick, Robert 'To the Virgins, to Make Much of Time' Gather ye rosebuds while ye may, Old Time is still a-flying.

Hesse, Hermann *Siddhartha* In the shade of the house, in the sunshine on the river bank by the boats, in the shade of the sallow wood and the fig tree, Siddharta, the handsome Brahmin's son, grew up with his friend Govinda.

Higgins, Colin *Harold and Maude* Harold Chasen stepped up on the chair and placed the noose about his neck.

Hoban, Russell *Riddley Walker* On my naming day when I come 12 I gone front spear and kilt a wyld boar he parbly ben the las wyld pig on the Bundel.

Homer *The Odyssey* By now the other warriors, those that had escaped head-long ruin by sea or in a battle, were safely home.

Hopkins, Gerard Manley 'The Wreck of the Deutschland' Thou mastering me . . .

Hughes, Thomas *Tom Brown's Schooldays* The Browns have been illustrious by the pen of Thackeray and the pencil of Doyle.

Hugo, Victor *The Hunchback of Notre-Dame* It was three hundred forty-eight years, six months, and nineteen days ago today that the citizens of Paris were awakened by the pealing of all the bells in the triple precincts of the City, the University, and the Town.

Hugo, Victor *Les Misérables* In 1815, M. Charles-François-Bienvenu Myriel was Bishop of D—.

Hurston, Zora Neale *Their Eyes Were Watching God* Ships at a distance have every man's wish on board.

Huxley, Aldous *Brave New World* A squat gray building of only thirty-four stories. Over the main entrance the words CENTRAL LONDON HATCHERY AND CONDITIONING CENTRE, and in a shield the World State's motto, Community, Identity, Stability.

Huxley, Aldous *Crome Yellow* Along this particular stretch of line, no express had ever passed.

Irving, John *The Hotel New Hampshire* The summer my father bought the bear, none of us was born – we weren't even conceived: not Frank, the oldest; not Fanny, the loudest; not me, the next; and not the youngest of us, Lilly and Egg.

Irving, John *A Prayer for Owen Meany* I am doomed to remember a boy with a wrecked voice – not because of his voice, or because he was the smallest person I ever knew, or even because he was the instrument of my mother's death, but because he is the reason I believe in God; I am a Christian because of Owen Meany.

Irving, John *The World According to Garp* Garp's mother, Jenny Fields, was arrested in Boston in 1942 for wounding a man in a movie theater.

Jacques, Brian *Redwall* Mathias cut a comical figure as he hobbled his way along the cloisters, with his large sandals flip-flopping and his tail peeping from beneath the baggy folds of an oversized novice's habit.

James, Henry *The Turn of the Screw* The story had held us, round the fire, sufficiently breathless, but except the obvious remark that it was gruesome, as, on Christmas Eve in an old house, a strange tale should essentially be, I remember no comment uttered till somebody happened to say that it was the only case he had met in which such a visitation had fallen on a child.

L
I
T
E
R
A
T
U
R
E

Jong, Erica *Fear of Flying* There were 117 psychoanalysts on the Pan Am flight to Vienna and I'd been treated by at least six of them.

Jonson, Ben 'To Celia' Drink to me only with thine eyes: and I will pledge with mine.

Joyce, James *Dubliners* There was no hope for him this time: it was the third stroke.

Joyce, James *Portrait of the Artist as a Young Man* Once upon a time and a very good time it was there was a moocow coming down along the road and this moocow that was coming down along the road met a nicens little boy named baby tuckoo.

Joyce, James *Ulysses* Stately plump Buck Mulligan came from the stairhead, bearing a bowl of lather on which a mirror and a razor lay crossed.

Juster, Norton *The Phantom Tollbooth* There was a boy named Milo who didn't know what to do with himself . . .

Kafka, Franz 'Metamorphosis' As Gregor Samsa awoke one morning from uneasy dreams, he found himself transformed into a giant insect.

Kafka, Franz *The Castle* It was late in the evening when K. arrived.

Kafka, Franz *The Trial* Someone must have been telling lies about Joseph K, for without having done anything wrong he was arrested one fine morning.

Keats, John 'La Belle Dame Sans Merci' Oh, What can ail thee, knight at arms Alone and palely loitering.

Keats, John *Hyperion* Deep in the shady sadness of a vale . . .

Keats, John 'On First Looking into Chapman's Homer' Much have I travell'd in the realms of gold, And many goodly states and kingdoms seen.

Keats, John 'To Autumn' Season of mists and mellow fruitfulness, close bosom-friend of the maturing sun.

Kennedy, William *Quinn's Book* I, Daniel Quinn, neither the first nor the last of a line of such Quinn's, set eyes on Maud the wondrous on a late December day in 1849 on the banks of the river of the aristocrats and paupers, just as the great courtesan Magdalena Colón, also known as La Última, a woman whose presence turned men into spittling, masturbating pigs, boarded a skiff to carry her across the river's icy water from Albany to Greenbush, her first stop en route to the city of Troy, a community of iron, where later that evening she was scheduled to enact, yet again, her role as the lascivious Lais, that fabled prostitute who spurned Demosthenes' gold and yielded free to Diogenes, the virtuous, impecunious tub-dweller.

Kidd, Sue *The Secret Life of Bees* At night I would lie in bed and watch the show, how bees squeezed through the cracks of my bedroom wall . . .

King, Stephen *Carrie* Nobody was really surprised when it happened, not really, not on the subconscious level where savage things grow.

King, Stephen *Cujo* Not so long ago, a monster came to the small town of Castle Rock, Maine.

Kingsolver, Barbara *The Bean Trees* I have been afraid of putting air in a tire ever since I saw a tractor tire blow up and throw Newt Hardbines's father over the top of the Standard Oil sign.

Kingsolver, Barbara *Pigs in Heaven* Women on their own run in Alice's family.

Kipling, Rudyard 'Gunga Din' You may talk o'gin and beer, when you're quartered safe out 'ere.

Kipling, Rudyard 'If' If you can keep your head when all about you are losing theirs and blaming it on you.

Kipling, Rudyard *The Jungle Book* It was seven o'clock of a very warm evening in the Seeonee hills when Father Wolf woke up from his day's rest, scratched himself, yawned, and spread out his paws one after the other to get rid of the sleepy feeling in their tips.

Kipling, Rudyard *Kim* He sat in defiance of municipal orders, astride the gun of Zam-Zammeh on her brick platform opposite the old Ajaibgher – the Wonder House, as the natives called the Lahore Museum.

Kipling, Rudyard *Stalky and Co* In summer all right-minded boys built huts in the furze-hill behind the College – little lairs whittled out of the heart of the prickly bushes, full of stumps, odd root-ends, and spikes, but, since they were strictly forbidden, palaces of delight.

Knowles, John *A Separate Peace* I went back to the Devon School not long ago, and found it looking oddly newer than when I was a student there fifteen years before.

Kosinski, Jerzy *The Painted Bird* In the first weeks of World War II, in the fall of 1939, a six year old boy from a large city in Eastern Europe was sent by his parents, like thousands of other children, to the shelter of a distant village.

Kundera, Milan *The Unbearable Lightness of Being* The idea of eternal return is a mysterious one, and Nietzsche has often perplexed other philosophers with it: to think that everything recurs as we once experienced it, and that the recurrence itself recurs ad infinitum! What does this mad myth signify?

L'Engle, Madeline *A Wrinkle In Time* It was a dark and stormy night.

Lawrence, DH *Lady Chatterley's Lover* Ours is essentially a tragic age, so we refuse to take it tragically.

Lawrence, DH *Sons and Lovers* 'The Bottoms' succeeded to 'Hell Row'.

Lawrence, DH *Women In Love* Ursula and Gudrun Brangwen sat one morning in the window-bay of their father's house in Beldover, working and talking.

Le Carré, John *The Honourable Schoolboy* Afterwards, in the dusty little corners where London's secret servants drink together, there was argument about where the Dolphin case history should really begin.

Le Carré, John *The Russia House* In a broad Moscow street not two hundred yards from the Leningrad station, on the upper floor of an ornate and hideous hotel built by Stalin in the style known to Muscovites as Empire During the Plague, the British Council's first ever audio fair for the teaching of the English language and the spread of British culture was grinding to its excruciating end.

Le Carré, John *The Spy Who Came in from the Cold* The American handed Leamas another cup of coffee and said, 'Why don't you go back and sleep? We can ring you if he shows up.'

Le Carré, John *Tinker, Tailor, Soldier, Spy* The truth is, if old Major Dover hadn't dropped dead at Taunton races Jim would never have come to Thursgood's at all.

Lee, Harper *To Kill a Mockingbird* When he was nearly thirteen, my brother Jem got his arm badly broken at the elbow.

Le Guin, Ursula *The Dispossessed* There was a wall.

Le Guin, Ursula *The Left Hand of Darkness* I'll make my report as if I told a story, for I was taught as a child on my homeworld that Truth is a matter of the imagination.

Leroux, Gaston *The Phantom of the Opera* It was the evening on which MM. Debienne and Poligny, the managers of the Opera, were giving a last gala performance to mark their retirement.

Levin, Ira *Rosemary's Baby* Rosemary and Guy Woodhouse had signed a lease on a five-room apartment in a geometric white house on First Avenue when they received word, from a woman named Mrs. Cortez, that a four-room apartment in Bramford had become available.

Lewis, CS *The Lion, the Witch and the Wardrobe* Once there were four children whose names were Peter, Susan, Edmond, and Lucy.

Lewis, CS *Surprised By Joy* I was born in the winter of 1898 at Belfast, the son of a solicitor and of a clergyman's daughter.

Lewis, Sinclair *Babbitt* The tower of Zenith aspired above the morning mist; austere towers of steel and cement and limestone, sturdy as cliffs and delicate as silver rods.

Lewis, Sinclair *Elmer Gantry* Elmer Gantry was drunk. He was eloquently drunk, lovingly and pugnaciously drunk.

Lewis, Sinclair *Main Street* This is America – a town of a few thousand, in a region of wheat and corn and dairies and little groves. The town is, in our tale, called 'Gopher Prairie, Minnesota.' But its Main Street is the continuation of Main Streets everywhere.

London, Jack *The Call of the Wild* Buck did not read the newspapers or he would have known that trouble was brewing.

Longfellow, Henry Wadsworth *The Song of Hiawatha* Should you ask me, whence these stories?

Longfellow, Henry Wadsworth 'The Village Blacksmith' Under a spreading chestnut tree The village smithy stands.

Lovecraft, HP *The Call Of Cthulhu* The most merciful thing in the world, I think, is the inability of the human mind to correlate all its contents.

Macaulay, Rose *The Towers of Trebizond* 'Take my camel dear', said my aunt Dot, as she climbed down from this animal on her return from High Mass.

McCloskey, Robert *Make Way for Ducklings* Mr. and Mrs. Mallard were looking for a place to live.

McCullers, Carson *The Heart Is a Lonely Hunter* In the town there were two mutes, and they were always together.

McCullough, Colleen *The First Man in Rome* Having no personal commitment to either of the new consuls, Gaius Julius Caesar and his son simply tacked themselves onto the procession which started nearest to their own house, the procession of the senior consul, Marcus Minucius Rufus.

McCullough, Colleen *The Thorn Birds* On December 8th, 1915, Meggie Cleary had her fourth birthday.

McCullough, Colleen *Caesar's Women* Brutus, I don't like the look of your skin. Come here to the light, please.

MacDonald, Betty *Mrs. Piggle Wiggle* I expect I might as well begin by telling you about Mrs. Piggle-Wiggle.

McEwan, Ian *Enduring Love* The beginning is simple to mark.

McKenna, Richard *The Sand Pebbles* Hello, ship, Jake Holman said under his breath.

McMillan, Terry *Waiting to Exhale* Right now I'm supposed to be all geeked up because I'm getting ready for a New Year's Eve party that some guy named Lionel invited me to.

McMurtry, Larry *Terms of Endearment* The success of a marriage invariably depends on the woman, Mrs. Greenway said.

Malamud, Bernard *The Fixer* From the small crossed window of his room above the stable in the brickyard, Yakov Bok saw people in their long overcoats running somewhere early that morning, everybody in the same direction.

Mann, Thomas *Buddenbrooks* And – and – what comes next? Oh, yes, yes, what the dickens does come next? C'est la question, ma très chère demoiselle! Frau Consul Buddenbrooks shot a glance at her husband and came to the rescue of her daughter.

Marks, Leo 'Code Poem for the French Resistance' The life that I have is all that I have, And the life that I have is yours.

Márquez, Gabriel García *One Hundred Years of Solitude* Many years later, as he faced the firing squad, Colonel Aureliano Buendía was to remember that distant afternoon when his father took him to discover ice.

Martel, Yann *Life of Pi* My suffering left me sad and gloomy.

Marvell, Andrew 'To His Coy Mistress' Had we but world enough, and time, This coyness, Lady, were no crime.

Masefield, John 'Sea-Fever' I must go down to the seas again, to the lonely sea and the sky, And all I ask is a tall ship and a star to steer her by . . .

Maugham, W Somerset *Of Human Bondage* The day broke grey and dull.

Melville, Herman *Billy Budd* In the time before steamships, or then more frequently than now, a stroller along the docks of any considerable sea-port would occasionally have his attention arrested by a group of bronzed mariners, man-of-war's men or merchant-sailors in holiday attire ashore on liberty.

Melville, Herman *Moby-Dick* Call me Ishmael.

Metalious, Grace *Peyton Place* Indian summer is like a woman. Ripe, hotly passionate, but fickle, she comes and goes as she pleases so that one is never sure whether she will come at all, nor for how long she will stay.

Michener, James A *The Source* On Tuesday the freighter steamed through the Straits of Gibraltar and for five days plowed eastward through the Mediterranean, past islands and peninsulas rich in history, so that on Saturday night the steward advised Dr. Cullinane, 'If you wish an early sight of the Holy Land you must be up at dawn.'

Miller, Henry *Tropic of Cancer* I am living at the Villa Borghese. There is not a crumb of dirt anywhere nor a chair misplaced. We are alone here and we are dead.

Miller Jr, Walter *A Canticle for Leibowitz* Brother Francis Gerard of Utah might never have discovered the blessed documents, had it not been for the pilgrim with girded loins who had appeared during that young novice's Lenten fast in the desert.

Milton, John *Lycidas* Yet once more, O ye laurels, and once more, Ye myrtles brown, with ivy never sere.

LITERATURE

Milton, John 'On His Blindness' When I consider how my light is spent, Ere half my days, in this dark world and wide.

Milton, John *Paradise Lost* Of man's first disobedience, and the fruit Of that forbidden tree, whose mortal taste Brought death into the world, and all our woe, With loss of Eden.

Mitchell, Margaret *Gone with the Wind* Scarlett O'Hara was not beautiful, but men seldom realized it when caught by her charm as the Tarleton twins were.

Montgomery, Lucy Maud *Anne of Green Gables* Mrs. Rachel Lynde lived just where the Avonlea main road dipped down into a little hollow.

Morrison, Toni *Beloved* 124 was spiteful.

Morrison, Toni *Sula* In that place, where they tore the night shade and blackberry patches from their roots to make room for the Medallion City Golf Course, there was once a neighborhood.

Nabokov, Vladimir *Lolita* Lolita, light of my life, fire of my loins.

Naylor, Gloria *The Women of Brewster Place* Brewster Place was the bastard child of several clandestine meetings between the alderman of the sixth district and the managing director of the Unico Realty Company.

Niven, Larry *Ringworld* In the night time heat of Beirut in one of a row of general address transfer booths, Louis Wu flicked into reality.

Norton, Mary *The Borrowers* It was Mrs May who first told me about them.

Oates, Joyce Carol *Because It Is Bitter, and Because It Is My Heart* Little Red Garlock, sixteen years old, skull smashed soft as a rotted pumpkin and body dumped into the Cassadaga River near the foot of Pitt Street, must not have sunk as deep as he'd been intended to sink, or floated as far.

Oates, Joyce Carol *Bellefleur* It was many years ago in that dark, chaotic, unfathomable pool of time before Germaine's birth (nearly twelve months before her birth), on a night in late September stirred by innumerable frenzied winds, like spirits contending with one another.

Oates, Joyce Carol *Expensive People* I was a child murderer.

O'Connor, Flannery *The Violent Bear It Away* Francis Marion Tarwater's uncle had been dead for only half a day when the boy got too drunk to finish digging his grave.

Orwell, George *1984* It was a bright cold day in April, and the clocks were striking thirteen.

Owen, Wilfred 'Anthem for Doomed Youth' What passing-bells for these who die as cattle?

Pasternak, Boris *Doctor Zhivago* On they went, singing 'Rest Eternal,' and whenever they stopped, their feet, the horses, and the gusts of wind seemed to carry on their singing.

Paterson, Katherine *Bridge to Terabitha* Ba-room, ba-room, ba-room, baripity, baripity, baripity, baripity – Good.

Piercy, Marge *Small Change* Beth was looking in the mirror of her mother's vanity.

Piper, Watty *The Little Engine That Could* Chug, chug, chug. Puff, puff, puff. Ding-dong, ding-dong.

Plath, Sylvia *The Bell Jar* It was a queer, sultry summer, the summer they electrocuted the Rosenbergs, and I didn't know what I was doing in New York.

Pohl, Frederik *Gateway* My name is Robinette Broadhead, in spite of which I am male.

Pope, Alexander *The Dunciad* The Mighty Mother, and her Son, who brings The Smithfield muses to the ear of kings, I sing.

Porter, Katherine Anne *Ship of Fools* August, 1931 – The port town of Veracruz is a little purgatory between land and sea.

Portis, Charles *True Grit* People do not give it credence that a fourteen-year-old girl could leave home and go off in the wintertime to avenge her father's blood.

Potok, Chaim *The Chosen* For the first fifteen years of our lives, Danny and I lived within five blocks of each other and neither of us knew of the other's existence.

Puzo, Mario *The Godfather* Amerigo Bonasera sat in New York Criminal Court Number 3 and waited for justice; vengeance on the men who had so cruelly hurt his daughter.

Pynchon, Thomas *Gravity's Rainbow* A screaming comes across the sky.

Rand, Ayn *Atlas Shrugged* Who is John Galt?.

Remarque, Erich Maria *All Quiet on the Western Front* We are five miles behind the front.

Renault, Mary *The King Must Die* The Citadel of Troizen, where the Palace stands, was built by giants before anyone remembers.

Rey, HA *Curious George* This is George. He lived in Africa.

Robbins, Tom *Even Cowgirls Get the Blues* Amoebae leave no fossils.

Robbins, Tom *Jitterbug Perfume* The beet is the most intense of vegetables.

Robbins, Tom *Still Life with Woodpecker* In the last quarter of the twentieth century, at a time when Western civilization was declining too rapidly for comfort and yet too slowly to be exciting, much of the world sat on the edge of an increasingly expensive theater seat, waiting – with various combinations of dread, hope, and ennui – for something momentous to occur.

Robinson, Marilynne *Housekeeping* My name is Ruth. I grew up with my sister, Lucille, under the care of my grandmother,.

Rölvaag, OE *Giants in the Earth* Bright, clear sky over a plain so wide that the rim of the heavens cut down on it around the entire horizon.

Roth, Philip *Portnoy's Complaint* She was so deeply imbedded in my consciousness that for the first year of school I seemed to have believed that each of my teachers was my mother in disguise.

Rushdie, Salman *The Satanic Verses* To be born again, sang Gibreel Farishta tumbling from the heavens, 'first you have to die'.

Salinger, JD *The Catcher in the Rye* If you really want to hear about it, the first thing you'll probably want to know is where I was born, and what my lousy childhood was like.

Schaefer, Jack *Shane* He rode into our valley in the summer of '89.

Scott, Paul *The Day of the Scorpion* Ex-Chief Minister Mohammed Ali Kasim was arrested at his home in Ranpur at 5am on August 9th 1942 by a senior English police officer who arrived in a car, with a motorcycle escort, two armed guards and a warrant for his detention under the Defence of India Rules.

Scott, Sir Walter *Old Mortality* 'Most Readers,' says the Manuscript of Mr Pattieson, 'must have witnessed with delight the joyous burst which attends the dismissing of a village-school on a fine summer evening.'

Sebold, Alice *The Lovely Bones* My name was Salmon, like the fish; first name, Susie.

Segal, Erich *Love Story* What can you say about a 25 year old girl who died?

Selden, George *The Cricket in Times Square* A mouse was looking at Mario. The mouse's name was Tucker.

Service, Robert *The Shooting of Dan McGrew* A bunch of the boys were whooping it up in the Malarnute saloon.

Sewell, Anna *Black Beauty* The first place that I can well remember was a large pleasant meadow with a pond of clear water in it.

Sharpe, Tom *The Midden* It was Timothy Bright's ambition to make a fortune.

Shaw, Irwin *Rich Man, Poor Man* Mr. Donnelly, the track coach, ended the day's practice early because Henry Fuller's father came down to the high-school field to tell Henry that they had just got a telegram from Washington announcing that Henry's brother had been killed in action in Germany.

Shelley, Mary *Frankenstein* You will rejoice to hear that no disaster has accompanied the commencement of an enterprise which you have regarded with such evil forebodings.

Shelley, Percy Bysshe 'Ozymandias of Egypt' I met a traveller from an antique land . . .

Sholokhov, Mikhail *And Quiet Flows the Don* The Melekhov farm was right at the end of the Tatarsk village.

Shute, Nevil *On the Beach* Lt Commander Peter Holmes of the Royal Australian Navy woke soon after dawn.

Simak, Clifford *City* Gramp Stevens sat in a lawn chair, watching the mower at work, feeling the warm, soft sunshine seep into his bones.

Simak, Clifford *Way Station* The noise was ended now. The smoke drifted like thin gray wisps of fog above the tortured earth and the shattered fences.

Sims, George R *In the Workhouse – Christmas Day* It is Christmas Day in the Workhouse.

Singer, Isaac Bashevis *Shosha* I was brought up on three dead languages – Hebrew, Aramaic, and Yiddish (some consider the last not a language at all) – and in a culture that developed in Babylon: the Talmud.

Smith, Betty *A Tree Grows in Brooklyn* Serene was a word you could put to Brooklyn, New York.

Smith, Dodie *101 Dalmatians* Not long ago, there lived in London a young married couple of Dalmatian dogs named Pongo and Misses Pongo.

Solzhenitsyn, Alexander *The Gulag Archipelago* How do people get to this clandestine Archipelago?

Sontag, Susan *Death Kit* Diddy the Good was taking a business trip.

Spencer, Scott *Endless Love* When I was seventeen and in full obedience to my heart's most urgent commands, I stepped far from the pathway of normal life and in a moment's time ruined everything I loved – I loved so deeply, and when the love was interrupted, when the incorporeal body of love shank back in terror and my own body was locked away, it was hard for others to believe that a life so new could suffer so irrevocably.

Spenser, Edmund *The Faerie Queene* A Gentle Knight was pricking on the plaine.

Steinbeck, John *Cannery Row* Cannery Row in Monterey in California is a poem, a stink, a grating noise, a quality of light, a tone, a habit, a nostalgia, a dream.

Steinbeck, John *The Grapes of Wrath* To the red country and part of the gray country of Oklahoma, the last rains came gently, and they did not cut the scarred earth.

Steinbeck, John *Of Mice and Men* A few miles south of Soledad, the Salinas River drops in close to the hill-side bank and runs deep and green.

Steinbeck, John *The Pearl* Kino awakened in the near dark.

Stevenson, Robert Louis *The Strange Case of Dr Jekyll and Mr Hyde* Mr. Utterson the lawyer was a man of a rugged countenance, that was never lighted by a smile; cold, scanty and embarrassed.

Stevenson, Robert Louis *Kidnapped* I will begin the story of my adventures with a certain morning early in the month of June, the year of grace 1751, when I took the key for the last time out of the door of my father's house.

Stevenson, Robert Louis *Treasure Island* Squire Trelawney, Dr. Livesey, and the rest of these gentlemen having asked me to write down the whole particulars about Treasure Island.

Stevenson, RL & L Osbourne *The Wrong Box* How very little does the amateur, dwelling at home at ease, comprehend the labours and perils of the author.

Stewart, Mary *The Crystal Cave* I am an old man now, but then I was already past my prime when Arthur was crowned King.

Stoker, Bram *Dracula* 3 May. Bistritz. – Left Munich at 8:35 P.M., on 1st May, arriving at Vienna early next morning; should have arrived at 6:46, but the train was an hour late. Buda-Pesth seems a wonderful place, from the glimpse which I got from the train and the little I could walk through the streets.

Stone, Irving *Lust for Life* Monsieur Van Gogh, it's time to wake up.

Stout, Rex *The Hand in Glove* It was not surprising that Sylvia Raffray, on that Saturday in September, had occasion for discourse with various men, none of them utterly ordinary, and with one remarkable young woman; it was not surprising that all this happened without any special effort on Sylvia's part, for she was rich, personable to an extreme, an orphan, and six months short of twenty-one years.

Stowe, Harriet Beecher *Uncle Tom's Cabin* Late in the afternoon of a chilly day in February, two gentlemen were sitting alone over their wine, in a well-furnished dining parlour, in the town of P——, in Kentucky.

Sturgeon, Theodore *More Than Human* The idiot lived in a black and gray world, punctuated by the white lightning of hunger and the flickering of fear.

Styron, William *The Confessions of Nat Turner* To the public – The late insurrection in Southampton has greatly excited the public mind and led to a thousand idle, exaggerated and mischievous reports.

Swift, Jonathan *Gulliver's Travels* My father had a small estate in Nottinghamshire; I was the third of five sons.

Tan, Amy *The Hundred Secret Senses* My sister Kwan believes she has yin eyes.

Tan, Amy *The Joy Luck Club* My father asked me to be the fourth corner at the Joy Luck Club.

Thackeray, William M *Vanity Fair* While the present century was in its teens, and on one sunshiny morning in June, there drove up to the great iron gate of Miss Pinkerton's academy for young ladies, on Chiswick Mall, a large family coach, with two fat horses in blazing harness, driven by a fat coachman in a three cornered hat and wig, at the rate of four miles an hour.

Theroux, Paul *The Mosquito Coast* We drove past Tiny Polski's mansion house to the main road, and then the five miles into Northampton, Father talking the whole way about savages and the awfulness of America – how it got turned into a dope-taking, door-locking, ulcerated danger zone of rabid scavengers and criminal millionaires and moral sneaks.

Thomas, Dylan *Under Milk Wood* To begin at the beginning, It is spring, moonless night in the small town, starless and bible-black . . .

Thompson, Flora *Lark Rise to Candleford* The hamlet stood on a gentle rise in the flat, wheat-growing north-east corner of Oxfordshire.

Thoreau, Henry David *Walden* When I wrote the following pages, or rather the bulk of them, I lived alone, in the woods, a mile from any neighbor, in a house which I had built myself, on the shore of Walden Pond, in Concord, Massachusetts, and earned my living by the labor of my hands only.

Thurber, James *The Thirteen Clocks* Once upon a time, in a gloomy castle on a lonely hill, where there were thirteen clocks that wouldn't go, there lived a cold, aggressive Duke, and his niece, the Princess Saralinda.

Tolkien, JRR *The Hobbit* In a hole in the ground there lived a hobbit.

Tolstoy, Leo *Anna Karenina* All happy families are alike, but an unhappy family is unhappy after its own fashion.

Tolstoy, Leo *War and Peace* Well, Prince, so Genoa and Lucca are now just family estates of the Buonapartes.

Travers, PL *Mary Poppins* If you want to find Cherry Tree Lane all you have to do is ask a policeman at the crossroads.

Twain, Mark *The Adventures of Huckleberry Finn* You don't know about me, without you have read a book by the name of *The Adventures of Tom Sawyer*, but that ain't no matter.

Twain, Mark *The Adventures of Tom Sawyer* TOM!

Tyler, Anne *Breathing Lessons* Maggie and Ira Moran had to go to a funeral in Deer Lick, Pennsylvania.

Undset, Sigrid *Kristin Lavransdatter* When the lands and goods of Ivar Gjesling the younger, of Sundbu, were divided after his death in 1306, his lands in Sil of Gudbrandsdal fell to his daughter Ragnfrid and her husband Lavrans Björngulfsön.

Updike, John *Rabbit at Rest* Standing amid the tan, excited post-Christmas crowd at the Southwest Florida Regional Airport, Rabbit Angstrom has a funny sudden feeling that what he has come to meet, what's floating in unseen about to land, is not his son Nelson and daughter-in-law Pru and their two children but something more ominous and intimately his: his own death, shaped vaguely like an airplane.

Updike, John *Rabbit Is Rich* Running out of gas, Rabbit Angstrom thinks as he stands behind the summer-dusty windows of the Springer Motors display.

Updike, John *Rabbit Redux* Men emerge pale from the little printing plant at four sharp, ghosts for an instant, blinking, until the outdoor light overcomes the look of constant indoor light clinging to them.

Updike, John *Rabbit, Run* Boys are playing basketball around a telephone pole with a backboard bolted to it.

Uris, Leon *Exodus* The airplane plip-plopped down the runway to a halt before the big sign: WELCOME TO CYPRUS.

Verne, Jules *Around the World in 80 Days* Mr Phileas Fogg lived, in 1872, at No. 7, Savile Row, Burlington Gardens, the house in which Sheridan died in 1814.

Vidal, Gore *Creation* I am blind. But I am not deaf. Becuase of the incompleteness of my misfortune, I was obliged yesterday to listen for nearly six hours to a self-styled historian whose account of what the Athenians call 'the Persian Wars' was nonsense of a sort that were I less old and more privileged, I would have risen in my seat at the Odeon and scandalized all Athens by answering him.

Vidal, Gore *Lincoln* Elihu B. Washburne opened his gold watch.

Vidal, Gore *Myra Breckinridge* I am Myra Breckinridge whom no man will ever possess.

Virgil *Aeneid* I sing of arms and the man.

Voltaire *Candide* In the country of Westphalia, in the castle of the most noble Baron of Thunder-ten-tronckh, lived a youth whom Nature had endowed with a most sweet disposition.

Vonnegut, Kurt *Breakfast of Champions* This is a tale of a meeting of two lonesome, skinny, fairly old white men on a planet which was dying fast.

Vonnegut, Kurt *Cat's Cradle* Call me Jonah.

Vonnegut, Kurt *Slapstick* To whom it may concern: It is springtime.

Vonnegut, Kurt *Slaughterhouse-Five* All this happened, more or less.

Walker, Alice *The Color Purple* You better not never tell nobody but God.

Walker, Alice *Possessing the Secret of Joy* I did not realize for a long time that I was dead.

Waller, Robert *The Bridges of Madison County* On the morning of August 8, 1965, Robert Kincaid locked the door to his small two-room apartment on the third floor of a rambling house in Bellingham, Washington.

Warren, Robert Penn *A Place To Come To* I was the only boy, or girl either, in the public school in the town of Dugton, Claxford County, Alabama, whose father had ever got killed in the middle of the night standing up in the front of his wagon to piss on the hindquarters of one of a span of mules and, being drunk, pitching forward on his head, still hanging onto his dong, and hitting the pike in such a position and condition that both the left front and left rear wheels of the wagon rolled, with perfect precision, over his unconscious neck, his having passed out being, no doubt, the reason he took the fatal plunge in the first place.

Waugh, Evelyn *Brideshead Revisited* When I reached C Company lines, which were at the top of the hill, I paused and looked back at the camp, just coming into full view before me through the grey mist of early morning.

Waugh, Evelyn *Scoop* While still a young man, John Courteney Boot had, as his publisher proclaimed, 'achieved an assured and enviable position in contemporary letters'.

Wells, HG *The Island of Doctor Moreau* I do not propose to add anything to what has already been written concerning the loss of the 'Lady Vain'.

Wells, HG *The Time Machine* The Time Traveller (for so it will be convenient to speak of him) was expounding a recondite matter to us.

Wells, HG *The War of the Worlds* No one would have believed in the last years of the nineteenth century that this world was being watched keenly and closely by intelligences greater than man's and yet as mortal as his own; that as men busied themselves about their various concerns they were scrutinised and studied, perhaps almost as narrowly as a man with a microscope might scrutinise the transient creatures that swarm and multiply in a drop of water.

Welty, Eudora *The Optimist's Daughter* A nurse held the door open for them. Judge McKelva going first, then his daughter Laurel, then his wife Fay, they walked into the windowless room where the doctor would make his examination.

Wharton, Edith *Ethan Frome* I had the story, bit by bit, from various people, and, as generally happens in such cases, each time it was a different story.

White, EB *Charlotte's Web* Where's Papa going with that ax? said Fern to her mother as they were setting the table for breakfast.

White, EB *Stuart Little* When Mrs. Frederick C. Little's second son arrived, everybody noticed that he was not much bigger than a mouse.

Wibberley, Leonard *The Mouse That Roared* The Duchy of Grand Fenwick lies in a precipitous fold of the northern Alps and embraces in its tumbling landscape portions of three valleys, a river, one complete mountain with an elevation of two thousand feet and a castle.

Wilde, Oscar *The Ballad of Reading Gaol* He did not wear his scarlet coat.

Wilde, Oscar *The Picture of Dorian Gray* The studio was filled with the rich odour of roses, and when the light summer wind stirred amidst the trees of the garden there came through the open door the heavy scent of the lilac, or the more delicate perfume of the pink-flowering thorn.

Wilder, Thornton *The Bridge of San Luis Rey* On Friday noon, July the twentieth, 1714, the finest bridge in all Peru broke and precipitated five travelers into the gulf below.

Wolfe, Thomas *You Can't Go Home Again* It was the hour of twilight on a soft spring day toward the end of April in the year of Our Lord 1929, and George Webber leaned his elbows on the sill of his back window and looked out at what he could see of New York.

Wolfe, Thomas *Look Homeward, Angel* A destiny that leads the English to the Dutch is strange enough; but one that leads from Epsom into Pennsylvania, and thence into the hills that shut in Altamont over the proud coral cry of the cock, and the soft stone smile of the angel, is touched by that dark miracle of chance which makes new magic in a dusty world.

Woolf, Virginia *Orlando* He – for there could be no doubt of his sex, though the fashion of the time did something to disguise it – was in the act of slicing at the head of a Moor which swung from the rafters.

Wordsworth, William *The Prelude* Oh there is blessing in this gentle breeze.

Wouk, Herman *The Winds of War* Commander Victor Henry rode a taxi-cab home from the Navy building on Constitution Avenue, in a gusty gray March rainstorm that matched his mood.

Wright, Richard *Native Son* Brrrrrrriiiiiiiiiiiiiiiiiiiiiiiinng! An alarm clock clanged in the dark and silent room. A bed spring creaked. A woman's voice sang out impatiently. 'Bigger, shut that thing off!'

Wyndham, John *The Day of the Triffids* When a day that you happen to know is Wednesday starts off by sounding like Sunday, there is something seriously wrong somewhere.

Wyss, Johann *The Swiss Family Robinson* For many days we had been tempest-tossed.

Yeats, WB 'When You are Old' When you are old and grey and full of sleep, And nodding by the fire, take down this book . . .

Zelazny, Roger *Lord of Light* His followers called him Mahasamatman and said he was a god. He preferred to drop the Maha- and the -atman, however, and called himself Sam.

L
I
T
E
R
A
T
U
R
E

NB: This is another section where it is only possible to list a good cross-section of works rather than a fully comprehensive catalogue. It is hoped that many of the better-known openings are included, as well as some more obscure but interesting ones. In the cases of works written in a foreign language and translated into English, the wording will vary according to the translator.

Closing Words of Books and Poems

Arnold, Matthew 'Dover Beach' Swept with confused alarms of struggle and flight, where ignorant armies clash by night.

Arnold, Matthew 'The Scholar Gipsy' Shy traffickers, the dark Iberians come, And on the beach undid his corded bales.

Asimov, Isaac *I Robot* She died last month at the age of Eighty Two.

Austen, Jane *Emma* But, in spite of these deficiencies, the wishes, the hopes, the confidence, the predictions of the small band of true friends who witnessed the ceremony, were fully answered in the perfect happiness of the union.

Austen, Jane *Lady Susan* I confess that I can pity only Miss Manwaring, who coming to town and putting herself to an expense in clothes, which impoverished her for two years, on purpose to secure him, was defrauded of her due by a woman ten years older than herself.

Austen, Jane *Mansfield Park* Fanny had never been able to approach but with some painful sensation of restraint or alarm, soon grew as dear to her heart, and as thoroughly perfect in her eyes, as everything else within the view and patronage of Mansfield Park had long been.

Austen, Jane *Northanger Abbey* I leave it to be settled by whomsoever it may concern, whether the tendency of this work be altogether to recommend parental tyranny or reward filial disobedience.

Austen, Jane *Persuasion* She gloried in being a sailor's wife, but she must pay the tax of quick alarm for belonging to that profession which is, if possible, more distinguished in its domestic virtues than in its national importance.

Austen, Jane *Pride and Prejudice* And they were both ever sensible of the warmest gratitude towards the persons who, by bringing her into Derbyshire, had been the means of uniting them.

Austen, Jane *Sanditon* It was impossible not to feel him hardly used; to be obliged to stand back in his own house and see the best place by the first constantly occupied by Sir Harry Denham.

Austen, Jane *Sense and Sensibility* Between Barton and Delaford, there was that constant communication which strong family affection would naturally dictate; and among the merits and the happiness of Elinor and Marianne, let it not be ranked as the least considerable, that though sisters and living almost within sight of each other, they could live without disagreement between themselves, or producing coolness between their husbands.

Austen, Jane *The Watsons* Emma was of course un-influenced, except to greater esteem for Elizabeth, by such representations – and the visitors departed without her.

Bellow, Saul *Henderson the Rain King* I guess I felt it was my turn now to move, and so went running – leaping, leaping, pounding, and tingling over the pure white lining of the gray Arctic silence.

Bennett, Arnold *Clayhanger* He braced himself to the exquisite burden to life.

Bennett, Arnold *The Old Wives' Tale* She glanced at the soup plate, and, on the chance that it might after all contain something worth inspection, she awkwardly balanced on her old legs and went to it again.

Brontë, Anne *Agnes Grey* And now I think I have said sufficient.

Brontë, Anne *The Tenant of Wildfell Hall* Till then, farewell, Gilbert Markham Staningley, June 10th 1847.

Brontë, Charlotte *Jane Eyre* Amen; even so come, Lord Jesus.

Brontë, Charlotte *The Professor* Papa, Come!

Brontë, Charlotte *Villette* Madame Walravens fulfilled her ninetieth year before she died. Farewell.

Brontë, Emily *Wuthering Heights* I lingered around them under that benign sky; watched the moths fluttering among the heath and harebells, listening to the soft wind breathing through the grass, and wondered how anyone could ever imagine unquiet slumbers for the sleepers in that quiet earth.

Buchan, John *The Thirty-Nine Steps* But I had done my best service, I think, before I put on khaki.

Carey, Peter *Jack Maggs* Affectionately Inscribed to Percival Clarence Buckle, A man of letters, A patron of the arts.

Carroll, Lewis *Alice's Adventures in Wonderland* And how she would feel with all their simple sorrows, and find a pleasure in all their simple joys, remembering her own child-life, and the happy summer days.

Carroll, Lewis *Through the Looking Glass* But the provoking kitten only began on the other paw, and pretended it hadn't heard the question. Which do *you* think it was?

Cervantes, Miguel de *Don Quixote* Farewell.

Clarke, Arthur C *2001* But he would think of something.

Cleland, John *Fanny Hill* I shall see you soon, and in the meantime think candidly of me, and believe me ever, madam, Yours, etc, etc, etc.

Collins, Wilkie *The Moonstone* Who can tell?

Conrad, Joseph *Lord Jim* While he waves his hand sadly at his butterflies.

Conrad, Joseph *An Outcast of the Islands* And Almayer, who stood waiting, with a smile of tipsy attention on his lips, heard no other answer.

Cookson, Catherine *The Maltese Angel* Oh, let me cry. Let me cry, my love.

Cookson, Catherine *The Year of the Virgins* Listen to me, Flo Coulson, your mother loves me. Do you hear that? Your mother loves me. Everything comes to him who waits. Your mother loves me.

Cooper, James Fenimore *The Pioneers* Who are opening the way for the march of the Nation across the Continent.

Defoe, Daniel *Robinson Crusoe* And here, resolving to harass myself no more, I am preparing for a longer journey than all these, having lived 72 years, a life of infinite variety, and learn'd sufficiently to know the value of retirement, and the blessing of ending our days in peace.

Dickens, Charles *David Copperfield* Oh Agnes, Oh my soul, so may thy face be by me when I close my life indeed; so may I, when realities are melting from me like the shadows which I now dismiss, still find thee near me, pointing upward!

Dickens, Charles *Great Expectations* And had given her a heart to understand what my heart used to be.

Dickens, Charles *Oliver Twist* These, and a thousand looks and smiles, and turns of thought and speech – I would fain recall them every one.

Dickens, Charles *Oliver Twist (supplementary)* I believe it none the less because that nook is in a church, and she was weak and erring.

Dickens, Charles *A Tale of Two Cities* It is a far, far better thing that I do, than I have ever done: it is a far, far better rest that I go to, than I have ever known.

Dostoevsky, Fyodor *Crime and Punishment* That might be the subject of a new story, but our present story is ended.

Doyle, Arthur Conan *The Hound of the Baskervilles* We can stop at Mancini's for a little dinner on the way.

Dumas, Alexander *The Three Musketeers* The opinion of those who thought themselves the best informed was that he was boarded and lodged in some royal castle at the expense of his generous eminence.

Fielding, Henry *Tom Jones* Who doth not most gratefully bless the day when Mr Jones was married to Sophia.

Greene, Graham *Brighton Rock* She walked rapidly in the thin June sunlight towards the worst horror of all.

Harris, Robert *Fatherland* Then he tugged the gun from his waistband, checked to make sure it was loaded and moved towards the silent trees.

Hartley, LP *Eustace and Hilda* But the cold crept onwards and he did not wake.

Heller, Joseph *Catch-22* The knife came down missing him by inches, and he took off.

Hughes, Thomas *Tom Brown's School Days* We can come to the knowledge of him in whom alone, the love and the tenderness, and the purity, and the strength, the courage, and the wisdom of all these, dwell for ever and ever in perfect fullness.

Huxley, Aldous *Crome Yellow* He climbed into the hearse.

Le Carré, John *The Honourable Schoolboy* And nor does Guillam, for George's sake.

Le Carré, John *The Russia House* It's going to be alright Harry, he assured me as he showed me off the premises. Tell them that. Spying is waiting.

Lewis, CS *The Lion, The Witch and The Wardrobe* But if the Professor was right it was only the beginning of the adventures of Narnia.

Lewis, Sinclair *Arrowsmith* We'll plug along on it for two or three years, and maybe we'll get something permanent – and probably we'll fail!

Longfellow, Henry Wadsworth 'The Village Blacksmith' Thus on its sounding anvil shaped Each burning deed and thought.

Longfellow, Henry Wadsworth 'The Wreck of the Hesperus' Christ saves us all from a death like this, on the reef of Norman's woe.

Lowry, Malcolm *Under the Volcano* Somebody threw a dead dog after him down the ravine.

Martel, Yann *Life of Pi* Very few castaways can claim to have survived so long at sea as Mr Patel, and none in the company of an adult Bengal tiger.

Marvell, Andrew 'To His Coy Mistress' Thus though we cannot make our Sun, stand still, yet we will make him run.

McEwan, Ian *Enduring Love* So now, Rachael said. Tell Leo as well. Say it again slowly, that thing about the river.

Melville, Herman *Billy Budd* I am sleepy, and the oozy weeds about me twist.

Milton, John *On His Blindness* They also serve who only stand and wait.

Mitchell, Margaret *Gone With the Wind* After all, Tomorrow is another day.

O'Brien, Flann *At Swim-Two-Birds* He went home one evening and drank three cups of tea with three lumps of sugar in each, cut his jugular with a razor three times and scrawled with a dying hand on a picture of his wife, goodbye, goodbye, goodbye.

Scott, Paul *The Day of the Scorpion* She closed her eyes as perhaps Susan was doing, even now, and after a while felt the quietness of her own happiness and grace welling up inside her; and smiled, ignoring the rain that seemed to be falling on her face.

Service, Robert 'The Shooting of Dan McGrew' The woman that kissed him and pinched his poke, was the lady that's known as Lou.

Sewell, Anna *Black Beauty* I am still in the orchard at Birtwick standing with my old friends under the apple trees.

Shaw, Irwin *The Young Lions* Because he knew he had to deliver Noah Ackerman, personally, to Captain Green.

Solzhenitsyn, Alexander *One Day in the Life of Ivan Denisovich* The three extra days were because of the leap years.

Steel, Danielle *Kaleidoscope* He held her tightly in his arms and she knew he was telling the truth. 'Everything's going to be all right now.'

Steel, Danielle *Star* Home at last. Together.

Swift, Jonathan *Gulliver's Travels* And therefore, I here entreat those who have any tincture of this absurd vice, that they will not presume to appear in my sight.

Thompson, Flora *Lark Rise to Candleford* They were spun of love and kinship and cherished memories.

Tolstoy, Leo *War and Peace* In the present case, it is an essential to surmount a consciousness of an unreal freedom and to recognise a dependence not perceived by our senses.

Tremain, Rose *Restoration* Before I have grown too frail to climb the stairs – I shall bring you back.

Twain, Mark *The Adventures of Tom Sawyer* And if I git to be a reg'lar ripper of a robber, and everybody talking 'bout it, I reckon she'll be proud she snaked me in out of the wet.

Waugh, Evelyn *Brideshead Revisited* 'You're looking unusually cheerful today,' said the second-in-command.

Wilde, Oscar *The Ballad of Reading Gaol* The coward does it with a kiss, The brave man with a sword.

Wood, Mrs Henry *East Lynne* Oh Barbara, never forget – never forget that the only way to ensure peace in the end, is to strive always to be doing right, unselfishly, under God.

Wyndham, John *The Day of the Triffids* Until we have wiped the last one of them from the face of the land they have usurped.

L I T E R A T U R E

NB: This section is much shorter than the opening lines, merely because closing lines tend to be less memorable than opening lines, and consequently, rarely crop up in any form of quiz.

Index of Books (in title order)

(* denotes author's first book)

Book	Author	Book	Author
An American Tragedy	Theodore Dreiser	The Borrowers	Mary Norton
An Evil Cradling	Brian Keenan	The Bostonians	Henry James
And Quiet Flows the Don	Mikhail Sholokhov	The Bottle Factory Outing	Beryl Bainbridge
Angel Pavement	JB Priestley	The Box of Delights	John Masefield
Angela's Ashes	Frank McCourt	Boyhood	Leo Tolstoy
Angels & Demons	Dan Brown	The Boys from Brazil	Ira Levin
Animal Farm	George Orwell	Branded Man	Catherine Cookson
Anna Karenina	Leo Tolstoy	Brave New World	Aldous Huxley
Anna of the Five Towns	Arnold Bennett	Bravo Two Zero	Andy McNab
Anne of Green Gables*	LM Montgomery	Breakfast at Tiffany's	Truman Capote
Antic Hay	Aldous Huxley	Breaking Hearts	Simon Gray
Any Old Iron	Anthony Burgess	The Bride of Lammermoor	Walter Scott
Appassionata	Jilly Cooper	Brideshead Revisited	Evelyn Waugh
Armageddon	Leon Uris	The Bridesmaid	Ruth Rendell
Around the World in 80 Days	Jules Verne	The Bridge of San Luis Rey	Thornton Wilder
As I Lay Dying	William Faulkner	The Bridge on the River Kwai	Pierre Boulle
At Mrs Lippincote's*	Elizabeth Taylor	The Bridges of Madison	Robert James Waller
Atlas Shrugged	Ayn Rand	County	
Atonement	Ian McEwan	Bridget Jones's Diary:	Helen Fielding
August 1914	Alexander	A Novel	
	Solzhenitsyn	A Brief History of Time	Stephen Hawking
The Awakening	Kate Chopin	Brigadier Gerard, The Exploits of	Arthur Conan Doyle
An Awfully Big Adventure	Beryl Bainbridge	Brighton Rock	Graham Greene
The Bad Place	Dean R Koontz	The British Museum Is Falling	David Lodge
The Ballad of Peckham Rye	Muriel Spark	Down	
The Ballad of the Sad Café	Carson McCullers	Broca's Brain	Carl Sagan
Bambi	Felix Salten	The Broker	John Grisham
Barchester Towers	Anthony Trollope	The Brothers Karamazov	Fyodor Dostoyevsky
Barnaby Rudge	Charles Dickens	The Buccaneers	Edith Wharton
Baron Münchhausen	RE Raspe	Buddenbrooks*	Thomas Mann
The Battle of the Books	Jonathan Swift	The Buddha of Suburbia	Hanif Kureishi
The Beach	Alex Garland	Bulldog Drummond	Herman Cyril McNeile
Beasts and Superbeasts	Hector Hugh Munro		(Sapper)
	(Saki)	Busman's Honeymoon	Dorothy L Sayers
Beau Geste	PC Wren	The Cabala*	Thornton Wilder
The Beautiful and Damned	F Scott Fitzgerald	Cakes and Ale	William Somerset
The Beauty Myth	Naomi Wolf		Maugham
Behind the Scenes at the	Kate Atkinson	Call for the Dead*	John Le Carré
Museum		Call of the Wild	Jack London
Belinda	Maria Edgeworth	The Call of Wings	Agatha Christie
The Bell Jar	Sylvia Plath	Camilla	Fanny Burney
Beloved	Toni Morrison	The Camomile Lawn	Mary Wesley
Bend in the River	VS Naipaul	Campbell's Kingdom	Ralph Hammond
Bend Sinister	Vladimir Nabokov		Innes
Ben Hur	Lew Wallace	Cancer Ward	Alexander
Best Friends	Jacqueline Wilson		Solzhenitsyn
Beware of Pity	Stefan Zweig	Candide	Voltaire
The BFG	Roald Dahl	The Canterbury Tales	Geoffrey Chaucer
Biggles	Capt. WE Johns	The Captain and the Kings	Taylor Caldwell
The Big Sleep	Raymond Chandler	Captain Corelli's Mandolin	Louis de Bernières
Big Sur	Jack Kerouac	Captain Slaughterboard	Mervyn Peake
Billy Budd	Herman Melville	Drops Anchor*	
Billy Bunter	Frank Richards	The Carpetbaggers	Harold Robbins
Billy Liar	Keith Waterhouse	The Carpet People*	Terry Pratchett
Birds of Prey	Wilbur Smith	The Case of the Velvet Claws	Earl Stanley Gardner
Birdsong	Sebastian Faulks	The Castle	Franz Kafka
Black Ajax	George MacDonald	The Castle of Otranto	Horace Walpole
	Fraser	Castle Rackrent*	Maria Edgeworth
Black Beauty	Anna Sewell	The Casuarina Tree	William Somerset
The Black Prince	Iris Murdoch		Maugham
The Black Stallion	Walter Farley	Cat and Mouse	Günther Grass
The Blinder	Barry Hines	Catch-22	Joseph Heller
Bliss, and other stories	Katherine Mansfield	The Catcher in the Rye*	JD Salinger
The Bloody Ground	Bernard Cornwell	Catherine Herself*	James Hilton
Blott on the Landscape	Tom Sharpe	Catriona	Robert Louis
The Blue Angel	Heinrich Mann		Stevenson
Bluebeard	Charles Perrault	The Cauldron	Colin Forbes
Bondage of Love	Catherine Cookson	Cause Celeb	Helen Fielding
The Bonfire of the Vanities	Tom Wolfe	The Caves of Steel	Isaac Asimov
Bonjour Tristesse	Françoise Sagan	Cecilia	Fanny Burney
The Book of Nonsense	Edward Lear	A Celebration of Mass	Pope John Paul II

Book	Author	Book	Author
The Celestine Prophecy	James Redfield	Dangerous Love	Ben Okri
Central Line (short story)	Maeve Binchy	The Dangling Man*	Saul Bellow
Centuries	Nostradamus	Daniel Deronda	George Eliot
A Certain Justice	PD James	Dark Carnival*	Ray Bradbury
Charity	Len Deighton	The Dark Frontier*	Eric Ambler
Charlie and the Chocolate Factory	Roald Dahl	Darkness at Noon	Arthur Koestler
		Dark Shadows Falling	Joe Simpson
Charlotte's Friends	Sarah Kennedy	The Darling Buds of May	HE Bates
Chatterton	Peter Ackroyd	David Copperfield	Charles Dickens
Chérie	Colette	The Da Vinci Code	Dan Brown
Childhood	Leo Tolstoy	The Day of the Jackal	Frederick Forsyth
Childhood	Maxim Gorky	The Day of the Locust	Nathanael West
Children of the New Forest	Capt. Frederick Marryat	The Day of the Triffids*	John Wyndham
		A Dead Cert	Dick Francis
The Children of Violence	Doris Lessing	Dead Man Walking	Sister Helen Prejean
Child Whispers*	Enid Blyton	Dead Souls	Nikolai Gogol
Chitty Chitty Bang Bang	Ian Fleming	Death Comes for the Archbishop	Willa Cather
Chocolat	Joanne Harris		
Chomolungma Sings the Blues	Ed Douglas	Death in the Afternoon	Ernest Hemingway
		Death in Venice	Thomas Mann
Christmas Carol, A	Charles Dickens	Death Is Now My Neighbour	Colin Dexter
Chronicles of Thomas Covenant	Stephen Donaldson	The Decameron	Giovanni Boccaccio
		Deception Point	Dan Brown
Cider With Rosie	Laurie Lee	Decline and Fall*	Evelyn Waugh
The Citadel	AJ Cronin	The Decline and Fall of the Roman Empire	Edward Gibbon
The City and the Stars	Arthur C Clarke		
Clarissa	Samuel Richardson	Deliverance	James Dickey
Claudia	Arnold Zweig	Demon Seed	Dean Koontz
Claudine (series)	Colette	Denis Duval (unfinished)	WM Thackeray
Clayhanger	Arnold Bennett		
A Clockwork Orange	Anthony Burgess	The Descent of Man	Charles Darwin
The Cloister and the Hearth	Charles Reade	Desperate Remedies*	Thomas Hardy
Close Relations	Deborah Moggach	Desperation	Stephen King
Coastliners	Joanne Harris	The Devil Rides Out	Dennis Wheatley
Cocaine Nights	JG Ballard	The Devils of Loudun	Aldous Huxley
Cold Mountain	Charles Frazier	The Dharma Bums	Jack Kerouac
The Collector	John Fowles	Diana: Her New Life	Andrew Morton
Colonel Sun	Robert Markham	The Diary of a Madman	Nikolai Gogol
The Color Purple	Alice Walker	The Diary of Anne Frank	Anne Frank
La Comédie Humaine	Honoré de Balzac	The Diary of a Nobody	George and Weedon Grossmith
The Comforters	Muriel Spark		
The Commitments*	Roddy Doyle	Digital Fortress*	Dan Brown
Common Sense	Thomas Paine	Discworld	Terry Pratchett
Confessions of an English Opium Eater	Thomas De Quincey	Doctor Doolittle	Hugh Lofting
		Doctor Faustus	Thomas Mann
Coningsby	Benjamin Disraeli	Doctor Kildare	Max Brand
A Cool Million	Nathanael West	Doctor Sax	Jack Kerouac
Coral Island	RM Ballantyne	Doctor Zhivago	Boris Pasternak
The Corridors of Power	CP Snow	The Dog It Was That Died*	Alan Coren
The Count of Monte Cristo	Alexandre Dumas (Père)	The Dogs of War	Frederick Forsyth
		Dog Years	Günther Grass
The Country Diary of an Edwardian Lady	Edith Holden	Don Quixote	Miguel Cervantes
		The Doors of Perception	Aldous Huxley
The Country Girls	Edna O'Brien	Double Act	Jacqueline Wilson
Cover Her Face*	PD James	Double Indemnity	James M Cain
Cranford	Mrs Elizabeth Gaskell	Down Among the Women	Fay Weldon
		Down and Out in Paris and London	George Orwell
Credo	Melvyn Bragg		
Crime and Punishment	Fyodor Dostoyevsky	Dracula	Bram Stoker
The Crocodile Bird	Ruth Rendell	Dracula Unbound	Brian Aldiss
Crome Yellow	Aldous Huxley	The Dream Life of Balso Snell	Nathanael West
Cross of St George	Alexander Kent	The Dream Merchants*	Harold Robbins
The Cruel Sea	Nicholas Monsarrat	The Dressmaker	Beryl Bainbridge
Cry, the Beloved Country	Alan Paton	The Drowned World*	JG Ballard
A Cure for Cancer	Michael Moorcock	The Dubliners	James Joyce
Curtain	Agatha Christie	Dune	Frank Herbert
Daisy Miller	Henry James	Eagle Has Landed	Jack Higgins
Dame's Delight*	Margaret Forster	Earthly Powers	Anthony Burgess
A Dance to the Music of Time (12 volumes)	Anthony Powell	East of Eden	John Steinbeck
		Eating People Is Wrong*	Malcolm Bradbury
Dangerous Davies	Leslie Thomas	Eats, Shoots & Leaves	Lynne Truss

LITERATURE

Book	Author	Book	Author
Ecstasy	Irvine Welsh	For Want of a Nail*	Melvyn Bragg
The Eleventh Commandment	Jeffrey Archer	For Whom the Bell Tolls	Ernest Hemingway
Emily	Jilly Cooper	Foucault's Pendulum	Umberto Eco
Eminent Victorians	Lytton Strachey	The Foundation Trilogy	Isaac Asimov
Emma	Jane Austen	The Fourth Estate	Jeffrey Archer
Empire of the Sun	JG Ballard	The Fourth Protocol	Frederick Forsyth
The End of Alice	AM Homes	The Foxglove Saga*	Auberon Waugh
Enduring Love	Ian McEwan	Framley Parsonage	Anthony Trollope
Enemies of the System	Brian Aldiss	Frankenstein*	Mary Shelley
The English Assassin	Michael Moorcock	Frankenstein Unbound	Brian Aldiss
English Journey	Beryl Bainbridge	The French Lieutenant's	John Fowles
The English Patient	Michael Ondaatje	Woman	
Erewhon	Samuel Butler	Frenchman's Creek	Daphne Du Maurier
Esther Waters	George Moore	From Doon with Death*	Ruth Rendell
Ethan Frome	Edith Wharton	From Here to Eternity	James Jones
Eugene Onegin	Alexander Pushkin	Full Circle: A Pacific Journey	Michael Palin
Evelina*	Fanny Burney	Funeral in Berlin	Len Deighton
Evening Class	Maeve Binchy	Fungus the Bogeyman	Raymond Briggs
Evening in Byzantium	Irwin Shaw	Furnace	Muriel Gray
Every Man for Himself	Beryl Bainbridge	The Game	AS Byatt
Excalibur	Bernard Cornwell	Game, Set and Match	Len Deighton
The Executioner's Song	Norman Mailer	Gamesmanship	Stephen Potter
Executive Orders	Tom Clancy	The Garden of Eden	Ernest Hemingway
Exodus	Leon Uris	The Garden Party & Other	Katherine Mansfield
The Exorcist	William Peter Blatty	Stories	
The Expedition of	Tobias Smollett	Gargantua	François Rabelais
Humphrey Clinker		The Garrick Year	Margaret Drabble
Eyeless in Gaza	Aldous Huxley	Gaudy Night	Dorothy L Sayers
Eye of the Tiger	Wilbur Smith	Gentlemen Marry Brunettes	Anita Loos
Fahrenheit 451	Ray Bradbury	Gentlemen Prefer Blondes	Anita Loos
Fair Stood the Wind for	HE Bates	George's Marvellous Medicine	Roald Dahl
France		Georgy Girl	Margaret Forster
A Fairytale of New York	JP Donleavy	Germinal	Émile Zola
Faith	Len Deighton	Get Shorty	Elmore Leonard
'The Fall of the House of	Edgar Allan Poe	Ghost	Danielle Steele
Usher'		The Ghost in the Machine	Arthur Koestler
Fame Is the Spur	Howard Spring	The Ghost Road	Pat Barker
Famous Five	Enid Blyton	Gigi	Colette
Fanfarlo	Charles Baudelaire	Gil Blas	Alain Le Sage
Fanny Hill	John Cleland	The Ginger Man*	JP Donleavy
Fanshawe*	Nathaniel Hawthorne	Giovanni's Room	James Baldwin
Farewell, My Lovely	Raymond Chandler	The Gladiators	Arthur Koestler
A Farewell to Arms	Ernest Hemingway	The Glass Bead Game	Herman Hesse
Far from the Madding Crowd	Thomas Hardy	The Glass Key	Dashiell Hammett
The Fatal Englishman	Sebastian Faulks	Glubbslyme*	Jacqueline Wilson
Father Brown stories	GK Chesterton	The Go-Between	LP Hartley
Fathers and Sons	Ivan Turgenev	The Godfather	Mario Puzo
The Fat Woman's Joke*	Fay Weldon	The God of Small Things	Arundhati Roy
Fear and Loathing in Las	Hunter S Thompson	God's Little Acre	Erskine Caldwell
Vegas		The Golden Apples of the	Ray Bradbury
Fear Is the Key	Alistair MacLean	Sun	
Fear of Flying	Erica Jong	The Golden Bowl	Henry James
Feet of Clay	Terry Pratchett	Gone With the Wind	Margaret Mitchell
Felix Holt	George Eliot	Goodbye Mr Chips	James Hilton
Felix in the Underworld	John Mortimer	Goodbye to Berlin	Christopher
Fever Pitch*	Nick Hornby		Isherwood
The Fiend's Delight	Ambrose Bierce	The Good Companions	JB Priestley
Fifty Years of Europe	Jan Morris	The Good Earth	Pearl Buck
Filthy Lucre	Beryl Bainbridge	The Good Soldier Svejk	Jaroslav Hasek
The Final Programme	Michael Moorcock	Good Wives	Louisa May Alcott
Finnegans Wake	James Joyce	The Gormenghast Trilogy	Mervyn Peake
First Among Equals	Jeffrey Archer	Go Tell It on the Mountain	James Baldwin
The First Circle	Alexander	Grapefruit	Yoko Ono
	Solzhenitsyn	The Grapes of Wrath	John Steinbeck
First Love, Last Rites*	Ian McEwan	The Grass is Singing*	Doris Lessing
First Men in the Moon	HG Wells	Gravity's Rainbow	Thomas Pynchon
The Fisher King	Anthony Powell	Great Apes	Will Self
Flanimals*	Ricky Gervais	Great Expectations	Charles Dickens
The Flute-Player	DM Thomas	The Great Fire of London*	Peter Ackroyd
The Fog	James Herbert	The Great Gatsby	F Scott Fitzgerald
Forsyte Saga	John Galsworthy	The Green Hat	Michael Arlen

LITERATURE

Book	Author
King Solomon's Ring	Konrad Lorenz
A Kiss Before Dying	Ira Levin
The Kraken Wakes	John Wyndham
Lace	Shirley Conran
La Chartreuse de Parme	Stendhal
Lady Chatterley's Lover	DH Lawrence
The Lady in the Lake	Raymond Chandler
The Lady of the Camellias	Alexander Dumas (Fils)
The Lark	Edith Nesbit
Lark Rise to Candleford	Flora Thompson
The Last Continent	Terry Pratchett
The Last Days of Pompeii	Edward Bulwer-Lytton
The Last Enemy	Richard Hillary
The Last Juror	John Grisham
The Last of the Mohicans	James Fenimore Cooper
Last Orders	Graham Swift
The Last Testament of Oscar Wilde	Peter Ackroyd
The Last Tycoon	F Scott Fitzgerald
La Symphonie Pastorale	André Gide
Leather-Stocking stories	James Fenimore Cooper
The Legend of Sleepy Hollow	Washington Irving
Le Rouge et le Noir	Stendhal
Les Misérables	Victor Hugo
The Liar	Stephen Fry
The Life and Loves of a She-Devil	Fay Weldon
Life at the Top	John Braine
The Life of Charlotte Brontë	Mrs Elizabeth Gaskell
Light a Penny Candle*	Maeve Binchy
The Light That Failed	Rudyard Kipling
Lily Hart	Charlotte Brontë
The Lion and the Unicorn	George Orwell
The Lion, the Witch and the Wardrobe	CS Lewis
Little Book of Calm	Paul Wilson
Little Dorritt	Charles Dickens
The Little Drummer Girl	John Le Carré
Little Lord Fauntleroy	Frances Hodgson Burnett
Little Men	Louisa May Alcott
The Little Minister	JM Barrie
Little Red Riding Hood	Charles Perrault
Little Women	Louisa May Alcott
Liza of Lambeth*	William Somerset Maugham
Lola Rose	Jacqueline Wilson
Lolita	Vladimir Nabokov
London: The Novel	Edward Rutherfurd
The Loneliness of the Long-Distance Runner	Alan Sillitoe
The Long and the Short and the Tall	Willis Hall
Long Walk to Freedom	Nelson Mandela
Longitude	Dava Sobel
Looking for Mr Goodbar	Judith Rossner
The Looking-Glass War	John Le Carré
The Loom of Youth*	Alec Waugh
Lord Jim	Joseph Conrad
Lord of the Flies*	William Golding
The Lord of the Rings (Trilogy)	JRR Tolkien
Lorna Doone	RD Blackmore
Lost Continent: Travels in Small Town America	Bill Bryson
Lost Horizon	James Hilton

Book	Author
The Lost World of the Kalahari	Laurens Van Der Post
The Lost World	Michael Crichton
The Lost World	Arthur Conan Doyle
Love in a Cold Climate	Nancy Mitford
Love in Another Town	Barbara Taylor Bradford
Love in the Time of Cholera	Gabriel García Márquez
Love on the Dole	Walter Greenwood
Love Story	Eric Segal
The L-Shaped Room	Lynne Reid Banks
The Luck of Barry Lyndon	WM Thackeray
Lucky Jim*	Kingsley Amis
Lust for Life	Irving Stone
The Macdermots of Ballycloran*	Anthony Trollope
Madame Bovary	Gustave Flaubert
Mad Cows	Kathy Lette
Made in America	Bill Bryson
The Magic Mountain	Thomas Mann
The Magus	John Fowles
The Maid of Buttermere	Melvyn Bragg
Maigret	Georges Simenon
Making History	Stephen Fry
The Maltese Falcon	Dashiell Hammett
The Man from the North*	Arnold Bennett
A Man Lay Dead*	Ngaio Marsh
The Man Who Listens to Horses	Monty Roberts
Man Who Was Thursday	GK Chesterton
The Man Who Watched the Trains Go By	Georges Simenon
Manhattan Transfer	John Dos Passos
Mansfield Park	Jane Austen
The Martian	George Du Maurier
Martin Chuzzlewit*	Charles Dickens
Mary Barton*	Elizabeth Gaskell
The Mary Deare	Ralph Hammond Innes
Mary Poppins	PL Travers
The Mask of Dimitrios	Eric Ambler
Maskerade	Terry Pratchett
Master and Commander	Patrick O'Brian
The Master and Margarita	Mikhail Bulgakov
Matilda	Roald Dahl
The Mayor of Casterbridge	Thomas Hardy
Meet the Tiger	Leslie Charteris
Melincourt	Thomas Love Peacock
Memoirs of a Fox-Hunting Man	Siegfried Sassoon
The Memory Game	Nicci French
Men Are from Mars, Women Are from Venus	John Gray
Men at Arms	Terry Pratchett
Message from Malaga	Helen MacInnes
The Metamorphosis	Franz Kafka
Metroland	Julian Barnes
The Midden	Tom Sharpe
Midnight Cowboy	James Herlihy
Midnight's Children	Salman Rushdie
The Midwich Cuckoos	John Wyndham
Miguel Street	VS Naipaul
Mildred Pierce	James M Cain
The Mill on the Floss	George Eliot
Miss Lonelyhearts	Nathanael West
Moby-Dick	Herman Melville
Moll Flanders	Daniel Defoe
A Month in the Country	Ivan Turgenev
The Moon and Sixpence	William Somerset Maugham

LITERATURE

Book	Author	Book	Author
Poldark	Winston Graham	Riotous Assembly*	Tom Sharpe
Popcorn	Ben Elton	Rip Van Winkle	Washington Irving
Porterhouse Blue	Tom Sharpe	Rites of Passage	William Golding
Portnoy's Complaint	Philip Roth	Road Rage	Ruth Rendell
The Portrait of a Lady	Henry James	The Roads to Freedom (Trilogy)	Jean-Paul Sartre
Portrait of the Artist as a Young Dog	Dylan Thomas	The Road to Wigan Pier	George Orwell
		Robinson Crusoe	Daniel Defoe
Portrait of the Artist as a Young Man	James Joyce	Rob Roy	Walter Scott
		Rockets Galore	Compton Mackenzie
The Poseidon Adventure	Paul Gallico	The Adventures of Roderick Random	Tobias Smollett
Possession	AS Byatt		
The Postman Always Rings Twice	James M Cain	Rogue Justice	Geoffrey Household
		Rogue Male	Geoffrey Household
The Power and the Glory	Graham Greene	Romola	George Eliot
Prater Violet	Christopher Isherwood	Rookwood	William Harrison Ainsworth
A Prayer for Owen Meany	John Irving	Room at the Top	John Braine
Precaution*	James Fenimore Cooper	A Room with a View	EM Forster
		Rosemary's Baby	Ira Levin
Prelude	Katherine Mansfield	Runaway Jury	John Grisham
Prelude to Space*	Arthur C Clarke	Rupert of Hentzau	Anthony Hope
The President's Daughter	Jack Higgins	Rural Rides	William Cobbett
Prester John	John Buchan	The Sailor Who Fell from Grace with the Sea	Yukio Mishima
Pretend You Don't See Her	Mary Higgins Clark		
Pride and Prejudice	Jane Austen	The Saint	Leslie Charteris
The Prime of Miss Jean Brodie	Muriel Spark	Salammbô	Gustave Flaubert
		Salar the Salmon	Henry Williamson
Prime Time	Joan Collins	Salmagundi	Washington Irving
The Prince	Niccolò Machiavelli	Sard Harker	John Masefield
Princess Daisy	Judith Krantz	The Satanic Verses	Salman Rushdie
Princess in Love	Anna Pasternak	Saturday	Ian McEwan
The Prisoner of Zenda	Anthony Hope	Saturday Night and Sunday Morning*	Alan Sillitoe
The Professor	Charlotte Brontë		
Promiscuities	Naomi Wolf	Say Cheese and Die Again!	RL Stine
Prozac Nation	Elizabeth Wurtzel	The Scarlatti Inheritance	Robert Ludlum
Psychology, the Science of Mind and Behaviour	Richard D Gross	The Scarlet Letter	Nathaniel Hawthorne
		The Scarlet Pimpernel	Baroness Orczy
Public Good	Thomas Paine	The Screwtape Letters	CS Lewis
Puss in Boots	Charles Perrault	The Sea, The Sea	Iris Murdoch
A Question of Proof	Rex Stout	Sea-Wolf	Jack London
A Question of Upbringing (first of A Dance to the Music of Time)	Anthony Powell	The Second Sex	Simone de Beauvoir
		Secret Diary of Adrian Mole Aged 13¾*	Sue Townsend
Quo Vadis	Henry Sienkiewicz	The Secret Garden	Frances Hodgson Burnett
Rabbit Tetralogy	John Updike		
The Radiant Way	Margaret Drabble	The Secret Life of Walter Mitty	James Thurber
Raffles	EW Hornung	The Secret Seven	Enid Blyton
The Ragged Trousered Philanthropists	Robert Tressell	The Seed and the Sower	Laurens Van Der Post
The Ragman's Daughter	Alan Sillitoe	Seize the Day	Saul Bellow
The Railway Children	Edith Nesbit	The Selfish Gene	Richard Dawkins
The Rainbow	DH Lawrence	Sense and Sensibility*	Jane Austen
The Rainmaker	John Grisham	The Sentinel	Arthur C Clarke
Raj Quartet	Paul Scott	Seventh Avenue	Norman Bogner
The Rats	James Herbert	79 Park Avenue	Harold Robbins
The Razor's Edge	William Somerset Maugham	Shadow Baby	Margaret Forster
		Shadow of a Sun*	AS Byatt
Rebecca	Daphne Du Maurier	Sharpe's Devil	Bernard Cornwell
The Red Badge of Courage	Stephen Crane	She	Henry Rider Haggard
The Remains of the Day	Kazuo Ishiguro		
Remembrance Day	Brian Aldiss	The Shipping News	E Annie Proulx
Remembrance of Things Past (novel cycle in 7 parts)	Marcel Proust	Shogun	James Clavell
		A Short History of Nearly Everything	Bill Bryson
Remote Control*	Andy McNab		
The Return of the Native	Thomas Hardy	Shout at the Devil	Wilbur Smith
The Rhinemann Exchange	Robert Ludlum	The Sign of Four	Arthur Conan Doyle
Riceyman Steps	Arnold Bennett	Silas Marner	George Eliot
Riders of the Purple Sage	Zane Grey	The Silence of the Lambs	Thomas Harris
Right Ho, Jeeves	PG Wodehouse	The Silmarillion	JRR Tolkien
The Rights of Man	Thomas Paine	The Simisola	Ruth Rendell
Ring of Bright Water	Gavin Maxwell	Sins	Judith Gould

LITERATURE

Book	Author	Book	Author
Typee*	Herman Melville	What's Become of Waring?	Anthony Powell
Ulysses	James Joyce	What's Bred in the Bone	Robertson Davies
The Unbearable Bassington	Hector Hugh Munro (Saki)	Wheels	Arthur Hailey
		When Eight Bells Toll	Alistair Maclean
The Unbearable Lightness of Being	Milan Kundera	When the Lion Feeds*	Wilbur Smith
		When the Wind Blows	Raymond Briggs
Uncle Remus stories	Joel Chandler Harris	Where Eagles Dare	Alistair Maclean
Uncle Tom's Cabin	Harriet Beecher Stowe	Whisky Galore	Compton Mackenzie
		The White Company	Arthur Conan Doyle
Under the Greenwood Tree	Thomas Hardy	White Eagles Over Serbia	Lawrence Durrell
Under the Net*	Iris Murdoch	White Fang	Jack London
Under the Volcano	Malcolm Lowry	The White Hotel	DM Thomas
Under Western Eyes	Joseph Conrad	The White Peacock*	DH Lawrence
Unnatural Exposure	Patricia Cornwell	Whose Body?	Dorothy L Sayers
The Upstart	Catherine Cookson	A Wide Field	Günther Grass
Utopia	Thomas More	Wild Swans	Jung Chang
V	Thomas Pynchon	Wilhelm Meister's Apprenticeship	Johann Goethe
Valperga	Mary Shelley	Wilhelm Meister's Travels	Johann Goethe
The Van	Roddy Doyle	Wilt	Tom Sharpe
Vanity Fair: A Novel Without a Hero	WM Thackeray	The Wind in the Willows	Kenneth Grahame
		A Window in Thrums	JM Barrie
Vathek	William Beckford	The Winds of War	Herman Wouk
Vicar of Wakefield	Oliver Goldsmith	Winnie-the-Pooh	AA Milne
Vicky Angel	Jacqueline Wilson	Winnie-the-Pooh: Now We Are Six	AA Milne
Victory	John Williams		
Villette	Charlotte Brontë	Winsome Winnie	Stephen Leacock
The Virginians	WM Thackeray	The Witches of Eastwick	John Updike
The Virgin Soldiers*	Leslie Thomas	The Witching Hour	Anne Rice
A Vision of Battlements*	Anthony Burgess	With These Hands	Pam Ayers
Visitors	Anita Brookner	Witness for the Prosecution	Agatha Christie
Vivien Grey*	Benjamin Disraeli	The Woman in White	Wilkie Collins
The Voyage Out*	Virginia Woolf	The Woman Who Walked into Doors	Roddy Doyle
Walden, or Life in the Woods	Henry Thoreau		
War and Peace	Leo Tolstoy	Women in Love	DH Lawrence
The Warden	Anthony Trollope	The Wonderful Adventures of	Selma Lagerlöf Nils
The War of the Worlds	HG Wells	Worrals of the WAAF	Capt. WE Johns
Washington Square	Henry James	Worst Fears	Fay Weldon
The Wasp Factory	Iain Banks	A Wreath of Roses	Elizabeth Taylor
The Water-Babies	Charles Kingsley	Wreckers Must Breathe	Ralph Hammond Innes
Watership Down	Richard Adams		
Waverley	Walter Scott	Wuthering Heights	Emily Brontë
The Way of All Flesh	Samuel Butler	The X Files	Les Martin
A Weekend with Claud*	Beryl Bainbridge	A Year in Cricklewood	Alan Coren
Weir of Hermiston	Robert Louis Stevenson	A Year in Provence	Peter Mayall
		Year of the Tiger	Jack Higgins
The Well of Loneliness	Radcliffe Hall	The Young Fur Traders	RM Ballantyne
Westward Ho!	Charles Kingsley	The Young Man*	Stephen Potter
What America Means to Me	Pearl Buck	Youth	Leo Tolstoy
What Did You Do in the War, Mummy	Mavis Nicholson	Zen and the Art of Motorcycle Maintenance	Robert Pirsig
What Katy Did	Susan Coolidge		

NB: The list above is a good cross-section of popular works, but by no means comprehensive. Many popular books are included and some interesting less-known works. For ease of reference, the list is re-sorted below by author.

Index of Books By Author

(* denotes author's first book)

Author	Book	Author	Book
Paul Ableman	I Hear Voices	Richard Adams	Watership Down
Peter Ackroyd	Chatterton	William Harrison Ainsworth	Rookwood
	The Great Fire of London*	Louisa May Alcott	Little Men
	Hawksmoor		Good Wives
	The Last Testament of Oscar Wilde		Little Women
Douglas Adams	Hitchhiker's Guide to the Galaxy*	Brian Aldiss	Dracula Unbound
			Enemies of the System
			Frankenstein Unbound

Author	Book	Author	Book
	Greybeard	Aphra Behn	Oroonoko
	Helliconia Trilogy	William Beckford	Vathek
	Non-Stop	Saul Bellow	The Actual
	Remembrance Day		Dangling Man*
Eric Ambler	The Dark Frontier*		Seize the Day
	The Mask of Dimitrios		Herzog
Kingsley Amis	Jake's Thing		Humboldt's Gift
	Lucky Jim*	Peter Benchley	Jaws
	The Old Devils	Arnold Bennett	Riceyman Steps
	One Fat Englishman		Anna of the Five Towns
	Stanley and the Women		The Old Wives' Tale
	Take a Girl Like You		Clayhanger
	That Uncertain Feeling		The Man from the North*
Martin Amis	Night Train	Louis de Bernières	Captain Corelli's Mandolin
Jeffrey Archer	The Eleventh Commandment	Ambrose Bierce	The Fiend's Delight
	First Among Equals		An Occurence at Owl Creek Bridge
	The Fourth Estate	Maeve Binchy	Evening Class
	Not a Penny More, Not a Penny Less*		Light a Penny Candle*
Michael Arlen	The Green Hat		'Central Line' (short story)
	Piracy	RD Blackmore	Lorna Doone
Isaac Asimov	The Foundation Trilogy	William Peter Blatty	The Exorcist
	The Caves of Steel	Enid Blyton	Child Whispers*
	I, Robot		Noddy
Kate Atkinson	Behind the Scenes at the Museum		The Famous Five
			The Secret Seven
Margaret Atwood	Alias Grace	Giovanni Boccaccio	The Decameron
	The Handmaid's Tale	Norman Bogner	Seventh Avenue
Jane Austen	Emma	Pierre Boulle	The Bridge on the River Kwai
	Mansfield Park		Planet of the Apes
	Northanger Abbey	Malcolm Bradbury	Eating People Is Wrong*
	Persuasion		The History Man
	Pride and Prejudice	Ray Bradbury	Dark Carnival*
	Sense and Sensibility*		Fahrenheit 451
Pam Ayres	With These Hands		The Golden Apples of the Sun
Richard Bach	Jonathan Livingston Seagull		The Toynbee Convector
Enid Bagnold	National Velvet	Barbara Taylor Bradford	Love In Another Town
Beryl Bainbridge	An Awfully Big Adventure	Melvyn Bragg	Credo
	The Bottle Factory Outing		For Want of a Nail*
	The Dressmaker		The Maid of Buttermere
	English Journey		A Time to Dance
	Every Man for Himself	John Braine	Life at the Top
	Filthy Lucre		Room at the Top
	Sweet William		Stay With Me Till Morning
	A Weekend with Claud*	Max Brand	Doctor Kildare
James Baldwin	Go Tell It on the Mountain	Celia Brayfield	Harvest
	Giovanni's Room	Raymond Briggs	Fungus the Bogeyman
	Just Above My Head		Mother Goose Treasury
RM Ballantyne	Coral Island		The Snowman
	The Young Fur Traders		The Strange House*
JG Ballard	Cocaine Nights		When the Wind Blows
	High Rise	Anthelme Brillat-Savarin	The Physiology of Taste
	Empire of the Sun	Vera Brittain	Testament of Experience
	The Drowned World*		Testament of Friendship
Honoré de Balzac	La Comédie Humaine		Testament of Youth
Iain Banks	The Wasp Factory	Anne Brontë	Agnes Grey*
Lynne Reid Banks	The L-Shaped Room		The Tenant of Wildfell Hall
Pat Barker	The Ghost Road	Charlotte Brontë	Jane Eyre
Julian Barnes	Metroland		Lily Hart
JM Barrie	The Little Minister		The Professor
	A Window in Thrums		Villette
HE Bates	The Two Sisters *	Emily Brontë	Wuthering Heights
	Fair Stood the Wind for France	Anita Brookner	Altered States
	The Jacaranda Tree		Hôtel du Lac
	The Darling Buds of May		A Start in Life*
			Visitors
Charles Baudelaire	La Fanfarlo	Dan Brown	Angels & Demons
			The Da Vinci Code

LITERATURE

Author	Book
	Deception Point
	Digital Fortress*
Bill Bryson	Lost Continent: Travels in Small Town America
	Made In America
	Neither Here Nor There
	Notes from a Small Island
	A Short History of Nearly Everything
John Buchan	Greenmantle
	Huntingtower
	Prester John
	The Thirty-Nine Steps
	The Three Hostages
Pearl Buck	The Good Earth
	A House Divided
	What America Means to Me
Mikhail Bulgakov	The Master and Margarita
Edward Bulwer-Lytton	The Last Days of Pompeii
John Bunyan	The Pilgrim's Progress
Anthony Burgess	Any Old Iron
	A Clockwork Orange
	Earthly Powers
	Inside Mr Enderby
	Time for a Tiger*
	A Vision of Battlements*
Melvin Burgess	Junk
Frances Hodgson Burnett	Little Lord Fauntleroy
	The Secret Garden
Fanny Burney	Camilla
	Cecilia
	Evelina*
Edgar Rice Burroughs	Tarzan
Wiliam Burroughs	The Naked Lunch
Samuel Butler	Erewhon
	The Way of All Flesh
AS Byatt	The Game
	Possession
	Shadow of a Sun*
	Still Life
James M Cain	Double Indemnity
	Mildred Pierce
	The Postman Always Rings Twice
Erskine Caldwell	God's Little Acre
	Tobacco Road
Taylor Caldwell	The Captain and the Kings
Naomi Campbell	Swan
Albert Camus	The Outsider
	The Plague
Truman Capote	Breakfast at Tiffany's
	Other Voices, Other Rooms*
Lorenzo Carcaterra	Sleepers
John Le Carré	Call For the Dead*
	The Little Drummer Girl
	The Looking-Glass War
	The Night Manager
	Our Game
	A Small Town in Germany
	The Spy Who Came in from the Cold
	The Tailor of Panama
	Tinker, Tailor, Soldier, Spy
Lewis Carroll	Alice's Adventures In Wonderland
	Through the Looking Glass

Author	Book
Barbara Cartland	Jigsaw*
Willa Cather	Death Comes for the Archbishop
	O Pioneers!
Miguel Cervantes	Don Quixote
Raymond Chandler	The Big Sleep
	Farewell, My Lovely
	The High Window
	The Lady in the Lake
Jung Chang	Wild Swans
Henri Charrière	Papillon
Leslie Charteris	Meet the Tiger
	The Saint
Geoffrey Chaucer	The Canterbury Tales
GK Chesterton	The Napoleon of Notting Hill
	The Innocence of Father Brown
	The Man Who Was Thursday
Kate Chopin	The Awakening
Agatha Christie	The Call of Wings
	Curtain
	Hound of Death
	The Murder of Roger Ackroyd
	The Mysterious Affair at Styles
	Witness for the Prosecution
Tom Clancy	Executive Orders
Arthur C Clarke	The City and the Stars
	The Nine Billion Names of God
	Prelude to Space*
	The Sentinel
	3001: The Final Odyssey
	2001: A Space Odyssey
	2061: Odyssey Three
	2010: Odyssey Two
Mary Higgins Clark	Pretend You Don't See Her
James Clavell	King Rat
	Noble House
	Shogun
John Cleland	Fanny Hill
William Cobbett	Rural Rides
Colette	Chérie
	Claudine (series)
	Gigi
Jackie Collins	Hollywood Wives
Joan Collins	Prime Time
Wilkie Collins	The Moonstone
	The Woman in White
William Congreve	Incognita, or Love and Duty Reconciled*
Joseph Connolly	Stuff
Joseph Conrad	Almayer's Folly*
	Heart of Darkness
	Lord Jim
	The Nigger of the Narcissus
	Nostromo
	An Outcast of the Islands
	Under Western Eyes
Shirley Conran	Lace
	Superwoman
Benjamin Constant	Adolphe
Catherine Cookson	Bondage of Love
	Branded Man

LITERATURE

Author	Book	Author	Book
	Stark*	Mrs Elizabeth Gaskell	Cranford
Nicholas Evans	The Horse Whisperer		The Life of Charlotte
Walter Farley	The Black Stallion		Brontë
James T Farrell	Studs Lonigan Trilogy		Mary Barton*
Howard Fast	The Immigrants		North and South
Sebastian Faulks	Birdsong	Ricky Gervais	Flanimals*
	The Fatal Englishman	Edward Gibbon	The Decline and Fall of
William Faulkner	Absalom, Absalom !		the Roman Empire
	As I Lay Dying	André Gide	La Symphonie Pastorale
	Soldiers' Pay*	Johann Goethe	The Sorrows of Young
	The Sound and the Fury		Werther
Helen Fielding	Bridget Jones's Diary:		Wilhem Meister's
	A Novel		Apprenticeship
	Cause Celeb		Wilhem Meister's Travels
Henry Fielding	Amelia	Nikolai Gogol	Dead Souls
	The History of Tom Jones,		The Diary of a Madman
	A Foundling		The Overcoat
	Joseph Andrews	William Golding	Lord of the Flies*
F Scott Fitzgerald	The Beautiful and		Pincher Martin
	Damned		Rites of Passage
	The Great Gatsby	Oliver Goldsmith	The Vicar of Wakefield
	The Last Tycoon	Ivan Goncharov	Oblomov
	Tender Is the Night	Maxim Gorky	Childhood
	This Side of Paradise*		Mother
Gustave Flaubert	Madame Bovary		My Universities
	Salammbô	Judith Gould	Sins
Ian Fleming	Chitty Chitty Bang Bang	Winston Graham	Poldark
	James Bond series	Kenneth Grahame	The Wind in the Willows
Ken Follett	The Third Twin	Günther Grass	Cat and Mouse
Michael Foot	The Pen and the Sword		Dog Years
Colin Forbes	The Cauldron		The Tin Drum*
CS Forester	The African Queen		A Wide Field
	The Happy Return	Robert Graves	I, Claudius
	Hornblower series	John Gray	Men are From Mars,
	Payment Deferred*		Women are From
Helen Forrester	Mourning Doves		Venus
EM Forster	Howards End	Muriel Gray	Furnace
	A Passage to India	Simon Gray	Breaking Hearts
	A Room With A View	Graham Greene	Brighton Rock
Margaret Forster	Dame's Delight*		The Heart of the Matter
	Georgy Girl		The Honorary Consul
	Mother, Can You Hear		Our Man in Havana
	Me?		The Power and the Glory
	Shadow Baby		Stamboul Train
Frederick Forsyth	The Day of the Jackal		The Third Man
	The Dogs of War	Walter Greenwood	Love on the Dole
	The Fourth Protocol	Zane Grey	Riders of the Purple Sage
	Icon	Brothers Grimm	Snow White and the
	The Odessa File		Seven Dwarfs
John Fowles	The Collector	John Grisham	The Broker
	The French Lieutenant's		The Last Juror
	Woman		The Partner
	The Magus		The Pelican Brief
Dick Francis	Dead Cert		The Rainmaker
Anne Frank	The Diary of Anne Frank		Runaway Jury
Antonia Fraser	Gunpowder Plot: Terror	Richard D Gross	Psychology, the Science
	and Faith in 1605		of Mind and Behaviour
Charles Frazier	Cold Mountain	George and Weedon	The Diary of a Nobody
Nicci French	The Memory Game	Grossmith	
Stephen Fry	Making History	Henry Rider Haggard	Allan Quatermain
	The Liar*		King Solomon's Mines
Jostein Gaarder	Sophie's World		She
Paul Gallico	Jenny	Arthur Hailey	Airport
	The Poseidon Adventure		Hotel
	The Snow Goose		Wheels
John Galsworthy	The Forsyte Saga	Radcliffe Hall	The Well of Loneliness
Earl Stanley Gardner	The Case of the Velvet	Willis Hall	The Long and the Short
	Claws		and the Tall
	Perry Mason	Dashiell Hammett	The Glass Key
Alex Garla	The Beach		The Maltese Falcon
Jill Gascoigne	Just Like a Woman		The Thin Man

LITERATURE

Author	Book	Author	Book
	Kangaroo		The Garden Party, and
	Lady Chatterley's Lover		other stories
	The Plumed Serpent		Prelude
	The Rainbow	Robert Markham	Colonel Sun
	Sons and Lovers	(aka Kingsley Amis)	The James Bond Dossier
	The White Peacock*	Howard Marks	Mr Nice
	Women in Love	Gabriel García Márquez	Love in the Time of
Stephen Leacock	Winsome Winnie		Cholera
Edward Lear	A Book of Nonsense		One Hundred Years of
Harper Lee	To Kill A Mockingbird		Solitude
Laurie Lee	Cider With Rosie	Capt. Frederick Marryat	Children of the New
Elmore Leonard	Get Shorty		Forest
Alain Le Sage	Gil Blas		Mr Midshipman Easy
Doris Lessing	The Children of Violence		Peter Simple
	The Grass is Singing*	Ngaio Marsh	A Man Lay Dead*
Kathy Lette	Mad Cows		Overture to Death
Primo Levi	If This Is A Man	Les Martin	The X Files
Ira Levin	The Boys from Brazil	John Masefield	The Box of Delights
	A Kiss Before Dying		Sard Harker
	Rosemary's Baby	William Somerset	Cakes and Ale
	The Stepford Wives	Maugham	The Casuarina Tree
CS Lewis	The Lion, the Witch and		Liza of Lambeth*
	the Wardrobe		The Moon and Sixpence
	Out of the Silent Planet		Of Human Bondage
	The Screwtape Letters		The Razor's Edge
Richard Llewellyn	How Green Was My	Armistead Maupin	Tales of the City
	Valley	Gavin Maxwell	Ring of Bright Water
David Lodge	The British Museum Is		Harpoon at a Venture
	Falling Down	Peter Mayall	A Year in Provence
	The Picturegoers*	John McCarthy and Jill	Some Other Rainbow
	Therapy	Morrell	
Hugh Lofting	Doctor Doolittle	Mary McCarthy	The Group
Jack London	The Call of the Wild	Frank McCourt	Angela's Ashes
	The Sea-Wolf	Carson McCullers	The Heart Is a Lonely
	White Fang		Hunter*
Anita Loos	Gentlemen Marry		The Ballad of the Sad
	Brunettes		Café
	Gentlemen Prefer	Ian McEwan	Amsterdam
	Blondes		Atonement
Konrad Lorenz	King Solomon's Ring		Enduring Love
Malcolm Lowry	Under the Volcano		First Love, Last Rites*
Robert Ludlum	The Rhinemann		Saturday
	Exchange	Andy McNab	Bravo Two Zero
	The Scarlatti Inheritance		Immediate Action
Colleen McCullough	The Thorn Birds		Remote Control*
George MacDonald Fraser	Black Ajax	Herman Cyril McNeile	Bulldog Drummond
Niccolò Machiavelli	The Prince	(Sapper)	
Helen MacInnes	Message from Malaga	Herman Melville	Billy Budd
Compton Mackenzie	The Passionate		Moby-Dick
	Elopement*		Typee*
	Rockets Galore	Grace Metalious	Peyton Place
	Whisky Galore	James Michener	Tales of the South
Alistair Maclean	Fear Is the Key		Pacific*
	The Guns of Navarone	John Stuart Mill	The Subjection of
	HMS Ulysses*		Women
	Ice Station Zebra		The System of Logic
	When Eight Bells Toll	Henry Miller	Tropic of Cancer
	Where Eagles Dare		Tropic of Capricorn
Norman Mailer	Tough Guys Don't Dance		Nexus
	The Naked and the	AA Milne	Now We Are Six
	Dead*		Winnie-the-Pooh
	The Executioner's Song	Yukio Mishima	The Sailor Who Fell from
	An American Dream		Grace with the Sea
Thomas Malory	Le Morte D'Arthur	Margaret Mitchell	Gone With the Wind
Nelson Mandela	Long Walk to Freedom	Nancy Mitford	Love in a Cold Climate
Heinrich Mann	The Blue Angel	Deborah Moggach	Close Relations
Thomas Mann	Buddenbrooks*	Nicholas Monsarrat	The Cruel Sea
	Death in Venice		The Story of Esther
	Doctor Faustus		Costello
	The Magic Mountain	LM Montgomery	Anne of Green Gables*
Katherine Mansfield	Bliss, and other stories	Michael Moorcock	A Cure for Cancer

LITERATURE

Author	Book	Author	Book
Harold Robbins	79 Park Avenue	Henry Sienkiewicz	Quo Vadis?
	The Carpetbaggers	Alan Sillitoe	Loneliness of the Long-Distance Runner
	The Dream Merchants*		
	Never Love a Stranger		The Ragman's Daughter
	A Stone For Danny Fisher		Saturday Night and Sunday Morning*
Monty Roberts	The Man Who Listens to Horses	Georges Simenon	Maigret
			The Man Who Watched the Trains Go By
Judith Rossner	Looking for Mr Goodbar	Joe Simpson	Dark Shadows Falling
Philip Roth	American Pastoral		Touching the Void
	Portnoy's Complaint	Upton Sinclair	Jungle, The
JK Rowling	Harry Potter and the Chamber of Secrets	Wilbur Smith	Birds of Prey
			Eye of the Tiger
	Harry Potter and the Goblet of Fire		Shout at the Devil
			When the Lion Feeds*
	Harry Potter and the Philosopher's Stone	Tobias Smollett	The Adventures of Roderick Random
	Harry Potter and the Prisoner of Azkaban		The Adventures of Peregrine Pickle
Arundhati Roy	The God of Small Things		The Expedition of Humphrey Clinker
Damon Runyon	Guys and Dolls	CP Snow	The Corridors of Power
Salman Rushdie	Grimus*		Strangers and Brothers
	Midnight's Children	Dava Sobel	Longitude
	The Moor's Last Sigh	Alexander Solzhenitsyn	August 1914
	The Satanic Verses		Cancer Ward
Edward Rutherfurd	London: The Novel		The First Circle
Marquis de Sade	Justine		The Gulag Archipelago
Carl Sagan	Broca's Brain		The Oak and the Calf
Françoise Sagan	Bonjour Tristesse		One Day in the Life of Ivan Denisovich*
JD Salinger	The Catcher in the Rye*		
Felix Salten	Bambi	Muriel Spark	The Ballad of Peckham Rye
Jean-Paul Sartre	In Camera		
	Nausea		The Comforters
	Roads to Freedom Trilogy		The Prime of Miss Jean Brodie
Siegfried Sassoon	Memoirs of a Fox-Hunting Man		
Dorothy L Sayers	Busman's Honeymoon	Mickey Spillane	I, The Jury
	Gaudy Night	Howard Spring	Fame Is the Spur
	Murder Must Advertise		My Son, My Son
	The Nine Tailors	Johanna Spyri	Heidi
	Whose Body?	Danielle Steele	Ghost
Ernst Schumacher	Small Is Beautiful	John Steinbeck	East of Eden
Paul Scott	Raj Quartet		The Grapes of Wrath
Sir Walter Scott	The Abbot		Of Mice and Men
	The Bride of Lammermoor		Tortilla Flat
	The Heart of Midlothian	Stendhal	La Chartreuse de Parme
	Ivanhoe		Le Rouge et le Noir
	Kenilworth	Julia Stephenson	Pandora's Diamond
	Rob Roy	Laurence Sterne	The Life and Opinions of Tristram Shandy
	Tales of My Landlord		
	The Talisman	Robert Louis Stevenson	Catriona
	Waverley		Kidnapped
Eric Segal	Love Story		The Strange Case of Dr Jekyll and Mr Hyde
Will Self	Great Apes		
Paul Sellers	Alphabats		Weir of Hermiston
Robert Service	Ploughman of the Moon	RL Stine	Say Cheese and Die Again!
	Harper of Heaven		
Vikram Seth	A Suitable Boy	Bram Stoker	Dracula
Anna Sewell	Black Beauty	Irving Stone	The Agony and the Ecstasy
Tom Sharpe	Blott on the Landscape		
	Midden		Lust for Life
	Porterhouse Blue	Rex Stout	A Question of Proof
	Riotous Assembly*	Harriet Beecher Stowe	Uncle Tom's Cabin
	Wilt	Lytton Strachey	Eminent Victorians
Irwin Shaw	Evening in Byzantium	Robert Smith Surtees	Jorrocks's Jaunts and Jollities
Mary Shelley	Frankenstein*		
	Valperga		Mr Sponge's Sporting Tour
Mikhail Sholokhov	And Quiet Flows the Don	Patrick Susskind	Perfume
Nevil Shute	On the Beach	Graham Swift	Last Orders
	A Town Like Alice	Jonathan Swift	The Battle of the Books

LITERATURE

Author	Book	Author	Book
	Night and Day	Johann Wyss	The Swiss Family
	To the Lighthouse		Robinson
	The Voyage Out*	Émile Zola	Germinal
Herman Wouk	The Winds of War		J'Accuse
PC Wren	Beau Geste		Nana
Peter Wright	Spycatcher		Thérèse Raquin
Elizabeth Wurtzel	Prozac Nation	Arnold Zweig	Claudia
John Wyndham	The Day of the Triffids*	Stefan Zweig	Beware of Pity
	The Kraken Wakes		Kaleidoscope
	The Midwich Cuckoos		

Books: General Information

The Admirable Crichton   Master: Lord Loam. Ship: The Bluebell.

Alexandria Quartet   Justine, Balthazar, Mountolive, Clea (who had her right hand cut off to save her from drowning after it was pinned underwater by a harpoon gun).

Alice in Wonderland   In the croquet game, the mallets were flamingoes and the balls were hedgehogs.

The Anglo-Saxon Chronicle   Early record in English of events in England from the arrival of Christianity to 1154, surviving in seven manuscripts and begun about 890, possibly by Alfred the Great. Entries include the arrival of Hengist and Horsa, the story of Cynewulf and Cyneheard, and Alfred's last series of Danish wars. One famous passage is a poem about the battle of Brunanburh (937). The chronicle was expanded and continued, particularly in the late 16th and early 17th century.

Animal Farm   The manor farm was owned by Mr Jones, Napoleon the pig became the leader, Boxer was the horse.

Anna Karenina   Anna's death: She threw herself under a train.

Anne of Green Gables   Prince Edward Island was the setting for Anne Shirley's adventures.

Antic Hay   Title comes from a line in Edward II by Christopher Marlowe.

Around the World in 80 Days   Central character is Phileas Fogg and his valet is Passepartout. They start and finish at the Reform Club in London. The Indian Widow is Aouda.

Baedeker Books   Named after Karl Baedeker of Essen (1801–59), who started the issue of the famous guidebooks in Koblenz. The tradition was continued by his son Fritz, who transferred the business to Leipzig. The term 'Baedeker raids' was applied to the deliberate bombing in the Second World War of provincial cities of great historic and cultural significance, such as Bath, Exeter and Norwich.

Bildungsroman (lit. education novel)   Novels portraying a person's formative years, a favourite genre with German authors. Agathon (1766) is considered the first example, but Goethe's Wilhelm Meister's Apprenticeship (1796) is outstanding.

Bleak House   Court case was Jarndyce v Jarndyce, the rag and bone man was Krook (who died of spontaneous combustion).

Book of the Century   Lord of the Rings was voted Book of the Century in a survey of 25,000 people carried out in 1997 by Channel 4 and Waterstone's.

Bookshop   First WH Smith: Euston Station.

The Borrowers   The Names: Pod, Homily, Arrietty.

Bradshaw's Railway Guide   First published in 1839 in the form of Railway Time Tables by George Bradshaw (1801–53), a Quaker printer and engraver. These developed into Bradshaw's Monthly Railway Guide in 1841 and continued to be published until May 1961.

Brave New World   Title from The Tempest by William Shakespeare.

The Brothers Karamazov   Alyosha, Dmitry, Ivan, Smolykov.

Cakes and Ale   Title from a line in Twelfth Night by William Shakespeare.

The Call of the Wild   Dog's name Buck.

Candide   Dr Pangloss's famous quote: 'All is for the best in the best of possible worlds.'

Canterbury Tales   The pilgrims met at the Tabard Inn, Southwark. The host on the pilgrimage was Harry Bailly. The summoner's tale tells of a corrupt mendicant friar who is tricked into accepting a donation of a fart.

Catch-22   Set in Pianosa in the Mediterranean. Captain Yossarian had the predicament. Kid Sampson died: cut in half by a low-flying aircraft. Catch-22 is the predicament faced by US bomber crews: You don't have to fly any more missions if you're crazy, but if you ask to be grounded you prove you're not crazy.

The Catcher in the Rye   Central character Holden Caulfield.

Children's Laureate   Quentin Blake became the first in 1999, Anne Fine replacing him in May 2001. Michael Morpurgo became the third holder in May 2003 and Jacqueline Wilson the fourth in May 2005.

Clayhanger Trilogy   Clayhanger, Hilda, Lessways, These Twain. A fourth novel, The Roll Call, is loosely connected to the trilogy.

Cold Comfort Farm   Cows' names: Aimless, Feckless, Graceless, Pointless.

The Corridors of Power   War Minister was Roger Quaife.

The Count of Monte Cristo   The Count was Edmond Dantès, imprisoned in the Château d'If. He inherited a fortune left by Abbé Faria.

Crime and Punishment   Crime: murder of a female pawnbroker. Criminal: Raskolnikov. Investigating Inspector: Petrovitch.

David Copperfield   Headmaster of Salem House School: Mr Creakle. Aunt: Betsy Trotwood. Wives: Dora Spenlow and Agnes Wickfield.

Death in Venice   Gustav von Aschenbach dies of cholera.

Dickens   Only novel with female narrator: Bleak House.

Doctor Zhivago   Title character: Dr Yuri Zhivago. Wife: Tania Gromeko. Lover: Lara Antipova.

Dombey and Son   Captain Cuttle's famous quote: 'When found, make a note of.'

Don Quixote   Horse: Rosinante. Squire: Sancho Panza. Lady: Dulcinea.

East of Eden   Based on the story of Cain and Abel.

Emma   Emma Woodhouse marries Mr Knightley.

Every Man For Himself   Story of the *Titanic* disaster told by Morgan, a well connected young man.

Fair Stood the Wind for France   Title from 'Ballad of Agincourt' by Michael Drayton.

Far from the Madding Crowd   Bathsheba Everdene marries Sergeant Troy and Gabriel Oak. Title from 'Elegy Written in a Country Church-yard' by Thomas Gray.

Feet of Clay   Main character Commander Sir Samuel Vimes, head of Ankh-Morpork City Guard.

Finnegans Wake   Central character is Humphrey Chimpden Earwicker, a publican; the action takes place during one night.

Forsyte Saga Trilogy   *A Man of Property, In Chancery, To Let.*

For Whom the Bell Tolls   Title from a sermon by John Donne.

Foundation Trilogy   *Foundation, Foundation and Empire,* Se*cond Foundation.*

Gargantua and Pantagruel   Published under name 'Alcofri bas Nasier' (anagram of François Rabelais).

George Smiley   First appeared in *Call for the Dead.*

Glass of Blessings (Barbara Pym)   Title from 'The Pulley' by George Herbert.

Gone with the Wind   Scarlett O'Hara marries Charles Hamilton, Frank Kennedy, Rhett Butler.

Gothic Novel: 1st   *The Castle of Otranto* by Horace Walpole (1764).

Grapes of Wrath   The Joad family – Tom, Al, Noah, Ruthie, Winfield and Rosasharn leave Oklahoma for California.

Gravity's Rainbow   Central character Tyrone Slothrop.

The Great Gatsby   Jay Gatsby loves Daisy Buchanan, cousin of narrator Nick Carraway.

Gulliver's Travels   Horses: Houyhnyms. Humans: Yahoos. Lands visited: Lilliput, Brobdingnag, Laputa, Blefuscu. Subtitle: 'Travels into Several Remote Nations of the World'.

Hardy's last novel   *Jude the Obscure.*

Harleian Manuscripts   Collection of manuscripts made by Robert Harley, first earl of Oxford (1661–1724). It consisted of over 50,000 books, 350,000 pamphlets, and 7,000 manuscripts of biblical texts and other historical data. The manuscripts were bought by Parliament in 1753 and placed in the British Museum. They are now housed in the British Library.

Harry Potter Books   Illustrated by Mary Grandpré. First in the series titled *Harry Potter and the Sorcerer's Stone* in the USA.

Heavy Metal   Phrase coined by William Burroughs in *The Naked Lunch.*

Helliconia Trilogy   *Helliconia Spring, Helliconia Summer, Helliconia Winter.*

The History Man   Title character Howard Kirk.

Howard's End   House owners Mr and Mrs Wilcox.

Incunabula   Books printed before 1501 (means 'swaddling clothes').

Interior Monologue   Extended representation in prose or verse of a character's unspoken thoughts, memories and impressions, rendered as if directly overheard by the reader without the intervention of a summarising narrator.

Ivanhoe   Love interest: Lady Rowena.

James Bond books not by Fleming   *Colonel Sun* and *The James Bond Dossier* by Kingsley Amis, writing as Robert Markham.

Jane Eyre   Mr Rochester lives at Thornfield Hall. Jane's school is Lowood. Jane's bullying cousin is John Reed. Her home until aged 10 is Gateshead Hall. Dedicated to William Makepeace Thackeray.

The Jewel in the Crown   First novel in the Raj Quartet. Plot revolves around the alleged rape in the Bibighar Gardens of Daphne Manners.

Jude the Obscure   Jude Fawley aspires to go to Christminster (Oxford), but fails to get into Sarcophagus College.

Kidnapped   Central character is David Balfour. His friend is the Jacobite Alan Breck. The ship that is meant to take David to the Carolina is the *Covenant.*

Kipps   Central character Arthur Kipps. Occupation: draper's assistant.

The Last Tycoon   Allegedly based on the Hollywood film producer Irving Thalberg.

Leather-Stocking stories   Hero: Natty Bumppo, also called 'Hawkeye', 'Pathfinder' and 'Deerslayer'. The Last of the Mohicans was Uncas and his father was Chingachgook.

Little Lord Fauntleroy   Title character: Cedric Errol.

Little Women   They are the March sisters: Amy, Beth, Jo and Meg.

Lolita   Title character: Dolores Haze.

The Longest Journey (EM Forster)   Title from *Epipsychidion* by Percy Bysshe Shelley.

Look Homeward, Angel (Thomas Wolfe)   from *Lycidas* by John Milton.

The Lord of the Rings   Setting: Middle Earth. Hobbit: Bilbo Baggins. Bilbo's nephew: Frodo. Maker of the One Ring: Sauron. Sauron's land: Mordor. Wizard: Gandalf. Gandalf's horse: Shadowfax. Books in the trilogy: *The Fellowship of the Ring, The Two Towers, The Return of the King.*

Madame Bovary   Title character née Emma Rouault.

Mansfield Park   Heroine Fanny Price.

The Mayor of Casterbridge   Mayor: First Michael Henchard then Donald Farfrae. Setting: Wessex. 'Casterbridge' is Dorchester. Henchard sells his wife and daughter for five guineas.

The Memory Game   Nicci Gerrard and Sean French are co-writers.

The Mill on the Floss   Central characters: Tom and Maggie Tulliver. Setting: Dorlcote Mill.

Mirror Crack'd From Side to Side (Agatha Christie)   Title from 'The Lady of Shalott' by Alfred Lord Tennyson.

Moby Dick   Captain: Ahab. Narrator: Ishmael. Ship: Pequod.

The Moon and Sixpence   Inspired by the life of Paul Gauguin.

The Moonstone   Title is the name of a diamond.

Morse   Christian name Endeavour (revealed in *Death Is Now My Neighbour*).

Mort   Main character, Mort, is Death's hopelessly inept teenage apprentice.

Mr Weston's Good Wine (TF Powys)   Title from *Emma,* by Jane Austen.

My Son, My Son   Original title *Oh Absalom.*

LITERATURE

Nicholas Nickleby Nicholas marries Madeline Bray. School: Dotheboys Hall. Schoolmaster: Wackford Squeers. Friend: Smike.

The Nine Tailors Are church bells that cause Geoffrey Deacon's death.

Nineteen Eighty-Four Hero: Winston Smith. His lover: Julia (junior member of the anti-Sex League). Britain depicted as Airstrip One (part of Oceania).

Northanger Abbey Heroine Catherine Morland.

Our Mutual Friend Title character: John Harmon. Marries: Bella Wilfe. Villain: Silas Wegg the peg-leg.

Pale Fire (Nabokov) Title from *Timon of Athens* by William Shakespeare.

A Passage to India Setting: Chandrapore. Central characters: Dr Aziz and Cyril Fielding. Aziz accused of rape by Adela Quested.

Peter Rabbit's father Killed and made into a pie by Mrs McGregor.

The Pickwick Papers Cricket match: All-Muggleton v Dingley Dell.

The Pilgrim's Progress Hero: Christian. Castle: Doubting. Giant: Despair. Goal: Celestial City.

The Portrait of a Lady Title character Isabel Archer.

Power and the Glory Set in Mexico.

The Prime of Miss Jean Brodie Art teacher: Teddy Lloyd.

The Prince and the Pauper Title characters – Prince: Edward, Prince of Wales, later Edward VI; Pauper: Tom Canty.

Prison: authors in
Brendan Behan for IRA activities.

William Blake in Chichester for fighting with a soldier.

John Bunyan in Bedford gaol for preaching without a licence.

Daniel Defoe after writing *The Shortest Way with Dissenters* (a satire on High Church attitudes to religious nonconformism).

John Donne in the Fleet for marrying Anne Moore (a minor) in 1576. Hence his comment: 'John Donne – Anne Donne – Undone.'

Fyodor Dostoyevsky was condemned to death for belonging to a revolutionary organisation but was reprieved and served 4 years hard labour in Siberia.

Ben Jonson was imprisoned for killing Gabriel Spenser, but after pleading benefit of clergy was merely branded on the left thumb.

Ezra Pound was charged with treason for delivering radio broadcasts on behalf of the Axis powers during the Second World War, but was found unfit to plead and instead imprisoned in an asylum.

Alexander Solzhenitsyn spent 8 years in a prison camp for criticising Stalin's conduct of the war against Nazi Germany.

Oscar Wilde was imprisoned for 2 years in Reading Gaol for homosexual offences. He wrote *De Profundis* while incarcerated, not *The Ballad of Reading Gaol*.

The Prisoner of Zenda Title character: King Rudolf. Kingdom: Ruritania. Imprisoned by: Duke Michael.

Quentin Durward Marries Isabelle de Croye.

Rabbit Tetralogy *Rabbit, Run*; *Rabbit Redux*; *Rabbit Is Rich*; *Rabbit at Rest*.

The Railway Children Names: Peter, Phyllis, Roberta.

The Raj Quartet *The Jewel in the Crown*, *The Day of the Scorpion*, *A Division of the Spoils*, *The Towers of Silence*.

The Red and The Black (Stendhal's *Le Rouge et le Noir*). Colours symbolise respectively the Army and the Church.

The Red Badge of Courage Set in the American Civil War.

Rip Van Winkle Set in the Catskill Mountains. Rip sleeps for 20 years.

Room 101 In Orwell's *Nineteen Eighty-Four*, this room contained rats used to help interrogate Winston Smith, as they were his great fear.

The Scarlet Letter Central character: Hester Prynne. The Scarlet Letter: A for Adultery.

The Scarlet Pimpernel Title character: Sir Percy Blakeney.

Scriblerus Club Literary group including Swift, Pope, Gay, Arbuthnot and Thomas Parnell, which met from January to July 1714 to 'ridicule all the false tastes in learning'. Martinos Scriblerus was a pseudonym occasionally used by Pope.

The Seed and the Sower Filmed as *Merry Christmas Mr Lawrence*.

Sense and Sensibility Characters who represent these quallities: Sense – Elinor Dashwood. Sensibility – Marianne Dashwood.

Sherlock Holmes Landlady: Mrs Hudson.

Shogun Central character: John Blackthorne.

Slaughterhouse-Five Hero: Billy Pilgrim.

Sons and Lovers Son: Paul Morel.

The Sound and the Fury Title from: *Macbeth* by William Shakespeare. Family: Benjy, Caddy, Jason and Quentin Compson.

Spanish Civil War Served as stretcher bearer: WH Auden (for the Republicans).

The Spy Who Came in from the Cold Title character: Leamas.

Stammered Somerset Maugham.

Steppenwolf Central character: Harry Haller.

Stream of Consciousness Term coined in William James's (1842–1910) *Principles of Psychology* (1890) and used to describe the continuity of impressions and thoughts in the human mind. The literary sense of the term was introduced in 1918 by May Sinclair (1863–1946) in a review of early volumes of Dorothy Richardson's (1873–1957) novel sequence *Pilgrimage* (1915–38) and is a method for representing the aforementioned psychological principle in unpunctuated or fragmentary forms of interior monologue.

The Sun Also Rises Source of the term: 'The Lost Generation'.

Swiss Family Robinson Johann David Wyss wrote the story and his son Johann Rudolf completed and edited it. The Robinsons' names: Fritz, Ernest, Franz and Jack.

Sword of Honour Trilogy *Men at Arms*, *Officers and Gentlemen*, *Unconditional Surrender*.

The Tailor of Panama Tailor: Harry Pendel.

The Tale of Two Cities Cities: Paris and London. Sentenced to guillotine: Charles Darnay. Sacrificed himself in Darnay's place: Sydney Carton.

Tender Is the Night Title from 'Ode to a Nightingale' by John Keats.

Tess of the D'Urbervilles Tess marries Angel Clare.

The Thirty-Nine Steps Hannay's servant: Paddock.

Three Men in a Boat Title characters: George, Harris, Montmorency (Dog).

Thrums Name given in JM Barrie to disguise Kirriemuir, his home town.

The Tin Drum Hero: Oskar Matzerath (a dwarf).

Tobacco Road Sharecropper: Jeeter Lester. Jeeter's wife: Ada.

Tom Jones Tom's wife: Sophia Western. Her servant: Mrs Honour.

The Trial Central character: Joseph K.

The Turn of the Screw Children: Miles and Flora. Ghosts: Miss Jessel and Peter Quint.

2001: A Space Odyssey Book based on the film of the same name.

Ulysses Central characters: Leopold and Molly Bloom and Stephen Daedalus. Set during 18 hours in Dublin on 16 June 1904.

Uncle Tom's Cabin Slave owner: Simon Legree.

Unnatural Exposure Plot: Bodies are being dumped in rubbish and bin men demand stress counselling.

Vanity Fair Central character: Becky Sharp marries: Rawdon Crawley. Becky's friend: Amelia Sedley. she marries: (1) George Osborne; (2) Captain Dobbin. School: Miss Pinkerton's. Illustrated by: W.M. Thackeray.

Victory (John Williams) Set during Tony Blair's campaign for the 1997 election (pictures by Tom Stoddart).

Villette Villette is a city based on Brussels.

The Water-Babies Set in Vendale.

Watership Down Rabbits Bigwig, Fiver, General Woundwort, Hazel.

The Well of Loneliness Originally banned for lesbian content.

Westward Ho! Hero: Amyas Leigh. His love: Rose of Torridge.

What Katy Did Heroine's full name: Katy Carr.

Whisky Galore Setting: Great and Little Todday.

Whitbread Awards: Man and Wife Michael Frayn and Claire Tomalin became the first married couple to win Whitbread Awards, in 2003.

White Fang offspring of a wolf-dog and a dog.

WH Smith *The End of Alice*, banned for its content of child abuse

The Wind in the Willows Characters: Badger, Mole, Toad, Water Rat.

Winnie-the-Pooh Title character: Edward (Pooh). Boy: Christopher Robin. Donkey: Eeyore. Elephant: Heffalump. Kidnapped baby: Roo (kangaroo). Illustrator: EH Shepard.

Woman publishers Virago (run by women for women).

Women in Love Gudrun Brangwen and Gerald Crich were based on Katherine Mansfield and John Middleton Murry.

Wuthering Heights Narrated by Mr Lockwood and Nelly Deane.

Wyss, Johann Rudolf Wrote the Swiss National Anthem 'Rufst du mein Vaterland'.

Zuleika Dobson (Max Beerbohm) Servant: Mélisande.

Jane Austen's Characters
(of her six completed novels)

Jane Austen was born in 1775 and died at Winchester, aged 42, in the summer of 1817, having lived a quiet, uneventful life. One of eight children, she lived in the rectory at Steventon until she was 16, when her family moved to Bath. Her father died in 1805 and she remained unmarried, spending the rest of her life with her mother and sister, Cassandra, initially in Southampton, then in Chawton in Hampshire. She was well-read and her favourite writer, Dr Johnson, is quoted in several of her works.

Emma: Completed in 1815 and published in 1816. The novel was dedicated to the Prince Regent. The Churchills' estate in Yorkshire is Enscombe, the Bateses lived in Highbury and the Woodhouse residence was in Hartfield, Highbury.

Abbot, Misses The two Abbots (first names unknown), students at Mrs Goddard's school.

Abdy, John Son of Old John, ostler and head man at the Crown.

Abdy, Old John For 27 years clerk to the late Reverend Bates.

Bates, Miss Hetty Daughter of Reverend Bates and Mrs Bates, sister to Miss Jane Bates, aunt to Jane Fairfax. The town chatterbox, but has a sweet and kind nature and is loved by all though being neither married, rich nor pretty. She is insulted by Emma at Box Hill and true to her nature takes no offence, but this teaches Emma a valuable lesson.

Bates, Miss Jane Youngest daughter of Reverend Bates and Mrs Bates, sister to Miss Hetty Bates. Married Lieutenant Fairfax, who died in battle; Jane herself died soon after giving birth to Jane Fairfax.

Bates, Mrs Old, deaf widowed mother of Miss Jane Bates and Miss Hetty Bates.

Bates, Reverend Father to Miss Jane Bates and Miss Hetty Bates.

Bickerton, Miss Betty Parlour border at Mrs Goddard's school. She and Harriet are attacked by gypsies while out walking and Miss Bickerton flees, leaving Harriet to fend for herself.

Bird, Mrs Friend of Augusta Hawkins.

Bragge, Mr Cousin of Mr Suckling.

Bragge, Mrs Cousin of Mr Suckling. Mrs Elton offers Jane Fairfax a position with Mrs Bragge.

Braithwaite family Friends of Mr and Mrs Churchill.

Brown, Mrs Friend of Augusta Hawkins.

Campbells Colonel and Mrs Campbell and their daughter. Friends of Lieutenant Fairfax and patron of Jane Fairfax. Miss Campbell marries Mr Dixon and Jane then leaves to become a governess.

Churchill, Frank Foppish son of Captain Weston and Miss Churchill, adopted by his aunt and uncle, Mr and Mrs Churchill of Enscombe. Meets Jane Fairfax in Weymouth and enters into a secret engagement. A charming and attractive man who flirts with Emma to allay suspicion of his secret, but eventually agrees to marry Jane.

Churchill, Miss Mr Churchill's sister. Married Captain Weston and had a son, Frank Weston Churchill.

Churchill, Mr and Mrs Of Enscombe in Yorkshire, although also having a home in Richmond. The aunt and uncle of Frank Weston Churchill, whom they fostered when Miss Churchill/Weston died. Mrs Churchill died in Richmond and Mr Churchill allows Frank to marry Jane Fairfax.

Coles Mr and Mrs Cole are nouveaux riches and

although they have 'been settled some years in Highbury', Emma continues to think of them as inferior until they hold a party and she is dismayed to find all her friends are going.

Cooper, Mrs James   Friend of Augusta Hawkins.

Cox family   Lower-class family in Highbury although William was a lawyer, as was his father. They are friends of the Bateses and the Eltons.

Dixon, Mr   Of Balycraig, Ireland. Once saved Jane Fairfax from drowning and Emma imagines they are in love. Frank Churchill teased Jane with the name 'Dixon'. Mr Dixon marries Miss Campbell.

Elton, Mr Philip   Vicar of Highbury who falls in love with Emma, although she wants him to marry Harriet. He is offended at this suggestion and leaves Highbury. He meets Miss Augusta Hawkins while staying at the White Hart in Bath and marries her. On his return to Highbury he is now smug and resentful and he and his new wife never miss a chance to slight Emma.

Fairfax, Jane   Orphaned daughter of Lieutenant Fairfax and Miss Jane Bates. Niece of Miss Hetty Bates. Meets Frank Churchill in Weymouth and becomes engaged secretly. She is then employed by Mrs Smallridge as governess. Disliked by Emma Woodhouse initially although for no good reason at all, she eventually marries Frank.

Fairfax, Lieutenant   Father of Jane Fairfax and husband of Jane Bates. He died in battle soon after his daughter was born.

Farmer Mitchell   Provides Mr Weston with umbrellas.

Ford, Mrs   Highbury shopkeeper.

Gilberts   The two Gilberts, Mrs and Miss, are Highbury residents mentioned in chapter 29.

Goddard, Mrs   Owner of school for girls in Highbury at which Harriet Smith attends. Harriet boards with Mrs Goddard.

Graham, Mr   Friend of Mr John Knightley.

Green, Mr   Friend of Augusta Hawkins at Bath.

Hannah   Servant at Randalls, the nearby estate of Hartfield. She is the daughter of James the Hartfield coachman.

Harry   Servant at Donwell Abbey.

Hawkins, Miss Augusta   Sister of Selina. A conceited social climber who meets Mr Elton at Bath and marries him. She shares a mutual dislike of Emma. Refers to her husband as Mr E of 'Caro Sposo'.

Hawkins, Miss Selina   Sister to Augusta. She marries Mr Suckling.

Hodges, Mrs   Housekeeper at Donwell Abbey.

Hughes family   Residents of Highbury.

James   The trusted coachman for the Woodhouse family at Hartfield.

Jeffereys, Miss   see Partridge, Miss Clara.

Knightley, Bella and Emma   Daughters of Isabella Woodhouse and John Knightley. Nieces of Emma Woodhouse.

Knightley, George   Son of Isabella Woodhouse and John Knightley. Nephew of Emma Woodhouse.

Knightley, Henry   Oldest son of Isabella Woodhouse and John Knightley. Nephew of Emma Woodhouse.

Knightley, Isabella   Daughter of Henry Woodhouse and shares his concern about illness. Her mother died when she was about 12 years old. She is about seven years older than her sister Emma. She is married to Mr John Knightley and lives in London.

Knightley, Master John   Youngest son of Isabella Woodhouse and John Knightley. Nephew of Emma Woodhouse.

Knightley, Mr George   Brother of John Knightley. A kind and honest man who was not scared to point

out Emma's shortcomings. George is also the most attractive man in the novel and eventually marries Emma.

Knightley, Mr John   Of Brunswick Square. George Knightley's brother. Married to Isabella Woodhouse.

Larkins, William   Mr Knightley's property manager; the manager of Donwell Abbey.

Martin family   Of Abbey Mill Farm. Mr and Mrs Martin and their son Robert and daughters Elizabeth (and one other). Harriet stays with them and forms a friendship with Robert. Emma persuades her that the Martins are socially inferior and there is a period of difficulty before Harriet comes to her senses and marries Robert.

Martin, Elizabeth   Sister of Robert Martin who breaks the ice between her brother and Harriet Smith, thus allowing them to marry.

Martin, Robert   Promises Harriet Smith to read two books, *Romance of the Forest* by Anne Radcliffe and *The Children of the Abbey* by Regina Maria Roche. He eventually marries Harriet after being turned down initially.

Milmans   Now Mrs Bird and Mrs James Cooper.

Nash, Miss   Head teacher at Mrs Goddard's school who sang the praises of Mr Elton.

Otways   Highbury residents referred to in chapter 46.

Partridge, Miss Clara   Friend of Mrs Elton. Sometimes called Miss Jeffereys.

Patty   Maid to Mrs and Miss Bates.

Perry, Mr   Apothecary at Highbury.

Perry, Mrs   Wife of the apothecary at Highbury. They have several children.

Prince, Miss   Teacher at Mrs Goddard's school.

Richardson, Miss   Teacher at Mrs Goddard's school.

Saunders, John   Miss Bates considers taking her mother's spectacles to him to fix.

Serle   Cook at Hartfield.

Smallridge, Mrs   Friend of Sucklings and Bragges, offered Jane Fairfax a governess position.

Smith, Harriet   A boarder at Mrs Goddard's. Her favourite book is *The Vicar of Wakefield* and she is delighted that Robert Martin has read it. Her keepsake box has the words 'most precious treasures' written on the silver tissue wrapping. After refusing Robert Martin's proposal of marriage and then having several romantic adventures, she eventually sees sense and marries him.

Stokes, Mrs   Referred to by Emma in chapters 29 and 38 at the Crown Inn at Highbury.

Suckling, Mr   Of Maple Grove, near Bristol. A rich and cultured man who marries Selina Hawkins, the sister of Mrs Elton. He is often mentioned by Mrs Elton in the hope of elevating herself.

Taylor, Anne   Governess to Emma at Hartfield, where she was employed for 16 years. She marries Mr Weston at the start of the novel. A kind and friendly woman who was more of a friend than a teacher to Emma.

Tom   Servant at Randalls.

Tupman   Upstart who settled near the Suckling home of Maple Grove.

Wallis, Mrs   Bakes apples for Miss Bates.

Weston, Captain Mr   Of Randalls near Hartfield. Frank Churchill is his son from his first marriage. His second marriage is to Miss Anne Taylor. He is a good friend of Emma's.

Wingfield, Mr   Isabella Knightley's apothecary in London.

Woodhouse, Emma   Daughter of Henry Woodhouse and sister to Isabella Knightley. Her mother died when she was about five years old. She is the central character of the novel. She is nearly 21 years old and is beautiful, clever and rich, with true hazel eyes, and according to Mrs Weston 'is the picture of grown-up health'. She is however a snob; she befriends Harriet Smith with intention to improve her and invents various romantic liaisons for her. She is also a gossip and invents an affair between Jane Fairfax and Mr Dixon, before insulting Miss Bates at Box Hill and being rebuked by George Knightley. This causes a re-examination of her previous conduct. She changes her ways and is rewarded by marrying George.

Woodhouse, Mr Henry   Of Hartfield, Highbury. Father of Isabella Knightley and Emma Woodhouse. A chronic hypochondriac whose favourite dish was 'gruel, gruel, gruel'.

Wright   Housekeeper at the vicarage.

Mansfield Park: **Completed in 1813 and first published in 1814. Often cited as the least romantic of Austen's novels but acutely socially aware, focusing as it does on the slave trade and the British aristocracy's propensity to exploit their social inferiors.**

Anderson, Miss   Younger sister of Charles Anderson. Described as Miss Anderson of the Aylmers, of Twickenham.

Anderson, Mr Charles   Friend of Tom Bertram.

Aylmers   Reside in Twickenham. Maria Rushworth (née Bertram) stays with them and Charles Crawford visits.

Baddeley   Sir Thomas Bertram's butler.

Bertram, Edmund   Younger son of Sir Thomas and Lady Bertram. As he is not the heir to Mansfield Park, he is groomed to be a clergyman. He is good-natured and is the only Bertram to show kindness to Fanny Price. He is initially smitten with Mary Crawford before turning his attentions towards Fanny Price and eventually marrying her.

Bertram, Julia   The Bertrams' younger daughter. Shares her sister's temperament and personality although, as she is younger and less beautiful, she is not so self-assured. She tends to follow Maria around and upon her sister's elopement she runs away with Yates, her brother Tom's friend.

Bertram, Lady Maria   Née Ward (sister to Mrs Norris and Mrs Frances Price). She is the wife of Sir Thomas, mother to the Bertram children and aunt to Fanny Price. She is neurotic, lazy and an incorrigible hypochondriac who values attractiveness over other, more lasting qualities.

Bertram, Maria   The Bertrams' older daughter. Vain and arrogant of manner, she treats Fanny Price badly and marries the equally odious Mr Rushworth for his wealth.

Bertram, Sir Thomas   Baronet and Member of Parliament. Married to Maria Ward. They have four children: Tom, Edmund, Maria and Julia. He takes on Fanny Price, the child of his sister-in-law who has fallen on difficult times. Sir Thomas is a stern but kind man. He is also the owner of Mansfield Park. The novel tells of the departure of Sir Thomas to the West Indies and the moral decline of his household into a series of inappropriate relationships and forbidden theatricals. Sir Thomas owns slaves on his plantations in the Caribbean but a series of disasters ensue to show him the error of his ways.

Bertram, Tom   The Bertrams' older son and heir to Mansfield Park. He is a hard-drinking party-goer who gets into debt, for which Edmund suffers. His lifestyle eventually catches up with him and he nearly dies from an illness caused by his excessive drinking.

Crawford, Admiral   Uncle of Henry and Mary Crawford, whom he brings up after their parents die. His wife dies, and his mistress moves in with him.

Uses his influence to help William Price secure his lieutenant's commission.

Crawford, Henry   Brother of Mary Crawford. He is an attractive but unprincipled man who initially woos Fanny Price; both Maria and Julia Bertram fall under his spell too. Maria marries but Henry runs off with her, although their relationship ends badly.

Crawford, Mary   Sister of Henry Crawford. Mary is as passionate as her brother and equally lacking in principle. She is a free spirit; Edmund Bertram falls in love with her and nearly proposes.

Ellis   Maid of the Bertrams, attends Maria and Julia.

Grant, Dr   45 years old. Succeeds Mr Norris as Rector of Mansfield. Brother-in-law to Henry and Mary Crawford. Made Dean of Westminister, but dies there in a fit of apoplexy brought on after three large dinners.

Grant, Mrs   Half-sister of Henry and Mary Crawford. Wife of Dr Grant, the second parson at Mansfield. She lives in the Rectory but after her husband dies she lives with Mary Crawford.

Harding, Mr   Old friend of Sir Thomas Bertram. Warns of, and later informs him of Maria (Bertram) Rushworth's and Henry Crawford's elopement. His attempts to prevent a scandal are thwarted by the elder Mrs Rushworth.

Holford, Mrs   Acquaintance of Tom Bertram. It is at her house that he is embarrassed by Miss Anderson.

Jackson, Christopher   Carpenter who is prevented from profiting from the dismantling of the stage and scenery during the amateur theatricals episode.

Jackson, Dick   Son of Christopher. Prevented from profiting from the dismantling of the stage and scenery. Mentioned in chapter 15.

Lee, Miss   Governess to Maria and Julia Bertram, and to Fanny Price.

Nanny   Mrs Norris's servant and chief counsellor.

Norris, Mrs   Oldest of the three Ward sisters. She married a clergyman and settled at Mansfield Parsonage until widowed and moving to a smaller house. She has no children and is an officious busybody, always endeavouring to derive glory from her association with the Bertram family. She is cruel to Fanny Price, whom she is always reminding of her 'place' in the family.

Norris, Reverend   Friend of Sir Thomas Bertram, marrying his sister-in-law Miss Ward. Sir Thomas gives him a living at Mansfield, later becomes ill and dies.

Price, Betsy   Youngest child of Lieutenant and Frances Price. Fanny's youngest sister is five years old.

Price, Charles   Youngest son of Lieutenant and Frances Price. Fanny's youngest brother is eight years old.

Price, Fanny   Central character of the novel. Oldest daughter of Lieutenant and Mrs Fanny Price. Her parents, unable to support nine children, send her off to live with her aunt Lady Maria Bertram and her rich husband Sir Thomas Bertram, at Mansfield Park. She falls in love and marries her cousin Edmund Bertram, although first subject to proposals from the slick Henry Crawford.

Price, Mary   Daughter of Lieutenant and Frances Price. Is about four years old when Fanny leaves home, but dies a few years later. Gives Susan a silver knife.

Price, Mr   Officer in the Marines, who was prone to a drink or two. After 11 years he was disabled from active service and lived in Portsmouth. He married Frances Ward, their children being: William, Fanny, Mary (deceased), Susan, John and Richard, Tom, Charles, and Betsy.

LITERATURE

Price, Mrs Frances   Youngest of three Ward sisters (Lady Maria Bertram and Mrs Norris being the other two). She married Lieutenant Price of the Marines to disoblige her family, causing a rift with Mrs Norris. Lives in Portsmouth with her disabled husband. Children: William, Fanny, Mary (deceased), Susan, John, Richard, Tom, Charles, Sam and Betsy.

Price, Susan   Third daughter of Lieutenant and Frances Price. Fanny's younger sister is 14 years old when she moves to Mansfield Park, where she takes Fanny's place as Lady Bertram's companion.

Price, Tom   Son of Lieutenant and Frances Price. Nine years old. Fanny helped care for him before her departure to Mansfield Park.

Price, William   Oldest child of Lieutenant and Frances Price, and favourite brother of Fanny. Joins the Royal Navy, serves as midshipman with Captain Marshall. In his attempt to woo Fanny, Henry Crawford arranges a promotion to second lieutenant for William.

Ravenshaw, Lord   Owner of Ecclesford in Cornwall where a large house party is held, and *Lovers' Vows* is staged (called off upon the death of his grandmother).

Rebecca   The Prices' slovenly and lazy upper servant.

Repton, Mr Humphrey   A landscape gardener and improver of estates. Mr Rushworth considers hiring him, at the rate of five guineas a day. Humphrey Repton was of course a notable real-life landscapist of the day.

Rushworth, Mr   Wealthy landowner but thoroughly idiotic and lacking in personality. He marries Maria Bertram.

Sneyd, Mr   Tom Bertram's friend who lives in Ramsgate with Mrs Sneyd his mother, and his two sisters.

Sneyd, Mrs   Mother of Mr, Miss and Augusta Sneyd.

Stornoway, Lady   Née Ross. Former intimate friend of Mary Crawford, although the two have not been close for thre years. Is attracted to Henry Crawford. Later jilts a young officer in the Blues and marries Lord Stornoway.

Stornoway, Lord   Husband of Lady Stornoway.

Yates, Mr   Friend of Tom Bertram, who proposes the amateur theatricals at Mansfield Park. He shows an interest in Julia Bertram and eventually elopes with her.

***Northanger Abbey*: Published posthumously in 1818, it is the shortest of Austen's six major works. The novel was completed in 1799 and pokes fun at the existing fashion for the Gothic novel typified in the works of Ann Radcliffe, particularly *The Mysteries of Udolpho*. The novel was originally called *Susan* but Austen renamed the heroine and the book. Northanger Abbey is the home of the Tilney family in Bath.**

Alice   In chapter 28 Eleanor asks Catherine to write to her 'Direct to me at Lord Longtown's, and, I must ask it, under cover to Alice.'

Allen, Mr and Mrs   Mr and Mrs Allen live in Fullerton. They are older and wealthier than the Morlands and treat Catherine Morland as a daughter. They invite Catherine to go to Bath with them. Mr Allen spends most of his time playing cards in Bath while his wife splashes her time either shopping, knitting or talking to Mrs Thorpe.

Andrews, Miss   A friend of Isabella Thorpe, described in chapter 6 as 'a sweet girl, one of the sweetest creatures in the world'. She is a great fan of Gothic novels and appears to have read them all.

Hughes, Mrs   A lady who is a member of Henry and Eleanor's party at the ball in the Upper Rooms, Bath.

Hunt, Captain   An admirer of Isabella Thorpe. Mentioned in chapter 6: 'I told Captain Hunt, at one of our assemblies this winter, that if he was to ask me to tease me all night, I would dance with him unless he would allow Miss Andrews to be as beautiful as an angel.'

Morland, Catherine   The 17-year-old heroine of the novel. Having spent her formative years in her family's modest home in Fullerton reading Gothic novels, she lets her imagination run riot when she stays with the Tilney family at Northanger Abbey. She believes General Tilney murdered his wife and although she has a kind and intelligent nature, it becomes apparent that her inexperience makes her a bad reader of people. After overcoming the embarrassment of suspecting his father of murder, Catherine is eventually betrothed to Henry.

Morland, George   One of Catherine Morland's youngest siblings, a child of six.

Morland, Harriet   The youngest in the Morland family, a four-year-old girl who vies with little George in being the first to welcome Catherine home from her adventures.

Morland, James   Catherine Morland's oldest brother who is a fellow student of John Thorpe at Oxford University. He is a good-natured but inexperienced young man, who becomes engaged to Isabella Thorpe but breaks it off when she begins to flirt with Frederick Tilney.

Morland, Mr   Father of the Morland clan. He was a clergyman in Fullerton and appears briefly at the beginning and end of the novel.

Morland, Mrs   Wife of the clergyman. A sensible soul, who does not insist on her daughters being accomplished in spite of incapacity or distaste.

Morland, Richard   The heroine's second oldest brother – a young man who would apparently have to do without cravats if he were entirely dependent on the love-sick Catherine for that article of dress.

Morland, Sarah (Sally)   Catherine Morland's 16-year-old sister who, being a young lady of common gentility, has naturally altered her name as far as she can, from Sally to Sarah.

Skinner, Dr   Mentioned in chapter 8 as having stayed with his family at the pump rooms in Bath for some three months.

Thorpe, Anne   One of Mrs Thorpe's two younger daughters. Although not as beautiful as Isabella, she does very well by pretending to be as handsome, imitating her air, and dressing in the same style.

Thorpe, Edward   One of three sons of Mrs Thorpe. He attended Merchant Taylors.

Thorpe, Isabella   One of three daughters of Mrs Thorpe and sister of John Thorpe. She is beautiful but shallow and as such a perfect friend for Catherine Morland. She is a master of artifice and is able to charm all and sundry, but eventually Catherine sees her for the malicious gossip she is, as do her romantic interests James Morland and Frederick Tilney.

Thorpe, John   The arrogant and boastful brother of Isabella Thorpe, and the would-be suitor of Catherine Morland. He attended Oxford University.

Thorpe, Mrs   A former schoolfellow and intimate of Mrs Allen's. She is the widowed mother of Isabella and their natures are similar.

Thorpe, William   Another young Thorpe sibling. This one is at sea, but like his more academic brothers, and according to his mother (in chapter 6), he too is apparently beloved and respected by all who know him!

Tilney, Eleanor Henry's younger sister. A shy, quiet young woman who shares her brother's interest in reading.

Tilney, Frederick A dashing captain in the 12th Light Dragoons, oldest brother of Henry and Eleanor. He flirts with Isabella Thorpe, which leads her to break off her engagement to James Morland, but then abandons her in Bath.

Tilney, General The authoritarian father of Henry, Frederick and Eleanor. A widower who takes great pride in his home, Northanger Abbey, which he refurbished himself. He is material and as such is concerned that his children marry well. He is also gruff and overbearing which makes Catherine Morland think poorly of him, to the extent of suspecting him of murder.

Tilney, Henry The hero of the novel. A 26-year-old parson in the village of Woodston. He is intelligent, witty and charming, and nurtures Catherine through her fantasies. Her true nature shines through in the end and Henry falls in love with her.

Persuasion: **Completed in 1816 during her second phase of writing. As in the case of *Northanger Abbey*, *Persuasion* was published posthumously by Austen's brother Henry in 1818.**

Benwick, Captain Formerly first lieutenant of the *Laconia*. He was engaged to Fanny Harville, who died the preceding summer while he was at sea. Later attracted to Anne Elliot, he falls in love with and becomes engaged to Louisa Musgrove. Captain Benwick is a sensitive man who loves poetry.

Brand, Admiral Brother of Captain Frederick Wentworth. Disliked by Mrs Croft because he 'got away some of my best men' (as relayed by Admiral Croft). He has the curacy of Monksford, but later moves out of the county, marries and has a parish in Shropshire.

Brigden, Captain A friend of Admiral Croft, mentioned in chapter 18.

Carteret, Miss Daughter of Lady Dalrymple: 'So plain and so awkward, that she would never had been tolerated in Camden Place but for her birth'.

Clay, Mrs Penelope Elizabeth Elliot's gold-digging friend. Both Anne and Lady Russell are concerned about her romantic designs on Sir Walter while staying at Bath. She is a divorcee with two children.

Croft, Admiral Sir Walter is persuaded to lease Kellynch Hall to the admiral and his wife.

Croft, Mrs Sophia Wife of Admiral Croft.

Dalrymple, Lady An Irish viscountess. Mother of the Honourable Miss Carteret and cousin of Sir Walter Elliot. She takes a house for three months at Laura Place, Bath, and Sir Walter writes to her in the hope of patching up old wounds.

Dalrymple, Viscount Husband of Viscountess Dalrymple. His death before the beginning of the novel has caused some friction between the Dalrymples and the Elliots as Sir Walter did not send a letter of condolence to the viscountess due to his own life-threatening illness.

Drew, Sir Archibald Friend of Admiral Croft who mistook Anne Elliot for the Admiral's wife while walking the streets of Bath. He has a grandson, mentioned in chapter 18.

Durands Visitors to Bath, mentioned in chapter 21.

Elliot, Anne The central character of the novel. Two years younger than her sister, Elizabeth. Both Elizabeth and her father Sir Walter show her little affection but she is the favourite of Lady Russell, who convinced her to break her engagement with Captain Wentworth eight years ago when she was 19, due to his limited funds. Anne visits her sister, Mary, at Uppercross, and is very loving to her two children, Charles and Walter. Anne meets Captain Wentworth on the street. They exchange pleasantries and then deeper thoughts and feelings, realise they are in love and are eventually married.

Elliot, Elizabeth Oldest daughter of Sir Walter Elliot. She is 29 at the beginning of the novel and runs the house, Kellynch Hall. Sir Walter, Mrs Clay and she go to reside in Bath while the unwanted Anne goes to visit her hypochondriacal sister Mary at the Musgroves' residence, Uppercross.

Elliot, Lady Elizabeth Wife of Sir Walter and mother of Elizabeth, Anne and Mary. She died 14 years before the novel begins. Lady Elliot was the daughter of James Stevenson of South Park, Gloucester.

Elliot, Mary Youngest daughter of Sir Walter. Married to Charles Musgrove. They live at Uppercross with their two children. Mary is a hypochondriac.

Elliot, Mrs Granddaughter of a butcher, daughter of a glazier. Her wealth attracts William Walter Elliot who marries her. She dies after an unhappy marriage.

Elliot, Sir Walter Of Kellynch Hall, Somersetshire. Baronet. Sir Walter is 54 years old at the beginning of the novel. His wife, Elizabeth, died 14 years before the novel begins. Father of Elizabeth, Anne and Mary. To manage his debts he is forced to leave Kellynch Hall and move to more humble quarters at Camden Place, Bath.

Elliot, Sir Walter The Second Elliot, grandfather of Mr William Elliot.

Elliot, William Walter Grandson and presumed heir of Sir Walter Elliot (the Second). Recently widowed, he begins to have designs on Anne Elliot, causing Captain Wentworth to feel jealous pangs. Mrs Smith informs Anne of Elliot's true and despicable nature. He is the nephew of the first Sir Walter.

Frankland, Mrs Friend of Lady Russell. Visitor to Bath.

Harville, Captain Resident of Lyme. Friend of Captain Frederick Wentworth. Mr and Mrs Harville have three children.

Harville, Mrs Wife of Captain Harville. Anne looks upon their union as an example of a happy marriage.

Hayter, Charles Oldest son of the Hayters. Non-resident curate. Has an understanding with, and marries his cousin, Henrietta Musgrove, after securing a church living.

Hayter, Mr Henry Owner of Winthrop. Husband of Mrs Musgrove's sister. They have a son, Charles, and two daughters.

Hayter, Mrs Mrs Musgrove's sister. Wife of Henry and mother of a son, Charles, and two daughters.

Jeeves Servant of the Crofts who drove their carriage.

Jemima Servant of the Musgroves at Uppercross.

Musgrove, Charles Elder son of Charles and Mary Musgrove (née Elliot).

Musgrove, Charles Oldest child of Charles and Mary Musgrove. Married to Mary Elliot. They live at Uppercross with their two children, Charles (little) and Walter.

Musgrove, Mr Charles The elder Charles Musgrove is the owner of Uppercross Hall, Somerset. Second only to Sir Walter Elliot in the neighbourhood. His children include Charles, Richard (Dick), Henrietta, Louisa, Mary, and several younger ones, Harry being the youngest son.

Musgrove, Louisa Second daughter of Charles (elder) and Mrs Musgrove, 19 years old.

Musgrove, Mary Youngest daughter of Sir Walter Elliot. Marries Charles Musgrove (the younger) after

LITERATURE

he is refused by her sister Anne. Mother of Charles and Walter. She is a hypochondriac.

Musgrove, Mrs Mary   Wife of the elder Charles Musgrove. Always had a special connection with Captain Frederick Wentworth as he was the commander in charge of her late son, Dick.

Musgrove, Richard   Dick Musgrove is the good-for-nothing but now deceased son of the elder Charles Musgrove and Mary Musgrove.

Musgrove, Walter   Younger son of Charles and Mary Musgrove (née Elliot), aged two at the beginning of the novel.

Rooke, Nurse   Sister of Mrs Smith's landlady.

Russell, Lady   Wife of the late Sir Henry Russell. She was the close friend of Lady Elliot and continues to support her daughters after Lady Elliot's death. She is Anne's godmother and treats her with more affection than other members of the Elliot family.

Russell, Sir Henry   Lady Russell's late husband.

Shepherd, Mr   Trusted family advisor of the Elliots. Helps Lady Russell draw up a plan for ways that Sir Walter Elliot can save money.

Smith, Mrs   Née Hamilton. Friend of Anne Elliot at school. Later Anne finds her again in Bath, widowed, impoverished and crippled, and helps her after finding out that it was Mr William Walter Elliot who put her into debt and refused to help her after her husband died.

Speed, Mrs   Landlady at Mrs Smith's lodgings in Bath.

Wallis, Colonel   Friend of Mr Elliot, 'a highly respectable man, perfectly the gentleman'.

Wentworth, Captain   Brother of Edward Wentworth and Sophia Croft. Captain Frederick Wentworth has been in love with Anne Elliot but Lady Russell persuaded Anne to break off the relationship due to his limited means. Eventually Lady Russell concedes she was wrong in her judgement of him and, now in a healthier financial position, he lets Anne know of his feelings for her in a letter and finally marries her.

Wentworth, Edward   Brother of Captain Frederick Wentworth and Sophia Croft. He has the curacy of Monksford but later moves out of the county, marries and has a parish in Shropshire.

***Pride & Prejudice*: Completed in 1797, under the title *First Impressions*, and published in 1813. The imaginary places mentioned in the novel include Longbourn, Herts (residence of the Bennets), Netherfield Park, Herts (residence of the Bingleys), Pemberley, Derbyshire (residence of Fitzwilliam Darcy).**

Annesley, Mrs   Companion to Miss Georgiana Darcy. A genteel, agreeable looking woman.

Bennet, Catherine (Kitty)   The fourth Bennet sister. Kitty tends to follow Lydia's lead in whatever she does.

Bennet, Elizabeth   Second oldest of the five Bennet sisters and the central character of the novel. She is quick-witted, intelligent, bold and attractive (with particularly fine eyes). She prides herself on being a good judge of character but in reality her vanity often clouds her judgement. After a stormy relationship she eventually marries Mr Fitzwilliam Darcy. Jane Austen called Elizabeth 'as delightful a creature as ever appeared in print'.

Bennet, Jane   Oldest of the five Bennet sisters and foil to Elizabeth's more rash deliberations. Jane is the model of the perfect older sister: beautiful, kind and loving, with unerring good sense. Marries Charles Bingley at the end of the novel.

Bennet, Lydia   The youngest of the Bennet sisters and the favourite of her mother, whose frivolous nature she mirrors. Elopes with George Wickham despite his involvement with Mary King.

Bennet, Mary   The third Bennet sister, who is described as 'the only plain one in the family'. Annoys Elizabeth with her unaccomplished singing in front of Mr Darcy.

Bennet, Mr   Father of the five Bennet sisters, and long-suffering husband of a foolish woman. A kindly, intelligent man who settles for an easy life to the cost of his youngest daughter's honour.

Bennet, Mrs   Mother of the five Bennet sisters. A shrewish woman who is intent on marrying off her five daughters.

Bingley, Charles   The amiable and good-tempered man who rents Netherfield Park at the beginning of the novel. Father of Caroline and Louisa Hurst. He marries Jane Bennet by the end of the book and moves out of the neighbourhood.

Bingley, Miss Caroline   Charles Bingley's unmarried sister. She is arrogant and superficial but unlike Darcy has no redeeming virtues, always ridiculing the poor manners of the Bennet children.

Carter, Captain   Member of the regiment in Meryton.

Chamberlayne, Mr   Member of the regiment in Meryton.

Collins, Rev. William   Clergyman and Mr Bennet's cousin who is in line to inherit Longbourn when Mr Bennet dies. A rather comical fellow, prone to making long rambling speeches on nothing but what he feels will elevate him in the esteem of the listener.

Darcy, Georgiana   Fitzwilliam Darcy's younger sister who has all of her brother's virtues but none of his aloofness.

Darcy, Lady Anne   Born Lady Anne Fitzwilliam; Lady Catherine de Bourgh's sister and Mr Darcy's mother.

Darcy, Mr (the elder)   Fitzwilliam Darcy's father, who died approximately five years before the novel begins.

Darcy, Mr Fitzwilliam   Wealthy aristocrat and owner of Pemberley. At the beginning of the novel he is very conscious of class difference but falls in love with Elizabeth Bennet because she refuses to treat him as anything but an equal. He begins to judge people by their character rather than their social standing. He eventually marries Elizabeth.

Dawson   Lady Catherine's maid.

De Bourgh, Anne   Lady Catherine's sickly daughter who is pampered by her mother.

De Bourgh, Catherine   Mr Collins' patron and Mr Darcy's aunt. Extremely wealthy and aristocratic, she likes the world to know of her superior standing. Her shallowness helps Darcy to mend his ways.

De Bourgh, Sir Lewis   Lady Catherine's late husband.

Denny, Captain   A member of the regiment in Meryton and friend of George Wickham.

Fitzwilliam, Colonel   Mr Darcy's cousin who accompanies Elizabeth Bennet during her stay with the Collinses and confides to her that he must marry for money as he is a second son.

Forster, Colonel   Head of the regiment stationed at Meryton. A decent man who suffers great guilt when Lydia Bennet elopes with George Wickham.

Forster, Harriet   Colonel Forster's wife who befriends Lydia Bennet and invites her to spend the summer with them in Brighton, from where Lydia elopes with Wickham.

Gardiner, Mr Edward   Brother of Mrs Bennet who works as a merchant and, unlike the aristocrats who live off the interest of their land, is seen as of inferior class. Darcy eventually overcomes his prejudice towards the working class by perceiving the decency of Mr Gardiner.

Gardiner, Mrs Mr Gardiner's wife who tends to act as a mother-figure for Elizabeth and Jane Bennet. She brings Jane to London with her in order to ease her heartbreak over Bingley's failure to return to Netherfield. She also gives good counsel to Elizabeth with regard to Wickham's intentions.

Gouldings, The Residents of Haye-Park. Only William Goulding is mentioned: 'we overtook William Goulding in his curricle', chapter 51.

Grantley, Miss An acquaintance of Miss Caroline Bingley.

Haggerston, Mr Mr Gardiner's attorney.

Harrington, Harriet Acquaintance of Mrs Forster and Lydia Bennet in Brighton.

Harrington, Miss 'Pen' Acquaintance of Mrs Forster and Lydia Bennet in Brighton.

Hill, Mrs Housekeeper at Longbourn.

Hurst, Mr Husband of Charles Bingley's sister Louisa. Does nothing but eat and play cards.

Hurst, Mrs Louisa Charles Bingley's married sister who has a similarly abhorrent nature to her unmarried sister.

Jenkinson, Mrs Anne de Bourgh's companion.

John Both Collinses and Gardiners have a servant named John.

Jones, Mr The apothecary at Meryton.

King, Miss Mary Heiress to 10,000 pounds who was courted by Wickham.

Long, Mrs The Bennets' neighbour who has two nieces.

Lucas, Charlotte Elizabeth's friend who is intent on marrying for security and avails herself of the intentions of the Reverend Collins.

Lucas, Lady Sir William's wife and mother of Charlotte and Maria.

Lucas, Maria Charlotte Lucas's younger sister who travels with her father and Elizabeth Bennet when visiting Charlotte.

Lucas, Sir William Friend and neighbour of the Bennets who loves nothing better than to talk of his knighthood.

Metcalfe, Lady Acquaintance of Lady Catherine.

Morris, Mr The man who shows Netherfield Park to Mr Bingley.

Nicholls, Mrs The housekeeper at Netherfield.

Philips, Mr The husband of Mrs Bennet's sister. An attorney in Meryton.

Philips, Mrs Mrs Bennet's sister who lives in Meryton (where the soldiers are based) and consequently is often visited by the Bennet sisters.

Pope, Miss Governess in Lady Metcalf's family.

Pratt, Mr Member of the regiment at Meryton.

Reynolds, Mrs Housekeeper at Pemberley.

Richard, Mr An employee of Mr Philips – Lydia mentions that he will join the regiment if her uncle lets him go.

Robinson, Mr Man who, at the Assembly Ball, asked Mr Bingley which girl he thought the handsomest.

Sarah A maid.

Stone, Mr Mr Gardiner's clerk.

Watson, Miss A resident of Meryton whom the soldiers visited.

Webbs, The Miss Acquaintances of Lady Catherine.

Wickham, George An officer in the regiment stationed at Meryton. Initially favoured by Elizabeth Bennet to be a good and amiable man but events contrive to show his true character to be deceitful and mercenary. After forming a liaison with Mary King, he eventually elopes with Lydia Bennet.

Wickham, Old Mr Father of George and steward to the late Mr Darcy.

Younge, Mrs Former governess of Georgiana Darcy who informs Darcy of the whereabouts of Wickham and Lydia.

Sense and Sensibility: **Written in 1797 and published in 1811, her first published novel was financed by Austen herself after both *Northanger Abbey* and *Pride and Prejudice* were rejected by a publisher. Her brother Henry and sister Cassandra were instrumental in convincing Austen to publish the novel, originally entitled *Elinor and Marianne*.**

Betsy Dashwoods' servant at Norland Park and Barton Park.

Betty Mrs Jennings' maid.

Brandon, Colonel Of Delaford in Dorsetshire. A 35-year-old former military officer who was stationed in India. His stern exterior hides a soft heart. Marries Marianne Dashwood and becomes less stern.

Careys A family in Newton, near Barton Park. Friends of the Middletons.

Cartwright Mrs Jennings' servant, mentioned in chapter 26.

Clarke, Mrs An 'intimate acquaintance' of Mrs Jennings.

Courtland, Lord Friend of Robert Ferrars. Robert disapproves of all three of his building plans, and suggests a cottage instead.

Dashwood, Elinor At 19 the oldest and wisest of the daughters of Mrs Dashwood and Henry, often sacrificing her own happiness in order to maintain the family's status quo. Marries Edward Ferrers and lives at Delaford where she is eventually joined by Marianne and the colonel.

Dashwood, Fanny Daughter of Mrs Ferrars, sister of Edward and Robert Ferrars, married John Dashwood and has a more miserly temperament even than he.

Dashwood, Harry John and Fanny Dashwood's spoilt four-year-old son.

Dashwood, Henry Of Stanhill and Norland Park, Sussex. By his first wife he had one son, John; by his second, three daughters, Elinor, Marianne and Margaret. He dies at the beginning of the novel, leaving his son his estate and ensuring his daughters are forced to accept an invitation from Sir John Middleton to Barton Cottage.

Dashwood, John Son of Henry Dashwood. Mean and miserly to his three half-sisters. Married to Fanny Ferrars, with one son, Harry, four years old.

Dashwood, Margaret Henry and Mrs Dashwood's youngest daughter. At 13 years old she is at a difficult age and although she aspires to Marianne's romantic inclinations her sounder sense prevails.

Dashwood, Marianne Henry and Mrs Dashwood's second daughter. Two years younger than Elinor and lacking her discretion and calm. After falling and hurting her ankle is carried home by the rakish Willoughby who shares her love of the arts. Willoughby lets her down in love, and she eventually marries Colonel Brandon and lives happily at Delaford.

Dashwood, Mrs Mother of Elinor, Marianne and Margaret. She is close to her daughters but hopes to see them married off.

Davies, Dr Discussed in chapter 32 as a possible beau of Anne Steele.

Dennison, Mrs Mrs Dennison mistakes Elinor and Marianne for their brother's guests in chapter 36.

Donavan, Mr Apothecary who attends Charlotte Palmer's baby in chapter 37.

LITERATURE

Elliott, Lady   Elliott's wife who can't entertain for want of space.

Elliott, Sir   Robert Ferrars' friend who lives in a cottage near Dartford.

Ellisons   Miss Grey's guardians.

Ferrars, Edward   The 23-year-old brother of Fanny but with a very different nature. Shy and retiring with a kind heart, he eventually marries Elinor Dashwood.

Ferrars, Mrs   Of Park Street. Mother of Edward, Robert and Fanny. A bad-tempered woman who ironically disowns her benevolent son, Edward.

Ferrars, Robert   Edward's brother and husband of Lucy Steele. Arrogant of manner but beloved of his mother.

Godby, Miss   Told Miss Sparks that nobody in their senses could expect Mr Ferrars to give up a woman like Miss Morton, chapter 38.

Grey, Sophia   John Willoughby's wife, whom he married in preference to Marianne Dashwood as she was wealthier.

Harris, Dr   Helps to cure Marianne Dashwood during her illness at Cleveland.

Henshawe, Biddy   Aunt of Miss Grey who 'married a very wealthy man'.

Jennings, Mrs   Of Berkeley-street, a jolly but vulgar widow who makes endless jokes about potential suitors for Elinor and Marianne. The mother of Lady Mary Middleton and Charlotte Palmer.

Middleton, Anna-Maria   Sir John Middleton's daughter, about three years old.

Middleton, John   Sir John Middleton's son, about six years old.

Middleton, Lady Mary   Daughter of Mrs Jennings, sister of Charlotte Palmer, and wife of Sir John Middleton. A vain and proper woman who does not share her husband's gregarious nature.

Middleton, Sir John   Owner of Barton Park in Devonshire, and as such, the Dashwoods' landlord. A gregarious man who is forever inviting the Dashwoods to his neighbouring property, Barton Cottage. Married to Mary Jennings.

Middleton, William   Sir John Middleton's son.

Morton, Miss   Only daughter of Lord Morton. She was first supposed to marry Edward Ferrars, then his brother Robert, but ends up with neither.

old Gibson   Former resident of East Kingham Farm, the property 'immediately adjoining' Norland Park, who is alluded to in chapter 33.

Palmer, Charlotte   Daughter of Mrs Jennings. Married to Thomas Palmer; forever apologising for her husband's ill manners to all and sundry and seemingly blind to his shortcomings.

Palmer, Thomas   Of Cleveland in Somerset, and Hanover Square. Married Charlotte Jennings. Very disagreeable nature.

Pratt, Mr   Of Longstaple, uncle of the Steeles.

Richardson, Mrs   Friend of Anne Steele, appearing in chapter 38.

Robert, Sir   Edward and Robert Ferrars' and Fanny Dashwood's uncle.

Rose, Mr   One of Anne Steele's beaus; clerk to Mr Simpson in Exeter, mentioned in chapter 21.

Sharpe, Martha   Friend of Anne Steele who shared her habit of eavesdropping as portrayed in chapter 38.

Simpson, Mr   Exeter resident; employer of Mr Rose, mentioned in chapter 21.

Smith, Mrs   Of Allenham Court in Devonshire. Willoughby's aunt, who does not appear in the novel but disinherits her nephew and sends him to London when she hears of the plight of Miss Williams.

Sparks, Miss   Referred to in gossip with Miss Godby about Mr Ferrars' giving up of Lucy Steele as being quite reasonable, in chapter 38.

Steele, Anne (Nancy)   Sister of Lucy Steele, nearly 30 years old and 'never succeeded in catching the Doctor'. A distant cousin of Mrs Jennings who becomes a guest at Barton Cottage and gains the approval of Lady Middleton through flattery towards her and her children.

Steele, Lucy   Anne Steele's younger sister, Mr Pratt's niece. Marginally smarter than her sister and a bit of an opportunist. Marries Robert Ferrars.

Taylor, Mrs   Mrs Jennings' friend and the main source for news about Miss Grey.

Thomas   Dashwoods' servant at Norland Park and Barton Park.

Walker, Miss   Acquaintance of Mrs Taylor, mentioned in chapter 30.

Westons   Friends of Mrs Jennings in London, mentioned in chapter 20.

Williams, Eliza   Colonel Brandon's adopted daughter of a woman he once held in great affection. She does not appear in the novel, but her seduction by Willoughby, and eventual abandonment by him, are integral to the plot.

Willoughby, John   Of Combe Magna in Somerset; 25-year-old, roguish young man who loves art and literature but is ultimately reckless and deceitful. Husband of Sophia Grey whom he married for money after disappointing Marianne Dashwood.

Charles Dickens's Characters (the Novels)

Barnaby Rudge: **fifth published novel (1841), originally as serial in weekly magazine *Master Humphrey's Clock***

Benjamin   Member of the Prentice Knights with Simon Tappertit.

Chester, Edward   Son of John, eventually overcomes the opposition of his father and marries Emma Haredale. The couple relocate to the West Indies.

Chester, Sir John   Father of Edward, tries to prevent Edward's marriage to Emma Haredale. Becomes a member of Parliament. Killed in a duel by Emma's uncle Geoffrey.

Cobb, Tom   Friend of John Willet at the Maypole Inn.

Daisy, Solomon   Clerk and bell-ringer at the parish church in Chigwell. Friend of John Willet at the Maypole Inn. Daisy tells the story of Reuben Haredale's murder.

Dennis, Ned   Executioner at Tyburn, becomes involved in the Gordon Riots and is executed.

Fielding, Sir John   Blind half-brother of novelist Henry Fielding. Magistrate at Bow Street. Dickens has him at the scene of the Gordon Riots when, in fact, Fielding was on his deathbed at the time of the riots.

Gashford   Lord George Gordon's hypocritical secretary. He urges the rioters to exact revenge on Geoffrey Haredale, who had exposed his treacherous ways. He abandons Lord Gordon when the riots are suppressed by soldiers and becomes a government spy.

Gordon, Lord George   1751–93 Historical figure and leader of the Gordon (anti-Catholic) Riots of 1780.

Grip   Barnaby Rudge's pet raven, who carried his

head on one side and seemed to embody the spirit of all-knowingness with his sound unwitting advice.

Grueby, John Loyal servant of Lord George Gordon who tries to isolate Gordon from the rioters when the protest turns to violence.

Haredale, Emma Daughter of the murdered Reuben and niece of Geoffrey. She eventually marries Edward Chester.

Haredale, Geoffrey Brother of the murdered Reuben and uncle of Emma. Suspected of being responsible for the murder of his brother, he spends his life in pursuit of the real killer. A Catholic, his house is burned in the Gordon Riots. He fights a duel with Sir John Chester.

Haredale, Reuben Brother of Geoffrey, father of Emma. Murdered before the story begins.

Hugh Ostler at the Maypole. Joins the rioters in London and is later hanged. Revealed to be the son of Sir John Chester.

Langdale Kindly vintner and distiller in Holborn based on an historical figure. The Catholic Langdale shelters Geoffrey Haredale from the rioters. His home and warehouse are burned in the riots, his stores of spirits are consumed by the mob.

Miggs, Miss Maid in the Varden household. Comically allies with Martha Varden against her husband. Miggs aids the rioters when they attempt to capture Gabriel. She is discharged after the riots and becomes a jailer in a women's prison.

Parkes, Phil Friend of John Willet at the Maypole Inn.

Philips Constable who the Lord Mayor of London suggests might help to protect Langdale during the Gordon Riots.

Rudge, Barnaby Main character, a simple but good-hearted boy who unwittingly gets involved in the Gordon Riots when he falls into bad company. He is later arrested and sentenced to death but gains reprieve through the help of Gabriel Varden.

Rudge, Barnaby Sr Father of Barnaby and husband of Mary. He was the Steward at the Warren and murdered his employer, Reuben Haredale. He went into hiding after the murder and resurfaces years later trying to extort money from his wife. He is finally captured by Geoffrey Haredale.

Rudge, Mary Barnaby's mother, goes to great lengths to keep Barnaby away from his father who has murdered Reuben Haredale.

Stagg Blind member of the Prentice Knights with Simon Tappertit. He joins Barnaby Rudge Sr trying to extort money from Mary Rudge. Killed when he tries to run from officers arresting Hugh, Barnaby, and Rudge Sr.

Tappertit, Simon Locksmith Gabriel Varden's apprentice, who is in love with Gabriel's daughter, Dolly. He becomes a leader of the rioters during the Gordon Riots and during the fighting loses his slender legs, long his pride and joy.

Varden, Dolly Daughter of Gabriel and Martha, friend of Emma Haredale, loved by Joe Willet, whom she eventually marries.

Varden, Gabriel Honest locksmith and owner of the Golden Key where Simon Tappertit is apprenticed. Father of Dolly and long-suffering husband of Martha. He is a friend of Barnaby's mother and, after the Gordon Riots, helps clear Barnaby's name.

Varden, Martha Overbearing wife of Gabriel, mother of Dolly. A woman of 'uncertain temper' and a fanatical Protestant, her fanaticism is tempered after the riots when she witnesses the heroics of her husband.

Willet, Joe Son of John who resents his father's

treatment of him. He joins the army and loses an arm in the American Revolution. Later he marries Dolly Varden. The couple become proprietors of the rebuilt Maypole Inn.

Willet, John Proprietor of the Maypole Inn and father of Joe. Father and son quarrel when John treats the adult Joe as a child and Joe leaves, joining the army. John witnesses the destruction of the Maypole by the rioters. He is later reconciled with his son.

Bleak House: **ninth novel published in 20 monthly parts between March 1852 and September 1853**

Badger, Bayham Doctor, cousin of Kenge, to whom Richard Carstone is apprenticed. Badger's wife Laura talks incessantly about her two former husbands, Captain Swosser and Professor Dingo.

Bagnet Family Musical, military family headed by Matthew, an old army friend of George Rouncewell. Bagnet's wife, the old girl, knows Matthew so well that he always calls upon her to supply his opinion. The Bagnet children, Quebec, Malta and Woolwich, are named after the bases where the family have been stationed. Matthew is guarantor to George's loan from Smallweed. When Smallweed calls in the debt George is forced to deliver a document Smallweed needs to help Tulkinghorn learn Lady Dedlock's secret.

Barbary, Miss Godmother who raises Esther Summerson. Later found to be Esther's aunt, the sister of Lady Dedlock.

Bogsby, James George 'Highly respectable' landlord of the Sol's Arms.

Boodle, Lord Politician who attends Sir Leicester Dedlock's social gatherings. Like Buffy he speculates on governmental machinations, including Coodle, Doodle and so on through the alphabet up to Quoodle.

Boythorn, Lawrence Friend of John Jarndyce whom Dickens based on writer Walter Savage Landor (1775-1864)

Bucket, Inspector Detective in charge of finding Tulkinghorn's murderer. After Lady Dedlock's disappearance Sir Leicester hires Bucket to find her. He later uncovers the will that is instrumental in clearing up the Jarndyce and Jarndyce Chancery case.

Buffy, the Right Hon. William MP who attends Sir Leicester Dedlock's social gatherings. Like Lord Boodle he speculates on governmental machinations, including Cuffy, Duffy and so on through the alphabet up to Puffy.

Carstone, Richard Ward of John Jarndyce and a party to the case of Jarndyce and Jarndyce. He marries Ada Clare and later dies when his health declines as the estate he hopes to acquire is consumed in court costs.

Chadband, Reverend Typical Dickensian hypocritical reverend, admonishing Jo in the spirit while he starves. Marries the former Mrs Rachael.

Clare, Ada Ward of John Jarndyce, friend of Esther Summerson, cousin of Richard Carstone, whom she marries but is soon widowed.

Darby Police constable on duty in Tom-all-Alone's, who accompanies Inspector Bucket and Mr Snagsby

Dedlock, Lady Honoria Wife of Sir Leicester Dedlock and, unknown to her husband, mother of Esther Summerson. A tainted woman who lives a life of lies. When Tulkinghorn, the family lawyer, learns the secret she runs away and is found dead by Esther at the gates of the cemetery in which Esther's father, Captain Hawdon, lies buried.

Dedlock, Sir Leicester Husband of Lady Dedlock, a

baronet who is 20 years older than his wayward wife. Owner of Chesney Wold, and guardian of the status quo.

Dedlock, Volumnia Poor relation of Sir Leicester Dedlock. 'Rouged and necklaced' hanger-on at Chesney Wold.

Dingo, Professor Mrs Bayham Badger's second husband, who was said to have been 'of European reputation'.

Doyce, Daniel Smith and engineer who has perfected the ultimate invention, involving a very curious secret process, but is constantly thwarted by the government in his attempt to get it developed. The invention goes unexplained.

Flite, Miss A slightly mad old woman who is a regular attendant at the court of Chancery, expecting to receive a favourable judgement in a case that no one is sure has ever existed.

Gridley Known as the 'Man from Shropshire' and another casualty of Chancery.

Grub, Mr President of the Umbugology and Ditchwaterisics session at the second meeting of the Mudfog Association.

Grubble, Mr Landlord of the Dedlock Arms, who never wore a coat except at church. His wife was a beautiful woman who broke her ankle but it never healed.

Guppy, William Clerk for Kenge and Carboy. Proposes marriage to Esther Summerson, which she refuses. Guppy is involved in the investigation of Lady Dedlock's secret.

Hawdon, Captain *See* Nemo.

Hortense, Mademoiselle Lady Dedlock's French maid. She is dismissed in favour of Rosa and aids Tulkinghorn in discovering Lady Dedlock's secret. When Tulkinghorn spurns her she murders him. Hortense is based on Mrs Manning, a murderer whose execution Dickens witnessed in 1849.

Jarndyce, John Owner of Bleak House and party in the Chancery suit of Jarndyce and Jarndyce. He adopts Esther Summerson, who becomes close friends with John's cousins, Ada Clare and Richard Carstone. John hates the lawsuit which has gone on for so long with no end in sight. Richard, however, becomes totally consumed by the case, hoping it will make him his fortune. This obsession causes Carstone and Jarndyce to suffer a falling out. Jarndyce falls in love with Esther and asked her to marry him, but although she originally consents, she subsequently falls in love with Allan Woodcourt.

Jellyby, Caroline (Caddy) Neglected daughter of Mrs Jellyby and acts as her personal secretary ('I'm pen and ink to ma'). Caddy leaves home and marries Prince Turveydrop.

Jellyby, Mrs Mrs Jellyby is involved in many causes and charities but neglects her large family. Dickens modelled Mrs Jellyby on Caroline Chisholm.

Jellyby, Peepy Little brother of Caddy and son of Mrs Jellyby whose clothes were either too big or too small.

Jenny Brickmaker's wife, befriended by Esther Summerson after Jenny's child dies. Later exchanges coats with Lady Dedlock, throwing Bucket off in his pursuit of Lady Dedlock as she flees following the revealing of her secret.

Jo The crossing sweeper. When Jo shows Lady Dedlock the haunts of Captain Hawdon, lawyer Tulkinghorn has Jo kept moving from place to place. He befriends Esther Summerson at Bleak House and communicates smallpox to Charlie, and then Esther. Jo later dies at George's Shooting Gallery.

Jobling, Tony (Weevle) Friend of Guppy who takes

Nemo's room at Krook's after Nemo's death. Jobling and Guppy discover the spectacular death of Krook and are temporary celebrities, drinking for free at the Sol's Arms.

Kenge Solicitor for John Jarndyce in the firm Kenge and Carboy. Known as 'Conversation Kenge'.

Krook Drunken and illiterate proprietor of a rag and bottle shop. Known as the 'Lord Chancellor', Krook collects court documents. A will instrumental in the Jarndyce and Jarndyce court case is found among his holdings by Mr Smallweed, who inherits Krook's possessions following his demise by spontaneous combustion. Krook is Mrs Smallweed's brother.

Lord Chancellor A high legal figure in the Court of Chancery (of course).

Mooney Beadle who is summoned to Krook's home on Hawdon's (Nemo's) death and gives evidence at the inquest.

Neckett, Charlotte (Charley) Daughter of sheriff's officer Neckett. When her father dies Charley cares for her two younger siblings, Emma and Tom. Charley becomes Esther Summerson's maid, nursing Esther through smallpox. She later marries a miller.

Neckett, Mr Sheriff's officer who arrests debtors and delivers them to Coavin's sponging house (temporary debtor's prison). Thus Skimpole gives Neckett the nickname 'Coavinses'. Neckett dies leaving three orphans: Charlotte (Charley), Emma and Tom.

Nemo Alias of Captain Hawdon (Nemo is Latin for 'nobody'). Nemo is doing some law copying for Snagsby and is a boarder in Krook's rag and bottle shop when he dies of an opium overdose. He is later found to be the former lover of Lady Dedlock and the father of Esther Summerson.

Pardiggle, Mrs Associate of Mrs Jellyby in her charitable works.

Quale, Mr Part of Mrs Jellyby's circle of friends, although interested in Caddy Jellyby. Eventually weds Miss Wisk.

Rachael, Mrs Esther Summerson's nurse. Later marries Reverend Chadband.

Rosa Personal maid to Lady Dedlock after Hortense is dismissed. Marries Mrs Rouncewell's grandson.

Rouncewell, George Son of the Dedlock's housekeeper Mrs Rouncewell. George ran away to join the army and cut himself off from his mother. After leaving the army he buys a shooting gallery in London with money borrowed from Smallweed. Smallweed pressures George to give over examples of Captain Hawdon's handwriting in order to help Tulkinghorn learn Lady Dedlock's secret. Charged with the murder of Tulkinghorn by Bucket, later George is exonerated of the crime and is reunited with his mother.

Rouncewell, Mrs Longtime housekeeper of Chesney Wold, home of Sir Leicester Dedlock. Mother of George and another son, who is an important ironmaster in northern England.

Skimpole, Harold Friend of John Jarndyce who claims he is a mere child who understands nothing of money, and through this smooth act manages to have everyone else pay his way through life. Dickens modelled Skimpole on Leigh Hunt.

Smallweed, Mr Joshua Grandfather Smallweed is a usurer to whom Rouncewell owes money. Smallweed uses this leverage to obtain from George a sample of Nemo's handwriting in an attempt to help Tulkinghorn learn Lady Dedlock's secret. Also in the Smallweed family are grandmother – Krook's sister, at whom grandfather throws cushions when she mentions money – and the twin grandchildren, Bartholomew and Judy.

Snagsby Law stationer near Chancery Lane who hires Nemo to do some copy work. Snagsby's wife is a zealous supporter of Rev. Chadband.

Squod, Phil George Rouncewell's ugly little assistant at the shooting gallery. Formerly a travelling tinker.

Summerson, Esther Principal character in the story and one of the narrators. She is brought up an orphan by her aunt, Miss Barbary. On her aunt's death she is adopted by John Jarndyce and becomes companions to his wards, Ada Clare and Richard Carstone. It is revealed that Esther is the illegitimate daughter of Captain Hawdon and Lady Dedlock. John Jarndyce falls in love with her and asks her to marry him. She consents out of respect for Jarndyce, but during the engagement she falls in love with Allan Woodcourt.

Tangle, Mr Barrister who is the leading living authority on the case of Jarndyce v Jarndyce having read nothing else since his schooldays.

Tulkinghorn, Mr Family lawyer to the Dedlocks. When he finds out Lady Dedlock's secret past, and tries to gain from it, he is murdered by Lady Dedlock's former maid, Hortense.

Turveydrop, Mr Owner of a dance academy on Newman Street and a 'model of deportment'.

Turveydrop, Prince Son of Mr Turveydrop, owner of a dance academy. Prince, named for the Prince Regent, gives dancing lessons and supports his father.

Vholes Richard Carstone's solicitor in Symond's Inn, recommended by Skimpole, who lures Richard deeper into the Chancery case that will ultimately lead to Richard's despair and death.

Wisk, Miss Feminist who eventually accepts Mr Quale as her husband.

Woodcourt, Allan A young surgeon who falls in love with Esther Summerson before going away as ship's doctor to India. On his return to England he learns that Esther is engaged to John Jarndyce. When Jarndyce learns that Esther is in love with Woodcourt he releases her to marry him.

A Christmas Carol: **Christmas book published December 1843 by Chapman and Hall; illustrated by John Leech; too short to be classified as a novel and perhaps more correctly categorised as a novella**

Belle Scrooge's former fiancée, whom he had forgotten until reminded by the Ghost of Christmas Past.

Cratchit, Bob Long-suffering clerk of Ebenezer Scrooge and father of Tiny Tim. Bob endures his employer's mistreatment until Scrooge, reformed by the visit of the three spirits, raises his salary and vows to help his struggling family.

Cratchit, Caroline Wife of Bob and mother of four children, Peter, Belinda, Martha and the youngest, Tiny Tim.

Cratchit, Tiny Tim Crippled son of Bob Cratchit. The forecast of Tim's death by the Ghosts of Christmas Present and Future is instrumental in Scrooge's reformation, after which Tim is afforded proper medical attention and is cured.

Dilber, Mrs A laundress whom Ebenezer Scrooge meets in his vision of Christmas Future, selling his belongings after his death.

Fan Scrooge's sister, mother of his nephew Fred. She has died before the story begins, but lives again in the 'shadows' shown to Scrooge by the Ghost of Christmas Past.

Fezziwig, Mr Scrooge was apprenticed to 'Old Fezziwig' after he left school. Scrooge visits his old employer with the Ghost of Christmas Past and is reminded of what a kind, generous man he was.

Fezziwig, Mrs Wife of the merchant 'Old Fezziwig'.

Fred Ebenezer Scrooge's nephew who is ignored in his invitation to Scrooge to attend Christmas dinner, but the Ghost of Christmas Present shows Fred saying some good-natured things about his uncle.

Ghost of Christmas Future Shows Scrooge the demise of Tiny Tim and of himself, leading to Scrooge's reformation.

Ghost of Christmas Past Shows Scrooge his lonely and difficult childhood and gradual decline into the miser he will become.

Ghost of Christmas Present Shows Scrooge the joy that Christmas brings, both at the poor household of the Cratchits and at the home of his nephew Fred.

Joe A fence (seller of stolen goods).

Marley, Jacob Scrooge's former partner, who died seven Christmas Eves ago. Jacob, in life, was a penny-pinching miser like Scrooge and is suffering for it in the afterlife. His ghost comes to haunt Scrooge, hoping to change Scrooge's life and therefore help him to avoid Marley's fate.

Scrooge, Ebenezer Probably Dickens' best-known character, the miserly Scrooge, with his familiar cry of 'Bah, Humbug!', is visited by the ghost of his former partner, Jacob Marley, who sends three more spirits in hopes of reforming Scrooge's heartless and penny-pinching ways. It is a tough assignment for them and he fights the inevitable, but he is eventually transformed into a benevolent humanitarian.

Topper, Mr A bachelor who is a guest at Fred's Christmas dinner.

Wilkins, Dick Scrooge's fellow apprentice at Mr Fezziwig's.

David Copperfield: **eighth novel published in 20 monthly parts between May 1849 and November 1850**

Babley, Richard *See* Mr Dick.

Bailey, Captain Army officer who makes David Copperfield jealous by dancing with the eldest Miss Larkins.

Barkis A carrier between Blunderstone and Yarmouth. He marries Clara Peggotty. Famous quote: 'Barkis is willing', denoting his desire to marry Peggotty.

Charley The 'dreadful old man' who owns a marine shop at Chatham. David Copperfield sells his jacket to Charley for eighteen pence.

Chestle, Mr Elderly Kentish hop-grower, who marries the eldest Miss Larkins.

Chillip, Doctor Attends Mrs Copperfield at David's birth.

Copperfield, Clara Mother of David Copperfield. A widow when David is born, she later is lured into marriage by Edward Murdstone, who destroys her spirit. She dies along with her newborn son while David is away at school.

Copperfield, David Main character and narrator of the story, modelled after Dickens's life. Begins life with his widowed mother and their maid, Peggotty. When his mother marries Mr Murdstone his life becomes miserable. He is sent to Creakle's school, where he meets Steerforth and Traddles. After the death of his mother he goes to work at Murdstone and Grinby and is lodged with the Micawbers. David runs away to live with his aunt Betsey Trotwood in Dover. He marries Dora Spenlow and then Agnes Wickfield.

Creakle, Mr Severe headmaster of Salem House Academy, where David first goes to school. He was based on William Jones, headmaster of Wellington Academy, which Dickens attended from 1825 to 1827.

Creakle, Mrs Mr Creakle's wife (unnamed). They have a daughter (unnamed also) who attracts David and Steerforth.

Crewler, Reverend Horace A curate in Devonshire. Father of Sophy Crewler.

Crewler, Sophy Daughter of the Reverend Horace Crewler and fiancée of Tommy Traddles.

Crupp, Mrs David Copperfield's brandy-loving landlady at the Adelphi.

Dartle, Rosa Companion to Mrs Steerforth, possessively attached to Steerforth, who has marked her face when a child by throwing a hammer in a fit of temper. Rosa hates Little Em'ly for running away with Steerforth.

Demple, George A doctor's son and fellow pupil of David Copperfield at Salem House.

Dick, Mr Kite-making, memoir-writing companion to Betsey Trotwood, who gives good advice but is not all there. Mr Dick's real name was Richard Babley but he was always referred to as plain Mr Dick. His insight is uncanny and he becomes a friend of David's.

Em'ly, Little Mr Peggotty's niece and David's childhood friend. She is later engaged to Ham but is lured away by the charms of Steerforth. Mr Peggotty is heartbroken and searches for her, finally finding her when Steerforth tires of her and she leaves him. She later emigrates to Australia with her uncle.

Endell, Martha A girl whose ruin foreshadows Little Em'ly's and helps to prevent her falling into the same trap. She eventually emigrates to Australia with Little Em'ly, Mr Peggotty and Mrs Gummidge.

Fibbitson, Mrs Elderly inmate of the almshouses where Mrs Mell lives.

Gummidge, Mrs Widow of Mr Peggotty's former partner in a boat concern, who had died very poor. She lives with Mr Peggotty and later emigrates to Australia with him.

Heep, Uriah A hypocritical clerk of Mr Wickfield's who is continually citing his humbleness. He deviously plots to ruin Wickfield but is later undone by Mr Wilkins Micawber. On their first meeting, David describes him as 'a red-haired person – a youth of fifteen, as I take it now, but looking much older – whose hair was cropped as close as the closest stubble; who had hardly any eyebrows, and no eyelashes'.

Jip Dora Spenlow's pet spaniel, whose name was short for Gypsy. He dies at David Copperfield's feet at the very moment of Dora's death.

Joram Assistant to Mr Omer in his capacity as the Yarmouth undertaker, who, after marrying Omer's daughter, Minnie, becomes a partner in the business.

Jorkins, Mr Partner of Francis Spenlow in the firm of proctors where David Copperfield is articled. Jorkins is largely unseen, although Spenlow finds it expedient to refer to his opinion to justify his own conduct.

Kidgerbury, Mrs Domestic help of David and Dora, described as 'the oldest inhabitant of Kentish Town who went out charring'.

Larkins Family Mr Larkins and his two daughters, the youngest Miss Larkins and the eldest Miss Larkins. The eldest Miss Larkins would be about 30 years old when David, as a young 17-year-old, had a crush on her.

Littimer Manservant to Steerforth, involved in the concealment of the elopement of Steerforth and Emily. He is later guilty of embezzlement and is captured with the help of Miss Mowcher. David says of him: 'I believe there never existed in his station a more respectable-looking man. He was taciturn, soft-footed, very quiet in his manner, deferential, observant, always at hand when wanted, and never near when not wanted; but his great claim to consideration was his respectability'.

Maldon, Jack Annie Strong's cousin, who goes to India; he may have been dishonourable in his intentions to Annie without her reciprocating.

Mealy Potatoes Boy who works at Murdstone and Grinby's warehouse, whose name derived from the complexion of his skin.

Mell, Charles Assistant schoolmaster at Salem House Academy. David Copperfield befriends Mell and finds that his mother lives in an almshouse, which he innocently relates to Steerforth. Steerforth uses this information to discredit Mell and have him dismissed. Mell later emigrates to Australia and becomes headmaster at Colonial Salem House Grammar School in Port Middlebay.

Micawber, Emma Long-suffering wife of Mr Micawber, whom she swears she will never leave despite his financial difficulties. David describes her as 'a thin and faded lady, not at all young, with a baby at her breast. This baby was one of twins; and I may remark here that I hardly ever, in all my experience of the family, saw both the twins detached from Mrs Micawber at the same time. One of them was always taking refreshment'.

Micawber, Wilkins David lodges at his home. Always in debt and waiting for 'something to turn up', he ends up in debtor's prison. On his release he has various occupations but is eventually employed at Mr Wickfield's office, where he exposes the deeds of Uriah Heep. In gratitude for this his debts are paid and he emigrates to Australia, where he prospers. Famous quote: 'Annual income £20, annual expenditure £19 19/6, result, happiness. Annual income £20, annual expenditure £20 0/6d, result, misery'.

Mills, Julia Friend and confidante of Dora Spenlow and David's go-between during his courtship with Dora. She later goes to live in India.

Mowcher, Miss Steerforth's friend; a dwarf who sells cosmetics; his relations with her give the reader insight into the pity that dominates Steerforth's character (which includes self-pity).

Murdstone, Edward Second husband of Clara Copperfield whom David dislikes. He is a stern disciplinarian with a violent nature, who sends David off to Salem House School and later consigns him to the warehouse of Murdstone and Grinby.

Murdstone, Jane The equally stern sister of Edward Murdstone who moves in with David and his mother after her marriage to Murdstone.

Omer, Minnie Daughter of Mr Omer, who marries his foreman, Joram.

Omer, Mr Draper, tailor, haberdasher and furnisher, who resided in Yarmouth and arranged the funeral of Clara Murdstone and her baby son.

Peggotty, Clara David's devoted nurse and sister to Daniel Peggotty. After the death of David's mother she is discharged and marries Barkis. When Barkis dies she goes to live with David and Betsey Trotwood.

Peggotty, Daniel Crotchety fisherman brother of Clara. He lives in an overturned boat on the beach at Yarmouth with Little Em'ly, Ham and Mrs Gummidge. When Em'ly abandons them to elope with Steerforth,

Daniel vows to find her. Steerforth later leaves Em'ly and she is reunited with Daniel. At the end of the novel Daniel, Em'ly and Mrs Gummidge resettle in Australia.

Peggotty, Ham Orphaned nephew of Daniel Peggotty and fiancé of Little Em'ly. A fisherman and boatbuilder. He drowns trying to rescue Steerforth. 'He was a huge, strong fellow of six feet high, broad in proportion, and round-shouldered; but with a simpering boy's face and curly light hair that gave him quite a sheepish look.'

Shepherd, Miss Boarder at Misses Nettingall's educational establishment and a brief early romantic fixation of young David Copperfield.

Spenlow, Dora Daughter of David's employer, Francis Spenlow. She and David are married and David tries to teach her to keep house, but she has no head for it. She becomes ill with an unspecified illness and dies young.

Spenlow, Francis Proctor at Doctor's Commons where David is apprenticed. David says of him: 'He was a little light-haired gentleman, with undeniable boots, and the stiffest of white cravats and shirt-collars. He was buttoned up mighty trim and tight, and must have taken a great deal of pains with his whiskers, which were accurately curled.'

Steerforth, James Friend of David, whom he often calls 'Daisy', at the Salem House school where his engaging charm makes him everyone's favourite. David later runs into him again in London and he accompanies David on a trip to Yarmouth, where he charms Little Em'ly into eloping with him. They go abroad and Steerforth soon tires of Em'ly and deserts her. He is later drowned in a shipwreck where Ham Peggotty, from whom Steerforth stole Em'ly away, dies trying to save him.

Strong, Annie Young wife of Dr Strong who has a strong affiliation to Jack Maldon.

Strong, Dr David's teacher who is writing a dictionary; his wife is much younger and David's observance of their relationship shapes his early doubts about marriage.

Tiffey, Mr Chief clerk at Spenlow and Jorkins, who tells David Copperfield of Mr Spenlow's accidental death.

Tipp Carman at Murdstone and Grinby's, who addressed David Copperfield as 'David' whereas the other workers referred to him as 'the little gent' or 'the young Suffolker'.

Topsawyer According to a story told to David Copperfield at the inn in Yarmouth, Topsawyer ordered a glass of ale like that ordered by David, drank it and fell dead.

Traddles, Tommy Downtrodden pupil with David Copperfield and Steerforth at Salem House. David's best friend and best man at David's wedding to Dora Spenlow. He later becomes a lawyer and marries Sophy Crewler.

Trotwood, Betsey David Copperfield's great aunt. David runs away from London, when he is installed at Murdstone and Grinby's warehouse, and goes to Dover to live with Betsey. She helps David get a start in life and, when she loses her fortune, goes to London to live with David.

Wickfield, Agnes Childhood friend of David Copperfield and daughter of Betsey Trotwood's lawyer. Becomes David's wife after the death of Dora.

Wickfield, Mr Father of Agnes and lawyer to Betsey Trotwood. His overindulgence of wine causes him to be vulnerable to the schemes of Uriah Heep, who becomes his partner and attempts to ruin him.

Yawler Friend of Tommy Traddles at Salem House 'with his nose on one side'.

***Dombey and Son*: seventh novel, published in monthly parts by Bradbury and Evans, from October 1846 to April 1848**

Bagstock, Joe Dombey's friend who sets him up with Edith Granger.

Blimber, Cornelia Prim and proper daughter of Dr and Mrs Blimber.

Blimber, Dr Pompous and pedantic headmaster of the school in Brighton where Paul Dombey was a pupil.

Blimber, Mrs Proud and devoted wife of Dr Blimber who feigned learnedness.

Bokum, Mrs Widow, and 'dearest friend' of Mrs MacStinger. She kept a close eye on Captain Bunsby on his way to his wedding to Mrs MacStinger in case he attempted escape.

Briggs One of Paul Dombey's fellow pupils at Doctor Blimber's school.

Brogley, Mr The 'sworn broker and appraiser' who took possession of The Wooden Midshipman after Solomon Gills fell into debt.

Brown, Conversation Acquaintance of Cousin Feenix, who was a 'four-bottle man at the Treasury Board'.

Brown, Good Mrs An ugly old rag and bone vendor and mother of Alice Marwood (Brown). She kidnaps Florence Dombey and steals her clothes.

Bunsby, Captain Jack Commander of the *Cautious Clara* and friend of Captain Cuttle, who marries Mrs MacStinger.

Burgess and Co. Mr Toots's tailors, who were 'fash'nable but very dear'.

Carker, Harriet Takes pity on Alice Marwood, who at first shuns her when she finds out that she is James Carker's sister but eventually becomes her friend. Harriet marries Mr Morfin.

Carker, James Manager at Dombey and Son who is employed to convey messages to Edith but not content with seducing her also contrives to bring the firm to ruin. Blessed with a set of extremely white teeth, he is the brother of John and Harriet Carker. He is eventually killed under a train whilst in flight from Dombey.

Carker, John Referred to as Carker the Junior, due to his lowly position, although in actual fact is older than James by nearly three years. John stole money from the firm but was kept on by Dombey, although his brother never lets him forget the indiscretion. John is devoted to his sister Harriet.

Chick, Louisa Sister of Paul Dombey Snr and friend to Mrs Tox. Her famous quote is 'make an effort'.

Chick, Mr Husband of Louisa Chick and therefore Mr Dombey's brother-in-law.

Cuttle, Captain Seafaring friend of Sol Gills, whose shop he cares for when Sol goes in search of his lost nephew, Walter Gay. His famous quote is 'When found, make a note of'.

Daws, Mary Young kitchen-maid in Paul Dombey's household.

Diogenes Dog owned by the Blimber family originally but given to Florence Dombey by Toots, with the Blimbers' blessing.

Dombey, Florence Neglected daughter of Paul Dombey and sister of little Paul, whom she nurses in his illness. She marries Walter Gay and eventually cares for her bankrupt and invalid father.

Dombey, Paul Jnr The long-hoped-for heir to the house of Dombey and Son. His mother dies at his birth, leaving him a frail and sickly child. His father sends him to Brighton in the care of Mrs Pipchin, hoping the sea air will bolster his failing health. He lives only six years.

Dombey, Paul Snr Powerful head of the House of Dombey shipping firm. He wants a son and when a daughter (Florence) is born he despises her. His second child, a son (Paul), is weak and sickly and dies a child. Paul's first wife dies with the birth of Paul Jnr and he remarries.

Feenix, Cousin Referred to as 'Cousin' although in actuality a Lord. He is nephew to Cleopatra Skewton.

Flowers Cleopatra Skewton's personal maid.

Game Chicken, The Pugilist employed by Mr Toots in the 'cultivation of those gentle arts which refine and humanise existence'.

Gay, Walter Sol Gill's nephew, he is employed in the house of Dombey and Son. When Walter befriends Florence Dombey her father is displeased and sends him to the firm's branch in Barbados. The ship in which he sails is lost and Sol goes to search for him.

Gills, Solomon Uncle of Walter Gay and owner of a ship's chandler shop called 'The Wooden Midshipman'. When Walter's ship is lost at sea Solomon goes in search of him, leaving the care of the shop to his friend, Captain Cuttle.

Glubb, Old Old, crab-faced man who influences Paul Dombey with his stories of fish and sea monsters.

Granger, Colonel First husband of Edith Granger.

Granger, Edith Paul Dombey's second wife is the widow of Colonel Granger and the daughter of Mrs Skewton. She marries Dombey but does not love him. She later elopes with John Carker, a manager at Dombey's firm, to punish her husband.

Howler, the Rev. Melchisedech Officiates at the wedding of Captain Bunsby and Mrs MacStinger.

MacStinger, Mrs Captain Cuttle's irascible landlady, who is a widow with three children: Charles (known as Chowley), Juliana and Alexander.

Marwood, Alice Good Mrs Brown's daughter, who was John Carker's mistress and Edith's cousin.

Morfin, Mr The assistant manager of Dombey and Son who marries Harriet Carker.

Nipper, Susan Florence's companion who speaks her mind and later marries Mr Toots.

Pankey, Miss Young lady who is the only other boarder at Mrs Pipchin's when Paul Dombey lives there.

Perch, Mr Timid messenger in the firm of Dombey and Son.

Pipchin, Mrs Keeper of 'an infantine Boarding House of a very select description' in Brighton.

Rob the Grinder Robin Toodle, who has a miscreant youth then works at first for Captain Cuttle and then James Carker.

Skewton, Cleopatra Mother of Edith Granger. She dies after having a stroke.

Toodle, Mr Husband of Polly Toodle and father of Rob the Grinder. He is a stoker on the railway and later an engine driver.

Toodle, Polly Little Paul Dombey's nurse, known in the Dombey household as Richards, dismissed when she takes Paul to visit her family in a poorer section of London. She re-enters the story when Captain Cuttle asks her to look after Sol Gill's Shop 'The Wooden Midshipman'.

Toots, Mr A student at Dr Blimber's school who loves Florence but marries Susan.

Tox, Lucretia Close friend of Mrs Chick, Paul Dombey Snr's sister. She has hopes to marry Paul Snr after his first wife dies. Paul marries Mrs Granger instead, breaking Miss Tox's heart, but she stays loyal to him through later hardships.

Withers Mrs Skewton's page, who pushes her around in her wheelchair.

Great Expectations: thirteenth novel published in 36 weekly parts in 1860 / 1861

Avenger, The Pip's name for Pepper, a servant boy hired by him. Pip has such a hard time finding things to keep him busy 'that I sometimes sent him to Hyde Park Corner to see what o'clock it was.'

Barley, Clara Herbert Pocket's secret sweetheart. She is secret because Herbert knows his mother would say she is below his 'station'. She's actually a sweet, fairy-like girl who takes care of her dying drunk of a father.

Barley, Old Bill Clara's father, an unseen 'sad old rascal' who used to be a ship's purser.

Biddy A kind, intelligent girl Pip's age who works for Mr Wopsle's great aunt at the school. Later, she comes to work for Joe, taking care of Mrs Joe Gargery. She loves Pip but he ignores her as his expectations are realised. When Pip eventually realises he loves her too it is too late as she has married Joe.

Black Bill A prisoner Wemmick recognises in Newgate Prison 'behind the cistern' when he takes Pip on a visit to the prison.

Brandley, Mrs Friend of Miss Havisham, whom Estella boarded with at Richmond.

Camilla Ageing relative of Miss Havisham who doesn't have an inch of love for the woman but is greedy for her money. She buzzes around Miss Havisham like a sycophantic fly. Matthew Pocket's sister.

Compeyson Con man who deceives Miss Havisham to get her money and then leaves her at the altar. He is an accomplice of Magwitch in the original prison break. He later exposes Magwitch and accidentally drowns when Magwitch is recaptured.

Drummle, Bentley Pip's fellow student at Matthew Pocket's. He marries Estella for her money and abuses her. He is killed when kicked by a horse that he has mistreated.

Estella Pip meets Estella at Satis House and falls in love with her, but she is cruel to him. Pip goes to London and becomes a gentleman and continues to adore Estella, but she warns him that she is incapable of love. She later marries Bentley Drummle, who mistreats her and she leaves him. Drummle dies and Estella and Pip meet two years later and vow to remain together.

Gargery, Joe Blacksmith, friend and adoptive father to Pip. Joe is also the husband of Pip's sister, Georgiana Mary, who mistreats him as badly as she does Pip. After his wife's death Joe comes to London and nurses Pip through an illness. Later he marries Pip's friend Biddy.

Gargery, Mrs Joe Wife of Joe Gargery and sister of Pip; a bitter, angry woman who brings up Pip 'by hand' – that is, she whips him whenever she can, often employing 'the tickler'. She is ultimately beaten to death by Orlick.

Georgiana Ageing relative of Miss Havisham.

Handel Herbert Pocket's affectionate name for Pip.

Havisham, Miss A very rich and grim old woman who lives in seclusion at Satis House. She is the adopted mother of Estella, whom she teaches to break men's hearts to avenge her own misfortune at being left at the altar by Compeyson years before. She continues to wear her wedding dress and even keeps the mouldy wedding cake. Pip goes to Miss Havisham's to play and meets and falls in love with Estella. Pip believes Miss

Havisham is his secret benefactor as he goes to London and becomes a gentleman. She dies in a house fire.

Hubble, Mr and Mrs Simple, silly folks from Pip's village. Mr Hubble is a wheelwright.

Jaggers Lawyer who serves Miss Havisham and Magwitch, as he specialises in getting convicts light sentences. It is through Jaggers that Pip receives the benefits of the great expectations that he assumes are from Miss Havisham but in reality are from the convict Magwitch.

Magwitch, Abel A convict whom Pip helps in the marshes after his escape from the prison ship. He is recaptured and transported to Australia, where he gains a fortune which he secretly uses to increase Pip's 'expectations'. He secretly returns to England as Provis and confronts Pip with the secret source of his good fortune. Magwitch is recaptured and dies before he can be executed. Magwitch is also the father of Estella.

Molly Jaggers' housekeeper, Magwitch's wife and Estella's mother.

Orlick, Dolge Joe Gargery's journeyman blacksmith, he quarrels with Mrs Joe and later attacks her, leaving her with injuries of which she later dies. He falls in with a bad lot and tries to murder Pip.

Pip (Philip Pirrip) The narrator as well as the protagonist of the story. Pip is an orphan being raised by his sister, Mrs Joe Gargery, and her husband, Joe Gargery, a blacksmith.

Pocket, Herbert Pip goes to London and meets Herbert, who he discovers is the 'pale young gentleman' with whom he fought at Miss Havisham's as a child. Pip and Herbert become best friends and share chambers at Barnard's Inn and at the Temple. Herbert helps teach Pip 'city manners'. Pip helps Herbert become a partner in the firm of Clarriker and Co., which enables Pocket to marry Clara Barley.

Pocket, Matthew Father of Herbert and cousin of Miss Havisham. He is the only one of Miss Havisham's relatives who speaks honestly of her and has been banished from her presence. Matthew is Pip's tutor in London. He has no control over his large family and has a habit of pulling himself up by his hair in frustration. Pip tells Miss Havisham of Matthew's good character and she leaves him 4,000 pounds in her will. Matthew's wife, Belinda, is obsessed with social position, having been the daughter of a knight.

Pocket, Sarah Ageing relative of Miss Havisham.

Pumblechook, Uncle Joe's uncle, a well-to-do corn-chandler in the village. He considers himself upper-class and is actually a bombastic fool: 'A large hard-breathing middle-aged slow man, with a mouth like a fish, dull staring eyes, and sandy hair standing upright on his head, so that he looked as if he had just been all but choked'.

Raymond, Cousin Ageing relative of Miss Havisham.

Skiffins, Miss Very partial to the Aged Wemmick and eventually marries John Wemmick at a church in Camberwell Green.

Startop Student and boarder of Matthew Pocket. He is a good friend of Pip's.

Trabb Tailor who makes Pip a new suit of clothes before he goes to London, also in charge of the mourners at Pip's sister's funeral.

Trabb's Boy Assistant to Trabb, the tailor, who terrorises Pip. He later leads Herbert to the limekiln to rescue Pip from Orlick.

Wemmick, John Jagger's confidential clerk, friend of Pip (in private) who lives in a delightfully strange

house with 'an aged parent'. 'A dry man, rather short in stature, with a square wooden face, whose expression seemed to have been imperfectly chipped out with a dull-edged chisel.'

Wemmick, 'The Aged' Wemmick's elderly, and quite deaf, relative (commonly held to be Wemmick's father, but not described as such by Dickens). The Aged lives with Wemmick in his castle and is quite happy when you nod at him.

Whimple, Mrs Landlady of the house where Old Barley and his daughter Clara had lodgings.

Wopsle's Great-Aunt A 'ridiculous old lady' who runs the so-called school in town out of a cottage.

Wopsle, Mr Parish clerk, friend of the Gargerys. He aspires to enter the Church and preach in the pulpit but instead becomes an actor with the stage name of Waldengarver. Pip sees him perform *Hamlet* in London.

Hard Times: tenth novel, written for *Household Words* from April to August 1854

Bitzer A student in Gradgrind's school of hard facts. Later a light porter in Bounderby's bank.

Blackpool, Stephen A worker in Bounderby's mill. His wife is a drunk and he befriends Rachael, but falls out with his employer and leaves to look for work elsewhere. He is accused of robbing the bank, and before his name is cleared he falls down a well and dies. Later he is cleared with the discovery that the robbery was committed by young Tom Gradgrind.

Bounderby, Josiah Coketown Banker, mill owner and 'self-made man', abandoned as a child. His story is exposed as a sham when Mrs Pegler, his loving mother whom he has discarded, is found. Bounderby marries his friend Gradgrind's daughter Louisa and later discards her.

Childers, EWB Young man who is an equestrian in Sleary's Circus. He marries Sleary's daughter Josephine and has a son, who at three years old is, according to Sleary, 'The Little Wonder of Thcolathtic Equitation'.

Gordon, Emma Tightrope-walker, who comforts Sissy Jupe when her father vanishes.

Gradgrind, Adam Smith and Malthus The two youngest sons of Thomas Gradgrind, named by their father after famous political economists.

Gradgrind, Louisa Oldest daughter of Thomas and like him a victim of utilitarianism. She marries Bounderby, whom she doesn't love. She later leaves her husband and returns to her father.

Gradgrind, Mrs Wife of Thomas and mother of their five children.

Gradgrind, Thomas A mill owner retired from business and father of Louisa and Tom. He runs a school and emphasises the importance of facts and figures over fancy to his students and his children. By the end of the story he learns that facts and figures must be tempered by love and forbearance.

Gradgrind, Tom Son of Thomas, nicknamed 'The Whelp' by Harthouse. He is employed at Bounderby's bank, from which he later steals; the blame is set on Stephen Blackpool. He finally leaves the country with the aid of Sleary and his circus troupe.

Harthouse, James A Parliamentary candidate visiting Coketown, he befriends Tom Gradgrind in an attempt to seduce his sister Louisa, who is in an unhappy marriage to Bounderby. As a result of the attempted seduction Louisa runs home to her father, refuses to return to her husband, and is later disowned by him.

Jupe, Cecilia (Sissy) Daughter of Signor Jupe, a clown in Sleary's Circus, who is deserted by her father and taken in by Gradgrind. She befriends Louisa.

Kidderminster   Small boy with an old face, who played the part of Childers's infant son in 'his daring vaulting act as the Wild Huntsman of the North American Prairies'.

M'Choakumchild   Schoolmaster in Gradgrind's school where fancy and imagination are discouraged in favour of hard facts.

Merrylegs   Signor Jupe's highly trained performing dog which makes its way to Sleary's Circus at Chester following Jupe's disappearance and dies at Sleary's feet.

Pegler, Mrs   Revealed at the end of the story to be Bounderby's loving mother, exposing as a sham his claim to be a 'self-made man', who raised himself in the streets.

Rachael   Friend of Stephen Blackpool, who loves her but cannot gain release from his drunken wife. She defends Stephen when he is accused of theft from the bank.

Slackbridge   Rabble-rousing trade union delegate who persuades the Coketown millworkers to shun Stephen Blackpool.

Sladdery, Mr   Fashionable London librarian who boasts of having a high connection.

Sleary   Proprietor of Sleary's Circus. Speaks with a lisp ('People mutht be amuthed'). He helps Tom Gradgrind escape abroad after the bank robbery.

Sparsit, Mrs   Housekeeper of Bounderby with aristocratic connections. She is a busybody, causing dissension between Bounderby and his wife Louisa Gradgrind.

Little Dorrit: eleventh novel, published in 1857

Bangham, Mrs   Charwoman and messenger at the Marshalsea Prison who attended Mrs Dorrit at the birth of Amy.

Barnacle, Tite   A senior official in the Circumlocution Office, where everything goes round in circles, and nothing ever gets done.

Barroneau, Madame   The widow whom Rigaud married and was accused of murdering, although his version of events is that she leapt over a cliff-top after a violent quarrel.

Casby, Christopher   Formerly town-agent to Tite Barnacle. His benevolent appearance leads to him being referred to as the 'last of the Patriarchs'. Father of Flora Finchina.

Charlotte   The 'false young friend' of Miss Wade when they were schoolgirls.

Chivery, John and Young John   The two sons of the turnkey at the Marshalsea. John Chivery was dubbed the 'sentimental son' whilst Young John loves Amy Dorrit and assists in finding her father's fortune.

Chivery, Mr and Mrs John   John Chivery was a turnkey at the Marshalsea Prison who never opened his mouth 'without occasion'. His wife ran a tobacconist shop.

Clennam, Arthur   Returns to England from abroad, where he has spent years with his father in the family business. On his father's death he falls out with his mother and gives up his share of the business. He befriends Amy Dorrit at the Marshalsea and becomes business partner to Daniel Doyce. After losing everything in a banking scam by Merdle he is himself imprisoned in the Marshalsea. His health fails and Amy cares for him in the prison. The novel ends with Arthur and Amy's marriage.

Clennam, Mrs   Invalid mother of Arthur, with whom she has a falling-out over the family business. She

avoids a blackmail scheme by Rigaud/Blandois when her tumbledown house tumbles down on him.

Dawes, Mary   Nurse in the poor nobleman's household where Miss Wade was employed as a governess.

Dorrit, Amy   Title character, daughter of William Dorrit, born in the Marshalsea debtors' prison. She works for Mrs Clennam and befriends Arthur. Her father inherits a fortune and they leave the prison and travel abroad. After her father's death she discovers that the fortune has been lost in a banking scam. She nurses Arthur in the Marshalsea when his fortune is lost in the same banking scam, and eventually marries him.

Dorrit, Edward (Tip)   Ne'er-do-well brother of Amy Dorrit and son of Edward Dorrit.

Dorrit, Fanny   Sister of Amy. A dancer with social aspirations, Fanny marries Mr Sparkler, stepson of Mr Merdle. Fanny and Sparkler lose everything in the Merdle banking scam.

Dorrit, Frederick   Brother of William, uncle of Fanny, Edward and Amy. He plays clarionet in a small-time theatre. He is due an inheritance but the knowledge is kept from him by the intrigues of Mrs Clennam.

Dorrit, William   Father of Amy, Fanny and Edward, and long-time inmate of the Marshalsea debtors' prison. He inherits an estate and leaves the prison, travelling in style with his daughters. After his death Amy learns that his fortune has been lost in the Merdle banking scam.

Doyce, Daniel   Inventor of an unspecified mechanical wonder which he is unable to get a patent for in the Circumlocution Office. He enters a partnership with Arthur Clennam, who loses the firm's money in the Merdle scandal. Doyce later sells the invention abroad and returns to liberate Arthur from the Marshalsea.

Finching, Flora   Former sweetheart of Arthur Clennam who reappears 20 years later, 'grown to be very broad, and short of breath'. Dickens modelled the character of Flora after his own early sweetheart, Maria Beadnell, who reappears later in Dickens's life but not quite the way he remembered her.

Flintwinch, Ephraim   Brother of Jeremiah whose looks are almost identical.

Flintwinch, Jeremiah   Mrs Clennam's clerk to whom her son Arthur relinquishes his share of the family business.

Flintwinch, Mrs Jeremiah, née Affery   Wife of Mrs Clennam's clerk who sees the evil doings of the house in dreams.

Gowan, Henry   Arthur Clennam first meets him when Gowan is idly tossing stones into the Thames. The always affable Henry marries Pet Meagles.

Haggage, Doctor   Prisoner who attends at the birth of Amy Dorrit.

Jenkinson   Messenger in the Circumlocution Office.

Lion   Henry Gowan's Newfoundland dog, who dies by poison probably administered by Blandois.

Maggy   Simple-minded granddaughter of Mrs Bangham.

Meagles, Mr and Mrs   Kind-hearted retired banker Mr Meagles, his wife and daughter Minnie 'Pet', befriend Arthur Clennam, Amy Dorrit and Daniel Doyce. The Meagleses adopt Tattycoram from the Foundling Hospital.

Merdle, Mr and Mrs   Mr Merdle is an unscrupulous banker. Investing in his enterprises ruins the Dorrits, Arthur Clennam and others. Merdle commits suicide when his fraud is uncovered. Mrs Merdle is the mother of Mr Sparkler by a previous marriage.

Mr F's Aunt   Companion to Flora Finching (aunt to her

late husband) and one of the funniest characters in Dickens. Dickens describes her as 'an amazing little old woman, with a face like a staring wooden doll too cheap for expression, and a stiff yellow wig perched unevenly on the top of her head, as if the child who owned the doll had driven a tack through it anywhere, so that it only got fastened on'. She has a great propensity for uttering totally nonsensical barbs.

Pancks   Clerk and rent collector for Mr Casby. He assists in finding William Dorrit's fortune. A comical character who does everything 'with a puff and a snort'.

Plornish, Mr   A simple, good-natured plasterer.

Rigaud/Blandois   Villain of the novel. Rigaud attempts to blackmail Mrs Clennam and has her house fall and crush him for his efforts.

Slingo   Dealer in horses who vowed to give Tip Dorrit 'a berth' on his release from the Marshalsea.

Sparkler, Mr Edmund   Son of Mrs Merdle by her first marriage. Edmund is one of the Lords of the Circumlocution Office and marries Fanny Dorrit.

Tattycoram/Harriet Beadle   Adopted by the Meagleses from the Foundling Hospital, Harriet is given the name Tattycoram and is maid to the Meagleses daughter, Pet. She exhibits fits of temper and is counselled by Mr Meagles to 'count five and twenty'.

Wade, Miss   Dark figure who lures Tattycoram away from the kind-hearted Meagles.

Wobbler, Mr   Member of the Secretarial Department of the Circumlocution Office.

Martin Chuzzlewit: sixth novel published in 1843–4 as *The Life and Adventures of Martin Chuzzlewit*

Bailey, Christopher   Impish 'small boy with a large red head, and no nose to speak of' who worked as boot-boy and porter at Mrs Todgers's Commercial Boarding House.

Brick, Jefferson   War correspondent on the *New York Rowdy Journal*.

Buffum, Oscar   One of the deputation who arranges the 'le-vee' in honour of Elijah Pogram at the National Hotel in an American town.

Bullamy   Porter at the offices of Montague Tigg's fraudulent Anglo-Bengalee Disinterested Loan and Assurance Company. Following Tigg's murder Bullamy and Crimple make off with the firm's money.

Chiggle   An 'immortal' American sculptor who made a statue of Elijah Pogram.

Choke, General Cyrus   American swindler, who introduces Martin Chuzzlewit to Scadder.

Chollop, Major Hannibal   American 'worshipper of freedom', who meets Martin Chuzzlewit and Mark Tapley in Eden.

Chuzzlewit, Jonas   Son of Anthony Chuzzlewit, he kills his father to gain his inheritance, marries Mercy Pecksniff and, through his cruelty, breaks her spirit. He murders Tigg and, on the way to prison, kills himself.

Chuzzlewit, Martin   Grandson of Martin Sr. He has a falling-out with his grandfather over his love for Mary Graham. Becomes a pupil of Pecksniff who, because of pressure from the grandfather, throws young Martin out.

Chuzzlewit, Old Martin   Grandfather of Martin, cousin of Pecksniff, brother of Anthony, uncle of Jonas. Martin is suspicious of his hypocritical relatives, chiefly Pecksniff, whose hypocrisy Martin exposes and is reconciled with his grandson, young Martin.

Crimple, David   Officer at the offices of Montague Tigg's Anglo-Bengalee Disinterested Loan and Assurance Company. He and Bullamy steal the firm's money after Tigg's murder.

Diver, Colonel   Editor of the *New York Rowdy Journal*.

Dunkle, Doctor Ginery   A 'gentleman of great poetical elements' who acts as the spokesman of the committee that welcomes Elijah Pogram.

Fips, Mr   Lawyer in Austin Friars, who was secretly commissioned by Old Martin to employ Tom Pinch to arrange and catalogue books at £100 per year.

Gamp, Sarah   A midwife, nurse and 'layer-out' of the dead. She is a fixture in the story and appears to be much more concerned with her own creature comforts than those of her patients.

Gill, Mrs   Client of Mrs Gamp, who could calculate exactly when the birth of her babies was due.

Graham, Mary   Mary cares for old Martin Chuzzlewit with the knowledge that she will not profit from Martin's wealth after his death. Chuzzlewit's grandson Martin falls in love with Mary, which displeases his grandfather, who disinherits young Martin but eventually gives them his blessing to marry.

Harris, Mrs   Sarah Gamp's alluded-to but unseen friend. Betsey Prig expresses disbelief as to her existence.

Hominy, Mrs   Pretentious so-called philosopher and authoress whom Martin Chuzzlewit meets in America.

Izzard, Mr   Member of the committee that welcomes Elijah Pogram.

Jinkins, Mr   Boarder at Mrs Todgers's who, although talking of splendid things, was a fish-salesman's book-keeper.

Jobling, Doctor John   Doctor who attended Anthony Chuzzlewit and Lewsome and who became the medical officer of the Anglo-Bengalee Disinterested Loan and Life Assurance Company.

Kedgick, Captain   Landlord of the National Hotel in an American town.

Kettle, La Fayette   Secretary of the Watertoast Association, whom Martin Chuzzlewit encounters on his travels to Eden.

Lewsome   Young surgeon attended by Doctor Jobling and nursed by Sarah Gamp during a serious illness.

Lupin, Mrs   Landlady of the Blue Dragon who eventually marries Mark Tapley.

Mould, Mr   Undertaker whose countenance often belied the seriousness of his job.

Nadgett   Inquiry agent employed at a salary of £1 per week by Tigg's fraudulent company. Discovers Jonas Chuzzlewit's intention to poison Anthony Chuzzlewit and later Jonas's guilt in the murder of Tigg, by fishing his blood-stained clothes from the river.

Pecksniff, Seth   Sanctimonious surveyor and architect, and one of the biggest hypocrites in fiction. A cousin of old Martin Chuzzlewit and the father of Mercy and Charity.

Pinch, Tom   Devoted admirer and assistant to Pecksniff. A kindly, sweet-tempered fellow, completely blind to Pecksniff's hypocrisy despite a multitude of evidence of it. He finally becomes aware of Pecksniff's true character and is dismissed.

Pogram, Hon. Elijah   American Congressman who meets Martin Chuzzlewit on a steamboat on the way back from Eden.

Prig, Mrs Betsey   Nurse who is a friend and colleague of Sarah Gamp and who comically doubts the existence of Mrs Harris.

Scadder, Zephania   Agent of the Eden Land Corporation who is introduced to Martin Chuzzlewit by Cyrus Choke.

Tacker   Chief mourner for Mr Mould the undertaker.

LITERATURE

Tamaroo Slow-witted old woman who replaced Young Bailey at Todgers's.

Tapley, Mark Ostler at the Blue Dragon Inn and servant to young Martin Chuzzlewit. He accompanies Martin to America and later marries Mrs Lupin, the Blue Dragon's landlady. The inn is renamed The Jolly Tapley.

Tigg, Montague Disreputable adventurer, who changes his name to Tigg Montague. Tigg discovers the murderous intentions of Jonas Chuzzlewit via his agent, Nadgett, and is killed by Jonas.

Todgers, Mrs Proprietor of a Commercial Boarding House in London in which she welcomes Charity and Mercy Pecksniff despite her rule of only receiving gentlemen boarders.

Wolf, Mr One of Montague Tigg's guests at a dinner attended by Jonas Chuzzlewit.

The Mystery of Edwin Drood: **fifteenth novel unfinished at Dickens's death in 1870**

Bazzard Clerk to Hiram Grewgious who writes an unproduced tragedy, 'The Thorn of Anxiety'. Grewgious admits that Bazzard has a strange power over him.

Billickin, Mrs London landlady of Rosa Bud and her chaperone, Miss Twinkleton. She insists on using the title 'Billickin' in business matters, fearing being taken advantage of because she is a woman. Mrs Billickin and Miss Twinkleton take a comical dislike for one another.

Brobity, Miss The owner of a school in Cloisterham. Miss Brobity married Mr Sapsea.

Bud, Rosa Betrothed to Edwin Drood in childhood, they later agree that they cannot marry. Edwin disappears and John Jasper declares his love for Rosa. In terror she flees to London to her guardian, Grewgious. 'The pet pupil of the Nuns' House is Miss Rosa Bud, of course called Rosebud; wonderfully pretty, wonderfully childish, wonderfully whimsical'.

Chinaman, Jack Keeper of a London opium den in competition with Princess Puffer's den.

Crisparkle, Septimus Minor canon of Cloisterham Cathedral. 'Mr Crisparkle, Minor Canon, early riser, musical, classical, cheerful, kind, good-natured, social, contented, and boy-like'. He takes Neville Landless as a pupil and helps Neville flee to London when suspicion is cast on him for the disappearance of Edwin Drood.

Datchery, Dick Mysterious visitor to Cloisterham whose 'white head was unusually large, and his shock of white hair was unusually thick and ample'. Datchery keeps an eye on John Jasper after the disappearance of Edwin Drood. The true identity of Datchery is one of the most contested points of the uncompleted mystery.It is widely believed that Datchery is one of the characters in the book in disguise; most likely candidates include Neville, Bazzard, Tartar, Grewgious, Helena, or even Edwin Drood himself.

Deputy (Winks) Boy hired by Durdles to throw stones at him when he is wandering drunk at night. 'Sometimes the stones hit him, and sometimes they miss him, but Durdles seems indifferent to either fortune. The hideous small boy, on the contrary, whenever he hits Durdles, blows a whistle of triumph through a jagged gap, convenient for the purpose in the front of his mouth, where half his teeth are wanting; and whenever he misses him, yelps out "Mulled agin!"'

Drood, Edwin He is an orphan and had been betrothed by his father to Rosa Bud since early childhood. Later Edwin and Rosa rebel against the arrangement. Rosa is also wooed by Edwin's uncle John Jasper. Edwin turns up missing and his watch is found in the river. Jasper hints suspicion of Neville Landless in the disappearance when the novel stops short with the death of Dickens in 1870.

Durdles Drunken stonemason who engraves tombstones for Cloisterham Cathedral. John Jasper is interested in Durdles's ability to tap on the tombs and discover their contents. Durdles hires Deputy to throw stones at him when he catches him wandering about drunk at night. No man is better known in Cloisterham.

Giggles, Miss Pupil at Miss Twinkleton's school who is described as 'so deficient in sentiment' that she professes to pull faces at any young man paying homage.

Grewgious, Hiram Guardian of Rosa Bud. He is upset at John Jasper's advances to Rosa and finds her lodging in London at an apartment owned by Mrs Billickin. He later investigates the disappearance of Edwin Drood and is suspicious of Jasper. 'An angular man with no conversational powers' is how he describes himself.

Honeythunder, Luke Loud, overbearing philanthropist and guardian of Neville and Helena Landless.

Jasper, John Uncle of Edwin Drood who has an opium habit. He cares for his nephew but harbours secret feelings for Edwin's fiancée Rosa Bud. Edwin disappears and the story ends prematurely with Dickens's death, but many believe that it was Jasper who killed Edwin Drood. 'Mr Jasper is a dark man of some six-and-twenty, with thick, lustrous, well-arranged black hair and whiskers. He looks older than he is, as dark men often do. His voice is deep and good, his face and figure are good, his manner is a little sombre.' He is said to be capable of mesmerism.

Landless, Helena Twin sister of Neville who, as the story ends prematurely, is falling in love with Canon Crisparkle.

Landless, Neville Twin brother of Helena. He and his sister are brought to Cloisterham by their guardian, Mr Honeythunder. Neville is attracted to Rosa Bud and, being set up by Jasper, quarrels with Edwin Drood. After Drood's disappearance Jasper casts blame on Neville, who has no alibi and flees to London with his sister.

Puffer, Princess Old hag who runs the London opium den that John Jasper frequents.

Sapsea, Thomas Pompous auctioneer turned mayor of Cloisterham. 'The purest Jackass in Cloisterham.'

Tartar Retired navy man and friend of Crisparkle. He befriends Neville in London and works with Grewgious and Crisparkle in protecting Neville from John Jasper.

Tisher, Mrs Miss Twinkleton's assistant at the school for girls at Nun's House.

Tope, Mr Chief verger and showman of Cloisterham Cathedral. His wife acts as John Jasper's housekeeper.

Twinkleton, Miss Principal of a school for girls at Nun's House in Cloisterham (Cloisterham was based on Rochester) where Rosa Bud and Helena Landless attend. She is assisted by Mrs Tisher. Miss Twinkleton later becomes Rosa's chaperone in London.

Nicholas Nickleby: **third published novel (1839) as** *The Life and Adventures of Nicholas Nickleby*

Alphonse Mrs Wititterly's page whose appearance belied his name.

Bolder Pupil at Dotheboys Hall whose father was 'two pound ten short' in the payment of his fees.

Bonney, Mr The promoter of The United Metropolitan Hot Muffin and Crumpet Baking and Punctual Delivery Company.

Bravassa, Miss Beautiful actress in Mr Crummles's company.

Bray, Madeline Cares for her selfish invalid father who tries to sell her in marriage to his creditor Arthur Gride, assisted by Ralph Nickleby. Her father dies and the scheme is exposed. She marries Nicholas at the end of the story.

Bray, Walter Father of Madeline whose sudden death on the morning of his daughter's sham of a wedding day prevents the marriage.

Brooker, Mr Ralph Nickleby's former clerk, who took charge of his employer's son and named him Smike. On returning to England following an eight-year sentence of transportation he reveals Smike's real identity.

Browdie, John Bluff Yorkshire corn factor and stalwart friend of Nicholas Nickleby and Smike. He marries Matilda Price.

Browndock, Miss Mr Nickleby's cousin's sister-in-law.

Bulph, Mr Pilot in whose house the Crummleses live when they visit Portsmouth.

Cheeryble Brothers Charles and Edwin (Ned). Benevolent businessmen who employ and befriend Nicholas Nickleby and his family.

Cheeryble, Frank Nephew of the Cheeryble twins, who marries Kate Nickleby.

Chowser, Colonel Disreputable acquaintance of Ralph Nickleby. He was a Colonel 'of the Militia . . . and the race-courses'.

Crummles, Mr Vincent Manager of a touring acting company who hires Nicholas Nickleby and Smike and becomes their friend.

Dibabs, Jane Former acquaintance of Mrs Nickleby, who cites her as an example of a woman who 'married a man who was a great deal older than herself'.

Dick Blind blackbird owned by Tim Linkinwater and kept in the Cheeryble Brothers' counting-house.

Folair, Mr Pantomimist in Mr Crummles's touring company.

Gallanbile, Mr MP who seeks a cook through the General Agency Office which Nicholas also uses.

Gride, Arthur Old miserly character who tries to buy a marriage to Madeline Bray with the help of her father.

Grudden, Mrs General helper at the Crummles's touring company who could turn her hand to anything.

Hawk, Sir Mulberry Friend of Ralph Nickleby who has lecherous designs on Kate and assaults her. Hawk is a man of fashion and a gambler. He shoots and kills Lord Frederick Verisopht in a duel.

Kenwigs Family Mr Kenwigs was a turner in ivory and he and his family lodged in the same house as Newman Noggs.

Knag, Miss Madame Mantalini's forewoman who ultimately becomes the proprietor of the business.

Knag, Mortimer Brother of Miss Knag, who works as an ornamental stationer and small circulating library keeper in a street off the Tottenham Court Road.

La Creevy, Miss Miniature painter in the Strand. The Nicklebys lease lodging from her briefly and she becomes their faithful friend. In the end she marries the Cheeryble Brothers' old clerk, Tim Linkinwater.

Ledbrook, Miss Actress in Mr Crummles's touring company and a friend of Miss Snevellici.

Lillyvick, Mr Collector of water rates, and Mrs Kenwig's uncle, who marries Henrietta Petowker.

Linkinwater, Tim Faithful clerk to the Cheeryble Brothers and friend of the Nicklebys. He marries Miss La Creevy.

Mantalini, Madame Milliner and dressmaker who employs Kate Nickleby. Her business is ruined by her husband's extravagances and is transferred to Miss Knag.

Mantalini, Mr Husband of Madame Mantalini who ultimately separates from her and becomes bankrupt and imprisoned where he is taken by a laundress to turn a mangle in a cellar. 'My life is one demd horrid grind.'

Nickleby, Kate Sister of Nicholas. She is placed by her uncle, Ralph Nickleby, with Madame Mantalini. She is the object of the undesirable attentions of some of the evil-minded clients of her uncle, who is using her to his advantage.

Nickleby, Mrs Mother of Nicholas and Kate. Absent-minded and self-absorbed, she continues to 'put on airs' even in the reduced situation of her family after the financial ruin and death of her husband. The character is heavily drawn from Dickens's mother.

Nickleby, Nicholas Brother to Kate, nephew of Ralph, and the principal character of the story. Hoping to provide support for his mother and sister after the death of his father, he turns to his uncle Ralph for assistance.

Nickleby, Ralph Uncle to Nicholas and Kate (and later we find, father of Smike). A rich and miserly moneylender who feigns to help his late brother's family but, in reality, tries to humiliate Nicholas and use Kate to his own advantage.

Noggs, Newman Once a well-to-do gentleman but he squanders his money and is reduced to serving Ralph Nickleby as clerk. He befriends Nicholas and eventually helps him escape the designs of Ralph.

Petowker, Miss Henrietta Actress at the Theatre Royal, Drury Lane, who meets Mr Lillyvick at the Kenwigs' home and marries him.

Price, Matilda Miller's daughter, who marries John Browdie.

Pupker, Sir Matthew The chairman of The United Metropolitan Hot Muffin and Crumpet Baking and Punctual Delivery Company.

Sliderskew, Peg Arthur Gride's housekeeper who steals a box of documents from her master, including a will relating to Madeline Bray's inheritance. Peg is apprehended for the theft and sentenced to transportation.

Smike Abandoned at Dotheboys Hall in the care of the evil Squeers, Smike is mistreated for years before being rescued by Nicholas. He later dies from the treatment he received as a child. After his death it is discovered that he was Ralph Nickleby's son.

Snevellici, Miss Actress in Mr Crummles's touring company and a friend of Miss Ledbrook.

Squeers, Wackford Proprietor of Dotheboys Hall, he took in boys who were not wanted by their families and mistreated them. Nicholas Nickleby becomes his assistant master but sees the way he treats his charges, gives him a sound thrashing, and leaves.

Timberry, Snittle Actor who presides at Vincent Crummles's farewell dinner before the family leaves for America.

Tix, Tom Broker who takes possession of the Mantalinis' business.

Verisopht, Lord Frederick Young nobleman in Ralph Nickleby's circle who is killed in a duel with Sir Mulberry Hawk.

Wititterly, Henry and Julia Married couple living in Cadogan Place, Sloane Street. Kate Nickleby was employed briefly as Mrs Wititterly's companion.

LITERATURE

Wrymug, Mrs A 'genteel female' who is a client at the General Agency Office.

The Old Curiosity Shop: fourth published novel in 1841

Barbara 'Little servant-girl', 'very tidy, modest and demure, but very pretty too'.

Brass, Sally Sister and partner of Quilp's unscrupulous attorney, Sampson Brass. She is the mother of the Marchioness, the below-stairs maid.

Brass, Sampson 'An attorney of no good repute', Brass served as Daniel Quilp's lawyer. He helps Quilp get the Curiosity Shop from Nell's grandfather and when he tries to help Quilp frame Kit Nubbles he is undone with the help of his clerk Dick Swiveller.

Cheggs, Mr and Miss Friends of Sophy Wackles, the sweetheart of Dick Swiveller. Mr Cheggs is a market gardener, who eventually marries Sophy, much to the chagrin of Dick.

Codlin and Short Proprietors of a travelling Punch and Judy show that Nell and her grandfather meet on their travels through the English countryside.

Edwards, Miss Student-teacher at Miss Monflathers' Boarding and Day Establishment who lodged for nothing but also received no pay.

Foxey Revered father of Sally and Sampson Brass. His maxim was 'always suspect everybody'.

Grinder, Mr A travelling entertainer who followed behind a couple in Highland dress on stilts, with a drum on his back.

Jarley, Mrs Proprietor of a travelling waxworks who employs Nell and her grandfather. When the grandfather schemes to steal from Mrs Jarley, in order to support a gambling habit, Nell persuades him that they should take to the road again.

Jiniwin, Mrs Mrs Quilp's mother, who has many unsuccessful verbal run-ins with Daniel Quilp.

Monflathers, Miss Head of the Boarding and Day Establishment in the town where Mrs Jarley sets up her waxwork exhibition.

Nell's Grandfather Owner of the Old Curiosity Shop. He has a secret gambling habit, hoping to make a fortune for his granddaughter. He borrows money to gamble from Quilp. When he cannot pay he takes Nell and escapes London to the country. When Nell dies he is heart-broken.

Nubbles, Kit Kit is shop boy at the Curiosity Shop owned by Nell's grandfather.

Quilp, Daniel An evil dwarf who lends money to Nell's grandfather who gambles it away and flees London with Nell in an attempt to avoid Quilp. Quilp attempts to find the pair as they travel through the country. Later Quilp is pursued by the police and, lost in the fog, he drowns in the Thames.

Single Gentleman, The Mysterious lodger of the Brasses who is trying to find Nell and her grandfather. He is revealed to be the brother of the grandfather and finds the pair shortly before his brother's death.

Slum, Mr Tallish gentleman who composes verses to advertise products for a fee.

Sweet William Travelling conjuror met by Little Nell and her grandfather at the Jolly Sandboys.

Swiveller, Dick Friend of Fred Trent who has designs to marry Fred's sister Nell Trent but is encouraged to wait until Nell has inherited her grandfather's money. When Nell and her grandfather leave London Swiveller is befriended by Quilp, who helps him gain employment.

The Marchioness Dick Swiveller's nickname for the little servant kept locked below stairs by the Brasses. Swiveller later marries her.

Trent, Fred Nell's brother, a gambler, would like to get his hands on his grandfather's money through his friend Dick Swiveller.

Trent, Nelly Known as Little Nell, she is the principal character in the story. She lives with her grandfather, when he falls into the clutches of Daniel Quilp she helps him escape London. The hardships endured during their wanderings are too much for the delicate Nell.

Wackles, Sophy First love of Dick Swiveller. Swiveller reluctantly leaves her and enters into a scheme, hatched by Nell's brother Fred Trent, to marry Nell and inherit the grandfather's money. Sophy marries Cheggs, a market gardener.

Whisker Self-willed pony who, from being the most obstinate and opinionated pony on the face of the earth, was, in Kit Nubbles's hands, the meekest and most tractable of animals.

Oliver Twist: second published novel, originally in Bentley's Miscellany between February 1837 and April 1839 in 24 monthly instalments

Artful Dodger, The See Jack Dawkins.

Bates, Charley Member of Fagin's band of thieves. He mends his ways after Fagin is captured.

Bedwin, Mrs A 'motherly old lady' who is Mr Brownlow's housekeeper.

Betsy (Bet) Prostitute and friend of Nancy. Goes mad after identifying Nancy's body.

Blathers Bow Street Runner (London policeman) who, along with Duff, investigates the attempted robbery of the Maylie home.

Brittles Despite being over 30 years old, described as a 'lad of all work' residing at Mrs Maylie's.

Brownlow, Mr Adopts Oliver after he is charged with pickpocketing. He later establishes Oliver's true identity.

Bull's-eye Bill Sikes's white shaggy dog who falls to his death at the same time as Sikes accidentally hangs himself on Jacob's Island, Bermondsey.

Bumble, Mr Beadle at the workhouse where Oliver is born. He mistreats the residents in his care and becomes the symbol of Dickens's distaste for the workhouse system. Bumble names the foundling Twist due to his coming next alphabetically after the last 'Swabble'. In fact he says the next one will be 'Unwin' and then 'Vilkins'. He marries Mrs Corney and later is disgraced and becomes a resident in the same workhouse. Famous quote when told by Mr Brownlow that the law supposes that your wife acts under your directions: 'If the law supposes that, then the law is a ass . . . a idiot.'

Charlotte Maidservant to Mr and Mrs Sowerberry. She is very partial to Noah Claypole, whom she feeds with oysters.

Chickweed, Conkey According to Blathers, he was a publican who carried out a fake burglary on himself, althought the crime was detected by Jem Spyers.

Chitling, Tom Member of Fagin's gang and Betsy's sweetheart.

Claypole, Noah Assistant at Sowerberry's with whom Oliver fights. Noah later joins Fagin's band and spies on Nancy. After Fagin's capture he testifies against him and becomes an informer for the police.

Corney, Mrs Matron of the workhouse where Oliver is born. She marries Bumble, making him miserable. The Bumbles are disgraced and end up as paupers in the workhouse they once ruled over.

Dawkins, Jack The most successful and interesting of Fagin's thieves. He shows Oliver the ropes of the pickpocket game and is later captured and sentenced to transportation. Dawkins is better known as The Artful Dodger.

Duff Bow Street Runner (London policeman) who, along with Blathers, investigates the attempted robbery of the Maylie home.

Fagin A crafty old Jew who runs a thieves' school near Field Lane in Saffron Hill. Oliver falls in with Fagin's band when he runs away from the workhouse. When Fagin attempts to help Monks destroy Oliver's reputation he is arrested and executed at Newgate.

Fleming, Agnes Mother of Oliver, whom she gives birth to out of wedlock with Edwin Leeford and subsequently dies at the workhouse. Agnes is also the sister of Rose Maylie.

Gamfield, Mr Cruel chimney sweep who does not let the safety of his sweeps concern him. 'Even if they've stuck in a chimbley, roasting their feet makes 'em struggle to hextricate themselves.'

Grimwig, Mr Cantankerous friend of Mr Brownlow. Quote: 'I'll eat my head!'

Kags Robber who was in the house on Jacob's Island when Bill Sikes sought refuge there.

Leeford, Edward Villainous son of Edwin and half-brother of Oliver Twist who plots with Fagin to corrupt Oliver, in which case Leeford will inherit all of their father's property. After the plan is foiled Leeford is forced to emigrate to America, where he dies in prison. Leeford is referred to as Monks.

Leeford, Edwin Father of Oliver, whom he has fathered out of wedlock with Agnes Fleming. Also father of Edward (Monks) from a previous marriage. Edwin has died before the story begins.

Losberne, Dr Impetuous doctor who treats Oliver and Rose in illness. A friend of the Maylie family.

Mann, Mrs Matron of a workhouse farm where Oliver is raised until he is nine years old.

Maylie, Harry Son of Mrs Maylie, he marries Rose.

Maylie, Mrs Mother of Harry and the adopted mother of Rose.

Maylie, Rose A poor girl adopted by Mrs Maylie. She and Mr Brownlow endeavour to help Oliver through Nancy. When Nancy's conversation with Rose on London Bridge is overheard by Claypole, Nancy is murdered by Sikes. She later marries Harry.

Monks *See* Edward Leeford.

Nancy Prostitute and member of Fagin's band of thieves. Befriends Oliver and is eventually murdered by Sikes trying to help Oliver escape Fagin's clutches.

Sally, Old Old hag present at Oliver's birth. She steals the locket and ring from Oliver's mother as she lies dying.

Sikes, Bill A vicious thief working on the fringes of Fagin's band of pickpockets. He uses Oliver in an attempt to burgle the Brownlow home. When Nancy tries to help Oliver she is found out by Fagin who relates the information to Sikes. He murders Nancy, and later hangs himself by accident while trying to escape a hue-and-cry.

Slout Master of the workhouse where Oliver was born, replaced by Mr Bumble following his death.

Sowerberry, Mr Undertaker to whom Oliver is apprenticed. Oliver is mistreated and runs away to London.

Spyers, Jem Bow Street Runner who detected the deception of Conkey Chickweed's fake burglary.

Twist, Oliver Principal character in the story. He is born in a workhouse, where he is mistreated by Bumble, the beadle (quote: 'Please sir, may I have some more?'). He is apprenticed to Sowerberry, the undertaker, and runs away to London where he falls in with Fagin.

***Our Mutual Friend*: fourteenth novel, published in 1865**

Blight Mortimer Lightwood's office boy, often referred to as 'young Blight'.

Blogg, Mr Beadle who permits Betty Higden to adopt Sloppy

Boffin, Mrs Henrietta Noddy Boffin's wife, who, unlike her husband, enjoyed the good life.

Boffin, Nicodemus John Harmon's servant. When John's son is supposed drowned, Boffin and his wife inherit the Harmon fortune, for a time.

Boots and Brewer Guests at the Veneerings' social gatherings.

Dolls, Mr Father of Jenny Wren, whose real name is Cleaver but is called Mr Dolls by Eugene Wrayburn.

Gliddery, Bob Pot-boy at the Six Jolly Fellowship Porters.

Goody, Mrs The Reverend Mr Milvey suggests that the Boffins adopt her grandchild but his wife disagrees, as she is an 'inconvenient woman, who drank eleven cups of tea the previous Christmas, and grumbled all the time'.

Handford, Julius Alias taken by John Harmon in order to investigate his own supposed drowning.

Harmon, John Son of a wealthy dust contractor and heir to his fortune if he agrees to marry Bella Wilfer. He is away from England when his father dies, and on the way home he is supposed drowned in a case of mistaken identity.

Headstone, Bradley A schoolteacher and master of the boys department of a school on the borders of Kent and Surrey. He becomes obsessed with Lizzie Hexam. Lizzie wants nothing to do with him and he becomes jealous.

Hexam, Charley Brother of Lizzie and son of Gaffer, who becomes Bradley Headstone's pupil.

Hexam, Gaffer Waterman, father of Lizzie, who plies the Thames looking for dead bodies. He finds a body thought to be John Harmon, the central character in the story.

Hexam, Lizzie Daughter of waterman Gaffer Hexam and sister of Charley. She is opposed to her father's business of combing the Thames looking for drowned bodies but is true to him. When her father drowns she goes to live with Jenny Wren. Eventually she marries Eugene Wrayburn.

Higden, Betty Almost 80 years old but still very active. She keeps 'a Minding School' for children.

Kibble, Jacob Fellow-passenger with John Harmon on the voyage from the Cape to London.

Lightwood, Mortimer A lawyer, too lazy to take on much work, and friend of Eugene Wrayburn. His only clients are the Boffins, which puts him in the middle of much of the story.

Milvey, Mrs Margaretta Wife of the Reverend Milvey and mother of their six children.

Milvey, the Reverend Frank The Boffins' clergyman, whom they consult when they decide to adopt an orphan.

Potterson, Miss Abbey Proprietor of the Six Jolly Fellowship Porters, on the Thames.

Riah 'An old Jewish man, in an ancient coat, long of skirt and wide of pocket' who fronts a money-lending business. He befriends Lizzie Hexam and Jenny Wren.

Riderhood, Rogue Waterman and former partner of Gaffer Hexam who tries to pin blame on Gaffer for the Harmon murder to gain a reward. Riderhood later becomes a lock-keeper and tries to blackmail Bradley Headstone after Bradley tries to murder Eugene Wrayburn.

LITERATURE

Rokesmith, John   Alias used by John Harmon when he is employed as secretary to the Boffins.

Sloppy   Orphan boy adopted by Betty Higden and given the job of turning the mangle at her Minding School.

Tootle, Tom   Gentleman who tells Miss Abbey Potterson that a man has been run down in a wherry, by a foreign steamer, on the Thames. The man turns out to be Rogue Riderhood.

Veneering, Hamilton & Anastasia   High society couple at whose frequent dinner parties the story of John Harmon is discovered. Hamilton buys his way into Parliament and is later bankrupt and the couple flee to France.

Venus, Mr   Taxidermist and dealer in bones and skeletons who owned a 'little dark greasy' shop in Clerkenwell.

Wegg, Silas   Rascally street vendor hired by Mr Boffin to read to him. Wegg is illiterate and makes the stories up as he goes along. After installing himself in the Boffin household he goes about trying to get a piece of the Boffin fortune.

Wilfer, Bella   Girl specified in old Harmon's will as the one that his son John should marry in order to gain his inheritance. When John disappears and is presumed drowned she is left 'a widow without ever being married'. She leaves her home and goes to live with the Boffins.

Williams, William   Regular customer of Miss Abbey Potterson at the Six Jolly Fellowship Porters.

Wrayburn, Eugene   Lawyer and friend of Mortimer Lightwood. 'If there is a word in the dictionary under any letter from A to Z that i abominate, it is energy.' He becomes interested in the Harmon case and meets Lizzie Hexam and falls in love with her. She loves him also but tries to distance herself from him because they come from different classes of society.

Wren, Jenny aka Fanny Cleaver   Crippled dolls' dressmaker with whom Lizzie Hexam lives after the death of her father. She helps Lizzie escape London when pursued by Headstone and Wrayburn.

Pickwick Papers: first published novel and serialised between April 1836 and November 1837 as *The Posthumous Papers of the Pickwick Club*

Allen, Arabella   Sister of Benjamin, who attempted to marry her to his friend Bob Sawyer. Arabella eventually marries Nathaniel Winkle.

Allen, Benjamin   Medical student and close friend of Bob Sawyer.

Bagman, The   Appears twice in the novel, first at the Peacock, Eatanswill, and then at the Bush Inn, Bristol, reciting a story on each occasion: 'The Bagman's Story' and 'The Bagman's Uncle'.

Bantam, Angelo Cyrus   Master of Ceremonies at Bath.

Bardell, Mrs Martha   Mr Pickwick's landlady in Goswell Street.

Betsy   Mrs Raddle's dirty and slipshod maid.

Bladud, Prince   Legendary founder of Bath, the subject of 'The True Legend of Prince Bladud' that Mr Pickwick reads in his bedroom.

Boffer   A Stock Exchange broker, on whose probable methods and timing of committing suicide Wilkins Flasher and Frank Simmery placed bets.

Boldwig, Captain   'Little fierce man in a stiff black neckerchief and blue surtout', who discovered Mr Pickwick asleep in a wheelbarrow on his land.

Bolo, Miss   Mr Pickwick's whist partner whilst at Bath, who 'went straight home in a flood of tears, and a sedan chair' due to his bad play.

Brooks   Pieman who could 'make pies out o'

anything' including cats. He lodged at Sam Weller's.

Brown   The Muggleton shoemaker, whose name on Rachael Wardle's shoes, which had been left with Sam Weller for cleaning, showed Mr Wardle that she was staying at the White Hart.

Budger, Mrs   Elderly widow with whom Mr Jingle dances at the Rochester ball, in Mr Winkle's dress-suit, to the jealous fury of Doctor Slammer, who consequently challenges the unfortunate Winkle to a duel.

Bulder, Colonel   Head of the Rochester garrison who attends the charity ball also attended by the Pickwickians. Bulder also commands the military review at Chatham when Mr Pickwick gets in the way.

Bullman   Plaintiff in the case discussed by Dodson and Fogg's clerks in the hearing of Mr Pickwick and Sam Weller.

Burton, Thomas   Member of the Brick Lane Branch of the United Grand Junction Ebenezer Temperance Association. 'Purveyor of cat's meat to the Lord Mayor and Sheriffs, and several members of the Common Council.'

Buzfuz, Sergeant   Bullying counsel for Mrs Bardell, who is a wicked caricature of a type of histrionic advocate frequently encountered in those days.

Charley   Dishevelled, red-headed pot-boy at the Magpie and Stump where Mr Pickwick and Sam Weller go in search of Mr Lowten.

Cripps, Tom   Errand-boy to Benjamin Allen and Bob Sawyer.

Crookey   Servant at Namby's sponging-house.

Dodson and Fogg   Mrs Bardell's attorneys who commit her to prison for non-payment of their costs.

Dowler, Mr and Mrs   Army officer and his wife who travelled with Mr Pickwick to Bath.

Dumkins, Mr   A formidable cricketer who played for the All-Muggleton club.

Fizkin, Horatio   Buff candidate in the Eatanswill election, who was defeated by the Honourable Samuel Slumkey.

Flasher, Wilkins   A Stock Exchange broker who, with Frank Simmery, placed bets on Boffer's probable methods and timing of committing suicide.

Groffin, Thomas   Chemist, who attempts, unsuccessfully, to be excused jury duty in the case of Bardell v Pickwick.

Grub, Gabriel   Subject of 'The Story of the Goblins who stole a Sexton' as told by Mr Wardle.

Grundy, Mr   Gentleman who refuses to oblige the company with a song at the Magpie and Stump where Mr Pickwick and Sam Weller have arranged to meet Mr Lowten.

Harris   Greengrocer in whose shop the Bath footmen hold their party.

Humm, Mr Anthony   President of the Brick Lane Branch of the United Grand Junction Ebenezer Temperance Association.

Hunt   Head gardener to Captain Boldwig, who is receiving orders from his master when the appearance of Mr Pickwick asleep in a wheelbarrow on his land is brought to the attention of Boldwig.

Isaac   A 'shabby man in black leggings' who accompanies Mr Jackson when he arrests Mrs Bardell.

Jackson, Mr   Dodson and Fogg's clerk who arrests Mrs Bardell and serves the Pickwickians with subpoenas to attend the trial.

Jingle, Alfred   A wandering rascal who befriends Mr Pickwick and accompanies the group to the Wardle home at Dingley Dell. He entices Miss Rachael to elope with him and is run down and bought off by Rachael's brother. Pickwick eventually exposes Jingle, who uses the alias of Charles Fitz-Marshall when tricking Pickwick into thinking he is planning another elopement.

Jinkins, Mr Suitor of the widow in 'The Bagman's Story'.

Jinks, Mr Dishevelled-looking clerk who worked for Mr Nupkins as the magistrate's adviser.

Lowten, Mr Mr Perker's clerk who first meets Mr Pickwick after singing a comic song at the Magpie and Stump.

Muzzle Mr Nupkins's footman who challenges Job Trotter to a fight over the affections of the cook.

Namby, Mr Sheriff's deputy of Bell Alley, Coleman Street, who arrests Mr Pickwick at the suit of Mrs Bardell.

Nupkins, Mr George Magistrate in attendance on the Pickwickian expedition to Ipswich.

Perker, Mr Mr Wardle's lawyer at Gray's Inn, who looks after Mr Pickwick's interests in the case of Bardell v Pickwick.

Pickwick, Samuel Founder and Chairman of the Pickwick Club. Pickwick, along with his friends Tupman, Snodgrass and Winkle and his servant Sam Weller, travel around England in search of adventure. Pickwick is one of Dickens's most loved characters.

Porkenham Family Close friends of the Nupkins family. George Nupkins is horrified at the possibility that they might know the true identity of Captain Fitz-Marshall.

Roker, Tom Turnkey at the Fleet, who shows Mr Pickwick his accommodation for the next three months.

Samba, Quanko Bowler in the West Indies cricket match described by Alfred Jingle at Dingley Dell. He apparently bowled Jingle out but never recovered from his exertions and died.

Sawyer, Bob Medical student and close friend of Benjamin Allen. 'Sawyer, late Nockemorf', who eventually gains a medical appointment in India.

Simmery, Frank A Stock Exchange broker, who, with Wilkins Flasher, placed bets on Boffer's probable methods and timing of committing suicide.

Skimpin, Mr Sergeant Buzfuz's assistant during the trial of Bardell v Pickwick.

Slammer, Dr Surgeon who is infuriated when Alfred Jingle, wearing Nathaniel Winkle's coat, dances with Mrs Budger, and consequently challenges Winkle to a duel, but discovers the mistaken identity before any damage is done.

Slasher, Dr Surgeon at St Bartholomew's Hospital, who was said to be the best operator alive. 'Took a boy's leg out of the socket last week, boy ate five apples and a gingerbread cake exactly two minutes after it was all over, boy said that he wouldn't lie there to be made game of and he'd tell his mother if they didn't begin.'

Slumkey, the Hon. Samuel Blue candidate in the Eatanswill election, who defeated Horatio Fizkin.

Slurk, Mr Editor of the *Eatanswill Independent* who has a furious quarrel with a rival editor.

Snodgrass, Augustus A member of the Pickwick Club and party to the adventures of Pickwick's travels. He falls in love with Emily Wardle and marries her at the end of the story.

Snubbin, Sergeant Mr Pickwick's counsel for defence in the trial of Bardell v Pickwick, who proves out of his depth against the redoubtable Sergeant Buzfuz.

Struggles, Mr Extremely passionate but unsuccessful bowler for the Dingley Dell cricket team.

Trotter, Job Servant to Alfred Jingles who has a couple of run-ins with Sam Weller, who takes a dislike to him, not least because he has a habit of calling him Mr Walker.

Trundle, Mr Partner of Isabel Wardle in a game of cards and ultimately becomes her partner in marriage.

Tupman, Tracy A member of the Pickwick Club, and travelling companion to Mr Pickwick in the story's adventures.

Upwitch, Richard Greengrocer who was a jury member in the trial of Bardell v Pickwick.

Wardle, Emily Daughter of Mr Wardle and niece of Rachael, who marries Augustus Snodgrass.

Wardle, Isabella Daughter of Mr Wardle and niece of Rachael, who marries Mr Trundle.

Wardle, Mr Yeoman farmer and owner of Manor Farm at Dingley Dell. Pickwick and his friends visit Manor Farm frequently. Wardle's daughter marries Pickwickian Augustus Snodgrass. Jingle tries to elope with Miss Rachael, Wardle's sister, but is caught and bought off.

Wardle, Rachael Sister of Mr Wardle who was persuaded to elope by Mr Jingle but is accosted by Mr Pickwick at the White Hart Inn and Jingle is bought off for £120.

Weller, Sam Mr Pickwick's servant is one of the most popular characters in Dickens's works. He counsels his master with Cockney wisdom and is thoroughly devoted to Pickwick. Sam has an unfortunate habit of transposing Ws and Vs to comical effect.

Weller, Tony Samuel's father, Tony Weller, is equally entertaining, also having the same unfortunate habit of transposing Ws and Vs to comical effect.

Whiffers, Mr Footman who resigns at the 'swarry' at Bath because the requirement for him to eat cold meat was a manly outrage.

Wicks, Mr One of Dodson and Fogg's clerks.

Wildspark, Tom Tony Weller's example of the importance of an alibi 'Ve got Tom Vildspark off that 'ere manslaughter, with a alleybi, ven all the bigvigs to a man said as nothing couldn't save him.'

Wilkins Gardener to Captain Boldwig, who brings to the attention of his master the appearance of Mr Pickwick asleep in a wheelbarrow on his land.

Winkle, Nathaniel Member of the Pickwick Club and travelling companion to Pickwick and his friends. He marries Arabella Allen, which upsets his father. Later Winkle's father comes to London and sees his daughter-in-law for himself, and is reconciled to the marriage.

Wugsby, Mrs Colonel One of the ladies that Mr Pickwick plays cards with at Bath.

A Tale of Two Cities: twelfth novel, serialised in *All the Year Round* in weekly parts from April to November 1859

Carton, Sydney Lawyer who is able to get a charge of treason reversed for Charles Darnay due to a strong physical resemblance. He later takes Darnay's place at the guillotine. Quote: 'It is a far, far better thing I do than I have ever done.'

Cruncher, Jerry Messenger for Tellson's Bank who moonlights as a grave robber.

Darnay, Charles Nephew of Marquis St Evrémonde. He is tried for treason in London and is acquitted due to his resemblance to Sydney Carton. He marries Lucie Manette, daughter of Dr Manette. He

LITERATURE

returns to Paris to help a friend imprisoned there and is arrested once more.

Defarge, Ernest   Husband of Madame Defarge and keeper of a wine shop in Paris. He is a leader among the revolutionaries.

Defarge, Madame Thérèse   Wife of wine-shop keeper Ernest Defarge, and a leader among the revolutionaries. She records enemies of the Republic in her knitting. She accidentally shoots herself dead in a struggle with Miss Pross in Paris.

Foulon, Joseph-François   Unscrupulous financier of the ancien régime who is seized by a mob and decapitated.

Gabelle, Théophile   Postmaster in the village of St Evrémonde who is arrested when the French Revolution begins. Dickens named the character after the salt tax imposed in the pre-revolutionary days.

Jacques   Name by which several of the French revolutionaries are known. Defarge is 'Jacques Four'.

Lorry, Jarvis   A clerk in Tellson's bank who is instrumental in bringing Dr Manette, who is imprisoned in Paris, back to England. He returns to Paris to look after the bank's interest after the Revolution starts and while there helps Lucie and Charles Darnay in their predicament.

Manette, Dr Alexandre   A prisoner in the Bastille in Paris for eighteen years. He is released and accompanies his daughter, Lucie, and Jarvis Lorry to England. He returns to Paris after the outbreak of the Revolution and, as a former prisoner, is able to secure Darnay's release.

Manette, Lucie   Daughter of Dr Manette. She is taken to Paris by Jarvis Lorry when her father is released from prison. She marries Charles Darnay but is adored from afar by Sydney Carton, who feels unfit for her. Darnay and Lucie have a daughter, also named Lucie. When Darnay is imprisoned in Paris by the revolutionaries Carton takes his place at the guillotine, thereby fulfilling his promise to help Lucie.

Pross, Miss   Lucie Manette's loyal maid. In the end of the novel she struggles with Madame Defarge and Defarge is killed in the scuffle.

Pross, Solomon/John Barsad   Miss Pross's brother, who sneaks Carton into the prison to trade places with Darnay.

Stryver, Mr   Solicitor friend of Sydney Carton who helps to defend Charley Darnay from the charges of treason.

'Vengeance, The'   Fiery woman friend of Madame Defarge who regularly attended the executions at the guillotine.

Plays and Playwrights

(* denotes playwright's first play)

Playwright	Play
Aeschylus (c. 525–456 BC)	Oresteia Trilogy
	The Persians
	Prometheus Bound
	Seven Against Thebes
	Suppliants
Edward Albee (1928–)	The American Dream
	A Delicate Balance
	Three Tall Women
	Tiny Alice
	Who's Afraid of Virginia Woolf?
	The Zoo Story
Maxwell Anderson (1888–1959)	Anne of the Thousand Days
Jean Anouilh (1910–87)	Antigone
	Becket
	Eurydice
	The Lark (L'Alouette)
	L'Hermine*
	L'Invitation au Château
	Thieves' Carnival
	Waltz of the Toreadors
John Arden (1930–)	All Fall Down*
	Ironhand
	Live Like Pigs
	Serjeant Musgrave's Dance
	Vandaleur's Folly
	The Workhouse Donkey
Aristophanes (c448–388 BC)	The Acharnians
	The Birds
	Clouds
	Ecclesiazusae
	The Frogs
	The Knights
	Lysistrata
	The Peace
	Plutus
	Thesmophoriazusae
	The Wasps
W H Auden (1907–73)	The Ascent of F6
	The Dance of Death
Alan Ayckbourn (1939–)	Absent Friends
	Absurd Person Singular
	Bedroom Farce
	Boy Who Fell into a Book
	By Jeeves
	Callisto 5
	A Chorus of Disapproval
	Comic Potential
	Communicating Doors
	Damsels in Distress
	Drowning on Dry Land
	How the Other Half Loves
	Jeeves
	Joking Apart
	Just Between Ourselves
	Living Together
	Man of the Moment
	Mr Whatnot*
	The Norman Conquests
	Relatively Speaking
	Round and Round the Garden
	Season's Greetings
	Sisterly Feelings

Playwright	Play
	A Small Family Business
	Snake in the Grass
	Sugar Daddies
	Table Manners
	Ten Times Table
	Time and Time Again
	Time of My Life
	Way Upstream
	Woman in Mind
J M Barrie (1860–1937)	The Admirable Crichton
	The Boy David (last)
	Dear Brutus
	Mary Knows
	Peter Pan
	Quality Street
	Walker, London*
	What Every Woman Knows
H E Bates (1905–74)	The Last Bread
Pierre Beaumarchais (1732–99)	The Barber of Seville
	Eugénie*
	The Marriage of Figaro
Samuel Beckett (1906–89)	Breath
	Endgame
	Happy Days
	Ill Seen Ill Said
	Not I
	Waiting for Godot
Brendan Behan (1923–64)	The Hostage
	The Quare Fellow*
Aphra Behn (1640–89)	The Feigned Courtizans
	The Forced Marriage
	The Rover
Alan Bennett (1934–)	An Englishman Abroad
	Forty Years On*
	Getting On
	Habeas Corpus
	The History Boys
	Kafka's Dick
	The Madness of George III
	The Old Country
	On the Margin (1st TV play)
	A Question of Attribution
	Talking Heads
Alan Bleasdale (1946–)	Are You Lonesome Tonight?
	Boys from the Blackstuff
	Having a Ball
	It's a Madhouse
	The Monocled Mutineer
	No More Sitting on the Old School Bench*
	On the Ledge
Simon Block	Chimps
Edward Bond (1934–)	Early Morning
	Narrow Road to the Deep North
	The Pope's Wedding*
Dion Boucicault (c. 1820–90)	The Colleen Bawn
	The Corsican Brothers
	London Assurance (written under name of Lee Morton)
	The Octoroon
	The Shaughraun
Bertolt Brecht (1898–1956)	Baal
	The Caucasian Chalk Circle

LITERATURE

Playwright	Play	Playwright	Play
	Drums in the Night*		Relative Values
	Fear and Misery in the Third Reich		This Happy Breed
			The Vortex
	The Good Woman of Setzuan	John Dryden (1631–1700)	All for Love
			The Indian Emperor
	Mother Courage		Marriage à-la-Mode
	The Preventable Rise of Arturo Ui		The Rival Ladies
			The State of Innocence
	The Threepenny Opera	Alexander Dumas (Fils)	Camille
Abe Burrows (1910–85)	Cactus Flower	(1824–95)	
Jim Cartwright (1958–)	Bed	T S Eliot (1888–1965)	The Cocktail Party
	Hard Fruit		The Confidential Clerk
	The Rise and Fall of Little Voice		The Elder Statesman
			The Family Reunion
	Road*		Murder in the Cathedral
Anton Chekhov (1860–1904)	The Bear		The Rock
	The Cherry Orchard		Sweeney Agonistes*
	Ivanov*	Ben Elton (1959–)	Blast from the Past
	The Island of Sakhalin		Gasping*
	The Seagull		Popcorn
	The Three Sisters		Silly Cow
	Uncle Vanya	George Etherege (c. 1635–92)	The Comical Revenge, or Love in a Tub
	The Wood Demon		The Man of Mode, or Sir Fopling Flutter
Caryl Churchill (1938–)	The Ants*		She Would If She Could
	Cloud Nine	Euripides (c. 484–406 BC)	Alcestis*
	Fen		Andromache
	Icecream		The Bacchae
	Light Shining in Buckinghamshire		Electra
			Hecuba
	Lives of the Great Poisoners		Helen
	A Number		Hippolytus
	Serious Money		Ion
	Softcops		Iphigenia in Aulis
	Top Girls		Iphigenia in Tauris
Jean Cocteau (1889–1963)	L'Aigle à deux têtes		Medea
	Les Mariés de la Tour Eiffel		The Phoenician Women
	Orpheus		The Trojan Women
William Congreve (1670–1729)	The Double Dealer	George Farquhar (c. 1677–1707)	The Beaux' Stratagem
	Love for Love		The Constant Couple
	The Mourning Bride		Love and a Bottle*
	The Old Bachelor*		The Recruiting Officer
	The Way of the World	Georges Feydeau (1862–1921)	An Absolute Turkey
Pierre Corneille (1606–84)	Andromède		A Flea in her Ear
	Le Cid		Hotel Paradiso
	Cinna		Ladies' Tailor*
	Clitandre		Pig in a Poke
	La Galerie du Palais	Eduardo de Filippo (1900–84)	Filumena
	Horace		La Grande Magia
	The Liar (Le Menteur)		Saturday, Sunday, Monday
	Mélite*	Alistair Foot and Anthony Marriot	No Sex Please, We're British
	La Mort de Pompée		
	Nicomède	John Ford (c. 1586–1640)	The Broken Heart
	Polyeucte		The Lady's Trial
	Pulchérie		The Lover's Melancholy
	Rodogune		Perkin Warbeck
	Théodore		'Tis Pity She's a Whore
	La Veuve	Dario Fo (1926–)	The Accidental Death of an Anarchist
Noël Coward (1899–1973)	Bitter Sweet		
	Blithe Spirit	Michael Frayn (1933–)	Alphabetical Order
	Cavalcade		Benefactors
	Design for Living		Clouds
	Easy Virtue		Copenhagen
	Fallen Angels		Donkeys' Years
	Hay Fever		Here
	I'll Leave it to You*		Look, Look
	Nude with Violin		Make and Break
	Peace in Our Time		Noises Off
	Post Mortem		The Sandboy
	Present Laughter		The Two of Us*
	Private Lives		

Playwright	Play	Playwright	Play
Brian Friel (1929–)	Dancing at Lughnasa		Sleeping Dog
	The Enemy Within		Spoiled
	Faith Healer		Stagestruck
	The Freedom of the City		Two Sundays
	Molly Sweeney		Wise Child*
	Philadelphia, Here I Come!	John Guare (1938–)	The House of Blue Leaves
	Translations		Six Degrees of Separation
	Wonderful Tennessee	Patrick Hamilton (1904–62)	Gaslight (aka: Angel Street)
Christopher Fry (1907–)	The Boy With a Cart		Rope (US title: Rope's End)
	Curtmantle	Christopher Hampton (1946–)	After Mercer
	The Lady's Not for Burning		Les Liaisons Dangereuses
	A Phoenix Too Frequent		The Philanthropist
	Thursday's Child		Savages
	The Tower		Total Eclipse
	Venus Observed		Treats
John Galsworthy (1867–1933)	The Silver Box		When Did You Last See My Mother?*
	The Skin Game		
Jean Genet (1910–86)	The Balcony	David Hare (1947–)	The Absence of War
	The Maids		Knuckle
	The Screens		Licking Hitler (TV play)
John Godber (1956–)	April in Paris		Man Above Men (TV play)
	Big Trouble in the Little Bedroom		Murmuring Judges
			Racing Demon
	Bouncers		The Secret Rapture
	Happy Families		Slag*
	Happy Jack	Richard Harris (1934–)	The Business of Murder
	Lucky Sods		Dead Guilty
	The Office Party		The Maintenance Man
	On a Night Like This		Outside Edge
	On the Piste		Stepping Out
	Salt of the Earth	Harold Harwood (1874–1959)	The Grain of Mustard Seed
	September in the Rain		
	Shakers	Ronald Harwood (1934–)	After the Lions
	Teechers		Another Time
	Up 'N' Under		Country Matters*
Johann W von Goethe (1749–1832)	Götz von Berlichingen		The Dresser
	Die Mitschuldigen		Goodbye Kiss
	Egmont		The Handyman
	Erwin und Elmire		Mahler's Conversion
	Faust (Parts I & II)		Poison Pen
	Iphigenie auf Tauris		Reflected Glory
	Torquato Tasso		Taking Sides
Nikolai Gogol (1809–52)	The Inspector General	Victor Hugo (1802–85)	Angelo
			Cromwell
William Golding (1911–93)	The Brass Butterfly		Hernani
			Lucrèce Borgia
Oliver Goldsmith (1728–74)	She Stoops to Conquer		Marie Tudor
			Marion Delorme
Maxim Gorky (1868–1936)	The Lower Depths		Le Roi s'amuse
			Ruy Blas
Harley Granville Barker (1877–1946)	The Madras House	Henrik Ibsen (1828–1906)	An Enemy of the People
	The Marrying of Ann Leete		Catiline*
	The Voysey Inheritance		A Doll's House
	Waste		Ghosts
Simon Gray (1936–)	Butley		Hedda Gabler
	Cell Mates		John Gabriel Borkman
	The Common Pursuit		Love's Comedy
	Dog Days		The Master Builder
	Dutch Uncle		Peer Gynt
	Hidden Laughter		The Wild Duck
	The Idiot	Eugène Ionesco (1912–94)	The Bald Prima Donna
	Japes		Rhinoceros
	The Late Middle Classes		The Lesson
	Life Support	Alfred Jarry (1873–1907)	Ubu Roi
	Molly		
	Old Masters	Terry Johnson (1955–)	Dead Funny
	Otherwise Engaged		Hitchcock Blonde
	Plaintiffs and Defendants		Hysteria
	Quartermaine's Terms		Imagine Drowning
	The Rear		Insignificance
	Simply Disconnected		Unsuitable for Adults

LITERATURE

Playwright	Play
Ben Jonson (1572–1637)	The Alchemist
	Bartholomew Fair
	Catiline
	Cynthia's Revels
	Every Man in His Humour
	Every Man Out of His Humour
	The Poetaster
	The Sad Shepherd (unfinished)
	Sejanus
	The Silent Woman
	Volpone
Tom Kempinski (1938–)	Duet for One
	Separation
Joseph Kesselring (1902–67)	Arsenic and Old Lace
Thomas Kyd (1558–94)	The Spanish Tragedy
Mike Leigh (1943–)	Abigail's Party
	Babies Grow Old
	Big Basil
	The Box Play*
	Greek Tragedy
	Individual Fruit Pies
	My Parents Have Gone to Carlisle
	Nuts in May
Alain-René Lesage (1668–1747)	Turcaret
Ira Levin (1929–)	Deathtrap
	Veronica's Room
Frederick Lonsdale (1881–1954)	Aren't We All?
	Canaries Sometimes Sing
	The Last of Mrs Cheyney
	On Approval
Federico García Lorca (1898–1936)	Blood Wedding
	The House of Bernarda Alba
	Yerma
Compton Mackenzie (1883–1972)	The Gentleman in Grey
Maurice Maeterlinck (1862–1949)	The Blue Bird
	La Princesse Maleine
	Mary Magdalene
	Pelléas et Mélisande
David Mamet (1947–)	American Buffalo
	The Cryptogram
	Duck Variations
	Glengarry Glen Ross
	A Life in the Theater
	Oleanna
	Sexual Perversity in Chicago
	The Shawl
	Speed-the-Plow
Christopher Marlowe (1564–93)	Doctor Faustus
	Edward II
	The Jew of Malta
	The Massacre at Paris
	Tamburlaine the Great
Conor McPherson (1971–)	The Weir
Thomas Middleton (c. 1570–1627)	Blurt
	The Changeling (with William Rowley)
	A Game at Chess
	Master Constable
	The Spanish Gypsy (with William Rowley)
	Women Beware Women
Arthur Miller (1915–2005)	After the Fall
	All My Sons*
	Broken Glass

Playwright	Play
	The Crucible
	Danger: Memory!
	Death of a Salesman
	The Last Yankee
	The Man Who Had All the Luck
	The Price
	The Ride Down Mount Morgan
	A View from the Bridge
Molière (1622–1673)	The Blue-Stockings
	Le Bourgeois Gentilhomme
	The Impostor
	Le Malade Imaginaire
	Le Misanthrope
	The Miser
	The School for Wives
	Tartuffe
Nicholas Monsarrat (1910–79)	The Visitors
John Mortimer (1923–)	The Dock Brief
	A Voyage Round My Father
Peter Nichols (1927–)	Ben Spray
	Born in the Gardens
	Chez Nous
	Daddy Kiss It Better
	A Day in the Death of Joe Egg*
	Forget-Me-Not Lane
	The Freeway
	The Heart of the Country
	The National Health
	Passion Play
	A Piece of My Mind
	Poppy
	Privates on Parade
	So Long Life
	Walk on the Grass (first TV play)
	When the Wind Blows
Edna O'Brien (1932–)	Flesh and Blood
	Madame Bovary
	Virginia
Sean O'Casey (1880–1964)	The Bishop's Bonfire
	Cockadoodle Dandy
	Juno and the Paycock
	The Plough and the Stars
	The Shadow of a Gunman
	The Silver Tassie
Clifford Odets (1906–63)	Awake and Sing!
	Golden Boy
	Till the Day I Die
	Waiting for Lefty
Eugene O'Neill (1888–1953)	Ah, Wilderness
	Anna Christie
	Beyond the Horizon
	Desire under the Elms
	The Emperor Jones
	The Great God Brown
	The Hairy Ape
	The Iceman Cometh
	Lazarus Laughed
	Long Day's Journey into Night
	Marco Millions
	Mourning Becomes Electra
	Strange Interlude
	A Touch of the Poet
	The Web*
Joe Orton (1933–67)	Entertaining Mr Sloane*
	The Erpingham Camp

Playwright	Play	Playwright	Play
	Loot	Edmond Rostand	Chantecler
	The Ruffian on the Stair	(1868–1918)	Cyrano de Bergerac
	What the Butler Saw	William Rowley	A New Wonder: A Woman
John Osborne	The Entertainer	(c. 1585–1642)	Never Vext
(1929–94)	Epitaph for George Dillon	Willy Russell	Blind Scouse Trilogy*
	The Hotel in Amsterdam	(1947–)	Blood Brothers
	Inadmissible Evidence		Boy with Transistor Radio
	Jill and Jack (TV play)		Breezeblock Park
	Look Back in Anger		Educating Rita
	Luther		I Read the News Today (radio)
	A Patriot for Me		John, Paul, George
	West of Suez (TV play)		Ringo . . . and Bert
Arthur Wing Pinero	The Cabinet Minister		King of the Castle (TV play)
(1855–1934)	Dandy Dick		One for the Road
	The Gay Lord Quex		Our Day Out
	His House in Order		Shirley Valentine
	The Magistrate		Stags and Hens
	Mid-Channel	Jean-Paul Sartre	In Camera
	The Profligate	(1905–80)	The Condemned of Altona
	The Schoolmistress	James Saunders	The Ark*
	The Second Mrs Tanqueray	(1925–2004)	Bodies
	The Squire		Making It Better
	Trelawny of the 'Wells'		Next Time I'll Sing to You
	£200 a Year*		Retreat
Harold Pinter	Betrayal		A Scent of Flowers
(1930–)	The Birthday Party	Friedrich von Schiller	Demetrius (unfinished)
	The Caretaker	(1759–1805)	Don Carlos
	The Homecoming		The Maid of Orleans
	Hothouse		Maria Stuart
	Moonlight		The Robbers*
	No Man's Land		Wallenstein Trilogy
	One for the Road		William Tell
	Other Places	Anthony Shaffer	The Case of the Oily
	The Room*	(1926–2001)	Levantine
Luigi Pirandello	Come Tu Mi Vuoi		Murderer
(1867–1936)	Enrico IV		Sleuth
	Six Characters in Search of	Peter Shaffer	Amadeus
	an Author	(1926–)	Black Comedy
Sylvia Plath	Three Women		Equus
(1932–63)			Five-Finger Exercise*
JB Priestley	Dangerous Corner*		The Gift of the Gorgon
(1894–1984)	I Have Been Here Before		Lettice and Lovage
	An Inspector Calls		The Private Ear
	Laburnum Grove		The Public Eye
	The Linden Tree		The Royal Hunt of the Sun
	Time and the Conways		Yonadab
	When We Are Married	George Bernard Shaw	Androcles and the Lion
Alexander Pushkin	Boris Godunov	(1856–1950)	Arms and the Man
(1799–1837)			Back to Methuselah
Jean Racine	Alexandre le Grand		Caesar and Cleopatra
(1639–99)	Andromaque		Candida
	Athalie		Captain Brassbound's
	Bajazet		Conversion
	Bérénice		The Devil's Disciple
	Britannicus		The Doctor's Dilemma
	Esther		Getting Married
	Iphigénie		Heartbreak House
	La Thébaïde, ou Les Frères		John Bull's Other Island
	ennemis		Major Barbara
	Mithridate		Man and Superman
	Phèdre		The Millionairess
Terence Rattigan	Adventure Story		Mrs Warren's Profession
(1911–77)	The Browning Version		Pygmalion
	Cause Célèbre		Saint Joan
	The Deep Blue Sea		Widowers' Houses
	Flare Path		You Never Can Tell
	French Without Tears	Sam Shepard	Buried Child
	Harlequinade	(1943–)	Cowboys*
	Ross		The Curse of the Starving
	Separate Tables		Class
	The Winslow Boy		Dog and Rocking Chair

LITERATURE

Playwright	Play	Playwright	Play
	Eyes for Consuela		The March on Russia
	Fool for Love		Mother's Day
	A Lie of the Mind		The Restoration of Arnold
	The Rock Garden		Middleton*
	Simpatico		Sisters
	The Tooth of Crime	August Strindberg	The Creditors
	True West	(1849–1912)	The Dance of Death
Richard Brinsley	The Critic		A Dream Play
Sheridan	Jupiter		The Father
(1751–1816)	The Rivals		Master Olof
	St Patrick's Day		Miss Julie
	The School for Scandal		To Damascus
R C Sherriff	Home at Seven	J M Synge	In the Shadow of the Glen
(1896–1975)	Journey's End*	(1871–1909)	The Playboy of the Western
Alan Sillitoe (1928–)	All Citizens Are Soldiers		World
and Ruth Fainlight			Riders to the Sea
(1931–)			The Tinker's Wedding
Neil Simon	Barefoot in the Park		The Well of the Saints
(1927–)	Biloxi Blues	Peter Terson (1932–)	Zigger Zagger
	California Suite	Brandon Thomas	Charley's Aunt
	Come Blow Your Horn*	(1856–1914)	
	The Gingerbread Lady	Dylan Thomas	Under Milk Wood
	The Good Doctor	(1914–53)	
	Last of the Red Hot Lovers	John Vanbrugh	The Confederacy
	Little Me	(1664–1726)	The Provok'd Husband
	Lost in Yonkers		The Provok'd Wife
	The Odd Couple		(both above completed by
	Plaza Suite		Colley Cibber)
	The Prisoner of Second		The Relapse, or Virtue in
	Avenue		Danger
	Promises, Promises	John Webster	The Devil's Law Case
	The Sunshine Boys	(1580–1625)	The Duchess of Malfi
	Sweet Charity		The White Devil
	They're Playing Our Song	Frank Wedekind	Earth Spirit
Sophocles	Ajax	(1864–1918)	Pandora's Box
(c. 496–405 BC)	Antigone		Spring Awakening
	Electra	Arnold Wesker	Annie Wobbler
	Ichneutae	(1932–)	Chicken Soup With Barley
	Oedipus at Colonus		Chips With Everything
	Oedipus Rex		I'm Talking About
	Philoctetes		Jerusalem
	Trachiniae		The Kitchen
Tom Stoppard	After Magritte		Roots
(1937–)	Albert's Bridge (radio)	Peter Whelan (1931–)	The Accrington Pals*
	Dirty Linen		The Bright and Bold Design
	The Dissolution of Dominic		Clay
	Boot (radio)		Divine Right
	Enter a Free Man		The Herbal Bed
	Indian Ink		Nativity
	The Invention of Love		A Russian in the Woods
	Jumpers		The School of Night
	M Is for Moon Among Other		Shakespeare Country
	Things (radio)	Hugh Whitemore	The Best of Friends
	Night and Day	(1936–)	Breaking the Code
	Professional Foul (TV play)		It's Ralph
	The Real Inspector Hound		Pack of Lies
	Rosencrantz and		Stevie*
	Guildenstern Are Dead	Oscar Wilde	The Duchess of Padua
	Separate Peace (first TV play)	(1854–1900)	An Ideal Husband
	Travesties		The Importance of Being
	A Walk on the Water*		Ernest
Tom Stoppard and	Every Good Boy Deserves		Lady Windermere's Fan
André Previn (1929–)	Favour		Salome
David Storey	The Changing Room		A Woman of No Importance
(1933–)	The Contractor	Thornton Wilder	The Angel that Troubled the
	Cromwell	(1897–1975)	Waters
	Early Days		The Long Christmas Dinner
	The Farm		The Matchmaker
	Home		Our Town
	In Celebration		The Skin of Our Teeth
	Life Class		The Trumpet Shall Sound

Playwright	Play	Playwright	Play
Tennessee Williams (1911–83)	Battle of Angels* Camino Real Cat on a Hot Tin Roof The Glass Menagerie The Night of the Iguana The Rose Tattoo A Streetcar Named Desire	William Wycherley (1640–1716)	Suddenly Last Summer Sweet Bird of Youth The Country Wife The Gentleman Dancing Master The Plain Dealer

Plays and Playwrights (in Play Order)

(for playwrights' dates see previous section)

Play	Playwright	Play	Playwright
Abigail's Party	Mike Leigh	Athalie	Jean Racine
The Absence of War	David Hare	Awake and Sing	Clifford Odets
Absent Friends	Alan Ayckbourn	Baal	Bertolt Brecht
An Absolute Turkey	Georges Feydeau	Babies Grow Old	Mike Leigh
Absurd Person Singular	Alan Ayckbourn	The Bacchae	Euripides
The Accidental Death of an Anarchist	Dario Fo	Back to Methuselah	George Bernard Shaw
The Accrington Pals*	Peter Whelan	Bajazet	Jean Racine
The Acharnians	Aristophanes	The Balcony	Jean Genet
The Admirable Crichton	J M Barrie	The Bald Prima Donna	Eugène Ionesco
Adventure Story	Terence Rattigan	The Barber of Seville	Pierre Beaumarchais
After Magritte	Tom Stoppard	Barefoot in the Park	Neil Simon
After Mercer	Christopher Hampton	Bartholomew Fair	Ben Jonson
After the Fall	Arthur Miller	Battle of Angels*	Tennessee Williams
After the Lions	Ronald Harwood	The Bear	Anton Chekhov
Ah, Wilderness	Eugene O'Neill	The Beaux' Stratagem	George Farquhar
Ajax	Sophocles	Becket	Jean Anouilh
Albert's Bridge (radio)	Tom Stoppard	Bed	Jim Cartwright
Alcestis*	Euripides	Bedroom Farce	Alan Ayckbourn
The Alchemist	Ben Jonson	Ben Spray	Peter Nichols
Alexandre le Grand	Jean Racine	Benefactors	Michael Frayn
All Citizens Are Soldiers	Alan Sillitoe and Ruth Fainlight	Bérénice	Jean Racine
		The Best of Friends	Hugh Whitemore
All Fall Down*	John Arden	Betrayal	Harold Pinter
All for Love	John Dryden	Beyond the Horizon	Eugene O'Neill
All My Sons*	Arthur Miller	Big Basil	Mike Leigh
Alphabetical Order	Michael Frayn	Big Trouble in the Little Bedroom	John Godber
Amadeus	Peter Shaffer		
American Buffalo	David Mamet	Biloxi Blues	Neil Simon
The American Dream	Edward Albee	The Birds	Aristophanes
An Enemy of the People	Henrik Ibsen	The Birthday Party	Harold Pinter
An Englishman Abroad	Alan Bennett	The Bishop's Bonfire	Sean O'Casey
Androcles and the Lion	George Bernard Shaw	Bitter Sweet	Noël Coward
Andromache	Euripides	Black Comedy	Peter Shaffer
Andromaque	Jean Racine	Blast From the Past	Ben Elton
Andromède	Pierre Corneille	Blind Scouse Trilogy*	Willy Russell
The Angel that Troubled the Waters	Thornton Wilder	Blithe Spirit	Noël Coward
		Blood Brothers	Willy Russell
Angelo	Victor Hugo	Blood Wedding	Federico García Lorca
Anna Christie	Eugene O'Neill	The Blue Bird	Maurice Maeterlinck
Anne of the Thousand Days	Maxwell Anderson	The Blue-Stockings	Molière
		Blurt	Thomas Middleton
Annie Wobbler	Arnold Wesker	Bodies	James Saunders
Another Time	Ronald Harwood	Boris Godunov	Alexander Pushkin
Antigone	Jean Anouilh	Born in the Gardens	Peter Nichols
Antigone	Sophocles	Bouncers	John Godber
The Ants*	Caryl Churchill	Le Bourgeois Gentilhomme	Molière
April in Paris	John Godber		
Are You Lonesome Tonight?	Alan Bleasdale	The Box Play*	Mike Leigh
		The Boy David (last)	J M Barrie
Aren't We All?	Frederick Lonsdale	Boy Who Fell into a Book	Alan Ayckbourn
The Ark*	James Saunders	The Boy with a Cart	Christopher Fry
Arms and the Man	George Bernard Shaw	Boy with Transistor Radio	Willy Russell
Arsenic and Old Lace	Joseph Kesselring	Boys from the Blackstuff	Alan Bleasdale
The Ascent of F6	W H Auden and Christopher Isherwood	The Brass Butterfly	William Golding
		Breaking the Code	Hugh Whitemore
		Breath	Samuel Beckett

LITERATURE

Play	Playwright	Play	Playwright
Breezeblock Park	Willy Russell	The Corsican Brothers	Dion Boucicault
The Bright and Bold Design	Peter Whelan	Country Matters*	Ronald Harwood
		The Country Wife	William Wycherley
Britannicus	Jean Racine	Cowboys*	Sam Shepard
Broken Glass	Arthur Miller	The Creditors	August Strindberg
The Broken Heart	John Ford	The Critic	Richard Brinsley Sheridan
The Browning Version	Terence Rattigan	Cromwell	David Storey
Buried Child	Sam Shepard	Cromwell	Victor Hugo
The Business of Murder	Richard Harris	The Crucible	Arthur Miller
Butley	Simon Gray	The Cryptogram	David Mamet
By Jeeves	Alan Ayckbourn	The Curse of the Starving Class	Sam Shepard
The Cabinet Minister	Arthur Wing Pinero		
Cactus Flower	Abe Burrows	Curtmantle	Christopher Fry
Caesar and Cleopatra	George Bernard Shaw	Cynthia's Revels	Ben Jonson
California Suite	Neil Simon	Cyrano de Bergerac	Edmond Rostand
Callisto 5	Alan Ayckbourn	Daddy Kiss It Better	Peter Nichols
Camille	Alexander Dumas (Fils)	Damsels in Distress	Alan Ayckbourn
Camino Real	Tennessee Williams	The Dance of Death	W H Auden
Canaries Sometimes Sing	Frederick Lonsdale	The Dance of Death	August Strindberg
Candida	George Bernard Shaw	Dancing at Lughnasa	Brian Friel
Captain Brassbound's Conversion	George Bernard Shaw	Dandy Dick	Arthur Wing Pinero
		Dangerous Corner*	J B Priestley
The Caretaker	Harold Pinter	Danger: Memory!	Arthur Miller
The Case of the Oily Levantine	Anthony Shaffer	A Day in the Death of Joe Egg*	Peter Nichols
Cat on a Hot Tin Roof	Tennessee Williams	Dead Funny	Terry Johnson
Catiline*	Henrik Ibsen	Dead Guilty	Richard Harris
Catiline	Ben Jonson	Dear Brutus	J M Barrie
The Caucasian Chalk Circle	Bertolt Brecht	Death of a Salesman	Arthur Miller
		Deathtrap	Ira Levin
Cause Célèbre	Terence Rattigan	The Deep Blue Sea	Terence Rattigan
Cavalcade	Noël Coward	A Delicate Balance	Edward Albee
Cell Mates	Simon Gray	Demetrius (unfinished)	Friedrich von Schiller
The Changeling	Thomas Middleton and William Rowley	Design for Living	Noël Coward
		Desire under the Elms	Eugene O'Neill
The Changing Room	David Storey	The Devil's Disciple	George Bernard Shaw
Chantecler	Edmond Rostand	The Devil's Law Case	John Webster
Charley's Aunt	Brandon Thomas	Dirty Linen	Tom Stoppard
The Cherry Orchard	Anton Chekhov	The Dissolution of Dominic Boot (radio)	Tom Stoppard
Chez Nous	Peter Nichols		
Chicken Soup With Barley	Arnold Wesker	Divine Right	Peter Whelan
		The Dock Brief	John Mortimer
Chimps	Simon Block	The Doctor's Dilemma	George Bernard Shaw
Chips With Everything	Arnold Wesker	Dog and Rocking Chair	Sam Shepard
A Chorus of Disapproval	Alan Ayckbourn	Dog Days	Simon Gray
Le Cid	Pierre Corneille	A Doll's House	Henrik Ibsen
Cinna	Pierre Corneille	Don Carlos	Friedrich von Schiller
Claude Gueux	Victor Hugo	Donkeys' Years	Michael Frayn
Clay	Peter Whelan	The Double Dealer	William Congreve
Clitandre	Pierre Corneille	Doctor Faustus	Christopher Marlowe
Cloud Nine	Caryl Churchill	A Dream Play	August Strindberg
Clouds	Aristophanes	The Dresser	Ronald Harwood
Clouds	Michael Frayn	Drowning on Dry Land	Alan Ayckbourn
Cockadoodle Dandy	Sean O'Casey	Drums in the Night*	Bertolt Brecht
The Cocktail Party	T S Eliot	The Duchess of Malfi	John Webster
The Colleen Bawn	Dion Boucicault	The Duchess of Padua	Oscar Wilde
Come Blow Your Horn*	Neil Simon	Duck Variations	David Mamet
		Duet for One	Tom Kempinski
Come Tu Mi Vuoi	Luigi Pirandello	Dutch Uncle	Simon Gray
Comic Potential	Alan Ayckbourn	Early Days	David Storey
The Comical Revenge, or Love in a Tub	Sir George Etherege	Early Morning	Edward Bond
		Earth Spirit	Frank Wedekind
The Common Pursuit	Simon Gray	Easy Virtue	Noël Coward
Communicating Doors	Alan Ayckbourn	Ecclesiazusae	Aristophanes
The Condemned of Altona	Jean-Paul Sartre	Educating Rita	Willy Russell
		Edward II	Christopher Marlowe
The Confederacy	John Vanbrugh	Egmont	Johann Wolfgang von Goethe
The Confidential Clerk	T S Eliot		
The Constant Couple	George Farquhar	The Elder Statesman	T S Eliot
The Contractor	David Storey	Electra	Euripides
Copenhagen	Michael Frayn	Electra	Sophocles

Play	Playwright	Play	Playwright
The Emperor Jones	Eugene O'Neill	Greek Tragedy	Mike Leigh
Endgame	Samuel Beckett	Habeas Corpus	Alan Bennett
The Enemy Within	Brian Friel	The Hairy Ape	Eugene O'Neill
Enrico IV	Luigi Pirandello	The Handyman	Ronald Harwood
Enter a Free Man	Tom Stoppard	This Happy Breed	Noël Coward
The Entertainer	John Osborne	Happy Days	Samuel Beckett
Entertaining Mr Sloane*	Joe Orton	Happy Families	John Godber
Epitaph for George Dillon	John Osborne	Happy Jack	John Godber
Equus	Peter Shaffer	Hard Fruit	Jim Cartwright
The Erpingham Camp	Joe Orton	Harlequinade	Terence Rattigan
Erwin und Elmire	Johann Wolfgang von Goethe	Having a Ball	Alan Bleasdale
		Hay Fever	Noël Coward
Esther	Jean Racine	The Heart of the Country	Peter Nichols
Eugénie*	Pierre Beaumarchais	Heartbreak House	George Bernard Shaw
Eurydice	Jean Anouilh	Hecuba	Euripides
Every Good Boy Deserves Favour	Tom Stoppard and André Previn	Hedda Gabler	Henrik Ibsen
		Helen	Euripides
Every Man in his Humour	Ben Jonson	The Herbal Bed	Peter Whelan
Every Man Out of his Humour	Ben Jonson	Here	Michael Frayn
		Hernani	Victor Hugo
Eyes For Consuela	Sam Shepard	Hidden Laughter	Simon Gray
Faith Healer	Brian Friel	Hippolytus	Euripides
Fallen Angels	Noël Coward	His House in Order	Arthur Wing Pinero
The Family Reunion	T S Eliot	The History Boys	Alan Bennett
The Farm	David Storey	Hitchock Blonde	Terry Johnson
The Father	August Strindberg	Home	David Storey
Faust (Parts I & II)	Johann Wolfgang von Goethe	Home at Seven	R C Sherriff
		The Homecoming	Harold Pinter
Fear and Misery in the Third Reich	Bertolt Brecht	Horace	Pierre Corneille
		The Hostage	Brendan Behan
The Feigned Courtizans	Aphra Behn	The Hotel in Amsterdam	John Osborne
Fen	Caryl Churchill	Hotel Paradiso	Georges Feydeau
Filumena	Eduardo de Filippo	Hothouse	Harold Pinter
Five-Finger Exercise*	Peter Shaffer	The House of Bernarda Alba	Federico García Lorca
Flare Path	Terence Rattigan		
A Flea in her Ear	Georges Feydeau	The House of Blue Leaves	John Guare
Flesh and Blood	Edna O'Brien		
Fool for Love	Sam Shepard	How the Other Half Loves	Alan Ayckbourn
The Forced Marriage	Aphra Behn	Hysteria	Terry Johnson
Forget-Me-Not Lane	Peter Nichols	I Have Been Here Before	J B Priestley
Forty Years On*	Alan Bennett	I Read the News Today (radio)	Willy Russell
The Freedom of the City	Brian Friel		
The Freeway	Peter Nichols	Icecream	Caryl Churchill
French Without Tears	Terence Rattigan	The Iceman Cometh	Eugene O'Neill
The Frogs,	Aristophanes	Ichneutae	Sophocles
La Galerie du Palais	Pierre Corneille	An Ideal Husband	Oscar Wilde
A Game at Chess	Thomas Middleton	The Idiot	Simon Gray
Gaslight (aka: Angel Street)	Patrick Hamilton	I'll Leave it to You*	Noël Coward
		Ill Seen Ill Said	Samuel Beckett
Gasping*	Ben Elton	I'm Talking About Jerusalem	Arnold Wesker
The Gay Lord Quex	Arthur Wing Pinero		
The Gentleman Dancing Master	William Wycherley	Imagine Drowning	Terry Johnson
		The Importance of Being Ernest	Oscar Wilde
The Gentleman in Grey	Compton Mackenzie		
Getting Married	George Bernard Shaw	The Impostor	Molière
Getting On	Alan Bennett	In Camera	Jean-Paul Sartre
Ghosts	Henrik Ibsen	In Celebration	David Storey
The Gift of the Gorgon	Peter Shaffer	In the Shadow of the Glen	J M Synge
The Gingerbread Lady	Neil Simon	Inadmissible Evidence	John Osborne
The Glass Menagerie	Tennessee Williams	The Indian Emperor	John Dryden
Glengarry Glen Ross	David Mamet	Indian Ink	Tom Stoppard
Golden Boy	Clifford Odets	Individual Fruit Pies	Mike Leigh
The Good Doctor	Neil Simon	Insignificance	Terry Johnson
Goodbye Kiss	Ronald Harwood	An Inspector Calls	J B Priestley
The Good Woman of Setzuan	Bertolt Brecht	The Inspector General	Nikolai Gogol
		The Invention of Love	Tom Stoppard
Götz von Berlichingen	Johann W von Goethe	L'Invitation au Château	Jean Anouilh
The Grain of Mustard Seed	Harold Harwood	Ion	Euripides
		Iphigenia in Aulis	Euripides
La Grande Magia	Eduardo de Filippo	Iphigenia in Tauris	Euripides
The Great God Brown	Eugene O'Neill	Iphigénie	Jean Racine

Play	Playwright	Play	Playwright
Iphigenie auf Tauris	Johann Wolfgang von Goethe	Loot	Joe Orton
		Lost in Yonkers	Neil Simon
Ironhand	John Arden	Love and a Bottle*	George Farquhar
The Island of Sakhalim	Anton Chekov	Love for Love	William Congreve
It's a Madhouse	Alan Bleasdale	The Lover's Melancholy	John Ford
It's Ralph	Hugh Whitemore	Love's Comedy	Henrik Ibsen
Ivanov*	Anton Chekhov	The Lower Depths	Maxim Gorky
Japes	Simon Gray	Lucky Sods	John Godber
Jeeves	Alan Ayckbourn	Lucrèce Borgia	Victor Hugo
The Jew of Malta	Christopher Marlowe	Luther	John Osborne
Jill and Jack (TV play)	John Osborne	Lysistrata	Aristophanes
John Bull's Other Island	George Bernard Shaw	M Is for Moon Among Other Things (radio)	Tom Stoppard
John Gabriel Borkman	Henrik Ibsen		
John, Paul, George, Ringo . . . and Bert	Willy Russell	Madame Bovary	Edna O'Brien
		The Madness of George III	Alan Bennett
Joking Apart	Alan Ayckbourn		
Journey's End*	R C Sherriff	The Madras House	Harley Granville Barker
Jumpers	Tom Stoppard	The Magistrate	Arthur Wing Pinero
Juno and the Paycock	Sean O'Casey	Mahler's Conversion	Ronald Harwood
Jupiter	Richard Brinsley Sheridan	The Maid of Orleans	Friedrich von Schiller
Just Between Ourselves	Alan Ayckbourn	The Maids	Jean Genet
Kafka's Dick	Alan Bennett	The Maintenance Man	Richard Harris
King of the Castle (TV play)	Willy Russell	Major Barbara	George Bernard Shaw
		Make and Break	Michael Frayn
The Kitchen	Arnold Wesker	Making It Better	James Saunders
The Knights	Aristophanes	Le Malade Imaginaire	Molière
Knuckle	David Hare	Man Above Men (TV play)	David Hare
La Princess Maleine	Count Maurice Maeterlinck		
Laburnum Grove	J B Priestley	Man and Superman	George Bernard Shaw
Ladies' Tailor*	Georges Feydeau	The Man of Mode, or Sir Fopling Flutter	George Etherege
Lady Windermere's Fan	Oscar Wilde		
The Lady's Not for Burning	Christopher Fry	Man of the Moment	Alan Ayckbourn
The Lady's Trial	John Ford	The Man Who Had All the Luck	Arthur Miller
L'Aigle à deux têtes	Jean Cocteau		
The Lark (L'Alouette)	Jean Anouilh	The March on Russia	David Storey
The Last Bread	H E Bates	Marco Millions	Eugene O'Neill
Last of Mrs Cheyney	Frederick Lonsdale	Marie Tudor	Victor Hugo
The Last of the Red Hot Lovers	Neil Simon	Marion Delorme	Victor Hugo
		The Marriage of Figaro	Pierre Beaumarchais
The Last Yankee	Arthur Miller	Marriage à-la-Mode	John Dryden
The Late Middle Classes	Simon Gray	The Marrying of Ann Leete	Harley Granville Barker
Lazarus Laughed	Eugene O'Neill		
Les Mariés de la Tour Eiffel	Jean Cocteau	Mary Knows	J M Barrie
		Mary Magdalene	Maurice Maeterlinck
Les Liaisons Dangereuses	Christopher Hampton	Maria Stuart	Friedrich von Schiller
		The Massacre at Paris	Christopher Marlowe
The Lesson	Eugène Ionesco	The Master Builder	Henrik Ibsen
Lettice and Lovage	Peter Shaffer	Master Constable	Thomas Middleton
L'Hermine*	Jean Anouilh	Master Olof	August Strindberg
The Liar (Le Menteur)	Pierre Corneille	The Matchmaker	Thornton Wilder
Licking Hitler (TV play)	David Hare	Medea	Euripides
A Lie of the Mind	Sam Shepard	Mélite	Pierre Corneille
Life Class	David Storey	Mid-Channel	Arthur Wing Pinero
A Life in the Theater	David Mamet	The Millionairess	George Bernard Shaw
Life Support	Simon Gray	Le Misanthrope	Molière
Light Shining in Buckinghamshire	Caryl Churchill	The Miser	Molière
		Miss Julie	August Strindberg
The Linden Tree	J B Priestley	Mithridate	Jean Racine
Little Me	Neil Simon	Die Mitschuldigen	Johann Wolfgang von Goethe
Live Like Pigs	John Arden		
Lives of the Great Poisoners	Caryl Churchill	Molly	Simon Gray
		Molly Sweeney	Brian Friel
Living Together	Alan Ayckbourn	The Monocled Mutineer	Alan Bleasdale
London Assurance	Dion Boucicault	Moonlight	Harold Pinter
The Long Christmas Dinner	Thornton Wilder	La Mort de Pompée	Pierre Corneille
		Mother Courage	Bertolt Brecht
Long Day's Journey into Night	Eugene O'Neill	Mother's Day	David Storey
		Mourning Becomes Electra	Eugene O'Neill
Look Back in Anger	John Osborne		
Look, Look	Michael Frayn	The Mourning Bride	William Congreve

Play	Playwright	Play	Playwright
Mr Whatnot*	Alan Ayckbourn	A Piece of My Mind	Peter Nichols
Mrs Warren's Profession	George Bernard Shaw	Pig in a Poke	Georges Feydeau
Murder in the Cathedral	T S Eliot	The Plain Dealer	William Wycherley
Murderer	Anthony Shaffer	Plaintiffs and Defendants	Simon Gray
Murmuring Judges	David Hare	The Playboy of the	J M Synge
My Parents Have Gone	Mike Leigh	Western World	
to Carlisle		Plaza Suite	Neil Simon
Narrow Road to the	Edward Bond	The Plough and the	Sean O'Casey
Deep North		Stars	
The National Health	Peter Nichols	Plutus	Aristophanes
Nativity	Peter Whelan	The Poetaster	Ben Jonson
A New Wonder: A Woman	William Rowley	Poison Pen	Ronald Harwood
Never Vext		Polyeucte	Pierre Corneille
Next Time I'll Sing to You	James Saunders	Popcorn	Ben Elton
Nicomède	Pierre Corneille	The Pope's Wedding*	Edward Bond
Night and Day	Tom Stoppard	Poppy	Peter Nichols
The Night of the Iguana	Tennessee Williams	Post Mortem	Noël Coward
No Man's Land	Harold Pinter	Present Laughter	Noël Coward
No More Sitting on the	Alan Bleasdale	The Preventable Rise	Bertolt Brecht
Old School Bench*		of Arturo Ui	
No Sex Please, We're	Alistair Foot and Anthony	The Price	Arthur Miller
British	Marriot	The Prisoner of Second	Neil Simon
Noises Off	Michael Frayn	Avenue	
Norman Conquests	Alan Ayckbourn	The Private Ear	Peter Shaffer
Not I	Samuel Beckett	Private Lives	Noël Coward
Nude with Violin	Nöel Coward	Privates on Parade	Peter Nichols
A Number	Caryl Churchill	Professional Foul	Tom Stoppard
Nuts in May	Mike Leigh	(TV play)	
The Octoroon	Dion Boucicault	The Profligate	Arthur Wing Pinero
The Odd Couple	Neil Simon	Prometheus Bound	Aeschylus
Oedipus at Colonus	Sophocles	Promises, Promises	Neil Simon
Oedipus Rex	Sophocles	The Provok'd Husband	John Vanbrugh (completed
The Office Party	John Godber		by Colley Cibber)
The Old Bachelor*	William Congreve	The Provok'd Wife	John Vanbrugh (completed
The Old Country	Alan Bennett		by Colley Cibber)
Old Masters	Simon Gray	The Public Eye	Peter Shaffer
Oleanna	David Mamet	Pulchérie	Pierre Corneille
On a Night Like This	John Godber	Pygmalion	George Bernard Shaw
On Approval	Frederick Lonsdale	Quality Street	J M Barrie
On the Ledge	Alan Bleasdale	The Quare Fellow*	Brendan Behan
On the Margin	Alan Bennett	Quartermaine's Terms	Simon Gray
(first TV play)		A Question of Attribution	Alan Bennett
On the Piste	John Godber	Racing Demon	David Hare
One for the Road	Harold Pinter	The Real Inspector	Tom Stoppard
One for the Road	Willy Russell	Hound	
Oresteia Trilogy	Aeschylus	The Rear	Simon Gray
Orpheus	Jean Cocteau	The Recruiting Officer	George Farquhar
Other Places	Harold Pinter	Reflected Glory	Ronald Harwood
Otherwise Engaged	Simon Gray	The Relapse	John Vanbrugh
Our Day Out	Willy Russell	Relative Values	Noël Coward
Our Town	Thornton Wilder	Relatively Speaking	Alan Ayckbourn
Outside Edge	Richard Harris	The Restoration of	David Storey
Pack of Lies	Hugh Whitemore	Arnold Middleton*	
Pandora's Box	Frank Wedekind	Retreat	James Saunders
Passion Play	Peter Nichols	Rhinoceros	Eugène Ionesco
A Patriot for Me	John Osborne	The Ride Down	Arthur Miller
The Peace	Aristophanes	Mount Morgan	
Peace in Our Time	Noël Coward	Riders to the Sea	J M Synge
A Piece of My Mind	Peter Nichols	The Rise and Fall of	Jim Cartwright
Peer Gynt	Henrik Ibsen	Little Voice	
Pelléas et Mélisande	Count Maurice Maeterlinck	The Rival Ladies	John Dryden
Perkin Warbeck	John Ford	The Rivals	Richard Brinsley
The Persians	Aeschylus		Sheridan
Peter Pan	J M Barrie	Road	Jim Cartwright
Phèdre	Jean Racine	The Robbers*	Friedrich von Schiller
Philadelphia Here I Come	Brian Friel	The Rock Garden	Sam Shepard
The Philanthropist	Christopher Hampton	The Rock	T S Eliot
Philoctetes	Sophocles	Rodogune	Pierre Corneille
The Phoenician Women	Euripides	Le Roi s'amuse	Victor Hugo
A Phoenix Too Frequent	Christopher Fry	The Room*	Harold Pinter

LITERATURE

Play	Playwright	Play	Playwright
Roots	Arnold Wesker	Slag*	David Hare
Rope (US title: Rope's End)	Patrick Hamilton	Sleeping Dog	Simon Gray
		Sleuth	Anthony Shaffer
The Rose Tattoo	Tennessee Williams	A Small Family Business	Alan Ayckbourn
Rosencrantz and Guildenstern Are Dead	Tom Stoppard	Snake in the Grass	Alan Ayckbourn
		So Long Life	Peter Nichols
Ross	Terence Rattigan	Softcops	Caryl Churchill
Round and Round the Garden	Alan Ayckbourn	The Spanish Gypsy	Thomas Middleton and William Rowley
The Rover	Aphra Behn	The Spanish Tragedy	Thomas Kyd
The Royal Hunt of the Sun	Peter Shaffer	Speed-the-Plow	David Mamet
		Spoiled	Simon Gray
The Ruffian on the Stair*	Joe Orton	Spring Awakening	Frank Wedekind
A Russian in the Woods	Peter Whelan	The Squire	Arthur Wing Pinero
Ruy Blas	Victor Hugo	Stagestruck	Simon Gray
The Sad Shepherd (unfinished)	Ben Jonson	Stags and Hens	Willy Russell
		State of Innocence	John Dryden
Saint Joan	George Bernard Shaw	Stepping Out	Richard Harris
Saint Patrick's Day	Richard Brinsley Sheridan	Stevie*	Hugh Whitemore
Salome	Oscar Wilde	Strange Interlude	Eugene O'Neill
Salt of the Earth	John Godber	A Streetcar Named Desire	Tennessee Williams
The Sandboy	Michael Frayn		
Saturday, Sunday, Monday	Eduardo de Filippo	Suddenly Last Summer	Tennessee Williams
Savages	Christopher Hampton	Sugar Daddies	Alan Ayckbourn
A Scent of Flowers	James Saunders	The Sunshine Boys	Neil Simon
The School for Scandal	Richard Brinsley Sheridan	Suppliants	Aeschylus
The School for Wives	Molière	Sweeney Agonistes*	T S Eliot
The Schoolmistress	Arthur Wing Pinero	Sweet Bird of Youth	Tennessee Williams
The School of Night	Peter Whelan	Sweet Charity	Neil Simon
The Screens	Jean Genet	Table Manners	Alan Ayckbourn
The Seagull	Anton Chekhov	Taking Sides	Ronald Harwood
Season's Greetings	Alan Ayckbourn	Talking Heads	Alan Bennett
The Second Mrs Tanqueray	Arthur Wing Pinero	Tamburlaine the Great	Christopher Marlowe
		Tartuffe	Molière
The Secret Rapture	David Hare	Teechers	John Godber
Sejanus	Ben Jonson	La Thébaïde, ou Les Frères ennemis	Jean Racine
Separate Peace (first TV Play)	Tom Stoppard		
		Ten Times Table	Alan Ayckbourn
Separate Tables	Terence Rattigan	Théodore	Pierre Corneille
Separation	Tom Kempinski	Thesmophoriazusae	Aristophanes
September in the Rain	John Godber	They're Playing Our Song	Neil Simon
Sergeant Musgrave's Dance	John Arden		
		Thieves' Carnival	Jean Anouilh
Serious Money	Caryl Churchill	The Three Sisters	Anton Chekhov
Seven Against Thebes	Aeschylus	Three Tall Women	Edward Albee
Sexual Perversity in Chicago	David Mamet	Three Women	Sylvia Plath
		The Threepenny Opera	Bertolt Brecht
The Shadow of a Gunman	Sean O'Casey	Thursday's Child	Christopher Fry
		Till the Day I Die	Clifford Odets
Shakers	John Godber	Time and the Conways	J B Priestley
Shakespeare Country	Peter Whelan	Time and Time Again	Alan Ayckbourn
The Shaughraun	Dion Boucicault	Time of My Life	Alan Ayckbourn
The Shawl	David Mamet	The Tinker's Wedding	J M Synge
She Stoops to Conquer	Oliver Goldsmith	Tiny Alice	Edward Albee
She Would If She Could	George Etherege	'Tis Pity She's a Whore	John Ford
Shirley Valentine	Willy Russell	To Damascus	August Strindberg
The Silent Woman	Ben Jonson	The Tooth of Crime	Sam Shepard
Silly Cow	Ben Elton	Top Girls	Caryl Churchill
The Silver Box	John Galsworthy	Torquato Tasso	Johann Wolfgang von Goethe
The Silver Tassie	Sean O'Casey		
Simpatico	Sam Shepard	Total Eclipse	Christopher Hampton
Simply Disconnected	Simon Gray	A Touch of the Poet	Eugene O'Neill
Single Spies	Alan Bennett	The Tower	Christopher Fry
Sisterly Feelings	Alan Ayckbourn	Trachiniae	Sophocles
Sisters	David Storey	Translations	Brian Friel
Six Characters in Search of an Author	Luigi Pirandello	Travesties	Tom Stoppard
		Treats	Christopher Hampton
Six Degrees of Separation	John Guare	Trelawny of the 'Wells'	Arthur Wing Pinero
		The Trojan Women	Euripides
The Skin Game	John Galsworthy	True West	Sam Shepard
The Skin of Our Teeth	Thornton Wilder	The Trumpet Shall Sound	Thornton Wilder

Play	Playwright	Play	Playwright
Turcaret	Alain-René Lesage	Way Upstream	Alan Ayckbourn
£200 a Year*	Arthur Wing Pinero	The Web*	Eugene O'Neill
The Two of Us*	Michael Frayn	The Weir	Conor McPherson
Two Sundays	Simon Gray	The Well of the Saints	J M Synge
Ubu Roi	Alfred Jarry	West of Suez (TV play)	John Osborne
Uncle Vanya	Anton Chekhov	What Every Woman	J M Barrie
Under Milk Wood	Dylan Thomas	Knows	
Unsuitable for Adults	Terry Johnson	What the Butler Saw	Joe Orton
Up 'N' Under	John Godber	When Did You Last See	Christopher Hampton
Vandaleur's Folly	John Arden	My Mother?*	
Venus Observed	Christopher Fry	When the Wind Blows	Peter Nichols
Veronica's Room	Ira Levin	When We Are Married	J B Priestley
La Veuve	Pierre Corneille	The White Devil	John Webster
A View from the Bridge	Arthur Miller	Who's Afraid of Virginia	Edward Albee
Virginia	Edna O'Brien	Woolf ?	
The Visitors	Nicholas Monsarrat	Widowers' Houses	George Bernard Shaw
Volpone (The Fox)	Ben Jonson	The Wild Duck	Henrik Ibsen
The Vortex	Noël Coward	William Tell	Friedrich von Schiller
A Voyage Round My	John Mortimer	The Winslow Boy	Terence Rattigan
Father		Wise Child*	Simon Gray
The Voysey Inheritance	Harley Granville Barker	Woman in Mind	Alan Ayckbourn
Waiting for Godot	Samuel Beckett	A Woman of No	Oscar Wilde
Waiting for Lefty	Clifford Odets	Importance	
Walk on the Grass	Peter Nichols	Women Beware Women	Thomas Middleton
(first TV Play)		Wonderful Tennessee	Brian Friel
A Walk on the Water*	Tom Stoppard	The Wood Demon	Anton Chekhov
Walker, London*	J M Barrie	The Workhouse Donkey	John Arden
Wallenstein Trilogy	Friedrich von Schiller	Yerma	Federico García Lorca
Waltz of the Toreadors	Jean Anouilh	Yonadab	Peter Shaffer
The Wasps	Aristophanes	You Never Can Tell	George Bernard Shaw
Waste	Harley Granville-Barker	Zigger Zagger	Peter Terson
The Way of the World	William Congreve	The Zoo Story	Edward Albee

Theatre: General Information

After the Fall   Central character: Quentin. Former wife: Maggie (modelled on Marilyn Monroe).

Arms and the Man   Setting: Bulgaria. Family: Petkoffs.

Banned by Lord Chamberlain   *Early Morning* by Edward Bond (1968) was the last play to be banned by the Lord Chamberlain, whose office was abolished on 26 Sept. 1968.

The Birthday Party   Party for: Stanley. Boarding house owners: Meg and Petey.

The Blue Bird   Children: Mytyl and Tyltyl.

Broadway theatre named after   Neil Simon is the only living American playwright to be so honoured.

Camille   Central character Marguerite Gautier.

Candida   Candida's husband: Reverend Morell. Poet: Marchbanks.

The Caretaker   Title character Davies.

Cat on a Hot Tin Roof   Title character: Maggie Pollitt. Husband: Brick. Location: St Louis.

Cell Mates   Took over from Stephen Fry: Simon Ward.

Charley's Aunt   Title character: Donna Lucia d'Alvadores. Charley's surname: Wykeham.

Chips with Everything   Setting: RAF.

Comedy   Meaning: Revel-song.

Comedy of Intrigue   Founder: Sir George Etherege.

Death of a Salesman   Salesman: Willie Loman.

Doll's House   Doll's name: Nora. Nora's husband: Torvald Helmer.

Entertainer   Title character   Archie Rice.

Equus   Psychiatrist: Dysart. Stableboy: Alan Strang.

The Gingerbread Lady   Filmed as: *Only When I Laugh.*

The Glass Menagerie   Family: Wingfields.

Hedda Gabler   Husband: Professor George Tessman.

The Iceman Cometh   Salesman: Hickey. Setting: Harry Hope's saloon (NY).

The Importance of Being Ernest   Title character: Jack Worthing (real name Ernest Moncrieff). Governess: Miss Prism. Jack found in handbag at station. Left in baby's place: novel. Algernon Moncrieff's fictional friend: Bunbury.

In Camera   Setting: Hell. Characters: Garcin, Estelle, Inez.

The Inspector General   Impostor: Khlestakov.

Japanese theatre   Two main types: Nō (lit: talent) was developed in the 14th century from a court dance and the acrobatics of the sarugaku troupes. Kabuki (lit: singing and dancing art) was developed in the 17th century and was originally only performed by women. The costumes worn come from the Edo period (1603–1868).

The Jew of Malta   Title character: Barabas.

Journey's End   Setting: First World War.

Jumpers   Professor: George Moore. George's Wife: Dotty.

Juno and the Paycock   Paycock: Jack Boyle.

Killed by Tortoise   Aeschylus was allegedly killed when an eagle dropped a tortoise on his head.

Killed fellow actor in duel   Ben Jonson.

Le Bourgeois Gentilhomme   Title character: Monsieur Jourdain.

Lady Windermere's Fan   Mother: Mrs Erlynne.

The Lady's Not for Burning   Setting: Cool Clary.

Famous Lines   Brazil, where the nuts come from (*Charley's Aunt*).

He is the very pineapple of politeness (Mrs Malaprop in *The Rivals*).

Heav'n has no rage, like love to hatred burn'd,
Nor Hell a fury, like a woman scorned (*The Mourning Bride*).

Music hath charms to soothe a savage breast (*The Mourning Bride*).

Our civil community is founded on the pestiferous soil of falsehood (Dr Stockman in *An Enemy of the People*).

Very flat, Norfolk (*Private Lives*).

The Long Day's Journey into Night   Family: Tyrones.

Look Back in Anger   Central character: Jimmy Porter. Jimmy's wife: Alison.

Lyceum   Managed by Sir Henry Irving 1878–99.

The Maids   Title characters: Claire and Solange.

Le Misanthrope   Title character: Alceste.

The Miser   Lead character: Harpagon.

Mourning Becomes Electra   Based on the Oresteia Trilogy by Aeschylus.

Norman Conquests   *Table Manners*, *Round and Round the Garden*, *Living Together*.

Oresteia Trilogy (Aeschylus)   *Agamemnon*, *Choephoroe* (*The Libation-Bearers*), *Eumenides*.

Peter Pan   Children: John, Michael and Wendy Darling. Hook educated at Eton. Dog: Nana.

Phèdre   Based on *Hippolytus* by Euripides.

The Playboy of the Western World   Title character: Christie Mahon.

Prison   Written in: *Our Lady of the Flowers* by Jean Genet.

Private Lives   Written for Gertrude Lawrence.

Pushkin's 'Little Tragedies'   *Mozart and Salieri*, *The Covetous Knight*, *The Stone Guest*, *The Feast during the Plague*.

Pygmalion   Professor: Henry Higgins. Flowergirl: Eliza Doolittle. Higgins home: Wimpole St. Scandal over: use of the word 'bloody'.

The Quare Fellow   Set in a Dublin prison.

The Rivals   Rivals: Captain Absolute (Ensign Beverley) and Sir Lucius O'Trigger (Bob Acres). Setting: Bath. Lady: Lydia Languish. Her Aunt: Mrs Malaprop.

Roots   Central character: Beatie Bryant. Setting: Norfolk.

Seagull   Central characters: Irina, Nina, Trigorin the novelist.

Second Mrs Tanqueray   Title character: Paula Ray.

She Stoops to Conquer   Central character: Marlow. Marlow's love: Miss Hardcastle.

State of Innocence   Based on *Paradise Lost* by John Milton.

A Streetcar Named Desire   Central character: Blanche Du Bois. Blanche's sister: Stella. Stella's husband: Stanley Kowalsky. Setting: New Orleans.

Sturm und Drang (Storm and Stress)   German literary movement that preceded Romanticism, taking its name from the play by Max Klinger *Der Wirrwarr, oder Sturm und Drang*.

Subtitle   *Man and Superman*   'A Comedy and a Philosophy'.

Theatre of Cruelty   Name given by Antonin Artaud to his use of lighting effects, screams and oversized puppets to induce audience reaction, as in *Les Cenci*.

Theatre of Fact   Aka Documentary Theatre: a German movement founded in the early 1960s by Rolf Hochuth, Peter Weiss and Heinar Kipphardt, highlighting the political propaganda of post-Second World War Germany.

Theatre of the Absurd   Name given to the pessimistic vision of humanity struggling vainly to find a purpose as depicted in works by Beckett (*Waiting for Godot*), Ionesco (*The Bald Soprano*), and such diverse dramatists as Jean Genet, Arthur Adamov and Harold Pinter.

The Three Sisters   Title characters: Irina, Masha, Olga.

Tragedy   Meaning: goat-song.

Travesties   Setting: Zurich.

Volpone   Servant: Mosca.

Waiting for Godot   Tramps: Vladimir (Didi), Estragon (Gogo).

Waiting for Lefty   Title character: Lefty Costello.

Wallenstein Trilogy   *Wallensteins Lager*, *Die Piccolomini*, *Wallensteins Tod*.

The Way of the World   Central characters: Mirabell, Millamant, Lady Wishford.

Wesker Trilogy   *Chicken Soup with Barley*, *Roots*, *I'm Talking About Jerusalem*.

What the Butler Saw   Setting: Psychiatrist's clinic.

The Winslow Boy   Based on Archer–Shee case.

Theatres of the British Isles

(excluding London, see separate section; English unless stated otherwise)

Aberdeen, Capitol (Sco)	Bath, Rondo Studio Theatre	Blackpool, Opera House
Aberdeen, His Majesty's Theatre (Sco)	Bath, Theatre Royal	Bolton, Albert Hall
Aberdeen, Music Hall (Sco)	Belfast, The Grand Opera House (Ire)	Bolton, Octagon
Aldeburgh, Snape Maltings	Belfast, Group Theatre (Ire)	Bournemouth, Pavilion Theatre
Alnwick, Playhouse	Belfast, Lyric Theatre (Ire)	Bradford, Alhambra Theatre
Andover, Cricklade Theatre	Belfast, Waterfront (Ire)	Bradford, St George's Hall
Andover, Winton Studio Theatre	Bexhill, De La Warr Pavilion	Brighton, Brighton Centre
Armagh, The Marketplace Theatre (Ire)	Birmingham, Alexandra	Brighton, Dome
Averham, Robin Hood Theatre	Birmingham, Crescent	Brighton, Gardner Arts Centre
Aylesbury, Limelight Theatre	Birmingham, Hippodrome	Brighton, Komedia Theatre
Barnstaple, Queens Theatre	Birmingham, Repertory Theatre	Brighton, Theatre Royal
Basildon, Towngate Theatre	Birmingham, Symphony Hall	Bristol, Colston Hall
Basingstoke, The Anvil	Blackburn, King George's Hall	Bristol, Hippodrome
Basingstoke, Haymarket	Blackburn, Opera House	Bristol, Old Vic Theatre
	Blackpool, Grand Theatre	Bristol, Theatre Royal (oldest in Britain: built 1766)

Bromley, Churchill Theatre
Bury St Edmunds, Theatre Royal
Buxton, Opera House
Cambridge, ADC Theatre
Cambridge, Arts Theatre
Cambridge, Corn Exchange
Canterbury, Gulbenkian Theatre
Canterbury, Marlowe Theatre
Cardiff, New Theatre (Wal)
Cardiff, St David's Hall (Wal)
Cardiff, Sherman Theatre (Wal)
Carlisle, Sands Centre
Carshalton, Charles Cryer Studio
  Theatre
Chatham, Theatre Royal
Cheltenham, Everyman Theatre
Cheltenham, Playhouse Theatre
Chester, Gateway Theatre
Chesterfield, Pomegranate Theatre
Chichester, Festival Theatre
Chichester, Minerva Studio
Cockermouth, Kirkgate Centre
Colchester, Mercury Theatre
Coleraine, Riverside Theatre (Ire)
Cork, Cork Opera House (Ire)
Cork, Everyman Palace Theatre (Ire)
Cork, Granary Theatre (Ire)
Cork, Half Moon Theatre (Ire)
Cork, Savoy Theatre (Ire)
Coventry, Belgrade Theatre
Coventry, Warwick Arts Centre
Crawley, The Hawth
Crewe, Lyceum
Croydon, Fairfield Hall & Ashcroft
  Theatre
Croydon, Warehouse Theatre
Darlington, Civic Theatre – Arts
  Centre
Derby, Assembly Rooms
Derby, Playhouse Theatre
Dublin, Abbey Theatre (Ire)
Dublin, Andrews Theatre (Ire)
Dublin, Dublin Gate Theatre (Ire)
Dublin, Gaiety Theatre (Ire)
Dublin, Olympia Theatre (Ire)
Dublin, Peacock Theatre (Ire)
Dublin, Tivoli Theatre (Ire)
Dumfries, Theatre Royal (Sco)
Eastbourne, Congress Theatre
Eastbourne, Devonshire Park
  Theatre
Eastbourne, Winter Garden
Edinburgh, Festival Theatre (Sco)
Edinburgh, Gilded Balloon (Sco)
Edinburgh, King's Theatre (Sco)
Edinburgh, Playhouse (Sco)
Edinburgh, Royal Lyceum Theatre
  (Sco)
Edinburgh, Traverse (Sco)
Eltham, Bob Hope Theatre
Exeter, Northcott Theatre
Felixstowe, Spa Pavilion Theatre
Galway, Blackbox Theatre (Ire)
Galway, Druid Theatre (Ire)
Glasgow, Citizens Theatre (Sco)
Glasgow, Pavilion Theatre (Sco)
Glasgow, Royal Concert Hall (Sco)
Glasgow, Theatre Royal (Sco)
Glasgow, Tramway (Sco)
Glasgow, Tron Theatre (Sco)
Glyndebourne, Opera House
Grimsby, Auditorium

Great Yarmouth, Britannia Theatre
Great Yarmouth, New Wellington
  Theatre
Great Yarmouth, St George's
  Theatre
Guildford, Civic Theatre
Guildford, Yvonne Arnaud Theatre
Halifax, Victoria Theatre
Hanley, The Royal
Hastings, The Stables
Hastings, White Rock Theatre
High Wycombe, Wycombe Swan
  Theatre
Hitchin, The Queen Mother Theatre
Hornchurch, Queen's Theatre
Harrogate, Harrogate Theatre
Huddersfield, Lawrence Batley
  Theatre
Hull, Donald Roy Theatre
Hull, Hull Arena
Hull, Hull City Hall
Hull, Hull Truck Theatre
Ifield, Barn Theatre
Ilford, Kenneth More Theatre
Ilfracombe, The Landmark Theatre
Inverness, Eden Court Theatre (Sco)
Isle of Man, Gaiety Theatre
Ipswich, Corn Exchange
Ipswich, New Wolsey Theatre
Ipswich, Regent Theatre
Ipswich, Sir John Mills Theatre
Keswick, Theatre By The Lake
Lancaster, Dukes Playhouse
Lancaster, Grand Theatre
Lancaster, Nuffield Theatre
Leeds, City Varieties
Leeds, Grand Theatre
Leeds, West Yorkshire Playhouse
Leicester, De Montfort Hall
Leicester, Haymarket Theatre
Leicester, Phoenix Arts
Liverpool, Empire
Liverpool, Everyman Theatre
Liverpool, Neptune Theatre
Liverpool, Playhouse
Liverpool, Royal Court Theatre
Liverpool, Royal Phillharmonic Hall
Liverpool, St George's Hall
Llandudno, North Wales Theatre
  (Wal)
Manchester, Apollo
Manchester, Bridgewater Hall
Manchester, Contact Theatre
Manchester, Library Theatre
Manchester, Lowry Centre
Manchester, Palace Theatre-Opera
  House
Manchester, Royal Exchange
  Theatre
Mansfield, Palace Theatre
Milton Keynes, Milton Keynes
  Theatre
Mold, Theatre Clwyd (Wal)
Mull, Little Theatre (Sco)
Newark, Palace Theatre
Newbury, Corn Exchange
Newbury, Watermill Theatre
Newcastle, Opera House
Newcastle, Playhouse
Newcastle, Theatre Royal
Newcastle-under-Lyme, New Vic
  Theatre

Northampton, Derngate Theatre
Northampton, Royal Theatre
Norwich, The Maddermarket
Norwich, Playhouse
Norwich, Theatre Royal
Nottingham, Lace Market Theatre
Nottingham, Playhouse
Nottingham, Royal Centre
Nottingham, Theatre Royal
Oldham, Coliseum Theatre
Oldham, Sixth Form College Theatre
Oxford, Apollo Theatre
Oxford, Old Fire Station
Oxford, Playhouse Theatre
Perth, Perth Theatre (Sco)
Peterborough, Key Theatre
Pitlochry, Festival Theatre (Sco)
Plymouth, Drum Theatre
Plymouth, Mayflower
Plymouth, Theatre Royal
Poole, The Lighthouse
Porthcurno (Cornwall), Minack
  (open-air)
Portsmouth, Guildhall
Portsmouth, New Theatre Royal
Preston, Guildhall & Charter Theatre
Reading, The Hexagon
Reading, The Mill at Sonning
Redhill, Harlequin
Rhyl, Pavilion Theatre (Wal)
St Helens, Theatre Royal
Salford, The Lowry
Salisbury, Playhouse
Scarborough, Futurist Theatre
Scarborough, Spa Theatre
Scarborough, Stephen Joseph
  Theatre
Sheffield, City Hall
Sheffield, Crucible
Sheffield, Lyceum
Sligo, Hawk's Well Theatre (Ire)
South Shields, Custom House
Southampton, The Gantry
Southampton, The Mayflower
Southampton, The Nuffield Theatre
Southsea, Kings Theatre
Stevenage, Gordon Craig Theatre
Stoke-on-Trent, New Victoria
  Theatre
Stoke-on-Trent, The Royal
Stoke-on-Trent, Victoria Hall
Stratford-upon-Avon, The Other
  Place
Stratford-upon-Avon, Royal
  Shakespeare Theatre
Stratford-upon-Avon, Swan Theatre
Sunderland, Empire Theatre
Swansea, Grand Theatre (Wal)
Swindon, Wyvern Theatre
Tamworth, Arts Centre
Taunton, Brewhouse Theatre
Tewkesbury, Roses Theatre
Torquay, Princess Theatre
Truro, Hall For Cornwall
Wakefield, Theatre Royal & Opera
  House
Warrington, Parr Hall
Watford, Palace Theatre
Wavendon, The Stables
Wellingborough, The Castle
Weymouth, Pavilion
Winchester, Theatre Royal

LITERATURE

Windsor, Theatre Royal
Woking, Ambassadors / New
  Victoria
Wolverhampton, Arena
Wolverhampton, Grand Theatre

Worcester, Swan Theatre
Worthing, Connaught Theatre
Worthing, Northbrook Theatre
Worthing, Pavilion Theatre
Wythenshaw, Forum Theatre

York, Barbican
York, Grand Opera House
York, Theatre Royal

Poetry: By Poet

Peter Ackroyd
(1949–)

Anna Akhmatova
(1889–66)
Matthew Arnold
(1822–88)

Margaret Atwood
(1939–)
W H Auden
(1907–73)

Richard Harris Barham
(1788–1845)
Charles Baudelaire
(1821–67)
Hilaire Belloc
(1870–1953)

John Betjeman
(1906–84)

Laurence Binyon
(1869–1943)
William Blake
(1757–1827)

Aleksandr Blok
(1880–1921)

Country Life
London Lickpenny
Ouch
Anno Domini
White Flock
Dover Beach
Empedocles on Etna
The Forsaken Merman
The Scholar Gypsy
Sohrab and Rustum
The Strayed Reveller
Thyrsis
Tristram and Iseult
The Circle Game
In the Secular Night
About the House
The Age of Anxiety
Another Time
City Without Walls
The Double Man
Homage to Clio
In Memory of W.B. Yeats
Look, Stranger!
Miss Gee
New Year Letter
Night Mail
On This Island
The Orators
Paid on Both Sides
The Shield of Achilles
Spain
Stop All the Clocks
The Ingoldsby Legends
The Jackdaw of Rheims
Les Fleurs du mal

The Bad Child's Book of
  Beasts
Cautionary Tales
Matilda
Continual Dew
Death in Leamington
A Few Late
  Chrysanthemums
Highland Low
The Metropolitan Railway
Mount Zion
New Bats in Old Belfries
A Nip in the Air
Old Lights for New Chancels
A Subaltern's Love Song
For the Fallen
Tristram's End
Jerusalem
Milton
The Sick Rose
Songs of Experience
Songs of Innocence
The Tyger
Nocturnal Hours
The Rose and the Cross
The Scythians
Songs About the Lady Fair

Edmund Blunden
(1896–1974)

Wilfrid Scawen Blunt
(1840–1922)
Gordon Bottomley
(1874–1948)
Robert Bridges
(1844–1930)

Emily Brontë
(1818–48)

Rupert Brooke
(1887–1915)

Elizabeth Barrett
Browning
(1806–61)

Robert Browning
(1812–89)

John Bunyan
(1628–88)
Robert Burns
(1759–96)

The Twelve
Almswomen
Bonadventure
Pastorals
Undertones of War
The Waggoner
The Old Squire

Poems of Thirty Years
To Ironfounders and Others
Eros and Psyche
The Growth of Love
London Snow
October
Prometheus the Firegiver
The Spirit of Man
The Testament of Beauty
Gondal
Last Lines
Plead for Me
Remembrance
To Imagination
1914
The Old Vicarage,
  Grantchester
The Soldier
Aurora Leigh
The Battle of Marathon
Casa Guidi Windows
The Cry of the Children
How Do I Love Thee?
Poems before Congress
The Seraphim
Sonnets from the
  Portuguese
Andrea del Sarto
Bells and Pomegranates
Childe Roland to the Dark
  Tower Came
Fra Lippo Lippi
Home Thoughts From
  Abroad
Home-Thoughts, from the
  Sea
How They Brought the Good
  News from Ghent to Aix
Men and Women
My Last Duchess
Paracelsus
Pauline
The Pied Piper of Hamelin
Pippa Passes
Rabbi Ben Ezra
The Ring and the Book
Soliloquy of the Spanish
  Cloister
Sordello
The Pilgrim

Address to a Mouse
Auld Lang Syne
Comin' Through the Rye
The Cotter's Saturday Night

	Death and Doctor Hornbook		The Rime of the Ancient
	Despondency		Mariner
	Desolate and Pale	William Cory	Heraclitus
	Moonlight	(1823–92)	Ionica
	Epistle to Davie	William Cowper	John Gilpin
	Ae Fond Kiss	(1731–1800)	The Task
	For a' that and a' that	George Crabbe	The Borough
	Halloween	(1754–1832)	The Village
	The Holy Fair	Hart Crane	The Bridge
	Holy Willie's Prayer	(1899–1932)	White Buildings
	The Jolly Beggars	Dante Alighieri	Banquet
	Kilmarnock Poems	(1265–1321)	Canzoniere
	The Lament		The Divine Comedy
	A Red, Red Rose	W H Davies	Leisure
	Scots Musical Museum	(1871–1940)	Money
	Tam O'Shanter		School's Out
	To a Field Mouse		A Soul's Destroyer
	The Twa Herds	Emily Dickinson	A Bird Came Down the Walk
Samuel Butler	Hudibras	(1830–86)	A Narrow Fellow in the
(1612–80)			Grass
Lord Byron	Beppo		Parting
(1788–1824)	Childe Harold's Pilgrimage	Austin Dobson	At the Sign of the Lyre
	The Destruction of	(1840–1921)	A Fancy From Fontenelle
	Sennacherib		Proverbs in Porcelain
	Don Juan		Vignettes in Rhyme
	Hours of Idleness	John Donne	Anniversaries
	Lara	(c. 1572–1631)	The Canonization
	The Prisoner of Chillon		The Exstasie
	She Walks in Beauty		The Good-Morrow
	The Siege of Corinth		Metempsychosis
	The Vision of Judgment		A Nocturnall upon St Lucies
	We'll Go No More A-Roving		Day
Luis de Camoes	The Lusiads		Song
(1524–1580)	Rimas		The Sun Rising
Roy Campbell	The Flaming Terrapin		A Valediction: Forbidding
(1901–1957)	Flowering Rifle		Mourning
	Soldier's Reply to the Poet	Ernest Dowson	Decorations
	The Wayzgoose	(1867–1900)	Non Sum Qualis Eram
Thomas Campbell	Gertrude of Wyoming		Vitae Sumina Brevis
(1777–1844)		John Dryden	Absalom and Achitophel
Lewis Carroll	The Hunting of the Snark	(1631–1700)	Alexander's Feast
(1832–98)	Jabberwocky		Annus Mirabilis: The Year of
	Phantasmagoria and other		Wonders, 1666
	Poems		Astræ Redux
	The Walrus and the		Fables, Ancient and
	Carpenter		Modern
Sydney Carter	Lord of the Dance		The Hind and the Panther
(1915–)			The Medal
Charles Causley	Farewell, Aggie Weston		Religio Laici
(1917–2003)	Figure of 8		A Song for St Cecilia's Day
	RIJP		Sylvia the Fair
	Survivor's Leave	T S Eliot	Ash Wednesday
	Underneath the Water	(1888–1965)	Four Quartets
	Union Street		Gerontion
	The Young Man of Cury		The Hollow Men
Thomas Chatterton	The Rowley Poems		The Journey of the Magi
(1752–70)			The Love Song of J. Alfred
Geoffrey Chaucer	The Canterbury Tales		Prufrock
(c. 1343–1400)	Troilus and Criseyde		The Waste Land
G K Chesterton	The Donkey	Ralph Waldo Emerson	Brahma
(1874–1936)	Greybeards at Play	(1803–82)	Give All to Love
	The Wild Knight		May–Day
John Clare	First Love		The Problem
(1793–1864)	The Rural Muse	William Empson	The Gathering Storm
	The Shepherd's	(1906–84)	
	Calendar	Quintus Ennius	Annales
	Village Minstrel	(239–169 BC)	
Samuel Taylor	The Ancient Mariner	Gavin Ewart	Poets
Coleridge (1772–1834)	Christabel	(1916–95)	
	Dejection: An ode	Edward Fitzgerald	The Rubaiyat of Omar
	Kubla Khan	(1809–83)	Khayyam (translation from
	Ode to France		Persian)

LITERATURE

James Elroy Flecker *The Bridge of Fire*
(1884–1915)   *The Golden Journey to*
                        Samarkand
                     The Old Ships
Robert Lee Frost   *After Apple-Picking*
(1874–1963)   *Birches*
                     A Boy's Will
                     The Death of the Hired Man
                     Dust of Snow
                     Fire and Ice
                     A Further Range
                     The Gift Outright
                     A Lone Striker
                     Mountain Interval
                     Mowing
                     Neither Out Far Nor In Deep
                     New Hampshire
                     North of Boston
                     The Oven Bird
                     Pan With Us
                     The Silken Tent
                     Steeple Bush
                     Stopping by Woods on a
                        Snowy Evening
                     The Tuft of Flowers
                     West-Running Brook
                     A Witness Tree
Jean Genet   *Chant Secret*
(1910–86)
Allen Ginsberg   *Empty Mirror*
(1926–97)   *Howl**
                     Kaddish
                     Planet News
                     Reality Sandwiches
Johann Wolfgang   *Erlkönig*
  von Goethe   *Kennst du das Land*
(1749–1832)   *Roman Elegies*
Oliver Goldsmith   *The Deserted Village*
(1728–74)   *Elegy on the Death of a Mad*
                        Dog
                     The Traveller
Robert Graves   *Fairies and Fusiliers*
(1895–1985)   *Over the Brazier*
                     A Slice of Wedding Cake
Thomas Gray   *The Bard*
(1716–71)   *The Descent of Odin*
                     Elegy Written in a Country
                        Churchyard
                     The Fatal Sisters
                     Ode on a Distant Prospect of
                        Eton College
                     The Progress of Poesy
Graham Greene   *Bubbling April*
(1904–91)
Julian Grenfell   *Into Battle*
(1888–1915)
William Hamilton   *Last Dying Words of Bonny*
(1665–1751)   *Heck*
William Hamilton   *The Braes of Yarrow*
(1704–54)
Thomas Hardy   *The Darkling Thrush*
(1840–1928)   *The Dynasts*
                     Wessex Poems
                     Winter Words
Seamus Heaney   *Beowulf* (translation)
(1929–)   *Field Work*
                     Death of a Naturalist
                     Door into the Dark
                     Haw Lantern
                     Seeing Things
                     The Spirit Level (collection)
                     Sweeney's Flight

Felicia Hemans   *Casabianca*
(1793–1835)   *The Landing of the Pilgrim*
                        Fathers
William Henley   *England, My England*
(1849–1903)   *For England's Sake*
                     Hawthorn and Lavender
                     In Hospital
                     Invictus
                     A Song of Speed
                     Song of the Sword
Robert Herrick   *Cherry-Ripe*
(1591–1674)   *Delight in Disorder*
                     To the Virgins, To Make
                        Much of Time
                     Upon Julia's Clothes
Friedrich Hölderlin *Friedensfeier (Celebration of*
(1770–1843)   *Peace)*
Homer   *The Iliad*
(8th century BC)   *The Odyssey*
Thomas Hood   *Autumn, Ode to*
(1799–1845)   *The Dream of Eugene*
                        Aram
                     Faithless Sally Brown
                     Lycus the Centaur
                     National Tales
                     Ruth
                     The Song of the Shirt
                     Tim Turpin
                     Whims and Oddities
Gerard Manley Hopkins *Felix Randal*
(1844–89)   *Pied Beauty*
                     The Windhover
                     The Wreck of the
                        Deutschland
A E Housman   *Epitaph on an Army of*
(1859–1936)   *Mercenaries*
                     Fancy's Knell
                     Last Poems
                     More Poems
                     A Shropshire Lad
Ted Hughes   *Birthday Letters* (collection)
(1930–98)   *Cave Birds*
                     Crow
                     The Hawk in the Rain
                     Lupercal
                     Moortown
                     The Remains of Elmet
                     Wodwo
Victor Hugo   *Les Châtiments*
(1802–85)   *Les Contemplations*
James Leigh Hunt   *Abou Ben Adhem*
(1784–1859)   *Jenny Kissed Me*
                     Juvenilia
                     The Nile
Henrik Ibsen   *Brand*
(1828–1906)
Elizabeth Jennings   *The Animals' Arrival*
(1926–2001)   *Lucidities*
                     One Flesh
                     Relationships
                     Song for a Birth or a Death
                     A Way of Looking
Samuel Johnson   *London*
(1709–84)   *The Vanity of Human Wishes*
Ben Jonson   *Drink to Me Only With Thine*
(1572–1637)   *Eyes*
                     To Celia
John Keats   *Endymion*
(1795–1821)   *The Eve of St Agnes*
                     Grecian Urn, Ode on a
                     Hymn to Pan
                     Hyperion

Isabella or the Pot of Basil
La Belle Dame Sans Merci
Lamia
Ode on Melancholy
Ode to a Nightingale
On First Looking into
  Chapman's Homer
Ode to Psyche
To Autumn

Rudyard Kipling
(1865–1936)
The Ballad of East and West
Barrack-Room Ballads
The Betrothed
Cities and Thrones and
  Powers
The Female of the Species
The Gods of the Copybook
  Headings
Gunga Din
If
Mandalay
The Way Through the
  Woods
The White Man's Burden

Walter Savage Landor Gebir
(1775–1864) Rose Aylmer
William Langland Piers Plowman
(c. 1322–1400)
Philip Larkin Church Going
(1922–85) High Windows
The North Ship
This Be the Verse
The Whitsun Weddings

Emma Lazarus Admetus
(1849–87) By the Waters of Babylon
The New Colossus

Edward Lear The Owl and the Pussycat
(1812–88)
Laurie Lee April Rise
(1914–97) The Bloom of Candles
My Many–Coated Man
The Sun My Monument

Cecil Day Lewis Beechen Vigil
(1904–72) Overtures to Death
C S Lewis Dymer
(1898–1963)
Henry Wadsworth The Belfry of Bruges
Longfellow The Courtship of Miles
(1807–82)   Standish
Evangeline
Excelsior
Kalevala
The Golden Legend
The Song of Hiawatha
Paul Revere's Ride
The Skeleton in Armour
The Village Blacksmith
Voices of the Night
Wayside Inn, Tales of a
The Wreck of the Hesperus

Federico García Lorca Canciones
(1898–1936) Romancero Gitano
Richard Lovelace To Althea
(1618–57) To Lucasta, On Going to the
  Wars
Hugh MacDiarmid A Drunk Man Looks at the
(1892–1978)   Thistle
Sangschaw
Louis MacNeice Autumn Sequel
(1907–63) Bagpipe Music
Blind Fireworks
The Burning Perch
Solstices

Stéphane Mallarmé L'Après-midi d'un Faune
(1842–98)
Osip Mandelstam Kamen Stone
(1891–1938) Tristia
Walter de la Mare The Listeners
(1873–1956) O Lovely England
Peacock Pie
Silver
Songs of Childhood
The Veil
Leo Marks (1920–2001) Code Poem for the French
  Resistance
Christopher Marlowe Come Live With Me and Be
(1564–93)   My Love
Hero and Leander
  (unfinished)
The Passionate Shepherd to
  His Love
Andrew Marvell The Definition of Love
(1621–78) The Garden
An Horatian Ode
To His Coy Mistress
John Masefield Cargoes
(1878–1967) Dauber
The Everlasting Mercy
Gallipoli
Nan
Reynard the Fox
Sea Fever
Shakespeare
The Widow in the Bye-Street
Vladimir Mayakovsky The Backbone Flute
(1894–1930) A Cloud in Trousers
150,000,000
John McCrae In Flanders Fields
(1872–1918)
William McGonagall Poetic Gems
(1830–1902) The Tay Bridge Disaster
Alice Meynell Renouncement
(1847–1922) The Shepherdess
John Milton At a Solemn Music
(1608–74) Comus
De Doctrina Christiana
Il Penseroso
L'Allegro
Let Us with a Gladsome
  Mind
Lycidas
Nativity Ode
On His Blindness
On the Late Massacre in
  Piedmont
Paradise Lost
Paradise Regained
Samson Agonistes
E G Moll Returned Soldier
(1900–93)
Clement Moore A Visit from St Nicholas
(1779–1863)
Thomas Moore Irish Melodies
(1779–1852) Lalla Rookh
The Last Rose of Summer
The Light of Other Days
Pete Morgan My Enemies Have Sweet
(1939–)   Voices
Edwin Muir Chorus of the Newly Dead
(1887–1959) The Confirmation
Journeys and Places
The Labyrinth
Ogden Nash Bed Riddance
(1902–71) I'm a Stranger Here Myself
Versus

LITERATURE

Henry Newbolt (1862–1938)	The Death of Admiral Blake Drake's Drum The Island Race Songs of the Sea	Francis Quarles (1592–1644) Manuel Quintana (1772–1857)	Argalus and Parthenia Divine Fancies Al combate de Trafalgar
Cardinal J H Newman (1801–90)	The Dream of Gerontius	Rainer Maria Rilke (1875–1926)	Die Sonnette an Orpheus
Alfred Noyes (1880–1958)	Drake The Flower of Old Japan The Forest of Wild Thyme Forty Singing Seamen The Highwayman The Torchbearers	Arthur Rimbaud (1854–91)	Le Bateau ivre (The Drunken Boat) Les Illuminations
		Pierre de Ronsard (1524–85)	Amours Le Bocage
Arthur O'Shaughnessy (1844–81)	An Epic of Women Lays of France Music and Moonlight Ode (We Are The Music-Makers) Songs of a Worker	Isaac Rosenberg (1890–1918)	On Receiving News of the War Trench Poems
		Christina Rossetti (1830–94)	A Birthday Goblin Market A Pageant The Prince's Progress Remember Uphill
Wilfred Owen (1893–1918)	Anthem For Doomed Youth Disabled Dulce et Decorum Est		
Francis Palgrave (1824–97)	Idylls and Songs	Dante Gabriel Rossetti (1828–82)	The Blessed Damozel The House of Life The King's Tragedy The White Ship
Boris Pasternak (1890–1960)	Above the Barriers Lieutenant Shmidt		
Coventry Patmore (1823–96)	Amelia The Toys The Unknown Eros The Victories of Love	Siegfried Sassoon (1886–1967)	Aftermath Attack Counter-Attack Everyone Sang The Old Huntsman
George Peele (1556–96)	A Farewell to Arms	Alan Seeger (1888–1916)	Rendezvous
Sylvia Plath (1932–63)	Ariel The Colossus Crossing the Water A Winter Ship Winter Trees	Robert Service (1874–1958)	Rhymes of a Rolling Stone The Shooting of Dan McGrew
		William Shakespeare (1564–1616)	Let Me Not to the Marriage of True Minds (Sonnet 116) Shall I Compare Thee to a Summer's Day (Sonnet 18)
Edgar Allan Poe (1809–49)	Annabel Lee The Bells Eureka Israfel Lenore The Raven Tamerlane To My Mother		
		P B Shelley and Elizabeth Shelley Percy Bysshe Shelley (1792–1822)	Original Poetry by Victor and Cazire Adonais Alastor Epipsychidion Hellas Julian and Maddalo Love's Philosophy To Naples Ode to the West Wind Ozymandias of Egypt Prometheus Unbound Queen Mab To a Skylark To Liberty The Witch of Atlas
Alexander Pope (1688–1744)	The Dunciad Eloisa to Abelard An Epistle to Doctor Arbuthnot An Essay on Man Of the Use of Riches The Rape of the Lock Windsor Forest		
Ezra Pound (1885–1972)	A Lume Spento The Cantos Exultations Homage to Sextus Propertius Hugh Selwyn Mauberley If This Be Treason Pisan Cantos Quia Pauper Amavi Umbra		
		Sir Philip Sidney (1554–86) Alan Sillitoe (1928–)	Arcadia Astrophel and Stella Marmalade Jim at the Farm The Rats and Other Poems Snow on the North Side of Lucifer Storm Sun Before Departure Tides and Stone Walls
John Pudney (1909–77)	For Johnny		
Alexander Pushkin (1799–1837)	The Bronze Horseman Egyptian Nights Eugene Onegin Poltava The Prisoner of the Caucasus The Robber Brothers Ruslan and Lyudmilla Tzigani	Stevie Smith (1902–71)	Not Waving But Drowning
		Charles Hamilton Sorley (1895–1915) Robert Southey (1774–1843)	All the Hills and Vales Along Marlborough The Battle of Blenheim Bishop Bruno Bishop Hatto The Inchcape Rock The Old Man's Comforts

Muriel Spark (1918–) — The Fanfarlo

Edmund Spenser (c. 1552–99) — The Faerie Queene / Mother Hubberds Tale / The Shepheardes Calender

James Stephens (1882–1950) — The Crock of Gold / In the Poppy Field / Insurrections

Robert Louis Stevenson (1850–94) — A Child's Garden of Verses / A London Sabbath Morn / Underwoods / The Vagabond / The Woodman

John Still (1543–1608) — Jolly Good Ale and Old

Rabindranath Tagore (1861–1941) — The Crescent Moon / Gitanjali / The Golden Boat / Manasi

Ann Taylor (1782–1866) and Jane Taylor (1783–1824) — Twinkle Twinkle Little Star

Alfred, Lord Tennyson (1809–92) — The Charge of the Light Brigade / Crossing the Bar / Idylls of the King / In Memoriam / The Lady of Shalott / Locksley Hall / The Lotos-Eaters / Maud / Oenone / The Princess / The Revenge / Rizpah / Timbuctoo / To Virgil / Ulysses

William Makepeace Thackeray (1811–63) — The Sorrows of Werther

Dylan Thomas (1914–53) — After the Funeral / Altarwise by Owl-Light / And Death Shall Have No Dominion / Deaths and Entrances / Do Not Go Gentle into That Good Night / Especially When the October Wind / In Country Sleep / In the White Giant's Thigh / I See the Boys of Summer / Light Breaks Where No Sun Shines / Over Sir John's Hill / Poem in October / We Lying by Seasand

Edward Thomas (1878–1917) — Adlestrop

Henry David Thoreau (1817–62) — Independence / Smoke

Rose Thorpe (1850–1939) — Curfew Must Not Ring Tonight

John Updike (1932–) — The Carpentered Hen and Other Tame Creatures

Paul Valéry (1871–1945) — La Jeune Parque

Edward de Vere 17th Earl of Oxford (1550–1604) — What Cunning Can Express

Emile Verhaeren (1855–1916) — Les Débâcles / Les Flamandes / La Multiple Splendeur

Paul Verlaine (1844–96) — La Bonne Chanson / Fêtes Galantes / Sagesse

François Villon (1431–1463) — Ballade des pendus / Le Grand Testament / Le Petit Testament

Virgil (70–19 BC) — The Aeneid / The Bucolics / The Georgics (or Art of Husbandry)

Vincent Voiture (1597–1648) — Vers de Société

Voltaire (1694–1778) — La Henriade

Walt Whitman (1819–92) — Drum-Taps / Leaves of Grass / O Captain! My Captain! / Song of Myself / When Lilacs Last in the Dooryard Bloom'd

John Greenleaf Whittier (1807–92) — At Sundown / Barbara Frietchie / The Battle Autumn of 1862 / In War Time / Laus deo / Snow-bound

Oscar Wilde (1854–1900) — The Ballad of Reading Gaol / Ravenna / To Milton

Tennessee Williams (1911–83) — The Summer Belvedere / In the Winter of Cities

William Wordsworth (1770–1850) — The Affliction of Margaret / The Borderers / To the Cuckoo / Daffodils / Ode to Duty / The Excursion / Guilt and Sorrow / Intimations of Immortality / I Wandered Lonely as a Cloud / The Lucy Poems / My Heart Leaps Up / Nutting / The Prelude / Resolution and Independence / She Was a Phantom of Delight / The Solitary Reaper / Tintern Abbey / Upon Westminster Bridge / Vaudracour and Julia

W B Yeats (1865–1939) — Brown Penny / Byzantium / Ego Dominus Tuus / He Wishes For the Cloths of Heaven / An Irish Airman Foresees His Death / The Lake Isle of Innisfree / Sailing to Byzantium / When You Are Old

Sergey Yesenin (1895–1925) — The Black Man / Confessions of a Hooligan / Desolate and Pale Moonlight / Moscow of the Taverns

Yevgeny Yevtushenko (1933–) — Babi Yar / Heavy Soils / Ivan the Terrible / A Wave of the Hand / Zima Junction

LITERATURE

Poetry: By Poem

(for poets' dates see previous section)

Abou Ben Adhem	James Leigh Hunt	*Barrack-Room Ballads*	Rudyard Kipling
About the House	W H Auden	*Le Bateau Ivre*	Arthur Rimbaud
Above the Barriers	Boris Pasternak	*The Battle Autumn*	John Greenleaf Whittier
Absalom and Achitophel	John Dryden	*of 1862*	
Address to a Mouse	Robert Burns	*The Battle of Blenheim*	Robert Southey
Adlestrop	Edward Thomas	*The Battle of Marathon*	Elizabeth Barrett
Admetus	Emma Lazarus		Browning
Adonais	Percy Bysshe Shelley	*Bed Riddance*	Ogden Nash
The Aeneid	Virgil	*Beechen Vigil*	Cecil Day Lewis
The Affliction of Margaret	William Wordsworth	*The Belfry of Bruges*	Henry Wadsworth
L'Allegro	John Milton		Longfellow
After Apple-Picking	Robert Lee Frost	*Bells and Pomegranates*	Robert Browning
Aftermath	Siegfried Sassoon	*The Bells*	Edgar Allan Poe
After the Funeral	Dylan Thomas	*Beppo*	Lord George Byron
The Age of Anxiety	W H Auden	*The Betrothed*	Rudyard Kipling
Alastor	Percy Bysshe Shelley	*Birches*	Robert Lee Frost
Al Combate de Trafalgar	Manuel Quintana	*A Bird Came Down the*	Emily Dickinson
Alexander's Feast	John Dryden	*Walk*	
All the Hills and Vales	Charles Hamilton	*A Birthday*	Christina Rossetti
Along	Sorley	*Bishop Bruno*	Robert Southey
Almswomen	Edmund Blunden	*Bishop Hatto*	Robert Southey
Altarwise by Owl-Light	Dylan Thomas	*The Black Man*	Sergey Yesenin
To Althea	Richard Lovelace	*The Blessèd Damozel*	Dante Gabriel Rossetti
Amelia	Coventry Patmore	*Blind Fireworks*	Louis MacNeice
Amours	Pierre de Ronsard	*On His Blindness*	John Milton
And Death Shall Have	Dylan Thomas	*The Bloom of Candles*	Laurie Lee
No Dominion		*Le Bocage*	Pierre de Ronsard
Andrea del Sarto	Robert Browning	*Bonadventure*	Edmund Blunden
The Animals' Arrival	Elizabeth Jennings	*La Bonne Chanson*	Paul Verlaine
Annabel Lee	Edgar Allan Poe	*The Borderers*	William Wordsworth
Annales	Quintus Ennius	*The Borough*	George Crabbe
Anniversaries	John Donne	*A Boy's Will*	Robert Lee Frost
Anno Domini	Anna Akhmatova	*The Braes of Yarrow*	William Hamilton
Annus Mirabilis:	John Dryden	*Brahma*	Ralph Waldo Emerson
The Year of Wonders,		*Brand*	Henrik Ibsen
1666		*The Bridge of Fire*	James Elroy Flecker
Another Time	W H Auden	*The Bridge*	Hart Crane
Anthem For Doomed	Wilfred Owen	*The Bronze Horseman*	Alexander Pushkin
Youth		*Brown Penny*	W B Yeats
April Rise	Laurie Lee	*Bubbling April*	Graham Greene
Arcadia	Sir Philip Sidney	*The Bucolics*	Virgil
Argalus and Parthenia	Francis Quarles	*The Burning Perch*	Louis MacNeice
Ariel	Sylvia Plath	*By the Waters of Babylon*	Emma Lazarus
Ash Wednesday	T S Eliot	*Byzantium*	W B Yeats
Astræ Redux	John Dryden	*Canciones*	Federico Garcia Lorca
Astrophel and Stella	Sir Philip Sidney	*The Canonization*	John Donne
At a Solemn Music	John Milton	*The Canterbury Tales*	Geoffrey Chaucer
At Sundown	John Greenleaf Whittier	*The Cantos*	Ezra Pound
Attack	Siegfried Sassoon	*Canzoniere*	Dante Alighieri
At the Sign of the Lyre	Austin Dobson	*Cargoes*	John Masefield
Auld Lang Syne	Robert Burns	*Carpentered Hen and*	John Updike
Aurora Leigh	Elizabeth Barrett	*Other Tame Creatures*	
	Browning	*Casa Guidi Windows*	Elizabeth Barrett Browning
Autumn Sequel	Louis MacNeice	*Casabianca*	Felicia Hemans
Babi Yar	Yevgeny Yevtushenko	*Cautionary Tales*	Hilaire Belloc
The Backbone Flute	Vladimir Mayakovsky	*Cave Birds*	Ted Hughes
The Bad Child's Book of	Hilaire Belloc	*Chant Secret*	Jean Genet
Beasts		*The Charge of the Light*	Alfred, Lord Tennyson
Bagpipe Music	Louis MacNeice	*Brigade*	
Ballade des pendus	François Villon	*Cherry-Ripe*	Robert Herrick
Ballad of East and West	Rudyard Kipling	*Childe Harold's*	Lord Byron
The Ballad of Reading	Oscar Wilde	*Pilgrimage*	
Gaol		*Childe Roland to the*	Robert Browning
Banquet	Dante Alighieri	*Dark Tower Came*	
Barbara Frietchie	John Greenleaf Whittier	*A Child's Garden of*	Robert Louis Stevenson
The Bard	Thomas Gray	*Verses*	

Chorus of the Newly Dead	Edwin Muir
Christabel	Samuel Taylor Coleridge
The Circle Game	Margaret Atwood
Cities and Thrones and Powers	Rudyard Kipling
City Without Walls	W H Auden
A Cloud in Trousers	Vladimir Mayakovsky
Code Poem for the French Resistance	Leo Marks
The Colossus	Sylvia Plath
Come Live With Me and Be My Love	Christopher Marlowe
Comin' Through the Rye	Robert Burns
Comus	John Milton
Confessions of a Hooligan	Sergey Yesenin
The Confirmation	Edwin Muir
Continual Dew	John Betjeman
The Cotter's Saturday Night	Robert Burns
Counter-Attack	Siegfried Sassoon
Country Life	Peter Ackroyd
The Courtship of Miles Standish	Henry Wadsworth Longfellow
The Crescent Moon	Rabrindranath Tagore
The Crock of Gold	James Stephens
Crossing the Bar	Alfred, Lord Tennyson
Crossing the Water	Sylvia Plath
Crow	Ted Hughes
The Cry of the Children	Elizabeth Barrett Browning
Curfew Must Not Ring Tonight	Rose Thorpe
Daffodils	William Wordsworth
The Darkling Thrush	Thomas Hardy
Dauber	John Masefield
Death and Doctor Hornbook	Robert Burns
Death in Leamington	John Betjeman
The Death of Admiral Blake	Henry Newbolt
Death of a Naturalist	Seamus Heaney
The Death of the Hired Man	Robert Lee Frost
Deaths and Entrances	Dylan Thomas
Decorations	Ernest Dowson
The Definition of Love	Andrew Marvell
De Doctrina Christiana	John Milton
Dejection: An Ode	Samuel Taylor Coleridge
Delight in Disorder	Robert Herrick
The Descent of Odin	Thomas Gray
The Deserted Village	Oliver Goldsmith
Desolate and Pale Moonlight	Robert Burns
Despondency	Robert Burns
Destruction of Sennacherib	Lord Byron
Disabled	Wilfred Owen
The Divine Comedy	Dante Alighieri
Divine Fancies	Francis Quarles
Don Juan	Lord George Byron
The Donkey	G K Chesterton
Do Not Go Gentle into That Good Night	Dylan Thomas
Door into the Dark	Seamus Heaney
The Double Man	W H Auden
Dover Beach	Matthew Arnold
Drake	Alfred Noyes
Drake's Drum	Henry Newbolt
The Dream of Gerontius	Cardinal J H Newman
Drink to Me Only with Thine Eyes	Ben Jonson
Drum-Taps	Walt Whitman
The Drunken Boat	Arthur Rimbaud
A Drunk Man Looks at the Thistle	Hugh MacDiarmid
Dulce et Decorum Est	Wilfred Owen
The Dunciad	Alexander Pope
Dust of Snow	Robert Lee Frost
Duty, Ode to	William Wordsworth
Dymer	C S Lewis
The Dynasts	Thomas Hardy
Ego Dominus Tuus	W B Yeats
Egyptian Nights	Alexander Pushkin
Elegy on the Death of a Mad Dog	Oliver Goldsmith
Elegy Written in a Country Churchyard	Thomas Gray
Eloisa to Abelard	Alexander Pope
Empedocles on Etna	Matthew Arnold
Empty Mirror	Allen Ginsberg
Endymion	John Keats
England, My England	William Henley
An Epic of Women	Arthur O'Shaughnessy
Epipsychidion	Percy Bysshe Shelley
Epistle to Davie	Robert Burns
An Epistle to Doctor Arbuthnot	Alexander Pope
Epitaph on an Army of Mercenaries	A E Housman
Erlkönig	Johann Wolfgang von Goethe
Eros and Psyche	Robert Bridges
Especially When the October Wind	Dylan Thomas
An Essay on Man	Alexander Pope
Eugene Aram	Thomas Hood
Eugene Onegin	Alexander Pushkin
Eureka	Edgar Allan Poe
Evangeline	Henry Wadsworth Longfellow
The Eve of St Agnes	John Keats
The Everlasting Mercy	John Masefield
Everyone Sang	Siegfried Sassoon
Excelsior	Henry Wadsworth Longfellow
The Excursion	William Wordsworth
The Exstasie	John Donne
Exultations	Ezra Pound
Fables, Ancient and Modern	John Dryden
The Faerie Queene	Edmund Spenser
Fairies and Fusiliers	Robert Graves
Faithless Sally Brown	Thomas Hood
A Fancy From Fontenelle	Austin Dobson
Fancy's Knell	A E Housman
Fanfarlo	Muriel Spark
Farewell, Aggie Weston	Charles Causley
A Farewell to Arms	George Peele
The Fatal Sisters	Thomas Gray
Felix Randal	Gerard Manley Hopkins
The Female of the Species	Rudyard Kipling
Fêtes Galantes	Paul Verlaine
A Few Late Chrysanthemums	John Betjeman
Field Work	Seamus Heaney
Figure of 8	Charles Causley
Fire and Ice	Robert Lee Frost
First Love	John Clare
The Flaming Terrapin	Roy Campbell
Flowering Rifle	Roy Campbell
The Flower of Old Japan	Alfred Noyes
Ae Fond Kiss	Robert Burns

For a' that and a' that	Robert Burns
For England's Sake	William Henley
For Johnny	John Pudney
For the Fallen	Laurence Binyon
The Forest of Wild Thyme	Alfred Noyes
The Forsaken Merman	Matthew Arnold
Forty Singing Seamen	Alfred Noyes
Four Quartets	T S Eliot
Fra Lippo Lippi	Robert Browning
Friedensfeier (celebration of peace)	Friedrich Hölderlin
A Further Range	Robert Lee Frost
Gallipoli	John Masefield
The Garden	Andrew Marvell
The Gathering Storm	William Empson
Gebir	Walter Savage Landor
The Georgics (or Art of Husbandry)	Virgil
Gerontion	T S Eliot
Gertrude of Wyoming	Thomas Campbell
The Gift Outright	Robert Lee Frost
Gitanjali	Rabindranath Tagore
Give All to Love	Ralph Waldo Emerson
Goblin Market	Christina Rossetti
The Gods of the Copybook	Rudyard Kipling
The Golden Boat	Rabindranath Tagore
The Golden Journey to Samarkand	James Elroy Flecker
The Golden Legend	Henry Wadsworth Longfellow
Gondal	Emily Brontë
The Good Morrow	John Donne
Le Grand Testament	François Villon
Greybeards at Play	G K Chesterton
The Growth of Love	Robert Bridges
Guilt and Sorrow	William Wordsworth
Gunga Din	Rudyard Kipling
Halloween	Robert Burns
Haw Lantern	Seamus Heaney
The Hawk in the Rain	Ted Hughes
Hawthorn and Lavender	William Henley
He Wishes For the Cloths of Heaven	W B Yeats
Heavy Soils	Yevgeny Yevtushenko
Hellas	Percy Bysshe Shelley
La Henriade	Voltaire
Heraclitus	William Cory
Hero and Leander (unfinished)	Christopher Marlowe
The Song of Hiawatha	Henry Wadsworth Longfellow
High and Low	John Betjeman
The Highwayman	Alfred Noyes
High Windows	Philip Larkin
The Hind and the Panther	John Dryden
The Hollow Men	T S Eliot
The Holy Fair	Robert Burns
Holy Willie's Prayer	Robert Burns
Homage to Clio	W H Auden
Homage to Sextus Propertius	Ezra Pound
Home-Thoughts, from Abroad	Robert Browning
Home-Thoughts, from the Sea	Robert Browning
An Horatian Ode	Andrew Marvell
Hours of Idleness	Lord Byron
The House of Life	Dante Gabriel Rossetti
How Do I Love Thee?	Elizabeth Barrett Browning
Howl*	Allen Ginsberg
How They Brought the Good News from Ghent to Aix	Robert Browning
Hudibras	Samuel Butler
Hugh Selwyn Mauberley	Ezra Pound
The Hunting of the Snark	Lewis Carroll
Hymn to Pan	John Keats
Hyperion	John Keats
I See the Boys of Summer	Dylan Thomas
I Wandered Lonely as a Cloud	William Wordsworth
Idylls and Songs	Francis Palgrave
Idylls of the King	Alfred, Lord Tennyson
If	Rudyard Kipling
If This Be Treason	Ezra Pound
The Iliad	Homer
Il Penseroso	John Milton
I'm a Stranger Here Myself	Ogden Nash
To Imagination	Emily Brontë
The Inchcape Rock	Robert Southey
In Country Sleep	Dylan Thomas
Independence	Henry David Thoreau
The Ingoldsby Legends	Richard Harris Barham
In Flanders Field	John McCrae
In Hospital	William Henley
In Memoriam	Alfred, Lord Tennyson
In Memory of W.B. Yeats	W H Auden
Insurrections	James Stephens
In the Poppy Fields	James Stephens
In the Secular Night	Margaret Atwood
In the White Giant's Thigh	Dylan Thomas
Intimations of Immortality	William Wordsworth
Into Battle	Julian Grenfell
Invictus	William Henley
In War Time	John Greenleaf Whittier
Ionica	William Cory
An Irish Airman Foresees His Death	W B Yeats
Irish Melodies	Thomas Moore
Isabella or the Pot of Basil	John Keats
The Island Race	Henry Newbolt
Israfel	Edgar Allan Poe
Ivan the Terrible	Yevgeny Yevtushenko
Jabberwocky	Lewis Carroll
The Jackdaw of Rheims	Richard Harris Barham
Le Jardin des Tuileries	Oscar Wilde
Jenny Kissed Me	James Leigh Hunt
Jerusalem	William Blake
La Jeune Parque	Paul Valéry
John Gilpin	William Cowper
The Jolly Beggars	Robert Burns
Jolly Good Ale and Old	John Still
The Journey of the Magi	T S Eliot
Journeys and Places	Edwin Muir
Julian and Maddalo	Percy Bysshe Shelley
Juvenilia	James Leigh Hunt
Kaddish	Allen Ginsberg
Kamen	Osip Mandelstam
Kalevala	Henry Wadsworth Longfellow
Kennst du das Land	Johann Wolfgang von Goethe
Kilmarnock Poems	Robert Burns
The King's Tragedy	Dante Gabriel Rossetti
Kubla Khan	Samuel Taylor Coleridge
L'Après-midi d'un Faune	Stéphane Mallarmé
La Belle Dame Sans Merci	John Keats
La Nymphe de la Seine	Jean Racine
The Labyrinth	Edwin Muir
The Lady of Shalott	Alfred, Lord Tennyson
The Lake Isle of Innisfree	W B Yeats

LITERATURE

Ouch	Peter Ackroyd	Returned Soldier	E G Moll
The Oven Bird	Robert Lee Frost	The Revenge	Alfred, Lord Tennyson
Over Sir John's Hill	Dylan Thomas	Reynard the Fox	John Masefield
Over the Brazier	Robert Graves	Rhymes of a Rolling Stone	Robert Service
Overtures to Death	Cecil Day Lewis	RIJP	Charles Causley
The Owl and the Pussycat	Edward Lear	Rimas	Luis de Camoes
		The Rime of the Ancient Mariner	Samuel Taylor Coleridge
Ozymandias	Percy Bysshe Shelley		
A Pageant	Christina Rossetti	The Ring and the Book	Robert Browning
Paid on Both Sides	W H Auden	Rizpah	Alfred, Lord Tennyson
Pan With Us	Robert Lee Frost	The Robber Brothers	Alexander Pushkin
Paracelsus	Robert Browning	Romancero Gitano	Federico Garcia Lorca
Paradise Lost	John Milton	Roman Elegies	Johann Wolfgang von
Paradise Regained	John Milton		Goethe
Parting	Emily Dickinson	The Rose and the Cross	Aleksandr Blok
The Passionate Shepherd to His Love	Christopher Marlowe	Rose Aylmer	Walter Savage Landor
		The Rowley Poems	Thomas Chatterton
Pastorals	Edmund Blunden	The Rubaiyat of Omar Khayyam (translation from Persian)	Edward Fitzgerald
Pauline	Robert Browning		
Paul Revere's Ride	Henry Wadsworth Longfellow		
		The Rural Muse	John Clare
Peacock Pie	Walter De La Mare	Ruslan and Lyudmila	Alexander Pushkin
Le Petit Testament	François Villon	Ruth	Thomas Hood
Petits Poèmes en prose	Charles Baudelaire	Sagesse	Paul Verlaine
Phantasmagoria and other Poems	Lewis Carroll	Sailing to Byzantium	W B Yeats
		Samson Agonistes	John Milton
Pied Beauty	Gerard Manley Hopkins	Sangschaw	Hugh MacDiarmid
The Pied Piper of Hamelin	Robert Browning	The Scholar Gypsy	Matthew Arnold
		School's Out	W H Davies
Piers Plowman	William Langland	Scots Musical Museum	Robert Burns
The Pilgrim	John Bunyan	The Scythians	Aleksandr Blok
Pippa Passes	Robert Browning	Sea-Fever	John Masefield
Pisan Cantos	Ezra Pound	Seeing Things	Seamus Heaney
Planet News	Allen Ginsberg	The Seraphim	Elizabeth Barrett Browning
Plead for Me	Emily Brontë	Shakespeare	John Masefield
Poem in October	Dylan Thomas	Shall I Compare Thee to a Summer's Day? (Sonnet 18)	William Shakespeare
Poems before Congress	Elizabeth Barrett Browning		
		She Walks in Beauty	Lord Byron
Poems of Thirty Years	Gordon Bottomley	She Was a Phantom of Delight	William Wordsworth
Poetic Gems	William McGonagall		
Poets	Gavin Ewart	The Shephearde's Calender	Edmund Spenser
Poltava	Alexander Pushkin		
Prelude	William Wordsworth	The Shepherdess	Alice Meynell
The Prince's Progress	Christina Rossetti	The Shepherdes Calendar	John Clare
The Princess	Alfred, Lord Tennyson		
The Prisoner of Chillon	Lord Byron	The Shield of Achilles	W H Auden
The Prisoner of the Caucasus	Alexander Pushkin	The Shooting of Dan McGrew	Robert Service
The Problem	Ralph Waldo Emerson	A Shropshire Lad	A E Housman
The Progress of Poesy	Thomas Gray	The Sick Rose	William Blake
Prometheus the Firegiver	Robert Bridges	The Siege of Corinth	Lord Byron
Prometheus Unbound	Percy Bysshe Shelley	The Silken Tent	Robert Lee Frost
Proverbs in Porcelain	Austin Dobson	Silver	Walter de la Mare
Queen Mab	Percy Bysshe Shelley	The Skeleton in Armour	Henry Wadsworth Longfellow
Quia Pauper Amavi	Ezra Pound		
Rabbi Ben Ezra	Robert Browning	A Slice of Wedding Cake	Robert Graves
The Rape of the Lock	Alexander Pope	Smoke	Henry David Thoreau
The Rats and Other Poems	Alan Sillitoe	Snow-bound	John Greenleaf Whittier
		Snow on the North Side of Lucifer	Alan Sillitoe
The Raven	Edgar Allan Poe		
Ravenna	Oscar Wilde	Sohrab and Rustum	Matthew Arnold
Reality Sandwiches	Allen Ginsberg	Soldier's Reply to the Poet	Roy Campbell
A Red, Red Rose	Robert Burns		
Relationships	Elizabeth Jennings	The Soldier	Rupert Brooke
Religio Laici	John Dryden	Soliloquy of the Spanish Cloister	Robert Browning
The Remains of Elmet	Ted Hughes		
Remember	Christina Rossetti	The Solitary Reaper	William Wordsworth
Remembrance	Emily Brontë	Solstices	Louis MacNeice
Rendezvous	Alan Seeger	Song	John Donne
Renouncement	Alice Meynell	Song for a Birth or a Death	Elizabeth Jennings
Resolution and Independence	William Wordsworth		

L
I
T
E
R
A
T
U
R
E

The Witch of Atlas	Percy Bysshe Shelley	The Wreck of the	Henry Wadsworth
A Witness Tree	Robert Lee Frost	Hesperus	Longfellow
Wodwo	Ted Hughes	The Young Man of Cury	Charles Causley
The Woodman	Robert Louis Stevenson	Zima Junction	Yevgeny Yevtushenko
The Wreck of the Deutschland	Gerard Manley Hopkins		

Poetry: General Information

alexandrine Iambic or trochaic hexameter (line of 12 syllables or 6 feet) with, usually, a caesura (break) at the 6th syllable.

allegory Narrative or description in prose or verse with an underlying meaning or moral message as in *The Faerie Queene* or *The Pilgrim's Progress.*

apocope Omission of the final letter, syllable or sound of a word, e.g. the poetic use of th' instead of the.

assonance Use of the same or similar vowel sounds close together for the sake of euphony, memorability or emotional effect, e.g. 'And deep asleep he seemed'.

asylum, committed to John Clare from 1837 until his death.

W H Auden Friend and collaborator: Christopher Isherwood.

The Ballad of Reading Gaol Famous extract: 'And all men kill the thing they love, by all let this be heard, Some do it with a bitter look, Some with a flattering word. The coward does it with a kiss, The brave man with a sword!'

ballade Poem of three eight-line stanzas, rhyming ababbcbc, and one four-line *envoi* (final stanza) rhyming bcbc, with a refrain at the end of each of its four sections. François Villon was a great exponent of the ballade in French, Hilaire Belloc in English.

Bastille Imprisoned for a year in 1717: Voltaire (François Marie Arouet).

bathos Anticlimax or sudden descent, intended or not, from the sublime to the commonplace, e.g. the last 2 lines of Tennyson's *Enoch Arden*: 'And when they buried him the little port, Had seldom seen a costlier funeral.'

Beat Poets Lawrence Ferlinghetti, Allen Ginsberg, Jack Kerouac, Gregory Corso.

Belloc Many of his works illustrated by G K Chesterton.

The Betrothed Extract: A woman is only a woman, but a good cigar is a Smoke.

Elizabeth Barrett Browning Pet name: She was affectionately known as 'My Little Portuguese' by her husband Robert Browning.

Brunanburh Poem in Old English, included in four manuscripts of the *Anglo-Saxon Chronicle* under the year 937 and dealing with the battle of that name.

catachresis Misuse or incorrect application of a word, e.g. 'chronic' to mean 'severe', or 'refute' to mean 'deny'.

Christian Poet First English: Caedmon.

Clerihew Comic biographical poem in the form of a quatrain with lines of various length, rhyming aabb, named after its inventor Edmund Clerihew Bentley (1875–1956). Example: The Art of Biography is different from Geography. Geography is about maps, Biography is about chaps.

dithyramb Song or poem in honour of Dionysus.

The Donkey Describes itself as 'the devil's walking parody On all four-footed things'.

Dover Beach First lines 'The sea is calm tonight The tide is full.'

duels Ben Jonson killed fellow actor Gabriel Spencer. To defend his wife's honour, Alexander challenged and was killed by Baron d'Anthès.

Dymer C S Lewis published this work under the name of Clive Hamilton.

Elegy Written in a Country Churchyard Opening: 'The curfew tolls the knell of parting day, The lowing herd wind slowly o'er the lea . . .' Extract: 'Far from the madding crowd's ignoble strife . . .'

elision Suppression of a vowel or syllable in verse for the sake of metrical correctness, e.g. 'ta'en' (one syllable) replacing 'taken' (two).

enjambement Running-on of one line of verse into another without a grammatical break, e.g.: 'Nay, but this dotage of our general's / O'erflows the measure . . .' (*Antony and Cleopatra*).

epigram Pointed, witty saying or verse that may be aphoristic, sarcastic, complimentary or amusing.

euphuism Highly elaborate prose style as found in John Lyly's *Euphues* (1580).

The Exeter Book Important manuscript containing Old English poetry, copied about 940 and given by Bishop Leofric (d. 1072) to Exeter Cathedral. The best-known poems include *The Wanderer, The Seafarer, Widsith, The Ruin, Wulf and Eadwacer, The Wife's Lament, The Husband's Message* and *Resignation.*

Four Quartets (T S Eliot) *Burnt Norton, East Coker, The Dry Salvages, Little Gidding.*

The Four Boileau, La Fontaine, Molière, Racine.

Georgian Poets Writing during the reign of *George V*: Lascelles Abercrombie, Hilaire Belloc, Rupert Brooke, W H Davies, Ernest Dowson, John Drinkwater, James Elroy Flecker, Robert Graves, Ralph Hodgson, John Masefield, Walter de la Mare, Harold Monro, Siegfried Sassoon, Sir John Squire, Edward Thomas.

Gertrude of Wyoming Poem by Thomas Campbell in Spenserian stanzas, published 1809. Describes the destruction of the settlement of Wyoming in Pennsylvania by a force of Indians.

The Golden Treasury of best songs and Lyrical poems in the English language Editor: Francis Palgrave edited the classic book of poetic works (1861) with the help of his friend Tennyson, but controversially omitted all of William Blake's poems.

Griffin Poetry Prize Inaugurated in 2001 in Canada. $40,000 awarded to best Canadian collection and $40,000 to best international collection.

haiku Japanese verse form of seventeen syllables in three lines of five, seven and five syllables, encapsulating an idea, image or mood.

Home-Thoughts, From Abroad Opening: 'Oh, to be in England Now that April's there . . .'

Imagism Poetic movement and theory (1909–17) which emphasised direct treatment of subject-matter, extreme economy of language and the rhythm of phrases rather than the rhythm of regular metres. Poets include Richard Aldington, HD, F S Flint, James Joyce, Amy Lowell and Ezra Pound.

Keats's epitaph By himself: 'Here lies one whose name was writ in water.'

Kubla Khan Sacred river: Alph.

Lake Poets Wordsworth, Coleridge and Southey.

Leisure Opening: 'What is this life if, full of care, We have no time to stand and stare?'

limerick Five-line nonsense verse popularised by Edward Lear and following a rhyming scheme of aabba. Example: There was a young lady of Wilts Who walked up to Scotland on stilts When they said it was shocking To show so much stocking She answered 'Then what about kilts?'

The Listeners First line: '"Is there anybody there?" said the traveller . . .'

Maud Classic lines: 'Come into the garden, Maud, For the black bat, night, has flown . . .'

Metaphysical Poets A group of English poets of the 17th century, who include John Donne, George Herbert, Henry Vaughan, Richard Crashaw and Andrew Marvell (term first used by Samuel Johnson, possibly influenced by a phrase of Dryden's).

metre Measure of lines of verse which in English is basically accentual, determined by stress, each group of syllables, usually two or three, forms a metrical unit called a foot.

Milton called Athens 'Mother of arts and eloquence'.

The New Colossus Lines from this sonnet, inscribed on the Statue of Liberty: 'Give me your tired, your poor, Your huddled masses, yearning to breathe free, The wretched refuse of your teeming shore. Send these, the homeless, tempest-tost to me, I lift my lamp beside the golden door'.

Night Mail Opening: 'This is the Night Mail crossing the Border, Bringing the cheque and the postal order.'

Ode on a Distant Prospect of Eton College Extract: 'Ye distant spires, ye antique towers . . .'

Ode to Autumn Opening: 'Season of mists and mellow fruitfulness, Close bosom-friend of the maturing sun'.

Old English poem, 1st *Beowulf* (probably composed orally in the 8th century; written down in 10th century).

The Old Vicarage, Grantchester Details: Contains German and Greek lines (Jeffrey Archer purchased the property).

On his Blindness First line: 'When I consider how my light is spent'.

Ozymandias First line: 'I met a traveller from an antique land . . .'

pathetic fallacy The ascription of human emotions to non-human objects and phenomena, e.g. 'the cruel sea'.

The Pilgrim's Progress Extract: 'The name of the Slough was Despond'.

Pléiade, La Group of seven French poets and writers of the 16th century, led by Pierre de Ronsard. The name was taken from that given by the Alexandrian critics to seven tragic poets of the reign of Ptolemy III Philadelphus (285–246 BC). The other six members of La Pléiade were Joachim du Bellay, Jean-Antoine de Baïf, Jean Dorat, Rémy Belleau, Etienne Jodelle and Pontis de Tyard.

Poet Laureate Deposed: John Dryden, who became a Catholic in 1685 and was deposed in 1689 after the Glorious Revolution. Longest in office: Alfred, Lord Tennyson (1850–92).

Pott's disease Suffered by Alexander Pope, who was only 4' 6" tall.

prisoner poets François Villon – for his various criminal activities. James Leigh Hunt: 2 years (1813–15) for libelling the Prince Regent. Jean Genet: for theft, male prostitution, and other crimes. Richard Lovelace: in 1642, for being a Royalist.

The Rape of the Lock Two Catholic families quarrel after a male member of one steals a lock of hair from a female member of the other.

Sally Brown **(Thomas Hood)** Extract: 'They went and told the sexton, and The sexton toll'd the bell'.

Sea Fever Opening: 'I must go down to the seas again, to the lonely sea and the sky, And all I ask is a tall ship and a star to steer her by . . .'

Shall I compare thee to a summer's day Next lines: 'Thou art more lovely and more temperate. Rough winds do shake the darling buds of May, And summer's lease hath all too short a date . . .'

The Soldier First line: 'If I should die think only this of me'.

Song **(John Donne)** First line: 'Go and catch a falling star . . .'

Songs of Childhood Published by Walter de la Mare using the pseudonym Walter Ramal.

sonnets Three basic types: Spenserian, Shakespearian and Petrarchan.

Spasmodic School Term coined by William Aytoun (1813–65) in his *Firmilian, or The Student of Badajoz* (1854) as an attack on the intensely melodramatic poems of such as P J Bailey, J W Marston, S T Dobell and Alexander Smith.

Spenserian stanza Eight iambic pentameters followed by one iambic hexameter, rhyming ababbcbcc.

spondee Metrical foot consisting of two long or stressed syllables.

The Star-Spangled Banner By Francis Scott Key (1779–1843). First line: 'Oh say can you see by the dawn's early light . . .'

Stella (from *Astrophel and Stella*) Thought to be Penelope Devereux.

A Subaltern's Love-song Beloved: Miss Joan Hunter Dunn. Towns mentioned: Aldershot and Camberley. Car mentioned: Hillman.

Tennyson quotes 'In the Spring a young man's fancy lightly turns to thoughts of love.'
'Man is the hunter; woman is his game . . .'
''Tis better to have loved and lost Than never to have loved at all.'

tercet Three-line stanza, particularly as used in terza rima.

terza rima Verse-form of three-line stanzas rhyming aba, bcb, cdc, and so on, usually iambic pentameters, e.g. *Ode to the West Wind*.

To a Field Mouse Opening: 'Wee, sleekit, cow'rin', tim'rous beastie, O what a panic's in thy breastie ! Extract: 'The best laid schemes o' mice an' men. Gang aft a-gley'.

To a Skylark Opening: 'Hail to thee, blithe Spirit'!

To the Virgins, To Make Much of Time First line: 'Gather ye rosebuds while ye may . . .'

Transcendentalists A mid 19th-century New England movement of writers, poets and philosophers who believed in the unity of all creation, the innate goodness of man and the supremacy of insight over logic and experience. Notable adherents were Ralph Waldo Emerson and Henry David Thoreau.

Upon Westminster Bridge Opening: 'Earth has not anything to show more fair . . .'

The Village Blacksmith Opening: Under the spreading chestnut tree The village smithy stands . . .'

A Visit from St Nicholas Opening: ''Twas the night before Christmas . . .'

LITERATURE

Whitbread Literary Award Winners

	Category	Title	Author
1971	Novel	*The Destiny Waltz*	Gerda Charles
	Biography	*Henrik Ibsen*	Michael Meyer
	Poetry	*Mercia Hymns*	Geoffrey Hill
1972	Novel	*The Bird of Night*	Susan Hill
	Biography	*Trollope*	James Pope-Hennessy
	Children's book	*The Diddakoi*	Rumer Godden
1973	Novel	*The Chip-Chip Gatherers*	Shiva Naipaul
	Biography	*CB: A Life of Sir Henry Campbell-Bannerman*	John Wilson
	Children's book	*The Butterfly Ball & the Grasshopper's Feast*	Alan Aldridge and William Plomer
1974	Novel	*The Sacred and Profane Love Machine*	Iris Murdoch
	Biography	*Poor Dean Brendan*	Andrew Boyle
	Children's book (joint)	*How Tom Beat Captain Najork and His Hired Sportsmen*	Russell Hoban and Quentin Blake
		The Emperor's Winding Sheet	Jill Paton Walsh
1975	Novel	*Docherty*	William McIlvanney
	Autobiography	*In Our Infancy*	Helen Corke
	First book	*The Improbable Puritan: A Life of Bulstrode Whitelocke*	Ruth Spalding
1976	Novel	*The Children of Dynmouth*	William Trevor
	Biography	*Elizabeth Gaskell*	Winifred Gerin
	Children's book	*A Stitch in Time*	Penelope Lively
1977	Novel	*Injury Time*	Beryl Bainbridge
	Biography	*Mary Curzon*	Nigel Nicolson
	Children's book	*No End to Yesterday*	Shelagh Macdonald
1978	Novel	*Picture Palace*	Paul Theroux
	Biography	*Lloyd George: The People's Champion*	John Grigg
	Children's book	*The Battle of Bubble and Squeak*	Philippa Pearce
1979	Novel	*The Old Jest*	Jennifer Johnston
	Autobiography	*About Time*	Penelope Mortimer
	Children's novel	*Tulku*	Peter Dickinson
1980	Novel & Book of the Year	*How Far Can You Go?*	David Lodge
	Biography	*On the Edge of Paradise: A.C. Benson the Diarist*	David Newsome
	Children's novel	*John Diamond*	Leon Garfield
1981	Novel	*Silver's City*	Maurice Leitch
	Biography	*Monty: The Making of a General*	Nigel Hamilton
	Children's novel	*The Hollow Land*	Jane Gardam
	First novel	*A Good Man in Africa*	William Boyd
1982	Novel	*Young Shoulders*	John Wain
	Biography	*Bismarck*	Edward Crankshaw
	Children's novel	*The Song of Pentecost*	W J Corbett
	First novel	*On the Black Hill*	Bruce Chatwin
1983	Novel	*Fools of Fortune*	William Trevor
	Biography (joint)	*Vita*	Victoria Glendinning
		King George V	Kenneth Rose
	Children's novel	*The Witches*	Roald Dahl
	First novel	*Flying to Nowhere*	John Fuller
1984	Novel	*Kruger's Alp*	Christopher Hope
	Biography	*T.S. Eliot*	Peter Ackroyd
	Children's novel	*The Queen of the Pharisees' Children*	Barbara Willard
	First novel	*A Parish of Rich Women*	James Buchan
	Short story	*Tomorrow is Our Permanent Address*	Diane Rowe
1985	Novel	*Hawksmoor*	Peter Ackroyd
	Biography	*Hugh Dalton*	Ben Pimlott
	Children's novel	*The Nature of the Beast*	Janni Howker
	First novel	*Oranges Are Not the Only Fruit*	Jeanette Winterson
	Poetry & Book of the year	*Elegies*	Douglas Dunn
1986	Novel & Book of the Year	*An Artist of the Floating World*	Kazuo Ishiguro
	Biography	*Gilbert White*	Richard Mabey
	Children's novel	*The Coal House*	Andrew Taylor
	First novel	*Continent*	Jim Crace
	Poetry	*Stet*	Peter Reading
1987	Novel	*The Child in Time*	Ian McEwan
	Biography & Book of the Year	*Under the Eye of the Clock*	Christopher Nolan

	Category	Title	Author
	First novel	*The Other Garden*	Francis Wyndham
	Poetry	*The Haw Lantern*	Seamus Heaney
1988	Novel	*The Satanic Verses*	Salman Rushdie
	Biography	*Tolstoy*	A N Wilson
	Children's novel	*Awaiting Developments*	Judy Allen
	First novel & Book of the Year	*The Comforts of Madness*	Paul Sayer
	Poetry	*The Automatic Oracle*	Peter Porter
1989	Novel	*The Chymical Wedding*	Lindsay Clarke
	Biography and Book of theYear	*Coleridge: Early Visions*	Richard Holmes
	Children's novel	*Why Weeps the Brogan?*	Hugh Scott
	First novel	*Gerontius*	James Hamilton
	Poetry	*Shibboleth*	Michael Donaghy
1990	Novel & Book of the Year	*Hopeful Monsters*	Nicholas Mosley
	Biography	*A.A. Milne: His Life*	Ann Thwaite
	Children's novel	*A.K.*	Peter Dickinson
	First novel	*The Buddha of Suburbia*	Hanif Kureishi
	Poetry	*Daddy, Daddy*	Paul Durcan
1991	Novel	*The Queen of the Tambourine*	Jane Gardam
	Biography & Book of the Year	*A Life of Picasso*	John Richardson
	Children's novel	*Harvey Angell*	Diana Hendry
	First novel	*Alma Cogan*	Gordon Burn
	Poetry	*Gorse Fires*	Michael Longley
1992	Novel	*Poor Things*	Alasdair Gray
	Biography	*Trollope*	Victoria Glendinning
	Children's novel	*The Great Elephant Chase*	Gillian Cross
	First novel & Book of the Year	*Swing Hammer Swing!*	Jeff Torrington
	Poetry	*The Gaze of the Gorgon*	Tony Harrison
1993	Novel & Book of the Year	*Theory of War*	Joan Brady
	Biography	*Philip Larkin*	Andrew Motion
	Children's novel	*Flour Babies*	Anne Fine
	First novel	*Saving Agnes*	Rachel Cusk
	Poetry	*Mean Time*	Carol Ann Duffy
1994	Novel & Book of the Year	*Felicia's Journey*	William Trevor
	Biography	*The Married Man*	Brenda Maddox
	Children's novel	*Gold Dust*	Geraldine McCaughrean
	First novel	*The Longest Memory*	Fred D'Aguiar
	Poetry	*Out of Danger*	James Fenton
1995	Novel	*The Moor's Last Sigh*	Salman Rushdie
	Biography	*Gladstone*	Roy Jenkins
	Children's novel	*The Wreck of the Zanzibar*	Michael Morpurgo
	First novel & Book of the Year	*Behind the Scenes at the Museum*	Kate Atkinson
	Poetry	*Gunpowder*	Bernard O'Donoghue
1996	Novel	*Every Man for Himself*	Beryl Bainbridge
	Biography	*Thomas Cranmer: A Life*	Diarmaid MacCulloch
	First novel	*The Debt to Pleasure*	John Lancaster
	Poetry & Book of the Year	*The Spirit Level*	Seamus Heaney
	Children's Book of the Year	*The Tulip Touch*	Anne Fine
1997	Novel	*Quarantine*	Jim Crace
	Biography	*Victor Hugo*	Graham Robb
	First novel	*The Ventriloquist's Tale*	Pauline Melville
	Poetry & Book of the Year	*Tales from Ovid*	Ted Hughes
	Children's Book of the Year	*Aquila*	Andrew Norriss
1998	Novel	*Leading the Cheers*	Justin Cartwright
	Biography	*Georgiana, Duchess of Devonshire*	Amanda Foreman
	First novel	*The Last King of Scotland*	Giles Foden
	Children's Book of the Year	*Skellig*	David Almond
	Poetry & Book of the Year	*Birthday Letters*	Ted Hughes
1999	Novel	*Music and Silence*	Rose Tremain
	Biography	*Berlioz: Servitude and Greatness*	David Cairns
	First novel	*White City Bloc*	Tim Lott
	Children's Book of the Year	*Harry Potter and the Prisoner of Azkaban*	J K Rowling
	Poetry & Book of the Year	*Beowulf*	Seamus Heaney
2000	Novel & Book of the Year	*English Passengers*	Mathew Kneale
	Biography	*Bad Blood: A memoir*	Lorna Sage
	First novel	*White Teeth*	Zadie Smith
	Children's Book of the Year	*Coram Bay*	Jamila Gavin
	Poetry	*The Asylum Dance*	John Burnside
2001	Novel	*Twelve Bar Blues*	Patrick Neate
	Biography	*Selkirk's Island*	Diana Souhami
	First novel	*Something Like A House*	Sid Smith

LITERATURE

Category	Title	Author
Children's Book & Book of the Year	The Amber Spyglass	Philip Pullman
Poetry	Bunny	Selima Hill
2002 Novel	Spies	Michael Frayn
Biography & Book of the Year	Samuel Pepys: The Unequalled Self	Claire Tomalin
First Novel	The Song of Names	Norman Lebrecht
Children's Book of the Year	Saffy's Angel	Hilary McKay
Poetry	The Ice Age	Paul Farley
2003 Novel & Book of the Year	The Curious Incident of the Dog in the Night-Time	Mark Haddon
Biography	Orwell: The Life	D J Taylor
First Novel	Vernon God Little	D B C Pierre
Children's Book of the Year	The Fire-Eaters	David Almond
Poetry	Landing Light	Don Paterson
2004 Novel & Book of the Year	Small Island	Andrea Levy
Biography	My Heart Is My Own: The Life of Mary Queen of Scots	John Guy
First Novel	Eve Green	Susan Fletcher
Children's Book of the Year	Not the End of the World	Geraldine McCaughrean
Poetry	Corpus	Michael Symmons

Pulitzer Prize for Fiction

Year	Book	Author	Year	Book	Author
1918	His Family	Ernest Poole	1954	No Award	
1919	The Magnificent Ambersons	Booth Tarkington	1955	A Fable	William Faulkner
1920	No Award		1956	Andersonville	Mackinlay Kantor
1921	The Age of Innocence	Edith Wharton	1957	No Award	
1922	Alice Adams	Booth Tarkington	1958	A Death in the Family	James Agee
1923	One of Ours	Willa Cather	1959	The Travels of Jamie McPheeters	Robert Lewis Taylor
1924	The Able McLaughlins	Margaret Wilson			
1925	So Big	Edna Ferber	1960	Advise and Consent	Allen Drury
1926	Arrowsmith	Sinclair Lewis	1961	To Kill a Mockingbird	Harper Lee
1927	Early Autumn	Louis Bromfield	1962	The Edge of Sadness	Edwin O'Connor
1928	The Bridge at San Luis Rey	Thornton Wilder	1963	The Reivers	William Faulkner
1929	Scarlet Sister Mary	Julia Peterkin	1964	No Award	
1930	Laughing Boy	Oliver LaFarge	1965	The Keepers of the House	Shirley Ann Grau
1931	Years of Grace	Margaret Ayer Barnes	1966	Collected Stories of Katherine Anne Porter	Katherine Anne Porter
1932	The Good Earth	Pearl S Buck	1967	The Fixer	Bernard Malamud
1933	The Store	T S Stribling			
1934	Lamb in his Bosom	Caroline Miller	1968	The Confessions of Nat Turner	William Styron
1935	Now in November	Josephine Winslow Johnson	1969	House Made of Dawn	N Scott Momaday
1936	Honey in the Horn	Harold L Davis	1970	Collected Stories	Jean Stafford
1937	Gone with the Wind	Margaret Mitchell	1971	No Award	
1938	The Late George Apley	John Phillips Marquand	1972	Angle of Repose	Wallace Stegner
			1973	The Optimist's Daughter	Eudora Welty
1939	The Yearling	Marjorie Kinnan Rawlings	1974	No Award	
			1975	The Killer Angels	Michael Shaara
1940	The Grapes of Wrath	John Steinbeck	1976	Humboldt's Gift	Saul Bellow
1941	No Award		1977	No Award	
1942	In This Our Life	Ellen Glasgow	1978	Elbow Room	James Alan McPherson
1943	Dragon's Teeth	Upton Sinclair			
1944	Journey in the Dark	Martin Flavin	1979	The Stories of John Cheever	John Cheever
1945	A Bell for Adano	John Hersey			
1946	No Award		1980	The Executioner's Song	Norman Mailer
1947	All the King's Men	Robert Penn Warren	1981	A Confederacy of Dunces	John Kennedy Toole
1948	Tales of the South Pacific	James A Michener	1982	Rabbit is Rich	John Updike
			1983	The Color Purple	Alice Walker
1949	Guard of Honor	James Gould Cozzens	1984	Ironweed	William Kennedy
1950	The Way West	A B Guthrie Jr	1985	Foreign Affairs	Alison Lurie
1951	The Town	Conrad Richter	1986	Lonesome Dove	Larry McMurty
1952	The Caine Mutiny	Herman Wouk	1987	A Summons to Memphis	Peter Taylor
1953	The Old Man and the Sea	Ernest Hemingway	1988	Beloved	Toni Morrison
			1989	Breathing Lessons	Anne Tyler

Year	Book	Author	Year	Book	Author
1990	The Mambo Kings Play Songs of Love	Oscar Hijuelos	1998	American Pastoral	Philip Roth
1991	Rabbit at Rest	John Updike	1999	The Hours	Michael Cunningham
1992	A Thousand Acres	Jane Smiley	2000	Interpreteur of Maladies	Jhumpa Lahiri
1993	A Good Scent from a Strange Mountain	Robert Olen Butler	2001	The Amazing Adventures of Kavalier & Clay	Michael Chabon
1994	The Shipping News	E Annie Proulx	2002	Empire Falls	Richard Russo
1995	The Stone Diaries	Carol Shields	2003	Middlesex	Jeffrey Eugenides
1996	Independence Day	Richard Ford			
1997	Martin Dressler: Tale of an American Dreamer	Steven Millhauser	2004	The Known World	Edward P Jones

Booker Prize for Fiction

Year	Book	Author	Year	Book	Author
1969	Something to Answer For	P H Newby	1985	The Bone People	Keri Hulme
1970	The Elected Member	Bernice Rubens	1986	The Old Devils	Kingsley Amis
1971	In a Free State	V S Naipaul	1987	Moon Tiger	Penelope Lively
1972	G	John Berger	1988	Oscar and Lucinda	Peter Carey
1973	The Siege of Krishnapur	J G Farrell	1989	The Remains of the Day	Kazuo Ishiguro
1974	The Conservationist Holiday	Nadine Gordimer Stanley Middleton (joint)	1990	Possession	A S Byatt
			1991	The Famished Road	Ben Okri
			1992	Sacred Hunger The English Patient	Barry Unsworth Michael Ondaatje (joint)
1975	Heat and Dust	Ruth Prawer Jhabvala	1993	Paddy Clarke Ha Ha Ha	Roddy Doyle
1976	Saville	David Storey	1994	How Late it Was, How Late	James Kelman
1977	Staying On	Paul Scott	1995	The Ghost Road	Pat Barker
1978	The Sea, The Sea	Iris Murdoch	1996	Last Orders	Graham Swift
1979	Offshore	Penelope Fitzgerald	1997	The God of Small Things	Arundhati Roy
			1998	Amsterdam	Ian McEwan
1980	Rites of Passage	William Golding	1999	Disgrace	J M Coetzee
1981	Midnight's Children	Salman Rushdie	2000	The Blind Assassin	Margaret Atwood
1982	Schindler's Ark	Thomas Keneally	2001	True History of the Kelly Gang	Peter Carey
1983	The Life and Times of Michael K	J M Coetzee	2002	Life of Pi	Yann Martel
			2003	Vernon God Little	D B C Pierre
1984	Hotel Du Lac	Anita Brookner	2004	The Line of Beauty	Alan Hollinghurst

NB: The Man Booker Prize is awarded for a novel by a citizen of the UK, Eire, South Africa, or any Commonwealth country, with the proviso that it was first published in Britain.

Orange Prize for Fiction

The Orange Award was launched in January 1996 and is restricted to female novelists. As well as the annual prize of £30,000 the winner receives a bronze figurine created by Griznel Niven known as the 'Betsie'.

Winners	Year	Title
Helen Dunmore	1996	A Spell of Winter
Anne Michaels	1997	Fugitive Pieces
Carol Shields	1998	Larry's Party
Suzanne Berne	1999	A Crime in the Neighbourhood
Linda Grant	2000	When I Lived in Modern Times
Kate Grenville	2001	The Idea of Perfection
Ann Patchett	2002	Bel Canto
Valerie Martin	2003	Property
Andrea Levy	2004	Small Island

LITERATURE

Fictional Literary Characters

(except Dickens and Shakespeare)

Captain Absolute	*The Rivals*
Captain Ahab	*Moby-Dick*
Roderick Alleyn	created by Ngaio Marsh
Charlie Allnutt	*The African Queen*
Squire Allworthy	*Tom Jones*
Andy Capp	drawn by Reg Smythe
Andy Pandy	created by Maria Bird
Harry Angstrom	the Rabbit Tetralogy
Lara Antipova	*Doctor Zhivago*
Aouda	*Around the World in 80 Days*
John Appleby	created by Michael Innes
Isobel Archer	*The Portrait of a Lady*
Jack Aubrey	*Master and Commander* (& others)
Steve Austin	*Cyborg* (by Martin Caidin)
Ayesha	*She*
Dr Aziz	*A Passage to India*
Babar	created by Jean de Brunhoff
Badger	*The Wind in the Willows*
Bilbo Baggins	*The Hobbit, Lord of the Rings*
David Balfour	*Kidnapped*
The Baron (John Mannering)	created by Anthony Morton (John Creasey)
Oliver Barrett IV	*Love Story*
Bastable Family	*The Treasure-Seekers* (by E Nesbit)
Batman	created by Bob Kane
Dr Jim Bayliss	*All My Sons*
Bazarov	*Fathers and Sons*
Belinda	*The Rape of the Lock*
Elizabeth Bennet	*Pride and Prejudice*
Inspector Bertozzo	*Accidental Death of an Anarchist*
Rev. Edmund Bertram	*Mansfield Park*
Sir Thomas Bertram	*Mansfield Park*
Margot Beste-Chetwynde	*Decline and Fall*
Big Daddy	*Cat on a Hot Tin Roof*
Bigwig (rabbit)	*Watership Down*
Ernie Bilko	created by Nat Hiken
Mr Bingley	*Pride and Prejudice*
John Blackthorne	*Shogun*
Modesty Blaise	created by Peter O'Donnell
Sir Percy Blakeney	*The Scarlet Pimpernel*
Colonel Blimp	created by David Low
Leopold Bloom	*Ulysses*
Prince Andrey Bolkonsky	*War and Peace*
James Bond	created by Ian Flemming
Bosinney	*The Forsyte Saga*
Boxer the Horse	*Animal Farm*
Jack Boyle	*Juno and the Paycock*
Lady Bracknell	*The Importance of Being Ernest*
Ben Braddock	*The Graduate*
Colonel Brandon	*Sense and Sensibility*
Alan Breck	*Kidnapped*
Brer Rabbit	the Uncle Remus stories
Dorothea Brooke	*Middlemarch*
Father Brown	created by G K Chesterton
Pinkie Brown	*Brighton Rock*
Beatrice Bryant	*Roots*
Daisy Buchanan	*The Great Gatsby*
Charlie Bucket	*Charlie and the Chocolate Factory*
Buck (the Dog)	*The Call of the Wild*
Natty Bumppo	the Leatherstocking stories
Albert Campion	created by Margery Allingham
Tom Canty	*The Prince and the Pauper*
Sir Danvers Carew	*Dr Jekyll and Mr Hyde*
William Carey	*Of Human Bondage*
Katy Carr	*What Katy Did*
Captain Cat	*Under Milk Wood*
Anne Catherick	*The Woman in White*
Catherine	*The Bell*
Holden Caulfield	*The Catcher in the Rye*
Jenny Cavillieri	*Love Story*
Professor Challenger	*The Lost World*
Canon Chasuble	*The Importance of Being Ernest*
Chauntecleer (the hen)	*Nun's Priest's Tale*
Jack Chesney	*Charley's Aunt*
Harvey Cheyne	*Captains Courageous*
Chichikov	*Dead Souls*
Chingachgook	the Leatherstocking stories
Mr Charles Chipping	*Goodbye, Mr Chips*
Christian	*The Pilgrim's Progress*
Frank Churchill	*Emma*
Petty Officer Claggart	*Billy Budd*
Angel Clare	*Tess of the D'Urbervilles*
Eric Claudin	*The Phantom of the Opera*
Darius Clayhanger (printer)	*Clayhanger*
Clegg	*The Collector*
Robert James Colley	*Rites of Passage*
Compson family	*The Sound and the Fury* and *Absalom, Absalom!*
Hugh Conway	*Lost Horizon*
Mr Crawford	*Mansfield Park*
Guy Crouchback	*Men at Arms*
Lenina Crowne	*Brave New World*
Isabelle de Croye	*Quentin Durward*
Sergeant Cuff	*The Moonstone*
Curdie (miner)	*The Princess and the Goblin*
Stephen Daedalus	*Ulysses*
Adam Dalgleish	created by P D James
Edmond Dantès	*Count of Monte Christo*
Mrs Danvers	*Rebecca*
Dapper	*The Alchemist*
Mr Fitzwilliam Darcy	*Pride and Prejudice*
Dashwood family	*Sense and Sensibility*
Anne Deever	*All My Sons*
Danny Deever	*Barrack-Room Ballads*
Maxim De Winter	*Rebecca*
James Dixon	*Lucky Jim*
Captain Dobbin	*Vanity Fair*
Eliza Doolittle	*Pygmalion*
Paul Drake	created by Erle Stanley Gardner
Abel Drugger	*The Alchemist*
Blanche Du Bois	*A Streetcar Named Desire*
Lady Dulcinea	*Don Quixote*
Auguste Dupin	created by Edgar Allan Poe
Albus Dumbledore	Harry Potter books
Dudley Dursley	Harry Potter books
Catherine Earnshaw	*Wuthering Heights*
Humphrey Chimpden Earwicker	*Finnegans Wake*
Eeyore	*Winnie-the-Pooh*
Montague Egg	created by Dorothy L Sayers
Anne Elliot	*Persuasion*

Sir Walter Elliot	*Persuasion*	Victoria Jones	*Bhowani Junction* (John
Mrs Erlynne	*Lady Windermere's Fan*		Masters)
Cedric Errol	*Little Lord Fauntleroy*	Robert Jordan	*For Whom the Bell Tolls*
Esmeralda	*The Hunchback of Notre*	Monsieur Jourdain	*Le Bourgeois Gentilhomme*
	Dame	Joseph K	*The Trial*
Estragon	*Waiting for Godot*	Alyosha Karamazov	*The Brothers Karamazov*
Etienne	*Germinal*	Dmitri Karamazov	*The Brothers Karamazov*
Bathsheba Everdene	*Far from the Madding Crowd*	Ivan Karamazov	*The Brothers Karamazov*
Face	*The Alchemist*	Chris Keller	*All My Sons*
Jane Fairfax	*Emma*	Frank Kennedy	*Gone With the Wind*
Jude Fawley	*Jude the Obscure*	Khlestakov	*The Inspector General*
Gervase Fenn	created by Edmund Crispin	Kipps (draper's	*Kipps*
Cyril Fielding	*A Passage to India*	assistant)	
Fiver	*Watership Down*	Howard Kirk	*The History Man*
Pegeen Flaherty	*The Playboy of the Western*	Joseph Knecht	*The Glass Bead Game*
	World		(aka *Magister Ludi*)
Flashman	*Tom Brown's Schooldays*	Mr Knightley	*Emma*
Henry Fleming	*The Red Badge of Courage*	Kostoglotov	*Cancer Ward*
Phileas Fogg	*Around the World in 80 Days*	Stanley Kowalsky	*A Streetcar Named Desire*
Fossil family	*Ballet Shoes* (Noel	Lydia Languish	*The Rivals*
	Streatfeild)	Leamas	*The Spy Who Came in from*
Frodo	*The Lord of the Rings*		*the Cold*
Archdeacon Frollo	*The Hunchback of Notre*	Simon Legree	*Uncle Tom's Cabin*
	Dame	Amyas Leigh	*Westward Ho!*
Gandalf	*The Lord of the Rings*	Jeeter Lester	*Tobacco Road*
James Gatz	*The Great Gatsby*	Adrian Leverkühn	*Doctor Faustus*
(Jay Gatsby)		(composer)	
Marguerite Gautier	*Camille*	Levin	*Anna Karenina*
Gerard	*The Cloister and the Hearth*	Ligia	*Quo Vadis?*
Inspector Ghote	created by H R F Keating	Teddy Lloyd	*The Prime of Miss Jean*
Roderick Glossop	the Jeeves stories		*Brodie*
(psychiatrist)		Lord Loam	*The Admirable Crichton*
Anthony Gloster	*The Mary Gloster* (Kipling)	Willy Loman	*Death of a Salesman*
(shipowner)		Lovewit	*The Alchemist*
Holly Golightly	*Breakfast at Tiffany's*	Frank Lubey	*All My Sons*
Gollum	*The Lord of the Rings*	Lucky	*Waiting for Godot*
Hermione Granger	Harry Potter books	Tertius Lydgate	*Middlemarch*
Cordelia Gray	created by P D James	(surgeon)	
Grendel	*Beowulf*	Lt Macaulay	*Bhowani Junction* (John
Jack Grey	*Pale Fire*		Masters)
Joan Griffin	*The Invisible Man*	Christie Mahon	*The Playboy of the Western*
Clyde Griffiths	*An American Tragedy*		*World*
Captain Grimes	*Decline and Fall*	Major Major	*Catch-22*
Tania Gromeko	*Doctor Zhivago*	Mrs Malaprop	*The Rivals*
Gunga Din	created by Rudyard Kipling	Draco Malfoy	Harry Potter books
Tod Hackett	*The Day of the Locust*	Captain Charles	*Lost Horizon*
Harry Haller	*Steppenwolf*	Mallison	
Basil Hallward	*The Picture of Dorian Gray*	Daphne Manners	*The Jewel in the Crown*
Charles Hamilton	*Gone With the Wind*	Stephen Maturin	created by Patrick O'Brian
Richard Hannay	*The Thirty-Nine Steps*	Oskar Matzerath	*The Tin Drum*
Miss Hardcastle	*She Stoops to Conquer*	Oliver Mellors	*Lady Chatterley's Lover*
Hawkeye	the Leatherstocking stories	Merrylegs (pony)	*Black Beauty*
Bill Haydon (spy)	*Tinker, Tailor, Soldier, Spy*	Messala	*Ben Hur*
Dolores Haze	*Lolita*	Duke Michael	*The Prisoner of Zenda*
Hazel (rabbit)	*Watership Down*	Mildew	*Fungus the Bogeyman*
Nora Helmer	*A Doll's House*	Millamant	*The Way of the World*
Michael Henchard	*The Mayor of Casterbridge*	George Milton	*Of Mice and Men*
Frederic Henry	*A Farewell to Arms*	Minnehaha	*Hiawatha*
Hickey	*The Iceman Cometh*	Mirabell	*The Way of the World*
Henry Higgins	*Pygmalion*	Mold	*Fungus the Bogeyman*
Charles Highway	*The Rachel Papers*	Mole	*The Wind in the Willows*
Bridget Hitler	*Young Adolf* by Beryl	Algernon Moncrieff	*The Importance of Being*
	Bainbridge		*Ernest*
Captain Hook	*Peter Pan*	Montmorency	*Three Men in a Boat*
Houyhnhnms (horses)	*Gulliver's Travels*	(the dog)	
Humbert Humbert	*Lolita*	Dr Monygham	*Nostromo*
Humpty Dumpty	*Through the Looking Glass*	Paul Morel	*Sons and Lovers*
Injun Joe	*Tom Sawyer*	Dean Moriarty	*On the Road*
Mrs Jennings	*Sense and Sensibility*	Catherine Morland	*Northanger Abbey*
Mrs Jessel	*The Turn of the Screw*	Mother's Younger	*Ragtime* (E L Doctorow)
Tom Joad	*The Grapes of Wrath*	Brother	
Jocasta	*Oedipus the King*	Mowgli	*The Jungle Book*

L
I
T
E
R
A
T
U
R
E

Matthew Mugg (catsmeat man)	*Doctor Dolittle*	Archie Rice	*The Entertainer*
Prince Myshkin	*The Idiot*	Rico Bandello	*Little Caesar* (W R Burnett)
Mytyl	*The Blue Bird*	John Ridd	*Lorna Doone*
Nana	*Peter Pan*	Sir Colenso Ridgeon	*The Doctor's Dilemma*
Napoleon the Pig	*Animal Farm*	Rikki Tikki Tavi	*The Jungle Book*
Nawab of Satipur	*Heat and Dust* (Ruth Prawer Jhabvala)	Christopher Robin	*Winnie-the-Pooh*
		Fanny Robin	*Far from the Madding Crowd*
Nayland-Smith	*Fu Manchu*	Mr Rochester	*Jane Eyre*
Captain Nemo	*Twenty Thousand Leagues Under the Sea*	Mildred Rodgers	*Of Human Bondage*
		Rose of Torridge	*Westward Ho!*
Norah Nesbit	*Of Human Bondage*	Emma Rouault	*Madame Bovary*
Gabriel Oak	*Far from the Madding Crowd*	Lady Rowena	*Ivanhoe*
Kitty Oblonsky	*Anna Karenina*	Roxane	*Cyrano de Bergerac*
Julia O'Brien	*Nineteen Eighty-Four*	Nicholas Rubashov	*Darkness at Noon*
Mrs Ogmore-Pritchard	*Under Milk Wood*	King Rudolf	*The Prisoner of Zenda*
O-Lan	*The Good Earth*	Mrs Rushworth	*Mansfield Park*
Oompa Loompas	*Charlie and the Chocolate Factory*	Captain Charles Ryder	*Brideshead Revisited*
		Iris Aroon St Charles	*Good Behaviour* (Molly Keane)
George Osborne	*Vanity Fair*		
Mr Palmer	*Sense and Sensibility*	Sauron	*The Lord of the Rings*
Doctor Pangloss	*Candide*	Rose Sayer	*The African Queen*
Panurge	*Gargantua and Pantagruel*	Scamper	*The Secret Seven*
Sancho Panza	*Don Quixote*	Basil Seal	*Black Mischief*
Passepartout	*Around the World in 80 Days*	Amelia Sedley	*Vanity Fair*
Paul Pennyfeather	*Decline and Fall*	John Francis Shade	*Pale Fire*
Pertelote (the cock)	*The Nun's Priest's Tale*	Shadowfax (horse)	*The Lord of the Rings*
Ronald Osprey Petrefact	*Ancestral Vices* (Tom Sharpe)	Shalimar	*The Arabian Nights*
		Becky Sharp	*Vanity Fair*
Petrovitch	*Crime and Punishment*	Anne Shirley	*Anne of Green Gables*
Alexander Petrovsky	*Russian Hide-and-Seek* (Kingsley Amis)	Napoleon Bonaparte Simpson	*The Spectacles* (Edgar Allan Poe)
Aunt Peturia	Harry Potter books	Saleem Sinai	*Midnight's Children*
Phaedrus	*Zen and the Art of Motorcycle Maintenance*	Dr Slop	*Tristram Shandy*
		Obadiah Slope	*Barchester Towers*
Piggy	*Lord of the Flies*	Tyrone Slothrop	*Gravity's Rainbow*
Billy Pilgrim	*Slaughterhouse-Five*	Lennie Small	*Of Mice and Men*
Captain Pissani	*Accidental Death of an Anarchist*	Pavel Smedyakov	*The Brothers Karamazov*
		George Smiley	created by John le Carré
Maggie Pollitt	*Cat on a Hot Tin Roof*	Smith	*Loneliness of the Long Distance Runner*
Polynesia (parrot)	*Doctor Dolittle*		
Ernest Pontifex	*The Way of All Flesh*	Winston Smith	*Nineteen Eighty-Four*
Jimmy Porter	*Look Back in Anger*	Lady Sneerwell	*The School for Scandal*
Claude (Mustard) Pott	created by P G Wodehouse	Julian Sorel	*The Red and the Black*
Harry Potter	Harry Potter books	Bertie Stanhope	*Barchester Towers*
Pozzo	*Waiting for Godot*	Steerpike	*Titus Groan*
Ford Prefect	*The Hitchhiker's Guide to the Galaxy*	Alan Strang	*Equus*
		Subtle	*The Alchemist*
Private Prewitt	*From Here to Eternity*	Joseph Surface	*The School for Scandal*
Fanny Price	*Mansfield Park*	Svengali	*Trilby*
Dr Primrose	*The Vicar of Wakefield*	Tadzio	*Death in Venice*
Miss Prism	*The Importance of Being Ernest*	John Tanner	*Man and Superman*
		Tatiana	*Eugene Onegin*
Dr Proudie	*Barchester Towers*	Lady Teazle	*The School for Scandal*
Mrs Proudie	*Barchester Towers*	Professor George Tessman	*Hedda Gabler*
Hester Prynne	*The Scarlet Letter*		
Pushmi-Pullyu (two-headed llama)	*Doctor Dolittle*	Becky Thatcher	*Tom Sawyer*
		Henry Tilney	*Northanger Abbey*
Roger Quaife	*The Corridors of Power*	Timmy	*The Famous Five*
Quasimodo	*The Hunchback of Notre Dame*	Tinker Bell	*Peter Pan*
		Tiresias	*Oedipus the King*
Queen of Hearts	*Alice's Adventures in Wonderland*	Toad	*The Wind in the Willows*
		Uncle Toby	*Tristram Shandy*
Adela Quested	*A Passage to India*	Kenneth Marchal Toomey	*Earthly Powers*
Quint	*The Turn of the Screw*		
Ralph	*Lord of the Flies*	Topsy	*Uncle Tom's Cabin*
Elwin Ransome	*Perelandra* by C S Lewis	Rev. John Treherne	*The Admirable Crichton*
Raskolnikov	*Crime and Punishment*	Trigorin	*The Seagull*
Paul Ray	*The Second Mrs Tanqueray*	Trilby (artist's model)	*Trilby*
Red Queen	*Through the Looking Glass*	Disko Troop	*Captains Courageous*
Ignatius J Reilly	*Confederacy of Dunces* (John K Toole)	Sergeant Troy	*Far from the Madding Crowd*
		Maggie Tulliver	*The Mill on the Floss*
		Tom Tulliver	*The Mill on the Floss*

Tweedledum and Tweedledee	*Through the Looking Glass*	Mr Weston	*Emma*
Tyltyl	*The Blue Bird*	Reg Wexford	created by Ruth Rendell
Uncas	the Leatherstocking stories	Ann Whitefield	*Man and Superman*
Andrew Undershaft (arms maker)	*Major Barbara*	White Queen	*Through the Looking Glass*
Jean Valjean	*Les Misérables*	Mr Wickham	*Pride and Prejudice*
Piet van der Valk	created by Nicolas Freeling	Ashley Wilkes	*Gone With the Wind*
Harriet Vane	created by Dorothy L Sayers	Aaron Winthrop	*Silas Marner*
Uncle Vernon	Harry Potter books	Willy Nilly	*Under Milk Wood*
Vladimir	*Waiting for Godot*	Willy Wonka	*Charlie and the Chocolate Factory*
Gustav Von Aschenbach	*Death in Venice*	Nero Wolfe	created by Rex Stout
Voldemort	Harry Potter books	Emma Woodhouse	*Emma*
Count Vronsky	*Anna Karenina*	Ernest Wooley	*The Admirable Crichton*
Alice Walker	*The Color Purple*	Wormold	*Our Man in Havana*
The Walrus and the Carpenter	*Through the Looking Glass*	Jack Worthing	*The Importance of Being Ernest*
Wang Lung	*The Good Earth*	General Woundwort (rabbit)	*Watership Down*
Maria Ward	*Mansfield Park*	Charles Wykeham	*Charley's Aunt*
Water Rat	*The Wind in the Willows*	Yahoos (humans)	*Gulliver's Travels*
Ronald Weasley	Harry Potter books	Mary Yellan	*Jamaica Inn*
Captain Wentworth	*Persuasion*	Captain Yossarian	*Catch-22*
Sophia Western	*Tom Jones*	Falther Zossima	*The Brothers Karamazov*

Chaucer's Canterbury Pilgrims

1	The Knight's Tale		13	The Physician's Tale
2	The Miller's Tale		14	The Pardoner's Tale
3	The Reeve's Tale		15	The Shipman's Tale
4	The Cook's Tale		16	The Prioress's Tale
5	The Man of Law's Tale		17	Chaucer's Tale of Sir Thopas
6	The Wife of Bath's Tale		18	Chaucer's Tale of Melibeus
7	The Friar's Tale		19	The Monk's Tale
8	The Summoner's Tale		20	The Nun's Priest's Tale
9	The Clerk's Tale		21	The Second Nun's Tale
10	The Merchant's Tale		22	The Canon's Yeoman's Tale
11	The Squire's Tale		23	The Manciple's Tale
12	The Franklin's Tale		24	The Parson's Tale

NB: The Canterbury Tales was an unfinished collection of tales told in the course of a pilgrimage to Thomas Becket's shrine at Canterbury. In addition to the 22 story-tellers listed above, the party included a dyer, weaver, arrowmaker, haberdasher, carpenter, ploughman and guidesman, making a total of 29. Chaucer himself may be included as a pilgrim to give a definitive total of 30.

Mr Men and Little Misses

Mr Men

1 Mr Bounce is round and yellow and very cuddly. He is forever turning somersaults while landing on his head.
2 Mr Brave proves that looks can be deceiving, bespectacled and yellow-looking but utterly fearless.
3 Mr Bump is always having accidents of all sorts, and so is always wrapped in bandages from his latest injury.
4 Mr Busy always has something to do, and like Mr Rush this blue character simply cannot relax.
5 Mr Chatterbox never ever stops talking, not even for a moment. It is impossible to get a word in edgeways.
6 Mr Cheeky is extremely rude. When he meets people in the street he insults them unashamedly. (Not one of the original 43 characters but introduced in 2001 as a result of a nationwide competition to celebrate the 30th anniversary of their birth. Gemma Almond, 8, from Shropshire won the competition.)
7 Mr Cheerful is always looking on the bright side of life and is there to cheer you up when you are down.
8 Mr Christmas was not one of the original 43 Mr Men books but was created for a Christmas special.
9 Mr Clever is wide-eyed and bespectacled, and of course knows absolutely everything.
10 Mr Clumsy means well but really is very clumsy indeed, so don't let him near Mr Bump's children.
11 Mr Daydream is in a world of his own most of the time, his imagination running rife.
12 Mr Dizzy lives in a land where pigs and elephants are clever, and he just can't get his head around it all.
13 Mr Forgetful is big and blue and egg-shaped and very very absent-minded.
14 Mr Funny lives in a teapot-shaped house, and drives a shoe-shaped car. He is a practical joker par excellence.
15 Mr Fussy likes things to be neat and tidy, and even irons his shoelaces. He is green and fastidious.
16 Mr Greedy is the greediest person alive. When he comes to visit, make sure there's no food lying around!
17 Mr Grumble is never content. On a lovely day he hates the hot sun, and when it snows he's too cold!
18 Mr Grumpy is always in a bad mood, no matter what. He can't stand it when other people have fun.

LITERATURE

19   Mr Happy lives in Happyland where everyone and everything is always happy. Big and yellow with a grin to match.
20   Mr Impossible really can do the impossible! Mauve in colour, there is nothing up his sleeve!
21   Mr Jelly is scared of everything and anything. The quivering red blob is also known as Mr Nervous.
22   Mr Lazy likes nothing more than to do absolutely nothing. He'll laze about in the sun all day if he can.
23   Mr Mean is not very nice really. He's tall and slim but with short arms and long pockets.
24   Mr Messy needs to get his act together. His garden is overgrown and his washing up is never done.
25   Mr Mischief is a bigger practical joker than Mr Fun. He is always sniggering over his latest prank.
26   Mr Muddle just can't get things right, so if you meet him in the morning, he'll say 'Good Afternoon!'
27   Mr Noisy is always shouting. He's utterly incapable of talking quietly.
28   Mr Nonsense looks like a clown and acts like one, his big red nose protruding from a nonsensical grin.
29   Mr Nosey is incapable of minding his own business. His long green nose is taller than himself.
30   Mr Perfect is as his name implies. He has a perfect house with a perfect garden and his lawn is always perfect.
31   Mr Quiet can't stand noisy people or places. Unfortunately he lives in Loudland and it's very trying for him.
32   Mr Rush is always in a hurry and this mauve, triangular-faced flash is heading for a fall unless he slows down.
33   Mr Silly is just plain daft! Even his large red hat is pulled down over his eyes so he cannot see properly.
34   Mr Skinny is long, yellow and as skinny as a rake – literally! Perhaps he should help Mr Messy with his garden!
35   Mr Slow is in no hurry. His moustachioed face gives him a distinguished look . . . but don't rush him!
36   Mr Small really is very tiny, his little red features barely discernible unless you are looking down!
37   Mr Sneeze lives in Coldland, and always has a cold and a very red nose and a blue face from all his sneezing.
38   Mr Snow is the personification of all the snowmen you have ever made in wintertime.
39   Mr Strong can lift entire buildings. He eats a lot of eggs, too, to keep his strength up. He is Big and Square.
40   Mr Tall is as tall as a cliff. He has very long legs, so he can walk a long way very very quickly.
41   Mr Tickle likes to tickle people but his long arms can make breakfast while lying in bed! He was the first Mr Man.
42   Mr Topsy-Turvy reads books upside-down and has a clock that goes anti-clockwise. He greets people he meets by saying 'Morning Good' and he also wears his hat upside-down.
43   Mr Uppity is an outrageous snob, although his black topper makes him look rather distinguished and dapper.
44   Mr Worry is always deep in thought, with a deep frown upon his round blue face.
45   Mr Wrong just can't get things right. He can't even choose a pair of gloves of the same colour!

Little Misses

1   Little Miss Bossy can't stop ordering people around and shouting at them. When she says jump you jump.
2   Little Miss Brainy is the female counterpart of Mr Clever.
3   Little Miss Busy is always busy cleaning the house, shopping, gardening, cooking. She never stops!
4   Little Miss Chatterbox is the female counterpart of Mr Chatterbox and is equally talkative.
5   Little Miss Contrary is always deep in thought but will never agree about anything!
6   Little Miss Curious cannot help but have an inquiring mind.
7   Little Miss Dotty lives in nonsenseland, where Mr Silly and Mr Nonsense live, and she is equally dotty.
8   Little Miss Fickle changes her mind constantly and who knows what or where the mood takes her.
9   Little Miss Fun is a party animal! She's always ready to go out and have fun somewhere.
10   Little Miss Giggles can't stop giggling. She giggles so much that when she's around, everyone else starts too!
11   Little Miss Greedy is as greedy as Mr Greedy. In the earliest books she was also called Little Miss Plump.
12   Little Miss Helpful tries her hardest to be as helpful as she possibly can be. She really does try . . . so hard!
13   Little Miss Late is never on time and punctuality is certainly not her byword.
14   Little Miss Lucky doesn't seem quite as lucky as her name implies, but things always come out all right in the end.
15   Little Miss Magic can do magic! I suppose Mr Impossible would be her male equivalent
16   Little Miss Naughty is very naughty and her naughty ways do not make her very many friends!
17   Little Miss Neat can't stand any sort of mess. She is bespectacled, round and green.
18   Little Miss Quick doesn't hang around at all, and whatever she does she does it very quickly indeed.
19   Little Miss Scatterbrain is very absent-minded and her male equivalent would be Mr Forgetful.
20   Little Miss Shy is very unassuming and would rather be left alone so I won't embarrass her any longer.
21   Little Miss Somersault has very long legs and is very gymnastic. She is forever turning somersaults.
22   Little Miss Splendid looks a little aloof but is quite splendid really although a little prim and proper.
23   Little Miss Star is round and blue with lovely green shoes. She is a real star through and through.
24   Little Miss Stubborn will not listen. No matter how silly her ideas are she is determined to follow them through.
25   Little Miss Sunshine is a vision in yellow and her beaming smile is sure to cheer the hardest heart.
26   Little MissTidy is not green like Little Miss Neat but yellow, and she doesn't wear glasses either.
27   Little Miss Tiny is very small indeed. In fact she is smaller than Mr Small!
28   Little Miss Trouble cannot help but find trouble. She is the female equivalent of Mr Mischief.
29   Little Miss Twins do everything in pairs, and say things twice twice. They live in Twoland. The Little Miss Twins were inspired by Roger Hargreaves's twin daughters.
30   Little Miss Wise is the person to consult if you want some sound advice, as she is very wise indeed.

Note

Mr Men and Little Misses received six new friends 15 years after the death of their creator Roger Hargreaves. His son penned the tales of Mr Cool, Mr Rude, Mr Good, Little Miss Bad, Little Miss Scary and Little Miss Whoops. Adam Hargreaves took over the running of the Mr Men empire after his father died of a stroke in 1988 at the age of 53. Adam had been the original inspiration for the books when he asked his father what a tickle looked like. The result was Mr Tickle, the first in a series which went on to sell over 100 million copies worldwide. The first four new books were published in April 2003 and the two others in September 2003. The books were written by Adam, but he still credited his father as author to keep his father's memory alive.

Poets Laureate

John Dryden (1668-88)	William Wordsworth (1843–50)
Thomas Shadwell (1688–92)	Alfred, Lord Tennyson (1850–92)
Nahum Tate (1692–1715)	Alfred Austin (1896–1913)
Nicholas Rowe (1715–18)	Robert Bridges (1913–30)
Laurence Eusden (1718–30)	John Masefield (1930–67)
Colley Cibber (1730–57)	Cecil Day-Lewis (1968–72)
William Whitehead (1757–85)	Sir John Betjeman (1972–84)
Thomas Wharton (1785–90)	Ted Hughes (1984–1998)
Henry James Pye (1790–1813)	Andrew Motion (1999–)
Robert Southey (1813–43)	

NB: Ben Jonson was the first to be granted a pension as poet, to James I (1616), and in 1630 Charles I added an annual butt of canary wine, which was discontinued by Henry Pye who preferred money. Sir William Davenant succeeded Jonson but the position was only made official in 1668. William Whitehead appointed after Thomas Gray declined the honour. Similarly Alfred, Lord Tennyson became laureate after Samuel Rogers declined.

Servants (and Masters)

Lugg	Campion	Françoise	Marcel Family
Bunter	Lord Peter Wimsey		(*Remembrance of Things*
Miss Lemon	Poirot		*Past*)
Mrs Hudson	Sherlock Holmes	Anatole	Aunt Dahlia (Jeeves stories)
Reginald Jeeves	Bertie Wooster	Mary Ann	White Rabbit
Launcelot Gobbo	Shylock	Eurycleia	Ulysses
Passepartout	Phileas Fogg	Feers	Madame Ranevsky (*Cherry*
Sancho Panza	Don Quixote		*Orchard*)
Mélisande	Zuleika Dobson	Mrs Honour	Sophia Western (*Tom Jones*)
Paddock	Richard Hannay	Corporal Trim	Uncle Toby (*Tristram Shandy*)

Other Literary Prizewinners in 2004

Agatha (mystery award)	Best Novel: *Letter From Home* by Carolyn Hart
Anthony Award	Created in 1986 and named after Anthony Boucher (William Anthony Parker White), well-known writer and critic. The award is for an outstanding mystery novel and was won in 2004 by Laura Lippman (*Every Secret Thing*)
Arthur C Clarke (science fiction)	Best Novel published in Britain: *Quicksilver* by Neal Stephenson
Betty Trask Prize	For first novels in English, published in the UK, by Commonwealth citizens under the age of 35. The £8,000 first prize in 2004 went to Louise Dean for *Becoming Strangers*
Crime Writers Association	Gold Dagger (Fiction): *Blacklist* by Sara Paretsky
Edgar Allan Poe Awards	Awarded by the Mystery Writers of America (MWA), the 2004 award going to Ian Rankin for *Resurrection Men*
Hugo (science fiction)	Best US novel: *Paladin of Souls* by Lois McMaster Bujold
Kate Greenaway Medal (children's illustration)	*Ella's Big Chance* by Shirley Hughes
Nestlé Smarties Prize	Awarded by the Youth Libraries Group to the most outstanding children's book published in the UK across three age groups.
	Age 0–5 *Biscuit Bear* by Mini Grey
	Age 6–8 *Fergus Crane* by Paul Stewart and Chris Riddell
	Age 9–11 *Spilled Water* by Sally Grindley
Samuel Johnson Prize	Established in December 1998. The £30,000 prize is awarded to non-fiction works published in the UK between 1 January and 30 April of the year of the prize. The 2004 winner was Anna Funder for *Stasiland: Stories From Behind the Berlin Wall*

LONDON

Theatres

Name	Address	Post	Details
Adelphi	Strand	WC2	Opened by John Scott in 1806 and originally called the Sans Pareil. First performance on 17 November 1806, *The Rout*, recitations by Miss Jane M Scott. Present auditorium built in 1930. Recently showing *Chicago* (Olivier Award: Best Musical 1998).
Albery	St Martin's Lane	WC2	Designed in 1903 by W G R Sprague and called the New Theatre till 1923. Recently showing *Hecuba* (by Euripides).
Aldwych	Aldwych	WC2	Designed 1905 by W G R Sprague. Home of Ben Travers farces 1925–33. Recently showing *Fame: The Musical* (by David de Silva).
Almeida	Almeida St	N1	Fringe theatre recently showing *Hedda Gabler* (by Henrik Ibsen).
Apollo	Shaftesbury Ave	W1	Designed in 1901 by Lewen Sharp. Recently showing *A Life in the Theatre* (by David Mamet).
Apollo Victoria	Victoria	SW1	Opened in 1930 as a cinema; theatre since 1979. Recently showing *Starlight Express* from 27 March 1984–12 January 2002 and since 6 July 2004 *Saturday Night Fever*.
Arts	Strand	WC2	Opened in 1927 as an avant-garde theatre challenging the censorial constraints of the Lord Chamberlain's Office. Recently showing *Immodesty Blaize and Walter's Burlesque!*
Barbican (and Pit)	Silk St	EC2	Opened in 1982, since when the London Symphony Orchestra has been in residence at Barbican Hall. Also home of the Royal Shakespeare Company.
Bloomsbury	Off Tottenham Ct Rd	WC1	Fringe theatre that shows a wide spectrum of work.
Bridewell	Bride Lane	EC4	Fringe theatre.
Bush	Shepherd's Bush	W12	Fringe theatre founded in 1972.
Cambridge	Earlham St	WC2	Designed in 1930. Recently showing *Grease* (transferred from the Dominion) and since 28 October 2002 *Our House* (by Tim Firth).
Coliseum	St Martin's Lane	WC2	Largest theatre in the West End, seating nearly 2,500. Interior designed in 1904 by Frank Matcham. Home of the English National Opera since 1968.
Comedy	Panton St	SW1	Designed in 1881 by Thomas Verity. Recently showing *Whose Life is it Anyway?* (by Brian Clark).
Criterion	Piccadilly	W1	Current home of the Reduced Shakespeare Company. Designed in 1874 by Thomas Verity.
Dominion	Tottenham Ct Rd	WC1	Built 1929 by William and T R Millburn. Recently showing *We Will Rock You* (by Ben Elton).
Donmar Warehouse	Earlham St	WC2	Recently showing *The Wild Duck* (by Henrik Ibsen).
Drury Lane Theatre Royal	Catherine St	WC2	Designed in 1812 by Benjamin Wyatt. Designed in 1929 by Ewen Barr. Recently showing *The Producers* (by Mel Brooks).
Duchess	Catherine St	WC2	Recently showing *The Birthday Party* (by Harold Pinter).
Duke of York's	St Martin's Lane	WC2	Designed by Walter Emden in 1892 and called the Trafalgar Square till 1895. Recently showing *The Dresser* (by Ronald Harwood).
Fortune	Russell St	WC2	Designed in 1924 by Ernest Schaufelberg. Recently showing *The Woman in Black*.
Gaiety	Strand	WC2	Opened in 1868 and had England's first electric lighting system in 1878.
Garrick	Charing Cross Road	WC2	Designed by Walter Emden and C J Phipps in 1889. Recently showing *Elmina's Kitchen* (by Kwame Kwei-Armah).
Gate (Prince Albert Pub)	Pembridge Rd	W11	Reputation for high-quality productions of neglected European classics.
Gielgud	Shaftesbury Ave	W1	Designed 1906 by W G R Sprague. Originally the Hick's Theatre: then the Globe (1909–95). Recently showing *Some Girls* (by Neil LaBute).
Greenwich	Crooms Hill	SE10	Open since 1969 in reconstructed Victorian music hall.
Hackney Empire	Mare St	E8	Designed by Frank Matcham (1854–1920), was most famous music hall at turn of last century. After being used as television studio and bingo hall, it has reverted to its music-hall roots since its refurbishment and reopening in 2002. The Bullion Room and the Acorn (seating 60) are two small auditoriums within the complex. Has gained a fine reputation for giving young black talent a chance to express itself.
Hampstead Theatre Club	Swiss Cottage	NW3	Fringe theatre.
Her Majesty's	Haymarket	SW1	Original building designed by Sir John Vanbrugh in 1705; present theatre designed 1896 by C J Phipps. Recently showing *Phantom of the Opera*.
King's Head	Upper St	N1	Founded as a pub theatre in 1970.

Name	Address	Post	Details
Lyceum	Wellington St	WC2	Designed by James Payne in 1771. Recently showing *Lion King* (songs by Elton John and Tim Rice).
Lyric	King St Hammersmith	W6	Designed in 1979. Usually performances of planned short-season runs.
Lyric	Shaftesbury Ave	W1	Designed in 1888 by C J Phipps. Recently showing *Death of a Salesman* (by Arthur Miller).
Mayfair	Mayfair Hotel	W1	Part of the hotel complex.
Mermaid	Puddle Dock	EC4	Founded in 1959 by Sir Bernard Miles.
New Ambassadors	West St	WC2	Designed in 1913 by W G R Sprague. Ivor Novello made debut here in *Deburau*. Recently showing *Someone Who'll Watch Over Me* (by Frank McGuinness).
New End	New End	NW3	Fringe theatre.
New London	Drury Lane	WC2	Designed in 1973 by Paul Turkovic. Recently showing *Joseph And The Amazing Technicolor Dreamcoat.*
Old Vic	Waterloo Rd	SE1	Designed 1818 by Rudolf Cabanel. Currently owned by the Old Vic Theatre Trust 2000 Ltd. Recently showing *The Philadelphia Story.*
Palace	Cambridge Circus	WC2	Built by T E Collcutt and G H Holloway, opened in 1891 as The Royal English Opera House showing Sir Arthur Sullivan's *Ivanhoe.* Recently showing *The Woman In White.*
Palladium	Argyll St	WC1	Opened in 1910 as a music hall. Recently showing *Chitty Chitty Bang Bang.*
Peacock	Portugal St	WC2	Sadler's Wells theatre. Recently Showing *Opus Cactus* (by the Momix Dance Company).
Phoenix	Charing Cross Road	WC2	Designed by Giles Gilbert Scott and Bertie Crewe and opened in 1930. Recently showing *Blood Brothers* (by Willy Russell).
Piccadilly	Denman St	W1	Designed in 1928 by Bertie Crewe and Edward Stone. Recently showing *Guys and Dolls.*
Players	Off Villiers St	SW1	Several locations since 1936. Now situated underneath Charing Cross arches.
Playhouse	Northumberland Ave	WC2	Designed by Sefton Parry in 1882. Recently showing *House of Desires* (by Sor Juana Ines de la Cruz).
Prince Edward	Old Compton St	W1	Opened in 1930. Recently showing *Mary Poppins.*
Prince of Wales	Coventry St	W1	Designed 1937 by Robert Cromie. Recently showing *Mamma Mia!*
Queen's	Shaftesbury Ave	W1	Interior designed 1907 by W G R Sprague, new exterior redesigned by Bryan Westwood and Hugh Casson after bomb damage in 1940, reopened 1959. Recently showing *Les Miserables.*
Regent's Park (open air)	Regent's Park	NW1	Founded in 1932. Stages annual productions of *A Midsummer Night's Dream.*
Royal Court Downstairs	Sloane Square	SW3	Recently showing *Topdog/Underdog* (by Suzan-Lori Parks).
Royal Court Upstairs	Sloane Square	SW3	Recently showing *Food Chain* (by Mick Mahoney).
Royal National Theatre	South Bank	SE1	Designed by Denys Lasdun, opened 1976. Three auditoriums, the Olivier (large and open-spaced), the Lyttelton (proscenium arched) and the Cottesloe (small but flexible).
Royal Opera	Bow St	WC2	Designed by Edward Shepherd in 1732. Redesigned by E M Barry in 1858 and called The Covent Garden Opera Company. Renamed the Royal Opera House in 1968.
Sadler's Wells	Rosebery Ave	EC1	Opened in 1683 by Thomas Sadler. A studio theatre, the Lilian Baylis, was opened in 1998.
Savoy	Strand	WC2	Designed in 1881 by C J Phipps and financed by Richard D'Oyly Carte for the production of Gilbert and Sullivan Operas. First public building to be lit by electricity, although the Gaiety theatre had experimented in 1878. Recently showing *Blithe Spirit* (by Noel Coward).
Shaftesbury	Shaftesbury Ave	WC1	Designed in 1911 by Bertie Crewe. Recently showing *The Far Pavilions.*
Shakespeare's Globe	Southwark	SE1	Sam Wanamaker's dream of a theatre for all was opened in 1997 with Mark Rylance playing Henry V.
St Martin's	West St	WC2	Designed in 1916 by W G R Sprague. Recently showing *The Mousetrap.*
Strand	Aldwych	WC2	Designed 1905 by W G R Sprague. Recently showing *The Rat Pack.*
Theatre Royal, Haymarket	Haymarket	SW1	Built in 1821 by John Nash. Recently showing *Acorn Antiques: the Musical.*
Theatre Royal, Stratford	Gerry Raffles Square	E15	Built in 1884 by James George Buckle.
Tricycle	Kilburn High Rd	NW6	Fringe theatre.
Unicorn	Great Newport St	WC2	Presently a travelling company following the closure of its theatre in Great Newport Street.
Vaudeville	Strand	WC2	Designed by C J Phipps 1870. Recently showing *Stomp* (by Luke Cresswell and Steve McNicholas).

L
O
N
D
O
N

Name	Address	Post	Details
Venue	Leicester Square	WC2	Opened in November 2001, the brainchild of Adam Kenwright. Was specifically designed to show the musical *Taboo*, based on the life of pop singer Boy George. Recently showing *Round the Horne . . . Revisited 2*.
Victoria Palace	Victoria St	SW1	Designed in 1911 by Frank Hatcham. Recently showing *Billy Elliot: The Musical*.
Westminster	Palace St	SW1	Possibly the nearest theatre to Buckingham Palace.
Whitehall	Whitehall	SW1	Built in 1930. Formerly to the design of E A Stone. Known for its farces. Recently renamed the Trafalgar. Recently showing *Losing Louis*.
Wyndham's	Charing Cross Road	WC2	Designed by W G R Sprague and opened in 1899. Recently showing *As You Like It* (by William Shakespeare).
Young Vic	The Cut	SE1	Built in 1970. Recently showing *Hobson's Choice* (by Harold Brighouse).

NB: Notable London fringe theatres (and pubs) not listed above include Half Moon, Old Red Lion, Orange Tree, Bird's Nest, Landor, Hen & Chickens, Pentameters, Albany, Etcetera, Oval House, Pleasance, Richmond (The Green) and Riverside Studios.

Statues

Site	Person(s) Depicted
Albert Hall (SW7)	*Prince Albert* by Joseph Durham (1863).
Bank of England (EC2)	Stone statues of *Sir John Soane* by Sir William Reid Dick (1937) and *King William III* by Sir Henry Cheere (1735).
Banqueting House, Whitehall (SW1)	Lead bust of *Charles I* by unknown sculptor.
Belgrave Square (SW1)	Bronze of *Simon Bolivar* by Hugo Daini (1974).
Birdcage Walk (SW1)	Bronze of *Field Marshal Earl Alexander of Tunis* by James Butler (1985).
Bloomsbury Square, (WC1)	*Charles James Fox* by Richard Westmacott (1816).
Cannon St (EC4)	Bronze mask of *Winston Churchill* by Frank Dobson (1959) over the entrance to Bracken House.
Carey St / Serle St (WC2)	Stone figure of *Sir Thomas More* by Robert Smith (1866).
Carlton Gardens (SW1)	Bronze of *General Charles de Gaulle* and *George VI* by William McMillan.
Cavendish Square (W1)	Bronze of *William George Bentinck* by Thomas Campbell (1851).
Charing Cross Rd (WC2)	Bronze of *Sir Henry Irving* by Thomas Brock (1910) by the St Martin's Place side of the National Portrait Gallery.
Chelsea Embankment (SW3)	Bronze of *Thomas Carlyle* by Sir Joseph Boehm (1882); seated bronze of *Sir Thomas More* by L Cubitt Bevis (1969).
Chelsea Hospital (SW3)	*Bronze of King Charles II in Roman Costume*, by Grinling Gibbons (1676).
Chiswick House (W4)	Stone figure of *Inigo Jones* by John Rysbrack (1729).
City Rd (EC1)	*John Wesley* by John Adams-Acton (1891).
Cockspur St (SW1)	Bronze equestrian of *George III* by Matthew Cotes Wyatt.
Commercial Rd (E1)	Bronze of *Clement Attlee* by Frank Forster (1988) outside Limehouse Library.
Cornhill (No 32) EC3	Mahogany carving of *The Brontë sisters in Conversation with William Makepeace Thackeray* by Walter Gilbert (1939).
Crystal Palace Park (SE19)	Marble bust of *Sir Joseph Paxton* by W F Woodington (1869).
Downing St (SW1)	*Mountbatten* outside Foreign Office.
Euston Station (NW1)	Bronze of *Robert Stephenson* by Baron Marochetti (1871).
Festival Hall (SE1)	Bronze of *Frederic Chopin*, beside the Festival Hall, by B Kubica (1975).
Fleet St (EC4)	Stone of *Elizabeth I* by William Kerwin (1586) over the vestry porch of St Dunstan in the West. This is the oldest statue of a monarch in London and, in fact, the oldest outdoor statue of any kind.
Fleet St (Nos 143–4) EC4	Stone of *Mary, Queen of Scots*, placed by an admirer, Sir John Tollemache Sinclair (1880).
Greenwich Park (SE10)	Samuel Nixon's Foggit Tor granite of *William IV*, erected in King William IV St in 1844 and moved to present site in 1938.
Grosvenor Gardens (SW1)	Bronze equestrian of *Marechal Foch* by G. Mallisard (1930).
Grosvenor Square (W1)	Bronze of *F.D. Roosevelt* by Sir William Reid Dick; bronze of *General Dwight D. Eisenhower* by Robert Dean (1989).
Guildhall (EC2)	Limewood carvings of mythical giants, *Gog and Magog*, by David Evans, replacing those burned in 1940.
Hamilton Gardens (W1)	Bronze of *George Gordon Byron* by Richard Belt (1880).
Hanover Square (W1)	Bronze of *William Pitt the Younger* by Francis Chantrey (1831).
Highgate Cemetery (N6)	Bronze of *Karl Marx* by Laurence Bradshaw (1956).
Holborn Circus (EC1)	Equestrian bronze of *Prince Albert* by Charles Bacon (1874).
Horse Guards Parade (SW1)	Bronze of *Field Marshal Earl Kitchener* by John Tweed (1926); bronze equestrian of *Field Marshal Viscount Wolseley* by Sir William Goscombe John (1920).

Site	Person(s) Depicted
Houses of Parliament (SW1)	Equestrian bronze of *Richard I* in Old Palace Yard by Carlo Marochetti (1861); bronze of *Oliver Cromwell* outside Westminster Hall by Sir Hamo Thornycroft (1899). Statue of *George VI* stands opposite the *Richard I* outside the grounds and was sculpted by William Reid Dick (1947).
Hyde Park Corner (SW1)	Bronze of *The Duke of Wellington* on his horse, Copenhagen, by J E Boehm (1888).
Kensington Gardens (SW7)	Bronze of *Sir Winston and Lady Churchill* by Oscar Nemon (1981) situated near Hyde Park Gate; seated statue of *Queen Victoria* by her daughter, Princess Louise (1893); Albert Memorial designed by George Gilbert Scott, with seated statue of Albert begun by Baron Marochetti and completed in 1876 by John Foley.
Kensington Palace (W8)	Bronze of *William III* by Heinrich Baucke (1907) presented by Kaiser Wilhelm II to his uncle, Edward VII.
King Charles Street (SW1)	Bronze figure of *Robert Clive* by John Tweed (1912).
King Edward Street (EC1)	Granite figure of *Sir Rowland Hill*, founder of the Penny Post, by R Onslow Ford (1881).
Leicester Square: Centre (WC2)	Marble of *William Shakespeare* by Giovanni Fontana (1874); bronze of *Charlie Chaplin* by John Doubleday (unveiled by Ralph Richardson in 1981).
Leicester Square: Gates (WC2)	Memorial gates, to *John Hunter* by Thomas Woolner, *Isaac Newton* by William Calder Marshall, *Joshua Reynolds* by Henry Weekes (all 1874) and *William Hogarth* by Joseph Durham (1875), all of whom have commemorative busts.
The Mall (near Admiralty Arch, SW1)	Bronze of *Captain James Cook* by Sir Thomas Brock (1914). Seated marble statue of Queen Victoria by Sir Thomas Brock (1911).
Marylebone Rd (NW1)	Bronze of *John Fitzgerald Kennedy* by Jacques Lipchitz (1965).
Millbank (SW1)	Bronze of *Sir John Everett Millais* by Sir Thomas Brock (1904).
Old Bailey (EC4)	Gilt of *Justice* by F W Pomeroy (1907).
Park Crescent (W1)	Bronze of *Edward Augustus, Duke of Kent* (Queen Victoria's father) by S S Gahagen (1827).
Park Lane (W1)	*Achilles* (20' bronze cast in 1822 by Sir Richard Westmacott) 'Erected by the women of England to Arthur, Duke of Wellington and his brave companions in arms'.
Parliament Square (SW1)	Bronzes of *George Canning*, in a toga, by Richard Westmacott (1832); *Sir Robert Peel* by Matthew Noble (1876); *Field Marshal Jan Christian Smuts* by Jacob Epstein (1958); *Abraham Lincoln* (copy of the statue by Augustus Saint-Gaudens in Chicago); *Winston Churchill* by Ivor Roberts Jones (1973); *Benjamin Disraeli* by Mario Raggi (1883); *Lord Palmerston* by Thomas Woolner (1876).
Piccadilly Circus (W1)	*Shaftesbury Memorial Fountain*, better known as *Eros* although Alfred Gilbert's 1893 aluminium statue in fact depicts *The Angel of Christian Charity*, in honour of Lord Shaftesbury himself.
Pimlico Gardens (SW1)	Stone of *William Huskisson* in a Roman toga, by John Gibson (1836).
Prudential Assurance (Holborn EC1)	Cupronised plaster bust of *Charles Dickens* by Percy Fitzgerald (1907).
Red Lion Square (WC1)	Bronze bust of *Bertrand Russell* by Marcelle Quinton (1980).
Royal Exchange (EC2)	Equestrian bronze of *Wellington* begun by Francis Chantrey & completed by Henry Weekes (1844); and stone figure of *Richard Whittington* by J E Carew (1845).
Royal Geographical Society, Kensington Gore (SW7)	Bronzes of *David Livingstone* by T B Huxley-Jones (1953) and *Sir Ernest Shackleton* by C Sarjeant Jagger (1932).
St Bartholomew's Hospital (EC1)	Stone figure of *Henry VIII*, the founder, by Francis Bird (1702) stands over the gateway.
St Giles Cripplegate	Memorial statue of *John Milton* by Montford (1904).
St James's Square (SW1)	*William III*, equestrian bronze by John Bacon the Elder (1808).
St Martin's Place (WC2)	Marble statue of *Edith Cavell* by Sir George Frampton (1920). Famous inscription reads: 'Patriotism is not enough. I must have no hatred or bitterness for anyone.'
St Thomas's Hospital (SE1)	Statue of *Sir Robert Clayton*, the hospital's benefactor. The only outdoor stone statue by Grinling Gibbons.
Savoy Place (WC2)	Bronze of *Michael Faraday* by J H Foley (1889) situated outside the Institution of Electrical Engineers.
Soho Square (W1)	Stone statue of *King Charles II* by Caius Gabriel Cibber once owned by W S Gilbert.
Somerset House, Strand (WC2)	Baroque fountain in bronze, including a figure of *King George III* by John Bacon the Elder (1788).
South Africa House (Trafalgar Square)	Large stone figure of *Bartholomew Diaz* by Coert Steynberg (1934).
South Square, Gray's Inn (WC1)	*Francis Bacon* by F W Pomeroy (1912).
Strand (WC2)	Bronzes of *Air Chief Marshal Lord Dowding* and *Sir Arthur 'Bomber' Harris* by Faith Winter (1988) opposite St Clement Danes, the RAF church, *William Gladstone* by Sir Hamo Thorneycroft (1905) and *Dr Samuel Johnson* by Percy Fitzgerald (1910).
Tavistock Square (WC1)	Bronze of *Mahatma Gandhi* by Fredda Brilliant (unveiled by Harold Wilson in 1968).
Tooting Broadway (SW17)	Bronze of *King Edward VII* by L F Roselieb (1911).

LONDON

Site	Person(s) Depicted
Trafalgar Square (WC2)	Bronzes outside National Gallery of *George Washington* by Jean-Antoine Houdon and *James II* in Roman dress by Grinling Gibbons; *Sir Henry Havelock* by William Behnes (1861); bronze equestrians of *George IV* by Sir Francis Chantrey (1834) and *Charles I* by Hubert Le Sueur (1633); *Nelson's column* (170′ 2″), with statue of Nelson by E H Bailey (1843) and Landseer's lions cast in 1868 from guns recovered from the wreck of the *Royal George*. On the north wall of the Square are bronze busts of Admirals *Lord Beatty* by William McMillan (1984), *Lord Cunningham*, by Franta Belsky (1967) and *Lord Jellicoe* by Sir Charles Wheeler (1948).
University College London (WC1)	Bronze tablet and medallion of *Richard Trevithick* by L S Merrifield (1933).
Victoria Embankment (WC2)	*Isambard Kingdom Brunel* by Carlo Marochetti (1877); *Cleopatra's Needle* (68 ½').
Victoria Embankment Gardens (WC2)	Bronzes of *John Stuart Mill* by Thomas Woolner (1878); *Robert Burns* by Sir John Steel (1884); *Sir Arthur Sullivan* by W Goscombe John (1903), with a mourning female on the plinth; *Robert Raikes* by Sir Thomas Brock (1880).
Victoria Tower Gardens, Westminster (SW1)	*Burghers of Calais* by Rodin, copy (installed 1915) of original in Calais, created 1895. Emmeline and Christabel Pankhurst by A G Walker (1930).
Waterloo Place (SW1)	*Duke of York Column* memorial to Frederick, 2nd son of George III, statue by Sir Richard Westmacott 1834; bronze equestrian of *King Edward VII* by Sir Bertram Mackennal (1922); bronze of *Captain Robert Falcon Scott* by Lady Scott (1915); *Florence Nightingale* by Walker.
Westminster Bridge (SE1)	Thomas Thornycroft's *Boadicea* at the north-eastern end.
Whitehall (SW1)	Bronzes of *Sir Walter Raleigh* by William McMillan (1959); *Field Marshal Montgomery of Alamein* by Oscar Nemon (unveiled by Queen Mother in 1980); *Field Marshal the Viscount Alanbrooke* and *Field Marshal the Viscount Slim*, both by Ivor Roberts Jones.
Woodford Green (E18)	Bronze of *Winston Churchill* by David McFall (unveiled by Field Marshal Montgomery in October 1959).
Woolwich, Royal Arsenal (SE18)	Stone figure of *Wellington* by Thomas Milnes (1848).

Bridges

From East to West	Type	Opened	
Queen Elizabeth II	Road	1991	Clockwise route of M25; the Dartford Tunnel is the anti-clockwise route.
Tower	Road	1894	Built by John Wolfe-Barry to a design by Sir Horace Jones, the furthest bridge downstream in London.
London	Road	1831	Rebuilt by John Rennie but moved to Lake Havasu City, Arizona, in 1967; new bridge opened by Queen Elizabeth II, 16 March 1973.
Alexandra	Rail	1866	Cannon St in the north to Clink St in the south.
Southwark	Road	1819	Built by John Rennie; rebuilt 1921.
Millennium	Foot	2000	Built by an amalgamation of Norman Foster, Anthony Caro and Ove Enge. Links St Paul's Cathedral and the Tate Modern.
Blackfriars	Rail	1864	Upper Thames St in the north to Southwark St in the south.
Blackfriars	Road	1769	Rebuilt 1869 and widened 1910.
Waterloo	Road	1817	Built by John Rennie but rebuilt by LCC between 1937 and 1944 to plans of Sir Giles Gilbert Scott, opened by Herbert Morrison 1945.
Hungerford	Rail & Foot	1863	Suspension bridge built by Brunel 1845 but rebuilt 1863 as Rail & Foot bridge designed by Sir John Hawkshaw.
Westminster	Road	1750	Leads from Westminster Abbey and Houses of Parliament to the former County Hall and St Thomas' Hospital. The bridge was rebuilt in 1862.
Lambeth	Road	1862	Leads from Millbank in the north to Lambeth Palace. Rebuilt in 1932.
Vauxhall	Road	1816	Leads from Millbank in the north to Kennington Lane. Rebuilt in 1906.
Grosvenor	Rail	1860	Rebuilt 1967.
Chelsea	Road	1934	Built 1858 but rebuilt as suspension bridge 1934 and widened 1937.
Albert	Road	1873	Restructured by Sir Joseph Bazalgette in 1884 and strengthened 1973.
Battersea	Road	1772	Built of wood by Henry Holland and rebuilt by Bazalgette 1890.
Battersea	Rail	1863	
Wandsworth	Road	1873	Rebuilt 1940.
Putney	Rail	1889	
Putney	Road	1729	Rebuilt by Bazalgette 1886.
Hammersmith	Road	1827	Rebuilt by Bazalgette 1887 and the first London suspension bridge.
Barnes	Rail & Foot	1849	Restructured 1893.
Chiswick	Road	1933	Built by Sir Herbert Baker and Alfred Dryland.
Kew	Rail	1869	

From East to West	Type	Opened	
Kew	Road	1759	Rebuilt and renamed The King Edward VII Bridge 1903.
Richmond Lock	Foot	1894	
Twickenham	Road	1933	
Richmond	Rail	1848	Restructured 1908.
Richmond	Road	1777	Widened 1937.
Teddington Lock	Foot	1889	
Kingston	Road	1828	Widened 1914.
Hampton Court	Road	1753	Replaced by iron bridge 1865 and rebuilt 1933.

Postal Areas

E1	Whitechapel	SW1	Belgravia	EC4	Fleet St
E2	Bethnal Green	SW2	Brixton		
E3	Bow	SW3	Chelsea	SE1	Southwark
E4	Chingford	SW4	Clapham	SE2	Abbey Wood
E5	Clapton	SW5	Earls Court	SE3	Blackheath
E6	East Ham	SW6	Fulham	SE4	Brockley
E7	Forest Gate	SW7	South Kensington	SE5	Camberwell
E8	Hackney	SW8	South Lambeth	SE6	Catford
E9	Homerton	SW9	Stockwell	SE7	Charlton
E10	Leyton	SW10	West Brompton	SE8	Deptford
E11	Leytonstone	SW11	Battersea	SE9	Eltham
E12	Manor Park	SW12	Balham	SE10	Greenwich
E13	Plaistow	SW13	Barnes	SE12	Lee
E14	Poplar	SW14	Mortlake	SE13	Lewisham
E15	Stratford	SW15	Putney	SE14	New Cross
E16	Victoria Docks	SW16	Streatham	SE15	Peckham
E17	Walthamstow	SW17	Tooting	SE16	Rotherhithe
E18	South Woodford	SW18	Wandsworth	SE17	Walworth
		SW19	Wimbledon	SE18	Woolwich
N1	Islington	SW20	West Wimbledon	SE19	Norwood
N2	East Finchley			SE20	Anerley
N3	Finchley (Church End)	W1	Mayfair	SE21	Dulwich
N4	Finsbury Park	W2	Paddington	SE22	East Dulwich
N5	Highbury	W3	Acton	SE23	Forest Hill
N6	Highgate	W4	Chiswick	SE24	Herne Hill
N7	Holloway	W5	Ealing	SE25	South Norwood
N8	Hornsey	W6	Hammersmith	SE26	Sydenham
N9	Lower Edmonton	W7	Hanwell	SE27	West Norwood
N10	Muswell Hill	W8	Kensington	SE28	Thamesmead
N11	New Southgate	W9	Maida Vale		
N12	North Finchley	W10	North Kensington	NW1	Camden Town
N13	Palmers Green	W11	Notting Hill	NW2	Cricklewood
N14	Southgate	W12	Shepherds Bush	NW3	Hampstead
N15	South Tottenham	W13	West Ealing	NW4	Hendon
N16	Stoke Newington	W14	West Kensington	NW5	Kentish Town
N17	Tottenham			NW6	Kilburn
N18	Upper Edmonton	WC1	Bloomsbury	NW7	Mill Hill
N19	Upper Holloway	WC2	St James	NW8	Marylebone
N20	Whetstone			NW9	Kingsbury
N21	Winchmore Hill	EC1	Finsbury	NW10	Willesden
N22	Wood Green	EC2	City	NW11	Golders Green
		EC3	Spitalfields		

LONDON

General Information

Admiralty Arch (SW1)   Built in 1910 to the design of Sir Aston Webb (who also designed the façade of Buckingham Palace) and consisting of 3 identical arches. Situated where the Mall leads into Trafalgar Square.

Alexandra Palace (N22)   Sited in Muswell Hill and built in 1875 by Meeson and Johnson.

Alsop, William   Designer of North Greenwich Jubilee Line Station.

Art galleries   Tate Gallery, Millbank; Tate Modern, Bankside; National Gallery, Trafalgar Square; National Portrait Gallery, St Martin's Place; Wallace Collection, W1; Courtauld Institute, Strand; Sir John Soane's Museum, Lincoln's Inn Fields; William Morris Gallery, Forest Rd, E17; Queen's Gallery in Buckingham Palace; Dulwich Picture Gallery built by Sir John Soane 1811–13, England's oldest public art gallery.

Banqueting House   Designed by Inigo Jones in 1622 and the only part of Whitehall Palace still standing.

Belfast, HMS (SE1)   Built in 1939 and situated at Symon's Wharf in Vine Lane, this 11,000-ton cruiser, the largest ever built was opened to the public in 1971.

Big Ben   Housed in St Stephen's Tower within the Houses of Parliament (Palace of Westminster) Big Ben, weighing in at 13.5 tons, is the name of the large bell housed in the clock tower and named after, either Benjamin Caunt, a popular boxer of the day (1858), or more likely Sir Benjamin Hall, the Chief Commissioner of Works.

Billingsgate Market (EC3)   Fish market in Lower Thames St, in use for over 7 centuries, which closed on 16 Jan 1982.

Billingsgate Market (E14)   Opened on the Isle of Dogs 3 days after the original market closed.

Birdcage Walk (SW1)   Here stood the aviary of James I.

Birkbeck College (WC1)   Founded in 1823 as the London mechanics' Institution. Took its present name in 1907 and became part of the University of London in 1920. Situated in Malet Street.

Bishop of London, first   St Mellitus, c. AD 604.

Blackfriars Bridge   Roberto Calvi, an Italian banker, found hanging beneath it on 19 June 1982.

Blue Plaques   William Ewart had the idea of using these to commemorate famous people, and Lord Byron was the first to have a plaque conferred on the house where he was born in Holles St, Westminster.

British Library   Formed in 1973 from the amalgamation of the British Museum Library, National Central Library and National Lending Library. Now situated at St Pancras.

British Museum (WC1)   Founded in 1753, initially to house the collection of Hans Sloane (1660–1753), it was opened to the public in 1759 at Montague House. The present museum was built on the same site in 1823–47 to a design of Robert Smirke. The ethnographical department of the museum is called The Museum of Mankind. Among the best known of the museum's treasures are the Elgin Marbles, Portland Vase, Mildenhall Treasure, Rosetta Stone, Sutton Hoo, Lewis Chessman, and the Lindow Man. Recent millennium renovations include the museum's inner courtyard, hidden from the public for 150 years being turned into the 'Great Court'

covered with a spectacular glass and steel roof designed by Norman Foster.

British Telecom Tower   Designed by Eric Bedford and stands 580' high with a 40' mast giving an overall height of 620'. Originally called the Post Office Tower and nowadays simply the Telecom Tower.

Burghers of Calais replica   Sited in Victoria Tower Gardens.

Canary Wharf Tower   Designed by Cesar Pelli and at 850 feet exceeds the British Telecom Tower as Britain's tallest structure. Officially called No. 1 Canada Square.

Centre of London   Charing Cross is now used as the point for measuring distances to other places.

Charing Cross Station (WC2)   Situated just off the Strand and designed by Sir John Hawkshaw in 1864.

Clink Street (SE1)   Site of the Bishop of Winchester's London estate and synonymous with the name of his Ecclesiastical prison.

Clubs   Boodle's; Brooks's; Carlton; White's (all situated in St James's St, SW1); Beefsteak; Garrick; Pratt's (all the waiters are called George); Reform (Pall Mall), Athenaeum, Portland, Savile, Travellers, Groucho.

Coal Tax   Christopher Wren's 50 new churches were paid for by a tax on coal entering London.

Cockneys   Must be born within the sound of the church bells of St Mary le Bow.

Concert halls: famous   Barbican Hall; Royal Festival Hall & Queen Elizabeth Hall; Royal Albert Hall; Wigmore Hall; London Coliseum; Royal Opera House.

Congestion charge   From 17 February 2003 motorists driving into central London pay £5 (due to rise to £8 in July 2005) for the privilege!

Courtauld Institute of Art   Owned by the University of London and situated at Somerset House on the Strand.

Covent Garden Market (WC2)   London's main wholesale fruit, flower and vegetable market. Congestion in Central London caused its closure in 1974 after 340 years trading. The New Covent Garden Market was opened immediately at the former railway yard at Nine Elms, Battersea.

Denmark St   Aka Tin Pan Alley; home of the music publishing industry.

Docklands Light Railway   Opened in 1987 and now extended from the Isle of Dogs to Bank.

Drainage system   Designed by Joseph Bazalgette between 1859 and 1875 and still serving as the basis of London's sewage system.

Eel Pie Island, Twickenham   Joined to the mainland by an old rickety concrete bridge, about 3' wide. Made famous in the 1960s when the Rolling Stones played a concert there.

Football clubs: oldest   Fulham (formed in 1879); Leyton Orient (1881); Spurs (1882); QPR (1885); Millwall (1885); Arsenal (1886); Brentford (1889); Wimbledon (1889); West Ham (1900); Chelsea (1905); Crystal Palace (1905); Charlton (1905).

Fringe theatres (not listed in main table)   Arcola; Artsdepot; Barons Court; Blue Elephant; Brockley Jack; Bull; Camden People's; Chelsea; Chicken Shed; Clapham Common; Diorama; Etcetera; Finborough; Hanover Grand; Hen and Chickens;

Hoxton Hall; Jackson's Lane; Laban; Little Angel; Menier; Millfield Arts; North Garden; Oval House; Pentameters; Pleasance; Questors; Roundhouse; Shaw; Southwark Playhouse; Stratford Circus; Tabard; Theatre 503; Tristan Bates; Union; Warehouse; Waterman's; White Bear.

Fulham Palace Official residence of the Bishop of London until 1973.

Greater London Consists of 31 boroughs and the cities of Westminster and London.

Greater London Council Created in 1965, but abolished in 1986. Originally called the London County Council, formed 1889.

Greenwich Palace (SE10) Built by Humphrey Deele of Gloucester in 1426 and now the site of the Royal Naval Hospital.

Gun salutes A salute of 62 guns is fired at the Tower of London on the birthdays of HRH Prince Philip, HM Queen Elizabeth, the Queen Mother and HM the Queen, who also has a 62-gun salute on accession and coronation day. A 42-gun salute is fired at the Tower of London and Hyde Park on other state occasions, e.g. opening and dissolution of Parliament, the birth of a royal infant, or a royal procession through London.

Hampton Court Maze Constructed for William and Mary (1690).

Highgate Hill Dick Whittington supposedly 'turned' here and became Lord Mayor.

Hyde Park Corner (SW1) Historic entrance to London from the west via the tollgate through Kensington and Knightsbridge.

Imperial War Museum Opened in 1920, and since 1935 occupying the remaining part of the old Bethlehem Royal Hospital, opened in 1815.

Livery Companies Craft guilds set up to promote the various trades of London. The Weavers are the oldest established guild whilst the Mercers are thought of as the senior guild. At present there are 102 city guilds, The Water Conservators being the latest set up in 2000.

Lloyd's of London Insurance underwriting corporation functional since the late 17th century, housed since 1986 in a headquarters designed by Richard Rogers.

London Eye Situated on the South Bank between the Hungerford and Westminster bridges. The British Airways London Eye is administered by the Tussauds Group. The diameter of the wheel is 135 metres (450 feet) and the architects were David Marks and Julia Barfield. The eye is also known as The Millennium Wheel.

London Gazette Henry Muddiman started it in 1665. It is published on Tuesdays and Fridays, as the official organ of Britain's government. It was known as the *Oxford Gazette* for the first 23 bulletins.

London Stone Now set in the wall of the Bank of China, Cannon St, and possibly once used by the Romans as a measuring point.

Marble Arch Designed by John Nash to commemorate Nelson's victories, erected on side of Buckingham Palace in 1827, moved to Hyde Park in 1851.

Marylebone Road Site of Madame Tussaud's and the Planetarium.

May Day Parade Traditional parade through Hyde Park.

Mayor Ken Livingstone (as at April 2005).

Monument (EC2) Contains 311 steps and commemorates the nearby spot in Pudding Lane where the Great Fire started in 1666. Designed by Christopher Wren, the total height is 202 feet.

Museum: Childhood Situated in Bethnal Green. Administered by the Victoria and Albert Museum, opened in 1872.

Museum of London (EC2) Opened in 1976 and illustrating the history of London from prehistoric times to the present day.

Museum: Wellington Apsley House, Hyde Park Corner. Administered by the Victoria and Albert Museum.

National History Museum (SW7) Situated near the V & A Museum in Cromwell Rd and opened in 1881 to a design of Alfred Waterhouse. Merged with the Ecological Museum in 1985.

National Maritime Museum (SE10) Founded in 1932.

New Scotland Yard (SW1) Metropolitan Police HQ situated near Victoria Street since 1967. The previous Scotland Yard building on the North Bank near Westminster Bridge was completed by Norman Shaw in 1890, after the original building at the top of Whitehall was damaged by a Fenian bomb in 1884.

Oldest club White's, founded 1693.

Oldest theatre The Theatre Royal, Drury Lane, its present auditorium being built in 1812.

Palace of Westminster (SW1) The first palace was built for Edward the Confessor, not completed till 1858, but after the fire of 1834 its replacement was designed to become the home of both Houses of Parliament. Charles Barry's design was preferred to 96 other entrants, and he brought in Augustus Pugin to provide the Gothic interiors. The House of Commons was rebuilt by Giles Gilbert Scott after the bombing of 1941. St Stephen's Tower tops the Commons building, whilst the Victoria Tower stands at the southern end, at the other extreme from Big Ben.

Parks (central London) Green, Hyde, Regent's, St James's, Kensington Gardens.

Pelicans Live in St James's Park.

Peter Pan Statue in Kensington Gardens sculpted by George Frampton in 1912.

Petticoat Lane (E1) East London's long-established Sunday market (8am to 2pm) on Middlesex Street. Originally called Hog Lane Market in the 15th century. Given the name Petticoat Lane around 1600 because of its clothes stalls.

Piccadilly Circus Junction of Haymarket, Regent St, Piccadilly, Shaftesbury Avenue, Coventry Street.

Planetarium Opened in 1958 in Marylebone Rd, next to Madame Tussaud's.

Pool of London A reach of Thames consisting of two parts: the Lower running from Limekiln Creek to Cherry Garden Pier, and the Upper, from Cherry Garden Pier to London Bridge. Tower Bridge divides the two.

Queen's House, Greenwich Started by Inigo Jones during the reign of James I, as a gift to his wife Anne of Denmark; eventually completed in 1640. Now the centrepiece of the National Maritime Museum.

Ratcliff Highway Murders Seven victims were murdered in 2 incidents on this street in present-day Stepney in Dec. 1811. John Williams, a lodger at the Pear Tree public house, was arrested but hanged himself before his trial. The incident was a spur to the eventual forming of the Metropolitan Police in 1829.

Richard II Oldest painting of an English monarch from life (late 14th century), in Westminster Abbey.

LONDON

Roman Gates of London Wall   Aldgate; Aldersgate; Bishopsgate; Cripplegate; Ludgate; Newgate.

Royal Academy   Founded by Joshua Reynolds in 1768, and originally site at Somerset House. Established in 1868 at Burlington House. Piccadilly Sackler Galleries added in 1990 by Norman Foster.

Royal Courts of Justice   Designed by George Street in 1868 and situated on the north side of the Strand, the courts hear civil cases and criminal appeals. Opened by Queen Victoria in 1882 the Supreme Court is made up of the High Court, Court of Appeal and Crown Court. The High Court has 3 divisions: Queen's Bench, Family and Chancery. There are over 150 judges in the Royal Courts of Justice, a corridor known as the Chicken Run, and a recent wing named after St Thomas More. A tributary of the River Fleet is reputed to run under the building.

Royal Exchange (EC3)   Founded by Thomas Gresham in 1566 as the 'Bourse' and proclaimed the Royal Exchange by Elizabeth I in 1570. First building destroyed in the Great Fire in 1666; second burned down in 1838; third completed 1842.

Royal National Theatre   Building on the South Bank opened in 1976 and designed by Denys Lasdun. Lyttelton was 1st of the 3 auditoria to open, followed by the Olivier and Cottesloe.

Science Museum (SW7)   Originally housed in the Victoria and Albert Museum but moved into its own building, across Exhibition Road, in 1913. The museum is the world's pre-eminent museum of science, medicine and technology. The Wellcome Wing, designed by Richard MacCormac, was opened in 2000 in partnership with the Wellcome Trust, Science Museum, and the Heritage Lottery Fund.

St James's Palace (SW1)   Built by Henry VIII.

St Paul's Cathedral   The new St Paul's Cathedral was built by Sir Christopher Wren between 1675 and 1710. The frescoes depicting the life of St Paul, above the Whispering Gallery on the underside of the dome are by James Thornhill. In the lower part of the south-west tower stands William Kempster's Geometrical Staircase and the clock room in the upper part houses Great Tom, the largest of three bells. The original St Paul's was built in 604 in the reign of St Ethelbert of Kent, the first Christian king in England, only to be destroyed by fire soon after. Two more rebuildings took place, culminating in the destruction by the Great Fire of 1666, when the only monument to survive was that of John Donne, the poet, who had been Dean of St Paul's for the last 10 years of his life. From pavement to the top of the cross on the tower of the dome, St Paul's is 365 feet high.

Silent Change   Annual ceremony to admit the new Lord Mayor.

Smithfield Market (EC1)   London's largest meat market which, although in decline, employs its own police force.

Somerset House   Designed by Sir William Chambers in the late 18th century and situated on the Strand.

Stock Exchange (EC2)   The new Stock Exchange opened in June 1973, replacing a building opened in 1888.

Strawberry Hill   Horace Walpole's Twickenham residence, built in 1748 and much extended, which is now the Roman Catholic St Mary's College of Higher Education.

Thames   No native name is known before Julius Caesar called the river 'Tamesis'. After Kent it is the oldest place name in England. Since 1996 it has been controlled by the Environment Agency.

Thames Embankments   Victoria Embankment on the north side of the river, running from Westminster to Blackfriars, the Albert Embankment on the south side from Westminster Bridge to Vauxhall, and the Chelsea Embankment, from Chelsea Bridge to Battersea Bridge were constructed by Sir J W Bazalgette.

Thames tunnels   The first tunnel under the Thames, completed in 1843, and linking Wapping and Rotherhithe, was called the 'Thames Tunnel' and is still in existence as a railway tunnel. The oldest road tunnel is the old Blackwall, opened in 1897; other road tunnels include the new Blackwall (1967), Rotherhithe (1908), and Dartford (1963 and 1980). The only foot tunnel still in existence runs from Greenwich to the Isle of Dogs.

Thames reaches   Starting from the mouth and proceeding upriver, the reaches are: Sea Reach (Yantlet Creek to West Blyth Buoy); Lower Hope (to Coalhouse Point); Gravesend (to Tilburyness); Northfleet Hope (to Broadness); St Clement's or Fiddlers' (to Stoneness); Long (to Dartford Creek); Erith Rands (to Coalharbour Point); Erith (to Jenningtree Point); Halfway (to Crossness); Barking (to Tripcock Point); Gallions (to Woolwich Hoba Wharf); Woolwich (to Lyle Park); Bugsby's (to Blackwell Point); Blackwall (to Dudgeon's Dock); Greenwich (to Deptford Creek); Limehouse (to Limekiln Creek); Lower Pool (to Cherry Garden Pier); Upper Pool (to London Bridge); London Bridge to Westminster Bridge and Westminster Bridge to Vauxhall Bridge (both nameless); Nine Elms (to Chelsea Bridge); Chelsea (to Battersea Bridge); Battersea (to Wandsworth Bridge); Wandsworth (to Putney Bridge); Barn Elms (to Hammersmith Bridge); Chiswick (to Chiswick Ferry); Corney (to Barnes Railway Bridge); and Mortlake (to Kew Bridge).

Theatre: largest   Coliseum.

Tower of London: first foundation   White Tower built by Gundul, bishop of Rochester, between 1078 and 1098.

Tower of London: Crown Jewels first housed   During reign of Henry III.

Tower of London: last beheading   Simon Fraser, Lord Lovat, in 1747. Last execution: Joseph Jacobs (15 Aug 1941).

Tower of London: last Monarch to occupy   James I.

Tower of London: Towers   Beauchamp; Bell; Bloody; Bowyer; Brick; Broad Arrow; Byward; Constable; Cradle; Devereux; Develin; Flint; Lanthorn; Martin; Middle; Salt; St Thomas's; Wakefield; Wardrobe (no longer standing); Well; White (the oldest).

Underground   First stretch of underground electric railway between City and Stockwell opened in 1890. John Fowler and Sir Benjamin Baker engineered the work.

Other British Underground systems in Glasgow, Liverpool, and Newcastle.

Metropolitan Railway, using steam locomotives, opened in 1863 and ran from Paddington to Farringdon St. Harry Beck (1902–74) redesigned the map in 1931 and his use of straight lines and a colour-coding system for the different lines is still in use.

Underground Map   Albert Stanley, Lord Ashfield, issued first map in 1908. The present colour-coded map was implemented in 1933 from a design by Harry Beck.

Unknown Warrior's Tomb   Westminster Abbey.

Victoria and Albert Museum (SW7)   The national museum of fine and applied art and design. Founded in 1852, and moved to its present site in 1857, being known then as the South Kensington Museum. The building was designed by Aston Webb and given its current name in 1899.

Wallace Collection   Art collection in Hertford House, Manchester Square, W1. Most famous work: *The Laughing Cavalier*.

Wardour St   Once used as a term to denote the British film industry.

Westminster Abbey: founder   St Edward the Confessor.

Westminster Abbey: Nave   At the end of the Nave, just in front of the Great West Door, is a memorial to Winston Churchill and nearby is the grave of the Unknown Warrior, commemorating those who were killed in WW1. The graves and memorials in the Nave include those of David Livingstone, David Lloyd George, Clement Attlee, Ramsay MacDonald, Isaac Newton, Lord and Lady Baden-Powell and F D Roosevelt.

Westminster Abbey: Poets' Corner   Graves and memorials of most of the major English poets and some writers and musicians. The foremost tomb is that of Geoffrey Chaucer, the first to be buried there, and the foremost memorial is that of William Shakespeare. Among the 20th-century poets commemorated are W H Auden, Dylan Thomas and T S Eliot. Gerard Manley Hopkins (1844–89),

although buried in Glasnevin Cemetery, Dublin, has a commemorative plaque. Samuel Johnson, Charles Dickens and G F Handel are also buried there, and Oscar Wilde has been commemorated on floor and window.

Westminster Abbey: Royal Tombs   Elizabeth I; Mary I; Edward the Confessor; Henry VII; James I; Edward VI; George II; Henry III; Edward I; Edward III; Richard II; Henry V; Anne; Charles II; William III; Mary II and Mary Stewart; Queen of Scotland and France.

Westminster Abbey: Tomb of Elizabeth & Mary   Latin inscription on their tomb reads: 'Consorts both in throne and grave, here sleep we two sisters, Elizabeth and Mary, in the hope of one resurrection.'

Westminster Cathedral (SW1)   Roman Catholic Cathedral in Francis St, SW1, built of brick and Portland stone, to the design of John Francis Bentley and completed in 1903.

Westminster Hall   Built by William Rufus between 1097 and 1099, home of the Royal Courts of Justice till they moved to the Strand in 1882, and incorporated in the Houses of Parliament.

White Lodge   Built in 1727–8 in Richmond Park and formerly a royal residence, it is now the Royal Ballet School.

Whitehall Palace   Tudor Palace much used by Henry VIII (died there in 1547) but William III found the river air exacerbated his asthma so transferred the royal residence to Kensington Palace. Only the Banqueting House, a later addition, survived the fire that destroyed the palace in 1698.

Zoo   Founded by Sir Stamford Raffles; opened in 1828 after his death. Aviary designed by Lord Snowdon and opened in 1965.

L
O
N
D
O
N

MEDICINE

Medical Discoveries

Discovery	Date	Discoverer	Nationality
adrenal gland: function of	1856	Alfred Vulpian	French
adrenalin	1901	Jokichi Takamine	Japanese
AIDS	1981	Lost Angeles scientists	American
antisepsis	1865	Joseph Lister	British
blood circulation	1628	William Harvey	British
blood groups	1901	Karl Landsteiner	Austrian
chloroform	1847	James Simpson	British
chromosomes	1888	Thomas Morgan	American
corpuscles, red	1684	Antoni van Leeuwenhoek	Dutch
cortisone	1934	Edward Kendall	American
diabetes, cause of	1901	Eugene Opic	American
diphtheria bacillus	1884	Edwin Klebs and Friedrich Löffler	German
DNA, structure of	1953	Francis Crick and James Watson	British/American
Down's Syndrome, cause of	1959	Dr Jerome, Lejeune	French
electro-encephalogram	1929	Hans Berger	German
endorphins	1975	Hughes, Guillemin	American
enzymes	1833	Anselme Payen, Jean-François Persoz	French
ether as anaesthetic	1846	William Morton	American
heparin	1915	Jay McLean	American
heredity	1865	Gregor Mendel	Austrian
HIV virus, isolated	1983	Luc Montagnier (among others)	French
insulin, isolated	1921	F G Banting, C H Best, J J R McLeod	Canadian
interferon	1957	A Isaacs, J Lindemann	UK/Swiss
leprosy bacillus	1869	Gerhard Hansen	Norwegian
microbes	1762	M A Plenciz	Austrian
morphine	1805	Friedrich Sertürner	German
nitrous oxide	1776	Joseph Priestley	British
nucleic acid	1869	J F Miescher	Swiss
penicillin	1928	Alexander Fleming	British
protozoa	1675	Antoni van Leeuwenhoek	Dutch
rabies vaccination	1885	Louis Pasteur	French
Rhesus factor	1939	Karl Landsteiner, A S Wiener	Austrian
scurvy, treatment of	1740	James Lind	British
sleeping sickness transmission	1895	David Bruce	British
smallpox vaccination	1796	Edward Jenner	British
streptomycin	1943	Selman Waksman	American
tomography	1915	André Bocage	French
tuberculosis bacillus	1882	Robert Koch	German
typhus bacillus	1880	Karl Eberth	German
vitamin A	1913	E McCollum, M Davis, T Osborne, L Mendel	American
vitamin B (niacin)	1913	Casimir Funk	Polish
vitamin B1 (thiamin)	1897	Christiaan Eijkman	Dutch
vitamin B2 (riboflavin)	1933	R Kuhn, A von Szent-Gyorgi, J Wagner-Jauregg	Austrian/ Hungarian/ Austrian
vitamin B3	1937	Madden, Strong, Wooley, Elvehjem	British/American
vitamin B5	1933	R J Williams	American
vitamin B6	1936	Birch, A von Szent-Gyorgi	US/Hungarian
vitamin B9	1938	Day	British
vitamin B12	1937	G R Minot, W P Murphy	British
vitamin C (isolated)	1928	A von Szent-Gyorgi	Hungarian
vitamin D (isolated)	1924	Steenbock, Hess, Weinstock	German
vitamin E	1923	H M Evans, Bishop	American
vitamin K1	1934	Carl Peter Henrik Dam	Danish
vitamins, necessity of	1906	Sir Frederick Hopkins	British
X-rays	1892	Heinrich Hertz	German
X-rays, properties of	1895	Wilhelm Röntgen	German
yellow fever, mosquito transmission	1881	Ronald Ross	British

Bones in the Human Body

skull

occipital	1
parietal – 1 pair	2
sphenoid	1
ethmoid	1
inferior nasal conchae – 1 pair	2
frontal – 1 pair fused	1
nasal – 1 pair	2
lacrimal – 1 pair	2
temporal – 1 pair	2
maxilla – 1 pair	2
zygomatic – 1 pair	2
vomer	1
palatine – 1 pair	2
mandible – 1 pair fused	1
	22

arms

upper arm:	humerus – 1 pair	2
lower arm:	radius –1 pair	2
	ulna – 1 pair	2
carpus:	scaphoid – 1 pair	2
	lunate – 1 pair	2
	triquetral – 1 pair	2
	pisiform – 1 pair	2
	trapezium – 1 pair	2
	trapezoid – 1 pair	2
	capitate – 1 pair	2
	hamate – 1 pair	2
metacarpals – 5 pairs		10
phalanges:	1st digit – 2 pairs	4
	2nd digit – 3 pairs	6
	3rd digit – 3 pairs	6
	4th digit – 3 pairs	6
	5th digit – 3 pairs	6
		60

hip bones (pelvic girdle)

ilium fused with ischium and pubis – 1 pair	2

ears

malleus	2
incus	2
stapes	2
	6

vertebrae

cervical	7
thoracic	12
lumbar	5
sacral – 5 fused to form sacrum	1
coccyx – fused joint	1
	26

ribs

true ribs – 7 pairs	14
false ribs – 5 pairs (2 floaters)	10
	24

sternum

manubrium	1
sternebrae	1
xiphisternum	1
	3

throat

hyoid	1

pectoral girdle

clavicle – 1 pair	2
scapula – 1 pair	2
	4

legs

upper leg:	femur – 1 pair	2
lower leg:	tibia – 1 pair	2
	fibula – 1 pair	2
tarsus:	talus – 1 pair	2
	calcaneus – 1 pair	2
	navicular – 1 pair	2
	medial cuneiform – 1 pair	2
	intermediate cuneiform – 1 pair	2
	lateral cuneiform – 1 pair	2
	cuboid – 1 pair	2
metatarsals – 5 pairs		10
phalanges	1st digit – 2 pairs	4
	2nd digit – 3 pairs	6
	3rd digit – 3 pairs	6
	4th digit – 3 pairs	6
	5th digit – 3 pairs	6
		58

Total

skull	22
arms	60
hips	2
ears	6
vertebrae	26
ribs	24
sternum	3
throat	1
pectoral girdle	4
legs	58
	206

MEDICINE

General Information

abdomen   contains most of the digestive system. It is the biggest cavity in the body, extending from underneath the diaphragm to the groin area and bounded at the back of the body by the spine, and round its upper sides by the ribs. The abdomen contains the alimentary canal, liver, spleen, kidneys and pancreas.

acid in stomach   hydrochloric.

acupuncture   Traditional acupuncture is based on the principle that our health is dependent on the bal-anced functioning of the body's motivating energy, known as Qi (ch'i). This Qi flows throughout the body, but is concentrated in channels beneath the skin, known as meridians. The aim of treatment is to restore the balance between the equal and opposite qualities of Qi, namely the Yin and Yang.

The Human body is composed of 12 meridians that mirror themselves on the left and right side of the body. Each of these meridians contains / is a part of muscles, tendons, ligaments and a surrounding facia that stretches all along the meridian, a bit like a string of sausages. From childhood there were times when we felt that powerful emotions would overwhelm us. We learnt to suppress these overwhelming emotions by contracting muscles within us. These contractions become habitual and are thought to have an effect on the body structure affecting bone alignment in the joints, spine and cranium. When the body structure is distorted (extremely common) nerves can get pinched or stretched, internal body organs become distorted, hormonal glands under- or overproduce, joints can wear out quicker, and various muscles and tendons may become shortened or overstretched. Stress is the most common cause of this distortion, but there are other common factors that will also affect our health and well-being. These include diet, drugs and lack of appropriate exercise.

Acupuncture treats the body as a whole – the physical, mental (emotional) & psychic (spirit) levels, not only the disease or ailment. It is an ancient art of healing developed over thousands of years and works by stimulating the Qi and eliminating all toxins from the body. This is achieved by stimulation of specific energy points. Acupuncture can be done without needle – laser, electro-acupuncture, finger pressure (shiatsu) or ultrasound. It is not a substitute for conventional medicine but acts to compliment it. It was popularised in the Western world in 1972 following Richard Nixon's visit to China and his championing of its benefits.

There are hundreds of acupuncture points throughout the body, but here is a list of the main 12 meridians:

(1) the Lung Channel of Hand, (2) the Large Intestine Channel of Hand, (3) the Stomach Channel of Foot, (4) the Spleen Channel of Foot, (5) the Heart Channel of Hand, (6) the Small Intestine Channel of Hand, (7) the Urinary Bladder Channel of Foot, (8) the Kidney Channel of Foot, (9) the Pericardium Channel of Hand, (10) the Triple Burner Channel of Hand, (11) the Gall Bladder Channel of Foot, (12) the Liver Channel of Foot.

Notes: The lungs (Yin) and large intestine (Yang) are paired organs. Their opening is the nose, and they govern skin and hair. The main function of the large intestine is the metabolism of water and the passing of water. The spleen (Yin) and the stomach (Yang) are paired organs. Their opening is the mouth and they control the flesh and the limbs.The spleen is the main organ of digestion. Its function is to transport nutrients and regulate the blood (keep it within the channels). It is responsible for the transformation of food into nourishment. The stomach receives food while the spleen transports nutrients. The stomach moves things downward while the spleen moves things upward.

The heart (Yin) and the small intestine (Yang) are paired organs. Their point of entry is the tongue. They control the blood vessels and are reflected in the face. The heart governs the blood vessels and is responsible for moving blood through them. It also stores the spirit, and is the organ usually associated with mental processes.The major function of the small intestine is to separate waste material from the nutritious elements in food. The nutritious elements are then distributed throughout the body and the waste is sent on to the large intestine. The kidneys (Yin) and the urinary bladder (Yang) are paired organs. Their opening is the urethra. They control the bones, marrow, and brain, and their health is

reflected in the hair of the head. The kidneys store Original Essence (Yuan Jing) and are therefore responsible for growth, development, and reproductive functions. They play the primary role in water metabolism and control the body's liquids, and also hold the body's most basic Yin and Yang. The main function of the urinary bladder is to transform fluids into urine and excrete it from the body. The pericardium (Yin) and the triple burner (Yang) are paired organs. Though the pericardium has no separate physiological functions, it is generally mentioned with regard to the delirium induced by high fevers. The triple burner is regarded as 'having a name but no form' but is considered to be an organ that coordinates all the functions of water metabolism.

The liver (Yin) and the gall bladder (Yang) are considered paired organs. Their point of entry is the eyes. They control the sinews (muscles and joints), and their health is reflected in the finger and toe nails. The main task of the liver is spreading and regulating Qi throughout the entire body. Its unique character is flowing and free, so depression or frustration can disturb its functioning. In addition, the liver is responsible for storing blood when the body is at rest. This characteristic, together with its control over the lower abdomen, makes it the most critical organ in terms of women's menstrual cycle and sexuality. The main function of the gall bladder is storing and excreting the bile produced by the liver.

adrenal glands glands that produce adrenalin, which prepares the body for stress by increasing heart rate and blood pressure. They also produce cortisone, which has a variety of metabolic effects.

allergy term used by Clemens von Pirquet (1874–1929) in 1906 following his observations of the skin reaction to his test for tuberculosis.

allopathy treatment of disease by conventional means – i.e. with drugs having opposite effects to the symptoms (opposite of homoeopathy).

Alzheimer's disease serious disorder of the brain manifesting itself in premature senility. Named after the German neurologist Alois Alzheimer (1864–1915), who first identified it.

analeptic drug restores and invigorates.

anaphylaxis an extreme, often life-threatening reaction to an antigen, e.g. to a bee sting, due to hypersensitivity following an earlier dose.

anaplasty medical name for plastic surgery.

anatomy The science of the bodily structure of animals and plants.

angioplasty surgical technique for restoring normal blood flow through an artery by means of laser therapy or insertion of a balloon into the narrowed section.

artery tubular thick-walled muscular vessel that conveys oxygenated blood from the heart, the largest being the aorta.

Asperger's syndrome mild variant of autism diagnosed in 1994. Sufferers may have extraordinary compensating talents, e.g. musical prodigy Joseph Erber (born 1984).

axilla anatomical name for the armpit.

biology the study of living organisms.

blepharitis inflammation of the eyelids.

blood: circulation time 23 seconds on average.

blood content in body varies slightly, but average man has 12 pts (5.6 litres) and woman 7 pts (3.3 litres), making the average 9 pints in general. An approximate calculation for adults is 60 millilitres per kilogram of body weight.

blood groups A, B, AB, O. Blood groups may also be divided into Rhesus negative and positive. The most common group is O, which is universally given, and AB can receive from any group.

blood pressure: readings systolic is highest blood pressure reading; diastolic is lowest. Abnormally high or low conditions are called hypertension and hypotension respectively.

body builds the classification system is called somatotype and consists of: ectomorph (tall), endomorph (fat), mesomorph (muscular).

bones consist mainly of collagen, calcium phosphate and inorganic salts, mainly hydroxyapatite. The smallest is the stapes and the largest the femur. The only non-connected bone is the hyoid in the throat.

bradycardia abnormally slow heart action.

brain the brain contains 10,000 million nerve cells, each of which has a potential 25,000 inter-connections with other cells. Average weight of the brain is 3lb (1.4 kg). The left side is the rational side.

calcaneus heel bone.

cells the smallest cell in the human body is the male sperm, the largest is the female ovum.

central nervous system brain and spinal cord (vertebrates).

Chinese restaurant syndrome the so-called illness caused by monosodium glutamate. There is no evidence that the symptoms of dizziness and headaches affect more than a tiny proportion of people.

cholangiography X-ray examination of the bile ducts used to locate obstructions.

cholecystography X-ray examination of the gall bladder used to detect the presence of gall stones.

chromosomes there are 23 pairs in the human body, the female having two X sex chromosomes while the male has one XY pair. They carry the gene sequence and, therefore, full genetic blueprint.

collagen protein of great tensile strength present in bones, cartilage, tendons, ligaments and the skin.

colostrum mother's first breast-product after a birth before milk flow begins. Contains antibodies that bring important immunities.

comedo medical name for a blackhead.

conjunctivitis aka pink eye.

cornea convex transparent membrane that forms the forward covering of the eyeball; it is the only part of the body devoid of blood supply.

couéism form of auto-suggestion propagated by Emile Coué (1857–1926). A key phrase was: 'Every day, and in every way, I am becoming better and better.'

coxa (aka innominate bone) hip bone or joint (contrast ilium).

Crohn's disease chronic inflammatory disease of the intestines, especially the colon and ileum, causing ulcers and fistulae. Named after B B Crohn, US pathologist (1874–1983).

crural of the leg.

cubital of the forearm.

dentine calcified tissue of tooth.

diaphragm dome-shaped muscular partition that separates the abdominal and thoracic cavities.

disease: most widespread tooth and gum disease.

Down's syndrome: cause extra chromosome (three number 21s instead of the usual two, hence the medical name, Trisomy 21).

Economo's disease trypanosomiasis (sleeping sickness).

English disease aka bronchitis.

enuresis Involuntary urination.

epiglottis thin cartilaginous flap that covers the entrance to the larynx during swallowing, preventing food from entering the trachea.

epilepsy: categories petit mal, grand mal, psychomotor.

epistaxis a nose bleed.

erysipelas aka St Anthony's Fire.

erythrocyte red blood cell that contains the pigment haemoglobin and transports oxygen and carbon dioxide to and from the tissues.

eye chart, standard Snellen chart.

folic acid another name for vitamin B.

gall bladder muscular membranous sac; its function is to store and concentrate bile, a fluid that is received from the liver and is important in digestion. In humans, it is situated on the underside of the liver and is pear-shaped and expendable, with a capacity of about 1.7 fluid ounces (50 ml).

gland: largest the liver.

glandular fever infectious viral disease characterised by swelling of the lymph glands and prolonged lassitude. Aka infectious mononucleosis.

Government Chief Medical Officer Professor Liam Donaldson.

Graves disease exophthalmic goitre with characteristic swelling of the neck and protrusion of the eyes, resulting from an overactive thyroid gland.

haemoglobin red oxygen-carrying protein containing iron and present in the red blood cells of vertebrates.

haemophilia male-only disease that prevents the blood from clotting. Women may be carriers. Aka Royal Disease.

hallux big toe.

hardest substance in body tooth enamel.

Harefield Britain's leading hospital for heart and heart-and-lung operations, situated 20 miles west of London.

hemicrania migraine.

hernia the projection of an organ through the lining of the cavity in which it is normally situated. The two most common forms of hernia are femoral (upper thigh) and inguinal (groin).

heroin: made from morphine, an opium derivative.

herpes zoster shingles, an acute painful inflammation of the nerve ganglia, with a skin eruption, often forming a girdle around the waist, and caused by the same virus as chickenpox.

homoeopathy treatment of disease by minute doses of drugs that in a healthy person would produce symptoms of the disease. Opposite of allopathy.

hormones: female sex oestrogen and progesterone.

hospice movement: founder Dame Cicely Saunders.

housemaid's knee inflammation and swelling of the bursa in front of the kneecap, often caused by continual kneeling on hard surfaces. Aka prepatellar bursitis.

humerus bone extending from the shoulder to the elbow.

humours obsolete name for the four chief fluids of the body, i.e. blood, phlegm, yellow bile and black bile, that were once thought to determine a person's physical and mental qualities. Aka cardinal humours.

Hurler's syndrome defect in metabolism resulting in mental retardation, a protruding abdomen and bone deformities, including an abnormally large head. Aka gargoylism.

MEDICINE

hypermetropia   the condition of having long sight.

illium   bone forming the upper part of each half of the human pelvis (contrast coxa).

inferiority complex   named by Alfred Adler.

innominate bone (aka coxa)   bone formed from the fusion of the ilium, ischium and pubis, aka the hip bone.

insulin: gland that produces   pancreas (in cells called the islets of Langerhans).

interferon   proteins made by cells in response to virus infection.

iridology   diagnosis by examination of the iris of the eye (used mainly in alternative medicine).

iris   the coloured muscular diaphragm that surrounds and controls the size of the pupil.

jaw bones   maxilla (upper jaw), mandible (lower jaw).

joints: lubricating fluid   synovial fluid.

keloid/cheloid   overgrown scar tissue.

kidney   organ that maintains water balance and expels metabolic wastes. The kidneys consist of two series of specialised tubules that empty into two collecting ducts, the Wolffian ducts. The two kidneys are positioned on the back wall of the abdomen.

kissing disease   glandular fever.

kyphosis   excessive outward curvature of the thoracic spine causing hunching of the back.

larynx   cartilaginous and muscular hollow organ forming part of the air passage to the lungs. Aka Adam's apple, voice-box.

Lassa fever   acute and often fatal febrile viral haemorrhagic disease of tropical Africa, named from the village in Nigeria where first reported.

Legionnaires' disease   form of bacterial pneumonia first identified after an outbreak at an American Legion meeting in Philadelphia in 1976 and spread by water droplets through air-conditioning systems and similar devices.

leucocyte   colourless amoeboid cell of blood and lymph, containing a nucleus and important in fighting disease. Aka white blood cell/white corpuscle.

leucoderma (aka vitiligo)   skin condition characterized by loss of melanin pigmentation.

leucoma   a white opacity in the cornea of the eye.

leucotomy   surgical cutting of white nerve fibres within the brain, especially prefrontal lobotomy.

leukaemia   malignant disease in which the bone marrow and other blood-forming organs produce too many leucocytes.

ligament   short band of tough flexible fibrous connective tissue linking bones together.

ligature   tie or bandage used in surgery for a bleeding artery.

lingua   the tongue.

lipids   organic compounds that are esters of fatty acids and are found in blood, cell membranes and elsewhere.

lithotomy   surgical removal of a calculus (stony secretion) from the bladder or urinary tract.

lithotripsy   removal of a calculus from the bladder or urinary tract by means of ultrasound techniques that shatter the stone so that fragments passs naturally from the body.

liver   largest organ in the human body, composed of a spongy mass of wedge-shaped lobes that has numerous metabolic and secretory functions. It is tucked beneath the diaphragm, protected from damage by the lower ribs of the right side. Its average weight is 3 to 4 lb (1.36 to 1.81 kg).

liver: functions   production of bile to emulsify fat in the bowel. Reception of all the products of food absorption and the subsequent release as energy sources. Carbohydrates are stored as glycogen, and the liver uses insulin from the pancreas to control the body's glucose level. Purification of blood. Production of proteins needed for blood clotting.

liver transplants: hospital   Addenbrooke's Hospital near Cambridge was the pioneer.

lordosis   inward curvature of the spine.

lungs   the 700 million air sacs are called alveoli, and the right lung is heavier than the left.

lunula   crescent-shaped white area at the base of the fingernail.

Lyme disease   form of arthritis caused by spirochaete bacteria transmitted by ticks. Named after a town in Connecticut, USA, where an outbreak occurred in 1975.

Mantoux test   intradermal tuberculin test named after French physician Charles Mantoux 1877–1947.

mastoid process   conical prominence on the temporal bone behind the ear, to which muscles are attached.

Ménière's syndrome   inner ear disorder characterised by ringing in ear, dizziness and impaired hearing.

miner's disease   pneumoconiosis (caused by inhalation of coal dust).

mnemonic   for nerves in the superorbital tissue: Lazy French Tarts Lie Naked In Anticipation (Lacrimal, Frontal, Trochlear, Lateral, Nasociliary, Internal, Abduceris).

mons pubis   rounded mass of fatty tissue lying over the joint of the pubic bones.

mons veneris   rounded mass of fatty tissue on a woman's abdomen above the vulva (Latin: Mount of Venus).

Moorfields   (London EC1) Britain's leading hospital specialising in eye injuries.

MRSA   general term for a group of bacteria that are penicillin-resistant. It particularly attacks the weak and infirm and is prevalent in hospital environments among patients with open wounds.

Munchausen's syndrome   medical name for feigned symptoms brought on with a view to gaining admission into hospital.

Munchausen's syndrome by proxy   mental condition in which a person seeks attention by inducing illness in another person, especially a child. Named after R E Raspe's literary hero.

muscae volitantes   moving black specks seen before the eyes, caused by opaque fragments floating in the vitreous humour ('floaters') or a defect in the lens.

muscle: not attached at both ends   tongue.

muscles: smile or frown debate   although smiling is more beneficial to one's wellbeing, in fact, frowning uses more muscles.

myeloid tissue   term for bone marrow, found in the or spinal cord and elsewhere.

myopia   short-sightedness.

naevus   birthmark in the form of a raised red patch on the skin.

nosology   branch of medical science dealing with the classification of diseases.

obstetrics   of or relating to childbirth and associated processes.

oedema   condition characterised by an excess of watery fluid collecting in the cavities or tissues of the body. Aka dropsy.

oesophagus   part of the alimentary canal between the pharynx and the stomach. Aka gullet.

olfactory of or relating to the sense of smell.

organs: largest the skin is the largest and heaviest organ of the human body, but the largest and heaviest organ within the human body is the liver.

Paget's cancer cancer of the nipple and surrounding tissue. Named after Sir James Paget (1814–99) the English surgeon and pathologist who described this disease.

Paget's disease chronic disease of the bones characterised by inflammation and deformation. Aka *osteitis deformans*.

pancreas gland secreting the hormone insulin, which regulates glucose levels in the body. Deficiency of insulin causes diabetes mellitus (sugar diabetes). The pancreas lies across the upper part of the abdomen, in front of the spine and on top of the aorta and the vena cava (the body's main artery and vein). The basic structures in the pancreas are the acini, collections of secreting cells round the blind end of a small duct. Among the acini are small groups of cells called the 'islets of Langerhans'. These constitute the whole 'other life' of the pancreas as an endocrine organ secreting the insulin required by the body to control its sugar level. The pancreas also has an exocrine gland which produces essential alkali in the form of sodium bicarbonate to neutralise the acidic content of the stomach.

pathology study of causes and nature of diseases.

phlebitis inflammation of a vein.

phlegm: medical name sputum.

plasma clear yellowish fluid portion of blood or lymph in which the corpuscles and cells are suspended.

prescription charge from 1 April 2003 £6.30p.

purkinje effect As light intensity decreases red objects are perceived to fade faster than blue objects of similar brightness.

radius outer and slightly shorter of the two bones of the forearm.

retina light-sensitive portion of the eyeball.

retrovir brand name of zidovudine (AZT), used in treating HIV and AIDS.

rubella German measles.

rubeola medical name for measles.

Schick test identifies susceptibility to diphtheria.

sclera the white part of the eye.

sex change operation: first George (Christine) Jorgensen (1952).

Siamese twins: called after most famous conjoined twins to survive into adulthood: Chang and Eng (1811–74), born in Siam.

singultus hiccup.

skin accounts for 16% of the body's weight and has an average surface area of 2,800 sq in (18,000 sq cm); as such, it is the largest and heaviest organ of the human body.

spleen main function is to act as a filter for the blood and to make antibodies. It lies just below the diaphragm at the top of the left-hand side of the abdomen. It is normally about 5 inches (13 cm) long and weighs about ½ lb (240 g) and lies along the line of the 10th rib.

Stockholm syndrome psychological term for process of bonding between hostage and captors.

Stoke Mandeville Britain's leading hospital for the treatment of spinal injuries.

stomach capacity about 2–2½ pints (0.94–1.18 litres).

stomatology study of mouth diseases.

strabismus medical name for a squint.

syncope technical name for a faint.

talipes club foot.

talus the ankle bone.

teeth By the age of 2–3 a child will usually have a complete set of 20 deciduous (milk) teeth. A full set of 32 permanent teeth develops after the age of six. The front four teeth in each jaw are called incisors, the next two are the canines (eyeteeth), the next four are premolars (the hindmost being the third molar or wisdom teeth), the outer teeth are called molars.

teeth: mnemonic 4 canines ('dogs' 4 letters)
8 incisors (8 letters in word)
8 premolars (8 letters in word)
12 molars (remaining teeth)
C is before I and M in alphabet and premolar implies that they come before molars.

tendon cord or strand of strong fibrous tissue attaching a muscle to a bone.

testes two glands that produce sperms and the male hormone testosterone.

test tube baby: first Louise Brown in 1978 (doctors were Steptoe and Edwards).

thalassotherapy ancient medical treatment of lying in sea water.

thorax anatomical name for the chest.

thyroid gland situated in the neck in front of the windpipe. Controls the metabolism.

tincture medicinal extract in a solution of alcohol.

tongue medical name lingua. Studding the tongue are many small projections called papillae. Inside these are some 9,000 taste buds which respond to only four basic tastes i.e. sweet, sour, salt and bitter.

Tourette's syndrome neurological disorder characterised by tics, involuntary vocalisation, and in some cases the compulsive utterance of obscenities. The syndrome is named after French neurologist Gilles de la Tourette.

trachea the windpipe.

trachoma contagious disease of the eye with inflamed granulation on the inner surface of the lids, caused by chlamydiae.

trench foot medical condition prevalent throughout the First World War caused by standing around in cold, wet and unsanitary conditions and in severe cases resulting in amputation of the feet.

trismus variety of tetanus with tonic spasms of the jaw muscles causing the mouth to remain tightly closed. Aka lockjaw.

ulna inner and longer of the two bones of the forearm.

urticaria hives or nettle rash.

varicella chickenpox.

variola smallpox.

vascular relating to blood vessels.

venereal disease: most common gonorrhea.

vitiligo (aka leucoderma) skin disease characterised by loss of melanin pigmentation.

vitamin term coined by Casimir Funk (1884–1967) in 1911 for the unidentified substances present in food that could prevent the diseases scurvy, beriberi and pellagra.

Wasserman test: used for testing for syphilis.

white death tuberculosis.

yellow fever tropical virus disease with fever and jaundice, transmitted by the mosquito and often fatal.

M
E
D
I
C
I
N
E

Phobias

Term	Meaning	Term	Meaning	Term	Meaning
abluto	bathing	copro	faeces	keno	void
acaro	itching	cremno	precipices	keraunothneto	fall of man-made satellites
acero	sourness	cryo	ice, frost	kineso	motion
achulo	darkness	cymo	sea swell	kineto	motion
acro	heights	cyno	dogs	klepto	stealing
aero	air	cyprido	venereal disease	koni	dust
agora	open spaces	demo	crowds	kopo	fatigue
aichuro	points	demono	demons	kristallo	ice
ailuro	cats	dendro	trees	kypho	stooping
akoustico	sound	dermato	skin	lachano	vegetables
alektoro	chickens	dermatosio	skin disease	lalo	stuttering
algo	pain	didaskaleino	school	leuko	white
amaka	carriages	dike	justice	limno	lakes
amatho	dust	dipso	drinking	linono	string
amaxo	vehicles	dora	fur	logo	words
ambulo	walking	dromo	crossing streets	lysso	insanity
amycho	being scratched	dysmorpho	deformity	maieusio	pregnancy
andro	men	eisoptro	mirror	mania	insanity
anemo	wind	electro	electricity	mastigo	flogging
angino	narrowness	eleuthero	freedom	mechano	machinery
anglo	England and the English	emeto	vomiting	melano	black
anthro	flowers	enete	pins	melo	music
anthropo	man	entomo	insects	merintho	being bound
antlo	flood	eoso	dawn	metallo	metals
apeiro	infinity	eremo	solitude	meteoro	meteors
api	bees	ergasio	surgery	metro	poetry
arachno	spiders	erythro	blushing	mono	being alone
astheno	weakness	frigo	being cold	musico	music
astra	lightning	gallo	France and the French	muso	mice
ataxio	disorder	gato	cats	myso	dirt or contamination
ate	ruin	gameto	marriage		
atelo	imperfection	gelio	laughter	myxo	slime
aulo	flute	genio	chins	necro	corpses
aurora	Northern Lights	geno	sex	negro	black people
automyso	being dirty	genu	knees	nelo	glass
bacilli	microbes	gephyro	crossing bridges	neo	newness
ballisto	missiles	geuma	taste	nepho	clouds
baro	gravity	gnosio	knowledge	nosema	illness
baso	walking	grapho	writing	noso	disease
batho	depth	gymno	nudity	nycto	darkness
batracho	reptiles	gyno	women	ochlo	crowds
belone	needles	hade	Hell	ocho	vehicles
blenno	slime	haemato	blood	odonto	teeth
bronto	thunder	halo	speaking	oiko	home
caino	novelty	hamartio	sin	olfacto	smell
carcino	cancer	haphe	being touched	ombro	rain
cardio	heart condition	hapto	touch	ommeta	eyes
carno	meat	harpaxo	robbers	oneiro	dreams
cathiso	sitting	hedono	pleasure	ophidio	snakes
catoptro	mirrors	helmintho	worms	ornitho	birds
chaeto	hair	hiero	sacred things	osmo	odours
cheima	cold	hippo	horses	osphresio	body odours
chero	cheerfulness	hodo	travel	ostracono	shellfish
chiono	snow	homichlo	fog	ourano	Heaven
chrometo	money	homo	homosexuals	paedo	children or dolls
chromo	colour	horme	shock	panto	everything
chrono	duration	hyalinopygo	glass bottoms	paralipo	neglect of duty
chronometro	clocks	hydro	water	paraskavedekatria	Friday the 13th
cibo	food	hygro	dampness		
crystallo	crystals	hypegia	responsibility	partheno	girls
claustro	closed spaces	hypno	sleep	patho	disease
clino	going to bed	hypso	high places	patroio	heredity
cnido	stings	ideo	ideas	peccato	sinning
coito	sexual intercourse	io	rust	pediculo	lice
		kakorraphia	failure	pelado	bald people
cometo	comets	katagelo	ridicule	penia	poverty

phago	swallowing	**scio**	shadows	**terdeka**	the number 13
phasmo	ghosts	**scoliono**	school	**thaaso**	sitting
phengo	daylight	**scopo**	being stared at	**thalasso**	sea
phobo	fears	**seia**	flash	**thanato**	death
phono	speaking aloud or noise	**sela**	flashes	**theo**	God
		sidero	stars	**thermo**	heat
photo	light	**siderodromo**	travelling by train	**thixo**	touching
phronemo	thinking			**toco**	childbirth
phthisio	tuberculosis	**sino**	China	**toxi**	poison
phyllo	leaves	**sito**	food	**traumato**	injury
pnigero	smothering	**sopho**	learning	**tremo**	trembling
pogono	beards	**sperma**	germs	**trichopatho**	hair
poine	punishment	**spermato**	semen	**triskaideka**	the number 13
poly	many things	**sphekso**	wasps	**trypano**	injections
potamo	rivers	**staso**	standing	**xantho**	yellow
poto	alcohol	**stygio**	hell	**xeno**	foreigners
pterono	feathers	**syphilo**	syphilis	**zelo**	jealousy
pyro	fire	**tacho**	speed	**zoo**	animals
rhabdo	being beaten	**tapho**	graves and being buried alive		
russo	Russia				
rypo	soiling				
satano	Satan	**terato**	monsters		

MILITARY

Operations: Military and Social

Accolade   Unfulfilled 1943 plan for capture of Rhodes and other Aegean islands.

Acrobat   Original name for Operation Torch and the name used in the 1943 film *Tunisian Victory*, it was the planned British operation to advance from Cyrenaica to Tripoli, 1941.

Adlertag (Eagle Day)   Start of main German air offensive on 13 August 1940, which led to the Adlerangriff (German plan for Battle of Britain).

A Go   Japanese plan for a counterattack against possible US recapture of the Marianas during 1944.

Alaric   First German codename for their possible military takeover in Italy.

Allied Force   Began on 24 March 1999 when United States military forces, acting with Nato allies, commenced air strikes against Serbian military targets in the former Yugoslavia. The multinational force was tasked by Nato to bring an end to crimes committed by the Federal Republic of Yugoslavia against ethnic Albanians in the southern province of Kosovo. On 20 June 1999 Operation Allied Force was officially terminated. This was in response to the departure of all FRY military and police forces from Kosovo in compliance with the Military Technical Agreement, which was signed by the Commander of KFOR and representatives of the FRY Government on 9 June 1940.

Alpen Veilchen (Alpine Violet)   Proposed plan for Italians to break out from Albania into Greece. Cancelled on 19 January 1940.

Anakim   First Allied plan for amphibious reconquest of Burma, abandoned in 1943.

Anton   German occupation of Vichy France on 11 November 1942, first codenamed Attila.

Anvil   Original codename for Allied landing on the French coast between Toulon and Cannes, later changed to Dragoon.

Aphrodite   American scheme to load surplus bombers with explosives and fly them to the south coast of Britain, where the two-man crew would bail out and another plane would guide the plane to crash into a V-1 site. Joe Kennedy, elder brother of JFK, was blown up on a test run over Norfolk.

Apostle I   Allied return to Norway on 10 May 1945.

Arcadia   Codename for the conference between Churchill and F.D. Roosevelt in Washington, 22 December 1941–14 January 1942.

Aufbau Ost   Prior to Barbarossa, this was the German buildup in the east.

Autumn Mist (Herbstnebel)   Codename for the Ardennes Offensive (Battle of the Bulge) in 1944.

Avalanche   US and British forces landing in the Gulf of Salerno causing the Germans to withdraw to the Gustav Line across the peninsula north of Naples, 9–19 September 1943.

Avonmouth   Failed Allied expedition to Narvik May–June 1940.

Axis (Achse)   Originally called 'Alaric', the disarming of the Italian army after their surrender to the Germans on 8 September 1943.

Babylon   7 June 1981, destruction of Osirak nuclear reactor in Iraq by Israeli F16s.

Badr   6 October 1973, Arab assault in Yom Kippur War.

Bagration   Successful Soviet offensive in the central part of the German-occupied Russian Front, 23 June–29 August 1944.

Barbarossa   German invasion of the USSR on 22 June 1941, supported by Romanian troops.

Battleaxe   15 June 1941, the first British offensive into 'Hellfire' (Halfaya) Pass, which failed to recapture Tobruk.

Baytown   British landing at Reggio, 3 September 1943, and advance into the south-west Italian mainland, reaching Auletta on 19 September and Potenza on 20 September.

Bernhard   Failed German plan to flood Britain with forged money during the Second World War, by means of an air drop, and thereby ruin the British economy.

Bigot   Security classification for Normandy landing planning documents.

Birdcage   Airborne leaflet drop on POW camps in the Far East announcing Japanese surrender.

Blackbuck 1   1 May 1982, bombing of Port Stanley runway by a Vulcan bomber.

Blackcock   XII British Corps attack at Roermond, southeast Holland, 16–26 January 1945.

Black (Schwarz)   The German occupation of Italy in 1943.

Blue Book   Following an unexplained UFO sighting in Roswell, New Mexico, in 1947 the US Air Force set up a study group code-named Project Sign. Of the 147 reported sightings all but 12 were explained. A further rush of sightings prompted the set up of Project Grudge on 11 February 1949. The USAF attempted to explain every UFO sighting but of the 273 official sightings, 231 were classed as unidentified. In March 1952 Project Grudge went public as Project Blue Book and for the next 17 years remained the USAF's official UFO Study Program. Investigations ceased in 1969 as the US government advised the USAF that the project was no longer justifiable.

Bluecoat   Normandy Operation of 30 July 1944, which concerned the initial British diversionary breakout from their American boundary, followed by the US 3rd Army, under Patton, breaking through the German defences at Avranches, the gateway from Normandy into Brittany.

Bodenplatte   Luftwaffe offensive operation against Allied airfields in north-western Europe during December 1944.

Bodyguard   Overall codename for multiple Allied deception tactics in 1944, but usually associated with the diversionary operation to deceive the Germans into thinking that the invasion was to be Kent-based and aimed at the Pas de Calais. Originally codenamed Jael.

Bolero   The build up of US troops in the UK in 1942.

Bolo   During Vietnam War, an ambush operation by American F-4 fighters, flying like bombers, which knocked out 7 North Vietnamese Migs in one go.

Brassard   Allied amphibious landings launched from Corsica on Elba, 17 June 1944.

Brevity   15 May 1941, the first British offensive into Hellfire Pass.

Buckshot Planned British attack in Libya, May 1942.

Bumblebee Anti-burglary device instigated by the Metropolitan Police on 1 June 1993 and sponsored by Yellow Pages. Bumblebee has several aspects to its 'sting'. The aim is to target known burglars in an effort to 'fight back' against criminals. In 1995 the Bumblebee Imaging System was implemented whereby stolen property recovered by the police can be matched against photographs supplied by the victim. Bumblebee has also run a campaign to make people aware that covert police patrols are carried out at car boot sales. Another key factor in Bumblebee operations is the personalisation of belongings. The increase in computer and mobile phone companies having tracing methods has meant their products are no longer worth stealing.

Cartwheel Phase One US troops recapture important islands in the Solomon Island Group from 1 July to 25 November 1943.

Cartwheel Phase Two US and Australian forces invasion of north-east New Guinea from 4 September 1943 to 23 March 1944.

Catapult 3 July 1940, British naval attack on French fleet at Mers-el-Kebir, destroying or damaging most of its ships to prevent them from falling into German or Italian hands.

Catherine British plan for forcing a passage into the Baltic to aid Poland, before the country's invasion by Germany and the Soviet Union in September 1939.

Cedar Falls The US clearance of Vietcong from Iron Triangle, Vietnam, in 1967.

Centaur Crackdown on Britain's 'black economy' by Customs and Excise from 1985 onwards. Lester Piggott was a famous catch.

Cerberus Channel dash of the German ships *Scharnhorst, Prinz Eugen* and *Gneisenau* from Brest to Germany in February 1942.

Chariot 27–28 March 1942, British Commando raid on St Nazaire to destroy the Normandie Dock.

Charnwood Normandy operation of 7 July 1944: attack north of Caen following a massive RAF bombardment.

Chastise British bombers led by Wing-Commander Guy Gibson attacked three dams in the Ruhr region of Germany in May 1943, using the spinning or 'bouncing' bombs designed by Barnes Wallis. Two dams were breached. Aka the Dambusters' Raid.

Cheshire British equivalent of Operation 'Provide Promise', i.e. the RAF flights into Sarajevo.

Chicken Little Abortive attempt to predict time and place of Skylab's return to Earth in 1979.

Chromite 15 September 1950, General MacArthur's successful amphibious landing at Inchon during the Korean War.

Clean Hands Launched by Milan magistrates in February 1992 to halt corruption in the city, especially collusion between the Mafia and the Christian Democratic Party.

Cobra Allied Normandy USAAF breakout of July 25 1944, following massive bombardment by USAAF.

Cockade Part of Allied deception plan to convince Germans that invasion of Europe would be anywhere but Normandy in summer of 1944. Brittany, northern Norway and the Pas de Calais were false objectives.

Colossus First British airborne operation (unsuccessful), Tragino viaduct, Campagne, Italy, on 10 February 1941.

Compass 9 December 1940, British 8th Army attack at Sidi Barrani, Egypt, which began the destruction of the Italian 10th Army.

Corkscrew Allied operations against the Mediterranean island of Pantelleria in June 1943.

Coronet Proposed US invasion of Japanese island of Honshu in March 1946 overtaken by Japanese surrender the year before.

Corporate British recapture of the Falklands in May/June 1982.

Countryman Investigation into alleged corruption in the Metropolitan Police.

Cromwell Not an operation but a British codeword for 'Invasion Imminent' used from 1940.

Crossbow Operation using fighters, anti-aircraft batteries and barrage balloons against German V-1 flying bombs in 1944, and later to bomb the V-2 rocket launch sites.

Crusader The 8th Army's first offensive (as 8th Army) in Libya, 18 November to 12 December 1941.

Culverin Allied plan for recapture of northern Sumatra in 1943 – never carried out.

Deliberate Force Nato's air campaign against Bosnian Serbs from 30 August to 14 Sepember 1995.

Deny Flight UN denial of Bosnian airspace to warring parties, began on 12 April 1993. On 28 February 1994 four Bosnian Serb warplanes violating the no-fly zone were shot down by Nato aircraft. This was the first military engagement ever undertaken by the UN/NATO Alliance.

Desert Sabre Official name for the ground war in the Persian Gulf January–February 1991, although US media often used the term 'Desert Sword'.

Desert Shield US-led multinational force, whose establishment was formally announced on 9 November 1990 and whose aim was to secure the withdrawal of Iraqi troops from Kuwait.

Desert Storm Air offensive launched by US-led allied forces on the night of 17 January 1991 against targets in Iraq and Iraqi-occupied Kuwait. The campaign lasted until 27 February 1991.

Detachment US capture of the Japanese island of Iwo Jima from 19 February to 1 March 1945.

Diadem Allied offensive that began on 11 May 1944, and broke the German Gustav Line, capturing Rome on 4 June 1944.

Dickens The 3rd Battle of Cassino, Italy, 15 March 1944. The original codename was Bradman, a cricket reference.

Diver British anti-V-1 measures.

Downfall Projected Allied invasion of mainland Japan, planned for 1 November 1945 and never carried out.

Dragoon Launched on 15 August 1944; Allied invasion of southern France, subsequent to Operation Anvil. When the US 7th Army and the French 1st Army landed on the French Riviera the Americans drove through the Alps to take Grenoble, while the French took Marseilles and advanced up the Rhône valley to rejoin the Americans near Lyons and move northeastward into Alsace in September 1944.

Dracula Liberation of Rangoon completed on 3 May1945.

Dynamo Evacuation of Anglo-French forces from Dunkirk, 26 May to 4 June 1940.

Eclipse Proposed dropping of Allied airborne army on Berlin in April 1945.

Edelweiss German Army Group A's operations against Baku area of the Caucasus during the summer of 1942.

MILITARY

Eisenhammer   Planned Luftwaffe attack on Soviet power stations during February 1945.

El Dorado Canyon   14 April 1986, 24 USAF F-111 bombers attacked Tripoli in reprisal raid.

Epsom   Normandy operation in the last 5 days of June 1944, a british move to outflank Caen from the West.

Eureka   Codename for the Tehran conference of November 1943 between Churchill, Roosevelt and Stalin.

Exporter   British and Free French invasion of Vichy-ruled Lebanon and Syria from 8 June to 12 July 1941.

Felix   Proposed German plan to capture Gibraltar and the Canary and Cape Verde Islands with Spanish aid in November 1940. Spain's neutrality ruled it out.

Firebrand   Allied occupation of Corsica, largely by Free French forces, from September to October 1943.

Flash   Codename for attempt on Hitler's life in March 1943 when a bomb placed in his plane by Fabian von Schlabrendorff failed to explode.

Flintlock   US invasion of Marshall Islands and Kwajalein Atoll from 31 January to 7 February 1944.

Forager   US invasion of the Marianas between J11 and 26 June 1944.

Fortitude, North and South   Deception campaigns to suggest that invasion of Northern Europe would be directed at either Norway or the Pas de Calais in 1944.

Freeborn   8th Army provision for withdrawal to Egyptian frontier in 1941.

Frequent Wind   US evacuation of Saigon, Vietnam, in April 1975.

Fritz   Initial plan for German invasion of the Soviet Union in December 1940, precursor of Barbarossa.

Fuller   Attempt to prevent the German warships *Scharnhorst* and *Gneisenau* escaping from Brest in December 1943.

Full Flow   Greatest UK exercise since 1945 involving transfer of 57,000 troops from UK to Germany for Lionheart/Cold Fire exercises; began 3 September 1984.

Galvanic   US occupation of Tarawa, Makin and Apamama, in the Gilbert Islands, on 20–21 November 1943.

Gemsbock   Anti-partisan drive in Greece, July 1944.

Gomorrah   RAF fire-storm raid on Hamburg, 25 July 1943, when anti-radar chaff, codenamed 'Window', was used for the first time.

Goodwood   Normandy offensive of 18 July 1944: an attack by the British Second Army south-east of Caen following massive bombardment by RAF.

Granby   British contribution to the Gulf War from Operation Desert Storm to the ceasefire on 11 April 1991.

Granite   US offensive operations in the Central Pacific, beginning March 1944.

Grapeshot   Allied attack on German-occupied northern Italy in 1944.

Grenade   Operation that linked Lieutenant General William Simpson's 9th US Army to the Canadian offensive against the lower Rhine (Operation Veritable) in February 1945.

Gymnast   Proposed British landings in Tunisia and Algeria in 1941, superseded by Torch.

Hammer   Proposed Allied attack on Trondheim, central Norway, April 1940, abandoned as impracticable.

Hercules   Proposed German airborne invasion of Malta in the spring of 1942 involving airborne and sea landings. The operation was cancelled.

Horrido   German anti-partisan drive in Yugoslavia during the spring of 1944.

Husky   US and British troops landing in Sicily on 10 July 1943; total occupation achieved by 17 August 1943.

Icarus   Proposed German invasion of Iceland in 1940; not carried out.

Iceberg   US capture of Okinawa from 1 April to 22 June 1945.

I Go   Japanese codename for naval counter-offensive in the Pacific during April 1943.

I – Go Sakusen   Japanese air offensive in south-west Pacific, 7 to 16 April 1945 (aka Operation A).

Iltis   German anti-partisan drive in Greece during March 1944.

Infatuate   Allied operation to capture Walcheren Island in the Scheldt estuary on 1–18 November 1944.

Irma   Media term for the airlift of some 40 people seriously injured in the war in Bosnia-Herzegovina to hospitals in the UK, Sweden and Italy in August 1993. Named after Irma Hadzimuratovic, a wounded 5-year-old whose plight was given huge media coverage after Prime Minister John Major arranged for her flight out of Sarajevo.

Ironclad   British occupation of Diego Suarez, Madagascar, 8 May 1942.

Isabella (Ilona)   Abortive German plans to occupy Atlantic coasts of Spain and Portugal in 1941.

Jael   See Bodyguard.

Jericho   RAF Mosquito raid on Amiens jail to release Resistance prisoners, 18 February 1944.

Joint Guardian   In the aftermath of Operation Allied Force the Joint Guardian operation continues to pursue the ultimate goal of a peaceful multi-ethnic and democratic Kosovo. The original five-point plan of Allied Force was to stop the Serb offensive, force a Serb withdrawal, establish democratic self-government in Kosovo, allow a Nato-led peacekeeping force and to allow the safe return of Kosovar Albanian refugees.

Jubilee   Disastrous Anglo-Canadian amphibious raid on Dieppe on 19 August 1942.

Junction City   Only US para assault of Vietnam War, 22 February–14 May 1967.

Jupiter   Projected Allied invasion of northern Norway in 1942; not carried out.

Just Cause   Code name for the US military invasion of Panama between 20 December 1989 and 13 February 1990. It saw the first operational use of the stealth bomber.

Ka Go   Japanese reinforcement of Guadalcanal in August 1942 resulting in the battle of the Eastern Solomons.

Kathleen   A German-planned invasion of Ireland in the summer of 1940, with the support of the IRA. Preparing work on this plan was made by the IRA themselves, but aborted.

Konstantin   German operation to seize control of Italian-controlled Balkans during September 1943.

Koralle   German anti-partisan drive in Greece during July 1944.

Kreuzoller   German anti-partisan drive in Greece during August 1944.

Kugelblitz   German anti-partisan drive in Yugoslavia during latter half of 1943.

Kutuzov   Soviet counter-offensive in the Kursk salient of July 1943.

Leopard German assault on the island of Leros, Greece, in 1943.

Lightfoot General Montgomery's plan for the breakthrough phase of the 2nd Battle of El Alamein, 23 October 1942. It failed to break the German defences.

Lila German operation to seize the French fleet at Toulon. They found the fleet scuttled on 27 November 1942.

Limerick British attack in Libya, June 1942.

Linebacker II The 1972 Christmas bombing offensive against North Vietnam by US B-52 bombers.

Little Saturn Soviet offensive against the German relief forces trying to break through to the encircled 6th Army at Stalingrad, launched on 16 December 1942.

Lumberjack Advances by US First Army to the Rhine at Cologne and by US Third Army further south in February 1945.

Lustre British transfer of forces from Western Desert to Greece in March 1941.

Luttich German attempt to cut off the Americans breaking out of Normandy by attacking at Mortain 17 August 1944.

Magic Name given to the overall US Intelligence programme before and during the Second World War devoted to breaking Japanese codes.

Magic Carpet Airlift of some 50,000 Jews from Yemen to Israel in the late 1940s and early 1950s.

Magician Codename for the Metropolitan Police Flying Squad operation to foil the world's biggest armed robbery at the Millennium Dome in London. Armed with smoke bombs, ammonia and a nail gun, the gang crashed into the building in a stolen JCB. Their aim was to steal the DeBeers Millennium Diamonds, worth between £200 and £350 million. The police had known about the attempted robbery for months and duly arrested the five robbers on 7 November 2000. The men were sentenced on 18 February 2002; two received 18 years, two 15 years and one five years.

Magnet Codename for the arrival of US forces in Northern Ireland in February 1942.

Mailfist Planned Allied recapture of Singapore, in 1945.

Manhattan District Cover name for the USA's atomic bomb project begun in June 1942.

Mannah Dropping of food supplies to occupied Holland by RAF in April and May 1945. Also codename for British intervention in the Greek civil war in October 1944.

Marita German assault on Yugoslavia and Greece in May 1941.

Maritime Monitor Royal Navy blockade of Serbia.

Market Garden The disastrous Allied airborne attack near Arnhem on 17 September 1944 which failed to link up with the British Second Army. Market was the airborne operation in which Allied paratroops were to seize key river crossings in advance of Second Army's tanks. Garden was the ground phase.

Menace Failed Anglo-Free French attempt to capture Vichy Dakar in West Africa with help from De Gaulle in September 1940.

Mercury German airborne assault on Crete in May 1941.

Midsummer Night's Dream Probing attack by Rommel in Libya, 14 September 1941.

Millennium RAF Bomber Command's 30/31 May 1942, 1,000-bomber raid on Cologne.

Mincemeat Aka The Man Who Never Was. Precursor of Operation Husky, whereby the aim was to deceive the German general staff into believing the proposed Allied attack on Sicily was, in fact, to be on Sardinia and Corsica in the west and the Greek mainland in the east. The deception was the plan of two relatively junior officers, Squadron Leader Sir Archibald Cholmondley and intelligence officer Lt Cmdr Ewen Montagu. It was Cholmondley who first suggested planting a series of subtle clues on a dead body and ensuring the Germans would be privy to this information, and it was Montagu who gave the plan its feasibility. The dead body, whose true identity was never revealed, was given the name of Captain (acting major) William Martin of the Royal Marines, and his mode of death was a plane crash at sea off the Spanish coast, where the Abwehr (German Intelligence) was known to be very active. The plan was a total success and 'Husky' gave the Allies control of the Mediterranean.

Mongoose Operation launched by President John F Kennedy and his brother Robert Kennedy, the Attorney-General, in December 1961, with the aim of overthrowing Fidel Castro of Cuba.

Moonlight Sonata German air-raid on Coventry on 14 and 15 November 1940.

Moses Secret airlift of Ethiopian Jews, or Falashas, to Israel from refugee camps in Sudan 1984–5.

Musketeer Anglo-French assault on Suez on 5 November 1956, first ever use of helicopters in amphibious landing.

Myth Soviet investigation into the death of Hitler in 1946, with aim of ensuring that he was in fact dead.

Neptun German anti-partisan drive, Greece 1944.

Neptune Naval side of Operation Overlord, involving 7,000 Allied ships.

No Ball Air attacks on German rocket-launching sites in 1944–5.

Noble Eagle American military operation to eliminate terrorist networks around the world. The ongoing assault on terrorism was launched in response to the terrorist attack on the World Trade Center on 11 September 2001. More than 35,000 military reservists were activated in the first year to support homeland defence as part of the campaign.

Nordlicht (Northern Lights) German operation against Leningrad during the summer of 1942.

Nordwind German counter-attack in Alsace (west of Strasbourg) in January 1945.

Oak Rescue of former prime minister Benito Mussolini from captivity in the Abruzzi mountains on 12 September 1943 by a small German force under Otto Skorzeny.

Olive Allied attack on the Gothic Line, Italy, in August 1944.

Olympic Proposed Allied plan to invade Kyushu in October 1945, precursor of projected Operation Downfall, the assault on Japan itself.

Ore The ongoing investigation into paedophilia via the Internet. The police have been able to track down downloaders of child pornography, via their credit card details, and specifically target those that have regular contact with children. So far the operation has unmasked over a thousand offenders in the UK, many of whom live a middle-class suburban lifestyle ranging from businessmen to pop musicians.

Overcast US plan launched in July 1945 to spirit German weapon scientists away from Europe to work in US laboratories.

MILITARY

Overlord Code name for the Allied invasion of Normandy in 1944. Originally planned for May, the day finally chosen was 5 June but the operation was delayed 24 hours by bad weather.

Panther German anti-partisan drive in Yugoslavia during spring of 1944.

Paperclip American project authorised by Harry S Truman in September 1946 whereby a selection of German scientists was brought to America to work on behalf of the US Government during the 'Cold War' following the end of the Second World War.

Paraquat British recapture of South Georgia from Argentina on 25 April 1982.

Peace for Galilee Codename for Israel's full-scale invasion of Lebanon in June 1982, launched with aim of eradicating the PLO from Lebanon.

Pedestal British convoy to supply Malta in August 1942, involving 2 battleships (*Nelson* and *Rodney*), 3 aircraft carriers (*Victorious* and *Eagle* were sunk and *Indomitable* damaged), 2 ferry carriers (*Argus* and *Furious* carrying Spitfires), to Malta, 14 merchantmen (9 sunk, 5 arrived, including tanker, *Ohio* which was literally dragged into Malta sandwiched between 2 destroyers.

Pegasus 15 April 1968, relief by US and South Vietnamese forces of Khe Sanh combat base, Vietnam, besieged since mid-January.

Plan Blue (Fall Blau) Originally, the name given to a 1938 study from the Luftwaffe about aerial warfare in England, but more commonly the German offensive in southern Russia in the spring of 1942. Aka 'Case Blue'.

Plan Green (Fall Grün) In 1937 the plan to attack and occupy Czechoslovakia, which was executed without resistance in May 1938, after the Munich conference. In 1940 it was the name given to the plan for a frontal attack on the Maginot Line, later called Fall Braun.

Plan Red (Fall Rot) In 1935 Fall Rot was a study to defend against a surprise attack by France while defending the borders against Czechoslovakia and Poland. The 1937 version of Fall Rot included offensive operations against Czechoslovakia with the aim of preventing a prolonged two-front war. In 1940 it was the second part of the western campaign; after the destruction of the British Expeditionary Force and the northern army of France, it was, with Fall Braun, the attack on the rest of the French army, which was still entrenched in the Maginot Line.

Plan White (Fall Weiss) German invasion of Poland in September 1939. Aka 'Case White'.

Plan Yellow (Fall Gelb) German assault in the Low Countries and France launched on10 May 1940. Aka 'Case Yellow'.

Platinum Part of 'Barbarossa' comprising operations towards Murmansk in the north.

Plunder Montgomery's crossing of the Rhine at the head of the 21st Army Group on 23 March 1945.

Pointblank Bombing campaign against German military, industrial and economic targets from May 1943.

Polar Bear German assault on the island of Kos, Greece, in 1943.

Provide Assistance Codename for the US relief operation launched on 23 July1994 to deliver humanitarian relief to Rwandan refugees in Zaïre, prompted by an outbreak of cholera, aka Operation Support Hope.

Provide Comfort Code name for an emergency relief programme announced by Western allied forces on 16 April 1991, for the besieged Kurdish population of northern Iraq.

Provide Promise USAF flights into Sarajevo during conflict. Began on 2 July 1992 with 21 nations forming a coalition to resupply a war-ravaged Sarajevo. The longest humanitarian airlift in history ended on 9 January 1996.

Puma Proposed British operation to seize Canary Islands in 1941.

Punishment German air attacks on Yugoslav capital of Belgrade from 6 to 8 April 1941.

Quadrant Codename of the Quebec conference of August 1943, attended by Churchill and Roosevelt.

Rankin Allied plans for return to European continent. Rankin A involved possible return in advance of scheduled Normandy invasion, B was response in case of German withdrawal from France or Norway, C in case of German unconditional surrender.

Ratweek RAF and Yugoslav partisans launch attacks on roads and railways intending to prevent German withdrawal from Yugoslavia, September 1944.

Reckless US operation against Hollandia, New Guinea, in April 1944.

Regenbogen (Rainbow) Scuttling of German U-boats at the end of the Second World War. 231 scuttled during May 1945.

Restore Hope Codename given to the December 1992 deployment of a US-led 35,000-strong multinational force in Somalia to ensure the safe delivery of international aid to Somalis who were starving as a result of the year-long civil war.

Rhine Exercise The one and only cruise of the German battleship *Bismarck* from19 to 27 May 1941, when she sank in the Bay of Biscay.

Rhubarb RAF Fighter Command sweeps over the English Channel and occupied French coastline from late 1940 onwards.

Richard German plan for intervention in Spain in the event of a Republican victory in the Civil War.

Ring Soviet operation to destroy encircled German 6th Army at Stalingrad in January 1943.

Rösselsprung (Knight's Move) German attack on Tito's HQ, Hvar, Yugoslavia, 25 May 1944.

Rolling Thunder Programme of sustained US bombing of North Vietnam mounted by administration of President Lyndon Johnson, March 1965–November 1968.

Rosario Argentine invasion of the Falkland Islands on 3 April 1982.

Roundup Allied plan to land in France between the Somme and the Seine (Dieppe and Le Havre) in spring 1943 by 30 US and 18 British divisions; replaced by Overlord.

Rumpelkammer (Junk Room) German V1 campaign against UK 1944–5.

Rumyantsev Soviet counter-offensive following Operation Citadel, August 1943, mounted at southern end of the Kursk salient.

Salmon Trap Abortive German plan to cut Murmansk railway in 1942.

Sandstone Codename for the US Army's nuclear testing series of 1948.

Schneesturm (Snowstorm) German anti-partisan drive in Yugoslavia late 1943.

Scorcher British occupation of Crete after withdrawal from Greece, May–June 1941.

Sea-Lion Proposed German invasion of England in 1940.

Sextant Cairo conference held just before and after the British–Soviet–US Tehran conference. At Cairo were US, British and Chinese heads of state, November and December 1943.

Sharp Guard Nato-WEU restriction on shipping to the Federal Republic of Yugoslavia in 1994.

Sheepskin Invasion of Anguilla in March 1969 by 300 British troops and 50 police to restore British rule from St Kitts-Nevis.

Shingle Amphibious landing at Anzio, 22 January 1944, sealed off by Germans until Operation Diadem broke through the Gustav Line.

Sho Go (Victory) Japanese defence plan in the summer of 1944, embracing several plans which could be put into effect once the axis of Allied advance became clear. Plan 1 provided for the defence of the Philippines, Plan 2 for the defence of Formosa and the Ryukyus, Plan 3 for the defence of Japan itself, Plan 4 for the defence of the Kuriles and Hokkaido. After Plan 1 was triggered, the Battle of Leyte Gulf ensued.

Shrapnel Abortive British plan of 1940 to seize the Cape Verde Islands in the event of Spain entering the war on Germany's side and threatening Gibraltar.

Sickle Cover name for the build-up of the US Eighth Air Force in Britain from 1942.

Slapstick British landing at Taranto on the heel of Italy and advance along the coast towards the German Gustav Line 9 September–30 November 1943.

Sledgehammer Proposed British–American contingency plan to invade Normandy and Brittany in Autumn 1942 if the Soviet Union appeared about to collapse.

Source British midget submarine attack on German battleship *Tirpitz*, 22 September 1943.

Spring Canadian breakout in Normandy July 1944, coordinated with Operations Goodwood and Cobra.

Starfish British deception plan early in the Second World War to simulate the effects of marker incendiaries dropped by bombers, and lure German bombers away from real targets.

Starkey Allied invasion practice in English Channel, September 1943, part of the Cockade deception plan.

Starvation US naval operation, launched in March 1945, to mine Japan's home waters.commenced March.

Steinadler German anti-partisan drive in Greece during July 1944.

Steinbock (Ibex) Luftwaffe bombing attacks on Britain in the spring of 1944.

Stosser German parachute operations during the Ardennes Offensive in 1944.

Strangle Air attacks destroying German communications in Italy before Operation Diadem in March 1944.

Student The German occupation of Rome in 1943. Part of Operation Black.

Sunrise Secret negotiations with the German command in Italy for surrender of German forces in May 1945.

Supercharge I British break-out in the 2nd Battle of El Alamein 2–4 November 1942.

Super-Gymnast Plan for an Allied landing in north-west Africa in 1942, which evolved into Operation Torch.

Symbol Anglo–American Casablanca Conference 14–23 January 1943.

Taxable RAF drop window off the Pas de Calais, as diversion for D-Day, 5–6 June 1944.

Terminal Allied conference at Potsdam 16 July to 2 August 1945.

Thunderbolt 3 July 1976, Israeli commando raid to release hostages of hijacked Palestinian terrorists to Entebbe. Thunderbolt was also codename in the Second World War for Luftwaffe cover for 'Cerberus'.

Thunderclap Plan favoured by 'Bomber' Harris for an all-out bombing assault on Germany, as a war winning *coup de grâce*, applied in particular to the bombing of Dresden in February 1945.

Tidal Wave USAAF bombing of the oil refineries at Ploesti, Romania, 1 August 1943.

Tiger British fast convoy loaded with war material which passed the length of the Mediterranean during May 1941, bringing tanks and fighter planes to the 8th Army in Egypt.

Torch Final codename for Allied landings in north-west Africa, 8 November 1942.

Totalize Normandy Operation of 7 Aug 1944, concerning Canadian attack towards Falaise, Normandy, aiming to link with US forces closing in from the south to trap German troops concentrated southward in the 'Falaise pocket'.

Tractable Canadian follow-up attack towards Falaise of 14 August 1944, an extension of Totalize.

Trident Anglo–American summit conference, Washington 12–25 May 1943. Operation Trident is also the name of a Metropolitan Police initiative begun in March 1998 to end a spate of shootings among the black communities in London.

Turquoise Codename for the French military operation in Rwanda launched on 23 June 1994 following the death in a plane crash of President Juvenal Habyarimana and the violence that followed.

Typhoon (Taifun) German push to capture Moscow, September–December 1941.

U Go Japanese drive on India, from Burma in March 1944.

UNOSOM II The aftermath of Operation Restore Hope in Somalia in 1994.

Uphold Democracy 19 September 1994, USA ousting of Haitian Junta in favour of exiled President Jean-Bertrand Aristide.

Uranus Soviet attack which trapped the Germans 6th Army in Stalingrad, November 1942.

Urgent Fury Codename for the military invasion of the Caribbean island of Grenada in October 1983 by 7,000 US Marines in order to rescue medical students embroiled in political chaos following the murder of PM Maurice Bishop by hardline Stalinists.

Valkyrie Codeword for anti-Nazi uprising planned to follow the failed assassination attempt on Adolf Hitler by Claus von Stauffenberg on 20 July 1944.

Varsity Airborne assault that accompanied Montgomery's crossing of the Rhine on 24 March 1945.

Velvet Unrealised offer made late in 1942, to base 20 Anglo–American air force squadrons in Soviet Caucasus.

Vengeance Assassination of Admiral Yamamoto, Japanese naval commander in chief, by American P-38 fighters on 18 April 1943.

Veritable Opening of the Allied Rhineland campaign on 8 February 1945 with Canadians driving south from Nijmegen in the Netherlands to capture land between the Rhine and Maas and so clear German troops from the west bank of the Upper Rhine.

Vittles US name for Berlin Airlift, 26 June 1948 to 30 September 1949.

Vulcan   Final Allied offensive in Tunisia, 6 May 1943.

Warden   RAF flights over northern Iraq, post Gulf War.

Watch on the Rhine   The German counter-offensive in the Ardennes commencing 16 December 1944, aka the Battle of the Bulge.

Watchtower   7 August 1942, US capture of airstrip on Guadalcanal and the naval and seaplane base Tulagi in Solomon Isles, leading to a 6-month campaign to expel the Japanese from Guadalcanal.

Weiss 1 and 2   German anti-partisan drive in Bosnia, February 1943.

Weser Exercise   The German invasion of Norway in April 1940.

Wilfred   Proposed British plan to mine neutral Norwegian waters in April 1940, which was pre-empted by German invasion of Norway, though not before one minefield was laid.

Winter Storm   General Von Manstein's unsuccessful operation to relieve Germany's encircled 6th Army at Stalingrad, December 1942.

Wolf   German anti-partisan drive in Yugoslavia in the spring of 1944.

Zeppelin   Abortive German plot to assassinate Stalin in July 1944.

Zipper   Projected British assault on Japanese-occupied Malaya in 1945, which was pre-empted by their surrender.

Zitadelle   German attack that led to the Battle of Kursk (central Russia) in July 1943, the largest tank battle in history.

Zorba   Codename for the ongoing investigation into Freemasonry within the Police Force.

General Information

aerobatics team: RAF   Red Arrows.

army: European country without one   Liechtenstein.

army: largest   China.

bugle calls   Reveille (first), Last Post (Penultimate), Lights Out (Last).

concentration camp: first   British in the Boer War.

decorations: highest UK civilian   George Cross.

decorations: highest UK military   Victoria Cross.

Foreign Legion   Founded by King Louis-Philippe (1831) as an aid to controlling French colonial possessions. The Legion's unofficial motto is *Legio Patria Nostra* (The Legion is Our Fatherland). Its monthly magazine is called *Képi Blanc* (White Kepi). Its HQ was formerly in Sidi Ben Abbas (Algeria) but is now in Aubagne, near Marseilles.

guards regiments   Grenadiers, Coldstream, Scots, Irish and Welsh.

home guard: original name   Local Defence Volunteers.

Household Cavalry regiments   Life Guards, Blues and Royals.

Marines: attached to   Admiralty (although classified as soldiers). The Royal Marines were founded in 1664.

Monty's double   Clifford James.

National Service   Commencing in 1947 and initially for men of 18+ and for a two-year term (lowered to 18 months); abolished in 1960. Last recruits passed out in 1962.

Officer Training School: Army   Sandhurst.

Officer Training School: Navy   Dartmouth.

Officer Training School: RAF   Cranwell.

Parachute Regiment: nickname   Red Devils.

private army: only force allowed in UK   Duke of Atholl Highlanders.

RAF: formed   Initially the Royal Flying Corps formed 13 May (1912) but amalgamated with the Royal Naval Air Service on 1 Apil 1918 to form the RAF.

salutes   Queen's Birthday 62 guns, opening of Parliament 42 guns.

SAS (Special Air Service): Founder   David Stirling.

Special Forces equivalents   Delta Force (US), SAS and SBS (Britain), Spetznaz (Russia).

US Air Force Academy (Colorado Springs)   Founded in 1954 and is the Officer Training School for the US Air Force.

US Marines: founded   1775.

US Military Academy (West Point)   Founded in 1802 and is the Officer Training School for the US Army.

US Naval Academy (Annapolis)   Founded in 1845 and is the Officer Training School for the US Navy and Marine Corps.

Victoria Cross: most won in a single action   Eleven at Rorke's Drift (22 January 1879) during the Zulu Wars.

Comparative Ranks in the Armed Forces

OFFICERS

Royal Navy	Army	RAF
Admiral of the Fleet	Field Marshal	Marshal of the Royal Air Force
Admiral	General	Air Chief Marshal
Vice-Admiral	Lieutenant-General	Air Marshal
Rear-Admiral	Major-General	Air Vice-Marshal
Commodore	Brigadier	Air Commodore
Captain	Colonel	Group Captain
Commander	Lieutenant-Colonel	Wing Commander
Lt-Commander	Major	Squadron Leader
Lieutenant	Captain	Flight Lieutenant
Sub-Lieutenant	Lieutenant	Flying Officer
Acting Sub-Lieutenant	Second Lieutenant	Pilot Officer

NONCOMMISSIONED OFFICERS

Fleet Chief Petty Officer	Warrant Officer Class 1	Warrant Officer
	Warrant Officer Class 2	
Chief Petty Officer	Staff Sergeant	Flight Sergeant/Chief Technician
Petty Officer	Sergeant	Sergeant
Leading Rate	Corporal	Corporal
	Lance-Corporal	

Battles

Battle	War	Date	Details
Aachen	Second World War	21 Oct. 1944	Eight-day battle culminating in Allies capturing first major German city in the war.
Abensberg	Napoleonic Wars	20 Apr. 1809	French and Bavarians under Napoleon defeat Austrians under Archduke Charles.
Aberdeen	English Civil War	13 Sept. 1644	Royalists under marquis of Montrose defeated the Covenanters under Lord Burleigh.
Aboukir Bay/Nile	French Revolutionary Wars	1 Aug. 1798	Nelson destroyed 11 French ships in harbour, nullifying Napoleon's Egyptian land successes.
Abraham, Plains of	Seven Years' War	13 Sept. 1759	British secured Quebec; British and French leaders' James Wolfe and Marquis de Montcalm, were killed.
Actium	Second Triumvirate War	2 Sept. 31 BC	Octavian defeated Antony and Cleopatra on a promontory in Acarnania, Greece.
Adrianople	Roman/Visigoth War	9 Aug. AD 378	The Visigoth Fritigern defeated Romans led by Emperor Valens.
Adowa/Adwa	Italian Invasion of Ethiopia	1 Mar. 1896	King Menelik II's decisive defeat of General Baratieri forced Treaty of Addis Ababa on Italy, October 1896.
Adwalton Moor	English Civil War	30 June 1643	Royalists under the earl of Newcastle defeated Lord Fairfax's parliamentarians.
Aegospotami	Peloponnesian War	405 BC	The final battle of the Peloponnesian War in which the fleets of the two Greek rival powers fought a sea battle in the Hellespont and the Spartan leader Lysander using better tactics eventually defeated the Athenians under Conon.
Agincourt	Hundred Years' War	25 Oct. 1415	Henry V's archers laid foundations for defeat of French, under Constable Charles d'Albret.
Alamo	Texan/Mexican War	6 Mar. 1836	Col. Travis, Jim Bowie and Davy Crockett were among 183 Texans killed by Santa Anna's Mexican troops.
Åland	Great Northern War	July 1714	Russian fleet under Apraksin and Peter the Great defeated the Swedes under Ehrenskjold.
Alarcos	Spanish/Muslim Wars	18 July 1195	Moors under Yakub el Mansur defeated Spaniards under Alfonso VIII of Castile.
Aleppo	Tatar Invasion of Syria	11 Nov. 1400	Tatars under Tamerlane defeated Turks under the Syrian Emirs.
Alesia	Gallic Wars	c. 52 BC	Romans under Julius Caesar defeated Gauls under Vercingetorix.
Alexandria	British invasion of Egypt	21 Mar. 1801	British under Sir Ralph Abercromby (killed) defeated French under General Menou.
Algeciras Bay	French Revolutionary Wars	8 July 1801	Two sea battles between British under Saumarez and French under Linois; the first was indecisive but the second won a victory for Saumarez.
Alicante	War of Spanish Succession	29 June 1706	Admiral Sir George Byng commanded a fleet of 5 ships that attacked the city walls causing severe damage.
Aliwal	First Anglo-Sikh War	28 Jan. 1846	General Sir Harry Smith led a joint British/Indian force to victory against Sikhs.
Alkmaar	Eighty Years' War	8 Oct. 1573	Siege was laid, 21 August 1573, by 1,000 Spaniards but Dutch defended successfully.
Alma	Crimean War	20 Sept. 1854	Indecisive battle between Russian and a joint British/French/Turkish army.
Alnwick	Anglo-Scottish Wars	13 Nov. 1093	Malcolm Canmore, king of Scotland, and his son Edward were both slain.

MILITARY

Battle	War	Date	Details
Alsen	Schleswig-Holstein War	29 June 1864	In this last engagement of the war, the Prussians defeated the Danes.
Amphipolis	Peloponnesian War	422 BC	Indecisive attempt by the Athenians under Cleon to recapture Amphipolis from the Spartans.
Ankara	Ottoman Wars	20th July 1402	Mongols under Tamerlane defeated Ottomans under the sultan Bayezid I.
Antietam	US Civil War	17 Sept. 1862	A decisive battle that halted the Confederates in their advance on Maryland.
Antioch	First Crusade	3 June 1098	Siege started on 21 October 1097; Saracens held out against crusaders for 7 months.
Antwerp	Eighty Years' War	4 Nov. 1576	Known as the Spanish Fury; Sancho d'Avila's Spaniards slaughtered 8,000 Walloons.
Anzio	Second World War	22 Jan. 1944	A surprise landing near Rome by nearly 50,000 British/American troops.
Appomattox	US Civil War	9 Apr. 1865	Confederate army was surrounded in the Court House and Lee surrendered to Grant.
Arausio	Teutonic Wars	105 BC	Germanic tribes defeated Romans under Quintus Servilius Caepio and Gnaeus Mallius Maximus.
Arbela	Alexander's Asiatic Wars	1 Oct. 331 BC	Macedonians defeated Persians under Darius, making Alexander master of Asia.
Arcot	Carnatic War	Aug. 1751	Robert Clive captured fortress and held it for 7 weeks, delaying French advance in India.
Ardennes	Second World War	16 Jan. 1945	Aka Battle of the Bulge (coined by Churchill), the last German offensive on the Western Front.
Armada	Anglo-Spanish War	July 1588	Spanish Armada of 130 ships defeated by English fleet of 197, under Lord Howard.
Arnhem	Second World War	17 Sept. 1944	While airborne US troops secured bridges over Maas and Waal, British Arnhem landing severely defeated.
Arques	French Religious Wars	21 Sept. 1589	Henry of Navarre, later King Henry IV, led Huguenots to victory against Catholic League.
Arsuf	Third Crusade	7 Sept. 1191	King Richard I gained notable tactical victory against the Saracens.
Ascalon/Ashqelon	First Crusade	19 Aug. 1099	Crusaders under Godefroi de Bouillon gained a victory against Saracens under Kilidj Arslan.
Ashdown	Danish invasion of Britain	8 Jan. 871	King Ethelred of Wessex aided by Alfred the Great defeated the Danes.
Ashingdon	Danish invasion of Britain	18 Oct. 1016	Canute of Denmark defeated Edmund Ironside, which led to him becoming King.
Aspern	Napoleonic Wars	22 May 1809	French retreated to the island of Lobau in the Danube; they had few supplies and Napoleon rejected his generals' advice to retreat. Napoleon's first defeat, by an Austrian army.
Aughrim	War of English Succession	12 July 1691	William III's army led by Godert de Ginkel scattered a Jacobite army in Galway.
Auldearn	English Civil War	9 May 1645	Royalists under the marquis of Montrose defeated Covenanters east of Nairn.
Austerlitz	Napoleonic Wars	2 Dec. 1805	Aka Battle of the Three Emperors (Russian, French, Austrian). Napoleon defeated Kutuzov.
Bāhādurpur	Mughal Civil War	24 Feb 1658	Conflict between the four sons of Shāh Jehan, Mughal emperor of India, over the succession. The shah's second son, Shujā, set himself up as the governor of Bengal but was defeated in battle by the son of Dārā Shikoh, the eldest son of Shah Jehan. The third son, Aurangzeb, later executed his nephew, Sulaymān Shikoh.
Balaclava	Crimean War	25 Oct. 1854	Allied victory over the Russians, but disastrous charge of British Light Brigade prompted General Bosquet to say 'This is not war.'
Ball's Bluff	US Civil War	21 Oct. 1861	Confederates under General Evans defeated Union army under General Stone.
Baltimore	War of 1812	11 Sept. 1814	British under General Ross (killed) defeated Americans under General Winder.
Bannockburn	Scottish Independence	24 June 1314	Robert the Bruce defeated English invaders under King Edward II.
Barāri Ghāt	Afghan-Marāthā War	9 Jan. 1760	Afghan army under Ahmad Shāh Durrāni defeated the Marāthās under Dattāji Sindhia (died).
Barnet	Wars of the Roses	14 Apr. 1471	Yorkists under King Edward IV defeated Lancastrians under earl of Warwick (killed).

Battle	War	Date	Details
Beachy Head	War of English Succession	29–30 June 1690	English and Dutch under Lord Torrington defeated by French under Tourville.
Belleau Wood	First World War	6 June 1918	First major US – German clash of the war, a hard-won victory by General Bundy over Ludendorff.
Bellevue	Franco-Prussian War	18 Oct. 1870	Marshal Bazaine was driven back from Metz by Germans.
Berwick	Scottish Independence	28 Mar. 1296	Edward I's troops killed thousands after John de Balliol's refusal to supply men for Gascon War.
Beymaroo	First British-Afghan War	23 Nov.1841	General Elphinstone allowed only 1 gun for Brigadier Shelton to dislodge Afghans.
Bismarck	Second World War	27 May 1941	After sinking the cruiser *Hood*, Lutjens' battleship was sunk near Brest by British torpedo planes and warships.
Blenheim	War of Spanish Succession	13 Aug. 1704	Duke of Marlborough and Eugene of Savoy defeated French under Marshal Tallard in Bavarian town.
Blood River	Afrikaner-Zulu War	16 Dec. 1838	Zulus under King Dingaan (Dingane) were routed by the Transvaal Boers.
Blore Heath	Wars of the Roses	23 Sept. 1459	Yorkists under the earl of Salisbury dispersed Lancastrians under Lord Audley.
Borodino	Napoleonic Wars	7 Sept. 1812	Napoleon paved the way for his triumphant march on Moscow by defeating Kutuzov.
Bosworth Field	Wars of the Roses	21 Aug. 1485	Henry, Duke of Richmond, later Henry VII, defeated and killed Richard III to end wars.
Boudicca	Roman invasion of Britain	AD 61	Suetonius routed Queen Boudicca of the Iceni, who took poison on the battlefield.
Boyne	War of English Succession	1 July 1690	Decisive battle of the war; William III defeated James II.
Brandywine	US War of Independence	11 Sept. 1777	British under General Howe forced George Washington's troops to retreat.
Breitenfeld	Thirty Years' War	17 Sept. 1631	First major Protestant victory of the war, in which the Roman Catholic Habsburg emperor Ferdinand II and the Catholic League under Johan Isaclaes Graf von Tilly were defeated by the Swedish-Saxon army under King Gustavus II Adolphus of Sweden.
Brill	Eighty Years' War	1 Apr. 1572	De La Marck's *Wetergeuzen* (sea beggars) took Dutch port from Spain to gain first Dutch victory of war.
Britain	Second World War	June 1940 –Apr. 1941	German air raids intended to prepare for invasion of Britain but repulsed by RAF
Bronkhurst Spruit	First Boer War	20 Dec. 1880	Opening engagement of the war, a British column of 259 was ambushed and defeated.
Bull Run (Manassas) (First)	US Civil War	21July 1861	Beauregard defeated McDowell's Union army, Confederate General Jackson gained nickname 'Stonewall'.
Bull Run (Manassas) (Second)	US Civil War	29–30 Aug. 1862	Confederates Lee and Jackson routed troops under General Pope.
Bunker Hill	US War of Independence	17 June 1775	British troops under Howe gained Breed's Hill and Bunker Hill but suffered heavy losses.
Burgos	Peninsular War	19 Sept.–22 Oct. 1812 10–12 June 1813	Duke of Wellington twice laid siege to Burgos. The first attempt against the French garrison was disastrous and 2,000 Allied troops were killed, while the French lost 600. In a second, decisive attempt the city was captured within two days.
Burlington Heights	War of 1812	5 May 1813	British under Col. Proctor attacked by Clay but eventually gained the day.
Bussaco	Peninsular War	27 Sept. 1810	Wellington defeated pursuing French army under Marshals Masséna and Ney.
Buxar/Baksar	British/Bengal War	23 Oct.1764	Major Munro's victory over a confederation of Indian pirates gave the East India Company control of Bengal and Bihar.
Cadiz	Anglo-Spanish War	29 Apr. 1587	Drake destroyed over 100 ships in his famous singeing of the Spanish king's beard.
Caer Caradoc	Roman invasion of Britain	AD 50	Romans under Ostorius Scapula defeated Caratacus, king of the British tribe of Trinovantes.
Calais	Anglo-French Wars	6 Jan. 1558	Last English stronghold in France lost, causing Mary I to say 'When I am dead and opened, you shall find Calais will be writ on my heart'.

MILITARY

Battle	War	Date	Details
Cambodia	Vietnamese invasion	7 Jan. 1979	Vietnamese army captured Phnom Penh and formed People's Republic of Kampuchea.
Cambrai	First World War	20 Nov.– 7 Dec. 1917	Brig.-Gen. Elles led world's first massed tank attack: dramatic breakthrough but soon reversed.
Camden	US War of Independence	16 Aug. 1780	British under Cornwallis defeated Americans under General Gates.
Camperdown	French Revolutionary Wars	11 Oct.1797	British fleet under Duncan intercepted and routed a Dutch convoy on its way to support a French invasion of Ireland.
Campo Santo	War of Austrian Succession	8 Feb. 1743	Indecisive battle between Spaniards under Mortemar and Imperialists under Count Traum.
Camulodunum	Second Roman invasion of Britain	c. AD 43	Romans under Emperor Claudius accepted surrender of local tribes after defeat on the Medway.
Cannae	Second Punic War	3 Aug. 216 BC	Hannibal gained a devastating victory over Romans under Varro due to superior cavalry.
Cape Matapan	Second World War	28 Mar. 1941	Small British fleet sank six or seven Italian ships off Cape Matapan, Greece (aka Cape Tainaron).
Cape St Vincent	French Revolutionary Wars	14 Feb. 1797	Spaniards were totally defeated by fleet of Sir John Jervis, who was made earl of St Vincent.
Carabobo	Latin American Wars	24 June 1921	South American rebels under Antonio Simon Bolivar defeated Spanish royalists under General La Torre.
Carbisdale	English Civil War	27 Apr. 1650	Marquis of Montrose captured by parliamentary force and executed the following month.
Carchemish	Syrian War	605 BC	Babylonian troops led by Crown Prince Nebuchadrezzar II captured Carchemish from the Egyptians.
Carlisle	Jacobite Rebellion of '45	9 Nov. 1745	Young Pretender, Charles Edward Stuart, Bonny Prince Charlie, defeated duke of Cumberland.
Carrhae	Roman/Mesopotamia War	53 BC	Romans under Marcus Licinius Crassus (killed) invaded Mesopotamia but were defeated by the Parthians.
Carrical	Seven Years' War	2 Aug. 1758	British under Admiral Pocock defeated French under Comte d'Ache but with few gains.
Cartagena	War of Austrian Succession	9 Mar. 1741	Port blockaded by British under Admiral Vernon but extensive losses forced his withdrawal.
Cassino	Second World War	Jan./May 1944	Fierce and protracted battle during which Allies blew up the Benedictine monastery, 15 February, believing it to be German-occupied.
Castillon	Hundred Years' War	17 July 1453	John Talbot, earl of Shrewsbury, was killed, and the English lost Gascony, in the last battle of the war.
Cedar Creek	US Civil War	19 Oct. 1864	Union General Sheridan defeated Confederates under General Early.
Cedar Mountain	US Civil War	9 Aug. 1862	Union Corps under Banks attacked Confederates under Jackson but forced to withdraw.
Cerignola	Franco-Spanish Wars	28 Apr. 1503	Spanish under Cordoba defeated French troops under Louis XII.
Chaeronea	Philippan Campaigns	338 BC	Macedonian army under Philip II defeated the joint Theban/Athenian army.
Chaldiran	Ottoman Wars	23 Aug.1514	Ottomans under Sultan Selim I defeated Safavid army under Shah Esma'il northeast of Lake Van.
Châlons	Attila Conquests	451 AD	Aka Battle of the Catalaunian Plains. Joint force of Romans and Visigoths defeated the Huns under Attila.
Chevy Chase	Scottish Independence	15 Aug. 1388	Aka Otterburn. Henry Percy's (Hotspurs) superior forces were soundly beaten by Scots.
Chickahominy	US Civil War	3 June 1864	General Lee's Confederates soundly repulsed Union attacks under Grant.
Chippenham	Danish Invasion of Britain	Jan. 878	Danes under Guthrum attacked King Alfred on 12th Night; he was forced to hide at Athelney.
Chongju	Russo-Japanese War	Apr. 1904	First land battle of war; Cossacks were driven back with few losses.
Chorillos	Peruvian-Chilean War	13 Jan. 1861	Chileans comprehensively defeated Peruvians.
Christianople	Danish-Swedish Wars	Autumn 1611	First military exploit of the 16-year-old King Gustavus Adolphus of Sweden was a total success.

Battle	War	Date	Details
Chrysler's Farm	War of 1812	11 Nov. 1813	British under Colonel Morrison defeated Americans under General Boyd.
Ciudad Rodrigo	Peninsular War	8 Jan. 1812	Decisive battle 54 miles south-west of Salamanca. Wellington ordered an assault on the border fortress that eventually succeeded, but 600 Allied troops were killed, including General Robert Craufurd.
Cold Harbour	US Civil War	3 June 1864	Grant's frontal attack on entrenched Confederate forces repulsed but counter-assault was disastrously defeated by Lee.
Colenso	Second Boer War	15 Dec. 1899	Sir Redvers Buller's first move to relieve Ladysmith repelled by Gen. Botha.
Copenhagen	French Revolutionary Wars	2 Apr. 1801	Nelson turned his blind eye to Admiral Hyde Parker's signal to retire and gained the day.
Coral Sea	Second World War	8 May 1942	Naval conflict fought mainly by aircraft from carriers. US carrier *Lexington* lost, but Japanese withdrew.
Coronel	First World War	1 Nov. 1914	Von Spee's *Scharnhorst* and *Gneisenau* sank the British ships *Monmouth* and *Good Hope*.
Corunna	Peninsular War	16 Jan. 1809	French under Marshal Soult defeated by British under Sir John Moore (killed).
Crécy	Hundred Years' War	26 Aug. 1346	Edward III's archers and cannon defeated French cavalry under Philip VI.
Cropredy Bridge	English Civil War	29 June 1644	Royalists under Charles I defeated Sir William Waller's parliamentarians near Banbury.
Cross Keys	US Civil War	8 June 1862	Confederates under Ewell fought successful rearguard action against Fremonts' Federals.
Cuba	Castro Revolt	26 July 1953	Fidel and Raul Castro led unsuccessful raid on armoury at Santiago and were imprisoned.
Culloden	Jacobite Rebellion of '45	16 Apr. 1746	Aka Drumossie Moor. Duke of Cumberland earned epithet 'Butcher' for treatment of Jacobite Rebels after his crushing victory.
Custoza (First)	Italian War of Independence	24 July 1848	Crushing defeat for the forces of Charles Albert, king of Sardinia-Piedmont by the Austrian veteran Field Marshal Joseph Radetzky.
Custoza (Second)	Italian War of Independence	24 June 1866	An 80,000-man Austrian army under Archduke Albert defeated a 120,000-man Italian army under Victor Emmanuel II.
Cyprus	Turkish Invasion	20 July 1974	Turkey invaded northern Cyprus and established a beachhead around Kyrenia.
D-Day	Second World War	6 June 1944	The launching of Operation Overlord, the Allied Invasion of Normandy, was a major turning point of the war.
Dettingen	War of Austrian Succession	27 June 1743	Anglo-Austrian-German victory over French; the last occasion that a British sovereign (George II) led his troops into battle.
Diamond Hill	Second Boer War	11 June 1900	Lord Roberts attacked General Botha near Pretoria and drove him from his position.
Dien Bien Phu	French-Vietnamese War	13 Mar.–7 May 1954	General Giap's siege and capture of key stronghold ended French power in Indochina and caused partition of Vietnam.
Dieppe	Second World War	19 Aug. 1942	Daytime Allied raid testing German Atlantic defences; 2nd Canadian Division suffered terrible losses.
Dingaan's Day	Afrikaner-Zulu War	16 Dec. 1838	Zulus under Dingaan were routed by the Transvaal Boers.
Dominica	US War of Independence	12 Apr. 1782	Aka Battle of Les Saintes. Admiral Rodney defeated French fleet, preserved British hold on Jamaica.
Dorylaeum	First Crusade	1 July 1097	Victory for Crusaders under Bohemond and Raymond of Toulouse over Seljuk Turks.
Douro	Peninsular War	12 May 1809	Wellington crossed the Douro and drove Marshal Soult's French troops out of Oporto.
Dover	Anglo-Dutch Wars	29 Nov. 1652	Dutch fleet under van Tromp victorious over Admiral Blake's English fleet at Dover and at Dungeness shortly after.
Dresden	Napoleonic Wars	26 Aug. 1813	Napoleon victorious over Russians, Prussians and Austrians.
Ebro River	Spanish Civil War	July–Nov. 1938	General Franco's Nationalists won a counter-offensive against Republicans under Modesto.

MILITARY

Battle	War	Date	Details
Edgecote	Wars of the Roses	26 July 1469	Lancastrian victory over Yorkists under the earl of Pembroke.
Edgehill	English Civil War	24 Oct. 1642	Indecisive first battle of Civil War between Charles I and parliamentarians under earl of Essex.
El Alamein	Second World War	Oct.–Nov. 1942	Montgomery's 8th Army drove Germans out of Egypt.
Elands River	Second Boer War	4 Aug. 1900	Australians under Col. Hore held out under fire until relieved by Kitchener.
Empingham	Wars of the Roses	12 Mar. 1470	Aka Losecoat Field. King Edward IV routed Sir Robert Welles's rebels.
Entholm	Northern Wars	11 June 1676	Swedes were defeated by Danish fleet under Admiral van Tromp.
Erbach	French Revolutionary Wars	15 May 1800	French under Sainte-Suzanne held out against Austrians under General Baron Kray.
Evesham	Second Barons' War	4 Aug. 1265	Prince Edward defeated the Barons, killed Simon de Montfort and restored Henry III.
Eylau	Napoleonic Wars	7–8 Feb. 1807	Indecisive battle between French troops under Napoleon and a joint Russian and Prussian army under Leonty Leontyevich Bennigsen.
Falkirk (First)	Scottish Independence	22 July 1298	English under Edward I defeated Scots under Sir William Wallace, who became a fugitive.
Falkirk (Second)	Jacobite Rebellion of '45	17 Jan. 1746	Jacobite army under Charles Edward Stuart (Young Pretender) defeated royalist forces under Henry Hawley.
Falkland Islands	First World War	8 Dec. 1914	Sturdee's squadron sank most of German Pacific squadron under von Spee (died).
Falkland Islands	British-Argentine War	2 Apr. 1982	Argentinian armed forces under General Galtieri invaded Falklands. On 3 April South Georgia was taken and on 5 April Rear Adm. Sandy Woodward led task force to free islands. On May 2 the *General Belgrano* was sunk by the sub *Conqueror*, and on 4 May the destroyer *Sheffield* was hit, and sank on 10 May. On 21 May 5,000 troops under Major-Gen. Jeremy Moore went ashore at Port San Carlos, and Argentinian surrender terms were eventually signed on 14 June, 10 weeks and 3 days after invasion.
Ferrybridge	Wars of the Roses	28 Mar. 1461	Lancastrians under Lord Clifford defeated Yorkists under Lord Fitzwalter (killed).
Fisher's Hill	US Civil War	22 Sept. 1864	Union force under Sheridan defeated Confederates under General Early.
Five Forks	US Civil War	1 Apr.1865	Sheridan and Warren defeated Pickett's Confederates causing Lee's withdrawal from Richmond and surrender at Appomattox on 9 April.
Flodden	Anglo-Scottish Wars	9 Sept. 1513	English under the earl of Surrey (Thomas Howard) defeated Scots under James IV (killed).
Fontenoy	War of Austrian Succession	11 May 1745	French under Marshal de Saxe repulsed duke of Cumberland's abortive drive to relieve Tournai.
Formigny	Hundred Years' War	15 Apr. 1450	French under the comte de Clermont defeated English under Kyrielle, restoring Normandy to France.
Fort Frontenac	Seven Years' War	27 Aug. 1758	Colonel Bradstreet defeated French under Noyan, who lost control of Lake Ontario.
Gebora	Peninsular War	19 Feb. 1811	Spaniards under Mendizabal were routed by French under Marshal Soult.
Gettysburg	US Civil War	1–3 July 1863	Greatest battle of the war between Meade's army of the Potomac and Lee's army of Virginia. Only a narrow Union victory, but it stopped Lee's invasion of the North.
Gibraltar	War of Spanish Succession	24 July 1704	British and Dutch fleet under Sir George Rooke defeated Spanish under marquis de Salinas and took Gibraltar.
Gitschin	Seven Weeks' War	29 June 1866	Prussians under Prince Frederick Charles defeated Austrians and Saxons under Clam-Gallas.
Glorious 1st of June	French Revolutionary Wars	1 June1794	Aka Ushant. British under Lord Howe defeated French and sank the *Vengeur*.

Battle	War	Date	Details
Golden Spurs	Flemish War	11 July 1302	Aka Courtrai. Untrained Flemish guild workers defeated French cavalry in Flanders and took their spurs as a trophy of their victory.
Graf Spee	Second World War	17 Dec. 1939	The pride of the German fleet, the pocket battle ship Graf Spee was scuttled by Captain Hans Langsdorf after being harried by three British cruisers Achilles, Ajax and Exeter and forced into Montevideo harbour. The Uruguayan government ordered the ship to sea but, rather than face a certain defeat, Hitler himself ordered the scuttling and Langsdorf shot himself.
Granada	Moorish Wars	Jan. 1492	Moors under Boabdil were defeated and the city came under Catholic rule of Ferdinand II of Aragon and Isabella I of Castille.
Grant's Hill	Seven Years' War	14 Sept. 1758	Major Grant with 800 Highlanders defeated by French under de Ligneris at Fort Duquesne.
Gravelines	Franco-Spanish Wars	13 July 1558	Spanish under comte d'Egmont, backed by an English fleet, defeated French under Marshal de Thermes.
Guadalajara	Spanish Civil War	8 Mar. 1937	Republicans defeated Nationalists under Franco and Italian Fascists under General Roatta.
Guadalcanal	Second World War	Aug. 1942–Jan. 1943	Americans eventually gained victory over Japanese after 5 months' fighting on land and sea.
Guadeloupe	French Revolutionary Wars	3 July 1794	Sir John Jervis captured island but it was recaptured by the French on 10 December.
Guilford Courthouse	US War of Independence	15 Mar. 1781	British under Lord Cornwallis defeated Americans under General Greene.
Halidon Hill	Scottish Independence	19 July 1333	English troops under Edward III defeated Scottish forces attempting to relieve Berwick-upon-Tweed.
Han Ko/Hangö	Great Northern War	4–6 Aug. 1714	Peter the Great commanded a fleet against Swedes, the first major Russian victory at sea.
Harfleur	Hundred Years' War	Aug.–Sept. 1415	English under Henry V defeated the French troops after a 6-week siege of the port.
Harpers Ferry	US Civil War	15 Sept. 1862	Confederates under General Thomas Stonewall Jackson forced Union garrison to surrender.
Hastings	Norman Conquest	14 Oct. 1066	Aka Battle of Senlac Hill. Harold II of England (killed) defeated by William, duke of Normandy.
Hedgeley Moor	Wars of the Roses	25 Apr. 1464	Yorkist Lord Montagu routed Lancastrians under Margaret of Anjou and Ralph Percy (killed).
Heligoland	Napoleonic Wars	31 Aug. 1807	British squadron under Admiral Thomas Russell captured island from Danes.
Heligoland Bight	First World War	28 Aug. 1914	Admiral Beatty's battle cruiser Lion sank the German cruisers Mainz and Koln.
Heliopolis	French Revolutionary Wars	20 Mar. 1800	Turks in Egypt under Ibrahim Bey routed by French under General Kléber.
Herrings	Hundred Years War	12 Feb. 1429	Sir John Fastolfe defeated the comte de Clermont at Rouvray.
Hexham	Wars of the Roses	15 May 1464	Yorkists under Lord Montagu defeated and executed duke of Somerset.
Homildon Hill	Scottish Independence	14 Sept. 1402	English troops under Sir Henry Percy (Hotspur) defeated the Scots under the 4th earl of Douglas.
Hydaspes	Alexander's Asiatic Wars	326 BC	Fourth and last pitched battle fought by Alexander the Great during his Asiatic Campaign. Despite overwhelming numerical superiority of the Persian army led by Porus, and the 200 elephants that Porus had at his disposal, Alexander's tactical genius won the day.
Hyderabad	Conquest of Sind	24 Mar. 1843	British under Sir Charles Napier defeated Baluchis under Shir Mohammed.
Ilipa	Second Punic War	206 BC	Romans under Publius Cornelius Scipio (Africanus) defeated Carthaginians under Hasdrubal. Gisco and Mago in the Spanish town near Seville.
Imola	French Revolutionary Wars	3 Feb. 1797	French and Italian troops under Marshal Victor defeated Papal troops under General Colli.
Imphal	Second World War	29 Mar. 1944	Japanese troops besieged the city of Imphal in

Battle	War	Date	Details
			Assam, north-east India.
Inchon	Korean War	15 Sept. 1950	Amphibious landing by General Almond's X Corps drove the North Korean troops inland and seized Kimpo airfield.
Ingogo River	First Boer War	8 Feb. 1881	Boers defeated a small British column of 5 companies, 4 guns and a mounted force.
Inhlobane Mountain	Zulu War	28 Mar. 1879	British force of 1,300 under Cols Buller and Russell defeated by Zulus.
Inkerman	Crimean War	5 Nov. 1854	Russians under Prince Menshikov defeated by Franco-British troops under Raglan.
Ipsus	Macedonian-Egyptian War	301 BC	The combined forces of Lysimachus king of Thrace and Seleucus I Nicator of Babylon defeated the Macedonian army under Antigonus (killed) and his son Demetrius.
Isandhlwana	Zulu War	22 Jan. 1879	Six companies of 24th Regiment under Col. Durnford overwhelmed by Zulus under Matyana.
Issus	Alexander's Asiatic War	333 BC	Alexander the Great defeated Persians under King Darius.
Ivry	French Religious Wars	14 Mar. 1590	Henry IV's Huguenots defeated Catholic League under duc de Mayenne.
Iwo Jima	Second World War	19 Feb. 1945	General Schmidt's US V Amphibious Corps assaulted and secured the small island (8 sq miles) by 26 March.
Jajau	Mughal Civil War	12 June 1707	Family conflict to decide the successor to the Mughal emperor Aurangzeb; eventually his eldest surviving son Bahādur Shāh succeeded after a bloody battle with his brother Azam Shāh.
Jarnac	French Religious Wars	13 Mar. 1569	Catholics under the duke of Anjou defeated Huguenots under the prince de Condé.
Jena	Napoleonic Wars	14 Oct. 1806	Napoleon defeated the prince of Hohenlohe's Prussian army.
Jutland	First World War	31 May 1916	(Aka Skagerrak) Only major clash betwen British and German fleets in the war. British lost two ships, but German High Seas fleet did not seek battle thereafter.
Kadesh	Egyptian/Hittite War	1299 BC	Seeking to recapture the Syrian city of Kadesh, Ramses II engaged the Hittite leader Muwatallis without success and was forced to retreat; the Hittites moving southward into Damascus.
Kambula	Zulu War	29 Mar. 1879	British under Colonel Wood defeated Zulus under Cetewayo.
Karbalā	Muslim Wars	10 Oct. 680	Husayn ibn Ali, grandson of the Prophet Muhammad was defeated and killed by an army sent by the Umayyad Caliph Yazid I.
Karnāl	Mughal Civil Wars	24 Feb. 1739	Persian forces under Nāder Shāh defeated the Mughals under Emperor Muhammad Shāh.
Kemendine	First Burma War	10 June 1824	British under Sir Archibald Campbell defeated Burmese troops.
Khartoum	British-Sudan Campaign	26 Jan. 1885	General Gordon killed defending the city against the Mahdi after Beresford's troops were delayed.
Killiecrankie	Jacobite Rising	27 July 1689	Highland Jacobites under 'Bonny' Dundee defeated William III's troops under General Mackay, but Dundee's death undid the victory.
Kilsyth	English Civil War	15 Aug. 1645	Royalists under marquis of Montrose defeated Covenanters under General Baillie.
Kimberley	Second Boer War	15 Oct. 1899	Gen. French relieved town on 15 Feb. 1900 from Boer siege led by General Cronje.
Kioge	Northern War	July 1677	Danish fleet under Admiral Juel defeated Swedes under Admiral Horn.
Kissingen	Seven Weeks War	10 July 1866	Prussians under General Falkstein defeated Bavarians under General Zoller.
Kiu-lien-Cheng	Russo-Japanese War	1 May 1904	Japanese under Marshal Kuroki defeated Russians under General Sassulitch.
Königgrätz	Seven Weeks War	3 July 1866	Aka Battle of Sadowa. Decisive battle of the conflict in which Helmuth von Moltke's Prussian army defeated the Austrian army led

Battle	War	Date	Details
			by General Benedek, which led to Austria's exclusion from a Prussian-dominated Germany. The war was formally concluded on 23 August 1866 by the Treaty of Prague. Bismarck's alliance with Italy meant Venetia was ceded to the Italians.
Kosovo	Byzantine Wars	June 1389	Battle fought at Kosovo Polje (Field of the Blackbirds) between Serbs under Prince Lazar and Turks under Sultan Murad I, who gained a hard-fought victory.
Kursk Salient	Second World War	5–13 July 1943	Largest tank battle of the war, in which Russians smashed massive German offensive.
Ladysmith	Second Boer War	2 Nov. 1899	Sir George White defended against Boers until Redvers Buller relieved town 27 Feb. 1900.
Laings Nek	First Boer War	28 Jan. 1881	British under Gen Colley repulsed by Boers.
Lake Erie	War of 1812	10 Sept. 1813	Master Commandant Oliver Hazard Perry's fleet of 9 ships engaged 6 British warships under Captain Robert Heriot Barclay and although having to transfer from his flagship *Lawrence* to its sister ship *Niagara*, Perry sailed directly into the British line and firing broadsides as he went eventually forced the British to surrender.
Lake Trasimeno	Second Punic War	217 BC	The Carthaginian General Hannibal defeated the Roman army under Gaius Flaminius (killed) on the north shore of the Italian lake.
Landau	War of Spanish Succession	29 July 1702	French under de Melac lost the fortress to Prince Louis of Baden.
Langport	English Civil War	10 July 1645	Parliamentarians under Thomas Fairfax defeated Royalists under Lord Goring.
Langside	Anti-Marian Uprising	13 May 1568	Mary Queen of Scots's army was defeated by earl of Moray; Mary escaped to England.
Lansdowne	English Civil War	5 July 1643	Royalists under Sir Ralph Hopton defeated parliamentarians under Sir William Waller.
La Rochelle	Hundred Years' War	1372	A Castilian fleet under Bocanegra, acting in support of the French, defeated the English under Pembroke.
Lauffeld	War of Austrian Succession	2 July 1747	French under Marshal Saxe defeated allied Austrian and British army under Cumberland.
Leck	Thirty Years' War	5 Apr. 1632	Gustavus Adolphus's Swedish/German army defeated Imperialists under Tilly (mortally wounded).
Leghorn	Anglo-Dutch Wars	31 Mar. 1653	Admiral Van Gelen (killed) destroyed 6 English ships commanded by Commodore Appleton.
Leipzig	Napoleonic Wars	16–19 Oct. 1813	Napoleon defeated, and forced into decisive retreat, by Coalition of Blücher, Schwarzenberg and Bernadotte.
Le Mans	Franco-Prussian War	10–11 Jan. 1871	French under Chanzy were completely routed by Germans under Prince Frederick Charles.
Leningrad	Second World War	15 Jan. 1944	(Now St Petersburg) Russians relieved the 30-month blockade of the city after 5 days' fighting.
Lepanto	Cyprus War	7 Oct. 1571	Last major battle using oared ships brought decisive victory for the Holy League fleet under Don John of Austria over Ottoman Turks.
Leuctra	Boeotian-Athenian War	371 BC	Boeotian army under Epaminondas defeated a Spartan army under King Cleombrotus.
Lewes	English Barons' War	14 May 1264	Simon de Montfort defeated Henry III and Prince Edward and signed the Mise of Lewes.
Lexington	US War of Independence	19 Apr. 1775	First battle of the war resulted in minor victory for British troops under Lt-Col. Francis Smith.
Leyte Gulf	Second World War	24–26 Oct. 1944	Biggest ever naval battle. United States defeated Japanese comprehensively, losing 6 ships to Japan's 28.
Liaoyang	Russo-Japanese War	25 Aug.–3 Sept. 1904	Japanese army under Marshal Oyama forced Russians under General Kuropatkin to retreat.
Lille	War of Spanish Succession	12 Aug. 1708	French under Marshal de Boufflers surrendered to Prince Eugene on 25 Oct. 1708.
Lindley	Second Boer War	27 May 1900	Colonel Spragge surrendered to superior Boer force.
Little Bighorn	Sioux Rising	25 June 1876	Col. Custer (killed) and his 7th US Cavalry

MILITARY

Battle	War	Date	Details
			wiped out by Sioux and Cheyenne warriors under Sitting Bull.
Loudoun Hill	Scottish Independence	10 May 1307	Robert the Bruce defeated earl of Pembroke's cavalry by his spearmen's steadfastness.
Lucknow	Indian Mutiny	June–Nov. 1857	Siege relieved by General Sir Colin Campbell.
Lundy's Lane	War of 1812	25 July 1814	Americans under General Brown unsuccessfully attacked British under Sir George Drummond.
Lützen	Thirty Years' War	16 Nov. 1632	Indecisive battle in which Gustavus II Adolphus of Sweden lost his life while engaging the Habsburg forces of Albrecht von Wallenstein.
Madrid	Spanish Civil War	7 Nov. 1936	Nationalists under General Mola attacked the Republican forces of General Miaja causing the government to flee to Valencia.
Mafeking	Second Boer War	Oct. 1899	Colonel Baden-Powell resisted Boers under General Cronje in siege not raised till 17 May 1900.
Magdeburg	Thirty Years' War	Mar. 1631	Imperialists under Field Marshal Tilly besieged the city and von Falkenberg was killed.
Magenta	Italian Independence Wars	4 June 1859	French under General MacMahon defeated Austrians under Marshal Gyulai.
Majuba Hill	First Boer War	27 Feb. 1881	Boers under General Joubert defeated British under Sir George Colley (killed).
Maldon	Danish Invasion of Britain	AD 991	Danish army under Tryggvason defeated Anglo-Saxons under Brithnoth.
Malplaquet	War of Spanish Succession	11 Sept. 1709	German and British forces under Marlborough defeated French under Villars in costly victory.
Malvern Hill	US Civil War	1 July 1862	Union repelled fierce Confederate attacks during 7 days' battle.
Mantineia	Peloponnesian War	418 BC	Spartan forces under King Agis defeated the Athenians.
Manzikert	Anatolian Wars	AD 1071	Byzantines under the emperor Romanus IV Diogenes were defeated by the Seljuq Turks led by Sultan Alp-Arslan.
Marathon	Persian-Greek Wars	Sept. 490 BC	Athenians under Miltiades, 10,000 in number, defeated 50,000 Persians.
Marengo	French Revolutionary Wars	14 June 1800	Napoleon with aid of General Desaix (killed) defeated Austrians under General Mélas.
Margate	Hundred Years' War	24 Mar. 1387	Earls of Arundel and Nottingham repelled invasion threat from Franco-Castilian force.
Marne	First World War	6–9 Sept. 1914 and July 1918	Two bloody battles. In both cases the Germans were forced to retreat.
Marston Moor	English Civil War	2 July 1644	Prince Rupert's royalists defeated by Cromwell's Ironsides under Fairfax and Manchester.
Medellín	Peninsular War	28 Mar. 1809	French under Marshal Victor comprehensively defeated Spanish under Cuesta.
Medway	Second invasion of Britain	c. AD 43	Romans under Emperor Claudius defeated Britons under Caratacus and his brother Togodumnus (died)
Megiddo	Palestinian War	c.1468 BC	The Palestinian town of Megiddo was captured by the Egyptian king Thutmosis III.
Metauro River	Second Punic War	207 BC	Romans under Marcus Livius Salinator and Claudius Nero defeated Carthaginians under Hasdrubal (died), the brother of Hannibal.
Midway	Second World War	3–6 June 1942	In battle fought mainly by aircraft, Japanese attack on US base repelled, US carrier *Yorktown* lost, but 4 Japanese carriers sunk.
Missolonghi (First)	Greek War of Independence	Jan. 1823	The Ottomans were forced to withdraw after failing to take the key fortress of Missolonghi (Mesolóngion).
Missolonghi (Second)	Greek War of Independence	23 Apr. 1826	Joint Turkish/Egyptian forces under Ibrahim Pasha defeated a smalll Greek garrison under Mavrocordatos.
Mohács	Ottoman Wars	29 Aug. 1526	Turks under Suleyman I defeated Hungarians under Louis II.
Molinos del Rey	Peninsular War	21 Dec. 1808	French under General St Cyr defeated Spanish under Reding.
Monongahela	French-Indian War	9 July 1755	British army under General Edward Braddock was routed by the joint French and Indian

Battle	War	Date	Details
			forces under Captain Daniel de Beaujeu and, after his death, by Captain Jean Dumas. The survivors of the battle near Fort Duquesne (Pittsburgh) included George Washington.
Mons Lactarius	Ostrogoth War	AD 553	Byzantine General Narses defeated the Goths under Teias (died), near Naples, Italy.
Morat	Swiss-Burgundy War	22 June 1476	Victory for the Swiss Confederation over the Burgundians under Charles the Bold.
Morgarten	Swiss War of Independence	15 Nov. 1315	Swiss Confederation's first military success against the Austrians under Leopold I.
Mortimer's Cross	Wars of the Roses	2 Feb. 1461	Edward, duke of York, defeated Lancastrians under earls of Pembroke and Wiltshire.
Mukden	Russo-Japanese War	19 Feb.–10 Mar. 1905	Russian stronghold in Manchuria that finally fell to the Japanese.
Munda	Roman Civil War	45 BC	Decisive battle of the Roman Civil War when Julius Caesar conclusively defeated the Pompeians.
Mylae	First Punic War	260 BC	Romans destroyed 50 Carthaginian ships.
Näfels	Swiss War of Independence	9 Apr. 1388	Major victory for the newly formed Swiss Confederation in its struggle against Habsburg overlordship. Albert III of Austria advanced with an army against Glarus, a district that had adhered to the confederacy in 1352 but had been restored to the Habsburgs in 1355. The rebels, reinforced by troops from Schwyz, at first repelled the attack but then made a successful counter-attack on the heights of Näfels.
Nahāvand	Arabian Wars	AD 642	Arab forces under Nu'mān defeated Sāsānian troops under Firuzan.
Nancy	Swiss-Burgundy War	1477	Victory for the Swiss Confederation over the Burgundians under Charles the Bold (died).
Nanjing	Chinese Civil War	22 Apr. 1949	Communists captured Chiang Kai-shek's Nationalist capital, enabling communists under Mao Zedong to take control of China.
Naseby	English Civil War	14 June 1645	Parliamentarians under Fairfax routed Prince Rupert's royalists.
Nashville	US Civil War	15–16 Dec. 1864	Union army under General Thomas defeated Confederates under General Hood.
Navarino	Greek War of Independence	20 Oct. 1827	Last action between wooden ships. Britain, France and Russia defeated Turks and Egyptians.
Nemea	Corinthian War	394 BC	After the victory of Sparta in the Peloponnesian War against Athens it maintained its military superiority against a coalition of troops from Thebes, Corinth, Athens and Argos, largely due to their skill in hoplite warfare (use of heavy infantry).
Neva River	Swedish Holy War	15 July 1240	Novgorod army under Prince Alexander Yaroslavich defeated the Swedes under earl Birger on the banks of the Neva. Yaroslavich was given the name Nevsky in honour of his victory.
Neville's Cross	Anglo-Scottish Wars	17 Oct. 1346	Scots under David II routed by Henry de Percy and Ralph de Neville.
Newbury (First)	English Civil War	20 Sept. 1643	Charles I failed to prevent the parliamentarians under the earl of Essex from marching to London.
Newbury (Second)	English Civil War	27 Oct. 1644	Charles I's inconclusive encounter with parliamentary force under the earl of Manchester spurred formation of the New Model Army.
New Orleans	War of 1812	Jan. 1815	Andrew Jackson defeated English force under General Sir Edward Pakenham (killed).
New Orleans	US Civil War	Apr. 16th 1862	Union fleet under Commodore Farragut bombarded Forts Jackson and forced surrender of city.
Niagara	Seven Years' War	June 1759	British under General Prideaux (killed) besieged the Canadian fort and William Johnson successfully repulsed Ligneris.

Battle	War	Date	Details
Nicopolis	Ottoman Wars	25 Sept. 1396	Turks under Sultan Bayezid I defeated a Christian Allied army under Sigismund, king of Hungary.
Nile/Aboukir Bay	French Revolutionary Wars	1–2 Aug. 1798	French fleet destroyed and Admiral Brueys killed by Nelson, checking Napoleon's plans in Middle East.
Nong Sa Rai	Thai War of Independence	1593	The final battle between the Thai troops under Prince Naresuen and Burmese troops under King Nanda Bayin. The Burmese Crown Prince was slain by Naresuen and Thai independence was safe for 150 years.
Nördlingen	Thirty Years' War	5–6 Sept. 1634	Decisive victory for the Holy Roman Empire and Spain under Matthias Gallas over the Swedish army led by Gustav Karlsson Horn and Bernhard of Saxe-Weimar, which led to the dissolution of the Heilbronn alliance and forced Cardinal Richelieu to bring France into the war.
Northampton	Wars of the Roses	10 July 1460	Earl of March, later Edward IV, routed the Lancastrians, captured Henry VI and executed supporters, including Buckingham and Shrewsbury.
Novara	Italian War of Independence	23 Mar. 1849	Austrian troops under Marshal Joseph Radetzky routed Piedmontese army.
Okinawa	Second World War	1 Apr.–21 June 1945	US amphibious landing met fierce and protracted resistance inland, losing over 7,000 men to Japan's 100,000 killed. US and Japanese commanders Bruckner and Ushiima.
Omdurman	British-Sudan Campaigns	2 Sept. 1898	General Kitchener destroyed the Mahdi's army. Last full-scale cavalry charge by 21st Lancers, including Winston Churchill.
Opequan	US Civil War	19 Sept. 1864	Confederates under General Early defeated by General Sheridan and Lt-Col. George Custer.
Oporto	Peninsular War	28 Mar. 1809	French under Marshal Soult defeated Portuguese under Lima and Pareiras.
Orléans	Hundred Years' War	12 Oct. 1428–8 May 1429	Decisive siege in which English were forced to withdraw after Joan of Arc captured key siege forts.
Oswego	Seven Years' War	11 Aug. 1756	French under marquis of Montcalm took English fort held by Col. Mercer (killed).
Otterburn	Scottish Independence	15 Aug. 1388	Aka Chevy Chase. Scots under earls Douglas (killed) and Murray defeated Henry Percy (Hotspur).
Oudenarde	War of Spanish Succession	11 July 1708	British and Imperialists under Marlborough and Prince Eugene defeated French under Ventome and Burgundy.
Palo Alto	Mexican War	8 May 1846	First clash of the Mexican War in which the Americans under General Zachary Taylor defeated the Mexican army under General Mariano Arista.
Panipat (First)	Indian Wars	21 Apr. 1526	Mughal chief Bābur defeated Sultan Ibrāhim Lodo of Delhi (died).
Panipat (Second)	Indian Wars	5 Nov. 1556	Bayram Khān, the guardian of Mughal emperor Akbar, defeated the Hindu General Hemu.
Panipat (Third)	Indian Wars	14 Jan. 1761	Afghan chief Ahmad Shāh Durrāni defeated the Marāthā army under the Bhāo Sahib.
Parma	War of Polish Succession	29 June 1734	French under Marshal de Coigny defeated Imperialists under Count Claudius de Mercy (killed).
Passchendaele	First World War	30 Oct. 1917	Aka 3rd Battle of Ypres. Canadian 3rd and 4th Division and British pushed back Germans but suffered heavy casualties.
Patay	Hundred Years War	18 June 1429	French under Joan of Arc and duc d'Alençon defeated English under Talbot and Fastolfe.
Pea Ridge	US Civil War	6–8 Mar. 1862	Aka Elk Horn Tavern. First key Union victory west of Mississippi. Confederate General Ben McCulloch killed.
Pearl Harbor	Second World War	7 Dec. 1941	Japanese carrier-based planes attacked US Pacific fleet without declaring war, sank 19 ships. USA forced into the war.
Pharsalus	Roman Civil War	48 BC	Julius Caesar defeated the much larger force of Pompey. Caesar, who had only minor losses,

Battle	War	Date	Details
			exclaimed 'Hoc voluerunt' ('They would have it so').
Philippi	Brutus' Rebellion	42 BC	Republicans under Brutus and Cassius (both committed suicide) defeated by Octavian and Mark Antony, exposing Rome to autocratic rule.
Pichincha	Latin-American Wars	24 May 1822	South American rebels under Antonio José de Sucre overcame Spanish royalists.
Pinkie Cleugh	Anglo-Scottish Wars	10 Sept. 1547	Scots under the earls of Arran and Huntly defeated by English under Protector Somerset.
Plains of Abraham	Seven Years' War	13 Sept. 1759	French under Montcalm defeated by Wolfe and lost Quebec. Both generals killed.
Plassey	Seven Years' War	23 June 1757	British under Robert Clive defeated nawab of Bengal and assured East India Company's rule there.
Poitiers	Hundred Years' War	19 Sept. 1356	English archers under Edward the Black Prince defeated French under King John II.
Plataea	Persian-Greek Wars	479 BC	Greeks under Pausanias won a decisive victory over the Persians under Mardonius.
Port Arthur	Sino-Japanese War	21 Nov. 1894	(Now called Lushun.) Japanese defeated Chinese with very few casualties.
Port Arthur	Russo-Japanese War	8 Feb. 1904	Japanese fleet attacked Russian squadron without declaring war. Japan eventually won the port after almost a year's fighting (treaty of Portsmouth).
Preston	English Civil War	17–19 Aug. 1648	Cromwell's Roundheads defeated royalists under duke of Hamilton and Sir Marmaduke Langdale, ending the Second Civil War.
Preston	Jacobite Rebellion 1715	13 Nov. 1715	General Will Thomas's royalists defeated Jacobites under Thomas Forster.
Prestonpans	Jacobite Rebellion 1745	21 Sept. 1745	Aka Gladsmuir. Jacobites under Young Pretender Charles Edward Stuart defeated royalists in a 10-minute battle.
Princeton	US War of Independence	3 Jan. 1777	Americans under George Washington defeated British under Cornwallis.
Pydna	Third Macedonian War	22 June 168 BC	Romans under Lucius Aemilius Paullus defeated the Macedonians under king Perseus.
Pyramids	French Revolutionary Wars	21 July 1798	Napoleon defeated Mamelukes under Murad Bey and went on to occupy Cairo.
Quatre Bras	Napoleon's Hundred Days	16 June 1815	Marshal Ney engaged Wellington, causing his withdrawal to Waterloo.
Quebec	Seven Years' War	27 June 1759	First of two battles of Seven Years' War, which decided the future of Canada.
Queenston Heights	War of 1812	13 Oct. 1812	British in Canada under General Brock (killed) defeated Americans under General Van Rensselaer.
Quiberon Bay	Seven Years' War	20 Nov. 1759	British fleet under Admiral Hawke defeated French under Marshal de Conflans.
Radcot Bridge	Richard II's Barons' War	20 Dec. 1387	Earl of Derby, later Henry IV, defeated Richard II's supporter Robert de Vere, earl of Oxford.
Ramillies	War of Spanish Succession	23 May 1706	British and Imperialists under Marlborough defeated French under Villeroi.
Rieti	Italian War of Independence	7 Mar. 1821	Austrians defeated Pepe's Neapolitans, entered Naples and reinstated Ferdinand IV on throne.
Rio Salado		30 Oct. 1340	Castilian forces under Alfonso XI and Portuguese forces under Alfonso IV defeated Muslim Marinids of North Africa.
River Plate	Second World War	13 Dec. 1939	The battle in Uruguayan waters between British and German warships ended on 17 December with the scuttling of the German pocket battleship *Graf Spee*
Roanoke Island	US Civil War	7 Feb. 1862	Union General Burnside defeated Confederates under General Wise.
Rocroi	Thirty Years War	19 May 1643	French army under the Duc d'Enghien (later known as the Great Condé) routed a Spanish army under Don Francisco de Melo, ending the Spanish ascendancy in Europe.
Rorke's Drift	Zulu-British War	22 Jan. 1879	Lts Chard and Bromhead led a company from 24th Regiment to repulse numerically far superior Zulu attack. 11 VCs awarded.

MILITARY

Battle	War	Date	Details
Ruhr Pocket	Second World WarI	1 Apr. 1945	US 9th Army surrounded remnants of Field Marshal Model's Army Group B, causing mass surrender and Model's suicide.
Sadowa	Seven Weeks' War	3 July 1866	See Königgrätz.
Sahagun	Peninsular War	21 Dec. 1808	Decisive British cavalry victory over the French 133 miles north-east of Salamanca. Henry Paget (Lord Uxbridge) led the 15th Hussars against General Debelle's cavalry fleeing from the 10th Hussars under General Slade. Debelle mistook the British cavalry for inferior Spanish troops and engaged them in battle. Debelle and half his men escaped but left behind at least 120 killed and more than 160 captured. Paget lost two men.
St Albans (First)	Wars of the Roses	22 May 1455	First battle in these wars. Duke of York defeated Lancastrians. Henry VI captured. Northumberland and Somerset killed.
St Albans (Second)	Wars of the Roses	17 Feb. 1461	Lancastrians under Margaret of Anjou defeated Yorkists and released Henry VI.
Saintes	US War of Independence	12 Apr. 1782	British under Admiral Sir George Rodney gained a decisive naval victory in the West Indies over a French fleet under the Comte de Grasse.
Salamanca	Peninsular War	22 July 1812	Wellington's Allied army defeated Marshal Auguste Marmont's force, the main French army in Spain.
Salamis (First)	Persian-Greek Wars	480 BC	Greeks under Themistocles won a naval victory over the Persians under Xerxes.
Salamis (Second)	Macedonian-Egyptian War	306 BC	Demetrius I Poliorcetes of Macedonia won a naval encounter with the Egyptians under Ptolemy I.
Salerno	Second World War	Sept. 1943	In Allied amphibious landing, 5th Army reinforced by US 82nd Airborne and British 7th Armoured took port and had entered Naples by 1 October.
Samaria	Palestinian War	722 BC	The capital of the Hebrew kingdom of Israel was destroyed by the Assyrians under Sargon II.
Samugarh	Mughal Civil War	29 May 1658	Decisive battle of the struggle for the Mughal throne between Aurangzeb and Murād Bakhsh, the third and fourth sons of Shah Jehan, on the one side, and the eldest son, Dārā Shikoh, on the other. Aurangzeb ultimately triumphed and began his long rule as emperor.
San Jacinto	Texan Rising	21 Apr. 1836	General Houston defeated Mexicans under Santa Anna, which led to admission of Texas to US states 1845.
Santa Cruz (First)	Anglo-Spanish Wars	1657	British fleet under Robert Blake destroyed the harboured Spanish fleet.
Santa Cruz (Second)	Anglo-Spanish Wars	1797	Horatio Nelson lost his right arm during his unsuccessful assault on the Tenerife port.
Saratoga (First)	US War of Independence	19 Sept. 1777	Aka Battle of Freeman's Farm. British army under General Burgoyne unsuccessfully attempted to gain access to Albany.
Saratoga (Second)	US War of Independence	7 Oct. 1777	Aka Battle of Bemis Heights or Second Battle of Freeman's Farm. General Burgoyne's continued engagement of American troops was thwarted by General Benedict Arnold.
Saratoga (Third)	US War of Independence	17 Oct. 1777	Decisive battle of the war whereby the British army under General Burgoyne was defeated by the Americans under Gates; the outcome encouraged the French into the war.
Sauchie Burn	Barons' Rebellion	18 June 1488	James III of Scotland (killed) defeated by rebel barons under the earl of Angus.
Sedan	Franco-Prussian War	1 Sept.1870	General von Moltke's German Army defeated French, Emperor Napoleon III surrendered, French Second Empire fell.
Sedgemoor	Monmouth's Rebellion	6 July 1685	Royal troops under the earl of Feversham defeated James, duke of Monmouth.
Selby	English Civil War	11 Apr. 1644	Sir Thomas Fairfax defeated royalists under Col. John Bellasis.

Battle	War	Date	Details
Seringapatam	Fourth Mysore War	1799	British army under Richard Wellesley defeated the Indians under Tipu Sultan (died).
Sevastopol	Crimean War	Sept. 1854–Sept. 1855	Successful Allied siege of Russian naval base.
Seven Days battle	US Civil War	26 June–2 July 1862	Confederates under General Lee staved off Union campaign to capture Richmond after a week-long series of battles.
Sevenoaks	Cade's Rebellion	18 June 1450	Rebels under Jack Cade defeated royal troops under Sir Humphrey Stafford (died).
Shanghai	Sino-Japanese War	8 Aug. 1937	Chinese defended this port for three months but eventually succumbed to Japanese.
Shannon and Chesapeake	War of 1812	1 June 1813	British frigate Shannon under Capt. Broke captured US frigate Chesapeake under Capt. Lawrence (killed).
Sheerness	Anglo-Dutch Wars	7 June 1667	Dutch fleet under Admiral de Ruyter sailed up the Medway to Upnor Castle and sank 7 ships.
Sheriffmuir	Jacobite Rebellion 1715	13 Nov. 1715	Indecisive battle between 10,000 Jacobite rebels under the earl of Mar and 3,300 loyalist Scots under the duke of Argyll.
Shiloh	US Civil War	6–7 Apr. 1862	Major engagement with even casualties, but Confederates under General Johnston (killed) eventually left the field to Grant's Federal troops.
Shirogawa	Satsuma Rebellion	24 Sept. 1876	Imperial army under Prince Taruhito defeated rebels under Takamori Saigo (killed).
Shrewsbury	Percy's Rebellion	21 July 1403	Royalists under Henry IV defeated Henry Percy (Hotspur), who was killed in battle.
Six Day War	Israeli–Arab War	5–10 June 1967	Victory over United Arab Republic, Syria and Jordan brought Israel control of Golan Heights, West Bank, Gaza Strip, Sinai Peninsula and the Old City of Jerusalem.
Sluys	Hundred Years' War	24 June 1340	English archers under Edward III defeated French in the Zwyn estuary in the main naval engagement of the war.
Solferino	Italian War of Independence	24 June 1859	Indecisive but bloody battle that led to the peace of Villafranca and the Austrian loss of Lombardy to Italy.
Solway Moss	Anglo-Scottish Wars	25 Nov. 1542	Scots under Oliver Sinclair were routed by English under Thomas Dacre and John Musgrave.
Somme	First World War	1 July–19 Nov.	Franco-British offensive cost over 1 million casualties, made small territory gains. First tank attack of war on 15 Sept. In 1918 Germans made the Somme target for their last offensive.
Stamford Bridge	Norse Invasion of Britain	25 Sept. 1066	English under Harold II defeated Norsemen under Harold Hardrada and Tostig (both killed).
Stirling Bridge	Scottish Independence	11 Sept. 1297	Scots under Sir William Wallace defeated the invading English under the earl of Surrey.
Stoke	Lambert Simnel's Rebellion	16 June 1487	Royal troops under Henry VII defeated rebels under John de la Pole, earl of Lincoln.
Talavera	Peninsular War	28 July 1809	Arthur Wellesley was made Viscount Wellington after defeating the French under King Joseph Bonaparte and Marchand Jourdan.
Tālikota	Muslim Wars	Jan. 1565	Muslim sultans of Bijāpur, Bidar, Ahmadnagar, and Golconda defeated the forces of the Hindu raja of Vijayanagar.
Tearless Battle	Spartan Wars	368 BC	Arcadians attempted to cut off Spartan army under Archidamus but no Spartans were killed.
Tel-el-Kebir	Egyptian Revolt	13 Sept. 1882	Sir Garnet Wolseley defeated Egyptian nationalists under Arabi Pasha.
Teutoburg Forest	German-Roman War	AD 9	The Germanic Cherusci tribe, led by the young German prince Arminius, ambushed and slaughtered the Roman army under General Quinctilius Varus (committed suicide).
Tewkesbury	Wars of the Roses	4 May 1471	Yorkists under Edward IV defeated Lancastrians under Queen Margaret and Somerset. Prince Edward, son of Henry VI (killed).
Thapsus	Roman Civil War	6 Feb. 46 BC	Romans under Julius Caesar slaughtered the troops of Quintus Metellus Scipio, the father-in-law of Pompey the Great, and within weeks had conquered the rest of Roman Africa.

MILITARY

Battle	War	Date	Details
Thermopylae	Third Persian Invasion	19 Aug. 480 BC	Spartans and Thespians under Leonidas defeated by Persians under Xerxes.
Thorn	Great Northern War	22 Sept. 1702	Swedes under Charles XII defeated Poles and elected Stanislas Leszczynski king of Poland.
Tinchebrai	Norman Civil War	28 Sept. 1106	English under Henry I defeated his brother duke Robert of Normandy, annexing Normandy.
Toulon	French Revolutionary Wars	Aug.–Dec. 1793	Notable for being the engagement that earned Napoleon Bonaparte his reputation as a military tactician when he forced the withdrawal of the Anglo-Spanish fleet.
Tours/Poitiers	Muslim Invasion of France	10 Oct. 732	Franks under Charles Martel defeated Saracens under Abderrahman Ibn Abdillah (killed), halting Moorish conquest of Europe.
Towton	Wars of the Roses	29 Mar. 1461	Edward IV defeated Lancastrians under Henry VI and was crowned on 28 June.
Trafalgar	Napoleonic Wars	21 Oct. 1805	British fleet under Nelson (died) and Collingwood defeated Spanish and French under Villeneuve, losing no ships and capturing half of the enemy's.
Trenton	US War of Independence	26 Dec. 1776	Notable as the first success of George Washington in open warfare.
Tsushima Strait	Russo-Japanese War	27–28 May 1905	Admiral Togo routed Russian fleet under Rozlidestrenski, making first use of naval radio.
Ulm	Napoleonic Wars	20 Oct. 1805	Napoleon defeated Austrians under General Baron Mack von Leiberich (court-martialled).
Ulundi	Zulu-British War	4 July 1879	Final battle of the Anglo-Zulu War, in which Cetshwayo (Cetewayo) was defeated and taken prisoner.
Ushant			See Glorious 1st of June.
Valmy	French Revolutionary Wars	20 Sept. 1792	French under Dumouriez and Kellerman defeated Prussians under Duke of Brunswick.
Verdun	First World War	21 Feb.–20 Dec. 1916	German General von Falkenhayn's war of attrition against French, with combined casualties of over 650,000 and no conclusive outcome.
Vienna	Ottoman Wars	July–Sept. 1683	The Siege of Vienna by the Turks against the Habsburg Holy Roman Emperor Leopold I. On 12 September a combined force led by John III Sobieski defeated the Turks.
Vinegar Hill	Irish Rebellion	21 June 1798	Irish loyalists under General Lake defeated Catholic rebels under Father Murphy.
Virginia Capes	US War of Independence	5 Sept. 1781	French naval victory over a British fleet under Admiral Thomas Graves near Chesapeake Bay.
Vitoria	Peninsular War	21 June 1813	British under Wellington defeated French and expelled Joseph Bonaparte from Spain.
Vyborg	Russo-Finnish War	24 Apr. 1918	General Mannerheim's Finnish White Army defeated Bolsheviks.
Wakefield	Wars of the Roses	30 Dec. 1460	Lancastrians under Somerset defeated Yorkists under Richard of York (killed).
Wandiwāsh	Seven Years' War	22 Jan. 1760	British under Sir Eyre Coote defeated the French under the Comte de Lally in what was the decisive battle in the Anglo-French conflict in southern India.
Warburg	Seven Years' War	31 July 1760	French under Chevalier du Muy forced to retire by joint Prussian/British force.
Waterloo	Napoleon's Hundred Days	18 June 1815	Wellington aided by Prussians under Blücher defeated Napoleon who abdicated on 22 June.
Worcester	English Civil War	3 Sept. 1651	Last pitched battle of civil war in which Cromwell defeated royalists under Charles II.
Yarmuk River	Palestinian Wars	20 Aug. 636	Arabian army under Khālid ibn al-Walid defeated a Byzantine army under Theodorus.
Yom Kippur	Israeli-Arab War	6–24 Oct. 1973	Syrian and Egyptian surprise offensive along Golan Heights and Suez Canal defeated after heavy fighting.
Yorktown	US War of Independence	19 Oct. 1781	General Cornwallis forced to surrender to US and French troops, ending war.
Ypres (First)	First World War	14 Oct.1914	General von Falkenhayn's push to reach ports of Calais and Dunkirk halted by the British Expeditionary Force under Sir John French.

Battle	War	Date	Details
Ypres (Second)	First World War	22 Apr.–late May 1915	General Falkenhayn used lethal chlorine gas for the first time, causing many Allied deaths and advancing about 3 miles.
Ypres (Third)	First World War		See Passchendaele.
Zama	Second Punic War	202 BC	Carthaginians under Hannibal were defeated by Romans under Scipio Africanus in final battle of this war.
Zenta	Ottoman Wars	11 Sept. 1697	Ottoman army under Sultan Mustafa II was engaged by an Austrian army under Prince Eugene of Savoy while crossing the Tisza river and comprehensively defeated.
Zutphen	Dutch War of Independence	22 Sept. 1586	Spanish victory over English force under Leicester notable for death of Sir Philip Sidney.

MUSIC: CLASSICAL

Opera: Précis of Plots

Aida (Verdi, 1871) Aida, a captive Ethiopian princess, is servant to the Egyptian princess Amneris. Both are in love with General Radamès, who loves Aida. Radamès goes to war against the Ethiopians, defeats them and is given Amneris's hand in marriage, but Radames is suspected of having betrayed his country in trying to help Aida and sentenced to death. Aida conceals herself in the tomb where both of them are buried alive, while above them, Amneris prays.

The Barber of Seville (Rossini, 1816) Count Almaviva, aided by his barber Figaro, is pursuing Rosina. Her guardian, Bartolo, who wants to marry her himself, tries to stop them but is unsuccessful, and Rosina marries the count.

The Bartered Bride (Smetana, 1866) Marenka loves Jenik, whose parents want to marry her to the halfwit son of Micha. Jenik is offered money to give her up, and accepts on condition she marries Micha's eldest son. This turns out to be Jenik himself; Marenka can marry him after all.

La Bohème (Puccini, 1896) Mimi, who is consumptive, falls in love with a Bohemian poet, Rodolfo, and for a while they live together, but constant quarrels drive them apart. Then Rodolfo's friends discover that Mimi is dying and bring her to him, but it is too late and she dies in his arms.

Carmen (Bizet, 1875) The soldier Don José deserts the army to follow the gypsy girl Carmen, who leaves him for the toreador Escamillo. Mad with jealousy, Don José follows her to the bullring and kills her.

Cavalleria Rusticana (Mascagni, 1890) Brokenhearted because her lover, Turiddu, has abandoned her for another woman, Santuzza tells the other woman's husband what is going on. He kills Turiddu in a duel.

The Coronation of Poppaea (Monteverdi, 1643) Emperor Nero resolves to marry his mistress Poppaea. One by one, he murders everyone who stands in their way until Poppaea is crowned empress.

Così fan tutte (Mozart, 1790) The sisters Fiordiligi and Dorabella swear to be faithful to their lovers Ferrando and Guglielmo, so to try their fidelity the latter pretend to go off to the wars. But they return in disguise and each proceeds to make advances to the other's girl, who both respond. The men then reveal their disguise, but forgive their wayward sweethearts, and both couples are reunited.

Don Giovanni (Mozart, 1787) Foiled in his attempts to seduce Donna Anna, the libertine Don Giovanni (aka Don Juan) kills her father, the Commendatore. Anna and her fiancé Don Ottavio vow to avenge him. They are joined by Donna Elvira, another former victim of the Don. In a gesture of defiance, Don Giovanni has confronted a statue of the Commendatore and invited him to dinner. The Commendatore duly accepts, arrives at the Don's house and drags him down to hell.

Eugene Onegin (Tchaikovsky, 1879) Tatyana, young and open-hearted, falls in love with the worldly Eugene Onegin and confesses her feelings, but he rejects her. Years later they meet again and this time he falls in love with her, but by now she is married and, though still attracted to him, sends him away for ever.

Falstaff (Verdi, 1893) Shakespeare's fat knight, Sir John Falstaff, is simultaneously wooing two wives of Windsor, Mistress Ford and Mistress Page, who discover what he is up to and contrive to pay him back, but Falstaff eventually takes it in good part and the opera finishes with a happy ending for a young couple involved in the plotting – Nannetta Ford and her lover, Fenton.

Faust (Gounod, 1859) Faust has been given back his youth by the devil, Mephistopheles, so he can pursue the beautiful Marguerite. They fall in love and she has a child, but Faust then deserts her. She kills the child and is condemned to death. Faust returns to save her, but he is too late, and she dies and is borne to heaven.

Fidelio (Beethoven, 1805) When Florestan is unjustly imprisoned, his wife Leonora disguises herself as a young man called Fidelio and gets a job inside the prison, from where she succeeds in getting him freed.

The Flying Dutchman (Wagner, 1843) A Dutch sea captain has been condemned by the Devil to sail the seas for ever, unless he can find a woman who will love him until death. Once in every seven years he is allowed to land in search of her. He meets Senta, who declares her love for him, but leaves her owing to a misunderstanding, whereupon she throws herself into the sea and drowns, thus freeing him.

Gloriana (Britten, 1953) The libretto was based on Lytton Strachey's *Elizabeth and Essex* and concerns the decline of Essex in the affections of Queen Elizabeth. The opening act tells of a fight between Essex and Lord Montjoy at the court of Elizabeth. They are rebuked, but the rebellious nature of Essex is recognised by the Queen. Essex is appointed Deputy of Ireland and given the charge of subduing Tyrone, but fails miserably. On his return to England the disgraced Essex rebels and is arrested as a traitor. At his trial at Whitehall, Essex is given a death sentence, which is eventually signed by Elizabeth after an injudicious word from Lady Rich. The final act depicts the Queen reflecting on her life to the audience.

Lohengrin (Wagner, 1850) The heroine, Elsa, falsely accused, will lose her life if she cannot find a champion. When one appears (Lohengrin, a knight searching for the Holy Grail), he agrees to defend her so long as she never asks his name. Eventually they marry, but an enemy dupes her into asking her husband's name. Now she has broken her vow and he leaves her for ever.

Lucia di Lammermoor (Donizetti, 1835) Lucy Ashton is in love with Edgar, but is tricked by her brother into marrying someone else. On her wedding night she goes mad and kills her husband. When he learns of her subsequent death, Edgar kills himself.

Madame Butterfly (Puccini, 1904) The American naval Lieutenant Pinkerton has married the innocent Japanese girl Cio-Cio-San. He regards the arrangements as only temporary and leaves her when the time comes, but she loves him and longs for his return. When he does, with an American wife, Butterfly promises to give him their child and then kills herself.

The Magic Flute (Mozart, 1791) This is a contest between Good (the high priest Sarastro) and Evil (the Queen of the Night). Prince Tamino falls in love with the Queen of the Night's daughter, Pamina, and has to undergo many tests and temptations, helped by a gift of a magic flute, before he conquers Evil and wins the hand of his beloved.

Manon (Massenet, 1884) Manon Lescaut and the Chevalier Des Grieux fall in love and run away together, but she prefers luxury to poverty and leaves him for a rich man. She is eventually deported for being a prostitute. Des Grieux follows her, but she is overwhelmed by her suffering and dies in his arms.

The Marriage of Figaro (Mozart, 1786) Figaro, barber to the womanising Count Almaviva, is about to be married to Susanna, the countess's maid, but discovers the count has designs on her. Figaro, Susanna, the countess and her page Cherubino hatch a plot to unmask the count, and all ends happily with the wedding of Figaro and Susanna.

The Mastersingers of Nuremberg (Wagner, 1868) The Mastersingers of Nuremberg are to hold a song contest, the prize being the hand of Eva. The knight Walther arrives, falls in love with Eva and decides to compete, coached by Hans Sachs the cobbler. Although his rival Beckmesser does his best to discredit him, he wins both the contest and Eva.

Norma (Bellini,1831) The Druid priestess Norma has had two children by the Roman general Pollione, who has now fallen in love with a younger priestess, Adalgisa. Norma incites a Gallo-Roman war, Pollione is captured and sentenced to death, and they both go to be sacrificed together.

Otello (Verdi, 1887) Otello, the Moor of Venice, is tricked by the evil Iago into believing his wife, Desdemona, has been unfaithful to him. In a fit of jealousy he kills her, learns the truth, then kills himself.

I Pagliacci (Leoncavallo, 1893) A troupe of strolling players enact a real-life drama. The clown, Canio, does not know that his wife, Nedda, is having an affair with Silvio, a villager, although he is suspicious. At that night's performance, in which Canio plays a jealous husband, reality gets the better of him, the play becomes a real quarrel, and he stabs both Nedda and Silvio to death.

The Pearl Fishers (Bizet, 1863) Pearl fishers Zurga and Nadir have long loved the priestess, Leila, but have vowed not to let this destroy their friendship. Then Leila arrives to conduct a religious ceremony, and she and Nadir confess their love. They are discovered and sentenced to death. Zurga helps them escape but loses his own life as a result.

Peter Grimes (Britten, 1945) The lone fisherman, Peter Grimes, is an outsider in the East Coast fishing community where he lives. Already under suspicion after the mysterious death of his young apprentice, when a second boy dies unaccountably, Grimes is forced to take to sea and drowns himself.

Rigoletto (Verdi, 1851) The hunchback jester Rigoletto has helped his master, the Duke of Mantua, to seduce the daughter of the courtier Monterone, who curses him. The duke believes that Rigoletto has a mistress (actually his daughter), Gilda, and seduces her. In revenge, Rigoletto plots to have the duke murdered, but the plot misfires and Gilda is killed instead. The curse has been fulfilled.

The Ring Cycle (Wagner, 1876) *The Rhinegold*: The magic Rhinegold is at the bottom of the River Rhine, guarded by the Rhinemaidens. Alberich, the wicked dwarf, steals it and makes a ring from it to become all-powerful. Meanwhile, the god Wotan is looking for money to pay for his castle of Valhalla and plots to steal the gold. He tricks Alberich into parting with it, but it is cursed and results in a death. *The Valkyrie*: Wotan has fathered nine warrior-maidens, the Valkyries; his favourite is Brünnhilde. He also has a son and a daughter, Siegmund and Sieglinde, who were separated at birth. In a storm, Siegmund takes shelter in a hut where Sieglinde lives with her husband Hunding. The two fall in love and run away but are pursued by Hunding, who kills Siegmund. Brünnhilde carries Siegmund off to Valhalla in defiance of her father, who condemns her to sleep in a ring of fire until a hero comes to rescue her. *Siegfried*: Sieglinde has died giving birth to a son, Siegfried, who has been brought up by the dwarf Mime in the hope that he will one day get the Ring back. With the help of Wotan and Brünnhilde, Siegfried is led to the magic rock where he awakes Brünnhilde and they fall in love. *Twilight of the Gods*: Siegfried has taken the Ring from the dragon that was guarding it and now gives it to Brünnhilde while he goes in search of further adventure. He reaches the Hall of the Gibichungs, who hope to marry him to their sister Gutrune. Although Brünnhilde comes with the Ring to rescue him, he is killed. Brünnhilde builds a funeral pyre for him and climbs on to it herself. The Rhinemaidens arrive in a flood and snatch back the Ring, while Valhalla is consumed in flames. It is the end of the gods.

Der Rosenkavalier (Strauss, 1911) The young Count Octavian is having an affair with an older woman, the Marschallin, although she knows it cannot last. Octavian is sent to bear a silver rose as a symbol of the forthcoming marriage of the beautiful young Sophie von Faninal to a much older man, Baron Ochs. The two young people fall in love, their elders realise that it is better to let them go, and Octavian and Sophie face a future together.

Ruslan and Lyudmila (Glinka, 1842) Svyetozar is hosting a wedding celebration for his daughter Lyudmila, who is betrothed to the knight Ruslan. The bard Bayan sings but foretells ill fortune for the newly-weds. A thunderclap followed by total darkness interrupts the festivities. Light returns but Lyudmila has disappeared. Lyudmila's former suitors search in vain. Ruslan encounters the wise magician Finn, who tells him of Lyudmila's abduction by the evil dwarf Chernomor. Ruslan acquires a magic sword and challenges Chernomor to a duel. The dwarf casts a sleeping spell on Lyudmila before encountering Ruslan, who defeats him by cutting off his beard, the source of power. Ruslan awakens Lyudmila with a magic ring.

The Tales of Hoffmann (Offenbach, 1881) The poet Hoffmann relates the stories of the three loves of his life, all destroyed by the same evil genius. First, there is Olympia, who, he does not realize until too late, is only a mechanical doll. Then the courtesan Giulietta, who leaves him for another, and finally Antonia, a pure young girl who knows she will die if she tries to sing but is tricked into doing so. The story of loss is about to be repeated with the opera singer Stella, and Hoffmann is left alone to drown his sorrows in beer.

MUSIC CLASSICAL

Tosca (Puccini, 1900)   The opera singer Floria Tosca is loved by the political agitator Cavaradossi and desired by the evil police chief Scarpia. Cavaradossi is arrested, but Scarpia promises Tosca he will free him if she agrees to give herself to him. She kills Scarpia, but he has tricked her and Cavaradossi is shot, whereupon Tosca throws herself to her death from the prison battlements.

La Traviata (The Fallen Woman) (Verdi, 1853)   Violetta, a courtesan, has fallen in love with a young aristocrat, Alfredo, but Alfredo's father begs her to break off the relationship as it will bring disgrace to his family, and she goes back to her old life. Alfredo confronts and denounces her, but she is dying of consumption, and when, too late, he returns to her side, she dies in his arms.

Tristan und Isolde (Wagner, 1865)   Isolde is to be married to King Mark of Cornwall and his nephew Tristan is sent to fetch her, but the two fall in love. After the wedding they meet, but they are discovered and Tristan is wounded. Isolde comes to him as he dies, then herself falls lifeless over his body.

Il Trovatore (The Troubadour) (Verdi, 1853)   Leonora is being serenaded by a mysterious troubador, regarded as a rival by Count di Luna, who is in love with her. The troubador turns out to be Manrico, apparently the son of the gypsy Azucena. But Azucena explains that years ago, in revenge for the agony of seeing her mother burned to death, she threw the Count's abducted baby brother into the flames – but by mistake threw her own baby instead. Manrico and Leonora run away but are pursued by the Count, who imprisons Manrico. Leonora agrees to marry the Count as the price of Manrico's freedom, but then kills herself. The Count executes Manrico, then is told by Azucena that he has killed his own brother.

Turandot (Busoni, 1917)   The cruel Chinese princess Turandot will marry only if a suitor prince can solve her three riddles. If he cannot, he will die. An unknown prince answers the riddles correctly but tells her that if she can discover his name by morning, he will agree to die. Turandot tortures the slave girl Liu, who knows the name but will not reveal it, and Liu eventually dies. The prince tells Turandot his name. It is 'Love,' and she accepts him as her husband.

NB: The above is only a small selection of operas but offers a flavour of the moods and emotions that can be explored in others.

Composers
(Chronological order)

Name	Principal works	Details
Hildegard of Bingen 1098–1179	Church music departing from traditional plainsong style	Saint and abbess
Pérotin c. 1160–c. 1205	Christmas and St Stephen's Day graduals (1198, 1199)	aka Perotinus Magnus; maître de chapelle at Notre Dame; exponent of *ars antiqua*
Adam de la Halle c. 1250–?1306	*Le jeu de Robin et de Marion* anticipated the genre of opéra comique	Aka Adam the Hunchback; born Arras, France and died in Naples; court musician of the Comte d'Artois
Machaut, Guillaume de c. 1300–c.1377	*Messe de Notre Dame* (for four violins); *Voir Dit* (Tale of Truth), collection of ballads; 23 motets	Born and died in Reims; leading French composer of free-flowing *ars nova* style of 14th century; canon of Reims Cathedral
Landini, Francesco c. 1325–1397	Various madrigals; over 140 ballads	Born and died in Florence; blinded in youth from smallpox; noted for 'Landini Cadence' in which sixth degree octave is inserted between leading note and octave
Dunstable, John c. 1390–1453	Masses and motets	Aka Dunstaple; internationally renowned in his day
Du Fay, Guillaume c. 1400–1474	8 masses; 87 motets; 59 French chansons	Composed earliest requiem mass; possibly originated Fauxbourdon style; canon of Cambrai
Ockeghem, Johannes c. 1430–1495	14 masses; 10 motets; 20 chansons	Born Flanders and died Tours; composer to 3 successive French kings: Charles VII, Louis XI, Charles VIII
Josquin des Prés c. 1445–1521	18 masses; 100 motets	Born Picardy and died Hainault; Luther called him 'Master of the Notes'
Isaac, Heinrich c. 1450–1517	36 masses; 'Innsbruck I Must Leave You' (song) reworked by J.S. Bach and Brahms	Born Brabant and died Florence; taught in household of Medici family
Taverner, John c. 1490–1545	8 masses (inc. *Westron Wynde*); other church music	Occasionally alleged to have given up music to persecute Catholics under Thomas Cromwell; subject of opera by Peter Maxwell Davies
Cabezón, Antonio de c. 1510–1566	'El Caballero variation'	Born Burgos and died Madrid; blind from birth
Tallis, Thomas c. 1510–1585	'Spem in alium nunquam habui' (In no other is my Hope) (motet)	Elizabeth I granted monopoly of sheet music to Tallis and William Byrd

MUSIC CLASSICAL

Name	Principal works	Details
Gabrieli, Andrea c. 1510–1586	7 masses and numerous motets	Born and died in Venice
Palestrina, Giovanni 1525–1594	Over 100 masses and 250 motets, including *Stabat Mater*	Took his name from his birthplace; lost his family in Italian plague
Lassus, Orlande 1532–1594	Wrote some 2,000 madrigals, motets, chansons, canzonas, masses, lieder, etc.	Born at Mons, died at Munich; preceded Palestrina as chapelmaster of Papal Church of St John Lateran, Rome
Byrd, William 1543–1623	Prolific composer and pioneer of madrigals but also composed motets, masses and music for organ and virginals, his most famous work being the collection of 42 virginal pieces *My Lady Nevells Book*	Pupil of Thomas Tallis and favoured by Queen Elizabeth despite being a Catholic; granted monopoly of all sheet music in England along with Tallis
Victoria Tomás Luis de 1548–1611	Composed in a similar style to that of Palestrina but distinguished by his use of Spanish melody. His total output consisted of church music including the motets *Vexilla Regis* and *Magnum Mysterium*, the acclaimed *Officium Hebdonadae Sanctae*, and the Requiem Mass composed at the death of Empress Maria	Spanish composer, born in Avila; studied for priesthood in Rome and in 1576 became chaplain to the widowed Empress Maria, sister of Philip II, returning with her to Madrid in 1583 to the convent of the Descalzas Reales, where he remained as choirmaster until his death
Morley, Thomas 1557–1602	Father of the English madrigal who edited the collection *The Triumphs of Oriana*; his last work was *The First Book of Ayres*	Pupil of Byrd who became organist at St Paul's Cathedral and Gentleman of the Chapel Royal in 1592
Sweelinck, Jan Piterszoon 1562–1621	Wrote over 250 vocal works and 70 for keyboard. His fantasias were the first example of fully worked-out fugues. He founded the North German school which later included Diderik Buxtehude and J S Bach	Dutch composer, organist and harpsichordist. Succeeded his father as organist of the Oude Kerk (old church), Amsterdam in 1580, a position he held until his death
Bull, John c. 1562–1628	Although Bull's reputation was as a performer rather than a composer, he, along with William Byrd and Orlando Gibbons, published the first book of keyboard music in England, the aptly named *Parthenia* (Maidenhood), 1611. his other works include the virginal pieces *Walsingham* and *God Save the King*, although the attribution of our present National Anthem to Bull is perhaps not from this piece but a later untitled work	English musician. Appointed organist in the Queen's Chapel in 1586 and became the first music lecturer at Gresham College in 1597, and organist to James I in 1607. His Catholicism led him to flee England in 1613 to become organist of the Chapel Royal, Brussels and in 1615 became organist at Antwerp Cathedral, where he remained until his death
Dowland, John 1562–1626	Published 87 songs as well as *Lachrimae* (1604), 21 dance pieces containing 7 pavanes, all beginning with the theme of Dowland's song 'Flow my tears'	Lutenist and singer/songwriter for the king of Denmark (1598–1606) and Lord Howard de Walden (1606–12) as well as Anne of Denmark and Charles I
Monteverdi, Claudio 1567–1643	First opera *La Favola d'Orfeo* (1607) is earliest opera in the regular repertoire; last opera: *L'Incoronazione di Poppea* (1642); many operas lost; other works listed in tables	Son of a barber/surgeon who wed the singer Claudia Cattaneo; he was a pupil of Ingegneri and was patronised by the duke of Mantua; took holy orders for a short time
Gibbons, Orlando 1583–1625	Composer of madrigals, e.g. 'The Silver Swan', and anthems, e.g. 'This is the Record of John'; also contributed to the first book of keyboard music printed in England, *Parthenia*	Organist of Chapel Royal from 1604 and Westminster Abbey from 1623
Frescobaldi, Girolamo	In 1612 he published 12 fantasias, and in 1624 a collection of 10 ricercari,	Italian virtuoso organist, born in Ferrara. Became organist

Composer	Dates		
	1583–1643	five canzoni and 11 capriccios. Frescobaldi was a strong influence of the German Baroque school through the work of his pupils Froberger and Tunder	at St Peter's, Rome, where 30,000 people are said to have attended his first performance
Schütz, Heinrich	1585–1672	*Christmas Oratorio*; settings of the Passion	German composer and organist who studied law and was one of Bach's influences
Froberger, Johann Jakob	1616–67	Froberger was the first important German composer for the harpsichord and a leading light of early Baroque music	German composer, born in Stuttgart. He became a court organist in Vienna, 1637, and later that year travelled to Rome to study under Frescobaldi
Lully, Jean-Baptiste	1632–1687	Composed 20 operas and ballets, including *Alceste* (1684), *Psyché* (1678), *Roland* (1685), *Armide et Rénaud* (1686), *Achille et Polixène* (posthumous collaboration with Colasse) and *Le Bourgeois Gentilhomme* (collaboration with Molière)	Italian-born but took French nationality in 1661; from 1664 collaborated with Molière in series of comedy-ballets which were forerunners of French opera; danced role of the Mufti in *Le Bourgeois Gentilhomme*; died accidentally by stabbing himself in the foot with long pole used to conduct (wound turned gangrenous)
Buxtehude, Diderik	c. 1637–1707	20 cantatas, of which the cycle of seven *Membra Jesu Nostri*, are the most famous. He also wrote toccatas, preludes, fugues and chaconnes. Most of his harpsichord music has been lost	Danish organist and composer. In 1688 he became organist of Mary's Church, Lübeck, where his fame spread throughout Northern Germany. Handel visited him in 1703 and in 1705 J S Bach was known to have walked the 200 miles from Arnstadt to hear him play
Blow, John	1649–1708	Wrote over 100 anthems and 13 services but best known work was masque *Venus and Adonis* (1682)	One of the first choirboys of Chapel Royal after Restoration and organist at Westminster Abbey (1668–79), preceding Henry Purcell
Corelli, Arcangelo	1653–1713	First composition: Sonata for Violin and Lute. 60 sonatas (48 trio and 12 solo) 12 Concerti Grossi (published posthumously) the most famous being his *Christmas Concerto*	Italian violinist, conductor and composer. From 1687 he was under the patronage of Cardinal Pamphili. Corelli was a skilled conductor and is often thought of as a pioneer of modern orchestral direction
Purcell, Henry	1659–1695	Only opera *Dido and Aeneas* (1683); fantasias for strings (1680); 'My Heart is Inditing' for Coronation of James II (1685); semi-operas include *The Fairy Queen*, *King Arthur*, *The Tempest* and the unfinished *The Indian Queen*	Succeeded Matthew Locke as composer to the king's violins and John Blow as organist of Westminster Abbey (1679); in 1682 became one of the three organists of the Chapel Royal
Scarlatti, Alessandro	1660–1725	First of 115 operas *Gli Equivoci*; his greatest considered to be *Mitridate Eupatore* (1707); only comic opera *Il Trionfo dell'Onore* (1718); last opera *La Griselda* (1721)	Founder of Neapolitan School of composers; father of Domenico Scarlatti
Couperin, François	1668–1733	Composed 230 harpsichord pieces, also chamber music	Wrote textbook *The Art of Touching the Keyboard*; known as 'Couperin the Great' on account of quantity of musicians in the family
Vivaldi, Antonio	1678–1741	First opera *Ottone in Villa* (1713); first Venetian opera *Orlando Finto Pazzo*, best known opera *Orlando Furioso* (1727); most famous work *The Four*	Nicknamed the Red Priest after taking holy orders in 1703; taught violin at Ospedale della Pietà, an orphanage, from

MUSIC CLASSICAL

Name	Principal works	Details
Telemann, Georg Philipp 1681–1767	*Seasons* (1725); most famous oratorio *Juditha Triumphans* (1716)	1703; died and buried in a pauper's grave in Vienna; Peter Ryom catalogued works, Leipzig, 1974 with prefix RV (Ryom Verzeichnis)
	Often considered the most prolific of all composers with 600 overtures and 44 passions to his name as well as 40 operas (best known being *Pimpinone*, 1725)	German composer and organist who had no formal training but studied Lully and André Campra; appointed Kantor at the Thomaskirche, Leipzig, in preference to J S Bach
Bach, Johann Sebastian 1685–1750	Orchestral and keyboard works include: *Brandenburg Concertos (Nos 1–6)* (1717); *The Well-Tempered Klavier* (48 preludes and fugues); *Goldberg Variations* (30 variations on original theme); English suites and French suites, as well as the unfinished *Die Kunst der Fuge* (The Art of Fugue); famous oratorios include *St John Passion, St Matthew Passion* and *Christmas Oratorio*	Born Eisenach and died in Leipzig; orphaned at age of 10 and lived with elder brother at Ohrdruf; married his cousin Maria Barbara Bach in 1707 and after her death in 1720 married Anna Magdalena Wilcken (December 1721); almost totally blind during last year of life; Wagner described his work as 'The most stupendous miracle in all music'; catalogues have BWV nos (Bach Werke Verzeichnis)
Scarlatti, Domenico 1685–1757	About 550 harpsichord sonatas; also operas and oratorios	Long-time friend of Handel; powerful influence on modern keyboard technique
Handel, George Frederick 1685–1759	First opera *Almira* (1705) and last *Deidamia* (1740); other notable operas include *Agrippina* (1709), *Rinaldo* (1711), *Teseo* (1712), *Radamisto* (1720), *Tamerlano* (1724), *Orlando* (1733), *Ariodante* (1735), *Alcina* (1735), *Berenice* (1737), *Serse* (1738); orchestral works include *Water Music* (1717) and *Music for Royal Fireworks* (1749) played in Green Park to mark the Peace of Aix-la-Chapelle; oratorios include *Esther* (1732), *Athalia* (1733), *Alexander's Feast* (1736), *Israel in Egypt* (1739), *Messiah* (1741), *Judas Maccabaeus* (1746); church music includes *Dettingen Te Deum* (1743), *Chandos Anthems* (1718), *Zadok the Priest* (1737); other famous work is 5th Harpsichord Suite, nicknamed *The Harmonious Blacksmith* (1720)	Born in Halle and died in London; son of a barber/surgeon; studied law until his father died; became English citizen in 1726; received pension of £200 p.a. for life from Queen Anne (1712), which was increased to £600 by King George I for whom he wrote his famous *Water Music* suite in 1717; blind for last 7 years of his life and aided by his agent and friend, John Christopher Smith
Arne, Thomas Augustine 1710–1778	First opera was *Rosamond* (1733); composed settings for Shakespeare songs including 'Under the Greenwood Tree', 'Where the Bee Sucks' and 'Blow Blow thou Winter Wind'; most famous work is 'Rule Britannia', originally written for *The Masque of Alfred*	Born and died in London; son of an upholsterer and educated at Eton; his sister was famous actress Mrs Cibber; son Michael wrote 'The Lass with a delicate air'; married a singer, Cecilia Young (1736)
Boyce, William 1711–1779	Most famously associated with the song 'Heart of Oak', composed in 1759 for pantomime *Harlequin's Invasion* to words by David Garrick; 8 symphonies and 12 overtures	Master of the King's Musick from 1755
Gluck, Christoph Willibald 1714–1787	First opera *Artaserse* (1741); best known opera is *Orfeo et Eurydice* (1762); other operas include *La Clemenza di Tito* (1752), *Alceste* (1767) and *Armide* (1777); his best-known ballet is *Don Juan* (1761); opera comiques include *The Pilgrimage to Mecca*	Born Erasbach, Germany and died in Vienna; German composer under patronage of Prince Lobkowitz in his formative years; in 1754 Empress Maria Theresa appointed him opera Kapellmeister to court theatre in Vienna

Haydn, Franz Joseph
1732–1809

Composed 104 numbered symphonies; Symphony in D Major No 96 is called the 'Miracle' because it was thought that after its first performance the audience flocking to applaud him escaped injury when a chandelier fell on their empty seats. In fact, this incident occurred on 2 February 1795 while his 102nd Symphony was playing; composed 20 operas, the first *La Canterina* 1766 and the last *Orfeo ed Euridice* (1791); other works include numerous masses, cantatas, oratorios, concertos and chamber music

Austrian-born son of a farmer-wheelwright; precocious talent as a child; from 1761 was patronised by Prince Paul Esterházy, working as Vice-Kapellmeister at Eisenstadt, Hungary; mutual admiration for Mozart influenced his work from 1781; Beethoven was his pupil for a short period; regarded as the father of the symphony only because of his prolific output; his works are often given Hob nos, after Anthony van Hoboken (1887–1983), who catalogued them

Cimarosa, Domenico
1749–1801

First of 65 operas was *Le Stravaganze del Conti* (1772); best known opera *The Secret Marriage* (1792); other operas include *Artaserse* (1784), *Penelope* (1795) and *L'Apprensivo Raggirato* (1798); also wrote 30 keyboard sonatas

Court composer to Catherine II of Russia; in 1791 succeeded Salieri as Kapellmeister to Leopold II in Vienna; sentenced to death in 1799 for supporting French Republican army but reprieved on condition he left Naples

Mozart, Wolfgang Amadeus
1756–1791

First operas was *Apollo et Hyacinthus* (1767); other operas include *Bastien und Bastienne* (1768), *Idomeneo* (1780), *The Marriage of Figaro* (1786), *Don Giovanni* (1787), *Così fan tutte* (1789), *Die Zauberflöte* (The Magic Flute) (1791); last opera *La Clemenza di Tito* (1791); of the 41 symphonies the last 3 were composed in a matter of a few weeks; also wrote numerous orchestral pieces and concertos for both piano and violin as well as horn concertos, string quartets, 40 songs and many sonatas; *Eine Kleine Nachtmusik* (1787) is a popular orchestral piece, being theme tune for *Brain of Britain* quiz

Born in Salzburg and died in Vienna; Johannes Chrysostomus Wolfgangus Theophilus was baptismal name; son of Leopold, Vice-Kapellmeister to Prince Archbishop of Salzburg; sister was Maria Anna (Nannerl; 1751–1829); in Rome in 1769 he heard Allegri's *Miserere* and wrote it out from memory; married Constance Weber in August 1782; his *Requiem Mass* for Count von Walsegg was completed after his death by Franz Süssmayr; work was catalogued by Ludwig von Köchel, an Austrian botanist and mineralogist

Beethoven, Ludwig van
1770–1827

Only opera *Fidelio* (1805) was originally called *Leonora*; nine complete symphonies, but Dr Barry Cooper, a music lecturer at Aberdeen University, has pieced together, from sketches, a 10th Symphony by making projections of existing themes; composed 32 piano sonatas, including No. 14 in C sharp minor (*Moonlight*) and No. 15 in D major (*Pastoral*); best-known piano concerto was No. 5 (*Emperor*); numerous songs, sonatas and masses; one violin concerto

Born in Bonn and buried in Central Friedhof, Vienna; father was court singer to the elector of Cologne; dedicated his 3rd Symphony to Napoleon but retracted it on hearing he had made himself emperor; learned he was going deaf in 1798; mystery cloaks identity of his 'Immortal Beloved', although Antonie Brentano is a candidate as he dedicated his *Diabelli Variations* to her; freedom of Vienna bestowed on him in 1815

Paganini, Niccolò
1782–1840

Six violin concertos remain but various others lost; composed many variations on existing works, such as *God Save the King*, an aria from *La Cenerentola* and *Witches' Dance*, based on an air by Süssmayr; popular work is *Variations on a Theme of Rossini* and *24 Caprices*; also wrote 12 sonatas for violin and guitar

Born in Genoa, died of cancer of the larynx in Nice; regarded as greatest genius of the violin; successful gambler who owned a casino and lent money to struggling musicians, e.g. Berlioz; Mephistophelean looks fostered stories of satanic powers

Weber, Carl Maria
1786–1826

First of 9 operas *Das Waldmädchen* (1800); other operas include *Silvana* (1810), *Abu Hassan* (1811), *Der Freischütz* (1821), *Euryanthe* (1823) and his final opera *Oberon* (1826); also composed symphonies, songs and masses

Born Eutin in Oldenburg, Germany, the son of a musician and actor-manager; died of tuberculosis while staying with Sir George Smart in his Great Portland St home and re-buried in Dresden in 1844

Meyerbeer, Giacomo
1791–1864

First opera *Jephtas Gelübde* (1812). Other notable operas include *Robert le Diable* (1831), *Les Huguenots* (1836), *Le Prophète* (1940), *L'Etoile du Nord*

German operatic composer, born in Berlin and originally named Jakob Liebmann Beer. He was a child prodigy pianist, playing

MUSIC CLASSICAL

Name	Principal works	Details
	(1854) and *L'Africaine* (1864). Also wrote oratorio, marches, songs, and church music	a Mozart concerto at the age of 11. Meyerbeer's pageant-like operas were attacked by the anti-Semitism of Wagner
Rossini, Gioachino Antonio 1792–1868	First of 35 operas was *Demetrio e Polibio* (1806); best-known operas include *Tancredi* (1813), *Otello* (1816), *Elizabeth of England* (1815), *La Gazza Ladra*, *Cinderella* (1817) and his last opera *William Tell* (1829); also composed cantatas, sonatas and orchestral works although retired completely from opera as a result of neurasthenia; late works include *Petite Messe Solennelle* and a variety of pieces he called 'Sins of my Old Age'; notable prodigy: 6 string sonatas date from his early teens	Born Pesaro in Italy, died in Paris; buried in Père Lachaise cemetery, but reinterred in Florence in 1887; son of a trumpeter and a singer; married soprano Isabella Colbran (1821) and then after divorcing her, Olympe Pélissier; court composer to Charles X of France in 1825; famous for his 'Samedi Soirs' performances; a gourmand:Tournedos Rossini is named after him; nicknamed Monsieur Crescendo
Schubert, Franz Peter 1797–1828	Wrote 9 numbered symphonies although 7th and 8th were unfinished, as were some unnumbered ones; first opera *Des Teufels Lustschloss* (1814); prolific output included over 600 songs of which 144 were written in 1815 (8 in one day); some popular songs include 'Death and the Maiden (1817), the *Winterreise* (Winter Journey) song cycle (1827) and settings of Shakespearean songs. e.g: 'Who is Sylvia?' and 'Hark, Hark the Lark', also notable Goethe settings; of his oratorios, *Lazarus* (1820), his setting of psalm 23, is best known, although 'Wanderier Fantasy' is popular; unusually did not compose any concertos	Born and died in Vienna, buried near to Beethoven at Währing, and later exhumed and reburied in the Central Cemetery of Vienna; father was schoolmaster and his first teacher; the celebrated baritone Michael Vogl sang many of his lieder; Schubert was a torchbearer at Beethoven's funeral in 1827; his works were catalogued by Otto Deutsch
Donizetti, Gaetano 1797–1848	First opera *Il Pigmalione* (1816); other operas include *Enrico di Borgogna* (1818), *Zoraide di Grenate* (1822), *Ann Boleyn* (1830), *Lucretia Borgia* (1833), *Lucia di Lammermoor* (1835), *Mary Stuart* (1835), *Roberto Devereux* (1837), *Don Pasquale* (1843) and (last) *Dom Sébastien* (1843); also wrote church music, string quartets and symphonies	Born and died in Bergamo; joined the Austrian army and composed in his spare time until 1822 when he left and became full-time composer; became insane in later life due to syphilis
Bellini, Vincenzo 1801–1835	First opera *Adelson e Salvini* (1825); others include *The Sleepwalker* (1831), *Norma* (1831) and, last opera, *I Puritani* (1835)	Born in Catania, Sicily, died in Puteaux, near Paris, reinterred in Catania 1876; studied under Niccolò Zingarelli at San Sebastiano in Naples
Berlioz, Hector 1803–1869	Operas: *Benvenuto Cellini* (1837), *Les Troyens* (1858) and *Béatrice et Bénédict* (1862); famous orchestral works include *Waverley* (1828), *King Lear* (1831), *Le Corsaire* (1831), *Rob Roy* (1832), *Harold in Italy* (1834), *Symphonie Funèbre et Triomphale* (1840); best known work is *Symphony Fantastique* (1830); famous dramatic cantata is *The Damnation of Faust*	Born Grenoble and died in Paris; son of a provincial doctor but dropped out of medical school for a music career; married Irish actress Harriet Smithson (1833); Paganini paid him 20,000 francs for *Harold in Italy*; formed liaison with singer Marie Recio (1841)
Strauss the Elder, Johann 1804–1849	Composed 251 works of which 152 were waltzes; *Radetzky March* (1848), named after an Austrian field-marshal, easily his best known work	Born and died (scarlet fever) in Vienna
Glinka, Mikhail 1804–1857	Two operas *Life for the Tsar* (1836) – aka Ivan Susanin – and *Ruslan and Lyudmila* (1842); orchestral works include *Kamarinskaya* (1848) and *Night in Madrid* (1848)	Born in Smolensk and died in Berlin; first Russian composer to be recognised outside Russia; worked in Communications Ministry 1824–8

Composer	Works	Biography
Mendelssohn, Felix 1809–1847	Twelve early string symphonies, also 5 mature symphonies and concertos (e.g. for violin); dramatic works include *Midsummer Night's Dream* and the unfinished opera *Lorelei*; best known oratorios *Elijah* (1846) and *St Paul* (1836); hymns include 'Hear My Prayer' (1844), which contains the section 'O for the Wings of a Dove'	Born Hamburg and died in Leipzig, probably due to overwork and blow of sister's death; grandson of philosopher Moses Mendelssohn; wrote *Hebrides Overture* (aka *Fingal's Cave*) after visit to Britain in 1829; eldest sister was Fanny, a piano virtuoso; at 12 became friend of the 72-year-old Goethe
Chopin, Frédéric 1810–1849	Piano works include the 'Funeral March' Sonata (1837), *Krakowiak Rondo* (1828) and *Là ci darem variations*; famous for his nocturnes, preludes, mazurks, études, written for solo piano; Waltz in D flat, known as the Minute Waltz	Born in Zelazowa Wola, Poland, of French father and Polish mother, died in Paris; all works involve a piano; though a piano virtuoso, gave only about 30 public performances; lover of novelist George Sand (1837–47)
Schumann, Robert 1810–1856	Only opera *Genoveva* (1849); incidental music to Byron's verse-drama *Manfred* 1849; 4 symphonies, songs and song-cycles, and numerous piano pieces, including *Abegg Variations* (dedicated to Meta Abegg and written using notes of her surname in 1830)	Born in Zwickau and died in Endenich; studied law at Leipzig and Heidelberg; married Clara Wieck in 1840; attempted suicide in 1854 by throwing himself in the Rhine and was committed to an asylum
Liszt, Franz 1811–1886	One opera *Don Sanche* (1825) in collaboration with Ferdinando Paer; 2 symphonies *Faust* (1857) and *Dante* (1856); piano works include 19 composed 'Hungarian Rhapsodies', 1846–85, *Années de pèlerinage* (1848–77) and concertos; symphonic poems include *Les Préludes* (1848), *Orpheus* (1854), *Prometheus* (1850) and *Hamlet* (1858); also composed numerous études, songs and oratorios	Born Raiding in Hungary, died in Bayreuth; child prodigy who gave first piano recital aged 9; lived with Countess Marie d'Agoult from 1833 and had 3 children, one of whom, Cosima, first married Hans Bülow and then Wagner; Kapellmeister at Weiner court 1848–59, and championed Wagner and Berlioz; in 1865 he took minor orders and became Abbé Liszt
Wagner, Richard 1813–1883	Composed only 1 symphony, in C (1832); first opera *Die Feen* (The Fairies 1834) although he did compose earlier work *Die Hochzeit* but destroyed it; other operas include *Rienzi*, *The Flying Dutchman*, *Lohengrin*, *Tannhäuser*, *Der Ring des Nibelungen*, *The Mastersingers of Nuremberg* and *Parsifal* (his last); the opera *Tristan und Isolde* reflected his emotional turmoil over Mathilde Wesendonck; orchestral works include overture based on 'Rule, Britannia', *Faust* overture, *Siegfried Idyll* and concert overture *Polonia*; also composed *7 Songs From Goethe's Faust*, as well as many books on music; pioneer of the Leitmotiv	Born Leipzig and died in Venice, buried at Wahnfried; attended school in Dresden and Thomasschule in Leipzig; married actress Minna Planer in 1836 but had affair with Mathilde Wesendonck; King Ludwig of Bavaria became his patron; Minna died in 1866 and he started affair with Cosima, wife of Hans Bülow, who bore him 2 daughters (Isolde and Eva); Cosima's marriage was annulled in 1869 and she gave birth to Wagner's son, Siegfried; Wagner and Cosima were married in 1870
Verdi, Giuseppe 1813–1901	First opera *Oberto, Conte di San Bonifacio* (1838) although an earlier one, *Rocester*, is lost; other operas include *Nabucco* (1841), *Ernani* (1843), *Attila* (1846), *Macbeth* (1847), *Luisa Miller* (1849), *Stiffelio* (1850), *Rigoletto* (1851), *Il Trovatore* (1852), *Otello* (1886) and *Falstaff* (1892); Verdi's *Requiem* composed in memory of poet Manzoni and played at funeral of Diana, Princess of Wales (1997)	Born Parma, died in Milan leaving bulk of his money to a home he had founded for elderly musicians; innkeeper's son first taught by local organist Antonio Barezzi, a wholesaler whose daughter he married; between 1838 and 1840 his wife and 2 children died; married soprano, Giuseppina Strepponi in 1859; in 1860, after Italian independence from Austria, elected deputy in first National Parliament
Gounod, Charles 1818–1893	First opera *Sapho* (1851); best known *Faust* (1859); 3 symphonies and various oratorios and cantatas; also *Funeral March of a Marionette* (1872)	Born in Paris, died in St Cloud; won Grand Prix de Rome in 1839; studied for priesthood but chose a life in music
Offenbach, Jacques 1819–1880	First opera *Die Rheinnixen* (1864); only grand opera *The Tales of Hoffmann* (1881); only ballet *Le Papillon* (1860); operettas include *Orpheus in the*	Born in Deutz, near Cologne, and died in Paris; son of a cantor in Cologne synagogue; surname Offenbach came from the

MUSIC CLASSICAL

Name	Principal works	Details
	Underworld (1858), La Belle Hélène (1864) and Daphnis et Chloé (1860)	name of family's home town
Bruckner, Anton 1824–1896	Ten symphonies, last unfinished; masses in D Minor (1864), E Minor (1869) and F Minor (1872) as well as cantatas and chamber music; many works edited by composer and others, and exist in various versions	Born in Ansfelden, died in Vienna; virtuoso organist; first (unnumbered) symphony written in his late thirties
Smetana, Bedrich 1824–1884	First opera The Brandenburgers in Bohemia (1863); other operas include The Bartered Bride (1866), The Secret (1878), The Kiss (1876) and Two Widows (1874); cycle of 6 symphonic poems, Má Vlast (My Country) 1874–9)	Born in Litomyšl, died in Prague; regarded as founder of Czech music; active in founding national opera house; venereal disease caused deafness and later insanity
Strauss the Younger, Johann 1825–1899	Composed nearly 400 waltzes of which the best known include Blue Danube, Tales from the Vienna Woods (1868), Roses From the South (1880) and Emperor Waltz (1888); most famous operetta Die Fledermaus (The Bat 1874); also composed various polkas and an unfinished ballet, Cinderella (completed by Joseph Bayer)	Born and died in Vienna; worked as a bank clerk in early career; known as the Waltz King; in 1848 revolution supported opposite side to his father
Borodin, Alexander 1833–1887	Only opera Prince Igor left unfinished and completed by Rimsky-Korsakov and Alexander Glazunov; 3 symphonies, the 3rd completed by Glazunov; 2 string quartets; tone poem In The Steppes of Central Asia; music used in Forrest and Wright's musical Kismet	Born and died in St Petersburg; illegitimate son of Russian prince; doctor and professor of chemistry; feminist who founded a school of medicine for women
Brahms, Johannes 1833–1897	Four symphonies and 4 concertos; orchestral works include Tragic Overture (1880), Academic Festival Overture (1880) and Variations on a Theme by Haydn (1873); key choral works, German Requiem (1866) and Schickalslied (1871); no operas, but nearly 200 songs as well as chamber music, organ works and piano works, including Variations on a Theme by Paganini (1866)	Born in Hamburg, died in Vienna; son of professional double-bass player; hailed as genius by Schumann in essay 'New Paths' 1853 and succeeded him as teacher to Princess Friederike of Lippe-Detmold
Saint–Saëns, Camille 1835–1921	First opera La Princesse Jaune (1872); most famous opera Samson and Delilah (1868); 3 symphonies (2 other symphonies were withdrawn); symphonic poems include Danse Macabre (1874); popular orchestral piece Carnival of the Animals (1886), its performance forbidden in the composer's lifetime (movement 13, 'The Swan', most popular piece); also composed Variations on a Theme of Beethoven (1874) and Polonaise for 2 pianos; various oratorios and masses include Psalm 150 (1907); 5 piano concertos, No. 2 best known	Born in Paris and died in Algiers; symphony No. 3 dedicated to Liszt's memory; wrote coronation march for Edward VII, 1902; Carnival of the Animals in 14 movements i.e. 'Royal March of the Lion', 'Hens & Cocks', 'Wild Asses', 'Tortoises', 'The Elephant', 'Kangaroos', 'Aquarium', 'Persons with Long Ears', 'Cuckoo in the Depths of Woods', 'Aviary', 'Pianists', 'Fossils', 'The Swan', 'Finale'; the tortoises are represented by the can-can in slow motion, the 'Dance of the Sylphs' on double-basses for the elephant and the fossils is a parody of Danse Macabre
Bizet, Georges 1838–1875	First opera Le Docteur Miracle (1856); last and most famous opera Carmen (1874); one symphony; orchestral suite L'Arlésienne	Born in Paris, died in Bougival; entered Paris Conservatory at age 9; Won Grand Prix de Rome in 1857
Mussorgsky, Modest 1839–1881	First opera Salammbô (unfinished); Boris Godunov (1869) only completed opera, piano works Pictures at an Exhibition; orchestral A Night on the Bare Mountain	Born in Karevo, Pskov, died in St Petersburg; one of the Russian 5 or Mighty Handful (the others: Balakirev, Cui, Borodin, Rimsky-Korsakov)

Tchaikovsky, Pyotr
1840–1893

First opera *Voyevoda* (1868); others include *Eugene Onegin* (1879) and *The Queen of Spades* (1890); last opera *Yolanta* (1891); 3 ballets *Swan Lake* (1876), *Sleeping Beauty* (1889) and *Nutcracker* (1892); other works include 6 symphonies, 2 piano concertos, a violin concerto, a number of tone poems including *Romeo and Juliet* and *Italian Caprice*, as well as an unnumbered *Manfred Symphony* (1885); *Rococo Variations* for cello and orchestra

Born in Votkinsk, died in St Petersburg of cholera, although he may have taken poison to avoid a homosexual scandal; read Law in St Petersburg and became civil servant; married Antonina Miliukova 1877 but left her a month later and attempted suicide in his guilt; Countess Nadezhda von Meck was his patron although they never met (it is said that he crossed the street once to avoid a meeting); it is said that he used to hold his head while conducting, lest it fall off!

Dvořák, Antonín
1841–1904

Opera *Alfred* (1870); best-known *Rusalka* (1900); last opera *Armida* (1903); 9 symphonies, including No. 9 in E Minor, *From the New World*, and other cello concertos

Born in Nelahozeves, Bohemia, died in Prague; son of a village butcher; joined National Theatre of Prague as viola player in 1866

Sullivan, Arthur
1842–1900

Only grand opera *Ivanhoe* (1890); composed tune for hymn 'Onward Christian Soldiers'; 14 operettas in collaboration with W.S. Gilbert; songs include 'The Lost Chord'; first operetta *Cox and Box* (1866, librettist Burnand); last operetta *The Emerald Isle* left unfinished (completed by Edward German to Basil Hood's libretto); oratorios include *The Prodigal Son* (1869); cantatas include *Kenilworth* (1864); composed a symphony in E (the 'Irish'); incidental music to various Shakespeare plays

Born in Lambeth and died, appropriately, on St Cecilia's Day, at Westminster; son of Irish bandmaster at Sandhurst; first to win Mendelssohn Scholarship of the Royal Academy of Music, 1856; knighted in 1883; *Thespis* in 1871 was 1st collaboration with Gilbert; Savoy Theatre, opened during run of *Patience*, specialized in Gilbert and Sullivan; the two fell out during a run of *The Gondoliers* supposedly over a choice of carpet for the theatre; they were reconciled for *Utopia Ltd* and *The Grand Duke* (1896)

Grieg, Edvard
1843–1907

Orchestral works include *Peer Gynt Suite* (1875), *Lyric Suite* (1904) and *Holberg Suite* (1884); wrote *Norwegian Dances* (4 hands) and numerous songs for piano; 1 symphony, 1 piano concerto

Born and died in Bergen; married his cousin, soprano Nina Hagerup, in 1867 when he also founded the Norwegian Academy of Music; Ibsen commissioned incidental music to *Peer Gynt*

Rimsky-Korsakov, Nikolay
1844–1908

First opera *The Maid of Pskov* (aka: *Ivan the Terrible*) 1872; last opera (of 14) *The Golden Cockerel* (1907); 3 symphonies – first major Russian symphonies; famous orchestral works include *Spanish Caprice* (1887) and *Sheherazade* (1888)

Born in Tikhvin, died in Lyubensk; navy cadet as child, hoping to become a sailor; slow movement of 1st Symphony written off Gravesend; wrote 1st opera whilst serving as a naval lieutenant; edited *100 Russian Folk-Songs* 1877

Janáček, Leoš
1854–1928

First opera *Šárka* (1888); others *Jenůfa* (1904) and *From the House of the Dead* (1930: his last); Glagolitic Mass; rhapsody *Taras Bulba*; 2 string quartets; song-cycle *Diary of One Who Disappeared*

Born in Moravia, died in Moravská, Ostrava; Czech composer who had his success late in life; inspired by an affair with Kamila Stösslova

Elgar, Edward
1857–1934

Composed 2 symphonies and an unfinished 3rd; cantata, *The Dream of Gerontius* (1900); orchestral works *Pomp and Circumstance* marches (1901–30), *Enigma Variations* (1899); Violin Concerto in B Minor (1910); Cello Concerto in E Minor (1919); unfinished opera *The Spanish Lady*

Born in Broadheath, Worcestershire, died in Worcester; son of an organist and music shop proprietor in Worcester; married General's daughter Caroline Roberts who died in 1920; knighted in 1904 as first English composer of international repute since Purcell

MUSIC CLASSICAL

Name	Principal works	Details
Puccini, Giacomo 1858–1924	First opera *Le Villi* (The Willis) 1883; best-known opera *Manon Lescaut* (1893), *La Bohème* (1896), *Tosca* (1900), *Madame Butterfly* (1904), *Turandot* (unfinished, but completed by Franco Alfano)	Born in Lucca, Italy, died in Brussels; came from a long line of church musicians
Mahler, Gustav 1860–1911	Ten symphonies (one unfinished, completed by Deryck Cooke, 1st 8 of which Mahler conducted first performances); song symphony *Song of the Earth* (1909); song-cycle *Kindertotenlieder* (1904); cantata *Das Klagende Lied* (1880); only opera was completion of Weber's *The Three Pintos*	Born in Kalist, Bohemia, died in Vienna; brilliant conductor who headed Hamburg Opera from 1891; then Vienna State Opera, New York Metropolitan Opera, New York Philharmonic; converted from Judaism to Roman Catholicism 1897; married musician Alma Schindler in 1902
Debussy, Achille-Claude 1862–1918	Most famous opera *Pelléas et Mélisande*; orchestral works *Prélude à l'après-midi d'un Faune* (1894); *La Mer* (1905); *Nocturnes* (1899)	Born in St Germain-en-Laye, died (cancer) in Paris; won Prix de Rome in 1884 with cantata *L'Enfant prodigue*; influenced by Javanese gamelan music at Paris Exposition; as well as by impressionist painters; married Lily Texier 1899 but left her 5 years later for a singer, Emma Bardac and married her in 1908; part of *La Mer* written in Eastborne
Delius, Frederick 1862–1934	First opera *Irmelin* (1892); last opera *Fennimore and Gerda* (1910); others *The Magic Fountain* (1895), *Koanga* (1897), *A Village Romeo and Juliet* (1901), and *Margot-la-Rouge* (1902); orchestral pieces *Brigg Fair* (1907), *On Hearing the First Cuckoo in Spring* (1912); choral works *Sea Drift* (1909), *A Mass of Life* (1909); various Norwegian songs, as well as concertos, piano pieces and melodramas	Born in Bradford, Yorkshire, died in Grez-sur-Loing; reinterred in May 1935 at Limpsfield, Surrey; until 1904 composed under name of Fritz Delius; influenced by lasting friendship with Grieg; married Jelka Rosen 1903 and lived near Fontainebleau; became blind (probably due to syphilis) and continued composing helped by a young Yorkshire musician, Eric Fenby
Szymanowski, Karol 1882–1937	Operas *Hagith* (1913), *King Roger* (1924); 4 symphonies, 2 violin concertos, 2 ballets; voices and orchestra *Love Songs of Hafiz* (1911), *Stabat Mater* (1926); violin and piano, *Myths* (1915); also songs	Born in Tymoslowska, Ukraine, died in Lausanne; leading figure at turn of century in composer's association 'Young Poland in Music'; later influenced both by Stravinsky and by folk music of Tatra Mountains
Strauss, Richard 1864–1949	First of 15 operas *Guntram* (1893); others *Salome* (1905), *Electra* (1909), *Der Rosenkavalier* (1911), *Die Frau ohne Schatten* (1919); last opera *Capriccio* (1941); ballets include *Josephslegende* (1914); tone poems include *Till Eulenspiegel*, *Don Quixote* and *Also sprach Zarathustra*	Born in Munich, died in Garmisch-Partenkirchen; son of a horn player in Munich Court Orchestra; married soprano Pauline de Ahna, 1894; became Austrian citizen in 1947
Dukas, Paul 1865–1935	One opera *Ariane et Barbe-Bleu* (1906); 1 ballet *La Péri* (1912); most famous work, symphonic poem *The Sorcerer's Apprentice* (1897); 1 symphony, 1 piano sonata	Born and died in Paris; never prolific, he burned at least 15 years of unpublished work before he died; helped Saint-Saëns complete Guiraud's opera *Frédégonde*
Sibelius, Jean 1865–1957	Tone poem *Finlandia* became voice of his country; others *En Saga* (1901), *The Swan of Tuonela* (1893); 7 symphonies, 1 violin concerto	Born in Hämeenlinna (Tavastehus), died in Järvenpää; received State pension for life in 1897 to free him to compose; 5th Symphony written on his 50th birthday; did not compose for the last 27 years of his life

Nielsen, Karl
1865–1931

Six symphonies for violin, flute and clarinet; concertos, string quartets, piano music, songs; operas: *Saul and David* (1902), *Maskarade* (1906)

Born in Nøotre-Lyndelse, Denmark, died in Copenhagen; wife a sculptor; developed 'progressive tonality' in which a work may change its key as it develops; in 5th symphony, sidedrummer is instructed to improvise so as to halt progress of orchestra

Satie, Erik
1866–1925

Three ballets *Parade* (1917), *Mercure*, and *Relâche* (1924). Parade was scored for typewriters, airplane propellers, sirens, ticker-tape, steamship whistle and lottery wheel. A marionette opera *Geneviève de Brabant* (1899). Piano pieces, include *Trois morceaux en forme de poire* (Three pear-shaped pieces) a work for four hands (1903) and *Gymnopédies* (1888) a trio of piano pieces Nos 1 and 3 orchestrated by Debussy and No. 2 by Roland-Manuel.

French composer and pianist, born in Honfleur, of a French father and Scottish mother. In 1893, he had a stormy affair with the artist Suzanne Valadon but lived as a recluse for some years. Satie parodied the orthodoxy and stiffness of established music using whimsical titles and musical directions. He was a major influence on many French composers including Debussy, Ravel and 'Les Six'

Vaughan Williams, Ralph
1872–1958

First opera *Hugh the Drover* (1914); last *The Pilgrim's Progress* (1951); orchestral works *In the Fen Country* (1904), *Fantasia on a Theme by Thomas Tallis* (1910); 9 symphonies, also concertos, ballets, songs and chamber music

Born in Down Ampney, Gloucestershire, died in London; lived in Dorking in Surrey 1929–53

Rachmaninoff, Sergei
1873–1943

Three symphonies; 4 piano concertos, notably the 2nd in C minor; *Rhapsody on a Theme of Paganini* (1934) for piano and orchestra; many piano pieces; first opera *Aleko* (1892), last *Monna Vanna* (1907)

Born in Semyonovo, Starorussky, died in Beverly Hills; virtuoso pianist; became US citizen in 1943; lifelong friend of the celebrated bass Chaliapin; underwent hypnosis when experiencing creative block – 2nd piano concerto dedicated to hypnotist

Holst, Gustav
1874–1934

Best known for orchestral suite *The Planets* (1918); also for orchestra: *Egdon Heath* (1927), *Book Green Suite* (1933); first opera *Savitri* (1908), last opera *The Wandering Scholar* (1930)

Born in Cheltenham, died in London; worked as trombonist for Carl Rosa Opera (1898–1900); learned Sanskrit to translate hymns from *Rig Veda*

Schoenberg, Arnold
1874–1951

First opera (the monodrama): *Erwartung* (1909), last *Moses and Aron* (19051) other significant works include: *Gurrelieder, Pierrot Lunaire, A Survivor from Warsaw* and *Verklarte Nacht*

Revolutionised music to reach atonality and serialism; had a phobia about the number 13, and 'Moses and Aron' is spelled thus so as to only have 12 letters; teacher of Webern and Berg; became a US citizen in 1941

Ives, Charles
1874–1954

Four symphonies and the so-called first orchestral set (New England Symphony); 'Universe' Symphony was never completed in his lifetime but Johnny Reinhard completed it and performed it in 1996; also wrote the song 'Shall We Gather at the River'

Born in Danbury, Connecticut, died in New York; wrote symphony while at Yale; formed his own insurance company (1907); 3rd symphony won Pulitzer Prize (1947)

Ravel, Maurice
1875–1937

Operas: *L'Heure Espagnole* (1907), *L'Enfant et les Sortilèges* (1925); ballets: *Daphnis et Chloé* (1911), *Boléro* (1928); 2 piano concertos (written simultaneously); also for piano: *Pavane pour une infante défunte* (1899), *Le Tombeau de Couperin* (1917); chamber music

Born in Ciboure, died in Paris; orchestrated Mussorgsky's *Pictures at an Exhibition*; repeated failure to win Prix de Rome led to resignation of director of Paris Conservatoire, which awards it

Respighi, Ottorino
1879–1936

Roman trilogy of symphonic poems: *Pines of Rome, Fountains of Rome, Roman Festivals*; also *Three Botticelli Pictures*; concertos and operas

Born in Bolgna, died in Rome; studied under Rimsky-Korsakov in St Petersburg and Max Binch in Berlin

MUSIC CLASSICAL

Name	Principal works	Details
Bridge, Frank 1879–1941	One opera: *The Christmas Rose* (1929). Orchestral suite *The Sea* (1911) String Quartets: *Sir Roger de Coverley* (1922), *Scherzo Phantastick* (1901), and *Sally in our Alley* (1916)	Born in Brighton, died in Eastbourne; English composer, conductor, violist and violinist. In 1927 taught the 14-year-old Benjamin Britten. Conducted the New Symphony Orchestra from its inception at Covent Garden. Best known for his string quartets
Ireland, John 1879–1962	Orchestral prelude *The Forgotten Rite* (1913). Symphonic rhapsody *Mai-Dun* (1921); the title refers to the prehistoric Dorset fortification, Maiden Castle. Comic overture *Satyricon* 1946); Tone poem *Sea Fever* (1913)	English composer and pianist, born in Bowden, Cheshire, and died in Washington, West Sussex. Established his reputation with his Violin Sonata in A (1917) but is best remembered for his settings of poems by Hardy, Housman and Masefield
Bartók, Béla 1881–1945	*Music for Strings, Percussion and Celesta* (1936); *Concerto for Orchestra* (1943); only opera *Duke Bluebeard's Castle* (1911); ballets: *The Wooden Prince* (1911) and *The Miraculous Mandarin* (1919); 3 piano concertos; 2 violin concertos; 6 string quartets	Born in Nagyszentmiklós, Hungary (now Romania), died (leukaemia) in New York; dedicated collector of Hungarian and other East European folk music; anti-Nazi who emigrated to USA in 1940
Kodály, Zoltán 1882–1967	Three operas *Háry János* (1926), *Spinning Room* (1932), and *Czinka Panna* (1948). Choral and orchestral work *Psalmus Hungaricus* (1923) was based on text of Psalm 55 and commissioned for the 50th anniversary of the union of Buda and Pest. Two sets of Hungarian dances for orchestra *Marosszék Dances* (1930) and *Dances of Galánta* (1933)	Hungarian composer born in Kecskemét and died in Budapest. Wrote collections of folksongs with Béla Bartók between 1906 and 1921, although these were not published until 1951 as *Corpus Musicae Popularis Hungariae*. He carried out reforms in musical education and developed an evolutionary system of training and sight-singing
Stravinsky, Igor 1882–1971	Ballets include *The Firebird* (1910), *Petrushka* (1911), *The Rite of Spring* (1913), *Agon* (1953); first opera *The Nightingale* (1909), last *The Rake's Progress* (1951); important works in all the major forms include *Symphony of Psalms* (1930), *Ebony Concerto* (1946), *Septet* (1953), *Threni* (1958)	Born Oranienbaum, died New York; most influential classical composer of 20th century; became French citizen 1934, American 1945; first performance of *The Rite of Spring* in Paris caused famous riot by unattentive listeners
Webern, Anton 1883–1945	String quartet (1938); *Variations* for orchestra (1940); 3 cantatas; 1 symphony	Studied under Schoenberg and became rigorous exponent of serial music; born in Vienna, died in Mittersill after being shot accidentally by American sentry
Bax, Arnold 1883–1953	One ballet *Between Dusk and Dawn* (1917); seven symphonies. orchestral tone poem *Tintagel* (1919) first performed 1920; other orchestral works include *November Woods* (1917) and *Mourning Song* (1946)	Born in Streatham and died in Cork; English composer and pianist; master of the Kings/Queens; Music 1942–53. Knighted in 1937. His autobiography *Farewell My Youth* (1943) is an acclaimed work
Varèse, Edgard 1883–1965	Orchestral works include *Amériques* (1921), *Octandre* (1923) *Intégrales* (1925), *Arcana* (1927) and *Ionisation* (1931). Known for his experimental use of instrument combinations and unconventional percussion. His *Désert* (1954) employs tape-recorded sound; concentrated on electronic music later	French composer and conductor, born in Paris and died in New York. Became an American citizen in 1926. He organised the international Composers' Guild in 1921 and co-founded the Pan-American Association of Composers in 1927
Berg, Alban 1885–1935	Two operas, *Wozzeck* (1922) and *Lulu* (1935); *Lyric Suite* for string quartet (1926); violin concerto (1935)	Born and died in Vienna (insect bite); quit civil servant career to compose; *Lulu* completed by Friedrich Cerha, many years after Berg's death, due to reluctance of his widow
Prokofiev, Sergey 1891–1953	Seven symphonies, also concerti and string quartets; symphonic tale *Peter and the Wolf* (1936); ballets include *The Buffoon* (1920), *Age of Steel* (1926),	Born Sontsovka, died in Moscow; lived in Paris 1920–33; wrote film scores, e.g. *Lieutenant Kijé* and *Alexander Nevsky*; died

Romeo and Juliet (1936); operas include *The Gambler* (1917), *Love for Three Oranges* (1919), *War and Peace* (1943)

on the same day as Stalin

Bliss, Arthur
1891–1975

First opera *The Olympians* (1949); last opera *Tobias and the Angel* (1960); first ballet *Checkmate* (1937); last ballet *The Lady of Shalott* (1958); first symphony: *Colour Symphony*

Born and died in London; wrote music for Korda's film based on H G Wells's *Things to Come*; knighted in 1950; became master of the Queen's Musick in 1953

Hindemith, Paul
1895–1963

Operas include *Murder, the Hope of Women* (1919), *Mathis der Maler* (1935), *The Long Christmas Dinner* (1960); ballets: *Der Dämon* (1922), *Nobilissima Visione* (1938), *Hérodiade* (1944); several symphonies; a wealth of string quartets and sonatas

Born in Hannau, died in Frankfurt; married Gertrud Rottenberg in 1924; satirical opera *News of the Day* (1929) featured soprano singing in her bath; founded a music school in Ankara; associated with Gebrauchsmusik ('utility' music, written for some social purpose)

Gershwin, George
1898–1937

First 'hit' song was 'Swanee' (1919); 1 opera: *Porgy and Bess*; *Rhapsody in Blue* for piano, jazz band and orchestra (1924); tone poem for *An American in Paris* (1928)

Born in Brooklyn, NY, died in Beverly Hills, California; turned pro musician aged 14; many collaborations with his elder brother, lyricist Ira Gershwin

Poulenc, Francis
1899–1963

First opera: *Les Mamelles de Tirésias* (1944), last *La Voix Humaine* (1958); ballet *Les Biches* (1923); solo piano works, concertos, sonatas and many songs; church music including *Gloria* and *Stabat Mater*

Born and died in Paris; had independent income (related to family in Rhône-Poulenc pharmaceuticals); longtime companion of baritone Pierre Bernac

Copland, Aaron
1900–1990

First ballet *Grohg* (1925); others *Billy the Kid* (1938), *Rodeo* (1942), *Appalachian Spring* (1944); 5 symphonies; orchestral work *El Salon Mexico* (1936); only opera *The Tender Land* (1954)

Born in Brooklyn, NY, died in New York; symphony finale based on *Fanfare for the Common Man*

Walton, William
1902–1983

Two symphonies; 4 concertos; oratorio *Belshazzar's Feast* (1931); 2 operas *Troilus and Cressida* (1954) and *The Bear* (1967); first ballet *The First Shoot* (1935)

Born in Oldham, died in Forio d'Ischia; son of choirmaster and singing teacher; wrote *Façade* to accompany Edith Sitwell; film scores include *First of the Few* and *Henry V*

Tippett, Michael
1905–1998

First opera *The Midsummer Marriage* (1955), also *The Knot Garden* (1969), *The Ice Break* (1976), last *New Year* (1989); 4 symphonies, 5 string quartets, concertos etc.; oratorio *A Child of Our Time* includes negro spirituals

Born and died in London; wrote own libretti; committed pacifist – acted as page-turner for Britten and Pears while imprisoned in Wormwood Scrubs as conscientious objector

Shostakovich, Dmitry
1906–1975

Fifteen symphonies, 15 string quartets, 6 concertos; piano preludes; first opera *The Nose* (1928); first ballet *The Age of Gold* (1930)

Born in St Petersburg, died in Moscow; twice severely criticised for formalism by Stalinist regime; fire fighter in Nazi siege of Leningrad 1941; wrote much film music

Messiaen, Olivier
1908–1992

One symphony *Turangalîla* (premiered by Bernstein, 1948); *L'Ascension* for orchestra (1935); much organ music; 1 opera *St Francis of Assisi*

Born in Avignon, died in Paris; many works inspired by birdsong; *Quartet for the End of Time* (1941) written and premiered in POW camp

Carter, Elliott
1908–

Ballets *Pocahontas* (1939), *The Minotaur* (1947); concertos and symphonic works; many sonatas; *Night Fantasies* for piano (1980); 3 string quartets

Born in New York; encouraged by Ives; studied under Nadia Boulanger in Paris 1932–5

Barber, Samuel
1910–1981

Three operas and three symphonies; two ballets *Medea* (1946), revised as *Cave of the Heart* in 1947, and *Souvenirs* (1952); tone poem *Knoxville: Summer of 1915* (1947)

American composer and pianist; born in West Chester, Pennsylvania, and died in New York. Reputation made with his tone poem based on Arnold's 'Dover Beach' (1931)

MUSIC CLASSICAL

Name	Principal works	Details
Britten, Benjamin 1913–1976	First opera *Paul Bunyan* (1941); others include *Peter Grimes* (1945), *Billy Budd* (1951), *The Turn of the Screw* (1954) and last *Death in Venice* (1973); *Variations on a Theme of Frank Bridge* for string orchestra (1937); *War Requiem* for choir and orchestra (1961); only ballet *The Prince of the Pagodas* (1956)	Born at Lowestoft on St Cecilia's Day (22 Nov.) and died at Aldeburgh; lifelong friendship with Peter Pears; founded Aldeburgh Festival in 1948; became Lord Britten of Aldeburgh in 1976; first composer to be created life peer
Lutoslawski, Witold 1913–1994	Four symphonies; *Concerto for Orchestra* (1954); concertos for violin, cello, etc.; *Venetian Games* for orchestra (1961)	Warsaw café pianist in Second World War; regularly wrote controlled aleatory music, leaving certain things to chance; refused to write opera as could not see why people should sing rather than talk
Bernstein, Leonard 1918–1990	Three symphonies, 1 violin concerto (called *Serenade*); operas, *Trouble in Tahiti*, later became part of *A Quiet Place*; musicals: *On the Town, West Side Story, Candide*	Born in Lawrence, Massachusetts, died in New York; celebrated conductor and teacher; wrote film music for *On the Waterfront* (1954)
Simpson, Robert 1921–1997	11 symphonies; two piano sonatas *Variations and Finale on a Theme of Haydn* (1948) and *Variations and Finale on a Theme of Beethoven* (1990)	English composer, musicologist and author; on BBC music staff 1951–80. Wrote books on several composers, including Carl Nielsen, Anton Bruckner and Jean Sibelius
Arnold, Malcolm 1921–	Nine symphonies; ballets: *Homage to the Queen* (1953), *Rinaldo and Armida* (1955) and *Electra* (1963); concert overture *Beckus the Dandipratt* (1948)	Born in Northampton; English composer, trumpeter, and conductor. Like Richard Rodney Bennett composed several film scores including *The Bridge on the River Kwai*; knighted in 1993
Boulez, Pierre 1921–	*Le Marteau sans Maître* for voice and chamber orchestra (1957); *Pli Selon Pli* for voice and orchestra (1962); *Eclats/Multiples* (1976)	Born in Montbrison; leader of French 12-tone music school; once suggested burning down opera houses, but now conducts in them regularly; continually revises a small number of works
Ligeti, György 1923–	Opera *Le Grand Macabre* (1978), *Kammerkonzert* (1970); 2 string quartets, piano études; various orchestral works	Born in Discőszentmáron; left Hungary in 1956; music used in film *2001*, though he only found out when he went to see it; one work is for 100 metronomes
Berio, Luciano 1925–2003	Orchestral music; many pieces for voice and various instruments include *Circles* (1960); operas include *La Vera Storia* (1982); most famous work *Sinfonia* (1969)	Exponent of serial and electronic music; one movement of *Sinfonia* mixes a movement of Mahler's *Resurrection* with much other music and spoken text
Henze, Hans Werner 1926–	Nine symphonies; prolific in most musical forms; first opera *Das Wundertheater* (1949), others include *Boulevard Solitude* (1951), *The Bassarids* (1965), *The English Cat* (1983); latest opera *Venus and Adonis* (1997)	Born in Gütersloh; equally at home with atonal, aleatory and conventional techniques; much influenced by Italy, living there for some years; many works have left-wing inspiration
Stockhausen, Karlheinz 1928–	Many works for varying ensembles, e.g. *Gruppen* for 3 orchestras and *Stimmung* for singers and tape; piano pieces, also electronic music; ongoing operatic project: *Licht* (cycle of 7 operas each linked to a day of the week)	Born in Mödrath, near Cologne; studied under Frank Martin, Messiaen and Milhaud; experimental works include a string quartet for players in helicopters

Rautavaara, Einojuhani
1928–

Operas include *Vincent* (based on Van Gogh); latest opera *Aleksis Kivi* (1997); 7 symphonies, concertos, etc.

Born in Helsinki; a number of works invoke angels; *Cantus Arcticus* is a concerto for birds (recorded) and orchestra

Sondheim, Stephen
1930–

First musical *Saturday Night* (1957, but premiered in 1998); also *A Funny Thing Happened on the Way to the Forum* (1962), *Company* (1970), *A Little Night Music* (1973), *Pacific Overtures* (1976), *Sweeney Todd* (1979), *Passion* (1995), *Bounce* (2003)

Born in New York; writes lyrics and music; wrote lyrics for *West Side Story* and *Gypsy*; writes film scores, plays and film scripts; works often presented by opera companies

Górecki, Henryk
1933–

Three symphonies – the 3rd (*Symphony of Sorrowful Songs*) catapulted him to fame; also 2 string quartets, *Lerchenmusik, Kleines Requiem für ein Polka*, etc.

Born in Czernice, Poland; earlier work in a much more modern style; now exploring medieval influences

Maxwell Davies, Peter
1934–

Eight symphonies as of 2005; 10 Strathclyde Concertos for Scottish Chamber Orchestra, among other concertos; first opera *Taverner* (1970), latest *The Doctor of Myddfai* (1996); other works include the tone poem *Mavis in Las Vegas* and *Mr Emmet Takes a Walk*. Recent works include *Naxos Quartet No. 6* (2005) and *Military March* (2005)

Born in Salford, very prolific; lives in Orkney (since 1970), many works inspired by Orcadian writer George Mackay Brown; surname is really Davies; universally known as Max; his 8th symphony, 'Antarctic Symphony' was composed after visiting the Antarctic peninsula between 20 December 1997 and 8 January 1998. His works are catalogued by his manager Judy Arnold and are therefore known by 'J' numbers

Birtwistle, Harrison
1934–

First opera *Punch and Judy* (1967), latest *The Last Supper* (2000); and one ballet: *Pulsefield* (1977); *Pulse Shadow* 1996) for soprano, ensemble (and strings);

Born in Accrington; *Panic* (concertante work for saxophone and drum kit) commissioned for last night of centenary Prom season 1995; co-founded Pierrot Players with Maxwell Davies; knighted in 1998

Schnittke, Alfred
1934–1998

Eight symphonies, several concerti, including concerti grossi; first opera *Life with an Idiot* (1992), *The Eleventh Commandment* (1962), latest *Gesualdo* (1994); ballets include *Peer Gynt* (1986); also *Faust* cantata

Born in Engels, USSR, died in Hamburg; Russian-born of German origin; name linked to 'polystylism', where many styles of music appear in one piece; symphony No. 5 is also Concerto Grosso No. 4

Pärt, Arvo
1935–

Three symphonies, plus concerti; choral works include *St John's Passion* (1982), *Miserere* (1989) and *Berlin Mass* (1991)

Born in Paide, Estonia; emigrated to West Berlin in 1982; his early works were influenced by Shostakovich but developed his own austere style. Specialises in religious texts

Bennett, Richard Rodney
1936–

Four operas; *The Ledge* (1961), *The Mines of Sulphur* (1965), *Penny for a Song* (1966), *Victory* (1969); ballets: *Jazz Calendar* (1964) and *Isadora* (1981); setting of poems by Kathleen Raine for soprano, chorus and orchestra *Spells* (1974). Presently working on 'Reflections of a Scottish Folksong', a piece to celebrate the late Queen Mother

Born in Broadstairs, Kent; English composer and pianist educated at the Royal Academy of Music and in Paris under Pierre Boulez; ventured into the jazz field with his 1964 ballet *Jazz Calendar*, and followed this with *Jazz Pastoral* (1969); knighted in 1998.

Tavener, John
1944–

Operas include *Thérèse* (1979), *Mary of Egypt* (1992); many works for various instrumental groupings; *The Whale* (1967) was in the first ever concert by London Sinfonietta; cello and strings piece *The Protecting Veil* (1987); choral work: *We Shall See Him as He Is* (1990), *Song for Athene* (sung at the funeral of Diana, Princess of Wales)

Born in London; recent work pervaded by religious sentiment of Russian Orthodox Church which he joined in 1977; claims descent from John Taverner. He was knighted in 2000

MUSIC CLASSICAL

Name	Principal works	Details
Adams, John 1947–	First operas *Nixon in China* (1987), *The Death of Klinghoffer* (1991), Ballets include *Shaker Loops* (1978), *Grand Pianola Music* (1982) and *The Chairman Dances* (1985). Most famous orchestral work: *Harmonium* (1981)	Born in Worcester, Massachusetts. Originally known as a minimalist but more recently has broadened his style and has consequently emerged as one of the best-known and most often performed American composers
Martland, Steven 1958–	Most famous orchestral work to date *Babi Yar* (1983); ensemble piece *Remembering Lennon* (1981)	English composer born in Liverpool; professed aim 'to return music to the streets'. His trademark flat-top haircut and Bermuda shorts, and his touring 'band' give him popular appeal to a wider audience
Adès, Thomas 1971–	*Chamber Symphony* (1990) first performed in 1993; *Five Eliot Landscapes* (1990); *The Origin of the Harp* (1994); *The Premises Are Alarmed* (1996) for the opening of the Bridgewater Hall in which the Halle was conducted by Kent Nagano; *Powder Her Face* (1995) Chamber Opera; *Asyla* (1997)	English composer and pianist; second in piano section of the BBC Young Musician of the Year in 1989; graduated from Cambridge in 1992 with a double-starred first and established himself as a leading light both as a virtuoso and composer; Made his Proms debut in 1998 and the following year conducted the BBC Symphony Orchestra in the London premiere of *Asyla*

Operatic Characters (by character)

Character	Opera	Composer	Role
Abdallo	Nabucco	Verdi	Nabucco's officer
Abdullah	Oberon	Weber	Pirate
Abigaille	Nabucco	Verdi	Nabucco's adopted daughter
Abimelech	Samson et Dalila	Saint-Saëns	Satrap of Gaza
Abraham	Háry János	Kodály	Innkeeper
Adalgisa	Norma	Bellini	Temple virgin
Adele	Die Fledermaus	Johann Strauss II	Eisenstein's maid
Adelma	Turandot	Busoni	Turandot's slave
Admetus	Alceste	Gluck	Alceste's husband
Adriano	Rienzi	Wagner	Colonna's son
Aegisth	Elektra	Richard Strauss	Klytemnestra's lover
Aeneas	Dido and Aeneas	Purcell	Trojan general
Agathe	Der Freischütz	Weber	Cuno's daughter
Ahmed	Marouf	Rabaud	Pastry cook
Aida	Aida	Verdi	Ethiopian princess
Alberich	Der Ring des Nibelungen	Wagner	Nibelung dwarf
Albert Herring	Albert Herring	Britten	Greengrocer's assistant
Albrecht von Brandenburg	Mathis der Maler	Hindemith	Archbishop of Mainz
Alceste	Alceste	Gluck	Wife of Admetus
Alcindoro	La Bohème	Puccini	Musetta's escort
Alfio	Cavalleria Rusticana	Mascagni	Teamster
Don Alfonso	Così fan tutte	Mozart	Don
Alfonso d'Este	Lucrezia Borgia	Donizetti	Lucrezia's third husband
Alfonso XI	La Favorita	Donizetti	King of Castile
Alfredo Germont	La Traviata	Verdi	Violetta's lover (a singer)
Ali	Marouf	Rabaud	Marouf's friend
Alice/Alisa	Lucia di Lammermoor	Donizetti	Lucy's companion
Alice Ford	Falstaff	Verdi	Citizen of Windsor
Alidoro	La Cenerentola	Rossini	Philosopher and magician
Almaviva	The Barber of Seville	Rossini	Count
Almaviva	The Marriage of Figaro	Mozart	Count
Emperor Altoum	Turandot	Puccini	Turandot's father
Don Alvaro	La Forza del Destino	Verdi	Leonora's lover
Alwa	Lulu	Berg	Writer
Amaryllus	The Poisoned Kiss	Vaughan Williams	Empress's son
Ambrogio	The Barber of Seville	Rossini	Bartolo's servant
Amelia	A Masked Ball	Verdi	Riccardo's lover, wife of Renato
Amfortas	Parsifal	Wagner	King of the Grail
Amina	The Sleepwalker	Bellini	The sleepwalking girl
Amneris	Aida	Verdi	Egyptian princess
Amonasro	Aida	Verdi	Aida's father (King of Ethiopia)
Amor	Orfeo ed Euridice	Gluck	God of love
Andromaque	The Trojans (Les Troyens)	Berlioz	Hector's widow
Angèle	The Tsar Has His Photograph Taken	Weill	Photographer
Angelica	The Poisoned Kiss	Vaughan Williams	Tormentilla's maid
Angelina	La Cenerentola	Rossini	Don Magnifico's step-daughter, Cinderella
Donna Anna	Don Giovanni	Mozart	Don Ottavio's fiancée
Annina	Der Rosenkavalier	Richard Strauss	Valzacchi's partner
Annina	La Traviata	Verdi	Violetta's confidante
Annius	La Clemenza di Tito	Mozart	Patrician
Antonio	The Marriage of Figaro	Mozart	Gardener
Apollyon	The Pilgrim's Progress	Vaughan Williams	Fallen angel
Arbace	Idomeneo	Mozart	Idomeneo's confidante
Mr Archdale	Porgy and Bess	Gershwin	White man
Arthur Bucklaw/Arturo	Lucia di Lammermoor	Donizetti	Lord
Arthur Jones	Billy Budd	Britten	Seaman
Ashby	The Girl of the Golden West	Puccini	Wells-Fargo agent
Avosmediano	Palestrina	Pfitzner	Bishop of Cadiz
Azucena	Il Trovatore	Verdi	Gypsy woman
Baba the Turk	The Rake's Progress	Stravinsky	Bearded lady
Babekan	Oberon	Weber	Saracen prince
Balthasar Zorn	The Mastersingers of Nuremberg	Wagner	Mastersinger and pewterer
Balthazar	La Favorita	Donizetti	Superior of the monastery
Barak	Turandot	Busoni	Servant

Character	Opera	Composer	Role
Barak	*Die Frau ohne Schatten*	Richard Strauss	Dyer
Barbarina	*The Marriage of Figaro*	Mozart	Antonio's daughter
Barnaba	*La Gioconda*	Ponchielli	Spy
Baron Ochs	*Der Rosenkavalier*	Richard Strauss	Sophie's would-be suitor
Baroncelli	*Rienzi*	Wagner	Roman citizen
Bartolo	*The Barber of Seville*	Rossini	Rosina's guardian
Basilio	*The Barber of Seville*	Rossini	Singing teacher
Don Basilio	*The Marriage of Figaro*	Mozart	Organist
Bayan	*Ruslan and Lyudmila*	Glinka	Bard
Sixtus Beckmesser	*The Mastersingers of Nuremberg*	Wagner	Mastersinger and town clerk
Beelzebub	*Doktor Faust*	Busoni	Spirit voice
Belinda	*Dido and Aeneas*	Purcell	Lady in waiting
Lady Bellows	*Albert Herring*	Britten	Elderly autocrat
Ben Budge	*The Beggar's Opera*	Pepusch	Highwayman
Benôit	*La Bohème*	Puccini	Landlord
Beppe	*I Pagliacci*	Leoncavallo	Harlequin
Berta	*The Barber of Seville*	Rossini	Housekeeper
Bess	*Porgy and Bess*	Gershwin	Porgy's mistress, formerly Crown's
Betty Doxy	*The Beggar's Opera*	Pepusch	Lady of the town
Bianca	*The Rape of Lucretia*	Britten	Nurse
Bianca	*La Rondine*	Puccini	Magda's friend
Lady Billows	*Albert Herring*	Britten	Elderly autocrat
Billy Budd	*Billy Budd*	Britten	Seaman and stammerer
Billy Jackrabbit	*The Girl of the Golden West*	Puccini	Red indian
Biterolf	*Tannhäuser*	Wagner	Knight
Dr Blind	*Die Fledermaus*	Johann Strauss II	Eisenstein's attorney
Bob Boles	*Peter Grimes*	Britten	Fisherman
Boniface	*Le Jongleur de Notre Dame*	Massenet	Cook
The Bonze	*Madame Butterfly*	Puccini	Priest
Brangäne	*Tristan und Isolde*	Wagner	Isolde's maid
Brünnhilde	*Der Ring des Nibelungen*	Wagner	Valkyrie
Brutus Jones	*Emperor Jones*	Gruenberg	Escaped convict, tribal ruler
Bussy	*Zazà*	Leoncavallo	Journalist
Calaf	*Turandot*	Busoni	Suitor to Turandot
Calaf	*Turandot*	Puccini	Suitor to Turandot
Canio	*I Pagliacci*	Leoncavallo	Pagliaccio (clown)
Wolfgang Capito	*Mathis der Maler*	Hindemith	Councillor
Cardillac	*Cardillac*	Hindemith	Goldsmith
Don Carlos	*Don Carlos*	Verdi	Heir to Spanish throne
Don Carlos	*Ernani*	Verdi	King of Castile
Carmen	*Carmen*	Bizet	Gypsy
Carolina	*The Secret Marriage*	Cimarosa	Geronimo's daughter
Cascart	*Zazà*	Leoncavallo	Music-hall performer
Cassio	*Otello*	Verdi	Lieutenant
Catarina	*Madame Sans-Gêne*	Giordano	Laundress
Cavaradossi	*Tosca*	Puccini	Painter
Sir Robert Cecil	*Gloriana*	Britten	Secretary to the Council
Celio	*The Love for Three Oranges*	Prokofiev	Magician
Cesare Angelotti	*Tosca*	Puccini	Escaped political prisoner
Charlemagne	*Oberon*	Weber	Emperor of the Franks
Charles Gérard	*Andrea Chénier*	Giordano	Revolutionary leader
Chernomor	*Ruslan and Lyudmila*	Glinka	An evil dwarf
Cherubino	*The Marriage of Figaro*	Mozart	Page
Chevalier des Grieux	*Manon*	Massenet	Manon's love
Chochenille	*The Tales of Hoffmann*	Offenbach	Spalanzani's servant
Chorèbe	*The Trojans (Les Troyens)*	Berlioz	Cassandra's lover
Christine	*Intermezzo*	Richard Strauss	Storch's wife
Chrysothemis	*Elektra*	Richard Strauss	Elektra's sister
Cio-Cio-San	*Madame Butterfly*	Puccini	Pinkerton's wife
Cirillo	*Fedora*	Giordano	Coachman
Claggart	*Billy Budd*	Britten	Master-at-arms
Claison	*Capriccio*	Richard Strauss	Actress
Clara	*Porgy and Bess*	Gershwin	Jake's wife
Princess Clarissa	*The Love for Three Oranges*	Prokofiev	King's niece
Clorinda	*La Cenerentola*	Rossini	Don Magnifico's daughter
Clotilde	*Norma*	Bellini	Norma's friend
Mrs Coaxer	*The Beggar's Opera*	Pepusch	Lady of the town
Comtesse de Coigny	*Andrea Chénier*	Giordano	Madeleine's mother
Cola Rienzi	*Rienzi*	Wagner	Papal legate
Collatinus	*The Rape of Lucretia*	Britten	Soldier
Colline	*La Bohème*	Puccini	Philosopher

Character	Opera	Composer	Role
Commendatore	Don Giovanni	Mozart	Donna Anna's father
Comte de Grieux	Manon	Massenet	Chevalier's father
Conrad Nachtigall	The Mastersingers of Nuremberg	Wagner	Mastersinger and bucklemaker
Coppelius	The Tales of Hoffmann	Offenbach	Scientist
Count de Luna	Il Trovatore	Verdi	Count of aragon
Crébillon	La Rondine	Puccini	Perichaud's friend
Creon	Oedipus Rex	Stravinsky	Jocasta's brother
Crown	Porgy and Bess	Gershwin	Stevedore
Don Curzio	The Marriage of Figaro	Mozart	Lawyer
Daland	The Flying Dutchman	Wagner	Sea captain
El Dancairo	Carmen	Bizet	Smuggler
Dandini	La Cenerentola	Rossini	Valet
Daniello	Johnny Spielt Auf	Krenek	Artist
Dansker	Billy Budd	Britten	Seaman
Dapertutto	The Tales of Hoffmann	Offenbach	Sorcerer
The Dark Fiddler	A Village Romeo and Juliet	Delius	Real owner of land
David	The Mastersingers of Nuremberg	Wagner	Hans Sachs' apprentice
David	L'Amico Fritz	Mascagni	Rabbi
de Bretigny	Manon	Massenet	A nobleman
Désiré	Fedora	Giordano	Valet
Despina	Così fan tutte	Mozart	Maid
Dickson	La Dame Blanche	Boieldieu	Tenant of the White Lady
Dido	Dido and Aeneas	Purcell	Queen of Carthage
Dimitri	Fedora	Giordano	Groom
Dipsacus	The Poisoned Kiss	Vaughan Williams	Magician
Dolly Trull	The Beggar's Opera	Pepusch	Lady of the town
Donald	Billy Budd	Britten	Seaman
Donner	Der Ring des Nibelungen	Wagner	Norse god
Dorabella	Così fan tutte	Mozart	Fiordiligi's sister
Douphol	La Traviata	Verdi	Baron
Duclou	Zazà	Leoncavallo	Stage manager
Mme Dufresne	Zazà	Leoncavallo	Milio's wife
Dumas	Andrea Chénier	Giordano	President of the tribunal
Earl of Essex	Gloriana	Britten	The Queen's favorite
Principessa Eboli	Don Carlos	Verdi	Lady-in-waiting
Edgar/Edgardo	Lucia di Lammermoor	Donizetti	Edgar of Ravenswood
Edmondo	Manon Lescaut	Puccini	Student
Elettra	Idomeneo	Mozart	Greek princess
Elektra	Elektra	Richard Strauss	Agamemnon's daughter
Elisabeth	Tannhäuser	Wagner	Hermann's niece
Elizabeth of England	Gloriana	Britten	Queen of England
Elisetta	The Secret Marriage	Cimarosa	Geronimo's older daughter
Ellen Orford	Peter Grimes	Britten	Schoolteacher
Elvino	The Sleepwalker	Bellini	Farmer, Amina's love
Elvira	Ernani	Verdi	Ernani's beloved
Donna Elvira	Don Giovanni	Mozart	Lady from Burgos
Enzo	La Gioconda	Ponchielli	Sea captain
Erda	Der Ring des Nibelungen	Wagner	Earth goddess
Ernesto	Don Pasquale	Donizetti	Don Pasquale's nephew
Eroshka	Prince Igor	Borodin	Gudok player
Escamillo	Carmen	Bizet	Bullfighter
Esmerelda	The Bartered Bride	Smetana	Dancer
Estrella	Háry János	Kodály	Lady-in-waiting
Euridice	Orfeo ed Euridice	Gluck	Orfeo's wife
Eva	The Mastersingers of Nuremberg	Wagner	Pogner's daughter
Fafner	Der Ring des Nibelungen	Wagner	Giant, builder of Valhalla
Dr Falke	Die Fledermaus	Johann Strauss II	Eisenstein's Friend
Faninal	Der Rosenkavalier	Richard Strauss	Sophie's father
Farfarello	The Love for Three Oranges	Prokofiev	A devil
Farlaf	Ruslan and Lyudmila	Glinka	Warrior, suitor to Lyudmila
Fasolt	Der Ring des Nibelungen	Wagner	Giant, builder of Valhalla
Fata Morgana	The Love for Three Oranges	Prokofiev	Witch
Fatima	Oberon	Weber	Reiza's companion
Fatimah	Marouf	Rabaud	Marouf's wife
Fenena	Nabucco	Verdi	Nabucco's daughter
Fenton	Falstaff	Verdi	In Love with Nanetta
Feodor	Boris Godunov	Mussorgsky	Son of Boris Godunov
Ferrando	Così fan tutte	Mozart	Dorabella's fiancé
Ferrando	Il Trovatore	Verdi	Captain of the Guard
Fidalma	The Secret Marriage	Cimarosa	Geronimo's sister
Figaro	The Barber of Seville	Rossini	Barber

M
U
S
I
C

C
L
A
S
S
I
C
A
L

Character	Opera	Composer	Role
Figaro	*The Marriage of Figaro*	Mozart	Servant to Almaviva
Filch	*The Beggar's Opera*	Pepusch	Pickpocket
Filipievna	*Eugene Onegin*	Tchaikovsky	Nurse
Finn	*Ruslan and Lyudmila*	Glinka	Wizard
Fiordiligi	*Così fan tutte*	Mozart	Dorabella's sister
Fiorello	*The Barber of Seville*	Rossini	Servant
Flamand	*Capriccio*	Richard Strauss	Musician
Flavio	*Norma*	Bellini	Centurion
Florestan	*Fidelio*	Beethoven	Spanish nobleman
Flosshilde	*Der Ring des Nibelungen*	Wagner	Rhinemaiden
Frank Ford	*Falstaff*	Verdi	Alice's husband
Frank	*Die Fledermaus*	Johann Strauss II	Prison governor
Frantz	*The Tales of Hoffmann*	Offenbach	Crespel's servant
Frasquita	*Carmen*	Bizet	Gypsy
Frasquita	*Der Corregidor*	Wolf	Tio Lucas' wife
Frazier	*Porgy and Bess*	Gershwin	Catfish Row 'lawyer'
Freia	*Der Ring des Nibelungen*	Wagner	Goddess of youth and beauty
Fricka	*Der Ring des Nibelungen*	Wagner	Wotan's wife
Fritz Kothner	*The Mastersingers of Nuremberg*	Wagner	Mastersinger and baker
Froh	*Der Ring des Nibelungen*	Wagner	Norse god
Frosch	*Die Fledermaus*	Johann Strauss II	Jailer
Gallanthus	*The Poisoned Kiss*	Vaughan Williams	Amaryllus's sister
Mr Gedge	*Albert Herring*	Britten	Vicar
Geneviève	*Pelléas et Mélisande*	Debussy	Mother of Pelléas
Gennaro	*Lucrezia Borgia*	Donizetti	Venetian nobleman, Lucrezia's son
Gennaro	*The Jewels of the Madonna*	Wolf-Ferrari	Blacksmith
Georges Brown	*La Dame Blanche*	Boieldieu	English officer
Gérald	*Lakmé*	Delibes	English officer
Gerhilde	*Der Ring des Nibelungen*	Wagner	Valkyrie
Geronimo	*The Secret Marriage*	Cimarosa	Citizen of Bologna
Gertrude	*Hänsel and Gretel*	Humperdinck	Mother of Hansel and Gretel
Gilda	*Rigoletto*	Verdi	Rigoletto's daughter
La Gioconda	*La Gioconda*	Ponchielli	Street singer, Enzo's love
Giorgetta	*Il Tabarro*	Puccini	Michele's wife
Godfrey	*Lohengrin*	Wagner	Elsa's brother
Golaud	*Pelléas et Mélisande*	Debussy	Arkel's grandson
Gorislava	*Ruslan and Lyudmila*	Glinka	Ratmir's lover
Goro	*Madame Butterfly*	Puccini	Marriage broker
Grech	*Fedora*	Giordano	Policeman
Prince Gremin	*Eugene Onegin*	Tchaikovsky	General
Grigorij	*Boris Godunov*	Mussorgsky	False Dimitri
Grimgerde	*Der Ring des Nibelungen*	Wagner	Valkyrie
Gubetta	*Lucrezia Borgia*	Donizetti	Servant to Lucrezia
Guglielmo	*Così fan tutte*	Mozart	Fiordiligi's fiancé
Gunther	*Der Ring des Nibelungen*	Wagner	Hagen's half-brother
Gutrune	*Der Ring des Nibelungen*	Wagner	Gunther's sister
Gzak	*Prince Igor*	Borodin	Polovtsian Khan
Hadji	*Lakmé*	Delibes	Nilakantha's servant
Hagen	*Der Ring des Nibelungen*	Wagner	Alberich's Descendant
Hans Foltz	*The Mastersingers of Nuremberg*	Wagner	Mastersinger and coppersmith
Hans Sachs	*The Mastersingers of Nuremberg*	Wagner	Mastersinger and cobbler
Hans Schwarz	*The Mastersingers of Nuremberg*	Wagner	Mastersinger and stocking weaver
Happy	*The Girl of the Golden West*	Puccini	Miner
Haroun al Rashid	*Oberon*	Weber	Caliph of Baghdad
Harry Paddington	*The Beggar's Opera*	Pepusch	Highwayman
Helmwige	*Der Ring des Nibelungen*	Wagner	Valkyrie
Henry Ashton	*Ennio Lucia di Lammermoor*	Donizetti	Lord of Lammermoor
Hermann	*Tannhäuser*	Wagner	Landgrave of Thuringia
Hermann	*The Tales of Hoffmann*	Offenbach	Student
Hermann Ortel	*The Mastersingers of Nuremberg*	Wagner	Mastersinger and soap boiler
Herod	*Salome*	Richard Strauss	Ruler of Galileo
Herodias	*Salome*	Richard Strauss	Herod's wife
Hob	*The Poisoned Kiss*	Vaughan Williams	Servant of Dipsacus
Hoffmann	*The Tales of Hoffmann*	Offenbach	Poet
Hunding	*Der Ring des Nibelungen*	Wagner	Siegmund's enemy
Hylas	*The Trojans (Les Troyens)*	Berlioz	Trojan sailor
Idamente	*Idomeneo*	Mozart	Idomeneo's son
Idomeneo	*Idomeneo*	Mozart	King of Crete
Ighino	*Palestrina*	Pfitzner	Palestrina's son
Prince Igor	*Prince Igor*	Borodin	Prince of Seversk
Ilia	*Idomeneo*	Mozart	Trojan princess

Character	Opera	Composer	Role
Ilka	Háry János	Kodály	Háry's fiancée
Incredible	Andrea Chénier	Giordano	Spy
Iopas	The Trojans (Les Troyens)	Berlioz	Poet
Irene	Rienzi	Wagner	Rienzi's sister
Isolde	Tristan und Isolde	Wagner	Irish princess
Jacquino	Fidelio	Beethoven	Rocco's assistant
Jago	Ernani	Verdi	Silva's squire
Jake	Porgy and Bess	Gershwin	Fisherman
Aunt Jane	Hugh the Drover	Vaughan Williams	Sister of the constable
Jaroslavna	Prince Igor	Borodin	Prince Igor's wife
Jean	Le Jongleur de Notre Dame	Massenet	A poor juggler
Jemmy Twitcher	The Beggar's Opera	Pepusch	Highwayman
Jenik	The Bartered Bride	Smetana	Micha's son
Jenny	La Dame Blanche	Boieldieu	Dickson's wife
Jenny Diver	The Beggar's Opera	Pepusch	Lady of the night
Jim	Porgy and Bess	Gershwin	Cotton picker
Jocasta	Oedipus Rex	Stravinsky	Wife of Oedipus
Joe	The Girl of the Golden West	Puccini	Miner
John	Peter Grimes	Britten	Peter's apprentice
John the Butcher	Hugh the Drover	Vaughan Williams	Mary's fiancé
John the Baptist	Salome	Richard Strauss	Jewish prophet
Johnny	Johnny Spielt Auf	Krenek	Artist
Don José	Carmen	Bizet	Corporal in the Guard
Juan Lopez	Der Corregidor	Wolf	Mayor
Judith	Duke Bluebeard's Castle	Bartók	Bluebeard's last wife
Junius	The Rape of Lucretia	Britten	Roman general
Justizrat	Intermezzo	Richard Strauss	Storch's friend
Kammersänger	Intermezzo	Richard Strauss	Storch's friend
Kate	Madame Butterfly	Puccini	Pinkerton's wife
Kathinka	The Bartered Bride	Smetana	Marenka's mother
Kecal	The Bartered Bride	Smetana	Marriage broker
King of Clubs	The Love for Three Oranges	Prokofiev	Ruler of the kingdom
Klingsor	Parsifal	Wagner	Magician
Kontchak	Prince Igor	Borodin	Polovtsian Khan
Kontchakovna	Prince Igor	Borodin	Kontchak's daughter
Kruschev	Boris Godunov	Mussorgsky	Boyard
Kundry	Parsifal	Wagner	Bewitched woman
Kunz Vogelgesang	The Mastersingers of Nuremberg	Wagner	Mastersinger and furrier
Kurvenal	Tristan und Isolde	Wagner	Tristan's retainer
Lakmé	Lakmé	Delibes	Nilakantha's daughter
Larina	Eugene Onegin	Tchaikovsky	Tatyana's mother
Larkens	The Girl of the Golden West	Puccini	Miner
Lartigen	Zazà	Leoncavallo	Monologist
Lawrence	The Wreckers	Smyth	Lighthouse keeper
Leandro	The Love for Three Oranges	Prokofiev	King of Spades and PM
Lenski	Eugene Onegin	Tchaikovsky	Olga's fiancé
Leonara di Gusman	La Favorita	Donizetti	King's mistress
Leonora	Il Trovatore	Verdi	Beloved of Manrico
Leonora	Fidelio	Beethoven	Florestan's wife
Leporello	Don Giovanni	Mozart	Servant
Lescaut	Manon	Massenet	A gambler
Lillas Pastia	Carmen	Bizet	Innkeeper
Lily	Porgy and Bess	Gershwin	Strawberry woman
Lindorf	The Tales of Hoffmann	Offenbach	Councillor of Nuremberg
Linette	The Love for Three Oranges	Prokofiev	Princess hidden in an orange
Lisette	La Rondine	Puccini	Magda's maid
Liù	Turandot	Puccini	Slave girl
Lob	The Poisoned Kiss	Vaughan Williams	Assistant of Dipsacus
Lockit	The Beggar's Opera	Pepusch	Jailer
Lodovico	Otello	Verdi	Venetian ambassador
Loge	Der Ring des Nibelungen	Wagner	Norse god
Lohengrin	Lohengrin	Wagner	Parsifal's son
Lola	Cavalleria Rusticana	Mascagni	Alfio's wife
Lorek	Fedora	Giordano	Surgeon
Loris Ipanov	Fedora	Giordano	Count
Lucia	The Rape of Lucretia	Britten	Lucretia's attendant
Lucretia	Palestrina	Pfitzner	Palestrina's wife
Lucretia	The Rape of Lucretia	Britten	Wife of Collatinus
Lucrezia Borgia	Lucrezia Borgia	Donizetti	Duchess of Ferrara
Lucy/Lucia	Lucia di Lammermoor	Donizetti	Ashton's sister
Lucy Lockit	The Beggar's Opera	Pepusch	Jailer's daughter

Character	Opera	Composer	Role
Luigi	Il Tabarro	Puccini	Stevedore, Giorgetta's father
Lulu	Lulu	Berg	Prostitute
Luther	The Tales of Hoffmann	Offenbach	Innkeeper
Lyudmila	Ruslan and Lyudmila	Glinka	A noblewoman
Macheath	The Beggar's Opera	Pepusch	Highwayman
MacIrton	La Dame Blanche	Boieldieu	Justice of the Peace
Mad Margaret	Ruddigore	Sullivan	Mad woman
Maddalena	Rigoletto	Verdi	Sparafucile's sister
Madeleine de Coigny	Andrea Chénier	Giordano	In love with Andrea Chénier
Madelon	Andrea Chénier	Giordano	Old woman
Maffio Orsini	Lucrezia Borgia	Donizetti	Lucrezia's enemy
Magda	La Rondine	Puccini	Rambaldo's mistress
Magdalena	The Mastersingers of Nuremberg	Wagner	Nurse
Don Magnifico	La Cenerentola	Rossini	Baron of Montflagon
Mahomet	Der Rosenkavalier	Richard Strauss	Negro page
Dr Malatesta	Don Pasquale	Donizetti	Don Pasquale's friend
Maliella	The Jewels of the Madonna	Wolf-Ferrari	Gennaro's adopted sister
Mallika	Lakmé	Delibes	Lakmé's slave
Mama Lucia	Cavalleria Rusticana	Mascagni	Turiddu's mother
Manon	Manon	Massenet	Lescaut's cousin
Manrico	Il Trovatore	Verdi	Troubador
Duke of Mantua	Rigoletto	Verdi	Nobleman
Manuela	Der Corregidor	Wolf	Maid
Manz	A Village Romeo and Juliet	Delius	Farmer
Marcellina	Fidelio	Beethoven	Rocco's daughter
Marcellina	The Marriage of Figaro	Mozart	Housekeeper
Marcello	La Bohème	Puccini	Painter
Marco	Zazà	Leoncavallo	Dufresne's butler
Marenka	The Bartered Bride	Smetana	In love with Jenik
Marguerite	La Dame Blanche	Boieldieu	Servant
Marguérite	Faust	Gounod	Beloved of Faust
Maria	Porgy and Bess	Gershwin	Cookshop keeper
Marianne	Der Rosenkavalier	Richard Strauss	Sophie's duenna
Marie	Wozzeck	Berg	Prostitute
Marie-Louise	Háry János	Kodály	Napoleon's second wife
Marina Mnishek	Boris Godunov	Mussorgsky	Daughter of Voyevode of Sandomir
Mario Cavaradossi	Tosca	Puccini	Painter
King Marke	Tristan und Isolde	Wagner	King of Cornwall
Marlardot	Zazà	Leoncavallo	Music-Hall owner
Marouf	Marouf	Rabaud	Shoemaker
Marschallin	Der Rosenkavalier	Richard Strauss	Princess
Martha Schwerlein	Faust	Gounod	Marguérite's neighbour
Marti	A Village Romeo and Juliet	Delius	Farmer
Cavaliere Marullo	Rigoletto	Verdi	Courtier
Mary	Hugh the Drover	Vaughan Williams	Constable's daughter
Marzci	Háry János	Kodály	Marie's coachman
Masetto	Don Giovanni	Mozart	Peasant
Mat of the Mint	The Beggar's Opera	Pepusch	Highwayman
Mathieu	Andrea Chénier	Giordano	Waiter
Mathis	Mathis der Maler	Hindemith	Painter (Grünewald)
Matteo Borsa	Rigoletto	Verdi	Courtier
Matteo del Sarto	Arlecchino	Busoni	Tailor
Max	Johnny Spielt Auf	Krenek	Composer
Mélisande	Pelléas et Mélisande	Debussy	Golaud's wife
Melot	Tristan und Isolde	Wagner	Courtier
Melusine	Háry János	Kodály	Countess
Mercedes	Carmen	Bizet	Gypsy
Micaela	Carmen	Bizet	Village girl
Micha	The Bartered Bride	Smetana	Jenik's father
Michele	Il Tabarro	Puccini	Barge owner
Michelin	Zazà	Leoncavallo	Journalist
Milio Dufresne	Zazà	Leoncavallo	Zaza's lover
Mime	Der Ring des Nibelungen	Wagner	A Nibelung
Mimi	La Bohème	Puccini	Seamstress
Minnie	The Girl of the Golden West	Puccini	Barmaid
Dr Miracle	The Tales of Hoffmann	Offenbach	Doctor
Missail	Boris Godunov	Mussorgsky	Vagrant
Mistrust	The Pilgrim's Progress	Vaughan Williams	Neighbour
Molly Brazen	The Beggar's Opera	Pepusch	Lady of the town
Monostatos	The Magic Flute	Mozart	Servant

Character	Opera	Composer	Role
Montano	Otello	Verdi	Otello's predecessor
Morales	Carmen	Bizet	Officer of the Guard
Augustin Moser	The Mastersingers of Nuremberg	Wagner	Mastersinger and tailor
Muff	The Bartered Bride	Smetana	Comedian
Musetta	La Bohème	Puccini	In love with Marcello
Nabucco	Nabucco	Verdi	Nebuchadnezzar, King of Babylon
Naina	Ruslan and Lyudmila	Glinka	Witch
Namouna	Oberon	Weber	Fatima's grandmother
Nancy	Albert Herring	Britten	Baker's assistant
Nanetta	Falstaff	Verdi	Ford's daughter
Narbal	The Trojans (Les Troyens)	Berlioz	Dido's minister
Narraboth	Salome	Richard Strauss	Captain of the Guard
Natalia	Zazà	Leoncavallo	Zazà's maid
Nathanael	The Tales of Hoffmann	Offenbach	Student
Ned Keene	Peter Grimes	Britten	Apothecary
Nedda	I Pagliacci	Leoncavallo	Canio's wife
Nick	The Girl of the Golden West	Puccini	Bartender
Nicklaus	The Tales of Hoffmann	Offenbach	Hoffmann's friend
Nicola	Fedora	Giordano	Footman
Nicoletta	The Love for Three Oranges	Prokofiev	Princess hidden in an orange
Nilakantha	Lakmé	Delibes	Brahmin priest
Nimming Ned	The Beggar's Opera	Pepusch	Highwayman
Ninetta	The Love for Three Oranges	Prokofiev	Princess hidden in an orange
Norina	Don Pasquale	Donizetti	Widow
Norma	Norma	Bellini	Druid priestess
Norman	Lucia di Lammermoor	Donizetti	Follower of Ashton
Obstinate	The Pilgrim's Progress	Vaughan Williams	Neighbour
Octavian	Der Rosenkavalier	Richard Strauss	Bearer of the Rose
Oedipus	Oedipus Rex	Stravinsky	King of Thebes
Olga	Eugene Onegin	Tchaikovsky	Tatiana's sister
Olivier	Capriccio	Richard Strauss	Poet
Olympia	The Tales of Hoffmann	Offenbach	Mechanical doll
One-Arm	Die Frau ohne Schatten	Richard Strauss	Barak's brother
One-Eye	Die Frau ohne Schatten	Richard Strauss	Barak's brother
Orest	Elektra	Richard Strauss	Elektra's brother
Orfeo	Orfeo ed Euridice	Gluck	Singer-poet
Orlovsky	Die Fledermaus	Johann Strauss II	Rich Russian
Oroveso	Norma	Bellini	Norma's father
Ortlinde	Der Ring des Nibelungen	Wagner	Valkyrie
Ortrud	Lohengrin	Wagner	Wife of Frederick
Oscar	A Masked Ball	Verdi	Riccardo's page
Ovlour	Prince Igor	Borodin	Polovtsian traitor
Palestrina	Palestrina	Pfitzner	Composer
Pamina	The Magic Flute	Mozart	Daughter of Queen of the Night
Pang	Turandot	Puccini	Lord of Provisions
Pantalone	Turandot	Busoni	Minister
Pantaloon	The Love for Three Oranges	Prokofiev	King's friend
Panthée	The Trojans (Les Troyens)	Berlioz	Priest
Paolino	The Secret Marriage	Cimarosa	Carolina's secret husband
Paolo Orsini	Rienzi	Wagner	Patrician
Papagena	The Magic Flute	Mozart	Destined to be Papageno's wife
Papageno	The Magic Flute	Mozart	Bird catcher
Parpignol	La Bohème	Puccini	Toy vendor
Parsifal	Parsifal	Wagner	Knight of the Holy Grail
Peachum	The Beggar's Opera	Pepusch	Fence
Pelléas	Pelléas et Mélisande	Debussy	Arkel's grandson
Périchaud	La Rondine	Puccini	Rambaldo's friend
Peter	Porgy and Bess	Gershwin	Honey-man
Peter	Hänsel and Gretel	Humperdinck	Father of Hansel and Gretel
Peter Grimes	Peter Grimes	Britten	Fisherman
Pilgrim	The Pilgrim's Progress	Vaughan Williams	Pilgrim
Pimen	Boris Godunov	Mussorgsky	Hermit
Ping	Turandot	Puccini	Chinese Grand Chancellor
Lt Pinkerton	Madame Butterfly	Puccini	Lt in US Navy
Pittichinaccio	The Tales of Hoffmann	Offenbach	Giulietta's admirer
Don Pizarro	Fidelio	Beethoven	Prison governor
Pliable	The Pilgrim's Progress	Vaughan Williams	Neighbour
Veit Pogner	The Mastersingers of Nuremberg	Wagner	Mastersinger and goldsmith (Eva's father)
Pollione	Norma	Bellini	Proconsul of Rome

MUSIC CLASSICAL

Character	Opera	Composer	Role
Polly Peachum	The Beggar's Opera	Pepusch	Peachum's daughter, Macheath's wife
Polyxène	The Trojans (Les Troyens)	Berlioz	Priam's daughter
Pong	Turandot	Puccini	Lord of the Imperial Kitchen
Porgy	Porgy and Bess	Gershwin	A crippled beggar
Priam	The Trojans (Les Troyens)	Berlioz	King of Troy
Prince	Lulu	Berg	Traveller in Africa
Prince	The Love for Three Oranges	Prokofiev	Hypochondriac
Prunier	La Rondine	Puccini	Poet
Publius	La Clemenza di Tito	Mozart	Captain of Praetorian Guard
Queen Mother of Samarkand	Turandot	Busoni	Negress
Rafaele	The Jewels of the Madonna	Wolf-Ferrari	Leader of the Camorra
Raimondo	Rienzi	Wagner	Papal legate
Rambaldo	La Rondine	Puccini	Banker
Ramfis	Aida	Verdi	High priest
Don Ramiro	La Cenerentola	Rossini	Prince of Salerno
Jack Rance	The Girl of the Golden West	Puccini	Sheriff
Rangoni	Boris Godunov	Mussorgsky	Jesuit
Ratmir	Ruslan and Lyudmila	Glinka	Suitor to Lyudmila
Raymond/ Raimondo	Lucia di Lammermoor	Donizetti	Chaplain, Lucy's tutor
Mr Redburn	Billy Budd	Britten	First lieutenant
Red Whiskers	Billy Budd	Britten	Impressed seaman
Reinmar von Zweter	Tannhäuser	Wagner	Knight
Reiza	Oberon	Weber	Haroun el Rashid's daughter
El Remondado	Carmen	Bizet	Smuggler
Renato	A Masked Ball	Verdi	Riccardo's secretary
Repela	Der Corregidor	Wolf	Valet to magistrate
Rhadames	Aida	Verdi	Captain of the Guard
Riccardo	A Masked Ball	Verdi	Governor of Louisiana
Riedinger	Mathis der Maler	Hindemith	Rich Lutheran
Rigoletto	Rigoletto	Verdi	Gilda's father, a jester
Rocco	Fidelio	Beethoven	Chief jailer
Rodolfo	La Bohème	Puccini	Poet
Rosalinda	Die Fledermaus	Johann Strauss II	Eisenstein's wife
Rose	Lakmé	Delibes	An English lady
Rosina	The Barber of Seville	Rossini	Dr Bartolo's ward
Rossweisse	Der Ring des Nibelungen	Wagner	Valkyrie
Roucher	Andrea Chénier	Giordano	Andrea's friend
Ruggero	La Rondine	Puccini	Son of Rambaldo's childhood friend
Ruslan	Ruslan and Lyudmila	Glinka	Suitor to Lyudmila
Rustighello	Lucrezia Borgia	Donizetti	Alfonso's henchman
Sali	A Village Romeo and Juliet	Delius	Mary's daughter
Salome	Salome	Richard Strauss	Daughter of Herodias
Santuzza	Cavalleria Rusticana	Mascagni	In love with Turiddu
Sarastro	The Magic Flute	Mozart	High priest
Baron Scarpia	Tosca	Puccini	Chief of police
Dr Schön	Lulu	Berg	Editor
Senta	The Flying Dutchman	Wagner	Daland's daughter
Sharpless	Madame Butterfly	Puccini	US consul in Nagasaki
Sid	Albert Herring	Britten	Butcher's assistant
Siegfried	Der Ring des Nibelungen	Wagner	Son of Siegmund and Sieglunde
Sieglunde	Der Ring des Nibelungen	Wagner	Siegmund's twin sister
Siegmund	Der Ring des Nibelungen	Wagner	Mortal son of Wotan
Silvano	A Masked Ball	Verdi	A young sailor
Silvio	I Pagliacci	Leoncavallo	In love with Nedda
Sophie	Der Rosenkavalier	Richard Strauss	Daughter of von Faninal
Spalanzani	The Tales of Hoffmann	Offenbach	Inventor
Sportin' Life	Porgy and Bess	Gershwin	Dope dealer
Stella	The Tales of Hoffmann	Offenbach	Opera singer
Robert Storch	Intermezzo	Richard Strauss	Musical conductor
Suky Tawdry	The Beggar's Opera	Pepusch	Lady of the town
Susan B Anthony	The Mother of Us All	Thomson	American suffragette
Susanna	The Marriage of Figaro	Mozart	Maid
Suzuki	Madame Butterfly	Puccini	Servant
Suzy	La Rondine	Puccini	Magda's friend
Svyetor	Ruslan and Lyudmila	Glinka	Lyudmila's father
Talpa	Il Tabarro	Puccini	Stevedore
Tannhäuser	Tannhäuser	Wagner	Knight
Tatiana	Eugene Onegin	Tchaikovsky	In love with Eugene
Telramund	Lohengrin	Wagner	Count of Brabant

Character	Opera	Composer	Role
Thisbe	La Cenerentola	Rossini	Don Magnifico's daughter
Timorous	The Pilgrim's Progress	Vaughan Williams	Neighbour
Tinca	Il Tabarro	Puccini	Stevedore
Tio Lucas	Der Corregidor	Wolf	Miller
Tiresias	Oedipus Rex	Stravinsky	Blind soothsayer
Titurel	Parsifal	Wagner	Father of Amfortas
Titus	La Clemenza di Tito	Mozart	Emperor of Rome
Tom Rakewell	The Rake's Progress	Stravinsky	The Rake
Tonio	I Pagliacci	Leoncavallo	Clown
Tonuelo	Der Corregidor	Wolf	Court messenger
Tormentilla	The Poisoned Kiss	Vaughan Williams	Daughter of Dipsacus
Tosca	Tosca	Puccini	Singer
Toto	Zazà	Leoncavallo	Dufresne's child
Mrs Trapes	The Beggar's Opera	Pepusch	Tally woman
Trim	The Girl of the Golden West	Puccini	Miner
Tristan	Tristan und Isolde	Wagner	Cornish knight
Trouble	Madame Butterfly	Puccini	Cio-Cio-San's child
Truchsess von Waldburg	Mathis der Maler	Hindemith	Leader of the army
Trulove	The Rake's Progress	Stravinsky	Anne's father
Princess Turandot	Turandot	Puccini	Daughter of Altoum
Turiddu	Cavalleria Rusticana	Mascagni	Soldier
Ulrica	A Masked Ball	Verdi	Fortune teller
Ulrich Eisslinger	The Mastersingers of Nuremberg	Wagner	Mastersingers and grocer
Mr Upfold	Albert Herring	Britten	Mayor
Ursula	Mathis der Maler	Hindemith	Riedinger's daughter
Valzacchi	Der Rosenkavalier	Richard Strauss	Scandalmonger
Varlaam	Boris Godunov	Mussorgsky	Vagrant
Vasek	The Bartered Bride	Smetana	Micha's second son
Venus	Tannhäuser	Wagner	Supernatural seductress
Captain Vere	Billy Budd	Britten	Ship's captain
Violetta Valery	La Traviata	Verdi	Courtesan
Vitellia	La Clemenza di Tito	Mozart	Daughter of deposed emperor
Vitellozzo	Lucrezia Borgia	Donizetti	Nobleman
Miss Vixen	The Beggar's Opera	Pepusch	Lady of the town
Vizier	Marouf	Rabaud	Sultan's adviser
Vladimir Igorevitch	Prince Igor	Borodin	Igor's son
Vladimir Yaroslavovitch	Prince Igor	Borodin	Yaroslavna's brother
Vreli	A Village Romeo and Juliet	Delius	Marti's daughter
Jake Wallace	The Girl of the Golden West	Puccini	Minstrel
Sir Walter Raleigh	Gloriana	Britten	Courtier
Walter von Stolzing	The Mastersingers of Nuremberg	Wagner	Franconian knight
Walther von der Vogelweide	Tannhäuser	Wagner	Knight
Waltraute	Der Ring des Nibelungen	Wagner	Valkyrie
Watchful	The Pilgrim's Progress	Vaughan Williams	Porter
Wellgunde	Der Ring des Nibelungen	Wagner	Rhine maiden
Woglinde	Der Ring des Nibelungen	Wagner	Rhine maiden
Wolfram	Tannhäuser	Wagner	Knight
Wotan	Der Ring des Nibelungen	Wagner	Norse god
Wowkle	The Girl of the Golden West	Puccini	Billy's squaw
Wozzeck	Wozzeck	Berg	Soldier
Xenia	Boris Godunov	Mussorgsky	Boris Godunov's daughter
Yamadori	Madame Butterfly	Puccini	Rich Japanese
Yniold	Pelléas et Mélisande	Debussy	Golaud's son
Yvette	La Rondine	Puccini	Magda's friend
Yvonne	Jonny Spielt Auf	Krenek	Chambermaid
Zaccaria	Nabucco	Verdi	High Priest of Jerusalem
Zazà	Zazà	Leoncavallo	Music-hall singer
Zerlina	Don Giovanni	Mozart	Engaged to Matteo
Zuniga	Carmen	Bizet	Captain of the Guard

MUSIC CLASSICAL

Operatic Characters (by opera)

Opera	Composer	Character	Role
Aida	Verdi	Aida	Ethiopian princess
		Amneris	Egyptian princess
		Amonasro	Aida's father (King of Ethiopia)
		Ramfis	High priest
		Rhadames	Captain of the Guard
Albert Herring	Britten	Albert Herring	Greengrocer's assistant
		Lady Bellows	Elderly autocrat
		Mr Gedge	Vicar
		Mr Upfold	Mayor
		Nancy	Baker's assistant
		Sid	Butcher's assistant
Alceste	Gluck	Admetus	Alceste's husband
		Alceste	Wife of Admetus
L'Amico Fritz	Mascagni	David	Rabbi
Andrea Chénier	Giordano	Charles Gérard	Revolutionary leader
		Comtesse de Coigny	Madeleine's mother
		Dumas	President of the tribunal
		Incredible	Spy
		Madeleine de Coigny	In love with Andrea Chénier
		Madelon	Old woman
		Mathieu	Waiter
		Roucher	Andrea's friend
Arlecchino	Busoni	Matteo del Sarto	Tailor
The Barber of Seville	Rossini	Almaviva	Count
		Ambrogio	Bartolo's servant
		Bartolo	Rosina's guardian
		Basilio	Singing teacher
		Berta	Housekeeper
		Figaro	Barber
		Fiorello	Servant
		Rosina	Dr Bartolo's ward
The Bartered Bride	Smetana	Esmerelda	Dancer
		Jenik	Micha's son
		Kathinka	Marenka's mother
		Kecal	Marriage broker
		Marenka	In love with Jenik
		Micha	Jenik's father
		Muff	Comedian
		Vasek	Micha's second son
The Beggar's Opera	Pepusch	Ben Budge	Highwayman
		Betty Doxy	Lady of the town
		Dolly Trull	Lady of the town
		Filch	Pickpocket
		Harry Paddington	Highwayman
		Jemmy Twitcher	Highwayman
		Jenny Diver	Lady of the night
		Lockit	Jailer
		Lucy Lockit	Jailer's daughter
		Macheath	Highwayman
		Mat of the Mint	Highwayman
		Miss Vixen	Lady of the town
		Molly Brazen	Lady of the town
		Mrs Coaxer	Lady of the town
		Mrs Trapes	Tally woman
		Nimming Ned	Highwayman
		Peachum	Fence
		Polly Peachum	Peachum's daughter, Macheath's wife
		Suky Tawdry	Lady of the town
Billy Budd	Britten	Arthur Jones	Seaman
		Billy Budd	Seaman and stammerer
		Captain Vere	Ship's captain
		Claggart	Master-at-arms
		Dansker	Seaman
		Donald	Seaman
		Mr Redburn	First lieutenant
		Red Whiskers	Impressed seaman

Opera	Composer	Character	Role
La Bohème	Puccini	Alcindoro	Musetta's escort
		Benoît	Landlord
		Colline	Philosopher
		Marcello	Painter
		Mimi	Seamstress
		Musetta	In love with Marcello
		Parpignol	Toy Vendor
		Rodolfo	Poet
Boris Godunov	Mussorgsky	Feodor	Son of Boris Godunov
		Grigorij	False Dimitri
		Kruschev	Boyar
		Marina Mnishek	Daughter of Voyevode Sandomir
		Missail	Vagrant
		Pimen	Hermit
		Rangoni	Jesuit
		Varlaam	Vagrant
		Xenia	Boris Godunov's daughter
Capriccio	Richard Strauss	Claison	Actress
		Flamand	Musician
		Olivier	Poet
Cardillac	Hindemith	Cardillac	Goldsmith
Carmen	Bizet	Carmen	Gypsy
		Don José	Corporal in the Guard
		El Dancairo	Smuggler
		El Remondado	Smuggler
		Escamillo	Bullfighter
		Frasquita	Gypsy
		Lillas Pastia	Innkeeper
		Mercedes	Gypsy
		Micaela	Village girl
		Morales	Officer of the Guard
		Zuniga	Captain of the Guard
Cavalleria Rusticana	Mascagni	Alfio	Teamster
		Lola	Alfio's wife
		Mama Lucia	Turiddu's mother
		Santuzza	In love with Turiddu
		Turiddu	Soldier
La Cenerentola	Rossini	Alidoro	Philosopher and magician
		Angelina	Don Magnifico's stepdaughter, Cinderella
		Clorinda	Don Magnifico's daughter
		Dandini	Valet
		Don Magnifico	Baron of Montflagon
		Don Ramiro	Prince of Salerno
		Thisbe	Don Magnifico's daughter
La Clemenza di Tito	Mozart	Annius	Patrician
		Publius	Captain of Praetorian Guard
		Titus	Emperor of Rome
		Vitellia	Daughter of deposed emperor
Der Corregidor	Wolf	Frasquita	Tio Lucas' wife
		Juan Lopez	Mayor
		Manuela	Maid
		Repela	Valet to magistrate
		Tio Lucas	Miller
		Tonuelo	Court messenger
Così fan tutte	Mozart	Despina	Maid
		Don Alfonso	Don
		Dorabella	Fiordiligi's sister
		Ferrando	Dorabella's fiancé
		Fiordiligi	Dorabella's sister
		Guglielmo	Fiordiligi's fiancé
La Dame Blanche	Boieldieu	Dickson	Tenant of the White Lady
		Georges Brown	English officer
		Jenny	Dickson's wife
		MacIrton	Justice of the Peace
		Marguerite	Servant
Dido and Aeneas	Purcell	Aeneas	Trojan general
		Belinda	Lady-in-waiting
		Dido	Queen of Carthage
Don Carlos	Verdi	Don Carlos	Heir to Spanish throne
		Principessa Eboli	Lady in waiting

Opera	Composer	Character	Role
Don Giovanni	Mozart	Commendatore	Donna Anna's father
		Donna Anna	Don Ottavio's fiancée
		Donna Elvira	Lady from Burgos
		Leporello	Servant
		Masetto	Peasant
		Zerlina	Engaged to Matteo
Don Pasquale	Donizetti	Dr Malatesta	Don Pasquale's friend
		Ernesto	Don Pasquale's nephew
		Norina	Widow
Duke Bluebeard's Castle	Bartók	Judith	Bluebeard's last wife
Elektra	Richard Strauss	Aegisth	Klytemnestra's lover
		Chrysothemis	Elektra's sister
		Elektra	Agamemnon's daughter
		Orest	Elektra's brother
Emperor Jones	Gruenberg	Brutus Jones	Escaped convict, tribal leader
Ernani	Verdi	Don Carlos	King of Castile
		Elvira	Ernani's beloved
		Jago	Silva's squire
Eugene Onegin	Tchaikovsky	Filipievna	Nurse
		Prince Gremin	General
		Larina	Tatyana's mother
		Lenski	Olga's fiancé
		Olga	Tatiana's sister
		Tatiana	In love with Eugene
Falstaff	Verdi	Alice Ford	Citizen of Windsor
		Fenton	In love with Nanetta
		Frank Ford	Alice's husband
		Nanetta	Ford's daughter
Faust	Gounod	Marguérite	Beloved of Faust
		Martha Schwerlein	Marguérite's neighbour
La Favorita	Donizetti	Alfonso XI	King of Castile
		Balthazar	Superior of the monastery
		Leonara di Gusman	King's mistress
Fedora	Giordano	Cirillo	Coachman
		Désiré	Valet
		Dimitri	Groom
		Grech	Policeman
		Lorek	Surgeon
		Loris Ipanov	Count
		Nicola	Footman
Fidelio	Beethoven	Don Pizarro	Prison governor
		Florestan	Spanish nobleman
		Jacquino	Rocco's assistant
		Leonora	Florestan's wife
		Marcellina	Rocco's daughter
		Rocco	Chief jailer
Die Fledermaus	Johann Strauss II	Adele	Eisenstein's maid
		Dr Blind	Eisenstein's attorney
		Dr Falke	Eisenstein's friend
		Frank	Prison governor
		Frosch	Jailer
		Orlovsky	Rich Russian
		Rosalinda	Eisenstein's wife
The Flying Dutchman	Wagner	Daland	Sea captain
		Senta	Daland's daughter
Die Frau ohne Schatten	Richard Strauss	Barak	Dyer
		One-Arm	Barak's brother
		One-Eye	Barak's brother
La Forza del Destino	Verdi	Don Alvaro	Leonora's lover
Der Freischütz		Agathe	Cuno's daughter
La Gioconda	Ponchielli	Barnaba	Spy
		Enzo	Sea captain
		La Gioconda	Street singer, Enzo's love
The Girl of the Golden West		Ashby	Wells-Fargo agent
		Billy Jackrabbit	Red Indian
		Happy	Miner
		Jack Rance	Sheriff
		Jake Wallace	Minstrel
		Joe	Mine
		Larkens	Miner
		Minnie	Barmaid

Opera	Composer	Character	Role
		Nick	Bartender
		Trim	Miner
		Wowkle	Billy's squaw
Gloriana	Britten	Earl of Essex	The Queen's favourite
		Elizabeth of England	Queen of England
		Sir Robert Cecil	Secretary to the Council
		Sir Walter Raleigh	Courtier
Hänsel and Gretel	Humperdinck	Gertrude	Mother of Hansel and Gretel
		Peter	Father of Hansel and Gretel
Háry János	Kodály	Abraham	Innkeeper
		Estrella	Lady-in-waiting
		Ilka	Háry's fiancée
		Marie-Louise	Napoleon's second wife
		Marzci	Marie's coachman
		Melusine	Countess
Hugh the Drover	Vaughan Williams	Aunt Jane	Sister of the constable
		John the Butcher	Mary's fiancé
		Mary	Constable's daughter
Idomeneo	Mozart	Arbace	Idomeneo's confidante
		Elettra	Greek princess
		Idamente	Idomeneo's son
		Idomeneo	King of Crete
		Ilia	Trojan princess
Intermezzo	Richard Strauss	Christine	Storch's wife
		Justizrat	Storch's friend
		Kammersänger	Storch's friend
		Robert Storch	Musical conductor
The Jewels of the Madonna	Wolf-Ferrari	Gennaro	Blacksmith
		Maliella	Gennaro's adopted sister
		Rafaele	Leader of the Camorra
Le Jongleur de Notre Dame	Massenet	Boniface	Cook
Jonny Spielt Auf	Krenek	Daniello	Artist
(Jonny Plays on)		Jonny	Artist
		Max	Composer
		Yvonne	Chambermaid
Lakmé	Delibes	Gérald	English officer
		Hadji	Nilakantha's servant
		Lakmé	Nilakantha's daughter
		Mallika	Lakmé's slave
		Nilakantha	Brahmin priest
		Rose	An English lady
Lohengrin		Godfrey	Elsa's brother
		Lohengrin	Parsifal's son
		Ortrud	Wife of Frederick
		Telramund	Count of Brabant
The Love for Three Oranges	Prokofiev	Celio	Magician
		Farfarello	A devil
		Fata Morgana	Witch
		King of Clubs	Ruler of the kingdom
		Leandro	King of Spades and prime minister
		Linette	Princess hidden in an orange
		Nicoletta	Princess hidden in an orange
		Ninetta	Princess hidden in an orange
		Pantaloon	King's friend
		Prince	Hypochondriac
		Princess Clarissa	King's niece
Lucia di Lammermoor	Donizetti	Alice/Alisa	Lucia's companion
		Arthur Bucklaw/Arturo	Lord
		Henry Ashton/Enrico	Lorn of Lammermoor
		Edgar/Edgardo	Edgar of Ravenswood
		Norman/Normando	Follower of Ashton
		Raymond/Raimondo	Chaplain, Lucy's tutor
Lucrezia Borgia	Donizetti	Alfonso d'Este	Duke of Ferrara, Lucrezia's third husband
		Gennaro	Venetian nobleman, Lucrezia's son
		Gubetta	Servant to Lucrezia
		Lucrezia Borgia	Duchess of Ferrara
		Maffio Orsini	Lucrezia's enemy
		Rustighello	Alfonso's henchman
		Vitellozzo	Nobleman, Gennaro's friend

MUSIC CLASSICAL

Opera	Composer	Character	Role
Lulu	Berg	Alwa	Writer
		Dr Schön	Editor
		Lulu	Prostitute
		Prince	Traveller in Africa
Madame Butterfly	Puccini	The Bonze	Priest
		Cio-Cio-San	A geisha, Pinkerton's wife
		Goro	Marriage broker
		Kate	Pinkerton's American wife
		Lt Pinkerton	Lieutenant in US Navy
		Sharpless	US consul in Nagasaki
		Suzuki	Servant
		Trouble	Cio-Cio-San's child
		Yamadori	Rich Japanese
Madame Sans-Gêne	Giordano	Catarina	Laundress
The Magic Flute	Mozart	Monostatos	Servant
		Pamina	Daughter of Queen of the Night
		Papagena	Destined to be Papageno's wife
		Papageno	Bird catcher
		Sarastro	High priest
Manon	Massenet	Chevalier des Grieux	Manon's love
		Comte des Grieux	Chevalier's father
		de Bretigny	A nobleman
		Lescaut	A gambler
		Manon	Lescaut's cousin
Marouf	Rabaud	Ahmed	Pastry cook
		Ali	Marouf's friend
		Fatimah	Marouf's wife
		Marouf	Shoemaker
		Vizier	Sultan's adviser
The Marriage of Figaro	Mozart	Almaviva	Count
		Antonio	Gardener
		Barbarina	Antonio's daughter
		Cherubino	Page
		Don Basilio	Organist
		Don Curzio	Lawyer
		Figaro	Servant to Almaviva
		Marcellina	Housekeeper
		Susanna	Maid
A Masked Ball	Verdi	Amelia	Riccardo's love, wife of Renato
		Oscar	Riccardo's page
		Renato	Riccardo's secretary
		Riccardo	Governor of Louisiana
		Silvano	A young sailor
		Ulrica	Fortune teller
The Mastersingers of Nuremberg	Wagner	Augustin Moser	Mastersinger and tailor
		Balthasar Zorn	Mastersinger and pewterer
		Sixtus Beckmesser	Mastersinger and town clerk
		Conrad Nachtigall	Mastersinger and bucklemaker
		David	Hans Sachs's apprentice
		Eva	Pogner's daughter
		Fritz Kothner	Mastersinger and baker
		Hans Foltz	Mastersinger and coppersmith
		Hans Sachs	Mastersinger and cobbler
		Hans Schwarz	Mastersinger and stocking weaver
		Hermann Ortel	Mastersinger and soap boiler
		Kunz Vogelgesang	Mastersinger and furrier
		Magdalena	Nurse
		Ulrich Eisslinger	Mastersinger and grocer
		Veit Pogner	Mastersinger and goldsmith (Eva's father)
		Walter von Stolzing	Franconian knight
Mathis der Maler	Hindemith	Albrecht von Brandenburg	Archbishop of Mainz
		Mathis	Painter (Grünewald)
		Riedinger	Rich Lutheran
		Truchsess von Waldburg	Leader of the army
		Ursula	Riedinger's daughter
		Wolfgang Capito	Councillor
The Mother of Us All	Thomson	Susan B Anthony	American suffragette
Nabucco	Verdi	Abdallo	Nabucco's officer
		Abigaille	Nabucco's adopted daughter

Opera	Composer	Character	Role
		Fenena	Nabucco's daughter
		Nabucco	Nebuchadnezzar, King of Babylon
		Zaccaria	High Priest of Jerusalem
Norma	Bellini	Adalgisa	Temple virgin
		Clotilde	Norma's friend
		Flavio	Centurion
		Norma	Druid priestess
		Oroveso	Norma's father
		Pollione	Proconsul of Rome
Oberon	Weber	Abdullah	Pirate
		Babekan	Saracen prince
		Charlemagne	Emperor of the Franks
		Fatima	Reiza's companion
		Haroun al Rashid	Calif of Baghdad
		Namouna	Fatima's grandmother
		Reiza	Haroun el Rashid's daughter
Oedipus Rex	Stravinsky	Creon	Jocasta's brother
		Jocasta	Wife of Oedipus
		Oedipus	King of Thebes
		Tiresias	Blind soothsayer
Orfeo et Euridice	Gluck	Amor	God of love
		Euridice	Orfeo's wife
		Orfeo	Singer poet
Otello	Verdi	Cassio	Lieutenant
		Lodovico	Venetian ambassador
		Montano	Otello's predecessor
I Pagliacci	Leoncavallo	Beppe	Harlequin
		Canio	Pagliaccio (clown)
		Nedda	Canio's wife
		Silvio	In love with Nedda
		Tonio	Clown
Palestrina	Pfitzner	Avosmediano	Bishop of Cadiz
		Ighino	Palestrina's son
		Lucretia	Palestrina's wife
		Palestrina	Composer
Parsifal	Wagner	Amfortas	King of the Grail
		King Titurel	Father of Amfortas
		Klingsor	Magician
		Kundry	Bewitched woman
		Parsifal	Knight of the Holy Grail
Pelléas et Mélisande	Debussy	Geneviève	Mother of Pelléas
		Golaud	Arkel's grandson
		Mélisande	Golaud's wife
		Pelléas	Arkel's grandson
		Yniold	Golaud's son
Peter Grimes	Britten	Bob Boles	Fisherman
		Ellen Orford	Schoolteacher
		John	Peter's apprentice
		Ned Keene	Apothecary
		Peter Grimes	Fisherman
The Pilgrim's Progress	Vaughan Williams	Apollyon	Fallen angel
		Mistrust	Neighbour
		Obstinate	Neighbour
		Pilgrim	Pilgrim
		Pliable	Neighbour
		Timorous	Neighbour
		Watchful	Porter
The Poisoned Kiss	Vaughan Williams	Amaryllus	Empress's son
		Angelica	Tormentilla's maid
		Dipsacus	Magician
		Gallanthus	Amaryllus's sister
		Hob	Servant of Dipsacus
		Lob	Assistant of Dipsacus
		Tormentilla	Daughter of Dipsacus
Porgy and Bess	Gershwin	Bess	Porgy's mistress, formerly Crown's
		Clara	Jake's wife
		Crown	Stevedore
		Frazier	Catfish Row 'lawyer'
		Jake	Fisherman
		Jim	Cotton picker
		Lily	Strawberry woman

MUSIC CLASSICAL

Opera	Composer	Character	Role
		Maria	Cookshop keeper
		Mr Archdale	White man
		Peter	Honey-man
		Porgy	A crippled beggar
		Sportin' Life	Dope dealer
Prince Igor	Borodin	Eroshka	Gudok player
		Gzak	Polovtsian Khan
		Jaroslavna	Prince Igor's wife
		Kontchak	Polovtsian Khan
		Kontchakovna	Kontchak's daughter
		Ovlour	Polovtsian traitor
		Prince Igor	Prince of Seversk
		Vladimir Igorevitch	Igor's son
		Vladimir Yaroslavovitch	Yaroslavna's brother
The Rake's Progress	Stravinsky	Baba the Turk	Bearded lady
		Tom Rakewell	The Rake
		Trulove	Anne's father
The Rape of Lucretia	Britten	Bianca	Nurse
		Collatinus	Soldier
		Junius	Roman general
		Lucia	Lucretia's attendant
		Lucretia	Wife of Collatinus
Rienzi	Wagner	Adriano	Colonna's son
		Baroncelli	Roman citizen
		Cola Rienzi	Papal legate
		Irene	Rienzi's sister
		Paolo Orsini	Patrician
		Raimondo	Papal legate
Rigoletto	Verdi	Cavaliere Marullo	Courtier
		Duke of Mantua	Nobleman
		Gilda	Rigoletto's daughter
		Maddalena	Sparafucile's sister
		Matteo Borsa	Courtier
		Rigoletto	Gilda's father, a jester
Der Ring des Nibelungen	Wagner	Alberich	Nibelung dwarf
		Brünnhilde	Valkyrie
		Donner	Norse god
		Erda	Earth goddess
		Fafner	Giant, builder of Valhalla
		Fasolt	Giant, builder of Valhalla
		Flosshilde	Rhinemaiden
		Freia	Goddess of youth and beauty
		Fricka	Wotan's wife
		Froh	Norse god
		Gerhilde	Valkyrie
		Grimgerde	Valkyrie
		Gunther	Hagen's half-brother
		Gutrune	Gunther's sister
		Helmwige	Valkyrie
		Hunding	Siegmund's enemy
		Loge	Norse god
		Mime	A Nibelung
		Ortlinde	Valkyrie
		Rossweisse	Valkyrie
		Siegfried	Son of Siegmund and Sieglunde
		Sieglunde	Siegmund's twin sister
		Siegmund	Mortal son of Wotan
		Waltraute	Valkyrie
		Wellgunde	Rhine maiden
		Woglinde	Rhine maiden
		Wotan	Norse god
La Rondine	Puccini	Bianca	Magda's friend
		Crébillon	Perichaud's friend
		Lisette	Magda's maid
		Magda	Salon owner, Rambaldo's mistress
		Périchaud	Rambaldo's friend
		Prunier	Poet
		Rambaldo	Banker
		Ruggero	Son of Rambaldo's childhood friend
		Suzy	Magda's friend
		Yvette	Magda's friend

Opera	Composer	Character	Role
Der Rosenkavalier	Richard Strauss	Annina	Valzacchi's partner
		Baron Ochs	Sophie's would-be suitor
		Faninal	Sophie's father
		Mahomet	Negro page
		Marianne	Sophie's duenna
		Marschallin	Princess
		Octavian	Bearer of the Rose
		Sophie	Daughter of Faninal
		Valzacchi	Scandalmonger
Ruddigore	Sullivan	Mad Margaret	Mad woman
Ruslan and Lyudmila	Glinka	Bayan	Bard
		Chernomor	An evil dwarf
		Farlaf	Warrior
		Finn	Wizard
		Gorislava	Ratmir's lover
		Lyudmila	a noblewoman
		Naina	Witch
		Ratmir	Knight, suitor to Lyudmila
		Ruslan	Suitor to Lyudmila
		Svyetozer	Lyudmila's father
Salome	Richard Strauss	Herod	Ruler of Galilee
		Herodias	Herod's wife
		John the Baptist	Jewish prophet
		Narraboth	Captain of the Guard
		Salome	Daughter of Herodias
Samson et Dalila	Saint-Saëns	Abimielech	Satrap of Gaza
The Secret Marriage	Cimarosa	Carolina	Geronimo's daughter
		Elisetta	Geronimo's older daughter
		Fidalma	Geronimo's sister
		Geronimo	Citizen of Bologna
		Paolino	Carolina's secret husband
The Sleepwalker (La Sonnambula)	Bellini	Amina	The sleepwalking girl
		Elvino	Farmer
Il Tabarro	Puccini	Giorgetta	Michele's wife
		Luigi	Stevedore, Giorgetta's lover
		Michele	Barge owner
		Talpa	Stevedore
		Tinca	Stevedore
The Tales of Hoffmann	Offenbach	Chochenille	Spalanzani's servant
		Coppelius	Scientist
		Dapertutto	Sorcerer
		Dr Miracle	Doctor
		Frantz	Crespel's servant
		Hermann	Student
		Hoffmann	Poet
		Lindorf	Councillor of Nuremberg
		Luther	Innkeeper
		Nathanael	Student
		Nicklaus	Hoffmann's friend
		Olympia	Mechanical doll
		Pittichinaccio	Giulietta's admirer
		Spalanzani	Inventor
		Stella	Opera singer
Tannhäuser	Wagner	Biterolf	Knight
		Elisabeth	Hermann's niece
		Hermann	Landgrave of Thuringia
		Reinmar von Zweter	Knight
		Tannhäuser	Knight
		Venus	Supernatural seductress
		Walther von der Vogelweide	Knight
		Wolfram	Knight
Tosca	Puccini	Baron Scarpia	Chief of Police
		Cavaradossi	Painter
		Cesare Angelotti	Escaped political prisoner
		Mario Cavaradossi	Painter
		Tosca	Singer
La Traviata	Verdi	Alfredo Germont	Violetta's lover (a singer)
		Annina	Violetta's confidante
		Douphol	Baron
		Violetta Valery	Courtesan

MUSIC CLASSICAL

Opera	Composer	Character	Role
Tristan und Isolde	Wagner	Brangäne	Isolde's maid
		Isolde	Irish princess
		King Marke	King of Cornwall
		Kurvenal	Tristan's retainer
		Melot	Courtier
		Tristan	Cornish knight
The Trojans (Les Troyens)	Berlioz	Andromaque	Hector's widow
		Chorèbe	Cassandra's lover
		Hylas	Trojan sailor
		Iopas	Poet
		Narbal	Dido's minister
		Panthée	Priest
		Polyxène	Priam's daughter
		Priam	King of Troy
Il Trovatore	Verdi	Azucena	Gypsy woman
		Count de Luna	Count of Aragon
		Ferrando	Captain of the Guard
		Manrico	Troubadour
		Leonora	Beloved of Manrico
The Tsar Has His Photograph Taken	Weill	Angèle	Photographer
Turandot	Busoni	Adelma	Turandot's slave
		Barak	Servant
		Calaf	Suitor to Turandot
		Pantalone	Minister
		Queen Mother of Samarkand	Negress
Turandot	Puccini	Calaf	Suitor to Turandot
		Emperor Altoum	Turandot's father
		Liù	Slave girl
		Pang	Lord of Provisions
		Ping	Chinese Grand Chancellor
		Pong	Lord of the Imperial Kitchen
		Princess Turandot	Daughter of Altoum
A Village Romeo and Juliet	Delius	The Dark Fiddler	Real owner of land
		Manz	Farmer
		Marti	Farmer
		Sali	Manz's daughter
		Vreli	Marti's daughter
Wozzeck	Berg	Marie	Prostitute
		Wozzeck	Soldier
The Wreckers	Smyth	Lawrence	Lighthouse keeper
Zazà	Leoncavallo	Bussy	Journalist
		Cascart	Music-hall performer
		Duclou	Stage manager
		Mme Dufresne	Milio's wife
		Lartigen	Monologist
		Marco	Dufresne's butler
		Marlardot	Music-hall owner
		Michelin	Journalist
		Milio Dufresne	Zaza's lover
		Natalia	Zazà's maid
		Toto	Dufresne's child
		Zazà	Music-hall singer

Operas and Operettas

Operas and operettas	Composer	First performance	Librettist	General information
Adriana Lecouvreur	Francesco Cilea	1902 Milan	Colautti	
L'Africaine	Giacomo Meyerbeer	1865 London, Paris, New York	Scribe	
Ägyptische Helena	Richard Strauss	1928 Dresden	Hofmannsthal	
Aida	Giuseppe Verdi	1871 Cairo	Ghislanzoni	
Akhnaten	Philip Glass	1984 Stuttgart	Glass (Richard Riddell, Robert Israel and Shalom Goldman helped with the libretto)	
Albert Herring	Benjamin Britten	1947 Glyndebourne	Crozier	
Alceste	Christoph Gluck	1767 Vienna	Calzabigi	
Aleko	Sergei Rachmaninov	1893 Moscow	Nemirovich-Danchenko	
Alfred	Thomas Arne	1740 London	Thomson and Mallet	Contains song 'Rule, Britannia'
Almira	George Frederick Handel	1705 Hamburg	Feustking	Handel's first opera
Alzira	Giuseppe Verdi	1845 Naples	Cammarano	
Amahl and the Night Visitors	Gian Carlo Menotti	1951 New York	Menotti	First opera written for TV
Amelia Goes to the Ball	Gian Carlo Menotti	1937 Berlin	Menotti	
L'Amico Fritz	Pietro Mascagni	1891 Rome	Daspuro	
Amleto (Hamlet)	Franco Faccio	1865 Genoa	Boito	
Andrea Chénier	Umberto Giordano	1896 Milan	Illica	
Aniara	Karl-Birger Blomdahl	1959 Stockholm	Lindegren	
Anne Boleyn	Gaetano Donizetti	1830 Milan	Romani	
Antar	Gabriel Dupont	1921 Paris	Dupont	
Antony and Cleopatra	Samuel Barber	1966 New York (Met)	Zeffirelli and Barber	
Arabella	Richard Strauss	1933 Dresden	Hofmannsthal	
Ariadne auf Naxos	Richard Strauss	1916 Vienna	Hofmannsthal	
Ariane et Barbe-bleu	Paul Dukas	1907 Paris	Maeterlinck	
Arlecchino (Harlequin)	Ferruccio Busoni	1917 Zurich	Busoni	
Armide	Christoph Gluck	1777 Paris	Quinault	
Artaxerxes	Thomas Arne	1762 London	Metastasio	
At the Boar's Head	Gustav Holst	1925 Manchester	Holst	
The Barber of Seville	Giovanni Paisiello	1782 St Petersburg	Petrosellini	
The Barber of Seville	Gioachino Rossini	1816 Rome	Sterbini	Based on Beaumarchais comedy
The Bartered Bride	Bedrich Smetana	1866 Prague	Sabina	
The Bassarids	Hans Werner Henze	1966 Salzburg	Auden and Kallman	
The Bear	William Walton	1967 Aldeburgh	Dehn	
Beatrice Cenci	Berthold Goldschmidt	1988 London	Esslin	Prizewinner in Festival of Britain Competition 1951
Béatrice et Bénédict	Hector Berlioz	1862 Baden-Baden	Berlioz	
The Beautiful Galathea	Franz von Suppe	1865 Vienna	Henrion	
The Beggar's Opera	Christoph Pepusch	1728 London	Gay	
Belfagor	Ottorino Respighi	1923 Milan	Morselli and Gaustalla	
Belisario	Gaetano Donizetti	1836 Venice	Cammarano	
La Belle Hélène	Jacques Offenbach	1864 Paris	Meilhac and Halévy	

MUSIC CLASSICAL

Operas and operettas	Composer	First performance		Librettist	General information
The Bells of Corneville	Robert Planquette	1877	Paris and New York	Clairville and Gabet	
Benvenuto Cellini	Hector Berlioz	1838	Paris	Wailly and Barbier	
Berenice	George Frederick Handel	1737	London	Salvi	
Billy Budd	Benjamin Britten	1951	London	Forster and Crozier	Ship: HMS *Indomitable*
The Black Mask	Krzysztof Penderecki	1986	Salzburg	Kupfer and Penderecki	
Blond Eckbert	Judith Weir	1994	London	Weir	
Boccaccio	Franz von Suppé	1879	Vienna	Zell and Génée	
La Bohème	Ruggiero Leoncavallo	1897	Venice	Leoncavallo	Title translates as *La Bohème*, though not the same story
La Bohème	Giacomo Puccini	1896	Turin	Giacosa and Illica	
The Bohemian Girl	Michael Balfe	1843	London	Bunn	
Boris Godunov	Modeste Mussorgsky	1874	St Petersburg	Mussorgsky	
Boulevard Solitude	Hans Werner Henze	1952	Hanover	Henze and Weil	
Die Brautwahl	Ferruccio Busoni	1912	Hamburg	Busoni, after Hoffmann	
The Burning Fiery Furnace	Benjamin Britten	1966	Orford	Plomer	
The Caliph of Baghdad	François Boieldieu	1800	Paris	Saint-Just	
La Calisto	Pietro Francesco Cavalli	1651	Venice	Faustini	
La Campana Sommersa	Ottorino Respighi	1927	Hamburg	Guastalla	Title translates as *The Submerged Bell*
Candide	Leonard Bernstein	1956	Boston	Hellmann	
El Capitán	John Philip Sousa	1896	New York and Boston	Klein	
Capriccio	Richard Strauss	1942	Munich	Krauss and Strauss	
I Capuleti e i Montecchi	Vincenzo Bellini	1830	Venice	Romani	The Capulets and the Montagues, i.e. Romeo and Juliet
Cardillac	Paul Hindemith	1926	Dresden	Lion	
Caritas	Robert Saxton	1991	Wakefield	Wesker	
Carmen	Georges Bizet	1875	Paris	Meilhac and Halévy	Carmen dies by stabbing (at the hands of Don José)
Castor and Pollux	Jean-Philippe Rameau	1737	Paris	Bernard	
The Catiline Conspiracy	Iain Hamilton	1974	Stirling	Hamilton	
Cavalleria Rusticana	Pietro Mascagni	1890	Rome	Menasci and Targioni-Tozzetti	
Cendrillon (Cinderella)	Nicolò Isouard	1810	Paris	Étienne	
Cendrillon (Cinderella)	Jules Massenet	1899	Paris	Henry Cain	
La Cenerentola (Cinderella)	Gioachino Rossini	1817	Rome	Ferretti	
Chérubin	Jules Massenet	1905	Monte Carlo	Henry Cain and Francis de Croisset	The story of Cherubino after the marriage of Figaro
Cheryomushki	Dmitry Shostakovich	1959	Moscow	Mass and Chervinsky	Shostakovich's only operetta
The Chocolate Soldier	Oscar Straus	1908	Vienna	Jacobson and Bernauer	Based on G B Shaw's play *Arms and the Man*
Christmas Eve	Nikolay Rimsky-Korsakov	1895	St Petersburg	Rimsky-Korsakov	Based on Gogol story
Le Cid	Jules Massenet	1885	Paris	D'Ennery, Gallet and Blau	
La Clemenza di Tito	Wolfgang Amadeus Mozart	1791	Prague	Metastasio	Mozart's last opera
Comedy on the Bridge	Bohuslav Martinů	1937	Prague (Radio)	Martinu	
Conchita	Riccardo Zandonai	1911	Milan	Vaucaire and Zangarini	
Confessions of a Justified Sinner	Thomas Wilson	1976	York	John Currie	Based on the novel by James Hogg
The Consul	Gian Carlo Menotti	1950	Philadelphia	Menotti	The Consul represents bureaucratic red tape

Operas and operettas	Composer	First performance		Librettist	General information
Le Coq d'Or	Nikolay Rimsky-Korsakov	1909	Moscow	Belsky	Rimsky-Korsakov's 14th and last opera
The Coronation of Poppaea	Claudio Monteverdi	1643	Venice	Busenello	Monteverdi's last opera
Der Corregidor (The Magistrate)	Hugo Wolf	1896	Mannheim	Mayreder	Based on The Three-Cornered Hat by Alarcón
Il Corsaro	Giuseppe Verdi	1848	Trieste	Piave	Based on Byron's poem The Corsair
Così fan tutte	Wolfgang Amadeus Mozart	1790	Vienna	da Ponte	Role of Fiordiligi long regarded as unsingable
The Count of Luxemburg	Franz Lehár	1909	Vienna	Wilner and Bodanzky	
Cox and Box	Arthur Sullivan	1867	London	Burnand	
The Cunning Little Vixen	Leoš Janáček	1924	Brno	Janáček	
Curlew River	Benjamin Britten	1964	Orford	Plomer	A church parable
Dafne	Jacopo Peri	1598	Florence	Rinuccini	Generally regarded to be the earliest opera
Dalibor	Bedrich Smetana	1868	Prague	Spindler	Translation of German text by Joseph Wenzig
La Dame Blanche (White Lady)	François Boieldieu	1825	Paris	Scribe	Based on Scott's The Monastery and Guy Mannering
Danton's Death	Gottfried Von Einem	1947	Salzburg	Blacher and Von Einem	Based on drama by Büchner
Daphne	Richard Strauss	1938	Dresden	Gregor	
Dardanus	Jean-Philipe Rameau	1739	Paris	De La Bruyère	
The Daughter of the Regiment	Gaetano Donizetti	1840	Paris	Saint-Georges and Bayard	
David	Darius Milhaud	1954	Jerusalem	Lunel	
Day of Peace (Friedenstag)	Richard Strauss	1938	Munich	Gregor	
Death in Venice	Benjamin Britten	1973	Aldeburgh	Myfanwy Piper	
Debora e Jaéle	Ildebrando Pizzetti	1922	Milan	Pizzetti	
Deidamia	George Frederick Handel	1741	London	Rolli	Handel's last opera
The Deserted Island	Franz Joseph Haydn	1779	Esterháza	Metastasio	Also the title of an opera by G Scarlatti
Les Deux Journées (The Two Days)	Luigi Cherubini	1800	Paris	Bouilly	Known in Britain as The Water Carrier
Les Dialogues des Carmélites	Francis Poulenc	1957	Milan, Paris, San Francisco	Lavery	
Dido and Aeneas	Henry Purcell	1689	Chelsea	Nahum Tate	
A Dinner Engagement	Lennox Berkeley	1954	Aldeburgh	Paul Dehn	
Doctor Miracle	Georges Bizet	1857	Paris	Battu and Halévy	Joint winner of the Offenbach Prize with Lecocq
Doctor Miracle	Charles Lecocq	1857	Paris	Battu and Halévy	Joint winner of the Offenbach Prize with Bizet
The Doctor of Myddfai	Peter Maxwell Davies	1996	Cardiff	Pountney	
Doktor Faust	Ferruccio Busoni	1925	Dresden	Busoni	Completed after Busoni's death by Jarnach
Dollar Princess	Leo Fall	1907	Vienna	Willner and Grünbaum	
Don Carlos	Giuseppe Verdi	1867	Paris	Méry and Du Locle	Also known as Don Carlo
Don Giovanni	Wolfgang Amadeus Mozart	1787	Prague	Da Ponte	Based on Bertati's Don Juan (1775)
Don Pasquale	Gaetano Donizetti	1843	Paris and London	Ruffini	
Don Quixote	Jules Massenet	1910	Monte Carlo	Henry Cain	
The Duenna	Roberto Gerhard	1949	BBC Radio	Gerhard and Hassall	Based on Sheridan work
The Duenna	Sergey Prokofiev	1946	Leningrad	Prokofiev and Mendelson	Based on Sheridan work
Duke Bluebeard's Castle	Béla Bartók	1918	Budapest	Béla Balázs	
Duke of Alba	Gaetano Donizetti	1882	Rome	Scribe	Completed by Salvi
The Dwarf (Der Zwerg)	Alexander Zemlinsky	1922	Cologne	G C Klaren	Based on Oscar Wilde's The Birthday of the Infanta
Edgar	Giacomo Puccini	1889	Milan	Fontana	
Einstein on the Beach	Philip Glass	1976	Avignon	Knowles, Childs, Johnson	Composed in collaboration with Robert Wilson
Electrification of the Soviet Union	Nigel Osborne	1987	Glyndebourne	Craig Raine	Based on Pasternak's 'Last Summer and 'Spectorsky'

MUSIC CLASSICAL

Operas and operettas	Composer	First performance		Librettist	General information
Elegy for Young Lovers	Hans Werne Henze	Schwetzingen	1961	Auden and Kallman	
Elektra	Richard Strauss	Dresden	1909	Hofmannsthal	
L'Elisir d'Amore	Gaetano Donizetti	Milan	1832	Romani	
Elizabeth, Queen of England	Gioachino Rossini	Naples	1815	Giovanni Schmidt	Based on Sophia Lee's novel The Recess
The Emerald Isle	Arthur Sullivan	London (Savoy)	1901	Basil Hood	Posthumous comic opera completed by Edward German
The Emperor Jones	Louis Gruenberg	New York	1933	de Jaffa	
L'Enfant et les Sortilèges	Maurice Ravel	Monte Carlo	1925	Colette	
The English Cat	Hans Werner Henze	Schwetzingen	1983	Edward Bond	
Ernani	Giuseppe Verdi	Venice	1844	Piave	Based on Victor Hugo's play Hernani
Esclarmonde	Jules Massenet	Paris	1889	Blau and de Gramont	
L'Étoile (The Star)	Emmanuel Chabrier	Paris	1877	Leterrier and Vanloo	
L'Étoile du Nord (The North Star)	Giacomo Meyerbeer	Paris	1854	Scribe	
Eugene Onegin	Pyotr Tchaikovsky	Moscow	1879	Shilovsky and Tchaikovsky	
Euryanthe	Carl Maria Weber	Vienna	1823	Helmina von Chézy	
The Excursions of Mr Brouček	Leoš Janáček	Prague	1920	Janáček	
The Fair Maid of Perth	Georges Bizet	Paris	1867	St George and Adenis	Based on Sir Walter Scott's play of the same name
The Faithful Shepherd	George Frederick Handel	London	1712	Rossi	Based on Guarini's play
The Fall of the House of Usher	Claude Debussy	New Haven	1977	Debussy	Based on Edgar Allan Poe work but left unfinished and reconstructed by W Harwood
Falstaff	Giuseppe Verdi	Milan	1893	Boito	Verdi's last opera
Fanny Robin	Edward Harper	Edinburgh	1975	Harper	Based on Wessex poems and Far From the Madding Crowd
Faust	Ludwig Spohr	Prague	1816	J K Bernard	Not based on Goethe's Faust
Faust	Charles Gounod	Paris	1859	Barbier and Carré	Based on Carré's Faust et Marguerite and Goethe's Faust
La Favola d'Orfeo	Claudio Monteverdi	Mantua	1607	Striggio	
La Favorite	Gaetano Donizetti	Paris	1840	Royer, Vaëz and Scribe	
Fedora	Umberto Giordano	Milan	1898	Colautti	Based on Sardou's play of the same name
Die Feen (The Fairies)	Richard Wagner	Munich	1888	Wagner	Wagner's first opera
Fennimore and Gerda	Frederick Delius	Frankfurt	1919	Delius	Delius's 6th and last opera
Der Ferne Klang	Franz Schreker	Frankfurt	1912	Schreker	
La Fiamma	Ottorino Respighi	Rome	1934	Guastalla	
Fidelio, or the Triumph of Married Love	Ludwig van Beethoven	Vienna	1805	Josef Sonnleithner	Beethoven's only opera
Fidelity Rewarded	Franz Joseph Haydn	Esterháza	1781	G Lorenzi	
The Fiery Angel	Sergey Prokofiev	Paris	1954	Prokofiev	Prokofiev's Symphony No. 3 uses themes from this opera
La Finta Giardiniera (The Feigned Garden Girl)	Wolfgang Amadeus Mozart	Munich	1775	Uncertain	Mozart's first significant opera
Die Fledermaus (The Bat)	Johann Strauss II	Vienna and New York	1874	Hafner and Genée	Opera in 3 acts although often played in one
The Flying Dutchman	Richard Wagner	Dresden	1843	Wagner	
Die Frau ohne Schatten	Richard Strauss	Vienna	1919	Hofmannsthal	English title: The Woman without a Shadow
From One Day to the Next	Arnold Schoenberg	Frankfurt	1930	Max Blonda	Max Blonda was Gertrud Schoenberg
From the House of the Dead	Leoš Janáček	Brno	1930	Janáček	Based on Dostoyevsky's novel

Operas and operettas	Composer	First performance		Librettist	General information
The Gambler	Sergey Prokofiev	1929	Brussels	Prokofiev	Based on Dostoyevsky's short story
The Gamblers	Dmitry Shostakovich	1978	Leningrad	Shostakovich	Unfinished opera completed by Krzysztof Meyer
Gawain	Harrison Birtwistle	1991	London	David Harsent	
Genoveva	Robert Schumann	1850	Leipzig	Reinick and Schumann	Also the name of an opera by Detlev Müller-Siemens
Gesualdo	Alfred Schnittke	1994	Vienna	Bletschacher	Based on life of the composer Gesualdo
Der Gewaltige Hahnrei	Berthold Goldschmidt	1992	Berlin	Goldschmidt	Composed in 1930
Gianni Schicchi	Giacomo Puccini	1918	New York	Forzano	The third part of Puccini's Il Trittico
La Gioconda	Amilcare Ponchielli	1876	Milan	'Tobia Gorrio' (Arrigo Boito)	Contains the ballet Dance of the Hours (Act 3)
Un Giorno di Regno	Giuseppe Verdi	1840	Milan	Romani	
The Girl of the Golden West (La Fanciulla del West)	Giacomo Puccini	1910	New York (Met)	Civinini and Zangarini	Based on Belasco's play The Girl of the Golden West
Giuditta	Franz Lehár	1934	Vienna	Knepler and Löhner	Lehár's only opera
Gloriana	Benjamin Britten	1953	London	W Plomer	Commissioned for coronation of Elizabeth II
Golem	John Casken	1989	London	Casken and Audi	
Golem	Larry Sitsky	1993	Sydney	Larry Sitsky	Aka: 'The King of Barataria'
The Gondoliers	Arthur Sullivan	1889	London	W S Gilbert	
Götterdämmerung (The Twilight of the Gods)	Richard Wagner	1876	Bayreuth	Wagner	Final opera in his tetralogy Der Ring des Nibelungen
The Government Inspector	Werner Egk	1957	Schwetzingen	Egk	Based on Gogol's story
The Grand Duke	Arthur Sullivan	1896	London and Berlin	W S Gilbert	Aka: 'The Statutory Duel'
Grande Duchesse de Gérolstein	Jacques Offenbach	1867	Paris, New York & London	Meilhac and Halévy	
The Grand Macabre	György Ligeti	1978	Stockholm	Meschke	
Greek	Mark-Anthony Turnage	1988	Munich	Turnage and Jonathan Moore	Based on Berkoff's play Greek
The Greek Passion	Bohuslav Martinů	1961	Zurich	Martinů and Kazantzakis	Based on Kazantzakis novel Christ Recrucified
Griséldis	Jules Massenet	1901	Paris	Silvestre and Morand	Based on a story in Boccaccio's Decameron
The Growing Castle	Malcolm Williamson	1968	Dynevor	Williamson	Based on Strindberg's dream play
Guntram	Richard Strauss	1894	Weimar	Strauss	Strauss's first opera
Gwendoline	Emmanuel Chabrier	1886	Brussels	Mendès	
The Gypsy Baron (Zigeunerbaron)	Johann Strauss II	1885	Vienna	Schnitzer	
Halka	Stanislaw Moniuszko	1848	Vilnius (Wilno)	Wolski	
Hamlet (3 acts)	Humphrey Searle	1968	Hamburg	Searle	
Hamlet (5 acts)	Ambroise Thomas	1868	Paris	Barbier and Carré	Other operas on the subject by Scarlatti, Gasparini, Mercadante, Grandi, Szokolay
Hans Heiling	Heinrich Marschner	1833	Berlin	Devrient	
Hänsel and Gretel	Engelbert Humperdinck	1893	Weimar	Adelheid Wette	Based on the story by the Brothers Grimm
The Happy Prince	Malcolm Williamson	1965	Farnham	Williamson	
Harmony of the World	Paul Hindemith	1957	Munich	Hindemith	Based on life of Johann Kepler
Henry VIII	Camille Saint-Saëns	1883	Paris	Détroyat and Silvestre	
Hérodiade	Jules Massenet	1881	Brussels	Millet and Grémont	
L'Heure Espagnole	Maurice Ravel	1911	Paris	Franc-Nohain	
Higglety Pigglety Pop!	Oliver Knussen	1985	Glyndebourne	Knussen and Sendak	
Hin und Zurück (There and Back)	Paul Hindemith	1927	Baden Baden	Schiffer	
Hippolyte et Aricie	Jean-Philippe Rameau	1733	Paris	Abbé Pellegrin	

Operas and operettas	Composer	First performance		Librettist	General information
Historia von D. Johann Fausten	Alfred Schnittke	Hamburg	1995	Morgener and Schnittke	
HMS Pinafore	Arthur Sullivan	London	1878	W S Gilbert	Aka: 'The Lass That Loved a Sailor'
The Horseman	Aulis Sallinen	Savonlinna	1975	Haavikko	
Hugh the Drover	Ralph Vaughan Williams	London	1924	Harold Child	Aka: 'Love in the Stocks'
Les Huguenots	Giacomo Meyerbeer	Paris	1836	Scribe and Deschamps	
The Ice Break	Michael Tippett	Covent Garden	1977	Tippett	
Idomeneo, King of Crete	Wolfgang Amadeus Mozart	Munich	1781	G B Varesco	
Imeneo	George Frederick Handel	London	1740	Anonymous	
The Immortal Hour	Rutland Boughton	Glastonbury	1914	Boughton	
Importance of Being Earnest	Mario Castelnuovo-Tedesco	New York	1975	Castelnuovo-Tedesco	
L'Incoronazione di Poppea	Claudio Monteverdi	Venice	1642	Busenello	
The Indian Queen	Henry Purcell	London	1695	Dryden and R Howard	Concerns Mexican–Peruvian rivalry
Inès de Castro	James MacMillan	Edinburgh	1996	Clifford	
L'Infedeltà delusa (Deceit Outwitted)	Franz Joseph Haydn	Eszterháza	1773	Coltellini	
Intermezzo	Richard Strauss	Dresden	1924	Strauss	Two main characters portrayed are Strauss and his wife
Intolleranza	Luigi Nono	Venice	1961	Nono	
The Invisible City of Kitezh	Nikolay Rimsky-Korsakov	St Petersburg	1907	Belsky	
Iolanthe	Arthur Sullivan	London and New York	1882	W S Gilbert	Aka: 'The Peer and the Peri'
Iphigénie en Aulide	Christoph Gluck	Paris	1774	Du Roullet	
Iphigénie en Tauride	Christoph Gluck	Paris	1778	Guillard and Du Roullet	
Iris	Pietro Mascagni	Rome	1898	Illica	
Irish Legend	Werner Egk	Salzburg	1955	Egk	Based on W B Yeats's 'Countess Cathleen'
Irmelin	Frederick Delius	Oxford	1953	Delius	
The Italian Girl in Algiers	Gioachino Rossini	Venice	1813	Anelli	Libretto taken from Mosca's opera of the same name
Ivan IV	Georges Bizet	Bordeaux	1951	F H Leroy and H Trianon	Originally written for Gounod
Ivanhoe	Arthur Sullivan	London	1891	J Sturgis	Based on Sir Walter Scott's novel
The Jacobin	Antonin Dvořák	Prague	1889	M Cervinková-Riegrová	
Jenůfa	Leoš Janáček	Brno	1904	Janáček	Retains title of 'Her Foster-Daughter' in Czech Republic
Jérusalem	Giuseppe Verdi	Paris	1847	Royer and Vaëz	
The Jewels of the Madonna	Ermanno Wolf-Ferrari	Berlin	1911	Golisciani and Zangarini	
The Jewess (La Juive)	Jacques Halévy	Paris	1835	Scribe	
Joan of Arc	Giuseppe Verdi	Milan	1845	Solera	
Le Jongleur de Notre Dame	Jules Massenet	Monte Carlo	1902	Léna	
Jonny Spielt Auf	Ernst Krenek	Leipzig	1927	Krenek	
The Journey to Rheims	Gioachino Rossini	Paris	1825	Balocchi	Full title: *The Journey to Rheims or Inn of the Golden Lily*
Judith	Arthur Honegger	Monte Carlo	1926	R Morax	
Judith	Eugene Goossens	London and Philadelphia	1929	Arnold Bennett	
Juha	Aarre Merikanto	Finland	1958	Ackté and Aho	
Julien	Gustave Charpentier	Paris	1913	Charpentier	Sequel to *Louise*
Julietta	Bohuslav Martinů	Prague	1938	Martinů	

Operas and operettas	Composer	First performance		Librettist	General information
Julius Caesar in Egypt	George Frederick Handel	1724	London	N F Haym	Numerous other operas on the theme of Julius Caesar
The Jumping Frog of Calaveras County	Lukas Foss	1950	Indiana	J Karsavina	Based on Mark Twain story
Der Junge Lord (The Young Lord)	Hans Werner Henze	1965	Berlin	I Bachmann	
Der Kaiser von Atlantis	Viktor Ullmann	1943	Terezin	Kien	Premiere in Terezin prison camp banned
Kashchey the Immortal	Nikolay Rimsky-Korsakov	1902	Moscow	Rimsky-Korsakov	
Kate and the Devil	Antonin Dvořák	1899	Prague	A Wenig	
Katerina Izmaylova	Dmitry Shostakovich	1934	Moscow	A Preys and Shostakovich	Revision of Lady Macbeth of the Mtsensk District
Die Kathrin	Erich Korngold	1939	Stockholm	Korngold	
Katya Kabanova	Leoš Janáček	1921	Brno	Janáček	Based on Ostrovsky's play The Storm
Khovanshchina (The Khovansky Affair)	Modest Mussorgsky	1886	St Petersburg	V Stasov and Mussorgsky	Completed by Rimsky-Korsakov
King Arthur, or the British Worthy	Henry Purcell	1691	London	Dryden	Semi-opera, but in reality a play with extensive music
The King Goes Forth to France	Aulis Sallinen	1984	Savonlinna	P Haavikko	
The King of Lahore	Jules Massenet	1877	Paris	L Gallet	
The King of Ys	Édouard-Victor-Antoine Lalo	1888	Paris	Blau	
King Priam	Michael Tippett	1962	Coventry	Tippett	Based on Homer's Iliad
King Roger	Karol Szymanowski	1926	Warsaw	J Iwaszkiewicz	
The King's Children	Engelbert Humperdinck	1897	Munich and London	Ernst Rosmer	Rosmer the pseudonym of Else Bernstein-Porges
The Kiss	Bedrich Smetana	1876	Prague	E Krásnohorská	Based on story by Joanna Muzakova
Die Kluge (The Clever Girl)	Carl Orff	1943	Frankfurt	Orff	Aka The Wise Woman
The Knot Garden	Michael Tippett	1970	Covent Garden	Tippett	
Koanga	Frederick Delius	1904	Elberfeld	C F Keary	Based on G W Gable's novel The Grandissimes
König Hirsch (King Stag)	Hans Werner Henze	1956	Berlin	H von Cramer	
Lady Macbeth of Mtsensk District	Dmitry Shostakovich	1963	Leningrad	A Preys and Shostakovich	See Katerina Izmaylova
Lakmé	Léo Delibes	1883	Paris and Chicago	Gondinet and Gille	
The Lambton Worm	R Sherlaw Johnson	1978	Oxford	Anne Ridler	
The Land of Smiles	Franz Lehár	1923	Vienna	L Herzer and F Löhner	
The Last Temptations	Joonas Kokkonen	1975	Helsinki	L Kokkonen	Based on life of Finnish evangelist Paavo Ruotsalainen
Lear	Aribert Reimann	1978	Munich	Claus Henneberg	
The Legend of Tsar Sultan	Nikolay Rimsky-Korsakov	1900	Moscow	Belsky	Based on Pushkin poem; contains 'The Flight of the Bumble Bee'
Leonora, or Married Love	Pierre Gaveaux	1798	Paris	J N Bouilly	
Let's Make An Opera	Benjamin Britten	1949	Aldeburgh	Eric Crozier	
Das Liebesverbot	Richard Wagner	1836	Magdeburg	Wagner	Based on Shakespeare's Measure for Measure
Life for the Tsar	Mikhail Glinka	1836	St Petersburg	Baron Yegor Rosen	
Life with an Idiot	Alfred Schnittke	1992	Amsterdam	Erofeyev	
The Light Cavalry	Franz von Suppé	1866	Vienna	C Costa	
The Lighthouse	Peter Maxwell Davies	1980	Edinburgh	Davies	
Linda di Chamounix	Gaetano Donizetti	1842	Vienna	Rossi	
The Lodger	Phyllis Tate	1960	London	David Franklin	
Lodoiska	Luigi Cherubini	1791	Paris	Fillette-Loraux	
Lohengrin	Richard Wagner	1850	Weimar	Wagner	Liszt was the conductor at the first performance

Operas and operettas

Operas and operettas	Composer	First performance	Librettist	General information
I Lombardi	Giuseppe Verdi	1843 Milan	Solera	
The Long Christmas Dinner	Paul Hindemith	1961 Mannheim	Thornton Wilder	
Louise	Gustave Charpentier	1900 Paris	Charpentier	
The Love for Three Oranges	Sergey Prokofiev	1921 Chicago	Prokofiev	
The Love of Danae	Richard Strauss	1952 Salzburg	J Gregor	
The Love of the Three Kings	Italo Montemezzi	1913 La Scala	Benelli	
Lowland (Tiefland)	Eugen D'Albert	1903 Prague	R Lothar	
Lucia di Lammermoor	Gaetano Donizetti	1835 Naples	Cammarano	Based on Scott's novel *Bride of Lammermoor* (1819)
Lucio Silla	Wolfgang Amadeus Mozart	1772 Milan	G da Gamerra	
Lucrezia Borgia	Gaetano Donizetti	1833 Milan	Romani	
Luisa Miller	Giuseppe Verdi	1849 Naples	Cammarano	
Lulu	Alban Berg	1937 Zurich	Berg	
Macbeth	Giuseppe Verdi	1847 Florence	Piave	
Macbeth	Ernest Bloch	1910 Paris	Edmond Fleg	
Macbeth	Lawrance Collingwood	1934 London	Collingwood	
Madame Angot's Daughter	Charles Lecocq	1872 Brussels	Clairville, Siraudin and Koning	
Madame Butterfly	Giacomo Puccini	1904 Milan	Giacosa and Illica	Based on Belasco's play
Madame Sans-Gêne	Umberto Giordano	1915 New York and Turin	Simoni	
Maddalena	Sergey Prokofiev	1978 Manchester	Prokofiev	
The Magic Flute	Wolfgang Amadeus Mozart	1791 Vienna	Schikaneder	
The Magic Fountain	Frederick Delius	1977 London	Delius	Completed by Edward Downes
The Magic Island (Die Zauberinsel)	Heinrich Sutermeister	1942 Dresden	Sutermeister	Based on Shakespeare's *The Tempest*
The Maid of Orleans	Pyotr Tchaikovsky	1881 St Petersburg	Tchaikovsky	
The Maid of Pskov	Nikolay Rimsky-Korsakov	1873 St Petersburg	Rimsky-Korsakov	
The Makropoulos Affair	Leoš Janáček	1926 Brno	Janáček	Based on Karel Čapek's play
Les Mamelles de Tirésias	Francis Poulenc	1947 Paris	Poulenc	Based on Apollinaire play
Manon	Jules Massenet	1884 Paris	Meilhac and Gille	
Manon Lescaut	Giacomo Puccini	1893 Turin	Giacosa, Illica, Ricordi, Praga and Oliva	Based on Prévost's novel *Manon Lescaut*
Margot la Rouge	Frederick Delius	1981 BBC Radio	Rosenval	Composed 1902
Maria di Rohan	Gaetano Donizetti	1843 Vienna	Cammarano	
Maria Golovin	Gian Carlo Menotti	1958 Brussels and New York	Menotti	
Maria Stuarda	Gaetano Donizetti	1835 Milan	G Bardari	Based on Schiller's play
Maritana	Vincent Wallace	1845 London	E Fitzball	
Marouf	Henri Rabaud	1914 Paris	Népoty	
The Marriage	Bohuslav Martinů	1954 Hamburg	Martinů	First airing was on American television (NBC) in 1953
The Marriage	Modest Mussorgsky	1917 Petrograd	Mussorgsky	
The Marriage of Figaro	Wolfgang Amadeus Mozart	1786 Vienna	Da Ponte	Based on Beaumarchais play
Martha, or Richmond Fair	Friedrich von Flotow	1847 Vienna	W Friedrich	
The Martyrdom of St Magnus	Peter Maxwell Davies	1977 Kirkwall	Davies	First performance, St Magnus Cathedral, Kirkwall, Orkney
Mary of Egypt	John Tavener	1992 Aldeburgh	Mother Thekla	
Mary, Queen of Scots	Thea Musgrave	1977 Edinburgh	Musgrave	Also the name of a ballet by John McCabe

Operas and operettas	Composer	First performance		Librettist	General information
The Mask of Orpheus	Harrison Birtwistle	1986	London	Peter Zinovieff	
Maskarade	Carl Nielsen	1906	Copenhagen	V Andersen	
A Masked Ball	Giuseppe Verdi	1859	Rome	Antonio Somma	
I Masnadieri (The Robbers)	Giuseppe Verdi	1847	London	Maffei	
Master Peter's Puppet Show	Manuel de Falla	1923	Seville	Falla	Based on incident in Cervantes' Don Quixote
The Mastersingers of Nuremberg	Richard Wagner	1868	Munich	Wagner	
Mathis der Maler (Matthias the Painter)	Paul Hindemith	1938	Zurich	Hindemith	Based on life of Matthias Grünewald
Mavra	Igor Stravinsky	1922	Paris	Kochno	
May Night	Nikolay Rimsky-Korsakov	1880	St Petersburg	Rimsky-Korsakov	Based on Gogol story
Mazeppa	Pyotr Tchaikovsky	1884	Moscow	Tchaikovsky and Burenin	
Medea (Médée)	Luigi Cherubini	1797	Paris	F B Hoffman	
The Medium	Gian Carlo Menotti	1946	Columbia University	Menotti	
Mephistopheles	Arrigo Boito	1868	Milan	Boito	Based on Goethe's Faust
Merrie England	Edward German	1902	London (Savoy)	Basil Hood	
The Merry Widow	Franz Lehár	1905	Vienna	V Léon and L Stein	Widow's name is Hanna Glawari
The Merry Wives of Windsor	Otto Nicolai	1849	Berlin	S H Mosenthal	
The Midsummer Marriage	Michael Tippett	1955	London	Tippett	
A Midsummer Night's Dream	Benjamin Britten	1960	Aldeburgh	Pears and Britten	
Mignon	Ambroise Thomas	1866	Paris	Barbier and Carré	Based on Goethe's novel Wilhelm Meisters Lehrjahre
The Mikado	Arthur Sullivan	1885	London	W S Gilbert	Aka: The Town of Titipu
The Mines of Sulphur	Richard Rodney Bennett	1965	London	Beverley Cross	
Mireille	Charles Gounod	1864	London and Paris	Carré	
The Miserly Knight	Sergei Rachmaninov	1906	Moscow	Rachmaninov	
Miss Donnithorne's Maggot	Peter Maxwell Davies	1974	Adelaide	Randolph Stow	
Miss Julie	Ned Rorem	1965	New York	Kenward Elmslie	Based on Strindberg's play
Miss Julie	William Alwyn	1976	Broadcast	Alwyn	Other version by Rorem and Bibalo
Mitridate, Rè di Ponto	Wolfgang Amadeus Mozart	1770	Milan	V A Cigna-Santi	
Mlada	Nikolay Rimsky-Korsakov	1892	St Petersburg	Rimsky-Korsakov	
Monday From Light	Karlheinz Stockhausen	1988	Milan	Stockhausen	
Monsieur Beaucaire	André Messager	1919	Birmingham	Lonsdale and Ross	Based on Booth Tarkington's story
The Moon (Der Mond)	Carl Orff	1939	Munich	Orff	
Moses in Egypt	Gioachino Rossini	1818	Naples	A L Tottola	
Moses und Aron	Arnold Schoenberg	1954	Hamburg	Schoenberg	
The Mother (Matka)	Alois Hába	1931	Munich	Hába	
The Mother of Us All	Virgil Thomson	1947	New York	Stein	Gertrude Stein and Virgil Thomson are characters
Mozart and Salieri	Nikolay Rimsky-Korsakov	1898	Moscow	Rimsky-Korsakov	
La Muette de Portici	Daniel Auber	1828	Paris	Scribe and Delavigne	Aka: Masaniello
Nabucco (Nebuchadnezzar)	Giuseppe Verdi	1842	Milan	T Solera	
La Navarraise	Jules Massenet	1894	Covent Garden	Jules Claretie and Henri Cain	
Nelson	Lennox Berkeley	1953	London	Alan Pryce-Jones	
Nero (Nerone)	Arrigo Boito	1924	Milan	Boito	
Nero (Nerone)	Pietro Mascagni	1935	Milan	Targioni-Tozzetti	
Neues vom Tage (News of the Day)	Paul Hindemith	1929	Berlin	Marcellus Schiffer	

Operas and operettas

	Composer	First performance		Librettist	General information
New Year	Michael Tippett	1989	Houston	Tippett	
A Night at the Chinese Opera	Judith Weir	1987	Cheltenham	Weir	
The Night Bell	Gaetano Donizetti	1836	Naples	Donizetti	
A Night in Paris	Frederick Delius	1982	London	Rosenval	
A Night in Venice	Johann Strauss II	1883	Berlin	F Zell (Camillo Walzel) and Génée	
The Nightingale (Le Rossignol)	Igor Stravinsky	1914	Paris and London	Stravinsky and S Mitusov	
Nixon in China	John Adams	1987	Houston	Alice Goodman	
Norma	Vincenzo Bellini	1831	Milan	Romani	
The Nose	Dmitry Shostakovich	1930	Leningrad	Zamyatin, Yunin, Preys	Based Gogol story. Shostakovich wrote part of libretto
Notre Dame	Franz Schmidt	1914	Vienna	Leopold Wilk and Schmidt	
Noye's Fludde	Benjamin Britten	1958	Aldeburgh	Britten	Based on Chester miracle play
Oberon, or the Elf-King's Oath	Carl Maria Weber	1826	Covent Garden	J R Planché	
L'Oca del Cairo	Wolfgang Amadeus Mozart	1860	Frankfurt	Varesco	Unfinished opera buffa
Oedipus	George Enescu	1936	Paris	E Fleg	
Oedipus Rex	Igor Stravinsky	1927	Paris	J Cocteau	From Sophocles
The Olympians	Arthur Bliss	1949	London	J B Priestley	
The Opera Ball	Richard Heuberger	1898	Vienna	Léon and Waldeberg	Contains the aria 'Geh'n wir in's Chambre séparée'
The Oracle	Franco Leoni	1905	Covent Garden	C Zanoni	Based on story The Cat and the Cherub by C B Fernald
Orfeo ed Euridice	Christoph Gluck	1762	Vienna	Calzabigi	
Orlando	George Frederick Handel	1733	London	Anon	Based on Ariosto's 16th-century poem, Orlando Furioso
Orlando Furioso	Antonio Vivaldi	1727	Venice	Braccioli	
Orlando Paladino	Franz Joseph Haydn	1782	Eszterháza	N Porta	
Orpheus in the Underworld	Jacques Offenbach	1858	Paris	Crémieux and Halévy	
Osud (Fate)	Leoš Janáček	1958	Brno	Janáček	Janáček and Fedora Bartosová
Otello	Giuseppe Verdi	1887	Milan	Boito	
Ottone	George Frederick Handel	1723	London	N Haym	
Our Man in Havana	Malcolm Williamson	1963	London	Sidney Gilliat	Based on Graham Greene's novel
Padmâvatî	Albert Roussel	1923	Paris	L Laloy	Opera-ballet
I Pagliacci	Ruggiero Leoncavallo	1892	Milan	Leoncavallo	Famous aria 'Vesti la giubba' ('On with the motley') refers to clown's attire
Palestrina	Hans Pfitzner	1917	Munich	Pfitzner	
Paradise Lost	Krzysztof Penderecki	1978	Chicago	Christopher Fry	Based on Milton's poem
Paris and Helen	Christoph Gluck	1770	Vienna	Calzabigi	
Parisian Life (La Vie Parisienne)	Jacques Offenbach	1866	Paris	Meilhac and Halévy	
Parsifal	Richard Wagner	1882	Bayreuth	Wagner	Wagner's last opera
Partenope	George Frederick Handel	1730	London	Stampiglia	
Patience	Arthur Sullivan	1881	London	W S Gilbert	Aka: Bunthorne's Bride
Paul Bunyan	Benjamin Britten	1941	New York	W H Auden	
The Pearl Fishers	Georges Bizet	1863	Paris	Cormon and Carré	Action set in Ceylon (Sri Lanka)

Operas and operettas	Composer	First performance		Librettist	General information
Penelope	Rolf Liebermann	1954	Salzburg	H Strobel	Based on the story of Ulysses' wife in Homer's Odyssey
Pénélope	Gabriel Fauré	1913	Monte Carlo and Paris	René Fauchois	
A Penny For a Song	Richard Rodney Bennett	1967	London	Colin Graham	
The Perfect Fool	Gustav Holst	1923	Covent Garden	Holst	
Peter Grimes	Benjamin Britten	1945	London	Montagu Slater	Based on George Crabbe's poem 'The Borough'
Peter Schmoll and his Neighbours	Carl Maria Weber	1803	Augsburg	Joseph Türk	
The Pilgrim's Progress	Ralph Vaughan Williams	1951	Covent Garden	Vaughan Williams	Christian's name in Bunyan's novel is changed to Pilgrim
The Pirate	Vincenzo Bellini	1827	Milan	Romani	
The Pirates of Penzance	Arthur Sullivan	1879	Paignton, Devon, and New York	W S Gilbert	Aka: The Slave of Duty
The Poacher or the Voice of Nature	Albert Lortzing	1842	Leipzig	Lortzing	
The Poisoned Kiss	Ralph Vaughan Williams	1936	London and Cambridge	Evelyn Sharp	Aka: The Empress and the Necromancer
Polly	Christoph Pepusch	1777	London	John Gay	
Porgy and Bess	George Gershwin	1935	Boston and New York	DuBose Heyward and Ira Gershwin	
Powder her Face	Thomas Adès	1995	Cheltenham	Philip Hensher	Shown on British television on Christmas Day 1999
Il Prigioniero (The Prisoner)	Luigi Dallapiccola	1949	Italy	Dallapiccola	
Prima Donna	Arthur Benjamin	1949	London	Cedric Cliffe	
Prima la Musica e Poe le Parole	Antonio Salieri	1786	Vienna	Casti	
Prince Igor	Alexander Borodin	1890	St Petersburg	Borodin	First performed in double bill with Mozart's Der Schauspieldirektor Completed by Rimsky-Korsakov and Glazunov
The Prince of Homburg	Hans Werner Henze	1960	Hamburg	Bachmann	
Princess Ida	Arthur Sullivan	1884	London and Boston	W S Gilbert	Aka: Castle Adamant
The Prodigal Son	Benjamin Britten	1968	Orford	Plomer	A church parable
Le Prophète	Giacomo Meyerbeer	1849	Paris and London	Scribe	
Punch and Judy	Harrison Birtwistle	1968	Aldeburgh	Stephen Pruslin	
Purgatory	Gordon Crosse	1966	Cheltenham	W B Yeats	
I Puritani (di Scozia)	Vincenzo Bellini	1835	London and Paris	C Pepoli	Bellini's last opera
I Quattro Rusteghi (The Four Rustics)	Ermanno Wolf-Ferrari	1906	Munich	Sugano and Pizzolato	
The Queen of Sheba	Károly Goldmark	1875	Vienna	S H Mosenthal	
The Queen of Spades (Pique Dame)	Pyotr Tchaikovsky	1890	St Petersburg	M Tchaikovsky and Pyotr Tchaikovsky	
Quiet Flows the Don	Ivan Dzerzhinsky	1935	Leningrad	Dzerzhinsky	
A Quiet Place	Leonard Bernstein	1983	Houston	S Wadsworth	Revised in 3 acts incorporating Bernstein's Trouble in Tahiti
Radamisto	George Frederick Handel	1720	London	N Haym	
The Rajah's Diamond	Alun Hoddinott	1979	BBC TV	Myfanwy Piper	
The Rake's Progress	Igor Stravinsky	1951	Venice	Chester Kallman and W H Auden	
The Rape of Lucretia	Benjamin Britten	1946	Glyndebourne	Ronald Duncan	
The Red Line	Aulis Sallinen	1978	Helsinki	Sallinen	
Regina	Marc Blitzstein	1949	New Haven	Blitzstein	Based on Lillian Hellman's play The Little Foxes

MUSIC CLASSICAL

Operas and operettas	Composer	First performance	Librettist	General information
Il Rè Pastore (The Shepherd King)	Wolfgang Amadeus Mozart	1775 Salzburg	Metastasio	
Resurrection	Peter Maxwell Davies	1987 Darmstadt	Maxwell Davies	
Das Rheingold (The Rhine Gold)	Richard Wagner	1869 Munich	Wagner	Became the prologue to the The Ring cycle
Richard the Lionhearted	André Grétry	1784 Paris	M J Sedaine	
Riders to the Sea	Ralph Vaughan Williams	1937 London	J M Synge	Faithful setting of Synge's play
Rienzi	Richard Wagner	1842 Dresden	Wagner	Based on Bulwer-Lytton's novel
Rigoletto	Giuseppe Verdi	1851 Venice	Piave	Based on Hugo's play Le Roi s'Amuse
Rinaldo	George Frederick Handel	1711 London	Rossi	Handel's first opera in England
Der Ring des Nibelungen	Richard Wagner	1876 Bayreuth	Wagner	
Der Ring des Polykrates	Erich Korngold	1916 Hamburg	J Korngold	Composed 1914
The Rise and Fall of the City of Mahagonny	Kurt Weill	1930 Leipzig	Brecht	
The Rising of the Moon	Nicholas Maw	1970 Glyndebourne	Beverley Cross	
Il Ritorno d'Ulisse in Patria	Claudio Monteverdi	1640 Venice	G Badoaro	English title: Ulysses' Return to His Native Land
Robert Devereux, Earl of Essex	Gaetano Donizetti	1837 Naples	Cammarano	
Robert the Devil	Giacomo Meyerbeer	1831 Paris	Scribe and Delavigne	
Rodelinda	George Frederick Handel	1725 London	Salvi and Haym	
Le Roi l'a dit	Léo Delibes	1873 Paris	Gondinet	
Le Roi malgré lui	Emmanuel Chabrier	1887 Paris	De Najac and Buroni	
Romeo and Juliet	Charles Gounod	1867 Paris, London and NY	Barbier and Carré	
Romeo and Juliet	Heinrich Sutermeister	1940 Dresden	Sutermeister	
La Rondine (The Swallow)	Giacomo Puccini	1917 Monte Carlo	Giuseppe Adami	Adapted from a German libretto by Alfred Lillner and Heinze Reichart
Der Rosenkavalier	Richard Strauss	1911 Dresden	Hofmannsthal	
The Royal Hunt of the Sun	Iain Hamilton	1977 London	Hamilton	Based on Peter Shaffer's play
Ruddigore	Arthur Sullivan	1887 London and New York	W S Gilbert	Aka: The Witch's Curse
Rusalka	Alexander Dargomyzhsky	1856 St Petersburg	Dargomyzhsky	
Rusalka	Antonin Dvořák	1901 Prague	J Kvapil	
Ruslan and Lyudmila	Mikhail Glinka	1842 St Petersburg	Shirkov and Bakhturin	Based on Pushkin's poem
Ruth	Lennox Berkeley	1956 London	Crozier	
Sadko	Nikolay Rimsky-Korsakov	1898 Moscow	Rimsky-Korsakov, Stasov and Belsky	
St François d'Assise	Olivier Messiaen	1983 Paris	Messiaen	Messiaen's only opera
The Saint of Bleecker Street	Gian Carlo Menotti	1954 New York	Menotti	
Salome	Antoine Mariotte	1908 Lyons	Oscar Wilde	Based on Oscar Wilde's play
Salome	Richard Strauss	1905 Dresden	Hedwig Lachmann	Based on Wilde's play
Samson et Dalila	Camille Saint-Saëns	1877 Weimar	Lemaire	
Sapho	Jules Massenet	1897 Paris	Cain and Bernède	
Sárka	Zdeněk Fibich	1897 Prague	Schulzová	
Sárka	Leoš Janáček	1925 Brno	Zeyer	
Saturday from Light	Karlheinz Stockhausen	1984 Milan	Stockhausen	
Saul and David	Carl Nielsen	1902 Copenhagen	Christiansen	
Der Schauspieldirektor (The Impresario)	Wolfgang Amadeus Mozart	1786 Vienna	G Stephanie	
Schwanda the Bagpiper	Jaromir Weinberger	1927 Prague	Kares and Brod	

Operas and operettas	Composer	First performance	Librettist	General information
Die Schweigsame Frau	Richard Strauss	1935 Dresden	Stefan Zweig	Translates as 'The Silent Woman'
The Secret	Bedřich Smetana	1878 Prague	Krásnohorská	
The Secret Marriage	Domenico Cimarosa	1792 Vienna	G Bertati	
Semele	John Eccles	1964 Oxford	Congreve	Based on Ovid's *Metamorphoses* Includes aria 'Where'er you walk'
Semele	George Frederick Handel	1744 London	Congreve	
Semiramide	Gioachino Rossini	1823 Venice	G Rossi	Many other operas based on Voltaire's *Sémiramis*
Semyon Kotko	Sergey Prokofiev	1940 Moscow	Prokofiev	
The Short Life (La Vida Breve)	Manuel De Falla	1913 Nice	Fernández Shaw	
The Sicilian Vespers	Giuseppe Verdi	1855 Paris	Scribe and Duveyrier	
The Siege of Corinth	Gioachino Rossini	1826 Paris	Balocchi and Soumet	
Siegfried	Richard Wagner	1876 Bayreuth	Wagner	Third part of *Der Ring das Nibelungen*
Sigurd	Ernest Reyer	1884 Brussels and London	Du Locle and Blau	
The Silken Ladder	Gioachino Rossini	1812 Venice	G M Foppa	
Simon Boccanegra	Giuseppe Verdi	1857 Venice	Piave and Montanelli	
Sir John in Love	Ralph Vaughan Williams	1929 London	Vaughan Williams	'Greensleeves' is sung by Mistress Ford in Act 3
The Sleepwalker	Vincenzo Bellini	1831 Milan and London	Romani	Italian title: *La Sonnambula*
The Small Venetian Square	Ermanno Wolf-Ferrari	1936 Milan	Ghisalberti	
The Snow Maiden (Snegurochka)	Nikolay Rimsky-Korsakov	1882 St Petersburg	Rimsky-Korsakov	
Die Soldaten (The Soldiers)	Bernd Alois Zimmermann	1965 Cologne	Zimmermann and Bernd Alois	
Son and Stranger	Felix Mendelssohn	1851 Leipzig	Klingemann	German title: *Die Heimkehr aus der Fremde*
The Sorcerer	Arthur Sullivan	1877 London	W S Gilbert	
Sorochintsy Fair	Modest Mussorgsky	1913 Moscow	Mussorgsky	Unfinished opera based on Gogol story
The Spanish Lady	Edward Elgar	Never performed	Elgar	Incomplete. Based on Jonson's *The Devil Is an Ass*
Stiffelio	Giuseppe Verdi	1850 Trieste	Piave	
The Stone Guest	Alexander Dargomyzhsky	1872 St Petersburg	Pushkin	Same story as *Don Giovanni*
The Story of a Real Man	Sergey Prokofiev	1948 Leningrad	Mira Mendelson and Prokofiev	
La Straniera	Vincenzo Bellini	1829 Milan	Romani	
Suor Angelica (Sister Angelica)	Giacomo Puccini	1918 New York	Forzano	The second part of Puccini's *Il Trittico*
Susanna's Secret	Ermanno Wolf-Ferrari	1909 Munich	Zangarini and Golisciani	Secret is that Susanna smokes
Il Tabarro (The Cloak)	Giacomo Puccini	1918 New York	Adami	The first part of Puccini's *Il Trittico*
A Tale of Two Cities	Arthur Benjamin	1957 London	Cedric Cliffe	
The Tales of Hoffmann	Jacques Offenbach	1881 Paris	Barbier and Carré	Three acts: Olympia, Antonia and Giulietta ('Barcarolle' in Act 3)
Tamerlane (Tamerlano)	George Frederick Handel	1724 London	N F Haym	
The Taming of the Shrew	Hermann Goetz	1874 Mannheim	J V Widmann	
Tancredi	Gioachino Rossini	1813 Venice	Rossi	
Tannhäuser	Richard Wagner	1845 Dresden	Wagner	Full title: *Tannhäuser and the Singing Contest on the Wartburg*
Taras Bulba	Arturo Berutti	1895 Buenos Aires	Berutti	
Taverner	Peter Maxwell Davies	1972 Covent Garden	Maxwell Davies	
The Telephone	Gian Carlo Menotti	1947 New York	Menotti	
The Tempest (Der Sturm)	Frank Martin	1956 Vienna	Martin	

MUSIC CLASSICAL

Operas and operettas	Composer	First performance	Librettist	General information
The Tender Land	Aaron Copland	1954 New York	H Everett	
Thais	Jules Massenet	1894 Paris	L Gallet	Based on Anatole France novel (1890)
Theseus (Teseo)	George Frederick Handel	1713 London	N F Haym	
Thespis	Arthur Sullivan	1871 London	W S Gilbert	Aka: The Gods Grown Old
The Thieving Magpie	Gioachino Rossini	1817 Milan	Gherardini	Italian title: La Gazza Ladra
The Threepenny Opera	Kurt Weill	1928 Berlin	Brecht	Based on The Beggar's Opera by John Gay and Christoph Pepusch
Tom Jones	Edward German	1907 London and Manchester	Thompson and Courtneidge	
Tom Jones	Stephen Oliver	1976 Snape	Oliver	
Tom Jones	François Philidor	1765 Paris	Poinsinet and Davesne	
Tosca	Giacomo Puccini	1900 London and Rome	Giacosa and Illica	Based on Sardou's play
Die Tote Stadt (The Dead City)	Erich Korngold	1920 Hamburg and Cologne	Paul Schott	Paul Schott is the pseudonym for Erich Korngold and his father Julius Korngold
The Travelling Companion	Charles Villiers Stanford	1925 Liverpool	Henry Newbolt	
La Traviata (The Fallen Woman)	Giuseppe Verdi	1853 Venice	Piave	Based on Dumas fils' novel Lady of the Camellias collaboration
The Trial (Der Prozess)	Gottfried von Einem	1953 Salzburg	Blacher and H von Cramer	From Franz Kafka's novel
Trial by Jury	Arthur Sullivan	1875 London	W S Gilbert	Only grand opera produced by the
Tristan und Isolde	Richard Wagner	1865 Munich	Wagner	
Troilus and Cressida	William Walton	1954 Covent Garden	Christopher Hassall	Based on Chaucer's story, as opposed to Shakespeare's
The Trojans (Les Troyens)	Hector Berlioz	1863 Paris	Berlioz	
Trouble in Tahiti	Leonard Bernstein	1952 New York	Bernstein	
Il Trovatore (The Troubadour)	Giuseppe Verdi	1853 Rome	Cammarano and Bardare	Fourth act completed by Bardare, after death of Cammarano
The Tsarevich (Der Zarewitsch)	Franz Lehár	1927 Berlin	Reichart and Jenbach	
The Tsar Has His Photograph Taken	Kurt Weill	1928 Leipzig	Kaiser	
The Tsar's Bride	Nikolay Rimsky-Korsakov	1899 Moscow	L A Mey	Adaptation of L A Mey's play, extra scene by Tumenev
Turandot	Ferruccio Busoni	1917 Zurich	Busoni	Based on Gozzi's play
Turandot (unfinished)	Giacomo Puccini	1926 Milan	Adami and Simoni	Final scene completed by Franco Alfano
Il Turco in Italia	Gioachino Rossini	1814 Milan	Romani	
The Turn of the Screw	Benjamin Britten	1954 Venice and London	Myfanwy Piper	Based on Henry James's story
The Twin Brothers	Franz Schubert	1820 Vienna	G von Hofmann	
The Two Widows	Bedrich Smetana	1874 Prague	Emanuel Züngel	
Ulisse	Luigi Dallapiccola	1968 Berlin	Dallapiccola	Based on Homer
Ulysses	Reinhard Keiser	1722 Copenhagen	F M Lersner	Based on Homer
Ulysses	John C Smith	1733 London	S Humphreys	
Utopia Limited	Arthur Sullivan	1893 London	W S Gilbert	Aka: The Flowers of Progress
Vakula the Smith	Pyotr Tchaikovsky	1876 St Petersburg	Y Polonsky	Based on Gogol's story Christmas Eve
The Valkyrie (Die Walküre)	Richard Wagner	1870 Munich	Wagner	The Valkyrie is Brünnhilde
The Vampire	Heinrich Marschner	1828 Leipzig	W A Wohlbrück	Based on John Polidori's story 'The Vampyre'
Vanessa	Samuel Barber	1958 New York	Menotti	Based on Dinesen's Seven Gothic Tales
Venus and Adonis	John Blow	1683 London	Anon	
La Vera Constanza (True Constancy)	Franz Joseph Haydn	1779 Esterháza	F Puttini	

Operas and operettas	Composer	First performance		Librettist	General information
Véronique	André Messager	1898	Paris	Vanloo and Duval	
Das Verratene Meer (The Sea Betrayed)	Hans Werner Henze	1990	Berlin	Treichel	
La Vestale	Gaspare Spontini	1807	Paris	De Jouy	
Victory	Richard Rodney Bennett	1970	Covent Garden	Beverley Cross	Based on Joseph Conrad's novel
A Village Romeo and Juliet	Frederick Delius	1907	Berlin	Delius	
Le Villi (The Willis)	Giacomo Puccini	1884	Milan	F Fontana	
Violanta	Erich Korngold	1916	Munich	Müller	
The Violins of Saint-Jacques	Malcolm Williamson	1966	London	William Chappell	
The Visit of the Old Lady	Gottfried von Einem	1971	Vienna	Dürrenmatt	
The Voice of Ariadne	Thea Musgrave	1974	Snape Maltings	A Elguera	
La Voix Humaine (The Human Voice)	Francis Poulenc	1959	Paris	Cocteau	
La Wally	Alfredo Catalani	1892	Milan	Illica	
The Wandering Scholar	Gustav Holst	1934	Liverpool	Clifford Bax	
War and Peace	Sergey Prokofiev	1944	Moscow	Mira Mendelson and Prokofiev	
Wat Tyler	Alan Bush	1974	Sadler's Wells	Nancy Bush	
We Come to the River	Hans Werner Henze	1976	London	Edward Bond	
The Wedding of the Camacho	Felix Mendelssohn	1827	Berlin	F Voight	Based on an episode in Don Quixote
Werther	Jules Massenet	1892	Vienna	Blau, Milliet, Hartmann	Based on Goethe's novel The Sorrows of Young Werther
Where the Wild Things Are	Oliver Knussen	1980	Brussels	Maurice Sendak and Knussen	
William Tell	Gioachino Rossini	1829	Paris	De Jouy and Bis	André Grétry and B A Weber composed operas on same subject
The World on the Moon	Franz Joseph Haydn	1777	Eszterháza	Goldoni	
Wozzeck	Alban Berg	1925	Berlin	Berg	
The Wreckers	Ethel Smyth	1906	Leipzig	'H B' (Harry Brewster) Laforestier	
Das Wunder der Heliane	Erich Korngold	1927	Hamburg	Müller	
Wuthering Heights	Bernard Herrmann	1982	Portland, Oregon	Lucille Fletcher	
Xerxes (Serse)	George Frederick Handel	1738	London	Stampiglia	
Yan Tan Tethera	Harrison Birtwistle	1986	London	T Harrison	
The Yeomen of the Guard	Arthur Sullivan	1888	London and NY	W S Gilbert	Aka: The Merryman and his Maid
Yolanta (Iolanta)	Pyotr Tchaikovsky	1892	St Petersburg	M Tchaikovsky	
Zampa, or the Marble Bride	Ferdinand Hérold	1831	Paris	Mélesville	
Zar und Zimmermann	Albert Lortzing	1837	Leipzig	Lortzing	English translation: Tsar and Carpenter
Zazà	Ruggiero Leoncavallo	1900	Milan	Leoncavallo	

Operatic Suicides and Deaths

Character	Opera	Composer	Method
Aida	Aida	Verdi	Conceals herself in vault in which her lover is immured so as to share his death.
Andrey	Khovanshchina	Mussorgsky	Climbs a funeral pyre and perishes in the flames.
Brünnhilde	Götterdämmerung	Wagner	Rides her horse Grane on to Siegfried's funeral pyre.
Carmen	Carmen	Bizet	Stabbed by Don José.
Cio-Cio-San	Madame Butterfly	Puccini	Commits hara-kiri.
Cleopatra	Antony and Cleopatra	Barber	Presses an asp to her bosom.
Dido	Dido and Aeneas	Purcell	Stabs herself and mounts a funeral pyre.
Edgardo	Lucia di Lammermoor	Donizetti	Stabs himself with a dagger at Lucia's tomb.
Ernani	Ernani	Verdi	Stabs himself in fulfilment of a pledge to die when his enemy, Silva, sounds his horn.
Fenella	La Muette de Portici	Auber	Throws herself into the sea when she learns that her brother Masaniello has been killed.
Gioconda	La Gioconda	Ponchielli	Stabs herself to frustrate the lust of the spy Barnaba.
Gwendoline	Gwendoline	Chabrier	Stabs herself to join her Danish lover, Harald, in death.
Herman	Queen of Spades (Pique Dame)	Tchaikovsky	Stabs himself when he sees the ghost of an old countess whose death he has caused.
Iris	Iris	Mascagni	Throws herself into a sewer after unjustly being accused of becoming a geisha.
Katerina Ismailova	Lady Macbeth of Mtsensk District	Shostakovich	Drowns herself in a river en route to a Siberian prison camp.
La Wally	La Wally	Catalani	Throws herself from a precipice during an avalanche in the Alps.
Lakmé	Lakmé	Delibes	Poisons herself with the juice of an exotic flower when she loses her lover, Gerald.
Leonora	Il Trovatore	Verdi	Takes poison from a ring and swallows it rather than submit to the Count di Luna.
Liù	Turandot	Puccini	Stabs herself rather than reveal under torture the name of the Unknown Prince, Calaf.
Magda Sorel	The Consul	Menotti	Seals her kitchen and turns on the gas.
Manfredo	The Love of Three Kings	Montemezzi	Deliberately kisses the poisoned lips of his murdered wife Fiora in her tomb.
Marfa	Khovanshchina	Mussorgsky	Climbs a funeral pyre and perishes in the flames.
Margared	Le Roi d'Ys	Lalo	Leaps from precipice in remorse for aiding enemies to open dikes that protect city from sea.
Mizgir	The Snow Maiden (Snegurochka)	Rimsky-Korsakov	Flings himself into a lake when his beloved Snow Maiden is melted by a ray of sunlight.
Otello	Otello	Verdi	Stabs himself with a dagger following his murder of Desdemona.
Pollione	Norma	Bellini	Joins the Druid priestess on her funeral pyre.
Salome	Hérodiade	Massenet	Stabs herself upon learning that John the Baptist has been executed.
Selika	L'Africaine	Meyerbeer	Inhales the perfume of the manchinel tree, deadly to all who breathe it.
Seneca	L'Incoronazione di Poppea	Monteverdi	Opens his veins in the bath at the command of Emperor Nero.
Sister Angelica	Suor Angelica	Puccini	Swallows a poisonous potion she has concocted from the herbs in her convent's garden.
Tosca	Tosca	Puccini	Leaps to her death from parapet of the castle of Sant' Angelo in Rome after her lover is shot.
Violetta	La Traviata	Verdi	Dies of consumption.
Werther	Werther	Massenet	Shoots himself with a pistol.
Wozzeck	Wozzeck	Berg	Stabs his wife then walks into a pond and drowns.

Opera: General Information

aria (air) Solo vocal piece in A-B-A form.

bleeding chunks Operatic extracts played out of context. Term coined by Sir Donald Tovey.

burletta A comic operetta.

Camerata Society of 16th-century Florentine poets and musicians who developed opera.

canon Counterpoint in which one melodic strand gives the rule to another.

cantata Musical setting of a text, often religious, consisting of arias and choruses interspersed with recitatives.

canticle Bible hymn, other than a psalm, used in church liturgy.

cantor 1) Leading singer in a synagogue. 2) Director of music in Lutheran Church.

caoine (pronounced 'keen') Irish funeral song accompanied by wailing.

castrato Male soprano or contralto whose voice was preserved by castration before puberty.

'Catalogue Aria' Nickname for Leporello's aria in Act 1 Scene 2 of Mozart's *Don Giovanni* in which he recounts to Donna Elvira a list of his master Don Giovanni's conquests.

coloratura Word applied both to a florid virtuoso aria and to the voice required for such a passage.

Don Giovanni: conquests Italian 640, German 231, French 100, Turkish 91, Spanish 1003 = 2,065 (according to Leporello, although in the opera he has none).

English National Opera Assumed name in 1974, six years after moving into Coliseum in St Martin's Lane from previous London HQ at Sadler's Wells, Rosebery Avenue.

Gilbert and Sullivan: row over Librettist and composer fell out over choice of carpet for the Savoy.

Gluck and Piccinni war Divided Paris into French and Italian opera fans in the 1770s.

grand opera Opera on a large scale, usually entirely sung.

intermezzo Instrumental interlude used in course of an opera or play. Term also used for short opera performed between the acts of a larger one.

La Scala, Milan Built in 1778 and named after Regina della Scala, wife of a Duke of Milan. The opera house (lit. the staircase) opened on 3 August 1778 with operas of Salieri.

The Legend of Tsar Saltan Orchestral interlude 'The Flight of the Bumble Bee' appears in Act 3.

leitmotif (leading theme) Recurring theme written for a specific character or event in opera or television and film music.

libretto The words of any vocal piece such as an oratorio, but particularly the text of an opera.

'Love-Death' Wagner's name given to love duet in Act 2 of *Tristan und Isolde*, although more generally regarded as Isolde's aria at end of Act 3.

Mastersingers: thirteen Sixtus Beckmesser – Town Clerk, Fritz Kothner – Baker, Balthasar Zorn – Pewterer, Ulrich Eisslinger – Grocer, Hans Sachs – Cobbler, Veit Pogner – Goldsmith, Kunz Vogelgesang – Furrier, Conrad Nachtigal – Bucklemaker, Augustin Mosler – Tailor, Hermann Ortel – Soap boiler, Hans Schwarz – Stocking weaver, Hans Foltz – Coppersmith, Walther von Stolzing – Unemployed.

Moody-Manners Opera Co Touring opera company formed in 1898 by Charles Manners and his wife Fanny Moody but disbanded in 1916.

***opera buffa* (Fr. *opera bouffe*)** Comic opera; the opposite of *opera seria*.

opéra-comique 1) Second opera house of Paris; originally opened 1715; has a history of name changes and re-location; it is currently known as Salle Favart. 2) Term describing opera with spoken dialogue.

operetta Light opera, sometimes of a comic nature, e.g. Gilbert and Sullivan operettas.

overture Introductory music for an opera, oratorio or ballet.

Paris Opéra (Académie de Musique) Latest building opened in 1875 and commonly known as Garnier or Salle Garnier, after its architect. After the opening of the Opéra Bastille in 1990, the Garnier Opéra is now used mainly for ballet. The term Paris Opéra is now used to mean the Garnier and the Bastille.

pasticcio/pastiche Opera in which each act is by a different composer. Although these terms are often used synonymously, pastiche describes a work written in the style of another period or manner.

patter song Rapid, sometimes tongue-twisting song often found in comic opera and now in pop music.

polo Andalusian folk song accompanied with dance and performed in 3/8 with syncopations and vocal coloraturas on words, e.g. 'Ole' and 'Ay', as performed in several operas.

prima donna (first lady) Most important female singer in an opera.

prologue Introductory piece that presents the background for an opera.

Puccini: unfinished opera *Turandot* (completed by Franco Alfano).

Rhinemaidens: three Flosshilde, Wellgunde, Woglinde.

Singspiel German light opera with spoken dialogue.

soubrette Soprano comedienne.

surtitle A printed translation of part of the text of an opera, usually projected on a screen above the stage. This innovation was first used on 21 January 1983 by the Canadian Opera company for *Electra*.

travesti Term used to describe operatic roles whereby character parts are sung by the opposite gender, e.g. Cherubino in *The Marriage of Figaro* or Prince Orlofsky in *Die Fledermaus*. Such parts are often called breeches or trouser-roles.

Turandot: three riddles What is born each night and dies each dawn ... hope. What flickers red and is warm like a flame, yet is not fire ... blood. What is like ice but burns ... Turandot.

TV opera: first *Amahl and the Night Visitors* (Magi) by Menotti (1951).

Valkyries Brünnhilde, Gerhilde, Grimgerde, Helmwige, Ortlinde, Rossweise, Schwertleite, Siegrune, Waltraute.

Venice Opera House Teatro La Fenice, opened in 1792 and destroyed by fire 1836, rebuilt 1837 but seriously damaged again in 1996.

voice registers Chest, head and middle voice; so called because the notes seem to come from these areas.

MUSIC CLASSICAL

Hymns, Anthems, Songs and Ballads

Abide With Me Henry Francis Lyte.

America the Beautiful Katherine Lee Bates (words); Samuel Augustus Ward (music).

America (My Country 'tis of Thee) Samuel Francis Smith (tune of 'God Save the Queen').

Annie Laurie William Douglas. First line: Maxwelton's braes are bonnie, where early fa's the dew.

Auld Lang Syne Robert Burns.

Battle Hymn of the Republic Julia Ward Howe. First line: Mine eyes have seen the glory of the coming of the Lord (tune of 'John Brown's body')

Beer Barrel Polka (Roll out the barrel) Tune by Jaromir Vejvoda.

Caller Herrin' Tune by Nathaniel Gow blends fishwives' cry with bells of St Andrew's Church; words by Lady Nairne.

Calm Sea and Prosperous Voyage J W Goethe.

The Campbells are Coming Anon.

Columbia, the Gem of the Ocean Thomas à Becket (1808–90).

Eternal Father, Strong To Save William Whiting (words); J B Dykes (music); aka 'The Navy's Hymn'. First line, 'O thou who bidd'st the ocean deep'.

Evening Hymn Purcell (music); Fuller (words). First line, 'Now that the sun hath veiled his light'.

The Flowers that Bloom in the Springtime W S Gilbert (words); Arthur Sullivan (music).

For the Fallen 3rd movement of Elgar's choral work *Spirit of England* with words by Laurence Binyon.

Funiculì Funiculà Luigi Denza's song composed for the opening of the Naples funicular railway in 1880.

General William Booth Enters into Heaven Ives (music); Vachel Lindsay (words).

Girl I Left Behind Me, The Played in the British Army on occasions of departure and sometimes known as 'Brighton Camp'.

God Bless the Prince of Wales Henry Brinley Richards (music); Ceiriog Hughes (words).

God Preserve the Emperor Francis (Emperor's Hymn) Lorenz Haschka (words); Haydn (music); known as 'Austria' in hymn-books and became Austrian anthem. The German anthem 'Deutschland über Alles' adopted the tune.

Greensleeves Old English tune popularly attributed to Henry VIII but no evidence of this is available, although it may have been written during his reign. Mentioned by Shakespeare in *The Merry Wives of Windsor* and tune used by Holst in *St Paul's Suite* and by Busoni in *Turandot*.

Habañera Cuban song and dance of African origins, which became popular in Spain. Famous example is the habañera in Bizet's *Carmen*.

Happy Birthday to You Composed in USA by Mildred Hill and published by Clayton F Summy as 'Good Morning to All'.

Hark, the Herald Angels Sing Words by Charles Wesley.

Hear My Prayer Hymn by Mendelssohn containing section 'O for the wings of a dove'.

Heart of Oak Written by actor David Garrick in 1759 to music by William Boyce. It was a topical song from the pantomime *Harlequin's Invasion* and commemorated the British victories at Minden, Quiberon Bay and Quebec.

Home, Sweet Home Henry Bishop composed the music (1821) and the words were by J H Payne.

Internationale Socialist song composed by P Degeyter to words by Eugène Pottier; it was the official anthem of Communist Russia until 1 January 1944 and often confused with 'The Red Flag'.

Jerusalem Music by Hubert Parry (1916); words by William Blake.

Jubilate Psalm 100 (Anglican service), alternative to Benedictus; set to music by various composers.

Keel Row Quoted by Debussy in the 3rd movement of his *Images*. This song, of unknown origin, first appeared in a collection of favourite Scots tunes and is principally identified with the North-east of England.

keen (caoine) Irish funeral song with wailing. Represented in Vaughan Williams's opera *Riders to the Sea*.

Land of Hope and Glory Finale of Elgar's *Coronation Ode* with words by A C Benson. The tune adapts the melody of the trio section of *Pomp and Circumstance March* No. 1 in D.

Land of My Fathers (Hen Wlad fy Nhadau) National anthem of Wales (words by Evan James; music by his son James); originally called 'Glan Rhondda'.

Lass of Richmond Hill James Hook (music); L McNally (words). The song refers to Richmond in Yorkshire.

Last Rose of Summer, The Adaption of R A Millihin's 'The Groves of Barley' by Thomas Moore (1779-1852), famously heard in Friedrich von Flotow's opera *Martha*.

Let Us Garlands Bring Song-cycle by Gerald Finzi to words by Shakespeare, first performed in 1942 for the 70th birthday of Vaughan Williams. The five songs are 1) 'Come Away Death', 2) 'Who Is Sylvia?' 3) 'Fear No More the Heat O' the Sun', 4) 'O Mistress Mine', 5) 'It Was a Lover and His Lass'.

Lilliburlero Song of unknown origin, which is the tune of Northern Ireland's 'Orange' party, set to different words as 'Protestant Boys'.

Lincoln, the Great Commoner Song by Charles Ives; words by Edwin Markham.

Londonderry Air Irish folk tune first published in the Petrie collection of 1855, the most famous words being those of 'Danny Boy' by F E Weatherly.

The Lost Chord Song by Arthur Sullivan composed in 1877 in sorrow at his brother's death.

Magnificat Canticle of the Virgin Mary, 'My Soul Doth Magnify the Lord', as it appears in St Luke's Gospel. Latin name is the first word of the Vulgate translation, i.e. Magnificat anima mea Dominum.

La Marseillaise French national anthem, words and music by Claude Rouget de Lisle; written in 1792 under the title 'War Song for the Rhine Army'. Famously quoted in Tchaikovsky's *1812 Overture*.

Nearer, My God, to Thee Hymn existing in British and American versions, both set to verses by Sarah Flower Adams. The English version was composed by John Dykes, and the American version is sung to the tune 'Bethany,' by Lowell Mason.

O Canada! Canadian national anthem; originally a hymn in honour of St John the Baptist; music composed by Calixa Lavallée in 1880.

O Come All Ye Faithful John Francis Wade wrote both the words and music in the early 1740s.

O God, Our Help in Ages Past Based on Psalm 90 by Isaac Watts to a tune by William Croft, this hymn is particularly associated with Remembrance Day services.

Old Folks at Home   By Stephen Foster. First line: 'Way down upon the Swanee River, far, far away'.

Onward, Christian Soldiers   Reverend Sabine Baring-Gould published the words in 1868 and Arthur Sullivan the music in 1871.

Pammelia (All Honey)   First collection of rounds, catches and canons published in England, by T Ravenscroft in 1609.

Rock of Ages, Cleft For Me   Hymn; words by Reverend Augustus Montague Toplady; music by Richard Redhead.

Rule, Britannia!   Music by Thomas Arne to words of James Thomson and first played in *The Masque of Alfred* at Maidenhead on 1 August 1740. It has become a nationalistic English anthem and is also often considered to be the hidden theme of Elgar's *Enigma Variations*.

St Anne   English hymn tune of uncertain origin but possibly composed by William Croft. It is usually sung to the words 'O God, Our Help in Ages Past'.

Seven Gypsy Songs   Dvořák (music), Heyduk (words). 1) 'My Song Resounds', 2) 'My Triangle is Singing', 3) 'Silent the Woods', 4) 'Songs My Mother Taught Me', 5) 'Sound the Fiddle', 6) 'Clean Cotton Clothes', 7) 'To the Heights of Tatra'.

Sheep May Safely Graze   Air by J S Bach subsequently arranged by several composers, notably William Walton in *The Wise Virgins*.

Simple Gifts   Shaker hymn composed by Joseph Brackett (1848) and quoted by Copland in *Appalachian Spring*.

Song of Destiny (Schicksalslied)   Brahms (music); Hölderlin (words).

Song of the Fates (Gesang der Farzen)   Brahms (music); Goethe (words).

The Star-Spangled Banner   National anthem of USA. Words by Francis Scott Key (1814), written during the war of 1812, and music adapted from John Stafford Smith's *Anacreon in Heaven*.

Sumer is Icumen In (Summer is coming in)   Dating from *c.* 1240 and often quoted as the oldest extant canon. Aka 'The Reading Rota' as the author is thought to have been John of Fornsete, a monk of Reading Abbey.

Tea for Two   Song by Vincent Youmans, written for *No, No, Nanette* (1925). An orchestral version by Shostakovich (1928) was given the name 'Tahiti Trot'.

'Tis the Last Rose of Summer   Old Irish air originally called 'Castle Hyde'.

While Shepherds Watched Their Flocks   Words by Nahum Tate.

Ballets

Name	Music by	Choreographer	First performance	
The Age of Gold	Dmitry Shostakovich	Kaplan and Vaynonen	1930	Leningrad
Agon	Igor Stravinsky	Balanchine	1957	Los Angeles
El Amor brujo (Love the Magician)	Manuel de Falla	Falla (as pantomime) La Argentinita (as ballet in 1931)	1915	Madrid
Apollo Musagetes (Apollo, Leader of the Muses)	Igor Stravinsky	Bolm	1928	Washington
		Balanchine	1928	Paris
Appalachian Spring	Aaron Copland	Martha Graham	1944	Washington
L'Après-midi d'un faune	Claude Debussy	Nijinsky	1912	Paris
		Robbins	1946	New York
Bacchus and Ariadne	Albert Roussel	Lifar	1931	Paris
La Bayadère	Léon Minkus	Petipa	1877	St Petersburg
Les Biches	Francis Poulenc	Nijinskaya	1924	Monte Carlo
Billy the Kid	Aaron Copland	Loring	1938	Chicago
Boléro	Maurice Ravel	Nijinskaya	1928	Paris
The Bolt	Dmitry Shostakovich	Lopokov	1931	Leningrad
La Boutique Fantastique	Ottorino Respighi (arr. of Rossini's music)	Massine	1919	London
The Box of Toys	Claude Debussy	André Hellé	1919	Paris
Caroline Mathilde	Peter Maxwell Davies	Flindt	1991	Amsterdam
Checkmate	Arthur Bliss	de Valois	1937	Paris
Cinderella	Sergey Prokofiev	Ashton	1948	Moscow
Coppélia	Léo Delibes	Saint-Léon	1870	Paris
La Création du Monde	Darius Milhaud	Börlin	1923	Paris
The Creatures of Prometheus	Ludwig van Beethoven	Viganò	1801	Vienna
		Ashton	1970	Bonn
Daphnis et Chloé	Maurice Ravel	Fokine	1912	Paris
		Ashton	1957	London
Les Deux Pigeons	André Messager	Mérante	1886	Paris
Don Quixote	Léon Minkus	Petipa	1869	St Petersburg
Edward II	John McCabe	Bintley	1996	Stuttgart
Façade	William Walton	Ashton	1931	London
The Fairy's Kiss	Igor Stravinsky	Nijinskaya	1928	Paris
		MacMillan	1980	London
Fall River Legend	Morton Gould	de Mille	1948	New York
Fancy Free	Leonard Bernstein	Robbins	1944	New York
Le Festin de l'araignée (Spider's Banquet)	Albert Roussel	Staats	1913	Paris

Name	Music by	Choreographer	First Performance	
La Fille mal gardée (The Unchaperoned Girl)	John Lanchbery (arr. of Ferdinand Hérold's music)	Ashton	1960	London
Firebird	Igor Stravinsky	Fokine	1910	Paris
The Four Temperaments	Paul Hindemith	Balanchine	1946	New York
Gaîté Parisienne	Manuel Rosenthal (arr. of Offenbach's music)	Massine	1938	Monte Carlo
Gayane	Aram Khachaturian	Anisimova	1942	Leningrad
Giselle, or the Wilis	Adolphe Adam	Coralli and Perrot	1841	Paris
		Petipa	1884	St Petersburg
The Good-Humoured Ladies	Domenico Scarlatti (arr. by Tommasini)	Massine	1917	Rome
The Haunted Ballroom	Geoffrey Toye	de Valois	1934	London
Homage to the Queen	Malcolm Arnold	Ashton	1953	London (Coronation Night)
Horoscope	Constant Lambert	Ashton	1938	London
Jeux (Games)	Claude Debussy	Nijinsky	1913	Paris
Josephslegende (Legend of Joseph)	Richard Strauss	Fokine	1914	London and Paris
Madame Chrysanthème	Alan Rawsthorne	Ashton	1955	London
Les Mariés de la Tour Eiffel	Les Six (excluding Durey)	Börlin	1921	Paris
Miracle in the Gorbals	Arthur Bliss	Helpmann	1944	London
Miss Julie	Andrzej Panufnik	MacMillan	1970	Stuttgart
Nobilissima Visione	Paul Hindemith	Massine	1938	Monte Carlo
Nutcracker	Pyotr Tchaikovsky	Ivanov	1892	St Petersburg
Ondine (Undine)	Hans Werner Henze	Ashton	1958	London
Orpheus	Igor Stravinsky	Balanchine	1948	New York
Parade	Erik Satie	Massine	1917	Paris
Le Pas d'Acier	Sergey Prokofiev	Massine	1927	Paris
Paul Bunyan	William Bergsma	Ballet for puppets	1939	San Francisco
Peer Gynt	Alfred Schnittke	Neumeier	1986	Hamburg
The Peri	Paul Dukas	Clustine	1912	Paris
Perséphone	Igor Stravinsky	Jooss	1934	Paris
		Ashton	1962	London
Les Petits Riens	Wolfgang Amadeus Mozart	Jean Noverre	1778	Paris
Petrushka	Igor Stravinsky	Fokine	1911	Paris
Pineapple Poll	Arthur Sullivan (arr. by Mackerras)	Cranko	1951	Sadler's Wells
The Prince of the Pagodas	Benjamin Britten	Cranko	1957	Covent Garden
		MacMillan	1995	London
The Prodigal Son	Sergey Prokofiev	Balanchine	1929	Paris
Pulcinella	Igor Stravinsky	Massine	1920	Paris
The Rake's Progress	Gavin Gordon	de Valois	1935	London
Raymonda	Alexander Glazunov	Petipa	1898	Paris
The Rite of Spring	Igor Stravinsky	Nijinsky	1913	London and Paris
		MacMillan	1962	London
Rodeo	Aaron Copland	de Mille	1942	New York
Romeo and Juliet	Sergey Prokofiev	Psota	1938	Brno
		MacMillan	1965	London
Salome	Peter Maxwell Davies	Flindt	1978	Copenhagen
The Sanguine Fan	Edward Elgar	Hynd (1976 revival)	1917	London
Scaramouche	Jean Sibelius	Walbom	1922	Copenhagen
Scheherazade	Nikolay Rimsky-Korsakov	Fokine	1910	Paris
Schlagobers (Whipped Cream)	Richard Strauss	Kröller	1924	Vienna and Breslau
The Seven Deadly Sins	Kurt Weill	Balanchine	1933	Paris
The Sleeping Beauty	Pyotr Tchaikovsky	Petipa	1890	St Petersburg
The Song of the Earth	Gustav Mahler	MacMillan	1965	London
Spartacus	Aram Khachaturian	Jacobson	1956	Leningrad
Le Spectre de la Rose	Carl Maria Weber	Fokine	1911	Monte Carlo
The Stone Flower	Sergey Prokofiev	Lavrovsky	1954	Moscow
Swan Lake	Pyotr Tchaikovsky	Reisinger	1877	Moscow
		Petipa and Ivanov	1895	St Petersburg
Les Sylphides	Frederic Chopin	Mérante	1876	Paris
Sylvia, ou La Nymph de Diane	Léo Delibes	Fokine	1907	St Petersburg
		Ashton	1952	London
The Tales of Hoffmann	Jacques Offenbach (arr. Lanchbery)	Darrell	1973	London
The Three-Cornered Hat	Manuel de Falla	Massine	1919	London
Tiresias	Constant Lambert	Ashton	1951	London
The Triumph of Neptune	Lord Berners	Balanchine	1926	London
La Ventana	Holm Lumbye	Bournonville	1854	Copenhagen

Name	Music by	Choreographer	First Performance	
A Wedding Bouquet	Lord Berners	Ashton	1936	London
The Wedding (Les Noces)	Igor Stravinsky	Nijinskaya	1923	Paris
The Wise Virgins	William Walton	Ashton	1940	Sadler's Wells
The Wooden Prince	Bela Bartók	Balázs	1917	Budapest

NB: Where ballets have been re-choreographed, both original and better-known modern versions are listed.

Ballet: General Information

ballet: first *Balet Comique de la Royne* (Paris 1581), produced by violinist Balthasar de Beaujoyeux.

Ballets Russes Founded in Paris in 1909 by Serge Diaghilev (Mikhail Fokine was his choreographer).

ballet terms Jeté – leap from one foot to another; arabesque – one leg raised behind and arms extended; entrechat – leap while striking heels together; pirouette – rapid whirling round on the point of one foot.

Bolshoi Theatre (Great Theatre) Oldest theatre in Moscow, originally called the Petrovsky, built by Maddox (1780), home of the Bolshoi Ballet.

classic ballet: first *Le Bourgeois Gentilhomme* (1670).

comédie-ballet French musico-dramatic entertainment devised by Molière and Lully in the late 17th century.

corps de ballet The ballet troupe excluding the principal dancers.

Dance Theatre of Harlem Founded by Arthur Mitchell (1968); first black classical ballet company; presented season at Covent Garden 1981.

defections from USSR Mikhail Baryshnikov while dancing with the Kirov in Toronto (1974); Natalia Makarova while dancing with the Kirov in London (1972); Rudolf Nureyev while dancing with the Kirov in Paris (1961).

La Fille mal gardée (The Unchaperoned Girl) Adaptation of a work based on French songs and airs originally produced in Bordeaux 1789.

Marie Taglioni (1804–1884) First ballerina to dance on points and to wear a tutu.

professional ballet dancer: first female La Fontaine in Lully's *Le Triomphe de l'Amour* at the Paris Opera House 1681.

Pulcinella Scenes and costumes by Picasso.

ritual dances: four dances (The Midsummer Marriage) 'The Earth in Autumn', 'Waters in Winter', 'Air in Spring', 'Fire in Summer'.

Ritual Fire Dance From Falla's *El Amor brujo* (*Love the Magician*).

Royal Ballet Name bestowed by Royal Charter in 1956 on the former Sadler's Wells Ballet, Covent Garden. Touring company originally known as Sadler's Wells Royal Ballet is now based in Birmingham and since 1991 is known as Birmingham Royal Ballet.

Le Spectre de la Rose Weber's *Invitation to the Dance* used as musical score.

Dance Types

allemande German dance, moderately paced in 4/4 rhythm, and performed in a cheerful fashion.

anglaise English country dance in quick duple metre.

apache French dance, often violent, imitating a Parisian gangster and his girlfriend.

badinage Playful dance or dance movement of a suite.

beguine Sensuous Latin ballroom dance originating in the Caribbean and danced to a bolero rhythm.

bergamasque (bergomask) Peasant dance of Bergamo, Italy, resembling a tarantella.

black bottom Popular dance of the late 1920s, originally in North America, involving lively rotation of the hips.

bolero Spanish dance in triple rhythm, said to have been invented in Cadiz around 1780.

bossa-nova Brazilian variation of the samba.

bourrée French dance, in quadruple time, performed in a lively style very like the gavotte.

branle French country dance of the 15th century characterised by a swaying motion and performed in a linked circle.

break dance Energetic solo dance frequently involving spinning on the floor on the back or head; originating in the USA in the 1980s.

cachucha Andalusian dance in triple metre similar to a bolero, for solo dancer.

cakewalk Popularised in the 1890s when black slaves parodied the white method of dance, a cake being awarded to best dancers.

calinda Negro dance, which was basis for an orchestral dance-interlude by Delius in his second opera *Koanga*.

calypso West Indian folk dance but better known in its sung form.

canaries Old 17th-century dance similar to a gigue and so called because it imitated Canary Island rituals.

can-can Boisterous Parisian dance of quadrille pattern originating in Algeria in the 1830s.

carmagnole Round dance, popular in the French Revolutionary period.

cha-cha-cha Cuban dance developed from the mambo in early 1950s.

chaconne Slow and dignified dance, probably originating in Spain.

Charleston Fast foxtrot named after Charleston, South Carolina, and popularised in New York in 1922.

conga Latin American dance of three steps and kick to the side, performed in chain with hands on the next person's hips.

cotillon Lively French formation dance of the 18th century similar to a quadrille.

courante   From the French meaning 'running', a courante is moderate to lively in pace, with shifting rhythms.

csárdás   Hungarian dance in two sections: 1) Slow and melancholy, 2) quick and lively.

cushion dance   Dance where one partner dropped a cushion before the other, who then knelt on it and bestowed a kiss on the bearer.

danse champêtre   French rustic dance performed in the open air.

divertissement   Dance or ballet with or without lyric, included in an opera or play to add variety.

ezcudantza   Basque festival dance for two performers with accompaniment of pipe and tabor.

fandango   Old Spanish courtship dance in triple time.

farandole   French line dance in 6/8 time usually to the accompaniment of galoubet and tambourin.

flamenco   Spanish dance with lively toe and heel steps, usually accompanied by guitar and castanets.

foxtrot   Ballroom dance in quadruple time combining short and long steps in various sequences, originated in North America in the early 20th century.

funk   Style of popular dance music of US black origin, popularised by singers such as James Brown. The staccato body movements follow the heavy syncopation of the music.

galliard   Spirited dance popular in Tudor times, performed in a gay, rollicking manner, in triple time.

galop (galopade)   Mid-19th-century dance with lively rhythm, executed with hopping movements.

gavotte   French dance in 4/4 time, starting on the third beat of the bar.

gigue   Formal dance for two in the 16th and 17th centuries; derived from the jig and usually with violin accompaniment.

gitana   Spanish gypsy dance.

gopak   Lively Russian folk dance in duple time.

guajira   Spanish dance with alternating rhythm between 6/8 and 3/4.

guaracha   Spanish and Mexican folk dance in two sections, one in triple time and the other in duple. Dancer usually plays guitar.

habañera   Cuban dance named after the city of Havana. Performed in 2/4 time.

halling   Norwegian dance possibly originating in the Hallingdal. It is a frantic dance accompanied by Hardanger fiddle and other violins.

hanacca   Moravian dance in simple triple time; a sort of quick polonaise.

haute danse   Old term for a dance where feet are lifted, as opposed to *basse danse* in which they stay close to the floor.

hay   Traditional country dance for two or more partners, with interweaving steps.

hob-and-nob   Scottish country dance (1745) tune developed into 'The Campbells are Coming'.

hopak (gopak)   Ukrainian folk dance, once for men only but later danced by couples. Steps are improvised but in 2/4 time.

hornpipe   Lively English sailors' dance in 4/4 time.

jabo/jaleo   Spanish dance for solo performer in a slow triple rhythm.

jarabe   Spanish tap dance.

jig   Lively British folk dance, usually in 6/8 time.

jitterbug   Energetic dance, popular in the 1940s, performed chiefly to swing music.

jive   Lively and jerky dance performed to jazz and, later, to rock and roll, popular in the 1940s and 1950s. Nowadays a generic term for any lively dance.

joropo   Latin dance in rapid 3/4 time.

jota   Spanish dance in rapid triple time with castanets and accompanied by guitar and voice.

krakoviak   Polish dance from Krakow district, in lively 2/4 time.

kujawiak   Polish dance for two, slower variant of the mazurka.

lambada   Fast erotic Brazilian dance in which couples frequently touch hips. (lit: A beating)

lancer   Quadrille for 8 or 16 pairs, popular in 19th-century England.

Ländler   Traditional couple dance of Bavaria and Alpine Austria which greatly influenced the evolution of the waltz.

lezginka   Dance of the Lezghins, a Muslim tribe on the Iran border.

loure   French dance, similar to a gigue but slower and graver, usually with bagpipe accompaniment.

malagueña   Spanish dance from Málaga and Murcia, similar to fandango and exported to Mexico by Spanish settlers.

mambo   Latin American ballroom dance.

matelotte   Dutch sailors' dance similar to hornpipe but danced in clogs, with arms interlinked behind the dancers' backs.

maxixe   Brazilian dance, precursor of the tango.

mazurka   Polish national dance in triple time.

merengue   Latin American ballroom dance.

minuet   Stately court dance of 17th century in triple time. The style was adopted by classical composers in suites and overtures, and as third movement of symphonies and quartets.

morris   English folk dance for men with accompaniment of fiddle, tabor, pipe, concertina and accordion, long associated with Whitsuntide. The dancers wear bells on their knees and often represent characters, e.g. the Fool or the Queen of the May.

musette   Dance with a drone bass accompaniment.

nachtanz (after-dance)   Term applied to the second of the two dance tunes which were commonly paired from the 15th to 16th centuries, i.e. pavane and salliard, sarabande and gigue, and passamezzo and salfarello.

new Jack swing   Type of funk dance, often with rap.

paso doble   Spanish dance with double steps in rapid 2/4 time.

passacaglia   Almost indistinguishable from the chaconne in its slow triple-time steps.

passamezzo   Italian dance of the 16th and 17th centuries, similar to pavane but faster and less serious.

passepied   Lively minuet of Breton origin in triple time and popular in the 17th century.

pavane   Slow, stately dance of Spanish origin, often danced in conjunction with the galliard.

polka   Bohemian dance, popular in 19th century and comprising three steps and a hop in fast duple time.

polonaise   Polish dance in 3/4 time performed as a march in a ceremonial style.

polska   Scandinavian dance in simple triple time that derives from the Mazurka and dates from the union of the Polish and Swedish crowns (1587).

quadrille   Square dance in five movements, for four or more couples.

quick-step   Fast version of the foxtrot. Also a lively march in 2/4, also known as a quick march.

rant   Old English 17th-century dance of the jig variety, originating in the north of England and Scotland.

redowa   Bohemian dance resembling the Polish mazurka.

rigaudon (rigadoon)   Light and graceful dance performed in 4/4 time and in a lively spirit, originating in Provence.

rondeña   Fandango of southern Spain, named after Ronda in Andalusia.

rueda   Spanish round dance in quintuple time, popular in Castile.

rumba   Cuban dance in 8/8 time, originating in the 1920s and extending into the jazz age and into ballroom dancing.

running set   English folk dance still popular in the Appalachian mountains of America.

salsa   Latin American dance style combining Latin rhythms with rock.

saltarello   Traditional Italian dance usually in compound duple time and as the name suggests incorporates a series of jumps and leaps.

samba   Lively, modern ballroom dance from Brazil, developed from the maxixe. The samba was popularized in Britain in the 1940s and 1950s by Edmundo Ros.

saraband(e)   Originating in 17th century Spain and performed in slow, dignified triple metre.

sardana   National dance of Catalonia performed to the accompaniment of the fluvial.

schottische (Scottish)   A 19th-century German dance resembling a slow polka. Introduced to England in 1848 and known as the 'German polka'.

seguidilla   Andalusian national dance in fast triple metre.

Sir Roger de Coverley   English country dance of uncertain origin.

springer   Norwegian folk dance in 3/4 time.

Strathspey   Scottish dance, slower than a reel, in 4/4 time using the Scotch snap rhythm.

tango   Syncopated, faster version of habañera, originating in Argentina *c.* 1900; characterised by long gliding steps and sudden pauses.

tarantella   Neapolitan peasant dance in 6/8 time.

tirana   Spanish song/dance in 6/8 time, usually to guitar accompaniment; popular in Andalusia.

torch Dance (Fackeltanz)   More often a torchlight procession to music, usually performed at weddings.

trepak   Quick Russian dance in 2/4 time, most often associated with Cossacks.

veleta (valeta)   Ballroom dance in triple-time. (Lit. weather-vane)

verbunkos   Hungarian soldiers' dance used in the late 18th century to attract recruits for the army.

volta   Lively Italian dance resembling a galliard and popular in the 16th and 17th centuries. Aslo known as lavolta. Britten's *Gloriana* includes a volta.

waltz   Developed from the ländler around 1800 and performed in triple time whilst couples spin around the dance floor.

zamba   Argentinian scarf dance (originated in Peru) in 6/8 time.

zapateado   Spanish dance in triple time, characterised by rhythmic heel stamping.

zortziko   Basque folk dance in 5/4 time, similar to the rueda.

zydeco   Style of popular dance music that mixes cajun and Afro-Caribbean with rhythm and blues.

Organ Stops

Two types are flue pipes and reed pipes. Pipes may vary from 32 feet in length to less than an inch, giving the organ a range of nine octaves, larger than any other instrument. Below are listed some common stops.

Aeolina	Eighteenth	Jubal	Octavin	Seventeenth
Amoroso	Eleventh	Jula	Oiseau	Seventy-first
Bassoon	Eoline	Jungfernstime	Open Diapason	Third
Bible-Regal	Fernflöte (Distant	Keen Strings	Ottavina	Thirty-first
Bird Whistle	Flute)	Keraulophon	Parade Drum	Thunder
Block-flute	Fifteenth	Kerophone	Parforce	Tibia
Canary	Flageolet	Kleine Mixture	Pfeife	Twelfth
Carillon	Flûte à Pavillon	Koppel	Phoneuma	Tympani
Celesta	Forty-third	Labial Oboe	Piano	Ucceli
Clarabella	Furniture	Largo	Piccolo	Unda Maris (Wave
Clarinet Flute	Gamba	Larigot	Plein Jeu	of the Sea)
Clarion	Gedackt	Ludwigtone	Point-Flute	Untersatz
Cor de Nuit	Gemshorn	Magnaton	Portunal	Vidula
Corno di Bassetto	Grave Mixture	Major Bass	Quadragesima	Viola di Samba
Corno Dolce	Grobregal	Major Flute	Quincena	Vox Angelica
Cornopean	Hahn	Marimba	Quint	Vox Humana
Cor-Oboe	Harmonic Bass	Melodia	Racket	Wald Quint
Cremona	Harmonic Flute	Melophone	Rain	Woodland Flute
Crumhorn	Harmonic Piccolo	Mixture Stop	Reed Flute	Xylophone
Cuckoo	Harp	Montre	Resultant	Zauberflöte
Cymbel	Hautboy	Musette	Sackbut	Ziflot
Diaphone	Hohlflöte	Night Horn	Sadt	Zimbelstern
Docena	Horn Diapason	Nightingale	Salamine	Zünk
Doppelflöte	Hummel	Nineteenth	Salicional	
Dulciana Mixture	Infra Bass	Ninth	Scarf	
Duophone	Italian Principal	None	Septime	
Echo Gamba	Iula	Oboe	Serpent	

MUSIC CLASSICAL

Ballet Dancers and Choreographers

Alvin Ailey Jr (1931–89)	Mats Elk (1945–)	Mikhail Mordkin (1880–1944)
Alicia Alonso (1921–)	Garth Fagan (1940–)	Bronislava Nijinska (1891–1972)
Frederick Ashton (1904–88)	Suzanne Farrell (1945–)	Vaclav Nijinsky (1890–1950)
George Balanchine (1904–83)	Mikhail Fokine (1880–1942)	Alwin Nikolais (1910–93)
Mikhail Baryshnikov (1948–)	Margot Fonteyn (1919–91)	Rudolf Nureyev (1939–93)
Maurice Béjart (1927–)	William Forsythe (1949–)	Gideon Obarzanek (1966–)
Svetlana Beriosova (1932–98)	Loie Fuller (1862–1928)	Anna Pavlova (1885–1931)
David Bintley (1957–)	Martha Graham (1894–1991)	Marius Petipa (1818–1910)
Carlo de Blaisis (1795–1878)	Beryl Grey (1927–)	Roland Petit (1924–)
August Bournonville (1805–79)	Carlotta Grisi (1819–99)	Maya Plisetskya (1925–)
Darcy Bussell (1969–)	Sylvie Guillem (1965–)	Jerome Robbins (1918–98)
Maria Anna de Camargo (1710–70)	Hanya Holm (1893–1992)	Marie Sallé (1707–56)
Enrico Cecchetti (1850–1928)	Doris Humphrey (1895–1958)	Antoinette Sibley (1939–)
Harold Christensen (1904–89)	Kurt Jooss (1901–79)	Maria Taglioni (1808–84)
Lew Christensen (1909–84)	Tamara Karsavina (1885–1978)	Glen Tetley (1926–)
John Cranko (1927–73)	Gelsey Kirkland (1952–)	Twyla Tharp (1941–)
Birgit Cullberg (1908–99)	Jirì Kylàn (1947–)	Antony Tudor (1908–87)
Merce Cunningham (1919–)	Rudolf von Laban (1879–1958)	Galina Ulanova (1910–98)
Patrick Delcroix (1963–)	Serge Lifar (1905–86)	Ninette de Valois (1898–2001)
Agnes De Mille (1905–93)	Paul Lightfoot (1966–)	Auguste Vestris (1760–1842)
Charles-Louis Didelot (1797–1837)	Kenneth MacMillan (1929–1992)	Gaetano Vestris (1729–1808)
Anton Dolin (1904–83)	Natalia Makarova (1940–)	Charles Weidman (1901–75)
Anthony Dowell (1943–)	Hans van Manen (1932–)	Mary Wigman (1886–1973)
Nacho Duato (1957–)	Alicia Markova (1910–2004)	
Isadora Duncan (1878–1927)	Léonide Massine (1896–1979)	

Orchestral Positions
(can vary with conductor's preference)

Section	Position
First violins	Left of conductor and to the right of second violins
Second violins	Left of first violins and in front but slightly left of conductor
Cellos	Right of conductor and to the left of the violas
Violas	Right of cellos and in front but slightly right of the conductor
Double basses	Behind the violas and cellos
Trumpets	Behind the double basses and double bassoons
Horns	Behind the clarinets and bassoons
Harp	Behind the bass clarinet and in front of percussion
Piccolo	Left of second violin and in front of bass clarinet
Flutes	Left of piccolo and in front of clarinets
Cor anglais	Right of double basses and back of violas
Oboes	Right of cor anglais and left of the flutes
Bassoons	Behind the oboes and in front of the horns
Double bassoon	Behind the cor anglais and in front of the trumpets
Clarinets	Behind the flutes and in front of the horns
Bass clarinet	Behind the piccolo and to the left of second violins
Percussion	Behind the harp and to the right of timpani
Timpani	Behind the horns and between percussion and trombones
Trombones	Behind horns and trumpets
Tuba	Behind trumpets and to the left of trombones

NB: All positions are viewed relative to the section and not the front.

Master of the King's/Queen's Music

1625	Nicholas Lanier		1848	George Frederick Anderson
1666	Louis Grabu		1870	William George Cusins
1674	Nicholas Staggins		1893	Walter Parratt
1700	John Eccles		1924	Edward Elgar
1735	Maurice Greene		1934	Walford Davies
1755	William Boyce		1942	Arnold Bax
1779	John Stanley		1953	Arthur Bliss
1786	William Parsons		1975	Malcolm Williamson (died 2 March 2003)
1817	William Shield		2004	Peter Maxwell Davies
1834	Christian Kramer			

Classical Works

Music	Composer
Abegg Variations	Robert Schumann
Academic Festival Overture	Johannes Brahms
An Alpine Symphony	Richard Strauss
Also sprach Zarathustra (Thus Spake Zoroaster)	Richard Strauss
Alto Rhapsody	Johannes Brahams
The Apostles (oratorio)	Edward Elgar
Appassionata Sonata	Ludwig van Beethoven
Archduke Trio	Ludwig van Beethoven
Ariana a Naxos (cantata)	Franz Joseph Haydn
The Art of Fugue	Johann Sebastian Bach
Asrael (symphony)	Josef Suk
Aurora's Wedding	Pyotr Tchaikovsky
Bergomask Suite	Claude Debussy
Brandenburg Concertos	Johann Sebastian Bach
El Capitán (march)	John Philip Sousa
Capriccio Espagnol	Nikolay Rimsky-Korsakov
Carmina Burana (part 1 of Trionfi trilogy)	Carl Orff
Carnaval	Robert Schumann
Carnival	Antonín Dvořák
The Carnival of Animals	Camille Saint-Saëns
Catulli Carmina (cantata)	Carl Orff
Caucasian Sketches	Mikhail Ippolitov-Ivanov
Celtic Requiem	John Tavener
Chagall Windows	John McCabe
Chamber Symphony (name of two works)	Arnold Schoenberg
Chandos Anthems	George Frederick Handel
A Child of Our Time	Sir Michael Tippett
The Childhood of Christ	Hector Berlioz
Children's Corner	Claude Debussy
A Children's Overture	Roger Quilter
Christmas Oratorio	Johann Sebastian Bach
Clair de Lune	Claude Debussy
The Cloud Messenger	Gustav Holst
Cockaigne (In London Town)	Edward Elgar
Colonel Bogey	Kenneth Alford
Colour Symphony	Arthur Bliss
Concertino Pastorale	John Ireland
Construction in Metal (name of three works)	John Cage
Coronation Mass	Wolfgang Amadeus Mozart
Coronation Ode	Edward Elgar
The Creation	Franz Joseph Haydn
Crown Imperial	William Walton
The Crown of India	Edward Elgar
The Crucifixion	John Stainer
The Curlew (song cycle)	Peter Warlock
The Damnation of Faust	Hector Berlioz
Dance of Death (Totentanz)	Franz Liszt
Danse Macabre	Camille Saint-Saëns
Dante Symphony	Franz Liszt
Davidde Penitente	Wolfgang Amadeus Mozart
Death and the Maiden	Franz Schubert
Death and Transfiguration	Richard Strauss
The Death of Cleopatra	Hector Berlioz
Deborah	George Frederick Handel
Diabelli Variations	Ludwig van Beethoven
The Dream of Gerontius	Edward Elgar
Ebony Concerto	Igor Stravinsky

Music	Composer
Éclats (Fragments)	Pierre Boulez
Egdon Heath	Gustav Holst
Eight Songs for a Mad King	Peter Maxwell Davies
Eine Kleine Nachtmusik (A Little Night Music)	Wolfgang Amadeus Mozart
Elegy For JFK	Igor Stravinsky
Elijah Oratorio	Felix Mendelssohn
Emperor March (Kaisermarsch)	Richard Wagner
Emperor Waltz	Johann Strauss II
The Enclosed Garden	Gabriel Fauré
L'Enfant prodigue (cantata)	Claude Debussy
An English Suite	Parry, Hubert
España	Emmanuel Chabrier
Esther	George Frederick Handel
Façade	William Walton
The Fair Melusina	Felix Mendelssohn
Fanfare for the Common Man	Aaron Copland
Fantasia on a Theme by Thomas Tallis	Ralph Vaughan Williams
Fantasia on a Theme of Handel	Michael Tippett
Fantasia on Christmas Carols	Ralph Vaughan Williams
Fantasia on Greensleeves	Ralph Vaughan Williams
Faust Overture	Richard Wagner
Fêtes galantes	Claude Debussy
Finlandia	Jean Sibelius
Fireworks	Igor Stravinsky
Fireworks Music	George Frederick Handel
Five Tudor Portraits	Ralph Vaughan Williams
The Flight of the Bumble Bee	Nikolay Rimsky-Korsakov
Four Last Songs	Richard Strauss
Four Sea Interludes	Benjamin Britten
The Four Seasons	Antonio Vivaldi
Four Serious Songs	Johannes Brahms
French Suites	Johann Sebastian Bach
Froissart	Edward Elgar
From Stone to Thorn	Peter Maxwell Davies
From the Diary of Virginia Woolf	Dominick Argento
Funeral March of a Marionette	Charles Gounod
The Garden of Fand	Arnold Bax
Gaspard de la Nuit	Maurice Ravel
A German Requiem	Johannes Brahms
The Girl With the Flaxen Hair	Claude Debussy
Gold and Silver (waltz)	Franz Lehár
The Golden Spinning Wheel	Antonín Dvořák
Golliwogg's Cakewalk	Claude Debussy
Good Friday Music	Richard Wagner
Gymnopédies	Erik Satie
Gypsy Songs (Zigeunerlieder)	Johannes Brahms
Habañera	Maurice Ravel
Hail to the Chief	James Sanderson
Hamlet (fantasy overture)	Pyotr Tchaikovsky
Hamlet (symphonic poem)	Franz Liszt

Music	Composer	Music	Composer
Harold in Italy	Hector Berlioz	Lady Radnor's Suite	Hubert Parry
L'Heure Espagnole (The Spanish Hour)	Maurice Ravel	Land of the Mountain and the Flood	Hamish MacCunn
Hiawatha	Samuel Coleridge-Taylor	The Lark Ascending	Ralph Vaughan Williams
Hodie (On This Day)	Ralph Vaughan Williams	The Last Sleep of the Virgin	Jules Massenet
Holberg Suite	Edvard Grieg		
The Holy Boy	John Ireland	Late Swallows	Frederick Delius
Holy Sonnets of John Donne	Benjamin Britten	Lazarus (oratorio)	Franz Schubert
		The Legend of St Elizabeth	Franz Liszt
L'Horizon chimérique	Gabriel Fauré	Lélio, or the Return to Life	Hector Berlioz
Hungarian Dances	Johannes Brahms	Lie Strewn the White Flocks (pastoral)	Arthur Bliss
Hungarian Rhapsodies	Franz Liszt		
The Hymn of Jesus	Gustav Holst	Lieutenant Kijé	Sergey Prokofiev
Hymn of Paradise	Herbert Howells	The Light of Life	Edward Elgar
Hymn to St Magnus	Peter Maxwell Davies	A Lincoln Portrait	Aaron Copland
Hymns from the Rig Veda	Gustav Holst	Little Suite	Claude Debussy
Iberia	Isaac Albéniz	Little Symphony	Charles Gounod
Imaginary Landscape	John Cage	A London Overture	John Ireland
In a Summer Garden	Frederick Delius	A London Symphony	Ralph Vaughan Williams
Indian Diary	Ferruccio Busoni	The Love Feast of the Apostles	Richard Wagner
Indian Fantasy	Ferruccio Busoni		
In Honour of the City	George Dyson	Love-Dreams (Liebesträume)	Franz Liszt
In Honour of the City of London	William Walton		
		Love-Song Waltzes	Johannes Brahms
In the Faery Hills	Arnold Bax	The Magic Island	William Alwyn
In the South	Edward Elgar	Makrokosmos	George Crumb
In the Steppes of Central Asia	Alexander Borodin	Mantra	Karlheinz Stockhausen
		The Mask of Time	Michael Tippett
Invitation to the Dance	Carl Maria Weber	Mass of Christ the King	Malcolm Williamson
In Windsor Forest	Ralph Vaughan Williams	A Mass of Life	Frederick Delius
Irish Symphony	Hamilton Harty	Má Vlast (My Country)	Bedřich Smetana
Islamey	Mily Balakirev	Mazeppa	Franz Liszt
The Island of Joy	Claude Debussy	Memento Vitae (Memory of Life)	Thea Musgrave
The Isle of the Dead	Sergei Rachmaninov		
Israel in Egypt	George Frederick Handel	Mephisto Waltzes	Franz Liszt
Israel Symphony	Ernest Bloch	La Mer (The Sea)	Claude Debussy
Italian Caprice	Pyotr Tchaikovsky	Messiah (oratorio)	George Frederick Handel
Italian Serenade	Hugo Wolf	Metamorphosen	Richard Strauss
Jacob's Ladder	Arnold Schoenberg	A Midsummer Night's Dream (1826)	Felix Mendelssohn
Jamaican Rumba	Arthur Benjamin		
Jeux d'Eau (Fountains)	Maurice Ravel	A Midsummer Night's Dream	Carl Orff (1939)
Jeux d'Enfants (Children's Games)	Georges Bizet		
		Mikrokosmos	Béla Bartók
Joan of Arc at the Stake (oratorio)	Arthur Honegger	The Miraculous Mandarin	Béla Bartók
		Mládí (Youth)	Leoš Janáček
Joan of Arc at the Stake (concert aria)	Franz Liszt	Moby Dick (cantata)	Bernard Herrmann
		Moby Dick (concertato)	Peter Mennin
Johannesburg Festival Overture	William Walton	Moby Dick (symphonic poem)	Douglas Moore
Joshua	George Frederick Handel	Morning Heroes	Arthur Bliss
Judas Maccabaeus	George Frederick Handel	Mother Goose Suite	Maurice Ravel
Judith (oratorio)	Thomas Arne (1761)	Name Day (Namensfeier)	Ludwig van Beethoven
Judith (oratorio)	Hubert Parry (1888)	Natural Histories	Maurice Ravel
Judith Triumphant	Antonio Vivaldi	New England Holidays	Charles Ives
Kakadu Variations	Ludwig van Beethoven	Night and Dreams	Franz Schubert
Kamarinskaya (Wedding Song)	Mikhail Glinka	Night on the Bare Mountain	Modest Mussorgsky
Karelia Suite	Jean Sibelius	Noble and Sentimental Waltzes	Maurice Ravel
Kinderscenen (Scenes From Childhood)	Robert Schumann		
		The Noonday Witch	Antonín Dvořák
King David	Arthur Honegger	Norfolk Rhapsody	Ralph Vaughan Williams
The Kingdom (oratorio)	Edward Elgar	North Country Sketches	Frederick Delius
King of Prussia Quartets	Wolfgang Amadeus Mozart	Nursery Suite	Edward Elgar
		The Oceanides	Jean Sibelius
King Stephen	Ludwig van Beethoven	Ode For St Cecilia's Day	Henry Purcell (1683–92)
Kontakte (Contacts)	Karlheinz Stockhausen	Ode For St Cecilia's Day	George Frederick Handel (1739)
Lachrimae	John Dowland		
Lachrymae	Benjamin Britten	Ode For St Cecilia's Day	Hubert Parry (1889)
Lady in the Dark	Kurt Weill	Ode to Death	Gustav Holst
The Lady of Shalott	Maurice Jacobson	Ode to Napoleon Bonaparte	Arnold Schoenberg
The Lady of Shalott	Phyllis Tate		

Music	Composer	Music	Composer
Odyssey	Nicholas Maw	Russian Easter Festival Overture	Nikolay Rimsky-Korsakov
Oiseaux Exotiques	Olivier Messiaen		
Omar Khayyám	Granville Bantock	Rustic Wedding	Károly Goldmark
On Hearing the First Cuckoo in Spring	Frederick Delius	Rustle of Spring	Christian Sinding
		St Anthony Variations	Johannes Brahms
Orb and Sceptre March	William Walton	St John Passion	Johann Sebastian Bach
Organ Solo Mass	Wolfgang Amadeus Mozart	St Ludmila	Antonín Dvořák
		St Matthew Passion	Johann Sebastian Bach
Orpheus	Franz Liszt	St Nicolas	Benjamin Britten
Othello	Antonín Dvořák	St Paul	Felix Mendelssohn
An Oxford Elegy	Ralph Vaughan Williams	St Paul's Suite	Gustav Holst
Pacific 231	Arthur Honegger	St Thomas Wake	Peter Maxwell Davies
Pan and Syrinx	Carl Nielsen	Samson (oratorio)	George Frederick Handel
Papillons (Butterflies)	Robert Schumann		
Paradise Lost (cantata)	Christopher Steel	Sarnia	John Ireland
Pavane	Gabriel Fauré	Satyricon	John Ireland
Pavane For a Dead Infanta	Maurice Ravel	Scapino	William Walton
Peacock Variations	Zoltán Kodály	Scaramouche	Darius Milhaud
Peasant Cantata	Johann Sebastian Bach	Scenes from the Bavarian Highlands	Edward Elgar
Peer Gynt	Edvard Grieg		
Pelléas et Mélisande	Gabriel Fauré	Scenes From the Saga of King Olaf	Edward Elgar
Pelléas et Mélisande	Arnold Schoenberg		
Pelléas et Mélisande	Jean Sibelius	Scottish Fantasy	Max Bruch
Peter and the Wolf	Sergey Prokofiev	Scythian Suite	Sergey Prokofiev
Phaëton	Camille Saint-Saëns	The Sea	Frank Bridge
Phoebus and Pan	Johann Sebastian Bach	Sea Drift	Frederick Delius
Pierrot Lunaire	Arnold Schoenberg	Sea Fever	John Ireland
Pines of Rome	Ottorino Respighi	Sea Pictures	Edward Elgar
The Planets	Gustav Holst	The Seasons	Franz Joseph Haydn
The Pleasure Dome of Kubla Khan	Charles Griffes	Serenade for Tenor, Horn and Strings	Benjamin Britten
Poet & Peasant Overture	Franz von Suppé	Severn Suite	Edward Elgar
Pohjola's Daughter	Jean Sibelius	Sheherazade	Nikolay Rimsky-Korsakov (1889)
Polovtsian Dances	Alexander Borodin		
Portsmouth Point	William Walton	Shéhérazade	Maurice Ravel (1904)
Prélude à l'Après-midi d'un faune	Claude Debussy	Shepherd Fennel's Dance	Balfour Gardiner
		Shylock	Gabriel Fauré
Préludes	Claude Debussy	Siegfried Idyll	Richard Wagner
Les Préludes	Ferencz Liszt	Simple Symphony	Benjamin Britten
Procession	Karlheinz Stockhausen	Slavonic Dances	Antonín Dvořák
The Prodigal Son	Benjamin Britten	Slavonic Rhapsodies	Antonín Dvořák
The Prodigal Son	Claude Debussy	The Soldier's Tale	Igor Stravinsky
The Prodigal Son (oratorio)	Arthur Sullivan	A Song for the Lord Mayor's Table	William Walton
Prometheus	Franz Liszt	The Song of Sorrow	Gustav Mahler
Queen Mary's Funeral Music	Henry Purcell	The Song of the Earth	Gustav Mahler
		Song of the Flea	Modest Mussorgsky
Quiet City	Aaron Copland	Song of the High Hills	Frederick Delius
Radetzky March	Johann Strauss the Elder	Song of the Young Boys	Karlheinz Stockhausen
Raft of the Medusa, The	Hans Werner Henze	Songs Without Words	Felix Mendelssohn
Rakastava (The Lover)	Jean Sibelius	Songs and Dances of Death	Modest Mussorgsky
Ramifications	György Ligeti		
Rapsodie Espagnole	Franz Liszt	Songs My Mother Taught Me	Antonín Dvořák
Rapsodie Espagnole (including Habañera)	Maurice Ravel		
		Songs of Travel	Ralph Vaughan Williams
Renard (The Fox)	Igor Stravinsky	The Sorcerer's Apprentice (based on Goethe poem)	Paul Dukas
Rhapsody in Blue	George Gershwin		
Rhapsody on a Theme of Paganini	Sergei Rachmaninov		
		The Spectre's Bride	Antonín Dvořák
Roman Festivals	Ottorino Respighi	The Spirit of England	Edward Elgar
Romeo and Juliet (fantasy overture)	Pyotr Tchaikovsky	Spitfire Prelude and Fugue	William Walton
		A Spring Symphony	Benjamin Britten
Romeo and Juliet (symphony)	Hector Berlioz	Spring (Printemps)	Claude Debussy
		The Starlight Express	Edward Elgar
Roses From the South	Johann Strauss II	La Stravaganza (The Extraordinary)	Antonio Vivaldi
Le Rouet d'Omphale	Camille Saint-Saëns		
Rugby	Arthur Honegger	Street Corner	Alan Rawsthorne
Ruins of Athens	Ludwig van Beethoven	Such a Day, Such a Night	Francis Poulenc
Rule, Britannia! (from the masque Alfred)	Thomas Arne	Suite bergamasque	Claude Debussy
		Summer Night on the River	Frederick Delius
Running Set	Ralph Vaughan Williams		

MUSIC CLASSICAL

Music	Composer
Summer's Last Will and Testament	Constant Lambert
The Swan of Tuonela	Jean Sibelius
Swan Song	Franz Schubert
The Swan-Turner	Paul Hindemith
Symphonia Domestica	Richard Strauss
Symphonic Dances	Sergei Rachmaninov
Symphonic Metamorphosis of Themes by Weber	Paul Hindemith
Symphonie Espagnole	Édouard-Victor-Antoine Lalo
Symphonie Fantastique	Hector Berlioz
Symphonie Funèbre et Triomphale	Hector Berlioz
Symphonies of Wind Instruments	Igor Stravinsky
Symphony in Three Movements	Igor Stravinsky
Symphony of Psalms	Igor Stravinsky
Syrinx	Claude Debussy
Tahiti Trot	Dmitry Shostakovich
Tales from the Vienna Woods	Johann Strauss II
Tam O'Shanter	Malcolm Arnold
Taras Bulba	Leoš Janáček
The Tempest	Pyotr Tchaikovsky (1873)
The Tempest	Jean Sibelius (1925)
Theodora	George Frederick Handel
Three Pear-Shaped Pieces	Erik Satie
Three Places in New England	Charles Ives
Three Screaming Popes	Mark-Anthony Turnage
Till Eulenspiegel	Richard Strauss
Tintagel	Arnold Bax
To the Children	Sergei Rachmaninov
The Tomb of Couperin	Maurice Ravel
Tragic Overture	Johannes Brahms
Transcendental Studies	Franz Liszt
Turandot	Carl Maria Weber
Tzigane (Gypsy)	Maurice Ravel

Music	Composer
Ultimos Ritos (Last Rites)	John Tavener
Ulysses (cantata)	Mátyás Seiber
The Unanswered Question	Charles Ives
Universal Prayer	Andrzej Panufnik
Vallée d'Obermann (Obermann Valley)	Franz Liszt
La Valse (The Waltz)	Maurice Ravel
Valse Triste (Sad Waltz)	Jean Sibelius
Variations on a Rococo Theme	Pyotr Tchaikovsky
Variations on a Theme by Haydn	Johannes Brahms
Variations on a Theme of Frank Bridge	Benjamin Britten
Variations on a Theme of Hindemith	William Walton
Venetian Games	Witold Lutoslawski
A Vision of Aeroplanes	Ralph Vaughan Williams
The Vision of Judgement	Peter Racine Fricker
The Vision of St Augustine	Michael Tippett
Visions Fugitives (Fleeting Visions)	Sergey Prokofiev
The Wand of Youth	Edward Elgar
War Requiem	Benjamin Britten
The Wasps	Ralph Vaughan Williams
Water Music	George Frederick Handel
The Water Sprite	Antonín Dvořák
Wedding Day at Troldhaugen	Edvard Grieg
Welles Raises Kane	Bernard Herrmann
The Whale	John Tavener
The White Peacock	Charles Griffes
Wine	Alban Berg
Winterreise (Winter Journey)	Franz Schubert
The Wood Dove	Antonín Dvořák
The Young Person's Guide to the Orchestra	Benjamin Britten
Zyklus (Cycle)	Karlheinz Stockhausen

Musical Instructions

a cappella In the chapel style (unaccompanied).

accarezzevole Caressingly.

accelerando Becoming faster.

ad libitum At will, improvised.

adagietto Not quite as slow as adagio.

adagio At ease. Slow tempo between largo (slower) and andante (faster).

adagissimo Very slow.

addolorato Sorrowfully.

à demi-jeu With half the power.

à demi-voix With half the voice, whispered.

affábile Gently, pleasingly.

afflito Sorrowfully, mournfully, sadly.

affrettando Hurrying.

allegramente Brightly, gaily.

allegretto Moderately quick.

allegro Quick.

ancora Repeat, again.

andante Moving along, flowing (slowish but not slow).

andantino Diminutive of andante although nowadays usually means a little faster.

arcato Bowed.

arpeggio Playing of the notes of a chord individually in quick succession.

ballabile In a dance style.

bariolage Rapid alternation of open and stopped strings in violin playing.

barré Playing a chord on the guitar with finger across all strings raising their pitch equally.

bisbigliando Both hands playing adjacent strings of harp repeatedly pianissimo.

bouche fermée Closed-mouth singing, i.e. humming.

brio Vigour, spirit.

calando Diminishing gradually – softer and slower.

calcando Quickening gradually (literally, trampling).

col legno With the wood; using the stick part of the bow to strike the string.

common time 4/4 metre.

comodo Leisurely, moderate speed.

con brio With vigour.

con fuoco With fire; using both force and speed.

con lancio With verve.

con sordini On stringed instruments – with mutes; on keyboard instruments – with dampers.

coperti   Covered; relates to drums being muted by being covered with a cloth.

crescendo   Becoming louder.

da capo   From the beginning (literally, from the head).

dal segno   From the sign, meaning return to the sign and repeat.

diminuendo   Becoming quieter.

diminution   Opposite of augmentation, i.e shortening of the time-values of notes of melodic parts.

dolce   Sweet, with an implication of 'soft'.

forte   Loudly.

fortissimo   Very loudly.

gedämpft (damped)   Therefore muted for strings and horns; muffled for drums; soft-pedalled for piano.

giocoso   Merry, playful.

grazioso   Graceful.

jeté (flung)   Bowing technique whereby the upper part of the bow is bounced on the string.

larghetto   Slow tempo, a little faster than largo.

largo   Broad, slow tempo.

legato   Smoothly, with no breaks between successive notes.

lento   Slow.

maestoso   Majestically or stately.

martelé (hammered)   Playing the violin with short strokes and never lifting the bow from the strings.

mezza voce   Subdued tone between piano and forte (literally, middle voice).

moderato   Moderate pace.

morendo   Dying away, fading.

muta   Direction to change keys, frequently found in timpani and horn parts.

piacere (pleasure)   At the performer's discretion.

pianissimo (pp)   Very soft.

pianississimo (ppp)   Very, very soft.

piano (p)   Soft.

pianoforte   Soft-loud.

pizzicato (pinched)   On string instruments, plucking the string.

poco a poco   Little by little, gradually.

portamento   Carrying, i.e. the carrying of the sound from one note to another (very legato).

portato   Halfway between staccato and legato.

prestissimo   Very, very fast; the fastest tempo.

presto   Fast.

rake   On guitar, dragging the pick across muted strings in an arpeggiated fashion.

rallentando   Becoming gradually slower.

ritardando   Delaying, becoming gradually slower.

rubato (robbed)   Freely slowing down and speeding up the tempo without changing the basic pulse.

saltato (saltando)   Bowing technique where the bow is bounced lightly on the string. Means 'jumping'.

scherzando (scherzhaft)   Playful, light-hearted.

scherzo   Piece in a lively tempo; 'joke'.

sostenuto   Sustained.

sotto voce   Under the voice, in a quiet soft voice.

spiccato (detached)   Bouncing the bow on the strings.

stringendo   Tightening, increasing the tension by hurrying the tempo.

strophic   Describes a song that has identical music in each verse.

subito   Suddenly, at once.

sul ponticello   On the bridge: playing a stringed instrument with the bow as near as possible to the bridge.

sul tasto   Instruction to take the bow over the fingerboard. Means 'on the fingerboard'.

sur la touche   Bow over the fingerboard. Means 'on the touch', synonymous with *sul tasto*.

susurrando   Whispering, murmuring.

tacet   Stop playing and be silent.

tutti (all)   Instruction for the whole orchestra to play.

una corda   One string, i.e. the use of the soft pedal which causes the hammers of a piano to.strike only one string per note instead of three.

vibrato   Rapid alteration of pitch or intensity of a note to impart 'expression'.

vivace   Vivacious, i.e. fast and lively.

MUSIC CLASSICAL

Names and Nicknames of Symphonies

The Age of Anxiety	Bernstein's Symphony No. 2
Alleluiasymphonie	Haydn's Symphony No. 30 in C
America	Bloch's 'Epic Rhapsody' Symphony (1926)
Andante Cantabile	Tchaikovsky's Symphony No. 5 in E minor (2nd movement)
Antar	Rimsky-Korsakov's Symphony No. 2 Op. 9 (Oriental Suite)
Antarctica	Vaughan Williams's Symphony No. 7
Apocalyptic	Bruckner's Symphony No. 7
Asrael	Suk's Symphony No. 2 in C minor Op. 27
Babi Yar	Shostakovich's Symphony No. 13 in B flat minor Op. 113
The Bear (L'Ours)	Haydn's Symphony No. 82 in C
The Bells of Zlonice	Dvořák's Symphony No. 1 in C minor Op. 3
The Bell	Khachaturian's Symphony No. 2 in A minor
The Camp Meeting	Ives's Symphony No. 3
Capricieuse	Berwald's Symphony No. 2
Celestial Railroad	Ives's Symphony No. 4, 2nd movement, fantasy piece for piano
Cello Symphony	Britten's Opus 68 Symphony dedicated to Rostropovich
La Chasse (The Hunt)	Haydn's Symphony No. 73 in D
Choral	Beethoven's Symphony No. 9 in D minor Op. 125
Christmas	Haydn's Symphony No. 26 in D minor
Classical	Prokofiev's Symphony No. 1 in D Op. 25
Clock	Haydn's Symphony No. 101 in D
Decoration Day	Ives's 2nd Movement of his 'New England Holidays'
Deliciae Basiliensis	Honegger's Symphony No. 4
The Distraught Man	Haydn's Symphony No. 60 in C major

The Divine Poem	Scriabin's Symphony No. 3 in C minor Op. 43
Le Double	Dutilleux's Symphony No. 3
Dreams of Gandalf	Sallinen's Symphony No. 7
Drumroll	Haydn's Symphony No. 103 in E flat
Eroica	Beethoven's Symphony No. 3 in E flat major
Espansiva (Expansive)	Nielsen's Symphony No. 3
Fantaisies	Martinu's Symphony No. 6
Farewell (Abschied)	Haydn's Symphony No. 45 in F sharp minor
Fate	Beethoven's Symphony No. 5 in C minor Op. 67
Fate	Tchaikovsky's Symphony No. 4 in F minor Op. 36
Festive	Smetana's Symphony in E
Fire	Haydn's Symphony No. 59 in A
First of May	Shostakovich's Symphony No. 3 in E flat Op. 20
Four Seasons	Malipiero's Symphony No. 1
The Four Temperaments	Nielsen's Symphony No. 2 in C minor Op. 16
Fourth of July	Ives's 3rd Movement of his 'New England Holidays'
From a New Zealand Diary	Sallinen's Symphony No. 6
From the New World	Dvořák's Symphony No. 9 (formerly No. 5) in E minor
Funeral March	Beethoven's Symphony No. 3 in E flat Op. 55 (2nd movement)
Gothic	Havergal Brian's Symphony No. 1 in D minor
Great C Major	Schubert's Symphony No. 9 in C major
Great G Minor	Mozart's Symphony No. 40 in G minor, K550
Haffner	Mozart's Symphony No. 35 in D, K385
Heavenly Length	Schubert's Symphony No. 9 in C major
The Hen	Haydn's Symphony No. 83 in G minor
Holidays	Ives's Symphony (1904–13)
Horn Signal	Haydn's Symphony No. 31 in D
The Hunt (La Chasse)	Haydn's Symphony No. 73 in D
Hydriotaphia	Alwyn's Symphony No. 5
Hymn of Praise	Mendelssohn's Symphony No. 2 in B flat Op. 52
Ilya Murometz	Glière's Symphony No. 3
Imperial	Haydn's Symphony No. 53 in D
The Inextinguishable	Nielsen's Symphony No. 4, Op. 29
Irish	Stanford's Symphony No. 3 in F minor Op. 28
Irish	Sullivan's Symphony in E minor
Israel	Bloch's Symphony (1916)
Italian	Mendelssohn's Symphony No. 4 in A major Op. 90
Jeremiah	Bernstein's Symphony No. 1
Jupiter	Mozart's Symphony No. 41 in C major, K551
Kaddish	Bernstein's Symphony No. 3
Lamentations	Haydn's Symphony No. 26 in D minor
Largo	Dvořák's Symphony No. 5 (No. 9) in E minor (2nd movement)
Loudon	Haydn's Symphony No. 69 in C
Leningrad	Shostakovich's Symphony No. 7 in C major Op. 60
Linz	Mozart's Symphony No. 36 in C, K425
Little C Major	Schubert's Symphony No. 6 in C major
Little G Minor	Mozart's Symphony No. 25 in G minor, K183
Little Russian	Tchaikovsky's Symphony No. 2 in C minor Op. 17
Liturgique	Honegger's Symphony No. 3
Lobgesang (Hymn of Praise)	Mendelssohn's Symphony No. 2 in B flat Op. 52
London	Vaughan Williams's Symphony No. 2
London	Haydn's Symphony No. 104 in D
London Symphonies	Haydn's Symphonies Nos 93–104
Maria Theresia	Haydn's Symphony No. 48 in C
Mathis der Maler	Hindemith's Symphony (1934)
Le Matin (Morning)	Haydn's Symphony No. 6 in D
Mercury	Haydn's Symphony No. 43 in E flat
Michelangelo	Kancheli's Symphony No. 4
Le Midi (Noon)	Haydn's Symphony No. 7 in C
Military	Haydn's Symphony No. 100 in G
Miracle	Haydn's Symphony No. 96 in D
Mysterious Mountain	Hovahness' Symphony No. 2 Op. 132
New England Holidays	Ives's Symphony (1904–13)
New World	Dvořák's Symphony No. 9 (formerly No. 5) in E minor
1917 Symphony	Shostakovich's Symphony No. 12 in D minor
Nordic	Hanson's Symphony No. 1 in E minor Op. 21
Die Nullte	Bruckner's Symphony No. 0 in D minor
October	Shostakovichs' Symphony No. 2 in B major Op. 14
Ode to Joy	Beethoven's Symphony No. 9 in D Op. 125 (4th movement)
Organ	Saint-Saëns' Symphony No. 3 in C minor
L'Ours (The Bear)	Haydn's Symphony No. 82 in C
Oxford	Haydn's Symphony No. 92 in G

Palindrome	Haydn's Symphony No. 47 in G
Paris	Mozart's Symphony No. 31 in D, K297
Paris Symphonies	Haydn's Symphonies Nos 82–87
La Passione	Haydn's Symphony No. 49 in F minor
Pastoral	Beethoven's Symphony No. 6 in F major
Pastoral	Vaughan Williams's Symphony No. 3
Pathétique	Tchaikovsky's Symphony No. 6 in B minor Op. 74
The Philosopher	Haydn's Symphony No. 22 in E flat
Pittsburgh	Hindemith's Symphony (1958)
Polish	Tchaikovsky's Symphony No. 3 in D Op. 29
La Poule (The Hen)	Haydn's Symphony No. 83 in G minor
Prague	Mozart's Symphony No. 38 in D, K504
Reformation	Mendelssohn's Symphony No. 5 in D minor
La Reine (The Queen)	Haydn's Symphony No. 85 in B flat
Requiem	Hanson's Symphony No. 4 Op. 34
Resurrection	Mahler's Symphony No. 2 in C minor
Resurrection	Rubbra's Symphony No. 9
Rhenish	Schumann's Symphony No. 3 in E flat major Op. 97
Romantic	Bruckner's Symphony No. 4 in E Flat major
Romantic	Hanson's Symphony No. 2 Op. 30
La Roxelane	Haydn's Symphony No. 63 in C major
Rustic Wedding	Goldmark's Symphony Op. 26
St Florian	Schnittke's Symphony No. 2
Salomon	Haydn's Symphony No. 104 in D
Salomon Symphonies	Haydn's Symphonies Nos 93–104
Schoolmaster	Haydn's Symphony No. 55 in E flat
Scotch (Scottish)	Mendelssohn's Symphony No. 3 in A minor Op. 56
Sea	Hanson's Symphony No. 7
Sea	Vaughan Williams's Symphony No. 1 in C
The Seasons	Spohr's Symphony No. 9 in B minor
Serena	Hindemith's Symphony (1946)
Sérieuse	Berwald's Symphony No. 1
Das Siegeslied	Brian's Symphony No. 4
Simple	Britten's Symphony Op. 4
Simple	Nielsen's Symphony No. 6
Sinfonia Antarctica	See Antarctica
Sinfonia Boreale	Holmboe's Symphony No. 8
Sinfonia da Requiem	Britten's Symphony Op. 20
Sinfonia di Sfere	Panufnik's Symphony No. 5
Sinfonia Elegiaca	Malipiero's Symphony No. 2
Sinfonia Elegiaca	Panufnik's Symphony No. 2
Sinfonia Mistica	Panufnik's Symphony No. 6
Sinfonia Rustica	Holmboe's Symphony No. 3
Sinfonia Rustica	Panufnik's Symphony No. 1
Sinfonia Sacra	Holmboe's Symphony No. 4
Sinfonia Sacra	Panufnik's Symphony No. 3
Sinfonia Sacra	Rubbra's Symphony No. 9
Sinfonia Votiva	Panufnik's Symphony No. 8
Singulière	Berwald's Symphony No. 3 in C minor
Le Soir (Evening)	Haydn's Symphony No. 8 in G
Song in the Night	Szymanowski's Symphony No. 3
Spring	Schumann's Symphony No. 1 in B flat Op. 38
Stimmen Verstummen	Gubaildulina's Symphony (1986)
Study	Bruckner's Symphony in F minor
Summer Music	Mathias's Symphony No. 2
Surprise	Haydn's Symphony No. 94 in G major
Symphony of a Thousand	Mahler's Symphony No. 8 in E flat major
Tempest	Haydn's Symphony No. 8 in G, Fourth movement
Tempora Mutantur	Haydn's Symphony No. 64 in A
Thanksgiving Day	Ives's 4th movement of his 'New England Holidays'
Titan	Mahler's Symphony No. 1 in D major
To the Memory of Lenin	Shostakovich's Symphony No. 12 in D minor Op. 112
Tragic	Schubert's Symphony No. 4 in C minor
Trauer (Mourning)	Haydn's Symphony No. 44 in E minor
Di Tre Re	Honegger's Symphony No. 5
Triumph	Smetana's Symphony in E
Ukrainian	Tchaikovsky's Symphony No. 2 in C minor
Unfinished	Schubert's Symphony No. 8 in B minor
Vigil	MacMillan's Symphony (1997)
Wagner	Bruckner's Symphony No. 3 in D minor
Washington Mosaics	Sallinen's Symphony No. 5
Washington's Birthday	Ives's 1st movement of his 'New England Holidays'

MUSIC CLASSICAL

Waves	Kernis' Symphony No. 1
Winter Daydreams	Tchaikovsky's Symphony No. 1 in G minor Op. 13
The Year 1905	Shostakovich's Symphony No. 11 in G minor Op. 103
The Year 1917	Shostakovich's Symphony No. 12 in D minor Op. 112

Names and Nicknames of Symphonies (by composer)

Alwyn's Symphony No. 5	*Hydriotaphia*
Beethoven's Symphony No. 3 in E flat major	*Eroica*
Beethoven's Symphony No. 3 in E flat Op. 55 (2nd movement)	*Funeral March*
Beethoven's Symphony No. 5 in C minor Op. 67	*Fate*
Beethoven's Symphony No. 6 in F major	*Pastoral*
Beethoven's Symphony No. 9 in D minor Op. 125	*Choral*
Beethoven's Symphony No. 9 in D Op. 125 (4th movement)	*Ode to Joy*
Bernstein's Symphony No. 1	*Jeremiah*
Bernstein's Symphony No. 2	*The Age of Anxiety*
Bernstein's Symphony No. 3	*Kaddish*
Berwald's Symphony No. 1	*Sérieuse*
Berwald's Symphony No. 2	*Capricieuse*
Berwald's Symphony No. 3 in C major	*Singulière*
Bloch's 'Epic Rhapsody' Symphony (1926)	*America*
Bloch's Symphony (1916)	*Israel*
Brian's Symphony No. 1 in D minor	*Gothic*
Brian's Symphony No. 4	*Das Siegeslied*
Britten's Op. 68 dedicated to Rostropovich	*Cello Symphony*
Britten's Symphony Op. 20	*Sinfonia da Requiem*
Britten's Symphony Op. 4	*Simple*
Bruckner's Symphony in F minor	*Study*
Bruckner's Symphony No. 0 in D minor	*Die Nullte*
Bruckner's Symphony No. 3 in D minor	*Wagner*
Bruckner's Symphony No. 4 in E flat major	*Romantic*
Bruckner's Symphony No. 7	*Apocalyptic*
Dutilleux's Symphony No. 3	*Le Double*
Dvořák's Symphony No. 1 in C minor Op. 3	*The Bells of Zlonice*
Dvořák's Symphony No. 5 (No. 9) in E minor (2nd movement)	*Largo*
Dvořák's Symphony No. 9 (formerly No. 5) in E minor	*From the New World*
Glière's No. 3	*Ilya Murometz*
Goldmark's Symphony Op. 26	*Rustic Wedding*
Gubaildulina's Symphony (1986)	*Stimmen Verstummen*
Hanson's Symphony No. 1 in E minor Op. 21	*Nordic*
Hanson's Symphony No. 2 Op. 30	*Romantic*
Hanson's Symphony No. 4 Op. 34	*Requiem*
Hanson's Symphony No. 7	*Sea*
Haydn's Symphony No. 6 in D	*Le Matin (Morning)*
Haydn's Symphony No. 7 in C	*Le Midi (Noon)*
Haydn's Symphony No. 8 in G	*Le Soir (Evening)*
Haydn's Symphony No. 8 in G (4th movement)	*Tempest*
Haydn's Symphony No. 22 in E flat	*The Philosopher*
Haydn's Symphony No. 26 in D minor	*Christmas*
Haydn's Symphony No. 26 in D minor	*Lamentation*
Haydn's Symphony No. 30 in C	*Alleluiasymphonie*
Haydn's Symphony No. 31 in D	*Horn Signal*
Haydn's Symphony No. 43 in E flat	*Mercury*
Haydn's Symphony No. 44 in E minor	*Trauer (Mourning)*
Haydn's Symphony No. 45 in F sharp minor	*Farewell (Abschied)*
Haydn's Symphony No. 47 in G	*Palindrome*
Haydn's Symphony No. 48 in C	*Maria Theresia*
Haydn's Symphony No. 49 in F minor	*La Passione*
Haydn's Symphony No. 53 in D	*Imperial*
Haydn's Symphony No. 55 in E flat	*Schoolmaster*
Haydn's Symphony No. 59 in A	*Fire*
Haydn's Symphony No. 60 in C major	*The Distraught Man*
Haydn's Symphony No. 63 in C major	*La Roxolane*
Haydn's Symphony No. 64 in A	*Tempora Mutantur*
Haydn's Symphony No. 69 in C	*Laudon*
Haydn's Symphony No. 73 in D	*The Hunt (La Chasse)*
Haydn's Symphonies Nos 82–87	*Paris Symphonies*
Haydn's Symphony No. 82 in C	*The Bear (L'Ours)*
Haydn's Symphony No. 83 in G minor	*The Hen (La Poule)*
Haydn's Symphony No. 85 in B flat	*La Reine (The Queen)*

Haydn's Symphony No. 92 in G	Oxford
Haydn's Symphonies Nos 93–104	London Symphonies
Haydn's Symphonies Nos 93–104	Salomon Symphonies
Haydn's Symphony No. 94 in G major	Surprise
Haydn's Symphony No. 96 in D	Miracle
Haydn's Symphony No. 100 in G	Military
Haydn's Symphony No. 101 in D	Clock
Haydn's Symphony No. 103 in E flat	Drumroll
Haydn's Symphony No. 104 in D	London
Haydn's Symphony No. 104 in D	Salomon
Hindemith's Symphony (1934)	Mathis der Maler
Hindemith's Symphony (1946)	Serena
Hindemith's Symphony (1958)	Pittsburgh
Holmboe's Symphony No. 3	Sinfonia Rustica
Holmboe's Symphony No. 4	Sinfonia Sacra
Holmboe's Symphony No. 8	Sinfonia Boreale
Honegger's Symphony No. 3	Liturgique
Honegger's Symphony No. 4	Deliciae Basiliensis
Honegger's Symphony No. 5	Di Tre Re
Hovahness' Symphony No. 2 Op. 132	Mysterious Mountain
Ives's 1st movement of his 'New England Holidays'	Washington's Birthday
Ives's 2nd movement of his 'New England Holidays'	Decoration Day
Ives's 3rd movement of his 'New England Holidays'	Fourth of July
Ives's 4th movement of his 'New England Holidays'	Thanksgiving Day
Ives's Symphony No. 3	The Camp Meeting
Ives's Symphony No. 4, 2nd movement; fantasy piece for piano	Celestial Railroad
Ives's Symphony (1904–13)	Holidays
Ives's Symphony (1904–13)	New England Holidays
Kanchell's Symphony No. 4	Michelangelo
Kernis's Symphony No. 1	Waves
Khachaturian's Symphony No. 2 in A minor	The Bell
MacMillan's Symphony (1997)	Vigil
Mahler's Symphony No. 1 in D major	Titan
Mahler's Symphony No. 2 in C minor	Resurrection
Mahler's Symphony No. 8 in E flat major	Symphony of a Thousand
Malipiero's Symphony No. 1	Four Seasons
Malipiero's Symphony No. 2	Sinfonia Elegiaca
Martinu's Symphony No. 6	Fantaisies
Mathias's Symphony No. 2	Summer Music
Mendelssohn's Symphony No. 2 in B flat Op. 52	Lobgesang (Hymn of Praise)
Mendelssohn's Symphony No. 3 in A minor Op. 56	Scotch (Scottish)
Mendelssohn's Symphony No. 4 in A major Op. 90	Italian
Mendelssohn's Symphony No. 5 in D minor	Reformation
Mozart's Symphony No. 25 in G minor, K183	Little G Minor
Mozart's Symphony No. 31 in D, K297	Paris
Mozart's Symphony No. 35 in D, K385	Haffner
Mozart's Symphony No. 36 in C, K425	Linz
Mozart's Symphony No. 38 in D, K504	Prague
Mozart's Symphony No. 40 in G minor, K550	Great G Minor
Mozart's Symphony No. 41 in C major, K551	Jupiter
Nielsen's Symphony No. 2 in C minor Op. 16	The Four Temperaments
Nielsen's Symphony No. 3	Espansiva (Expansive)
Nielsen's Symphony No. 4, Op. 29	The Inextinguishable
Nielsen's Symphony No. 6	Simple
Panufnik's Symphony No. 1	Sinfonia Rustica
Panufnik's Symphony No. 2	Sinfonia Elegiaca
Panufnik's Symphony No. 3	Sinfonia Sacra
Panufnik's Symphony No. 5	Sinfonia di Sfere
Panufnik's Symphony No. 6	Sinfonia Mistica
Panufnik's Symphony No. 8	Sinfonia Votiva
Prokofiev's Symphony No. 1 in D Op. 25	Classical
Rimsky-Korsakov's Symphony No. 2 Op. 9 (Oriental Suite)	Antar
Rubbra's Symphony No. 9	Resurrection
Rubbra's Symphony No. 9	Sinfonia Sacra
Saint-Saëns's Symphony No. 3 in C minor	Organ
Sallinen's Symphony No. 5	Washington Mosaics
Sallinen's Symphony No. 6	From a New Zealand Diary
Sallinen's Symphony No. 7	Dreams of Gandalf
Schnittke's Symphony No. 2	St Florian
Schubert's Symphony No. 4 in C minor	Tragic
Schubert's Symphony No. 6 in C major	Little C Major
Schubert's Symphony No. 8 in B minor	Unfinished

MUSIC CLASSICAL

Schubert's Symphony No. 9 in C major	*Great C Major*
Schubert's Symphony No. 9 in C major, D944	*Heavenly Length*
Schubert's Symphony No. 1 in B flat Op. 38	*Spring*
Schubert's Symphony No. 3 in E flat major Op. 97	*Rhenish*
Scriabin's Symphony No. 3 in C minor Op. 43	*The Divine Poem*
Shostakovich's Symphony No. 2 in B major Op. 14	*October*
Shostakovich's Symphony No. 3 in E flat Op. 20	*First of May*
Shostakovich's Symphony No. 7 in C major Op. 60	*Leningrad*
Shostakovich's Symphony No. 11 in G minor Op. 103	*The Year 1905*
Shostakovich's Symphony No. 12 in D minor Op. 112	*The Year 1917*
Shostakovich's Symphony No. 12 in D minor Op. 12	*To the Memory of Lenin*
Shostakovich's Symphony No. 13 in B flat minor Op. 113	*Babi Yar*
Smetana's Symphony in E	*Festive/Triumph*
Spohr's Symphony No. 9 in B minor	*Seasons*
Stanford's Symphony No. 3 in F minor Op. 28	*Irish*
Suk's Symphony No. 2 in C minor Op. 27	*Asrael*
Sullivan's Symphony in E minor	*Irish*
Szymanowski's Symphony No. 3	*Song in the Night*
Tchaikovsky's Symphony No. 1 in G minor Op. 13	*Winter Daydreams*
Tchaikovsky's Symphony No. 2 in C minor Op. 17	*Little Russian/Ukrainian*
Tchaikovsky's Symphony No. 3 in D Op. 29	*Polish*
Tchaikovsky's Symphony No. 4 in F minor Op. 36	*Fate*
Tchaikovsky's Symphony No. 6 in B minor Op. 74	*Pathétique*
Vaughan Williams's Symphony No. 1 in C	*Sea*
Vaughan Williams's Symphony No. 2	*London*
Vaughan Williams's Symphony No. 3	*Pastoral*
Vaughan Williams's Symphony No. 7	*Antarctica*

Nicknames of Classical Works

Actus Tragicus	Bach's church cantata No. 106 ('God's time is the best')
Adieux Sonata	Beethoven's Piano Sonata No. 26 in E flat major, which he called 'The Farewell'
African	Saint-Saën's Piano Concerto No. 5
Air on the G String	Wilhelmj's arrangement of Bach Suite for Orchestra No. 3 in D (2nd movement)
American Quartet	Dvořák's String Quartet in F Op. 96
Andante Cantabile	Tchaikovsky's String Quartet No. 1 in D Op. 11 (2nd movement)
Appassionata Sonata	Beethoven's Piano Sonata No. 23 in F minor Op. 57
Archduke Trio	Beethoven's Piano Trio in B flat Op. 97, dedicated to Archduke Rudolf of Austria
Arpeggione	Schubert's Sonata in A minor for cello and piano
Basle Concerto	Stravinsky's Concerto in D for strings
Battle Symphony	Beethoven's orchestral work 'Wellington's Victory' Op. 91
The Bell	Haydn's String Quartet in D minor Op. 76 No. 2
The Bird	Haydn's String Quartet in C Op. 33 No. 3
The Black Mass	Scriabin's Piano Sonata No. 9 in F Op. 68
Black-key Étude	Chopin's Étude in G flat major for piano Op. 10 No. 5
Brandenburg Concertos	Bach's 6 concertos for various instruments, BWV 1046–1051
Bridal Chorus	Wagner's chorus from Act 3 of *Lohengrin*
Butterfly	Chopin's Étude in G flat for piano Op. 25 No. 9
Cat Waltz	Chopin's Waltz in F for piano Op. 34 No. 3
Cat's Fugue	Scarlatti's Fugue in G minor for harpsichord
La Chasse	Haydn's String Quartet in B flat Op. 1 No. 1
Chopsticks	Anonymous quick waltz tune for piano, first published in London 1877
Coffee Cantata	Bach's Cantata No. 211
Colas Breugnon	Kabalevsky's opera *The Craftsman of Clamecy*
Concord Sonata	Ives's Piano Sonata No. 2
Contemplation of Nothing Serious	Ives's orchestral piece *Central Park in the Dark in the Good Old Summertime*
Coronation Concerto	Mozart's Piano Concerto No. 26 in D, K537
The Cuckoo and the Nightingale	Handel's second set of six concertos for organ and orchestra
Dance Before the Golden Calf	Schoenberg's climax of Act 2 of his opera *Moses und Aron*
Dance of the Blessed Spirits	Gluck's slow dance in Act 2 of *Orfeo ed Euridice*, noted for its flute solo
Dance of the Comedians	Smetana's dance episode in Act 3 of *The Bartered Bride*, featuring clowns
Dance of the Hours	Episode, frequently played separately, in Act 3 of Ponchielli's *La Gioconda* and representing the conflict between darkness and light
Dance of the Seven Veils	Dance episode during Strauss's opera *Salome*
Dance of the Sylphs	Berlioz's orchestral episode during *La Damnation de Faust*, which forms part of Faust's dream on the banks of the Elbe

Dance of the Tumblers	Rimsky-Korsakov's episode during *The Snow Maiden* in which acrobats dance for the Tsar Berendey
Dead March in Saul	Handel's Funeral March from the oratorio *Saul*
Death and the Maiden	Schubert's String Quartet No. 14 in D minor
Dettingen Te Deum	Handel's *Te Deum* in D
Devil's Trill	Tartini's Violin Sonata in G minor
Diabelli Variations	Beethoven's 33 variations on a waltz by Diabelli in C for piano Op. 120
The Difficult Decision	Beethoven's String Quartet in F Op. 135 (4th movement)
Dissonance Quartet	Mozart's String Quartet No. 19 in C major, K465
Dog Waltz	Chopin's Waltz in D flat for piano Op. 64 No. 1
Dominicus Mass	Mozart's Mass in C, K66
Donkey Quartet	Haydn's String Quartet in D minor Op. 76 No. 2
Dorian Toccata and Fugue	Bach Toccata and Fugue in D minor for organ, BWV 538
A Dream	Haydn's String Quartet in F Op. 50 No. 5 (2nd movement)
Dumbarton Oaks	Stravinsky's Concerto in E flat for chamber ensemble
Dumky Trio	Dvořák's Piano Trio in E minor Op. 90
Ebony	Stravinsky's Concerto for clarinet and jazz band
Edward	Brahms's Ballade in D minor for piano Op. 10 No. 1
Eine Kleine Nachtmusik	Mozart's Divertimento in G for strings, K525
Eine Kleine Trauermusik	Schubert's Nonet in E flat minor for wind instuments
Elegy	Massenet's orchestral selection in E minor from his opera *Les Érinnyes*
Elvira Madigan	Mozart's Piano Concerto No. 21 in C
Emperor Concerto	Beethoven's Piano Concerto No. 5 in E flat major Op. 73
Emperor Quartet	Haydn's String Quartet in C major Op. 76 No. 3
English Suites	Bach's 6 Suites for harpsichord, BWV 806-811
Erdödy Quartets	Haydn's 6 String Quartets
Eroica Variations	Beethoven's 15 Variations and fugue on an Original Theme in E flat major Op. 76 Nos 75–80 for piano
Eyeglass Duo	Beethoven's Duo in E flat for viola and cello
Fall of Warsaw	Chopin's Étude in C minor for piano Op. 10 No. 12
Il Favorito	Vivaldi's Violin Concerto in E minor Op. 11 No. 2
Fiddle Fugue	Bach's Fugue in D minor for organ, BWV 539
Fifths	Haydn's String Quartet in D minor Op. 76 No. 2
Fingal's Cave	Mendelssohn's Overture for orchestra Op. 26, originally named *The Lonely Island*
The Forty-eight	Bach's *Well-Tempered Clavier*
The Four Seasons	Vivaldi's 4 Violin Concertos Op. 8 Nos 1–4
The Four Temperaments	Hindemith's Theme and Variations for string and piano: melancholic, sanguine, phlegmatic, choleric
French Suites	Bach's 6 Suites for harpsichord, BWV 812–817
The Frog	Haydn's String Quartet in D Op. 50 No. 6
From My Life	Smetana's String Quartets No. 1 in E minor (especially) and No. 2 in D minor
Funeral Anthem	Handel's anthem in G minor, *The Ways of Zion Do Mourn*
Funeral March	Chopin's Piano Sonata No. 2 in B flat minor Op. 35 (3rd movement)
Funeral March	Beethoven's Piano Sonata No. 12 in A flat Op. 26 (3rd movement)
Für Elise	Beethoven's Bagatelle in A minor for piano
Il Gardellino	Vivaldi's Flute Concerto in D Op. 10 No. 3
Gassenhauer Trio	Beethoven's Trio in B flat for clarinet, cello and piano Op. 11
German Suites	Bach's set of 6 keyboard partitas
Ghost Trio	Beethoven's Piano Trio in D major Op. 70 No. 1
The Girl With Enamel Eyes	Delibes 3-act ballet *Coppelia*
Goldberg Variations	Bach's Aria with Diverse Variations for harpsichord, BWV 988
Golden Sonata	Purcell's Sonata in F for two violins, viola da gamba and organ
Grand Duo	Schubert's Sonata in C major for piano (4 hands)
Grande Valse Brillante	Chopin's Waltz in E flat for piano Op. 18
Grazer Fantasie	Schubert's Fantasy in C for piano
Great Fugue	Beethoven's Fugue in B flat major for String Quartet Op. 133
Great Organ Mass	Haydn's Mass in E flat, Hob. XXII:4
Grief	Chopin's Étude in E for piano Op. 10 No. 3
Gypsy Rondo	Haydn's Piano Trio in G, Hob. XV:25 (3rd movement)
Haffner Serenade	Mozart's Suite in D major for orchestra, K250
Hallelujah Chorus	Handel's Chorus in D from his oratorio *Messiah*, No. 44
Hallelujah Concerto	Handel's Organ Concerto in B flat Op. 106
Hammerklavier	Beethoven's Piano Sonata No. 29 in B flat major Op. 106
Handel Variations	Brahms's Variations and Fugue on a Theme by Handel in B flat for Piano
Handel's Largo	Handel's aria 'Ombre mai fù', from his opera *Serse* (*Xerxes*)
Harmonious Blacksmith	Handel's Harpsichord Suite No. 5 in E (4th movement) Air with 5 variations
Harmonious Inspiration	Vivaldi's 12 concertos for various instruments Op. 3
Harmony Mass	Haydn's Mass No. 12 in B flat, H XXII:14
Harp Étude	Chopin's Étude in A flat for piano Op. 25 No. 1
Harp Quartet	Beethoven's String Quartet in E flat major Op. 74
Haydn Quartets	Mozart's 6 String Quartets Op. 10, K387–465

MUSIC CLASSICAL

Haydn Variations	Brahms's Variations on a Theme by Joseph Haydn in B flat
The Hebrides	Mendelssohn's Overture for orchestra Op. 26
Heiliger Dankgesang	Beethoven's String Quartet in A minor Op. 132 (3rd movement)
Heiligmesse	Haydn's Mass in B flat, Hob. XXII:10
Hexenmenuet	Haydn's String Quartet in D minor Op. 76 No. 2 (3rd movement)
Hoffmeister Quartet	Mozart's String Quartet in D, K499
Hornpipe (aka Lark)	Haydn's String Quartet in D Op. 64 No. 5
Hornpipe Concerto	Handel's Concerto Grosso in B minor Op. 6, No. 12
Horn Trio	Brahms's Trio in E flat for violin, horn and piano Op. 40
Horseman (aka The Rider)	Haydn's String Quartet in G minor Op. 74 No. 3
Housatonic at Stockbridge	Ives's 'Three Places in New England' (3rd movement)
Humoresque	Dvořák's piano piece in G flat Op. 101 No. 7
Hunt Cantata	Bach Cantata 208 'Was mir behagt, ist nur die munter Jagd!'
The Hunt	Mozart's String Quartet No. 17 in B flat, K458
The Hunt	Haydn's String Quartet in B flat Op. 1 No. 1
Imperial Mass	Haydn's Mass No. 9 in D minor, Hob. XXII:11
Italian Concerto	Bach's Concerto for solo harpsichord, BWV 971
Jesu, Joy of Man's Desiring	Bach's chorale prelude from Cantata 147, 'Herz und Mund und Tat und Leben'
Jeunehomme Concerto	Mozart's Piano Concerto in E flat Op. 33 No. 2
Jig Fugue	Bach's Fugue in G for organ, BWV 577
The Joke	Haydn's String Quartet in E flat Op. 33 No. 2
Jungfernquartette	Haydn's 6 String Quartets Op. 33
Kaiser (aka Emperor)	Haydn's String Quartet in C Op. 76 No. 3
Kamennoi-Ostrov	Rubinstein's piece for piano in F sharp No. 22
Kettledrum Mass (Paukenmesse)	Haydn's Mass No. 7 in C major, Hob. XXII:9
Kreutzer Sonata	Beethoven's Violin Sonata No. 9 in A major Op. 47
Kreutzer Sonata Quartet	Janáček's String Quartet No. 1
Lark (aka Hornpipe)	Haydn's String Quartet in D Op. 64 No. 5
Late Quartets	Beethoven's String Quartets Op. 127, 130–133 and 135
Liebestraum	Liszt's Nocturne in A flat for piano; No. 3 of 3 of that title
Little Fugue in G Minor	Bach's Fugue for organ, BWV 578
Little Organ Mass	Haydn's Mass in B flat No. 5, Hob. XXII:7
Lobkowitz Quartets	Haydn's 2 String Quartets Op. 77 Nos 81–82
La Malinconia	Beethoven's String Quartet in B flat Op. 18 No. 6 (4th movement)
Manzoni Requiem	Verdi's Requiem, in memory of poet Alessandro Manzoni
Marche Militaire	Schubert's March in D for piano duet Op. 51 No. 1
Mariazell Mass	Haydn's Mass in C, Hob. XXII:8
Mass in Time of War	Haydn's Mass No. 7 in C, Hob. XXII:9
Mazeppa Études	Liszt's Transcendental Études for piano No. 4
Meditation	Massenet's selection in D for violin and orchestra from the opera Thaïs
Melody in F	Rubinstein's Piano Piece No. 1 of 2 melodies Op. 3
Military Polonaise	Chopin's Polonaise in A for piano Op. 40 No. 1
Minuet in G	Beethoven's 6 Minuets, WoO 10 No. 2
Minuet in G	Paderewski's Minuet for piano Op. 14 No. 1
Minuet in G	Bach's 'Notebook for Anna Magdalena Bach', 1st selection
Minute Waltz	Chopin's Waltz in D flat for piano Op. 64 No. 1
Missa Solemnis	Beethoven's Mass in D Op. 123
Moonlight Sonata	Beethoven's Piano Sonata No. 14 in C sharp minor Op. 27 No. 2
The Mount of Olives	Beethoven's Oratorio Christ on the Mount of Olives Op. 85
Mozartiana	Tchaikovsky's Suite No. 4 for orchestra
A Musical Joke	Mozart's Divertimento in F for chamber ensemble, K522
Muss es sein? Es muss sein! Es muss sein!	Beethoven's String Quartet in F major Op. 135 (4th movement)
Nelson Mass	Haydn's Mass No. 9 in D minor, Hob. XXII:11
New England	Ives's first orchestral set
Nicolai Mass	Haydn's Mass in G, Hob. XXII:6
Organ Solo Mass	Mozart's Mass in C, K259
Paganini Études	Liszt's 6 Études for piano on themes of Paganini
Paganini Variations	Brahms's Variations on a Theme of Paganini in A minor for piano
Pastoral Sonata	Beethoven's Piano Sonata No. 15 in D major Op. 28
Pastoral Symphony	Handel's interlude from his oratorio Messiah, No. 13
Pathétique	Beethoven's Piano Sonata No. 8 in C minor Op. 13
Paukenmesse (Kettledrum Mass)	Haydn's Mass in C major, Hob. XXII:9
Peasant Cantata	Bach's Cantata 212 'Mer hahn en neue Oberkeet'
Pomp and Circumstance	Elgar's March in D major, from a set of 5 with that title, Op. 39 No. 1
Posthorn Serenade	Mozart's Serenade in D for orchestra, K320
Prelude in C	Bach's Well-Tempered Clavier Volume I, 1st selection
Prelude in C sharp minor	Rachmaninoff's Prelude for piano, Op. 3 No. 2
Prussian Quartets	Mozart's 3 String Quartets, K575, 589, 590
Prussian Quartets	Haydn's 6 String Quartets Op. 50 Nos 1–6
Quartetto Serioso	Beethoven's String Quartet in F minor Op. 95
Quartettsatz	Schubert's String Quartet No. 12 in C minor

Quintenquartett	Haydn's String Quartet in D minor Op. 76 No. 2
Rage over a Lost Penny	Beethoven's Rondo a Capriccio in G for piano Op. 129
Raindrop Prelude	Chopin's Prelude in D flat for piano Op. 28 No. 15
Rain Sonata	Brahms's Violin Sonata No. 1 in G Op. 78
Ratswahl Cantata	Bach's Cantata 71, 'Gott ist mein König'
Razor Quartet	Haydn's String Quartet in F minor Op. 55 No. 2
Razumovsky Quartets	Beethoven's 3 String Quartets Op. 59
Recitative	Haydn's String Quartet in G Op. 17 No. 5
Reliquie Sonata	Schubert's Piano Sonata No. 13 in C
Rêve Angélique	Rubinstein's piano piece in F sharp No. 22 from Kamennoi-Ostrov
Revolutionary Étude	Chopin's Étude in C minor for piano Op. 10 No. 12
The Rider (aka Horseman)	Haydn's String Quartet in G minor Op. 74 No. 3
Rondo a Capriccio	Beethoven's Piano Sonata in G Op. 129
Rondo alla Turca	Mozart's Piano Sonata in A, K331 (3rd movement)
Russian Quartets	Haydn's 6 String Quartets Op. 33 Nos 1–6
Russian Quartets	Beethoven's 3 String Quartets Op. 59
St Anne Fugue	Bach's Fugue in E flat for organ, BWV 552
St Anthony Chorale	Haydn's Divertimento in B flat for wind, instruments II:46 (2nd movement)
St Cecilia Mass	Haydn's Mass in C, XXII:5
St Joseph Mass	Haydn's Mass in E flat, Hob. XXII:4
Gli Scherzi	Haydn's 6 String Quartets Op. 33 Nos 37–42
Scherzoso	Beethoven's String Quartet in B flat Op. 130
Schübler Chorales	Bach's 6 Chorale Preludes for organ, BWV 645–50
Serenade	Haydn's String Quartet in F Op. 3 No. 5
Sheep May Safely Graze	Bach's Cantata 208, 'Was mir behagt ist nur die muntre Jagd'
Shepherd Boy Étude	Chopin's Étude in A flat for piano Op. 25 No. 1
Six-Four-Time Mass	Haydn's Mass in G, Hob. XXII:6
Solemn Vespers	Mozart's Vesperae Solennes de Confessore in C, K339
Sonata Facile	Mozart's Piano Sonata in C, K545
Sonata quasi una Fantasia	Beethoven's Piano Sonata No. 13 in E flat and No. 14 in C sharp minor
Spatzenmesse	Mozart's Mass in G, K220
Spaur Mass	Mozart's Mass in C, K258
Spring Sonata	Beethoven's Violin and Piano Sonata No. 5 in F Op. 24
Spring Song	Mendelssohn's 'Lied ohne Worte' (Song Without Words)
La Stravaganza	Vivaldi's 12 Violin Concertos Op. 4
Street Song Trio	Beethoven's Trio in B flat for clarinet, cello and piano Op. 11
Sun Quartets	Haydn's 6 String Quartets Op. 20 Nos 1–6
Sunrise Quartet	Haydn's String Quartet in B flat Op. 76 No. 4
Swedish Rhapsody	Alfvén's Midsommarvaka for orchestra Op. 19
Tempest	Beethoven's Piano Sonata No. 17 in D
Theresia Mass	Haydn's Mass No. 10 in B flat, Hob. XXII:12
Three Places in New England	Ives's first orchestral set
Timpani Mass	Haydn's Mass in C, Hob. XXII:9
To the Memory of an Angel	Berg's Violin Concerto
The Torrent	Chopin's Étude in C sharp Minor for piano Op. 10 No. 4
Tost Quartets	Haydn's 12 String Quartets Op. 54, 55, and 64
Trauer-Ode	Bach's Cantata 198, 'Lass, Fürstin, lass noch einen Strahl'
Ein Traum	Haydn's String Quartet in F Op. 50 No. 5 (2nd movement)
Triangle Concerto	Liszt's Piano Concerto No. 1 in E flat
Triple Concerto	Beethoven's Concerto in C for piano, violin and cello Op. 56
Tristesse	Chopin's Étude in E for piano Op. 10 No. 3
Trout Quintet	Schubert's Quintet in A for piano, violin, viola, cello and double bass
Trumpet Tune	Purcell's harpsichord piece in C
Trumpet Voluntary	Jeremiah Clarke's instrumental piece in D
Turkish March	Beethoven's incidental music to The Ruins of Athens for orchestra
Turkish Rondo	Mozart's Piano Sonata in A, K331 (3rd movement)
Twinkle Twinkle Variations	Mozart's Variation on 'Ah, vous dirai-je, maman' in C for piano
Two-Cello Quintet	Schubert's String Quintet in C Op. 163
Utrecht Jubilate	Handel's Jubilate in D
Utrecht Te Deum	Handel's Te Deum in D
Villanelle	Chopin's Étude in G flat for piano Op. 25 No. 9
Voces Intimae (Friendly Voices)	Sibelius' String Quartet in D minor Op. 56
Waisenhausmesse	Mozart's Mass in C minor, K139
Waldstein	Beethoven's Piano Sonata No. 21 in C major Op. 53
Wedding March	Mendelssohn's incidental music to A Midsummer Night's Dream for orchestra Op. 61 (9th movement)
Wedge Fugue	Bach's Fugue in E minor for organ
The White Mass	Scriabin's Piano Sonata No. 7 in F sharp Op. 64
Wind-Band Mass	Haydn's Mass No. 12 in B flat, Hob. XXII:14
Winter Wind Étude	Chopin's Etude in A minor for piano Op. 25 No. 11
Witches' Minuet	Haydn's String Quartet in D minor Op. 76 No. 2 (3rd movement)
WTC	Bach's Well-Tempered Clavier

MUSIC CLASSICAL

General Information

acciaccatura   A short grace note played simultaneously with the principal note and released immediately.

Aldeburgh Festival   Founded by Benjamin Britten in 1948, held in Aldeburgh, Suffolk, with concert hall, the Maltings, at nearby Snape.

Amati family   Violin makers in Cremona, 16th–18th century. Nicola Amati taught Stradivari and Guarneri.

arpeggio   Chord spread, i.e. notes played one after the other as on the harp.

Ars Antiqua (Old Art)   Refers to music of 12th and 13th centuries derived from the school of Paris.

Ars Nova (New Art)   Style of music developed in 14th-century France and Italy. Term coined by Philippe de Vitry.

attempted suicide: Debussy's wife   Rosalie 'Lily' Texier shot herself during a bout of depression.

attempted suicide: Tchaikovsky   Walked into the freezing River Neva at dead of night following his disastrous marriage in 1877.

Aurora's Wedding   Divertissement of last act of *Sleeping Beauty*, sometimes performed separately.

bagatelle   Short, plain composition especially for pianoforte e.g. Für Elise.

Baroque   Musical era roughly from 1600 to around 1750.

Battle Symphony   Beethoven's orchestral work *Wellington's Victory* Op. 91 (includes 'Rule, Britannia!' and 'God Save the King').

berceuse   Lullaby.

Boehm system   Theobald Boehm (1794–1881) devised an acoustically superior system of placing and sizing the holes in the flute, and of using the keys to cover them, now universally used.

Bond   Popular all-girl classical combo. Its four members are Haylie Ecker (1st violin), Eos Chater (2nd violin), Tania Davis (viola) and Gay-Yee Westerhoff (cello). Haylie and Tania are native Australians, Eos is Welsh and Gay-Yee is English.

Boosey and Hawkes Ltd   London music publishers (amalgamated 1930).

Boston Symphony Orchestra   Founded in October 1881 by Henry Lee Higginson.

Brahms: personal motto   *Frei aber Froh* (free but happy). He used the initial letters as the thematic structure of his 3rd Symphony.

Brandenburg Concertos   Bach's 6 Concerti Grossi dedicated to Christian Ludwig, Margrave of Brandenburg.

brindisi   Drinking song usually accompanying a toast.

Canterbury degrees (Lambeth degrees)   Music degrees conferred traditionally by the Archbishop of Canterbury.

capriccio   Musical composition that has original and unexpected effects. Janáček and Stravinsky both wrote works called 'Capriccio'.

Carnegie Hall   Largest concert-hall in New York, designed by W B Tuthill and opened in 1891.

castrato   Male soprano castrated before puberty to preserve the voice.

cataloguers of works   Schubert – Deutsch; Haydn – Hoboken; Scarlatti – Kirkpatrick (Longo numbers are also still used); Mozart – Köchel; Vivaldi – Ryom (Pincherle & Fanna also catalogued works); J S Bach – Schmieder (used initials BWV: Bach-Werke-Verzeichnis); Liszt – both R and S numbers; Nielsen – FS (Fog and Schousboe); Frank Bridge – H numbers; Holmboe – Rapoport (M for Meta numbers, after Holmboe's wife); Bartók – Sz numbers; Beethoven – Kinsky (used WoO numbers for works without an opus) and Hess (used Hn numbers for other works); Purcell – Zimmerman; Handel – Baselt (HMV numbers); Dvorak – Burghauser; Donizetti – Inzaghi; Chopin – Brown.

catch   Type of round whose words may sound comical when sung. A catch club was formed in London in 1761.

chamber music   Term coined by Charles Burney in 1805 to describe music not intended for the church, theatre or public concert room, but now applied to ensemble music written for small groups, such as string quartets.

Cheltenham Festival   Music festival started in 1945 as Festival of British Contemporary Music but since 1969 drawing music from international sources.

J. & W. Chester Ltd   Music publishers founded in Brighton (1874) and specialising in Russian and other foreign composers.

Chetham's School of Music   Founded in 1656, by a bequest from Humphrey Chetham (1580–1653), situated in Long Millgate, Manchester; Chetham's is Britain's only full-scale music school for children, with over 280 boys and girls aged 8–18.

Chicago Symphony Orchestra   Founded in 1891 by Theodore Thomas; it is the third oldest orchestra in USA.

children: most born to one composer   Twenty to J S Bach.

Children's Corner   Six piano pieces dedicated by Debussy to his daughter: 1) Dr Gradus ad Parnassum, 2) Jimbo's Lullaby, 3) Serenade for the Doll, 4) Snow is Dancing, 5) The Little Shepherd, 6) Golliwogg's Cakewalk.

clam   Playing a wrong note in a performance.

Classic FM: top 100, most popular work   Max Bruch's 1st Violin Concerto (1996 and 1997).

Classical Period   Ranges from the late 18th to the early 19th century.

Colour Symphony (Arthur Bliss): movements   The four movements: *Purple, Red, Blue* and *Green*.

Composers' Guild of Great Britain   Founded in 1944 to protect the rights of composers; affiliated to the Society of Authors. First president was Vaughan Williams.

concerto   Work, usually in three movements, which contrasts and integrates a solo instrument with the orchestra.

conductor with 36 names   Louis Julien (1812–60) was sponsored at his baptism by 36 members of the local philharmonic society.

coronach (corranach)   Funeral dirge of Ireland and Highland Scotland.

Crossover Chart   Established in 1996 and includes popular light classical pieces.

deaf composers   Beethoven, Fauré, Smetana.

deaf percussionist   Evelyn Glennie.

Diabelli Variations   Beethoven's Thirty-Three Variations on a Waltz by Diabelli.

Dido's Lament   Aria from Act 3 of Purcell's *Dido and Aeneas*, played annually at Remembrance Day service at the Cenotaph and beginning with the words 'When I am laid in earth'.

The Divine Poem Scriabin's Symphony No. 3 in C minor Op. 43 (three movements entitled *Struggles*, *Delights* and *Divine Play*).

Dvořák: son-in-law Josef Suk.

Early Music Consort Founded by David Munrow in 1967 to perform Renaissance and medieval music on original instruments.

Edinburgh Festival Founded in 1947 with Rudolf Bing as director. Three-week festival of music held in August–September now teems with other arts and entertainments.

Eighteen-Twelve (1812) Concert overture Op. 49 by Tchaikovsky commemorating the defeat of Napoleon's Grande Armée on its retreat from Moscow. It incorporates 'La Marseillaise'.

English Chamber Orchestra Founded in 1948 as the Goldsbrough Orchestra (after its founder); present name adopted in 1960.

English Folk Dance and Song Society Amalgamation in 1932 of Folk Song Society (founded 1898) and English Folk Dance Society (founded 1911); HQ in Cecil Sharp House, London, NW1 7AY.

Enigma Variations: **musical portraits** 1) Lady Elgar (C.A.E.); 2) Hew Steuart-Powell (H.D.S.-P.); 3) RB Townshend (R.B.T.); 4) W. Meath Baker (W.M.B.); 5) Richard P. Arnold (R.P.A.); 6) Isabel Fitton (Ysobel); 7) A. Troyte Griffith (Troyte); 8) Winifred Norbury (W.N.); 9) AJ Jaeger (Nimrod); 10) Dora Penny (Dorabella); 11) GR Sinclair (G.R.S.); 12) Basil Nevinson (B.G.N.); 13) Lady Mary Lygon; 14) Elgar (E.D.U.).

Estampes (*Engravings*) Three piano pieces by Debussy: *Pagodas*, *Evening in Granada*, and *Gardens in the Rain*.

étude (study) Composition intended to test and extend the performer's technique.

eurhythmics Method invented by Émile Jaques-Dalcroze (1865–1950) for expressing rhythmical aspect of music through gymnastic exercises.

Faust Symphony (Liszt) Movements portray three characters: *Faust*, *Gretchen* and *Mephistopheles*.

Fireworks Music Handel wrote the music to celebrate the Peace of Aix-La-Chapelle (1749); first played in Green Park, London.

First Post British Army bugle call, a summons back to the barracks, sounded at 9.30 p.m.

The Five (aka The Mighty Handful) Russian composers Balakirev, Borodin, Cui, Mussorgsky and Rimsky-Korsakov.

Frankfurt Group English composers who were pupils of Iwan Knorr in the 1890s; they were Norman O'Neill, Roger Quilter, Cyril Scott and Balfour Gardiner.

funeral marches Famous ones include the 3rd movement of Chopin's 2nd piano sonata; Handel's Dead March in *Saul*; 2nd movement of Beethoven's *Eroica*; Siegfried's Funeral March from Wagner's *Götterdämmerung*.

Gagliano family 18th-century family of violin-makers from Naples. Key members: Alessandro, his sons, Niccolò and Gennaro, and grandsons Ferdinando and Giuseppe.

gamelan A kind of orchestra widespread in south-east Asia, especially Indonesia, whose range of percussion includes gongs, drums, marimbas and chimes.

Gebrauchsmusik (utility music) Term associated in the 1920s with works by Hindemith, Weill and Krenek, influenced by Brecht and designed for social and educational purposes.

Gesamtkunstwerk Wagner's term for a dramatic work in which drama, music, poetry, song and painting would be united into a single artistic whole.

glee Vocal music for three or four parts, unaccompanied and homophonic, popular in late 18th- and early 19th-century England.

Goldberg Variations J S Bach's 30 variations on a theme for two-manual harpsichord.

Grove, Sir George English music writer (1820–1900) who, after training as a civil engineer, turned to musical studies and compiled *Grove's Dictionary of Music and Musicians*, then published in 4 volumes, now expanded into 20.

Guarneri Quartet American string quartet formed in 1964 in Vermont. Members are Arnold Steinhardt and John Dally (violins), Michael Tree (viola) and Peter Wiley (cello), who replaced founding member David Soyer in 2000.

Hail to the Chief March traditionally played at formal American events to announce the arrival of the President, first used at the inauguration of Martin Van Buren in 1837. The words came from Sir Walter Scott's *Lady of the Lake* but are no longer used. Derived from an old Gaelic tune, the melody was adapted by the English composer, James Sanderson (1769–1841) for a scene in Scott's play.

hairpins Nickname for the signs < (crescendo) and > (diminuendo).

Hallé Orchestra Founded in 1857 by Charles Hallé and based in Manchester. Sir John Barbirolli was the principal conductor from 1943 to his death in 1970. Kent Nagano has been the conductor since 1992.

Haydn's Symphony No. 45 Haydn directed his musicians to gradually leave the stage during the last movement, hence the nickname 'Farewell'.

Henry Wood: pseudonym Paul Klenovsky was the cryptic name (Klen means maple tree) under which Wood transcribed for orchestra Bach's Toccata and Fugue in D minor.

Hexameron Six variations for piano on a march from Bellini's *I Puritani*, each written by a different composer/pianist, i.e. Liszt, Pixis, Herz, Thalberg, Czerny and Chopin, each of whom played his variation at the first performance of the work in a charity concert in Paris in 1837 (first of the super groups one might say!). Liszt later added orchestral accompaniments and played whole series at recitals.

humoresque Humorous or capricious instrumental piece. Famous examples are by Dvorák and Schumann.

Images Title used by Debussy for two works: 1) *Images* for Orchestra, including *Gigues*, *Ibéria* and *Rondes de Printemps*; 2) two sets for solo piano: *Reflets dans l'eau*, *Hommage à Rameau*, *Movement*, *Cloches à travers les feuilles*, *Et la lune descend sur le temple qui fut* and *Poissons d'or*.

Jena Symphony A work found by Fritz Stein in 1909 in Jena, Germany, and linked until 1957 with Beethoven; it turned out that Friedrich Witt was the composer.

La Jeune France (Young France) Group of four French composers (Yves Baudrier, André Jolivet, Daniel Lesur and Olivier Messiaen) who resolved in Paris in 1936 to carry out 'a return to the human' in composition.

MUSIC CLASSICAL

jubilate   Hymn of praise, usually based on Psalm 100 (in Roman Catholic Psalter, Psalm 99).

Juilliard Quartet   Founded by William Schuman in New York in 1946; the line-up as at April 2001 is Joel Smirnoff and Ronald Copes (violins), Samuel Rhodes (viola) and Joel Krosnick (cello).

K numbers   Named after the cataloguers of two composers: Mozart – Ludwig von Köchel; Scarlatti – Ralph Kirkpatrick.

karaoke (empty orchestra)   Singing along with recorded accompaniment.

Kneller Hall   Headquarters, founded in 1857 at Twickenham, Middlesex, of Royal Military School of Music.

La Scala (The Staircase)   Milan opera house built in 1778 on the site of a church founded in the 18th century by Regina della Scala, wife of a Duke of Milan.

Last Post   British Army bugle call sounded at 10 p.m. that ends the day. It is customary to play the Last Post at military funerals.

Leeds Piano Competition   Established in 1963 by Fanny Waterman and Marion Thorpe and held triennially. The first winner was Michael Roll, and many placed pianists have won international reputations, notably Peter Donohoe, who was placed sixth in 1981.

Leitmotiv   Term first used by A W Ambrose (c.1865) in an article about Wagner's operas and Liszt's symphonic poems; it was later used by F W Jähns, to denote a short and recurrent musical figure standing for an idea or character.

Les Six   Term coined by Henri Collet in 1920 to describe the avant-garde French composers Georges Auric (1899–1983), Louis Durey (1888–1979), Arthur Honegger (1892–1955), Darius Milhaud (1892–1974), Francis Poulenc (1899–1963) and Germaine Tailleferre (1892–1983).

Leventritt Competition   International competition alternately for pianists and violinists, established in 1939 by Leventritt Foundation, New York. Winner's prize consists of engagements with prominent orchestras and offer of recording contract.

Lincoln Center for the Performing Arts   New York arts centre consisting of Metropolitan Opera House, Avery Fisher Hall, Juilliard School and various theatres and societies.

London Philharmonic Orchestra   Founded by Sir Thomas Beecham in 1932.

London Symphony Orchestra   Founded by players who seceded from Henry Wood's Queen's Hall orchestra in 1904 and run by its own members ever since.

Má Vlast   Cycle of 6 symphonic poems by Smetana: 1) *The High Citadel* (*Vysehrad*); 2) *River Moldau* (*Vltava*); 3) *Sàrka*; 4) *From Bohemia's Meadows and Forests* (*Z Ceskych Luhu a Haju*); 5) *Tabor*; 6) *Blánik* (*The Valhalla of the Hussite heroes*).

madrigal   Song form for two or more voices developed in 13th- and 14th-century Italy, most often secular and unaccompanied; revived and enhanced during the Renaissance into an expressive, polyphonic form introduced into Elizabethan England.

Manchester School   Name given to group of composers (Maxwell Davies, Harrison Birtwistle, Alexander Goehr and John Ogdon) taught in Manchester by Richard Hall in the late 1950s.

masque   Courtly entertainment that evolved in 17th-century England, incorporating music, acting and spectacular costumes and scenery.

Mighty Handful (aka The Five)   Alternative name for 'The Five' (coined by Vladimir Stasov).

minimalism   Style of music that developed in the 1960s, involving repetition of short musical motifs in simple harmonic idiom. Prominent members include Philip Glass, Steve Reich and Terry Riley.

minuet   Movement (usually the 3rd) in sonatas and symphonies of the classical period, derived from the dance of the same name.

Miserere   Psalm 51 (50 in Roman Catholic Psalter) set to music by various composers.

most prolific composer   Georg Philipp Telemann is often assigned this title; among his output are over 600 overtures, 44 Passions, 40 operas and numerous other works.

motet   Choral composition, generally on a sacred text.

motif   Short melodic pattern or musical idea that runs throughout a piece.

Mourning Music (***Trauermusik***)   Paul Hindemith work composed within hours of the death of George V in 1936.

Mozart: wrote down on first hearing   Gregorio Allegri's *Miserere* was supposedly sacrosanct to the Vatican; Mozart went to a service there and went home and wrote it down from memory, thereby risking excommunication. It is however very likely that Mozart had heard the piece on at least one occasion prior to his visit to Rome.

Mozart's Piano Concerto No. 21 in C   Given nickname of 'Elvira Madigan' in 1967 because it was the theme tune of the film of that name.

Mozart's Piano Concerto No. 26 in D   Given nickname of 'Coronation' because it was played at King Leopold II of Prussia's coronation.

Mozart's String Quartets 14–19   Dedicated to Haydn with the words 'I send my six sons to you'.

Mozart: work falsely attributed to   *Adélaide* violin concerto. In 1977 Marius Casadesus admitted he composed it.

musical epochs   Medieval 600–1425; Renaissance 1425–1600; Baroque 1600–1750; Classical 1750–1825; Romantic 1820–80; Post-Romantic 1880–1910; Modern since 1910; some historians also identify a Nationalist epoch 1860–1910 and an Impressionist epoch 1890–1920.

musique concrète   Music composed by manipulating recorded sounds, especially natural sounds rather than electronic.

National Gallery Recitals   During the Second World War Dame Myra Hess founded and directed a series of lunchtime recitals, which became very popular and helped to sustain morale.

New Symphony Orchestra   London orchestra founded by Sir Thomas Beecham in 1905 and became Royal Albert Hall Orchestra in 1920 and later disbanded.

New York Philharmonic Orchestra   Oldest US symphony orchestra, founded in 1842 as Philharmonic Society of New York; merged with New York Symphony Orchestra in 1928 to become Philharmonic Symphony Orchestra of New York; now known as the NYPO.

nocturne   Night-piece, serenade.

notes of the scale: English to Italian   A=la, B=si, C=do, D=re, E=mi, F=fa, G=sol.

octet   A group of 8 musicians, or a piece of music written for such a group. A string octet is usually a double string quartet.

opus (work) Opus numbers are used to designate the order in which a given composer's works were written or published.

oratorio Musical setting for voices and orchestra of a text based on the Scriptures or an epic theme. Could be described as an opera without staging, scenery or costumes.

Parthenia Title of the first book of keyboard music printed in England (1611), collecting pieces by William Byrd, John Bull and Orlando Gibbons.

pastorale Either a musical play based on a rustic subject, or a composition with rustic overtones.

Performing Right Society Association of composers, authors, and music publishers founded in Britain in 1914 to collect royalties for non-dramatic public performance and broadcasting of members' works.

Philharmonia Orchestra English symphony orchestra founded in 1945 by Walter Legge.

piano quartet Piano, violin, viola and cello.

piano quintet Usually string quartet plus piano.

piano trio Piano, violin, and cello.

Pictures at an Exhibition Mussorgsky's versions in music of 10 pictures displayed at a memorial exhibition for Russian artist Victor Hartmann: 1) *The Gnome*; 2) *The Old Castle*; 3) *Tuileries*; 4) *Bydlo* (a farm cart); 5) *Unhatched Chickens*; 6) *Samuel Goldenberg and Shmuyle*; 7) *Market-Place at Limoges*; 8) *Catacombs*; 9) *Baba-Yaga (The Hut on Fowl's Legs)*; 10) *The Great Gate of Kiev*.

Pierrot Players Instrument ensemble founded in 1967 by Maxwell Davies and Harrison Birtwistle, regrouped to form the Fires of London in 1970 before disbanding in 1987.

Pomp and Circumstance Elgar's title (taken from Act 3 of *Othello*) for his set of five marches for symphony orchestra, the first of which was the basis for 'Land of Hope and Glory' (words by A C Benson).

Pre-classical Term applied to composers such as C P E Bach who are considered to be later than baroque and leading to the 'Classical' style of Haydn and Mozart.

Promenade Concerts Although promenade concerts (at which listeners could saunter around) were put on in London as early as 1838, it was not until 1895 that they became a regular annual feature when Robert Newman began a series at Queen's Hall with Henry Wood as conductor. Wood's name became synonymous with the Proms, and after his death in 1944, Malcolm Sargent became principal conductor (1948–67). Royal Albert Hall became venue in 1941 on the destruction of Queen's Hall.

Proms: centenary 1995; Harrison Birtwistle composed *Panic*.

Proms: last four directors Sir William Glock, Robert Ponsonby, Sir John Drummond and, the present incumbent, Nicholas Kenyon.

Queen's Hall Once London's chief concert hall, situated in Langham Place, opened in 1893 and destroyed by fire in 1941, following a Nazi bombing raid.

rāga Indian musical form that represents a mood, concept or occasion by one of many patterns of notes presented as an ascending and descending scale used as a basis for improvisation.

Ring Cycle Full title *Der Ring des Nibelungen (The Ring of the Nibelung)*. Often referred to as the tetralogy although Wagner himself called the first opera, *Das Rheingold*, the prologue. After it comes *Die Walküre (The Valkyrie)*, followed by *Siegfried* and finally, *Götterdämmerung (Twilight of the Gods)*.

Royal Academy of Music Founded in London in 1822 and situated in Tenterden Street but moved to Marylebone Road in 1912. The RAM has about 700 students and 150 staff.

Royal College of Music Founded in 1882 but moved to its present site at Prince Consort Road, South Kensington in 1894.

Royal Philharmonic Orchestra Founded in 1946 by Sir Thomas Beecham, who was principal conductor until his death in 1961.

St Louis Symphony Orchestra Founded in March 1881, the second oldest symphony orchestra in the USA.

Scottish Chamber Orchestra Founded in 1974 with headquarters in Queen's Hall, Edinburgh.

secular music Any music that is not sacred music.

septet Make-up varies, but typical format would be violin, viola, French horn, clarinet, bassoon, cello and double bass.

sextet Group of 6 musicians; a string sextet usually two each of violins, violas and cellos.

sonata Instrumental composition usually in three or four movements for unaccompanied piano or, more rarely, for another stringed instrument with piano accompaniment.

stanza One of a number of sections of a song, two or more lines long, characterised by a common metre, rhyme and number of lines.

string quartet Violins (1st and 2nd), viola and cello.

string quintet String quartet with added viola or cello.

string trio Violin, viola and cello.

Sturm und Drang (Storm and Stress) Term applied to a period (*c.*1760–80) of great emotional intensity in German literature and music. Musically, it is particularly associated with F J Haydn's works around the time of his Symphonies 40–59.

Suite bergamasque Piano suite by Debussy, its 4 movements: *Prélude, Menuet, Clair de Lune*, and *Passepied*.

symphonic structure In the Classical model, 4 movements: 1) a fast sonata; 2) a slow movement; 3) a minuet scherzo; 4) a fast movement, mostly a rondo.

Tchaikovsky Piano Competition Quadrennial competition first held in Moscow in 1954. Famous winners include Van Cliburn, John Ogdon, Vladimir Ashkenazy.

Three Bs Bach, Beethoven, Brahms (term coined by Hans von Bülow).

Three Choirs Festival Annual meeting that rotates among the 3 cathedral choirs of Gloucester, Hereford and Worcester, held almost continuous since the early 18th century.

tonic sol-fa System of sight-singing and notation devised by Sarah Ann Glover in England in the 1840s, though much the same system had been introduced in the USA by D Sower in 1832.

toy symphony Term for a symphony in which toy instruments are used as well as strings and piano; the most popular example is a work by Leopold Mozart, with toy instruments now thought to have been added by Michael Haydn.

train wreck Colloquial term for what happens when the parts in an ensemble collide because the musicians are not playing together.

MUSIC CLASSICAL

The Triumphs of Oriana   Collection of 5- and 6-part English madrigals by 24 composers assembled by Thomas Morley in 1601 in honour of Elizabeth I.

trumpet voluntary   Piece that imitates a trumpet but is, in fact, played using a similar sounding organ stop. The best known version is a transcription by Henry Wood of a piece originally ascribed to Purcell but now credited to Jeremiah Clarke. He called it 'The Prince of Denmark's March', but Wood's title has superseded Clarke's.

Tuning of Strings   Cello: C, G, D, A (octave lower than the viola). Violin: G, D, A, E. Double-bass: E, A, D, G. Banjo: 4 strings C, G, D, A; 5 strings G, D, G, B, D. Viola: C, G, D, A (5th lower than violin).

Tweedledum and Tweedledee   Name coined by John Byrom (1692–1763) to satirise the public feuding between composers G F Handel and G Bononcini.

violinists: known for revealing garments   Vanessa Mae, Anne-Sophie Mutter, Linda Lampenius.

Wagner's patron   Ludwig II, King of Bavaria (1845–86).

The Walk to the Paradise Garden   Intermezzo before concluding scene of Delius's opera *A Village Romeo and Juliet*. The Paradise Garden is actually a public house.

Wedding March   Played at the end of Act 4 of Mendelssohn's *Midsummer Night's Dream* and traditionally used on exit from the church. The Bridal Chorus from *Lohengrin* commonly announces the entry.

Wigmore Hall   London concert hall in Wigmore Street, opened in 1901 as Bechstein Hall.

WoO   Werk ohne Op. zahl (work without opus number): system of catalogue numbers used to identify composer's works that lack opus numbers.

woodwind quintet   Usually flute, clarinet, oboe, French horn and bassoon.

Musical Instruments

accordion   Invented by Friedrich Buschmann of Berlin in 1822.

Aeolian harp   Box and strings that sound when hit by a current of air.

aeolina   Mouth organ.

angelica   Instrument of the lute family with 16 or 17 strings.

arpeggione   Six-stringed cello invented by G Staufer of Vienna in 1823. Aka *guitare d'amour*.

aulos   Double-reed wind instrument of ancient Greece.

autoharp   Zither on which chord keys are pressed by one hand and strings strummed by the other.

Bach trumpet   Valveless trumpet in either C or D.

backfall   Part of an organ that connects the rods to the keyboard.

bagpipes   Ancient instrument popular throughout the world but particularly identified with Scotland. The Scottish Highland bagpipe has two tenor drones and a bass drone, tuned an octave apart. The chanter is the pipes that plays the tune. Versions of the bagpipe around the world include the Bulgarian *gaida*, the *cornemuse* of France and Belgium, the *gaita* of northwestern Spain and the Irish Uilleann pipes.

balalaika   Russian three-stringed instrument of the lute family with a triangular belly and moveable frets on the arm. The balalaika was developed in the 18th century from the *domra*.

bamboula   West Indian tambourine.

bandoneon   Argentinian variant of the accordion.

baritone horn   Brass instrument in B flat, related to the euphonium with a smaller bore and 3 valves.

baryton   Stringed instrument similar to viola da gamba but with sympathetic strings. Played by Prince Esterházy (Haydn's patron); it has made a revival in recent years.

Basque drum   Tambourine.

bassanello   Shawm-like woodwind instrument, no longer played.

bassoon   Bass member of the double-reed oboe family, pitched in C.

bell lyra   Type of portable glockenspiel.

bissex   Twelve-string guitar invented in 1770 by Vanhecke.

bodhran   Irish frame drum played with a double-ended stick.

bombard   Alto-pitched shawm.

bombardon   Form of bass tuba with 3 piston valves.

boobams   Percussion instrument using a varying number of bamboo tubes.

bottleneck   Tube that fits over a finger on the fretting hand used for slide-guitar playing.

bouzouki   Greek fretted string instrument with a long neck and 4 sets of strings.

cabaca/cabasa   Latin American percussion instrument, around or pear-shaped gourd covered with beads and fitted with a handle.

calliope   Literally meaning 'beautiful-voiced' after the Muse of epic poetry; US name for a steam-driven organ.

campanelle   Glockenspiel.

canale   Psaltery.

canntaireachd   Ancient Highland bagpipe notation, using syllables to represent a group of notes.

carillon   Alternative name for glockenspiel, so called by Handel in 1739 when he first used the instrument in *Saul*.

castanets   Twin cup-shaped clappers; name derives from the Spanish *castaña*, chestnut wood.

celesta   Small keyboard instrument patented by Auguste Mustel in 1886 and famously used in Tchaikovsky's 'Dance of the Sugar Plum Fairy'.

cello: full name   Violoncello.

cembalo   Short for clavicembalo, the Italian word for harpsichord.

cetera   Zither.

chalumeau   Forerunner of the clarinet with 6 to 8 finger-holes.

chanterelle   The E string on a violin, or the highest string on any instrument in the violin or lute family.

charivari   Cacophonous, extemporised music produced with any household utensil or object that will make a noise.

chitarrone   Lute similar to a theorbo but longer.

choke cymbal: aka   High-hat cymbal.

chromatic harp   Harp built by Pleyel in 1897; equipped with a string for every semitone, it needed no pedals.

cimbalom Form of dulcimer native to Hungary, made up of a box on which strings are hit with mallets.

cittern A 15th-century forerunner of the lute with metal strings tuned in pairs and plucked.

clapper Striker in the middle of a bell.

clarinet Single-reed woodwind instrument developed by J C Denner of Nuremberg in the late 17th century.

clàrsach Ancient small Celtic harp having brass strings instead of gut or nylon ones.

clavecin Harpsichord.

claves Cuban percussion instruments consisting of round wooden sticks that are stuck together.

clavichord/clarichord Small keyboard instrument invented in 14th century. Aka manichord or chekker.

colascione European version of oriental long-necked lute popular in the Tudor period.

colophony Bow rosin (named after Colophon in Asia Minor, the source of the best rosin).

concertina Invented by Charles Wheatstone in 1829 as the 'Symphonium'. Similar to accordion but no keyboard.

console Part of organ by which the musician operates the instrument.

cor anglais French for English horn, but in fact an alto oboe; invented by Ferlandis of Bergamo.

cor de chasse Hunting horn developed in France in 17th century.

cornopean Late 19th-century brass instrument similar to a trumpet.

crembalum Type of Jew's harp.

crook Tube inserted into a brass instrument to lengthen its tube and change its pitch.

crotales Ancient Greek percussion instrument in form of a rattle or clapper.

crumhorn Early and widely used Renaissance double-reed instrument. Name means 'curved horn'.

crwth Welsh medieval instrument with 6 strings, a bowed lyre.

cuckoo Two-note wind instrument imitating the bird.

damper Felt piece that damps the vibration of the string on a piano until the key is depressed.

didjeridu (didgeridoo) Native Australian wind instrument, which allows player to breathe through nose while playing.

digitorium Small keyboard machine usually having 5 keys, which are sprung more severely than usual so as to strengthen fingers. Invented by Myer Marks in the mid-19th century.

domra Type of early balalaika with a round body and two or three metal strings tuned a fourth apart.

double bass: aka Bull-fiddle, doghouse.

Dudelsack German form of bagpipe.

dulcimer Ancient instrument with wire strings stretching over a shallow box which are struck with rods.

dulcitone Instrument similar to celesta but with steel tuning forks instead of steel plates.

duplex-coupler piano Invented by Emanuel Moór in 1921; has 2 keyboards, upper tuned an octave higher.

electronde Electronic instrument invented by Martin Taubman in 1933, like the theramin but can create staccato effect.

embouchure Mouthpiece of a brass instrument.

emicon Electric instrument invented in USA in 1931 and producing notes from air in graded chromatic scale.

English flute: aka Recorder.

English horn Alto oboe, pitched a 5th lower and having a conical shape and bulbous bell.

euphonium Tenor tuba in B flat. Also name of instrument made of glass plates and rods by Ernst Chladni in 1790.

fagotto Bassoon.

fipple Mouthpiece for all wind instruments.

flageolet Small type of recorder.

flexatone Patented in 1922 and consisting of a flexible metal sheet suspended in a wire frame with handle. Shaking produces a tremolo sound.

flugelhorn Brass instrument in the cornet family but with a wider bore and larger bell.

flûte à bec (beak flute) Type of recorder.

French harp Harmonica.

French horn Coiled brass wind intrument extending to 11ft when uncoiled with a bell of 14in diameter. Early form supposedly introduced to the orchestra by Lully; modern form uses valves introduced in the 1820s.

frog On bowed instruments, the end of the bow that is held in the hand. Aka nut.

Geigenwerk Type of hurdy-gurdy invented in Nuremberg in 1575 by Hans Haiden.

gekkin Japanese instrument with circular body like banjo but with 9 frets and 4 strings tuned in pairs.

gemshorn Type of flute made of horn, not used since 16th century. Aka chamois horn.

gittern Medieval ancestor of guitar.

glockenspiel (lit. bell play) Musical instrument consisting of hanging metal bars, which are struck with a hammer.

gong Ancient percussion instrument first found in China, a metal disc generally with upturned edges, usually with indefinite pitch but sometimes tuned.

grelots Little bells, e.g. sleigh bells, used as percussion.

gusla One-stringed bowed instrument long popular in Slavonic cultures.

gusli Ancient Russian instrument of the zither family.

harmonica Mouth organ with metal reeds, first produced by Friedrich Buschman of Berlin in 1821 as the 'Mundäoline'. The two main types of harmonicas are the chromatic and the diatonic. The chromatic harmonica is preferred by blues players such as Bob Dylan and Neil Young. The diatonic harmonica has a wider range and more suited to the virtuoso such as Larry Adler.

harmonium Small portable reed organ perfected by Alexandre Debain of Paris in the early 1840s.

harp Forty-seven-stringed instrument whose modern orchestral version with a pedal mechanism was developed by Sébastien Érard.

harpsichord Wing-shaped keyboard instrument in which the strings are mechanically plucked rather that struck with a hammer.

hautbois French name for oboe, (lit. 'high wood').

Hawaiian guitar Ukulele (also nickname of steel guitar) introduced by the Portuguese.

heckelphone Double-reed, baritone oboe with a conical bore and bulbous bell.

helicon Tuba with a circular construction that can be wrapped around the body for marching bands.

hellertion Electric instrument developed in Frankfurt in 1936 by Bruno Helberger and Peter Lertes, similar to Theremin but with a range of 6 octaves.

hitschiriki Japanese instrument like a bamboo flute with 7 finger-holes and 2 thumb-holes.

hityokin Japanese vertical flute made of bamboo.

MUSIC CLASSICAL

hornpipe   Wind instrument with a single reed and a cow's horn fitted on the end.

hummel   Swedish zither.

hurdy-gurdy   Medieval instrument resembling a viol but whose sound is produced by friction of hand-cranked wooden wheel on strings that could be stopped by keys.

huruk   Hourglass-shaped Indian drum.

hydraulis   Ancient instrument, aka water organ, supposedly invented in Greece by Ktesibios in the 3rd century BC.

idiophone   Term used for instrument whose own material makes a characteristic sound such as castanets, gongs, bells, etc.

Irish harp   Small harp played while held in the lap.

Japanese fiddle   One-stringed instrument played by street performers.

Jew's harp   Folk instrument consisting of a metal frame that contains a flexible strip of metal. The frame is held between the player's teeth while the metal strip is twanged.

kazoo   Short tube open at both ends, with a vibrating membrane in between, played by humming into it; a kind of mirliton.

kin   Japanese string instrument, a small koto.

kithara   Ancient but sophisticated Greek lyre, which is finger plucked.

klavier   Keyboard instrument (with strings).

knollhorn   Soft-sounding herald horn from the mid-western region of the US.

Korean temple block   Oriental addition to the 20th-century dance-band drummer's equipment, constituting a skull-shaped hollow block of wood, in several sizes, and struck with a drumstick.

koto   Japanese instrument resembling a zither, with 7 to 13 silk strings plucked by the fingers.

lira   A 16th-century string instrument with drones, played with a bow.

loure   French bagpipe.

lute   Ancient musical instrument with a pear-shaped belly and a long, fretted fingerboard and played like a modern guitar.

lutherie   The art of making string instruments – not only lutes, but also guitars and the violin family.

luthier   One who practises lutherie.

lyra (lyre)   Ancient Greek instrument with a 4-sided frame, encompassing strings attached from a soundbox to a crossbar. Played like a harp.

machete   Portuguese 4-string folk guitar.

mandocello   Bass mandolin.

mandola/mandora   Small, early precursor of the lute and mandolin with 9 frets and up to 6 strings.

mandolin   Instrument in the lute family, fretted and with 8 wire strings tuned in four pairs, G, D, A, E.

maracas   Latin American percussion instrument consisting of two seed-filled gourds, which are shaken by handles.

mardakion   Accordion-like instrument from the mid-west US.

marimba   African percussion instrument introduced to Latin America, a deeper pitched version of the xylophone with metal resonators.

m'bira   African 'thumb piano' made up of a number of metal or cane tongues held in position with a bar attached to a box or board. The free ends are twanged with the thumbs.

mellophone   Variation of the French horn constructed for marching.

melodeon   Related to the concertina, with 10 treble keys on the right, bellows and 4 bass keys on the left.

metallophone   Percussion instrument consisting of tuned metal bars arranged in single or double rows.

mirliton   Instrument containing a membrane to modify a sound made when the player hums or sings into or against it.

monochord   Musical instrument with one string, used for determining the ratios of musical intervals.

Moog synthesizer   Earliest commercial, voltage-controlled synthesizer, invented by Robert Moog in 1965.

mouth organ   The term covers many instruments with metal reeds but nowadays is synonymous with the harmonica.

musetta   Bellows-operated French bagpipe popular in the court of Louis XIV.

mute   Device usually conical in shape, that muffles a brass instrument's sound.

nightingale   Toy instrument used in by Scarlatti in an oratorio by Scarlatti and by Leopold Mozart in his *Toy Symphony*.

nose flute   Originating in Polynesia, a bamboo flute blown through the nostrils.

nut   On bowed instruments, device fitted on to the end of the bow that is held in the hand, and used to adjust the bow's tension.

oboe   Double-reed woodwind instrument with a conical bore in C and a natural scale of D.

oboe d'amore   Slightly bigger than the normal oboe, with a pear-shaped bell, and pitched a minor third lower.

ocarina (little goose)   Small, round, wind instrument with finger holes, and made out of clay or porcelain; so named by Giuseppe Donati in mid-1800s; aka sweet potato.

oliphant   Small medieval horn made from an elephant's tusk.

ondes Martenot   Electronic keyboard instrument developed by Maurice Martenot in the 1920s; shaped like a spinet.

ophicleide   Large, brass, keyed bass bugle played in the upright position, developed from the serpent (name is Greek for 'serpent with keys') but displaced by the bass tuba.

panharmonicon   Mechanical orchestra invented by Johann Maelzel in 1805; inspiration of Beethoven's *Battle Symphony*.

panpipes (aka syrinx)   Ancient wind instrument consisting of several pipes of graduated lengths bound together.

pegbox   Box at the end of the neck on string instruments into which the pegs that adjust the strings are inserted.

phagotum   Type of bellows-blown bagpipe invented by Canon Afranio of Ferrara in the early 1500s.

pianoforte   Full name of the piano, with 88 keys, first made in Florence around 1700 by Bartolomeo Cristofori; name is Italian for soft-loud.

pianola   Player piano manufactured in the early 1900s by the Aeolian Corporation; the first of the kind was the Welte-Mignon.

piccolo   Small flute that sounds an octave higher than written (piccolo in C) or, less often, a minor ninth higher than written (piccolo in D flat).

point   Tip of the bow of a string instrument.

poliphant   Thirty-seven-stringed instrument of early 17th century; a cross between harp, lute and theorbo.

posthorn Cylindrical, valveless straight horn used by coachmen and mailcarriers to announce arrival.

psaltery Ancient string instrument, similar to the dulcimer.

purfling Decorative strip inlaid around the edges of a string instrument.

pyiba Pear-shaped, four-stringed, ancient Chinese lute.

racket Double-reed instrument consisting of short, thick cylinder of wood drilled along its length with a bore-holes connected into a single air channel.

raspa Cuban percussion instrument made out of gourd with notches that are scraped with a stick.

ratamacue Drum rudiment consisting of an alternating-hand sticking pattern.

ratchet/rattle Percussion instrument with a cogwheel that strikes one or more metal or wooden projections when twirled.

rebab An ancient North African and Middle Eastern short-necked fiddle with two strings.

rebec Small, pear-shaped, medieval bowed instrument, a development of the Arab rebab, with a short neck and three to five strings.

recorder End-blown wooden flute without keys, with a tapering bore.

reed(s) Clarinet is a single-reed instrument; oboe and bassoon are double-reed.

regal Portable reed organ of the 16th century.

Rhodes piano Electric piano developed by Harold Rhodes.

rhythmicon Keyboard percussion instrument using photoelectric cell and devised by Lev Theremin and Henry Cowell in 1931.

rosin Block of hardened tree resin that is rubbed across the bow hairs to enhance the friction.

rote (rotta) Lyre-type instrument from the Middle Ages.

sackbut Renaissance name for the slide trombone, which then had a smaller bell and narrower bore.

saddle On guitar, a thin strip of ivory, bone or plastic set into the bridge.

saltbox Charivari instrument used by flipping the lid and beating the side with a rolling pin or spoon.

samisen Flat-backed, long-necked lute from Japan with a skin-covered belly and three silk strings.

sarangi Northern Indian fiddle with short, thick neck and 3 to 4 bowed strings plus sympathetic strings.

sarod Indian instrument usually having 6 main strings and 12 to 15 sympathetic strings.

sarrusophone Double-reed woodwind instrument related to the oboe but made of brass, invented by French bandleader Sarrus in 1856.

saxophone Single-reed family of instruments, usually metal but sometimes plastic, invented by Adolphe Sax around 1840 and patented in 1846.

scordatura Changing the tuning of one or more strings from their standard pitch.

scroll Ornamental curled portion at the end of the pegbox on instruments of the violin family.

Scruggs picking Banjo finger-picking style developed by Earl Scruggs, using the thumb and two fingers.

serpent S-curved wooden horn with a conical bore, finger holes and a cup-shaped mouthpiece.

seven-string guitar Has an extra, high A string.

shakuhachi End-blown bamboo flute from Japan.

shawm Family of high-pitched, double-reed woodwind instruments of the Middle Ages; precursors of the oboe.

sheng Chinese mouth organ made up of wind chamber fitted with pipes with reeds that vibrate.

shofar Ancient Hebrew ceremonial wind instrument made of a ram's horn.

simandl bow For string basses; a bow configured to be held with the palm up.

sistrum Ancient percussion instrument made up of metal disc rattles threaded on rods.

sitar Long-necked Indian lute with moveable arched frets, a gourd resonator close to the pegboard, and 3 to 7 strings, below which are sympathetic strings, often as many as 12. Made popular in the West by Ravi Shankar.

skirl On bagpipe, the sounds made by the upper pipes.

sousaphone Tuba that encircles the body and made specifically for John Philip Sousa's band.

spinet Small Renaissance keyboard instrument with a plucking action like a harpsichord.

steel drums Made out of various-sized oil drums, with deeply incised patterns with different pitches.

stick, Chapman Electric 10-stringed (5 bass and 5 guitar) instrument that utilises tapping technique on strings.

swell Mechanical device on some keyboard instruments for adjusting the volume of sound.

switch Percussion instrument, made up of wires bound at one end, that is struck against the hand.

sympathetic string String that vibrates in an instrument without being plucked in response to the vibrations of strings that are plucked, or to a percussion impact.

tablas Asymmetrical pair of conical, tuned, wooden Indian drums, beaten with the hands.

tabor Earliest form of the snare drum, which evolved into a military instrument.

talon The nut end of the bow used to play string instruments.

tambour Type of drum.

tambourine Percussion instrument of Arab origin consisting of a small, shallow, circular drum with metal discs inserted into its frame. The discs are known as jingles.

tambur(a) Long-necked, round-bodied lute. Indian tamburas have 4 strings, drones and a moveable ivory bridge to adjust pitch; Balkan tamburas are fretted.

tam-tam Large, flat, thin metal saucer suspended on a frame and struck with a soft beater.

theorbo Sixteenth-century arch-lute with numerous stopped and unstopped strings attached to separate pegbox.

Theremin Electronic instrument developed by Lev Theremin (1920); the hands do not touch the instrument but produce oscillations when they move around the antenna.

ti tzu Chinese flute with 6 finger-holes and a 7th hole covered with thin membrane whose vibration dictates the tone.

timbrel Ancient Middle Eastern tambourine, and its medieval European descendant.

tin whistle High-pitched, end-blown Irish flute with 6 holes, made out of metal.

tonette Wood or plastic end-blown flute with finger-holes.

tremolo arm Device that changes the pitch of the strings by moving the bridge with a type of spring action.

trombone Brass instrument, larger than a trumpet, and with a sliding tube to extend notes.

MUSIC CLASSICAL

trumpet Brass wind instrument consisting of a long tubular central piece with a cup-shaped mouth-piece and wide, bell-shaped base. A trumpet has three valves.

tuba Bass instrument patented by W Wieprecht and Moritz in Berlin (1835).

tubular bells Percussion instrument in the form of suspended tubes, tuned to the diatonic scale, and struck with a hammer.

tuning-fork Two-pronged metal instrument invented in 1711 by the trumpeter John Shore. The pure tone that it emits when set vibrating helps to give the pitch to singers or instruments.

uilleann pipes Irish bagpipes worked by bellows held under one arm.

ukelele (ukulele) Four-stringed instrument developed in Hawaii in the 1870s from a kind of Portugese guitar

upright piano Piano in which strings are vertical. John Isaac Hawkins of Philadelphia first built iron-framed uprights in 1800.

vibraphone (vibes) Xylophone with metal bars and a wide vibrato effect produced by electrically operated fans.

vihuela Six-string Spanish instrument of the 1600s that looks like a guitar but is tuned as a lute.

vina Indian stringed instrument, those from northern India having a long stick-like unfretted fingerboard resting on two resonating gourds, those from southern India having a much broader

fingerboard and a wooden body in place of one of the gourds.

viola da braccio Tenor viol played under the arm.

viola da gamba Bass viol played between the knees.

viola d'amore Unfretted tenor instrument with 7 strings and 7 to 14 sympathetic strings.

violin Treble stringed instrument with 4 strings tuned to G, D, A, E.

violoncello Tenor stringed instrument of the violin family, played between the knees, using bass clef, with 4 strings tuned to C, G, D, A.

virginal Small, soft-sounding harpsichord of the 16th and 17th centuries, with one string to a note.

Wagner tuba Invented by Richard Wagner specifically for his *Ring Cycle*; look is more of a horn than a tuba.

whammy bar Another name for tremolo arm.

woodwind Recorders, flutes, clarinets, saxophones, oboes, piccolos, cor anglais and bassoons (lowest pitch).

xylophone (lit. wood sound) Percussion instrument consisting of graduated, tuned wooden bars played by being struck with a hammer.

xylorimba Combination of xylophone and marimba.

zither Family of plucked string instruments including the dulcimer, hummel, koto, autoharp and psaltery, where the (up to 45) strings run the entire length of a flat body.

Famous Musicians

Bassoonists
Archie Camden
John Hebden
D Kern Holoman
Jacques Hotteterre
Edwin James
John Lampe
William Waterhouse

Cellists
Hugo Becker
Luigi Boccherini
Anner Bylsma
Pablo Casals
Gaspar Cassadó
Mischel Cherniavsky
Myung-Wha Chung
Robert Cohen
Christopher Coin
Karl Davidoff
Jean Louis Dufort
Jean Pierre Dufort
Jacqueline Du Pré
Maurice Eisenberg
Emanuel Feuermann
Amaryllis Fleming
Pierre Fournier
Auguste Franchomme
Carl Fuchs
Karine Georgian
Georg Goltermann
Bernard Greenhouse
Natalia Gutman
Lynn Harrell
Beatrice Harrison
Nicola Haym

John Hebden
Thomas Igloi
Steven Isserlis
Giuseppe Maria
  Jacchini
Ivor James
Antonio Janigro
Hans Kindler
Ralph Kirshbaum
Anton Kraft
Nicolaus Kraft
Robert Lindley
Julian Lloyd Webber
Martin Lovett
Antonio Lysy
Yo-Yo Ma
Enrico Mainardi
Mischa Maisky
António Meneses
Howard Mitchell
May Mukle
André Navarra
Charles Neate
Zara Nelsova
Arto Noras
Vladimir Orloff
Siegfried Palm
Stephen Paxton
Boris
  Pergamenschikov
Gregor Piatigorsky
Alfredo Piatti
Anthony Pini
William Pleeth
David Popper
Julius Rietz

Bernhard Romberg
Leonard Rose
Mstislav Rostropovich
Milos Sádlo
Felix Salmond
Samuil Samosud
Heinrich Schiff
Johann Schlick
Georg Schnéevoigt
Mátyás Seiber
Adrien François Servais
Raphael Sommer
William Henry Squire
János Starker
Guilhermina Suggia
Paul Tortelier
Arturo Toscanini
Christopher Van
  Kampen
Alfred Wallenstein
Raphael Wallfisch
Moray Welsh
August Wenzinger
Gay-Yee Westerhoff
Hanus Wihan

Clarinettists
John Adams
Heinrich Bärmann
Jack Brymer
Louis Cahuzac
Benny Goodman
Woody Herman
Janet Hilton
Emma Johnson
Reginald Kell

Thea King
Hyacinth Klosé
Henry Lewis
Richard Mühlfeld
Gervase de Peyer
Artie Shaw
Anton Stadler
Richard Stolzman
Morton Subotnick
Frederick Thurston
Bernard Walton

Double Bass
Giovanni Bottesini
Ida Carroll
Eugene Cruft
Domenico Dragonetti
Barry Guy
Gary Karr
Franz Kotzwara
Serge Koussevitzky

Flautists
Richard Adeney
Bruno Bartoletti
Michel Blavet
Theobald Boehm
Giulio Briccialdi
Franz Doppler
Karl Doppler
Louis François
  Fleury
James Galway
Severino Gazzelloni
Geoffrey Gilbert
Dave Heath

Hans-Joachim
  Koellreutter
Hans-Martin Linde
Johann Bernhard
  Logier
Edward McGuire
Susan Milan
Gareth Morris
Marcel Moyse
Aurèle Nicolet
Johann Quantz
Jean-Pierre Rampal
Elaine Shaffer
Fritz Spiegl
Adolf Terschak
David Van Vactor

French Horn
Hermann Baumann
Aubrey Brain
Dennis Brain
Alan Civil
Anthony Halstead
David Pyatt
Barry Tuckwell

Guitarists
Julian Bream
Leo Brouwer
Cornelius Cardew
Ferdinando Carulli
Mauro Giuliani
Peter Katona
Zoltan Katona
Miguel Llobet
Carlos Montoya
Gaspar Sanz
Andrés Segovia
Philip Selby
Fernando Sor
Francisco Tárrega
Jason Vieaux
John Williams
Narciso Yepes

Harpists
Osian Ellis
Félix Godefroid
Marie Goossens
Sidonie Goossens
Alphonse Hasselmans
Ursula Holliger
Alfred Holý
Maria Korchinska
Johann Krumpholtz
François Naderman
Elias Parish-Alvars
John Parry
Nansi Richards
Marisa Robles
Carlos Salzédo
Marcel Tournier
Nicanor Zabaleta

Horns
Johannes Amon
David Amram
Adolph Borsdorf
Alan Civil
Louis-François Dauprat
John Denison
Heinrich Domnich

Anton Joseph Hampel
Maurice Handford
Ifor James
Ignaz Leutgeb
Giovanni Punto
Timothy Reynish
Franz Joseph Strauss
Barry Tuckwell

Mouth Organists
Larry Adler
Tommy Reilly

Oboists
Evelyn Barbirolli (née
  Rothwell)
Neil Black
Janet Craxton
John Cruft
Johann Fischer
Leon Goossens
Heinz Holliger
John Lancie
Ludwig August Lebrun
Charles Mackerras
Jean-Claude Malgoire
Friedrich Ramm
Ray Still
Edo de Waart

Organists
Herbert Andrews
Jennifer Bate
Jonathan Battishill
William Best
E Power Biggs
John Birch
John Blitheman
John Blow
Léon Boëllmann
Georg Böhm
Kevin Bowyer
John Dykes Bower
Ernest Bullock
Charles Burney
John Camidge
Matthew Camidge
Thomas Camidge
Melville Cook
George Cunningham
Carlo Curley
John Danby
Thurston Dart
Christopher Dearnley
William Done
Maurice Dupré
Hermann Finck
Grattan Flood
Virgil Fox
Alfred Gaul
Nicolas Gigault
Eugène Gigout
Johann Goldberg
John Goss
Alan Gray
Nicolas de Grigny
Douglas Guest
George Guest
Christopher Herrick
Edward Hopkins
Karl Friedrich Horn
Francis Jackson

Geraint Jones
Johann Kerll
Jacob Kirckman
Leonhard Kleber
Carlmann Kolb
Johann Krebs
Jean Langlais
Philip Ledger
Edwin Lemare
Henry Ley
Gaston Litaize
Charles Lloyd
Vincent Lübeck
David Lumsden
André Marchal
Louis Marchand
Giovanni Martini
Olivier Messiaen
Georg Monn
James Nares
Edward Naylor
Martin Neary
Sydney Nicholson
Thomas Noble
Vincent Novello
Herbert Oakeley
Boris Ord
Johann Pachelbel
Jane Parker-Smith
Peter Pears
Simon Preston
Daniel Purcell
Henry Purcell
James Pyne
Helmuth Rilling
Edward Rimbault
Alec Robertson
Douglas Robinson
Lionel Rogg
Cyril Rootham
Barry Rose
Bernard Rose
Francisco de Salinas
Sir Malcolm Sargent
Heinrich Scheidemann
Samuel Scheidt
Albert Schweitzer
John Scott
George Sinclair
Johann Staden
Paul Steinitz
Leopold Stokowski
Karl Straube
Herbert Sumsion
Richard Terry
George Thalben-Ball
David Titterington
Thomas Trotter
David Tudor
Franz Tunder
Denis Vaughan
Louis Vierne
Helmut Walcha
William Walond
Henry Watson
Gillian Weir
Charles Wesley
Allan Wicks
Charles-Marie Widor
David Willcocks
Charles Lee Williams
Malcolm Williamson

Arthur Wills
Philipp Wolfrum
Leslie Woodgate
Henry Wood
Pietro Alessandro Yon
Pietro Ziani

Percussionists
James Blades
Evelyn Glennie
Stomu Yamashita

Pianists
Jacques Abram
Joaquin Achucarro
Thomas Ades
Daniel Adni
Roy Agnew
Martha Argerich
Vladimir Ashkenazy
Stefan Askenase
Victor Babin
Gina Bachauer
Paul Badura-Skoda
Daniel Barenboim
Hans Barth
Ethel Bartlett
Harold Bauer
Malcolm Bilson
Christian Blackshaw
Marc Blitzstein
Michel Block
Susan Bradshaw
Alfred Brendel
Yefim Bronfman
Bruno Canino
Teresa Carreño
Jean Casadesus
Robert Marcel
  Casadesus
Shura Cherkassky
Aldo Ciccolini
Van Cliburn
Harriet Cohen
Elizabeth Coolidge
Imogen Cooper
Joseph Cooper
Alfred Cortot
Johann Cramer
Paul Crossley
Clifford Curzon
Karl Czerny
György Cziffra
Michel Dalberto
Edward Dannreuther
Bella Davidovich
Peter Donohoe
Ania Dorfmann
Barry Douglas
Karl Engel
John Field
Margaret Fingerhut
Rudolf Firkusny
Annie Fischer
Edwin Fischer
Leon Fleisher
Myers Foggin
Andor Foldes
Hubert Foss
Ian Fountain
Fou Ts'ong
Philip Fowke

MUSIC CLASSICAL

Homero Francesch
Samson François
Peter Frankl
Justus Frantz
Géza Frid
Ignaz Friedman
Benjamin Frith
Liza Fuchsova
Ossip Gabrilowitsch
Irwin Gage
Andrei Gavrilov
Walter Gieseking
Emil Gilels
Arabella Goddard
Leopold Godowsky
Anthony Goldstone
Richard Goode
Glenn Gould
Gary Graffman
Percy Grainger
Arthur de Greef
Gordon Green
Horacio Gutiérrez
Monique Haas
Ingrid Haebler
Charles Hallé
Mark Hambourg
Paul Hamburger
Iain Hamilton
Clara Haskil
Claude Helffer
Clifton Helliwell
Myra Hess
Rolf Hind
Alfred Hipkins
Ludwig Hoffman
Vladimir Horowitz
Colin Horsley
Louis Horst
Mieczyslaw Horszowski
Stephen Hough
Andrew Imbrie
John Ireland
Edward Isaacs
Leonard Isaacs
Michael Isador
Martin Isepp
Eugene Istomin
Paul Jacobs
Byron Janis
Grant Johannesen
Graham Johnson
Eileen Joyce
Terence Judd
Jeffrey Kahane
Joseph Kalichstein
Friedrich Kalkbrenner
William Kapell
Jean-Rodolphe Kars
Julius Katchen
Peter Katin
Mindru Katz
Wilhelm Kempff
John Kirkpatrick
Evgeny Kissin
Bernhard Klee
Walter Klien
Karl Klindworth
Zoltán Kocsis
Alfons Kontarsky
Aloys Kontarsky
Lili Kraus

Katia Labèque
Marielle Labèque
Frederic Lamond
Alicia de Larrocha
Philip Ledger
Yvonne Lefébure
Theodor Leschetizky
Oscar Levant
Raymond Lewenthal
Hans Leygraf
Josef Lhévinne
Rosina Lhévinne
John Lill
Eugene List
Kathleen Long
Marguérite Long
Alessandro Longo
Yvonne Loriod
Radu Lupu
Moura Lympany
Alexei Lyubimov
Joanna McGregor
Witold Malcuzynski
Leopold Mannes
Tobias Matthay
Denis Matthews
Florence May
Fanny Mendelssohn
Hephzibah Menuhin
Frank Merrick
Noel Mewton-Wood
Nina Milkina
Benno Moiseiwitsch
Federico Mompou
David Money
Stephen Montague
Gerald Moore
Angus Morrison
Ignaz Moscheles
Charles Neate
Marc Neikrug
Ivor Newton
Joaquin Nin
David Owen Norris
Lev Oborin
Noriko Ogawa
John Ogdon
Garrick Ohlsson
Mercedes Olivera
Georges Onslow
Ursula Oppens
Rafael Orozco
Leslie Orrey
Cristina Ortiz
George Osborne
Cécile Ousset
Vladimir Ovchinikov
Vladimir de Pachmann
Ignacy Jan Paderewski
Kun Woo Paik
Maria von Paradis
   (blind)
Jon Kimura Parker
Eric Parkin
Geoffrey Parsons
Güher Pekinel
Süher Pekinel
Leonard Pennario
Murray Perahia
Vlado Perlemuter
Egon Petri
Nikolai Petrov

Isidor Philipp
Maria-João Pires
Johann Peter Pixis
Artur Pizarro
Barbara von Ployer
Ivo Pogorelich
Maurizio Pollini
Jean-Bernard Pommier
Viktoria Postnikova
Leff Pouishnoff
Ferdinand Praeger
André Previn
Stephen Pruslin
Gwenneth Pryor
Anne Queffélec
Ruth Railton
Thomas Rajna
Dezsö Ránki
Clarence Raybould
Julius Reubke
Robert Riefling
Ferdinand Ries
Bernard Roberts
Rae Robertson
Pascal Rogé
Michael Roll
Martin Roscoe
Charles Rosen
Moriz Rosenthal
Mstislav Rostropovich
Anton Rubinstein
Arthur Rubinstein
Nikolay Rubinstein
Mikhail Rudy
Christian Rummel
Walter Rummel
Harold Rutland
Vasily Safonov
Harold Samuel
György Sándor
Jesús Maria Sanromá
Vasily Sapellnikov
Sir Malcolm Sargent
Irene Scharrer
Xaver Scharwenka
Ernest Schelling
Heinrich Schenker
Andras Schiff
Allan Schiller
Artur Schnabel
Karl Ulrich Schnabel
Irina Schnittke
Clara Schumann
Phyllis Sellick
Yitkin Seow
Peter Serkin
Rudolf Serkin
Shulamith Shafir
William Shakespeare
Howard Shelley
Maxim Shostakovich
Béla Siki
Constantin Silvestri
Abbey Simon
Leonard Slatkin
Jan Smeterlin
Cyril Smith
Ronald Smith
Yonty Solomon
Georg Solti
Peter Stadlen
Bernhard Stavenhagen

Wilhelm Stenhammar
Ronald Stevenson
Soulima Stravinsky
Walter Susskind
Roberto Szidon
Carl Tausig
André Tchaikowsky
Boris Tchaikovsky
Alec Templeton
Sigismond Thalberg
Jean-Yves Thibaudet
Michael Tilson Thomas
Martino Tirimo
Donald Tovey
Valerie Tryon
Norman Tucker
David Tudor
Rosalyn Tureck
Mitsuko Uchida
Sergio Varella-Cid
Tamás Vásáry
Bálint Vazsonyi
Isabelle Vengerova
Adela Verne
Mathilde Verne
Roger Vignoles
Ricardo Viñes
Lucille Wallace
Peter Wallfisch
Fanny Waterman
Sydney Watson
André Watts
Daniel Wayenberg
Joseph Weingarten
Erik Werba
Jósef Wieniawski
Earl Wild
David Wilde
Malcolm Williamson
Paul Wittgenstein
Roger Woodward
Enloc Wu
Friedrich Wührer
Marie Wurm
Jürg Wyttenbach
Théophile Ysaye
Carlo Zecchi
Géza Zichy
Alexander Ziloti
Krystian Zimerman
Jan Zimmer
Agnes Zimmermann

Trumpeters
Maurice André
Malcolm Arnold
Ernest Hall
Håkan Hardenberger
Philip Jones
Humphrey Lyttelton
Johann Petzold
Gerard Schwarz
Crispian Steel-Perkins
Edward Tarr
John Wilbraham

Tuba
Eleazar de Carvalho

Violists
Yuri Bashmet
Tania Davis

Paul Doktor
Watson Forbes
Rivka Golani
Karel Hába
Nobuko Imai
Allan Pettersson
Jean Pougnet
William Primrose
Frederick Riddle
Hermann Ritter
Peter Schidlof
Bernard Shore
Lionel Tertis
Walter Trampler
Efrem Zimbalist

Violinists
Joseph Achron
Delphin Alard
Pierre Amoyal
Jelly Arányi
Alexandre-Joseph Artôt
Thomas Baltzar
John Banister
Angel Barrios
Richard Barth
Yuri Bashmet
Rudolf Baumgartner
Hugh Bean
Paul Beard
Boris Belkin
Joshua Bell
Norbert Brainin
George Bridgetower
Adolph Brodsky
Ole Bull
Alfredo Campoli
John Carrodus
Marius Casadesus
Arthur Catterall
Eos Chater
Levon Chilingiran
Kyung-Wha Chung
Raymond Cohen
Béla Dekany
Gioconda De Vito
Augustine Dumay
Haylie Ecker
John Ella
Mischa Elman
Devy Erlih
Adila Fachiri
Carlo Farina
Alfonso Ferrabosco
Christian Ferras
Michael Festing
Carl Flesch
Giovanni Fontana
Zino Francescatti
Miriam Fried
Joseph Fuchs

Mayumi Fujikawa
Ivan Galamian
Saschko Gawriloff
André Gertler
Rivka Golani
Szymon Goldberg
Stephane Grappelli
Hyam Greenbaum
Sidney Griller
Frederick Grinke
Ida Haendel
Marie Hall
Jascha Heifetz
Joseph Hellmesberger
Willy Hess
Ulf Hoelscher
Karl Hoffmann
Ralph Holmes
Henry Holst
Yuzuko Horigome
Jenö Hubay
Bronislaw Huberman
Monica Huggett
Shizuka Ishikawa
Feliks Janiewicz
Joseph Joachim
Leila Josefowicz
Joseph Kaminski
Mark Kaplan
Louis Kaufman
Hans Keller
Nigel Kennedy
Willem Kes
Isabelle van Keulen
Young-Uck Kim
Pawel Kochánski
Leonid Kogan
Franz Kotzwara
Fritz Kreisler
Gidon Kremer
Rodolphe Kreutzer
Wenzel Krumpholtz
Oleg Krysa
Jan Kubelik
Sigiswald Kuijken
Georg Kulenkampff
Franz Lamotte
Linda Lampenius
Jaime Laredo
Cho-Liang Lin
Tasmin Little
Alan Loveday
Mark Lubotsky
Anne Macnaghten
Vanessa Mae
André Mangeot
Mantovani
Alessandro Marcello
Silvia Marcovici
Johanna Martzy
Joseph Massart

Nicola Matteis
Eduard Melkus
Isolde Menges
Yehudi Menuhin
Goto Midori
Stoika Milanova
Nathan Milstein
Shlomo Mintz
Lydia Mordkovitch
Viktoria Mullova
Charles Munch
Anne-Sophie Mutter
Pietro Nardini
Yfrah Neaman
Wilma Neruda
Ginette Neveu
Sigmund Nissel
David Oistrakh
Igor Oistrakh
Raphael Oleg
Frantisek Ondncek
Igor Ozim
Niccolò Paganini
Manoug Parikian
György Pauk
Edith Peinemann
Itzhak Perlman
George Frederic Pinto
Adolf Pollitzer
Jean Pougnet
Maud Powell
William Primrose
Gaetano Pugnani
Giovanni Punto
Michael Rabin
John Ravenscroft
Ede Reményi
Vadim Repin
Ruggiero Ricci
Franz Anton Ries
Hubert Ries
Alexander Ritter
Andreas Jakob
  Romberg
Arnold Rosé
Carl Rosiers
Max Rostal
Christian Rummel
George Saint-George
Prosper Sainton
Johann Peter Salomon
Albert Sammons
Eugene Sarbu
Emile Sauret
Rosario Scalero
Anton Schindler
Alexander Schneider
Wolfgang Schneiderhan
Jaap Schröder
Franz Schubert
Ignaz Schuppanzigh

Otakar Sevcik
Emily Shinner
Oscar Shumsky
Joseph Silverstein
Dmitry Sitkovetzky
Camillo Sivori
Nikolay Sokoloff
Paolo Spagnoletti
Albert Spalding
Theodore Spiering
Johann Wenzel Stamitz
Simon Standage
Isaac Stern
Julius Stern
Frederick Stock
George Stratton
Josef Suk
Zoltán Székely
Henryk Szeryng
Josef Szigeti
Gabor Takács-Nagy
Václav Talich
Giuseppe Tartini
Vilmos Tátrai
Charles Taylor
Arve Tellefsen
Emil Telmányi
Henri Temianka
Klaus Tennstedt
Carlo Tessarini
Jacques Thibaud
César Thomson
Luigi Tomasini
Giuseppe Torelli
Yan Pascal Tortelier
Roman Totenberg
Berthold Tours
Chrétien Urhan
Tibór Varga
Sándor Végh
Maxim Vengerov
Henri Verbrugghen
Henri Vieuxtemps
H. Waldo Warner
Joseph Miroslav Weber
Henryk Wieniawski
Wanda Wilkomirska
Marie Wilson
Michael Zacharewitsch
Christian Zacharias
Zvi Zeitlin
Jakob Zeugheer
Efrem Zimbalist
Frank Peter Zimmermann
Louis Zimmermann
Yossi Zivoni
Olive Zorian
Pinchas Zukerman
Paul Zukofsky

MUSIC CLASSICAL

Famous Singers

Sopranos
Aïno Ackté
Roberta Alexander
Jeannine Altmeyer
Elly Ameling
Marie Angel

Sheila Armstrong
Martina Arroyo
Florence Austral
Lilian Bailey
Isobel Baillie
Josephine Barstow

Kathleen Battle
Hildegard Behrens
Elizabeth Billington
Judith Blegen
Hannelore Bode
Barbara Bonney

Lucrezia Bori
Inge Borkh
Gré Brouwenstijn
Norma Burrowes
Montserrat Caballé
Teresa Cahill

Maria Callas
Emma Calvé
Maria Caniglia
Maria Caradori-Allan
Margherita Carosio
Katharina Cavalieri
Maria Cebotari
Maria Chiara
Charlotte Church
Gina Cigna
Mimi Coertse
Isabella Colbran
Elizabeth Connell
Mary Costa
Régine Crespin
Joan Cross
Lella Cuberli
Maud Cunitz
Toti Dal Monte
Suzanne Danco
Barbara Daniels
Gloria Davy
Anne Dawson
Lynne Dawson
Lisa Della Casa
Joséphine De Reszke
Emmy Destinn
Libuse Domaninska
Helen Donath
Dorothy Dorow
Dorothy Dow
Elizabeth Duparc
Denise Duval
Noël Eadie
Jean Eaglen
Emma Eames
Florence Easton
Christiane Eda-Pierre
Mary Ellis
Anne Evans
Carole Farley
Geraldine Farrar
Eileen Farrell
Helen Field
Sylvia Fischer
Kirsten Flagstad
Mirella Freni
Elizabeth Fretwell
Marya Freund
Marta Fuchs
Johanna Gadski
Amelita Galli-Curci
Mary Garden
Lesley Garrett
Catherine Gayer
Mechthild Gessendorf
Sona Ghazarian
Christel Goltz
Jill Gomez
Linda Esther Gray
Silvia Greenberg
Giulia Grisi
Reri Grist
Edita Gruberova
Nora Gruhn
Elisabeth Grümmer
Hilde Gueden
Nancy Gustafson
Marie Gutheil-Schoder
Alison Hagley
Joan Hammond
Heather Harper

Eiddwen Harrhy
Kathryn Harries
Elizabeth Harwood
Minnie Hauk
Cynthia Haymon
Lorna Haywood
Frieda Hempel
Elvira de Hidalgo
Judith Howarth
Karen Huffstodt
Rita Hunter
Maria Ivogün
Gundula Janowitz
Maria Jeritza
Sumi Jo
Eva Johannson
Gwyneth Jones
Ava June
Sena Jurinac
Raina Kabaivanska
Kiri Te Kanawa
Julie Kaufmann
Adelaide Kemble
Barbra Kemp
Yvonne Kenny
Adele Kern
Emma Kirkby
Dorothy Kirsten
Katharina Klafsky
Anny Konetzni
Hilde Konetzni
Annelies Kupper
Selma Kurz
Dora Labbette
Aloysia Lange
Nanny Larsén-Todsen
Magda Laszló
Marjorie Lawrence
Evelyn Lear
Lilli Lehmann
Liza Lehmann
Lotte Lehmann
Frida Leider
Adèle Leigh
Hellen Lemmens
Tiana Lemnitz
Mary Lewis
Miriam Licette
Caterina Ligendza
Jenny Lind
Berit Lindholm
Wilma Lipp
Pilar Lorengar
Victoria de Los Angeles
Felicity Lott
Germaine Lubin
Pauline Lucca
Sylvia McNair
Catherine Malfitano
Mathilde Mallinger
Blanche Marchesi
Lois Marshall
Margaret Marshall
Eva Marton
Valerie Masterson
Amalie Materna
Edith Mathis
Karita Mattila
Johanna Meier
Nellie Melba
Janine Micheau
Julia Migenes

Zinka Milanov
Anna von Mildenburg
Audrey Mildmay
Aprile Millo
Nelly Miricioiu
Martha Mödl
Anna Moffo
Fanny Moody
Grace Moore
Elsie Morison
Edda Moser
Maria Müller
Carol Neblett
Judith Nelson
Mignon Nevada
Agnes Nicholls
Birgit Nilsson
Christine Nilsson
Alda Noni
Elizabeth Norberg
Lillian Nordica
Jessye Norman
Clara Novello
Jarmila Novotná
Magda Olivero
Elaine Padmore
Felicity Palmer
Euphrosyne Parepa
Anne Pashley
Giuditta Pasta
Adelina Patti
Rose Pauly
Fanny Persiani
Roberta Peters
Helga Pilarczyk
Rosalind Plowright
Deborah Polaski
Lily Pons
Rosa Ponselle
Lucia Popp
Leontyne Price
Margaret Price
Yvonne Printemps
Ana Pusar
Ashley Putnam
Louisa Pyne
Rosa Raisa
Hildegard Ranczak
Judith Raskin
Aulikki Rautawaara
Delia Reinhardt
Maria Reining
Elisabeth Rethberg
Esther Réthy
Katia Ricciarelli
Margaret Ritchie
Faye Robinson
Joan Rodgers
Amanda Roocroft
Annaliese Rothenberger
Hermine Rudersdorff
Leonie Rysanek
Hilde Sadek
Sibyl Sanderson
Sylvia Sass
Bidú Sayão
Marianne Schech
Erna Schlüter
Elisabeth Schumann
Vera Schwarz
Elisabeth Schwarzkopf
Graziella Sciutti

Renata Scotto
Nadine Secunde
Irmgard Seefried
Meta Seinemeyer
Marcella Sembrich
Luciana Serra
Ellen Shade
Honor Sheppard
Margaret Sheridan
Amy Shuard
Margarethe Siems
Anja Silja
Dorothy Silk
Beverly Sills
Jeannette Sinclair
Victoria Sladen
Oda Slobodskaya
Elisabeth Söderström
Henriette Sontag
Elena Souliotis
Maria Stader
Eleanor Steber
Hanny Steffek
Sophie Stehle
Anna Steiger
Teresa Stich-Randall
Lilian Stiles Allen
Teresa Stolz
Anna Storace
Rosina Storchio
Teresa Stratas
Rita Streich
Cheryl Studer
Rosa Sucher
Elsie Suddaby
Susan Sunderland
Joan Sutherland
Helena Tattermuschová
Renata Tebaldi
Giusto Tenducci (male)
Milka Ternina
Margarete
  Teschemacher
Eva Tetrazzini
Luisa Tetrazzini
Maggie Teyte
Thérèse Tietjens
Pauline Tinsley
Anna Tomowa-Sintow
Helen Traubel
Carrie Tubb
Eva Turner
Dawn Upshaw
Viorica Ursuleac
Leontina Vaduva
Benita Valente
Anita Välkki
Ninon Vallin
Carol Vaness
Julia Varady
Astrid Varnay
Elizabeth Vaughan
Galina Vishnevskaya
Jennifer Vyvyan
Johanna Wagner
Yoko Watanabe
Claire Watson
Janice Watson
Lilian Watson
Aloysia Weber
Gillian Webster
Lucie Weidt

Ljuba Welitsch
Ruth Welting
Catherine Wilson
Marie Wittich
Sophie Wyss
Rachel Yakar
Mara Zampieri
Ruth Ziesak
Teresa Zylis-Gara

Mezzo-sopranos

Janet Baker
Agnes Baltsa
Cecilia Bartoli
Teresa Berganza
Faustina Bordoni
Olga Borodina
Marianne Brandt
Marie Brema
Grace Bumbry
Sally Burgess
Majorano Caffarelli
Sarah Jane Cahier
Susanna Cibber
Katherine Ciesinski
Cynthi Clarey
Girolamo Crescentini
Claire Croiza
Janice De Gaetani
Astra Desmond
Oralia Dominguez
Nancy Evans
Maria Ewing
Brigitte Fassbaender
Linda Finnie
Muriel Forster
Elena Gerhardt
Rita Gorr
Bernadette Greevy
Giuditta Grisi
Barbara Hendricks
Jane Henschel
Alfreda Hodgson
Grace Hoffman
Elisabeth Höngen
Marilyn Horne
Anne Howells
Eirian James
Della Jones
Fiona Kimm
Louise Kirkby-Lunn
Gillian Knight
Nadezda Kniplová
Kathleen Kuhlmann
Lotte Lenya
Marjana Lipovsek
Martha Lipton
Jean Madeira
Maria Malibran
Mathilde Marchesi
Waltraud Meier
Susanne Mentzer
Kerstin Meyer
Yvonne Minton
Diana Montague
Ann Murray
Hyacinth Nicholls
Elena Obraztsova
Maria Olczewska
Anne Sofie von Otter
Rosa Papier
Anna Pollak

Florence Quivar
Eva Randová
Nell Rankin
Regina Resnik
Anna Reynolds
Jean Rigby
Vera Rozsa
Trudeliese Schmidt
Hanna Schwarz
Constance Shacklock
Mitsuko Shirai
Giulietta Simionato
Monica Sinclair
Doris Soffel
Frederica von Stade
Risë Stevens
Ebe Stignani
Conchita Supervia
Gladys Swarthout
Klara Takács
Blanche Thebom
Kerstin Thorborg
Jennie Tourel
Zélia Trebelli
Tatiana Troyanos
Lucia Valentini-Terrani
Josephine Veasey
Shirley Verrett
Pauline Viardot-Garcia
Sieglinde Wagner
Edyth Walker
Penelope Walker
Sarah Walker
Carolyn Watkinson
Lucie Weidt
Eugenia Zareska
Delores Ziegler

Counter-tenors

James Bowman
Michael Chance
Alfred Deller
Jochen Kowalski
Andreas Scholl

Contraltos

Muriel Brunskill
Clara Butt
Giovanni Carestini
Kathleen Ferrier
Birgit Finnilä
Maureen Forrester
Louise Homer
Mary Jarred
Sigrid Onegin
Norma Procter
Gladys Ripley
Charlotte Sainton-Dolby
Ernestine
  Schumann-Heink
Antoinette Sterling
Caroline Unger
Lucia Elizabeth Vestris
Mary Wakefield
Helen Watts

Baritones

Thomas Allen
Pasquale Amato
Ettore Bastianini
Pierre Bernac
John Brownlee

Sesto Bruscantini
Renato Bruson
Delme Bryn-Jones
Renato Capecchi
Piero Cappuccilli
Clive Carey
Ulrik Cold
Brian Cooke
Peter Dawson
Giuseppe De Luca
Willi
  Domgraf-Fassbänder
Geraint Evans
Keith Falkner
David Ffrangcon-Davies
Dietrich Fischer-Dieskau
Lucien Fugère
Peter Glossop
Tito Gobbi
John Goss
Franz Grundheber
Hakan Hagegard
Derek Hammond-Stroud
Thomas Hampson
Percy Heming
Thomas Hemsley
Roy Henderson
George Henschel
Jason Howard
Neil Howlett
Gerhard Hüsch
Dmitri Hvorostovsky
Jorma Hynninen
Richard Jackson
Herbert Janssen
Phillip Joll
Dimitri Kharitonov
Peter Knapp
Otakar Kraus
Tom Krause
Jean-Louis Lassalle
Sergei Leiferkus
François Le Roux
George London
Benjamin Luxon
Donald McIntyre
James Maddalena
Victor Maurel
Donald Maxwell
Michael Maybrick
Yury Mazurok
Robert Merrill
Johannes Messchaert
Dennis Noble
John Noble
Alan Opie
Rolando Panerai
Charles Panzéra
Kostas Paskalis
Antonio Pini-Corsi
Juan Pons
Hermann Prey
Gino Quilico
Louis Quilico
Frederick Ranalow
John Rawnsley
Theodor Reichmann
Maurice Renaud
Marko Rothmüller
Titta Ruffo
Kennerley Rumford
Karel Salomon

Mario Sammarco
Charles Santley
Heinrich Schlusnus
Andreas Schmidt
Paul Schöffler
Antonio Scotti
William Shimell
John Shirley-Quirk
Paolo Silveri
Knut Skram
Russell Smythe
Gérard Souzay
Oley Speaks
Mariano Stabile
Thomas Stewart
Richard Stilwell
Julius Stockhausen
Jonathan Summers
Giuseppe Taddei
Carlo Tagliabue
Antonio Tamburini
Lawrence Tibbett
Alan Titus
Hermann Uhde
Theodor Uppman
Giuseppe Valdengo
Anton Van Rooy
Ramón Vinay
Michael Vogl
Eberhard Wächter
Ian Wallace
Jess Walters
William Warfield
Leonard Warren
Bernd Weikl
Willard White
Clarence Whitehill
David Wilson-Johnson
Ingvar Wixell
Ekkerhard Wlaschiha
Gregory Yurisich
Giorgio Zancanaro

Tenors

Valentin Adamberger
John Aler
John Alexander
Luigi Alva
Max Alvary
Francisco Araiza
John Beard
Karl Beck
Kim Begley
Jussi Björling
Beno Blachut
Rockwell Blake
Dino Borgioli
Stuart Burrows
José Carreras
Enrico Caruso
Richard Cassilly
Graham Clark
John Coates
Vinson Cole
Peter Cornelius
Jean Cox
Charles Craig
Richard Crooks
Hugues Cuénod
Arthur Davies
Ben Davies
Ryland Davies

Tudor Davies
Mario Del Monaco
François Delsarte
Fernando De Lucia
Gregory Dempsey
Jean De Reszke
Anton Dermota
Plácido Domingo
Nigel Douglas
Ronald Dowd
Warren Ellsworth
Poul Elming
Gervase Elwes
Karl Erb
Bruce Ford
Paul Frey
Manuel del Garcia
Nicolai Gedda
Giuseppe Giacomelli
Beniamino Gigli
Reiner Goldberg
Karl Graun
Donald Grobe
Jerry Hadley
Ben Heppner
Martyn Hill
Joseph Hislop
Werner Hollweg
Hans Hopf
Walter Hyde
Hermann Jadlowker
Neil Jenkins
Siegfried Jerusalem
Edward Johnson
Parry Jones
Manfred Jung
Michael Kelly
Jan Kiepura
Waldemar Kmentt
Heinrich Knote
Alfredo Kraus
Werner Krenn
David Kuebler
Charles Kullman
Gary Lakes
Philip Langridge
Mario Lanza
Giacomo Lauri-Volpi
Jeffrey Lawton
Richard Leech
Keith Lewis
Richard Lewis
Luis Lima
Edward Lloyd
Max Lorenz
Veriano Lucheti

John McCormack
James McCracken
Giovanni Mario
Giovanni Martinelli
Yury Marusin
Helmut Melchert
Lauritz Melchior
Chris Merritt
Thomas Moser
Frank Mullings
Heddle Nash
Angelo Neumann
Albert Niemann
Adolphe Nourrit
Karl Oestvig
Alexander Oliver
Joseph O'Mara
Juan Oncina
Dennis O'Neill
Ian Partridge
Julius Patzak
Luciano Pavarotti
Peter Pears
Jan Peerce
Aureliano Pertile
Alfred Piccaver
Vilém Pribyl
Josef Protschka
Anton Raaff
Torsten Ralf
Thomas Randle
Sims Reeves
Alberto Remedios
David Rendall
Kenneth Riegel
Anthony Rolfe Johnson
Vladimir Rosing
Helge Roswaenge
Robert Rounseville
Giovanni-Battista
  Rubini
Thomas Salignac
Giovanni-Battista
  Sbriglia
Benedikt Schack
Aksel Schiotz
Tito Schipa
Erik Schmedes
Ludwig Schnorr
Rudolf Schock
Peter Schreier
Peter Seiffert
William Shakespeare
George Shirley
Léopold Simoneau
Leo Slezak

Fritz Soot
Gerhard Stolze
Kurt Streit
Ludwig Suthaus
Set Svanholm
Ferruccio Tagliavini
Francesco Tamagno
Enrico Tamberlik
Richard Tauber
John Templeton
Jess Thomas
Joseph Tichatschek
Richard Tucker
Fritz Uhl
Ragnar Ulfung
Georg Unger
Gerhard Unger
Jon Vickers
Ramón Vinay
Heinrich Vogl
Joseph Ward
Russell Watson
Spas Wenkoff
Walter Widdop
Steuart Wilson
Gösta Winbergh
Wolfgang Windgassen
Hermann Winkelmann
Hermann Winkler
Ludwig Wüllner
Fritz Wunderlich
Alexander Young
Heinz Zednik
Giovanni Zenatello
Ivo Zidek

Castrato
Domenico Annibali
Majorano Caffarelli
Girolano Crescentini
Carlo Farinelli
Gaetano Guadagni
Domenico Mustafa
Senesino

Bass
Donald Adams
Paul Bender
Kurt Böhme
Kim Borg
Fyodor Chaliapin
Boris Christoff
Henry Cooke
Stafford Dean
Otto Edelmann
Signor Foli

David Franklin
Gottlob Frick
Manuel Garcia
Nicolai Ghiaurov
Nicola Ghiuselev
Josef Greindl
Paul Hillier
Robert Holl
Gwynne Howell
Marcel Journet
Manfred Jungwirth
Alexander Kipnis
Paul Knüpfer
Luigi Lablache
Charles Manners
Josef von Manowarda
Kurt Moll
Paolo Montarsolo
Yevgeny Nesterenko
Robert Newman
Siegmund Nimsgern
Ezio Pinza
Pol Plançon
Paul Plishka
Robert Radford
Ruggero Raimondi
Karl Ridderbusch
Michael Rippon
Paul Robeson
Forbes Robinson
Nicola Rossi-Lemeni
Joseph Rouleau
Kurt Rydl
Matti Salminen
Manfred Schenk
Andrew Shore
Cesare Siepi
Hans Sotin
Roger Soyer
Horace Stevens
Fyodor Stravinsky
Mihály Székely
Italo Tajo
Martti Talvela
Bryn Terfel
David Thomas
John Tomlinson
Richard Van Allan
José Van Dam
Norman Walker
Gustavus Waltz
David Ward
Ludwig Weber
Nicola Zaccaria

Conductors

Claudio Abbado
Komei Abe
Hermann Abendroth
Maurice Abravanel
Byron Adams
John Adams
Kurt Adler
Peter Adler
Yuri Ahronovitch
Gerd Albrecht
John Alldis

Antonio Almeida
Petr Altricher
Carl Alwin
Gilbert Amy
Karel Ancerl
Géza Anda
Karsten Andersen
Martin André
Volkmar Andreae
Paul Angerer
Enrique Arbós

Richard Armstrong
Vladimir Ashkenazy
David Atherton
Moshe Atzmon
Daniel Barenboim
Thomas Beecham
Jiri Belohlavek
Richard Bernas
Leonard Bernstein
Henry Bishop
Stanley Black

Richard Blackford
Nadia Boulanger
Pierre Boulez
Adrian Boult
Martyn Brabbins
Joly Braga-Santos
Nicholas Braithewaite
Warwick Braithwaite
Max Bruch
Hans Bülow
Fritz Busch

Ferruccio Busoni
Basil Cameron
Philip Cannon
Guido Cantelli
André Caplet
Franco Capuana
John Carewe
Mosco Carner
Jean-Claude
  Casadesus
Fritz Cassirer
Aldo Ceccato
Zdenek Chalabala
Harry Christophers
Myung-Whun Chung
Nicholas Cleobury
Stephen Cleobury
André Cluytens
Albert Coates
James Conlon
Emil Cooper
Michael Costa
Robert Craft
John Crosby
Edric Cundell
William Cusins
Henryk Czyz
Frank Damrosch
Leopold Damrosch
Walter Damrosch
Paul Daniel
Oskar Danon
Stephen Darlington
Dennis Russell Davies
Andrew Davis
Colin Davis
Jacques Delacôte
Norman Del Mar
Gaetano Delogu
John DeMain
Neville Dilkes
Christoph von Dohnányi
Antal Dorati
Clive Douglas
Edward Downes
Sian Edwards
Karl Elmendorff
Alberto Erede
Mark Ermler
Franco Faccio
Bryan Fairfax
Charles Farncombe
Robert Farnon
Vladimir Fedoseyev
Frederick Fennell
Arthur Fiedler
Max Fiedler
Adam Fischer
Ivan Fischer
Anatole Fistoulari
Grzegorz Fitelberg
Claus Peter Flor
Lawrence Foster
Myer Fredman
Ferenc Fricsay
Oskar Fried
Lionel Friend
Janos Fürst
Wilhelm Furtwängler
Piero Gamba
John Eliot Gardiner
Valery Gergiev

Alexander Gibson
Michael Gielen
Carlo Maria Giulini
Jane Glover
Daniel Godfrey
Walter Goehr
Georg Göhler
Vladimir Golschmann
Reginald Goodall
Roy Goodman
Ron Goodwin
Eugene Goossens
  (Belg.)
Eugene Goossens (Fr.)
Eugene Goossens (GB)
Hans Graf
Michael Graubart
Noah Greenberg
Bohumil Gregor
Charles Groves
Hermann Grunebaum
Marco Guidarini
Karl Haas
Robert Haas
François Habeneck
Alan Hacker
Hartmut Haenchen
Bernard Haitink
Charles Hallé
Louis Halsey
Simon Halsey
Maurice Handford
Vernon Handley
Nikolaus Harnoncourt
Trevor Harvey
László Heltay
Philippe Herreweghe
Bernard Herrmann
Alfred Hertz
Leslie Heward
Richard Hickox
Alfred Hill
Jun'ichi Hirokami
Irwin Hoffman
Christopher Hogwood
Heinrich Hollreiser
Imogen Holst
Bo Holten
Anthony Hopkins
John Hopkins
Jascha Horenstein
Milan Horvat
Anthony Hose
Elgar Howarth
Owain Arwel Hughes
Donald Hunt
George Hurst
Eliahu Inbal
Michiyoshi Inoue
Ernest Irving
Robert Irving
José Iturbi
Hiroyuki Iwaki
René Jacobs
Reginald Jacques
Jussi Jalas
Marek Janowski
Arvid Jansons
Mariss Jansons
Neeme Järvi
Paavo Järvi
Graeme Jenkins

Newell Jenkins
Eugen Jochum
Jullien Joly
Simon Joly
Enrique Jordá
Armin Jordan
James Judd
Louis Julien
Jürgen Jürgens
Robert Kajanus
Okko Kamu
Herbert von Karajan
Jacek Kasprzyk
Bernard Keeffe
Christopher Keene
Joseph Keilberth
Rudolf Kempe
Paul van Kempen
István Kertész
Willem Kes
Hans Kindler
Robert King
Bernhard Klee
Carlos Kleiber
Erich Kleiber
Otto Klemperer
Paul Kletzki
Berislav Klobucar
Hans Knappertsbusch
Kazuhiro Koizumi
Kyril Kondrashin
Franz Konwitschny
Kazimierz Kord
Zdenek Kosler
André Kostelanetz
Serge Koussevitzky
Jiri Kout
Karel Kovarovic
Clemens Krauss
Yakov Kreizberg
Jan Krenz
Henry Krips
Josef Krips
Jaroslav Krombholc
Karl Krueger
Rafael Kubelik
Gustav Kuhn
Efrem Kurtz
Franz Lachner
Charles Lamoureux
Michael Lankester
Joseph Lanner
Lars-Erik Larsson
Eduard Lassen
Ashley Lawrence
Alexander Lazarev
Philip Ledger
Michel Legrand
György Lehel
Erich Leinsdorf
Lawrence Leonard
Raymond Leppard
Hermann Levi
James Levine
Anthony Lewis
Henry Lewis
András Ligeti
Andrew Litton
Grant Llewellyn
David Lloyd-Jones
James Lockhart
Alain Lombard

Jesus Lopez-Cobos
James Loughran
Ferdinand Löwe
John Lubbock
Leighton Lucas
Leopold Ludwig
Alexandre Luigini
Peter Maag
Lorin Maazel
Zdenek Macal
Denis McCaldin
Nicholas McGegan
Charles Mackerras
Ernest MacMillan
Fritz Mahler
Gustav Mahler
Jerzy Maksymiuk
Jean-Claude Malgoire
Nikolay Malko
Luigi Mancinelli
August Manns
Mantovani
Gino Marinuzi
Neville Marriner
Odaline de la Martinez
Jean Martinon
Giuseppe Martucci
Diego Masson
Kurt Masur
Eduardo Mata
Lovro von Matacic
Muir Mathieson
John Mauceri
Peter Maxwell Davies
Zubin Mehta
Willem Mengelberg
Herbert Menges
Howard Mitchell
Bernardino Molinari
Francesco
  Molinari-Pradelli
Pierre Monteux
Kenneth Montgomery
Rudolf Moralt
Wyn Morris
Felix Mottl
Evgeny Mravinsky
Karl Muck
Michael Mudie
Leopoldo Mugnone
Charles Munch
Karl Münchinger
Riccardo Muti
Kent Nagano
Garcia Navarro
Boyd Neel
John Nelson
Woldemar Nelsson
Frantisek Neumann
Václav Neumann
Roy Newsome
Harry Newstone
Arthur Nikisch
Roger Norrington
David Oistrakh
Sakari Oramo
Eugene Ormandy
Tadaaki Otaka
Willem van Otterloo
Seiji Ozawa
Ettore Panizza
Paul Paray

Alain Paris
Andrew Parrott
Jules-Étienne
  Pasdeloup
Giuseppe Patanè
Bernhard Paumgartner
Emil Paur
Wilfrid Pelletier
Murray Perahia
Libor Pesek
Zoltán Peskó
Trevor Pinnock
Percy Pitt
Michel Plasson
Giorgio Polacco
Egon Pollak
John Poole
Frederik Prausnitz
Georges Prêtre
André Previn
Fernando Previtali
Brian Priestman
Klaus Pringsheim
John Pritchard
Felix Prohaska
Eve Queler
Peter Raabe
Ruth Railton
Karl Rankl
Simon Rattle
Clarence Raybould
Ernest Read
Hans Redlich
Leopold Reichwein
Fritz Reiner
Edouard van Remoortel
Timothy Reynish
Hans Richter
Karl Anton
  Rickenbacher
Kathleen Riddick
Hugo Rignold
Helmuth Rilling
Carlo Rizzi
James Robertson
Christopher Robinson
Stanford Robinson
Arthur Rodzinski
Landon Ronald
Karl Rosa
Hans Rosbaud
Albert Rosen
Joseph Rosenstock
Antoni Ros Marbá
Mario Rossi
Mstislav Rostropovich
Walter Rothwell
Tony Rowe
Witold Rowicki
Gennady
  Rozhdestvensky
Julius Rudel

Max Rudolf
Christian Rummel
Donald Runnicles
John Rutter
Paul Sacher
Vasily Safonov
Karel Salomon
Esa-Pekka Salonen
Samuil Samosud
Kurt Sanderling
Nello Santi
Gabriele Santini
Nino Sanzogno
Jukka-Pekka Saraste
Sir Malcolm Sargent
Wolfgang Sawallisch
Franz Schalk
Xaver Scharwenka
Hermann Scherchen
Heinrich Schiff
Anton Schindler
Thomas Schippers
Erich Schmid
Ole Schmidt
Hans Schmidt-Isserstedt
Georg Schnéevoigt
Alexander Schneider
Max Schönherr
Michael Schonwandt
Hans-Hubert Schönzeler
Peter Schreier
Ernst von Schuch
Ignaz Schuppanzigh
Carl Schuricht
Gerard Schwarz
Rudolf Schwarz
Claudio Scimone
Christopher Seaman
Uri Segal
Leif Segerstam
Karel Sejna
Jerzy Semkow
Tullio Serafin
Robert Shaw
Howard Shelley
Maxim Shostakovich
Oscar Shumsky
Joseph Silverstein
Constantin Silvestri
Geoffrey Simon
Yury Simonov
Vassily Sinaisky
George Sinclair
Dmitri Sitkovetsky
Stanislaw
  Skrowaczewski
Leonard Slatkin
Nicolas Slonimsky
Alexander Smallens
George Smart
Váslav Smetácek
Nicholas Smith

Ethel Smyth
Nikolay Sokoloff
Georg Solti
Marc Soustrot
Theodore Spiering
Peter Stadlen
Simon Standage
Bernhard Stavenhagen
Erwin Stein
Fritz Stein
Horst Stein
Emil Steinbach
Fritz Steinbach
Pinchas Steinberg
William Steinberg
Markus Stenz
Fritz Stiedry
Frederick Stock
Leopold Stokowski
Josef Stransky
George Stratton
Karl Straube
Eduard Strauss I
Eduard Strauss II
Richard Strauss
Igor Stravinsky
Simon Streatfeild
Wolfgang Stresemann
Frank van der Stucken
Otmar Suitner
Walter Susskind
Yevgeny Svetlanov
Hans Swarowsky
Ward Swingle
Tadeusz Sygietynski
Georg Szell
Eugen Szenkar
Michel Tabachnik
Anu Tali
Václav Talich
Egisto Tango
Jeffrey Tate
Vilem Tausky
Pyotr Tchaikovsky
Yuri Temirkanov
Klaus Tennstedt
Richard Terry
Christian Thielemann
Michael Tilson Thomas
Theodore Thomas
Bryden Thomson
Heinz Tietjen
Martino Tirimo
Paul Tortelier
Yan Pascal Tortelier
Arturo Toscanini
Geoffrey Toye
Barry Tuckwell
Rosalyn Tureck
Martin Turnovsky
Erik Tuxen
Heinz Unger

Eduard Van Beinum
André Vandernoot
Osmo Vanska
Silvio Varviso
Tamás Vásáry
Denis Vaughan
Sándor Végh
Henri Verbrugghen
Gilbert Vinter
Jaroslav Vogel
Hans Vonk
Edo de Waart
Roger Wagner
Siegfried Wagner
Alfred Wallenstein
Bruno Walter
Günter Wand
Volker Wangenheim
Guy Warrack
Akeo Watanabe
Sydney Watson
Joseph Miroslav Weber
Martin Wegelius
Bruno Weil
Felix Weingartner
George Weldon
Walter Weller
Franz Welser-Möst
August Wenzinger
Ian Whyte
Günther Wich
Allan Wicks
Mark Wigglesworth
David Wilde
Stephen Wilkinson
Jósef Wilkomirski
David Willcocks
Malcolm Williamson
Antoni Wit
Albert Wolff
Hugh Wolff
Henry Wood
David Wooldridge
Barry Wordsworth
Franz Wüllner
Jürg Wyttenbach
Arvid Yansons
Simone Young
Eugène Ysaye
Takuo Yuasa
Lothar Zagrosek
Carlo Zecchi
Hans Zender
Jakob Zeugheer
Alexander Ziloti
David Zinman
Pinchas Zukerman
Paul Zukofsky
Herman Zump

MUSIC: POP

Show and Film Songs: by Song

Song	Show/Film	Song	Show/Film
Ac-cent-tchu-ate the Positive	Here Come the Waves	All Through the Night	Anything Goes
Adelaide	Guys and Dolls	All Time High	Octopussy
Afraid to Dream	You Can't Have Everything	All You Need Is Love	Yellow Submarine
		Almost Like Being in Love	Brigadoon
After the Ball	The Jolson Story	Always	Christmas Holiday
	A Trip to Chinatown (show)		Blue Skies
	Lillian Russell	Always True to You in My Fashion	Kiss Me Kate
After You Get What You Want You Don't Want it	There's No Business Like Showbusiness	Among My Souvenirs	The Best Years of Our Lives
Again	Road House		Paris
Ain't Got a Dime to My Name	Road to Morocco	And This Is My Beloved	Kismet
Ain't Got No – I Got Life	Hair	Animal Crackers in My Soup	Curly Top
Ain't It a Shame About Mame	Rhythm on the River	The Anniversary Song	The Jolson Story
Ain't Misbehavin'	Atlantic City	Another Brick in the Wall	The Wall
	Gentlemen Marry Brunettes	Another Suitcase in Another Hall	Evita (show)
	You Were Meant For Me	Anything You Can Do	Annie Get Your Gun
	Hot Chocolates (show)	Any Time's Kissing Time	Chu Chin Chow
	The Strip	Anywhere I Wander	Hans Christian Andersen
	Follow the Band		
	Stormy Weather	April in Paris	April in Paris
Ain't She Sweet?	You Were Meant For Me		Paris Holiday
	You're My Everything		Both Ends of the Candle
Alabamy Bound	With a Song in My Heart	April Played the Fiddle	If I Had My Way
	Broadway	April Showers	The Jolson Story
	The Great American Broadcast		Jolson Sings Again
	Show Business		The Eddie Duchin Story
Alexander's Ragtime Band	Alexander's Ragtime Band		April Showers
	There's No Business Like Show Business	Aquarius	Hair
		Arriverderci Darling	The Seven Hills of Rome
Alice Blue Gown	Irene	As I Love You	The Big Beat
All Alone	Alexander's Ragtime Band	As Long As He Needs Me	Oliver
		As Time Goes By	Everybody's Welcome (show)
All God's Chillun Got Rhythm	A Day at the Races		Casablanca
All I Ask of You	Phantom of the Opera (show)	At Last	Sun Valley Serenade
			The Glenn Miller Story
All I Do Is Dream of You	Sadie McKee		Orchestra Wives
	Broadway Melody of 1936	At Long Last Love	At Long Last Love
	The Boy Friend		You Never Know (show)
	Singin' in the Rain	Auf Wiederseh'n	The Blue Paradise
All My Loving	A Hard Day's Night		Deep in My Heart
All of Me	Meet Danny Wilson	Avalon	The Benny Goodman Story
	Lady Sings the Blues		The Jolson Story
All of You	Silk Stockings		Both Ends of the Candle
All or Nothing At All	Weekend Pass		
All Over the Place	Sailors Three		
All the Things You Are	Broadway Rhythm	Baby Doll	The Belle of New York
	Because You're Mine	Baby Face	Glorifying the American Girl
	Till The Clouds Roll By		Jolson Sings Again
All the Time in the World	On Her Majesty's Secret Service		Thoroughly Modern Millie
All the Way (1957)	The Joker Is Wild		

Song	Show/Film	Song	Show/Film
Baby I Don't Care	Jailhouse Rock	Blue Skies	Glorifying the
Baby It's Cold Outside (1949)	Neptune's Daughter		American Girl
Bachelor Boy	Summer Holiday		The Jazz Singer
Bali Ha'i	South Pacific		Blue Skies
Basin Street Blues	The Glenn Miller Story		Alexander's Ragtime
	The Strip		Band
Baubles, Bangles and Beads	Kismet		White Christmas
Be a Clown	The Pirate	Boogie Woogie Bugle Boy	Swingtime Johnny
	Singin' in the Rain		Buck Privates
	(show)	Boots and Saddle	Call of the Canyon
Beale Street Blues	St Louis Blues	Born Free (1966)	Born Free
	It's Trad, Dad	The Boys in the Backroom	Destry Rides Again
Beat Out Dat Rhythm	Carmen Jones	Brazil	The Eddie Duchin
on a Drum			Story
Beautiful Dreamer	Swanee River		The Girl He Left
Be-Bop-A-Lula	The Girl Can't Help It		Behind
Be Careful, It's My Heart	Holiday Inn		Saludos Amigos
Because the Night	That Summer	The Breeze and I	Cuban Pete
Begin the Beguine	Broadway Melody of	Bright Eyes	Watership Down
	1940	Broken Hearted	The Best Things in Life
	Night and Day		Are Free
	Jubilee (show)	Brother, Can You Spare	Americana
Beginner's Luck	Shall We Dance	a Dime?	
Bei Mir Bist Du Schön	Love, Honour and	Buckle Down, Winsocki	Best Foot Forward
	Behave	Burlington Bertie from Bow	Mother Wore Tights
Be My Love	Looking For Love		Star
	The Toast of New	Bushel and a Peck	Guys and Dolls (show)
	Orleans	Bustopher Jones	Cats (show)
The Best Things In Life	The Best Things In Life	But Beautiful	Road to Rio
Are Free	Are Free	But Not for Me	Girl Crazy
	Good News	Buttons and Bows	The Paleface
Bewitched, Bothered	Pal Joey		Son of Paleface
and Bewildered		Button Up Your Overcoat	Follow Through
Bibbidi-Bobbidi-Boo	Cinderella		The Best Things in Life
Bidin' My Time	Girl Crazy		Are Free
	Rhapsody in Blue	Bye Bye Blackbird	Pete Kelly's Blues
	The Glenn Miller Story		The Eddie Cantor
Big Spender	Sweet Charity		Story
Bill	Showboat		Rainbow Round My
	The Man I Love		Shoulder
	Both Ends of the	By Strauss	An American in Paris
	Candle		The Show Is On (show)
The Birth of the Blues	Painting the Clouds	By the Light of the Silvery	The Jolson Story
	with Sunshine	Moon	Two Weeks with Love
	The Best Things in Life		The Birth of the Blues
	Are Free		Sunbonnet Sue
	The Birth of the Blues	By the Sleepy Lagoon	Sleepy Lagoon
The Black Bottom	George White's		
	Scandals (show)	Ça C'est l'Amour	Les Girls
	A Star Is Born	California, Here I Come	Lucky Boy
The Black Hills of Dakota	Calamity Jane		Jolson Sings Again
Bless Yore Beautiful Hide	Seven Brides for		With a Song in My
	Seven Brothers		Heart
Blow, Gabriel, Blow	Anything Goes		You're My Everything
Blueberry Hill	The Singing Hill		The Jolson Story
Blue Moon	This Could Be the Night		Rose of Washington
	Words and Music		Square
	Kiss Them for Me	Call Me	American Gigolo
	Grease	Call Me Irresponsible (1963)	Papa's Delicate
	Torch Song		Condition
	With a Song in My	Candy Kisses	Down Dakota Way
	Heart	Can I Forget You	High, Wide and
Blues in the Night	The Birth of the Blues		Handsome

Song	Show/Film	Song	Show/Film
The Canoe Song	Sanders of the River		Oh Kay (show)
Can't Buy Me Love	A Hard Day's Night		Both Ends of the Candle
Can't Help Falling in Love	Blue Hawaii		
Can't Help Lovin' Dat Man	Both Ends of the Candle		Tea for Two
	Show Boat	Do I Love You Because You're Beautiful	Cinderella (show)
	Till The Clouds Roll By	Do I Love You, Do I	Night and Day
Carolina in the Morning	The Dolly Sisters		DuBarry Was a Lady
	Jolson Sings Again	Doin' What Comes Naturally	Annie Get Your Gun
	April Showers	Do I Worry	Pardon My Sarong
	I'll See You in My Dreams	Dominique	The Singing Nun
		The Donkey Serenade	The Firefly
C'est Magnifique	Can-Can	Don't Cry for Me, Argentina	Evita
C'est Si Bon	Latin Quarter (show)	Don't Ever Leave Me	Sweet Adeline
	New Faces		Both Ends of the Candle
Charmaine	Sunset Boulevard		
The Charm of You	Anchors Aweigh	Don't Fence Me In	Don't Fence Me In
Chattanooga Choo Choo	The Glenn Miller Story		Hollywood Canteen
	Springtime in the Rockies	Don't It Make My Brown Eyes Blue	Convoy
	Sun Valley Serenade	Don't Laugh at Me	Trouble in Store
Chattanooga Shoeshine Boy	Indian Territory	Don't Rain on My Parade	Funny Girl
Cheek to Cheek	Top Hat	Do-Re-Mi	The Sound of Music
Cheerful Little Earful	Sweet and Low (show)	Down among the Sheltering Palms	That Midnight Kiss
Chica Chica Boom Chic	That Night in Rio		Some Like It Hot
Chim Chim Cheree (1964)	Mary Poppins	Do You Know Where You're Going To?	Mahogany
Clap Hands, Here Comes Charley	Funny Lady		
		The Drinking Song	The Student Prince
Clap Yo' Hands	Oh Kay (show)	Duelling Banjos	Deliverance
	Rhapsody in Blue		
	Funny Face	Edelweiss	The Sound of Music
Climb Ev'ry Mountain	The Sound of Music	Eleanor Rigby	Yellow Submarine
Close as Pages in a Book	Up in Central Park	Embraceable You	An American in Paris
A Cock-Eyed Optimist	South Pacific		Girl Crazy
Colonel Bogey March	The Bridge on the River Kwai		Nancy Goes to Rio
			Rhapsody in Blue
Come and Get It	The Magic Christian		Sincerely Yours
Come Back to Sorrento	Paramount on Parade		With a Song in My Heart
Consider Yourself	Oliver		
The Continental (1934)	The Gay Divorcee	Emotions	The Stud
Cool Water	Hands across the Water	Empty Chairs at Empty Tables	Les Misérables (show)
		The Entertainer	The Sting
A Couple of Swells	Easter Parade	Evergreen	A Star is Born
		Everybody's Doing It	The Fabulous Dorseys
Dance to the Music	Woodstock		Alexander's Ragtime Band
Dancing in the Street	Cooley High		
Dancing on the Ceiling	Evergreen		Easter Parade
Dat's Love	Carmen Jones	Everybody's Talkin'	Midnight Cowboy
Day by Day	Godspell	Everything's Coming Up Roses	Gypsy
Days of Wine and Roses (1962)	Days of Wine and Roses	Ev'ry Time We Say Goodbye	Seven Lively Arts (show)
The Deadwood Stage	Calamity Jane	Experiment	Nymph Errant (show)
Dear Little Cafe	Bitter-Sweet	Eye of the Tiger	Rocky III
Deep in the Heart of Texas	With a Song in My Heart		
		Falling in Love Again	The Blue Angel
	Hi Neighbour	Falling in Love with Love	The Boys from Syracuse
Delta Lady	Mad Dogs and Englishmen		
		Fame	Fame
Diamonds Are a Girl's Best Friend	Gentlemen Prefer Blondes	Fascinating Rhythm	Girl Crazy
			Lady, Be Good!
Ding Dong the Witch Is Dead	The Wizard of Oz		Rhapsody in Blue
D.I.V.O.R.C.E.	Five Easy Pieces		Singin' in the Rain (show)
Do Do Do	Star		

MUSIC POP

Song	Show/Film
Feather Your Nest	Tip Top (show)
Feed the Birds	Mary Poppins
A Fellow Needs a Girl	Allegro (show)
Fever	Hey Boy! Hey Girl!
Five Foot Two, Eyes of Blue	Has Anybody Seen My Gal?
Flash Bang Wallop	Half a Sixpence (show)
Flashdance – What a Feeling (1983)	Flashdance
A Foggy Day	A Damsel in Distress
Foggy Mountain Breakdown	Bonnie and Clyde
The Folks Who Live on the Hill	High, Wide and Handsome
For All We Know (1970)	Lovers and Other Strangers
For Every Man There's a Woman	Casbah
For You, for Me, for Everyone	The Shocking Miss Pilgrim
French Military Marching Song	The Desert Song
Friendship	DuBarry Was a Lady
From the Top of Your Head	Two for Tonight
Genie with the Light Brown Lamp	Aladdin and His Wonderful Lamp
The Gentleman is a Dope	Allegro (show)
Get Me to the Church on Time	My Fair Lady
Get Out and Get Under	Hullo Tango (show) The Pleasure Seekers (show)
Get Out of Town	Leave It to Me (show)
Getting to Know You	The King and I
Gigi (1958)	Gigi
The Gipsy in Me	Anything Goes (show)
Give Me the Moonlight	Hullo America The Dolly Sisters
The Glory of Love	Karate Kid II
God on High	Les Misérables
Gonna Build a Mountain	Stop the World – I Want To Get Off
Good Morning Starshine	Hair
Goodnight, Sweetheart	The Big Broadcast of 1936 You Were Meant for Me
Happy Days Are Here Again	Chasing Rainbows Rain or Shine
Happy Holiday	Holiday Inn
Happy Talk	South Pacific
Harry Lime Theme	The Third Man
Have You Met Miss Jones	Gentlemen Marry Brunettes
Have Yourself a Merry Little Christmas	Meet Me in St Louis
The Heat Is On	Beverly Hills Cop
Hello, Hello, Who's Your Lady Friend?	The Story of Vernon and Irene Castle
Hello, Young Lovers	The King and I
Help	Help! John, Paul, George, Ringo and Bert

Song	Show/Film
Here Comes the Sun	John, Paul, George, Ringo and Bert
Here in My Arms	Tea for Two
Hernando's Hideaway	The Pajama Game
Hi-Diddle-Dee-Dee (An Actor's Life For Me)	Pinocchio
High Hopes (1959)	Hole in the Head
High Noon (1952)	High Noon
Hold the Line	Yesterday's Heroes
Honeysuckle Rose	Thousands Cheer Tin Pan Alley
Hong Kong Blues	To Have and Have Not
Hopelessly Devoted to You	Grease
Hound Dog	Grease
How Are Things in Glocca Morra	Finian's Rainbow
How Could You Believe Me?	Wedding Bells
How High the Moon?	Two for the Show
How Long Has This Been Going On	Funny Face Rosalie (show)
How to Handle a Woman	Camelot
I Cain't Say No	Oklahoma!
I Concentrate on You	Broadway Melody of 1940
I Could Have Danced All Night	My Fair Lady
I Could Write a Book	Pal Joey
Ida, Sweet as Apple Cider	Babes in Arms The Eddie Cantor Story Incendiary Blonde
I Didn't Know What Time It Was	Pal Joey Too Many Girls
I'd Do Anything	Oliver
I Don't Know How to Love Him	Jesus Christ Superstar
I Feel Pretty	West Side Story
If Ever I Would Leave You	Camelot
If I Didn't Care	The Great American Broadcast
If I Had a Talking Picture of You	The Best Things In Life Are Free Sunny Side Up
If I Loved You	Carousel
If I Ruled The World	Pickwick (show)
If I Were A Bell	Guys and Dolls
If I Were A Rich Man	Fiddler on the Roof
I Get a Kick Out of You	Anything Goes Night and Day Sunny Side of the Street
I Got Plenty of Nuttin'	Porgy and Bess
I Got Rhythm	Girl Crazy Rhapsody in Blue An American in Paris
I Got the Sun in the Morning	Annie Get Your Gun
I Hate Men	Kiss Me, Kate
I Just Called to Say I Love You (1984)	Woman in Red
I Know Him So Well	Chess (show)
I Like to Recognize the Tune	Too Many Girls (show) Meet the People

Song	Show/Film	Song	Show/Film
I'll Be with You in Apple Blossom Time	Buck Privates		I'll See You In My Dreams
I'll Build a Stairway to Paradise	Rhapsody in Blue		Incendiary Blonde
	Stop Flirting (show)		Show Business
	An American in Paris	It Might As Well Be Spring (1945)	State Fair
	George White's Scandals of 1922 (show)	It's a Hap-Hap-Happy Day	Gulliver's Travels
I'll Never Fall in Love Again	Promises, Promises (show)	It's a Lovely Day Today	Call Me Madam
		It's All Right with Me	Can-Can
I'll See You Again	Bitter-Sweet	It's d'Lovely	Anything Goes
I'll See You in My Dreams	Follow the Boys		The Fleet's Lit Up (show)
	I'll See You In My Dreams		Red Hot and Blue (show)
	Pardon My Rhythm	It's Easy to Remember	Mississippi
I Love a Piano	Easter Parade	It's Only a Paper Moon	Too Young to Know
I Love Paris	Can-Can		Take a Chance
I Love You (Archer and Thompson)	Little Jesse James (show)	I've Been a Bad Bad Boy	Privilege
		I've Got a Crush on You	Three for the Show
	The Sun Also Rises		Meet Danny Wilson
I Love You (Porter)	Mexican Hayride		Strike Up the Band (show)
I Love You, Samantha	High Society		Both Ends of the Candle
I'm Always Chasing Rainbows	The Dolly Sisters		
	Oh, Look (show)		
	The Ziegfeld Girl	I've Got a Gal in Kalamazoo	Kiss Them for Me
I'm Forever Blowing Bubbles	On Moonlight Bay		Orchestra Wives
I'm Free	Tommy	I've Got Five Dollars	Gentlemen Marry Brunettes
I'm Getting Sentimental over You	DuBarry Was a Lady		
I'm Gonna Wash that Man Right out of My Hair	South Pacific	I've Got My Eyes on You	Broadway Melody of 1940
		I've Got You on My Mind	The Gay Divorcee
I'm in Love With a Wonderful Guy	South Pacific	I've Got You under My Skin	Born to Dance
			Night and Day
I'm Looking over a Four-Leaf Clover	The Jazz Singer		This Could Be the Night
	Jolson Sings Again	I've Grown Accustomed to Her Face	My Fair Lady
I'm Riding for a Fall	Thank Your Lucky Stars	I Wanna Be Loved by You	Gentleman Marry Brunettes
I'm Sitting on Top of the World	I'll Cry Tomorrow		
	The Jolson Story		Good Boy (show)
	Love Me Or Leave Me		Some Like It Hot
	The Singing Fool		Three Little Words
The Impossible Dream	Man of La Mancha	I Want to Be Happy	No, No, Nanette
Indian Love Call	One Night of Love		Tea for Two
	Rose Marie	I Whistle a Happy Tune	The King and I
Inka Dinka Doo	The Great Schnozzle	I Wish I Didn't Love You So	The Perils of Pauline
	This Time for Keeps	I Wish I Were in Love Again	Babes in Arms (show)
	Two Girls and a Sailor		
In the Cool, Cool, Cool of the Evening (1951)	Here Comes the Groom		Words and Music
		I Wonder Who's Kissing Her Now	I Wonder Who's Kissing Her Now
In the Mood	The Glenn Miller Story		
	Sun Valley Serenade		Moonlight in Havana
In the Still of the Night	Night and Day		Prince for Tonight (show)
	Rosalie		The Time, the Place and the Girl
I Remember You	The Fleet's In		
Irresistible You	Broadway Rhythm	I Won't Dance	Lovely to Look At
Isn't It Kinda Fun	State Fair		Roberta
Isn't It Romantic?	Love Me Tonight		Till the Clouds Roll By
Isn't This a Lovely Day	Top Hat	I Yi Yi Yi I Like You Very Much	That Night in Rio
It Ain't Necessarily So	Porgy and Bess		
I Talk to the Trees	Paint Your Wagon		
It Could Happen to You	And the Angels Sing		
It Had to Be You	Her Kind of Man	The James Bond Theme	Doctor No

M
U
S
I
C

P
O
P

Song	Show/Film	Song	Show/Film
Jean	The Prime of Miss Jean Brodie	Liza	An American in Paris
Jeepers Creepers	Going Places		George White's Scandals of 1945
Jenny	Lady in the Dark Star		The Jolson Story
Jezebel	The Seven Hills of Rome		The Man I Love
			Rhapsody in Blue
Johnny One Note	Words and Music Babes in Arms (show)		Show Girl (show)
			Starlift
Jolly Holiday	Mary Poppins	Long Ago and Far Away	Cover Girl
June in January	Here Is My Heart		Till the Clouds Roll By
June Is Busting Out All Over	Carousel	Looking for a Boy	Tip-Toes (show)
Just in Time	Bells Are Ringing	Look of Love	Casino Royale
Just One of Those Things	Can-Can	Louise	Innocents of Paris
	The Eddie Duchin Story		The Stooge
	Jubilee (show)	Love Changes Everything	Aspects of Love (show)
	Lullaby of Broadway	Love in Bloom	She Loves Me Not
	Night and Day	Love Is a Many-Splendored Thing	Grease
	Panama Hattie		Love Is a Many-Splendored Thing
	Young at Heart	Love Is Sweeping the Country	Of Thee I Sing (show)
Keep the Home Fires Burning	Variety Jubilee	Love Steals Your Heart	The Wicked Lady
Keep Young and Beautiful	Roman Scandals	Love Thy Neighbour	We're Not Dressing
Kiss in Your Eyes	The Emperor Waltz	Love Walked In	Rhapsody in Blue
Knockin' on Heaven's Door	Pat Garrett and Billy the Kid		The Goldwyn Follies
		Luck Be a Lady Tonight	Guys and Dolls
		Lucky in Love	Good News
The Lady Is a Tramp	Babes in Arms (show)		The Best Things in Life Are Free
	Pal Joey	Lucy in the Sky with Diamonds	John, Paul, George, Ringo and Bert
	Words and Music	Lullaby of Broadway	Gold Diggers of 1935
The Lambeth Walk	Me and My Girl		Lullaby of Broadway
Lara's Theme (aka Somewhere My Love)	Dr Zhivago	Lulu's Back in Town	Broadway Gondolier
The Last Time I Saw Paris	Paris Holiday	Lydia the Tattooed Lady	At the Circus
	Till the Clouds Roll By Lady, Be Good!	Mack the Knife	The Threepenny Opera (show)
Lavender Blue	So Dear to My Heart		Satchmo the Great
Leaning on a Lamp Post	Me and My Girl Feather Your Nest	Mad About the Boy	Words and Music (show)
Let Me Be Loved	The James Dean Story		Set to Music (show)
Let's Be Buddies	Black Vanities (show) Panama Hattie	Make Believe	Till the Clouds Roll By
Let's Call the Whole Thing Off	Shall We Dance?		Show Boat
Let's Do It (Let's Fall in Love)	Night and Day	The Man I Love	Both Ends of the Candle
	Can-Can		The Eddy Duchin Story
	Wake Up and Dream (show)		Lady Sings the Blues
	Paris (show)		The Man I Love
Let's Face the Music and Dance	Follow the Fleet		Rhapsody in Blue
Let's Go Fly a Kite	Mary Poppins		Sincerely Yours
Let's Hear It for the Boy	Footloose		Will o' the Whispers (show)
Life Is Just a Bowl of Cherries	George White's Scandals		Young at Heart
	The Best Things In Life Are Free	The March of the Siamese Children	The King and I
Little April Shower	Bambi		
Little Girl Blue	Jumbo		
A Little Of What You Fancy	Variety Jubilee	Maria	West Side Story
Living Doll	Serious Charge		

Song	Show/Film	Song	Show/Film
Marta	*The Big Broadcast*	Oh, What a Beautiful Morning	*Oklahoma!*
Maybe	*Oh Kay* (show)	Oh, What a Circus	*Evita*
Me and My Shadow	*Hold That Ghost*	Oh, You Beautiful Doll	*Wharf Angel*
Memories Are Made of This	*The Seven Hills of Rome*		*Oh, You Beautiful Doll*
Memory	*Cats* (show)		*The Story of Vernon and Irene Castle*
Memo to Turner	*Performance*		*For Me and My Gal*
Mimi	*Love Me Tonight*	Ol' Man River	*Show Boat*
	Pepe		*Till the Clouds Roll By*
Minnie the Moocher	*The Big Broadcast*	Once upon a Dream	*Play it Cool*
Miss Otis Regrets	*Hi Diddle Diddle* (show)	One Night in Bangkok	*Chess* (show)
	Night and Day	Only a Rose	*The Vagabond King*
Mister Snow	*Carousel*	Only You	*Rock around the Clock*
Mona Lisa (1950)	*After Midnight*	On the Atchison, Topeka and Santa Fe	*The Harvey Girls*
Moonlight Becomes You	*Road to Morocco*		
Moon River (1961)	*Breakfast at Tiffany's*	On the Beach	*Wonderful Life*
The More I See You	*The Diamond Horseshoe*	On the Good Ship Lollipop	*Bright Eyes*
		On the Street Where You Live	*My Fair Lady*
The Most Beautiful Girl in the World	*Jumbo*	On the Sunny Side of the Street	*Swing Parade of 1946*
			Is Everybody Happy
Most Gentlemen Don't Like Love	*Black Velvet* (show)		*Both Ends of the Candle*
	Leave it to Me (show)		*The Benny Goodman Story*
Mountain Greenery	*Words and Music*		
Mr Mistoffolees	*Cats* (show)		*The Eddie Duchin Story*
Mrs Robinson	*The Graduate*		*On the Sunny Side of the Street*
Music, Maestro, Please	*These Foolish Things* (show)		
Music of the Night	*Phantom of the Opera* (show)	Our Love Is Here to Stay	*An American in Paris*
			The Goldwyn Follies
My Baby Just Cares for Me	*Whoopee*		*Lady Sings the Blues*
My Favourite Things	*Sound of Music*		
My Funny Valentine	*Pal Joey*	Out of My Dreams	*Oklahoma!*
	Babes in Arms (show)	Over My Shoulder	*Evergreen*
	Gentlemen Marry Brunettes	Over the Rainbow (1939)	*The Wizard of Oz*
My Heart Belongs to Daddy	*Let's Make Love*	Pack up Your Troubles in Your Old Kit Bag	*Her Soldier Boy* (show)
	Love Thy Neighbour		
	Night and Day		*Wait Till the Sun Shines Nellie*
My Heart Stood Still	*Words and Music*		
	A Connecticut Yankee	People Will Say We're in Love	*Oklahoma!*
My One and Only	*Funny Face*	The Physician	*Nymph Errant* (show)
My Resistance Is Low	*Las Vegas Story*		*Star*
My Romance	*Jumbo*	Pinball Wizard	*Tommy*
My Sin	*The Best Things in Life Are Free*	Please Do It Again	*The French Doll* (show)
			Thoroughly Modern Millie
The Nearness of You	*Romance in the Dark*		*Rhapsody in Blue*
Never on Sunday (1960)	*Never on Sunday*		*Mayfair and Montmartre* (show)
New York, New York	*On the Town*		
Nice Work If You Can Get it	*An American in Paris*	The Power of Love	*Back to the Future*
	A Damsel in Distress	Practically Perfect	*Mary Poppins* (show)
Night and Day	*Lady on a Train*	Put It There, Pal	*Road to Utopia*
	The Gay Divorcee	Puttin' on the Ritz	*Blue Skies*
	Night and Day		*Idiot's Delight*
	Reveille with Beverley		*Puttin' on the Ritz*
The Night They Invented Champagne	*Gigi*	Que Sera, Sera (1956)	*The Man Who Knew Too Much*
Nobody Does It Better	*The Spy Who Loved Me*		
Oh, Lady Be Good	*Lady, Be Good!*	Raindrops Keep Falling on My Head	*Butch Cassidy and the Sundance Kid*
	Rhapsody in Blue		

Song	Show/Film	Song	Show/Film
Red Sails in the Sunset	Province Town Follies (show)		Broadway Rhythm
			Pete Kelly's Blues
Return to Sender	Girls! Girls! Girls!		Somebody Loves Me
Rhapsody in Blue	The King of Jazz		Lullaby of Broadway
	Rhapsody in Blue		Rhapsody in Blue
Rhythm of Life	Sweet Charity	Some Day	The Vagabond King
Rhythm of the Rain	The Man from the Folies Bergère	Some Day My Prince Will Come	Snow White and the Seven Dwarfs
The Riff Song	The Desert Song	Some Enchanted Evening	South Pacific
Right Back Where We Started From	The World is Full of Married Men	Someone to Watch over Me	Rhapsody in Blue
			Young at Heart
River Kwai March	The Bridge on the River Kwai		Three for the Show
			Both Ends of the Candle
Road Runner	Cooley High		
Rock around the Clock	Rock around the Clock		Beau James
	The Blackboard Jungle		Star
Roll Along, Prairie Moon	Here Comes the Band	Something's Coming	West Side Story
		Somewhere	West Side Story
Say You, Say Me (1985)	White Nights	Sonny Boy	The Singing Fool
Second-Hand Rose	Funny Girl		Jolson Sings Again
	My Man		The Best Things in Life Are Free
	The Ziegfeld Follies of 1921 (show)	Soon	Strike Up the Band (show)
The Second Time Around	High Time		
Secret Love (1953)	Calamity Jane	A Spoonful of Sugar	Mary Poppins
Send in the Clowns	A Little Night Music (show)	Spring Is Here	I Married an Angel
		Stardust	The Eddie Duchin Story
September Song	Knickerbocker Holiday		
	Pepe	Stay as Sweet as You Are	College Rhythm
	September Affair	Staying Alive	Saturday Night Fever
Seventy-Six Trombones	Music Man	Straighten Up and Fly Right	Here Comes Elmer
The Shadow of Your Smile (1965)	The Sandpiper		On Stage Everybody
		Strange Music	Song of Norway
Shaft (1971)	Shaft	Stranger in Paradise	Kismet
Shall We Dance?	The King and I	Strangers in the Night	A Man Could Get Killed
The Sheik of Araby	Make it Snappy (show)		
	Tin Pan Alley	Suicide Is Painless	M.A.S.H.
She Loves You	A Hard Day's Night	Summer Nights	Grease
She's So Beautiful	Time	Summertime	Porgy and Bess
Ship Without a Sail	Heads Up	Sunny Disposish	Americana (show)
Shoes with Wings On	The Barkleys of Broadway	Sunrise Sunset	Fiddler on the Roof
		Supercalifragilisticexpiali-docious	Mary Poppins
Short'nin' Bread	Jericho		
Sing For Your Supper	The Boys from Syracuse	The Surrey with the Fringe on Top	Oklahoma!
Singin' in the Rain	Hollywood Revue of 1929	Swanee	Jolson Sings Again
			Sinbad (show)
	Little Nellie Kelly		Rhapsody in Blue
	Singin' in the Rain		Jigsaw (show)
Sit Down You're Rocking the Boat	Guys and Dolls		The Glorious Days (show)
			The Jolson Story
Slap That Bass	Shall We Dance?		Sincerely Yours
Slaughter on Tenth Avenue	On Your Toes		A Star Is Born
	Words and Music		
Smoke Gets in Your Eyes	Roberta	Sweeping the Clouds Away	Paramount on Parade
	Till the Clouds Roll By	Sweet and Lowdown	Tip-Toes (show)
	Lovely to Look At	Sweet Georgia Brown	Some Like It Hot
So Am I	Lady Be Good! (show)	Sweet Leilani (1937)	Waikiki Wedding
		Swingin' on a Star (1944)	Going My Way
So in Love	Kiss Me Kate	S'Wonderful	Funny Face
Somebody Loves Me	George White's Scandals of 1924 (show)		Rhapsody in Blue
			An American in Paris
			Starlift

Song	Show/Film	Song	Show/Film
Take My Breath Away (1986)	Top Gun	The Ugly Duckling	Hans Christian
Talk to the Animals (1967)	Doctor Dolittle		Andersen
Tara's Theme	Gone with the Wind	Up Where We Belong (1982)	An Officer and a
Tea for Two	With a Song in My		Gentleman
	Heart		
	Sincerely Yours	Varsity Drag	Good News
	Jazz on a Summer's		
	Day	Wanderin' Star	Paint Your Wagon
	Tea for Two	Wanting You	The New Moon
	No, No, Nanette	Watch the Birdie	Hellzapoppin
Thank Heaven for Little Girls	Gigi	The Way We Were (1973)	The Way We Were
Thanks for the Memory (1938)	The Big Broadcast of	The Way You Look Tonight	Swing Time
	1938	(1936)	
That Certain Feeling	Tip-Toes (show)	We Kiss in the Shadow	The King and I
	That Certain Feeling	Welcome to My Dream	Road to Utopia
That Old Black Magic	Star Spangled Rhythm	Well, Did You Evah?	High Society
	Radio Stars on Parade		DuBarry Was a Lady
	Here Come the		(show)
	Waves	We'll Gather Lilacs	Lilacs in the Spring
	Meet Danny Wilson		Perchance to Dream
That's Amore	The Caddy		(show)
That's Entertainment	The Band Wagon	We're in the Money	Painting the Clouds
That's for Me	State Fair		with Sunshine
There Is Nothing Like a Dame	South Pacific		Gold Diggers of
There's A Small Hotel	On Your Toes (show)		1933
	Words and Music	What is This Thing Called	Starlift
	Pal Joey	Love?	Wake Up and Dream
There's No Business Like	There's No Business		Night and Day
Show Business	Like Show Business		The Eddie Duchin
	Annie Get Your Gun		Story
They All Laughed	Shall We Dance?	Whatever Lola Wants	What Lola Wants
They Call the Wind Maria	Paint Your Wagon		Damn Yankees (show)
They Can't Take That Away	The Barkleys of	What Kind of Fool Am I?	Stop the World – I
From Me	Broadway		Want to Get Off
	Shall We Dance?	What'll I Do?	Alexander's Ragtime
This Can't Be Love	Words and Music		Band
	The Boys from	When I Fall in Love	Istanbul
	Syracuse		One Minute to Zero
	Jumbo	When I Grow Too Old to	The Night is Young
This Is My Song	Countess from Hong	Dream	Deep in My Heart
	Kong	When I Take My Sugar to Tea	Monkey Business
This Nearly Was Mine	South Pacific	When the Going Gets Tough	Jewel of the Nile
Thou Swell	A Connecticut Yankee	When the Red Red Robin	I'll Cry Tomorrow
	Words and Music		Has Anybody Seen My
Three Coins in the Fountain	Three Coins in the		Gal?
(1954)	Fountain		The Jolson Story
Till There Was You	Music Man	When Will I See You Again?	Black Joy
Time of My Life (1987)	Dirty Dancing	When You're Smiling	Meet Danny Wilson
Together	The Best Things in Life	When You Wish upon A Star	Pinocchio
	Are Free	Where or When	Words and Music
	Since You Went Away		Babes In Arms
To-Kay	Bitter-Sweet	Where's That Rainbow?	Words and Music
To Keep My Love Alive	A Connecticut Yankee	Where the Blue of the Night	The Big Broadcast
	(show)	Whistle While You Work	Snow White and the
Tonight	West Side Story		Seven Dwarfs
Too Darn Hot	Kiss Me Kate	White Christmas	White Christmas
Trail of the Lonesome Pine	Way Out West		Blue Skies
The Trolley Song	Meet Me in St Louis		Holiday Inn
True Love	High Society	Who's Sorry Now?	Three Little Words
Tubular Bells	The Exorcist		A Night in Casablanca
Tutti Frutti	Don't Knock the	Who Wants to Be a Millionaire?	High Society
	Rock	Why Can't You Behave?	Kiss Me, Kate
Two Little Blue Birds	Sunny		

M
U
S
I
C

P
O
P

Song	Show/Film	Song	Show/Film
Why Do I Love You?	Show Boat	Home to	About
Why Was I Born?	Sweet Adeline (show)	You'll Never Know (1943)	Hello, 'Frisco, Hello
Wind beneath My Wings	Beaches	You'll Never Walk Alone	Carousel
Windmills of Your Mind (1968)	The Thomas Crown Affair	You Light up My Life (1977)	You Light Up My Life
		You Made Me Love You	Broadway Melody of 1938
Wish Me Luck As You Wave Me Goodbye	Shipyard Sally		Wharf Angel
With a Little Bit of Luck	My Fair Lady		The Jolson Story
With a Little Help from My Friends	Woodstock		Syncopation
	Stardust		Jolson Sings Again
	All This and World War II		Love Me Or Leave Me
	Sgt Pepper's Lonely Hearts Club Band	You Make Me Feel So Young	I'll Get By
	Yellow Submarine		Three Little Girls in Blue
With a Song in My Heart	Words and Music	You Must Have Been a Beautiful Baby	Hard to Get
	With a Song in My Heart		My Dream Is Yours
	This Is The Life		The Eddie Cantor Story
	Spring Is Here	Younger Than Springtime	South Pacific
	Painting the Clouds with Sunshine	You're the Cream in My Coffee	The Cockeyed World
	Young Man of Music		The Best Things in Life Are Free
With Every Breath I Take	Here Is My Heart	You're the One That I Want	Grease
Won't You Come Home Bill Bailey?	The Five Pennies	You're the Top	Night and Day
			Anything Goes
Woodchoppers' Ball	What's Cooking?	You Started Something	Moon over Miami
Wooden Heart	G.I. Blues	You Stepped out of a Dream	The Ziegfeld Girl
Wouldn't It Be Loverly	My Fair Lady	You Took Advantage of Me	Present Arms
Wunderbar	Kiss Me, Kate		On Your Toes (show)
			A Star Is Born
Yes Sir, That's My Baby	The Eddie Cantor Story Broadway (show)	You've Lost That Lovin' Feelin'	Stardust
You Are Beautiful	Flower Drum Song	Zip-a-dee-doo-dah (1947)	Song of the South
You'd Be So Nice to Come	Something to Shout	Zorba's Dance	Zorba the Greek

Show and Film Songs: by Show or Film

Show/Film	Song	Show/Film	Song
A Connecticut Yankee	My Heart Stood Still Thou Swell	All This and World War II	With a Little Help from My Friends
A Connecticut Yankee (show)	To Keep My Love Alive	Allegro (show)	A Fellow Needs a Girl
A Damsel in Distress	A Foggy Day Nice Work If You Can Get It		The Gentleman Is a Dope
A Day at the Races	All God's Chillun Got Rhythm	A Man Could Get Killed	Strangers in the Night
		American Gigolo	Call Me
After Midnight	Mona Lisa (1950)	Americana	Brother, Can You Spare a Dime
A Hard Day's Night	All My Loving	Americana (show)	Sunny Disposish
	Can't Buy Me Love	An American in Paris	By Strauss
	She Loves You		Embraceable You
Aladdin and His Wonderful Lamp	Genie With the Light Brown Lamp		I Got Rhythm
Alexander's Ragtime Band	Alexander's Ragtime (1970) Band		I'll Build a Stairway to Paradise
	All Alone		Liza
	Blue Skies		Nice Work If You Can Get It
	Everybody's Doing It		Our Love Is Here to Stay
	What'll I Do		S'Wonderful
A Little Night Music (show)	Send in the Clowns	A Night in Casablanca	Who's Sorry Now?

Show/Film	Song	Show/Film	Song
An Officer and a Gentleman	Up Where We Belong (1982)	Black Joy	When Will I See You Again?
Anchor's Aweigh	The Charm of You	Black Vanities (show)	Let's Be Buddies
And the Angels Sing	It Could Happen to You	Black Velvet (show)	Most Gentlemen Don't Like Love
Annie Get Your Gun	Anything You Can Do		
	Doin' What Comes Naturally	Blue Hawaii	Can't Help Falling in Love
	I Got the Sun in the Morning	Blue Skies	Always
	There's No Business Like Show Business		Blue Skies
			Puttin' on the Ritz
Anything Goes	All Through the Night		White Christmas
	Blow, Gabriel, Blow	Bonnie and Clyde	Foggy Mountain Breakdown
	I Get a Kick out of You		
	It's d'Lovely	Born Free	Born Free (1966)
	You're the Top	Born to Dance	I've Got You under My Skin
Anything Goes (show)	The Gipsy in Me		
April in Paris	April in Paris	Both Ends of the Candle	April in Paris
April Showers	April Showers		Avalon
	Carolina in the Morning		Bill
Aspects of Love (show)	Love Changes Everything		Can't Help Loving Dat Man
A Star Is Born	Evergreen (1976)		Do Do Do
	The Black Bottom		Don't Ever Leave Me
	Swanee		I've Got a Crush on You
	You Took Advantage of Me		The Man I Love
			On the Sunny Side of the Street
Atlantic City	Ain't Misbehavin'		Someone to Watch Over Me
At Long Last Love	At Long Last Love		
A Trip to Chinatown (show)	After the Ball	Breakfast at Tiffany's	Moon River (1961)
At the Circus	Lydia the Tattooed Lady	Bridge on the River Kwai	Colonel Bogey March
		Brigadoon	Almost Like Being in Love
Babes in Arms	Ida, Sweet as Apple Cider	Bright Eyes	On the Good Ship Lollipop
	Where or When		
Babes in Arms (show)	I Wish I Were in Love Again	Broadway	Alabamy Bound
		Broadway (show)	Yes, Sir, That's My Baby
	Johnny One Note	Broadway Gondolier	Lulu's Back in Town
	The Lady Is a Tramp	Broadway Melody of 1936	All I Do Is Dream of You
	My Funny Valentine	Broadway Melody of 1938	You Made Me Love You
Back to the Future	The Power of Love	Broadway Melody of 1940	Begin the Beguine
Bambi	Little April Shower		I Concentrate on You
The Band Wagon	That's Entertainment		I've Got My Eyes on You
The Barkleys of Broadway	They Can't Take That Away from Me	Broadway Rhythm	All the Things You Are
			Irresistible You
	Shoes With Wings On		Somebody Loves Me
Beaches	Wind beneath My Wings	Buck Privates	Boogie Woogie Bugle Boy
Beau James	Someone to Watch over Me		I'll Be with You in Apple Blossom Time
Because You're Mine	All the Things You Are		
The Belle of New York	Baby Doll	Butch Cassidy and the Sundance Kid	Raindrops Keep Falling On My Head
Bells Are Ringing	Just in Time		
Best Foot Forward	Buckle Down, Winsocki		
The Best Things in Life Are Free	The Best Things in Life are Free	Calamity Jane	The Black Hills of Dakota
			The Deadwood Stage
Beverly Hills Cop	The Heat Is On		Secret Love (1953)
Birth of the Blues	Blues in the Night	Call Me Madam	It's a Lovely Day Today
	By the Light of the Silvery Moon	Call of the Canyon	Boots and Saddle
		Camelot	How to Handle a Woman
Bitter-Sweet	Dear Little Cafe		If Ever I Would Leave You
	I'll See You Again		
	To-Kay		
The Blackboard Jungle	Rock around the Clock		

Show/Film	Song	Show/Film	Song
Can-Can	C'est Magnifique	DuBarry Was a Lady	Do I Love You, Do I
	I Love Paris		Friendship
	It's All Right with Me		I'm Getting Sentimental
	Just One of Those		over You
	Things	DuBarry Was a Lady (show)	Well, Did You Evah?
	Let's Do It (Let's Fall in		
	Love)	Easter Parade	A Couple of Swells
Careless Lady	All of Me		Everybody's Doing It
Carmen Jones	Beat Out Dat Rhythm		I Love a Piano
	on a Drum	Evergreen	Dancing on the Ceiling
	Dat's Love		Over My Shoulder
Carousel	If I Loved You	Everybody's Welcome (show)	As Time Goes By
	June Is Busting Out All	Evita	Don't Cry For Me,
	Over		Argentina
	Mister Snow		Oh, What a Circus
	You'll Never Walk Alone	Evita (show)	Another Suitcase in
Casablanca	As Time Goes By		Another Hall
Casbah	For Every Man There's		
	Woman	Fame	Fame (1980)
Casino Royale	The Look of Love	Feather Your Nest	Leaning on a Lamp Post
Cats	Bustopher Jones	Fiddler on the Roof	Sunrise, Sunset
	Mr Mistofolees		If I Were a Rich Man
	Memory	Finian's Rainbow	How Are Things in
Chasing Rainbows	Happy Days Are Here		Glocca Morra?
	Again	Five Easy Pieces	D.I.V.O.R.C.E.
Chess (show)	I Know Him So Well	Flashdance	Flashdance – What a
	One Night in Bangkok		Feeling (1983)
Christmas Holiday	Always	Flower Drum Song	You Are Beautiful
Chu Chin Chow	Any Time's Kissing	Follow the Band	Ain't Misbehavin'
	Time	Follow The Boys	I'll See You in My
Cinderella	Bibbidi-Bobbidi-Boo		Dreams
Cinderella (show)	Do I Love You Because	Follow the Fleet	Let's Face the Music
	You're Beautiful?		and Dance
College Rhythm	Stay as Sweet as You	Follow Through	Button Up Your
	Are		Overcoat
Convoy	Don't It Make My Brown	Footloose	Let's Hear It for the Boy
	Eyes Blue	For Me and My Gal	Oh, You Beautiful Doll
Cooley High	Dancing in the Street	Funny Face	Clap Yo' Hands
	Road Runner		How Long Has This
Countess from Hong Kong	This Is My Song		Been Going On?
Cover Girl	Long Ago and Far Away		My One and Only
Cuban Pete	The Breeze and I		S'Wonderful
Curly Top	Animal Crackers in My	Funny Girl	Don't Rain on My
	Soup		Parade
			Second-Hand Rose
Damn Yankees (show)	Whatever Lola Wants	Funny Lady	Clap Hands, Here
Days of Wine and Roses	Days of Wine and		Comes Charley
	Roses (1962)		
Deep in My Heart	Auf Wiederseh'n	Gentlemen Marry Brunettes	Have You Met Miss
	When I Grow Too Old to		Jones
	Dream		I Wanna Be Loved by
Deliverance	Duelling Banjos		You
Destry Rides Again	The Boys in the		I've Got Five Dollars
	Backroom		My Funny Valentine
Dirty Dancing	Time of My Life (1987)		Ain't Misbehavin'
Doctor Dolittle	Talk to the Animals	Gentlemen Prefer Blondes	Diamonds Are a Girl's
	(1967)		Best Friend
Doctor No	The James Bond Theme	George White's Scandals	Life Is Just a Bowl of
Don't Fence Me In	Don't Fence Me In		Cherries
Don't Knock the Rock	Tutti Frutti	George White's Scandals of	I'll Build a Stairway To
Down Dakota Way	Candy Kisses	1922 (show)	Paradise
Dr Zhivago	Lara's Theme (aka	George White's Scandals of	Somebody Loves Me
	Somewhere My Love)	1924 (show)	

Show/Film	Song	Show/Film	Song
George White's Scandals of 1945	Liza		When the Red Red Robin
George White's Scandals (show)	The Black Bottom	*Heads Up*	Ship Without a Sail
G.I. Blues	Wooden Heart	*Hello, 'Frisco, Hello*	You'll Never Know (1943)
Gigi	Gigi (1958)	*Hellzapoppin*	Watch the Birdie
	The Night They Invented Champagne	*Help!*	Help
	Thank Heaven for Little Girls	*Here Comes Elmer*	Straighten Up and Fly Right
Girl Crazy	Bidin' My Time	*Here Comes the Band*	Roll Along, Prairie Moon
	But Not for Me	*Here Comes the Groom*	In the Cool, Cool, Cool of the Evening
	Embraceable You		
	Fascinating Rhythm	*Here Come the Waves*	That Old Black Magic
	I Got Rhythm		Ac-cent-tchu-ate the Positive
Girls! Girls! Girls!	Return to Sender		
Glorifying the American Girl	Baby Face	*Here Is My Heart*	June in January
	Blue Skies		With Every Breath I Take
Godspell	Day by Day		
Going My Way	Swingin' on a Star (1944)	*Her Kind of Man*	It Had to Be You
		Her Soldier Boy (show)	Pack Up Your Troubles in Your Old Kit Bag
Going Places	Jeepers Creepers		
Gold Diggers of 1933	We're in the Money	*Hey Boy! Hey Girl!*	Fever
Gold Diggers of 1935	Lullaby of Broadway	*Hi Diddle Diddle* (show)	Miss Otis Regrets
Gone with the Wind	Tara's Theme	*High Noon*	High Noon (1952)
Good Boy (show)	I Wanna Be Loved by You	*High Society*	I Love You, Samantha
Good News	The Best Things in Life Are Free		True Love
			Well, Did You Evah?
	Lucky in Love		Who Wants to Be a Millionaire?
	Varsity Drag	*High Time*	The Second Time Around
Grease	Blue Moon		
	Hopelessly Devoted to You	*High, Wide and Handsome*	Can I Forget You
			The Folks Who Live on the Hill
	Hound Dog		
	Love Is a Many-Splendored Thing	*Hi Neighbour*	Deep in the Heart of Texas
	Summer Nights	*Hold That Ghost*	Me and My Shadow
	You're the One That I Want	*Hole in the Head*	High Hopes (1959)
		Holiday Inn	Be Careful, It's My Heart
Gulliver's Travels	It's A Hap-Hap-Happy Day		Happy Holiday
Guys and Dolls	Adelaide		White Christmas (1942)
	If I Were a Bell	*Hollywood Canteen*	Don't Fence Me In
	Luck Be a Lady Tonight	*Hollywood Revue of 1929*	Singin' in the Rain
	Sit Down You're Rocking the Boat	*Hot Chocolates* (show)	Ain't Misbehavin'
		Hullo America	Give Me the Moonlight
Guys and Dolls (show)	Bushel and a Peck	*Hullo Tango* (show)	Get Out and Get Under
Gypsy	Everything's Coming Up Roses		
		Idiot's Delight	Puttin' on the Ritz
		If I Had My Way	April Played the Fiddle
Hair	Ain't Got No – Got Life	*I'll Cry Tomorrow*	I'm Sitting on Top of the World
	Aquarius		
	Good Morning Starshine		When the Red Red Robin
Half a Sixpence (show)	Flash Bang Wallop	*I'll Get By*	You Make Me Feel So Young
Hands across the Water	Cool Water		
Hans Christian Andersen	Anywhere I Wander	*I'll See You in My Dreams*	Carolina in the Morning
	The Ugly Duckling		I'll See You in My Dreams
Hard to Get	You Must Have Been a Beautiful Baby		It Had to Be You
Has Anybody Seen My Gal?	Five Foot Two, Eyes of Blue	*I Married an Angel*	Spring Is Here

M
U
S
I
C

P
O
P

Show/Film	Song	Show/Film	Song
Incendiary Blonde	Ida, Sweet as Apple Cider	Knickerbocker Holiday	September Song
	It Had to Be You	Lady, Be Good!	Fascinating Rhythm
Indian Territory	Chattanoogie Shoeshine Boy		The Last Time I Saw Paris (1941)
Innocents of Paris	Louise		Oh, Lady Be Good
Irene	Alice Blue Gown	Lady, Be Good (show)	So Am I
Is Everybody Happy	On the Sunny Side of the Street	Lady in the Dark	Jenny
		Lady on a Train	Night and Day
Istanbul	When I Fall in Love	Lady Sings the Blues	All of Me
It's Trad, Dad	Beale Street Blues		The Man I Love
I Wonder Who's Kissing Her Now	I Wonder Who's Kissing Her Now		Our Love Is Here to Stay
		Las Vegas Story	My Resistance Is Low
Jailhouse Rock	Baby I Don't Care	Latin Quarter (show)	C'est Si Bon
Jazz on a Summer's Day	Tea for Two	Leave It to Me (show)	Get Out of Town
The Jazz Singer	I'm Looking Over a Four-Leaf Clover		Most Gentlemen Don't Like Love
Jericho	Short'nin' Bread	Les Misérables	Empty Chairs at Empty Tables
Jesus Christ Superstar	I Don't Know How to Love Him		God on High
Jewel of the Nile	When the Going Gets Tough	Les Girls	Ça C'est l'Amour
Jigsaw (show)	Swanee	Let's Make Love	My Heart Belongs to Daddy
John, Paul, George, Ringo and Bert	Help	Lilacs in the Spring	We'll Gather Lilacs
	Here Comes the Sun	Lillian Russell	After the Ball
	Lucy in the Sky with Diamonds	Little Jesse James (show)	I Love You (Archer and Thompson)
Jolson Sings Again	April Showers	Little Nellie Kelly	Singin' in the Rain
	Baby Face	Looking for Love	Be My Love
	California, Here I Come	Love, Honour and Behave	Bei Mir Bist Du Schön
	Carolina in the Morning	Love Is a Many-Splendored Thing	Love is a Many-Splendored Thing
	I'm Looking Over a Four-Leaf Clover	Lovely to Look At	I Won't Dance
	Sonny Boy		Smoke Gets in Your Eyes
	Swanee	Love Me Or Leave Me	I'm Sitting on Top of the World
	You Made Me Love You		You Made Me Love You
Jubilee (show)	Begin the Beguine	Love Me Tonight	Isn't It Romantic?
	Just One of Those Things		Mimi
		Lovers and Other Strangers	For All We Know (1970)
Jumbo	Little Girl Blue	Love Thy Neighbour	My Heart Belongs to Daddy
	The Most Beautiful Girl in the World		
	My Romance	Lucky Boy	California, Here I Come
	This Can't Be Love	Lullaby of Broadway	Just One of Those Things
Karate Kid II	The Glory of Love		Somebody Loves Me
Kismet	And This Is My Beloved		Lullaby of Broadway (1935)
	Baubles, Bangles and Beads		
	Stranger in Paradise	Mad Dogs and Englishmen	Delta Lady
Kiss Me, Kate	Always True to You in My Fashion	Mahogany	Do You Know Where You're Going To?
	I Hate Men	Make It Snappy (show)	The Sheik of Araby
	So in Love	Man of La Mancha	The Impossible Dream
	Too Darn Hot		
	Why Can't You Behave?	Mary Poppins	Chim Chim Cheree (1964)
	Wunderbar		
Kiss Them for Me	Blue Moon		
	I've Got a Gal in Kalamazoo		

Show/Film	Song	Show/Film	Song
	Feed the Birds		Miss Otis Regrets
	Jolly Holiday		My Heart Belongs to Daddy
	Let's Go Fly a Kite		Night and Day
	A Spoonful of Sugar		What Is This Thing Called Love
	Supercalifragilisticexpialidocious		You're the Top
Mary Poppins (show)	Practically Perfect	No, No, Nanette	I Want To Be Happy
M.A.S.H.	Suicide Is Painless		Tea for Two
Mayfair and Montmartre (show)	Please Do it Again	Nymph Errant (show)	Experiment
Me and My Girl	The Lambeth Walk		The Physician
	Leaning on a Lamp Post		
Meet Danny Wilson	All of Me	Octopussy	All Time High
	I've Got a Crush on You	Of Thee I Sing (show)	Love Is Sweeping the Country
	That Old Black Magic		
	When You're Smiling	Oh Kay (show)	Clap Yo' Hands
Meet Me in St Louis	Have Yourself a Merry Little Christmas		Do Do Do
			Maybe
	The Trolley Song	Oh, Look (show)	I'm Always Chasing Rainbows
Meet the People	I Like to Recognise the Tune	Oh, You Beautiful Doll	Oh You Beautiful Doll
Mexican Hayride	I Love You (Porter)	Oklahoma!	I Cain't Say No
Midnight Cowboy	Everybody's Talkin'		Oh What a Beautiful Morning
Mississippi	It's Easy to Remember		
Monkey Business	When I Take My Sugar to Tea		Out of My Dreams
			People Will Say We're in Love
Moonlight in Havana	I Wonder Who's Kissing Her Now		The Surrey With the Fringe On Top
Moon over Miami	You Started Something		
Mother Wore Tights	Burlington Bertie from Bow	Oliver	As Long As He Needs Me
Music Man	Seventy-Six Trombones		Consider Yourself
	Till There Was You		I'd Do Anything
My Dream Is Yours	You Must Have Been Beautiful Baby	One Minute to Zero	When I Fall in Love
		One Night of Love	Indian Love Call
My Fair Lady	Get Me to the Church On Time	On Her Majesty's Secret Service	All the Time in the World
	I Could Have Danced All Night	On Moonlight Bay	I'm Forever Blowing Bubbles
	I've Grown Accustomed to Her Face	On Stage Everybody	Straighten Up and Fly Right
	On the Street Where You Live	On the Sunny Side of the Street	On the Sunny Side of the Street
	With a Little Bit of Luck	On the Town	New York, New York
	Wouldn't It Be Loverly	On Your Toes	Slaughter on Tenth Avenue
My Man	Second-Hand Rose		
		On Your Toes (show)	There's a Small Hotel
Nancy Goes to Rio	Embraceable You		You Took Advantage of Me
Neptune's Daughter	Baby It's Cold Outside (1949)	Orchestra Wives	At Last
			I've Got a Gal in Kalamazoo
Never on Sunday	Never on Sunday (1960)		
New Faces	C'est Si Bon	Painting the Clouds with Sunshine	The Birth of the Blues
Night and Day	Begin the Beguine		We're in the Money
	Do I Love You, Do I		With a Song in My Heart
	I Get a Kick out of You	Paint Your Wagon	I Talk to the Trees
	In the Still of the Night		They Call the Wind Maria
	I've Got You under My Skin		Wanderin' Star
	Just One of Those Things	Pal Joey	Bewitched, Bothered and Bewildered
	Let's Do It (Let's Fall in Love)		

M U S I C   P O P

Show/Film	Song	Show/Film	Song
	I Could Write a Book		I'll Build a Stairway to
	I Didn't Know What Time		Paradise
	It Was		Liza
	The Lady is a Tramp		Love Walked In
	My Funny Valentine		The Man I Love
	There's a Small Hotel		Oh, Lady Be Good
Panama Hattie	Just One of Those		Please Do It Again
	Things		Rhapsody in Blue
	Let's Be Buddies		Somebody Loves Me
Papa's Delicate Condition	Call Me Irresponsible		Someone to Watch over
	(1963)		Me
Paramount on Parade	Come Back to Sorrento		Swanee
	Sweeping the Clouds		S'Wonderful
	Away	Rhythm on the River	Ain't It a Shame about
Pardon My Rhythm	I'll See You in My		Mame
	Dreams	Road House	Again
Pardon My Sarong	Do I Worry	Road to Morocco	Ain't Got a Dime to My
Paris	Among My Souvenirs		Name
Paris (show)	Let's Do it (Let's Fall in		Moonlight Becomes You
	Love)		But Beautiful
Paris Holiday	April in Paris	Road to Rio	But Beautiful
	The Last Time I Saw	Road to Utopia	Put It There, Pal
	Paris		Welcome to My Dream
Pat Garrett and Billy the Kid	Knockin' on Heaven's	Roberta	I Won't Dance
	Door		Smoke Gets in Your
Pepe	Mimi		Eyes
	September Song	Rock around the Clock	Only You
Perchance to Dream (show)	We'll Gather Lilacs		Rock around the Clock
Performance	Memo to Turner	Rocky III	Eye of the Tiger
Pete Kelly's Blues	Bye Bye Blackbird	Romance in the Dark	The Nearness of You
	Somebody Loves Me	Roman Scandals	Keep Young and
Phantom of the Opera (show)	All I Ask of You		Beautiful
	Music of the Night	Rosalie	In the Still of the Night
Pickwick (show)	If I Ruled the World	Rosalie (show)	How Long Has This
Pinocchio	Hi-Diddle-Dee-Dee (An		Been Going On
	Actor's Life For Me)	Rose Marie	Indian Love Call
	When You Wish upon a	Rose of Washington Square	California, Here I
	Star (1940)		Come
Play It Cool	Once upon a Dream	Sadie McKee	All I Do Is Dream of
Porgy and Bess	I Got Plenty of Nuttin'		You
	It Ain't Necessarily So	Sailors Three	All Over the Place
	Summertime	St Louis Blues	Beale Street Blues
Present Arms	You Took Advantage of	Saludos Amigos	Brazil
	Me	Sanders of the River	The Canoe Song
Prince for Tonight (show)	I Wonder Who's Kissing	Satchmo the Great	Mack the Knife
	Her Now	Saturday Night Fever	Staying Alive
Privilege	I've Been a Bad Bad Boy	September Affair	September Song
Promises, Promises (show)	I'll Never Fall in Love	Sergeant Pepper's Lonely	With a Little Help from
	Again	Hearts Club Band	My Friends
Province Town Follies (show)	Red Sails in the Sunset	Serious Charge	Living Doll
Puttin' on the Ritz	Puttin' on the Ritz	Set to Music (show)	Mad about the Boy
		Seven Brides for	Bless Yore Beautiful
Radio Stars on Parade	That Old Black Magic	Seven Brothers	Hide
Rain or Shine	Happy Days Are Here	The Seven Hills of Rome	Arriverderci Darling
	Again		Jezebel
Rainbow Round My Shoulder	Bye Bye Blackbird		Memories are Made of
Red Hot and Blue (show)	It's d'Lovely		This
Reveille with Beverley	Night and Day	Seven Lively Arts (show)	Ev'ry Time We Say
Rhapsody in Blue	Bidin' My Time		Goodbye
	Clap Yo' Hands	Shaft	Shaft (1971)
	Embraceable You	Shall We Dance?	Beginner's Luck
	Fascinating Rhythm		Let's Call the Whole
	I Got Rhythm		Thing Off

Show/Film	Song	Show/Film	Song
	Slap That Bass	Spring Is Here	With a Song in My Heart
	They All Laughed	Springtime in the Rockies	Chattanooga Choo Choo
	They Can't Take That Away from Me		
She Loves Me Not	Love in Bloom	Star	Burlington Bertie from Bow
Shipyard Sally	Wish Me Luck As You Wave Me Goodbye		Do Do Do
Show Boat	Bill		Jenny
	Can't Help Loving Dat Man		The Physician
	Make Believe		Someone to Watch over Me
	Ol' Man River	Stardust	With a Little Help from My Friends
	Why Do I Love You?		You've Lost That Lovin' Feelin'
Show Business	Alabamy Bound		
	It Had to Be You		
Show Girl (show)	Liza	Starlift	Liza
Silk Stockings	All of You		S'Wonderful
Sinbad (show)	Swanee		What Is This Thing Called Love?
Sincerely Yours	Embraceable You		
	The Man I Love	Star Spangled Rhythm	That Old Black Magic
	Swanee	State Fair	Isn't It Kinda Fun
	Tea for Two		It Might As Well Be Spring (1945)
Since You Went Away	Together		That's For Me
Singin' in the Rain	All I Do Is Dream of You	Stop Flirting (show)	I'll Build a Stairway to Paradise
	Singin' in the Rain		
Singin' in the Rain (show)	Be a Clown	Stop the World – I Want To Get Off	What Kind of Fool Am I?
	Fascinating Rhythm		
Sleepy Lagoon	By the Sleepy Lagoon		
Snow White and the Seven Dwarfs	Some Day My Prince Will Come		Gonna Build a Mountain
	Whistle While You Work	Stormy Weather	Ain't Misbehavin'
So Dear to My Heart	Lavender Blue	Strike Up the Band (show)	I've Got a Crush on You
Somebody Loves Me	Somebody Loves Me		Soon
Some Like It Hot	Down among the Sheltering Palms	Summer Holiday	Bachelor Boy
	Sweet Georgia Brown	Sunbonnet Sue	By the Light of the Silvery Moon
	I Wanna Be Loved by You	Sunny	Two Little Blue Birds
Something to Shout About	You'd Be So Nice to Come Home to	Sunny Side of the Street	I Get a Kick Out of You
Song of Norway	Strange Music	Sunny Side Up	If I Had a Talking Picture of You
Song of the South	Zip-a-dee-doo-dah (1947)		
Son of Paleface	Buttons and Bows	Sunset Boulevard	Charmaine
The Sound of Music	Climb Ev'ry Mountain	Sun Valley Serenade	At Last
	Do-Re-Mi		Chattanooga Choo Choo
	Edelweiss		In the Mood
	My Favourite Things		
South Pacific	Bali Ha'i	Swanee River	Beautiful Dreamer
	A Cock-Eyed Optimist	Sweet Adeline	Don't Ever Leave Me
	Happy Talk	Sweet Adeline (show)	Why Was I Born?
	I'm Gonna Wash That Man Right Out of My Hair	Sweet and Low (show)	Cheerful Little Earful
		Sweet Charity	Big Spender
	I'm in Love with a Wonderful Guy		Rhythm of Life
	Some Enchanted Evening	Swing Parade of 1946	On the Sunny Side of the Street
	There Is Nothing Like A Dame	Swing Time	The Way You Look Tonight (1936)
	This Nearly Was Mine	Swingtime Johnny	Boogie Woogie Bugle Boy
	Younger Than Springtime	Syncopation	You Made Me Love You

MUSIC POP

Show/Film	Song	Show/Film	Song
Take a Chance	It's Only a Paper Moon		Yes Sir, That's My
Tea for Two	Do Do Do		Baby
	Here in My Arms		You Must Have Been a
	I Want to Be Happy		Beautiful Baby
	Tea for Two	The Eddie Duchin Story	April Showers
Thank Your Lucky Stars	I'm Riding for a Fall		Brazil
That Certain Feeling	That Certain Feeling		Just One of Those
That Midnight Kiss	Down among the		Things
	Sheltering Palms		On the Sunny Side of
That Night in Rio	Chica Chica Boom Chic		the Street
	I Yi Yi Yi Yi I Like You		Stardust
	Very Much		What Is This Thing
That Summer	Because the Night		Called Love?
The Benny Goodman Story	Avalon		The Man I Love
	On the Sunny Side of	The Emperor Waltz	Kiss in Your Eyes
	the Street	The Exorcist	Tubular Bells
The Best Things in Life	The Birth of the Blues	The Fabulous Dorseys	Everybody's Doing It
Are Free	Broken Hearted	The Firefly	The Donkey Serenade
	Button Up Your	The Five Pennies	Won't You Come Home
	Overcoat		Bill Bailey
	If I Had a Talking Picture	The Fleet's In	I Remember You
	of You	The Fleet's Lit Up (show)	It's d'Lovely
	Life is Just a Bowl of	The French Doll (show)	Please Do It Again
	Cherries	The Gay Divorcee	The Continental
	Lucky in Love		I've Got You on My
	My Sin		Mind
	Sonny Boy		Night and Day
	Together	The Girl Can't Help It	Be-Bop-A-Lula
	You're the Cream in My	The Girl He Left Behind	Brazil
	Coffee	The Glenn Miller Story	At Last
The Best Years of Our Lives	Among My Souvenirs		Basin Street Blues
The Big Beat	As I Love You		Bidin' My Time
The Big Broadcast	Marta		Chattanooga Choo
	Minnie the Moocher		Choo
	Where the Blue of the		In the Mood
	Night	The Glorious Days (show)	Swanee
The Big Broadcast of 1936	Goodnight, Sweetheart	The Goldwyn Follies	Love Walked In
The Big Broadcast of 1938	Thanks for the Memory		Our Love Is Here to
	(1938)		Stay
The Blue Angel	Falling in Love Again	The Graduate	Mrs Robinson
The Blue Paradise	Auf Wiederseh'n	The Great American	Alabamy Bound
The Boy Friend	All I Do Is Dream of	Broadcast	
	You		If I Didn't Care
The Boys from Syracuse	Falling in Love with	The Great Schnozzle	Inka Dinka Doo
	Love	The Harvey Girls	On the Atchison, Topeka
	Sing for Your Supper		and Santa Fe
	This Can't Be Love	The James Dean Story	Let Me Be Loved
The Bridge on the River Kwai	River Kwai March	The Jazz Singer	Blue Skies
The Caddy	That's Amore	The Joker Is Wild	All the Way (1957)
The Cockeyed World	You're the Cream in My	The Jolson Story	After the Ball
	Coffee		The Anniversary Song
The Desert Song	French Military		April Showers
	Marching		Avalon
	Song		By the Light of the
	The Riff Song		Silvery Moon
The Diamond Horseshoe	The More I See You		California, Here I
The Dolly Sisters	Carolina in the Morning		Come
	Give Me the Moonlight		I'm Sitting on Top of the
	I'm Always Chasing		World
	Rainbows		Liza
The Eddie Cantor Story	Bye Bye Blackbird		Swanee
	Ida, Sweet as Apple		When the Red Red
	Cider		Robin

Show/Film	Song	Show/Film	Song
	You Made Me Love You	The Vagabond King	Only a Rose
The King and I	Getting to Know You		Some Day
	The March of the Siamese Children	The Wall	Another Brick in the Wall
	Hello, Young Lovers	The Way We Were	The Way We Were (1973)
	I Whistle a Happy Tune	The Wicked Lady	Love Steals Your Heart
	Shall We Dance?	The Wizard of Oz	Over the Rainbow (1939)
	We Kiss in the Shadow		
The King of Jazz	Rhapsody in Blue	The World Is Full of Married Men	Right Back Where We Started From
The Magic Christian	Come and Get It		
The Man from the Folies Bergere	Rhythm of the Rain	The Ziegfeld Follies of 1921 (show)	Second-Hand Rose
The Man I Love	Bill	The Ziegfeld Girl	I'm Always Chasing Rainbows
	Liza		You Stepped Out of a Dream
	The Man I Love		
The Man Who Knew Too Much	Que Sera, Sera (1956)	There's No Business Like Show Business	Alexander's Ragtime Band
The New Moon	Wanting You		There's No Business Like Show Business
The Night Is Young	When I Grow Too Old to Dream		After You Get What You Want You Don't Want It
The Pajama Game	Hernando's Hideaway	These Foolish Things (show)	Music, Maestro, Please
The Paleface	Buttons and Bows	This Could Be the Night	I've Got You under My Skin
The Perils of Pauline	I Wish I Didn't Love You So		
The Pirate	Be a Clown		Blue Moon
The Pleasure Seekers (show)	Get Out and Get Under	This Is the Life	With a Song in My Heart
The Prime of Miss Jean Brodie	Jean	This Time for Keeps	Inka Dinka Doo
The Sandpiper	The Shadow of Your Smile (1965)	Thoroughly Modern Millie	Baby Face
			Please Do It Again
The Seven Hills of Rome	Arriverderci Darling	Thousands Cheer	Honeysuckle Rose
	Memories Are Made of This	Three Coins in the Fountain	Three Coins in the Fountain (1954)
The Shocking Miss Pilgrim	For You, for Me, for Everyone	Three for the Show	I've Got a Crush on You
The Show Is On (show)	By Strauss		Someone to Watch over Me
The Singing Fool	I'm Sitting on Top of the World	Three Little Girls in Blue	You Make Me Feel So Young
	Sonny Boy	Three Little Words	I Wanna Be Loved by You
The Singing Hill	Blueberry Hill		
The Singing Nun	Dominique		Who's Sorry Now?
The Spy Who Loved Me	Nobody Does It Better	Till the Clouds Roll By	Long Ago and Far Away
The Sting	The Entertainer		All the Things You Are
The Stooge	Louise		Can't Help Loving Dat Man
The Story of Vernon and Irene Castle	Hello, Hello, Who's Your Lady Friend?		I Won't Dance
	Oh, You Beautiful Doll		The Last Time I Saw Paris
The Strip	Ain't Misbehavin'		Make Believe
	Basin Street Blues		Ol' Man River
The Stud	Emotions		Smoke Gets in Your Eyes
The Student Prince	The Drinking Song		
The Sun Also Rises	I Love You (Archer and Thompson)	Time	She's So Beautiful
		Tin Pan Alley	Honeysuckle Rose
The Third Man	Harry Lime Theme		The Sheik of Araby
The Thomas Crown Affair	Windmills of Your Mind (1968)	Tip-Toes (show)	Looking for a Boy
			Sweet and Lowdown
The Threepenny Opera (show)	Mack the Knife		That Certain Feeling
The Time, the Place and the Girl	I Wonder Who's Kissing Her Now	Tip Top (show)	Feather Your Nest
The Toast of New Orleans	Be My Love	To Have and Have Not	Hong Kong Blues

M
U
S
I
C

P
O
P

Show/Film	Song	Show/Film	Song
Tommy	I'm Free		Tea for Two
	Pinball Wizard		Alabamy Bound
Too Many Girls	I Didn't Know What		Blue Moon
	Time It Was		With a Song in My
Too Many Girls (show)	I Like to Recognize the		Heart
	Tune	The Wizard of Oz	Ding Dong the Witch Is
Too Young to Know	It's Only a Paper Moon		Dead
Top Gun	Take My Breath Away		Over the Rainbow
	(1986)		(1939)
Top Hat	Cheek to Cheek	Woman in Red	I Just Called to Say I
	Isn't This a Lovely Day		Love You
Torch Song	Blue Moon	Wonderful Life	On the Beach
Trouble in Store	Don't Laugh at Me	Woodstock	Dance to the Music
Two for the Show	How High the Moon?		With a Little Help from
Two for Tonight	From the Top of Your		My Friends
	Head	Words and Music	Slaughter on Tenth
Two Girls and a Sailor	Inka Dinka Doo		Avenue
Two Weeks with Love	By the Light of the		Blue Moon
	Silvery Moon		I Wish I Were in Love
			Again
Up in Central Park	Close As Pages in a		Johnny One Note
	Book		The Lady Is a Tramp
			Mountain Greenery
Variety Jubilee	Keep the Home Fires		My Heart Stood Still
	Burning		There's a Small Hotel
	A Little of What You		This Can't Be Love
	Fancy		Thou Swell
			Where or When
			Where's That
Waikiki Wedding	Sweet Leilani (1937)		Rainbow?
Wait Till the Sun Shines,	Pack Up Your Troubles		With a Song in My
Nellie	in Your Old Kit Bag		Heart
Wake Up and Dream	What Is This Thing	Words and Music (show)	Mad about the Boy
	Called Love?	Yellow Submarine	All You Need Is Love
Wake Up and Dream (show)	Let's Do It (Let's Fall in		Eleanor Rigby
	Love)		With a Little Help from
Watership Down	Bright Eyes		My Friends
Way Out West	Trail of the Lonesome	Yesterday's Heroes	Hold the Line
	Pine	You Can't Have Everything	Afraid to Dream
Wedding Bells	How Could You Believe	You Light Up My Life	You Light Up My Life
	Me?		(1977)
Weekend Pass	All or Nothing at All	You Never Know (show)	At Long Last Love
We're Not Dressing	Love Thy Neighbour	Young at Heart	Just One of Those
West Side Story	I Feel Pretty		Things
	Maria		The Man I Love
	Something's Coming		Someone to Watch over
	Somewhere		Me
	Tonight	Young Man of Music	With a Song in My
Wharf Angel	Oh, You Beautiful Doll		Heart
	You Made Me Love	You're My Everything	Ain't She Sweet?
	You		California, Here I
What Lola Wants	Whatever Lola Wants		Come
What's Cooking?	Woodchoppers' Ball	You Were Meant for Me	Ain't Misbehavin'
White Christmas	Blue Skies		Ain't She Sweet?
	White Christmas		Goodnight, Sweetheart
White Nights	Say You, Say Me (1985)	Zorba the Greek	Zorba's Dance
Whoopee	My Baby Just Cares for		
	Me		
Will o' the Whispers (show)	The Man I Love,		
With a Song in My Heart	California, Here I Come		
	Deep in the Heart of		
	Texas		
	Embraceable You		

Dubbed Singing Voice of Well-Known Actors

Actor	Voice and film
Ann Blyth	Gogi Grant (Both Ends of the Candle)
Audrey Hepburn	Marni Nixon (My Fair Lady)
Christopher Plummer	Bill Lee (Sound of Music)
Cyd Charisse	India Adams (The Band Wagon)
Deborah Kerr	Marni Nixon (King and I)
Diahann Carroll	Bernice Peterson (Carmen Jones)
Dorothy Dandridge	Marilyn Horne (Carmen Jones)
Edmund Purdom	Mario Lanza (The Student Prince)
Franco Nero	Gene Merlina (Camelot)
Harry Belafonte	LeVerne Hutcherson (Carmen Jones)
Jean Seberg	Anita Gordon (Paint Your Wagon)
Jeanne Crain	Anita Ellis (Gentlemen Marry Brunettes)
Joan Leslie	Louanne Hogan (Rhapsody in Blue)
Joe Adams	Marvin Hayes (Carmen Jones)
John Kerr	Bill Lee (South Pacific)
Juanita Hall	Muriel Smith (South Pacific)
Larry Parks	Al Jolson (The Jolson Story)
Lucille Bremer	Trudy Erwin (Till the CloudsRoll By)
Natalie Wood	Marni Nixon (West Side Story)
Ned Beatty	Vernon Midgley (Hear My Song)
Peter O'Toole	Simon Gilbert (Man of La Mancha)
Richard Beymer	Jim Bryant (West Side Story)
Rita Moreno	Leona Gordon (King and I)
Rita Moreno	Betty Wand (West Side Story)
Rossano Brazzi	Giorgio Tozi (South Pacific)
Sophia Loren	Renata Tebaldi (Aida)
Susan Hayward	Jane Froman (With a Song inMy Heart)
Vera-Ellen	Carole Richards (Call Me Madam)

M
U
S
I
C

P
O
P

Theme Songs or Signature Tunes

Song/Tune	Artiste	Song/Tune	Artiste
Back to Those Happy Days	Herman Darewski	Everybody Loves Somebody	Dean Martin
Be My Love	Mario Lanza	Give Me the Moonlight	Frankie Vaughan
Because of You	Tony Bennett	Give My Regards to	George M Cohen
Begin the Beguine	Leslie (Hutch) Hutchinson	Broadway	
		Goodbye (closing theme)	Benny Goodman
Bei Mir Bist Du Schön	Andrews Sisters	Goodnight	Cavan O'Connor
Bewitched Bothered and Bewildered	Bill Snyder	Goodnight, Sweetheart (closing theme)	Ray Noble
Bill	Helen Morgan	Here's to the Next Time	Henry Hall
Blue Flame (opening theme)	Woody Herman	How High the Moon	Les Paul and Mary Ford
Bugle Call Rag	Harry Roy	Hurry on Down	Nellie Lutcher
Ciribiribin	Harry James	Ida, Sweet as Apple Cider	Eddie Cantor
Clap Hands Here Comes Charlie	Charlie Kunz	I Do Like to Be Beside the Seaside	Reginald Dixon
Cocktails for Two	Carl Brisson	I Don't Care	Eva Tanguay
Coquette	Guy Lombardo	If I Didn't Care	Ink Spots
Cry	Johnnie Ray	I Got Rhythm	Ethel Merman
Cuban Love Song	Edmundo Ros	I'll See You Again	Noël Coward
Dancing Time	Oscar Rabin	I'll See You in My Dreams	Tony Martin
Darling, Je Vous Aime Beaucoup	Hildegarde	I Love a Lassie	Harry Lauder
		I'm Getting Sentimental Over You	Tommy Dorsey
Dear Old Southland	Layton and Johnstone		
Deep Forest	Earl Hines	Inka Dinka Doo	Jimmy Durante
Dinah	Dinah Shore	In the Mood	Joe Loss
Don't Laugh at Me	Norman Wisdom	I Used to Sigh for the Silvery Moon	G H Elliott (Chocolate-coloured Coon)
Dream	The Pied Pipers		
Dream Along with Me	Perry Como	J'Attendrai	Jean Sablon

Song/Tune	Artiste	Song/Tune	Artiste
Just an Old-Fashioned Girl	Eartha Kitt	Some of These Days	Sophie Tucker
Just Like a Melody from Out of the Sky	Jay Wilbur	Somebody Stole My Gal	Billy Cotton
		So Rare (closing theme)	Jimmy Dorsey
La Mer	Charles Trenet	So Tired	Russ Morgan
Leaning on a Lamp Post	George Formby	Speak to Me of Love	Lucienne Boyer
Let's Dance (opening theme)	Benny Goodman	Stage Coach	Eric Winstone
Life Is Nothing without Music	Fred Hartley	Stormy Weather	Lena Horne
Louise	Maurice Chevalier	Straighten Up and Fly Right	Nat King Cole
Love in Bloom	Jack Benny	Sugar Blues	Clyde McCoy
Love Is Like a Violin	Ken Dodd	Summertime	Bob Crosby
Lullaby of Broadway	George Shearing	Sunrise Serenade	Frankie Carle
Makin' Whoopee	Eddie Cantor	Sweet and Lovely	Russ Columbo
Mañana Is Soon Enough For Me	Peggy Lee	Take Me to Your Heart Again	Edith Piaf
		Take the 'A' Train	Duke Ellington
Marigold	Billy Mayerl	Tenderly	Rosemary Clooney
Marta	Arthur Tracy (The Street Singer)	Thanks for the Memory	Bob Hope
		That Old Black Magic	Stanley Black
			Billy Daniels
Minnie the Moocher	Cab Calloway		
Moonlight Serenade	Glenn Miller	That's What I Like about the South	Phil Harris
Mother Machree	John MacCormack		
Music, Maestro, Please	Harry Leader	The Dicky Bird Hop	Ronald Gourlay
My Blue Heaven	Gene Austin	The Donkey Serenade	Monte Rey
My Heart Belongs to Daddy	Mary Martin	The Jolly Brothers	Albert Whelan
My Mammy	Al Jolson	The Sweetest Music This Side of Heaven	Maurice Winnick
My Time Is Your Time	Rudy Vallee		
Near You	Francis Craig	The Very Thought of You (opening theme)	Ray Noble
Nightmare	Artie Shaw		
Oh Monah	Lew Stone	The Wheel of Fortune	Kay Starr
O Mein Papa	Eddie Calvert	Tumbling Tumbleweeds	Sons of the Pioneers
One O'Clock Jump	Count Basie	We'll Be Together Again	Frankie Laine
On the Air	Carroll Gibbons	What's New	Billy Butterfield
Over the Rainbow	Judy Garland	When Day Is Done	Ambrose
Paper Doll	Mills Brothers	When It's Sleepy Time Down South	Louis Armstrong
Rags, Bottles or Bones	Syd Walker		
Red Sails in the Sunset	Suzette Tarri	When My Baby Smiles At Me	Ted Lewis
Rhapsody in Blue	Paul Whiteman		
Rose of Washington Square	Fanny Brice	When the Moon Comes Over the Mountain	Kate Smith
Sally	Gracie Fields		
Say It With Music	Jack Payne	When You're Smiling	George Elrick
Sentimental Journey	Les Brown	Where the Blue of the Night	Bing Crosby
She's My Lovely	Billy Ternent	Whispering	Roy Fox
Shine On Harvest Moon	Nora Bayes	Woodchoppers' Ball	Woody Herman
Skyliner	Charlie Barnet	You're Dancing on My Heart	Victor Sylvester
Sleepy Serenade	Cyril Stapleton	Yours	Vera Lynn
Smoke Rings	Glen Gray		

NB: The theme tunes or signature tunes above are the ones the people themselves considered to be so, and not always the one most readily identifiable with the artist. For example, few would consider 'Yours' to be more identifiable with Vera Lynn than 'The White Cliffs of Dover'. Similarly, 'Take Me To Your Heart Again' is certainly not the most famous Edith Piaf song.

It is probably a good idea at this stage to lay to rest once and for all the most common source of frustration for quiz players on the topic of signature tunes, i.e. is Glenn Miller's signature tune 'In the Mood' or 'Moonlight Serenade'? The problem arises because 'In the Mood' was one of Glenn Miller's most popular tunes and was featured in both *Sun Valley Serenade* and *The Glenn Miller Story*; however, Glenn Miller himself composed 'Moonlight Serenade' and always considered this to be his signature tune. Joe Loss did, in fact, record 'In the Mood' and subsequently adopted it as his signature.

TV and Radio Theme Tunes

Programme	Tune (and/or composer)	Programme	Tune (and/or composer)
Absolutely Fabulous	'This Wheel's on Fire' by Julie Driscoll	Great Antiques Hunt	Theme tune by the Brodsky Quartet
Angel	Theme tune performed by Darling Violetta	Harry's Game	Theme by Clannad
The Archers	'Barwick Green' (from My Native Heath) suite written in 1922 by Arthur Wood	Have Gun, Will Travel	'The Ballad of the Paladin'
		Hawaii Five O	Music by Morton Stevens
		Horse of the Year Show	Mozart's 'A Musical Joke'
Auf Wiedersehen Pet	'That's Living Alright' (sung by Joe Fagin)	Howards Way	Theme tune by Simon May
The Avengers	Theme by Laurie Johnson	Howards Way: vocal version	'Always There' by Marti Webb
Big Brother	Theme tune by Element Four (aka Paul Oakenfold and Andy Gray)	I'm Sorry I'll Read That Again	'The Angus Prune Tune'
Billy Cotton Band Show	'Somebody Stole My Gal'	Inspector Morse	Theme tune by Barrington Pheloung
Blake's 7	Music by Dudley Simpson	Ironside	Theme by Quincy Jones
Blue Peter	'Barnacle Bill the Sailor' by Robison and Luther (famous adaptation by Mike Oldfield)	Jason King	Theme by Laurie Johnson
		Juke Box Jury	'Hit and Miss' by John Barry
		Just a Minute	Minute Waltz by Chopin
Bonanza	Music by David Rose	The Killing Game	'Tom Hark' by the Piranhas
Bootsie and Snudge	'Pop Goes the Weasel'		
Brain of Britain	Mozart's Eine kleine Nachtmusik	Kojak	Theme by Billy Goldenberg
Buffy the Vampire Slayer	Theme written and performed by rock band Nerf Herder	Life and Times of David Lloyd George	'Chi Mai' by Ennio Morricone
		Light of Experience	Theme by Doina De Jale
Captain Pugwash	'Hornblower' (played on the accordion by Tommy Edwards)	The Lone Ranger	William Tell Overture by Rossini
Crossroads	Theme by Tony Hatch and later adapted by Paul McCartney	M.A.S.H.	'Suicide Is Painless' by Mash
		Mastermind	'Approaching Menace' by Neil Richardson
Dad's Army	'Who Do You Think You're Kidding, Mr Hitler?' sung by Bud Flanagan	Match of the Day	Drum Majorette
		Miami Vice	'Miami Vice Theme' and 'Crockett's Theme' (both by Jan Hammer)
Danger Man	Music by Edwin Astley		
Desert Island Discs	'By the Sleepy Lagoon' by Eric Coates	Minder	'I Could Be So Good For You' by Pat Waterman and Gerard Kenny
Doctor Kildare	'Three Stars Will Shine Tonight' (vocal version by Richard Chamberlain)	Mission Impossible	Theme by Lalo Schifrin
		Mistral's Daughter	'Only Love' (sung by Nana Mouskouri)
Dr Who	Theme by Ron Grainer	Monty Python's Flying Circus	'Liberty Bell' by John Paul Souza
The Dukes of Hazzard	Theme tune by Waylon Jennings		
		Moonlighting	'Moonlighting Theme' by Al Jarreau
EastEnders	Theme tune by Simon May		
EastEnders: vocal version	'Anyone Can Fall in Love' sung by Anita Dobson	Neighbours	Theme by Tony Hatch
		Noddy	Paul K Joyce
Equaliser	Theme tune by Stewart Copeland	No Honestly	'No Honestly' by Lynsey de Paul
Friends	'I'll Be There For You' by The Rembrandts	Onedin Line	Spartacus by Khatchaturian
Grand Prix	BBC – 'The Chain' by Fleetwood Mac	One Foot in the Grave	Composed and sung by Eric Idle

Programme	Tune (and/or composer)	Programme	Tune (and/or composer)
Owen MD	'Sleepy Shores' by Johnny Pearson	Test Match Special	'Soul Limbo' by Booker T & The MGs
Perry Mason	Theme by Fred Steiner	That Was the Week That Was	Sung by Millicent Martin
The Persuaders	Music by John Barry		
The Prisoner	Music by Ron Grainer	The Third Man	'Harry Lime Theme' by Anton Karas
Prisoner Cell Block H	'On the Inside' (sung by Lynne Hamilton)	Tinker, Tailor, Soldier, Spy	Nunc Dimittis, arranged by Geoffrey Burgon
Protectors	'Avenues and Alleyways' by Tony Christie	Top of the Pops	'Yellow Pearl' by Phil Lynott (co-written by Lynott and Ray Davies); 'Whole Lotta Love' by CCS (instrumental version of Led Zeppelin song); 'The Wizard' by Paul Hardcastle
Randall and Hopkirk (Deceased)	Music by Edwin Astley		
Rawhide	Theme sung by Frankie Laine		
Ready Steady Go!	'Wipe Out' (The Surfaris); '5-4-3-2-1' (Manfred Mann)	Top Secret	'Sucu Sucu'
The Saint	Music by Edwin Astley	Two-Way Family Favourites	'With a Song in My Heart' by Richard Rodgers
The Seven Faces of Woman	'She' (sung by Charles Aznavour)		
The Sky at Night	At the Castle Gate by Sibelius (from Pelléas et Mélisande)	Van Der Valk	'Eye Level' by Simon Park
		What the Papers Say	From the Cornish Dances by Malcolm Arnold
The Snowman	'Walking in the Air' (sung by Aled Jones)		
South Bank Show	Variations on a Theme of Paganini by Julian Lloyd Webber	X Files	Music by Mark Snow
		Yes Honestly	'Yes Honestly' by Georgie Fame
Star Trek	Music by Alexander Courage		
Stingray	'Aquamarina' (sung by Garry Miller)	Z Cars	'Theme from Z Cars' aka 'Johnny Todd' by the Johnny Keating Orchestra
Supergran	Theme composed and sung by Billy Connolly		

Eurovision Song Contest Winners

Year	Song	Country (and Singer)	UK Entry	UK Posn
1956	Refrain	Switzerland (Lys Assia)	No entry	
1957	Net Als Toen	Holland (Corry Brokken)	All (Patricia Breden)	6th
1958	Dors, Mon Amour	France (André Claveau)	No entry	
1959	Een Beetje	Holland (Teddy Scholten)	Sing Little Birdie (Pearl Carr and Teddy Johnson)	2nd
1960	Tom Pillibi	France (Jacqueline Boyer)	Looking High, High, High (Bryan Johnson)	2nd
1961	Nous, les Amoureux	Luxembourg (Jean-Claude Pascal)	Are You Sure (Allisons)	2nd
1962	Un Premier Amour	France (Isabelle Aubret)	Ring-a-ding Girl (Ronnie Carroll)	4th
1963	Dansevise	Denmark (Grethe Jorgen Ingmann)	Say Wonderful Things (Ronnie Carroll)	4th
1964	Non Ho L'Eta (This Is My Prayer)	Italy (Gigliola Cinquetti)	I Say the Little Things (Matt Monro)	2nd
1965	Poupée de Cire, Poupée de Son	Luxembourg (France Gall)	I Belong (Kathy Kirby)	2nd
1966	Merci Chérie	Austria (Udo Jurgens)	A Man without Love (Kenneth McKellar)	7th
1967	Puppet on a String	UK (Sandie Shaw)	Puppet on a String	1st
1968	La La La	Spain (Massiel)	Congratulations (Cliff Richard)	2nd
1969	Viva Cantando	Spain (Salome)	Boom Bang-A-Bang	1st
	Boom Bang-A-Bang	UK (Lulu)		
	De Troubadour	Holland (Lennie Kuhr)		
	Un Jour Un Enfant	France (Frida Boccara)		

Year	Song	Country (and Singer)	UK Entry	UK Posn
1970	All Kinds of Everything	Ireland (Dana)	Knock Knock (Mary Hopkin)	2nd
1971	Un Banc, Un Arbre, Une Rue	Monaco (Séverine)	Jack in the Box (Clodagh Rodgers)	4th
1972	Après Toi (Come What May)	Luxembourg (Vicky Leandros)	Beg, Steal or Borrow (New Seekers)	2nd
1973	Tu Te Reconnaîtras (Wonderful Dream)	Luxembourg (Anne-Marie David)	Power to all our Friends (Cliff Richard)	3rd
1974	Waterloo	Sweden (Abba)	Long Live Love (Olivia Newton-John)	4th
1975	Ding A Dong	Holland (Teach In)	Let Me Be the One (Shadows)	2nd
1976	Save Your Kisses for Me	UK (Brotherhood of Man)	Save Your Kisses For Me	1st
1977	L'Oiseau et L'Enfant	France (Marie Myriam)	Rock Bottom (Lynsey de Paul)	2nd
1978	A-ba-ni-bi	Israel (Izhar Cohen and the Alpha-Beta)	The Bad Old Days (Coco)	11th
1979	Hallelujah	Israel (Milk and Honey featuring Gali Atari)	Mary Ann (Black Lace)	7th
1980	What's Another Year?	Ireland (Johnny Logan)	Love Enough for Two (Prima Donna)	3rd
1981	Making Your Mind Up	UK (Buck's Fizz)	Making Your Mind Up	1st
1982	Ein Bisschen Frieden (A Little Peace)	Germany (Nicole)	One Step Further (Bardo)	7th
1983	Si la Vie Est Cadeau	Luxembourg (Corinne Hermes)	I'm Never Giving Up (Sweet Dreams)	6th
1984	Diggi loo-Diggi Ley	Sweden (Herreys)	Love Games (Belle and the Devotions)	7th
1985	La Det Swinge (Let it Swing)	Norway (Bobbysocks)	Love Is (Vikki)	4th
1986	J'aime la Vie	Belgium (Sandra Kim)	Runner in the Night (Ryder)	7th
1987	Hold Me Now	Ireland (Johnny Logan)	Only the Light (Rikki)	13th
1988	Ne Partez Pas Sans Moi	Switzerland (Celine Dion)	Go (Scott Fitzgerald)	2nd
1989	Rock Me	Yugoslavia (Riva)	Why Do I Always Get It Wrong (Live Report)	2nd
1990	Insieme:1992	Italy (Toto Cutugno)	Give a Little Love Back to the World (Emma)	6th
1991	Fångad Av En Stormvind	Sweden (Carola)	A Message to Your Heart (Samantha Janus)	10th
1992	Why Me?	Ireland (Linda Martin)	One Step Out of Time (Michael Ball)	2nd
1993	In Your Eyes	Ireland (Niamh Kavanagh)	Better the Devil You Know (Sonia)	2nd
1994	Rock 'n' Roll Kids	Ireland (Paul Harrington and Charlie McGettigan)	We Will Be Free (Lonely Symphony) (Frances Ruffelle)	10th
1995	Nocturne	Norway (Secret Garden)	Love City Groove (Love City Groove)	10th
1996	The Voice	Ireland (Eimear Quinn)	Just a Little Bit (Gina G)	8th
1997	Love Shine a Light	UK (Katrina and the Waves)	Love Shine a Light	1st
1998	Diva	Israel (Dana International)	Where Are You? (Imaani)	2nd
1999	Take Me to Your Heaven	Sweden (Charlotte Nilsson)	Say It Again (Precious)	12th
2000	Fly on the Wings of Love	Denmark (Olsen Brothers)	Don't Play That Song Again (Nikki French)	16th
2001	Everybody	Estonia (Tanel Pader and Dave Benton)	No Dream Impossible (Lindsay Dracass)	15th
2002	I Wanna	Latvia (Marija Naumova)	Come Back (Jessica Garlick)	3rd equal
2003	Every Way That I Can	Turkey (Sertab Erener)	Cry Baby (Jemini)	Last
2004	Wild Dances	Ukraine (Ruslana)	Hold onto Our Love (James Fox)	16th
2005	My Number One	Greece (Helena Paparizou)	Touch My Fire (Javine Hylton)	22nd

MUSIC POP

Classical-based Pop Tunes

Baubles, Bangles and Beads Adapted from the String Quartet in D major by Alexander Borodin

Beat Out Dat Rhythm on a Drum Based on 'The Gypsy Song' from the opera *Carmen* by Georges Bizet

Can Can (Bad Manners) Adapted from *Orpheus in the Underworld* by Jacques Offenbach

Can't Help Falling in Love Based on *Plaisir d'Amour* by Giovanni Martini

Capstick Comes Home Based on Dvořák's Symphony No. 9 in E minor (2nd movement, Largo)

Danny Boy Lyrics by Frederick Weatherly (1848–1929) and based on 'The Londonderry Air'

Dat's Love Based on 'Habañera' from the opera *Carmen* by Georges Bizet

Fanfare for the Common Man (ELP) Based on Aaron Copland's orchestral piece of the same name

Hello Muddah, Hello Fadduh Adapted from 'Dance of the Hours', Act 3 of *La Gioconda* by Amilcare Ponchielli

Hot Diggity Adapted from *España* (Spanish Rhapsody) by Emmanuel Chabrier

I Believe in Father Christmas Adapted from the *Lieutenant Kijé Suite*, Op. 60 by Sergei Prokofiev

I'd Climb the Highest Mountain Based on *Humoresque* Opus 101 No. 7 by Antonín Dvořák

If I Had Words Adapted from the 3rd movement of Symphony No. 3 Op. 78 by Charles Camille Saint-Saëns

If You Are But a Dream Adapted from *Romance* in E flat by Anton Rubinstein

I'm Always Chasing Rainbows Adapted from *Fantaisie Impromptu* in C sharp minor Op. 66 by Frederic Chopin

In An Eighteenth-century Drawing Room Adapted from Piano Sonata No. 3 in C by Wolfgang Amadeus Mozart

Joybringer Adapted from the 4th movement of *The Planets Suite* Op. 32 by Gustav Holst ('Jupiter – Bringer of Jollity')

Kiss in Your Eyes Adapted from *Une Chambre séparée* by Richard Heuberger

Lamp Is Low Adapted from *Pavane pour une infante défunte* by Maurice Ravel

Land of Hope and Glory Based on *Pomp and Circumstance March* No. 1 by Edward Elgar

Like I Do Adapted from 'Dance of the Hours', Act 3 of *La Gioconda* by Amilcare Ponchielli

Moon Love Based on the 2nd movement of Tchaikovsky's Symphony No. 5

More Than Love Adapted from the 2nd movement of the Sonata for Piano No. 8 in C minor, Op. 13 by Ludwig van Beethoven

My Reverie Based on Debussy's *Rêverie*

Narcissus Adapted from the *Water Scenes Suite*, Op. 13 No. 4 by Ethelbert Nevin

Nut Rocker Adapted from the March from *Casse-noisette Suite*, Op. 71 by Tchaikovsky

On the Isle of May Based on Tchaikovsky's Andante Cantabile

Our Love Based on Tchaikovsky's *Romeo and Juliet Overture*

Question and Answer Adapted from *Petite Suite de Concert*, Op. 77 by Samuel Coleridge-Taylor

River Kwai March Based on 'Colonel Bogey March' by Kenneth Alford

Rodrigo's Concerto An arrangement of the 2nd movement of the *Concerto for Guitar and Orchestra in D major* by Joaquin Rodrigo

Sabre Dance Adapted from *Gayaneh Ballet* by Aram Khatchaturian

So Deep Is the Night Adapted from Etude in E minor, Op. 10 No. 3 by Frédéric Chopin

Song of India Adapted from *Chanson indoue* by Nikolai Rimsky-Korsakov

The Story of a Starry Night Based on the 1st movement of Symphony No. 6 by Tchaikovsky

Strange Music Adapted from *Wedding-Day in Troldhaugen* by Edvard Grieg

Stranger in Paradise Adapted from a theme of the *Polovtsian Dances* by Alexander Borodin

Suddenly (Tony Bennett) Adapted from *Une Chambre Séparée* by Richard Heuberger

Surrender (Elvis Presley) Adapted from 'Torna A Surriento' by Ernesto De Curtis

The Things I Love Based on Melodie in E flat major, Op. 42 No 3 by Tchaikovsky

Till the End of Time Based on Chopin's Polonaise No. 6 in A flat for piano

Toccata and Fugue (Vanessa Mae) Variation of a Toccata and Fugue by Johann Sebastian Bach

Under the Lilac Bough From the musical *Lilac Time*, based on various pieces of music of Franz Schubert

Wagon Wheels Adapted from the 2nd movement of Dvorak's Symphony No. 9 in E minor

Wild Horses Based on 'Wilder Reiter' by Robert Schumann

Wooden Heart Adapted from the German folk song 'Muss I denn'

Composers of Pop Songs and Tunes

Song	Composer	Song	Composer
Alexander's Ragtime Band	Irving Berlin	Automatically Sunshine	William 'Smokey' Robinson
Alfie	Burt Bacharach and Hal David		
All along the Watchtower	Bob Dylan	Baby I Don't Care	Leiber and Stoller
All of You	Cole Porter	Bad To Me	Lennon and McCartney
All the Young Dudes	David Bowie	Batdance	Prince
Alternate Title	Mickey Dolenz	Beautiful Dreamer	Stephen Foster
Always Something There To Remind Me	Burt Bacharach and Hal David	Begin the Beguine	Cole Porter
		Boat That I Row, The	Neil Diamond
And I Love You So	Don McLean	Born Free	Don Black and John Barry
Anything You Can Do	Irving Berlin	Bright Eyes	Mike Batt

Song	Composer	Song	Composer
Bring it on Home to Me	Sam Cooke	Halfway to Paradise	Gerry Goffin and Carole King
Brown Eyed Handsome Man	Chuck Berry	Happy Holiday	Irving Berlin
		A Hard Rain's Gonna Fall	Bob Dylan
Carnival Is Over	Tom Springfield	Have I Told You Lately	Van Morrison
Chain Reaction	Bee Gees	Help Me Make It through The Night	Kris Kristofferson
Chantilly Lace	J P Richardson (The Big Bopper)	Hey, Good Looking	Hank Williams
Cheek to Cheek	Irving Berlin	Hopelessly Devoted to You	John Farrar
Close to You	Burt Bacharach and Hal David	The Hustle	Van McCoy
Come and Get It	Paul McCartney	I Don't Wanna Fight	Lulu
A Couple of Swells	Irving Berlin	I Don't Want to Talk About it	Cat Stevens and Danny Whitten
Cupid	Sam Cooke	If Not for You	Bob Dylan
Dancing in the Street	Marvyn Gaye and William Stevenson	I Get a Kick Out of You	Cole Porter
		I Got Plenty of Nuttin'	George and Ira Gershwin
Dancing on a Saturday Night	Barry Blue and Lynsey De Paul	I Got Rhythm	George and Ira Gershwin
		I Got the Sun in the Morning	Irving Berlin
The Day I Met Marie	Hank Marvin		
Dick-A-Dum Dum (Kings Road)	Jim Dale	I Just Don't Know What to do with Myself	Burt Bacharach and Hal David
Do They Know It's Christmas?	Bob Geldof and Midge Ure	I'll Keep You Satisfied	Lennon and McCartney
		I'll Never Fall in Love Again	Burt Bacharach and Hal David
Do You Know Where You're Going To?	Gerry Goffin and Michael Masser	I'll Never Fall in Love Again (Tom Jones)	Lonnie Donegan and Jimmie Currie
Do You Love Me	Berry Gordy Jr	I Love You, Samantha	Cole Porter
Do You Want To Know a Secret	Lennon and McCartney	I'm a Believer	Neil Diamond
		I'm a Tiger	Marty Wilde and Ronnie Scott
Doctorin' the Tardis	Gary Glitter, Ron Grainer, Chapman and Chinn	I'm into Something Good	Gerry Goffin and Carole King
Doin' What Comes Naturally	Irving Berlin		
Don't Cry Out Loud	Carole Bayer Sager and Peter Allen	I Say a Little Prayer	Burt Bacharach and Hal David
		I Shot the Sheriff	Bob Marley
Don't Give Up On Us	Tony Macaulay	Isn't This a Lovely Day	Irving Berlin
Don't Sleep in the Subway	Tony Hatch and Jackie Trent	It Doesn't Matter Anymore	Paul Anka
		It Don't Mean a Thing	Duke Ellington and Irving Mills
Easter Parade	Irving Berlin		
Eloise	Paul Ryan	It Might as Well Rain until September	Gerry Goffin and Carole King
Fascinating Rhythm	George and Ira Gershwin	It's All in the Game	Charles Dawes and Carl Sigman
First Cut Is the Deepest	Cat Stevens	I've Got You under My Skin	Cole Porter
Floy Joy	William 'Smokey Robinson'	I Wanna Be Your Man	Lennon and McCartney
For the Good Times	Kris Kristofferson	I Will Drink the Wine	Paul Ryan
Genie with the Light Brown Lamp	Marvin, Welch, Bennett, Rostill (Shadows)	Jackie Wilson Said	Van Morrison
		Jambalaya	Hank Williams
Georgy Girl	Jim Dale and Tom Springfield	The James Bond Theme	Monty Norman
		Just Like a Woman	Bob Dylan
Giving It All Away	Leo Sayer and David Courtney	Killing Me Softly with His Song	Charles Fox and Norman Gimbel
Goldfinger	Tony Newley, John Barry and Leslie Bricusse	Knockin' on Heaven's Door	Bob Dylan
Goodbye	Lennon and McCartney	Lady	Lionel Richie
Goodbye (Mary Hopkin)	Lennon and McCartney	The Lady is a Tramp	Rodgers and Hart
Got to Get You into My Life	Lennon and McCartney	Leaning on a Lamp Post	Noel Gay
Grease	Barry Gibb	Leavin' on a Jet Plane	John Denver
A Groovy Kind of Love	Carole Bayer Sager and Tony Wine	Legend of the Glass Mountain	Nino Rota

M
U
S
I
C

P
O
P

Song	Composer
Let's Call the Whole Thing Off	George and Ira Gershwin
Let's Do It (Let's Fall in Love)	Cole Porter
Let's Face the Music and Dance	Irving Berlin
Little Bit Me, Little Bit You	Neil Diamond
Living Doll	Lionel Bart
The Locomotion	Gerry Goffin and Carole King
Love and Marriage	Sammy Cahn and Jimmy Van Heusen
MacArthur Park	Jim Webb
Mack the Knife	Weill, Brecht, Blitzstein
Mad about the Boy	Noël Coward
Mad Dogs and Englishmen	Noël Coward
Magic Moments	Burt Bacharach and Hal David
Mama Told Me Not to Come	Randy Newman
The Man Who Sold the World	David Bowie
The March of the Siamese Children	Richard Rodgers
Mighty Quinn	Bob Dylan
Miss Otis Regrets	Cole Porter
Mr Tambourine Man	Bob Dylan
Money (That's What I Want)	Berry Gordy Jr and Janie Bradford
Mrs Brown You've Got a Lovely Daughter	Trevor Peacock
My Guy	William 'Smokey' Robinson
My Heart Belongs to Daddy	Cole Porter
My Resistance Is Low	Hoagy Carmichael and Harold Adamson
Needles and Pins	Sonny Bono and Jack Nitzche
A Nice Cup Of Tea	A P Herbert
Night and Day	Cole Porter
Nothing Compares 2 U	Prince
Oh, Carol	Neil Sedaka and Howard Greenfield
Oh No, Not My Baby	Gerry Goffin and Carole King
Photograph	Ringo Starr and George Harrison
Pink Cadillac	Bruce Springsteen
The Purple People Eater	Sheb Wooley
Puttin' on the Ritz	Irving Berlin
Rhapsody in Blue	George Gershwin
River Kwai March	Malcolm Arnold
Roamin' in the Gloamin'	Harry Lauder
Rocket Man	Elton John and Bernie Taupin
Roll Over Beethoven	Chuck Berry
Running Bear	J P Richardson (The Big Bopper)

Song	Composer
Saving All My Love for You	Gerry Goffin and Michael Masser
September Song	Maxwell Anderson and Kurt Weill
Simon Smith and His Amazing Dancing Bear	Randy Newman
Something's Gotten Hold of My Heart	Roger Cook and Roger Greenaway
Something Tells Me	Roger Cook and Roger Greenaway
Sophisticated Lady	Duke Ellington, Irving Mills and Mitchell Parish
Step Inside Love	Lennon and McCartney
The Stripper	David Rose
S'Wonderful	George and Ira Gershwin
Take Five	Paul Desmond and Lola Brubeck
Take Good Care of My Baby	Gerry Goffin and Carole King
Tara's Theme	Max Steiner
Tears of a Clown	Smokey Robinson, Stevie Wonder, Henry Cosby
This Guy's in Love With You	Burt Bacharach and Hal David
This is My Song	Charlie Chaplin
This Wheel's on Fire	Bob Dylan and Rick Danko
Throw Down A Line	Hank B Marvin
To Keep My Love Alive	Rodgers and Hart
To Know Him is To Love Him	Phil Spector
To Love Somebody	Barry and Robin Gibb
Too Darn Hot	Cole Porter
Trains and Boats and Planes	Burt Bacharach and Hal David
True Love	Cole Porter
Twenty-Four Hours from Tulsa	Burt Bacharach and Hal David
Twisting the Night Away	Sam Cooke
Up on the Roof	Gerry Goffin and Carole King
Up Where We Belong	Buffy St Marie, Jack Nitzche, William Jennings
We Are the World	Michael Jackson and Lionel Richie
Well, Did You Evah?	Cole Porter
What'll I Do	Irving Berlin
What's New, Pussycat?	Burt Bacharach and Hal David
When I'm Dead and Gone	Gallagher and Lyle
When I Need You	Carole Bayer Sager and Albert Hammond
Wherever I Lay My Hat	Marvin Gaye and Norman Whitfield
A Whiter Shade of Pale	Keith Richard and Gary Brooker
Who Wants to Be a Millionaire	Cole Porter

Song	Composer	Song	Composer
Wichita Lineman	Jim Webb	Woodstock	Joni Mitchell
Wild Thing	Chip Taylor	A World Without Love	Lennon and McCartney
Wild World	Cat Stevens	Wunderbar	Cole Porter
Will You Love Me Tomorrow	Gerry Goffin and Carole King		
		You Make Me Feel So Young	Mack Gordon and Joseph Myrow
A Winter's Tale	Mike Batt		
Wired for Sound	B A Robertson and Alan Tarney	Your Cheating Heart	Hank Williams
		You're the One That I Want	John Farrar
Without You	Peter Ham and Tony Evans (Badfinger)	You're the Top	Cole Porter
		You've Got Your Troubles	Roger Cook and Roger Greenaway
Woman in Love	Barry and Robin Gibb		

Derivations of Names

Group	Derivation	Where from
Abba (1972)	The initials of of its members' Christian names	Sweden/Norway
Adam and the Ants (1977)	Adopted his surname as collective name for his group of four	London
A-Ha (1982)	Keyboardist Mags Furuholmen chose name as it was a universally accepted expression	Norway
Alice Cooper (1965)	Spelt out by a ouija board	USA
America (1967)	Met at London school; all 3 members were sons of US Air Force officers stationed in UK	USA
Archies (1967)	Named after a popular CBS cartoon series based on John Goldwater comic book characters	USA
Art of Noise (1983)	The name of an Italian futurist manifesto	UK
Aswad (1983)	Arabic for 'Black'	UK
Bachman–Turner Overdrive (1973)	Added name of a trucking magazine, *Overdrive*, to those of its founding members	Canada
Bad Company (1973)	From a Jeff Bridges film	UK
Bangles (1981)	Forced to change name from the Bangs because of existing band	Los Angeles
Bauhaus (1980)	Named after the German art movement	UK
Bay City Rollers (1970)	Chosen by sticking pin in map of USA and pricking Bay City	UK
Bee Gees (1959)	From the initials of their founder Barry Gibb. There is no substance to the myth that a racetrack promoter (Bill Goode) and a DJ (Bill Gates) inspired the name	Australia
B-52's	Southern US nickname for a bouffant hairstyle adopted by its female members	Georgia
Blondie (1975)	Lead singer's hair colour	New York
Boomtown Rats (1978)	Originally Nightlife Thugs; changed name to phrase in Woody Guthrie biography *Bound For Glory*	Dublin
Bread (1968)	Chosen after they were stuck behind a Wonder Bread truck in a traffic jam	Los Angeles
Buffalo Springfield (1966)	A make of steamroller	California
Canned Heat (1966)	From 1928 song by Mississipi bluesman Tommy Johnson, 'Canned Heat Blues'	Los Angeles
Captain And Tennille (1971)	Mike Love of the Beach Boys called Daryl Dragon 'Captain Keyboards' and the name stuck; other member Toni Tennille	San Francisco
CCS (1970)	Collective Consciousness Society, a collaboration between Alexis Korner, Mickie Most and John Cameron	UK
Clannad (1981)	Gaelic for 'Family'	Ireland
Commodores (1968)	Random choice from dictionary (nearly called the Commodes, so they say)	USA
Cream (1966)	Thought themselves the best so named themselves accordingly	UK
Creedence Clearwater Revival (1968)	Creedence was a friend of the band and Clearwater came from a beer commercial	USA
Crystals (1961)	After Crystal Bates, daughter of their first songwriter, Leroy Bates	USA
Cult (1982)	Originally called Southern Death Cult, taken from a newspaper headline	UK
Cure (1976)	Originally called the Easy Cure, a stock phrase of the day	Crawley
Damned (1976)	From the Dracula-style fancy dress worn by lead singer Dave Vanian	UK
Deacon Blue (1987)	From a Steely Dan record	UK
Dead Kennedys (1978)	Name was designed to shock, as it refers to the Kennedy brothers John and Robert	San Francisco
Deep Purple (1968)	Chosen as a contrast to Vanilla Fudge, on whom they based their early music	UK
Def Leppard (1977)	Corruption of Deaf Leopard, proposed by band's lead singer Joe Elliott	Sheffield

Group	Derivation	Where from
Depeche Mode (1980)	From a French fashion magazine, meaning 'Fast Fashion'	UK
Devo (1972)	From video *Truth about De-evolution*, award winner at Ann Arbor Film Festival	Akron, Ohio
Dexy's Midnight Runners (1978)	Slang term for the pep pill Dexedrine	Birmingham
Dire Straits (1977)	From the financial plight of the group when formed	UK
Doobie Brothers (1970)	After 'doobie' the Californian nickname for a marijuana cigarette	San Jose, California
Doors (1965)	From Aldous Huxley book *The Doors of Perception* (Huxley took title from Blake work)	Los Angeles
Dr Feelgood (1971)	From 1962 US hit 'Doctor Feel-Good' by bluesman Piano Red	UK
Dr Hook (1968)	Prompted by the eye patch (as in Captain Hook) worn by lead singer Ray Sawyer	New Jersey
Duran Duran (1978)	First gig was at Barbarella's in Birmingham so used a name from the Jane Fonda film	Birmingham
Earth, Wind and Fire (1969)	Singer and drummer Maurice White named band after 3 of the ancient elements	USA
The Easybeats	From a BBC Light programme pop show hosted by Brian Matthew	USA
Echo and the Bunnymen (1977)	Echo was the nickname for their drum machine, which was replaced by Pete de Freitas	Liverpool
Eurythmics (1977)	Named in 1980 after 'Rhythm Gymnastics' style devised by Emile Jaques-Dalcroze	UK
Everything But the Girl (1982)	Took their misleading name from a local second-hand furniture store	Hull
Faces (1969)	Steve Marriot left the Small Faces to form Humble Pie and the 'Small' was dropped	London
Fairport Convention (1967)	After the house, 'Fairport', in which its guitarist Simon Nicol lived in Muswell Hill	London
Faith No More (1980)	After a greyhound on which they had a bet	Los Angeles
Fifth Dimension (1966)	Originally called Versatiles changed name to reflect being beyond the 4th dimension	Los Angeles
Fine Young Cannibals (1984)	From the Robert Wagner/Natalie Wood film *All the Fine Young Cannibals*	UK
Fixx (1980)	Originally called the Portraits but changed it to Fix then to Fixx because of drug slur	UK
Fleetwood Mac (1967)	From 2 members, drummer Mick Fleetwood and bassist John McVie	UK
Flock of Seagulls (1979)	From cult novel by Richard Bach, *Jonathan Livingstone Seagull* (1970)	Liverpool
Frankie Goes to Hollywood (1980)	Headline in *Variety* magazine about Sinatra moving from Las Vegas to Hollywood	Liverpool
G4 (2004)	All four members are graduates of the Guildhall School of Music. Name derives from Guildhall and the number in the band	UK
Genesis (1965)	Originally Garden Wall; Jonathan King renamed them in 1967 as they were being 'born'	London
Grateful Dead (1963)	Said to come from an Egyptian prayer book	San Francisco
Guess Who (1965)	Forerunner of Bachman–Turner Overdrive; name based on British band The Who	Canada
Guns N' Roses (1985)	Combination of former guitarist Tracii Guns and the lead singer's assumed name	Los Angeles
Harpers Bizarre (1963)	Variation on the magazine *Harper's Bazaar* (*Harper's and Queen*)	San Francisco
Headgirl (1981)	Motorhead and Girlschool united for one-hit wonder 'The St Valentine's Day Massacre'	UK
Heaven 17 (1980)	Named after a group in Anthony Burgess's novel *A Clockwork Orange*	Sheffield
Herman's Hermits (1961)	The Herman was derived from Sherman, the flying squirrel in *Rocky and Bullwinkle Show*	Manchester
Hollies (1962)	Tribute to Buddy Holly	Manchester
Hot Chocolate (1969)	Named by an agent from the Apple record company as a pun on their colour and style	London
Human League (1977)	From a science-fiction computer game	Sheffield
Humble Pie (1969)	Superstars Frampton and Marriott named band to contrast with their pop idol status	London
Icehouse (1980)	Originally Flowers; changed name to that of their 1st album so as not to clash with existing group	Sydney
INXS (1977)	Originally called Farriss Brothers after 3 members but changed to a pun on In Excess	Australia

Group	Derivation	Where from
Iron Maiden (1976)	From a medieval instrument of torture	London
Jefferson Airplane (1965)	Hippie jargon for a paper match split at one end to hold a reefer; subsequently changed name to Jefferson Starship (1974) then Starship (1985)	San Francisco
Jesus and Mary Chain (1983)	After Alan McGee's club in London, where they performed early hits	Scotland
Jethro Tull (1967)	From the famous agriculturist, author of *Horse Hoeing Husbandry*	Blackpool
Joy Division (1977)	Nazi slang term for a military brothel	UK
Judas Priest (1973)	From Bob Dylan song, 'Ballad of Frankie Lee and Judas Priest'	Birmingham
Kaiser Chiefs (2003)	Named after a successful South African football team	Leeds
Kajagoogoo (1983)	Supposedly from original surname of film director Elia Kazan 'Kazanjoglou'	UK
KC and the Sunshine Band (1973)	Named after founder Harry Wayne Casey	Florida
Kinks (1963)	Named by pop impresario Larry Page, based on 'Kinky', a vogue word of swinging London	London
Kraftwerk (1970)	German for power plant referring to their electronic synthesisers	Düsseldorf
Level 42 (1980)	From the answer to the meaning of life in Douglas Adams's *The Hitch Hiker's Guide to the Galaxy*	UK
Lovin' Spoonful (1965)	From a line in a song by bluesman John Hurt	USA/Canada
Lynyrd Skynyrd (1966)	Named after the gym teacher who had expelled them from school	Jacksonville, Florida
Madness (1976)	From a Prince Buster song	UK
Mamas and the Papas (1965)	Named from 2 married couples in group, John and Michelle Phillips and Cass Elliot and John Hendricks	New York
Manhattan Transfer (1969)	From novel by Jon Dos Passos	New York
McFly (2002)	Named after the schoolboy hero of the film *Back to the Future*	UK
Men at Work (1979)	From road sign 'Danger Men at Work'	Melbourne
Metallica (1981)	Adopted a name to suit their particular type of rock music	Los Angeles
Mindbenders (1965)	The name of a Dirk Bogarde film	UK
Mothers of Invention (1965)	Originally called the Muthers but changed to echo proverb 'necessity is the . . .'	Los Angeles
Motley Crue (1981)	Play on phrase motley crew, which was an apt name for their bizarre appearance	USA
Motorhead (1975)	Song written by Ian 'Lemmy' Kilminster for Hawkwind, group he was sacked from	UK
Mott the Hoople (1968)	From an obscure novel by Willard Manus published in 1967	Hereford
Move (1966)	From the 5 members various moves from their prior bands	Birmingham
New Kids on the Block (1984)	Named by manager Maurice Starr as a white equivalent to his other band, New Edition	Massachusetts
New Order (1980)	After suicide of Ian Curtis, Joy Division became New Order, which was also a Nazi term	UK
Pet Shop Boys (1981)	Named by its members for friends who worked in an Ealing pet shop	London
Pink Floyd (1965)	Named as tribute to bluesmen Pink Anderson and Floyd Council	London
Planxty (1972)	From an Irish folk dance	Ireland
Platters (1953)	Black American group took their name from the slang term for gramophone records	Los Angeles
Poco (1968)	Originally called Pogo after a comic strip but forced to amend it when creator objected	Los Angeles
Pogues (1983)	Original name was Pogue Mahone ('Kiss my arse'); changed after BBC banned them	UK/Ireland
Pretenders (1978)	Named by Chrissie Hynde after a Platters hit, 'The Great Pretender'	UK/USA
Pretty Things (1963)	After the Bo Diddley hit 'Pretty Thing'	Sidcup, Kent
Procul Harum (1967)	Originally called the Paramounts, said to have been renamed after someone's cat	Southend, Essex

Group	Derivation	Where from
Psychedelic Furs (1977)	From Velvet Underground hit 'Venus in Furs'	London
R.E.M. (1980)	Although an abbreviation for rapid eye movement, the name was arbitrarily arrived at	Athens, Georgia
REO Speedwagon (1967)	From an early make of fire engine, Ransom E. Olds Speedwagon	Champaign, Illinois
Righteous Brothers (1962)	Originally called Paramours; took their name from the slang for excellent performers	Anaheim, California
Rolling Stones (1962)	From the Muddy Waters song 'Rolling Stone'	London
Ronettes (1959)	From the nickname of Veronica Bennett (Ronnie), one of the founder members	New York
Roxy Music (1971)	Based on the Roxy cinema chain	London
Run DMC (1982)	Nicknames of their 2 lead singers, Joseph 'Run' Simmons and Darryl 'D' McDaniels	New York
Scissor Sisters (1999)	From the interlocking sexual position of lesbians	New York
Scritti Politti (1977)	Based on the Italian phrase for 'political writings'	Leeds
Searchers (1961)	Named after the John Wayne film	Liverpool
Selecter (1979)	From the 'B' side of their debut single 'Gangsters', written by Noel Davies	Coventry
Sex Pistols (1975)	Malcolm McLaren named them after his boutique 'Sex' and Shakespeare character	London
Shadows (1959)	Originally called the Drifters; Jet Harris changed name in a Ruislip pub in 1959	London
Shakatak (1980)	From a local boutique	London
Shakespears Sister (1989)	From a Smiths' song (spelt wrongly)	UK
Shalamar (1977)	Named after the Shalimar Gardens near Lahore in Pakistan	Los Angeles
Shirelles (1957)	Name based on their lead singer Shirley Owens	Passaic, New Jersey
Showaddywaddy (1973)	From 'Bop bop showaddywaddy' backing of 'Little Darlin' by the Diamonds	Leicester
Simple Minds (1977)	Self-deprecatory name adopted during the Punk era	Glasgow
Simply Red (1985)	Named after the red hair of its lead singer Mick Hucknall	Manchester
Slade (1969)	Originally Ambrose Slade among other names, shortened to Slade in 1969	Wolverhampton
Smiths (1982)	Suggests the anonymity its members are said to have sought	Manchester
Soft Cell (1979)	Pun on 'soft sell', a term used for selling by inducement	Leeds
Soft Machine (1966)	After the William Burroughs novel of 1961	Canterbury
Spandau Ballet (1979)	Name derived from 2 contrasting words as an oxymoron to give effect	London
Split Enz (1972)	Originally called Split Ends after hair that has split, but changed spelling in 1975	Auckland, NZ
Squeeze (1974)	From a Velvet Underground Album	London
Steeleye Span (1969)	Name adopted from the traditional Lincolnshire ballad 'Horkston Grange'	UK
Steely Dan (1972)	Name of steam-powered dildo in novel The Naked Lunch by William Burroughs	Los Angeles
Steppenwolf (1968)	From the Herman Hesse novel	USA/Canada
Stone Roses (1980)	Originally played as Patrol and English Rose; chose similar name to Rolling Stones	Manchester
Stranglers (1974)	Originally the Guildford Strangler; shortened name when gaining following	Guildford
Strawbs (1967)	Originally the Strawberry Hill Boys, from the area of London they were from	London
Supertramp (1969)	From the W H Davies book Autobiography of a Super-tramp	London
Supremes (1959)	Originally called the Primettes as they supported the Primes (Temptations)	Detroit
Sweet (1966)	Originally called Wainwright's Gentlemen then Sweetshop	UK
Swinging Blue Jeans (1958)	Originally called Bluegenes; changed name on gaining sponsorship from jeans company	Liverpool

MUSIC POP

Group	Derivation	Where from
Take That (1994)	From the caption beside a Madonna poster	UK
Talking Heads (1975)	From the television jargon for a kind of static presentation	New York
Teardrop Explodes (1978)	From a caption in a Marvel science fiction comic	Liverpool
Tears for Fears (1981)	From Arthur Janov's book on primal therapy *Prisoners of Pain*	UK
Ten cc (10cc) (1972)	Named by Jonathan King, because the average male semen ejaculation was 9 cc	Manchester
Ten Thousand Maniacs (1981)	Name resulted from mishearing of film title *12,000 Maniacs*	Jamestown, New York
Ten Years After (1965)	Originally called Jaybirds changed name in 1966 on 10th anniversary of rock 'n' roll	Nottingham
The The (1980)	Parody of the many rock groups whose name begins with 'The'	London
Thin Lizzy (1969)	From 'Tin Lizzy', colloquial name for an old car	Dublin
Thompson Twins (1977)	From the characters in the Tintin cartoons by Hergé	Sheffield
Three Dog Night (1968)	Australian expression for a cold night when 3 dogs are needed to keep warm	USA
Toto (1978)	Corruption of real name of lead singer, Toteaux, to give the name of dog in *The Wizard of Oz*	Los Angeles
T'Pau (1986)	Carol Decker named group from the high priestess of Vulcan, a character in *Star Trek*	London
U2 (1977)	Said to be suggestive of the words 'You too'	Dublin
UB40 (1978)	From designation of Unemployment Benefit form	Birmingham
Ultravox (1976)	Name means 'beyond the voice', but may also refer to founder John Foxx	London
Velvet Underground (1965)	From the title of a pornographic publication	London
Wet Wet Wet (1986)	From a lyric on a Scritti Politti record	UK
X (1977)	From group's lead singer Exene Cervenka, nicknamed X	Los Angeles
XTC (1977)	Suggests 'ecstasy', but last 2 letters are initials of their drummer Terry Chambers	Swindon
Yardbirds (1963)	From the jazzman Charlie Parker, nicknamed Yardbird	Kingston-upon-Thames
Yazoo (1982)	From an early blues record label	UK

Singles

(number in brackets = top chart position)

NB: The listings below include all Top 10 singles released between the inception of the UK charts in November 1952 and 31 December 2004.
Other records that did not make the Top 10, but are notable for some other reason, are also included. Solo artistes are listed by surname.
The alphabetical listing of song titles includes the year of release of the single after the artiste's name. Other information is given where appropriate.

Title	Group/Artiste	Title	Group/Artiste
Abacab (9)	Genesis (1981)	Ain't Misbehavin' (3)	Tommy Bruce & The Bruisers (1960)
Abba-Esque EP (1)	Erasure (1992)		
ABC (8)	Jackson 5 (1970)	Ain't No Doubt (1)	Jimmy Nail (1992)
Abracadabra (2)	Steve Miller Band (1982)	Ain't No Love (Ain't No Use) (3)	Sub Sub and Melanie Williams (1993)
Abraham Martin And John (9)	Marvin Gaye (1970)		
Absolute Beginners (2)	David Bowie (1986)	Ain't No Mountain High Enough (6)	Diana Ross (1970)
Absolute Beginners (4)	Jam (1981)		
Absolutely Everybody (7)	Vanessa Amorosi (2000)	Ain't No Pleasing You (2)	Chas & Dave (1982)
		Ain't No Stoppin' Us (8)	DJ Luck & MC Neat featuring JJ (2000)
Absolutely Fabulous (6)	Pet Shop Boys (1994)		
		Ain't No Stoppin' Us Now (5)	McFadden & Whitehead (1979)
Accidents (46) second and only other hit	Thunderclap Newman (1970)		
		Ain't No Sunshine (8)	Michael Jackson (1972)
Achilles Heel (re-issue) (8)	Toploader (2000)		
Achy Breaky Heart (3) first hit	Billy Ray Cyrus (1992)	Ain't Nobody (1)	LL Cool J (1997)
		Ain't Nobody (8)	Course (1997)
Activ 8 (Come With Me) (3)	Altern 8 (1991)	Ain't Nobody (8)	Rufus & Chaka Khan (1984)
Addam's Groove (4)	MC Hammer (1991)		
		Ain't Nobody Better (10)	Inner City (1989)
Addicted To Bass (2)	Puretone (2002)	Ain't Nobody (remix) (6)	Rufus & Chaka Khan (1989)
Addicted To Love (5)	Robert Palmer (1986)		
		Ain't Nothing Goin' On But The Rent (5)	Gwen Guthrie (1986)
Addictive (3)	Truth Hurts featuring Rakim (2002)		
		Ain't Talkin' 'Bout Dub (7)	Apollo Four Forty (1997)
Adelante (2)	Sash (2000)		
Adoration Waltz (9)	David Whitfield (1957)	Ain't That A Shame (7) first hit	Pat Boone (1955)
		Ain't That Funny (8)	Jimmy Justice (1962)
Affirmation (8)	Savage Garden (2000)		
		Ain't That Just The Way (6)	Lutricia McNeal (1997)
Africa (3)	Toto (1983)		
African Waltz (9)	Johnny Dankworth (1961)	Air Hostess (2)	Busted (2004)
		Air That I Breathe, The (2)	Hollies (1974)
Afrika Shox (7)	Leftfield / Bambaataa (1999)	Air That I Breathe, The (6)	Simply Red (1998)
		Airport (4)	Motors (1978)
After The Love Has Gone (4)	Earth Wind & Fire (1979)	Airwave (10)	Rank 1 (2000)
		Aisha (9)	Death In Vegas (2000)
After The Love Has Gone (5)	Steps (1999)		
After You're Gone/Sacred Trust (2) first hit	One True Voice (2002)	Albatross (1)	Fleetwood Mac (1968)
		Albatross (re-issue) (2)	Fleetwood Mac (1973)
Agadoo (2)	Black Lace (1984)		
Again (6)	Janet Jackson (1993)	Alcoholic (10)	Starsailor (2001)
		Alfie (9)	Cilla Black (1966)
Against All Odds (1)	Mariah Carey & Westlife (2000)	Alice I Want You Just For Me (9)	Full Force (1985)
		Alive (5)	S Club (2002)
Against All Odds (Take A Look At Me Now) (2)	Phil Collins (1984)	Alive And Kicking (7)	Simple Minds (1985)
		All About Lovin' You (9)	Bon Jovi (2003)
Ain't Gonna Bump No More (With No Big Fat Woman) (2)	Joe Tex (1977)	All About Us (3)	Peter Andre (1997)
		All Alone Am I (7)	Brenda Lee (1963)
Ain't Got No – I Got Life / Do What You Gotta Do (2)	Nina Simone (1968)	All Along The Watchtower (5)	Jimi Hendrix Experience (1968)
Ain't It Fun (9)	Guns 'N' Roses (1993)		
		All Around My Hat (5)	Steeleye Span (1975)
Ain't It Funny (3)	Jennifer Lopez (2001)		
		All Around The World (1)	Oasis (1998)
Ain't It Funny (remix) (4)	Jennifer Lopez (2002)	All Around The World (1)	Lisa Stansfield (1989)
		All Because Of You (6)	Geordie (1973)

Title	Group/Artiste	Title	Group/Artiste
All By Myself (6)	Celine Dion (1996)		(1957)
All Cried Out (8)	Alison Moyet (1984)	All Star Hit Parade (2)	Various Artists
All Day And All Of The Night (2)	Kinks (1964)		(1956)
All Day And All Of The Night (7)	Stranglers (1988)	All Stood Still (8)	Ultravox (1981)
All Falls Down (10)	Kanye West	All That I Need (1)	Boyzone (1998)
	featuring Syleena	All That She Wants (1) first hit	Ace Of Base (1993)
	Johnson (2004)	All The Love In The World (10)	Dionne Warwick
All For Love (2)	Bryan Adams, Rod		(1982)
	Stewart & Sting	All The Small Things (2)	Blink 182 (2000)
	(1994)	All The Things She Said (9)	Simple Minds (1986)
All For You (3)	Janet Jackson	All The Things She Said (1)	Tatu (2003)
	(2001)	All The Time And Everywhere (9)	Dickie Valentine
All 4 Love (5)	Color Me Badd		(1953)
	(1991)	All The Way From Memphis (10)	Mott The Hoople
All Hooked Up (7)	All Saints (2001)		(1973)
		All The Way (re-entry) (3)	Frank Sinatra (1957)
All I Ask Of You (3)	Cliff Richard and	All The Young Dudes (3)	Mott The Hoople
	Sarah Brightman		(1972)
	(1986)	All This Time (1)	Michelle (2004)
All I Ever Need Is You (8)	Sonny & Cher (1972)	All Time High (75)	Rita Coolidge (1983)
All I Have (2)	Jennifer Lopez	All Together Now (4)	Farm (1990)
	featuring LL Cool J	All Together Now 2004 (5)	Farm featuring SFX
	(2003)		Boys Choir (2004)
All I Have To Do Is Dream (3)	Bobbie Gentry &	All You Good Good People EP (8)	Embrace (1997)
	Glen Campbell	All You Need Is Love (1)	Beatles (1967)
	(1969)	Ally's Tartan Army (6)	Andy Cameron
All I Have To Do Is Dream /	Everly Brothers		(1978)
Claudette (1)	(1958)	Almaz (4)	Randy Crawford
All I Have To Give (2)	Backstreet Boys		(1986)
	(1998)	Almost There (2)	Andy Williams
All I Really Want To Do (4)	Byrds (1965)		(1965)
All I Really Want To Do (9)		Almost Unreal (7)	Roxette (1993)
first solo hit	Cher (1965)	Alone (5)	Bee Gees (1997)
All I See Is You (9)	Dusty Springfield	Alone (8)	Petula Clark (1957)
	(1966)	Alone (3)	Heart (1987)
All I Wanna Do (4)	Sheryl Crow (1994)	Alone (7)	Lasgo (2002)
All I Wanna Do (4)	Dannii Minogue	Alone Again (Naturally) (3)	Gilbert O'Sullivan
	(1997)		(1972)
All I Wanna Do Is Make Love	Heart (1990)	Alone Without You (8)	King (1985)
To You (8)		Alphabet Street (9)	Prince (1988)
All I Want (2)	Mis-Teeq (2001)	Alright (6)	Jamiroquai (1997)
All I Want For Christmas Is	Mariah Carey (1994)	Alright / Time (2)	Supergrass (1995)
You (2)		Alright Alright Alright (3)	Mungo Jerry (1973)
All I Want Is You (4)	911 (1998)	Also Sprach Zarathustra	Deodato (1973)
All I Want Is You (4)	U2 (1989)	(2001) (7)	
All In My Head (7)	Kosheen (2003)	Alternate Title (2)	Monkees (1967)
All Kinds Of Everything (1) first hit	Dana (1970)	Always (3)	Atlantic Starr (1987)
All Mine (8)	Portishead (1997)	Always (2)	Bon Jovi (1994)
All My Life (5)	Foo Fighters (2002)	Always (4)	Erasure (1994)
All My Life (8)	K-Ci & JoJo (1998)	Always And Forever /	Heatwave (1978)
All My Love (6)	Cliff Richard (1967)	Mind Blowing Decisions	
All Night Holiday (20)	Russ Abbot (1985)	(remix) (9)	
All Night Long (5)	Rainbow (1980)	Always Be My Baby (3)	Mariah Carey (1996)
All Night Long (All Night) (2)	Lionel Richie (1983)	Always Breaking My Heart (8)	Belinda Carlisle
(All Of A Sudden) My	Paul Anka (1959)		(1996)
Heart Sings (10)		Always Come Back To Your	Samantha Mumba
All Of Me Loves All Of You (4)	Bay City Rollers	Love (3)	(2001)
	(1974)	Always Look On The Bright	Monty Python
All Of My Heart (5)	ABC (1982)	Side Of Life (3)	(1991)
All Of My Life (9)	Diana Ross (1974)	Always On My Mind (1)	Pet Shop Boys
All Or Nothing (4)	O-Town (2001)		(1987)
All Or Nothing (1)	Small Faces (1966)	Always On My Mind (9)	Elvis Presley (1972)
All Out Of Love /	H & Claire (2002)	Always On Time (6)	Ja Rule featuring
Beauty And The Beast (10)			Ashanti (2002)
All Over (2)	Lisa Maffia (2003)	Always There (6)	Incognito featuring
All Right Now (2)	Free (1970)		Jocelyn Brown
All Right Now (remix) (8)	Free (1991)		(1991)
All Rise (4) first hit	Blue (2001)	Always Yours (1)	Gary Glitter (1974)
All She Wants Is (9)	Duran Duran (1989)	Am I That Easy To Forget (3)	Engelbert
All Shook Up (re-entry) (1)	Elvis Presley with		Humperdinck
	The Jordanaires		(1968)

Title	Group/Artiste	Title	Group/Artiste
AM To PM (3)	Christina Milian (2002)	Another Chance (1)	Roger Sanchez (2001)
Amateur Hour (7)	Sparks (1974)	Another Day (9)	Lemar (2004)
Amazing (4)	George Michael (2004)	Another Day (2)	Paul McCartney (1971)
Amazing Grace (5)	Judy Collins (1970)	Another Day (7)	Whigfield (1994)
Amazing Grace (1)	Pipes & Drums & Military Band Of The Royal Scots Dragoon Guards (1972)	Another Day In Paradise (5)	Brandy & Ray J (2001)
		Another Day In Paradise (2)	Phil Collins (1989)
America: What Time Is Love (4)	KLF (1992)	Another Lover (9)	Dane (2001)
American Dream (55) first and only hit	Crosby, Stills, Nash and Young (1989)	Another Night (2)	MC Sar & The Real McCoy (1994)
American Dream (3)	Jakatta (2001)	Another One Bites The Dust (5)	Queen featuring Wyclef Jean, Pras Michel and Free (1998)
American Idiot (3)	Green Day (2004)		
American Life (2)	Madonna (2003)		
American Pie (1)	Madonna (2000)	Another One Bites The Dust (7)	Queen (1980)
American Pie (2) first hit	Don McLean (1972)	Another Rock And Roll Christmas (7)	Gary Glitter (1984)
Americanos (4)	Holly Johnson (1989)	Another Step (Closer To You) (6)	Kim Wilde & Junior (1987)
Amigo (9)	Black Slate (1980)	Another Suitcase In Another Hall (7)	Madonna (1997)
Amnesia (10)	Chumbawamba (1998)		
Amoureuse (13) first hit	Kiki Dee (1973)	Answer Me (9) first hit	Barbara Dickson (1976)
An American Trilogy (8)	Elvis Presley (1972)	Answer Me (1)	Frankie Laine (1953)
An Everlasting Love (10)	Andy Gibb (1978)	Answer Me (1)	David Whitfield (1953)
An Innocent Man (8)	Billy Joel (1984)		
Anarchy In The UK (38) first hit	Sex Pistols (1976) re-issued 1992 (No. 33)	Ant Rap (3)	Adam & The Ants (1981)
		Ante Up (7)	MOP featuring Busta Rhymes (2001)
And I Love You So (3)	Perry Como (1973)		
And The Beat Goes On (2)	Whispers (1980)	Anthem, The (10)	Good Charlotte (2003)
And The Heavens Cried (6)	Anthony Newley (1961)	Antmusic (EP) (2)	Adam & The Ants (1980)
Anfield Rap (Red Machine In Full Effect) (3)	Liverpool FC (1988)	Any Dream Will Do (1)	Jason Donovan (1991)
Angel (5)	Madonna (1985)	Any Old Iron (21) first hit	Peter Sellers (1957) re-issue reached No. 17
Angel (1)	Shaggy featuring Rayvon (2001)		
Angel (4)	Simply Red (1996)	Any Way That You Want Me (8)	Troggs (1966)
Angel / What Made Milwaukee Famous (Has Made A Loser Out Of Me) (4)	Rod Stewart (1972)	Anyone Can Fall In Love (4)	Anita Dobson (1986)
		Anyone Of Us (Stupid Mistake) (1)	Gareth Gates (2002)
Angel Eyes (4)	Roxy Music (1979)	Anyone Who Had A Heart (1)	Cilla Black (1964)
Angel Eyes / Voulez Vous (3)	Abba (1979)	Anything (5)	Culture Beat (1994)
Angel Eyes (Home And Away) (5)	Wet Wet Wet (1987)	Anything (2)	3T (1996)
Angel Face (4)	Glitter Band (1974)	Anything For You (10)	Gloria Estefan and The Miami Sound Machine (1988)
Angel Fingers (1)	Wizzard (1973)		
Angel Of Harlem (9)	U2 (1988)		
Angel Of Mine (4)	Eternal (1997)	Anything Is Possible / Evergreen (1)	Will Young (2002)
Angel Street (8)	M People (1998)	Anytime You Need A Friend (8)	Mariah Carey (1994)
Angela Jones (7)	Michael Cox (1960)		
Angelo (1)	Brotherhood Of Man (1977)	Anyway Anyhow Anywhere (10)	Who (1965)
Angels (4)	Robbie Williams (1997)	Anywhere For You (4)	Backstreet Boys (1997)
Angie (5)	Rolling Stones (1973)	Anywhere Is (7)	Enya (1995)
Angie Baby (5)	Helen Reddy (1975)	Apache (1)	Shadows (1960)
Animal (6)	Def Leppard (1987)	Apeman (5)	Kinks (1970)
Animal Nitrate (7)	Suede (1993)	Applejack (4)	Jet Harris & Tony Meehan (1963)
Annie I'm Not Your Daddy (2)	Kid Creole & The Coconuts (1982)		
Annie's Song (1)	John Denver (1974)	April Love (7)	Pat Boone (1957)
Annie's Song (3)	James Galway (1978)	April Skies (8)	Jesus & Mary Chain (1987)
Anniversary Waltz – Part 1, The (2)	Status Quo (1990)	Are Friends Electric (1)	Tubeway Army (1979)
Another Brick In The Wall Part II (1)	Pink Floyd (1979)	Are You Gonna Go My Way (4)	Lenny Kravitz (1993)

M
U
S
I
C

P
O
P

Title	Group/Artiste	Title	Group/Artiste
Are You Lonesome Tonight (1)	Elvis Presley with The Jordanaires (1961)	Baby Baby (5)	Corona (1995)
		Baby Baby (4)	Frankie Lymon & Teenagers (1957)
Are You Ready For Love (1)	Elton John (2003)	Baby Baby (2)	Amy Grant (1991)
Are You Ready To Rock (8)	Wizzard (1974)	Baby Boy (2)	Beyonce featuring Sean Paul (2003)
Are You Sure (2)	Allisons (1961)		
Aria (5)	Mr Acker Bilk, his Clarinet & Strings (1976)	Baby Boy (4)	Big Brovaz (2003)
		Baby Can I Hold You / Shooting Star (2)	Boyzone / Stephen Gately (1997)
		Baby Come Back (1)	Pato Banton (1994)
Arms Around The World (4)	Louise (1997)	Baby Come Back (1)	Equals (1968)
Arms Of Mary (5)	Sutherland Brothers & Quiver (1976)	Baby Come On Over (5)	Samantha Mumba (2001)
Army Of Me (10)	Björk (1995)	Baby Don't Change Your Mind (4)	Gladys Knight & The Pips (1977)
Around The World (5)	Bing Crosby (1957)		
Around The World (5)	Daft Punk (1997)	Baby Face (2)	Little Richard (1959)
Around The World (7)	East 17 (1994)	Baby I Don't Care (3)	Transvision Vamp (1989)
Around The World (8)	Gracie Fields (1957)		
Around The World (4)	Ronnie Hilton (1957)	Baby I Don't Care (6)	Jennifer Ellison (2003)
Art For Art's Sake (5)	10CC (1975)		
Arthur's Theme (Best That You Can Do) (7)	Christopher Cross (1982)	Baby I Know (10)	Rubettes (1977)
		Baby I Love You (8)	Dave Edmunds (1973)
As (4)	George Michael & Mary J Blige (1999)		
		Baby I Love You (3)	Jennifer Lopez (2004)
As I Love You (re-entry) (1)	Shirley Bassey (1959)	Baby I Love You (8)	Ramones (1980)
		Baby I Love Your Way (2)	Big Mountain (1994)
As Long As He Needs Me (2)	Shirley Bassey (1960)	Baby I Love Your Way – Freebird (6)	Will To Power (1989)
As Long As You Love Me (3)	Backstreet Boys (1997)	Baby It's You (7)	Beatles (1995)
		Baby It's You (8)	JoJo featuring Bow Wow (2004)
As Tears Go By (9)	Marianne Faithfull (1964)		
		Baby Jane (1)	Rod Stewart (1983)
As Time Goes By (5)	Dooley Wilson (1977)	Baby Jump (re-entry) (1)	Mungo Jerry (1971)
		Baby Let Me Take You Home (21) first hit	Animals (1964)
As Usual (5)	Brenda Lee (1964)		
As You Like It (5)	Adam Faith (1962)	Baby Love (1)	Supremes (1964)
Ashes To Ashes (1)	David Bowie (1980)	Baby Make It Soon (9)	Marmalade (1969)
At My Most Beautiful (10)	REM (1999)	Baby Now That I've Found You (1)	Foundations (1967)
At Night (6)	Shakedown (2002)	Baby One More Time (1)	Britney Spears (1999)
At The Club / Saturday Night At The Movies (re-entry) (3)	Drifters (1972)		
		Baby Please Don't Go (10)	Them (1965)
		Babycakes (1)	3 Of A Kind (2004)
At The Hop (3)	Danny & The Juniors (1958)	Babylon (5)	David Gray (2000)
		Babylon's Burning (7) first hit	Ruts (1979)
Atlantis (2)	Shadows (1963)	Baby's Got A Temper (5)	Prodigy (2002)
Atmosphere (7)	Russ Abbot (1984)	Back For Good (1)	Take That (1995)
Atomic (1)	Blondie (1980)	Back Here (re-issue) (5)	BBMak (2001)
Attention To Me (9)	Nolans (1981)	Back Home (1)	England World Cup Squad (1970)
Auf Weidersehen (10)	Vera Lynn (1952)		
Australia (7)	Manic Street Preachers (1996)	Back In My Life (4)	Alice Deejay (1999)
		Back Off Boogaloo (2)	Ringo Starr (1972)
Autobahn (11) first hit	Kraftwerk (1975)	Back Street Luv (4) first and only hit	Curved Air (1971)
Automatic (2)	Pointer Sisters (1984)		
		Back To Life (However Do You Want Me) (1)	Soul II Soul featuring Caron Wheeler (1989)
Automatic High (2)	S Club Juniors (2002)		
Automatic Lover (4)	Dee D Jackson (1978)	Back To The Sixties (4)	Tight Fit (1981)
		Back Together Again (3)	Roberta Flack & Donny Hathaway (1980)
Automatically Sunshine (10)	Supremes (1972)		
Autumn Almanac (3)	Kinks (1967)	Backstage (4)	Gene Pitney (1966)
Avenging Angels (6)	Space (1998)	Bad (3)	Michael Jackson (1987)
Axel F (2)	Harold Faltermeyer (1985)		
		Bad Actress (10)	Terrorvision (1996)
Axel F / Keep Pushin' (7)	Clock (1995)	Bad Bad Boy (10)	Nazareth (1973)
Ay Ay Ay Ay Moosey (10)	Modern Romance (1981)	Bad Boy (7)	Marty Wilde (1959)
		Bad Boys (2)	Wham! (1983)
B With Me (5)	Mis-Teeq (2002)	Bad Day (8)	REM (2003)
Babe (6)	Styx (1980)	Bad Girl (10)	Madonna (1993)
Babe (1)	Take That (1993)	Bad Intentions (4)	Dr Dre featuring Knoc-Turn'al (2002)
Babooshka (5)	Kate Bush (1980)		

Title	Group/Artiste	Title	Group/Artiste
Bad Moon Rising (1)	Creedence Clearwater Revival (1969)	Batdance (2)	Prince (1989)
		Battle (10)	Wookie featuring Lain (2000)
Bad To Me (1)	Billy J Kramer And The Dakotas (1963)	Battle Of New Orleans (2)	Lonnie Donegan & His Skiffle Group (1959)
Bad Touch, The (4)	Bloodhound Gang (2000)	Be Alone No More (6) first hit	Another Level (1998)
Bag It Up (1)	Geri Halliwell (2000)	Be Careful (7)	Sparkle featuring R Kelly (1998)
Baggy Trousers (3)	Madness (1980)		
Bailamos (4)	Enrique Iglesias (1999)	Be Cool (7)	Paffendorf (2002)
Baker Street (3) first hit	Gerry Rafferty (1978)	Be Faithful (1)	Fatman Scoop featuring The Crooklyn Clan (2003)
Baker Street (2)	Undercover (1992)	Be Mine (4)	Lance Fortune (1960)
Ball Of Confusion (7)	Temptations (1970)	Be My Baby (6)	Vanessa Paradis (1992)
Ball Park Incident (6) first hit	Wizzard (1972)		
Ballad Of Bonnie And Clyde (1)	Georgie Fame (1967)	Be My Baby (4)	Ronettes (1963)
		Be My Girl (2)	Jim Dale (1957)
Ballad Of Davy Crockett (2)	Bill Hayes (1956)	Be Quick Or Be Dead (2)	Iron Maiden (1992)
Ballad Of Davy Crockett, The (3)	Tennessee Ernie Ford (1956)	Be The First To Believe (6) first hit	A1 (1999)
Ballad Of John And Yoko (1)	Beatles (1969)		
Ballad Of Paladin (10)	Duane Eddy (1962)	Be There (8)	UNKLE featuring Ian Brown (1999)
Ballad Of Tom Jones, The (4)	Space with Cerys of Catatonia (1998)	Beat Dis (2) first and biggest hit	Bomb The Bass (1988)
Ballroom Blitz, The (2)	Sweet (1973)	Beat Goes On (11) first hit	All Seeing I, The (1998)
Bamboogie (2)	Bamboo (1998)		
Banana Boat Song (8) first hit	Shirley Bassey (1957)	Beat It (3)	Michael Jackson (1983)
Banana Boat Song (Day-O) (2) first hit	Harry Belafonte (1957)	Beat Mama (9)	Cast (1999)
		Beat Surrender (1)	Jam (1982)
Banana Republic (3)	Boomtown Rats (1980)	Beat The Clock (10)	Sparks (1979)
		Beatles Movie Medley (10)	Beatles (1982)
Banana Rock (9)	Wombles (1974)	Beatnik Fly (8)	Johnny & The Hurricanes (1960)
Banana Splits (7)	Dickies (1979)		
Band Of Gold (6) first and only hit	Don Cherry (1956)	Beautiful (10)	Matt Darey with Marcella Woods (2002)
Band Of Gold (1)	Freda Payne (1970)	Beautiful (1)	Christina Aguilera (2003)
Band On The Run (3)	Paul McCartney & Wings (1974)		
Bang Bang (2) first hit	B A Robertson (1979)	Beautiful Day (1)	U2 (2000)
		Beautiful Ones (8)	Suede (1996)
Bang Bang (My Baby Shot Me Down) (3)	Cher (1966)	Beautiful Stranger (2)	Madonna (1999)
		Beauty And The Beast (9) first hit	Celine Dion & Peabo Bryson (1992)
Bangers And Mash (22)	Peter Sellers and Sophia Loren (1961)	Because I Got High (1)	Afroman (2001)
		Because I Love You (The Postman Song) (6)	Stevie B (1991)
Bangin' Man (3)	Slade (1974)		
Bangla-Desh (10)	George Harrison (1971)	Because Of You (3)	Scanty Sandwich (2000)
Banks Of The Ohio (6)	Olivia Newton-John (1971)	Because The Night (5)	Patti Smith Group (1978)
Banner Man (3)	Blue Mink (1971)	Because They're Young (2)	Duane Eddy (1960)
Barbados (1)	Typically Tropical (1975)	Because We Want To (1) first hit	Billie (1998)
		Because You Loved Me (5)	Celine Dion (1996)
Barbara Ann (3)	Beach Boys (1966)	Because You're Mine (3)	Mario Lanza (1952)
Barber's Adagio For Strings (4)	William Orbit (1999)	Because You're Mine (6)	Nat 'King' Cole (1952)
Barbie Girl (1) first hit	Aqua (1997)		
Barcelona (2)	Freddy Mercury & Montserrat Caballé (1987)	Because You're Mine (re-entry) (10)	Nat 'King' Cole (1953)
		Bed Sitter (4)	Soft Cell (1981)
Barcelona (re-issue) (2)	Freddy Mercury & Montserrat Caballé (1992)	Beds Are Burning (48) first hit	Midnight Oil (1988)
		Beds Are Burning (re-issue) (6)	Midnight Oil (1989)
Barrel Of A Gun (4)	Depeche Mode (1997)	Bedshaped (10)	Keane (2004)
		Bedtime Story (4)	Madonna (1995)
Bartender And The Thief, The (3)	Stereophonics (1998)	Beetlebum (1)	Blur (1997)
		Before (7)	Pet Shop Boys (1996)
Basket Case (7)	Green Day (1995)	Beg Steal Or Borrow (2)	New Seekers (1972)
Bat Out Of Hell (re-issue) (8)	Meat Loaf (1993)	Begin The Beguine (1)	Julio Iglesias (1981)

M
U
S
I
C

P
O
P

Title	Group/Artiste	Title	Group/Artiste
Behind A Painted Smile (5)	Isley Brothers (1969)	Big Seven (8)	Judge Dread (1972)
Behind The Groove (6)	Teena Marie (1980)	Big Ship (8)	Cliff Richard (1969)
Being Boiled (6)	Human League (1982)	Billie Jean (1)	Michael Jackson (1983)
Being Brave (10)	Menswear (1996)	Bills Bills Bills (6)	Destiny's Child (1999)
Being Nobody (3)	Richard X vs Liberty X (2003)	Billy Don't Be A Hero (1)	Paper Lace (1974)
Being With You (1)	Smokey Robinson (1981)	Bimbo (7)	Ruby Wright (1954)
		Bionic Santa (10)	Chris Hill (1976)
Belfast (8)	Boney M (1977)	Bird Dog (2)	Everly Brothers (1958)
Belfast Child (1)	Simple Minds (1989)	Bird Of Paradise (6)	Snowy White (1983)
Believe (1)	Cher (1998)	Birdhouse In Your Soul (6)	They Might Be Giants (1990)
Believe In Me (8)	Utah Saints (1993)		
Belissima (4)	DJ Quicksilver (1997)	Birdie Song (The Birdie Dance) (2)	Tweets (1981)
		Bitch (6)	Meredith Brooks (1997)
Bell Bottom Blues (4) first hit	Alma Cogan (1954)		
Ben (7)	Michael Jackson (1972)	Bits And Pieces (2)	Dave Clark Five (1964)
Ben (5)	Marti Webb (1985)	Bitter Sweet Symphony (2)	Verve (1997)
Bend It (2)	Dave Dee, Dozy, Beaky, Mick & Tich (1966)	Bitterest Pill (I Ever Had To Swallow) (2)	Jam (1982)
Bend Me Shape Me (3)	Amen Corner (1968)	Black And White (6)	Greyhound (1971)
Bernadette (8)	Four Tops (1967)	Black Betty (7)	Ram Jam (1977)
Best Disco In Town, The (10)	Ritchie Family (1976)	Black Coffee (1)	All Saints (2000)
Best In Me (8)	Let Loose (1995)	Black-Eyed Boy (5)	Texas (1997)
Best Of Me, The (2)	Cliff Richard (1989)	Black Hills Of Dakota (7)	Doris Day (1954)
Best Of My Love (4)	Emotions (1977)	Black Is Black (2)	La Belle Epoque (1977)
Best Thing That Ever Happened To Me (7)	Gladys Knight & The Pips (1975)	Black Is Black (2)	Los Bravos (1966)
Best Things In Life Are Free (remix), The (7)	Luther Vandross & Janet Jackson (1995)	Black Night (2) first hit	Deep Purple (1970)
		Black Or White (1)	Michael Jackson (1991)
Best Things In Life Are Free, The (2)	Luther Vandross & Janet Jackson with BBD and Ralph Tresvant (1992)	Black Skin Blue-Eyed Boys (9)	Equals (1970)
		Black Suits Comin' (Nod Ya Head) (3)	Will Smith featuring Tra-Knox (2002)
Best Years Of Our Lives (4)	Modern Romance (1982)	Black Superman (Muhammad Ali) (7)	Johnny Wakelin & Kinshasa Band (1975)
Best, The (5)	Tina Turner (1989)	Black Velvet (2)	Alannah Myles (1990)
Betcha By Golly Wow (13) first hit	Stylistics (1972)	Blackberry Way (1)	Move (1968)
Bette Davis Eyes (10) first and biggest hit	Kim Carnes (1981)	Blame It On The Boogie (4) first hit	Big Fun (1989)
Better Best Forgotten (2)	Steps (1999)	Blame It On The Boogie (8)	Jacksons (1978)
Better Day (9)	Ocean Colour Scene (1997)	(Blame It) On The Pony Express (7)	Johnny Johnson & The Bandwagon (1970)
Better Love Next Time (8)	Dr Hook (1980)		
Better Off Alone (2)	DJ Jurgen presents Alice DeeJay (1999)	Blame It On The Weatherman (1)	B*Witched (1999)
		Blanket On The Ground (6)	Billie Jo Spears (1975)
Better The Devil You Know (2)	Kylie Minogue (1990)	Blaze Of Glory (13) first solo hit	Jon Bon Jovi (1990)
Better Watch Out (10)	Ant & Dec (1996)	Bless You (5)	Tony Orlando (1961)
Beyond The Stars (8)	David Whitfield (1955)	Blind Vision (10)	Blancmange (1983)
Big Apple (8)	Kajagoogoo (1983)	Blinded By The Light (6)	Manfred Mann's Earth Band (1976)
Big Bad John (2)	Jimmy Dean (1961)		
Big Big World (5)	Emilia (1998)	Blinded By The Lights (10)	Streets (2004)
Big Boys Don't Cry / Rockin' Robin (10)	Lolly (1999)	Blinded By The Sun (7)	Seahorses (1997)
		Block Rockin' Beats (1)	Chemical Brothers (1997)
Big Brother UK TV Theme (4)	Element Four (2000)	Blockbuster (1)	Sweet (1973)
Big Fun (4)	Gap Band (1986)	Blood On The Dancefloor (1)	Michael Jackson (1997)
Big Fun (8) first hit	Inner City (1988)		
Big Hunk O' Love, A (4)	Elvis Presley with The Jordanaires (1959)	Blood Sweat And Tears (6)	V (2004)
		Bloodnok's Rock 'N' Roll Call / Ying Tong Song (3)	Goons (1956)
Big In Japan (8) first and only hit	Alphaville (1984)	Blossom Fell, A (10)	Ronnie Hilton (1955)
Big Love (9)	Fleetwood Mac (1987)	Blossom Fell, A (3)	Nat 'King' Cole (1955)
Big Man (2)	Four Preps (1958)		
Big Mistake (2)	Natalie Imbruglia (1998)	Blossom Fell, A (9)	Dickie Valentine (1955)

Title	Group/Artiste
Blow The House Down (10)	Living In A Box (1989)
Blow Ya Mind (6)	Lock 'N' Load (2000)
Blowing Wild (2)	Frankie Laine (1954)
Blue Angels (6)	Pras (1998)
Blue Bayou / Mean Woman Blues (3)	Roy Orbison (1963)
Blue (Da Ba Dee) (1)	Eiffel 65 (1999)
Blue Eyes (8)	Elton John (1982)
Blue Eyes (3)	Don Partridge (1968)
Blue Guitar (8)	Justin Hayward & John Lodge (1975)
Blue Is The Colour (5)	Chelsea FC (1972)
Blue Jean (6)	David Bowie (1984)
Blue Monday (re-entry) (9)	New Order (1983)
Blue Monday (remix) (3)	New Order (1988)
Blue Moon (1)	Marcels (1961)
Blue Moon (9)	Elvis Presley (1956)
Blue Moon / Only You (9)	John Alford (1996)
Blue Room (8)	Orb (1992)
Blue Savannah (3)	Erasure (1990)
Blue Star (The Medic Theme) (2)	Cyril Stapleton Orchestra (1955)
Blue Suede Shoes (10)	Carl Perkins (1956)
Blue Suede Shoes (9)	Elvis Presley (1956)
Blue Tango (8)	Ray Martin Orchestra (1952)
Blue Tango (re-entry) (10)	Ray Martin Orchestra (1952)
Blue Velvet (2)	Bobby Vinton (1990)
Blueberry Hill (re-entry) (6)	Fats Domino (1956)
Blurred (6)	Pianoman (1996)
Blurry (8)	Puddle Of Mudd (2002)
Bo Diddley (4)	Buddy Holly (1963)
Boat That I Row, The (6)	Lulu (1967)
Bobby's Girl (3)	Susan Maughan (1962)
Body And Soul (9)	Mai Tai (1985)
Body Groove (3)	Architechs featuring Nana (2000)
Body II Body (5)	Samantha Mumba (2000)
Body Talk (4)	Imagination (1981)
Bodyshakin' (3)	911 (1997)
Bohemian Like You (re-issue) (5)	Dandy Warhols (2001)
Bohemian Rhapsody (1)	Queen (1975)
Bohemian Rhapsody (re-issue) / These Are The Days Of Our Lives (1)	Queen (1991)
Bomb Diggy (6)	Another Level (1999)
Bomb! (These Sounds Fall Into My Mind) (5)	Bucketheads (1995)
Boney M Megamix (7)	Boney M (1992)
Boogie Nights (2)	Heatwave (1977)
Boogie Oogie Oogie (3)	A Taste Of Honey (1978)
Boogie Wonderland (4)	Earth Wind & Fire with The Emotions (1979)
Book Of Days (10)	Enya (1992)
Book Of Love (8)	Mudlarks (1958)
Book (re-entry), The (10)	David Whitfield (1954)
Book, The (5)	David Whitfield (1954)
Boom Bang-A-Bang (2)	Lulu (1969)
Boom Boom Boom (1)	Outhere Brothers (1995)

Title	Group/Artiste
Boom Boom Boom Boom (1)	Vengaboys (1999)
Boom! Shake The Room (1)	Jazzy Jeff & The Fresh Prince (1993)
Boombastic (1)	Shaggy (1995)
Bootie Call (1)	All Saints (1998)
Bootylicious (2)	Destiny's Child (2001)
Bop Bop Baby (5)	Westlife (2002)
Borderline (2)	Madonna (1986)
Born Free (6)	Vic Reeves & The Roman Numerals (1994)
Born in England (9)	Twisted X (2004)
Born Slippy (2)	Underworld (1996)
Born To Be Alive (10)	Patrick Hernandez (1979)
Born To Be With You (8)	Chordettes (1956)
Born To Be With You (5)	Dave Edmunds (1973)
Born To Make You Happy (1)	Britney Spears (2000)
Born To Try (3)	Delta Goodrem (2003)
Born Too Late (5)	Poni-Tails (1958)
Born With A Smile On My Face (2) first hit	Stephanie De Sykes with Rain (1974)
Boss Drum (4)	Shamen (1992)
Both Sides Now (14) first hit	Judy Collins (1970)
Both Sides Of The Story (7)	Phil Collins (1993)
Boulevard Of Broken Dreams (5)	Green Day (2004)
Bouncer, The (7)	Kicks Like A Mule (1992)
Bound 4 Da Reload (Casualty) (1)	Oxide & Neutrina (2000)
Bow Wow (That's My Name) (6)	Lil Bow Wow (2001)
Boxer Beat (3)	Jo Boxers (1983)
Boxer, The (6)	Simon & Garfunkel (1969)
Boy From New York City (2)	Darts (1978)
Boy From Nowhere, A (2)	Tom Jones (1987)
Boy Is Mine, The (2)	Brandy & Monica (1998)
Boy Named Sue, A (4)	Johnny Cash (1969)
Boy You Knock Me Out (3)	Tatyana Ali featuring Will Smith (1999)
Boys (7)	Britney Spears featuring P Williams (2002)
Boys Are Back In Town, The (8)	Thin Lizzy (1976)
Boys Cry (8)	Eden Kane (1964)
Boys Keep Swinging (7)	David Bowie (1979)
Boys Of Summer, The (2)	DJ Sammy (2003)
Boys (Summertime Love) (3)	Sabrina (1988)
Brand New Key (4)	Melanie (1972)
Brass In Pocket (1)	Pretenders (1979)
Break Away (6)	Beach Boys (1969)
Break My Stride (4)	Matthew Wilder (1984)
Break The Rules (8)	Status Quo (1974)
Breakaway (4)	Tracey Ullman (1983)
Breakdance Party (9)	Break Machine (1984)
Breakfast At Tiffany's (1)	Deep Blue Something (1996)
Breakfast In America (9)	Supertramp (1979)
Breakfast In Bed (6)	UB40 featuring Chrissie Hynde (1988)
Breakin' ... There's No Stopping Us Now (5)	Ollie & Jerry (1984)

M
U
S
I
C

P
O
P

Title	Group/Artiste	Title	Group/Artiste
Breakin' Down The Walls Of Heartache (4)	Johnny Johnson & The Bandwagon (1968)	Buddy/The Magic Number (7) biggest hit	De La Soul (1989)
Breaking Up Is Hard To Do (3)	Partridge Family (1972)	Buffalo Gals (9)	Malcolm McLaren and The World Famous Supreme Team (1982)
Breaking Up Is Hard To Do (7)	Neil Sedaka (1962)		
Breakout (4)	Swing Out Sister (1986)	Buffalo Soldier (4)	Bob Marley & The Wailers (1983)
Breakthru (7)	Queen (1989)	Buffalo Stance (3) first hit	Neneh Cherry (1988)
Breath Of Life (8)	Erasure (1992)	Bug A Boo (9)	Destiny's Child (1999)
Breathe (1)	Blu Cantrell featuring Sean Paul (2003)		
Breathe (1)	Prodigy (1996)	Buggin' Me (6)	True Steppers with Dane Bowers (2000)
Breathe Again (2)	Toni Braxton (1994)		
Breathe Easy (4)	Blue (2004)	Build Me Up Buttercup (2)	Foundations (1968)
Breathless (1)	Corrs (2000)	Bullet In The Gun (2000 remix) (7)	Planet Perfecto (2000)
Breathless (8)	Jerry Lee Lewis (1958)		
Breeze And I, The (5)	Caterina Valente (1955)	Bulls On Parade (8)	Rage Against The Machine (1996)
Breeze On By (8)	Donny Osmond (2004)	Bump N' Grind (8)	R Kelly (1995)
		Bump, The (3)	Kenny (1974)
Bridge Of Sighs, The (9) first hit	David Whitfield (1953)	Bunsen Burner (9)	John Otway (2002)
		Buona Sera (7)	Acker Bilk & His Paramount Jazz Band (1960)
Bridge Over Troubled Water (1)	Simon & Garfunkel (1970)		
Bridget The Midget (Queen of the Blues) (2)	Ray Stevens (1971)	Burn (1)	Usher (2004)
		Burning Bridges (On And Off And On Again) (5)	Status Quo (1988)
Bright Eyes (1)	Art Garfunkel (1979)		
Brimful Of Asha (remix) (1)	Cornershop (1998)	Burning Down The House (7)	Tom Jones & The Cardigans (1999)
Bring A Little Water Sylvie/ Dead Or Alive (7)	Lonnie Donegan & His Skiffle Group (1956)	Burning Heart (5)	Survivor (1986)
		Burning Love (7)	Elvis Presley (1972)
Bring It All Back (1) first hit	S Club 7 (1999)	Bus Stop (5)	Hollies (1966)
Bring It On / My Lover's Prayer (5)	Alistair Griffin featuring Robin Gibb (2004)	Business (6)	Eminem (2003)
		But I Do (3)	Clarence 'Frogman' Henry (1961)
Bring It On Home To Me (7)	Animals (1965)	Butterfingers (re-entry) (8)	Tommy Steele (1957)
Bring Me Edelweiss (5)	Edelweiss (1989)	Butterfly (3)	Crazy Town (2001)
Bring Me To Life (1)	Evanescence (2003)	Butterfly (1) first hit	Andy Williams (1957)
Bring The Noise (14) biggest hit	Anthrax featuring Chuck D (1991)	By The Way (2)	Red Hot Chili Peppers (2002)
Bring Your Daughter ... To The Slaughter (1)	Iron Maiden (1991)	Bye Bye Baby (1)	Bay City Rollers (1975)
Bringing On Back The Good Times (9)	Love Affair (1969)	Bye Bye Baby (7)	TQ (1999)
		Bye Bye Bye (3)	N Sync (2000)
Britannia Rag (re-entry) (5)	Winifred Atwell (1953)	Bye Bye Love (6) first hit	Everly Brothers (1957)
British Hustle / Peace On Earth (8)	Hi Tension (1978)	C U When You Get There (3)	Coolio featuring 40 Thevz (1997)
Brits 1990, The (2)	Various Artists (1990)	Ca Plane Pour Moi (8)	Plastic Bertrand (1978)
Broken Bones (8)	Love Inc (2003)	Calendar Girl (8)	Neil Sedaka (1961)
Broken Down Angel (9)	Nazareth (1973)	California Dreamin' (re-entry) (9)	Mamas & The Papas (1997)
Broken Hearted Melody (7)	Sarah Vaughan (1959)	California Love (6)	2Pac featuring Dr Dre (1996)
Broken Silence (9)	So Solid Crew (2003)	California Man (7)	Move (1972)
Broken Wings (6)	Art & Dotty Todd (1953)	Call Me (1)	Blondie (1980)
		Call Me (2)	Spagna (1987)
Broken Wings (4)	Mr Mister (1985)	(Call Me) Number One (2)	Tremeloes (1969)
Broken Wings (re-entry) (1)	Stargazers (1953)	Call On Me (1)	Eric Prydz (2004)
Brontosaurus (7)	Move (1970)	Call Up The Groups (3) first hit	Barron Knights with Duke D'Mond (1964)
Brother Louie (7)	Hot Chocolate (1973)		
Brother Louie (4)	Modern Talking (1986)	Call, The (8)	Backstreet Boys (2001)
Brown Sugar/Bitch/Let It Rock (2)	Rolling Stones (1971)	Calling (7)	Geri Halliwell (2001)
Brown-eyed Handsome Man (3)	Buddy Holly (1963)	Calling All The Heroes (6)	It Bites (1986)
Bubblin' (9)	Blue (2004)	Calling Occupants Of Interplanetary Craft (9)	Carpenters (1977)
Buck Rogers (5)	Feeder (2001)		

Title	Group/Artiste	Title	Group/Artiste
Calling Your Name (4)	Marilyn (1983)	Can't Take My Eyes Off You (4)	Boystown Gang (1982)
Camels (9)	Santos (2001)	Can't Take My Eyes Off You (5)	Andy Williams (1968)
Camouflage (4)	Stan Ridgway (1986)	Can't Wait Another Minute (7)	Five Star (1986)
Can Can (3)	Bad Manners (1981)	Can't You See That She's	Dave Clark Five
Can Can You Party (8)	Jive Bunny & The Mastermixers (1990)	Mine (10)	(1964)
Can I Play With Madness (3)	Iron Maiden (1988)	Captain Beaky / Wilfred The Weasel (5)	Keith Michell (1980)
Can I Take You Home Little Girl (10)	Drifters (1975)	Captain Of Her Heart, The (8)	Double (1986)
Can I Touch You ... There (6)	Michael Bolton (1995)	Car 67 (7)	Driver 67 (1978)
		Car Wash (9) first hit	Rose Royce (1976)
Can The Can (1)	Suzi Quatro (1973)	Car Wash (4)	Christina Aguilera featuring Missy Elliott (2004)
Can We Fix It? (1)	Bob The Builder (2000)		
Can You Feel It (6)	Jacksons (1981)	Cara Mia (1)	David Whitfield with Mantovani (1954)
Can You Feel It / Hip To Hip (5)	V (2004)		
Can You Feel The Force (5)	Real Thing (1979)	Caramel (9)	City High featuring Eve (2002)
Can You Forgive Her (7)	Pet Shop Boys (1993)	Caravan Of Love (1)	Housemartins (1986)
Candida (9) first hit	Dawn (1971)	Careless Hands (6)	Des O'Connor (1967)
Candle In The Wind 97 / Something About The Way You Look Tonight (1)	Elton John (1997)	Careless Whisper (1) first solo hit	George Michael (1984)
		Caribbean Disco Show, The (8)	Lobo (1981)
Candle In The Wind (re-issue) (5)	Elton John (1988)	Caribbean Queen (No More Love On The Run) (6)	Billy Ocean (1984)
Candy (2)	Mandy Moore (2000)		
Candy (6)	New Edition (1983)		
Candy Girl (1)	Brian Poole & The Tremeloes (1964)	Carnation (6) B side of Going Underground	Liam Gallagher and Steve Craddock (1999)
Candy Man (6)			
		Carnaval De Paris (5)	Dario G (1998)
Canned Heat (4)	Jamiroquai (1999)	Carnival (72) first hit	Cardigans (1995)
Can't Be With You Tonight (2)	Judy Boucher (1987)	Carnival Girl (9)	Texas featuring Kardinal Offishall (2003)
Can't Buy Me Love (1)	Beatles (1964)		
Can't Fight The Moonlight (1)	LeAnn Rimes (2000)	Carnival Is Over, The (1)	Seekers (1965)
Can't Get By Without You (2)	Real Thing (1976)	Carolina Moon / Stupid Cupid (1)	Connie Francis (1958)
Can't Get By Without You (The Second Decade Remix) (6)	Real Thing (1986)		
		Caroline (5)	Status Quo (1973)
Can't Get Enough (8)	Soulsearcher (1999)	Carrie (4)	Cliff Richard (1980)
Can't Get Enough (10)	Raghav (2004)	Carrie-Anne (3)	Hollies (1967)
Can't Get Enough Of Your Love Babe (8)	Barry White (1974)	Carry Me Home (9)	Gloworm (1994)
		Cars (1)	Gary Numan (1979)
Can't Get It Back (8)	Mis-Teeq (2003)	Cartoon Heroes (7)	Aqua (2000)
Can't Get Used To Losing You (3)	Beat (1983)	Casanova (9)	Levert (1987)
		Case Of The Ex (3)	Mya (2001)
Can't Get Used To Losing You (2)	Andy Williams (1963)	Cassius (7)	Cassius 1999 (1999)
Can't Get You Out Of My Head (1)	Kylie Minogue (2001)	Cast Your Fate To The Wind (5)	Sounds Orchestral (1964)
Can't Give You Anything (But My Love) (1)	Stylistics (1975)	Castles In The Sky (3)	Ian Van Dahl (2001)
Can't Help Falling In Love (4)	Stylistics (1976)	Cat Amongst The Pigeons / Silent Night (2)	Bros (1988)
Can't Help Falling In Love (3)	Andy Williams (1970)	Cat Crept In, The (2)	Mud (1974)
Can't Hold Us Down (6)	Christina Aguilera featuring Lil' Kim (2003)	Catch A Falling Star (9)	Perry Como (1958)
		Catch The Wind (4) first hit	Donovan (1965)
Can't I (9)	Nat 'King' Cole (1953)	Catch Us If You Can (5)	Dave Clark Five (1965)
Can't I (re-entry) (6)	Nat 'King' Cole (1953)	Cathy's Clown (1)	Everly Brothers (1960)
Can't I (re-entry) (10)	Nat 'King' Cole (1953)	Cats In The Cradle (7)	Ugly Kid Joe (1993)
		Caught In A Moment (8)	Sugababes (2004)
Can't Keep This Feeling In (10)	Cliff Richard (1998)	Caught In The Middle (2)	A1 (2002)
Can't Nobody (5)	Kelly Rowland (2003)	Caught Out There (4)	Kelis (2000)
Can't Shake The Feeling (8)	Big Fun (1989)	Causing A Commotion (4)	Madonna (1987)
Can't Stand Losing You (re-release) (2)	Police (1979)	Cecilia (4)	Suggs and Louchie Lou & Michie One (1996)
Can't Stand Me Now (2)	Libertines (2004)		
Can't Stay Away From You (7)	Gloria Estefan & Miami Sound Machine (1989)	Celebration (7)	Kool & The Gang (1980)
		Centerfold (3)	J Geils Band (1982)

MUSIC
POP

Title	Group/Artiste	Title	Group/Artiste
Certain Smile, A (4)	Johnny Mathis (1958)	Chocolate Salty Balls (1)	Chef (1998)
C'est La Vie (1) first hit	B*Witched (1998)	Choose Life (6)	PF Project featuring Ewan McGregor (1997)
C'est La Vie (3)	Robbie Nevil (1986)		
Cha Cha Slide (1)	DJ Casper (2004)	Chorus (3)	Erasure (1991)
Chain Gang (9)	Sam Cooke (1960)	Chosen Few, The (7)	Dooleys (1979)
Chain Gang (9)	Jimmy Young (1956)	Christmas Alphabet (1)	Dickie Valentine (1955)
Chain Reaction (1)	Diana Ross (1986)		
Chain Reaction / One For Sorrow (remix) (2)	Steps (2001)	Christmas Island (8)	Dickie Valentine (1956)
Chains (6) first and biggest hit	Tina Arena (1994)	Christmas Time (Don't Let The Bells End) (2)	Darkness (2003)
Chance (9)	Big Country (1983)		
Change (10)	Lisa Stansfield (1991)	Church Of The Poison Mind (2)	Culture Club (1983)
		Cigarettes And Alcohol (7)	Oasis (1994)
Change (4)	Tears For Fears (1983)	Cinderella Rockefella (1)	Esther & Abi Ofarim (1968)
Change Would Do You Good, A (8)	Sheryl Crow (1997)	Cindy Incidentally (2)	Faces (1973)
		Cindy Oh Cindy (5)	Eddie Fisher (1956)
Changes (3)	2Pac (1999)	Circle In The Sand (4)	Belinda Carlisle (1988)
Changes (1)	Ozzy & Kelly Osbourne (2003)		
		Circle, The (6)	Ocean Colour Scene (1996)
Changing Partners (10)	Bing Crosby (1954)		
Changing Partners (4)	Kay Starr (1954)	Circles (4)	New Seekers (1972)
Changing Partners (re-entry) (9)	Bing Crosby (1954)	Circus, The (6)	Erasure (1987)
Changingman, The (7)	Paul Weller (1995)	Clair (1)	Gilbert O'Sullivan (1972)
Chanson D'Amour (1)	Manhattan Transfer (1977)		
		Clairvoyant, The (6)	Iron Maiden (1988)
Chant No. 1 (I Don't Need This Pressure On) (3)	Spandau Ballet (1981)	Clap Back / Reigns (9)	Ja Rule (2003)
		Clapping Song, The (6)	Shirley Ellis (1965)
Charlie Brown (6)	Coasters (1959)	Classic (8)	Adrian Gurvitz (1982)
Charly (3) first hit	Prodigy (1991)		
Charmaine (6) first hit	Bachelors (1963)	Classical Gas (9)	Mason Williams (1968)
Charmless Man (5)	Blur (1996)		
Chase The Sun (5)	Planet Funk (2001)	Cleanin' Out My Closet (4)	Eminem (2002)
Ch-Check It Out (8)	Beastie Boys (2004)	Clementine (8)	Bobby Darin (1960)
Check Out The Groove (10)	Bobby Thurston (1980)	Clementine (3)	Mark Owen (1997)
		Cleopatra's Theme (3) first hit	Cleopatra (1998)
Check This Out (6)	LA Mix (1988)	Clint Eastwood (4)	Gorillaz (2001)
Cheeky Song (Touch My Bum) (2)	Cheeky Girls (2002)	Clocks (9)	Coldplay (2003)
Chequered Love (4)	Kim Wilde (1981)	Close The Door (6)	Stargazers (1955)
Cherish (4)	Kool & The Gang (1985)	Close (To The Edit) (8) first hit	Art Of Noise (1984)
Cherish (3)	Madonna (1989)	Close To You (9)	Marti Pellow (2001)
Cherish/Could It Be Forever (2) first hit	David Cassidy (1972)	Close To You (7)	Maxi Priest (1990)
		Closer Than Close (4)	Rosie Gaines (1997)
Cherry Pink And Apple Blossom White (1)	Eddie Calvert (1955)	Closer to Me (4)	Five (2001)
		Closest Thing To Crazy, The (10)	Katie Melua (2003)
Cherry Pink And Apple Blossom White (1)	Perez 'Prez' Prado (King of the Mambo) (1955)	Cloud Lucky Seven (2)	Guy Mitchell (1953)
		Cloud Number 9 (6)	Bryan Adams (1999)
		Clouds Across The Moon (6)	Rah Band (1985)
Chi Mai (The Theme From The Life And Times Of Lloyd George) (2)	Ennio Morricone (1981)	Club Tropicana (4)	Wham! (1983)
		C'Mon Everybody (6)	Eddie Cochran (1959)
Chicka Boom (5)	Guy Mitchell (1953)	C'Mon Everybody (3)	Sex Pistols (1979)
Chicka Boom (re-entry) (4)	Guy Mitchell (1954)	Co-Co (2)	Sweet (1971)
Chicken Song, The (1)	Spitting Image (1986)	Coco Jamboo (8)	Mr President (1997)
		Cognoscenti Vs Intelligentsia (4)	Cuban Boys (1999)
Child (3)	Mark Owen (1996)	Cold As Ice (4)	MOP (2001)
Children (2)	Robert Miles (1996)	Colette (9)	Billy Fury (1960)
Children Of The Revolution (2)	T Rex (1972)	Colourblind (1)	Darius (2002)
Child's Prayer, A (7)	Hot Chocolate (1975)	Colours (4)	Donovan (1965)
		Combine Harvester (Brand New Key) (1)	Wurzels (1976)
China Girl (2)	David Bowie (1983)		
China In Your Hand (1)	T'Pau (1987)	Come And Get It (4) first and biggest hit	Badfinger (1970)
China Tea (5)	Russ Conway (1959)		
		Come And Stay With Me (4)	Marianne Faithfull (1965)
Chiquitita (2)	Abba (1979)		
Chirpy Chirpy Cheep Cheep (1)	Middle Of The Road (1971)	Come As You Are (9)	Beverley Knight (2004)
		Come As You Are (9)	Nirvana (1992)
Chocolate (6)	Kylie Minogue (2004)	Come Baby Come (3)	K7 (1993)
Chocolate Box (9)	Bros (1989)		

Title	Group/Artiste	Title	Group/Artiste
Come Back And Shake Me (3)	Clodagh Rodgers (1969)	Computer Love / The Model (re-entry) (1)	Kraftwerk (1981)
Come Back And Stay (4)	Paul Young (1983)	Concrete And Clay (1)	Unit Four Plus Two
Come Back Brighter (8)	Reef (1997)		(1965)
Come Back Darling (10)	UB40 (1998)	Condemnation (9)	Depeche Mode
Come Back My Love (2)	Darts (1978)		(1993)
Come Back To What You Know (6)	Embrace (1998)	Confessin' (1)	Frank Ifield (1963)
		Confessions Part II / My Boo (5)	Usher (2004)
Come Get Some (7)	Rooster (2004)	Confide In Me (2)	Kylie Minogue (1994)
Come In Out Of The Rain (8)	Wendy Moten (1994)	Confusion / Last Train To	Electric Light
Come Into My Life (7)	Joyce Sims (1988)	London (8)	Orchestra (1979)
Come Into My World (8)	Kylie Minogue (2002)	Congratulations (1)	Cliff Richard (1968)
		Constantly (4)	Cliff Richard (1964)
Come Live With Me (5)	Heaven 17 (1983)	Contact (6)	Edwin Starr (1979)
Come On (21) first hit	Rolling Stones (1963)	Controversy (5)	Prince (1993)
		Conversations (7)	Cilla Black (1969)
Come On Eileen (1)	Dexy's Midnight Runners (1982)	Convoy (2)	C W McCall (1976)
		Convoy G.B. (4)	Laurie Lingo & The
Come On England (2)	England's Barmy Army (2004)		Dipsticks (1976)
		Cool For Cats (2)	Squeeze (1979)
Come On Over (10)	Kym Marsh (2003)	Cool Water (2)	Frankie Laine (1955)
Come On Over Baby (All I Want Is You) (8)	Christina Aguilera (2000)	Cornflake Girl (4)	Tori Amos (1994)
		Coronation Rag (re-entry) (5)	Winifred Atwell (1953)
Come On Let's Go (10)	Tommy Steele (1958)		
		Cosmic Girl (6)	Jamiroquai (1996)
Come On Over To My Place (re-issue) (9)	Drifters (1972)	Cotton Eye Joe (1)	Rednex (1994)
		Cottonfields (5)	Beach Boys (1970)
Come On You Reds (1)	Manchester United Football Club (1994)	Could Have Told You So (6)	Halo James (1989)
		Could I Have This Kiss Forever (7)	Whitney Houston & Enrique Iglesias (2000)
Come Outside (1)	Mike Sarne with Wendy Richard (1962)		
		Could It Be Forever / Cherish (2) first hit	David Cassidy (1972)
Come Play With Me (10)	Wedding Present (1992)	Could It Be I'm Falling In Love (5)	David Grant & Jaki Graham (1985)
Come Prima (2)	Marino Marini & His Quartet (1958)	Could It Be Magic (3)	Take That (1992)
		Could You Be Loved (5)	Bob Marley & The Wailers (1980)
Come Softly To Me (6)	Fleetwoods (1959)		
Come Softly To Me (9)	Frankie Vaughan & The Kaye Sisters (1959)	Couldn't Get It Right (10)	Climax Blues Band (1976)
		Could've Been (4)	Tiffany (1988)
Come Tomorrow (4)	Manfred Mann (1965)	Counting Teardrops (4)	Emile Ford & The Checkmates (1960)
Come Undone (4)	Robbie Williams (2003)		
Come What May (2)	Vicky Leandros (1972)	Country House (1)	Blur (1995)
		Country Roads (7)	Hermes House Band (2001)
Come With Me (2)	Puff Daddy featuring Jimmy Page (1998)	Cover Girl (4)	New Kids On The Block (1990)
Come With Me (6)	Special D (2004)	Coward Of The County (1)	Kenny Rogers (1980)
Come With Us / The Test (14)	Chemical Brothers (2002)	Cowpuncher's Cantata (11) first hit	Max Bygraves (1952)
Comes A-Long A-Love (1)	Kay Starr (1952)		
Comfortably Numb (10)	Scissor Sisters (2004)	Cowpuncher's Cantata (re-entry) (6)	Max Bygraves (1953)
Coming Around (5)	Travis (2000)	Cowpuncher's Cantata (re-entry) (8)	Max Bygraves (1953)
Coming Around Again (10)	Carly Simon (1987)	Cowpuncher's Cantata (re-entry) (10)	Max Bygraves (1953)
Comin' Home (16) first solo hit	Eric Clapton (1969)		
Coming Home Now (4)	Boyzone (1996)	Coz I Luv You (1)	Slade (1971)
Coming Up (2)	Paul McCartney (1980)	Crackers International EP (2)	Erasure (1988)
		Cracklin' Rosie (3) first hit	Neil Diamond (1970)
Common People (2)	Pulp (1995)	Cradle Of Love (2)	Johnny Preston (1960)
Communication (Somebody Answer The) (5)	Mario Piu (1999)		
		Crash (5)	Primitives (1988)
Complete (4)	Jaimeson (2003)	Crashed The Wedding (1)	Busted (2003)
Complex (6)	Gary Numan (1979)	Crazy (5)	Seal (1990)
		Crazy Crazy Nights (4)	Kiss (1987)
Complicated (3)	Avril Lavigne (2002)	Crazy For You (2)	Let Loose (1994)
Compliments On Your Kiss (2)	Red Dragon with Brian & Tony Gold (1994)	Crazy For You (2)	Madonna (1985)
		Crazy For You (remix) (2)	Madonna (1991)

MUSIC POP

Title	Group/Artiste	Title	Group/Artiste
Crazy Horses (2)	Osmonds (1972)	D.I.V.O.R.C.E. (1) first hit	Billy Connolly (1975)
Crazy In Love (1)	Beyonce (Knowles) (2003)	Da Da Da (2)	Trio (1982)
Crazy Little Party Girl (7)	Aaron Carter (1998)	Da Doo Ron Ron (5)	Crystals (1963)
Crazy Little Thing Called Love (2)	Queen (1979)	Da Funk / Musique (7)	Daft Punk (1997)
Crazy Love (10)	M J Cole (2000)	Da Ya Think I'm Sexy? (10)	Girls Of FHM (2004)
Crazy Rap (10)	Afroman (2002)	Da Ya Think I'm Sexy? (7)	N-Trance featuring Rod Stewart (1997)
Crazy (remix) (6)	Mark Morrison (1996)	Da Ya Think I'm Sexy? (1)	Rod Stewart (1978)
Creep (7)	Radiohead (1993)	Daddy Cool (6) first hit	Boney M (1976)
Creep (re-entry), The (10)	Ken Mackintosh Orchestra (1954)	Daddy Cool / The Girl Can't Help It (6) first hit	Darts (1977)
Creep (re-issue) (6)	TLC (1996)	Daddy's Home (2)	Cliff Richard (1981)
Creeque Alley (9)	Mamas & The Papas (1967)	Dance Away (2)	Roxy Music (1979)
Criticize (4)	Alexander O'Neal (1987)	Dance Dance Dance (Yowsah Yowsah Yowsah) (6) first hit	Chic (1977)
Crockett's Theme (2)	Jan Hammer (1987)	Dance For Me (6)	Sisqo (2001)
Crocodile Rock (5)	Elton John (1972)	Dance Into The Light (9)	Phil Collins (1996)
Crocodile Shoes (4)	Jimmy Nail (1994)	Dance Little Lady Dance (6)	Tina Charles (1976)
Cross My Broken Heart (6)	Sinitta (1988)	Dance On (1)	Shadows (1962)
Crossroads (1)	Blazin' Squad (2002)	Dance The Night Away (4)	Mavericks (1998)
Crown, The (6)	Gary Byrd & The GB Experience (1983)	Dance To The Music (7)	Sly & The Family Stone (1968)
Cruel Summer (8)	Ace Of Base (1998)	Dance With Guitar Man (4)	Duane Eddy & The Rebelettes (1962)
Cruel Summer (8)	Bananarama (1983)	Dance With Me (10)	Debelah Morgan (2001)
Cruise Into Christmas (10)	Jane McDonald (1998)	Dance With The Devil (3)	Cozy Powell (1973)
Crunch, The (6)	Rah Band (1977)	Dance (With U) (2)	Lemar (2003)
Crush (4)	Jennifer Paige (1998)	Dance Yourself Dizzy (2)	Liquid Gold (1980)
Crush On You (9)	Aaron Carter (1997)	Dancin' Party (4)	Showaddywaddy (1977)
Crush On You (5)	Jets (1987)	Dancing In The City (3)	Marshall Hain (1978)
Cry (2)	Kym Marsh (2003)	Dancing In The Dark (re-entry) (4)	Bruce Springsteen (1985)
Cry For Help (7)	Rick Astley (1991)	Dancing In The Moonlight (remix) (7)	Toploader (2000)
Cry Just A Little Bit (3)	Shakin' Stevens (1983)	Dancing In The Street (1)	David Bowie & Mick Jagger (1985)
Cry Me A River (2)	Justin Timberlake (2003)	Dancing In The Street (re-issue) (4)	Martha Reeves & The Vandellas (1969)
Cry Wolf (5)	A-Ha (1986)	(Dancing) On A Saturday Night (2) first and biggest hit	Barry Blue (1973)
Cryin' In The Rain (6)	Everly Brothers (1962)	Dancing On The Ceiling (7)	Lionel Richie (1986)
Crying (1)	Don McLean (1980)	Dancing On The Floor (Hooked On Love) (10)	Third World (1981)
Crying Game, The (5)	Dave Berry (1964)	Dancing Queen (1)	Abba (1976)
Crying In The Chapel (1)	Elvis Presley with The Jordanaires (1965)	Dancing Tight (4)	Galaxy featuring Phil Fearon (1983)
Crying In The Chapel (re-entry) (7)	Lee Lawrence (1953)	Dancing With Tears In My Eyes (3)	Ultravox (1984)
Crying Over You (11) only other hit	Ken Boothe (1974)	Dancing With The Captain (8)	Paul Nicholas (1976)
Crystal (8)	New Order (2001)	Danger Games (8)	Pinkees (1982)
Cubik / Olympic (10)	808 State (1990)	Danger High Voltage (2)	Electric Six (2003)
Cuddly Toy (re-issue) (4)	Roachford (1989)	Daniel (4)	Elton John (1973)
Cuff Of My Shirt (9)	Guy Mitchell (1954)	Darlin' (6)	Frankie Miller (1978)
Cult Of Snap (8)	Snap (1990)	Dat (6)	Pluto Shervington (1976)
Cum On Feel The Noize (1)	Slade (1973)	Daughter Of Darkness (5)	Tom Jones (1970)
Cumberland Gap (1)	Lonnie Donegan & His Skiffle Group (1957)	Davy's On The Road Again (6)	Manfred Mann's Earth Band (1978)
Cumberland Gap (10)	Vipers Skiffle Group (1957)	Day After Day (10)	Badfinger (1972)
Cupid (7)	Sam Cooke (1961)	Day And Night (1)	Billie Piper (2000)
Cupid (6)	Johnny Nash (1969)	Day I Met Marie, The (10)	Cliff Richard (1967)
Cupid – I've Loved You For A Long Time (4)	Detroit Spinners (1980)	Day The Rains Came, The (1)	Jane Morgan (1958)
Curtain Falls (4)	Blue (2004)	Day Trip To Bangor (Didn't We Have A Lovely Time) (3)	Fiddler's Dram (1979)
Cut Some Rug / Castle Rock (7)	Bluetones (1996)		
Cutter, The (8)	Echo And The Bunnymen (1983)		
D.I.S.C.O. (2)	Ottowan (1980)		

Title	Group/Artiste	Title	Group/Artiste
Day Tripper / We Can Work It Out (1)	Beatles (1965)	Devil You Know, The (10)	Jesus Jones (1993)
Day We Caught The Train, The (4)	Ocean Colour Scene (1996)	Devil's Answer, The (4)	Atomic Rooster (1971)
Day We Find Love, The (4)	911 (1997)	Diamonds (1)	Jet Harris & Tony Meehan (1963)
Day Without Love, A (6)	Love Affair (1968)	Diana (1) first hit	Paul Anka (1957)
Daydream (2)	Lovin' Spoonful (1966)	Diane (1)	Bachelors (1964)
Daydream Believer (5)	Monkees (1967)	Diary Of Horace Wimp, The (8)	Electric Light Orchestra (1979)
Daydreamer / The Puppy Song (1)	David Cassidy (1973)	Did You Ever (2)	Nancy Sinatra & Lee Hazlewood (1971)
Daydreamin' (6)	Tatyana Ali (1998)	Die Another Day (3)	Madonna (2002)
Days Of Pearly Spencer, The (4)	Marc Almond (1992)	Different Beat, A (1)	Boyzone (1996)
Daysleeper (6)	REM (1998)	Different Corner, A (1)	George Michael (1986)
D-Days (10)	Hazel O'Connor (1981)	Dilemma (1)	Nelly featuring Kelly Rowland (2002)
De Do Do Do De Da Da Da (5)	Police (1980)	Dime And A Dollar (8)	Guy Mitchell (1954)
Dead End Street (5)	Kinks (1966)	Dime And A Dollar (re-entry) (8)	Guy Mitchell (1954)
Dead From The Waist Down (7)	Catatonia (1999)	Dip It Low (2)	Christina Milian (2004)
Dead Giveaway (8)	Shalamar (1983)		
Dead Ringer For Love (5)	Meat Loaf (1981)	Dirty (1)	Christina Aguilera featuring Redman (2002)
Dean And I, The (10)	10CC (1973)		
Dear Jessie (5)	Madonna (1989)	Dirty Cash (2)	Adventures Of Stevie V (1990)
Dear John (10)	Status Quo (1982)		
Dear Lonely Hearts (4)	Nat 'King' Cole (1962)	Dirty Diana (4)	Michael Jackson (1988)
Dear Prudence (3)	Siouxsie & The Banshees (1983)		
		Disappointed (6)	Electronic (1992)
Death Of A Clown (3)	Dave Davies (1967)	Disco Connection (10)	Isaac Hayes (1976)
Debora / One Inch Rock (re-issue) (7)	Tyrannosaurus Rex (1972)	Disco Duck (Part One) (6)	Rick Dees & His Cast Of Idiots (1976)
December 1963 (Oh What A Night) (1)	Four Seasons (1976)	Disco Stomp (6)	Hamilton Bohannon (1975)
Deck Of Cards (re-entry) (5)	Wink Martindale (1963)	Disco 2000 (7)	Pulp (1995)
		Disco's Revenge (9)	Gusto (1996)
Dedicated Follower Of Fashion (4)	Kinks (1966)	Discotheque (1)	U2 (1997)
Dedicated To The One I Love (2)	Mamas & The Papas (1967)	Distant Drums (1)	Jim Reeves (1966)
Dedicated To The One I Love (6)	Bitty McLean (1994)	Divine Emotions (8)	Narada (1988)
Deep (5)	East 17 (1993)	Dizzy (1)	Tommy Roe (1969)
Deep Deep Trouble (7)	Simpsons featuring Bart & Homer (1991)	Dizzy (1)	Vic Reeves & The Wonder Stuff (1991)
Deeper And Deeper (6)	Madonna (1992)	DJ (3)	H & Claire (2002)
Deeper Love, A (5)	Aretha Franklin (1994)	DJ / Stop (9)	Jamelia (2004)
Deeper Shade Of Blue (4)	Steps (2000)	Do Anything You Wanna Do (9)	Eddie & The Hotrods (1977)
Deeper Underground (1)	Jamiroquai (1998)		
Deepest Blue (7)	Deepest Blue (2003)	Do I Do (10)	Stevie Wonder (1982)
Deeply Dippy (1)	Right Said Fred (1992)		
		Do It Again (1)	Beach Boys (1968)
Delaware (3)	Perry Como (1960)	Do It Do It Again (9)	Raffaella Carra (1978)
Delilah (2)	Tom Jones (1968)		
Delilah (7)	Sensational Alex Harvey Band (1975)	Do Nothing / Maggie's Farm (4)	Specials (1980)
		Do That To Me One More Time (7)	Captain & Tennille (1980)
Delta Lady (10)	Joe Cocker (1969)	Do The Bartman (1)	Simpsons (1991)
Dem Girlz (I Don't Know Why) (10)	Oxide & Neutrino featuring Kowdean (2002)	Do The Conga (10)	Black Lace (1984)
		(Do) The Hucklebuck (5)	Coast To Coast (1981)
Denis (2) first hit	Blondie (1978)	(Do The) Spanish Hustle (10)	Fatback Band (1976)
Desiderata (7)	Les Crane (1972)	Do They Know It's Christmas (1)	Band Aid (1984)
Design For Life, A (2)	Manic Street Preachers (1996)	Do They Know It's Christmas (1)	Band Aid II (1989)
		Do They Know It's Christmas (re-entry) (3)	Band Aid (1985)
Desire (1)	U2 (1988)	Do They Know It's Christmas? (1)	Band Aid 20 (2004)
Detroit City (8)	Tom Jones (1967)	Do U Still (7)	East 17 (1996)
Devil Gate Drive (1)	Suzi Quatro (1974)	Do Wah Diddy (9)	DJ Otzi (2001)
Devil In Disguise (1)	Elvis Presley with The Jordanaires (1963)	Do Wah Diddy Diddy (1)	Manfred Mann (1964)
Devil Woman (9)	Cliff Richard (1976)		
Devil Woman (5)	Marty Robbins (1962)		

M
U
S
I
C

P
O
P

Title	Group/Artiste	Title	Group/Artiste
Do What You Do (6)	Jermaine Jackson (1985)	Don't Bring Me Down (6)	Animals (1966)
Do Ya Do Ya (Wanna Please Me) (10)	Samantha Fox (1986)	Don't Bring Me Down (3)	Electric Light Orchestra (1979)
Do You Feel My Love (8)	Eddy Grant (1980)	Don't Bring Me Down (10)	Pretty Things (1964)
Do You Know (6)	Michelle Gayle (1997)	Don't Call Me Baby (re-issue) (1)	Madison Avenue (2000)
Do You Know (I Go Crazy) (8)	Angel City (2004)	Don't Cry (8)	Guns 'N' Roses (1991)
Do You Know The Way To San Jose (8)	Dionne Warwick (1968)	Don't Cry Daddy (8)	Elvis Presley (1970)
Do You Love Me (1)	Brian Poole & The Tremeloes (1963)	Don't Cry For Me Argentina (1)	Julie Covington (1976)
Do You Love Me (30) first hit	Dave Clark Five (1963)	Don't Cry For Me Argentina (3)	Madonna (1996)
		Don't Cry For Me Argentina (5)	Shadows (1978)
Do You Mind (1)	Anthony Newley (1960)	Don't Do It Baby (9)	Mac & Katie Kissoon (1975)
Do You Really Like It (1)	DJ Pied Piper & Master of Ceremonies (2001)	Don't Ever Change (5)	Crickets (1962)
		Don't Forbid Me (2)	Pat Boone (1957)
Do You Really Want To Hurt Me (1) first hit	Culture Club (1982)	Don't Forget To Remember (2)	Bee Gees featuring Colin Peterson (1969)
Do You See The Light (Looking For) (10)	Snap featuring Niki Harris (1993)	Don't Get Me Wrong (10)	Pretenders (1986)
Do You Wanna Dance (7)	Barry Blue (1973)	Don't Give Me Your Life (2)	Alex Party (1995)
Do You Wanna Touch Me? (Oh Yeah) (2)	Gary Glitter (1973)	Don't Give Up (1)	Chicane featuring Bryan Adams (2000)
Do You Want Me (5)	Salt-N-Pepa (1991)	Don't Give Up (9)	Peter Gabriel & Kate Bush (1986)
Do You Want To Know A Secret (2)	Billy J Kramer And The Dakotas (1963)	Don't Give Up On Us (1)	David Soul (1976)
		Don't Go (3)	Yazoo (1982)
Doctor Doctor (3)	Thompson Twins (1984)	Don't Go Breaking My Heart (1)	Elton John & Kiki Dee (1976)
Doctor Jones (1)	Aqua (1998)	Don't Go Breaking My Heart (7)	Elton John & RuPaul (1994)
Doctor My Eyes (9)	Jackson 5 (1973)		
Doctorin' The House (6)	Coldcut with Yazz & Plastic Population (1988)	Don't It Make My Brown Eyes Blue (5)	Crystal Gayle (1977)
		Don't Knock The Rock (7)	Bill Haley & His Comets (1957)
Doctorin' The Tardis (1)	Timelords (1988)	Don't Know Much (2)	Linda Ronstadt with Aaron Neville (1989)
Doctor's Orders (7)	Sunny (1974)		
Does Your Chewing Gum Lose Its Flavour (On The Bedpost Overnight) (3)	Lonnie Donegan & His Skiffle Group (1959)	Don't Laugh At Me (3)	Norman Wisdom (1954)
Does Your Mother Know (4)	Abba (1979)	Don't Leave Me (6)	Blackstreet (1997)
Doesn't Really Matter (5)	Janet Jackson (2000)	Don't Leave Me This Way (5)	Harold Melvin & The Bluenotes (1977)
Dog Eat Dog (4)	Adam & The Ants (1980)	Don't Leave Me This Way (1)	Communards (1986)
Doin' The Do (7)	Betty Boo (1990)	Don't Let Go (3)	David Sneddon (2003)
Doing Alright With The Boys (6)	Gary Glitter (1975)		
Dolce Vita (5)	Ryan Paris (1983)	Don't Let Go (Love) (5)	En Vogue (1997)
Dolly My Love (10)	Moments (1975)	Don't Let It Die (2)	Hurricane Smith (1971)
Dolphins Were Monkeys (5)	Ian Brown (2000)		
Dominique (7)	Singing Nun (Soeur Sourire) (1963)	Don't Let Me Be Misunderstood (3)	Animals (1965)
		Don't Let Me Down / You And I (2)	Will Young (2002)
Domino Dancing (7)	Pet Shop Boys (1988)	Don't Let Me Get Me (6)	Pink (2002)
Don Quixote (10)	Nik Kershaw (1985)	Don't Let The Stars Get In Your Eyes (1) first hit	Perry Como (1953)
Donald Where's Your Troosers (re-issue) (4)	Andy Stewart (1989)	Don't Let The Sun Catch You Crying (6)	Gerry & The Pacemakers (1964)
Donna (2) first hit	10CC (1972)	Don't Let The Sun Go Down On Me (1)	George Michael with Elton John (1991)
Donna (3)	Marty Wilde (1959)	Don't Look Any Further (9)	M People (1993)
Don't (2)	Elvis Presley with The Jordanaires (1958)	Don't Look Back In Anger (1)	Oasis (1996)
		Don't Make Me Wait (10)	911 (1996)
		Don't Make My Baby Blue (10)	Shadows (1965)
Don't Answer Me (6)	Cilla Black (1966)	Don't Marry Her (8)	Beautiful South (1996)
Don't Be A Stranger (3)	Dina Carroll (1993)		
Don't Be Cruel (42) first hit	Bobby Brown (1988)		
Don't Be Stupid (You Know I Love You) (5)	Shania Twain (2000)		
Don't Blame Me (8)	Frank Ifield (1964)	Don't Miss The Partyline (7)	Bizz Nizz (1990)
Don't Break My Heart (3)	UB40 (1985)	Don't Need The Sun To Shine (To Make Me Smile) (9)	Gabrielle (2001)

Title	Group/Artiste	Title	Group/Artiste
Don't Pay The Ferryman (48) first hit	Chris De Burgh (1982)	Double Dutch (3)	Malcolm McLaren (1983)
Don't Play Your Rock 'N' Roll To Me (8)	Smokie (1975)	Dove (I'll Be Loving You) (9)	Moony (2002)
Don't Speak (1)	No Doubt (1997)	Down Boy (2)	Holly Valance (2002)
Don't Stand So Close To Me (1)	Police (1980)	Down Deep Inside (Theme From The Deep) (5)	Donna Summer (1977)
Don't Stay Away Too Long (3)	Peters & Lee (1974)	Down Down (1)	Status Quo (1974)
Don't Stop (3)	ATB (1999)	Down 4 U (4)	Irv Gotti Presents (2002)
Don't Stop Me Now (9)	Queen (1979)		
Don't Stop Movin' (5)	Livin' Joy (1996)	Down On The Beach Tonight (7)	Drifters (1974)
Don't Stop Movin' (1)	S Club 7 (2001)	Down On The Street (9)	Shakatak (1984)
Don't Stop The Music (7)	Yarbrough & Peoples (1980)	Down To Earth (3)	Curiosity Killed The Cat (1986)
Don't Stop Till You Get Enough (3)	Michael Jackson (1979)	Down Under (1)	Men At Work (1983)
Don't Stop (Wiggle Wiggle) (1)	Outhere Brothers (1995)	Down Yonder (8)	Johnny & The Hurricanes (1960)
Don't Take Away The Music (4)	Tavares (1976)	Downhearted (3)	Eddie Fisher (1953)
Don't Talk Just Kiss (3)	Right Said Fred with Jocelyn Brown (1991)	Downtown (2)	Petula Clark (1964)
		Downtown (remix) (10)	Petula Clark (1988)
		Downtown Train (10)	Rod Stewart (1990)
Don't Talk To Him (2)	Cliff Richard & The Shadows (1963)	Dr Beat (6)	Miami Sound Machine (1984)
Don't Talk To Me About Love (7)	Altered Images (1983)	Dr Kiss Kiss (8)	5000 Volts (1976)
Don't Tell Me (8)	Blancmange (1984)	Dr Love (4)	Tina Charles (1976)
Don't Tell Me (5)	Avril Lavigne (2004)	Dragnet (7)	Ray Anthony (1953)
Don't Tell Me (4)	Madonna (2000)	Dragnet (re-entry) (9)	Ted Heath Orchestra (1953)
Don't That Beat All (8)	Adam Faith (1962)	Dragostea Din Tei (3)	O-Zone (2004)
Don't Think I'm Not (9)	Kandi (2000)	Drama! (4)	Erasure (1989)
Don't Think You're The First (10)	Coral (2003)	Dreadlock Holiday (1)	10CC (1978)
Don't Throw Your Love Away (1)	Searchers (1964)	Dream Baby (2)	Roy Orbison (1962)
Don't Treat Me Like A Child (3) first hit	Helen Shapiro (1961)	Dream Lover (1)	Bobby Darin (1959)
		Dream On (6)	Depeche Mode (2001)
Don't Turn Around (5)	Ace Of Base (1994)	Dream To Me (9)	Dario G (2001)
Don't Turn Around (1)	Aswad (1988)	Dreamboat (1)	Alma Cogan (1955)
Don't Walk Away (7)	Jade (1993)	Dreamer (remix) (1)	Livin' Joy (1995)
Don't Wanna Let You Go (9)	Five (2000)	Dreamin' (5)	Johnny Burnette (1960)
Don't Wanna Lose This Feeling (5)	Dannii Minogue (2003)	Dreamin' (8)	Cliff Richard (1980)
Don't Wanna Lose You (6)	Gloria Estefan (1989)	Dreaming (2)	Blondie (1979)
		Dreaming (9)	Glen Goldsmith (1988)
Don't Want To Forgive Me Now (7)	Wet Wet Wet (1995)	Dreaming (10)	Ruff Driverz presents Arrola (1998)
Don't Waste My Time (8)	Paul Hardcastle featuring Carol Kenyon (1986)	Dreaming Of Me (57) first hit	Depeche Mode (1981)
Don't Worry (5)	Appleton (2003)	Dreamlover (9)	Mariah Carey (1993)
Don't Worry (2) first solo hit	Kim Appleby (1990)	Dreams (6)	Corrs (1998)
Don't Worry Be Happy (2)	Bobby McFerrin (1988)	Dreams (1)	Gabrielle (1993)
		Dream's A Dream, A (6)	Soul II Soul (1990)
Don't You (Forget About Me) (7)	Simple Minds (1985)	Dreams Can Tell A Lie (10)	Nat 'King' Cole (1956)
Don't You Love Me (3)	Eternal (1997)		
Don't You Rock Me Daddy-O (4)	Lonnie Donegan & His Skiffle Group (1957)	Dress You Up (5)	Madonna (1985)
		Drifting Away (9)	Lange featuring Skye (2002)
Don't You Rock Me Daddy-O (10)	Vipers Skiffle Group (1957)	Drinking In L.A. (re-issue) (3)	Bran Van 3000 (1999)
Don't You Think It's Time (6)	Mike Berry & The Outlaws (1963)	Drive (5)	Cars (1984)
Don't You Want Me (6)	Felix (1992)	Drive (re-entry) (4)	Cars (1985)
Don't You Want Me (1)	Human League (1981)	Drive-In Saturday (3)	David Bowie (1973)
		Driven By You (6)	Brian May (1991)
Don't You Want Me (remix) (10)	Felix (1995)	Driving In My Car (4)	Madness (1982)
Doo Wap (That Thing) (3)	Lauryn Hill (1998)	Drop Dead Gorgeous (7)	Republica (1997)
Doodah! (7)	Cartoons (1999)	Drop It Like It's Hot (10)	Snoop Dogg featuring Pharrell (2004)
Dooms Night (8)	Azzido Da Bass (2000)		
Doop (1)	Doop (1994)	Drop The Boy (2)	Bros (1988)
Double Barrel (1) first hit	Dave & Ansil Collins (1971)	Drops Of Jupiter (Tell Me) (10)	Train (2001)
		Drowned World (Substitute For Love) (10)	Madonna (1998)

MUSIC POP

Title	Group/Artiste	Title	Group/Artiste
Drowning (4)	Backstreet Boys (2002)	Emma (3)	Hot Chocolate (1974)
Drowning In Berlin (9)	Mobiles (1982)	Emotion (3)	Destiny's Child (2001)
Drugs Don't Work, The (1)	Verve (1997)		
Dry County (9)	Bon Jovi (1994)	Emotional Rescue (9)	Rolling Stones (1980)
Dry Your Eyes (1)	Streets (2004)	Encore Une Fois (2)	Sash (1997)
Dub Be Good To Me (1)	Beats International with Lindy Layton (1990)	End Is The Beginning Is The End, The (10)	Smashing Pumpkins (1997)
		End Of The Line (5)	Honeyz (1998)
Dude (7)	Beenie Man (2004)	End Of The Road (1)	Boyz II Men (1992)
Dude (Looks Like A Lady) (20) first hit; first release 1987, No 45	Aerosmith (1990)	Endless Love (3)	Luther Vandross & Mariah Carey (1994)
Duke Of Earl (6)	Darts (1979)	Endless Love (7)	Diana Ross & Lionel Richie (1981)
Dumb (3)	411 (2004)		
Dyna-Mite (4)	Mud (1973)	Endless Sleep (4) first hit	Marty Wilde (1958)
Dy-Na-Mi-Tee (5)	Ms Dynamite (2002)	Endlessly (28) first and biggest hit	Brook Benton (1959)
D'You Know What I Mean? (1)	Oasis (1997)		
Each Time (2)	E-17 (1998)	England's Irie (6)	Black Grape, Joe Strummer & Keith Allen (1996)
Each Time You Break My Heart (5)	Nick Kamen (1986)		
Early In The Morning (8)	Vanity Fare (1969)	English Country Garden (5)	Jimmie Rodgers (1962)
Earth Angel (4)	Crew Cuts (1955)		
Earth Dies Screaming, The/ Dream A Lie (10)	UB40 (1980)	Enjoy The Silence (6)	Depeche Mode (1990)
Earth Song (1)	Michael Jackson (1995)	Enjoy The Silence 04 (7)	Depeche Mode (2004)
Easy (9)	Commodores (1977)	Enjoy Yourself (5)	A+ (1999)
Easy Lover (1)	Philip Bailey duet with Phil Collins (1985)	Enola Gay (8)	Orchestral Manoeuvres In The Dark (1980)
Eat You Alive (10)	Limp Bizkit (2003)	Enter Sandman (5)	Metallica (1991)
Ebb Tide (9)	Frank Chacksfield (1954)	Erase / Rewind (7)	Cardigans (1999)
		Erasure-ish (25) first hit	Björn Again (1992)
Ebeneezer Goode (1)	Shamen (1992)	Ernie (The Fastest Milkman In The West) (1)	Benny Hill (1971)
Ebony And Ivory (1)	Paul McCartney with Stevie Wonder (1982)	Erotica (3)	Madonna (1992)
		Escape (3)	Enrique Iglesias (2002)
E-Bow The Letter (4)	REM (1996)		
Echo Beach (10)	Martha & The Muffins (1980)	Escaping (3)	Dina Carroll (1996)
		Especially For You (3)	Denise & Johnny (1998)
Ecuador (2)	Sash featuring Rodriguez (1997)	Especially For You (1)	Kylie Minogue & Jason Donovan (1988)
Edelweiss (2)	Vince Hill (1967)		
Edge Of Heaven, The / Where Did Your Heart Go (1)	Wham! (1986)	Et Les Oiseaux Chantaient (And The Birds Were Singing) (4)	Sweet People (1980)
Egyptian Reggae (5)	Jonathan Richman & Modern Lovers (1977)	Eternal Flame (1)	Atomic Kitten (2001)
		Eternal Flame (1)	Bangles (1989)
Eighteen Strings (9)	Tinman (1994)	Eternally (8)	Jimmy Young (1953)
Eighteen With A Bullet (7)	Pete Wingfield (1975)	Eternity / The Road To Mandalay (1)	Robbie Williams (2001)
Eighth Day (5)	Hazel O'Connor (1980)	Eton Rifles, The (3)	Jam (1979)
		European Female (9)	Stranglers (1983)
Einstein A Go-Go (5)	Landscape (1981)	Evapor 8 (6)	Altern 8 (1992)
Elected (4)	Alice Cooper (1972)	Eve Of Destruction (3)	Barry McGuire (1965)
Election Day (7) first hit	Arcadia (1985)		
Electric Avenue (2)	Eddy Grant (1983)	Eve Of War (remix), The (3)	Jeff Wayne's War Of The Worlds (1989)
Electric Avenue (remix) (5)	Eddy Grant (2001)		
Electrical Storm (5)	U2 (2002)		
Electricity (5)	Suede (1999)	Even After All (10)	Finley Quaye (1997)
Elenore (7)	Turtles (1968)	Even Better Than The Real Thing (remix) (8)	U2 (1992)
Elephant Stone (8)	Stone Roses (1990)		
		Even The Bad Times Are Good (4)	Tremeloes (1967)
Elevation (3)	U2 (2001)		
Eloise (3)	Damned (1986)	Ever Fallen In Love (9)	Fine Young Cannibals (1987)
Eloise (2)	Barry Ryan (1968)		
Elusive Butterfly (5)	Val Doonican (1966)	Ever Fallen In Love (With Someone You Shouldn't've) (12) biggest hit	Buzzcocks (1978)
Elusive Butterfly (5)	Bob Lind (1966)		
Embarrassment (4)	Madness (1980)		

Title	Group/Artiste	Title	Group/Artiste
Evergreen/Anything Is Possible (1)	Will Young (2002)	(Everything I Do) I Do It For You (7)	Fatima Mansions (1992)
Everlasting Love (5)	Cast From Casualty (1998)	Everything I Have Is Yours (re-entry) (8)	Eddie Fisher (1953)
Everlasting Love (1)	Love Affair (1968)	Everything I Own (1) first hit	Ken Boothe (1974)
Evermore (3)	Ruby Murray (1955)	Everything I Own (1) first solo hit	Boy George (1987)
Every Beat Of My Heart (2)	Rod Stewart (1986)		
Every Breath You Take (1)	Police (1983)	Everything Is Alright (Uptight) (10)	C J Lewis (1994)
Every Day Hurts (3)	Sad Cafe (1979)		
Every Day (I Love You More) (2)	Jason Donovan (1989)	Everything Is Beautiful (6) first hit	Ray Stevens (1970)
		Everything Must Change (9)	Paul Young (1984)
Every Day Of My Life (5)	Malcolm Vaughan (1955)	Everything Must Go (5)	Manic Street Preachers (1996)
Every Little Step (6)	Bobby Brown (1989)	Everything's Alright (9)	Mojos (1964)
		Everything's Gonna Be Alright (5)	Sweetbox (1998)
Every Little Thing She Does Is Magic (1)	Police (1981)	Everytime (1)	Britney Spears (2004)
		Everytime / Ready Or Not (3)	A1 (1999)
Every Loser Wins (1)	Nick Berry (1986)	Everytime You Need Me (3)	Fragma featuring Maria Rubia (2001)
Every Morning (10)	Sugar Ray (1999)		
Every Time You Go Away (4)	Paul Young (1985)	Everywhere (4)	Fleetwood Mac (1988)
Everybody (6)	Clock (1995)		
Everybody (4)	Hear'Say (2001)	Evil Hearted You / Still I'm Sad (3)	Yardbirds (1965)
Everybody (7)	Progress presents The Boy Wunda (1999)	Evil That Men Do, The (5)	Iron Maiden (1988)
		Evil Woman (10)	Electric Light Orchestra (1976)
Everybody (9)	Tommy Roe (1963)	Ev'rywhere (3)	David Whitfield (1955)
Everybody (Backstreet's Back) (3)	Backstreet Boys (1997)		
		Excerpt From A Teenage Opera (1)	Keith West (1967)
Everybody Dance (9)	Chic (1978)		
Everybody Get Together (8)	Dave Clark Five (1970)	Ex-Factor (4)	Lauryn Hill (1999)
		Exodus (Theme From 'Exodus') (6)	Ferrante & Teicher (1961)
Everybody Get Up (2)	Five (1998)		
Everybody Gonfi-Gon (7)	Two Cowboys (1994)	Experiments With Mice (7)	Johnny Dankworth (1956)
Everybody Hurts (7)	REM (1993)	Express Yourself (5)	Madonna (1989)
Everybody In The Place (EP) (2)	Prodigy (1992)	Extended Play EP (7)	Bryan Ferry (1976)
Everybody Knows (2)	Dave Clark Five (1967)	Exterminate (2)	Snap featuring Niki Harris (1993)
Everybody Wants To Rule The World (2)	Tears For Fears (1985)	Eye Level (re-entry) (1)	Simon Park Orchestra (1973)
Everybody Wants To Run The World (5)	Tears For Fears (1986)	Eye Of The Tiger (1)	Survivor (1982)
		Eyes On You (6)	Jay Sean featuring Rishi Rich Project (2004)
Everybody's Changing (4)	Keane (2004)		
Everybody's Free (To Feel Good) (6)	Rozalla (1991)	F**k It (I Don't Want You Back) (1)	Eamon (2004)
		F.L.M. (7)	Mel & Kim (1987)
Everybody's Free (To Wear Sunscreen) (1)	Baz Luhrmann (1999)	F.U.R.B. (F U Right Back) (1)	Frankee (2004)
		Fable (7)	Robert Miles (1996)
Everybody's Got To Learn Sometime (5)	Korgis (1980)	Fabulous (8)	Charlie Gracie (1957)
(Everybody's Got To Learn Sometime) I Need Your Loving (3)	Baby D (1995)	Faces (8)	2 Unlimited (1993)
		Fade To Grey (8)	Visage (1980)
Everybody's Laughing (10)	Phil Fearon & Galaxy (1984)	Fairground (1)	Simply Red (1995)
		Fairytale Of New York (2)	Pogues featuring Kirsty MacColl (1987)
Everybody's Somebody's Fool (5)	Connie Francis (1960)		
Everyday (5)	Bon Jovi (2002)	Faith (2)	George Michael (1987)
Everyday (3)	Slade (1974)		
Everyday I Love You (3)	Boyzone (1999)	Faith Can Move Mountains (7)	Johnnie Ray & The Four Lads (1952)
Everyday Is Like Sunday (9)	Morrissey (1988)		
Everyone Says Hi (20)	David Bowie (2002)	Faith Can Move Mountains (re-entry) (9)	Johnnie Ray & The Four Lads (1953)
Everyone's Gone To The Moon (4)	Jonathan King (1965)	Faith Can Move Mountains (re-entry) (10)	Nat 'King' Cole (1953)
Everything (6)	Mary J Blige (1997)	Faith Can Move Mountains (re-entry) (9)	Johnnie Ray & The Four Lads (1953)
Everything About You (3) first hit	Ugly Kid Joe (1992)		
Everything Changes (1)	Take That (1994)	Faith Can Move Mountains (11) first hit	Jimmy Young (1953)
Everything Counts (6)	Depeche Mode (1983)		
Everything I Am (6)	Plastic Penny (1968)	Fall In Love With You (2)	Cliff Richard & The Shadows (1960)
(Everything I Do) I Do It For You (1)	Bryan Adams (1991)		
		Fallin' (3)	Alicia Keys (2001)

M
U
S
I
C

P
O
P

Title	Group/Artiste	Title	Group/Artiste
Falling (7)	Julie Cruise (1990)	Ferry 'Cross The Mersey (1)	Christians, Holly
Falling (9)	Roy Orbison (1963)		Johnson, Paul
Falling Apart At The Seams (9)	Marmalade (1976)		McCartney,
Falling In Love Again (8)	Eagle-Eye Cherry		Gerry Marsden &
	(1998)		Stock Aitken
Falling Into You (10)	Celine Dion (1996)		Waterman (1989)
Fame (1)	Irene Cara (1982)	Fever (5)	Peggy Lee with Jack
Familiar Feeling (10)	Moloko (2003)		Marshall's Music
Family Affair (8)	Mary J Blige (2001)		(1958)
Fancy Pants (4)	Kenny (1975)	Fever (6)	Madonna (1993)
Fanfare For The Common	Emerson Lake &	Fields Of Fire (400 Miles) (10)	Big Country (1983)
Man (2) only hit	Palmer (1977)	first hit	
Fantastic Day (9)	Haircut 100 (1982)	50:50 / Lullaby (5)	Lemar (2003)
Fantasy (2)	Appleton (2002)	Figaro (1)	Brotherhood Of Man
Fantasy (5)	Black Box (1990)		(1978)
Fantasy (4)	Mariah Carey (1995)	Fighter (3)	Christina Aguilera
Fantasy Island (5)	Tight Fit (1982)		(2003)
Far Far Away (2)	Slade (1974)	Fill Me In (1)	Craig David (2000)
Farewell – Bring It On Home	Rod Stewart (1974)	Filmstar (9)	Suede (1997)
To Me / You Send Me (7)		Final Countdown, The (1)	Europe (1986)
Farewell Is A Lonely Sound (8)	Jimmy Ruffin (1970)	Finally Found (4)	Honeyz (1998)
Farewell My Summer Love (7)	Michael Jackson	Finally (re-issue) (2)	Ce Ce Peniston
	(1984)		(1992)
Fascinating Rhythm (9)	Bass-O-Matic (1990)	Find My Love (7)	Fairground Attraction
Fashion (5)	David Bowie		(1988)
	(1980)	Find The Time (7)	Five Star (1986)
Fast Car (5)	Tracy Chapman	Fine Time (9)	Yazz (1989)
	(1988)	Finest Dreams (8)	Richard X featuring
Fast Food Song (2)	Fast Food Rockers		Kelis (2003)
	(2003)	Finger Of Suspicion (1)	Dickie Valentine with
Fast Love (1)	George Michael		The Stargazers
	(1996)		(1954)
Fat Lip (8)	Sum 41 (2001)	Fings Ain't Wot They Used To	Max Bygraves (1960)
Fat Neck (10)	Black Grape (1996)	Be (5)	
Father (10)	LL Cool J (1998)	Fire (1)	Crazy World Of
Father And Son (2)	Boyzone (1995)		Arthur Brown
Father And Son (2)	Ronan Keating &		(1968)
	Yusuf Islam (2004)	Fire (35) first hit	U2 (1981)
Fattie Bum Bum (8)	Carl Malcolm (1975)	Fire Brigade (3)	Move (1968)
Favourite Shirts (Boy Meets	Haircut 100 (1981)	Firestarter (1)	Prodigy (1996)
Girl) (4)		Firewire (9)	Cosmic Gate (2001)
Favourite Things (2)	Big Brovaz (2003)	First Cut Is The Deepest (18)	P P Arnold (1967)
FBI (6)	Shadows (1961)	first hit	
Fear Of The Dark (live) (8)	Iron Maiden (1993)	First Night, The (6)	Monica (1998)
Feel (4)	Robbie Williams	First Of May (6)	Bee Gees (1969)
	(2002)	First Of The Gang To Die (6)	Morrissey (2004)
Feel Good (7)	Phats & Small	First Time, The (1)	Robin Beck (1988)
	(1999)	first and only hit	
Feel Good Time (3)	Pink featuring	First Time, The (5)	Adam Faith with The
	William Orbit (2003)		Roulettes (1963)
Feel It (1)	Tamperer featuring	Fit But You Know It (4)	Streets (2004)
	Maya (1998)	Five Colours In Her Hair (1)	McFly (2004)
Feel It Boy (9)	Beenie Man featuring	5-4-3-2-1 (5) first hit	Manfred Mann (1964)
	Janet (2002)	Five Live EP (1)	George Michael,
(Feel Like) Heaven (6)	Fiction Factory		Queen, Lisa
	(1984)		Stansfield (1993)
Feel So Good (10)	Mase (1997)	5-7-0-5 (8)	City Boy (1978)
Feel So Real (5)	Steve Arrington	Fix (7)	Blackstreet (1997)
	(1985)	Flap Your Wings / My Place (1)	Nelly (2004)
Feel The Beat (5)	Darude (2000)	Flash (5)	BBE (1997)
Feel The Need In Me (4) first hit	Detroit Emeralds	Flash (10)	Queen (1980)
	(1973)	Flashdance (3)	Deep Dish (2004)
Feelings (4)	Morris Albert (1975)	Flashdance ... What A Feeling (2)	Irene Cara (1983)
Feels Like Heaven (5)	Urban Cookie	Flat Beat (1)	Mr Oizo (1999)
	Collective (1993)	Flava (1)	Peter Andre (1996)
Feels Like I'm In Love (1)	Kelly Marie (1980)	Flawless (7)	Ones (2001)
Feels So Good (5)	Melanie B (2001)	Flawless (Go To The City) (8)	George Michael
Feet Up (2) first hit	Guy Mitchell (1952)		(2004)
Fernando (1)	Abba (1976)	Flip Reverse (2)	Blazin' Squad (2003)
Ferry 'Cross The Mersey (8)	Gerry & The	Flirtation Waltz (re-entry) (10)	Winifred Atwell
	Pacemakers (1964)		(1953)

Title	Group/Artiste	Title	Group/Artiste
Float On (1)	Floaters (1977)	Forever Love (1) first solo hit	Gary Barlow (1996)
Floral Dance, The (2) first and only hit	Brighouse & Rastrick Brass Band (1977)	Forget Me Not (3)	Eden Kane (1962)
Floral Dance (21) first and only hit	Terry Wogan (1978)	Forget Me Not (7)	Vera Lynn (1952)
		Forget Me Not (re-entry) (5)	Vera Lynn (1952)
Flowers (2)	Sweet Female Attitude (2000)	Forget Me Nots (8)	Patrice Rushen (1982)
Flowers In The Rain (2)	Move (1967)	Forgot About Dre (7)	Dr Dre featuring Eminem (2000)
Floy Joy (9)	Supremes (1972)		
Fly Away (1)	Lenny Kravitz (1999)	Forgotten Town (22) first hit	Christians (1987)
Fly By II (6)	Blue (2002)	48 Crash (3)	Suzi Quatro (1973)
Fly On The Wings Of Love (8)	XTM & DJ Chucky presents Annia (2003)	Found A Cure (6)	Ultra Naté (1998)
		Found That Soul (9)	Manic Street Preachers (2001)
Fly, The (1)	U2 (1991)		
Flying (4)	Cast (1996)	Four Bacharach And David Songs EP (2)	Deacon Blue (1990)
Flying Without Wings (1)	Westlife (1999)	Four From Toyah EP (4)	Toyah (1981)
Fog On The Tyne (Revisited) (2)	Gazza & Lindisfarne (1990)	Four Letter Word (6)	Kim Wilde (1988)
		Four Minute Warning (4)	Mark Owen (2003)
Folk Singer, The (4)	Tommy Roe (1963)	4 My People (5)	Missy Elliott (2002)
Follow Da Leader (5)	Nigel & Marvin (2002)	4 Seasons Of Loneliness (10)	Boyz II Men (1997)
		Fox On The Run (5)	Manfred Mann (1968)
Follow Me (3)	Uncle Kracker (2001)		
Follow The Rules (9)	Livin' Joy (1996)	Fox On The Run (2)	Sweet (1975)
Follow You Follow Me (7)	Genesis (1978)	Frankie (1)	Sister Sledge (1985)
Food For Thought/King (4) first hit	UB40 (1980)	Freak Like Me (1)	Sugababes (2002)
		Freak Me (1)	Another Level (1998)
Fool Again (1)	Westlife (2000)	Free (7)	DJ Quicksilver (1997)
Fool (If You Think It's Over) (30) first hit	Chris Rea		
		Free (4)	Ultra Naté (1997)
Fool No More (4)	S Club 8 (2003)	Free (1) first hit	Deniece Williams (1977)
Fool Such As I, A/I Need Your Love Tonight (1)	Elvis Presley with The Jordanaires (1959)	Free As A Bird (2)	Beatles (1995)
		Free Me (7)	Cast (1997)
		Free Me (5)	Emma (2003)
Fool To Cry (6)	Rolling Stones (1976)	Freed From Desire (3)	Gala (1997)
Foolish (4)	Ashanti (2002)	Freedom (1)	Wham! (1984)
Foolish Beat (9)	Debbie Gibson (1988)	Freedom (2) first hit	Robbie Williams (1996)
Foot Tapper (1)	Shadows (1963)	Freedom Come Freedom Go (6)	Fortunes (1971)
Footloose (6)	Kenny Loggins (1984)	Freeek! (7)	George Michael (2002)
Footsee (9)	Wigan's Chosen Few (1975)	Freestyler (2)	Bomfunk MCs (2000)
Footsteps (4)	Steve Lawrence (1960)	Freight Train (5)	Charles McDevitt Skiffle Group and Nancy Whiskey (1957)
For All We Know (6)	Shirley Bassey (1971)		
For America (10)	Red Box (1986)	French Kiss (2)	Lil' Louis (1989)
For Lovers (7)	Wolfman featuring Pete Doherty (2004)	French Kissin' In The USA (8)	Deborah Harry (1986)
		Fresh! (6)	Gina G (1997)
For Once In My Life (3)	Stevie Wonder (1968)	Friday I'm In Love (6)	Cure (1992)
For The Good Times (7)	Perry Como (1973)	Friday On My Mind (6)	Easybeats (1966)
For Whom The Bell Tolls (4)	Bee Gees (1993)	Friday's Child (4)	Will Young (2004)
(For You) I'll Do Anything You Want Me To (5)	Barry White (1975)	Friend Or Foe (9)	Adam Ant (1982)
		Friendly Persuasion (3)	Pat Boone (1956)
For Your Babies (9)	Simply Red (1992)	Friends (8)	Arrival (1970)
For Your Eyes Only (8)	Sheena Easton (1981)	Friends And Neighbours (re-entry) (3)	Billy Cotton & His Band (1954)
		Friends Forever (5)	Thunderbugs (1999)
For Your Love (3)	Yardbirds (1965)	Frightened City (3)	Shadows (1961)
Forest, A (31)	Cure (1980)	From A Distance (6)	Bette Midler (1991)
Forever (6)	Damage (1996)	From A Jack To A King (2)	Ned Miller (1963)
Forever (6)	N-Trance (2002)	From A Window (10)	Billy J Kramer And The Dakotas (1964)
Forever (8)	Roy Wood (1973)		
Forever And Ever (1)	Slik (1976)	From Me To You (1)	Beatles (1963)
Forever And For Always (6)	Shania Twain (2003)	From New York To L.A. (6)	Patsy Gallant (1977)
Forever Autumn (5)	Jeff Wayne's War Of The Worlds featuring Justin Hayward (1978)	From The Heart (6)	Another Level (1999)
		From The Underworld (6)	Herd (1967)
		From This Moment On (9)	Shania Twain (1998)

Title	Group/Artiste	Title	Group/Artiste
Frontin' (6)	Pharrell Williams featuring Jay-Z (2003)	Get It On (1)	T Rex (1971)
		Get Lost (10)	Eden Kane (1961)
Frozen (1)	Madonna (1998)	Get Off Of My Cloud (1)	Rolling Stones (1965)
Frozen Orange Juice (10)	Peter Sarstedt (1969)	Get Outta My Dreams Get Into	
Full Metal Jacket (I Wanna Be Your Drill Instructor) (2)	Abigail Mead & Nigel Goulding (1987)	My Car (3)	Billy Ocean (1988)
		Get Over You / Move This Mountain (3)	Sophie Ellis-Bextor (2002)
Funeral Pyre (4)	Jam (1981)	Get Ready (10)	Temptations (1969)
Funkin' For Jamaica (N.Y.) (10)	Tom Browne (1980)	Get Ready For This (2)	2 Unlimited (1991)
Funky Gibbon / Sick Man Blues (4)	Goodies (1975)	Get The Girl! Kill The Baddies! (9)	Pop Will Eat Itself (1993)
Funky Moped / Magic Roundabout (5) first and only hit	Jasper Carrott (1975)	Get The Message (8)	Electronic (1991)
		Get The Party Started (2)	Pink (2002)
Funky Town (8)	Pseudo Echo (1987)	Get Up And Boogie (7)	Silver Convention (1976)
Funky Weekend (10)	Stylistics (1976)		
Funkytown (2)	Lipps Inc (1980)	Get Up (Before The Night Is Over) (2)	Technotronic featuring Ya Kid K (1990)
Funny Familiar Forgotten Feeling (7)	Tom Jones (1967)		
Funny Funny (13) first hit	Sweet (1971)	Get UR Freak On (4)	Missy Elliott (2001)
Funny How Love Can Be (8)	Ivy League (1965)	Get-A-Way (4)	Maxx (1994)
G.H.E.T.T.O.U.T. (10)	Changing Faces (1997)	Gett Off (4)	Prince & The New Power Generation (1991)
G.L.A.D. (10)	Kim Appleby (1991)		
Gambler (4)	Madonna (1985)	Gettin' Jiggy Wit It (3)	Will Smith (1998)
Gamblin' Man / Putting On The Style (1)	Lonnie Donegan & His Skiffle Group (1957)	Ghetto Child (7)	Detroit Spinners (1973)
		Ghetto Heaven (10)	Family Stand (1990)
Game Of Love (2)	Wayne Fontana & The Mindbenders (1965)	Ghetto Romance (7)	Damage (2000)
		Ghetto Superstar (2)	Pras Michel, Ol' Dirty Bastard and Mya (1998)
Games People Play (6)	Joe South (1969)		
Games Without Frontiers (4)	Peter Gabriel (1980)	Ghost Town (1)	Specials (1981)
Gangsta Lovin' (6)	Eve featuring Alicia Keys (2002)	Ghostbusters (2)	Ray Parker Jr (1984)
		Ghosts (5)	Japan (1982)
Gangsta's Paradise (1)	Coolio featuring LV (1995)	Giddy-Up-A-Ding-Dong (4)	Freddie Bell & The Bellboys (1956)
Gangster Trippin' (3)	Fatboy Slim (1998)	Gift Of Christmas, The (9) first and only hit	Childliners (1995)
Gangsters (6)	Special AKA (1979)		
Garden Of Eden (1)	Frankie Vaughan (1957)	Gigi (8)	Billy Eckstine (1959)
Gay Bar (5)	Electric Six (2003)	Gilly Gilly Ossenfeffer Katzenellen Bogen By The Sea (7)	Max Bygraves (1954)
Gaye (8)	Clifford T Ward (1973)		
		Gimme All Your Lovin' (10)	ZZ Top (1984)
Gee Baby (4)	Peter Shelley (1974)	Gimme Dat Ding (6)	Pipkins (1970)
Gee Whiz It's You (4)	Cliff Richard & The Shadows (1961)	Gimme Gimme Gimme (a man after midnight) (3)	Abba (1979)
Genie In A Bottle (1)	Christina Aguilera (1999)	Gimme Hope Jo'Anna (7)	Eddy Grant (1988)
		Gimme Little Sign (8)	Brenton Wood (1967)
Genie In A Bottle / Save Yourself (10)	Speedway (2003)	Gimme Some Loving (2)	Spencer Davis Group (1966)
Geno (1)	Dexy's Midnight Runners (1980)	Gimme Some More (5)	Busta Rhymes (1999)
Gentle On My Mind (2)	Dean Martin (1969)	Gimme The Light (remix) (5)	Sean Paul (2003)
Georgy Girl (3)	Seekers (1967)	Gin House Blues (12) first hit	Amen Corner (1967)
Get A Life (3)	Soul II Soul (1989)		
Get Away (1)	Georgie Fame & The Blue Flames (1966)	Ginny Come Lately (5)	Brian Hyland (1962)
		Girl All The Bad Guys Want (8)	Bowling For Soup (2002)
Get Back (1)	Beatles with Billy Preston (1969)	Girl Can't Help It, The/Daddy Cool (6) first hit	Darts (1977)
Get Busy (4)	Sean Paul (2003)	Girl Can't Help It, The (9)	Little Richard (1957)
Get Dancing (8) first hit	Disco Tex & Sex-O-Lettes (1974)	Girl Crazy (7)	Hot Chocolate (1982)
Get Down (1)	Gilbert O'Sullivan (1973)	Girl Don't Come (3)	Sandie Shaw (1964)
		Girl I'm Gonna Miss You (2)	Milli Vanilli (1989)
Get Down On It (3)	Kool & The Gang (1981)	Girl Is Mine, The (8)	Michael Jackson & Paul McCartney (1982)
Get Get Down (5)	Paul Johnson (1999)		
Get Here (4)	Oleta Adams (1991)	Girl Like You, A (4)	Edwyn Collins (1995)
Get It (10)	Darts (1979)		

Title	Group/Artiste	Title	Group/Artiste
Girl Like You, A (3)	Cliff Richard & The Shadows (1961)	Go Away Little Girl (6)	Mark Wynter (1962)
Girl Of My Best Friend, The (9)	Elvis Presley with The Jordanaires (1976)	Go (Before You Break My Heart) (8)	Gigliola Cinquetti (1974)
		Go Let It Out (1)	Oasis (2000)
Girl On TV (6)	Lyte Funkie Ones (2000)	Go Now (1) first hit	Moody Blues (1964)
		Go On Move (7)	Reel 2 Real with The Mad Stuntman (1994)
Girl You Know It's True (3)	Milli Vanilli (1988)		
Girlfriend (1)	Billie (1998)	Go West (2)	Pet Shop Boys (1993)
Girlfriend (10)	B2K (2003)		
Girlfriend (2)	N Sync (2002)	Go Wild In The Country (7)	Bow Wow Wow (1982)
Girlfriend (8)	Pebbles (1988)		
Girlie Girlie (7)	Sophia George (1985)	God Gave Rock And Roll To You (4)	Kiss (1992)
Girls (3)	Moments & Whatnauts (1975)	God Is A DJ (6)	Faithless (1998)
		God Only Knows (2)	Beach Boys (1966)
Girls And Boys (5)	Blur (1994)	God Save The Queen (2)	Sex Pistols (1977)
Girls And Boys (6)	Good Charlotte (2003)	Goin' Down (4)	Melanie C (1999)
		Goin' Home (4)	Osmonds (1973)
Girls Girls Girls (7)	Sailor (1976)	Going Back (10)	Dusty Springfield (1966)
Girls Just Want To Have Fun (2)	Cyndi Lauper (1984)		
Girls Like Us (7)	B15 Project with Chrissy D & Lady G (2000)	Going Back To My Roots (4)	Odyssey (1981)
		Going Back To My Roots / Rich In Paradise (9)	FPI Project present Rich In Paradise and Paolo Dini (1989)
Girls On Film (5)	Duran Duran (1981)		
Girls Talk (4)	Dave Edmunds (1979)		
		Going For Gold (8)	Shed Seven (1996)
Give A Little Love (1)	Bay City Rollers (1975)	Going In With My Eyes Open (2)	David Soul (1977)
Give A Little Love (7)	Daniel O'Donnell (1998)	Going Nowhere (9)	Gabrielle (1993)
		Going Out (5)	Supergrass (1996)
Give In To Me (2)	Michael Jackson (1993)	Going Under (8)	Evanescence (2003)
Give It Away (9)	Red Hot Chili Peppers (1994)	Going Underground / Carnation (6)	Buffalo Tom / Liam Gallagher & Steve Cradock (1999)
Give It Away (9)	Deepest Blue (2004)		
Give It To You (5)	Jordan Knight (1999)		
Give It Up (1)	KC & The Sunshine Band (1983)	Going Underground / Dreams Of Children (1)	Jam (1980)
Give It Up (re-entry) (5)	Goodmen (1993)	Gold (10)	Artist Formerly Known As Prince (1995)
Give Me A Little More Time (5)	Gabrielle (1996)		
Give Me A Reason (9)	Triple Eight (2003)		
Give Me Back My Heart (4)	Dollar (1982)	Gold (2)	Spandau Ballet (1983)
Give Me Just A Little More Time (3) first hit	Chairmen Of The Board (1970)	Golden Brown (2)	Stranglers (1982)
		Golden Lights (21) second and only other hit	Twinkle (1965)
Give Me Just A Little More Time (2)	Kylie Minogue (1992)		
		Golden Touch (9)	Razorlight (2004)
Give Me Love (Give Me Peace On Earth) (8)	George Harrison (1973)	Golden Years (8)	David Bowie (1975)
		Golden Years EP, The (8)	Motorhead (1980)
Give Me The Night (7)	George Benson (1980)	Goldeneye (10)	Tina Turner (1995)
		Goldfinger (5)	Ash (1996)
Give Me Your Word (1)	Tennessee Ernie Ford (1955)	Gone Till November (3)	Wyclef Jean (1998)
Give Peace A Chance (2)	John Lennon & The Plastic Ono Band (1969)	Gonna Get Along Without You Now (8)	Viola Wills (1979)
Giving It All Away (5) first solo hit	Roger Daltrey (1973)	Gonna Make You A Star (1)	David Essex (1974)
Glad All Over (1)	Dave Clark Five (1963)	Gonna Make You An Offer You Can't Refuse (8)	Jimmy Helms (1973)
Glad It's All Over / Damned On 45 (6)	Captain Sensible (1984)	Gonna Make You Sweat (Everybody Dance Now) (3)	C & C Music Factory (1990)
Glass Of Champagne, A (2)	Sailor (1975)	Goo Goo Barabajagal (Love Is Hot) (12)	Jeff Beck (1969) biggest hit
Globetrotter (5)	Tornados (1963)	Good Enough (4)	Dodgy (1996)
		Good Golly Miss Molly (8)	Little Richard (1958)
Gloria (6)	Laura Branigan (1982)	Good Heart, A (1)	Feargal Sharkey (1985)
Glorious (4)	Andreas Johnson (2000)	Good Life (4)	Inner City (1988)
		Good Life (Buena Vida) (remix) (10)	Inner City (1999)
Glory Of Love (3)	Peter Cetera (1986)		
Glow Worm (10)	Mills Brothers (1953)	Good Luck Charm (1)	Elvis Presley with
Go (10)	Moby (1991)		

MUSIC POP

Title	Group/Artiste	Title	Group/Artiste
	The Jordanaires (1962)	Gotta Pull Myself Together (9)	Nolans (1980)
Good Morning Freedom (10)	Blue Mink (1970)	Gotta Tell You (2)	Samantha Mumba (2000)
Good Morning Judge (5)	10CC (1977)		
Good Morning Starshine (6)	Oliver (1969)	Govinda (7)	Kula Shaker (1996)
Good Old Arsenal (16) first hit	Arsenal FC First Team Squad (1971)	Granada (10)	Frankie Laine (1954)
		Granada (re-entry) (9)	Frankie Laine (1954)
Good Old Rock 'N' Roll (7)	Dave Clark Five (1969)	Grand Coolie Dam (6)	Lonnie Donegan & His Skiffle Group (1958)
Good The Bad And The Ugly, The (1)	Hugo Montenegro (1968)	Grand Piano (9)	Mixmaster (1989)
Good Thing (8)	Eternal (1996)	Grandad (1)	Clive Dunn (1970)
Good Thing (7)	Fine Young Cannibals (1989)	Grandma's Party (9)	Paul Nicholas (1976)
		Gravel Pit (6)	Wu-Tang Clan (2000)
Good Thing Going (We've Got A Good Thing Going) (4)	Sugar Minott (1981)	Gravity (7)	Embrace (2004)
		Grease (3)	Frankie Valli (1978)
Good Times (5)	Chic (1979)	Grease Megamix (3)	John Travolta & Olivia Newton-John (1990)
Good Timin' (1)	Jimmy Jones (1960)		
Good Tradition (10) first hit	Tanita Tikaram (1988)	Great Balls Of Fire (1)	Jerry Lee Lewis (1957)
Good Vibrations (1)	Beach Boys (1966)	Great Beyond, The (3)	REM (2000)
Good Year For The Roses, A (6)	Elvis Costello (1981)	Great Pretender, The / Only You (5) first hit	Platters (1956)
Goodbye (2)	Mary Hopkin (1969)		
Goodbye (1)	Spice Girls (1998)	Great Pretender, The (4)	Freddie Mercury (1987)
Goodbye Jimmy Goodbye (10)	Ruby Murray (1959)		
Goodbye My Love (2)	Glitter Band (1975)	Great Pretender, The (9)	Jimmy Parkinson (1956)
Goodbye My Love (4)	Searchers (1965)		
Goodbye Sam Hello Samantha (6)	Cliff Richard (1970)	Greatest Love Of All (8)	Whitney Houston (1986)
Goodbye Stranger (9)	Pepsi & Shirlie (1987)	Green Door (8)	Jim Lowe (1956)
		Green Door (1)	Shakin' Stevens (1981)
Goodbye Yellow Brick Road (6)	Elton John (1973)		
Goodness Gracious Me (4)	Peter Sellers and Sophia Loren (1960)	Green Door (2)	Frankie Vaughan (1956)
		Green Green Grass Of Home (1)	Tom Jones (1966)
Goodnight Girl (1)	Wet Wet Wet (1992)	Green Leaves Of Summer, The (7)	Kenny Ball & His Jazzmen (1962)
Goodnight Midnight (4)	Clodagh Rodgers (1969)	Green Manalishi (With The Two Pronged Crown), The (10)	Fleetwood Mac (1970)
Goodnight Tonight (5)	Wings (1979)		
Goody Two Shoes (1)	Adam Ant (1982)		
Google Eye (10)	Nashville Teens (1964)	Green Onions (7)	Booker T & The MG's (1979)
Gossip Folks (9)	Missy Elliott featuring Ludacris (2003)	Green Tambourine (7)	Lemon Pipers (1968)
		Grey Day (4)	Madness (1981)
		Groove Is In The Heart / What Is Love (2)	Deee-Lite (1990)
Got My Mind Set On You (2)	George Harrison (1987)		
Got Some Teeth (8)	Obie Trice (2003)	Groove, The (7)	Rodney Franklin (1980)
Got The Feelin' (3)	Five (1998)		
Got 'Til It's Gone (6)	Janet Jackson (1997)	Groovejet (If This Ain't Love) (1)	Spiller (2000)
Got To Be Certain (2)	Kylie Minogue (1988)	Groover, The (4)	T Rex (1973)
Got To Be There (5)	Michael Jackson (1972)	Groovin' (8)	Young Rascals (1967)
Got To Get It (4)	Culture Beat (1993)	Groovin' With Mr Bloe (2)	Mr Bloe (1970)
Got To Get You Into My Life (6)	Cliff Bennett & The Rebel Rousers (1966)	Groovin' (You're The Best Thing) / Big Boss Groove (5)	Style Council (1984)
		Groovy Kind Of Love, A (1)	Phil Collins (1988)
Got To Give It Up (7)	Marvin Gaye (1977)	Groovy Kind Of Love, A (2)	Mindbenders (1966)
Got To Have Your Love (2)	Liberty X (2002)	Groovy Train (6)	Farm (1990)
Got To Have Your Love (4)	Mantronix featuring Wondress (1990)	Guaglione (2)	Perez 'Prez' Prado & His Orchestra (1995)
Gotham City (9)	R Kelly (1997)	Guantanamera (7)	Sandpipers (1966)
Gotta Be You (10)	3T (1997)	Gudbuy T'Jane (2)	Slade (1972)
Gotta Get Thru This (1)	Daniel Bedingfield (2001)	Guess I Was A Fool (5)	Another Level (1998)
		Guiding Star (9)	Cast (1997)
Gotta Have Something In The Bank Frank (8)	Frankie Vaughan & The Kaye Sisters (1957)	Guilty (2)	Blue (2003)
		Guilty (10)	Pearls (1974)
		Guilty Conscience (5)	Eminem featuring Dr Dre (1999)
Gotta Have Something In The Bank Frank (8)	Kaye Sisters (1957)		
		Guitar Boogie Shuffle (10)	Bert Weedon (1959)

Title	Group/Artiste	Title	Group/Artiste
Guitar Tango (4)	Shadows (1962)	Happy Xmas (War Is Over) (4)	John Lennon, Yoko Ono & The Plastic Ono Band with The Harlem Community Choir (1972)
Guns Don't Kill People Rappers Do (3)	Goldie Lookin Chain (2004)		
Gym And Tonic (1)	Spacedust (1998)		
Gypsies Tramps And Thieves (4)	Cher (1971)	Happy Xmas (War Is Over) (re-entry) (2)	John Lennon, Yoko Ono & The Plastic Ono Band with The Harlem Community Choir (1980)
Gypsy Woman (La Da Dee) (2)	Crystal Waters (1991)		
H.A.P.P.Y. Radio (9)	Edwin Starr (1979)		
Ha Ha Said The Clown (4)	Manfred Mann (1967)		
Half A Heart (8)	H & Claire (2002)	Happy Xmas (War Is Over) (5)	Idols (2003)
Half As Much (3) first hit	Rosemary Clooney (1952)	Hard Day's Night, A (1)	Beatles (1964)
		Hard Day's Night, A (14)	Peter Sellers (1965)
Halfway Down The Stairs (7)	Muppets (1977)	Hard Habit To Break (8)	Chicago (1984)
Halfway To Paradise (3)	Billy Fury (1961)	Hard Headed Woman (2)	Elvis Presley with The Jordanaires (1958)
Hallelujah (5)	Milk & Honey featuring Gali Atari (1979)		
Hallelujah Freedom (10)	Junior Campbell (1972)	Hard Knock Life (Ghetto Anthem) (2)	Jay-Z (1998)
Hallowed Be Thy Name (live) (9)	Iron Maiden (1993)	Hard Rain's Gonna Fall, A (10) first solo hit	Bryan Ferry (1973)
Halo (10)	Texas (1997)		
Hammer To the Heart (6)	Tamperer featuring Maya (2000)	Hard To Say I'm Sorry (7)	Az Yet featuring Peter Cetera (1997)
Hand On Your Heart (1)	Kylie Minogue (1989)	Hard To Say I'm Sorry (4)	Chicago (1982)
Handbags And Gladrags (4)	Stereophonics (2001)	Harder I Try, The (2)	Brother Beyond (1988)
Hands Clean (12)	Alanis Morissette (2002)	Hardest Part Is The Night (68) first hit	Bon Jovi (1985)
Hands Off – She's Mine (9)	Beat (1980)	Harlem Shuffle (7) first and only hit	Bob & Earl (1969)
Hands To Heaven (4)	Breathe (1988)		
Hands Up (Give Me Your Heart) (3)	Ottowan (1981)	Harvest For The World (8)	Christians (1988)
		Harvest For The World (10)	Isley Brothers (1976)
Handy Man (3)	Jimmy Jones (1960)	Haters (8)	So Solid Crew presents Mr Shabz (2002)
Hang On In There Baby (3)	Johnny Bristol (1974)		
Hang On In There Baby (3)	Curiosity (1992)		
Hang On Sloopy (5)	McCoys (1965)	Hats Off To Larry (6)	Del Shannon (1961)
Hang On To Your Love (8)	Jason Donovan (1990)	Have A Cheeky Christmas (10)	Cheeky Girls (2003)
		Have A Drink On Me (8)	Lonnie Donegan & His Group (1961)
Hangin' Tough (1)	New Kids On The Block (1990)		
		Have A Nice Day (5)	Stereophonics (2001)
Hanging On The Telephone (5)	Blondie (1978)		
Hanky Panky (2)	Madonna (1990)	Have I The Right (6)	Dead End Kids (1977)
Happenin' All Over Again (4)	Lonnie Gordon (1990)		
		Have I The Right (1)	Honeycombs (1964)
Happening, The (6)	Supremes (1967)	Have I Told You Lately (5)	Rod Stewart (1993)
Happy (8)	MN8 (1995)	Have You Ever (1)	S Club 7 (2001)
Happy Birthday (2)	Altered Images (1981)	Have You Ever Been In Love (10)	Leo Sayer (1982)
		Have You Ever Really Loved A Woman (4)	Bryan Adams (1995)
Happy Birthday (2)	Stevie Wonder (1981)		
		Have You Seen Her (3)	Chi-Lites (1972)
Happy Birthday Sweet Sixteen (3)	Neil Sedaka (1961)	Have You Seen Her (8)	MC Hammer (1990)
		Have You Seen Her / Oh Girl (re-issue) (5)	Chi-Lites (1975)
Happy Days And Lonely Nights (6)	Ruby Murray (1955)		
		Have You Seen Your Mother Baby Standing In The Shadow (5)	Rolling Stones (1966)
Happy Hour (3)	Housemartins (1986)		
Happy Jack (3)	Who (1966)		
Happy People / U Saved Me (6)	R Kelly (2004)	Hawkeye (7)	Frankie Laine (1955)
Happy Talk (1) first hit	Captain Sensible (1982)	Hazard (3)	Richard Marx (1992)
		He Ain't Heavy He's My Brother (3)	Hollies (1969)
Happy To Be On An Island In The Sun (5)	Demis Roussos (1975)		
		He Ain't Heavy He's My Brother (re-issue) (1)	Hollies (1988)
Happy Together (10)	Jason Donovan (1991)		
		He Ain't No Competition (6)	Brother Beyond (1988)
Happy Wanderer (Der Fröhliche Wanderer) (2)	Obernkirchen Children's Choir (1954)		
		He Wasn't Man Enough (5)	Toni Braxton (2000)
		Head Over Feet (7)	Alanis Morissette (1996)
Happy Wanderer (Der Fröhliche Wanderer) (re-entry) (8)	Obernkirchen Children's Choir (1954)		
		Heal The World (2)	Michael Jackson (1992)
Happy Whistler, The (8)	Don Robertson (1956)	Hear The Drummer (Get Wicked) (3)	Chad Jackson (1990)

Title	Group/Artiste	Title	Group/Artiste
Heard It All Before (9)	Sunshine Anderson (2001)	Help! (1)	Beatles (1965)
Heart (1)	Pet Shop Boys (1988)	Here And Now / You'll Be Sorry (4)	Steps (2001)
Heart And Soul (75)	Cilla Black with Dusty Springfield (1993)	Here Comes My Baby (4)	Tremeloes (1967)
		Here Comes Summer (1)	Jerry Keller (1959)
		Here Comes That Feeling (5)	Brenda Lee (1962)
Heart And Soul (4) first hit	T'Pau (1987)	Here Comes The Hotstepper (4)	Ini Kamoze (1995)
Heart Full Of Soul (2)	Yardbirds (1965)	Here Comes The Night (2)	Them (1965)
Heart Of A Man, The (5)	Frankie Vaughan (1959)	Here Comes The Rain Again (8)	Eurythmics (1984)
		Here Comes The Sun (10)	Steve Harley (1976)
Heart Of A Teenage Girl, The (10)	Craig Douglas (1960)	Here 4 One (6)	Blazin' Squad (2004)
		Here I Am (5)	Bryan Adams (2002)
Heart Of Asia (3)	Watergate (2000)		
Heart Of Glass (1)	Blondie (1979)	Here I Go Again (4)	Hollies (1964)
Heart Of Gold (10)	Neil Young (1972)	Here I Go Again (remix) (9)	Whitesnake (1987)
Heart Of My Heart (7)	Max Bygraves (1954)	Here I Stand (10)	Bitty McLean (1994)
Heart On My Sleeve (6)	Gallagher & Lyle (1976)	Here In My Heart (1)	Al Martino (1952)
		Here It Comes Again (4)	Fortunes (1965)
Heartache (2)	Pepsi & Shirlie (1987)	Here It Comes Again (7)	Melanie C (2003)
		Here We Go Round The Mulberry Bush (8)	Traffic (1967)
Heartache Avenue (7)	Maisonettes (1982)		
Heartaches By The Number (re-entry) (5)	Guy Mitchell (1959)	Here With Me (4)	Dido (2001)
		Here's Where The Story Ends (7)	Tin Tin Out featuring Shelley Nelson (1998)
Heartbeat (2)	Nick Berry (1992)		
Heartbeat (3) first hit	Ruby Murray (1954)		
Heartbeat (7)	Showaddywaddy (1975)	Hernando's Hideaway (1)	Johnston Brothers (1955)
		Hero (7)	Mariah Carey (1993)
Heartbeat / Tragedy (1)	Steps (1998)	Hero (1)	Enrique Iglesias (2002)
Heartbreak Hotel (2) first hit	Elvis Presley (1956)		
Heartbreak Hotel / Hound Dog (re-issue) (10)	Elvis Presley (1971)	Hero (4)	Chad Kroeger featuring Josey Scott (2002)
Heartbreaker (5)	Mariah Carey featuring Jay-Z (1999)		
		Heroes And Villains (8)	Beach Boys (1967)
		Hersham Boys (6)	Sham 69 (1979)
Heartbreaker (2)	Dionne Warwick (1982)	He's Gonna Step On You Again (4)	John Kongos (1971)
		He's In Town (3)	Rockin' Berries (1964)
Heart-Shaped Box (5)	Nirvana (1993)		
Heatseeker (12) biggest hit	AC/DC (1988)	He's Misstra Know It All (10)	Stevie Wonder (1974)
Heaven (1)	DJ Sammy & Yanou featuring Do (2002)		
		He's So Fine (16) first hit	Chiffons (1963)
Heaven For Everyone (2)	Queen (1995)	He's The Greatest Dancer (6)	Sister Sledge (1979)
Heaven Is A Halfpipe (4)	OPM (2001)	Hey Baby (2)	No Doubt (2002)
Heaven Is A Place On Earth (1) first hit	Belinda Carlisle (1987)	Hey Baby (Unofficial World Cup Remix) (10)	DJ Otzi (2002)
Heaven Knows I'm Miserable Now (10)	Smiths (1984)	Hey Baby (Uuh, Aah) (1)	DJ Otzi (2001)
		Hey Boy Hey Girl (3)	Chemical Brothers (1999)
Heaven Must Be Missing An Angel (4) first hit	Tavares (1976)		
		Hey Child (3)	East 17 (1997)
Heaven Must Have Sent You (3)	Elgins (1971)	Hey DJ I Can't Dance To That Music You're Playing (7)	Beatmasters featuring Betty Boo (1989)
Heaven's What I Feel (4)	Gloria Estefan (1998)		
		Hey Dude (2)	Kula Shaker (1996)
Hell Raiser (2)	Sweet (1973)	Hey Girl (10)	Small Faces (1966)
Hello (1)	Lionel Richie (1984)		
Hello Goodbye (1)	Beatles (1967)	Hey Girl Don't Bother Me (1)	Tams (1971)
Hello Hello I'm Back Again (2)	Gary Glitter (1973)	Hey Joe (6)	Jimi Hendrix Experience (1967)
Hello Hurray (6)	Alice Cooper (1973)		
Hello Little Girl (9)	Fourmost (1963)	Hey Joe (1)	Frankie Laine (1953)
Hello Mary Lou / Travellin' Man (2)	Ricky Nelson (1961)	Hey Jude (1)	Beatles (1968)
Hello Suzie (4)	Amen Corner (1969)	Hey Little Girl (2)	Del Shannon (1962)
Hello This Is Joanie (The Telephone Answering Machine Song) (6)	Paul Evans (1978)	Hey Ma (8)	Cam'ron featuring Juelz Santana (2003)
Hello, Dolly! (4)	Louis Armstrong and the All Stars (1964)	Hey Mamma (6)	Black Eyed Peas (2004)
Help / La Na Nee Nee Noo Noo (3)	Bananarama (1989)		
		Hey Matthew (9)	Karel Fialka (1987)
Help Me Make It Through The Night (6)	John Holt (1974)	Hey Music Lover (6)	S Express (1989)
		Hey Now (Girls Just Want To Have Fun) (4)	Cyndi Lauper (1994)
Help The Aged (8)	Pulp (1997)		
Help Yourself (5)	Tom Jones (1968)	Hey Paula (8)	Paul & Paula (1963)

Title	Group/Artiste	Title	Group/Artiste
Hey Rock And Roll (2) first hit	Showaddywaddy (1974)	Hold Me Now (2)	Johnny Logan (1987)
Hey Sexy Lady (10)	Shaggy (2002)	Hold Me Now (4)	Thompson Twins (1983)
Hey There (4)	Rosemary Clooney (1955)		
Hey There (5)	Johnnie Ray (1955)	Hold Me Thrill Me Kiss Me (3)	Muriel Smith (1953)
(Hey There) Lonely Girl (4)	Eddie Holman (1974)	Hold Me Thrill Me Kiss Me Kill Me (2)	U2 (1995)
Hey Whatever (4)	Westlife (2003)	Hold Me Tight (5) first hit	Johnny Nash (1968)
Hey Ya! (3)	Outkast (2003)	Hold My Hand (1)	Don Cornell (1954)
(Hey You) The Rocksteady Crew (6)	Rocksteady Crew (1983)	Hold On (5) first hit	En Vogue (1990)
Hey! Baby (2)	Bruce Channel (1962)	Hold On (6)	Wilson Phillips (1990)
Hi Hi Hi / C Moon (5)	Wings (1972)	Hold On Me (10)	Phixx (2003)
Hi Ho Silver (5)	Jim Diamond (1986)	Hold On Tight (4)	Electric Light Orchestra (1981)
Hi-Ho Silver Lining (14) first hit	Jeff Beck (1967)		
Hidden Agenda (10)	Craig David (2003)	Hold On To My Love (7)	Jimmy Ruffin (1980)
Hide U (6)	Kosheen (2001)	Hold Tight (4)	Dave Dee, Dozy, Beaky, Mick & Tich (1966)
Hideaway (10)	Dave Dee, Dozy, Beaky, Mick & Tich (1966)		
		Hold Your Head Up (5) first and biggest hit	Argent (1972)
Hideaway (9)	De'Lacy (1995)	Holding Back The Years (2)	Simply Red (1986)
Hi-Fidelity (5)	Kids From Fame (1982)	Holding On For You (5)	Liberty X (2002)
		Holding Out For A Hero (2)	Bonnie Tyler (1985)
High (8)	Cure (1992)	Hole In My Shoe (2)	Neil (1984)
High (4)	Lighthouse Family (1998)	Hole In My Shoe (2)	Traffic (1967)
		Hole In The Ground (9) first hit	Bernard Cribbins (1962)
High Class Baby (7)	Cliff Richard with The Drifters (1958)	Hole In The Head (1)	Sugababes (2003)
High Energy (5)	Evelyn Thomas (1984)	Holiday (6)	Madonna (1984)
		Holiday Rap (6)	MC Miker G & Deejay Sven (1986)
High Hopes (re-entry) (6)	Frank Sinatra (1959)	Holiday (re-entry) (2)	Madonna (1985)
High In The Sky (6)	Amen Corner (1968)	Holiday (re-issue) (5)	Madonna (1991)
High Life (8)	Modern Romance (1983)	Holidays In The Sun (8)	Sex Pistols (1977)
		Holler / Let Love Lead The Way (1)	Spice Girls (2000)
High Noon (Do Not Forsake Me) (7) first hit	Frankie Laine (1952)		
		Hollywood (2)	Madonna (2003)
High Time (4)	Paul Jones (1966)	Holy Cow (6)	Lee Dorsey (1966)
High Voltage / Points Of Authority (9)	Linkin Park (2002)	Holy Smoke (3)	Iron Maiden (1990)
		Homburg (6)	Procol Harum (1967)
Higher Ground (8)	UB40 (1993)	Home Lovin' Man (7)	Andy Williams (1970)
Higher State Of Consciousness (8)	Josh Wink (1995)	Homely Girl (5)	Chi-Lites (1974)
		Homely Girl (6)	UB40 (1989)
Higher State Of Consciousness (remix) (7)	Josh Wink (1996)	Homeward Bound (9)	Simon & Garfunkel (1966)
Hillbilly Rock Hillbilly Roll (7)	Woolpackers (1996)	Homing Waltz (9)	Vera Lynn (1952)
Hindu Times, The (1)	Oasis (2002)	Honey (3)	Mariah Carey (1997)
Hip To Hip / Can You Feel It (5)	V (2004)	Honey (2)	Bobby Goldsboro (1968)
Hippy Chick (re-entry) (8)	Soho (1991)		
Hippy Hippy Shake (2)	Swinging Blue Jeans (1963)	Honey Come Back (4)	Glen Campbell (1970)
History (8)	Mai Tai (1985)	Honey Honey (10)	Sweet Dreams (1974)
History / Ghosts (5)	Michael Jackson (1997)	Honey (re-issue) (2)	Bobby Goldsboro (1975)
Hit And Miss (10)	John Barry Seven (1960)	Honey To The Bee (3)	Billie (1999)
		Hong Kong Garden (7)	Siouxsie & The Banshees (1978)
Hit 'Em High (The Monstars' Anthem) (8)	B Real / Busta Rhymes / Coolio / LL Cool J / Method Man (1997)	Honky Tonk Women (1)	Rolling Stones (1969)
		Hooked On Classics (2)	Royal Philharmonic Orchestra (1981)
Hit Me With Your Rhythm Stick (1)	Ian Dury & The Blockheads (1978)	Hooray Hooray (It's A Cheeky Holiday) (3)	Cheeky Girls (2003)
Hit That Perfect Beat (3)	Bronski Beat (1985)	Hooray Hooray It's A Holi-Holiday (3)	Boney M (1979)
Hit The Road Jack (6)	Ray Charles (1961)		
Hold Back The Night (5)	Trammps (1975)	Hoots Mon (1)	Lord Rockingham's XI (1958)
Hold Me (3)	P J Proby (1964)		
Hold Me Close (1)	David Essex (1975)	Hopelessly Devoted To You (2)	Olivia Newton-John (1978)
Hold Me In Your Arms (10)	Rick Astley (1989)		

MUSIC POP

Title	Group/Artiste	Title	Group/Artiste
Horny (5)	Mark Morrison (1996)	How Wonderful You Are (2)	Gordon Haskell (2001)
Horny (2)	Mousse T vs Hot 'N' Juicy (1998)	How You Remind Me (4)	Nickelback (2002)
Horse With No Name (re-entry) (3)	America (1972)	Howzat (4)	Sherbet (1976)
Hot Diggity (Dog Ziggity Boom) (4)	Perry Como (1956)	Human (8)	Human League (1986)
Hot In Herre (4)	Nelly (2002)	Human Nature (10)	Gary Clail On U-Sound System (1994)
Hot Love (1)	T Rex (1971)		
(Hot S**t) Country Grammar (7)	Nelly (2000)	Human Nature (8)	Madonna (1995)
Hot Stuff (9)	Arsenal FC (1998)	Humpin' Around (remix) (8)	Bobby Brown (1995)
Hot Toddy (6)	Ted Heath Orchestra (1953)	Hundred Mile High City (4)	Ocean Colour Scene (1997)
Hotel (3)	Cassidy featuring R Kelly (2004)	Hundred Pounds Of Clay, A (9)	Craig Douglas (1961)
Hotel California (8)	Eagles (1977)	Hungry Like The Wolf (5)	Duran Duran (1982)
Hotlegs / I Was Only Joking (5)	Rod Stewart (1978)	Hunting High And Low (5)	A-Ha (1986)
Hound Dog (2)	Elvis Presley (1956)	Hurdy Gurdy Man (4)	Donovan (1968)
House Arrest (3)	Krush (1987)	Hurry Up Harry (10)	Sham 69 (1978)
House Nation (re-entry) (8)	Housemaster Boyz and The Rude Boy Of The House (1987)	Hurt (4)	Manhattans (1976)
		Hurt So Good (4)	Susan Cadogan (1975)
House Of Fun (1)	Madness (1982)	Husan (7)	Bhangra Knights vs Husan (2003)
House Of Love (10) first hit	East 17 (1992)		
House Of The Rising Sun (1)	Animals (1964)	Hush (2)	Kula Shaker (1997)
House Of The Rising Sun (4)	Frijid Pink (1970)	Hustle, The (3)	Van McCoy & Soul City Symphony (1975)
House That Jack Built, The (4)	Alan Price Set (1967)		
House That Jack Built, The (9)	Tracie (1983)	Hymn To Her (8)	Pretenders (1986)
Housecall (remix) (8)	Shabba Ranks featuring Maxi Priest (1993)	Hyperballad (8)	Björk (1996)
		Hypnotize (10)	Notorious BIG (1997)
How About That! (4)	Adam Faith (1960)	I Ain't Gonna Stand For It (10)	Stevie Wonder (1980)
How Am I Supposed To Live Without You (3) first hit	Michael Bolton (1990)	I Am A Cider Drinker (Paloma Blanca) (3)	Wurzels (1976)
How Bizarre (5)	OMC (1996)	I Am Blessed (7)	Eternal (1995)
How 'Bout Us (5) first and only hit	Champaign (1981)	I Am The Law (32) first hit	Anthrax (1987)
		I Am The Beat (6)	Look (1980)
How Can I Be Sure (1)	David Cassidy (1972)	I Am ... I Said (4)	Neil Diamond (1971)
How Can I Love You More (remix) (8)	M People (1996)	I Beg Your Pardon (5)	Kon Kan (1989)
		I Begin To Wonder (2)	Dannii Minogue (2003)
How Can We Be Lovers (10)	Michael Bolton (1990)	I Believe (2)	Bachelors (1964)
		I Believe (11) first hit	Marcella Detroit (1994)
How Come (4)	D12 (2004)	I Believe (6)	EMF (1991)
How Come, How Long (10)	Babyface featuring Stevie Wonder (1997)	I Believe (1)	Frankie Laine (1953)
		I Believe / Up On The Roof (1)	Robson & Jerome (1995)
How Deep Is Your Love (3)	Bee Gees (1977)	I Believe I Can Fly (1)	R Kelly (1997)
How Deep Is Your Love (9)	Dru Hill (1998)	I Believe In A Thing Called Love (2)	Darkness (2003)
How Deep Is Your Love (1)	Take That (1996)	I Believe In Christmas (9)	Tweenies (2001)
How Do I Live (7)	LeAnn Rimes (1998)	I Believe In Father Christmas (2)	Greg Lake (1975)
How Do You Do It (1)	Gerry & The Pacemakers (1963)	I Believe (In Love) (8)	Hot Chocolate (1971)
How Do You Want Me To Love You? (10)	911 (1998)	I Believe (re-issue) (7)	Happy Clappers (1995)
(How Does It Feel To Be) On Top Of The World (9)	England United (1998)	I Believe In You (2)	Kylie Minogue (2004)
How High (6)	Charlatans (1997)	I Believe My Heart (2)	Duncan James & Keedie (2004)
How Many Tears (10)	Bobby Vee (1961)		
(How Much Is) That Doggie In The Window (9)	Patti Page (1953)	I Belong To You (6)	Gina G (1996)
		I Breathe Again (5)	Adam Rickett (1999)
(How Much Is) That Doggie In The Window (1)	Lita Roza (1953)	I Can Do It (7)	Rubettes (1975)
		I Can Hear Music (10)	Beach Boys (1969)
How Much Love (10)	Leo Sayer (1977)	I Can Hear The Grass Grow (5)	Move (1967)
How Soon (10)	Henry Mancini Orchestra (1964)	I Can Help (6)	Billy Swan (1974)
		I Can Make You Feel Good (8)	Kavana (1997)
How Will I Know (5)	Whitney Houston (1986)	I Can Make You Feel Good (7)	Shalamar (1982)
		I Can Only Disappoint U (8)	Mansun (2000)

Title	Group/Artiste	Title	Group/Artiste
I Can Prove It (8)	Phil Fearon (1986)	I Don't Want To (9)	Toni Braxton (1997)
I Can See Clearly Now (5)	Johnny Nash (1972)	I Don't Want To Miss A Thing (4)	Aerosmith (1998)
I Can See For Miles (10)	Who (1967)	I Don't Want To Put A Hold	Berni Flint (1977)
I Can't Break Down (2)	Sinead Quinn (2003)	On You (3)	
I Can't Control Myself (2)	Troggs (1966)	I Don't Want To Talk About It (3)	Everything But The
I Can't Dance (7)	Genesis (1992)		Girl (1988)
I Can't Explain (8) first hit	Who (1965)	I Don't Want To Talk About It /	Rod Stewart (1977)
(I Can't Get No) Satisfaction (1)	Rolling Stones	First Cut Is The Deepest (1)	
	(1965)	I Drove All Night (7)	Cyndi Lauper (1989)
I Can't Go For That	Daryl Hall & John	I Drove All Night (7)	Roy Orbison (1992)
(No Can Do) (8)	Oates (1982)	I Eat Cannibals Part 1 (8)	Toto Coelo (1982)
(I Can't Help) Falling In Love	UB40 (1993)	I Feel Fine (1)	Beatles (1964)
With You (1)		I Feel For You (1)	Chaka Khan (1984)
I Can't Help Myself (7)	Lucid (1998)	I Feel For You (9)	Bob Sinclair (2000)
I Can't Help Myself	Four Tops (1970)	I Feel Like Buddy Holly (7)	Alvin Stardust (1984)
(re-issue) (10)		I Feel Love (1)	Donna Summer
I Can't Leave You Alone (9)	George McCrae		(1977)
	(1974)	I Feel Love (re-issue) (8)	Donna Summer
I Can't Let Go (2)	Hollies (1966)		(1995)
I Can't Let Maggie Go (8)	Honeybus (1968)	I Feel Love (medley) (3)	Bronski Beat with
I Can't Read You (6)	Daniel Bedingfield		Marc Almond
	(2003)		(1985)
I Can't Stand It (7)	Captain Hollywood	I Feel The Earth Move (7)	Martika (1989)
	Project (1990)	I Feel You (1)	Peter Andre (1996)
I Can't Stand The Rain (5)	Eruption (1978)	I Feel You (8)	Depeche Mode
I Can't Stand Up For Falling	Elvis Costello (1980)		(1993)
Down (4)		I Finally Found Someone (10)	Barbra Streisand &
I Can't Stop Lovin' You	Leo Sayer (1978)		Bryan Adams
(Though I Try) (6)			(1997)
I Can't Stop Loving You (1)	Ray Charles (1962)	I Found Lovin' (7)	Fatback Band (1987)
I Can't Take The Power (7)	Off-Shore (1990)	I Found Lovin' (9)	Steve Walsh (1987)
I Can't Tell A Waltz From	Alma Cogan (1954)	I Found Someone (5)	Cher (1987)
A Tango (6)		I Get A Kick Out Of You (7)	Gary Shearston
I Can't Tell The Bottom From	Hollies (1970)		(1974)
The Top (7)		I Get A Little Sentimental	New Seekers (1974)
I Can't Wait (2)	Nu Shooz (1986)	Over You (5)	
I Close My Eyes And Count	Dusty Springfield	I Get Around (7)	Beach Boys (1964)
To Ten (4)	(1968)	I Get Lonely (5)	Janet Jackson
I Could Be Happy (7)	Altered Images		(1998)
	(1981)	I Get So Lonely (5)	Nat 'King' Cole & The
I Could Be So Good For You (3)	Dennis Waterman		Four Knights (1954)
	with The Dennis	I Get So Lonely (re-entry) (10)	Nat 'King' Cole & The
	Waterman Band		Four Knights (1954)
	(1980)	I Get The Sweetest Feeling (9)	Jackie Wilson (1972)
I Could Easily Fall (In Love	Cliff Richard & The	I Get The Sweetest Feeling/	Jackie Wilson (1987)
With You) (9)	Shadows (1964)	(Your Love Keeps	
I Couldn't Live Without	Petula Clark (1966)	Lifting Me) Higher and Higher	
Your Love (6)		(re-issue) (3)	
I Did What I Did For Maria (2)	Tony Christie (1971)	I Get Weak (10)	Belinda Carlisle
I Didn't Know I Loved You	Gary Glitter (1972)		(1988)
(Til I Saw You Rock 'N' Roll) (4)		I Go Ape (9) first hit	Neil Sedaka (1959)
I Didn't Mean To Turn You On (9)	Robert Palmer (1986)	I Go To Sleep (7)	Pretenders (1981)
I Die: You Die (6)	Gary Numan (1980)	I Got 5 On It (3)	Luniz (1996)
I Don't Believe In If Anymore (8)	Roger Whittaker	I Got You Babe (1)	Sonny & Cher (1965)
	(1970)	I Got You Babe (1)	UB40 featuring
I Don't Care (7)	Shakespears Sister		Chrissie Hynde
	(1992)		(1985)
I Don't Know Anybody Else (4)	Black Box (1990)	I Got You Babe / Soda Pop (5)	Avid Merrion, Davina
I Don't Know Why (7)	Eden Kane (1962)		McCall & Patsy
I Don't Like Mondays (1)	Boomtown Rats		Kensit (2004)
	(1979)	I Guess That's Why They Call It	Elton John (1983)
I Don't Wanna Dance (1)	Eddy Grant (1982)	The Blues (5)	
I Don't Wanna Fight (7)	Tina Turner (1993)	I Have A Dream (2)	Abba (1979)
I Don't Wanna Get Hurt (7)	Donna Summer	I Have A Dream / Seasons In	Westlife (1999)
	(1989)	The Sun (1)	
I Don't Wanna Know (1)	Mario Winans	I Have Forgiven Jesus (10)	Morrissey (2004)
	featuring Enya &	I Have Nothing (3)	Whitney Houston
	P Diddy (2004)		(1993)
I Don't Wanna Lose You (8)	Tina Turner (1989)	I Haven't Stopped Dancing Yet (9)	Pat & Mick (1989)
I Don't Want A Lover (8)	Texas (1989)	I Hear You Knocking (1)	Dave Edmunds
I Don't Want Our Loving To Die (5)	Herd (1968)		(1970)

MUSIC

POP

Title	Group/Artiste	Title	Group/Artiste
I Hear You Now (8)	Jon & Vangelis (1980)	I Need Love (8)	LL Cool J (1987)
I Heard It Through The Grapevine (1)	Marvin Gaye (1969)	I Need You (3)	BVSMP (1988)
		I Need You (10)	Deuce (1995)
I Heard It Through The Grapevine (re-issue) (8)	Marvin Gaye (1986)	I Need Your Lovin' (8)	Alyson Williams (1989)
I Hope You Dance (2)	Ronan Keating (2004)	I Only Have Eyes For You (1)	Art Garfunkel (1975)
I Just Called To Say I Love You (1)	Stevie Wonder (1984)	I Only Wanna Be With You (4)	Bay City Rollers (1976)
I Just Can't Help Believing (6)	Elvis Presley (1971)	I Only Want To Be With You (4) first hit	Dusty Springfield (1963)
I Just Can't Stop Loving You (1)	Michael Jackson (1987)	I Only Want To Be With You (4)	Tourists (1979)
(I Just) Died In Your Arms Tonight (4)	Cutting Crew (1986) first hit	I Owe You Nothing (1)	Bros (1988)
		I Pretend (1)	Des O'Connor (1968)
I Just Don't Have The Heart (3)	Cliff Richard (1989)	I Put A Spell On You (9)	Alan Price Set (1966)
I Just Don't Know What To Do With Myself (3)	Dusty Springfield (1964)	I Put A Spell On You (re-issue) (8)	Sonique (2000)
I Just Wanna Be Loved (4)	Culture Club (1998)		
I Just Want To Make Love To You (5)	Etta James (1996)	I Quit (4)	Bros (1988)
		I Quit (8)	Hepburn (1999)
I Knew I Loved You (10)	Savage Garden (1999)	I Remember Elvis Presley (The King Is Dead) (4)	Danny Mirror (1977)
I Knew You Were Waiting (For Me) (1)	Aretha Franklin & George Michael (1987)	I Remember You (1)	Frank Ifield (1962)
		I Saw Him Standing There (8)	Tiffany (1988)
I Know Him So Well (1)	Elaine Paige & Barbara Dickson (1985)	I Saw Mommy Kissing Santa Claus (3)	Jimmy Boyd (1953)
I Know What You Want (3)	Busta Rhymes & Mariah Carey featuring The Flipmode Squad (2003)	I Saw Mommy Kissing Santa Claus (re-entry) (6)	Beverley Sisters (1953)
		I Say A Little Prayer (4)	Aretha Franklin (1968)
		I Second That Emotion (9)	Japan (1982)
I Know Where It's At (4) first hit	All Saints (1997)	I See A Star (8)	Mouth & Macneal (1974)
I Like It (1)	Gerry & The Pacemakers (1963)	I See The Moon (1)	Stargazers (1954)
I Like It (9)	Narcotic Thrust (2004)	I Shot The Sheriff (9)	Eric Clapton (1974)
		I Shot The Sheriff (2)	Warren G (1997)
I Like To Move It (5)	Reel 2 Real With The Mad Stuntman (1994)	I Should Be So Lucky (1) first hit	Kylie Minogue (1988)
		I Should Have Known Better (1)	Jim Diamond (1984)
I Lost My Heart To A Starship Trooper (6)	Sarah Brightman & Hot Gossip (1978)	I Shoulda Loved Ya (8)	Narada Michael Walden (1980)
I Love It When We Do (5)	Ronan Keating (2002)	I Still Believe (3)	Ronnie Hilton (1954)
		I Still Believe In You (7)	Cliff Richard (1992)
I Love My Radio (My Deejay's Radio) (6)	Taffy (1987)	I Still Haven't Found What I'm Looking For (6) biggest hit	Chimes (1990)
I Love Rock 'N' Roll (4)	Joan Jett & The Blackhearts (1982)	I Still Haven't Found What I'm Looking For (6)	U2 (1987)
I Love The Sound Of Breaking Glass (7)	Nick Lowe (1978)	I Surrender (3)	Rainbow (1981)
		I Swear (2)	All-4-One (1994)
I Love The Way You Love Me (2)	Boyzone (1998)	I Think I Love You (10)	Kaci (2002)
I Love To Love (1) first hit	Tina Charles (1976)	I Think I'm Paranoid (9)	Garbage (1998)
I Love You (1)	Cliff Richard & The Shadows (1960)	I Think Of You (5)	Merseybeats (1964)
		I Think We're Alone Now (1)	Tiffany (1988)
I Love You (10)	Donna Summer (1977)	I Touch Myself (10)	Divinyls (1991)
		I Try (7)	Macy Gray (1999)
I Love You Always Forever (5)	Donna Lewis (1996)	I Turn To You (1)	Melanie C (2000)
I Love You Baby (3)	Paul Anka (1957)	I Understand (5)	Freddie & The Dreamers (1964)
I Love You Because (5)	Jim Reeves (1964)		
I Love You Love Me Love (1)	Gary Glitter (1973)	I Wanna Be A Hippy (6)	Technohead (1996)
I Love You Smile (2)	Shanice (1992)	I Wanna Be The Only One (1)	Eternal featuring BeBe Winans (1997)
I Luv U Baby (remix) (2)	Original (1995)		
I Miss You (8)	Blink 182 (2004)	I Wanna Be U (6)	Chocolate Puma (2001)
I Miss You (9)	Haddaway (1993)	I Wanna Be Your Lover (41) first hit	Prince (1980)
I Must Be Seeing Things (6)	Gene Pitney (1965)		
I Need A Girl (Part One) (4)	P Diddy featuring Usher & Loon (2002)	I Wanna Be Your Man (12)	Rolling Stones (1963)
		I Wanna Dance Wit Choo (6)	Disco Tex & Sex-O-Lettes (1975)
I Need A Lover Tonight (7)	Ken Doh (1996)	I Wanna Dance With Somebody (Who Loves Me) (1)	Whitney Houston (1987)

Title	Group/Artiste	Title	Group/Artiste
I Wanna Do It With You (8)	Barry Manilow (1982)	I Wish It Could Be Christmas Everyday (4)	Wizzard (1973)
(I Wanna Give You) Devotion (2)	Nomad (1991)	I Wish It Would Rain Down (7)	Phil Collins (1990)
I Wanna Go Home (The Wreck Of The John 'B') (5)	Lonnie Donegan & Wally Stott Orchestra (1960)	I Wonder (4)	Dickie Valentine (1955)
I Wanna Hold Your Hand (9)	Dollar (1979)	I Wonder Why (2)	Showaddywaddy (1978)
(I Wanna) Love My Life Away (26) first hit	Gene Pitney (1961)	I Wonder Why (5)	Curtis Stigers (1992)
I Wanna Love You Forever (7)	Jessica Simpson (2000)	I Won't Change You (9)	Sophie Ellis-Bextor (2004)
I Wanna Sex You Up (1) first hit	Color Me Badd (1991)	I Won't Forget You (3)	Jim Reeves (1964)
I Wanna Stay With You (6)	Gallagher & Lyle (1976)	I Won't Last A Day Without You / Goodbye To Love (9)	Carpenters (1972)
I Want Candy (9)	Bow Wow Wow (1982)	I Won't Let The Sun Go Down On Me (re-issue) (2)	Nik Kershaw (1984)
I Want It All (3)	Queen (1989)	I Won't Let You Down (3)	PhD (1982)
I Want It That Way (1)	Backstreet Boys (1999)	I Won't Run Away (7)	Alvin Stardust (1984)
I Want Love (9)	Elton John (2001)	I Wouldn't Trade You For The World (4)	Bachelors (1964)
(I Want To Be) Elected (9)	Mr Bean and The Smear Campaign with Bruce Dickinson (1992)	I.O.U. (2)	Freeez (1983)
		Ice Ice Baby (1)	Vanilla Ice (1990)
		Ice In The Sun (8)	Status Quo (1968)
I Want To Be Free (8)	Toyah (1981)	I'd Do Anything For Love (But I Won't Do That) (1)	Meat Loaf (1993)
I Want To Break Free (3)	Queen (1984)		
I Want To Hold Your Hand (1)	Beatles (1963)	I'd Lie For You (And That's The Truth) (2)	Meat Loaf (1995)
I Want To Know What Love Is (1)	Foreigner (1984)		
I Want To Stay Here (3)	Steve & Eydie (1963)	I'd Like To Teach The World To Sing (1)	New Seekers (1971)
I Want To Wake Up With You (1)	Boris Gardiner (1986)	I'd Love You To Want Me (5)	Lobo (1974)
I Want You Back (1) first hit	Melanie B featuring Missy 'Misdemeanor' Elliott (1998)	I'd Never Find Another You (5)	Billy Fury (1961)
		I'd Rather Jack (8)	Reynolds Girls (1989)
		Idle Gossip (3)	Perry Como (1954)
		If (1)	Telly Savalas (1975)
I Want You Back (5)	Bananarama (1988)	If Anyone Finds This I Love You (4)	Ruby Murray with Anne Warren (1955)
I Want You Back (4)	Cleopatra (1998)		
I Want You Back (2)	Jackson 5 (1970)	If I Can't / Them Thangs (10)	50 Cent / G-Unit (2004)
I Want You Back (5)	N Sync (1999)		
I Want You Back (remix) (8)	Michael Jackson & The Jackson 5 (1988)	If I Can't Have You (4)	Yvonne Elliman (1978)
		If I Could Turn Back The Hands Of Time (3)	R Kelly (1999)
I Want You For Myself (2)	Another Level / Ghostface Killah (1999)	If I Could Turn Back Time (6)	Cher (1989)
		If I Didn't Care (9)	David Cassidy (1974)
I Want Your Love (10)	Atomic Kitten (2000)	If I Give My Heart To You (4)	Doris Day (1954)
I Want Your Love (4)	Chic (1979)	If I Give My Heart To You (re-entry) (3)	Joan Regan (1954)
I Want Your Love (5)	Transvision Vamp (1988)	If I Had A Hammer (4)	Trini Lopez (1963)
I Want Your Sex (3)	George Michael (1987)	If I Had Words (3)	Scott Fitzgerald and Yvonne Keely with The St Thomas More School Choir (1978)
I Was Kaiser Bill's Batman (5)	Whistling Jack Smith (1967)		
I Was Made For Dancin' (4)	Leif Garrett (1979)		
I Was Made To Love Her (5)	Stevie Wonder (1967)	If I Let You Go (1)	Westlife (1999)
I (Who Have Nothing) (6)	Shirley Bassey (1963)	If I Never See You Again (3)	Wet Wet Wet (1997)
I Will (4)	Ruby Winters (1977)	If I Only Had Time (3)	John Rowles (1968)
I Will Always Love You (1)	Whitney Houston (1992)	If I Said You Have A Beautiful Body Would You Hold It Against Me (3)	Bellamy Brothers (1979)
I Will Always Love You (6)	Rik Waller (2002)		
I Will Come To You (5)	Hanson (1997)	If I Told You That (9)	Whitney Houston & George Michael (2000)
I Will Return (5)	Springwater (1971)		
I Will Survive (16)	Arrival (1970)		
I Will Survive (1)	Gloria Gaynor (1979)	If I Was (1)	Midge Ure (1985)
I Will Survive (remix) (5)	Gloria Gaynor (1993)	If I Were A Carpenter (9)	Bobby Darin (1966)
I Wish (5)	Stevie Wonder (1976)	If I Were A Carpenter (7)	Four Tops (1968)
		If I Were A Rich Man (9)	Topol (1967)
(I Wish I Knew How It Would Feel To Be) Free / One (6)	Lighthouse Family (2001)	If It Happens Again (9)	UB40 (1984)
		If It Makes You Happy (9)	Sheryl Crow (1996)

Title	Group/Artiste	Title	Group/Artiste
If Not For You (7) first hit	Olivia Newton-John (1971)	I'll Be There For You – You're All I Need To Get By (10)	Method Man featuring Mary J Blige (1995)
If Not You (5)	Dr Hook (1976)		
If Only I Could (3)	Sydney Youngblood (1989)	I'll Be There For You (re-entry) (5)	Rembrandts (1997)
(If Paradise Is) Half As Nice (1)	Amen Corner (1969)	I'll Be There For You (Theme From Friends) (3)	Rembrandts (1995)
If She Should Come To You (4)	Anthony Newley (1960)	I'll Be Your Angel (9)	Kira (2003)
If The Kids Are United (9)	Sham 69 (1978)	I'll Be Your Baby Tonight (6)	Robert Palmer & UB40 (1990)
If The Whole World Stopped Loving (3)	Val Doonican (1967)	I'll Come When You Call (6)	Ruby Murray (1955)
If There's Any Justice (3)	Lemar (2004)	I'll Find My Way Home (6)	Jon & Vangelis (1981)
If Tomorrow Never Comes (1)	Ronan Keating (2002)	I'll Fly For You (9)	Spandau Ballet (1984)
If Ya Gettin' Down (2)	Five (1999)	I'll Get By (10)	Shirley Bassey (1961)
If You Believe (re-entry) (7)	Johnnie Ray (1955)		
If You Buy This Record Your Life Will Be Better (3)	Tamperer featuring Maya (1998)	I'll Keep You Satisfied (4)	Billy J Kramer And The Dakotas (1963)
If You Can't Give Me Love (4)	Suzi Quatro (1978)		
If You Can't Stand The Heat (10)	Bucks Fizz (1982)	I'll Make Love To You (5)	Boyz II Men (1994)
If You Come Back (1)	Blue (2001)	I'll Never Break Your Heart (re-issue) (8)	Backstreet Boys (1996)
If You Come To Me (3)	Atomic Kitten (2003)		
If You Don't Know Me By Now (9)	Harold Melvin & The Bluenotes (1973)	I'll Never Fall In Love Again (1)	Bobbie Gentry (1969)
If You Don't Know Me By Now (2)	Simply Red (1989)	I'll Never Fall In Love Again (2)	Tom Jones (1967)
If You Ever (2)	East 17 featuring Gabrielle (1996)	I'll Never Find Another You (1) first hit	Seekers (1965)
If You Go Away (8)	Terry Jacks (1974)	I'll Never Get Over You (4)	Johnny Kidd & The Pirates (1963)
If You Go Away (9)	New Kids On The Block (1991)	I'll Pick A Rose For My Rose (10)	Marv Johnson (1969)
If You Gotta Go Go Now (2)	Manfred Mann (1965)		
If You Gotta Make A Fool Of Somebody (3)	Freddie & The Dreamers (1963)	I'll Remember (Theme From 'With Honours') (7)	Madonna (1994)
If You Had My Love (4)	Jennifer Lopez (1999)	I'll Say Forever My Love (7)	Jimmy Ruffin (1970)
If You Leave Me Now (1)	Chicago (1976)	I'll Stand By You (10)	Pretenders (1994)
If You Let Me Stay (7) first hit	Terence Trent D'Arby (1987)	I'll Stand By You (1)	Girls Aloud (2004)
		I'll Stop At Nothing (4)	Sandie Shaw (1965)
If You Love Me (8)	Brownstone (1995)	I'll Take You Home Again Kathleen (7)	Slim Whitman (1957)
If You Only Let Me In (6)	MN8 (1995)		
If You Think You Know How To Love Me (3)	Smokie (1975)	I'm A Believer (3)	EMF & Reeves & Mortimer (1995)
If You Tolerate This Your Children Will Be Next (1)	Manic Street Preachers (1998)	I'm A Believer (1)	Monkees (1967)
		I'm A Boy (2)	Who (1966)
If You Wanna Party (9)	Molella with The Outhere Brothers (1995)	I'm A Clown / Some Kind Of Summer (3)	David Cassidy (1973)
		I'm A Man (8) first hit	Chicago (1970)
If You Were With Me Now (4)	Kylie Minogue & Keith Washington (1991)	I'm A Man (9)	Spencer Davis Group (1967)
		I'm A Man Not A Boy (7)	North & South (1997)
If You're Looking For A Way Out (6)	Odyssey (1980)	I'm A Slave For You (4)	Britney Spears (2001)
If You're Not The One (1)	Daniel Bedingfield (2002)	I'm A Tiger (9)	Lulu (1968)
Ignition (remix) (1)	R Kelly (2003)	I'm a Wonderful Thing Baby (4)	Kid Creole & The Coconuts (1982)
Iko Iko (10)	Natasha (1982)		
Il Silenzio (8)	Nini Rosso (1965)	I'm Alive (1)	Hollies (1965)
I'll Be (9)	Foxy Brown featuring Jay-Z (1997)	I'm Alive (6)	Stretch 'N' Vern present Maddogg (1996)
I'll Be Back (5) first and only hit	Arnee & The Terminators (1991)	(I'm Always Hearing) Wedding Bells (5)	Eddie Fisher (1955)
I'll Be Home (1)	Pat Boone (1956)	(I'm Always Touched By Your) Presence Dear (10)	Blondie (1978)
I'll Be Loving You (Forever) (5)	New Kids On The Block (1990)	I'm Coming Home (2)	Tom Jones (1967)
I'll Be Missing You (1)	Puff Daddy & Faith Evans with 112 (1997)	I'm Crying (8)	Animals (1964)
		I'm Doing Fine Now (4)	Pasadenas (1992)
I'll Be Satisfied (10)	Shakin' Stevens (1982)	I'm Easy / Be Aggressive (3)	Faith No More (1993)
I'll Be There (2)	Mariah Carey (1992)	I'm Every Woman (4)	Whitney Houston (1993)
I'll Be There (7)	Emma (2004)		
I'll Be There (4)	Jackson 5 (1970)	I'm Every Woman (remix) (8)	Chaka Khan (1989)

Title	Group/Artiste	Title	Group/Artiste
I'm Free (5)	Soup Dragons (1990)	I'm Walking Behind You (1)	Eddie Fisher with Hugo Winterhalter's Orchestra and Sally Sweetland (1953)
I'm Gonna Be Alright (3)	Jennifer Lopez (2002)		
I'm Gonna Be Strong (2)	Gene Pitney (1964)		
I'm Gonna Get Me A Gun (6)	Cat Stevens (1967)	I'm With You (7)	Avril Lavigne (2003)
I'm Gonna Get You (3)	Bizarre Inc featuring Angie Brown (1992)	I'm Your Angel (3)	Celine Dion & R Kelly (1998)
I'm Gonna Getcha Good (4)	Shania Twain (2002)	I'm Your Baby Tonight (5)	Whitney Houston (1990)
I'm Gonna Make You Love Me (3)	Diana Ross & The Supremes and The Temptations (1969)	I'm Your Man (1)	Wham! (1985)
		I'm Your Man (2)	Shane Richie (2003)
I'm Gonna Make You Mine (2)	Lou Christie (1969)	Imagine (6)	John Lennon (1975)
I'm Gonna Run Away From You (4)	Tami Lynn (1971)	Imagine (re-entry) (1)	John Lennon (1980)
		Imagine (re-issue) (3)	John Lennon (1999)
I'm Gonna Tear Your Playhouse Down (9)	Paul Young (1984)	Imitation Of Life (6)	REM (2001)
		Immortality (5)	Celine Dion with The Bee Gees (1998)
I'm In Heaven (9)	Jason Nevins / UKNY featuring Holly James (2003)	In A Broken Dream (3)	Python Lee Jackson (1972)
I'm In The Mood For Dancing (3)	Nolans (1979)	In A Golden Coach (3)	Billy Cotton & His Band (1953)
I'm Into Something Good (1)	Herman's Hermits (1964)	In A Golden Coach (7)	Dickie Valentine (1953)
I'm Leaving It (All) Up To You (2)	Donny & Marie Osmond (1974)	In All The Right Places (8)	Lisa Stansfield (1993)
I'm Like A Bird (5)	Nelly Furtado (2001)	In Betweenies, The / Father Christmas Do Not Touch Me (7)	Goodies (1974)
I'm Looking Out The Window / Do You Want To Dance (2)	Cliff Richard with Norrie Paramor / Cliff Richard & The Shadows (1962)	In Da Club (3)	50 Cent (2003)
		In Demand (6)	Texas (2000)
I'm Mandy Fly Me (6)	10CC (1976)	In Dreams (6)	Roy Orbison (1963)
I'm Not A Girl Not Yet A Woman (2)	Britney Spears (2002)	In Dulce Jubilo / On Horseback (4)	Mike Oldfield (1975)
I'm Not In Love (1)	10CC (1975)	In My Defence (8)	Freddie Mercury (1992)
I'm Not Scared (7)	Eighth Wonder (1988)	In My Eyes (9)	Milk Inc (2002)
I'm On Fire (4)	5000 Volts (1975)	In My Own Time (4)	Family (1971)
I'm On Fire / Born In The USA (5)	Bruce Springsteen (1985)	In My Place (2)	Coldplay (2002)
		In Our Lifetime (4)	Texas (1999)
I'm Only Sleeping / Off On Holiday (7)	Suggs (1995)	In Summer (5)	Billy Fury (1963)
		In The Air Tonight (2) first solo hit	Phil Collins (1981)
I'm Outta Love (6)	Anastacia (2000)	In The Air Tonight (remix) (4)	Phil Collins (1988)
I'm Over You (2)	Martine McCutcheon (2000)	In The Army Now (2)	Status Quo (1986)
		In The Bad Bad Old Days (8)	Foundations (1969)
I'm Real (4)	Jennifer Lopez (2001)	In The Closet (8)	Michael Jackson (1992)
I'm Right Here (5)	Samantha Mumba (2002)	In The Country (6)	Cliff Richard & The Shadows (1966)
I'm Still In Love With You (6)	Sean Paul featuring Sasha (2004)	In The End (8)	Linkin Park (2001)
		In The Ghetto (2)	Elvis Presley (1969)
I'm Still Standing (4)	Elton John (1983)	In The Middle (8)	Sugababes (2004)
I'm Still Waiting (1)	Diana Ross (1971)	In The Middle Of Nowhere (8)	Dusty Springfield (1965)
I'm Stone In Love With You (10)	Johnny Mathis (1975)	In The Name Of The Father (8)	Black Grape (1995)
I'm Stone In Love With You (9)	Stylistics (1972)	In The Navy (2)	Village People (1979)
I'm Telling You Now (2)	Freddie & The Dreamers (1963)	In The Shadows (3)	Rasmus (2004)
I'm The Leader Of The Gang (I Am) (1)	Gary Glitter (1973)	In The Summertime (1) first hit	Mungo Jerry (1970)
		In The Summertime (5)	Shaggy featuring Rayvon (1995)
I'm The Lonely One (8)	Cliff Richard & The Shadows (1964)	In The Year 2525 (Exordium And Terminus) (1)	Zager & Evans (1969) only hit
I'm The One (2)	Gerry & The Pacemakers (1964)	In These Arms (9)	Bon Jovi (1993)
		In Thoughts Of You (9)	Billy Fury (1965)
I'm The Urban Spaceman (5)	Bonzo Dog Doo-Dah Band (1968)	In Too Deep (6)	Belinda Carlisle (1996)
I'm Too Sexy (2) first hit	Right Said Fred (1991)	In Yer Face (9)	808 State (1991)
		In Your Arms (Rescue Me) (8)	Nu Generation (2000)
I'm Walking Backwards For Christmas / Bluebottle Blues (4)	Goons (1956)	In Your Eyes (7)	George Benson (1983)

Title	Group/Artiste	Title	Group/Artiste
In Your Eyes (3)	Kylie Minogue (2002)	Isn't She Lovely (4)	David Parton (1977)
In Your Room (8)	Depeche Mode (1994)	Israelites (1)	Desmond Dekker & Aces (1969)
In Zaire (4)	Johnny Wakelin (1976)	Israelites (re-issue) (10)	Desmond Dekker (1975)
Incommunicado (6)	Marillion (1987)	It Ain't What You Do It's The Way That You Do It (4)	Fun Boy Three & Bananarama (1982)
Incredible (remix) (8)	M-Beat featuring General Levy (1994)	It Began In Afrika (8)	Chemical Brothers (2001)
Incredible (What I Meant To Say) (9)	Darius (2003)	It Can't Be Right (8)	2play featuring Raghav & Naila Boss (2004)
Independent Women Part 1 (1)	Destiny's Child (2000)	It Didn't Matter (9)	Style Council (1987)
Indian Love Call (7)	Slim Whitman (1955)	It Doesn't Have To Be This Way (5)	Blow Monkeys (1987)
Indian Reservation (3)	Don Fardon (1970)	It Doesn't Matter (3)	Wyclef Jean (2000)
Indiana Wants Me (2)	R Dean Taylor (1971)	It Doesn't Matter Anymore (1)	Buddy Holly (1959)
Infinite Dreams (6)	Iron Maiden (1989)	It Don't Come Easy (4)	Ringo Starr (1971)
Infinity (5)	Guru Josh (1990)	It Feels So Good (remix) (1)	Sonique (2000)
Informer (2)	Snow (1993)	It Hurts So Much (8)	Jim Reeves (1965)
Inner Smile (6)	Texas (2001)	It Is Time To Get Funky (9)	D Mob (1989)
Innocent Eyes (9)	Delta Goodrem (2003)	It Keep Rainin' (Tears From Eyes) (2)	Bitty McLean (1993)
Innuendo (1)	Queen (1991)	It Miek (7)	Desmond Dekker & Aces (1969)
Insania (3)	Peter Andre (2004)	It Might As Well Rain Until September (3)	Carole King (1962)
Insanity (3)	Oceanic (1991)	It Must Be Him (2) first and biggest hit	Vikki Carr (1967)
Insatiable (8)	Darren Hayes (2002)	It Must Be Love (4)	Madness (1981)
Inside (1)	Stiltskin (1994)	It Must Be Love (re-issue) (6)	Madness (1992)
Inside Out (3)	Odyssey (1982)	It Must Have Been Love (3)	Roxette (1990)
Insomnia (3)	Faithless (1996)	It Must Have Been Love (re-issue) (10)	Roxette (1993)
Instant Karma (5)	John Lennon & The Plastic Ono Band (1970)	It Only Takes A Minute (9)	One Hundred Ton And A Feather (1976)
Instant Replay (8)	Dan Hartman (1978)	It Only Takes A Minute (7)	Take That (1992)
Instant Replay (10)	Yell! (1990)	It Only Took A Minute (6)	Joe Brown & The Bruvvers (1962)
Instinction (10)	Spandau Ballet (1982)	It Should Have Been Me (5)	Yvonne Fair (1976)
Interesting Drug (9)	Morrissey (1989)	It Started With A Kiss (5)	Hot Chocolate (1982)
Intergalactic (5)	Beastie Boys (1998)	It Takes More (7)	Ms Dynamite (2002)
International Bright Young Thing (7)	Jesus Jones (1991)	It Takes Scoop (9)	Fatman Scoop featuring The Crooklyn Clan (2004)
Into The Groove (1)	Madonna (1985)		
Into The Valley (10)	Skids (1979)	It Takes Two (5)	Rod Stewart & Tina Turner (1990)
Intuition (7)	Linx (1981)	It Wasn't Me (1)	Shaggy featuring Rikrok (2001)
Invisible (7)	D-Side (2003)		
Invisible Sun (2)	Police (1981)	Itchycoo Park (3)	Small Faces (1967)
Invisible Touch (live) (7)	Genesis (1992)	Itchycoo Park (re-issue) (9)	Small Faces (1975)
Ire Feelings (Skanga) (9)	Rupie Edwards (1974)	It'll Be Me (2)	Cliff Richard & The Shadows (1962)
Irish Blood English Heart (3)	Morrissey (2004)	It's A Fine Day (5)	Opus III (1992)
Irish Rover, The (8)	Pogues & The Dubliners (1987)	It's A Hard Life (6)	Queen (1984)
Irish Son (6)	Brian McFadden (2004)	It's A Heartache (4)	Bonnie Tyler (1977)
Iron Lion Zion (5)	Bob Marley & The Wailers (1992)	It's A Love Thing (9)	Whispers (1981)
Is It Cos I'm Cool (9)	Mousse T featuring Emma Lanford (2004)	It's A Miracle (4)	Culture Club (1984)
		It's A Sin (1)	Pet Shop Boys (1987)
Is There Anybody Out There (5)	Bassheads (1991)	It's All Coming Back To Me Now (3)	Celine Dion (1996)
Is There Something I Should Know (1)	Duran Duran (1983)	It's All Gravy (9)	Romeo featuring Christina Milian (2002)
Is This Love (9)	Bob Marley & The Wailers (1978)		
Is This Love (9)	Whitesnake (1987)	It's All In The Game (1)	Tommy Edwards (1958)
Is This Love? (3)	Alison Moyet (1986)	It's All In The Game (5)	Four Tops (1970)
Island In The Sun (3)	Harry Belafonte (1957)		
Island Of Dreams (5)	Springfields (1962)		
Islands In The Stream (7)	Kenny Rogers & Dolly Parton (1983)		
Isle Of Innisfree (3) first hit	Bing Crosby (1952)		
Isn't It A Wonder (2)	Boyzone (1997)		

Title	Group/Artiste	Title	Group/Artiste
It's All In The Game (2)	Cliff Richard & The Shadows (1963)	It's The Way You Make Me Feel / Too Busy Thinking 'Bout My Baby (2)	Steps (2001)
It's All Over (9)	Cliff Richard (1967)	It's Time For Love (5)	Chi-Lites (1975)
It's All Over Now (1)	Rolling Stones (1964)	It's Too Late (8)	Dina Carroll (1991)
It's Almost Tomorrow (1) first and only hit	Dreamweavers (1956)	It's Too Late (6)	Carole King (1971)
It's Alright (3)	East 17 (1993)	It's Too Late (8)	Quartz introducing Dina Carroll (1991)
It's Alright (5)	Pet Shop Boys (1989)	It's Too Soon To Know (7)	Pat Boone (1958)
It's Been So Long (4)	George McCrae (1975)	It's Wonderful (To Be Loved By You) (6)	Jimmy Ruffin (1970)
It's Different For The Girls (5)	Joe Jackson (1980)	It's Written In The Stars (7)	Paul Weller (2002)
It's For You (7)	Cilla Black (1964)	It's You (9)	Freddie Starr (1974)
It's Four In The Morning (3)	Faron Young (1972)	It's Your Life (5)	Smokie (1977)
It's Getting Better (8)	Mama Cass (1969)	Itsy Bitsy Teeny Weeny Yellow Polka Dot Bikini (1)	Bombalurina (1990)
It's Goin' Down (7)	X-Ecutioners (2002)	Itsy Bitsy Teeny Weeny Yellow Polka Dot Bikini (8)	Brian Hyland (1960)
It's Gonna Be A Cold Cold Christmas (4)	Dana (1975)	I've Been A Bad Bad Boy (5)	Paul Jones (1967)
It's Gonna Be Me (9)	N Sync (2000)	I've Been Losing You (8)	A-Ha (1986)
It's Good News Week (5)	Hedgehoppers Anonymous (1965)	I've Been Thinking About You (2)	Londonbeat (1990)
It's Grim Up North (10)	Justified Ancients Of Mu Mu (1991)	I've Got A Little Puppy (4)	Smurfs (1996)
It's Impossible (4)	Perry Como (1971)	I've Got A Little Something For You (2)	MN8 (1995)
It's In His Kiss (6)	Linda Lewis (1975)	I've Got You (6)	Martine McCutcheon (1999)
It's Late (3)	Ricky Nelson (1959)	I've Got You Under My Skin (4)	Frank Sinatra with Bono (1993)
It's Like That (1)	Run DMC vs Jason Nevins (1998)	I've Gotta Get A Message To You (1)	Bee Gees (1968)
It's Love (Trippin') (6)	Goldtrix presents Andrea Brown (2002)	(I've Had) The Time Of My Life (6)	Bill Medley & Jennifer Warnes (1987)
It's My Life (7)	Animals (1965)	(I've Had) The Time Of My Life (re-entry) (8)	Bill Medley & Jennifer Warnes (1990)
It's My Life (3)	Bon Jovi (2000)	I've Lost You (9)	Elvis Presley (1970)
It's My Life (2)	Dr Alban (1992)	I've Never Been To Me (1)	Charlene (1982)
It's My Party (9)	Lesley Gore (1963)	I've Told Every Little Star (7)	Linda Scott (1961)
It's My Party (1)	Dave Stewart with Barbara Gaskin (1981)	I've Waited So Long (3)	Anthony Newley (1959)
It's No Good (5)	Depeche Mode (1997)	Jack In The Box (7)	Moments (1977)
It's Not Right But It's OK (3)	Whitney Houston (1999)	Jack In The Box (4)	Clodagh Rodgers (1971)
It's Not Unusual (1) first hit	Tom Jones (1965)	Jack Mix II / III (4)	Mirage (1985)
It's Now Or Never (1)	Elvis Presley with The Jordanaires (1960)	Jack Mix IV (8)	Mirage (1987)
It's Oh So Quiet (4)	Björk (1995)	Jack That House Built, The (6)	Jack 'N' Chill (1988)
It's OK (3)	Atomic Kitten (2002)	Jack Your Body (1)	Steve 'Silk' Hurley (1987)
It's Only Love (29)	Bryan Adams & Tina Turner (1985)	Jackie (22) first solo hit	Scott Walker (1967)
It's Only Love / Beyond The Reef (3)	Elvis Presley (1980)	Jackie Wilson Said (I'm In Heaven When You Smile) (5)	Dexy's Midnight Runners (1982)
It's Only Make Believe (4)	Glen Campbell (1970)	Jailhouse Rock (1)	Elvis Presley (1958)
It's Only Make Believe (10)	Child (1978)	James Bond Theme (Moby's Re-Version) (8)	Moby (1997)
It's Only Make Believe (10)	Billy Fury (1964)	James Dean (I Wanna Know) (4)	Daniel Bedingfield (2002)
It's Only Make Believe (1) first hit	Conway Twitty (1958)	Jamming / Punky Reggae Party (9)	Bob Marley & The Wailers (1977)
It's Only Rock And Roll (10)	Rolling Stones (1974)	January (1)	Pilot (1975)
It's Over (10)	Clock (1997)	Japanese Boy (1)	Aneka (1981)
It's Over (8)	Funk Masters (1983)	Jarrow Song (6)	Alan Price (1974)
It's Over (10)	Level 42 (1987)	Jazz It Up (7)	Reel 2 Real (1996)
It's Over (1)	Roy Orbison (1964)	Je Ne Sais Pas Pourquoi (2)	Kylie Minogue (1988)
It's Raining (2)	Darts (1978)	Je T'Aime (Moi Non Plus) (9)	Judge Dread (1975)
It's Raining (10)	Shakin' Stevens (1981)	Je T'Aime ... Moi Non Plus (2)	Jane Birkin & Serge Gainsbourg (1969)
It's Raining Men (1)	Geri Halliwell (2001)	Je T'Aime ... Moi Non Plus (re-issue) (1)	Jane Birkin & Serge Gainsbourg (1969)
It's Raining Men (3)	Weather Girls (1984)	Jealous Guy (1)	Roxy Music (1981)

MUSIC POP

Title	Group/Artiste	Title	Group/Artiste
Jealous Mind (1)	Alvin Stardust (1974)	Jump To The Beat (8)	Dannii Minogue (1991)
Jealousy (2)	Billy Fury (1961)		
Jean Genie, The (2)	David Bowie (1972)	Jumpin' (6)	Liberty X (2003)
Jeans On (3)	David Dundas (1976)	Jumpin' Jumpin' (5)	Destiny's Child (2000)
Jeepster (2)	T Rex (1971)		
Jennifer Eccles (7)	Hollies (1968)	Jumping Jack Flash (1)	Rolling Stones (1968)
Jennifer Juniper (5)	Donovan (1968)		
Jenny From The Block (3)	Jennifer Lopez (2002)	Jungle Rock (3)	Hank Mizell (1976)
		Just A Girl (re-issue) (3)	No Doubt (1997)
Jerusalem (10)	Fat Les 2000 (2000)	Just A Little (1)	Liberty X (2002)
Jesamine (2)	Casuals (1968)	Just A Step From Heaven (8)	Eternal (1994)
Jesse Hold On (4)	B*Witched (1999)	Just An Illusion (2)	Imagination (1982)
Jesus To A Child (1)	George Michael (1996)	Just Another Day (5)	Jon Secada (1992)
		Just Around The Hill (8)	Sash (2000)
Jet (7)	Paul McCartney & Wings (1974)	Just Can't Get Enough (8)	Depeche Mode (1981)
Jig A Jig (7)	East Of Eden (1971)	Just Don't Want To Be Lonely (9)	Freddie McGregor (1987)
Jilted John (4) first and only hit	Jilted John (1978)		
Jingle Bell Rock (7)	Max Bygraves (1959)	Just For You (10)	Glitter Band (1974)
Jive Talkin' (5)	Bee Gees (1975)	Just For You (8)	M People (1997)
Jive Talkin' (7)	Boogie Box High (1987)	Just Got Lucky (7)	Jo Boxers (1983)
		Just Like A Pill (1)	Pink (2002)
Joan Of Arc (5)	Orchestral Manoeuvres In The Dark (1981)	Just Like A Woman (10)	Manfred Mann (1966)
		Just Like Eddie (5)	Heinz (1963)
Joanna (7)	Scott Walker (1968)	(Just Like) Starting Over (1)	John Lennon (1980)
Joanna / Tonight (2)	Kool & The Gang (1984)	Just Looking (4)	Stereophonics (1999)
Joe Le Taxi (3)	Vanessa Paradis (1988)	Just Lose It (1)	Eminem (2004)
		Just Loving You (6)	Anita Harris (1967)
John And Julie (6)	Eddie Calvert (1955)	Just My Imagination (Running Away With Me) (8)	Temptations (1971)
Johnny Come Home (8)	Fine Young Cannibals (1985)	Just One Look (2)	Hollies (1964)
Johnny Reggae (3)	Piglets (1971)	Just One More Night (8)	Yellow Dog (1978)
Johnny Remember Me (1)	John Leyton (1961)	Just One Smile (8)	Gene Pitney (1966)
Johnny Will (4)	Pat Boone (1961)	Just Say No (5)	Grange Hill Cast (1986)
Join In And Sing Again (9)	Johnston Brothers (1955)	Just The Two Of Us (2)	Will Smith (1998)
Join Together (9)	Who (1972)	Just The Way I'm Feeling (10)	Feeder (2003)
Joker, The (1)	Steve Miller Band (1990)	Just The Way You Are (8)	Milky (2002)
		Just Walkin' In The Rain (8)	Johnnie Ray (1956)
Jolene (7)	Dolly Parton (1976)	Just What I Always Wanted (8)	Mari Wilson (1982)
Journey, The (3)	911 (1997)	Just When I Needed You Most (8)	Randy Vanwarmer (1979)
Joy (4)	Soul II Soul (1992)		
Joy And Pain (10)	Donna Allen (1989)	Just Who Is The Five O'Clock Hero (8)	Jam (1982)
Joybringer (9)	Manfred Mann's Earth Band (1973)	Justified And Ancient (2)	KLF with Tammy Wynette (1991)
Joyride (4)	Roxette (1991)	Justify My Love (2)	Madonna (1990)
Judy In Disguise (With Glasses) (3)	John Fred & The Playboy Band (1968)	Ka-Ching (8)	Shania Twain (2003)
Judy Teen (5)	Cockney Rebel (1974)	Karma Chameleon (1)	Culture Club (1983)
		Karma Police (8)	Radiohead (1997)
Juke Box Jive (3)	Rubettes (1974)	Kate Bush On Stage EP (10)	Kate Bush (1979)
Julia Says (3)	Wet Wet Wet (1995)	Kayleigh (2)	Marillion (1985)
		(Keep Feeling) Fascination (2)	Human League (1983)
Julie Ann (10)	Kenny (1975)		
Julie Do Ya Love Me (8)	White Plains (1970)	Keep Me A Secret (5)	Ainslie Henderson (2003)
Juliet / Tell Me Girl (What Are You Gonna Do) (1)	Four Pennies (1964)	Keep On Dancin' (8)	Gary's Gang (1979)
		Keep On Dancing (9) first hit	Bay City Rollers (1971)
Jump (2)	Girls Aloud (2003)		
Jump (2)	Kris Kross (1992)	Keep On Jumpin' (7)	Lisa Marie Experience (1996)
Jump (7)	Van Halen (1984)		
Jump Around (re-issue) / Top O' The Morning (8)	House Of Pain (1993)	Keep On Jumpin' (8)	Todd Terry with Martha Wash and Jocelyn Brown (1996)
Jump (For My Love) (6)	Pointer Sisters (1984)		
Jump They Say (9)	David Bowie (1993)	Keep On Loving You (7)	REO Speedwagon (1981)
Jump To The Beat (3)	Stacy Lattisaw (1980)	Keep On Movin' (1)	Five (1999)

Title	Group/Artiste	Title	Group/Artiste
Keep On Moving (5)	Soul II Soul featuring Caron Wheeler (1989)	Kiss Me (4)	Stephen 'Tin Tin' Duffy (1985)
Keep On Running (1)	Spencer Davis Group (1965)	Kiss Me Honey Honey Kiss Me (3)	Shirley Bassey (1958)
Keep On Walkin' (10)	Ce Ce Peniston (1992)	Kiss (re-entry) (5)	Dean Martin (1953)
Keep Searchin' (We'll Follow The Sun) (3)	Del Shannon (1965)	Kiss The Girl (9)	Peter Andre (1998)
		Kiss The Rain (4)	Billie Myers (1998)
Keep The Faith (5)	Bon Jovi (1992)	Kiss (When The Sun Don't Shine) (3)	Vengaboys (1999)
Kernkraft 400 (2)	Zombie Nation (2000)	Kiss You All Over (6)	Exile (1978)
Ketchup Song (Asereje), The (1)	Las Ketchup (2002)	Kisses Sweeter Than Wine (7)	Jimmie Rodgers (1957)
Kevin Carter (9)	Manic Street Preachers (1996)	Kisses Sweeter Than Wine (8)	Frankie Vaughan (1957)
Kewpie Doll (9)	Perry Como (1958)	Kissin' Cousins (10)	Elvis Presley with The Jordanaires (1964)
Kewpie Doll (10)	Frankie Vaughan (1958)		
Key The Secret, The (2)	Urban Cookie Collective (1993)	Kissin In The Back Row Of The Movies (2)	Drifters (1974)
Key To My Life (3)	Boyzone (1995)	Kites (9)	Simon Dupree & The Big Sound (1967)
Kids (2)	Robbie Williams & Kylie Minogue (2000)	Klubbhopping (10)	Klubbheads (1996)
		Knee Deep In The Blues (3)	Guy Mitchell (1957)
Kids In America (2) first hit	Kim Wilde (1981)	Knock Knock Who's There (2)	Mary Hopkin (1970)
Kid's Last Fight, The (3)	Frankie Laine (1954)		
Killamangiro (8)	Babyshambles (2004)	Knock On Wood (10)	David Bowie (1974)
Killer (1)	Adamski (1990)	Knock On Wood (6)	Amii Stewart (1979)
Killer (4)	ATB (2000)	Knock On Wood / Light My Fire (remix) (7)	Amii Stewart (1985)
Killer (EP) (8)	Seal (1991)		
Killer On The Loose (10)	Thin Lizzy (1980)	Knock Out (8)	Triple Eight (2003)
Killer Queen (2)	Queen (1974)	Knock Three Times (1)	Dawn (1971)
Killing Me Softly (1)	Fugees (1996)	Knocked It Off (8)	B A Robertson (1979)
Killing Me Softly With His Song (6)	Roberta Flack (1973)		
Killing Moon (9)	Echo And The Bunnymen (1984)	Knockin' On Heaven's Door (2)	Guns 'N' Roses (1992)
Killing Of Georgie (Parts 1 And 2), The (2)	Rod Stewart (1976)	Knockin' On Heaven's Door / Throw These Guns Away (1)	Dunblane (1996)
		Knowing Me Knowing You (1)	Abba (1977)
Kind Of Magic, A (3)	Queen (1986)	Kon-Tiki (1)	Shadows (1961)
Kinda Love (8)	Darius (2004)	Koochy (4)	Armand Van Helden (2000)
King / Food For Thought (4) first hit	UB40 (1980)		
		Kowalski (8)	Primal Scream (1997)
King Creole (2)	Elvis Presley with The Jordanaires (1958)	Kung Fu Fighting (8)	Bus Stop featuring Carl Douglas (1998)
King Of My Castle (1)	Wamdue Project (1999)		
		Kung Fu Fighting (1)	Carl Douglas (1974)
King Of Rock 'N' Roll, The (7)	Prefab Sprout (1988)	Kung-Fu (9)	187 Lockdown (1998)
King Of The Cops (6)	Billy Howard (1975)		
King Of The Road (1)	Roger Miller (1965)	La Bamba (1)	Los Lobos (1987)
King Of The Road (EP) (9)	Proclaimers (1990)	La Dee Dah (4)	Jackie Dennis (1958)
Kings Of The Wild Frontier (2)	Adam & The Ants (1981)		
		La Isla Bonita (1)	Madonna (1987)
Kingston Town (4)	UB40 (1990)	La La La Hey Hey (7)	Outhere Brothers (1995)
Kinky Afro (5)	Happy Mondays (1990)		
		La Mer (Beyond The Sea) (8)	Bobby Darin (1960)
Kinky Boots (5)	Patrick MacNee & Honor Blackman (1990)	La Primavera (3)	Sash (1998)
		Labelled With Love (4)	Squeeze (1981)
		Labour Of Love (6)	Hue & Cry (1987)
Kiss (5)	Art Of Noise featuring Tom Jones (1988)	Ladies Knight (9)	Kool & The Gang (1979)
		Ladies Night (8)	Atomic Kitten featuring Kool and the Gang (2003)
Kiss (9)	Dean Martin (1953)		
Kiss (6)	Prince & The Revolution (1986)	Lady D'Arbanville (8)	Cat Stevens (1970)
Kiss And Say Goodbye (4)	Manhattans (1976)	Lady Eleanor (3)	Lindisfarne (1972)
Kiss From A Rose (re-issue) / I'm Alive (4)	Seal (1995)	Lady (Hear Me Tonight) (1)	Modjo (2000)
		Lady In Red, The (1)	Chris De Burgh (1986)
Kiss Kiss (1)	Holly Valance (2002)		
Kiss Me (4)	Sixpence None The Richer (1999)	Lady Lynda (6)	Beach Boys (1979)
		Lady Madonna (1)	Beatles (1968)

MUSIC
POP

Title	Group/Artiste	Title	Group/Artiste
Lady Marmalade (1)	Christina Aguilera, Lil' Kim, Mya & Pink (2001)	Leader Of The Pack (re-issue) (7)	Shangri-Las (1976)
		Lean On Me (3)	Club Nouveau (1987)
Lady Rose (5)	Mungo Jerry (1971)	Lean On Me (7)	Mud (1976)
Lady Willpower (5)	Union Gap featuring Gary Puckett (1968)	Lean On Me (Ah-Li-Ayo) (3)	Red Box (1985)
		Learnin' The Blues (2)	Frank Sinatra with Nelson Riddle (1955)
Ladyboy Is Mine, The (10)	Stuntmasters (2001)		
Lambada (4)	Kaoma (1989)	Leave A Light On (4)	Belinda Carlisle (1989)
Lamplight (7)	David Essex (1973)		
Land Of Make Believe, The (9)	Allstars (2002)	Leave A Little Love (8)	Lulu (1965)
Land Of Make Believe, The (1)	Bucks Fizz (1981)	Leave (Get Out) (2)	JoJo (2004)
Larger Than Life (5)	Backstreet Boys (1999)	Leave Home (17) first hit	Chemical Brothers (1995)
Last Christmas / Everything She Wants (2)	Wham! (1984)	Leave Me Alone (2)	Michael Jackson (1989)
Last Christmas (re-issue) (6)	Wham! (1985)	Leave Right Now (1)	Will Young (2003)
Last Farewell, The (2)	Roger Whittaker (1975)	Leave Them All Behind (9)	Ride (1992)
		Leavin' On A Jet Plane (2)	Peter Paul & Mary (1970)
Last Goodbye / Be With You (2)	Atomic Kitten (2002)		
Last Kiss, The (6)	David Cassidy (1985)	Leaving New York (5)	REM (2004)
		Leeds United (10)	Leeds United FC (1972)
Last Night In Soho (8)	Dave Dee, Dozy, Beaky, Mick & Tich (1968)	Left Outside Alone (3)	Anastacia (2004)
		Left To My Own Devices (4)	Pet Shop Boys (1988)
Last Night On Earth (10)	U2 (1997)	Legacy EP (7)	Mansun (1998)
Last Night Was Made For Love (4)	Billy Fury (1962)	Legend Of Xanadu (1)	Dave Dee, Dozy, Beaky, Mick & Tich (1968)
Last Of The Famous International Playboys (6)	Morrissey (1989)		
		Lenny (10)	Supergrass (1995)
Last One Standing (8)	Girl Thing (2000)	Les Bicyclettes De Belsize (5)	Engelbert Humperdinck (1968)
Last Resort (3)	Papa Roach (2001)		
Last Thing On My Mind (6)	Steps (1998)	Lessons In Love (3)	Level 42 (1986)
Last Thing On My Mind (5)	Ronan Keating & Leann Rimes (2004)	Let 'Em In (2)	Wings (1976)
		Let Forever Be (9)	Chemical Brothers (1999)
Last Time, The (1)	Rolling Stones (1965)	Let It Be (2)	Beatles (1970)
Last Train Home (8)	Lostprophets (2004)	Let It Be (1)	Ferry Aid (1987)
Last Train To San Fernando (2)	Johnny Duncan & Blue Grass Boys (1957)	Let It Rain (10)	East 17 (1995)
		Let It Rock / Memphis Tennessee (6)	Chuck Berry (1963)
Last Train To Trancentral (2)	KLF (1991)	Let Love Be Your Energy (10)	Robbie Williams (2001)
Last Waltz, The (1)	Engelbert Humperdinck (1967)	Let Me Be Your Fantasy (1)	Baby D (1994)
Lately (6)	Samantha Mumba (2001)	(Let Me Be Your) Teddy Bear (3)	Elvis Presley with The Jordanaires (1957)
Lately (6)	Lisa Scott-Lee (2003)		
Lately (3)	Stevie Wonder (1981)	Let Me Blow Ya Mind (4)	Eve featuring Gwen Stefani (2001)
Laugh At Me (9)	Sonny (1965)	Let Me Clear My Throat (8)	DJ Kool (1997)
Laughing Gnome, The (6)	David Bowie (1973)	Let Me Entertain You (3)	Robbie Williams (1998)
Launch, The (2)	DJ Jean (1999)		
Lavender (5)	Marillion (1985)	Let Me Go Lover (9) (first hit)	Teresa Brewer with The Lancers (1955)
Lay All Your Love On Me (7)	Abba (1981)		
Lay All Your Love On Me (3)	Racey (1978)	Let Me Go Lover (10)	Kathy Kirby (1964)
Lay Down Your Arms (1)	Anne Shelton (1956)	Let Me Go Lover (3)	Dean Martin (1955)
Lay Lady Lay (5)	Bob Dylan (1969)	Let Me Go Lover (5)	Ruby Murray (1955)
Layla (7)	Derek & The Dominoes (1972)		
Layla (re-issue) (4)	Derek & The Dominoes (1982)	Let Me In (2)	Osmonds (1973)
		Let Me Kiss You (8)	Morrissey (2004)
Lazy (9)	Suede (1997)	Let Me Live (9)	Queen (1996)
Lazy (2)	X-Press 2 featuring David Byrne (2002)	Let Me Show You (5)	Camisra (1998)
		Let Me Try Again (5)	Tammy Jones (1975)
Lazy Days (8)	Robbie Williams (1997)	Let The Beat Control Your Body (6)	2 Unlimited (1994)
Lazy River (2)	Bobby Darin (1961)	Let The Heartaches Begin (1) first hit	Long John Baldry (1967)
Lazy Sunday (2)	Small Faces (1968)		
Le Freak (7)	Chic (1978)	Let The Music Play (9)	Barry White (1975)
Leader Of The Pack (re-issue) (3)	Shangri-Las (1972)	Let There Be Drums (3)	Sandy Nelson (1961)

Title	Group/Artiste	Title	Group/Artiste
Let There Be Love (6)	Simple Minds (1991)	Letter From America (3)	Proclaimers (1987)
Let Your Head Go / This Groove (3)	Victoria Beckham (2004)	Letter To You, A (10)	Shakin' Stevens (1984)
Let Your Love Flow (7) first hit	Bellamy Brothers (1976)	Letter, The (5)	Box Tops (1967)
		Licence To Kill (6)	Gladys Knight (1989)
Let Your Yeah Be Yeah (5)	Pioneers (1971)	Lie To Me (10)	Bon Jovi (1995)
Let's All Chant (8)	Michael Zager Band (1978)	Life (8)	Des'ree (1998)
		Life (6)	Haddaway (1993)
Let's Dance (1)	David Bowie (1983)	Life Ain't Easy (4)	Cleopatra (1998)
Let's Dance (1)	Five (2001)	Life For Rent (8)	Dido (2003)
Let's Dance (2)	Chris Montez (1962)	Life Got Cold (3)	Girls Aloud (2003)
Let's Dance (re-entry) (9)	Chris Montez (1972)	Life Is A Flower (5)	Ace Of Base (1998)
Let's Get Ready To Rhumble (9)	PJ & Duncan (1994)	Life Is A Minestrone (7)	10CC (1975)
Let's Get Rocked (2)	Def Leppard (1992)	Life is A Rollercoaster (1)	Ronan Keating (2000)
Let's Get Serious (8)	Jermaine Jackson (1980)	Life Is Too Short Girl (9)	Sheer Elegance (1976)
Let's Get Together Again (8)	Glitter Band (1974)	Life Less Ordinary, A (10)	Ash (1997)
Let's Get Together No. 1 (6)	Big Ben Banjo Band (1954)	Life On Mars (3)	David Bowie (1973)
		Lifeline (7)	Spandau Ballet (1982)
Let's Go All The Way (3)	Sly Fox (1986)	Lifestyles Of The Rich And Famous (8)	Good Charlotte (2003)
Let's Go Crazy / Take Me With You (7)	Prince & The Revolution (1985)	Lift Me Up (1)	Geri Halliwell (1999)
Let's Go Round Again (10)	Louise (1997)	Lifted (4)	Lighthouse Family (1996)
Let's Go To San Francisco (4)	Flowerpot Men (1967)	Light My Fire (7)	Clubhouse featuring Carl (1994)
Let's Groove (3)	Earth Wind & Fire (1981)	Light My Fire (6)	Jose Feliciano (1968)
Let's Hang On! (4)	Four Seasons featuring The Sound Of Frankie Valli (1965)	Light My Fire (1)	Will Young (2002)
		Light My Fire / 137 Disco Heaven (medley) (5)	Amii Stewart (1979)
Let's Have A Ball (4)	Winifred Atwell (1957)	Light My Fire (re-issue) (7)	Doors (1991)
Let's Have A Ding Dong (3)	Winifred Atwell (1955)	(Light Of Experience) Doina De Jale (4)	Georghe Zamfir (1976)
Let's Have A Party (2)	Winifred Atwell (1953)	Light Of My Life (8) first hit	Louise (1995)
Let's Have A Quiet Night In (8)	David Soul (1977)	Like A Baby (10)	Len Barry (1966)
Let's Have Another Party (1)	Winifred Atwell (1954)	Like A Prayer (3)	Madhouse (2002)
		Like A Prayer (1)	Madonna (1989)
Let's Hear It For The Boy (2)	Deniece Williams (1984)	Like A Rolling Stone (4)	Bob Dylan (1965)
		Like A Rose (6)	A1 (2000)
Let's Make A Night To Remember (10)	Bryan Adams (1996)	Like A Virgin (3)	Madonna (1984)
		Like Clockwork (6)	Boomtown Rats (1978)
Let's Party (1)	Jive Bunny & The Mastermixers (1989)	Like Glue (3)	Sean Paul (2003)
		Like I Do (3)	Maureen Evans (1962)
Let's Put It All Together (9)	Stylistics (1974)	Like I Love You (2)	Justin Timberlake (2002)
Let's Spend The Night Together/ Ruby Tuesday (3)	Rolling Stones (1967)	Like I've Never Been Gone (3)	Billy Fury (1963)
Let's Stay Together (7)	Al Green (1972)	Like Sister And Brother (7)	Drifters (1973)
Let's Stay Together (6)	Tina Turner (1983)	Like To Get To Know You Well (4)	Howard Jones (1984)
Let's Stick Together (Let's Work Together) (4)	Bryan Ferry (1976)	Lily The Pink (1)	Scaffold (1968)
Let's Talk About Sex (2)	Salt-N-Pepa featuring Psychotropic (1991)	Lily Was Here (6)	Dave A Stewart with Candy Dulfer (1990)
		Lion Sleeps Tonight, The (1)	Tight Fit (1982)
		Lipstick On Your Collar (3)	Connie Francis (1959)
Let's Think About Living (6)	Bob Luman (1960)	Liquid Dreams (3)	O-Town (2001)
Let's Try Again / Didn't I Blow Your Mind (8)	New Kids On The Block (1990)	Liquidator (9)	Harry J Allstars (1969)
Let's Twist Again / The Twist (re-issue) (5)	Chubby Checker (1975)	Listen To What The Man Said (6)	Wings (1975)
		Listen To Your Heart (10)	Sonia (1989)
Let's Twist Again (remix) (2)	Chubby Checker (1961)	Listen To Your Heart / Dangerous (6)	Roxette (1990)
Let's Wait Awhile (3)	Janet Jackson (1987)	Little Arrows (3)	Leapy Lee (1968)
		Little Bird / Love Song For A Vampire (3)	Annie Lennox (1993)
Let's Walk Thata-Way (4)	Doris Day & Johnnie Ray (1953)	Little Bit Me A Little Bit You, A (3)	Monkees (1967)
Let's Work Together (2)	Canned Heat (1970)	Little Bit More, A (2)	Dr Hook (1976)

Title	Group/Artiste	Title	Group/Artiste
Little Bit More, A (1)	911 (1999)	Living Doll (1)	Cliff Richard & The Drifters (1959)
Little Bit Of Lovin' (8)	Kele Le Roc (1998)		
Little Bit Of Luck, A (9)	DJ Luck & MC Neat (1999)	Living Doll (1)	Cliff Richard & The Young Ones with Hank Marvin (1986)
Little Bit Of Soap, A (5)	Showaddywaddy (1978)	Living In A Box (5)	Living In A Box (1987)
Little Bitty Tear, A (9)	Burl Ives (1962)		
Little By Little / She Is Love (2)	Oasis (2002)	Living In America (5)	James Brown (1986)
Little Children (1)	Billy J Kramer And The Dakotas (1964)	Living In The Past (3)	Jethro Tull (1969)
		Living Next Door To Alice (5)	Smokie (1976)
Little Darlin' (3)	Diamonds (1957)	Living Next Door To Alice (Who The F**K Is Alice) (3)	Smokie featuring Roy 'Chubby' Brown (1995)
Little Devil (9)	Neil Sedaka (1961)		
Little Donkey (3)	Nina & Frederick (1960)	Living On My Own (1)	Freddie Mercury (1993)
Little Drummer Boy (6)	Beverley Sisters (1959)	Living On The Ceiling (7)	Blancmange (1982)
		Living On Video (9)	Trans X (1985)
Little Fluffy Clouds (10)	Orb (1993)	Living Years, The (2)	Mike & The Mechanics (1989)
Little L (5)	Jamiroquai (2001)		
Little Less Conversation, A (1)	Elvis vs JXL (2002)	LK (Carolina Carol Bela) (17)	DJ Marky & XRS with Stamina MC (2002)
Little Lies (5)	Fleetwood Mac (1987)		
Little Love And Understanding, A (10)	Gilbert Becaud (1975)	L-L-Lucy (10)	Mud (1975)
		Loadsamoney (4)	Harry Enfield (1988)
Little Loving, A (6)	Fourmost (1964)	Loco (5)	Fun Lovin' Criminals (2001)
Little Man (4)	Sonny & Cher (1966)		
Little Miss Lonely (8)	Helen Shapiro (1962)	Loco In Acapulco (7)	Four Tops (1988)
		Locomotion (5)	Orchestral Manoeuvres In The Dark (1984)
Little More Love, A (4)	Olivia Newton-John (1978)		
Little Peace, A (1)	Nicole (1982)	Loco-Motion, The (2)	Little Eva (1962)
Little Red Monkey (10)	Frank Chacksfield (1953)	Loco-Motion, The (2)	Kylie Minogue (1988)
		Logical Song, The (2)	Scooter (2002)
Little Red Rooster (1)	Rolling Stones (1964)	Logical Song, The (7)	Supertramp (1979)
		Lola (2)	Kinks (1970)
Little Respect, A (4)	Erasure (1988)	Lola's Theme (1)	Shapeshifters (2004)
Little Respect, A (3)	Wheatus (2001)	Lollipop (6)	Chordettes (1958)
Little Shoemaker, The (7) first hit	Petula Clark (1954)	Lollipop (2)	Mudlarks (1958)
Little Things (5)	Dave Berry (1965)	London Nights (2)	London Boys (1989)
Little Things Mean A Lot (1)	Kitty Kallen (1954)	Lone Ranger, The (5)	Quantum Jump (1979)
Little Time, A (1)	Beautiful South (1990)		
		Loneliness (1)	Tomcraft (2003)
Little Town Flirt (4)	Del Shannon (1963)	Lonely (6)	Peter Andre (1997)
Little White Bull (6)	Tommy Steele (1959)	Lonely Boy (3)	Paul Anka (1959)
		Lonely Bull, The (3)	Herb Alpert & The Tijuana Brass (1963)
Little Willy (4)	Sweet (1972)		
Live And Let Die (5)	Guns 'N' Roses (1991)	Lonely Pup (In A Christmas Shop) (4)	Adam Faith with The Children (1960)
Live And Let Die (9)	Paul McCartney & Wings (1973)	Lonely This Christmas (1)	Mud (1974)
		Long And Winding Road, The / Suspicious Minds (1)	Will Young & Gareth Gates (2002)
Live Forever (10)	Oasis (1994)		
Live In Trouble (7)	Barron Knights (1977)	Long Goodbye, The (3)	Ronan Keating (2003)
Live Is Life (6)	Opus (1985)		
Live It Up (3)	Mental As Anything (1987)	Long-Haired Lover From Liverpool (1)	Little Jimmy Osmond (1972)
Live Like Horses (9)	Elton John & Luciano Pavarotti (1996)	Long Hot Summer / Paris Match (3)	Style Council (1983)
		Long Live Love (1)	Sandie Shaw (1965)
Live The Dream (7)	Cast (1997)	Long Tall Glasses (4)	Leo Sayer (1974)
Live To Tell (2)	Madonna (1986)	Long Tall Sally (3)	Little Richard (1957)
Live Together (10)	Lisa Stansfield (1990)	Long Train Runnin (7)	Doobie Brothers (1993)
Liverpool Lou (7)	Scaffold (1974)		
Livin' It Up (re-issue) (5)	Ja Rule featuring Case (2002)	Look At Me (2) first solo hit	Geri Halliwell (1999)
		Look At That Girl (1)	Guy Mitchell (1953)
Livin' La Vida Loca (1)	Ricky Martin (1999)	Look Away (7)	Big Country (1986)
Livin' On A Prayer (4)	Bon Jovi (1986)	Look For A Star (7)	Garry Mills (1960)
Livin' Thing (4)	Electric Light Orchestra (1976)	Look Homeward Angel (7)	Johnnie Ray (1957)
		Look Mama (10)	Howard Jones (1985)
Living Daylights, The (5)	A-Ha (1987)	Look Of Love, The (4)	ABC (1982)

Title	Group/Artiste	Title	Group/Artiste
Look Of Love, The (9)	Madonna (1987)	Love Don't Live Here Anymore (2)	Rose Royce (1978)
Look Through Any Window (4)	Hollies (1965)	Love Grows (Where My Rosemary Goes) (1)	Edison Lighthouse (1970)
Look Wot You Dun (4)	Slade (1972)	Love Guaranteed (7)	Damage (1997)
Look, The (7) first hit	Roxette (1989)	Love Hangover (10)	Diana Ross (1976)
Lookin' Through The Windows (9)	Jackson 5 (1972)	Love Hurts (4)	Jim Capaldi (1975)
Looking After No. 1 (11) first hit	Boomtown Rats (1977)	Love I Lost, The (3)	West End featuring Sybil (1993)
Looking For Love (8)	Karen Ramirez (1998)	Love In An Elevator (13)	Aerosmith (1989)
Looking Through The Eyes Of Love (9)	Partridge Family starring David Cassidy (1973)	Love In The First Degree (3)	Bananarama (1987)
Looking Through The Eyes Of Love (3)	Gene Pitney (1965)	Love Is A Many-Splendoured Thing (2)	Four Aces featuring Al Alberts (1955)
Loop Di Love (4)	Shag (1972)	Love Is A Stranger (6)	Eurythmics (1983)
Loop-De-Loop (5)	Frankie Vaughan (1963)	Love Is All Around (5)	Troggs (1967)
		Love Is All Around (1)	Wet Wet Wet (1994)
Lorelei (10)	Lonnie Donegan (1960)	Love Is Contagious (7)	Taja Seville (1988)
		Love Is In The Air (5)	John Paul Young (1978)
Lose My Breath (2)	Destiny's Child (2004)	Love Is Life (6)	Hot Chocolate (1970)
Lose Yourself (1)	Eminem (2002)	Love Is Like A Violin (8) first hit	Ken Dodd (1960)
Losing My Mind (6)	Liza Minnelli (1989)	Love Is Like Oxygen (9)	Sweet (1978)
Losing You (10)	Brenda Lee (1963)	Love Is Only A Feeling (5)	Darkness (2004)
Losing You (9)	Dusty Springfield (1964)	Love Is The Drug (2)	Roxy Music (1975)
		Love Is The Law (3)	Seahorses (1997)
Lost For Words (9)	Ronan Keating (2003)	(Love Is) The Tender Trap (2)	Frank Sinatra (1956)
Lost In France (9) first hit	Bonnie Tyler (1976)	Love Kills (10)	Freddie Mercury (1984)
Lost In Music (remix) (4)	Sister Sledge (1984)	Love Letters (4)	Ketty Lester (1962)
Lost In Space (4)	Apollo Four Forty (1998)	Love Letters (4)	Alison Moyet (1987)
Lost In Space (6)	Lighthouse Family (1998)	Love Letters (6)	Elvis Presley (1966)
Lost John / Stewball (2)	Lonnie Donegan Skiffle Group (1956)	Love Letters In The Sand (2)	Pat Boone (1957)
		Love Like A Man (10)	Ten Years After (1970)
Lost Without You (4)	Delta Goodrem (2003)	Love Like You And Me (10)	Gary Glitter (1975)
Loungin' (7)	LL Cool J (1996)	Love Machine (3)	Miracles (1976)
Love Action (I Believe In Love) (3)	Human League (1981)	Love Machine (2)	Girls Aloud (2004)
		Love Makes The World Go Round (6)	Perry Como (1958)
Love Ain't Gonna Wait For You / Say Goodbye (2)	S Club (2003)	Love Me (6)	Yvonne Elliman (1976)
Love Ain't Here Anymore (3)	Take That (1994)	Love Me Do (17) first hit	Beatles (1962)
Love And Affection (10) first and biggest hit	Joan Armatrading (1976)	Love Me Do (re-entry) (4)	Beatles (1982)
		Love Me For A Reason (2) first hit	Boyzone (1994)
Love And Kisses (8)	Dannii Minogue (1991)	Love Me For A Reason (1)	Osmonds (1974)
		Love Me Forever (5)	Marion Ryan (1958)
Love And Marriage (3)	Frank Sinatra (1956)	Love Me Like I Love You (4)	Bay City Rollers (1976)
Love And Pride (2)	King (1985)	Love Me Love My Dog (3)	Peter Shelley (1975)
Love And Understanding (10)	Cher (1991)	Love Me Or Leave Me (8)	Sammy Davis Jr (1955)
Love At First Sight (2)	Kylie Minogue (2002)		
Love Can Build A Bridge (1)	Cher, Chrissie Hynde, Neneh Cherry and Eric Clapton (1995)	Love Me Tonight (9)	Tom Jones (1969)
		Love Missile F1-11 (3)	Sigue Sigue Sputnik (1986)
Love Can't Turn Around (10)	Farley 'Jackmaster' Funk and Jessie Saunders (1986)	Love Of A Lifetime (9)	Honeyz (1999)
		Love Of My Life (9)	Dooleys (1977)
		Love Of Richard Nixon, The (2)	Manic Street Preachers (2004)
Love Cats, The (7)	Cure (1983)	Love Of The Common People (9)	Nicky Thomas (1970)
Love Changes Everything (2) first hit	Michael Ball (1989)	Love Of The Common People (2)	Paul Young (1983)
		Love Of The Loved (35) first hit	Cilla Black (1963)
Love Changes Everything (2)	Climie Fisher (1988)	Love On A Mountain Top (10)	Robert Knight (1973)
Love City Groove (7) first and only hit	Love City Groove (1995)	Love On The Line (6)	Blazin' Squad (2002)
		Love On Your Side (9)	Thompson Twins (1983)
Love Come Down (7)	Evelyn 'Champagne' King (1982)	Love Plus One (3)	Haircut 100 (1982)
Love Doesn't Have To Hurt (4)	Atomic Kitten (2003)	Love Really Hurts Without You (2)	Billy Ocean (1976)
Love Don't Cost A Thing (1)	Jennifer Lopez (2001)	Love Resurrection (10)	Alison Moyet (1984)
Love Don't Live Here Anymore (3)	Jimmy Nail (1985)	Love Rollercoaster (7)	Red Hot Chili Peppers (1997)

M
U
S
I
C

P
O
P

Title	Group/Artiste	Title	Group/Artiste
Love Shack (2)	B-52's (1990)	Lullaby (9)	Shawn Mullins (1999)
Love Shine A Light (3)	Katrina & The Waves (1997)	Luv Me Luv Me (5)	Shaggy (2001)
Love Song / Alive And Kicking (re-issues) (6)	Simple Minds (1992)	Luv U Better (7)	LL Cool J (2002)
Love Spreads (2)	Stone Roses (1994)	Luvstruck (9)	Southside Spinners (2000)
Love Story (Vs Finally) (8)	Layo & Bushwacka (2003)	Lyin' Eyes (23)	Eagles (1975)
Love Theme From A Star Is Born (Evergreen) (3)	Barbra Streisand (1977)	Ma Baker (2)	Boney M (1977)
Love Theme From The Thornbirds (10)	Juan Martin (1984)	Ma (He's Making Eyes At Me) (2)	Johnny Otis Show (1957)
Love To Hate You (4)	Erasure (1991)	Ma (He's Making Eyes At Me) (10)	Lena Zavaroni (1974)
Love To Love You Baby (4) first hit	Donna Summer (1976)	Macarena (2)	Los Del Rio (1996)
Love Town (6)	Booker Newbury III (1983)	Macarthur Park (4)	Richard Harris (1968)
Love Train (4)	Holly Johnson (1989)	Macarthur Park (5)	Donna Summer (1978)
Love Train (9)	O'Jays (1973)	Machine Gun (20) first hit	Communards (1974)
Love Will Save The Day (10)	Whitney Houston (1988)	Mack The Knife (1)	Bobby Darin (1959)
Love Won't Wait (1)	Gary Barlow (1997)	Mad About You (9)	Bruce Ruffin (1972)
Love Worth Waiting For, A (2)	Shakin' Stevens (1984)	Mad Passionate Love (6)	Bernard Bresslaw (1958)
Love X Love (10)	George Benson (1980)	Mad World (3) first hit	Tears For Fears (1982)
Love You Like Mad (7)	VS (2004)	Mad World (1)	Michael Andrews featuring Gary Jules (2003)
Love You Save, The (7)	Jackson 5 (1970)	Madame Helga (4)	Stereophonics (2003)
Love ... Thy Will Be Done (9)	Martika (1991)	Maggie May (1)	Rod Stewart (1971)
Lovefool (2)	Cardigans (1997)	Magic Fly (2)	Space (1977)
Lovely Day (7)	Bill Withers (1978)	Magic Moments (1)	Perry Como (1958)
Lovely Day (remix) (4)	Bill Withers (1988)	Magic Number, The / Buddy (7) biggest hit	De La Soul (1989)
Lover's Concerto, A (5)	Toys (1965)	Magic Roundabout/Funky Moped (5)	Jasper Carrott (1975)
Lovers Of The World Unite (7)	David & Jonathan (1966)	Magical Mystery Tour EP (2)	Beatles (1967)
Love's Been Good To Me (8)	Frank Sinatra (1969)	Mah Na Mah Na (8)	Piero Umiliani (1977)
Love's Got A Hold On My Heart (2)	Steps (1999)	Maid Of Orleans (The Waltz Joan Of Arc) (4)	Orchestral Manoeuvres In The Dark (1982)
Love's Gotta Hold On Me (4)	Dollar (1979)	Main Title Theme From Man With The Golden Arm (9)	Billy May Orchestra (1956)
Love's Just A Broken Heart (5)	Cilla Black (1966)	Make It A Party (7)	Winifred Atwell (1956)
Love's Theme (10)	Love Unlimited Orchestra (1974)	Make It Easy On Yourself (1)	Walker Brothers (1965)
Love's Unkind (3)	Donna Summer (1977)	Make It Good (11)	A1 (2002)
Lovesick Blues (1)	Frank Ifield (1962)	Make It Soon (9)	Tony Brent (1953)
Lovestruck (10)	Madness (1999)	Make It Soon (re-entry) (9)	Tony Brent (1953)
Lovin' Each Day (2)	Ronan Keating (2001)	Make It With You (5)	Bread (1970)
Lovin' Is Easy (6)	Hear'Say (2002)	Make It With You (7)	Let Loose (1996)
Lovin' Things (6) first hit	Marmalade (1968)	Make Love To Me (8)	Jo Stafford (1954)
Loving You (2)	Minnie Riperton (1975)	Make Luv (1)	Room 5 featuring Oliver Cheatham (2003)
LSF (10)	Kasabian (2004)		
LSI (6)	Shamen (1992)	Make Me An Island (3)	Joe Dolan (1969)
Lucille (10)	Little Richard (1957)	Make Me Smile (Come Up And See Me) (1)	Steve Harley & Cockney Rebel (1975)
Lucille (1)	Kenny Rogers (1977)		
Lucille / So Sad (to watch good love go bad) (4)	Everley Brothers (1960)	Make The World Go Away (8) first hit	Eddy Arnold (1966)
Lucky (5)	Britney Spears (2000)	Makin' Love (9)	Floyd Robinson (1959)
Lucky Lips (4)	Cliff Richard & The Shadows (1963)	Making Up Again (7)	Goldie (1978)
Lucky Man (7)	Verve (1997)	Making Your Mind Up (1) first hit	Bucks Fizz (1981)
Lucky Number (3)	Lene Lovich (1979)	Male Stripper (4)	Man 2 Man meet Man Parrish (1987)
Lucky Stars (3)	Dean Friedman (1978)		
Lucy In The Sky With Diamonds (10)	Elton John (1974)	Malt And Barley Blues (5)	McGuinness Flint (1971)
Lullaby (5)	Cure (1989)	Mama (5)	Dave Berry (1966)

Title	Group/Artiste	Title	Group/Artiste
Mama (4)	Genesis (1983)	Massachusetts (1)	Bee Gees (1967)
Mama – Who Da Man? (3)	Richard Blackwood (2000)	Masses Against The Classes, The (1)	Manic Street Preachers (2000)
Mama / Robot Man (2)	Connie Francis (1960)	Master And Servant (9)	Depeche Mode (1984)
Mama / Who Do You Think You Are (1)	Spice Girls (1997)	Masterblaster (Jammin') (2)	Stevie Wonder (1980)
Mama Told Me Not To Come (4)	Tom Jones & The Stereophonics (2000)	Masterblaster 2000 (5)	DJ Luck & MC Neat featuring JJ (2000)
Mama Told Me Not To Come (3)	Three Dog Night (1970)	Matchstalk Men And Matchstalk Cats And Dogs (1) first and only hit	Brian & Michael (1978)
Mama Used To Say (7)	Junior (1982)	Material Girl (3)	Madonna (1985)
Mama Weer All Crazee Now (1)	Slade (1972)	Matinee (8)	Franz Ferdinand (2004)
Mambo Italiano (1)	Rosemary Clooney & The Mellomen (1954)	Matthew And Son (2)	Cat Stevens (1967)
		May I Have The Next Dream With You (8)	Malcolm Roberts (1968)
Mambo No 5 (1)	Bob The Builder (2001)	May You Always (9)	Joan Regan (1959)
Mambo No 5 (A Little Bit Of ...) (1)	Lou Bega (1999)	Maybe (12)	Enrique Iglesias (2002)
Mamma Mia (1)	Abba (1975)	Maybe (6)	Emma (2003)
Man From Laramie, The (1)	Jimmy Young (1955)	Maybe Baby (4)	Crickets (1958)
Man Of Mystery / The Stranger (5)	Shadows (1960)	Maybe That's What It Takes (3)	Alex Parks (2003)
Man Of The World (2)	Fleetwood Mac (1969)	Maybe Tomorrow (3)	Stereophonics (2003)
Man On Fire / Wanderin' Eyes (6)	Frankie Vaughan (1957)	Me Against The Music (2)	Britney Spears featuring Madonna (2003)
Man On The Edge (10)	Iron Maiden (1995)	Me And My Life (4)	Tremeloes (1970)
Man (Uh-Huh) (7)	Rosemary Clooney (1954)	Me And You And A Dog Named Boo (4)	Lobo (1971)
Man Who Sold The World, The (3)	Lulu (1974)	Me And You Versus The World (9)	Space (1996)
Man With The Child In His Eyes (6)	Kate Bush (1978)	Me Julie (2)	Shaggy & Ali G (2002)
Man Without Love, A (2)	Engelbert Humperdinck (1968)	Me No Pop (32)	Kid Creole and the Coconuts (1981)
Man! I Feel Like A Woman (3)	Shania Twain (1999)	Me The Peaceful Heart (9)	Lulu (1968)
Manchild (5)	Neneh Cherry (1989)	Mean Streak (10)	Cliff Richard & The Drifters (1959)
Mandy (9)	Eddie Calvert (1958)		
Mandy (1)	Westlife (2003)	Measure Of A Man / With A Little Help From My Friends (1)	Sam & Mark (2004)
Maneater (6)	Daryl Hall & John Oates (1982)	Meet Me On The Corner (2)	Max Bygraves (1955)
Manic Monday (2) first hit	Bangles (1986)	Meet Me On The Corner (5)	Lindisfarne (1972)
Marblehead Johnson (7)	Bluetones (1996)	(Meet) The Flintstones (3)	BC-52s (1994)
March Of The Siamese Children (4)	Kenny Ball & His Jazzmen (1962)	Megablast / Don't Make Me Wait (6)	Bomb The Bass featuring Merlin & Antonia / Lorraine & Lose (1988)
Marcheta (8) first hit	Karl Denver (1961)		
Marguerita Time (3)	Status Quo (1983)	Megamix (6)	Technotronic (1990)
Maria (1)	Blondie (1999)	Mellow Yellow (8)	Donovan (1967)
Maria (8)	P J Proby (1965)	Melody Of Love (10)	Ink Spots (1955)
Maria Elena (5)	Los Indios Tabajaras (1963)	Melting Pot (3) first hit	Blue Mink (1969)
Maria Maria (6)	Santana featuring The Product G&B (2000)	Memories Are Made Of This (5)	Dave King featuring The Keynotes (1956)
Marie (9)	Bachelors (1965)	Memories Are Made Of This (1)	Dean Martin (1956)
(Marie's The Name) His Latest Flame / Little Sister (1)	Elvis Presley (1961)	Memory (6)	Elaine Paige (1981)
Marjorine (48) first hit	Joe Cocker (1968)		
Marrakesh Express (17) first and only hit	Crosby, Stills and Nash (1969)	Memphis Tennessee (19) first hit	Dave Berry (1963)
Martha's Harbour (10)	All About Eve (1988)	Men In Black (1) first hit	Will Smith (1997)
Mary Had A Little Boy (8)	Snap (1990)	Mercy Mercy Me – I Want You (9)	Robert Palmer (1991)
Mary Had A Little Lamb (9)	Wings (1972)	Merry Christmas Everyone (1)	Shakin' Stevens (1985)
Mary's Boy Child (1)	Harry Belafonte (1957)	Merry Gentle Pops (9)	Barron Knights with Duke D'Mond (1965)
Mary's Boy Child / Oh My Lord (1)	Boney M (1978)		
Mary's Boy Child (re-entry) (10)	Harry Belafonte (1958)	Merry Xmas Everybody (1)	Slade (1973)
Mary's Prayer (3)	Danny Wilson (1988)	Mess Of Blues, A (2)	Elvis Presley with The Jordanaires (1960)
Mas Que Nada (10)	Echobeatz (1998)		
Mass Destruction (7)	Faithless (2004)	Message In A Bottle (1)	Police (1979)

M
U
S
I
C

P
O
P

Title	Group/Artiste	Title	Group/Artiste
Message To You Rudy, A / Nite Club (10)	Specials featuring Rico (1979)	Missing You (3)	Chris De Burgh (1988)
Message Understood (6)	Sandie Shaw (1965)	Missing You (9)	John Waite (1984)
Message, The (8)	Grandmaster Flash & The Furious Five (1982)	Mississippi (1)	Pussycat (1976)
		Mistletoe And Wine (1)	Cliff Richard (1988)
Metal Guru (1)	T Rex (1972)	Misty (2)	Ray Stevens (1975)
Mexicali Rose (8)	Karl Denver (1961)	Misty Blue (5)	Dorothy Moore (1976)
Mexico (15)	Long John Baldry (1968)		
		Misunderstood (8)	Robbie Williams (2004)
MFEO (8)	Kavana (1997)		
Mi Chico Latino (1)	Geri Halliwell (1999)	Mixed Up World (7)	Sophie Ellis-Bextor (2003)
Miami (3)	Will Smith (1998)		
Miami Hit Mix / Xmas Through Your Eyes (8)	Gloria Estefan (1992)	Mmm Mmm Mmm Mmm (2) first hit	Crash Test Dummies (1994)
Miami Vice Theme (5)	Jan Hammer (1985)	Mmmbop (1)	Hanson (1997)
Michael (1)	Highwaymen (1961)	Mo Money Mo Problems (6)	Notorious BIG featuring 112 (1997)
Michael Row The Boat / Lumbered (6)	Lonnie Donegan & His Group (1961)		
Michelle (1)	Overlanders (1966)	Moan And Groan (7)	Mark Morrison (1997)
Mickey (2)	Toni Basil (1982)		
Mickey (4)	Lolly (1999)	Mobile (4)	Ray Burns with Eric Jupp and Orchestra (1955)
Midas Touch (8)	Midnight Star (1986)		
Midlife Crisis (10)	Faith No More (1992)	Mockingbird Hill (10)	Migil Five (1964)
		Modern Girl (8)	Sheena Easton (1980)
Midnight In Chelsea (4)	Jon Bon Jovi (1997)		
Midnight In Moscow (2)	Kenny Ball & His Jazzmen (1961)	Modern Love (2)	David Bowie (1983)
		Moi ... Lolita (9)	Alizee (2002)
Midnight Rider (10)	Paul Davidson (1975)	Moments In Soul (7)	JT & The Big Family (1990)
Midnight Train To Georgia (10)	Gladys Knight & The Pips (1976)	Mona (2)	Craig McLachlan & Check 1-2 (1990)
Mighty Joe (43) second and only other hit	Shocking Blue (1970)	Mona Lisa (5)	Conway Twitty (1959)
Mighty Quinn (1)	Manfred Mann (1968)	Monday Monday (3)	Mamas & The Papas (1966)
Milk (10)	Garbage featuring Tricky (1996)	Money (5)	Flying Lizards (1979)
		Money (5)	Jamelia featuring Beenie Man (2000)
Milk And Alcohol (9)	Dr Feelgood (1979)		
Milkshake (2)	Kelis (2004)	Money For Nothing (4)	Dire Straits (1985)
Millennium (1)	Robbie Williams (1998)	Money Honey (3)	Bay City Rollers (1975)
		Money Money Money (3)	Abba (1976)
Millennium Prayer, The (1)	Cliff Richard (1999)	Money's Too Tight (To Mention) (13)	Simply Red (1985) first hit
Million Love Songs, A (7)	Take That (1992)		
Millionaire (3)	Kelis featuring Andre 3000 (2004)	Monkey Spanner (7) only other hit	Dave & Ansel Collins (1971)
Mind Of It's Own, A (6)	Victoria Beckham (2002)	Monsieur Dupont (6)	Sandie Shaw (1969)
Minute You're Gone, The (1)	Cliff Richard (1965)	Monster Mash (3)	Bobby 'Boris' Pickett & the Crypt-Kickers (1973)
Miracles (10)	Pet Shop Boys (2003)		
Mirror In The Bathroom (4)	Beat (1980)		
Mirror Man (2)	Human League (1982)	Montego Bay (3) first hit	Bobby Bloom (1970)
		Mony Mony (7)	Billy Idol (1987)
Mirror Mirror (4)	Dollar (1981)	Mony Mony (1)	Tommy James & The Shondells (1968)
Mirror Mirror (9)	Pinkerton's Assorted Colours (1966)	Moody Blue (6)	Elvis Presley (1977)
Misfit (7)	Curiosity Killed The Cat (1987)	Moon River (1)	Danny Williams (1961)
Misfit (6)	Amy Studt (2003)	Moonglow / Theme From Picnic (7)	Morris Stoloff (1956)
Miss Independent (6)	Kelly Clarkson (2003)	Moonlight Shadow (4)	Mike Oldfield featuring Maggie Reilly (1983)
Miss Perfect (5)	Abs featuring Nodesha (2003)		
Miss Sarajevo (6)	Passengers (1995)	Moonlighting (2)	Leo Sayer (1975)
Miss You / Far Away Eyes (3)	Rolling Stones (1978)	Moonlighting Theme (8)	Al Jarreau (1987)
		Moonshine Sally (10)	Mud (1975)
Miss You Like Crazy (2)	Natalie Cole (1989)	More (10)	Perry Como (1956)
Miss You Nights / Tonight (3)	Westlife (2003)	More (4)	Jimmy Young (1956)
Mis-Shapes / Sorted For E's And Wizz (2)	Pulp (1995)	More And More Party Pops (5)	Russ Conway (1959)
		More I See You, The (3)	Chris Montez (1966)
Missing (remix) (3)	Everything But The Girl (1994)	More More More (5)	Andrea True Connection (1976)

Title	Group/Artiste	Title	Group/Artiste
More More More (3)	Rachel Stevens (2004)	Movin' Too Fast (2)	Artful Dodger & Romina Johnson (2000)
More Party Pops (10)	Russ Conway (1958)		
More Than A Woman (1)	Aaliyah (2002)	Moving (9)	Supergrass (1999)
More Than A Woman (2)	911 (1998)	Moving On Up (2)	M People (1993)
More Than A Woman (7)	Tavares (1978)	Mozart Symphony No. 40 in	Waldo De Los Rios
More Than Ever (Coma Prima) (5)	Malcolm Vaughan with The Mike Sammes Singers (1958)	G Minor (5)	(1971)
		Mr Blobby (1)	Mr Blobby (1993)
		Mr Blue Sky (6)	Electric Light Orchestra (1978)
More Than I Can Say (2)	Leo Sayer (1980)		
More Than I Can Say / Staying In (4)	Bobby Vee (1961)	Mr Brightside (10)	Killers (2004)
		Mr Hankey The Christmas Poo (4)	Mr Hankey (1999)
More Than I Needed To Know (5)	Scooch (2000)	Mr Loverman (re-issue) (3)	Shabba Ranks (1993)
More Than In Love (2)	Kate Robbins & Beyond (1981)		
		Mr Sandman (11) first hit	Chordettes (1954)
More Than This (5)	Emmie (1999)	Mr Sandman (9)	Four Aces featuring Al Alberts (1955)
More Than This (6)	Roxy Music (1982)		
More Than Words (2)	Extreme (1991)	Mr Sandman (5)	Dickie Valentine (1954)
More To This World (8)	Bad Boys Inc (1994)		
		Mr Sleaze (3)	Stock Aitken Waterman (1987)
More You Ignore Me The Closer I Get, The (8)	Morrissey (1994)		
		Mr Soft (8)	Cockney Rebel (1974)
Morning Has Broken (9)	Cat Stevens (1972)		
Morning Side Of The Mountain (5)	Donny & Marie Osmond (1974)	Mr Tambourine Man (1) first hit	Byrds (1965)
		Mr Vain (1)	Culture Beat (1993)
Morningtown Ride (2)	Seekers (1966)	Mr Wendal / Revolution (4)	Arrested Development (1993)
Most Beautiful Girl In The World, The (1)	Artist Formerly Known As Prince (1994)		
		Mr Wonderful (5)	Peggy Lee (1957)
		Mr Writer (5)	Stereophonics (2001)
Most Beautiful Girl, The (2)	Charlie Rich (1974)		
Most Girls (5)	Pink (2000)	Mrs Robinson (4)	Simon & Garfunkel (1968)
Mother And Child Reunion (5) first solo hit	Paul Simon (1972)		
		Mrs Robinson (EP) (9)	Simon & Garfunkel (1969)
Mother Nature And Father Time (7)	Nat 'King' Cole (1953)		
		Ms Grace (1)	Tymes (1974)
Mother Of Mine (2)	Neil Reid (1972)	Ms Jackson (2)	Outkast (2001)
Motorhead Live (6)	Motorhead (1981)	(Mucho Mambo) Sway (2)	Shaft (1999)
Motown Song, The (10)	Rod Stewart with The Temptations (1991)	Mulder And Scully (3)	Catatonia (1998)
		Mull Of Kintyre / Girls' School (1)	Wings (1977)
		Multiplication (5)	Bobby Darin (1961)
Mouldy Old Dough (1)	Lieutenant Pigeon (1972)	Mundian To Bach Ke (5)	Panjabi MC (2003)
		Murder On The Dancefloor (2)	Sophie Ellis-Bextor (2001)
Moulin Rouge (1)	Mantovani & His Orchestra (1953)		
		Musclebound / Glow (10)	Spandau Ballet (1981)
Moulin Rouge (re-entry) (10)	Mantovani & His Orchestra (1953)		
		Music (1)	Madonna (2000)
Mountain Greenery (re-entry) (4)	Mel Tormé (1956)	Music (3)	John Miles (1976)
Move Any Mountain (remix) (4)	Shamen (1991)	Music And Lights (5)	Imagination (1982)
Move Away (7)	Culture Club (1986)	Music Gets The Best Of Me (14)	Sophie Ellis Bextor (2002)
Move Closer (1)	Phyllis Nelson (1985)		
		Music Is My Radar (10)	Blur (2000)
Move It (2) first hit	Cliff Richard and The Drifters (1958)	Music Of The Night, The (7)	Michael Crawford (1987)
Move Mania (8)	Sash featuring Shannon (1998)	Music Of Torvill And Dean EP, The (9)	Richard Hartley & Mike Reed Orchestra (1984)
Move Move Move (The Red Tribe) (6)	1996 Manchester Utd FA Cup Squad (1996)		
		Music Sounds Better With You (2)	Stardust (1998)
		Music To Watch Girls By (9)	Andy Williams (1999)
Move On Baby (7)	Cappella (1994)	Music's No Good Without You, The (8)	Cher (2001)
Move Over Darling (8)	Doris Day (1964)		
Move Over Darling (8)	Tracey Ullman (1983)	Must Be The Music (8)	Joey Negro featuring Taka Boom (2000)
Move Ya Body (6)	Nina Sky (2004)	Must To Avoid, A (6)	Herman's Hermits (1965)
Move Your Body (3)	Eiffel 65 (2000)		
Move Your Body (Elevation) (7)	Xpansions (1991)	My All (4)	Mariah Carey (1998)
Move Your Feet (3)	Junior Senior (2003)	My Baby Just Cares For Me (5)	Nina Simone (1987)
		My Baby Loves Lovin' (9)	White Plains (1970)
Movies (5)	Alien Ant Farm (2002)	My Band (2)	D12 (2004)
Moviestar (5)	Stereophonics (2004)	My Best Friend's Girl (3) first and biggest hit	Cars (1978)

Title	Group/Artiste	Title	Group/Artiste
My Boo / Confessions Part II (5)	Usher (2004)	My Old Piano (5)	Diana Ross (1980)
My Boy (5)	Elvis Presley (1974)	My One Temptation (7)	Mica Paris (1988)
My Boy Lollipop (2)	Millie (1964)	My Perfect Cousin (9)	Undertones (1980)
My Brother Jake (4)	Free (1971)	My Place / Flap Your Wings (1)	Nelly (2004)
My Camera Never Lies (1)	Bucks Fizz (1982)	My Prayer (9)	Gerry Monroe (1970)
My Cherie Amour (4)	Stevie Wonder (1969)	My Prayer (4)	Platters (1956)
My Coo-Ca-Choo (2) first hit	Alvin Stardust (1973)	My Prerogative (6)	Bobby Brown (1988)
My Culture (9)	1 Giant Leap featuring Maxi Jazz and Robbie Williams (2002)	My Prerogative (3)	Britney Spears (2004)
		My Pretty One (6)	Cliff Richard (1987)
		My Resistance Is Low (3)	Robin Sarstedt (1976)
My Destiny (7)	Lionel Richie (1992)	My Sentimental Friend (2)	Herman's Hermits (1969)
My Ding-A-Ling (1)	Chuck Berry (1972)		
My Dixie Darling (10)	Lonnie Donegan & His Skiffle Group (1957)	My September Love (re-entry) (3)	David Whitfield (1956)
		My Sharona (6)	Knack (1979)
My Ever Changing Moods (5)	Style Council (1984)	My Ship Is Coming In (3)	Walker Brothers (1965)
My Eyes Adored You (5)	Frankie Valli (1975)		
My Favourite Mistake (9)	Sheryl Crow (1998)	My Simple Heart (9)	Three Degrees (1979)
My Favourite Waste Of Time (3)	Owen Paul (1986)		
My Friend (3)	Frankie Laine (1954)	My Son My Son (1)	Vera Lynn with The Frank Weir Orchestra (1954)
My Friend Stan (2)	Slade (1973)		
My Friend The Sea (7)	Petula Clark (1961)		
My Generation (2)	Who (1965)	My Special Angel (3)	Malcolm Vaughan (1957)
My Girl (3)	Madness (1980)		
My Girl Lollipop (My Boy Lollipop) (9)	Bad Manners (1982)	My Star (5)	Ian Brown (1998)
		My Sweet Lord (1)	George Harrison (1971)
My Girl (re-issue) (2)	Temptations (1992)		
My Guy (5)	Mary Wells (1964)	My Sweet Lord (re-issue) (1)	George Harrison (2002)
My Happiness (4)	Connie Francis, David Rose Orchestra (1959)	My Toot Toot (6)	Denise La Salle (1985)
		My True Love (9)	Jack Scott (1958)
My Happy Ending (5)	Avril Lavigne (2004)	My Vision (6)	Jakatta featuring Seal (2002)
My Heart Has A Mind Of It's Own (3)	Connie Francis (1960)		
		My Way (10)	Dorothy Squires (1970)
My Heart Will Go On (1)	Celine Dion (1998)		
My Immortal (7)	Evanescence (2003)	My Way (6)	Limp Bizkit (2001)
My Kind Of Girl (5)	Matt Monro (1961)	My Way (9)	Elvis Presley (1977)
My Little Lady (6)	Tremeloes (1968)	My Way (5)	Frank Sinatra (1969)
My Little One (6)	Marmalade (1971)	My Way Of Thinking / I Think It's Going To Rain (6)	UB40 (1980)
My Love (4)	Petula Clark (1966)		
My Love (8)	Kele Le Roc (1999)	My Weakness Is None Of Your Business (9)	Embrace (1998)
My Love (9)	Paul McCartney & Wings (1973)		
		Mysterious Girl (2)	Peter Andre featuring Bubbler Ranx (1996)
My Love (1)	Westlife (2000)		
My Love (5)	Julio Iglesias featuring Stevie Wonder (1988)	Mysterious Girl (re-issue) (1)	Peter Andre (2004)
		Mysterious Times (2)	Sash featuring Tina Cousins (1998)
My Love And Devotion (10)	Doris Day (1952)		
My Love For You (9)	Johnny Mathis (1960)	Na Na Hey Hey Kiss Him Goodbye (5)	Bananarama (1983)
My Love Is Your Love (2)	Whitney Houston (1999)	Na Na Hey Hey Kiss Him Goodbye (9)	Steam (1970)
My Lover's Prayer / Bring It On (5)	Alistair Griffin featuring Robin Gibb (2004)	Na Na Is The Saddest Word (5)	Stylistics (1975)
		Na Na Na (10)	Cozy Powell (1974)
		Nairobi (3)	Tommy Steele (1958)
My Lovin' (4)	En Vogue (1992)		
My Mind's Eye (4)	Small Faces (1966)	Naked (5)	Louise (1996)
My Name Is (2) first hit	Eminem (1999)	Naked In The Rain (4)	Blue Pearl (1990)
My Name Is Jack (8)	Manfred Mann (1968)	Name Of The Game, The (1)	Abba (1977)
		Nancy Boy (4)	Placebo (1997)
My Name Is Prince (7)	Prince & The New Power Generation (1992)	Nathan Jones (5)	Supremes (1971)
		National Express (8)	Divine Comedy (1999)
My Neck My Back (Lick It) (4)	Khia (2004)	Native New Yorker (5) first hit	Odyssey (1977)
My Oh My (6)	Aqua (1998)	Natural (6)	Peter Andre (1997)
My Oh My (2)	Slade (1983)	Natural (3)	S Club 7 (2000)
My Old Man's A Dustman (Ballad Of A Refuse Disposal Officer) (1)	Lonnie Donegan & His Group (1960)	Natural Born Bugie (4)	Humble Pie (1969)
		Natural Sinner (6)	Fair Weather (1970)

Title	Group/Artiste	Title	Group/Artiste
Naughty Girl (10)	Beyonce (2004)	Next Episode, The (3)	Dr Dre featuring Snoop Dogg (2001)
Naughty Lady Of Shady Lane (6)	Ames Brothers (1955)		
Naughty Lady Of Shady Lane (5)	Dean Martin (1955)	Next Time, The / Bachelor Boy (1)	Cliff Richard and The Shadows (1962)
Neanderthal Man (2)	Hotlegs (1970)	Nice Guy Eddie (10)	Sleeper (1996)
Need You Tonight (2)	INXS (1988)	Night Birds (9)	Shakatak (1982)
Needin' U (8)	David Morales presents The Face (1998)	Night Chicago Died, The (3)	Paper Lace (1974)
		Night Fever (1)	Bee Gees (1978)
Needles And Pins (1)	Searchers (1964)	Night Games (6)	Graham Bonnet (1981)
Needles And Pins (10)	Smokie (1977)		
Nellie The Elephant (4)	Toy Dolls (1984)	Night Has A Thousand Eyes, The (3)	Bobby Vee (1963)
Nelson Mandela (9)	Special AKA (1984)		
Nessaja (4)	Scooter (2002)	Night Of Fear (2) first hit	Move (1967)
Nessun Dorma (2)	Luciano Pavarotti (1990)	Night Owl (5)	Gerry Rafferty (1979)
		Night They Drove Old Dixie Down, The (6)	Joan Baez (1971)
Never / These Dreams (re-issue) (8)	Heart (1988)	Night To Remember, A (5)	Shalamar (1982)
Never Be The Same Again (1)	Melanie C with Lisa Left Eye Lopes (2000)	Night, The (7)	Frankie Valli & The Four Seasons (1975)
Never Can Say Goodbye (4)	Communards (1987)	Nights In White Satin (re-entry) (9)	Moody Blues (1972)
Never Can Say Goodbye (2) first hit	Gloria Gaynor (1974)	Nights On Broadway (6)	Candi Staton (1977)
		Nightshift (3)	Commodores (1985)
Never Do A Tango With An Eskimo (6)	Alma Cogan (1955)	Nikita (3)	Elton John (1985)
		911 (9)	Wyclef Jean featuring Mary J Blige (2000)
Never Ending Song Of Love (2)	New Seekers (1971)		
Never Ending Story (4)	Limahl (1984)		
Never Ever (1)	All Saints (1997)	9pm (Till I Come) (1)	ATB (1999)
Never Felt Like This Before (8)	Shaznay Lewis (2004)	Nine Times Out Of Ten (3)	Cliff Richard & The Shadows (1960)
Never Forget (1)	Take That (1995)		
Never Gonna Give You Up (1) first hit	Rick Astley (1987)	9 To 5 (3)	Sheena Easton (1980)
Never Gonna Leave Your Side (1)	Daniel Bedingfield (2003)	Nineteen (1)	Paul Hardcastle (1985)
		19 / 2000 (6)	Gorillaz (2001)
Never Gonna Give You Up (6)	Musical Youth (1983)	1999 / Little Red Corvette (re-issue) (2)	Prince (1985)
Never Gonna Let You Go (7)	Tina Moore (1997)		
Never Had A Dream Come True (1)	S Club 7 (2000)	1999 (re-entry) (10)	Prince (1999)
		Nineteenth Nervous Breakdown (2)	Rolling Stones (1966)
Never Had A Dream Come True (6)	Stevie Wonder (1970)	99 Red Balloons (1)	Nena (1984)
Never Knew Love Like This Before (4)	Stephanie Mills (1980)	99 Ways (5)	Tab Hunter (1957)
		No Arms Can Ever Hold You (7)	Bachelors (1964)
Never Leave You (Uh Oooh Uh Oooh) (2)	Lumidee (2003)	No Charge (1)	J J Barrie (1976)
		No Diggity (9)	Blackstreet (1996)
Never Let Her Slip Away (5)	Andrew Gold (1978)	No Doubt About It (2)	Hot Chocolate (1980)
Never Let Her Slip Away (5)	Undercover (1992)	No Fronts (9)	Dog Eat Dog (1996)
Never Let You Down (7)	Honeyz (1999)	No Good Advice (2)	Girls Aloud (2003)
Never Never (4)	Assembly (1983)	No Good 4 Me (6)	Oxide & Neutrino featuring Megaman (2000)
Never Never Never (8)	Shirley Bassey (1973)		
		No Good (Start The Dance) (4)	Prodigy (1994)
Never Say Goodbye (9)	Karl Denver (1962)	No Honestly (7)	Lynsey De Paul (1974)
Never Too Late (4)	Kylie Minogue (1989)		
Never Trust A Stranger (7)	Kim Wilde (1988)	No Letting Go (3)	Wayne Wonder (2003)
New Beginning / Bright Eyes (3)	Stephen Gately (2000)		
		No Limit (1)	2 Unlimited (1993)
New Beginning (Mamba Seyra) (8)	Bucks Fizz (1986)	No Matter How I Try (5)	Gilbert O'Sullivan (1971)
New Day Has Come, A (7)	Celine Dion (2002)	No Matter What (5)	Badfinger (1971)
New Direction (2)	S Club Juniors (2002)	No Matter What (1)	Boyzone (1998)
		No Milk Today (7)	Herman's Hermits (1966)
New England, A (7)	Kirsty MacColl (1985)		
New Moon On Monday (9)	Duran Duran (1984)	No More (6)	A1 (2001)
New Song (3) first hit	Howard Jones (1983)	No More (Baby I'Ma Do Right) (6)	3LW (2001)
New Years Day (10)	U2 (1983)	No More Drama (9)	Mary J Blige (2002)
New York Groove (9)	Hello (1975)	No More Heroes (8)	Stranglers (1977)
New York Mining Disaster 1941 (12) first hit	Bee Gees (1967)	No More (I Can't Stand It) (8)	Maxx (1994)
		No More I Love Yous (2)	Annie Lennox (1995)

Title	Group/Artiste	Title	Group/Artiste
No More Lonely Nights (2)	Paul McCartney (1984)	Nothing's Gonna Stop Us Now (1)	Starship (1987)
No More Mr Nice Guy (10)	Alice Cooper (1973)	Notorious (7)	Duran Duran (1986)
No More Tears (Enough Is Enough) (3)	Donna Summer & Barbra Streisand (1979)	November Rain (4)	Guns 'N' Roses (1992)
		Novocaine For The Soul (10)	Eels (1997)
No More The Fool (5)	Elkie Brooks (1986)	Now (3)	Al Martino (1953)
No No No (5) first hit	Destiny's Child (1998)	Now Is The Time (5)	Jimmy James & The Vagabonds (1976)
No One But You (3)	Billy Eckstine (1954)	Now That We Found Love (2)	Heavy D & The Boyz (1991)
No One Is Innocent / My Way (7)	Sex Pistols (1978)		
No One Quite Like Grandma (1)	St Winifred's School Choir (1980)	Now That We've Found Love (10)	Third World (1978)
		Now Those Days Are Gone (8)	Bucks Fizz (1982)
No Other Love (1)	Ronnie Hilton (1956)	N-R-G (12) first hit	Adamski (1990)
No Particular Place To Go (3)	Chuck Berry (1964)	Nu Flow (3)	Big Brovaz (2002)
No Regrets (9) first solo hit	Midge Ure (1982)	Nuff Vibes EP (5)	Apache Indian (1993)
No Regrets (7)	Walker Brothers (1976)		
		Number 1 (6)	Tweenies (2000)
No Regrets / Antmusic (4)	Robbie Williams (1998)	Numero Uno (9)	Starlight (1989)
		Nut Rocker (1)	B Bumble and the Stingers (1962)
No Scrubs (3)	TLC (1999)		
No Son Of Mine (6)	Genesis (1991)	Nutbush City Limits (4)	Ike & Tina Turner (1973)
No Surprises (4)	Radiohead (1998)		
No Woman No Cry (2)	Fugees (1996)	03 Bonnie & Clyde (2)	Jay-Z featuring Beyonce Knowles (2003)
No Woman No Cry (re-entry) (8)	Bob Marley & The Wailers (1981)		
Nobody Does It Better (7)	Carly Simon (1977)	O L'Amour (7)	Dollar (1987)
		O Superman (2)	Laurie Anderson (1981)
Nobody I Know (10)	Peter & Gordon (1964)	O.T.B (On The Beach) / Reachers Of Civilisation (4)	York (2000)
Nobody Knows (4)	Tony Rich Project (1996)	Ob-La-Di Ob-La-Da (1)	Marmalade (1968)
		Oblivious (47) first hit	Aztec Camera (1983)
Nobody Needs Your Love (2)	Gene Pitney (1966)	Obsession (5) first and only hit	Animotion (1985)
Nobody Told Me (6)	John Lennon (1984)	Obvious (3)	Westlife (2004)
Nobody Wants To Be Lonely (4)	Ricky Martin & Christina Aguilera (2001)	Obviously (1)	McFly (2004)
		Off The Wall (7)	Michael Jackson (1979)
Nobody's Child (6)	Karen Young (1969)		
Nobody's Darlin' But Mine (4)	Frank Ifield (1963)	Oh Babe What Would You Say? (4)	Hurricane Smith (1972)
Nobody's Diary (3)	Yazoo (1983)	Oh Baby I... (4)	Eternal (1994)
Nobody's Fool (9)	Haircut 100 (1982)	Oh Boy (3)	Crickets (1957)
North Country Boy (4)	Charlatans (1997)	Oh Boy (1)	Mud (1975)
Northern Lights (10)	Renaissance (1978)	Oh Boy (The Mood I'm In) (8)	Brotherhood Of Man (1977)
Northern Star (4)	Melanie C (1999)		
Not A Dry Eye In The House (7)	Meat Loaf (1996)	Oh Carol (3)	Neil Sedaka (1959)
Not Fade Away (3)	Rolling Stones (1964)	Oh Carol (5)	Smokie (1978)
Not Gonna Get Us (7)	Tatu (2003)	Oh Carolina (1) first hit	Shaggy (1993)
Not In Love (5)	Enrique featuring Kelis (2004)	Oh Diane (9)	Fleetwood Mac (1982)
Not Over Yet (6)	Grace (1995)	Oh Happy Day (2)	Edwin Hawkins Singers (1969)
Not Over Yet (9)	Diana Ross (1999)		
Not Such An Innocent Girl (6)	Victoria Beckham (2001)	Oh Happy Day (4)	Johnston Brothers (1953)
(Nothin' Serious) Just Buggin' (7)	Whistle (1986)		
Nothing (9)	A (2002)	Oh Julie (1)	Shakin' Stevens (1982)
Nothing Can Divide Us (5)	Jason Donovan (1988)	Oh Lori (8)	Alessi (1977)
		Oh Mein Papa (1) first hit	Eddie Calvert (1953)
Nothing Compares 2 U (1)	Sinead O'Connor (1990)		
		Oh My Papa (9)	Eddie Fisher (1954)
Nothing Else Matters (6)	Metallica (1992)	Oh My Papa (re-entry) (10)	Eddie Fisher (1954)
Nothing Hurts Like Love (3)	Daniel Bedingfield (2004)	Oh No Not My Baby (6)	Rod Stewart (1973)
		Oh Pretty Woman (1)	Roy Orbison (1964)
Nothing Lasts Forever (8)	Echo And The Bunnymen (1997)	Oh Well (2)	Fleetwood Mac (1969)
Nothing Really Matters (7)	Madonna (1999)	Oh What A Circus (3)	David Essex (1978)
Nothing Rhymed (8) first hit	Gilbert O'Sullivan (1970)	Oh Yeah (6)	Ash (1996)
		Oh Yeah (On The Radio) (5)	Roxy Music (1980)
Nothing's Gonna Change My Love For You (1)	Glenn Madeiros (1988)	Oh Yes! You're Beautiful (2)	Gary Glitter (1974)
Nothing's Gonna Stop Me Now (8)	Samantha Fox (1987)	Ohh! What A Life (10)	Gibson Brothers (1979)

Title	Group/Artiste	Title	Group/Artiste
Oi (8)	Platinum 45 featuring More Fire Crew (2002)	One Day I'll Fly Away (2)	Randy Crawford (1980)
OK (7)	Big Brovaz (2003)	One Day In Your Life (1)	Michael Jackson (1981)
OK? (10)	Julie Covington, Rula Lenska, Charlotte Cornwell and Sue Jones-Davies (1977)	One For Sorrow (2)	Steps (1998)
		One In Ten (7)	UB40 (1981)
		One Kiss From Heaven (9)	Louise (1996)
		One Love (3)	Blue (2002)
		One Love (8)	Prodigy (1993)
Okay! (4)	Dave Dee, Dozy, Beaky, Mick & Tich (1967)	One Love (4)	Stone Roses (1990)
		One Love / People Get Ready (5)	Bob Marley & The Wailers (1984)
Ol' Rag Blues (9)	Status Quo (1983)	One Man Band (6)	Leo Sayer (1974)
Old Before I Die (2)	Robbie Williams (1997)	One Minute Man (10)	Missy Elliott featuring Ludacris (2001)
Older / I Can Make You Love Me (3)	George Michael (1997)		
Oldest Swinger In Town (6)	Fred Wedlock (1981)	One Moment In Time (1)	Whitney Houston (1988)
Ole Ola (Mulher Brasilieira) (4)	Rod Stewart and Scottish World Cup Football Squad '78 (1978)	One More Chance (5)	Michael Jackson (2003)
		One More Night (4)	Phil Collins (1985)
		One More Time (2)	Daft Punk (2000)
Oliver's Army (2)	Elvis Costello & The Attractions (1979)	One More Try (8)	George Michael (1988)
On A Carousel (4)	Hollies (1967)	One Nation Under A Groove (9)	Funkadelic (1978)
On A Night Like This (2)	Kylie Minogue (2000)	One Night / I Got Stung (1)	Elvis Presley (1959)
On A Ragga Tip (2)	SL2 (1992)	One Night In Heaven (6)	M People (1993)
On A Saturday Night (45) only other hit	Terry Dactyl and the Dinosaurs (1973)	One Night Stand (5)	Mis-Teeq (2001)
		One Of These Nights (23) first hit	Eagles (1975)
On A Slow Boat To China (3)	Emile Ford & The Checkmates (1960)	One Of Us (3)	Abba (1981)
		One Of Us (6)	Joan Osborne (1996)
On Her Majesty's Secret Service (7)	Propellerheads / David Arnold (1997)	One Shining Moment (10)	Diana Ross (1992)
		One Step Beyond (7)	Madness (1979)
On My Knees (4)	411 featuring Ghostface Killah (2004)	One Step Closer (2)	S Club Juniors (2002)
		One Step Further (2)	Bardo (1982)
On My Own (2)	Patti LaBelle & Michael McDonald (1986)	One Step Too Far (6)	Faithless featuring Dido (2002)
		One Sweet Day (6)	Mariah Carey & Boyz II Men (1995)
On My Radio (8)	Selecter (1979)		
On Our Own (Theme from Ghostbusters II) (4)	Bobby Brown (1989)	One To Another (3)	Charlatans (1996)
		1-2-3 (3) first hit	Len Barry (1965)
On The Beach (7)	Cliff Richard & The Shadows (1964)	1-2-3 (9)	Gloria Estefan & Miami Sound Machine (1988)
On The Inside (3)	Lynne Hamilton (1989)		
On The Radio (7)	Martine McCutcheon (2001)	1-2-3-4 Get With The Wicked (10)	Richard Blackwood (2000)
On The Rebound (1)	Floyd Cramer (1961)	1-2-3 O'Leary (4)	Des O'Connor (1968)
On The Road Again (8) first hit	Canned Heat (1968)	One Vision (7)	Queen (1985)
On The Ropes (EP) (10)	Wonder Stuff (1993)	One Way Love (9)	Cliff Bennett & The Rebel Rousers (1964)
On The Street Where You Live (1)	Vic Damone (1958)		
On Your Own (5)	Blur (1997)	One Way Ticket (9)	Eruption (1979)
Once Around The Block (46)	Badly Drawn Boy (1999)	One Week (5)	Barenaked Ladies (1999)
Once Upon A Dream (7)	Billy Fury (1962)	One Wild Night (10)	Bon Jovi (2001)
Once Upon A Long Ago (10)	Paul McCartney (1987)	One, The (8)	Backstreet Boys (2000)
One (7)	U2 (1992)	One, The (10)	Elton John (1992)
One And One (3)	Robert Miles featuring Maria Nayler (1996)	Onion Song (9)	Marvin Gaye & Tammi Terrell (1969)
One And One Is One (3)	Medicine Head (1973)	Only Fools (Never Fall In Love) (10)	Sonia (1991)
One And Only, The (1)	Chesney Hawkes (1991)	Only Living Boy In New Cross, The (7)	Carter The Unstoppable Sex Machine (1992)
One By One (7)	Cher (1996)		
One Day At A Time (1)	Lena Martell (1979)	Only Love (2)	Nana Mouskouri (1986)

Title	Group/Artiste	Title	Group/Artiste
Only One I Know, The (9) first hit	Charlatans (1990)	Out Of Space / Ruff In The Jungle Bizness (5)	Prodigy (1992)
Only One Road (8)	Celine Dion (1995)	Out Of The Blue (9)	Delta Goodrem (2004)
Only One Woman (5)	Marbles (1968)		
Only Rhyme That Bites, The (10)	MC Tunes vs 808 State (1990)	Out Of Time (1)	Chris Farlowe (1966)
		Out Of Time (5)	Blur (2003)
Only Sixteen (1)	Craig Douglas (1959)	Out Of Touch (7)	Uniting Nations (2004)
Only The Lonely (re-entry) (1)	Roy Orbison (1960)		
Only Thing That Looks Good On Me Is You, The (6)	Bryan Adams (1996)	Out Of Your Mind (2)	True Steppers, with Dane Bowers and Victoria Beckham (2000)
Only Way Is Up, The (1)	Yazz & The Plastic Population (1988)		
Only Way Out, The (10)	Cliff Richard (1982)	Outside (2)	George Michael (1998)
Only When You Leave (3)	Spandau Ballet (1984)	Outside Of Heaven (1)	Eddie Fisher (1953)
Only Yesterday (2)	Carpenters (1975)	Over Under Sideways Down (10)	Yardbirds (1966)
Only You (1)	Flying Pickets (1983)	Over You (5)	Roxy Music (1980)
Only You (3)	Hilltoppers (1956)	Overload (6)	Sugababes (2000)
Only You / The Great Pretender (5)	Platters (1956)	Overprotected (4)	Britney Spears (2002)
Only You (4)	Praise (1991)	Oxygene Part IV (4)	Jean-Michel Jarre (1977)
Only You (2)	Yazoo (1982)		
Only You Can (3)	Fox (1975)	P.I.M.P. (5)	50 Cent (2003)
Ooh Aah ... Just A Little Bit (1)	Gina G (1996)	Pacific (10)	808 State (1989)
Ooh La La (2)	Wiseguys (1999)	Pain Killer (5)	Turin Brakes (2003)
Ooh La La La (Let's Go Dancin') (6)	Kool & The Gang (1982)	Paint It Black (1)	Rolling Stones (1966)
Ooh Stick You! (8)	Daphne & Celeste (2000)	Painter Man (10)	Boney M (1979)
		Pale Shelter (5)	Tears For Fears (1983)
Ooh To Be Ah (7)	Kajagoogoo (1983)		
Ooh-Wakka-Doo-Wakka-Day (8)	Gilbert O'Sullivan (1972)	Paloma Blanca (10)	George Baker Selection (1975)
Ooops (42) first hit	Björk (1991)	Pandora's Box (7)	Orchestral Manoeuvres In The Dark (1991)
Oops (Oh My) (5)	Tweet (2002)		
Oops Up (5)	Snap (1990)		
Oops Up Side Your Head (6)	Gap Band (1980)	Pandora's Kiss (5)	Louise (2003)
Oops! ... I Did It Again (1)	Britney Spears (2000)	Papa Don't Preach (1)	Madonna (1986)
		Papa Don't Preach (3)	Kelly Osbourne (2002)
Open Arms (4)	Mariah Carey (1996)		
Open Road (7)	Gary Barlow (1997)	Papa's Got A Brand New Pigbag (3)	Pigbag (1982)
Open You Mind (7)	Usura (1993)		
Open Your Heart (6)	Human League (1981)	Paper Plane (8)	Status Quo (1973)
		Paper Roses (7)	Kaye Sisters (1960)
Open Your Heart (9)	M People (1995)		
Open Your Heart (4)	Madonna (1986)	Paper Roses (2)	Marie Osmond (1973)
Opera Song, The (Brave New World) (3)	Jurgen Vries featuring CMC (2003)	Paper Sun (5)	Traffic (1967)
		Paperback Writer (1)	Beatles (1966)
Operation Blade (Bass In The Place) (5)	Public Domain (2000)	Paradise City (6)	Guns 'N' Roses (1989)
Opposites Attract (2)	Paula Abdul with The Wild Pair (1990)	Paralysed (8)	Elvis Presley (1957)
		Paranoid (4) first and biggest hit	Black Sabbath (1970)
Ordinary World (5)	Aurora featuring Naimee Coleman (2000)	Paranoid Android (3)	Radiohead (1997)
		Parisienne Walkways (8)	Gary Moore (1979)
Ordinary World (6)	Duran Duran (1993)	Parklife (10)	Blur (1994)
Original Prankster (6)	Offspring (2000)	Part Of The Union (2)	Strawbs (1973)
Orinoco Flow (1)	Enya (1988)	Part-Time Lover (3)	Stevie Wonder (1985)
Orville's Song (4)	Keith Harris & Orville (1982)	Party (2)	Elvis Presley with The Jordanaires (1957)
Ossie's Dream (Spurs Are On Their Way To Wembley) (5)	Tottenham Hotspur FA Cup Final Squad (1981)		
Our Favourite Melodies (9)	Craig Douglas (1962)	Party Fears Two (9) first and biggest hit	Associates (1982)
		Party For Two (10)	Shania Twain featuring Mark McGrath (2004)
Our House (5)	Madness (1982)		
Our Lips Are Sealed (7)	Fun Boy Three (1983)		
Out In The Fields (5)	Gary Moore & Phil Lynott (1985)	Party People ... Friday Night (5)	911 (1997)
		Party Pops (24) first hit	Russ Conway (1957)
Out Of Reach (4)	Gabrielle (2001)	Party's Over, The (9)	Lonnie Donegan (1962)

Title	Group/Artiste	Title	Group/Artiste
Pasadena (4)	Temperance Seven (1961)	Phatt Bass (9)	Warp Brothers vs Aquagen (2000)
Pass And Move (It's The Liverpool Groove) (4)	Liverpool FC & The Boot Room Boyz (1996)	Phenomenon (9)	LL Cool J (1997)
		Phorever People (5)	Shamen (1992)
Pass It On (5)	Coral (2003)	Photograph (8)	Ringo Starr (1973)
Pass That Dutch (10)	Missy Elliott (2003)	Physical (7)	Olivia Newton-John (1981)
Pass The Dutchie (1)	Musical Youth (1982)		
Passengers (5)	Elton John (1984)	Piano Party (10)	Winifred Atwell (1959)
Passion (remix) (6)	Gat Decor (1996)		
Patches (2)	Clarence Carter (1970)	Pick A Part That's New (4)	Stereophonics (1999)
Patience (10)	Guns 'N' Roses (1989)	Pick Up The Pieces (6) first and biggest hit	Average White Band (1975)
Patricia (8)	Perez Prado & His Orchestra (1958)	Pick Up The Pieces (8)	Hudson-Ford (1973)
		Pickin' A Chicken (9) first and only hit	Eve Boswell with Glen Somer Orchestra (1955)
Peace (8)	Sabrina Johnston (1991)		
Peace In Our Time (8)	Cliff Richard (1993)	Picture Of You (2)	Boyzone (1997)
Peace On Earth / Little Drummer Boy (3)	David Bowie & Bing Crosby (1982)	Picture Of You, A (2)	Joe Brown & The Bruvvers (1962)
Peaches (8)	Presidents of the United States of America (1996)	Picture This (12)	Blondie (1978)
		Pictures Of Lily (4)	Who (1967)
		Pictures Of Matchstick Men (7) first hit	Status Quo (1968)
Peaches / Go Buddy Go (8)	Stranglers (1977)		
Peacock Suit (5)	Paul Weller (1996)	Pie Jesu (3)	Sarah Brightman & Paul Miles-Kingston (1985)
Pearl In The Shell (7)	Howard Jones (1984)		
Pearl's A Singer (8) first hit	Elkie Brooks (1977)	Piece Of My Heart (7)	Shaggy featuring Marsha (1997)
Peek-A-Boo (7)	New Vaudeville Band (1967)	Pieces Of Me (4)	Ashlee Simpson (2004)
Peggy Sue (6)	Buddy Holly (1957)	Pied Piper (5)	Crispian St Peters (1966)
Penny Lane / Strawberry Fields Forever (2)	Beatles (1967)		
People Are People (4)	Depeche Mode (1984)	Pied Piper (11) second and only other hit	Bob and Marcia (1971)
		Pinball Wizard (7)	Elton John (1976)
People Everyday (2)	Arrested Development (1992)	Pinball Wizard (4)	Who (1969)
		Pink Cadillac (5)	Natalie Cole (1988)
People Hold On (4)	Lisa Stansfield vs Dirty Rotten Scoundrels (1997)	Pipes Of Peace (1)	Paul McCartney (1983)
		Pitchin' (In Every Direction) (6)	Hi-Gate (2000)
People Like You People Like Me (5)	Glitter Band (1976)	Place Your Hands (6)	Reef (1996)
		Planet Earth (12) first hit	Duran Duran (1981)
Pepe (2)	Duane Eddy (1961)	Play (3)	Jennifer Lopez (2001)
Pepper Box (6)	Peppers (1974)		
Perfect (1)	Fairground Attraction (1988)	Play Me Like You Play Your Guitar (9)	Duane Eddy & The Rebelettes (1975)
Perfect Day (1)	Various Artists (1997)	Play That Funky Music (10)	Vanilla Ice (1991)
		Play That Funky Music (7)	Wild Cherry (1976)
Perfect Gentleman (4)	Wyclef Jean (2001)	Played A Live (The Bongo Song) (6)	Safri Duo (2001)
Perfect Moment (1)	Martine McCutcheon (1999)		
		Playing With Knives (4)	Bizarre Inc (1991)
Perfect 10 (2)	Beautiful South (1998)	Please (7)	U2 (1997)
		Please Come Home For Christmas (7)	Bon Jovi (1994)
Perfect Year, The (5)	Dina Carroll (1993)		
Perfidia (4)	Ventures (1960)	Please Don't Fall In Love (7)	Cliff Richard (1983)
Perseverance (5)	Terrorvision (1996)	Please Don't Go (3)	KC & The Sunshine Band (1979)
Personality (6)	Anthony Newley (1959)	Please Don't Go (4)	No Mercy (1997)
		Please Don't Go (3)	Donald Peers (1968)
Personality (9)	Lloyd Price (1959)	Please Don't Go / Game Boy (1)	KWS (1992)
Peter Gunn (8)	Art Of Noise featuring Duane Eddy (1986)	Please Don't Make Me Cry (10)	UB40 (1983)
		Please Don't Tease (1)	Cliff Richard & The Shadows (1960)
Peter Gunn Theme (6)	Duane Eddy (1959)		
Petite Fleur (9)	Chris Barber's Jazz Band (1959)	Please Don't Turn Me On (4)	Artful Dodger featuring Lifford (2000)
Phantom Of The Opera, The (7)	Sarah Brightman & Steve Harley (1986)	Please Forgive Me (2)	Bryan Adams (1993)
		Please Help Me I'm Falling (9)	Hank Locklin (1960)
		Please Mr Postman (2)	Carpenters (1975)
		Please Please Me (2)	Beatles (1963)

MUSIC

POP

Title	Group/Artiste	Title	Group/Artiste
Please Stay (10)	Kylie Minogue (2000)	Pretty Vacant (6)	Sex Pistols (1977)
Please Tell Him That I Said Hello (8)	Dana (1975)	Price Of Love, The (2)	Everly Brothers (1965)
Poetry In Motion (1)	Johnny Tillotson (1960)	Pride (In The Name Of Love) (3)	U2 (1984)
Point Of View (3)	DB Boulevard (2002)	Prince Charming (1)	Adam & The Ants (1981)
Poison (45)	Bardot (2001)	Princess In Rags (9)	Gene Pitney (1965)
Poison (2)	Alice Cooper (1989)	Private Emotion (9)	Ricky Martin featuring Meja (2000)
Poison Arrow (6)	ABC (1982)		
Poison Ivy (7)	Lambrettas (1980)		
Pool Hall Richard / I Wish It Would Rain (8)	Faces (1973)	Private Investigations (2)	Dire Straits (1982)
Poor Little Fool (4)	Ricky Nelson (1958)	Private Number (8)	Judy Clay & William Bell (1968)
Poor Man's Son (5)	Rockin' Berries (1965)	Private Number (3)	911 (1999)
Poor Me (1)	Adam Faith (1960)	Prize Of Gold (6)	Joan Regan (1955)
Poor People Of Paris (1)	Winifred Atwell (1956)	Problems (6)	Everly Brothers (1959)
Pop (9)	N Sync (2001)	Professional Widow (remix) (1)	Tori Amos (1997)
Pop Go The Workers (5)	Barron Knights with Duke D'Mond (1965)	Promise Me (3)	Beverley Craven (1991)
Pop Muzik (2)	M (1979)	Promised Land (9)	Elvis Presley (1975)
Pop Ya Colla (2)	Usher (2001)	Promises (6)	Ken Dodd (1966)
Popcorn (5)	Hot Butter (1972)	Promises (38) first hit	Take That (1991)
Poppa Piccolino (2)	Diana Decker (1953)	Proper Crimbo (4)	Bo Selecta (2003)
Poppa Piccolino (re-entry) (5)	Diana Decker (1954)	Protect Your Mind (For The Love Of A Princess) (4)	DJ Sakin & Friends (1999)
Porcelain (5)	Moby (2000)		
Portrait Of My Love (3)	Matt Monro (1960)	Proud Mary (8) first hit	Creedence Clearwater Revival (1969)
Portsmouth (3)	Mike Oldfield (1976)		
Positively Fourth Street (8)	Bob Dylan (1965)	Proud One, The (5)	Osmonds (1975)
Power Of A Woman (5)	Eternal (1995)	Prove Your Love (8)	Taylor Dayne (1988)
Power Of Good-Bye / Little Star, The (6)	Madonna (1998)	Pub With No Beer, A (3)	Slim Dusty (1959)
Power Of Love, The / Do You Believe In Love (re-issue) (9)	Huey Lewis & The News (1986)	Public Image (9)	Public Image Ltd (1978)
Power Of Love, The (re-issue) (6)	Frankie Goes To Hollywood (2000)	Pump Up The Jam (2)	Technotronic featuring Felly (1989)
Power Of Love, The (re-issue) (10)	Frankie Goes To Hollywood (1993)	Pump Up The Volume / Anitina (The First Time) (1)	Marrs (1987)
Power Of Love, The (4)	Celine Dion (1994)	Puppet On A String (1)	Sandie Shaw (1967)
Power Of Love, The (1)	Frankie Goes To Hollywood (1984)	Puppy Love (1) first solo hit	Donny Osmond (1972)
Power Of Love, The (1)	Jennifer Rush (1985)	Puppy Love / Sleigh Ride (6)	S Club Juniors (2002)
Power Rangers (3)	Mighty Morphin Power Rangers (1994)	Pure And Simple (1)	Hear'Say (2001)
Power To All Our Friends (4)	Cliff Richard (1973)	Pure Morning (4)	Placebo (1998)
Power To The People (7)	John Lennon & The Plastic Ono Band (1971)	Pure Shores (1)	All Saints (2000)
		Purple Haze (3)	Jimi Hendrix Experience (1967)
Power, The (1) first hit	Snap (1990)	Purple Pills / Purple Hills (2)	D12 (2001)
Praise You (1)	Fatboy Slim (1999)	Purple Rain (8)	Prince & The Revolution (1984)
Pray (8)	MC Hammer (1990)	Purple People Eater, The (12)	Sheb Wooley (1958)
Pray (1)	Take That (1993)	Push It (9)	Garbage (1998)
Praying For Time (6)	George Michael (1990)	Push It / Tramp (2)	Salt-N-Pepa (1988)
Pretend (2)	Nat 'King' Cole (1953)	Push The Feeling On (remix) (3)	Nightcrawlers featuring John Reid (1995)
Pretend (4)	Alvin Stardust (1981)		
Pretty Blue Eyes (4)	Craig Douglas (1960)	Pushbike Song, The (2)	Mixtures (1971)
		Puss 'N' Boots (5)	Adam Ant (1983)
Pretty Flamingo (1)	Manfred Mann (1966)	Put Em High (6)	Stonebridge featuring Therese (2004)
Pretty Fly (For A White Guy) (1)	Offspring (1999)		
Pretty Good Year (7)	Tori Amos (1994)	Put The Needle On It (7)	Dannii Minogue (2002)
Pretty Green Eyes (2)	Ultrabeat (2003)		
Pretty Little Angel Eyes (5)	Showaddywaddy (1978)	Put Your Arms Around Me (10)	Texas (1997)
		Put Your Hands Together (7)	D Mob (1990)
Pretty Little Black-Eyed Susie (2)	Guy Mitchell (1953)	Put Your Head On My Shoulder (7)	Paul Anka (1959)
Pretty Paper (6)	Roy Orbison (1964)		

Title	Group/Artiste	Title	Group/Artiste
Put Your Love In Me (10)	Hot Chocolate (1977)	Rat Race / Rude Boys Outa Jail (5)	Specials (1980)
Putting On The Style / Gambling Man (1)	Lonnie Donegan (1957)	Rat Trap (1)	Boomtown Rats (1978)
Pyjamarama (10)	Roxy Music (1973)	Rave On (5)	Buddy Holly (1958)
Pyramid Song (5)	Radiohead (2001)	Raving I'm Raving (2)	Shut Up & Dance (1992)
Quarter To Three (7)	Gary US Bonds (1961)	Rawhide (6)	Frankie Laine (1959)
Que Sera Mi Vida (5)	Gibson Brothers (1979)	Ray Of Light (2)	Madonna (1998)
		Reach (2)	S Club 7 (2000)
Queen Of Clubs (7)	KC & The Sunshine Band (1974)	Reach For The Stars / Climb Ev'ry Mountain (1)	Shirley Bassey (1961)
Queen Of My Heart (1)	Westlife (2001)	Reach Out I'll Be There (1)	Four Tops (1966)
Queen Of New Orleans (10)	Jon Bon Jovi (1997)	Reach Up (Papa's Got A Brand New Pig Bag) (6)	Perfecto Allstarz (1995)
Question (2)	Moody Blues (1970)	(Reach Up For The) Sunrise (5)	Duran Duran (2004)
Quiereme Mucho (Yours) (3)	Julio Iglesias (1982)	Ready Or Not (5)	Course (1997)
Quit Playing Games (With My Heart) (2)	Backstreet Boys (1997)	Ready Or Not (1)	Fugees (1996)
		Ready Willing And Able (7)	Doris Day (1955)
Rabbit (8)	Chas & Dave (1980)	Real Gone Kid (8)	Deacon Blue (1988)
Race With The Devil (8)	Gun (1968)		
Race, The (7)	Yello (1988)	Real Good Time (7)	Alda (1998)
Rachel (10)	Al Martino (1953)	Real Love (4)	Beatles (1996)
Rachmaninoff's Variation On A Theme (9)	Winifred Atwell (1954)	Real Love (8)	Time Frequency (1993)
Radancer (6)	Marmalade (1972)	Real Slim Shady, The (1)	Eminem (2000)
Radar Love (7)	Golden Earring (1973)	Real Thing, The (1)	Tony Di Bart (1994)
Radio (1)	Robbie Williams (2004)	Real Thing, The (9)	Lisa Stansfield (1997)
Radio Gaga (2)	Queen (1984)	Real Thing, The (6)	2 Unlimited (1994)
Rag Doll (2)	Four Seasons featuring Frankie Valli (1964)	Real Things (4)	Javine (2003)
		Real To Me (1)	Brian McFadden (2004)
Ragamuffin Man (8)	Manfred Mann (1969)	Real Wild Child (Wild One) (10)	Iggy Pop (1986)
		Real World (9)	D-Side (2003)
Rage Hard (4)	Frankie Goes To Hollywood (1986)	Really Free (27) first hit	John Otway and Wild Willy Barrett (1977)
Rags To Riches (9)	Elvis Presley (1971)	Really Saying Something (5)	Bananarama with Fun Boy Three (1982)
Rags To Riches (re-entry) (3)	David Whitfield (1954)		
Rain (7)	Madonna (1993)	Reason (8)	Ian Van Dahl (2002)
Rain (7)	Status Quo (1976)	Reasons To Be Cheerful (Part 3) (3)	Ian Dury & The Blockheads (1979)
Rain And Tears (29)	Aphrodite's Child (1968)	Reason To Believe (19) first hit	Rod Stewart (1971)
Rain Or Shine (2)	Five Star (1986)	Rebel Rebel (5)	David Bowie (1974)
Rain Rain Rain (8)	Frankie Laine, The Four Lads and The Buddy Cole Quartet (1954)	Rebel Yell (6)	Billy Idol (1985)
		Red Alert (5)	Basement Jaxx (1999)
Rain, The (4)	Oran 'Juice' Jones (1986)	Red Balloon (7)	Dave Clark Five (1968)
Rain (Supa Dupa Fly), The (first hit)	Missy 'Misdemeanor' Elliott (1997)	Red Blooded Woman (5)	Kylie Minogue (2004)
Rainbow (3)	Marmalade (1970)	Red Dress (7)	Alvin Stardust (1974)
Rainbow Valley (5)	Love Affair (1968)	Red Letter Day, A (9)	Pet Shop Boys (1997)
Raincloud (6)	Lighthouse Family (1997)	Red Light Spells Danger (2)	Billy Ocean (1977)
Raindrops Keep Falling On My Head (10)	Sacha Distel (1970)	Red Red Wine (1)	UB40 (1983)
		Red River Rock (3)	Johnny & The Hurricanes (1959)
Rainy Day Women Nos 12 And 35 (7)	Bob Dylan (1966)	Reet Petite (The Sweetest Girl In Town) (6)	Jackie Wilson (1957)
Ramblin' Rose (5)	Nat 'King' Cole (1962)	Reet Petite (The Sweetest Girl In Town) (re-issue) (1)	Jackie Wilson (1986)
Ramona (4)	Bachelors (1964)	Reflections (5)	Diana Ross & The Supremes (1967)
Randy (9)	Blue Mink (1973)		
Rapper's Delight (3)	Sugarhill Gang (1979)	Reflections Of My Life (3)	Marmalade (1969)
		Reflex, The (1)	Duran Duran (1984)
Rapture (5)	Blondie (1981)	Reggae Tune (10)	Andy Fairweather-Low (1974)
Rapture (2)	IIO (2001)		
Rasputin (2)	Boney M (1978)	Regret (4)	New Order (1993)

MUSIC POP

Title	Group/Artiste	Title	Group/Artiste
Regulate (5)	Warren G & Nate Dogg (1994)	Rhythm Of The Night (4)	DeBarge (1985)
		Rhythm Of The Night, The (2)	Corona (1994)
Reigns / Clap Back (9)	Ja Rule (2003)	Rhythm Of The Rain (5)	Cascades (1963)
Relax (1) first hit	Frankie Goes To Hollywood (1983)	Rhythm Of The Rain (9)	Jason Donovan (1990)
Relax (re-issue) (5)	Frankie Goes To Hollywood (1993)	Richard III (2)	Supergrass (1997)
Release Me (1)	Engelbert Humperdinck (1967)	Ricochet (8)	Joan Regan & The Squadronaires (1953)
Relight My Fire (1)	Take That featuring Lulu (1993)	Ricochet (re-entry) (9)	Joan Regan & The Squadronaires (1954)
Remember Me (8)	Blue Boy (1997)	Riddle, The (3)	Nik Kershaw (1984)
Remember Me (7)	Diana Ross (1971)	Ride A White Swan (2)	T Rex (1970)
Remember Me This Way (3)	Gary Glitter (1974)	Ride It (4)	Geri (2004)
Remember (Sha-La-La) (6)	Bay City Rollers (1974)	Ride Like The Wind (3)	East Side Beat (1991)
Remember The Time / Come Together (3)	Michael Jackson (1992)	Right Now 2004 / Someone Like Me (8)	Atomic Kitten (2004)
Remember You're A Womble (3)	Wombles (1974)	Ride On Time (1) first hit	Black Box (1989)
Remember You're Mine / There's A Goldmine In The Sky (5)	Pat Boone (1957)	Ride Wit Me (3)	Nelly featuring City Spud (2001)
		Riders In The Sky (8)	Ramrods (1961)
Reminisce / Where The Story Ends (8)	Blazin' Squad (2003)	Right Back Where We Started From (8)	Maxine Nightingale (1975)
Renaissance (5)	M People (1994)	Right Back Where We Started From (4)	Sinitta (1989)
Rendezvous (8)	Craig David (2001)	Right By Your Side (10)	Eurythmics (1983)
Rendez-Vu (4)	Basement Jaxx (1999)	Right Here (3)	SWV (1993)
		Right Here Right Now (2)	Fatboy Slim (1999)
Renegade Master '98 (remix) (3)	Wildchild (1998)	Right Here Waiting (2)	Richard Marx (1989)
Rent (8)	Pet Shop Boys (1987)	Right In The Night (Fall In Love With Music) (re-issue) (10)	Jam & Spoon featuring Plavka (1995)
Renta Santa (10)	Chris Hill (1975)	Right Now (10) first hit	Atomic Kitten (1999)
Re-Offender (7)	Travis (2003)	Right Said Fred (10)	Bernard Cribbins (1962)
Requiem (4)	London Boys (1989)		
Re-Rewind The Crowd Say Bo Selecta (2)	Artful Dodger featuring Craig David (1999)	Ring My Bell (1) first and only hit	Anita Ward (1979)
Rescue Me (3)	Madonna (1991)	Ring Ring (Ha Ha Hey) (10)	De La Soul (1991)
Rescue Me (8)	Ultra (1999)	Rio (9)	Duran Duran (1982)
Respect (10)	Aretha Franklin (1967)	Rip It Up (4)	Bill Haley & His Comets (1956)
Respect Yourself (7)	Bruce Willis (1987)	Rip It Up (8)	Orange Juice (1983)
Respectable (1)	Mel & Kim (1987)	Rise (1)	Gabrielle (2000)
Resurrection (3)	PPK (2001)	Rise & Fall (2)	Craig David featuring Sting (2003)
Resurrection Shuffle, The (3)	Ashton Gardner & Dyke (1971)		
Return Of Django / Dollar In The Teeth (5)	Upsetters (1969)	Rise And Fall Of Flingel Bunt, The (5)	Shadows (1964)
Return Of The Los Palmas Seven, The (7)	Madness (1981)	Rise To The Occasion (10)	Climie Fisher (1987)
Return Of The Mack (1)	Mark Morrison (1996)	River Deep Mountain High (3)	Ike & Tina Turner (1966)
Return To Innocence (3)	Enigma (1994)	River Of Dreams, The (3)	Billy Joel (1993)
Return To Me (2)	Dean Martin (1958)	River, The (3)	Ken Dodd (1965)
Return To Sender (1)	Elvis Presley with The Jordanaires (1962)	Riverdance (9)	Bill Whelan and Anuna and RTE Concert Orchestra (1994)
Reunited (4)	Peaches & Herb (1979)	Rivers Of Babylon / Brown Girl In The Ring (1)	Boney M (1978)
Reverence (10)	Faithless (1997)	Road Rage (5)	Catatonia (1998)
Reverence (10)	Jesus & Mary Chain (1992)	Road To Hell (Part 2), The (10)	Chris Rea (1989)
Reverend Black Grape (9)	Black Grape (1995)	Road To Nowhere (6)	Talking Heads (1985)
Reward (6)	Teardrop Explodes (1981)	Robert De Niro's Waiting (3)	Bananarama (1984)
Rhinestone Cowboy (4)	Glen Campbell (1975)	Robin Hood (10)	Gary Miller (1956)
		Robin (The Hooded Man) (42)	Clannad (1984)
Rhythm Is A Dancer (1)	Snap (1992)	Rocafella (13)	Cam'ron featuring Juelz Santana (2002)
Rhythm Is A Mystery (3)	K-Klass (1991)		
Rhythm Of My Heart (3)	Rod Stewart (1991)		

Title	Group/Artiste	Title	Group/Artiste
Rock A Hula Baby / Can't Help Falling in Love(1)	Elvis Presley with The Jordanaires (1962)	Roll On / This Is How We Do It (7)	Mis-Teeq (2002)
Rock And Roll (Parts 1 And 2) (2)	Gary Glitter (1972)	Roll Over Beethoven (6)	Electric Light Orchestra (1973)
Rock And Roll Waltz (1)	Kay Starr (1956)	Roll Over Lay Down (9)	Status Quo (1975)
Rock Around The Clock (re-entry) (1)	Bill Haley & His Comets (1955)	Roll With It (2)	Oasis (1995)
Rock Around The Clock (re-entry) (5)	Bill Haley & His Comets (1956)	Rollercoaster (1)	B*Witched (1998)
Rock DJ (1)	Robbie Williams (2000)	Rollin' (1)	Limp Bizkit (2001)
		Rollin' Home (9)	Status Quo (1986)
Rock Island Line (8) first hit	Lonnie Donegan Skiffle Group (1956)	Rolling Stone (5)	David Essex (1975)
		Romeo (6)	Basement Jaxx (2001)
Rock Me Amadeus (1)	Falco (1986)	Romeo (3)	Petula Clark (1961)
Rock Me Gently (2)	Andy Kim (1974)	Romeo (3)	Romeo Dunn (2002)
Rock My Heart (9)	Haddaway (1994)	Romeo (4)	Mr Big (1977)
Rock 'N' Roll (8)	Status Quo (1981)	Romeo And Juliet (8)	Dire Straits (1981)
Rock 'N' Roll Damnation (24) first hit	AC/DC (1978)	Roobarb And Custard (7)	Shaft (1991)
		Room In Your Heart (5)	Living In A Box (1989)
Rock 'N' Roll Winter (6)	Wizzard (1974)	Room On The 3rd Floor (5)	McFly (2004)
Rock On (3) first hit	David Essex (1973)	Rose Garden (3)	Lynn Anderson (1971)
Rock The Boat (4)	Forrest (1983)		
Rock The Boat (6)	Hues Corporation (1974)	Rose Marie (1) first hit	Slim Whitman (1955)
		Roses (4)	Outkast (2004)
Rock This Town (9)	Stray Cats (1981)	Roses Are Red (3)	Ronnie Carroll (1962)
Rock Wit U (Awww Baby) (7)	Ashanti (2003)		
Rock With You (7)	Michael Jackson (1980)	Roses Are Red (8)	Mac Band with McCampbell Brothers (1988)
Rock Your Baby (8)	KWS (1992)	Rosie (4)	Don Partridge (1968)
Rock Your Baby (1) first hit	George McCrae (1974)	Rotterdam (5)	Beautiful South (1996)
Rock Your Body (2)	Justin Timberlake (2003)	Roulette (1)	Russ Conway (1959)
Rock-A-Beatin' Boogie (4)	Bill Haley & His Comets (1955)	Round And Round (9)	Jaki Graham (1985)
		Round Round (1)	Sugababes (2002)
Rock-A-Billy (1)	Guy Mitchell (1957)	Roussos Phenomenon EP, The (1)	Demis Roussos (1976)
Rockafeller Shank, The (6)	Fatboy Slim (1998)		
Rockaria! (9)	Electric Light Orchestra (1977)	Rubber Ball (4) first hit	Bobby Vee (1961)
		Rubber Ball (9)	Marty Wilde (1961)
Rocket (6)	Mud (1974)	Rubber Bullets (1)	10CC (1973)
Rocket Man (2)	Elton John (1972)	Rubberneckin' (remix) (5)	Elvis Presley (2003)
Rockin' All Over The World (3)	Status Quo (1977)	Ruby Don't Talk Your Love To Town (2)	Kenny Rogers & The First Edition (1969)
Rockin' Around The Christmas Tree (6)	Brenda Lee (1962)		
		Ruby Tuesday (9)	Melanie (1970)
Rockin' Around The Christmas Tree (3)	Mel & Kim (1987)	Ruby Tuesday / Let's Spend The Night Together (3)	Rolling Stones (1967)
Rockin' Good Way, A (5)	Shakin' Stevens & Bonnie Tyler (1984)	Rumble In The Jungle (3)	Fugees featuring A Tribe Called Quest, Busta Rhymes and Forte (1997)
Rockin' Over The Beat (9)	Technotronic featuring Ya Kid K (1990)		
		Run (5)	Snow Patrol (2004)
Rockin' Robin (3)	Michael Jackson (1972)	Run Away (6)	MC Sar & The Real McCoy (1995)
Rockin' Roll Baby (6)	Stylistics (1974)	Run Baby Run (10)	Newbeats (1971)
Rockin' Through The Rye (3)	Bill Haley & His Comets (1956)	Run For Home (10)	Lindisfarne (1978)
		Run Run Away (7)	Slade (1984)
Rocking Goose (3)	Johnny & The Hurricanes (1960)	Run Run Run (6)	Jo Jo Gunne (1972)
		Run To Him (6)	Bobby Vee (1961)
Rockit (8)	Herbie Hancock (1983)	Run To Me (9)	Bee Gees (1972)
Rocks / Funky Jam (7)	Primal Scream (1994)	Run To The Hills (7)	Iron Maiden (1982)
		Run To The Hills (re-issue) (9)	Iron Maiden (2002)
Rodrigo's Guitar Concerto De Aranjuez (3)	Manuel & The Music Of The Mountains (1976)	Run To The Sun (6)	Erasure (1994)
		Run To You (11) first hit	Bryan Adams (1985)
		Run To You (3)	Rage (1992)
Rok Da House (5)	Beatmasters with The Cookie Crew (1988)	Runaway (2)	Corrs (1999)
		Runaway (6)	Janet Jackson (1995)
		Runaway (1) first hit	Del Shannon (1961)
Roll Away The Stone (8)	Mott The Hoople (1973)	Runaway Boys (9)	Stray Cats (1980)
		Runaway Train (re-entry) (7)	Soul Asylum (1993)

MUSIC POP

Title	Group/Artiste	Title	Group/Artiste
Runner, The (10)	Three Degrees (1979)	Satisfaction (2)	Benny Benassi presents The Biz (2003)
Running Bear (1)	Johnny Preston (1960)	Satisfy You (8)	Puff Daddy featuring R Kelly (2000)
Running In The Family (6)	Level 42 (1987)	Saturday Love (6)	Cherelle with Alexander O'Neal (1985)
Running Scared (9)	Roy Orbison (1961)		
Running Up That Hill (3)	Kate Bush (1985)		
Running With The Night (9)	Lionel Richie (1983)	Saturday Night (6)	Suede (1997)
Rush Rush (6)	Paula Abdul (1991)	Saturday Night (1)	Whigfield (1994)
Rushes (5)	Darius (2002)	Saturday Night's Alright For	Elton John (1973)
S Club Party (2)	S Club 7 (1999)	Fighting (7)	
S**t On You (10)	D12 (2001)	Savage, The (10)	Shadows (1961)
S.O.S. (6)	Abba (1975)	Save A Prayer (2)	Duran Duran (1982)
Sabre Dance (5)	Love Sculpture (1968)	Save Me (4)	Dave Dee, Dozy, Beaky, Mick & Tich (1966)
Sacred Trust / After You're Gone (2) first hit	One True Voice (2002)		
Sacrifice (re-issue) / Healing Hands (1)	Elton John (1990)	Save Our Love (8)	Eternal (1994)
		Save The Best For Last (3)	Vanessa Williams (1992)
Sad Songs (Say So Much) (7)	Elton John (1984)		
Sad Sweet Dreamer (1)	Sweet Sensation (1974)	Save The Last Dance For Me (2)	Drifters (1960)
		Save Tonight (6) first and biggest hit	Eagle-Eye Cherry (1998)
Saddle Up (9) first and only hit	David Christie (1982)		
Sadness Part 1 (1)	Enigma (1990)	Save Your Kisses For Me (1)	Brotherhood Of Man (1976)
Safety Dance, The (6)	Men Without Hats (1983)		
		Save Your Love (1)	Renee & Renato (1982)
Sail On (8)	Commodores (1979)		
Sailing (1)	Rod Stewart (1975)	Save Yourself / Genie In A Bottle (10)	Speedway (2003)
Sailing On The Seven Seas (3)	Orchestral Manoeuvres In The Dark (1991)	Saved By The Bell (2)	Robin Gibb (1969)
		Saving All My Love For You (1) first hit	Whitney Houston (1985)
Sailing (re-entry) (3)	Rod Stewart (1976)		
Sailor (1)	Petula Clark (1961)	Saviour's Day (1)	Cliff Richard (1990)
Sailor (10)	Anne Shelton (1961)	Say A Little Prayer (10)	Bomb The Bass featuring Maureen (1988)
Saint, The (3)	Orbital (1997)		
Saints Rock 'N' Roll, The (5)	Bill Haley & His Comets (1956)		
Sale Of The Century (10)	Sleeper (1996)	Say Cheese (10)	Fast Food Rockers (2003)
Sally (4)	Gerry Monroe (1970)	Say Goodbye / Love Ain't Gonna Wait For You (2)	S Club (2003)
Salsoul Nugget (If U Wanna) (6)	M & S presents The Girl Next Door (2001)	Say Hello Wave Goodbye (3)	Soft Cell (1982)
		Say I Won't Be There (5)	Springfields (1963)
Saltwater (6)	Julian Lennon (1991)	Say I'm Your No.1 (7)	Princess (1985)
Saltwater (6)	Chicane with Maire Brennan of Clannad (1999)	Say It Again (6)	Precious (1999)
		Say It Again (7)	Jermaine Stewart (1988)
Salva Mea (remix) (9)	Faithless (1996)	Say It Isn't So (10)	Bon Jovi (2000)
Sam (6)	Olivia Newton-John (1977)	Say It Isn't So (4)	Gareth Gates (2003)
		Say My Name (3)	Destiny's Child (2000)
Samba De Janeiro (8)	Bellini (1997)	Say Say Say (2)	Paul McCartney & Michael Jackson (1983)
Same Old Brand New You (1)	A1 (2000)		
San Bernadino (7)	Christie (1970)		
San Franciscan Nights (7)	Eric Burdon & The Animals (1967)	Say What You Want (3)	Texas (1997)
San Francisco (Be Sure To Wear Some Flowers In Your Hair) (1)	Scott McKenzie (1967)	Say What You Want / Insane (re-recording) (4)	Texas featuring The Wu-Tang Clan (1998)
		Say Wonderful Things (6)	Ronnie Carroll (1963)
Sanctify Yourself (10)	Simple Minds (1986)	Say You Love Me (7)	Simply Red (1998)
Sandstorm (8)	Cast (1996)	Say You Say Me (8)	Lionel Richie (1985)
Sandstorm (3)	Darude (2000)	Say You'll Be Mine (1)	Spice Girls (1996)
Sandy (2)	John Travolta (1978)	Say You'll Be Mine / Better The Devil You Know (4)	Steps (1999)
Santa Bring My Baby Back (To Me) (7)	Elvis Presley (1957)	Say You're Mine Again (10)	June Hutton with Axel Stordahl (1953)
Santa Claus Is Comin' To Town / My Hometown (9)	Bruce Springsteen (1985)	Say You're Mine Again (re-entry) (6)	June Hutton with Axel Stordahl (1953)
Santa's List (5)	Cliff Richard (2003)		
Santo Natale (2)	David Whitfield (1954)	Scandalous (2)	Mis-Teeq (2003)
Satan (3)	Orbital (1997)	Scarlett O'Hara (2)	Jet Harris & Tony Meehan (1963)
Satellite Of Love 04 (10)	Lou Reed (2004)		

Title	Group/Artiste	Title	Group/Artiste
Scatman (3)	Scatman John (1995)	Seven Days And One Week (3)	BBE (1996)
		Seven Drunken Nights (7)	Dubliners (1967)
Scatman's World (10)	Scatman John (1995)	Seven Little Girls Sitting In The Back Seat (3)	Avons (1959)
School Day (Ring! Ring! Goes The Bell) (24) first hit	Chuck Berry (1957)		
School's Out (1) first hit	Alice Cooper (1972)	Seven Lonely Days (re-entry) (6)	Gisele McKenzie (1953)
Scientist, The (10)	Coldplay (2002)	7 Nation Army (7)	White Stripes (2003)
Scotch On The Rocks (8)	Band Of The Black Watch (1975)	Seven Seas Of Rye (10) first hit	Queen (1974)
Scream (3)	Michael Jackson & Janet Jackson (1995)	7 Seconds (3)	Youssou N'Dour featuring Neneh Cherry (1994)
Scream If You Wanna Go Faster (8)	Geri Halliwell (2001)	Seven Tears (1)	Goombay Dance Band (1982)
Se A Vide (That's The Way Life Is) (8)	Pet Shop Boys (1996)	7 Ways To Love (8)	Cola Boy (1991)
		Sex On The Beach (2)	T-Spoon (1998)
Sea Of Love (3)	Marty Wilde (1959)	Sexbomb (3)	Tom Jones & Mousse T (2000)
Sealed With A Kiss (1)	Jason Donovan (1989)		
		Sexcrime (Nineteen Eighty-Four) (4)	Eurythmics (1984)
Sealed With A Kiss (3)	Brian Hyland (1962)		
Sealed With A Kiss (re-issue) (7)	Brian Hyland (1975)	Sexed Up (10)	Robbie Williams (2003)
Search For The Hero (9)	M People (1995)		
Searchin' (30) first hit	Coasters (1957)	(Sexual) Healing (4)	Marvin Gaye (1982)
Searchin' (I Gotta Find A Man) (6)	Hazell Dean (1984)	Sexy Eyes (4)	Dr Hook (1980)
Searchin' My Soul (10)	Vonda Shepard (1998)	Sexy MF / Strollin' (4)	Prince & The New Power Generation (1992)
Searching (4)	China Black (1994)	Sha La La (3)	Manfred Mann (1964)
Seaside Shuffle (2)	Terry Dactyl & The Dinosaurs (1972)	Sha La La La Lee (3)	Small Faces (1966)
		Shackles (Praise You) (5)	Mary Mary (2000)
Seasons In The Sun (1)	Terry Jacks (1974)	Shaddup You Face (1)	Joe Dolce Music Theatre (1981)
Secret (5)	Madonna (1994)		
Secret Love (5)	Bee Gees (1991)	Shake Rattle And Roll (4) first hit	Bill Haley & His Comets (1954)
Secret Love (1)	Doris Day (1954)		
Secret Love (4)	Kathy Kirby (1963)	Shake Ur Body (7)	Shy FX & T Power featuring Di (2002)
Secret Lovers (10)	Atlantic Starr (1986)		
Secrets (9)	Eternal (1996)	Shake Ya Tailfeather (10)	Nelly / P Diddy / Murphy Lee (2003)
Secrets That You Keep, The (3)	Mud (1975)		
See Emily Play (6)	Pink Floyd (1967)	Shake You Down (6)	Gregory Abbott (1986)
See It In A Boy's Eyes (5)	Jamelia (2004)		
See My Baby Jive (1)	Wizzard (1973)	Shake Your Body (Down To The Ground) (4)	Jacksons (1979)
See My Friend (10)	Kinks (1965)		
See The Day (3)	Dee C Lee (1985)	Shake Your Head (4)	Was (Not Was) (1992)
See Ya (6)	Atomic Kitten (2000)		
See You (6)	Depeche Mode (1982)	Shake Your Love (7)	Debbie Gibson (1988)
		Shakespeare's Way With Words (10)	One True Voice (2003)
See You Later Alligator (7)	Bill Haley & His Comets (1956)	Shakin' All Over (1)	Johnny Kidd & The Pirates (1960)
Self Control (5)	Laura Branigan (1984)	Shakin' Stevens EP, The (2)	Shakin' Stevens (1982)
Semi-Detached Suburban Mr James (2)	Manfred Mann (1966)	Shalala Lala (5)	Vengaboys (2000)
		Shame Shame Shame (6)	Shirley & Company (1975)
Send In The Clowns (6)	Judy Collins (1975)		
Senses Working Overtime (10)	XTC (1982)	Shang-A-Lang (2)	Bay City Rollers (1974)
Sentinel (10)	Mike Oldfield (1992)		
Senza Una Donna (Without A Woman) (4)	Zucchero & Paul Young (1991)	Shape Of My Heart (4)	Backstreet Boys (2000)
		Shapes Of Things (3)	Yardbirds (1966)
Separate Lives (4)	Phil Collins & Marilyn Martin (1985)	Sharing You (10)	Bobby Vee (1962)
		Shattered Dreams (5)	Johnny Hates Jazz (1987)
September (3)	Earth Wind & Fire (1978)		
		Shazam! (4)	Duane Eddy (1960)
Serenade (re-entry) (8)	Slim Whitman (1956)	She (1)	Charles Aznavour (1974)
Serious (8)	Donna Allen (1987)		
Sesame's Treet (2)	Smart Es (1992)	She Bangs (3)	Ricky Martin (2000)
Set Adrift On Memory Bliss (3)	PM Dawn (1991)	She Believes (In Me) (2)	Ronan Keating (2004)
Set Me Free (7)	Jaki Graham (1986)		
Set Me Free (9)	Kinks (1965)	She Don't Let Nobody (4)	Chaka Demus & Pliers (1993)
Set You Free (remix) (2)	N-Trance (1995)		
Set You Free (2nd remix) (4)	N-Trance (2001)	She Drives Me Crazy (5)	Fine Young Cannibals (1989)
Setting Sun (1)	Chemical Brothers (1996)		
7 Days (1)	Craig David (2000)		

Title	Group/Artiste	Title	Group/Artiste
She Loves You (1)	Beatles (1963)	Show Me The Meaning Of Being Lonely (3)	Backstreet Boys (2000)
She Makes My Day (6)	Robert Palmer (1988)	Show Me The Way (10)	Peter Frampton (1976)
She Makes My Nose Bleed (9)	Mansun (1997)	Show Me You're A Woman (8)	Mud (1975)
She Means Nothing To Me (9)	Phil Everly / Cliff Richard (1983)	Show Must Go On, The (2) first hit	Leo Sayer (1973)
She Wants To Dance With Me (6)	Rick Astley (1988)	Show You The Way To Go (1)	Jacksons (1977)
She Wants To Move (5)	NERD (2004)	Show, The (7)	Doug E Fresh & The Get Fresh Crew (1985)
She Wants You (3)	Billie (1998)		
She Wears My Ring (3)	Solomon King (1968)		
She Wears Red Feathers (1)	Guy Mitchell (1953)	Showing Out (Get Fresh At The Weekend) (3)	Mel & Kim (1986)
She Will Be Loved (4)	Maroon 5 (2004)		
She'd Rather Be With Me (4)	Turtles (1967)	Shuffle, The (4)	Van McCoy (1977)
Sheffield Grinder/Capstick Comes Home, The (3)	Tony Capstick (1981)	Shut Up (7)	Madness (1981)
		Shut Up (2)	Black Eyed Peas (2003)
Sheila (3) first hit	Tommy Roe (1962)		
Sheila Take A Bow (10)	Smiths (1987)	Shut Up And Forget About It (9)	Dane (2001)
Sherry (10) first and only hit	Adrian Baker (1975)	Shut Your Mouth (20)	Garbage (2002)
Sherry (8)	Four Seasons (1962)	Shy Boy (4)	Bananarama (1982)
She's A River (9)	Simple Minds (1995)	Shy Guy (2)	Diana King (1995)
She's A Star (9)	James (1997)	Sick And Tired (4)	Anastacia (2004)
She's Got Claws (6)	Gary Numan (1981)	Side By Side (7)	Kay Starr (1953)
She's Got That Vibe (3)	R Kelly (1994)	Side Saddle (1)	Russ Conway (1959)
She's Leaving Home (1)	Billy Bragg with Cara Tivey (1988)	Sideshow (3)	Barry Biggs (1976)
		Sight For Sore Eyes (6)	M People (1994)
She's Not You (1)	Elvis Presley with The Jordanaires (1962)	Sign O' The Times (10)	Prince (1987)
		Sign Of The Times (3)	Belle Stars (1983)
		Sign Your Name (2)	Terence Trent D'Arby (1988)
She's On It (10)	Beastie Boys (1987)		
She's Out Of My Life (3)	Michael Jackson (1980)	Sign, The (2)	Ace Of Base (1994)
		Signature Tune Of 'The Army Game', The (5)	Michael Medwin, Bernard Bresslaw, Alfie Bass and Leslie Fyson (1958)
She's The One / It's Only Us (1)	Robbie Williams (1999)		
Shindig (6)	Shadows (1963)		
Shine (5)	Aswad (1994)	Silence Is Easy (9)	Starsailor (2003)
Shine A Little Love (6)	Electric Light Orchestra (1979)	Silence Is Golden (1)	Tremeloes (1967)
		Silence (remixes) (3)	Delirium featuring Sarah McLachlan (2000)
Shine On (8)	Degrees Of Motion featuring Biti (1994)		
Shining Light (8)	Ash (2001)	Silent Night (8)	Bing Crosby (1952)
Shiny Happy People (6)	REM (1991)	Silhouettes (3)	Herman's Hermits (1965)
Ship Of Fools (6)	Erasure (1988)		
Shirley (6)	Shakin' Stevens (1982)	Silhouettes (10)	Cliff Richard (1990)
		Silly Games (2)	Janet Kay (1979)
Shocked (6)	Kylie Minogue (1991)	Silly Love Songs (2)	Wings (1976)
Shoop Shoop Song (It's In His Kiss), The (1)	Cher (1991)	Silly Thing (6)	Sex Pistols (1979)
		Silver Dream Machine (4)	David Essex (1980)
Shoot Me With Your Love (7)	D:Ream (1995)	Silver Lady (1)	David Soul (1977)
Shooting Star (3)	Flip & Fill (2002)	Silver Machine (3)	Hawkwind (1972)
Shortsharpshock EP (9)	Therapy? (1993)	Silver Star (3)	Four Seasons (1976)
Shotgun Wedding (6) first and only hit	Roy C (1966)	Simon Says (2)	1910 Fruitgum Co (1968)
Shotgun Wedding (re-issue) (8)	Roy C (1972)	Simon Smith and his Amazing Dancing Bear (4)	Alan Price Set (1967)
Should I Stay Or Should I Go (re-issue) (1)	Clash (1991)	Simon Templar / Two Pints Of Lager And A Packet Of Crisps Please (7)	Splodgeness-abounds (1980)
Shoulda Woulda Coulda (10)	Beverley Knight (2002)		
		Simple Game (3)	Four Tops (1971)
Shout (10)	Ant & Dec (1997)	Since I Don't Have You (10)	Guns 'N' Roses (1994)
Shout (7)	Louchie Lou & Michie One (1993)		
		Since Yesterday (5)	Strawberry Switchblade (1984)
Shout (8)	Lulu (1986)		
Shout (7) first hit	Lulu & The Luvvers (1964)	Since You've Been Gone (6)	Rainbow (1979)
		Sing (3)	Travis (2001)
Shout (4)	Tears For Fears (1984)	Sing Baby Sing (3)	Stylistics (1975)
		Sing For The Moment (6)	Eminem (2003)
Shout To The Top (7)	Style Council (1984)	Sing It Back (4)	Moloko (1999)
Show, The (2)	Girls Aloud (2004)	Sing Me (8)	Brothers (1977)
Show Me Heaven (1)	Maria McKee (1990)	Sing Our Own Song (5)	UB40 (1986)
Show Me Love (8)	Robyn (1998)	Singing The Blues (1)	Guy Mitchell (1956)
Show Me Love (6)	Robin S (1993)		
Show Me Love (remix) (9)	Robin S (1997)		

Title	Group/Artiste	Title	Group/Artiste
Singing The Blues (1)	Tommy Steele (1956)	Smurf Song, The (2)	Father Abraham & Smurfs (1978)
Single (3)	Natasha Bedingfield (2004)	Snake (10)	R Kelly featuring Big Trigger (2003)
Sir Duke (2)	Stevie Wonder (1977)	Snap Megamix (10)	Snap (1991)
Sister (10)	Bros (1989)	Snooker Loopy (6)	Matchroom Mob with Chas & Dave (1986)
Sister Jane (9)	New World (1972)		
Sisters Are Doin' It For Themselves (9)	Eurythmics & Aretha Franklin (1985)	Snoopy Vs The Red Baron (4)	Hotshots (1973)
Sit Down (2)	James (1991)	Snoopy Vs The Red Baron (8)	Royal Guardsmen (1967)
Sit Down (remix) (7)	James (1998)	Snot Rap (9)	Kenny Everett (1983)
(Sittin' On) The Dock Of The Bay (3)	Otis Redding (1968)	Snow Coach (7)	Russ Conway (1959)
Sitting Down Here (5)	Lene Marlin (2000)	So Cold The Night (8)	Communards (1986)
Six Teens, The (9)	Sweet (1974)	So Confused (6)	2play featuring Raghav & Jucxi (2004)
6 Underground (remix) (9)	Sneaker Pimps (1997)		
16 Bars (7)	Stylistics (1976)	So Emotional (5)	Whitney Houston (1987)
Sixteen Reasons (9)	Connie Stevens (1960)	So Good (3)	Boyzone (1995)
Sixteen Tons (10)	Frankie Laine (1956)	So Good To Be Back Home Again (8)	Tourists (1980)
Sixteen Tons (1)	Tennessee Ernie Ford (1956)	So Hard (4)	Pet Shop Boys (1990)
68 Guns (17) first and biggest hit	Alarm (1983)	So Lonely (8)	Jakatta (2002)
Size Of A Cow, The (5)	Wonder Stuff (1991)	So Lonely (6)	Police (1980)
Sk8er Boi (8)	Avril Lavigne (2003)	So Long Baby (10)	Del Shannon (1961)
Skin Deep (7)	Duke Ellington (1954)	So Macho / Cruising (2)	Sinitta (1986)
		So Pure (3)	Baby D (1996)
Skin Deep (9)	Ted Heath Orchestra (1954)	So Why So Sad (8)	Manic Street Preachers (2001)
Skweeze Me Pleeze Me (1)	Slade (1973)	So Yesterday (9)	Hilary Duff (2003)
Sky (2)	Sonique (2000)	So You Win Again (1)	Hot Chocolate (1977)
Sky High (9)	Jigsaw (1975)		
Skye Boat Song, The (10)	Roger Whittaker & Des O'Connor (1986)	So Young (6)	Corrs (1998)
		Soda Pop / I Got You Babe (5)	Avid Merrion, Davina McCall & Patsy Kensit (2004)
Slam Dunk (Da Funk) (10)	Five (1997)		
Slam Jam (4)	WWF Superstars (1992)	Softly As I Leave You (10)	Matt Monro (1962)
		Softly Softly (1)	Ruby Murray (1955)
Slave To Love (10)	Bryan Ferry (1985)	Softly Whispering I Love You (4)	Congregation (1971)
Sledgehammer (4)	Peter Gabriel (1986)	Soldier Blue (7)	Buffy St Marie (1971)
Sleeping Satellite (1)	Tasmin Archer (1992)	Soley Soley (5)	Middle Of The Road (1971)
Sleeping With The Light On (3)	Busted (2003)		
Sleepy Shores (8)	Johnny Pearson Orchestra (1971)	Solid (3)	Ashford & Simpson (1985)
Slight Return (2)	Bluetones (1996)	Solid Gold Easy Action (2)	T Rex (1972)
Slightest Touch, The (4)	Five Star (1987)	Solitaire (4)	Andy Williams (1973)
Sloop John B (2)	Beach Boys (1966)	Solitary Man (9)	Him (2004)
Slow (1)	Kylie Minogue (2003)	Solomon Bites The Worm (10)	Bluetones (1998)
Slow Down (10)	John Miles (1977)	Solsbury Hill (10)	Erasure (2003)
Slow Jamz (3)	Twista (2004)	Some Girls (2)	Racey (1979)
Slowhand (10)	Pointer Sisters (1981)	Some Girls (9)	Ultimate Kaos (1994)
		Some Girls (2)	Rachel Stevens (2004)
Smack My Bitch Up (8)	Prodigy (1997)		
Smalltown Boy (3) first hit	Bronski Beat (1984)	Some Kinda Fun (10)	Chris Montez (1963)
Smarty Pants (9)	First Choice (1973)		
Smells Like Teen Spirit (7)	Nirvana (1991)	Some Might Say (1)	Oasis (1995)
Smile (2)	Nat 'King' Cole (1954)	Some Of Your Lovin' (8)	Dusty Springfield (1965)
Smoke (5)	Natalie Imbruglia (1998)	Some People (3)	Cliff Richard (1987)
		Somebody Help Me (1)	Spencer Davis Group (1966)
Smoke Gets In Your Eyes (1)	Platters (1959)		
Smooth (3)	Santana featuring Rob Thomas (2000)	Somebody Stole My Gal (6)	Johnnie Ray (1953)
		Somebody Stole My Gal (re-entry) (6)	Johnnie Ray (1953)
Smooth Criminal (3)	Alien Ant Farm (2001)	Somebody To Love (2)	Queen (1976)
		Somebody To Love (3)	Boogie Pimps (2004)
Smooth Criminal (8)	Michael Jackson (1988)	Somebody's Watching Me (6)	Rockwell (1984)
		Someday (4)	Eternal (1996)

M
U
S
I
C

P
O
P

Title	Group/Artiste	Title	Group/Artiste
Someday (9)	Ricky Nelson (1958)	Somewhere Only We Know (3)	Keane (2004)
Someday (6)	Nickelback (2003)	Somewhere Out There (8)	Linda Ronstadt &
Someday I'll Be Saturday Night (7)	Bon Jovi (1995)		James Ingram
Someday (I'll Come Back) (10)	Lisa Stansfield		(1987)
	(1992)	Somewhere Somehow (7)	Wet Wet Wet (1995)
Someone (6)	Johnny Mathis	Son Of A Gun (remix) (6)	JX (1995)
	(1959)	Son Of A Preacher Man (9)	Dusty Springfield
Someone Else's Baby (2)	Adam Faith (1960)		(1968)
Someone Like Me / Right Now	Atomic Kitten (2004)	Son Of Hickory Holler's Tramp (2)	O C Smith (1968)
2004 (8)		Son Of My Father (1) first hit	Chicory Tip (1972)
Someone Else's Roses (5)	Joan Regan (1954)	Song For Guy (4)	Elton John (1978)
Someone Like You (10)	Russell Watson &	Song For The Lovers, A (3)	Richard Ashcroft
	Faye Tozer (2002)		(2000)
Someone Loves You Honey (9)	Lutricia McNeal	Song For Whoever (2) first hit	Beautiful South
	(1998)		(1989)
Someone Someone (2)	Brian Poole & The	Song Of The Dreamer (10)	Johnnie Ray (1955)
	Tremeloes (1964)	Song 2 (2)	Blur (1997)
Someone's Looking At You (4)	Boomtown Rats	Songbird (3)	Oasis (2003)
	(1980)	Sorrow (3)	David Bowie (1973)
Somethin' Is Goin' On (9)	Cliff Richard (2004)	Sorrow (4)	Merseys (1966)
Somethin' Stupid (1)	Robbie Williams &	Sorry I'm A Lady (8)	Baccara (1978)
	Nicole Kidman	Sorry Seems To Be The	Blue featuring Elton
	(2001)	Hardest Word (1)	John (2002)
Somethin' Stupid (1)	Nancy Sinatra &	Sorry Suzanne (3)	Hollies (1969)
	Frank Sinatra	Sound (9)	James (1991)
	(1967)	Sound And Vision (3)	David Bowie (1977)
Something (4)	Shirley Bassey	Sound Of Drums (3)	Kula Shaker (1998)
	(1970)	Sound Of Silence, The (3)	Bachelors (1966)
Something (4)	Lasgo (2002)	Sound Of The Underground (1)	Girls Aloud (2002)
Something / Come Together (4)	Beatles (1969)	first hit	
Something About You (6)	Level 42 (1985)	Southern Freeez (8)	Freeez (1981)
Something Beautiful (3)	Robbie Williams	Souvenir (3)	Orchestral
	(2003)		Manoeuvres In
Something Better Change /	Stranglers (1977)		The Dark (1981)
Straighten Out (9)		Sowing The Seeds Of Love (5)	Tears For Fears
Something 'Bout You Baby I	Status Quo (1981)		(1989)
Like (9)		Space Jungle, The (7)	Adamski (1990)
Something Changed (10)	Pulp (1996)	Space Oddity (5)	David Bowie (1969)
Something Deep Inside (4)	Billie Piper (2000)	Space Oddity (re-issue) (1)	David Bowie (1975)
Something Else / Friggin' In The	Sex Pistols (1979)	Spaceman (1) first hit	Babylon Zoo (1996)
Riggin' (3)		Spanish (8)	Craig David (2003)
Something For The Pain (8)	Bon Jovi (1995)	Spanish Eyes (re-issue) (5)	Al Martino (1973)
Something Goin' On (5)	Todd Terry (1997)	Spanish Flea (3)	Herb Alpert & The
Something Good (4)	Utah Saints (1992)		Tijuana Brass
Something In The Air (1)	Thunderclap		(1965)
	Newman (1969)	Spanish Harlem (14)	Aretha Franklin
(Something Inside) So Strong (4)	Labi Siffre (1987)		(1971)
Something Old Something	Fantastics (1971)	Speak Like A Child (4)	Style Council (1983)
New (9)		Speak To Me Pretty (3)	Brenda Lee (1962)
Something Tells Me (Something	Cilla Black (1971)	Special AKA Live EP, The (1)	Special AKA (1980)
Is Gonna Happen Tonight) (3)		Special Brew (3)	Bad Manners (1980)
Something's Burning (8)	Kenny Rogers & The	Special Years, The (7)	Val Doonican (1965)
	First Edition (1970)	Speechless (9)	D-Side (2003)
Something's Gotten Hold Of	Marc Almond	Speedy Gonzales (2)	Pat Boone (1962)
My Heart (1)	featuring Gene	Spice Up Your Life (1)	Spice Girls (1997)
	Pitney (1989)	Spin The Black Circle (10)	Pearl Jam (1994)
Something's Gotten Hold Of	Gene Pitney (1967)	Spinning Around (1)	Kylie Minogue (2000)
My Heart (5)		Spinning The Wheel (2)	George Michael
Something's Happening (6)	Herman's Hermits		(1996)
	(1968)	Spirit In The Sky (1)	Dr & The Medics
Sometimes (2)	Erasure (1986)		(1986)
Sometimes (3)	Britney Spears	Spirit In The Sky (1)	Gareth Gates
	(1999)		featuring The
Somewhere (9)	Pet Shop Boys		Kumars (2003)
	(1997)	Spirit In The Sky (1)	Norman Greenbaum
Somewhere (6)	P J Proby (1964)		(1970)
Somewhere Along The Way (3)	Nat 'King' Cole	Splish Splash (18) first hit	Bobby Darin (1958)
first hit	(1952)	Splish Splash (7)	Charlie Drake (1958)
Somewhere I Belong (10)	Linkin Park (2003)	Squeeze Box (10)	Who (1976)
Somewhere In My Heart (3)	Aztec Camera	S-S-Single Bed (4)	Fox (1976)
	(1988)	St Anger (9)	Metallica (2003)

Title	Group/Artiste	Title	Group/Artiste
St Elmo's Fire (Man In Motion) (6)	John Parr (1985)	Stayin' Alive (2)	N-Trance featuring Ricardo Da Force (1995)
St Therese Of The Roses (re-entry) (3)	Malcolm Vaughan (1956)		
St Valentine's Day Massacre EP (5)	Motorhead & Girlschool (1981)	Steal My Sunshine (8)	Len (1999)
Staccato's Theme (4)	Elmer Bernstein (1959)	Steam (7)	East 17 (1994)
		Steam (10)	Peter Gabriel (1993)
Stagger Lee (7)	Lloyd Price (1959)	Step Back In Time (4)	Kylie Minogue (1990)
Stairway Of Love (3)	Michael Holliday (1958)	Step By Step (2)	New Kids On The Block (1990)
Stairway To Heaven (8)	Far Corporation (1985)	Step Inside Love (8)	Cilla Black (1968)
Stairway To Heaven (7)	Rolf Harris (1993)	Step Off (Part 1) (8)	Grandmaster Melle Mel & Furious Five (1984)
Stairway To Heaven (8)	Neil Sedaka (1960)		
Stan (1)	Eminem (2000)	Step On (5)	Happy Mondays (1990)
Stand And Deliver (1)	Adam & The Ants (1981)	Steppin' Out (6)	Joe Jackson (1983)
		Stereotype / International Jet Set (6)	Specials (1980)
Stand By Me (2)	Oasis (1997)		
Stand By Me (re-issue) (1)	Ben E King (1987)	Stereotypes (7)	Blur (1996)
Stand By Your Man (1) first hit	Tammy Wynette (1975)	Stick It Out (4)	Right Said Fred & Friends (1993)
Stand Tough (7)	Point Break (2000)	Still (4)	Commodores (1979)
Stand Up For Your Love Rights (2)	Yazz (1988)	Still D.R.E. (6)	Dr Dre featuring Snoop Doggy Dogg (2000)
Stand Up Tall (10)	Dizzee Rascal (2004)		
Standing In The Road (4)	Blackfoot Sue (1972)		
Standing In The Shadows Of Love (6)	Four Tops (1967)	Still On Your Side (8)	BBMak (2001)
		Still Water (Love) (10)	Four Tops (1970)
Standing On The Corner (4)	King Brothers (1960)	Stillness In Time (9)	Jamiroquai (1995)
Star Guitar (8)	Chemical Brothers (2002)	Stole (2)	Kelly Rowland (2003)
		Stolen (4)	Jay Sean (2004)
Star People '97 (2)	George Michael (1997)	Stomp (6)	Brothers Johnson (1980)
Star 69 (10)	Fatboy Slim (2001)	Stomp (1)	Steps (2000)
Star Trekkin' (1)	Firm (1987)	Stoned Love (3)	Supremes (1971)
Star Wars Theme / Cantina Band (7)	Meco (1977)	Stonk, The (1)	Hale & Pace & The Stonkers (1991)
Stardust (7)	David Essex (1974)	Stool Pigeon (7)	Kid Creole & The Coconuts (1982)
Staring At The Sun (3)	U2 (1997)		
Starlight (2)	Supermen Lovers with Mani Hoffman (2001)	Stop (4)	Sam Brown (1989)
		Stop (2)	Spice Girls (1998)
		Stop Crying Your Heart Out (2)	Oasis (2002)
Starmaker (3)	Kids From Fame (1982)	Stop In The Name Of Love (7)	Supremes (1965)
		Stop Living The Lie (1)	David Sneddon (2003)
Starman (10)	David Bowie (1972)		
Starry Eyed (1)	Michael Holliday (1960)	Stop Sign (10)	Abs (2003)
		Stop Stop Stop (2)	Hollies (1966)
Starry-Eyed Surprise (6)	Oakenfold (2002)	Stop The Cavalry (3)	Jona Lewie (1980)
Stars (8)	Simply Red (1991)	Stop The Rock (10)	Apollo Four Forty (1999)
Stars On 45 (2)	Starsound (1981)		
Stars On 45 Vol.2 (2)	Starsound (1981)	Storm In A Teacup (7)	Fortunes (1972)
Start (1)	Jam (1980)	Story Of My Life, The (1)	Michael Holliday (1958)
Start Me Up (7)	Rolling Stones (1981)		
Starting Together (2)	Su Pollard (1986)	Story Of My Life (9)	Kristian Leontiou (2004)
State Of Mind (8)	Holly Valance (2003)		
Stay (4)	Eternal (1993)	Story Of The Blues, The (3)	Wah (1982)
Stay (8)	Hollies (1963)	Story Of Tina, The (10)	Al Martino (1954)
Stay (2)	Sash featuring La Trec (1997)	Straight From The Heart (9)	Doolally (1999)
		Straight Up (3)	Paula Abdul (1989)
Stay (1)	Shakespears Sister (1992)	Stranded (3)	Lutricia McNeal (1998)
Stay Another Day (1)	East 17 (1994)	Strange And Beautiful (7)	Aqualung (2002)
Stay (Faraway So Close) (4)	U2 (1993)	Strange Currencies (9)	REM (1995)
Stay (I Missed You) (6)	Lisa Loeb & Nine Stories (1994)	Strange Kind Of Woman (8)	Deep Purple (1971)
		Strange Lady In Town (6)	Frankie Laine (1955)
Stay On These Roads (5)	A-Ha (1988)	Strange Little Girl (7)	Stranglers (1982)
Stay Out Of My Life (9)	Five Star (1987)	Stranger In Moscow (4)	Michael Jackson (1996)
Stay Together (3)	Suede (1994)		
Stay With Me (6)	Faces (1971)	Stranger In Paradise (1) first hit	Tony Bennett (1955)
Stay With Me (Baby) (10)	Rebecca Wheatley (2000)	Stranger In Paradise (6)	Four Aces featuring Al Alberts (1955)
Stayin' Alive (4)	Bee Gees (1978)	Stranger In Paradise (6)	Tony Martin (1955)

Title	Group/Artiste	Title	Group/Artiste
Stranger On The Shore (2)	Acker Bilk with Leon Young Strings (1961)	Sugar Town (8)	Nancy Sinatra (1967)
Strangers In The Night (1)	Frank Sinatra (1966)	Sugarbush (8)	Doris Day & Frankie Laine (1952)
Strawberry Fair (3)	Anthony Newley (1960)	Sugarbush (re-entry) (8)	Doris Day & Frankie Laine (1952)
Strawberry Fields Forever (3)	Candy Flip (1990)	Sukiyaki (10)	Kenny Ball & His Jazzmen (1963)
Streak, The (1)	Ray Stevens (1974)		
Street Dance (3)	Break Machine (1984)	Sukiyaki (6)	Kyu Sakamoto (1963)
Street Life (5)	Crusaders (1979)	Sultana (5)	Titanic (1971)
Street Life (9)	Roxy Music (1973)	Sultans Of Swing (8) first hit	Dire Straits (1979)
Street Spirit (Fade Out) (5)	Radiohead (1996)	Summer Holiday (1)	Cliff Richard and The Shadows (1963)
Street Tuff (3)	Rebel MC & Double (1989)	Summer In The City (8)	Lovin' Spoonful (1966)
Streets Of London (2)	Ralph McTell (1974)		
Streets Of Philadelphia (2)	Bruce Springsteen (1994)	Summer Night City (5)	Abba (1978)
		Summer Nights (10)	Marianne Faithfull (1965)
Strong (4)	Robbie Williams (1999)	Summer Nights (1)	John Travolta & Olivia Newton-John (1978)
Strong Enough (5)	Cher (1999)		
Stronger (7)	Britney Spears (2000)	Summer Of Love (8)	Lonyo (2000)
Stronger / Angels With Dirty Faces (7)	Sugababes (2002)	Summer Of My Life (7)	Simon May (1976)
		Summer Set (5) first hit	Acker Bilk and his Paramount Jazz Band (1960)
Strummin' (52) first hit	Chas and Dave (1978)		
Strut Your Funky Stuff (10)	Frantique (1979)	Summer Son (5)	Texas (1999)
Stuck (9)	Stacie Orrico (2003)	Summer Sunshine (6)	Corrs (2004)
Stuck In A Moment You Can't Get Out Of (2)	U2 (2001)	Summer (The First Time) (9)	Bobby Goldsboro (1973)
Stuck In The Middle (4)	Louise (2001)	Summerlove Sensation (3)	Bay City Rollers (1974)
Stuck In The Middle With You (8)	Stealer's Wheel (1973)	Summertime (7)	Another Level featuring TQ (1999)
Stuck On You (3)	Elvis Presley with The Jordanaires (1960)	Summertime (8)	Jazzy Jeff & The Fresh Prince (1991)
Stuck On You (9)	Trevor Walters (1984)	Summertime Blues (18) first hit	Eddie Cochran (1958)
Stupid Cupid / Carolina Moon (1)	Connie Francis (1958)	Summertime City (4)	Mike Batt (1975)
Stupid Girl (4)	Garbage (1996)	Summertime Of Our Lives (5)	A1 (1999)
Stutter (7)	Joe (2001)	Sun Ain't Gonna Shine Anymore, The (1)	Walker Brothers (1966)
Stutter Rap (No Sleep 'Til Bedtime) (4)	Morris Minor & The Majors (1987)	Sun Always Shines On TV, The (1)	A-Ha (1985)
Substitute (2)	Clout (1978)	Sun And The Rain, The (5)	Madness (1983)
Substitute (8)	Liquid Gold (1980)	Sun Arise (3)	Rolf Harris (1962)
Substitute (5)	Who (1966)	Sun Goes Down (Living It Up), The (10)	Level 42 (1983)
Substitute (re-issue) (7)	Who (1976)		
Subterranean Homesick Blues (9)	Bob Dylan (1965)	Sun Hits The Sky (10)	Supergrass (1997)
Suburbia (8)	Pet Shop Boys (1986)	Sun Is Shining (3)	Bob Marley vs Funkstar De Luxe (1999)
Such A Night (1)	Johnnie Ray (1954)		
Sucu Sucu (9)	Laurie Johnson (1961)	Sunchyme (2)	Dario G (1997)
		Sunday Girl (1)	Blondie (1979)
Suddenly (3)	Angry Anderson (1988)	Sunday Morning Call (4)	Oasis (2000)
		Sundown (4)	S Club 8 (2003)
Suddenly (4)	Billy Ocean (1985)	Sunlight (8)	DJ Sammy (2003)
Suddenly There's A Valley (7)	Petula Clark (1955)	Sunny (3)	Boney M (1977)
Suddenly You Love Me (6)	Tremeloes (1968)	Sunny (10)	Boogie Pimps (2004)
Suedehead (5) first hit	Morrissey (1988)	Sunny Afternoon (1)	Kinks (1966)
Sugar And Spice (2)	Searchers (1963)	Sunrise (7)	Simply Red (2003)
Sugar Baby Love (1) first hit	Rubettes (1974)	Sunset (Bird Of Prey) (9)	Fatboy Slim (2000)
Sugar Candy Kisses (3)	Mac & Katie Kissoon (1975)	Sunshine (9)	Gabrielle (1999)
		Sunshine (3)	Gareth Gates (2003)
Sugar Me (5) first hit	Lynsey De Paul (1972)	Sunshine (3)	Twista (2004)
		Sunshine After The Rain (10)	Elkie Brooks (1977)
Sugar Moon (6)	Pat Boone (1958)	Sunshine After The Rain, The (4)	Berri (1995)
Sugar Sugar (1) first and only hit	Archies (1969)	Sunshine Girl (8)	Herman's Hermits (1968)

Title	Group/Artiste	Title	Group/Artiste
Sunshine Of Your Smile, The (9)	Mike Berry (1980)	Sweet Surrender (6)	Wet Wet Wet (1989)
Sunshine On A Rainy Day (re-mix) (4)	Zoe (1991)	Sweet Talkin' Guy (re-issue) (4)	Chiffons (1972)
Sunshine Superman (2)	Donovan (1966)	Sweet Talkin' Woman (6)	Electric Light Orchestra (1978)
Super Trouper (1)	Abba (1980)	Sweetest Smile (8)	Black (1987)
Superfly Guy (5)	S Express (1988)	Sweetest Thing (3)	U2 (1998)
Superman (Gioca Jouer) (9)	Black Lace (1983)	Sweetness (4)	Michelle Gayle (1994)
Supermarioland (8)	Ambassadors Of Funk with MC Mario (1992)	Sweets For My Sweet (3)	C J Lewis (1994)
Supernature (8)	Cerrone (1978)	Sweets For My Sweet (1) first hit	Searchers (1963)
Superstar (3)	Jamelia (2003)	Swing The Mood (1)	Jive Bunny & The Mastermixers (1989)
Supreme (4)	Robbie Williams (2000)		
Sure (1)	Take That (1994)	Swing Your Daddy (4)	Jim Gilstrap (1975)
Surfin' USA (34) first hit	Beach Boys (1963)	Swingin' Shepherd Blues (3)	Ted Heath Orchestra (1958)
Surrender (10)	Diana Ross (1971)		
Surrender (7)	Swing Out Sister (1987)	Swinging On A Star (7)	Big Dee Irwin (1963)
		Swiss Maid (2)	Del Shannon (1962)
Surrender (Torna Surriento) (1)	Elvis Presley with The Jordanaires (1961)	Swords Of A Thousand Men (6)	Ten Pole Tudor (1981)
Surrender Your Love (7)	Nightcrawlers featuring John Reid (1995)	Sylvia (4)	Focus (1973)
		Sylvia's Mother (2) first hit	Dr Hook (1972)
		Sympathy For The Devil (9)	Guns 'N' Roses (1995)
Surround Yourself With Sorrow (3)	Cilla Black (1969)	Synth And Strings (8)	Yomanda (1999)
Survivor (1)	Destiny's Child (2001)	System Addict (3)	Five Star (1986)
Susan's House (9)	Eels (1997)	Taboo (10)	Glamma Kid featuring Shola Ama (1999)
Suspicion (9)	Elvis Presley (1976)		
Suspicious Minds (8)	Fine Young Cannibals (1986)	Tahiti (8)	David Essex (1983)
		Tainted Love (5)	Marilyn Manson (2002)
Suspicious Minds (2)	Elvis Presley (1969)	Tainted Love (1)	Soft Cell (1981)
Suspicious Minds / The Long and Winding Road (1)	Will Young and Gareth Gates (2002)	Tainted Love (5)	Soft Cell / Marc Almond (1991)
		Take A Chance On Me (1)	Abba (1978)
Sven Sven Sven (7)	Bell & Spurling (2001)	(Take A Little) Piece Of My Heart (9)	Erma Franklin (1992)
Swallowed (7)	Bush (1997)	Take A Look Around (Theme From MI 2) (3) first hit	Limp Bizkit (2000)
Swamp Thing (3)	Grid (1994)		
Sway (6)	Dean Martin (1954)	Take Five (6)	Dave Brubeck Quartet (1961)
Swear It Again (1) first hit	Westlife (1999)		
Sweat (A La La La La Long) (re-entry) (3)	Inner Circle (1993)	Take Good Care Of My Baby (3)	Bobby Vee (1961)
		Take Good Care Of Yourself (9)	Three Degrees (1975)
Swedish Rhapsody (2)	Mantovani & His Orchestra (1953)	Take It To The Limit (12)	Eagles (1976)
Swedish Rhapsody (10)	Ray Martin Orchestra (1953)	Take Me Bak 'Ome (1)	Slade (1972)
		Take Me Home (2) first hit	Sophie Ellis-Bextor (2001)
Swedish Rhapsody (re-entry) (4)	Ray Martin Orchestra (1953)		
Sweet Caroline (8)	Neil Diamond (1971)	Take Me I'm Yours (19) first hit	Squeeze (1978)
Sweet Child O' Mine (remix) (6)	Guns 'N' Roses (1989)	Take Me Out (3)	Franz Ferdinand (2004)
Sweet Dream (7)	Jethro Tull (1969)	Take Me There (7)	Blackstreet & Mya featuring Mase and Blinky Blink (1998)
Sweet Dreams (Are Made Of This) (2)	Eurythmics (1983)		
Sweet Dreams My LA Ex (2)	Rachel Stevens (2003)	Take Me To The Clouds Above (1)	LMC vs U2 (2004)
		Take Me To The Mardi Gras (7)	Paul Simon (1973)
Sweet Harmony (8)	Beloved (1993)	Take Me To Your Heart (8)	Rick Astley (1988)
Sweet Inspiration (10)	Johnny Johnson & The Bandwagon (1970)	Take My Breath Away (1) first hit	Berlin (1986)
		Take My Breath Away (5)	Emma Bunton (2001)
Sweet Like Chocolate (1)	Shanks & Bigfoot (1999)	Take My Breath Away (re-entry) (3)	Berlin (1990)
Sweet Little Mystery (5)	Wet Wet Wet (1987)	Take My Heart (9)	Al Martino (1952)
Sweet Love 2K (3)	Fierce (2000)	Take On Me (1)	A1 (2000)
Sweet Lullaby (10)	Deep Forest (1994)	Take On Me (2) first hit	A-Ha (1985)
Sweet Nothin's (4)	Brenda Lee (1960)	Take That Look Off Your Face (3)	Marti Webb (1980)
Sweet Old-Fashioned Girl (3)	Teresa Brewer (1956)	Take These Chains From My Heart (5)	Ray Charles (1963)
Sweet Soul Music (7)	Arthur Conley (1967)	Take Your Shoes Off (3)	Cheeky Girls (2003)

M
U
S
I
C

P
O
P

Title	Group/Artiste	Title	Group/Artiste
Take Your Time (10)	Mantronix featuring Wondress (1990)	Tell Me When (7) first and biggest hit	Applejacks (1964)
Taken For Granted (10)	Sia (2000)	Tell Me When (6)	Human League (1995)
Takes Two To Tango (6) first hit	Louis Armstrong (1952)	Tell Me Why (The Riddle) (7)	Paul Van Dyk featuring Saint Etienne (2000)
Talk About Our Love (6)	Brandy featuring Kanye West (2004)		
Talk Of The Town (8)	Pretenders (1980)	Telstar (1)	Tornados (1962)
Talking In Your Sleep / Love Me (6)	Martine McCutcheon (1999)	Temma Harbour (6)	Mary Hopkin (1970)
		Temple Of Love (3)	Sisters Of Mercy (1992)
Tammy (2)	Debbie Reynolds (1957)	Temptation (1)	Everly Brothers (1961)
Tap Turns On The Water (5)	CCS (1971)		
Tarzan Boy (3) first and only hit	Baltimora (1985)	Temptation (2)	Heaven 17 (1983)
Taste Of Aggro, A (3)	Barron Knights (1978)	Temptation (remix) (4)	Heaven 17 (1992)
		10538 Overture (9)	Electric Light Orchestra (1972)
Tattva (4)	Kula Shaker (1996)		
Tea For Two Cha Cha (3)	Tommy Dorsey Orchestra and Warren Covington (1958)	Tender (2)	Blur (1999)
		Tenderly (10)	Nat 'King' Cole (1954)
		Tennessee Wig Walk (4)	Bonnie Lou (1954)
Teacher / The Witches Promise (4)	Jethro Tull (1970)	Tequila (5)	Champs (1958)
		Tequila (2)	Terrorvision (1999)
Tear Fell, A (2)	Teresa Brewer (1956)	Terry (4) first hit	Twinkle (1964)
Teardrop (10)	Massive Attack (1998)	Terrys Theme From Limelight (3)	Ron Goodwin Orchestra (1953)
		Terry's Theme From Limelight (2)	Frank Chacksfield (1953)
Teardrops (5)	Shakin' Stevens (1984)	Tetris (6) first and only hit	Doctor Spin (1992)
Teardrops (3)	Womack & Womack (1988)	Tha Crossroads (8)	Bone Thugs-N-Harmony (1996)
Tearin' Up My Heart (9)	N Sync (1999)	Thank Abba For The Music (4)	Steps, Tina Cousins, Cleopatra, B*Witched and Billie (1999)
Tears (1)	Ken Dodd (1965)		
Tears I Cried, The (8)	Glitter Band (1975)		
Tears In Heaven (5)	Eric Clapton (1992)		
Tears Of A Clown / Ranking Full Stop (6)	Beat (1979)	Thank God I Found You (10)	Mariah Carey (2000)
		Thank U (5)	Alanis Morissette (1998)
Tears Of A Clown, The (1)	Smokey Robinson & The Miracles (1970)		
		Thank U Very Much (4) first hit	Scaffold (1967)
		Thank You (3)	Dido (2001)
Tears On My Pillow (1)	Kylie Minogue (1990)	Thank You (2)	Jamelia (2004)
		Thanks For The Memory (Wham Bam Thank You Mam) (7)	Slade (1975)
Tears On My Pillow (1)	Johnny Nash (1975)		
Tease Me (3) first hit	Chaka Demus & Pliers (1993)	That Don't Impress Me Much (3)	Shania Twain (1999)
Teddy Bear (4)	Red Sovine (1981)	That Girl (3)	McFly (2004)
Teen Beat (9)	Sandy Nelson (1959)	That Girl Belongs To Yesterday (7)	Gene Pitney (1964)
Teenage Dirtbag (2)	Wheatus (2001)	That Look In Your Eye (5)	Ali Campbell (1995)
Teenage Kicks (31) first hit	Undertones (1978)	That Ole Devil Called Love (2)	Alison Moyet (1985)
Teenage Rampage (2)	Sweet (1974)	That Same Old Feeling (5)	Pickettywitch (1970)
Teenager On Love, A (2)	Marty Wilde (1959)	That Sounds Good To Me (4)	Jive Bunny & The Mastermixers (1990)
Telegram Sam (1)	T Rex (1972)		
Telephone Line (8)	Electric Light Orchestra (1977)	That'll Be The Day (1) first hit	Crickets (1957)
		That's All Right (re-issue) (3)	Elvis Presley (2004)
Telephone Man (6)	Meri Wilson (1977)		
Teletubbies Say Eh-Oh! (1)	Teletubbies (1997)	That's Amore (2)	Dean Martin and Dick Stabile Orchestra (1954)
Tell Her About It (4)	Billy Joel (1983)		
Tell Him (10)	Billie Davis (1963)		
Tell Him (3)	Barbra Streisand & Celine Dion (1997)	That's Livin' Alright (3)	Joe Fagin (1984)
		That's My Home (7)	Mr Acker Bilk & his Paramount Jazz Band (1961)
Tell Him (6)	Hello (1974)		
Tell It To My Heart (3) first hit	Taylor Dayne (1988)		
Tell It To My Heart (9)	Kelly Llorenna (2002)	That's The Way (I Like It) (4)	KC & The Sunshine Band (1975)
Tell Laura I Love Her (1)	Ricky Valance (1960)	That's The Way It Is (10)	Mel & Kim (1988)
Tell Me (4)	Melanie B (2000)	That's The Way Love Goes (2)	Janet Jackson (1993)
Tell Me A Story (5)	Jimmy Boyd (1953)		
Tell Me A Story (5)	Jimmy Boyd & Frankie Laine (1953)	That's The Way Love Is (8)	Ten City (1989)
		That's What Friends Are For (8)	Deniece Williams (1977)
Tell Me What He Said (2)	Helen Shapiro (1962)		

Title	Group/Artiste	Title	Group/Artiste
That's What I Like (1)	Jive Bunny & The Mastermixers (1989)	There's A Whole Lot Of Loving (2)	Guys & Dolls (1975)
		(There's) Always Something There To Remind Me (1) first hit	Sandie Shaw (1964)
That's What Love Will Do (3)	Joe Brown & The Bruvvers (1963)	There's No Other Way (8)	Blur (1991)
That's You (10)	Nat 'King' Cole (1960)	There's Nothing I Won't Do (4)	JX (1996)
Them Girls Them Girls (5)	Zig & Zag (1994)	These Are The Times (4)	Dru Hill (1999)
Them Thangs / If I Can't (10)	50 Cent / G-Unit (2004)	These Boots Are Made For Walking (1)	Nancy Sinatra (1966)
Theme For a Dream (3)	Cliff Richard & The Shadows (1961)	These Days (7)	Bon Jovi (1996)
Theme From A Summer Place (2)	Percy Faith & his Orchestra (1960)	These Words (1)	Natasha Bedingfield (2004)
Theme From A Threepenny Opera (Mack The Knife) (8)	Louis Armstrong and his All-Stars (1956)	They Don't Care About Us (4)	Michael Jackson (1996)
Theme From Dixie (7)	Duane Eddy (1961)	They Don't Know (3)	So Solid Crew (2001)
Theme From Harry's Game (5) first hit	Clannad (1982)	They Don't Know (2)	Tracey Ullman (1983)
Theme From M.A.S.H. (Suicide Is Painless) (7)	Manic Street Preachers (1992)	(They Long To Be) Close To You (6) first hit	Carpenters (1970)
Theme From M.A.S.H. (Suicide Is Painless) (1)	MASH (1980)	They're Coming To Take Me Away Ha-Haaa! (4)	Napoleon XIV (1966)
Theme From Mahogany (Do You Know Where You're Going To) (5)	Diana Ross (1976)	Thieves In The Temple (7)	Prince (1990)
		Thing Called Love, A (4)	Johnny Cash (1972)
Theme From Mission Impossible (7)	Adam Clayton and Larry Mullen (1996)	Things (2)	Bobby Darin (1962)
Theme From New York New York (re-issue) (4)	Frank Sinatra (1986)	Things Can Only Get Better (6)	Howard Jones (1985)
Theme From S-Express (1)	S-Express (1988)	Things Can Only Get Better (remix) (1)	D:Ream (1994)
Theme From Shaft (4)	Isaac Hayes (1971)	Things I've Seen (6)	Spooks (2001)
Theme From The Deerhunter (Cavatina) (9)	Shadows (1979)	Things That Make You Go Hmmm ... (4)	C & C Music Factory (1991)
Theme From The Legion's Last Patrol (4)	Ken Thorne Orchestra (1963)	Things We Do For Love, The (6)	10CC (1976)
		Think Of You (7)	Whigfield (1995)
Theme From The Threepenny Opera (9)	Dick Hyman Trio (1956)	Think Twice (1)	Celine Dion (1994)
		Thinking About Your Love (4)	Kenny Thomas (1991)
Theme From Z Cars (8)	Johnny Keating Orchestra (1962)	Thinking It Over (5)	Liberty (2001)
		This Ain't A Love Song (6)	Bon Jovi (1995)
Then He Kissed Me (2)	Crystals (1963)	This Charming Man (re-issue) (8)	Smiths (1992)
Then I Kissed Her (4)	Beach Boys (1967)	This Corrosion (7)	Sisters Of Mercy (1987)
There Are More Questions Than Answers (9)	Johnny Nash (1972)	This Groove / Let Your Head Go (3)	Victoria Beckham (2004)
There But For Fortune (8)	Joan Baez (1965)	This Guy's In Love With You (3)	Herb Alpert (1968)
There By The Grace Of God (6)	Manic Street Preachers (2002)	This Is A Call (5)	Foo Fighters (1995)
		This Is It (10)	Dannii Minogue (1993)
There Goes My Everything (2)	Engelbert Humperdinck (1967)	This Is It (9)	Melba Moore (1976)
There Goes My Everything (6)	Elvis Presley (1971)	This Is My Song (1)	Petula Clark (1967)
There Goes My First Love (3)	Drifters (1975)	This Is My Song (2)	Harry Secombe (1967)
There Goes The Fear (3)	Doves (2002)		
There Is A Mountain (8)	Donovan (1967)	This Is Not A Love Song (5)	Public Image Ltd (1983)
There It Is (5)	Shalamar (1982)		
There Must Be A Reason (9)	Frankie Laine (1954)	This Is Tomorrow (9)	Bryan Ferry (1977)
There Must Be A Way (7)	Frankie Vaughan (1967)	This Little Bird (6)	Marianne Faithfull (1965)
		This Love (3)	Maroon 5 (2004)
There Must Be An Angel (Playing With My Heart) (1)	Eurythmics (1985)	This Old Heart Of Mine (4)	Rod Stewart (1975)
There There (4)	Radiohead (2003)	This Old Heart Of Mine (Is Weak For You) (3)	Isley Brothers (1968)
There There My Dear (7)	Dexy's Midnight Runners (1980)	This Ole House (4)	Billie Anthony with Eric Jupp Orchestra (1954)
There You Go (6)	Pink (2000)		
There You'll Be (3)	Faith Hill (2001)	This Ole House (1)	Rosemary Clooney (1954)
There's A Ghost In My House (3)	R Dean Taylor (1974)		
There's A Heartache Following Me (6)	Jim Reeves (1964)	This Ole House (1)	Shakin' Stevens (1981)
There's A Kind Of Hush (7)	Herman's Hermits (1967)	This One's For The Children (9)	New Kids On The Block (1990)

MUSIC POP

Title	Group/Artiste	Title	Group/Artiste
This Time I Know It's For Real (3)	Donna Summer (1989)	Time After Time (3)	Cyndi Lauper (1984)
This Time (We'll Get It Right) / England We'll Fly The Flag (2)	England World Cup Squad (1982)	Time (Clock Of The Heart) (3)	Culture Club (1982)
		Time Drags By (10)	Cliff Richard & The Shadows (1966)
This Town Ain't Big Enough For Both Of Us (2)	Sparks (1974)	Time Has Come, The (4)	Adam Faith (1961)
This Used To Be My Playground (3)	Madonna (1992)	Time Is Now, The (2)	Moloko (2000)
		Time Is Running Out (8)	Muse (2003)
This Wheel's On Fire (5)	Julie Driscoll, Brian Auger & The Trinity (1968)	Time Is Tight (4)	Booker T & The MG's (1969)
Thong Song (3)	Sisqo (2000)	Time To Burn (3)	Storm (2000)
Thorn In My Side (5)	Eurythmics (1986)	Time To Say Goodbye (Con Te Partiro) (2)	Sarah Brightman & Andrea Bocelli (1997)
Those Were The Days (1)	Mary Hopkin (1968)		
Thought I'd Died And Gone To Heaven (8)	Bryan Adams (1992)	Time Warp (remix), The (7)	Damian (1989)
		Times They Are A-Changin' (9) first hit	Bob Dylan (1965)
Thousand Miles, A (6)	Vanessa Carlton (2002)	Tin Soldier (9)	Small Faces (1967)
		Tipsy (4)	J-Kwon (2004)
Three Bells, The (6)	Browns (1959)	Tired Of Being Alone (4)	Al Green (1971)
Three Coins In The Fountain (5)	Four Aces featuring Al Alberts (1954)	Tired Of Waiting For You (1)	Kinks (1965)
		To Be Or Not To Be (9)	B A Robertson (1980)
Three Coins In The Fountain (1)	Frank Sinatra (1954)	To Be With You (3)	Mr Big (1992)
3 Is Family (9)	Dana Dawson (1995)	To Be With You Again (10)	Level 42 (1987)
3 Lions (1)	Baddiel & Skinner and Lightning Seeds (1996)	To Cut A Long Story Short (5) first hit	Spandau Ballet (1980)
		To Earth With Love (10)	Gay Dad (1999)
		To Know Him Is To Love Him (2)	Teddy Bears (1958)
3 Lions '98 (1)	Baddiel & Skinner and Lightning Seeds (1998)	To Know You Is To Love You (5)	Peter & Gordon (1965)
		To Live And Die In L.A. (10)	Makaveli (1997)
Three Little Pigs (5)	Green Jelly (1993)	To Love Somebody (5)	Nina Simone (1969)
Three Steps To Heaven (1)	Eddie Cochran (1960)	To Love Somebody (8)	Jimmy Somerville (1990)
Three Steps To Heaven (2)	Showaddywaddy (1975)	To The Moon And Back (3)	Savage Garden (1998)
Three Times A Lady (1)	Commodores (1978)	To You I Belong (1)	B*Witched (1998)
3 x 3 EP (10)	Genesis (1982)	Tobacco Road (6)	Nashville Teens (1964)
3AM / Thunderbirds (1)	Busted (2004)		
3AM Eternal (1)	KLF featuring Children of The Revolution (1991)	Toca's Miracle (1)	Fragma (2000)
		Toccata (5)	Sky (1980)
		Together (6)	Connie Francis (1961)
Thriller (10)	Michael Jackson (1983)	Together (8)	P J Proby (1964)
Through The Barricades (6)	Spandau Ballet (1986)	Together Again (4)	Janet Jackson (1997)
Through The Rain (8)	Mariah Carey (2002)	Together Forever (2)	Rick Astley (1988)
Through The Wire (9)	Kanye West (2004)	Together In Electric Dreams (3)	Giorgio Moroder & Phil Oakey (1984)
Throw Down The Line (7)	Cliff Richard & Hank Marvin (1969)	Together We Are Beautiful (1)	Fern Kinney (1980)
Thunder (4)	East 17 (1995)	Tokoloshe Man (4)	John Kongos (1971)
Thunder In The Mountains (4)	Toyah (1981)	Tokyo Melody (9)	Helmut Zacharias (1964)
Thunderbirds / 3AM (1)	Busted (2004)		
Thunderbirds Are Go (5)	FAB featuring MC Parker (1990)	Tom Dooley (5)	Kingston Trio (1958)
Ticket To Ride (1)	Beatles (1965)	Tom Dooley (3)	Lonnie Donegan & His Skiffle Group (1958)
Tide Is High (Get The Feeling), The (1)	Atomic Kitten (2002)		
		Tom Hark (2)	Elias & His Zigzag Jive Flutes (1958)
Tide Is High, The (1)	Blondie (1980)	Tom Hark (6)	Piranhas (1980)
Tie a Yellow Ribbon Round the Old Oak Tree (1)	Dawn featuring Tony Orlando (1973)	Tom Tom Turnaround (6)	New World (1971)
Tie Me Kangaroo Down Sport (9) first hit	Rolf Harris (1960)	Tom Traubert's Blues (Waltzing Matilda) (6)	Rod Stewart (1992)
Tiger Feet (1)	Mud (1974)	Tomboy (10)	Perry Como (1959)
(Til) I Kissed You (2)	Everly Brothers (1959)	Tomorrow (8)	Johnny Brandon, The Phantoms, and Norman Warren (1955)
Till (2)	Tom Jones (1971)		
Till The End Of The Day (8)	Kinks (1965)		
Tilt Ya Head Back (5)	Nelly & Christina Aguilera (2004)	Tomorrow (9)	Sandie Shaw (1966)
Time (9)	Craig Douglas (1961)	Tomorrow's (Just Another Day) / Madness (Is All In My Mind) (8)	Madness (1983)

Title	Group/Artiste	Title	Group/Artiste
Tom's Diner (2)	DNA featuring Suzanne Vega (1990)	Toxygene (4)	Orb (1997)
		Toy Balloons (7)	Russ Conway (1961)
		Toy Boy (4)	Sinitta (1987)
Tonight (3)	New Kids On The Block (1990)	Toy Soldiers (5)	Martika (1989)
Tonight / Miss You Nights (3)	Westlife (2003)	Tracks Of My Tears, The (9)	Smokey Robinson & The Miracles (1969)
Tonight I Celebrate My Love (2)	Peabo Bryson & Roberta Flack (1983)	Tracy (4)	Cufflinks (1969)
		Tragedy (1)	Bee Gees (1979)
Tonight I'm Yours (Don't Hurt Me) (8)	Rod Stewart (1981)	Trail Of The Lonesome Pine, The (2)	Laurel & Hardy with The Avalon Boys (1975)
Tonight Tonight (7)	Smashing Pumpkins (1996)	Train Of Thought (8)	A-Ha (1986)
Tonight's The Night (Gonna Be Alright) (5)	Rod Stewart (1976)	Trains and Boats and Planes (4)	Burt Bacharach (1965)
Too Bad (9)	Nickelback (2002)	Trapped (3)	Colonel Abrams (1985)
Too Blind To See It (5)	Kym Sims (1991)	Trash (3)	Suede (1996)
Too Busy Thinking 'Bout My Baby (5)	Marvin Gaye (1969)	Travellers Tune (5)	Ocean Colour Scene (1997)
Too Close (1)	Blue (2001)	Travellin' Band (8)	Creedence Clearwater Revival (1970)
Too Funky (4)	George Michael (1992)		
Too Good To Be Forgotten (5)	Amazulu (1986)	Travellin' Light (1)	Cliff Richard & The Shadows (1959)
Too Good To Be Forgotten (10)	Chi-Lites (1974)		
Too Hot (9)	Coolio (1996)	Tribal Dance (4)	2 Unlimited (1993)
Too Late For Goodbyes (6)	Julian Lennon (1984)	Tribute (Right On) (5)	Pasadenas (1988)
Too Lost In You (10)	Sugababes (2003)	Trick Me (2)	Kelis (2004)
Too Many Broken Hearts (1)	Jason Donovan (1989)	Trip To Trumpton, A (6)	Urban Hype (1992)
Too Much (2)	Bros (1989)	Trippin' (8)	Mark Morrison (1996)
Too Much (6)	Elvis Presley with The Jordanaires (1957)	Trouble (10)	Coldplay (2000)
		Trouble (7)	Pink (2003)
Too Much (1)	Spice Girls (1997)	True (1)	Spandau Ballet (1983)
Too Much Heaven (3)	Bee Gees (1978)		
Too Much Love Will Kill You (5)	Brian May (1992)	True (4)	Jaimeson featuring Angel Blu (2003)
Too Much Too Little Too Late (3)	Johnny Mathis & Deniece Williams (1978)	True Blue (1)	Madonna (1986)
		True Faith (4)	New Order (1987)
Too Nice To Talk To (7)	Beat (1980)	True Faith (remix) (9)	New Order (1994)
Too Shy (1)	Kajagoogoo (1983)	True Love (4)	Bing Crosby & Grace Kelly (1956)
Too Soon To Know (3)	Roy Orbison (1966)		
Too Young (5)	Donny Osmond (1972)	True Love (2)	Elton John – duet with Kiki Dee (1993)
Too Young To Die (10)	Jamiroquai (1993)		
Too Young To Go Steady (8)	Nat 'King' Cole (1956)	True Love Never Dies (re-issue) (7)	Flip & Fill featuring Kelly Llorenna (2002)
Top Of The World (2)	Brandy featuring Mase (1998)	True Love Ways (8)	Cliff Richard (1983)
Top Of The World (5)	Carpenters (1973)	True Love Ways (2)	Peter & Gordon (1965)
Torch (2)	Soft Cell (1982)	Truly (6)	Lionel Richie (1982)
Torn (2)	Natalie Imbruglia (1997)	Truly Madly Deeply (4)	Savage Garden (1998)
Torn Between Two Lovers (4)	Mary MacGregor (1977)	Try Again (5)	Aaliyah (2000)
Tossing And Turning (3)	Ivy League (1965)	Try Me Out (6)	Corona (1995)
Total Eclipse Of The Heart (5)	Nicki French (1995)	Tu M'Aimes Encore (To Love Me Again) (7)	Celine Dion (1995)
Total Eclipse Of The Heart (1)	Bonnie Tyler (1983)		
Touch Me (1)	Rui Da Silva featuring Cassandra (2001)	Tubthumping (2)	Chumbawamba (1997)
Touch Me (3)	49ers (1989)	Tumbling Dice (5)	Rolling Stones (1972)
Touch Me (All Night Long) (5)	Cathy Dennis (1991)	Tunnel Of Love (10)	Fun Boy Three (1983)
Touch Me (I Want Your Body) (3) first hit	Samantha Fox (1986)	Turn (8)	Travis (1999)
		Turn Around (3)	Phats & Small (1999)
Touch Me In The Morning (9)	Diana Ross (1973)	Turn Back Time (1)	Aqua (1998)
Touch Too Much, A (8)	Arrows (1974)	Turn It On Again (8)	Genesis (1980)
Tower Of Strength (1)	Frankie Vaughan (1961)	Turn It Up / Fire It Up (2)	Busta Rhymes (1998)
Town Called Malice / Precious (1)	Jam (1982)	Turn Me On (2)	Kevin Lyttle (2003)
Toxic (1)	Britney Spears (2004)	Turn Off The Light (4)	Nelly Furtado (2001)

MUSIC POP

Title	Group/Artiste	Title	Group/Artiste
Turn On Tune In Cop Out (re-issue) (3)	Freak Power (1995)		The Mindbenders (1964)
Turn The Music Up (8)	Players Association (1979)	Un Banc Un Arbre Une Rue (9)	Severine (1971)
		(Un Dos Tres) Maria (6)	Ricky Martin (1997)
Turning Japanese (3)	Vapors (1980)	Una Paloma Blanca (5)	Jonathan King (1975)
Turtle Power (1)	Partners In Kryme (1990)	Unbelievable (3)	EMF (1990)
		Un-Break My Heart (2)	Toni Braxton (1996)
Tusk (6)	Fleetwood Mac (1979)	Unbreakable (1)	Westlife (2002)
		Unchained Melody (10) first and only hit	Les Baxter his Chorus and Orchestra (1955)
Tweedle Dee (4)	Little Jimmy Osmond (1973)		
Tweedle Dee Tweedle Dum (2)	Middle Of The Road (1971)	Unchained Melody (1)	Gareth Gates (2002)
Twelfth Of Never, The (1)	Donny Osmond (1973)	Unchained Melody (2)	Al Hibbler (1955)
		Unchained Melody (1)	Jimmy Young (1955)
Twelfth Of Never, The (8)	Cliff Richard (1964)	Unchained Melody/(There'll Be Bluebirds Over) The White Cliffs Of Dover (1)	Robson & Jerome (1995)
12:51 (7)	Strokes (2003)		
20th Century Boy (3)	T Rex (1973)		
Twenty Four Hours From Tulsa (5)	Gene Pitney (1963)	Unchained Melody (re-issue) (1)	Righteous Brothers (1990)
Twenty Four Seven (6)	Artful Dodger featuring Melanie Blatt (2001)	Uncle John From Jamaica (6)	Vengaboys (2000)
		Under Pressure (1)	Queen & David Bowie (1981)
Twenty Tiny Fingers (4)	Stargazers (1955)	Under The Boardwalk (2)	Bruce Willis (1987)
25 Or 6 To 4 (7)	Chicago (1970)	Under The Bridge / Lady Marmalade (1)	All Saints (1998)
21 Questions (6)	50 Cent (2003)		
21 Seconds (1)	So Solid Crew (2001)	Under The Bridges Of Paris (7)	Eartha Kitt (1955)
		Under The Bridges Of Paris (6)	Dean Martin (1955)
Twilight Time (3)	Platters (1958)	Under The Moon Of Love (1)	Showaddywaddy (1976)
Twilight Zone (2)	2 Unlimited (1992)		
Twist And Shout (1)	Chaka Demus & Pliers (1993)	Under The Thumb (10)	Amy Studt (2003)
		Under Your Thumb (3)	Godley & Creme (1981)
Twist And Shout (10)	Deacon Blue (1991)		
Twist And Shout (4) first hit	Brian Poole & The Tremeloes (1963)	Underneath Your Clothes (3)	Shakira (2002)
		Underwater Love (4)	Smoke City (1997)
Twist And Shout (4)	Salt-N-Pepa (1988)	Undivided Love (5)	Louise (1996)
Twist In My Sobriety (22)	Tanita Tikaram (1988)	Unforgettable Fire, The (6)	U2 (1985)
		Union Of The Snake (3)	Duran Duran (1983)
Twist (Yo Twist), The (2)	Fat Boys & Chubby Checker (1988)	United States Of Whatever (10)	Liam Lynch (2002)
		United We Stand (10) first hit	Brotherhood Of Man (1970)
Twistin' The Night Away (6)	Sam Cooke (1962)		
2 Become 1 (1)	Spice Girls (1996)	Universal, The (5)	Blur (1995)
Two Can Play That Game (re-entry) (3)	Bobby Brown (1995)	Unleash The Dragon (6)	Sisqo (2000)
		Unpretty (6)	TLC (1999)
2 Faced (3)	Louise (2000)	Unpretty (6)	Metallica (1996)
2-4-6-8 Motorway (5) first hit	Tom Robinson Band (1977)	Until It Sleeps (5)	Metallica (1996)
		Until It's Time For You To Go (5)	Elvis Presley (1972)
		Until The End Of Time (4)	2Pac (2001)
Two Hearts (6)	Phil Collins (1988)	Until The Time Is Through (2)	Five (1998)
Two In A Million / You're My Number One (2)	S Club 7 (1999)	Unwritten (6)	Natasha Bedingfield (2004)
Two Kinds Of Teardrops (5)	Del Shannon (1963)	Up And Down (4)	Vengaboys (1998)
Two Little Boys (1)	Rolf Harris (1969)	Up Around The Bend (3)	Creedence Clearwater Revival (1970)
Two Princes (3)	Spin Doctors (1993)		
2 Times (2)	Ann Lee (1999)		
Two Tribes (1)	Frankie Goes To Hollywood (1984)	Up Middle Finger (7)	Oxide & Neutrino (2001)
U And Me (10)	Cappella (1994)	Up On The Roof (10)	Kenny Lynch (1962)
U Can't Touch This (3)	MC Hammer (1990)	Up The Junction (2)	Squeeze (1979)
U Got It Bad (5)	Usher (2001)	Up The Ladder To The Roof (6)	Supremes (1970)
U Got 2 Let The Music (2)	Cappella (1993)	Up To The Wildstyle (10)	Porn Kings vs DJ Supreme (1999)
U Know What's Up (2)	Donell Jones (2000)		
U Make Me Wanna (4)	Blue (2003)	Up Town Top Ranking (1) first and only hit	Althia & Donna (1977)
U R The Best Thing (remix) (4)	D:Ream (1994)		
U Remind Me (3)	Usher (2001)	Up Up And Away (6)	Johnny Mann Singers (1967)
U Saved Me / Happy People (6)	R Kelly (2004)		
U Sure Do (re-entry) (4)	Strike (1995)	Up Where We Belong (7)	Joe Cocker & Jennifer Warnes (1983)
Ugly (7)	Bubba Sparxxx (2001)		
Ugly Duckling, The (10)	Mike Reid (1975)	Upside Down (10)	A Teens (2001)
Uh La La La (10)	Alexia (1998)	Upside Down (2)	Diana Ross (1980)
Um Um Um Um Um Um (5)	Wayne Fontana &	Uptown Girl (1)	Billy Joel (1983)

Title	Group/Artiste	Title	Group/Artiste
Uptown Girl (1)	Westlife (2001)	Walk On By (7)	Gabrielle (1997)
Use It Up And Wear It Out (1)	Odyssey (1980)	Walk On By (6)	Sybil (1990)
Vacation (10)	Connie Francis (1962)	Walk On By (5)	Leroy Van Dyke (1962)
Valentine (9)	T'Pau (1988)	Walk On By (9)	Dionne Warwick (1964)
Vaya Con Dios (7)	Les Paul & Mary Ford (1953)	Walk On The Wild Side (10)	Lou Reed (1973)
Venus (8)	Bananarama (1986)	Walk On Water (10)	Milk Inc (2002)
Venus (4)	Don Pablo's Animals (1990)	Walk Right Back / Ebony Eyes (1)	Everly Brothers (1961)
Venus (8) first hit	Shocking Blue (1970)	Walk Right In (10)	Rooftop Singers (1963)
Venus In Blue Jeans (4)	Mark Wynter (1962)	Walk Right Now (7)	Jacksons (1981)
Vertigo (1)	U2 (2004)	Walk Tall (3) first hit	Val Doonican (1964)
Victim Of Love (7)	Erasure (1987)	Walk The Dinosaur (10)	Was (Not Was) (1987)
Victims (3)	Culture Club (1983)		
Video Killed The Radio Star (1) first hit	Buggles (1979)	Walk This Way (8)	Run DMC (1986)
		Walk With Me (10)	Seekers (1966)
Vienna (2)	Ultravox (1981)	Walkaway (9)	Cast (1996)
Vienna Calling (10)	Falco (1986)	Walkin' (7)	CCS (1971)
View To A Kill, A (2)	Duran Duran (1985)	Walkin' Back To Happiness (1)	Helen Shapiro (1961)
Vincent (1)	Don McLean (1972)		
Vindaloo (2)	Fat Les (1998)	Walkin' Miracle, A (6)	Limmie & The Family Cookin (1974)
Virginia Plain (4) first hit	Roxy Music (1972)		
Virtual Insanity (3)	Jamiroquai (1996)	Walkin' To Missouri (9) first hit	Tony Brent (1952)
Vision Of Love (9) first hit	Mariah Carey (1990)	Walkin' To Missouri (re-entry) (7)	Tony Brent (1953)
Visions (7)	Cliff Richard (1966)	Walking Away (3)	Craig David (2000)
Viva Bobby Joe (6)	Equals (1969)	Walking In The Air (5)	Aled Jones (1985)
Viva Forever (1)	Spice Girls (1998)	Walking In The Rain (7)	Modern Romance (1983)
Viva La Radio (6)	Lolly (1999)		
Viva Las Vegas (10)	ZZ Top (1992)	Walking In The Rain (10)	Partridge Family starring David Cassidy (1973)
Vogue (1)	Madonna (1990)		
Voice In The Wilderness (2)	Cliff Richard & The Shadows (1960)		
Voice Within, The (9)	Christina Aguilera (2003)	Walking On Broken Glass (8)	Annie Lennox (1992)
		Walking On Sunshine (10)	Bad Manners (1981)
Volare (2)	Dean Martin (1958)	Walking On Sunshine (8)	Katrina & The Waves (1985)
Volare (10)	Domenico Modugno (1958)		
		Walking On Sunshine (4)	Rocker's Revenge (1982)
Voodoo Chile (1)	Jimi Hendrix Experience (1970)	Walking On The Moon (1)	Police (1979)
Voyage Voyage (5)	Desireless (1988)	Walking Wounded (6)	Everything But The Girl (1996)
Wait (7)	Robert Howard & Kym Mazelle (1989)		
		Wall Street Shuffle, The (10)	10CC (1974)
		Walls Come Tumbling Down (6)	Style Council (1985)
Waiting For A Girl Like You (8)	Foreigner (1981)	Waltz Away Dreaming (10)	Toby Bourke with George Michael (1997)
Waiting For A Star To Fall (9)	Boy Meets Girl (1988)		
Waiting For An Alibi (9)	Thin Lizzy (1979)	Wanderer, The (10)	Dion (1962)
Waiting For The Train (7)	Flash & The Pan (1983)	Wanderer, The (7)	Status Quo (1984)
		Wanderin' Eyes (6)	Charlie Gracie (1957)
Waiting For Tonight (5)	Jennifer Lopez (1999)	Wand'rin' Star (1)	Lee Marvin (1970)
Wake Me Up Before You Go Go (1)	Wham! (1984)	Wanna Be Startin' Something (8)	Michael Jackson (1983)
Wake Up Boo! (9)	Boo Radleys (1995)	Wannabe (1) first hit	Spice Girls (1996)
Wake Up Little Susie (2)	Everly Brothers (1957)	Wanted (4)	Perry Como (1954)
		Wanted (3)	Dooleys (1979)
Walk Away (4)	Matt Monro (1964)	Wanted (re-entry) (4)	Al Martino (1954)
Walk Away From Love (10)	David Ruffin (1976)	War (3)	Edwin Starr (1970)
Walk Away Renee (3)	Four Tops (1967)	War Baby (6)	Tom Robinson (1983)
Walk Don't Run (8)	Ventures (1960)		
Walk Hand In Hand (2)	Tony Martin (1956)	War Of Nerves (7)	All Saints (1998)
Walk In The Black Forest, A (3)	Horst Jankowski (1965)	War Song, The (2)	Culture Club (1984)
Walk Like A Panther '98 (10)	The All Seeing I, with Tony Christie (1999)	Warpaint (5)	Brook Brothers (1961)
Walk Like An Egyptian (3)	Bangles (1986)	Watching Me Watching You (10)	David Grant (1983)
Walk Of Life (2)	Dire Straits (1986)	Watching The Detectives (15) first hit	Elvis Costello (1977)
Walk On (5)	U2 (2001)	Water Water / Handful Of Songs (5)	Tommy Steele (1957)

M U S I C   P O P

Title	Group/Artiste	Title	Group/Artiste
Waterfalls (9)	Paul McCartney (1980)	We Will Make Love (2)	Russ Hamilton (1957)
Waterfalls (4)	TLC (1995)	We Will Rock You (1)	Five & Queen (2000)
Waterloo (1) first hit	Abba (1974)	Weak In The Presence Of	Alison Moyet (1987)
Waterloo Sunset (2)	Kinks (1967)	Beauty (6)	
Way, The (Put Your Hand In My Hand) (5)	Divine Inspiration (2003)	Wear My Ring Around Your Neck (3)	Elvis Presley with The Jordanaires (1958)
Way Down (1)	Elvis Presley (1977)	Weather With You (7)	Crowded House (1992)
Way Down Yonder In New Orleans (3)	Freddy Cannon (1960)	Wedding Bells (7)	Godley & Creme (1981)
Way I Am, The (8)	Eminem (2000)		
Way It Used To Be, The (3)	Engelbert Humperdinck (1969)	Wedding, The (3)	Julie Rogers (1964)
Way Of Life (6)	Family Dogg (1969)	Wee Rule (6)	Wee Papa Girl Rappers (1988)
Way To Your Love, The (1)	Hear'Say (2001)	Weekend, The (7)	Michael Gray (2004)
Way We Were, The / Try To Remember (4)	Gladys Knight & The Pips (1975)	Welcome Home (1)	Peters & Lee (1973)
Way You Make Me Feel, The (3)	Michael Jackson (1987)	Welcome To My World (6)	Jim Reeves (1963)
		Welcome To the Cheap Seats (EP) (8)	Wonder Stuff (1992)
Way You Make Me Feel, The (6)	Ronan Keating (2000)	(Welcome) To The Dance (5)	Des Mitchell (2000)
Way You Move, The (7)	Outkast featuring Sleepy Brown (2004)	Welcome To The Pleasure Dome (2)	Frankie Goes To Hollywood (1985)
		Welcome To Tomorrow (6)	Snap featuring Summer (1994)
Wayward Wind (9)	Gogi Grant (1956)	We'll Bring The House Down (10)	Slade (1981)
Wayward Wind (1)	Frank Ifield (1963)	We'll Find Our Day (17) only other hit	Stephanie De Sykes (1975)
Wayward Wind (8)	Tex Ritter (1956)		
We All Follow Man United (10)	Manchester United Football Club (1985)	Well I Ask You (1)	Eden Kane (1961)
		We're All Alone (6) first hit	Rita Coolidge (1977)
We All Stand Together (3)	Paul McCartney & The Frog Chorus (1984)	We're Going To Ibiza! (1)	Vengaboys (1999)
		We're Gonna Do It Again (6)	Manchester Utd Football Squad & Stryker (1995)
We Are (8)	Ana Johnsson (2004)		
We Are Detective (7)	Thompson Twins (1983)	We're On The Ball (3)	Ant & Dec (2002)
		We're Through (7)	Hollies (1964)
We Are Family (8)	Sister Sledge (1979)	West End Girls (1) first hit	Pet Shop Boys (1985)
We Are Family (remix) (5)	Sister Sledge (1993)		
We Are Glass (5)	Gary Numan (1980)	Westside (4)	TQ (1999)
We Are The Champions (2)	Queen (1977)	Wet Dream (10) first and only hit	Max Romeo (1969)
We Are The World (1)	USA For Africa (1985)	We've Got It Goin' On (3)	Backstreet Boys (1996)
We Call It Acieed (3)	D Mob (1988)	We've Got Tonight (4)	Ronan Keating featuring Lulu (2002)
We Can Work It Out / Day Tripper (1)	The Beatles (1965)		
We Close Our Eyes (5) first hit	Go West (1985)	Wham Rap (8)	Wham! (1983)
We Come 1 (3)	Faithless (2001)	What (3)	Soft Cell (1982)
We Didn't Start The Fire (7)	Billy Joel (1989)	What A Difference A Day Made (6)	Esther Phillips (1975)
We Do It (5)	R & J Stone (1976)		
We Don't Have To ... (2)	Jermaine Stewart (1986)	What A Girl Wants (3)	Christina Aguilera (2000)
We Don't Need Another Hero (Thunderdome) (3)	Tina Turner (1985)	What A Waste (9) first hit	Ian Dury & The Blockheads (1978)
We Don't Talk Anymore (1)	Cliff Richard (1979)	What A Wonderful World / Cabaret (1)	Louis Armstrong Orchestra & Chorus / Louis Armstrong and his All-Stars (1968)
We Got A Love Thang (6)	Ce Ce Peniston (1992)		
We Gotta Get Out Of This Place (2)	Animals (1965)		
We Have A Dream (5)	Scotland World Cup Squad (1982)	What About Us (4)	Brandy (2002)
		What Am I Gonna Do (3)	Rod Stewart (1983)
We Have All The Time In The World (3)	Louis Armstrong (1994)	What Am I Gonna Do With You (5)	Barry White (1975)
We Just Be Dreamin' (3)	Blazin' Squad (2003)		
We Like To Party! (Vengabus) (3)	Vengaboys (1999)	What Are You Doing Sunday (3)	Dawn featuring Tony Orlando (1971)
We Love You / Dandelion (8)	Rolling Stones (1967)		
We Shall Overcome (26) first hit	Joan Baez (1965)	What Became Of The Likely Lads (9)	Libertines (2004)
We Should Be Together (10)	Cliff Richard (1991)		
We Take Mystery (To Bed) (9)	Gary Numan (1982)	What Becomes Of The Broken Hearted (10)	Jimmy Ruffin (1966)
(We Want) The Same Thing (6)	Belinda Carlisle (1990)		

Title	Group/Artiste	Title	Group/Artiste
What Becomes Of The Broken Hearted/Saturday Night At The Movies / You'll Never Walk Alone (1)	Robson & Jerome (1996)	What's Love Got To Do With It (2)	Warren G featuring Adina Howard (1996)
What Becomes Of The Broken Hearted (re-issue) (4)	Jimmy Ruffin (1974)	What's Love Got To Do With It (3)	Tina Turner (1984)
What Can I Do (3)	Corrs (1998)	What's Luv (4)	Fat Joe featuring Ashanti (2002)
What Can I Say (10)	Boz Scaggs (1977)	What's So Different (10)	Ginuwine (1999)
What Can You Do For Me (10)	Utah Saints (1991)	What's The Colour Of Money (7)	Hollywood Beyond (1986)
What Do I Do (5)	Phil Fearon & Galaxy (1984)	What's The Frequency Kenneth (9)	REM (1994)
What Do I Get (37) first hit	Buzzcocks (1978)	What's Up (6)	DJ Miko (1994)
What Do I Have To Do (6)	Kylie Minogue (1991)	What's Up (2)	4 Non Blondes (1993)
What Do You Want (1)	Adam Faith (1959)		
What Do You Want To Make Those Eyes At Me For (1)	Emile Ford & The Checkmates (1959)	What's Your Flava (8)	Craig David (2002)
		Whatta Man (7)	Salt-N-Pepa with En Vogue (1994)
What Do You Want To Make Those Eyes At Me For (5)	Shakin' Stevens (1987)	Wheels (8)	String-A-Longs (1961)
What Have I Done To Deserve This (2)	Pet Shop Boys & Dusty Springfield (1987)	When (1)	Kalin Twins (1958)
		When (3)	Showaddywaddy (1977)
What Have You Done For Me Lately (3)	Janet Jackson (1986)	When A Child Is Born (1)	Johnny Mathis (1976)
What I Am (2)	Tin Tin Out featuring Emma Bunton (1999)	When A Man Loves A Woman (8)	Michael Bolton (1991)
		When A Man Loves A Woman (4)	Percy Sledge (1966)
		When A Man Loves A Woman (re-issue) (2)	Percy Sledge (1987)
What I Go To School For (3)	Busted (2002)	When A Woman (6)	Gabrielle (2000)
What If (6)	Kate Winslet (2001)	When Doves Cry (10)	Ginuwine (1997)
What Is Love (2)	Haddaway (1993)	When Doves Cry (4)	Prince (1984)
What Is Love (2)	Howard Jones (1983)	When Forever Has Gone (2)	Demis Roussos (1976)
What It Feels Like For A Girl (7)	Madonna (2001)	When I Fall In Love (2)	Nat 'King' Cole (1957)
What I've Got In Mind (4)	Billie Jo Spears (1976)	When I Fall In Love (4)	Donny Osmond (1973)
What Kinda Boy You Looking For Girl (10)	Hot Chocolate (1983)	When I Fall In Love / My Arms Keep Missing You (2)	Rick Astley (1987)
What Makes A Man (2)	Westlife (2000)	When I Fall In Love (re-issue) (4)	Nat 'King' Cole (1987)
What My Heart Wants To Say (5)	Gareth Gates (2002)		
What Now My Love (5)	Shirley Bassey (1962)	When I Grow Up (9)	Garbage (1999)
What The World Is Waiting For / Fool's Gold (8)	Stone Roses (1989)	When I Lost You (6)	Sarah Whatmore (2002)
What Time Is Love (5)	KLF with Children of The Revolution (1990)	When I Need You (5)	Will Mellor (1998)
		When I Need You (1)	Leo Sayer (1977)
		When I Said Goodbye / Summer Of Love (5)	Steps (2000)
What Took You So Long (1)	Emma Bunton (2001)	When I Think Of You (10)	Janet Jackson (1986)
What Would I Be (2)	Val Doonican (1966)	When I'm Dead And Gone (2)	McGuinness Flint (1970)
What Would You Do (3)	City High (2001)		
What You Got (4)	Abs (2002)	When I'm Good And Ready (5)	Sybil (1993)
What You Waiting For (4)	Gwen Stefani (2004)	When Johnny Comes Marching Home / Made You (5)	Adam Faith with John Barry Orchestra (1960)
What You're Made Of (7)	Lucie Silvas (2004)		
What You're Proposing (2)	Status Quo (1980)	When Julie Comes Around (10)	Cufflinks (1970)
What'd I Say (10)	Jerry Lee Lewis (1961)	When Love And Hate Collide (2)	Def Leppard (1995)
Whatever (3)	Oasis (1994)	When Love Comes To Town (6)	U2 with B B King (1989)
Whatever I Do (Wherever I Go) (4)	Hazell Dean (1984)		
Whatever Will Be Will Be (1)	Doris Day (1956)	When Mexico Gave Up The Rumba (6)	Mitchell Torok (1956)
Whatever You Want (4)	Status Quo (1979)	When My Little Girl Is Smiling (9)	Craig Douglas (1962)
Whatever U Want (9)	Christina Milian featuring Joe Budden (2004)	When My Little Girl Is Smiling (9)	Jimmy Justice (1962)
		When She Was My Girl (3)	Four Tops (1981)
What's Another Year (1)	Johnny Logan (1980)	When The Girl In Your Arms Is The Girl In Your Heart (3)	Cliff Richard with the Norrie Paramor Orchestra (1961)
What's Going On (6)	Artists Against Aids Worldwide (2001)		
What's It Gonna Be?! (6)	Busta Rhymes featuring Janet (1999)	When The Going Gets Tough (1)	Boyzone (1999)
		When The Going Gets Tough The Tough Get Going (1)	Billy Ocean (1986)

M
U
S
I
C

P
O
P

Title	Group/Artiste	Title	Group/Artiste
When The Heartache Is Over (10)	Tina Turner (1999)	Wherever I Lay My Hat (That's My Home) (1) first hit	Paul Young (1983)
When The Lights Go Out (4)	Five (1998)		
When We Dance (9)	Sting (1994)	Wherever You Will Go (3)	Calling (2002)
When We Were Young (10)	Bucks Fizz (1983)	Which Way You Goin' Billy (7)	Poppy Family (1970)
When Will I Be Famous (2)	Bros (1988)	Whiskey In The Jar (6) first hit	Thin Lizzy (1973)
When Will I Be Loved (4)	Everly Brothers (1960)	Whispering Grass (1)	Windsor Davies & Don Estelle (1975)
When Will I See You Again (1)	Three Degrees (1974)	Whistle Song (Blow My Whistle B***h) (5)	DJ Aligator Project (2002)
When Will You Say I Love You (3)	Billy Fury (1963)	White Christmas (5)	Bing Crosby (1977)
When You Ask About Love (4)	Matchbox (1980)	White Christmas (6)	Mantovani & His Orchestra (1952)
When You Believe (4)	Mariah Carey & Whitney Houston (1998)	White Flag (2)	Dido (2003)
		White Horses (10)	Jacky (1968)
When You Come Back To Me (2)	Jason Donovan (1989)	White Lines (Don't Do It) (7)	Grandmaster & Melle Mel (1984)
When You Look At Me (3)	Christina Milian (2002)	White Sport Coat, A (6)	King Brothers (1957)
		White Wedding (6)	Billy Idol (1985)
When You Lose The One You Love (7)	David Whitfield with Mantovani (1955)	Whiter Shade Of Pale, A (1)	Procol Harum (1967)
		Who Am I (10)	Beenie Man (1998)
When You Say Nothing At All (1)	Ronan Keating (1999)	Who Am I / This Is It! (5)	Adam Faith (1961)
		Who Are We (6)	Ronnie Hilton (1956)
(When You Say You Love Somebody) In The Heart (7)	Kool & The Gang (1984)	Who Do You Love Now (Stringer) (3)	Riva featuring Dannii Minogue (2001)
When You Tell Me That You Love Me (2)	Diana Ross (1991)	Who Feels Love? (4)	Oasis (2000)
		Who Found Who (10)	Jellybean featuring Elisa Fiorillo (1987)
When You Walk In The Room (3)	Searchers (1964)		
When You're Gone (3)	Bryan Adams featuring Melanie C (1998)	Who Is It (10)	Michael Jackson (1992)
		Who Killed Bambi (6)	Ten Pole Tudor (1979)
When You're In Love With A Beautiful Woman (1)	Dr Hook (1979)	Who Let The Dogs Out (2)	Baha Men (2000)
		Who Loves You (6)	Four Seasons (1975)
(When You're) Young And In Love (7)	Flying Pickets (1984)	Who Needs Love Like That (10)	Erasure (1992)
		Who The Hell Are You (10)	Madison Avenue (2000)
Whenever Wherever (2)	Shakira (2002)		
Whenever You Need Somebody (3)	Rick Astley (1987)	Whodunit (5)	Tavares (1977)
		Whole Again (1)	Atomic Kitten (2001)
Where Are You Baby (3)	Betty Boo (1990)	Whole Lotta Love (3)	Goldbug (1996)
Where Are You Now (My Love) (1)	Jackie Trent (1965)	Whole Lotta Shakin' Goin' On (8)	Jerry Lee Lewis (1957)
Where Did Our Love Go (8)	Donnie Elbert (1972)		
Where Did Our Love Go (3) first hit	Supremes (1964)	Whole Lotta Woman (1)	Marvin Rainwater (1958)
(Where Do I Begin) Love Story (4)	Andy Williams (1971)	Whole Of The Moon (re-issue), The (3)	Waterboys (1991)
Where Do You Go (2)	No Mercy (1997)	Whoomph! (There It Is) (4)	Clock (1995)
Where Do You Go To My Lovely (1)	Peter Sarstedt (1969)	Whoops Now / What'll I Do (9)	Janet Jackson (1995)
Where Is The Love (1)	Black Eyed Peas (2003)	Who's David? (1)	Busted (2004)
		Who's In The House (8)	Beatmasters featuring Merlin (1989)
Where Love Lives (remix) (9)	Alison Limerick (1996)		
Where The Boys Are / Baby Roo (5)	Connie Francis (1961)	Who's Leaving Who (4)	Hazell Dean (1988)
		Who's Sorry Now (1)	Connie Francis (1958)
Where The Story Ends / Reminisce (8)	Blazin' Squad (2003)	Who's That Girl (3)	Eurythmics (1983)
Where The Streets Have No Name (4)	U2 (1987)	Who's That Girl (6)	Eve (2001)
		Who's That Girl (1)	Madonna (1987)
Where The Streets Have No Name (Can't Take My Eyes Off You) / How Can You Expect To Be Taken Seriously (4)	Pet Shop Boys (1991)	Why (10)	Glamma Kid (1999)
		Why (5)	Annie Lennox (1992)
		Why (8)	Mis-Teeq (2001)
		Why (1)	Anthony Newley (1960)
Where The Wind Blows (2)	Frankie Laine (1953)	Why (3)	Donny Osmond (1972)
Where Will The Baby's Dimple Be (6)	Rosemary Clooney and Mellomen, with the Buddy Cole Quartet (1955)	Why (10)	Carly Simon (1982)
		Why (2)	3T featuring Michael Jackson (1996)
Where's The Love (4)	Hanson (1997)	Why? (6)	Bronski Beat (1984)
Where's Your Head At? (9)	Basement Jaxx (2001)	Why Can't I Wake Up With You (2)	Take That (1993)

Title	Group/Artiste	Title	Group/Artiste
Why Can't This Be Love (8)	Van Halen (1986)	Wishing (If I Had A Photograph Of You) (10)	A Flock Of Seagulls (1982)
Why Do Fools Fall In Love (1)	Frankie Lymon & Teenagers (1956)	Wishing On A Star (10)	Fresh 4 featuring Lizz E (1989)
Why Do Fools Fall In Love (4)	Diana Ross (1981)	Wishing On A Star (3)	Rose Royce (1978)
Why Does It Always Rain On Me? (10)	Travis (1999)	Wishing Well (7)	Free (1973)
Why Don't You Get A Job? (2)	Offspring (1999)	Wishing Well (4)	Terence Trent D'Arby (1987)
Why Oh Why Oh Why (6)	Gilbert O'Sullivan (1973)	Wishing You Were Somehow Here Again (7)	Sarah Brightman (1987)
Wichita Lineman (7) first hit	Glen Campbell (1969)	Witch Doctor (2)	Cartoons (1999)
Wicked Game (10)	Chris Isaak (1990)	Witch Doctor (5)	Don Lang & His Frantic Five (1958)
Wicker Man, The (9)	Iron Maiden (2000)	Witch Queen Of New Orleans, The (2)	Redbone (1971)
Wide Boy (9)	Nik Kershaw (1985)		
Wide-Eyed And Legless (6)	Andy Fairweather-Low (1975)	Witch, The (8)	Rattles (1970)
Wiggle It (3)	2 In A Room (1991)	With A Girl Like You (1)	Troggs (1966)
Wig-Wam Bam (4)	Sweet (1972)	With A Little Help From Friends (10)	Young Idea (1967)
Wild Boys (2)	Duran Duran (1984)	With A Little Help From My Friends (1)	Joe Cocker (1968)
Wild In The Country / I Feel So Bad (4)	Elvis Presley with The Jordanaires (1961)	With A Little Help From My Friends (1)	Wet Wet Wet (1988)
Wild One (7)	Bobby Rydell (1960)	With A Little Help From My Friends / Measure Of A Man (1)	Sam & Mark (2004)
Wild One, The (7)	Suzi Quatro (1974)	With A Little Luck (5)	Wings (1978)
Wild Side Of Life (9)	Status Quo (1976)	With All My Heart (4)	Petula Clark (1957)
Wild Thing (2) first hit	Troggs (1966)	With My Own Eyes (10)	Sash (2000)
Wild West Hero (6)	Electric Light Orchestra (1978)	With Or Without You (4)	U2 (1987)
Wild Wild West (2)	Will Smith featuring Dru Hill (1999)	With You (7)	Jessica Simpson (2004)
Wild Wind (2)	John Leyton (1961)	With You I'm Born Again (2)	Billy Preston & Syreeta (1979)
Wild World (8)	Jimmy Cliff (1970)		
Wild World (5)	Maxi Priest (1988)	Without Love (10)	Tom Jones (1969)
Wildest Dreams (6)	Iron Maiden (2003)	Without Me (1)	Eminem (2002)
Will I Ever (7)	Alice Deejay (2000)	Without You (1)	Mariah Carey (1994)
Will I? (5)	Ian Van Dahl (2001)	Without You (1)	Nilsson (1972)
Will 2K (2)	Will Smith (1999)	Woman (9)	Neneh Cherry (1996)
Will You (8)	Hazel O'Connor (1981)	Woman (1)	John Lennon (1981)
Will You Be There (9)	Michael Jackson (1993)	Woman In Love (1)	Barbra Streisand (1980)
Will You Love Me Tomorrow (4)	Shirelles (1961)	Woman In Love (3)	Three Degrees (1979)
Wimoweh (4)	Karl Denver (1962)		
Winchester Cathedral (4)	New Vaudeville Band (1966)	Woman In Love, A (1)	Frankie Laine (1956)
Wind Beneath My Wings (3)	Steven Houghton (1997)	Woman Trouble (6)	Artful Dodger & Robbie Craig with Craig David (2000)
Wind Beneath My Wings (5)	Bette Midler (1989)	Woman (Uh-Huh) (7)	Jose Ferrer (1954)
Wind Cries Mary, The (6)	Jimi Hendrix Experience (1967)	Wombling Merry Christmas (2)	Wombles (1974)
Wind Me Up (Let Me Go) (2)	Cliff Richard & The Shadows (1965)	Wombling Song, The (4) first hit	Wombles (1974)
Wind Of Change (2)	Scorpions (1991)	Wonder Of You, The (1)	Elvis Presley (1970)
Windmills Of Your Mind (8)	Noel Harrison (1969)	Wonderful (1)	Ja Rule featuring R Kelly & Ashanti (2004)
Wings Of A Dove (2)	Madness (1983)		
Winner Takes It All, The (1)	Abba (1980)	Wonderful Christmastime (6)	Paul McCartney (1979)
Winter In July (7)	Bomb The Bass (1991)	Wonderful Copenhagen (5)	Danny Kaye (1953)
Winter World Of Love (7)	Engelbert Humperdinck (1969)	Wonderful Land (1)	Shadows (1962)
		Wonderful Life (8)	Black (1987)
Winter's Tale, A (2)	David Essex (1982)	Wonderful Time Up There, A (2)	Pat Boone (1958)
Winter's Tale, A (6)	Queen (1995)	Wonderful Tonight (3)	Damage (1997)
Wipe Out (5)	Surfaris (1963)	Wonderful World (7)	Herman's Hermits (1965)
Wipeout (2)	Fat Boys & The Beach Boys (1987)	Wonderful World Beautiful People (6) first hit	Jimmy Cliff (1969)
Wired For Sound (4)	Cliff Richard (1981)	Wonderful World Of The Young (8)	Danny Williams (1962)
Wish You Were Here (8)	Eddie Fisher (1953)		
Wishful Thinking (9)	China Crisis (1984)	Wonderful World (re-issue) (2)	Sam Cooke (1986)
Wishing (10)	Buddy Holly (1963)	Wonderland (8)	Big Country (1984)
Wishing I Was Lucky (6)	Wet Wet Wet (1987)	Wondrous Stories (7) first hit	Yes (1977)

MUSIC POP

Title	Group/Artiste	Title	Group/Artiste
Wonderwall (2)	Mike Flowers Pops (1995)	Years May Come Years May Go (7)	Herman's Hermits (1970)
Wonderwall (2)	Oasis (1995)	Yeh Yeh (1)	Georgie Fame & The Blue Flames (1964)
Won't Get Fooled Again (9)	Who (1971)		
Won't Take It Lying Down (7)	Honeyz (2000)	Yellow (4)	Coldplay (2000)
Won't Talk About It (9)	Beats International (1990)	Yellow River (1) first hit	Christie (1970)
		Yellow Rose Of Texas (2)	Mitch Miller (1955)
Wood Beez (Pray Like Aretha Franklin) (10)	Scritti Politti (1984)	Yellow Submarine / Eleanor Rigby (1)	Beatles (1966)
Wooden Heart (1)	Elvis Presley (1961)	Yes (8)	McAlmont & Butler (1995)
Woodstock (1)	Matthews Southern Comfort (1970)		
		Yes I Will (9)	Hollies (1965)
Woo-Hah!! Got You All In Check (8)	Busta Rhymes (1996)	Yes My Darling Daughter (10)	Eydie Gorme (1962)
		Yes Sir I Can Boogie (1)	Baccara (1977)
Word Girl, The (6)	Scritti Politti featuring Ranking Ann (1985)	Yes Tonight Josephine (1)	Johnnie Ray (1957)
		Yesterday (8)	Beatles (1966)
Word Up (3)	Cameo (1986)	Yesterday (8)	Matt Monro (1965)
Word Up (8)	Gun (1994)	Yesterday (4)	Wet Wet Wet (1997)
Words (8)	Bee Gees (1968)	Yesterday Has Gone (4)	Cupid's Inspiration (1968)
Words (1)	Boyzone (1996)		
Words (2)	F R David (1983)	Yesterday Man (3)	Chris Andrews (1965)
Words Are Not Enough/I Know Him So Well (5)	Steps (2001)	Yesterday Once More (2)	Carpenters (1973)
		Yesterdays / November Rain (8)	Guns 'N' Roses (1992)
Wordy Rappinghood (7)	Tom Tom Club (1981)	Yester-Me Yester-You Yesterday (2)	Stevie Wonder (1969)
Work It (6)	Missy Elliott (2002)		
Work It (7)	Nelly featuring Justin Timberlake (2003)	Ying Tong Song (re-issue) (9)	Goons (1973)
		You (2)	S Club 7 (2002)
		You (10)	Ten Sharp (1992)
Work It Out (7)	Beyonce (2002)	You Ain't Seen Nothing Yet (2)	Bachman-Turner Overdrive (1974)
Work Rest And Play EP (6)	Madness (1980)		
Work That Body (7)	Diana Ross (1982)	You Always Hurt The One You Love (6)	Clarence 'Frogman' Henry (1961)
Workaholic (4)	2 Unlimited (1992)		
Working In A Coalmine (8)	Lee Dorsey (1966)	You Are Alive (4)	Fragma (2001)
Working My Way Back To You / Forgive Me Girl (1)	Detroit Spinners (1980)	You Are Everything (5)	Diana Ross & Marvin Gaye (1974)
World (9)	Bee Gees (1967)		
World In Motion (1)	Englandneworder (1990)	You Are My Destiny (6)	Paul Anka (1958)
		You Are My World (30)	Communards (1985)
World Of Our Own (1)	Westlife (2002)	You Are Not Alone (1)	Michael Jackson (1995)
World Of Our Own, A (3)	Seekers (1965)		
World Without Love, A (1) first hit	Peter & Gordon (1964)	You Are The Sunshine Of My Life (7)	Stevie Wonder (1973)
World's Greatest, The (4)	R Kelly (2002)	You Belong To Me (1)	Jo Stafford (1952)
Would I Lie To You (1)	Charles & Eddie (1992)	You Better You Bet (9)	Who (1981)
		You Came (3)	Kim Wilde (1988)
Would You? (3)	Touch & Go (1998)	You Can Call Me Al (4)	Paul Simon (1986)
Wouldn't Change A Thing (2)	Kylie Minogue (1989)	You Can Do It (2)	Ice Cube featuring Mack 10 & MS Toi (2004)
Wouldn't It Be Good (4)	Nik Kershaw (1984)		
Wrapped Around Your Finger (7)	Police (1983)	You Can Do Magic (3)	Limmie & The Family Cookin (1973)
Written In The Stars (10)	Elton John & LeAnn Rimes (1999)	You Can Get It If You Really Want (2)	Desmond Dekker (1970)
Wrong (8)	Everything But The Girl (1996)	You Can Never Stop Me Loving You (10)	Kenny Lynch (1963)
Wrong Impression (10)	Natalie Imbruglia (2002)	You Can't Hurry Love (1)	Phil Collins (1982)
		You Can't Hurry Love (3)	Supremes (1966)
Wuthering Heights (1) first hit	Kate Bush (1978)	You Could Be Mine (3)	Guns 'N' Roses (1991)
Xanadu (1)	Olivia Newton-John and ELO (1980)	You Do Something To Me (9)	Paul Weller (1995)
X-Files (8)	DJ Dado (1996)	You Don't Bring Me Flowers (5)	Barbra & Neil (1978)
X-Files, The (2)	Mark Snow (1996)	You Don't Care About Us (5)	Placebo (1998)
X Gon' Give It To Ya (6)	DMX (2003)	You Don't Have To Be A Baby To Cry (6)	Caravelles (1963)
Y Viva Espana (4)	Sylvia (1974)		
Y.M.C.A. (1)	Village People (1978)	You Don't Have To Be A Star (To Be In My Show) (7)	Marilyn McCoo & Billy Davis Jr (1977)
Yeah (1)	Usher featuring Lil' Jon & Ludacris (2004)	You Don't Have To Go (3)	Chi-Lites (1976)
		You Don't Have To Say You Love Me (5)	Guys & Dolls (1976)
Year 3000 (2)	Busted (2003)		

Title	Group/Artiste	Title	Group/Artiste
You Don't Have To Say You Love Me (9)	Elvis Presley (1971)	You Really Got Me (1)	Kinks (1964)
You Don't Have To Say You Love Me (1)	Dusty Springfield (1966)	You Rock My World (2)	Michael Jackson (2001)
You Don't Know (1)	Helen Shapiro (1961)	You Said No (1)	Busted (2003)
You Don't Know Me (9)	Ray Charles (1962)	You See The Trouble With Me (1)	Black Legend (2000)
You Don't Know Me (1)	Armand Van Helden (1999)	You See The Trouble With Me (2)	Barry White (1976)
		You Send Me (29) first hit	Sam Cooke (1958)
You Don't Love Me (No No No) (3)	Dawn Penn (1994)	You Sexy Thing (2)	Hot Chocolate (1975)
(You Drive Me) Crazy (5)	Britney Spears (1999)	You Sexy Thing (re-issue) (6)	Hot Chocolate (1997)
You Drive Me Crazy (2)	Shakin' Stevens (1981)	You Sexy Thing (remix) (10)	Hot Chocolate (1987)
		You Should Be Dancing (5)	Bee Gees (1976)
You Gave Me Love (10)	Crown Heights Affair (1980)	You Should Be ... (3)	Blockster (1999)
You Get What You Give (5)	New Radicals (1999)	You Should Really Know (8)	The Pirates featuring Enya, Shola Ama, Naila Boss & Ishani (2004)
You Got It (3)	Roy Orbison (1989)		
You Got It (The Right Stuff) (1)	New Kids On The Block (1989)	You Showed Me (8)	Lightning Seeds (1997)
You Got Soul (6)	Johnny Nash (1969)	You Spin Me Round (Like A Record) (1)	Dead Or Alive (1985)
You Got The Love (4)	Source featuring Candi Staton (1991)	You Stole The Sun From My Heart (5)	Manic Street Preachers (1999)
You Got The Love (3) (re-entry)	Source featuring Candi Staton (1997)	You Take Me Up (2)	Thompson Twins (1984)
		You To Me Are Everything (1) first hit	Real Thing (1976)
U Got 2 Know (6)	Cappella (1993)	You To Me Are Everything (The Decade Remix 76–86) (5)	Real Thing (1986)
You Got What It Takes (7)	Marv Johnson (1960)	You Wear It Well (1)	Rod Stewart (1972)
You Got What It Takes (2)	Showaddywaddy (1977)	You Were Made For Me (3)	Freddie & The Dreamers (1963)
You Gotta Be (re-issue) (10)	Des'ree (1999)	You Were On My Mind (2)	Crispian St Peters (1966)
(You Gotta) Fight For Your Right (To Party) (11) first hit	Beastie Boys (1987)	You Were Right (9)	Badly Drawn Boy (2002)
You Had Me (9)	Joss Stone (2004)	You Win Again (1)	Bee Gees (1987)
You Have Been Loved / The Strangest Thing '97 (2)	George Michael (1997)	You Won't Find Another Fool Like Me (1)	New Seekers (1973)
You Held The World In Your Arms (9)	Idlewild (2002)	You Won't Forget About Me (7)	Dannii Minogue vs Flower Power (2004)
You Just Might See Me Cry (2)	Our Kid (1976)		
You Keep It All In (8)	Beautiful South (1989)	You You You (6)	Alvin Stardust (1974)
You Keep Me Hangin' On (8)	Supremes (1966)	You'll Answer To Me (5)	Cleo Laine (1961)
You Keep Me Hangin' On (2)	Kim Wilde (1986)	You'll Never Find Another Love Like Mine (10)	Lou Rawls (1976)
You Little Thief (5)	Feargal Sharkey (1986)	You'll Never Know (6)	Shirley Bassey (1961)
You Make It Move (26) first hit	Dave Dee, Dozy, Beaky, Mick & Tich (1965)	You'll Never Stop Me From Loving You (1) first hit	Sonia (1989)
You Make Me Feel Brand New (2)	Stylistics (1974)	You'll Never Walk Alone (1)	Crowd (1985)
You Make Me Feel Like Dancing (2)	Leo Sayer (1976)	You'll Never Walk Alone (1)	Gerry & The Pacemakers (1963)
You Make Me Feel Brand New (7)	Simply Red (2003)	You'll See (5)	Madonna (1995)
You Make Me Feel (Mighty Real) (5)	Jimmy Somerville (1990)	Young And Foolish (10)	Edmund Hockridge (1956)
You Make Me Feel (Mighty Real) (8)	Sylvester (1978)	Young At Heart (8)	Bluebells (1984)
		Young At Heart (re-issue) (1)	Bluebells (1993)
You Make Me Sick (9)	Pink (2001)	Young At Heart (12) first hit	Frank Sinatra (1954)
You Make Me Wanna (1)	Usher (1998)	Young Gifted And Black (5)	Bob & Marcia (1970)
You Might Need Somebody (4)	Shola Ama (1997)	Young Girl (1)	Union Gap featuring Gary Puckett (1968)
You Must Have Been A Beautiful Baby (10)	Bobby Darin (1961)	Young Girl (re-issue) (6)	Gary Puckett & The Union Gap (1974)
You Must Love Me (10)	Madonna (1996)	Young Guns (Go For It) (3) first hit	Wham! (1982)
You Need Hands / Tulips From Amsterdam (3)	Max Bygraves with The Clark Brothers (1958)	Young Hearts Run Free (2) first hit	Candi Staton (1976)
You Needed Me (1)	Boyzone (1999)	Young Love (1)	Tab Hunter (1957)
You Only Tell Me You Love Me When You're Drunk (8)	Pet Shop Boys (2000)	Young Love (1)	Donny Osmond (1973)
		Young Lovers (9)	Paul & Paula (1963)

MUSIC

POP

Title	Group/Artiste	Title	Group/Artiste
Young New Mexican Puppeteer, The (6)	Tom Jones (1972)	You're The First The Last My Everything (1)	Barry White (1974)
Young Ones, The (1)	Cliff Richard & The Shadows (1962)	You're The One I Love (3)	Shola Ama (1997)
Young Parisians (9)	Adam & The Ants (1980)	You're The One That I Want (1)	John Travolta & Olivia Newton-John (1978)
Your Christmas Wish (8)	Smurfs (1996)	You're The One That I Want (re-issue) (4)	John Travolta & Olivia Newton-John (1998)
Your Game (3)	Will Young (2004)		
Your Love Is King (6)	Sade (1984)	You're The Voice (6)	John Farnham (1987)
Your Loving Arms (remix) (6)	Billie Ray Martin (1995)	You've Got A Friend (9)	Brand New Heavies (1997)
Your Song (7)	Elton John (1971)	You've Got A Friend (4)	James Taylor (1971)
Your Song (4)	Elton John & Alessandro Safina (2002)	You've Got It Bad (7)	Ocean Colour Scene (1996)
Your Woman (1)	White Town (1997)	You've Got Me Dangling On A String (5)	Chairmen of the Board (1970)
You're A Lady (3)	Peter Skellern (1972)	You've Got Your Troubles (2)	Fortunes (1965)
You're A Superstar (7)	Love Inc (2002)	You've Lost That Lovin' Feelin' (2)	Cilla Black (1965)
You're All That Matters To Me (6)	Curtis Stigers (1992)	You've Lost That Lovin' Feelin' (1) first hit	Righteous Brothers (1965)
You're Driving Me Crazy (1)	Temperance Seven (1961)		
You're Gone (7)	Marillion (2004)	You've Lost That Lovin' Feelin' (re-issue) (3)	Righteous Brothers (1990)
You're Gorgeous (3)	Babybird (1996)		
(You're) Having My Baby (6)	Paul Anka featuring Odia Coates (1974)	You've Lost That Lovin' Feelin' (re-issue) (10)	Righteous Brothers (1969)
		Yummy Yummy Yummy (5)	Ohio Express (1968)
You're History (7)	Shakespears Sister (1989)	Zabadak! (3)	Dave Dee, Dozy, Beaky, Mick & Tich (1967)
You're In My Heart (3)	Rod Stewart (1977)		
You're Makin' Me High (7)	Toni Braxton (1996)	Zambesi (2) first and only hit	Lou Busch and his Orchestra (1956)
You're More Than A Number In My Little Red Book (5)	Drifters (1976)		
You're Moving Out Today (6) only hit	Carole Bayer Sager (1977)	Zambesi (17) second and only other hit	Piranhas featuring Boring Bob Grover
		Zephyr Song, The (11)	Red Hot Chili Peppers (2002)
You're My Best Friend (7)	Queen (1976)		
You're My World (1)	Cilla Black (1964)	Ziggy Stardust (15) biggest hit	Bauhaus (1982)
You're No Good (3)	Swinging Blue Jeans (1964)	Zing A Little Zong (10)	Bing Crosby & Jane Wyman (1952)
You're Not Alone (1)	Olive (1997)	Zombie (14)	Cranberries (1994)
You're Sixteen (3)	Johnny Burnette (1961)	Zoom (2)	Fat Larry's Band (1982)
You're Sixteen (4)	Ringo Starr (1974)	Zorba's Dance (6)	Marcello Minerbi (1965)
You're So Vain (3)	Carly Simon (1972)		
You're Still The One (10) first hit	Shania Twain (1998)		

Singles: by Group/Artiste

Group/Artiste	Title	Group/Artiste	Title
A	Nothing (9)		Dancing Queen (1)
A Flock Of Seagulls	Wishing (If I Had A Photograph Of You) (10)		Does Your Mother Know (4)
			Fernando (1)
A1	Be The First To Believe (6)		Gimme Gimme Gimme (A Man After Midnight) (3)
	Caught In The Middle (2)		
	Everytime / Ready Or Not (3)		I Have A Dream (2)
	Like A Rose (6)		Knowing Me Knowing You (1)
	Make It Good (11)		
	No More (6)		Lay All Your Love On Me (7)
	Same Old Brand New You (1)		Mamma Mia (1)
	Summertime Of Our Lives (5)		Money Money Money (3)
	Take On Me (1)		Name Of The Game, The (1)
A Teens	Upside Down (10)		One Of Us (3)
A Tribe Called Quest	Rumble In The Jungle (3)		S.O.S. (6)
A+	Enjoy Yourself (5)		Summer Night City (5)
Aaliyah	More Than A Woman (1)		Super Trouper (1)
	Try Again (5)		Take A Chance On Me (1)
Abba	Angel Eyes / Voulez Vous (3)		Waterloo (1)
	Chiquitita (2)		Winner Takes It All, The (1)

Group/Artiste	Title
Abbot, Russ	All Night Holiday (20)
	Atmosphere (7)
Abbott, Gregory	Shake You Down (6)
ABC	All Of My Heart (5)
	Look Of Love, The (4)
	Poison Arrow (6)
Abdul, Paula	Opposites Attract (2)
	Rush Rush (6)
	Straight Up (3)
Abrams, Colonel	Trapped (3)
Abs	Stop Sign (10)
	What You Got (4)
Abs featuring	Miss Perfect (5)
Nodesha	
AC/DC	Heatseeker (12)
	Rock 'N' Roll Damnation (24)
Ace Of Base	All That She Wants (1)
	Cruel Summer (8)
	Don't Turn Around (5)
	Life Is A Flower (5)
	Sign, The (2)
Aces	Israelites (1)
	It Miek (7)
Adam & The Ants	Ant Rap (3)
	Antmusic (EP) (2)
	Dog Eat Dog (4)
	Kings Of The Wild Frontier (2)
	Prince Charming (1)
	Stand And Deliver (1)
	Young Parisians (9)
Adams, Bryan	All For Love (2)
	Cloud Number 9 (6)
	Don't Give Up (1)
	(Everything I Do) I Do It For You (1)
	Have You Ever Really Loved A Woman (4)
	Here I Am (5)
	I Finally Found Someone (10)
	It's Only Love (29)
	Let's Make A Night To Remember (10)
	Only Thing That Looks Good On Me Is You, The (6)
	Please Forgive Me (2)
	Run To You (11)
	Thought I'd Died And Gone To Heaven (8)
	When You're Gone (3)
Adams, Oleta	Get Here (4)
Adamski	Killer (1)
	N-R-G (12)
	Space Jungle, The (7)
Adventures Of Stevie V	Dirty Cash (2)
Aerosmith	Dude (Looks Like A Lady) (20)
	I Don't Want To Miss A Thing (4)
	Love In An Elevator (13)
Afroman	Because I Got High (1)
	Crazy Rap (10)
Aguilera, Christina	Beautiful (1)
	Come On Ever Baby (All I Want Is You) (8)
	Dirrty (1)
	Fighter (3)
	Genie In A Bottle (1)
	Lady Marmalade (1)
	Nobody Wants To Be Lonely (4)
	Voice Within, The (9)
	What A Girl Wants (3)

Group/Artiste	Title
Aguilera, Christina featuring Lil' Kim	Can't Hold Us Down (6)
Aguilera, Christina featuring Missy Elliott	Car Wash (4)
A-Ha	Cry Wolf (5)
	Hunting High And Low (5)
	I've Been Losing You (8)
	Living Daylights, The (5)
	Stay On These Roads (5)
	Sun Always Shines On TV, The (1)
	Take On Me (2)
	Train Of Thought (8)
Alan Price Set	House That Jack Built, The (4)
	I Put A Spell On You (9)
	Simon Smith And His Amazing Dancing Bear (4)
Alarm	68 Guns (17)
Albert, Morris	Feelings (4)
Alberts, Al	Love Is A Many Splendoured Thing (2)
	Mr Sandman (9)
	Stranger In Paradise (6)
	Three Coins In The Fountain (5)
Alda	Real Good Time (7)
Alessi	Oh Lori (8)
Alex Party	Don't Give Me Your Life (2)
Alexia	Uh La La La (10)
Alford, John	Blue Moon / Only You (9)
Ali, Tatyana	Boy You Knock Me Out (3)
	Daydreamin' (6)
Alien Ant Farm	Movies (5)
	Smooth Criminal (3)
Alizee	Moi ... Lolita (9)
All About Eve	Martha's Harbour (10)
All Saints	All Hooked Up (7)
	Black Coffee (1)
	Bootie Call (1)
	I Know Where It's At (4)
	Never Ever (1)
	Pure Shores (1)
	Under The Bridge / Lady Marmalade (1)
	War Of Nerves (7)
All Seeing I, The	Beat Goes On (11)
	Walk Like A Panther '98 (10)
Allen, Donna	Joy And Pain (10)
	Serious (8)
Allen, Keith	England's Irie (6)
All-4-One	I Swear (2)
Allisons	Are You Sure (2)
Allstars	Land Of Make Believe, The (9)
Almond, Marc	Days Of Pearly Spencer, The (4)
	I Feel Love (medley) (3)
	Something's Gotten Hold Of My Heart (1)
	Tainted Love (5)
Alpert, Herb	Lonely Bull, The (3)
	Spanish Flea (3)
	This Guy's In Love With You (3)
Alphaville	Big In Japan (8)
Altered Images	Don't Talk To Me About Love (7)
	Happy Birthday (2)
	I Could Be Happy (7)
Altern 8	Activ 8 (Come With Me) (3)
	Evapor 8 (6)
Althia & Donna	Up Town Top Ranking (1)
Ama, Shola	Taboo (10)
	You Might Need Somebody (4)

Group/Artiste	Title	Group/Artiste	Title
	You're The One I Love (3)		We're On The Ball (3)
Amazulu	Too Good To Be Forgotten (5)	Ant, Adam	Friend Or Foe (9)
Ambassadors Of Funk	Supermarioland (8)		Goody Two Shoes (1)
Amen Corner	Bend Me Shape Me (3)		Puss 'N' Boots (5)
	Gin House Blues (12)	Anthony, Billie	This Ole House (4)
	Hello Suzie (4)	Anthrax	Bring The Noise (14)
	High In The Sky (6)		I Am The Law (32)
	(If Paradise Is) Half As Nice (1)	Anuna	Riverdance (9)
America	Horse With No Name (re-entry)	Apache Indian	Nuff Vibes EP (5)
	(3)	Aphrodite's Child	Rain And Tears (29)
Ames Brothers	Naughty Lady Of Shady Lane (6)	Apollo Four Forty	Ain't Talkin' 'Bout Dub (7)
Amorosi, Vanessa	Absolutely Everybody (7)		Lost In Space (4)
Amos, Tori	Cornflake Girl (4)		Stop The Rock (10)
	Pretty Good Year (7)	Appleby, Kim	Don't Worry (2)
	Professional Widow (remix) (1)		G.L.A.D. (10)
Anastacia	I'm Outta Love (6)	Applejacks	Tell Me When (7)
	Left Outside Alone (3)	Appleton	Don't Worry (5)
	Sick And Tired (4)		Fantasy (2)
Anderson, Angry	Suddenly (3)	Aqua	Barbie Girl (1)
Anderson, Laurie	O Superman (2)		Cartoon Heroes (7)
Anderson, Lynn	Rose Garden (3)		Doctor Jones (1)
Anderson, Sunshine	Heard It All Before (9)		My Oh My (6)
Andre, Peter	All About Us (3)		Turn Back Time (1)
	Flava (1)	Aquagen	Phatt Bass (9)
	I Feel You (1)	Aqualung	Strange And Beautiful (7)
	Insania (3)	Arcadia	Election Day (7)
	Kiss The Girl (9)	Archer, Tasmin	Sleeping Satellite (1)
	Lonely (6)	Archies	Sugar Sugar (1)
	Mysterious Girl (2)	Architechs	Body Groove (3)
	Mysterious Girl (re-issue) (1)	Arena, Tina	Chains (6)
	Natural (6)	Argent	Hold Your Head Up (5)
Andrea True	More More More (5)	Armatrading, Joan	Love And Affection (10)
Connection		Armstrong, Louis	Hello, Dolly! (4)
Andrews, Chris	Yesterday Man (3)		Takes Two To Tango (6)
Andrews, Michael	Mad World (1)		Theme From A Threepenny
featuring Gary Jules			Opera (Mack The Knife) (8)
Aneka	Japanese Boy (1)		We Have All The Time In The
Angel City	Do You Know (I Go Crazy) (8)		World (3)
Animals	Baby Let Me Take You Home		What A Wonderful World /
	(21)		Cabaret (1)
	Bring It On Home To Me (7)	Arnee & The	I'll Be Back (5)
	Don't Bring Me Down (6)	Terminators	
	Don't Let Me Be Misunderstood	Arnold, David	On Her Majesty's Secret
	(3)		Service (7)
	House Of The Rising Sun (1)	Arnold, Eddy	Make The World Go Away (8)
	I'm Crying (8)	Arnold, P P	First Cut Is The Deepest (18)
	It's My Life (7)	Arrested	Mr Wendal /
	San Franciscan Nights (7)	Development	Revolution (4)
	We Gotta Get Out Of This		People Everyday (2)
	Place (2)	Arrington, Steve	Feel So Real (5)
Animotion	Obsession (5)	Arrival	Friends (8)
Anka, Paul	(All Of A Sudden) My Heart		I Will Survive (16)
	Sings (10)	Arrows	Touch Too Much, A (8)
	Diana (1)	Arsenal FC	Hot Stuff (9)
	I Love You Baby (3)	Arsenal FC First	Good Old Arsenal (16)
	Lonely Boy (3)	Team Squad	
	Put Your Head On My Shoulder	Art & Dotty Todd	Broken Wings (6)
	(7)	Art Of Noise	Close (To The Edit) (8)
	You Are My Destiny (6)		Kiss (5)
	(You're) Having My Baby (6)		Peter Gunn (8)
Another Level	Be Alone No More (6)	Artful Dodger	Movin' Too Fast (2)
	Bomb Diggy (6)		Please Don't Turn Me On (4)
	Freak Me (1)		Re-Rewind The Crowd Say Bo
	From The Heart (6)		Selecta (2)
	Guess I Was A Fool (5)		Twenty Four Seven (6)
	I Want You For Myself (2)		Woman Trouble (6)
	Summertime (7)	Artists Against Aids	What's Going On (6)
Ant & Dec	Better Watch Out (10)	Worldwide	
	Let's Get Ready To Rhumble (9)	Ash	Goldfinger (5)
	Shout (10)		Life Less Ordinary, A (10)

Group/Artiste	Title
	Oh Yeah (6)
	Shining Light (8)
Ashanti	Always On Time (6)
	Foolish (4)
	Rock Wit U (Awww Baby) (7)
	What's Luv (4)
Ashcroft, Richard	Song For The Lovers, A (3)
Ashford & Simpson	Solid (3)
Ashton Gardner & Dyke	Resurrection Shuffle, The (3)
Assembly	Never Never (4)
Associates	Party Fears Two (9)
Astley, Rick	Cry For Help (7)
	Hold Me In Your Arms (10)
	Never Gonna Give You Up (1)
	She Wants To Dance With Me (6)
	Take Me To Your Heart (8)
	Together Forever (2)
	When I Fall In Love / My Arms Keep Missing You (2)
	Whenever You Need Somebody (3)
Aswad	Don't Turn Around (1)
	Shine (5)
ATB	Don't Stop (3)
	Killer (4)
	9pm (Till I Come) (1)
Atlantic Starr	Always (3)
	Secret Lovers (10)
Atomic Kitten	Eternal Flame (1)
	I Want Your Love (10)
	If You Come To Me (3)
	It's OK (3)
	Last Goodbye / Be With You (2)
	Love Doesn't Have To Hurt (4)
	Right Now (10)
	See Ya (6)
	Someone Like Me / Right Now 2004 (8)
	Tide Is High (Get The Feeling), The (1)
	Whole Again (1)
Atomic Kitten featuring Kool and the Gang	Ladies Night (8)
Atomic Rooster	Devil's Answer, The (4)
Attractions	Oliver's Army (2)
Atwell, Winifred	Britannia Rag (re-entry) (5)
	Coronation Rag (re-entry) (5)
	Flirtation Waltz (re-entry) (10)
	Let's Have A Ball (4)
	Let's Have A Ding Dong (3)
	Let's Have A Party (2)
	Let's Have Another Party (1)
	Make It A Party (7)
	Piano Party (10)
	Poor People Of Paris (1)
	Rachmaninoff's Variation On A Theme (9)
Auger, Brian	This Wheel's On Fire (5)
Aurora	Ordinary World (5)
Avalon Boys	Trail Of The Lonesome Pine, The (2)
Average White Band	Pick Up The Pieces (6)
Avid Merrion, Davina McCall & Patsy Kensit	I Got You Babe / Soda Pop (5)

Group/Artiste	Title
Avons	Seven Little Girls Sitting In The Back Seat (3)
Axel Stordahl	Say You're Mine Again (10)
	Say You're Mine Again (re-entry) (6)
Az Yet	Hard To Say I'm Sorry (7)
Aznavour, Charles	She (1)
Aztec Camera	Oblivious (47)
	Somewhere In My Heart (3)
Azzido Da Bass	Dooms Night (8)
B Bumble and the Stingers	Nut Rocker (1)
B15 Project	Girls Like Us (7)
B2K	Girlfriend (10)
B Real	Hit 'Em High (The Monstars' Anthem) (8)
B*Witched	Blame It On The Weatherman (1)
	C'est La Vie (1)
	Jesse Hold On (4)
	Rollercoaster (1)
	Thank Abba For The Music (4)
	To You I Belong (1)
B, Melanie	Feels So Good (5)
	I Want You Back (1)
	Tell Me (4)
B, Stevie	Because I Love You (The Postman Song) (6)
Baby D	(Everybody's Got To Learn Sometime) I Need Your Loving (3)
	Let Me Be Your Fantasy (1)
	So Pure (3)
Babybird	You're Gorgeous (3)
Babyface	How Come, How Long (10)
Babylon Zoo	Spaceman (1)
Babyshambles	Killamangiro (8)
Baccara	Sorry I'm A Lady (8)
	Yes Sir I Can Boogie (1)
Bacharach, Burt	Trains and Boats and Planes (4)
Bachelors	Charmaine (6)
	Diane (1)
	I Believe (2)
	I Wouldn't Trade You For The World (4)
	Marie (9)
	No Arms Can Ever Hold You (7)
	Ramona (4)
	Sound Of Silence, The (3)
	You Ain't Seen Nothing Yet (2)
Bachman-Turner Overdrive	
Backstreet Boys	All I Have To Give (2)
	Anywhere For You (4)
	As Long As You Love Me (3)
	Call, The (8)
	Drowning (4)
	Everybody (Backstreet's Back) (3)
	I Want It That Way (1)
	I'll Never Break Your Heart (re-issue) (8)
	Larger Than Life (5)
	One, The (8)
	Quit Playing Games (With My Heart) (2)
	Shape Of My Heart (4)
	Show Me The Meaning Of Being Lonely (3)

Group/Artiste	Title
	We've Got It Goin' On (3)
Bad Boys Inc	More To This World (8)
Bad Manners	Can Can (3)
	My Girl Lollipop (My Boy Lollipop) (9)
	Special Brew (3)
	Walking On Sunshine (10)
Baddiel & Skinner	3 Lions (1)
	3 Lions '98 (1)
Badfinger	Come And Get It (4)
	Day After Day (10)
	No Matter What (5)
Badly Drawn Boy	Once Around The Block (46)
	You Were Right (9)
Baez, Joan	Night They Drove Old Dixie Down, The (6)
	There But For Fortune (8)
	We Shall Overcome (26)
Baha Men	Who Let The Dogs Out (2)
Bailey, Philip	Easy Lover (1)
Baker Selection, George	Paloma Blanca (10)
Baker, Adrian	Sherry (10)
Ball, Kenny & His Jazzmen	Green Leaves Of Summer, The (7)
	March Of The Siamese Children (4)
	Midnight In Moscow (2)
	Sukiyaki (10)
Ball, Michael	Love Changes Everything (2)
Baltimora	Tarzan Boy (3)
Bambaataa	Afrika Shox (7)
Bamboo	Bamboogie (2)
Bananarama	Cruel Summer (8)
	Help (3)
	I Want You Back (5)
	It Ain't What You Do It's The Way That You Do It (4)
	Love In The First Degree (3)
	Na Na Hey Hey Kiss Him Goodbye (5)
	Really Saying Something (5)
	Robert De Niro's Waiting (3)
	Shy Boy (4)
	Venus (8)
Band Aid	Do They Know It's Christmas (1)
	Do They Know It's Christmas (re-entry) (3)
Band Aid II	Do They Know It's Christmas (1)
Band Aid 20	Do They Know It's Christmas? (1)
Band Of The Black Watch	Scotch On The Rocks (8)
Bangles	Eternal Flame (1)
	Manic Monday (2)
	Walk Like An Egyptian (3)
Banton, Pato	Baby Come Back (1)
Barber's Jazz Band, Chris	Petite Fleur (9)
Bardo	One Step Further (2)
Bardot	Poison (45)
Barenaked Ladies	One Week (5)
Barlow, Gary	Forever Love (1)
	Love Won't Wait (1)
	Open Road (7)
Barron Knights	Call Up The Groups (3)
	Live In Trouble (7)
	Merry Gentle Pops (9)

Group/Artiste	Title
	Pop Go The Workers (5)
	Taste Of Aggro, A (3)
Barry, John	As You Like It (5)
	How About That! (4)
	When Johnny Comes Marching Home / Made You (5)
Barry, Len	Like A Baby (10)
	1-2-3 (3)
Basement Jaxx	Red Alert (5)
	Rendez-Vu (4)
	Romeo (6)
	Where's Your Head At? (9)
Basil, Toni	Mickey (2)
Bass, Alfie	Signature Tune Of 'The Army Game', The (5)
Bassey, Shirley	As I Love You (re-entry) (1)
	As Long As He Needs Me (2)
	Banana Boat Song (8)
	For All We Know (6)
	I (Who Have Nothing) (6)
	I'll Get By (10)
	Kiss Me Honey Honey Kiss Me (3)
	Never Never Never (8)
	Reach For The Stars / Climb Ev'ry Mountain (1)
	Something (4)
	What Now My Love (5)
	You'll Never Know (6)
Bassheads	Is There Anybody Out There (5)
Bass-O-Matic	Fascinating Rhythm (9)
Batt, Mike	Summertime City (4)
Bauhaus	Ziggy Stardust (15)
Baxter, Les	Unchained Melody (10)
Bay City Rollers	All Of Me Loves All Of You (4)
	Bye Bye Baby (1)
	Give A Little Love (1)
	I Only Wanna Be With You (4)
	Keep On Dancing (9)
	Love Me Like I Love You (4)
	Money Honey (3)
	Remember (Sha-La-La) (6)
	Shang-A-Lang (2)
	Summerlove Sensation (3)
BBD	Best Things In Life Are Free, The (2)
BBE	Flash (5)
	Seven Days And One Week (3)
BBMak	Back Here (re-issue) (5)
	Still On Your Side (8)
BC-52s	(Meet) The Flintstones (3)
Beach Boys	Barbara Ann (3)
	Break Away (6)
	Cottonfields (5)
	Do It Again (1)
	God Only Knows (2)
	Good Vibrations (1)
	Heroes And Villains (8)
	I Can Hear Music (10)
	I Get Around (7)
	Lady Lynda (6)
	Sloop John B (2)
	Surfin' USA (34)
	Then I Kissed Her (4)
	Wipeout (2)
Beastie Boys	Ch-Check It Out (8)
	Intergalactic (5)
	She's On It (10)
	(You Gotta) Fight For Your Right (To Party) (11)

Group/Artiste	Title	Group/Artiste	Title
Beat	Can't Get Used To Losing You (3)	Bedingfield, Natasha	Single (3)
	Hands Off – She's Mine (9)		These Words (1)
	Mirror In The Bathroom (4)		Unwritten (6)
	Tears Of A Clown / Ranking Full Stop (6)	Bee Gees	Alone (5)
			Don't Forget To Remember (2)
	Too Nice To Talk To (7)		First Of May (6)
Beatles	All You Need Is Love (1)		For Whom The Bell Tolls (4)
	Baby It's You (7)		How Deep Is Your Love (3)
	Ballad Of John And Yoko (1)		Immortality (5)
	Beatles Movie Medley (10)		I've Gotta Get A Message To You (1)
	Can't Buy Me Love (1)		
	Day Tripper / We Can Work It Out (1)		Jive Talkin' (5)
			Massachusetts (1)
	Free As A Bird (2)		New York Mining Disaster 1941 (12)
	From Me To You (1)		
	Get Back (1)		Night Fever (1)
	Hard Day's Night, A (1)		Run To Me (9)
	Hello Goodbye (1)		Secret Love (5)
	Help! (1)		Stayin' Alive (4)
	Hey Jude (1)		Too Much Heaven (3)
	I Feel Fine (1)		Tragedy (1)
	I Want To Hold Your Hand (1)		Words (8)
	Lady Madonna (1)		World (9)
	Let It Be (2)		You Should Be Dancing (5)
	Love Me Do (17)		You Win Again (1)
	Love Me Do (re-entry) (4)	Beenie Man	Dude (7)
	Magical Mystery Tour EP (2)		Feel It Boy (9)
	Paperback Writer (1)		Money (5)
	Penny Lane / Strawberry Fields Forever (2)		Who Am I (10)
		Bega, Lou	Mambo No 5 (A Little Bit Of ...) (1)
	Please Please Me (2)	Belafonte, Harry	Banana Boat Song (2)
	Real Love (4)		Island In The Sun (3)
	She Loves You (1)		Mary's Boy Child (1)
	Something / Come Together (4)		Mary's Boy Child (re-entry) (10)
	Ticket To Ride (1)	Bell & Spurling	Sven Sven Sven (7)
	Yellow Submarine / Eleanor Rigby (1)	Bell, William	Private Number (8)
		Bellamy Brothers	If I Said You Have A Beautiful Body Would You Hold It Against Me (3)
	Yesterday (8)		
Beatmasters	Hey DJ I Can't Dance To That Music You're Playing (7)		
			Let Your Love Flow (7)
	Rok Da House (5)	Belle Stars	Sign Of The Times (3)
	Who's In The House (8)	Bellini	Samba De Janeiro (8)
Beats International	Dub Be Good To Me (1)	Beloved	Sweet Harmony (8)
	Won't Talk About It (9)	Bennett, Tony	Stranger In Paradise (1)
Beautiful South	Don't Marry Her (8)	Benny Benassi presents The Biz	Satisfaction (2)
	Little Time, A (1)		
	Perfect 10 (2)	Benson, George	Give Me The Night (7)
	Rotterdam (5)		In Your Eyes (7)
	Song For Whoever (2)		Love X Love (10)
	You Keep It All In (8)	Benton, Brook	Endlessly (28)
Becaud, Gilbert	Little Love And Understanding, A (10)	Berlin	Take My Breath Away (1)
			Take My Breath Away (re-entry) (3)
Beck, Jeff	Goo Goo Barabajagal (Love Is Hot) (12)		
		Bernard Ebbinghouse Orchestra	It's All Over (9)
	Hi-Ho Silver Lining (14)		
Beck, Robin	The First Time (1)	Bernstein, Elmer	Staccato's Theme (4)
Beckham, Victoria	Mind Of It's Own, A (6)	Berri	Sunshine After The Rain, The (4)
	Not Such An Innocent Girl (6)		
	Out Of Your Mind (2)	Berry, Chuck	Let It Rock / Memphis Tennessee (6)
	This Groove / Let Your Head Go (3)		
			My Ding-A-Ling (1)
Bedingfield, Daniel	Gotta Get Thru This (1)		No Particular Place To Go (3)
	I Can't Read You (6)		School Day (Ring! Ring! Goes The Bell) (24)
	If You're Not The One (1)		
	James Dean (I Wanna Know) (4)	Berry, Dave	Crying Game, The (5)
			Little Things (5)
	Never Gonna Leave Your Side (1)		Mama (5)
	Nothing Hurts Like Love (3)		Memphis Tennessee (19)

M
U
S
I
C

P
O
P

Group/Artiste	Title	Group/Artiste	Title
Berry, Mike	Sunshine Of Your Smile, The (9)	Black Grape	England's Irie (6)
Berry, Nick	Every Loser Wins (1)		Fat Neck (10)
	Heartbeat (2)		In The Name Of The Father (8)
Beverley Sisters	I Saw Mommy Kissing Santa Claus (re-entry) (6)		Reverend Black Grape (9)
		Black Lace	Agadoo (2)
	Little Drummer Boy (6)		Do The Conga (10)
Beyonce	Naughty Girl (10)		Superman (Gioca Jouer) (9)
	Work It Out (7)	Black Legend	You See The Trouble With Me (1)
Beyonce (Knowles)	Crazy In Love (1)	Black Sabbath	Paranoid (4)
Beyonce featuring Sean Paul	Baby Boy (2)	Black Slate	Amigo (9)
		Black, Cilla	Alfie (9)
B-52's	Love Shack (2)		Anyone Who Had A Heart (1)
Bhangra Knights vs Husan	Husan (7)		Conversations (7)
			Don't Answer Me (6)
Big Ben Banjo Band	Let's Get Together No. 1 (6)		Heart and Soul (75)
Big Brovaz	Baby Boy (4)		It's For You (7)
	Favourite Things (2)		Love Of The Loved (35)
	Nu Flow (3)		Love's Just A Broken Heart (5)
	OK (7)		Something Tells Me (Something Is Gonna Happen Tonight) (3)
Big Country	Chance (9)		
	Fields Of Fire (400 Miles) (10)		
	Look Away (7)		Step Inside Love (8)
	Wonderland (8)		Surround Yourself With Sorrow (3)
Big Dee Irwin	Swinging On A Star (7)		
Big Fun	Blame It On The Boogie (4)		You're My World (1)
	Can't Shake The Feeling (8)		You've Lost That Lovin' Feelin' (2)
Big Mountain	Baby I Love Your Way (2)		
Bigfoot	Sweet Like Chocolate (1)	Blackfoot Sue	Standing In The Road (4)
Biggs, Barry	Sideshow (3)	Blackman, Honor	Kinky Boots (5)
Bilk, Mr Acker	Aria (5)	Blackstreet	Don't Leave Me (6)
	Buona Sera (7)		Fix (7)
	Stranger On The Shore (2)		No Diggity (9)
	Summer Set (5)		Take Me There (7)
	That's My Home (7)	Blackwood, Richard	Mama – Who Da Man? (3)
Bill Haley & His Comets	Don't Knock The Rock (7)		1-2-3-4 Get With The Wicked (10)
	Rip It Up (4)		
	Rock Around The Clock (re-entry) (1)	Blancmange	Blind Vision (10)
			Don't Tell Me (8)
	Rock Around The Clock (re-entry) (5)		Living On The Ceiling (7)
		Blatt, Melanie	Twenty-Four Seven (6)
	Rock-A-Beatin' Boogie (4)	Blazin' Squad	Crossroads (1)
	Rockin' Through The Rye (3)		Flip Reverse (2)
	Saints Rock 'N' Roll, The (5)		Here 4 One (6)
	See You Later Alligator (7)		Love On The Line (6)
	Shake Rattle And Roll (4)		Reminisce / Where The Story Ends (8)
Billie	Because We Want To (1)		
	Girlfriend (1)		We Just Be Dreamin' (3)
	Honey To The Bee (3)		Where The Story Ends / Reminisce (8)
	She Wants You (3)		
	Thank Abba For The Music (4)	Blige, Mary J	As (4)
Birkin, Jane	Je T'Aime ... Moi Non Plus (2)		Everything (6)
	Je T'Aime ... Moi Non Plus (re-issue) (1)		Family Affair (8)
			I'll Be There For You – You're All I Need To Get By (10)
Biti	Shine On (8)		
Bizarre Inc	I'm Gonna Get You (3)		911 (9)
	Playing With Knives (4)		No More Drama (9)
Bizz Nizz	Don't Miss The Partyline (7)	Blink 182	All The Small Things (2)
Björk	Army Of Me (10)		I Miss You (8)
	Hyperballad (8)	Blinky Blink	Take Me There (7)
	It's Oh So Quiet (4)	Blockster	You Should Be ... (3)
	Ooops (42)	Blondie	Atomic (1)
Björn Again	Erasure-ish (25)		Call Me (1)
Black	Sweetest Smile (8)		Denis (2)
	Wonderful Life (8)		Dreaming (2)
Black Box	Fantasy (5)		Hanging On The Telephone (5)
	I Don't Know Anybody Else (4)		Heart Of Glass (1)
	Ride On Time (1)		(I'm Always Touched By Your) Presence Dear (10)
Black Eyed Peas	Hey Mamma (6)		
	Shut Up (2)		Maria (1)
	Where Is The Love (1)		Picture This (12)

Group/Artiste	Title	Group/Artiste	Title
	Rapture (5)		Say A Little Prayer (10)
	Sunday Girl (1)		Winter In July (7)
	Tide Is High, The (1)	Bombalurina	Itsy Bitsy Teeny Weeny Yellow
Bloodhound Gang	Bad Touch, The (4)		Polka Dot Bikini (1)
Bloom, Bobby	Montego Bay (3)	Bomfunk MCs	Freestyler (2)
Blow Monkeys	It Doesn't Have To Be This	Bon Jovi	All About Lovin' You (9)
	Way (5)		Always (2)
Blue	All Rise (4)		Dry County (9)
	Breathe Easy (4)		Everyday (5)
	Bubblin' (9)		Hardest Part Is The
	Curtain Falls (4)		Night (68)
	Fly By II (6)		In These Arms (9)
	Guilty (2)		It's My Life (3)
	If You Come Back (1)		Keep The Faith (5)
	One Love (3)		Lie To Me (10)
	Sorry Seems To Be The		Livin' On A Prayer (4)
	Hardest Word (1)		One Wild Night (10)
	Too Close (1)		Please Come Home For
	U Make Me Wanna (4)		Christmas (7)
Blue Boy	Remember Me (8)		Say It Isn't So (10)
Blue Flames	Get Away (1)		Someday I'll Be Saturday Night
	Yeh Yeh (1)		(7)
Blue Grass Boys	Last Train To San Fernando (2)		Something For The Pain (8)
Blue Mink	Banner Man (3)		These Days (7)
	Good Morning Freedom (10)		This Ain't A Love Song (6)
	Melting Pot (3)	Bon Jovi, Jon	Blaze Of Glory (13)
	Randy (9)		Midnight In Chelsea (4)
Blue Pearl	Naked In The Rain (4)		Queen Of New Orleans (10)
Blue, Barry	(Dancing) On A Saturday Night	Bone Thugs-N-	Tha Crossroads (8)
	(2)	Harmony	
	Do You Wanna Dance (7)	Boney M	Belfast (8)
Bluebells	Young At Heart (8)		Boney M Megamix (7)
	Young At Heart (re-issue) (1)		Daddy Cool (6)
Bluenotes	Don't Leave Me This Way (5)		Hooray Hooray It's A Holi-
	If You Don't Know Me By Now		Holiday (3)
	(9)		Ma Baker (2)
Bluetones	Cut Some Rug / Castle Rock (7)		Mary's Boy Child – Oh My Lord (1)
	Marblehead Johnson (7)		Painter Man (10)
	Slight Return (2)		Rasputin (2)
	Solomon Bites The Worm (10)		Rivers Of Babylon / Brown Girl
Blur	Beetlebum (1)		In The Ring (1)
	Charmless Man (5)		Sunny (3)
	Country House (1)	Bonnet, Graham	Night Games (6)
	Girls And Boys (5)	Bono	I've Got You Under My Skin (4)
	Music Is My Radar (10)	Bonzo Dog Doo-Dah	I'm The Urban Spaceman (5)
	On Your Own (5)	Band	
	Out Of Time (5)	Boo Radleys	Wake Up Boo! (9)
	Parklife (10)	Boo, Betty	Doin' The Do (7)
	Song 2 (2)		Hey DJ I Can't Dance To That
	Stereotypes (7)		Music You're Playing (7)
	Tender (2)		Where Are You Baby (3)
	There's No Other Way (8)	Boogie Box High	Jive Talkin' (7)
	Universal, The (5)	Boogie Pimps	Somebody To Love (3)
Bo Selecta	Proper Crimbo (4)		Sunny (10)
Bob & Earl	Harlem Shuffle (7)	Booker Newbury III	Love Town (6)
Bob and Marcia	Pied Piper (11)	Booker T & The MG's	Green Onions (7)
	Young Gifted And Black (5)		Time Is Tight (4)
Bob The Builder	Can We Fix It? (1)	Boomtown Rats	Banana Republic (3)
	Mambo No 5 (1)		I Don't Like Mondays (1)
Bocelli, Andrea	Time To Say Goodbye (Con Te		Like Clockwork (6)
	Partiro) (2)		Looking After No. 1 (11)
Bohannon, Hamilton	Disco Stomp (6)		Rat Trap (1)
Bolton, Michael	Can I Touch You ... There (6)		Someone's Looking At
	How Am I Supposed To Live		You (4)
	Without You (3)	Boone, Pat	Ain't That A Shame (7)
	How Can We Be Lovers (10)		April Love (7)
	When A Man Loves A Woman		Don't Forbid Me (2)
	(8)		Friendly Persuasion (3)
Bomb The Bass	Beat Dis (2)		I'll Be Home (1)
	Megablast / Don't Make Me		It's Too Soon To Know (7)
	Wait (6)		Johnny Will (4)

MUSIC POP

Group/Artiste	Title	Group/Artiste	Title
	Love Letters In The Sand (2)		Love Me For A Reason (2)
	Remember You're Mine /		No Matter What (1)
	There's A Goldmine In The		Picture Of You (2)
	Sky (5)		So Good (3)
	Speedy Gonzales (2)		When The Going Gets Tough
	Sugar Moon (6)		(1)
	Wonderful Time Up There, A (2)		Words (1)
Boot Room Boyz	Pass And Move (It's The		You Needed Me (1)
	Liverpool Groove) (4)	Bragg, Billy	She's Leaving Home (1)
Boothe, Ken	Crying Over You (11)	Bran Van 3000	Drinking In L.A. (re-issue) (3)
	Everything I Own (1)	Brand New Heavies	You've Got A Friend (9)
Bootzilla Orchestra	Double Dutch (3)	Brandon, Johnny	Tomorrow (8)
Boris Pickett & Crypt-	Monster Mash (3)	Brandy	Another Day In Paradise (5)
Kickers			Boy Is Mine, The (2)
Boswell, Eve	Pickin' A Chicken (9)		Top Of The World (2)
Boucher, Judy	Can't Be With You Tonight (2)		What About Us (4)
Boulevard, DB	Point Of View (3)	Brandy featuring	Talk About Our Love (6)
Bourke, Toby	Waltz Away Dreaming (10)	Kanye West	
Bow Wow Wow	Go Wild In The Country (7)	Branigan, Laura	Gloria (6)
	I Want Candy (9)		Self Control (5)
Bowers, Dane	Buggin' Me (6)	Braxton, Toni	Breathe Again (2)
	Out Of Your Mind (2)		He Wasn't Man Enough (5)
Bowie, David	Absolute Beginners (2)		I Don't Want To (9)
	Ashes To Ashes (1)		Un-Break My Heart (2)
	Blue Jean (6)		You're Makin' Me High (7)
	Boys Keep Swinging (7)	Bread	Make It With You (5)
	China Girl (2)	Break Machine	Breakdance Party (9)
	Dancing In The Street (1)		Street Dance (3)
	Drive-In Saturday (3)	Breathe	Hands To Heaven (4)
	Everyone Says Hi (20)	Brent, Tony	Make It Soon (9)
	Fashion (5)		Make It Soon (re-entry) (9)
	Golden Years (8)		Walkin' To Missouri (9)
	Jean Genie, The (2)		Walkin' To Missouri (re-entry) (7)
	Jump They Say (9)	Bresslaw, Bernard	Mad Passionate Love (6)
	Knock On Wood (10)		Signature Tune Of 'The Army
	Laughing Gnome, The (6)		Game', The (5)
	Let's Dance (1)	Brewer, Teresa	Let Me Go Lover (9)
	Life On Mars (3)		Sweet Old-Fashioned Girl (3)
	Modern Love (2)		Tear Fell, A (2)
	Peace On Earth / Little	Brian & Michael	Matchstalk Men And Matchstalk
	Drummer Boy (3)		Cats And Dogs (1)
	Rebel Rebel (5)	Brighouse & Rastrick	Floral Dance, The (2)
	Sorrow (3)	Brass Band	
	Sound And Vision (3)	Brightman, Sarah	All I Ask Of You (3)
	Space Oddity (5)		I Lost My Heart To A Starship
	Space Oddity (re-issue) (1)		Trooper (6)
	Starman (10)		Phantom Of The Opera, The (7)
	Under Pressure (1)		Pie Jesu (3)
Bowling For Soup	Girl All The Bad Guys Want		Time To Say Goodbye (Con Te
	(8)		Partiro) (2)
Box Tops	Letter, The (5)		Wishing You Were Somehow
Boy Meets Girl	Waiting For A Star To Fall (9)		Here Again (7)
Boyd, Jimmy	I Saw Mommy Kissing Santa	Bristol, Johnny	Hang On In There Baby (3)
	Claus (3)	Bronski Beat	Hit That Perfect Beat (3)
	Tell Me A Story (5)		I Feel Love (medley) (3)
Boystown Gang	Can't Take My Eyes Off You (4)		Smalltown Boy (3)
Boyz II Men	End Of The Road (1)		Why? (6)
	4 Seasons Of Loneliness (10)	Brook Brothers	Warpaint (5)
	I'll Make Love To You (5)	Brooks, Elkie	No More The Fool (5)
	One Sweet Day (6)		Pearl's A Singer (8)
Boyzone	All That I Need (1)		Sunshine After The Rain (10)
	Baby Can I Hold You /	Brooks, Meredith	Bitch (6)
	Shooting Star (2)	Bros	Cat Amongst The Pigeons /
	Coming Home Now (4)		Silent Night (2)
	Different Beat, A (1)		Chocolate Box (9)
	Everyday I Love You (3)		Drop The Boy (2)
	Father And Son (2)		I Owe You Nothing (1)
	I Love The Way You Love Me		I Quit (4)
	(2)		Sister (10)
	Isn't It A Wonder (2)		Too Much (2)
	Key To My Life (3)		When Will I Be Famous (2)

Group/Artiste	Title	Group/Artiste	Title
Brother Beyond	Harder I Try, The (2)		Don't Give Up (9)
	He Ain't No Competition (6)		Kate Bush On Stage EP (10)
Brotherhood Of Man	Angelo (1)		Man With The Child In His
	Figaro (1)		Eyes (6)
	Oh Boy (The Mood I'm In) (8)		Running Up That Hill (3)
	Save Your Kisses For Me (1)		Wuthering Heights (1)
	United We Stand (10)	Busted	Air Hostess (2)
Brothers	Sing Me (8)		Crashed The Wedding (1)
Brothers Johnson	Stomp (6)		Sleeping With The Light On (3)
Brown, Angie	I'm Gonna Get You (3)		3AM / Thunderbirds (1)
Brown, Bobby	Don't Be Cruel (42)		What I Go To School For (3)
	Every Little Step (6)		Who's David? (1)
	Humpin' Around (remix) (8)		Year 3000 (2)
	My Prerogative (6)		You Said No (1)
	On Our Own (Theme from	Buzzcocks	Ever Fallen In Love (With
	Ghostbusters II) (4)		Someone You Shouldn't've)
	Two Can Play That Game (re-		(12)
	entry) (3)		What Do I Get (37)
Brown, Foxy	I'll Be (9)	BVSMP	I Need You (3)
Brown, Ian	Be There (8)	Bygraves, Max	Cowpuncher's Cantata (re-
	Dolphins Were Monkeys (5)		entry) (6)
	My Star (5)		Cowpuncher's Cantata (re-
Brown, James	Living In America (5)		entry) (8)
Brown, Jocelyn	Always There (6)		Cowpuncher's Cantata (re-
	Don't Talk Just Kiss (3)		entry) (10)
	Keep On Jumpin' (8)		Fings Ain't Wot They Used To
Brown, Roy 'Chubby'	Living Next Door To Alice		Be (5)
	(Who The F**K Is Alice) (3)		Gilly Gilly Ossenfeffer
Brown, Sam	Stop (4)		Katzenellen Bogen
Browne, Tom	Funkin' For Jamaica (N.Y.) (10)		By The Sea (7)
Browns	Three Bells, The (6)		Heart Of My Heart (7)
Brownstone	If You Love Me (8)		Jingle Bell Rock (7)
Brubeck Quartet,	Take Five (6)		Meet Me On The Corner (2)
Dave			You Need Hands / Tulips From
Bruce, Tommy	Ain't Misbehavin' (3)		Amsterdam (3)
Bruisers	Ain't Misbehavin' (3)	Byrd, Gary	Crown, The (6)
Bryson, Peabo	Beauty And The Beast (9)	Byrds	All I Really Want To Do (4)
	Tonight I Celebrate My Love (2)		Mr Tambourine Man (1)
Bubbler Ranx	Mysterious Girl (2)	Byrne, David	Lazy (2)
Bucketheads	Bomb! (These Sounds Fall Into	C & C Music Factory	Gonna Make You Sweat
	My Mind), The (5)		(Everybody Dance Now) (3)
Bucks Fizz	If You Can't Stand The Heat		Things That Make You Go
	(10)		Hmmm ... (1)
	Land Of Make Believe,	C J Lewis	Everything Is Alright (Uptight)
	The (1)		(10)
	Making Your Mind Up (1)		Sweets For My Sweet (3)
	My Camera Never Lies (1)	C W McCall	Convoy (2)
	New Beginning (Mamba Seyra)	C, Melanie	Goin' Down (4)
	(8)		Here It Comes Again (7)
	Now Those Days Are Gone (8)		I Turn To You (1)
	When We Were Young (10)		Never Be The Same Again (1)
Buddy Cole & his	Hey There (4)		Northern Star (4)
Orchestra			When You're Gone (3)
	This Ole House (1)	C, Roy	Shotgun Wedding (6)
Buddy Cole Quartet	Rain Rain Rain (8)		Shotgun Wedding (re-issue) (8)
	Where Will The Baby's Dimple	Caballé, Montserrat	Barcelona (2)
	Be (6)		Barcelona (re-issue) (2)
Buffalo Tom	Going Underground / Carnation	Cadogan, Susan	Hurt So Good (4)
	(6)		Wherever You Will Go (3)
Buggles	Video Killed The Radio Star (1)	Calvert, Eddie	Cherry Pink And Apple
Bunton, Emma	Take My Breath Away (5)		Blossom White (1)
	What I Am (2)		John And Julie (6)
	What Took You So Long (1)		Mandy (9)
Burdon, Eric	San Franciscan Nights (7)		Oh Mein Papa (1)
Burl Ives	Little Bitty Tear, A (9)	Cameo	Word Up (3)
Burnette, Johnny	Dreamin' (5)	Cameron, Andy	Ally's Tartan Army (6)
	You're Sixteen (3)	Camisra	Let Me Show You (5)
Burns, Ray	Mobile (4)	Campbell, Ali	That Look In Your Eye (5)
Bus Stop	Kung Fu Fighting (8)	Campbell, Glen	All I Have To Do Is Dream (3)
Bush	Swallowed (7)		Honey Come Back (4)
Bush, Kate	Babooshka (5)		It's Only Make Believe (4)

MUSIC

POP

Group/Artiste	Title	Group/Artiste	Title
	Rhinestone Cowboy (4)		I Won't Last A Day Without You
	Wichita Lineman (7)		/ Goodbye To Love (9)
Campbell, Junior	Hallelujah Freedom (10)		Only Yesterday (2)
Cam'ron	Rocafella (13)		Please Mr Postman (2)
Cam'ron featuring	Hey Ma (8)		(They Long To Be) Close To
Juelz Santana			You (6)
Candy Flip	Strawberry Fields Forever (3)		Top Of The World (5)
Canned Heat	Let's Work Together (2)		Yesterday Once More (2)
	On The Road Again (8)	Carr, Vikki	It Must Be Him (2)
Cannon, Freddy	Way Down Yonder In New	Carra, Raffaella	Do It Do It Again (9)
	Orleans (3)	Carroll, Dina	Don't Be A Stranger (3)
Cantrell, Blu featuring	Breathe (1)		Escaping (3)
Sean Paul			It's Too Late (8)
Capaldi, Jim	Love Hurts (4)		Perfect Year, The (5)
Cappella	Move On Baby (7)	Carroll, Ronnie	Roses Are Red (3)
	U And Me (10)		Say Wonderful Things (6)
	U Got 2 Let The Music (2)	Carrott, Jasper	Funky Moped / Magic
	U Got 2 Know (6)		Roundabout (5)
Capstick, Tony	Sheffield Grinder / Capstick	Cars	Drive (5)
	Comes Home, The (3)		Drive (re-entry) (4)
Captain	Do That To Me One More Time		My Best Friend's Girl (3)
	(7)	Carter The	Only Living Boy In New Cross,
Captain Hollywood	I Can't Stand It (7)	Unstoppable	The (7)
Project		Sex Machine	
Captain Sensible	Glad It's All Over / Damned On	Carter, Aaron	Crazy Little Party Girl (7)
	45 (6)		Crush On You (9)
	Happy Talk (1)	Carter, Clarence	Patches (2)
Cara Tivey	She's Leaving Home (1)	Cartoons	Doodah! (7)
Cara, Irene	Fame (1)		Witch Doctor (2)
	Flashdance ... What A Feeling	Cascades	Rhythm Of The Rain (5)
	(2)	Case	Livin' It Up (re-issue) (5)
Caravelles	You Don't Have To Be A Baby	Cash, Johnny	Boy Named Sue, A (4)
	To Cry (6)		Thing Called Love, A (4)
Cardigans	Burning Down The House (7)	Cass, Mama	It's Getting Better (8)
	Carnival (72)	Cassandra	Touch Me (1)
	Erase / Rewind (7)	Cassidy featuring	Hotel (3)
	Lovefool (2)	R Kelly	
Carey, Mariah	Against All Odds (1)	Cassidy, David	Breaking Up Is Hard To Do (3)
	All I Want For Christmas Is You		Could It Be Forever / Cherish
	(2)		(2)
	Always Be My Baby (3)		Daydreamer / The Puppy Song
	Anytime You Need A Friend (8)		(1)
	Dreamlover (9)		How Can I Be Sure (1)
	Endless Love (3)		If I Didn't Care (9)
	Fantasy (4)		I'm A Clown / Some Kind Of
	Heartbreaker (5)		Summer (3)
	Hero (7)		Last Kiss, The (6)
	Honey (3)	Cassius 1999	Cassius (7)
	I'll Be There (2)	Cast	Beat Mama (9)
	My All (4)		Flying (4)
	One Sweet Day (6)		Free Me (7)
	Open Arms (4)		Guiding Star (9)
	Thank God I Found You (10)		Live The Dream (7)
	Through The Rain (8)		Sandstorm (8)
	Vision Of Love (9)		Walkaway (9)
	When You Believe (4)	Cast From Casualty	Everlasting Love (5)
	Without You (1)	Casuals	Jesamine (2)
Carl	Light My Fire (7)	Catatonia	Dead From The Waist Down
Carlisle, Belinda	Always Breaking My Heart (8)		(7)
	Circle In The Sand (4)		Mulder And Scully (3)
	Heaven Is A Place On Earth		Road Rage (5)
	(1)	Caterina Valente	Breeze And I, The (5)
	I Get Weak (10)	CCS	Tap Turns On The Water (5)
	In Too Deep (6)		Walkin' (7)
	Leave A Light On (4)	Ce Ce Peniston	Finally (re-issue) (2)
	(We Want) The Same Thing (6)		Keep On Walkin' (10)
Carlton, Vanessa	Thousand Miles, A (6)		We Got A Love Thang (6)
Carnes, Kim	Bette Davis Eyes (10)	Cerrone	Supernature (8)
Carpenters	Calling Occupants Of	Cerys of Catatonia	Ballad Of Tom Jones, The (4)
	Interplanetary Craft (9)	Cetera, Peter	Glory Of Love (3)

Group/Artiste	Title
	Hard To Say I'm Sorry (7)
Chacksfield, Frank	Ebb Tide (9)
	Little Red Monkey (10)
	Terry's Theme From Limelight (2)
Chairmen Of The Board	Give Me Just A Little More Time (3)
	You've Got Me Dangling On A String (5)
Chaka Demus & Pliers	She Don't Let Nobody (4)
	Tease Me (3)
	Twist And Shout (1)
Champaign	How 'Bout Us (5)
Champs	Tequila (5)
Changing Faces	G.H.E.T.T.O.U.T. (10)
Channel, Bruce	Hey! Baby (2)
Chapman, Tracy	Fast Car (5)
Charlatans	How High (6)
	North Country Boy (4)
	One To Another (3)
	Only One I Know, The (9)
Charlene	I've Never Been To Me (1)
Charles & Eddie	Would I Lie To You (1)
Charles McDevitt Skiffle Group	Freight Train (5)
Charles, Ray	Hit The Road Jack (6)
	I Can't Stop Loving You (1)
	Take These Chains From My Heart (5)
	You Don't Know Me (9)
Charles, Tina	Dance Little Lady Dance (6)
	Dr Love (4)
	I Love To Love (1)
Chas and Dave	Ain't No Pleasing You (2)
	Rabbit (8)
	Snooker Loopy (6)
	Strummin' (52)
Check 1-2	Mona (2)
Checker, Chubby	Let's Twist Again / The Twist (re-issue) (5)
	Let's Twist Again (remix) (2)
	Twist (Yo Twist), The (2)
Checkmates	Counting Teardrops (4)
	On a Slow Boat To China (3)
	What Do You Want To Make Those Eyes At Me For (1)
Cheeky Girls	Cheeky Song (Touch My Bum) (2)
	Have A Cheeky Christmas (10)
	Hooray Hooray (It's A Cheeky Holiday) (3)
	Take Your Shoes Off (3)
Chef	Chocolate Salty Balls (1)
Chelsea FC	Blue Is The Colour (5)
Chemical Brothers	Block Rockin' Beats (1)
	Come With Us / The Test (14)
	Hey Boy Hey Girl (3)
	It Began In Afrika (8)
	Leave Home (17)
	Let Forever Be (9)
	Setting Sun (1)
	Star Guitar (8)
Cher	All I Ever Need Is You (8)
	All I Really Want To Do (9)
	Bang Bang (My Baby Shot Me Down) (3)
	Believe (1)
	Gypsies Tramps And Thieves (4)
	I Found Someone (5)
	I Got You Babe (1)

Group/Artiste	Title
	If I Could Turn Back Time (6)
	Little Man (4)
	Love And Understanding (10)
	Love Can Build A Bridge (1)
	Music's No Good Without You, The (8)
	One By One (7)
	Shoop Shoop Song (It's In His Kiss), The (1)
	Strong Enough (5)
Cherelle	Saturday Love (6)
Cherry, Don	Band Of Gold (6)
Cherry, Eagle-Eye	Falling In Love Again (8)
	Save Tonight (6)
Cherry, Neneh	Buffalo Stance (3)
	Love Can Build A Bridge (1)
	Manchild (5)
	7 Seconds (3)
	Woman (9)
Chic	Dance Dance Dance (Yowsah Yowsah Yowsah) (6)
	Everybody Dance (9)
	Good Times (5)
	I Want Your Love (4)
	Le Freak (7)
Chicago	Hard Habit To Break (8)
	Hard To Say I'm Sorry (4)
	If You Leave Me Now (1)
	I'm A Man (8)
	25 Or 6 To 4 (7)
Chicane	Don't Give Up (1)
	Saltwater (6)
Chicory Tip	Son Of My Father (1)
Chiffons	Sweet Talkin' Guy (re-issue) (4)
Child	It's Only Make Believe (10)
Childliners	Gift Of Christmas, The (9)
Children	Lonely Pup (In A Christmas Shop) (4)
Children of The Revolution	3AM Eternal (1)
	What Time Is Love (5)
Chi-Lites	Have You Seen Her (3)
	Have You Seen Her / Oh Girl (re-issue) (5)
	Homely Girl (5)
	It's Time For Love (5)
	Too Good To Be Forgotten (10)
	You Don't Have To Go (3)
Chimes	I Still Haven't Found What I'm Looking For (6)
China Black	Searching (4)
China Crisis	Wishful Thinking (9)
Chocolate Puma	I Wanna Be U (6)
Chordettes	Born To Be With You (8)
	Lollipop (6)
	Mr Sandman (11)
Chrissy D and Lady G	Girls Like Us (7)
Christians	Ferry 'Cross The Mersey (1)
	Harvest For The World (8)
Christie	San Bernadino (7)
	Yellow River (1)
Christie, David	Saddle Up (9)
Christie, Lou	I'm Gonna Make You Mine (2)
Christie, Tony	I Did What I Did For Maria (2)
	Walk Like A Panther '98 (10)
Chumbawamba	Amnesia (10)
	Tubthumping (2)
Cinquetti, Gigliola	Go (Before You Break My Heart) (8)
City Boy	5-7-0-5 (8)

Group/Artiste	Title	Group/Artiste	Title
City High	Caramel (9)		Mr Soft (8)
	What Would You Do (3)	Coelo, Toto	I Eat Cannibals Part 1 (8)
City Spud	Ride Wit Me (3)	Cogan, Alma	Bell Bottom Blues (4)
Clannad	Robin (The Hooded Man) (42)		Dreamboat (1)
	Theme From Harry's Game (5)		I Can't Tell A Waltz From A
Clapton, Eric	Comin' Home (16)		Tango (6)
	I Shot The Sheriff (9)		Never Do A Tango With An
	Love Can Build A Bridge (1)		Eskimo (6)
	Tears In Heaven (5)	Cola Boy	7 Ways To Love (8)
Clark Brothers	You Need Hands / Tulips From	Coldcut	Doctorin' The House (6)
	Amsterdam (3)	Coldplay	Clocks (9)
Clark, Petula	Alone (8)		In My Place (2)
	Downtown (2)		Scientist, The (10)
	Downtown (remix) (10)		Trouble (10)
	I Couldn't Live Without Your		Yellow (4)
	Love (6)	Cole, Natalie	Miss You Like Crazy (2)
	Little Shoemaker, The (7)		Pink Cadillac (5)
	My Friend The Sea (7)	Coleman, Naimee	Ordinary World (5)
	My Love (4)	Collins, Edwyn	Girl Like You, A (4)
	Romeo (3)	Collins, Judy	Amazing Grace (5)
	Sailor (1)		Both Sides Now (14)
	Suddenly There's A Valley (7)		Send In The Clowns (6)
	This Is My Song (1)	Collins, Phil	Against All Odds (Take A Look
	With All My Heart (4)		At Me Now) (2)
Clarkson, Kelly	Miss Independent (6)		Another Day In Paradise (2)
Clash	Should I Stay Or Should I Go		Both Sides Of The Story (7)
	(re-issue) (1)		Dance Into The Light (9)
Clay, Judy	Private Number (8)		Easy Lover (1)
Clayton, Adam	Theme From Mission		Groovy Kind Of Love, A (1)
	Impossible (7)		I Wish It Would Rain Down (7)
Cleopatra	Cleopatra's Theme (3)		In The Air Tonight (2)
	I Want You Back (4)		In The Air Tonight (remix) (4)
	Life Ain't Easy (4)		One More Night (4)
	Thank Abba For The Music (4)		Separate Lives (4)
Cliff Bennett & The	Got To Get You Into My Life (6)		Two Hearts (6)
Rebel Rousers			You Can't Hurry Love (1)
	One Way Love (9)	Color Me Badd	All 4 Love (5)
Cliff, Jimmy	Wild World (8)		I Wanna Sex You Up (1)
	Wonderful World Beautiful	Commodores	Easy (9)
	People (6)		Nightshift (3)
Climax Blues Band	Couldn't Get It Right (10)		Sail On (8)
Clock	Axel F / Keep Pushin' (7)		Still (4)
	Everybody (6)		Three Times A Lady (1)
	It's Over (10)	Communards	Don't Leave Me This Way (1)
	Whoomph! (There It Is) (4)		Machine Gun (20)
Clooney, Rosemary	Half As Much (3)		Never Can Say Goodbye (4)
	Hey There (4)		So Cold The Night (8)
	Mambo Italiano (1)		You Are My World (30)
	Man (Uh-Huh) (7)	Como, Perry	And I Love You So (3)
	This Ole House (1)		Catch A Falling Star (9)
	Where Will The Baby's Dimple		Delaware (3)
	Be (6)		Don't Let The Stars Get In Your
Clout	Substitute (2)		Eyes (1)
Club Nouveau	Lean On Me (3)		For The Good Times (7)
Clubhouse	Light My Fire (7)		Hot Diggity (Dog Ziggity Boom)
Coast To Coast	(Do) The Hucklebuck (5)		(4)
Coasters	Charlie Brown (6)		Idle Gossip (3)
	Searchin' (30)		It's Impossible (4)
Coates, Odia	(You're) Having My Baby (6)		Kewpie Doll (9)
Cochran, Eddie	C'Mon Everybody (6)		Love Makes The World Go
	Summertime Blues (18)		Round (6)
	Three Steps To Heaven (1)		Magic Moments (1)
Cocker, Joe	Delta Lady (10)		More (10)
	Marjorine (48)		Tomboy (10)
	Up Where We Belong (7)		Wanted (4)
	With A Little Help From My	Company	Shame Shame Shame (6)
	Friends (1)	Congregation	Softly Whispering I Love You
Cockney Rebel	Judy Teen (5)		(4)
	Make Me Smile (Come Up And	Conley, Arthur	Sweet Soul Music (7)
	See Me) (1)	Connolly, Billy	D.I.V.O.R.C.E. (1)

Group/Artiste	Title
Conway, Russ	China Tea (5)
	More And More Party Pops (5)
	More Party Pops (10)
	Party Pops (24)
	Roulette (1)
	Side Saddle (1)
	Snow Coach (7)
	Toy Balloons (7)
Cooke, Sam	Chain Gang (9)
	Cupid (7)
	Twistin' The Night Away (6)
	Wonderful World (re-issue) (2)
	You Send Me (29)
Cookie Crew	Rok Da House (5)
Cool J, LL	Ain't Nobody (1)
	Father (10)
	Hit 'Em High (The Monstars' Anthem) (8)
	I Need Love (8)
	Loungin' (7)
	Luv U Better (7)
	Phenomenon (9)
Coolidge, Rita	All Time High (75)
	We're All Alone (6)
Coolio	C U When You Get There (3)
	Gangsta's Paradise (1)
	Hit 'Em High (The Monstars' Anthem) (8)
	Too Hot (9)
Cooper, Alice	Elected (4)
	Hello Hurray (6)
	No More Mr Nice Guy (10)
	Poison (2)
	School's Out (1)
Coral	Don't Think You're The First (10)
	Pass It On (5)
	Summer Sunshine (6)
Cornell, Don	Hold My Hand (1)
Cornershop	Brimful Of Asha (remix) (1)
Cornwell, Charlotte	OK? (10)
Corona	Baby Baby (5)
	Rhythm Of The Night, The (2)
	Try Me Out (6)
Corrs	Breathless (1)
	Dreams (6)
	Runaway (2)
	So Young (6)
	What Can I Do (3)
Cosmic Gate	Firewire (9)
Costello, Elvis	Good Year For The Roses, A (6)
	I Can't Stand Up For Falling Down (4)
	Oliver's Army (2)
Cotton, Billy & His Band	Friends And Neighbours (re-entry) (3)
	In A Golden Coach (3)
Course	Ain't Nobody (8)
	Ready Or Not (5)
Cousins, Tina	Mysterious Times (2)
	Thank Abba For The Music (4)
Covington, Julie	Don't Cry For Me Argentina (1)
	OK? (10)
Cox, Michael	Angela Jones (7)
Cradock, Steve	Going Underground / Carnation (6)
Craig, Robbie	Woman Trouble (6)
Cramer, Floyd	On The Rebound (1)
Cranberries	Zombie (14)

Group/Artiste	Title
Crane, Les	Desiderata (7)
Crash Test Dummies	Mmm Mmm Mmm Mmm (2)
Craven, Beverley	Promise Me (3)
Crawford, Michael	Music Of The Night, The (7)
Crawford, Randy	Almaz (4)
	One Day I'll Fly Away (2)
Crazy Town	Butterfly (3)
Crazy World Of Arthur Brown	Fire (1)
Creedence Clearwater Revival	Bad Moon Rising (1)
	Proud Mary (8)
	Travellin' Band (8)
	Up Around The Bend (3)
Crew Cuts	Earth Angel (4)
Cribbins, Bernard	Hole In The Ground (9)
	Right Said Fred (10)
Crickets	Don't Ever Change (5)
	Maybe Baby (4)
	Oh Boy (3)
	That'll Be The Day (1)
Crosby, Stills and Nash	Marrakesh Express (17)
Crosby, Stills, Nash and Young	American Dream (55)
Crosby, Bing	Around The World (5)
	Changing Partners (10)
	Changing Partners (re-entry) (9)
	Isle Of Innisfree (3)
	Peace On Earth / Little Drummer Boy (3)
	Silent Night (8)
	True Love (4)
	White Christmas (5)
	Zing A Little Zong (10)
Cross, Christopher	Arthur's Theme (Best That You Can Do) (7)
Crow, Sheryl	All I Wanna Do (4)
	Change Would Do You Good, A (8)
	If It Makes You Happy (9)
	My Favourite Mistake (9)
Crowd	You'll Never Walk Alone (1)
Crowded House	Weather With You (7)
Crown Heights Affair	You Gave Me Love (10)
Cruise, Julie	Falling (7)
Crusaders	Street Life (5)
Crystals	Da Doo Ron Ron (5)
	Then He Kissed Me (2)
Cuban Boys	Cognoscenti Vs Intelligentsia (4)
Cufflinks	Tracy (4)
	When Julie Comes Around (10)
Cult Of Ant	Better Watch Out (10)
Culture Beat	Anything (5)
	Got To Get It (4)
	Mr Vain (1)
Culture Club	Church Of The Poison Mind (2)
	Do You Really Want To Hurt Me (1)
	I Just Wanna Be Loved (4)
	It's A Miracle (4)
	Karma Chameleon (1)
	Move Away (7)
	Time (Clock Of The Heart) (3)
	Victims (3)
	War Song, The (2)
Cupid's Inspiration	Yesterday Has Gone (4)
Cure	A Forest (31)
	Friday I'm In Love (6)
	High (8)
	Love Cats, The (7)

MUSIC

POP

Group/Artiste	Title	Group/Artiste	Title
	Lullaby (5)		Love Is Only A Feeling (5)
Curiosity	Hang On In There Baby (3)	Darts	Boy From New York City (2)
Curiosity Killed	Down To Earth (3)		Come Back My Love (2)
The Cat	Misfit (7)		Daddy Cool / The Girl Can't
Curved Air	Back Street Luv (4)		Help It (6)
Cutting Crew	(I Just) Died In Your Arms		Duke Of Earl (6)
	Tonight (4)		Get It (10)
Cyril Stapleton	Blue Star (The Medic Theme)		It's Raining (2)
Orchestra	(2)	Darude	Feel The Beat (5)
Cyrus, Billy Ray	Achy Breaky Heart (3)		Sandstorm (3)
D Mob	It Is Time To Get Funky (9)	Dave & Ansil Collins	Double Barrel (1)
	Put Your Hands Together (7)		Monkey Spanner (7)
	We Call It Acieed (3)	Dave Clark Five	Bits And Pieces (2)
D12	How Come (4)		Can't You See That She's Mine
	My Band (2)		(10)
	Purple Pills / Purple Hills (2)		Catch Us If You Can (5)
	S**t On You (10)		Do You Love Me (30)
D:Ream	Shoot Me With Your Love (7)		Everybody Get Together (8)
	Things Can Only Get Better		Everybody Knows (2)
	(remix) (1)		Glad All Over (1)
	U R The Best Thing (remix) (4)		Good Old Rock 'N' Roll (7)
Da Force, Ricardo	Stayin' Alive (2)		Red Balloon (7)
Da Silva, Rui	Touch Me (1)	Dave Dee, Dozy,	Bend It (2)
Dactyl, Terry and the	On A Saturday Night (45)	Beaky, Mick and	Hideaway (10)
Dinosaurs	Seaside Shuffle (2)	Tich	Hold Tight (4)
Daft Punk	Around The World (5)		Last Night In Soho (8)
	Da Funk / Musique (7)		Legend Of Xanadu (1)
	One More Time (2)		Okay! (4)
Dale, Jim	Be My Girl (2)		Save Me (4)
Daltrey, Roger	Giving It All Away (5)		You Make It Move (26)
Damage	Forever (6)		Zabadak! (3)
	Ghetto Romance (7)	David & Jonathan	Lovers Of The World Unite (7)
	Love Guaranteed (7)	David Rose & His	My Happiness (4)
	Wonderful Tonight (3)	Orchestra	
Damian	Time Warp (remix), The (7)	David Whitfield &	Adoration Waltz (9)
Damned	Eloise (3)	Roland Shaw	
Damone, Vic	On The Street Where You Live	David, Craig	Fill Me In (1)
	(1)		Hidden Agenda (10)
Dana	All Kinds Of Everything (1)		Rendezvous (8)
	It's Gonna Be A Cold Cold		Re-Rewind The Crowd Say Bo
	Christmas (4)		Selecta (2)
	Please Tell Him That I Said		7 Days (1)
	Hello (8)		Spanish (8)
Dane	Another Lover (9)		Walking Away (3)
	Shut Up And Forget About It (9)		What's Your Flava (8)
Dankworth, Johnny	African Waltz (9)		Woman Trouble (6)
	Experiments With Mice (7)	David, Craig	Rise & Fall (2)
Danny &	At The Hop (3)	featuring Sting	
The Juniors		David, F R	Words (2)
Daphne & Celeste	Ooh Stick You! (8)	Davidson, Paul	Midnight Rider (10)
Darey, Matt	Beautiful (10)	Davies, Dave	Death Of A Clown (3)
Darin, Bobby	Clementine (8)	Davies, Windsor	Whispering Grass (1)
	Dream Lover (1)	Davis Jr, Billy	You Don't Have To Be A Star
	If I Were A Carpenter (9)		(To Be In My Show) (7)
	La Mer (Beyond The Sea) (8)	Davis Jr, Sammy	Love Me Or Leave Me (8)
	Lazy River (2)	Davis, Billie	Tell Him (10)
	Mack The Knife (1)	Dawn	Candida (9)
	Multiplication (5)		Knock Three Times (1)
	Splish Splash (18)		Tie A Yellow Ribbon Round The
	Things (2)		Old Oak Tree (1)
	You Must Have Been A		What Are You Doing Sunday (3)
	Beautiful Baby (10)	Dawson, Dana	3 Is Family (9)
Darius	Colourblind (1)	Day, Doris	Black Hills Of Dakota (7)
	Incredible (What I Meant To		If I Give My Heart To You (4)
	Say) (9)		Let's Walk Thata-Way (4)
	Kinda Love (8)		Move Over Darling (8)
	Rushes (5)		My Love And Devotion (10)
Darkness	Christmas Time (Don't Let The		Ready Willing And Able (7)
	Bells End) (2)		Secret Love (1)
	I Believe In A Thing Called Love		Sugarbush (8)
	(2)		Sugarbush (re-entry) (8)

Group/Artiste	Title
	Whatever Will Be Will Be (1)
Dayne, Taylor	Prove Your Love (8)
	Tell It To My Heart (3)
De Burgh, Chris	Don't Pay The Ferryman (48)
	Lady In Red, The (1)
	Missing You (3)
De La Soul	Magic Number, The / Buddy (7)
	Ring Ring (Ha Ha Hey) (10)
De Paul, Lynsey	No Honestly (7)
	Sugar Me (5)
De Sykes, Stephanie	Born With A Smile On My Face (2)
	We'll Find Our Day (17)
Deacon Blue	Four Bacharach And David Songs EP (2)
	Real Gone Kid (8)
	Twist And Shout (10)
Dead End Kids	Have I The Right (6)
Dead Or Alive	You Spin Me Round (Like A Record) (1)
Dean, Hazell	Searchin' (I Gotta Find A Man) (6)
	Whatever I Do (Wherever I Go) (4)
	Who's Leaving Who (4)
Dean, Jimmy	Big Bad John (2)
Death In Vegas	Aisha (9)
DeBarge	Rhythm Of The Night (4)
Dec	Better Watch Out (10)
Decker, Diana	Poppa Piccolino (2)
	Poppa Piccolino (re-entry) (5)
Dee C Lee	See The Day (3)
Dee D Jackson	Automatic Lover (4)
Dee, Kiki	Amoureuse (13)
	Don't Go Breaking My Heart (1)
	True Love (2)
Deee-Lite	Groove Is In The Heart / What Is Love (2)
Deejay, Alice	Back In My Life (4)
	Will I Ever (7)
Deejay, Sven	Holiday Rap (6)
Deep Blue Something	Breakfast At Tiffany's (1)
Deep Dish	Flashdance (3)
Deep Forest	Sweet Lullaby (10)
Deep Purple	Black Night (2)
	Strange Kind Of Woman (8)
Deepest Blue	Deepest Blue (7)
	Give It Away (9)
Def Leppard	Animal (6)
	Let's Get Rocked (2)
	When Love And Hate Collide (2)
Degrees Of Motion	Shine On (8)
Dekker, Desmond	Israelites (1)
	Israelites (re-issue) (10)
	It Miek (7)
	You Can Get It If You Really Want (2)
De'Lacy	Hideaway (9)
Delirium	Silence (remixes) (3)
Denise & Johnny	Especially For You (3)
Dennis, Cathy	Touch Me (All Night Long) (5)
Dennis, Jackie	La Dee Dah (4)
Denver, John	Annie's Song (1)
Denver, Karl	Marcheta (8)
	Mexicali Rose (8)
	Never Say Goodbye (9)
	Wimoweh (4)
Deodato	Also Sprach Zarathustra (2001) (7)

Group/Artiste	Title
Depeche Mode	Barrel Of A Gun (4)
	Condemnation (9)
	Dream On (6)
	Dreaming Of Me (57)
	Enjoy The Silence (6)
	Enjoy The Silence 04 (7)
	Everything Counts (6)
	I Feel You (8)
	In Your Room (8)
	It's No Good (5)
	Just Can't Get Enough (8)
	Master And Servant (9)
	People Are People (4)
	See You (6)
Derek & The Dominoes	Layla (7)
	Layla (re-issue) (4)
Desireless	Voyage Voyage (5)
Des'ree	Life (8)
	You Gotta Be (re-issue) (10)
Destiny's Child	Bills Bills Bills (6)
	Bootylicious (2)
	Bug A Boo (9)
	Emotion (3)
	Independent Women Part 1 (1)
	Jumpin' Jumpin' (5)
	Lose My Breath (2)
	No No No (5)
	Say My Name (3)
	Survivor (1)
Detroit, Marcella	I Believe (11)
Detroit Emeralds	Feel The Need In Me (4)
Detroit Spinners	Cupid – I've Loved You For A Long Time (4)
	Ghetto Child (7)
	Working My Way Back To You / Forgive Me Girl (1)
Deuce	I Need You (10)
Dexy's Midnight Runners	Come On Eileen (1)
	Geno (1)
	Jackie Wilson Said (I'm In Heaven When You Smile) (5)
	There There My Dear (7)
Di	Shake Ur Body (7)
Di Bart, Tony	Real Thing, The (1)
Diamond, Jim	Hi Ho Silver (5)
	I Should Have Known Better (1)
Diamond, Neil	Cracklin' Rosie (3)
	I Am ... I Said (4)
	Sweet Caroline (8)
	You Don't Bring Me Flowers (5)
Diamonds	Little Darlin' (3)
Dick Stabile & his Orchestra	That's Amore (2)
Dickies	Banana Splits (7)
Dickinson, Bruce	(I Want To Be) Elected (9)
Dickson, Barbara	Answer Me (9)
	I Know Him So Well (1)
Dido	Here With Me (4)
	Life For Rent (8)
	One Step Too Far (6)
	Thank You (3)
	White Flag (2)
Dini, Paolo	Going Back To My Roots / Rich In Paradise (9)
Dinosaurs	Seaside Shuffle (2)
Dion	Wanderer, The (10)
Dion, Celine	All By Myself (6)
	Beauty And The Beast (9)
	Because You Loved Me (5)
	Falling Into You (10)

MUSIC

POP

Group/Artiste	Title	Group/Artiste	Title
	I'm Your Angel (3)	Dollar	Give Me Back My Heart (4)
	Immortality (5)		I Wanna Hold Your Hand (9)
	It's All Coming Back To Me Now (3)		Love's Gotta Hold On Me (4)
	My Heart Will Go On (1)		Mirror Mirror (4)
	New Day Has Come, A (7)		O L'Amour (7)
	Only One Road (8)	Domino, Fats	Blueberry Hill (re-entry) (6)
	Power Of Love, The (4)	Don Lang & His	Witch Doctor (5)
	Tell Him (3)	Frantic Five	
	Think Twice (1)	Don Pablo's Animals	Venus (4)
	Tu M'Aimes Encore (To Love Me Again) (7)	Donegan, Lonnie	Battle Of New Orleans (2)
Dire Straits	Money For Nothing (4)		Bring A Little Water Sylvie / Dead Or Alive (7)
	Private Investigations (2)		Cumberland Gap (1)
	Romeo And Juliet (8)		Does Your Chewing Gum Lose Its Flavour (On The Bedpost Overnight) (3)
	Sultans Of Swing (8)		
	Walk Of Life (2)		Don't You Rock Me Daddy-O (4)
Dirty Rotten Scoundrels	People Hold On (4)		Gamblin' Man / Putting On The Style (1)
Disco Tex	Get Dancing (8)		Grand Coolie Dam (6)
	I Wanna Dance Wit Choo (6)		Have A Drink On Me (8)
Distel, Sacha	Raindrops Keep Falling On My Head (10)		I Wanna Go Home (The Wreck Of The John 'B') (5)
Divine Comedy	National Express (8)		Lorelei (10)
Divine Inspiration	Way, The (Put Your Hand In My Hand) (5)		Lost John / Stewball (2)
			Michael Row The Boat / Lumbered (6)
Divinyls	I Touch Myself (10)		My Dixie Darling (10)
Dizzee Rascal	Stand Up Tall (10)		My Old Man's A Dustman (Ballad Of A Refuse Disposal Officer) (1)
DJ Aligator Project	Whistle Song (Blow My Whistle B***h), The (5)		
DJ Casper	Cha Cha Slide (1)		Party's Over, The (9)
DJ Dado	X-Files (8)		Rock Island Line (8)
DJ Jean	Launch, The (2)		Tom Dooley (3)
DJ Jurgen presents Alice DeeJay	Better Off Alone (2)	Donovan	Catch The Wind (4)
			Colours (4)
DJ Kool	Let Me Clear My Throat (8)		Hurdy Gurdy Man (4)
DJ Luck & MC Neat	Ain't No Stoppin Us (8)		Jennifer Juniper (5)
	Little Bit Of Luck, A (9)		Mellow Yellow (8)
	Masterblaster 2000 (5)		Sunshine Superman (2)
DJ Marky & XRS	LK (Carolina Carol Bela) (17)		There Is A Mountain (8)
DJ Miko	What's Up (6)	Donovan, Jason	Any Dream Will Do (1)
DJ Otzi	Do Wah Diddy (9)		Especially For You (1)
	Hey Baby (Unofficial World Cup Remix) (10)		Every Day (I Love You More) (2)
	Hey Baby (Uuh, Aah) (1)		Hang On To Your Love (8)
DJ Pied Piper & The MC	Do You Really Like It (1)		Happy Together (10)
DJ Quicksilver	Belissima (4)		Nothing Can Divide Us (5)
	Free (7)		Rhythm Of The Rain (9)
DJ Sakin & Friends	Protect Your Mind For The Love Of A Princess) (4)		Sealed With A Kiss (1)
			Too Many Broken Hearts (1)
DJ Sammy	Boys Of Summer, The (2)		When You Come Back To Me (2)
	Heaven (1)		
	Sunlight (8)	Doobie Brothers	Long Train Runnin' (7)
DJ Supreme	Up To The Wildstyle (10)	Doolally	Straight From The Heart (9)
DMX	X Gon' Give It To Ya (6)	Dooleys	Chosen Few, The (7)
DNA	Tom's Diner (2)		Love Of My Life (9)
Do	Heaven (1)		Wanted (3)
Dobson, Anita	Anyone Can Fall In Love (4)	Doonican, Val	Elusive Butterfly (5)
Doctor Spin	Tetris (6)		If The Whole World Stopped Loving (3)
Dodd, Ken	Love Is Like A Violin (8)		
	Promises (6)		Special Years, The (7)
	River, The (3)		Walk Tall (3)
	Tears (1)		What Would I Be (2)
Dodgy	Good Enough (4)	Doop	Doop (1)
Dog Eat Dog	No Fronts (9)	Doors	Light My Fire (re-issue) (7)
Dogg, Nate	Regulate (5)	Dorsey, Lee	Holy Cow (6)
Doh, Ken	I Need A Lover Tonight (7)		Working In A Coalmine (8)
Dolan, Joe	Make Me An Island (3)	Double	Captain Of Her Heart, The (8)
Dolce Music Theatre, Joe	Shaddup You Face (1)	Doug E Fresh & Get Fresh Crew	Show, The (7)

Group/Artiste	Title
Douglas, Carl	Kung Fu Fighting (1)
	Kung Fu Fighting (8)
Douglas, Craig	Heart Of A Teenage Girl, The (10)
	Hundred Pounds Of Clay, A (9)
	Only Sixteen (1)
	Our Favourite Melodies (9)
	Pretty Blue Eyes (4)
	Time (9)
	When My Little Girl Is Smiling (9)
Doves	There Goes The Fear (3)
Dr & The Medics	Spirit In The Sky (1)
Dr Alban	It's My Life (2)
Dr Dre	Bad Intentions (4)
	California Love (6)
	Forgot About Dre (7)
	Guilty Conscience (5)
	Next Episode, The (3)
	Still D.R.E. (6)
Dr Feelgood	Milk And Alcohol (9)
Dr Hook	Better Love Next Time (8)
	If Not You (5)
	Little Bit More, A (2)
	Sexy Eyes (4)
	Sylvias Mother (2)
	When You're In Love With A Beautiful Woman (1)
Drake, Charlie	Splish Splash (7)
Dreamers	I Understand (5)
	If You Gotta Make A Fool Of Somebody (3)
	I'm Telling You Now (2)
	You Were Made For Me (3)
Dreamweavers	It's Almost Tomorrow (1)
Drifters	At The Club / Saturday Night At The Movies (3)
	Can I Take You Home Little Girl (10)
	Come On Over To My Place (re-issue) (9)
	Down On The Beach Tonight (7)
	High Class Baby (7)
	Kissin In The Back Row Of The Movies (2)
	Like Sister And Brother (7)
	Living Doll (1)
	Mean Streak (10)
	Move It (2)
	Save The Last Dance For Me (2)
	There Goes My First Love (3)
	You're More Than A Number In My Little Red Book (5)
Driscoll, Julie	This Wheel's On Fire (5)
Driver 67	Car 67 (7)
Dru Hill	How Deep Is Your Love (9)
	These Are The Times (4)
	Wild Wild West (2)
D-Side	Invisible (7)
	Real World (9)
	Speechless (9)
Dubliners	Irish Rover, The (8)
	Seven Drunken Nights (7)
Duff, Hilary	So Yesterday (9)
Duffy, Stephen 'Tin Tin'	Kiss Me (4)
Duke D'Mond	Call Up The Groups (3)
	Merry Gentle Pops (9)
	Pop Go The Workers (5)

Group/Artiste	Title
Dulfer, Candy	Lily Was Here (6)
Dunblane	Knockin' On Heaven's Door / Throw These Guns Away (1)
Duncan James & Keedie	I Believe My Heart (2)
Duncan, Johnny	Last Train To San Fernando (2)
Dundas, David	Jeans On (3)
Dunn, Clive	Grandad (1)
Dunn, Romeo	Romeo (3)
Duran Duran	All She Wants Is (9)
	Girls On Film (5)
	Hungry Like The Wolf (5)
	Is There Something I Should Know (1)
	New Moon On Monday (9)
	Notorious (7)
	Ordinary World (6)
	Planet Earth (12)
	(Reach Up For The) Sunrise (5)
	Reflex, The (1)
	Rio (9)
	Save A Prayer (2)
	Union Of The Snake (3)
	View To A Kill, A (2)
	Wild Boys (2)
Dusty, Slim	Pub With No Beer, A (3)
Dylan, Bob	Lay Lady Lay (5)
	Like A Rolling Stone (4)
	Positively Fourth Street (8)
	Rainy Day Women Nos 12 And 35 (7)
	Subterranean Homesick Blues (9)
	Times They Are A-Changin' (9)
Dynamite, Ms	Dy-Na-Mi-Tee (5)
	It Takes More (7)
E-17	Each Time (2)
Eagles	Hotel California (8)
	Lyin' Eyes (23)
	One Of These Nights (23)
	Take It To The Limit (12)
Eamon	F**k It (I Don't Want You Back) (1)
Earth Wind & Fire	After The Love Has Gone (4)
	Let's Groove (3)
	September (3)
Earth Wind & Fire with Emotions	Boogie Wonderland (4)
East Of Eden	Jig A Jig (7)
East 17	Around The World (7)
	Deep (5)
	Do U Still (7)
	Hey Child (3)
	House Of Love (10)
	If You Ever (2)
	It's Alright (3)
	Let It Rain (10)
	Stay Another Day (1)
	Steam (7)
	Thunder (4)
East Side Beat	Ride Like The Wind (3)
Easton, Sheena	For Your Eyes Only (8)
	Modern Girl (8)
	9 To 5 (3)
Easybeats	Friday On My Mind (6)
Echo And The Bunnymen	Cutter, The (8)
	Killing Moon (9)
	Nothing Lasts Forever (8)
Echobeatz	Mas Que Nada (10)
Eckstine, Billy	Gigi (8)
	No One But You (3)

M
U
S
I
C

P
O
P

Group/Artiste	Title	Group/Artiste	Title
	Circus, The (6)	Ellis-Bextor, Sophie	Get Over You / Move This
	Crackers International EP (2)		Mountain (3)
	Drama! (4)		I Won't Change You (9)
	Little Respect, A (4)		Mixed Up World (7)
	Love To Hate You (4)		Murder On The Dancefloor (2)
	Run To The Sun (6)		Music Gets The Best Of Me
	Ship Of Fools (6)		(14)
	Sometimes (2)		Take Me Home (2)
	Victim Of Love (7)	Ellison, Jennifer	Baby I Don't Care (6)
	Who Needs Love Like That (10)	Embrace	All You Good Good People EP
Eddie & The Hotrods	Do Anything You Wanna Do (9)		(8)
Eddy, Duane	Ballad Of Paladin (10)		Come Back To What You Know
	Because They're Young (2)		(6)
	Dance With Guitar Man (4)		Gravity (7)
	Pepe (2)		My Weakness Is None Of Your
	Peter Gunn (8)		Business (9)
	Peter Gunn Theme (6)	Emerson Lake &	Fanfare For The Common Man
	Play Me Like You Play Your	Palmer	(2)
	Guitar (9)	EMF	I Believe (6)
	Shazam! (4)		I'm A Believer (3)
	Theme From Dixie (7)		Unbelievable (3)
Edelweiss	Bring Me Edelweiss (5)	Emilia	Big Big World (5)
Edison Lighthouse	Love Grows (Where My	Eminem	Business (6)
	Rosemary Goes) (1)		Cleanin' Out My Closet (4)
Edmunds, Dave	Baby I Love You (8)		Forgot About Dre (7)
	Born To Be With You (5)		Guilty Conscience (5)
	Girls Talk (4)		Just Lose It (1)
	I Hear You Knocking (1)		Lose Yourself (1)
Edwards, Rupie	Ire Feelings (Skanga) (9)		My Name Is (2)
Edwards, Tommy	It's All In The Game (1)		Real Slim Shady, The (1)
Eels	Novocaine For The Soul (10)		Sing For The Moment (6)
	Susan's House (9)		Stan (1)
Eiffel 65	Blue (Da Ba Dee) (1)		Way I Am, The (8)
	Move Your Body (3)		Without Me (1)
808 State	Cubik / Olympic (10)	Emma	Free Me (5)
	In Yer Face (9)		I'll Be There (7)
	Only Rhyme That Bites, The (10)		Maybe (6)
	Pacific (10)	Emmie	More Than This (5)
Eighth Wonder	I'm Not Scared (7)	Emotions	Best Of My Love (4)
Eirc Jupp & His	Mobile (4)		Boogie Wonderland (4)
Orchestra		En Vogue	Don't Let Go (Love) (5)
Elbert, Donnie	Where Did Our Love Go (8)		Hold On (5)
Electric Light	Confusion / Last Train To		My Lovin' (4)
Orchestra	London (8)		Whatta Man (7)
	Diary Of Horace Wimp, The (8)	Enfield, Harry	Loadsamoney (4)
	Don't Bring Me Down (3)	England United	(How Does It Feel To Be) On
	Evil Woman (10)		Top Of The World (9)
	Hold On Tight (4)	England World Cup	Back Home (1)
	Livin' Thing (4)	Squad	This Time (We'll Get It Right) /
	Mr Blue Sky (6)		England We'll Fly The Flag (2)
	Rockaria! (9)	Englandneworder	World In Motion (1)
	Roll Over Beethoven (6)	England's Barmy	Come On England (2)
	Shine A Little Love (6)	Army	
	Sweet Talkin' Woman (6)	Enigma	Return To Innocence (3)
	Telephone Line (8)		Sadness Part 1 (1)
	10538 Overture (9)	Enrique featuring	Not In Love (5)
	Wild West Hero (6)	Kelis	
	Xanadu (1)	Enya	Anywhere Is (7)
Electric Six	Danger High Voltage (2)		Book Of Days (10)
	Gay Bar (5)		Orinoco Flow (1)
Electronic	Disappointed (6)	Equals	Baby Come Back (1)
	Get The Message (8)		Black Skin Blue-Eyed Boys (9)
Element Four	Big Brother UK TV Theme (4)		Viva Bobby Joe (6)
Elgins	Heaven Must Have Sent You	Erasure	Abba-Esque EP (1)
	(3)		Always (4)
Elias & His Zigzag	Tom Hark (2)		Blue Savannah (3)
Jive Flutes			Breath Of Life (8)
Elliman, Yvonne	If I Can't Have You (4)		Chorus (3)
	Love Me (6)		Solsbury Hill (10)
Ellington, Duke	Skin Deep (7)	Eric Jupp & His	This Ole House (4)
Ellis, Shirley	Clapping Song, The (6)	Orchestra	

Group/Artiste	Title	Group/Artiste	Title
Eric Rodgers & His Orchestra	You Need Hands / Tulips From Amsterdam (3)		Lucille / So Sad (To Watch Good Love Go Bad) (4)
Eruption	I Can't Stand The Rain (5)		Price Of Love, The (2)
	One Way Ticket (9)		Problems (6)
Essex, David	Gonna Make You A Star (1)		Temptation (1)
	Hold Me Close (1)		(Til) I Kissed You (2)
	Lamplight (7)		Wake Up Little Susie (2)
	Oh What A Circus (3)		Walk Right Back / Ebony Eyes (1)
	Rock On (3)		When Will I Be Loved (4)
	Rolling Stone (5)	Everly, Phil	She Means Nothing To Me (9)
	Silver Dream Machine (4)	Everything But The Girl	I Don't Want To Talk About It (3)
	Stardust (7)		Missing (remix) (3)
	Tahiti (8)		Walking Wounded (6)
	Winter's Tale, A (2)		Wrong (8)
Estefan, Gloria	Anything For You (10)	Exile	Kiss You All Over (6)
	Can't Stay Away From You (7)	Extreme	More Than Words (2)
	Don't Wanna Lose You (6)	FAB	Thunderbirds Are Go (5)
	Heaven's What I Feel (4)	Faces	Cindy Incidentally (2)
	Miami Hit Mix / Christmas Through Your Eyes (8)		Pool Hall Richard / I Wish It Would Rain (8)
	1-2-3 (9)		Stay With Me (6)
Estelle, Don	Whispering Grass (1)	Fagin, Joe	That's Livin' Alright (3)
Esther & Abi Ofarim	Cinderella Rockefella (1)	Fair Weather	Natural Sinner (6)
Eternal	Angel Of Mine (4)	Fair, Yvonne	It Should Have Been Me (5)
	Don't You Love Me (3)	Fairground Attraction	Find My Love (7)
	Good Thing (8)		Perfect (1)
	I Am Blessed (7)	Fairweather-Low, Andy	Reggae Tune (10)
	I Wanna Be The Only One (1)		Wide-Eyed And Legless (6)
	Just A Step From Heaven (8)	Faith No More	I'm Easy / Be Aggressive (3)
	Oh Baby I ... (4)		Midlife Crisis (10)
	Power Of A Woman (5)	Faith, Adam	As You Like It (5)
	Save Our Love (8)		Don't That Beat All (8)
	Secrets (9)		First Time, The (5)
	Someday (4)		How About That! (4)
	Stay (4)		Lonely Pup (In A Christmas Shop) (4)
Europe	Final Countdown, The (1)		Poor Me (1)
Eurythmics	Here Comes The Rain Again (8)		Someone Else's Baby (2)
	Love Is A Stranger (6)		Time Has Come, The (4)
	Right By Your Side (10)		What Do You Want (1)
	Sexcrime (Nineteen Eighty-Four) (4)		When Johnny Comes Marching Home / Made You (5)
	Sisters Are Doin' It For Themselves (9)		Who Am I / This Is It! (5)
	Sweet Dreams (Are Made Of This) (2)	Faithfull, Marianne	As Tears Go By (9)
	There Must Be An Angel (Playing With My Heart) (1)		Come And Stay With Me (4)
	Thorn In My Side (5)		Summer Nights (10)
	Who's That Girl (3)		This Little Bird (6)
Evanescence	Bring Me To Life (1)	Faithless	God Is A DJ (6)
	Going Under (8)		Insomnia (3)
	My Immortal (7)		Mass Destruction (7)
Evans, Faith	I'll Be Missing You (1)		One Step Too Far (6)
Evans, Maureen	Like I Do (3)		Reverence (10)
Evans, Paul	Hello This Is Joanie (The Telephone Answering Machine Song) (6)		Salva Mea (remix) (9)
			We Come 1 (3)
Eve	Caramel (9)	Falco	Rock Me Amadeus (1)
	Gangsta Lovin' (6)		Vienna Calling (10)
	Let Me Blow Ya Mind (4)	Faltermeyer, Harold	Axel F (2)
	Who's That Girl (6)	Fame, Georgie	Ballad Of Bonnie And Clyde (1)
Evelyn 'Champagne' King	Love Come Down (7)		Get Away (1)
			Yeh Yeh (1)
Everett, Kenny	Snot Rap (9)	Family	In My Own Time (4)
Everly Brothers	All I Have To Do Is Dream / Claudette (1)	Family Dogg	Way Of Life (6)
		Family Stand	Ghetto Heaven (10)
	Bird Dog (2)	Fantastics	Something Old Something New (9)
	Bye Bye Love (6)		
	Cathy's Clown (1)	Far Corporation	Stairway To Heaven (8)
	Cryin' In The Rain (6)	Fardon, Don	Indian Reservation (3)
		Farley 'Jackmaster' Funk	Love Can't Turn Around (10)

MUSIC POP

Group/Artiste	Title	Group/Artiste	Title
Farlowe, Chris	Out Of Time (1)		Rise To The Occasion (10)
Farm	All Together Now (4)	Fisher, Eddie	Cindy Oh Cindy (5)
	Groovy Train (6)		Downhearted (3)
Farm featuring SFX Boys Choir	All Together Now 2004 (5)		Everything I Have Is Yours (re-entry) (8)
Farnham, John	You're The Voice (6)		(I'm Always Hearing) Wedding Bells (5)
Fast Food Rockers	Fast Food Song (2)		I'm Walking Behind You (1)
	Say Cheese (10)		Oh My Papa (1)
Fat Boys	Twist (Yo Twist), The (2)		Oh My Papa (re-entry) (10)
	Wipeout (2)		Outside Of Heaven (1)
Fat Joe	What's Luv (4)		Wish You Were Here (8)
Fat Larry's Band	Zoom (2)	Fitzgerald, Scott	If I Had Words (3)
Fat Les	Vindaloo (2)	Five	Closer to Me (4)
Fat Les 2000	Jerusalem (10)		Don't Wanna Let You Go (9)
Fatback Band	(Do The) Spanish Hustle (10)		Everybody Get Up (2)
	I Found Lovin' (7)		Got The Feelin' (3)
Fatboy Slim	Gangster Trippin' (3)		If Ya Gettin' Down (2)
	Praise You (1)		Keep On Movin' (1)
	Right Here Right Now (2)		Let's Dance (1)
	Rockafeller Shank, The (6)		Slam Dunk (Da Funk) (10)
	Star 69 (10)		Until The Time Is Through (2)
	Sunset (Bird Of Prey) (9)		We Will Rock You (1)
Father Abraham	Smurf Song, The (2)		When The Lights Go Out (4)
Fatima Mansions	(Everything I Do) I Do It For You (7)	Five Star	Can't Wait Another Minute (7)
			Find The Time (7)
Fatman Scoop featuring The Crooklyn Clan	Be Faithful (1)		Rain Or Shine (2)
	It Takes Scoop (9)		Slightest Touch, The (4)
			Stay Out Of My Life (9)
Fearon, Phil	Dancing Tight (4)		System Addict (3)
	Everybody's Laughing (10)	5000 Volts	Dr Kiss Kiss (8)
	I Can Prove It (8)		I'm On Fire (4)
	What Do I Do (5)	Flack, Roberta	Back Together Again (3)
Feeder	Buck Rogers (5)		Killing Me Softly With His Song (6)
	Just The Way I'm Feeling (10)		
Feliciano, Jose	Light My Fire (6)		Tonight I Celebrate My Love (2)
Felix	Don't You Want Me (6)	Flash & The Pan	Waiting For The Train (7)
	Don't You Want Me (remix) (10)	Fleetwood Mac	Albatross (1)
Felly	Pump Up The Jam (2)		Albatross (re-issue) (2)
Ferrante & Teicher	Exodus (Theme From 'Exodus') (6)		Big Love (9)
			Everywhere (4)
Ferrer, Jose	Woman (Uh-Huh) (7)		Green Manalishi, The (With The Two-Pronged Crown) (10)
Ferry Aid	Let It Be (1)		Little Lies (5)
Ferry, Bryan	Extended Play EP (7)		Man Of The World (2)
	Hard Rain's Gonna Fall, A (10)		Oh Diane (9)
	Let's Stick Together (Let's Work Together) (4)		Oh Well (2)
	Slave To Love (10)		Tusk (6)
	This Is Tomorrow (9)	Fleetwoods	Come Softly To Me (6)
Fialka, Karel	Hey Matthew (9)	Flint, Berni	I Don't Want To Put A Hold On You (3)
Fiction Factory	(Feel Like) Heaven (6)		
Fiddler's Dram	Day Trip To Bangor (Didn't We Have A Lovely Time) (3)	Flip & Fill	Shooting Star (3)
			True Love Never Dies (re-issue) (7)
Fields, Gracie	Around The World (8)		
Fierce	Sweet Love 2K (3)	Floaters	Float On (1)
50 Cent	In Da Club (3)	Flowerpot Men	Let's Go To San Francisco (4)
	P.I.M.P. (5)	Flowers Pops, Mike	Wonderwall (2)
	21 Questions (6)	Flying Lizards	Money (5)
50 Cent / G-Unit	If I Can't / Them Thangs (10)	Flying Pickets	Only You (1)
Fine Young Cannibals	Ever Fallen In Love (9)		(When You're) Young And in Love (7)
	Good Thing (7)		
	Johnny Come Home (8)	Focus	Sylvia (4)
	She Drives Me Crazy (5)	Fontana, Wayne	Game Of Love (2)
	Suspicious Minds (8)		Um Um Um Um Um Um (5)
Fiorillo, Elisa	Who Found Who (10)	Foo Fighters	All My Life (5)
Firm	Star Trekkin' (1)		This Is A Call (5)
First Choice	Smarty Pants (9)	Ford, Emile	Counting Teardrops (4)
First Edition	Ruby Don't Talk Your Love To Town (2)		On a Slow Boat To China (3)
	Something's Burning (8)		What Do You Want To Make Those Eyes At Me For (1)
Fisher, Climie	Love Changes Everything (2)	Ford, Mary	Vaya Con Dios (7)

Group/Artiste	Title	Group/Artiste	Title
Foreigner	I Want To Know What Love Is (1)		You Are Alive (4)
	Waiting For A Girl Like You (8)	Frampton, Peter	Show Me The Way (10)
Forrest	Rock The Boat (4)	Francis, Connie	Carolina Moon / Stupid Cupid (1)
Forte	Rumble In The Jungle (3)		Everybody's Somebody's Fool (5)
Fortune, Lance	Be Mine (4)		
Fortunes	Freedom Come Freedom Go (6)		Lipstick On Your Collar (3)
	Here It Comes Again (4)		Mama / Robot Man (2)
	Storm In A Teacup (7)		My Happiness (4)
	You've Got Your Troubles (2)		My Heart Has A Mind Of It's Own (3)
40 Thevz	C U When You Get There (3)		Together (6)
49ers	Touch Me (3)		Vacation (10)
Foundations	Baby Now That I've Found You (1)		Where The Boys Are / Baby Roo (5)
	Build Me Up Buttercup (2)		Who's Sorry Now (1)
	In The Bad Bad Old Days (8)	Frank Weir Orchestra	My Son My Son (1)
Four Aces	Love Is A Many-Splendoured Thing (2)	Frankee	F.U.R.B. (F U Right Back) (1)
	Mr Sandman (9)	Frankie Goes To Hollywood	Power Of Love (re-issue), The (6)
	Stranger In Paradise (6)		Power Of Love (re-issue), The (10)
	Three Coins In The Fountain (5)		Power Of Love, The (1)
Four Knights	I Get So Lonely (5)		Rage Hard (4)
	I Get So Lonely (re-entry) (10)		Relax (1)
Four Lads	Faith Can Move Mountains (7)		Relax (re-issue) (5)
	Faith Can Move Mountains (re-entry) (9)		Two Tribes (1)
	Rain Rain Rain (8)		Welcome To The Pleasure Dome (2)
4 Non Blondes	What's Up (2)	Franklin, Aretha	Deeper Love, A (5)
411	Dumb (3)		I Knew You Were Waiting (For Me) (1)
411 featuring Ghostface Killah	On My Knees (4)		I Say A Little Prayer (4)
Four Pennies	Juliet / Tell Me Girl (What Are You Gonna Do) (1)		Respect (10)
			Sisters Are Doin' It For Themselves (9)
Four Preps	Big Man (2)		Spanish Harlem (14)
Four Seasons	December 1963 (Oh What A Night) (1)	Franklin, Erma	(Take A Little) Piece Of My Heart (9)
	Let's Hang On! (4)	Franklin, Rodney	Groove, The (7)
	Night, The (7)	Frantique	Strut Your Funky Stuff (10)
	Rag Doll (2)	Franz Ferdinand	Matinee (8)
	Sherry (8)		Take Me Out (3)
	Silver Star (3)	Freak Power	Turn On Tune In Cop Out (re-issue) (3)
	Who Loves You (6)		
Four Tops	Bernadette (8)	Freddie	I Understand (5)
	I Can't Help Myself (re-issue) (10)		If You Gotta Make A Fool Of Somebody (3)
	If I Were A Carpenter (7)		I'm Telling You Now (2)
	It's All In The Game (5)		You Were Made For Me (3)
	Loco In Acapulco (7)	Freddie Bell & The Bellboys	Giddy-Up-A-Ding-Dong (4)
	Reach Out I'll Be There (1)		
	Simple Game (3)	Free	All Right Now (2)
	Standing In The Shadows Of Love (6)		All Right Now (remix) (8)
	Still Water (Love) (10)		Another One Bites The Dust (5)
	Walk Away Renee (3)		My Brother Jake (4)
	When She Was My Girl (3)		Wishing Well (7)
Fourmost	Hello Little Girl (9)	Freeez	I.O.U. (2)
	Little Loving, A (6)		Southern Freeez (8)
Fox	Only You Can (3)	French, Nicki	Total Eclipse Of The Heart (5)
	S-S-Single Bed (4)	Fresh 4	Wishing On A Star (10)
Fox, Samantha	Do Ya Do Ya (Wanna Please Me) (10)	Fresh Prince	Boom! Shake The Room (1)
			Summertime (8)
	Nothing's Gonna Stop Me Now (8)	Friedman, Dean	Lucky Stars (3)
		Frijid Pink	House Of The Rising Sun (4)
	Touch Me (I Want Your Body) (3)	Frog Chorus	We All Stand Together (3)
FPI Project	Going Back To My Roots / Rich In Paradise (9)	Fugees	Killing Me Softly (1)
			No Woman No Cry (2)
Fragma	Everytime You Need Me (3)		Ready Or Not (1)
	Toca's Miracle (1)		Rumble In The Jungle (3)
		Full Force	Alice I Want You Just For Me (9)

Group/Artiste	Title
Fun Boy Three	It Ain't What You Do It's The Way That You Do It (4)
	Our Lips Are Sealed (7)
	Really Saying Something (5)
	Tunnel Of Love (10)
Fun Lovin' Criminals	Loco (5)
Funk Masters	It's Over (8)
Funkadelic	One Nation Under A Groove (9)
Funkstar De Luxe	Sun Is Shining (3)
Furious Five	Message, The (8)
	Step Off (Part 1) (8)
Furtado, Nelly	I'm Like A Bird (5)
	Turn Off The Light (4)
Fury, Billy	Colette (9)
	Halfway To Paradise (3)
	I'd Never Find Another You (5)
	In Summer (5)
	In Thoughts Of You (9)
	It's Only Make Believe (10)
	Jealousy (2)
	Last Night Was Made For Love (4)
	Like I've Never Been Gone (3)
	Once Upon A Dream (7)
	When Will You Say I Love You (3)
Fyson, Leslie	Signature Tune Of 'The Army Game', The (5)
G, Ali	Me Julie (2)
G, Dario	Carnaval De Paris (5)
	Dream To Me (9)
	Sunchyme (2)
G, Gina	Fresh! (6)
	I Belong To You (6)
	Ooh Aah ... Just A Little Bit (1)
G, Warren	I Shot The Sheriff (2)
	Regulate (5)
	What's Love Got To Do With It (2)
Gabriel, Peter	Don't Give Up (9)
	Games Without Frontiers (4)
	Sledgehammer (4)
	Steam (10)
Gabrielle	Don't Need The Sun To Shine (To Make Me Smile) (9)
	Dreams (1)
	Give Me A Little More Time (5)
	Going Nowhere (9)
	If You Ever (2)
	Out Of Reach (4)
	Rise (1)
	Sunshine (9)
	Walk On By (7)
	When A Woman (6)
Gaines, Rosie	Closer Than Close (4)
Gainsbourg, Serge	Je T'Aime ... Moi Non Plus (2)
	Je T'Aime ... Moi Non Plus (re-issue) (1)
Gala	Freed From Desire (3)
Galaxy	Dancing Tight (4)
	Everybody's Laughing (10)
	What Do I Do (5)
Gali Atari	Hallelujah (5)
Gallagher & Lyle	Heart On My Sleeve (6)
	I Wanna Stay With You (6)
Gallagher, Liam	Going Underground / Carnation (6)
Gallagher, Liam & Steve Cradock	Carnation (6)
Gallant, Patsy	From New York To L.A. (6)
Galway, James	Annie's Song (3)

Group/Artiste	Title
Gap Band	Big Fun (4)
	Oops Up Side Your Head (6)
Garbage	I Think I'm Paranoid (9)
	Milk (10)
	Push It (9)
	Shut Your Mouth (20)
	Stupid Girl (4)
	When I Grow Up (9)
Gardiner, Boris	I Want To Wake Up With You (1)
Garfunkel, Art	Bright Eyes (1)
	I Only Have Eyes For You (1)
Garrett, Leif	I Was Made For Dancin' (4)
Gary Clail On U-Sound System	Human Nature (10)
Gary US Bonds	Quarter To Three (7)
Gary's Gang	Keep On Dancin' (8)
Gaskin, Barbara	It's My Party (1)
Gat Decor	Passion (remix) (6)
Gately, Stephen	Baby Can I Hold You / Shooting Star (2)
	New Beginning / Bright Eyes (3)
Gates, Gareth	Anyone Of Us (Stupid Mistake) (1)
	Long And Winding Road, The / Suspicious Minds (1)
	Say It Isn't So (4)
	Sunshine (3)
	Unchained Melody (1)
	What My Heart Wants To Say (5)
Gates, Gareth featuring The Kumars	Spirit In The Sky (1)
Gay Dad	To Earth With Love (10)
Gaye, Marvin	Abraham Martin And John (9)
	Got To Give It Up (7)
	I Heard It Through The Grapevine (1)
	I Heard It Through The Grapevine (re-issue) (8)
	Onion Song (9)
	(Sexual) Healing (4)
	Too Busy Thinking 'Bout My Baby (5)
	You Are Everything (5)
Gayle, Crystal	Don't It Make My Brown Eyes Blue (5)
Gayle, Michelle	Do You Know (6)
	Sweetness (4)
Gaynor, Gloria	I Will Survive (1)
	I Will Survive (remix) (5)
	Never Can Say Goodbye (2)
Gazza	Fog On The Tyne (Revisited) (2)
GB Experience	Crown, The (6)
General Levy	Incredible (remix) (8)
Genesis	Abacab (9)
	Follow You Follow Me (7)
	I Can't Dance (7)
	Invisible Touch (live) (7)
	Mama (4)
	No Son Of Mine (6)
	3 x 3 EP (10)
	Turn It On Again (8)
Gentry, Bobbie	All I Have To Do Is Dream (3)
	I'll Never Fall In Love Again (1)
Geordie	All Because Of You (6)
George, Boy	Everything I Own (1)
George, Sophia	Girlie Girlie (7)
Gerry & The Pacemakers	Don't Let The Sun Catch You Crying (6)
	Ferry Cross The Mersey (8)

Group/Artiste	Title	Group/Artiste	Title
	How Do You Do It (1)	Goldsmith, Glen	Dreaming (9)
	I Like It (1)	Goldtrix presents	It's Love (Trippin') (6)
	I'm The One (2)	Andrea Brown	
	You'll Never Walk Alone (1)	Good Charlotte	Anthem, The (10)
Ghostface Killah	I Want You For Myself (2)		Girls And Boys (6)
Gibb, Andy	An Everlasting Love (10)		Lifestyles Of The Rich And
Gibb, Robin	Saved By The Bell (2)		Famous (8)
Gibson Brothers	Ohh! What A Life (10)	Goodies	Funky Gibbon / Sick Man Blues
	Que Sera Mi Vida (5)		(4)
Gibson, Debbie	Foolish Beat (9)		In Betweenies, The / Father
	Shake Your Love (7)		Christmas Do Not Touch
Gilstrap, Jim	Swing Your Daddy (4)		Me (7)
Ginuwine	What's So Different (10)	Goodmen	Give It Up (re-entry) (5)
	When Doves Cry (10)	Goodrem, Delta	Born To Try (3)
Giorgio Moroder	Together In Electric Dreams (3)		Innocent Eyes (9)
Girl Thing	Last One Standing (8)		Lost Without You (4)
Girls Aloud	I'll Stand By You (1)		Out Of The Blue (9)
	Jump (2)	Goodwin, Ron	Terry's Theme From Limelight (3)
	Life Got Cold (3)	Orchestra	
	Love Machine (2)	Goombay Dance	Seven Tears (1)
	No Good Advice (2)	Band	
	Show, The (2)	Goons	Bloodnok's Rock 'N' Roll Call /
	Sound Of The Underground (1)		Ying Tong Song (3)
Girls Of FHM	Da Ya Think I'm Sexy? (10)		I'm Walking Backwards For
Girlschool	St Valentine's Day Massacre		Christmas / Bluebottle Blues
	EP (5)		(4)
Glamma Kid	Taboo (10)		Ying Tong Song (re-issue) (9)
	Why (10)	Gordon, Lonnie	Happenin' All Over Again (4)
Glen Somers & His	Pickin' A Chicken (9)	Gore, Lesley	It's My Party (9)
Orchestra		Gorillaz	Clint Eastwood (4)
Glitter Band	Angel Face (4)		19 / 2000 (6)
	Goodbye My Love (2)	Gorme, Eydie	Yes My Darling Daughter (10)
	Just For You (10)	Goulding, Nigel	Full Metal Jacket
	Let's Get Together Again (8)		(I Wanna Be Your Drill
	People Like You People Like		Instructor) (2)
	Me (5)	Grace	Not Over Yet (6)
	Tears I Cried, The (8)	Gracie, Charlie	Fabulous (8)
Glitter, Gary	Always Yours (1)		Wanderin' Eyes (6)
	Another Rock And Roll	Graham, Jaki	Could It Be I'm Falling In Love
	Christmas (7)		(5)
	Do You Wanna Touch Me? (Oh		Round And Round (9)
	Yeah) (2)		Set Me Free (7)
	Doing Alright With The Boys (6)	Grandmaster	White Lines (Don't Do It) (7)
	Hello Hello I'm Back Again (2)	Grandmaster Flash	Message, The (8)
	I Didn't Know I Loved You	Grandmaster Melle	Step Off (Part 1) (8)
	(Til I Saw You Rock 'N'	Mel	
	Roll) (4)	Grange Hill Cast	Just Say No (5)
	I Love You Love Me Love (1)	Grant, Amy	Baby Baby (2)
	I'm The Leader Of The Gang (I	Grant, David	Could It Be I'm Falling In Love
	Am) (1)		(5)
	Love Like You And Me (10)		Watching Me Watching You
	Oh Yes! You're Beautiful (2)		(10)
	Remember Me This Way (3)	Grant, Eddy	Do You Feel My Love (8)
	Rock And Roll (Parts 1 And 2)		Electric Avenue (2)
	(2)		Electric Avenue (remix) (5)
Gloworm	Carry Me Home (9)		Gimme Hope Jo'Anna (7)
Go West	We Close Our Eyes (5)		I Don't Wanna Dance (1)
Godley & Creme	Under Your Thumb (3)	Grant, Gogi	Wayward Wind (9)
	Wedding Bells (7)	Gray, David	Babylon (5)
Gold, Andrew	Never Let Her Slip Away (5)	Gray, Macy	I Try (7)
Gold, Brian	Compliments On Your Kiss (2)	Gray, Michael	Weekend, The (7)
Gold, Tony	Compliments On Your Kiss	Green, Al	Let's Stay Together (7)
	(2)		Tired Of Being Alone (4)
Goldbug	Whole Lotta Love (3)	Green Day	American Idiot (3)
Golden Earring	Radar Love (7)		Basket Case (7)
Goldie	Making Up Again (7)		Boulevard Of Broken Dreams
Goldie Lookin Chain	Guns Don't Kill People Rappers		(5)
	Do (3)	Green Jelly	Three Little Pigs (5)
Goldsboro, Bobby	Honey (2)	Greenbaum, Norman	Spirit In The Sky (1)
	Honey (re-issue) (2)	Greyhound	Black And White (6)
	Summer (The First Time) (9)	Grid	Swamp Thing (3)

MUSIC POP

Group/Artiste	Title
Griffin, Alistair featuring Robin Gibb	Bring It On / My Lover's Prayer (5)
Gun	Race With The Devil (8)
	Word Up (8)
Guns 'N' Roses	Ain't It Fun (9)
	Don't Cry (8)
	Knockin' On Heaven's Door (2)
	Live And Let Die (5)
	November Rain (4)
	Paradise City (6)
	Patience (10)
	Since I Don't Have You (10)
	Sweet Child O' Mine (remix) (6)
	Sympathy For The Devil (9)
	Yesterdays / November Rain (8)
	You Could Be Mine (3)
Guru Josh	Infinity (5)
Gurvitz, Adrian	Classic (8)
Gusto	Disco's Revenge (9)
Guthrie, Gwen	Ain't Nothing Goin' On But The Rent (5)
Guys & Dolls	There's A Whole Lot Of Loving (2)
	You Don't Have To Say You Love Me (5)
H & Claire	All Out Of Love / Beauty And The Beast (10)
	DJ (3)
	Half A Heart (8)
Haddaway	I Miss You (9)
	Life (6)
	Rock My Heart (9)
	What Is Love (2)
Haircut 100	Fantastic Day (9)
	Favourite Shirts (Boy Meets Girl) (4)
	Love Plus One (3)
	Nobody's Fool (9)
Hale & Pace & The Stonkers	Stonk, The (1)
Hall, Daryl & John Oates	I Can't Go For That (No Can Do) (8)
	Maneater (6)
Halliwell, Geri	Bag It Up (1)
	Calling (7)
	It's Raining Men (1)
	Lift Me Up (1)
	Look At Me (2)
	Mi Chico Latino (1)
	Ride It (4) billed as 'Geri'
	Scream If You Wanna Go Faster (8)
Halo James	Could Have Told You So (6)
Hamilton, Lynne	On The Inside (3)
Hamilton, Russ	We Will Make Love (2)
Hammer, Jan	Crockett's Theme (2)
	Miami Vice Theme (5)
Hancock, Herbie	Rockit (8)
Hanson	I Will Come To You (5)
	Mmmbop (1)
	Where's The Love (4)
Happy Clappers	I Believe (re-issue) (7)
Happy Mondays	Kinky Afro (5)
	Step On (5)
Hardcastle, Paul	Don't Waste My Time (8)
	Nineteen (1)
Harlem Community Choir	Happy Xmas (War Is Over) (4)
	Happy Xmas (War Is Over) (re-entry) (2)

Group/Artiste	Title
Harley, Steve	Here Comes The Sun (10)
	Make Me Smile (Come Up And See Me) (1)
	Phantom Of The Opera, The (7)
Harris, Anita	Just Loving You (6)
Harris, Jet	Applejack (4)
	Diamonds (1)
	Scarlett O'Hara (2)
Harris, Niki	Do You See The Light (Looking For) (10)
	Exterminate (2)
Harris, Richard	Macarthur Park (4)
Harris, Rolf	Stairway To Heaven (7)
	Sun Arise (3)
	Tie Me Kangaroo Down Sport (9)
	Two Little Boys (1)
Harrison, George	Bangla-Desh (10)
	Give Me Love (Give Me Peace On Earth) (8)
	Got My Mind Set On You (2)
	My Sweet Lord (1)
	My Sweet Lord (re-issue) (1)
Harrison, Noel	Windmills Of Your Mind (8)
Harry J Allstars	Liquidator (9)
Harry, Deborah	French Kissin' In The USA (8)
Hartley, Richard	Music Of Torvill And Dean EP, The (9)
Hartman, Dan	Instant Replay (8)
Haskell, Gordon	How Wonderful You Are (2)
Hathaway, Donny	Back Together Again (3)
Hawkes, Chesney	One And Only, The (1)
Hawkins Singers, Edwin	Oh Happy Day (2)
Hawkwind	Silver Machine (3)
Hayes, Bill	Ballad Of Davy Crockett (2)
Hayes, Darren	Insatiable (8)
Hayes, Isaac	Disco Connection (10)
	Theme From Shaft (4)
Hayward, Justin	Blue Guitar (8)
	Forever Autumn (5)
Hazlewood, Lee	Did You Ever (2)
Hear'Say	Everybody (4)
	Lovin' Is Easy (6)
	Pure And Simple (1)
	Way To Your Love, The (1)
Heart	All I Wanna Do Is Make Love To You (8)
	Alone (3)
	Never / These Dreams (re-issue) (8)
Heatwave	Always And Forever / Mind Blowing Decisions (remix) (9)
	Boogie Nights (2)
Heaven 17	Come Live With Me (5)
	Temptation (2)
	Temptation (remix) (4)
Heavy D & The Boyz	Now That We Found Love (2)
Hedgehoppers Anonymous	It's Good News Week (5)
Heinz	Just Like Eddie (5)
Hello	New York Groove (9)
	Tell Him (6)
Helms, Jimmy	Gonna Make You An Offer You Can't Refuse (8)
Henderson, Ainslie	Keep Me A Secret (5)
Hendrix Experience, Jimi	All Along The Watchtower (5)
	Hey Joe (6)
	Purple Haze (3)
	Voodoo Chile (1)

Group/Artiste	Title	Group/Artiste	Title
	Wind Cries Mary, The (6)		It Doesn't Matter Anymore (1)
Henry Mancini	How Soon (10)		Peggy Sue (6)
Orchestra			Rave On (5)
Henry, Clarence	But I Do (3)		Wishing (10)
'Frogman'	You Always Hurt The One You	Hollywood Beyond	What's The Colour Of Money
	Love (6)		(7)
Hepburn	I Quit (8)	Holman, Eddie	(Hey There) Lonely Girl (4)
Herd	From The Underworld (6)	Holt, John	Help Me Make It Through The
	I Don't Want Our Loving To Die		Night (6)
	(5)	Honeybus	I Can't Let Maggie Go (8)
Herman's Hermits	I'm Into Something Good (1)	Honeycombs	Have I The Right (1)
	Must To Avoid, A (6)	Honeyz	End Of The Line (5)
	My Sentimental Friend (2)		Finally Found (4)
	No Milk Today (7)		Love Of A Lifetime (9)
	Silhouettes (3)		Never Let You Down (7)
	Something's Happening (6)		Won't Take It Lying Down (7)
	Sunshine Girl (8)	Hopkin, Mary	Goodbye (2)
	There's A Kind Of Hush (7)		Knock Knock Who's There (2)
	Wonderful World (7)		Temma Harbour (6)
	Years May Come Years May		Those Were The Days (1)
	Go (7)	Hot Butter	Popcorn (5)
Hermes House Band	Country Roads (7)	Hot Chocolate	Brother Louie (7)
Hernandez, Patrick	Born To Be Alive (10)		Child's Prayer, A (7)
Hi Tension	British Hustle / Peace On Earth		Emma (3)
	(8)		Girl Crazy (7)
Hibbler, Al	Unchained Melody (2)		I Believe (In Love) (8)
Hi-Gate	Pitchin' (In Every Direction) (6)		It Started With A Kiss (5)
Highwaymen	Michael (1)		Love Is Life (6)
Hill, Benny	Ernie (The Fastest Milkman In		No Doubt About It (2)
	The West) (1)		Put Your Love In Me (10)
Hill, Chris	Bionic Santa (10)		So You Win Again (1)
	Renta Santa (10)		What Kinda Boy You Looking
Hill, Faith	There You'll Be (3)		For Girl (10)
Hill, Lauryn	Doo Wap (That Thing) (3)		You Sexy Thing (2)
	Ex-Factor (4)		You Sexy Thing (re-issue) (6)
Hill, Vince	Edelweiss (2)		You Sexy Thing (remix) (10)
Hilltoppers	Only You (3)	Hot Gossip	I Lost My Heart To A Starship
Hilton, Ronnie	Around The World (4)		Trooper (6)
	Blossom Fell, A (10)	Hot 'N' Juicy	Horny (2)
	I Still Believe (3)	Hotlegs	Neanderthal Man (2)
	No Other Love (1)	Hotshots	Snoopy Vs The Red Baron (4)
	Who Are We (6)	Houghton, Steven	Wind Beneath My Wings (3)
Him	Solitary Man (9)	House Of Pain	Jump Around (re-issue) / Top
Hockridge, Edmund	Young And Foolish (10)		O' The Morning (8)
Hoffman, Mani	Starlight (2)	Housemartins	Caravan Of Love (1)
Holliday, Michael	Stairway Of Love (3)		Happy Hour (3)
	Starry Eyed (1)	Housemaster Boyz	House Nation (re-entry) (8)
	Story Of My Life, The (1)	Houston, Whitney	Could I Have This Kiss Forever
Hollies	Air That I Breathe, The (2)		(7)
	Bus Stop (5)		Greatest Love Of All (8)
	Carrie-Anne (3)		How Will I Know (5)
	He Ain't Heavy He's My Brother		I Have Nothing (3)
	(3)		I Wanna Dance With
	He Ain't Heavy He's My Brother		Somebody (Who Loves Me)
	(re-issue) (1)		(1)
	Here I Go Again (4)		I Will Always Love You (1)
	I Can't Let Go (2)		If I Told You That (9)
	I Can't Tell The Bottom From		I'm Every Woman (4)
	The Top (7)		I'm Your Baby Tonight (5)
	I'm Alive (1)		It's Not Right But It's OK (3)
	Jennifer Eccles (7)		Love Will Save The Day (10)
	Just One Look (2)		My Love Is Your Love (2)
	Look Through Any Window (4)		One Moment In Time (1)
	On A Carousel (4)		Saving All My Love For You (1)
	Sorry Suzanne (3)		So Emotional (5)
	Stay (8)		When You Believe (4)
	Stop Stop Stop (2)	Howard, Adina	What's Love Got To Do With It
	We're Through (7)		(2)
	Yes I Will (9)	Howard, Billy	King Of The Cops (6)
Holly, Buddy	Bo Diddley (4)	Hudson-Ford	Pick Up The Pieces (8)
	Brown-eyed Handsome Man (3)	Hue & Cry	Labour Of Love (6)

Group/Artiste	Title
Hues Corporation	Rock The Boat (6)
Huey Lewis & The News	Power Of Love / Do You Believe In Love (re-issue), The (9)
Hugo Winterhalter's Orchestra	Downhearted (3)
	I'm Walking Behind You (1)
	Wish You Were Here (8)
	Cindy Oh Cindy (5)
	Everything I Have Is Yours (re-entry) (8)
	(I'm Always Hearing) Wedding Bells (5)
	Oh My Papa (9)
	Oh My Papa (re-entry) (10)
	Outside Of Heaven (1)
Human League	Being Boiled (6)
	Don't You Want Me (1)
	Human (8)
	(Keep Feeling) Fascination (2)
	Love Action (I Believe In Love) (3)
	Mirror Man (2)
	Open Your Heart (6)
	Tell Me When (6)
Humble Pie	Natural Born Bugie (4)
Humperdinck, Engelbert	Am I That Easy To Forget (3)
	Last Waltz, The (1)
	Les Bicyclettes De Belsize (5)
	Man Without A Love, A (2)
	Release Me (1)
	There Goes My Everything (2)
	Way It Used To Be, The (3)
	Winter World Of Love (7)
Hunter, Tab	99 Ways (5)
	Young Love (1)
Hutton, June	Say You're Mine Again (10)
	Say You're Mine Again (re-entry) (6)
Hyland, Brian	Ginny Come Lately (5)
	Itsy Bitsy Teeny Weeny Yellow Polka Dot Bikini (8)
	Sealed With A Kiss (3)
	Sealed With A Kiss (re-issue) (7)
Hyman Trio, Dick	Theme From The Threepenny Opera (9)
Hynde, Chrissie	Breakfast In Bed (6)
	I Got You Babe (1)
	Love Can Build A Bridge (1)
Ian Dury & The Blockheads	Hit Me With Your Rhythm Stick (1)
	Reasons To Be Cheerful (Part 3) (3)
	What A Waste (9)
Ice Cube featuring Mack 10 & MS Toi	You Can Do It (2)
Idlewild	You Held The World In Your Arms (9)
Idol, Billy	Mony Mony (7)
	Rebel Yell (6)
	White Wedding (6)
Idols	Happy Xmas (War Is Over) (5)
Ifield, Frank	Confessin' (1)
	Don't Blame Me (8)
	I Remember You (1)
	Lovesick Blues (1)
	Nobody's Darlin' But Mine (4)
	Wayward Wind (1)
Iglesias, Enrique	Bailamos (4)
	Could I Have This Kiss Forever (7)

Group/Artiste	Title
	Escape (3)
	Hero (1)
	Maybe (12)
Iglesias, Enrique featuring Kelis	Not In Love (5) billed as 'Enrique'
Iglesias, Julio	Begin The Beguine (1)
	My Love (5)
	Quiereme Mucho (Yours) (3)
IIO	Rapture (2)
Ike	Nutbush City Limits (4)
	River Deep Mountain High (3)
Imagination	Body Talk (4)
	Just An Illusion (2)
	Music And Lights (5)
Imbruglia, Natalie	Big Mistake (2)
	Smoke (5)
	Torn (2)
	Wrong Impression (10)
Incognito	Always There (6)
Ingram, James	Somewhere Out There (8)
Ink Spots	Melody Of Love (10)
Inner Circle	Sweat (A La La La La La Long) (re-entry) (3)
Inner City	Ain't Nobody Better (10)
	Big Fun (8)
	Good Life (4)
	Good Life (Buena Vida) (remix) (10)
INXS	Need You Tonight (2)
Iron Maiden	Be Quick Or Be Dead (2)
	Bring Your Daughter ... To The Slaughter (1)
	Can I Play With Madness (3)
	Clairvoyant, The (6)
	Evil That Men Do, The (5)
	Fear Of The Dark (live) (8)
	Hallowed Be Thy Name (live) (9)
	Holy Smoke (3)
	Infinite Dreams (6)
	Man On The Edge (10)
	Run To The Hills (7)
	Run To The Hills (re-issue) (9)
	Wicker Man, The (9)
	Wildest Dreams (6)
Irv Gotti Presents	Down 4 U (4)
Isaak, Chris	Wicked Game (10)
Isley Brothers	Behind A Painted Smile (5)
	Harvest For The World (10)
	This Old Heart Of Mine (Is Weak For You) (3)
It Bites	Calling All The Heroes (6)
Ivy League	Funny How Love Can Be (8)
	Tossing And Turning (3)
J Geils Band	Centerfold (3)
J J Barrie	No Charge (1)
J, Ray	Another Day In Paradise (5)
Ja Rule	Always On Time (6)
	Clap Back / Reigns (9)
	Livin' It Up (re-issue) (5)
Ja Rule featuring R Kelly & Ashanti	Wonderful (1)
Jack Marshall's Music	Fever (5)
Jack 'N' Chill	Jack That House Built, The (6)
Jacks, Terry	If You Go Away (8)
	Seasons In The Sun (1)
Jackson 5	ABC (8)
	Doctor My Eyes (9)
	I Want You Back (2)
	I Want You Back (remix) (8)
	I'll Be There (4)

Group/Artiste	Title
	Lookin' Through The Windows (9)
	Love You Save, The (7)
Jackson, Chad	Hear The Drummer (Get Wicked) (3)
Jackson, Janet	Again (6)
	All For You (3)
	Best Things In Life Are Free (remix), The (7)
	Best Things In Life Are Free, The (2)
	Doesn't Really Matter (5)
	Got 'Til It's Gone (6)
	I Get Lonely (5)
	Let's Wait Awhile (3)
	Runaway (6)
	Scream (3)
	That's The Way Love Goes (2)
	Together Again (4)
	What Have You Done For Me Lately (3)
	When I Think Of You (10)
	Whoops Now / What'll I Do (9)
Jackson, Jermaine	Do What You Do (6)
	Let's Get Serious (8)
Jackson, Joe	It's Different For The Girls (5)
	Steppin' Out (6)
Jackson, Michael	Ain't No Sunshine (8)
	Bad (3)
	Beat It (3)
	Ben (7)
	Billie Jean (1)
	Black Or White (1)
	Blood On The Dancefloor (1)
	Dirty Diana (4)
	Don't Stop Till You Get Enough (3)
	Earth Song (1)
	Farewell My Summer Love (7)
	Girl Is Mine, The (8)
	Give In To Me (2)
	Got To Be There (5)
	Heal The World (2)
	History / Ghosts (5)
	I Just Can't Stop Loving You (1)
	I Want You Back (remix) (8)
	In The Closet (8)
	Leave Me Alone (2)
	Off The Wall (7)
	One Day In Your Life (1)
	One More Chance (5)
	Remember The Time / Come Together (3)
	Rock With You (7)
	Rockin' Robin (3)
	Say Say Say (2)
	Scream (3)
	She's Out Of My Life (3)
	Smooth Criminal (8)
	Stranger In Moscow (4)
	They Don't Care About Us (4)
	Thriller (10)
	Wanna Be Startin' Something (8)
	Way You Make Me Feel, The (3)
	Who Is It (10)
	Why (2)
	Will You Be There (9)
	You Are Not Alone (1)

Group/Artiste	Title
	You Rock My World (2)
Jacksons	Blame It On The Boogie (8)
	Can You Feel It (6)
	Shake Your Body (Down To The Ground) (4)
	Show You The Way To Go (1)
	Walk Right Now (7)
Jacky	White Horses (10)
Jade	Don't Walk Away (7)
Jagger, Mick	Dancing In The Street (1)
Jaimeson	Complete (4)
Jaimeson featuring Angel Blu	True (4)
Jakatta	American Dream (3)
	My Vision (6)
	So Lonely (8)
Jam	Absolute Beginners (4)
	Beat Surrender (1)
	Bitterest Pill (I Ever Had To Swallow), The (2)
	Eton Rifles, The (3)
	Funeral Pyre (4)
	Going Underground / Dreams Of Children (1)
	Just Who Is The Five O'Clock Hero (8)
	Start (1)
	Town Called Malice / Precious (1)
Jam & Spoon	Right In The Night (Fall In Love With Music) (re-issue) (10)
Jamelia	DJ / Stop (9)
	Money (5)
	See It In A Boy's Eyes (5)
	Superstar (3)
	Thank You (2)
James	She's A Star (9)
	Sit Down (2)
	Sit Down (remix) (7)
	Sound (9)
James, Etta	I Just Want To Make Love To You (5)
James, Tommy	Mony Mony (1)
Jamiroquai	Alright (6)
	Canned Heat (4)
	Cosmic Girl (6)
	Deeper Underground (1)
	Little L (5)
	Love Foolosophy (14)
	Stillness In Time (9)
	Too Young To Die (10)
	Virtual Insanity (3)
Janet	Feel It Boy (9)
	What's It Gonna Be?! (6)
Jankowski, Horst	Walk In The Black Forest, A (3)
Japan	Ghosts (5)
	I Second That Emotion (9)
Jarre, Jean-Michel	Oxygene Part IV (4)
Jarreau, Al	Moonlighting Theme (8)
Javine	Real Things (4)
Jay Sean	Stolen (4)
Jay Sean featuring Rishi Rich Project	Eyes On You (6)
Jay-Z	Hard Knock Life (Ghetto Anthem) (2)
	Heartbreaker (5)
	I'll Be (9)
Jay-Z featuring Beyonce Knowles	03 Bonnie & Clyde (2)
Jazzy Jeff	Boom! Shake The Room (1)

Group/Artiste	Title
	Summertime (8)
Jean, Wyclef	Another One Bites The Dust (5)
	Gone Till November (3)
	It Doesn't Matter (3)
	911 (9)
	Perfect Gentleman (4)
Jeff Wayne's War Of The Worlds	Eve Of War (remix), The (3)
	Forever Autumn (5)
Jellybean	Who Found Who (10)
Jesus & Mary Chain	April Skies (8)
	Reverence (10)
Jethro Tull	Living In The Past (3)
	Sweet Dream (7)
	Teacher / The Witches Promise (4)
Jets	Crush On You (5)
Jigsaw	Sky High (9)
Jilted John	Jilted John (4)
Jimmy Boyd & Frankie Laine	Tell Me A Story (5)
Jimmy James & The Vagabonds	Now Is The Time (5)
Jive Bunny & The Mastermixers	Can Can You Party (8)
	Let's Party (1)
	Swing The Mood (1)
	That Sounds Good To Me (4)
	That's What I Like (1)
JJ	Ain't No Stoppin Us (8)
	Masterblaster 2000 (5)
J-Kwon	Tipsy (4)
Jo Boxers	Boxer Beat (3)
	Just Got Lucky (7)
Jo Jo Gunne	Run Run Run (6)
Joan Jett & The Blackhearts	I Love Rock 'N' Roll (4)
Joe	Stutter (7)
Joe Brown & The Bruvvers	It Only Took A Minute (6)
	Picture Of You, A (2)
	That's What Love Will Do (3)
Joel, Billy	An Innocent Man (8)
	River Of Dreams, The (3)
	Tell Her About It (4)
	Uptown Girl (1)
	We Didn't Start The Fire (7)
John Barry Seven	Hit And Miss (10)
John Fred & Playboy Band	Judy In Disguise (With Glasses) (3)
John, Elton	Are You Ready For Love (1)
	Blue Eyes (8)
	Candle In The Wind 97 / Something About The Way You Look Tonight (1)
	Candle In The Wind (re-issue) (5)
	Crocodile Rock (5)
	Daniel (4)
	Don't Go Breaking My Heart (1)
	Don't Go Breaking My Heart (7) with RuPaul & Kiki Dee
	Don't Let The Sun Go Down On Me (1)
	Goodbye Yellow Brick Road (6)
	I Guess That's Why They Call It The Blues (5)
	I Want Love (9)
	I'm Still Standing (4)
	Live Like Horses (9)
	Lucy In The Sky With Diamonds (10)
	Nikita (3)

Group/Artiste	Title
	One, The (10)
	Passengers (5)
	Pinball Wizard (7)
	Rocket Man (2)
	Sacrifice (re-issue) / Healing Hands (re-issue) (1)
	Sad Songs (Say So Much) (7)
	Saturday Night's Alright For Fighting (7)
	Song For Guy (4)
	Sorry Seems To Be The Hardest Word (1)
	True Love (2)
	Written In The Stars (10)
	Your Song (4) with Alessandro Safina
	Your Song (7)
Johnny & The Hurricanes	Beatnik Fly (8)
	Down Yonder (8)
	Red River Rock (3)
	Rocking Goose (3)
Johnny Hates Jazz	Shattered Dreams (5)
Johnny Johnson & The Bandwagon	(Blame It) On The Pony Express (7)
	Breakin' Down The Walls Of Heartache (4)
	Sweet Inspiration (10)
Johnny Keating Orchestra	Theme From Z Cars (8)
Johnny Kidd & The Pirates	I'll Never Get Over You (4)
	Shakin' All Over (1)
Johnny Pearson Orchestra	Sleepy Shores (8)
Johnson, Andreas	Glorious (4)
Johnson, Holly	Americanos (4)
	Ferry 'Cross The Mersey (1)
	Love Train (4)
Johnson, Laurie	Sucu Sucu (9)
Johnson, Marv	I'll Pick A Rose For My Rose (10)
	You Got What It Takes (7)
Johnson, Paul	Get Get Down (5)
Johnson, Romina	Movin' Too Fast (2)
Johnsson, Ana	We Are (8)
Johnston Brothers	Hernando's Hideaway (1)
	Join In And Sing Again (9)
	Oh Happy Day (4)
Johnston, Sabrina	Peace (8)
JoJo	Leave (Get Out) (2)
JoJo featuring Bow Wow	Baby It's You (8)
Jon & Vangelis	I Hear You Now (8)
	I'll Find My Way Home (6)
Jones, Aled	Walking In The Air (5)
Jones, Donell	U Know What's Up (2)
Jones, Howard	Like To Get To Know You Well (4)
	Look Mama (10)
	New Song (3)
	Pearl In The Shell (7)
	Things Can Only Get Better (6)
	What Is Love (2)
Jones, Jesus	Devil You Know, The (10)
	International Bright Young Thing (7)
Jones, Jimmy	Good Timin' (1)
	Handy Man (3)
Jones, Oran 'Juice'	Rain, The (4)
Jones, Paul	High Time (4)
	I've Been A Bad Bad Boy (5)
Jones, Tammy	Let Me Try Again (5)

Group/Artiste	Title	Group/Artiste	Title
Jones, Tom	Boy From Nowhere, A (2)	Kaye, Danny	Wonderful Copenhagen (5)
	Burning Down The House (7)	KC & The Sunshine	Give It Up (1)
	Daughter Of Darkness (5)	Band	Please Don't Go (3)
	Delilah (2)		Queen Of Clubs (7)
	Detroit City (8)		That's The Way (I Like It) (4)
	Funny Familiar Forgotten	K-Ci & JoJo	All My Life (8)
	Feeling (7)	Keane	Bedshaped (10)
	Green Green Grass Of Home		Everybody's Changing (4)
	(1)		Somewhere Only We Know (3)
	Help Yourself (5)	Keating, Johnny	Don't That Beat All (8)
	I'll Never Fall In Love Again (2)	Keating, Ronan	I Hope You Dance (2)
	I'm Coming Home (2)		I Love It When We Do (5)
	It's Not Unusual (1)		If Tomorrow Never Comes (1)
	Kiss (5)		Life is A Rollercoaster (1)
	Love Me Tonight (9)		Long Goodbye, The (3)
	Mama Told Me Not To		Lost For Words (9)
	Come (4)		Lovin' Each Day (2)
	Sexbomb (3)		She Believes (In Me) (2)
	Till (2)		Way You Make Me Feel, The
	Without Love (10)		(6)
	Young New Mexican		We've Got Tonight (4)
	Puppeteer, The (6)		When You Say Nothing At All
Jones-Davies, Sue	OK? (10)		(1)
JT & The Big Family	Moments In Soul (7)	Keating, Ronan &	Last Thing On My Mind (5)
Judge Dread	Big Seven (8)	Leann Rimes	
	Je T'Aime (Moi Non Plus) (9)	Keating, Ronan &	Father And Son (2)
Junior	Another Step (Closer To You)	Yusuf Islam	
	(6)	Keely, Yvonne	If I Had Words (3)
	Mama Used To Say (7)	Keith Harris & Orville	Orville's Song (4)
Junior Senior	Move Your Feet (3)	Kelis	Caught Out There (4)
Justice, Jimmy	Ain't That Funny (8)		Milkshake (2)
	When My Little Girl Is Smiling		Trick Me (2)
	(9)	Kelis featuring	Millionaire (3)
Justified Ancients	It's Grim Up North (10)	Andre 3000	
Of Mu Mu		Keller, Jerry	Here Comes Summer (1)
JX	Son Of A Gun (remix) (6)	Kelly, Grace	True Love (4)
	There's Nothing I Won't Do (4)	Kelly, R	Be Careful (7)
JXL	Little Less Conversation, A (1)		Bump 'N' Grind (8)
K7	Come Baby Come (3)		Gotham City (9)
Kaci	I Think I Love You (10)		Happy People / U Saved Me (6)
Kajagoogoo	Big Apple (8)		I Believe I Can Fly (1)
	Ooh To Be Ah (7)		If I Could Turn Back The Hands
	Too Shy (1)		Of Time (3)
Kalin Twins	When (1)		Ignition (remix) (1)
Kallen, Kitty	Little Things Mean A Lot (1)		I'm Your Angel (3)
Kamen, Nick	Each Time You Break My Heart		Satisfy You (8)
	(5)		She's Got That Vibe (3)
Kamoze, Ini	Here Comes The Hotstepper		U Saved Me / Happy People (6)
	(4)		World's Greatest, The (4)
Kandi	Don't Think I'm Not (9)	Kelly, R featuring	Snake (10)
Kane, Eden	Boys Cry (8)	Big Trigger	
	Forget Me Not (3)	Ken Mackintosh	Creep (re-entry), The (10)
	Get Lost (10)	Orchestra	
	I Don't Know Why (7)	Ken Thorne	Theme From The Film The
	Well I Ask You (1)	Orchestra	Legion's Last Patrol (4)
Kaoma	Lambada (4)	Kenny	Bump, The (3)
Kasabian	LSF (10)		Fancy Pants (4)
Kate Robbins &	More Than In Love (2)		Julie Ann (10)
Beyond		Kenyon, Carol	Don't Waste My Time (8)
Katrina & The Waves	Love Shine A Light (3)	Kershaw, Nik	Don Quixote (10)
	Walking On Sunshine (8)		I Won't Let The Sun Go Down
Kavana	I Can Make You Feel Good (8)		On Me (2)
	MFEO (3)		Riddle, The (3)
Kay, Janet	Silly Games (2)		Wide Boy (9)
Kaye Sisters	Come Softly To Me (9)		Wouldn't It Be Good (4)
	Gotta Have Something In The	Keynotes	Memories Are Made Of This (5)
	Bank Frank (8)	Keys, Alicia	Fallin' (3)
	Gotta Have Something In The		Gangsta Lovin' (6)
	Bank Frank (8) with Frankie	Khan, Chaka	Ain't Nobody (8)
	Vaughan		Ain't Nobody (remix) (6)
	Paper Roses (7)		I Feel For You (1)

Group/Artiste	Title	Group/Artiste	Title
	I'm Every Woman (remix) (8)	Knight, Robert	Love On A Mountain Top (10)
Khia	My Neck My Back (Lick It) (4)	Knoc-Turn'al	Bad Intentions (4)
Kicks Like A Mule	Bouncer, The (7)	Kon Kan	I Beg Your Pardon (5)
Kid Creole & The	Annie I'm Not Your Daddy (2)	Kongos, John	He's Gonna Step On You Again
Coconuts	I'm a Wonderful Thing Baby (4)		(4)
	Me No Pop (32)		Tokoloshe Man (4)
	Stool Pigeon (7)	Kool & The Gang	Celebration (7)
Kidman, Nicole	Somethin' Stupid (1)		Cherish (4)
Kids From Fame	Hi-Fidelity (5)		Get Down On It (3)
	Starmaker (3)		Joanna / Tonight (2)
Killers	Mr Brightside (10)		Ladies Knight (9)
Kim, Andy	Rock Me Gently (2)		Ooh La La La (Let's Go
King	Alone Without You (8)		Dancin') (6)
	Love And Pride (2)		(When You Say You Love
King Brothers	Standing On The Corner (4)		Somebody) In The Heart (7)
	White Sport Coat, A (6)	Korgis	Everybody's Got To Learn
King, B B	When Love Comes To Town (6)		Sometime (5)
King, Ben E	Stand By Me (re-issue) (1)	Kosheen	All In My Head (7)
King, Carole	It Might As Well Rain Until		Hide U (6)
	September (3)	Kowdean	Dem Girlz (I Don't Know Why)
	It's Too Late (6)		(10)
King, Dave	Memories Are Made Of This (5)	Kraftwerk	Autobahn (11)
King, Diana	Shy Guy (2)		Computer Love / The Model
King, Jonathan	Everyone's Gone To The Moon		(re-entry) (1)
	(4)	Kramer, Billy J and	Bad To Me (1)
	Una Paloma Blanca (5)	The Dakotas	Do You Want To Know A Secret
King, Solomon	She Wears My Ring (3)		(2)
Kingston Trio	Tom Dooley (5)		From A Window (10)
Kinks	All Day And All Of The Night (2)		I'll Keep You Satisfied (4)
	Apeman (5)		Little Children (1)
	Autumn Almanac (3)	Kravitz, Lenny	Are You Gonna Go My Way (4)
	Dead End Street (5)		Fly Away (1)
	Dedicated Follower Of Fashion	Kris Kross	Jump (2)
	(4)	Kroeger, Chad	Hero (4)
	Lola (2)	Krush	House Arrest (3)
	See My Friend (10)	Kula Shaker	Govinda (7)
	Set Me Free (9)		Hey Dude (2)
	Sunny Afternoon (1)		Hush (2)
	Till The End Of The Day (8)		Sound Of Drums (3)
	Tired Of Waiting For You (1)		Tattva (4)
	Waterloo Sunset (2)	KWS	Please Don't Go / Game Boy
	You Really Got Me (1)		(1)
Kinney, Fern	Together We Are Beautiful (1)		Rock Your Baby (8)
Kinshasa Band	Black Superman (Muhammad	Kyu Sakamoto	Sukiyaki (6)
	Ali) (7)	La Belle Epoque	Black Is Black (2)
Kira	I'll Be Your Angel (9)	LA Mix	Check This Out (6)
Kirby, Kathy	Let Me Go Lover (10)	La Na Nee Nee Noo	Help (3)
	Secret Love (4)	Noo	
Kiss	Crazy Crazy Nights (4)	La Salle, Denise	My Toot Toot (6)
	God Gave Rock And Roll To	La Trec	Stay (2)
	You (4)	LaBelle, Patti	On My Own (2)
Kitt, Eartha	Under The Bridges Of Paris (7)	Lain	Battle (10)
K-Klass	Rhythm Is A Mystery (3)	Laine, Cleo	You'll Answer To Me (5)
KLF	America: What Time Is Love (4)	Laine, Frankie	Answer Me (1)
	Justified And Ancient (2)		Blowing Wild (2)
	Last Train To Trancentral (2)		Cool Water (2)
	3AM Eternal (1)		Granada (10)
	What Time Is Love (5)		Granada (re-entry) (9)
Klubbheads	Klubbhopping (10)		Hawkeye (7)
Knack	My Sharona (6)		Hey Joe (1)
Knight, Beverley	Come As You Are (9)		High Noon (Do Not Forsake
	Shoulda Woulda Coulda (10)		Me) (7)
Knight, Gladys	Baby Don't Change Your Mind		I Believe (1)
	(4)		Kid's Last Fight, The (3)
	Best Thing That Ever		My Friend (3)
	Happened To Me (7)		Rain Rain Rain (8)
	Licence To Kill (6)		Rawhide (1)
	Midnight Train To Georgia (10)		Sixteen Tons (10)
	Way We Were, The / Try To		Strange Lady In Town (6)
	Remember (4)		Sugarbush (8)
Knight, Jordan	Give It To You (5)		Sugarbush (re-entry) (8)

Group/Artiste	Title	Group/Artiste	Title
	There Must Be A Reason (9)		(Just Like) Starting Over (1)
	Where The Wind Blows (2)		Nobody Told Me (6)
	Woman In Love, A (1)		Power To The People (7)
Lake, Greg	I Believe In Father Christmas (2)		Woman (1)
Lambrettas	Poison Ivy (7)	Lennon, Julian	Saltwater (6)
Lancers	Let Me Go Lover (9)		Too Late For Goodbyes (6)
Landscape	Einstein A Go-Go (5)	Lennox, Annie	Little Bird / Love Song For A Vampire (3)
Lange	Drifting Away (9)		No More I Love Yous (2)
Lanza, Mario	Because You're Mine (3)		Walking On Broken Glass (8)
Las Ketchup	Ketchup Song (Asereje), The (1)		Why (5)
Lasgo	Alone (7)	Lenska, Rula	OK? (10)
	Something (4)	Leon Young String Chorale	Stranger On The Shore (2)
Lattisaw, Stacy	Jump To The Beat (3)	Leontiou, Kristian	Story Of My Life (9)
Lauper, Cyndi	Girls Just Want To Have Fun (2)	Lester, Ketty	Love Letters (4)
	Hey Now (Girls Just Want To Have Fun) (4)	Let Loose	Best In Me (8)
	I Drove All Night (7)		Crazy For You (2)
	Time After Time (3)		Make It With You (7)
Laurel & Hardy	Trail Of The Lonesome Pine, The (2)	Level 42	It's Over (10)
Laurie Lingo & The Dipsticks	Convoy G.B. (4)		Lessons In Love (3)
			Running In The Family (6)
Lavigne, Avril	Complicated (3)		Something About You (6)
	Don't Tell Me (5)		Sun Goes Down (Living It Up), The (10)
	I'm With You (7)		To Be With You Again (10)
	My Happy Ending (5)	Levert	Casanova (9)
	Sk8er Boi (8)	Lewie, Jona	Stop The Cavalry (3)
Lawrence, Lee	Crying In The Chapel (re-entry) (7)	Lewis, Donna	I Love You Always Forever (5)
		Lewis, Linda	It's In His Kiss (6)
Lawrence, Steve	Footsteps (4)	Lewis, Shaznay	Never Felt Like This Before (8)
Layo & Bushwacka	Love Story (Vs Finally) (8)	Leyton, John	Johnny Remember Me (1)
Layton, Lindy	Dub Be Good To Me (1)		Wild Wind (2)
Le Roc, Kele	Little Bit Of Lovin' (8)	Libertines	Can't Stand Me Now (2)
	My Love (8)		What Became Of The Likely Lads (9)
Leandros, Vicky	Come What May (2)	Liberty X	Got To Have Your Love (2)
Lee Lewis, Jerry	Breathless (8)		Don't Tell Me (5)
	Great Balls Of Fire (1)		Holding On For You (5)
	What'd I Say (10)		Jumpin' (6)
	Whole Lotta Shakin' Goin' On (8)		Just A Little (1)
			Thinking It Over (5)
Lee, Ann	2 Times (2)	Lieutenant Pigeon	Mouldy Old Dough (1)
Lee, Brenda	All Alone Am I (7)	Lifford	Please Don't Turn Me On (4)
	As Usual (5)	Lighthouse Family	High (4)
	Here Comes That Feeling (5)		(I Wish I Knew How It Would Feel To Be) Free / One (6)
	Losing You (10)		Lifted (4)
	Rockin' Around The Christmas Tree (6)		Lost In Space (6)
	Speak To Me Pretty (3)		Raincloud (6)
	Sweet Nothin's (4)	Lightning Seeds	3 Lions (1)
Lee, Leapy	Little Arrows (2)		3 Lions '98 (1)
Lee, Peggy	Fever (5)		You Showed Me (8)
	Mr Wonderful (5)	Lil Bow Wow	Bow Wow (That's My Name) (6)
Leeds United FC	Leeds United (10)	Lil' Kim	Lady Marmalade (1)
Leftfield	Afrika Shox (7)	Lil' Louis	French Kiss (2)
Lemar	Another Day (9)	Limahl	Never Ending Story (4)
	Dance (With U) (2)	Limerick, Alison	Where Love Lives (remix) (9)
	50:50 / Lullaby (5)	Limmie & The Family Cookin	Walkin' Miracle, A (6)
	If There's Any Justice (3)		
Lemon Pipers	Green Tambourine (7)		You Can Do Magic (3)
Len	Steal My Sunshine (8)	Limp Bizkit	Eat You Alive (10)
Lennon, John	Give Peace A Chance (2)		My Way (6)
	Happy Xmas (War Is Over) (4)		Rollin' (1)
	Happy Xmas (War Is Over) (re-entry) (2)		Take A Look Around (Theme From MI 2) (3)
	Imagine (6)	Lind, Bob	Elusive Butterfly (5)
	Imagine (re-entry) (1)	Lindisfarne	Fog On The Tyne (Revisited) (2)
	Imagine (re-issue) (3)		Lady Eleanor (3)
	Instant Karma (5)		Meet Me On The Corner (5)

Group/Artiste	Title
	Run For Home (10)
Linkin Park	High Voltage / Points Of Authority (9)
	In The End (8)
	Somewhere I Belong (10)
Linx	Intuition (7)
Lipps Inc	Funkytown (2)
Liquid Gold	Dance Yourself Dizzy (2)
	Substitute (8)
Lisa Left Eye Lopes	Never Be The Same Again (1)
Lisa Loeb	Stay (I Missed You) (6)
Lisa Marie Experience	Keep On Jumpin' (7)
Little Eva	Loco-Motion, The (2)
Little Richard	Baby Face (2)
	Girl Can't Help It, The (9)
	Good Golly Miss Molly (8)
	Long Tall Sally (3)
	Lucille (10)
Liverpool FC	Anfield Rap (Red Machine In Full Effect) (3)
	Pass And Move (It's The Liverpool Groove) (4)
Livin' Joy	Don't Stop Movin' (5)
	Dreamer (remix) (1)
	Follow The Rules (9)
Living In A Box	Blow The House Down (10)
	Living In A Box (5)
	Room In Your Heart (5)
Lizz E	Wishing On A Star (10)
Llorenna, Kelly	Tell It To My Heart (9)
	True Love Never Dies (re-issue) (7)
LMC vs U2	Take Me To The Clouds Above (1)
Lobo	Caribbean Disco Show, The (8)
	I'd Love You To Want Me (5)
	Me And You And A Dog Named Boo (4)
Lock 'N' Load	Blow Ya Mind (6)
Locklin, Hank	Please Help Me I'm Falling (9)
Lodge, John	Blue Guitar (8)
Logan, Johnny	Hold Me Now (2)
	What's Another Year (1)
Loggins, Kenny	Footloose (6)
Lolly	Big Boys Don't Cry / Rockin' Robin (10)
	Mickey (4)
	Viva La Radio (6)
London Boys	London Nights (2)
	Requiem (4)
London Philharmonic Orchestra	True Love Ways (8)
Londonbeat	I've Been Thinking About You (2)
Long John Baldry	Let The Heartaches Begin (1)
	Mexico (15)
Lonyo	Summer Of Love (8)
Look	I Am The Beat (6)
Loon	I Need A Girl (Part One) (4)
Lopez, Jennifer	Ain't It Funny (4)
	Ain't It Funny (remix) (4)
	Baby I Love You (3)
	If You Had My Love (4)
	I'm Gonna Be Alright (3)
	I'm Real (4)
	Jenny From The Block (3)
	Love Don't Cost A Thing (1)
	Play (3)
	Waiting For Tonight (5)
Lopez, Jennifer featuring LL Cool J	All I Have (2)

Group/Artiste	Title
Lopez, Trini	If I Had A Hammer (4)
Lord Rockingham's XI	Hoots Mon (1)
Loren, Sophia	Goodness Gracious Me (4)
Lorraine & Lose	Megablast / Don't Make Me Wait (6)
Los Bravos	Black Is Black (2)
Los Del Rio	Macarena (2)
Los Indios Tabajaras	Maria Elena (5)
Los Lobos	La Bamba (1)
Lostprophets	Last Train Home (8)
Lou Busch	Zambesi (2)
Lou, Bonnie	Tennessee Wig Walk (4)
Louchie Lou	Cecilia (4)
	Shout (7)
Louise	Arms Around The World (4)
	Let's Go Round Again (10)
	Light Of My Life (8)
	Naked (4)
	One Kiss From Heaven (9)
	Pandora's Kiss (5)
	Stuck In The Middle (4)
	2 Faced (3)
	Undivided Love (5)
Love Affair	Bringing On Back The Good Times (3)
	Day Without Love, A (6)
	Everlasting Love (1)
	Rainbow Valley (5)
Love City Groove	Love City Groove (7)
Love Inc	Broken Bones (8)
	You're A Superstar (7)
Love Sculpture	Sabre Dance (5)
Love Unlimited Orchestra	Love's Theme (10)
Lovich, Lene	Lucky Number (3)
Lovin' Spoonful	Daydream (2)
	Summer In The City (8)
Lowe, Jim	Green Door (8)
Lowe, Nick	I Love The Sound Of Breaking Glass (7)
Lucid	I Can't Help Myself (7)
Ludacris	One Minute Man (10)
	Rollout (My Business) (20)
Luhrmann, Baz	Everybody's Free (To Wear Sunscreen) (1)
Lulu	Boat That I Row, The (6)
	Boom Bang-A-Bang (2)
	I'm A Tiger (9)
	Leave A Little Love (8)
	Man Who Sold The World, The (3)
	Me, The Peaceful Heart (9)
	Relight My Fire (1)
	Shout (7)
	Shout (8) remake
	We've Got Tonight (4)
Luman, Bob	Let's Think About Living (6)
Lumidee	Never Leave You (Uh Oooh Uh Oooh) (2)
Luniz	I Got 5 On It (3)
Luvvers	Shout (7)
LV	Gangsta's Paradise (1)
Lymon, Frankie & Teenagers	Baby Baby (4)
	Why Do Fools Fall In Love (1)
Lynch, Kenny	Up On The Roof (10)
	You Can Never Stop Me Loving You (10)
Lynch, Liam	United States Of Whatever (10)
Lynn, Tami	I'm Gonna Run Away From You (4)
Lynn, Vera	Auf Wiedersehen (10)

M
U
S
I
C

P
O
P

Group/Artiste	Title
	Do Wah Diddy Diddy (1)
	5-4-3-2-1 (5)
	Fox On The Run (5)
	Ha Ha Said The Clown (4)
	If You Gotta Go Go Now (2)
	Just Like A Woman (10)
	Mighty Quinn (1)
	My Name Is Jack (8)
	Pretty Flamingo (1)
	Ragamuffin Man (8)
	Semi-Detached Suburban Mr James (2)
	Sha La La (3)
Manfred Mann's Earth Band	Blinded By The Light (6)
	Davy's On The Road Again (6)
	Joybringer (9)
Manhattan Transfer	Chanson D'Amour (1)
Manhattans	Hurt (4)
	Kiss And Say Goodbye (4)
Manic Street Preachers	Australia (7)
	Design For Life, A (2)
	Everything Must Go (5)
	Found That Soul (9)
	If You Tolerate This Your Children Will Be Next (1)
	Kevin Carter (9)
	Love Of Richard Nixon, The (2)
	Masses Against The Classes, The (1)
	So Why So Sad (8)
	Theme From M.A.S.H. (Suicide Is Painless) (7)
	There By The Grace Of God (6)
	You Stole The Sun From My Heart (5)
Manilow, Barry	I Wanna Do It With You (8)
Mann Singers, Johnny	Up Up And Away (6)
Manson, Marilyn	Tainted Love (5)
Mansun	I Can Only Disappoint U (8)
	Legacy EP (7)
	She Makes My Nose Bleed (9)
Mantovani & His Orchestra	Cara Mia (1)
	Moulin Rouge (1)
	Moulin Rouge (re-entry) (10)
	Swedish Rhapsody (2)
	When You Lose The One You Love (7)
	White Christmas (6)
Mantronix	Got To Have Your Love (4)
	Take Your Time (10)
Manuel and The Music Of The Mountains	Rodrigo's Guitar Concerto De Aranjuez (3)
Marbles	Only One Woman (5)
Marcels	Blue Moon (1)
Marie, Kelly	Feels Like I'm In Love (1)
Marie, Teena	Behind The Groove (6)
Marillion	Incommunicado (6)
	Kayleigh (2)
	Lavender (5)
	You're Gone (7)
Marilyn	Calling Your Name (4)
Marino Marini & His Quartet	Come Prima (2)
Marley, Bob	Sun Is Shining (3)
Marley, Bob, & The Wailers	Buffalo Soldier (4)
	Could You Be Loved (5)
	Iron Lion Zion (5)

Group/Artiste	Title
	Is This Love (9)
	Jamming / Punky Reggae Party (9)
	No Woman No Cry (re-entry) (8)
	One Love / People Get Ready (5)
Marlin, Lene	Sitting Down Here (5)
Marmalade	Baby Make It Soon (9)
	Falling Apart At The Seams (9)
	Lovin' Things (6)
	My Little One (6)
	Ob-La-Di Ob-La-Da (1)
	Radancer (6)
	Rainbow (3)
	Reflections Of My Life (3)
Maroon 5	She Will Be Loved (4)
	This Love (3)
Marrs	Pump Up The Volume / Anitina (The First Time) (1)
Marsden, Gerry	Ferry 'Cross The Mersey (1)
Marsh, Kym	Come On Over (10)
	Cry (2)
Marsha	Piece Of My Heart (7)
Marshall Hain	Dancing In The City (3)
Martell, Lena	One Day At A Time (1)
Martha & The Muffins	Echo Beach (10)
Martika	I Feel The Earth Move (7)
	Love ... Thy Will Be Done (9)
	Toy Soldiers (5)
Martin, Billie Ray	Your Loving Arms (remix) (6)
Martin, Dean	Gentle On My Mind (2)
	Kiss (9)
	Kiss (re-entry) (5)
	Let Me Go Lover (3)
	Memories Are Made Of This (1)
	Naughty Lady Of Shady Lane (5)
	Return To Me (2)
	Sway (6)
	That's Amore (2)
	Under The Bridges Of Paris (6)
	Volare (2)
Martin, Juan	Love Theme From The Thornbirds (10)
Martin, Marilyn	Separate Lives (4)
Martin, Ricky	Livin' La Vida Loca (1)
	Nobody Wants To Be Lonely (4)
	Private Emotion (9)
	She Bangs (3)
	(Un Dos Tres) Maria (6)
Martin, Tony	Stranger In Paradise (6)
	Walk Hand In Hand (2)
Martindale, Wink	Deck Of Cards (re-entry) (5)
Martino, Al	Here In My Heart (1)
	Now (3)
	Rachel (10)
	Spanish Eyes (re-issue) (5)
	Story Of Tina, The (10)
	Take My Heart (9)
	Wanted (re-entry) (4)
Marvin, Hank	Living Doll (5)
	Throw Down The Line (7)
Marvin, Lee	Wand'rin' Star (1)
Marx, Richard	Hazard (3)
	Right Here Waiting (2)
Mary, Mary	Shackles (Praise You) (5)
Mase	Feel So Good (10)
	Take Me There (7)
	Top Of The World (2)

Group/Artiste	Title	Group/Artiste	Title
MASH	Theme From M.A.S.H. (Suicide Is Painless) (1)		Rock Your Baby (1)
Massive Attack	Teardrop (10)	McCutcheon, Martine	I'm Over You (2)
Master Of Ceremonies	Do You Really Like It (1)		I've Got You (6)
			On The Radio (7)
Matchbox	When You Ask About Love (4)		Perfect Moment (1)
Matchroom Mob	Snooker Loopy (6)		Talking In Your Sleep / Love Me (6)
Mathis, Johnny	Certain Smile, A (4)	McDonald, Jane	Cruise Into Christmas (10)
	I'm Stone In Love With You (10)	McDonald, Michael	On My Own (2)
	My Love For You (9)	McFadden, Brian	Irish Son (6)
	Someone (6)		Real To Me (1)
	Too Much Too Little Too Late (3)	McFadden & Whitehead	Ain't No Stoppin' Us Now (5)
	When A Child Is Born (1)	McFerrin, Bobby	Don't Worry Be Happy (2)
Matthews Southern Comfort	Woodstock (1)	McFly	Five Colours In Her Hair (1)
			Obviously (1)
Maughan, Susan	Bobby's Girl (3)		Room On The 3rd Floor (5)
Maureen	Say A Little Prayer (10)		That Girl (3)
Mavericks	Dance The Night Away (4)	McGregor, Ewan	Choose Life (6)
Maxi Jazz	My Culture (9)	McGregor, Freddie	Just Don't Want To Be Lonely (9)
Maxx	Get-A-Way (4)		
	No More (I Can't Stand It) (8)	McGuinness Flint	Malt And Barley Blues (5)
May Orchestra, Billy	Main Title Theme From Man With The Golden Arm (9)		When I'm Dead And Gone (2)
		McGuire, Barry	Eve Of Destruction (3)
May, Brian	Driven By You (6)	McKee, Maria	Show Me Heaven (1)
	Too Much Love Will Kill You (5)	McKenzie, Gisele	Seven Lonely Days (re-entry) (6)
May, Simon	Summer Of My Life (7)		
Maya	Feel It (1)	McKenzie, Scott	San Francisco (1)
	Hammer To the Heart (6)	McLachlan, Craig	Mona (2)
	If You Buy This Record Your Life Will Be Better (3)	McLachlan, Sarah	Silence (remixes) (3)
		McLaren, Malcolm	Buffalo Gals (9)
Mazelle, Kym	Wait (7)		Double Dutch (3)
M-Beat	Incredible (remix) (8)	McLean, Bitty	Dedicated To The One I Love (6)
MC Hammer	Addam's Groove (4)		
	Have You Seen Her (8)		Here I Stand (10)
	Pray (8)		It Keep Rainin' (Tears From Eyes) (2)
	U Can't Touch This (3)	McLean, Don	American Pie (2)
MC Mario	Supermarioland (8)		Crying (1)
MC Miker G	Holiday Rap (6)		Vincent (1)
MC Neat	Little Bit Of Luck, A (9)	McNeal, Lutricia	Ain't That Just The Way (6)
MC Parker	Thunderbirds Are Go (5)		Someone Loves You Honey (9)
MC Sar	Another Night (2)		Stranded (3)
	Run Away (6)	McTell, Ralph	Streets Of London (2)
MC Tunes	Only Rhyme That Bites, The (10)	Mead, Abigail	Full Metal Jacket (I Wanna Be Your Drill Instructor) (2)
McAlmont & Butler	Yes (8)		
McCampbell Brothers	Roses Are Red (8)	Meat Loaf	Bat Out Of Hell (re-issue) (8)
McCartney, Paul	Another Day (2)		Dead Ringer For Love (5)
	Band On The Run (3)		I'd Do Anything For Love (But I Won't Do That) (1)
	Coming Up (2)		
	Ebony And Ivory (1)		I'd Lie For You (And That's The Truth) (2)
	Ferry 'Cross The Mersey (1)		
	Girl Is Mine, The (8)		Not A Dry Eye In The House (7)
	Jet (7)		
	Live And Let Die (9)	Meco	Star Wars Theme / Cantina Band (7)
	My Love (9)		
	No More Lonely Nights (2)	Medeiros, Glenn	Nothing's Gonna Change My Love For You (1)
	Once Upon A Long Ago (10)		
	Pipes Of Peace (1)	Medicine Head	One And One Is One (3)
	Say Say Say (2)	Medley, Bill	(I've Had) The Time Of My Life (6)
	Waterfalls (9)		
	We All Stand Together (3)		(I've Had) The Time Of My Life (re-entry) (8)
	Wonderful Christmastime (6)		
McCoo, Marilyn	You Don't Have To Be A Star (To Be In My Show) (7)	Medwin, Michael	Signature Tune Of 'The Army Game', The (5)
McCoy, Van	Hustle, The (3)	Meehan, Tony	Applejack (4)
	Shuffle, The (4)		Diamonds (1)
McCoys	Hang On Sloopy (5)		Scarlett O'Hara (2)
McCrae, George	I Can't Leave You Alone (9)	Megaman	No Good 4 Me (6)
	It's Been So Long (4)	Meja	Private Emotion (9)

M
U
S
I
C

P
O
P

Group/Artiste	Title	Group/Artiste	Title
Mel & Kim	F.L.M. (7)		Star People '97 (2)
	Respectable (1)		Too Funky (4)
	Rockin' Around The Christmas Tree (3)		Waltz Away Dreaming (10)
	Showing Out (Get Fresh At The Weekend) (3)		You Have Been Loved / The Strangest Thing '97 (2)
	That's The Way It Is (10)	Michel, Pras	Another One Bites The Dust (5)
Melanie	Brand New Key (4)		Ghetto Superstar That Is What
	Ruby Tuesday (9)		You Are (2)
Melle Mel	White Lines (Don't Do It) (7)	Michell, Keith	Captain Beaky / Wilfred The Weasel (5)
Mellomen	Mambo Italiano (1)	Michelle	All This Time (1)
	Where Will The Baby's Dimple Be (6)	Michie One	Cecilia (4)
Mellor, Will	When I Need You (5)		Shout (7)
Melua, Katie	Closest Thing To Crazy, The (10)	Middle Of The Road	Chirpy Chirpy Cheep Cheep (1)
			Soley Soley (5)
Melvin, Harold	Don't Leave Me This Way (5)		Tweedle Dee Tweedle Dum (2)
	If You Don't Know Me By Now (9)	Midler, Bette	From A Distance (6)
			Wind Beneath My Wings (5)
Men At Work	Down Under (1)	Midnight Oil	Beds Are Burning (re-issue) (6)
Men Without Hats	Safety Dance, The (6)	Midnight Star	Midas Touch (8)
Menswear	Being Brave (10)	Mighty Morphin	Anything For You (10)
Mental As Anything	Live It Up (3)	Power Rangers	
Mercury, Freddie	Great Pretender, The (4)	Migil Five	Mockingbird Hill (10)
	In My Defence (8)	Mike & The	Living Years, The (2)
	Living On My Own (1)	Mechanics	
	Love Kills (10)	Mike Berry &	Don't You Think It's Time (6)
Mercury, Freddy	Barcelona (2)	The Outlaws	
	Barcelona (re-issue) (2)	Miles, John	Music (3)
Meri Wilson	Telephone Man (6)		Slow Down (10)
Merlin	Who's In The House (8)	Miles, Robert	Children (2)
Merlin & Antonia	Megablast / Don't Make Me Wait (6)		Fable (7)
			One And One (3)
Merseybeats	I Think Of You (5)	Miles-Kingston, Paul	Pie Jesu (3)
Merseys	Sorrow (4)	Milian, Christina	AM to PM (3)
Metallica	Enter Sandman (5)		Dip It Low (2)
	Nothing Else Matters (6)		It's All Gravy (9)
	St Anger (9)		When You Look At Me (3)
	Until It Sleeps (5)	Milian, Christina	Whatever U Want (9)
Method Man	Hit 'Em High (The Monstars' Anthem) (8)	featuring Joe Budden	
		Milk & Honey	Hallelujah (5)
	I'll Be There For You – You're All I Need To Get By (10)	Milk Inc	In My Eyes (9)
			Walk On Water (10)
Miami Sound Machine	Anything For You (10)	Milky	Just The Way You Are (8)
	Can't Stay Away From You (7)	Millard Thomas	Banana Boat Song (2)
	Dr Beat (6)	Miller Band, Steve	Abracadabra (2)
	1-2-3 (9)		Joker, The (1)
Michael Reed Orchestra	Music Of Torvill And Dean EP, The (9)	Miller, Frankie	Darlin' (6)
		Miller, Gary	Robin Hood (10)
Michael, George	Amazing (4)	Miller, Ned	From A Jack To A King (2)
	As (4)	Miller, Roger	King Of The Road (1)
	Careless Whisper (1)	Milli Vanilli	Girl I'm Gonna Miss You (2)
	Different Corner, A (1)		Girl You Know It's True (3)
	Don't Let The Sun Go Down On Me (1)	Millie	My Boy Lollipop (2)
		Mills Brothers	Glow Worm (10)
	Faith (2)	Mills, Garry	Look For A Star (7)
	Fast Love (1)	Mills, Stephanie	Never Knew Love Like This Before (4)
	Five Live EP (1)		
	Flawless (Go To The City) (8)	Mindbenders	Game Of Love (2)
	Freeek! (7)		Groovy Kind Of Love, A (2)
	I Knew You Were Waiting (For Me) (1)		Um Um Um Um Um Um (5)
		Minerbi, Marcello	Zorba's Dance (6)
	I Want Your Sex (3)	Minnelli, Liza	Losing My Mind (6)
	If I Told You That (9)	Minogue, Dannii	All I Wanna Do (4)
	Jesus To A Child (1)		Don't Wanna Lose This Feeling (5)
	Older / I Can Make You Love Me (3)		I Begin To Wonder (2)
	One More Try (8)		Jump To The Beat (8)
	Outside (2)		Love And Kisses (8)
	Praying For Time (6)		Put The Needle On It (7)
	Spinning The Wheel (2)		This Is It (10)

Group/Artiste	Title	Group/Artiste	Title
	Who Do You Love Now (Stringer) (3)		Heartaches By The Number (re-entry) (5)
Minogue, Dannii vs Flower Power	You Won't Forget About Me (7)		Knee Deep In The Blues (3)
Minogue, Kylie	Better The Devil You Know (2)		Look At That Girl (1)
	Can't Get You Out Of My Head (1)		Pretty Little Black-Eyed Susie (2)
	Chocolate (6)		Rock-A-Billy (1)
	Come Into My World (8)		She Wears Red Feathers (1)
	Confide In Me (2)	Mixmaster	Singing The Blues (1)
	Especially For You (1)	Mixtures	Grand Piano (9)
	Give Me Just A Little More Time (2)	Mizell, Hank	Pushbike Song, The (2)
	Got To Be Certain (2)	MN8	Jungle Rock (3)
	Hand On Your Heart (1)		Happy (8)
	I Believe In You (2)		If You Only Let Me In (6)
	I Should Be So Lucky (1)		I've Got A Little Something For You (2)
	If You Were With Me Now (4)	Mobiles	Drowning In Berlin (9)
	In Your Eyes (3)	Moby	Go (10)
	Je Ne Sais Pas Pourquoi (2)		James Bond Theme (Moby's Re-Version) (8)
	Kids (2)		Porcelain (5)
	Loco-Motion, The (2)	Modern Romance	Ay Ay Ay Ay Moosey (10)
	Love At First Sight (2)		Best Years Of Our Lives (4)
	Never Too Late (4)		High Life (8)
	On A Night Like This (2)		Walking In The Rain (7)
	Please Stay (10)	Modern Talking	Brother Louie (4)
	Red Blooded Woman (5)	Modjo	Lady (Hear Me Tonight) (1)
	Shocked (6)	Modugno, Domenico	Volare (10)
	Slow (1)	Mojos	Everything's Alright (9)
	Spinning Around (1)	Molella	If You Wanna Party (9)
	Step Back In Time (4)	Moloko	Familiar Feeling (10)
	Tears On My Pillow (1)		Sing It Back (4)
	What Do I Have To Do (6)		Time Is Now, The (2)
	Wouldn't Change A Thing (2)	Moments	Dolly My Love (10)
Minott, Sugar	Good Thing Going (We've Got A Good Thing Going) (4)		Girls (3)
			Jack In The Box (7)
Miracles	Love Machine (3)	Monica	Boy Is Mine, The (2)
	Tears Of A Clown, The (1)		First Night, The (6)
	Tracks Of My Tears, The (9)	Monkees	Alternate Title (2)
Mirage	Jack Mix II / III (4)		Daydream Believer (5)
	Jack Mix IV (8)		I'm A Believer (1)
Mirror, Danny	I Remember Elvis Presley (The King Is Dead) (4)		Little Bit Me A Little Bit You, A (3)
Missy Elliott	4 My People (5)	Monro, Matt	My Kind Of Girl (5)
	Get UR Freak On (4)		Portrait Of My Love (3)
	One Minute Man (10)		Softly As I Leave You (10)
	Pass That Dutch (10)		Walk Away (4)
	Rain (Supa Dupa Fly), The (16)		Yesterday (8)
	Work It (6)	Monroe, Gerry	My Prayer (9)
Missy Elliott featuring Ludacris	Gossip Folks (9)		Sally (4)
Missy 'Misdemeanor' Elliott	Don't You Think It's Time (6)	Montenegro, Hugo	Good The Bad And The Ugly, The (1)
		Montez, Chris	Let's Dance (2)
Mis-Teeq	All I Want (2)		Let's Dance (re-entry) (9)
	B With Me (5)		More I See You, The (3)
	Can't Get It Back (8)		Some Kinda Fun (10)
	One Night Stand (5)	Monty Python	Always Look On The Bright Side Of Life (3)
	Roll On / This Is How We Do It (7)	Moody Blues	Go Now (1)
	Scandalous (2)		Nights In White Satin (re-entry) (9)
	Why (8)		Question (2)
Mitch Miller	Yellow Rose Of Texas (2)	Moony	Dove (I'll Be Loving You) (9)
Mitchell, Des	(Welcome) To The Dance (5)	Moore, Dorothy	Misty Blue (5)
Mitchell, Guy	Chicka Boom (5)	Moore, Gary	Out In The Fields (5)
	Chicka Boom (re-entry) (4)		Parisienne Walkways (8)
	Cloud Lucky Seven (2)	Moore, Mandy	Candy (6)
	Cuff Of My Shirt (9)	Moore, Melba	This Is It (9)
	Dime And A Dollar (8)	Moore, Tina	Never Gonna Let You Go (7)
	Dime And A Dollar (re-entry) (8)	MOP	Ante Up (7)
	Feet Up (2)		Cold As Ice (4)

Group/Artiste	Title	Group/Artiste	Title
Morales, David	Needin' U (8)		Lean On Me (7)
More Fire Crew	Oi (8)		L-L-Lucy (10)
Morgan, Debelah	Dance With Me (10)		Lonely This Christmas (1)
Morgan, Jane	Day The Rains Came, The (1)		Moonshine Sally (10)
Morissette, Alanis	Hands Clean (12)		Oh Boy (1)
	Head Over Feet (7)		Rocket (6)
	Thank U (5)		Secrets That You Keep, The (3)
Morricone, Ennio	Chi Mai (Theme From TV		Show Me You're A Woman (8)
	Series The Life And Times Of		Tiger Feet (1)
	Lloyd George) (2)	Mudlarks	Book Of Love (8)
Morris Minor	Stutter Rap (No Sleep 'Til		Lollipop (2)
	Bedtime) (4)	Mullen, Larry	Theme From Mission
Morrison, Mark	Crazy (remix) (6)		Impossible (7)
	Horny (5)	Mullins, Shawn	Lullaby (9)
	Moan And Groan (7)	Mumba, Samantha	Always Come Back To Your
	Return Of The Mack (1)		Love (3)
	Trippin' (8)		Baby Come On Over (5)
Morrissey	Everyday Is Like Sunday (9)		Body II Body (5)
	First Of The Gang To Die (6)		Gotta Tell You (2)
	I Have Forgiven Jesus (10)		I'm Right Here (5)
	Interesting Drug (9)		Lately (6)
	Irish Blood English Heart (3)	Mungo Jerry	Alright Alright Alright (3)
	Last Of The Famous		Baby Jump (re-entry) (1)
	International Playboys (6)		In The Summertime (1)
	Let Me Kiss You (8)		Lady Rose (5)
	More You Ignore Me The	Muppets	Halfway Down The Stairs (7)
	Closer I Get, The (8)	Murray, Ruby	Evermore (3)
	Suedehead (5)		Goodbye Jimmy Goodbye (10)
Mortimer, Bob	I'm A Believer (3)		Happy Days And Lonely Nights
Moten, Wendy	Come In Out Of The Rain (8)		(6)
Motorhead	Golden Years EP, The (8)		Heartbeat (3)
	Motorhead Live (6)		If Anyone Finds This I Love You
	St Valentine's Day Massacre		(4)
	EP (5)		I'll Come When You Call (6)
Motors	Airport (4)		Let Me Go Lover (5)
Mott The Hoople	All The Way From Memphis		Softly Softly (1)
(10)		Muse	Time Is Running Out (8)
	All The Young Dudes (3)	Musical Youth	Never Gonna Give You Up (6)
	Roll Away The Stones (8)		Pass The Dutchie (1)
Mouskouri, Nana	Only Love (2)	Mya	Case Of The Ex (3)
Mousse T	Horny (2)		Ghetto Superstar That Is What
	Sexbomb (3)		You Are (2)
Mousse T featuring	Is It Cos I'm Cool (9)		Lady Marmalade (1)
Emma Lanford			Take Me There (7)
Mouth	I See A Star (8)	Myers, Billie	Kiss The Rain (4)
Move	Blackberry Way (1)	Myles, Alannah	Black Velvet (2)
	Brontosaurus (7)	N Sync	Bye Bye Bye (3)
	California Man (7)		Girlfriend (2)
	Fire Brigade (3)		I Want You Back (5)
	Flowers In The Rain (2)		It's Gonna Be Me (9)
	I Can Hear The Grass Grow (5)		Pop (9)
	Night Of Fear (2)		Tearin' Up My Heart (9)
Moyet, Alison	All Cried Out (8)	Nail, Jimmy	Ain't No Doubt (1)
	Is This Love? (3)		Crocodile Shoes (4)
	Love Letters (4)		Love Don't Live Here Anymore
	Love Resurrection (10)		(3)
	That Ole Devil Called Love (2)	Nana	Body Groove (3)
	Weak In The Presence Of	Napoleon XIV	They're Coming To Take Me
	Beauty (6)		Away Ha-Haaa! (4)
Mr Bean	(I Want To Be) Elected (9)	Narada	Divine Emotions (8)
Mr Big	Romeo (4)	Narada Michael	I Shoulda Loved Ya (8)
	To Be With You (3)	Walden	
Mr Blobby	Mr Blobby (1)	Narcotic Thrust	I Like It (9)
Mr Bloe	Groovin' With Mr Bloe (2)	Nash, Johnny	Cupid (6)
Mr Hankey	Mr Hankey The Christmas Poo		Hold Me Tight (5)
	(4)		I Can See Clearly Now (5)
Mr Mister	Broken Wings (4)		Tears On My Pillow (1)
Mr Oizo	Flat Beat (1)		There Are More Questions
Mr President	Coco Jamboo (8)		Than Answers (9)
Mud	Cat Crept In, The (2)		You Got Soul (6)
	Dyna-Mite (4)	Nashville Teens	Google Eye (10)

Group/Artiste	Title	Group/Artiste	Title
	Tobacco Road (6)		Step By Step (2)
Nat 'King' Cole	Because You're Mine (6)		This One's For The Children (9)
	Because You're Mine (re-entry) (10)		Tonight (3)
			You Got It (The Right Stuff) (1)
	Blossom Fell, A (3)	New Order	Blue Monday (re-entry) (9)
	Can't I (9)		Blue Monday (remix) (3)
	Can't I (re-entry) (6)		Crystal (8)
	Can't I (re-entry) (10)		Regret (4)
	Dear Lonely Hearts (4)		True Faith (4)
	Dreams Can Tell A Lie (10)		True Faith (remix) (9)
	Faith Can Move Mountains (re-entry) (10)	New Power Generation	Gett Off (4)
			My Name Is Prince (7)
	I Get So Lonely (5)		Sexy MF / Strollin' (4)
	I Get So Lonely (re-entry) (10)	New Radicals	You Get What You Give (5)
	Mother Nature And Father Time (7)	New Seekers	Beg Steal Or Borrow (2)
			Circles (4)
	Pretend (2)		I Get A Little Sentimental Over You (5)
	Ramblin' Rose (5)		
	Smile (2)		I'd Like To Teach The World To Sing (1)
	Somewhere Along The Way (3)		
	Tenderly (10)		Never Ending Song Of Love (2)
	That's You (10)		You Won't Find Another Fool Like Me (1)
	Too Young To Go Steady (8)		
	When I Fall In Love (2)	New Vaudeville Band	Peek-A-Boo (7)
	When I Fall In Love (re-issue) (4)		Winchester Cathedral (4)
Natasha	Iko Iko (10)	New World	Sister Jane (9)
Nayler, Maria	One And One (3)		Tom Tom Turnaround (6)
Nazareth	Bad Bad Boy (10)	Newbeats	Run Baby Run (10)
	Broken Down Angel (9)	Newley, Anthony	And The Heavens Cried (6)
N'Dour, Youssou	7 Seconds (3)		Do You Mind (1)
Negro, Joey	Must Be The Music (8)		If She Should Come To You (4)
Neil	Hole In My Shoe (2)		I've Waited So Long (3)
Nelly	Dilemma (1)		Personality (6)
	Flap Your Wings / My Place (1)		Strawberry Fair (3)
	Hot In Herre (4)		Why (1)
	(Hot S**t) Country Grammar (7)	Newton-John, Olivia	Banks Of The Ohio (6)
	Ride Wit Me (3)		Grease Megamix (3)
Nelly & Christina Aguilera	Tilt Ya Head Back (5)		Hopelessly Devoted To You (2)
			If Not For You (7)
Nelly / P Diddy / Murphy Lee	Shake Ya Tailfeather (10)		Little More Love, A (4)
			Physical (7)
Nelly featuring Justin Timberlake	Work It (7)		Sam (6)
			Summer Nights (1)
Nelson Riddle & His Orchestra	Learnin' The Blues (2)		Xanadu (1)
			You're The One That I Want (1)
Nelson, Phyllis	Move Closer (1)		You're The One That I Want (re-issue) (4)
Nelson, Ricky	Hello Mary Lou / Travellin' Man (2)		
		Nicholas, Paul	Dancing With The Captain (8)
	It's Late (3)		Grandma's Party (9)
	Poor Little Fool (4)	Nickelback	How You Remind Me (4)
	Someday (9)		Someday (6)
Nelson, Sandy	Let There Be Drums (3)		Too Bad (9)
	Teen Beat (9)	Nicole	Little Peace, A (1)
Nelson, Shelley	Here's Where The Story Ends (7)	Nigel & Marvin	Follow Da Leader (5)
		Nightcrawlers	Push The Feeling On (remix) (3)
Nena	99 Red Balloons (1)		Surrender Your Love (7)
NERD	She Wants To Move (5)	Nightingale, Maxine	Right Back Where We Started From (8)
Nevil, Robbie	C'est La Vie (3)		
Neville, Aaron	Don't Know Much (2)	Nilsson	Without You (1)
Nevins, Jason	It's Like That (1)	Nina & Frederick	Little Donkey (3)
Nevins, Jason / UKNY featuring Holly James	I'm In Heaven (9)	Nina Sky	Move Ya Body (6)
		911	All I Want Is You (4)
			Bodyshakin' (3)
New Edition	Candy Girl (1)		Day We Find Love, The (4)
New Kids On The Block	Cover Girl (4)		Don't Make Me Wait (10)
	Hangin' Tough (1)		How Do You Want Me To Love You? (10)
	If You Go Away (9)		
	I'll Be Loving You (Forever) (5)		Journey, The (3)
	Let's Try Again / Didn't I Blow Your Mind (8)		Little Bit More, A (1)
			More Than A Woman (2)

M
U
S
I
C

P
O
P

Group/Artiste	Title	Group/Artiste	Title
	Party People ... Friday Night (5)		Love Really Hurts Without You (2)
	Private Number (3)		Red Light Spells Danger (2)
Nine Stories	Stay (I Missed You) (6)		Suddenly (4)
1910 Fruitgum Co	Simon Says (2)		When The Going Gets Tough The Tough Get Going (1)
Nirvana	Come As You Are (9)		
	Heart-Shaped Box (5)	Oceanic	Insanity (3)
	Smells Like Teen Spirit (7)	O'Connor, Des	Careless Hands (6)
N-Joi	Anthem (8)		I Pretend (1)
No Doubt	Don't Speak (1)		1-2-3 O'Leary (4)
	Hey Baby (2)		Skye Boat Song, The (10)
	Just A Girl (re-issue) (3)	O'Connor, Hazel	D-Days (10)
No Mercy	Please Don't Go (4)		Eighth Day (5)
	Where Do You Go (2)		Will You (8)
Nolans	Attention To Me (9)	O'Connor, Sinead	Nothing Compares 2 U (1)
	Gotta Pull Myself Together (9)	O'Donnell, Daniel	Give A Little Love (7)
	I'm In The Mood For Dancing (3)	Odyssey	Going Back To My Roots (4)
Nomad	(I Wanna Give You) Devotion (2)		If You're Looking For A Way Out (6)
North & South	I'm A Man Not A Boy (7)		Inside Out (3)
Notorious BIG	Hypnotize (10)		Native New Yorker (5)
	Mo Money Mo Problems (6)		Use It Up And Wear It Out (1)
N-Trance	Da Ya Think I'm Sexy? (7)	Off-Shore	I Can't Take The Power (7)
	Forever (6)	Offspring	Original Prankster (6)
	Set You Free (remix) (2)		Pretty Fly (For A White Guy) (1)
	Set You Free (2nd remix) (4)		Why Don't You Get A Job? (2)
	Stayin' Alive (2)	Ohio Express	Yummy Yummy Yummy (5)
Nu Generation	In Your Arms (Rescue Me) (8)	O'Jays	Love Train (9)
Nu Shooz	I Can't Wait (2)	Ol' Dirty Bastard	Ghetto Superstar That Is What You Are (2)
Numan, Gary	Cars (1)		
	Complex (6)	Oldfield, Mike	In Dulce Jubilo / On Horseback (4)
	I Die: You Die (6)		
	She's Got Claws (6)		Moonlight Shadow (4)
	We Are Glass (5)		Portsmouth (3)
	We Take Mystery (To Bed) (9)		Sentinel (10)
Oakenfold	Starry-Eyed Surprise (6)	Olive	You're Not Alone (1)
Oakey, Phil	Together In Electric Dreams (3)	Oliver	Good Morning Starshine (6)
Oasis	All Around The World (1)	Ollie & Jerry	Breakin' ... There's No Stopping Us Now (5)
	Cigarettes And Alcohol (7)		
	Don't Look Back In Anger (1)	OMC	How Bizarre (5)
	D'You Know What I Mean? (1)	187 Lockdown	Kung-Fu (9)
	Go Let It Out (1)	1 Giant Leap	My Culture (9)
	Hindu Times, The (1)	One Hundred Ton and a Feather	It Only Takes A Minute (9)
	Little By Little / She Is Love (2)		
	Live Forever (10)	112	I'll Be Missing You (1)
	Roll With It (2)		Mo Money Mo Problems (6)
	Some Might Say (1)	One True Voice	Sacred Trust / After You're Gone (2)
	Songbird (3)		
	Stand By Me (2)		Shakespeare's Way With Words (10)
	Stop Crying Your Heart Out (2)		
	Sunday Morning Call (4)	O'Neal, Alexander	Criticize (4)
	Whatever (3)		Saturday Love (6)
	Who Feels Love? (4)	Ones	Flawless (7)
	Wonderwall (2)	Ono, Yoko	Happy Xmas (War Is Over) (4)
Obernkirchen Children's Choir	Happy Wanderer (Der Fröhliche Wanderer) (2)		Happy Xmas (War Is Over) (re-entry) (2)
	Happy Wanderer (Der Fröhliche Wanderer) (re-entry) (8)		Instant Karma (5)
		OPM	Heaven Is A Halfpipe (4)
Obie Trice	Got Some Teeth (8)	Opus	Live Is Life (6)
Ocean Colour Scene	Better Day (9)	Opus III	It's A Fine Day (5)
	Circle, The (6)	Orange Juice	Rip It Up (8)
	Day We Caught The Train, The (4)	Orb	Blue Room (8)
			Little Fluffy Clouds (10)
	Hundred Mile High City (4)		Toxygene (4)
	Traveller's Tune (5)	Orbison, Roy	Blue Bayou / Mean Woman Blues (3)
	You've Got It Bad (7)		
Ocean, Billy	Caribbean Queen (No More Love On The Run) (6)		Dream Baby (2)
			Falling (9)
	Get Outta My Dreams Get Into My Car (3)		I Drove All Night (7)
			In Dreams (6)
			It's Over (1)

Group/Artiste	Title	Group/Artiste	Title
	Oh Pretty Woman (1)	Outhere Brothers	Boom Boom Boom (1)
	Only The Lonely (re-entry) (1)		Don't Stop (Wiggle Wiggle) (1)
	Pretty Paper (6)		If You Wanna Party (9)
	Running Scared (9)		La La La Hey Hey (7)
	Too Soon To Know (3)	Outkast	Hey Ya! (3)
	You Got It (3)		Ms Jackson (2)
Orbit, William	Barber's Adagio For Strings (4)		Roses (4)
Orbital	Saint, The (3)	Outkast featuring	Way You Move, The (7)
	Satan (3)	Sleepy Brown	
OMD	Enola Gay (8)	Overlanders	Michelle (1)
	Joan Of Arc (5)	Owen, Mark	Child (3)
	Locomotion (5)		Clementine (3)
	Maid Of Orleans (The Waltz		Four Minute Warning (4)
	Joan Of Arc) (4)	Oxide & Neutrina	Bound 4 Da Reload (Casualty)
	Pandora's Box (7)		(1)
	Sailing On The Seven Seas (3)	Oxide & Neutrino	Up Middle Finger (7)
	Souvenir (3)	Oxide & Neutrino	Dem Girlz (I Don't Know Why)
Original	I Luv U Baby (remix) (2)	with Kowdean	(10)
Orlando, Tony	Bless You (5)	Oxide & Neutrino with	No Good 4 Me (6)
	Tie A Yellow Ribbon Round The	Megaman	
	Old Oak Tree (1)	O-Zone	Dragostea Din Tei (3)
	What Are You Doing Sunday	Paffendorf	Be Cool (7)
	(3)	Page, Jimmy	Come With Me (2)
Orrico, Stacie	Stuck (9)	Page, Patti	(How Much Is) That Doggie In
Osborne, Joan	One Of Us (6)		The Window (3)
Osbourne, Kelly	Papa Don't Preach (3)	Paige, Elaine	I Know Him So Well (1)
Osbourne,	Changes (1)		Memory (6)
Ozzy & Kelly		Paige, Jennifer	Crush (4)
Osmond, Donny	Breeze On By (8)	Palmer, Robert	Addicted To Love (5)
	I'm Leaving It (All) Up To You		I Didn't Mean To Turn You On
	(2)		(9)
	Morning Side Of The Mountain		I'll Be Your Baby Tonight (6)
	(5)		Mercy Mercy Me – I Want You
	Puppy Love (1)		(9)
	Too Young (5)		She Makes My Day (6)
	Twelfth Of Never, The (1)	Panjabi MC	Mundian To Bach Ke (5)
	When I Fall In Love (4)	Papa Roach	Last Resort (3)
	Why (3)	Paper Lace	Billy Don't Be A Hero (1)
	Young Love (1)		Night Chicago Died, The (3)
Osmond, Little Jimmy	Long-Haired Lover From	Paradis, Vanessa	Be My Baby (6)
	Liverpool (1)		Joe Le Taxi (3)
	Tweedle Dee (4)	Paramount Jazz Band	Buona Sera (7)
Osmond, Marie	I'm Leaving It (All) Up To You		Summer Set (5)
	(2)		That's My Home (7)
	Morning Side Of The Mountain	Paris, Mica	My One Temptation (7)
	(5)	Paris, Ryan	Dolce Vita (5)
	Paper Roses (2)	Parker Jr, Ray	Ghostbusters (2)
Osmonds	Crazy Horses (2)	Parkinson, Jimmy	Great Pretender, The (9)
	Goin' Home (4)	Parks, Alex	Maybe That's What It Takes (3)
	Let Me In (2)	Parr, John	St Elmo's Fire (Man In Motion)
	Love Me For A Reason (1)		(6)
	Proud One, The (5)	Partners In Kryme	Turtle Power (1)
O'Sullivan, Gilbert	Alone Again (Naturally) (3)	Parton, David	Isn't She Lovely (4)
	Clair (1)	Parton, Dolly	Islands In The Stream (7)
	Get Down (1)		Jolene (7)
	No Matter How I Try (5)	Partridge Family	Breaking Up Is Hard To Do (3)
	Nothing Rhymed (8)		Looking Through The Eyes Of
	Ooh-Wakka-Doo-Wakka-Day		Love (9)
	(8)		Walking In The Rain (10)
	Why Oh Why Oh Why (6)	Partridge, Don	Blue Eyes (3)
Otis Show, Johnny	Ma (He's Making Eyes At Me)		Rosie (4)
	(2)	Pasadenas	I'm Doing Fine Now (4)
O-Town	All Or Nothing (4)		Tribute (Right On) (5)
	Liquid Dreams (3)	Passengers	Miss Sarajevo (6)
Ottowan	D.I.S.C.O. (2)	Pat & Mick	I Haven't Stopped Dancing Yet
	Hands Up (Give Me Your		(9)
	Heart) (3)	Paul & Paula	Hey Paula (8)
Otway, John	Bunsen Burner (9)		Young Lovers (9)
Otway, John & Wild	Really Free (27)	Paul, Les	Vaya Con Dios (7)
Willy Barrett		Paul, Owen	My Favourite Waste Of Time
Our Kid	You Just Might See Me Cry (2)		(3)

M
U
S
I
C

P
O
P

Group/Artiste	Title	Group/Artiste	Title
Paul, Sean	Get Busy (4)		Turn Around (3)
	Gimme The Light (remix) (5)	PhD	I Won't Let You Down (3)
	Like Glue (3)	Phillips, Esther	What A Difference A Day Made (6)
Paul, Sean featuring Sasha	I'm Still In Love With You (6)		
Pavarotti, Luciano	Live Like Horses (9)	Phixx	Hold On Me (10)
	Nessun Dorma (2)	Pianoman	Blurred (6)
Payne, Freda	Band Of Gold (1)	Pickettywitch	That Same Old Feeling (5)
Peaches & Herb	Reunited (4)	Pigbag	Papa's Got A Brand New Pigbag (3)
Pearl Jam	Spin The Black Circle (10)		
Pearls	Guilty (10)	Piglets	Johnny Reggae (3)
Pebbles	Girlfriend (8)	Pilot	January (1)
Peers, Donald	Please Don't Go (3)	Pink	Don't Let Me Get Me (6)
Pellow, Marti	Close To You (9)		Get The Party Started (2)
Penn, Dawn	You Don't Love Me (No No No) (3)		Just Like A Pill (1)
			Lady Marmalade (1)
Peppers	Pepper Box (6)		Most Girls (5)
Pepsi & Shirlie	Goodbye Stranger (9)		There You Go (6)
	Heartache (2)		Trouble (7)
Percy Faith & His Orchestra	Half As Much (3)		You Make Me Sick (9)
	Theme From A Summer Place (2)	Pink featuring William Orbit	Feel Good Time (3)
Perez Prado & His Orchestra	Patricia (8)	Pink Floyd	Another Brick In The Wall Part II (1)
Perez 'Prez' Prado Orchestra	Cherry Pink And Apple Blossom White (1)		See Emily Play (6)
	Guaglione (2)	Pinkees	Danger Games (8)
Perfecto Allstarz	Reach Up (Papa's Got A Brand New Pig Bag) (6)	Pinkerton's Assorted Colours	Mirror Mirror (9)
Perkins, Carl	Blue Suede Shoes (10)	Pioneers	Let Your Yeah Be Yeah (5)
Pet Shop Boys	Absolutely Fabulous (6)	Piper, Billie	Day And Night (1)
	Always On My Mind (1)		Something Deep Inside (4)
	Before (7)	Pipes and Drums of the Royal Scots Dragoon Guards	Amazing Grace (1)
	Can You Forgive Her (7)		
	Domino Dancing (7)		
	Go West (2)	Pipkins	Gimme Dat Ding (6)
	Heart (1)	Pips	Baby Don't Change Your Mind (4)
	It's A Sin (1)		
	It's Alright (5)		Best Thing That Ever Happened To Me (7)
	Left To My Own Devices (4)		
	Miracles (10)		Midnight Train To Georgia (10)
	Red Letter Day, A (9)		Way We Were, The / Try To Remember (4)
	Rent (8)		
	Se A Vide (That's The Way Life Is) (8)	Piranhas	Tom Hark (6)
			Zambesi (17)
	So Hard (4)	Pirates, f. Enya, Shola Ama, Naila Boss & Ishani	You Should Really Know (8)
	Somewhere (9)		
	Suburbia (8)		
	West End Girls (1)		
	What Have I Done To Deserve This (2)	Pitney, Gene	Backstage (4)
			I Must Be Seeing Things (6)
	Where The Streets Have No Name (Can't Take My Eyes Off You) / How Can You Expect To Be Taken Seriously (4) You Only Tell Me You Love Me When You're Drunk (8)		(I Wanna) Love My Life Away (26)
			I'm Gonna Be Strong (2)
			Just One Smile (8)
			Looking Through The Eyes Of Love (3)
Peter & Gordon	Nobody I Know (10)		Nobody Needs Your Love (2)
	To Know You Is To Love You (5)		Princess In Rags (9)
			Something's Gotten Hold Of My Heart (1) with Marc Almond
	True Love Ways (2)		
	World Without Love, A (1)		Something's Gotten Hold Of My Heart (5)
Peter Paul & Mary	Leavin' On A Jet Plane (2)		
Peters & Lee	Don't Stay Away Too Long (3)		That Girl Belongs To Yesterday (7)
	Welcome Home (1)		
Peterson, Colin	Don't Forget To Remember (2)		Twenty-Four Hours From Tulsa (5)
PF Project	Choose Life (6)		
Phantoms	Tomorrow (8)	Piu, Mario	Communication (Somebody Answer The) (5)
Pharrell Williams featuring Jay-Z	Frontin' (6)	PJ & Duncan	Let's Get Ready To Rhumble (9)
Phats & Small	Feel Good (7)	Placebo	Nancy Boy (4)
			Pure Morning (4)
			You Don't Care About Us (5)

Group/Artiste	Title	Group/Artiste	Title
Planet Funk	Chase The Sun (5)		Burning Love (7)
Planet Perfecto	Bullet In The Gun (2000 remix) (7)		Crying In The Chapel (1)
			Devil In Disguise (1)
Plastic Bertrand	Ca Plane Pour Moi (8)		Don't (2)
Plastic Ono Band	Give Peace A Chance (2)		Don't Cry Daddy (8)
	Happy Xmas (War Is Over) (4)		Fool Such As I / I Need Your
	Happy Xmas (War Is Over) (re-entry) (2)		Love Tonight, A (1)
			Girl Of My Best Friend, The (9)
	Instant Karma (5)		Good Luck Charm (1)
	Power To The People (7)		Hard-Headed Woman (2)
Plastic Penny	Everything I Am (6)		Heartbreak Hotel (2)
Plastic Population	Doctorin' The House (6)		Heartbreak Hotel / Hound Dog
	Only Way Is Up, The (1)		(re-issue) (10)
Platinum 45	Oi (8)		Hound Dog (2)
Platters	Great Pretender / Only You, The (5)		I Just Can't Help Believing (6)
			In The Ghetto (2)
	My Prayer (4)		It's Now Or Never (1)
	Smoke Gets In Your Eyes (1)		It's Only Love / Beyond The
	Twilight Time (3)		Reef (3)
Plavka	Right In The Night (Fall In Love With Music) (re-issue) (10)		I've Lost You (9)
			Jailhouse Rock (1)
Players Association	Turn The Music Up (8)		King Creole (2)
PM Dawn	Set Adrift On Memory Bliss (3)		Kissin' Cousins (10)
Pogues	Fairytale Of New York (2)		(Let Me Be Your) Teddy Bear
	Irish Rover, The (8)		(3)
Point Break	Stand Tough (7)		Little Less Conversation, A (1)
Pointer Sisters	Automatic (2)		Love Letters (6)
	Jump (For My Love) (6)		(Marie's The Name) His Latest
	Slowhand (10)		Flame / Little Sister (1)
Police	Can't Stand Losing You (re-release) (2)		Mess Of Blues, A (2)
			Moody Blue (6)
	De Do Do Do De Da Da Da (5)		My Boy (5)
	Don't Stand So Close To Me (1)		My Way (9)
			One Night / I Got Stung (1)
	Every Breath You Take (1)		Paralysed (8)
	Every Little Thing She Does Is Magic (1)		Party (2)
			Promised Land (9)
	Invisible Sun (2)		Rags To Riches (9)
	Message In A Bottle (1)		Return To Sender (1)
	So Lonely (6)		Rock A Hula Baby / Can't Help
	Walking On The Moon (1)		Falling In Love (1)
	Wrapped Around Your Finger (7)		Rubberneckin' (remix) (5)
			Santa Bring My Baby Back (To
Pollard, Su	Starting Together (2)		Me) (7)
Poni-Tails	Born Too Late (5)		She's Not You (1)
Poole, Brian	Candy Man (6)		Stuck On You (3)
	Do You Love Me (1)		Surrender (Torna Surriento) (1)
	Someone Someone (2)		Suspicion (9)
	Twist And Shout (4)		Suspicious Minds (2)
Pop Will Eat Itself	Get The Girl! Kill The Baddies! (9)		That's All Right (re-issue) (3)
			There Goes My Everything (6)
Pop, Iggy	Real Wild Child (Wild One) (10)		Too Much (6)
Poppy Family	Which Way You Goin' Billy (7)		Until It's Time For You To Go
Porn Kings	Up To The Wildstyle (10)		(5)
Portishead	All Mine (8)		Way Down (1)
Powell, Cozy	Dance With The Devil (3)		Wear My Ring Around Your
	Na Na Na (10)		Neck (3)
PPK	Resurrection (3)		Wild In The Country / I Feel So
Praise	Only You (4)		Bad (4)
Pras	Blue Angels (6)		Wonder Of You, The (1)
Precious	Say It Again (6)		Wooden Heart (1)
Prefab Sprout	King Of Rock 'N' Roll, The (7)		You Don't Have To Say You
Presidents Of The United States	Peaches (8)		Love Me (9)
		Preston, Billy	Get Back (1)
Presley, Elvis	All Shook Up (re-entry) (1)		With You I'm Born Again (2)
	Always On My Mind (9)	Preston, Johnny	Cradle Of Love (2)
	An American Trilogy (8)		Running Bear (1)
	Are You Lonesome Tonight (1)	Pretenders	Brass In Pocket (1)
	Big Hunk O' Love, A (4)		Don't Get Me Wrong (10)
	Blue Moon (9)		Hymn To Her (8)
	Blue Suede Shoes (9)		I Go To Sleep (7)

Group/Artiste	Title	Group/Artiste	Title
	I'll Stand By You (10)		Satisfy You (8)
	Talk Of The Town (8)	Pulp	Common People (2)
Pretty Things	Don't Bring Me Down (10)		Disco 2000 (7)
Price, Alan	Jarrow Song (6)		Help The Aged (8)
Price, Lloyd	Personality (9)		Mis-Shapes / Sorted For E's
	Stagger Lee (7)		And Wizz (2)
Priest, Maxi	Close To You (7)		Something Changed (10)
	Housecall (remix) (8)	Puretone	Addicted To Bass (2)
	Wild World (5)	Pussycat	Mississippi (1)
Primal Scream	Kowalski (8)	Python Lee Jackson	In A Broken Dream (3)
	Rocks / Funky Jam (7)	Quantum Jump	Lone Ranger, The (5)
Primitives	Crash (5)	Quartz introducing	It's Too Late (8)
Prince	Alphabet Street (9)	Dina Carroll	
	Batdance (2)	Quatro, Suzi	Can The Can (1)
	Controversy (5)		Devil Gate Drive (1)
	Gett Off (4)		48 Crash (3)
	Gold (10)		If You Can't Give Me Love (4)
	I Wanna Be Your Lover (41)		Wild One, The (7)
	Kiss (6)	Quaye, Finley	Even After All (10)
	Let's Go Crazy / Take Me With	Queen	Another One Bites The Dust (5)
	You (7)		Another One Bites The Dust (7)
	Most Beautiful Girl In The		Bohemian Rhapsody (1)
	World, The (1)		Bohemian Rhapsody (re-issue)
	My Name Is Prince (7)		/ These Are The Days Of Our
	1999 / Little Red Corvette (re-		Lives (1)
	issue) (2)		Breakthru (7)
	1999 (re-entry) (10)		Crazy Little Thing Called Love
	Purple Rain (8)		(2)
	Sexy MF / Strollin' (4)		Don't Stop Me Now (9)
	Sign O' The Times (10)		Five Live EP (1)
	Thieves In The Temple (7)		Flash (10)
	When Doves Cry (4)		Heaven For Everyone (2)
Princess	Say I'm Your No.1 (7)		I Want It All (3)
Proby, P J	Hold Me (3)		I Want To Break Free (3)
	Maria (8)		Innuendo (1)
	Somewhere (6)		It's A Hard Life (6)
	Together (8)		Killer Queen (2)
Proclaimers	King Of The Road (EP) (9)		Kind Of Magic, A (3)
	Letter From America (3)		Let Me Live (9)
Procol Harum	Homburg (6)		One Vision (7)
	Whiter Shade Of Pale, A (1)		Radio Gaga (2)
Prodigy	Baby's Got A Temper (5)		Seven Seas Of Rye (10)
	Breathe (1)		Somebody To Love (2)
	Charly (3)		Under Pressure (1)
	Everybody In The Place (EP)		We Are The Champions (2)
	(2)		We Will Rock You (1)
	Firestarter (1)		Winter's Tale, A (6)
	No Good (Start The Dance) (4)		You're My Best Friend (7)
	One Love (8)	Quinn, Sinead	I Can't Break Down (2)
	Out Of Space / Ruff In The	Quiver	Arms Of Mary (5)
	Jungle Bizness (5)	R & J Stone	We Do It (5)
	Smack My Bitch Up (8)	Racey	Lay All Your Love On Me (3)
Product G&B	Maria Maria (6)		Some Girls (2)
Progress presents	Everybody (7)	Radiohead	Creep (7)
Boy Wunda			Karma Police (8)
Propellerheads	On Her Majesty's Secret		No Surprises (4)
	Service (7)		Paranoid Android (3)
Prydz, Eric	Call On Me (1)		Pyramid Song (5)
Pseudo Echo	Funky Town (8)		Street Spirit (Fade Out) (5)
Psychotropic	Let's Talk About Sex (2)		There There (4)
Public Domain	Operation Blade (Bass In The	Rafferty, Gerry	Baker Street (3)
	Place) (5)		Night Owl (5)
Public Image Ltd	Public Image (9)	Rage	Run To You (3)
	This Is Not A Love Song (5)	Rage Against The	Bulls On Parade (8)
Puckett, Gary	Lady Willpower (5)	Machine	
	Young Girl (1)	Raghav	Can't Get Enough (10)
	Young Girl (re-issue) (6)	Rah Band	Clouds Across The Moon (6)
Puddle Of Mudd	Blurry (8)		Crunch, The (6)
Puff Daddy	Come With Me (2)	Rainbow	All Night Long (5)
	I Need A Girl (Part One) (4)		I Surrender (3)
	I'll Be Missing You (1)		Since You've Been Gone (6)

Group/Artiste	Title
Rainwater, Marvin	Whole Lotta Woman (1)
Rakim	Addictive (3)
Ram Jam	Black Betty (7)
Ramirez, Karen	Looking For Love (8)
Ramones	Baby I Love You (8)
Ramrods	Riders In The Sky (8)
Rank 1	Airwave (10)
Ranking Ann	Word Girl, The (6)
Ranks, Shabba	Housecall (remix) (8)
	Mr Loverman (re-issue) (3)
Rasmus	In The Shadows (3)
Rattles	Witch, The (8)
Rawls, Lou	You'll Never Find Another Love Like Mine (10)
Ray Anthony	Dragnet (7)
Ray Martin Orchestra	Blue Tango (8)
	Blue Tango (re-entry) (10)
	Swedish Rhapsody (10)
	Swedish Rhapsody (re-entry) (4)
Ray, Johnnie	Faith Can Move Mountains (7)
	Faith Can Move Mountains (re-entry) (9)
	Hey There (5)
	If You Believe (re-entry) (7)
	Just Walkin' In The Rain (1)
	Let's Walk Thata-Way (4)
	Look Homeward Angel (7)
	Somebody Stole My Gal (6)
	Somebody Stole My Gal (re-entry) (6)
	Song Of The Dreamer (10)
	Such A Night (1)
	Yes Tonight Josephine (1)
Rayvon	Angel (1)
	In The Summertime (5)
Razorlight	Golden Touch (9)
Rea, Chris	Fool (If You Think It's Over) (30)
	Road To Hell (Part 2), The (10)
Real McCoy	Another Night (2)
	Run Away (6)
Real Thing	Can You Feel The Force (5)
	Can't Get By Without You (2)
	Can't Get By Without You (The Second Decade Remix) (6)
	You To Me Are Everything (1)
	You To Me Are Everything (The Decade Remix 76-86) (5)
Rebel MC & Double	Street Tuff (3)
Rebelettes	Dance With Guitar Man (4)
	Play Me Like You Play Your Guitar (9)
Red Box	For America (10)
	Lean On Me (Ah-Li-Ayo) (3)
Red Dragon	Compliments On Your Kiss (2)
Red Hot Chili Peppers	By The Way (2)
	Give It Away (9)
	Love Rollercoaster (7)
	Zephyr Song, The (11)
Redbone	Witch Queen Of New Orleans, The (2)
Redding, Otis	(Sittin' On) The Dock Of The Bay (3)
Reddy, Helen	Angie Baby (5)
Redman	Dirrty (1)
Rednex	Cotton Eye Joe (1)
Reed, Lou	Satellite Of Love 04 (10)
	Walk On The Wild Side (10)
Reef	Come Back Brighter (8)

Group/Artiste	Title
	Place Your Hands (6)
Reel 2 Real	Go On Move (7)
	I Like To Move It (5)
	Jazz It Up (7)
Reeves, Jim	Distant Drums (1)
	I Love You Because (5)
	I Won't Forget You (3)
	It Hurts So Much (8)
	There's A Heartache Following Me (6)
	Welcome To My World (6)
Reeves, Martha	Dancing In The Street (re-issue) (4)
Reeves, Vic	Born Free (6)
	Dizzy (1)
	I'm A Believer (3)
Regan, Joan	If I Give My Heart To You (re-entry) (3)
	May You Always (9)
	Prize Of Gold (6)
	Ricochet (8)
	Ricochet (re-entry) (9)
	Someone Else's Roses (5)
Reid, John	Push The Feeling On (remix) (3)
	Surrender Your Love (7)
Reid, Mike	Ugly Duckling, The (10)
Reid, Neil	Mother Of Mine (2)
Reilly, Maggie	Moonlight Shadow (4)
REM	At My Most Beautiful (10)
	Bad Day (8)
	Daysleeper (6)
	E-Bow The Letter (4)
	Everybody Hurts (7)
	Great Beyond, The (3)
	Imitation Of Life (6)
	Leaving New York (5)
	Shiny Happy People (6)
	Strange Currencies (9)
	What's The Frequency Kenneth (9)
Rembrandts	I'll Be There For You (re-entry) (5)
	I'll Be There For You (Theme From Friends) (3)
Renaissance	Northern Lights (10)
Renee & Renato	Save Your Love (1)
REO Speedwagon	Keep On Loving You (7)
Republica	Drop Dead Gorgeous (7)
Revolution	Kiss (6)
	Let's Go Crazy / Take Me With You (7)
	Purple Rain (8)
Reynolds Girls	I'd Rather Jack (8)
Reynolds, Debbie	Tammy (2)
Rhymes, Busta	Ante Up (7)
	Gimme Some More (5)
	Hit 'Em High (The Monstars' Anthem) (8)
	Rumble In The Jungle (3)
	Turn It Up / Fire It Up (2)
	What's It Gonna Be?! (6)
	Woo-Hah!! Got You All In Check (8)
Rhymes, Busta & Mariah Carey featuring The Flipmode Squad	I Know What You Want (3)
Rich In Paradise	Going Back To My Roots / Rich In Paradise (9)
Rich Project, Tony	Nobody Knows (4)
Rich, Charlie	Most Beautiful Girl, The (2)

M
U
S
I
C

P
O
P

Group/Artiste	Title	Group/Artiste	Title
Richard X featuring Kelis	Finest Dreams (8)		When The Girl In Your Arms Is The Girl In Your Heart (3)
Richard X vs Liberty X	Being Nobody (3)		Wind Me Up (Let Me Go) (2)
			Wired For Sound (4)
Richard, Cliff	All I Ask Of You (3)		Young Ones, The (1)
	All My Love (6)	Richard, Wendy	Come Outside (1)
	Best Of Me, The (2)	Richie, Lionel	All Night Long (All Night) (2)
	Big Ship (8)		Dancing On The Ceiling (7)
	Can't Keep This Feeling In (10)		Endless Love (7)
	Carrie (4)		Hello (1)
	Congratulations (1)		My Destiny (7)
	Constantly (4)		Running With The Night (9)
	Daddy's Home (2)		Say You Say Me (8)
	Day I Met Marie, The (10)		Truly (6)
	Devil Woman (9)	Richie, Shane	I'm Your Man (2)
	Don't Talk To Him (2)	Richman, Jonathan	Egyptian Reggae (5)
	Dreamin' (8)	Rick Dees & His Cast Of Idiots	Disco Duck (Part One) (6)
	Fall In Love With You (2)		
	Gee Whiz It's You (4)	Rickett, Adam	I Breathe Again (5)
	Girl Like You, A (3)	Rico	Message To You Rudy, A / Nite Club (10)
	Goodbye Sam Hello Samantha (6)		
		Ride	Leave Them All Behind (9)
	High Class Baby (7)	Ridgway, Stan	Camouflage (4)
	I Could Easily Fall (In Love With You) (9)	Right Said Fred	Deeply Dippy (1)
			Don't Talk Just Kiss (3)
	I Just Don't Have The Heart (3)		I'm Too Sexy (2)
	I Love You (1)	Right Said Fred & Friends	Stick It Out (4)
	I Still Believe In You (7)		
	I'm Looking Out The Window / Do You Want To Dance (2)	Righteous Brothers	Unchained Melody (re-issue) (1)
			You've Lost That Lovin' Feelin' (1)
	I'm The Lonely One (8)		
	In The Country (6)		You've Lost That Lovin' Feelin' (re-issue) (3)
	It'll Be Me (2)		
	It's All In The Game (2)		You've Lost That Lovin' Feelin' (re-issue) (10)
	It's All Over (9)		
	Living Doll (1)	Rikrok	It Wasn't Me (1)
	Living Doll (1) with The Young Ones	Rimes, LeAnn	Can't Fight The Moonlight (1)
			How Do I Live (7)
	Lucky Lips (4)		Written In The Stars (10)
	Mean Streak (10)	Riperton, Minnie	Loving You (2)
	Millennium Prayer, The (1)	Ritchie Family	Best Disco In Town, The (10)
	Minute You're Gone, The (1)	Ritter, Tex	Wayward Wind (8)
	Mistletoe And Wine (1)	Riva	Who Do You Love Now (Stringer) (3)
	Move It (2)		
	My Pretty One (6)	Roachford	Cuddly Toy (re-issue) (4)
	Next Time / Bachelor Boy, The (1)	Robbins, Marty	Devil Woman (5)
		Robert Howard	Wait (7)
	Nine Times Out Of Ten (3)	Roberts, Malcolm	May I Have The Next Dream With You (8)
	On The Beach (7)		
	Only Way Out, The (10)	Robertson, B A	Bang Bang (2)
	Peace In Our Time (8)		Knocked It Off (8)
	Please Don't Fall In Love (7)		To Be Or Not To Be (9)
	Please Don't Tease (1)	Robertson, Don	Happy Whistler, The (8)
	Power To All Our Friends (4)	Robinson, Floyd	Makin' Love (9)
	Santa's List (5)	Robinson, Smokey	Being With You (1)
	Saviour's Day (1)		Tears Of A Clown, The (1)
	She Means Nothing To Me (9)		Tracks Of My Tears, The (9)
	Silhouettes (10)	Robinson, Tom	War Baby (6)
	Some People (3)	Robson & Jerome	I Believe / Up On The Roof (1)
	Somethin' Is Goin' On (9)		Unchained Melody / (There'll Be Bluebirds Over) The White Cliffs Of Dover (1)
	Summer Holiday (1)		
	Theme For a Dream (3)		
	Throw Down The Line (7)		What Becomes Of The Broken Hearted / Saturday Night At The Movies / You'll Never Walk Alone (1)
	Time Drags By (10)		
	Travellin' Light (1)		
	True Love Ways (8)		
	Twelfth Of Never, The (8)	Robyn	Show Me Love (8)
	Visions (7)	Rocker's Revenge	Walking On Sunshine (4)
	Voice In The Wilderness (2)	Rockin' Berries	He's In Town (3)
	We Don't Talk Anymore (1)		Poor Man's Son (5)
	We Should Be Together (10)		

Group/Artiste	Title
Rocksteady Crew	(Hey You) The Rocksteady Crew (6)
Rockwell	Somebody's Watching Me (6)
Rodgers, Clodagh	Come Back And Shake Me (3)
	Goodnight Midnight (4)
	Jack In The Box (4)
Rodgers, Jimmie	English Country Garden (5)
	Kisses Sweeter Than Wine (7)
Rodriguez	Ecuador (2)
Roe, Tommy	Dizzy (1)
	Everybody (9)
	Folk Singer, The (4)
	Sheila (3)
Rogers, Julie	Wedding, The (3)
Rogers, Kenny	Coward Of The County (1)
	Islands In The Stream (7)
	Lucille (1)
	Ruby Don't Talk Your Love To Town (2)
	Something's Burning (8)
Rolling Stones	Angie (5)
	Brown Sugar / Bitch / Let It Rock (2)
	Come On (21)
	Emotional Rescue (9)
	Fool To Cry (6)
	Get Off My Cloud (1)
	Have You Seen Your Mother Baby Standing In the Shadow (5)
	Honky Tonk Women (1)
	(I Can't Get No) Satisfaction (1)
	I Wanna Be Your Man (12)
	It's All Over Now (1)
	It's Only Rock And Roll (10)
	Jumping Jack Flash (1)
	Last Time, The (1)
	Let's Spend The Night Together / Ruby Tuesday (3)
	Little Red Rooster (1)
	Miss You / Far Away Eyes (3)
	Nineteenth Nervous Breakdown (2)
	Not Fade Away (3)
	Paint It Black (1)
	Start Me Up (7)
	Tumbling Dice (5)
	We Love You / Dandelion (8)
Roman Numerals	Born Free (6)
Romeo	It's All Gravy (9)
Romeo, Max	Wet Dream (10)
Ronettes	Be My Baby (4)
Ronstadt, Linda	Don't Know Much (2)
	Somewhere Out There (8)
Rooftop Singers	Walk Right In (10)
Room 5 featuring Oliver Cheatham	Make Luv (1)
Rooster	Come Get Some (7)
Ross, Diana	Ain't No Mountain High Enough (6)
	All Of My Life (9)
	Chain Reaction (1)
	Endless Love (7)
	I'm Gonna Make You Love Me (3)
	I'm Still Waiting (1)
	Love Hangover (10)
	My Old Piano (5)
	Not Over Yet (9)
	One Shining Moment (10)
	Reflections (5)

Group/Artiste	Title
	Remember Me (7)
	Surrender (10)
	Theme From Mahogany (Do You Know Where You're Going To) (5)
	Touch Me In The Morning (9)
	Upside Down (2)
	When You Tell Me That You Love Me (3)
	Why Do Fools Fall In Love (4)
	Work That Body (7)
	You Are Everything (5)
Rosso, Nini	Il Silenzio (8)
Roulettes	First Time, The (5)
Roussos, Demis	Happy To Be On An Island In The Sun (5)
	Roussos Phenomenon EP, The (1)
	When Forever Has Gone (2)
Rowland, Kelly	Can't Nobody (5)
	Dilemma (1)
	Stole (2)
Rowles, John	If I Only Had Time (3)
Roxette	Almost Unreal (7)
	It Must Have Been Love (3)
	It Must Have Been Love (re-issue) (10)
	Joyride (4)
	Listen To Your Heart / Dangerous (6)
	Look, The (7)
Roxy Music	Angel Eyes (4)
	Dance Away (2)
	Jealous Guy (1)
	Love Is The Drug (2)
	More Than This (6)
	Oh Yeah (On The Radio) (5)
	Over You (5)
	Pyjamarama (10)
	Street Life (9)
	Virginia Plain (4)
Royal Guardsmen	Snoopy Vs The Red Baron (8)
Royal Philharmonic Orchestra	All I Ask Of You (3)
	Hooked On Classics (2)
Royce, Rose	Car Wash (9)
	Love Don't Live Here Anymore (2)
	Wishing On A Star (3)
Roza, Lita	(How Much Is) That Doggie In The Window (1)
Rozalla	Everybody's Free (To Feel Good) (6)
RTE Concert Orchestra	Riverdance (9)
Rubettes	Baby I Know (10)
	I Can Do It (7)
	Juke Box Jive (3)
	Sugar Baby Love (1)
Rubia, Maria	Everytime You Need Me (3)
Ruff Driverz presents Arrola	Dreaming (10)
Ruffin, Bruce	Mad About You (9)
Ruffin, David	Walk Away From Love (10)
Ruffin, Jimmy	Farewell Is A Lonely Sound (8)
	Hold On To My Love (7)
	I'll Say Forever My Love (7)
	It's Wonderful (To Be Loved By You) (6)
	What Becomes Of The Broken Hearted (10)

Group/Artiste	Title
	What Becomes Of The Broken Hearted (re-issue) (4)
Rufus	Ain't Nobody (8)
	Ain't Nobody (remix) (6)
Run DMC	It's Like That (1)
	Walk This Way (8)
RuPaul	Don't Go Breaking My Heart (7)
Rush, Jennifer	Power Of Love, The (1)
Rushen, Patrice	Forget Me Nots (8)
Ruts	Babylon's Burning (7)
Ryan, Barry	Eloise (2)
Ryan, Marion	Love Me Forever (5)
Rydell, Bobby	Wild One (7)
S Club	Alive (5)
	Love Ain't Gonna Wait For You / Say Goodbye (2)
S Club 8	Fool No More (4)
	Sundown (4)
S Club Juniors	Automatic High (2)
	New Direction (2)
	One Step Closer (2)
	Puppy Love / Sleigh Ride (6)
S Club 7	Bring It All Back (1)
	Don't Stop Movin' (1)
	Have You Ever (1)
	Natural (3)
	Never Had A Dream Come True (1)
	Reach (2)
	S Club Party (2)
	Two In A Million / You're My Number One (2)
	You (2)
S Express	Hey Music Lover (6)
	Superfly Guy (5)
	Theme From S'Express (1)
S, Robin	Show Me Love (6)
	Show Me Love (remix) (9)
Sabrina	Boys (Summertime Love) (3)
Sad Cafe	Every Day Hurts (3)
Sade	Your Love Is King (6)
Safina, Alessandro	Your Song (4)
Safri Duo	Played A Live (The Bongo Song) (6)
Sager, Carole Bayer	You're Moving Out Today (6)
Sailor	Girls Girls Girls (7)
	Glass Of Champagne, A (2)
Saint Etienne	Tell Me Why (The Riddle) (7)
Sally Sweetland (soprano)	I'm Walking Behind You (1)
Salt-N-Pepa	Do You Want Me (5)
	Let's Talk About Sex (2)
	Push It / Tramp (2)
	Twist And Shout (4)
	Whatta Man (7)
Sam & Mark	Measure Of A Man / With A Little Help From My Friends (1)
Sanchez, Roger	Another Chance (1)
Sandpipers	Guantanamera (7)
Santana	Maria Maria (6)
	Smooth (3)
Santana, Juelz	Rocafella (13)
Santos	Camels (9)
Sarne, Mike	Come Outside (1)
Sarstedt, Peter	Frozen Orange Juice (10)
	Where Do You Go To My Lovely (1)
Sarstedt, Robin	My Resistance Is Low (3)
Sash	Adelante (2)
	Ecuador (2)

Group/Artiste	Title
	Encore Une Fois (2)
	Just Around The Hill (8)
	La Primavera (3)
	Move Mania (8)
	Mysterious Times (2)
	Stay (2)
	With My Own Eyes (10)
Saunders, Jessie	Love Can't Turn Around (10)
Savage Garden	Affirmation (10)
	I Knew I Loved You (10)
	To The Moon And Back (3)
	Truly Madly Deeply (4)
Savalas, Telly	If (1)
Sayer, Leo	Have You Ever Been In Love (10)
	How Much Love (10)
	I Can't Stop Lovin' You (Though I Try) (6)
	Long Tall Glasses (4)
	Moonlighting (2)
	More Than I Can Say (2)
	One Man Band (6)
	Show Must Go On, The (2)
	When I Need You (1)
	You Make Me Feel Like Dancing (2)
Scaffold	Lily The Pink (1)
	Liverpool Lou (7)
	Thank U Very Much (4)
Scaggs, Boz	What Can I Say (10)
Scanty Sandwich	Because Of You (3)
Scatman John	Scatman (3)
	Scatman's World (10)
Scissor Sisters	Comfortably Numb (10)
Scooch	More Than I Needed To Know (5)
Scooter	Logical Song, The (2)
	Nessaja (4)
Scorpions	Wind Of Change (2)
Scott, Jack	My True Love (9)
Scott, Josey	Hero (4)
Scott, Linda	I've Told Every Little Star (7)
Scott-Lee, Lisa	Lately (6)
Scottish World Cup Football Squad	Ole Ola (Mulher Brasilieira) (4)
	We Have A Dream (5)
Scritti Politti	Wood Beez (Pray Like Aretha Franklin) (10)
	Word Girl, The (6)
Seahorses	Blinded By The Sun (7)
	Love Is The Law (3)
Seal	Crazy (2)
	Killer (EP) (8)
	Kiss From A Rose (re-issue) / I'm Alive (4)
	My Vision (6)
Searchers	Don't Throw Your Love Away (1)
	Goodbye My Love (4)
	Needles And Pins (1)
	Sugar And Spice (2)
	Sweets For My Sweet (1)
	When You Walk In The Room (3)
Secada, Jon	Just Another Day (5)
Secombe, Harry	This Is My Song (2)
Sedaka, Neil	Breaking Up Is Hard To Do (7)
	Calendar Girl (8)
	Happy Birthday Sweet Sixteen (3)
	I Go Ape (9)
	Little Devil (9)

Group/Artiste	Title	Group/Artiste	Title
	Oh Carol (3)		Wonderful Land (1)
	Stairway To Heaven (8)		Young Ones, The (1)
Seekers	Carnival Is Over, The (1)	Shaft	(Mucho Mambo) Sway (2)
	Georgy Girl (3)		Roobarb And Custard (7)
	I'll Never Find Another You (1)	Shag	Loop Di Love (4)
	Morningtown Ride (2)	Shaggy	Angel (1)
	Walk With Me (10)		Boombastic (1)
	World Of Our Own, A (3)		Hey Sexy Lady (10)
Selecter	On My Radio (8)		In The Summertime (5)
Sellers, Peter	Any Old Iron (17)		It Wasn't Me (1)
	Bangers And Mash (22)		Luv Me Luv Me (5)
	Goodness Gracious Me (4)		Me Julie (2)
	Hard Day's Night, A (14)		Oh Carolina (1)
Sensational Alex	Delilah (7)		Piece Of My Heart (7)
Harvey Band		Shakatak	Down On The Street (9)
Severine	Un Banc Un Arbre Une Rue (9)		Night Birds (9)
Sex Pistols	Anarchy In The UK (33)	Shakedown	At Night (6)
	C'Mon Everybody (3)	Shakespears Sister	I Don't Care (7)
	God Save The Queen (2)		Stay (1)
	Holidays In The Sun (8)		You're History (7)
	No One Is Innocent / My Way	Shakira	Underneath Your Clothes (3)
	(7)		Whenever Wherever (2)
	Pretty Vacant (6)	Shalamar	Dead Giveaway (8)
	Silly Thing (6)		I Can Make You Feel
	Something Else / Friggin' In		Good (7)
	The Riggin' (3)		Night To Remember, A (5)
Sex-O-Lettes	Get Dancing (8)		There It Is (5)
	I Wanna Dance Wit Choo (6)	Sham 69	Hersham Boys (6)
Shadows	Apache (1)		Hurry Up Harry (10)
	Atlantis (2)		If The Kids Are United (9)
	Dance On (1)	Shamen	Boss Drum (4)
	Don't Cry For Me Argentina (5)		Ebeneezer Goode (1)
	Don't Make My Baby Blue (10)		LSI (6)
	Don't Talk To Him (2)		Move Any Mountain (remix) (4)
	Fall In Love With You (2)		Phorever People (5)
	FBI (6)	Shangri-Las	Leader Of The Pack (re-issue)
	Foot Tapper (1)		(3)
	Frightened City (3)		Leader Of The Pack (re-issue)
	Gee Whiz It's You (4)		(7)
	Girl Like You, A (3)	Shanice	I Love You Smile (2)
	Guitar Tango (4)	Shanks	Sweet Like Chocolate (1)
	I Could Easily Fall (In Love	Shannon	Move Mania (8)
	With You) (9)	Shannon, Del	Hats Off To Larry (6)
	I Love You (1)		Hey Little Girl (2)
	I'm Looking Out The Window /		Keep Searchin' (We'll Follow
	Do You Want To Dance (2)		The Sun) (3)
	I'm The Lonely One (8)		Little Town Flirt (4)
	In The Country (6)		Runaway (1)
	It'll Be Me (2)		So Long Baby (10)
	It's All In The Game (2)		Swiss Maid (2)
	Kon-Tiki (1)		Two Kinds Of Teardrops (5)
	Lucky Lips (4)	Shapeshifters	Lola's Theme (1)
	Man Of Mystery / The Stranger	Shapiro, Helen	Don't Treat Me Like A Child (3)
	(5)		Little Miss Lonely (8)
	Next Time / Bachelor Boy, The		Tell Me What He Said (2)
	(1)		Walkin' Back To Happiness (1)
	Nine Times Out Of Ten (3)		You Don't Know (1)
	On The Beach (7)	Sharkey, Feargal	Good Heart, A (1)
	Please Don't Tease (1)		You Little Thief (5)
	Rise And Fall Of Flingel Bunt,	Shaw, Sandie	Girl Don't Come (3)
	The (5)		I'll Stop At Nothing (4)
	Savage, The (10)		Long Live Love (1)
	Shindig (6)		Message Understood (6)
	Summer Holiday (1)		Monsieur Dupont (6)
	Theme For a Dream (3)		Puppet On A String (1)
	Theme From The Deerhunter		(There's) Always Something
	(Cavatina) (9)		There To Remind Me (1)
	Time Drags By (10)		Tomorrow (9)
	Travellin' Light (1)	Shearston, Gary	I Get A Kick Out Of You (7)
	Voice In The Wilderness (2)	Shed Seven	Going For Gold (8)
	Wind Me Up (Let Me Go) (2)	Sheer Elegance	Life Is Too Short Girl (9)

M
U
S
I
C

P
O
P

Group/Artiste	Title	Group/Artiste	Title
Shelley, Peter	Gee Baby (4)		You Make Me Feel Brand
	Love Me Love My Dog (3)		New (7)
Shelton, Anne	Lay Down Your Arms (1)	Simpson, Ashlee	Pieces Of Me (4)
	Sailor (10)	Simpson, Jessica	I Wanna Love You Forever (7)
Shepard, Vonda	Searchin' My Soul (10)		With You (7)
Sherbet	Howzat (4)	Simpsons	Do The Bartman (1)
Shervington, Pluto	Dat (6)	Simpsons featuring	Deep Deep Trouble (7)
Shirelles	Will You Love Me Tomorrow (4)	Bart & Homer	
Shirley	Shame Shame Shame (6)	Sims, Joyce	Come Into My Life (7)
Shocking Blue	Mighty Joe (43)	Sims, Kym	Too Blind To See It (5)
	Venus (8)	Sinatra, Frank	All The Way (re-entry) (3)
Shondells	Mony Mony (1)		High Hopes (re-entry) (6)
Showaddywaddy	Dancin' Party (4)		I've Got You Under My Skin (4)
	Heartbeat (7)		Learnin' The Blues (2)
	Hey Rock And Roll (2)		Love And Marriage (3)
	I Wonder Why (2)		(Love Is) The Tender Trap (2)
	Little Bit Of Soap, A (5)		Love's Been Good To Me (8)
	Pretty Little Angel Eyes (5)		My Way (5)
	Three Steps To Heaven (2)		Somethin' Stupid (1)
	Under The Moon Of Love (1)		Strangers In The Night (1)
	When (3)		Theme From New York New
	You Got What It Takes (2)		York (re-issue) (4)
Shut Up & Dance	Raving I'm Raving (2)		Three Coins In The Fountain
Shy FX & T Power	Shake Ur Body (7)		(1)
Sia	Taken For Granted (10)		Young At Heart (12)
Siffre, Labi	(Something Inside) So Strong	Sinatra, Nancy	Did You Ever (2)
	(4)		Somethin' Stupid (1)
Sigue Sigue Sputnik	Love Missile F1-11 (3)		Sugar Town (8)
Silvas, Lucie	What You're Made Of (7)		These Boots Are Made For
Silver Convention	Get Up And Boogie (7)		Walking (1)
Simon & Garfunkel	Boxer, The (6)	Sinclair, Bob	I Feel For You (9)
	Bridge Over Troubled Water (1)	Singing Nun	Dominique (7)
	Homeward Bound (9)	(Soeur Sourire)	
	Mrs Robinson (4)	Sinitta	Cross My Broken Heart (6)
	Mrs Robinson (EP) (9)		Right Back Where We Started
Simon Dupree &	Kites (9)		From (4)
The Big Sound			So Macho / Cruising (2)
Simon Park Orchestra	Eye Level (re-entry) (1)		Toy Boy (4)
Simon, Carly	Coming Around Again (10)	Siouxsie & The	Dear Prudence (3)
	Nobody Does It Better (7)	Banshees	Hong Kong Garden (7)
	Why (10)	Sisqo	Dance For Me (6)
	You're So Vain (3)		Thong Song (3)
Simon, Paul	Mother And Child Reunion (5)		Unleash The Dragon (6)
	Take Me To The Mardi Gras (7)	Sister Sledge	Frankie (1)
	You Can Call Me Al (4)		He's The Greatest Dancer (6)
Simone, Nina	Ain't Got No – I Got Life /		Lost In Music (remix) (4)
	Do What You Gotta Do (2)		We Are Family (8)
	My Baby Just Cares For Me (5)		We Are Family (remix) (5)
	To Love Somebody (5)	Sisters Of Mercy	Temple Of Love (3)
Simple Minds	Alive And Kicking (7)		This Corrosion (7)
	All The Things She Said (9)	Sixpence None	Kiss Me (4)
	Belfast Child (1)	The Richer	
	Don't You (Forget About Me)	Skellern, Peter	You're A Lady (3)
	(7)	Skids	Into The Valley (10)
	Let There Be Love (6)	Sky	Toccata (5)
	Love Song / Alive And Kicking	Skye	Drifting Away (9)
	(re-issues) (6)	SL2	On A Ragga Tip (2)
	Sanctify Yourself (10)	Slade	Bangin' Man (3)
	She's A River (9)		Coz I Luv You (1)
Simply Red	Air That I Breathe, The (6)		Cum On Feel The Noize (1)
	Angel (4)		Everyday (3)
	Fairground (1)		Far Far Away (2)
	For Your Babies (9)		Gudbuy T'Jane (2)
	Holding Back The Years (2)		Look Wot You Dun (4)
	If You Don't Know Me By Now		Mama Weer All Crazee Now
	(2)		(1)
	Money's Too Tight (To Mention)		Merry Xmas Everybody (1)
	(13)		My Friend Stan (2)
	Say You Love Me (7)		My Oh My (2)
	Stars (8)		Run Run Away (7)
	Sunrise (7)		Skweeze Me Pleeze Me (1)

Group/Artiste	Title
	Take Me Bak 'Ome (1)
	Thanks For The Memory (Wham Bam Thank You Mam) (7)
	We'll Bring The House Down (10)
Sledge, Percy	When A Man Loves A Woman (4)
	When A Man Loves A Woman (re-issue) (2)
Sleeper	Nice Guy Eddie (10)
	Sale Of The Century (10)
Slik	Forever And Ever (1)
Sly & The Family Stone	Dance To The Music (7)
Sly Fox	Let's Go All The Way (3)
Small Faces	All Or Nothing (1)
	Hey Girl (10)
	Itchycoo Park (3)
	Itchycoo Park (re-issue) (9)
	Lazy Sunday (2)
	My Mind's Eye (4)
	Sha La La La Lee (3)
	Tin Soldier (9)
Smart Es	Sesame's Treet (2)
Smashing Pumpkins	End Is The Beginning Is The End, The (10)
	Tonight Tonight (7)
Smear Campaign	(I Want To Be) Elected (9)
Smith Group, Patti	Because The Night (5)
Smith, Hurricane	Don't Let It Die (2)
	Oh Babe What Would You Say? (4)
Smith, Muriel	Hold Me Thrill Me Kiss Me (3)
Smith, O C	Son Of Hickory Holler's Tramp (2)
Smith, Will	Black Suits Comin' (Nod Ya Head) (3)
	Boy You Knock Me Out (3)
	Gettin' Jiggy Wit It (3)
	Just The Two Of Us (2)
	Men In Black (1)
	Miami (3)
	Wild Wild West (2)
	Will 2K (2)
Smiths	Heaven Knows I'm Miserable Now (10)
	Sheila Take A Bow (10)
	This Charming Man (re-issue) (8)
Smoke City	Underwater Love (4)
Smokie	Don't Play Your Rock 'N' Roll To Me (8)
	If You Think You Know How To Love Me (3)
	It's Your Life (5)
	Living Next Door To Alice (5)
	Living Next Door To Alice (Who The F**K Is Alice) (3)
	Needles And Pins (10)
	Oh Carol (5)
Smurfs	I've Got A Little Puppy (4)
	Smurf Song, The (2)
	Your Christmas Wish (8)
Snap	Cult Of Snap (8)
	Do You See The Light (Looking For) (10)
	Exterminate (2)
	Mary Had A Little Boy (8)
	Oops Up (5)
	Power, The (1)
	Rhythm Is A Dancer (1)

Group/Artiste	Title
	Snap Megamix (10)
	Welcome To Tomorrow (6)
Sneaker Pimps	6 Underground (remix) (9)
Sneddon, David	Don't Let Go (3)
	Stop Living The Lie (1)
Snoop Dogg	Next Episode, The (3)
Snoop Dogg featuring Pharrell	Drop It Like It's Hot (10)
Snoop Doggy Dogg	Still D.R.E. (6)
Snow	Informer (2)
Snow, Mark	X-Files, The (2)
Snow Patrol	Run (5)
So Solid Crew	Broken Silence (9)
	They Don't Know (3)
	21 Seconds (1)
So Solid Crew presents Mr Shabz	Haters (8)
Soft Cell	Bed Sitter (4)
	Say Hello Wave Goodbye (3)
	Tainted Love (1)
	Tainted Love (5) with Marc Almond
	Torch (2)
	What (3)
Soho	Hippy Chick (re-entry) (8)
Somerville, Jimmy	To Love Somebody (8)
	You Make Me Feel (Mighty Real) (5)
Sonia	Listen To Your Heart (10)
	Only Fools (Never Fall In Love) (10)
	You'll Never Stop Me From Loving You (1)
Sonique	I Put A Spell On You (re-issue) (8)
	It Feels So Good (remix) (1)
	Sky (2)
Sonny	All I Ever Need Is You (8)
	I Got You Babe (1)
	Laugh At Me (9)
	Little Man (4)
Soul Asylum	Runaway Train (re-entry) (7)
Soul City Symphony	Hustle, The (3)
Soul II Soul	Back To Life (However Do You Want Me) (1)
	Dream's A Dream, A (6)
	Get A Life (3)
	Joy (4)
	Keep On Moving (5)
Soul, David	Don't Give Up On Us (1)
	Going In With My Eyes Open (2)
	Let's Have A Quiet Night In (8)
	Silver Lady (1)
Soulsearcher	Can't Get Enough (8)
Sounds Orchestral	Cast Your Fate To The Wind (5)
Soup Dragons	I'm Free (5)
Source	You Got The Love (3)
	You Got The Love (4)
South, Joe	Games People Play (6)
Southside Spinners	Luvstruck (9)
Sovine, Red	Teddy Bear (4)
Space	Avenging Angels (6)
	Ballad Of Tom Jones, The (4)
	Magic Fly (2)
	Me And You Versus The World (9)
Spacedust	Gym And Tonic (1)
Spagna	Call Me (2)
Spandau Ballet	Chant No. 1 (I Don't Need This Pressure On) (3)

M
U
S
I
C

P
O
P

Group/Artiste	Title	Group/Artiste	Title
	Gold (2)	Spooks	Things I've Seen (6)
	I'll Fly For You (9)	Springfield, Dusty	All I See Is You (9)
	Instinction (10)		Going Back (10)
	Lifeline (7)		Heart and Soul (75)
	Musclebound / Glow (10)		I Close My Eyes And Count To Ten (4)
	Only When You Leave (3)		I Just Don't Know What To Do With Myself (3)
	Through The Barricades (6)		
	To Cut A Long Story Short (5)		I Only Want To Be With You (4)
	True (1)		In The Middle Of Nowhere (8)
Sparkle	Be Careful (7)		Losing You (9)
Sparks	Amateur Hour (7)		Some Of Your Lovin' (8)
	Beat The Clock (10)		Son Of A Preacher Man (9)
	This Town Ain't Big Enough For Both Of Us (2)		What Have I Done To Deserve This (2)
Sparxxx, Bubba	Ugly (7)		You Don't Have To Say You Love Me (1)
Spears, Billie Jo	Blanket On The Ground (6)		
	What I've Got In Mind (4)	Springfields	Island Of Dreams (5)
Spears, Britney	Baby One More Time (1)		Say I Won't Be There (5)
	Born To Make You Happy (1)	Springsteen, Bruce	Dancing In The Dark (re-entry) (4)
	Boys (7)		
	Everytime (1)		I'm On Fire / Born In The USA (5)
	I'm A Slave For You (4)		
	I'm Not A Girl Not Yet A Woman (2)		Santa Claus Is Comin' To Town / My Hometown (9)
	Lucky (5)		Streets Of Philadelphia (2)
	My Prerogative (3)	Springwater	I Will Return (5)
	Oops ... I Did It Again (1)	Squadronaires	Ricochet (8)
	Overprotected (4)		Ricochet (re-entry) (9)
	Sometimes (3)	Squeeze	Cool For Cats (2)
	Stronger (7)		Labelled With Love (4)
	Toxic (1)		Take Me I'm Yours (19)
	(You Drive Me) Crazy (5)		Up The Junction (2)
Spears, Britney featuring Madonna	Me Against The Music (2)	Squires, Dorothy	My Way (10)
		St Marie, Buffy	Soldier Blue (7)
Special AKA	Gangsters (6)	St Peters, Crispian	Pied Piper (5)
	Nelson Mandela (9)		You Were On My Mind (2)
	Special AKA Live EP, The (1)	St Thomas More School Choir	If I Had Words (3)
Special D	Come With Me (6)		
Specials	Do Nothing / Maggie's Farm (4)	St Winifred's School Choir	No One Quite Like Grandma (1)
	Ghost Town (1)		
	Message To You Rudy / Nite Club, A (10)	Stafford, Jo	Make Love To Me (8)
			You Belong To Me (1)
	Rat Race / Rude Boys Outa Jail (5)		Stomp (1)
			Thank Abba For The Music (4)
	Stereotype / International Jet Set (6)		When I Said Goodbye / Summer Of Love (5)
Speedway	Genie In A Bottle / Save Yourself (10)		Words Are Not Enough / I Know Him So Well (5)
Spencer Davis Group	Gimme Some Loving (2)	Stamina MC	LK (Carolina Carol Bela) (17)
	I'm A Man (9)	Stanley Black & His Orchestra	Book (re-entry), The (10)
	Keep On Running (1)		
	Somebody Help Me (1)		Book, The (5)
Spice Girls	Goodbye (1)		Rags To Riches (re-entry) (3)
	Holler / Let Love Lead The Way (1)	Stansfield, Lisa	All Around The World (1)
			Change (10)
	Mama / Who Do You Think You Are (1)		Five Live EP (1)
			In All The Right Places (8)
	Say You'll Be Mine (1)		Live Together (10)
	Spice Up Your Life (1)		People Hold On (4)
	Stop (2)		Real Thing, The (9)
	Too Much (1)		Someday (I'll Come Back) (10)
	2 Become 1 (1)	Stardust	Music Sounds Better With You (2)
	Viva Forever (1)		
	Wannabe (1)	Stardust, Alvin	I Feel Like Buddy Holly (7)
Spiller	Groovejet (If This Ain't Love) (1)		I Won't Run Away (7)
			Jealous Mind (1)
Spin Doctors	Two Princes (3)		My Coo-Ca-Choo (2)
Spitting Image	Chicken Song, The (1)		Pretend (4)
Splodgenessabounds	Simon Templar / Two Pints Of Lager And A Packet Of Crisps Please (7)		Red Dress (7)
			You You You (6)
		Stargazers	Broken Wings (re-entry) (1)

Group/Artiste	Title	Group/Artiste	Title
	Close The Door (6)		Heartbeat / Tragedy (1)
	Finger Of Suspicion (1)		Here And Now / You'll Be Sorry (4)
	I See The Moon (1)		It's The Way You Make Me Feel / Too Busy Thinking 'Bout My Baby (2)
	Twenty Tiny Fingers (4)		
Starlight	Numero Uno (9)		
Starr, Edwin	Contact (6)		
	H.A.P.P.Y. Radio (9)		Last Thing On My Mind (6)
	War (3)		Love's Got A Hold On My Heart (2)
Starr, Freddie	It's You (9)		
Starr, Kay	Changing Partners (4)		One For Sorrow (2)
	Comes A-Long A-Love (1)		Say You'll Be Mine / Better The Devil You Know (4)
	Rock And Roll Waltz (1)		
	Side By Side (7)	Stereophonics	Bartender And The Thief, The (3)
Starr, Ringo	Back Off Boogaloo (2)		
	It Don't Come Easy (4)		Handbags And Gladrags (4)
	Photograph (8)		Have A Nice Day (5)
	You're Sixteen (4)		Just Looking (4)
Starsailor	Alcoholic (10)		Madame Helga (4)
	Silence Is Easy (9)		Mama Told Me Not Come (4)
Starship	Nothing's Gonna Stop Us Now (1)		Maybe Tomorrow (3)
			Mr Writer (5)
Starsound	Stars On 45 (2)		Moviestar (5)
	Stars On 45 Vol.2 (2)		Pick A Part That's New (4)
Staton, Candi	Nights On Broadway (6)	Steve & Eydie	I Want To Stay Here (3)
	You Got The Love (4)	Steve 'Silk' Hurley	Jack Your Body (1)
	You Got The Love (re-entry) (3)	Stevens, Cat	I'm Gonna Get Me A Gun (6)
	Young Hearts Run Free (2)		Lady D'Arbanville (8)
Status Quo	Anniversary Waltz – Part 1, The (2)		Matthew And Son (2)
			Morning Has Broken (9)
	Break The Rules (8)	Stevens, Connie	Sixteen Reasons (9)
	Burning Bridges (On And Off And On Again) (5)	Stevens, Rachel	More More More (3)
			Some Girls (2)
	Caroline (5)		Sweet Dreams My LA Ex (2)
	Dear John (10)	Stevens, Ray	Bridget The Midget (The Queen Of The Blues) (2)
	Down Down (1)		
	Ice In The Sun (8)		Everything Is Beautiful (6)
	In The Army Now (2)		Misty (2)
	Marguerita Time (3)		Streak, The (1)
	Ol' Rag Blues (9)	Stevens, Shakin'	Cry Just A Little Bit (3)
	Paper Plane (8)		Green Door (1)
	Pictures Of Matchstick Men (7)		I'll Be Satisfied (10)
	Rain (7)		It's Raining (10)
	Rock 'N' Roll (8)		Letter To You, A (10)
	Rockin' All Over The World (3)		Love Worth Waiting For, A (2)
	Roll Over Lay Down (9)		Merry Christmas Everyone (1)
	Rollin' Home (9)		Oh Julie (1)
	Something 'Bout You Baby I Like (9)		Rockin' Good Way, A (5)
			Shakin' Stevens EP, The (2)
	Wanderer, The (7)		Shirley (6)
	What You're Proposing (2)		Teardrops (5)
	Whatever You Want (4)		This Ole House (1)
	Wild Side Of Life (9)		What Do You Want To Make Those Eyes At Me For (5)
Stealer's Wheel	Stuck In The Middle With You (8)		
			You Drive Me Crazy (2)
Steam	Na Na Hey Hey Kiss Him Goodbye (9)	Stewart, Amii	Knock On Wood (6)
			Knock On Wood / Light My Fire (remix) (7)
Steele, Tommy	Butterfingers (re-entry) (8)		
	Come On Let's Go (10)		Light My Fire / 137 Disco Heaven (medley) (5)
	Little White Bull (6)		
	Nairobi (3)	Stewart, Andy	Donald Where's Your Troosers (re-issue) (4)
	Singing The Blues (1)		
	Water Water / Handful Of Songs (1)	Stewart, Dave	It's My Party (1)
		Stewart, Dave A	Lily Was Here (6)
Steeleye Span	All Around My Hat (5)	Stewart, Jermaine	Say It Again (7)
Stefani, Gwen	Let Me Blow Ya Mind (4)		We Don't Have To ... (2)
	What You Waiting For (4)	Stewart, Rod	All For Love (2)
Steps	After The Love Has Gone (5)		Angel / What Made Milwaukee Famous (Has Made A Loser Out Of Me) (4)
	Better Best Forgotten (2)		
	Chain Reaction / One For Sorrow (remix) (2)		
			Baby Jane (1)
	Deeper Shade Of Blue (4)		Da Ya Think I'm Sexy? (1)

Group/Artiste	Title
	Da Ya Think I'm Sexy? (7) with N-Trance
	Downtown Train (10)
	Every Beat Of My Heart (2)
	Farewell – Bring It On Home To Me / You Send Me (7)
	Have I Told You Lately (5)
	Hotlegs / I Was Only Joking (5)
	I Don't Want To Talk About It / First Cut Is The Deepest (1)
	It Takes Two (5)
	Killing Of Georgie (Parts 1 And 2), The (2)
	Maggie May (1)
	Motown Song, The (10)
	Oh No Not My Baby (6)
	Ole Ola (Mulher Brasilieira) (4)
	Reason to Believe (19)
	Rhythm Of My Heart (3)
	Sailing (1)
	Sailing (re-entry) (3)
	This Old Heart Of Mine (4)
	Tom Traubert's Blues (Waltzing Matilda) (6)
	Tonight I'm Yours (Don't Hurt Me) (8)
	Tonight's The Night (Gonna Be Alright) (5)
	What Am I Gonna Do (3)
	You Wear It Well (1)
	You're In My Heart (3)
Stigers, Curtis	I Wonder Why (5)
	You're All That Matters To Me (6)
Stiltskin	Inside (1)
Sting	All For Love (2)
	When We Dance (9)
Stock Aitken Waterman	Ferry 'Cross The Mersey (1)
	Mr Sleaze (3)
Stoloff, Morris	Moonglow / Theme From Picnic (7)
Stone, Joss	You Had Me (9)
Stone Roses	Elephant Stone (8)
	Love Spreads (2)
	One Love (4)
	What The World Is Waiting For / Fool's Gold (8)
Stonebridge featuring Therese	Put Em High (6)
Storm	Time To Burn (3)
Stranglers	All Day And All Of The Night (7)
	European Female (9)
	Golden Brown (2)
	No More Heroes (8)
	Peaches / Go Buddy Go (8)
	Something Better Change / Straighten Out (9)
	Strange Little Girl (7)
Strawberry Switchblade	Since Yesterday (5)
Strawbs	Part Of The Union (2)
Stray Cats	Rock This Town (9)
	Runaway Boys (9)
Streets	Blinded By The Lights (10)
	Dry Your Eyes (1)
	Fit But You Know It (4)
Streisand, Barbra	I Finally Found Someone (10)
	Love Theme From A Star Is Born (Evergreen) (3)
	No More Tears (Enough Is Enough) (3)
	Tell Him (3)

Group/Artiste	Title
	Woman In Love (1)
	You Don't Bring Me Flowers (5)
Stretch 'N' Vern present Maddogg	I'm Alive (6)
Strike	U Sure Do (re-entry) (4)
String-A-Longs	Wheels (8)
Strokes	12:51 (7)
Strummer, Joe	England's Irie (6)
Stryker	We're Gonna Do It Again (6)
Studt, Amy	Misfit (6)
	Under The Thumb (10)
Stuntmasters	Ladyboy Is Mine, The (10)
Style Council	Groovin' (You're The Best Thing) / Big Boss Groove (5)
	It Didn't Matter (9)
	Long Hot Summer / Paris Match (5)
	My Ever Changing Moods (5)
	Shout To The Top (7)
	Speak Like A Child (4)
	Walls Come Tumbling Down (6)
Stylistics	Betcha By Golly Wow (13)
	Can't Give You Anything (But My Love) (1)
	Can't Help Falling In Love (4)
	Funky Weekend (10)
	I'm Stone In Love With You (9)
	Let's Put It All Together (9)
	Na Na Is The Saddest Word (5)
	Rockin' Roll Baby (6)
	Sing Baby Sing (3)
	16 Bars (7)
	You Make Me Feel Brand New (2)
Styx	Babe (6)
Sub Sub	Ain't No Love (Ain't No Use) (3)
Suede	Animal Nitrate (7)
	Beautiful Ones (8)
	Electricity (5)
	Filmstar (9)
	Lazy (9)
	Saturday Night (6)
	Stay Together (3)
	Trash (3)
Sugababes	Caught In A Moment (8)
	Freak Like Me (1)
	Hole In The Head (1)
	In The Middle (8)
	Overload (6)
	Round Round (1)
	Stronger / Angels With Dirty Faces (7)
	Too Lost In You (10)
Sugar Ray	Every Morning (10)
Sugarhill Gang	Rapper's Delight (3)
Suggs	Cecilia (4)
	I'm Only Sleeping / Off On Holiday (7)
Sum 41	Fat Lip (8)
Summer	Welcome To Tomorrow (6)
Summer, Donna	Down Deep Inside (Theme From The Deep) (5)
	I Don't Wanna Get Hurt (7)
	I Feel Love (1)
	I Feel Love (re-issue) (8)
	I Love You (10)
	Love To Love You Baby (4)
	Love's Unkind (3)
	Macarthur Park (5)
	No More Tears (Enough Is Enough) (3)

Group/Artiste	Title	Group/Artiste	Title
	This Time I Know It's For Real (3)		Telegram Sam (1)
Sunny	Doctor's Orders (7)		20th Century Boy (3)
Supergrass	Alright / Time (2)	Taffy	I Love My Radio (My Deejay's Radio) (6)
	Going Out (5)	Taja Seville	Love Is Contagious (7)
	Lenny (10)	Taka Boom	Must Be The Music (8)
	Moving (9)	Take That	Babe (1)
	Richard III (2)		Back For Good (1)
	Sun Hits The Sky (10)		Could It Be Magic (3)
Supermen Lovers	Starlight (2)		Everything Changes (1)
Supertramp	Breakfast In America (9)		How Deep Is Your Love (1)
	Logical Song, The (7)		It Only Takes A Minute (7)
Supremes	Automatically Sunshine (10)		Love Ain't Here Anymore (3)
	Baby Love (1)		Million Love Songs, A (7)
	Floy Joy (9)		Never Forget (1)
	Happening, The (6)		Pray (1)
	I'm Gonna Make You Love Me (3)		Promises (38)
	Nathan Jones (5)		Relight My Fire (1)
	Reflections (5)		Sure (1)
	Stoned Love (3)		Why Can't I Wake Up With You (2)
	Stop In The Name Of Love (7)	Talking Heads	Road To Nowhere (6)
	Up The Ladder To The Roof (6)	Tamperer	Feel It (1)
	Where Did Our Love Go (3)		Hammer To The Heart (6)
	You Can't Hurry Love (3)		If You Buy This Record Your Life Will Be Better (3)
	You Keep Me Hangin' On (8)	Tams	Hey Girl Don't Bother Me (1)
Surfaris	Wipe Out (5)	Taste Of Honey, A	Boogie Oogie Oogie (3)
Survivor	Burning Heart (5)	Tatu	All The Things She Said (1)
	Eye Of The Tiger (1)		Not Gonna Get Us (7)
Sutherland Brothers	Arms Of Mary (5)	Tavares	Don't Take Away The Music (4)
Swan, Billy	I Can Help (6)		Heaven Must Be Missing An Angel (4)
Sweet	Ballroom Blitz, The (2)		More Than A Woman (7)
	Blockbuster (1)		Whodunit (5)
	Co-Co (2)	Taylor, James	You've Got A Friend (4)
	Fox On The Run (2)	Taylor, R Dean	Indiana Wants Me (2)
	Funny Funny (13)		There's A Ghost In My House (3)
	Hell Raiser (2)		
	Little Willy (4)	Teardrop Explodes	Reward (6)
	Love Is Like Oxygen (9)	Tears For Fears	Change (4)
	Six Teens, The (9)		Everybody Wants To Rule The World (2)
	Teenage Rampage (2)		
	Wig-Wam Bam (4)		Everybody Wants To Run The World (5)
Sweet Dreams	Honey Honey (10)		
Sweet Female Attitude	Flowers (2)		Mad World (3)
Sweet People	Et Les Oiseaux Chantaient (And The Birds Were Singing) (4)		Pale Shelter (5)
			Shout (4)
Sweet Sensation	Sad Sweet Dreamer (1)		Sowing The Seeds Of Love (5)
Sweetbox	Everything's Gonna Be Alright (5)	Technohead	I Wanna Be A Hippy (6)
		Technotronic	Get Up (Before The Night Is Over) (2)
Swing Out Sister	Breakout (4)		
	Surrender (7)		Megamix (6)
Swinging Blue Jeans	Hippy Hippy Shake (2)		Pump Up The Jam (2)
	You're No Good (3)		Rockin' Over The Beat (9)
SWV	Right Here (3)	Ted Heath Orchestra	Dragnet (re-entry) (9)
Sybil	Love I Lost, The (3)		Hot Toddy (6)
	Walk On By (6)		Skin Deep (9)
	When I'm Good And Ready (5)		Swingin' Shepherd Blues (3)
Sylvester	You Make Me Feel (Mighty Real) (8)	Teddy Bears	To Know Him Is To Love Him (2)
Sylvia	Y Viva Espana (4)	Teletubbies	Teletubbies Say Eh-Oh! (1)
Syreeta	With You I'm Born Again (2)	Temperance Seven	Pasadena (4)
T Rex	Children Of The Revolution (2)		You're Driving Me Crazy (1)
	Get It On (1)	Temptations	Ball Of Confusion (7)
	Groover, The (4)		Get Ready (10)
	Hot Love (1)		I'm Gonna Make You Love Me (3)
	Jeepster (2)		
	Metal Guru (1)		Just My Imagination (Running Away With Me) (8)
	Ride A White Swan (2)		
	Solid Gold Easy Action (2)		Motown Song, The (10)

M
U
S
I
C

P
O
P

Group/Artiste	Title	Group/Artiste	Title
	My Girl (re-issue) (2)		Woman In Love (3)
10CC	Art For Art's Sake (5)	Three Dog Night	Mama Told Me Not To Come (3)
	Dean And I, The (10)		
	Donna (2)	3 Of A Kind	Babycakes (1)
	Dreadlock Holiday (1)	3LW	No More (Baby I'Ma Do Right) (6)
	Good Morning Judge (5)		
	I'm Mandy Fly Me (6)	3T	Anything (2)
	I'm Not In Love (1)		Gotta Be You (10)
	Life Is A Minestrone (7)		Why (2)
	Rubber Bullets (1)	Thunderbugs	Friends Forever (5)
	Things We Do For Love, The (6)	Thunderclap Newman	Accidents (46)
			Something In The Air (1)
	Wall Street Shuffle, The (10)	Thurston, Bobby	Check Out The Groove (10)
Ten City	That's The Way Love Is (8)	Tiffany	Could've Been (4)
Ten Pole Tudor	Swords Of A Thousand Men (6)		I Saw Him Standing There (8)
	Who Killed Bambi (6)		I Think We're Alone Now (1)
Ten Sharp	You (10)	Tight Fit	Back To The Sixties (4)
Ten Years After	Love Like A Man (10)		Fantasy Island (5)
Tennessee Ernie Ford	Ballad Of Davy Crockett, The (3)		Lion Sleeps Tonight, The (1)
	Give Me Your Word (1)	Tijuana Brass	Lonely Bull, The (3)
	Sixteen Tons (1)		Spanish Flea (3)
Tennille	Do That To Me One More Time (7)	Tikaram, Tanita	Good Tradition (10)
			Twist In My Sobriety (22)
Terrell, Tammi	Onion Song (9)	Tillotson, Johnny	Poetry In Motion (1)
Terrorvision	Bad Actress (10)	Timberlake, Justin	Cry Me A River (2)
	Perseverance (5)		Like I Love You (2)
	Tequila (2)		Rock Your Body (2)
Terry, Todd	Keep On Jumpin' (8)	Time Frequency	Real Love (8)
	Something Goin' On (5)	Timelords	Doctorin' The Tardis (1)
Tex, Joe	Ain't Gonna Bump No More (With No Big Fat Woman) (2)	Tin Tin Out	Here's Where The Story Ends (7)
Texas	Black-Eyed Boy (5)		What I Am (2)
	Halo (10)	Tinman	Eighteen Strings (9)
	I Don't Want A Lover (8)	Titanic	Sultana (5)
	In Demand (6)	TLC	Creep (re-issue) (6)
	In Our Lifetime (4)		No Scrubs (3)
	Inner Smile (6)		Unpretty (6)
	Put Your Arms Around Me (10)		Waterfalls (4)
	Say What You Want (3)	Tom Robinson Band	2-4-6-8 Motorway (5)
	Say What You Want / Insane (re-recording) (4)	Tom Tom Club	Wordy Rappinghood (7)
		Tomcraft	Loneliness (1)
	Summer Son (5)	Tommy Dorsey Orchestra	Tea For Two Cha Cha (3)
Texas featuring Kardinal Offishall	Carnival Girl (9)	Tony Osborne & His Orchestra	Around The World (8)
Them	Baby Please Don't Go (10)		
	Here Comes The Night (2)	Tony Scott's Orchestra	Banana Boat Song (2)
Therapy?	Shortsharpshock EP (9)		
They Might Be Giants	Birdhouse In Your Soul (6)	Toploader	Achilles Heel (re-issue) (8)
Thin Lizzy	Boys Are Back In Town, The (8)		Dancing In The Moonlight (remix) (7)
	Killer On The Loose (10)	Topol	If I Were A Rich Man (9)
	Waiting For An Alibi (9)	Tormé, Mel	Mountain Greenery (re-entry) (4)
	Whiskey In The Jar (6)		
Third World	Dancing On The Floor (Hooked On Love) (10)	Tornados	Globetrotter (5)
			Telstar (1)
	Now That We've Found Love (10)	Torok, Mitchell	When Mexico Gave Up The Rumba (6)
Thomas, Evelyn	High Energy (5)	Toto	Africa (3)
Thomas, Kenny	Thinking About Your Love (4)	Tottenham Hotspur FC	Ossie's Dream (Spurs Are On Their Way To Wembley) (5)
Thomas, Nicky	Love Of The Common People (9)		
Thomas, Rob	Smooth (3)	Touch & Go	Would You? (3)
Thompson Twins	Doctor Doctor (3)	Tourists	I Only Want To Be With You (4)
	Hold Me Now (4)		So Good To Be Back Home Again (8)
	Love On Your Side (9)		
	We Are Detective (7)	Toy Dolls	Nellie The Elephant (4)
	You Take Me Up (2)	Toyah	Four From Toyah EP (4)
Three Degrees	My Simple Heart (9)		I Want To Be Free (8)
	Runner, The (10)		Thunder In The Mountains (4)
	Take Good Care Of Yourself (9)	Toys	Lover's Concerto, A (5)
	When Will I See You Again (1)	Tozer, Faye	Someone Like You (10)

Group/Artiste	Title	Group/Artiste	Title
T'Pau	China In Your Hand (1)		Let's Stay Together (6)
	Heart And Soul (4)		Nutbush City Limits (4)
	Valentine (9)		River Deep Mountain High (3)
TQ	Bye Bye Baby (7)		We Don't Need Another Hero
	Summertime (7)		(Thunderdome) (3)
	Westside (4)		What's Love Got To Do With It
Tracie	House That Jack Built, The (9)		(3)
Traffic	Here We Go Round The		When The Heartache Is Over
	Mulberry Bush (8)		(10)
	Hole In My Shoe (2)	Turtles	Elenore (7)
	Paper Sun (5)		She'd Rather Be With Me (4)
Train	Drops Of Jupiter (Tell Me) (10)	Twain, Shania	Don't Be Stupid (You Know I
Tra-Knox	Black Suits Comin' (Nod Ya		Love You) (5)
	Head) (3)		Forever And For Always (6)
Trammps	Hold Back The Night (5)		From This Moment On (9)
Trans X	Living On Video (9)		I'm Gonna Getcha Good (4)
Transvision Vamp	Baby I Don't Care (3)		Ka-Ching (8)
	I Want Your Love (5)		Man! I Feel Like A Woman
Travis	Coming Around (5)		(3)
	Re-Offender (7)		That Don't Impress Me Much
	Sing (3)		(3)
	Turn (8)		You're Still The One (10)
	Why Does It Always Rain On	Twain, Shania	Party For Two (10)
	Me? (10)	featuring	
Travolta, John	Grease Megamix (3)	Mark McGrath	
	Sandy (2)	Tweenies	I Believe In Christmas (9)
	Summer Nights (1)		Number 1 (6)
	You're The One That I Want (1)	Tweet	Oops (Oh My) (5)
	You're The One That I Want	Tweets	Birdie Song (The Birdie Dance)
	(re-issue) (4)		(2)
Tremeloes	(Call Me) Number One (2)	Twinkle	Golden Lights (21)
	Candy Man (6)		Terry (4)
	Do You Love Me (1)	Twista	Slow Jamz (3)
	Even The Bad Times Are Good		Sunshine (3)
	(4)	Twisted X	Born in England (9)
	Here Comes My Baby (4)	Twitty, Conway	It's Only Make Believe (1)
	Me And My Life (4)		Mona Lisa (5)
	My Little Lady (6)	Two Cowboys	Everybody Gonfi-Gon (7)
	Silence Is Golden (1)	2 In A Room	Wiggle It (3)
	Someone Someone (2)	2Pac	California Love (6)
	Suddenly You Love Me (6)		Changes (3)
	Twist And Shout (4)		Until The End Of Time (4)
Trent D'Arby, Terence	If You Let Me Stay (7)	2play featuring	So Confused (6)
	Sign Your Name (2)	Raghav & Jucxi	
	Wishing Well (4)	2play featuring	It Can't Be Right (8)
Trent, Jackie	Where Are You Now (My Love)	Raghav & Naila Boss	
	(1)	2 Unlimited	Faces (8)
Tresvant, Ralph	Best Things In Life Are Free,		Get Ready For This (2)
	The (2)		Let The Beat Control Your
Tricky	Milk (10)		Body (6)
Trinity	This Wheel's On Fire (5)		No Limit (1)
Trio	Da Da Da (2)		Real Thing, The (6)
Triple Eight	Give Me A Reason (9)		Tribal Dance (4)
	Knock Out (8)		Twilight Zone (2)
Troggs	Any Way That You Want Me (8)		Workaholic (4)
	I Can't Control Myself (2)	Tyler, Bonnie	Holding Out For A Hero (2)
	Love Is All Around (5)		It's A Heartache (4)
	Wild Thing (2)		Lost In France (9)
	With A Girl Like You (1)		Rockin' Good Way, A (5)
True Steppers	Buggin' Me (6)		Total Eclipse Of The Heart (1)
	Out Of Your Mind (2)	Tymes	Ms Grace (1)
Truth Hurts	Addictive (3)	Typically Tropical	Barbados (1)
T-Spoon	Sex On The Beach (2)	Tyrannosaurus Rex	Debora / One Inch Rock (re-
Tubeway Army	Are Friends Electric (1)		issue) (7)
Turin Brakes	Pain Killer (5)	UB40	Breakfast In Bed (6)
Turner, Tina	Best, The (5)		Come Back Darling (10)
	Goldeneye (10)		Don't Break My Heart (3)
	I Don't Wanna Fight (7)		Earth Dies Screaming / Dream
	I Don't Wanna Lose You (8)		A Lie, The (10)
	It Takes Two (5)		Higher Ground (8)
	It's Only Love (29)		Homely Girl (6)

MUSIC POP

Group/Artiste	Title	Group/Artiste	Title
	(I Can't Help) Falling In Love With You (1)		Fire (35)
	I Got You Babe (1)		Fly, The (1)
	If It Happens Again (9)		Hold Me Thrill Me Kiss Me Kill Me (2)
	I'll Be Your Baby Tonight (6)		I Still Haven't Found What I'm Looking For (6)
	King / Food For Thought (4)		Last Night On Earth (10)
	Kingston Town (4)		New Years Day (10)
	My Way Of Thinking / I Think It's Going To Rain (6)		One (7)
	One In Ten (7)		Please (7)
	Please Don't Make Me Cry (10)		Pride (In The Name Of Love) (3)
	Red Red Wine (1)		Staring At The Sun (3)
	Sing Our Own Song (5)		Stay (Faraway So Close) (4)
Ugly Kid Joe	Cats In The Cradle (7)		Stuck In A Moment You Can't Get Out Of (2)
	Everything About You (3)		Sweetest Thing (3)
Ullman, Tracey	Breakaway (4)		Unforgettable Fire, The (6)
	Move Over Darling (8)		Vertigo (1)
	They Don't Know (2)		Walk On (5)
Ultimate Kaos	Some Girls (9)		When Love Comes To Town (6)
Ultra	Rescue Me (8)		Where The Streets Have No Name (4)
Ultra Naté	Found A Cure (6)		With Or Without You (4)
	Free (4)	V	Blood Sweat And Tears (6)
Ultrabeat	Pretty Green Eyes (2)		Can You Feel It / Hip To Hip (5)
Ultravox	All Stood Still (8)	Valance, Holly	Down Boy (2)
	Dancing With Tears In My Eyes (3)		Kiss Kiss (1)
			State Of Mind (8)
	Vienna (2)	Valance, Ricky	Tell Laura I Love Her (1)
Umiliani, Piero	Mah Na Mah Na (8)	Valentine, Dickie	All The Time And Everywhere (9)
Uncle Kracker	Follow Me (3)		Blossom Fell, A (9)
Undercover	Baker Street (2)		Christmas Alphabet (1)
	Never Let Her Slip Away (5)		Christmas Island (8)
Undertones	My Perfect Cousin (9)		Finger Of Suspicion (1)
	Teenage Kicks (31)		I Wonder (4)
Underworld	Born Slippy (2)		In A Golden Coach (7)
Union Gap	Lady Willpower (5)		Mr Sandman (5)
	Young Girl (1)	Valli, Frankie	Grease (3)
	Young Girl (re-issue) (6)		Let's Hang On! (4)
Unit Four Plus Two	Concrete And Clay (1)		My Eyes Adored You (5)
Uniting Nations	Out Of Touch (7)		Night, The (7)
UNKLE	Be There (8)		Rag Doll (2)
Upsetters	Return Of Django / Dollar In The Teeth (5)	Van Dahl, Ian	Castles In The Sky (3)
Urban Cookie Collective	Feels Like Heaven (5)		Reason (8)
	Key The Secret, The (2)		Will I? (5)
Urban Hype	Trip To Trumpton, A (6)	Van Dyk, Paul	Tell Me Why (The Riddle) (7)
Ure, Midge	If I Was (1)	Van Dyke, Leroy	Walk On By (5)
	No Regrets (9)	Van Halen	Jump (7)
USA For Africa	We Are The World (1)		Why Can't This Be Love (8)
Usher	Burn (1)	Van Helden, Armand	Koochy (4)
	Confessions Part II / My Boo (5)		You Don't Know Me (1)
	I Need A Girl (Part One) (4)	Vandellas	Dancing In The Street (re-issue) (4)
	Pop Ya Colla (2)	Vandross, Luther	Best Things In Life Are Free (remix), The (7)
	U Got It Bad (5)		Best Things In Life Are Free, The (2)
	U Remind Me (3)		Endless Love (3)
	You Make Me Wanna (1)	Vanilla Ice	Ice Ice Baby (1)
Usher featuring Lil' Jon & Ludacris	Yeah (1)		Play That Funky Music (10)
Usura	Open Your Mind (7)	Vanity Fare	Early In The Morning (8)
Utah Saints	Believe In Me (8)	Vanwarmer, Randy	Just When I Needed You Most (8)
	Something Good (4)	Vapors	Turning Japanese (3)
	What Can You Do For Me (10)	Various Artists	All Star Hit Parade (2)
U2	All I Want Is You (4)		Brits 1990, The (2)
	Angel Of Harlem (9)		Perfect Day (1)
	Beautiful Day (1)	Vaughan, Frankie	Come Softly To Me (9)
	Desire (1)		Garden Of Eden (1)
	Discotheque (1)		
	Electrical Storm (5)		
	Elevation (3)		
	Even Better Than The Real Thing (remix) (8)		

Group/Artiste	Title	Group/Artiste	Title
	Gotta Have Something In The Bank Frank (8)	Ward, Clifford T	Gaye (8)
	Green Door (2)	Warhols, Dandy	Bohemian Like You (re-issue) (5)
	Heart Of A Man, The (5)	Warnes, Jennifer	(I've Had) The Time Of My Life (6)
	Kewpie Doll (10)		(I've Had) The Time Of My Life (re-entry) (8)
	Kisses Sweeter Than Wine (8)		Up Where We Belong (7)
	Loop-De-Loop (5)	Warp Brothers	Phatt Bass (9)
	Man On Fire / Wanderin' Eyes (6)	Warren, Anne	If Anyone Finds This I Love You (4)
	There Must Be A Way (7)	Warwick, Dionne	All The Love In The World (10)
	Tower Of Strength (1)		Do You Know The Way To San
Vaughan, Malcolm	Every Day Of My Life (5)		Jose (8)
	My Special Angel (3)		Heartbreaker (2)
	St Therese Of The Roses (re-entry) (3)		Walk On By (9)
Vaughan, Sarah	Broken Hearted Melody (7)	Was (Not Was)	Shake Your Head (4)
Vee, Bobby	How Many Tears (10)		Walk The Dinosaur (10)
	More Than I Can Say / Staying In (4)	Wash, Martha	Keep On Jumpin' (8)
		Washington, Keith	If You Were With Me Now (4)
	Night Has A Thousand Eyes, The (3)	Waterboys	Whole Of The Moon (re-issue), The (3)
	Rubber Ball (4)	Watergate	Heart Of Asia (3)
	Run To Him (6)	Waterman, Dennis	I Could Be So Good For You (3)
	Sharing You (10)		
	Take Good Care Of My Baby (3)	Waters, Crystal	Gypsy Woman (La Da Dee) (2)
Vega, Suzanne	Tom's Diner (2)	Watson, Russell	Someone Like You (10)
Vengaboys	Boom Boom Boom Boom (1)	Weather Girls	It's Raining Men (3)
	Kiss (When The Sun Don't Shine) (3)	Webb, Marti	Ben (5)
			Take That Look Off Your Face (3)
	Shalala Lala (5)		
	Uncle John From Jamaica (6)	Wedding Present	Come Play With Me (10)
	Up And Down (4)	Wedlock, Fred	Oldest Swinger In Town (6)
	We Like To Party! (Vengabus) (3)	Wee Papa Girl Rappers	Wee Rule (6)
	We're Going To Ibiza! (1)	Weedon, Bert	Guitar Boogie Shuffle (10)
Ventures	Perfidia (4)	Weller, Paul	Changingman, The (7)
	Walk Don't Run (8)		It's Written In The Stars (7)
Verve	Bitter Sweet Symphony (2)		Peacock Suit (5)
	Drugs Don't Work, The (1)		You Do Something To Me (9)
	Lucky Man (7)	Wells, Mary	My Guy (5)
Village People	In The Navy (2)	West End	Love I Lost, The (3)
	Y.M.C.A. (1)	West, Kanye	Through The Wire (9)
Vinton, Bobby	Blue Velvet (2)	West, Kanye featuring	All Falls Down (10)
Vipers Skiffle Group	Cumberland Gap (10)	Syleena Johnson	
	Don't You Rock Me Daddy-O (10)	West, Keith	Excerpt From A Teenage Opera (2)
Vries, Jurgen featuring CMC	Opera Song, The (Brave New World) (3)	Westlife	Against All Odds (1)
			Bop Bop Baby (5)
Visage	Fade To Grey (8)		Flying Without Wings (1)
VS	Love You Like Mad (7)		Fool Again (1)
Wah	Story Of The Blues, The (3)		Hey Whatever (4)
Waite, John	Missing You (9)		I Have A Dream / Seasons In
Wakelin, Johnny	Black Superman (Muhammad Ali) (7)		The Sun (1)
			If I Let You Go (1)
	In Zaire (4)		Mandy (1)
Waldo De Los Rios	Mozart Symphony No. 40 in G Minor (5)		Miss You Nights / Tonight (3)
			My Love (1)
Walker Brothers	Make It Easy On Yourself (1)		Obvious (3)
	My Ship Is Coming In (3)		Queen Of My Heart (1)
	No Regrets (7)		Swear It Again (1)
	Sun Ain't Gonna Shine Anymore, The (1)		Unbreakable (1)
			Uptown Girl (1)
Walker, Scott	Jackie (22)		What Makes A Man (2)
	Joanna (7)		World Of Our Own (1)
Waller, Rik	I Will Always Love You (6)	Wet Wet Wet	Angel Eyes (Home And Away) (5)
Wally Stott Orchestra	I Wanna Go Home (The Wreck Of The John 'B') (5)		Don't Want To Forgive Me Now (7)
Walsh, Steve	I Found Lovin' (9)		Goodnight Girl (1)
Walters, Trevor	Stuck On You (9)		If I Never See You Again (3)
Wamdue Project	King Of My Castle (1)		
Ward, Anita	Ring My Bell (1)		

M
U
S
I
C

P
O
P

Group/Artiste	Title	Group/Artiste	Title
	Julia Says (3)	Whitman, Slim	I'll Take You Home Again
	Love Is All Around (1)		Kathleen (7)
	Somewhere Somehow (7)		Indian Love Call (7)
	Sweet Little Mystery (5)		Rose Marie (1)
	Sweet Surrender (6)		Serenade (re-entry) (8)
	Wishing I Was Lucky (6)	Whittaker, Roger	I Don't Believe In If Anymore
	With A Little Help From My		(8)
	Friends (1)		Last Farewell, The (2)
	Yesterday (4)		Skye Boat Song, The (10)
Wham!	Bad Boys (2)	Who	Anyway Anyhow Anywhere (10)
	Club Tropicana (4)		Happy Jack (3)
	Edge Of Heaven / Where Did		I Can See For Miles (10)
	Your Heart Go, The (1)		I Can't Explain (8)
	Freedom (1)		I'm A Boy (2)
	I'm Your Man (1)		Join Together (9)
	Last Christmas / Everything		My Generation (2)
	She Wants (2)		Pictures Of Lily (4)
	Last Christmas (re-issue) (6)		Pinball Wizard (4)
	Wake Me Up Before You Go		Squeeze Box (10)
	Go (1)		Substitute (5)
	Wham Rap (8)		Substitute (re-issue) (7)
	Young Guns (Go For It) (3)		Won't Get Fooled Again (9)
Whatmore, Sarah	When I Lost You (6)		You Better You Bet (9)
Whatnauts	Girls (3)	Wigan's Chosen Few	Footsee (9)
Wheatley, Rebecca	Stay With Me (Baby) (10)	Wild Cherry	Play That Funky Music (7)
Wheatus	Little Respect, A (3)	Wild Pair	Opposites Attract (2)
	Teenage Dirtbag (2)	Wildchild	Renegade Master '98 (remix) (3)
Wheeler, Caron	Back To Life (However Do You	Wilde, Kim	Another Step (Closer To You) (6)
	Want Me) (1)		Chequered Love (4)
	Keep On Moving (5)		Four Letter Word (6)
Whelan, Bill	Riverdance (9)		Kids In America (2)
Whigfield	Another Day (7)		Never Trust A Stranger (7)
	Saturday Night (1)		You Came (3)
	Think Of You (7)		You Keep Me Hangin' On (2)
Whiskey, Nancy	Freight Train (5)	Wilde, Marty	Bad Boy (7)
Whispers	And The Beat Goes On (2)		Donna (3)
	It's A Love Thing (9)		Endless Sleep (4)
Whistle	(Nothin' Serious) Just Buggin' (7)		Rubber Ball (9)
Whistling Jack Smith	I Was Kaiser Bill's Batman (5)		Sea Of Love (3)
White Plains	Julie Do Ya Love Me (8)		Teenager On Love, A (2)
	My Baby Loves Lovin' (9)	Wilder, Matthew	Break My Stride (4)
White Stripes	7 Nation Army (7)	Will To Power	Baby I Love Your Way –
White Town	Your Woman (1)		Freebird (2)
White, Barry	Can't Get Enough Of Your Love	Williams, Alyson	I Need Your Lovin' (8)
	Babe (8)	Williams, Andy	Almost There (2)
	(For You) I'll Do Anything You		Butterfly (1)
	Want Me To (5)		Can't Get Used To Losing You
	Let The Music Play (9)		(2)
	What Am I Gonna Do With You		Can't Help Falling In Love (3)
	(5)		Can't Take My Eyes Off You (5)
	You See The Trouble With Me		Home Lovin' Man (7)
	(2)		Music To Watch Girls By (9)
	You're The First The Last My		Solitaire (4)
	Everything (1)		(Where Do I Begin) Love Story
White, Snowy	Bird Of Paradise (6)		(4)
Whitesnake	Here I Go Again (remix) (9)	Williams, Danny	Moon River (1)
	Is This Love (9)		Wonderful World Of The Young
Whitfield, David	Answer Me (1)		(8)
	Beyond The Stars (8)	Williams, Deniece	Free (1)
	Book (re-entry), The (10)		Let's Hear It For The Boy (2)
	Book, The (5)		That's What Friends Are For (8)
	Bridge Of Sighs (9)		Too Much Too Little Too Late (3)
	Cara Mia (1)	Williams, Mason	Classical Gas (9)
	Ev'rywhere (3)	Williams, Melanie	Ain't No Love (Ain't No Use) (3)
	My September Love (re-entry)	Williams, P	Boys (7)
	(3)	Williams, Robbie	Angels (4)
	Rags To Riches		Come Undone (4)
	(re-entry) (3)		Eternity / The Road To
	Santo Natale (2)		Mandalay (1)
	When You Lose The One You		Feel (4)
	Love (7)		Freedom (2)

M
U
S
I
C

P
O
P

Group/Artiste	Title	Group/Artiste	Title
	Rockin' Over The Beat (9)	Young, Paul	Come Back And Stay (4)
Yanou	Heaven (1)		Every Time You Go Away (4)
Yarbrough & Peoples	Don't Stop The Music (7)		Everything Must Change (9)
Yardbirds	Evil Hearted You / Still I'm Sad (3)		I'm Gonna Tear Your Playhouse Down (9)
	For Your Love (3)		Love Of The Common People (2)
	Heart Full Of Soul (2)		Senza Una Donna (Without A Woman) (4)
	Over Under Sideways Down (10)		Wherever I Lay My Hat (That's My Home) (1)
	Shapes Of Things (3)		
Yazoo	Don't Go (3)		
	Nobody's Diary (3)	Young, Will	Anything Is Possible / Evergreen (1)
	Only You (2)		Don't Let Me Down / You And I (2)
Yazz	Doctorin' The House (6)		
	Fine Time (9)		Friday's Child (4)
	Only Way Is Up, The (1)		Leave Right Now (1)
	Stand Up For Your Love Rights (2)		Light My Fire (1)
Yell!	Instant Replay (10)		Long And Winding Road, The / Suspicious Minds (1)
Yello	Race, The (7)		Your Game (3)
Yellow Dog	Just One More Night (8)		
Yes	Wonderous Stories (7)	Youngblood, Sydney	If Only I Could (3)
Yomanda	Synth And Strings (8)	Zacharias, Helmut	Tokyo Melody (9)
York	O.T.B (On The Beach) / Reachers Of Civilisation (4)	Zager & Evans	In The Year 2525 (Exordium And Terminus) (1)
Young Idea	With A Little Help From Friends (10)	Zager Band, Michael	Let's All Chant (8)
		Zamfir, Georghe	(Light Of Experience) Doina De Jale (4)
Young Ones	Living Doll (1)		
Young Rascals	Groovin' (8)	Zavaroni, Lena	Ma (He's Making Eyes At Me) (10)
Young, Faron	It's Four In The Morning (3)		
Young, Jimmy	Chain Gang (9)	Zig & Zag	Them Girls Them Girls (5)
	Eternally (8)	Zoe	Sunshine On A Rainy Day (re-mix) (4)
	Faith Can Move Mountains (11)		
	Man From Laramie, The (1)	Zombie Nation	Kernkraft 400 (2)
	More (4)	Zucchero	Senza Una Donna (Without A Woman) (4)
	Unchained Melody (1)		
Young, John Paul	Love Is In The Air (5)	ZZ Top	Gimme All Your Lovin' (10)
Young, Karen	Nobody's Child (6)		Viva Las Vegas (10)
Young, Neil	Heart Of Gold (10)		

The 1000 Number One UK Singles

(The following is a list of every No. 1 record from the inception of the charts
until the end of March 2005)

	Artist	Song	Date
1	Al Martino	Here In My Heart	14 Nov 1952
2	Jo Stafford	You Belong To Me	16 Jan 1953
3	Kay Starr	Comes A-Long A-Love	23 Jan 1953
4	Eddie Fisher	Outside Of Heaven	30 Jan 1953
5	Perry Como	Don't Let The Stars Get In Your Eyes	6 Feb 1953
6	Guy Mitchell	She Wears Red Feathers	13 Mar 1953
7	Stargazers	Broken Wings	10 Apr 1953
8	Lita Roza	(How Much Is) That Doggie In The Window	17 Apr 1953
9	Frankie Laine	I Believe	24 Apr 1953
10	Eddie Fisher	I'm Walking Behind You	26 June 1953
11	Mantovani	Song from 'The Moulin Rouge'	14 Aug 1953
12	Guy Mitchell	Look At That Girl	11 Sept 1953
13	Frankie Laine	Hey Joe	23 Oct 1953
14	David Whitfield	Answer Me	6 Nov 1953
15	Frankie Laine	Answer Me	13 Nov 1953
16	Eddie Calvert	Oh Mein Papa	8 Jan 1954
17	Stargazers	I See The Moon	12 Mar 1954
18	Doris Day	Secret Love	16 Apr 1954
19	Johnnie Ray	Such A Night	30 Apr 1954
20	David Whitfield	Cara Mia	2 July 1954
21	Kitty Kallen	Little Things Mean A Lot	10 Sept 1954
22	Frank Sinatra	Three Coins In The Fountain	17 Sept 1954

	Artist	Song	Date
23	Don Cornell	Hold My Hand	8 Oct 1954
24	Vera Lynn	My Son My Son	5 Nov 1954
25	Rosemary Clooney	This Ole House	26 Nov 1954
26	Winifred Atwell	Let's Have Another Party	3 Dec 1954
27	Dickie Valentine	Finger Of Suspicion	7 Jan 1955
28	Rosemary Clooney	Mambo Italiano	14 Jan 1955
29	Ruby Murray	Softly, Softly	18 Feb 1955
30	Tennessee Ernie Ford	Give Me Your Word	11 Mar 1955
31	Perez 'Prez' Prado & His Orchestra	Cherry Pink And Apple Blossom White	29 Apr 1955
32	Tony Bennett	Stranger In Paradise	13 May 1955
33	Eddie Calvert	Cherry Pink And Apple Blossom White	27 May 1955
34	Jimmy Young	Unchained Melody	24 June 1955
35	Alma Cogan	Dreamboat	15 July 1955
36	Slim Whitman	Rose Marie	29 July 1955
37	Jimmy Young	The Man From Laramie	14 Oct 1955
38	Johnston Brothers	Hernando's Hideaway	11 Nov 1955
39	Bill Haley & His Comets	Rock Around The Clock	25 Nov 1955
40	Dickie Valentine	Christmas Alphabet	16 Dec 1955
41	Tennessee Ernie Ford	Sixteen Tons	20 Jan 1956
42	Dean Martin	Memories Are Made Of This	17 Feb 1956
43	Dream Weavers	It's Almost Tomorrow	16 Mar 1956
44	Kay Starr	Rock And Roll Waltz	30 Mar 1956
45	Winifred Atwell	Poor People Of Paris	13 Apr 1956
46	Ronnie Hilton	No Other Love	4 May 1956
47	Pat Boone	I'll Be Home	15 June 1956
48	Frankie Lymon & The Teenagers	Why Do Fools Fall in Love	20 July 1956
49	Doris Day	Whatever Will Be Will Be (Que Sera, Sera)	10 Aug 1956
50	Anne Shelton	Lay Down Your Arms	21 Sept 1956
51	Frankie Laine	A Woman In Love	19 Oct 1956
52	Johnnie Ray	Just Walking In The Rain	16 Nov 1956
53	Guy Mitchell	Singing The Blues	4 Jan 1957
54	Tommy Steele	Singing The Blues	11 Jan 1957
55	Frankie Vaughan	The Garden Of Eden	25 Jan 1957
56	Tab Hunter	Young Love	22 Feb 1957
57	Lonnie Donegan	Cumberland Gap	12 Apr 1957
58	Guy Mitchell	Rock-A-Billy	17 May 1957
59	Andy Williams	Butterfly	24 May 1957
60	Johnnie Ray	Yes Tonight Josephine	7 June 1957
61	Lonnie Donegan	Puttin' On The Style / Gamblin' Man	28 June 1957
62	Elvis Presley	All Shook Up	12 July 1957
63	Paul Anka	Diana	30 Aug 1957
64	The Crickets	That'll Be The Day	1 Nov 1957
65	Harry Belafonte	Mary's Boy Child	22 Nov 1957
66	Jerry Lee Lewis	Great Balls Of Fire	10 Jan 1958
67	Elvis Presley	Jailhouse Rock	24 Jan 1958
68	Michael Holliday	The Story Of My Life	14 Feb 1958
69	Perry Como	Magic Moments	28 Feb 1958
70	Marvin Rainwater	Whole Lotta Woman	25 Apr 1958
71	Connie Francis	Who's Sorry Now	16 May 1958
72	Vic Damone	On The Street Where You Live	27 June 1958
73	Everly Brothers	All I Have To Do Is Dream / Claudette	4 July 1958
74	Kalin Twins	When	22 Aug 1958
75	Connie Francis	Carolina Moon / Stupid Cupid	26 Sept 1958
76	Tommy Edwards	All In The Game	7 Nov 1958
77	Lord Rockingham's XI	Hoots Mon	28 Nov 1958
78	Conway Twitty	It's Only Make Believe	19 Dec 1958
79	Jane Morgan	The Day The Rains Came	23 Jan 1959
80	Elvis Presley	I Got Stung / One Night	30 Jan 1959
81	Shirley Bassey	As I Love You	20 Feb 1959
82	The Platters	Smoke Gets In Your Eyes	20 Mar 1959
83	Russ Conway	Side Saddle	27 Mar 1959
84	Buddy Holly	It Doesn't Matter Anymore	24 Apr 1959
85	Elvis Presley	A Fool Such As I / I Need Your Love Tonight	15 May 1959
86	Russ Conway	Roulette	19 June 1959
87	Bobby Darin	Dream Lover	3 July 1959
88	Cliff Richard	Living Doll	31 July 1959
89	Craig Douglas	Only Sixteen	11 Sept 1959
90	Jerry Keller	Here Comes Summer	9 Oct 1959
91	Bobby Darin	Mack The Knife	16 Oct 1959
92	Cliff Richard	Travellin' Light	30 Oct 1959
93	Adam Faith	What Do You Want	4 Dec 1959

MUSIC POP

	Artist	Song	Date
94	Emile Ford & The Checkmates	What Do You Want To Make Those Eyes At Me For	18 Dec 1959
95	Michael Holliday	Starry Eyed	29 Jan 1960
96	Anthony Newley	Why	5 Feb 1960
97	Adam Faith	Poor Me	10 Mar 1960
98	Johnny Preston	Running Bear	17 Mar 1960
99	Lonnie Donegan	My Old Man's A Dustman	31 Mar 1960
100	Anthony Newley	Do You Mind	28 Apr 1960
101	Everly Brothers	Cathy's Clown	5 May 1960
102	Eddie Cochran	Three Steps To Heaven	23 June 1960
103	Jimmy Jones	Good Timin'	7 July 1960
104	Cliff Richard	Please Don't Tease	28 July 1960
105	Johnny Kidd & The Pirates	Shakin' All Over	4 Aug 1960
106	Shadows	Apache	25 Aug 1960
107	Ricky Valance	Tell Laura I Love Her	29 Sept 1960
108	Roy Orbison	Only The Lonely	20 Oct 1960
109	Elvis Presley	It's Now Or Never	3 Nov 1960
110	Cliff Richard	I Love You	29 Dec 1960
111	Johnny Tillotson	Poetry In Motion	12 Jan 1961
112	Elvis Presley	Are You Lonesome Tonight	26 Jan 1961
113	Petula Clark	Sailor	23 Feb 1961
114	Everly Brothers	Walk Right Back / Ebony Eyes	2 Mar 1961
115	Elvis Presley	Wooden Heart	23 Mar 1961
116	The Marcels	Blue Moon	4 May 1961
117	Floyd Cramer	On The Rebound	18 May 1961
118	The Temperance Seven	You're Driving Me Crazy	25 May 1961
119	Elvis Presley	Surrender	1 June 1961
120	Del Shannon	Runaway	29 June 1961
121	Everly Brothers	Temptation	20 July 1961
122	Eden Kane	Well I Ask You	3 Aug 1961
123	Helen Shapiro	You Don't Know	10 Aug 1961
124	John Leyton	Johnny Remember Me	31 Aug 1961
125	Shirley Bassey	Reach For The Stars / Climb Ev'ry Mountain	21 Sept 1961
126	Shadows	Kon Tiki	5 Oct 1961
127	The Highwaymen	Michael	12 Oct 1961
128	Helen Shapiro	Walkin' Back To Happiness	19 Oct 1961
129	Elvis Presley	His Latest Flame	9 Nov 1961
130	Frankie Vaughan	Tower Of Strength	7 Dec 1961
131	Danny Williams	Moon River	28 Dec 1961
132	Cliff Richard	The Young Ones	11 Jan 1962
133	Elvis Presley	Can't Help Falling In Love / Rock-A-Hula Baby	22 Feb 1962
134	Shadows	Wonderful Land	22 Mar 1962
135	B Bumble & The Stingers	Nut Rocker	17 May 1962
136	Elvis Presley	Good Luck Charm	24 May 1962
137	Mike Sarne with Wendy Richard	Come Outside	28 June 1962
138	Ray Charles	I Can't Stop Loving You	12 July 1962
139	Frank Ifield	I Remember You	26 July 1962
140	Elvis Presley	She's Not You	13 Sept 1962
141	Tornados	Telstar	4 Oct 1962
142	Frank Ifield	Lovesick Blues	8 Nov 1962
143	Elvis Presley	Return To Sender	13 Dec 1962
144	Cliff Richard	The Next Time / Bachelor Boy	3 Jan 1963
145	Shadows	Dance On	24 Jan 1963
146	Jet Harris & Tony Meehan	Diamonds	31 Jan 1963
147	Frank Ifield	Wayward Wind	21 Feb 1963
148	Cliff Richard	Summer Holiday	14 Mar 1963
149	Shadows	Foot Tapper	29 Mar 1963
150	Gerry & The Pacemakers	How Do You Do It?	11 Apr 1963
151	Beatles	From Me To You	2 May 1963
152	Gerry & The Pacemakers	I Like It	20 June 1963
153	Frank Ifield	Confessin' (That I Love You)	18 July 1963
154	Elvis Presley	(You're The) Devil In Disguise	1 Aug 1963
155	Searchers	Sweets For My Sweet	8 Aug 1963
156	Billy J Kramer & The Dakotas	Bad To Me	22 Aug 1963
157	Beatles	She Loves You	12 Sept 1963
158	Brian Poole & The Tremeloes	Do You Love Me	10 Oct 1963
159	Gerry & The Pacemakers	You'll Never Walk Alone	31 Oct 1963
160	Beatles	I Want To Hold Your Hand	12 Dec 1963
161	Dave Clark Five	Glad All Over	16 Jan 1964
162	Searchers	Needles And Pins	30 Jan 1964
163	Bachelors	Diane	20 Feb 1964
164	Cilla Black	Anyone Who Had A Heart	27 Feb 1964

	Artist	Song	Date
165	Billy J Kramer & The Dakotas	Little Children	19 Mar 1964
166	Beatles	Can't Buy Me Love	2 Apr 1964
167	Peter & Gordon	A World Without Love	23 Apr 1964
168	Searchers	Don't Throw Your Love Away	7 May 1964
169	Four Pennies	Juliet	21 May 1964
170	Cilla Black	You're My World	28 May 1964
171	Roy Orbison	It's Over	25 June 1964
172	Animals	The House Of The Rising Sun	9 July 1964
173	Rolling Stones	It's All Over Now	16 July 1964
174	Beatles	A Hard Day's Night	23 July 1964
175	Manfred Mann	Do Wah Diddy Diddy	13 Aug 1964
176	Honeycombs	Have I The Right	27 Aug 1964
177	Kinks	You Really Got Me	10 Sept 1964
178	Herman's Hermits	I'm Into Something Good	24 Sept 1964
179	Roy Orbison	Oh Pretty Woman	8 Oct 1964
180	Sandie Shaw	(There's) Always Something There To Remind Me	22 Oct 1964
181	Supremes	Baby Love	19 Nov 1964
182	Rolling Stones	Little Red Rooster	3 Dec 1964
183	Beatles	I Feel Fine	10 Dec 1964
184	Georgie Fame & The Blue Flames	Yeah Yeah	14 Jan 1965
185	Moody Blues	Go Now!	28 Jan 1965
186	Righteous Brothers	You've Lost That Loving Feeling	4 Feb 1965
187	Kinks	Tired Of Waiting For You	18 Feb 1965
188	Seekers	I'll Never Find Another You	25 Feb 1965
189	Tom Jones	It's Not Unusual	11 Mar 1965
190	Rolling Stones	The Last Time	18 Mar 1965
191	Unit Four Plus Two	Concrete And Clay	8 Apr 1965
192	Cliff Richard	The Minute You're Gone	15 Apr 1965
193	Beatles	Ticket To Ride	22 Apr 1965
194	Roger Miller	King Of The Road	13 May 1965
195	Jackie Trent	Where Are You Now (My Love)	20 May 1965
196	Sandie Shaw	Long Live Love	27 May 1965
197	Elvis Presley	Crying In The Chapel	17 June 1965
198	Hollies	I'm Alive	24 June 1965
199	Byrds	Mr Tambourine Man	22 July 1965
200	Beatles	Help!	5 Aug 1965
201	Sonny & Cher	I Got You Babe	26 Aug 1965
202	Rolling Stones	(I Can't Get No) Satisfaction	9 Sept 1965
203	Walker Brothers	Make It Easy On Yourself	23 Sept 1965
204	Ken Dodd	Tears	30 Sept 1965
205	Rolling Stones	Get Off Of My Cloud	4 Nov 1965
206	Seekers	The Carnival Is Over	25 Nov 1965
207	Beatles	Day Tripper / We Can Work It Out	16 Dec 1965
208	Spencer Davis Group	Keep On Running	20 Jan 1966
209	Overlanders	Michelle	27 Jan 1966
210	Nancy Sinatra	These Boots Are Made For Walking	17 Feb 1966
211	Walker Brothers	The Sun Ain't Gonna Shine Anymore	17 Mar 1966
212	Spencer Davis Group	Somebody Help Me	14 Apr 1966
213	Dusty Springfield	You Don't Have To Say You Love Me	28 Apr 1966
214	Manfred Mann	Pretty Flamingo	5 May 1966
215	Rolling Stones	Paint It Black	26 May 1966
216	Frank Sinatra	Strangers In The Night	2 June 1966
217	Beatles	Paperback Writer	23 June 1966
218	Kinks	Sunny Afternoon	7 July 1966
219	Georgie Fame & The Blue Flames	Getaway	21 July 1966
220	Chris Farlowe	Out Of Time	28 July 1966
221	Troggs	With A Girl Like You	4 Aug 1966
222	Beatles	Yellow Submarine / Eleanor Rigby	18 Aug 1966
223	Small Faces	All Or Nothing	15 Sept 1966
224	Jim Reeves	Distant Drums	22 Sept 1966
225	Four Tops	Reach Out I'll Be There	27 Oct 1966
226	Beach Boys	Good Vibrations	17 Nov 1966
227	Tom Jones	Green Green Grass Of Home	1 Dec 1966
228	Monkees	I'm A Believer	19 Jan 1967
229	Petula Clark	This Is My Song	16 Feb 1967
230	Engelbert Humperdinck	Release Me	2 Mar 1967
231	Frank Sinatra & Nancy Sinatra	Somethin' Stupid	13 Apr 1967
232	Sandie Shaw	Puppet On A String	27 Apr 1967
233	Tremeloes	Silence Is Golden	18 May 1967
234	Procol Harum	A Whiter Shade Of Pale	8 June 1967
235	Beatles	All You Need Is Love	19 July 1967

MUSIC POP

	Artist	Song	Date
236	Scott McKenzie	San Francisco (Be Sure To Wear Some Flowers In Your Hair)	9 Aug 1967
237	Engelbert Humperdinck	The Last Waltz	6 Sept 1967
238	Bee Gees	Massachusetts	11 Oct 1967
239	Foundations	Baby Now That I've Found You	8 Nov 1967
240	Long John Baldry	Let The Heartaches Begin	22 Nov 1967
241	Beatles	Hello Goodbye	6 Dec 1967
242	Georgie Fame	The Ballad Of Bonnie And Clyde	24 Jan 1968
243	Love Affair	Everlasting Love	31 Jan 1968
244	Manfred Mann	The Mighty Quinn	14 Feb 1968
245	Esther & Abi Ofarim	Cinderella Rockefella	28 Feb 1968
246	Dave Dee, Dozy, Beaky, Mick & Tich	Legend Of Xanadu	20 Mar 1968
247	Beatles	Lady Madonna	27 Mar 1968
248	Cliff Richard	Congratulations	10 Apr 1968
249	Louis Armstrong	What A Wonderful World / Cabaret	24 Apr 1968
250	Union Gap featuring Gary Puckett	Young Girl	22 May 1968
251	Rolling Stones	Jumpin' Jack Flash	19 June 1968
252	Equals	Baby Come Back	3 July 1968
253	Des O'Connor	I Pretend	24 July 1968
254	Tommy James & The Shondells	Mony Mony	31 July 1968
255	Crazy World of Arthur Brown	Fire	14 Aug 1968
256	Beach Boys	Do It Again	28 Aug 1968
257	Bee Gees	I've Gotta Get A Message To You	4 Sept 1968
258	Beatles	Hey Jude	11 Sept 1968
259	Mary Hopkin	Those Were The Days	25 Sept 1968
260	Joe Cocker	With A Little Help From My Friends	6 Nov 1968
261	Hugo Montenegro Orchestra	The Good The Bad And The Ugly	13 Nov 1968
262	Scaffold	Lily The Pink	11 Dec 1968
263	Marmalade	Ob-La-Di Ob-La-Da	1 Jan 1969
264	Fleetwood Mac	Albatross	29 Jan 1969
265	Move	Blackberry Way	5 Feb 1969
266	Amen Corner	(If Paradise Is) Half As Nice	12 Feb 1969
267	Peter Sarstedt	Where Do You Go To My Lovely?	26 Feb 1969
268	Marvin Gaye	I Heard It Through The Grapevine	26 Mar 1969
269	Desmond Dekker & The Aces	Israelites	16 Apr 1969
270	Beatles	Get Back	23 Apr 1969
271	Tommy Roe	Dizzy	4 June 1969
272	Beatles	The Ballad Of John And Yoko	11 June 1969
273	Thunderclap Newman	Something In The Air	2 July 1969
274	Rolling Stones	Honky Tonk Women	23 July 1969
275	Zager & Evans	In The Year 2525 (Exordium And Terminus)	30 Aug 1969
276	Creedence Clearwater Revival	Bad Moon Rising	20 Sept 1969
277	Jane Birkin & Serge Gainsbourg	Je T'Aime ... Moi Non Plus	11 Oct 1969
278	Bobbie Gentry	I'll Never Fall In Love Again	18 Oct 1969
279	Archies	Sugar Sugar	25 Oct 1969
280	Rolf Harris	Two Little Boys	20 Dec 1969
281	Edison Lighthouse	Love Grows (Where My Rosemary Goes)	31 Jan 1970
282	Lee Marvin	Wand'rin' Star	7 Mar 1970
283	Simon & Garfunkel	Bridge Over Troubled Water	28 Mar 1970
284	Dana	All Kinds Of Everything	18 Apr 1970
285	Norman Greenbaum	Spirit In The Sky	2 May 1970
286	England World Cup Squad	Back Home	16 May 1970
287	Christie	Yellow River	6 June 1970
288	Mungo Jerry	In The Summertime	13 June 1970
289	Elvis Presley	The Wonder Of You	1 Aug 1970
290	Smokey Robinson & The Miracles	Tears Of A Clown	12 Sept 1970
291	Freda Payne	Band Of Gold	19 Sept 1970
292	Matthews Southern Comfort	Woodstock	31 Oct 1970
293	Jimi Hendrix	Voodoo Chile	21 Nov 1970
294	Dave Edmunds	I Hear You Knocking	28 Nov 1970
295	Clive Dunn	Grandad	9 Jan 1971
296	George Harrison	My Sweet Lord	30 Jan 1971
297	Mungo Jerry	Baby Jump	6 Mar 1971
298	T Rex	Hot Love	20 Mar 1971
299	Dave & Ansil Collins	Double Barrel	1 May 1971
300	Dawn	Knock Three Times	15 May 1971
301	Middle Of The Road	Chirpy Chirpy Cheep Cheep	19 June 1971
302	T Rex	Get It On	24 July 1971
303	Diana Ross	I'm Still Waiting	21 Aug 1971
304	Tams	Hey Girl Don't Bother Me	18 Sept 1971
305	Rod Stewart	Maggie May	9 Oct 1971

	Artist	Song	Date
306	Slade	Coz I Luv You	13 Nov 1971
307	Benny Hill	Ernie (The Fastest Milkman In The West)	11 Dec 1971
308	New Seekers	I'd Like To Teach The World To Sing (In Perfect Harmony)	8 Jan 1972
309	T Rex	Telegram Sam	5 Feb 1972
310	Chicory Tip	Son Of My Father	19 Feb 1972
311	Nilsson	Without You	11 Mar 1972
312	The Pipes & Drums & Military Band of The Royal Scots Dragoon Guards	Amazing Grace	15 Apr 1972
313	T Rex	Metal Guru	20 May 1972
314	Don McLean	Vincent	17 June 1972
315	Slade	Take Me Bak 'Ome	1 July 1972
316	Donny Osmond	Puppy Love	8 July 1972
317	Alice Cooper	School's Out	12 Aug 1972
318	Rod Stewart	You Wear It Well	2 Sept 1972
319	Slade	Mama Weer All Crazee Now	9 Sept 1972
320	David Cassidy	How Can I Be Sure	30 Sept 1972
321	Lieutenant Pigeon	Mouldy Old Dough	14 Oct 1972
322	Gilbert O'Sullivan	Clair	11 Nov 1972
323	Chuck Berry	My Ding-A-Ling	25 Nov 1972
324	Little Jimmy Osmond	Long Haired Lover From Liverpool	23 Dec 1972
325	Sweet	Blockbuster	27 Jan 1973
326	Slade	Cum On Feel The Noize	3 Mar 1973
327	Donny Osmond	The Twelfth Of Never	31 Mar 1973
328	Gilbert O'Sullivan	Get Down	7 Apr 1973
329	Dawn featuring Tony Orlando	Tie A Yellow Ribbon Round The Old Oak Tree	21 Apr 1973
330	Wizzard	See My Baby Jive	19 May 1973
331	Suzi Quatro	Can The Can	16 June 1973
332	10CC	Rubber Bullets	23 June 1973
333	Slade	Skweeze Me Pleeze Me	30 June 1973
334	Peters & Lee	Welcome Home	21 July 1973
335	Gary Glitter	I'm The Leader Of The Gang (I Am)	28 July 1973
336	Donny Osmond	Young Love	25 Aug 1973
337	Wizzard	Angel Fingers	22 Sept 1973
338	Simon Park Orchestra	Eye Level	29 Sept 1973
339	David Cassidy	Daydreamer / The Puppy Song	27 Oct 1973
340	Gary Glitter	I Love You Love Me Love	17 Nov 1973
341	Slade	Merry Xmas Everybody	15 Dec 1973
342	New Seekers	You Won't Find Another Fool Like Me	19 Jan 1974
343	Mud	Tiger Feet	26 Jan 1974
344	Suzi Quatro	Devil Gate Drive	23 Feb 1974
345	Alvin Stardust	Jealous Mind	9 Mar 1974
346	Paper Lace	Billy Don't Be A Hero	16 Mar 1974
347	Terry Jacks	Seasons In The Sun	6 Apr 1974
348	Abba	Waterloo	4 May 1974
349	Rubettes	Sugar Baby Love	18 May 1974
350	Ray Stevens	The Streak	15 June 1974
351	Gary Glitter	Always Yours	22 June 1974
352	Charles Aznavour	She	29 June 1974
353	George McCrae	Rock Your Baby	27 July 1974
354	Three Degrees	When Will I See You Again	17 Aug 1974
355	Osmonds	Love Me For A Reason	31 Aug 1974
356	Carl Douglas	Kung Fu Fighting	21 Sept 1974
357	John Denver	Annie's Song	12 Oct 1974
358	Sweet Sensation	Sad Sweet Dreamer	19 Oct 1974
359	Ken Boothe	Everything I Own	26 Oct 1974
360	David Essex	Gonna Make You A Star	16 Nov 1974
361	Barry White	You're The First, The Last, My Everything	7 Dec 1974
362	Mud	Lonely This Christmas	21 Dec 1974
363	Status Quo	Down Down	18 Jan 1975
364	Tymes	Ms Grace	25 Jan 1975
365	Pilot	January	1 Feb 1975
366	Steve Harley & Cockney Rebel	Make Me Smile (Come Up And See Me)	22 Feb 1975
367	Telly Savalas	If	8 Mar 1975
368	Bay City Rollers	Bye Bye Baby	22 Mar 1975
369	Mud	Oh Boy	3 May 1975
370	Tammy Wynette	Stand By Your Man	17 May 1975
371	Windsor Davies & Don Estelle	Whispering Grass	7 June 1975
372	10CC	I'm Not In Love	28 June 1975
373	Johnny Nash	Tears On My Pillow	12 July 1975
374	Bay City Rollers	Give A Little Love	19 July 1975

MUSIC POP

	Artist	Song	Date
375	Typically Tropical	Barbados	9 Aug 1975
376	Stylistics	Can't Give You Anything (But My Love)	16 Aug 1975
377	Rod Stewart	Sailing	6 Sept 1975
378	David Essex	Hold Me Close	4 Oct 1975
379	Art Garfunkel	I Only Have Eyes For You	25 Oct 1975
380	David Bowie	Space Oddity	8 Nov 1975
381	Billy Connolly	D.I.V.O.R.C.E.	22 Nov 1975
382	Queen	Bohemian Rhapsody	29 Nov 1975
383	Abba	Mamma Mia	31 Jan 1976
384	Slik	Forever And Ever	14 Feb 1976
385	Four Seasons	December '63 (Oh, What A Night)	21 Feb 1976
386	Tina Charles	I Love To Love (But My Baby Loves To Dance)	6 Mar 1976
387	Brotherhood Of Man	Save Your Kisses For Me	27 Mar 1976
388	Abba	Fernando	8 May 1976
389	J J Barrie	No Charge	5 June 1976
390	Wurzels	Combine Harvester (Brand New Key)	12 June 1976
391	Real Thing	You To Me Are Everything	26 June 1976
392	Demis Roussos	The Roussos Phenomenon EP (main track: Forever And Ever)	17 July 1976
393	Elton John & Kiki Dee	Don't Go Breaking My Heart	24 July 1976
394	Abba	Dancing Queen	4 Sept 1976
395	Pussycat	Mississippi	16 Oct 1976
396	Chicago	If You Leave Me Now	13 Nov 1976
397	Showaddywaddy	Under The Moon Of Love	4 Dec 1976
398	Johnny Mathis	When A Child Is Born (Soleado)	25 Dec 1976
399	David Soul	Don't Give Up On Us	15 Jan 1977
400	Julie Covington	Don't Cry For Me Argentina	12 Feb 1977
401	Leo Sayer	When I Need You	19 Feb 1977
402	Manhattan Transfer	Chanson D'Amour	12 Mar 1977
403	Abba	Knowing Me Knowing You	2 Apr 1977
404	Deniece Williams	Free	7 May 1977
405	Rod Stewart	I Don't Want To Talk About It / First Cut Is The Deepest	21 May 1977
406	Kenny Rogers	Lucille	18 June 1977
407	Jacksons	Show You The Way To Go	25 June 1977
408	Hot Chocolate	So You Win Again	2 July 1977
409	Donna Summer	I Feel Love	23 July 1977
410	Brotherhood Of Man	Angelo	20 Aug 1977
411	Floaters	Float On	27 Aug 1977
412	Elvis Presley	Way Down	3 Sept 1977
413	David Soul	Silver Lady	8 Oct 1977
414	Baccara	Yes Sir I Can Boogie	29 Oct 1977
415	Abba	The Name Of The Game	5 Nov 1977
416	Wings	Mull Of Kintyre / Girls' School	3 Dec 1977
417	Althia & Donna	Up Town Top Ranking	4 Feb 1978
418	Brotherhood Of Man	Figaro	11 Feb 1978
419	Abba	Take A Chance On Me	18 Feb 1978
420	Kate Bush	Wuthering Heights	11 Mar 1978
421	Brian & Michael	Matchstalk Men And Matchstalk Cats And Dogs	8 Apr 1978
422	Bee Gees	Night Fever	29 Apr 1978
423	Boney M	Rivers Of Babylon / Brown Girl In The Ring	13 May 1978
424	John Travolta & Olivia Newton John	You're The One That I Want	17 June 1978
425	Commodores	Three Times A Lady	19 Aug 1978
426	10CC	Dreadlock Holiday	23 Sept 1978
427	John Travolta & Olivia Newton John	Summer Nights	30 Sept 1978
428	Boomtown Rats	Rat Trap	18 Nov 1978
429	Rod Stewart	Da Ya Think I'm Sexy	2 Dec 1978
430	Boney M	Mary's Boy Child / Oh My Lord	9 Dec 1978
431	Village People	Y.M.C.A.	6 Jan 1979
432	Ian Dury & The Blockheads	Hit Me With Your Rhythm Stick	27 Jan 1979
433	Blondie	Heart Of Glass	3 Feb 1979
434	Bee Gees	Tragedy	3 Mar 1979
435	Gloria Gaynor	I Will Survive	17 Mar 1979
436	Art Garfunkel	Bright Eyes	14 Apr 1979
437	Blondie	Sunday Girl	26 May 1979
438	Anita Ward	Ring My Bell	16 June 1979
439	Tubeway Army	Are 'Friends' Electric	30 June 1979
440	Boomtown Rats	I Don't Like Mondays	28 July 1979
441	Cliff Richard	We Don't Talk Anymore	25 Aug 1979
442	Gary Numan	Cars	22 Sept 1979
443	Police	Message In A Bottle	29 Sept 1979

	Artist	Song	Date
444	Buggles	Video Killed The Radio Star	20 Oct 1979
445	Lena Martell	One Day At A Time	27 Oct 1979
446	Dr Hook	When You're In Love With A Beautiful Woman	17 Nov 1979
447	Police	Walking On The Moon	8 Dec 1979
448	Pink Floyd	Another Brick In The Wall	15 Dec 1979
449	Pretenders	Brass In Pocket	19 Jan 1980
450	Specials	The Special AKA Live EP (main track: Too Much Too Young)	2 Feb 1980
451	Kenny Rogers	Coward Of The County	16 Feb 1980
452	Blondie	Atomic	1 Mar 1980
453	Fern Kinney	Together We Are Beautiful	15 Mar 1980
454	Jam	Going Underground / Dreams Of Children	22 Mar 1980
455	Detroit Spinners	Working My Way Back To You / Forgive Me Girl	12 Apr 1980
456	Blondie	Call Me	26 Apr 1980
457	Dexy's Midnight Runners	Geno	3 May 1980
458	Johnny Logan	What's Another Year	17 May 1980
459	MASH	Suicide Is Painless (Theme from M*A*S*H)	31 May 1980
460	Don McLean	Crying	21 June 1980
461	Olivia Newton John & Electric Light Orchestra	Xanadu	12 July 1980
462	Odyssey	Use It Up And Wear It Out	26 July 1980
463	Abba	The Winner Takes It All	9 Aug 1980
464	David Bowie	Ashes To Ashes	23 Aug 1980
465	Jam	Start	6 Sept 1980
466	Kelly Marie	Feels Like I'm In Love	13 Sept 1980
467	Police	Don't Stand So Close To Me	27 Sept 1980
468	Barbra Streisand	Woman In Love	25 Oct 1980
469	Blondie	The Tide Is High	15 Nov 1980
470	Abba	Super Trouper	29 Nov 1980
471	John Lennon	(Just Like) Starting Over	20 Dec 1980
472	St Winifred's School Choir	There's No One Quite Like Grandma	27 Dec 1980
473	John Lennon	Imagine	10 Jan 1981
474	John Lennon	Woman	7 Feb 1981
475	Joe Dolce Music Theatre	Shaddap You Face	21 Feb 1981
476	Roxy Music	Jealous Guy	14 Mar 1981
477	Shakin' Stevens	This Ole House	28 Mar 1981
478	Bucks Fizz	Making Your Mind Up	18 Apr 1981
479	Adam & The Ants	Stand And Deliver	9 May 1981
480	Smokey Robinson	Being With You	13 June 1981
481	Michael Jackson	One Day In Your Life	27 June 1981
482	Specials	Ghost Town	11 July 1981
483	Shakin' Stevens	Green Door	1 Aug 1981
484	Aneka	Japanese Boy	29 Aug 1981
485	Soft Cell	Tainted Love	5 Sept 1981
486	Adam & The Ants	Prince Charming	19 Sept 1981
487	Dave Stewart & Barbara Gaskin	It's My Party	17 Oct 1981
488	Police	Every Little Thing She Does Is Magic	14 Nov 1981
489	Queen & David Bowie	Under Pressure	21 Nov 1981
490	Julio Iglesias	Begin The Beguine (Volver A Empezar)	5 Dec 1981
491	Human League	Don't You Want Me	12 Dec 1981
492	Bucks Fizz	Land Of Make Believe	16 Jan 1982
493	Shakin' Stevens	Oh Julie	30 Jan 1982
494	Kraftwerk	The Model / Computer Love	6 Feb 1982
495	Jam	Town Called Malice / Precious	13 Feb 1982
496	Tight Fit	The Lion Sleeps Tonight	6 Mar 1982
497	Goombay Dance Band	Seven Tears	27 Mar 1982
498	Bucks Fizz	My Camera Never Lies	17 Apr 1982
499	Paul McCartney & Stevie Wonder	Ebony And Ivory	24 Apr 1982
500	Nicole	A Little Peace	15 May 1982
501	Madness	House Of Fun	29 May 1982
502	Adam Ant	Goody Two Shoes	12 June 1982
503	Charlene	I've Never Been To Me	26 June 1982
504	Captain Sensible	Happy Talk	3 July 1982
505	Irene Cara	Fame	17 July 1982
506	Dexy's Midnight Runners	Come On Eileen	7 Aug 1982
507	Survivor	Eye Of The Tiger	4 Sept 1982
508	Musical Youth	Pass The Dutchie	2 Oct 1982
509	Culture Club	Do You Really Want To Hurt Me	23 Oct 1982
510	Eddy Grant	I Don't Wanna Dance	13 Nov 1982
511	Jam	Beat Surrender	4 Dec 1982
512	Renee & Renato	Save Your Love	18 Dec 1982

MUSIC

POP

	Artist	Song	Date
513	Phil Collins	You Can't Hurry Love	15 Jan 1983
514	Men At Work	Down Under	29 Jan 1983
515	Kajagoogoo	Too Shy	19 Feb 1983
516	Michael Jackson	Billie Jean	5 Mar 1983
517	Bonnie Tyler	Total Eclipse Of The Heart	12 Mar 1983
518	Duran Duran	Is There Something I Should Know	26 Mar 1983
519	David Bowie	Let's Dance	9 Apr 1983
520	Spandau Ballet	True	30 Apr 1983
521	New Edition	Candy Girl	28 May 1983
522	Police	Every Breath You Take	4 June 1983
523	Rod Stewart	Baby Jane	2 July 1983
524	Paul Young	Wherever I Lay My Hat	23 July 1983
525	K C & The Sunshine Band	Give It Up	13 Aug 1983
526	UB40	Red Red Wine	3 Sept 1983
527	Culture Club	Karma Chameleon	24 Sept 1983
528	Billy Joel	Uptown Girl	5 Nov 1983
529	Flying Pickets	Only You	10 Dec 1983
530	Paul McCartney	Pipes Of Peace	14 Jan 1984
531	Frankie Goes To Hollywood	Relax	28 Jan 1984
532	Nena	99 Red Balloons	3 Mar 1984
533	Lionel Richie	Hello	24 Mar 1984
534	Duran Duran	The Reflex	5 May 1984
535	Wham!	Wake Me Up Before You Go-Go	2 June 1984
536	Frankie Goes To Hollywood	Two Tribes	16 June 1984
537	George Michael	Careless Whisper	18 Aug 1984
538	Stevie Wonder	I Just Called To Say I Love You	8 Sept 1984
539	Wham!	Freedom	20 Oct 1984
540	Chaka Khan	I Feel For You	10 Nov 1984
541	Jim Diamond	I Should Have Known Better	1 Dec 1984
542	Frankie Goes To Hollywood	The Power Of Love	8 Dec 1984
543	Band Aid**	Do They Know It's Christmas	15 Dec 1984
544	Foreigner	I Want To Know What Love Is	19 Jan 1985
545	Elaine Paige & Barbara Dickson	I Know Him So Well	9 Feb 1985
546	Dead Or Alive	You Spin Me Round (Like A Record)	9 Mar 1985
547	Philip Bailey & Phil Collins	Easy Lover	23 Mar 1985
548	USA For Africa	We Are The World	20 Apr 1985
549	Phyllis Nelson	Move Closer	4 May 1985
550	Paul Hardcastle	19	11 May 1985
551	Crowd	You'll Never Walk Alone	15 June 1985
552	Sister Sledge	Frankie	29 June 1985
553	Eurythmics	There Must Be An Angel (Playing With My Heart)	27 July 1985
554	Madonna	Into The Groove	3 Aug 1985
555	UB40 & Chrissie Hynde	I Got You Babe	31 Aug 1985
556	David Bowie & Mick Jagger	Dancing in the Street	7 Sept 1985
557	Midge Ure	If I Was	5 Oct 1985
558	Jennifer Rush	The Power Of Love	12 Oct 1985
559	Feargal Sharkey	A Good Heart	16 Nov 1985
560	Wham!	I'm Your Man	30 Nov 1985
561	Whitney Houston	Saving All My Love For You	14 Dec 1985
562	Shakin' Stevens	Merry Christmas Everyone	28 Dec 1985
563	Pet Shop Boys	West End Girls	11 Jan 1986
564	A-Ha	The Sun Always Shines On TV	25 Jan 1986
565	Billy Ocean	When The Going Gets Tough, The Tough Get Going	8 Feb 1986
566	Diana Ross	Chain Reaction	8 Mar 1986
567	Cliff Richard & The Young Ones	Living Doll	29 Mar 1986
568	George Michael	A Different Corner	19 Apr 1986
569	Falco	Rock Me Amadeus	10 May 1986
570	Spitting Image	The Chicken Song	17 May 1986
571	Doctor & The Medics	Spirit In The Sky	7 June 1986
572	Wham!	The Edge Of Heaven	28 June 1986
573	Madonna	Papa Don't Preach	12 July 1986
574	Chris De Burgh	The Lady In Red	2 Aug 1986
575	Boris Gardiner	I Want To Wake Up With You	23 Aug 1986
576	Communards	Don't Leave Me This Way	13 Sept 1986
577	Madonna	True Blue	11 Oct 1986
578	Nick Berry	Every Loser Wins	18 Oct 1986
579	Berlin	Take My Breath Away	8 Nov 1986
580	Europe	The Final Countdown	6 Dec 1986
581	Housemartins	Caravan Of Love	20 Dec 1986
582	Jackie Wilson	Reet Petite	27 Dec 1986
583	Steve 'Silk' Hurley	Jack Your Body	24 Jan 1987

	Artist	Song	Date
584	George Michael & Aretha Franklin	I Knew You Were Waiting (For Me)	7 Feb 1987
585	Ben E King	Stand By Me	21 Feb 1987
586	Boy George	Everything I Own	14 Mar 1987
587	Mel & Kim	Respectable	28 Mar 1987
588	Ferry Aid	Let It Be	4 Apr 1987
589	Madonna	La Isla Bonita	25 Apr 1987
590	Starship	Nothing's Gonna Stop Us Now	9 May 1987
591	Whitney Houston	I Wanna Dance With Somebody (Who Loves Me)	6 June 1987
592	The Firm	Star Trekkin'	20 June 1987
593	Pet Shop Boys	It's A Sin	4 July 1987
594	Madonna	Who's That Girl	25 July 1987
595	Los Lobos	La Bamba	1 Aug 1987
596	Michael Jackson	I Just Can't Stop Loving You	15 Aug 1987
597	Rick Astley	Never Gonna Give You Up	29 Aug 1987
598	M/A/R/R/S	Pump Up The Volume / Anitina (The First Time I See She Dance)	3 Oct 1987
599	Bee Gees	You Win Again	17 Oct 1987
600	T'Pau	China In Your Hand	14 Nov 1987
601	Pet Shop Boys	Always On My Mind	19 Dec 1987
602	Belinda Carlisle	Heaven Is A Place On Earth	16 Jan 1988
603	Tiffany	I Think We're Alone Now	30 Jan 1988
604	Kylie Minogue	I Should Be So Lucky	20 Feb 1988
605	Aswad	Don't Turn Around	26 Mar 1988
606	Pet Shop Boys	Heart	9 Apr 1988
607	S'Express	Theme from S'Express	30 Apr 1988
608	Fairground Attraction	Perfect	14 May 1988
609	Wet Wet Wet / Billy Bragg with Cara Tivey	With A Little Help From My Friends / She's Leaving Home	21 May 1988
610	Timelords	Doctorin' The Tardis	18 June 1988
611	Bros	I Owe You Nothing	25 June 1988
612	Glenn Medeiros	Nothing's Gonna Change My Love For You	9 July 1988
613	Yazz & The Plastic Population	The Only Way Is Up	6 Aug 1988
614	Phil Collins	A Groovy Kind Of Love	10 Sept 1988
615	Hollies	He Ain't Heavy He's My Brother	24 Sept 1988
616	U2	Desire	8 Oct 1988
617	Whitney Houston	One Moment In Time	15 Oct 1988
618	Enya	Orinoco Flow (Sail Away)	29 Oct 1988
619	Robin Beck	The First Time	19 Nov 1988
620	Cliff Richard	Mistletoe & Wine	10 Dec 1988
621	Kylie Minogue & Jason Donovan	Especially For You	7 Jan 1989
622	Marc Almond with Gene Pitney	Something's Gotten Hold Of My Heart	28 Jan 1989
623	Simple Minds	Belfast Child	25 Feb 1989
624	Jason Donovan	Too Many Broken Hearts	11 Mar 1989
625	Madonna	Like A Prayer	25 Mar 1989
626	Bangles	Eternal Flame	15 Apr 1989
627	Kylie Minogue	Hand On Your Heart	13 May 1989
628	Gerry Marsden, Paul McCartney, Holly Johnson & The Christians	Ferry 'Cross The Mersey	20 May 1989
629	Jason Donovan	Sealed With A Kiss	10 June 1989
630	Soul II Soul featuring Caron Wheeler	Back To Life	24 June 1989
631	Sonia	You'll Never Stop Me Loving You	22 July 1989
632	Jive Bunny & The Mastermixers	Swing The Mood	5 Aug 1989
633	Black Box	Ride On Time	9 Sept 1989
634	Jive Bunny & The Mastermixers	That's What I Like	21 Oct 1989
635	Lisa Stansfield	All Around The World	11 Nov 1989
636	New Kids On The Block	You Got It (The Right Stuff)	25 Nov 1989
637	Jive Bunny & The Mastermixers	Let's Party	16 Dec 1989
638	Band Aid II**	Do They Know It's Christmas	23 Dec 1989
639	New Kids On The Block	Hangin' Tough	16 Jan 1990
640	Kylie Minogue	Tears On My Pillow	27 Jan 1990
641	Sinead O'Connor	Nothing Compares 2 U	3 Feb 1990
642	Beats International	Dub Be Good To Me	3 Mar 1990
643	Snap	The Power	31 Mar 1990
644	Madonna	Vogue	14 Apr 1990
645	Adamski	Killer	12 May 1990
646	EnglandNewOrder	World In Motion	9 June 1990
647	Elton John	Sacrifice / Healing Hands	23 June 1990
648	Partners In Kryme	Turtle Power	28 July 1990
649	Bombalurina	Itsy Bitsy Teeny Weeny Yellow Polka Dot Bikini	25 Aug 1990
650	Steve Miller Band	The Joker	15 Sept 1990
651	Maria McKee	Show Me Heaven	29 Sept 1990

M
U
S
I
C

P
O
P

	Artist	Song	Date
652	Beautiful South	A Little Time	27 Oct 1990
653	Righteous Brothers	Unchained Melody	3 Nov 1990
654	Vanilla Ice	Ice Ice Baby	1 Dec 1990
655	Cliff Richard	Saviour's Day	22 Dec 1990
656	Iron Maiden	Bring Your Daughter To The Slaughter	5 Jan 1991
657	Enigma	Sadness Part 1	19 Jan 1991
658	Queen	Innuendo	26 Jan 1991
659	KLF	3AM Eternal	2 Feb 1991
660	Simpsons	Do The Bartman	16 Feb 1991
661	Clash	Should I Stay Or Should I Go	9 Mar 1991
662	Hale & Pace	The Stonk	23 Mar 1991
663	Chesney Hawkes	The One And Only	30 Mar 1991
664	Cher	Shoop Shoop Song (It's In His Kiss)	4 May 1991
665	Color Me Badd	I Wanna Sex You Up	8 June 1991
666	Jason Donovan	Any Dream Will Do	29 June 1991
667	Bryan Adams	(Everything I Do) I Do It For You	13 July 1991
668	U2	The Fly	2 Nov 1991
669	Vic Reeves & The Wonder Stuff	Dizzy	9 Nov 1991
670	Michael Jackson	Black Or White	23 Nov 1991
671	George Michael & Elton John	Don't Let The Sun Go Down On Me	7 Dec 1991
672	Queen	Bohemian Rhapsody / These Are The Days Of Our Lives	21 Dec 1991
673	Wet Wet Wet	Goodnight Girl	25 Jan 1992
674	Shakespears Sister	Stay	22 Feb 1992
675	Right Said Fred	Deeply Dippy	18 Apr 1992
676	KWS	Please Don't Go / Game Boy	9 May 1992
677	Erasure	Abba-esque EP	13 June 1992
678	Jimmy Nail	Ain't No Doubt	18 July 1992
679	Snap	Rhythm Is A Dancer	8 Aug 1992
680	Shamen	Ebeneezer Goode	19 Sept 1992
681	Tasmin Archer	Sleeping Satellite	17 Oct 1992
682	Boyz II Men	End Of The Road	31 Oct 1992
683	Charles & Eddie	Would I Lie To You	21 Nov 1992
684	Whitney Houston	I Will Always Love You	5 Dec 1992
685	2 Unlimited	No Limit	13 Feb 1993
686	Shaggy	Oh Carolina	20 Mar 1993
687	Bluebells	Young At Heart	3 Apr 1993
688	George Michael & Queen with Lisa Stansfield	Five Live (EP)	1 May 1993
689	Ace Of Base	All That She Wants	22 May 1993
690	UB40	(I Can't Help) Falling In Love With You	12 June 1993
691	Gabrielle	Dreams	26 June 1993
692	Take That	Pray	17 July 1993
693	Freddie Mercury	Living On My Own	14 Aug 1993
694	Culture Beat	Mr Vain	28 Aug 1993
695	Jazzy Jeff & The Fresh Prince (Will Smith)	Boom! Shake The Room	25 Sept 1993
696	Take That featuring Lulu	Relight My Fire	9 Oct 1993
697	Meat Loaf	I'd Do Anything For Love (But I Won't Do That)	23 Oct 1993
698	Mr Blobby	Mr Blobby	11 Dec 1993
699	Take That	Babe	18 Dec 1993
700	Chaka Demus & Pliers	Twist & Shout	8 Jan 1994
701	D:Ream	Things Can Only Get Better	22 Jan 1994
702	Mariah Carey	Without You	19 Feb 1994
703	Doop	Doop	19 Mar 1994
704	Take That	Everything Changes	9 Apr 1994
705	Prince	The Most Beautiful Girl In The World	23 Apr 1994
706	Tony Di Bart	The Real Thing	7 May 1994
707	Stiltskin	Inside	14 May 1994
708	Manchester United 1994 Football Squad	Come On You Reds	21 May 1994
709	Wet Wet Wet	Love Is All Around	4 June 1994
710	Whigfield	Saturday Night	17 Sept 1994
711	Take That	Sure	15 Oct 1994
712	Pato Banton (with Robin & Ali Campbell)	Baby Come Back	29 Oct 1994
713	Baby D	Let Me Be Your Fantasy	26 Nov 1994
714	East 17	Stay Another Day	10 Dec 1994
715	Rednex	Cotton Eye Joe	14 Jan 1995
716	Celine Dion	Think Twice	4 Feb 1995

	Artist	Song	Date
717	Cher, Chrissie Hynde, Neneh Cherry & Eric Clapton	Love Can Build A Bridge	25 Mar 1995
718	Outhere Brothers	Don't Stop (Wiggle Wiggle)	1 Apr 1995
719	Take That	Back For Good	8 Apr 1995
720	Oasis	Some Might Say	6 May 1995
721	Livin' Joy	Dreamer	13 May 1995
722	Robson Green & Jerome Flynn	Unchained Melody / White Cliffs Of Dover	20 May 1995
723	Outhere Brothers	Boom Boom Boom	8 July 1995
724	Take That	Never Forget	5 Aug 1995
725	Blur	Country House	26 Aug 1995
726	Michael Jackson	You Are Not Alone	9 Sept 1995
727	Shaggy	Boombastic	23 Sept 1995
728	Simply Red	Fairground	30 Sept 1995
729	Coolio featuring LV	Gangsta's Paradise	28 Oct 1995
730	Robson & Jerome	I Believe / Up On The Roof	11 Nov 1995
731	Michael Jackson	Earth Song	9 Dec 1995
732	George Michael	Jesus To A Child	20 Jan 1996
733	Babylon Zoo	Spaceman	27 Jan 1996
734	Oasis	Don't Look Back In Anger	2 Mar 1996
735	Take That	How Deep Is Your Love	9 Mar 1996
736	Prodigy	Firestarter	30 Mar 1996
737	Mark Morrison	Return Of The Mack	20 Apr 1996
738	George Michael	Fastlove	4 May 1996
739	Gina G	Ooh Aah ... Just A Little Bit	25 May 1996
740	Baddiel, Skinner & Lightning Seeds	Three Lions	1 June 1996
741	Fugees	Killing Me Softly	8 June 1996
742	Gary Barlow	Forever Love	20 July 1996
743	Spice Girls	Wannabe	27 July 1996
744	Peter Andre	Flava	14 Sept 1996
745	Fugees	Ready Or Not	21 Sept 1996
746	Deep Blue Something	Breakfast At Tiffany's	5 Oct 1996
747	Chemical Brothers	Setting Sun	12 Oct 1996
748	Boyzone	Words	19 Oct 1996
749	Spice Girls	Say You'll Be There	26 Oct 1996
750	Robson & Jerome	What Becomes Of The Broken Hearted / Saturday Night At The Movies / You'll Never Walk Alone	9 Nov 1996
751	Prodigy	Breathe	23 Nov 1996
752	Peter Andre	I Feel You	7 Dec 1996
753	Boyzone	A Different Beat	14 Dec 1996
754	Dunblane	Knockin' On Heaven's Door / Throw These Guns Away	21 Dec 1996
755	Spice Girls	2 Become 1	28 Dec 1996
756	Tori Amos	Professional Widow (It's Got To Be Big)	18 Jan 1997
757	White Town	Your Woman	25 Jan 1997
758	Blur	Beetlebum	1 Feb 1997
759	LL Cool J	Ain't Nobody	8 Feb 1997
760	U2	Discotheque	15 Feb 1997
761	No Doubt	Don't Speak	22 Feb 1997
762	Spice Girls	Mama / Who Do You Think You Are	15 Mar 1997
763	Chemical Brothers	Block Rockin' Beats	5 Apr 1997
764	R Kelly	I Believe I Can Fly	12 Apr 1997
765	Michael Jackson	Blood On The Dance Floor	3 May 1997
766	Gary Barlow	Love Won't Wait	10 May 1997
767	Olive	You're Not Alone	17 May 1997
768	Eternal featuring Bebe Winans	I Wanna Be The One	31 May 1997
769	Hanson	MmmBop	7 June 1997
770	Puff Daddy & Faith Evans	I'll Be Missing You	28 June 1997
771	Oasis	D'You Know What I Mean	19 July 1997
772	Will Smith	Men In Black	16 Aug 1997
773	Verve	The Drugs Don't Work	13 Sept 1997
774	Elton John	Candle In The Wind '97 / Something About The Way You Look Tonight	20 Sept 1997
775	Spice Girls	Spice Up Your Life	25 Oct 1997
776	Aqua	Barbie Girl	1 Nov 1997
777	Various Artists*	Perfect Day	29 Nov 1997
778	Teletubbies	Teletubbies Say Eh-oh!	13 Dec 1997
779	Spice Girls	Too Much	27 Dec 1997
780	All Saints	Never Ever	17 Jan 1998
781	Oasis	All Around The World	24 Jan 1998
782	Usher	You Make Me Wanna ...	31 Jan 1998
783	Aqua	Doctor Jones	7 Feb 1998
784	Celine Dion	My Heart Will Go On	21 Feb 1998

MUSIC

POP

	Artist	Song	Date
785	Cornershop	Brimful Of Asha	28 Feb 1998
786	Madonna	Frozen	7 Mar 1998
787	Run DMC vs Jason Nevins	It's Like That	21 Mar 1998
788	Boyzone	All That I Need	2 May 1998
789	All Saints	Under The Bridge / Lady Marmalade	9 May 1998
790	Aqua	Turn Back Time	16 May 1998
791	Tamperer featuring Maya	Feel It	30 May 1998
792	B*Witched	C'est La Vie	6 June 1998
793	Baddiel, Skinner & Lightning Seeds	Three Lions '98	20 June 1998
794	Billie	Because We Want To	11 July 1998
795	Another Level	Freak Me	18 July 1998
796	Jamiroquai	Deeper Underground	25 July 1998
797	Spice Girls	Viva Forever	1 Aug 1998
798	Boyzone	No Matter What	15 Aug 1998
799	Manic Street Preachers	If You Tolerate This Your Children Will Be Next	5 Sept 1998
800	All Saints	Bootie Call	12 Sept 1998
801	Robbie Williams	Millennium	19 Sept 1998
802	Melanie B featuring Missy Elliott	I Want You Back	26 Sept 1998
803	B*Witched	Rollercoaster	3 Oct 1998
804	Billie	Girlfriend	17 Oct 1998
805	Spacedust	Gym And Tonic	24 Oct 1998
806	Cher	Believe	31 Oct 1998
807	B*Witched	To You I Belong	19 Dec 1998
808	Spice Girls	Goodbye	26 Dec 1998
809	Chef	Chocolate Salty Balls (PS I Love You)	2 Jan 1999
810	Steps	Heartbeat / Tragedy	9 Jan 1999
811	Fatboy Slim	Praise You	16 Jan 1999
812	911	A Little Bit More	23 Jan 1999
813	Offspring	Pretty Fly (For A White Guy)	30 Jan 1999
814	Armand Van Helden featuring Duane Harden	You Don't Know Me	6 Feb 1999
815	Blondie	Maria	13 Feb 1999
816	Lenny Kravitz	Fly Away	20 Feb 1999
817	Britney Spears	Baby One More Time	27 Feb 1999
818	Boyzone	When The Going Gets Tough	13 Mar 1999
819	B*Witched	Blame It On The Weatherman	27 Mar 1999
820	Mr Oizo	Flat Beat	3 Apr 1999
821	Martine McCutcheon	Perfect Moment	17 Apr 1999
822	Westlife	Swear It Again	1 May 1999
823	Backstreet Boys	I Want It That Way	15 May 1999
824	Boyzone	You Needed Me	22 May 1999
825	Shanks & Bigfoot	Sweet Like Chocolate	29 May 1999
826	Baz Luhrmann	Everybody's Free (To Wear Sunscreen)	12 June 1999
827	S Club 7	Bring It All Back	19 June 1999
828	Vengaboys	Boom Boom Boom Boom	26 June 1999
829	ATB	9PM (Till I Come)	3 July 1999
830	Ricky Martin	Livin' La Vida Loca	17 July 1999
831	Ronan Keating	When You Say Nothing At All	7 Aug 1999
832	Westlife	If I Let You Go	21 Aug 1999
833	Geri Halliwell	Mi Chico Latino	28 Aug 1999
834	Lou Bega	Mambo No 5	4 Sept 1999
835	Vengaboys	We're Going To Ibiza	18 Sept 1999
836	Eiffel 65	Blue (Da Ba Dee)	25 Sept 1999
837	Christina Aguilera	Genie In A Bottle	16 Oct 1999
838	Westlife	Flying Without Wings	30 Oct 1999
839	Five	Keep On Movin'	6 Nov 1999
840	Geri Halliwell	Lift Me Up	13 Nov 1999
841	Robbie Williams	She's The One / It's Only Us	20 Nov 1999
842	Wamdue Project	King Of My Castle	27 Nov 1999
843	Cliff Richard	Millennium Prayer	4 Dec 1999
844	Westlife	I Have A Dream / Seasons In The Sun	25 Dec 1999
845	Manic Street Preachers	The Masses Against The Classes	22 Jan 2000
846	Britney Spears	Born To Make You Happy	29 Jan 2000
847	Gabrielle	Rise	5 Feb 2000
848	Oasis	Go Let It Out	19 Feb 2000
849	All Saints	Pure Shores	26 Feb 2000
850	Madonna	American Pie	11 Mar 2000
851	Chicane featuring Bryan Adams	Don't Give Up	18 Mar 2000
852	Geri Halliwell	Bag It Up	25 Mar 2000
853	Melanie C with Lisa 'Left Eye' Lopes	Never Be The Same Again	1 Apr 2000
854	Westlife	Fool Again	8 Apr 2000

	Artist	Song	Date
855	Craig David	Fill Me In	15 Apr 2000
856	Fragma	Toca's Miracle	22 Apr 2000
857	Oxide & Neutrino	Bound 4 Da Reload (Casualty)	6 May 2000
858	Britney Spears	Oops! ... I Did It Again	13 May 2000
859	Madison Avenue	Don't Call Me Baby	20 May 2000
860	Billie Piper	Day & Night	27 May 2000
861	Sonique	It Feels So Good	3 June 2000
862	Black Legend	You See The Trouble With Me	24 June 2000
863	Kylie Minogue	Spinning Around	1 July 2000
864	Eminem	Real Slim Shady	8 July 2000
865	Corrs	Breathless	15 July 2000
866	Ronan Keating	Life Is A Rollercoaster	22 July 2000
867	Five and Queen	We Will Rock You	29 July 2000
868	Craig David	7 Days	5 Aug 2000
869	Robbie Williams	Rock DJ	12 Aug 2000
870	Melanie C	I Turn To You	19 Aug 2000
871	Spiller	Groovejet (If This Ain't Love)	26 Aug 2000
872	Madonna	Music	2 Sept 2000
873	A1	Take On Me	9 Sept 2000
874	Modjo	Lady (Hear Me Tonight)	16 Sept 2000
875	Mariah Carey & Westlife	Against All Odds	30 Sept 2000
876	All Saints	Black Coffee	14 Oct 2000
877	U2	Beautiful Day	21 Oct 2000
878	Steps	Stomp	28 Oct 2000
879	Spice Girls	Holler / Let Love Lead The Way	4 Nov 2000
880	Westlife	My Love	11 Nov 2000
881	A1	Same Old Brand New You	18 Nov 2000
882	LeAnn Rimes	Can't Fight The Moonlight	25 Nov 2000
883	Destiny's Child	Independent Women Part 1	2 Dec 2000
884	S Club 7	Never Had A Dream Come True	9 Dec 2000
885	Eminem	Stan	16 Dec 2000
886	Bob The Builder	Can We Fix It	23 Dec 2000
887	Rui Da Silva featuring Cassandra	Touch Me	13 Jan 2001
888	Jennifer Lopez	Love Don't Cost A Thing	20 Jan 2001
889	Limp Bizkit	Rollin'	27 Jan 2001
890	Atomic Kitten	Whole Again	10 Feb 2001
891	Shaggy featuring Rikrok	It Wasn't Me	10 Mar 2001
892	Westlife	Uptown Girl	17 Mar 2001
893	Hear'Say	Pure And Simple	24 Mar 2001
894	Emma Bunton	What Took You So Long	14 Apr 2001
895	Destiny's Child	Survivor	28 Apr 2001
896	S Club 7	Don't Stop Movin'	5 May 2001
897	Geri Halliwell	It's Raining Men	12 May 2001
898	DJ Pied Piper	Do You Really Like It	2 June 2001
899	Shaggy featuring Rayvon	Angel	9 June 2001
900	Christina Aguilera with Lil' Kim, Mya & Pink	Lady Marmalade	30 June 2001
901	Hear'Say	The Way To Your Love	7 July 2001
902	Roger Sanchez	Another Chance	14 July 2001
903	Robbie Williams	Eternity / The Road To Mandalay	21 July 2001
904	Atomic Kitten	Eternal Flame	4 Aug 2001
905	So Solid Crew	21 Seconds	18 Aug 2001
906	Five	Let's Dance	25 Aug 2001
907	Blue	Too Close	8 Sept 2001
908	Bob The Builder	Mambo No 5	15 Sept 2001
909	DJ Otzi	Hey Baby	22 Sept 2001
910	Kylie Minogue	Can't Get You Out Of My Head	29 Sept 2001
911	Afroman	Because I Got High	27 Oct 2001
912	Westlife	Queen of My Heart	17 Nov 2001
913	Blue	If You Come Back	24 Nov 2001
914	S Club 7	Have You Ever	1 Dec 2001
915	Daniel Bedingfield	Gotta Get Thru This	8 Dec 2001
916	Robbie Williams & Nicole Kidman	Somethin' Stupid	22 Dec 2001
917	Aaliyah	More Than A Woman	19 Jan 2002
918	George Harrison	My Sweet Lord	26 Jan 2002
919	Enrique Iglesias	Hero	2 Feb 2002
920	Westlife	World Of Our Own	2 Mar 2002
921	Will Young	Anything Is Possible / Evergreen	9 Mar 2002
922	Gareth Gates	Unchained Melody	30 Mar 2002
923	Oasis	The Hindu Times	27 Apr 2002
924	Sugababes	Freak Like Me	4 May 2002

	Artist	Song	Date
925	Holly Valance	Kiss Kiss	11 May 2002
926	Ronan Keating	If Tomorrow Never Comes	18 May 2002
927	Liberty X	Just A Little	25 May 2002
928	Eminem	Without Me	1 June 2002
929	Will Young	Light My Fire	8 June 2002
930	Elvis vs JXL	A Little Less Conversation	22 June 2002
931	Gareth Gates	Anyone Of Us (Stupid Mistake)	20 July 2002
932	Darius	Colourblind	10 Aug 2002
933	Sugababes	Round Round	24 Aug 2002
934	Blazin' Squad	Crossroads	31 Aug 2002
935	Atomic Kitten	The Tide Is High (Get The Feeling)	7 Sept 2002
936	Pink	Just Like A Pill	28 Sept 2002
937	Will Young & Gareth Gates	The Long And Winding Road / Suspicious Minds	5 Oct 2002
938	Las Ketchup	The Ketchup Song (Asereje)	19 Oct 2002
939	Nelly featuring Kelly Rowland	Dilemma	26 Oct 2002
940	DJ Sammy & Yanou featuring Do	Heaven	9 Nov 2002
941	Westlife	Unbreakable	16 Nov 2002
942	Christina Aguilera	Dirrty	23 Nov 2002
943	Daniel Bedingfield	If You're Not The One	7 Dec 2002
944	Eminem	Lose Yourself	14 Dec 2002
945	Blue featuring Elton John	Sorry Seems To Be The Hardest Word	21 Dec 2002
946	Girls Aloud	Sound Of The Underground	28 Dec 2002
947	David Sneddon	Stop Living The Lie	25 Jan 2003
948	Tatu	All The Things She Said	8 Feb 2003
949	Christina Aguilera	Beautiful	8 Mar 2003
950	Gareth Gates	Spirit In The Sky	22 Mar 2003
951	Room 5 featuring Oliver Cheatham	Make Luv	5 Apr 2003
952	Busted	You Said No	3 May 2003
953	Tomcraft	Loneliness	10 May 2003
954	R Kelly	Ignition	17 May 2003
955	Evanescence	Bring Me To Life	14 June 2003
956	Beyonce	Crazy In Love	12 July 2003
957	Daniel Bedingfield	Never Gonna Leave Your Side	2 Aug 2003
958	Blu Cantrell featuring Sean Paul	Breathe	9 Aug 2003
959	Elton John	Are You Ready For Love?	6 Sept 2003
960	Black Eyed Peas	Where Is The Love?	13 Sept 2003
961	Sugababes	Hole In The Head	25 Oct 2003
962	Fatman Scoop	Be Faithful	1 Nov 2003
963	Kylie Minogue	Slow	15 Nov 2003
964	Busted	Crashed The Wedding	22 Nov 2003
965	Westlife	Mandy	29 Nov 2003
966	Will Young	Leave Right Now	6 Dec 2003
967	Kelly & Ozzy Osbourne	Changes	20 Dec 2003
968	Michael Andrews featuring Gary Jules	Mad World	27 Dec 2003
969	Michelle McManus	All This Time	17 Jan 2004
970	LMC vs U2	Take Me To The Clouds Above	7 Feb 2004
971	Sam & Mark	With A Little Help From My Friends / Measure Of A Man	21 Feb 2004
972	Busted	Who's David	28 Feb 2004
973	Peter Andre	Mysterious Girl	6 Mar 2004
974	Britney Spears	Toxic	13 Mar 2004
975	DJ Casper	Cha Cha Slide	20 Mar 2004
976	Usher	Yeah	27 Mar 2004
977	McFly	Five Colours In Her Hair	10 Apr 2004
978	Eamon	F**k It (I Don't Want You Back)	24 Apr 2004
979	Frankee	F.U.R.B. (F U Right Back)	22 May 2004
980	Mario Winans featuring Enya & P Diddy	I Don't Wanna Know	12 June 2004
981	Britney Spears	Everytime	26 June 2004
982	McFly	Obviously	3 July 2004
983	Usher	Burn	10 July 2004
984	Shapeshifters	Lola's Theme	24 July 2004
985	The Streets	Dry Your Eyes	31 July 2004
986	Busted	Thunderbirds / 3AM	7 Aug 2004
987	3 Of A Kind	Babycakes	21 Aug 2004
988	Natasha Bedingfield	These Words	28 Aug 2004
989	Nelly	My Place / Flap Your Wings	11 Sept 2004
990	Brian McFadden	Real To Me	18 Sept 2004
991	Eric Prydz	Call On Me	25 Sept 2004
992	Robbie Williams	Radio	16 Oct 2004
993	Ja Rule featuring R Kelly & Ashanti	Wonderful	6 Nov 2004

	Artist	Song	Date
994	Eminem	Just Lose It	13 Nov 2004
995	U2	Vertigo	20 Nov 2004
996	Girls Aloud	I'll Stand By You	27 Nov 2004
997	Band Aid 20**	Do They Know It's Christmas	11 Dec 2004
998	Steve Brookstein	Against All Odds	8 Jan 2005
999	Elvis Presley	Jailhouse Rock	15 Jan 2005
1000	Elvis Presley	I Got Stung / One Night	22 Jan 2005
1001	Ciara featuring Petey Pablo	Goodies	29 Jan 2005
1002	Elvis Presley	It's Now Or Never	5 Feb 2005
1003	Eminem	Like Toy Soldiers	12 Feb 2005
1004	U2	Sometimes You Can't Make It On Your Own	19 Feb 2005
1005	Jennifer Lopez	Get Right	26 Feb 2005
1006	Nelly featuring Tim McGraw	Over And Over	5 Mar 2005
1007	Stereophonics	Dakota	12 Mar 2005
1008	McFly	All About You / You've Got A Friend	19 Mar 2005
1009	Tony Christie featuring Peter Kay	(Is This The Way To) Amarillo	26 Mar 2005

The 1000 Number One UK Singles by Artist

Artist	Song	Date	No
A1	Take On Me	09 Sept 2000	873
	Same Old Brand New You	18 Nov 2000	881
Aaliyah	More Than A Woman	19 Jan 2002	917
Abba	Waterloo	04 May 1974	348
	Mamma Mia	31 Jan 1976	383
	Fernando	08 May 1976	388
	Dancing Queen	04 Sept 1976	394
	Knowing Me Knowing You	02 Apr 1977	403
	The Name Of The Game	05 Nov 1977	415
	Take A Chance On Me	18 Feb 1978	419
	The Winner Takes It All	09 Aug 1980	463
	Super Trouper	29 Nov 1980	470
Ace Of Base	All That She Wants	22 May 1993	689
Adam & The Ants	Stand And Deliver	09 May 1981	479
	Prince Charming	19 Sept 1981	486
	Goody Two Shoes	12 June 1982	502
Adams, Bryan	(Everything I Do) I Do It For You	13 July 1991	667
Adamski	Killer	12 May 1990	645
Afroman	Because I Got High	27 Oct 2001	911
Aguilera, Christina	Genie In A Bottle	16 Oct 1999	837
	Lady Marmalade	30 June 2001	900
	Dirrty	23 Nov 2002	942
	Beautiful	08 Mar 2003	949
A-Ha	The Sun Always Shines On TV	25 Jan 1986	564
All Saints	Never Ever	17 Jan 1998	780
	Under The Bridge / Lady Marmalade	09 May 1998	789
	Bootie Call	12 Sept 1998	800
	Pure Shores	26 Feb 2000	849
	Black Coffee	14 Oct 2000	876
Almond, Marc with Gene Pitney	Something's Gotten Hold Of My Heart	28 Jan 1989	622
Althia & Donna	Up Town Top Ranking	04 Feb 1978	417
Amen Corner	(If Paradise Is) Half As Nice	12 Feb 1969	266
Amos, Tori	Professional Widow (It's Got To Be Big)	18 Jan 1997	756
Andre, Peter	Flava	14 Sept 1996	744
	I Feel You	07 Dec 1996	752
	Mysterious Girl	06 Mar 2004	973
Andrews, Michael	Mad World	27 Dec 2003	968
Aneka	Japanese Boy	29 Aug 1981	484
Animals	The House Of The Rising Sun	09 July 1964	172
Anka, Paul	Diana	30 Aug 1957	63
Another Level	Freak Me	18 July 1998	795
Aqua	Barbie Girl	01 Nov 1997	776
	Doctor Jones	07 Feb 1998	783
	Turn Back Time	16 May 1998	790
Archer, Tasmin	Sleeping Satellite	17 Oct 1992	681
Archies	Sugar Sugar	25 Oct 1969	279
Armstrong, Louis	What A Wonderful World / Cabaret	24 Apr 1968	249

MUSIC POP

Artist	Song	Date	No
Astley, Rick	Never Gonna Give You Up	29 Aug 1987	597
Aswad	Don't Turn Around	26 Mar 1988	605
ATB	9PM (Till I Come)	03 July 1999	829
Atomic Kitten	Whole Again	10 Feb 2001	890
	Eternal Flame	04 Aug 2001	904
	The Tide Is High (Get The Feeling)	07 Sept 2002	935
Atwell, Winifred	Let's Have Another Party	03 Dec 1954	26
	Poor People Of Paris	13 Apr 1956	45
Aznavour, Charles	She	29 June 1974	352
B Bumble & The Stingers	Nut Rocker	17 May 1962	135
B*Witched	C'est La Vie	06 June 1998	792
	Rollercoaster	03 Oct 1998	803
	To You I Belong	19 Dec 1998	807
	Blame It On The Weatherman	27 Mar 1999	819
Baby D	Let Me Be Your Fantasy	26 Nov 1994	713
Babylon Zoo	Spaceman	27 Jan 1996	733
Baccara	Yes Sir I Can Boogie	29 Oct 1977	414
Bachelors	Diane	20 Feb 1964	163
Backstreet Boys	I Want It That Way	15 May 1999	823
Baddiel, Skinner & Lightning Seeds	Three Lions	01 June 1996	740
	Three Lions '98	20 June 1998	793
Bailey, Philip	Easy Lover	23 Mar 1985	547
Baldry, Long John	Let The Heartaches Begin	22 Nov 1967	240
Band Aid**	Do They Know It's Christmas	15 Dec 1984	543
Band Aid 20**	Do They Know It's Christmas	11 Dec 2004	997
Band Aid II**	Do They Know It's Christmas	23 Dec 1989	638
Bangles	Eternal Flame	15 Apr 1989	626
Banton, Pato (with Robin & Ali Campbell)	Baby Come Back	29 Oct 1994	712
Barlow, Gary	Forever Love	20 July 1996	742
	Love Won't Wait	10 May 1997	766
Barrie, J J	No Charge	05 June 1976	389
Bassey, Shirley	As I Love You	20 Feb 1959	81
	Reach For The Stars / Climb Ev'ry Mountain	21 Sept 1961	125
Bay City Rollers	Bye Bye Baby	22 Mar 1975	368
	Give A Little Love	19 July 1975	374
Beach Boys	Good Vibrations	17 Nov 1966	226
	Do It Again	28 Aug 1968	256
Beatles	From Me To You	02 May 1963	151
	She Loves You	12 Sept 1963	157
	I Want To Hold Your Hand	12 Dec 1963	160
	Can't Buy Me Love	02 Apr 1964	166
	A Hard Day's Night	23 July 1964	174
	I Feel Fine	10 Dec 1964	183
	Ticket To Ride	22 Apr 1965	193
	Help!	05 Aug 1965	200
	Day Tripper / We Can Work It Out	16 Dec 1965	207
	Paperback Writer	23 June 1966	217
	Yellow Submarine / Eleanor Rigby	18 Aug 1966	222
	All You Need Is Love	19 July 1967	235
	Hello Goodbye	06 Dec 1967	241
	Lady Madonna	27 Mar 1968	247
	Hey Jude	11 Sept 1968	258
	Get Back	23 Apr 1969	270
	The Ballad Of John And Yoko	11 June 1969	272
Beats International	Dub Be Good To Me	03 Mar 1990	642
Beautiful South	A Little Time	27 Oct 1990	652
Beck, Robin	The First Time	19 Nov 1988	619
Bedingfield, Daniel	Gotta Get Thru This	08 Dec 2001	915
	If You're Not The One	07 Dec 2002	943
	Never Gonna Leave Your Side	02 Aug 2003	957
Bedingfield, Natasha	These Words	28 Aug 2004	988
Bee Gees	Massachusetts	11 Oct 1967	238
	I've Gotta Get A Message To You	04 Sept 1968	257
	Night Fever	29 Apr 1978	422
	Tragedy	03 Mar 1979	434
	You Win Again	17 Oct 1987	599
Bega, Lou	Mambo No 5	04 Sept 1999	834
Belafonte, Harry	Mary's Boy Child	22 Nov 1957	65
Bennett, Tony	Stranger In Paradise	13 May 1955	32
Berlin	Take My Breath Away	08 Nov 1986	579

Artist	Song	Date	No
Berry, Chuck	My Ding-A-Ling	25 Nov 1972	323
Berry, Nick	Every Loser Wins	18 Oct 1986	578
Beyonce	Crazy In Love	12 July 2003	956
Billie (Piper)	Because We Want To	11 July 1998	794
	Girlfriend	17 Oct 1998	804
	Day & Night	27 May 2000	860
Birkin, Jane & Serge Gainsbourg	Je T'Aime … Moi Non Plus	11 Oct 1969	277
Black Box	Ride On Time	09 Sept 1989	633
Black Eyed Peas	Where Is The Love?	13 Sept 2003	960
Black Legend	You See The Trouble With Me	24 June 2000	862
Black, Cilla	Anyone Who Had A Heart	27 Feb 1964	164
	You're My World	28 May 1964	170
Blazin' Squad	Crossroads	31 Aug 2002	934
Blondie	Heart Of Glass	03 Feb 1979	433
	Sunday Girl	26 May 1979	437
	Atomic	01 Mar 1980	452
	Call Me	26 Apr 1980	456
	The Tide Is High	15 Nov 1980	469
	Maria	13 Feb 1999	815
Blue	Too Close	08 Sept 2001	907
	If You Come Back	24 Nov 2001	913
	Sorry Seems To Be The Hardest Word	21 Dec 2002	945
Bluebells	Young At Heart	03 Apr 1993	687
Blur	Country House	26 Aug 1995	725
	Beetlebum	01 Feb 1997	758
Bob The Builder	Can We Fix It	23 Dec 2000	886
	Mambo No 5	15 Sept 2001	908
Bombalurina	Itsy Bitsy Teeny Weeny Yellow Polka Dot Bikini	25 Aug 1990	649
Boney M	Rivers Of Babylon / Brown Girl In The Ring	13 May 1978	423
	Mary's Boy Child / Oh My Lord	09 Dec 1978	430
Boomtown Rats	Rat Trap	18 Nov 1978	428
	I Don't Like Mondays	28 July 1979	440
Boone, Pat	I'll Be Home	15 June 1956	47
Boothe, Ken	Everything I Own	26 Oct 1974	359
Bowie, David	Space Oddity	08 Nov 1975	380
	Ashes To Ashes	23 Aug 1980	464
	Under Pressure	21 Nov 1981	489
	Let's Dance	09 Apr 1983	519
	Dancing In The Street	07 Sept 1985	556
Boy George	Everything I Own	14 Mar 1987	586
Boyz II Men	End Of The Road	31 Oct 1992	682
Boyzone	Words	19 Oct 1996	748
	A Different Beat	14 Dec 1996	753
	All That I Need	02 May 1998	788
	No Matter What	15 Aug 1998	798
	When The Going Gets Tough	13 Mar 1999	818
	You Needed Me	22 May 1999	824
Bragg, Billy with Cara Tivey	She's Leaving Home	21 May 1988	609
Brian & Michael	Matchstalk Men And Matchstalk Cats And Dogs	08 Apr 1978	421
Brookstein, Steve	Against All Odds	08 Jan 2005	998
Bros	I Owe You Nothing	25 June 1988	611
Brotherhood Of Man	Save Your Kisses For Me	27 Mar 1976	387
	Angelo	20 Aug 1977	410
	Figaro	11 Feb 1978	418
Bucks Fizz	Making Your Mind Up	18 Apr 1981	478
	Land Of Make Believe	16 Jan 1982	492
	My Camera Never Lies	17 Apr 1982	498
Buggles	Video Killed The Radio Star	20 Oct 1979	444
Bunton, Emma	What Took You So Long	14 Apr 2001	894
Bush, Kate	Wuthering Heights	11 Mar 1978	420
Busted	You Said No	03 May 2003	952
	Crashed The Wedding	22 Nov 2003	964
	Who's David	28 Feb 2004	972
	Thunderbirds / 3AM	07 Aug 2004	986
Byrds	Mr Tambourine Man	22 July 1965	199
Calvert, Eddie	Oh Mein Papa	08 Jan 1954	16
	Cherry Pink And Apple Blossom White	27 May 1955	33
Cantrell, Blu featuring Sean Paul	Breathe	09 Aug 2003	958
Captain Sensible	Happy Talk	03 July 1982	504
Cara, Irene	Fame	17 July 1982	505
Carey, Mariah	Without You	19 Feb 1994	702

MUSIC POP

Artist	Song	Date	No
	Against All Odds	30 Sept 2000	875
Carlisle, Belinda	Heaven Is A Place On Earth	16 Jan 1988	602
Cassidy, David	How Can I Be Sure	30 Sept 1972	320
	Daydreamer / The Puppy Song	27 Oct 1973	339
Chaka Demus & Pliers	Twist & Shout	08 Jan 1994	700
Charlene	I've Never Been To Me	26 June 1982	503
Charles & Eddie	Would I Lie To You	21 Nov 1992	683
Charles, Ray	I Can't Stop Loving You	12 July 1962	138
Charles, Tina	I Love To Love (But My Baby Loves To Dance)	06 Mar 1976	386
Chef	Chocolate Salty Balls (PS I Love You)	02 Jan 1999	809
Chemical Brothers	Setting Sun	12 Oct 1996	747
	Block Rockin' Beats	05 Apr 1997	763
Cher	Shoop Shoop Song (It's In His Kiss)	04 May 1991	664
	Love Can Build A Bridge	25 Mar 1995	717
	Believe	31 Oct 1998	806
Cherry, Neneh	Love Can Build A Bridge	25 Mar 1995	717
Chicago	If You Leave Me Now	13 Nov 1976	396
Chicane featuring Bryan Adams	Don't Give Up	18 Mar 2000	851
Chicory Tip	Son Of My Father	19 Feb 1972	310
Christians	Ferry 'Cross The Mersey	20 May 1989	628
Christie	Yellow River	06 June 1970	287
Christie, Tony featuring Peter Kay	(Is This The Way To) Amarillo	26 Mar 2005	1009
Ciara featuring Petey Pablo	Goodies	29 Jan 2005	1001
Clapton, Eric	Love Can Build A Bridge	25 Mar 1995	717
Clark, Petula	Sailor	23 Feb 1961	113
	This Is My Song	16 Feb 1967	229
Clash	Should I Stay Or Should I Go	09 Mar 1991	661
Clooney, Rosemary	This Ole House	26 Nov 1954	25
	Mambo Italiano	14 Jan 1955	28
Cochran, Eddie	Three Steps To Heaven	23 June 1960	102
Cocker, Joe	With A Little Help From My Friends	06 Nov 1968	260
Cogan, Alma	Dreamboat	15 July 1955	35
Collins, Phil	You Can't Hurry Love	15 Jan 1983	513
	Easy Lover	23 Mar 1985	547
	A Groovy Kind Of Love	10 Sept 1988	614
Color Me Badd	I Wanna Sex You Up	08 June 1991	665
Commodores	Three Times A Lady	19 Aug 1978	425
Communards	Don't Leave Me This Way	13 Sept 1986	576
Como, Perry	Don't Let The Stars Get In Your Eyes	06 Feb 1953	5
	Magic Moments	28 Feb 1958	69
Connolly, Billy	D.I.V.O.R.C.E.	22 Nov 1975	381
Conway, Russ	Side Saddle	27 Mar 1959	83
	Roulette	19 June 1959	86
Coolio featuring LV	Gangsta's Paradise	28 Oct 1995	729
Cooper, Alice	School's Out	12 Aug 1972	317
Cornell, Don	Hold My Hand	08 Oct 1954	23
Cornershop	Brimful Of Asha	28 Feb 1998	785
Corrs	Breathless	15 July 2000	865
Covington, Julie	Don't Cry For Me Argentina	12 Feb 1977	400
Cramer, Floyd	On The Rebound	18 May 1961	117
Crazy World of Arthur Brown	Fire	14 Aug 1968	255
Creedence Clearwater Revival	Bad Moon Rising	20 Sept 1969	276
Crickets	That'll Be The Day	01 Nov 1957	64
Crowd	You'll Never Walk Alone	15 June 1985	551
Culture Beat	Mr Vain	28 Aug 1993	694
Culture Club	Do You Really Want To Hurt Me	23 Oct 1982	509
	Karma Chameleon	24 Sept 1983	527
D:Ream	Things Can Only Get Better	22 Jan 1994	701
Damone, Vic	On The Street Where You Live	27 June 1958	72
Dana	All Kinds Of Everything	18 Apr 1970	284
Darin, Bobby	Dream Lover	03 July 1959	87
	Mack The Knife	16 Oct 1959	91
Darius	Colourblind	10 Aug 2002	932
Dave & Ansil Collins	Double Barrel	01 May 1971	299
Dave Clark Five	Glad All Over	16 Jan 1964	161
Dave Dee, Dozy, Beaky, Mick & Tich	Legend Of Xanadu	20 Mar 1968	246
David, Craig	Fill Me In	15 Apr 2000	855
	7 Days	05 Aug 2000	868
Davies, Windsor	Whispering Grass	07 June 1975	371
Dawn	Knock Three Times	15 May 1971	300
	Tie A Yellow Ribbon Round The Old Oak Tree	21 Apr 1973	329

Artist	Song	Date	No
Day, Doris	Secret Love	16 Apr 1954	18
	Whatever Will Be Will Be (Que Sera, Sera)	10 Aug 1956	49
De Burgh, Chris	The Lady In Red	02 Aug 1986	574
Dead Or Alive	You Spin Me Round (Like A Record)	09 Mar 1985	546
Dee, Kiki	Don't Go Breaking My Heart	24 July 1976	393
Deep Blue Something	Breakfast At Tiffany's	05 Oct 1996	746
Dekker, Desmond & The Aces	Israelites	16 Apr 1969	269
Denver, John	Annie's Song	12 Oct 1974	357
Destiny's Child	Independent Women Part 1	02 Dec 2000	883
	Survivor	28 Apr 2001	895
Detroit Spinners	Working My Way Back To You / Forgive Me Girl	12 Apr 1980	455
Dexy's Midnight Runners	Geno	03 May 1980	457
	Come On Eileen	07 Aug 1982	506
Di Bart, Tony	The Real Thing	07 May 1994	706
Diamond, Jim	I Should Have Known Better	01 Dec 1984	541
Dickson, Barbara	I Know Him So Well	09 Feb 1985	545
Dion, Celine	Think Twice	04 Feb 1995	716
	My Heart Will Go On	21 Feb 1998	784
DJ Casper	Cha Cha Slide	20 Mar 2004	975
DJ Otzi	Hey Baby	22 Sept 2001	909
DJ Pied Piper	Do You Really Like It	02 June 2001	898
DJ Sammy & Yanou feat. Do	Heaven	09 Nov 2002	940
Doctor & The Medics	Spirit In The Sky	07 June 1986	571
Dodd, Ken	Tears	30 Sept 1965	204
Dolce, Joe Music Theatre	Shaddap You Face	21 Feb 1981	475
Donegan, Lonnie	Cumberland Gap	12 Apr 1957	57
	Puttin' On The Style / Gamblin' Man	28 June 1957	61
	My Old Man's A Dustman	31 Mar 1960	99
Donovan, Jason	Especially For You	07 Jan 1989	621
	Too Many Broken Hearts	11 Mar 1989	624
	Sealed With A Kiss	10 June 1989	629
	Any Dream Will Do	29 June 1991	666
Doop	Doop	19 Mar 1994	703
Douglas, Carl	Kung Fu Fighting	21 Sept 1974	356
Douglas, Craig	Only Sixteen	11 Sept 1959	89
Dr Hook	When You're In Love With A Beautiful Woman	17 Nov 1979	446
Dream Weavers	It's Almost Tomorrow	16 Mar 1956	43
Dunblane	Knockin' On Heaven's Door / Throw These Guns Away	21 Dec 1996	754
Dunn, Clive	Grandad	09 Jan 1971	295
Duran Duran	Is There Something I Should Know	26 Mar 1983	518
	The Reflex	05 May 1984	534
Dury, Ian & The Blockheads	Hit Me With Your Rhythm Stick	27 Jan 1979	432
Eamon	F**k It (I Don't Want You Back)	24 Apr 2004	978
East 17	Stay Another Day	10 Dec 1994	714
Edison Lighthouse	Love Grows (Where My Rosemary Goes)	31 Jan 1970	281
Edmunds, Dave	I Hear You Knocking	28 Nov 1970	294
Edwards, Tommy	All In The Game	07 Nov 1958	76
Eiffel 65	Blue (Da Ba Dee)	25 Sept 1999	836
Electric Light Orchestra	Xanadu	12 July 1980	461
Eminem	Real Slim Shady	08 July 2000	864
	Stan	16 Dec 2000	885
	Without Me	01 June 2002	928
	Lose Yourself	14 Dec 2002	944
	Just Lose It	13 Nov 2004	994
	Like Toy Soldiers	12 Feb 2005	1003
England World Cup Squad	Back Home	16 May 1970	286
EnglandNewOrder	World In Motion	09 June 1990	646
Enigma	Sadness Part 1	19 Jan 1991	657
Enya	Orinoco Flow (Sail Away)	29 Oct 1988	618
	I Don't Wanna Know	12 June 2004	980
Equals	Baby Come Back	03 July 1968	252
Erasure	Abba-esque EP	13 June 1992	677
Essex, David	Gonna Make You A Star	16 Nov 1974	360
	Hold Me Close	04 Oct 1975	378
Estelle, Don	Whispering Grass	07 June 1975	371
Eternal featuring Bebe Winans	I Wanna Be The One	31 May 1997	768
Europe	The Final Countdown	06 Dec 1986	580
Eurythmics	There Must Be An Angel (Playing With My Heart)	27 July 1985	553
Evanescence	Bring Me To Life	14 June 2003	955
Evans, Faith	I'll Be Missing You	28 June 1997	770

Artist	Song	Date	No
Everly Brothers	All I Have To Do Is Dream / Claudette	04 July 1958	73
	Cathy's Clown	05 May 1960	101
	Walk Right Back / Ebony Eyes	02 Mar 1961	114
	Temptation	20 July 1961	121
Fairground Attraction	Perfect	14 May 1988	608
Faith, Adam	What Do You Want	04 Dec 1959	93
	Poor Me	10 Mar 1960	97
Falco	Rock Me Amadeus	10 May 1986	569
Fame, Georgie	Yeah Yeah	14 Jan 1965	184
	Getaway	21 July 1966	219
	The Ballad Of Bonnie And Clyde	24 Jan 1968	242
Farlowe, Chris	Out Of Time	28 July 1966	220
Fatboy Slim	Praise You	16 Jan 1999	811
Fatman Scoop	Be Faithful	01 Nov 2003	962
Ferry Aid	Let It Be	04 Apr 1987	588
Firm, The	Star Trekkin'	20 June 1987	592
Fisher, Eddie	Outside Of Heaven	30 Jan 1953	4
	I'm Walking Behind You	26 June 1953	10
Five	Keep On Movin'	06 Nov 1999	839
	We Will Rock You	29 July 2000	867
	Let's Dance	25 Aug 2001	906
Fleetwood Mac	Albatross	29 Jan 1969	264
Floaters	Float On	27 Aug 1977	411
Flying Pickets	Only You	10 Dec 1983	529
Ford, Emile & The Checkmates	What Do You Want To Make Those Eyes At Me For	18 Dec 1959	94
Ford, Tennessee Ernie	Give Me Your Word	11 Mar 1955	30
	Sixteen Tons	20 Jan 1956	41
Foreigner	I Want To Know What Love Is	19 Jan 1985	544
Foundations	Baby Now That I've Found You	08 Nov 1967	239
Four Pennies	Juliet	21 May 1964	169
Four Seasons	December '63 (Oh, What A Night)	21 Feb 1976	385
Four Tops	Reach Out I'll Be There	27 Oct 1966	225
Fragma	Toca's Miracle	22 Apr 2000	856
Francis, Connie	Who's Sorry Now	16 May 1958	71
	Carolina Moon / Stupid Cupid	26 Sept 1958	75
Frankee	F.U.R.B. (F U Right Back)	22 May 2004	979
Frankie Goes To Hollywood	Relax	28 Jan 1984	531
	Two Tribes	16 June 1984	536
	The Power Of Love	08 Dec 1984	542
Franklin, Aretha	I Knew You Were Waiting (For Me)	07 Feb 1987	584
Fugees	Killing Me Softly	08 June 1996	741
	Ready Or Not	21 Sept 1996	745
Gabrielle	Dreams	26 June 1993	691
	Rise	05 Feb 2000	847
Gardiner, Boris	I Want To Wake Up With You	23 Aug 1986	575
Garfunkel, Art	I Only Have Eyes For You	25 Oct 1975	379
	Bright Eyes	14 Apr 1979	436
Gates, Gareth	Unchained Melody	30 Mar 2002	922
	Anyone Of Us (Stupid Mistake)	20 July 2002	931
	The Long And Winding Road / Suspicious Minds	05 Oct 2002	937
	Spirit In The Sky	22 Mar 2003	950
Gaye, Marvin	I Heard It Through The Grapevine	26 Mar 1969	268
Gaynor, Gloria	I Will Survive	17 Mar 1979	435
Gentry, Bobbie	I'll Never Fall In Love Again	18 Oct 1969	278
Gerry & The Pacemakers	How Do You Do It?	11 Apr 1963	150
	I Like It	20 June 1963	152
	You'll Never Walk Alone	31 Oct 1963	159
Gina G	Ooh Aah ... Just A Little Bit	25 May 1996	739
Girls Aloud	Sound Of The Underground	28 Dec 2002	946
	I'll Stand By You	27 Nov 2004	996
Glitter, Gary	I'm The Leader Of The Gang (I Am)	28 July 1973	335
	I Love You Love Me Love	17 Nov 1973	340
	Always Yours	22 June 1974	351
Goombay Dance Band	Seven Tears	27 Mar 1982	497
Grant, Eddy	I Don't Wanna Dance	13 Nov 1982	510
Greenbaum, Norman	Spirit In The Sky	02 May 1970	285
Hale & Pace	The Stonk	23 Mar 1991	662
Haley, Bill & His Comets	Rock Around The Clock	25 Nov 1955	39
Halliwell, Geri	Mi Chico Latino	28 Aug 1999	833
	Lift Me Up	13 Nov 1999	840

Artist	Song	Date	No
	Bag It Up	25 Mar 2000	852
	It's Raining Men	12 May 2001	897
Hanson	MmmBop	07 June 1997	769
Hardcastle, Paul	19	11 May 1985	550
Harden, Duane	You Don't Know Me	06 Feb 1999	814
Harley, Steve & Cockney Rebel	Make Me Smile (Come Up And See Me)	22 Feb 1975	366
Harris, Jet & Tony Meehan	Diamonds	31 Jan 1963	146
Harris, Rolf	Two Little Boys	20 Dec 1969	280
Harrison, George	My Sweet Lord	30 Jan 1971	296
	My Sweet Lord	26 Jan 2002	918
Hawkes, Chesney	The One And Only	30 Mar 1991	663
Hear'Say	Pure And Simple	24 Mar 2001	893
	The Way To Your Love	07 July 2001	901
Hendrix, Jimi	Voodoo Chile	21 Nov 1970	293
Herman's Hermits	I'm Into Something Good	24 Sept 1964	178
Highwaymen	Michael	12 Oct 1961	127
Hill, Benny	Ernie (The Fastest Milkman In The West)	11 Dec 1971	307
Hilton, Ronnie	No Other Love	04 May 1956	46
Holliday, Michael	The Story Of My Life	14 Feb 1958	68
	Starry Eyed	29 Jan 1960	95
Hollies	I'm Alive	24 June 1965	198
	He Ain't Heavy He's My Brother	24 Sept 1988	615
Holly, Buddy	It Doesn't Matter Anymore	24 Apr 1959	84
Honeycombs	Have I The Right	27 Aug 1964	176
Hopkin, Mary	Those Were The Days	25 Sept 1968	259
Hot Chocolate	So You Win Again	02 July 1977	408
Housemartins	Caravan Of Love	20 Dec 1986	581
Houston, Whitney	Saving All My Love For You	14 Dec 1985	561
	I Wanna Dance With Somebody (Who Loves Me)	06 June 1987	591
	One Moment In Time	15 Oct 1988	617
	I Will Always Love You	05 Dec 1992	684
Hugo Montenegro Orchestra	The Good The Bad And The Ugly	13 Nov 1968	261
Human League	Don't You Want Me	12 Dec 1981	491
Humperdinck, Engelbert	Release Me	02 Mar 1967	230
	The Last Waltz	06 Sept 1967	237
Hurley, Steve 'Silk'	Jack Your Body	24 Jan 1987	583
Hynde, Chrissie	I Got You Babe	31 Aug 1985	555
	Love Can Build A Bridge	25 Mar 1995	717
Ifield, Frank	I Remember You	26 July 1962	139
	Lovesick Blues	08 Nov 1962	142
	Wayward Wind	21 Feb 1963	147
	Confessin' (That I Love You)	18 July 1963	153
Iglesias, Enrique	Hero	02 Feb 2002	919
Iglesias, Julio	Begin The Beguine (Volver A Empezar)	05 Dec 1981	490
Iron Maiden	Bring Your Daughter To The Slaughter	05 Jan 1991	656
Ja Rule featuring R Kelly & Ashanti	Wonderful	06 Nov 2004	993
Jacks, Terry	Seasons In The Sun	06 Apr 1974	347
Jackson, Michael	One Day In Your Life	27 June 1981	481
	Billie Jean	05 Mar 1983	516
	I Just Can't Stop Loving You	15 Aug 1987	596
	Black Or White	23 Nov 1991	670
	You Are Not Alone	09 Sept 1995	726
	Earth Song	09 Dec 1995	731
	Blood On The Dance Floor	03 May 1997	765
Jacksons	Show You The Way To Go	25 June 1977	407
Jagger, Mick	Dancing in the Street	07 Sept 1985	556
Jam	Going Underground / Dreams Of Children	22 Mar 1980	454
	Start	06 Sept 1980	465
	Town Called Malice / Precious	13 Feb 1982	495
	Beat Surrender	04 Dec 1982	511
James, Tommy & The Shondells	Mony Mony	31 July 1968	254
Jamiroquai	Deeper Underground	25 July 1998	796
Jazzy Jeff & The Fresh Prince (Will Smith)	Boom! Shake The Room	25 Sept 1993	695
Jive Bunny & The Mastermixers	Swing The Mood	05 Aug 1989	632
	That's What I Like	21 Oct 1989	634
	Let's Party	16 Dec 1989	637
Joel, Billy	Uptown Girl	05 Nov 1983	528
John, Elton	Don't Go Breaking My Heart	24 July 1976	393
	Sacrifice / Healing Hands	23 June 1990	647
	Don't Let The Sun Go Down On Me	07 Dec 1991	671

Artist	Song	Date	No
	Candle In The Wind '97 / Something About The Way You Look Tonight	20 Sept 1997	774
	Sorry Seems To Be The Hardest Word	21 Dec 2002	945
	Are You Ready For Love?	06 Sept 2003	959
Johnson, Holly	Ferry 'Cross The Mersey	20 May 1989	628
Johnston Brothers	Hernando's Hideaway	11 Nov 1955	38
Jones, Jimmy	Good Timin'	07 July 1960	103
Jones, Tom	It's Not Unusual	11 Mar 1965	189
	Green Green Grass Of Home	01 Dec 1966	227
Jules, Gary	Mad World	27 Dec 2003	968
K C & The Sunshine Band	Give It Up	13 Aug 1983	525
Kajagoogoo	Too Shy	19 Feb 1983	515
Kalin Twins	When	22 Aug 1958	74
Kallen, Kitty	Little Things Mean A Lot	10 Sept 1954	21
Kane, Eden	Well I Ask You	03 Aug 1961	122
Keating, Ronan	When You Say Nothing At All	07 Aug 1999	831
	Life Is A Rollercoaster	22 July 2000	866
	If Tomorrow Never Comes	18 May 2002	926
Keller, Jerry	Here Comes Summer	09 Oct 1959	90
Kelly Marie	Feels Like I'm In Love	13 Sept 1980	466
Kelly, R	I Believe I Can Fly	12 Apr 1997	764
	Ignition	17 May 2003	954
Khan, Chaka	I Feel For You	10 Nov 1984	540
Kidd, Johnny & The Pirates	Shakin' All Over	04 Aug 1960	105
Kidman, Nicole	Somethin' Stupid	22 Dec 2001	916
King, Ben E	Stand By Me	21 Feb 1987	585
Kinks	You Really Got Me	10 Sept 1964	177
	Tired Of Waiting For You	18 Feb 1965	187
	Sunny Afternoon	07 July 1966	218
Kinney, Fern	Together We Are Beautiful	15 Mar 1980	453
KLF	3AM Eternal	02 Feb 1991	659
Kraftwerk	The Model / Computer Love	06 Feb 1982	494
Kramer, Billy J & The Dakotas	Bad To Me	22 Aug 1963	156
	Little Children	19 Mar 1964	165
Kravitz, Lenny	Fly Away	20 Feb 1999	816
KWS	Please Don't Go / Game Boy	09 May 1992	676
Laine, Frankie	I Believe	24 Apr 1953	9
	Hey Joe	23 Oct 1953	13
	Answer Me	13 Nov 1953	15
	A Woman In Love	19 Oct 1956	51
Las Ketchup	The Ketchup Song (Asereje)	19 Oct 2002	938
Lennon, John	(Just Like) Starting Over	20 Dec 1980	471
	Imagine	10 Jan 1981	473
	Woman	07 Feb 1981	474
Lewis, Jerry Lee	Great Balls Of Fire	10 Jan 1958	66
Leyton, John	Johnny Remember Me	31 Aug 1961	124
Liberty X	Just A Little	25 May 2002	927
Lieutenant Pigeon	Mouldy Old Dough	14 Oct 1972	321
Lightning Seeds	Three Lions	01 June 1996	740
	Three Lions '98	20 June 1998	793
Lil' Kim	Lady Marmalade	30 June 2001	900
Limp Bizkit	Rollin'	27 Jan 2001	889
Livin' Joy	Dreamer	13 May 1995	721
LL Cool J	Ain't Nobody	08 Feb 1997	759
LMC vs U2	Take Me To The Clouds Above	07 Feb 2004	970
Logan, Johnny	What's Another Year	17 May 1980	458
Lopes, Lisa 'Left Eye'	Never Be The Same Again	01 Apr 2000	853
Lopez, Jennifer	Love Don't Cost A Thing	20 Jan 2001	888
	Get Right	26 Feb 2005	1005
Lord Rockingham's XI	Hoots Mon	28 Nov 1958	77
Los Lobos	La Bamba	01 Aug 1987	595
Love Affair	Everlasting Love	31 Jan 1968	243
Luhrmann, Baz	Everybody's Free (To Wear Sunscreen)	12 June 1999	826
Lulu	Relight My Fire	09 Oct 1993	696
Lymon, Frankie & The Teenagers	Why Do Fools Fall in Love	20 July 1956	48
Lynn, Vera	My Son My Son	05 Nov 1954	24
Madison Avenue	Don't Call Me Baby	20 May 2000	859
Madness	House Of Fun	29 May 1982	501
Madonna	Into The Groove	03 Aug 1985	554
	Papa Don't Preach	12 July 1986	573
	True Blue	11 Oct 1986	577

Artist	Song	Date	No
	La Isla Bonita	25 Apr 1987	589
	Who's That Girl	25 July 1987	594
	Like A Prayer	25 Mar 1989	625
	Vogue	14 Apr 1990	644
	Frozen	07 Mar 1998	786
	American Pie	11 Mar 2000	850
	Music	02 Sept 2000	872
Manchester United 1994 Football Squad	Come On You Reds	21 May 1994	708
Manfred Mann	Do Wah Diddy Diddy	13 Aug 1964	175
	Pretty Flamingo	05 May 1966	214
	The Mighty Quinn	14 Feb 1968	244
Manhattan Transfer	Chanson D'Amour	12 Mar 1977	402
Manic Street Preachers	If You Tolerate This Your Children Will Be Next	05 Sept 1998	799
	The Masses Against The Classes	22 Jan 2000	845
Mantovani	Song from 'The Moulin Rouge'	14 Aug 1953	11
Marcels	Blue Moon	04 May 1961	116
Marmalade	Ob-La-Di Ob-La-Da	01 Jan 1969	263
M/A/R/R/S	Pump Up The Volume / Anitina (The First Time I See She Dance)	03 Oct 1987	598
Marsden, Gerry	Ferry 'Cross The Mersey	20 May 1989	628
Martell, Lena	One Day At A Time	27 Oct 1979	445
Martin, Dean	Memories Are Made Of This	17 Feb 1956	42
Martin, Ricky	Livin' La Vida Loca	17 July 1999	830
Martino, Al	Here In My Heart	14 Nov 1952	1
Marvin, Lee	Wand'rin' Star	07 Mar 1970	282
MASH	Suicide Is Painless (Theme from M*A*S*H)	31 May 1980	459
Mathis, Johnny	When A Child Is Born (Soleado)	25 Dec 1976	398
Matthews Southern Comfort	Woodstock	31 Oct 1970	292
McCartney, Paul	Ebony And Ivory	24 Apr 1982	499
	Pipes Of Peace	14 Jan 1984	530
	Ferry 'Cross The Mersey	20 May 1989	628
McCrae, George	Rock Your Baby	27 July 1974	353
McCutcheon, Martine	Perfect Moment	17 Apr 1999	821
McFadden, Brian	Real To Me	18 Sept 2004	990
McFly	Five Colours In Her Hair	10 Apr 2004	977
	Obviously	03 July 2004	982
	All About You / You've Got A Friend	19 Mar 2005	1008
McGraw, Tim	Over And Over	05 Mar 2005	1006
McKee, Maria	Show Me Heaven	29 Sept 1990	651
McKenzie, Scott	San Francisco (Be Sure To Wear Some Flowers In Your Hair)	09 Aug 1967	236
McLean, Don	Vincent	17 June 1972	314
	Crying	21 June 1980	460
McManus, Michelle	All This Time	17 Jan 2004	969
Meat Loaf	I'd Do Anything For Love (But I Won't Do That)	23 Oct 1993	697
Medeiros, Glenn	Nothing's Gonna Change My Love For You	09 July 1988	612
Mel & Kim	Respectable	28 Mar 1987	587
Melanie B	I Want You Back	26 Sept 1998	802
Melanie C	Never Be The Same Again	01 Apr 2000	853
	I Turn To You	19 Aug 2000	870
Men At Work	Down Under	29 Jan 1983	514
Mercury, Freddie	Living On My Own	14 Aug 1993	693
Michael, George	Careless Whisper	18 Aug 1984	537
	A Different Corner	19 Apr 1986	568
	I Knew You Were Waiting (For Me)	07 Feb 1987	584
	Don't Let The Sun Go Down On Me	07 Dec 1991	671
	Five Live (EP)	01 May 1993	688
	Jesus To A Child	20 Jan 1996	732
	Fastlove	04 May 1996	738
Middle Of The Road	Chirpy Chirpy Cheep Cheep	19 June 1971	301
Miller, Roger	King Of The Road	13 May 1965	194
Miller, Steve Band	The Joker	15 Sept 1990	650
Minogue, Kylie	I Should Be So Lucky	20 Feb 1988	604
	Especially For You	07 Jan 1989	621
	Hand On Your Heart	13 May 1989	627
	Tears On My Pillow	27 Jan 1990	640
	Spinning Around	01 July 2000	863
	Can't Get You Out Of My Head	29 Sept 2001	910
	Slow	15 Nov 2003	963
Missy Elliott	I Want You Back	26 Sept 1998	802

MUSIC POP

Artist	Song	Date	No
Mitchell, Guy	She Wears Red Feathers	13 Mar 1953	6
	Look At That Girl	11 Sept 1953	12
	Singing The Blues	04 Jan 1957	53
	Rock-A-Billy	17 May 1957	58
Modjo	Lady (Hear Me Tonight)	16 Sept 2000	874
Monkees	I'm A Believer	19 Jan 1967	228
Moody Blues	Go Now!	28 Jan 1965	185
Morgan, Jane	The Day The Rains Came	23 Jan 1959	79
Morrison, Mark	Return Of The Mack	20 Apr 1996	737
Move	Blackberry Way	05 Feb 1969	265
Mr Blobby	Mr Blobby	11 Dec 1993	698
Mr Oizo	Flat Beat	03 Apr 1999	820
Mud	Tiger Feet	26 Jan 1974	343
	Lonely This Christmas	21 Dec 1974	362
	Oh Boy	03 May 1975	369
Mungo Jerry	In The Summertime	13 June 1970	288
	Baby Jump	06 Mar 1971	297
Murray, Ruby	Softly, Softly	18 Feb 1955	29
Musical Youth	Pass The Dutchie	02 Oct 1982	508
Mya	Lady Marmalade	30 June 2001	900
Nail, Jimmy	Ain't No Doubt	18 July 1992	678
Nash, Johnny	Tears On My Pillow	12 July 1975	373
Nelly	Dilemma	26 Oct 2002	939
	My Place / Flap Your Wings	11 Sept 2004	989
	Over And Over	05 Mar 2005	1006
Nelson, Phyllis	Move Closer	04 May 1985	549
Nena	99 Red Balloons	03 Mar 1984	532
New Edition	Candy Girl	28 May 1983	521
New Kids On The Block	You Got It (The Right Stuff)	25 Nov 1989	636
	Hangin' Tough	16 Jan 1990	639
New Seekers	I'd Like To Teach The World To Sing (In Perfect Harmony)	08 Jan 1972	308
	You Won't Find Another Fool Like Me	19 Jan 1974	342
Newley, Anthony	Why	05 Feb 1960	96
	Do You Mind	28 Apr 1960	100
Newton John, Olivia	You're The One That I Want	17 June 1978	424
	Summer Nights	30 Sept 1978	427
	Xanadu	12 July 1980	461
Nicole	A Little Peace	15 May 1982	500
Nilsson	Without You	11 Mar 1972	311
911	A Little Bit More	23 Jan 1999	812
No Doubt	Don't Speak	22 Feb 1997	761
Numan, Gary	Cars	22 Sept 1979	442
Oasis	Some Might Say	06 May 1995	720
	Don't Look Back In Anger	02 Mar 1996	734
	D'You Know What I Mean	19 July 1997	771
	All Around The World	24 Jan 1998	781
	Go Let It Out	19 Feb 2000	848
	The Hindu Times	27 Apr 2002	923
Ocean, Billy	When The Going Gets Tough, The Tough Get Going	08 Feb 1986	565
O'Connor, Des	I Pretend	24 July 1968	253
O'Connor, Sinead	Nothing Compares 2 U	03 Feb 1990	641
Odyssey	Use It Up And Wear It Out	26 July 1980	462
Ofarim, Esther & Abi	Cinderella Rockefella	28 Feb 1968	245
Offspring	Pretty Fly (For A White Guy)	30 Jan 1999	813
Olive	You're Not Alone	17 May 1997	767
112	I'll Be Missing You	28 June 1997	770
Orbison, Roy	Only The Lonely	20 Oct 1960	108
	It's Over	25 June 1964	171
	Oh Pretty Woman	08 Oct 1964	179
Osbourne, Kelly	Changes	20 Dec 2003	967
Osbourne, Ozzy	Changes	20 Dec 2003	967
Osmond, Donny	Puppy Love	08 July 1972	316
	The Twelfth Of Never	31 Mar 1973	327
	Young Love	25 Aug 1973	336
Osmond, Little Jimmy	Long Haired Lover From Liverpool	23 Dec 1972	324
Osmonds	Love Me For A Reason	31 Aug 1974	355
O'Sullivan, Gilbert	Clair	11 Nov 1972	322
	Get Down	07 Apr 1973	328
Outhere Brothers	Don't Stop (Wiggle Wiggle)	01 Apr 1995	718

Artist	Song	Date	No
	Boom Boom Boom	08 July 1995	723
Overlanders	Michelle	27 Jan 1966	209
Oxide & Neutrino	Bound 4 Da Reload (Casualty)	06 May 2000	857
P Diddy	I Don't Wanna Know	12 June 2004	980
Pablo, Petey	Goodies	29 Jan 2005	1001
Paige, Elaine	I Know Him So Well	09 Feb 1985	545
Paper Lace	Billy Don't Be A Hero	16 Mar 1974	346
Partners In Kryme	Turtle Power	28 July 1990	648
Payne, Freda	Band Of Gold	19 Sept 1970	291
Perez 'Prez' Prado & His Orchestra	Cherry Pink And Apple Blossom White	29 Apr 1955	31
Pet Shop Boys	West End Girls	11 Jan 1986	563
	It's A Sin	04 July 1987	593
	Always On My Mind	19 Dec 1987	601
	Heart	09 Apr 1988	606
Peter & Gordon	A World Without Love	23 Apr 1964	167
Peters & Lee	Welcome Home	21 July 1973	334
Pilot	January	01 Feb 1975	365
Pink	Lady Marmalade	30 June 2001	900
	Just Like A Pill	28 Sept 2002	936
Pink Floyd	Another Brick In The Wall	15 Dec 1979	448
Pipes & Drums & Military Band of The Royal Scots Dragoon Guards	Amazing Grace	15 Apr 1972	312
Platters	Smoke Gets In Your Eyes	20 Mar 1959	82
Police	Message In A Bottle	29 Sept 1979	443
	Walking On The Moon	08 Dec 1979	447
	Don't Stand So Close To Me	27 Sept 1980	467
	Every Little Thing She Does Is Magic	14 Nov 1981	488
	Every Breath You Take	04 June 1983	522
Poole, Brian & The Tremeloes	Do You Love Me	10 Oct 1963	158
Presley, Elvis	All Shook Up	12 July 1957	62
	Jailhouse Rock	24 Jan 1958	67
	I Got Stung / One Night	30 Jan 1959	80
	A Fool Such As I / I Need Your Love Tonight	15 May 1959	85
	It's Now Or Never	03 Nov 1960	109
	Are You Lonesome Tonight	26 Jan 1961	112
	Wooden Heart	23 Mar 1961	115
	Surrender	01 June 1961	119
	His Latest Flame	09 Nov 1961	129
	Can't Help Falling In Love / Rock-A-Hula Baby	22 Feb 1962	133
	Good Luck Charm	24 May 1962	136
	She's Not You	13 Sept 1962	140
	Return To Sender	13 Dec 1962	143
	(You're The) Devil In Disguise	01 Aug 1963	154
	Crying In The Chapel	17 June 1965	197
	The Wonder Of You	01 Aug 1970	289
	Way Down	03 Sept 1977	412
	A Little Less Conversation	22 June 2002	930
	Jailhouse Rock	15 Jan 2005	999
	I Got Stung / One Night	22 Jan 2005	1000
	It's Now Or Never	05 Feb 2005	1002
Preston, Johnny	Running Bear	17 Mar 1960	98
Pretenders	Brass In Pocket	19 Jan 1980	449
Prince	The Most Beautiful Girl In The World	23 Apr 1994	705
Procol Harum	A Whiter Shade Of Pale	08 June 1967	234
Prodigy	Firestarter	30 Mar 1996	736
	Breathe	23 Nov 1996	751
Prydz, Eric	Call On Me	25 Sept 2004	991
Puff Daddy	I'll Be Missing You	28 June 1997	770
Pussycat	Mississippi	16 Oct 1976	395
Quatro, Suzi	Can The Can	16 June 1973	331
	Devil Gate Drive	23 Feb 1974	344
Queen	Bohemian Rhapsody	29 Nov 1975	382
	Under Pressure	21 Nov 1981	489
	Innuendo	26 Jan 1991	658
	Bohemian Rhapsody / These Are The Days Of Our Lives	21 Dec 1991	672
	Five Live (EP)	01 May 1993	688
	We Will Rock You	29 July 2000	867
Rainwater, Marvin	Whole Lotta Woman	25 Apr 1958	70
Ray, Johnnie	Such A Night	30 Apr 1954	19
	Just Walking In The Rain	16 Nov 1956	52

M
U
S
I
C

P
O
P

Artist	Song	Date	No
	Yes Tonight Josephine	07 June 1957	60
Real Thing	You To Me Are Everything	26 June 1976	391
Rednex	Cotton Eye Joe	14 Jan 1995	715
Reeves, Jim	Distant Drums	22 Sept 1966	224
Reeves, Vic & The Wonder Stuff	Dizzy	09 Nov 1991	669
Renee & Renato	Save Your Love	18 Dec 1982	512
Richard, Cliff	Living Doll	31 July 1959	88
	Travellin' Light	30 Oct 1959	92
	Please Don't Tease	28 July 1960	104
	I Love You	29 Dec 1960	110
	The Young Ones	11 Jan 1962	132
	The Next Time / Bachelor Boy	03 Jan 1963	144
	Summer Holiday	14 Mar 1963	148
	The Minute You're Gone	15 Apr 1965	192
	Congratulations	10 Apr 1968	248
	We Don't Talk Anymore	25 Aug 1979	441
	Living Doll	29 Mar 1986	567
	Mistletoe And Wine	10 Dec 1988	620
	Saviour's Day	22 Dec 1990	655
	Millennium Prayer	04 Dec 1999	843
Richie, Lionel	Hello	24 Mar 1984	533
Right Said Fred	Deeply Dippy	18 Apr 1992	675
Righteous Brothers	You've Lost That Loving Feeling	04 Feb 1965	186
	Unchained Melody	03 Nov 1990	653
Rimes, LeAnn	Can't Fight The Moonlight	25 Nov 2000	882
Robinson, Smokey	Being With You	13 June 1981	480
Robinson, Smokey & The Miracles	Tears Of A Clown	12 Sept 1970	290
Robson & Jerome	I Believe / Up On The Roof	11 Nov 1995	730
	Unchained Melody / White Cliffs Of Dover	20 May 1995	722
	What Becomes Of The Broken Hearted / Saturday Night At The Movies / You'll Never Walk Alone	09 Nov 1996	750
Roe, Tommy	Dizzy	04 June 1969	271
Rogers, Kenny	Lucille	18 June 1977	406
	Coward Of The County	16 Feb 1980	451
Rolling Stones	It's All Over Now	16 July 1964	173
	Little Red Rooster	03 Dec 1964	182
	The Last Time	18 Mar 1965	190
	(I Can't Get No) Satisfaction	09 Sept 1965	202
	Get Off Of My Cloud	04 Nov 1965	205
	Paint It Black	26 May 1966	215
	Jumpin' Jack Flash	19 June 1968	251
	Honky Tonk Women	23 July 1969	274
Room 5 featuring Oliver Cheatham	Make Luv	05 Apr 2003	951
Ross, Diana	I'm Still Waiting	21 Aug 1971	303
	Chain Reaction	08 Mar 1986	566
Roussos, Demis	The Roussos Phenomenon EP (main track: Forever And Ever)	17 July 1976	392
Rowland, Kelly	Dilemma	26 Oct 2002	939
Roxy Music	Jealous Guy	14 Mar 1981	476
Roza, Lita	(How Much Is) That Doggie In The Window	17 Apr 1953	8
Rubettes	Sugar Baby Love	18 May 1974	349
Rui Da Silva featuring Cassandra	Touch Me	13 Jan 2001	887
Run DMC vs Jason Nevins	It's Like That	21 Mar 1998	787
Rush, Jennifer	The Power Of Love	12 Oct 1985	558
S Club 7	Bring It All Back	19 June 1999	827
	Never Had A Dream Come True	09 Dec 2000	884
	Don't Stop Movin'	05 May 2001	896
	Have You Ever	01 Dec 2001	914
Sam & Mark	With A Little Help From My Friends / Measure Of A Man	21 Feb 2004	971
Sanchez, Roger	Another Chance	14 July 2001	902
Sarne, Mike with Wendy Richard	Come Outside	28 June 1962	137
Sarstedt, Peter	Where Do You Go To My Lovely?	26 Feb 1969	267
Savalas, Telly	If	08 Mar 1975	367
Sayer, Leo	When I Need You	19 Feb 1977	401
Scaffold	Lily The Pink	11 Dec 1968	262
Searchers	Sweets For My Sweet	08 Aug 1963	155
	Needles And Pins	30 Jan 1964	162
	Don't Throw Your Love Away	07 May 1964	168
Seekers	I'll Never Find Another You	25 Feb 1965	188

Artist	Song	Date	No
	The Carnival Is Over	25 Nov 1965	206
S'Express	Theme from S'Express	30 Apr 1988	607
Shadows	Apache	25 Aug 1960	106
	Kon Tiki	05 Oct 1961	126
	Wonderful Land	22 Mar 1962	134
	Dance On	24 Jan 1963	145
	Foot Tapper	29 Mar 1963	149
Shaggy	Oh Carolina	20 Mar 1993	686
	Boombastic	23 Sept 1995	727
	It Wasn't Me	10 Mar 2001	891
	Angel	09 June 2001	899
Shakespears Sister	Stay	22 Feb 1992	674
Shamen	Ebeneezer Goode	19 Sept 1992	680
Shanks & Bigfoot	Sweet Like Chocolate	29 May 1999	825
Shannon, Del	Runaway	29 June 1961	120
Shapeshifters	Lola's Theme	24 July 2004	984
Shapiro, Helen	You Don't Know	10 Aug 1961	123
	Walkin' Back To Happiness	19 Oct 1961	128
Sharkey, Feargal	A Good Heart	16 Nov 1985	559
Shaw, Sandie	(There's) Always Something There To Remind Me	22 Oct 1964	180
	Long Live Love	27 May 1965	196
	Puppet On A String	27 Apr 1967	232
Shelton, Anne	Lay Down Your Arms	21 Sept 1956	50
Showaddywaddy	Under The Moon Of Love	04 Dec 1976	397
Simon & Garfunkel	Bridge Over Troubled Water	28 Mar 1970	283
Simon Park Orchestra	Eye Level	29 Sept 1973	338
Simple Minds	Belfast Child	25 Feb 1989	623
Simply Red	Fairground	30 Sept 1995	728
Simpsons	Do The Bartman	16 Feb 1991	660
Sinatra, Frank	Three Coins In The Fountain	17 Sept 1954	22
	Strangers In The Night	02 June 1966	216
	Somethin' Stupid	13 Apr 1967	231
Sinatra, Nancy	These Boots Are Made For Walking	17 Feb 1966	210
	Somethin' Stupid	13 Apr 1967	231
Sister Sledge	Frankie	29 June 1985	552
Slade	Coz I Luv You	13 Nov 1971	306
	Take Me Bak 'Ome	01 July 1972	315
	Mama Weer All Crazee Now	09 Sept 1972	319
	Cum On Feel The Noize	03 Mar 1973	326
	Skweeze Me Pleeze Me	30 June 1973	333
	Merry Xmas Everybody	15 Dec 1973	341
Slik	Forever And Ever	14 Feb 1976	384
Small Faces	All Or Nothing	15 Sept 1966	223
Smith, Will	Men In Black	16 Aug 1997	772
Snap	The Power	31 Mar 1990	643
	Rhythm Is A Dancer	08 Aug 1992	679
Sneddon, David	Stop Living The Lie	25 Jan 2003	947
So Solid Crew	21 Seconds	18 Aug 2001	905
Soft Cell	Tainted Love	05 Sept 1981	485
Sonia	You'll Never Stop Me Loving You	22 July 1989	631
Sonique	It Feels So Good	03 June 2000	861
Sonny & Cher	I Got You Babe	26 Aug 1965	201
Soul II Soul featuring Caron Wheeler	Back To Life	24 June 1989	630
Soul, David	Don't Give Up On Us	15 Jan 1977	399
	Silver Lady	08 Oct 1977	413
Spacedust	Gym & Tonic	24 Oct 1998	805
Spandau Ballet	True	30 Apr 1983	520
Spears, Britney	Baby One More Time	27 Feb 1999	817
	Born To Make You Happy	29 Jan 2000	846
	Oops! ... I Did It Again	13 May 2000	858
	Toxic	13 Mar 2004	974
	Everytime	26 June 2004	981
Specials	The Special AKA Live EP	02 Feb 1980	450
	Ghost Town	11 July 1981	482
Spencer Davis Group	Keep On Running	20 Jan 1966	208
	Somebody Help Me	14 Apr 1966	212
Spice Girls	Wannabe	27 July 1996	743
	Say You'll Be There	26 Oct 1996	749
	2 Become 1	28 Dec 1996	755
	Mama / Who Do You Think You Are	15 Mar 1997	762
	Spice Up Your Life	25 Oct 1997	775

Artist	Song	Date	No
	Too Much	27 Dec 1997	779
	Viva Forever	01 Aug 1998	797
	Goodbye	26 Dec 1998	808
	Holler / Let Love Lead The Way	04 Nov 2000	879
Spiller	Groovejet (If This Ain't Love)	26 Aug 2000	871
Spitting Image	The Chicken Song	17 May 1986	570
Springfield, Dusty	You Don't Have To Say You Love Me	28 Apr 1966	213
St Winifred's School Choir	There's No One Quite Like Grandma	27 Dec 1980	472
Stafford, Jo	You Belong To Me	16 Jan 1953	2
Stansfield, Lisa	All Around The World	11 Nov 1989	635
	Five Live (EP)	01 May 1993	688
Stardust, Alvin	Jealous Mind	09 Mar 1974	345
Stargazers	Broken Wings	10 Apr 1953	7
	I See The Moon	12 Mar 1954	17
Starr, Kay	Comes A-Long A-Love	23 Jan 1953	3
	Rock And Roll Waltz	30 Mar 1956	44
Starship	Nothing's Gonna Stop Us Now	09 May 1987	590
Status Quo	Down Down	18 Jan 1975	363
Steele, Tommy	Singing The Blues	11 Jan 1957	54
Steps	Heartbeat / Tragedy	09 Jan 1999	810
	Stomp	28 Oct 2000	878
Stereophonics	Dakota	12 Mar 2005	1007
Stevens, Ray	The Streak	15 June 1974	350
Stevens, Shakin'	This Ole House	28 Mar 1981	477
	Green Door	01 Aug 1981	483
	Oh Julie	30 Jan 1982	493
	Merry Christmas Everyone	28 Dec 1985	562
Stewart, Dave & Barbara Gaskin	It's My Party	17 Oct 1981	487
Stewart, Rod	Maggie May	09 Oct 1971	305
	You Wear It Well	02 Sept 1972	318
	Sailing	06 Sept 1975	377
	I Don't Want To Talk About It / First Cut Is The Deepest	21 May 1977	405
	Da Ya Think I'm Sexy	02 Dec 1978	429
	Baby Jane	02 July 1983	523
Stiltskin	Inside	14 May 1994	707
Streets	Dry Your Eyes	31 July 2004	985
Streisand, Barbra	Woman In Love	25 Oct 1980	468
Stylistics	Can't Give You Anything (But My Love)	16 Aug 1975	376
Sugababes	Freak Like Me	04 May 2002	924
	Round Round	24 Aug 2002	933
	Hole In The Head	25 Oct 2003	961
Summer, Donna	I Feel Love	23 July 1977	409
Supremes	Baby Love	19 Nov 1964	181
Survivor	Eye Of The Tiger	04 Sept 1982	507
Sweet	Blockbuster	27 Jan 1973	325
Sweet Sensation	Sad Sweet Dreamer	19 Oct 1974	358
T Rex	Hot Love	20 Mar 1971	298
	Get It On	24 July 1971	302
	Telegram Sam	05 Feb 1972	309
	Metal Guru	20 May 1972	313
Tab Hunter	Young Love	22 Feb 1957	56
Take That	Pray	17 July 1993	692
	Relight My Fire	09 Oct 1993	696
	Babe	18 Dec 1993	699
	Everything Changes	09 Apr 1994	704
	Sure	15 Oct 1994	711
	Back For Good	08 Apr 1995	719
	Never Forget	05 Aug 1995	724
	How Deep Is Your Love	09 Mar 1996	735
Tamperer featuring Maya	Feel It	30 May 1998	791
Tams	Hey Girl Don't Bother Me	18 Sept 1971	304
Tatu	All The Things She Said	08 Feb 2003	948
Teletubbies	Teletubbies Say Eh-oh!	13 Dec 1997	778
Temperance Seven	You're Driving Me Crazy	25 May 1961	118
10CC	Rubber Bullets	23 June 1973	332
	I'm Not In Love	28 June 1975	372
	Dreadlock Holiday	23 Sept 1978	426
Three Degrees	When Will I See You Again	17 Aug 1974	354
3 Of A Kind	Babycakes	21 Aug 2004	987
Thunderclap Newman	Something In The Air	02 July 1969	273

Artist	Song	Date	No
Tiffany	I Think We're Alone Now	30 Jan 1988	603
Tight Fit	The Lion Sleeps Tonight	06 Mar 1982	496
Tillotson, Johnny	Poetry In Motion	12 Jan 1961	111
Timelords	Doctorin' The Tardis	18 June 1988	610
Tomcraft	Loneliness	10 May 2003	953
Tornados	Telstar	04 Oct 1962	141
T'Pau	China In Your Hand	14 Nov 1987	600
Travolta, John	You're The One That I Want	17 June 1978	424
	Summer Nights	30 Sept 1978	427
Tremeloes	Silence Is Golden	18 May 1967	233
Trent, Jackie	Where Are You Now (My Love)	20 May 1965	195
Troggs	With A Girl Like You	04 Aug 1966	221
Tubeway Army	Are 'Friends' Electric	30 June 1979	439
Twitty, Conway	It's Only Make Believe	19 Dec 1958	78
2 Unlimited	No Limit	13 Feb 1993	685
Tyler, Bonnie	Total Eclipse Of The Heart	12 Mar 1983	517
Tymes	Ms Grace	25 Jan 1975	364
Typically Tropical	Barbados	09 Aug 1975	375
U2	Desire	08 Oct 1988	616
	The Fly	02 Nov 1991	668
	Discotheque	15 Feb 1997	760
	Beautiful Day	21 Oct 2000	877
	Vertigo	20 Nov 2004	995
	Sometimes You Can't Make It On Your Own	19 Feb 2005	1004
UB40	Red Red Wine	03 Sept 1983	526
	I Got You Babe	31 Aug 1985	555
	(I Can't Help) Falling In Love With You	12 June 1993	690
Union Gap featuring Gary Puckett	Young Girl	22 May 1968	250
Unit Four Plus Two	Concrete And Clay	08 Apr 1965	191
Ure, Midge	If I Was	05 Oct 1985	557
USA For Africa	We Are The World	20 Apr 1985	548
Usher	You Make Me Wanna ...	31 Jan 1998	782
	Yeah	27 Mar 2004	976
	Burn	10 July 2004	983
Valance, Holly	Kiss Kiss	11 May 2002	925
Valance, Ricky	Tell Laura I Love Her	29 Sept 1960	107
Valentine, Dickie	Finger Of Suspicion	07 Jan 1955	27
	Christmas Alphabet	16 Dec 1955	40
Van Helden, Armand	You Don't Know Me	06 Feb 1999	814
Vanilla Ice	Ice Ice Baby	01 Dec 1990	654
Various Artists*	Perfect Day	29 Nov 1997	777
Vaughan, Frankie	The Garden Of Eden	25 Jan 1957	55
	Tower Of Strength	07 Dec 1961	130
Vengaboys	Boom Boom Boom Boom	26 June 1999	828
	We're Going To Ibiza	18 Sept 1999	835
Verve	The Drugs Don't Work	13 Sept 1997	773
Village People	Y.M.C.A.	06 Jan 1979	431
Walker Brothers	Make It Easy On Yourself	23 Sept 1965	203
	The Sun Ain't Gonna Shine Anymore	17 Mar 1966	211
Wamdue Project	King Of My Castle	27 Nov 1999	842
Ward, Anita	Ring My Bell	16 June 1979	438
Westlife	Swear It Again	01 May 1999	822
	If I Let You Go	21 Aug 1999	832
	Flying Without Wings	30 Oct 1999	838
	I Have A Dream / Seasons In The Sun	25 Dec 1999	844
	Fool Again	08 Apr 2000	854
	Against All Odds	30 Sept 2000	875
	My Love	11 Nov 2000	880
	Uptown Girl	17 Mar 2001	892
	Queen Of My Heart	17 Nov 2001	912
	World Of Our Own	02 Mar 2002	920
	Unbreakable	16 Nov 2002	941
	Mandy	29 Nov 2003	965
Wet Wet Wet	With A Little Help From My Friends	21 May 1988	609
	Goodnight Girl	25 Jan 1992	673
	Love Is All Around	04 June 1994	709
Wham!	Wake Me Up Before You Go-Go	02 June 1984	535
	Freedom	20 Oct 1984	539
	I'm Your Man	30 Nov 1985	560
	The Edge Of Heaven	28 June 1986	572
Whigfield	Saturday Night	17 Sept 1994	710

MUSIC

POP

Artist	Song	Date	No
White Town	Your Woman	25 Jan 1997	757
White, Barry	You're The First, The Last, My Everything	07 Dec 1974	361
Whitfield, David	Answer Me	06 Nov 1953	14
	Cara Mia	02 July 1954	20
Whitman, Slim	Rose Marie	29 July 1955	36
Williams, Andy	Butterfly	24 May 1957	59
Williams, Danny	Moon River	28 Dec 1961	131
Williams, Deniece	Free	07 May 1977	404
Williams, Robbie	Millennium	19 Sept 1998	801
	She's The One / It's Only Us	20 Nov 1999	841
	Rock DJ	12 Aug 2000	869
	Eternity / The Road To Mandalay	21 July 2001	903
	Somethin' Stupid	22 Dec 2001	916
	Radio	16 Oct 2004	992
Wilson, Jackie	Reet Petite	27 Dec 1986	582
Winans, Mario	I Don't Wanna Know	12 June 2004	980
Wings	Mull Of Kintyre / Girls' School	03 Dec 1977	416
Wizzard	See My Baby Jive	19 May 1973	330
	Angel Fingers	22 Sept 1973	337
Wonder, Stevie	Ebony And Ivory	24 Apr 1982	499
	I Just Called To Say I Love You	08 Sept 1984	538
Wurzels	Combine Harvester (Brand New Key)	12 June 1976	390
Wynette, Tammy	Stand By Your Man	17 May 1975	370
Yazz & The Plastic Population	The Only Way Is Up	06 Aug 1988	613
Young, Jimmy	Unchained Melody	24 June 1955	34
	The Man From Laramie	14 Oct 1955	37
Young, Paul	Wherever I Lay My Hat	23 July 1983	524
Young, Will	Anything Is Possible / Evergreen	09 Mar 2002	921
	Light My Fire	08 June 2002	929
	The Long And Winding Road / Suspicious Minds	05 Oct 2002	937
	Leave Right Now	06 Dec 2003	966
Zager & Evans	In The Year 2525 (Exordium And Terminus)	30 Aug 1969	275

*The artists on the 777th No. 1, 'Perfect Day', were the BBC Symphony Orchestra with Andrew Davis, Thomas Allen, Brett Anderson (Suede), Laurie Anderson, Joan Armatrading, Bono (U2), David Bowie, Boyzone, Brodsky Quartet, Ian Broudie (Lightning Seeds), Burning Spear, Robert Cray, Evan Dando (Lemonheads), Dr John, Gabrielle, Lesley Garrett, Emmylou Harris, Huey Morgan (Fun Lovin' Criminals), Elton John, Tom Jones, Shane McGowan, Courtney Pine, Lou Reed, Skye (Morcheeba), Heather Small (M People), Suzanne Vega, Visual Ministry Orchestra, Sheona White, Tammy Wynette.

**The artists on Band Aid were Keren Woodward, Sarah Dallin, Siobhan Fahey (Bananarama); Bob Geldof, Johnny Fingers, Simon Crowe, Pete Briquette (Boomtown Rats); David Bowie; Phil Collins; Boy George, Jon Moss (Culture Club); Simon Le Bon, Nick Rhodes, Andy Taylor, John Taylor, Roger Taylor (Duran Duran); Holly Johnson (Frankie Goes to Hollywood); Martin Ware, Glenn Gregory (Heaven 17); Robert 'Kool' Bell, James Taylor, Dennis Thomas (Kool and the Gang); Marilyn; Paul McCartney; George Michael; Jody Watley (Shalimar); Tony Hadley, John Keeble, Gary Kemp, Martin Kemp, Steve Norman (Spandau Ballet); Francis Rossi, Rick Parfitt (Status Quo); Sting; Adam Clayton, Bono (U2); Midge Ure, Chris Cross (Ultravox); Paul Weller; Paul Young.

The artists on Band Aid II were Bananarama, Big Fun, Bros, Cathy Dennis, D Mob, Jason Donovan, Kevin Godley, Glen Goldsmith, Kylie Minogue, The Pasadenas, Chris Rea, Cliff Richard, Jimmy Somerville, Sonia, Lisa Stansfield, Technotronic, Wet Wet Wet.

The artists on Band Aid 20 were Damon Albarn (made the tea); Tim Wheeler (Ash); Daniel Bedingfield; Natasha Bedingfield; James Bourne, Mattie Jay, Charlie Simpson (Busted); Chris Martin (Coldplay); Ed Graham, Dan Hawkins, Justin Hawkins, Frankie Poullain (The Darkness); Dido; Ms Dynamite; Grant Nichols (Feeder); Bob Geldof; Neil Hannon (The Divine Comedy); Jamelia; Tom Chaplin, Richard Hughes, Tim Rice-Oxley (Keane); Beverley Knight; Lemar; Shaznay Lewis; Paul McCartney; Madonna; Katie Melua; Roisin Murphy (Moloko); Skye (Morcheeba); Jonny Greenwood, Thom Yorke (Radiohead); Dizzee Rascal; Richard Colburn, Gary Lightbody, Mark McClell, John Quinn (Snow Patrol); Rachel Stevens; Joss Stone; Keisha Buchanan, Mutya Buena, Heidi Range (The Sugababes); Danny Goffey (Supergrass); Ben Carrigan, Connor Deasy, Kevin Horan, Padraic MacMahon, Daniel Ryan (The Thrills); Andy Dunlop, Fran Healy, Dougie Payne, Neil Primrose (Travis); Olly Knights, Gail Paradjanian (Turin Brakes); Bono, The Edge (U2); Midge Ure; Robbie Williams; Will Young.

The featured artists in the original recording with their lyrics are as follows: (Paul Young) It's Christmas time, There's no need to be afraid. At Christmas time, We let in light and we banish shade (Boy George) And in our world of plenty We can spread a smile of joy, Throw your arms around the world at Christmas time (George Michael) But say a prayer, Pray for the other ones, At Christmas time it's hard (Simon Le Bon) But when you're having fun, There's a world outside your window (Sting) And it's a world of dread and fear, Where the only water flowing is (Bono joins in) The bitter sting of fears, And the Christmas bells that are ringing, Are clanging chimes of doom (Bono only) Well, tonight thank God it's them instead of you (All) And there won't be snow in Africa this Christmas time, The greatest gift they'll get this year is life, Where nothing ever grows, No rain or river flows, Do they know it's Christmas time at all? Feed the world, Let them know it's Christmas time, Feed the world, Do they know it's Christmas time at all? (Paul Young) Here's to you raise a glass for everyone, Here's to them underneath the burning sun, Do they know it's Christmas time at all? (All) chorus repeat.

Christmas No. 1s

1952	Here in My Heart – Al Martino	1980	There's No One Quite Like Grandma – St Winifred's School Choir
1953	Answer Me – Frankie Laine		
1954	Let's Have Another Party – Winifred Atwell	1981	Don't You Want Me – Human League
1955	The Christmas Alphabet – Dickie Valentine.	1982	Save Your Love – Renee and Renato
1956	Just Walkin' in the Rain – Johnnie Ray	1983	Only You – Flying Pickets
1957	Mary's Boy Child – Harry Belafonte	1984	Do They Know It's Christmas – Band Aid
1958	It's Only Make Believe – Conway Twitty	1985	Merry Christmas Everyone – Shakin' Stevens
1959	What Do You Want to Make Those Eyes at Me For – Emile Ford and the Checkmates	1986	Reet Petite – Jackie Wilson
1960	I Love You – Cliff Richard and the Shadows	1987	Always on My Mind – Pet Shop Boys
1961	Moon River – Danny Williams	1988	Mistletoe and Wine – Cliff Richard
1962	Return to Sender – Elvis Presley	1989	Do They Know It's Christmas? – Band Aid II
1963	I Want to Hold Your Hand – Beatles	1990	Saviour's Day – Cliff Richard
1964	I Feel Fine – Beatles	1991	Bohemian Rhapsody / These Are the Days of Our Lives – Queen
1965	Day Tripper/We Can Work It Out – Beatles		
1966	Green Green Grass of Home – Tom Jones	1992	I Will Always Love You – Whitney Houston
1967	Hello Goodbye – Beatles	1993	Mr. Blobby – Mr. Blobby
1968	Lily the Pink – Scaffold	1994	Stay Another Day – East 17
1969	Two Little Boys – Rolf Harris	1995	Earth Song – Michael Jackson
1970	I Hear You Knockin' – Dave Edmunds	1996	2 Become 1 – Spice Girls
1971	Ernie (The Fastest Milkman in the West) – Benny Hill	1997	Too Much – Spice Girls
		1998	Goodbye – Spice Girls
1972	Long Haired Lover from Liverpool – Little Jimmy Osmond	1999	I Have a Dream/Seasons in the Sun – Westlife
1973	Merry Xmas Everybody – Slade	2000	Can We Fix It – Bob The Builder
1974	Lonely This Christmas – Mud	2001	Somethin' Stupid – Robbie Williams and Nicole Kidman
1975	Bohemian Rhapsody – Queen		
1976	When a Child Is Born – Johnny Mathis	2002	Sound Of The Underground – Girls Aloud
1977	Mull of Kintyre/Girls' School – Wings	2003	Mad World – Michael Andrews featuring Gary Jules
1978	Mary's Boy Child – Boney M		
1979	Another Brick in the Wall – Pink Floyd	2004	Do They Know It's Christmas? – Band Aid 20

LPs

Title	Group/artiste	Title	Group/artiste
Abacab	Genesis	Attack of the Grey Lantern	Mansun
Abbey Road	Beatles	Auberge	Chris Rea
According to My Heart	Jim Reeves	Autobahn	Kraftwerk
Achtung Baby	U2	Automatic for the People	R.E.M.
Actually	Pet Shop Boys	Avalon	Roxy Music
Adrenalize	Def Leppard	Babylon and On	Squeeze
Affection	Lisa Stansfield	Back in Black	AC/DC
Afterburner	ZZ Top	Back to Front (1)	Gilbert O'Sullivan (1972)
Aftermath	Rolling Stones		
The Age of Consent	Bronski Beat	Back to Front (1)	Lionel Richie (1992)
Agent Provocateur	Foreigner	Bad	Michael Jackson
Aja	Steely Dan	Bagsy Me	Wannadies
Aladdin Sane	David Bowie	Band of Gypsies	Jimi Hendrix
Album of the Year	Faith No More	Band on the Run	Wings
Alf	Alison Moyet	Batman	Prince
All Change	Cast	Bat Out Of Hell	Meat Loaf
All Things Must Pass	George Harrison	Before the Rain	Eternal
Ancient Heart	Tanita Tikaram	Beggars Banquet	Rolling Stones
Andromeda Heights	Prefab Sprout	Be Here Now (1)	Oasis
Another Time, Another Place	Bryan Ferry	Behind the Mask	Fleetwood Mac
Anthem	Toyah	Big Bang	We've Got a Fuzzbox and We're Gonna Use it
The Anvil	Visage		
Appetite for Destruction	Guns 'N' Roses		
Are You Experienced?	Jimi Hendrix Experience	Big River	Jimmy Nail
		Billion Dollar Babies	Alice Cooper
Are You Gonna Go My Way	Lenny Kravitz	Black Tie White Noise	David Bowie
Argus	Wishbone Ash	Blast	Holly Johnson
Armed Forces	Elvis Costello	Blonde on Blonde	Bob Dylan
Arrival	Abba	Blondes Have More Fun	Rod Stewart
Astral Weeks	Van Morrison	Blood on the Dance Floor (1)	Michael Jackson
Atlantic Crossing	Rod Stewart	Blood Sugar Sex Magik	Red Hot Chili Peppers
Atom Heart Mother	Pink Floyd		

Title	Group/artiste	Title	Group/artiste
Bloody Tourists	10cc	Discovery	Electric Light Orchestra
Blue for You	Status Quo		
Blue Is the Colour	Beautiful South	Disraeli Gears	Cream
Blue Sky on Mars	Matthew Sweet	Diva	Annie Lennox
Bookends	Simon and Garfunkel	The Division Bell	Pink Floyd
Both Sides	Phil Collins	Dizzy Heights	Lightning Seeds
Boys and Girls	Bryan Ferry	Do It Yourself	The Seahorses
Breakfast In America	Supertramp	Don't Be Cruel	Bobby Brown
Breathless	Kenny G	Don't Believe the Truth	Oasis
Bridge of Spies	T'Pau	Don't Shoot Me, I'm Only the Piano Player	Elton John
Bridge Over Troubled Water	Simon and Garfunkel		
British Steel	Judas Priest	Dookie	Green Day
Brothers in Arms	Dire Straits	Double Fantasy	John Lennon
Buddah and the Chocolate Box	Cat Stevens	Down Drury Lane to Memory Lane	One Hundred and One Strings
Bursting at the Seams	Strawbs	Drag	kd lang
Business as Usual	Men at Work	Dreamland	Robert Miles
Cafe Bleu	Style Council	Dreams Are Nothin' More Than Wishes	David Cassidy
Call off the Search	Kafie Melva		
Can't Slow Down	Lionel Richie	Dr Feelgood	Motley Crue
Captain Fantastic and the Brown Dirt Cowboy	Elton John	Duke	Genesis
		Eat to the Beat	Blondie
Captain Paralytic and the Brown Ale Cowboy	Mike Harding	Electric Ladyland	Jimi Hendrix Experience
Caribou	Elton John	Electric Warrior	T Rex
Carry On up the Charts	Beautiful South	Elegantly Wasted	INXS
Catch Bull at Four	Cat Stevens	Eliminator	ZZ Top
China Town	Thin Lizzy	Emergency on Planet Earth	Jamiroquai
Chorus	Erasure	Emotional Rescue	Rolling Stones
Circle of One	Oleta Adams	Endless Flight	Leo Sayer
The Circus	Erasure	English Settlement	X-Ray Specs
Cloud Nine	George Harrison	Enjoy Yourself	Kylie Minogue
Colour	Christians	Every Good Boy Deserves Favour	Moody Blues
The Colour and the Shape	Foo Fighters		
Colour By Numbers	Culture Club	Every Picture Tells a Story	Rod Stewart
The Colour of My Love	Celine Dion	Everybody Else Is Doing it, So Why Can't We	Cranberries
Come On Over	Shania Twain		
Coming Up	Suede	Everything Changes	Take That
Communiqué	Dire Straits	Everything Must Go	Manic Street Preachers
Connected	Stereo MCs		
Conscience	Womack and Womack	Exile on Main Street	Rolling Stones
		Extra Virgin	Olive
Conversation Peace	Stevie Wonder	Façades	Sad Cafe
Cosmo's Factory	Creedence Clearwater Revival	Face Value	Phil Collins
		Falling Into You	Celine Dion
		Fantastic!	Wham!
Cracked Rear View	Hootie and the Blowfish	Faster Than the Speed of Night	Bonnie Tyler
Crazy You	G.U.N.	The Fat of the Land (1)	The Prodigy
Cricklewood Green	Ten Years After	Fear of the Dark	Iron Maiden
Crime of the Century	Supertramp	Fever In Fever Out	Luscious Jackson
Crocodiles	Echo and the Bunnymen	The Final Cut	Pink Floyd
		Fireball	Deep Purple
Cross of Changes	Enigma	Flaming Pie (1)	Paul McCartney
Crossroads	Tracy Chapman	Flesh and Blood	Roxy Music
Cuts Both Ways	Gloria Estefan	Flowers in the Dirt	Paul McCartney
Dancin' in the Key of Life	Steve Arrington	Flying Colours	Chris De Burgh
Dangerous	Michael Jackson	Fog on the Tyne	Lindisfarne
Dare	Human League	Foreign Affair	Tina Turner
Dark Side of the Moon	Pink Floyd	Forever	Damage
A Day at the Races	Queen	Forever Changes	Love
Daydream	Mariah Carey	461 Ocean Boulevard	Eric Clapton
Days of Future Passed	Moody Blues	Four Symbols	Led Zeppelin
Destination Anywhere	Jon Bon Jovi	Foxtrot	Genesis
Destiny	Gloria Estefan	Fresh	Gina G
Devil Without a Cause	Kid Rock	Fresh Cream	Cream
Diamond Dogs	David Bowie	From the Cradle	Eric Clapton
Diamond Life	Sade	The Game	Queen
A Different Beat	Boyzone	Germ Free Adolescents	X-Ray Specs
Different Class	Pulp	Ghost in the Machine	Police
Dig Your Own Hole	Chemical Brothers	The Gift	Jam

Title	Group/artiste	Title	Group/artiste
Give Me the Reason	Luther Vandross	It's Great When You're ... Straight Yeah!	Black Grape
Glittering Prize	Simple Minds	I've Been Expecting You	Robbie Williams
Goat's Head Soup	Rolling Stones	Jagged Little Pill	Alanis Morissette
Going for the One	Yes	Jam	Little Angels
Going to a Go-Go	Smokey Robinson and the Miracles	John Wesley Harding	Bob Dylan
Gold Blade	Hometurf	Jollification	Lightning Seeds
Goodbye	Cream	The Joshua Tree	U2
Goodbye Cruel World	Elvis Costello	Journey Through the Secret Life of Plants	Stevie Wonder
Goodbye Yellow Brick Road	Elton John		
Goodnight Vienna	Ringo Starr	Journey to the Centre of the Earth	Rick Wakeman
Graceland	Paul Simon		
Graffiti Bridge	Prince	Ju Ju	Siouxsie and the Banshees
A Grand Don't Come For Free	The Streets		
The Great Escape	Blur	Junction Seven	Steve Winwood
Great Expectations	Tasmin Archer	K	Kula Shaker
The Great Rock 'N' Roll Swindle	Sex Pistols	Kaleidoscope	Siouxsie and the Banshees
Guilty	Barbra Streisand		
Happy Nation	Ace of Base	Kavana	Kavana
Harvest	Neil Young	Keep the Faith	Bon Jovi
Headquarters	Monkees	Kimono My House	Sparks
The Healing Game	Van Morrison	Kings of the Wild Frontier	Adam Ant
Hearsay	Alexander O'Neal	Koo Koo	Debbie Harry
Heaven and Hell	Vangelis	L	Steve Hillage
Heavy Soul (1)	Paul Weller	Labour of Love	UB40
Hedgehog Sandwich	Not the 9 O'Clock News Cast	La Passione	Chris Rea
		Ladies and Gentlemen	George Michael
Hello	Status Quo	The Last Waltz	The Band
Help!	Beatles	L.A. Woman	Doors
Hergest Ridge	Mike Oldfield	Legend	Bob Marley and the Wailers
High on the Happy Side	Wet Wet Wet		
Highway 61 Revisited	Bob Dylan	Let It Bleed	Rolling Stones
History – Past Present and Future Book	Michael Jackson	Let's Talk About Love	Celine Dion
		The Lexicon of Love	ABC
Hit	Wannadies	Lie	Charles Manson
Hopes and Fears	Keane	Life	Simply Red
Horses	Patti Smith	Life After Death	Notorious B.I.G.
Hotel California	Eagles	Life Thru a Lens	Robbie Williams
Hot Rats	Frank Zappa	Lil' Darlin'	Thomas Ribeiro
Hounds of Love	Kate Bush	The Lion and the Cobra	Sinead O'Connor
Houses of the Holy	Led Zeppelin	Little Creatures	Talking Heads
Human Racing	Nik Kershaw	Live at the BBC	Beatles
Human's Lib	Howard Jones	Live in the City of Light	Simple Minds
Human Touch	Bruce Springsteen	Liverpool	Frankie Goes to Hollywood
Hunky Dory	David Bowie		
Hunting High and Low	A-Ha	Living in Oz	Rick Springfield
The Hurting	Tears for Fears	Living in the Material World	George Harrison
Hypnotised	Undertones	Living in the Past	Jethro Tull
Hysteria (1)	Def Leppard	The Lone Ranger	Suggs
Hysteria (3)	Human League	Love at the Greek	Neil Diamond
I Am	Earth Wind and Fire	Love de Luxe	Sade
I Do Not Want What I Haven't Got	Sinead O'Connor	Love Hurts	Cher
		Love over Gold	Dire Straits
If the Beatles Had Read Hunter ... The Singles	Wonder Stuff	Lovesexy	Prince
		Machine Head	Deep Purple
The Immaculate Collection	Madonna	Mad Dogs and Englishmen	Joe Cocker
In Blue	Corrs	Made in Heaven	Queen
In It for the Money	Supergrass	Magic and Medicine (1)	The Coral
Innervisions	Stevie Wonder	Make It Big	Wham!
An Innocent Man	Billy Joel	Makin' Movies	Dire Straits
The Innocents	Erasure	Manifesto	Roxy Music
Innuendo	Queen	The Man Who	Travis
In Search of the Lost Chord	Moody Blues	Meat is Murder	Smiths
In Square Circle	Stevie Wonder	Meaty, Beaty, Big and Bouncy	Who
In Through the Out Door	Led Zeppelin		
Into the Gap	Thompson Twins	Medusa	Annie Lennox
Invisible Touch	Genesis	Middle of Nowhere (1)	Hanson
I Say I Say I Say	Erasure	Millennium	Backstreet Boys
I Should Coco	Supergrass	The Miracle	Queen
It Doesn't Matter Anymore	Supernaturals	Mirror Ball	Neil Young
It's Better to Travel	Swing Out Sister	Misplaced Childhood	Marillion

Title	Group/artiste	Title	Group/artiste
Missing ... Presumed Having a Good Time	Notting Hillbillies	Outlandos d'Amour	Police
		Oxygene	Jean-Michel Jarre
Mondo Bongo	Boomtown Rats	Parallel Lines	Blondie
Monster	R.E.M.	Paranoid	Black Sabbath
The More Things Change	Machine Head	Parklife	Blur
Morning Glory	Oasis	Pastpresent	Clannad
Mother Nature Calls	Cast	Pearl	Janis Joplin
Mr Fantasy	Traffic	Pearls	Elkie Brooks
Mr Wonderful	Fleetwood Mac	Pet Sounds	Beach Boys
Mud Slide Slim and the Blue Horizon	James Taylor	Phuq	Wildhearts
		Physical Graffiti	Led Zeppelin
Music Box	Mariah Carey	Picture This	Wet Wet Wet
Music for the Jilted Generation	Prodigy	Pieces of You	Jewel
Music from Big Pink	The Band	Pills 'N' Thrills and Bellyaches	Happy Mondays
My Aim Is True	Elvis Costello	Pin-Ups	David Bowie
Naked	Talking Heads	Piper at the Gates of Dawn	Pink Floyd
Nashville Skyline	Bob Dylan	Pisces, Aquarius, Capricorn and Jones Ltd	Monkees
Natural	Peter Andre		
Never a Dull Moment	Rod Stewart	Play (1)	Moby
Never for Ever	Kate Bush	The Pleasure Principle	Gary Numan
Nevermind	Nirvana	Pocketful of Kryptonite	Spin Doctors
Never Mind the Bollocks Here's the Sex Pistols	Sex Pistols	Pop	U2
		Popped in Souled Out	Wet Wet Wet
New Boots and Panties!!	Ian Dury & the Blockheads	Porcupine	Echo and the Bunnymen
A New Flame	Simply Red		
New Jersey	Bon Jovi	Pornography	Cure
A New World Record	Electric Light Orchestra	Postcard	Mary Hopkin
		Pot Luck	Elvis Presley
A Night at the Opera	Queen	Presence	Led Zeppelin
Night Birds	Shakatak	Private Collection	Cliff Richard
Night Flight to Venus	Boney M	Private Dancer	Tina Turner
Nightfreak and the Sons of Becker	The Coral	Promises and Lies	UB40
		Prophets, Seers and Sages	T Rex
A Night on the Town	Rod Stewart	Protection	Massive Attack
Night Owl	Gerry Rafferty	Pulse	Pink Floyd
Nine Lives	Aerosmith	Pump	Aerosmith
1982	Status Quo	Pump Up the Jam	Technotronic
Nobody Else	Take That	Push	Bros
A Nod's as Good as a Wink To a Blind Horse	Faces	A Question of Balance	Moody Blues
		Quick Step and Side Kick	Thompson Twins
No Fences	Garth Brooks	Rage	T'Pau
No Jacket Required	Phil Collins	Rage in Eden	Ultravox
No More Heroes	Stranglers	Ram	Paul and Linda McCartney
No Need to Argue	Cranberries		
No Parlez	Paul Young	Rattle and Hum	U2
No Sleep till Hammersmith	Motorhead	The Raw and the Cooked	Fine Young Cannibals
No Strings Attached	'N Sync	Real Things	2 Unlimited
Nothing Like the Sun	Sting	Red River Valley	Slim Whitman
The Number of the Beast	Iron Maiden	Regatta de Blanc	Police
Ocean Drive	Lighthouse Family	Reload	Tom Jones
Oceans of Fantasy	Boney M	Reminiscing	Buddy Holly and the Crickets
Odds and Sods	Who		
Off the Wall	Michael Jackson	Replicas	Tubeway Army
Ogden's Nut Gone Flake	Small Faces	Republic	New Order
OK Computer (1)	Radiohead	Return of the Space Cowboy	Jamiroquai
Old New Borrowed and Blue	Slade	Return to Fantasy	Uriah Heep
Older	George Michael	Revenge	Eurythmics
Once Upon a Star	Bay City Rollers	Revolver	Beatles
Once Upon a Time	Simple Minds	Rhythm of the Saints	Paul Simon
One Hot Minute	Red Hot Chili Peppers	The Riddle	Nik Kershaw
On Every Street	Dire Straits	Rising from the East	Bally Sagoo
On the Level	Status Quo	Roping the Wind	Garth Brooks
On the Threshold of a Dream	Moody Blues	Rubber Soul	Beatles
Only Human	Dina Carroll	Rumours	Fleetwood Mac
Only Yesterday	Carpenters	Rum, Sodomy and the Lash	Pogues
Ooh-La-La	Faces	Runaway Horses	Belinda Carlisle
Open Road (1)	Gary Barlow	Said and Done	Boyzone
Original Pirate Material	The Streets	Saturday Night	Zhane
Our Favourite Shop	Style Council	Savage	Eurythmics
Out of Time	R.E.M.	Scary Monsters and Super Creeps	David Bowie

Title	Group/artiste	Title	Group/artiste
Script for a Jester's Tear	Marillion	Synchronicity	Police
The Secret of Association	Paul Young	Take Two	Robson and Jerome
The Seeds of Love	Tears for Fears	Tales from Topographic Oceans	Yes
Sensational	Michelle Gayle		
Sentimental Journey	Ringo Starr	Talk On Corners	Corrs
Sergeant Pepper's Lonely Hearts Club Band	Beatles	Talking Back to the Night	Steve Winwood
		Talking Book	Stevie Wonder
Seven and the Ragged Tiger	Duran Duran	Talking with the Taxman about Poetry	Billy Bragg
Seventh Son of a Seventh Son	Iron Maiden		
Share My World	Mary J. Blige	Tango in the Night	Fleetwood Mac
Shaved Fish	John Lennon	Tanx	T Rex
Shelter	Brand New Heavies	Tapestry	Carole King
Shepherd Moons	Enya	A Tapestry of Dreams	Charles Aznavour
She's So Unusual	Cyndi Lauper	Tarkus	Emerson, Lake and Palmer
She's the Boss	Mick Jagger		
Silk and Steel	Five Star	Tears and Laughter	Johnny Mathis
Singles	Alison Moyet	Tease Me	Chaka Demus and Pliers
The Six Wives of Henry VIII	Rick Wakeman		
Sleeping with the Past	Elton John	Teaser and the Firecat	Cat Stevens
The Slider	T Rex	Technique	New Order
Slippery When Wet	Bon Jovi	Telekon	Gary Numan
Slowhand	Eric Clapton	Tell Me on a Sunday	Marti Webb
Smiler	Rod Stewart	Tellin' Stories	The Charlatans
The Smoker You Drink The Player You Get	Joe Walsh	10	Wet Wet Wet
		Ten	Pearl Jam
So	Peter Gabriel	Ten Good Reasons	Jason Donovan
So Far So Good	Bryan Adams	Tennis	Chris Rea
Solitude Standing	Suzanne Vega	The Man and His Music	Sam Cooke
So Long So Wrong	Alison Krauss and Union Station	Thriller	Michael Jackson
		Through the Barricades	Spandau Ballet
Some Friendly	Charlatans	Thunder and Lightning	Thin Lizzy
So Much for the City	The Thrills	Time for Healing	Sounds of Blackness
Song Bird	Eva Cassidy	Timeless	Sarah Brightman
The Song Remains the Same	Led Zeppelin	To the Extreme	Vanilla Ice
Songs About Jane	Maroon 5	To the Faithful Departed	Cranberries
Songs in the Key of Life	Stevie Wonder	Touch	Eurythmics
Songs of Faith and Devotion	Depeche Mode	Tragic Kingdom	No Doubt
The Soul Cages	Sting	Transformer	Lou Reed
Soul Provider	Michael Bolton	Travelling without Moving	Jamiroquai
Sound of Lies	The Jayhawks	Trout Mask Replica	Captain Beefheart and his Magic Band
Sparkle in the Rain	Simple Minds		
Spartacus	Farm	True Stories	Talking Heads
Speak and Spell	Depeche Mode	Tubular Bells	Mike Oldfield
Spellbound	Paula Abdul	Tuesday Night Music Club	Sheryl Crow
Spirits Having Flown	Bee Gees	Tug of War	Paul McCartney
Sports Car	Judie Tzuke	Tunnel of Love	Bruce Springsteen
Standing Stone	Paul McCartney	Turn Back the Clock	Johnny Hates Jazz
Stand Up	Jethro Tull	Turn It Upside Down	Spin Doctors
Stanley Road	Paul Weller	Tusk	Fleetwood Mac
Staring at the Sun	U2	12 Gold Bars	Status Quo
Stars	Simply Red	21 Today	Cliff Richard
Station to Station	David Bowie	U.F. Orb	Orb
Stay on These Roads	A-Ha	Ultra	Depeche Mode
Steel Wheels	Rolling Stones	Under the Pink	Tori Amos
Steeltown	Big Country	The Unforgettable Fire	U2
Step by Step	New Kids on the Block	Universal Soldier	Donovan
		Up	Right Said Fred
Sticky Fingers	Rolling Stones	Upstairs at Eric's	Yazoo
Still Crazy after All These Years	Paul Simon	Urban Hymns (1)	Verve
		Use Your Illusion	Guns 'N' Roses
Still Waters	Bee Gees	Vauxhall and I	Morrissey
Stranded	Roxy Music	Very	Pet Shop Boys
The Stranger	Billy Joel	Viva Hate	Morrissey
Street Fighting Years	Simple Minds	Voice of Love	Diana Ross
String of Hits	Shadows	Voices from the Holy Land	Aled Jones
Stripped	Rolling Stones	Voodo Lounge	Rolling Stones
Stupidity	Dr Feelgood	Voulez-Vous	Abba
Supernatural	Santana	Wake Up!	Boo Radleys
Surrealistic Pillow	Jefferson Airplane	Waking Up the Neighbours	Bryan Adams
Sweet Baby James	James Taylor	Walking Wounded	Everything But the Girl
Symbol	Prince	Walthamstow	East 17

MUSIC POP

Title	Group/artiste	Title	Group/artiste
Wanted	Yazz	White Feathers	Kajagoogoo
War	U2	White on Blonde	Texas
Water Sign	Chris Rea	The Whole Story	Kate Bush
Watermark	Enya	Wicked Game	Chris Isaak
We All Had Doctors' Papers	Max Boyce	Wild!	Erasure
We Can Make It	Peters and Lee	Wild Wood	Paul Weller
We Can't Dance	Genesis	Wish	Cure
We Have All the Time in the World	Louis Armstrong	Wish You Were Here	Pink Floyd
		Women and Captain First	Captain Sensible
We Too Are One	Eurythmics	Words of Love	Buddy Holly and the Crickets
Welcome to the Pleasuredome	Frankie Goes to Hollywood	Wu-Tang Forever	Wu-Tang Clan
Welcome to Wherever You Are	INXS	You and Me Both	Yazoo
Whatever You Want	Status Quo	Young Americans	David Bowie
When the World Knows Your Name	Deacon Blue	Your Secret Love	Luther Vandross
		You Showed Me	Lightning Seeds
Where We Belong	Boyzone	Youthquake	Dead or Alive
Whipped Cream and Other Delights	Herb Alpert and the Tijuana Brass	Zenyatta Mondatta	Police
		Zooropa	U2

Nationalities of Pop Groups and Soloists

Abba Sweden and Norway
AC/DC UK and Australia
Adamski UK
Air Supply UK and Australia
Alphaville Germany
Aneka UK
Angry Anderson Australia
Anthrax USA
Aphrodite's Child Greece
Aqua Denmark
Babyshambles UK
Baccara Spain
Basia Poland
Belle Stars UK
Black Box Italy
Boney M Jamaica, Antilles, Montserrat
Boris Gardiner Jamaica
Cappella Italy
Cardigans Sweden
Catatonia Wales
Champs Boys France
Chicory Tip UK
Coral UK
Crowded House Australia and New Zealand
Curved Air UK
Cutting Crew UK and Canada
Danny Mirror Holland
Darts UK
Deee-Lite USA, Russia and Japan
Del Amitri UK
Eddy Grant Guyana
Edmund Hockridge Canada
Emile Ford UK
Enigma Germany and Romania
Enya Ireland
Europe Sweden
Father Abraham Holland
Fleetwood Mac UK and USA
Foreigner UK and USA
Fox UK and USA
FPI Project Italy
Franz Ferdinand Scotland
Funkadelic USA
Gallagher and Lyle UK
Gibson Brothers Martinique
Go-Gos USA
Golden Earring Holland
Greyhound Jamaica

Guess Who Canada
Hawkwind UK (German dancer)
Helmut Zacharias Germany
Hothouse Flowers Ireland
Human Resource Holland
Icehouse New Zealand
Incognito UK and France
Inner Circle Jamaica
Jam and Spoon Germany
Jam Machine Italy
Jam Tronik Germany
Jan Hammer Czechoslovakia
John Farnham Australia
John Parr UK
John Paul Young Australia
JT and the Big Family Italy
Kaoma France
Keane UK
Kraftwerk Germany
Lobo (70s band) USA
Lobo (80s band) Holland
Mai Tai Holland
Manfred Mann South Africa
M/A/R/R/S UK
Martha and the Muffins Canada
Martika USA
McFly UK
Men at Work Australia
Men Without Hats Canada
Mental As Anything Australia
Metallica USA and Denmark
Mezzoforte Iceland
Midnight Oil Australia
Milk and Honey Israel
Millie Jamaica
Milli Vanilli France and Germany
Mixmaster Italy
Modern Talking Germany
Mouth and MacNeal Holland
New Seekers UK
Norman Greenbaum USA
Opus Austria
Ottawan France
Pasadenas UK
Patsy Gallant Canada
Peppers France
Percy Faith Canada
Perez Prado Cuba

Plastic Bertrand Belgium
Poppy Family Canada
Praga Khan Belgium
Prefab Sprout UK
Pseudo Echo Australia
Python Lee Jackson Australia
Rob 'N' Raz (featuring Leila K) Sweden
Roxette Sweden
Rozalla Zimbabwe
Rush Canada
Shocking Blue Holland
Silver Convention Germany and USA
Snap Germany and USA
Soeur Sourire (Singing Nun) Belgium
Spagna Italy
Split Enz New Zealand and UK
Starlight Italy
Starsound Holland

Stereophonics Wales
Sweet People France
Sylvia Sweden
Teach-In Holland
Technotronic Belgium
Ten Sharp Holland
Third World Jamaica
Thomas Dolby UK
Thompson Twins New Zealand and UK
Thrills Ireland
2 Unlimited Holland
Vanessa Paradis France
Van Halen Holland and USA
Whigfield Denmark
Wigan's Chosen Few USA
Yello Switzerland
Zucchero Italy
Zutons UK

Composition of Pop Groups

A1
Ben Adams
Christian Ingebrigtsen
Paul Marazzi
Mark Read

ABBA
Benny Andersson
Agnetha Fältskog
Anni-Frid Lyngstad
Björn Ulvaeus
Swedish group except for the Norwegian brunette
Anni-Frid Lyngstad

ABC
Martin Fry – Vocals
Mark Lickley – Bass
Dave Robinson – Drums
Steve Singleton – Saxophone
Mark White – Guitar

AC/DC
Dave Evans – Vocals (left 1977)
Mark Evans – Bass
Brian Johnson – Vocals (replaced Bon Scott)
Phil Rudd – Drums (Left in 1982)
Bon Scott – Vocals (previously drums, died 1980)
Chris Slade
Cliff Williams (replaced Dave Evans)
Simon Wright (replaced Phil Rudd)
Angus Young – Lead Guitar
Malcolm Young – Guitar

Ace of Base
Jonas 'Joker' Berggren
Jenny Berggren
Linn Berggren
Ulf 'Buddha' Ekberg

Adam and the Ants
Matthew Ashman – Guitar and Piano
Dave Barbe 'Barbarossa' – Drums
Johnny Bivouac – Guitar
Stuart Goddard (Adam) – Lead Vocals and Guitar
Jordan – Vocals
Andy Warren – Bass

Aerosmith
Jimmy Crespo – Guitar (joined after Whitfield left)
Rick Dufay – Guitar (joined after Whitfield left)
Tom Hamilton – Bass
Joey Kramer – Drums
Joe Perry – Guitar
Ray Tabano – Guitar (replaced by Brad Whitfield)
Steve Tyler – Lead Vocals
Brad Whitfield – Guitar (left in 1980)

A-Ha
Magne Furuholmen – Keyboards, Guitar, Backing Vocals
Morten Harket – Lead Vocals
Paul Waaktaar-Savoy – Guitar and Backing Vocals

Airforce
Ginger Baker – Drums and Percussion
Graham Bond – Saxophone
Rick Grech – Bass and Violin
Jeanette Jacobs – Vocals
Remi Kabaka – Percussion
Denny Laine – Guitar
Steve Winwood – Guitar, Keyboards and Vocals
Chris Wood – Saxophone and Flute

Alarm, The
Eddie MacDonald – Guitar and Vocals
Mike Peters – Bass and Vocals
Dave Sharp – Guitar and Vocals
Mark Taylor – Keyboards
Nigel Twist – Drums

All Saints
Natalie Appleton
Nicole Appleton
Melanie Blatt
Shaznay Lewis

Altered Images
Michael 'Tich' Anderson – Drums
Caesar – Guitar
Claire Grogan – Vocals
Tony McDaid – Guitar
Johnny McElhone – Bass

MUSIC POP

Amazulu
Sharon Bailey – Percussion
Lesley Beach – Saxophone
Debbie Evans – Drums
Clare Henny – Bass
Rose Minor – Vocals
Margo Sagov – Guitar

Amen Corner
Dennis Bryon – Drums
Andy Fairweather Lowe – Guitar and Lead Vocals
Alan Jones – Saxophone
Neil Jones – Guitar
Mike Smith – Saxophone
Clive Taylor – Bass
Blue Weaver – Guitar

Animals
Vic Briggs – Bass
George Bruno – Keyboards and Vocals
Eric Burdon – Vocals
Charles 'Chas' Chandler – Bass
Luke Francis – Guitar and Vocals
Barry Jenkins – Drums and Percussion
Danny McCullough – Bass, Guitar and Vocals
Zoot Money – Organ
Alan Price – Piano and Vocals
Dave Rowberry – Organ
Andy Somers – Guitar
John Steele – Drums
Hilton Valentine – Guitar
John Weider – Guitar, Violin and Bass

Another Level
Mark Baron
Dane Bowers
Bobak Kianoush
Wayne Williams

Aphrodite's Child
Silver Koulouris – Guitar and Percussion
Vangelis Papathanassiou – Keyboards, Flute and Vocals
Demis Roussos – Vocals
Lucas Sideras – Drums and Vocals

Aqua
René Dif – Bald-headed Vocalist Claus Noreen
Lene Nystrom – Lead Vocalist
Soren Rasted
Danish group except for Nystrom, who is Norwegian

Argent
Rod Argent – Keyboards and Vocals
Russ Ballard – Guitar, Piano and Vocals
Jim Grimaldi – Guitar
Robert Henrit – Drums and Percussion
Jim Rodford – Bass and Vocals
John Verity – Guitar and Vocals

Art of Noise
Anne Dudley – Keyboards
JJ Jeczalik – Keyboards

Ash
Mark Hamilton – Bass
Charlotte Hatherly – Guitar
Rick 'Rock' McMurray – Drums
Tim Wheeler – Vocals, Guitar

Asia
Geoff Downes – Keyboards
Steve Howe – Guitar

Greg Lake – Vocals and Bass
Mandy Meyer – Guitar
Carl Palmer – Drums
John Payne – Vocals and Bass
Al Pitrelli – Guitar
John Wetton – Vocals and Bass

Aswad
Donnal Benjamin – Guitar and Vocals
Brinsley Forde – Guitar and Vocals
Tony Gadd – Bass
Angus 'Drummie Zeb' Gaye – Drums
Donald 'Dee' Griffiths – Guitar
Courtney Hemmings – Keyboards
Bunny McKenzie – Harmonica and Vocals
Candy McKenzie – Vocals
George 'Ras' Oban – Bass
Tony Robinson – Bass and Keyboards

Atomic Kitten
Jenny Frost
Natasha Hamilton
Liz McLarnon
Kerry McFadden (née Katona) – replaced by Jenny Frost

Atomic Rooster
Steve Bolton – Guitar
John Cann – Guitar and Vocals
Vincent Crane – Keyboards and Vocals
Chris Farlowe – Vocals
Pete Frenchy – Vocals
Paul Hammond – Drums and Percussion
Johnny Mandala – Guitar
Carl Palmer – Drums and Percussion
Ric Parnell – Drums and Percussion

Average White Band
Roger Ball – Keyboards and Saxophone
Malcolm Duncan – Saxophone
Alan Gorrie – Vocals
Robbie Mcintosh – Drums and Percussion
Onnie Mcintyre – Guitar and Vocals
Hamish Stuart – Bass, Guitar and Vocals

Aztec Camera
Roddy Frame – Guitar and Vocals
Dave Mulholland – Drums
Campbell Owens – Bass

B-52s, The
Fred Schneider – Keyboards and Vocals
Kate Pierson – Organ and Vocals
Keith Strickland – Drums
Cindy Wilson – Guitar and Vocals
Ricky Wilson – Guitar

Babyshambles
Gemma Clarke – Drums (left in 2005)
Pete Doherty – Guitar and Vocals
Adam Ficek – Drums (replaced Gemma Clarke)
Drew McConnell – Bass
Patrick Walden – Guitar

Bachelors
Con Cluskey
Declan Cluskey
John Stokes

Backstreet Boys
Nick Carter
Howie Dorough
Brian Littrell

AJ McLean
Kevin Richardson

Bad Manners
Buster Bloodvessel – Vocals
Louis Cook – Guitar and Vocals
Dave Farren – Bass
Paul Hyman – Trumpet
Chris Kane – Tenor Sax
Andrew Marson – Alto Sax
Alan Sayag – Harmonica and Vocals
Martin Stewart – Keyboards
Brian Tuitt – Drums

Badfinger
Tom Evans – Bass, Guitar and Vocals
Mike Gibbons – Drums
Pete Ham – Vocals
Joey Molland – Guitar and Vocals

Bananarama
Sarah Dallin
Siobhan Fahey (left 1987 and formed
  Shakespears Sister)
Jacquie O'Sullivan (1988-1991)
Keren Woodward

Band, The
Rick Danko – Bass and Vocals
Levon Helm – Drums, Keyboards and Vocals
Garth Hudson – Accordion, Keyboards and
  Saxophone
Robbie Robertson – Guitar, Keyboards and
  Vocals

Band of Gypsies, The
Billy Cox – Bass
Jimi Hendrix – Guitar and Vocals
Buddy Miles – Drums

Bangles, The
Lyne Elklnad – Guitar, Vocals
  (replaced by Susanna Hoffs)
Susanna Hoffs – Vocals, Rhythm Guitar
Amanda Mills – Vocals, Bass
  (replaced by Annette Zilinkas)
Debbi Peterson – Vocals, Drums
Vicki Peterson – Vocals, Lead Guitar
Michael 'Mickis' Steele – Bass and Vocals
Annette Zilinkas – Bass, Harmonica

Bardot
Belinda Chapple
Sophie Monk
Sally Polyhronas
Katie Underwood (left in May 2001)
Tiffany Wood
Winners of the Australian 'Popstars', disbanded in
  May 2002

Barron Knights, The
Barron Anthony – Vocals
Butch Baker – Guitar and Vocals
Dave Ballinger – Drums
Duke D'Mond – Vocals
Peanuts Langford – Guitar and Vocals

Bay City Rollers
Eric Faulkner – Guitar, Mandolin and Vocals
Alan Longmuir – Accordion, Bass, Piano and
  Vocals
Derek Longmuir – Drums and Percussion

Les McKeown – Guitar and Lead Vocals
Ian Mitchell – Guitar and Vocals
Stuart Wood – Bass, Guitar, Piano and Vocals

Beach Boys
Glen Campbell – Guitar and Vocals
Blondie Chapman
Ricky Fataar
Al Jardine – Rhythm Guitar and Vocals
Bruce Johnstone
Mike Love – Lead Vocals
David Marks
John Stamos
Brian Wilson – Vocals, Keyboard and Bass
Carl Wilson – Vocals and Guitar
Dennis Wilson – Drums

Beastie Boys
Michael Diamond
Adam Horowitz
Adam Yauch

Beatles, The
Pete Best – Drums
George Harrison – Lead Guitar and Vocals
John Lennon – Vocals, Guitar and Piano
Paul McCartney – Vocals, Bass, Guitar and Piano
Ringo Starr – Drums
Stu Sutcliffe – Guitar and Vocals
Brian Epstein – Manager (died in 1967)

Beautiful South
Jacqui Abbot – Vocals
Briana Corrigan – Vocals (replaced by Jacqui Abbot
  in 1994)
Paul Heaton – Vocals
David Hemmingway – Drums
David Rotheray – Guitar
David Stead – Drums
Sean Welch – Bass

Bee Gees
Barry Gibb
Maurice Gibb (died 12 Jan 2003)
Robin Gibb

Bellamy Brothers, The
David Bellamy – Vocals
Howard Bellamy – Vocals
Richard Bennett – Guitar
King Errison – Percussion
Alan Estes – Drums
Emory Gordy – Bass

B*witched
Lindsay Armaou
Edele Lynch
Keavy Lynch
Sinead O'Carroll

Big Brother and the Holding Company
Peter Albin – Bass and Vocals
Sam Andrew – Guitar and Vocals
David Getz – Drums and Vocals
James Gurley – Guitar and Vocals
Janis Joplin – Lead Vocals

Big Country
Stuart Adamson – Lead Vocals and Guitar (died
  2001)
Pat Ahern – Drums
Mark Brzezicki – Drums

Tony Butler – Bass and Vocals
Bruce Watson – Guitar and Vocals

Björn Again
Benny Anderwear
Agnetha Falstart
Frida Longstokin
Bjorn Volvo-us
Australian tribute-band backed by Ola Drumkitt and
Rutger Sonofagunn

Black Box
Daniele Davoli – Lead Vocals
Mirko Limoni
Valeno Semplici

Black Sabbath
Vinnie Apice – Drums
Terry 'Geezer' Butler – Bass
Ian Gillan – Vocals
Glen Hughes – Vocals
Tony Iommi – Guitar
Ronnie James – Vocals (replaced by Ian Gillan)
Geoff Nicols – Keyboards
Ozzy Osbourne – Vocals and Harmonica
(replaced by James)
Cozy Powell – Drums
Eric Singer – Drums
Dave Spitz – Bass
Rick Wakeman – Keyboard
Bill Ward – Drums

Blazin' Squad
DJ Tommy B
Flava
MC Freek
Kenzie
Krazy
Melo-D
Reepa
Rocky B
Spike-E
Strider

Blind Faith
Ginger Baker – Drums
Eric Clapton – Lead Guitar
Rick Grech – Bass and Violin
Steve Winwood – Vocals

Blodwyn Pig
Mick Abrahams – Guitar and Vocals
Ron Berg – Drums and Percussion
Jack Lancaster – Cornet, Saxophone and Violin
Andy Pile – Bass

Blondie
Clement Burke – Drums
Paul Carbonara – Guitar
James Destri – Keyboard
Leigh Foxx – Bass
Debbie Harry – Lead Vocals
Nigel Harrison – Bass
Frank Infante – Guitar
Chris Stein – Guitar

Blood, Sweat and Tears
Dave Bergeron – Trombone and Tuba
David Clayton-Thomas – Vocals
Bobby Colomby – Drums
Jim Fielder – Bass
Jerry Hyman – Trombone

Steve Katz – Guitar, Harmonica and Vocals
Tom Klatka – Trumpet
Al Kooper – Guitar, Keyboards and Vocals
Jerry La Croix – Saxophone and Vocals
Fred Lipsius – Saxophone and Piano
Ron McLure – Bass
Dick Nalligan – Keyboards
Alan Rubin – Trumpet
Lou Soloff – Trumpet
William Tillman – Saxophone
George Wadenius – Guitar
Larry Willis – Keyboards
Chuck Winfield – Trumpet

Blue
Anthony Costa
Duncan James
Lee Ryan
Simon Webbe

Blur
Damon Albarn – Lead Vocals and Keyboards
Graham Coxon – Guitar
Alex James – Bass
Dave Rowntree – Drums

Bon Jovi
Jon Bon Jovi – Lead Vocals and Guitar
Richie Sambora – Lead Guitar
Dave Bryan – Keyboardist
Tico Torres – Drums
Alec John Such – Bass
(replaced by Hugh McDonald)
Hugh McDonald – Bass

Boney M
Marcia Barrett
Bobby Farrell
Liz Mitchell
Maisie Williams

Bonzo Dog Doo-Dah Band
Vernon Dudley Bowhay-Nowell – Percussion
Glen Colson – Drums
Neil Innes – Guitar, Piano and Vocals
Rodney Slater – Saxophone
Larry 'Legs' Smith – Drums
Roger Ruskin Spear – Percussion, Saxophone,
Trumpet
Sam Spoons – Acoustic Bass and Percussion
Vivian Stanshall – Lead Vocals and Various
Instruments

Boomtown Rats
Pete Briquette – Bass and Vocals
Gerry Cott – Guitar
Simon Crowe – Drums and Vocals
Johnny Fingers – Keyboards
Bob Geldof – Lead Vocals
Gary Roberts – Guitar and Vocals

Bow Wow Wow
Matthew Ashman – Guitar and Vocals
Dave Barbe 'Barbarossa' – Drums
Leigh Gorman – Bass and Vocals
Annabella Lu-Win – Lead Vocals

Boyz II Men
Mike McCaryl
Nathan Morris
Wanya Morris
Shawn Stockman

Boyzone
Keith Duffy
Stephen Gately
Mikey Graham
Ronan Keating
Shane Lynch

Bread
Mike Botts – Drums and Percussion
David Gates – Lead Vocals, Guitar, Keyboards,
    Violin, Bass
James Griffin – Guitar, Keyboards and Vocals
Larry Knechtel – Harmonica (replaced Rob Royer)
Rob Royer – Vocals, Guitar and Keyboards

Bronski Beat
Steve Bronski – Keyboards
John Foster – Vocals (replaced Jimmy Somerville in
    1986)
Jimmy Somerville – Lead Vocals
Larry Steinbeck – Keyboards

Bros
Matt Goss
Luke Goss
Craig Logan

Brotherhood of Man
Tony Burrows
    (founder member left before Eurovision success)
Sue Glover
    (founder member left before Eurovision success)
Johnny Goodison
    (founder member left before Eurovision success)
Roger Greenaway
    (founder member left before Eurovision success)
Martin Lee (Eurovision winner)
Sunny Leslie
    (founder member left before Eurovision success)
Lee Sheriden (Eurovision winner)
Nicky Stevens (Eurovision winner)
Sandra Stevens (Eurovision winner)
Russell Stone
    (founder member left before Eurovision success)
Tony Burrows was also lead singer with The Ivy
League, White Plains, Flowerpot Men, Pipkins and
Edison Lighthouse

Bucks Fizz
Jay Aston
Cheryl Baker
Bobby G (real name Robert Gubby)
Mike Nolan
Shelley Preston (replaced Jay Aston in 1985)
David Van Day (ex Dollar) replaced Mike Nolan in
1995 but then formed another version of the band
with Nolan, whilst Bobby G continued as the only
founder member of his version. When Nolan left after
a dispute with Van Day, Bobby G sued for improper
use of name and although it was originally found in
favour of Van Day in 2001 the verdict was set aside
out of court in 2002 and Bobby G was given the
proprietary use of the group's name whilst the other
version is now called David Van Day's Bucks Fizz.

Buffalo Springfield
Richie Furay – Guitar and Vocals
Doug Hastings – Vocals
Dewey Martin – Drums
Jim Messina – Bass and Vocals
Bruce Palmer – Bass
Stephen Stills – Guitar and Piano
Neil Young – Guitar and Vocals

Buggles
Geoff Downes – Keyboards
Trevor Horn – Vocals and Various Instruments

Busted
Charlie Simpson
Matt Jay
James Bourne

Buzzcocks
Garth Davies – Bass
Howard Deveto – Vocals
Steve Diggle – Bass and Guitar
Steve Garvey – Bass
John Maher – Drums
Pete Shelley – Guitar and Vocals

Byrds, The
Skip Battin
Gene Clark
    (co-founder but left in 1966 and died in 1991)
Michael Clarke – Drums
    (founding member, died in 1993)
David Crosby – Guitar and Vocals
John Guerin
Chris Hillman – Bass and Mandolin
    (founding member)
Kevin Kelley
Roger McGuinn – Lead Vocals and Guitar
    (founding member)
Gene Parsons – Drums (replaced David Crosby)
Gram Parsons – Guitar
Clarence White – Guitar
John York
Two of the five founding members have
now died, but the other three get together
with various combinations of the above-
named musicians to perform as The Byrds,
although the last gig by the original five was
in 1991.

Calling, The
Alex Band – Lead Vocals
Aaron Kamin – Guitar
Billy Mohler – Bass
Nate Wood – Drums
Sean Woolstenhulme – Guitar

Captain and Tennille
Daryl Dragon – Keyboards
Toni Tennille – Lead Vocals

Carpenters, The
Karen Carpenter – Vocals and Drums
Richard Carpenter – Vocals and Piano

Catatonia
Paul Jones – Bass
Dafydd Ieuan – Drums
    (left 1995 to join Super Furry Animals)
Cerys Matthews – Lead Vocals
Clancy Pegg – Keyboard (left in 1995)
Owen Powell – Guitar
    (joined after Ieuan and Pegg left)
Aled Richards – Drums (replaced Dafydd
    Ieuan)
Mark Roberts – Guitar

Chairmen of the Board
General Norman Johnson – Lead Vocals
Ken Knox – Saxophone
Danny Woods – Vocals

Charlatans
John Baker – Guitar
Martin Blunt – Bass
  (nervous breakdown after Baker left)
Jon Brookes – Drums
Tim Burgess – Lead Vocals
Mark Collins – Guitar (replaced John Baker)
Rob Collins – Organ
  (died in a car crash 23 July 1996)
Tony Rogers – Keyboards

Chemical Brothers
Tom Rowlands
Ed Simons

Chic
Bernard Edwards – Bass (died 1996)
Nile Rodgers – Guitar

Chicago
DaWane Bailey
  (joined temporarily between 1991 and 1993)
Peter Cetera – Vocals & Bass
  (founding member left 1985)
Bill Champlin – Keyboards (joined in 1982)
Donnie Dacus – Guitar
  (replaced Kath after shooting accident)
Marty Grebb – Saxophone and Guitars
  (briefly played in 1981)
Keith Howland – Guitars (joined in 1995)
Tris Imboden – Drums
  (replaced Danny Seraphine in 1991)
Terry Kath – Guitar and Vocals
  (founding member died 1978)
Robert Lamm – Keyboard and Vocals
  (founding member)
Lee Loughnane – Trumpet and Percussion
  (founding member)
Laudir De Oliveira – Congas, Bongos and
  Percussion (1974–82)
James Pankow – Trombone (founding member)
Walter Parazaider (Walt Perry) – Saxophone
  (founding member)
Chris Pinnick – Guitar
  (replaced Dacus in 1980, left in 1981)
Jason Scheff – (replaced Peter Cetera in 1985)
Danny Seraphine – Drums and Percussion
  (founding member)
Steven Stills – Guitar (replaced by Chris Pinnick)
Originally named Chicago Transit Authority when
having their first hit 'I'm a Man' but forced to change
it after being threatened with legal action by Mayor
Richard Daley.

Clash, The
Terry Chimes – Drums
  (replaced by Topper Headon in 1977)
Topper Headon – Drums
Mick Jones – Guitar and Vocals
Paul Simonon – Bass
Joe Strummer – Lead Vocals and Guitar (died
  December 2002)

Cliff Richard and The Shadows
Cliff Richard – Vocals
See separate entry for The Shadows

Coldcut
Matt Black
Jonathan Moore

Coldplay
Guy Berryman – Bass
Jon Buckland – Guitar
Will Champion – Drums
Chris Martin – Lead Vocals, Keyboard

Commodores, The
William King – Trumpet
Ronald LaPread – Bass
Thomas McClary – Guitar
JD Nicholas –
  (formerly of Heatwave, replaced Lionel Richie)
Walter 'Clyde' Orange – Drums
Lionel Richie – Lead Vocals, Piano and Saxophone
Milan Williams – Keyboards

Communards
Richard Coles – Keyboard
Jimmy Somerville – Vocals

Coral, The
Paul Duffy – Bass and Saxophone
Nick Power – Keyboards and Vocals
Bill Ryder-Jones – Guitar and Trumpet
Ian Skelly – Drums
James Skelly – Lead Vocals
Lee Southall – Guitar and Vocals

Corrs, The
Andrea Corr – Lead Vocals
Caroline Corr – Drums and Vocals
Jim Corr – Guitar and Keyboard
Sharon Corr – Violin and Vocals

Cranberries
Mike Hogan – Bass
Noel Hogan – Guitarist (main song writer)
Feargal Lawler – Drums
Dolores O'Riordan – Lead Vocals

Cream
Peter 'Ginger' Baker – Drums
Jack Bruce – Bass and Vocals
Eric Clapton – Guitar and Vocals

Crickets
Jerry Allison – Drums
Sonny Curtis – Guitar and Vocals
  (joined in circa 1961)
Buddy Holly – Guitar and Lead Vocals
Joe B Mauldin – Bass
Niki Sullivan – Rhythm Guitar
  (founding member left in 1958)

Crowded House
Neil Finn (New Zealander founding member)
Tim Finn
  (songwriting brother of Neil joined band 1989–91)
Mark Hart – Guitarist (American joined in 1993)
Paul Hester – Drums (Australian founding member)
Craig Hooper – Guitar (founding member 1985–6)
Nick Seymour – Bass (Australian founding member)
Formed in 1985 as the Mullanes (founder Neil Finn's
middle name) but became Crowded House in 1986.
Disbanded 1996.

Culture Club
Mikey Craig – Bass
Boy George – Lead Vocals
Rob Hay – Guitar
Jon Moss – Drums

Cure, The
Andy Anderson – Drums
Perry Bamonte – Guitar
Jason Cooper – Drums
Michael Dempsey – Bass
Simon Gallup – Bass
Roger O'Donnell – Keyboards
Robert Smith – Guitar and Vocals
Porl Thompson – Guitar
Phil Thornalley – Bass
Lol Tolhurst – Keyboards
Boris Williams – Drums

Cutting Crew
Martin 'Frosty' Beedle – Drummer
Nick Van Eede – Lead Vocals
Colin Farley – Bass
Kevin MacMichael – Guitar

Damned, The
Brian James – Guitar
Rat Scabies – Drums
Captain Sensible – Bass
Dave Vanian – Vocals

Dave Clark Five
Dave Clark – Drums
Lenny Davidson Guitar
Rick Huxley – Guitar
Denis Payton – Saxophone
Mike Smith – Keyboards and Lead Vocals

Dave Dee, Dozy, Beaky, Mick and Tich
Ian Amey (Tich) – Guitar
Trevor Davies (Dozy) – Bass
John Dymond (Beaky) – Guitar
David Harman (Dave Dee) – Vocals
Michael Wilson (Mick) – Drums

Dawn
Telma Hopkins
Tony Orlando
Pam Vincent
Joyce Vincent-Wilson

Deacon Blue
Guy Barker – Trumpet
Pete Beachill – Trombone
Dave Bishop – Baritone Saxophone
Stuart Elliot – Bodhran
Mark Feltham – Harmonica
Simon Gardener – Trumpet
Graham Kelling – Guitar (founding member)
Lorraine Mcintosh – Vocals (founding member)
James Prime – Piano
Ricky Ross – Vocals (founding member)
Neil Sidwell – Trombone
Jamie Talbot – Baritone Saxophone
Phil Todd – Tenor Saxophone
Ewen Vernal – Bass
Douglas Vipond – Drums (founding member)
Chris White – Tenor Saxophone
Gavin Wright – Fiddle
Husband and wife team of Ricky Ross and Lorraine
Mcintosh played with various artists on LPs and the
above are mostly session musicians.

Deep Purple
Don Airey – Keyboards (joined in 2002)
Ritchie Blackmore – Guitar
(founder left 1975 returned 1989–92)

Tommy Bolin – Guitar and Vocals
(replaced Blackmore 1975)
David Coverdale – Guitar and Vocals
(replaced Gillan 1973–6)
Rod Evans – Vocals (founding member)
Ian Gillan – Vocals
(replaced Evans 1969 left, returned 1994)
Roger Glover – Bass
(replaced Nick Semper in June 1969)
Glenn Hughes – Bass
(replaced Roger Glover in 1973)
John Lord – Keyboards (founding member)
Steve Morse – Guitar (joined in 1994)
Ian Paice – Drums (founding member)
Joe Satriani – Guitar (1993–4)
Nick Semper – Bass (founding member)
Joe Lyn Turner – Vocals (1989-92)
Founded in 1968 as Roundabout but changed name
in April to Deep Purple

Def Leppard
Richard Allen – Drums (lost left arm in car accident)
Vivian Campbell – Guitar (replaced Steve Clark)
Steve Clark – Guitar joined in 1977, died 1991)
Phil Cohen – Guitar (replaced Pete Willis)
Joe Elliott – Vocals (joined in 1977)
Rick Savage – Bass
Pete Willis – Guitar (fired from the band for alcoholism)

Depeche Mode
Vince Clarke – Synthesiser
(replaced by Wilder in 1982)
Andy Fletcher – Keyboard and Backing Vocals
David Gahan – Lead Vocals
Martin Gore – Guitar, Keyboard and Backing Vocals
Alan Wilder – Keyboard, Piano and Drums
(left in 1995)

Destiny's Child
Beyonce Knowles
Kelly Rowland
Michelle Williams

Dexy's Midnight Runners
Kevin 'Billy' Adams – Guitar and Banjo
Kevin 'Al' Archer – Keyboards and Vocals
(founding member)
Mickey Billingham – Keyboards
Geoff Blythe – Tenor Saxophone
Steve Brennan – Violin
Andy 'Stoker' Growcott – Drums
(replaced Bobby Junlor)
Bobby Junior – Drums
Giorgio Kilkenny – Bass (replaced Steve Wynn)
Andy Leek – Keyboards
Roger MacDuff – Violin
Brian Maurice – Alto Saxophone
Helen O'Hara – Violin
Jim Paterson – Trombone
Kevin Rowlands – Lead Vocals (founding member)
Peter Saunders – Alto Saxophone
Seb Shelton – Drums
Paul Speare – Tenor Saxophone
Steve 'Babyface' Spooner – Alto Sax
(replaced Saunders)
Mick Talbot – Keyboards
Pete Williams – Bass
Steve Wynn – Bass

Dire Straits
John Illsley – Bass
Dave Knopfler – Guitar

MUSIC POP

Mark Knopfler – Lead Vocals and Guitar
Pick Withers – Drums

Dollar
Thereze Bazar
David Van Day

Doobie Brothers
Mike Hossack – Drums
Tom Johnston – Guitar
Keith Knudsen – Drums and Vocals
Michael McDonald – Vocals
John McFee – Guitar and Violin
Patrick Simmons – Guitar and Vocals

Drifters
Willie Ferbie
Ben E King
Rudy Lewis (died in 1964)
Clyde McPhatter (founder died in 1972)
Johnny Moore (died 1998)
Bill Pinkney (only living founding member in 1953)
Charlie Thomas
Andrew Thrasher
Gearhardt Thrasher
Since 1958 Pinkney has used the name The
Original Drifters to differentiate themselves from a
British group that became The Shadows

Duran Duran
Simon Le Bon – Lead Vocals
Nick Rhodes – Keyboards
Andy Taylor – Guitar
John Taylor – Bass
Roger Taylor – Drums

Eagles
Dan Felder – Guitar and Lead Vocals
Glenn Frey – Guitar, Piano, Keyboard and Vocals
Don Henley – Drums
Timothy B Schmit – Bass
Joe Walsh – Guitar, Organ and Vocals

Earth, Wind and Fire
Philip Bailey – Drums and Vocals (founding member)
Ronald Bautista – Guitar and Vocals
Michael Beal – Guitar and Harmonica
Leslie Drayton – Trumpet
Larry Dunn – Keyboards
Sonny Emory – Drums
Wade Flemons – Backing Vocals
John Graham – Guitar
Yackov Ben Israel – Conga and Percussion
Ralph Johnson – Drums
Ronnie Laws – Saxophone and Flute
Al McKay – Rhythm Guitar (founding member)
Sheldon Reynolds – Backing Vocals
Sherry Scot – Backing Vocals
Alexander Thomas – Trombone
Chet Washington – Tenor Saxophone
Fred White – Drums and Percussion
Maurice White – Drums and Vocals (founder 1970)
Verdine White – Bass
Don Whitehead – Keyboards and Backing Vocals
Andrew Woolfolk – Saxophone
Band's name derived from the astrological signs of
the three founding members

East 17
Terry Caldwell – Vocals
Brian Harvey – Lead Singer
John Hendy – Vocals
Tony Mortimer – Keyboards

Electric Light Orchestra
Michael De Albuquerque – Bass and Cello
Phil Bates – Guitar and Backing Vocals
Bev Bevan – Drums, Percussion and Backing
  Vocals
Louis Clark – Keyboards and Backing Vocals
Mike Edwards – Cello
Melvyn Gale – Cello
Wilf Gibson – Violin
Kelly Groucutt – Bass and Backing Vocals
Pete Haycock – Bass and Backing Vocals
Parthenon Huxley – Guitar and Backing Vocals
Mik Kaminski – Violin
Neil Lockwood – Backing Vocals
Jeff Lynne – Guitar, Keyboards and Vocals
Hugh McDowell – Cello
Richard Tandy – Piano, Harmonica and Backing
  Vocals
Eric Troyer – Keyboards and Backing Vocals
Colin Walker – Cello
Roy Wood – Guitar, Banjo, Sitar and Vocals

EMF
James Atkin – Lead Vocals
Derry Brownson – Keyboards
Mark Decloedt – Drums
Ian Dench – Guitar and Keyboards
Zac Foley – Bass

En Vogue
Terry Ellis
Cindy Herron-Braggs
Maxine Jones
Dawn Robinson (left in 1995)

Erasure
Andy Bell
Vince Clarke

Eternal
Easther Bennett
Vernette Bennett
Kelle Bryan
Louise Redknapp (née Nurding)

Eurythmics
Annie Lennox
Dave Stewart

Faces, The
Kenney Jones – Drums
Ronnie Lane – Bass
Ian McLagan – Keyboards
Rod Stewart – Lead Vocals
Ronnie Wood – Guitar and Backing Vocals
Following Marriott's defection to form Humble Pie in
1969, Ron Wood and Rod Stewart were brought in
and the Small Faces became The Faces

Fairground Attraction
Roy Dodds – Drums
Simon Edwards – Bass
Mark Nevin – Guitar
Eddi Reader – Lead Vocals

Feeder
Taka Hirose – Bass
Jon Lee – Drums
Grant Nicholas – Vocals, Guitar

Fine Young Cannibals
Andy Cox – Guitar
Roland Gift – Lead Vocals
David Steele – Bass

Five
Richard Abidin Breen 'Abs'
Jason Brown 'J'
Sean Conlon
Ritchie Neville
Scott Robinson

Five Star
Delroy Pearson
Deniece Pearson
Doris Pearson
Lorraine Pearson
Stedman Pearson

Fleetwood Mac
Lindsey Buckingham – Vocals and Guitar
   (joined in 1974)
Mick Fleetwood – Drums
Peter Green – Guitar
Christine McVie née Perfect – Keyboards and Vocals
John McVie – Bass
Stevie Nicks – Vocals

Foo Fighters
William Goldsmith – Drums
Dave Grohl – Vocals and Guitar
Nate Mendel – Bass
Pat Smear – Guitar

Foreigner
Thom Gimbel – Saxophone, Guitar
Lou Gramm – Lead Vocals
Jeff Jacobs – Piano, Vocals
Mick Jones – Guitar, Piano, Vocals
Mark Schulman – Drums
Bruce Turgon – Bass

Four Tops
Renaldo Benson
Abdul Fakir
Lawrence Payton
Levi Stubbs

Frankie Goes to Hollywood
Peter Gill – Drums
Holly Johnson – Lead Vocals
Nasher Nash – Guitar
Mark O'Toole – Bass
Paul Rutherford – Vocals

Frankie Lymon and the Teenagers
Sherman Garnet – Vocals
Frankie Lymon – Vocals
James Merchant – Vocals
Joe Negroni – Vocals
Herman Santiago – Vocals

Franz Ferdinand
Robert Hardy – Bass
Alexander Kapranos – Guitar and Vocals
Nicholas McCarthy – Guitar
Paul Thomson – Drums

Free
Andy Fraser – Bass
Simon Kirke – Drums
Paul Kossoff – Guitar
Paul Rodgers – Vocals

Fugees
Lauryn 'L' Hill
Wyclef 'Clef' Jean
Prakazrel 'Pras' Michel

Fun Boy Three
Lynval Golding – Guitar and Vocals
Terry Hall – Vocals
Neville Staples – Vocals

Fun Lovin' Criminals
Steve 'O' Borovini – Drums
   (left 1999 replaced by Jayson)
Maxwell 'Mackie' Jayson – Drums
Brian 'Fast, Fisty, etc' Leiser – Guitar
Huey 'DiFontaine' Morgan – Lead Vocals and Guitar

G4
Jonathan Ansell
Mike Christie
Matt Stiff
Ben Thapa

Genesis
Tony Banks – Keyboard
Phil Collins – Drums (joined in 1970, left in 1996)
Peter Gabriel – Lead Vocals (left in 1975)
Steve Hackett – Guitar (joined in 1970, left in 1977)
Anthony Philips – Guitar (left in 1970)
Mike Rutherford – Bass
John Silver – Drums (replaced by Collins)
Chris Stewart – Drums (replaced by John Silver)
Ray Wilson – Drums (replaced Phil Collins)

Gerry and the Pacemakers
Les Chadwick – Bass
Arthur Mack – Piano (replaced by Les Maguire)
Les Maguire – Piano
Freddie Marsden – Drums
Gerry Marsden – Lead Vocals and Guitar

Girls Aloud
Nadine Coyle
Sarah Harding
Nicola Roberts
Cheryl Tweedy
Kimberley Walsh
Girl Group formed through ITV's *Popstars: The Rivals*

Gladys Knight and the Pips
William Guest – Vocals
Gladys Knight – Lead Vocals
Merald Knight – Vocals
Edward Patten – Vocals

Go West
Peter Cox – Vocals
Richard Drummie – Guitar, Keyboards and Vocals

Green Day
Billie Joe Armstrong – Vocals and Guitar
Tre Cool – Drums
Mike Dirnt – Bass
John Kiffmeyer – Drums (replaced by Tre Cool)

Guns 'N' Roses
Steven Adler – Drums (replaced by Matt Sorum)
Duff 'Rose' McKagan – Bass
Dizzy Read – Keyboard (added in 1990)
Axl Rose – Lead Vocals
Slash – Guitar
Matt Sorum – Drums
Izzy Stradlin – Guitar

M
U
S
I
C

P
O
P

Happy Mondays
Bez – Percussion
Paul Davis – Keyboards
Mark 'Cow' Day – Guitar
Paul Ryder – Bass
Shaun Ryder – Vocals
Gary Whelan – Drums

Hawkwind
Dave Brock – Guitar and Vocals
Robert Calvert – Vocals
Ian 'Lemmy' Kilmister – Lead Vocals and Bass
Stacia – Dancer
Nik Turner – Saxophone and Flute
Memorable for Lemmy's vocals on 'Silver Machine'
and the nude gyrations of six-foot dancer Stacia

Hear'Say
Danny Foster
Mylenne Klass
Kim Marsh (left in 2001 and was replaced by
    Shentall)
Suzanne Shaw
Johnny Shentall
Noel Sullivan

Heaven 17
Glenn Gregory – Vocals
Ian Craig Marsh – Keyboards
    (previously in Human League)
Martin Ware – Keyboards
    (previously in Human League)
Carol Kenyon was the uncredited vocalist on
'Temptation'

Hollies, The
Bernard Calvert – Bass
    (replaced Eric Haydock in 1966)
Alan Clarke – Lead Vocals (founding member)
Bobby Elliott – Drums (replaced Rathbone in 1963)
Eric Haydock – Bass (founding member 1962–6)
Tony Hicks – Guitar (founding member)
Graham Nash – Guitar and Vocals
    (founder 1962–8, and 1983)
Don Rathbone – Drums (founding member 1962–3)
Mikael Rikfors – Lead Vocals
    (replaced Alan Clarke 1971–3)
Terry Sylvester – Guitar and Vocals
    (replaced Nash in 1968)
Founded in 1962

Hot Chocolate
Franklyn De Allie – Guitar
Errol Brown – Lead Vocals
Tony Connor – Drums
Larry Ferguson – Pianist
Harvey Hinsley – Guitar
Ian King – Drums (replaced by Tony Connor)
Patrick Olive – Percussionist
Tony Wilson – Bass (left in 1976)

Housemartins, The
Stan Cullimore – Bass
Norman Cook – Guitar
Paul Heaton – Vocals and Guitar
    (later formed Beautiful South)
David Hemmingway – Drums
    (later formed Beautiful South)
Ted Key – Guitar
    (replaced by Norman 'Fat Boy Slim' Cook)
Hugh Whitaker – Drums
    (replaced by David Hemmingway)

Hue and Cry
Greg Kane
Pat Kane

Huey Lewis and the News
Mario Cipollina – Bass
Johnny Colla – Guitar and Saxophone
Bill Gibson – Drums
Chris Hayes – Guitar
Sean Hopper – Keyboards
Huey Lewis – Lead Vocals

Human League, The
Ian Burden (joined in 1981)
Jo Callis – Synthesizer (joined in 1981)
Joanne Catherall
Ian Craig Marsh (left in 1980 to form Heaven 17)
Philip Oakley
Susan Anne Sulley
Martyn Ware (left in 1980 to form Heaven 17)
Adrian Wright – Synthesizer

Humble Pie
Dave 'Clem' Clempson – Guitar and Vocals
    (replaced Frampton)
Dave 'Bucket' Colwell (member of Humble Pie 2000)
Peter Frampton – Guitar and Vocals (left in 1971)
Steve Marriott – Guitar and Lead Vocals
Zoot Money – Keyboards
    (member of Humble Pie 2000)
Greg Ridley – Bass and Vocals
Jerry Shirley – Drums
Bob Tench – Guitar (member of Humble Pie 2000)

Il Divo
Urs Buhler – Tenor (Swiss)
Sebastien Izambard (French)
Carlos Marin – Baritone (Spanish)
David Miller – Tenor (American)

Ink Spots
Jerry Daniels (founding member)
Charles Fuqua (founding member)
Orville 'Hoppy' Jones (founding member)
Bill Kenny (replaced Jerry Daniels in 1936)
Jim 'Mr inkspots' Nabbie
    (replaced Kenny 1945, died 1992)
Ivory 'Deek' Watson (founding member)
Founded in 1932

Inspiral Carpets
Clint Boon – Organ
Craig Gill – Drums
Stephen Holt – Vocals
Graham Lambert – Guitar
David Swift – Bass

INXS
Michael Hutchence – Lead Vocals (died in 1997)
Garry Beers – Bass, Vocals
Andrew Farriss – Keyboard
Jon Farriss – Drums
Tim Farriss – Guitar
Kirk Pengilly – Guitar, Saxophone and Vocals

Isley Brothers
Ernie Isley – Drums, Guitar and Percussion
Marvin Isley – Bass and Percussion
O'Kelly Isley – Vocals
Ronald Isley – Vocals
Rudolph Isley – Vocals
Chris Jasper – Drums and Keyboards

Jackson Five
Jackie Jackson (born Sigmund Jackson)
Jermaine Jackson – Bass and Lead Vocals
Marlon Jackson
Michael Jackson – Lead Vocals
Randy Jackson – (replaced Jermaine 1976)
Tito Jackson (born Toriano Jackson) – Guitar

Jam, The
Rick Buckler – Drums (replaced David Waller in 1978)
Bruce Foxton – Bass
David Waller – Drums
Paul Weller – Vocals, Guitar

James
Tim Booth – Vocals
Saul Davies – Violin (added 1990)
Andy Diagram – Trumpet (added 1990)
Paul Gilbertson – Guitar
Jim Glennie – Bass
Larry Gott – Guitar (replaced Paul Gilbertson 1985)
Mark Hunter – Keyboard (added 1990)
Michael Kulas – Guitar (added 1999)
Adrian Oxaal – Guitar (added 1997)
David Baynton-Power – Drums (replaced Gavan Whelan 1990)
Gavan Whelan – Drums

Jamiroquai
Wallis Buchanan – Vibraphone
Nick Fyffe – (replaced Stuart Zender)
J (Jason) K (Kay) – Lead Vocals
Derrick McKenzie – Drums
Toby Smith – Keyboard
Stuart Zender – Bass (left October 1998)

Jethro Tull
Mick Abrahams – Guitar and Vocals
Ian Anderson – Flute, Guitar, Mandolin, Saxophone and Vocals
Barriemore Barlow – Drums (replaced Clive Bunker in 1971)
Clive Bunker – Drums
Glen Cornick – Bass
Martin Barre – Flute and Guitar
John Evan – Keyboards
John Glascock – Bass and Vocals (replaced Hammond, 1976)
Jeffrey Hammond – Bass (replaced Glen Cornick in 1971)
David Palmer – Keyboard

Kaiser Chiefs
Nick 'Peanuts' Baines – Keyboards
Nick Hodgson – Drums and Vocals
Simon Rix – Bass
Andrew 'Whitey' White – Guitar
Ricky Wilson – Lead Vocals

Keane
Tom Chaplin – Vocals
Richard Hughes – Drums
Tim Rice-Oxley – Keyboards

King Crimson
Robert Fripp – Guitar and Melotron
Michael Giles – Drums and Vocals
Greg Lake – Bass and Vocals
Ian McDonald – Flute, Keyboards and Saxophone

Kinks, The
Mick Avory – Drums
John Beecham – Trombone and Tuba
Laurie Brown – Vocals
Mike Cotton – Trumpet
John Dalton – Bass (left in 1976)
Dave Davies – Guitar, Vocals
Raymond Douglas Davies – Vocals, Guitar, Piano
John Gosling – Keyboards
Alan Holmes – Saxophone and Clarinet
Davy Jones – Saxophone and Clarinet
Peter Quaife – Bass
(left in 1969 and replaced by Dalton)

Kiss
Peter Criss – Drums and Vocals
Ace Frehley – Guitar and Vocals
Gene Simmons – Bass and Vocals
Paul Stanley – Guitar

Kool & The Gang
Clifford Adams – Trombone
Robert 'Kool' Bell – Bass
Robert 'The Captain' Bell – Keyboards and Saxophone
Gary Brown – Vocals
'Funky' George Brown – Drums
Skip Martin – Vocals
Odeen Mays – Vocals
Robert 'Spike' Mickens – Trumpet
Michael Ray – Trumpet
Pharoah Sanders
Charles 'Calydes' Smith – Guitar
James 'JT' Taylor – Vocals (joined in 1979, left after Toon)
Dennis 'DT' Thomas – Saxophone
Leon Thomas
Earl Toon Jnr – Vocals
(left and Taylor became front man)

Kraftwerk
Klaus Dinger
Wolfgang Flur – Electronic Drums
Thomas Homann (left the band)
Ralf Hutter – Organ
Eberhardt Khranemann – Bass (left the band)
Klaus Roeder – Guitar, Violin, Keyboards
Michael Rother – Guitar
Florian Schneider – Woodwind

Kula Shaker
Alonza Bevan – Bass
Jay Darlington – Keyboard
Crispian Mills – Lead Vocals
Paul Winterhart – Drums

Led Zeppelin
Jason Bonham – Drums (replaced his father in 1980)
John 'Bonzo' Bonham – Drums (died in 1980)
John Paul Jones – Bass
Jimmy Page – Lead Guitar
Robert Plant – Lead Vocals
Jimmy Page decided to reform the Yardbirds under the name of the New Yardbirds. Keith Moon commented that it would go down like a lead balloon, in fact, a Le(a)d Zeppelin.

Level 42
Boon Gould – Guitar
Phil Gould – Drums

MUSIC POP

Mark King – Bass and Vocals
Mark Lindup – Keyboards and Vocals

Libertines, The
Carl Barat – Vocals
Pete Doherty – Vocals and Guitar (fired in 2004)
John Hassall – Bass
Gary Powell – Drums
Anthony Rossomando – Guitar (replaced Doherty)

Liberty X
Michelle Heaton
Tony Lundon
Kevin Simm
Jessica Taylor
Kelli Young

Lighthouse Family, The
Tunde Baiyewu – Lead Vocals
Paul Tucker – Keyboards

Lightning Seeds
Ian Broudie – Lead Vocals and Guitar
Martyn Campbell – Bass
Paul Hemmings – Guitar
Ali Kane – Keyboards
    (replaced by Angie Pollock in 1996)
Angie Pollock – Keyboards
Mat Priest – Drums
Chris Sharrock – Drums
    (replaced by Mat Priest in 1996)

Limp Bizkit
Wes Borland – Guitar
Fred Durst – Lead Vocals
DJ Lethal (joined in 1996)
John Otto – Drums
Sam Rivers – Bass

Lonestar
Michael Britt – Guitar and Vocals
Richie McDonald – Lead Vocals
Keech Rainwater – Drums
Dean Sams – Keyboard and Vocals

Love Affair
Maurice Bacon – Drums
Rex Brayley – Guitar
Steve Ellis – Vocals
Morgan Fisher – Organ
Lynton Guest – Organ
Mick Jackson – Bass
A less well-known US band had the same name

Lynyrd Skynyrd
Bob Burns – Drums
Allen Collins – Guitar
Steve Gaines – Guitar
Ed King – Guitar
Billy Powell – Keyboards
Gary Rossington – Guitar
Leon Williams – Bass
Ronnie Van Zant – Vocals

M People
Paul Heard
Mike Pickering
Heather Small

Madness
Mike 'Barso' Barson – Keyboards
Mark 'Bedders' Bedford – Bass

Chris 'Chrissy Boy' Foreman – Guitar
Graham 'Suggs' McPherson – Lead Vocals
Carl 'Chas' Smash – Trumpet and Backing Vocals
Lee 'Kix' Thompson – Saxophone and Vocals
Daniel 'Woody' Woodgate – Drums and Percussion

Mamas and the Papas
Denny Doherty – Vocals
Mama Cass Elliot – Vocals
John Phillips – Guitar and Vocals
Michelle Phillips – Vocals

Manfred Mann
Michael D'Abo – Lead Vocals
    (replaced Paul Jones in 1966)
Mike Hugg – Drums and Percussion
Paul Jones – Lead Vocals
Tom McGuinness – Bass
Manfred Mann – Keyboards
Mike Vickers – Guitar

Manhattan Transfer
Tim Hauser
Laurel Masse
Alan Paul
Janis Siegel

Manic Street Preachers
James Dean Bradfield – Lead Vocals, Lead and
    Rhythm Guitar
Richey Edwards – Rhythm Guitar
    (went missing in 1995)
Sean Moore – Drums
Nicky Wire – Bass

Marillion
Fish – Vocals (left in 1988)
Steve Hogarth – Vocals (replaced Fish in 1989)
Mark Kelly – Keyboards
Ian Mosley – Drums
Mick Pointer – Drums
Steve Rothery – Guitar
Pete Trewavas – Bass

Marmalade
William 'Junior' Campbell – Guitar and Vocals
    (founding member)
Raymond Duffy – Drums (founding member)
Patrick Fairley – Guitar (founding member)
Dean Ford – Lead Vocals (founding member)
Graham Knight – Bass and Vocals
    (founding member)
Alan Whitehead – Drums (replaced Duffy in late 1966)
Founded in 1966 having previously been named
Dean Ford and the Gaylords

Martha Reeves and the Vandellas
Rosalind Ashford
Betty Kelly
Lols Reeves
Martha Reeves

McFly
Tom Fletcher – Guitar and Vocals
Danny Jones – Guitar and Vocals
Harry Judd – Drums
Dougie Poynter – Bass and Vocals

Middle of the Road
Phil Anderson – Guitar and Vocals
Ken Andrew – Drums and Vocals
    (founding member)

Eric Campbell-Lewis – Guitar (founding member)
Ian Campbell-Lewis – Guitar (founding member)
Sally Carr – Lead Vocals (founding member)
Shug Devun – Keyboards
Derek Hall – Guitar and Vocals
Neil Henderson – Bass and Vocals
Kenny McKay – Guitar and Vocals
Pat Monaghan – Guitar and Vocals

Mindbenders
Wayne Fontana – Lead Vocals
Graham Gouldman – Guitar
Paul Hancox – Drums
James O'Neill – Guitar
Eric Stewart – Guitar, Piano and Vocals

Mis-Teeq
Alesha Dixon
Su-Elise Nash
Sabrina Washington

Monkees, The
Mickey Dolenz – Drums and Vocals
Davy Jones – Tambourine and Vocals
Mike Nesmith – Guitar and Vocals
Peter Tork – Bass and Vocals

Moody Blues
Graeme Edge – Drums and Vocals
(founder member)
Justin Hayward – Guitar and Vocals
(replaced Laine)
Denny Laine – Guitar and Vocals
(founder member left, 1966)
John Lodge – Bass, Cello, Guitar and Vocals
Mike Pinder – Keyboards and Vocals
(founder member)
Ray Thomas – Reeds and Vocals
(founder member)
Clint Warwick – Guitar (founder member left in 1966)

Motorhead
Phil Campbell – Guitar
Mikkey Dee – Drums
Ian 'Lemmy' Kilmister – Lead Vocals and Bass

Mott the Hoople
Dale Griffin – Drums and Vocals
Ian Hunter – Piano, Guitar and Lead Vocals
Mick Ralphs – Guitar and Vocals
Overend Watts – Bass and Vocals

Move, The
Bev Bevan – Drums
Trevor Burton – Guitar and Vocals
Chris Kefford – Bass
Jeff Lynn – Guitar and Vocals
Rick Pride – Bass and Vocals
Carl Wayne – Guitar and Vocals
Roy Wood – Guitar, Banjo, Sitar and Vocals

Mud
Rob Davis
Les Gray
Dave Mount
Ray Stiles

Mugwumps
Denny Doherty – Vocals
Cass Elliot – Vocals
James Hendricks – Vocals
Zal Yanovsky – Guitar and Vocals

Mungo Jerry
Mike Cole – Bass
Ray Dorset – Vocals, Guitar
Colin Earl – Piano, Vocals
Paul King – Banjo, Guitar, Vocals

'N Sync
Lance Bass
JC Chasez
Joey Fatone
Chris Kirkpatrick
Justin Timberlake

Nazareth
Pete Agnew – Bass (founding member)
Manny Charlton – Guitar (founding member)
Zal Cleminson – Guitar (1979–81)
Ronnie Leahy – Keyboards
John Locke – Keyboards (replaced Zal Cleminson)
Dan McCafferty – Vocals (founding member)
Jimmy Murrison – Guitar
Bill Rankin – Guitar and Keyboards
(replaced Locke in 1981)
Darrell Sweet – Drummer (founding member)

New Christy Minstrels, The
Karen Black (better known nowadays as an actress)
Bob Buchanan
Gene Clark (left to join The Byrds)
Barry McGuire – Lead Vocals
Larry Ramos
Kenny Rogers – Vocals (1966–7)
Mike Settle
(left 1967 to start First Edition with Rogers)
Randy Sparks (founder of the group)

New Kids on the Block
Jonathan Knight
Jordan Knight
Joe McIntyre
Donnie Wahlberg
Danny Wood

New Seekers
Chris Barrington – Bass
(founding member left in 1970)
Peter Doyle (joined in 1970)
Eve Graham (founding member)
Sally Graham (founding member left in 1970)
Laurie Heath – Guitar (founding member left in 1970)
Marty Kristian (founding member)
Paul Layton (joined in 1970)
Peter Oliver (replaced Peter Doyle in 1973)
Lyn Paul (joined in 1970)
Keith Potger (founder but only played on one LP)

Nice, The
Brian 'Blinky' Davison – Drums
Keith Emerson – Keyboards
Lee Jackson – Bass
David O'List – Guitar and Vocals

Nickelback
Chad Kroeger – Vocals and Guitar
Mike Kroeger – Guitar
Ryan Peake – Guitar and Vocals
Ryan Vikedal – Bass

911
Lee Brennan
Jimmy Constable
Simon 'Spike' Dawbarn

MUSIC

POP

Nirvana
Kurt Cobain – Lead Vocals and Guitar (died in 1994)
David Grohl – Drums and Vocals
Chris Novoselic – Bass and Vocals

Oasis
Gem Archer – Guitar
  (replaced Paul Arthurs in 1999)
Paul 'Bonehead' Arthurs – Rhythm Guitar
Andy Bell – Bass (replaced Paul McGuigan)
Liam Gallagher – Vocals
Noel Gallagher – Vocals and Guitar
Tony McCarroll – Drums
Paul 'Guigsy' McGuigan – Bass
Alan White – Drums
  (replaced Tony McCarroll in 1994)

Ocean Colour Scene
Steve Craddock – Lead Guitar, Keyboards and
  Vocals
Simon Fowler – Lead Vocals, Guitar and Harmonica
Oscar Harrison – Drums and Vocals
Damon Minchela – Bass

O'Jays
Bill Isles
Eddie Levert
Bobby Massey
William Powell
Walter Williams
Formed in 1958 as the Mascots and became the
O'Jays in honour of Cleveland DJ Eddie O'Jay

One True Voice
Anton Gordon
Matt Johnson
Daniel Pearce
Keith Semple
Jamie Shaw
Vocal harmony group formed via ITV's *Popstars:
The Rivals*

Orchestral Manoeuvres in the Dark (OMD)
Malcolm Holmes – Keyboards
Dave Hughes – Drums and Percussion
Paul Humphreys – Keyboards
Andy McCluskey – Bass and Vocals

Osmonds, The
Donny Osmond
Alan Osmond
Little Jimmy Osmond
Wayne Osmond
Jay Osmond
Merrill Osmond

Pet Shop Boys
Chris Lowe
Neil Tennant – Lead Vocals

Peter, Paul and Mary
Paul Stookey – Guitar and Vocals
Mary Travers – Vocals
Peter Yarrow – Guitar and Vocals

Pink Floyd
Syd Barrett – Guitar and Vocals
Dave Gilmour – Guitar and Vocals
Nick Mason – Drums and Percussion
Roger Waters – Bass, Piano and Percussion
Rick Wright – Keyboards

Plastic Ono Band
Eric Clapton – Guitar
John Lennon – Vocals, Guitar and Piano
Yoko Ono – Vocals
Ringo Starr – Drums
Klaus Voorman – Bass
Alan White – Drums

Platters
Alex Hodge
David Lynch (died in 1981)
Herb Reed
Paul Robi (died in 1989)
Zola Taylor
Sonny Turner
Tony Williams (died in 1992)
Managed by Sam 'Buck' Ram

Pogues, The
James Feamley – Piano Accordion and Guitar
Jim Finer – Banjo and Mandolin
Darryl Hunt – Bass
Shane MacGowan – Lead Vocals
  (replaced by Joe Strummer)
Cait O'Riordan – Bass (replaced by Darryl Hunt)
Andrew Ranken – Drums
Peter 'Spidey' Stacy – Tin Whistle
Joe Strummer – Lead Vocals
Terry Woods

Police
Stewart Copeland – Drums
Sting (Gordon Sumner) – Lead Vocals and
  Bass
Andy Summers – Guitar
Miles Copeland – Manager

Pretenders, The
Martin Chambers – Drums
Pete Farndon – Bass (left 1982, died 1983)
Malcolm Foster – Bass (added 1983)
James Honeyman-Scott – Guitar
  (died in 1982)
Chrissie Hynde – Lead Vocals
Robbie McIntosh – Guitar (added 1983)

Proclaimers
Charlie Reid
Craig Reid

Procol Harum
Gary Brooker – Piano and Lead Vocals
Alan Cartwright – Bass
Chris Copping – Bass and Organ
Matthew Fisher – Guitar and Organ
Mick Grabham – Guitar
Bobby Harrison – Drums and Percussion
David Knights – Bass
Ray Royer – Guitar
Peter Solley – Organ
Robin Trower – Guitar and Vocals
BJ Wilson – Drums and Percussion

Prodigy
Graham 'Gizz' Butt – Guitar
Keith Flint – Lead Vocals
Liam Howlett – Keyboards
Alison 'Alli' MacInnes – Guitar
Sharky – Dancer and Backing Vocals
Leeroy Thornhill – Dancer
MC Maxim Reality (born Keith Palmer)

Public Image Ltd
Keith Levine – Guitar
John Lydon (Johnny Rotten) – Lead Vocals
Jim Walker – Drums
Jah Wobble – Bass

Pulp
Jarvis Cocker – Lead Vocals and Guitar
Peter Dalton – Keyboard
Wayne Furniss – Drums
Jamie Pinchbeck – Bass

Quarrymen, The
George Harrison – Lead Guitar and Vocals
John Lennon – Rhythm Guitar and Vocals
Paul McCartney – Bass and Vocals
Pete Best – Drums
Formed 1958 and became The Silver Beatles in
1959 when Tony Sheridan joined them. Whatever
became of them?

Queen
John Deacon – Bass
Brian May – Guitar and Vocals
Freddie Mercury (born Freddie Bulsara) – Vocals
   and Keyboard
Roger Taylor – Drums

Q-Tips, The
Stewart Blandmer – Saxophone and Vocals
Steve Farr – Saxophone and Vocals
Tony Hughes – Trumpet
Mick Pearl – Bass
Garth Watt Roy – Guitar and Vocals
Barry Watts – Drums
Paul Young – Guitar and Lead Vocals

Radiohead
Johnny Greenwood – Lead Guitar
Colin Greenwood – Bass
Ed O'Brien – Rhythm Guitar
Phil Selway – Drums
Thom Yorke – Lead Vocals and Rhythm Guitar

Rainbow
Don Airey – Keyboards (replaced David Stone)
Jimmy Bain – Bass (replaced Craig Gruber)
Ritchie Blackmore – Guitar
Graham Bonnet – Vocals
   (replaced Ronnie James Dio)
Tony Carey – Keyboards
   (replaced Mickey Lee Soule)
Mark Clarke – Bass (replaced Jimmy Bain)
Bob Daisley – Bass (replaced Mark Clarke)
Ronnie James Dio – Vocals
Gary Driscoll – Drums
Roger Glover – Bass (replaced Bob Daisley)
Craig Gruber – Bass
Cozy Powell – Drums (replaced Gary Driscoll)
Mickey Lee Soule – Keyboards
David Stone – Keyboards (replaced Tony Carey)

The Red Hot Chili Peppers
Flea (Michael Balzary) – Trumpet, Bass (founding
   member)
John Frusciante – (replaced Duane 'Blackbird'
   McKnight, left and rejoined)
Jack Irons – Drums (left to form What Is This)
Anthony Kiedis – Vocals (founding member)
Duane 'Blackbird' McKnight – Guitar (replaced Hillel
   Slovak)
Arik Marshall – Guitar (replaced John Frusciante)
Cliff Martinez – Bass
Dave Navarro – (replaced Jesse Tobias)

DH Peligro – Drums (formerly with Dead Kennedys)
Jack Sherman – Guitar
Hillel Slovak – Guitar (died 25 June 1988)
Chad Smith – Drums (replaced DH Peligro)
Jesse Tobias – Guitar (replaced Arik Marshall)
The Red Hot Chili Peppers were once known as
Tony Flow and the Miraculously Majestic Masters of
Mayhem

REM
Bill Berry – Drums (left in 1996)
Peter Buck – Lead Guitar, Mandolin and Banjo
Mike Mills – Bass, Keyboard
Michael Stipe – Lead Vocals and Guitar

Righteous Brothers
Bobby Hatfield
Bill Medley
Jimmy Walker (replaced Bill Medley in 1968)

Right Said Fred
Fred Fairbrass
Richard Fairbrass
Rob Manzoli

Rolling Stones, The
Mick Jagger – Lead Vocals
Brian Jones – Guitar (died in 1969)
Darryl Jones – Bass (joined in 1994)
Keith 'The Human Riff' Richards – Guitar
Ian Stewart – Piano (died 12 December 1985)
Mick Taylor – Guitar (1969–74)
Charlie Watts – Drums
Ron Wood – Bass (joined in 1975)
Bill Wyman – Bass (left in 1992)
Andrew Loog Oldham – Manager

Ronettes
Estelle Bennett
Veronica 'Ronnie' Bennett
Nedra Talley

Roxette
Marie Fredriksson – Vocals
Per Gessle – Guitar and Vocals

Roxy Music
Roger Bunn – Guitar
Brian Eno – Synthesizer
Bryan Ferry – Lead Vocals and Keyboards
John Gustafson – Bass (replaced Sal Maida)
Eddie Jobson – Keyboards
Rik Kenton – Bass (replaced Graham Simpson)
Andy MacKay – Saxophone
Sal Maida – Bass (replaced John Porter)
Phil Manzanera – Guitar
David O'List – Guitar
John Porter – Bass (replaced Rik Kenton)
Graham Simpson – Bass
David Skinner – Keyboards
Paul Thompson – Drums
Gary Tibbs – Bass (replaced John Wetton)
John Wetton – Bass

Rutles, The
Dirk McQuickly (Eric Idle)
Ron Nasty (Neil Innes)
Stig O'Hara (Ricky Fataar)
Barry Wom (John Halsey)
Leggy Mountbatten (Terence Bayler) – Manager
Spoof group invented by Eric Idle and Gary Weiss
and modelled on The Beatles. Had a minor hit in
actuality with 'I Must Be In Love'

M
U
S
I
C

P
O
P

S Club
Tina Barrett
Paul Cattermole (left 2002)
Jon Lee
Bradley McIntosh
Jo O'Meara
Hannah Spearritt
Rachel Stevens
Formerly known as S Club 7 until Paul Cattermole left

S Club Juniors
Aaron
Calvin
Daisy
Frankie
Hannah
Jay
Rochelle
Stacey

Salt-N-Pepa
Sandra 'Pepa' Denton
DJ Pamela Green
Cheryl 'Salt' James
DJ Dee Dee 'Spinderella' Roper (replaced Pamela Green)

Savage Garden
Darren Hayes – Lead Vocals
Daniel Jones – Guitar

Scaffold
John Gorman
Mike McGear
Roger McGough

Scissor Sisters
Babydaddy (Scott Hoffman) – Bass and Keyboards
Paddy Boom (Patrick Seacor) – Drums
Del Marquis (Derek Gruen) – Guitar
Ana Matronic (Ana Lynch) – Vocals
Jake Shears (Jason Sellards) – Lead Vocals

Searchers, The
Chris Curtis
Tony Jackson
John McNally
Mike Pinder

Seekers
Judith Durham – Vocal
Athol Guy – Bass
Keith Potger – Guitar
Bruce Woodley – Guitar

Sex Pistols
Paul Cook – Drums
Steve Jones – Guitar
Glen Matlock – Bass
   (replaced by Sid Vicious in 1977)
Wally Nightingale – Lead Vocals
Jonny Rotten – Vocals
Sid Vicious – Bass (died in 1979)
Malcolm McLaren – Manager
Reformed in 1996 for the 'Filthy Lucre' tour

Shadows, The
Brian Bennett – Drums (founding member)
Warren Bennett – Guitar and Keyboards (son of Brian)
John Farrar – Bass Guitar
   (replaced Alan Tarney in 1977)

Mo Foster – Bass (classed as an honorary Shadow)
Mark Griffiths – Bass (replaced Alan Jones in 1987)
Cliff Hall – Piano (from 1978 an honorary Shadow)
Jet Harris – Bass
   (replaced by Brian Locking in 1962)
Alan Hawkshaw – Piano and Keyboards (joined 1968)
Alan Jones – Bass
   (from 1977 an honorary Shadow)
Brian 'Licorice' Locking – Bass
   (left for religious reasons 1964)
Ben Marvin – Guitar (son of Hank)
Hank Marvin – Lead Guitar
Tony Meehan – Drums
   (replaced by Brian Bennett in 1961)
John Rostill – Bass Guitar
   (joined 1964, died in 1973)
Alan Tarney – Bass Guitar and Piano (1973–7)
Bruce Welch – Rhythm Guitar

Shakespears Sister
Marcella Detroit
Siobhan Fahey

Shalamar
Jeffrey Daniel
Howard Hewett
Jody Watley

Shamen, The
Colin Angus
Derek McKenzie (replaced by William Sinnott)
Keith McKenzie
William Sinnott (drowned in 1991)
Peter Stephenson
Richard 'Mr C' West

Simply Red
Tony Bowers – Bass
Mick 'Red' Hucknall – Lead Vocals
Chris Joyce – Drums
Tim Kellett – Brass, Keyboards
Fritz McIntyre – Keyboards
Sylvan Richardson – Guitar

Slade
Dave Hill – Lead Guitar and Backing Vocals
Noddy Holder – Lead Vocals and Guitar
Jim Lea – Bass and Violin
Don Powell – Drums

Small Faces
Kenney Jones – Drums
Ronnie Lane – Bass
Ian McLagan – Keyboards
Steve Marriott – Vocals and Guitar
Following Marriott's defection to form Humble Pie in 1969, Ron Wood and Rod Stewart were brought in and the Small Faces became The Faces

Smashing Pumpkins
Jimmy Chamberlin – Drums
Billy Corgan – Lead Vocals and Guitar
James Iha – Lead Guitar
Melissa Auf Der Maur – Bass
D'Arcy Wretzky – Bass (replaced by Melissa Auf Der Maur)

Smiths
Mike Joyce – Drums
Johnny Marr – Guitar
Stephen Morrissey – Vocals
Andy Rourke – Bass

Smokey Robinson and the Miracles
Bill Griffin – Vocals
Pete Moore – Vocals
Smokey Robinson – Lead Vocals
Bobby Rogers – Vocals
Ronny White – Vocals

So Solid Crew
Harvey
Lisa
Romeo
Band is reputed to have at least 30 transient members

Soft Cell
Marc Almond – Lead Vocals
Dave Ball – Synthesizer

Spandau Ballet
Tony Hadley – Lead Vocals
John Keeble – Drums
Gary Kemp – Guitar
Martin Kemp – Bass
Steve Norman – Guitar, Saxophone and Percussion
Steve Dagger – Manager

Spencer Davis Group
Spencer Davis – Guitar and Vocals (founding member)
Ray Fenwick – Guitar (replaced Phil Sawyer)
Eddie Hardin – Keyboards (replaced Phil Sawyer)
Phil Sawyer – Guitar and Keyboards (joined 1967 after Steve Winwood left)
Muff Winwood – Bass (founding member left in 1967)
Steve Winwood – Vocals, Guitar and Piano (founding member)
Peter York – Drums (founding member)
Steve Winwood left in 1967 to form Traffic

Spice Girls
Victoria Beckham (née Adams) 'Posh Spice'
Melanie 'B' Brown 'Scary Spice'
Emma Bunton 'Baby Spice'
Melanie 'C' Chisholm 'Sporty Spice'
Geri Halliwell 'Ginger Spice' (left the group in 1999)

Spinal Tap
Joe 'Mama' Bessemer – Drums (replaced Mick Shrimpton)
Peter James Bond (replaced Childs, spontaneously combusted)
Eric 'Stumpy Joe' Childs – Drums (died in 1974 after choking)
Ian Faith – Manager (replaced Hampton)
Glyn Hampton – Manager (left in 1975)
Ross MacLochness – Keyboards (replaced Denny Upham)
John 'Stumpy' Pepys – Drums (died in gardening accident 1969)
Jeanine Pettibone – Manager (replaced Ian Faith)
Ronnie Pudding – Bass
David St Hubbins (Michael McKean)
Viv Savage – Keyboards (replaced MacLochness)
Mick Shrimpton – Drums (replaced Bond but suffered same fate)
Ric Shrimpton – Drums (played in the 1992 revival group)
Derek Smalls (Harry Shearer) – Bass
Nigel Tufnel (Christopher Guest)
Denny Upham – Keyboards
CJ Vanston – Keyboards

(played in the 1992 revival group)
Fictitious group played by McKean, Guest and Shearer in the 1984 satirical film *This Is Spinal Tap*, although spawning minor hits such as 'Bitch School' and 'The Majesty of Rock'.

Squeeze
Paul Carrack – Keyboards and Vocals
Chris Difford – Guitar and Vocals
Paul Gunn – Drums (replaced by Gilson Lavis)
Jools Holland – Keyboards and Vocals
Gilson Lavis – Drums
Glenn Tilbrook – Guitar and Vocals
Miles Copeland – Manager (in the early days)

Status Quo
John Coghlan – Drums
Alan Lancaster – Bass
Roy Lynes – Keyboards
Rick Parfitt – Guitar and Vocals
Francis Rossi – Guitar and Vocals
The above are the five founding members, although various other musicians have played with the Quo over the years

Steps
Lee Latchford-Evans
Claire Richards
Lisa Scott-Lee
Faye Tozer
Ian 'H' Watkins

Stereophonics
Stuart Cable – Drummer
Kelly Jones – Lead Vocals and Guitar
Richard Jones – Bass

Stone Roses
Ian Brown – Vocals
Andy Couzens – Guitar
Pete Garner – Bass (replaced by Gary 'Mani' Mounfield)
Gary 'Mani' Mounfield – Bass
John Squire – Guitar
Simon Wolstencroft – Drums (replaced by Alan 'Reni' Wren)
Alan 'Reni' Wren – Drums

Stranglers, The
Jet Black – Drums
Jean-Jacques Burnel – Bass and Vocals
Hugh Cornwell – Guitar and Vocals
Dave Greenfield – Keyboards

Streets, The
Mike Skinner

Strokes, The
Julian Casablancas – Lead Vocals
Nikolai Fraiture – Bass
Albert Hammond Jr – Guitar
Fabrizio Moretti – Drums
Nick Valensi – Guitar

Suede
Brett Anderson – Lead Vocalist
Bernard Butler – Guitar (replaced by Richard Oakes)
Neil Codling – Keyboard, Vocals
Justine Frischmann – Guitar (left)
Simon Gilbert – Drums
Richard Oakes – Guitar
Mat Osman – Bass

MUSIC POP

Sugababes, The
Keisha Buchanan
Mutya Buena
Sioban Donaghy (left in 2001)
Heidi Range (replaced Sioban Donaghy)

Super Furry Animals
Huw 'Bunf' Bunford – Guitar and Vocals
Cian Ciaran – Keyboards
Dafydd Ieuan – Drums
Guto Pryce – Bass
Gruff Rhys – Lead Vocals and Guitar

Supergrass
Gaz Coombes – Lead Vocals and Guitar
Danny Goffey – Drums
Micky Quinn – Bass

Supertramp
Rick Davies – Keyboards, Harmonica and Vocals
Mark Hart – Keyboards and Vocals
John Helliwell – Keyboards and Saxophones
Cliff Hugo – Bass
Bob Sjebenberg – Drums
Jesse Sjebenberg – Keyboards, Guitar, Percussion and Vocals
Dougie Thompson – Bass
Lee Thornburg – Trumpet and Trombone
Carl Verheyen – Guitar and Vocals

Supremes
Florence Ballard
Cindy Birdsong
Diana Ross
Jean Terrell (joined after Ross left)
Mary Wilson (replaced by Birdsong on becoming Supremes)
Jean Terrell (joined after Ross left)
Originally called Primettes

Sweet
Brian Connolly – Vocals (founding member, died in 1997)
Steve Priest – Bass (founding member)
Andy Scott – Guitar
Mick Stewart – Guitar
Frank Torpey – Guitar (founding member)
Mick Tucker – Drums (founding member)
Phil Wainman – Drums

Take That
Gary Barlow – Lead Vocals, Piano and Composer
Howard Donald
Jason Orange
Mark Owen
Robbie Williams (left in 1995)
Disbanded in February 1996

Talking Heads
David Byrne – Guitar and Lead Vocals
Chris Frantz – Drums
Jerry Harrison – Guitar, Keyboards and Vocals
Martina Weymouth – Bass

Tears For Fears
Oleta Adams – Vocals
Roland Orzabal – Guitar, Keyboards and Vocals (founder)
Curt Smith – Bass and Vocals (founding member)
Ian Stanley – Keyboards
Basically a duo that became a one-man band when Curt Smith left in 1991

Temptations
Dennis Edwards
Mel Franklin
Eddie Kendricks
David Ruffin
Otis Williams
Paul Williams

10CC
Lol Creme – Guitar and Keyboards
Kevin Godley – Drums, Percussion and Vocals
Graham Gouldman – Bass, Guitar and Vocals
Eric Stewart – Guitar, Piano and Vocals

Ten Years After
Chick Churchill – Keyboards
Alvin Lee – Guitar and Vocals
Ric Lee – Drums and Percussions
Leo Lyons – Bass

Texas
Eddie Campbell – Keyboards
Richard Hynde – Drums
Stuart Kerr – Drums
Johnny McElhone – Bass
Ally McErlaine – Guitar
Tony McGovern – Guitar
Sharleen Spiteri – Lead Vocals and Guitar
Mykey Wilson – Drums

Them
Jim Armstrong – Sitar, Guitar and Drums
Peter Bardens – Organ
Ray Elliot – Organ, Flute, Saxophone
Billy Harrison – Guitar
David Harvey – Drums
Alan Henderson – Bass
John McAuley – Drums, Harmonica and Vocals
Ray Ken McPowell – Vocals
Van Morrison – Harmonica, Tenor Saxophone and Vocals

Thin Lizzy
Eric Bell – Guitar (founding member 1970–74)
Brian Downey – Drums (founding member 1970–83)
John DuCann – Guitar (January to April 1974)
Dave Flett – Guitar (1979–80)
Andy Gee – Guitar (January to April 1974)
Scott Gorham – Guitar (1974–83)
Phil Lynott – Bass and Vocals (founding member, died 1986)
Gary Moore – Guitar (January to April 1974 and 1977–9)
Mark Nauseef – Drums (1978–9)
Brian 'Robbo' Robertson – Guitar and Vocals ((1974–8)
Midge Ure – Guitar (1979–80)
Darren Wharton – Keyboards (1980-83)
Snowy White – Guitar (1980–82)
Eric Wrixon – Keyboards (founding member, 1970)

Thompson Twins
Tom Bailey – Synthesiser and Vocals
Chris Bell – Drums
Alannah Currie – Percussion, Saxophone and Vocals
Joe Leeway – Percussion
John Roog – Guitar
Matthew Seligman – Bass
Pete Todd – Guitar

Three Degrees
Sheila Ferguson
Valerie Holiday
Fayette Pinkney

Three Dog Night
Michael Allsup – Guitar
Jimmy Greenspoon – Keyboards
Danny Hutton – Vocals
Chuck Negren – Vocals
Joe Schermie – Bass
Floyd Sneed – Drums and Percussion
Cory Wells – Vocals

Thrills, The
Ben Carrigan – Drums
Conor Deasy – Vocals
Kevin Horan – Keyboards
Patraic McMahon – Bass
Daniel Ryan – Guitar

Thunderclap Newman
Speedy Keen – Drums, Guitar and Vocals
Jimmy McCulloch – Guitar
Andy Newman – Keyboards

TLC
Lisa 'Left-eye' Lopes (died in 2002)
Rozonda 'Chilli' Thomas
Tionne 'T-Boz' Watkins

Toploader
Julian Deane – Lead Guitar and Vocals
Rob Green – Drums
Dan Hipgrave – Rhythm and Acoustic Guitar
Matt Knight – Bass
Joseph Washbourn – Lead Vocals, Piano and Organ

T'Pau
Tim Burgess – Drums
Michael Chetwood – Keyboards
Carol Decker – Vocals
Paul Jackson – Bass
Ron Rogers – Guitar
Taj Wyzgowski – Guitar

Traffic
Reebop Kwaku Baah – Percussion
Barry Beckett – Keyboards
Jim Capaldi – Drums, Percussion and Vocals
Jim Gordon – Drums
Rick Grech – Bass and Violin
Roger Hawkins – Drums
David Hood – Bass
Dave Mason – Bass, Guitar, Sitar and Vocals
Steve Winwood – Lead Vocals, Guitar and Keyboard
Chris Wood – Flute, Organ, Percussion, Saxophone, Vocals)

Travelling Wilburys
Bob Dylan
George Harrison
Jeff Lynne
Roy Orbison
Tom Petty

Travis
Andy Dunlop – Lead Guitar
Fran Healey – Lead Vocals and Guitar
Douglas Payne – Bass
Neil Primrose – Drums

Tremeloes, The
Alan Blakely – Guitar
Dave Munden – Drums
Len 'Chip' Hawkes – Bass and Vocals
Rick West – Guitar
Formed 1959 and began life as backing group to Brian Poole. Signed by Decca in preference to The Beatles, who auditioned on the same day. When Poole went solo in 1966 they became equally successful in their own right.

T Rex
Miller Anderson – Guitar
Marc Bolan – Guitar and Vocals (died 1977)
Steve Currie – Bass
Dino Dines – Keyboards
Mickey Finn – Drums and Percussion
Herbie Flowers – Bass
Jack Green – Guitar
Gloria Jones – Vocals and Clarinet
Bill Legend – Drums
Dave Lutton – Drums
Tony Newman – Drums
Tyrone Scott – Keyboards
Steve 'Peregrine' Took – Percussion (replaced by Finn in 1969)
Tony Visconti
Formed in 1968 as Tyrannosaurus Rex but shortened to T Rex by the time of their first number one, 'Hot Love', in 1971

Troggs
Ronnie Bond – Drums and Percussion
Chris Britton – Guitar
Reg Presley – Lead Vocals
Peter Staples – Bass

2 Unlimited
Anita Doth (stage name of Anita Dells)
Ray Slijngaard

U2
Adam Clayton
Dave 'The Edge' Evans
Paul 'Bono' Hewson
Larry Mullen Jr

UB40
Astro – Trumpet, Vocals
James Brown – Drums
Ali Campbell – Lead Vocals
Robin Campbell – Guitar and Vocals
Earl Falconer – Bass and Vocals
Norman Hassan – Percussion and Vocals
Martin Meredith – Saxophone and Keyboards
Laurence Parry – Trumpet and Trombone
Brian Travers – Saxophone and Horn
Michael Virtue – Keyboards

Velvet Underground
Willie 'Loco' Alexander – (replaced Lou Reed)
John Cale – Vocals and various stringed instruments
Sterling Morrison – Guitar
Nico – Occasional Lead Singer (died 1988)
Lou Reed – Lead Vocals, Keyboards, Guitar
Maureen Tucker – Vocals, Guitar and Drums
Doug Yule – Vocals and Bass (replaced John Cale)

Vengaboys

DJ Dansky
DJ Delmundo
Denice
Kim
Robin
Roy
Yorick (replaced Robin in 1999)
Formed by Spanish DJs Dansky and Delmundo but
the four singer / dancers from Hungary, Trinidad,
Brazil and Holland became the live performers.
Vengaboys became the first Netherlands-based act
to score six successive Top 5 singles.

Verve

Richard Ashcroft – Lead Vocals and Guitar
Simon Jones – Bass
Nick McCable – Lead Guitar
Peter Salisbury – Drums
Simon Tang – Guitars, Keyboard

Village People

Eric Anzalone – Biker (replaced Glenn Hughes)
Alexander Briley – G.I.
David Hodo – Construction Worker
Glenn Hughes – Biker
Jeff Olson – Cowboy
Felipe Rose – Indian
Ray Simpson – Cop (replaced Victor Willis)
Victor Willis – Cop

Vixen

Janet 'Patricia' Gardner – Vocals
Laurie Hedlund – Drums
Tamara Ivanov – Rhythm Guitar
Pia Koko – Bass
Jan 'Lynn' Kuehnemund – Lead Guitar and Founder
Sharon 'Share' Pederson – Bass
   (replaced Pia Koko)
Maxine Petrucci – Bass (replaced Share Pederson)
Roxy Petrucci – Drums (replaced Laurie Hedlund)
Rana Ross – Bass (replaced Maxine Petrucci)
Gina Stile – Rhythm Guitar
   (replaced Tamara Ivanov)

Wailers

Aston Barrett – Bass, Guitar and Percussion
Carlton Barrett – Drums and Percussion
Tyrone Downie – Bass, Keyboards and Percussion
Bob Marley – Guitar, Percussion and Lead Vocals
   (died in 1981)
Alvin Patterson – Percussion
Earl Smith – Guitar and Percussion
I-Threes – Marcia Griffiths, Rita Marley, Judy Mowati
I-Threes were a vocal trio that backed Marley

Walker Brothers

Scott Engel (assumed the name Scott Walker)
Gary Leeds – Drums
John Maus – Guitar and Vocals
In fact none of the group were brothers or named
Walker

Was (Not Was)

Don Fagenson
David Weiss

Weather Girls

Izora Redman
Martha Wash

Weezer

Brian Bell – Guitar and Vocals
Rivers Cuomo – Lead Vocals and Rhythm Guitar
Matt Sharp – Bass and Vocals
Patrick Wilson – Drums

Westlife

Nicky Byrne
Klan Egan – Piano
Mark Feehily
Shane Filan – Lead Vocals
Bryan McFadden
Only act to reach number one with their first seven
releases, all entered at the top, and only band to
have four number ones in a single year.

Wet Wet Wet

Graeme Clark – Bass and Vocals
Tom Cunningham – Drums
Neil Mitchell – Keyboard and Vocals
Marti Pellow (born Mark McLoughlin) – Lead Vocals

Wham!

George Michael
Andrew Ridgeley

Whitesnake

Tommy Aldridge – Drums
Richard Bailey – Keyboards
Vivian Campbell – Guitar
Denny Carmassi – Drums
David Coverdale – Guitar and Vocals
Warren DeMartini – Guitar
David Dowle – Drums
Aynsley Dumber – Drums
Mel Galley – Guitar
Colin Hodgkinson – Bass
Brian Johnston – Keyboards
Jon Lord – Keyboards
Bernie Marsden – Guitar
Micky Moody – Guitar
Neil Murray – Bass
Ian Paice – Drums
Cozy Powell – Drums
Guy 'Starka' Pratt
Rudy Sarzo – Bass
Rick Serrate – Keyboards
Pete Solley – Keyboards
John Sykes – Guitar
Brett Tuggle – Keyboards
Steve Vai – Guitar
Adrian Vandenberg – Guitar

White Stripes, The

Jack White – Lead Vocals, Guitar and Piano
Meg White – Drums and Vocals

Who, The

Roger Daltrey – Lead Vocals
John Entwistle – Bass, Vocals, Piano and Brass
   (died in 2002)
Kenny Jones – Drums (replaced Keith Moon)
Keith Moon – Drums and Percussion
   (died in 1978)
Pete Townshend – Guitar, Organ, Synthesizer
   and Vocals

Wings

Geoff Britton – Drums
Joe English – Vocals, Drums
   (1975–6 replaced Sewell)
Denny Laine – Vocals, Keyboards, Guitar

Linda McCartney – Vocals, Keyboard (died in 1998)
Paul McCartney – Vocals, Piano, Bass
Jimmy McCulloch – Guitar and Vocals
Denny Sewell – Drums, Percussion and Vocals
(1971–5)

Wizzard
Mike Burney – Saxophone
Charlie Grima – Drums and Percussion
Bill Hunt – Keyboards
Hugh McDowell – Cello
Nick Pentelow – Saxophone
Rick Price – Bass and Vocals
Keith Smart – Drums
Roy Wood – Guitar and Vocals

Wu Tang Clan
Genius
Ghostface Killah
Inspectah Deck
Masta Killa
Method Man
Ol' Dirty Bastard
Raekwon
RZA
U-God

X-Ray Spex
Jak 'Airport' Stafford – Guitar
Paul Dean – Bass
Glyn Johns – Saxophone
Paul 'BP' Hurding – Drums
Lora Logic – Saxophone
Steve 'Rudi' Thompson – Saxophone
Poly Styrene – Vocals

Yardbirds
Jeff Beck – Lead Guitar
(replaced Eric Clapton in 1965)
Eric Clapton – Lead Guitar
(replaced Top Topham in 1963)
Chris Dreja – Guitar
(became bass after Samwell-Smith left)
Jim McCarty – Drums
Jimmy Page – Lead Guitar
(replaced Samwell-Smith in 1966)
Keith Relf – Lead Vocals and Harmonica
Paul Samwell-Smith – Bass
Anthony 'Top' Topham – Lead Guitar

Yazoo
Vince Clarke – Drum Machine, Guitar and Keyboards
Alison 'Alf' Moyet – Vocals

Yes
Jon Anderson – Vocals
(left briefly in 1980 but rejoined 1983)
Peter Banks – Guitar
Bill Bruford – Drums
Geoff Downes – Keyboards
(replaced Rick Wakeman 1980)
Trevor Horn – Guitar and Vocals
(replaced Anderson in 1980)
Steve Howe – Guitar
(replaced Peter Banks in 1970)
Tony Kaye – Organ
(1968–71 and then rejoined in 1983)
Patrick Moraz – Keyboards
(replaced Rick Wakeman 1974)
Trevor Rabin – Guitar joined in 1983)
Chris Squire – Bass
(remained with the band throughout)
Rick Wakeman – Keyboards
(1971–4, rejoined 1976–80)
Alan White – Drums (replaced Bill Bruford in 1972)

Zombies
Rod Argent – Clarinet, Keyboards, Violin and Vocals
Paul Atkinson – Guitar, Violin and Harmonica
Colin Blunstone – Guitar, Percussion and Vocals
Hugh Grundy – Drums
Chris White – Bass and Vocals

Zutons, The
Boyan Chowdhury – Guitar
Abi Harding – Saxophone
David McCabe – Vocals
Sean Payne – Drums
Russell Pritchard – Bass

ZZ Top
Frank Beard – Drums
Billy Gibbons – Vocals, Guitar
Dusty Hill – Bass
Ironically both Dusty Hill and Billy Gibbons sported
beards but Frank Beard was clean-shaven

M
U
S
I
C

P
O
P

General Information

album charts: first No. 1 *South Pacific, Original Soundtrack.*

album charts: started 1958.

album: top selling of 2004 *Scissor Sisters* (by the Scissor Sisters).

best-selling UK single 'Candle in the Wind '97' (by Elton John) sold 4.86 million.

B sides: famous 'I Talk to the Trees' by Clint Eastwood, B side of 'Wand'rin Star'; 'I Do it For You' by Fatima Mansions, B side of 'Theme from Mash' by Manic Street Preachers.

bongo player on 'Apache' Cliff Richard.

Booker T. and the M.G.s MG stands for Memphis Group.

charts: symbol indicating rise or fall Bullet.

cover crowd: 'Ferry 'Cross the Mersey' Christians,

Holly Johnson, Paul McCartney, Gerry Marsden and Stock Aitken Waterman.

David Bowie First TV appearance on *Gadzooks! It's All Happening* in 1965 with the Manish Boys who were nearly banned because of the length of Bowie's hair. Other groups he formed included King Bees, Kon-Rads, Feathers, Hype, and the Lower Third.

download chart 'Flying Without Wings' by Westlife was No. 1 in the first official download chart, announced on BBC Radio 1 on 1 September 2004.

Five Star: family name Pearson.

Madonna: father of children Carlos Leon, actor and personal trainer, Guy Ritchie, film director (husband).

missing star Richey Edwards of Manic Street Preachers went missing in 1995.

Monkees Advertisement in the Los Angeles *Daily Vanity* in September 1965 by Bob Rafelson and Bert Schneider led to the formation of the band. Of the 437 hopefuls who were auditioned, Stephen Stills, Charles Manson and Danny Hutton (later of Three Dog Night) were among those turned down.

most weeks on LP charts *Bat Out of Hell* (472 weeks to date but only reached No. 9).

No. 1 in LP charts throughout year *South Pacific, Original Soundtrack* (1959).

pop star thrown off plane in Germany Keith Flint of Prodigy.

single charts: first No. 1 'Here in My Heart' by Al Martino (November 1952).

single charts: started 14 November 1952 (12 records).

single: wrong name on label 'Elizabethan Reggae' by Boris Gardiner originally had 'Byron Lee' on label.

Spice Girls: nicknames Emma Bunton – Baby Spice, Mel Brown – Scary Spice, Mel Chisholm –

Sporty Spice, Victoria Adams – Posh Spice, Geri Halliwell – Ginger Spice.

Spice Girls: No. 1s Four of the five original members have had solo No. 1s, although Victoria Beckham's highest chart entry is at number two.

That's What Friends Are For Dionne Warwick and Friends featuring Elton John, Stevie Wonder and Gladys Knight.

1000th No. 1 'One Night' / 'I Got Stung' double A-side for Elvis Presley. Also became his 20th No. 1.

Top of the Pops: theme tunes 'Whole Lotta Love', 'Yellow Pearl' (Phil Lynott), 'The Wizard' (Paul Hardcastle), 'Get out of That' (Tony Gibber).

Vice-President of USA wrote: No. 1 Hit Charles Dawes adapted his 'Melodie' with Carl Sigman, which became 'It's all in the game'.

Vince Clarke: bands involved with Depeche Mode, Yazoo (with Alison Moyet) and Erasure (with Andy Bell).

Westlife: No. 1s First seven records all reached No. 1.

Previous Names of Groups

The Alarm Toilets, 17
America Daze
Applejacks Jaguars, Crestas
Badfinger Iveys
Bangles Supersonic Bangs, The Bangs
Bauhaus Bauhaus 1919
Beach Boys Carl and the Passions
Beatles Silver Beatles, Quarrymen, Beatals, Beat Brothers
Black Sabbath Earth
Boomtown Rats Nightlife Thugs
The Christians Natural High
The Commodores Mighty Mystics
The Cult Southern Death Cult
Culture Club In Praise of Lemmings, Sex Gang Children
The Cure The Easy Cure
Deep Purple Roundabout
Depeche Mode Composition of Sound
Dire Straits Cafe Racers
Doobie Brothers Pud
Dr Hook Chocolate Papers
Eurythmics The Catch, Tourists
Faces Quiet Melon, Small Faces
Family Farinas
Fifth Dimension Versatiles
The Fixx Portraits, The Fix
The Fourmost Blue Jays, Four Jays
The Four Seasons Variatones, Four Lovers
The Four Tops Four Aims
Frankie Goes to Hollywood Hollycaust
Freddie and the Dreamers Kingfishers
Genesis Garden Wall
Gerry and the Pacemakers Mars Bars
The Grateful Dead Warlocks
Herman's Hermits Heartbeats
Hollies Fourtones, Deltas
Human League Dead Daughters, Future
Icehouse Flowers
INXS Farriss Brothers

Led Zeppelin New Yardbirds, Birmingham Water Buffalo Society
Madness The Invaders
Mamas and the Papas The New Journeymen, Mugwumps
Manfred Mann Mann-Hugg Blues Brothers
Marillion Silmarillion
The Mission Sisters of Mercy
Mothers of Invention Muthers, Mothers
Mott the Hoople Silence
New Order Joy Division
Orchestral Manoeuvres in the Dark (OMD) VCL XL
Pogo Poco
Pogues Pogue Mahone
Procol Harum Paramounts
Righteous Brothers Paramours
Shadows Drifters
Simon and Garfunkel Tom and Jerry
Simply Red Frantic Elevators
Slade Ambrose Slade, 'N' Betweens
Sonny and Cher Caesar and Cleo
Spice Girls Touch (without Emma Bunton)
Split Enz Split Ends
Starship Jefferson Airplane, Jefferson Starship
Status Quo Spectres, Traffic Jam
Stone Roses Patrol, English Rose
Stranglers Guildford Stranglers
Strawbs Strawberry Hill Boys
Supremes Primettes
Sweet Wainwright's Gentlemen, Sweetshop
Swinging Blue Jeans Bluegenes
Talking Heads Portable Crushers, Vague Dots
Ten Years After Jaybirds
T Rex Tyrannosaurus Rex
Ultravox Zips, Innocents, London Soundtrack, Fire of London
Wham Executive (Paul Ridgeley and David Mortimer in line-up)
The Who High Numbers

MYTHOLOGY AND LEGEND

Deities

Role	Greek	Roman	Egyptian	Norse	Sumerian
Principal god	Zeus	Jupiter	Am(m)on	Odin	An
Principal goddess	Hera	Juno	Mut	Frigg	Inanna
Messenger of the gods	Hermes	Mercury	Thoth	Hermod	Uncertain
God of agriculture	Cronus	Saturn	Osiris	Uncertain	Emesh
Goddess of agriculture	Demeter	Ceres	Renenutet	Rindr	Nisaba
Goddess of childbirth	Eileithyia	Juno	Apet	Uncertain	Ninhursaga
Goddess of the dawn	Eos	Aurora	Uncertain	Uncertain	Anahita
God of the dead	Thanatos	Mors	Anubis	Odin	Nergal
Goddess of death	Hecate	Libitina	Nephthys	Hel	Uncertain
God of destruction	Ares	Mars	Seth	Uncertain	Uncertain
God of dreams	Morpheus	Morpheus	Uncertain	Uncertain	Uncertain
God of the Earth	Aesculapius	Aesculapius	Geb	Uncertain	Uncertain
Goddess of the Earth	Gaia	Tellus	Maat	Nerthus	Ki
God of fertility	Priapus	Faunus	Ing	Frey	Ninurta
Goddess of fertility	Artemis	Diana	Bastet	Gefjon	Inanna
God of fire	Hephaestus	Vulcan	Ptah	Loki	Gerra
Goddess of flowers	Hestia	Flora	Qudshu	Nanna	Uncertain
Goddess of health	Hygeia	Salus	Meresger	Uncertain	Nininsina Dazimus
Goddess of the hearth	Hestia	Vesta	Uncertain	Sigyn	Uncertain
God of heaven	Zeus	Jupiter	Ptah	Uncertain	An
Goddess of the hunt	Artemis	Diana	Neith	Skadi	Uncertain
Goddess of justice	Themis	Uncertain	Maat	Forseti	Uncertain
God of love	Eros	Cupid	Uncertain	Uncertain	Uncertain
Goddess of love	Aphrodite	Venus	Hathor	Freya	Inanna
Goddess of magic/ witchcraft	Hecate	Uncertain	Isis	Uncertain	Uncertain
God of marriage	Hymen	Hymen	Bes	Uncertain	Uncertain
God of the Moon	Apollo	Apollo	Neferhotep	Uncertain	Nanna
Goddess of the Moon	Selene	Luna	Isis	Mani	Ningal
Goddess of motherhood	Rhea	Ops	Taweret	Uncertain	Uncertain
God of music	Apollo	Apollo	Uncertain	Bragi	Uncertain
Goddess of night	Nyx	Uncertain	Nephthys	Nott	Uncertain
Goddess of peace	Irene	Pax	Uncertain	Uncertain	Uncertain
God of poetry	Apollo	Apollo	Thoth	Odin/Bragi	Uncertain
Goddess of the rainbow	Iris	Uncertain	Uncertain	Uncertain	Uncertain
God of the sea	Poseidon	Neptune	Nun	Aegir/Njord	Apsu
Goddess of the sea	Amphitrite	Salacia	Tefenet	Ran	Nammu
God of the sky	Uranus	Jupiter	Uncertain	Odin	An
Goddess of the sky	Hera	Juno	Nut	Uncertain	Inanna
God of sleep	Hypnos	Somnus	Uncertain	Uncertain	Uncertain
Goddess of spring	Persephone	Proserpine	Renpet	Uncertain	Ninkasi
God of the sun	Helios	Sol	Ra (Re)	Sol	Utu
God of thunder	Hephaestus	Jupiter	Seth	Thor	Adad
Goddess of truth	Themis	Justitia	Maat	Uncertain	Uncertain
God of the Underworld	Pluto/Hades	Orcus/Dis	Osiris	Villi	Endugukka
Goddess of the Underworld	Hecate	Proserpine	Hathor	Hel	Ereshkigal
Goddess of victory	Nike	Victoria	Apet	Uncertain	Uncertain
God of war	Ares	Mars	Seth	Tyr/Odin	Ninurta
Goddess of war	Athene	Minerva	Sekhmet	Uncertain	Inanna
God of water	Ganymede	Uncertain	Hapi	Uncertain	Enki
God of wine	Dionysus	Bacchus/Liber	Bes	Uncertain	Uncertain
God of wisdom	Apollo	Apollo	Thoth	Odin	Enki
Goddess of wisdom	Athene	Minerva	Neith	Uncertain	Hea
God of woods	Pan	Silvanus	Min	Uncertain	Ashnan
Goddess of youth	Hebe	Juventas	Renpet	Uncertain	Uncertain

Deities of Other Mythologies

Role	Babylonian	Hindu	Phoenician	Celtic	Aztec
King of the gods	Marduk	Indra	Kumarbi/El	Dagda	Tezcatlipoca
God of agriculture	Tammuz	Sita	Telepinu	Amaethon	Centeotl
Goddess of childbirth	Uncertain	Shashti	Ashtaroth	Brigit	Chihuacoatl
Goddess of the dawn	Aja	Ushas	Shachar	Uncertain	Uncertain
God of the Dead	Uncertain	Yama	Mot	Dagda	Mictlantecuhtli
Goddess of death	Uncertain	Kali	Uncertain	Morrígan	Mictlantecuhtli
God of destruction	Uncertain	Shiva	Uncertain	Balor	Itzlacoliuhqui
God of the Earth	Apsu	Uncertain	Uncertain	Dagda	Ometecuhtli
Goddess of the Earth	Tiamat	Pitthivi	Beruth	Danu	Coatlicue
God of fertility	Hadad	Dyaus	Baal	Cernunnos	Tlaloc
Goddess of fertility	Ishtar	Prithivi	Anath/Astarte	Danu	Chalchiuhtlicue
God of fire	Uncertain	Agni	Uncertain	Belenus	Xiuhtecuhtli
Goddess of flowers	Uncertain	Uncertain	Uncertain	Olwen	Xochiquetzal
God of heaven	Apsu	Dyaus	Anu	Uncertain	Ometeotl
Goddess of the hunt	Uncertain	Minakshi	Uncertain	Abnoba	Uncertain
God of love	Uncertain	Kama	Uncertain	Angus	Huehuecoyotl
Goddess of love	Ishtar	Rati	Astarte	Aine	Xochiquetzal
Goddess of magic/witchcraft	Uncertain	Dursa	Kamrusepa	Bodhbh	Malinalxochi
God of the Moon	Sin	Chandra	Yarikh	Uncertain	Uncertain
Goddess of the Moon	Anunitu	Candi	Nikkal	Arianrhod	Coyolxauhqui
Goddess of motherhood	Nintur	Devi	Hannahanna	Danu	Chalchiuhtlicue
God of music	Uncertain	Uncertain	Uncertain	Maponus	Macuilxochitl
Goddess of night	Uncertain	Ratri	Shalim	Uncertain	Itzlacoliuhqui
God of poetry	Uncertain	Uncertain	Uncertain	Ogma	Huitzilopochtli
God of the sea	Uncertain	Varuna	Yamm	Manannan	Uncertain
Goddess of the sea	Tiamat	Uncertain	Asherat	Don	Chalchiuhtlicue
God of the sky	Anu	Dyaus	Teshub	Camulus	Tlaloc
Goddess of the sky	Tiamat	Aditi	Shapash	Don	Uncertain
God of the sun	Shamash	Surya	Nergal	Lug	Tonatiuh
God of thunder	Hadad	Indra	Taru	Taranis	Tlaloc
God of war	Uncertain	Karttikeya	Astabis	Uncertain	Huitzilopochtli
Goddess of war	Ishtar	Durga	Astarte	Morrígan	Clhvacoatl
God of water	Ea	Varuna	Uncertain	Nechtan	Tlaloc
God of wine	Uncertain	Uncertain	Uncertain	Uncertain	Tepoztecatl
God of wisdom	Ea	Ganes(h)a	Uncertain	Uncertain	Uncertain
Goddess of wisdom	Uncertain	Uncertain	Uncertain	Sul	Uncertain

NB: There are a number of points that should be borne in mind when studying the above tables.

First, it should be remembered that in many instances there would be more than one representation of a god for a particular subject. For example, as well as Aegir, both Njord and Vili are often described as Norse gods of the sea. In all cases I have listed the main god who is usually identified with the subject.

Second, there is often a transposition of gods in some mythologies, and in particular the Middle East should be treated with some care. Babylonian mythology is often called Assyrian, Akkadian or Persian, while Phoenician can also be called Hittite as well as Assyrian and Akkadian.

Third, where there is controversy over an entry or there is no god who represents a subject, the word 'Uncertain' has been entered; this does not mean, for instance, that there was no Egyptian god of love but merely that there is not a single god who unequivocally fits the criteria of being both universally accepted and identifiable.

Groups

Muses (9)	of	Literal meaning	Pleiades (7)	7 against Thebes
Thalia	Comedy	Good cheer/plenty	Maia	Polynices
Clio	History	Fame	Taygete	Tydeus
Melpomene	Tragedy	Singing	Elektra	Adrastus
Urania	Astronomy	Celestial	Alkyone	Capaneus
Polyhymnia	Song and mime	Many songs	Asterope	Hippomedon
Erato	Love poetry	Lovely	Kelaino	Parthenopaeus
Euterpe	Lyric poetry	Joy	Merope	Amphiarus
Calliope	Epic poetry	Beautiful voice		
Terpsichore	Dance	Joyful dance		

Sages of India (7)

Atri
Bharadvaja
Gautama
Jamadagni
Kashyapa
Vasistha
Vishvamitra

Hills of Rome (7)

Capitoline
Quirinal
Viminal
Esquiline
Caelian
Aventine
Palatine

> Useful mnemonic:
> Can Queen Victoria Eat
> Cold Apple Pie?

Titans (12)

Brontes
Atlas
Astraeus
Cronus
Hyperion
Oceanus
Phoebe
Coeus
Helios
Arges
Rhea
Thema

> Useful mnemonic:
> BAA CHOP CHART

Underworld Rivers (5)

Cocytus (wailing)
Lethe (forgetfulness)
Acheron (grief)
Styx (hate)
Phlegethon (fire)

> Useful mnemonic:
> CLASP

Furies (3) (Erinyes or Eumenides)

Tisiphone (avenger of
murder)
Alecto (relentless)
Megaera (resentful)

> Useful mnemonic:
> Furies aren't TAMe

Graces (3) (Charites)

Euphrosyne (good cheer)
Aglaia (splendour or
bright one)
Thaleia (jollity)

> Useful mnemonic:
> Say Grace before you
> EAT

Fates (3) (Moerae)

Clotho (spun the thread of
life)
Atropos (cut off the thread
of life)
Lachesis (measured out
the thread of life)

> Useful mnemonic:
> CALI the fates in times
> of trouble

Gorgons (3)

Medusa
Euryale
Stheno

> Useful mnemonic:
> Medusa's hair was a
> MESs

Twelve Labours of Heracles

The killing of the Nemean lion Heracles beat the lion senseless and throttled it; he then skinned the lion with its own claws and donned the pelt to render himself invulnerable.

The killing of the Lernaean Hydra Iolaus cauterised the neck of the Hydra to prevent the two new heads growing each time that Heracles chopped off one of its nine heads.

The capture of the Hind on Mt Ceryneia Heracles chased the Hind for a year, for its golden horns and bronze hoofs. He blamed Eurystheus for its capture so as not to bring the wrath of Artemis on himself.

The capture of the Boar of Mt Erymanthus Heracles returned with the Boar to Tiryns, and Eurystheus hid in an urn at the sight of it.

The cleansing of the Augean stables Heracles cleaned the stables, which had not been cleaned in 30 years, by diverting the rivers Alpheus and Peneus through them.

The killing of the Birds of Lake Stymphalos Heracles scared the Birds from the trees with bronze castanets and shot them with arrows one by one.

The capture of the Cretan Bull Heracles captured the Bull and returned it to Greece.

The capture of the Mares of Diomedes Heracles slew Diomedes, fed him to the Mares and tamed them.

The capture of the Girdle of Hippolyte Heracles slew the queen of the Amazons and took the Girdle for Eurystheus' daughter.

The capture of Geryon's Cattle Heracles slew Geryon and returned to Greece with the Cattle.

The capture of the Apples of the Hesperides Heracles slew Ladon, the dragon that guarded the tree tended by the Hesperides, and took the Golden Apples (later returned by Athene).

The capture of Cerberus Heracles entered the underworld to capture the 3-headed dog.

General Information

Abderus Friend of Heracles in whose care Heracles left the mares of Diomedes. The horses ate him and Heracles founded a town in Thrace in his honour.

Abnoba The goddess of the hunt in the mythology of Gaul. Identified with the Roman Diana.

Acheloüs Greek river god, the son of Oceanus and Tethys.

Achilles Greek hero, born in Thessaly, son of Peleus and the goddess Thetis. When he was a baby his mother dipped him in the Styx, making him invulnerable save for his right heel, by which she held him.

Actaeon Greek hero, grandson of Cadmus, changed into a stag by Artemis and killed by his own hounds because he spied her bathing.

Admetus In Greek mythology the king of Pherae in Thessaly. Apollo served him for a year and introduced him to Alcestis.

Adonis Syrian god, the son of Myrrha and her father Cinyras. He was born from the bark of a tree and brought up by Persephone and forced to spend a third of his time with her and a third with Aphrodite. He was mortally wounded by a wild boar sent by a hostile god or goddess.

MYTHOLOGY AND LEGEND

Aeacus Son of Zeus and Aegina and king of the Myrmidones. The Myrmidones were originally ants, transformed into men by Zeus at the request of Aeacus. He had two sons, Peleus and Telamon, by his wife Endeis and was also the father of Phocus by a Nereid. Aeacus was one of the three judges of the Underworld.

Aeëtes In Greek mythology, the king of Colchis and possessor of the Golden Fleece sought by Jason.

Aegeus Greek king of Athens and father of Theseus by Aethra, daughter of Pittheus, king of Troezen. Aethra brought Theseus up secretly at her father's court, during which time Aegeus married Medea. When Theseus finally returned to his father's court, Medea fled. Before Theseus went to slay the Minotaur he and Aegeus agreed that he would hoist a white sail when returning to Athens to signal his success. On returning, Theseus forgot to do this and Aegeus, seeing a black sail on his son's ship, supposed him dead and, in grief, threw himself into the sea, henceforth called the Aegean.

Aegisthus In Greek mythology the seducer of Clytemnestra, the wife of his cousin Agamemnon, whom the two lovers conspired to kill. Agamemnon's son Orestes avenged the assassination by killing Aegisthus and Clytemnestra.

Aeneas Trojan hero, son of Aphrodite and Anchises, bravest of the Trojans after Hector and, according to some Roman lines of mythology, the founder of Rome. Aeneas was the lover of Dido, queen of Carthage.

Aeneid Virgil's unfinished epic poem in 12 volumes recounting the deeds of Aeneas, supposed ancestor of Emperor Augustus of Rome. The epic begins after the fall of Troy and ends with the defeat of Turnus the Rutulian prince and the subsequent marriage of Aeneas and Lavinia, the Latin princess.

Aeolus Greek god of the winds and son of Poseidon who gave Odysseus a sack containing all the winds.

Aesculapius Roman god of medicine. Greek counterpart is Asclepius.

Aesir Norse race of warlike gods, who lived in Asgardthey included Odin, Thor, Tyr, Baldu and Frigg (see Vanir).

Aetolus Conqueror of Aetolia. The son of Endymion, king of Elis, he was banished across the Corinthian Gulf after accidentally killing Apis in a chariot race.

Agamemnon Greek king of Argos, murdered by his wife Clytemnestra.

Aganippe Fountain at the foot of Mt Helicon, sacred to the Muses, who are sometimes called the Aganippides.

Ajax (the greater) Greek hero, a giant of a man, the son of Telamon. Killed himself in fury at not receiving Achille's armour after his death.

Ajax (the lesser) Greek hero, son of Oileus. Raped King Priam's daughter Cassandra on the altar of Athene.

Alcestis Greek heroine who saved her husband Admetus by offering her own life.

Alcheringa According to Australian aboriginal mythology, the Golden Age when the first ancestors were created.

Alcides Another name for Heracles, whose grandfather was reputed to be Alcaeus.

Alcmene Wife of Amphitrion, son of Alcaeus. Alcmene mothered Heracles by Zeus in the guise of her husband. Married Rhadamanthus after Amphitrion's death.

Alphito Greek barley goddess of Argos.

Amalthea She-goat. Zeus broke off one of Amalthea's horns to make the Cornucopia (Horn of Plenty).

Amazons Warrior women of Greek mythology who removed a breast to give free play to bow arm.

Amphitrion In Greek mythology king of Tiryns and husband of Alcmene.

Amphitrite Daughter of Nereus, leader of the Nereids. Mothered Triton by Poseidon.

Anchises According to Greek and Roman mythology, the Trojan father of Aeneas by Aphrodite.

Androcles Roman slave who aided and befriended a lion that later saved his life when he was thrown to the lions for attempting to escape.

Andromache In Greek mythology, the wife of Hector and slave of Neoptolemus.

Andromeda According to Greek mythology, daughter of king Cepheus and queen Cassiopeia; she was rescued by Perseus from a sea-monster and subsequently married him.

Angels Nine choirs divided into three ranks: Seraphim, Cherubim and Thrones; Dominions, Powers and Virtues; Principalities, Archangels and Angels.

Antaeus Libyan giant, son of Poseidon and Ge, who was an invincible wrestler until Hercules – realising he drew his strength from his mother, Earth – held him in the air and squeezed him to death.

Antigone In Greek mythology the daughter of Oedipus and Jocasta and sister of Ismene.

Anubis Egyptian god who guides souls to the world beyond. Often depicted with the head of a jackal.

Aphrodite Greek goddess of love and beauty and wife of Hephaestus.

Apis In Egyptian mythology, the sacred bull of Memphis, seen as an incarnation of Osiris.

Apollo Greek and Roman god of prophecy, music, youth, archery and healing, and son of Zeus and Leto (Jupiter and Latona in Roman myth).

Arachne According to Greek mythology, a weaver from Lydia who was changed into a spider by Athena.

Ares Greek god of war, son of Zeus and Hera and lover of Aphrodite.

Arethusa Greek goddess of springs and fountains.

Argo The 50-oared longship which carried Jason and the Argonauts to Colchis in their quest for the Golden Fleece.

Argonauts The band of heroes chosen by Jason to man the Argo and sail in search of the Golden Fleece. The Argonauts included Argus, Atalanta, Calais, Castor and Polydeuces, Heracles, Meleager, Orpheus, Peleus, Telamon and Zetes.

Argus (1) Greek watchman with 100 eyes who watched over Io but was killed by Hermes. His eyes were placed in the peacock's tail by Hera. (2) The faithful hound of Odysseus/Ulysses. (3) The builder of the Argo.

Ariadne In Greek mythology, the daughter of King Minos of Crete and wife of Dionysus after Theseus abandoned her.

Arjuna The Hindu god of dawn and charioteer of the sun, often identified with the Greek and Roman goddesses Eos and Aurora. Ajuna was also known as Rumra (lit. rosy).

Artemis Greek goddess of fertility and the hunt, daughter of Zeus and Leto and twin sister of Apollo.

Arthur Legendary British king, son of Uther Pendragon and Igraine, said to have lived in the 6th century. He was born in Tintagel and buried in Glastonbury; Arthur's court was at Camelot (Winchester, according to Malory's *Morte d'Arthur*).

Aruru One of the names of the Sumerian goddess of childbirth, Ninhursaga (lit. germ loosener).

Asclepius Greek god of healing.

Asgard In Norse mythology the realm of the gods in heaven and connected to the earth by the rainbow bridge, Bifrost, which was guarded by Heimdall.

Ask In Norse mythtology the ash tree from which man was hewn.

Asphodel, Plain of That part of Hades reserved for the great proportion of the dead. There they continued a shadowy existence in continuance of their former lives since they were bodiless. Contrast Elysium and Tartarus.

Ataentsic According to Iroquois and Huron mythology, the first woman and ancestor of the human race.

Atalanta Greek heroine who refused to marry any man unless he could beat her in a foot race. Milanion became her husband after Aphrodite helped him defeat her. Atalanta was the sole female Argonaut.

Aten Egyptian god; took the form of a solar disc.

Athene According to Greek mythology, the daughter of Zeus and Metis who sprang from her father's head fully armed. Among her titles was Parthenos (Virgin), from which the Parthenon was named.

Atlas Titan that bears up the earth. Son of Iapetus and Clymene and brother of Prometheus.

Attis Greek god of vegetation.

Autolycus Son of Hermes and Chione and grandfather of Odysseus.

Baba Yaga Witch or ogress in Slav mythology.

Bacchae Female followers of the cult of Bacchus or Dionysus.

Bacchus Roman mythological counterpart of the Greek Dionysus, god of wine and ecstasy.

Baldur Norse favourite of the gods and son of Odin and Frigg. Baldur was invulnerable to everything except mistletoe, and Loki tricked the blind god Hoder into throwing a mistletoe dart that killed him.

Balmung Siegfried's sword, according to the *Nibelungenlied*.

Basilisk Greek monster also called a Cockatrice, that killed with a stare.

Bastet According to Egyptian mythology, the cat-headed goddess of fertility, love and sex.

Befana Good fairy of Italian children who is supposed to fill their stockings with toys on Twelfth Night.

Belenus The Celtic god of healing and light, referred to as 'The Shining One'. He was in charge of the welfare of sheep and cattle. His wife is the goddess Belisama; they are often compared to the Roman Apollo and Minerva.

Bellerophon Greek hero who tamed Pegasus and killed the Chimera.

Bellona Greek goddess of war.

Beowulf Norse warrior prince who killed the man-eating monster Grendel in a wrestling match.

Bifrost In Norse mythology, the rainbow bridge that led from Asgard to Earth. Literally means quivering path.

Biton and Cleobis Sons of a priestess of Hera in Argos who drew their mother's chariot several miles to the goddess's temple when no oxen could be found.

Bor (Burr) Norse god who married the giantess Bestla. She bore him three sons, Odin, Villi and Vé.

Boreas Greek god of the north wind.

Bragi Norse god of poetry and music, son of Odin.

Briareus One of the Hecatoncheires. Aka Aegaeon.

Brigit Celtic goddess of the poetic arts, childbirth and divination.

Bunyip In Australian aboriginal mythology, monster who was the source of evil.

Cadmus In Greek mythology, the son of Agenor, king of Phoenicia and grandson of Poseidon. When Zeus carried off his sister Europa, he went to look for her but was told by the Delphic oracle to relinquish the search and to follow a magical cow. Where the cow lay down he was to found a city, the future city of Thebes. Cadmus married Harmonia.

Caishen Chinese god of wealth.

Calais Twin brother of Zetes. The winged sons of Boreas and Oreithyia, they accompanied the Argonauts and drove off the Harpies.

Calchas Renegade Trojan seer who helped the Greeks at Troy and foretold that Troy would not fall without Achilles' presence and that the sacrifice of Iphigenia was necessary to secure a favourable wind.

Callisto Daughter of Lycaon, who became one of Artemis's huntresses. She bore Arcas to Zeus, who sought to conceal their affair from his wife Hera by turning Callisto into a bear.

Calypso (Hidden) Nymph of the island of Ogygia who tended Odysseus there for 8 years until Zeus ordered him home to Ithaca.

Cassandra Greek heroine given the gift of prophecy by Apollo with the proviso that, although telling the truth, she would not be believed.

Cassiopeia Wife of Cepheus and mother of Andromeda.

Castor and Pollux Roman counterpart of Castor and Polydeuces.

Castor and Polydeuces Aka the Dioscuri, sons of Zeus and Leda. Castor was an expert horseman and Polydeuces was the best boxer in Greece. Some versions have the mortal Castor as son of Tyndareus (Leda lay with both Zeus and Tyndareus). They were transformed into the Gemini constellation

Centaur In Greek mythology the hybrid offspring of

MYTHOLOGY AND LEGEND

Centaurus, son of Ixion, and the mares of Mt Pelion in Thessaly.

Cepheus In Greek mythology, the husband of Cassiopeia and father of Andromeda.

Cerberus According to Greek mythology, the three-headed dog that guards the entrance to the Underworld. Offspring of Echidna and Typhon.

Chac Maya god of rain and lightening.

Chaos In Greek creation myth, Chaos was the infinite space existing before creation, from which Ge (the Earth) sprang.

Charon According to Greek mythology, the ferryman of the underworld. Offspring of Erebos and Nyx. Greeks to this day place a coin in the mouth of corpses to pay for the ferry charge.

Charybdis Greek mythological monster resembling a giant whirlpool which infested the Strait of Messina together with Scylla.

Chimera Greek monster with the head of lion, the body of a goat and the tail of a serpent. Offspring of Echidna and Typhon.

Chiron Centaur who was untypically wise and civilised. When Chiron died he became the constellation Sagittarius.

Circe Greek sorceress who turned Odysseus's men into swine. Daughter of Helios and Perse.

Clytemnestra Greek twin sister of Helen and wife of Agamemnon.

Conán the Bald According to Celtic mythology, a warrior and follower of the hero Finn Mac Cumhall. Conán was the son of Morna and brother of Goll.

Conchobar Celtic king of Ulster and illegitimate son of Nessa, queen of Ulster, and the druid Cathbhadh.

Consus Roman god of seed sowing.

Cressida According to Greek mythology, she deserted Troilus, a Trojan prince, for Diomedes.

Cretan bull Magnificent white bull sent by Poseidon to Minos for sacrifice. Minos's wife Pasiphaë so admired the bull that she had Daedalus construct a hollow cow for her to get inside and mate with the bull – that was how she came to bear the Minotaur. The bull was captured by Heracles, freed by Eurystheus and finally recaptured by Theseus at Marathon and sacrificed to Athene.

Croesus Last king of Lydia, famous for his vast wealth.

Cronus Greek god of agriculture and father of Zeus.

Cuchulainn In Celtic mythology the legendary Irish hero, called the 'Hound of Culann' because, having accidentally slain the watchdog of the smith, Culann, he subsequently took the animal's place as penance. He was brought up in the court of King Conchobar of Ulster, whose kingdom he defended against all invaders. Cuchulainn's parents were the sun god Lug, and Dechtire, the wife of an Ulster chieftain. Although Cuchulainn was a handsome youth, in battle he would turn into a frenzied monster, with one eye receding into his head while the other stood out huge and red on his cheek. Cuchulainn's wife was Emer, daughter of the chieftain Forgall. Women continued to fall in love with Cuchulainn after his marriage, and his eventual death was as a result of rebuffing the war goddess Morrigan, who assaulted him with innumerable foes.

Cupay In the mythology of the Peruvian Inca people, the god of death. He is sometimes known as Supay.

Cybele Greek goddess of the earth and lover of Attis.

Cyclops One-eyed giants descended from Gaia and Uranus. Polyphemus is most famous for his capture of Odysseus, who blinded him.

Daedalus In Greek mythology the greatest of mortal craftsmen who made wings out of wax and feathers for himself and his son Icarus to escape imprisonment in the Cretan labyrinth. However, Icarus flew too near the sun and fell to his death when the wax melted.

Damocles Member of the court of Dionysius I, tyrant of Syracuse. Cicero tells how the tyrant had him eat a sumptuous dinner while a sword was suspended by a hair over his head, to show him the limits of rank and power.

Danu (Dana) The Celtic earth-mother goddess, also identified with fertility, wisdom and the wind. In Welsh versions she is known as Don and is associated with the air and the sea.

Daphne Greek heroine turned into a laurel bush to evade Apollo.

Daphnis Son of Hermes and a nymph. The originator of pastoral poetry.

Deianeira Greek princess, the daughter of King Oenus and Queen Althaea of Aetolia, and the second wife of Heracles, whom she killed by mistake when she smeared his garment with a centaur's poisonous blood, thinking it was a love charm.

Deidamia Maiden who fell in love with Achilles and bore him Neoptolemus.

Deirdre According to Irish legend, she killed herself after being forced to marry King Conchobar.

Delphi Site of Apollo's Dorian shrine and oracle, the most famous centre of his worship.

Deucalion Greek hero, son of Prometheus, who repopulated the earth with his wife Pyrrha after Zeus's flood.

Devi (Mahadevi) In Hindu mythology the wife of S(h)iva. Originally there were several goddesses acknowledged as the wives of S(h)iva by different Hindu castes, but eventually they merged into the one manifestation, Devi. Other forms of Devi include, Bhairavi, Chandi, Durga, Gauri (Jagadgauri), Jaganmata, Kali, Parvati, Sati and Uma.

Dian-Cecht The Celtic god of medicine and healing, and the grandfather of the sun god Lug.

Dido Greek heroine, daughter of the King of Tyre, who founded Carthage. Virgil told of her suicide when abandoned by her lover, Aeneas.

Dioscuri (sons of Zeus) Zeus had intercourse with Leda in the form of a swan and she produced two eggs. From one came Castor and Clytemnestra and from the other came Polydeuces and Helen.

Draupnir Odin's magic ring.

Dryad In classical mythology a tree-nymph, sometimes called a hamadryad, which was supposed to die when the tree died. Oak trees were usually favoured by dryads.

Durga In Hindu mythola a fierce form of Devi who was born fully grown and beautiful; she was immediately armed by the gods and sent forth against the buffalo demon Mahisha. Although blessed with beautiful golden skin, Durga had a fixed, menacing expression and rode upon a tiger. In each of her 10 hands she held one of the god's weapons, i.e. Agni's flaming dart, Indra's thunderbolt, Kubera's club, Shesha's garland of snakes, S(h)iva's trident, Surya's quiver and arrow, Varuna's conch shell, Vayu's bow, Vishnu's discus and Yama's iron rod.

Echidna In Greek mythology, she was the offspring of the earth goddess Gaia and her brother Tartarus. Echidna had the upper body of a nymph and the lower body of a serpent.

Echo Greek nymph who pined away till she was only a voice for the love of Narcissus.

Edda Norse collection of mythological and heroic lays. Also the title of a manual of mythology compiled by the Icelandic historian Snorri Sturluson (1178–1241).

Egeria Roman goddess of fountains and childbirth.

Electra Daughter of Agamemnon and Clytemnestra, and sister of Orestes and Iphegenia.

Electryon Son of Perseus and Andromeda, king of Mycenae and father of Alcmene, the wife of Amphitrion.

Elysian Fields (Elysium) Greek mythological paradise to which the great and virtuous went after death.

Embla In Norse mythology the elm tree from which woman was hewn.

Endymion King of Elis who was visited by Selene while sleeping in a cave and forced into an endless sleep so she could admire his beauty.

Enlil In Sumerian mythology one of the triad of creator-gods with Enki and An.

Epeius Cowardly son of Panopeus who built the Trojan horse.

Epigoni Greek sons of the 7 against Thebes who succeeded in destroying the city.

Epimetheus In Greek mythology, the brother of Prometheus and husband of Pandora.

Epona Roman goddess of horses.

Erebus (Darkness) Son of Chaos and father of Aether and Hemera by Night, his sister.

Eros (Desire) Greek god of love, the offspring of Aphrodite and Ares.

Eshmun The Phoenician god of healing, identified with the Greek Asclepius and Roman Aesculapius.

Europa According to Greek mythology, the daughter of King Agenor and Queen Telephassa of Phoenicia. Zeus wooed Europa as a bull and had intercourse with her in the guise of an eagle. She bore him three sons: Minos, Rhadamanthus and Sarpedon. Europa married the Cretan king Asterius.

Eurus South-east wind, son of Astraeus and Eos.

Eurydice Greek dryad, wife of Orpheus. She was lost forever after Orpheus looked back to make sure she was following as he led her out of Hades.

Eurystheus King of the Argolid region of the Peloponnese, son of King Sthenelus and Queen Nicippe of Mycenae. Heracles was sentenced to serve him for 12 years as penance for killing his wife, Megara. Eurystheus subsequently set him the twelve labours.

Fafnir In Germanic mythology a dragon who guarded the Nibelung hoard of treasure.

Fauna Roman goddess of fertility.

Faunus Roman god of crops, herds and woodlands.

Fenrir In Norse mythology a monstrous wolf who was the offspring of Loki.

Ferghus Irish hero of superhuman size and strength. King of Ulster before Conchobar, Ferghus was the lover of Nessa, the mother of Conchobar.

Feronia Roman goddess of spring flowers.

Fides Roman god of honesty.

Finn mac Cumhal Irish hero who possessed the gift of foresight when biting his thumb.

Fintan In Irish mythology the salmon of knowledge, which Finn mac Cumhal tasted accidentally. He burned his thumb on the flesh as he turned it on a spit. Once he sucked the thumb he became a sage.

Fjorgyn Norse goddess, mother of Thor.

Fortuna Roman goddess of chance and fate.

Frey Norse god of fertility.

Freyja Norse goddess of love, twin sister of Frey.

Frigg Norse goddess of fertility, wife of Odin.

Ganesha Hindu god depicted with the head of an elephant; the offspring of Parvati, the wife of S(h)iva.

Ganymede Greek god of rain and cupbearer to the gods; the son of King Tros of Troy.

Garang The first man according to the Dinka people of the Sudan.

Genius Roman protective god, one for every individual, group and State.

Geryon Three-bodied monster living on the island of Erythia who owned cattle guarded by Eurytion.

Gilgamesh Sumerian king of Uruk, son of the goddess Ninsun and a mortal. His story is told in the Gilgamesh epic, the oldest extant work of literature (c. 2000 BC), which tells of his search for the secret of eternal life.

Gimli In Norse mythology the highest heavenly abode that was not consumed in Ragnarok.

Ginnungagap In Norse mythology the 'Yawning Gap' or primeval emptiness, which held all the potential energy of creation.

Glaucus (1) King of Corinth, son of Sisyphus and Merope and father of Bellerophon. He fed his horses on human flesh but Aphrodite caused them to devour Glaucus himself because he mocked her.

Glaucus (2) Grandson of Bellerophon who fought for the Trojans and was slain by Ajax.

Glaucus (3) Son of Minos and Pasiphaë who was drowned in a barrel of honey.

Glaucus (4) Boeotian fisherman who pursued Scylla and was turned into a sea god on eating a magic herb.

Golden Age Concept of the Greek poet Hesiod, who listed Golden, Silver, Bronze and Iron as the four ages of man in his *Works and Days*.

Golden Bough A gift Aeneas had to take to Proserpina before he could enter the underworld.

Golden Fleece Fleece of the golden ram of Colchis, kept by King Aeëtes of Colchis and guarded by an unsleeping dragon.

Gorgons Three sisters – Eurydale, Medusa and Scheno – offspring of Phorcys and Ceto. Medusa was the mortal sister killed by Perseus. The Gorgons were the sisters of the Graiae.

MYTHOLOGY AND LEGEND

Götterdämmerung Literally means 'Twilight of the Gods'; in Germanic mythology the equivalent of the Norse final battle, Ragnarok.

Graces Daughters of Zeus and the sea nymph Eurynome.

Graiae In Greek mythology, three sisters who had one eye and one tooth between them; sisters of the Gorgons.

Great Mother of the Gods Oriental and Greco-Roman deity, known as Cybele in Latin literature. Her full Roman name was Mater Deum Magna Idaea (Great Idaean Mother of the Gods). Her Phrygian name was Agdistis or Dindymus.

Griffin Greek monster with lion's body and eagle's head and wings.

Gula In Babylonian mythology the goddess of healing corresponding to the Sumerian Bau.

Hades In Greek mythology the son of Cronus and Rhea, and brother of Zeus and Poseidon. The three brothers drew lots for their realms and Hades drew the underworld. Although this nether world was not originally given a name, it became known by the name of its chief god Hades (unseen). The god Hades was also known as Pluto (rich), and the Roman equivalent was Dis or Orcus. The realm of Hades can be sub-divided into Elysium, Tartarus and the Plain of Asphodel.

Hamadryad See Dryad.

Hanuman In Indian mythology the monkey that became the most loyal companion of Rama and his consort Sita.

Harpies Greek spirits with heads of women and bodies of birds.

Hebe Greek goddess of youth and spring, daughter of Zeus and Hera, and wife of Heracles after his death.

Hecate Greek goddess of the underworld and daughter of Coeus and Phoebe.

Hector According to Greek mythology, the bravest Trojan and son of Priam; the brother of Paris and husband of Andromache. Killed by Achilles.

Hecuba Wife of King Priam of Troy and mother of Hector, Paris, Troilus and Cassandra.

Heimdall Norse god, and guardian of the bridge, Bifrost. Born of nine mothers.

Hekatoncheires (100 hands) In Greek mythology, the name of three giants with 100 hands and 50 heads each: Briareus, Cottus and Gyges. They were the offspring of Gaia and Uranus.

Helen Greek heroine, daughter of Zeus and Leda, sister of Clytemnestra and Castor and Pollux.

Hephaestus Son of Zeus and Hera who was thrown from Olympia by his mother and landed in the sea. Hephaestus made the armour for Achilles.

Hera Greek goddess of marriage and childbirth and queen of the gods.

Heracles Greek hero who performed the Twelve Labours of Eurystheus. Offspring of Zeus and Alcmene.

Hercules Roman equivalent of Heracles.

Hermaphroditus Son of Hermes and Aphrodite. Salmacis embraced him so closely that they became fused as one, with a woman's breasts and a man's genitals.

Hermes Son of Zeus and Maia. Hermes invented the lyre soon after birth.

Hermione Daughter of Helen and Menelaus.

Hermod Norse god, son of Odin.

Hero Greek high priestess and lover of Leander, who swam the Hellespont every night to see her but was eventually drowned causing Hero to throw herself in the sea.

Hesperides In Greek mythology, the daughters of the evening star who guarded the Golden Apples together with the dragon Ladon.

Hindu myth and religion Of all the world's leading mythologies, by far the most complex and expansive are Hindu beliefs. Even the term 'mythology' does not sit easily with a body of culture that is still revered today. It is beyond the scope of this work to trace the roots of Hindu beliefs and philosophy with its many tributaries, which themselves form a whole, separate strata of mythology. Many of the gods have personifications under differing names, and others have re-incarnations (avatars), which may bring with them a whole new substrata of mythology. Hindu mythology does not lend itself to fall comfortably within the table of comparative gods, indeed, the choice of Indra as principal god, or king of the gods, can only be loosely adhered to as a comparative to Zeus or Jupiter. Hindu mythology can be further divided into pre-Vedic, late-Vedic, post-Vedic, pre-Aryan post-Aryan and Classical, all of which has its own version of the creation. In the late-Vedic period, c.1200 BC, Brahma might have been considered the most important Hindu god, but he was gradually eclipsed by Vishnu and S(h)iva. Strict adherence to the Veda would place Prajapati (Lord of Creatures) as the creator god. In another version, the Prajapatis are the 10 'mind-born' children of Brahma. The traditional Trimurti of Brahma, Vishnu and S(h)iva, would be considered the most important Hindu gods, but it is true to say that Indra is the equivalent of Zeus in Greek mythology or Jupiter in Roman.

Hippolyte Queen of the Amazons and sister of Antiope.

Hoder Blind Norse god who killed Baldur.

Horus Egyptian god of light with a falcon's head, son of Osiris and Isis.

Huitzilopochtli Chief Aztec god, linked with the sun, fire, war and human sacrifice.

Hyacinthus Peloponnesian youth loved by Apollo who was killed when the jealous Zephyrus diverted a discus to hit him.

Hydra Greek monster usually depicted with 9 heads; slain by Heracles.

Hyperion Greek Titan, son of Uranus and Gaia.

Iapetus Greek Titan, father of Prometheus and Atlas, grandfather of Deucalion.

Icarus Son of Daedalus; he flew too near the sun while escaping from Crete and fell into the Aegean Sea and drowned.

Idavold In Norse mythology the playground of the gods.

Idomeneus King of Crete who contributed 100 ships to the expedition against Troy.

Idunn Norse goddess of the golden apples of youth, wife of Bragi.

Iliad Homer's epic poem on the siege of Troy.

Imhotep The Egyptian god of medicine and healing.

Io Greek heroine turned into a heifer by Zeus to save her from the wrath of Hera.

Iphigenia Daughter of Agamemnon and Clytemnestra, sacrificed by her father at Aulis to gain a favourable wind for the Greek fleet sailing to Troy.

Isis Egyptian goddess of magic and mother of Horus.

Ismene Daughter of Oedipus and Jocasta. She followed her father and her sister, Antigone, into exile.

Isthmian Games Quadrennial games held at Corinth in honour of Poseidon.

Ithaca Island home of Odysseus, one of the Ionian Islands.

Ixion Greek king of Thessaly who was the first to murder a kinsman, his father-in-law; he was bound to a wheel of fire in Tartarus for trying to rape Hera.

Janus Roman god of entrances, travel and the dawn, depicted as a man with two faces.

Jason Son of Aeson, the Aeolian King of Iolcos. Aeson's half-brother Pelias usurped the throne and Queen Alcimede was forced to smuggle her son to safety, entrusting him to the care of Chiron, the centaur. Jason returned to Iolcos to regain his father's kingdom and was told by Pelias that he would step down in return for the golden fleece of a ram, which hung from a tree in Colchis, and was guarded by a dragon. Jason engaged Argus to build a large galley for the journey and successfully attained his goal with the help of some legendary Greek heroes. During his adventures he married the sorceress Medea, but whether he ever attained the throne of Iolcos is doubtful. Jason eventually died when the decaying prow of the Argo fell on him.

Jimmu-tenno Legendary first Emperor of Japan, aka Kamu-yamato-iware-biko.

Jocasta Wife of King Laius and mother of Oedipus.

Jotunheim In Norse mythology the land of the race of giants, said to lie among the roots of Yggdrasil.

Jumala Finnish supreme god.

Juno Roman goddess of marriage, childbirth and light, and queen of the gods.

Jupiter Originally a Roman sky god, but then regarded by the Romans as *Dies Pater* (Father Day), and later still became the Roman equivalent of Zeus.

Kama Hindu god of love and pleasure.

Khnum Egyptian goddess of creation.

Khonsou Egyptian god, son of Ammon.

Kvasir Norse god of wisdom.

Laertes King of Ithaca and father of Odysseus by Anticleia.

Lakshmi In Hindu mythology, also known as Sri, attained importance as the consort of Vishnu under each of his incarnations; when he became Rama she was faithful Sita, and when he became Krishna she became his wife, Rukmini.

Lapithes Mythological race that fought a famous war with the centaurs.

Lares Roman gods of the house and fertility.

Leander Mythical youth of Abydos who drowned while swimming the Hellespont to meet Hero.

Leda Seduced by Zeus in the form of a swan and gave birth to Helen and Polydeuces in one egg and Castor and Clytemnestra in another. Other versions record that Helen and Polydeuces were children of Zeus and that Castor and Clytemnestra were children of her husband, Tyndareus.

Leviathan Sea monster mentioned in the book of Job, resembling a crocodile.

Liber Pater Roman god of agriculture and human fertility.

Libitina Roman goddess of funeral rites.

Lilith Demonic first wife of Adam in Hebrew mytholgy.

Lohengrin In Germanic legend, the son of Parsifal.

Loki Norse god of mischief.

Lorelei In German mythology a siren said to dwell on a rock at the edge of the Rhine, south of Koblenz, who lures boatmen to destruction.

Lud(d) Mythical king of Britain whose temple in Roman London was near St Paul's Cathedral. Ludd was also the name of a Celtic god of the sea.

Llyr (Lir) A Celtic god of waters and the sea; the father of Manannan.

Maat Egyptian goddess of sterility, truth and justice.

Mabinogion A collection of stories written in Welsh in medieval times, the principal source of ancient Welsh and British myths.

Macha In Celtic mythology a collective name for the trinity of war goddesses Macha, Morrígan and Nemain. As an individual, Macha was sometimes known as Dana (crow) or Badb (raven).

Mahabharata Sanskrit verse epic composed between 400 BC and AD 400. It relates a dynastic feud between the Pandavas and their cousins the Kauravas, respectively gods and demons.

Maia Roman goddess of fertility.

Manasa Serpent goddess of Hindu mythology.

Manitou Supreme deity of the Algonquian people of North America.

Manticore A fabulous monster with the body of a lion, the head of a man, porcupine's quills, and the tail or sting of a scorpion.

Marduk Supreme god of Babylon.

Mazda Persian god of wisdom.

Medea In Greek mythology a princess of Colchis and powerful sorceress; deserted by Jason after helping him to steal the Golden Fleece, she killed their two children.

Megara Daughter of King Creon of Thebes and first wife of Heracles, who killed her in a fit of madness caused by the goddess Hera.

Megingjord Name of Thor's belt, which magnifies his strength.

Meleager In Greek mythology the heir of King Oeneus of Calydon. The Fates appeared to his mother, Althaea, when he was seven days old, they pointed to a burning stick in the fireplace and told her that her son's life would last as long as the stick would burn. Althaea snatched the stick from the fire and hid it away. His father incurred the wrath of Artemis and she sent a wild boar to Calydon to ravage his crops. Meleager offered the boar's pelt and tusks to anyone who could deliver the death blow. Many of his fellow Argonauts joined the hunt, including Atalanta, who he was besotted

MYTHOLOGY AND LEGEND

by. Although Meleager himself delivered the final death thrust, he gave the pelt to Atalanta, which upset his two uncles. In a rage he killed them both, and his mother, seeing the corpses of her brothers, threw the stick into the fire, and Meleager's life drained away

Menelaus King of Sparta, younger brother of Agamemnon and husband of Helen.

Merope A Pleiad and wife of Sisyphus.

Metis In Greek mythology the daughter of Oceanus and Tethys and first wife of Zeus.

Mictlan Aztec land of the dead.

Midas Mythical king of Phygian. In one story, Apollo burdens him with ass's ears for fudging badly in a music contest. In another, he receives but manages to shed the gift of turning all he touches to gold.

Midgard In Norse mythology the dwelling place of mankind, formed from the body of the giant Ymir and linked to Asgard by Bifrost, the rainbow bridge.

Milo Champion wrestler in Greek mythology.

Mimir Norse giant who guarded the well of wisdom near the roots of Yggdrasil.

Minos In Greek mythology the son of Europa and Zeus and brother to Sarpedon and Rhadamanthys. Following a dispute with his two brothers, Minos succeeded to the throne of Crete. The issue of the succession was decided when, having prayed for a divine sign, Poseidon sent Minos a magnificent bull from the sea. However, because Minos neglected to sacrifice the bull, Poseidon cursed him, causing his wife, Pasiphaë, to fall madly in love with the creature. With the help of the craftsman Daedalus, Pasiphaë was able to satisfy her lust by hiding in a decoy cow. The offspring of this union was the Minotaur, a monster with the head of a bull but the body of a man. Minos commissioned Daedalus to construct a labyrinth to house the Minotaur, and each year 9 boys and 9 girls were brought from Athens as food for the monster. One year the Greek hero Theseus was chosen for sacrifice and slew the Minotaur with the help of Minos's daughter Ariadne, who supplied him with a thread to enable him to retrace his steps after the slaying. King Minos followed Daedalus to Sicily with his mind set on revenge, but Daedalus was warned of his presence and arranged for boiling oil to kill the king when he took a bath at Kamikos.

Minotaur Greek monster, son of Pasiphaë and a bull, kept in a labyrinth on Crete by King Minos.

Mithra(s) Persian god of light, justice and war.

Mjollnir Thor's hammer, said to cause lightning.

Mnemosyne Greek Titan who was the mother of all the Muses.

Morrígan Irish war goddess whose name means phantom queen; also the collective name of the trinity of war goddesses Macha, Morrígan and Nemain.

Muses Sacred to Mount Helicon. See listing on p. 993.

Myrmidons People of Aegina, created by Zeus for King Aeacus; some of them fought for Achilles at Troy.

Myth The term was first used by the Greek historian Herodotus (c.484 BC – c.420 BC) to describe a body of knowledge or beliefs that have no foundation in fact and so must be distinguished from history although recorded fact can take mythical proportions due to historical interpretation.

Nabu (Nebo) In Babylonian mythology, son of Marduk, and the scribe and herald of the gods.

Naiads Freshwater nymphs in Greek mythology.

Nanna Norse goddess, wife of Baldur.

Narcissus Greek hero whom Nemesis caused to fall in love with his own reflection.

Nataraja Title of the Hindu god S(h)iva, meaning lord of the dance.

Nehallenia Norse goddess of plenty.

Nemesis Greek goddess of destiny, the daughter of Oceanus.

Nereids Fifty beautiful sea nymphs, the daughters of Nereus and Doris, of whom the most famous were Amphitrite and Thetis.

Nereus Greek god of the sea.

Nessus Greek centaur whose blood caused the death of his killer, Heracles.

Nestor King of Pylos and only one of Neleus's 12 sons spared by Heracles. The oldest of the Greeks at Troy and the only one to return home without mishap.

Nibelung In German legend, any of the race of dwarfs who possessed a treasure hoard stolen by Siegfried.

Nibelungenlied Heroic epic of unknown authorship written in the early 13th centruy and based on German history and legend.

Niflheim In Norse mythology the abode of the dead, sometimes identified with hell.

Niobe In Greek mythology, queen of Thebes, wife of King Amphion and daughter of Tantalus and Dione.

Njord Norse god, father of Frey and Freyja.

Norns Norse goddesses of destiny: Urdr – the past, Verdandi – the present, and Skuld – the future.

Notus Greek mythology. South-west wind known to the Romans as Auster. Son of Astraeus and Eos.

Numa Pompilius Legendary second King of Rome who succeeded Romulus.

Nun In Egyptian mythology, the dark primeval ocean of chaos, which existed before the first gods.

Nymph Any one of a class of mythological, youthful female divinities inhabiting woods, springs, mountains or the sea. Although nymphs were not immortal, their life span was usually several thousand years.

Oceanid(e)s Greek sea-nymphs, daughters of Oceanus and Tethys.

Oceanus Greek god of the River Oceanus and son of Gaia and Uranus.

Odysseus (aka Ulysses) Greek hero, the son of Laertes and Anticlea, king and queen of Ithaca, a key figure in Homer's *Iliad* and central in the *Odyssey*.

Oedipus (swollen foot) Greek hero, king of Thebes, who inadvertently killed his father and married his mother.

Oisin In Celtic mythology, a warrior and poet, son of Finn mac Cumhall and Sadb.

Ops Roman goddess of the harvest, and consort of Saturn.

Oread A Greek mountain-nymph.

Orestes In Greek mythology the king of Argos and Sparta, son of Agamemnon and Clytemnestra.

Orion In Greek mythology a giant hunter, son of Poseidon and Euryale.

Orpheus Greek musician and poet, son of King Oeagrus of Thrace and Calliope. He married Eurydice, failed to rescue her from Hades after she was killed by a snake, and was finally torn to pieces by the women of Thrace.

Osiris Egyptian god of vegetation, brother of Seth and husband of Isis.

Otr Norse otter god.

Otus and Ephialtes Twin sons of Iphimedeia and Poseidon.

Pales Roman goddess of flocks.

Palladium Mythical statue of Athene given to Dardanus by Zeus to ensure the protection of Troy.

Pan Greek god of male sexuality, herds and woods.

Pandora In Greek mythology the first woman on earth. When her dowry box was opened it released all the world's ill and retained only hope.

Paris A prince of Troy, the son of Priam. He abducted Helen, the wife of Menelaus, so causing the Trojan War.

Parvati In Hindu mythology Parvati (the mountaineer) was one of the forms of Devi and as such, the mother of the elephant-headed god of wisdom, Ganes(h)a. Parvati became the golden-skinned Gauri.

Pasiphaë In Greek mythology the daughter of Helios and mother of the Minotaur.

Patroclus Greek warrior who, while wearing Achilles' armour, was killed by Hector during the siege of Troy.

Pegasus Greek winged horse that sprang from the body of Medusa after her death.

Pelasgus The first man, according to one version of the Greek creation myth.

Peleus In Greek mythology the King of Phythia in Thessaly. He married Thetis and fathered Achilles.

Penates Roman gods of food and drink.

Penelope The wife of Odysseus. During his long absence after the Trojan war, she tricked the suitors who were plaguing her to marry by unravelling a shroud every night, having promised to make her decision when she had finished weaving it.

Persephone Greek goddess of the underworld, corn and the spring.

Perse Daughter of Oceanus and wife of Helios, to whom she bore Circe, Pasiphaë, Aeëtes and Perses.

Perses (1) Son of Perseus and Andromeda. Said to have given his name to Persia.

Perses (2) Son of Helios and Perse and father of Hecate.

Perseus Greek hero, son of Zeus and Danaë; he slew the Gorgon Medusa and married Andromeda.

Phaeton Greek hero, son of Helios and Clymene. Killed by a thunderbolt from Zeus after losing control of the sun-chariot and endangering the safety of the world. Phaeton's body fell into the river Eridanus (Po).

Philoctetes Greek hero who killed Paris.

Pleiades In Greek mythology the 7 daughters of Atlas and Pleione.

Plutus Greek god of wealth.

Polybus In Greek mythology the king of Corinth, husband of Merope and adoptive father of Oedipus.

Pomona Roman goddess of fruit trees.

Portunus Roman god of husbands and harbours.

Poseidon Greek god of the sea and earthquakes.

Priam In Greek mythology the king of Troy, son of King Laomedon and Queen Strymo.

Priapus Son of Dionysus and Aphrodite, a fertility god, often portrayed with a grotesquely large phallus.

Procrustes (Stretcher) In Greek mythology an innkeeper who killed travellers on the road between Athens and Eleusis by lopping or stretching their bodies to fit his bed. Theseus killed him by decapitation.

Prometheus In Greek mythology a Titan, sometimes credited with making mankind out of clay. Because he stole fire from the gods and gave it to man, Zeus bound him to a rock for an eagle to peck out his liver, which always regrew because Prometheus was immortal.

Proserpine Roman goddess of the Underworld, corn and the spring.

Proteus Sea god, the son of Oceanus and Tethys. Proteus was a seer but would take any form to avoid questioning.

Psyche In Greek mythology the soul, often portrayed as a butterfly. Personified as a woman, she fell in love with Eros and suffered many ordeals before they were united.

Ptah Egyptian god of creation.

Pygmalion In Greek mythology the king of Cyprus who fell in love with Aphrodite and, because she would not lie with him, made an ivory image of her and laid it in his bed. Aphrodite brought the statue to life as Galatea.

Pyrrha Daughter of Epimetheus and Pandora and wife of Deucalion with whom she repopulated the earth after the flood.

Quetzalcoatl Toltec and Aztec god of vegetation and the wind, sometimes depicted as a bearded man wearing a mask, sometimes as a feathered serpent..

Quirinus Roman god of war, after whom a hill of Rome was named.

Ragnarok Final destruction of the Norse gods in a battle to the death with evil.

Ramayana One of the two great Sanskrit verse epics (along with the *Mahabharata*) dating back to the 3rd century BC, the story of Prince Rama, his struggle for the throne of Ajodhya, and his war with the demon Ravana to rescue his abducted wife Sita, with Hanuman's help

Remus See Romulus and Remus.

Rhadamanthus Son of Europa and Zeus and brother to Minos and Sarpedon. After death he became a judge in the underworld.

Rhea Greek goddess of motherhood; sister and wife of Cronus.

Rhesus Thracian king who helped the Trojans but was slain by Odysseus.

Rhiannon In Welsh Celtic mythology, the daughter of the King of the Otherworld and wife of Pwyll, prince of Dyfed.

Romulus and Remus Twin sons of Mars, and leg-

MYTHOLOGY AND LEGEND

endary founders of Rome.

Round Table   In Arthurian legend the great table of Camelot that seated King Arthur's knights. The Siege Perilous (dangerous seat) remained vacant because only the bringer of the Holy Grail could use it without coming to harm.

Rumina   Roman goddess of nursing mothers.

Sarpedon   In Greek mythology the son of Europa and Zeus and brother to Minos and Rhadamanthus.

Satyr   A Greek mythological creature, part man, part goat; the satyrs were followers of Dionysus.

Scaean (Left-Hand) Gate   Situated in the walls of Troy; the spot where Achilles fell.

Scylla   Greek sea monster; originally the daughter of Poseidon, she was turned into a monster by Amphitrite. In Strait of Messina located opposite Charybdis and depicted as snake with 6 heads that lived in a cave.

Sekmet   Egyptian goddess of power and battle, depicted with the head of a lioness.

Selene   Greek goddess of the moon, daughter of Hyperion and Thea; she was most notably the lover of Endymion.

Semiramis   In Assyrian mythology the wife of Ninus and co-founder with him of Nineveh.

Set   Egyptian god of evil.

Seven against Thebes   Greek champions – Adrasius, Amphiaraüs, Capaneus, Hippomedon, Parthenopaeus, Polynices and Tydeus – who failed to overthrow Eteocles from his Kingship.

Seven Kings of Rome   Romulus (753–715 BC), Numa Pompilius (715–673 BC), Tullius Hostilius (673–642 BC), Ancus Marcius (642–616 BC), Tarquin the Elder (616–579 BC), Servius Tullius (579–534 BC), Tarquinius Superbus (Proud Tarquin) (534–510 BC).

Shu   Egyptian god of Air.

Sibyl   Roman prophetess.

Sibylline Books   Roman tradition tells how a sibyl offered Tarquinius Priscus 9 prophetic books which he refused to buy at the price. She destroyed three and he still refused them; she burned three more and he took the remaining three at the price demanded for the nine. Special priests kept them and they were consulted only when the Senate authorised it in time of need. In 83 BC the originals were destroyed by fire. The original books instructed the Romans to convey the sacred stone of Cybele to Rome.

Sif   Norse goddess, wife of Thor.

Sigmund   In Germanic legend the son of Volsung who won the divine sword Gram by extracting it from a tree trunk.

Sigurd   In Germanic legend the son of Sigmund and Hjordis and owner of the horse, Grani.

Sigyn   Norse goddess, wife of Loki.

Silvanus   Roman god of trees and forests.

Siren   In Homer's *Odyssey* one of a group of creatures, half woman and half bird, who lure sailors to their death by their singing. Odysseus and the Argonauts withstood their fatal charms, the latter because Orpheus outsang them.

Sisyphus   In Greek mythology a Corinthian king destined in Hades to roll a large stone up a hill for evermore, only for it to keep rolling back when it reaches the top.

Skadi   In Norse mythology the wife of Njord.

Skan   Lakota god embodying the sky.

Sleipnir   Odin's 8-legged horse.

Sobek   Egyptian crocodile god.

Soma   In Hindu mythology an intoxicating drink. Soma was also an early god of the moon.

Spartoi (sown men)   Sprang up fully armed when Cadmus sowed the dragon's teeth and killed each other until five remained: Echion, Udaeus, Chthonius, Hyperenor and Pelorus.

Sphinx   Greek monster with a woman's head and lion's body.

Stentor   Greek herald during the Trojan War, famous for his very loud voice.

Stymphalian birds   In Greek mythology a flock of man-eating birds, which infested Lake Stymphalos in Arcadia. Killed by Heracles.

Surabhi   In Indian mythology a divine cow of plenty.

Syrinx   Greek nymph of Arcadia. She was pursued by Pan, who made the first pan-pipes from her embodiment, as turning into a bed of reeds was the only way she could escape him.

Tantalus   Greek mythological king of Sipylos in Lydia, who stole the food of the gods and was condemned to stand thirsty and hungry forever in a pool that receded when he bent down to drink, beneath fruit trees whose branches retreated when he reached to pick their fruit.

Tarpeian Rock   Named after Tarpeia, the traitor daughter of the keeper of the Roman citadel. Became the rock from which Roman traitors were thrown.

Tartarus   That part of Hades reserved for those that offended the gods during their lifetime.

Taweret   Egyptian protector goddess of women and children, often depicted as part crocodile, part lion and part hippopotamus.

Telamon   Son of Aeacus and brother of Peleus; Telamon fathered Ajax by Periboea.

Telemachus   Greek hero, son of Odysseus and Penelope.

Tenes   Son of Apollo who gave his name to the Greek island of Tenedos.

Themis   Daughter of Ge and Uranus and sister of Cronus. The wife of Zeus before Hera.

Theseus   Mythical Greek hero, king of Athens and son of King Aegeus and Queen Aethra; it was Theseus who defeated the Minotaur in its labyrinth home in Crete.

Thetis   Greek goddess and mother of Achilles.

Thunderbird   Totem figure of Native Americans from the north-west. Aka Skyamsen.

Tiresias   Legendary blind prophet of Thebes who had been both male and female and estimated that women had 9 times more pleasure during intercourse than men.

Tonalpohualli   Aztec sacred calendar consisting of 260 days which were divided into 20 weeks of 13 days.

Trimurti   Trinity of Hindu gods: Brahma(n) the Creator, Vishnu the Preserver and S(h)iva the Destroyer.

Tristan and Isolde   Celtic legend. Tristan was a harpist and Isolde was the daughter of the king of Ireland. They drank a love potion together by mistake and fell irretrievably in love.

Triton   Son of Poseidon and Amphitrite. He was a merman, the upper half human, the lower half fish. Triton used a conch shell trumpet to calm the waves.

Troilus   In Greek mythology, the young son of Priam, slain by Achilles. His romance with Cressida is a medieval invention.

Ull   Norse god and stepson of Thor.

Valhalla   In Norse mythology the great hall of Odin in Asgard, where warriors who died as heroes in battle dwelled eternally.

Valkyries   Norse warrior handmaidens to Odin.

Vanir   Norse race of benevolent gods including Njörd, Frey and Freyja. The Vanir warred with the Aesir and were eventually absorbed into their number.

Varuna   In Hindu mythology Varuna was at one time the upholder of heaven and earth and often associated with Surya as the creator of the sun. In post-Vedic mythology he became god of the seas and rivers.

Vertumnus   Roman god of fertility.

Vestal virgins   College of priestesses of the Roman cult of Vesta, the hearth goddess. Originally four of them; later 6 (generally considered as the number); and finally 7.

Vidar   Norse god, a son of Odin and slayer of the wolf Fenir.

Vishnu's Incarnations   The 10 avatars of Vishnu are 1. Matsya, 2. Kurma, 3. Varaha, 4. Narasinha, 5. Vamana 6. Paras(h)urama, 7. Ramachandra (Rama), 8. Krishna, 9. Buddha, 10. Kalki.

Völund   In Norse mythology, a smith and artificer and king of the elves. In Germanic legends he appears as Wieland; in English folklore as Wayland Smith.

Wyvern   Mythical beast with a dragon's head, a serpent's tail and a body with wings and two legs.

Yggdrasil   In Norse mythology, the ash tree that binds the heavens, earth and the underworld with its roots and branches. It shelters the remnants of humanity when Raganrok destroys the gods and sets the world on fire.

Ymir   The first being and forefather of all the Norse giants. Slain by Odin, who made the earth from his flesh, the water from his blood and the sky from his skull.

Zephyrus   West Wind, the son of Astraeus and Eus and father of Xanthus and Balius, the talking horses of Achilles. Roman counterpart was Favonius.

Zetes   Twin brother of Calais. Winged sons of Boreas and Oreithyia, they accompanied the Argonauts and drove off the Harpies.

Zeus's conquests   The supreme god of the Greek parthenon took many forms in his amorous pursuit of goddesses, nymphs and humans. See below.

Zeus's Conquests

Conquest	Form	Offspring
Alcmene	Amphitryon	Heracles
Antiope	Satyr	Amphion and Zetheus
Danaë	Shower of gold	Perseus
Demeter	Himself	Persephone
Europa	Bull and eagle	Minos, Sarpedon and Rhadamanthus
Eurynome	Himself	Graces
Ganymede	Eagle	None
Io	Cloud	Epaphos
Leda	Swan	Helen, Clytemnestra, Castor and Pollux
Leto	Quail	Apollo and Artemis
Maia	Himself	Hermes
Mnemosyne	Himself	Moses
Rhea	Serpent	None
Semele	Mortal	Dionysus
Thetis	Himself	None

MYTHOLOGY AND LEGEND

Famous Horses of Myth and History

Name	Owner	Horse's owner's identity
Arvak	Sol	Norse maiden
Abaster	Pluto	Greek god
Abatos	Pluto	Greek god
Abraxa	Aurora	Roman goddess
Actaeon	Helios	Greek sun god
Aethon	Helios	Greek sun god
Aeton	Pluto	Greek god
Al Borak	Mohammed	Founder of Islam
Alfana	Gradasso	Literary creation
Alsvid	Sol	Norse maiden
Amethea	Helios	Greek sun god
Arion	Hercules	Mythological hero
Arundel	Bevis of Hampton	Literary creation
Babieca	El Cid	Spanish hero
Balios	Achilles	Greek hero
Barbary Roan	Richard II	English king
Bayard	Renaud de Montauban	Legendary Frankish knight
Black Agnes	Mary Queen of Scots	Scottish queen
Black Bess	Dick Turpin	Literary creation
Brigliadoro	Orlando	Legendary character
Bronte	Helios	Greek sun god
Bucephalus (Ox-Head)	Alexander the Great	Macedonian ruler
Carman	Chevalier de Bayard	French knight
Celer	Lucius Verus	Roman emperor
Cerus	Adrastus	Mythological king of Argos
Champion	Gene Autry	TV cowboy
Comanche	US cavalry	Only survivor of Little Big Horn
Copenhagen	Duke of Wellington	Soldier and statesman
Cyllaros	Castor and Pollux	Roman mythological twins
Dapple	Sancho Panza	Literary character
Diablo	Cisco Kid	Literary creation
Dinos	Diomedes	Mythological king of Argos
Doublet	Princess Anne	Royal Olympian
Eos	Aurora	Roman goddess
Erythreos	Helios	Greek sun god
Ethon	Hector	Trojan hero
Fadda (mule)	Mohammed	Founder of Islam
Ferrant d'Espagne	Oliver	Legendary Frankish knight
Foxhunter	Colonel Harry Llewellyn	Olympic champion
Galathe	Hector	Trojan hero
Grani	Siegfried	German legendary character
Gringolet	Sir Gawain	Arthurian Knight
Grizzle	Dr Syntax	Literary creation
Haizum	Gabriel	Archangel
Harpagus	Castor and Pollux	Roman mythological twins
Hercules	The Steptoes	TV creation
Hippocampus	Neptune	Roman god
Hrimfaxi (Frost Mane)	Nott	Horse of Night (Norse myth)
Incitatus	Caligula	Roman emperor
Kantanka	Prince Gautama	The Buddha
Lampon	Diomedes	Mythological king of Argos
Lampos	Helios	Greek sun god
Lamri	King Arthur	Legendary Anglo-Saxon king
Marengo	Napoleon	French emperor
Marocco	Mr Banks	Elizabethan horseman
Marsala	Garibaldi	Italian patriot
Nonios	Pluto	Greek god
Pegasus	Bellerophon	Greek hero
Phaeton	Aurora	Roman goddess
Phallus (stallion)	Heraclius	Byzantine emperor
Phlegon	Helios	Greek sun god
Phrenicos	Hiero of Syracuse	Winner of 73rd olympiad
Podarge (Swift Foot)	Hector	Trojan hero
Purocis	Helios	Greek sun god
Ronald	Lord Cardigan	British soldier
Rosabelle	Mary Queen of Scots	Scottish queen
Rosinante	Don Quixote	Literary creation
Savoy	Charles VIII	French king
Scout	Tonto	TV creation
Sefton	British Army	Bomb victim
Shadowfax	Gandalf	Wizard in Lord of the Rings
Shibdiz	Chosroes II	Persian ruler
Silver	Lone Ranger	TV creation
Skinfaxi (Shining Mane)	Dagr	Horse of Day (Norse myth)
Sleipnir	Odin	Norse supreme god
Sorrel	William III	British king
Strymon	Xerxes	Persian king
Tachebrune	Ogier the Dane	Hero of chansons de geste
Tony	Tom Mix	Film cowboy
Topper	Hopalong Cassidy	Film cowboy
Trebizond	Guarinos	French knight at Roncesvalles
Trigger	Roy Rogers	TV cowboy
White Surrey	Richard III	English king
Xanthus	Achilles	Greek hero

Famous Dogs (Fact and Fiction)

Name	Owner or details
Arctophonos	Orion's dog (bear-killer)
Argos	Ulysses
Asta	*Thin Man* series
Blondie	Hitler
Boatswain	Lord Byron
Boot	Old English sheepdog in *The Perishers* (cartoon strip)
Bounce	Alexander Pope
Boy	Prince Rupert's dog, killed at Marston Moor
Bran	Finn mac Cumhal
Brutus	Landseer's greyhound (invader of the larder)
Cabal (Cavall)	King Arthur's favourite hound
Cerberus	Three-headed dog that guards Hades
Checkers	Richard Nixon
Daisy	Blondie
Danny	2003 Supreme Champion at Crufts. The Kennel name of the Pekinese is Yakee A Dangerous Liaison
Dash	Charles Lamb
Diamond	Isaac Newton
Digby	Biggest dog in the world in 1973 film
Dizzie	Michael Foot
Dougal	Character in *Magic Roundabout*
Dragon	Aubry of Montdidier
Flush	Elizabeth Barrett Browning
Freeway	Jonathan and Jennifer Hart
Gargittios	One of Geryon's dogs slain by Hercules
Geist	Matthew Arnold's dachshund
Gelert	Prince Llewellyn's greyhound
Giallo	Walter Savage Landor
Gnasher	Dennis the Menace
Goofy	Disney cartoon dog
Greyfriars Bobby	Watched over owner's grave for 14 years
Hamlet	Sir Walter Scott's black greyhound
Hodain (aka Leon)	Tristan
K9	Robot in *Dr Who*
Kaiser	Matthew Arnold's dachshund
Katmir	Dog of the Seven Sleepers
Laelaps	Procris
Laika	Fox terrier that was the first dog in space
Lassie	Actually a female dog named Pal
Luath	Cuchulainn
Luath	Robert Burns
Lucy	David Blunkett
Lufra	Douglas's hound in Scott's *Lady of the Lake*
Maera (Glistener)	Icarius
Maida	Sir Walter Scott's deerhound
Mathe	Richard II's greyhound
Montmorency	Three Men in a Boat
Nana	Darling family (*Peter Pan*)
Nigger	Guy Gibson
Nipper	Fox terrier logo for His Master's Voice (HMV)
Offa	David Blunkett
Olaf	Snoopy's brother
Orthos	One of Geryon's dogs slain by Hercules
Paddy	Harold Wilson
Pearl	Beryl the Peril
Peritas	Alexander the Great
Petra	*Blue Peter*
Pickles	Found the World Cup
Pluto	Disney cartoon dog
Ptoophagos	Orion's dog (glutton of Ptoon, in Boeotia)
Rin Tin Tin	Died in Jean Harlow's arms
Rufus	Sir Winston Churchill's poodle
Sandy	Little Orphan Annie
Scamper	Secret Seven
Sceolang	Finn mac Cumhal
Shep	John Noakes
Snoopy	Beagle in *Peanuts* (cartoon strip)
Snowy	Tintin
Soda	Chris Patten
Spike	Snoopy's brother
Spottie	*The Woodentops*
Theron	Roderick the Goth
Timmy	Famous Five member
Toby	Punch
Well'ard	Originally owned by Robbie Jackson in Eastenders. Dogs real name is Kyte
Whisky	Chris Patten
Won Ton Ton	Saved Hollywood in 1976 film

MYTHOLOGY AND LEGEND

NATURE

Living Creatures (except birds)

aardvark nocturnal mammal, inhabiting the grasslands of Africa south of the Sahara and feeding on ants and termites. It is the sole member of its family (Orycteropodidae) and order (Tubulidentata). Research by British, Chinese and South African scientists in 2003 reveals that the aardvark has the greatest number of features in common with other mammals, which makes it the closest living relative of our common ancestor. The aardvark is also called an ant bear. Sp.: *Orycteropus afer.*

aardwolf nocturnal mammal, inhabiting the plains of east and southern Africa, feeding on termites and insect larvae. Family: Hyaenidae (Hyenas) and Order: Carnivora. Sp.: *Proteles cristatus.*

abalone gastropod mollusc with a shallow, ear-shaped shell lined with mother-of-pearl. Gen.: *Haliotis.*

albacore long-finned tunny fish. Sp.: *Thunnus alalunga.*

alewife fish of the north-west Atlantic related to the herring. Sp.: *Alosa pseudoharengus.*

alligator either of two crocodilian reptiles of the family Alligatoridae (alligators and caymans) and distinguished from true crocodiles by their shorter and broader snouts. The American alligator (*Alligator mississippiensis*), the larger of the two species, can grow to a length of almost 6 metres, and the Chinese alligator (*Alligator sinensis*) to about a quarter of that length.

alpaca South American herbivore mammal of the Andes with long shaggy hair, related to the llama. Sp.: *Lama pacos.*

anchovy small marine food fish of the herring family. Sp.: *Engraulis encrasicholus.*

ant small social insect of the order Hymenoptera, typically living in organised colonies of winged males (drones), wingless sterile females (workers) and fertile females (queens). The body of an ant has three segments, i.e. head, abdomen and thorax. Family: Formicidae.

ant: Amazon ant which captures pupae of other ant species to raise as slaves. Gen.: *Polyergus.*

antelope bovid mammals of Africa and Asia that include bushbucks, elands, gnus, gazelles, impalas, springboks, dik-diks, blackbucks, oryxes, gerenuks and nilgai. Antelopes have unbranched horns, which they do not shed. Family: Boridae.

ape primates characterised by long arms and the absence of a tail. Great apes are the chimpanzee, gorilla and orang-utan (Family: Pongidae). Lesser apes are the various gibbons (Family: Hylobatidae).

argalis large Asiatic wild sheep with massive horns. Sp.: *Ovis ammon.*

armadillo nocturnal insect-eating but generally omnivorous edentate mammal native to the southern USA and Central and S. America, with large claws for digging and a body covered in bony plates, often rolling itself into a ball when threatened. They range from 3- to as many as 13-banded. Burmeister's and pink fairy armadillos are endangered species. Family: Dasypodidae.

axolotl aquatic newt-like salamander from Mexico, which in natural conditions retains its larval form for life but is able to breed. Name means 'water servant'. Sp.: *Ambystoma mexicanum.*

aye-aye nocturnal arboreal prosimian primate of Madagascar related to the lemurs. Sp.: *Daubentonia madagascariensis.*

babirusa wild hog with upturned tusks native to the Malay archipelago. Sp.: *Babyrousa babyrussa.*

baboon primate of the family Cercopithecidae, characterised by its fox-like muzzle and long tail. Gen.: *Papio.*

badger (American) stout-bodied carnivore with greyish to reddish coat and black facial stripes. Sp.: *Taxidea taxus.*

badger (Eurasian) stout-bodied carnivore with greyish coat and black and white facial stripes. All badgers are members of the family Mustelidae. Sp.: *Meles meles.*

badger (honey) aka ratel. Musteline mammal inhabiting wooded regions of Africa and Asia. Sp.: *Mellivora capensis.*

bandicoot any small, agile terrestrial marsupial of the family Peramelidae of Australia and New Guinea. Bandicoots typically have long, pointed muzzles, large ears and long tails, and feed mainly on small invertebrates.

bandicoot rat large, dark brown, burrowing rat of the family Muridae, order Rodentia, of India and Sri Lanka, sometimes known as a mole rat. The bandicoot rat makes a grunting noise similar to that of a pig. Sp.: *Bandicota indica.*

barnacle small marine crustacean of the subclass Cirripedia that, as an adult, lives head-down attached to rocks or the bottom of the hull of a ship.

barnacle: goose common barnacle found worldwide, living attached by a stalk to driftwood. Gen.: *Lepas.*

basking shark large slow-moving shark of the family Cetorhinidae, prone to swimming or floating at the surface with its mouth agape. The basking shark is the second largest shark after the whale shark, growing up to 14 metres in length. Sp.: *Cetorhinus maximus.*

bear large plantigrade, omnivorous mammal of the family Ursidae, order Carnivora. The smallest species is the Malaysian sun bear (*Helarctos malayanus*), and the largest is the Kodiak bear (*Ursus arctos middendorffi*).

beluga large kind of Russian sturgeon from which caviar is obtained. Sp.: *Huso huso.*

bib light brown European marine gadoid food fish. Aka pout. Sp.: *Gadus luscus.*

binturong arboreal civet of southern. Asia with a shaggy black coat and a prehensile tail. Sp.: *Arctictis binturong.*

bison: American ox-like grazing mammal with short-haired body and longer, darker hair on its head. Aka plains buffalo. Sp.: *Bison bison.*

black widow any venomous spider of the family Theridiidae, inhabiting warm climates throughout the world. The venom of the spider causes sharp pain and some muscle cramping but is usually only temporary and never fatal. The female is characterised by its dark colour and red hourglass marking on its abdomen. The males are rarely seen as they are often eaten by the female after mating. Black widows are known as button spiders in South Africa, redbacks in Australia and katipos in New Zealand. Gen.: *Latrodectus*.

bobcat   small Northern American lynx with a spotted, reddish-brown coat and a short tail. Sp.: *Felis rufus*.

bonito   one of several small, tuna-like marine food fishes of the family Scombridae (tunnies and mackerels) inhabiting warm Atlantic and Pacific waters. Gen.: *Sarda*.

boomslang   venomous tree-snake native to sub-Saharan Africa. Sp.: *Dispholidus typus*.

brachiosaurus   herbivorous dinosaurs, probably the largest land animals ever known (80 tons+). Gen.: *Brachiosaurus*.

brandling   red earthworm with rings of a brighter colour, which is often found in manure and used as fishing bait. Sp.: *Eisenia foetida*.

brown recluse   North American venomous spider with a dark brown body about 3 centimetres long with a distinct violin-shaped design on its back. Sp.: *Loxosceles reclusa*.

buffalo (African)   large, black, sparsely haired animal weighing up to 700kg. Sp.: *Syncerus caffer*.

buffalo (Indian)   aka water buffalo or carabao. South-east Asian domestic beast of burden weighing up to 1200kg. Sp.: *Bubalus bubalis*.

bullfrog   large frog native to North America and Mexico and known for its loud croak. Sp.: *Rana cateseiana*.

bumble-bee   large social bee with a loud hum. Aka humble-bee. Gen.: *Bombus*.

bummalo   small fish of south Asian coasts, dried and used as food, especially Bombay duck. Sp.: *Harpodon nehereus*.

bush baby   small nocturnal tree-dwelling African primate with very large eyes. Aka galago. Six species of the family Lorisidae.

cacomistle   raccoon-like animal of North America with a dark ringed tail. Sp.: *Bassariscus sumichrasti*.

callop   gold-coloured freshwater fish of Australia. Aka golden perch. Sp.: *Plectroplites ambiguus*.

camel: Arabian   camel with one hump native to the deserts of North Africa and the Near East (aka dromedary). Sp.: *Camelus dromedarius*.

camel: Bactrian   camel with two humps native to central Asia. Sp.: *Camelus bactrianus*.

capelin   small smeltlike fish of the North Atlantic used as food and as bait for catching cod. Sp.: *Mallotus villosus*.

capuchin   monkey of the family Cebidae, characterised by its head hair suggestive of a cowl. Gen.: *Cebus*.

capybara   very large, semi-aquatic rodent (up to 65 kg) native to South America east of the Andes. Sp.: *Hydrochoerus hydrochaeris*.

caracal   lynx native to Norht Africa and south-west. Asia. Sp.: *Felis caracal*.

caribou   large deer of Arctic regions of North America, having large branched antlers in the male and female, the only species of deer to do so. The caribou is known as a reindeer in Eurasia. Sp.: *Rangifer tarandus*.

carpenter ant   large ant which bores into wood to nest. Gen.: *Camponotus*.

cat: domestic   small feline mammal often kept as household pet. The cat is thought to have originated in Egypt. Unusual breeds include the Angora, which

is usually deaf, the Manx, which is tailless, and the Siamese, which has blue eyes. Cats move in the same way as the camel and giraffe, i.e. by moving first the front and back legs on one side, then the front and back legs on the other side. Most cats have 18 toes, 5 on the front foot and 4 on the back. Sp.: *Felis domesticus*.

cat: wild   feline mammal living in the wild. Sp.: *Felis silvestris*.

cattle   dairy breeds include Ayrshire, Danish Red, Friesian, Guernsey, Jersey and Kerry. Beef cattle include Aberdeen Angus, Blonde d'Aquitaine, Blue Grey, Charolais, Chianina, Devon, Galloway, Hereford, Highland, Limousin, Lincoln Red, Luing, Maine-Anjou, Shorthorn and Sussex. Dual-purpose breeds include Dexter, Meuse-Rhine-Ijssel, Red Poll, Dairy Shorthorn, Simmental, South Devon and Welsh Black. Gen.: *Bos*.

cavy   any small South American rodent of the family Caviidae, especially of the genus *Cavia*.

cayman (caiman)   reptile of the family Alligatoridae (alligators and caymans), inhabiting riverbanks of Central and South America.

centipede   carnivorous arthropod, having a body of between 14 and 190 segments, each bearing one pair of legs. The common house centipede, order Scutigerida, is 25 millimetres (1 inch) long with a black striped body and 15 pairs of legs. Class: Chilopoda.

chamois   agile goat-antelope native to the mountains of Europe and Asia. Sp.: *Rupicapra rupicapra*.

cheese-fly   small black fly that breeds in cheese. Sp.: *Piophila casei*.

cheetah   fastest-running feline with a leopard-like spotted coat and non-retractable claws. Sp.: *Acinonyx jubatus*.

chigger   tropical flea of which females burrow under people's skin, causing painful sores. Aka chigoe, sand flea and jigger. Sp.: *Tunga penetrans*.

chimpanzee   tailless primate of the family Pongidae, inhabiting forests and savannahs of tropical west and central Africa. The two species are the common chimpanzee (*Pan troglodytes*) and the pygmy chimpanzee (*Pan paniscus*).

chinchilla   small South American rodent of the family Chinchillidae, which is bred in captivity for its soft grey fur. Chinchillas resemble long-tailed rabbits, although their ears are smaller. Sp.: *Chinchilla laniger*.

Chinese water deer   along with the musk deer, one of only two species of deer that do not have antlers. Sp.: *Hyfropotes inermis*.

chipmunk   North American ground squirrel having alternate light and dark stripes running down the body. Gen.: *Tamias*.

cicada   any of 1,500 varieties of winged-insects of the order Homoptera. The dog-day cicada of the genus *Tibicen*, is typically 3 centimetres long with greenish head and wings, acting as a canopy over its abdomen and thorax. The so-called periodic cicadas of the genus *Magicicada*, including the 17-year and 13-year cicadas, are darker in colour and have red eyes.

civet   cat-like mammals of Africa and Southern Asia with spotted fur, noted for the powerful-smelling fluid from their anal glands from which they bear their name. Family: Viverridae.

clouded leopard   large spotted arboreal cat of South-east Asia. Sp.: *Neofelis nebulosa*.

coati   raccoon-like, omnivorous mammals of Central and South America with a long flexible snout and a long, usually ringed, tail. Gen.: *Nasua* and *Nasuella*.

coelacanth primitive lobe-finned fish of the Indian Ocean, thought to be many millions of years extinct until a living specimen was caught in 1938. Sp.: *Latimeria chalumnae*.

colugo see flying lemur.

coral any of a variety of invertebrate marine organisms of the phylum Cnidaria, class Anthozoa, characterised by having spikey, leathery or stonelike skeletons. Stony coral, of the order Madreporaria, form reefs and islands. Red coral, of the genus *Corallium*, also known as precious coral, is used to make ornaments and jewellery.

cougar see puma.

coyote aka prairie wolf. Predatory canine mammal of North America, smaller than the wolf. Sp.: *Canis latrans*.

crane-fly large two-winged flies with very long legs. Aka daddy-long-legs or leatherjacket. Family: Tipulidae.

crayfish small lobster-like freshwater crustacean. Aka spiny lobster. Gen.: *Astacus*.

cribo large, non-venomous American snake. Aka indigo snake or gopher snake. Sp.: *Drymarchon corais*.

crocodile any reptile of the family Crocodilidae, typically having a broad head, tapering snout, massive jaws, and a thick outer covering of boney scales. The salt water crocodile may grow up to 7 metres long and is the world's largest reptile. The sex of a crocodile is decided during incubation: a male is born if the egg is maintained at a constant 31.6 ° Celsius; hotter or colder and the sex is female. Gen.: *Crocodilus*.

crown of thorns starfish that feeds on coral polyps and has increasingly threatened Australia's Great Barrier Reef. The species can grow up to 50 centimetres, has numerous red spines and may have up to 19 arms. Sp.: *Acanthaster planci*.

dace freshwater fish related to the carp. Sp.: *Leuciscus leuciscus*.

death's-head hawk-moth Large dark hawk-moth with yellowish underwings and skull-like markings on the back of the thorax. Sp.: *Acherontia atropos*.

death-watch beetle small beetle which makes a sound like a watch ticking, once supposed to portend death, and whose larva bores in dead wood. Sp.: *Xestobium rufovillosum*.

deer any ruminant quadruped of the family Cervidae, distinguished in the male by the presence of deciduous branching horns or antlers, and in the young by the presence of spots. The furry covering of the newly formed antlers is given the name velvet.

devil's coach-horse large rove beetle. Sp.: *Ocypus olens*.

devil's darning needle alternative name for a dragonfly or damselfly. Order: Odonata.

dhole fierce canine pack-hunting mammal of the forests of central and South-east Asia. Sp.: *Cuon alpinus*.

dik-dik dwarf antelope native to Africa. Gen.: *Madoqua*.

dingo wild dog of the family Canidae, generally light brown in colour with long muzzle and bushy tail. The dingo, also known as the warrigal, can be found throughout mainland Australia and Tasmania. It is a scavenging carnivore and has a distinct howl but does not bark. Sp.: *Canis dingo*.

diplodocus four-legged plant-eating dinosaur with the longest known tail of all dinosaurs (11 metres). Gen.: *Diplodocus*.

dog domesticated carnivorous mammal. Sp.: *Canis familiaris*.

dolphin any of various marine cetacean mammals of the family Delphinidae, which are typically larger than porpoises but smaller than whales. The common dolphin is *Delphinus delphis*.

dolphin: bottle-nosed inhabiting all the world's oceans and named after its beak-like snout, which is shaped like a bottle and gives the impression of having a permanent smile. Sp.: *Tursiops truncatus*.

dormouse: common nocturnal squirrel-like rodent with bushy tail. Sp.: *Muscardinus avellanarius*.

dormouse (edible) aka fat dormouse. Largest of the dormice, once prized as food by the Romans. Sp.: *Glis glis*.

douroucouli nocturnal monkey of South America having large, staring eyes. Aka night monkey or owl monkey. Sp.: *Aotus trivirgatus*.

dragonet Any scaleless, spiny marine fish of the family Callionymidae, the males of which are brightly coloured.

dragonfly predatory insect of the suborder Anisoptera, order Odonata, having a large head and eyes, long slender body and two pairs of iridescent wings, which may have a span in excess of 15 centimetres. Sp.: *Libellula forensis*. Alternative names of the dragonfly include devil's darning needle and devil's arrow.

drosophila small fruit fly used extensively in genetic research because of its large chromosomes, numerous varieties and rapid rate of reproduction. Gen.: *Drosophila*.

duck-billed platypus amphibious egg-laying mammal of eastern Australia, having dense fur, a broad flat bill and tail and webbed feet. The platypus and echidna are the only two members of the order Monotremata, i.e. mammals that lay eggs. The male has a toxic horny spur on both hind legs, the venom of which is powerful enough to kill a dog and cause excruciating pain to humans. An excellent swimmer, the platypus has a buoyant body so always swims in a downward tract and is capable of being submerged for up to 10 minutes if resting. Sp.: *Ornithorhynchus anatinus*.

dugong large marine mammal of the order Sirenia, closely related to the manatee; the sole extant member of the family Dugongidae. The dugong is shorter than the manatee and darker skinned but has the same body shape. Manatees inhabit the waters of the Caribbean, South America and West Africa, while the dugongs are found in East African and Australian waters. Like the manatee, the dugong is also sometimes called a sea cow because of its grass-eating habits. Sightings of dugongs and manatees by early explorers gave rise to the mythology of mermaids and sirens. Sp.: *Dugong dugon*.

duiker mostly forest-dwelling African antelopes having a crest of long hair between their horns. Gen.: *Cephalophus* and *Sylvicapra*.

eagle ray large ray with long pointed pectoral fins. Family: Myliobatidae.

earth worm any of various species of ground worms of the phylum Annelida, class Oligochaeta, especially members of the genera *Lumbricus*, *Allolobophora* and *Eisenia*.

echidna egg-laying insectivorous mammals native to Australia and New Guinea, with a covering of spines, a long snout and long claws. Aka spiny anteater. Family: Tachyglossidae.

eel   teleost fish having long, snake-like body, smooth slimy skin and reduced fins. Gen.: *Anguilla*.

eland   antelope native to Africa, having spirally twisted horns. The giant eland is the largest of living antelopes. Gen.: *Taurotragus*.

elephant: African   larger of the two species of elephant. Sp.: *Loxodonta africana*.

elephant: Indian   smaller of the two species of elephant. Gen.: *Elephas maximus*.

emperor moth   large moth related to the silk moths with eye-spots on all four wings. Sp.: *Saturnia pavonia*.

eyra   reddish-brown variety of jaguarondi. Sp.: *Felis yagouaroundi*.

fallfish   freshwater fish of North America resembling the chub. Sp.: *Semotilus corporalis*.

fallow deer   small deer having a white-spotted reddish-brown coat in the summer. Sp.: *Dama dama*.

false gavial (gharial)   Southeast Asian reptile of the family Crocodilidae with long straight snout, giving the impression of being a gavial. Sp.: *Tomistoma schlegeli*.

fennec   smallest fox, native to North Africa and Arabia, having large pointed ears. Sp.: *Vulpes zerda*.

fer-de-lance   large, highly venomous pit viper of tropical South America and the West Indies. Sp.: *Bothrops atrox*.

ferret   domesticated albino variety of the polecat, bred for hunting rats and rabbits. Sp.: *Mustela putorius*.

fly   member of the insect order Diptera, containing over 85,000 species divided into the suborders Nematocera (midges, gnats, crane flies and mosquitoes), Brachycera (bee flies, robber flies and horse flies) and Cyclorrhapha (house flies, fruit flies, blow flies, and leafminers). Dipterans are distinguished from other insects (such as dragonflies and mayflies) by their wing structure, the so-called 'true' flies being characterised by the use of only one pair of wings for flight, the second pair becoming fixed and being used for balance. The smallest two-winged flies are midges, and the largest are robber flies of the family Asilidae, which can attain lengths of up to 8 centimetres.

flying fish   warm-water fish with wing-like pectoral fins for gliding through the air. Family: Exocoetidae.

flying fox   fruitbats with fox-like heads, largest species with wingspan approaching 2 metres. Family: Pteropodidae.

flying lemur   either of two lemur-like mammals of South-east Asia, having a membrane between the fore and hind limbs for gliding from tree to tree. Aka colugo. Gen.: *Cynocephalus*.

flying lizard   long-tailed lizard of S.E. Asia with elongated ribs supporting membranes for gliding. Gen.: *Draco*.

flying squirrel   any squirrel with skin joining the fore and hind limbs for gliding from tree to tree. Gen.: *Aeromys, Belomys, Eupetdurus, Glaucomys, Hylopetes, Petaurista, Petinomys, Pteromys, Pteromyscus, Trogopterus*.

fox   various members of the dog family, Canidae, typically small in stature with a bushy tail known as a brush. They include the African Sand, Bat-eared, Bengal, Black, Blanford's, Brant, Chama, Corsac, Hoary, Indian, Kit, Pale, Rüppell's, Samson, Sand, Silver, Steppe, Swift and Tibetan Sand. Gen.: *Vulpes, Dusicyon, Alopex, Otocyon*.

frog   several families of the order Anura, mainly insectivorous amphibians having a short, tailless body with long hind legs for hopping. The European common frog is Sp.: *Rana temporaria*.

furniture beetle   beetle whose larvae bore into wood and are known as 'woodworm'. Sp.: *Anobium punctatum*.

galago   see bush baby.

galliwasp   West Indian lizard. Sp.: *Diploglossus monotropis*.

garfish   marine fish having long, beak-like jaws with sharp teeth. Aka needlefish. Family: Belonidae.

gavial (gharial)   long-snouted reptile of the order Crocodilia, and the only species of the family Gavialidae. The gavial inhabits the rivers of northern India and grows to a length of up to 5 metres. Sp.: *Gavialis gangeticus*.

gazelle   antelope of Asia or Africa. Gen.: *Gazella, Antilope, Antidoreas, Procapra, Ammodoreas, Litocranius*.

gecko   nocturnal lizards found in warm climes, with adhesive feet for climbing purposes, the only lizards with voices. Family: Gekkonidae.

gelada   brownish baboon with a bare red patch on its chest, native to Ethiopia. Sp.: *Theropithecus gelada*.

gemsbok   large antelope of south-west and east Africa. Sp.: *Oryx gazella*.

genet (genette)   cat-like mammal native to Africa and Southern Europe with spotted fur and a long, ringed, bushy tail. Gen.: *Genetta*.

gerbil   various genera of mouse-like desert rodents. The species often kept as a pet is *Meriones unguiculatus*, the Mongolian gerbil.

gerenuk   antelope native to east Africa, with a very long neck and small head. Sp.: *Litocranius walleri*.

giant anteater   edentate (toothless) mammal of Central and South America with long snout used for feeding on termites. Sp.: *Myrmecophaga tridactyla*.

gila monster   venomous lizard of southwest USA and northwestern Mexico. The gila monster is stout-bodied with black and pink markings and grows to about 45 centimetres (18 inches). Sp.: *Heloderma suspectum*.

giraffe   ruminant mammal of Africa with a long neck and forelegs and a skin of dark patches separated by lighter lines. It is the tallest living animal (over 5 metres). Sp.: *Giraffa camelopardalis*.

gnu   two antelope species of the genus *Connochaetes*, native to southern Africa, Kenya, Tanzania and Zambia, with a large, erect head and brown stripes on the neck and shoulders. Aka wildebeest.

goat   males are called rams or billies and females are does or nannies. Domesticated breeds include Angora, Kashmir, Nubian, Saanen and Toggenburg. Sp.: *Capra hircus*.

goldfish   freshwater cyprinid fish of eastern Europe and Asia, especially China. Sp.: *Carassius auratus*.

gopher   burrowing rodents of the family Geomyidae native to North America, having food pouches on the cheeks. Aka pocket gopher.

gopher tortoise   tortoise native to southern USA, that excavates tunnels to shelter from the sun. Gen.: *Gopherus*.

gorilla   largest anthropoid ape, native to central Africa. Sp.: *Gorilla gorilla*.

gourami   large freshwater fish native to South-east Asia. Aka labyrinth fish. Sp.: *Osphronemus goramy*.

grampus   dolphin with a blunt snout and long, pointed black flippers. Aka Risso's dolphin. Sp.: *Grampus griseus*.

NATURE

grasshopper any orthopterous insect of the families Acrididae (short-horned grasshoppers) and Tettigoniidae (long-horned grasshoppers). The grasshopper frequents semi-arid regions and grasslands. Many species are green in colour, although some are brownish-grey with red or yellow markings. The upper hind legs of a grasshopper are elongated, and the males tend to produce a buzzing sound by rubbing the femur against its wings. The young of a grasshopper is called a nymph.

grayling silver-grey freshwater fish with a long, high dorsal fin. Gen.: *Thymallus*.

grayling butterfly having wings with grey undersides and bright eye-spots on the upper side. Sp.: *Hipparchia semele*.

greenbottle fly of the genus *Lucilia*, which lays eggs in the flesh of sheep.

grunion slender Californian silverside fish, which spawns on beaches. Sp.: *Leuresthes tenuis*.

gudgeon: common small European freshwater fish, often used as bait. Sp.: *Gobio gobio*.

guinea pig domesticated Southern American cavy kept as a pet or for research in biology. Sp.: *Cavia porcellus*.

haddock edible marine fish of the north Atlantic, similar to cod but smaller. Sp.: *Melanogrammus aeglefinus*.

hairstreak species of butterfly of the family Lycaenidae, distinguished by the hair-like markings on the underside of their wings. Usually brown or grey in colour but occasionally red and black. Gen.: *Callophrys*.

hamadryas large, powerful monkey of the plains and open-rock areas of southern Arabia and northeast Africa. Aka sacred baboon or Arabian baboon. Sp.: *Papio hamadryas*.

hamster: common Eurasian rodent of the subfamily Cricetinae, having a short tail and large cheek pouches for storing food. Sp.: *Cricetus cricetus*.

hamster: golden Eurasian rodent of the subfamily Cricetinae, having a short tail and large cheek pouches for storing food and often kept as a pet or as a laboratory animal. Sp.: *Mesocricetus auratus*.

hanuman Indian langur venerated by Hindus. Aka wanderoo. Sp.: *Semnopithecus entellus*.

hare larger than a rabbit, with longer ears, its habitat is called a form. Sp.: *Lepus europaeus*.

harp seal earless seal of the family Phocidae, found in the North Atlantic and Arctic oceans. The typical male is golden-grey with dark markings on its back and face and can grow up to 2 metres long and weigh in excess of 200 kilograms (440 pounds). A young harp seal is variously named bedlamer, beater or greyback, depending on its age and development. Sp.: *Pagophilus groenlandicus*.

hartebeest large African antelope with ringed horns bent back at the tips. Gen.: *Alcelaphus*.

harvest mouse small mouse with a prehensile tail, which nests in the stalks of growing grain. Sp.: *Micromys minutus*.

hedgehog Old World mammal of the order Insectivora with spiny back and very small tail. The common western European species is *Erinaceus europaeus*.

hellbender large, brownish-grey North American salamander measuring up to 75 centimetres in length, with a flat head, short stout legs and a wrinkled fold of skin down its sides. Sp.: *Cryptobranchus alleganiensis*.

hercules beetle large South American beetle with two horns extending from its head. Sp.: *Dynastes hercules*.

herring soft-finned fish of northern seas with elongated scaled body and smooth head. Sp.: *Clupea harengus*.

horned toad South-east Asian toads with horn-shaped extensions over the eyes. Family: Pelobatidae.

horned toad American lizard covered with spiny scales. Gen.: *Phrynosoma*.

hornet large wasp with brown and yellow striped body, capable of inflicting a severe sting. Sp.: *Vespa crabro*.

horseshoe bat bat of the Old World with a horseshoe-shaped ridge on the nose. Family: Rhinolophidae.

horseshoe crab large marine arthropod with a horseshoe-shaped shell and a long tail-spine. Gen.: *Limulus*.

house mouse very common grey mouse, which scavenges around human dwellings. Often kept as pets or used in laboratory experiments. Sp.: *Mus musculus*.

housefly fly of the family Muscidae, breeding in decaying organic matter and often entering houses. Sp.: *Musca domestica*.

hyena (spotted) long-legged, carnivorous, dog-like mammal of Africa. Aka laughing hyena. Sp.: *Crocuta crocuta*.

ibex wild goat of mountainous areas of Europe, north Africa and Asia, with a beard and thick, curved, ridged horns. Sp.: *Capra ibex*.

iguanodon large, herbivorous, long-tailed bipedal dinosaur of the Cretaceous period. Gen.: *Iguanodon*.

impala medium-size antelope of South and East Africa capable of long high jumps. Sp.: *Aepyceros melampus*.

indigo snake see cribo.

jackal four species of African or South Asian canine mammals of the genus *Canis*.

jackrabbit North American hare with long hind legs and large ears. The white-tailed jackrabbit is *Lepus townsendii*.

jaguar large feline mammal of south-west USA and Central and South America, similar to the leopard but with a shorter tail and larger spots on its coat. Sp.: *Panthera onca*.

jaguarondi North and South American small grey cat with short legs and long tail. Sp.: *Felis yagouaroundi*.

jellyfish marine coelenterate of the class Scyphozoa having an umbrella-shaped, jelly-like body and stinging tentacles.

kalong fruit-eating bat. Aka flying fox. Sp.: *Pteropus edulis*.

kangaroo any of up to 50 species of Australasian marsupial mammals of the family Macropodidae. Kangaroos may grow to a height in excess of 2.5 metres and leap a distance of over 13 metres in a single bound at a speed of 50 km per hour.

katipo venomous spider of New Zealand, usually black with a red or orange stripe on its abdomen. Sp.: *Latrodectus katipo*.

katydid orthopterous insect of the family Tettigoniidae (long-horned grasshopper). The katydid is usually coloured green and lives among the foliage of North American trees. Its name derives from the cry of 'katydid, katy didn't' which is heard throughout the night and produced by the insect rubbing its wings together.

kiang wild ass of a race native to Tibet with a thick furry coat, a subspecies of the Asiatic ass, *Equus hemionus*.

killer whale actually a kind of dolphin, with a black back, white belly and prominent dorsal fin. Sp.: *Orcinus orca*.

king cobra world's largest venomous snake (up to 5.5 metres), found from southern China to the Philippines and Indonesia. Aka hamadryad. Sp.: *Ophiophagus hannah*.

kinkajou nocturnal fruit-eating mammal of Central and South America, with a prehensile tail and a very long tail. Sp.: *Potos flavus*.

kissing gourami small, brightly coloured freshwater fish, a popular aquarium pet. Sp.: *Helostoma temminckii*.

koala slow-moving, arboreal marsupial of eastern Australia, having grey fur and feeding on eucalyptus leaves and bark. The koala is also known as a koala bear, although not related to the Ursidae family. It is the only animal apart from humans with unique fingerprints. Sp.: *Phascolarctos cinereus*.

kolinsky Siberian and Asian weasel with a rich brown coat. Sp.: *Mustela sibirica*.

Komodo dragon predatory lizard native to the East Indies, largest of all surviving lizards, reaching over 3 metres long. Sp.: *Varanus komodoensis*.

kouprey rare grey ox, native to forests in Indo-China. Sp.: *Bos sauveli*.

krait any venomous snake of the Asiatic genus *Bungarus*.

lamprey mostly parasitic, eel-like fish of the family Petromyzontidae, without scales, paired fins or jaws, but having a sucker mouth with horny teeth and a rough tongue.

land crab crab that lives in burrows inland and migrates in large numbers to the sea to breed. Sp.: *Cardisoma guanhumi*.

langur any of various agile arboreal Old World monkeys of the family Cercopithecidae.

laughing hyena see hyena (spotted).

leafcutter ant ant of tropical America, which cuts pieces from leaves to cultivate fungus. Gen.: *Atta*.

leafcutter bee solitary bee, which lines its nest with leaf fragments. Family: Megachilidae.

lemon shark member of the shark family Carcharhinidae breeding in western Atlantic waters. Have a short, blunt, rounded nose and feed on bony fish and molluscs. They grow up to 3.3 metres long.

lemon sole flatfish of the plaice family. Sp.: *Microstomus kitt*.

lemur any Madagascan prosimian primate of the family Lemuridae.

leopard large African or Asian feline mammal with either a black-spotted yellowish fawn or all-black coat. Aka panther. Sp.: *Panthera pardus*.

limpet marine gastropod mollusc with a shallow conical shell and a broad muscular foot that sticks tightly to rocks. The common limpet is *Patella vulgata*.

lion large predatory feline mammal of Africa and north-west India, often called the king of beasts. Sp.: *Panthera leo*.

llama South American ruminant related to the camel, kept as a beast of burden and for its soft woolly fleece. Sp.: *Lama glama*.

loach small, edible freshwater fish of the family Cobitidae.

locust orthopterous insect of the family Acrididae (short-horned grasshopper), which is prone to multiply quickly and migrate long distances in destructive swarms billions strong.

loris: slender and slow small slow-moving nocturnal tree-dwelling primates with small ears and a very short tail. The slender loris, *Loris tardigradus*, is found in southern India. The slow loris, *Nycticebus coucang*, is found in south-west Asia and the East Indies.

louse wingless insect parasitic on a wide range of birds and mammals. Those that infest the human hair and skin and transmit various diseases are *Pediculus humanus*.

lynx short-tailed cat inhabiting forests of Europe, Asia and North America. The lynx is distinguished by its tufted ears, hairy soles, broad short head and mottled fur. Sp.: *Felis lynx*.

macaque medium-sized monkey of the Old World genus *Macaca*, including the rhesus monkey and barbary ape, typically having a rather long face with cheek pouches.

mackerel (common) North Atlantic marine fish with a greenish-blue body, used for food. Sp.: *Scomber scombrus*.

magpie moth white geometrid moth with black and yellow markings whose caterpillars feed on fruit bushes. Sp.: *Abraxas grossulariata*.

Malayan stink badger aka teledu or skunk badger. Strong-smelling dark coat is key feature. Sp.: *Mydaus javanensis*.

mamba any venomous African snake of the genus *Dendroaspis*, especially the green and black mambas, *Dendroaspis angusticeps* and *Dendroaspis polylepis*.

mammoth large, extinct elephant of the Pleistocene period. Gen.: *Mammuthus*.

mammoth (woolly) large extinct elephant of the Pleistocene period having a hairy coat and long tusks. Sp.: *Mammuthus primigenius*.

manatee large, aquatic, plant-eating, sirenian mammal with paddle-like forelimbs, no hind limbs and a powerful tail. Aka sea cow. Gen.: *Trichechus*.

mandrill large West African baboon, the adult of which has a brilliantly coloured face and blue-coloured buttocks. Sp.: *Papio sphinx*.

mangabey various small long-tailed West and Central African monkeys of the genus *Cercocebus*. Named after a region of Madagascar.

marbled white whitish butterfly with black markings. Sp.: *Melanargia galathea*.

margay small wild Central and South American cat. Sp.: *Felis wiedii*.

markhor large, spiral-horned wild goat of Central Asia. Sp.: *Capra falconeri*.

marmoset tropical American monkeys having a long silky coat and a bushy tail. Gen.: *Callithrix*.

marmot burrowing, hibernating rodents of the squirrel family with a heavy-set body and short bushy tail, living in colonies in Europe, Asia and the Americas. Gen.: *Marmota*.

marten any weasel-like carnivore of the genus *Martes*, having valuable fur.

massasauga small North American rattlesnake named from corruption of Mississagi River, Ontario. Sp.: *Sistrurus catenatus*.

mastodon extinct, elephant-like proboscidean mammal common in the Miocene period. Gen.: *Mammut*.

NATURE

mayfly insects with an acquatic nymph and a fragile-winged adult, which lives only briefly in spring. Aka green drake. Order: Ephemeroptera.

meadow brown common brown butterfly with eye-spots on the upper wing. Sp.: *Maniola jurtina*.

megaloceros giant deer whose antlers had a 3.5 metre span; it lived in Eurasia during the last Ice Age. Gen.: *Megaloceros*.

megalosaurus flesh-eating dinosaur, the first to receive a scientific name. Gen.: *Megalosaurus*.

Mexican bearded lizard related to the gila monster and inhabiting the same territory, the Mexican bearded lizard is similar in colour but grows to about 80 centimetres (32 inches). Together they are the only species of poisonous lizards. Sp.: *Heloderma horridum*.

miller's thumb small, spiny, freshwater fish with a large head. Aka bullhead. Sp.: *Cottus gobio*.

millipede herbivorous arthropod of the class Diplopoda, which can have up to 200 pairs of legs.

mink: American semi-aquatic musteline mammal having slightly webbed feet, often hunted for their valuable fur. Sp.: *Mustela vison*.

mink: European slightly smaller version of the American mink. Sp.: *Mustela lutreola*.

mite small parasitic arachnid of the order Acarina, similar to ticks but distinguished by the lack of a sensory pit, known as Haller's organ, on the end segment of the first of four pairs of legs.

mola (ocean sunfish, headfish) large grey heavy ocean fish with short body, flattened sideways. Aka Sp.: *Mola mola*.

mole small burrowing mammals of the order Insectivora, family Talpidae, found in Europe, Asia and North America. The British mole is *Talpa europaeus*.

mongoose small predatory mammals of Africa, southern Europe and Asia, having long tail and brindled coat. Two sub-families: Galidinae and Herpestinae.

monkey any of numerous primates of a group including the families Cebidae (capuchins), Callithricidae (marmosets and tamarins) and Cercopithecidae (baboons and macaques), especially any of the long-tailed varieties.

moonfish see opah.

moose North American elk. Sp.: *Alces alces*.

mouf(f)lon wild mountain sheep of South Europe. Sp.: *Ovis musimon*.

mud puppy large, grey, neotenous aquatic salamander of eastern USA with conspicuous red feathery gills. Sp.: *Necturus maculosus*.

mudskipper any small goby of the family Periophthalmidae, found along the coasts of the Indian and Pacific oceans, able to leave the water and scramble over mud.

mulloway large Australian marine fish used as food. Sp.: *Argyrosomos hololepidotus*.

muntjac any small deer of the genus *Muntiacus*, native to South-east Asia, the male having tusks and small antlers.

musk deer three species of small Asian deer of the genus *Moschus*, having no antlers and in the male having long protruding canine teeth. The musk gland of the male is valued for its use in perfume and medicines.

musk ox large goat-antelope native to North America with a thick, shaggy coat and small, curved horns. Sp.: *Ovibos moschatus*.

muskellunge large North American pike particularly inhabiting the Great Lakes. Aka maskinonge. Sp.: *Esox masquinongy*.

muskrat large aquatic rodent of the vole tribe, native to North America, having a musky smell. Aka musquash. Gen.: *Ondata zibethicus*.

narwhal small Arctic whale, the male of which has a long, straight, spirally twisted tusk developed from one of its teeth. Sp.: *Monodon monoceros*.

natterjack toad of western Eurasia with a bright yellow stripe down its back and moving by running not hopping. Sp.: *Bufo calamita*.

newt any of more than 40 species of tailed amphibian of the order Urodela and family Salamandridae. Aquatic newts have smooth moist skins, while terrestrial species have rough skin and are known as efts. British newts are of the genera *Triturus* (tritons), the most common being the smooth newt (*Triturus vulgaris*).

nilgai large short-horned Indian antelope. Sp.: *Boselaphus tragocamelus*.

Norway lobster small European lobster or scampi. Aka Dublin Bay prawn. Sp.: *Nephrops norvegicus*.

numbat small western Australian termite-eating marsupial with a bushy tail and black and white striped back. Sp.: *Myrmecobius fasciatus*.

nurse shark Atlantic and Caribbean shark of the family Orectolobidae. Yellow-brown or grey-brown in colour and growing up to 4.2 metres, they are the most common hazard to divers although rarely fatally as their teeth are relatively small. Sp.: *Ginglymostoma cirratum*.

ocelot medium-size cat native to the Americas, having a deep yellow or orange coat with black striped and spotted markings. Sp.: *Felis pardalis*.

octopus any cephalopod mollusc of the order Octopoda, varying in size from 1 centimetre to almost 6 metres, with an armspan of almost 9 metres. Octopuses (or octopi) have 8 tentacles and eject an inky fluid when attacked. The largest species is the North Pacific octopus (*Octopus dofleini*) and the smallest is the Californian octopus (*Octopus micropyrsus*). The common octopus (*Octopus vulgaris*) reaches an average size of 1 metre. The octopus has the most complex brain of any invertebrate, having both long-term and short-term memories.

opah large, rare, deep-sea fish having a silver-blue back with white spots and crimson fins. Aka moonfish. Sp.: *Lampris guttatus*.

opossum any mainly tree-living marsupial of the family Didelphidae, native to North and South America, and having a prehensile tail and hind feet with an opposable thumb.

orang-utan large, red, long-haired, tree-living ape native to Borneo and Sumatra. Aka wild man of the woods. Sp.: *Pongo pygmaeus*.

orfe freshwater cyprinid fish of Europe that occurs in two colour varieties i.e. golden and silver. Orfes are often called goldfish. Sp.: *Idus idus*.

oribi small African grazing antelope having reddish-fawn back and white underparts. Sp.: *Ourebia ourebi*.

oryx large African antelope having long straight nearly upright horns. Gen.: *Oryx*.

otter freshwater carnivorous mammals of Europe, Asia, Africa and the Americas, with smooth fur and webbed feet. Sub-family Lutrinae.

ounce see snow leopard.

paddlefish primitive bony fish of the Mississippi and Yangtze rivers, leaden grey, with a long flat snout. Sp.: *Polyodon spathula* and *Psephurus gladius*

paddymelon (pademelon)   small wallaby of coastal scrubby regions of Australia. Gen.: *Thylogale*.

painted lady   orange-red butterfly with black and white spots. Sp.: *Cynthia cardui*.

panda: giant   large, rare, bear-like mammal native to certain mountain bamboo forests of China, having characteristic black and white markings. Sp.: *Ailuropoda melanoleuca*.

panda: red   Himalayan raccoon-like mammal with reddish-brown fur and a long, bushy tail. Sp.: *Ailurus fulgens*.

pangolin   various mammal species native to Asia and Africa covered with overlapping horny scales and having a small head with elongated snout and tongue, with which they feed on ants, and a tapering tail. Aka scaly anteater. Gen.: *Manus*.

peacock butterfly   butterfly with eye-like markings on its wings. Sp.: *Inachis io*.

pearl-oyster   any of various marine bivalve molluscs of the genus *Pinctada*, bearing pearls.

peccary   three species of American, wild, pig-like mammals of the family Tayassuidae. Sp.: *Tayassu tajacu*, *Tayassu pecari* and *Catagonus wagneri*.

Père David's deer   large, slender-antlered deer, named after Father A David, French missionary and naturalist (d. 1900). Sp.: *Elaphurus davidiensis*.

phalanger   any of various species of Australasian marsupial mammals of the family Phalangeridae, also known as possums on the Australian mainland and Tasmania.

plaice   European flatfish having a brown back with orange spots and a white underside, much used for food. Sp.: *Pleuronectes platessa*.

polar bear   white carnivorous bear of coastal regions of the North Pole. Sp.: *Ursus maritimus*.

polecat (European)   small, brownish-black, fetid flesh-eating mammal of the weasel family. Sp.: *Mustela putorius*.

porpoise   any of various marine cetacean mammals of the families Delphinidae and Phocoenidae, which are typically smaller than dolphins and with chubbier shape and blunter snout. Sp.: *Phocoena phocoena*.

possum   any member of the Phalangeridae family of marsupial mammals native to Australasia. Possums are tree-dwellers. The brush-tailed possum (*Trichosurus vulpecula*) is the most common marsupial in Australia.

potto   short-tailed prosimian primate, of the family Lorisidae, having vertebral spines protruding through its neck. The potto is often confused with the kinkajou, as it is a slow-moving, nocturnal, arboreal mammal.

prawn   any of various marine decapod crustaceans of the genera *Palaemon* and *Penaeus*, similar to shrimps but having two pairs of pincers.

pterodactyl   extinct flying reptile of the late Jurassic, having membranous wings supported on an elongated 4th digit. Gen.: *Pterodactylus*.

puma   largest American feline mammal, resembling a lion. It is the best jumper of the cat family. Aka cougar or mountain lion. Sp.: *Felis concolor*.

pygmy white-toothed shrew   smallest member of the mouse-like, long-snouted mammals of the family Soricidae. Sp.: *Suncus etruseus*.

quokka   small marsupial resembling a wallaby, primarily inhabiting Rottnest Island off the coast of Perth, Western Australia. Sp.: *Setonix brachyurus*.

rabbit   burrowing leporid mammal which is smaller than a hare and has much shorter ears. The European rabbit is *Oryctolagus cuniculus*.

raccoon   omnivorous mammal of the genus *Procyon* occupying diverse habitats in North and South America. It has a pointed muzzle, long tail and greyish-black fur with black bands around the tail and across the face. The common raccoon of North America is *Procyon lotor*.

ratel   see badger (honey).

red deer   forest-dweller of Europe and western to central Asia. Males are called harts and females, hinds. Harts with 12 tines are known as 'Royal' and one with 14 tines is a 'Wilson'. Sp.: *Cervus elaphus*.

reindeer   see caribou.

ring-tailed lemur   rock-dwelling lemur with elongated hind legs and a long tail with brown and white ringed markings. Sp.: *Lemur catta*.

Rocky Mountain goat   massive, yellowish-white goat-antelope inhabiting mountains in western North America. Sp.: *Oreamnos americanus*.

roe deer   small, graceful woodland deer of Eurasia, the males having small antlers and a reddish-brown summer coat. Sp.: *Capreolus capreolus*.

sable   marten of northern Asian and Japanese forests, with dark brown luxuriant fur. Sp.: *Martes zibellina*.

sabre-toothed tiger   extinct, lion-size mammal of the cat family (only distantly related to the tiger) with long, curved, upper canine teeth. Aka sabre-toothed cat. Gen.: *Smilodon*.

salamander   any tailed amphibian of the order Urodela that most commonly inhabit freshwater and damp woodlands. Salamanders resemble lizards but are related to newts in the family Salamandridae, and can be aquatic, semi-aquatic, or terrestrial. They are generally very small (10–15 centimetres) but giant salamanders may attain a length of up to 180 centimetres. The semi-aquatic Chinese giant salamander (*Andrias davidianus*) grows in excess of 1 metre but the largest salamander is the Japanese giant salamander (*Andrias japonicus*).

sand lizard   small, green-grey-brown Eurasian lizard with long clawed digits. Sp.: *Lacerta agilis*.

scorpion   arachnid of the order Scorpionida, having an elongated body and a segmented, upwardly curving tail that is tipped with a venomous stinger. During mating the male and female perform a courtship dance and after copulation the female often devours the male.

seal: eared   carnivorous pinniped (paddle-footed) aquatic mammal of the family Otariidae, which comes to shore to breed. Eared seals swim by 'rowing' with their front flippers and can turn their hindflippers forward to walk on land.

seal: elephant   large seal, the male having an inflatable snout. Aka sea elephant. Gen.: *Mirounga*.

seal: true   carnivorous pinniped (paddle-footed) aquatic mammal of the family Phocidae, which comes to shore to breed. They are earless, swim with their hindflippers, and hump along on land, unable to use their hindflippers as support.

sea lion   any of five species of eared seal of the South Atlantic and Pacific. The Californian sea lion (*Zalophus californianus*) is the species trained for circus performances.

sea squirt   any small primitive marine animal of the class Ascidiacea, having a sac-like body with openings through which water enters and leaves. Sea squirts are sedentary and sessile and can be found on coral reefs, pier pilings, ships' hulls, rocks and seashells. Peculiarly, they can be found on the backs of some species of crabs, while other species of crabs may dwell inside the cavities of a sea squirt.

serval slender feline mammal of the African savanna, having an orange-brown coat with black spots, large ears and long legs. Sp.: *Felis serval.*

shark any of the cartilaginous fish of the class Chondrichthyes with pointed snouts extending over a crescent-shaped mouth. Sharks do not have a swim bladder. There are more than 200 living species of shark including the hammerhead, mako, thresher, bull, bonnethead and Greenland. See also separate entries.

sheep any of various bovid mammals having ribbed horns and a narrow face. Domesticated breeds, genus *Ovis*, include Border Leicester, Cheviot, Clun Forest, Cobb 101, Cotswold, Dartmoor, Devon Longwool, Dorset Down, Dorset Horn, Exmoor Horned, Hampshire, Herdwick, Ile-de-France, Karakul, Kerry Hill, Leicester, Lincoln, The Lonk, Masham, Merino, Oxford, Rambouillet, Romney, Roscommon, Ryeland, Scottish Blackface, Shropshire, Southdown, Suffolk, Swaledale, Welsh Mountain, Wensleydale and Wiltshire Horned.

shrew small, mouse-like, long-snouted mammals of the order Insectivora, family Soricidae. The European common shrew is *Sorex araneus*. Aka shrewmouse.

shrew: elephant small, insect-eating mammals native to Africa, having a long snout and long hind limbs Family: Macroscelididae.

shrimp any of various marine decapod crustaceans of the genus *Crangon*, having a slender flattened body, long tail and a single pair of pincers. Although large shrimps in excess of 5 millimetres are sometimes called prawns, this is misleading as a prawn is a distinct species with two sets of pincers. The two most important shrimps are the common shrimp (*Crangon vulgaris*) and the edible shrimp (*Peneus setiferus*).

skunk American musteline mammals of the sub-family Mephitinae, typically having a black and white coat and bushy tail.They eject a foul-smelling fluid from the anal gland when attacked. The familiar striped skunk is *Mephitis mephitis*.

slender-tailed meerkat see suricate.

sloth shaggy-coated, arboreal edentate mammals of Central and South America that hang upside down by their arms. Three-toed sloths, genus *Bradypus*; two-toed sloths, genus *Choloepus*.

slow worm Eurasian legless lizard with brownish-grey, snake-like body. Sp.: *Anguis fragilis*.

snake (grass) non-venomous European snake having brownish-green body. Sp.: *Natrix natrix*.

snow leopard large, feline, mammal of mountainous regions of central Asia, having a long, pale brown coat marked with black rosettes. Aka ounce. Sp.: *Panthera uncia*.

solenodon rare, shrew-like, nocturnal mammal of the West Indies, having a long hairless tail and an elongated snout. Cuban species, *Solenodon cubanus*; Hispaniola species, *Solenodon paradoxus*.

spectacled bear solitary South American species of the family Ursidae and inhabiting mountainous terrain, which gives it an alternative name of Andean bear. It grows up to 180 centimetres long (6 feet) and has a dark brown coat, with whitish markings around its eyes and facial circumference. Sp.: *Tremarctos ornatus*.

sponge any member of primitive multicellular aquatic animals of the phylum Porifera, which have porous, baglike bodies with a skeleton of hard spicules or elastic fibres. The dried skeleton of sponges are procured for commercial purposes as bathroom sponges because of their ability to hold water.

squirrel (grey) grey-furred squirrel native to eastern North America but found worldwide. Sp.: *Sciurus carolinensis*.

squirrel (red) reddish-brown squirrel inhabiting woodlands of Europe and Asia. Sp.: *Sciurus vulgaris*.

starfish any echinoderm of the classes Asteroidea (sea stars) and Ophiuroidea (brittle stars), typically having a flat body and 5 tentacles, although some species may have many more.

stoat small, long-bodied carnivorous mammal of the weasel family having reddish-brown upper parts and a black-tipped tail and in northern areas turning white in winter, when it is known as ermine. Sp.: *Mustela erminea*.

sturgeon primitive bony fish of temperate waters of the northern hemisphere, valued as a source of caviar and isinglass. Family: Acipenseridae.

sugar glider Australian possum that glides from tree to tree by means of a fold of skin that joins its front and hind legs. The sugar glider is also known as the flying possum or flying phalanger. Sp.: *Petaurus breviceps*.

suricate southern African mongoose which has a lemur-like face. Aka slender-tailed meerkat. Sp.: *Suricata suricatta*.

swallowtail butterfly member of the subfamily Papilioninae, order Lepidoptera. Swallowtails are found worldwide and are named for the tail-like extensions of their hindwings. Gen.: *Papilio*.

taipan large highly venomous snake of north-east Australia, dark brown with a creamy-coloured head. Sp.: *Oxyuranus scutellatus*.

tapeworm any of various parasitic flatworms of the order Cestoda, which attack the liver and digestive tract of vertebrates.

tapir four species of forest-dwelling perissodactyl mammals of South and Central America and South-east Asia, having an elongated snout, three-toed hind legs and four-toed forelegs. Genus *Tapirus*.

tarpon large, silvery, game fish of warm Atlantic waters, having a compressed, scaled body. *Tarpon atlanticus* is the best-known species.

Tasmanian devil small, ferocious, carnivorous marsupial having black fur with pale markings, strong jaws and short legs. Aka ursine dasyure. Sp.: *Sarcophilus harrisi*.

Tasmanian wolf see thylacine.

tayra large, arboreal, musteline mammal of Central and South America, having a dark brown body and paler head. Sp.: *Eira barbata*.

teledu see Malayan stink badger.

tenrec: tailless small mammal of Madagascar (but largest insectivore), resembling a hedgehog or shrew. Sp.: *Tenrec ecaudatus*.

termite whitish, ant-like insect of the order Isoptera. The two main species are 'ground' termites and 'drywood' termites. Termites feed on cellulose, which is found in wood and wood products. They are social insects, and a typical colony would include workers, soldiers, winged reproductives, and a king and queen. The alternative name for a termite is 'white ant', although there are subtle differences between the body shape of an ant and a termite. An ant has a tapered abdomen, while that of a termite is straight. The ant also has bent antennae whereas the termites are straight. The winged reproductives are similar to flying ants, although their double wings are even in size while the ant's double wings are uneven in size.

terrapin web-footed chelonian reptile that lives on land or in fresh water. Family: Emydidae.

thylacine presumed extinct, dog-like carnivorous marsupial of Tasmania, having greyish-brown fur with dark vertical stripes on the back. Aka Tasmanian wolf. Sp.: *Thylacinus cynocephalus.*

tick small parasitic arachnid of the families Ixodidae and Nuttalliellidae (hard ticks) and Argasidae (soft ticks). Ticks dwell on the skin of warm-blooded animals and feed on the blood and tissues of their hosts.

tiger large Asian feline mammal with yellowy coat and black stripes. Sp.: *Panthera tigris.*

tiger shark large voracious shark of the family Carcharhinidae. Possess a reputation as a man-eater, but although undoubtedly capable of eating almost anything, in actuality they swim away from divers. Tiger sharks grow up to a length of 7.3 metres and have commercial use as a source of leather and liver oil. Sp.: *Galeocerdo cuvier.*

timber rattlesnake heavy-bodied snake with a broad head that is distinct from its narrow neck. The rattlesnake inhabits the prairies of North America, where it feeds on a variety of small mammals, which are killed by its venomous bite. Humans are not under threat from rattlesnakes as 60 per cent of all bites are dry, and even venomous bites rarely cause more than temporary discomfort. The rattlesnake is generally golden-brown with black markings except for the head, which is plain brown, and its rattler, at the tip of its tail, which is dark black. Sp.: *Crotalus horridus.*

toad anuran amphibian, secreting a poisonous fluid, similar to frogs but more terrestrial, having drier, warty skin. The Eurasian common toad is *Bufo bufo.*

tokay large (35 cm) grey gecko with orange and deep blue spots, of South-east Asia. Sp.: *Gekko gecko.*

tortoise herbivorous chelonian reptile found in warm regions worldwide except Australia. Family: Testudinidae.

tree frog arboreal frog of the family Hylidae, with sucker-like pads to aid in climbing. Tree frogs are also known as tree toads.

triceratops rhinoceros-like herbivorous dinosaur of the Cretaceous period, up to 9 metres long, having three horns and a short armoured neck frill. Gen.: *Triceratops.*

turtle aquatic chelonian reptiles with a flattened shell and flipper-like limbs for swimming. Several families of the order Chelonia.

Tyrannosaurus rex 14 metres long, 6 metres tall, flesh-eating dinosaur with relatively small 2-fingered hands. Gen.: *Tyrannosaurus.*

unau aka Linné's two-toed sloth. Sp.: *Choloepus didactylus.*

vervet small, yellowish-grey, African, long-tailed monkey. Sp.: *Cercopithecus aethiops.*

vicuña South American mammal of the high Andes related to the llama, with fine silky wool. Sp.: *Vicugna vicugna.*

viscacha large South American burrowing rodent related to the chinchillas. Gen.: *Lagidium* and *Lagostomus.*

vole (field) small, rodent of the family Cricetidae with stocky body, short tail and small ears. Sp.: *Microtus agrestis.*

vole (water) large amphibious vole of Eurasian river banks. Sp.: *Arvicola terrestris.*

wallaby (hare) small rodent-like herbivorous marsupial of Australia and New Guinea, family Macropodidae. Gen.: *Lagorchestes.*

wallaby (rock) herbivorous marsupial of Australia and New Guinea, resembling a small kangaroo, of the family Macropodidae. Gen.: *Protemnodon.*

walrus large, tusked, aquatic mammal of the Arctic, a bottom feeder – mainly on molluscs – related to the eared seals. Its family, Odobenidae, has only one species: *Odobenus rosmarus.*

wapiti big North American deer, which is now considered as a larger race of the red deer. Sp.: *Cervus canadensis.*

warble fly any of various flies of the genus *Hypoderma*, whose larvae infest the skin of cattle and horses.

warthog African wild pig with a large head, warty lumps on its face and large curved tusks. Sp.: *Phacochoerus aethiopicus.*

wasp stinging insect of the order Hymenoptera, with black and yellow stripes and a very thin waist.

water moccasin (cottonmouth) poisonous, semi-aquatic pit viper of south-eastern USA. Sp.: *Agkistrodon piscivorus.*

water opossum semi-aquatic tropical American opossum with dark-banded grey fur. Aka yapok. Sp.: *Chironectes minimus.*

weasel (European common) small, brown and white carnivorous mammal with a slender body, related to the stoat. Gen.: *Mustela nivalis.*

whale any of the larger marine mammals of the order Cetacea, having a streamlined body and horizontal tail, and breathing air through a blowhole on the head. Gen.: *Cetacea.*

whale shark large, tropical whale-like shark feeding close to the surface, mainly on plankton. It is however the world's largest living fish, attaining a maximum length of 16.9 metres. Sp.: *Rhincodon typus.*

white admiral mottled brown butterfly with a white splashed band down its wings. Sp.: *Limenitis camilla.*

wildcat wild cat of Eurasia and Africa with a grey and black coat and a bushy tail. Sp.: *Felis silvestris.*

wildebeest see gnu.

wisent the European bison. Sp.: *Bison bonasus.*

witch North Atlantic flatfish resembling the lemon sole. Sp.: *Glyptocephalus cynoglossus.*

wobbegong (spotted) carpet shark of the family Orectolobidae, inhabiting Australian waters and having a richly patterned brown and white skin. Sp.: *Orectolobus maculatus.*

wolf (grey) wild, flesh-eating mammal of the northern hemisphere, ancestor of the domestic dog. Gen.: *Canis lupus.*

wolf-fish large, voracious blenny of the North Atlantic. Family: Anarhichadidae.

wolverine large, musteline mammal of northern forests of Eurasia and North America, a predator and scavenger, having dark very thick water-resistant fur. Aka glutton. Sp.: *Gulo gulo.*

wombat (common) Australian bear-like terrestrial marsupial with coarse dark hair and small ears. Sp.: *Vombatus ursinus.*

wombat (hairy nosed) two marsupial species of Queensland and central south Australia, with fine grizzled fur and longer ears than the common wombat. Sp.: *Lasiorhinus krefftii* and *Lasiorhinus latifrons*.

woodchuck reddish-brown and grey North American burrowing marmot. Aka groundhog. Sp.: *Marmota monax*.

woodlouse small, terrestrial, isopod crustacean of the order Oniscoidae, feeding on rotten wood and plant matter, some of them (pill bugs) able to roll into a ball. The common woodlouse is *Oniscus asellus*.

yapok see water opossum.

yellowfin tuna fish of warm seas with yellowish fins, widely fished for food. Sp.: *Thunnus albacares*.

yellowtail game fish of coastal waters of southern California and Mexico, having a yellow tail fin. Sp.: *Seriola dorsalis*.

zebra (plains) African quadruped related to the ass and horse, with black and white stripes. Sp.: *Equus burchelli*.

zebu domestic humped ox of India, East Asia and Africa. Sp.: *Bos indicus*.

zorilla flesh-eating African mammal of the weasel family, aka African polecat. Sp.: *Ictonyx striatus*.

Miscellaneous Information

abranchiate having no gills.

amphibian: largest Japanese giant salamander.

anadromous of a fish (e.g. the salmon), swimming up a river from the sea to spawn.

anthrax fatal bacterial disease of sheep and cattle, transmissible to humans and affecting the skin and lungs; aka wool-sorters' disease.

ants: noses five.

apatosaurus: aka Brontosaurus.

ape: smallest gibbon (apes have no tails).

artiodactyl any placental ungulate mammal whose hoofs have an even number of toes – e.g. pigs, sheep, camels, deer, cattle, antelope and hippopotamuses.

batrachian of or relating to frogs or toads.

bees: eyes five.

braxy acute and usually fatal bacterial disease of sheep characterised by high fever, coma and inflammation of the fourth stomach, caused by infection with *Clostridium septicum*.

butterfly: largest Queen Alexandra's birdwing of Papua New Guinea has a wingspan of up to 25 centimetres (10 inches).

butterfly: tastes with back feet.

carnivore: largest the dinosaur Tyrannosaurus is the largest so far known; today the Kodiak bear is largest. The badger is the largest British carnivore.

carnivores: largest molars giant panda.

catadromous of a fish (e.g. the eel), swimming down a river to the sea to spawn.

chelonian reptiles including turtles, terrapins and tortoises, having upper and lower shells of bony plates – the carapace and plastron – covered with horny scales.

cladistics method of classifying animals and plants on the basis of shared characteristics that indicate the relative recency of common ancestry.

class major taxonomic division of animals that contain one or more orders e.g. Amphibia, Mammalia and Reptilia. The class Mammalia includes the orders Carnivora, Primates and Rodentia.

coarse fish any freshwater fish other than salmon and trout.

crab: lives in cast-off mollusc shell hermit crab.

cricket: ears situated on front legs.

crops: damage boll weevil (cotton); Colorado beetle (potato); locust (most vegetation); phylloxera (vine).

daddy-long-legs: aka cranefly or harvestman (US); the larvae are called leatherjackets.

death-watch beetle the ticking is caused by knocking its head against wood.

dinosaur: heaviest Brachiosaurus (up to 100 tons).

dinosaur: longest Diplodocus (up to 30 metres).

dog licences: year abolished 1988.

droppings deer – crotties, hare – currants, otter – spraints.

elephant: teeth number four.

elytron either of the two wing cases of a beetle.

family major taxonomic division of animals that contain one or more genera e.g. Canidae (dogs) and Felidae (cats). The family Canidae includes the genus *Vulpes* (foxes).

fish: fastest cosmopolitan sailfish.

fish: most poisonous stone fish.

fly: wings trues flies (including craneflies, gnat, mosquitos) have two; the four-winged caddis flies, dragonflies, etc., are not true flies.

genus major taxonomic division of animals that contain one or more species e.g. *Vulpes* (foxes). The genus *Vulpes* (foxes) includes the species *Vulpes bengalensis* (Bengal fox).

giant panda: related to raccoons (family Procyonidae).

glanders contagious and fatal disease of horses, mules and donkeys, caused by the bacterium *Actinobacillus mallei* and characterized by swellings below the jaw and mucous discharge from the nostrils.

hedgehog: fleas one hedgehog may have up to 500 fleas, but the hedgehog flea (*Archaeopsylla erinacei*) does not bite humans.

hedgehog: no. of spines usually about 5,000.

hinny offspring of a female donkey and a male horse.

horse: colours bay – brown with black mane and legs; chestnut – reddish-brown; dun – sandy with black mane; palomino – golden with pale mane; piebald – black and white; skewbald – brown and white; strawberry roan – chestnut and white.

insect: heaviest goliath beetle.

insects: segments head, abdomen, thorax (mnemonic: insects wear HATs).

invertebrate: largest giant squid.

kangaroo: name means 'I don't understand'.

kingdom any of the three groups into which natural objects may be divided i.e. animals, plants and minerals.

koala: name means 'no drink' (feeds on eucalyptus leaves).

lobster: colour Bluish but goes red when cooked.

louping-ill viral disease of animals, especially sheep, transmitted by ticks and causing staggering and jumping.

males give birth seahorse, from a pouch where the female deposits her eggs.

mallenders dry, scabby eruption behind a horse's knee.

metazoan any animal of the subkingdom Metazoa, having multicellular and differentiated tissues and comprising all animals except Protozoa and Parazoa (sponges).

mirror: response to the chimpanzee is the only animal, apart from humans, able to recognise itself in a mirror.

mule cross between a male horse and a donkey.

murrain infectious disease of cattle caused by parasites.

octopus: hearts three.

omasum the third stomach of a ruminant.

ophidian reptile of the suborder Serpentes, comprising snakes.

order Major taxonomic division of animals that contain one or more families e.g. Carnivora, Primates and Rodentia. The order Carnivore includes the families Canidae (dogs) and Felidae (cats).

pandas: born January (feed on bamboo shoots).

perissodactyl any placental ungulate mammal whose hoofs have an odd number of toes – e.g. horses, tapirs and rhinoceroses.

pets: legal age to buy in Britain 12 years old is the minimum legal age to purchase a pet.

phylum major taxonomic division of animals that contains one or more classes, e.g. Arthropoda and Chordata. The phylum Arthropoda includes the classes, Arachnids, Centipedes, Crustaceans and insects. The phylum Chordata includes the classes, Amphibia, Aves, Mammalia and Reptilia.

pinnipeds: definition carnivorous aquatic mammals with flippers for feet (name means wing-foot).

pismire Middle English name for an ant deriving from the smell of an anthill.

reproduces: young axolotl often reproduces before reaching adult stage itself.

rhinoceros: number of horns Indian and Javan, one; Black, Sumatran and White, two.

rodents: largest capybara (in world), beaver (in Europe), coypu (in UK).

ruminant herbivorous animal that chews the cud.

scrapie fatal disease of sheep and goats, a spongiform encephalopathy producing degeneration of the central nervous system, caused by changes in prion proteins.

sex: changes annually oyster.

silkworm: food mulberry leaves.

snake: heaviest South American anaconda.

spavin disease of a horse's hock with a hard bony swelling or excrescence.

species any of the taxonomic groups into which a

genus is divided; e.g. the genus *Vulpes* (foxes) has many different species, such as *Vulpes bengalensis* (Bengal fox) and *Vulpes pallida* (pale fox). Species are denoted by two words, the first being the genus and the second the species.

spider: eyes eight.

stomach: turns inside out starfish.

strangles acute bacterial disease of horses caused by infection with *Streptococcus equi*, characterised by inflammation of the mucous membranes of the respiratory tract. Aka equine distemper.

sunburn: suffers from the pig is the only non-human animal to suffer from sunburn.

taxonomy the branch of biology concerned with the classification of organisms into groups based on similarities of structure, origin and type. Carolus Linnaeus (1707–78) was the first person to structure principles for defining genera and species of organsims and to create a uniform system for naming them. The seven tiers of the hierarchy are kingdom, phylum, class, order, family, genus and species. The first six ranks use a single word to describe their members, but the names of species are binomial. Various intermediary divisions of the seven main ranks have been necessitated by the continuing discovery of new species: the prefixes sub-, super- and infra- are often applied to create new categories, and further tiers are established by using headings such as tribe or cohort. All intermediary divisions use a single word to describe their members, but subspecies become trinomial. Conventionally, the names of superfamilies end in 'oidea', families in idae', subfamilies in 'inae' and tribes in 'ini'.

taxonomy: mnemonic Kingdom, Phylum, Class, Order, Family, Genus, Species (Kent Play Cricket On Fridays, Girls Spectate).

turning sickness affliction of wildebeest whereby loss of balance faculties causes a never-ending walking in circles until death; it happens when bot-flies lay eggs in their nose and larvae find their way into the brain.

twins: consistent production armadillos and salamanders always give birth to twins.

ungulates all mammals with hoofs; they are divided into odd-toed (perissodactyl) and even-toed (artiodactyl).

vision: rear-view giraffes have ability to see behind them without turning.

woodlouse: legs fourteen.

WWF: symbol World Wide Fund for Nature symbol is a giant panda.

zoophyte plantlike animal, e.g. coral, sea anemone or sponge.

Gestation Periods

Animal	Days	Animal	Days	Animal	Days
aardvark	210	bear, grizzly	230	capybara	150
alpaca	345	polar bear	240	cat, domestic	52
anteater, giant	190	beaver	105	cattle	283
antelope	280	bison	280	chamois	165
armadillo	60–120	boar, wild	115	cheetah	95
ass	350	bobcat	63	chimpanzee	235
baboon	180	buffalo	310	civet	80
badger	100–360	bush baby	110–193	coati	77

Animal	Days	Animal	Days	Animal	Days
coyote	63	jackal	63	raccoon	63
deer, fallow	230	jaguar	100	rat, black	21
deer, musk	170	kangaroo	180–335	reindeer	225
dhole	61	koala	36	rhinoceros, black	450
dingo	63	lemming	21	seal, common	245
dog, domestic	60	lemur	60–160	seal, eared	360
dog, African wild	72	leopard	100	sea lion	350
dolphin	350	lion	110	sheep	148
dormouse	30	llama	360	shrew	18
dromedary	400	lynx	63	skunk	63
elephant, Asiatic	608	macaque	180	sloth	180–340
ermine	28	marmoset	150	squirrel	40
ferret	60	mink	50	tapir	370
fox, red	63	mole	35	tiger	103
gazelle	188	mongoose	60	vole	90
gerbil	28	moose	264	wallaby	40
gibbon	230	mouse	25	walrus	460
giraffe	460	narwhal	435	warthog	172
goat	150	ocelot	70	weasel	40
gorilla	260	opossum	12	whale	350
guinea pig	63	orang-utan	240	whale, beluga	435
hamster	25	otter	55	whale, sperm	435
hare	32	panda, giant	138	wolf	62
hare, mountain	50	pig	115	wolverine	270
hedgehog	30	porcupine	210	yak	258
hippopotamus	240	porpoise	183	zebra	340
horse	350	puma	93	zorilla	43
hyena	93	rabbit	30		

Maximum Life Spans

Species	Years	Species	Years	Species	Years
Marion's tortoise	152	slow-worm	54	giant panda	27
quahog	150	gorilla	53	red deer	26
man	123	domestic goose	50	tiger	26
spur thighed tortoise	116	Indian rhinoceros	49	grey squirrel	23
deep sea clam	100	European brown bear	47	domestic goat	20
killer whale	90	grey seal	46	blue sheep	20
sea anemone	90	blue whale	45	queen ant	18
European eel	88	goldfish	41	common rabbit	18
lake sturgeon	82	common boa	40	hedgehog	16
freshwater mussel	80	common toad	40	land snail	15
Asiatic elephant	78	Cape giraffe	36	guinea pig	14
tuatara	77	Bactrian camel	35	capybara	12
Andean condor	72	Hoffmann's sloth	34	tree shrew	11
African elephant	70	domestic cat	34	giant centipede	10
great eagle owl	68	canary	34	golden hamster	10
American alligator	66	American bison	33	fat dormouse	8
blue macaw	64	bobcat	32	millipede	7
horse	62	red kangaroo	30	house mouse	6
ostrich	62	domestic dog	29	moonrat	4
orang-utan	57	budgerigar	29	monarch butterfly	1
chimpanzee	56	lion	29	bedbug	0.5
pike	55	theraphosid spider	28	house fly	0.04
hippopotamus	54	domestic pig	27		

Animal Cries

Animal	Cry	Animal	Cry	Animal	Cry
apes	gibber	foxes	bark, yelp	owls	hoot, screech
asses	bray	frogs	croak		
bears	growl	geese	cackle, hiss	oxen	low, bellow
bees	hum	grasshoppers	chirp, pitter	parrots	talk
beetles	drone	guineafowls	come back	peacocks	scream
bitterns	boom	guineapigs	squeak	peewits	peewit
blackbirds	whistle	grouse	drum	pigs	grunt, squeak, squeal
blackcaps	chick-chack	hares	squeak		
bulls	bellow	hawks	scream		
calves	bleat	hens	cackle, cluck	pigeons	coo
cats	mew, purr, caterwaul, swear	horses	neigh, whinny	ravens	croak
				rooks	caw
				sheep	bleat, baa
chaffinches	chirp, pink	hyenas	laugh	snakes	hiss
chickens	peep	jays	chatter	sparrows	chirp
cocks	crow	kittens	mew	stags	bellow, call
cows	moo, low	lambs	bleat, baa	swallows	twitter
crows	caw	linnets	chuckle	swans (before death)	cry, sing
cuckoos	cuckoo	lions	roar, growl		
deer	bell	magpies	chatter	thrushes	whistle
dogs	bark, bay, howl, yelp	mice	squeak, squeal	tigers	roar, growl
				turkeys	gobble
doves	coo	monkeys	chatter, gibber	vultures	scream
ducks	quack			whitethroat	chirr
eagles	scream	nightingales	pipe, warble, jug-jug	wolves	howl
falcons	chant				
flies	buzz				

Animal Habitations

Animal	Habitation	Animal	Habitation	Animal	Habitation
ant	formicary, ant-hill	fox	earth, lair	rabbit	burrow, warren
		hare	form, down		
ape	tree-nest	horse	stable	spider	web
badger	set, earth	lion	den	squirrel	drey
bear	den, lair	mole	fortress	tiger	lair
beaver	lodge	mouse	hole, nest	wasp	vespiary, nest
bee	apiary, hive	otter	holt		
bird	nest, aviary	penguin	rookery	wolf	lair
eagle	eyrie				

Animals: Young

Animal	Young	Animal	Young	Animal	Young
ass	foal, hinny	fox	cub	pigeon	squab
bear	cub	frog	tadpole, froglet	pike	jack
beaver	kitten			rabbit	kit
cat	kitten	gnat	bloodworm	roe deer	kid
cod	codling	goat	kid	salmon	parr, smolt, grilse
cow	calf, heifer	goose	gosling		
crane-fly	leather jacket	grouse	poult	seal	pup
		hare	leveret	sheep	lamb
deer	fawn	hippopotamus	calf	squirrel	kitten
duck	duckling	horse	foal	swan	cygnet
eagle	eaglet	kangaroo	joey	whale	calf
eel	elver	lion	cub	zebra	foal
elephant	calf	otter	whelp		
fish	fry	pig	piglet		

Plants and Trees

abele the white poplar. Sp.: *Populus alba.*

alder betulaceous tree having toothed leaves and cone-like fruits. The bark is used in dying and tanning and the wood for bridges (as it resists underwater rot). Gen.: *Alnus.*

alfalfa leguminous plant with clover-like leaves and flowers, grown for fodder and as a salad vegetable. Aka lucerne. Sp.: *Medicago sativa.*

almond small rosaceous tree native to western Asia with pink flowers and green fruit containing edible nut. Sp.: *Prunus amygdalus.*

aloe vera Caribbean aloe yielding a gelatinous substance used in cosmetics as an emollient. Sp.: *Aloe vera.*

alsike species of clover named after Swedish town. Sp.: *Trifolium hybridum.*

anise umbelliferous plant having aromatic seeds. Sp.: *Pimpinella anisum.*

arum lily tall, lily-like, aroid plant found mainly in Southern Africa. Sp.: *Zantedeschia aethiopica.*

ash oleaceous tree with compound leaves, winged seeds and clusters of greenish flowers. Gen.: *Fraxinus.*

aspen poplar tree with especially tremulous leaves. Sp.: *Populus tremula.*

balsa bombacaceous tree of tropical America, distinguished by its very light wood. Sp.: *Ochroma lagopus.*

banyan moraceous tree of tropical India and the East Indies, having aerial roots that grow down from the branches into the soil, forming additional trunks. Sp.: *Ficus benghalensis.*

baobab African tree with an enormously thick trunk and large, edible, pulpy fruit hanging down on stalks. Sp.: *Adansonia digitata.*

barley erect, annual, temperate grass with short leaves and bristly flowers used for grain. Sp.: *Hordeum vulgares.*

bayberry North American shrub having aromatic leaves and bearing berries covered in a wax coating. Sp.: *Myrica cerifera and Myrica cerifera.*

beech hardwood tree having smooth, greyish bark. Gen.: *Fagus.*

bee orchid European and North Africa orchid with bee-shaped flowers. Sp.: *Ophrys apifera.*

betony purple-flowered plant. Sp.: *Stachys officinalis.*

bilberry hardy dwarf shrub of North Europe growing on heaths and mountains and having red drooping flowers and dark blue berries. Sp.: *Vaccinium myrtillus.*

birch hardwood, close-grained tree with thin, peeling bark. Gen.: *Betula.*

black bryony climbing plant with dark tubers and poisonous red berries. Sp.: *Tamus communis.*

black-eyed Susan flower with yellow petals and a dark centre. Gen.: *Rudbeckia.*

bladderwort aquatic plant whose leaves have small bladders for trapping and digesting insects. Gen.: *Utricularia.*

bladderwrack common brown seaweed with fronds containing air bladders that give buoyancy. Sp.: *Fucus vesiculosus.*

bleeding heart plant with heart-shaped, rose pink flowers hanging from an arched stem. Sp.: *Dicentra spectabilis.*

borage plant with bright blue flowers and hairy leaves used as flavouring. Sp.: *Borago officinalis.*

brookweed small, white-flowered plant of the primrose family growing in wet ground. Sp.: *Samolus valerandi.*

buckbean bog plant with white or pinkish hairy flowers. Sp.: *Menyanthes trifoliata.*

buckthorn (common) thorny shrub with berries formerly used as a cathartic. Sp.: *Rhamnus cathartica.*

buckwheat cereal plant with seeds used for fodder and for flour to make bread. Sp.: *Fagopyrum esculentum.*

burdock plant with prickly flowers and dock-like leaves. Gen.: *Arctium.*

busy Lizzie East African plant with abundant red, pink or white flowers, often grown as bedding or house plants. Sp.: *Impatiens walleriana.*

butterbur waterside plant with pale purple flowers and large, soft leaves formerly used to wrap butter. Gen.: *Petasites.*

buttercup yellow-flowered meadow plant of Europe and North America. Gen.: *Ranunculus.*

butterfly bush common name given to buddleia bush. Sp.: *Buddleia davidii.*

calabash tree evergreen tree, bearing fruit in the form of large gourds, native to tropical America. Sp.: *Crescentia cujete.*

calluna common heather native to Europe and North Africa. Sp.: *Calluna vulgaris.*

carambola small tree native to South-east Asia bearing golden-yellow ribbed fruit. Aka star fruit. Sp.: *Averrhoa carambola.*

cashew bushy evergreen tree native to Central and North America bearing kidney-shaped nuts attached to fleshy fruits. Sp.: *Anacardium occidentale.*

cassava (bitter) plant of the spurge family having starchy tuberous roots. Aka manioc tapioca. Sp.: *Manihot esculenta.*

catmint plant with downy leaves, purple-spotted white flowers, and a mint-like smell attractive to cats. Sp.: *Nepeta cataria.*

cedar coniferous tree having spreading branches, needle-like evergreen leaves and cones. Gen.: *Cedrus.*

celery pine Australasian tree with branchlets like celery leaves. Sp.: *Phyllocladus trichomanoides.*

charlock a wild mustard with yellow flowers. Sp.: *Sinapis arvensis.*

checkerberry North American evergreen shrub of the health family with spiny, scented leaves, white flowers and crimson fruits. Aka wintergreen. Sp.: *Gaultheria procumbens.*

cherry plum tree native to south-western Asia with solitary white flowers and red fruit. Sp.: *Prunus cerasifera.*

chervil umbelliferous plant with small white flowers; its aniseed flavoured leaves used as a herb for flavouring soup and salads. Sp.: *Anthriscus cereifolium.*

chestnut broad-leaved tree, which produces flowers in long catkins and nuts in a prickly bur. Gen.: *Castanea.*

chickpea leguminous plant with short, swollen pods containing yellow-beaked edible seed. Aka garbanza. Sp.: *Cicer arietinum.*

chicory blue-flowered plant cultivated for its salad

leaves and its root, which is ground for coffee. Sp.: *Cichorium intybus.*

Chinese water chestnut sedge with rushlike leaves arising from a corm, which is used as food. Sp.: *Eleocharis tuberosa.*

chives small allium with purple-pink flowers and dense tufts of long tubular leaves, which are used as a herb. Sp.: *Allium schoenoprasum.*

Christmas rose small, white-flowered, winter-blooming plant. Sp.: *Helleborus niger.*

cinchona evergreen trees of South America, of the madder family, having fragrant flowers; the bark of this tree contains quinine. Gen.: *Cinchona.*

cineraria plant cultivated for its bright flowers. Sp.: *Pericallis cruenta.*

cloudberry small mountain bramble with a white flower and an orange-coloured fruit. Sp.: *Rubus chamaemorus.*

coco de mer palm tree of the Seychelles producing a large fruit containing a two-lobed, edible nut (world's largest seed). Sp.: *Lodoicea maldivica.*

coltsfoot plant of the daisy family with large leaves and yellow flowers. Sp.: *Tussilago farfara.*

columbine an aquilegia with purple-blue flowers. Sp.: *Aquilegia vulgaris.*

cork oak evergreen Mediterranean oak. Sp.: *Quercus suber.*

cowbane poisonous plant found in marshes. Sp.: *Cicuta virosa.*

cow parsley hedgerow plant having lacelike umbels of flowers. Sp.: *Anthriscus sylvestris.*

cowslip primula with fragrant yellow flowers, which grows in pastures and meadows. Sp.: *Primula veris.*

cranesbill any of various plants of the genus *Geranium*, having pink or purple flowers and long, slender, beaked fruit.

cuckoo flower meadow plant with pale lilac flowers. Aka lady's smock. Sp.: *Cardamine pratensis.*

cuckoo pint wild arum with arrow-shaped leaves and scarlet berries. Sp.: *Arum maculatum.*

daffodil bulbous plant with a yellow, trumpet-shaped corona. Sp.: *Narcissus pseudonarcissus.*

daisy small, low-growing European plant having a rosette of white leaves and yellow centre. Sp.: *Bellis perennis.*

dawn redwood Chinese deciduous coniferous tree of a genus first known only from fossils. Sp.: *Metasequoia glyptostroboides.*

dead man's fingers species of orchid, *Orchis mascula.*

deadly nightshade highly poisonous plant with drooping purple flowers and black, cherry-like fruit. Sp.: *Atropa belladonna.*

death cap poisonous toadstool of deciduous woodland. Sp.: *Amanita phalloides.*

deodar Himalayan cedar with drooping branches bearing large barrel-shaped cones. Tallest of the cedar family. Sp.: *Cedrus deodara.*

destroying angel poisonous white toadstool. Sp.: *Amanita virosa.*

dewberry shrub with bluish fruit similar to a blackberry. Sp.: *Rubus caesius.*

dill umbelliferous herb with yellow flowers and aromatic seeds. Sp.: *Anethum graveolens.*

divi-divi tree native to tropical America, bearing curved pods, which are a source of tannin. Sp.: *Caesalpinia coriaria.*

dog's tooth violet plant of the Liliaceae family with speckled leaves, purple flowers and a toothed perianth. Sp.: *Erythronium dens-canis.*

Douglas fir large conifer over 100m tall of western North America. Sp.: *Pseudotsuga menziesii.*

doum palm tree with edible fruit. Sp.: *Hyphaene thebaica.*

dove's foot type of cranesbill. Sp.: *Geranium molle.*

dragon tree palm-like tree of the Canary Islands. Sp.: *Dracaena draco.*

durian large tree native to South-east Asia, bearing oval spiny fruit containing a creamy pulp with a fetid smell but an agreeable taste. Sp.: *Durio zibethinus.*

Dutchman's breeches plant of eastern North America with white flowers and finely divided leaves. Sp.: *Dicentra cucullaria.*

Dutchman's pipe climbing vine of eastern North America with hooked tubular flowers. Sp.: *Aristolochia durior.*

ebony tree with hard, dark wood often used for cabinetwork. Sometimes called persimmon. Sp.: *Diospyros ebenum.*

eglantine wild rose with small fragrant leaves and flowers. Sp.: *Rosa eglanteria.*

elm tree with serrated leaves and winged fruits (samaras), the wood being hard and heavy. Gen.: *Ulmus.*

endive curly-leaved plant used in salads. Sp.: *Cichorium endivia.*

eucalyptus myrtaceous tree native to Australia; species include blue gum and ironbark. Gen.: *Eucalyptus.*

false acacia the locust tree, often grown for ornament. Sp.: *Robinia pseudoacacia.*

felwort purple-flowered gentian. Sp.: *Gentianella amarella.*

fennel yellow-flowered umbelliferous plant with fragrant seeds and fine leaves used as flavourings. Sp.: *Foeniculum vulgare.*

fenugreek leguminous plant with aromatic seeds, which are often used in curry powder. Sp.: *Trigonella foenum-graecum.*

fern pteridophyte plant having roots, stems and fronds and reproducing by spores formed in structures (sori) on the fronds. Division: Pteridophyta (syn. Filicinophyta).

fever tree yellow-flowered southern African tree. Sp.: *Acacia xanthophloea.*

feverfew aromatic, bushy plant with feathery leaves and white, daisy-like flowers, used to treat migraine and formerly to reduce fever. Sp.: *Tanacetum parthenium.*

figwort plant of the genus *Scrophularia* with dull, purplish-brown flowers, once believed to be useful against scrofula.

flax-lily New Zealand plant of the agave family yielding valuable fibre. Sp.: *Phormium tenax.*

forget-me-not plant with small, yellow-eyed, bright blue flowers. Gen.: *Myosotis.*

foxglove tall plant with erect spikes of purple or white bell-shaped flowers. Sp.: *Digitalis purpurea.*

fraxinella aromatic plant of rue family having foliage that emits an ethereal inflammable oil. Aka burning bush. Sp.: *Dictamnus albus.*

gentian plants found in mountainous regions, having violet or blue trumpet-shaped flowers. Gen.: *Gentiana.*

gerbera any plant of the genus *Gerbera*, of Africa or Asia, especially the Transvaal daisy. Gen.: *Gerbera.*

N
A
T
U
R
E

germander any of various plants of the genus *Teucrium*, typically a mildly aromatic, white-felted perennial shrublet with a compact domed shape. The flowers, which appear between April and July, are reddish or purplish in colour. Germander was used in Cypriot folk-medicine as a cure for stomach ailments and jaundice.

germander speedwell creeping plant with german-der-like leaves and blue flowers. US name: bird's-eye speedwell. Sp.: *Veronica chamaedrys*.

ginger hot, spicy root, which can be powdered for use in cooking, or preserved in syrup, or candied. Sp.: *Zingiber officinale*.

gladiolus plants of *Iridaceae* family with sword-shaped leaves and brightly coloured flower spikes. Gen.: *Gladiolus*.

goatsbeard Eurasian plant with woolly stems and large heads of yellow-rayed flowers surrounded by large, green bracts. Sp.: *Tragopogon pratensis*.

goatsbeard American rosaceous plant with long spikes of small white flowers. Gen.: *Aruncus*.

goat's-rue Eurasian leguminous plant cultivated for its white, mauve or pinkish flowers. Sp.: *Galega officinalis*.

goat's-rue North American leguminous plant with pink-and-yellow flowers. Sp.: *Tephrosia virginiana*.

good King Henry weed of the goosefoot family. Sp.: *Chenopodium bonus-henricus*.

goosefoot plant that has small greenish flowers and leaves like the foot of a goose. Gen.: *Chenopodium*.

gopher North American tree, yielding yellowish tim-ber aka yellowwood. Not to be confused with the field gopher tree from which Noah's Ark was reput-edly built. Sp.: *Cladrastis lutea*.

grass monocotyledonous plants encompassing all the cereal plants as well as reeds and bamboos. Family *Gramineae*.

greenheart tropical American evergreen tree of the laurel family. Gen.: *Ocotea rodiaei*.

guaiacum trees native to tropical America with hard, dense, oily timber. Gen.: *Guaiacum*.

guava small tropical American tree bearing an edi-ble, pale orange fruit with pinky, juicy flesh. Sp.: *Psidium guajava*.

guelder rose deciduous shrub with round bunches of creamy-white flowers. Sp.: *Viburnum opulus*.

guernsey lily nerine, originally from South Africa, with large, pink, lily-like flowers. Sp.: *Nerine sarniensis*.

hare's-foot clover with soft hair around the flowers. Sp.: *Trifolium arvense*.

hart's tongue fern with narrow undivided fronds. Sp.: *Phyllitis scolopendrium*.

hawthorn thorny shrub or tree with white, red or pink blossom and small, dark red fruit or haws. Sp.: *Crataegus monogyna*.

hazel small tree bearing round brown edible nuts. Sp.: *Corylus avellana*.

henbane poisonous herbaceous plant with sticky hairy leaves and an unpleasant smell. Sp.: *Hyoscyamus niger*.

henna tropical shrub having small pink, red or white flowers; the reddish dye from its shoots and leaves is used to colour hair. Sp.: *Lawsonia inermis*.

herb Christopher white-flowered baneberry. Sp.: *Actaea spicata*.

herb Paris plant with a single flower and four leaves in a cross shape on an unbranched stem. Sp.: *Paris quadrifolia*.

herb Robert common cranesbill with red-stemmed

leaves and pink flowers. Sp.: *Geranium robertianum*.

holly evergreen tree with prickly leaves and red berries, often used as Christmas decorations. Gen.: *Ilex*.

hop climbing plant cultivated for the cones borne by the female, used in brewing. Sp.: *Humulus lupulus*.

hornbeam tree of the genus *Carpinus* with a smooth bark and a hard tough wood. Gen.: *Carpinus*.

horse chestnut Eurasian tree with palmate leaves and inedible nuts enclosed in a spiky bur (conkers). Sp.: *Aesculus hippocastanum*.

horse mushroom large, edible mushroom. Sp.: *Agaricus arvensis*.

horseradish cruciferous plant with long, lobed leaves. Sp.: *Armoracia rusticana*.

hortensia kind of hydrangea (distinct from lacecap) with large, round, infertile flower heads. Sp.: *Hydrangea macrophylla*.

huckleberry North American shrub with blue or black soft fruit. Gen.: *Gaylussacia*.

Iceland poppy Arctic poppy with white or yellow flowers. Sp.: *Papaver nudicaule*.

Indian hemp strong-smelling Asian moraceous plant. Aka marijuana, Cannabis. Sp.: *Cannabis indica*.

ivy climbing plants having lobed evergreen leaves and black, berry-like fruits. Gen.: *Hedera*.

jack-by-the-hedge white-flowered cruciferous plant of shady places. Sp.: *Alliaria petiolata*.

jackfruit East Indian tree bearing fruit resembling breadfruit. Sp.: *Artocarpus heterophyllus*.

japonica flowering shrub with round white, green or yellow, edible fruit and bright red flowers. Sp.: *Chaenomeles speciosa*.

jarrah the Western Australian mahogany gum tree. Sp.: *Eucalyptus marginata*.

jasmine oleaceous shrub or climbing plant whose fragrant flowers are used in perfumery. Gen.: *Jasminum*.

kangaroo paw Australian plant with irregular woolly flowers. Floral emblem of Western Australia. Sp.: *Anigozanthos manglesii*.

kangaroo vine evergreen climbing plant with serrat-ed leaves. Sp.: *Cissus antarctica*.

kidney vetch yellow-flavoured leguminous plant found in grassland. Aka lady's finger. Sp.: *Anthyllis vulneraria*.

knotweed fast-growing Japanese plant. Sp.: *Fallopia japonica*.

ladino large type of white clover native to Italy and cultivated for fodder. Sp.: *Trifolium repens*.

lamb's ears garden plant with whitish, woolly leaves. Sp.: *Stachys byzantina*.

lemon balm bushy plant with leaves smelling and tasting of lemon. Sp.: *Melissa officinalis*.

lemon geranium lemon-scented pelargonium. Sp.: *Pelargonium crispum*.

lemon verbena shrub with lemon-scented leaves. Aka lemon plant. Sp.: *Aloysia triphylla*.

leopard's bane any plant of the genus *Doronicum* with large, yellow, daisy-like flowers. Sp.: *Doronicum*.

live oak American evergreen tree. Sp.: *Quercus virginiana*.

loquat tree of the Rosaceae family, bearing small, yellow, egg-shaped fruit. Sp.: *Eriobotrya japonica*.

love-in-a-mist blue-flowered garden plant with many delicate green bracts. Sp.: *Nigella damascena*.

love-lies-bleeding   garden plant with drooping spikes of purple-red blooms. Sp.: *Amaranthus caudatus.*

lungwort   Eurasian plant with spotted leaves and clusters of blue or purple flowers. Sp.: *Pulmonaria officinalis.*

lungwort (sea)   boraginaceous plant of the northern temperate genus *Mertensia*, with drooping clusters of tubular, usually blue flowers. Aka oyster plant. Gen.: *Mertensia maritima.*

madder   plant with small yellow flowers and a red fleshy root. Gen.: *Rubia.*

mahogany   tropical tree yielding a hard, reddish-brown wood used for furniture making. Sp.: *Swietenia mahagoni.*

mandrake   poisonous plant with white, or purple flowers and large yellow fruit, having emetic and narcotic properties and possessing a root once thought to resemble the human form and to shriek when plucked. Sp.: *Mandragora officinarum.*

mangosteen   Malaysian tree bearing a white juicy-pulped fruit with a thick, reddish-brown rind. Sp.: *Garcinia mangostana.*

mangrove   any tropical tree or shrub of the genus *Rhizophora* growing in shore-mud with many tangled roots above ground. Gen.: *Rhizophora.*

Manila hemp   Philippine plant with a strong fibre used for rope-making. Sp.: *Musa textilis.*

manuka   small New Zealand tree with aromatic leaves and hard timber. Sp.: *Leptospermum scoparium.*

maple   any tree or shrub of the genus *Acer,* grown for shade, ornament, wood, or sugar.

marsh mallow   herbaceous plant, the roots of which were formerly used to make a sweet confection. Sp.: *Althaea officinalis.*

marsh marigold   golden-flowered plant, which grows in moist pastures. Sp.: *Caltha palustris.*

martagon   lily with small, purple, turban-like flowers. Sp.: *Lilium martagon.*

marvel of Peru   showy garden plant with flowers opening at dusk. Sp.: *Mirabilis jalapa.*

mayapple   American herbaceous plant bearing a yellow, egg-shaped fruit in May. Sp.: *Podophyllum peltatum.*

mayflower   In North America trailing arbutus that blooms in May. Sp.: *Epigaea repens.*

maz(z)ard   the wild sweet cherry of Europe. Sp.: *Prunus avium.*

meadow rue   plants of the buttercup family with small yellow or purple flowers. Gen.: *Thalictrum.*

meadow saffron   meadow plant resembling a crocus and producing lilac flowers in autumn, while still leafless. Sp.: *Colchicum autumnale.*

meadowsweet   plant of the Rosaceae family, common in meadows and damp places, with creamy-white fragrant flowers. Also the name of a North American plant of the genus *Spiraea.* Sp.: *Filipendula ulmaria.*

medlar   tree of the rose family bearing small brown apple-like fruits, which are best eaten when over-ripe. Sp.: *Mespilus germanica.*

mignonette   plants of the genus *Reseda,* some having aromatic grey-green flowers.

mimosa   Leguminous shrub having globular yellow flowers and sensitive leaflets, which droop when touched. Sp.: *Mimosa pudica.*

mistletoe   parasitic plant growing on apple and other trees and bearing white, glutinous berries in winter. Americans have a related plant of the genus *Phoradendron.* Sp.: *Viscum album.*

mock pennyroyal   North American aromatic plant. Sp.: *Hedeoma pulegioides.*

moneywort   trailing evergreen plant with round glossy leaves and yellow flowers. Sp.: *Lysimachia nummularia.*

monkey flower   short creeping plant with bright yellow flowers. Sp.: *Mimulus guttatus.*

monkey-puzzle   coniferous tree native to Chile with downward-pointing branches and small, close-set leaves. Aka Chile pine. Sp.: *Araucaria araucana.*

montbretia   hybrid plant of genus *Crocosmia* with bright, orange-yellow, trumpet-shaped flowers.

morning glory   any of various twining plants, with trumpet-shaped flowers, of the genus *Ipomoea.*

mother-in-law's tongue   plant with long, erect, pointed leaves. Sp.: *Sansevieria trifasciata.*

mung bean   leguminous plants of the genus *Vigna*, native to India and yielding a small bean used as food.

musk-rose   rambling rose with large, white flowers smelling of musk. Sp.: *Rosa moschata.*

musk thistle   nodding thistle whose flowers have a musky fragrance. Sp.: *Carduus nutans.*

musk tree   Australian tree with a musky smell. Sp.: *Olearia argyrophylla.*

mustard   plant eaten at the seedling stage, often with cress, and whose seeds are crushed and made into a paste and used as a spicy condiment. Sp.: *Sinapis alba.*

mustard   plant with slender pods and yellow flowers. Sp.: *Brassica nigra.*

myrtle   evergreen shrub with aromatic foliage and white flowers with purple-black ovoid berries. Sp.: *Myrtus communis.*

narcissus   yellow, orange or white flowered plants with crown surrounded by spreading segments. Gen.: *Narcissus*

nardoo   clover-like plant of Australian origin. Sp.: *Marsilea drummondii.*

nasturtium   Any cruciferous plant of the genus Nasturtium, including watercress. Trailing plants of the Americas with rounded edible leaves and bright orange, yellow or red flowers of the genus *Tropaeolum.*

nopal   cactus having yellow flowers and purple fruits, sometimes called prickly pear. Gen.: *Opuntia.*

oak   any tree of the genus *Quercus*, having lobed leaves and bearing acorns.

obeche   West African tree. Sp.: *Triplochiton scleroxylon.*

okra   African edible plant of the mallow family. Aka gumbo or ladies' fingers. Sp.: *Abelmoschus esculentus.*

orpin(e)   succulent, herbaceous, purple-flowered plant. Sp.: *Sedum telephium.*

ox-eye daisy   plant of the daisy family, with large white flowers with yellow centres. Sp.: *Leucanthemum vulgare.*

oxlip   woodland primula. Sp.: *Primula elatior.*

ox-tongue   plant of the daisy family with bright yellow flowers. Gen.: *Picris.*

palmyra   Asian palm with fan-shaped leaves used for matting. Sp.: *Borassus flabellifer.*

parsley   biennial herb with white flowers and crinkly aromatic leaves. Sp.: *Petroselinum crispum.*

parsley fern   fern with leaves like parsley. Sp.: *Cryptogramma crispa.*

passion flower   any climbing plant of the genus

NATURE

Passiflora with a flower that was supposed to suggest the instruments of the Crucifixion.

patchouli strongly scented south Asian shrub from which a perfume is made. Gen.: *Pogostemon.*

peanut leguminous plant bearing pods that ripen underground and contain seeds used as food and yielding oil. Sp.: *Arachis hypogaea.*

pedunculate oak a common oak in which clusters of acorns are borne on long stalks. Sp.: *Quercus robur.*

peepul (pipal) moraceous tree of tropical India and the East Indies, resembling the banyan, and thought of as sacred by Buddhists because the founder of the religion is said to have found enlightenment while sitting under its branches. Sp.: *Ficus religiosa.*

pennyroyal creeping mint cultivated for its supposed medicinal properties. Sp.: *Mentha pulegium.*

periwinkle tropical shrub native to Madagascar. Sp.: *Catharanthus roseus.*

periwinkle any of several Eurasian apocynaceous evergreen plants of the genus *Vinca*, having trailing stems and blue flowers. Aka creeping myrtle or trailing myrtle (USA).

pine coniferous evergreen with long, needle-shaped leaves and brown cones. Gen.: *Pinus.*

pinkster flower the pink azalea. Sp.: *Rhododendron periclymenoides.*

piripiri plant of the rose family native to New Zealand and having prickly burs. Sp.: *Acaena anserinifolia.*

poplar salicaceous tree with triangular leaves, light, soft wood and flowers borne in catkins. Gen.: *Populus.*

prickly pear cactus of the genus *Opuntia*, native to arid regions of America and bearing barbed bristles and large, pear-shaped, prickly fruits.

ragged robin pink-flowered campion with spiky, tattered-looking petals. Aka cuckoo flower. Sp.: *Lychnis flos-cuculi.*

rose shrub or climbing plant having prickly stems and fragrant flowers. Gen.: *Rosa.*

rowan tree with delicate pinnate leaves and scarlet berries. Sp.: *Sorbus aucuparia.*

rue dwarf shrub with bipinnate or tripinnate glaucous leaves and yellow flowers. Gen.: *Ruta.*

salsify Mediterranean plant having grass-like leaves, purple flower heads and a long, white edible taproot. Aka oyster plant or vegetable oyster. Sp.: *Tragopogon porrifolius.*

shaddock tree named after Captain Shaddoch who brought the seed to Barbados. Aka pomelo. Sp.: *Citrus maxima.*

shamrock most common shamrock is the wood sorrel, *Oxalis acetosella*, and this is the plant worn on St Patrick's Day. Other trifoliate shamrocks include black medic (*Medicago lupulina*) and white clover (*Trifolium repens*).

snake's head bulbous plant with bell-shaped, pendent flowers. Sp.: *Fritillaria meleagris.*

southernwood bushy kind of wormwood. Sp.: *Artemisia abrotanum.*

sweet marjoram one of two aromatic herbs (the other being wild marjoram) whose fresh dried leaves are used as a flavouring in cookery. Sp.: *Majorana hortensis.*

teak large, verbenaceous tree of East Indies yielding a hard, valuable yellow-brown wood. Sp.: *Tectona grandis.*

tobacco solanaceous plant having hairy leaves, and funnel-shaped, fragrant flowers. Gen.: *Nicotiana.*

tomatillo Mexican ground cherry bearing purplish, edible fruit. Sp.: *Physalis philadelphica.*

tomato plant of the nightshade family bearing glossy red or yellow pulpy edible fruit. Sp.: *Lycopersicon esculentum.*

toothwort parasitic plant with toothlike, root scales. Sp.: *Lathraea squamaria.*

toquilla palm-like tree native to South America. Sp.: *Carludovica palmata.*

trailing arbutus see mayflower.

Transvaal daisy plant of the Asteraceae family. Gen.: *Gerbera.*

traveller's joy wild clematis. Aka old man's beard. Sp.: *Clematis vitalba.*

tree mallow tall, woody-stemmed European mallow of cliffs and rocks. Sp.: *Lavatera arborea.*

tree tomato South American shrub with egg-shaped, red fruit. Sp.: *Cyphomandra betacea.*

tulip bulbous, spring-flowering plant of a variety of colours. The word tulip is derived from the Turkish *Tülbend*, meaning turban, from the shape of the expanded flower. Gen.: *Tulipa.*

tulip tree North American tree with tulip-like flowers and lobed leaves. Gen.: *Liriodendron tulipifera.*

tumbleweed plant of arid areas of North America and Australia. Its globular bush breaks off in late summer and is tumbled about by the wind, spreading its seed. Gen.: *Amaranthus alba.*

turmeric tropical Asian plant of the Zingiberaceae family, yielding aromatic rhizomes used as a spice and for yellow dye. Sp.: *Curcuma longa.*

umbrella plant African sedge having large umbrella-like whorls of slender leaves and widely grown as an ornamental water plant. Sp.: *Cyperus alternifolius.*

umbrella tree North American magnolia having long leaves clustered into an umbrella formation at the ends of the branches and unpleasant-smelling, white flowers. Sp.: *Magnolia tripetala.*

vetch plant largely used for silage and fodder. Sp.: *Vicia sativa.*

violet low-growing plant characterised by horizontal petals and purple, cordate leaves. Gen.: *Viola.*

viper's bugloss stiff bristly blue-flowered plant. Sp.: *Echium vulgare.*

wall fern an evergreen polypody with very large leaves. Sp.: *Polypodium vulgare.*

wallflower spring-flowering garden plant with fragrant yellow, orange-red or dark red flowers. Sp.: *Cheiranthus cheiri.*

wall germander European germander having two-lipped pinkish-purple flowers with a very small upper lip. Sp.: *Teucrium chamaedrys.*

wall rue small fern with leaves like rue, growing on walls and rocks. Aka spleewort. Sp.: *Asplenium ruta-muraria.*

walnut tree having aromatic leaves and drooping catkins, the nut of which contains a wrinkled edible kernel in two halves and enclosed in a green fruit. Gen.: *Juglans.*

wandering jew climbing plant with stemless, variegated leaves. Gen.: *Tradescantia albiflora.*

water chestnut aquatic plant bearing an edible seed. Sp.: *Trapa natans.*

water hyacinth tropical American aquatic plant which is a serious weed of waterways in warm countries. Sp.: *Eichhornia crassipes.*

watercress hardy perennial cress growing in running water, with pungent leaves used in salad. Sp.: *Nasturtium officinale.*

wayfaring tree white-flowered European and Asian shrub, common along roadsides, with berries turning from green through red to black. Sp.: *Viburnum lantana*.

wild marjoram one of two aromatic herbs (the other being sweet marjoram) whose fresh dried leaves are used as a flavouring in cookery. Sp.: *Origanum vulgare*.

wild pansy Eurasian plant having purple, yellow, and pale mauve spurred flowers, aka heartsease, love-in-idleness. Sp.: *Viola tricolor*.

willow white-wood tree with graceful flexible branches and catkins. Gen.: *Salix*.

wintergreen low-growing plants with drooping spikes of white, bell-shaped flowers. Gen.: *Pyrola*.

witch alder American shrub with leaves like that of the alder. Sp.: *Fothergilla gardenii*.

witch hazel North American shrub with yellow flowers, the leaves and bark used to treat bruises. Gen.: *Hamamelis virginiana*.

woad glaucous, yellow-flowered cruciferous plant formerly grown for its blue dye. Sp.: *Isatis tinctoria*.

wolfsbane various ranunculaceous plants with hooded purple or yellow flowers. Aka aconite, monkshood. Gen.: *Aconitum*.

wood anemone wild spring-flowering, anemone. Sp.: *Anemone nemorosa*.

woodruff white-flowered plant grown for the fragrance of its whorled leaves when dried or crushed. Sp.: *Galium odoratum*.

woody nightshade scrambling woody Eurasian plant with purple flowers and recurved petals with protruding cone of yellow anthers and poisonous, red, berry-like fruits. Aka bittersweet. Sp.: *Solanum dulcamara*.

wych elm Eurasian elm with large rough leaves and pliant branches. Sp.: *Ulmus glabra*.

yellow archangel Eurasian yellow-flowered nettle. Sp.: *Lamiastrum galeobdolon*.

yellow flag yellow-flowered iris with slender, sword-shaped leaves. Sp.: *Iris pseudacorus*.

yellow rattle yellow-flowered herb, which is partly parasitic. Sp.: *Rhinanthus minor*.

yellow toadflax plant with narrow leaves like flax and spurred yellow flowers. Sp.: *Linaria vulgaris*.

yerba buena (good herb) North American trailing plant with lilac flowers formally used by Californian Americans to make a medicinal tea. Sp.: *Satureja douglasii*.

yerba santa North American shrub whose leaves are used medicinally. Lit. 'holy herb'. Sp.: *Eriodictyon californicum*.

yew Dark-leaved evergreen coniferous tree having seeds enclosed in a fleshy red aril, and often planted in churchyards. Gen.: *Taxus*.

yiang-ylang / ilang-ilang. Malaysian tree from which a fragrant perfume is distilled. Sp.: *Cananga odorata*.

Yorkshire fog fodder grass. Sp.: *Holcus lanatus*.

yucca plant of Agavaceae family with woody stem and sword-shaped leaves. Aka Adam's needle. Gen.: *Yucca*.

Miscellaneous Information

agriculture: soilless hydroponics.

allogamy cross-fertilisation in plants.

angiosperm flower-producing plants that reproduce by seeds enclosed within a carpel, including herbaceous plants, herbs, shrubs, grasses and most trees.

carnations: types of self (one colour), fancy (multi-coloured), picotee (pale with darker edge).

carnivorous plants pitcher plant, sundew, venus fly trap.

deciduous conifer larch, swamp cypress.

Dutch elm disease disease of elms, often fatal, caused by the fungus *Ceratocystis ulmi* and spread by bark beetles.

entomophily pollination by insects.

entophyte plant growing inside a plant or animal.

epiphyte plant growing on another but not parasitic on it, e.g. a moss on a tree trunk.

fastest growth bamboo (about 38 cm, 15 inches a day).

flower parts female part: pistil male part: stamen Perfect flower: contains male and female parts. Stigma: mouth of the pistil, which receives the pollen in impregnation. Style: neck of the pistil, which contains the stigma. Ovary: swollen basal part of the pistil containg the ovules.

frond the compound leaf of a fern or a palm.

garden city: first Letchworth in Herts (1903), founded by Ebenezer Howard.

gymnosperm any of various plants having seeds unprotected by an ovary, including conifers, cycads and ginkgo.

halophyte plant adapted to saline conditions.

largest living thing a Californian redwood tree, *Sequoia sempervirens*, nicknamed the General Sherman (275 feet high and 1,385 tons in weight).

leaves: types of bract, stipule and pinnate.

mulch half-rotten vegetable matter used to prevent soil erosion.

nettle sting: cause formic acid.

oak apples: caused by wasp eggs.

oldest tree a bristlecone pine (*Pinus longaera*) nicknamed Old Methuselah. Approx 5,000 years old and situated in the White Mountains, California.

osmosis the passage of a solvent through a semipermeable membrane from a less concentrated to a more concentrated solution until both solutions are of the same concentration. Wilhelm Pfeffer, a German plant physiologist, first studied osmosis in 1877, although the term was introduced by the British chemist Thomas Graham in 1854. Osmosis is the method used by plants for water absorption.

pergola arbour or covered walk, formed of growing plants trained over trellis-work.

plant families apple – rose (Rosaceae); ash – olive (Oleaceae); asparagus – lily (Liliaceae); aubergine – nightshade (Solanum); avocado – laurel (Lauraceae); bamboo - grass (Gramineae); barley – grass (Gramineae); blackberry – rose (Rosaceae); bluebell – lily (Liliaceae); breadfruit – mulberry (Moraceae); broccoli – cabbage (Brassica); brussels sprout – cabbage (Brassica); buckwheat – dock (Polygonaceae); camellia – tea (Theaceae); carrot – parsley (Apiaceae); cauliflower – cabbage (Brassica); celery – parsley (Apiaceae); cherry – rose (Rosaceae); chives – lily (Liliaceae); cinnamon

– laurel (Lauraceae); coffee – madder (Rubiaceae); cork oak – beech (Fagacrab); cotton – mallow (Malvaceae); dandelion – daisy (Compositae); elder – honeysuckle (Caprifoliaceae); fig – mulberry (Moraceae); garlic – lily (Liliaceae); gooseberry – Grossulariaceae; guelder Rose – (Caprifoliaceae); hemlock – parsley (Apiaceae); hemp - mulberry (Moraceae); hop – mulberry (Moraceae); hyacinth – lily (Liliaceae); jasmine –olive (Oleaceae); Jerusalem artichoke – daisy (Compositae); knotgrass (Aka Allseed) – dock (Polygonaceae); leek – lily (Liliaceae); lemon – rue (Rutaceae); lettuce – daisy (Compositae); lilac – olive (Oleaceae); lime – rue (Rutaceae); maize – grass (Gramineae); marijuana – mulberry (Moraceae); mustard – cabbage (Brassica); okra – mallow (Malvaceae); onion – lily (Liliaceae); orange – rue (Rutaceae); parsnip – parsley (Apiaceae); peach – rose (Rosaceae); pear – rose (Rosaceae); plum – rose (Rosaceae); potato – nightshade (Solanum); privet – olive (Oleaceae); radish – cabbage (Brassica); rape – cabbage (Brassica); raspberry – rose (Rosaceae); rhubarb – dock (Polygonaceae); rye – grass (Gramineae); shallot – lily (Liliaceae); sorrel – dock (Polygonaceae); strawberry – rose (Rosaceae); swede – cabbage (Brassica); thistle – daisy (Compositae); tobacco – nightshade (Solanum); tomato – nightshade (Solanum); tulip – lily (Liliaceae); turnip – cabbage (Brassica); vanilla – orchid (Orchidaceae); wheat – grass (Gramineae).

plants: products from agar agar – seaweed; amber – pine tree resin; aspirin – willow tree (originally); atropine – deadly nightshade; cocaine – coca plant; cochineal – beetles; copra – coconut; digitalis – foxglove; frankincense (*Olibanum*) – tree bark resin (*Boswellia*); henna dye – leaves of henna plant; heroin – opium poppy; hessian – plant root; linen – spun flax; linseed oil – seeds of flax plant; madder – plant root; morphine – opium poppy; myrrh – myrrh tree resin; opium – opium poppy (*Papaver somniferum*); quinine – cinchona bark; raffia – palm; saffron – crocus; semolina – wheat; tapioca – cassava root; turmeric – curcuma plant; turpentine – coniferous trees (especially pine).

pomegranate: varieties paper-shell, Spanish ruby, wonderful.

roots: types of adventitious, aerial, climbing, contratile, lateral, pneumatophore, prop.

Royal Horticultural Society Founded in 1804 and in its centenary year of 1904 established Wisley as its Show Garden.

sacking: fibre used for jute.

scandents climbing plants.

sweet pea: from Sicily.

tallest tree Douglas fir.

taxonomy classification of living organisms into groups in an organised hierarchy. The largest group is the kingdom – e.g. Plants (Plantae); Animals (Animalia). Below the Kingdom; in descending order, come: Phylum, Class, Subclass; Order, Family, Genus, Species.

toadstool: most poisonous deathcap.

tomato: original name love apple.

tudor rose conventionalized 5-lobed figure of a rose; the white and the red rose were adopted as the symbols of the Houses of York and Lancaster during the Wars of the Roses.

tulip: named from the Turkish turban *Tülbend*.

underwater: grows rice.

vanilla: family orchid family.

variegation different colourings of a leaf.

xerophyte plant, such as cacti, that grows in dry conditions.

yucca tree: pollination only by the yucca moth, *Pronuba* (Tegetierila) *yuccasella*.

Alternative Names of Flowers, Plants and Trees

Aaron's beard	rose of Sharon	buckbean	bogbean
	althaea	burning bush	Fraxinella
adder's tongue	dogtooth violet	calla lily	arum lily
abele	white poplar	cardinal flower	scarlet lobelia
abelmosk	musk mallow	carnation	gillyflower
althaea	Aaron's beard	catmint	catnip
amaryllis	belladonna lily	catnip	catmint
antirrhinum	snapdragon	charlock	field mustard
aquilegia	columbine	checkerberry	wintergreen
arum lily	calla lily	Chile pine	monkey puzzle
Australian sword lily	kangaroo paw	Chinese eddo	elephant's ear
autumn crocus	meadow saffron	chionodoxa	glory-of-the-snow
baby's breath	gypsophila		
baobab	monkey bread tree	chlorophytum	spider plant
		clematis	traveller's joy
bayberry	wax myrtle	columbine	aquilegia
bergenia	elephant's ear	cow parsley	Queen Anne's lace
belladonna lily	amaryllis		
belladonna	deadly nightshade dwale	cowbane	water hemlock
		cowslip	marsh marigold (USA)
bluebell	wild hyacinth	cranberry	fen-berry
bog myrtle	sweet gale	creeping myrtle	periwinkle
bo tree	peepul	cuckoo flower	ragged Robin
bogbean	buckbean		lady's smock

cuckoo pint

dasheen
deadly nightshade
delphinium
dittany
dogtooth violet
dwale
eddo
eglantine

elephant's ear

fen-berry
field mustard
fleur-de-lis
fraxinella

French lilac

gas plant
gillyflower
ginkgo
gladiolus
glory-of-the-snow
goatsbeard (Eurasian plant)

goat's-rue (Eurasian plant)
golden chain
guaiacum
guelder Rose
gumbo
gypsophila
hawthorn

heartsease
Indian cress
iris
Jack-go-to-bed-at-noon

Jack-in-the-pulpit
Japanese quince
japonica

Johnny-jump-up (USA)
kangaroo paw

kidney vetch
kingcup
laburnum
ladies' fingers
lady's finger
lad's love
lady's smock
larkspur

jack-in-the-pulpit
lords and ladies
wake-Robin
elephant's ear
belladonna
larkspur
Fraxinella
adder's tongue
belladonna
elephant's ear
sweet brier
bergenia
Chinese eddo
eddo
dasheen
taro
cranberry
charlock
iris
dittany
burning bush
gas plant
goat's-rue
  (Eurasian
  plant)
fraxinella
carnation
maidenhair tree
sword lily
chionodoxa
Jack-go-to-bed-
  at-noon
French lilac
laburnum
lignum vitae
snowball tree
okra
baby's breath
may
quickthorn
whitethorn
Johnny-jump-up
  (USA)
love-in-idleness
wild pansy
nasturtium
fleur-de-lis
goatsbeard
  (Eurasian plant)
cuckoo pint
japonica
Japanese
  quince
heartsease
Australian sword
  lily
lady's finger
marsh marigold
golden chain
okra
kidney vetch
southernwood
cuckoo flower
delphinium

lignum vitae
lime tree
linden tree
livelong
lords and ladies
love-in-idleness
lungwort
maidenhair tree
mandrake
marsh marigold
marsh marigold (USA)
may
may apple
mayflower
meadow saffron

moneywort
monkey bread tree
monkey puzzle
mountain ash
musk mallow
naked boys
naked ladies
nasturtium
okra

old man's beard
orpin(e)
oyster-plant

pandanus
peepul
periwinkle

pink azalea
pinkster flower
Queen Anne's lace
quickthorn
ragged Robin
Rose of Sharon

rowan
salsify

scarlet lobelia
screw-pine
snapdragon
snowball tree
southernwood
spider plant
sweet brier
sweet gale
sword lily
taro
trailing arbutus
trailing myrtle
traveller's joy
vegetable oyster
Virginia creeper
wake-Robin
wandering sailor
water hemlock
wax myrtle

guaiacum
linden tree
lime tree
orpin(e)
cuckoo pint
heartsease
oyster-plant
ginkgo
may apple
kingcup
cowslip
hawthorn
mandrake
trailing arbutus
autumn crocus
naked ladies
naked boys
wandering sailor
baobab
Chile pine
rowan
abelmosk
meadow saffron
meadow saffron
Indian cress
gumbo
ladies' fingers
traveller's joy
livelong
lungwort
salsify
screw-pine
bo tree
creeping myrtle
trailing myrtle
pinkster flower
pink azalea
cow parsley
hawthorn
cuckoo flower
Aaron's beard
althaea
mountain ash
oyster-plant
vegetable oyster
cardinal flower
pandanus
antirrhinum
guelder rose
lad's love
chlorophytum
eglantine
bog myrtle
gladiolus
elephant's ear
mayflower
periwinkle
clematis
salsify
woodbine (USA)
cuckoo pint
moneywort
cowbane
bayberry

white poplar	abele	wintergreen	checkerberry
whitethorn	hawthorn	woodbine	wild
wild honeysuckle	woodbine		honeysuckle
wild hyacinth	bluebell	woodbine (USA)	Virginia creeper
wild pansy	heartsease	yellow rocket	winter cress
winter cress	yellow rocket		

NB: All the alternatives have been listed alphabetically for ease of reference.

County Flowers

Plantlife International launched a County Flowers campaign in 2002 asking members of the public to nominate a wild flower emblem for their designated areas. The English Bluebell topped the poll but was so far ahead of the competition that it was excluded as a choice. In addition to the present counties of England, the poll also included the traditional counties of Scotland, Wales and Northern Ireland (some of which are now Unitary Authorities), and several of the old English counties were also covered. A total of 50,000 people voted and the results were as follows.

ENGLAND

Bedfordshire: Bee orchid (*Ophrys apifera*). The mauve orchids mimic a bumblebee and are seen in disused quarries, on roadsides, even on waste ground in towns.

Berkshire: Summer snowflake (*Leucojum aestivum*). No longer officially a county but included in the survey. Because they grow beside the River Loddon, the tall-stemmed plants with drooping white flowers are known in the county as Loddon lilies.

Birmingham: Foxglove (*Digitalis purpurea*). Not a county as such but included in the survey. The tall purple flowers are found in parks and industrial wastelands. Tellingly perhaps, William Withering, the discoverer of the heart drug digitalis, which was derived from the foxglove, was chief physician at Birmingham General Hospital from 1775.

Bristol: Maltese cross (*Lychnis chalcedonica*). Not a county but included in the survey. Introduced to Britain in the 16th century, the delicate red petals can be seen in waste ground and on roadsides. It is known as the Flower of Bristol.

Buckinghamshire: Chiltern gentian (*Gentianella germanica*). Grows on the chalk downs of Buckinghamshire and flowers in the late summer.

Cambridgeshire: Pasqueflower (*Pulsatilla vulgaris*). Has been a famous Cambridgeshire flower since its discovery on the Gog Magog hills by John Ray in 1660. According to legend, the fluffy-stemmed purple plants grow on the graves of Viking warriors.

Cheshire: Cuckooflower (*Cardamine pratensis*). Also known as 'milkmaids'. It is a delicate flower of wet meadows and pond margins, befitting a county with more ponds than any other.

Cornwall: Cornish heath (*Erica vagans*). The lilac blooms are found on the Lizard moors in late summer, the only part of Britain where this shrub is found.

Cumbria: Grass-of-Parnassus (*Parnassia palustris*). The tallish white-petalled flowers appear on the county arms. Legend has it that the cattle of the gods of Mount Parnassus fed on the plant, and so it was given honorary status as a grass.

Derbyshire: Jacob's ladder (*Polemonium caeruleum*). The bright blue flowers and delicate ladder-shaped leaves of the wild plant are common in the Peak District and Yorkshire Dales.

Devon: Primrose (*Primula vulgaris*). The yellowy-white flowers have a strong presence in Devon's high-banked scenic country lanes. Local papermakers used to present little bunches to their customers to provide a 'breath of Devon'.

Dorset: Dorset heath (*Erica ciliaris*). This tall crimson heather is a defining species of Dorset's heathland and bogs.

Durham: Spring gentian (*Gentiana verna*). Even if Upper Teesdale had no other plant, botanical die-hards would flock there to see this deep-blue five-petalled favourite.

Essex: Common poppy (*Papaver rhoeas*). The unmistakable blood-red flowers still adorn cornfields in the county, though they are just as common on disturbed ground, especially on the chalk.

Gloucestershire: Wild daffodil (*Narcissus pseudonarcissus*). The county's golden triangle around the villages of Newent and Dymock is famous for its wild daffodils or Lent lilies. A 10-mile footpath known as 'The Daffodil Way' runs through the heart of Gloucestershire.

Hampshire: Dog rose (*Rosa canina*). Hampshire is rich in hedgerow roses and the lilac-petalled flower has long been the county's emblem.

Herefordshire: Mistletoe (*Viscum album*). No longer an official county but included in the survey. In Hereford, mistletoe grows on apple trees and hawthorns, from which it can be harvested as a winter crop.

Hertfordshire: Pasqueflower (*Pulsatilla vulgaris*). To be seen in abundance on the limestone hillsides; this popular flower was chosen by Cambridgeshire folk too.

Huntingdonshire: Water violet (*Hottonia palustris*). No longer a county in name but considered as such for the survey. The dainty five-petalled lilac flowers are hardier than they appear and can survive summer droughts.

Isle of Man: Fuchsia (*Fuchsia magellanica*). A Crown possession but included in the survey. On the island this exotic plant with its red shrimp-like blossom grows unusually tall.

Isle of Wight: Pyramidal orchid (*Anacamptis pyramidalis*). Not a county but included in the survey. The cone-shaped lilac plant abounds on the undercliff and across the island's hog's-back of chalk in June.

Isles of Scilly: Thrift (*Armeria maritima*). Part of the county of Cornwall but with its own flower. The lilac-coloured thrift can be seen on rocks and sea cliffs. The old threepenny bit used to have a depiction of thrift on the reverse.

Kent: Hop (*Humulus lupulus*). The pale green and white plants are unobtrusive climbers in hedgerows and thickets.

Lancashire: Red rose (*Rosa species*). The Red Rose county since the Middle Ages, when the House of Lancaster adopted the flower as its heraldic badge.

The true red rose of Lancashire is supposedly the red rose of the Mediterranean (*Rosa gallica*).

Leeds: **Bilberry** (*Vaccinium myrtillus*). Not a county but included in the survey. The bulbous purple berries are a symbol of the open air of the hills, especially around Bradford and Leeds.

Leicestershire: **Foxglove** (*Digitalis purpurea*). The foxglove helps to define Leicestershire's uplands, the woods and bracken swards of Charnwood Forest, but is scarce in the agricultural east of the county. Birmingham also chose the foxglove.

Lincolnshire: **Common dog violet** (*Viola riviniana*). Carpets the great limewoods of Bardney Forest near Lincoln. The term 'dog' denotes its lack of scent and is contrasted to 'sweet' violet.

Liverpool: **Sea holly** (*Eryngium maritimum*). Not a county but included in the survey. Its powder-blue cone-shaped flowers emerge in July, protected by prickly, wax-covered leaves.

London: **Rosebay willowherb** (*Epilobium angustifolium*). The tall purple flowers mingle with buddleias and Michaelmas daisies on railway banks, walls and waste ground.

Manchester: **Common cotton-grass** (*Eriophorum angustifolium*). Not a county but included in the survey. The white hairy plumes are an emblem of their boggy habitat and the wide open spaces.

Middlesex: **Wood anemone** (*Anemone nemorosa*). No longer a county but included in the survey. The long-stemmed pale-blue, white or pink unsymmetrical flowers are seen in woods and hedgebanks.

Newcastle upon Tyne: **Monkeyflower** (*Mimulus guttatus*). Not a county but included in the survey. From midsummer, the banks and shingles of the Tyne are bright with the yellowy-orange, red-spotted 'monkey faces' more common in rural Northumberland.

Norfolk: **Common poppy** (*Papaver rhoeas*). Original choice was Alexanders (*Smyrnium olusatrum*) but natives demanded a re-vote and out of five possible alternatives the poppy won. North Norfolk has long been known as 'poppyland'. Essex also chose the poppy as their county flower.

Northamptonshire: **Cowslip** (*Primula veris*). Frequently seen on road verges, quarries and railway banks, the tubular budded long-stemmed flowers adorned with beautiful orangey-yellow petals were chosen by three English counties.

Northumberland: **Bloody crane's-bill** (*Geranium sanguineum*). The vivid magenta flowers adorn coastal cliffs and dunes and spread inland on the rocks of the Whin Sill.

Nottingham: **Nottingham catchfly** (*Silene nutans*). Not a county but included in the survey. The spider-like flowers were once seen on the walls of the castle but since renovation are not to be found anywhere in Nottingham.

Nottinghamshire: **Autumn crocus** (*Crocus nudiflorus*). The tightly petalled purple flowers used to adorn the meadows of the Trent and were sold at Nottingham market.

Oxfordshire: **Fritillary** (*Fritillaria meleagris*). Some of the best-known fritillary fields are in Oxfordshire, along the flood-meadows of the Thames, the purple bells bowing on their snakey stalks.

Rutland: **Clustered bellflower** (*Campanula glomerata*). No longer a county but included in the survey. The familiar rich-blue flowers of the southern limestone are scarce in the county and therefore highly regarded.

Sheffield: **Wood crane's-bill** (*Geranium sylvaticum*). Not a county but included in the survey. A much-loved flower of old hay-meadows and damp, open woods near Sheffield, with its distinctive flowers the colour of runny blue ink.

Shropshire: **Round-leaved sundew** (*Drosera rotundifolia*). This crimson-leaved carnivore, with glues and acids to trap and devour careless insects, is a bog plant.

Somerset: **Cheddar pink** (*Dianthus gratianopolitanus*). Discovered on 'Chidderoks' 300 years ago, it grows in several places in the Mendip Hills but nowhere more profusely than the original site at Cheddar Gorge.

Staffordshire: **Heather** (*Calluna vulgaris*). Traditionally a Scottish flower but Staffordshire is proud of its heather moors, blooming purple beyond the Potteries and manufacturing towns.

Suffolk: **Oxlip** (*Primula elatior*). The signature flower of well-established woods on the East Anglian boulder clay. The apricot scents of the drooping yellow blooms made this a popular choice.

Surrey: **Cowslip** (*Primula veris*). In Surrey, cowslips grow in contrasting places – dry chalk downs and damp meadows. One of three English counties to insist upon the cowslip as their designated flower.

Sussex: **Round-headed rampion** (*Phyteuma orbiculare*). East and West Sussex are considered one county in the survey. Known as the Pride of Sussex, the sharp-blue flowers are common on the South Downs and bear resemblance to a many-tentacled jellyfish ready for its prey.

Warwickshire: **Honeysuckle** (*Lonicera periclymenum*). Honeysuckle is Shakespeare's 'woodbine', mentioned in *A Midsummer Night's Dream*, a play thought to have been set in the Forest of Arden.

Westmorland: **Alpine forget-me-not** (*Myosotis alpestris*). No longer a county but included in the survey. The blue flowers of this prettiest of forget-me-nots are confined in England to a few limestone hill-tops in the North Pennines.

Wiltshire: **Burnt orchid** (*Orchis ustulata*). This dwarf orchid belongs to the chalky core of Wiltshire, its white cone-shaped bloom turning pink and then dark red at the top.

Worcestershire: **Cowslip** (*Primula veris*). In parts of the county there are still small cowslip meadows hidden behind tall hedges. Locals call them 'cowslups'. One of three English counties to choose the cowslip as their preferred flower.

Yorkshire: **Harebell** (*Campanula rotundifolia*). For purposes of the survey Yorkshire was considered as a single county. It may appear surprising that the white rose was not chosen, but the blue and white blossom of the harebell matches the native folk for toughness and resilience, making it a perfect choice.

SCOTLAND

Aberdeenshire: **Bearberry** (*Arctostaphylos uva-ursi*). This red-berried trailing shrub is widespread at beautiful sites like the Muir of Dinnet.

Angus/Forfarshire: **Alpine catchfly** (*Lychnis alpina*). A single, remote hilltop of Angus boasts almost the whole British population of this pink alpine, although there are small areas of Cumbria where it is also seen.

Argyll: **Foxglove** (*Digitalis purpurea*). Seen on roadside banks in the mild, humid climate, foxgloves here look bigger and redder than those seen further south. Birmingham and Leicestershire also chose the foxglove.

Ayrshire: **Green-winged orchid** (*Orchis morio*). Vary from pink-purple to almost white, the upper petals

N
A
T
U
R
E

marked with dark veins and often suffused green. Unfortunately, although this beautiful flower is seen throughout the British Isles it is rare in Ayrshire.

Banffshire: Dark-red helleborine (Epipactis atrorubens). This rare and beautiful wild red orchid is a special plant of old Banff.

Berwickshire: Rock rose (Helianthemum nummularium). The five-petalled 'solflowers' form spectacular golden banks on some coastal cliffs in early summer.

Bute: Thrift (Armeria maritima). At its brightest and best on the rocky headlands and islands of the west coast. Bute shares the love of the thrift with the Isles of Scilly.

Caithness: Scots primrose (Primula scotica). Scots primrose grows on promontories on the north coast including the most northerly point of mainland Britain, Dunnet Head. The rich purple flower is native to Orkney and Pentland Firth but is found nowhere else.

Clackmannanshire: Opposite-leaved golden saxifrage (Chrysosplenium oppositifolium). Creeping plant characteristic of the shaded, wooded glens.

Cromarty: Spring cinquefoil (Potentilla neumanniana). This pretty five-petalled golden trailing flower reaches its northern limit on the sea cliffs.

Dumfriesshire: Harebell (Campanula rotundifolia). The true bluebell of Scotland, aka the 'cuckoo's shoe'. Also chosen, somewhat surprisingly, by Yorkshire.

Dunbartonshire: Lesser water-plantain (Baldellia ranunculoides). This pale pink-flowered aquatic brightens a few bays and shores of Loch Lomond, Scotland's first National Park.

East Lothian and Haddingtonshire: Viper's bugloss (Echium vulgare). Rich blue and black flower found on dry banks and dunes.

Edinburgh: Sticky catchfly (Lychnis viscaria). The pale purple flower has grown on rocks in Holyrood Park for at least 400 years.

Fife: Coralroot orchid (Corallorrhiza trifida). This pale yellow claw-fingered flower grows in quarries and disused railway lines.

Glasgow: Broom (Cytisus scoparius). The pale orange-brown vanilla-scented flowers of broom brighten many braes and railway lines.

Inverness-shire: Twinflower (Linnaea borealis). A shy species that creeps over the shady floor of mossy pinewoods, its drooping bell-shaped flowers hiding their inner beauty.

Kinross: Holy-grass (Hierochloe odorata). This delicate, scented grass grows on the banks of Loch Leven, the castle on a small island in the loch being the prison for a year of Mary, Queen of Scots.

Kirkcudbright: Bog rosemary (Andromeda polifolia). The delicate bulbous pink flowers are a particular feature of the much-reduced bogs of Galloway.

Lanarkshire: Dune helleborine (Epipactis leptochila). The county's coal 'bings' are home to two exotic orchids: the narrow-lipped or dune helleborine and Young's helleborine.

Moray: One-flowered wintergreen (Moneses uniflora). This star-shaped white plant needs mossy hollows in undisturbed pinewoods. Aka St Olaf's candle stick.

Nairn: Chickweed wintergreen (Trientalis europaea). This six-petalled white flower is not a true wintergreen but surprisingly, a relative of the primrose.

Orkney: Alpine bearberry (Arctostaphylos alpinus). The black berries amid the lightly veined leaves that turn red in autumn are in evidence on the path to the Old Man of Hoy rock stack.

Peebles: Cloudberry (Rubus chamaemorus). A miniature bramble of high places. The four-petalled, large white flowers with marmalade berries are hard to find but can be seen on the Pentland Hills.

Perthshire: Alpine gentian (Gentiana nivalis). This sweet 'gentian of the snows' is among the gems of Ben Lawers, the highest of the Perthshire hills.

Renfrewshire: Bogbean (Menyanthes trifoliata). A plant of dark, moorland waters, the bogbean's feathery flowers somewhat resemble an azalea.

Ross: Bog asphodel (Narthecium ossifragum). The golden spires of bog asphodel light up dark, peaty places after midsummer.

Roxburghshire: Maiden pink (Dianthus deltoides). Purple five-petalled scentless flower inhabiting dry banks and hill pastures.

Selkirkshire: Mountain pansy (Viola lutea). Largest of the native pansies, a flower of upland pastures, sheep and trout becks.

Shetland: Shetland mouse-ear (Cerastium nigrescens). This white ten-petalled flower is entirely confined to the island of Unst.

Stirlingshire: Scottish dock (Rumex aquaticus). Confined to the banks of Loch Lomond, the towering russet spires are sometimes called the Loch Lomond dock.

Sutherland: Grass-of-Parnassus (Parnassia palustris). Increasingly scarce elsewhere, this flower of wet flushes and hollows is still fairly common here. Also chosen by Cumbria.

West Lothian and Linlithgowshire: Common spotted orchid (Dactylorhiza fuchsii). The lilac spikes and red spotted leaves of this flower enliven many wild places in West Lothian.

Western Isles: Hebridean spotted orchid (Dactylorhiza fuchsii subspecies hebridensis). Believed to be a low-growing form of the much more widespread common spotted orchid, although more conical in shape and a richer lilac in colour.

Wigtownshire: Yellow iris (Iris pseudacorus). Known locally as 'segg' or 'sword-grass', a reference to the remarkable blade-like leaves. The flagging appearance belies a hardiness demanded by its habitat of wet fields and marshes.

WALES

Anglesey/Sir Fon: Spotted rock rose (Tuberaria guttata). Yellow five-petalled flower with distinct crimson spots near the base of each petal. Predominant on Anglesey's Holy Island.

Brecknockshire/Sir Frycheiniog: Cuckooflower (Cardamine pratensis). The delicate tall-stemmed lilac flowers appear in the meadows of Brecknock when the cuckoo returns in mid-April.

Caernarvonshire/Sir Gaernarfon: Snowdon lily (Lloydia serotina). The pride of Wales, unlike most alpines, blooms alone, and often out of reach, in rock crevices.

Cardiff/Caerdydd: Wild leek (Allium ampeloprasum). The lilac globes of the flowering wild leek were used to identify Welsh soldiers in battle against the English. The traditional emblem of Wales.

Cardiganshire/Ceredigion: Bog rosemary (Andromeda polifolia). A speciality of mid-west Wales, with delicate pink bells and rosemary-like foliage. Also chosen by Kirkcudbright.

Carmarthenshire/Sir Gaerfyddin: Whorled caraway (Carum verticillatum). Found on rough pasture, its frothy blossom symbolises the battle between conservation and intensive agriculture.

Denbighshire/Sir Ddinbych: Limestone woundwort (Stachys alpina). Grows among rocks by roadsides and is seen only in Denbigh and Gloucestershire.

Flintshire/Sir Fflint: Bell heather (Erica cinerea). Bell heather announces the brief blaze of colour that lights up the moors at the end of summer.

Glamorgan/Morgannwg: **Yellow whitlow grass** (*Draba aizoides*). Confined to cliffs and old walls on the Gower, this tiny cress flowers in the early spring.

Merioneth/Merionnydd: **Welsh poppy** (*Meconopsis cambrica*). The bright yellow Welsh poppy is a native of rocky gullies and stream sides in Merioneth.

Monmouthshire/Sir Fynwy: **Foxglove** (*Digitalis purpurea*). The foxglove is a common wayside flower in Gwent. Also chosen by Argyll, Birmingham and Leicestershire.

Montgomeryshire/Sir Drefaldwyn: **Spiked speedwell** (*Veronica spicata*). The tall, deep blue spikes of this rock plant are one of the celebrated rarities of Craig Breidden.

Pembrokeshire: **Thrift** (*Armeria maritima*). Thrift brightens up the county's coastline of headlands, rock arches and bays in May. Also chosen by the Isles of Scilly, Bute.

Radnorshire/Sir Faesyfed: **Radnor lily** (*Gagea bohemica*). Aka 'early-star-of-Bethlehem' and sometimes flowering as early as mid-winter.

NORTHERN IRELAND

Antrim: **Harebell** (*Campanula rotundifolia*). Known as the 'goblin's thimble' in Co. Antrim; legend has it that you pick it at your peril. Also chosen by Dumfriesshire and Yorkshire.

Armagh: **Cowbane** (*Cicula virosa*). As its name implies the plant is poisonous to cattle, and it is consequently slowly being eradicated.

Belfast: **Gorse** (*Ulex europaeus*). The bright yellow sweetly scented flowers are ever-present in heathland, waste ground, banks and coastal regions.

Derry: **Purple saxifrage** (*Saxifraga oppositifolia*). Inhabits cliff edges and rocks, and flowers early spring, often amid the lying snow.

Down: **Spring squill** (*Scilla verna*). The lilac petals of the squill inhabit coastal grasslands and cliffs.

Fermanagh: **Globeflower** (*Trollius europaeus*). The distinctive golden puffballs adorn the lake margins of west Fermanagh.

Tyrone: **Bog rosemary** (*Andromeda polifolia*). One of the special plants of the central Irish peat-bogs. Also chosen by Kirkcudbright and Cardiganshire.

Birds

alcid bird of the auk famil, Sp.: *Alcidae*.

Andean condor world's largest bird of prey with a wingspan of 3 metres and body weight of up to 15 kilograms. Sp.: *Vultur gryphus*.

avadavat: green and red South Asian waxbills (aka amadavat). Sp.: *Amandava formosa* and *Amandava amandava*.

avocet white bird with black-patterned head and back; its most notable feature is the upcurved bill. Sp.: *Recurvirostra avosetta*.

bateleur short-tailed African eagle. Sp.: *Terathopius ecaudatus*.

bean goose similar to the pink-footed goose but distinguished by its orange bill and feet. Sp.: *Anser fabalis*.

bee-eater exotic European bird with yellow throat and multi-coloured plumage. Sp.: *Merops apiaster*.

bittern bird of the heron family with a brown and buff plumage barred with black, and famous for its booming call. Sp.: *Botaurus stellaris*.

black grouse spectacular bird with a lyre-shaped tail, the cocks having black plumage and the hens, grey. The black grouse is famous for its courtship display during the mating season. Sp.: *Lyrurus tetrix*.

blackbird black bird of the thrush family having a yellow beak, the female having a dark brown plume. Sp.: *Turdus merula*.

blackcap small songbird, nicknamed 'the monk' in Germany because of its grey plumage and distinct black cap. Sp.: *Sylvia atricapilla*.

bobolink North American oriole originally called Bob o' Lincoln. Sp.: *Dolichonyx oryzivorus*.

boobook brown spotted owl, native to Australia and New Zealand. Sp.: *Ninox novaeseelandiae*.

booby tropical marine bird, similar to a gannet, with a straight, stout bill and white plumage with darker markings. Gen.: *Sula*.

bowerbird bird native to Australia and New Guinea; the males construct elaborate bowers of feathers, grasses and shells. Family *Ptilonorhynchidae*.

budgerigar small, green parakeet native to Australia, bred in coloured varieties and often kept as cage birds. Sp.: *Melopsittacus undulatus*.

bulbul Asian or African songbird of dull plumage with contrasting bright patches. Family *Pycnonotidae*.

bullfinch small plump finch with black head, grey-blue back and red breast. Sp.: *Pyrrhula pyrrhula*.

bunting: corn. seed-eating bird related to the finches with a streaked, sparrow-like plumage. Sp.: *Emberiza calandra*.

bustard: great large, mainly terrestrial bird with long neck, long legs and stout tapering body. Sp.: *Otis tarda*.

buzzard predatory bird of the hawk family with broad wings, well adapted for soaring flight. Sp.: *Buteo buteo*.

capercaillie largest of the grouse family and extinct in Britain from the late 18th until mid-19th century. Sp.: *Tetrao urogallus*.

cassowary large, flightless bird of Australia and the Malay Archipelago, with heavy body, stout legs, a wattled neck and a bony crest on its forehead. Gen.: *Casuarius*.

chaffinch common European finch, the male of which has a blue-grey head with pinkish cheeks and breast. Sp.: *Fringilla coelebs*.

chough large black bird of the crow family, seen in Europe, Asia and Africa, with a long, downward-curving red bill and red legs. Sp.: *Pyrrhocorax pyrrhocorax*.

chukar red-legged Eurasian partridge. Sp.: *Alectoris chukar*.

collared turtle dove similar to the turtle dove but with a black half moon on the back of its neck, which gives rise to the name. Sp.: *Streptopelia decaocto*.

coot resembles an oversized moorhen, although the breast is grey-black and the beak is white rather than yellow and red. Sp.: *Fulica atra*.

cormorant diving seabird with lustrous black plumage. Sp.: *Phalacrocorax carbo*.

corncrake rail with a rasping call, inhabiting grassland and nesting on the ground. Sp.: *Crex crex*.

cotinga any member of the large and varied New World tropical family Cotingidae, many with vivid plumage and unusually modified heel feathers.

cowbird North American oriole which often eats insects stirred up by grazing cattle and is known to lay its eggs in other birds' nests. Gen.: *Molothrus*.

crane long-legged, long-necked wading bird, which inhabits marshes and plains in most parts of the world except South America. Sp.: *Grus grus*.

crested lark often kept as a cage bird, not only for its own song but also for its ability to imitate the calls and cries of other birds. Sp.: *Galerida cristata*.

crossbill finch having a bill with crossed mandibles with which it opens pine cones. Gen.: *Loxia curvirostra*.

crow: carrion common predatory and scavenging European crow, similar to the rook but having a pure black bill. Sp.: *Corvus corone*.

crow: hooded highly intelligent bird with jet black and ashen grey plumage. Sp.: *Corvus cornix*.

cuckoo known as the harbinger of spring, the adult birds are slate blue-grey above, white underneath with dark grey barring. The cuckoo builds no nest of its own but parasitises other birds by laying in their nests. Sp.: *Cuculus canorus*.

curlew bird with brownish plumage that is barred and patterned, and bill that is long and slightly curved downwards. Sp.: *Numenius arquata*.

demoiselle small crane native to Asia and North Africa Sp.: *Anthropoides virgo*.

dipper diving bird of mountain streams. Aka water ouzel. Gen.: *Cinclus*.

dotterel small migratory plover named from the ease with which it is caught (word supposedly signifying stupidity). Sp.: *Eudromias morinellus*.

dowitcher wading bird breeding in North America and related to sandpipers. Gen.: *Limnodromus*.

drongo any insect-eating bird of the family Dicruridae, possessing a long, forked tail, native to Asia, Africa and Australia.

duiker long-tailed cormorant. Sp.: *Phalacrocorax africanus*.

dunlin long-billed sandpiper. Sp.: *Calidris alpina*.

dunnock small European songbird with brown and grey plumage. Sp.: *Prunella modularis*.

eagle large bird of prey with keen vision and powerful flight. Family Accipitridae.

eider sea duck of which the female's brownish plumage is the source of eiderdown, while the male plumage is white and black. Sp.: *Somateria mollissima*.

emu Australian flightless bird, second in size only to the ostrich, which it resembles, although the emu has three-toed feet as opposed to the ostriches' two-toed. Sp.: *Dromaius novaehollandiae*.

falcon any diurnal bird of prey of the family Falconidae, having long pointed wings and sometimes trained to hunt small game for sport.

fieldfare large Old World thrush having a pale grey head and rump, brown wings and back and a blackish tail. Sp.: *Turdus pilaris*.

finch any small seed-eating songbird of the family Fringillidae, including canaries, crossbills and chaffinches.

finch: zebra small Australian waxbill with black and white stripes on face, popular as a cage bird. Sp.: *Poephila guttata*.

frigate bird: magnificent seabird found in tropical seas, with a wide wingspan and deeply forked tail. Sp.: *Fregata magnificens*.

fulmar gull-like seabird, Britain's longest-lived bird, often reaching 40 years of age. Sp.: *Fulmarus glacialis*.

gadwall brownish-grey freshwater duck. Sp.: *Anas strepera*.

gannet heavily built marine bird, a spectacular diver for fish, having a long stout bill and typically white plumage with dark markings. Sp.: *Sula bassana*.

garganey small duck, the drake of which has a white stripe from the eye to the neck. Sp.: *Anas querquedula*.

gerfalcon (gyrfalcon) large falcon of cold northern regions. Sp.: *Falco rusticolus*.

glaucous gull large gull with typical brown and white speckled plumage, of Arctic coasts. Sp.: *Larus hyperboreus*.

go-away bird any of several touracos of the genus *Corythaixoides*.

godwit wading bird with long legs and a long, straight or slightly upcurved bill. Gen.: *Limosa*.

goldcrest smallest British and European bird, usually growing to a maximum of about 9cm (3½in), with an olive green plumage and yellow or orange crest. Sp.: *Regulus regulus*.

golden eagle large eagle with yellow-tipped head-feathers. Sp.: *Aquila chrysaetos*.

golden-eye black-and-white diving duck of northern waters. Sp.: *Bucephala clangula*.

golden-eye black-and-white diving duck, slightly larger than the above. Sp.: *Bucephala islandica*.

goldfinch exotically coloured bird with an unusual tinkling, twittering song, often compared to little bells. Sp.: *Carduelis carduelis*.

goosander large diving duck with a narrow serrated bill. Sp.: *Mergus merganser*.

goose any of various large waterbirds of the family Anatidae, with short legs, webbed feet and a broad bill.

goose: barnacle an Arctic goose which winters in northern Europe. Sp.: *Branta leucopsis*.

goose: Brent small migratory Arctic-breeding goose with black, grey and white plumage. Sp.: *Branta bernicla*.

goose: Canada wild goose with brownish-grey plumage and white cheeks and breast, native to northern America. Sp.: *Branta canadensis*.

goshawk large, short-winged hawk often used in falconry. Sp.: *Accipiter gentilis*.

great crested grebe large Old World grebe with a crest and ear-tufts. Sp.: *Podiceps cristatus*.

greenfinch finch with green and yellow plumage. Sp.: *Carduelis chloris*.

greylag goose native to Europe. Sp.: *Anser anser*.

grosbeak Any of various finches and cardinals having stout conical bills and brightly coloured plumage. The largest species is the pine grosbea,. *Pinicola enucleator*.

guillemot narrow-billed auk, nesting on cliffs or islands. Sp.: *Uria aalge*.

guinea fowl African fowl with slate-coloured white-spotted plumage. Sp.: *Numida meleagris*.

hammerhead heron-like African and Arabian marsh bird with a heavy black bill and an occipital crest. Sp.: *Scopus umbretta*.

harpy eagle South American crested bird of prey, one of the largest of eagles. Sp.: *Harpia harpyja*.

harrier any bird of prey of the genus *Circus* with long wings for swooping over the ground.

hawk any of various diurnal birds of prey of the family Accipitridae, having a characteristic curved beak, rounded short wings and a long tail.

heron: grey long-necked wading bird with a blue-grey plumage and yellow beak. Sp.: *Ardea cinerea.*

herring gull becomes progressively greyer as it matures and also changes colour from winter to summer. Sp.: *Larus argentatus.*

hobby small, long-winged falcon, which catches prey on the wing. Sp.: *Falco subbuteo.*

hoopoe Eurasian bird whose crest is held erect at moments of excitement. Sp.: *Upupa epops.*

hornbill tropical Old World bird with a horn-like excrescence on its large curved bill. Family Bucerotidae.

house martin black and white swallow-like bird, which builds a mud nest under the eaves of houses. Sp.: *Delichon urbica.*

ibis any wading bird of the family Threskiornithidae, with a long down-curved bill, long neck and long legs, and nesting in colonies.

Iceland gull although many spend the winter in Iceland the Iceland gull breeds in Greenland and north Alaska. Sp.: *Larus glaucoides.*

jabiru large black-necked stork of Central and South America, with mainly white plumage. Sp.: *Ephippiorhynchus mycteria.*

jacamar small insect-eating bird with partly iridescent plumage, of the tropical South American family Galbulidae.

jacana tropical wading bird with elongated toes and hind claws, which enable them to walk on floating leaves. Family Jacanidae.

jack snipe small snipe often seen in marshy areas. Sp.: *Lymnocryptes minimus.*

jackdaw small grey-headed crow often frequenting rooftops and nesting in tall buildings and noted for its inquisitiveness and magpie tendencies to thieve bright objects. Sp.: *Corvus monedula.*

Java sparrow waxbill native to Java and Bali. Sp.: *Padda oryzivora.*

jay brownish-pink bird of crow family, whose wings are decorated with flashes of blue. Sp.: *Garrulus glandarius.*

kaka large New Zealand parrot with olive-brown plumage. Sp.: *Nestor meridionalis.*

kestrel a resident of Great Britain and our most common true falcon; often mistaken for a sparrowhawk, but is a hoverer rather than a glider and is far less ferocious. Sp.: *Falco tinnunculus.*

killdeer large North American plover with a plaintive song. Sp.: *Charadrius vociferus.*

kingfisher slightly larger than the house sparrow and brilliantly plumed, the kingfisher is a swift flying, swooping bird that feeds on insects and small fish. Sp.: *Alcedo atthis.*

kittiwake small gull that nests on sea cliffs of the north Atlantic and Arctic oceans. Sp.: *Rissa tridactyla.*

kiwi flightless New Zealand birds with hairlike feathers and a long bill, nesting in burrows. Gen.: *Apteryx.*

knot small northern sandpiper with a short bill and grey plumage. Sp.: *Calidris canutus.*

lammergeier large vulture of Africa, central Asia and southern Europe, with a very large wingspan and dark, beard-like feathers on either side of its beak. Sp.: *Gypaetus barbatus.*

lapwing plover with black and white plumage, crested head, and a shrill cry. Sp.: *Vanellus vanellus.*

lesser whitethroat slightly smaller than its namesake and tends to be somewhat shyer. Sp.: *Sylvia curruca.*

limpkin wading marsh bird of the Americas whose name derives from its limping gait. Aka courlan. Sp.: *Aramus guarauna.*

linnet small European songbird; grey-brown plumage with red forehead and breast in summer; famous for its wide range of singing voice. Sp.: *Acanthis cannabina.*

little auk small Arctic auk. Sp.: *Plautus alle.*

little grebe small waterbird of the grebe family. Sp.: *Tachybaptus ruficollis.*

lory any of various brightly coloured Australasian and South-east Asian parrots of the subfamily Loriinae.

lorikeet any of various small brightly coloured parrots of the subfamily Loriinae.

lovebird any of various African and Madagascan parrots. Gen.: *Agapornis.*

lyre-bird either of two Australian birds of the family Menuridae, the male of which has a lyre-shaped tail.

macaw any long-tailed, brightly coloured parrot of the genus *Ara* or *Anodorhynchus,* native to South and Central America.

magpie black and white plumed bird of the crow family, often regarded as a pest by farmers as it has thieving tendencies, especially for bright shiny objects. Sp.: *Pica pica.*

magpie lark Australian bird of the family Grallinidae, in particular a common long-legged black and white bird, Sp.: *Grallina cyanoleuca.*

mallard duck which is common over most of the northern hemisphere, the drake having a bottle green head and rufous markings. The mallard is thought to be the ancestor of all domestic breeds of duck. Sp.: *Anas platyrhynchos.*

mandarin duck originally from eastern Asia but introduced in many other regions; although the female has typical looks, the drake is exotically coloured. Sp.: *Aix galericulata.*

Manx shearwater European oceanic bird with long slender wings and black and white plumage. Sp.: *Puffinus puffinus.*

marabou large West African stork whose down is used as a trimming for hats. Sp.: *Leptoptilos crumeniferus.*

meadow pipit common pipit native to Europe, Asia and Africa. Sp.: *Anthus pratensis.*

meadowlark North American songbirds with a yellow breast. Sp.: *Sturnella magna* and slightly smaller *Sturnella reglecta.*

merganser any of various diving fish-eating northern ducks of the genus *Mergus,* with a long narrow serrated hooked bill.

merlin small European or N. American falcon that hunts small birds. Sp.: *Falco columbarius.*

mistle (missel) thrush large thrush with a spotted breast that feeds on mistletoe berries. Sp.: *Turdus viscivorus.*

mockingbird long-tailed songbirds of the American family Mimidae noted as mimics of other birds' calls. The common mockingbird of the eastern USA is *Mimus polyglottos.*

Montagu's harrier slender migratory Eurasian bird of prey named after George Montagu 1751–1815, a British naturalist. Sp.: *Circus pygargus.*

moorhen waterside bird having black plumage with blue-green breast and a white line along the flanks. Sp.: *Gallinula chloropus.*

Muscovy musk duck   tropical American duck, having a small crest and red markings on its head. Sp.: *Cairina moschata*.

musk duck   Australian duck, having a musky smell. Sp.: *Biziura lobata*.

mutton-bird   various southern hemisphere birds of the genus *Puffinus*, especially the short-tailed shearwater. Sp.: *Puffinus tenuirostris*.

nightingale   loud songbird with dark brown plumage and lighter underparts. Sp.: *Luscinia megarhynchos*.

nightjar   nocturnal birds with a cryptic plumage and large eyes, which feed on insects. Sp.: *Caprimulgus*.

nutcracker   forest-dwelling Old World bird of the crow family, having speckled plumage. Sp.: *Nucifraga caryocatactes*.

nuthatch   small songbird that climbs up and down tree trunks and feeds on nuts and insects. Sp: Sitta europaea.

oriole: golden   yellow-plumed Eurasian bird with black wings and red beak. Sp.: *Oriolus oriolus*.

osprey   bird of prey with a dark back and whitish head and underparts praying on fish. Sp.: *Pandion haliaetus*.

ostrich   world's largest living bird can weigh in excess of 180 kilograms and stand 2.5 metres high. The ostrich can attain running speed of 40 mph, which it can sustain for up to 30 minutes. The ostrich lays the largest egg, weighing up to 2 kg and measuring 15 cm in diameter. Sp.: *Struthio camelus*.

ovenbird   any Central or South American bird of the family Furnariidae, which build domed nests out of clay or tunnel underground to lay their eggs.

owl: barn   type of owl that likes to nest in barns and other accessible rural buildings. Sp.: *Tyto alba*.

owl: eagle   large Eurasian owl with long ear-tufts. Sp.: *Bubo bubo*.

owl: horned   North American owl with hornlike feathers over the ears. Sp.: *Bubo virginianus*.

owl: little   small owl of Africa and Eurasia, with speckled plumage. Sp.: *Athene noctua*.

owl: long-eared   known for its peculiar barking cry, broken by 'yaps'; its long ears are in reality tufts of feathers. Sp.: *Asio otus*.

owl: tawny   familiar owl with rich brown plumage, barred and checked with darker bars and streaks. Sp.: *Strix aluco*.

oystercatcher   wading bird with black and white plumage and long laterally compressed orange-red bill. Sp.: *Haematopus ostralegus*.

partridge   game bird with light grey plumage, barred and streaked with chestnut. Sp.: *Perdix perdix*.

penguin   flightless seabird of the southern hemisphere with black upper parts and white underparts, and wings developed into scaly flippers for swimming underwater. Family Spheniscidae.

penguin: Adélie   Most common species of penguin. Sp.: *Pygoscelis adeliae*.

penguin: emperor   largest species of penguin, which can grow to a height of 120 cm (4 ft). Sp.: *Aptenodytes forsteri*.

penguin: fairy   smallest species of penguin, average height of 41 cm (16 in). Aka little blue penguin. Sp.: *Eudyptula minor*.

penguin: Galápagos   unlike the emperor and the Adélie, the Galápagos penguin is confined to the tropics of South America. Sp.: *Spheniscus mendiculus*.

penguin: gentoo   abundant in the Falkland and other Atlantic islands. Sp.: *Pygoscelis papua*.

peregrine falcon   powerful falcon, breeding on coastal cliffs and much used for falconry. Sp.: *Falco peregrinus*.

petrel   small wave-hanging seabirds, blackish with a white rump. Family: Hydrobihdar.

petrel: Wilson's   common petrel that breeds around Antarctica but is often seen in the Atlantic. Sp.: *Oceanites oceanicus*.

phalarope   any small wading bird or swimming bird of the family Phalaropodidae, with a straight bill and lobed feet.

pheasant   game bird introduced to Britain from its native home in south-eastern Europe and central Asia; the cock birds show a wide colour variation, with brown and buff common specimens, although some almost black birds have been sighted in recent years. Sp.: *Phasianus colchicus*.

pipit: tree   light brown plumed bird of the wagtail family. Sp.: *Anthus trivialis*.

plover: golden   a wader noted for its musical but sad rising whistle, the golden plover is a golden speckled colour with a white or sometimes black underparts. Sp.: *Pluvialis apricaria*.

plover: ringed   small chunky wader with brown plumage, white underparts and a black ring round the neck. Sp.: *Charadrius hiaticula*.

pochard   familiar diving duck, the male having silvery plumage with chestnut head and black underparts whilst the females are silvery-brown. Sp.: *Aythya ferina*.

ptarmigan   high mountain grouse whose grey-brown and black plumage changes to white in the winter. Sp.: *Lagopus mutus*.

puffin   Britain's most recognisable seabird, with its large multicoloured bill and awkward movement; the main colonies are in north Scotland, the largest on St Kilda, west of the Outer Hebrides. Sp.: *Fratercula arctica*.

quail   game bird, which looks like a miniature partridge although its plumage is a red-buff carrying streaks of cream and black. The quail is rarely sighted, due largely to its habit of taking refuge in grassland when spotted. Sp.: *Coturnix coturnix*.

quetzal   spectacular tree bird of central America, a member of the trogon family, with green back and crimson and white under parts; the male's green tail plumes grow to 60 cm (2 feet). Sp.: *Pharomachons mocinno*.

raven   large passerine bird of the crow family, having a large,straight, black bill, long, wedge-shaped tail and black plumage. Sp.: *Corvus corax*.

razorbill   common auk of the north Atlantic which typically nests in colonies on cliffs. Sp.: *Alca torda*.

red kite   once a common scavenger in the streets during Elizabethan and the early Stuart period, this bird of prey gradually died out but has been reintroduced into England and Wales. Sp.: *Milvus milvus*.

redpoll   soft striped brown plumed songbird of the finch family. Sp.: *Acanthis flammea*.

redstart   similar in size and habit to the robin, with a grey plumage and black throat. Sp.: *Phoenicurus phoenicurus*.

redstart: black   darker than its namesake but has similar feeding habits of taking insects, mainly on the wing. Sp.: *Phoenicurus ochruros*.

redwing   small European thrush, having a speckled breast, reddish flanks and brown back. Sp.: *Turdus iliacus*.

rhea either of two large flightless birds of South Africa, *Rhea americana* and *Pterocieia pennara*, similar to ostrich but hairy, three-toed feet.

ring ouzel thrush with a white crescent across its breast. Sp.: *Turdus torquatus.*

robin well-loved bird with brown plumage and red breast with yellow throat. Sp.: *Erithacus rubecula.*

roller beautifully coloured migrant from Africa. The plumage shows a brown back, with blue wing coverts, greenish-blue head, blue undersurface and purplish tail and wings. Sp.: *Coracias garrulus.*

rook most common member of the crow family, notable for its jet black plumage and depredations among the eggs of smaller birds. Sp.: *Corvus frugilegus.*

ruff Eurasian member of the sandpiper family. The males' communal dancing display is called 'lekking'. The female is called a reeve. Sp.: *Philomachus pugnax.*

Sabine's gull fork-tailed seabird breeding on islets and marshy tundra in Arctic Greenland, Alaska and northern Siberia. Sp.: *Larus sabini.*

sanderling small busy sandpiper of the genus *Calidris* that frequents sandy shores. Sp.: *Calidris alba.*

sand martin slightly smaller than the house martin, with dark brown plumage and a brown band across its white breast. Sp.: *Riparia riparia.*

sandpiper various smallish members of the family Scolopacidae, walkers with long legs and long slender bills, which includes the curlew, dunlin and snipe.

shag very similar to the cormorant but smaller and darker green, no white marking on face and more of a crest. Sp.: *Phalacrocorax aristotelis.*

shoveler duck with spoon-shaped bill, a blue patch on each wing, and in the male a green head, white breast and reddish-brown body. Sp.: *Anas clypeata.*

shrike: red-backed chestnut-backed bird with grey head and rump and black ear coverts. Aka butcher bird because it impales its prey on thorn-bushes for storage. Sp.: *Lanius collurio.*

siskin small finch with brownish-green back with yellow shades and black cap. Sp.: *Carduelis spinus.*

skua: Arctic smaller member of this predatory seabird genus with dark plumage and a hooked bill, all of them famous for harassing terns or gulls into dropping or disgorging fish they have caught. Sp.: *Stercorarius parasiticus.*

skua: great heavy, broad-winged seabird with brown plumage and wings with white bar on wings. Sp.: *Stercorarius skua.*

skylark like the cuckoo, this ground-dwelling songbird is often thought of as a harbinger of spring; it has a dull brown plumage with white ribbing. Sp.: *Alauda arvensis.*

smew merganser of north Europe and Asia with white plumage with black markings. Sp.: *Mergus albellus.*

snipe bird of the sandpiper family inhabiting marshy areas. Collective noun is a 'wisp'. Sp.: *Gallinago gallinago.*

snow bunting bunting of northern and arctic regions having a white plumage with dark markings on the wings, back and tail. Sp.: *Plectrophenax nivalis.*

social weaver small gregarious Old World passerine songbird of the chiefly African family Ploceidae, having a short thick bill and a dull plumage. The name derives from the bird's characteristic of building covered nests in trees and living in communities of hundreds. Sp.: *Philetairus socius.*

song thrush song bird with brown plumage and white underparts speckled with brown; its repetitive refrain sounds rather like 'Come out, come out, come out'. Sp.: *Turdus philomelos.*

sparrowhawk fiercest of our native hawks, identified by its rapid flight with long gliding intervals and sudden swoops on prey. Sp.: *Accipiter nisus.*

sparrow: house small common brown and grey bird which nests in the eaves and roofs of houses. Sp.: *Passer domesticus.*

spoonbill wading bird of warm regions, having white plumage and a long, horizontally flattened bill. Sp.: *Platalea leucorodia.*

spotted flycatcher sparrow-sized grey-brown bird with a whitish breast, able to catch insects in flight. Sp.: *Muscicapa striata.*

starling distinctly coloured bird with black, iridescently green-tinged plumage, white flecks throughout its cover, and a yellow beak. Sp.: *Sturnus vulgaris.*

stock dove similar to the wood-pigeon but smaller. Sp.: *Columba oenas.*

storm(y) petrel small petrel of the north Atlantic, Europe's smallest seabird. Sp.: *Hydrobates pelagicus.*

swallow streamlined insect-hunter with a distinctive blue sheen on the back and wings, chestnut throat and white breast. Sp.: *Hirunda rustica.*

swan: Bewick's smallest swan, rarely seen in England outside the Slimbridge Wildfowl Trust and the Ouse Washes. Sp.: *Cygnus columbianus.*

swan: mute commonest Eurasian swan, having white plumage and an orange-red bill with a swollen black base. Sp.: *Cygnus olor.*

swan: trumpeter large North American wild swan. Sp.: *Cygnus buccinator.*

swan: whooper black bill with yellow nose, most of Britain's winter whoopers are from Iceland. Sp.: *Cygnus cygnus.*

swift fast-flying bird with dark brown plumage; it is a summer bird in Britain and spends its winters in Africa. Sp.: *Apus apus.*

teal smallest of Europe's wintering ducks, appearing like a smaller wigeon. Sp.: *Anas crecca.*

tern graceful, slender-winged seabird that dives headlong after small fish. Gen.: *Sterna.*

tern: Arctic greyer than the common or sandwich tern, can be seen at close hand on the Farne Islands. Sp.: *Sterna paradisaea.*

tern: common most familiar tern, with grey-white plumage, black cap and red bill. Sp.: *Sterna hirundo.*

tern: little small tern distinguished from other terns by its yellow bill. Sp.: *Sterna albifrons.*

tern: roseate rare bird with white plumage, black cap and extremely long tail streamers. Sp.: *Sterna dougallii.*

tern: Sandwich largest of the terns found regularly in Britain, distinguished from other terns by its pale white plumage and black bill with yellow tip. Sp.: *Sterna sandvicensis.*

tit: bearded Eurasian songbird common in reed beds; it has a tawny back and tail and, in the male, a grey and black head. Sp.: *Panurus biarmicus.*

tit: blue gymnastic bird with bright blue cap and yellow underparts, often seen hanging upside down while hunting for food. Sp.: *Parus caeruleus.*

tit: crested chubby bird with dull brown plumage and white crest marked with black, in Britain restricted to the Scottish Highlands but more common on the Continent. Sp.: *Parus cristatus.*

tit: great Eurasian songbird with black-and-white head markings. Sp.: *Parus major.*

tit: long-tailed black and white plumed tit distinguished from other tits by its long tail. Sp.: *Aegithalos caudatus*.

tit: marsh grey-backed tit that inhabits woods and hedges. Sp.: *Parus palustris*.

tit: penduline southern European bird that derives its name from the hanging nest characteristic of the species. Sp.: *Remiz pendulinis*.

tit: willow Eurasian black-capped tit. Sp.: *Parus montanus*.

touraco (turaco) any brightly coloured crested arboreal African bird of the family Musophagidae.

tragopan tree-dwelling Asian pheasant; the male displays erect fleshy horns on its head. Gen.: *Tragopan*.

tree sparrow two distinct species. *Passer montanus* is a Eurasian sparrow inhabiting agricultural land. *Spizella arborea* is a North American sparrow-like bird of the bunting family, breeding on the edge of the tundra.

treecreeper small passerine songbirds of the family Certhiidae of the northern hemisphere, having a brown-and-white plumage and slender downward-curving bill. Named from their characteristic of creeping up trees to feed on insects. Gen.: *Certhia*.

turkey buzzard American vulture, unrelated to the Old World vultures, so called because of its bare reddish head and dark plumage. Sp.: *Cathartes aura*.

turtle dove small slim dove with thin neck, protruding round white head, deep chest and brownish-grey plumage with black marks. Sp.: *Streptopelia turtur*.

umbrella bird cotinga of tropical America, with a large, black, overhanging crest and a long feathered wattle. Gen.: *Cephalopterus*.

Victoria crowned pigeon large blue-crested pigeon of New Guinea. Sp.: *Goura victoria*.

vulture any of various large birds of prey of the distinct Old and New World families Accipitridae and Cathartidae, with the head and neck more or less bare of feathers, feeding mainly on carrion and reputed to gather with others in anticipation of a death.

wagtail: white terrestrial bird, named from the up and down waggings of the tail at each halt that accompany its short darting rushes in a zigzag course. Sp.: *Motacilla alba alba*.

wandering albatross very large white albatross of southern oceans, having very long and narrow black-tipped wings. Sp.: *Diomedea exulans*.

warbler: barred arrives in Europe, from Africa, later than the other warblers and rarely visits Britain. Sp.: *Sylvia nisoria*.

warbler: Cetti's named after an 18th-century Italian Jesuit; it is the only European passerine with 10 tail feathers, rather than 12. Sp.: *Cettia cetti*.

warbler: Dartford until recently Britain's only resident warbler; it was first described from Bexley Heath, near Dartford in Kent, in 1773. Sp.: *Sylvia undata*.

warbler: great reed migrant bird seen frequently in the reed beds of East Anglia and the southern coast. Sp.: *Acrocephalus arundinaceus*.

warbler: icterine migratory warbler with brownish plumage and olive green underparts. Sp.: *Hippolais icterina*.

warbler: reed inconspicuous bird with overall brown colouring with lighter underparts. Sp.: *Acrocephalus scirpaceus*.

water ouzel see dipper.

water rail highly nervous and secretive bird, more often heard than seen; it hides in its reed-bed home at the slightest disturbance. Sp.: *Rallus aquaticus*.

wattlebird various Australian honeyeaters with a wattle hanging from each cheek. Gen.: *Anthochaera* and *Melidectes*. Also various New Zealand songbirds of the family Callaeidae, with wattles hanging from the base of the bill, e.g. the saddleback. Sp.: *Creadion carunculatus*.

waxbill any small finch-like bird of the family Estrildidae, with a red bill resembling sealing wax in colour.

waxwing any of three species of crested perching birds of the genus *Bombycilla*, with small tips like red sealing wax to some wing feathers.

weka large flightless New Zealand rail. Sp.: *Gallirallus australis*.

whale-headed stork grey African stork with a large bill shaped like a clog. Sp.: *Balaeniceps rex*.

wheatear small northern thrush having a grey back, black wings and tail, white rump and pale brown underparts. Sp.: *Oenanthe oenanthe*.

whimbrel small migratory curlew with a striped crown and trilling call. Sp.: *Numenius phaeopus*.

whinchat Old World songbird having mottled brown-and-white plumage with pale cream underparts; it is a member of the subfamily of thrushes. Sp.: *Saxicola rubetra*.

white stork widely protected in Europe, a pure white bird with black wing tips and long red beak and legs. Sp.: *Ciconia ciconia*.

whitethroat warbler with greyish plumage, rusty wings and white underparts. Sp.: *Sylvia communis*.

wi(d)geon gregarious duck, the male of which has a reddish-brown head and chest, and grey and white back and wings. Sp.: *Anas penelope*.

woodchat shrike shrike of southern Europe, north Africa and the Middle East, having black and white plumage with a chestnut head. Sp.: *Lanius senator*.

woodcock any game bird of the genus *Scolopax* that inhabits woodlands. The common Eurasian species is *Scolopax rusticola*.

woodpecker any bird of the family Picidae that climbs and taps tree trunks in search of insects.

woodpecker: black largest of the European woodpeckers; the jet-black plumage is broken only by its red cap. Sp.: *Dryocopus martius*.

woodpecker: great spotted black and white plumage with a large red patch on the nape of the neck (male only); noted for its repeated drumming on the trunks of trees. Sp.: *Dendrocopos major*.

woodpecker: green large green and yellow European woodpecker with a red crown. Sp.: *Picus viridis*.

woodpecker: pileated large North American woodpecker with a red-topped head. Sp.: *Dryocopus pileatus*.

wood pigeon large pigeon, having white patches like a ring round its neck. Sp.: *Columba palumbus*.

wren small light brown bird famous for its building of more than one nest, the hen making her choice and the 'spares' used as roosting spots in bad weather. Sp.: *Troglodytes troglodytes*.

wryneck small bird of the woodpecker family, able to turn its head over its shoulder. Sp.: *Jynx torquilla*.

yellowhammer bunting of which the male has a yellow head, neck and breast. Sp.: *Emberiza citrinella*.

yellowlegs: greater and lesser two migratory sandpipers with yellow legs. Sp.: *Tringa melanoleuca* and *Tringa flavipes*.

Birds: Miscellaneous Information

altricial of a young bird or animal requiring care and feeding by the parents after hatching or birth

arctic tern: migrates to Antarctica

backwards-flying the hummingbird is the only bird that can fly backwards

beaks: characteristics insect-eating birds usually have pointed bills while carnivorous birds have hooked bills

bird: smallest bee hummingbird

bird of paradise: from New Guinea and nearby islands (birds of paradise hang upside down)

bird of prey: largest Andean condor

bird of prey: largest UK golden eagle

British bird: biggest mute swan

British bird: fastest runner pheasant (up to 21 mph)

British bird: highest flier whooper swans on migration have been sighted at 27,000 feet

British bird: largest egg mute swan

British bird: longest-lived Manx shearwater (29.82 years)

British bird: most common wren

British bird: smallest goldcrest

British bird: smallest egg goldcrest

British Isles: exclusive to red grouse and Scottish crossbill do not migrate and are found only in the UK

carinate of a bird having a keeled breastbone; opposite of ratite

deepest diving bird emperor penguin

drops bones on rocks to break the bearded vulture (lammergeyer)

ducks: sex that quacks only females

egg: smallest hummingbird

extinct birds dodo lived on the island of Mauritius and became extinct in the late 17th century; great auk or Atlantic pigeon became extinct in the mid-19th century; moa of New Zealand became totally extinct by early 19th century

falconry breeding and training of hawks for sporting purposes. The female is called a falcon, the male is a tiercel

fastest bird peregrine falcon has been timed at 217 mph during swoop as part of the courtship display. The golden eagle has reached speeds exceeding 150 mph during a vertical dive, but the fastest bird in level flight, with recorded speeds exceeding 110 mph, is the Alpine swift

fastest runner ostrich

first known bird archaeopteryx (name means 'ancient wing')

gizzard muscular thick-walled part of a bird's stomach, used for grinding food, usually with the help of grit

grallatorial of or relating to long-legged wading birds e.g. flamingos and storks (from Latin *grallator*, 'stiltwalker')

guano excrement of seabirds found on islands off South America, Africa and the West Indies and used as manure

hangs upside down birds of paradise of Papua New Guinea frequently adopt this position

largest birds ostrich is clearly the largest living bird (moas extinct); the largest flying bird is more contentious but is possibly the kori bustard of sub-Saharan Africa

longest migration Arctic tern (11,222 miles from Anglesey to Australia)

nests at end of riverbank tunnels kingfisher

nests in water crested grebe

New World: definition term used to differentiate between the time before and after the Americas were discovered. New World relates to the Americas: the western hemisphere

nostrils at tip of beak kiwi

Old World: definition term used to differentiate between the time before and after the Americas were discovered. The Old World consists of Europe, Asia and Africa: the eastern hemisphere

owl: smallest elf owl

painter of USA birds John Audubon

palmiped web-footed bird

ratite of a bird having a keelless breastbone and therefore unable to fly; opposite of carinate

sacred birds quetzal (Aztecs), ibis (Egyptians)

seabird: largest emperor penguin

smells when excited the hoopoe raises its crest when excited and emits a foul-smelling liquid

smell: keenest sense of kiwi

snail shells: breaks with stone thrush

sonar-equipped the guacharo, or oilbird, is capable of flying in total darkness in a similar way to bats

steals food in flight skua often steals food from other birds while in flight

strigiformes order of birds that solely includes owls

underwater: longest emperor penguin (up to 18 minutes)

underwater: walks dipper

web-footed bird: smallest petrel

white stork: UK breeding in 1416 a nest was found on St Giles Cathedral, Edinburgh, the only known UK breeding occurrence

wingspan: longest albatross, although the largest wings belong to the Andean condor

NATURE

Alternative or Poetic Names of Birds

adjutant bird	stork	blackcap	monk
aepyornis	elephant bird	black guillemot	puffinet
apteryx	kiwi	blue tit	tinnock
ash-coloured falcon	Montagu's harrier		tom tit
barn owl	yellow owl	bonxie	great skua
	white owl		skua
bearded tit	reedling	bullbat	nighthawk
blackbird	merle	bullfinch	nope

butcher bird	shrike (esp. red-backed)
chaffinch	sheld apple
corncrake	land rail
crow blackbird	grackle
cuckoo	gowk
cushat	wood pigeon
	ring dove
dabchick	little grebe
dipper	water crake
dunnock	hedge sparrow
elephant bird	aepyornis
fish hawk (North America)	osprey
frigate bird	man-of-war bird
goatsucker	nightjar
goldcrest	woodcock pilot
	golden-crested wren
golden-crested wren	goldcrest
gowk	cuckoo
grackle	crow blackbird
great grey shrike	white whisky john
great skua	bonxie
green cormorant	shag
greenfinch	green linnet
green linnet	greenfinch
green plover	lapwing
green woodpecker	yaffle
halcyon	kingfisher
hedge sparrow	dunnock
horned grebe	Slavonian grebe
kestrel	windhover
kingfisher	halcyon
kiwi	apteryx
kotuku	white heron
land rail	corncrake
lapwing	peewit (pewit)
	green plover
lark	laverock
laverock	lark
little grebe	dabchick
man-of-war bird	frigate bird
mavis	song thrush
merganser	sawbill
merle	blackbird
mock nightingale	sedge warbler
monk	blackcap
Montagu's harrier	ash-coloured falcon
moorhen	water hen
mosquito hawk	nighthawk
Mother Carey's chicken	storm petrel
mountain Linnet	twite
nighthawk	bullbat
	mosquito hawk
nightingale	philomel
nightjar	goatsucker (North America)
nope	bullfinch
osprey	fish hawk
peewit (pewit)	lapwing
philomel	nightingale
pipit	tit lark
puffin	sea parrot
puffinet	black guillemot
reedling	bearded tit
ring dove	cushat
robin	ruddock
ruddock	robin
sawbill	merganser
Scotch nightingale	sedge warbler
sea parrot	puffin
sedge warbler	Scotch nightingale
	mock nightingale
shag	green cormorant
sheld apple	chaffinch
shrike	butcher bird (esp. red-backed)
shoebill	whale-headed stork
skua	bonxie
Slavonian grebe	horned grebe
smew	white nun
song thrush	mavis
	throstle
stork	adjutant bird
storm petrel	Mother Carey's chicken
	witch
tawny owl	wood owl
throstle	song thrush
tinnock	blue tit
tit lark	pipit
tom tit	blue tit
turkey buzzard	turkey vulture
turkey vulture	turkey buzzard
twite	mountain linnet
water crake	dipper
water hen	moorhen
whale-headed stork	shoebill
white heron	kotuku
white nun	smew
white owl	barn owl
white whisky john	great grey shrike
windhover	kestrel
witch	storm petrel
woodcock pilot	goldcrest
wood owl	tawny owl
wood pigeon	cushat
yaffle	green woodpecker
yellow bunting	yellowhammer
yellowhammer	yellow bunting
yellow owl	barn owl

NB: For ease of reference, the alternatives have been listed alphabetically.

Collective Nouns

BY GROUPS

actors cast, company, troupe
aeroplanes flight, squadron, wing
angels host
antelopes herd
ants colony, army
apes shrewdness
arms pile
arrows sheaf, quiver
asparagus bundle
asses pace
badgers cete
barley crop
barracuda battery
baseball team
bass fleet
bears sleuth, sloth
beaters squad
beauties galaxy
beavers colony
bees swarm, grist
bells peal
birds flock
bishops bench
bitterns sedge, siege
bloodhounds sute
boars sounder
books library
bowls set
boy scouts jamboree
boys blush
bread batch, caste
bucks brace, leash
budgerigars chatter
butlers draught
camels caravan, flock
capercaillie tok
capitalists syndicate
cards pack, deck
cars fleet
cats clowder
cattle herd, drove
chickens brood
children class
chocolates box
choughs chattering
cigarettes packet
clams bed
clergy assemblage, convocation
clothes outfit
colts rag
coots covert
corn sheaf
cranes sedge, siege
cricket team eleven
crockery service
crows murder
cubs litter
curlews herd

dancers troupe
deer herd
dogs show, kennel
donkeys drove
dottrel trip
ducks (in flight) flush, pump, team
ducks (on ground) badelynge
ducks (in water) paddling
dunlins flight
eagles convocation
eels swarm
eggs clutch
elk gang
falcons cast
ferrets fesnyng, business
finches charm
firewood bundle
fish shoal
flamingos flurry, regiment
flies swarm
flowers bunch, bouquet, nosegay, posy
foresters stalk
foxes skulk, earth
frogs army, colony
fruit orchard
geese (in flight) skein
geese (on ground) gaggle
girls bevy
gnats swarm, cloud
goats herd, tribe, trip
goldfinches charm
goldfish troubling
golf-clubs set
grapes bunch, cluster
grass tuft
grouse (several broods) pack
grouse (single brood) covey
guardians board
guillemots bazaar
gulls colony
guns battery, park
hares down, husk
harpists melody
hawks cast
hay truss
hedgehogs array
hermits observance
herons sedge, siege
hooligans gang
horses haras
hounds pack, mute

hunters blast
hunting dogs cry
ibis crowd
islands archipelago, chain
jellyfish smuck
kangaroos troop
kittens kindle
knaves rayful
labourers gang
lapwings deceit
larks exaltation
leopards leap
lions pride
magistrates bench
magpies tiding, tittering
majors morbidity
mallards flush
mares stud
martens richesse
mice nest
minstrels troupe
moles labour
monkeys troop
mules barren
music library
musicians band, orchestra
nightingales watch
onions rope
owls parliament
oxbirds fling
oxen yoke, team
papers budget
parrots company
partridges covey
passenger pigeons roost
peacocks muster
pearls string, rope
peas pod
penguins rookery, colony
people assembly, clique, audience, community, congregation
pheasants nye
pictures exhibition
pigs litter, drove
plovers congregation, wing
plums basket
pochards rush
polecats chine
police posse, detachment
politicians caucus
porpoises school
poultry run

pups litter
quail bevy
rabbits nest
race horses string
rags bundle
ravens unkindness
rhinoceros crash
roes bevy
rooks clamour, building
ruffs hill
runners field
sailors crew, deck, watch
sails outfit
saints community
sandpipers fling
sardines family
savages horde
seals herd, pod
sergeants subtiltie
servants staff
sheep flock
sheldrakes dopping
ships fleet, flotilla
slaves gang
smelt quantity
snakes den, pit
snipe wisp, walk
soldiers detachment
spiders cluster, clutter
stamps collection
starlings murmuration
stars cluster, constellation
steps flight
sticks faggot
strawberries punnet
subalterns simplicity
swans herd, bevy
swifts flock
swine sounder, drift, dryet
swine (tame) doylt
teals spring
thieves gang
thrush mutation
tigers ambush
toads knot, knab
trees clump, orchard, spinney, thicket
troops brigade, division
trout hover
turkeys rafter
turtles bale, dole
turtle doves pitying
wasps nest
whales school, pod, gam
whelps litter

NATURE

whiskey case
whiting pod
wigeon company
wild cats dout

wildfowl plump, sord, sute
wine vintage

witches coven
wolves pack
women bevy

woodcock fall, plump
woodpeckers descent
worshippers congregation

BY NAMES

ambush tigers
archipelago islands
army frogs, ants
array hedgehogs
assemblage clergy
assembly people
audience people
badelynge ducks (on ground)
bale turtles
band musicians
barren mules
basket plums
batch bread
battery guns, barracuda
bazaar guillemots
bed clams
bench magistrates, bishops
bevy quail, girls, women, roes, swans
blast hunters
blush boys
board guardians
bouquet flowers
box chocolates
brace bucks
brigade troops
brood chickens
budget papers
building rooks
bunch grapes, flowers
bundle firewood, asparagus, rags
business ferrets
caravan camels
case whiskey
cast hawks, actors, falcons
caste bread
caucus politicians
cete badgers
chain islands
charm goldfinches
chatter budgerigars
chattering choughs
chine polecats
clamour rooks
class children
clique people
cloud gnats
clowder cats
clump trees
cluster grapes, spiders, stars

clutch eggs
clutter spiders
collection stamps
colony gulls, frogs, penguins, ants, beavers
community people, saints
company actors, wigeon, parrots
congregation people, plovers, worshippers
constellation stars
convocation eagles, clergy
coven witches
covert coots
covey partridges, grouse (single brood)
crash rhinoceros
crew sailors
crop barley
crowd ibis
cry hunting dog
deceit lapwings
deck cards, sailors
den snakes
descent woodpeckers
detachment soldiers, police
division troops
dole turtles
dopping sheldrakes
dout wild cats
down hares
doylt swine (tame)
draught butlers
drift swine
drove donkeys, cattle, pigs
dryet swine
earth foxes
eleven cricket team
exaltation larks quiver
exhibition pictures
faggot sticks
fall woodcock
family sardines
fesnyng ferrets
field runners
fleet cars, ships
flight dunlins, aeroplanes, steps
fling oxbirds, sandpipers
flock swifts, birds, sheep

flotilla ships
gaggle geese (on ground)
galaxy beauties
gam whales
gang labourers, hooligans, thieves, slaves, elk
gleam herring
grist bees
haras horses
herd deer, goats, cattle, curlews, antelopes, seals, swans
hill ruffs
horde savages
host angels
hover trout
husk hares
jamboree boy scouts
kennel dogs
kindle kittens
knab toads
knot toads
labour moles
leap leopards
leash bucks
library music, books
litter pups, whelps, pigs, cubs
melody harpists
morbidity majors
murder crows
murmuration starlings
muster peacocks
mutation thrush
mute hounds
nest mice, rabbits, wasps
nosegay flowers
nye pheasants
observance hermits
orchard fruit, trees
orchestra musicians
outfit sails, clothes
pace asses
pack hounds, cards, wolves, grouse (several broods)
packet cigarettes
paddling ducks (in water)
park guns
parliament owls
peal bells
pile arms
pit snakes

pitying turtle doves
plump woodcock, wildfowl
pod peas, whiting, whales, seals
posse police
posy flowers
pride lions
pump ducks (in flight)
punnet strawberries
quantity smelt
quiver arrows
rafter turkeys
rag colts
rayful knaves
richesse martens
rookery penguins
roost passenger pigeons
rope onions, pearls
run poultry
rush pochards
school porpoises, whales
sedge cranes, bitterns, herons
service cockery
set golf-clubs, bowls
sheaf corn, arrows
shoal fish
show dogs
shrewdness apes
siege bitterns, cranes, herons
simplicity subalterns
skein geese (in flight)
skulk foxes
sleuth bears
sloth bears
smuck jellyfish
sord wildfowl
sounder swine, boars
spinney trees
spring teals
squad beaters
squadron aeroplanes
staff servants
stalk foresters
string race horses, pearls
stud mares
subtiltie sergeants
sute bloodhounds, wildfowl
swarm gnats, bees, flies

syndicate capitalists
team ducks (in flight), baseball, oxen
thicket trees
tiding magpies
tittering magpies
tok capercaillie

tribe goats
trip goats
troop kangaroos, monkeys
troubling goldfish
troupe minstrels, actors, dancers
truss hay
tuft grass

unkindness ravens
vintage wine
walk snipe
watch sailors, nightingales
wing aeroplanes, plovers
wisp snipe
yoke oxen

NEWSPAPERS

National Newspapers

Name	Location	Founded	Details
Belfast News Letter	Belfast	1737	Britain's oldest surviving daily newspaper
Courier	Dundee	1816	Founded as the *Dundee Courier and Argus*
Daily Courant	London	1702	First successful daily newspaper
Daily Express	London	1900	Founded by C Arthur Pearson. Address: 10 Lower Thames St, London EC3R 6EN. Tel: 0871 434 1010
Daily Herald	London	1911	Merged into the *Sun* in 1964
Daily Mail	London	1896	Founded by Alfred Harmsworth (Lord Northcliffe). Address: 2 Derry St, Kensington, London W8 5TT. Tel: 020 7938 6000
Daily Mirror	London	1903	Founded by Alfred Harmsworth (Lord Northcliffe). Address: 1 Canada Square, Canary Wharf, London E14 5AP. Tel: 020 7293 3000
Daily Record	Glasgow	1895	Scottish equivalent of the *Daily Mirror* until the launch of the Scottish *Mirror*
Daily Sketch	London	1909	Merged into the *Daily Mail* in 1971
Daily Sport	Manchester	1989	Founded and owned by David Sullivan, David Gold and Ralph Gold
Daily Star	London	1978	Owned by United Newspapers (Express Group)
Daily Telegraph	London	1855	Amalgamated in 1937 with the *Morning Post*. Address: 1 Canada Square, Canary Wharf, London E14 5AP. Tel: 0161 848 0610
European	London	1990	Founded by Robert Maxwell and sold on Thursdays
Evening Standard	London	1827	Part of the 'Mail' Group of Newspapers
Financial News	London	1884	Merged with *Financial Times* in 1945
Financial Times	London	1888	Adopted its pink paper in 1893
Guardian	London	1821	Founded as the *Manchester Guardian* and became a daily in 1855. Address: 119 Farringdon Rd, London EC1R 3ER. Tel: 020 7278 2332
Herald	Glasgow	1783	Founded as *Glasgow Advertiser*, changed name to *Glasgow Herald* 1802–1992
Independent	London	1986	Originally part of the Mirror Group and founded by three *Daily Telegraph* journalists. Address: Independent House, 191 Marsh Wall, London E14 9RS. Tel: 020 7005 2000
Independent on Sunday	London	1990	Originally part of the Mirror Group
Mail on Sunday	London	1982	Sister paper to the *Daily Mail*
News of the World	London	1843	Founded by John Browne Bell. Address: 1 Virginia St, London E1 9XR. Tel: 020 7782 4000
Observer	London	1791	Founded by Irishman W S Bourne. Address: 119 Farringdon Rd, London EC1R 3ER. Tel: 020 7278 2332
People	London	1881	Founded to support the Conservative cause originally. Address: 1 Canada Square, Canary Wharf, London E14 5AP. Tel: 020 7293 3000
Press and Journal	Aberdeen	1748	Founded by James Chalmers as *Aberdeen's Journal*
Scotland on Sunday	Edinburgh	1988	Sister paper to the *Scotsman*
Scotsman	Edinburgh	1817	First non-London newspaper to open an office in Fleet Street
Sun	London	1964	Founded in 1911 as the *Daily Herald*. Address: 1 Virginia St, London E1 9XR. Tel: 020 7782 4100
Sunday Express	London	1918	Founded by Lord Beaverbrook
Sunday Mirror	London	1963	Founded by Harold Harmsworth as the *Sunday Pictorial* in 1915
Sunday Post	Glasgow	1914	Launched as the *Post Sunday Special*, it is the leading Scottish Sunday paper
Sunday Sport	Manchester	1986	Founded and owned by David Sullivan, David Gold and Ralph Gold

Name	Location	Founded	Details
Sunday Telegraph	London	1961	Sister paper to the *Daily Telegraph*. Address: 1 Canada Square, Canary Wharf, London E14 5AP. Tel: 020 7358 5000
Sunday Times	London	1822	Launched as *The New Observer* and then *The Independent Observer* in 1821
Times	London	1785	Founded by John Walter. Address: 1 Pennington St, London E1 9XN. Tel: 020 7782 5000
Today	London	1986	Founded by Eddie Shah

International Newspapers

(location and date founded)

ABC Madrid 1905
Al-Akhbar Cairo 1944
Apogevmatini Athens 1952
Avriani Athens 1980
Berlingske Tidende Copenhagen 1749
Bild am Sonntag Hamburg 1956
Boston American Boston 1904
B.T. Copenhagen 1916
Chicago Sun Chicago 1941
Corriere della Sera Milan 1876
Diario Popular Lisbon 1942
Ethnos Athens 1891
Evening Herald Dublin 1891
Evening Press Dublin 1954
Le Figaro Paris 1828
L'Humanité Paris 1904
Irish Independent Dublin 1905
Irish Times Dublin 1859
Izvestiya Petrograd 1917

La Lanterne Brussels 1944
La Libre Brussels 1884
Il Messaggero Rome 1878
Le Monde Paris 1944
Morgunbladid Reykavik 1913
Die Neue Zeitung Munich 1945
Neue Zürcher Zeitung Zurich 1789
New York Post New York 1801
New York Times New York 1851
New York World New York 1860
L'Osservatore Romano Vatican 1929
El Pais Madrid 1976
Plain Dealer Cleveland 1842
Politiken Copenhagen 1884
Pravda Moscow 1912
La Repubblica Rome 1976
Le Soir Brussels 1887
La Stampa Turin 1867

Süddeutsche Zeitung Munich 1945
Sunday Independent Dublin 1905
Sunday Press Dublin 1949
Sunday World Dublin 1973
Svenska Dagbladet Stockholm 1884
Tagesspiegel Berlin 1945
Tägliche Rundschau Berlin 1945
De Telegraaf Amsterdam 1893
Tribune Chicago 1847
La Vanguardia Barcelona 1881
Wall Street Journal New York 1889
Washington Post Washington DC 1877
Die Welt Hamburg 1945
Ya Madrid 1935

Regional Newspapers

Name	Location	Name	Location
Argus	Brighton	Evening Herald	Plymouth
Burton Mail	Burton-on-Trent	Evening Mail	Birmingham
Chronicle	Bath	Evening News	Bolton
Chronicle and Echo	Northampton		Cambridge
Courier and Advertiser	Dundee		Edinburgh
Citizen	Gloucester		Manchester
Daily Echo	Bournemouth		Norwich
Daily Examiner	Huddersfield		Scarborough
Daily Mail	Hull	Evening Post	Bristol
Daily Post	Liverpool		Nottingham
Daily Record	Glasgow		Reading
Dorset Echo	Weymouth		Wigan
East Anglian Daily Times	Ipswich	Evening Telegraph	Coventry
Eastern Daily Press	Norwich		Derby
Echo	Lincoln		Dundee
	Liverpool		Grimsby
	Sunderland		Peterborough
Essex Chronicle	Chelmsford		Scunthorpe
Evening Advertiser	Swindon	Evening Times	Glasgow
Evening Chronicle	Newcastle	Express and Echo	Exeter
	Oldham	Express Star	Wolverhampton
Evening Courier	Halifax	The Gazette	Blackpool
Evening Echo	Weymouth		South Shields
	Basildon	Gloucestershire Echo	Cheltenham
Evening Express	Aberdeen	Greenock Telegraph	Dunfermline (head office)
Evening Gazette	Colchester		
	Middlesbrough	Heartland Evening News	Nuneaton

Name	Location	Name	Location
Herald Express	Torquay	**Post**	Birmingham
Kent Today	Aylesford	**Sentinel**	Stoke
The Journal	Newcastle	**Shropshire Star**	Telford
Lancashire Evening Post	Preston	**South Wales Evening Post**	Swansea
Lancashire Evening Telegraph	Blackburn	**Southern Daily Echo**	Southampton
Mercury	Leicester	**Star**	Barnsley
News and Star	Carlisle		Doncaster
The News	Portsmouth		Sheffield
Northern Echo	Darlington	**Telegraph**	Belfast
Northamptonshire Evening Telegraph	Kettering	**Telegraph and Argus**	Bradford
		Western Daily Press	Bristol
Observer	Crawley	**Western Mail**	Cardiff
Oxford Mail	Oxford	**Western Morning News**	Plymouth
Paisley Daily Express	Glasgow	**Yorkshire Evening Post**	Leeds
		Yorkshire Post	Leeds

Editors (as at April 2005)

Daily Express   Peter Hill (previously Christopher Williams)

Daily Mail   Paul Dacre

Daily Mirror   Richard Wallace (previously Piers Morgan)

Daily Record   Bruce Waddell

Daily Sport   David Beevers

Daily Star   Dawn Neesom (previously Peter Hill)

Daily Star Sunday   Gareth Morgan

Daily Telegraph   Martin Newland (previously Charles Moore)

Evening Standard   Veronica Wadley (previously Max Hastings)

Financial Times   Andrew Gowers (previously Richard Lambert)

Guardian   Alan Rusbridger

Independent   Simon Kelner (previously Andrew Marr)

Independent on Sunday   Tristan Davies (previously Janet Street Porter)

Mail on Sunday   Peter Wright (previously Jonathan Holborow)

Metro   Kenny Campbell

News of the World   Andy Coulson (previously Rebekah Wade)

Observer   Roger Alton (previously Will Hutton, now Editor-in-Chief)

People   Mark Thomas (previously Neil Wallis)

Racing Post   Chris Smith (previously Alan Byrne)

Radio Times   Gill Hudson

Scottish Daily Mirror   Mike Graham

Spectator   Boris Johnson

Sun   Rebekah Wade (previously David Yelland)

Sunday Express   Martin Townshend (previously Michael Pilgrim)

Sunday Mail   Allan Rennie

Sunday Mirror   Tina Weaver (previously Colin Myler)

Sunday Sport   Paul Carter

Sunday Telegraph   Dominic Lawson

Sunday Times   John Witherow

Times   Robert Thomson

Vogue   Alexandra Shulman

Agony Aunts, Horoscopes, Crosswords

Agony Aunts

Virginia Ironside   *Independent*
Jane O'Gorman   *Daily Star*
Just Joan   *Daily Record*
Eve Pollard   *Daily Mirror*
Deidre Sanders   *Sun*
Kate Saunders   *Express*
Miriam Stoppard   *Daily Mirror*

Horoscopes

Jonathan Cainer   *Daily Mail*
Lynne Ewart   *Daily Record*
Russell Grant   *Daily Mirror*
Sally Kirkman   *Daily Star*
Marjorie Orr   *Express*
Mystic Meg   *Sun*

Shelley von Strunckel   *Evening Standard; Sunday Times*
Justin Toper   *Daily Express; Daily Star*
Peter Watson   *Daily Mail*

Crosswords

Peter Watson   *Daily Mail*
Aelred   *Independent*
Aquila   *Independent*
Araucaria   *Guardian*
Auctor   *Times*
Azed   *Observer*
Beelzebub   *Sunday Independent*
Bunthorne   *Guardian*
Columba   *Independent*

Enigmatist   *Guardian*
Gemini   *Guardian*
Mod   *Times*
Monk   *Independent*
Pasquale   *Guardian*
Paul   *Guardian*
Phi   *Independent*
Quixote   *Sunday Independent*
Rufus   *Guardian*
Spurios   *Independent*

Chess

Leonard Barden   *Evening Standard*
Raymond Keene   *Times*
Jon Speelman   *Independent*

Newspaper Cartoons and Cartoonist(s)

Alisdair   *Times*   Pugh and Way
Andy Capp   *Daily Mirror* and *Sunday Mirror*   Reg Smythe
As If   *Independent*   Sally Ann Lasson
Augusta   *Evening Standard*   Angus McGill and Dominic Poelsma
Austin   *Guardian*   Austin
Badlands   *Sun*   Steve McGarry
Beau Peep   *Daily Star*   Kettle and Christine
Ben and Katie   *Daily Star*   Doug Baker and Roca
Bill Caldwell (cartoonist)   *Daily Star*
Bogart   *Daily Mail*   Peter Plant
Bristow   *Evening Standard*   Frank Dickens
Clogger F.C.   *Daily Star*   Bill Caldwell
Colonel Blimp   *Evening Standard*   David Low
Dilbert   *Daily Telegraph* and *Express*   Scott Adams
Doonesbury   *Guardian*   Garry Trudeau
Dreadnoughts, The   *Sun*   Martin Fish
Faith, Hope and Sue   *Express*   Lisa Wild
Flatmates   *Daily Record*   Michael Atkinson
Flook (1949–84)   *Daily Mail*   Trog (Wally Fawkes)
Fred Basset   *Daily Mail*   Alex Graham
Gambols   *Express*   Barry Appleby
Garfield   *Evening Standard* and *Express*   Jim Davis
George & Lynne   *Sun*   Conrad and Gual
Giles   Daily and Sunday *Express*   Carl Ronald Giles
Grandad and the Lad   *Daily Record*   Bryan Walker
Griffin   *Express*   Griffin
Hagar the Horrible   *Sun*   Chris Browne
Heath   *Daily Telegraph*   Heath
Hector Breeze   *Express*   Hector Breeze
Horace   *Daily Mirror*   Kettle and Christine
I Don't Believe It   *Daily Mail*   Dick Millington
If   *Guardian*   Steve Bell

Jane   *Daily Mirror*   Norman Pett (originally)
The Johnsons   *Daily Express*   Peter Plant
Judge Dredd of 2000 AD   *Daily Star*   Smith and Rennie
Kipper Williams (cartoonist)   *Guardian*
Liberty Meadows   *Express*   Frank Cho
Livvy   *Sun*   Bob Maher
Mandy Capp   *Daily Mirror*   Carla Ostrer and Mahoney
Matt   *Daily Telegraph*   Matt Pritchett
Modesty Blaise (1963–2001)   *Evening Standard*   Peter O'Donnell
Paul Thomas   *Express*   Paul Thomas (untitled cartoon)
Peanuts   *Daily Mail*   Charles Schulz
Perishers   *Daily Mirror*   Bill Mevin and Maurice Dodd
Peter Brookes   *Times*   Peter Brookes (untitled cartoon)
Potto   *Evening Standard*   Frank Dickens
Psycops   *Sun*   Wilbur
Real Life   *Daily Mirror*   Johnston
Rupert Bear   *Express*   Mary Tourtel (1920–48)
Scorer   *Daily Mirror*   Tomlinson, Gillat and Pugh
Shuggie and Duggie   *Daily Record*   Bullimore and Anderson
Steve Bell (cartoonist)   *Guardian*
Striker   *Sun*   Pete Marsh
The Stringalongs   *Times* (originally)   Mark Boxer
Teenage Mum   *Daily Star*   Graham Hey
Tim   *Independent*
The Ultimate   *Daily Sport*   Paul Martin
Up and Running   *Daily Mail*   Gray and Shack
Weber Family   *Guardian*   Posy Simmonds
Wizard of Id   *Evening Standard*   Parker and Hart

NEWSPAPERS

General Information

Asahi Shimbun   Japan's leading newspaper has been produced 'untouched by human hands' since 24 September 1980.
***Avanti*: famous editor**   Benito Mussolini edited the Milan-based socialist paper from 1912 to 1914. Mussolini subsequently founded the newspaper *Il Popolo d'Italia* in 1914.
Beachcomber Column   Began in the *Daily Express* in 1917 under the name 'By the Way' its author inheriting the name 'Beachcomber', J B Morton wrote the column from 1924 to 1975 and the present author is William Hartston.
***Boy's Own*: founded**   in 1879 by the Religious Tract Society and ceased in 1967.
cartoon: first   drawn by John Wesley Jarvis in 1814 for the Washington Federal Republican.
cartoon: first   UK   'The Unknown Tongue' (printed in *Bell's New Weekly Messenger*) 8 Jan. 1832.
Children's Newspaper founded by Arthur Mee in 1919.
***Christian Science Monitor*: founder**   Mary Baker Eddy in Boston 1908.
clock on *Times* Diary page   always set on 4.30.
colour supplement: first   four-page section of the New York World 19 November 1893.
colour supplement: first   UK   Sunday Times Colour Section (became Sunday Times Magazine) 4 February 1962.
comic strip: first   *Yellow Kid* by R F Outcault (published in the *New York World* in 1896).
Corriere della Sera   although this newspaper translates as 'Evening Courier', it is a morning daily newspaper.
crossword puzzle: first   compiled by Liverpool-born Arthur Wynne (published in *New York World* Sunday 21 December 1913).
crossword puzzle: first UK   *Sunday Express* 2 November 1924.
crossword puzzle: first *Times*   1 February 1930 and compiled by Adrian Bell (father of ex-MP Martin Bell).
crusader logo   introduced on the *Express* by Lord Beaverbrook in 1930.
***Daily Express* column: famous**   'By the Way' (J B Morton under the name of 'Beachcomber').
famous sale   Max Aitken sold the Express group to Trafalgar House on 30 June 1977 (subsequently sold to United Newspapers 1985).

daily newspaper: first UK *The Perfect Diurnall* Feb. 1660 (*Daily Courant* of 1702 was first successful daily).

daily poem *Independent*.

Daily Sketch: merger in May 1971 the *Daily Sketch* merged into the *Daily Mail*.

Daily Telegraph editor: former W F (Bill) Deedes.

Daily Telegraph: news first published on front page 1969.

Daily Worker Communist newspaper founded in 1932. Name changed to *Morning Star* in 1966 but *Daily Worker* revived in 1992.

Der Spiegel the German news magazine was founded in 1947.

Edinburgh Gazette Scottish equivalent of the *London Gazette*, founded in 1699 and appearing twice a week.

Evening News: merger on 31 October 1980 the *Evening News* was merged into the *Evening Standard*.

evening newspaper: first *Dawks's News-Letter* (published in London) 23 June 1696.

famous columnists *Daily Mirror* political cartoonist Vicky and columnist Cassandra.

Foreign newspapers *El Pais* – Argentina, *Avanti* – Milan, *Exame* – Brazil, *Feral Tribune* – Croatia, *Hihon Keizai Shimbun* – Japan, *La Presse* – Quebec, *Moderna Tider* – Stockholm, *Qianshao* – Hong Kong.

founded as women's paper *Daily Mirror*.

Globe the British paper was suppressed in November 1915 for spreading false rumours about Lord Kitchener's resignation.

Good Housekeeping: founded the British magazine was founded in 1922, although the US version was founded much earlier.

Harijan: founder Mahatma Gandhi founded the Indian weekly publication in 1933.

Hearst, William Randolph: famous castle San Simeon, California.

Hearst: famous newspapers *Examiner* (1887 his first), *Morning Journal* (1895 later became *Journal-American*).

Hitler diaries extracts published by *Stern* magazine in May 1983 and considered authentic by historian Hugh Trevor-Roper, but later exposed as a fake produced by a dealer in Nazi memorabilia.

Independent: launched by Andreas Whittam-Smith and associates on 7 Oct. 1986 and subsequently acquired by a consortium led by Mirror Group Newspapers, 18 March 1994.

John Bull: date commenced 1906, although the character first appeared in 1712 in a pamphlet by John Arbuthnot (1667–1735).

The Liberator influential anti-slavery weekly newspaper of Abolitionist crusader William Lloyd Garrison between 1831 and 1865, published in Boston.

Life magazine: first published 1936 by Henry Luce, publisher of *Time*. *Life* magazine ceased on 29 December 1972 but was relaunched in October 1978.

Listener: founded by the BBC in 1929 and closed in January 1991.

London Daily News: founded by Robert Maxwell in February 1987 but it folded in July when the *Evening News* was temporarily relaunched.

London Gazette Government's bulletin in which official announcements are made. Founded in 1665 as the *Oxford Gazette* and appearing 4 times a week.

magazine: shortest title *Ms*, the American feminist magazine founded in 1972, may lay claim to that title.

Manchester Guardian: renamed In 1960 the *Manchester Guardian* was renamed *The Guardian*.

Marie-Claire: founded the French women's magazine was founded in 1954.

Messenger Group: launched by The free newspapers were launched by Eddie Shah in Warrington in 1983 and produced by non-union workers.

New Republic: founded by the American paper was founded by H D Croly in 1914.

New Society: founded the weekly sociology magazine was founded in 1962 and merged into the *New Statesman* in 1988.

newspaper: best-selling *News of the World* is Britain's largest-selling newspaper (approx 4.8 million).

newspaper: first *Acta Diurna* (Daily Events) dating from 59 BC and attributed to Julius Caesar.

newspaper: first surviving English *Weekly News* 1622. (Newspapers were printed before this date but none survive.)

New Statesman: founded by Beatrice and Sidney Webb in 1913 and aided by leading Fabians such as G B Shaw.

Now: founder the magazine was founded by James Goldsmith in September 1979 and ceased in March 1981.

page 3 girls: year started 1970.

People: famous libel case an article in 1909 alleged that chancellor David Lloyd George had committed adultery and had paid £20,000 to keep the case out of court.

Picture Post: first published 1938 and founded by Edward Hulton. It closed in 1957.

Playboy: founded by Hugh Hefner, December 1953.

Post: launched by Eddie Shah in November 1988 and folded after 33 issues.

Press Council: founded 1953 (replaced by the Press Complaints Commission 1 January 1991).

Private Eye: founded In February 1962 and saved from financial ruin by Peter Cook in April 1962.

Punch first published in 1841 and ceased production on 8 Aril 1992. Aka *The London Charivari*.

Radio Times: founded 1923.

Radio Times: first woman editor Sue Robinson.

Reader's Digest: founded DeWitt Wallace and his wife Lila Acheson published the first issue in Greenwich Village, New York 5 February 1922.

Scottish Daily News: founded launched by a workers' co-operative 5 May 1975 but closed in Oct. 1975 despite intervention by Robert Maxwell.

Sun: founded 15 September 1964 when the TUC sold its shares in the *Daily Herald*.

Sunday Correspondent: launched on 17 September 1989 and closed in Nov. 1990.

Sunday Herald: founded in 1915 and subsequently renamed the *Sunday Graphic*; closed down in 1960.

Tatler: founded by Richard Steele in 1709 and assisted by Joseph Addison until its closure in 1711. It was replaced by the non-political *Spectator* in 1711 but the name was revived in 1901 for an illustrated monthly magazine which is still published today.

Telegraph Group moved from Fleet Street to Docklands in 1987 and printed in London and new site (1986) in Manchester.

Time **magazine: founded by** Henry A Luce and Briton Hadden in 1923.

Times: **previous name** *Daily Universal Register* until 1788.

Times: **nickname** *The Thunderer* (the nickname of Thomas Barnes, editor of the *Times* 1817–41).

Times: **news first appeared on front page** 3 May 1966.

Today: **date commenced** launched by Eddie Shah 4 March 1986 as Britain's first full-colour, low-cost tabloid, its sales failed to achieve targets and it was subsequently sold to Tiny Rowland's Lonrho Co.

Wapping: exodus to *Times*, *Sunday Times*, *Sun* and *News of the World* moved overnight to a new plant in Wapping 25 Jan. 1986.

William Hickey column pen-name of Tom Driberg when writing for the *Daily Express* between 1928 and 1943. Having become an MP, Driberg later used the name as a columnist with the *Daily Mail* and *New Statesman*. The name derives from a famous 18th century diarist. The *Express* still has a Hickey column, although the 'William' has been dropped.

yellow journalism term coined to describe the sensationalistic reporting and frenzied promotional schemes adopted in the fierce circulation wars between William Randolph Hearst's *Journal* and Joseph Pulitzer's *World*.

NOBEL PRIZE WINNERS

	Physics	Chemistry	Literature	Medicine	Peace
1901	Wilhelm Röntgen (Ger.) Discovery of X-rays	Jacobus van't Hoff (Neth.) Laws of chemical dynamics and osmotic pressure	René Sully-Prudhomme (Fr.) Poet	Emil von Behring (Ger.) Work on serum therapy Pioneer in immunology	Jean Henri Dunant (Switz.) Frédéric Passy (Fr.)
1902	Hendrik Lorentz (Neth.) Pieter Zeeman (Neth.) Magnetism on radiation	Emil Fischer (Ger.) Work on sugar and purine syntheses	Theodor Mommsen (Ger.) Historian	Sir Ronald Ross (Brit.) Discovery of how malaria enters an organism	Elie Ducommun (Switz.) Charles Gobat (Switz.)
1903	Antoine-Henri Becquerel (Fr.) Pierre and Marie Curie (Fr.) Radioactivity	Svante Arrhenius (Swed.) Theory of electrolytic dissociation	Björnsterne Björnson (Nor.) Novelist, poet, dramatist	Niels Finsen (Den.) Phototherapy	Sir William Cremer (Brit.) Founder of Workmen's Peace Association
1904	Lord Rayleigh (Brit.) Discovery of argon	Sir William Ramsay (Brit.) Discovery of inert gases	Frédéric Mistral (Fr.), Poet J Echegaray Eizaguirre (Sp.)	Ivan Pavlov (Russ.) Physiology of digestion	Institute of International Law (founded 1873)
1905	Philipp Lenard (Ger.) Research on cathode rays	Adolf von Baeyer (Ger.) Work on organic dyes	H Sienkiewicz (Pol.) Novelist	Robert Koch (Ger.) Tuberculosis research	Bertha von Suttner (Austria)
1906	Sir J J Thomson (Brit.) Research into electrical conductivity of gases	Henri Moissan (Fr.) Isolation of fluorine Moissan furnace	Giosuè Carducci (Ita.) Poet	Camillo Golgi (Ita.) and S Ramon y Cajal (Sp.) Structure of nervous system	Theodore Roosevelt (US)
1907	A A Michelson (US) Spectroscopic and metrological investigations	Eduard Buchner (Ger.) Discovery of non-cellular fermentation	Rudyard Kipling (Brit.) Poet and novelist	Alphonse Laveran (Fr.) Discovery of the role of protozoa in diseases	Ernesto T Moneta (Ita.) Louis Renault (Fr.)
1908	Gabriel Lippman (Fr.) Photographic reproduction of colours	Lord Rutherford (Brit.) Disintegration of elements Chemistry of radioactivity	Rudolf Eucken (Ger.) Philosopher	Paul Ehrlich (Ger.) Ilya Mechnikov (Russ.) Work on immunity	Klas P Arnoldson (Swed.) Fredrik Bajer (Den.)
1909	Guglielmo Marconi (Ita.) Karl Braun (Ger.) Wireless telegraphy	Wilhelm Ostwald (Ger.) Pioneer work on catalysis, chemical equilibrium and reaction velocities	Selma Lagerlöf (Swed.) Novelist	Emil Kocher (Switz.) Physiology, pathology and surgery of thyroid gland	Baron d'Estournelles de Constant (Fr.) Auguste Beernaert (Belg.)
1910	J van Der Waals (Neth.) Gas and liquid equation	Otto Wallach (Ger.) Alicyclic combinations	Paul von Heyse (Ger.) Poet and novelist	Albrecht Kossel (Ger.) Cellular chemistry research	International Peace Bureau (founded 1891)

	Physics	Chemistry	Literature	Medicine	Peace
1911	Wilhelm Wien (Ger.) Discoveries regarding laws governing heat radiation	Marie Curie (Fr.) Discovered/isolated radium Discovered Polonium	Maurice Maeterlinck (Belg.) Dramatist	Allvar Gullstrand (Swed.) Work on dioptrics of the eye	Tobias Asser (Neth.) Alfred Fried (Austria)
1912	Nils Gustaf Dalén (Swed.) Invention of automatic regulators for lighting coastal beacons and light buoys	Victor Grignard (Fr.) Paul Sabatier (Fr.) Discovery of Grignard reagents and hydrogenating organic compounds	Gerhart Hauptmann (Ger.) Dramatist	Alexis Carrel (Fr.) Work on vascular suture Transplantation of organs	Elihu Root (US)
1913	H Kamerlingh Onnes (Neth.) Liquid helium production Low temperature properties	Alfred Werner (Switz.) Work on the linkage of atoms in molecules	Sir R Tagore (India) Poet	Charles Richet (Fr.) Work on anaphylaxis	Henri Lafontaine (Belg.)
1914	Max von Laue (Ger.) Discovery of diffraction of X-rays by crystals	Theodore Richards (US) Accurate determination of atomic weights of elements	no award	Robert Barany (Austria) Work on vestibular apparatus	no award
1915	Sir William Bragg (Brit.) Sir Lawrence Bragg (Brit.) Analysis of crystals by means of X-rays	Richard Willstätter (Ger.) Pioneer researches on plant pigments, especially chlorophyll	Romain Rolland (Fr.) Novelist	no award	no award
1916	no award	no award	V von Heidenstam (Swed.) Poet	no award	no award
1917	Charles Barkla (Brit.) Discovery of characteristic X-radiation of elements	no award	Karl Gjellerup (Den.) H Pontoppidan (Den.) Novelists	no award	International Red Cross Committee (founded 1863)
1918	Max Planck (Ger.) Elemental quantum theory	Fritz Haber (Ger.) Synthesis of ammonia	no award	no award	no award
1919	Johannes Stark (Ger.) Doppler effect in positive ions and spectral line division	no award	Carl Spitteler (Switz.) Poet and novelist	Jules Bordet (Belg.) Discoveries in regard to immunity	Woodrow Wilson (US)
1920	Charles Guillaume (Switz.) Discovery of anomalies in alloys	Walther Nernst (Ger.) Work in thermochemistry	Knut Hamsun (Nor.) Novelist	August Krogh (Den.) Discovery of capillary motor regulating mechanism	Léon Bourgeois (Fr.)

NOBEL PRIZE WINNERS

	Physics	Chemistry	Literature	Medicine	Peace
1921	Albert Einstein (Switz.) Services to theoretical physics	Frederick Soddy (Brit.) Chemistry of radioactive substances and occurrence and nature of isotopes	Anatole France (Fr.) Novelist	no award	Karl Branting (Swed.) Christian Louis Lange (Nor.)
1922	Niels Bohr (Den.) Investigation of atomic structure and radiation	Francis Aston (Brit.) Work with mass spectrograph	Jacinto Benavente y Martinez (Spa.) Dramatist	Archibald Hill (Brit.) Discovery relating to heat production in muscles	Fridtjof Nansen (Nor.)
1923	Robert Millikan (US) Work on elementary electric charge	Fritz Pregl (Austria) Method of microanalysis of organic substances	W B Yeats (Ire.) Poet	Sir F G Banting (Can.) J J R Macleod (Brit.) Discovery of insulin	no award
1924	Karl Siegbahn (Swed.) Work in X-ray spectroscopy	no award	Wladyslaw Reymont (Pol.) Novelist	Willem Einthoven (Neth.) Discovery of electro-cardiogram mechanism	no award
1925	James Franck (Ger.) Gustav Hertz (Ger.) Discovery of laws governing impact of electrons upon an atom	Richard Zsigmondy (Austria) Elucidation of hetero-geneous nature of colloidal solutions	George Bernard Shaw (Ire.) Dramatist	no award	Austen Chamberlain (Brit.) Charles G Dawes (US)
1926	Jean-Baptiste Perrin (Fr.) Work on discontinuous structure of matter	Theodor Svedberg (Swed.) Work on disperse systems	Grazia Deledda (Ita.) Novelist	Johannes Fibiger (Den.) Contributions to cancer research	Aristide Briand (Fr.) Gustav Stresemann (Ger.)
1927	Arthur Holly Compton (US) Discovery of wave change in diffused X-rays. Charles Wilson (Brit.) Visibility of electric particles	Heinrich Wieland (Ger.) Researches into the constitution of bile acids	Henri Bergson (Fr.) Philosopher	J Wagner-Jauregg (Austria) Work on malaria inoculation in dementia paralytica	Ferdinand Buisson (Fr.) Ludwig Quidde (Ger.)
1928	Owen Richardson (Brit.) Richardson's Law	Adolf Windaus (Ger.) Sterols + vitamin connection	Sigrid Undset (Nor.) Novelist	Charles Nicolle (Fr.) Work on typhus	no award
1929	Louis de Broglie (Fr.) Discovery of the wave nature of electrons	Sir Arthur Harden (Brit.) H von Euler-Chelpin (Swed.) Fermentation of sugars and connective enzymes	Thomas Mann (Ger.) Novelist	Christiaan Eijkman (Neth.) Antineuritic vitamin Sir F Hopkins (Brit.) Growth stimulating vitamins	Frank B Kellogg (US)
1930	Sir C Raman (India) Work on light diffusion	Hans Fischer (Ger.) Chlorophyll research	Sinclair Lewis (US) Novelist	Karl Landsteiner (US) Human blood grouping	Nathan Söderblom (Swed.)

	Physics	Chemistry	Literature	Medicine	Peace
1931	no award	Karl Bosch (Ger.) Friedrich Bergius (Ger.) High pressure methods	Erik Axel Karlfeldt (Swed.) Poet	Otto Warburg (Ger.) Discovery of nature and action of respiratory enzyme	Jane Addams (US) Nicholas Murray Butler (US)
1932	Werner Heisenberg (Ger.) Indeterminacy principle of quantum mechanics	Irving Langmuir (US) Discoveries in surface chemistry	John Galsworthy (Brit.) Novelist	Edgar D Adrian (Brit.) Sir C Sherrington (Brit.) Neuron investigations	no award
1933	P A M Dirac (Brit.) Erwin Schrödinger (Austria) Intro of wave equations in quantum mechanics	no award	Ivan Bunin (USSR) Novelist	Thomas Hunt Morgan (US) Heredity transmission functions of chromosomes	Sir Norman Angell (Brit.)
1934	no award	Harold Urey (US) Discovery of heavy hydrogen	Luigi Pirandello (Ita.) Dramatist	George R Minot (US) William P Murphy (US) George H Whipple (US) Anaemia treatments	Arthur Henderson (Brit.)
1935	Sir James Chadwick (Brit.) Discovery of the neutron	Frédéric Joliot-Curie (Fr.) Irène Joliot-Curie (Fr.) Radioactive element theory	no award	Hans Spemann (Ger.) Organizer effect in embryo	Carl von Ossietzky (Ger.)
1936	Victor Hess (Austria) Cosmic radiation discovery Carl Anderson (US) Positron discovery	Peter Debye (Neth.) Work on dipole moments and diffraction of X-rays and electrons in gases	Eugene O'Neill (US) Dramatist	Sir H H Dale (Brit.) Otto Loewi (Ger.) Work on chemical transmission of nerve impulses	Carlos S Lamas (Arg.)
1937	Clinton Davisson (US) George P Thomson (Brit.) Interference phenomenon in crystals irradiated by electrons	Walter Haworth (Brit.) Research on carbohydrates and vitamin C Paul Karrer (Switz.) Research on Carotenoids	Roger Martin du Gard (Fr.) Novelist	Albert Szent-Györgyi (Hung.) Work on biological combustion	Viscount Cecil of Chelwood (Brit.)
1938	Enrico Fermi (Ita.) Artificial radioactive element by neutron irradiation	Richard Kuhn (Ger.) Research on carotenoids (declined)	Pearl Buck (US) Novelist	Corneille Heymans (Belg.) Discovery of sinus role in respiration regulation	Nansen International Office for Refugees (founded 1931)
1939	Ernest Lawrence (US) Invented cyclotron	Adolf Butenandt (Ger.) Work on sexual hormones (declined) Leopold Ružička (Switz.) Polymethylenes research	Frans Eemil Sillanpää (Fin.) Novelist	Gerhard Domagk (Ger.) Antibacterial effect of Prontosil (declined)	no award

	Physics	Chemistry	Literature	Medicine	Peace
1940	no award	no award	no award	no award	no award
1941	no award	no award	no award	no award	no award
1942	no award	no award	no award	no award	no award
1943	Otto Stern (US) Discovery of the magnetic moment of the proton	George de Hevesy (Hung.) Use of isotopes as tracers in chemical research	no award	Henrik Dam (Den.) Discovery of vitamin K Edward A Doisy (US) Chemical nature of vitamin K	no award
1944	Isidor Rabi (US) Resonance method for registration of magnetic properties of atomic nuclei	Otto Hahn (Ger.) Discovery of the fission of heavy nuclei	J V Jensen (Den.) Novelist	Joseph Erlanger (US) Herbert S Gasser (US) Research on differentiated functions of nerve fibres	International Red Cross Committee (founded 1863)
1945	Wolfgang Pauli (Austria) Discovery of the exclusion principle	Artturi Virtanen (Fin.) Invention of fodder preservation method	Gabriela Mistral (Chile) Poet	Sir Alexander Fleming (Brit.) Ernst B Chain (Brit.) Lord Florey (Aus.) Penicillin discovery	Cordell Hull (US)
1946	Percy Bridgman (US) Discoveries in the domain of high-pressure physics	James Sumner (US) Wendell Stanley (US) John Northrop (US) Enzyme research	Herman Hesse (Switz.) Novelist	Hermann J Muller (US) Production of mutations by X-ray irradiation	Emily Greene Balch (US) John R Mott (US)
1947	Edward Appleton (Brit.) Discovery of Appleton layer in upper atmosphere	Robert Robinson (Brit.) Investigations on alkaloids and other plant products	André Gide (Fr.) Novelist and essayist	Carl F Cori (US) Gerty T Cori (US) Bernardo Houssay (Arg.) Glycogen conversion	American Friends Service Committee (US) Friends Service Council (London)
1948	Patrick Blackett (Brit.) Discoveries in the domain of nuclear physics analysis; serum proteins	Arne Tiselius (Swed.) Researches on electro-phoresis and adsorption	T S Eliot (Brit.) Poet and critic	Paul Müller (Switz.) Properties of DDT	no award
1949	Yukawa Hideki (Jap.) Prediction of the existence of mesons	William Giauque (US) Behaviour of substances at extremely low temps	William Faulkner (US) Novelist	Walter Rudolf Hess (Switz.) Middle brain function Antonio Egas Moniz (Port.) Leucotomy research	Lord Boyd-Orr (Brit.)
1950	Cecil Powell (Brit.) Photographic method of studying nuclear processes; discoveries about mesons	Otto Diels (Ger.) Kurt Alder (Ger.) Discovery and development of diene synthesis	Bertrand Russell (Brit.) Philosopher	Philip S Hench (US) Edward C Kendall (US) Tadeus Reichstein (Switz.) Cortex hormones research	Ralph Bunche (US)

	Physics	Chemistry	Literature	Medicine	Peace
1951	John Cockcroft (Brit.) Ernest Walton (Ire.) Atomic nuclei research	Edwin McMillan (US) Glenn Seaborg (US) Transuranium element work	Pär Lagerkvist (Swed.) Novelist	Max Theiler (SA) Yellow fever research	Léon Jouhaux (Fr.)
1952	Felix Bloch (US) Edward Purcell (US) Discovery of nuclear magnetic resonance in solids	Archer Martin (Brit.) Richard Synge (Brit.) Development of partition chromatography	François Mauriac (Fr.) Poet, novelist, dramatist	Selman A Waksman (US) Discovery of streptomycin	Albert Schweitzer (Alsace)
1953	Frits Zernike (Neth.) Method of phase contrast microscopy	Hermann Staudinger (Ger.) Work on macromolecules	Winston Churchill (Brit.) Historian and orator	Fritz A Lipman (US) H A Krebs (Brit.) Discovery of coenzyme A	George C Marshall (US)
1954	Max Born (Brit.) Wave functions studies Walther Bothe (Ger.) Coincidence method	Linus Pauling (US) Study of the nature of the chemical bond	Ernest Hemingway (US) Novelist	John F Enders (US) Thomas H Weller (US) Frederick Robbins (US) Polio virus in tissue culture	Office of the UN High Commisioner for Refugees (founded 1951)
1955	Willis Lamb Jnr (US) Hydrogen spectrum study Polykarp Kusch (US) Magnetic electron study	Vincent du Vigneaud (US) First synthesis of a polypeptide hormone	Halidor Laxness (Ice.) Novelist	Axel Hugo Theorell (Swed.) Nature and mode of action of oxidation enzymes	no award
1956	William Shockley (US) John Bardeen (US) Walter Brattain (US) Discovery of transistor effect	Nikolay Semyonov (USSR) Cyril Hinshelwood (Brit.) Work on the kinetics of chemical reactions	Juan Ramon Jimenez (Spa.) Poet	Werner Forssman (Ger.) Dickinson Richards (US) André F Cournand (US) Heart catheterisation	no award
1957	Tsung-Dao Lee (China) Chen Ning Yang (China) Principle of parity research	Alexander Todd (Brit.) Work on nucleotides and nucleotide coenzymes	Albert Camus (Fr.) Novelist and dramatist	Daniel Bovet (Ita.) Production of curare	Lester B Pearson (Can.)
1958	Pavel A Cherenkov (USSR) Ilya M Frank (USSR) Igor Y Tamm (USSR) Discovery and interpretation of Cherenkov effect	Frederick Sanger (Brit.) Determination of structure of the insulin molecule	Boris Pasternak (USSR) Novelist and poet (declined)	George W Beadle (US) Edward L Tatum (US) Joshua Lederberg (US) Research in genetics	Dominique G Pire (Belg.)
1959	Emilio Segrè (US) Owen Chamberlain (US) Antiproton research	Jaroslav Heyrovsky (Czech) Discovery + development of polarography	Salvatore Quasimodo (Ita.) Poet	Severo Ochoa (US) Arthur Kornberg (US) Nucleic acids research	Philip Noel-Baker (Brit.)

	Physics	Chemistry	Literature	Medicine	Peace
1960	Donald Glaser (US) Development of the bubble chamber	Willard Libby (US) Development of radio-carbon dating	Saint-John Perse (Fr.) Poet	Macfarlane Burnet (Aus.) Peter B Medawar (Brit.) Tissue transplant research	Albert Lutuli (SA)
1961	Robert Hofstadter (US) Atomic nucleon research Rudolf Mössbauer (Ger.) Mössbauer effect	Melvin Calvin (US) Study of chemical steps that take place during photosynthesis	Ivo Andrić (Yug) Novelist	Georg von Békésy (US) Functions of the inner ear	Dag Hammarskjöld (Swed.)
1962	Lev D Landau (USSR) Research into condensed state of matter	John C Kendrew (Brit.) Max F Perutz (Brit.) Hemoprotein research	John Steinbeck (US) Novelist	Francis H C Crick (Brit.) James D Watson (US) Maurice Wilkins (Brit.) DNA molecular structure	Linus Pauling (US)
1963	J H D Jensen (Ger.) Maria Goeppert Mayer (US) Eugene Paul Wigner (US) Atomic nuclei research	Giulio Natta (Ita.) Karl Ziegler (Ger.) Research into polymers in the field of plastics	George Seferis (Gre.) Poet	Sir John Eccles (Aus.) Alan Lloyd Hodgkin (Brit.) Andrew Huxley (Brit.) Nerve fibre research	International Red Cross and League of Red Cross (HQ of both in Geneva)
1964	Charles H Townes (US) Nikolay G Basov (USSR) Aleksandr Prokhorov (USSR) Maser/laser research	Dorothy Hodgkin (Brit.) Determining the structure of biochemical compounds used to control pernicious anaemia	Jean-Paul Sartre (Fr.) Philosopher and dramatist (declined)	Konrad Bloch (US) Feodor Lynen (Ger.) Cholesterol research	Martin Luther King Jr (US)
1965	Julian Schwinger (US) Richard Feynman (US) Tomonaga Shin'ichiro (Jap.) Quantum electrodynamics	Robert B Woodward (US) Synthesis of chlorophyll	Mikhail Sholokhov (USSR) Novelist	François Jacob (Fr.) Jacques Monod (Fr.) André Lwoff (Fr.) Body cells research	UN Children's Fund (founded 1946)
1966	Alfred Kastler (Fr.) Optical methods for studying Hertzian resonances in atoms	Robert S Mulliken (US) Research into electronic structure of molecules	Shmuel Yosef Agnon (Isr.) Nelly Sachs (Swed.) Novelist and poet	Charles B Huggins (US) Francis Peyton Rous (US) Cancer research	no award
1967	Hans A Bethe (US) Discoveries concerning the energy production of stars	Manfred Eigen (Ger.) Ronald G W Norrish (Brit.) George Porter (Brit.) Chemical reaction research	Miguel Angel Asturias (Guat.) Novelist	Haldan Keffer Hartline (US) George Wald (US) Ragnar A Granit (Swed.) Eye research	no award
1968	Luis W Alvarez (US) Discovered resonance states	Lars Onsager (US) Work on theory of thermo-dynamics of irreversible processes	Kawabata Yasunari (Jap.) Novelist	Robert W Holley (US) H Gobind Khorana (US) Marshall Nirenberg (US) Genetic code deciphering	René Cassin (Fr.)

	Physics	Chemistry	Literature	Medicine	Peace	Economics
1969	Murray Gell-Mann (US) Discoveries concerning the classification of elementary particles	Derek H R Barton (Brit.) Odd Hassel (Nor.) Organic compound research	Samuel Beckett (Ire.) Novelist and dramatist	Max Delbrück (US) Alfred D Hershey (US) Salvador E Luria (US) Research of viruses	International Labour Organization (founded 1919)	Ragnar Frisch (Nor.) Jan Tinbergen (Neth.) Work in econometrics
1970	Hannes Alfvén (Swed.) Louis Néel (Fr.) Work in magnetohydro-dynamics and magnetism	Luis Leloir (Arg.) Discovery of sugar nucleo-tides and their role in the biosynthesis of carbohydrates	A Solzhenitsyn (USSR) Novelist	Julius Axelrod (US) Bernard Katz (Brit.) Ulf von Euler (Swed.) Nerve transmission research	Norman Borlaug (US)	Paul Samuelson (US) Work in scientific analysis of economic theory
1971	Dennis Gabor (Brit.) Holography invention	Gerhard Herzberg (Can.) Molecule structure research	Pablo Neruda (Chile) Poet	Earl W Sutherland Jr (US) Action of hormones	Willy Brandt (Ger.)	Simon Kuznets (US) Economic growth of nations
1972	John Bardeen (US) Leon N Cooper (US) John R Schrieffer (US) Superconductivity theory	Christian B Anfinsen (US) Stanford Moore (US) William H Stein (US) Enzyme chemistry research	Heinrich Böll (Ger.) Novelist	Gerald M Edelman (US) Rodney Porter (Brit.) Research on the chemical structure of antibodies	no award	John Hicks (Brit.) Kenneth J. Arrow (US) Welfare theory and economic equilibrium theory
1973	Leo Esaki (Jap.) Ivar Giaever (US) Brian Josephson (Brit.) Superconductivity research	Ernst Fischer (Ger.) Geoffrey Wilkinson (Brit.) Organometallic chemistry	Patrick White (Aus.) Novelist	Karl von Frisch (Austria) Konrad Lorenz (Austria) Nikolaas Tinbergen (Neth.) Animal behaviour patterns	Henry Kissinger (US) Le Duc Tho (N. Viet.) (declined)	Wassily Leontief (US) Input analysis
1974	Sir Martin Ryle (Brit.) Antony Hewish (Brit.) Work in radio astronomy	Paul J Flory (US) Studies of long-chain molecules	Eyvind Johnson (Swed.) Harry Martinson (Swed.) Novelist and poet	Albert Claude (US) Christian R de Duve (Belg.) George E Palade (US) Cell structure research	Sato Eisaku (Jap.) Sean MacBride (Ire.)	Gunnar Myrdal (Swed.) Friedrich von Hayek (Brit.) Economic, social and institutional phenomena
1975	Aage Bohr (Den.) Ben R Mottelson (Den.) L James Rainwater (US) Atomic nucleus research paved way for nuclear fusion	J W Cornforth (Brit.) Vladimir Prelog (Switz.) Work in stereochemistry	Eugenio Montale (Ita.) Poet	Renato Dulbecco (US) Howard M Temin (US) David Baltimore (US) Tumour viruses research	Andrey D Sakharov (USSR)	Leonid Kantorovich (USSR) Tjalling Koopmans (US) Contribution to the theory of optimum allocation of resources
1976	Burton Richter (US) Samuel C C Ting (US) Elementary particles research	William Lipscomb (US) Structure of boranes	Saul Bellow (US) Novelist	Baruch Blumberg (US) D Carleton Gajdusek (US) Infectious diseases research	Mairead Corrigan (N. Ire.) Betty Williams (N. Ire.)	Milton Friedman (US) Consumption analysis and monetary theory

	Physics	Chemistry	Literature	Medicine	Peace	Economics
1977	Philip W Anderson (US) Sir Nevill Mott (Brit.) John H Van Vleck (US) Studies into behaviour of electrons in magnetic non-crystalline solids	Ilya Prigogine (Belg.) Widening the scope of thermodynamics	Vicente Aleixandre (Spa.) Poet	Rosalyn S Yalow (US) Roger Guillemin (US) Andrew Schally (US) Development of radio-immunoassay, research on pituitary hormones	Amnesty International (founded 1961)	Bertil Ohlin (Swed.) James Meade (Brit.) Contributions to theory of International trade
1978	Pyotr L Kapitsa (USSR) Invention of helium liquefier Robert W Wilson (US) Arno A Penzias (US) Discovery of cosmic microwave background radiation	Peter D Mitchell (Brit.) Formulation of a theory of energy transfer processes in biological systems	Isaac Bashevis Singer (US) Novelist	Werner Arber (Switz.) Daniel Nathans (US) Hamilton O Smith (US) Discovery of enzymes that fragment DNAs	Menachem Begin (Isr.) Anwar Sadat (Egy.)	Herbert A Simon (US) Decision-making processes in economic organisations
1979	Sheldon Glashow (US) Abdus Salam (Pak.) Steven Weinberg (US) Establishment of analogy between electromagnetism and subatomic particles	Herbert C Brown (US) Georg Wittig (Ger.) Introduction of compounds of boron and phosphorus in the synthesis of organic substances	Odysseus Elytis (Greece) Poet	Allan M Cormack (US) Godfrey N Hounsfield (Brit.) Development of computed axial tomography scan	Mother Teresa of Calcutta (India)	W Arthur Lewis (Brit.) Theodore W. Schultz (US) Analyses of economic processes in developing nations
1980	James W Cronin (US) Val L Fitch (US) Demonstration of simultaneous violation of both charge-conjugation + parity inversion symmetries	Paul Berg (US) 1st preparation of hybrid DNA Walter Gilbert (US) Frederick Sanger (Brit.) Development of chemical analysis of DNA structure	Czeslaw Milosz (US) Poet	Baruj Benacerraf (US) George D Snell (US) Jean Dausset (Fr.) Investigations of genetic control of the response of immunological system to foreign substances	Adolfo Pérez Esquivel (Arg.)	Lawrence R Klein (US) Development and analysis of empirical models of business fluctuations
1981	Kai M Siegbahn (Swed.) Nicolaas Bloembergen (US) Electron spectroscopy for chemical analysis Arthur L Schawlow (US) Applications of lasers in spectroscopy	Fukui Kenichi (Jap.) Roald Hoffmann (US) Orbital symmetry interpretation of chemical reactions	Elias Canetti (Bulg.) Novelist and essayist	Roger W Sperry (US) Functions of the cerebral hemispheres Torsten N Wiesel (Swed.) David H Hubel (US) Processing of visual information by the brain	Office of the United Nations High Commissioner for Refugees (founded 1951)	James Tobin (US) Empirical macro-economic theories
1982	Kenneth G Wilson (US) Analysis of continuous phase transitions	Aaron Klug (Brit.) Determination of structure of biological substances	Gabriel G Márquez (Col.) Novelist, journalist and social critic	Sune K Bergström (Swe.) Bengt I Samuelsson (Swe.) John R Vane (Brit.) Prostaglandins research	Alva Myrdal (Swed.) Alfonso G. Robles (Mex.)	George Stigler (US) Economic effects of governmental regulation

Year	Physics	Chemistry	Literature	Peace	Medicine	Economics
1983	S Chandrasekhar (US), William A Fowler (US) Research into stars	Henry Taube (Can.) Study of electron transfer reactions	William Golding (Brit.) Novelist	Lech Walesa (Pol.)	Barbara McLintock (US) Discovery of mobile plant genes affecting heredity	Gerard Debreu (US) Mathematical proof of supply and demand theory
1984	Carlo Rubbia (Ita.), Simon van der Meer (Neth.) Discovery of subatomic particles W and Z which supports electro weak theory	Bruce Merrifield (US) Development of a method of polypeptide synthesis	Jaroslav Seifert (Czech.) Poet	Desmond Tutu (SA)	Niels K Jerne (Den.), Georges J F Kohler (Ger.), Cesar Milstein (Arg.) Study of monoclonal antibodies	Richard Stone (Brit.) Development of national income accounting system
1985	Klaus von Klitzing (Ger.) Discovery of quantised Hall effect concerning exact measurement of electrical resistance	Herbert A Hauptman (US), Jerome Karle (US) Mapping chemical structure of small molecules	Claude Simon (Fr.) Novelist	International Physicians for the Prevention of Nuclear War (founded 1980)	Michael S Brown (US), Joseph L Goldstein (US) Cholesterol metabolism cell receptors	Franco Modigliani (US) Financial market theory and household savings
1986	Ernst Ruska (Ger.), Gerd Binnig (Ger.), Heinrich Rohrer (Switz.) Electron microscopes	Dudley Herschbach (US), Yuan T Lee (US), John C Polyani (Can.) Analytical methodology	Wole Soyinka (Nigeria) Playwright and poet	Elie Wiesel (Fr.)	Stanley Cohen (US), Rita Levi-Montalcini (Ita.) Discovery of regulatory agents concerning cell growths	James M Buchanan (US) Political theories advocating limited government role in the economy
1987	J Georg Bednorz (Ger.), K Alex Müller (Switz.) Discovery of new superconducting materials	Charles J Pedersen (US), Donald J Cram (US), Jean-Marie Lehn (Fr.) molecule development	Joseph Brodsky (US) Poet and essayist	Oscar Arias Sanchez (Costa Rica)	Tonegawa Susumu (Jap.) Study of genetic aspects of antibodies	Robert M Solow (US) Economic growth theory
1988	Leon Lederman (US), Melvin Schwartz (US), Jack Steinberger (US) Subatomic particle research	Johann Deisenhofer (Ger.), Robert Huber (Ger.), Hartmut Michel (Ger.) Photosynthesis research	Naguib Mahfouz (Egypt) Novelist	UN Peacekeeping Forces	James W Black (Brit.), Gertrude B Elion (US), George H Hitchings (US) Drug research	Maurice Allais (Fr.) Market theory
1989	Hans Dehmelt (US), Wolfgang Paul (Ger.), Norman Ramsey (US)	Sydney Altman (US), Thomas Cech (US) RNA research	Camilo Jose Cela (Spa.) Poet and novelist	Tenzin Gyatso (Tib.) Dalai Lama XIV	J Michael Bishop (US), Harold E Varmus (US)	Trygve Haavelmo (Nor.) Quantitative economics
1990	Jerome Friedman (US), Henry Kendall (US), Richard Taylor (Can.) Quark model theory	Elias James Corey (US) Retrosynthetic analysis	Octavio Paz (Mex.) Poet	Mikhail Gorbachev (Rus.)	Joseph E Murray (US), E Donnall Thomas (US)	Harry M Markowitz (US), Merton Miller (US), William Sharpe (US) Financial economic theory

	Physics	Chemistry	Literature	Medicine	Peace	Economics
1991	Pierre-Gilles de Gennes (Fr.) Superconductivity theory	Richard R Ernst (Switz.) Spectroscopy development	Nadine Gordimer (SA)	Erwin Neher (Ger.) Bert Sakmann (Ger.) Patch-clamp technique	Aung San Suu Kyi (Burma)	Ronald Coase (Brit.) Transaction cost theory
1992	George Charpak (Fr.) Elementary particle study	Rudolph A Marcus (US) Electron transfer	Derek Walcott (St Lucia) Poet	Edmond H Fischer (US) Edwin G Krebs (US) Protein regulation	Rigoberta Menchú (Guat.)	Gary S Becker (US) Microeconomic analysis
1993	Russell Hulse (US) Joseph Hooton Taylor (US) Discovery of new type of pulsar	Kary Banks Mullis (US) Polymerase chain reaction Michael Smith (Can.) Mutagenesis theory	Toni Morrison (US) Novelist	Richard Roberts (Brit.) Phillip Allen Sharp (US) Mosaic genes discovery	Nelson Mandela (SA) F W de Klerk (SA)	Robert Fugel (US) Douglas North (US) Quantitative methods as reasons for economic change
1994	Clifford Shull (US) Bertram Brockhouse (Can.) Study of neutron beams	George Olah (US) Carbocations	Kenzaburo Oe (Jap.) Novelist	Martin Rodbell (US) Alfred G Gilman (US) Discovery of G protein	Yasser Arafat (Pal.) Shimon Peres (Isr.) Yitzhak Rabin (Isr.)	John Nash (US) John Harsanyi (US) Reinhard Selten (Ger.) Games theory
1995	Martin L Pearl (US) Tau lepton discovery Frederick Reines (US) Neutrino detection	F Sherwood Rowland (US) Mario Molina (Mex.) Paul Crutzen (Ned.) Ozone layer research	Seamus Heaney (Ire.) Poet	Edward B Lewis (US) Eric F Wieschaus (US) C Nüsslein-Volhard (Ger.) Genes theory	Joseph Rotblat (Brit.) Pugwash Conferences on Science and World Affairs	Robert E Lucas (US) Macroeconomic analysis
1996	David M Lee (US) Douglas D Osheroff (US) Robert C Richardson (US) Discovery of superfluidity in helium-3	Harry Kroto (Brit.) Robert Curl (US) Richard Smalley (US) Discovery of C_{60} molecule	Wislawa Szymborska (Pol.) Poet	Peter C Doherty (Aus.) Rolf M Zinkernagel (Switz.)	Jose Ramos-Horta (E. Timor) Bishop Carlos Belo of Dili	James Mirrlees (Brit.) William Vickrey (Can.)
1997	Steven Chu (US) Claude Cohen-Tannoudji (Fr.) William D Phillips (US) Atom research	John Walker (Brit.) Paul Boyer (US) Jens Skou (Den.) Molecular biology research	Dario Fo (Ita.) Playwright	Stanley B Prusiner (US) Discovery of prions	Ms Jodie Williams (US) and International Campaign to Ban Landmines	Robert Merton (US) Myron Scholes (US) Fischer Black (US) Contribution to economic theory
1998	Robert B Laughlin (US) Horst L Stormer (Ger.) Daniel C Tsui (US) Quantum fluids	John Pople (Brit.) Walter Kohn (US) Quantum theory application to molecules	José Saramago (Port.) Novelist	Robert S Furghgott (US) Louis J Ignarro (US) Ferid Murad (US) Cardiovascular research	John Hume (N. Ire.) David Trimble (N. Ire.) For 'Good Friday' Agreement	Amartya Sen (India) Welfare economics
1999	Gerardus T Hooft (Neth.) Martinus J G Veltman (Neth.) Study of electro-weak interactions	Ahmed Zewai (Egypt) Femtosecond spectroscopy	Günter Grass (Ger.) Novelist	Günter Blobel (Ger.) Study of proteins	Médecins Sans Frontières (Belg.)	Robert A Mundell (Can.) Fiscal policy analysis

	Physics	Chemistry	Literature	Medicine	Peace	Economics
2000	Herbert Kroemer (Ger.), Zhores Alferov (Ger.) Developing semiconductor heterostructures; Jack S Kilby (US) Invention of the integrated circuit	Alan J Heeger (US), Alan G MacDiarmid (US), Hideki Shirakawa (Japan) Discovery of conductive polymers	Gao Xingjian (China)	Arvid Carlsson (Sweden), Paul Greengard (US), Eric Kandel (US) Research into signal transduction in the nervous system	Kim Dae Jung (S. Korea) Work in reconciliation with North Korea	James J Heckman (Ger.), Daniel L McFadden (US) Contribution to economic theory and analysis
2001	Eric A Cornell (US), Wolfgang Ketterle (Ger.), Carl E Wieman (US) Bose-Einstein condensation in dilute gases of alkali atoms and studies of the properties of the condensates	William S Knowles (US), Ryoji Noyori (Jap.) Work on chirally catalysed hydrogenation reactions; K Barry Sharpless (US) Work on chirally catalysed oxidation reactions	V S Naipaul (Trin.)	Leland H Hartwell (US), R Timothy Hunt (Brit.), Sir Paul M Nurse (Brit.) Discoveries of key regulators of the cell cycle	United Nations; Kofi Annan (Gha.) for their work for a better-organised and more peaceful world	George A Akerlof (US), A Michael Spence (US), Joseph E Stiglitz (US) Analyses of markets with asymmetric information
2002	Raymond Davis Jr (US), Masatoshi Koshiba (Jap.) Detection of cosmic neutrinos; Riccardo Giacconi (US) Discovery of cosmic X-ray sources	John B Fenn (US), Koichi Tanaka (Jap.) Soft desorption ionisation methods; Kurt Wüthrich (Switz.) Nuclear magnetic resonance spectroscopy	Imre Kertész (Hung.)	Sydney Brenner (Brit.), H Robert Horvitz (US), John E Sulston (Brit.) Study of genetic regulation of organ development and programmed cell death	Jimmy Carter (US) for his efforts to find peaceful solutions to international conflicts	Daniel Kahneman (Isr.) Application of psychological research into economic science; Vernon L Smith (US) Experiments in the study of alternative market mechanisms
2003	Alexei A Abrikosov (Rus.), Vitaly L Ginzburg (Rus.), Anthony J Leggett (Brit.) Pioneering contributions to the theory of superconductors and superfluids	Peter Agre (US), Roderick MacKinnon (US) Discoveries concerning channels in cell membranes	John M Coetzee (SA)	Paul C Lauterbur (US), Sir Peter Mansfield (Brit.) Discoveries concerning magnetic resonance imaging	Shirin Ebadi (Iran) For her efforts for democracy and human rights, particularly those of women and children	Robert F Engle III (US), Clive W J Granger (Brit.) Engle: methods of analysing economic time series with time-varying volatility; Granger: methods of analysing economic time series with common trends

	Physics	Chemistry	Literature	Medicine	Peace	Economics
2004	David J Gross (US) H David Politzer (US) Frank Wilczek (US) Discovery of asymptotic freedom in the theory of the strong interaction	Aaron Ciechanover (Isr.) Avram Hershko (Isr.) Irwin Rose (US) Discovery of ubiquitin-mediated protein degradation	Elfriede Jelinek (Austria)	Richard Axel (US) Linda B Buck (US) Discoveries of odorant receptors and the organisation of the olfactory system	Wangari Maathai (Ken.) For her contribution to sustainable development, democracy and peace	Finn E Kydland (Nor.) Edward C Prescott (US) Contributions to dynamic macroeconomics: the time consistency of economic policy and the driving forces behind business cycles

NB: Many of the award winners listed above have dual nationalities. The nationality given is therefore not necessarily the country of birth.

General Information
Royal Swedish Academy of Sciences awards the Physics, Chemistry and Economics Prizes.
Swedish Karolinska Institute awards the Medicine Prize.
Swedish Academy of Arts awards the Literature Prize.
The Peace Prize is awarded by a committee of 5 members of the Norwegian Storting.
Nils Dalen, the 1912 Nobel Prizewinner for Physics, was blinded in 1913 by an explosion whilst conducting an experiment.
William and Lawrence Bragg were the only father and son to win a prize when they were joint winners of the 1915 Physics Prize.
A woman has never won the Economics Prize.

ORGANISATIONS

Chief Executives or Chairmen (as at April 2005)

Abbey National Luqman Arnold (CE); Lord Burns (C)

Aberdeen Football Club Stuart Milne (C)

Adidas-Salomon Herbert Hainer (CE)

Alfred McAlpine Oliver Whitehead (C); Sir Ian Grice (CE)

Allders Brian Fidler (C)

Alliance & Leicester John R Windeler (C)

Allied Domecq Philip Bowman (CE); G J Robinson (C)

Ann Summers Jacqueline Gold (CE)

AOL Time Warner Dick Parsons (C); Dick Parsons (CE)

Arena Leisure Roger Withers (C); Ian Penrose (CE)

Arsenal Football Club P D Hill-Wood (C)

Arts Council Sir Christopher Frayling (C); Peter Hewitt (CE)

Aston Villa Football Club Herbert Douglas Ellis (C&CE)

Barclays Matthew W Barrett (C); John Varley (CE)

BAT (British American Tobacco) Jan du Plessis (C); Paul Adams (CE)

BBC Michael Grade (C)

Bhs Allan Leighton (C)

BMW Helmut Panke (CE)

BOC Tony Isaac (CE)

Body Shop Peter Saunders (CE); Adrian Bellamy (C)

Boeing Lew Platt (C)

Boosey & Hawkes John Minch (CE)

Boots Sir Nigel Rudd (C); Richard Baker (CE)

BP P D Sutherland (C); Lord Browne of Madingley (CE)

Bradford & Bingley Rod Kent (C); Steven Crawshaw (CE)

British Airways Willie Walsh (CE); Martin Broughton (C)

British Energy Adrian Montague (C)

British Midland Sir Michael Bishop (C)

British Telecom Sir Christopher Bland (C)

British Tourist Authority David Quarmby (C)

BSkyB James Murdoch (CE)

BUPA Bryan Nicholson (C)

Burger King Greg Brenneman (C&CE)

Cable & Wireless Richard Lapthorne (C); Francisco Caio (CE)

Cadbury Schweppes John Sunderland (C); Todd Stitzer (CE)

Camelot Sir Peter Middleton (C); Diane Thompson (CE)

Carpetright Lord Philip Charles Harris of Peckham (C)

Centrica Roy Gardner (CE); Roger Carr (C)

Channel 4 Kuke Johnson (C)

Chelsea Village Bruce Buck (C)

CNN Jim Walton (C)

Coca Cola Neville Isdell (C&CE)

Corus (formerly British Steel) Jim Leng (C)

Coutts and Company Lord Home (C); Gordon Pell (CE)

Covent Garden Market Authority Baroness Dean (C)

Daily Mail Viscount Rothermere IV (C); Charles Sinclair (CE)

Debenhams Rob Templeman (CE); John Lovering (C)

De La Rue Nicholas Brookes (C); Leo Quinn (CE)

Deutsche Bank Rolf Breuer (C)

De Vere Group Lord Daresbury (C); Carl Leaver (CE)

Diageo (Guinness & Grand Met) Lord Blyth (C); Paul Walsh (CE)

Dixons Sir John Collins (C); John Clare (CE)

Easyjet Sir Colin Chandler (C); Ray Webster (CE)

Economist Group, The Sir Robert Wilson (C); Helen Alexander (CE)

Egg Roberto Mendoza (C); Paul Gratton (CE)

EMAP Adam Broadbent (C); Tom Maloney (CE)

EMI Eric L Nicoli (C&CE)

Energis Archie Norman (C); John Pluthero (CE)

Eurotunnel PLC Jacques Gounon (C)

Financial Times Group David Bell (C); Olivier Fleurot (CE)

First Choice Holidays Michael Hodgkinson (C); Peter Long (CE)

Fitness First John Lovering (C); Mike Metcalf (CE)

France Telecom Didier Lombard (C&CE)

Fremantle Media Tony Cohen (CE)

Friends Provident D K Newbigging (C); K Satchell (CE)

Friends Reunited Stephen Pankhurst, Jason Porter, Julie Pankhurst (joint founders)

Geest Sir John Banham (C); Gareth Voyle (CE)

George Wimpey Peter Johnson (CE); John Robinson (C)

GKN Roy Brown (C); Kevin Smith (CE)

GlaxoSmithKline Sir Christopher Gent (C)

Greene King Timothy Bridge (C)

Guardian Media Group Paul Myers (C)

GUS Sir Victor Blank (C)

Halfords Rob Templeman (C); Ian McLeod (CE)

Hamleys Simon Burke (C)

Hanson PLC C D Collins (C); Alan Murray (CE)

Harrods Mohamed Al Fayed (C)

Hays R A Lawson (C); Colin Matthews (CE)

HBOS Lord Stevenson of Coddenham (C)

Hilton Group Sir Ian Robinson (C)

HMV Media Group Robin Miller (C); Alan Giles (CE)

House of Fraser John Coleman (CE)

HSBC John Bond (C)

Imperial Chemical Industries Peter Ellwood (C); John McAdam (CE)

Imperial Tobacco Derek Bonham (C); Gareth Davis (CE)

ITV Sir Peter Burt (C); Charles Allen (CE)

J D Wetherspoon Tim Martin (C)

Jessops Tim Brookes (CE)

J J B Sports David Whelan (C)

Johnson Matthey H Michael P Miles (C); Neil Carson (CE)

John Lewis Partnership Stuart Hampson (C&CE)

John Menzies William Thomson (C); Patrick Macdonald (CE)

J Sainsbury Sir Peter Davis (C)

Kellogg James M Jenness (C&CE)

Kenwood Appliances Colin Gordon (CE)

Kingfisher F H MacKay (C)

Lastminute.com Brian Collie (C)

Laura Ashley Khoo Kay Peng (C); Lilian Tan (CE)

Lego Mads Ovlisen (C); Jorgen Vig Knudstorp (CE)

Leicester City Football Club Jim McCahill (C)

Littlewoods James Ross (C)
Lloyds TSB Eric Daniels (CE)
London Stock Exchange Clara Furse (CE)
Manchester United PLC David Gill (CE)
Marks & Spencer Paul Myners (C); Stuart Rose (CE)
MFI John Hancock (CE)
Wm Morrison Ken Morrison (C)
Motorola Edward Zander (C&CE)
My Travel (formerly Airtours) Michael Beckett (C); Peter McHugh (CE)
National Westminster Bank Vicount Younger of Leckie (C)
Newcastle United PLC Freddy Shepherd (C)
News Corp K R Murdoch (C&CE)
Next Simon Wolfson (CE)
Nottingham Forest PLC Nigel Doughty (C)
Old Mutual PLC MJ Levett (C); Hasan Askari (CE)
Peacock Group Gavin Simonds (C)
Pearson PLC Marjorie Scardino (CE)
Pension Protection Fund Lawrence Churchill (C)
Pilkington Nigel Rudd (C); Stuart Chambers (CE)

Prudential Sir David Clementi (C); Mark Tucker (CE)
Rangers Football Club PLC John McClelland (C)
Rank Mike Smith (CE); Alun Cathcart (C)
Reuters Group Sir Christopher Hogg (C); T H Glocer (CE)
Rio Tinto R Leigh Clifford (CE); Paul Skinner (C)
Rolls-Royce PLC John Rose (CE); Simon Robertson (C)
Royal Bank of Scotland Fred Goodwin (CE); Sir George Mathewson (C)
Royal Doulton Hamish Grossart (C)
Royal Opera House Tony Hall (CE)
Ryanair Michael O'Leary (CE)
Safeway Steven A Burd (C&CE)
Sage Group Michael Jackson (C); Paul Walker (CE)
Sainsbury PLC Philip Hampton (C); Justin King (CE)
Scania Dr Bernd Pischetsrieder (C); Leif Östling (CE)
Scottish & Newcastle Brian Stewart (C); Tony Froggatt (CE)
Scottish Power Ian Russell (CE); Charles Miller Smith (C)

Signet Group James McAdam (C)
Somerfield John von Spreckelsen (C)
Sony Sir Howard Stringer (C&CE)
Sporting Index Richard Glynn (CE)
Tate and Lyle David Lees (C); Iain Ferguson (CE)
Taylor Woodrow Norman Askew (C); Iain Napier (CE)
Tesco Terry Leahy (CE); David Reid (C)
Tote Peter Jones (C)
Tottenham Hotspur PLC Daniel Levy (C)
Unilever Niall FitzGerald (C)
Virgin Group Sir Richard Branson (C)
Vodafone Lord MacLaurin of Knebworth (C); Arun Sarin (CE)
Wanadoo (formerly Freeserve) Olivier Sichel (C&CE)
Warner Chilcott John King (C); Roger Biossonneault (CE)
Wellcome Trust Sir Dominic Cadbury (C)
Wembley PLC Claes Hultman (C); Mark Elliott (CE)
Woolworths Trevor Bish-Jones (CE); Gerald Corbett (C)

Key: C = Chairman; CE = Chief Executive

Organisations, Movements and Bodies

ACP the 68 African, Caribbean and Pacific countries which have special trade relations with the European Union.

Action Directe leftwing French revolutionary group formed in 1979 and responsible for numerous bombings.

Agenda 21 blueprint for action adopted at the 1992 Earth Summit in Rio setting out requirements for sustainable development.

Aipac American Israel Public Affairs Committee, Israel's official lobbying arm in the USA and as such part of the influential US Jewish lobby. Based in Washington, DC.

Akali Dal supreme political organisation of the Indian Sikh community. Founded in December 1920 and based in the Punjab.

Alawi Islamic sub-sect signifying followers of the Caliph Ali, revered by Shias. Prominent in Syria, Lebanon and Turkey.

Alfaro Vive Carajo! translates as 'Alfaro Lives, Dammit!' Ecuadorean left-wing nationalist guerrilla group named in memory of the President 1895–1901, 1906–11.

Al-Fatah (Arabic: victory) Movement for the National Liberation of Palestine. Mainstream component of the PLO founded by Yasser Arafat in 1958.

Alpha 66 paramilitary group of anti-Castroites based in Miami. Formed in 1962 and named after its 66 founder members.

Al-Qaeda international terrorist group formed in the late 1980s by Osama bin Laden and Muhammad Atef and dedicated to opposing non-Islamic governments with force and violence.

Amazon Pact signed in July 1978 by Bolivia, Brazil, Colombia, Ecuador, Guyana, Peru, Surinam and Venezuela. Committed to preserving ecological balance of the Amazon region.

Amnesty International founded in 1961 by Peter Benenson and Sean Macbride Kropotkin, it - campaigns for the release of prisoners of conscience.

ANC African National Congress, South Africa's principal anti-apartheid organisation, banned 1960–90 but now the majority party in ruling coalition.

Angry Brigade small anarchistic group in the UK in existence in 1968–71, which carried out several bombings.

Anti-Nazi League leftwing organisation in the UK formed in the 1970s to combat racist parties and more recently the British National Party.

Anzus security pact between Australia, NZ and the USA signed in San Francisco on 1 September 1951. Initially formed as deterrent to Japan but no longer operational.

Apostles Cambridge University Conversation Society founded in 1820. Guy Burgess and Anthony Blunt were recruited from the Apostles by Soviet Intelligence.

Arab League organisation formed in 1945 originally for mutual economic aid but more recently dealing with the Middle East peace process.

ASEAN Association of South East Asian Nations. Founded in 1967, members include Indonesia, Malaysia, Singapore, Thailand, Philippines and Brunei.

Baader-Meinhof Gang extremist leftwing terrorist group active in Germany in the late 1960s; later became the Rote Armee Fraktion (RAF).

Ba'ath movement founded in Syria in the 1940s by Michel Aflaq with the aim of creating a single socialist Arab nation.

Band Aid charity formed by Bob Geldof and Midge Ure in December 1984 for the purpose of famine relief in Ethiopia.

BCCI Bank of Credit and Commerce International which collapsed in July 1991. Lord Justice Bingham criticised the Bank of England's supervisory role.

Benelux grouping of Belgium, Netherlands and Luxembourg for a mutually advantageous economic climate. Founded in 1932 by the Convention of Ouchy.

Black Berets élite paramilitary police force formed by the Soviet Interior Ministry in 1987. Aka Omon, they had a reputation for ruthlessness, especially in the Baltic States.

Black Sash South African liberal women's anti-apartheid organisation originally formed in 1955 as the Women's Defence of the Constitution League in response to the removal of the vote for coloureds. The black sash was worn as a peaceful protest against violation of rights.

Black September Palestinian terrorist group, named in memory of the Jordanian expulsion of Palestinians in Sepember 1970. Responsible for the Munich Olympic massacre of Israeli athletes.

B'Nai B'rith international Jewish organisation founded in 1843 and based in Washington, DC.

BND the German Federal Intelligence Service, founded in 1956 under the ex-Nazi Reinhard Gehlen and based in Munich.

Boss Bureau of State Security, a now defunct branch of the South African Intelligence Service. Founded in 1969 by PM J B Vorster.

Boundaries Commission UK body responsible for defining the boundaries of parliamentary constituencies.

Boys Brigade founded by William Smith in 1883.

Boys' Clubs although boys' clubs were in existence in major British cities in the 19th century, the National Association was founded in 1925.

BRA Bougainville Revolutionary Army, a guerrilla force fighting for independence for the mineral-rich island of Bougainville from the state of Papua New Guinea.

Brigate Rosse (Red Brigades) leftwing urban guerrillas responsible for a spate of kidnappings and bombings in the 1970s culminating in the murder of former PM Aldo Moro in 1978.

British Academy Established in 1901; its full title is 'British Academy for the Promotion of Historical, Philosophical and Philological Studies'.

British Council Established in 1934 and funded by the government for the purpose of representing British culture abroad. With offices in more than 80 countries, it arranges for visits by British artists, lecturers and performers, mounts exhibitions, teaches English and provides libraries of British books.

Brookings Institution Influential US think-tank based in Washington, DC, and comprised of distinguished figures from various fields.

Bruges Group Informal Conservative grouping of 'Eurosceptics', named from a speech made in the Belgian city of Bruges on 20 September 1988 by Margaret Thatcher.

Camorra Network of groups engaged in organised crime in the Naples region.

Caricom Caribbean Community and Common Market, an alliance of English-speaking Caribbean countries promoting economic, political and cultural unity.

Central African Federation Federation of the British colonies of Northern Rhodesia (Zambia), Southern Rhodesia (Zimbabwe) and Nyasaland (Malawi). Established in 1953 and dissolved in 1963.

Central Committee Leading organ in the Communist Party of the Soviet Union whose full members elected the powerful Politburo and secretariat.

CERM Centre d'Exploitation du Renseignement Militaire (Centre for Exploitation of Military intelligence). French internal security agency, formerly called Deuxième Bureau until 10 Dec. 1971.

CERN European Centre for Nuclear Research, a co-operative agency with 12 member countries founded in 1952 and located outside Geneva.

Charter 88 Pressure group in the UK that demands a new constitutional settlement guaranteeing political, civil and human rights.

Chetniks Serbian nationalist army of resistance led by Draza Mihailovic, which occupied parts of east and south Yugoslavia during the second world war. Term now applies to all Serb irregulars.

CHOGM Commonwealth Heads of Government Meeting, the main policy-making body of the Commonwealth. A CHOGM is convened every 2 years.

CIA Central Intelligence Agency, often referred to internally as 'The Company'. Its HQ is at Langley, Virginia.

Civic Forum Czech coalition of parties formed during the Velvet Revolution in November 1989 as the focus of democratic opposition to the communist regime.

Club of Rome non-governmental association of industrialists, policy analysts and scientists, seeking to bring their different perspectives to bear on problems of the global economy.

CND Campaign for Nuclear Disarmament, a British organisation which mobilised mass opposition to nuclear weapons in general and the UK's independent nuclear deterrent in particular. Founder members in 1958 include Bertrand Russell.

Comecon Informal name for the Council for Mutual Economic Assistance (CMEA), founded in 1949 as a response to the USA's Marshall Plan. Members included Warsaw Pact countries (excluding Albania) and Cuba, Mongolia and Vietnam.

Committee of 100 Militant offshoot of CND, formed in 1960 and headed by Bertrand Russell; its main weapon was 'sit down' protests.

Commonwealth of Nations Voluntary association of 53 independent states (Mozambique being latest member) which evolved from the British Empire, latterly concerned with postcolonial economic and cultural development. Originated with the 1931 Statute of Westminster. Elizabeth II is head of 16 Commonwealth states. Current (2005) Secretary-General is Don McKinnon, a former Foreign Minister of New Zealand.

Confederation of British Industry   CBI, formed in 1965 via merger of Federation of British Industries, British Employers' Confederation and National Association of British Manufacturers.

Congress   Bicameral legislature of the USA consisting of a 100-member senate elected for 6 years, with one third being renewed every 2 years, and a 435-member House of Representatives (lower chamber) elected for 2 years. Each state sends 2 senators to the upper house.

Contadora Group   Latin American peace initiative in Central America set up by Colombia, Mexico, Panama and Venezuela in January 1983; controversially recognises Nicaraguan Sandinistas.

Contras   Nicaraguan counter-revolutionary forces financed during the 1980s by the US Reagan administration, in part illegally, as revealed by the Iran–Contra affair. Many Contras offered allegiance to the dictator Anastasio Somoza, ousted in 1979.

Council of Europe   Intergovernmental organisation with its HQ in Strasbourg. Founded on 5 May 1949 to promote civil society and human rights.

CPLA   Cordillera People's Liberation Army, a guerrilla group operating in the Philippines until it signed a ceasefire with President Corazon Aquino on 13 Sept. 1986.

Creep   Committee to Re-elect the President. Established in advance of the November 1972 US Presidential elections, its aim was to re-elect Richard Nixon by orchestrating a dirty tricks campaign against his Democratic opponents, which ultimately led to the Watergate scandal.

Dáil Éireann   166-seat lower house of the legislature of Eire. Members are elected for 5-year term on the basis of proportional representation. Translates as 'Assembly of Ireland'.

Death Squads   Rightwing paramilitary groups often associated with conniving governments who assassinate those deemed a threat to the state. Term was coined in the 1960s in Brazil, when the police force used such squads, perhaps financed by the CIA.

Dergue   Military ruling body in Ethiopia between 1973 and 1991, most closely associated with the Marxist-Leninist regime of Lt-Col. Mengistu Haile Mariam.

Deuxième Bureau   French internal security agency run by the Ministry of the Interior and Administative Reform. Changed its name to CERM in 1971.

DGSE   Direction Générale de la Sécurité Extérieure (General Directorate for External Security), the French foreign secret service established on 4 April 1982.

Diet   Japanese bicameral legislature consisting of a House of Representatives (lower chamber) elected for a 4-year term and a House of Councillors (upper chamber), half of whose members are elected every years.

Dina   Chilean secret police serving the military junta during the 1970s.

DST   Direction de la Surveillance du Territoire. The French counterpart to the FBI or MI5.

Duma   The name of the parliament of Imperial Russia but now referring to the lower house of the new Russian parliament or Federal Assembly.

Earth Day   Annual worldwide effort on 22 April by pressure groups to focus public attention on environmental issues.

Earth Summit   World environmental conference also known as the UN Conference on Environment and Development (UNCED), held in Rio de Janeiro on 3–14 June 1992 and billed as the largest-ever gathering of world leaders.

EBRD   European Bank for Reconstruction and Development, founded in May 1990 by 39 countries (including USA and Soviet Union), plus the European Commission and the European Investment Bank. Conceived by French president François Mitterrand to aid the Eastern European transition to a market economy.

Economic and Social Council   ECOSOC, one of the 6 principal organs of the UN, established under Chapter X of the UN Charter, responsible for co-ordination of UN specialised agencies.

ECSC   European Coal and Steel Community, which brought Italy and Benelux countries into Franco-German co-operation framework of 1950 Schuman Plan, forerunner of EEC.

EEC   European Economic Community, founded under Treaty of Rome in March 1957 by France, Germany, Italy and Benelux countries; came into operation in January 1958.

EFTA   European Free Trade Association, set up in 1960 under the Stockholm Convention. Its 7 original members were UK, Denmark (left in 1973 to join the EC), Portugal (left 1986), Austria, Switzerland, Norway and Sweden.

EMS   European Monetary System, an arrangement for closer monetary co-operation within the EC, operational from March 1979.

EMU   European Monetary Union, dating back to the Werner report of 1971; works to promote the smooth operation of capital transfers within participating countries.

EOKA   National Organisation of Cypriot Fighters, Greek Cypriot movement which from 1955 until the independence of Cyprus in 1960 fought a guerrilla campaign against British rule.

ERM   Exchange Rate Mechanism, regarded as the core of the EMS but badly damaged when the UK and Italy pulled out as a result of Black Wednesday in September 1992.

ESA   European Space Agency, formed in 1973 as a result of the merger of the European Space Research Organisation and the European Launcher Development Organisation and committed to a European Space policy.

ETA   Basque Fatherland and Freedom, militant separatist organisation which fights for the independence of the Basque country from Spain.

EU   European Union, currently existing of 15 member states, the original 6 (Belgium, France, West Germany, Italy, Luxembourg, The Netherlands) plus Denmark, Eire, UK, Portugal, Spain, Greece, Austria, Sweden and Finland.

European Communities   more generally referred to as the EU since 1 November 1993, the date on which the Maastricht Treaty on the European Union came into force.

European Court of Justice   set up in Luxembourg under 1958 Treaty of Rome and responsible for ruling on whether EU member countries are acting in accord with Community Law.

European Parliament   one of 3 principal institutions of the EU, with the Council of Ministers and European Commission. Elections held every 5 years and parliament meets in Strasbourg.

Falange   Spain's rightwing nationalist party formed in 1937 by General Francisco Franco and formally abolished on 1 April 1977.

Falashas name assigned to Ethiopian Jews, which they themselves reject in favor of the name Beta Israel (House of Israel).

FAO Food and Agricultural Organisation, one of the largest of the UN specialised agencies founded in 1945, it aims to combat malnutrition and hunger.

Fascism a 20th-century ideology which has been interpreted as rightwing or centrist in orientation. Derived from the Latin fasces (bundle of rods sometimes including an axe used by Roman magistrates as a symbol of authority), term became prominent following Mussolini's 'March on Rome' in 1922.

FBI Federal Bureau of Investigation, part of the US Justice Department and deals with violations of federal law; has its HQ in Washington DC.

FCO Foreign and Commonwealth Office, UK government department responsible for external relations and representation. The FCO was created in 1968 through the merger of the original Foreign Office (formed in 1782) and the Commonwealth Office.

FLN Front de Libération Nationale (National Liberation Front), political organisation during Algeria's independence struggle (1954–62). Founded 1954 under leadership of Ahmed Ben Bella.

FLNC Front de Libération Nationale de la Corse (Corsican National Liberation Front). Formed in May 1976, it is a clandestine extremist group fighting for self-determination from France.

Force de Frappe independent French nuclear weapons strike force instigated by Charles de Gaulle in December 1960 as a protest at the special relationship between the UK and USA.

Four D's democratisation, disarmament, decartelisation and denazification, implemented against the defeated Germans by the Allies and agreed at Potsdam.

Friends of the Earth international environmental pressure group, originating in the USA as an offshoot of the Sierra Club. It supports research on environmental issues, lobbies policy makers, and has been most successful in increasing public awareness.

G7 Group of 7 most powerful industrialised countries: Canada, France, Germany, Italy, Japan, USA and the UK.

GCHQ Government Communications Headquarters, part of the UK intelligence machinery which provides government departments and military commands with signals intelligence. Established in 1946 as the successor to the Government Code and Cipher School.

Geneva Conventions body of international humanitarian laws adopted in Geneva on 12 August 1949 and endorsed by the UN, which are intended to protect and assist war victims.

Gleneagles Agreement the 1977 decision by Commonwealth heads of government to ban official sporting links with South Africa until the dismantling of apartheid. Named after the golf club in Scotland which was the venue for the meeting.

Gosplan Soviet Union's State Planning Committee established in 1921 to work out a single state economic plan and methods of implementing it.

Greenpeace environmental pressure group whose members, now organised internationally with a headquarters in Amsterdam, engage in non-violent action to disrupt environmentally damaging projects. Founded in 1971 when nuclear tests on Amchitka Island, Alaska were disrupted.

Grey Panthers US pressure group organised to promote the interests of the elderly and retired. Name derived humorously from the Black Panthers.

Guardian Angels US volunteer group founded in 1979 to fight crime in New York City. Wearing red berets, they have been accused of being vigilantes.

Gulag Soviet acronym, Chief Directorate of Labour Camps. Established in 1930, estimates put number of inmates in the 1940s at over 8 million, of whom 85% were political prisoners.

Haganah Jewish defence force which operated from 1920 until the creation of Israel in 1948 to defend Jewish settlements in Palestine.

Hallstein Doctrine West German policy in 1950s and 1960s of severing diplomatic relations with any state recognising East Germany and refusing relations with any communist country except the Soviet Union.

Hamas acronym for Islamic Resistance Movement, a radical islamic group operating in Israeli-occupied territories. Founded in February 1988 by Sheikh Ahmed Ismail Yassin.

harkis Algerian Muslim auxiliary soldiers in the service of the French army during the French occupation of Algeria 1938–62.

Hezbollah Party of God. The main fundamentalist, Shia movement in Lebanon, operating in the south against Israel.

Human Rights Watch US-based international human rights organisation, the second largest worldwide after Amnesty International. Originated in 1978 with HQ in New York.

IAEA International Atomic Energy Agency, autonomous organisation within the UN which aims to promote the peaceful use of nuclear energy; founded in 1957, and based in Vienna.

IBRD International Bank for Reconstruction and Development, a UN specialised agency more commonly known as the World Bank. Based in Washington, DC, and established in 1945 following the Bretton Woods conference, it is the largest single source of lending for development by its worldwide members.

ICAO International Civil Aviation Organisation, UN specialised agency which aims to establish international standards necessary for the safety and security of air transport.

ICRC International Committee of the Red Cross, founded in 1863 by Swiss philanthropist Henry Dunant after witnessing the battle of Solferino in 1859.

IMF International Monetary Fund, usually deemed synonymous with the World Bank, but to gain access to IBRD funds, member states must be members of the IMF.

Inkatha Zulu word meaning 'Mystical Coil', a reference to the coil worn by African women to help them carry heavy weights on their heads. Conservative South African organisation led by Chief Mangosuthu Buthelezi, founded in 1976 and based in Kwazulu-Natal.

International Court of Justice based at The Hague and founded in 1946, the ICJ is the principal judicial organ of the UN and is authorized to resolve disputes between UN member states. It is assisted by a governing body composed of 15 judges of differing nationalities, elected for a 9-year term.

Interpol International Criminal Police Organisation established in 1923 and based in Lyon.

IRA Irish Republican Army, currently the main militant republican movement in Northern Ireland, originally formed in 1919 to fight for Irish independence.

ORGANISATIONS

John Birch Society extreme rightwing group founded in the USA in 1958 by Robert H W Welch, its name deriving from an American intelligence worker killed by Chinese communists in 1945.

KGB Komitet Gosudarstvennoy Bezopasnosti (Committee of State Security), Soviet Union's security police established in 1954. The KGB was scrapped after the August coup of 1991 and replaced in Russia in Jan. 1994 by the Federal Counterintelligence Service.

Knesset The Israeli unicameral legislature, located in Jerusalem.

KNU Karen National Union, a guerrilla organisation in Myan Mar (Burma), which has fought for a separate Karen state since the late 1940s.

Ku Klux Klan US white racist paramilitary organisation with long history of violence against blacks. Established in Tennessee at the end of the US Civil War in 1865 and still active.

Lok Sabha lower house of the Indian Parliament; the upper chamber is the Rajya Sabah.

Mafia in Italy, the network of organised crime, including the Sicilian Mafia, the Neapolitan Camorra and the Calabrian 'Ndrangheta.

Matrix Churchill UK machine tool company at the centre of the events that led to the Scott inquiry established on 15 February 1996, into defence-related exports to Iraq. Paul Henderson, Trevor Abrahams and Peter Allen, executives of the Iraqi-owned Matrix Churchill, were arrested in October 1990 and charged with illegally exporting machine tools to Iraq. All three were acquitted and it emerged that Henderson had acted as an MI6 agent.

Mau Mau secret political society in Kenya which developed into a violent anti-colonial rebellion in the 1950s.

Médecins Sans Frontières founded in Paris by a group of French doctors in 1971 to provide emergency medical aid worldwide, it is funded by donations. MSF has offices in 20 countries worldwide, the international office being in Brussels.

MI5 the UK Security Service. The counterintelligence service was originally established in 1909 to assess and combat threats to UK security.

MI6 UK's Secret Intelligence Service. Formed in 1909, its role is to gather intelligence abroad in support of the government's security, defence, foreign and economic policies.

Monday Club right-wing grouping of the UK Conservative Party, formed in 1960. Established in reaction to Harold Macmillan's wind of change speech, the Club was characterised by support for the South African regime, and subsequently the Rhodesian UDI regime, by advocacy of voluntary repatriation of black Commonwealth immigrants, and by opposition to anti-apartheid activities such as sporting boycotts.

Moral Rearmament revivalist movement established in the UK in 1938 by the US-born Lutheran pastor Frank Buchman, which succeeded Buchman's previous 'Oxford Movement', based its teachings on the 4 absolutes of purity, unselfishness, honesty and love, and on the importance of 'life-change'.

Mossad the most important, powerful and prominent of the Israeli intelligence agencies. Founded in 1951 by Isser Harel, who served as its director until 1963, it concerns itself with matters of espionage, intelligence gathering and covert political operations in foreign countries.

Mujaheddin-I-Khalq lay guerrilla organisation representing leftwing Muslim groups in Iran. Founded in the early 1970s, it was banned after the Islamic Revolution for its espousal of a variant of Islamic socialism and its criticism of the regime of Ayatollah Khomeini.

NASA National Aeronautics and Space Administration, the US government agency created in 1958 to co-ordinate civilian activities in space.

National Front fringe UK racist party founded in 1967 from small neo-fascist groups, including League of Empire Loyalists, British National Party, and Racial Preservation Society.

National Health Service UK's state health care system. The architect of the service was Aneurin Bevan, health minister in the Labour government of Clement Attlee, drawing on the Beveridge Report of 1942 on the welfare state. The NHS was officially inaugurated on 5 July 1948.

National Trust National Trust for Places of Historic Interest or Natural Beauty, founded by Octavia Hill in 1895.

Nato North Atlantic Treaty Organisation, based in Brussels and formed in April 1949. Nato came into being during the Soviet blockade of Berlin, taking as its basic tenet that an armed attack on any Nato country would be seen as an attack on them all.

New Jewel Movement leftwing party founded in Grenada in 1973 which in 1979 overthrew the government of Sir Eric Gairy and set up a People's Revolutionary Government under PM Maurice Bishop.

1922 Committee body consisting of all Conservative back-bench MPs in the UK House of Commons. The name commemorates the decision in 1922, forced on the party leadership by Tory backbenchers, to bring down Lloyd George's coalition government. Sir Michael Spicer is the chairman as at the time of writing.

Non-Proliferation Treaty arms control agreement approved by the UN in June 1968 and effective from March 1970.

OECD Organisation for Economic Co-Operation and Development, formed in 1961 as the instrument for international co-operation among industrialised member states on economic and social policies. HQ in Paris.

Oireachtas bicameral legislature of the Republic of Ireland, comprising the 166-seat lower house, the Dáil Éireann, and the 60-seat upper house or Senate, the Seanad Éireann.

OPEC Organisation of Petroleum Exporting Countries, Established in Sept. 1960 by Iran, Iraq, Kuwait, Saudi Arabia and Venezuela, subsequently enlarged to include Qatar, Indonesia, Libya, Abu Dhabi, Algeria, Nigeria, Ecuador and Gabon. It aims to unify petroleum policies among member countries in order to ensure stable prices. Ecuador left OPEC in 1993.

Organisation of African Unity established in 1963 by 32 African countries to promote continental unity and solidarity of African states. Headquarters are in Addis Ababa, Ethiopia.

OSS Office for Strategic Services, US intelligence organisation which was the predecessor of the CIA. Established in June 1942.

Oxfam Oxford Committee for Famine Relief, founded in 1942 to aid women and children in Nazi-occupied Greece and based in Oxford, it now has 40 overseas field offices.

PDSA People's Dispensary for Sick Animals, founded by Mary Dickin in 1917.

Pearce Commission UK government body established in Nov. 1971 to investigate whether proposals to settle the dispute with Rhodesia over UDI (Unilateral Declaration of Independence) were acceptable to the Rhodesian people.

Pentagon HQ, in Arlington, VA, of the US Defense Department and the Departments of the Army, Navy and Airforce.

Phalange main rightwing Maronite Christian movement in Lebanon. The Phalangist Party and its militias spearheaded the Christian side in the Lebanese civil war 1975–91, during which they were allied with Israel.

PLO Palestine Liberation Organisation, founded in 1964 as spokesman for all matters concerning the Palestinian people. Yasser Arafat led the PLO between 1969 and 2004 and was succeeded on his death by Mahmoud Abbas (aka Abu Mazen).

Politburo key committee in the leadership structures of most communist parties, elected in the case of the Soviet Union by the central committee of the CPSU.

Quai d'Orsay term used for the French Ministry of Foreign Affairs, whose HQ is located in this street alongside the River Seine in Paris.

Radio Free Europe broadcasting operation covering the countries of Eastern and Central Europe, funded by the US government and operating from Munich under US management. Founded in 1949, it merged with Radio Liberty in 1976 and its aims are to broadcast non-partisan information.

Red Army Russian army formed in 1917 by the Bolsheviks and organised by Leon Trotsky to fight the anti-communist white armies.

Red Guards groups composed of students and schoolchildren in China who as 'Red Guards of the Cultural Revolution' had the task of unmasking revisionists and promoting Maoism. Emerging in 1966, the Red Guard operated for over a year before being disbanded.

Risorgimento the 19th-century movement for the political unification of Italy.

Royal Academy (of Arts) founded in 1768 at Somerset House but eventually moved to Burlington House. First president was Joshua Reynolds.

Royal Automobile Club founded in 1897 and responsible for many aspects of motoring safety and control.

Royal Exchange founded by Thomas Gresham in 1568 and home to various financial institutions. The present building was built by William Tite in 1844.

Royal Geographical Society founded in 1830 as the Geographical Society of London, it has been sited at Kensington Gore since 1912 in a house designed by Norman Shaw.

Royal Horticultural Society established in 1804 and awarded its royal charter in 1861, the RHS holds many shows but is primarily concerned with the Chelsea Flower Show held in Ranelagh Gardens since 1913. The Society has gardens at Wisley, Rosemoor near Great Torrington, Devon, and Hyde Hall, Essex.

Royal Institute of British Architects founded in 1834 under the patronage of William IV and given its Royal Charter in 1837. Membership in excess of 30,000; headquarters at Portland Place, London.

Royal Institution (of GB) established in 1799 by Count Rumford (Benjamin Thompson), this scientific organisation still has its headquarters in Albemarle St, London W1.

Royal Scottish Academy founded in 1826 and occupying a Greek Revival building in Edinburgh built by William Playfair.

Royal Society founded in 1660, early members included Christopher Wren and Samuel Pepys. Isaac Newton was president 1703–27.

SALT Strategic Arms Limitation Talks, held between USSR and USA 1969–79. Salt I, 1969–72, and Salt II, 1973–4, were between Nixon and Brezhnev and Salt II talks were concluded in 1979 by Carter and Brezhnev in Vienna, after which the SALT talks were renamed START.

Samaritans Founded by the Rev Chad Varah in November 1953. At this time Varah was Vicar of St Paul's, Clapham Junction, as well as being the scientific and astronautical consultant to Dan Dare in the *Eagle* comic strip. He was haunted by the suicide of a 14-year-old girl, who killed herself in 1935 when her periods started because she thought she had VD, and when the opportunity arose the helpline phone number of MAN 9000 was set up on 2 November 1953. In 1974 Chad Varah set up Befrienders International, the overseas equivalent of the Samaritans.

Sandinista leftwing Nicaraguan revolutionary movement that overthrew President Anastasio Somoza in 1979. Founded in 1961 and named in honour of Augusto César Sandino, the leader of a small peasant army that waged a campaign (1926–33) against the US occupation of Nicaragua.

SAVAK defunct Iranian security organisation established in 1957 with the aid of USA and Israeli intelligence services, and used to crush opposition to Mohammad Reza Shah Pahlavi.

Save the Children Fund founded by Eglantyne Jebb, an Englishwoman, who saw starving children in Austria (1919). The Princess Royal is the President.

Schengen Group European mainland countries within the EU which are party to the Schengen Agreement on abolishing border controls between their territories while improving police co-operation. The original group which met in Schengen in Luxembourg in June 1985 consisted of the Benelux countries and France and Germany; Spain and Portugal soon ratified the treaty, followed by Italy, Greece and Austria.

Securitate communist Romania's security police which mounted a brutal defence of the regime of Nicolae Ceausescu during the December 1989 revolution.

Sejm the lower house of the Polish National Assembly, comprising 460 directly elected members.

SHAPE Supreme Headquarters Allied Powers Europe, the NATO military HQ of Allied Command Europe. SHAPE was moved from Paris to near Mons in Belgium in 1967, after De Gaulle's decision to withdraw France from NATO.

Shin Bet the Israeli internal security agency, aka the General Security Service.

Sierra Club probably the world's first environmental pressure group, formed in 1892 in California by naturalist John Muir.

Sinn Fein (ourselves alone) prominent revolutionary party fighting initially for the republican independence of Ireland, and, since partition, for the reunification of the country.

Snowdrop Campaign founded after the killing of 16 children in Dunblane on 13 March 1996 and named after the only flower in bloom that day. The

ORGANISATIONS

campaign, backed by international film star Sean Connery, aims to ban civilian ownership of firearms.

Solidarity Polish trade union and opposition movement founded in 1980 by striking workers at the Gdansk shipyard. Its first leader was the future President Lech Walesa.

Stasi the Ministry of State Security of communist East Germany, which operated from 1950 to 1990.

Stern Gang British name for the Zionist guerrilla group founded in Palestine in 1940 by Abraham Stern and responsible till 1949 for several terrorist attacks.

Stormont the Northern Ireland parliament buildings in Belfast, the seat of the N.I. parliament from 1932 until the introduction of direct rule in 1972.

Tamil Tigers militant organisation formed in 1976 aiming to achieve and independent Tamil state in northern Sri Lanka.

TASS Soviet Union's state news agency.

Tontons Macoutes (from a Creole word meaning 'Uncle Knapsack', a bogeyman), the notorious Haitian right-wing secret police, set up in 1958 by Papa Doc Duvalier.

TUC Trades Union Congress, the key umbrella employees' organisation in the UK, founded in 1868.

Tulip Revolution Name given to the uprising in the former Soviet republic of Kyrgyzstan in March 2005. Many species of tulip are native to the mountains and steppes of Central Asia.

Tupamaros Uruguayan guerrilla group named after an 18th-century Peruvian Indian chief Tupac Amarú, and founded in 1962 by Raúl Antonaccio, an activist in sugar cane cutters' strikes. The group is still active today under the name 'National Liberation Movement'.

Tynwald parliament of the Isle of Man, a UK Crown Dependency. The principal chamber of Tynwald is the 24-member directly elected House of Keys. Tynwald celebrated its millennium in 1979; only the Althing of Iceland claims to be older (dating back to at least 930).

UN General Assembly established under Chapter IV of the UN Charter to act as the organisation's plenary body, representing all member states, it oversees the work of the UN's subsidiary bodies.

UN Secretariat listed in Chapter III of its Charter, the Secretariat, and the functions of the Secretary-General, are covered in detail in Chapter XV of the Charter. Elected by the Security Council. Secretariatship is usually for a term of 5 years with an automatic option to carry on unless vetoed by a member of the Council. Trygve Lie of Norway took office in Feb. 1946 and his term was extended until he resigned in November 1952, despite a Soviet veto. Other holders have been Dag Hammarskjöld of Sweden (April 1953 until his death in the Congo in September 1961), U Thant of Burma (1961–71), Kurt Waldheim of Austria (1972–81), Javier Pérez de Cuéllar of Peru (1982–91), Boutros Boutros-Ghali of Egypt (1 January 1992 – 1 January 1997, US vetoed continuation) and the incumbent Kofe Anan of Ghana.

UN Security Council established under Chapter V of the Charter, the Security Council has primary responsibility for the maintenance of international peace and security. It presently has 15 member states, 10 non-permanent members plus China, France, Russia, UK and USA, which are permanent members and carry power of veto.

UNESCO Paris-based UN Educational, Scientific and Cultural Organisation, founded in 1946 to promote international collaboration in those fields of endeavour. USA, UK and Singapore are not members at present after suggestions of financial mismanagement.

UNITA National Union for the Total Independence of Angola. Founded by Jonas Savimbi in March 1966, UNITA fought alongside the Popular Movement for the Liberation of Angola during the struggle against colonial rule, but following the Portuguese withdrawal in 1975 it began a rivalry with the MPLA, backed by South Africa and the USA and not yet concluded. Since the death of Savimbi in February 2002, UNITA has been led by Paulo Lukamba Gato.

United Arab Republic political union of Egypt and Syria proclaimed between 1958 and 1961. Egypt retained the title of UAR until 1971, when it took the name Arab Republic of Egypt.

United Nations Established on 24 Oct. 1945 with its HQ completed in New York in 1952, the UN replaced the inter-war League of Nations, and its 111 articles of the Charter were proposed at the San Francisco Conference from 25 April – 25 June 1945. Its 6 principal organs are the General Assembly, Security Council, Economic and Social Council, Trusteeship Council, International Court of Justice and the Secretariat. Membership has risen from 51 at inception to 191 as at 30 April 2005.

United Nations Budget Top 5 countries contributing to the UN are USA (24%), Japan (19%), Germany (8.4%), UK (5.96%), France (5.85%) as at 30 April 2005.

Universal Postal Union UN specialised agency based in Berne, Switzerland, first established in 1875 and taken over by the UN in 1948, charged with promoting international collaboration in postal services.

UNPROFOR UN Protection Force, established in January 1992 and dispatched to Croatia in March 1992 to monitor a ceasefire between Croatia and Krajina Serbs.

Velvet Revolution near-bloodless overthrow of Czech communist regime in November–December 1989 resulting in the ousting of the leader, Milos Jakes, and subsequent presidency of Vaclav Havel.

Warsaw Pact Warsaw Treaty Organisation, which was the communist counterpart to NATO during the cold war. Original signatories in May 1955 were Albania, Bulgaria, Czechoslovakia, East Germany, Hungary, Poland, Romania and the USSR. Albania withdrew in 1968 and following the collapse of communism in central and Eastern Europe the Warsaw Pact was dissolved in February 1991.

Women's Institute founded in 1897 at Stoney Creek, Canada.

World Health Organisation UN specialised agency based in Geneva and founded in 1948 with the aim of attaining the highest level of health for mankind.

World Wide Fund for Nature known until 1988 as the World Wildlife Fund, it was formed in 1961 and raises funds for a variety of conservation projects.

Yakuza Japanese criminal organisation comparable to US mafia-type syndicates.

PERFUME

Animal Sources

ambergris found floating on the sea (particularly the Indian Ocean) in oily grey lumps. It is excreted by the sperm whale after feeding on cuttlefish and is used as a base for perfumes.

castoreum comes from the follicles in the genital areas of both male and female beavers; used as a fixative.

civet comes from a pouch beneath the tails of both male and female civet cats; used as a fixative.

hyraceum excreted by the hyrax, a small rabbit-like animal found in the Middle East. It was used in ancient Arabic perfumes but is rarely used nowadays.

musk comes from the preputial follicle of the male musk deer. It is used as a fixative and is also thought to be an aphrodisiac. Chinese courtesans were fed bland foods perfumed with musk, so that when aroused the warmth of their bodies released the scent.

propolis a sticky brown fixative which bees collect from trees to use as a cement in their hives.

sweet hoof or onycha an ingredient of incense that comes from the shells of marine snails found around India and the Red Sea.

Plant, Mineral and Synthetic Sources

angelica root of the holy ghost (*Angelica archangelica*). It has a strong musky aroma.

bdellium myrrh (see also opoponax), an aromatic gum.

ben oil an essential oil from the winged seeds of the horseradish tree, used as a base oil for perfumes.

burning bush white dittany. The oil from the plant can vaporise in hot weather and catch fire without harming the plant itself. The fragrant essential oil is used in pot-pourri.

cherry pie heliotrope, used in pot-pourri and in modern perfumes such as 'Lou Lou' (Cacharel).

coumarin a white crystalline substance with a scent of new-mown hay, found in withered herbs and fruits. It is also manufactured synthetically from coal tar.

devil's dung asafoetida, a tall evil-smelling plant used as a fixative.

farnesol manufactured synthetically, but also found in musk. It gives a scent of lily of the valley.

frangipani the first plant to be named after a perfume. In 15th-century Rome, one of the Frangipani family made the perfume from orris, spices, civet and musk digested in wine alcohol. Later, French colonists in the West Indies found a bush (*Plumeria alba*) which had the same smell and named it frangipani.

galbanum small drops of it ooze from the stems of the giant fennel. It is mentioned in the Old Testament. It has a spicy-green scent with a hint of musk and is used in the 'top notes' of quality perfumes like Chanel No. 19.

handflower wallflower. The name 'handflower' comes from the practice, stemming from ancient Greece, of carrying the flowers in the hand as a nosegay during festivals.

indole the synthetic material derived from coal tar used to produce the scent of jasmine and neroli.

ionone the synthetic material used to make the scent of violets.

isoeugenol the synthetic material used to make the scent of carnations.

labdanum comes from rock-rose shrubs found around the Mediterranean; often gathered by combing the beards of goats which have browsed on the bushes. It was thought to have aphrodisiac qualities. Assyrian kings liked young women who had spent time soaking during a six-month period in baths of labdanum or bdellium, after six months soaking in myrrh.

linalol the synthetic material used to make the scents of lilac, lily and honeysuckle.

love-in-the-mist nigella, a hardy annual which grows to a height of about 1.5 m and has a fragrance of ambrette seeds.

malabathrum a dried aromatic leaf from a species of cinnamon, used by the Romans in the making of unguents.

muguet lily of the valley. It is used in many 'quality' perfumes such as 'Opium' (Yves St Laurent), and 'Florissa' (Floris). Its fragrance is manufactured synthetically as farnesol.

olibanum frankincense, a fragrant gum resin often used as an incense and, in perfumes, as a fixative.

opoponax myrrh (probably the Biblical myrrh collected from the land of Punt). Its oil, with a scent of fenugreek, is distilled from the yellowish lumps which occur on the plant. It is used mainly for incense and pot-pourri.

orris comes from iris roots; has a violet-like scent.

storax originally from the bark of the liquidamber tree which grows in Turkey, Asia Minor and Rhodes, but now manufactured synthetically. It has a smell of cinnamon, and is used as a fixative.

syringa lilac. The flowers are used mainly in pot-pourri, and its oil is used in 'quality' perfumes such as 'Chamade' (Guerlain), 'Florissa' (Floris) and 'Soir de Paris' (Bourjois).

verbena holy wort. The leaves have a lemon scent. It is used mainly in cosmetics and soaps and the leaves are sometimes dried for use in sachets.

Perfumes and Perfume Houses

Alliage	Estée Lauder (1972)	Knowing	Estée Lauder (1988)
Amarige	Givenchy (1991)	L'Aimant	Coty (1927)
Anaïs Anaïs	Cacharel (1978)	L'Air du Temps	Nina Ricci (1948)
Arpège	Lanvin (1927; relaunched 1994)	L'Egoïste	Chanel (1990)
		Le Jardin	Max Factor (1986)
Bal à Versailles	Jean Desprez (1962)	Lou Lou	Cacharel (1987)
Beautiful	Estée Lauder (1985)	Ma Griffe	Carven (1946)
Brut	Fabergé (1964)	Mon Parfum	Paloma Picasso / L'Oréal (1984)
Cabochard	Grès (1959)		
Calandre	Paco Rabanne (1969)	Must	Cartier (1981)
Chamade	Guerlain (1969)	Obsession	Calvin Klein (1985)
Charlie	Revlon (1973)	Old Spice	Shulton (1937)
Cheap and Chic	Moschino (1996)	Only	Julio Iglesias / Myrurgia (1989)
Chlöe	Lagerfeld (1975)		
Chypre	Coty (1917)	Opium	Yves St Laurent (1977)
CKOne	Calvin Klein (1994)	Paris	Yves St Laurent (1983)
Devin	Aramis (1978)	Parure	Guerlain (1975)
Diva	Ungaro (1983)	Pleasures	Estée Lauder (1996)
Drakkar Noir	Guy Laroche (1982)	Poême	Lancôme (1995)
Dune	Christian Dior (1991)	Poison	Christian Dior (1985)
Eau de Bonpoint	Annick Goutal (1989)	Polo	Ralph Lauren (1978)
Eau Sauvage	Dior (1966)	Red	Giorgio Beverly Hills (1989)
Eden	Cacharel (1994)		
Escape	Calvin Klein (1991)	Red Door	Elizabeth Arden (1990; relaunched 1996)
Eternity	Calvin Klein (1988)		
Fahrenheit	Dior (1988)	Rive Gauche	Yves St Laurent (1971)
Femme	Rochas (1944)	Samsara	Guerlain (1989)
Fidgi	Guy Laroche (1962)	Shalimar	Guerlain (1925)
Fleurs de Fleurs	Nina Ricci (1980)	Shocking	Schiaparelli (1936)
Gentleman	Givenchy (1974)	So Pretty	Cartier (1995)
Imprévu	Coty (1965)	Special No. 127	Floris (1890)
Intimate	Revlon (1955)	Trésor	Lancôme (1990)
Ivoire	Balmain (1979)	Tweed	Lenthéric (1933)
Jardins de Bagatelle	Guerlain (1983)	Vent Vert	Balmain (1947)
Je Reviens	Worth (1932)	Youth Dew	Estée Lauder (1953)
Jicky	Guerlain (1889)	Ysatis	Givenchy (1984)
Joy	Patou (1930)		

Notable Perfumes

aqua angeli   a perfumed water made from aloewood, nutmeg, clove, storax, benzoin and rosewater, first made for scenting the shirts of Louis XIV of France.

Chanel No. 5   named because the fragrance chosen by Coco Chanel from specimens supplied by Ernest Beauxs was sample No. 5. The first aldehyde perfume.

Chanel No. 19   named for Coco Chanel's birthday (19 August).

damask water   popular in 16th-century England. It is made mainly from rosewater.

Eau de Bonpoint   by Annick Goutal (1989). The first fragrance for babies.

eau-de-Cologne   first developed by Paul Feminis in Cologne in the early 18th century. Its main ingredients were lavender and citrus, neroli, bergamot and lemon. 4711 Mullhens of Cologne still uses the original formula.

Imperial Leather   first made in 1768 by Bayleys, the court perfumers in London, as a result of a challenge by the Russian Count Orloff, to make a perfume with the scent of worn leather. It became a favourite of Catherine the Great, under the name 'Eau de Cologne Impériale Russe'. Cussons took over Bayleys and renamed the perfume Imperial Russian Leather, but dropped 'Russian' in 1939.

L'Interdit   launched for Audrey Hepburn in 1957. It was Givenchy's first perfume. The name means 'the forbidden one' – forbidden, at first, to all but Audrey Hepburn, whose face graced the advertisement.

Jicky   the first 'modern' perfume, created in 1889 by Aimé Guerlain.

Joy   the most expensive perfume on the market soon after its manufacture by Jean Patou in 1930.

Only   launched in 1989 by Myrurgia in association with singer Julio Iglesias.

Special No. 127   created by Floris in 1890 for Grand Duke Orloff of Russia. No. 127 was the page in Floris' Book where he wrote formulae which were created uniquely for individual customers.

Vent Vert   launched in 1947 by Balmain. It was the first 'green' perfume.

Notable Perfumers

Baur Albert Baur was patenter of the first synthetic musk perfume, Musk Baur, in 1988.

Beaux Ernest Beaux developed the first aldehyde-based perfume, Chanel No. 5.

Carles Jean Carles, of Grasse, insured his nose for $1 million. His creations include 'Canoe' in 1935 (for Dana) and 'Shocking' in 1936 (for Schiaparelli). He founded the School of Perfumery in Grasse, Provence.

Farina Jean-Marie Farina opened a shop in Paris in 1806 to sell eau-de-Cologne. He sold his business in 1840 to Léonce Collas, who passed it on in 1862 to his cousins, Messrs Roger & Gallet.

Floris the oldest perfume house in the world, founded in 1730 as a barber's shop in Jermyn Street, London, by Juan Floris from Minorca.

Hermès arose from a harness-making, then glove-making business. Many of its perfumes are named after horse and carriage parts, for example 'Calèche' (a four-wheeled horse-drawn carriage).

Perkin William Perkin found out how to synthesise coumarin from coal tar, a much-used ingredient with a new-mown-hay fragrance. This was one of the first major discoveries in synthetic perfumery.

Miscellaneous

Abir perfumed powder used in India, usually sprinkled on linen. Its ingredients include sandalwood, aloes, cardamom, cloves, civet and rose.

Aldehyde a group of alcohol-derived chemicals which form other groups of chemicals known as benzoid compounds. Their discovery led to the manufacture of synthetic perfume ingredients.

chypre originally a famous Roman perfume made in Cyprus (hence the name). Nowadays used to describe perfumes with fresh top notes of bergamot, with other citrus ingredients such as neroli, lemon and orange, with middle notes of jasmin and rose and a base of oakmoss, with labdanum, storax, civet, patchouli and musk. The first modern chypre perfume was 'Chypre by Coty' (1917).

Cliff Richard: perfume brands Miss You Nights – a warm oriental scent containing rose, jasmine and ylang ylang, combined with sandalwood. Dream Maker – a floral scent, with notes of citrus fruits and a hint of peach.

khaluq an unguent made by early Arabs which men were forbidden to use.

kyphi an incense made by the ancient Egyptians, based on wine, honey, raisins, herbs, frankincense, myrrh and juniper berries.

kypros an ancient Greek perfume which contained wine and cardamon and a sweet-scented substance called aspalathus.

magma the dried dregs from unguent bottles which the ancient Greeks and Romans added to scented powders.

olla-podrida pot-pourri made by perfume-makers from their waste materials with which they mixed herbs and lavender and rose petals.

perfumer's organ not his or her nose! It is the work bench and surrounding ingredients and equipment.

pomander a solid ball of perfumed material, such as crushed petals bound with a gum. In Tudor times they were carried to mask unpleasant smells and to ward off infection. In the 16th century it became popular to make them from oranges with cloves pushed into them, then baked. People fastened them to their belts or wrists. Nowadays they are sometimes used to perfume wardrobes.

tussie-mussie a nosegay dating from Elizabethan times, when it was originally made from flowers and herbs chosen for their symbolic meanings, e.g. rosemary for remembrance, daisy for faithfulness etc.

unguent cone cone made from perfumed fat (usually ox-tallow), which was fixed on to the hair or head-dress so that it melted and ran down the hair and body, perfuming them as it did so.

P
E
R
F
U
M
E

Strengths and Forms of Perfume in Descending Order According to Strength

Concentration	Name
15–30% in high-grade alcohol	extrait
15–18% in 80–90% grade alcohol	eau de parfum
4–8% in alcohol	eau de toilette
3–5% in 70% alcohol/water	eau de Cologne
3% in 80% pure alcohol	eau fraiche

Containers

acerra small box used by the Romans to contain incense burned in temples.

alabastrum pot, usually made from alabaster, agate or onyx, used by the Romans to contain perfumed oils.

aryballos / ampulla small flask used by the ancient Greeks to contain perfumed oils, often carried hanging from the wrist by a small strap.

pouncet box box used since Elizabethan times to contain perfumed powders placed between bedlinen. Originally used to hold pumice stone which was needed in the preparation of parchment for writing.

vinaigrette small metal box whose inner lid was pierced, popular in 18th/19th-century Europe. It held a sponge soaked in aromatic vinegar and was used as a smelling bottle.

Founders

Amouage   The Hamood family of the Sultanate of Oman (1983).

Avon   David McConnell (1886), Suffern, California. He was a travelling book-salesman who liked to give his customers free gifts of inexpensive perfume. Originally called the California Perfume Co., its name changed to Avon (after Stratford-on-Avon) in 1959.

Cacharel   Jean Bosquet (1962), Paris. The name comes from a wild duck found in Provence.

Charles of the Ritz   Charles Jundt (1934), New York.

Coty   François Sputorno (1905), Paris.

Elizabeth Arden   Florence Graham (1910), New York. Name derived from the title of the book *Elizabeth and Her German Garden* by Elizabeth von Arnim.

Fragonard   Eugene Fuchs (1783), Grasse, Provence. Named after the painter Fragonard.

Lancôme   Armand Petitjean (1935), Paris.

Mary Chess   Grace Mary Chess Robinson (1932), London.

Revlon   Charles and Joseph Revson and Charles Lachmann (1932), Boston, originally to market nail varnish.

Perfume Families or Classification

Perfumes are usually classified according to seven 'family' groups which form a continuum from floral to fougère.

floral   mainly made from flower oils. These are light, daytime perfumes, e.g. 'Anaïs Anaïs' (Cacharel), 'L'Air du Temps' (Nina Ricci).

green   giving an impression of new-mown grass. Fresh-smelling perfumes which include among their ingredients mosses, ferns, citrus fruits and herbs, e.g. 'Alliage' (Estée Lauder), 'Chanel No. 19' (Chanel).

aldehydic   based on synthetic aldehydes. They range from floral through woody to powdery, e.g. 'Chanel No. 5' (Chanel), 'White Linen' (Estée Lauder).

chypre   their fragrance is floral or green but with a heavy base such as ambergris, e.g. 'Cabochard' (Grès), 'Chypre' (Coty).

oriental   their fragrance is spicy, strong and exotic and has a heavy sweetness which comes from ingredients such as musk, vanilla and sandalwood, e.g. 'Poison' (Christian Dior) and 'Opium' (Yves St Laurent).

tobacco / leather   they have a hint of tobacco, leather and woody aromas, e.g. 'Antaeus' (Chanel) and 'Cuir de Russie' (Chanel).

fougère   their fragrance is fresh, with a note of lavender, herbs, oakmoss, coumarin and new-mown hay, e.g. 'Drakkar Noir' (Guy Laroche), 'Brut' (Fabergé).

PHOTOGRAPHY

Photography and Cinematography

Ansel Easton Adams (1902–84) American photographer who co-founded Group f/64 with Edward Weston (1932) and helped set up the Department of Photography at the New York Museum of Modern Art (1940). His publications include *Taos Pueblo* (1930) and *Born Free and Equal* (1944).

Diane Arbus (1923–71) American photographer famous for her intense portraits of American social outcasts.

Eugène Atget (1857–1927) French photographer famous for recording the streets and scenes of old Paris; his unusual images of the commonplace inspired the Surrealists.

Richard Avedon (1923–2004) Photographer who made his name as a fashion photographer with *Harper's Bazaar*. His first sitter was Russian pianist-composer Sergei Rachmaninov.

David Royston Bailey (1938–) English photographer who started his professional life as a fashion photographer but developed as a portraitist during the 1960s, specialising in nudes. His 1965 collection *David Bailey's Box of Pin-ups* (1965) included pictures of celebrities of the day, from the Beatles to the Krays.

Billy Bitzer (1874–1944) US motion picture cameraman who, in partnership with the pioneer director D W Griffiths, developed camera techniques that set the standard for all future motion pictures. He was the first cameraman to use artificial lighting for his work, and his other innovations included the use of soft-focus photography, using a light-diffusion screen in front of the camera lens, the fade-out, and the iris shot, in which the frame is either gradually blacked out in a shrinking circle, thereby ending a scene, or gradually opened in a widening circle, beginning a scene.

Margaret Bourke-White (1904–71) American photo-journalist who was employed by *Fortune* magazine in 1929 and subsequently became staff photographer and associate editor on *Life* magazine (1936). She was the first woman photographer to be attached to the US armed forces, producing outstanding reports of the siege of Moscow in 1941, and the opening of the concentration camps in 1944. Bourke-White married the American author Erskine Caldwell in 1939 but was divorced in 1942.

Mathew Brady (1823–96) New York-born photographer famous for his record of the American Civil War with the Union armies.

Bill Brandt (1904–83) English photographer who studied with Man Ray in London before working for the Ministry of Information and recording conditions during the Blitz. Brandt subsequently found fame with his landscapes and nudes. His publications include *The English at Home* (1936), *Perspective of Nudes* (1961) and *Shadows of Light* (1966).

Brassaï (1899–1984) Professional name of Gyula Halász, the Hungarian-born French painter and photographer. His photography included the nightlife of 1930s Paris.

Henri Cartier-Bresson (1908–2004) French photographer who initially studied painting with André Lhote before working as an assistant to film director Jean Renoir. His publications include *The Decisive Moment* (1952) and *The Europeans* (1955).

Julia Margaret Cameron (1815–79) British photographer who pioneered portrait photography.

Louis Jacques Mandé Daguerre (1787–1851) French painter and physicist who invented the daguerreotype, i.e. the first practical process of photography. Though the first permanent photograph was made in 1826 by Niépce, it was of poor quality and required about 8 hours exposure time as opposed to Daguerre's process which took 20 to 30 minutes.

Terence Donovan (1936–96) London-born photographer and film director whose work covered a wide spectrum of contemporary life. He worked for *Vogue*, *Harpers & Queen*, *Elle*, and *Marie Claire*.

George Eastman (1854–1932) US manufacturer who introduced the Kodak camera (1888) and Brownie camera (1900). Contrary to popular belief he was unrelated to Linda Eastman.

Walker Evans (1903–75) American photographer who produced a powerful record of the faces, homes and lives of America's 1930s rural poor.

Roger Fenton (1819–69) English photographer who was famous for his Crimean War pictures.

William Henry Fox Talbot (1800–77) English chemist, linguist and photographer who in 1839 invented the photographic negative and whose *The Pencil of Nature* (1844) was the first photographic book.

William Friese-Greene (1855–1921) British photographer who is often credited with the invention of cinematography, although Thomas Edison would appear to have a stronger claim. Friese-Greene did however pioneer stereoscopic and colour cinematography, but once again lacked the technical knowledge necessary to bring his ideas to fruition. A 1951 feature film, *The Magic Box*, was based on his life.

John Heartfield (1891–1968) Originally named Helmut Herzfelde, German pioneer of the photomontage, e.g. *Hurrah, the Butter is Finished* (1935).

Lewis Wickes Hine (1874–1940) American photographer who studied sociology before making a photographic study of Ellis Island immigrants and child labourers. Hine worked for the American Red Cross in WW1 and recorded the construction of the Empire State Building in his survey *Men at Work* (1932).

James Wong Howe (1899–1976) Chinese-born American cinematographer who started work in 1917 as assistant cameraman to Cecil B De Mille and in 1922 became chief cameraman for *Famous Players*. Howe pioneered the use of the wide-angle lens, deep focus, and ceilinged sets to replicate shipboard claustrophobia. He won Oscars for his work on *The Rose Tattoo* (1955) and *Hud* (1963).

Yousuf Karsh (1908–2002) Armenian-born Canadian photographer who was appointed official portrait photographer to the Canadian government in 1935. His reputation was made with a 1941 portrait of Sir Winston Churchill, and he continued to photograph all the world's leading statesmen.

André Kertész (1894–1985) Hungarian-born American photographer famous for his pioneering use of the small hand-held camera, the well-observed social scene, the surreal figure study, still life, and later the fashion image.

Edwin Herbert Land (1909–91) US inventor and physicist whose invention of the Polaroid (one-step) process for developing and printing photographs culminated in a revolution in photography unparalleled since the advent of roll film.

Dorothea Lange (1895–1965) US photographer who started as a society photographer but became famous for her social records of migrant workers during the 1930s depression.

Lord Patrick Lichfield (1939–) British aristocratic photographer whose reputation was built around his royal photographs and his nude calendars.

Auguste Lumière (1862–1954), Louis Lumière (1864–1948) French chemist brothers who invented the first successful cine camera and projector (1895) and a process of colour photography. They also produced the first film newsreels, and the first movie, *La Sortie des usines Lumière* (1895).

László Moholy-Nagy (1895–1946) Hungarian-born American photographer famous for his constructivist-inspired, semi-abstract images, and his inspiring teaching at the Bauhaus.

Eadweard Muybridge (1830–1904) Original name Edward James Muggeridge. English photographer famous for his early experiments in capturing motion in photographic images and for his landscapes of the American West. Muybridge was employed by the railroad magnate Leland Stanford in 1872 to prove that during a particular moment in trotting, all four legs of a horse are off the ground simultaneously. His studies were interrupted while he was tried for the murder of his wife's lover, but after his acquittal he developed a special shutter that gave an exposure of 2/1,000 of a second which proved Stanford's theory.

Nadar (1820–1910) Professional name of Gaspard-Félix Tournachon, French artist and photographer whose Paris studio became a favourite haunt of the intelligentsia. In 1886 he produced the first photo interview, a series of 21 photographs of the centenarian scientist Eugène Chevreul, each captioned with the sitter's replies to Nadar's questions. He pioneered the use of aerial photographs for map-making and in 1858 took the first pictures from a balloon.

Joseph-Nicéphore Niépce (1765–1833) French inventor who was the first to make a permanent photographic image (1826).

Man Ray (1890–1976) American photographer, painter and film-maker, born Emanuel Rabinovich, who was a leading light in the development of Modernism. He founded the New York Dadaist movement with Marcel Duchamp and Francis Picabia before moving to Paris and working with René Clair. Man Ray pioneered the use of photographic images made without a camera, 'Rayographs'.

Henry Peach Robinson (1830–1901) English photographer who opened a studio at Leamington Spa in 1857 and specialised in images of costumed models and painted settings. He was a founder member of the Linked Ring (1892), a group of photographers seeking to excel in artistic creation.

Alexander Rodchenko (1891–1956) Soviet photographer and photomontagist who introduced 'New Photography' to post-revolutionary Russia.

Erich Salomon (1886–1944) German photojournalist who was master of the candid shot whereby he caught politicians and celebrities off guard for new magazines of the 1920s. He died in Auschwitz.

August Sander (1876–1964) German photographer celebrated for his ambitious project 'Man in the Twentieth Century', a picture of the doomed Weimar Republic through the faces of its people.

Aaron Siskind (1903–91) American photographer who began his career while teaching English in New York (1932). His subjects showed the usual American depiction of the depression of the 1930s, but unlike other documentaries of the period his *Dead End: The Bowery* and *Harlem Document* show as much concern for pure design as for the plight of the subjects. Siskind developed an abstract approach to his art and began photographing mundane subjects and architectural ruins. He became professor of photography at the Institute of Design of the Illinois Institute of Technology in Chicago (1951–71) and held a similar post at Rhode Island School of Design from 1971.

W Eugene Smith (1918–78) US photojournalist noted for his impassioned documentary photographs from around the world, seen mostly in *Life* magazine in the 1940s and 50s.

Edward Steichen (1879–1973) Luxembourg-born American photographer who became a member of the Linked Ring in England and made his reputation with his studies of the nude. In 1902 he co-founded the American Photo-Secession Group with Alfred Stieglitz. In WW1 he served as commander of the photographic division of the US army. In the 1920s Steichen developed a New Realism style and became heavily involved in fashion photography. He was head of US Naval Film Services during WW2, and director of photography at the New York Museum of Modern Art from 1945 to 1962, where he put on the 'Family of Man' exhibition in 1955.

Alfred Stieglitz (1864–1946) American photographer who founded the Photo-Secession Group in 1902 with Edward Steichen. He was a major figure in establishing photography as an art form and his gallery of modern art at 291 Fifth Avenue, NY, was the linchpin of his work.

Paul Strand (1890–1976) US photographer and documentary film-maker who studied under Lewis Hine. In 1933 he was appointed chief of photography and cinematography in the government Secretariat of Education in Mexico. Known for his still lifes, architectural studies and photographic books on regions of the world.

Edward Weston (1886–1958) American photographer who made his reputation in his Glendale studio but moved to Mexico in 1923, where he developed his modernist style. In 1932 he joined Ansel Adams and others in forming the 'straight photography' purists Group f/64 in California. His close-up studies of inanimate objects such as shells and vegetables exemplified his vision of detailed form and the richness of his control of tone. He produced notable landscapes of the Mojave Desert, and in 1937, with the first-ever award of a Guggenheim Fellowship to a photographer, travelled the American West before touring the Eastern States to illustrate an edition of Walt Whitman's *Leaves of Grass*.

Minor White (1908–76) American photographer and editor who was greatly influenced by Edward Weston and Alfred Stieglitz. In 1946 he moved to San Francisco and worked with Ansel Adams, whom he followed as director of the photographic department in the California School of Fine Art (1947–52). White was appointed professor of creative photography at the Massachusetts Institute of Technology (1965–76) and founded the periodicals *Aperture* and *Image*.

Garry Winogrand (1928–84) American photographer who created a highly influential brand of urban street photography, fusing the 'snapshot' approach with a sense of energy and crowded events in his images.

POLITICS

Country – Name of Governmental Chambers – Type of Government

NB The upper chambers of bicameral parliaments are listed first in this table, and the name of parliaments are the most commonly accepted, e.g. the parliament of Algeria is bicameral, the upper house being the Majlis el-Umma and the lower house the National Assembly. The combined assemblies are generally referred to as the Majlis (council). Parliaments are generally elected for a term of years but in some bicameral assemblies the two chambers may have differing lengths of term. In our example of Algeria, the lower house is elected for a five-year term but the upper house has a third of its members elected for six years, a third elected for three years, and the remaining third at the president's discretion. The membership is the statutory capacity as at January 2003.

Country	Name of Governmental Chambers	Name of Parliament	Years of Office
Afghanistan	Wolas Jirga (House of People) (249 members)	National Assembly	5
	Meshrano Jirga (House of Elders) (102 members)		varies
Albania	National Assembly (140 members)	People's Assembly	4
Algeria	Majlis el-Umma (Council of the Nation) (144 members)	Majlis	varies
	National Assembly (389 members)		5
Andorra	General Council of the Valleys (28 members)	General Council of the Valleys	4
Angola	National Assembly (223 members)	National Assembly	2–4
Anguilla	House of Assembly (11 members)	National Assembly	5
Antigua and Barbuda	Senate (17 members)	Parliament	varies
	House of Representatives (17 members)		5
Argentina	Senate (72 members)	Congress	varies
	Chamber of Deputies (257 members)		varies
Armenia	Azgayin Zhoghov (National Assembly) (131 members)	Azgayin Zhoghov	4
Aruba	Legislative Assembly (21 members)	Staten	4
Australia	Senate (76 members)	Federal Parliament	6
	House of Representatives (150 members)		3
Austria	Bundesrat (Federal Council) (64 members)	National Assembly	varies
	Nationalrat (National Council) (183 members)		4
Azerbaijan	Milli-Mejlis (National Council) (125 members)	Milli-Mejlis	varies
Bahamas	Senate (16 members)	Parliament	varies
	House of Assembly (40 members)		5
Bahrain	Consultative Council (40 members)	Majlis al-Shura	4
Bangladesh	Jatiya Sangsad (house of the nation) (300 members)	Jatiya Sangsad	5
Barbados	Senate (21 members)	Parliament	5
	House of Assembly (28 members)		5
Belarus	Council of the Republic (64 members)	National Assembly	5
	House of Representatives (110 members)		5
Belgium	Senate (71 members)	Federal Parliament	varies
	Chamber of Representatives (150 members)		4
Belize	Senate (12 members)	National Assembly	varies
	House of Representatives (29 members)		5
Benin	National Assembly (83 members)	National Assembly	4
Bermuda	Senate (11 members)	Parliament	varies
	House of Assembly (36 members)		5
Bhutan	Tshogdu (National Assembly) (154 members)	Tshogdu	3
Bolivia	Senate (27 members)	Congress	5
	Chamber of Deputies (130 members)		5
Bosnia-Herzegovina	Chamber of Peoples (15 members i.e. 5 Croat, 5 Muslim, 5 Serb)	National Assembly	2
	Chamber of Representatives (42 members)		2
Botswana	House of Chiefs (15 members)	National Assembly	5
	National Assembly (47 members)		5
Brazil	Senate (81 members)	Congress	8
	Chamber of Deputies (513 members)		4
Brunei	There are no political parties or elections, the Sultan ruling since a revolt in December 1962.		
Bulgaria	National Assembly (240 members)	National Assembly	4
Burkina Faso	Assembly of People's Deputies (111 members)	National Assembly	5
	Chamber of Representatives (178 members)		3
Burundi	National Assembly (220 members)	National Assembly	5
	Senate (54 members)		varies

Country	Name of Governmental Chambers	Name of Parliament	Years of Office
Cambodia	Senate (61 members)	National Assembly	5
	National Assembly (122 members)		5
Cameroon	National Assembly (180 members)	National Assembly	5
Canada	Senate (105 members)	Federal Parliament	varies
	House of Commons (301 members)		5
Cape Verde	National Assembly (72 members)	National Assembly	5
Central African Republic	National Assembly (109 members)	National Assembly	5
Chad	National Assembly (155 members)	National Assembly	4
Channel Islands (less Sark)	States of Deliberation (132 members)	The States	4
– Sark	Chief Pleas (5 members)	Chief Pleas	4
Chile	Senate (48 members)	Congress	8
	Chamber of Deputies (120 members)		4
China	National People's Congress (2,984 members)	National People's Congress	5
Colombia	Senate (102 members)	Congress	4
	House of Representatives (165 members)		4
Comoros	Senate (15 members)	Federal Assembly	6
	Legislative Council (42 members)		4
Congo, Dem. Rep. of the	New constitution yet to be finalised.	To be arranged	T. B. A.
Congo, Republic of the	Senate (66 members)	National Assembly	5
	National Assembly (137 members)		5
Costa Rica	Legislative Assembly (57 members)	Legislative Assembly	4
Côte d'Ivoire	National Assembly (225 members)	National Assembly	5
Croatia	Chamber of Counties (65 members)	Sabor (parliament)	4
	House of Representatives (151 members)		4
Cuba	National Assembly of People's Power (601 members)	National Assembly	5
Cyprus	House of Representatives (80 members)	Parliament	5
Czech Republic	Senate (81 members)	Federal Assembly	6
	Chamber of Deputies (200 members)		4
Denmark	Folketing (179 members including 2 for Greenland and the Faroes)	Folketing (parliament)	4
Djibouti	Chamber of Deputies (65 members)	National Assembly	5
Dominica	House of Assembly (30 members)	National Assembly	5
Dominican Republic	Senate (30 members)	Congress	4
	Chamber of Deputies (149 members)		4
East Timor	National Assembly (88 members)	National Assembly	T. B. A.
Ecuador	National Congress (121 members)	Congress	4
Egypt	Majlis Ash-Sha'Ab (People's Assembly) (454 members)	Majlis	5
El Salvador	Legislative Assembly (84 members)	Legislative Assembly	3
Equatorial Guinea	National Assembly (80 members)	National Assembly	5
Eritrea	Hagerawi Baito (National Assembly) (150 members)	Hagerawi Baito	4
Estonia	Riigikogu (National Assembly) (101 members)	Riigikogu	4
Ethiopia	Federation Council (108 members)	Parliament	5
	Council of People's Representatives (548 members)		5
Falkland Islands	Legislative Council (10 members)	Legislative Council	4
Faroe Islands	National Assembly (32 members)	Logting	4
Fiji Islands	Senate (32 members)	Parliament	varies
	House of Representatives (71 members)		5
Finland	Eduskunta (parliament) (200 members)	Eduskunta	4
France	Senate (321 members)	Parliament	varies
	National Assembly (577 members)		5
Gabon	Senate (91 members)	Parliament	6
	National Assembly (120 members)		5
Gambia	National Assembly (53 members)	National Assembly	5
Georgia	Parliament (235 members)	Parliament	4
Germany	Bundesrat (Federal Council) (69 members)	Parliament	varies
	Bundestag (Federal Assembly) (603 members)		4
Ghana	Parliament (230 members)	Parliament	4
Gibraltar	House of Assembly (18 members)	House of Assembly	4
Greece	Vouli Ton Ellinon (Chamber of Deputies) (300 members)	Vouli	4
Greenland	National Assembly (31 members)	Landstinget	4

Country	Name of Governmental Chambers	Name of Parliament	Years of Office
Grenada	Senate (13 members)	Parliament	5
	House of Representatives (15 members)		5
Guatemala	National Congress (113 members)	Congress	4
Guernsey	Parliament (45 members)	States of Deliberation	4
Guinea	National Assembly (114 members)	National Assembly	5
Guinea-Bissau	National People's Assembly (102 members)	National People's Assembly	4
Guyana	National Assembly (65 members)	National Assembly	5
Haiti	Senate (27 members)	National Assembly	6
	Chamber of Deputies (83 members)		4
Honduras	National Congress (128 members)	Congress	4
Hong Kong	Legislative Council (60 members)	Legislative Council	4
	Executive Council (19 members)		varies
Hungary	Országgyülés (National Assembly) (386 members)	Országgyülés	4
Iceland	Althingi (Parliament) (63 members)	Althingi	4
India	Rajya Sabha (Council of States) (245 members)	Sansad (Parliament)	6
	Lok Sabha (House of the People) (545 members)		5
Indonesia	Dewan Perwakilan Rakyat (H. of Representatives) (500 members)	Dewan Perwakilan Rakyat	5
Iran	Majles Shoraye Eslami (Islamic Ruling Council) (290 members)	Majles	4
Iraq	Majlis Watani (Council of the Nation) (250 members)	Majlis	4
Ireland	Seanad Eireann (Senate) (60 members)	Oireachtas (parliament)	5
	Dáil Eireann (House of Representatives) (166 members)		5
Israel	Knesset (Assembly) (120 members)	Knesset	4
Italy	Senate (315 members)	Parliament	5
	Chamber of Deputies (630 members)		5
Jamaica	Senate (21 members)	Parliament	5
	House of Representatives (60 members)		5
Japan	Sangiin (House of Councillors) (247 members)	Kokkai (Diet)	6
	Shugiin (House of Representatives) (480 members)		4
Jersey	Parliament (55 members)	Assembly of the States	varies
Jordan	Al-Aayan (Senate) (55 members)	Majlis Al-Umma	4
	Al-Nuwaab (House of Representatives) (110 members)		4
Kazakhstan	Senate (39 members)	Mazhilis	5
	Mazhilis (Council) (77 members)		5
Kenya	Bunge (National Assembly) (210 members)	Bunge	5
Kiribati	Maneaba Ni Maungatabu (House of Assembly) (41 members)	Unicameral	4
Korea North	Supreme People's Assembly (687 members)	National Assembly	5
Korea South	Kuk Hoe (National Assembly) (299 members)	Kuk Hoe	4
Kuwait	Majlis Al-Umma (Council of the Nation) (50 members)	Majlis	4
Kyrgyzstan	Suspended April 2005 Assembly of People's Representatives (70 members) Legislative Assembly (35 members)	Jogorku Kenesh (High Council)	5
Laos	Sapha Heng Xat (National Assembly) (109 members)	Sapha Heng Xat	5
Latvia	Saeima (Supreme Council) (100 members)	Saeima	4
Lebanon	Majlis Al-Nuwwab (Council of Deputies) (128 members)	Majlis	4
Lesotho	Senate (33 members)	Parliament	5
	National Assembly (120 members)		5
Liberia	Senate (26 members)	National Assembly	9
	House of Representatives (64 members)		6
Liechtenstein	Landtag (25 members)	Landtag	4
Lithuania	Seimas (Supreme Council) (141 members)	Seimas	4
Luxembourg	Chamber of Deputies (60 members)	Parliament	5
Macedonia	Sobranie (Assembly) (120 members)	Sobranie	4
Madagascar	National Assembly (150 members)	National Assembly	5
Malawi	National Assembly (193 members)	National Assembly	5

Country	Name of Governmental Chambers	Name of Parliament	Years of Office
Malaysia	Dewan Negara (Senate) (69 members)	Majlis	3
	Dewan Rakyat (House of Representatives) (193 members)		5
Maldives	Majlis (50 members)	Majlis	5
Mali	National Assembly (147 members)	National Assembly	5
Malta	Il-Kamra Tad-Deputati (House of Representatives) (65 members)	Il-Kamra Tad-Deputati	5
Man, Isle of	Legislative Council (11 members) House of Keys (24 members)	Tynwald	5
Marshall Islands	Nitijela (House of Assembly) (33 members)	Nitijela	4
Mauritania	Majlis-Al-Chouyoukh (Senate) (56 members)	National Assembly	6
	Al Jamiya-Al-Wataniya (National Assembly) (81 members)		5
Mauritius	National Assembly (70 members)	National Assembly	5
Mexico	Senate (128 members)	Congress	6
	Chamber of Deputies (500 members)		3
Micronesia (Federated States)	Congress (14 members, four of whom are elected for four years)	Congress	2
Moldova	Parliament (101 members)	Parliament	4
Monaco	National Council (24 members)	National Council	5
Mongolia	Ulsyn Ikh Khural (The Great Hural) (76 members)	Ulsyn Ikh Khural	4
Morocco	Majlis Nawab (Chamber of Representatives) (325 members)	Majlis	6
	Majlis al-Mustacharin (Chamber of Counsellors) (270 members)		9
Mozambique	People's Assembly (250 members)	National Assembly	5
Myanmar (Burma)	Constitutional Convention (706 members)	Constitutional Convention	T. B. A.
Namibia	National Council (26 members)	Parliament	6
	National Assembly (72 members)		5
Nauru	Parliament (18 members)	Parliament	3
Nepal	Rastriya Sabha (National Council) (60 members)	Parliament	6
	Pratinidhi Sabja (House of Representatives) (205 members)		5
Netherlands	First Chamber (75 members)	States General	4
	Second Chamber (150 members)		4
New Zealand	House of Representatives (120 members)	Parliament	3
Nicaragua	National Assembly (90 members)	National Assembly	6
Niger	National Assembly (113 members)	National Assembly	5
Nigeria	Senate (109 members)	National Assembly	4
	House of Representatives (360 members)		4
Norway	Lagting (25% of Storting membership)	Storting(et) (165 members)	4
	Odelsting (75% of Storting membership)		4
Oman	Majlis al Shura (Council of State) (83 members)	Majlis	4
	Majlis al-Dawla (58 members)		3
Pakistan	Senate (87 members)	Majlis-e-Shoora	3
	National Assembly (342 members)		4
Palau	Senate (14 members)	Olbiil Era Kelulau (Congress)	4
	House of Delegates (16 members)		4
Panama	Legislative Assembly (71 members)	Legislative Assembly	5
Papua New Guinea	National Parliament (109 members)	Parliament	5
Paraguay	Senate (45 members)	Congress	5
	Chamber of Deputies (80 members)		5
Peru	National Congress (120 members)	Congress	5
Philippines	Senate (24 members)	Congress	6
	House of Representatives (250 members)		3
Poland	Senate (100 members)	Sejm	4
	Sejm (Parliament) (460 members)		4
Portugal	Assembly of the Republic (230 members)	Assembly of the Republic	4
Qatar	No established parliament although the Amir is advised by a 30-member Council of Ministers		
Romania	Senate (140 members)	Parliament	4
	Chamber of Deputies (345 members)		4
Russia	Soviet Federation (178 members)	Federal Assembly	varies
	Duma (450 members)		4
Rwanda	National Transitional Assembly (53 members)	National Transitional Assembly	5
Saint Kitts and Nevis	National Assembly (14 members)	National Assembly	5

Country	Name of Governmental Chambers	Name of Parliament	Years of Office
Saint Lucia	Senate (11 members)	National Assembly	5
	National Assembly (18 members)		5
Saint Vincent and Grenadines	National Assembly (21 members)	National Assembly	5
Samoa	Legislative Assembly (49 members)	Legislative Assembly	5
San Marino	Consiglio grande e generale (60 members)	Consiglio grande e generale	5
São Tomé and Principe	National Assembly (55 members)	National Assembly	4
Saudi Arabia	Majlis al Shura (Council of State) (121 members)	Majlis	varies
Senegal	National Assembly (120 members)	National Assembly	5
Serbia and Montenegro	National Assembly (126 members)	National Assembly	2
Seychelles	National Assembly (34 members)	National Assembly	5
Sierra Leone	Parliament (124 members)	Parliament	5
Singapore	Parliament (84 members)	Parliament	5
Slovakia	National Council (150 members)	National Council	4
Slovenia	State Council (40 members)	National Assembly	5
	National Assembly (90 members)		4
Solomon Islands	Parliament (50 members)	Parliament	4
Somalia	National Assembly (245 members)	National Assembly	varies
South Africa	National Council of Provinces (90 members)	Volksraad	5
	Volksraad (National Assembly) (400 members)		5
Spain	Congress Senate (259 members)	Cortes Generales	4
	Congress of Deputies (350 members)		4
Sri Lanka	Parliament (225 members)	Parliament	6
Sudan	Majlis Watani (Council of the Nation) (360 members)	Majlis	4
Suriname	National Assembly (51 members)	National Assembly	5
Swaziland	Senate (30 members)	Libandla (Parliament)	5
	House of Assembly (65 members)		5
Sweden	Riksdag (349 members)	Riksdag(en)	4
Switzerland	Council of States (46 members)	Federal Assembly	4
	National Council (200 members)		4
Syria	Majlis Al-Chaab (250 members)	Majlis	4
Tadzhikstan	Majlisi Milliy (34 members)	Majlis Oli (Supreme Council)	5
	Majlisi Namoyandogon (63 members)		5
Taiwan	Yuan (225 members)	Yuan	3
Tanzania	Bunge (National Assembly) (296 members)	Bunge	5
Thailand	Wuthisapha (Senate) (200 members)	Rathasapha (Parliament)	6
	Saphaphuthan Ratsadon (National Assembly) (500 members)		4
Togo	National Assembly (81 members)	National Assembly	5
Tonga	Fale Alea (Legislative Assembly) (30 members)	Fale Alea	3
Trinidad and Tobago	Senate (31 members)	Parliament	5
	House of Representatives (36 members)		5
Tunisia	Majlis Al-Nuwwab (Council of Deputies) (182 members)	Majlis	5
Turkey	Millet Meclisi (National Assembly) (550 members)	Millet Meclisi	5
Turkmenistan	Mejlis (Council) (50 members)	Mejlis	5
Tuvalu	Parliament (15 members)	Parliament	4
Uganda	Parliament (303 members)	Parliament	5
Ukraine	Verkhovna Rada (Supreme Council) (450 members)	Verkhovna Rada	4
United Arab Emirates	Majlis Watani Itihad (Federal National Council) (360 members)	Majlis	2
United Kingdom	House of Lords (688 members as at 31 July 2002)	Parliament	varies
	House of Commons (659 members)		5
USA	Senate (Upper House of 100 members serve for 6 yrs)	Congress	6
	House of Representatives (435 members serve for 2 yrs)		2
Uruguay	Senate (31 members)	Congress	5
	Chamber of Deputies (99 members)		5
Uzbekistan	Senate (100 members)	Oliy Majlis	5
	Legislative Chamber (120 members)		5
Vanuatu	Parliament (52 members)	Parliament	4

Country	Name of Governmental Chambers	Name of Parliament	Years of Office
Venezuela	National Assembly (165 members)	National Assembly	5
Vietnam	Quoc Hoi (National Assembly) (500 members)	Quoc Hoi	5
Virgin Islands (US)	Senate (15 members)	Parliament	2
Yemen	Majlis Annowab (Council of Representatives) (301 members)	Majlis	6
	Shura Council (111 members)		varies
Yugoslavia	Vece Republika (Chamber of the Republics) (40 members)	Skupstina SRJ	5
	Vece Gradjana (Chamber of Citizens) (138 members)		4
Zambia	House of Assembly (150 members)	National Assembly	5
Zimbabwe	House of Assembly (150 members)	National Assembly	5

POLITICS

British Prime Ministers

Name	Term of Office	Party	Education	Constituency	Marriage(s)	Buried
1 Sir Robert Walpole (earl of Orford) (1676–1745)	1721–1742	Whig	Eton & Cambridge (King's)	Castle Rising (1701–2) King's Lynn (1702–42)	Catherine Shorter Maria Skerrett	Houghton, Norfolk
2 Sir Spencer Compton (earl of Wilmington) (1673–1743)	1742–1743	Whig	St Pauls & Oxford (Trinity)	Eye (Suffolk) (1698–1710) East Grinstead (1713–15) Sussex (1715–28)	Unmarried	Compton Wynates, Warwickshire
3 Henry Pelham (1695–1754)	1743–1754	Whig	Westminster & Oxford (Hart Hall)	Seaford (1717–22) Sussex (1722–54)	Catherine Manners	Laughton Church, nr Lewes, E. Sussex
4 Thomas Pelham-Holles (duke of Newcastle) (1693–1768)	1754–1756	Whig	Westminster & Cambridge (Clare)	House of Lords	Henrietta Godolphin	Laughton Church, nr Lewes, E. Sussex
5 William Cavendish (duke of Devonshire) (1720–1764)	1756–1757	Whig	private education	Derbyshire (1741–51)	Baroness Clifford	Derby Cathedral
6 Thomas Pelham-Holles (duke of Newcastle) (1693–1768)	1757–1762	Whig	Westminster & Cambridge (Clare)	House of Lords	Henrietta Godolphin	Laughton Church, nr Lewes, E. Sussex
7 John Stuart (earl of Bute) (1713–1792)	1762–1763	Tory	Eton	House of Lords	Mary Wortley-Montagu	Rothesay, Bute
8 George Grenville (1712–1770)	1763–1765	Whig	Eton & Oxford (Christ Church)	Buckingham (1741–70)	Elizabeth Wyndham	Wotton, Bucks
9 Charles Watson Wentworth (marquis of Rockingham) (1730–1782)	1765–1766	Whig	Westminster & Cambridge (St John's)	House of Lords	Mary Bright	York Minster
10 Augustus Henry Fitzroy (duke of Grafton) (1735–1811)	1766–1770	Whig	Westminster & Cambridge (Peterhouse)	Bury St Edmunds (1756)	Anne Liddell Elizabeth Wrottesley	Euston, Suffolk
11 Lord Frederick North (earl of Guildford) (1732–1792)	1770–1782	Tory	Eton, Oxford (Trinity), Leipzig	Banbury (1754–90)	Anne Speke	All Saints, Wroxton, Oxfordshire
12 Charles Watson Wentworth (marquis of Rockingham) (1730–1782)	1782	Whig	Westminster & Cambridge (St John's)	House of Lords	Mary Bright	York Minster
13 William Petty (earl of Shelburne) (1737–1805)	1782–1783	Whig	Oxford (Christ Church)	Chipping Wycombe (1760–61)	Sophia Carteret Louisa FitzPatrick	High Wycombe
14 William Henry Cavendish-Bentinck (duke of Portland) (1738–1809)	1783	Coalition	Eton & Oxford (Christ Church)	Weobly, Herefordshire (1761–2) (as Whig)	Dorothy Cavendish	St Marylebone, London
15 William Pitt the Younger (1759–1806)	1783–1801	Tory	Cambridge (Pembroke Hall)	Appleby (1781–1806)	Unmarried	Westminster Abbey
16 Henry Addington (Viscount Sidmouth) (1757–1844)	1801–1804	Tory	Cheam, Winchester, Lincoln's Inn & Oxford (Brasenose)	Devizes (1784–1805)	Ursula Mary Hammond Marianne Townshend	Mortlake
17 William Pitt the Younger (1759–1806)	1804–1806	Tory	Cambridge (Pembroke Hall)	Appleby (1781–1806)	Unmarried	Westminster Abbey
18 William Wyndham Grenville (1759–1834)	1806–1807	Coalition	Eton, Oxford (Christ Church), Lincoln's Inn	Buckingham (1782–4) Buckinghamshire (1784–90)	Anne Pitt	Burnham, Bucks
19 William Henry Cavendish-Bentinck (duke of Portland) (1738–1809)	1807–1809	Tory	Westminster & Oxford (Christ Church)	Weobly, Herefordshire (1761–2) (as Whig)	Dorothy Cavendish	St Marylebone, London
20 Spencer Perceval (1762–1812)	1809–1812	Tory	Harrow & Cambridge (Trinity)	Northampton	Jane Spencer-Wilson	Charlton

Name	Term of Office	Party	Education	Constituency	Marriage(s)	Buried
21 Robert Banks Jenkinson (earl of Liverpool) (1770–1828)	1812–1827	Tory	Charterhouse & Oxford (Christ Church)	Rye (1791–1803) elected for Appleby 1790 too young see note 4 below	Louisa Theodosia Hervey, Mary Chester	Hawkesbury
22 George Canning (1770–1827)	1827	Tory	Eton, Oxford (Christ Church), Lincoln's Inn		Joan Scott	Westminster Abbey
23 Frederick John Robinson (Viscount Goderich) (1782–1859)	1827–1828	Tory	Harrow, Cambridge (St John's), Lincoln's Inn	Carlow (1806–7) & Ripon (1807–27)	Sarah Hobart	Nocton, Lincs
24 Arthur Wellesley (duke of Wellington) (1769–1852)	1828–1830	Tory	Browns Seminary, King's Rd, Chelsea, Eton, Brussels & Angers Military Acad.	Rye (1806), Newport IOW (1807–9) St Michael (1807)	Catherine Pakenham	St Paul's Cathedral
25 Charles Grey (Earl Grey) (1764–1845)	1830–1834	Whig	Eton, Cambridge (Trinity) & Middle Temple	Northumberland (1786–1807) Appleby (1807), Tavistock (1807)	Mary Elizabeth Ponsonby	Howick House, Northumberland
26 Henry William Lamb (Viscount Melbourne) (1779–1848)	1834	Whig	Eton, Cambridge (Trinity), Glasgow, Lincoln's Inn	see n. 4 below	Caroline Ponsonby	Hatfield
27 Robert Peel (1788–1850)	1834–1835	Tory	Harrow, Oxford (Christ Church), Lincoln's Inn	see n. 4 below	Julia Floyd	Drayton Bassett
28 Henry William Lamb (Viscount Melbourne) (1779–1848)	1835–1841	Whig	Eton, Cambridge (Trinity), Glasgow, Lincoln's Inn	see n. 4 below	Caroline Ponsonby	Hatfield
29 Robert Peel (1788–1850)	1841–1846	Conservative	Harrow, Oxford (Christ Church), Lincoln's Inn	see n. 4 below	Julia Floyd	Drayton Bassett
30 John Russell (Earl Russell) (1792–1878)	1846–1852	Whig	Westminster & Edinburgh	see n. 4 below	Abigail Lister, Lady Frances Elliot	Chenies, Bucks
31 Edward George Stanley (earl of Derby) (1799–1869)	1852	Conservative	Eton & Oxford (Christ Church)	see n. 4 below	Emma Wilbraham-Bootle	Knowsley, Lancs
32 George Hamilton Gordon (earl of Aberdeen) (1784–1860)	1852–1855	Conservative (Peelite)	Harrow & Cambridge (St John's)	House of Lords	Catherine Hamilton, Harriet Douglas	Stanmore, Gtr London
33 Henry John Temple (Viscount Palmerston) (1784–1865)	1855–1858	Liberal	Harrow, Edinburgh, Cambridge (St John's)	see n. 4 below	Emile Lamb the Dowager Countess Cowper	Westminster Abbey
34 Edward George Stanley (earl of Derby) (1799–1869)	1858–1859	Conservative	Eton & Oxford (Christ Church)	see n. 4 below	Emma Wilbraham-Bootle	Knowsley, Lancs
35 Henry John Temple (Viscount Palmerston) (1784–1865)	1859–1865	Liberal	Harrow, Edinburgh, Cambridge (St John's)	see n. 4 below	Emile Lamb the Dowager Countess Cowper	Westminster Abbey
36 John Russell (Earl Russell) (1792–1878)	1865–1866	Liberal	Westminster & Edinburgh	see n. 4 below	Abigail Lister, Lady Frances Elliot	Chenies, Bucks
37 Edward George Stanley (earl of Derby) (1799–1869)	1866–1868	Conservative	Eton & Oxford (Christ Church)	see n. 4 below	Emma Wilbraham-Bootle	Knowsley, Lancs

POLITICS

Name	Term of Office	Party	Education	Constituency	Marriage(s)	Buried
38 Benjamin Disraeli (earl of Beaconsfield) (1804–1881)	1868	Conservative	Lincoln's Inn	Maidstone (1837–41), Shrewsbury (1841–7), Buckinghamshire (1847–76)	Mrs Wyndham Lewis née Mary Ann Evans	Hughenden Manor, Buckinghamshire
39 William Ewart Gladstone (1809–1898)	1868–1874	Liberal	Seaforth Vicarage, Eton, Oxford (Christ Church)	see n. 4 below	Catherine Glynne	Westminster Abbey
40 Benjamin Disraeli (earl of Beaconsfield) (1804–1881)	1874–1880	Conservative	Lincoln's Inn	Maidstone (1837–41), Shrewsbury (1841–7), Buckinghamshire (1847–76)	Mrs Wyndham Lewis née Mary Ann Evans	Hughenden Manor, Buckinghamshire
41 William Ewart Gladstone (1809–1898)	1880–1885	Liberal	Seaforth Vicarage, Eton, Oxford (Christ Church)	see n. 4 below	Catherine Glynne	Westminster Abbey
42 Robert Arthur Talbot Cecil (marquis of Salisbury) (1830–1903)	1885–1886	Conservative	Eton & Oxford (Christ Church)	Stamford (1853–68)	Georgiana Alderson	Hatfield
43 William Ewart Gladstone (1809–1898)	1886	Liberal	Seaforth Vicarage, Eton, Oxford (Christ Church)	see n. 4 below	Catherine Glynne	Westminster Abbey
44 Robert Arthur Talbot Cecil (marquis of Salisbury) (1830–1903)	1886–1892	Conservative	Eton & Oxford (Christ Church)	Stamford (1853–68)	Georgiana Alderson	Hatfield
45 William Ewart Gladstone (1809–1898)	1892–1894	Liberal	Seaforth Vicarage, Eton, Oxford (Christ Church)	see n. 4 below	Catherine Glynne	Westminster Abbey
46 Archibald Philip Primrose (earl of Rosebery) (1847–1929)	1894–1895	Liberal	Eton & Oxford (Christ Church)	House of Lords	Hannah de Rothschild	Dalmeny
47 Robert Arthur Talbot Cecil (marquis of Salisbury) (1830–1903)	1895–1902	Conservative	Eton & Oxford (Christ Church)	Stamford (1853–68)	Georgiana Alderson	Hatfield
48 Arthur Balfour (earl of Balfour) (1848–1930)	1902–1905	Conservative	Eton & Cambridge (Trinity)	Hertford (1874–85), E. Manchester (1885–1906), London (1906–22)	Unmarried	Whittinghame, East Lothian
49 Henry Campbell-Bannerman (1836–1908)	1905–1908	Liberal	Glasgow & Cambridge (Trinity)	Stirling (1868–1908)	Sarah Charlotte Bruce	Meigle, Scotland
50 Herbert Henry Asquith (earl of Oxford) (1852–1928)	1908–1916	Liberal	City of London & Oxford (Balliol)	East Fife (1886–1918), Paisley (1920–4)	Helen Kelsall Melland Emma Tennant	Sutton Courtney Church, Bucks
51 David Lloyd George (earl of Dwyfor) (1863–1945)	1916–1922	Coalition	Llanystumdwy Church School	Caernarvon (1890–1945)	Margaret Owen Frances Stevenson	Bank of River Dwyfor
52 Andrew Bonar Law (1858–1923)	1922–1923	Conservative	Gilbertfield in Hamilton & Glasgow High School	see n. 4 below	Annie Pitcairn Robley	Westminster Abbey
53 Stanley Baldwin (1867–1947) (Earl Baldwin of Bewdley)	1923–1924	Conservative	Harrow & Cambridge (Trinity)	Bewdley, Worcs (1908–37)	Lucy Ridsdale	Worcester Cathedral
54 James Ramsay MacDonald (1866–1937)	1924	Labour	Drainie Parish Board School	see n. 4 below	Margaret Gladstone	Spynie Churchyard, Lossiemouth
55 Stanley Baldwin (1867–1947) (Earl Baldwin of Bewdley)	1924–1929	Conservative	Harrow & Cambridge (Trinity)	Bewdley, Worcs (1908–37)	Lucy Ridsdale	Worcester Cathedral

Name	Term of Office	Party	Education	Constituency	Marriage(s)	Buried
56 James Ramsay MacDonald (1866–1937)	1929–1935	Labour	Drainie Parish Board School	see n. 4 below	Margaret Gladstone	Spynie Churchyard, Lossiemouth
57 Stanley Baldwin (1867–1947) (Earl Baldwin of Bewdley)	1935–1937	National	Harrow & Cambridge (Trinity)	Bewdley, Worcs (1908–37)	Lucy Ridsdale	Worcester Cathedral
58 Neville Chamberlain (1869–1940)	1937–1940	National	Rugby & Mason College (later Birmingham University)	Ladywood, Birmingham (1918–29) Edgbaston (1929–40)	Annie Vere Cole	Westminster Abbey (ashes)
59 Winston Leonard Spencer Churchill (1874–1965)	1940–1945	Coalition	Harrow & Royal Military College, Sandhurst	see n. 4 below	Clementine Ogilvy Hozier	Bladon, Oxfordshire
60 Clement Attlee (1883–1967)	1945–1951	Labour	Haileybury Coll. & Oxford (University)	Limehouse, Stepney (1922–50) West Walthamstow (1950–5)	Violet Millar	Westminster Abbey
61 Winston Leonard Spencer Churchill (1874–1965)	1951–1955	Conservative	Harrow & Royal Military College, Sandhurst	see n. 4 below	Clementine Ogilvy Hozier	Bladon, Oxfordshire
62 Anthony Eden (earl of Avon) (1897–1977)	1955–1957	Conservative	Eton & Oxford (Christ Church)	Warwick & Leamington (1923–57)	Beatrice Beckett Anne Spencer-Churchill	Alvediston, Wiltshire
63 Maurice Harold Macmillan (earl of Stockton) (1894–1986)	1957–1963	Conservative	Eton & Oxford (Balliol)	Stockton on Tees (1924–9 & 1931–45), Bromley (1945–64)	Dorothy Cavendish	Horsted Keynes
64 Alexander Frederick Douglas-Home (Lord Home of the Hirsel) (1903–1995)	1963–1964	Conservative	Eton & Oxford (Christ Church)	S. Lanark (1931–45), Lanark (1950–1), Kinross & West Perthshire (1963–74)	Elizabeth Alington	Coldstream
65 James Harold Wilson (1916–1995) (Lord Wilson of Rievaulx)	1964–1970	Labour	Milnsbridge, Royds Hall, Wirral, Oxford (Jesus)	Ormskirk (1945–50) Huyton (1950–83)	Gladys Mary Baldwin	Scilly Isles
66 Edward Heath (1916–)	1970–1974	Conservative	Chatham House, Ramsgate, Oxford (Balliol)	Bexley (1950–74), Bexley–Sidcup (1974–83), Old Bexley and Sidcup (1983–2001)	Unmarried	
67 James Harold Wilson (1916–1995) (Lord Wilson of Rievaulx)	1974–1976	Labour	Milnsbridge, Royds Hall, Wirral, Oxford (Jesus)	Ormskirk (1945–50) Huyton (1950–83)	Gladys Mary Baldwin	Scilly Isles
68 Leonard James Callaghan (Lord Callaghan of Cardiff) (1912–2005)	1976–1979	Labour	Portsmouth Northern Sec.	South Cardiff (1945–50), SE Cardiff (1950–83), Cardiff South and Penarth (1983–87)	Audrey Moulton	
69 Margaret Hilda Thatcher (1925–) (Baroness Thatcher of Kesteven)	1979–1990	Conservative	Kesteven & Grantham, Oxford (Somerville)	Finchley (1959–74), Barnet, Finchley (1974–92)	Denis Thatcher	
70 John Major (1943–)	1990–1997	Conservative	Rutlish Grammar	Huntingdon (1983 to present)	Norma Johnson	
71 Tony Blair (1953–)	1997–	Labour	Durham Choristers, Fettes (Edinburgh), Oxford (St John's)	Sedgefield (1983 to present)	Cherie Booth	

POLITICS

Notes

1 Prime Minister Although the office of prime minister is traditionally stated as commencing in 1721, in fact there were chief ministers given this label long before this date, and conversely there have been chief ministers subsequent to this date who did not bear the title of prime minister, e.g. William Pitt the Elder and Charles James Fox, in the mid- and late 18th century. To confuse matters further, Walpole was designated First Lord of the Treasury until 1730, as were some other future prime ministers of the 18th and 19th centuries. It was not until 1905 that the title of prime minister became official.

2 Party A second point of conjecture concerns the designation of the ruling party of the day. Until the first Electoral Reform Act of 1832 and the subsequent rise of the Conservative and Liberal parties, the government of the day was often a coalition of sorts, and the ruling party is given as the party of the prime minister in power, unless unaffiliated.

3 Chief ministers not listed above Sir William Pulteney, earl of Bath, actually kissed the hand of George II on 10 Feb. 1746, but within three days was unable to form a government. James Waldegrave kissed the hand of George II on 8 June 1757 but returned seals on 12 June, unable to form a ministry. Charles James Fox and his erstwhile enemy Lord North were the de facto heads of government in 1783, while the duke of Portland was merely the nominal prime minister. William Pitt the Elder, earl of Chatham, although not included in the table above, was in effect the prime minister from 1756 to 1761 during most of the Seven Years' War, although never taking up official office. From 1766 to 1768 Pitt was also Head of the Government but chose the secondary post of Lord Privy Seal; gout prevented him serving in anything but name for this second term.

4 Constituencies: See numbers in table above

(22) George Canning's constituencies: Newport IOW (1793–6 & 1806–7), Wendover (1796–1802), Tralee (1802–6), Hastings (1807–12), Liverpool (1812–23), Harwich (1823–6), Newport IOW (1826–7) & Seaford (1827).

(26) Viscount Melbourne's constituencies: Leominster (1806), Haddington Borough (1806–7), Portarlington (1807–12), Peterborough (1816–19), Hertfordshire (1819–26) Newport IOW (1827), Bletchingley (1827–8).

(27) Robert Peel's constituencies: Cashel (Tipperary) (1809–12), Chippenham (1812–17), Oxford University (1817–29), Westbury (1829–30), Tamworth (1830–50).

(30) Earl Russell's constituencies: Tavistock (1813–17, 1818–20, 1830–1), Huntingdonshire (1820–6), Bandon (1826–30), Devon (1831–2), South Devon (1832–5), Stroud (1835–41), London (1841–61).

(31) Earl of Derby's constituencies: Stockbridge (1822–6), Preston (1826–30), Windsor (1831–2), North Lancs (1832–44).

(33) Viscount Palmerston's constituencies: Newport IOW (1807–11), Cambridge University (1811–31), Bletchingley (1831–2), South Hants (1832–4), Tiverton (1835–65).

(39) William Gladstone's constituencies: Newark (1832–45 as Tory), Oxford University (1847–65 as Peelite until 1859 then Liberal), South Lancs (1865–8), Greenwich (1868–80), Midlothian (1880–95).

(52) Andrew Bonar Law's constituencies: Blackfriars, Glasgow (1900–6), Dulwich (1906–10), Bootle (1911–18), Central Glasgow (1918–23).

(54) Ramsay MacDonald's constituencies: Leicester (1906–18), Aberavon (1922–9), Seaham, Co. Durham (1929–31), Scottish Universities (1936–7).

(59) Winston Churchill's constituencies: Oldham (1900–6, Conservative until 1904 then Liberal), NW Manchester (1906–8), Dundee (1908–22), Epping (1924–45), Woodford, Essex (1945–64 as Conservative).

5 Miscellaneous information

(2) Sir Spencer Compton was a Tory until 1704.

(8) George Grenville was nicknamed the Gentle Shepherd.

(9) Charles Watson Wentworth repealed the Stamp Act.

(10) Augustus Henry Fitzroy, the duke of Grafton, was a victim of the pseudonymous Junius letters which attacked various government ministers in the London *Public Advertiser* (1769–72), although the identity of Junius remains unknown. Sir Philip Francis is a possible candidate. He was also a direct descendant of the illegitimate son of Charles II.

(11) Lord Frederick North became a Whig in 1783.

(13) William Petty, the earl of Shelburne, was nicknamed Malagrida, after a notorious scheming Jesuit. He sat in the English House of Lords in his father's English title of Baron Wycombe.

(18) William Wyndham Grenville's administration of February 1806–March 1807 was known as 'The Ministry of All the Talents' and comprised followers of Charles James Fox. Its greatest achievement was the abolition of slavery in March 1807. He was the son of George Grenville (PM 1763–65).

(20) Spencer Perceval was assassinated by John Bellingham in the lobby of the Commons.

(21) Robert Banks Jenkinson was created Lord Hawkesbury in 1803 and earl of Liverpool in 1808.

(22) George Canning fought a duel with Viscount Castlereagh on Putney Heath in September 1809 but was only slightly wounded.

(24) Arthur Wellesley, duke of Wellington, was known as Arthur Wesley until 1804.

(27) Robert Peel created the Metropolitan Police Force in 1829 and drafted the 'Tamworth Manifesto' which laid down the ideology and objectives of the party which became the Conservatives. He died after a fall from a horse.

(30) Abigail Lister, the wife of Lord John Russell, became Baroness Ribblesdale.

(31) Edward George Stanley, the earl of Derby, became a Tory in 1835 (previously a Whig).

(33) Henry John Temple, Viscount Palmerston, was a Tory until 1829, then a Whig, and finally a Liberal. He was the last Prime Minister to die in office.

(42) Robert Arthur Talbot Gascoyne-Cecil was also known as Viscount Cranborne.

(48) Arthur James Balfour was the son of James Balfour MP and his wife, the sister of the third marquess of Salisbury, later the Conservative Prime Minister.

(49) Henry Campbell-Bannerman died at 10 Downing Street, three weeks after resigning.
(50) Herbert Henry Asquith's administration was a coalition from 1915.
(52) Andrew Bonar Law was born in New Brunswick, Canada. His term of office was 209 days.
(53) Stanley Baldwin was related to Rudyard Kipling and Sir Edward Burne-Jones.
(59) Winston Churchill's first administration became Conservative from 23 May 1945.
(62) Anthony Eden's second wife was the niece of the former Prime Minister Winston Churchill.

6 William Pitt (the Elder) (1708–1778) Educated at Eton and Trinity College, Oxford. In 1735 he entered the House of Commons as member for the family borough of Old Sarum. In 1756 Pitt became nominally Secretary of State but was de facto Prime Minister from 1756 until October 1761. The King invited him to form a further government between 1766 and 1768 but he chose the secondary title of Lord Privy Seal while performing Prime Ministerial duties. Chronic gout caused a severe decline in his mental health and he died after making a speech in the House of Lords on 2 April 1778. His second son was William Pitt the Younger.

Members of Cabinet

(formed by the Rt. Hon. Tony Blair on 5 May 2005)

Tony Blair	Prime Minister, First Lord of the Treasury and Minister For the Civil Service
John Prescott	Deputy Prime Minister and First Secretary of State
Gordon Brown	Chancellor of the Exchequer
Jack Straw	Secretary of State for Foreign and Commonwealth Affairs
	Previous incumbent Robin Cook (May 1997 to June 2001)
Lord Falconer of Thoroton	Lord Chancellor and Secretary of State for Constitutional Affairs
Charles Clarke	Secretary of State for the Home Department
	Previous incumbents Jack Straw (May 1997 to June 2001) and David Blunkett (June 2001 to Dec 2004)
Ruth Kelly	Secretary of State for Education and Skills
	Previous incumbents David Blunkett (May 1997 to June 2001 when Education and Employment), Estelle Morris (June 2001 to Oct 2002) and Charles Clarke (Oct 2002 to Dec 2004)
Geoff Hoon	Leader of the House of Commons and Lord Privy Seal
	Previous incumbents Ann Taylor (May 1997 to July 1998), Margaret Beckett (July 1998 to June 2001), Robin Cook (June 2001 to Mar 2003) and Peter Hain (Mar 2003 to May 2005)
Alistair Darling	Secretary of State for Scotland
	Previous incumbents Donald Dewar (1997 to 1999) and Dr John Reid (May 1999 to Jan 2001)
Dr John Reid	Secretary of State for Defence
	Previous incumbents Lord George Robertson (May 1997 to Oct 1999) and Geoff Hoon (Oct 1999 to May 2005)
Patricia Hewitt	Secretary of State for Health
	Previous incumbents Frank Dobson (May 1997 to Oct 1999), Alan Milburn (Oct 1999 to June 2003) and Dr John Reid (June 2003 to May 2005)
Hilary Armstrong	Chief Whip and Parliamentary Secretary to the Treasury
	Previous incumbents Nick Brown (May 1997 to July 1998) and Ann Taylor (July 1998 to June 2001)
Tessa Jowell	Secretary of State for Culture, Media and Sport
	Previous incumbent Chris Smith (May 1997 to June 2001)
David Blunkett	Secretary of State for Work and Pensions
	Previous incumbents Harriet Harman (May 1997 to July 1998 when Social Security), Alistair Darling (July 1998 to May 2002 when Social Security), Andrew Smith (May 2002 to Sept 2004) and Alan Johnson (Sept 2004 to May 2005)
Peter Hain	Secretary of State for Northern Ireland
	Previous incumbents Mo Mowlam (May 1997 to Oct 1999), Peter Mandelson (Oct 1999 to Jan 2001), Dr John Reid (Jan 2001 to Oct 2002) and Paul Murphy (Oct 2002 to May 2005)
Peter Hain	Secretary of State for Wales
	Previous incumbents Ron Davies (May 1997 to 1998), Alun Michael (1998 to 1999) and Paul Murphy (1999 to 2002)
Hilary Benn	Secretary of State for International Development
	Previous incumbents Clare Short (June 2001 to May 2003), Baroness Amos (May to Oct 2003)
Baroness Amos	Leader of the House of Lords and Lord President of the Council
	Previous incumbents Lord Richard of Ammanford (May 1997 to July 1998), Baroness Jay of Paddington (July 1998 to June 2001) and Lord Williams of Mostyn (June 2001 to Sept 2003)
Alan Johnson	Secretary of State for Trade and Industry
	Previous incumbents Margaret Beckett (May 1997 to July 1998), Peter Mandelson (July to Dec 1998), Stephen Byers (Dec 1998 to June 2001), and Patricia Hewitt (June 2001 to May 2005)

POLITICS

Des Browne	Chief Secretary to the Treasury
	Previous incumbents Alistair Darling (May 1997 to July 1998), Stephen Byers (July to Dec 1998), Alan Milburn (Dec 1998 to Oct 1999), Andrew Smith (Oct 1999 to May 2002) and Paul Boateng (May 2002 to May 2005)
Margaret Beckett	Secretary of State for Environment, Food and Rural Affairs
	Previous incumbents Jack Cunningham (May 1997 to July 1998 when Agriculture, Fisheries and Food) and Nick Brown (July 1998 to June 2001 when Agriculture, Fisheries and Food)
Alistair Darling	Secretary of State for Transport
	Previous incumbent Dr John Reid (July 1998 to May 1999)
Ian McCartney	Minister without Portfolio and Party Chair
	Previous incumbent Dr John Reid (Oct 2002 to Mar 2003)
John Hutton	Chancellor of the Duchy of Lancaster (Minister for the Cabinet Office)
David Miliband	Minister of Communities and Local Government

also attending Cabinet meetings

Douglas Alexander	Minister of State for Europe in the Foreign and Commonwealth Office
Lord Grocott	Lords Chief Whip and Captain of the Gentlemen at Arms
Lord Goldsmith, QC	Attorney General

Departments of State and Ministers

Cabinet Office

Minister and Chancellor of the Duchy of Lancaster – The Rt. Hon. John Hutton, MP
Previous incumbents David Clark (May 1997 to July 1998), Dr Jack Cunningham (July 1998 to Oct 1999), Mo Mowlam (Oct 1999 to June 2001), Lord Macdonald of Tradeston (2001 to 2003), Douglas Alexander (2003 to 2004), Alan Milburn (2004 to 2005)
Minister without Portfolio and Party Chairman – The Rt. Hon. Ian McCartney, MP
Parliamentary Secretary – Jim Murphy, MP

Constitutional Affairs

Lord Chancellor and Secretary of State for Constitutional Affairs – Lord Falconer of Thoroton, QC
Minister of State – The Rt. Hon. Harriet Harman, QC, MP
Parliamentary Under-Secretaries – Baroness Ashton of Upholland and Bridget Prentice, MP

Culture, Media and Sport

Secretary of State – The Rt. Hon. Tessa Jowell, MP
Minister of State for Sport and Tourism – The Rt. Hon. Richard Caborn, MP
Parliamentary Under-Secretaries – David Lammy, MP, and James Purnell, MP

Defence

Secretary of State – The Rt. Hon. Dr John Reid, MP
Minister of State (Armed Forces) – The Rt. Hon. Adam Ingram, MP
Parliamentary Secretary of State – Don Touhig, MP
Parliamentary Under-Secretary of State – Lord Drayson

Education and Skills

Secretary of State – The Rt. Hon. Ruth Kelly, MP
Minister of State for Children – The Rt. Hon. Beverley Hughes, MP
Minister of State for Schools – The Rt. Hon. Jacqui Smith, MP
Minister of State for Universities – Bill Rammell, MP
Parliamentary Under-Secretaries of State – Lord Adonis, Maria Eagle, MP, and Phil Hope, MP

Environment, Food and Rural Affairs

Secretary of State – The Rt. Hon. Margaret Beckett, MP
Minister of State – Elliot Morley, MP
Parliamentary Under-Secretaries – Lord Bach, Ben Bradshaw, MP, and Jim Knight, MP

Foreign and Commonwealth Office

Secretary of State – The Rt. Hon. Jack Straw, MP
Minister for Europe – Douglas Alexander, MP
Minister for the Middle East – Dr Kim Howells, MP
Minister for Trade (also DTI) – Ian Pearson, MP
Parliamentary Under-Secretary of State – Lord Triesman

Health

Secretary of State – The Rt. Hon. Patricia Hewitt, MP
Ministers of State – The Rt. Hon. Jane Kennedy, MP, Lord Warner and Rosie Winterton, MP
Parliamentary Under-Secretaries of State – Liam Byrne, MP, and Caroline Flint, MP

Home Office

Secretary of State – The Rt. Hon. Charles Clarke, MP
Ministers of State – The Rt. Hon. Hazel Blears, MP, Tony McNulty, MP, and The Rt.
Hon. Baroness Scotland of Asthal, QC
Parliamentary Under-Secretaries – Andy Burnham, MP, Paul Goggins, MP, and Fiona
Mactaggart, MP

International Development

Secretary of State – The Rt. Hon. Hilary Benn, MP
Parliamentary Under-Secretary – Gareth Thomas, MP

Law Officers

Attorney General – Lord Goldsmith, QC
Solicitor General – The Rt. Hon. Mike O'Brien, MP
Advocate General for Scotland – Baroness Clark, QC

Northern Ireland Office

Secretary of State – The Rt. Hon. Peter Hain, MP
Ministers of State – David Hanson, MP, and Lord Rooker
Parliamentary Under-Secretaries of State – Angela Smith, MP, and
Shaun Woodward, MP

Office of the Deputy Prime Minister

Deputy Prime Minister and First Secretary of State – The Rt. Hon. John Prescott, MP
Minister for Local Government – Phil Woolas, MP
Minister for Housing and Planning – Yvette Cooper, MP
Parliamentary Under-Secretaries – Baroness Andrews OBE and Jim Fitzpatrick, MP

Privy Council Office

Leader of the House of Commons and Lord Privy Seal – The Rt. Hon.
Geoff Hoon, MP
Deputy Leader of the House of Commons (Parliamentary Secretary) –
Nigel Griffiths, MP

Scotland Office

Secretary of State – The Rt. Hon. Alistair Darling, MP
Parliamentary Under-Secretary – David Cairns, MP

Trade and Industry

Secretary of State – Alan Johnson
Minister for Energy and the Regions – The Rt. Hon. Alun Michael, MP
Minister for Energy – Malcolm Wicks, MP
Minister for Trade (also FCO) – Ian Pearson, MP
Parliamentary Under-Secretaries – Gerry Sutcliffe, MP, Barry Gardiner, MP, Lord
Sainsbury of Turville, and Meg Munn, MP (Reporting to the Rt. Hon. Tessa Jowell
MP on equality issues)

Transport

Secretary of State for Transport – Rt. Hon. Alistair Darling, MP
Minister for Transport – Dr Stephen Ladyman, MP
Parliamentary Under-Secretaries – Derek Twigg, MP, and Karen Buck, MP

Treasury

Prime Minister, First Lord of the Treasury and Minister for Civil Service – The Rt. Hon.
Tony Blair, MP
Chancellor of the Exchequer – The Rt. Hon. Gordon Brown, MP
Financial Secretary – The Rt. Hon. John Healey, MP
Paymaster General – The Rt. Hon. Dawn Primarolo, MP
Economic Secretary – Ivan Lewis, MP
Lords Commissioners – Vernon Coaker, MP, Gillian Merron, MP, Joan Ryan, MP, Tom
Watson, MP, Dave Watts, MP
Assistant Whips – Kevin Brennan, MP, Alan Campbell, MP, Ian Cawsey, MP, Tony
Cunningham, MP, Parmjit Dhanda, MP, Frank Roy, MP, Claire Ward, MP
Prime Minister's Parliamentary Private Secretary – The Rt. Hon. Keith Hill, MP

Welsh Office

Secretary of State – The Rt. Hon. Peter Hain, MP
Parliamentary Under-Secretary – Nick Ainger, MP

POLITICS

Work and Pensions

Secretary of State for Work and Pensions – The Rt. Hon. David Blunkett, MP
Minister for Work – The Rt. Hon. Margaret Hodge, MBE, MP
Minister for Pensions – The Rt. Hon. Stephen Timms, MP
Parliamentary Secretary of State – Lord Hunt of Kingsheath
Parliamentary Under-Secretaries of State – Anne McGuire, MP, and James Plaskitt, MP

Her Majesty's Household

Lord Chamberlain – The Rt. Hon. Lord Luce GCVO
Lord Steward – Duke of Abercorn
Master of the Horse – Lord Vestey
Mistress of the Robes – The Duchess of Grafton, GCVO
Deputy Chief Whip and Treasurer – Rt. Hon. Bob Ainsworth, MP
Comptroller – Thomas McAvoy, MP
Vice-Chamberlain – John Heppell, MP
Lord Chief Whip and Captain of the Honourable Corps of Gentlemen-At-Arms – Rt. Hon. Lord Grocott
Deputy Chief Whip (House of Lords) and Captain of the Queen's Yeomen of the Guard – Lord Davies of Oldham
Lords in Waiting – Lord Evans of Temple Guiting, Lord McKenzie of Luton, Lord Bassam of Brighton
Baronesses-in-Waiting – Baroness Crawley, Baroness Farrington of Ribbleton, Baroness Royall of Blaisdon
Second Church Estates Commissioner, representing Church Commissioners – Sir Stuart Bell, MP

Note
As at May 2005 the basic salary of Cabinet ministers was £130,347.
The Prime Minister's basic salary was £178,922 and the Lord Chancellor's £98,899 (although entitled to £207,736).
The First Minister of Scotland is Jack McConnell, representing Motherwell & Wishaw in the Scottish Parliament.
The First Minister of Wales is Rhodri Morgan, representing Cardiff West in the Welsh Assembly.
The Northern Ireland Assembly was suspended on 28 April 2003.

General Election Results by Candidate: 5 May 2005

Abbott, Diane	Hackney North & Stoke Newington	*Labour*
Adams, Gerry	Belfast West	*Sinn Fein*
Afriyie, Adam	Windsor	*Conservative*
Ainger, Nick	Carmarthen West & Pembrokeshire South	*Labour*
Ainsworth, Bob	Coventry North East	*Labour*
Ainsworth, Peter	Surrey East	*Conservative*
Alexander, Danny	Inverness, Nairn, Badenoch & Strathspey	*Liberal Democrat*
Alexander, Douglas	Paisley & Renfrewshire South	*Labour*
Allen, Graham	Nottingham North	*Labour*
Amess, David	Southend West	*Conservative*
Ancram, Michael	Devizes	*Conservative*
Anderson, David	Blaydon	*Labour*
Anderson, Janet	Rossendale & Darwen	*Labour*
Arbuthnot, James	Hampshire North East	*Conservative*
Armstrong, Hilary	Durham North West	*Labour*
Atkins, Charlotte	Staffordshire Moorlands	*Labour*
Atkinson, Peter	Hexham	*Conservative*
Austin, Ian	Dudley North	*Labour*
Austin, John	Erith & Thamesmead	*Labour*
Bacon, Richard	Norfolk South	*Conservative*
Bailey, Adrian	West Bromwich West	*Labour Co-op*
Baird, Vera	Redcar	*Labour*
Baker, Norman	Lewes	*Liberal Democrat*
Baldry, Tony	Banbury	*Conservative*
Balls, Ed	Normanton	*Labour Co-op*
Banks, Gordon	Ochil & Perthshire South	*Labour*
Barker, Greg	Bexhill & Battle	*Conservative*
Barlow, Celia	Hove	*Labour*
Baron, John	Billericay	*Conservative*
Barrett, John	Edinburgh West	*Liberal Democrat*
Barron, Kevin	Rother Valley	*Labour*
Battle, John	Leeds West	*Labour*
Bayley, Hugh	York, City of	*Labour*
Beckett, Margaret	Derby South	*Labour*
Begg, Anne	Aberdeen South	*Labour*

Beith, Alan	Berwick-upon-Tweed	*Liberal Democrat*
Bell, Sir Stuart	Middlesbrough	*Labour*
Bellingham, Henry	Norfolk North West	*Conservative*
Benn, Hilary	Leeds Central	*Labour*
Benton, Joe	Bootle	*Labour*
Benyon, Richard	Newbury	*Conservative*
Bercow, John	Buckingham	*Conservative*
Beresford, Sir Paul	Mole Valley	*Conservative*
Berry, Roger	Kingswood	*Labour*
Betts, Clive	Sheffield Attercliffe	*Labour*
Binley, Brian	Northampton South	*Conservative*
Blackman, Liz	Erewash	*Labour*
Blackman-Woods, Roberta	Durham, City of	*Labour*
Blair, Tony	Sedgefield	*Labour*
Blears, Hazel	Salford	*Labour*
Blizzard, Bob	Waveney	*Labour*
Blunkett, David	Sheffield Brightside	*Labour*
Blunt, Crispin	Reigate	*Conservative*
Bone, Peter	Wellingborough	*Conservative*
Borrow, David	Ribble South	*Labour*
Boswell, Tim	Daventry	*Conservative*
Bottomley, Peter	Worthing West	*Conservative*
Bradshaw, Ben	Exeter	*Labour*
Brady, Graham	Altrincham & Sale West	*Conservative*
Brake, Tom	Carshalton & Wallington	*Liberal Democrat*
Brazier, Julian	Canterbury	*Conservative*
Breed, Colin	Cornwall South East	*Liberal Democrat*
Brennan, Kevin	Cardiff West	*Labour*
Brokenshire, James	Hornchurch	*Conservative*
Brooke, Annette	Dorset Mid & Poole North	*Liberal Democrat*
Brown, Gordon	Kirkcaldy & Cowdenbeath	*Labour*
Brown, Lyn	West Ham	*Labour*
Brown, Nick	Newcastle upon Tyne East & Wallsend	*Labour*
Brown, Russell	Dumfries & Galloway	*Labour*
Browne, Des	Kilmarnock & Loudoun	*Labour*
Browne, Jeremy	Taunton	*Liberal Democrat*
Browning, Angela	Tiverton & Honiton	*Conservative*
Bruce, Malcolm	Gordon	*Liberal Democrat*
Bryant, Chris	Rhondda	*Labour*
Buck, Karen	Regent's Park & Kensington North	*Labour*
Burden, Richard	Birmingham Northfield	*Labour*
Burgon, Colin	Elmet	*Labour*
Burnham, Andy	Leigh	*Labour*
Burns, Simon	Chelmsford West	*Conservative*
Burrowes, David	Enfield Southgate	*Conservative*
Burstow, Paul	Sutton & Cheam	*Liberal Democrat*
Burt, Alastair	Bedfordshire North East	*Conservative*
Burt, Lorely	Solihull	*Liberal Democrat*
Butler, Dawn	Brent South	*Labour*
Butterfill, Sir John	Bournemouth West	*Conservative*
Byers, Stephen	Tyneside North	*Labour*
Byrne, Liam	Birmingham Hodge Hill	*Labour*
Cable, Dr Vincent	Twickenham	*Liberal Democrat*
Caborn, Richard	Sheffield Central	*Labour*
Cairns, David	Inverclyde	*Labour*
Calton, Patsy**	Cheadle	*Liberal Democrat*
Cameron, David	Witney	*Conservative*
Campbell, Alan	Tynemouth	*Labour*
Campbell, Gregory	Londonderry East	*Democratic Unionist*
Campbell, Sir Menzies	Fife North East	*Liberal Democrat*
Campbell, Ronnie	Blyth Valley	*Labour*
Carmichael, Alistair	Orkney & Shetland	*Liberal Democrat*
Carswell, Douglas	Harwich	*Conservative*
Cash, William	Stone	*Conservative*
Caton, Martin	Gower	*Labour*
Cawsey, Ian	Brigg & Goole	*Labour*
Challen, Colin	Morley & Rothwell	*Labour*
Chapman, Ben	Wirral South	*Labour*
Chaytor, David	Bury North	*Labour*
Chope, Christopher	Christchurch	*Conservative*
Clapham, Michael	Barnsley West & Penistone	*Labour*
Clappison, James	Hertsmere	*Conservative*

POLITICS

Clark, Greg	Tunbridge Wells	Conservative
Clark, Katy	Ayrshire North & Arran	Labour
Clark, Paul	Gillingham	Labour
Clarke, Charles	Norwich South	Labour
Clarke, Kenneth	Rushcliffe	Conservative
Clarke, Tom	Coatbridge, Chryston & Bellshill	Labour
Clegg, Nick	Sheffield Hallam	Liberal Democrat
Clelland, David	Tyne Bridge	Labour
Clifton-Brown, Geoffrey	Cotswold	Conservative
Clwyd, Ann	Cynon Valley	Labour
Coaker, Vernon	Gedling	Labour
Coffey, Ann	Stockport	Labour
Cohen, Harry	Leyton & Wanstead	Labour
Connarty, Michael	Linlithgow & Falkirk East	Labour
Conway, Derek	Old Bexley & Sidcup	Conservative
Cook, Frank	Stockton North	Labour
Cook, Robin	Livingston	Labour
Cooper, Rosie	Lancashire West	Labour
Cooper, Yvette	Pontefract & Castleford	Labour
Corbyn, Jeremy	Islington North	Labour
Cousins, Jim	Newcastle upon Tyne Central	Labour
Cox, Geoffrey	Devon West & Torridge	Conservative
Crabb, Stephen	Preseli Pembrokeshire	Conservative
Crausby, David	Bolton North East	Labour
Creagh, Mary	Wakefield	Labour
Cruddas, Jon	Dagenham	Labour
Cryer, Ann	Keighley	Labour
Cummings, John	Easington	Labour
Cunningham, Jim	Coventry South	Labour
Cunningham, Tony	Workington	Labour
Curry, David	Skipton & Ripon	Conservative
Curtis-Thomas, Claire	Crosby	Labour
Darling, Alistair	Edinburgh South West	Labour
Davey, Edward	Kingston & Surbiton	Liberal Democrat
David, Wayne	Caerphilly	Labour
Davidson, Ian	Glasgow South West	Labour Co-op
Davies, David	Monmouth	Conservative
Davies, Philip	Shipley	Conservative
Davies, Quentin	Grantham & Stamford	Conservative
Davis, David	Haltemprice & Howden	Conservative
Dean, Janet	Burton	Labour
Denham, John	Southampton Itchen	Labour
Dhanda, Parmjit	Gloucester	Labour
Dismore, Andrew	Hendon	Labour
Djanogly, Jonathan	Huntingdon	Conservative
Dobbin, Jim	Heywood & Middleton	Labour Co-op
Dobson, Frank	Holborn & St Pancras	Labour
Dodds, Nigel	Belfast North	Democratic Unionist
Doherty, Pat	Tyrone West	Sinn Fein
Donaldson, Jeffrey	Lagan Valley	Democratic Unionist
Donohoe, Brian	Ayrshire Central	Labour
Doran, Frank	Aberdeen North	Labour
Dorrell, Stephen	Charnwood	Conservative
Dorries, Nadine	Bedfordshire Mid	Conservative
Dowd, Jim	Lewisham West	Labour
Drew, David	Stroud	Labour Co-op
Duddridge, James	Rochford & Southend East	Conservative
Duncan Smith, Iain	Chingford & Woodford Green	Conservative
Duncan, Alan	Rutland & Melton	Conservative
Dunne, Philip	Ludlow	Conservative
Dunwoody, Gwyneth	Crewe & Nantwich	Labour
Durkan, Mark	Foyle	SDLP
Eagle, Angela	Wallasey	Labour
Eagle, Maria	Liverpool Garston	Labour
Efford, Clive	Eltham	Labour
Ellman, Louise	Liverpool Riverside	Labour Co-op
Ellwood, Tobias	Bournemouth East	Conservative
Engel, Natascha	Derbyshire North East	Labour
Ennis, Jeff	Barnsley East & Mexborough	Labour
Etherington, Bill	Sunderland North	Labour
Evans, Nigel	Ribble Valley	Conservative
Evennett, David	Bexleyheath & Crayford	Conservative

Fabricant, Michael	Lichfield	Conservative
Fallon, Michael	Sevenoaks	Conservative
Farrelly, Paul	Newcastle-under-Lyme	Labour
Farron, Tim	Westmorland & Lonsdale	Liberal Democrat
Featherstone, Lynne	Hornsey & Wood Green	Liberal Democrat
Field, Frank	Birkenhead	Labour
Field, Mark	Cities of London & Westminster	Conservative
Fisher, Mark	Stoke-on-Trent Central	Labour
Fitzpatrick, Jim	Poplar & Canning Town	Labour
Flello, Robert	Stoke-on-Trent South	Labour
Flint, Caroline	Don Valley	Labour
Flynn, Paul	Newport West	Labour
Follett, Barbara	Stevenage	Labour
Forth, Eric	Bromley & Chislehurst	Conservative
Foster, Don	Bath	Liberal Democrat
Foster, Michael	Hastings & Rye	Labour
Foster, Michael	Worcester	Labour
Fox, Dr Liam	Woodspring	Conservative
Francis, Dr Hywel	Aberavon	Labour
Francois, Mark	Rayleigh	Conservative
Fraser, Christopher	Norfolk South West	Conservative
Gale, Roger	Thanet North	Conservative
Galloway, George	Bethnal Green & Bow	Independent (Respect)
Gapes, Mike	Ilford South	Labour Co-op
Gardiner, Barry	Brent North	Labour
Garnier, Edward	Harborough	Conservative
Gauke, David	Hertfordshire South West	Conservative
George, Andrew	St Ives	Liberal Democrat
George, Bruce	Walsall South	Labour
Gerrard, Neil	Walthamstow	Labour
Gibb, Nick	Bognor Regis & Littlehampton	Conservative
Gibson, Dr Ian	Norwich North	Labour
Gidley, Sandra	Romsey	Liberal Democrat
Gildernew, Michelle	Fermanagh & South Tyrone	Sinn Fein
Gillan, Cheryl	Chesham & Amersham	Conservative
Gilroy, Linda	Plymouth Sutton	Labour Co-op
Godsiff, Roger	Birmingham Sparkbrook & Small Heath	Labour
Goggins, Paul	Wythenshawe & Sale East	Labour
Goldsworthy, Julia	Falmouth & Camborne	Liberal Democrat
Goodman, Helen	Bishop Auckland	Labour
Goodman, Paul	Wycombe	Conservative
Goodwill, Robert	Scarborough & Whitby	Conservative
Gove, Michael	Surrey Heath	Conservative
Gray, James	Wiltshire North	Conservative
Grayling, Chris	Epsom & Ewell	Conservative
Green, Damian	Ashford	Conservative
Greening, Justine	Putney	Conservative
Greenway, John	Ryedale	Conservative
Grieve, Dominic	Beaconsfield	Conservative
Griffith, Nia	Llanelli	Labour
Griffiths, Nigel	Edinburgh South	Labour
Grogan, John	Selby	Labour
Gummer, John	Suffolk Coastal	Conservative
Gwynne, Andrew	Denton & Reddish	Labour
Hague, William	Richmond (Yorks)	Conservative
Hain, Peter	Neath	Labour
Hall, Mike	Weaver Vale	Labour
Hall, Patrick	Bedford	Labour
Hamilton, David	Midlothian	Labour
Hamilton, Fabian	Leeds North East	Labour
Hammond, Philip	Runnymede & Weybridge	Conservative
Hammond, Stephen	Wimbledon	Conservative
Hancock, Mike	Portsmouth South	Liberal Democrat
Hands, Greg	Hammersmith & Fulham	Conservative
Hanson, David	Delyn	Labour
Harman, Harriet	Camberwell & Peckham	Labour
Harper, Mark	Forest of Dean	Conservative
Harris, Dr Evan	Oxford West & Abingdon	Liberal Democrat
Harris, Tom	Glasgow South	Labour
Harvey, Nick	Devon North	Liberal Democrat
Haselhurst, Sir Alan	Saffron Walden	Conservative
Havard, Dai	Merthyr Tydfil & Rhymney	Labour

POLITICS

Hayes, John	South Holland & The Deepings	*Conservative*
Heal, Sylvia	Halesowen & Rowley Regis	*Labour*
Heald, Oliver	Hertfordshire North East	*Conservative*
Healey, John	Wentworth	*Labour*
Heath, David	Somerton & Frome	*Liberal Democrat*
Heathcoat-Amory, David	Wells	*Conservative*
Hemming, John	Birmingham Yardley	*Liberal Democrat*
Henderson, Doug	Newcastle upon Tyne North	*Labour*
Hendrick, Mark	Preston	*Labour Co-op*
Hendry, Charles	Wealden	*Conservative*
Hepburn, Stephen	Jarrow	*Labour*
Heppell, John	Nottingham East	*Labour*
Herbert, Nick	Arundel & South Downs	*Conservative*
Hermon, Lady Sylvia	Down North	*Ulster Unionist*
Hesford, Stephen	Wirral West	*Labour*
Hewitt, Patricia	Leicester West	*Labour*
Heyes, David	Ashton-under-Lyne	*Labour*
Hill, Keith	Streatham	*Labour*
Hillier, Meg	Hackney South & Shoreditch	*Labour Co-op*
Hoban, Mark	Fareham	*Conservative*
Hodge, Margaret	Barking	*Labour*
Hodgson, Sharon	Gateshead East & Washington West	*Labour*
Hoey, Kate	Vauxhall	*Labour*
Hogg, Douglas	Sleaford & North Hykeham	*Conservative*
Hollobone, Philip	Kettering	*Conservative*
Holloway, Adam	Gravesham	*Conservative*
Holmes, Paul	Chesterfield	*Liberal Democrat*
Hood, Jimmy	Lanark & Hamilton East	*Labour*
Hoon, Geoff	Ashfield	*Labour*
Hope, Phil	Corby	*Labour Co-op*
Hopkins, Kelvin	Luton North	*Labour*
Horam, John	Orpington	*Conservative*
Horwood, Martin	Cheltenham	*Liberal Democrat*
Hosie, Stewart	Dundee East	*Scottish Nationalist*
Howard, Michael	Folkestone & Hythe	*Conservative*
Howarth, David	Cambridge	*Liberal Democrat*
Howarth, George	Knowsley North & Sefton East	*Labour*
Howarth, Gerald	Aldershot	*Conservative*
Howells, Dr Kim	Pontypridd	*Labour*
Hoyle, Lindsay	Chorley	*Labour*
Hughes, Beverley	Stretford & Urmston	*Labour*
Hughes, Simon	Southwark North & Bermondsey	*Liberal Democrat*
Huhne, Christopher	Eastleigh	*Liberal Democrat*
Humble, Joan	Blackpool North & Fleetwood	*Labour*
Hunt, Jeremy	Surrey South West	*Conservative*
Hurd, Nick	Ruislip Northwood	*Conservative*
Hutton, John	Barrow & Furness	*Labour*
Iddon, Dr Brian	Bolton South East	*Labour*
Illsley, Eric	Barnsley Central	*Labour*
Ingram, Adam	East Kilbride, Strathaven & Lesmahagow	*Labour*
Irranca-Davies, Huw	Ogmore	*Labour*
Jack, Michael	Fylde	*Conservative*
Jackson, Glenda	Hampstead & Highgate	*Labour*
Jackson, Stewart	Peterborough	*Conservative*
James, Sian	Swansea East	*Labour*
Jenkin, Bernard	Essex North	*Conservative*
Jenkins, Brian	Tamworth	*Labour*
Johnson, Alan	Hull West & Hessle	*Labour*
Johnson, Boris	Henley	*Conservative*
Johnson, Diana	Hull North	*Labour*
Jones, David	Clwyd West	*Conservative*
Jones, Helen	Warrington North	*Labour*
Jones, Kevan	Durham North	*Labour*
Jones, Dr Lynne	Birmingham Selly Oak	*Labour*
Jones, Martyn	Clwyd South	*Labour*
Jowell, Tessa	Dulwich & West Norwood	*Labour*
Joyce, Eric	Falkirk	*Labour*
Kaufman, Sir Gerald	Manchester Gorton	*Labour*
Kawczynski, Daniel	Shrewsbury & Atcham	*Conservative*
Keeble, Sally	Northampton North	*Labour*
Keeley, Barbara	Worsley	*Labour*
Keen, Alan	Feltham & Heston	*Labour Co-op*

Keen, Ann	Brentford & Isleworth	Labour
Keetch, Paul	Hereford	Liberal Democrat
Kelly, Ruth	Bolton West	Labour
Kemp, Fraser	Houghton & Washington East	Labour
Kennedy, Charles	Ross, Skye & Lochaber	Liberal Democrat
Kennedy, Jane	Liverpool Wavertree	Labour
Key, Robert	Salisbury	Conservative
Khabra, Piara	Ealing Southall	Labour
Khan, Sadiq	Tooting	Labour
Kidney, David	Stafford	Labour
Kilfoyle, Peter	Liverpool Walton	Labour
Kirkbride, Julie	Bromsgrove	Conservative
Knight, Greg	Yorkshire East	Conservative
Knight, Jim	Dorset South	Labour
Kramer, Susan	Richmond Park	Liberal Democrat
Kumar, Dr Ashok	Middlesbrough South & Cleveland East	Labour
Ladyman, Dr Stephen	Thanet South	Labour
Laing, Eleanor	Epping Forest	Conservative
Lait, Jacqui	Beckenham	Conservative
Lamb, Norman	Norfolk North	Liberal Democrat
Lammy, David	Tottenham	Labour
Lancaster, Mark	Milton Keynes North East	Conservative
Lansley, Andrew	Cambridgeshire South	Conservative
Law, Peter	Blaenau Gwent	Independent (Law)
Laws, David	Yeovil	Liberal Democrat
Laxton, Bob	Derby North	Labour
Lazarowicz, Mark	Edinburgh North & Leith	Labour Co-op
Leech, John	Manchester Withington	Liberal Democrat
Leigh, Edward	Gainsborough	Conservative
Lepper, David	Brighton Pavilion	Labour Co-op
Letwin, Oliver	Dorset West	Conservative
Levitt, Tom	High Peak	Labour
Lewis, Ivan	Bury South	Labour
Lewis, Dr Julian	New Forest East	Conservative
Liddell-Grainger, Ian	Bridgwater	Conservative
Lidington, David	Aylesbury	Conservative
Lilley, Peter	Hitchin & Harpenden	Conservative
Linton, Martin	Battersea	Labour
Lloyd, Tony	Manchester Central	Labour
Llwyd, Elfyn	Meirionnydd Nant Conwy	Plaid Cymru
Lord, Sir Michael	Suffolk Central & Ipswich North	Conservative
Loughton, Tim	Worthing East & Shoreham	Conservative
Love, Andy	Edmonton	Labour Co-op
Lucas, Ian	Wrexham	Labour
Luff, Peter	Worcestershire Mid	Conservative
Mackay, Andrew	Bracknell	Conservative
MacKinlay, Andrew	Thurrock	Labour
Maclean, David	Penrith & The Border	Conservative
MacNeil, Angus	Na h-Eileanan an Iar	Scottish Nationalist
MacShane, Denis	Rotherham	Labour
Mactaggart, Fiona	Slough	Labour
Mahmood, Khalid	Birmingham Perry Barr	Labour
Main, Anne	St Albans	Conservative
Malik, Shahid	Dewsbury	Labour
Malins, Humfrey	Woking	Conservative
Mallaber, Judy	Amber Valley	Labour
Mann, John	Bassetlaw	Labour
Maples, John	Stratford-on-Avon	Conservative
Marris, Robert	Wolverhampton South West	Labour
Marsden, Gordon	Blackpool South	Labour
Marshall, David	Glasgow East	Labour
Marshall-Andrews, Bob	Medway	Labour
Martin, Michael	Glasgow North East	Labour (speaker)
Martlew, Eric	Carlisle	Labour
Mates, Michael	Hampshire East	Conservative
Maude, Francis	Horsham	Conservative
May, Theresa	Maidenhead	Conservative
McAvoy, Tommy	Rutherglen & Hamilton West	Labour Co-op
McCabe, Stephen	Birmingham Hall Green	Labour
McCafferty, Christine	Calder Valley	Labour
McCarthy, Kerry	Bristol East	Labour
McCarthy-Fry, Sarah	Portsmouth North	Labour Co-op

POLITICS

McCartney, Ian	Makerfield	*Labour*
McCrea, Dr William	Antrim South	*Democratic Unionist*
McDonagh, Siobhain	Mitcham & Morden	*Labour*
McDonnell, Dr Alasdair	Belfast South	*SDLP*
McDonnell, John	Hayes & Harlington	*Labour*
McDougall, John	Glenrothes	*Labour*
McFadden, Pat	Wolverhampton South East	*Labour*
McFall, John	Dunbartonshire West	*Labour Co-op*
McGovern, Jim	Dundee West	*Labour*
McGrady, Eddie	Down South	*SDLP*
McGuinness, Martin	Ulster Mid	*Sinn Fein*
McGuire, Anne	Stirling	*Labour*
McIntosh, Anne	Vale of York	*Conservative*
McIsaac, Shona	Cleethorpes	*Labour*
McKechin, Ann	Glasgow North	*Labour*
McKenna, Rosemary	Cumbernauld, Kilsyth & Kirkintilloch East	*Labour*
McLoughlin, Patrick	Derbyshire West	*Conservative*
McNulty, Tony	Harrow East	*Labour*
Meacher, Michael	Oldham West & Royton	*Labour*
Meale, Alan	Mansfield	*Labour*
Mercer, Patrick	Newark	*Conservative*
Merron, Gillian	Lincoln	*Labour*
Michael, Alun	Cardiff South & Penarth	*Labour Co-op*
Milburn, Alan	Darlington	*Labour*
Miliband, David	South Shields	*Labour*
Miliband, Ed	Doncaster North	*Labour*
Miller, Andrew	Ellesmere Port & Neston	*Labour*
Miller, Maria	Basingstoke	*Conservative*
Milton, Anne	Guildford	*Conservative*
Mitchell, Andrew	Sutton Coldfield	*Conservative*
Mitchell, Austin	Great Grimsby	*Labour*
Moffatt, Laura	Crawley	*Labour*
Mole, Chris	Ipswich	*Labour*
Moon, Madeleine	Bridgend	*Labour*
Moore, Michael	Berwickshire, Roxburgh & Selkirk	*Liberal Democrat*
Moran, Margaret	Luton South	*Labour*
Morden, Jessica	Newport East	*Labour*
Morgan, Julie	Cardiff North	*Labour*
Morley, Elliot	Scunthorpe	*Labour*
Moss, Malcolm	Cambridgeshire North East	*Conservative*
Mountford, Kali	Colne Valley	*Labour*
Mudie, George	Leeds East	*Labour*
Mulholland, Greg	Leeds North West	*Liberal Democrat*
Mullin, Chris	Sunderland South	*Labour*
Mundell, David	Dumfriesshire, Clydesdale & Tweeddale	*Conservative*
Munn, Meg	Sheffield Heeley	*Labour Co-op*
Murphy, Conor	Newry & Armagh	*Sinn Fein*
Murphy, Denis	Wansbeck	*Labour*
Murphy, Jim	Renfrewshire East	*Labour*
Murphy, Paul	Torfaen	*Labour*
Murrison, Dr Andrew	Westbury	*Conservative*
Naysmith, Dr Doug	Bristol North West	*Labour Co-op*
Newmark, Brooks	Braintree	*Conservative*
Norris, Dan	Wansdyke	*Labour*
Oaten, Mark	Winchester	*Liberal Democrat*
O'Brien, Mike	Warwickshire North	*Labour*
O'Brien, Stephen	Eddisbury	*Conservative*
O'Hara, Eddie	Knowsley South	*Labour*
Olner, Bill	Nuneaton	*Labour*
Opik, Lembit	Montgomeryshire	*Liberal Democrat*
Osborne, George	Tatton	*Conservative*
Osborne, Sandra	Ayr, Carrick & Cumnock	*Labour*
Ottaway, Richard	Croydon South	*Conservative*
Owen, Albert	Ynys Mon	*Labour*
Paice, James	Cambridgeshire South East	*Conservative*
Paisley, Rev Ian	Antrim North	*Democratic Unionist*
Palmer, Dr Nick	Broxtowe	*Labour*
Paterson, Owen	Shropshire North	*Conservative*
Pearson, Ian	Dudley South	*Labour*
Pelling, Andrew	Croydon Central	*Conservative*
Penning, Michael	Hemel Hempstead	*Conservative*
Penrose, John	Weston-super-Mare	*Conservative*

Picking, Anne	East Lothian	*Labour*
Pickles, Eric	Brentwood & Ongar	*Conservative*
Plaskitt, James	Warwick & Leamington	*Labour*
Pope, Greg	Hyndburn	*Labour*
Pound, Stephen	Ealing North	*Labour*
Prentice, Bridget	Lewisham East	*Labour*
Prentice, Gordon	Pendle	*Labour*
Prescott, John	Hull East	*Labour*
Price, Adam	Carmarthen East & Dinefwr	*Plaid Cymru*
Primarolo, Dawn	Bristol South	*Labour*
Prisk, Mark	Hertford & Stortford	*Conservative*
Pritchard, Mark	Wrekin, The	*Conservative*
Prosser, Gwyn	Dover	*Labour*
Pugh, John	Southport	*Liberal Democrat*
Purchase, Ken	Wolverhampton North East	*Labour Co-op*
Purnell, James	Stalybridge & Hyde	*Labour*
Rammell, Bill	Harlow	*Labour*
Randall, John	Uxbridge	*Conservative*
Raynsford, Nick	Greenwich & Woolwich	*Labour*
Redwood, John	Wokingham	*Conservative*
Reed, Andy	Loughborough	*Labour Co-op*
Reed, Jamie	Copeland	*Labour*
Reid, Alan	Argyll & Bute	*Liberal Democrat*
Reid, Dr John	Airdrie & Shotts	*Labour*
Rifkind, Sir Malcolm	Kensington & Chelsea	*Conservative*
Riordan, Linda	Halifax	*Labour Co-op*
Robathan, Andrew	Blaby	*Conservative*
Robertson, Angus	Moray	*Scottish Nationalist*
Robertson, Hugh	Faversham & Kent Mid	*Conservative*
Robertson, John	Glasgow North West	*Labour*
Robertson, Laurence	Tewkesbury	*Conservative*
Robinson, Geoffrey	Coventry North West	*Labour*
Robinson, Iris	Strangford	*Democratic Unionist*
Robinson, Peter	Belfast East	*Democratic Unionist*
Rogerson, Dan	Cornwall North	*Liberal Democrat*
Rooney, Terry	Bradford North	*Labour*
Rosindell, Andrew	Romford	*Conservative*
Rowen, Paul	Rochdale	*Liberal Democrat*
Roy, Frank	Motherwell & Wishaw	*Labour*
Ruane, Chris	Vale of Clwyd	*Labour*
Ruddock, Joan	Lewisham Deptford	*Labour*
Ruffley, David	Bury St Edmunds	*Conservative*
Russell, Bob	Colchester	*Liberal Democrat*
Russell, Christine	Chester, City of	*Labour*
Ryan, Joan	Enfield North	*Labour*
Salmond, Alex	Banff & Buchan	*Scottish Nationalist*
Salter, Martin	Reading West	*Labour*
Sanders, Adrian	Torbay	*Liberal Democrat*
Sarwar, Mohammad	Glasgow Central	*Labour*
Scott, Lee	Ilford North	*Conservative*
Seabeck, Alison	Plymouth Devonport	*Labour*
Selous, Andrew	Bedfordshire South West	*Conservative*
Shapps, Grant	Welwyn Hatfield	*Conservative*
Shaw, Jonathan	Chatham & Aylesford	*Labour*
Sheerman, Barry	Huddersfield	*Labour Co-op*
Shepherd, Richard	Aldridge-Brownhills	*Conservative*
Sheridan, Jim	Paisley & Renfrewshire North	*Labour*
Short, Clare	Birmingham Ladywood	*Labour*
Simmonds, Mark	Boston & Skegness	*Conservative*
Simon, Sion	Birmingham Erdington	*Labour*
Simpson, Alan	Nottingham South	*Labour*
Simpson, David	Upper Bann	*Democratic Unionist*
Simpson, Keith	Norfolk Mid	*Conservative*
Singh, Marsha	Bradford West	*Labour*
Skinner, Dennis	Bolsover	*Labour*
Slaughter, Andrew	Ealing Acton & Shepherd's Bush	*Labour*
Smith, Andrew	Oxford East	*Labour*
Smith, Angela	Sheffield Hillsborough	*Labour*
Smith, Angela	Basildon	*Labour Co-op*
Smith, Geraldine	Morecambe & Lunesdale	*Labour*
Smith, Jacqui	Redditch	*Labour*
Smith, John	Vale of Glamorgan	*Labour*

Smith, Sir Robert	Aberdeenshire West & Kincardine	*Liberal Democrat*
Snelgrove, Anne	Swindon South	*Labour*
Soames, Nicholas	Sussex Mid	*Conservative*
Soulsby, Sir Peter	Leicester South	*Labour*
Southworth, Helen	Warrington South	*Labour*
Spellar, John	Warley	*Labour*
Spelman, Caroline	Meriden	*Conservative*
Spicer, Sir Michael	Worcestershire West	*Conservative*
Spink, Robert	Castle Point	*Conservative*
Spring, Richard	Suffolk West	*Conservative*
Squire, Rachel	Dunfermline & Fife West	*Labour*
Stanley, Sir John	Tonbridge & Malling	*Conservative*
Starkey, Phyllis	Milton Keynes South West	*Labour*
Steen, Sir Anthony	Totnes	*Conservative*
Stewart, Ian	Eccles	*Labour*
Stoate, Dr Howard	Dartford	*Labour*
Strang, Dr Gavin	Edinburgh East	*Labour*
Straw, Jack	Blackburn	*Labour*
Streeter, Gary	Devon South West	*Conservative*
Stringer, Graham	Manchester Blackley	*Labour*
Stuart, Gisela	Birmingham Edgbaston	*Labour*
Stuart, Graham	Beverley & Holderness	*Conservative*
Stunell, Andrew	Hazel Grove	*Liberal Democrat*
Sutcliffe, Gerry	Bradford South	*Labour*
Swayne, Desmond	New Forest West	*Conservative*
Swinson, Jo	Dunbartonshire East	*Liberal Democrat*
Swire, Hugo	Devon East	*Conservative*
Syms, Robert	Poole	*Conservative*
Tami, Mark	Alyn & Deeside	*Labour*
Tapsell, Sir Peter	Louth & Horncastle	*Conservative*
Taylor, Dari	Stockton South	*Labour*
Taylor, David	Leicestershire North West	*Labour Co-op*
Taylor, Dr Richard	Wyre Forest	*Independent (KHHC*)*
Taylor, Ian	Esher & Walton	*Conservative*
Taylor, Matthew	Truro & St Austell	*Liberal Democrat*
Teather, Sarah	Brent East	*Liberal Democrat*
Thomas, Gareth	Harrow West	*Labour Co-op*
Thornberry, Emily	Islington South & Finsbury	*Labour*
Thurso, John	Caithness, Sutherland & Easter Ross	*Liberal Democrat*
Timms, Stephen	East Ham	*Labour*
Tipping, Paddy	Sherwood	*Labour*
Todd, Mark	Derbyshire South	*Labour*
Touhig, Don	Islwyn	*Labour Co-op*
Tredinnick, David	Bosworth	*Conservative*
Trickett, Jon	Hemsworth	*Labour*
Truswell, Paul	Pudsey	*Labour*
Turner, Andrew	Isle of Wight	*Conservative*
Turner, Desmond	Brighton Kemptown	*Labour*
Turner, Neil	Wigan	*Labour*
Twigg, Derek	Halton	*Labour*
Tyrie, Andrew	Chichester	*Conservative*
Ussher, Kitty	Burnley	*Labour*
Vaizey, Ed	Wantage	*Conservative*
Vara, Shailesh	Cambridgeshire North West	*Conservative*
Vaz, Keith	Leicester East	*Labour*
Viggers, Peter	Gosport	*Conservative*
Villiers, Theresa	Chipping Barnet	*Conservative*
Vis, Rudi	Finchley & Golders Green	*Labour*
Walker, Charles	Broxbourne	*Conservative*
Wallace, Ben	Lancaster & Wyre	*Conservative*
Walley, Joan	Stoke-on-Trent North	*Labour*
Walter, Robert	Dorset North	*Conservative*
Waltho, Lynda	Stourbridge	*Labour*
Ward, Claire	Watford	*Labour*
Wareing, Robert	Liverpool West Derby	*Labour*
Waterson, Nigel	Eastbourne	*Conservative*
Watkinson, Angela	Upminster	*Conservative*
Watson, Tom	West Bromwich East	*Labour*
Watts, Dave	St Helens North	*Labour*
Webb, Professor Steve	Northavon	*Liberal Democrat*
Weir, Mike	Angus	*Scottish Nationalist*
Whitehead, Dr Alan	Southampton Test	*Labour*

Whittingdale, John	Maldon & Chelmsford East	*Conservative*
Wicks, Malcolm	Croydon North	*Labour*
Widdecombe, Ann	Maidstone & The Weald	*Conservative*
Wiggin, Bill	Leominster	*Conservative*
Willetts, David	Havant	*Conservative*
Williams, Alan	Swansea West	*Labour*
Williams, Betty	Conwy	*Labour*
Williams, Hywel	Caernarfon	*Plaid Cymru*
Williams, Mark	Ceredigion	*Liberal Democrat*
Williams, Roger	Brecon & Radnorshire	*Liberal Democrat*
Williams, Stephen	Bristol West	*Liberal Democrat*
Willis, Phil	Harrogate & Knaresborough	*Liberal Democrat*
Willott, Jenny	Cardiff Central	*Liberal Democrat*
Wills, Michael	Swindon North	*Labour*
Wilshire, David	Spelthorne	*Conservative*
Wilson, Rob	Reading East	*Conservative*
Wilson, Sammy	Antrim East	*Democratic Unionist*
Winnick, David	Walsall North	*Labour*
Winterton, Ann	Congleton	*Conservative*
Winterton, Sir Nicholas	Macclesfield	*Conservative*
Winterton, Rosie	Doncaster Central	*Labour*
Wishart, Peter	Perth & Perthshire North	*Scottish Nationalist*
Wood, Mike	Batley & Spen	*Labour*
Woodward, Shaun	St Helens South	*Labour*
Woolas, Phil	Oldham East & Saddleworth	*Labour*
Wright, David	Telford	*Labour*
Wright, Iain	Hartlepool	*Labour*
Wright, Jeremy	Rugby & Kenilworth	*Conservative*
Wright, Dr Tony	Cannock Chase	*Labour*
Wright, Tony	Great Yarmouth	*Labour*
Wyatt, Derek	Sittingbourne & Sheppey	*Labour*
Yeo, Tim	Suffolk South	*Conservative*
Young, Sir George	Hampshire North West	*Conservative*
Younger-Ross, Richard	Teignbridge	*Liberal Democrat*

*Kidderminster Hospital and Health Concern **Calton died three weeks after the General Election, and the ensuing bye-election was won by fellow Liberal Democrat Mark Hunter

General Election Results by Constituency: 5 May 2005

Aberavon	Francis, Dr Hywel	*Labour*
Aberdeen North	Doran, Frank	*Labour*
Aberdeen South	Begg, Anne	*Labour*
Aberdeenshire West & Kincardine	Smith, Sir Robert	*Liberal Democrat*
Airdrie & Shotts	Reid, Dr John	*Labour*
Aldershot	Howarth, Gerald	*Conservative*
Aldridge-Brownhills	Shepherd, Richard	*Conservative*
Altrincham & Sale West	Brady, Graham	*Conservative*
Alyn & Deeside	Tami, Mark	*Labour*
Amber Valley	Mallaber, Judy	*Labour*
Angus	Weir, Mike	*Scottish Nationalist*
Antrim East	Wilson, Sammy	*Democratic Unionist*
Antrim North	Paisley, Rev Ian	*Democratic Unionist*
Antrim South	McCrea, Dr William	*Democratic Unionist*
Argyll & Bute	Reid, Alan	*Liberal Democrat*
Arundel & South Downs	Herbert, Nick	*Conservative*
Ashfield	Hoon, Geoff	*Labour*
Ashford	Green, Damian	*Conservative*
Ashton-under-Lyne	Heyes, David	*Labour*
Aylesbury	Lidington, David	*Conservative*
Ayr, Carrick & Cumnock	Osborne, Sandra	*Labour*
Ayrshire Central	Donohoe, Brian	*Labour*
Ayrshire North & Arran	Clark, Katy	*Labour*
Banbury	Baldry, Tony	*Conservative*
Banff & Buchan	Salmond, Alex	*Scottish Nationalist*
Barking	Hodge, Margaret	*Labour*
Barnsley Central	Illsley, Eric	*Labour*
Barnsley East & Mexborough	Ennis, Jeff	*Labour*
Barnsley West & Penistone	Clapham, Michael	*Labour*
Barrow & Furness	Hutton, John	*Labour*
Basildon	Smith, Angela	*Labour Co-op*

POLITICS

Basingstoke	Miller, Maria	Conservative
Bassetlaw	Mann, John	Labour
Bath	Foster, Don	Liberal Democrat
Batley & Spen	Wood, Mike	Labour
Battersea	Linton, Martin	Labour
Beaconsfield	Grieve, Dominic	Conservative
Beckenham	Lait, Jacqui	Conservative
Bedford	Hall, Patrick	Labour
Bedfordshire Mid	Dorries, Nadine	Conservative
Bedfordshire North East	Burt, Alastair	Conservative
Bedfordshire South West	Selous, Andrew	Conservative
Belfast East	Robinson, Peter	Democratic Unionist
Belfast North	Dodds, Nigel	Democratic Unionist
Belfast South	McDonnell, Dr Alasdair	SDLP
Belfast West	Adams, Gerry	Sinn Fein
Berwickshire, Roxburgh & Selkirk	Moore, Michael	Liberal Democrat
Berwick-upon-Tweed	Beith, Alan	Liberal Democrat
Bethnal Green & Bow	Galloway, George	Independent (Respect)
Beverley & Holderness	Stuart, Graham	Conservative
Bexhill & Battle	Barker, Greg	Conservative
Bexleyheath & Crayford	Evennett, David	Conservative
Billericay	Baron, John	Conservative
Birkenhead	Field, Frank	Labour
Birmingham Edgbaston	Stuart, Gisela	Labour
Birmingham Erdington	Simon, Sion	Labour
Birmingham Hall Green	McCabe, Stephen	Labour
Birmingham Hodge Hill	Byrne, Liam	Labour
Birmingham Ladywood	Short, Clare	Labour
Birmingham Northfield	Burden, Richard	Labour
Birmingham Perry Barr	Mahmood, Khalid	Labour
Birmingham Selly Oak	Jones, Dr Lynne	Labour
Birmingham Sparkbrook & Small Heath	Godsiff, Roger	Labour
Birmingham Yardley	Hemming, John	Liberal Democrat
Bishop Auckland	Goodman, Helen	Labour
Blaby	Robathan, Andrew	Conservative
Blackburn	Straw, Jack	Labour
Blackpool North & Fleetwood	Humble, Joan	Labour
Blackpool South	Marsden, Gordon	Labour
Blaenau Gwent	Law, Peter	Independent (Law)
Blaydon	Anderson, David	Labour
Blyth Valley	Campbell, Ronnie	Labour
Bognor Regis & Littlehampton	Gibb, Nick	Conservative
Bolsover	Skinner, Dennis	Labour
Bolton North East	Crausby, David	Labour
Bolton South East	Iddon, Dr Brian	Labour
Bolton West	Kelly, Ruth	Labour
Bootle	Benton, Joe	Labour
Boston & Skegness	Simmonds, Mark	Conservative
Bosworth	Tredinnick, David	Conservative
Bournemouth East	Ellwood, Tobias	Conservative
Bournemouth West	Butterfill, Sir John	Conservative
Bracknell	Mackay, Andrew	Conservative
Bradford North	Rooney, Terry	Labour
Bradford South	Sutcliffe, Gerry	Labour
Bradford West	Singh, Marsha	Labour
Braintree	Newmark, Brooks	Conservative
Brecon & Radnorshire	Williams, Roger	Liberal Democrat
Brent East	Teather, Sarah	Liberal Democrat
Brent North	Gardiner, Barry	Labour
Brent South	Butler, Dawn	Labour
Brentford & Isleworth	Keen, Ann	Labour
Brentwood & Ongar	Pickles, Eric	Conservative
Bridgend	Moon, Madeleine	Labour
Bridgwater	Liddell-Grainger, Ian	Conservative
Brigg & Goole	Cawsey, Ian	Labour
Brighton Kemptown	Turner, Desmond	Labour
Brighton Pavilion	Lepper, David	Labour Co-op
Bristol East	McCarthy, Kerry	Labour
Bristol North West	Naysmith, Dr Doug	Labour Co-op
Bristol South	Primarolo, Dawn	Labour
Bristol West	Williams, Stephen	Liberal Democrat
Bromley & Chislehurst	Forth, Eric	Conservative

Bromsgrove	Kirkbride, Julie	*Conservative*
Broxbourne	Walker, Charles	*Conservative*
Broxtowe	Palmer, Dr Nick	*Labour*
Buckingham	Bercow, John	*Conservative*
Burnley	Ussher, Kitty	*Labour*
Burton	Dean, Janet	*Labour*
Bury North	Chaytor, David	*Labour*
Bury South	Lewis, Ivan	*Labour*
Bury St Edmunds	Ruffley, David	*Conservative*
Caernarfon	Williams, Hywel	*Plaid Cymru*
Caerphilly	David, Wayne	*Labour*
Caithness, Sutherland & Easter Ross	Thurso, John	*Liberal Democrat*
Calder Valley	McCafferty, Christine	*Labour*
Camberwell & Peckham	Harman, Harriet	*Labour*
Cambridge	Howarth, David	*Liberal Democrat*
Cambridgeshire North East	Moss, Malcolm	*Conservative*
Cambridgeshire North West	Vara, Shailesh	*Conservative*
Cambridgeshire South	Lansley, Andrew	*Conservative*
Cambridgeshire South East	Paice, James	*Conservative*
Cannock Chase	Wright, Dr Anthony	*Labour*
Canterbury	Brazier, Julian	*Conservative*
Cardiff Central	Willott, Jenny	*Liberal Democrat*
Cardiff North	Morgan, Julie	*Labour*
Cardiff South & Penarth	Michael, Alun	*Labour Co-op*
Cardiff West	Brennan, Kevin	*Labour*
Carlisle	Martlew, Eric	*Labour*
Carmarthen East & Dinefwr	Price, Adam	*Plaid Cymru*
Carmarthen West & Pembrokeshire South	Ainger, Nick	*Labour*
Carshalton & Wallington	Brake, Tom	*Liberal Democrat*
Castle Point	Spink, Robert	*Conservative*
Ceredigion	Williams, Mark	*Liberal Democrat*
Charnwood	Dorrell, Stephen	*Conservative*
Chatham & Aylesford	Shaw, Jonathan	*Labour*
Cheadle*	Calton, Patsy	*Liberal Democrat*
Chelmsford West	Burns, Simon	*Conservative*
Cheltenham	Horwood, Martin	*Liberal Democrat*
Chesham & Amersham	Gillan, Cheryl	*Conservative*
Chester, City of	Russell, Christine	*Labour*
Chesterfield	Holmes, Paul	*Liberal Democrat*
Chichester	Tyrie, Andrew	*Conservative*
Chingford & Woodford Green	Duncan Smith, Iain	*Conservative*
Chipping Barnet	Villiers, Theresa	*Conservative*
Chorley	Hoyle, Lindsay	*Labour*
Christchurch	Chope, Christopher	*Conservative*
Cities of London & Westminster	Field, Mark	*Conservative*
Cleethorpes	McIsaac, Shona	*Labour*
Clwyd South	Jones, Martyn	*Labour*
Clwyd West	Jones, David	*Conservative*
Coatbridge, Chryston & Bellshill	Clarke, Tom	*Labour*
Colchester	Russell, Bob	*Liberal Democrat*
Colne Valley	Mountford, Kali	*Labour*
Congleton	Winterton, Ann	*Conservative*
Conwy	Williams, Betty	*Labour*
Copeland	Reed, Jamie	*Labour*
Corby	Hope, Phil	*Labour Co-op*
Cornwall North	Rogerson, Dan	*Liberal Democrat*
Cornwall South East	Breed, Colin	*Liberal Democrat*
Cotswold	Clifton-Brown, Geoffrey	*Conservative*
Coventry North East	Ainsworth, Bob	*Labour*
Coventry North West	Robinson, Geoffrey	*Labour*
Coventry South	Cunningham, Jim	*Labour*
Crawley	Moffatt, Laura	*Labour*
Crewe & Nantwich	Dunwoody, Gwyneth	*Labour*
Crosby	Curtis-Thomas, Claire	*Labour*
Croydon Central	Pelling, Andrew	*Conservative*
Croydon North	Wicks, Malcolm	*Labour*
Croydon South	Ottaway, Richard	*Conservative*
Cumbernauld, Kilsyth & Kirkintilloch East	McKenna, Rosemary	*Labour*
Cynon Valley	Clwyd, Ann	*Labour*
Dagenham	Cruddas, Jon	*Labour*
Darlington	Milburn, Alan	*Labour*
Dartford	Stoate, Dr Howard	*Labour*

POLITICS

Daventry	Boswell, Tim	*Conservative*
Delyn	Hanson, David	*Labour*
Denton & Reddish	Gwynne, Andrew	*Labour*
Derby North	Laxton, Bob	*Labour*
Derby South	Beckett, Margaret	*Labour*
Derbyshire North East	Engel, Natascha	*Labour*
Derbyshire South	Todd, Mark	*Labour*
Derbyshire West	McLoughlin, Patrick	*Conservative*
Devizes	Ancram, Michael	*Conservative*
Devon East	Swire, Hugo	*Conservative*
Devon North	Harvey, Nick	*Liberal Democrat*
Devon South West	Streeter, Gary	*Conservative*
Devon West & Torridge	Cox, Geoffrey	*Conservative*
Dewsbury	Malik, Shahid	*Labour*
Don Valley	Flint, Caroline	*Labour*
Doncaster Central	Winterton, Rosie	*Labour*
Doncaster North	Miliband, Ed	*Labour*
Dorset Mid & Poole North	Brooke, Annette	*Liberal Democrat*
Dorset North	Walter, Robert	*Conservative*
Dorset South	Knight, Jim	*Labour*
Dorset West	Letwin, Oliver	*Conservative*
Dover	Prosser, Gwyn	*Labour*
Down North	Hermon, Lady Sylvia	*Ulster Unionist*
Down South	McGrady, Eddie	*SDLP*
Dudley North	Austin, Ian	*Labour*
Dudley South	Pearson, Ian	*Labour*
Dulwich & West Norwood	Jowell, Tessa	*Labour*
Dumfries & Galloway	Brown, Russell	*Labour*
Dumfriesshire, Clydesdale & Tweeddale	Mundell, David	*Conservative*
Dunbartonshire East	Swinson, Jo	*Liberal Democrat*
Dunbartonshire West	McFall, John	*Labour Co-op*
Dundee East	Hosie, Stewart	*Scottish Nationalist*
Dundee West	McGovern, Jim	*Labour*
Dunfermline & Fife West	Squire, Rachel	*Labour*
Durham, City of	Blackman-Woods, Roberta	*Labour*
Durham North	Jones, Kevan	*Labour*
Durham North West	Armstrong, Hilary	*Labour*
Ealing Acton & Shepherd's Bush	Slaughter, Andrew	*Labour*
Ealing North	Pound, Stephen	*Labour*
Ealing Southall	Khabra, Piara	*Labour*
Easington	Cummings, John	*Labour*
East Ham	Timms, Stephen	*Labour*
East Kilbride, Strathaven & Lesmahagow	Ingram, Adam	*Labour*
East Lothian	Picking, Anne	*Labour*
Eastbourne	Waterson, Nigel	*Conservative*
Eastleigh	Huhne, Christopher	*Liberal Democrat*
Eccles	Stewart, Ian	*Labour*
Eddisbury	O'Brien, Stephen	*Conservative*
Edinburgh East	Strang, Dr Gavin	*Labour*
Edinburgh North & Leith	Lazarowicz, Mark	*Labour Co-op*
Edinburgh South	Griffiths, Nigel	*Labour*
Edinburgh South West	Darling, Alistair	*Labour*
Edinburgh West	Barrett, John	*Liberal Democrat*
Edmonton	Love, Andy	*Labour Co-op*
Ellesmere Port & Neston	Miller, Andrew	*Labour*
Elmet	Burgon, Colin	*Labour*
Eltham	Efford, Clive	*Labour*
Enfield North	Ryan, Joan	*Labour*
Enfield Southgate	Burrowes, David	*Conservative*
Epping Forest	Laing, Eleanor	*Conservative*
Epsom & Ewell	Grayling, Chris	*Conservative*
Erewash	Blackman, Liz	*Labour*
Erith & Thamesmead	Austin, John	*Labour*
Esher & Walton	Taylor, Ian	*Conservative*
Essex North	Jenkin, Bernard	*Conservative*
Exeter	Bradshaw, Ben	*Labour*
Falkirk	Joyce, Eric	*Labour*
Falmouth & Camborne	Goldsworthy, Julia	*Liberal Democrat*
Fareham	Hoban, Mark	*Conservative*
Faversham & Kent Mid	Robertson, Hugh	*Conservative*
Feltham & Heston	Keen, Alan	*Labour Co-op*
Fermanagh & South Tyrone	Gildernew, Michelle	*Sinn Fein*

Fife North East	Campbell, Sir Menzies	*Liberal Democrat*
Finchley & Golders Green	Vis, Rudi	*Labour*
Folkestone & Hythe	Howard, Michael	*Conservative*
Forest of Dean	Harper, Mark	*Conservative*
Foyle	Durkan, Mark	*SDLP*
Fylde	Jack, Michael	*Conservative*
Gainsborough	Leigh, Edward	*Conservative*
Gateshead East & Washington West	Hodgson, Sharon	*Labour*
Gedling	Coaker, Vernon	*Labour*
Gillingham	Clark, Paul	*Labour*
Glasgow Central	Sarwar, Mohammad	*Labour*
Glasgow East	Marshall, David	*Labour*
Glasgow North	McKechin, Ann	*Labour*
Glasgow North East	Martin, Michael	*Labour* (speaker)
Glasgow North West	Robertson, John	*Labour*
Glasgow South	Harris, Tom	*Labour*
Glasgow South West	Davidson, Ian	*Labour Co-op*
Glenrothes	McDougall, John	*Labour*
Gloucester	Dhanda, Parmjit	*Labour*
Gordon	Bruce, Malcolm	*Liberal Democrat*
Gosport	Viggers, Peter	*Conservative*
Gower	Caton, Martin	*Labour*
Grantham & Stamford	Davies, Quentin	*Conservative*
Gravesham	Holloway, Adam	*Conservative*
Great Grimsby	Mitchell, Austin	*Labour*
Great Yarmouth	Wright, Tony	*Labour*
Greenwich & Woolwich	Raynsford, Nick	*Labour*
Guildford	Milton, Anne	*Conservative*
Hackney North & Stoke Newington	Abbott, Diane	*Labour*
Hackney South & Shoreditch	Hillier, Meg	*Labour Co-op*
Halesowen & Rowley Regis	Heal, Sylvia	*Labour*
Halifax	Riordan, Linda	*Labour Co-op*
Haltemprice & Howden	Davis, David	*Conservative*
Halton	Twigg, Derek	*Labour*
Hammersmith & Fulham	Hands, Greg	*Conservative*
Hampshire East	Mates, Michael	*Conservative*
Hampshire North East	Arbuthnot, James	*Conservative*
Hampshire North West	Young, Sir George	*Conservative*
Hampstead & Highgate	Jackson, Glenda	*Labour*
Harborough	Garnier, Edward	*Conservative*
Harlow	Rammell, Bill	*Labour*
Harrogate & Knaresborough	Willis, Phil	*Liberal Democrat*
Harrow East	McNulty, Tony	*Labour*
Harrow West	Thomas, Gareth	*Labour Co-op*
Hartlepool	Wright, Iain	*Labour*
Harwich	Carswell, Douglas	*Conservative*
Hastings & Rye	Foster, Michael	*Labour*
Havant	Willetts, David	*Conservative*
Hayes & Harlington	McDonnell, John	*Labour*
Hazel Grove	Stunell, Andrew	*Liberal Democrat*
Hemel Hempstead	Penning, Michael	*Conservative*
Hemsworth	Trickett, Jon	*Labour*
Hendon	Dismore, Andrew	*Labour*
Henley	Johnson, Boris	*Conservative*
Hereford	Keetch, Paul	*Liberal Democrat*
Hertford & Stortford	Prisk, Mark	*Conservative*
Hertfordshire North East	Heald, Oliver	*Conservative*
Hertfordshire South West	Gauke, David	*Conservative*
Hertsmere	Clappison, James	*Conservative*
Hexham	Atkinson, Peter	*Conservative*
Heywood & Middleton	Dobbin, Jim	*Labour Co-op*
High Peak	Levitt, Tom	*Labour*
Hitchin & Harpenden	Lilley, Peter	*Conservative*
Holborn & St Pancras	Dobson, Frank	*Labour*
Hornchurch	Brokenshire, James	*Conservative*
Hornsey & Wood Green	Featherstone, Lynne	*Liberal Democrat*
Horsham	Maude, Francis	*Conservative*
Houghton & Washington East	Kemp, Fraser	*Labour*
Hove	Barlow, Celia	*Labour*
Huddersfield	Sheerman, Barry	*Labour Co-op*
Hull East	Prescott, John	*Labour*
Hull North	Johnson, Diana	*Labour*

POLITICS

Hull West & Hessle	Johnson, Alan	*Labour*
Huntingdon	Djanogly, Jonathan	*Conservative*
Hyndburn	Pope, Greg	*Labour*
Ilford North	Scott, Lee	*Conservative*
Ilford South	Gapes, Mike	*Labour Co-op*
Inverclyde	Cairns, David	*Labour*
Inverness, Nairn, Badenoch & Strathspey	Alexander, Danny	*Liberal Democrat*
Ipswich	Mole, Chris	*Labour*
Isle of Wight	Turner, Andrew	*Conservative*
Islington North	Corbyn, Jeremy	*Labour*
Islington South & Finsbury	Thornberry, Emily	*Labour*
Islwyn	Touhig, Don	*Labour Co-op*
Jarrow	Hepburn, Stephen	*Labour*
Keighley	Cryer, Ann	*Labour*
Kensington & Chelsea	Rifkind, Sir Malcolm	*Conservative*
Kettering	Hollobone, Philip	*Conservative*
Kilmarnock & Loudoun	Browne, Des	*Labour*
Kingston & Surbiton	Davey, Edward	*Liberal Democrat*
Kingswood	Berry, Roger	*Labour*
Kirkcaldy & Cowdenbeath	Brown, Gordon	*Labour*
Knowsley North & Sefton East	Howarth, George	*Labour*
Knowsley South	O'Hara, Eddie	*Labour*
Lagan Valley	Donaldson, Jeffrey	*Democratic Unionist*
Lanark & Hamilton East	Hood, Jimmy	*Labour*
Lancashire West	Cooper, Rosie	*Labour*
Lancaster & Wyre	Wallace, Ben	*Conservative*
Leeds Central	Benn, Hilary	*Labour*
Leeds East	Mudie, George	*Labour*
Leeds North East	Hamilton, Fabian	*Labour*
Leeds North West	Mulholland, Greg	*Liberal Democrat*
Leeds West	Battle, John	*Labour*
Leicester East	Vaz, Keith	*Labour*
Leicester South	Soulsby, Sir Peter	*Labour*
Leicester West	Hewitt, Patricia	*Labour*
Leicestershire North West	Taylor, David	*Labour Co-op*
Leigh	Burnham, Andy	*Labour*
Leominster	Wiggin, Bill	*Conservative*
Lewes	Baker, Norman	*Liberal Democrat*
Lewisham Deptford	Ruddock, Joan	*Labour*
Lewisham East	Prentice, Bridget	*Labour*
Lewisham West	Dowd, Jim	*Labour*
Leyton & Wanstead	Cohen, Harry	*Labour*
Lichfield	Fabricant, Michael	*Conservative*
Lincoln	Merron, Gillian	*Labour*
Linlithgow & Falkirk East	Connarty, Michael	*Labour*
Liverpool Garston	Eagle, Maria	*Labour*
Liverpool Riverside	Ellman, Louise	*Labour Co-op*
Liverpool Walton	Kilfoyle, Peter	*Labour*
Liverpool Wavertree	Kennedy, Jane	*Labour*
Liverpool West Derby	Wareing, Robert	*Labour*
Livingston	Cook, Robin	*Labour*
Llanelli	Griffith, Nia	*Labour*
Londonderry East	Campbell, Gregory	*Democratic Unionist*
Loughborough	Reed, Andy	*Labour Co-op*
Louth & Horncastle	Tapsell, Sir Peter	*Conservative*
Ludlow	Dunne, Philip	*Conservative*
Luton North	Hopkins, Kelvin	*Labour*
Luton South	Moran, Margaret	*Labour*
Macclesfield	Winterton, Sir Nicholas	*Conservative*
Maidenhead	May, Theresa	*Conservative*
Maidstone & The Weald	Widdecombe, Ann	*Conservative*
Makerfield	McCartney, Ian	*Labour*
Maldon & Chelmsford East	Whittingdale, John	*Conservative*
Manchester Blackley	Stringer, Graham	*Labour*
Manchester Central	Lloyd, Tony	*Labour*
Manchester Gorton	Kaufman, Sir Gerald	*Labour*
Manchester Withington	Leech, John	*Liberal Democrat*
Mansfield	Meale, Alan	*Labour*
Medway	Marshall-Andrews, Bob	*Labour*
Meirionnydd Nant Conwy	Llwyd, Elfyn	*Plaid Cymru*
Meriden	Spelman, Caroline	*Conservative*
Merthyr Tydfil & Rhymney	Havard, Dai	*Labour*

Middlesbrough	Bell, Sir Stuart	*Labour*
Middlesbrough South & Cleveland East	Kumar, Dr Ashok	*Labour*
Midlothian	Hamilton, David	*Labour*
Milton Keynes North East	Lancaster, Mark	*Conservative*
Milton Keynes South West	Starkey, Phyllis	*Labour*
Mitcham & Morden	McDonagh, Siobhain	*Labour*
Mole Valley	Beresford, Sir Paul	*Conservative*
Monmouth	Davies, David	*Conservative*
Montgomeryshire	Opik, Lembit	*Liberal Democrat*
Moray	Robertson, Angus	*Scottish Nationalist*
Morecambe & Lunesdale	Smith, Geraldine	*Labour*
Morley & Rothwell	Challen, Colin	*Labour*
Motherwell & Wishaw	Roy, Frank	*Labour*
Na h-Eileanan an Iar	MacNeil, Angus	*Scottish Nationalist*
Neath	Hain, Peter	*Labour*
New Forest East	Lewis, Dr Julian	*Conservative*
New Forest West	Swayne, Desmond	*Conservative*
Newark	Mercer, Patrick	*Conservative*
Newbury	Benyon, Richard	*Conservative*
Newcastle-under-Lyme	Farrelly, Paul	*Labour*
Newcastle upon Tyne Central	Cousins, Jim	*Labour*
Newcastle upon Tyne East & Wallsend	Brown, Nick	*Labour*
Newcastle upon Tyne North	Henderson, Doug	*Labour*
Newport East	Morden, Jessica	*Labour*
Newport West	Flynn, Paul	*Labour*
Newry & Armagh	Murphy, Conor	*Sinn Fein*
Norfolk Mid	Simpson, Keith	*Conservative*
Norfolk North	Lamb, Norman	*Liberal Democrat*
Norfolk North West	Bellingham, Henry	*Conservative*
Norfolk South	Bacon, Richard	*Conservative*
Norfolk South West	Fraser, Christopher	*Conservative*
Normanton	Balls, Ed	*Labour Co-op*
Northampton North	Keeble, Sally	*Labour*
Northampton South	Binley, Brian	*Conservative*
Northavon	Webb, Professor Steve	*Liberal Democrat*
Norwich North	Gibson, Dr Ian	*Labour*
Norwich South	Clarke, Charles	*Labour*
Nottingham East	Heppell, John	*Labour*
Nottingham North	Allen, Graham	*Labour*
Nottingham South	Simpson, Alan	*Labour*
Nuneaton	Olner, Bill	*Labour*
Ochil & Perthshire South	Banks, Gordon	*Labour*
Ogmore	Irranca-Davies, Huw	*Labour*
Old Bexley & Sidcup	Conway, Derek	*Conservative*
Oldham East & Saddleworth	Woolas, Phil	*Labour*
Oldham West & Royton	Meacher, Michael	*Labour*
Orkney & Shetland	Carmichael, Alistair	*Liberal Democrat*
Orpington	Horam, John	*Conservative*
Oxford East	Smith, Andrew	*Labour*
Oxford West & Abingdon	Harris, Dr Evan	*Liberal Democrat*
Paisley & Renfrewshire North	Sheridan, Jim	*Labour*
Paisley & Renfrewshire South	Alexander, Douglas	*Labour*
Pendle	Prentice, Gordon	*Labour*
Penrith & The Border	Maclean, David	*Conservative*
Perth & Perthshire North	Wishart, Peter	*Scottish Nationalist*
Peterborough	Jackson, Stewart	*Conservative*
Plymouth Devonport	Seabeck, Alison	*Labour*
Plymouth Sutton	Gilroy, Linda	*Labour Co-op*
Pontefract & Castleford	Cooper, Yvette	*Labour*
Pontypridd	Howells, Dr Kim	*Labour*
Poole	Syms, Robert	*Conservative*
Poplar & Canning Town	Fitzpatrick, Jim	*Labour*
Portsmouth North	McCarthy-Fry, Sarah	*Labour Co-op*
Portsmouth South	Hancock, Mike	*Liberal Democrat*
Preseli Pembrokeshire	Crabb, Stephen	*Conservative*
Preston	Hendrick, Mark	*Labour Co-op*
Pudsey	Truswell, Paul	*Labour*
Putney	Greening, Justine	*Conservative*
Rayleigh	Francois, Mark	*Conservative*
Reading East	Wilson, Rob	*Conservative*
Reading West	Salter, Martin	*Labour*
Redcar	Baird, Vera	*Labour*

POLITICS

Redditch	Smith, Jacqui	*Labour*
Regent's Park & Kensington North	Buck, Karen	*Labour*
Reigate	Blunt, Crispin	*Conservative*
Renfrewshire East	Murphy, Jim	*Labour*
Rhondda	Bryant, Chris	*Labour*
Ribble South	Borrow, David	*Labour*
Ribble Valley	Evans, Nigel	*Conservative*
Richmond (Yorks)	Hague, William	*Conservative*
Richmond Park	Kramer, Susan	*Liberal Democrat*
Rochdale	Rowen, Paul	*Liberal Democrat*
Rochford & Southend East	Duddridge, James	*Conservative*
Romford	Rosindell, Andrew	*Conservative*
Romsey	Gidley, Sandra	*Liberal Democrat*
Ross, Skye & Lochaber	Kennedy, Charles	*Liberal Democrat*
Rossendale & Darwen	Anderson, Janet	*Labour*
Rother Valley	Barron, Kevin	*Labour*
Rotherham	MacShane, Denis	*Labour*
Rugby & Kenilworth	Wright, Jeremy	*Conservative*
Ruislip Northwood	Hurd, Nick	*Conservative*
Runnymede & Weybridge	Hammond, Philip	*Conservative*
Rushcliffe	Clarke, Kenneth	*Conservative*
Rutherglen & Hamilton West	McAvoy, Tommy	*Labour Co-op*
Rutland & Melton	Duncan, Alan	*Conservative*
Ryedale	Greenway, John	*Conservative*
Saffron Walden	Haselhurst, Sir Alan	*Conservative*
Salford	Blears, Hazel	*Labour*
Salisbury	Key, Robert	*Conservative*
Scarborough & Whitby	Goodwill, Robert	*Conservative*
Scunthorpe	Morley, Elliot	*Labour*
Sedgefield	Blair, Tony	*Labour*
Selby	Grogan, John	*Labour*
Sevenoaks	Fallon, Michael	*Conservative*
Sheffield Attercliffe	Betts, Clive	*Labour*
Sheffield Brightside	Blunkett, David	*Labour*
Sheffield Central	Caborn, Richard	*Labour*
Sheffield Hallam	Clegg, Nick	*Liberal Democrat*
Sheffield Heeley	Munn, Meg	*Labour Co-op*
Sheffield Hillsborough	Smith, Angela	*Labour*
Sherwood	Tipping, Paddy	*Labour*
Shipley	Davies, Philip	*Conservative*
Shrewsbury & Atcham	Kawczynski, Daniel	*Conservative*
Shropshire North	Paterson, Owen	*Conservative*
Sittingbourne & Sheppey	Wyatt, Derek	*Labour*
Skipton & Ripon	Curry, David	*Conservative*
Sleaford & North Hykeham	Hogg, Douglas	*Conservative*
Slough	Mactaggart, Fiona	*Labour*
Solihull	Burt, Lorely	*Liberal Democrat*
Somerton & Frome	Heath, David	*Liberal Democrat*
South Holland & The Deepings	Hayes, John	*Conservative*
South Shields	Miliband, David	*Labour*
Southampton Itchen	Denham, John	*Labour*
Southampton Test	Whitehead, Dr Alan	*Labour*
Southend West	Amess, David	*Conservative*
Southport	Pugh, John	*Liberal Democrat*
Southwark North & Bermondsey	Hughes, Simon	*Liberal Democrat*
Spelthorne	Wilshire, David	*Conservative*
St Albans	Main, Anne	*Conservative*
St Helens North	Watts, Dave	*Labour*
St Helens South	Woodward, Shaun	*Labour*
St Ives	George, Andrew	*Liberal Democrat*
Stafford	Kidney, David	*Labour*
Staffordshire Moorlands	Atkins, Charlotte	*Labour*
Stalybridge & Hyde	Purnell, James	*Labour*
Stevenage	Follett, Barbara	*Labour*
Stirling	McGuire, Anne	*Labour*
Stockport	Coffey, Ann	*Labour*
Stockton North	Cook, Frank	*Labour*
Stockton South	Taylor, Dari	*Labour*
Stoke-on-Trent Central	Fisher, Mark	*Labour*
Stoke-on-Trent North	Walley, Joan	*Labour*
Stoke-on-Trent South	Flello, Robert	*Labour*
Stone	Cash, William	*Conservative*

Stourbridge	Waltho, Lynda	*Labour*
Strangford	Robinson, Iris	*Democratic Unionist*
Stratford-on-Avon	Maples, John	*Conservative*
Streatham	Hill, Keith	*Labour*
Stretford & Urmston	Hughes, Beverley	*Labour*
Stroud	Drew, David	*Labour Co-op*
Suffolk Central & Ipswich North	Lord, Sir Michael	*Conservative*
Suffolk Coastal	Gummer, John	*Conservative*
Suffolk South	Yeo, Tim	*Conservative*
Suffolk West	Spring, Richard	*Conservative*
Sunderland North	Etherington, Bill	*Labour*
Sunderland South	Mullin, Chris	*Labour*
Surrey East	Ainsworth, Peter	*Conservative*
Surrey Heath	Gove, Michael	*Conservative*
Surrey South West	Hunt, Jeremy	*Conservative*
Sussex Mid	Soames, Nicholas	*Conservative*
Sutton & Cheam	Burstow, Paul	*Liberal Democrat*
Sutton Coldfield	Mitchell, Andrew	*Conservative*
Swansea East	James, Sian	*Labour*
Swansea West	Williams, Alan	*Labour*
Swindon North	Wills, Michael	*Labour*
Swindon South	Snelgrove, Anne	*Labour*
Tamworth	Jenkins, Brian	*Labour*
Tatton	Osborne, George	*Conservative*
Taunton	Browne, Jeremy	*Liberal Democrat*
Teignbridge	Younger-Ross, Richard	*Liberal Democrat*
Telford	Wright, David	*Labour*
Tewkesbury	Robertson, Laurence	*Conservative*
Thanet North	Gale, Roger	*Conservative*
Thanet South	Ladyman, Dr Stephen	*Labour*
Thurrock	MacKinlay, Andrew	*Labour*
Tiverton & Honiton	Browning, Angela	*Conservative*
Tonbridge & Malling	Stanley, Sir John	*Conservative*
Tooting	Khan, Sadiq	*Labour*
Torbay	Sanders, Adrian	*Liberal Democrat*
Torfaen	Murphy, Paul	*Labour*
Totnes	Steen, Sir Anthony	*Conservative*
Tottenham	Lammy, David	*Labour*
Truro & St Austell	Taylor, Matthew	*Liberal Democrat*
Tunbridge Wells	Clark, Greg	*Conservative*
Twickenham	Cable, Dr Vincent	*Liberal Democrat*
Tyne Bridge	Clelland, David	*Labour*
Tynemouth	Campbell, Alan	*Labour*
Tyneside North	Byers, Stephen	*Labour*
Tyrone West	Doherty, Pat	*Sinn Fein*
Ulster Mid	McGuinness, Martin	*Sinn Fein*
Upminster	Watkinson, Angela	*Conservative*
Upper Bann	Simpson, David	*Democratic Unionist*
Uxbridge	Randall, John	*Conservative*
Vale of Clwyd	Ruane, Chris	*Labour*
Vale of Glamorgan	Smith, John	*Labour*
Vale of York	McIntosh, Anne	*Conservative*
Vauxhall	Hoey, Kate	*Labour*
Wakefield	Creagh, Mary	*Labour*
Wallasey	Eagle, Angela	*Labour*
Walsall North	Winnick, David	*Labour*
Walsall South	George, Bruce	*Labour*
Walthamstow	Gerrard, Neil	*Labour*
Wansbeck	Murphy, Denis	*Labour*
Wansdyke	Norris, Dan	*Labour*
Wantage	Vaizey, Ed	*Conservative*
Warley	Spellar, John	*Labour*
Warrington North	Jones, Helen	*Labour*
Warrington South	Southworth, Helen	*Labour*
Warwick & Leamington	Plaskitt, James	*Labour*
Warwickshire North	O'Brien, Mike	*Labour*
Watford	Ward, Claire	*Labour*
Waveney	Blizzard, Bob	*Labour*
Wealden	Hendry, Charles	*Conservative*
Weaver Vale	Hall, Mike	*Labour*
Wellingborough	Bone, Peter	*Conservative*
Wells	Heathcoat-Amory, David	*Conservative*

POLITICS

Welwyn Hatfield	Shapps, Grant	*Conservative*
Wentworth	Healey, John	*Labour*
West Bromwich East	Watson, Tom	*Labour*
West Bromwich West	Bailey, Adrian	*Labour Co-op*
West Ham	Brown, Lyn	*Labour*
Westbury	Murrison, Dr Andrew	*Conservative*
Westmorland & Lonsdale	Farron, Tim	*Liberal Democrat*
Weston-super-Mare	Penrose, John	*Conservative*
Wigan	Turner, Neil	*Labour*
Wiltshire North	Gray, James	*Conservative*
Wimbledon	Hammond, Stephen	*Conservative*
Winchester	Oaten, Mark	*Liberal Democrat*
Windsor	Afriyie, Adam	*Conservative*
Wirral South	Chapman, Ben	*Labour*
Wirral West	Hesford, Stephen	*Labour*
Witney	Cameron, David	*Conservative*
Woking	Malins, Humfrey	*Conservative*
Wokingham	Redwood, John	*Conservative*
Wolverhampton North East	Purchase, Ken	*Labour Co-op*
Wolverhampton South East	McFadden, Pat	*Labour*
Wolverhampton South West	Marris, Robert	*Labour*
Woodspring	Fox, Dr Liam	*Conservative*
Worcester	Foster, Michael	*Labour*
Worcestershire Mid	Luff, Peter	*Conservative*
Worcestershire West	Spicer, Sir Michael	*Conservative*
Workington	Cunningham, Tony	*Labour*
Worsley	Keeley, Barbara	*Labour*
Worthing East & Shoreham	Loughton, Tim	*Conservative*
Worthing West	Bottomley, Peter	*Conservative*
Wrekin, The	Pritchard, Mark	*Conservative*
Wrexham	Lucas, Ian	*Labour*
Wycombe	Goodman, Paul	*Conservative*
Wyre Forest	Taylor, Dr Richard	*Independent (KHHC)*
Wythenshawe & Sale East	Goggins, Paul	*Labour*
Yeovil	Laws, David	*Liberal Democrat*
Ynys Mon	Owen, Albert	*Labour*
York, City of	Bayley, Hugh	*Labour*
Yorkshire East	Knight, Greg	*Conservative*

*Calton died three weeks after the General Election, and the ensuing bye-election was won by fellow Liberal Democrat Mark Hunter

Miscellaneous Information: After 2005 General Election

black Conservative MP: first	Adam Afriyie representing the Windsor constituency.
composition of the House of Commons (516 men, 129 women = 645) increased to 646 in June 2005	Labour 356 (257 men, 99 women), Conservatives 197 (180 men, 17 women), Liberal Democrats 62 (52 men, 10 women). Democratic Unionists 9 (8 men, 1 woman), Scottish Nationalists 6 (men), Sinn Fein 5 (4 men, 1 woman), Plaid Cymru 3 (men), SDLP 3 (men), Ulster Unionists 1 (woman). Independent 3 (men). Michael Martin (Speaker) does not vote in divisions except when the voting is tied. Due to the death of Jo Harrison, the Liberal Democrat candidate for Staffordshire South, no election took place on 5 May and the seat was contested at a 23 June by-election. Sir Patrick Cormack (Conservative) was returned as the MP.
husband and wife MPs	Ann and Nicholas Winterton; Julie Kirkbride and Andrew Mackay.
largest majority	Gerry Adams (Belfast West) had a majority of 19,315.
Muslim MP: first in the UK	Mohammad Sarwar (first elected Labour MP for Glasgow Govan in 1997).
first in England	Khalid Mahmood (first elected Labour MP for Birmingham Perry Barr in 2001).
first British-born	Shahid Malik (Labour MP for Dewsbury).
overseas born MPs	Paul Beresford (New Zealand), Piara Khabra (India), Khalid Mahmood (Pakistan), Mohammad Sarwar (Pakistan), Gisela Stuart (Germany), Rudi Vis (Holland).
percentage of vote	Labour 35.2%, Conservative 32.3%, Lib Dems 22%, Others 10.5%.
quickest result	Sunderland South result announced at 10.43pm, 45 secs slower than in 2001.
smallest majority	Laura Moffatt (Labour) defeated Henry Smith (Conservative) by 37 votes in Crawley.
sons of ex MP	Dominic Grieve is the son of Percy Grieve, former MP for Solihull. Hilary Benn is the son of Tony Benn, former MP for Chesterfield.
twins	Angela and Maria Eagle, MPs for Wallasey and Liverpool Garston.

PROVERBS

Biblical Proverbs (from the Book of Proverbs)

A wise man will hear, and will increase learning: and a man of understanding shall attain unto wise counsels (1.5).

Listen to the discipline of your father and do not forsake the law of your mother (1.8).

Happy is the man that has found wisdom, and the man that has discernment (3.13).

Do not hold back good from those to whom it is owing, when it happens to be in the power of your hand to do [it] (3.27).

Do not fabricate against your fellow man anything bad, when he is dwelling in a sense of security with you (3.29).

Do not quarrel with a man without cause, if he has rendered no bad to you (3.30).

Do not become envious of a man of violence, nor choose any of his ways (3.31).

Into the path of wicked ones do not enter, and do not walk straight on into the way of bad ones (4.14).

Remove from yourself the crookedness of speech, and the deviousness of lips put far away from yourself (4.24).

Smooth out the course of your foot, and may all your own ways be firmly established (4.26).

Go to the ant, see its ways and become wise (6.6).

Do not reprove a ridiculer, that he may not hate you. Give a reproof to a wise person and he will love you (9.8).

A wise son is one that makes a father rejoice, and a stupid son is the grief of his mother (10.1).

He that is walking in integrity will walk in security, but he that is making his ways crooked will make himself known (10.9).

Hatred is what stirs up contentions, but love covers over even all transgressions (10.12).

The tongue of the righteous person is choice silver, whilst the heart of the wicked one is worth little (10.20).

Deception is in the heart of those fabricating mischief, but those counselling peace have rejoicing (12.20).

A prudent man concealeth knowledge (12.23).

He that walketh with wise men shall be wise: but a companion of fools shall be destroyed (13.20).

He that spareth his rod hateth his son (13.24).

Pride goeth before destruction, and an haughty spirit before a fall (16.18).

General Proverbs

All roads lead to Rome.

An old poacher makes the best keeper.

Beauty is potent but money is omnipotent.

Better be stung by a nettle than pricked by a rose.

Between two stools one falls to the ground.

A bird in the hand is worth two in the bush.

Caesar's wife must be above suspicion.

Cards are the devil's books.

All cats are grey in the dark.

Caveat emptor (Let the buyer beware).

Diligence is the mother of good luck.

A drowning man will catch at a straw.

Enough is as good as a feast.

Every cloud has a silver lining.

Experience is the mistress of fools.

Faint heart never won fair lady.

A fair exchange is no robbery.

Fair words butter no parsnips.

Far fowls have fair feathers.

The folly of one man is the fortune of another.

A fool may ask more questions in an hour than a wise man can answer in seven years.

The fool wanders, the wise man travels.

Give a dog a bad name and hang him.

Go to bed with the lamb, and rise with the lark.

The hand that rocks the cradle rules the world.

He is a fool who makes his doctor his heir.

He should have a long spoon that sups with the devil.

He that sings on Friday will weep on Sunday.

He was a bold man that first ate an oyster.

A heavy purse makes a light heart.

A hedge between keeps friendship green.

If ifs and ans were pots and pans, there'd be no trade for tinkers.

If St Vitus's day [15 June] be rainy weather, it will rain for 30 days together.

If you run after two hares, you will catch neither.

If you sing before breakfast, you'll cry before night.

If you swear, you'll catch no fish.

Keep a thing seven years and you will find a use for it.

Knowledge is power.

A light purse makes a heavy heart.

Lose an hour in the morning and you'll be all day hunting for it.

A mackerel sky is never long dry.

Magpies: one's sorrow, two's mirth, three's a wedding, four's a birth, five's a christening, six a dearth, seven's heaven, eight is hell, and nine's the devil his ane sel'.

March comes in like a lion and goes out like a lamb.

Mighty oaks from little acorns grow.

Monday's child is fair of face,/Tuesday's child is full of grace,/Wednesday's child is full of woe,/Thursday's child has far to go,/Friday's child is loving and giving,/Saturday's child works hard for living. But the child who is born on the Sabbath day is lucky and happy and good and gay.

Nature abhors a vacuum.

Necessity is the mother of invention.

Needs must when the devil drives.

Never is a long day.

Never trouble trouble till trouble troubles you.

A nod is as good as a wink to a blind horse.

Out of debt, out of danger.

Penny wise, pound foolish.

Prevention is better than cure.

Procrastination is the thief of time

Promises and pie-crusts are made to be broken.

The proof of the pudding is in the eating.

Providence is better than rent.

Rain before seven, fine before eleven.

Red sky at night shepherd's delight, red sky in the morning shepherd's warning.

The road to hell is paved with good intentions.

Salmon and sermon have their season in Lent.

Save your breath to cool your porridge.

Sloth is the key to poverty.

Sneeze on a Monday you sneeze for danger, sneeze on a Tuesday you kiss a stranger, sneeze on a Wednesday you sneeze for a letter, sneeze on a Thursday for something better, sneeze on a Friday you sneeze for sorrow, sneeze on a Saturday see your sweetheart tomorrow, sneeze on a Sunday your safety seek, the devil will have you the whole of the week.

Spare the rod and spoil the child.

Speak well of your friend, of your enemy say nothing.

Still waters run deep.

A tale twice told is cabbage twice sold.

Talk of the devil, and he'll appear.

Tell that to the marines.

Thrift is good revenue.

Time and tide wait for no man.

Virtue is its own reward.

Virtue never grows old.

What can't be cured must be endured.

When the sun is highest he casts the least shadow.

When the wind is in the east it's good for neither man nor beast./When the wind is in the north the skilful fisher goes not forth./When the wind is in the south it blows the bait in the fish's mouth./When the wind is in the west the weather is at the best.

Who knows most says least.

Whom God wishes to destroy, he first makes mad (*Quos Deus vult perdere, prius dementat*).

A wild goose never laid a tame egg.

A wonder lasts but nine days.

You cannot make an omelette without breaking eggs.

You cannot make a silk purse out of a sow's ear.

You cannot teach an old dog new tricks.

Young men may die, old men must.

Zeal without knowledge is fire without light.

Zeal without prudence is frenzy.

NB Some of the proverbs above are corruptions of biblical proverbs. Others were coined by great thinkers and philosophers, and yet others have simply come into general usage through time.

QUOTATIONS

Quotations (in Alphabetical Order)

All Gaul is divided into three parts.	Julius Caesar
All hope abandon ye who enter. (from *Divine Comedy*)	Dante Alighieri
All is for the best in the best of possible worlds. (from *Candide*)	Voltaire
An archaeologist is the best husband any woman can have – the older she gets the more interested he is in her.	Agatha Christie
And so to bed.	Samuel Pepys
And therefore never send to know for whom the bell tolls; It tolls for thee.	John Donne
Arms and the man I sing. (from the *Aeneid*)	Virgil
Art for art's sake.	Victor Cousin
Attila the hen. (speaking about Margaret Thatcher)	Clement Freud
Balance of power.	Sir Robert Walpole
A bank is a place that will lend you money if you can prove that you don't need it.	Bob Hope
Because it's there. (when asked why he wanted to climb Mt Everest)	George Mallory
Better to err with Pope, than shine with Pye.	Lord George Byron
The bigger they come the harder they fall.	Robert Fitzsimmons
Blood is thicker than water.	Commodore Tattnall
The boy stood on the burning deck. (from 'Casablanca')	Felicia Hemans
Bread and circuses. (*Panem et circenses*, alluding to what the people desired)	Juvenal
The buck stops here.	Harry S Truman
A bumping pitch and a blinding light, an hour to play and the last man in.	Sir Henry Newbolt
Candy is dandy. But liquor is quicker.	Ogden Nash
Carthage must be destroyed.	Senator Cato
Cauliflower is nothing but cabbage with a college education. (from Pudd'nhead Wilson's calendar)	Mark Twain
The child is father of the man.	William Wordsworth
Claret is the liquor for boys, Port for men, but he who aspires to be a hero must drink brandy.	Dr Samuel Johnson
A classic is something that everybody wants to have read and nobody wants to read.	Mark Twain
A comedian does funny things; a good comedian does things funny.	Buster Keaton
The cook was a good cook as cooks go; and as cooks go she went.	Saki
Cough and the world coughs with you. Fart and you stand alone.	Trevor Griffiths
A desiccated calculating machine. (writing about Hugh Gaitskell)	Aneurin Bevan
The die is cast. (on crossing the Rubicon in 49 BC)	Julius Caesar
Don't count your chickens before they are hatched.	Aesop
Don't get mad, get even.	Senator Everett Dirksen
Don't one of you fire until you see the whites of their eyes. (at Bunker Hill in 1775)	US General Israel Putnam
Each man kills the thing he loves. (from *The Ballad of Reading Gaol*)	Oscar Wilde
Ears made him look like a taxi cab with both doors open. (writing about Clark Gable)	Howard Hughes
East is East and West is West and never the twain shall meet.	Rudyard Kipling
England is a nation of shopkeepers.	Napoleon Bonaparte
Eureka (I have found it).	Archimedes
Every man over forty is a scoundrel.	G B Shaw
Experience is the name everyone gives to his mistakes. (from *Lady Windermere's Fan*)	Oscar Wilde
Fair stood the wind for France.	Michael Drayton
Father, I cannot tell a lie, I did it with my little hatchet.	George Washington
The female of the species is more deadly than the male.	Rudyard Kipling
For fools rush in where angels fear to tread.	Alexander Pope
From the sublime to the ridiculous there is only one step. (after the retreat from Moscow in 1812)	Napoleon Bonaparte
Generals January and February. (referring to his chief allies against Britain and France in the Crimea)	Tsar Nicholas I
Genius is one per cent inspiration and ninety-nine per cent perspiration.	Thomas Alva Edison
The ghost in the machine.	Gilbert Ryle
Give a man a free hand and he'll run it all over you.	Mae West
Give me a lever long enough and I will move the world.	Archimedes
Give us the tools and we will finish the job.	Winston Churchill
Go and catch a falling star.	John Donne
Go West, young man, and grow up with the country.	Horace Greeley
God made the country, and man made the town.	William Cowper
God moves in a mysterious way, his wonders to perform.	William Cowper
God's in his heaven – all's right with the world.	Robert Browning
Golf is a good walk spoiled.	Mark Twain
The gondola of London. (referring to the hansom cab)	Benjamin Disraeli
Good Americans, when they die, go to Paris.	Thomas Gold Appleton

A grain, which in England is generally given to horses but in Scotland supports the people. (definition of oats)	Dr Samuel Johnson
That Great Cham of literature Samuel Johnson. (in a letter to John Wilkes)	Tobias Smollett
Great fleas have little fleas upon their backs to bite 'em, and little fleas have lesser fleas and so ad infinitum.	Augustus De Morgan
The greatest happiness of the greatest number.	Jeremy Bentham
He can run but he can't hide.	Joe Louis
He makes no friend who never made a foe.	Lord Alfred Tennyson
He nothing common did, or mean, Upon that memorable scene. ('An Horatian Ode upon Cromwell's Return from Ireland')	Andrew Marvell
He speaks to me as if I were a public meeting. (referring to William Gladstone)	Queen Victoria
Heaven has no rage like love to hatred turned, Nor hell a fury like a woman scorned.	William Congreve
Hell is other people.	Jean-Paul Sartre
Here Skugg lies snug as a bug in a rug.	Benjamin Franklin
History is bunk.	Henry Ford
The history of the world is but the biography of great men.	Thomas Carlyle
Hope springs eternal in the human breast.	Alexander Pope
How can they tell? (on being told Calvin Coolidge was dead)	Dorothy Parker
I am his Highness' dog at Kew; Pray tell me sir, whose dog are you?	Alexander Pope
I am just going outside and may be some time.	Capt. Lawrence Oates
I am the State (L'État, c'est moi).	Louis XIV
I awoke one morning and found myself famous.	Lord George Byron
I beseech you in the bowels of Christ, think it possible you may be mistaken.	Oliver Cromwell
I can resist everything except temptation. (from Lady Windermere's Fan)	Oscar Wilde
I fear the Greeks even when they bring gifts. (from the Aeneid)	Virgil
I have always thought that every woman should marry, and no man.	Benjamin Disraeli
I have been poor and I have been rich. Rich is better.	Sophie Tucker
I have nothing to declare but my genius. (at US customs)	Oscar Wilde
I have nothing to offer but blood, toil, tears and sweat.	Winston Churchill
I know I have the body of a weak and feeble woman, but I have the heart and stomach of a King.	Elizabeth I
I look upon the world as my parish.	John Wesley
I married beneath me, all women do.	Nancy Astor
I never trust a man unless I've got his pecker in my pocket.	Lyndon B Johnson
I think, therefore I am (cogito ergo sum).	René Descartes
I want to be the white man's brother, not his brother-in-law.	Martin Luther King
Ich bin ein Berliner.	John F Kennedy
I'd like that translated, if I may. (reacting to Nikita Khrushchev's banging of shoe on table at the UN)	Harold Macmillan
If God did not exist, it would be necessary to invent him.	Voltaire
If I have seen further it is by standing on the shoulders of giants.	Isaac Newton
If you can keep your head when all about you are losing theirs and blaming it on you. (from 'If')	Rudyard Kipling
If you can meet with triumph and disaster and treat those two impostors just the same (from 'If')	Rudyard Kipling
If you pay peanuts, you get monkeys.	Sir James Goldsmith
Ignorance is bliss.	Thomas Gray
Ignorance, Madam, pure ignorance. (when asked why he defined pastern as a knee of a horse in his dictionary).	Dr Samuel Johnson
I'm going to spend, spend, spend.	Viv Nicholson
I'm not really a Jew, just Jew-ish, not the whole hog. (Beyond the Fringe sketch)	Dr Jonathan Miller
I'm only a beer teetotaller not a champagne teetotaller. (from Candida)	G B Shaw
In my sport the quick are too often listed among the dead.	Jackie Stewart
In the future everyone will be famous for fifteen minutes.	Andy Warhol
In the long run we are all dead.	J M Keynes
In this country [England] it is good to kill an admiral from time to time, to encourage the others. (re: shooting of Byng)	Voltaire
In two words, Impossible.	Sam Goldwyn
Include me out.	Sam Goldwyn
Indomitable in retreat; invincible in advance; insufferable in victory. (writing of Field-Marshal Montgomery)	Winston Churchill
Into each life some rain must fall.	Henry Wadsworth Longfellow
Into the valley of death rode the six hundred.	Lord Alfred Tennyson
It is better to die on your feet than to live on your knees.	La Pasionaria
It is magnificent but it is not war. (referring to the Charge of the Light Brigade)	General Pierre Bousquet
It is true that liberty is precious – so precious that it must be rationed.	Lenin
It matters not how a man dies, but how he lives.	Dr Samuel Johnson
It's not the size of the dog in the fight – it's the size of the fight in the dog.	Dwight D Eisenhower
Keep a diary and one day it'll keep you.	Mae West
Kind hearts are more than coronets.	Lord Alfred Tennyson
Knowledge is Power.	Francis Bacon

The lady's not for turning.	Margaret Thatcher
The lamps are going out all over Europe.	Edward Gray
Laugh and the world laughs with you; Weep and you weep alone. (from her poem 'Solitude')	Ella Wheeler Wilcox
Let them eat cake.	Marie Antoinette
Let us never negotiate out of fear, but let us never fear to negotiate.	John F Kennedy
Lies, damned lies and statistics.	Benjamin Disraeli
The lion and the calf shall lie down together, but the calf won't get much sleep.	Woody Allen
A little learning is a dangerous thing.	Alexander Pope
Love is like the measles, we all have to go through it.	Jerome K Jerome
Love's young dream.	Thomas Moore
Macmillan's role as a poseur was itself a pose.	Harold Wilson
Mad is he? Then I hope he will bite some of my other generals. (on being told General Wolfe was mad)	George II
Man is born free; and everywhere he is in chains. (first line of *The Social Contract*)	Jean-Jacques Rousseau
Man is by nature a civic animal.	Aristotle
A man is only as old as the woman he feels.	Groucho Marx
Man is the hunter, woman is his game.	Lord Alfred Tennyson
A man who knows the price of everything and the value of nothing. (definition of a cynic)	Oscar Wilde
Manners maketh man.	William of Wykeham
Marriage is a wonderful invention, but then again, so is the bicycle repair kit.	Billy Connolly
The medium is the message.	Marshall McLuhan
The meek shall inherit the earth, but not its mineral rights.	J Paul Getty
Men seldom make passes at girls who wear glasses.	Dorothy Parker
A modest little man with much to be modest about. (writing of Clement Attlee)	Winston Churchill
The moving finger writes and having writ moves on.	Omar Khayyam
Mr Balfour's poodle. (referring to the House of Lords)	Lloyd George
Music hath charms to soothe the savage breast.	William Congreve
Never in the field of human conflict was so much owed by so many to so few. (referring to Battle of Britain pilots)	Winston Churchill
Never trust a man with short legs – brains too near their bottom.	Noël Coward
Nice guys finish last. (referring to his baseball team)	Leo Durocher
The night has a thousand eyes and the day but one.	Francis Bourdillon
No man but a blockhead ever wrote except for money.	Dr Samuel Johnson
No man is an island.	John Donne
No man is justified in doing evil on the ground of expediency.	Theodore Roosevelt
None but the brave deserves the fair.	John Dryden
Nothing is certain but death and taxes.	Benjamin Franklin
Nuts! (replying to von Manteuffel's surrender call during the Battle of the Bulge)	Brigadier General McAuliffe
O what a tangled web we weave when first we practise to deceive.	Sir Walter Scott
Oh liberty! what crimes are committed in your name!	Madame Roland
Old soldiers never die, they simply fade away.	General MacArthur
Once upon a midnight dreary, while I pondered weak and weary. (from 'The Raven')	Edgar Allan Poe
One man's wage rise is another man's price increase.	Harold Wilson
One swallow does not make a summer.	Aristotle
The only good Indians I ever saw were dead.	General Philip Sheridan
The only reason so many people showed up was to make sure that he was dead. (of Louis Mayer's funeral)	Sam Goldwyn
The only thing we have to fear is fear itself.	F D Roosevelt
Open my heart and you will see graved inside of it, 'Italy'.	Robert Browning
Patriotism is not enough. I must have no hatred or bitterness towards anyone.	Edith Cavell
Patriotism is the last refuge of a scoundrel.	Dr Samuel Johnson
Peace for our time. (on returning from Munich in 1938)	Neville Chamberlain
Peccavi. ('I have sinned' from a telegram sent after capturing Sind in 1834)	Sir Charles Napier
The pen is mightier than the sword.	Bulwer Lytton
A penny Punch and Judy show. (referring to television)	Winston Churchill
Politics is the art of the possible.	R A Butler
Power tends to corrupt and absolute power corrupts absolutely.	Lord Acton
Power without responsibility, the privilege of the harlot throughout the ages (referring to the press)	Stanley Baldwin
Procrastination is the thief of time.	Edward Young
Property is theft.	Pierre-Joseph Proudhon
The public be damned.	Cornelius Vanderbilt
Publish and be damned.	Duke of Wellington
Put your trust in God and keep your powder dry.	Oliver Cromwell
Quoth the Raven, 'Nevermore'. (from 'The Raven')	Edgar Allan Poe
Religion is the opium of the people.	Karl Marx
The remedy is worse than the disease.	Francis Bacon
Remember that time is money.	Benjamin Franklin

Reports of my death have been greatly exaggerated.	Mark Twain
A riddle wrapped in a mystery inside an enigma. (referring to the Soviet Union)	Winston Churchill
A Rose is a Rose is a Rose.	Gertrude Stein
The seagreen incorruptible. (referring to Robespierre)	Thomas Carlyle
The secret of success is sincerity, once you can fake that you've got it made.	Arthur Bloch
Seize the present day. (*carpe diem*)	Horace
She is the best man in England. (referring to Margaret Thatcher)	Ronald Reagan
A sheep in sheep's clothing. (writing of Clement Attlee)	Winston Churchill
Sic transit gloria mundi (So passes away the glory of the world).	Thomas à Kempis
A single death is a tragedy, a million deaths is a statistic.	Joseph Stalin
Speak softly and carry a big stick.	Theodore Roosevelt
Speech is silvern, Silence is golden.	Thomas Carlyle
Stone walls do not a prison make, Nor iron bars a cage. (from 'To Althea from Prison')	Richard Lovelace
Sweet Swan of Avon. (referring to William Shakespeare)	Ben Jonson
Television is an invention that permits you to be entertained in your living room by people you wouldn't have in your home.	Sir David Frost
Tell me the old, old story.	Katherine Hankey
There are two things no man will admit he can't do well: drive and make love.	Stirling Moss
There is no terror in a bang – only in the anticipation of it.	Alfred Hitchcock
There is properly no history; only biography.	Ralph Waldo Emerson
There never was a good war or a bad peace.	Benjamin Franklin
There's a sucker born every minute.	P T Barnum
There's no such thing as a free lunch. (also used by J K Galbraith)	Milton Friedman
They also serve who only stand and wait.	John Milton
Thy need is greater than mine. (on giving his water to a soldier at Zutphen)	Sir Philip Sydney
'Tis better to have loved and lost, than never to have loved at all. (from 'In Memoriam')	Lord Alfred Tennyson
To err is human, to forgive, divine.	Alexander Pope
The trouble with Freud is that he never played the Glasgow Empire Saturday night.	Ken Dodd
Turn on, Tune in, Drop out.	Timothy Leary
Unpleasant and unacceptable face of Capitalism. (referring to Lonrho)	Edward Heath
The unspeakable in pursuit of the uneatable. (referring to foxhunting)	Oscar Wilde
Variety's the spice of life.	William Cowper
Veni, Vidi, Vici (I came, I saw, I conquered). (from a letter written after his victory at Zela in Asia Minor)	Julius Caesar
A verbal contract isn't worth the paper it's written on.	Sam Goldwyn
War is hell.	General Sherman
Warts and everything.	Oliver Cromwell
We are American at puberty. We die French.	Evelyn Waugh
We are not amused.	Queen Victoria
We must indeed all hang together or, most assuredly, we shall all hang separately (on signing the Declaration of Independence)	Benjamin Franklin
A week is a long time in politics.	Harold Wilson
What you said hurt me very much. I cried all the way to the bank. (replying to critics)	Liberace
When a man is tired of London he is tired of life.	Dr Samuel Johnson
When a man knows he is to be hanged in a fortnight it concentrates his mind wonderfully.	Dr Samuel Johnson
When the eagles are silent the parrots begin to jabber.	Winston Churchill
Where law ends, tyranny begins.	William Pitt (1st Earl of Chatham)
Whoever is not against us is with us.	Janos Kadar
Will no one rid me of this turbulent priest? (referring to Thomas à Becket)	Henry II
The wind of change is blowing through the continent. (speaking to South African Parliament in 1960)	Harold Macmillan
Winning is not everything. It's the only thing.	Vince Lombardi
The wisest fool in Christendom. (speaking of James I of England and VI of Scotland)	Henry IV of France
A woman is only a woman, but a good cigar is a smoke. (from 'The Betrothed')	Rudyard Kipling
Women should be obscene and not heard.	John Lennon
Wonders will never cease.	Sir Henry Bate Dudley
The world must be made safe for democracy.	Woodrow Wilson
Worth seeing, yes; but not worth going to see. (speaking about the Giant's Causeway)	Dr Samuel Johnson
Would you buy a second-hand car from this man? (writing about Richard Nixon)	Mort Sahl
A writer of dictionaries, a harmless drudge. (definition of a lexicographer)	Dr Samuel Johnson
Ye distant spires, ye antique towers. (from 'Ode on a Distant Prospect of Eton')	Thomas Gray
You can fool all the people all of the time, and some of the people all the time, but you cannot fool all the people all of the time.	Abraham Lincoln
You can have it any colour as long as it's black.	Henry Ford
You can make a throne from bayonets but you can't sit on it long.	Boris Yeltsin
You're either part of the solution or part of the problem.	Eldridge Cleaver
You're not drunk if you can lie on the floor without holding on.	Dean Martin
Youth is wasted on the young.	G B Shaw

NB Details of the quotation are given in brackets above but will need to be cross-referenced if the alphabetical table by person is being used. The same caveat as in the 'Dying Sayings' applies. It is doubtful that many of these utterances were original thoughts; for instance, the Milton Friedman entry may have been a corruption of a phrase from a Robert Heinlein novel *The Moon Is a Harsh Mistress* and the MacArthur entry was almost certainly from a popular song of the 1920s. Some popular attributions, e.g. 'An Iron Curtain Descending', have also been omitted because of doubts about their origins.

Quotations (in Alphabetical Order by Person)

Acton, Lord	Power tends to corrupt and absolute power corrupts absolutely.
Aesop	Don't count your chickens before they are hatched.
Allen, Woody	The lion and the calf shall lie down together, but the calf won't get much sleep.
Antoinette, Marie	Let them eat cake.
Appleton, Thomas Gold	Good Americans, when they die, go to Paris.
Archimedes	*Eureka* (I have found it).
	Give me a lever long enough and I will move the world.
Aristotle	Man is by nature a civic animal.
	One swallow does not make a summer.
Astor, Nancy	I married beneath me, all women do.
Bacon, Francis	Knowledge is Power.
	The remedy is worse than the disease.
Baldwin, Stanley	Power without responsibility, the privilege of the harlot throughout the ages.
Barnum, P T	There's a sucker born every minute.
Bentham, Jeremy	The greatest happiness of the greatest number.
Bevan, Aneurin	A desiccated calculating machine.
Bloch, Arthur	The secret of success is sincerity, once you can fake that you've got it made.
Bonaparte, Napoleon	England is a nation of shopkeepers.
	From the sublime to the ridiculous there is only one step.
Bourdillon, Francis	The night has a thousand eyes and the day but one.
Bousquet, General Pierre	It is magnificent but it is not war.
Browning, Robert	God's in his heaven – all's right with the world.
	Open my heart and you will see graved inside of it, 'Italy'.
Butler, R A	Politics is the art of the possible.
Byron, Lord George	Better to err with Pope, than shine with Pye.
	I awoke one morning and found myself famous.
Caesar, Julius	All Gaul is divided into three parts.
	The die is cast.
	Veni, Vidi, Vici (I came, I saw, I conquered).
Carlyle, Thomas	Speech is silvern, Silence is golden.
	The history of the world is but the biography of great men.
	The seagreen incorruptible.
Cato, Senator	Carthage must be destroyed.
Cavell, Edith	Patriotism is not enough. I must have no hatred or bitterness towards anyone.
Chamberlain, Neville	Peace for our time.
Christie, Agatha	An archaeologist is the best husband any woman can have – the older she gets the more interested he is in her.
Churchill, Winston	A modest little man with much to be modest about.
	A penny Punch and Judy show.
	A riddle wrapped in a mystery inside an enigma.
	A sheep in sheep's clothing.
	Give us the tools and we will finish the job.
	I have nothing to offer but blood, toil, tears and sweat.
	Indomitable in retreat; invincible in advance; insufferable in victory.
	Never in the field of human conflict was so much owed by so many to so few.
	When the eagles are silent the parrots begin to jabber.
Cleaver, Eldridge	You're either part of the solution or part of the problem.
Congreve, William	Heaven has no rage like love to hatred turned, Nor hell a fury like a woman scorned.
	Music hath charms to soothe a savage breast.
Connolly, Billy	Marriage is a wonderful invention, but then again, so is the bicycle repair kit.
Cousin, Victor	Art for art's sake.
Coward, Noël	Never trust a man with short legs – brains too near their bottom.
Cowper, William	God made the country, and man made the town.
	God moves in a mysterious way, his wonders to perform.
	Variety's the spice of life.
Cromwell, Oliver	I beseech you in the bowels of Christ, think it possible you may be mistaken.
	Put your trust in God and keep your powder dry.
	Warts and everything.
Dante Alighieri	All hope abandon ye who enter.

QUOTATIONS

De Morgan, Augustus	Great fleas have little fleas upon their backs to bite 'em, and little fleas have lesser fleas and so ad infinitum.
Descartes, René	I think, therefore I am (*cogito ergo sum*).
Dirksen, Senator Everett	Don't get mad, get even.
Disraeli, Benjamin	I have always thought that every woman should marry, and no man.
	Lies, damned lies and statistics.
	The gondola of London.
Dodd, Ken	The trouble with Freud is that he never played the Glasgow Empire Saturday night.
Donne, John	And therefore never send to know for whom the bell tolls; it tolls for thee.
	Go and catch a falling star.
	No man is an island.
Drayton, Michael	Fair stood the wind for France.
Dryden, John	None but the brave deserves the fair.
Dudley, Sir Henry Bate	Wonders will never cease.
Durocher, Leo	Nice guys finish last.
Edison, Thomas Alva	Genius is one per cent inspiration and ninety-nine per cent perspiration.
Eisenhower, Dwight D	It's not the size of the dog in the fight – it's the size of the fight in the dog.
Elizabeth I	I know I have the body of a weak and feeble woman, but I have the heart and stomach of a King.
Emerson, Ralph Waldo	There is properly no history; only biography.
Fitzsimmons, Robert	The bigger they come the harder they fall.
Ford, Henry	History is bunk.
	You can have it any colour as long as it's black.
Franklin, Benjamin	Here Skugg lies snug as a bug in a rug.
	Nothing is certain but death and taxes.
	Remember that time is money.
	There never was a good war or a bad peace.
	We must indeed all hang together or, most assuredly, we shall all hang separately.
Freud, Clement	Attila the hen.
Friedman, Milton	There's no such thing as a free lunch.
Frost, Sir David	Television is an invention that permits you to be entertained in your living room by people you wouldn't have in your home.
George II	Mad is he? Then I hope he will bite some of my other generals.
George, Lloyd	Mr Balfour's poodle.
Getty, J Paul	The meek shall inherit the earth, but not its mineral rights.
Goldsmith, Sir James	If you pay peanuts, you get monkeys.
Goldwyn, Sam	A verbal contract isn't worth the paper it's written on.
	In two words, Impossible.
	Include me out.
	The only reason so many people showed up was to make sure that he was dead.
Gray, Thomas	Ignorance is bliss.
	Ye distant spires, ye antique towers.
Greeley, Horace	Go West, young man, and grow up with the country.
Grey, Edward	The lamps are going out all over Europe.
Griffiths, Trevor	Cough and the world coughs with you. Fart and you stand alone.
Hankey, Katherine	Tell me the old, old story.
Heath, Edward	Unpleasant and unacceptable face of Capitalism.
Hemans, Felicia	The boy stood on the burning deck.
Henry II	Will no one rid me of this turbulent priest?
Henry IV of France	The wisest fool in Christendom.
Hitchcock Alfred	There is no terror in a bang – only in the anticipation of it.
Hope, Bob	A bank is a place that will lend you money if you can prove that you don't need it.
Horace	Seize the present day (*carpe diem*).
Hughes, Howard	Ears made him look like a taxi cab with both doors open.
Jerome, Jerome K	Love is like the measles, we all have to go through it.
Johnson, Dr Samuel	A grain, which in England is generally given to horses but in Scotland supports the people.
	A writer of dictionaries, a harmless drudge.
	Claret is the liquor for boys, Port for men, but he who aspires to be a hero must drink brandy.
	Ignorance, Madam, pure ignorance.
	It matters not how a man dies, but how he lives.
	No man but a blockhead ever wrote except for money.
	Patriotism is the last refuge of a scoundrel.
	When a man is tired of London he is tired of life.
	When a man knows he is to be hanged in a fortnight it concentrates his mind wonderfully.
	Worth seeing, yes; but not worth going to see.
Johnson, Lyndon B	I never trust a man unless I've got his pecker in my pocket.
Jonson, Ben	Sweet Swan of Avon.
Juvenal	Bread and circuses (*Panem et circenses*).
Kadar, Janos	Whoever is not against us is with us.

Keaton, Buster	A comedian does funny things; a good comedian does things funny.
Kempis, Thomas à	*Sic transit gloria mundi* (so passes away the glory of the world).
Kennedy, John F	Ich bin ein Berliner.
	Let us never negotiate out of fear, but let us never fear to negotiate.
Keynes, J M	In the long run we are all dead.
Khayyam, Omar	The moving finger writes and having writ moves on.
King, Martin Luther	I want to be the white man's brother, not his brother-in-law.
Kipling, Rudyard	A woman is only a woman, but a good cigar is a smoke.
	East is East and West is West and never the twain shall meet.
	If you can keep your head when all about you are losing theirs and blaming it on you.
	If you can meet with triumph and disaster and treat those two impostors just the same.
	The female of the species is more deadly than the male.
Leary, Timothy	Turn on, Tune in, Drop out.
Lenin	It is true that liberty is precious – so precious that it must be rationed.
Lennon, John	Women should be obscene and not heard.
Liberace	What you said hurt me very much. I cried all the way to the bank.
Lincoln, Abraham	You can fool all the people some of the time, and some of the people all of the time, but you cannot fool all the people all the time.
Lombardi, Vince	Winning is not everything. It's the only thing.
Longfellow, Henry Wadsworth	Into each life some rain must fall.
Louis XIV	I am the State (*L'État, c'est moi*).
Louis, Joe	He can run but he can't hide.
Lovelace, Richard	Stone walls do not a prison make, Nor iron bars a cage.
Lytton, Bulwer	The pen is mightier than the sword.
MacArthur, General	Old soldiers never die, they simply fade away. (originally from a First World War song)
Macmillan, Harold	I'd like that translated, if I may.
	The wind of change is blowing through the continent.
Mallory, George	Because it's there.
Martin, Dean	You're not drunk if you can lie on the floor without holding on.
Marvell, Andrew	He nothing common did, or mean, Upon that memorable scene.
Marx, Groucho	A man is only as old as the woman he feels.
Marx, Karl	Religion is the opium of the people.
McAuliffe, Brigadier General	Nuts!
McLuhan, Marshall	The medium is the message.
Miller, Dr Jonathan	I'm not really a Jew, just Jew-ish, not the whole hog.
Milton, John	They also serve who only stand and wait.
Moore, Thomas	Love's young dream.
Moss, Stirling	There are two things no man will admit he can't do well: drive and make love.
Napier, Sir Charles	Peccavi (I have sinned).
Nash, Ogden	Candy is dandy. But liquor is quicker.
Newbolt, Sir Henry	A bumping pitch and a blinding light, an hour to play and the last man in.
Newton, Isaac	If I have seen further it is by standing on the shoulders of giants.
Nicholas I, Tsar	Generals January and February.
Nicholson, Viv	I'm going to spend, spend, spend.
Oates, Capt. Lawrence	I am just going outside and may be some time.
Parker, Dorothy	How can they tell?
	Men seldom make passes at girls who wear glasses.
Pasionaria, La	It is better to die on your feet than to live on your knees.
Pepys, Samuel	And so to bed.
Pitt, William (1st Earl of Chatham)	Where law ends, tyranny begins.
Poe, Edgar Allan	Once upon a midnight dreary, while I pondered weak and weary.
	Quoth the Raven, 'Nevermore'.
Pope, Alexander	A little learning is a dangerous thing.
	For fools rush in where angels fear to tread.
	Hope springs eternal in the human breast.
	I am his Highness' dog at Kew; Pray tell me sir, whose dog are you?
	To err is human, to forgive, divine.
Proudhon, Pierre-Joseph	Property is theft.
Putnam, US General Israel	Don't one of you fire until you see the whites of their eyes.
Reagan, Ronald	She is the best man in England.
Roland, Madame	Oh liberty! what crimes are committed in your name!
Roosevelt, F D	The only thing we have to fear is fear itself.
Roosevelt, Theodore	No man is justified in doing evil on the ground of expediency.
	Speak softly and carry a big stick.
Rousseau, Jean-Jacques	Man is born free, and everywhere he is in chains.
Ryle, Gilbert	The ghost in the machine.
Sahl, Mort	Would you buy a second-hand car from this man?
Saki	The cook was a good cook as cooks go; and as cooks go she went.

Sartre, Jean-Paul	Hell is other people.
Scott, Sir Walter	O what a tangled web we weave when first we practise to deceive.
Shaw, G B	Every man over forty is a scoundrel.
	I'm only a beer teetotaller not a champagne teetotaller.
	Youth is wasted on the young.
Sheridan, General Philip	The only good Indians I ever saw were dead.
Sherman, General	War is hell.
Sidney, Sir Philip	Thy need is greater than mine.
Smollett, Tobias	That great Cham of literature Samuel Johnson.
Stalin, Joseph	A single death is a tragedy, a million deaths is a statistic.
Stein, Gertrude	A Rose is a Rose is a Rose.
Stewart, Jackie	In my sport the quick are too often listed among the dead.
Tattnall, Commodore	Blood is thicker than water.
Tennyson, Lord Alfred	He makes no friend who never made a foe.
	Into the valley of death rode the six hundred.
	Kind hearts are more than coronets.
	Man is the hunter, woman is his game.
	'Tis better to have loved and lost, than never to have loved at all.
Thatcher, Margaret	The lady's not for turning.
Truman, Harry S	The buck stops here.
Tucker, Sophie	I have been poor and I have been rich. Rich is better.
Twain, Mark	A classic is something that everybody wants to have read and nobody wants to read.
	Cauliflower is nothing but cabbage with a college education.
	Golf is a good walk spoiled.
	Reports of my death have been greatly exaggerated.
Vanderbilt, Cornelius	The public be damned.
Queen Victoria	We are not amused.
	He speaks to me as if I were a public meeting.
Virgil	Arms and the man I sing.
	I fear the Greeks even when they bring gifts.
Voltaire	All is for the best in the best of possible worlds.
	If God did not exist, it would be necessary to invent him.
	In this country [England] it is good to kill an admiral from time to time, to encourage the others.
Walpole, Sir Robert	Balance of power.
Warhol, Andy	In the future everyone will be famous for fifteen minutes.
Washington, George	Father, I cannot tell a lie, I did it with my little hatchet.
Waugh, Evelyn	We are American at puberty. We die French.
Wellington, Duke of	Publish and be damned.
Wesley, John	I look upon the world as my parish.
West, Mae	Give a man a free hand and he'll run it all over you.
	Keep a diary and one day it'll keep you.
Wilcox, Ella Wheeler	Laugh and the world laughs with you; Weep and you weep alone.
Wilde, Oscar	A man who knows the price of everything and the value of nothing.
	Each man kills the thing he loves.
	Experience is the name everyone gives to his mistakes.
	I can resist everything except temptation.
	I have nothing to declare but my genius.
	The unspeakable in pursuit of the uneatable.
William of Wykeham	Manners maketh man.
Wilson, Harold	A week is a long time in politics.
	Macmillan's role as a poseur was itself a pose.
	One man's wage rise is another man's price increase.
Wilson, Woodrow	The world must be made safe for democracy.
Wordsworth, William	The child is father of the man.
Yeltsin, Boris	You can make a throne from bayonets but you can't sit on it long.
Young, Edward	Procrastination is the thief of time.

Nursery Rhymes

As I was going to St Ives I met a man with seven wives, each wife had seven sacks, each sack had seven cats, each cat had seven kits, kits, cats, sacks and wives, how many going to St Ives?

Baa baa black sheep have you any wool? Yes sir, yes sir, three bags full; one for the master, and one for the dame, and one for the little boy who lives down the lane.

Bobby Shafto's gone to sea, silver buckles on his knee,

he'll come back and marry me, bonny Bobby Shafto.

Dance to your daddy, my little babby, dance to your daddy, my little lamb; you shall have a fishy, in a little dishy, you shall have a fishy, when the boat comes in.

Ding, dong, bell, pussy's in the well. Who put her in? Little Johnny Green. Who pulled her out? Little Tommy Stout.

Doctor Foster went to Gloucester, in a shower of rain;

he stepped in a puddle, right up to his middle, and never went there again.

Georgie Porgie pudding and pie, kissed the girls and made them cry; when the boys came out to play, Georgie Porgie ran away.

Goosey, goosey gander, where shall I wander? Upstairs and downstairs, in my lady's chamber. There I met an old man who would not say his prayers, I took him by the left leg and threw him down the stairs.

Hark, hark, the dogs do bark, the beggars are coming to town; some in rags, and some in jags, and one in a velvet gown.

Hey diddle diddle, the cat and the fiddle, the cow jumped over the moon; the little dog laughed to see such sport, and the dish ran away with the spoon.

Hickory, dickory dock, the mouse ran up the clock. The clock struck one, the mouse ran down, hickory, dickory dock.

Humpty Dumpty sat on a wall, Humpty Dumpty had a great fall; all the king's horses and all the king's men couldn't put Humpty together again.

I had a little nut tree, nothing would it bear, but a silver nutmeg, and a golden pear.

If all the world were paper, and all the sea were ink, if all the trees were bread and cheese, what should we have to drink?

Jack be nimble, Jack be quick, Jack jump over the candle stick.

Jack Sprat could eat no fat, his wife could eat no lean, and so between them both, you see, they licked the platter clean.

Little Bo-Peep has lost her sheep, and doesn't know where to find them; leave them alone and they will come home, dragging their tails behind them.

Little Boy Blue, come blow your horn, the sheep's in the meadow, the cow's in the corn. Where is the boy who looks after the sheep? He's under a haystack fast asleep.

Little Jack Horner sat in the corner, eating a Christmas pie; he put in his thumb, and pulled out a plum, and said, What a good boy am I.

Little Miss Muffet sat on a tuffet, eating her curds and whey; along came a spider, who sat down beside her, and frightened Miss Muffet away.

Little Polly Flinders, sat among the cinders, warming her pretty little toes; her mother came and caught her, and whipped her little daughter, for spoiling her nice new clothes.

Little Tommy Tucker sings for his supper; what shall we give him? White bread and butter. How shall he cut it without a knife? How will he marry without a wife?

Lucy Locket lost her pocket, Kitty Fisher found it; not a penny was there in it, only ribbon round it.

Mary had a little lamb, its fleece was white as snow; and everywhere that Mary went the lamb was sure to go.

Mary, Mary, quite contrary, how does your garden grow? With silver bells and cockle shells, and pretty maids all in a row.

Old King Cole was a merry old soul, and a merry old soul was he; he called for his pipe, and he called for his bowl, and he called for his fiddlers three.

Old Mother Hubbard went to the cupboard, to fetch her poor dog a bone; but when she came there, the cupboard was bare, and so the poor dog had none.

On the twelfth day of Christmas my true love sent to me twelve lords a-leaping, eleven ladies dancing, ten pipers piping, nine drummers drumming, eight maids a-milking, seven swans a-swimming, six geese a-laying, five gold rings, four colly birds, three French hens, two turtle doves, and a partridge in a pear tree.

One, two, three, four, five, once I caught a fish alive; six, seven, eight, nine, ten, then I let it go again. Why did you let it go? Because it bit my finger so. Which finger did it bite? This little finger on the right.

Oranges and lemons, say the bells of St Clement's. You owe me five farthings, say the bells of St Martin's. When will you pay me? say the bells of Old Bailey. When I grow rich, say the bells of Shoreditch. When will that be? say the bells of Stepney. I'm sure I don't know, says the great bell at Bow. Here comes the candle to light you to bed, here comes a chopper to chop off your head.

Pat-a-cake, pat-a-cake baker's man, bake me a cake as fast as you can; pat it and prick it and mark it with B, put it in the oven for baby and me.

Pease porridge hot, pease porridge cold, pease porridge in the pot, nine days old.

Polly put the kettle on, Polly put the kettle on, Polly put the kettle on, we'll all have tea. Sukey take it off again, Sukey take it off again, Sukey take it off again, they've all gone away.

Pussy cat, pussy cat, where have you been? I've been to London to visit the Queen. Pussy cat, pussy cat, what did you there? I frightened a little mouse under her chair.

Ride a cock horse to Banbury Cross, to see a fine lady upon a white horse; rings on her fingers and bells on her toes, and she shall have music wherever she goes.

Ring-a-ring o'roses, a pocket full of posies, A-tishoo, A-tishoo, we all fall down.

Rub-a-dub-dub, three men in a tub, and how do you think they got there? The butcher, the baker, the candlestick maker, they all jumped out of a rotten potato, 'twas enough to make a man stare.

See-saw Margery Daw, Johnny shall have a new master; Johnny shall have but a penny a day, because he can't work any faster.

Simple Simon met a pieman, going to the fair; said Simple Simon to the pieman, let me taste your ware. Said the pieman to Simple Simon, show me first your penny; said Simple Simon to the pieman, indeed I have not any.

Sing a song of sixpence, a pocket full of rye; four and twenty blackbirds baked in a pie. When the pie was opened the birds began to sing; wasn't that a dainty dish to set before the king? The king was in his counting-house, counting out his money, the queen was in the parlour, eating bread and honey, the maid was in the garden, hanging out the clothes, along came a blackbird and pecked off her nose.

Solomon Grundy, born on Monday, christened on Tuesday, married on Wednesday, took ill on Thursday, worse on Friday, died on Saturday, buried on Sunday, this is the end of Solomon Grundy.

Taffy was a Welshman, Taffy was a thief, Taffy came to my house and stole a leg of beef. I went to Taffy's house, Taffy wasn't in, I jumped upon his Sunday hat, and poked it with a pin.

The Grand Old Duke of York, he had ten thousand men, he marched them up to the top of the hill, and he marched them down again; and when they were up they were up, and when they were down they were down, and when they were only halfway up, they were neither up nor down.

The man in the moon came down too soon, and asked the way to Norwich; he went by the south, and burnt his mouth, with supping cold plum porridge.

The north wind doth blow, and we shall have snow, and what will poor Robin do then, poor thing? He'll sit in a barn, and keep himself warm, and hide his head under his wing, poor thing.

The Queen of Hearts she made some tarts, all on a summer's day. The Knave of Hearts he stole the tarts, and took them clean away. The King of Hearts called for the tarts, and beat the knave full sore. The Knave of Hearts brought back the tarts, and vowed he'd steal no more.

There was a crooked man, who walked a crooked mile, he found a crooked sixpence against a crooked stile, he bought a crooked cat, which caught a crooked mouse, and they all lived together in a little crooked house.

There was a man lived in the moon, lived in the moon, lived in the moon, and his name was Aiken Drum, and he played upon a ladle, a ladle, a ladle.

There was an old woman who lived in a shoe, she had so many children she didn't know what to do; she gave them some broth without any bread, she whipped them all soundly and sent them to bed.

This little piggy went to market, this little piggy stayed at home, this little piggy had roast beef, this little piggy had none, and this little piggy went wee-wee-wee, all the way home.

Tom, Tom, the piper's son, stole a pig and away he run; the pig was eat, and Tom was beat, and Tom went howling down the street.

Twinkle, twinkle, little star, how I wonder what you are! Up above the world so high, like a diamond in the sky.

Wee Willie Winkie runs through the town, upstairs and downstairs in his night-gown, rapping at the window, crying through the lock, are the children all in bed, it's past eight o' clock.

What are little boys made of? . . . Snips and snails and puppy-dog tails. What are little girls made of? . . . Sugar and spice and all things nice.

Who killed Cock Robin? I, said the sparrow, with my bow and arrow, I killed Cock Robin. Who saw him die? I, said the fly, with my little eye, I saw him die.

Yankee Doodle came to town, riding on a pony; stuck a feather in his cap, and called it macaroni.

NB There are slight corruptions of wording in some nursery rhymes, usually dependent on region. For example, little boys can be made of 'frogs and snails'.

RELIGION

Popes

*Popes and antipopes		Dates	Original name, feast day or miscellaneous information
1	St Peter	To 64	feast day 29 June
2	St Linus	c. 67–76/79	feast day 23 September
3	St Anacletus	c. 76/79–88/91	feast day 26 April
4	St Clement I	c. 88/92–97/101	feast day 23 November
5	St Evaristus	c. 97–c107	feast day 6 October
6	St Alexander I	c. 105/9–115/19	feast day 3 May
7	St Sixtus I	c. 115–c125	feast day 3 April
8	St Telesphorus	c. 125–c136	feast day 5 January (Greek)
9	St Hyginus	c. 136–c140	feast day 11 January (Greek)
10	St Pius I	c. 140–c155	feast day 11 July
11	St Anicetus	c. 155–c166	feast day 17 April (Syria)
12	St Soter	c. 166–c175	feast day 22 April
13	St Eleutherius	c. 175–c189	feast day 26 May
14	St Victor I	c. 189–c199	feast day 28 July (African)
15	St Zephyrinus	c. 199–c217	feast day 26 August
16	St Calixtus I	217–222	feast day 14 October
17	Hippolytus	217–235	first antipope
18	St Urban I	222–230	feast day 25 May
19	St Pontian	230–235	feast day 19 November
20	St Anterus	235–236	feast day 3 January (Greek)
21	St Fabian	236–250	feast day 20 January
22	St Cornelius	251–253	feast day 16 September
23	Novatian	251	Novatianus (antipope)
24	St Lucius I	253–254	feast day 4 March
25	St Stephen I	254–257	feast day 2 August
26	St Sixtus II	257–258	feast day 6 August (Greek)
27	St Dionysius	259–268	feast day 6 December (Greek)
28	St Felix I	269–274	feast day 30 May
29	St Eutychian	275–283	feast day 7 December
30	St Gaius	283–296	feast day 22 April (Dalmatian)
31	St Marcellinus	296–304	feast day 26 April
32	St Marcellus I	308–309	feast day 16 January
33	St Eusebius	309–310	feast day 17 August (Greek)
34	St Miltiades	311–314	feast day 10 December
35	St Sylvester I	314–335	feast day 31 December
36	St Mark	336	feast day 7 October
37	St Julius I	337–352	feast day 12 April
38	Liberius	352–366	
39	Felix II	355–358	antipope 357–8
40	St Damasus I	366–384	feast day 11 December (Latin Mass)
41	Ursinus	366–367	Antipope
42	St Siricius	384–399	feast day 26 November
43	St Anastasius I	399–401	feast day 19 December
44	St Innocent I	401–417	feast day 28 July
45	St Zosimus	417–418	feast day 26 December (Greek)
46	St Boniface I	418–422	feast day 4 September
47	Eulalius	418–419	antipope
48	St Celestine I	422–432	feast day 27 July
49	St Sixtus III	432–440	feast day 28 March
50	St Leo I	440–461	feast day 11 April (Leo the Great)
51	St Hilary	461–468	feast day 28 February
52	St Simplicius	468–483	feast day 10 March
53	St Felix III	483–492	feast day 1 March
54	St Gelasius I	492–496	feast day 21 November
55	Anastasius II	496–498	
56	St Symmachus	498–514	feast day 19 July
57	Laurentius	498	antipope
58	Laurentius	501–505	antipope
59	St Hormisdas	514–523	feast day 6 August
60	St John I	523–526	feast day 27 May
61	Felix IV	526–530	feast day 30 January
62	Dioscorus	530	Egyptian
63	Boniface II	530–532	
64	John II	533–535	Mercurius (first pope to change name)

Popes and antipopes		Dates	Original name, feast day or miscellaneous information
65	St Agapetus I	535–536	feast day 22 April
66	St Silverius	536–537	feast day 20 June
67	Vigilius	537–555	
68	Pelagius I	556–561	
69	John III	561–574	Catelinus
70	Benedict I	575–579	
71	Pelagius II	579–590	
72	St Gregory I	590–604	feast day 12 March
73	Sabinian	604–606	
74	Boniface III	607	
75	St Boniface IV	608–615	
76	St Deusdedit	615–618	feast day 8 November (aka Adeodatus I)
77	Boniface V	619–625	
78	Honorius I	625–638	
79	Severinus	638–640	
80	John IV	640–642	Dalmatian
81	Theodore I	642–649	Jerusalem
82	St Martin I	649–655	feast day 12 November
83	St Eugenius I	654–657	feast day 2 June
84	St Vitalian	657–672	
85	Adeodatus II	672–676	
86	Donus	676–678	
87	St Agatho	678–681	feast day 10 January
88	St Leo II	681–683	feast day 3 July
89	St Benedict II	684–685	feast day 8 May
90	John V	685–686	Syrian
91	Conon	686–687	
92	St Sergius I	687–701	feast day 8 September
93	Theodore	687	antipope
94	Paschal	687	antipope
95	John VI	701–705	Greek
96	John VII	705–707	Greek
97	Sisinnius	708	
98	Constantine	708–715	
99	St Gregory II	715–731	feast day 11 February
100	St Gregory III	731–741	feast day 28 November (Syrian)
101	St Zacharias	741–752	feast day 15 March
102	Stephen II	752	died after two days
103	Stephen III	752–757	Papal States founder
104	St Paul I	757–767	feast day 28 June
105	Constantine II	767–768	antipope
106	Philip	768	antipope
107	Stephen IV	768–772	
108	Adrian I	772–795	
109	St Leo III	795–816	feast day 12 June (Crowned Charlemagne)
110	Stephen V	816–817	
111	St Paschal I	817–824	feast day 14 May
112	Eugenius II	824–827	
113	Valentine	827	feast day 14 February
114	Gregory IV	827–844	created 1 November All Saints day
115	John	844	antipope
116	Sergius II	844–847	
117	St Leo IV	847–855	feast day 17 July
118	Benedict III	855–858	
119	Anastasius	855	Anastasius the Librarian (antipope)
120	St Nicholas I	858–867	
121	Adrian II	867–872	
122	John VIII	872–882	crowned Charles the Fat Emperor
123	Marinus I	882–884	
124	St Adrian III	884–885	feast day 8 July
125	Stephen VI	885–891	
126	Formosus	891–896	
127	Boniface VI	896	
128	Stephen VII	896–897	
129	Romanus	897	
130	Theodore II	897	
131	John IX	898–900	
132	Benedict IV	900–903	
133	Leo V	903	
134	Christopher	903–904	antipope
135	Sergius III	904–911	

Popes and antipopes	Dates	Original name, feast day or miscellaneous information
136	Anastasius III	911–913	
137	Lando	913–914	
138	John X	914–928	
139	Leo VI	928	
140	Stephen VIII	929–931	
141	John XI	931–935	
142	Leo VII	936–939	
143	Stephen IX	939–942	
144	Marinus II	942–946	
145	Agapetus II	946–955	
146	John XII	955–964	Ottaviano (crowned Emperor Otto)
147	Leo VIII	963–965	
148	Benedict V	964–966	Benedict the Grammarian
149	John XIII	965–972	
150	Benedict VI	973–974	
151	Boniface VII	974	Franco (first term)
152	Benedict VII	974–983	
153	John XIV	983–984	Pietro Canepanova
154	Boniface VII	984–985	Franco (second term)
155	John XV	985–996	
156	Gregory V	996–999	Bruno of Carinthia (first German pope)
157	John XVI	997–998	Giovanni Filagato (antipope)
158	Sylvester II	999–1003	Gerbert of Aurillac (French)
159	John XVII	1003	Secco
160	John XVIII	1004–1009	Fasano
161	Sergius IV	1009–1012	Pietro Buccaporci
162	Gregory VI	1012	antipope
163	Benedict VIII	1012–1024	Teofilatto
164	John XIX	1024–1032	Romano (crowned Emperor Conrad II)
165	Benedict IX	1032–1044	Teofilatto (12 yrs old)
166	Sylvester III	1045	John of Sabina
167	Benedict IX	1045	Teofilatto (second term)
168	Gregory VI	1045–1046	Giovanni Graziano
169	Clement II	1046–1047	Suidger
170	Benedict IX	1047–1048	Teofilatto (third term)
171	Damasus II	1048	Poppo (Bavarian)
172	St Leo IX	1049–1054	feast day 19 April (aka Bruno of Egisheim)
173	Victor II	1055–1057	Gebhard of Hirschberg
174	Stephen X	1057–1058	Frederick of Lorraine
175	Benedict X	1058–1059	Giovanni Mincio (antipope)
176	Nicholas II	1058–1061	Gerard of Burgundy
177	Alexander II	1061–1073	Anselm of Baggio
178	Honorius II	1061–1072	Cadelo (antipope)
179	St Gregory VII	1073–1085	feast day 25 May 25 (aka Hildebrand)
180	Clement III	1080–1100	Guibert (antipope)
181	Victor III	1086–1087	feast day 16 September
182	Urban II	1088–1099	Odo of Lagery
183	Paschal II	1099–1118	Raniero
184	Theodoric	1100–1102	antipope
185	Albert/Aleric	1102	antipope
186	Sylvester IV	1105–1111	Maginulfo (antipope)
187	Gelasius II	1118–1119	Giovanni da Gaetan
188	Gregory VIII	1118–1121	Maurice Bourdin (antipope)
189	Calixtus II	1119–1124	Guy of Burgundy
190	Honorius II	1124–1130	Lamberto Scannabecchi
191	Celestine II	1124	Theobald Buccapecus
192	Innocent II	1130–1143	Gregorio Papareschi
193	Anacletus II	1130–1138	Pietro Pierleoni (antipope)
194	Victor IV	1138	Gregory Conti (antipope)
195	Celestine II	1143–1144	Guido de Castellis
196	Lucius II	1144–1145	Gherardo Caccianemici
197	Eugenius III	1145–1153	feast day 8 July (aka Bernard of Pisa)
198	Anastasius IV	1153–1154	Corrado di Suburra
199	Adrian IV	1154–1159	Nicholas Breakspear (only English pope)
200	Alexander III	1159–1181	Rolando Bandinelli
201	Victor IV	1159–1164	Ottaviano de Monticello (antipope)
202	Paschal III	1164–1168	Guido da Crema (antipope)
203	Calixtus III	1168–1178	John of Struma (antipope)
204	Innocent III	1179–1180	Lando di Sezze (antipope)
205	Lucius III	1181–1185	Ubaldo Allucingoli
206	Urban III	1185–1187	Uberto Crivelli

RELIGION

Popes and antipopes	Dates	Original name, feast day or miscellaneous information
207 Gregory VIII	1187	Alberto de Morra
208 Clement III	1187–1191	Paolo Scolari
209 Celestine III	1191–1198	Giacinto Bobo-Orsini
210 Innocent III	1198–1216	Lothair di Segni
211 Honorius III	1216–1227	Cencio Savelli
212 Gregory IX	1227–1241	Ugolino di Segni (excommunicated Frederick II)
213 Celestine IV	1241	Goffredo Castiglioni
214 Innocent IV	1243–1254	Sinibaldo Fieschi
215 Alexander IV	1254–1261	Rinaldo Deisegni
216 Urban IV	1261–1264	Jacques Pantaleon
217 Clement IV	1265–1268	Guido Fulcodi
218 Gregory X	1271–1276	Tebaldo Visconti
219 Innocent V	1276	feast day June 22nd (first Dominican pope)
220 Adrian V	1276	Ottobono Fieschi
221 John XXI	1276–1277	Pedro Hispano (Portuguese)
222 Nicholas III	1277–1280	Giovanni Orsini
223 Martin IV	1281–1285	Simon de Brion
224 Honorius IV	1285–1287	Giacomo Savelli
225 Nicholas IV	1288–1292	Girolamo Masci
226 St Celestine V	1294	feast day 19 May (first pope to abdicate)
227 Boniface VIII	1294–1303	Benedict Caetani
228 Benedict XI	1303–1304	feast day 7 July
229 Clement V	1305–1314	Bertrand de Got (Avignon from 1309)
230 John XXII	1316–1334	Jacques Duese (Babylonian Captivity 1309–77)
231 Nicholas V	1328–1330	Pietro Rainalducci (antipope)
232 Benedict XII	1334–1342	Jacques Fournier (Avignon)
233 Clement VI	1342–1352	Pierre Roger (Avignon)
234 Innocent VI	1352–1362	Etienne Aubert (Avignon)
235 Urban V	1362–1370	feast day 19 December (Avignon)
236 Gregory XI	1370–1378	Pierre de Beaufort (Avignon till 1377)
237 Urban VI	1378–1389	Bartolomeo Prignano (Western Schism 1378–1417)
238 Clement VII	1378–1394	Robert of Geneva (antipope)
239 Boniface IX	1389–1404	Pietro Tomacelli
240 Benedict XIII	1394–1423	Pedro de Luna (antipope)
241 Innocent VII	1404–1406	Cosimo de Migliorati
242 Gregory XII	1406–1415	Angelo Correr
243 Alexander V	1409–1410	Peter of Candia (antipope)
244 John XXIII	1410–1415	Baldassare Cossa (antipope)
245 Martin V	1417–1431	Oddone Colonna
246 Clement VIII	1423–1429	Gil Sanchez Munoz (antipope)
247 Benedict XIV	1425–1433	The Hidden Pope (counter antipope)
248 Eugenius IV	1431–1447	Gabriele Condulmer
249 Felix V	1439–1449	Amadeus VIII the Peaceful (antipope)
250 Nicholas V	1447–1455	Tommaso Parentucelli
251 Calixtus III	1455–1458	Alfonso di Borgia (uncle of Rodrigo)
252 Pius II	1458–1464	Enea Piccolomini
253 Paul II	1464–1471	Pietro Barbo
254 Sixtus IV	1471–1484	Francesco Dellarovere
255 Innocent VIII	1484–1492	Giovanni Battista Cibo
256 Alexander VI	1492–1503	Rodrigo Borgia (father of Lucretia)
257 Pius III	1503	Francesco Piccolomini
258 Julius II	1503–1513	Giuliano Dellarovere (patron of Michelangelo)
259 Leo X	1513–1521	Giovanni de Medici (excommunicated Luther 1521)
260 Adrian VI	1522–1523	Adrian Florenz Boeyens (only Dutch pope)
261 Clement VII	1523–1534	Giulio de Medici
262 Paul III	1534–1549	Alessandro Farnese (called Council of Trent)
263 Julius III	1550–1555	Giovanni del Monte
264 Marcellus II	1555	Marcello Cervini
265 Paul IV	1555–1559	Gian Pietro Carafa
266 Pius IV	1559–1565	Giovanni de Medici (concluded Council of Trent)
267 St Pius V	1566–1572	Antonio Ghislieri (excommunicated Elizabeth I 1570)
268 Gregory XIII	1572–1585	Ugo Boncompagni (Gregorian calendar)
269 Sixtus V	1585–1590	Felice Peretti (excommunicated Henry of Navarre)
270 Urban VII	1590	Giambattista Castagna
271 Gregory XIV	1590–1591	Niccolo Sfondrato
272 Innocent IX	1591	Giovanni Facchinetti
273 Clement VIII	1592–1605	Ippolito Aldobrandini
274 Leo XI	1605	Alessandro de Medici
275 Paul V	1605–1621	Camillo Borghese
276 Gregory XV	1621–1623	Alessandro Ludovisi
277 Urban VIII	1623–1644	Maffeo Barberini (patron of sculptor Bernini)

Popes and antipopes		Dates	Original name, feast day or miscellaneous information
278	Innocent X	1644–1655	Giovanni Pamphili
279	Alexander VII	1655–1667	Fabio Chigi
280	Clement IX	1667–1669	Giulio Rospiglioso
281	Clement X	1670–1676	Emilio Altieri
282	Innocent XI	1676–1689	feast day 13 August
283	Alexander VIII	1689–1691	Pietro Ottoboni
284	Innocent XII	1691–1700	Antonio Pignatelli
285	Clement XI	1700–1721	Giovanni Albani
286	Innocent XIII	1721–1724	Michelangelo dei Conti (recognised Old Pretender)
287	Benedict XIII	1724–1730	Pietro Maria Orsini
288	Clement XII	1730–1740	Lorenzo Corsini (condemned Freemasonry)
289	Benedict XIV	1740–1758	Prospero Lambertini
290	Clement XIII	1758–1769	Carlo Rezzonico
291	Clement XIV	1769–1774	Giovanni Ganganelli (dissolved Jesuits 1773)
292	Pius VI	1775–1799	Giannangelo Braschi
293	Pius VII	1800–1823	Barnaba Chiaramonti (revived Jesuits 1814)
294	Leo XII	1823–1829	Annibale Della Genga
295	St Pius VIII	1829–1830	Francesco Castiglioni
296	Gregory XVI	1831–1846	Bartolomeo Cappellari (Austrian)
297	Pius IX	1846–1878	Giovanni Mastai-Ferretti (longest reign, 32 yrs)
298	Leo XIII	1878–1903	Vincenzo Pecci
299	St Pius X	1903–1914	feast day 3 September (last to be canonised)
300	Benedict XV	1914–1922	Giacomo Della Chiesa
301	Pius XI	1922–1939	Ambrogio Damiano Ratti
302	Pius XII	1939–1958	Eugenio Maria Pacelli
303	John XXIII	1958–1963	Angelo Giuseppe Roncalli (second Vatican Council)
304	Paul VI	1963–1978	Giovanni Battista Montini (first to visit Asia)
305	John Paul I	1978	Albino Luciani (reigned 34 days)
306	John Paul II	1978–2005	Karol Wojtyla (Polish: first non-Italian since Adrian VI)
307	Benedict XVI	2005–	Joseph Alois Ratzinger (German; oldest at election since 1730)

Popes: Miscellaneous Information

antipope	an alternative claimant to the bishop of Rome who has just cause in disputing the papacy.		outside his own small circle. Felix X was the last elected antipope.
assassinated	26	last non-Italian	Adrian VI (1522) Dutch
boy pope	Benedict IX (12 yrs old)	last to be canonised	Pius X on 29 May 1954
Britain: first to visit	John Paul II (1982)	letters to churches	encyclicals
British Pope	Adrian IV (Nicholas Breakspear)	longest reign	Pius IX (32 yrs)
Cadaver Synod	Formosus (896) tried and executed after his death!	new pope: how known	White smoke from Vatican chimney
Celestine II	Theobald Buccapecus, elected pope in 1124, resigned after a few days and is often omitted in lists, hence the duplication.	non-existent pope	John XX, due to error in numbering in 10th century
		Pacem in Terris	encyclical of John XXIII (Peace on Earth)
Council of Trent	19th ecumenical council of RC Church; 1545–63 in northern Italy	Pilgrim Pope	Paul VI (because of his great travelling)
		pope's blessing	Urbi et Orbi (To the city and the world)
crushed to death	John XXI; ceiling of papal palace at Viterbo collapsed	pope: also called	Sovereign of Vatican City Vicar of Christ on Earth Bishop of Rome Patriarch of the West Primate of Italy
directives called	Papal Bull		
double name: first	John Paul I (named after two predecessors)	pope: elected by	College of Cardinals: two-thirds majority required
female pope	Joan (fictional)	pope: means	father
Humanae Vitae	encyclical of Paul VI condemning birth control (1968)	Redemptor Hominus	encyclical of John Paul II about respect for man
		Sacerdotalis Caelibatus	encyclical of Paul VI concerning priestly celibacy
Infallibility	doctrine promulgated in July 1870, reaffirmed 1973	throne	Sedes Gestatoria
John Paul II	archbishop of Cracow	Vatican Council: first	1869–70 (convoked by Pius IX)
last antipope	the count of Savoy took holy orders and set himself up as Clement XV in 1969 but was never recognised	Vatican Council: second	1962–65 (convoked by John XXIII)

RELIGION

Popes (Alphabetical Order)

1	Adeodatus II	672–676	69	Christopher	903–904
2	Adrian I	772–795	70	Clement I	c. 88/92–97/101
3	Adrian II	867–872	71	Clement II	1046–1047
4	Adrian III	884–885	72	Clement III	1080–1100
5	Adrian IV	1154–1159	73	Clement III	1187–1191
6	Adrian V	1276	74	Clement IV	1265–1268
7	Adrian VI	1522–1523	75	Clement V	1305–1314
8	Agapetus I	535–536	76	Clement VI	1342–1352
9	Agapetus II	946–955	77	Clement VII	1378–1394
10	Agatho	678–681	78	Clement VII	1523–1534
11	Albert/Aleric	1102	79	Clement VIII	1423–1429
12	Alexander I	c. 105/9–115/19	80	Clement VIII	1592–1605
13	Alexander II	1061–1073	81	Clement IX	1667–1669
14	Alexander III	1159–1181	82	Clement X	1670–1676
15	Alexander IV	1254–1261	83	Clement XI	1700–1721
16	Alexander V	1409–1410	84	Clement XII	1730–1740
17	Alexander VI	1492–1503	85	Clement XIII	1758–1769
18	Alexander VII	1655–1667	86	Clement XIV	1769–1774
19	Alexander VIII	1689–1691	87	Conon	686–687
20	Anacletus	c. 76/79–88/91	88	Constantine	708–715
21	Anacletus II	1130–1138	89	Constantine II	767–768
22	Anastasius	855	90	Cornelius	251–253
23	Anastasius I	399–401	91	Damasus I	366–384
24	Anastasius II	496–498	92	Damasus II	1048
25	Anastasius III	911–913	93	Deusdedit	615–618
26	Anastasius IV	1153–1154	94	Dionysius	259–268
27	Anicetus	c. 155–c. 166	95	Dioscorus	530
28	Anterus	235–236	96	Donus	676–678
29	Benedict I	575–579	97	Eleutherius	c. 175–c. 189
30	Benedict II	684–685	98	Eugenius I	654–657
31	Benedict III	855–858	99	Eugenius II	824–827
32	Benedict IV	900–903	100	Eugenius III	1145–1153
33	Benedict V	964–966	101	Eugenius IV	1431–1447
34	Benedict VI	973–974	102	Eulalius	418–419
35	Benedict VII	974–983	103	Eusebius	309–310
36	Benedict VIII	1012–1024	104	Eutychian	275–283
37	Benedict IX	1032–1044	105	Evaristus	c. 97–c. 107
38	Benedict IX	1045	106	Fabian	236–250
39	Benedict IX	1047–1048	107	Felix I	269–274
40	Benedict X	1058–1059	108	Felix II	355–358
41	Benedict XI	1303–1304	109	Felix III	483–492
42	Benedict XII	1334–1342	110	Felix IV	526–530
43	Benedict XIII	1394–1423	111	Felix V	1439–1449
44	Benedict XIII	1724–1730	112	Formosus	891–896
45	Benedict XIV	1425–1433	113	Gaius	283–296
46	Benedict XIV	1740–1758	114	Gelasius I	492–496
47	Benedict XV	1914–1922	115	Gelasius II	1118–1119
48	Benedict XVI	2005–	116	Gregory I	590–604
49	Boniface I	418–422	117	Gregory II	715–731
50	Boniface II	530–532	118	Gregory III	731–741
51	Boniface III	607	119	Gregory IV	827–844
52	Boniface IV	608–615	120	Gregory V	996–999
53	Boniface V	619–625	121	Gregory VI	1012
54	Boniface VI	896	122	Gregory VI	1045–1046
55	Boniface VII	974	123	Gregory VII	1073–1085
56	Boniface VII	984–985	124	Gregory VIII	1118–1121
57	Boniface VIII	1294–1303	125	Gregory VIII	1187
58	Boniface IX	1389–1404	126	Gregory IX	1227–1241
59	Calixtus I	217–222	127	Gregory X	1271–1276
60	Calixtus II	1119–1124	128	Gregory XI	1370–1378
61	Calixtus III	1168–1178	129	Gregory XII	1406–1415
62	Calixtus III	1455–1458	130	Gregory XIII	1572–1585
63	Celestine I	422–432	131	Gregory XIV	1590–1591
64	Celestine II	1124	132	Gregory XV	1621–1623
65	Celestine II	1143–1144	133	Gregory XVI	1831–1846
66	Celestine III	1191–1198	134	Hilary	461–468
67	Celestine IV	1241	135	Honorius I	625–638
68	Celestine V	1294	136	Honorius II	1061–1072

137	Honorius II	1124–1130	209	Marinus I	882–884
138	Honorius III	1216–1227	210	Marinus II	942–946
139	Honorius IV	1285–1287	211	Mark	336
140	Hormisdas	514–523	212	Martin I	649–655
141	Hyginus	c. 136–c. 140	213	Martin IV	1281–1285
142	Innocent I	401–417	214	Martin V	1417–1431
143	Innocent II	1130–1143	215	Miltiades	311–314
144	Innocent III	1179–1180	216	Nicholas I	858–867
145	Innocent III	1198–1216	217	Nicholas II	1058–1061
146	Innocent IV	1243–1254	218	Nicholas III	1277–1280
147	Innocent V	1276	219	Nicholas IV	1288–1292
148	Innocent VI	1352–1362	220	Nicholas V	1328–1330
149	Innocent VII	1404–1406	221	Nicholas V	1447–1455
150	Innocent VIII	1484–1492	222	Novatian	251
151	Innocent IX	1591	223	Paschal	687
152	Innocent X	1644–1655	224	Paschal I	817–824
153	Innocent XI	1676–1689	225	Paschal II	1099–1118
154	Innocent XII	1691–1700	226	Paschal III	1164–1168
155	Innocent XIII	1721–1724	227	Paul I	757–767
156	John	844	228	Paul II	1464–1471
157	John I	523–526	229	Paul III	1534–1549
158	John II	533–535	230	Paul IV	1555–1559
159	John III	561–574	231	Paul V	1605–1621
160	John IV	640–642	232	Paul VI	1963–1978
161	John V	685–686	233	Pelagius I	556–561
162	John VI	701–705	234	Pelagius II	579–590
163	John VII	705–707	235	Peter	to c. 64
164	John VIII	872–882	236	Philip	768
165	John IX	898–900	237	Pius I	c. 140–c. 155
166	John X	914–928	238	Pius II	1458–1464
167	John XI	931–935	239	Pius III	1503
168	John XII	955–964	240	Pius IV	1559–1565
169	John XIII	965–972	241	Pius V	1566–1572
170	John XIV	983–984	242	Pius VI	1775–1799
171	John XV	985–996	243	Pius VII	1800–1823
172	John XVI	997–998	244	Pius VIII	1829–1830
173	John XVII	1003	245	Pius IX	1846–1878
174	John XVIII	1004–1009	246	Pius X	1903–1914
175	John XIX	1024–1032	247	Pius XI	1922–1939
176	John XXI	1276–1277	248	Pius XII	1939–1958
177	John XXII	1316–1334	249	Pontian	230–235
178	John XXIII	1410–1415	250	Romanus	897
179	John XXIII	1958–1963	251	Sabinian	604–606
180	John Paul I	1978	252	Sergius I	687–701
181	John Paul II	1978–2005	253	Sergius II	844–847
182	Julius I	337–352	254	Sergius III	904–911
183	Julius II	1503–1513	255	Sergius IV	1009–1012
184	Julius III	1550–1555	256	Severinus	638–640
185	Lando	913–914	257	Silverius	536–537
186	Laurentius	498	258	Simplicius	468–483
187	Laurentius	501–505	259	Siricius	384–399
188	Leo I	440–461	260	Sisinnius	708
189	Leo II	681–683	261	Sixtus I	c115–c125
190	Leo III	795–816	262	Sixtus II	257–258
191	Leo IV	847–855	263	Sixtus III	432–440
192	Leo V	903	264	Sixtus IV	1471–1484
193	Leo VI	928	265	Sixtus V	1585–1590
194	Leo VII	936–939	266	Soter	c. 166–c. 175
195	Leo VIII	963–965	267	Stephen I	254–257
196	Leo IX	1049–1054	268	Stephen II	752
197	Leo X	1513–1521	269	Stephen III	752–757
198	Leo XI	1605	270	Stephen IV	768–772
199	Leo XII	1823–1829	271	Stephen V	816–817
200	Leo XIII	1878–1903	272	Stephen VI	885–891
201	Liberius	352–366	273	Stephen VII	896–897
202	Linus	c. 67–76/79	274	Stephen VIII	929–931
203	Lucius I	253–254	275	Stephen IX	939–942
204	Lucius II	1144–1145	276	Stephen X	1057–1058
205	Lucius III	1181–1185	277	Sylvester I	314–335
206	Marcellinus	296–304	278	Sylvester II	999–1003
207	Marcellus I	308–309	279	Sylvester III	1045
208	Marcellus II	1555	280	Sylvester IV	1105–1111

RELIGION

281	Symmachus	498–514		294	Urban VIII	1623–1644
282	Telesphorus	c. 125–c. 136		295	Ursinus	366–367
283	Theodore	687		296	Valentine	827
284	Theodore I	642–649		297	Victor I	c. 189–c. 199
285	Theodore II	897		298	Victor II	1055–1057
286	Theodoric	1100–1102		299	Victor III	1086–1087
287	Urban I	222–230		300	Victor IV	1138
288	Urban II	1088–1099		301	Victor IV	1159–1164
289	Urban III	1185–1187		302	Vigilius	537–555
290	Urban IV	1261–1264		303	Vitalian	657–672
291	Urban V	1362–1370		304	Zacharias	741–752
292	Urban VI	1378–1389		305	Zephyrinus	c. 199–c. 217
293	Urban VII	1590		306	Zosimus	417–418

General Information

Adam's first wife Lilith (according to Jewish folklore).

Adulterer's Bible edition of the Bible of 1631, with the misprinted commandment 'thou shalt commit adultery'. Aka Wicked Bible.

ahimsa law of Reverence for, and non-violence to, every form of life (Hindu, Buddhist and Jainist philosophy).

Angels: hierarchy of

1 Seraphim

2 Cherubim

3 Thrones

4 Dominations/Dominions

5 Virtues

6 Powers

7 Principalities

8 Archangels

9 Angels

Black Friars Dominicans (Friar Preachers are a mendicant order founded in 1215).

Black Monks Benedictines (established c. AD 535–540).

Buddhism founded by Siddhartha Gautama in the sixth century BC. Buddha means 'Enlightened One'. Two main divisions are Theravada Buddhism and Mahayana Buddhism.

The third minor division is Vajrayana or Tantric Buddhism.

The Buddha's teachings are described as the Four Noble Truths.

The Middle or Noble Eightfold Path is the finding of truth and leads to Nirvana.

The ten precepts include five for laymen, i.e. prohibiting killing, stealing, lying, sexual misconduct and drinking intoxicating liquor, and five for monastic novices, i.e. not to eat at certain hours, not to take part in festivals, not to use garlands or perfumes, not to use a luxurious bed and not to accept money for oneself. The birth of the Buddha is celebrated in the festival of Vesak/Wesak. The Buddha's first sermon is celebrated in the festival of Dhamma-cakka.

Cathari Manichean order that flourished in western Europe during the 12th and 13th centuries. The name derives from the Greek 'Katharos' meaning pure.

Christadelphians founded by John Thomas in 1848, although the name was adopted during the US Civil War.

Christian Scientists founded in Boston, Massachusetts, by Mary Baker Eddy (1879).

Church Army founded by Wilson Carlile (1882) in the slums of London.

Grey Friars Franciscans (founded c. 1207 and affiliated with the Poor Clares since 1212).

Hinduism originated about 4,000 years ago in the land of the Indus River.

The Veda is the most ancient body of religious literature.

The power of the Brahmans (priest class) is central to the belief.

Ahimsa is the doctrine of non-injury or the absence of the desire to harm.

Brahma (creator), Vishnu (protector) and Siva (destroyer and restorer) constitute the Trimurti.

Islam founded by Mohammed in AD 622 when he fled from Mecca to Medina (flight known as the Hegira).

Koran (Qur'ān) is regarded as the word of God given to Mohammed by the angel Gabriel.

Five pillars of Islamic faith are: the Shahādah – there is no god but God and Mohammed is the prophet of God; the salat – the five daily prayer sessions; the zakat – the tax that constitutes the giving of alms; the saum – fasting during daylight hours of Ramadan; hajj – the pilgrimage to Mecca that every Muslim should take at least once in their lifetime. The two major branches of Islam are the Sunnites (largest) and the Shi'ites.

Jainism founded in India in the sixth century BC by Mahavira. Jains practise Ahimsa.

Jehovah's Witnesses founded by Charles Taze Russell (1881).

Jerusalem centre of Islam, Judaism and Christianity. The Wailing Wall is sacred to the Jews, the Dome of the Rock is sacred to Muslims and Church of the Holy Sepulchre is sacred to Christians.

Jesse son of Obed, and father of David.

Judaism the body of Jewish civil and ceremonial law is contained in the Talmud, which comprises the Mishnah and the Gemara. The Hebrew Bible comprises 24 books. The civil calendar begins with the month of Tishri, the first day of which is the holiday of Rosh Hashana (New Year). Other Jewish holidays include Shavuot or Pentecost, which commemorates the revelation of the Torah (Law) at Sinai; Yom Kippur (Day of Atonement), which ends the ten days of penitence from Rosh Hashana; and Sukkot (Tabernacles), in remembrance of the Israelites' wanderings after the Exodus. Yom Kippur, Rosh Hashana, and Sukkot are celebrated in the Jewish month of Tishri. Purim celebrates the story of Esther and is celebrated in the month of Adar.

Israeli Jews are divided equally among Ashkenazi (Germanic) and Sephardic (strictly speaking, descendants of Spanish Jews pre-1492; more loosely, non-Ashkenazi), although the Ashkenazim constitute more than 80% of all Jews in the world.

Koran (Qur'an) Sacred book of Islam, regarded by Muslims as the final revelation of God to humankind, passed by the archangel Gabriel in Arabic to Muhammmad, the last of the prophets. It consists of 114 chapters (sūras) containing Christian and Arabic legend as well as Old and New Testament stories. The first translation into English was by George Sale in 1734, although Alexander Ross translated the Koran into English in 1649, but this was from a French translation.

Manich(a)eism religious order founded by the Persian prophet Mani (c. 216–274) based on the conflict between goodness and evil. Manicheism also describes any heretical philosophy involving dualistic doctrines.

Menorah seven-branched candelabrum that is now an emblem of Judaism and badge of Israel.

Methodism founded by John Wesley (1738).

Mormons aka Church of Jesus Christ of Latter-Day Saints, founded by Joseph Smith in 1830 and not Brigham Young, who merely led them to Salt Lake City, Utah, in 1847.

Panchen Lama one of the two great Lamas of Tibet. (The other is the Dalai Lama.)

Penitential Psalms seven psalms (i.e. 6, 32, 38, 51, 102, 130, 143) all expressing penitence.

Plymouth Brethren founded in Dublin by the Reverend John Nelson Darby (1827) and named after the Devon town.

Potiphar Pharaoh's official who bought Joseph as a slave.

Premonstratensians religious sect founded in the twelfth century by St Norbert.

religious journals Christian Scientists – *Citadel*, *Monitor*; Jehovah's Witnesses – *Watchtower*; Roman Catholics – *Tablet*, *Universe*, *Herald*; Salvation Army – *War Cry*.

Salvation Army founded by William Booth (1865) as the New Christian Mission; name changed in 1878. Motto: Blood and Fire.

Seven Sorrows of Mary
1 The prophecy of Simeon (that a sword would pierce her soul).
2 The flight into Egypt.
3 The loss of the holy child in Jerusalem.
4 Meeting with the Lord on the road to Calvary.
5 The Crucifixion (when she stood at the foot of the cross).
6 The Deposition (taking down of Christ from the cross).
7 The Entombment (burial of Christ).

Shakers founded by James Wardley and Jane Wardley (1747).

Shinto founded in Japan in the eighth century AD and divided into groups of which the best-known are Jinja and Kyoha.
The sacred texts are *Kojiki* and *Nihonshoki*.
Shinto literally means 'the teaching' or 'the way of the Gods'.

Sikhism founded by the Guru Nanak in the fifteenth century; the holy book is the Adi Granth.

Society of Friends founded by George Fox (1650); aka Quakers.

Society of Jesus founded by Ignatius Loyola (1534).

Stations of the Cross There are fourteen Stations of the Cross (aka Way of the Cross).They depict the final events in the Passion of Christ. Usually seen portrayed in churches but may also be found in cemeteries, hospitals and on mountainsides.
1 Jesus is condemned to death.
2 Jesus is made to bear his cross.
3 Jesus falls the first time.
4 Jesus meets his mother.
5 Simon of Cyrene is made to bear the cross.
6 Veronica wipes Jesus' face.
7 Jesus falls the second time.
8 Women of Jerusalem weep over Jesus.
9 Jesus falls the third time.
10 Jesus is stripped of his garments.
11 Jesus is nailed to the cross.
12 Jesus dies on the cross.
13 Jesus is taken down from the cross.
14 Jesus is placed in the sepulchre.

Ten Commandments listed in Exodus and Deuteronomy.
1 Thou shalt have no other gods before me.
2 Thou shalt not make any graven images or likeness of anything in Heaven.
3 Thou shalt not take the name of the Lord thy God in vain.
4 Remember the Sabbath day, to keep it holy.
5 Honour thy father and thy mother.
6 Thou shalt not kill.
7 Thou shalt not commit adultery.
8 Thou shalt not steal.
9 Thou shalt not bear false witness against thy neighbour.
10 Thou shalt not covet thy neighbour's house, wife, manservant, ox or ass.

Unification Church founded by the Reverend Sun Myung Moon (1954).

Visitation the visit of the Virgin Mary to her cousin Elizabeth, mother of John the Baptist.

White Friars Carmelites (mendicant order established c. 1155 and approved in 1226 by Pope Honorius III).

White Monks Cistercians (founded in 1098).

R
E
L
I
G
I
O
N

Archbishops of York

734	Egberht	928	Hrothweard	1041	Æthelric
767	Æthelberht	931	Wulfstan I	1051	Cynesige
780	Eanbald I	956	Osketel	1061	Ealdred
796	Eanbald II	971	Oswald	1070	Thomas I of Bayeux
808	Wulfsige	971	Edwald	1100	Gerard
837	Wigmund	992	Ealdwulf	1109	Thomas II
854	Wulfhere	1003	Wulfstan II	1119	Thurstan
900	Æthalbald	1023	Ælfric Puttoc	1143	William Fitzherbert

1147	Henry Murdac	1476	Lawrence Booth	1724	Lancelot Blackburn
1153	William Fitzherbert	1480	Thomas Rotherham	1743	Thomas Herring
1154	Roger of Pont l'Eveque	1501	Thomas Savage	1747	Matthew Hutton
1191	Geoffrey Plantagenet	1508	Christopher Bainbridge	1757	John Gilben
1215	Walter de Gray	1514	Thomas Wolsey	1761	Roben Hay Drumond
1256	Sewal de Bovill	1531	Edward Lee	1777	William Markham
1258	Godfrey Ludham	1545	Robert Holgate	1808	Edward Venables Vernon
1266	Walter Giffard	1555	Nicholas Heath		Harcourt
1279	William Wickwane	1561	Thomas Young	1847	Thomas Musgrave
1286	John Romanus	1570	Edmund Grindal	1860	Charles Thomas Longley
1298	Henry Newark	1577	Edwin Sandys	1863	William Thomson
1300	Thomas Corbridge	1589	John Piers	1891	William Connor Magee
1306	William Greenfield	1595	Matthew Hutton	1891	William Dalrymple
1317	William Melton	1606	Tobias Matthew		Maclagan
1342	William de la Zouche	1628	George Montaigne	1909	Cosmo Gordon Lang
1352	John Thoresby	1629	Samuel Harsnett	1929	William Temple
1374	Alexander Neville	1632	Richard Neile	1942	Cyril Forster Garbett
1388	Thomas Arundel	1641	John Williams	1956	Arthur Michael Ramsey
1396	Robert Waldby	1660	Accepted Frewen	1961	Frederick Donald Coggan
1398	Richard le Scrope	1664	Richard Sterne	1975	Stuart Yarwonh Blanch
1407	Henry Bowet	1683	John Dolben	1983	John Stapylton Habgood
1426	John Kempe	1688	Thomas Lamplugh	1995	David Michael Hope*
1452	William Booth	1691	John Sharp		
1464	George Nevill	1714	William Dawes		

*retired in March 2005 to become vicar of St Margaret's in Ilkley, Yorkshire

Patron Saints

accountants	Matthew	builders	Vincent Ferrer, Barbara, Thomas
actors	Genesius, Vitus		
advertising	Bernardino of Siena	cab-drivers	Fiacre
airmen	Our Lady of Loretto, Theresa	Canada	Joseph, Anne (mother of Mary)
animals	Francis of Assisi	cancer victims	Peregrine Laziosi
archers	Sebastian	caretakers	Joseph of Arimathea
architects	Thomas, Barbara	candle-makers	Ambrose
Argentina	Our Lady of Lujan	cavalry	Martin of Tours
army	Maurice	chaplains	John of Capistrano
artists	Luke	charcoal burners	Alexander
astronauts	Joseph of Cupertino	childbirth	Gerard Majella, Margaret of Antioch
astronomers	Dominic		
athletes	Sebastian	choirboys	Dominic Savio
Australia	Our Lady Help of Christians	church	Joseph
Austria	Leopold	carpenters	Joseph
authors	Francis of Sales	children	Nicholas
bakers	Elizabeth of Hungary, Nicholas of Torentino, Zita	chorea	Vitus
		civil servants	Thomas More
bankers	Matthew	clergy	Gabriel Possenti
barbers	Cosmas, Damian, Louis	coffin bearers	Joseph of Arimathea
bastards	John Francis Regis	colleges	Thomas Aquinas
battle	Archangel Michael	comedians	Vitus
beekeepers	Ambrose	condemned criminals	Dismas
beggars	Martin of Tours	cooks	Lawrence, Martha
Belgium	Joseph	craftsmen	Elegius
blacksmiths	Dunstan	crippled	Giles
Bolivia	Our Lady of Capucclana	Cuba	Our Lady of Charity
bookkeepers	Matthew	Cyprus	Barnabas
booksellers	John of God	Czech Republic	Wenceslas
Brazil	Peter of Alcantara	dairy workers	Bridgid of Ireland
brewers	Augustine of Hippo, Luke, Nicholas of Myra	dancers	Vitus
		deacons	Stephen
bricklayers	Stephen	deaf	Francis of Sales
brides	Nicholas of Myra	death	Archangel Michael, Margaret of Antioch
bridges	John Nepomucen		
broadcasters	Archangel Gabriel	Denmark	Asgar/Canute
Brussels	Michael	dentists	Apollonia
butchers	Anthony the Abbot, Luke, Adrian of Nicomedia	dieticians	Martha
		disabled	Giles
button-makers	Louis	disasters	Genevieve

doctors	Luke	Lisbon	Vincent
domestics	Zita	London	Paul
Dominican Republic	Our Lady of Mercy	lost articles	Anthony of Padua
doubters	Thomas	lost causes	Jude
drunkards	Martin of Tours	lovers	Valentine
dyers	Maurice	Madagascar	Vincent de Paul
earthquakes	Francis Borgia, Gregory the Wonderworker	Madrid	Isidore
		magistrates	Ferdinand III of Castile
ecologists	Francis of Assisi	Malta	Paul
eczema	Anthony the Abbot	marriage	John Francis Regis
Edinburgh	Giles	masons	Thomas
editors	John Bosco	mental illness	Dymphna
Egypt	Mark	messengers	Archangel Gabriel
El Salvador	Our Lady of Peace	metalworkers	Anastasius, Eligius
engineers	Patrick, Ferdinand III	Mexico	Joseph
England	George	midwives	Raymond Nonnatus
epilepsy	Dympna, Vitus	milliners	James the Greater
Europe	Cyril, Benedict	miners	Barbara, Anne (mother of Mary)
examination candidates	Joseph of Cupertino	Moscow	Boris
		motorcyclists	Our Lady of Grace
farmers	George, Isidore	motorists	Christopher, Frances of Rome
fathers	Joseph	motorways	John the Baptist
Finland	Henry	musicians/singers	Cecilia, Dunstan, Gregory
firemen	Florian	neurological disorders	Vitus
flying	Joseph of Cupertino		
fishermen	Peter, Andrew	New Zealand	Our Lady Help of Christians
Florence	John the Baptist	Norway	Olaf
florists	Dorothea, Therese	numismatists	Eligius
France	Denis	nurses	Agatha, Raphael, Camillus of Lellis
funeral directors	Joseph of Arimathea, Dismas		
gardeners	Adelard, Phocas, Tryphon, Dorothea, Fiacre	orphans	Ivo of Kermartin
		Oslo	Halivard
Germany	Boniface	painters	Luke
Glasgow	Kentigern (aka Mungo)	Pakistan	Thomas, Francis Xavier
goldsmiths	Dunstan	pallbearers	Joseph of Arimathea
gravediggers	Anthony, Joseph	Papua New Guinea	Archangel Michael
Greece	Andrew, Nicholas, Paul	paralysed	Giles
grocers	Michael	paratroopers	Archangel Michael
Guatemala	James the Greater	Paris	Geneviève
gunners	Barbara	pawnbrokers	Nicholas
haemorrhoids	Fiacre	perfumers	Nicholas of Myra
hairdressers	Martin of Porres	Peru	Joseph, Rose of Lima
Haiti	Our Lady of Perpetual Help	pilots	Mary, Our Lady of Loreto
headaches	Teresa of Avila, Denis	physicians	Luke
heart patients	John of God	pig herders	Anthony
hernia sufferers	Cathal	plasterers	Bartholomew
Holland	Willibrord	poets	Cecilia, David, Columbia
horseriders	Martin of Tours	Poland	Stanislaus, Casimir
horses	Eligius, Hippolytus	policemen	Michael
hospitals	John of God, Camillus de Lellis, Vincent de Paul	politicians	Thomas More
		poor	Anthony of Padua, Lawrence
hoteliers	Gentian, Amand	Portugal	George, Anthony
housewives	Anne, Martha, Zita	postal workers	Archangel Gabriel
Hungary	Stephen	pregnancy	Gerard Majella, Raymond Nonnatus
hunters	Eustace, Hubert		
ice skaters	Edwina	printers	Augustine of Hippo, John of God
Iceland	Olaf		
India	Our Lady of the Assumption	prison officers	Hippolytus
infantrymen	Maurice	quantity surveyors	Thomas
innkeepers	Amand, Martin of Tours, Gentian	Quebec	John the Baptist
Ireland	Patrick	rabies victims	Hubert
Italy	Francis of Assisi	radio	Archangel Gabriel
jewellers	Eligius (Eloi)	radiologists	Archangel Michael
Jordan	John the Baptist	Ripon	Wilfred
journalists	Francis of Sales	Rome	Peter
judges	John of Capistrano	Russia	Andrew, Nicholas
jumping	Venantius	sailors	Christopher, Cuthbert, Francis of Paolo, Dhocas
lame	Giles		
lawyers	Genesius, Ivo, Thomas More	scholars	Bede, Bridgit, Jerome
lepers	Giles	scientists	Albert
librarians	Jerome, Catherine of Alexandria	Scotland	Andrew
lighthouse keepers	Clement, Venerius	scouts	George

RELIGION

sculptors	Claude
secretaries	Genesius
shoemakers	Crispin
singers	Gregory
skiers	Bernard of Montjoux
skin diseases	Anthony
soldiers	George, Joan of Arc, Sebastian
South Africa	Our Lady of the Assumption
Spain	James
speleologists	Benedict
stamp collectors	Archangel Gabriel
statesmen	Thomas More
students	Thomas Aquinas
surgeons	Cosmas, Damian
Sweden	Bridget, Eric
swimmers	Adjutor
Switzerland	Nicholas
tailors	Homobonus
tax collectors	Matthew
teachers	Catherine, Gregory
teenagers	Maria Goretti
telecommunications	Archangel Gabriel

telephone	Gabriel
television	Clare
thieves	Dismas
throat disorders	Blaise
toothache	Apollonia
travellers	Christopher
undertakers	Dismas
unmarried women	Nicholas of Myra
venereal disease	Fiacre
Venice	Mark
vets	Eligius (Eloi)
Vietnam	Joseph
volcanoes	Agatha
Wales	David
West Indies	Gertrude
wine merchants	Amand, Vincent
wine growers	Vincent
wool combers	Blaise
workers	Joseph
writers	Francis of Sales
yachtsmen	Adjutor

NB Almost everyone, everything and everywhere can be included under the auspices of a patron saint. Sometimes the affiliation lies in historical events and sometimes in ancient folklore and, more frequently still, homage is often paid to a particular saint for convenience, for example, cab-drivers call on St Fiacre as their protector because the Hotel St Fiacre in Paris was the first establishment to offer coaches for hire. Confusion often arises in this field as to why a particular saint has been adopted by a particular group. For example, St Martin of Tours is identified with innkeepers and drunks but is often depicted as a young mounted soldier. It should also be noted that many occupations have more than one recognised patron saint, and extra care should therefore be taken when compiling questions on this subject. For example, do not ask who is the patron saint of soldiers unless you are prepared to accept any of the three possible answers.

Archbishops of Canterbury

1	Augustine	597–604	36	Anselm	1093–1109
2	Lawrence (Laurentius)	604–619	37	Ralph d'Escures	1114–22
3	Mellitus	619–624	38	William of Corbeil	1123–36
4	Justus	624–627	39	Theobald	1138–61
5	Honorius	627–653	40	Thomas à Becket	1162–70
6	Deusdedit	655–664	41	Richard of Dover	1174–84
7	Theodore (Theodorus) of Tarsus	668–690	42	Baldwin	1184–90
			43	Hubert Walter	1193–1205
8	Berhtwald (Beorhtweald)	693–731	44	Stephen Langton	1206–28
9	Tatwine	731–734	45	Richard le Grant	1229–31
10	Nothelm	735–739	46	Edmund Rich	1233–40
11	Cuthbert (Cuthbeorht)	740–760	47	Boniface of Savoy	1241–70
12	Bregowine (Breguwine)	761–764	48	Robert Kilwardby	1272–78
13	Jaenberht (Jaenbeorht)	765–792	49	John Pecham	1279–92
14	Aethelheard	793–805	50	Robert Winchelsey	1293–1313
15	Wulfred	805–832	51	Walter Reynolds	1313–27
16	Feologild	832	52	Simon Mepham	1327–33
17	Ceolnoth	833–870	53	John Stratford	1333–48
18	Aethelred	870–889	54	Thomas Bradwardine	1348–49
19	Piegmund	890–914	55	Simon Islip	1349–66
20	Aethelhelm	914–923	56	Simon Langham	1366–68
21	Wulfhelm	923–942	57	William Whittlesey	1368–74
22	Oda	942–958	58	Simon Sudbury	1375–81
23	Aelfsige	959	59	William Courtenay	1381–96
24	Beorhthelm	959	60	Thomas Arundel	1396–97
25	Dunstan	960–988	61	Roger Walden	1397–99
26	Aethelgar	988–990	60	Thomas Arundel (restored)	1399–1414
27	Sigeric Serio	990–994	62	Henry Chichele	1414–43
28	Aelfric	995–1005	63	John Stafford	1443–52
29	Aelfheah	1005–12	64	John Kempe	1452–54
30	Lyfing	1013–20	65	Thomas Bourchier	1454–86
31	Aethelnoth	1020–38	66	John Morton	1486–1500
32	Eadsige	1038–50	67	Henry Deane	1501–03
33	Robert of Jumièges	1051–52	68	William Warham	1503–32
34	Stigand	1052–70	69	Thomas Cranmer	1533–56
35	Lanfranc	1070–89	70	Reginald Pole	1556–58

71	Matthew Parker	1559–75		88	John Moore	1783–1805
72	Edmund Grindal	1575–83		89	Charles Manners Sutton	1805–28
73	John Whitgift	1583–1604		90	William Howley	1828–48
74	Richard Bancroft	1604–10		91	John Bird Sumner	1848–62
75	George Abbot	1611–33		92	Charles Thomas Longley	1862–68
76	William Laud	1633–45		93	Archibald Campbell Tait	1868–82
77	William Juxon	1660–63		94	Edward White Benson	1883–96
78	Gilbert Sheldon	1663–77		95	Frederick Temple	1896–1902
79	William Sancroft	1677–90		96	Randall Thomas Davidson	1903–28
80	John Tillotson	1691–94		97	Cosmo Gordon Lang	1928–42
81	Thomas Tenison	1694–1715		98	William Temple	1942–44
82	William Wake	1715–37		99	Geoffrey Francis Fisher	1945–61
83	John Potter	1737–47		100	Arthur Michael Ramsey	1961–74
84	Thomas Herring	1747–57		101	Frederick Donald Coggan	1974–80
85	Matthew Hutton	1757–58		102	Robert Alexander Runcie	1980–90
86	Thomas Secker	1758–68		103	George Carey	1990–2002
87	Frederick Cornwallis	1768–83		104	Rowan Williams	2002–

Miscellaneous Information

Archbishop of Canterbury: 100th	Arthur Michael Ramsey
Archbishop: remained bishop	Stigand remained bishop of Worcester
Aristotle philosophies: taught at Oxford	Edmund of Abingdon: first to do so
Augustine landed: where	Isle of Thanet AD 597
buried	SS Peter and Paul (later St Augustine's), Canterbury
converted King	King Aethelbert of Kent
founded church	Christ Church Canterbury
order of monks	Benedictines
Roman prior of	St Andrews Benedictine monastery
welcomed by	King Aethelbert of Kent
Bishop of London	Richard Chartres (132nd) since 26 January 1996
Book of Common Prayer: drew up	Thomas Cranmer
born on Greek island	Frederick Temple
Carthusian monk	Boniface of Savoy
Catholic archbishop: last	Reginald Pole
Charles I: ministered on scaffold	William Juxon
Edmund Rich: also known as	Edmund of Abingdon
English-born archbishop: first	Berhtwald
Father and son: only holders	Frederick and William Temple
Henry Chichele: founded	St John's and All Souls colleges at Oxford 1437
heresy: convicted of	Thomas Cranmer (burned at stake)
high treason: accused of	William Laud (beheaded on Tower Hill)
investiture controversy: resolved by	Synod of Rockingham (temporarily)
Lambeth Conference	decennial meeting of Anglican bishops
Lanfranc: originally trained as	lawyer
secured Crown for	William II (Rufus)
Laurentius' dream	dream of St Peter reminded him of his mission
Lombardy: born	Lanfranc and Anselm
Maidstone Hospital: founder	Boniface of Savoy
married Oliver Cromwell's niece	John Tillotson 1664
Mellitus: prayer legend	caused wind to divert fire from Canterbury church
Morton's Fork:	rich pay taxes; poor are considered to be concealing wealth
murdered in Canterbury Cathedral	Thomas à Becket
murdered during Peasant's Revolt	Simon Sudbury (first beheading on Tower Hill)
nicknames: John Whitgift	Little black husband (by Elizabeth I)
Matthew Parker	Nosey Parker
official residence	Lambeth Palace, and Old Palace Canterbury
ordination of women	promulgated in the General Synod in Feb. 1994.
pallium	a mantle, and symbol of papal approval of archiepiscopal appointment
Piers Gaveston excommunicated by	Robert Winchelsey
plague: died of	Thomas Bradwardine
plot against William I: detected	Lanfranc
position created by	Pope Gregory I
Primate of	All England
prior of Bec Benedictine monastery	Lanfranc, Anselm, Theobald
Protestant archbishop: first	Thomas Cranmer
published Antiquities of Greece	John Potter
Queen Elizabeth II: crowned	Geoffrey Fisher
refused oath of allegiance	William Sancroft: to William and Mary

R
E
L
I
G
I
O
N

Repton School: former headmasters	William Temple and Geoffrey Fisher
Richard I: governor in absentia	Hubert Walter
Rochester: first bishop of	St Justus
Scholasticism: founder of	St Anselm
Sheldonian Theatre, Oxford: built	Gilbert Sheldon
son-in-law of Archbishop Tait	Randall Thomas Davidson
St Dunstan: secured crown for	St Edward the Martyr AD 975
Stigand: excommunicated by	Pope Nicholas II 1059. Uncanonical behaviour caused Pope to support William I's invasion
succeeded Thomas Arnold at Rugby	Archibald Campbell Tait
Synod of Whitby 663/664	Northumbria decided to follow Roman Church
Tarsus: born in	Theodore
Theobald: patron of	Thomas à Becket, John of Salisbury, Vacarius
Thomas à Becket: also known as	Thomas of London
born	Cheapside, London
shrine despoiled by	Henry VIII
York: first bishop of	St Paulinus

The Bible

Genesis
God creates Adam from dust.
Garden of Eden planted.
Trees of Life and Knowledge.
Adam names all living beasts.
Eve is created from Adam's rib.
Serpent deceives Eve into eating forbidden fruit.
Birth of Cain and Abel.
Cain becomes tiller of the soil, and Abel a shepherd.
Cain kills Abel and when asked by the Lord as to his whereabouts replies, 'Am I my brother's keeper?'
Cain is 'marked' by God and flees to the land of Nod.
Cain's wife gives birth to a son, Enoch, and builds a city in his name.
Adam's third son Seth is fathered at the age of 130 and Adam dies at age 930.
Methuselah is sired by Enoch (descendant of Seth, not Cain) and lives for 969 years.
Methuselah sires Lamech who subsequently sires Noah.
Noah begets three sons: Shem, Ham, and Japheth. He was 500 years old.
God destroys man by bringing great flood but reprieves Noah.
Noah (aged 600) builds an ark of gopher wood (300 x 50 cubits, and 30 cubits high), three storeys in total.
God directs Noah to take aboard seven of each type of clean beast but just two of each unclean.
There were eight humans on the ark, i.e. Noah and his sons plus their wives.
Ark comes to rest on Mt Ararat.
Noah sends forth a raven and then a dove, which comes back with an olive leaf to show that the rains have ceased.
Noah becomes the first 'drunken man' after planting a vineyard.
Noah lives for 350 years after the flood and dies aged 950.
Noah's great grandson, Nimrod, begins to be a mighty one on the earth.
Nimrod's kingdom begins with Babel, Erech, Accad, Calneh and Shinar.
The whole earth is of one language, one speech.
After the tower of Babel is built, the Lord scatters the people abroad to confound their language.
The Lord calls unto Abram and blesses him.
Abram, with his wife Sarai and nephew Lot, journey into the land of Canaan.
Abram and Lot return from Egypt, after Sarai is taken by the Pharaoh.
Lot moves to live in Sodom, but the men of Sodom are wicked and sinners.
Then comes the 'Battle of the Kings'.
At the battle in the vale of Siddim, the kings of Sodom and Gomorrah are beaten and fall into slimepits.
Lot is taken prisoner by the victors.
Abram attacked at Hobah, and gains the release of Lot, all his goods, the women and the people.
Abram's wife Sarai cannot bear him children; she therefore gives Abram her maid Hagar, who bears him a child, Ishmael.
Abram is 86 years old when he fathers Ishmael.
The Lord renames Abram – Abraham.
The Lord makes a covenant with Abraham which states that every male child is to be circumcised at eight days old.
The Lord renames Sarai – Sarah.
At the age of 90, Sarah bears Abraham a son, Isaac.
Two angels come to see Lot at the gates of Sodom.
The men of Sodom are struck blind.

Lot, his wife and two daughters leave Sodom.

They are told not to look behind them.

Sodom and Gomorrah are destroyed by the Lord.

Lot's wife looks behind her and is turned into a pillar of salt.

Lot's two daughters get him drunk so that they may 'lie' with him to preserve his seed.

Lot's elder daughter has a son, Moab.

Lot's younger daughter also has a son called Ben-ammi.

Abraham tells Abimelech, king of Gerar, that Sarah is his sister, and she is taken by Abimelech.

Abraham casts Hagar and his son Ishmael away.

Abimelech makes a covenant with Abraham and returns to the land of the Philistines.

Abraham has his faith tested by the Lord.

Sarah dies at the age of 127.

A wife is sought for Isaac.

Abraham's servant finds and meets Rebekah.

Rebekah consents to go to Isaac; she then becomes his wife.

Abraham takes a second wife, Keturah.

Keturah bears him Zimran, Jokshan, Medan, Midian, Ishbak and Shuah.

Abraham dies aged 175.

Ishmael dies aged 137.

Ishmael has twelve sons – Nebajoth, Kedar, Adbeel, Mibsam, Mishma, Dumah, Massa, Hadar,
    Tems, Jetur, Naphish and Kedemah.

Rebekah gives birth to twins – Esau (a hunter) and Jacob (a tent-maker).

Esau sells his birthright to Jacob for a mess of pottage (bread and lentil stew).

Jacob deceives his father, Isaac, into believing that he is his brother Esau.

When Esau finds out about the deceit he threatens Jacob.

While searching for a wife, Jacob dreams of the ladder reaching from earth to the heavens.

Jacob dreams of the Angels of God ascending and descending on the ladder.

Jacob meets Rachel.

Jacob works for seven years in order to win Rachel.

Jacob takes both Rachel and her younger sister Leah as his wives.

Rachel is barren, but Leah bears Jacob a son, Reuben.

Leah later bears Simeon, Levi and Judah.

Rachel gives Jacob her handmaiden, Bilhah, to take as a wife.

Bilhah bears Dan and Naphtali.

Leah gives her maid, Zilpah, to Jacob to take as a wife.

Zilpah bears Gad and Asher.

Leah bears Jacob a fifth son, Issachar, a sixth, Zebulun, and a daughter, Dinah.

Rachel herself then conceives and bears a son, Joseph.

Jacob becomes very rich, with many cattle, maidservants, menservants, camels and asses.

Jacob has a vision at Mahanaim.

Jacob sends messengers to Esau, requesting his return to Laban.

Esau comes to meet him with 400 men.

Jacob sends a present to Esau of various animals.

When Jacob meets Esau, Jacob bows seven times.

Esau runs to meet Jacob, and embraces him. They both weep.

Jacob builds an altar at Shalem, and calls it El-elohe-Israel.

Dinah is defiled by Shechem, son of Hamor, the Hivite.

Simeon and Levi slay all the males of the city, and take Dinah from Shechem's house.

Jacob is unhappy with his sons, because the Canaanites and Perizzites will now rise against him.

God tells Jacob to move to Beth-el.

Jacob and his household journey to Beth-el, build an altar and call it El-beth-el.

Jacob is renamed Israel.

Rachel dies while giving birth to Benjamin.

While away from his household, Reuben lies with Bilhah, his father's concubine.

Jacob's sons now number twelve.

Jacob goes to his father, Isaac, at Hebron, where Isaac dies, aged 180.

Jacob favours Joseph over his brothers.

Joseph has dreams which cause his brothers to hate him.

At first Joseph's brothers plot to kill him.

Joseph's brothers sell him into slavery with the Ishmaelites.

The brothers dip Joseph's long garment in goat's blood, and take it to Jacob.

Jacob mourns his son's death.

Judah meets and takes the daughter of a Canaanite, named Shuah.

Shuah bears three sons: Er, Onan and Shelah.

Judah takes a wife for Er, whose name is Tamar.

Er displeases the Lord and He slays him.

Judah tells Onan to marry Tamar, his brother's widow.

Onan spills his seed on the ground; this displeases the Lord also and He slays Onan.

Judah tells Tamar to live in his house and wait until Shelah is grown.

Tamar deceives Judah into thinking she is a harlot.

When Judah hears that Tamar is pregnant, he orders her to be burnt.

She is spared when Judah realises he is the father of her child.

R
E
L
I
G
I
O
N

Tamar has twins, Pharez and Zarah.
Joseph is sold in Egypt to Potiphar, an officer of the Pharaoh.
Joseph is promoted to overseer.
Joseph's master's wife asks him to lie with her, but Joseph refuses.
She later pulls his garment off him and Joseph flees.
She lies to Potiphar, saying that Joseph came to her to force her to lie with him.
Joseph is imprisoned in the King's prison.
He interprets the dreams of the Pharaoh's officers.
After being in prison for two years, the Pharaoh has a dream and is told of Joseph.
Joseph interprets the Pharaoh's dream.
Joseph foretells the famine.
Joseph is released from prison and lives in the Pharaoh's house.
The famine is worldwide, but Egypt has stockpiled corn.
All the countries of the world come to Egypt to buy corn.
Jacob sends Joseph's brothers to Egypt to buy corn.
Joseph is now governor of the land.
His brothers come and bow before him.
Joseph recognises his brothers but they not him.
Joseph accuses his brothers of being spies.
Joseph supplies them with food and returns all their money to them.
At an inn the brothers realise that Joseph has returned their money.
Joseph insists that his brothers bring Benjamin to him.
Israel sends all the brothers to Egypt.
All the brothers are taken to Joseph's house for a feast.
Again Joseph fills their sacks with food and also returns their money.
Joseph puts his silver cup in the sack of Benjamin, the youngest brother.
Joseph's stewards find the silver cup and accuse the brothers of theft.
Judah petitions Joseph, asking that Benjamin be allowed to return to his father.
Joseph weeps and makes himself known to his brothers.
Pharaoh commands the brothers to bring back to Egypt all their families.
They tell Israel that Joseph is alive, but Israel does not believe them.
When Israel sees the wagons that Pharaoh has given to them, he believes.
Israel and his entire family return to Egypt to see Joseph.
Joseph meets his father at Goshen.
Israel is given Goshen by Pharaoh.
When people run out of money to buy bread, Joseph sells bread in exchange for livestock.
Joseph buys all the land of Egypt, except the land of the priests.
Joseph gives the people seed to grow their own crops.
The people must give one-fifth of their crops to Pharaoh.
Joseph takes his two sons, Manasseh and Ephraim, to Israel, where Israel blesses them.
Israel prophesies to his twelve sons, then dies, aged 147.
Israel insists that he be buried with his ancestors.
Pharaoh allows Joseph to travel to Canaan for the burial.
Afterwards Joseph and his brothers return to Egypt.
The brothers think that now Israel is dead, Joseph may seek retribution.
Joseph reassures them.
Joseph dies aged 110 and is buried in Egypt.

Exodus   Israel and his sons enter Egypt, each with his household.
Joseph is already in Egypt.
Their offspring multiply at an extraordinary rate until the land is filled with them.
A new king of Egypt becomes worried that the sons of Israel are growing so numerous.
The sons of Israel are oppressed.
The more they are oppressed, the more they multiply.
Eventually the Egyptians make the sons of Israel slaves.
The king of Egypt orders the Hebrew midwives, Shiphrah and Puah, to put to death any male child at
   birth.
Fearing God, the midwives disobey the Egyptian king.
Finally Pharaoh orders all his people to throw every newborn son into the River Nile.
A man from the house of Levi takes a daughter of Levi, and she becomes pregnant.
She conceals her son for three months.
She then places him in a basket, in the reeds, on the River Nile.
Pharaoh's daughter finds him, and realises he is a child of the Hebrews.
The child grows up and becomes a son to the daughter of Pharaoh.
She names him Moses.
Moses sees an Egyptian striking a Hebrew; he strikes the Egyptian down and kills him.
Pharaoh hears about it and tries to kill Moses.
Moses runs away to the land of Midian.
Moses meets the priest of Midian, who gives his daughter Zipporah to him.
Zipporah bears Moses a son, Gershom.
Moses becomes a shepherd.
While with the flock, Moses comes to Horeb. Here, an Angel appears to him in a flaming bush.

God speaks to Moses, instructing him to bring the sons of Israel out of Egypt.

Moses wants a sign that this is God.

God tells Moses to throw his rod on to the ground and it becomes a serpent.

God then tells Moses to grab the serpent by its tail, and it becomes a rod.

God gives Moses other signs, turning his hand into a leper's hand and restoring it and turning water from the Nile into blood.

Moses meets Aaron, his brother.

Moses returns to Egypt with his wife and family.

Moses and Aaron meet with the elders of the sons of Israel.

Moses and Aaron meet with Pharaoh and ask that the Hebrews may go into the wilderness for a festival.

Pharaoh refuses permission for the Hebrews to go into the wilderness.

Pharaoh makes the sons of Israel work harder.

The officers of the sons of Israel blame Moses and Aaron for this harsh treatment.

Moses promises to deliver the sons of Israel from this oppression.

Moses and Aaron again meet with Pharaoh; Moses is now 80 years old and Aaron 83.

Aaron throws down his rod in front of Pharaoh and it becomes a serpent.

The magic-practising priests of Egypt do the same thing.

Aaron's rod swallows their rods.

Moses meets Pharaoh on the bank of the Nile, strikes the water with his rod and turns the water into blood.

The magic-practising priests proceed to do the same thing.

Moses tells Pharaoh that unless the people are allowed to go into the wilderness, there will be a plague of frogs. Aaron waves his staff over the Nile and a plague of frogs come to land.

The magic-practising priests do the same thing.

Aaron strikes the dust of Egypt, and it all becomes a swarm of gnats.

The magic practising priests attempts to do the same but they fail.

Moses tells Pharaoh that if the people are not released into the wilderness, gadfly will infest every house.

Gadfly infest every house in Egypt.

Finally Pharaoh calls Moses and Aaron and tells them to take their people into the wilderness.

The gadfly disappear, so Pharaoh does not allow the people to go into the wilderness.

Moses tells Pharaoh that if the people are not released, a pestilence will strike every animal in Egypt.

Moses takes a handful of soot, throws it in the air, in sight of Pharaoh, and it becomes boils and blisters upon man and beast.

The magic-practising priests are unable to attempt to copy this because the boils are affecting them.

Moses again goes to Pharaoh and promises a hailstorm that will kill every man and beast in the field .

The next day, a storm of hail, thunder and lightning strikes Egypt.

Pharaoh now calls Moses and Aaron and release the people to go into the wilderness.

Once the storm stops, Pharaoh again refuses to release the people into the wilderness.

Moses and Aaron see Pharaoh and tell him that a plague of locusts will appear tomorrow unless the people are released.

Locusts covers all of the land of Egypt.

Moses stretches out his arm and darkness falls all over Egypt.

The firstborn of every family in Egypt is threatened with death.

Instructions for the feast of the Passover are given to Moses by the Lord.

At midnight, the firstborn of every man and every beast dies.

Finally Pharaoh tells the people to leave.

The exodus takes place.

The people of Israel reach the Red Sea.

A pillar of cloud by daytime and a pillar of fire by night lead them into the wilderness.

Pharaoh proceeds to give chase when he realises that the people are escaping.

When Pharaoh reaches the people they are camped by the sea.

Moses stretches his hand over the sea and it parts, allowing the sons of Israel to walk through the Red Sea. The Egyptians follows them into the Red Sea.

Moses again stretches his hand over the sea and the water returns to its normal state, drowning the Egyptians.

Moses leads the people into the wilderness for three days; they reach Marrah, but cannot drink the water because it is bitter.

The Lord directs Moses to a tree, which he throws into the water and the water becomes sweet.

At the wilderness of Sin, the sons of Israel begin to murmur against Moses and Aaron.

Quails arrive in the evening, and in the morning the wilderness is covered in bread.

By collecting double bread on the sixth day, and resting on the seventh, the Sabbath law is observed.

The sons of Israel eat the manna for 40 years.

At Massah, Moses is instructed to strike a stone with his rod, and water comes out of the rock.

The Amalekites attack the sons of Israel.

Moses instructs Joshua to choose men to go and fight the Amalekites.

Moses watches from the top of a hill.

When Moses lifts his rod, the Israelites are superior.

When Moses lowers his rod, the Amalekites are superior.

Moses' father-in-law, Jethro, along with his wife Zipporah, his two children, Gershom and Eliezer, and Moses' two sons, visits Moses in the wilderness.

Jethro adviseds Moses to appoint Judges.

Moses takes his advice.

The people go to meet their God on Mount Sinai.

The Lord calls Moses to the top of the mountain.

Moses then returns down the mountain to take Aaron back to the top with him.

Moses is given the Ten Commandments.

Rules on how slaves are treated, including 'eye for eye'.

Further rules covering theft, seduction, sorcery, bestiality, bribery and many more are given to Moses.

Three times a year the Israelites must celebrate a festival to the Lord.

Boundary of the 'promised land' is set, from the Red Sea to the Sea of the Philistines and from the wilderness to the river.

Moses goes up the mountain to receive the stone tablets.

Moses stays on the mountain for 40 days and 40 nights.

The people are instructed to build an ark of acacia wood, two and a half cubits in length, and one and a half cubits deep.

The ark must be overlaid with gold, both inside and outside.

The ark must have four gold rings, two either side.

The people must make two poles of acacia wood and overlay them with gold.

These poles go through the rings in order for the ark to be carried.

The poles must not be removed from the rings.

The commandments must be placed within the ark.

The people are instructed to build a tabernacle, with all its utensils.

The design of the garments to be worn by priests is given to Moses.

Instructions for the installation of priests are given.

Instructions for keeping the Sabbath are given.

When the Lord finishes speaking with Moses on Mount Sinai, he gives to Moses two tablets of stone.

The people are frustrated because Moses is on Mount Sinai for so long.

The people persuade Aaron to make a 'God' for them.

After melting down the people's jewellery, he makes a golden calf.

The making of the golden calf angers the Lord.

When Moses sees the golden calf, he is so angry he smashes the two tablets and destroys the golden calf.

Moses seeks out the loyal people and the sons of Levi gather themselves to him.

Moses sends the sons of Levi back into the camp to kill the sinners; they kill about 3,000.

Moses moves his tent outside the camp and calls it a tent of meeting.

Whenever Moses enters the tent, a pillar of cloud descends and stands at the entrance.

The Lord instructs Moses to carve out two tablets of stone and the Lord will rewrite the commandments.

The Lord will not allow Moses to see his face.

The Lord repeats the terms of the covenant between himself and the people of Israel.

Moses again comes down from Mount Sinai with the two tablets.

The people contribute gifts to the Lord.

Bezalel and Oholiab are selected for special teachings and wisdom.

The people begin to make the cloth and other finery for the tabernacle.

Once completed, the Lord's glory fills the tabernacle.

Leviticus   Instructions for offerings of animals and grain are given to the people of Israel.

All grain offerings must be seasoned with salt.

A young bull must be sacrificed for a sin of a priest.

A young goat must be sacrificed for a sin of a chieftain.

Other sins demand other offerings.

Even unintentional sins must be paid for with offerings.

The eating of fat or blood is forbidden.

Aaron and his sons are installed as priests.

Nadab and Abihu, sons of Aaron, make an offering to the Lord that was not prescribed.

Fire from heaven consumes both.

Instructions as to which animals and fish are clean or unclean are given.

Instructions for the purification of women are given.

Priests are to make leprosy tests; anybody with leprosy is declared unclean.

Garments worn by lepers are also unclean.

Instructions for offerings in the case of a cleansed leper are given.

Uncleanliness in the case of male and female discharges is explained.

Atonement Day procedures are given.

The laws regarding incest are given.

Similarly laws regarding sodomy and bestiality are given.

Laws regarding gleaning of crops are given.

Laws regarding slander, interbreeding, fruit trees and magic are given.

Similarly, laws regarding spiritism, respect of parents and adultery are given.

The law that priests are to be undefiled is explained.

Laws regarding Sabbath, Pentecost, Day of Atonement, festival of Booths and loaves of showbread explained.

The fiftieth year is to become a Jubilee.

The Jubilee year is also a year of restorations. For example, if a man sells his house, he must repurchase it in the fiftieth year.

Laws regarding the help to be given to the poor are explained.

Regarding the poor, money given must bear no usury or interest charges.

No idols or images of the Lord are to be worshipped.

The Lord explains the blessings that the people will enjoy if they keep his laws and commandments.

The Lord explains the chastisements that the people will suffer if they do not keep his laws and commandments.

Values are put on sanctifying your soul, animal, house, field, etc. to the Lord.

Numbers
(Numbers is Bemidbar in Hebrew and means 'In the wilderness'.)

The Lord tells Moses to register every male over 20 years of age.

The Lord also names the assembly; all are chieftains of the tribes of Israel.

The tribes are registered for the army.

All are registered except the Levites.

Moses is told to appoint the Levites over the tabernacle and all the utensils.

When the people set up camp, each tribe must camp with its (three-tribe) division.

Each tribe is designated a place to camp, starting with the (three-tribe) division of Judah eastmost.

The other tribes are designated a place in camp working westwards.

The tribe of Levi must minister to Aaron, and must keep their obligation to him.

Moses registers all the male Levites from the age of one month upwards.

Each of the families of Levi are given a task to perform regarding the tabernacle and the utensils.

Following instructions from Moses, all lepers, persons with discharges and anyone unclean are sent out of the camp.

A water test is explained, to test for jealousy.

If a man or woman takes a special vow to live as a Nazirite, they must stay away from grapes, wine and intoxicating liquor.

Also during the time of living as a Nazirite, no razor should touch a hair.

The further rules of the special vows of living as a Nazirite are explained.

The wording of the Lord's blessing is given to Moses. It is: May the Lord bless you and keep you, May the Lord make his face shine toward you and may he favour you, May the Lord lift up his face toward you and assign peace to you.

Having had all the laws and commandments explained to him, Moses now anoints the tabernacle.

All the chieftains make offerings of grain and cattle, of silver bowls, of other animals, which Moses accepts.

These offerings continue for eleven days.

On the twelfth day an offering by Naphtali is made; this is the inaugural offering at the altar.

The Lord tells Moses to instruct Aaron to light the seven lamps.

Moses is instructed to take the Levites among the people and cleanse them.

Instructions for the cleansing are given.

The Lord explains to Moses the preparation for the Passover.

The Lord instructs Moses to make two trumpets of silver.

These are to be used for convening the assembly or breaking up the camp.

If one trumpet is blown, the chieftains meet with Moses.

If two trumpets are blown, the whole assembly must meet with Moses.

On the twentieth day of the second month, of the third year, the cloud lifts and the people begin to leave the wilderness.

Moses asks Hobab to join the people going to Israel, but Hobab says that he wants to return to his own people.

Moses pleads with Hobab, and he joins Moses and the people.

Some of the people begin to complain about being in the wilderness.

This angers the Lord, and He sends down fire.

The people begin to cry for meat and fish.

Moses asks the Lord for help, because he feels he cannot cope.

The Lord tells Moses to select 70 of the oldest men, take them to the meeting tent, and He will place some of the spirit on them.

The spirit also falls on Eldad and Medad, who were not in the meeting tent, and they begin acting as prophets.

A wind blows quails from the coast to the camp.

Those people who showed selfish craving are slaughtered by the Lord.

Miriam and Aaron begin opposing Moses.

The Lord tells Moses to take Miriam and Aaron to the meeting tent, where He will speak with them.

The Lord is so angry that Miriam is struck with leprosy.

Moses pleads for mercy, and after seven days in quarantine, she is allowed back into the camp.

Moses sends out a man from each tribe, each a chieftain, to spy out the land of Canaan.

After 40 days they return to Moses; ten spies give bad reports.

The people begin to rebel.

The Lord is very angry that the people do not respect Him; He tells Moses that He will strike them with pestilence.

Moses pleads on their behalf.

The punishment for rebellion is to remain in the wilderness for 40 years.

Some of the people decide to leave the camp without Moses and the ark.

These people are defeated by the Amalekites and Canaanites.

Moses is instructed to tell the people of Isreal how they must render up burnt offerings on entering the promised land.

Moses is instructed to tell the people how they must atone for a sin by mistake.

Anyone who commits a deliberate sin must die.

A man collecting pieces of wood on the Sabbath is stoned to death.

Korah, Dathan and Abiram, together with 250 rebels, rise against Moses.

All the rebels are instructed to attend a meeting, each carrying a fire holder.

The earth swallows up Korah, Dathan and Abiram, their households and anything belonging to them.

A fire comes from the Lord and consumes the 250 rebels.

Some of the people still complain, so the Lord brings forth a scourge on them.

Moses tells Aaron to go among them and atone for their sins.

This Aaron does, and eventually stops the scourge.

This scourge kills 14,700 people.

A rod is taken from each of the twelve houses of Israel, placed in the meeting tent, and the Lord chooses one rod to bud.

Aaron's rod, for the house of Levi, has budded.

The Lord explains to Aaron the obligations of Levi.

Moses is instructed again regarding cleansing, especially regarding a man who dies in a tent.

The people move into the wilderness of Zin.

Here Miriam dies and is buried.

The people now have no water and reproach Moses and Aaron.

The Lord instructs Moses to strike a rock and water will come forth.

Moses strikes the rock twice and water enough for all the people and beasts comes forth.

These waters are called the Waters of Meribah.

Moses sends messengers to the king of Edom, to seek permission to pass through his land.

The king of Edom refuses.

The people turn away and travel to Mount Hor.

On Mount Hor, Moses strips Aaron of his clothes and places them on Eleazar (Aaron's son).

Aaron then dies.

The people weep for Aaron for 30 days.

The Canaanite king of Arad begins to attack the people and takes some captives.

The Lord intervenes and strikes down the Canaanites.

The people continue to trek around the land of Edom, but are not happy.

Some of the people rebel, so the Lord sends poisonous serpents among them and many die.

Moses is instructed to make a copper serpent and place it on a pole.

Anyone who was bitten by the serpents will look at the copper serpent and will live.

Moses sends messengers to Sihon, king of the Amorites, requesting permission to pass through his land.

Sihon refuses, and gathers his people and begins to fight the Israelites at Jahaz.

Sihon is defeated and the Israelites take possession of his land.

The Israelites now attack Ogm, the king of Bashan; they defeat him and take possession of his land.

Moab now grows very frightened of the Israelites.

Balak, the king of Moab, sends messengers to Balaam.

Balaam refuses to help.

Balak sends more messengers, more important messengers than at first.

Balaam goes with them to Balak, but on the journey meets with the Lord's angel, which only Balaam's she-ass sees.

Balaam beats his she-ass, and passes by the angel by walking in a field.

The angel reappears at a narrow place; again only Balaam's she-ass sees the angel.

Balaam beats his she-ass and he passes the angel by walking alongside the wall.

The angel reappears at a place where he cannot pass by; the she-ass lies down in the road.

Balaam beats his she-ass again.

The Lord makes the she-ass speak.

She asks Balaam, 'Why have you beaten me three times?'

Balaam says that if he had a sword he would have killed her.

The angel appears to Balaam and asks why he beats his she-ass.

Balaam continues his journey to Moab.

Balaam begins to speak the words that the Lord has put into his mouth.

He orders Balak to build seven altars.

He also orders him to provide seven bulls and seven rams.

A bull and a ram are offered on each altar.

Balaam refuses to help Balak.

Balaam proceeds to utter four proverbial statements, all the word of the Lord.

Balak is foiled.

Israel abides in Shittim and the people begin to commit whoredom with the daughters of Moab.

Israel joins himself unto Baal-peor and the anger of the Lord is blazed against him.
The Lord tells Moses to take the heads of the people and hang them up before him.
Zimri, a child of Israel, brings a Midianite woman into the sight of Moses.
Phinehas, son of Eleazar, son of Aaron, pierces both the man and woman and the plague is
    scourged.
The Lord tells Moses to vex the Midianites and smite them.
After the plague the Lord tells Moses and Eleazar to take the children of Israel, from 20 years
    onwards, out of Egypt.
Reuben and his descendants, numbering 250, are swallowed by the earth and become a sign.
The sons of Korah do not die.
Census is taken of eight more tribes and the land is divided.
Joshua is appointed to succeed Moses.
The procedures for various feast days and solemn days are established.
Moses equips an army to slay the Midianites.
The Lord speaks to Moses on the plains of Moab, by the Jordan at Jericho, and tells him to dwell
    in Canaan.

Deuteronomy   The fifth book of the Old Testament is written in the form of a farewell address by Moses to the
    Israelites before they enter the Promised Land of Canaan. The speeches recall Israel's past,
    reiterate laws and emphasise that observance of these laws is essential for the well-being of
    the people. The title Deuteronomy derives from the Greek meaning 'copy', although the Hebrew
    translation means 'words'.

Joshua   The book of Joshua was written while the people of Israel were exiles in Babylonia. It can be
    divided into three sections, i.e. the conquest of Canaan, the distribution of the land and
    Joshua's
    farewell address and death.
    This book contains the destruction of the Wall of Jericho.

Judges   The book of Judges was written at about the same time as the book of Joshua and the Judges
    were the leaders of Israel.
    Noteworthy events are the death of Joshua and the birth and death of Samson.

Ruth   The central character is a Moabite woman who marries the son of a Judaean couple living in Moab.
    Ruth moves to Judah with her mother-in-law, Naomi, and becomes the wife of Boaz. She bears
    Obed, the grandfather of David, although these events are thought to be doubtful.

Samuel,   Samuel anoints Saul as the first King of Israel and the book tells further of the exploits of his son
first book   Jonathan.
    The book continues with the story of David conquering Goliath and his great friendship with
    Jonathan.
    The book concludes with Abigail giving good counsel to David, Saul visiting the Witch of Endor,
    and the ultimate death of both Saul and Jonathan on Mount Gilboa.

Samuel,   David is anointed king at age 30. He rules for a further 40 years.
second book   David commits adultery with Bathsheba, the wife of Uriah the Hittite, and plots his death so he
    can marry her himself.
    The Lord sends Nathan, the anointer of David, to reprove him for his deed by telling him a
    parable of a ewe lamb.
    The Lord takes the life of the first-born of David and Bathsheba as penance.
    David and Bathsheba soon have another child, Solomon, and he is loved by the Lord.
    David's son Absalom plots the death of his brother Amnon, for forcing his sister Tamar.
    Absalom is killed during the civil war and is mourned by David.

Kings,   Zadok the Priest anoints Solomon as king.
first book   David eventually dies.
    The Lord appears to Solomon in a dream and grants a request and is pleased that he asks for
    wisdom.
    Solomon builds a great temple as a place of worship to the Lord and also a great house for himself.
    Queen of Sheba visits King Solomon and is impressed by his demeanour and they exchange
    gifts.
    Solomon's heart moves away from the Lord in his old age and he is told the kingship will be
    removed from his son.
    Solomon dies and is succeeded by his son, Rehoboam.
    The Lord's words come true as Jeroboam replaces Rehoboam as king of all Israel except Judah.
    The divided kingdom of Israel is eventually ruled by Ahab, son of Omri.
    Ahab takes Jezebel for a wife and sets up an altar to Baal in Samaria.
    Elijah the Tishbite informs Ahab there will be a drought and indeed no rain falls for 3½ years.
    Ahab tries to buy the vineyard of Naboth the Jezreelite but is refused.
    Ahab's wife Jezebel plots the death of Naboth to gain possession of his vineyard.
    Ahab is slain in battle with the Syrians.

R
E
L
I
G
I
O
N

Kings, second book	Elijah is taken up into heaven by a whirlwind and is succeeded by his pupil, Elisha. Jezebel is thrown out of a window and killed. Elisha dies and is buried; a dead man laid on his bones comes to life. The Lord is incensed by the Israelites and removes them, leaving only the tribe of Judah. Nebuchadnezzar II, the king of Babylon, destroys Jerusalem.
Chronicles, first book	The first book of Chronicles details genealogies from Adam up to and including the reign of David. The chronicler used the books of Samuel and Kings as his main source, although modifications were made.
Chronicles, second book	The second book of Chronicles details the reign of Solomon to the end of the Babylonian exile. The chronicler has ignored the northern kingdom of Samaria.
Ezra	Ezra continues the history of Israel from the end of the Babylonian exile. The chronicler details the rising of the Persian Empire from its first king, Cyrus the Great.
Nehemiah	The chronicler continues the story of Israel in the time of another Jewish leader, Nehemiah, who was released from captivity in *c.* 444 BC, during the reign of Artaxerxes, king of Persia. The rebuilding of Jerusalem is highlighted and the great wall is built.
Esther	Esther is the Jewish wife of the Persian King Ahasuerus (Xerxes I). Esther persuades the king to retract an order for the general annihilation of Jews throughout the Empire. The book explains how the feast of Purim came to be celebrated by the Jews, although the story is largely apocryphal.
Job	The book of Job is written in the form of a series of speeches whereby Job disputes with three friends and the Lord. Job proclaims his innocence and injustice of his suffering while his friends (Job's comforters) blame his sin. Job personifies poverty and patience.
Psalms	The book of Psalms consists of 150 sacred poems, which are meant to be sung. Usually divided into five sections, i.e. psalms 1–41, 42–72, 73–89, 90–106, 107–150. The best-known psalm is no. 23, 'The Lord is my Shepherd'. Psalm 51 is often called the 'Neck' verse as its recitation would save the neck of those claiming Benefit of Clergy. Although the authors are of doubtful origin, 73 psalms are attributed to David.
Proverbs	Book of wisdom with moral and ethical relevance, in a similar vein to the book of Job but with more finite thoughts. At the start of the text the proverbs are attributed to Solomon but it is known that many of them were written after his time.
Ecclesiastes	Another book of wisdom, which takes a fatalistic view of life and asks man not to question God's love. Once again the book alludes to Solomon as being the author, but this is doubtful because of chronologies in the text.
Song of Solomon	Collection of love poems spoken alternately by a man and a woman. This book is the festival scroll for Passover, which celebrates the Exodus of the Israelites from Egypt. The authorship is unknown and Solomon's name was added at a later date.
Isaiah	The prophet Isaiah, son of Amos, reflects on the blasphemy of his people in the eyes of the Lord. Isaiah calls for a return to the worship of the Lord and talks of 'beating swords into ploughshares'. Isaiah talks further of peace and his vision of the wolf residing with the lamb. Isaiah's prophecy of the falling of Babylon comes true.
Jeremiah	The Judaean prophet Jeremiah lived during the reign of King Josiah and his ministry lasted until the Babylonian conquest. Chapters 1–25 consist of prophecies against Judah and Jerusalem. Chapters 26–45 consist of narratives about Jeremiah and may have been composed by Baruch. Chapters 46–51 consist of prophecies against foreign nations and chapter 52 is a historical appendix.
Lamentations	The poems are laments over the destruction of Judah, Jerusalem and the Temple by the Babylonians in 586 BC. Lamentations is often called 'Lamentations of Jeremiah', although authorship is uncertain.
Ezekiel	The prophet Ezekiel was active during the first quarter of the sixth century BC. The book was written in exile and is valuable for understanding the lives of exiles in Babylon.

Daniel
Daniel interprets Nebuchadnezzar's dream.
Nebuchadnezzar throws Shadrach, Meshach and Abednego into a fiery furnace but the Lord
   sends an angel to help them.
Belshazzar holds a feast and Daniel interprets the writing on the wall, 'mene, mene, tekel, parsin'.
The interpretation means that the Lord has numbered the days of the Babylonian kingdom and it
   is to be divided.
King Darius reluctantly throws Daniel into the lions' den but the Lord sends an angel to help Daniel

Hosea
The last twelve books of the Old Testament bear the name of the minor prophets and are sometimes
   known as 'the Twelve'.
The first chapter is a biographical report of the prophet Hosea's marriage to Gomer, a harlot.
A similar marriage is described in Chapter 3, which is thought to allude to the Lord's love for Israel.

Joel
Joel reiterates the concept that salvation will come to Judah and Jerusalem only when the people
   turn to the Lord.

Amos
Amos, a Judaean prophet from Tekoa, was active during the reign of Jeroboam II.
Most of the chapters form a collection of individual sayings and reports of visions.
Much of the rest of the text is by way of a moral judgement on the rich and self-indulgent.
The book ends with a promise of restoration for Israel.

Obadiah
Shortest book of the Bible, with one chapter of 21 verses.
The book announces that the Day of Judgement is nigh for all nations and that Jews will be
   restored to their native land.

Jonah
The book of Jonah recounts the story of the prophet.
The Lord calls for Jonah to go to the Assyrian city of Nineveh to prophesy.
Jonah is concerned that the city will repent and be forgiven, and tries to escape his bidding.
Jonah is caught in a storm at sea while escaping and is thrown overboard at his own request.
The Lord appoints a great fish to swallow Jonah and he remains in the fish's maw for three days
   and nights.
Jonah prays for deliverance and is vomited out of the fish and once again told to go to Nineveh.
Jonah becomes angry as his fears of repentance are realised and he sits outside the city awaiting
   its destruction.
A plant springs up overnight to give him shelter from the heat but it is destroyed by a great worm.
Jonah is bitter about the destruction but the Lord chastises him for his care for a plant rather than
   people.

Micah
The Judaean prophet Micah was active during the last half of the eighth century BC.
Micah's threats and promises are a reiteration of many of the other minor prophets.

Nahum
The book is an oracle concerning Nineveh and is attributed to the vision of Nahum of Elkosh.
The fall of the city of Nineveh is the theme of the prophetic oracle.

Habakkuk
Similar to the book of Nahum; it is written in a liturgical style and portrays a moral theme.

Zephaniah
The dominant theme of the book is the 'Day of the Lord', which the prophet sees as imminent due
   to the sins of Judah.
The 'Humble' and 'Lowly' will be saved through purification by judgement.

Haggai
The book comprises four prophecies delivered over a four-month period in the second year of the
   reign of Darius I.

Zechariah
Chapters 1–8 contain the prophecies of Zechariah; the rest of the book is of unknown attribution.
Zechariah was active from 520 to 518 BC and was a contemporary of Haggai.
He shared the concern of Haggai that the Temple of Jerusalem must be rebuilt.

Malachi
Last of the twelve Old Testament books that bear the name of the minor prophets and, indeed,
   the last book of the OT.
The book comprises four chapters, each in the form of a question-and-answer discussion.
Malachi was probably written in the first half of the fifth century BC and its authorship is unknown.

NB The first five books of the Old Testament are usually called the Pentateuch, or Books of Moses. The contents of
the first four of these books have been catalogued in the order that the events took place in the text of the Bible. The
remaining books have important events highlighted but have no other great detail about them. The New Testament
has been dealt with in a similar manner. The author does not wish to upset any religious denomination and it should
be noted that texts can differ slightly from Bible to Bible. There are 39 books of the Old Testament and 27 of the New
Testament, totalling 66 in all.

R
E
L
I
G
I
O
N

New Testament

Matthew

The first of the four New Testament Gospels recounting the life and death of Jesus Christ.
Matthew, Mark and Luke are known as Synoptic Gospels, as they share a similar general view.
The Gospel was composed in Greek *c.* AD 70 and is traditionally attributed to the Apostle Matthew the tax-collector.
Chapters 5–7 describe Jesus's Sermon on the Mount, which includes the Beatitudes and the Lord's Prayer.

Mark

The Gospel is attributed to John Mark (Acts 12:12; 15:37), a disciple of Peter and associate of Paul.
Mark is the shortest and earliest of the four Gospels and was probably used by Matthew and Luke to compose their accounts.
More than 90 per cent of the content of Mark's Gospel appears in Matthew's and more than 50 per cent in the Gospel of Luke.

Luke

Luke was known as the beloved physician and was a close associate of the Apostle Paul.
Luke gives details of Jesus' infancy and the Ascension as well as Caesar Augustus' census.
Parables include the Good Samaritan and the Prodigal Son.

John

John was known as the beloved disciple of Jesus.
John's Gospel covers a different time span than the others, concentrating on Jesus' ministry in Judea.
John's account differs in that it does not record many of the symbolic acts of Jesus but rather portrays Jesus as God's son.

Acts of the Apostles

Acts was traditionally written by Luke, whose Gospel concludes where Acts begins, that is, with Christ's Ascension into heaven.
The early chapters describe the descent of the Holy Spirit on the Apostles at Pentecost, which was the birth of the Church.
Chapter 3 describes Peter's healing of a lame man and chapter 5 the death of Ananias for his false tongue.
Chapter 7 describes the stoning of Stephen.
Chapter 9 describes the healing of Aeneas by Peter and the conversion of Saul to Paul on the road to Damascus.
Chapters 27 and 28 describe Paul's shipwreck in Malta and his successful teaching in Rome.
The underlying theme is the spreading of Christianity to the Gentile world under the influence of the Holy Spirit.

Romans

The proper and full title of this book is 'The Epistle of Paul the Apostle to the Romans'.
The book was probably composed at Corinth in *c.* AD 57 and was addressed to the Christian Church at Rome.
The letter is largely a morality and cautionary tale but is considered important in Lutheran teaching.

Corinthians, first book

The proper and full title of this book is 'The First Letter of Paul the Apostle to the Corinthians'.
Written *c.* AD 53 at Ephesus, Asia Minor, and addresses the problems of the early years of the Church.
Paul begins his letter with a reminder that all are servants of Christ and stewards of the mysteries of God.
Paul goes on to address questions of immorality, marriage and celibacy as well as the worthy reception of the Eucharist.
In chapter 13 Paul explains that no gift of God has meaning unless accompanied by love.

Corinthians, second book

The proper and full title of this book is 'The Second Letter of Paul the Apostle to the Corinthians'.
Written *c.* AD 55 in Macedonia, possibly after an unsatisfactory visit by Paul to Corinth.
Paul urges the Corinthians to assist the poor of Jerusalem and is gratified when Titus reveals their repentance.

Galatians

The proper and full title of this book is 'The Letter of Paul the Apostle to the Galatians'.
In this book, Paul defends his credentials as a true Apostle of Jesus Christ.

Ephesians

The proper and full title of this book is 'The Letter of Paul the Apostle to the Ephesians'.
Traditionally supposed to have been written while Paul was in prison, but this is doubtful.
The text is in the form of an affirmation that there is one Lord, one faith, one baptism, one God and father of us all.

Philippians

The proper and full title of this book is 'The Letter of Paul the Apostle to the Philippians'.
There is more evidence that this letter was in fact written by Paul in prison (*c.* AD 62) than in the case of his letter to the Ephesians.
His address to the Macedonian people was probably stirred by thoughts of his own mortality as he pondered execution.

Colossians	The proper and full title of this book is 'The Letter of Paul the Apostle to the Colossians'. Addressed to Christians at Colossae, Asia Minor, whose congregation was founded by Epaphras. The letter is in the form of a reminder of God's love and a call for repentance for their wayward ways.
Thessalonians, first book	The proper and full title of this book is 'The First Letter of Paul the Apostle to the Thessalonians'. First letter was written after his co-worker, Timothy, returned from Thessalonia to report that the new converts were steadfast.
Thessalonians, second book	The proper and full title of this book is 'The Second Letter of Paul the Apostle to the Thessalonians'. The second letter explains that the final day will not come until after the Antichrist appears and proclaims himself God.
Timothy, first book	The proper and full title of this book is 'The First Letter of Paul the Apostle to Timothy'. The book deals with Church administration and the growth of heresies.
Timothy, second book	The proper and full title of this book is 'The Second Letter of Paul the Apostle to Timothy'. The letter urges Timothy to 'guard the truth that has been entrusted to you by the Holy Spirit'. The letter urges Timothy to visit soon, although the writer believes he is 'on the point of being sacrificed'.
Titus	The proper and full title of this book is 'The Letter of Paul the Apostle to Titus'. Titus was a close friend of Paul and was the organiser of the Church in Crete. The letter urges Titus to appoint worthy elders to positions of responsibility and to preach sound doctrine. The letter also warns against the disruptive influence of 'Jewish myths', especially those of the 'circumcision party'.
Philemon	The proper and full title of this book is 'The Letter of Paul the Apostle to Philemon'. The letter was written to Philemon, a wealthy Christian from Colossae, on behalf of Onesimus, Philemon's former slave.
Hebrews	The proper and full title of this book is 'The Letter of Paul the Apostle to the Hebrews'. The letter was addressed to a Christian community whose faith was faltering because of strong Jewish influences. The author concludes that Christianity is superior to Judaism.
James	The letter of James, a Christian Jew, is a moralistic reflection on early Jewish Christianity. The letter covers topics such as cursing, boasting, oaths, prayers, poverty and endurance under persecution.
Peter, first book	The first letter urges persecuted Christians to emulate the suffering Christ in their distress. He reminded them that after his Passion and death, Jesus rose from the dead and is now in glory.
Peter, second book	The second letter is principally concerned with the Second Coming of Christ. Peter also warns against false teachers, whose conduct is as immoral as their words are deceptive.
John, first book	The John in question is the disciple John the Evangelist, son of Zebedee. His first letter urges the Christian community to repudiate heretical teachings.
John, second book	The writer of both the second and the third letters calls himself 'presbyter', i.e. elder.
John, third book	Addressed to a certain Gaius and complaining of Diotrephes, who lies to put himself first.
Jude	The letter of Jude, brother of James and a servant of Jesus Christ, warns against false gods.
Revelation	The proper and full title of this book is 'The Revelation of St John the Divine'. Attributed to John, the beloved disciple, and possibly written at Patmos in the Aegean Sea. The number 7 is used in a symbolic sense to represent totality or perfection. Chapter 6 describes the Four Horsemen of the Apocalypse. Chapter 7 describes the 12 tribes of Israel, which were sealed 12,000 of each, totalling 144,000. Chapter 13 gives the number of the beast, i.e. 666. Chapter 14 describes the 144,000 virgins who will have their place in heaven.

RELIGION

SCIENCE

Chemical Elements

Name	Symbol	No.	Name source	Discovered or isolated by
actinium	Ac	89	beam	André-Louis Debierne 1899
aluminium	Al	13	alum	Hans Christian Oersted 1825
americium	Am	95	America	Glenn Seaborg, Ralph James, Leon Morgan and Albert Ghiorso at the University of Chicago 1944
antimony	Sb	51	antimonium	known to the ancients, its extraction from stibnite was first discovered by Basil Valentine c.1450, although its properties were first described by Nicholas Lémery in 1707
argon	Ar	18	inactive	Lord Rayleigh and W Ramsay 1894
arsenic	As	33	yellow orpiment	Albertus Magnus in the 13th century
astatine	At	85	unstable	Berkeley University, California, 1940
barium	Ba	56	heavy	Humphry Davy 1808
berkelium	Bk	97	university	Berkeley University, California, 1949
beryllium	Be	4	beryl	Nicolas Louis Vauquelin 1797
bismuth	Bi	83	uncertain	Basil Valentine 1450
boron	B	5	Arabic, buraq	Gay-Lussac, Thenard and Davy 1808
bromine	Br	35	stench	Antoine-Jérôme Balard 1826
cadmium	Cd	48	zinc ore	Friedrich Stromeyer 1817
caesium	Cs	55	silvery white	Robert Bunsen and G Kirchhoff 1860
calcium	Ca	20	lime	Humphry Davy 1808
californium	Cf	98	California	Berkeley University, California, 1950
carbon	C	6	charcoal	prehistoric
cerium	Ce	58	asteroid Ceres	Hisinger, Klaproth and Berzelius 1803
chlorine	Cl	17	greenish yellow	Humphry Davy 1810
chromium	Cr	24	colour	Nicolas Louis Vauquelin 1797
cobalt	Co	27	goblin	Georg Brandt 1735
copper	Cu	29	Cyprus	prehistoric
curium	Cm	96	Pierre and Marie Curie	Berkeley University, California, 1944
dysprosium	Dy	66	hard to get at	P E Lecoq de Boisbaudran 1886
einsteinium	Es	99	Einstein	Albert Ghiorso, Berkeley 1952
erbium	Er	68	Ytterby (Sweden)	Carl Gustav Mosander 1843
europium	Eu	63	Europe	Eugène-Anatole Demarçay 1901
fermium	Fm	100	Enrico Fermi	Albert Ghiorso, Berkeley 1952
fluorine	F	9	flowing	Henri Moissan 1886
francium	Fr	87	France	Marguerite Perey 1939
gadolinium	Gd	64	Johan Gadolin	P E Lecoq de Boisbaudran 1886
gallium	Ga	31	cock	P E Lecoq de Boisbaudran 1875
germanium	Ge	32	Germany	Clemens Winkler 1886
gold	Au	79	colour gold	prehistoric
hafnium	Hf	72	Copenhagen	Dirk Coster and G von Hevesy 1923
hahnium	Ha	105	Otto Hahn	disputed by Russia and USA
helium	He	2	sun	William Ramsay 1895
holmium	Ho	67	Stockholm	Soret, Delafontaine and Cleve 1878/9
hydrogen	H	1	water-producing	Cavendish 1766 but Lavoisier named it
indium	In	49	indigo	Ferdinand Reich and Theo Richter 1863
iodine	I	53	violet	Bernard Courtois 1811
iridium	Ir	77	rainbow (iris)	Smithson Tennant 1804
iron	Fe	26	Anglo-Saxon word	prehistoric
krypton	Kr	36	hidden	W Ramsay and Morris W Travers 1898
lanthanum	La	57	lie unseen	Carl Gustav Mosander 1839
lawrencium	Lr	103	Ernest Lawrence	Berkeley University, California, 1961
lead	Pb	82	Anglo-Saxon word	prehistoric
lithium	Li	3	stone	Johan August Arfvedson 1817
lutetium	Lu	71	Paris	Carl Auer von Welsbach and G Urbain 1907/8
magnesium	Mg	12	magnesia	Humphry Davy 1808
manganese	Mn	25	magnet	Carl W Scheele and Johan Gahn 1774
mendelevium	Md	101	D I Mendeleyev	Berkeley University, California, 1955
mercury	Hg	80	planet Mercury	prehistoric
molybdenum	Mo	42	lead	Peter Jacob Hjelm 1782
neodymium	Nd	60	new twin	Carl Auer von Welsbach 1885
neon	Ne	10	new	W Ramsay and Morris W Travers 1898
neptunium	Np	93	planet Neptune	Edwin McMillan and Philip Abelson 1940
nickel	Ni	28	copper demon	Baron Axel Frederik Cronstedt 1751

Name	Symbol	No.	Name source	Discovered or isolated by
niobium	Nb	41	Tantalus's daughter	discovered by Charles Hatchett 1801; first isolated by C W Blomstrand
nitrogen	N	7	nitre-forming	Daniel Rutherford 1772
nobelium	No	102	Nobel Inst. Stockholm	Berkeley University, California, 1958
osmium	Os	76	smell	Smithson Tennant 1804
oxygen	O	8	acid-producing	Scheele/Priestley 1772/4; Lavoisier name
palladium	Pd	46	asteroid Pallas	William Hyde Wollaston 1803
phosphorus	P	15	light-bringer	Hennig Brand 1669
platinum	Pt	78	silvery element	known to the ancients; first reported by A de Ulloa in South America 1736
plutonium	Pu	94	planet Pluto	Berkeley University, California, 1940
polonium	Po	84	Poland	Marie Curie 1898
potassium	K	19	potash	Humphry Davy 1807
praseodymium	Pr	59	green twin	Carl Auer von Welsbach 1885
promethium	Pm	61	Prometheus	Marinsky, Glendenin and Coryell 1947
protactinium	Pa	91	first actinium	Kasmir Fajans and D Göhring 1913
radium	Ra	88	ray	Pierre and Marie Curie and G Bemont 1898
radon	Rn	86	radium	F Dorn 1901
rhenium	Re	75	rhine	I Tacke, W Noddack and O Berg 1925
rhodium	Rh	45	rose	William Hyde Wollaston 1803
rubidium	Rb	37	dark red	R Bunsen and Gustav Kirchhoff 1861
ruthenium	Ru	44	Russia	Karl Klaus 1844 but named by G Osann in its impure form in 1827
rutherfordium	Rf	104	Ernest Rutherford	disputed by Soviet and US scientists
samarium	Sm	62	samarskite	P E Lecoq de Boisbaudran 1879
scandium	Sc	21	Scandinavia	Lars Nilson and Per Teodor Cleve 1879
selenium	Se	34	moon	Jons Jacob Berzelius 1817
silicon	Si	14	hard stone	Jons Jacob Berzelius 1824
silver	Ag	47	colour silver	prehistoric
sodium	Na	11	soda	Humphry Davy 1807
strontium	Sr	38	Strontian (Scotland)	Humphry Davy 1808
sulphur	S	16	sulphur	known to the ancients; first recognised as an element by Antoine Lavoisier 1777
tantalum	Ta	73	Tantalus	Anders Gustaf Ekeberg 1802
technetium	Tc	43	man-made	discovered by C Perrier and E G Segrè of Italy in a sample of molybdenum at Berkeley University, California, 1937
tellurium	Te	52	Earth	Franz J Müller von Reichenstein 1782
terbium	Tb	65	Ytterby (Sweden)	Carl Gustav Mosander 1843
thallium	Tl	81	green shoot	discovered by Sir William Crookes 1861
thorium	Th	90	Thor	Jons Jacob Berzelius 1828
thulium	Tm	69	Thule	Per Teodor Cleve 1879
tin	Sn	50	Anglo-Saxon word	prehistoric
titanium	Ti	22	Titans	discovered by William Gregor 1771; rediscovered by Martin Heinrich Klaproth (who gave it its present name) 1795
tungsten	W	74	heavy stone	Juan Jose and Fausto Elhuyar 1783
uranium	U	92	planet Uranus	Martin Heinrich Klaproth 1789
vanadium	V	23	Norse goddess	Nils Gabriel Sefström 1830
xenon	Xe	54	stranger	W Ramsay and Morris W Travers 1898
ytterbium	Yb	70	Ytterby (Sweden)	J C G de Marignac 1878
yttrium	Y	39	Ytterby (Sweden)	Johan Gadolin 1794
zinc	Zn	30	German word	known in China and India before 1500
zirconium	Zr	40	golden	discovered by Martin Heinrich Klaproth 1789; isolated by J J Berzelius in 1824

SCIENCE

Periodic Table of Elements

No.	Name	Symbol	Form	No.	Name	Symbol	Form
1	hydrogen	H	gas	10	neon	Ne	gas
2	helium	He	gas	11	sodium	Na	metallic solid
3	lithium	Li	metallic solid	12	magnesium	Mg	metallic solid
4	beryllium	Be	metallic solid	13	aluminium	Al	metallic solid
5	boron	B	metallic solid	14	silicon	Si	metallic solid
6	carbon	C	non-metallic solid	15	phosphorus	P	non-metallic solid
7	nitrogen	N	gas	16	sulphur	S	non-metallic solid
8	oxygen	O	gas	17	chlorine	Cl	gas
9	fluorine	F	gas	18	argon	Ar	gas

No.	Name	Symbol	Form	No.	Name	Symbol	Form
19	potassium	K	metallic solid	62	samarium	Sm	metallic solid
20	calcium	Ca	metallic solid	63	europium	Eu	metallic solid
21	scandium	Sc	metallic solid	64	gadolinium	Gd	metallic solid
22	titanium	Ti	metallic solid	65	terbium	Tb	metallic solid
23	vanadium	V	metallic solid	66	dysprosium	Dy	metallic solid
24	chromium	Cr	metallic solid	67	holmium	Ho	metallic solid
25	manganese	Mn	metallic solid	68	erbium	Er	metallic solid
26	iron	Fe	metallic solid	69	thulium	Tm	metallic solid
27	cobalt	Co	metallic solid	70	ytterbium	Yb	metallic solid
28	nickel	Ni	metallic solid	71	lutetium	Lu	metallic solid
29	copper	Cu	metallic solid	72	hafnium	Hf	metallic solid
30	zinc	Zn	metallic solid	73	tantalum	Ta	metallic solid
31	gallium	Ga	metallic liquid	74	tungsten	W	metallic solid
32	germanium	Ge	metalloid solid	75	rhenium	Re	metallic solid
33	arsenic	As	metalloid solid	76	osmium	Os	metallic solid
34	selenium	Se	non-metallic solid	77	iridium	Ir	metallic solid
35	bromine	Br	non-metallic liquid	78	platinum	Pt	metallic solid
36	krypton	Kr	gas	79	gold	Au	metallic solid
37	rubidium	Rb	radioactive semi-solid	80	mercury	Hg	metallic liquid
				81	thallium	Tl	metallic solid
38	strontium	Sr	metallic solid	82	lead	Pb	metallic solid
39	yttrium	Y	metallic solid	83	bismuth	Bi	metallic solid
40	zirconium	Zr	metallic solid	84	polonium	Po	radioactive solid
41	niobium	Nb	metallic solid	85	astatine	At	from bismuth
42	molybdenum	Mo	metallic solid	86	radon	Rn	gas
43	technetium	Tc	from molybdenum	87	francium	Fr	radioactive liquid
44	ruthenium	Ru	metallic solid	88	radium	Ra	radioactive solid
45	rhodium	Rh	metallic solid	89	actinium	Ac	from uranium
46	palladium	Pd	metallic solid	90	thorium	Th	metallic solid
47	silver	Ag	metallic solid	91	protactinium	Pa	from thorium
48	cadmium	Cd	metallic solid	92	uranium	U	metallic solid
49	indium	In	metallic solid	93	neptunium	Np	from plutonium
50	tin	Sn	metallic solid	94	plutonium	Pu	from uranium-238
51	antinomy	Sb	metallic solid	95	americium	Am	from plutonium
52	tellurium	Te	non-metallic solid	96	curium	Cm	from plutonium
53	iodine	I	solid but sublimates	97	berkelium	Bk	from americium
54	xenon	Xe	gas	98	californium	Cf	from cerium
55	caesium	Cs	metallic liquid	99	einsteinium	Es	from plutonium
56	barium	Ba	metallic solid	100	fermium	Fm	from plutonium
57	lanthanum	La	metallic solid	101	mendelevium	Md	from einsteinium
58	cerium	Ce	metallic solid	102	nobelium	No	from cerium
59	praseodymium	Pr	metallic solid	103	lawrencium	Lr	from californium
60	neodymium	Nd	metallic solid	104	rutherfordium	Rf	synthetic metal
61	promethium	Pm	from uranium	105	hahnium	Ha	from californium

Chemistry: General Information

atom and molecule: difference atoms are the smallest part of an element that can take part in a chemical reaction; molecules are the smallest particle of either an element or compound that can exist independently and at the same time keep the properties of the original substance, e.g. the smallest unit of water is the water molecule, which is made up of two atoms of hydrogen and one of oxygen.

atom: meaning indivisible.

chemical bonds there are two main types of chemical bonding, covalent and ionic, and two more specialised types, metallic and hydrogen bonding.

chemical groups there are various ways elements can be subdivided, the most common being metallic and non-metallic. Metallic elements, or their oxides, dissolve in acids to form positively charged ions called cations. Non-metallic elements can be further subdivided into the unreactive noble gases, the reactive halogens, and others.

chemical matter: three types compound, mixture or element.

chemistry: definition chemistry is the scientific study of substances.

isotopes atoms of a given element which have the same number of protons and electrons and the same chemical properties, but have a different number of neutrons in their nuclei, and consequently different atomic masses. Isotopes may be either stable or radioactive.

organic compounds all compounds that contain carbon. All other compounds are inorganic.

polymers polymers are long-chain molecules in which a group of atoms are repeated. They can be natural – e.g. cellulose, DNA, fats, proteins and starches – or artificial – e.g. nylon, polystyrene, polythene, PVC, and in fact all by-products of 'plastics'.

states of matter solid, liquid or gas.

sub-atomic particles chemical properties of elements depend on the structure of their atoms, which are made up of three sub-atomic particles, protons (positive charge), neutrons and electrons (negative charge). Protons and neutrons are situated in the nucleus of the atom and the electrons orbit this nucleus. The number of protons in the nucleus of an element determines the atomic number used in the periodic table.

sublimation　occurs when chemical matter changes directly from a solid to a gas without first melting into a liquid.

valency　property of atoms or groups, equal to the number of atoms of hydrogen that the atom or group will combine with or displace in forming compounds.

Geochemical Abundances of the Elements

		%		Mohs scale of hardness
Lithosphere	oxygen	46.60	1	talc
	silicon	27.72	2	gypsum
	aluminium	8.13	3	calcite
	iron	5.00	4	fluorite
			5	apatite
Hydrosphere	oxygen	85.70	6	orthoclase
	hydrogen	10.80	7	quartz
	chlorine	1.935	8	topaz
	sodium	1.078	9	corundum
			10	diamond
Halogens*	fluorine		**Noble gases†**	helium
	astatine			argon
	bromine			radon
	iodine			krypton
	chlorine			xenon
				neon

* Mnemonic: Fab(r)ic all end ine.

† Also called inert or rare gases.

NB The table listing the chemical elements in alphabetical order contains the name of the person who discovered or first isolated the element. This may be different from the person who first prepared the chemical, e.g. chlorine was first prepared (from hydrochloric acid and manganese dioxide) by Carl Wilhelm Scheele in 1774 and was considered a compound until Sir Humphry Davy showed that it could not in fact be decomposed and that muriatic (hydrochloric) acid consists of hydrogen and another true element that he named chlorine.

Mathematics: General Information

algebra　method of solving mathematical problems by the use of symbols when figures are inadequate due to their size or unknown nature.

angles　less than 90° = acute; more than 90° = obtuse; more than 180° = reflex.

Archimedes' principle　physical law of buoyancy stating that any body submerged in a fluid at rest is acted upon by an upward force equal to the weight of the fluid displaced.

binary numbers　a comparison of decimal and binary numbers (decimal first) 1 = 1, 2 = 10, 3 = 11, 4 = 100, 5 = 101, 6 = 110, 7 = 111, 8 = 1000, 9 = 1001, 10 = 1010.

books　Euclid – *Elements*; Bertrand Russell (in collaboration with A N Whitehead) – *Principia Mathematica*; Sir Isaac Newton – *Principia*.

calculus　branch of mathematics that permits the manipulation of continuously varying quantities. It is subdivided into integral and differential. Calculus (which is Latin for pebble) was independently invented by Gottfried Leibniz and Isaac Newton.

circle: parts of　*chord* = a line that joins two points of a circle; *diameter* = the longest chord of a circle; *radius* = point from centre of circle to perimeter; *sector* = portion of circle between centre and two points on perimeter; *segment* = portion of a circle

between a chord and the perimeter (it is important to know the distinction between a sector and a segment as this is an often-asked question). Circumference of a circle = 2 × pi × the radius (or pi × the diameter); the area of a circle = pi × radius².

complex number　number having a real and an imaginary part, e.g. 5 + 3i is a complex number.

coordinates　the technical names for graph coordinates are abscissa (the horizontal *x* coordinate) and ordinate (the vertical *y* coordinate).

cylinder　solid figure with straight sides and a circular section.
The area of a cylinder = 2 × pi × radius × height + 2 × pi × radius squared.
The volume = the area of the base × the height.

ellipse　an ellipse is a closed conic section with the appearance of a flattened circle. It is formed by an inclined plane that does not intersect the base of the cone.

factorial　the factorial of a number is the product of all the whole numbers inclusive between 1 and the number itself; the symbol is ! e.g. 6! = 1×2×3×4×5×6 = 720.

factors　a factor is a number that divides exactly into another number, e.g. 6 divides exactly into 48 eight times; thus both 6 and 8 are factors of 48.

Fibonacci numbers sequence of numbers in which each number is the sum of its two predecessors, e.g. 1, 1, 2, 3, 5, 8, 13, etc.

game theory branch of mathematics used to analyse competitive situations whose outcomes depend not only on one's own choices, and perhaps chance, but also on the choices made by other parties, or 'players'. Modern game theory was created practically at one stroke by the publication in 1944 of *Theory of Games and Economic Behaviour* by the mathematician John von Neumann and the economist Oskar Morgenstern.

geometry branch of mathematics concerned with the properties and relations of points, lines, surfaces, and solids. Euclid's *Elements*, written about 330 BC, is the definitive origin of the subject.

hexadecimal system base 16, uses digits 0–9 plus letters A–F to denote numbers 10 to 15.

imaginary number the square root of –1 is denoted by the letter i, so $i^2 = -1$; real multiples of i, such as 3i, 2.3i, etc., are known as imaginary numbers.

line: definition a line is length without breadth.

logarithms system invented by John Napier whereby multiplication and division of large numbers are made simple by substituting the operations of addition and subtraction.

matrix set of numbers arranged in rows and columns so as to form a rectangular array.
The numbers are called the elements, or entries, of the matrix.
The term matrix was introduced by the 19th-century English mathematician Arthur Cayley, who developed the algebraic aspect of matrices.

mean in a series of values in a distribution the mean is the average value of all the values: e.g. in a series such as 1, 4, 4, 5, 7, 9, 12 the mean would be 6.

median in a series of values in a distribution the median is the middle value in order of size: e.g. in a series such as 1, 4, 4, 5, 7, 9, 12 the median would be 5.

mode in a series of values in a distribution the mode is the most frequently occurring value: e.g. in a series such as 1, 4, 4, 5, 7, 9, 12 the mode would be 4.

numbers chiliad – 1,000; myriad – 10,000; lakh – 100,000; crore – 10,000,000; billion – 1,000,000,000,000 (USA 1,000,000,000); googol – one followed by a hundred noughts; googolplex – one followed by a googol of noughts.

octal system base 8; uses digits 0–7: e.g. 31 in base 10 would be 37 in base 8.

parabola curve formed by cutting a right circular cone with a plane parallel to the sloping side of the cone.

parallelogram quadrilateral with opposite pairs of sides equal in length and parallel. When all sides are of the same length it is known as a rhombus. The area of a parallelogram is base × height.

perfect numbers perfect numbers are equal to the sum of all their factors excluding the number itself, e.g. 6, whose factors are 1, 2, and 3. The first five perfect numbers are 6, 28, 496, 8,128, and 33,550,336.

pi (π) pi has been measured to many thousands of decimal places but to six places = 3.141592. It is a transcendental number.

polygons the sum of the interior angles = $(2n - 4) \times 90°$ where n = the number of sides. The sum of the exterior angles of any polygon = 360° regardless of the number of sides (an exterior angle of a polygon

is the angle between one side extended and the adjacent side): e.g. triangle = 180°; quadrilateral = 360°; pentagon = 540°; hexagon = 720°; octagon = 1080°; nonagon = 1260°; decagon = 1440°; hendecagon = 1620°; dodecagon = 1800°; icosagon = 3240°.

polyhedron solid figure with four or more plane faces.

prime number a natural number (over 1) that has no proper factors, i.e. which cannot be divided by any natural numbers other than itself and 1 – e.g. 2, 3, 5, 7, 11, 13, 17 ...

prism solid figure (polyhedron) with two equal polygonal faces in parallel planes, other faces being parallelograms. The volume of a prism = the area of either end × the perpendicular distance between the ends.

pyramid a solid figure whose base is a polygon and whose apex is joined to each vertex of the base. Therefore all its faces, apart from the base, are triangles. Any pyramid can be fitted inside a prism so that the base of the pyramid is one end of the prism, and the apex of the pyramid is on the other end of the prism. The volume of a pyramid on a rectangular base = ⅓ length × breadth × height.

Pythagoras' theorem in a right-angled triangle, the square of the hypotenuse is equal to the sum of the squares of the other two sides.

quadratic equation equation containing as its highest power the square of a single unknown variable.
General formula is $ax^2 + bx + c = 0$, in which a, b, and c are constants and only the coefficient a cannot equal 0.

rational number number that can be written in the form �娅 (a over b), where a and b are integers and b is not equal to zero.

reciprocal of a quantity, that quantity divided into 1; thus the reciprocal of 2 is ½.

rhombus diamond-shaped plane figure, a parallelogram with four equal sides and no right angles. The area of a rhombus = ½ the product of the diagonals.

simultaneous equations two or more algebraic equations that contain two or more unknown quantities and are simultaneously true, e.g. x + 3y = 6 and 3y – 2x = 4. The solution is to eliminate one of the variables by multiplying the first equation by 2 and adding the two equations to give 9y = 16.

sine in trigonometry, of an angle in a right-angled triangle, the ratio of the length of the side opposite the angle to the length of the hypotenuse.

sphere circular solid with all points on its surface the same distance from its centre. The surface area = 4 × pi × radius squared. Volume = ⅔ pi × radius cubed A little-known fact about the sphere is that the area of any zone of its curved surface lying between two parallel planes is exactly equal to the curved surface of the surrounding cylinder between the same two planes.

standard deviation in statistics, a measure of the variability (dispersion or spread) of any set of numerical values about their arithmetic mean. It is specifically defined as the square root of the arithmetic mean of the squared deviations.

tetrahedron solid figure with four triangular faces, i.e. a pyramid on a triangular base. The volume of a tetrahedron = ⅓ (the area of the triangular base x height).

topology branch of geometry which deals with those

properties of a figure which remain unchanged even when the figure is continuously transformed. A famous topological problem was to prove that only three colours are needed to produce a map to give adjoining areas different colours.

transcendental number   real number that is not a root of a polynomial equation with integer coefficients.

trapezium   four-sided plane figure quadrilateral with two parallel sides of unequal length. The area of a trapezium = ½ the sum of the parallel sides x the perpendicular distance between them. To find the area three measurements have to be taken, i.e. the height between the pair of parallel sides and the length of both of the parallel sides. If a and b are the two parallel sides the formula would be ½ (a + b)h.

triangle   Three-sided plane figure; *scalene* triangles

have no two sides equal; *isosceles* triangles have two equal sides and angles, *equilateral* triangles have three equal sides and angles. The area of a triangle = ½ base × height, however it is possible to calculate the area from the length of its sides using an Archimedean formula square root of (s(s − a) (s − b) (s − c)) where s = half the sum of the sides.

trigonometry   branch of mathematics which solves problems relating to plane and spherical triangles.

vector   physical quantity that has both magnitude and direction, such as velocity or acceleration of an object.

Venn diagrams   diagram representing a set or sets and the logical relationships between them. Sets are drawn as circles whose overlap contains elements that are common to both sets and thus represent a third set.

NB The information on mathematics is merely an overview of basic relevant information on the subject. No attempt has been made to show functions of matrices or calculus, for example, as these are beyond the scope of this book.

Physics: SI Units
(*Système International d'Unités*)

Base units

Quantity	Unit	Symbol	Definition
length	metre	m	1,650,763.73 wavelengths in vacuum of the red-orange light given out by the krypton-86 isotope.
mass	kilogram	kg	Mass of international prototype of the kilogram, at the Bureau International des Poids et Mesures at Sèvres, near Paris.
time	second	s	Duration of 9,192,631,770 periods of the radiation corresponding to the transition between the two hyperfine levels of the ground state of the caesium-133 atom.
electric current	ampere	A	That constant current which, if maintained in two straight parallel conductors of infinite length of negligible circular cross-section, and placed 1 metre apart in a vacuum, would produce between these conductors a force equal to 2×10^{-7} newtons per metre of length.
thermodynamic temperature	kelvin	K	The fraction $\frac{1}{273.16}$ of the thermodynamic temperature of the triple point of water. The triple point of water is the point where water, ice and water vapour are in equilibrium.
luminous intensity	candela	cd	The luminous intensity, in a given direction, of a source that emits monochromatic radiation of frequency 540×10^{12} Hz, and has a radiant intensity in that direction of $\frac{1}{683}$ watts per steradian.
amount of substance	mole	mol	Amount of substance of a system that contains as many elementary entities (atoms, molecules, ions, etc.) as there are atoms in 0.012 kilogram of carbon-12.

Supplementary units

plane angle	radian	rad	The plane angle between two radii of a circle that cut off on the circumference an arc equal in length to the radius.
solid angle	steradian	sr	The solid angle that, having its vertex in the centre of a sphere, cuts off an area of the surface of the sphere equal to that of a square having sides of length equal to the radius of the sphere.

S
C
I
E
N
C
E

Derived Units

Quantity	Unit	Symbol	Other SI Units
area	square metre	m^2	
volume	cubic metre	m^3	
velocity	metre per second	$m \cdot s^{-1}$	
angular velocity	radian per second	$rad\ s^{-1}$	
acceleration	metre per second squared	$m \cdot s^{-2}$	
angular acceleration	radian per second squared	$rad\ s^{-2}$	
frequency	hertz	Hz	s^{-1}
density	kilogram per cubic metre	$kg \cdot m^{-3}$	
momentum	kilogram metre per second	$kg \cdot m \cdot s^{-1}$	
angular momentum	kilogram metre squared per second	$kg \cdot m^2 \cdot s^{-1}$	
moment of inertia	kilogram metre squared	$kg \cdot m^2$	
force	newton	N	$kg \cdot m \cdot s^{-2}$
pressure (stress)	pascal	Pa	$N \cdot m^{-2} = kg \cdot m^{-1} \cdot s^{-2}$
work (energy)	joule	J	$N \cdot m = kg \cdot m^2 \cdot s^{-2}$
power	watt	W	$J \cdot s^{-1} = kg \cdot m^2 \cdot s^{-3}$
surface tension	newton per metre	$N \cdot m^{-1}$	$kg \cdot s^{-2}$
dynamic viscosity	newton second per metre squared	$N \cdot s \cdot m^{-2}$	$kg \cdot m^{-1} \cdot s^{-1}$
kinematic viscosity	metre squared per second	$m^2 \cdot s^{-1}$	
temperature	degree Celsius	$°C$	
thermal coefficient of linear expansion	per degree Celsius (or kelvin)	$°C^{-1}, K^{-1}$	
thermal conductivity	watt per metre degree Celsius	$W \cdot m^{-1} \cdot °C^{-1}$	$kg \cdot m \cdot s^{-3} \cdot °C^{-1}$
heat capacity	joule per kelvin	$J \cdot K^{-1}$	$kg \cdot m^2 \cdot s^{-2} \cdot K^{-1}$
specific heat capacity	joule per kilogram kelvin	$J \cdot kg^{-1} \cdot K^{-1}$	$m^2 \cdot s^{-2} K^{-1}$
specific latent heat	joule per kilogram	$J \cdot kg^{-1}$	$m^2\ s^{-2}$
electrical charge	coulomb	C	$A \cdot s$
electromotive force (potential difference)	volt	V	$W \cdot A^{-1} = kg \cdot m^2 \cdot s^{-3} \cdot A^{-1}$
electrical resistance	ohm	Ω	$V \cdot A^{-1} = kg \cdot m^2 \cdot s^{-3} \cdot A^{-2}$
electrical conductance	siemens	S	$A \cdot V^{-1} = kg^{-1} \cdot m^{-2} \cdot s^3 \cdot A^2$
electrical capacitance	farad	F	$A \cdot s \cdot V^{-1} = kg^{-1} \cdot m^{-2} \cdot s^4 \cdot A^2$
inductance	henry	H	$V \cdot s \cdot A^{-1} = kg \cdot m^2 \cdot s^{-2} \cdot A^{-2}$
magnetic flux	weber	Wb	$V \cdot s = kg \cdot m^2 \cdot s^{-2} \cdot A^{-1}$
magnetic flux density	tesla	T	$Wb \cdot m^{-2} = kg \cdot s^{-2} \cdot A^{-1}$
magnetomotive force	ampere	A	
luminous flux	lumen	Lm	$cd \cdot sr$
illumination	lux	Lx	$lm \cdot m^{-2} = cd \cdot sr \cdot m^{-2}$
radiation activity	becquerel	Bq	s^{-1}
radiation absorbed dose	gray	Gy	$J \cdot kg^{-1} = m^2 \cdot s^{-2}$

Physics: General Information

Avogadro's law law stating that equal volumes of gases at the same temperature and pressure contain equal numbers of molecules.

Avogadro's constant the number of atoms or molecules in one mole of a substance.

baryon subatomic particle that has a mass equal to or greater than that of a proton.

Bernoulli's principle the principle that in a liquid flowing through a pipe the pressure difference that accelerates the flow when the bore changes is equal to the product of half the density times the change of the square of the speed, provided friction is negligible. Named after Daniel Bernoulli, Swiss mathematician and physician 1700–82.

Coriolis effect an effect whereby a mass moving in a rotating system is accelerated perpendicular to its motion and to the axis of rotation, which helps to explain why wind patterns are clockwise in the northern hemisphere and anticlockwise in the southern. Named after French engineer G G Coriolis 1792–1843.

Doppler effect phenomenon observed for sound waves and electromagnetic radiation, characterised by a change in the apparent frequency of a wave as a result of relative motion between the observer and the source.

entropy measure of the unavailability of a system's thermal energy for conversion into mechanical work, often interpreted as a measure of the degree of disorder or randomness in the system.

fermion any of several subatomic particles with half-integral spin, e.g. nucleons.

Feynman diagram diagram of interactions between subatomic particles. Named after Richard Feynman, US physicist (1918–88).

Foucault's pendulum pendulum which rotates in relation to the Earth's surface and thus changes its plane in relation to the position of the Earth's rotational plane. The pendulum swings in a clockwise plane in the northern hemisphere and anticlockwise in the southern, and on the equator would therefore be stationary. This mathematical effect explains the trajectory of moving objects through the air. Named after Jean Bernard Foucault (1819–68), who set up the first pendulum.

General relativity Einstein's theory that the effects of acceleration and gravity were equivalent.

Heisenberg uncertainty principle principle that the momentum and position of a particle cannot both be precisely determined at the same time.

Latent heat heat required to convert a solid into a liquid or vapour, or a liquid into vapour, without change of temperature.

Matter: four fundamental forces interactions between matter can be explained by four forces.

1) Gravitational: weakest of the four forces, whereby masses mutually attract. Gravity is the force that holds solar systems and galaxies together.

2) Electromagnetic: force maintaining the magnetic field and the electron-nucleus structure of an atom.

3) Strong: about 100 times stronger than the electromagnetic force, it holds together the protons and neutrons within an atomic nucleus.

4) Weak: force associated with the radioactive beta-decay of some nuclei.

Matter: three fundamental states gas, solid, liquid.

Newton's three laws of motion 1) A body will remain stationary or travelling at a constant velocity unless it is acted upon by an external force.

2) The resultant force exerted on a body is directly proportional to the acceleration produced by the force and takes place in the direction of the force.

3) To every action there is an equal and opposite reaction.

Pauli exclusion principle the assertion that no two electrons in an atom can occupy the same energy state simultaneously, or in other words, that no two fermions can have the same quantum number. Named after Wolfgang Pauli, Austrian physicist (1900–58).

Physics: definition physics is the study of the basic laws that govern matter.

Quantum theory describes the behaviour of particles within atoms and the absorption and emission of electromagnetic radiation by matter in its various states.

Schrödinger's cat hypothetical situation whereby a cat is placed inside a box for one hour with a radioactive atom whose probability of decay is 50% per hour. If the atom decays a Geiger counter triggers a mechanism breaking a cyanide capsule and killing the cat. If the atom does not decay the cat remains alive. Quantum theory suggests that until the box is opened at the end of the hour, the cat is neither alive nor dead.

Special relativity states that nothing can exceed the speed of light, which is the same in all inertial time frames, and that all inertial time frames are equally good for carrying out experiments.

Thermodynamics: three laws 1) First law states that the total amount of energy in any closed system always remains the same.

2) Second law states that heat will always flow from a hotter object to a colder one and not the other way round.

3) Third law states that on approaching absolute zero, extracting energy from a system becomes increasingly harder.

Venturi tube device for measuring fluid flow, consisting of a tube so constricted that the pressure differential produced by fluid flowing through the constriction gives a measure of the rate of flow.

Wheatstone bridge apparatus for measuring electrical resistances by equalising the potential at two points of a circuit.

Young's modulus measure of elasticity equal to the ratio of the stress acting on a substance to the strain produced. Named after Thomas Young, English scientist (1773–1829).

Zeeman effect the splitting of the spectrum line into several components by a magnetic field. Named after Pieter Zeeman, Dutch physicist (1865–1943).

SCIENCE

SHAKESPEARE

Plays

1 All's Well That Ends Well
The Persons of The Play
The Dowager COUNTESS of Roussillon
BERTRAM, Count of Roussillon, her son
HELEN, an orphan, attending the Countess
LAVATCH, a clown, the Countess's servant
REYNALDO, the Countess's steward
PAROLES, Bertram's companion
LAFEU, an old lord
The KING of France

FIRST LORD DUMAINE
SECOND LORD DUMAINE, his brother
INTERPRETER, a French soldier
The DUKE of Florence
WIDOW Capilet
DIANA, her daughter
MARIANA, a friend of the widow
Lords, attendants, soldiers, citizens

Quotations

	Spoken by
A young man married is a man that's marr'd.	Paroles
From lowest place when virtuous things proceed.	King of France
I have an answer will serve all men.	Lavatch
Love all, trust a few, do wrong to none.	Countess of Roussillon
Oft expectation fails and most oft there where most it promises.	Helen
Our remedies oft in ourselves do lie which we ascribe to heaven.	Helen
Praising what is lost makes the remembrance dear.	King of France
The hind that would be mated by the lion must die for love.	Helen
The web of our life is of a mingled yarn.	First Lord Dumaine
There's a place and means for every man alive.	Paroles
'Twere all one that I should love a bright particular star.	Helen

Précis of plot
Helen, the daughter of a poor physician, Gerard de Narbonne, falls in love with Bertram, son of her guardian the Countess of Roussillon. Helen uses her magic to cure the King of France and as a reward he brings about the marriage of Helen and Bertram. The marriage is doomed to fail when Bertram takes flight to the Tuscan wars, and it is only consummated when Bertram seduces Helen in the guise of the Florentine maiden Diana.

Setting
France and Italy in the 14th century

2 Antony and Cleopatra
Mark ANTONY, Triumvir of Rome
Friends and followers of Antony:
VENTIDIUS
SILIUS
EROS
CAMIDIUS
SCARUS
DECRETAS
Domitius ENOBARBUS
DEMETRIUS
PHILO
SELEUCUS
Octavius CAESAR, Triumvir of Rome
OCTAVIA, his sister
Friends and followers of Caesar:
MAECENAS
AGRIPPA
TAURUS
DOLABELLA
THIDIAS
GALLUS
PROCULEIUS

LEPIDUS, Triumvir of Rome
Sextus POMPEY (Pompeius)

Friends of Pompey:
MENECRATES
MENAN
VARRIUS

CLEOPATRA, Queen of Egypt
Cleopatra's attendants:
CHARMIAN
IRAS
ALEXAS
DIOMED

MARDIAN, a eunuch

SOOTHSAYER
AMBASSADOR
MESSENGERS
BOY who sings
SENTRY and men of his WATCH
Men of the GUARD
EGYPTIAN
CLOWN
SERVANTS
SOLDIERS
Attendants, eunuchs, soldiers

Quotations

	Spoken by
Age cannot wither her, nor custom stale her infinite variety.	Enobarbus
Celerity is never more admired than by the negligent.	Cleopatra
Come thou monarch of the vine, plumpy Bacchus with pink eyne!	Boy (sung)
Dost thou not see my baby at my breast.	Cleopatra
Finish, good lady; the bright day is done, and we are for the dark.	Iras

Give me my robe, put on my crown; I have immortal longings in me.	Cleopatra
He wears the rose of youth upon him.	Antony
His biting is immortal; those that do die of it seldom or never recover.	Clown
His legs bestrid the ocean: his rear'd arm crested the world: his voice was properted.	Cleopatra
I am dying, Egypt, dying; only I here importune death a while until of many thousand kisses the poor last I lay upon thy lips.	Antony
I found you as a morsel cold upon dead Caesar's trencher.	Antony
I have yet room for six scotches more.	Scarus
I saw her once hop forty paces through the public street; and having lost her breath, she spoke, and panted, that she did make defect perfection.	Enobarbus
I wish you joy o' the worm.	Clown
If thou and nature can so gently part, the stroke of death is as a lover's pinch.	Cleopatra
In nature's infinite book of secrecy little can I read.	Soothsayer
In time we hate that which we often fear.	Charmian
It is well done, and fitting for a princess descended of so many royal kings.	Charmian
Let's have one other gaudy night.	Antony
My salad days, when I was green in judgement, cold in blood.	Cleopatra
Now boast thee, death, in thy possession lies a lass unparalleled.	Charmian
Out, fool – I forgive thee for a witch.	Charmian
O, wither'd is the garland of the war. The soldier's pole is fall'n: young boys and girls are level now with men. The odds is gone.	Cleopatra
Sometime we see a cloud that's dragonish, a vapour sometime like a bear or lion, a towered citadel, a pendant rock, a fork'd mountain, or blue promontory with trees upon't.	Antony
The barge she sat in, like a burnish'd throne, burn'd on the water.	Enobarbus
The nature of bad news infects the teller.	Messenger
There's beggary in the love that can be reckon'd.	Antony
Though I am mad I will not bite him. Call!	Cleopatra
Though it be honest, it is never good to bring bad news.	Cleopatra
To business that we love we rise betime, and go to't with delight	Antony
Unarm, Eros; the long day's task is done, and we must sleep	Antony
What's brave, what's noble, let's do it after the high Roman fashion, and make death proud to take us.	Cleopatra
Where's my serpent of old Nile.	Cleopatra

Précis of plot

The second triumvirate is disintegrating and Mark Antony becomes infatuated with Cleopatra, Queen of Egypt. The play tells of the sea fight between Antony and Octavius near Actium and Antony's subsequent suicide, believing Cleopatra dead. Cleopatra too commits suicide rather than be captured by Octavius.

Setting

Rome and Alexandria in the 1st century BC.

3 As You Like It

DUKE SENIOR, living in banishment	ORLANDO, Oliver's brother
ROSALIND, his daughter, later disguised as Ganymede	ADAM, a former servant of Sir Rowland
AMIENS, Lord attending on Duke Senior	DENIS, Oliver's servant
JAQUES, Lord attending on Duke Senior	SIR OLIVER MARTEXT, a country clergyman
TWO PAGES	CORIN, an old shepherd
DUKE FREDERICK	SILVIUS, a young shepherd, in love with Phoebe
CELIA, his daughter, later disguised as Aliena	PHOEBE, a shepherdess
LE BEAU, a courtier attending on Duke Frederick	WILLIAM, a countryman, in love with Audrey
CHARLES, Duke Frederick's wrestler	AUDREY, a goatherd, betrothed to Touchstone
TOUCHSTONE, a jester	HYMEN, God of marriage
OLIVER, eldest son of Sir Rowland de Bois	Lords, pages, and other attendants
JAQUES, Oliver's brother	

Quotations / **Spoken by**

All the world's a stage, and all the men and women merely players. They have their exits and their entrances and one man in his time plays many parts, his acts being seven ages.	Jaques
And rail'd on Lady Fortune in good terms	Jaques
And so, from hour to hour, we ripe and ripe, and then from hour to hour, we rot and rot; and thereby hangs a tale.	Jaques
An ill-favoured thing, sir, but mine own.	Touchstone
Ay, now am I in Ardenne; the more fool I. When I was at home I was in a better place; but travellers must be content.	Touchstone
Beauty provoketh thieves sooner than gold.	Rosalind
Blow, blow, thou winter wind, thou are not so unkind as man's ingratitude.	Amiens (sung)
But whate'er you are that in this desert inaccessible under the shade of melancholy boughs, lose and neglect the creeping hours of time.	Orlando

S
H
A
K
E
S
P
E
A
R
E

Chewing the food of sweet and bitter fancy.	Oliver
Dead shepherd, now I find thy saw of might, 'Who ever loved that loved not at first sight?'	Phoebe (quoting Marlowe's 'Hero and Leander')
Down on your knees, and thank heaven, fasting, for a good man's love.	Rosalind
Do you not know I am a woman? when I think I must speak, sweet, say on.	Rosalind
Every one fault seeming monstrous till his fellow-fault came to match it.	Rosalind
Fleet the time carelessly, as they did in the golden world.	Charles
For in my youth I never did apply hot and rebellious liquors to my blood	Adam
Hast any philosophy in thee, shepherd?	Touchstone
He that wants money, means and content is without three good friends.	Corin
He uses his folly like a stalking-horse and under the presentation of that he shoots his wit.	Duke Senior
How now, wit! whither wander you?	Celia
I am not a slut, though I thank the gods I am foul.	Audrey
I can suck melancholy out of a song, as a weasel sucks eggs.	Jaques
I do desire we may be better strangers.	Orlando
If ever – as that ever may be near – you meet in some fresh cheek the power of fancy, then shall you know the wounds invisible that love's keen arrows make.	
If it be true that good wine needs no bush 'tis true that a good play needs no epilogue.	Rosalind
If thou remember'st not the slightest folly that ever love did make thee run into, thou hast not loved.	Silvius
I had rather have a fool to make me merry than experience to make me sad.	Rosalind
I must have liberty withal, as large a charter as the wind, to blow on whom I please.	Jaques
It is a melancholy of mine own, compounded of many simples, extracted from many objects, and indeed the sundry contemplation of my travels, in which my often rumination wraps me in a most humorous sadness.	Jaques
It is meat and drink to me to see a clown.	Touchstone
It is to be all made of faith and service.	Silvius
It is to be all made of fantasy, all made of passion.	Silvius
It is to be all made of sighs and tears.	Silvius
Men are April when they woo, December when they wed, maids are May when they are maids, but the sky changes when they are wives.	Rosalind
Men have died from time to time and worms have eaten them, but not for love.	Rosalind
Most friendship is feigning, most loving mere folly.	Amiens (sung)
Motley's the only wear.	Jaques
My lungs began to crow like chanticleer, that fools should be so deep-contemplative, and I did laugh sans intermission an hour by his dial.	Jaques
My pride fell with my fortunes.	Rosalind
'No sir,' quoth he, 'Call me not fool till heaven hath sent me fortune' and then he drew a dial from his poke, and, looking on it with lack-lustre eye, says very wisely 'it is ten o' clock thus we may see,' quoth he, 'how the world wags.'	Jaques
No sooner met but they looked; no sooner looked but they loved; no sooner loved but they sighed; no sooner sighed but they asked one another the reason, no sooner knew the reason but they sought the remedy.	Rosalind
O, how bitter a thing it is to look into happiness through another man's eyes!	Orlando
O, how full of briers is this working-day world!	Rosalind
O Sir, we quarrel in print, by the book; as you have books for good manners. I will name you the degrees. The first, the Retort Courteous; the second, the Quip Modest; the third, the Reply Churlish; the fourth, the Reproof Valiant; the fifth, the Countercheck Quarrelsome; the sixth, the Lie with Circumstance; the seventh, the Lie Direct.	Touchstone
O wonderful, wonderful, and most wonderful! and yet again wonderful, and after that, out of all whooping!	Celia
Sans teeth, sans eyes, sans taste, sans everything.	Jaques
Speak, sad brow and true maid.	Rosalind
Sweep on, you fat and greasy citizens.	First Lord
Sweet are the uses of adversity, which like the toad, ugly and venomous, wears yet a precious jewel in its head; and this our life exempt from public haunt, finds tongues in trees, books in the running brooks, sermons in stones, and good in everything.	Duke Senior
The big round tears coursed one another down his innocent nose in piteous chase.	First Lord
The fair, the chaste and unexpressive she.	Orlando
The horn, the horn, the lusty horn is not a thing to laugh to scorn.	Lords (sung)
Therefore my age is as a lusty winter, frosty, but kindly.	Adam
The 'why' is plain as way to parish church.	Jaques
This is the very false gallop of the verses.	Touchstone
Thou mak'st a testament as worldlings do, giving thy sum of more to that which had too much.	First Lord
Time travels in divers paces with divers persons.	Rosalind

Truly, I would the gods had made thee poetical.	Touchstone
Truly thou art damned, like an ill-roasted egg all on one side.	Touchstone
Under the greenwood tree, who loves to lie with me, and turn his merry note, unto the sweet bird's throat, Come hither, come hither, come hither. Here shall he see: no enemy, but winter and rough weather.	Amiens (sung)
Very good orators, when they are out, they will spit.	Rosalind
We'll have a swashing and a martial outside, as many other mannish cowards have, that do outface it with their semblances.	Rosalind
Well said: that was laid on with a trowel.	Celia
We that are true lovers run into strange capers.	Touchstone
Who doth ambition shun and loves to live i' the sun seeking the food he eats and pleased with what he gets.	Chorus
Your 'if' is the only peacemaker; much virtue in 'if'.	Touchstone

Précis of plot

The story of the love between a high-born maiden, Rosalind, oppressed by her uncle Duke Frederick, who has usurped his elder brother's dukedom, and Orlando, the third and youngest son of Duke Frederick's enemy Sir Rowland de Bois, himself oppressed by his tyrannical elder brother Oliver. Sub-plots include the romantic liaisons between Touchstone and Audrey, Celia and Oliver, and Silvius and Phoebe.

Setting

The Forest of Arden (possibly Ardenne).

4 **The Comedy of Errors**

Solinus, DUKE of Ephesus	ANGELO, a goldsmith
EGEON, father of the Antipholus twins	BALTHASAR, a merchant
ANTIPHOLUS OF EPHESUS, Egeon's son	A COURTESAN
ANTIPHOLUS OF SYRACUSE, twin brother	Doctor PINCH, a schoolmaster and exorcist
DROMIO OF EPHESUS	MERCHANT OF EPHESUS
DROMIO OF SYRACUSE, his twin brother	SECOND MERCHANT, Angelo's creditor
ADRIANA, wife of Antipholus of Ephesus	EMILIA, an abbess at Ephesus
LUCIANA, her sister	Officers and attendants
NELL, Adriana's kitchen-maid	Jailer, messenger, headsman

Quotations	Spoken by
A wretched soul, bruised with adversity.	Adriana
The pleasing punishment that women bear.	Egeon

Précis of plot

The Comedy of Errors is a true farce, in as much as the unlikely situations stretch the imagination of the audience. But the play itself is probably the most classically constructed of any of Shakespeare's works. The action all takes place within a few hours and revolves around the mistaken identity of twin brothers and their bondmen, who also happen to be twins. The audience are further tested intellectually by the long-lost brothers sharing the same names as do their servants.

Setting

Ephesus circa 14th century.

5 **Coriolanus**

Caius MARTIUS, later surnamed CORIOLANUS	His LIEUTENANT
MENENIUS Agrippa	His SERVINGMEN
Titus LARTIUS, a General	CONSPIRATORS with Aufidius
COMINIUS, a General	Volscian LORDS
VOLUMNIA, Coriolanus' mother	Volscian CITIZENS
VIRGILIA, his wife	SOLDIERS in the Volscian army
YOUNG MARTIUS, his son	ADRIAN, a Roman
VALERIA, a chaste lady of Rome	NICANOR, a Volscian
SICINIUS Velutus, tribune	A Roman HERALD
Junius BRUTUS, tribune	MESSENGERS
CITIZENS of Rome	AEDILES
SOLDIERS in the Roman army	Gentlewoman, usher, Volscian Senators,
Tullus AUFIDIUS, General of the Volscian army	Roman Captains, officers and lictors

Quotations	Spoken by
Bid them wash their faces and keep their teeth clean.	Coriolanus
Chaste as the icicle that's candied by the frost from purest snow and hangs on Diana's temple.	Coriolanus
Hear you this Triton of the minnows?	Coriolanus
His nature is too noble for the world. He would not flatter Neptune for his trident.	Menenius
If you have writ your annals true, 'tis there that, like an eagle in a dove-cote, I fluttered your Volscians in Corioles. Alone I did it. 'Boy'!	Coriolanus

S
H
A
K
E
S
P
E
A
R
E

I thank you for your voices, thank you, your most sweet voices.　Third citizen
Look, sir, my wounds, I got them in my country's service when some certain of　Coriolanus
your brethren roar'd and ran from the noise of our own drums.
My gracious silence, hail!　Coriolanus
O, a kiss long as my exile, sweet as my revenge!　Coriolanus
You common cry of curs! whose breath I hate.　Coriolanus

Précis of plot
Caius Marcius is granted the cognomen of Coriolanus for his fearlessness in the Roman struggle against the neighbouring Volsci, but this brave but tyrannical warrior ultimately rebels and the subsequent intrigues form the basis of the plot.

Setting
Rome circa 5th century BC, Corioli, Antium.

6 Cymbeline, King of Britain
CYMBELINE, King of Britain
Princess INNOGEN, his daughter
GUIDERIUS, Cymbeline's son, known as Polydore
ARVIRAGUS, Cymbeline's son, known as Cadwal
QUEEN, Cymbeline's wife, Innogen's stepmother
Lord CLOTEN, the Queen's son
BELARIUS, a banished Lord, calling himself Morgan
CORNELIUS, a physician
HELEN, a lady attending on Innogen
Two LORDS, attending on Cloten
Two GENTLEMEN
Two British CAPTAINS
Two JAILERS
POSTHUMUS Leonatus, Innogen's husband
PISANIO, his servant
FILARIO, a friend of Posthumus

Filario's friends:
FRENCHMAN
DUTCHMAN
SPANIARD
GIACOMO, an Italian

Caius LUCIUS, ambassador, later General
Two Roman SENATORS
Roman TRIBUNES
Philharmonus, a SOOTHSAYER
JUPITER
Ghost of SICILIUS Leonatus, father of Posthumus
Ghost of the MOTHER of Posthumus
Ghosts of the BROTHERS of Posthumus
Lords attending Cymbeline, ladies attending the
Queen, musicians, messengers, soldiers

Quotations
Quotation	Spoken by
Fear no more the heat o' th' sun, nor the furious winter' rages. Thou thy worldly task hast done, home art gone and ta'en thy wages. Golden lads and girls all must, as chimney-sweepers, come to dust.	Guiderius
Hark, hark! the lark at heaven's gate sings, and Phoebus gins arise.	Musician (sung)
I have not slept one wink.	Pisanio
Prouder than rustling in unpaid-for silk.	Belarius
Slander, whose edge is sharper than the sword, whose tongue outvenoms all the worms of Nile, whose breath rides on the posting winds and doth belie all corners of the world.	Pisanio
The natural bravery of your isle, which stands as Neptune's park, ribbed and paled in, with banks unscalable and roaring waters.	Queen
There will be many Caesars, ere such another Julius. Britain's a world by itself, and we will nothing pay for wearing our own noses.	Cloten
Thersites body is as good as Ajax when neither is alive	Guiderius
The sceptre, learning, physic, must all follow this, and come to dust	Arviragus
Weariness can snore upon the flint, when resty sloth finds the down pillow hard.	Belarius
With fairest flowers whilst summer lasts and I live here Fidele, I'll sweeten thy sad grave; thou shalt not lack the flower that's like thy face, pale primrose, nor the azured harebell, like thy veins, no, nor the leaf of eglantine, whom not to slander, out-sweeten'd not thy breath.	Arviragus

Précis of plot
Cymbeline is a tragicomedy full of intrigues and sub-plots, the most notable concerning the wager between Giacomo and Posthumus regarding the chastity of Posthumus' wife Innogen. The subsequent 'death' and awakening of Innogen are central to the events that happily conclude this fantasy.

Setting
Britain and Rome circa 1st century AD.

NB Cymbeline's daughter's name is given in the folio as Imogen, but this is thought to be a misprint.

7 Hamlet

Prince HAMLET, son of King Hamlet and Queen Gertrude	Courtiers:
GHOST of Hamlet, late King of Denmark	VALTEMAND
KING CLAUDIUS, his brother	CORNELIUS
QUEEN GERTRUDE of Denmark, wife of Claudius	OSRIC
POLONIUS, a Lord	GENTLEMEN
LAERTES, son of Polonius	
OPHELIA, a daughter of Polonius	SAILOR
REYNALDO, servant of Polonius	PRIEST
FORTINBRAS, Prince of Norway	
A CAPTAIN in his army	HORATIO
AMBASSADORS from England	ROSENCRANTZ
PLAYERS, who play the Prologue, King and Queen, and	GUILDENSTERN
Lucianus, in 'The Mousetrap'	Soldiers:
Lords, messengers, attendants, guards, soldiers	FRANCISCO
followers of Laertes, sailors	BARNARDO
Two CLOWNS, gravedigger and his companion	MARCELLUS

Quotations

	Spoken by
A beast, that wants discourse of reason, would have mourned longer.	Hamlet
A certain convocation of political worms are e'en at him.	Hamlet
A countenance more in sorrow than in anger.	Horatio
A king of shreds and patches.	Hamlet
Alas, poor Yorick. I knew him, Horatio – a fellow of infinite jest, of most excellent fancy.	Hamlet
A little more than kin, and less than kind.	Hamlet
A man may fish with the worm that hath eat of a king, and eat of the fish that hath fed of that worm.	Hamlet
A man that fortune's buffets and rewards, hath ta'en with equal thanks.	Hamlet
And then it started like a guilty thing upon a fearful summons.	Horatio
And these few precepts in thy memory keep.	Polonius
And to my mind – though I am native here, and to the manner born, it is a custom more honoured in the breach than the observance.	Hamlet
Angels and ministers of grace defend us.	Hamlet
Assume a virtue, if you have it not.	Hamlet
A was a man. Take him for all in all, I shall not look upon his like again.	Hamlet
Ay, springes to catch woodcocks.	Polonius
Be all my sins remembered.	Hamlet
Beggar that I am, I am even poor in thanks.	Hamlet
Be somewhat scanter of your maiden presence.	Polonius
Be thou as chaste as ice, as pure as snow, thou shalt not escape calumny. Get thee to a nunnery, go, farewell.	Hamlet
Beware of entrance to a quarrel, but being in, bear't that the opposed may be aware of thee.	Polonius
Brevity is the soul of wit.	Polonius
But I am pigeon-liver'd and lack gall to make oppression bitter.	Hamlet
But I have that within which passeth show – these but the trappings and the suits of woe.	Hamlet
But in the gross and scope of my opinion, this bodes some strange eruption to our state.	Horatio
But, look, the morn, in russet mantle clad, walks o'er the dew of yon high eastern hill.	Horatio
But soft! methinks I scent the morning air.	Ghost
But that I am forbid to tell the secrets of my prison-house, I could a tale unfold.	Ghost
Come, give us a taste of your quality.	Hamlet
Cudgel thy brains no more about it.	First Clown
Cut off even in the blossoms of my sin.	Ghost
Do not, as some ungracious pastors do, show me the steep and thorny way to heaven.	Ophelia
Doubt thou the stars are fire; doubt that the sun doth move; doubt truth to be a liar; but never doubt I love.	Polonius
For this relief much thanks; tis bitter cold and I am sick at heart.	Francisco
Frailty thy name is woman.	Hamlet
Give it an understanding but no tongue.	Hamlet
Give me that man that is not passion's slave, and I will wear him in my heart's core, ay, in my heart of heart, as I do thee.	Hamlet
God's bodykins, man, much better. Use every man after his desert, and who should 'scape whipping?	Hamlet
Hath oped his ponderous and marble jaws.	Hamlet
His greatness weighed, his will is not his own.	Laertes
How now, a rat? dead for a ducat, dead.	Hamlet
I am but mad north-north-west; when the wind is southerly, I know a hawk from a handsaw.	Hamlet
I do not set my life at a pin's fee.	Hamlet
I doubt some foul play.	Hamlet

I have heard of your paintings too, well enough. God hath given you one face, and you make yourselves another.	Hamlet
I have thought some of nature's journeymen had made men and not made them well, they impersonated humanity so abominably.	Hamlet
Imperious Caesar, dead, and turn'd to clay. Might stop a hole to keep the wind away.	Hamlet
I must be cruel only to be kind.	Hamlet
In my mind's eye, Horatio.	Hamlet
In the dead waste and middle of the night.	Horatio
It goes so heavily with my disposition that this goodly frame, the earth, seems to me a sterile promontory.	Hamlet
It is not nor it cannot come to good. But break, my heart, for I must hold my tongue.	Hamlet
It out-Herods Herod.	Hamlet
It was as I have seen it in his life, a sable silver'd.	Horatio
It will discourse most excellent music.	Hamlet
I will speak daggers to her, but use none.	Hamlet
Look with what courteous action, it wafts you to a more removed ground.	Marcellus
Marry, this is miching *malhecho*. That means mischief.	Hamlet
More matter, with less art.	Queen Gertrude
Murder most foul, as in the best it is.	Ghost
Must, like a whore, unpack my heart with words.	Hamlet
My words fly up, my thoughts remain below.	King Claudius
Neither a borrower, nor a lender be.	Polonius
Now cracks a noble heart. Goodnight, sweet prince, and flight of angels sing thee to thy rest.	Horatio
O Hamlet, what a falling off was there!	Ghost
O, my offence is rank! it smells to heaven.	King Claudius
O my prophetic soul! mine uncle?	Hamlet
On fortune's cap we are not the very button.	Guildenstern
O, that this too too solid flesh would melt, thaw and resolve itself into a dew	Hamlet
O villain, villain, smiling, damned villain!	Hamlet
O, what a noble mind is here o'erthrown!	Ophelia
O, what a rogue and peasant slave am I.	Hamlet
Rest, rest, perturbed spirit!	Hamlet
Seems, madam? nay, it is; I know not 'seems'.	Hamlet
So excellent a king, that was, to this, Hyperion to a satyr: so loving to my mother, that he might not beteem the winds of heaven visit her face too roughly.	Hamlet
Some say that ever 'gainst that season comes, wherein our saviour's birth is celebrated, the bird of dawning singeth all night long.	Marcellus
Something is rotten in the state of Denmark.	Marcellus
Speak the speech, I pray you, as I pronounced it to you.	Hamlet
Still harping on my daughter.	Polonius
Suit the action to the word, the word to the action.	Hamlet
Take these again; for to the noble mind, rich gifts wax poor when givers prove unkind.	Ophelia
Tear a passion to tatters, to very rags, to split the ears of the groundlings.	Hamlet
That he is mad, 'tis true; 'tis true 'tis pity and pity 'tis 'tis true.	Polonius
The best actors in the world, either for tragedy, comedy, history pastoral, pastorical-comical, historical-pastoral, tragical-historical, tragical-comical-historical-pastoral, scene individable, or poem unlimited. Seneca cannot be too heavy, nor Plautus too light.	Polonius
The chariest maid is prodigal enough if she unmask her beauty to the moon.	Laertes
The glow-worm shows the matin to be near.	Ghost
The lady doth protest too much, methinks.	Queen Gertrude
The mobled queen.	Hamlet
The play, I remember, pleased not the million; 'twas caviare to the general.	Hamlet
The play's the thing wherein I'll catch the conscience of the King.	Hamlet
There are more things in heaven and earth, Horatio, than are dreamt of in your philosophy.	Hamlet
There is nothing either good or bad, but thinking makes it so.	Hamlet
There's rosemary, that's for remembrance. Pray, love, remember. And there is pansies; that's for thoughts.	Ophelia
The rest is silence. O, O, O, O!	Hamlet
These are but wild and whirling words, my lord.	Horatio
The time is out of joint. O cursed spite, that ever I was born to set it right.	Hamlet
They are the abstract and brief chronicles of the time.	Hamlet
This is the very coinage of your brain.	Queen Gertrude
This sweaty haste doth make the night joint-labourer with the day.	Marcellus
Though this be madness, yet there is method in't.	Polonius
Thou know'st 'tis common; all that lives must die.	Queen Gertrude
Thrift, thrift, Horatio! the funeral baked meats did coldly furnish forth the marriage tables.	Hamlet
'Tis now the very witching time of night, when churchyards yawn and hell itself breathes out contagion to this world.	Hamlet
To be, or not to be; that is the question: whether 'tis nobler in the mind to suffer the slings and arrows of outrageous fortune, or to take arms against a sea of troubles, and,	Hamlet

by opposing, end them. To die, to sleep – no more, and by a sleep to say we end the heartache and the thousand natural shocks that flesh is heir to – 'tis a consummation devoutly to be wished. To die, to sleep. To sleep, perchance to dream. Ay, there's the rub, for in that sleep of death what dreams may come when we have shuffled off this mortal coil must give us pause.

Unhand me, gentlemen; by heaven, I'll make a ghost of him that lets me.	Hamlet
Very like a whale.	Polonius
We do it wrong, being so majestical, to offer it the show of violence.	Marcellus
We know what we are, but know not what we may be.	Ophelia
What, frighted with false fire?	Hamlet
What may this mean, that thou, dead corpse, again in complete steel, revisit'st thus the glimpses of the moon, making night hideous.	Hamlet
What's Hecuba to him or he to Hecuba, that he should weep for her?	Hamlet
What should such fellows as I do, crawling between earth and heaven.	Hamlet
When sorrows come, they come not single spies, but in battalions.	King Claudius
Whether in sea or fire, in earth or air, the extravagant and erring spirit hies to his confine.	Horatio
While memory holds a seat in this distracted globe.	Hamlet
While one with moderate haste might tell a hundred.	Horatio
Whose sore task does not divide the Sunday from the week.	Marcellus
Why, let the stricken deer go weep, the hart ungalled play, for some must watch, while some must sleep, so runs the world away.	Hamlet
Why, she would hang on him, as if increase of appetite had grown by what it fed on.	Hamlet
With devotion's visage and pious action we do sugar o'er the devil himself.	Polonius
With one auspicious and one dropping eye, with mirth in funeral and with dirge in marriage.	King Claudius

Précis of plot
King Hamlet has been murdered by his brother Claudius, who has usurped the throne and married Gertrude, the King's widow. Prince Hamlet gains his revenge by feigning madness and ultimately killing his would-be assassins and Claudius.

Setting
Denmark.

8 Henry IV Part 1

KING HENRY IV	SIR JOHN Oldcastle
PRINCE HARRY, Prince of Wales, Henry's son	Edward (Ned) POINS
Lord JOHN OF LANCASTER, Henry's son	RUSSELL
Earl of WESTMORLAND	HARVEY
Sir Walter BLUNT	Earl of DOUGLAS
Earl of WORCESTER	FRANCIS, a drawer
Percy, Earl of NORTHUMBERLAND, his brother	VINTNER
Henry Percy, known as HOTSPUR, Northumberland's son	GADSHILL
Kate, LADY PERCY, Hotspur's wife	CARRIERS
Lord Edmund MORTIMER, called Earl of March	CHAMBERLAIN
LADY MORTIMER, his wife	OSTLER
OWAIN GLYNDWR, Lady Mortimer's father	TRAVELLERS
Mistress Quickly, HOSTESS of an Eastcheap inn	SHERIFF
Sir Richard VERNON	MESSENGERS
Scrope, ARCHBISHOP of York	SERVANT
SIR MICHAEL, member of the Archbishop's household	Lords and soldiers

Quotations

	Spoken by
A fellow of no mark nor likelihood.	King Henry
And such a deal of skimble-skamble stuff.	Hotspur
A plague of all cowards, I say.	Sir John
A plague of sighing and grief, it blows a man up like a bladder.	Sir John
Banish plump Jack, and banish all the world.	Sir John
By heaven, methinks it were an easy leap.	Hotspur
Came there a certain lord, neat and trimly dressed, fresh as a bridegroom, and his chin, new reaped, showed like a stubble-land at harvest-home. He was perfumed like a milliner, and 'twixt his finger and his thumb he held a pouncet-box, which ever and anon he gave his nose and took't away again.	Hotspur
Company, villainous company hath been the spoil of me.	Sir John
Domesday is near: die all, die merrily.	Hotspur
Farewell, the latter spring; farewell, All-hallown summer.	Prince Harry
He made me mad, to see him shine so brisk, and smell so sweet, and talk so like a waiting-gentlewoman, of guns and drums, and wounds, God save the mark! and telling me the sovereign'st thing on earth was parmacity for an inward bruise.	Hotspur
He was but as the cuckoo is in June, heard, not regarded.	King Henry
I am bewitched by the rogue's company.	Sir John
I am not in the role of common men.	Glyndwr

I am not yet of Percy's mind, the Hotspur of the North – he that kills me some six or seven dozen of Scots at a breakfast, washes his hands, and says to his wife, 'Fie upon this quiet life! I want work.'	Prince Harry
I could brain him with his lady's fan.	Hotspur
If all the year were playing holidays, to sport would be as tedious as to work.	Prince Harry
If reasons were as plentiful as blackberries.	Sir John
In those holy fields, over whose acres walk'd those blessed feet; which fourteen hundred years ago were nailed, for our advantage, on the bitter cross.	King Henry
I saw young Harry, with his beaver on.	Vernon
It would be argument for a week, laughter for a month, and a good jest forever.	Prince Harry
I understand thy kisses, and thou mine.	Mortimer
Let us be Diana's foresters, gentlemen of the shade, minions of the moon.	Sir John
Look down into the pomegranate, Ralph!	Francis
O, the blood more stirs to rouse a lion than to start a hare!	Hotspur
Old father antic, the law.	Sir John
So shaken as we are, so wan with care.	King Henry
O, thou hast damnable iteration, and art indeed able to corrupt a saint.	Sir John
O, monstrous! eleven buckram men grown out of two!	Prince Harry
Tell truth and shame the devil.	Hotspur
There lives not three good men unhanged in England, and one of them is fat and grows old.	Sir John
There's neither honesty, manhood, nor good fellowship in thee.	Sir John
'Tis my vocation, Hal. 'Tis no sin for a man to labour in his vocation.	Sir John
Two stars keep not their motion in one sphere	Prince Harry
What, in thy quips and thy quiddities.	Sir John
You rogue, they were bound every man of them, or I am a jew else, an Hebrew jew.	Sir John

Précis of plot
The main plot tells of the rebellions against King Henry by Worcester, Hotspur and Glyndwr. However, the sub-plots highlighting the characters of the young Prince Hal and the reprobate Sir John Oldcastle (Falstaff) lend the real substance to the play.

Setting
England in the early 15th century.

9 Henry IV Part 2

KING HENRY IV	Ensign PISTOL
PRINCE HARRY, later crowned King Henry V	PETO
PRINCE JOHN of Lancaster, Henry IV's son	DOLL TEARSHEET, a whore
SIR JOHN Falstaff	GOWER, a messenger
Bardolf	Sir John Blunt
Poins	Sir John Coleville
Falstaff's Page	Lord Hastings
Humphrey, Duke of GLOUCESTER, Henry IV's son	SNARE, a sergeant
Thomas, Duke of CLARENCE, Henry IV's son	FANG, a sergeant
Percy, Earl of NORTHUMBERLAND, of the rebels' party	Neville, Earl of WARWICK
NORTHUMBERLAND'S WIFE	Earl of SURREY
KATE, their son Hotspur's widow	Earl of WESTMORLAND
TRAVERS, Northumberland's servant	HARCOURT
MORTON, a bearer of news from Shrewsbury	Ralph MOULDY
Scrope, ARCHBISHOP of York	Simon SHADOW
Thomas, Lord MOWBRAY, the Earl Marshal	Thomas WART
MISTRESS QUICKLY, hostess of a tavern	Francis FEEBLE
PORTER of Northumberland's household	Peter BULLCALF
Robert SHALLOW, a country justice	DRAWERS
DAVY, Shallow's servant	BEADLES
SILENCE, a country justice	GROOMS
Sneak and other musicians	MESSENGER
Lord Chief Justice's men, soldiers and attendants	

Quotations

	Spoken by
A foutre for the world and worldlings base! I speak of Africa and golden joys.	Pistol
A joint of mutton, and any pretty little tiny kickshaws.	Shallow
A man can die but once.	Feeble
A rascally yea-forsooth knave.	Sir John
An habitation giddy and unsure, hath he that buildeth on the vulgar heart.	Archbishop of York
Away, you scullion, you rampallian, you fustilarian! I'll tickle your catastrophe.	Page
By my troth, captain, these are very bitter words.	Mistress Quickly
Death, as the psalmist saith, is certain to all; all shall die. How a good yoke of bullocks at Stamford fair?	Shallow
Even such a man, so faint, so spiritless, so dull, so dead in look, so woe-begone, drew Priam's curtain in the dead of night.	Northumberland
For my voice, I have lost it with hallowing and singing of anthems.	Sir John

He hath eaten me out of house and home.	Mistress Quickly
He was indeed the glass wherein the noble youth did dress themselves.	Lady Percy
I am not only witty in myself, but the cause that wit is in other men.	Sir John
I beseek you now, aggravate your choler.	Mistress Quickly
I can get no remedy against this consumption of the purse. Borrowing only lingers and lingers it out, but the disease is incurable.	Sir John
If I do, fillip me with a three-man beetle.	Sir John
Is it not strange that desire should so many years outlive performance.	Poins
I know thee not old man, fall to thy prayers.	King Harry
It was always yet the trick of our English nation, if they have a good thing, to make it too common.	Sir John
Let the end try the man.	Prince Harry
Lord, Lord, how subject we old men are to this vice of lying.	Sir John
O, sleep, O gentle sleep, nature's soft nurse, how have I frighted thee, that thou no more wilt weigh my eyelids down, and steep my senses in forgetfulness.	King Henry
Past and to come seems best; things present, worst.	Archbishop of York
Thou didst swear to me, upon a parcel-gilt goblet, sitting in my Dolphin-chamber, at the round table, by a sea coal fire, upon Wednesday in Wheeson week.	Mistress Quickly
Under which king, Besonian? speak, or die.	Pistol
Uneasy lies the head that wears a crown.	King Henry
We have heard the chimes at midnight, Master Shallow.	Sir John
We that are in the vanguard of our youth, I must confess, are wags too.	Sir John
Wilt thou upon the high and giddy mast, seal up the ship-boy's eyes, and rock his brains.	King Henry
With all appliances, and means to boot.	King Henry
Yet the first bringer of unwelcome news hath but a losing office, and his tongue sounds ever after as a sullen bell remembered knolling a departing friend.	Northumberland

Précis of plot

The plot of the first part of Henry IV is continued, although there are subtle changes made to certain characters and the historical content is not so highlighted. Hal is still plagued with rebellions, albeit from different spheres, but his anxieties over Prince Harry's behaviour are eventually alleviated in a touching scene, and this change of character is shown to the full in Harry's rejection of Sir John after his crowning.

Setting

England in the early 15th century.

10 Henry V

KING HARRY V of England, claimant to French throne	Sir Thomas ERPINGHAM
Duke of GLOUCESTER, the King's brother	John BATES
Duke of CLARENCE, the King's brother	Alexander COURT
Duke of EXETER, his uncle	Michael WILLIAMS
KING CHARLES VI of France	HERALD
ISABEL, his wife and queen	Duke of YORK
The DAUPHIN, their son and heir	SALISBURY
CATHERINE, their daughter	WESTMORLAND
Archbishop of CANTERBURY	WARWICK
ALICE, an old gentlewoman	Bishop of ELY
Richard, Earl of CAMBRIDGE	Sir Thomas GREY
Henry, Lord SCROPE of Masham	Duke of BOURBON
The CONSTABLE of France	Duke of ORLÉANS
MONTJOY, the French Herald	Duke of BERRI
GOVERNOR of Harfleur	Lord RAMBURES
French AMBASSADORS to England	Lord GRANDPRÉ
BOY, formerly Falstaff's page	Duke of BURGUNDY
HOSTESS, formerly Mistress Quickly, now Pistol's wife	PISTOL
Captain GOWER, an Englishman	NIM
Captain FLUELLEN, a Welshman	BARDOLPH
Captain MACMORRIS, an Irishman	CHORUS
Captain JAMY, a Scot	

Quotations

	Spoken by
All hell shall stir for this.	Pistol
And gentlemen in England now abed, shall think themselves accursed they were not here, and hold their manhoods cheap while any speaks, that fought with us upon Saint Crispin's day.	King Harry
And make your chronicle as rich with praise, as is the ooze and bottom of the sea.	Canterbury
As 'tis ever common that men are merriest when they are from home.	King Harry
Base is the slave that pays.	Pistol
But if it be a sin to covet honour, I am the most offending soul alive.	King Harry
Can this cock-pit hold the vasty fields of France? or may we cram, within this wooden O the very casques that did affright the air at Agincourt?	Chorus
Consideration like an angel came, and whipp'd the offending Adam out of him.	Canterbury
Cry, 'God for Harry! England and Saint George.'	King Harry

Every subject's duty is the king's; but every subject's soul is his own.	King Harry
For so work the honey-bees, creatures that by a rule in nature teach the act of order to a peopled kingdom.	Canterbury
For these fellows of infinite tongue, that can rhyme themselves into ladies' favours, they do always reason themselves out again.	King Harry
From camp to camp through the foul womb of night.	Chorus
He's in Arthur's bosom, if ever man went to Arthur's bosom.	Hostess
I dare not fight, but I will wink and hold out mine iron.	Nim
I see you stand like greyhounds in the slips.	King Harry
If he be not fellow with the best king, thou shalt find the best king of good fellows.	King Harry
If we are marked to die, we are enough to do our country loss; and if to live, the fewer men, the greater share of honour.	King Harry
I thought upon one pair of English legs did march three Frenchmen.	King Harry
Men of few words are the best men.	Boy
Now all the youth of England are on fire, and silken dalliance in the wardrobe lies.	Chorus
O that we now had here, but one ten thousand of those men in England that do no work today!	Warwick
Old men forget, yet all shall be forgot; but he'll remember with advantages, what feats he did that day.	King Harry
Once more unto the breach, dear friends, once more.	King Harry
On, on, you noblest English, whose blood is fet from fathers of war-proof. Fathers that, like so many Alexanders, have in these parts from morn til even fought, and sheathed their swords for lack of argument.	King Harry
Self love, my liege, is not so vile a sin as self neglecting.	Dauphin
Tennis balls, my liege.	Exeter
Then shall our names, familiar in his mouth as household words – Harry the King, Bedford and Exeter, Warwick and Talbot, Salisbury and Gloucester – be in their flowing cups, freshly remember'd.	King Harry
There is occasions and causes why and wherefore in all things.	Fluellen
There is some soul of goodness in these evils.	King Harry
This day is called the feast of Crispian. He that outlives this day and comes safe home will stand a-tiptoe when this day is named, and rouse him of the name of Crispian.	King Harry
Though patience be a tired mare, yet she will plod.	Nim
Trust none, for oaths are straws, men's faiths are wafer-cakes, and hold-fast is the only dog, my duck.	Pistol
Turn him to any cause of policy, the Gordian knot of it he will unloose.	Canterbury
We few, we happy few, we band of brothers.	King Harry

Précis of plot
The war against France dominates the play, although Shakespeare stayed loyal to many characters from the two parts of Henry IV to create comic diversion.

Setting
England and France 1414 to 1420.

11 Henry VI Part 1

KING HENRY VI	BASSET
Duke of GLOUCESTER, Lord Protector, uncle of Henry	A LAWYER
Duke of BEDFORD, regent of France	A LEGATE
Duke of EXETER	Earl of WARWICK
Bishop of WINCHESTER (later Cardinal), uncle of Henry	Earl of SALISBURY
Duke of SOMERSET	Earl of SUFFOLK
RICHARD PLANTAGENET, later DUKE OF YORK	Edmund MORTIMER
Duke of BURGUNDY, uncle of King Henry	Duke of ALENÇON
GENERAL of the French garrison at Bordeaux	BASTARD of Orléans
RENÉ, Duke of Anjou, King of Naples	Lord TALBOT
MARGARET, his daughter	JOHN Talbot
Sir William GLASDALE	COUNTESS of Auvergne
Sir Thomas GARGRAVE	MASTER GUNNER of Orléans
Sir John FASTOLF	A BOY, his son
Sir William LUCY	JOAN la Pucelle
CHARLES, Dauphin of France	A SHEPHERD, father of Joan
WOODVILLE, Lieutenant of the Tower of London	MAYOR of London
Porter, French sergeant, sentinels, scout, herald, officers	VERNON
Governor of Paris, fiends and soldiers, servingmen	
Messengers and keepers of the Tower of London	

Quotations

	Spoken by
And while I live, I'll ne'er fly from a man.	Joan
Between two hawks, which flies the higher pitch.	Warwick
Between two dogs, which hath the deeper mouth.	
Between two blades, which bears the better temper.	
Between two horses, which doth bear him best.	

Between two girls, which hath the merriest eye.
I have perhaps some shallow spirit of judgement.
Christ's mother helps me, else I were too weak.   Joan
Unbidden guests are often welcomest when they are gone.   Bedford

Précis of plot
The first part of Henry VI covers the period between the funeral of Henry V and the end of the Hundred Years
War, between England and France. As in many of the Shakespearian plays, the historical accuracy comes
second to the plot.

Setting
England 1422 to 1453.

12 Henry VI Part 2

KING HENRY VI and QUEEN MARGARET	Gloucester's SERVANTS
William de la Pole, Marquis, later Duke of SUFFOLK	Two SHERIFFS of London
Duke Humphrey of GLOUCESTER, the Lord Protector	Sir John STANLEY
Dame Eleanor Cobham, the DUCHESS of Gloucester	HERALD
CARDINAL BEAUFORT, Bishop of Winchester	Two MURDERERS
Duke of BUCKINGHAM	COMMONS
Duke of SOMERSET	CAPTAIN of a ship
Old Lord CLIFFORD and YOUNG CLIFFORD, his son	MASTER of that ship
Duke of YORK	The Master's MATE
EDWARD, Earl of March, the Duke's son	Walter WHITMORE
Crookback RICHARD, the Duke's son	Two GENTLEMEN
Earl of SALISBURY and Earl of WARWICK, his son	Jack CADE, a Kentishman
Emmanuel, the CLERK of Chatham	Dick the BUTCHER
Two or three PETITIONERS	Smith the WEAVER
Thomas HORNER, an armourer	A sawyer
PETER Thump, his man	JOHN
Three NEIGHBOURS, who drink to Horner	REBELS
Three PRENTICES, who drink to Peter	Sir Humphrey STAFFORD
Sir John HUME, a priest	STAFFORD'S BROTHER
John SOUTHWELL, a priest	Lord SAYE
Margery Jordan, a WITCH	Lord SCALES
Roger BOLINGBROKE, a conjurer	Matthew Gough
ASNATH, a spirit	A SERGEANT
Three or four CITIZENS of London	A BEADLE of Saint Albans
Simon SIMPCOX and SIMPCOX'S WIFE	Townsmen of Saint Albans
The MAYOR of Saint Albans	VAUX, a messenger
Alexander IDEN, who kills Cade	A POST
Aldermen of Saint Albans	MESSENGERS
Attendants, guards, servants, soldiers, falconers	A SOLDIER

Quotations

	Spoken by
Could I come near your beauty with my nails, I'd set my ten commandments in your face.	Duchess
Is not this a lamentable thing that of the skin of an innocent lamb should be made parchment? that parchment being scribbled o'er should undo a man?	Cade
Sir, he made a chimney in my father's house, and the bricks are alive at this day to testify.	Weaver
Smooth runs the water where the brook is deep.	Suffolk
The first thing we do let's kill all the lawyers.	Dick the Butcher
The gaudy, blabbing, and remorseful day, is crept into the bosom of the sea.	Captain
There shall be in England seven halfpenny loaves sold for a penny, the three-hooped pot shall have ten hoops and I will make it a felony to drink small beer.	Cade
Thou hast most traitorously corrupted the youth of the realm in erecting a grammar school; and, whereas before, our forefathers had no books but the score and tally, thou hast caused printing to be used and, contrary to the King, his crown and dignity, thou hast built a paper mill.	Cade
What stronger breastplate than a heart untainted.	King Henry

Précis of plot
The original title of this play was *The First Part of the Contention of the Two Famous Houses of York and
Lancaster*, and Shakespeare has stayed true, to a great extent, to this period of history, which includes the
Kentish rebellion led by Jack Cade, and ultimately leads to the Wars of the Roses.

Setting
England 1445 to 1455.

SHAKESPEARE

13 Henry VI Part 3

KING HENRY VI
QUEEN MARGARET
PRINCE EDWARD, their son
Duke of SOMERSET
Duke of EXETER
Earl of NORTHUMBERLAND
Earl of WESTMORLAND
Lord CLIFFORD
Lord Stafford
SOMERVILLE
Henry, young Earl of Richmond
A SOLDIER who has killed his father
A HUNTSMAN who guards King Edward
The divided House of Neville:
Earl of WARWICK
Marquis of MONTAGUE, his brother
Earl of OXFORD, their brother-in-law
Lord HASTINGS, their brother-in-law
Of the Duke of York's party:
Richard Plantagenet, Duke of YORK
EDWARD, Earl of March, his son, later KING EDWARD IV
LADY GRAY, a widow, later Edward's wife and queen
Earl RIVERS, Lady Gray's brother

GEORGE, later DUKE OF CLARENCE
RICHARD, later DUKE OF GLOUCESTER
Earl of RUTLAND, Edward's brother
Rutland's TUTOR, a chaplain
SIR JOHN Mortimer, York's uncle
Sir Hugh Mortimer, his brother
Duke of NORFOLK
Sir William Stanley
Earl of Pembroke
Sir John MONTGOMERY
A NOBLEMAN
Two GAMEKEEPERS
Three WATCHMEN
LIEUTENANT of the Tower

The French:
KING LOUIS
LADY BONA, his sister-in-law
Lord Bourbon, the French High Admiral

A SOLDIER who has killed his son
Mayor of Coventry
MAYOR of York
Aldermen of YORK
Soldiers, messengers and attendants

Quotations

	Spoken by
Didst thou never hear that things ill got had ever bad success?	King Henry
Down, down to hell, and say I sent thee thither.	Richard of Gloucester
Gives not the hawthorn bush a sweeter shade, to shepherds looking on their seely sheep, than doth a rich embroider'd canopy, to Kings that fear their subjects' treachery?	King Henry
My crown is in my heart, not on my head.	King Henry
O God! methinks it were a happy life, to be no better than a homely swain, to sit upon a hill, as I do now; to carve out dials quaintly, point by point, thereby to see the minutes how they run. How many makes the hour full complete, how many hours bring about the day, how many days will finish up the year, how many years a mortal man may live.	King Henry
Oh tiger's heart wrapp'd in a woman's hide!	York
Suspicion always haunts the guilty mind, the thief doth fear each bush an officer.	Richard of Gloucester

Précis of plot

This play chronicles the substantive episodes in the War of the Roses, although the usual Shakespearian anachronisms do not detract from the play's subtleties.

Setting

England 1455 to 1471.

14 Henry VIII (All Is True)

PROLOGUE
KING HENRY VIII
Duke of BUCKINGHAM
Lord ABERGAVENNY
Earl of SURREY
Duke of NORFOLK
Duke of SUFFOLK
LORD CHAMBERLAIN
LORD CHANCELLOR
Lord SANDS (aka Sir William Sands)
Sir Thomas LOVELL
Sir Anthony DENNY
Sir Henry GUILDFORD
CARDINAL WOLSEY
Two SECRETARIES
Buckingham's SURVEYOR
CARDINAL CAMPEIUS
GARDINER, King's secretary, later Bishop of Winchester
His PAGE
Thomas CROMWELL
CRANMER, Archbishop of Canterbury
QUEEN KATHERINE, later KATHERINE, Princess Dowager
GRIFFITH, her gentleman usher
PATIENCE, her waiting woman

Archbishop of Canterbury
Bishop of LINCOLN
Bishop of Ely
Bishop of Rochester
Bishop of Saint Asaph
Two priests
Serjeant-at-arms
Two noblemen
A CRIER
Appearing in the Coronation:
Three GENTLEMEN
Two judges
Choristers
Lord Mayor of London
Garter King of Arms
Marquis of Dorset
Four Barons of the Cinque Ports
Stokesley, Bishop of London
Old Duchess of Norfolk
Countesses

A MESSENGER
Lord CAPUTIUS
ANNE Boleyn

Other WOMEN
Six spirits who dance before Katherine in a vision
At Cranmer's trial:
A DOOR-KEEPER
Doctor BUTTS, the King's physician
Pursuivants, pages, footboys, grooms
BRANDON
SERJEANT-AT-ARMS
Sir Nicholas VAUX
Tipstaves, Halberdiers and common people
Appearing at the Legatine Court:
Two vergers
Ladies, gentlemen, a SERVANT, attendants

An OLD LADY
At the Christening:
A PORTER
His MAN
Two aldermen
Lord Mayor of London
GARTER King of Arms
Six noblemen
Old Duchess of Norfolk, godmother
Princess Elizabeth, the child
Marchioness Dorset, godmother

EPILOGUE
Two SCRIBES

Quotations

	Spoken by
A peace above all earthly dignities, a still and quiet conscience.	Cardinal Wolsey
Cromwell, I charge thee, fling away ambition. By that sin fell the angels.	Cardinal Wolsey
Had I but serv'd my God with half the zeal I served my King, he would not in mine age have left me naked to mine enemies.	Cardinal Wolsey
Heaven is above all yet – there sits a judge that no king can corrupt.	Queen Katherine
He gave his honours to the world again, his blessed part to heaven, and slept in peace.	Griffith
He was a man of an unbounded stomach.	Katherine
Love thyself last. Cherish those hearts that hate thee.	Cardinal Wolsey
He was a scholar, and a ripe and good one.	Griffith
Men's evil manners live in brass; their virtues we write in water	Griffith
So farewell – to the little good you bear me. Farewell, a long farewell, to all my greatness!	Cardinal Wolsey
So may he rest, his faults lie gently on him.	Katherine
Those twins of learning that he raised in you, Ipswich and Oxford.	Griffith
'Tis better to be lowly born, and range with humble livers in content, than to be perk'd up in a glistering grief and wear a golden sorrow.	Anne
Vain pomp and glory of this world, I hate ye!	Cardinal Wolsey

Précis of plot
The reign of Henry VIII from the opening description of the Field of the Cloth of Gold, of 1520, to the christening of Princess Elizabeth, in 1533.

Setting
England 1521 to 1533.

15 Julius Caesar

Julius CAESAR
CALPURNIA, his wife
Marcus BRUTUS, a noble Roman, opposed to Caesar
PORTIA, his wife
LUCIUS, his servant
Officers and soldiers in Brutus' army:
LUCILLIUS
MESSALA
VARRUS
CLAUDIO
YOUNG CATO
STRATO
VOLUMNIUS
FLAVIUS
DARDANIUS
CLITUS
Rulers of Rome after Caesar's death:
Mark ANTONY
OCTAVIUS Caesar
LEPIDUS

PINDARUS, Cassius' bondman
TITINIUS, an officer in Cassius' army
POPILLIUS Laena, a Senator
Senators, soldiers and attendants

ARTEMIDORUS
CINNA the Poet
Opposed to Caesar:
Caius CASSIUS
CASCA
TREBONIUS
DECIUS Brutus
METELLUS Cimber
CINNA
Caius LIGARIUS

FLAVIUS, a tribune
MURELLUS, a tribune
CICERO, a Senator
PUBLIUS, a Senator

A POET
GHOST of Caesar
A COBBLER
A CARPENTER
Other PLEBEIANS
A MESSENGER
SERVANTS
SOOTHSAYER

Quotations

	Spoken by
As Caesar loved me, I weep for him.	Brutus
As proper men as ever trod upon neat's leather have gone upon my handiwork.	Cobbler

SHAKESPEARE

Between the acting of a dreadful thing and the first motion, all the interim is like a phantasma, or a hideous dream.	Brutus
Beware the ides of March.	Soothsayer
But for your words, they rob the Hybla bees, and leave them honeyless.	Cassius
But I am constant as the Northern Star, of whose true fixed and resting quality, there is no fellow in the firmament.	Caesar
But when I tell him he hates flatterers; he says he does being then most flattered.	Decius
But yesterday the word of Caesar might have stood against the world. Now lies he there, and none so poor to do him reverence.	Antony
Caesar said to me 'Darest thou, Cassius, now leap in with me into this angry flood, and swim to yonder point?' Upon the word, accoutred as I was I plunged in and bade him follow.	Cassius
Cowards die many times before their deaths; the valiant never taste of death but once.	Caesar
Cry 'havoc' and let slip the dogs of war.	Antony
Et tu, Brute? – then fall Caesar.	Caesar (last words)
Fierce fiery warriors fight upon the clouds, in ranks and squadrons and right form of war.	Calpurnia
For Brutus is an honourable man; so are they all, all honourable men.	Antony
For he will never follow anything that other men begin.	Brutus
For I have neither wit, nor words, nor worth, action nor utterance, nor the power of speech, to stir men's blood.	Antony
Friends, Romans, countrymen, lend me your ears.	Antony
He reads much, he is a great observer, and he looks quite through the deeds of men.	Caesar
His life was gentle, and the elements so mixed in him that nature might stand up and say to all the world, 'This was a man'.	Antony
How hard it is for women to keep counsel!	Portia
How many ages hence, shall this our lofty scene be acted over, in states unborn and accents yet unknown.	Cassius
I am no orator as Brutus is; but as you know me all, a plain blunt man.	Antony
I am not gamesome; I do lack some part of that quick spirit that is in Antony.	Brutus
If you have tears, prepare to shed them now.	Antony
I had rather be a dog and bay the moon than such a Roman.	Brutus
Let me have men about me who are fat.	Caesar
Let's carve him as a dish fit for the gods.	Brutus
Lowliness is young ambition's ladder, whereto the climber upward turns his face; but when he once attains the upmost round, he then unto the ladder turns his back, looks in the clouds, scorning the base degrees by which he did ascend.	Brutus
Now in the name of all the gods at once, upon what meat doth this our Caesar feed, that he is grown so great?	Cassius
O judgement, thou art fled to brutish beasts, and men have lost their reasons!	Antony
O pardon me, thou bleeding piece of earth, that I am meek and gentle with these butchers!	Antony
See what a rent the envious Casca made.	Antony
Set honour in one eye and death i'th'other, and I will look on both indifferently.	Brutus
There is a tide in the affairs of men, which, taken at the flood, leads on to fortune.	Brutus
There was a Brutus once that would have brooked the eternal devil to keep his state in Rome, as easily as a king.	Cassius
This was the most unkindest cut of all.	Antony
This was the noblest Roman of them all.	Antony
Well, honour is the subject of my story. I cannot tell what you and other men think of this life; but, for my single self, I had as lief not be, as live to be in awe of such a thing as I myself.	Cassius
When beggars die, there are no comets seen; the heavens themselves blaze forth the death of princes.	Calpurnia
When love begins to sicken and decay, it useth an enforced ceremony.	Brutus
Why, he that cuts off twenty years of life, cuts off so many years of fearing death.	Casca
Why, man, he doth bestride the narrow world like a Colossus.	Cassius
Yet Brutus says he was ambitious, and Brutus is an honourable man.	Antony
Yond Cassius has a lean and hungry look. He thinks too much. Such men are dangerous.	Caesar
You are my true and honourable wife, as dear to me as are the ruddy drops that visit my sad heart.	Brutus
You blocks, you stones, you worse than senseless things!	Murellus

Précis of plot

The play depicts the events that led to the assassination of Julius Caesar and the aftermath thereof. As in many Shakespearian History plays, facts are often altered and rearranged in the interests of dramatic economy and effectiveness.

Setting

Rome, Sardis and near Philippi 44 to 42 BC.

16 King John

KING JOHN of England
QUEEN ELEANOR, his mother
LADY FALCONBRIDGE
Philip the BASTARD, later knighted as Richard Plantagenet,
her illegitimate son by King Richard I
Robert FALCONBRIDGE, her legitimate son
James GURNEY, her attendant
Lady BLANCHE of Spain, niece of King John
PRINCE HENRY, son of King John
HUBERT, a follower of King John
KING PHILIP of France
LOUIS THE DAUPHIN, his son
ARTHUR, Duke of Brittaine, nephew of King John
Lady CONSTANCE, his mother
Duke of AUSTRIA (Limoges)
CHÂTILLON, ambassador
Cardinal PANDOLF, a legate from the Pope
PETER OF POMFRET, a prophet
Lords, soldiers, attendants

Earl of SALISBURY
Earl of PEMBROKE
Earl of ESSEX
Lord BIGOT
A CITIZEN of Angers
HERALDS
EXECUTIONERS
MESSENGERS
SHERIFF

Quotations

Quotations	Spoken by
And oftentimes excusing of a fault doth make the fault the worser by th' excuse.	Pembroke
Another lean unwashed artificer cuts off his tale, and talks of Arthur's death.	Hubert
For courage mounteth with occasion.	Duke of Austria
Heat me these irons hot.	Hubert
Here is my throne; bid kings come bow to it.	Constance
How oft the sight of means to do ill deeds, make deeds ill done!	King John
Life is as tedious as a twice-told tale, vexing the dull ear of a drowsy man.	Louis the Dauphin
Lord of thy presence, and no land beside?	Queen Eleanor
Saint George that swinged the dragon, and e'er since sits on his horseback at mine hostess' door.	Bastard
This England never did, nor never shall, lie at the proud foot of a conqueror.	Bastard
To gild refined gold, to paint the lily.	Salisbury
When Fortune means to men most good, she looks upon them with a threatening eye.	Pandolf
Zounds! I was never so bethumped with words, since first I called my brother's father, dad.	Bastard

Précis of plot

Selected events from King John's reign are portrayed, although Shakespeare concentrates on Philip Falconbridge, the illegitimate son of Richard I, for his sub-plot; and significant events such as Magna Carta are ignored.

Setting

England and France 1199 to 1216.

17 King Lear

LEAR, King of Britain
GONERIL, Lear's eldest daughter
Duke of ALBANY, her husband
REGAN, Lear's second daughter
Duke of CORNWALL, her husband
CORDELIA, Lear's youngest daughter
King of FRANCE, a suitor of Cordelia
Duke of BURGUNDY, a suitor of Cordelia
Earl of KENT, later disguised as Caius
Earl of GLOUCESTER

EDGAR, later disguised as Tom o' Bedlam
EDMOND, bastard son of Gloucester
OLD MAN, Gloucester's tenant
Lear's FOOL
OSWALD, Goneril's steward
A SERVANT of Cornwall
A KNIGHT
A HERALD
A CAPTAIN
Gentlemen, servants, soldiers, attendants

Quotations

Quotations	Spoken by
And my poor fool is hanged. No, No, no life? Why should a dog, a horse, a rat have life and thou no breath at all?	Lear
As flies to wanton boys are we to the gods, they kill us for their sport	Gloucester
A still soliciting eye, and such a tongue.	Cordelia
Blow, winds, and crack your cheeks! rage, blow, you cataracts and hurricanoes, spout.	Lear
Drinks the green mantle of the standing pool.	Edgar
Fie, foe, and fum; I smell the blood of a British man.	Edgar
Fortune, good night; smile once more; turn thy wheel.	Kent
Howl, howl, howl, howl! O, you are men of stones.	Lear
How sharper than a serpent's tooth it is to have a thankless child.	Lear
I am a man more sinned against than sinning.	Lear
I have seen better faces in my time than stands on any shoulder that I see before me at this instant.	Kent

SHAKESPEARE

I have seen the day, with my good biting falchion.	Lear
I'll talk a word with this same learned Theban.	Lear
Ingratitude, thou marble-hearted fiend.	Lear
I tax you not, you elements, with unkindness.	Lear
Mastiff, greyhound, mongrel grim.	Edgar
My cue is villainous melancholy, with a sigh like Tom o' Bedlam.	Edmond
O, that way madness lies. Let me shun that.	Lear
Out-paramoured the Turk.	Edgar
Poor naked wretches, whereso'er you are.	Lear
Poor Tom's a-cold.	Edgar
So young and so untender?	Lear
Take physic, pomp, expose thyself to feel what wretches feel.	Lear
The gods are just, and of our pleasant vices, make instruments to plague us.	Edgar
The little dogs and all, Tray, Blanch, and sweetheart see, they bark at me.	Lear
The prince of darkness is a gentleman.	Edgar
These late eclipses in the sun and moon portend no good to us.	Gloucester
The wheel has come full circle.	Edmond
The worst is not so long as we can say 'This is the worst'.	Edgar
Things that love night, love not such nights as these.	Kent
This is the excellent foppery of the world; that when we are sick in fortune – often	Edmond
the surfeits of our own behaviour – we make guilty of our disasters the sun, the moon, and stars, as if we were villains by necessity, fools by heavenly compulsion, knaves, thieves, and treachers by spherical predominance, drunkards, liars, and adulterers by an enforced obedience of planetary influence; and all that we are evil in by a divine thrusting on.	
This is the foul fiend Flibbertigibbet; he begins at curfew, and walks 'til the first cock.	Edgar
Thou whoreson Z, thou unnecessary letter.	Kent
'Tis a naughty night to swim in.	Fool
Vex not his ghost, O let him pass.	Kent
You are not worth the dust which the rude wind blows in your face.	Albany

Précis of plot

The story of a king who, angry with the failure of his virtuous youngest daughter, Cordelia, to compete for his favour in a love-test, divides his kingdom between her two malevolent sisters. The sub-plot depicts Lear's madness and the blinding of Gloucester, as well as Edgar's loyalty to his father.

Setting

Britain.

18 Love's Labour's Lost

Ferdinand, KING of Navarre	BOYET
Lords attending on the King:	Two other LORDS
BIRON	COSTARD, a Clown
LONGUEVILLE	JAQUENETTA, a country wench
DUMAINE	Sir NATHANIEL, a curate
	HOLOFERNES, a schoolmaster
	Anthony DULL, a constable
PRINCESS of France	MERCADÉ, a messenger
Ladies attending on the Princess:	A FORESTER
ROSALINE	Don Adriano de ARMADO, a Spanish
KATHERINE	braggart
MARIA	MOTE, his page

Quotations

	Spoken by
A jest's prosperity lies in the ear of him that hears it, never in the tongue of him that makes it.	Rosaline
A lover's eyes will gaze an eagle blind; a lover's ear will hear the lowest sound.	Biron
At Christmas I no more desire a rose, than wish a snow in May's new-fangled mirth.	Biron
A very beadle to a humorous sigh.	Biron
Devise wit, write pen, for I am for whole volumes, in folio.	Armado
He draweth out the thread of his verbosity finer than the staple of his argument.	Holofernes
He hath never fed of the dainties that are bred in a book.	Nathaniel
In the posteriors of this day, which the rude multitude call the afternoon.	Armado
Light, seeking light, doth light of light beguile.	Biron
Remuneration – O, that's the Latin word for three-farthings.	Costard
Spite of cormorant devouring time.	King
Study is like the heavens' glorious sun, that will not be deep-searched with saucy looks. Small have continual plodders ever won, save base authority from others' books.	Biron
This wimpled, whining, purblind, wayward boy.	Biron
Why, all delights are vain; but that most vain, which with pain purchased, doth inherit pain.	Biron

Précis of plot

The young King of Navarre, and three of his friends, vow to devote the following three years to austere self-improvement, forgoing the company of women. The ensuing farce is both sophisticated and cleverly staged.

Setting

Navarre circa 14th century.

19 Macbeth

KING DUNCAN of Scotland	Scottish Thanes:
MALCOLM, King Duncan's son	LENNOX
DONALBAIN, King Duncan's son	ROSS
A CAPTAIN in Duncan's army	ANGUS
MACBETH, Thane of Glamis, later Thane Cawdor,	CAITHNESS
then King of Scotland	MENTEITH
LADY MACBETH, Macbeth's wife	
A DOCTOR, attending on Lady Macbeth	Six WITCHES
A Waiting-GENTLEWOMAN, attending on Lady Macbeth	An English DOCTOR
BANQUO, a Scottish Thane	A SPIRIT LIKE A CAT
FLEANCE, his son	Three APPARITIONS:
MACDUFF, Thane of Fife	an armed head
LADY MACDUFF, his wife	a bloody child
MACDUFF'S SON	a child crowned
SIWARD, Earl of Northumberland	Other SPIRITS
YOUNG SIWARD, his son	An OLD MAN
HECATE, Queen of the Witches	A MESSENGER
A PORTER at Macbeth's castle	MURDERERS
Three MURDERERS attending on Macbeth	SERVANTS
SEYTON, servant of Macbeth	soldiers, drummers
A show of eight kings, Lords and Thanes	

Quotations

	Spoken by
All the perfumes of Arabia will not sweeten this little hand.	Lady Macbeth
Angels are bright still, though the brightest fell.	Malcolm
Be innocent of the knowledge, dearest chuck.	Macbeth
Blow wind, come wrack, at least we'll die with harness on our back.	Macbeth
But screw your courage to the sticking-place, and we'll not fail.	Lady Macbeth
By the pricking of my thumbs, something wicked this way comes.	Second Witch
Canst thou not minister to a mind diseased.	Macbeth
Come what, come may, time and the hour runs through the toughest day.	Macbeth
Consider it not so deeply.	Lady Macbeth
Double, double, toil and trouble, fire burn, and cauldron bubble.	Three Witches
Hang out our banners on the outward walls.	Macbeth
How now, you secret, black, and midnight hags.	Macbeth
I am in blood stepped in so far that, should I wade no more, returning were as tedious as go o'er.	Macbeth
I dare do all that may become a man; who dares do more is none.	Macbeth
If you can look into the seeds of time, and say which grain will grow and which will not.	Banquo
I 'gin to be aweary of the sun.	Macbeth
I had most need of blessing, and Amen stuck in my throat.	Macbeth
I must become a borrower of the night, for a dark hour or twain.	Banquo
Infirm of purpose! give me the daggers.	Lady Macbeth
Is this a dagger which I see before me? the handle towards my hand? come let me clutch thee.	Macbeth
It was the owl that shrieked, the fatal bellman.	Lady Macbeth
I would applaud thee to the very echo.	Macbeth
Look like the innocent flower, but be the serpent under't.	Lady Macbeth
Might be the be-all and the end-all here.	Macbeth
Now good digestion wait on appetite, and health on both.	Macbeth
O, I could play the woman with mine eyes, and braggart with my tongue!	Macduff
Or have we eaten on the insane root, that takes the reason prisoner.	Banquo
Out, damned spot; out, I say.	Lady Macbeth
Shake off this downy sleep, death's counterfeit, and look on death itself!	Macduff
Sleep shall neither night nor day, hang upon his pent-house lid.	First Witch
Stands not within the prospect of belief.	Macbeth
That no compunctious visitings of nature shake my fell purpose.	Lady Macbeth
That which hath made them drunk hath made me bold.	Lady Macbeth
The attempt and not the deed confounds us.	Lady Macbeth
The earth hath bubbles, as the water has, and these are of them.	Banquo
The labour we delight in physics pain.	Macbeth
There's husbandry in heaven, their candles are all out.	Banquo
The Thane of Cawdor lives; why do you dress me in borrow'd robes.	

The weird sisters hand in hand.	Three Witches
This castle hath a pleasant seat; the air nimbly and sweetly recommends itself unto our gentle senses.	King Duncan
Throw physic to the dogs; I'll none of it.	Macbeth
To-morrow, and to-morrow, and to-morrow, creeps in this petty pace from day to day, to the last syllable of recorded time, and all our yesterdays have lighted fools the way to dusty death. Out, out, brief candle! Life's but a walking shadow, a poor player that struts and frets his hour upon the stage and then is heard no more: It is a tale told by an idiot, full of sound and fury, signifying nothing.	Macbeth
We have scotched the snake, not killed it.	Macbeth
What, all my pretty chickens and their dam, at one fell swoop.	Macduff
What are these, so wither'd and so wild in their attire, that look not like the inhabitants o' the earth, and yet are on't.	Banquo
What bloody man is that?	King Duncan
Who can be wise, amazed, temperate and furious, loyal and neutral, in a moment?	Macbeth
Yet I do fear thy nature; it is too full o'th' milk of human kindness.	Lady Macbeth
Yet who would have thought the old man to have had so much blood in him.	Lady Macbeth
Your face, my thane, is as a book where men may read strange matters.	Lady Macbeth

Précis of plot
A story of witchcraft, murder, and retribution, which can also be seen as a study in the philosophy and psychology of evil.

Setting
Scotland and England 1039 to 1057.

20 Measure for Measure

Vincentio, the DUKE of Vienna	A PROVOST
ANGELO, appointed his deputy	ELBOW, a simple constable
ESCALUS, an old Lord	A JUSTICE
CLAUDIO, a young gentleman	ABHORSON, an executioner
JULIET, betrothed to Claudio	BARNARDINE, a dissolute condemned
ISABELLA, Claudio's sister	prisoner
LUCIO, 'a fantastic'	MARIANA, betrothed to Angelo
Two other such GENTLEMEN	A BOY, attendant on Mariana
FROTH, a foolish gentleman	FRIAR PETER
MISTRESS OVERDONE, a bawd	FRANCESCA, a nun
POMPEY, her clownish servant	VARRIUS, a Lord, friend to the Duke
	Lords, officers, citizens, servants

Quotations	**Spoken by**
Ay, but to die, and go we know not where; to lie in cold obstruction, and to rot.	Claudio
But man, proud man, dressed in a little brief authority, most ignorant of what he's most assured, his glassy essence, like an angry ape, plays such fantastic tricks before high heaven as makes the angels weep.	Isabella
Condemn the fault, and not the actor of it.	Angelo
Every true man's apparel fits your thief.	Abhorson
Heaven doth with us as we with torches do.	Duke of Vienna
If I must die, I will encounter darkness as a bride, and hug it in my arms.	Claudio
I hold you as a thing enskied and sainted.	Lucio
No ceremony that to great ones 'longs. Not the king's crown, nor the deputed sword, the marshal's truncheon, nor the judge's robe, become them with one half so good a grace, as mercy does.	Isabella
O, it is excellent to have a giant's strength, but it is tyrannous to use it like a giant.	Isabella
Our doubts are traitors, and makes us lose the good we oft might win.	Lucio
Some rise by sin, and some by virtue fall.	Escalus
That in the captain's but a choleric word, which in the soldier is flat blasphemy.	Isabella
The jury passing on the prisoner's life, may in the sworn twelve have a thief or two, guiltier than him they try.	Angelo
The miserable have no other medicine; but only hope.	Claudio
They say, best men are moulded out of faults; and for the most, become much more the better, for being a little bad.	Mariana
This will last out a night in Russia, when nights are longest there.	Angelo
Virtue is bold, and goodness never fearful	Duke of Vienna

Précis of plot
The central action revolves around the dilemma of Isabella, a novice nun, whose brother is to be executed unless she succumbs to the attentions of Angelo. *Measure for Measure* is a morality play with similar sentiments to *The Merchant of Venice*, but is far more explicitly concerned with sex, and death.

Setting
Vienna circa 1500.

21 The Merchant of Venice

ANTONIO, a merchant of Venice
BASSANIO, his friend and Portia's suitor
LEONARDO, Bassanio's servant
LANCELOT, a clown and servant
GOBBO, his father
Prince of MOROCCO, Portia's suitor
Prince of ARAGON, Portia's suitor
PORTIA, an heiress
NERISSA, her waiting-gentlewoman
BALTHASAR, Portia's servant
STEFANO, Portia's servant
Jailer, attendants, servants, magnificoes of Venice

SHYLOCK, a Jew
JESSICA, his daughter
LORENZO
GRAZIANO
SALERIO
SOLANIO
DUKE of Venice
TUBAL, a Jew

Quotations

	Spoken by
A Daniel come to judgement, yea, a Daniel!	Shylock
All that glisters is not gold.	Morocco
And when I ope my lips, let no dog bark.	Graziano
But love is blind and lovers cannot see.	Jessica
But ships are but boards, sailors but men. There be land rats and water rats, water thieves and land thieves.	Shylock
How like a fawning publican he looks. I hate him for he is a Christian.	Shylock
How sweet the moonlight sleeps upon this bank!	Lorenzo
I am never merry when I hear sweet music	Jessica
I dote on his very absence.	Portia
If you prick us do we not bleed? If you tickle us do we not laugh? If you poison us do we not die? and if you wrong us shall we not revenge?	Shylock
It is a wise father that knows his own child.	Lancelot
I would not have given it for a wilderness of monkeys.	Shylock
Mislike me not for my complexion, the shadowed livery of the burnished sun.	Morocco
The quality of mercy is not strained. It droppeth as the gentle rain from heaven, upon the place beneath.	Portia
You call me misbeliever, cut-throat, dog, and spit upon my Jewish gaberdine.	Shylock
You taught me first to beg, and now methinks, you teach me how a beggar should be answered.	Portia

Précis of plot

The central plot involves an irascible Jewish money-lender and his efforts to exact full payment for a debt. The sub-plot involves the method of an heiress, Portia, of testing her suitors. The comedy is created by Shylock, the Jew's, strict adherence to the letter of the law and his ultimate downfall by being hoist by his own petard.

Setting

Venice and Belmont circa 14th century.

22 The Merry Wives of Windsor

MISTRESS Margaret PAGE
Master George PAGE, her husband
ANNE and WILLIAM Page, their children
MISTRESS Alice FORD
Master Frank FORD, her husband
Doctor CAIUS, a French physician
MISTRESS QUICKLY, his housekeeper
John RUGBY, his servant
Master FENTON, in love with Anne Page
Master Abraham SLENDER
Robert SHALLOW, his uncle, a justice
The HOST of the Garter Inn
Sir Hugh EVANS, a Welsh parson
Peter SIMPLE, Slender's servant
Children of Windsor, appearing as fairies

ROBIN, Sir John's page
JOHN, a servant
ROBERT, a servant
SIR JOHN Falstaff
BARDOLPH
PISTOL
NIM

Quotations

	Spoken by
A man of my kidney.	Sir John
Faith, thou hast some crotchets in thy head now.	Mistress Ford
Here will be an old abusing of God's patience and the King's English.	Mistress Quickly
I cannot tell what the dickens his name is.	Mistress Page
I have a kind of alacrity in sinking.	Sir John
I hope good luck lies in odd numbers.	Sir John
I will make a Star Chamber matter of it.	Shallow
O, what a world of vile ill-favoured faults.	Anne
There was the rankest compound of villainous smell that ever offended nostril.	Sir John
Vengeance of Jenny's case!	Mistress Quickly

We burn daylight. Here: read, read.	Mistress Ford
Why then, the world's mine oyster, which I with sword will open.	Pistol

Précis of plot
The central plot tells of Sir John Falstaff's unsuccessful attempts to seduce Mistress Page and Mistress Ford, and of the unfounded jealousy of Master Ford. The sub-plot revolves around the wooing of Anne Page and ultimate success of Master Fenton.

Setting
Windsor mid-15th century.

23 A Midsummer Night's Dream

THESEUS, Duke of Athens	SNUG, a joiner
HIPPOLYTA, Queen of the Amazons	Tom SNOUT, a Tinker
EGEUS, father of Hermia	
HERMIA, daughter of Egeus	Four Fairies:
LYSANDER, loved by Hermia	COBWEB
DEMETRIUS, suitor to Hermia	MOTE
HELENA, in love with Demetrius	MUSTARDSEED
OBERON, King of the Fairies	PEASEBLOSSOM
TITANIA, Queen of the Fairies	
ROBIN GOODFELLOW, a puck	
Peter QUINCE, a carpenter	
Nick BOTTOM, a weaver	
Francis FLUTE, a bellows-mender	
Robin STARVELING, a tailor	
Attendant Lords and fairies	

Quotations

	Spoken by
A calendar, a calendar! look in the almanac; find out moonshine, find out moonshine.	Bottom
A lion among ladies is a most dreadful thing; for there is not a more fearful wild-fowl than your lion living.	Bottom
A part to tear a cat in.	Bottom
A proper man, as one shall see in a summer's day.	Quince
And the imperial votaress passed on, in maiden meditation, fancy-free, yet marks I where the bolt of Cupid fell: It fell upon a little western flower, before milk-white, now purple with love's wound, and maidens call it love-in-idleness.	Oberon
Bless thee, Bottom! bless thee! thou art translated.	Quince
But earthlier happy is the rose distilled than that which, withering on the virgin thorn, grows, lives, and dies in single blessedness.	Theseus
He bravely broach'd his boiling bloody breast.	Quince (as prologue)
I am slow of study.	Snug
I have a reasonable good ear in music. Let's have the tongs and the bones.	Bottom
I have an exposition of sleep come upon me.	Bottom
I know a bank where the wild thyme blows, where oxlips and the nodding violet grows, quite over-canopied with luscious woodbine, with sweet musk-roses and with eglantine.	Oberon
Ill met by moonlight, proud Titania.	Oberon
I'll put a girdle round the earth in forty minutes.	Puck
I will roar you as gently as any sucking dove; I will roar you as 'twere any nightingale.	Bottom
Lord, what fools these mortals be.	Puck
Love looks not with the eyes, but with the mind; and therefore is wing'd Cupid painted blind.	Helena
Masters, spread yourselves.	Bottom
My hounds are bred out of the Spartan kind, so flew'd, so sanded, and their heads are hung, with ears that sweep away the morning dew; crook-knee'd, and dew-lapp'd like Thessalian bulls; slow in pursuit, but match'd in mouth like bells.	Theseus
Oh hell! to choose love by another's eyes.	Hermia
Or in the night, imagining some fear, how easy is a bush supposed a bear.	Theseus
She was a vixen when she went to school; and though she be but little, she is fierce.	Helena
Since once I sat upon a promontory, and heard a mermaid on a dolphin's back uttering such dulcet and harmonious breath that the rude sea grew civil at her song and certain stars shot madly from their spheres, to hear the sea-maid's music.	Oberon
So we grew together, like to a double cherry, seeming parted, but yet an union in partition; two lovely berries moulded on one stem.	Helena
Swift as a shadow, short as any dream, brief as the lightning in the collied night, that, in a spleen, unfolds both heaven and earth, and ere a man hath power to say 'Behold' the jaws of darkness do devour it up.	Lysander
That is the true beginning of our end.	Quince (as prologue)
The best in this kind are but shadows; and the worst are no worse, if imagination amend them.	Theseus
The course of true love never did run smooth.	Lysander

The iron tongue of midnight hath told twelve.	Theseus
The jaws of darkness do devour it up: so quick bright things come to confusion.	Lysander
The lover, all as frantic, sees Helen's beauty in a brow of Egypt. The poet's eye, in a fine frenzy rolling, doth glance from heaven to earth, from earth to heaven.	Theseus
The lunatic, the lover and the poet, are of imagination all compact.	Theseus
This is 'erc'les' vein.	Bottom
Very tragical mirth.	Lysander (reads)
What hempen homespuns have we swaggering here.	Puck

Précis of plot
Theseus, Duke of Athens, prepares to marry Hippolyta, Queen of the Amazons. The sub-plots include the tangled web of love between Lysander, Hermia, Demetrius and Helena, and the production of a play, *Pyramus and Thisbe* (based on Ovid's *Metamorphoses*), for the Duke's wedding.

Setting
Athens and a nearby wood.

24 Much Ado About Nothing
DON PEDRO, Prince of Aragon
BALTHASAR, attendant on Don Pedro, a singer
DON JOHN, the bastard brother of Don Pedro
BORACHIO, follower of Don John
CONRAD, follower of Don John
LEONATO, Governor of Messina
HERO, his daughter
BEATRICE, an orphan, his niece
ANTONIO, an old man, brother of Leonato
MARGARET, attendant on Hero
URSULA, attendant on Hero
DOGBERRY, constable in charge of Watch
VERGES, the Headborough, Dogberry's partner

BENEDICK, of Padua
CLAUDIO, of Florence
FRIAR Francis
A SEXTON
WATCHMEN
A BOY, serving Benedick
Attendants and messengers

Quotations	Spoken by
Are you good men and true?	Dogberry
But there was a star danced, and under that was I born.	Beatrice
Comparisons are odorous.	Dogberry
Disdain and scorn ride sparkling in her eyes.	Hero
Flat burglary, as ever was committed.	Dogberry
For there was never yet philosopher, that could endure the toothache patiently.	Leonato
Friendship is constant in all other things, save in the office and affairs of love.	Claudio
He hath indeed better bettered expectation.	Messenger
He is a very valiant trencherman, he has an excellent stomach.	Beatrice
He wears his faith but as the fashion of his hat.	Beatrice
I have a good eye, uncle, I can see a church by daylight.	Beatrice
I was not born under a rhyming planet.	Benedick
O that he were here to write me down an ass!	Dogberry
O, what men dare do! what men may do! what men daily do, not knowing what they do!	Claudio
Patch grief with proverbs, make misfortune drunk.	Leonato
Taming my wild heart to thy loving hand.	Beatrice
To be a well-favoured man is the gift of fortune, but to write and read comes by nature.	Dogberry
Well, everyone can master a grief but he that has it.	Benedick
What, my dear Lady Disdain! are you yet living?	Benedick
Yes, I thank God, I am as honest as any man living that is an old man and no honester than I.	Verges

Précis of plot
The central plot concerns Don John's deception whereby Claudio believes his beloved Hero unfaithful. However, the sub-plot of the relationship between Beatrice and Benedick adds the real substance to the play, and the gradual realisation of their love for each other has spawned countless works.

Setting
Messina in Sicily.

25 Othello
OTHELLO, the Moor of Venice
DESDEMONA, his wife
Michael CASSIO, his lieutenant
BIANCA, a courtesan, in love with Cassio
IAGO, the Moor's Ensign
EMILIA, Iago's wife
A CLOWN, servant of Othello
BRABANZIO, Desdemona's father, a senator

The DUKE of Venice
SENATORS of Venice
A HERALD
A MESSENGER

SHAKESPEARE

GRAZIANO, Brabanzio's brother
LODOVICO, kinsman of Brabanzio
RODERIGO, Venetian in love with Desdemona
MONTANO, Governor of Cyprus
Attendants, officers, sailors, gentlemen, musicians

Quotations

Quotations	Spoken by
A fellow almost damned in a fair wife, that never set a squadron in the field.	Iago
Alas, what ignorant sin have I committed?	Desdemona
And of the cannibals that each other eat, the Anthropophagi, and men whose heads do grow beneath their shoulders.	Othello
Be sure thou prove my love a whore. Be sure of it. Give me the ocular proof.	Othello
But I will wear my heart upon my sleeve, for daws to peck at.	Iago
But men are men, the best sometimes forgot.	Iago
But this denoted a foregone conclusion.	Othello
Excellent wretch! Perdition catch my soul.	Othello
He hath a daily beauty in his life that makes me ugly.	Iago
He that is robbed, not wanting what is stol'n, let him not know it and he's not robbed at all.	Othello
How poor are they that ha' not patience! what wound did ever heal but by degrees?	Iago
I am not merry, but I do beguile.	Desdemona
I do perceive here a divided duty.	Desdemona
If she be black, and thereto have a wit; she'll find a white that shall her blackness fit.	Iago
I have very poor and unhappy brains for drinking, I could well wish courtesy would invent some other custom of entertainment.	Cassio
I would have him nine years a-killing. A fine woman, a fair woman, a sweet woman.	Othello
Keep up your bright swords, for the dew will rust 'em.	Othello
My story being done, she gave me for my pains a world of kisses.	Othello
No hinge, nor loop to hang a doubt on.	Othello
O beware, my lord, of jealousy; it is the green-eyed monster which doth mock the meat it feeds on.	Iago
O God, that men should put an enemy in their mouths to steal away their brains.	Cassio
O most lame and impotent conclusion.	Desdemona
On horror's head horrors accumulate.	Othello
Potations pottle-deep.	Iago
Pride, pomp and circumstance of glorious war!	Othello
Reputation, reputation, reputation! O, I have lost my reputation! I have lost the immortal part of myself, and what remains is bestial.	Cassio
Silence that dreadful bell – It frights the isle from her propriety.	Othello
Take note, take note, O world, to be direct and honest is not safe.	Iago
Then must you speak of one that loved not wisely but too well.	Othello
'Tis neither here nor there.	Emilia
To mourn a mischief that is past and gone, is the next way to draw new mischief on.	Duke of Venice
To suckle fools, and chronicle small beer.	Iago
Your daughter and the Moor are now making the beast with two backs.	Iago
You are one of those that will not serve God, if the devil bids you.	Iago

Précis of plot

The story of a Moorish commander deluded by his ensign into believing that his young wife has been unfaithful to him with another soldier. By subtle innuendo and apparent physical proof, Iago convinces Othello that Desdemona has slept with Cassio, his lieutenant; his deceit results in tragedy.

Setting

Venice and Cyprus circa 1570.

26 Pericles, Prince of Tyre

John GOWER, the Presenter
ANTIOCHUS, King of Antioch
His DAUGHTER
PERICLES, Prince of Tyre
MARINA, Pericles' daughter
CLEON, governor of Tarsus
DIONIZA, his wife
LEONINE, a murderer
CERIMON, a physician of Ephesus
PHILEMON, his servant
KING SIMONIDES of Pentapolis
THAISA, his daughter
Three FISHERMEN, his subjects
Five PRINCES, suitors of Thaisa
LYSIMACHUS, Governor of Mytilene
Lords, ladies, pages, messengers, sailors and gentlemen

THALIART, a villain
HELICANUS
AESCHINES
A MARSHAL
LICHORIDA, Thaisa's nurse
A BAWD
A PANDER
BOULT, a leno
DIANA, Goddess of chastity

Quotations

Quotations	Spoken by
Master, I marvel how the fishes live in the sea.	Third Fisherman
Why, as men do a-land; the great ones eat up the little ones.	First Fisherman (reply)
O you gods! why do you make us love your goodly gifts and snatch them straight away?	Pericles
See where she comes, apparell'd like the spring!	Pericles
'Tis time to fear when tyrants seem to kiss.	Pericles

Précis of plot

Pericles, Prince of Tyre, flees from the court of the King of Antioch after solving a riddle that incriminates the King in an incestuous relationship with his daughter. The play chronicles the ensuing travels of Pericles and culminates in his reunion with his long lost daughter, Marina.

Setting

Antioch, Tyre, Tarsus, Pentapolis, Ephesus, Mitylene.

27 Richard II

KING RICHARD II	Followers of King Richard:
The QUEEN, his wife	GREEN
JOHN OF GAUNT, Duke of Lancaster, Richard's uncle	BAGOT
Harry BOLINGBROKE, his son, later HENRY IV	BUSHY
DUCHESS OF GLOUCESTER	
Duke of YORK, King Richard's uncle	Lord BERKELEY
DUCHESS OF YORK	Lord FITZWATER
Duke of AUMERLE, their son	Duke of SURREY
Thomas MOWBRAY, Duke of Norfolk	Lord WILLOUGHBY
	ABBOT OF WESTMINSTER
Of Bolingbroke's party:	Sir Piers EXTON
Percy, Earl of NORTHUMBERLAND	LORD MARSHAL
HARRY PERCY, his son	HERALDS
Lord ROSS	CAPTAIN of the Welsh army
Of King Richard's party:	LADIES attending the Queen
Earl of SALISBURY	GARDENER
BISHOP OF CARLISLE	Gardener's MEN
Sir Stephen SCROPE	Exton's MEN
	Lords, soldiers, attendants
KEEPER of the prison at Pomfret	
GROOM of King Richard's stable	

Quotations

Quotations	Spoken by
A jewel in a ten-times barred-up chest is a bold spirit in a loyal breast	Mowbray
Can sick men play so nicely with their names?	King Richard
For God's sake let us sit upon the ground, and tell sad stories of the death of kings: how some have been deposed; some slain in war; some haunted by the ghost they have deposed; some poisoned by their wives; some sleeping kill'd; all murder'd.	King Richard
How long a time lies in one little word!	Bolingbroke
Methinks I am a prophet new-inspired.	John of Gaunt
Mount, mount, my soul; thy seat is up on high, whilst my gross flesh sinks downward, here to die.	Richard (last words)
Not all the water in the rude rough sea, can wash the balm from an anointed king.	King Richard
O call back yesterday, bid time return.	Salisbury
Of comfort no man speak. Let's talk of graves, of worms and epitaphs.	King Richard
Peace shall go sleep with Turks and infidels.	Bishop of Carlisle
That which in mean men we entitle patience is pale cold cowardice in noble breasts.	Duchess of Gloucester
The daintiest last, to make the end most sweet.	Bolingbroke
Things sweet to taste prove in digestion sour.	John of Gaunt
This must my comfort be: the sun that warms you here shall shine on me.	Bolingbroke
This royal throne of kings, this sceptred isle, this earth of majesty, this seat of Mars, this other Eden, demi-paradise, this fortress built by nature for herself against infection and the hand of war, this happy breed of men, this little world, this precious stone set in the silver sea, which serves it in the office of a wall, or as a moat defensive to a house against the envy of less happier lands; this blessed plot, this earth, this realm, this England.	John of Gaunt
Truth hath a quiet breast.	Mowbray
We were not born to sue, but to command.	King Richard
You may my glories and my state depose, but not my griefs; still am I king of those.	Richard

Précis of plot

This tragical history play centres around the time of Richard's enforced abdication. The substance of the play is historically accurate, although elements of fiction do exist to some degree, for example, the murder of Richard by Sir Piers Exton.

Setting

England and Wales at the turn of the 15th century.

28 Richard III

KING EDWARD IV	Sir James BLUNT
DUCHESS OF YORK, his mother	Sir Walter HERBERT
PRINCE EDWARD, Edward IV's son	Duke of BUCKINGHAM
Richard, the young Duke of YORK, Edward IV's son	Duke of NORFOLK
George, Duke of CLARENCE	Sir Richard RATCLIFF
RICHARD, Duke of Gloucester, later KING RICHARD	Sir William CATESBY
Clarence's SON	Sir James TIRREL
Clarence's DAUGHTER	Two MURDERERS
QUEEN ELIZABETH, King Edward's wife	A PAGE
Anthony Woodville, Earl RIVERS, her brother	CARDINAL
Marquis of DORSET, her son	Bishop of ELY
Lord GRAY, her son	John, a PRIEST
Sir Thomas VAUGHAN	CHRISTOPHER, a priest
GHOST OF KING HENRY the Sixth	Earl of OXFORD
QUEEN MARGARET, his widow	Lord MAYOR of London
GHOST OF PRINCE EDWARD, his son	A SCRIVENER
LADY ANNE, Prince Edward's widow	Hastings, a PURSUIVANT
William, LORD HASTINGS, Lord Chamberlain	SHERIFF
Lord STANLEY, Earl of Derby, his friend	Aldermen and citizens
HENRY EARL OF RICHMOND, later KING HENRY VII	Attendants, two bishops,
Sir Robert BRACKENBURY, Lieutenant of the Tower	messengers and soldiers

Quotations

	Spoken by
A horse, a horse, my kingdom for a horse!	King Richard
And thus I clothe my naked villainy, with odd old ends stol'n forth of holy writ, and seem a saint, when I most play the devil.	Richard Gloucester
But soft, here come my executioners.	Richard Gloucester
High-reaching Buckingham grows circumspect.	King Richard
Now is the winter of our discontent, made glorious summer by this son of York.	Richard Gloucester
O coward conscience, how dost thou afflict me?	King Richard
Slave, I have set my life upon a cast, and I will stand the hazard of the die. I think there be six Richmonds in the field. Five have I slain today, instead of him. A horse, a horse, my kingdom for a horse.	King Richard (last words)
So wise so young, they say, do never live long.	Richard Gloucester
Their lips were four red roses on a stalk, and in their summer beauty kissed each other.	Tyrrell
Was ever woman in this humour wooed? Was ever woman in this humour won?	Richard Gloucester

Précis of plot

In this play, Shakespeare demonstrates a more complete artistic control of his historical material than in its predecessors, and historical events are freely manipulated in the interests of an overriding design. The play chronicles the period of about twelve years before Richard's reign, highlighting his bloody progress to the crown and his short two-year reign, culminating in his defeat at Bosworth.

Setting

England 1471 to 1485.

29 Romeo and Juliet

CHORUS	PETER
ROMEO	SAMSON
MONTAGUE, his father	GREGORY
MONTAGUE'S WIFE	Other SERVINGMEN
BENVOLIO, Montague's nephew	MUSICIANS
ABRAHAM, Montague's servingman	PETRUCCIO
BALTHASAR, Romeo's man	MERCUTIO
JULIET	PARIS
CAPULET, her father	PAGE to Paris
CAPULET'S WIFE	FRIAR LAURENCE
TYBALT, her nephew	FRIAR JOHN
His page	An APOTHECARY
Escalus, PRINCE of Verona	CHIEF WATCHMAN
Other CITIZENS OF THE WATCH	CAPULET'S COUSIN
Masquers, guests, gentlewomen, followers	Juliet's NURSE

Quotations

	Spoken by
A pair of star-crossed lovers take their life.	Chorus
A plague o' both your houses.	Mercutio
For you and I are past our dancing days.	Capulet
I do not bite my thumb at you sir, but I bite my thumb, sir.	Samson
Nay, I am the very pink of courtesy.	Mercutio
O happy dagger, this is thy sheath! there rust, and let me die.	Juliet (last words)

One pain is lessened by another's anguish.	Benvolio
O Romeo, Romeo, wherefore art thou Romeo.	Juliet
O then I see Queen Mab hath been with you.	Mercutio
Parting is such sweet sorrow.	Juliet
See how she leans her cheek upon her hand. O, that I were a glove upon that hand, that I might touch that cheek.	Romeo
Thus with a kiss I die.	Romeo (last words)
True, I talk of dreams, which are the children of an idle brain, begot of nothing but vain fantasy.	Mercutio
What's in a name? That which we call a rose by any other word would smell as sweet.	Juliet
When well-apparelled April on the heel of limping winter treads.	Capulet
With Rosaline, my ghostly father? No, I have forgot that name and that name's woe.	Romeo

Précis of plot
This play tells of the bitter feud between the Montagues and Capulets. Romeo, a Montague, falls in love with Juliet, a Capulet, but their love is doomed from the outset as death and tragedy befall both families.

Setting
Verona and Mantua early in the 14th century.

30 The Taming of the Shrew

In the Induction:	GREMIO, suitor of Bianca
CHRISTOPHER SLY, beggar and tinker	HORTENSIO, another suitor
A HOSTESS	TRANIO, a servant
A LORD	BIONDELLO, a servant
BARTHOLOMEW, his page	GRUMIO, a servant
HUNTSMEN, SERVANTS AND PLAYERS	CURTIS, a servant
In the play-within-the-play:	A WIDOW
BAPTISTA Minola, a gentleman of Padua	A TAILOR
KATHERINE, his elder daughter	A HABERDASHER
BIANCA, his younger daughter	An OFFICER
PETRUCHIO, a gentleman of Verona, suitor of Katherine	NATHANIEL, a servingman
VINCENTIO, Lucentio's father	PHILIP, a servingman
A PEDANT, schoolmaster from Mantua	JOSEPH, a servingman
Other servants of Baptista and Petruchio	PETER, a servingman
LUCENTIO, disguised as Cambio, a teacher	

Quotations
	Spoken by
And as the sun breaks through the darkest clouds, so honour peereth in the meanest habit.	Petruccio
A woman moved is like a fountain troubled, muddy, ill seeming, thick, bereft of beauty.	Katherine
No profit grows where is no pleasure ta'en.	Tranio
This is a way to kill a wife with kindness.	Petruccio

Précis of plot
The play has three main strands. The first shows how a drunken tinker, Christopher Sly, is made to believe himself a lord for whose entertainment a play is to be presented. The second strand is the central plot of the play performed for Sly, in which the shrewish Katherine is wooed, won, and tamed by the fortune-hunting Petruchio. The third strand involves Lucentio, Gremio, and Hortensio, all of them suitors for the hand of Katherine's sister, Bianca.

Setting
Padua and Petruchio's house circa 14th century.

31 The Tempest

PROSPERO, the rightful Duke of Milan	The MASTER of a ship
MIRANDA, his daughter	BOATSWAIN
ANTONIO, his brother, the usurping Duke of Milan	MARINERS
ALONSO, King of Naples	SPIRITS
SEBASTIAN, his brother	*The Masque*
FERDINAND, Alonso's son	Spirits appearing as:
GONZALO, an honest old counsellor of Naples	IRIS
ADRIAN, a Lord	CERES
FRANCISCO, a Lord	JUNO
ARIEL, an airy spirit attendant upon Prospero	Nymphs and reapers
CALIBAN, a savage and deformed native, who is also Prospero's slave	
TRINCULO, Alonso's jester	
STEFANO, Alonso's drunken butler	

Quotations
	Spoken by
A very ancient and fish-like smell.	Trinculo
Be not afeard. The isle is full of noises, sounds and sweet airs, that give delight and hurt not.	Caliban

S
H
A
K
E
S
P
E
A
R
E

Fie, what a spendthrift is he of his tongue!	Antonio
Full fathom five thy father lies. Of his bones are coral made.	Ariel (sung)
He that dies pays all debts.	Stefano
How beauteous mankind is! O brave new world, that has such people in't!	Miranda
In the dark backward and abyss of time?	Prospero
Knowing I loved my books, he furnished me from mine own library with volumes that	Prospero
I prize above my dukedom.	
Misery acquaints a man with strange bedfellows.	Trinculo
My library was dukedom large enough.	Prospero
They'll take suggestions as a cat laps milk.	Antonio
We are such stuff as dreams are made on, and our little life is rounded with a sleep.	Prospero
Where the bee sucks, there suck I.	Ariel
You taught me language, and my profit on't is I know how to curse.	Caliban

Précis of plot

The central plot of *The Tempest* is one of witchcraft and connivance. The action takes place on an island after a shipwreck, as Prospero explains to his daughter, Miranda, how they came to the island, some twelve years earlier, and how the shipwreck has brought his enemies, Alonso, King of Naples, and Prospero's own brother, Antonio, face to face with their wrongdoings. The action takes place within a few hours, as in *The Comedy of Errors*.

Setting

A small island off the coast of Tunis.

32 Timon of Athens

TIMON of Athens	FOOL
LUCILIUS, a servant	PAGE
An OLD ATHENIAN	CAPHIS
LORDS and SENATORS of Athens	ISIDORE'S SERVANT
VENTIDIUS, one of Timon's false friends	POET
ALCIBIADES, an Athenian Captain	PAINTER
APEMANTUS, a churlish philosopher	JEWELLER
One dressed as CUPID in the Masque	MERCHANT
LADIES dressed as Amazons in the Masque	Mercer
FLAVIUS, Timon's steward	LUCULLUS' SERVANT
FLAMINIUS, a servant	LUCIUS' SERVANT
SERVILIUS, a servant	TITUS' SERVANT
Other SERVANTS of Timon	HORTENSIUS' SERVANT
LUCULLUS, a flattering Lord	PHILOTUS' SERVANT
LUCIUS, a flattering Lord	PHRYNIA, a whore
SEMPRONIUS, a flatterring Lord	TIMANDRA, a whore
Three STRANGERS, one called Hostilius	The banditti, THIEVES
SOLDIER of Alcibiades' army	
Two of VARRO'S SERVANTS	
Messengers, attendants, soldiers	

Quotations	Spoken by
I wonder men dare trust themselves with men.	Apemantus
'Tis not enough to help the feeble up, but to support him after.	Timon

Précis of plot

Timon is a misanthrope because his friends flattered and sponged on him in prosperity but abandoned him in poverty. Timon finds gold once more and his friends return.

Setting

Athens and neighbouring woods.

33 Titus Andronicus

SATURNINUS, later Emperor	CAPTAIN
BASSIANUS, his brother	AEMILIUS
TITUS ANDRONICUS, general against the Goths	Sons of Titus:
SEMPRONIUS, kinsman of Titus	LUCIUS
VALENTINE, kinsman of Titus	QUINTUS
TAMORA, Queen of the Goths, wife of Saturninus	MARTIUS
Her sons:	MUTIUS
ALARBUS	
DEMETRIUS	
CHIRON	NURSE
AARON, a Moor, her lover	CLOWN
LAVINIA, daughter of Titus	
YOUNG LUCIUS, a boy, son of Lucius	
MARCUS ANDRONICUS, a tribune, Titus' brother	

PUBLIUS, his son
Senators, tribunes, Romans, Goths, soldiers and attendants

Quotations

	Spoken by
She is a woman, therefore may be wooed; she is a woman, therefore may be won; she is Lavinia, therefore must be loved.	Demetrius
Sweet mercy is nobility's true badge.	Tamora

Précis of plot

Tamora, Queen of the Goths, seeks revenge on her captor, Titus, for the ritual slaughter of her son, Alarbus; she achieves it when her other sons, Chiron and Demetrius, rape and mutilate Titus' daughter, Lavinia. Later, Titus himself seeks revenge on Tamora and her husband Saturninus, after Tamora's black lover, Aaron, has falsely led him to believe that he can save his sons' lives by allowing his own hand to be chopped off. Though he is driven to madness, Titus, with his brother Marcus and his last surviving son, Lucius, achieves a spectacular sequence of vengeance in which he cuts Tamora's sons' throats, serves their flesh baked in a pie to their mother, kills Lavinia to save her from her shame, and stabs Tamora to death. Then in rapid succession, Saturninus kills Titus and is himself killed by Lucius, who, as the new Emperor, is left with Marcus to bury the dead, to punish Aaron, and to 'heal' Rome.

Setting

Rome 4th century AD.

34 Troilus and Cressida

HELEN, wife of Menelaus, now living with Paris
ALEXANDER, servant of Cressida
Servants of Troilus, musicians
soldiers and attendants
Greeks:
AGAMEMNON, Commander-in-Chief
MENELAUS, his brother
NESTOR
ULYSSES
ACHILLES
PATROCLUS, his companion
DIOMEDES
AJAX
THERSITES
MYRMIDONS, soldiers of Achilles
Servants of Diomedes, soldiers
CASSANDRA, Priam's daughter, a prophetess
ANDROMACHE, wife of Hector
AENEAS, a commander
ANTENOR, a commander
PANDARUS, a Lord
CRESSIDA, his niece
CALCHAS, her father, who has joined the Greeks

PROLOGUE
Trojans:
PRIAM, King of Troy
His sons:
HECTOR
DEIPHOBUS
HELENUS, a priest
PARIS
TROILUS
MARGARETON, a bastard

Quotations

	Spoken by
For to be wise and love exceeds man's might.	Cressida
I am giddy. Expectation whirls me round. The imaginary relish is so sweet, that it enchants my sense.	Troilus
I have had my labour for my travail.	Pandarus
One touch of nature makes the whole world kin.	Ulysses
The baby figure of the giant mass of things to come at large.	Nestor
Welcome ever smiles, and farewell goes out sighing.	Ulysses

Précis of plot

The war between Greece and Troy has been provoked by the abduction of the Greek, Helen, by the Trojan hero Paris, son of King Priam. Shakespeare's play opens when the Greek forces, led by Menelaus' brother Agamemnon, have already been besieging Troy for seven years. Shakespeare concentrates on the opposition between the Greek hero Achilles and the Trojan Hector. Shakespeare also shows how the war, caused by one love affair, destroys another. The story of the love between the Trojan, Troilus, and the Grecian, Cressida, encouraged by her uncle Pandarus, and of Cressida's desertion of Troilus for the Greek Diomedes.

Setting

Troy and the Greek camp during the Trojan War.

35 Twelfth Night

ORSINO, Duke of Illyria
VALENTINE, attending Orsino
CURIO, attending Orsino
VIOLA, a lady, later disguised as Cesario

SIR ANDREW AGUECHEEK
MALVOLIO, Olivia's steward
FABIAN, a member of Olivia's household
FESTE, the clown, her jester
FIRST OFFICER

SHAKESPEARE

SEBASTIAN, her twin brother
ANTONIO, a sea-captain
OLIVIA, a Countess
MARIA, her waiting-gentlewoman
SIR TOBY BELCH, Olivia's kinsman

SECOND OFFICER
CAPTAIN
PRIEST
SERVANT of Olivia
Musicians, sailors, lords, attendants

Quotations

	Spoken by
Be not afraid of greatness. Some are born great, some achieve greatness, and some have greatness thrust upon 'em.	Malvolio
Cressida was a beggar.	Feste
Farewell, fair cruelty.	Viola
He does it with a better grace, but I do it more natural.	Sir Andrew
He plays o'th' viol-de-gamboys, and speaks three or four languages word for word without book.	Sir Toby
I am a great eater of beef, and I believe that does harm to my wit.	Sir Andrew
I am all the daughters of my father's house, and all the brothers too.	Viola
I am sure care's an enemy to life.	Sir Toby
If music be the food of love, play on.	Orsino
Is it a world to hide virtues in?	Sir Toby
Love sought is good, but given unsought, is better.	Olivia
Many a good hanging prevents a bad marriage.	Feste
My purpose is indeed a horse of that colour.	Maria
No more cakes and ale.	Sir Toby
Not to be a-bed after midnight is to be up betimes.	Sir Toby
O world, how apt the poor are to be proud!	Olivia
Still you keep o'th' windy side of the law.	Fabian
What is the opinion of Pythagoras concerning wildfowl?	Feste
Wherefore are these things hid?	Sir Toby
Why, this is very midsummer madness.	Olivia

Précis of plot

The main plot is of a shipwrecked girl, Viola, who, disguised as a boy, Cesario, serves a young Duke, Orsino, and undertakes love-errands on his behalf to a noble lady, Olivia, who falls in love with her but mistakenly betrothes herself to her twin brother Sebastian.

Setting

Illyria.

36 The Two Gentlemen of Verona

DUKE of Milan
SILVIA, his daughter
PROTEUS, a gentleman of Verona
LANCE, his clownish servant
VALENTINE, a gentleman of Verona
SPEED, his clownish servant
THURIO, a foolish rival to Valentine
EGLAMOUR, agent for Silvia in her escape

ANTONIO, father of Proteus
PANTHINO, his servant
JULIA, beloved of Proteus
LUCETTA, her waiting-woman
HOST, where Julia lodges
OUTLAWS
Servants and musicians

Quotations

	Spoken by
How use doth breed a habit in a man!	Valentine
I have no other but a woman's reason, I think him so because I think him so.	Lucetta
O heaven, were man but constant, he were perfect.	Proteus
Who is Silvia? What is she, that all our swains commend her?	Host (sung)

Précis of plot

This play tells of the friendship of Valentine and Proteus and the strain their relationship is put under when they both fall in love with Silvia, the daughter of the Duke of Milan.

Setting

Verona, Milan, and Mantua.

37 The Two Noble Kinsmen

THESEUS, Duke of Athens
HIPPOLYTA, Queen of the Amazons
EMILIA, her sister
PIRITHOUS, friend of Theseus
PALAMON, a noble kinsman
ARCITE, a noble kinsman
Hymen, God of marriage
ARTESIUS, an Athenian soldier
Three QUEENS, widows of kings killed in Thebes
VALERIUS, a Theban

PROLOGUE
A SERVANT
A BOY, who sings
A HERALD
MESSENGERS
A DOCTOR
EPILOGUE

WOMAN, attending Emilia
An Athenian GENTLEMAN
Six KNIGHTS, attending Arcite and Palamon
A JAILER, in charge of Theseus' prison
The WOOER of the jailer's daughter
Two FRIENDS of the jailer
Six COUNTRYMEN, one dressed as a baboon
GERALD, a schoolmaster
NELL, a country wench
Four other country wenches:
Fritz, Madeleine, Luce and Barbara
Timothy, a TABORER

Quotations   **Spoken by**
New plays and maidenheads are near akin.   Prologue
Your grief is written on your cheek.   Emilia

Précis of plot
This play is based on Chaucer's Knight's Tale, on which Shakespeare had already drawn for episodes of *A Midsummer Night's Dream*. It tells of the conflicting claims of love and friendship between Palamon and Arcite, the Two Noble Kinsmen of the title, who, as in *The Two Gentlemen of Verona*, both fall in love with the same woman, but unlike the earlier play, decide to fight for their love. The play is sometimes not listed as a Shakespearian play, as there is a body of thought that believes it to be, at best, a collaboration with John Fletcher; unlike *Henry VIII*, their other joint work, it was not listed in the 1623 folio of Shakespeare's works.

Setting
Athens.

38 The Winter's Tale

LEONTES, King of Sicily	A JAILER
HERMIONE, his wife	A MARINER
MAMILLIUS, his son	CAMILLO, a Lord
PERDITA, his daughter	ANTIGONUS, a Lord
POLIXENES, King of Bohemia	CLEOMENES, a Lord
FLORIZEL, his son, in love with Perdita, aka Doricles	DION, a Lord
ARCHIDAMUS, a Bohemian Lord	CLOWN, his son
AUTOLYCUS, a rogue, once in the service of Florizel	
PAULINA, Antigonus's wife	Other shepherds and shepherdesses
EMILIA, a lady attending on Hermione	Twelve countrymen disguised as satyrs
MOPSA, a shepherdess	Other Lords and gentlemen, ladies,
DORCAS, a shepherdess	Officers and servants at Leontes' court
SERVANT of the old shepherd	TIME, as chorus

Quotations   **Spoken by**
A sad tale's best for winter.   Mamillius
A snapper up of unconsidered trifles.   Autolycus
Exit, pursued by a bear.   Stage direction
For you there's rosemary and rue.   Perdita
Good sooth, she is the queen of curds and cream.   Camillo
I would there were no age between ten and three-and twenty, or that youth would   Old Shepherd
sleep out the rest; for there is nothing in the between but getting wenches with child,
wronging the ancientry, stealing, fighting.
Jog on, jog on, the footpath way.   Autolycus (sung)
Lawn as white as driven snow.   Autolycus (sung)
Let me have no lying. It becomes none but tradesmen.   Autolycus
We were as twinned lambs that did frisk i' th' sun, and bleat the one at th' other.   Polixenes
When daffodils begin to peer.   Autolycus (sung)

Précis of plot
The improbable tale of King Leontes' suspicions of his wife's adultery with King Polixenes, his childhood friend. Leontes expels his new-born daughter, Perdita, thinking her the fruit of this unholy alliance, and she is brought up as a shepherdess. Perdita falls in love with Florizel, son of Polixenes, her supposed father, but she is eventually re-united with her true father.

Setting
Sicily and Bohemia circa 14th century.

S
H
A
K
E
S
P
E
A
R
E

Chronology of Shakespeare's Plays

1589–92	*Henry VI* Parts 1, 2, and 3
1592–93	*Richard III, The Comedy of Errors*
1593–94	*Titus Andronicus, The Taming of the Shrew*
1594–95	*The Two Gentlemen of Verona, Love's Labour's Lost, Romeo and Juliet*
1595–96	*Richard II, A Midsummer Night's Dream*
1596–97	*King John, The Merchant of Venice*
1597–98	*Henry IV* Parts 1 and 2
1598–99	*Much Ado About Nothing, Henry V*
1599–1600	*Julius Caesar, As You Like It*
1600–01	*Hamlet, The Merry Wives of Windsor*
1601–02	*Twelfth Night, Troilus and Cressida*
1602–03	*All's Well That Ends Well*
1604–05	*Measure for Measure, Othello*
1605–06	*King Lear, Macbeth*
1606–07	*Antony and Cleopatra*
1607–08	*Coriolanus, Timon of Athens*
1608–09	*Pericles*
1609–10	*Cymbeline*
1610–11	*The Winter's Tale*
1611–12	*The Tempest*
1612–13	*Henry VIII, The Two Noble Kinsmen*

Other Works

1592–93	*Venus and Adonis* (narrative poem)
1593–94	*The Rape of Lucrece* (narrative poem)
1593–1600	*Sonnets* (154 in total)
1600–01	*The Phoenix and the Turtle* (67-line elegy)
1609 circa	*A Lover's Complaint* (329-line poem)
	Various poems (attributed)

Original Titles

Henry VI Part 2 – *The First Part of the Contention*
Henry VI Part 3 – *Richard Duke of York*
Henry VIII – *All Is True*

Full Titles

Cymbeline, King of Britain
Hamlet, Prince of Denmark
Othello, the Moor of Venice
Pericles, Prince of Tyre
Twelfth Night, or What You Will

NB Shakespeare is generally credited with having penned 37 plays, but it can be argued that this figure could perhaps be just as easily 36, or 38, depending on the treatment given to the final two works, *Henry VIII* and *The Two Noble Kinsmen*. These plays are thought to be collaborations between Shakespeare and John Fletcher, although only *Henry VIII* appears in the First Folio of 1623. Therefore, when one is asked which was the last play Shakespeare wrote, it is true to say that it would be impossible to give an unqualified answer unless the question is very specific. The last play wholly credited to Shakespeare is *The Tempest*; the last play cited in the First Folio is *Henry VIII*; and the last play that Shakespeare wrote ignoring these two provisos is *The Two Noble Kinsmen*. The author of this work was asked this question by Anne Robinson on *The Weakest Link* and she was not impressed when I informed her there were three possible answers. I referred her to my book but was quickly voted off.

It should also be noted that as well as doubts as to the degree of Shakespeare's involvement in one or two of the plays, there are also doubts as to their chronological order. There is evidence to suggest, for instance, that Shakespeare's first play was probably not *Henry VI* Part 1, but, *Henry VI* Part 2. However, an answer of *Henry VI* would seem to be the most equitable solution to this one.

Films Based on Shakespearian Works

A Thousand Acres – 1997	based on *King Lear* directed by Jocelyn Moorhouse
All Night Long – 1961	based on *Othello* directed by Basil Dearden
An Honourable Murder – 1959	based on *Julius Caesar* directed by Godfrey Grayson
Chimes at Midnight – 1966	based on *Henry V* directed by Orson Welles
Forbidden Planet – 1956	based on *The Tempest* directed by Fred M Wilcox
Kiss Me Kate – 1953	musical based on *The Taming of the Shrew* directed by George Sidney
Looking for Richard – 1996	based on *Richard III* directed by Al Pacino
Men of Respect – 1990	based on *Macbeth* directed by William Reilly
My Own Private Idaho – 1991	based on *Henry IV* directed by Gus Van Sant
Prospero's Books – 1991	based on *The Tempest* directed by Peter Greenaway
Ran – 1985	Japanese version of *King Lear* three sons cast instead of three daughters written and directed by Akira Kurosawa

Rosencrantz and Guildenstern Are Dead – 1990	based on *Hamlet*
	written and directed by Tom Stoppard
The Boys from Syracuse – 1940	musical based on *The Comedy of Errors*
	directed by Edward A Sutherland
Throne of Blood – 1957	Japanese version of *Macbeth*
	directed by Akira Kurosawa
West Side Story – 1961	based on *Romeo and Juliet*
	directed by Robert Wise

NB The list above includes only films that do not specifically mention the title of the Shakespeare work: e.g. *Joe Macbeth* is a gangster film that follows a very similar plot to *Men of Respect* but includes a reference to *Macbeth* in the title. There are many films that allude to characters in Shakespeare but do not follow the plot closely enough to be included here. The Orson Welles film *Chimes at Midnight* is sometimes called *Falstaff*.

General Information

As You Like It	seven ages of man: 1) infant; 2) schoolboy; 3) lover; 4) soldier; 5) justice; 6) old age; 7) second childhood.
born	23 April 1564 in Stratford-upon-Avon. This may or may not be the actual date, but St George's Day seemed apt.
children	three: Susanna, Judith and Hamnet. Susanna born 1582, and twins Hamnet and Judith born 1585. Hamnet died in 1596, aged 11½. Susanna married Dr John Hall and Judith married Thomas Quiney. Shakespeare's line ended in 1670 with the death of Elizabeth, Susanna's daughter.
christened	26 April 1564 at Holy Trinity Church, Stratford-upon-Avon.
chronicler	Francis Meres' *Palladis Tamia* listed Shakespeare's works up to 1598.
collaborators	John Fletcher and various others.
death	23 April 1616 in Stratford-upon-Avon. Shakespeare therefore, traditionally, died on his birthday, aged 52. There are no names on Shakespeare's gravestone, but these words:
	Good friend, for Jesus' sake forbear
	To dig the dust enclosed here.
	Blest be the man that spares these stones,
	And curst be he that moves my bones.
	Shakespeare's family erected a monument in Holy Trinity church, Stratford, 1623.
dedicatee	Henry Wriothesley, the 3rd Earl of Southampton, had the narrative poems *Venus and Adonis* and *The Rape of Lucrece* dedicated to him.
Falstaff, Sir John	based on Sir John Oldcastle, the Protestant martyr. Shakespeare was forced to change the name from Oldcastle to Falstaff after complaints from relatives. *Henry IV* Part 1 is here quoted using the original name. The original names of Sir John's associates Bardolph and Peto have also been listed in *Henry IV* Part 1 in their original form, i.e. Russell and Harvey.
father	John Shakespeare, a glover, wool dealer, and sometime Mayor; died 1601.
First Folio	John Heminges and Henry Condell produced First Folio 1623.
first play	*Henry VI* (see notes at end of plays).
great tragedy	the 'four great tragedies' are often listed as *Hamlet*, *King Lear*, *Macbeth*, and *Othello*.
home	bought 'New Place' Stratford in 1597 Bishopsgate, and also lived with a French Huguenot family called Mountjoy for a short while during 1604, at Cripplegate.
July: takes place in	*Romeo and Juliet*.
kin	William was one of eight children of which he was the third child and first son. Only three brothers and a sister survived infancy. William's brother Edmund was also an actor.
last play	*The Tempest*, *Henry VIII*, or *The Two Noble Kinsmen* (see notes at end of plays).
lines: most	Hamlet has the most lines spoken by any one character in a single play but is only third on the overall list if one takes into consideration other plays that a character may appear in. Richard III has more lines taking into account his appearances in *Henry VI*, but the most lines are spoken by Sir John Falstaff, if one considers that Shakespeare's folio of 1623 had by then changed the name of Sir John Oldcastle in *Henry IV* Part 1.
longest play	this can be contentious due to disputed passages, but taking the 1623 folio as the basis of the question, then *Hamlet* is longest followed by *Richard III*.
married	Anne Hathaway, a farmer's daughter, from Shottery, near Stratford, 28 November 1582. He was 18, she 26 and pregnant. Anne died in 1623.
mother	Mary Arden, from Wilmcote, Warwickshire; died in 1609.
portraits	Martin Droeshout's engraving of Shakespeare, first published on the title-page of the First Folio 1623, is one of only two likenesses of Shakespeare; the other is the bust of Shakespeare in his monument, designed by Gheerart Janssen. It is unclear whether these are true likenesses, as it was common practice of many artists to use stencils, and it is thought possible that Droeshout may have used a common stencil of the day, possibly that of Elizabeth I.
shortest play	given the criteria used for deciding the longest play, the shortest play is clearly *The Comedy of Errors*.
sobriquet	the Sweet Swan of Avon, coined by Ben Jonson.
sonnets	published in 1609 by Thomas Thorpe, and dedicated to 'Mr W.H.' The sonnets pertain to a

S
H
A
K
E
S
P
E
A
R
E

young man, a dark lady, and a rival poet. Sonnets 1 to 17 exhort a young man to marry; Sonnets 1 to 126 are all about a young man; Sonnets 127 to 154 are about the dark lady; Sonnet 126 is not in sonnet form, as it has only 12 lines.

theatres   Globe was built in 1599 on Bankside, south of the Thames. James Burbage founded the Lord Chamberlain's Company within the Globe and his son Richard Burbage was the principal actor. Shakespeare bought an interest in the Globe, and also a half share in the Blackfriars Theatre, in 1608, and from then on Shakespeare produced winter plays at the Blackfriars and summer plays at the Globe. The Lord Chamberlain's Men became the King's Men on James I's accession. Opposition to the King's Men came mainly from Edward Alleyne's 'Admiral's Men'. John Fletcher became chief dramatist of the King's Men after Shakespeare. Will Kempe was the leading comedy actor of the King's Men. Richard Tarleton was the leading comedy actor of the rival Admiral's Men. Forerunners of the Lord Chamberlain's Men were the Queen's Men. The Chamberlain's Men first performed at the 'Theatre', in Shoreditch, and then at the 'Curtain'. The Globe caught fire and was destroyed in 1613 during performance of *Henry VIII*.

First and Last Lines of Shakespeare's Plays

(C = Comedy   H = History   T = Tragedy)

Play	First line	Spoken by
C **All's Well That Ends Well**	In delivering my son from me I bury a second husband.	Dowager Countess of Roussillon
T **Antony and Cleopatra**	Nay, but this dotage of our General's o'erflows the measure.	Philo
C **As You Like It**	As I remember, Adam, it was upon this fashion.	Orlando
C **The Comedy of Errors**	Proceed, Solinus, to procure my fall.	Egeon
T **Coriolanus**	Before we proceed any further, hear me speak.	first Citizen
C **Cymbeline, King of Britain**	You do not meet a man but frowns.	first Gentleman
T **Hamlet**	Who's there?	Barnardo
H **Henry IV Part 1**	So shaken as we are, so wan with care.	King Henry IV
H **Henry IV Part 2**	Open your ears; for which of you will stop.	Rumour
H **Henry V**	O for a muse of fire.	Chorus (as Prologue)
H **Henry VI Part 1**	Hung be the heavens with black!	Bedford
H **Henry VI Part 2**	As by your high imperial majesty.	Suffolk
H **Henry VI Part 3**	I wonder how the King escaped our hands.	Warwick
H **Henry VIII (All Is True)**	I come no more to make you laugh.	Prologue
T **Julius Caesar**	Hence, home, you idle creatures, get you home.	Flavius
H **King John**	Now say, Châtillon, what would France with us?	King John
T **King Lear**	I thought the King had more affected the Duke of Albany than Cornwall.	Earl of Kent
C **Love's Labour's Lost**	Let fame, that all hunt after in their lives.	King Ferdinand
T **Macbeth**	When shall we three meet again? In thunder, lightning, or in rain?	First Witch
C **Measure for Measure**	Escalus.	Vincentio, Duke of Vienna
C **The Merchant of Venice**	In sooth, I know not why I am so sad.	Antonio
C **The Merry Wives of Windsor**	Sir Hugh, persuade me not. I will make a Star Chamber matter of it.	Shallow
C **A Midsummer Night's Dream**	Now, fair Hippolyta, our nuptial hour draws on apace.	Theseus
C **Much Ado About Nothing**	I learn in this letter that Don Pedro of Aragon comes this night to Messina.	Leonato
T **Othello**	Tush, never tell me!	Roderigo
C **Pericles, Prince of Tyre**	To sing a song that old was sung.	Gower, as Chorus
H **Richard II**	Old John of Gaunt, time-honoured Lancaster.	King Richard II
H **Richard III**	Now is the winter of our discontent.	Richard Gloucester
T **Romeo and Juliet**	Two households, both alike in dignity in fair Verona.	Chorus (as Prologue)
C **The Taming of the Shrew**	I'll feeze you, in faith.	Christopher Sly
C **The Tempest**	Boatswain!	Master of a ship
T **Timon of Athens**	Good day, sir.	Poet
T **Titus Andronicus**	Noble patricians, patrons of my right.	Saturninus
C **Troilus and Cressida**	In Troy there lies the scene. From isles of Greece.	Prologue
C **Twelfth Night**	If music be the food of love, play on.	Orsino
C **The Two Gentlemen of Verona**	Cease to persuade, my loving Proteus.	Valentine
C **The Two Noble Kinsmen**	New plays and maidenheads are near akin.	Prologue
C **The Winter's Tale**	If you shall chance, Camillo, to visit Bohemia.	Archidamus

Play	Last line	Spoken by
C **All's Well That Ends Well**	The bitter past, more welcome is the sweet.	The King of France (N.B. Epilogue follows)
T **Antony and Cleopatra**	High order in this great solemnity.	Octavius Caesar

Play	Last line	Spoken by
C **As You Like it**	Proceed, proceed. We'll so begin these rites as we do trust they'll end, in true delights.	Duke Senior (N.B. Epilogue follows)
C **The Comedy of Errors**	And now let's go hand in hand, not one before another.	Dromio of Ephesus
T **Coriolanus**	Yet he shall have a noble memory. Assist.	Aufidius
C **Cymbeline, King of Britain**	Ere bloody hands were washed, with such a peace.	Cymbeline
T **Hamlet**	Go, bid the soldiers shoot.	Fortinbras
H **Henry IV Part 1**	Let us not leave till all our own be won.	King Henry IV
H **Henry IV Part 2**	Come, will you hence?	Prince John (N.B. Epilogue follows)
H **Henry V**	And may our oaths well kept and prosp'rous be.	King Harry (N.B. Epilogue follows)
H **Henry VI Part 1**	But I will rule both her, the King, and realm.	Suffolk
H **Henry VI Part 2**	And more such days as these to us befall!	Warwick
H **Henry VI Part 3**	For here, I hope, begins our lasting joy.	King Edward IV
H **Henry VIII (All Is True)**	This little one shall make it holiday.	King Henry VIII (nb Epilogue follows)
T **Julius Caesar**	To part the glories of this happy day.	Octavius
H **King John**	If England to itself do rest but true.	Philip the Bastard
T **King Lear**	Shall never see so much, nor live so long.	Edgar
C **Love's Labour's Lost**	The words of Mercury are harsh after the songs of Apollo. You that way, we this way.	Armado
T **Macbeth**	Whom we invite to see us crowned at Scone.	Malcolm
C **Measure for Measure**	What's yet behind that's meet you all should know.	Vincentio, Duke of Vienna
C **The Merchant of Venice**	Well, while I live I'll fear no other thing so sore as keeping safe Nerissa's ring.	Graziano
C **The Merry Wives of Windsor**	For he tonight shall lie with Mistress Ford.	Master Ford
C **A Midsummer Night's Dream**	Meet me all by break of day.	Oberon (N.B. Epilogue follows)
C **Much Ado About Nothing**	Think not on him till tomorrow, I'll devise thee brave punishments for him. Strike up, pipers.	Benedick
T **Othello**	This heavy act with heavy heart relate.	Lodovico
C **Pericles, Prince of Tyre**	New joy wait on you. Here our play has ending.	Gower
H **Richard II**	In weeping after this untimely bier.	King Henry IV
H **Richard III**	That she may long live here, God say 'Amen'.	King Henry VII
T **Romeo and Juliet**	For never was a story of more woe than this of Juliet and her Romeo.	Escalus
C **The Taming of the Shrew,**	'Tis a wonder, by your leave, she will be tamed so.	Lucentio
C **The Tempest**	Please you, draw near.	Prospero (N.B. Epilogue follows)
T **Timon of Athens**	Let our drums strike.	Alcibiades
T **Titus Andronicus**	And being dead, let birds on her take pity.	Lucius
C **Troilus and Cressida**	Hope of revenge shall hide our inward woe.	Troilus
C **Twelfth Night**	And we'll strive to please you every day.	Feste
C **The Two Gentlemen of Verona**	One feast, one house, one mutual happiness.	Valentine
C **The Two Noble Kinsmen**	And bear us like the time.	Theseus (N.B. Epilogue follows)
C **The Winter's Tale**	We were dissevered. Hastily lead away.	Leontes

Shakespearian Characters

Character	Play	Character	Play
AARON, a Moor	*Titus Andronicus*	AESCHINES	*Pericles, Prince of Tyre*
ABERGAVENNY, Lord	*Henry VIII*	AGAMEMNON, commander in chief	*Troilus and Cressida*
ABHORSON, an executioner	*Measure for Measure*		
ABRAHAM, Montague's servingman	*Romeo and Juliet*	AGRIPPA	*Antony and Cleopatra*
		AGUECHEEK, Sir Andrew	*Twelfth Night*
ACHILLES	*Troilus and Cressida*	AJAX	*Troilus and Cressida*
ADAM, a former servant of Sir Rowland	*As You Like It*	ALARBUS, son of Tamora	*Titus Andronicus*
		ALBANY, Duke of, Goneril's husband	*King Lear*
ADRIAN, a Lord	*The Tempest*		
ADRIAN, a Roman	*Coriolanus*	ALCIBIADES, an Athenian Captain	*Timon of Athens*
ADRIANA	*The Comedy of Errors*		
AEDILES	*Coriolanus*	ALENÇON, Duke of	*Henry VI Part 1*
AEMILIUS	*Titus Andronicus*	ALEXANDER, servant of Cressida	*Troilus and Cressida*
AENEAS, a commander	*Troilus and Cressida*		

S
H
A
K
E
S
P
E
A
R
E

Character	Play	Character	Play
ALEXAS	Antony and Cleopatra	BARNARDINE	Measure for Measure
ALICE, an old gentlewoman	Henry V	BARNARDO	Hamlet
ALONSO, King of Naples	The Tempest	BARTHOLOMEW, a page	The Taming of the Shrew
AMIENS, Lord attending on Duke Senior	As You Like It		
		BASSANIO	The Merchant of Venice
ANDROMACHE, wife of Hector	Troilus and Cressida	BASSET	Henry VI Part 1
		BASSIANUS, Saturninus' brother	Titus Andronicus
ANGELO, a goldsmith	The Comedy of Errors	BASTARD of Orleans	Henry VI Part 1
ANGELO, appointed Vincentio's deputy	Measure for Measure	BATES, John	Henry V
ANGUS, a Thane	Macbeth	BAWD	Pericles, Prince of Tyre
ANNE, Lady	Richard III	BEADLE of Saint Albans	Henry VI Part 2
ANTENOR, a commander	Troilus and Cressida	BEATRICE, an orphan	Much Ado About Nothing
ANTIGONUS, a Lord	The Winter's Tale		
ANTIOCHUS, King of Antioch	Pericles, Prince of Tyre	BEAUFORT, Cardinal Bishop of Winchester	Henry VI Part 2
ANTIPHOLUS OF EPHESUS	The Comedy of Errors	BEDFORD, Duke of, regent of France	Henry VI Part 1
ANTIPHOLUS OF SYRACUSE	The Comedy of Errors	BELARIUS, a banished Lord	Cymbeline, King of Britain
ANTONIO, a merchant of Venice	The Merchant of Venice	BELCH, Sir Toby, Olivia's kinsman	Twelfth Night
ANTONIO, a sea-captain	Twelfth Night	BENEDICK, of Padua	Much Ado About Nothing
ANTONIO, an old man	Much Ado About Nothing		
		BENVOLIO, Montague's nephew	Romeo and Juliet
ANTONIO, father of Proteus	The Two Gentlemen of Verona	BERKELEY, Lord	Richard II
ANTONIO, Prospero's brother	The Tempest	BERRI, Duke of	Henry V
		BIANCA, a courtesan	Othello
ANTONY, Mark	Antony and Cleopatra, Julius Caesar	BIANCA, Baptista's youngest daughter	The Taming of the Shrew
APEMANTUS, a churlish philosopher	Timon of Athens	BIGOT, Lord	King John
		BIONDELLO, a servant	The Taming of the Shrew
APOTHECARY	Romeo and Juliet		
ARAGON, Prince of	The Merchant of Venice	BIRON	Love's Labour's Lost
ARCHBISHOP of York, Scrope	Henry IV Parts 1 and 2	BLANCHE, Lady, of Spain	King John
		BLUNT, Sir James	Richard III
ARCHIDAMUS, a Bohemian Lord	The Winter's Tale	BLUNT, Sir Walter	Henry IV Part 1
		BOATSWAIN	The Tempest
ARCITE, a noble kinsman	The Two Noble Kinsmen	BOLEYN, Anne	Henry VIII
ARIEL, an airy spirit	The Tempest	BOLINGBROKE, Harry, Duke of Hereford	Richard II
ARMADO, Don Adriano de	Love's Labour's Lost		
ARTEMIDORUS	Julius Caesar	BOLINGBROKE, Roger, a conjurer	Henry VI Part 2
ARTESIUS, an Athenian soldier	The Two Noble Kinsmen		
		BONA, Lady	Henry VI Part 3
ARTHUR, Duke of Brittaine	King John	BORACHIO, follower of Don John	Much Ado About Nothing
ARVIRAGUS	Cymbeline, King of Britain		
		BOTTOM, a weaver	A Midsummer Night's Dream
ASNATH, a spirit	Henry VI Part 2		
AUDREY, a goatherd	As You Like It	BOULT	Pericles, Prince of Tyre
AUFIDIUS, General	Coriolanus	BOURBON, Duke of	Henry V
AUMERLE, Duke of	Richard II	BOY who sings	Antony and Cleopatra
AUSTRIA (Limoges), Duke of	King John	BOY who sings	The Two Noble Kinsmen
		BOY, attendant on Mariana	Measure for Measure
AUSTRINGER	All's Well That Ends Well	BOY, formerly Falstaff's page	Henry V
AUTOLYCUS, a rogue	The Winter's Tale	BOY, serving Benedick	Much Ado About Nothing
BAGOT	Richard II		
BALTHASAR, a merchant	The Comedy of Errors	BOYET	Love's Labour's Lost
BALTHASAR, a singer	Much Ado About Nothing	BRABANZIO, a senator of Venice	Othello
BALTHASAR, Portia's servant	The Merchant of Venice	BRACKENBURY, Sir Robert	Richard III
		BRANDON	Henry VIII
BALTHASAR, Romeo's man	Romeo and Juliet	BRUTUS, Marcus, a noble Roman	Julius Caesar
BANDITTI, thieves	Timon of Athens		
BANQUO, a Scottish Thane	Macbeth	BRUTUS, tribune	Coriolanus
BAPTISTA MINOLA	The Taming of the Shrew	BUCKINGHAM, Duke of	Henry VIII
		BUCKINGHAM, Duke of	Henry VI Part 2 and Richard III
BARDOLPH	Henry IV Part 2 and Henry V		
		BULLCALF, Peter	Henry IV Part 2
	The Merry Wives of Windsor	BURGUNDY, Duke of	Henry V and Henry VI Part I

Character	Play
BURGUNDY, Duke of	King Lear
BUSHY	Richard II
BUTTS, the King's physician	Henry VIII
CADE, Jack	Henry VI Part 2
CAITHNESS, a Thane	Macbeth
CAIUS, a French physician	The Merry Wives of Windsor
CALCHAS, Cressida's father	Troilus and Cressida
CALIBAN, a deformed savage	The Tempest
CALPURNIA	Julius Caesar
CAMBRIDGE, Richard, Earl of	Henry V
CAMIDIUS	Antony and Cleopatra
CAMILLO, a Lord	The Winter's Tale
CANTERBURY, Archbishop of	Henry V
CANTERBURY, Archbishop of	Henry VIII
CAPHIS	Timon of Athens
CAPTAIN	King Lear
CAPTAIN	Titus Andronicus
CAPTAIN	Twelfth Night
CAPTAIN in Duncan's army	Macbeth
CAPTAIN of a ship	Henry VI Part 2
CAPTAIN of the Welsh army	Richard II
CAPULET'S COUSIN	Romeo and Juliet
CAPULET'S WIFE	Romeo and Juliet
CAPULET, Juliet's father	Romeo and Juliet
CAPUTIUS, Lord	Henry VIII
CARDINAL	Richard III
CARDINAL CAMPEIUS	Henry VIII
CARDINAL WOLSEY	Henry VIII
CARLISLE, Bishop of	Richard II
CARPENTER	Julius Caesar
CARRIERS	Henry IV Part 1
CASCA	Julius Caesar
CASSANDRA, a prophetess	Troilus and Cressida
CASSIO, Michael, a Lieutenant	Othello
CASSIUS	Julius Caesar
CATESBY, Sir William	Richard III
CATHERINE	Henry V
CELIA, later disguised as Aliena	As You Like It
CERES, a spirit	The Tempest
CERIMON, a physician of Ephesus	Pericles, Prince of Tyre
CHAMBERLAIN	Henry IV Part 1
CHARLES, Dauphin of France	Henry VI Part 1
CHARLES, Duke Frederick's wrestler	As You Like It
CHARMIAN	Antony and Cleopatra
CHÂTILLON, an ambassador	King John
CHIEF WATCHMAN	Romeo and Juliet
CHILDREN of WINDSOR	The Merry Wives of Windsor
CHIRON, son of Tamora	Titus Andronicus
CHRISTOPHER, a priest	Richard III
CICERO, a senator	Julius Caesar
CINNA the conspirator	Julius Caesar
CINNA the poet	Julius Caesar
CITIZENS OF THE WATCH	Romeo and Juliet
CLARENCE, Duke of	Henry V
CLARENCE, Duke of	Richard III
CLAUDIO	Julius Caesar
CLAUDIO, a young gentleman	Measure for Measure

Character	Play
CLAUDIO, of Florence	Much Ado About Nothing
CLEOMENES, a Lord	The Winter's Tale
CLEON, Governor of Tarsus	Pericles, Prince of Tyre
CLEOPATRA, Queen of Egypt	Antony and Cleopatra
CLIFFORD, Lord	Henry VI Part 3
CLIFFORD, Old Lord	Henry VI Part 2
CLIFFORD, the younger	Henry VI Part 2
CLITUS	Julius Caesar
CLOTEN, the Queens' son	Cymbeline, King of Britain
CLOWN	Antony and Cleopatra
CLOWN	Titus Andronicus
CLOWN, Autolycus' son	The Winter's Tale
CLOWN, servant of Othello	Othello
CLOWNS	Hamlet
COBBLER	Julius Caesar
COBHAM, Dame Eleanor	Henry VI Part 2
COBWEB	A Midsummer Night's Dream
COLEVILLE, Sir John	Henry IV Part 2
COMINIUS, a General	Coriolanus
CONRAD	Much Ado About Nothing
CONSTABLE of France	Henry V
CONSTANCE, Lady	King John
CORDELIA	King Lear
CORIN, an old shepherd	As You Like It
CORIOLANUS	Coriolanus
CORNELIUS	Hamlet
CORNELIUS, a physician	Cymbeline, King of Britain
CORNWALL, Duke of	King Lear
COSTARD, a Clown	Love's Labour's Lost
COUNTESS of Auvergne	Henry VI Part 1
COURT, Alexander	Henry V
COURTESAN	The Comedy of Errors
CRANMER, Archbishop of Canterbury	Henry VIII
CRESSIDA, Pandarus' niece	Troilus and Cressida
CRIER	Henry VIII
CROMWELL, Thomas	Henry VIII
CUPID	Timon of Athens
CURIO, attending Orsino	Twelfth Night
CURTIS, a servant	The Taming of the Shrew
CYMBELINE, King of Britain	Cymbeline, King of Britain
DARDANIUS	Julius Caesar
DAUPHIN, of France	Henry V
DAVY, Shallow's servant	Henry IV Part 2
DE LA POLE, William	Henry VI Part 2
DECIUS BRUTUS	Julius Caesar
DECRETAS	Antony and Cleopatra
DEIPHOBUS, son of Priam	Troilus and Cressida
DEMETRIUS	A Midsummer Night's Dream
DEMETRIUS	Antony and Cleopatra
DEMETRIUS	Titus Andronicus
DENIS, Oliver's servant	As You Like It
DENNY, Sir Anthony	Henry VIII
DESDEMONA	Othello
DIANA	All's Well That Ends Well
DIANA, Goddess of chastity	Pericles, Prince of Tyre
DICK the BUTCHER	Henry VI Part 2
DIOMED	Antony and Cleopatra
DIOMEDES	Troilus and Cressida
DION, a Lord	The Winter's Tale
DIONIZA, wife of Cleon	Pericles, Prince of Tyre

Character	Play
DOCTOR to Lady Macbeth	Macbeth
DOCTOR, an Englishman	Macbeth
DOGBERRY, the constable	Much Ado About Nothing
DOLABELLA	Antony and Cleopatra
DOLL TEARSHEET, a whore	Henry IV Part 2
DONALBAIN	Macbeth
DON JOHN	Much Ado About Nothing
DON PEDRO, Prince of Aragon	Much Ado About Nothing
DOOR-KEEPER	Henry VIII
DORCAS, a shepherdess	The Winter's Tale
DORSET, Marchioness of	Henry VIII
DORSET, Marquis of	Henry VIII
DORSET, Marquis of	Richard III
DOUGLAS, Earl of	Henry IV Part 1
DROMIO OF EPHESUS	The Comedy of Errors
DROMIO OF SYRACUSE	The Comedy of Errors
DULL, Anthony, a constable	Love's Labour's Lost
DUMAINE	Love's Labour's Lost
DUNCAN, King of Scotland	Macbeth
DUTCHMAN	Cymbeline, King of Britain
EDGAR, aka Tom o' Bedlam	King Lear
EDMOND	King Lear
EDWARD IV, King	Richard III
EDWARD, Earl of March	Henry VI Parts 2 and 3
EGEON, merchant of Syracuse	The Comedy of Errors
EGEUS, father of Hermia	A Midsummer Night's Dream
EGLAMOUR	The Two Gentlemen of Verona
EGYPTIAN	Antony and Cleopatra
ELBOW, a simple constable	Measure for Measure
ELIZABETH, Princess	Henry VIII
ELY, Bishop of	Henry V
ELY, Bishop of	Henry VIII
ELY, Bishop of	Richard III
EMILIA	The Two Noble Kinsmen
EMILIA, a lady	The Winter's Tale
EMILIA, an abbess	The Comedy of Errors
EMILIA, Iago's wife	Othello
EMMANUEL, Clerk of Chatham	Henry VI Part 2
ENOBARBUS, Domitius	Antony and Cleopatra
EROS	Antony and Cleopatra
ERPINGHAM, Sir Thomas	Henry V
ESCALUS, an old Lord	Measure for Measure
ESCALUS, Prince of Verona	Romeo and Juliet
ESSEX, Earl of	King John
EVANS, Sir Hugh, a Welsh parson	The Merry Wives of Windsor
EXETER, Duke of	Henry V
EXETER, Duke of	Henry VI Part 1
EXETER, Duke of	Henry VI Part 3
EXTON, Sir Piers	Richard III
FABIAN	Twelfth Night
FALCONBRIDGE, Lady	King John
FALCONBRIDGE, Robert	King John
FALSTAFF, Sir John	Henry IV Part 2
	The Merry Wives of Windsor
FANG, a sergeant	Henry IV Part 2
FASTOLF, Sir John	Henry VI Part 1
FEEBLE, Francis	Henry IV Part 2
FENTON, Master	The Merry Wives of Windsor
FERDINAND	The Tempest
FERDINAND, King of Navarre	Love's Labour's Lost
FESTE, the clown	Twelfth Night
FILARIO	Cymbeline, King of Britain
FIRST LORD DUMAINE	All's Well That Ends Well
FIRST OFFICER	Twelfth Night
FITZWATER, Lord	Richard II
FIVE PRINCES	Pericles, Prince of Tyre
FLAMINIUS, a servant	Timon of Athens
FLAVIUS	Timon of Athens
FLAVIUS, a tribune	Julius Caesar
FLEANCE	Macbeth
FLORENCE, Duke of	All's Well That Ends Well
FLORIZEL, aka Doricles	The Winter's Tale
FLUELLEN, Captain, a Welshman	Henry V
FLUTE, a bellows-mender	A Midsummer Night's Dream
FOOL	King Lear
FOOL	Timon of Athens
FORD, Master Frank	The Merry Wives of Windsor
FORD, Mistress Alice	The Merry Wives of Windsor
FORESTER	Love's Labour's Lost
FORTINBRAS, Prince of Norway	Hamlet
FRANCESCA, a nun	Measure for Measure
FRANCIS, a drawer	Henry IV Part 1
FRANCISCO	Hamlet
FRANCISCO, a Lord	The Tempest
FREDERICK, Duke	As You Like It
FRENCHMAN	Cymbeline, King of Britain
FRIAR FRANCIS	Much Ado About Nothing
FRIAR JOHN	Romeo and Juliet
FRIAR LAURENCE	Romeo and Juliet
FRIAR PETER	Measure for Measure
FROTH	Measure for Measure
GADSHILL	Henry IV Part 1
GALLUS	Antony and Cleopatra
GARDENER	Richard II
GARDINER, later Bishop of Winchester	Henry VIII
GARGRAVE, Sir Thomas	Henry VI Part 1
GARTER King of Arms	Henry VIII
GENERAL of French garrison	Henry VI Part 1
GEORGE, Duke of Clarence	Richard III
GEORGE, later Duke of Gloucester	Henry VI Part 3
GERALD, a schoolmaster	The Two Noble Kinsmen
GERTRUDE, Queen of Denmark	Hamlet
GHOST of Caesar	Julius Caesar
GHOST of Hamlet	Hamlet
GHOST of King Henry VI	Richard III
GHOST of Mother of Posthumus	Cymbeline, King of Britain
GHOST of Prince Edward	Richard III
GHOST of Sicilius Leonatus	Cymbeline, King of Britain
GHOSTS of brothers of Posthumus	Cymbeline, King of Britain
GIACOMO, an Italian	Cymbeline, King of Britain
GLASDALE, Sir William	Henry VI Part 1
GLOUCESTER, Duchess of	Richard II

Character	Play
GLOUCESTER, Duke Humphrey of	Henry VI Part 2
GLOUCESTER, Duke of	Henry V
GLOUCESTER, Duke of	Henry VI Part 1
GLOUCESTER, Earl of	King Lear
GLOUCESTER, Humphrey, Duke of	Henry IV Part 2
GOBBO	The Merchant of Venice
GONERIL	King Lear
GONZALO	The Tempest
GOODFELLOW, Robin, a puck	A Midsummer Night's Dream
GOUGH, Matthew	Henry VI Part 2
GOVERNOR of Harfleur	Henry V
GOWER, a messenger	Henry IV Part 2
GOWER, Captain, an Englishman	Henry V
GOWER, John, the Presenter	Pericles, Prince of Tyre
GRANDPRÉ, Lord	Henry V
GRAY, Lady	Henry VI Part 3
GRAY, Lord	Richard III
GRAZIANO	Othello
GRAZIANO	The Merchant of Venice
GREEN	Richard II
GREGORY	Romeo and Juliet
GREMIO	The Taming of the Shrew
GREY, Sir Thomas	Henry V
GRIFFITH, a gentleman usher	Henry VIII
GROOM of King Richard's stable	Richard II
GRUMIO, a servant	The Taming of the Shrew
GUIDERIUS, known as Polydore	Cymbeline, King of Britain
GUILDENSTERN	Hamlet
GUILDFORD, Sir Henry	Henry VIII
GURNEY, James	King John
HABERDASHER	The Taming of the Shrew
HAMLET, Prince	Hamlet
HARCOURT	Henry IV Part 2
HARVEY	Henry IV Part 1
HASTINGS, a pursuivant	Richard III
HASTINGS, Lord	Henry IV Part 2
HASTINGS, Lord	Henry VI Part 3
HECATE, Queen of Witches	Macbeth
HECTOR	Troilus and Cressida
HELEN	Cymbeline, King of Britain
HELEN	Troilus and Cressida
HELEN, an orphan	All's Well That Ends Well
HELENA	A Midsummer Night's Dream
HELENUS, a priest	Troilus and Cressida
HELICANUS	Pericles, Prince of Tyre
HENRY IV, King	Henry IV Parts 1 and 2
HENRY V, King	Henry V
HENRY VI, King	Henry VI Parts 1, 2 and 3
HENRY VIII, King	Henry VIII
HENRY, Earl of Richmond	Richard III
HENRY, Lord Scrope of Masham	Henry V
HERBERT, Sir Walter	Richard III
HERMIA	A Midsummer Night's Dream
HERMIONE	The Winter's Tale
HERO	Much Ado About Nothing
HIPPOLYTA, Queen of the Amazons	A Midsummer Night's Dream
HIPPOLYTA, Queen of the Amazons	The Two Noble Kinsmen
HOLOFERNES, a schoolmaster	Love's Labour's Lost
HORATIO	Hamlet
HORNER, Thomas, an armourer	Henry VI Part 2
HORTENSIO, a teacher	The Taming of the Shrew
HORTENSIUS' SERVANT	Timon of Athens
HOST of the Garter Inn	The Merry Wives of Windsor
HOST, where Julia lodges	The Two Gentlemen of Verona
HOSTESS, formerly Mistress Quickly	Henry V
HOTSPUR, Henry Percy	Henry IV Part 1
HUBERT	King John
HUME, Sir John, a priest	Henry VI Part 2
HUNTSMAN	Henry VI Part 3
HYMEN, God of marriage	The Two Noble Kinsmen
HYMEN, God of marriage	As You Like It
IAGO, the Moor's ensign	Othello
IDEN, Alexander	Henry VI Part 2
INNOGEN, Princess	Cymbeline, King of Britain
INTERPRETER, a French soldier	All's Well That Ends Well
IRAS	Antony and Cleopatra
IRIS, a spirit	The Tempest
ISABEL	Henry V
ISABELLA	Measure for Measure
ISIDORE'S SERVANT	Timon of Athens
JAILER	The Two Noble Kinsmen
JAILER'S BROTHER	The Two Noble Kinsmen
JAILER'S DAUGHTER	The Two Noble Kinsmen
JAMY, Captain, a Scot	Henry V
JAQUENETTA, a country wench	Love's Labour's Lost
JAQUES, Lord	As You Like It
JESSICA	The Merchant of Venice
JEWELLER	Timon of Athens
JOAN la Pucelle	Henry VI Part 1
JOHN	Henry VI Part 2
JOHN OF GAUNT, Duke of Lancaster	Richard II
JOHN OF LANCASTER	Henry IV Part 1
JOHN, a priest	Richard III
JOHN, a servant	The Merry Wives of Windsor
JOHN, King of England	King John
JOSEPH, a servingman	The Taming of the Shrew
JULIA	The Two Gentlemen of Verona
JULIET	Measure for Measure
JULIET	Romeo and Juliet
JULIUS CAESAR	Julius Caesar
JUNO, a spirit	The Tempest
JUPITER	Cymbeline, King of Britain
JUSTICE	Measure for Measure
KATE	Henry IV Part 2
KATE, Lady Percy	Henry IV Part 1
KATHERINE	Love's Labour's Lost
KATHERINE	The Taming of the Shrew

S
H
A
K
E
S
P
E
A
R
E

Character	Play	Character	Play
KEEPER of the prison	Richard II	MACDUFF, Thane of Fife	Macbeth
KENT, Earl of	King Lear	MACDUFF'S SON	Macbeth
KING CHARLES VI of France	Henry V	MACMORRIS, Captain	Henry V
		MAECENAS	Antony and Cleopatra
KING CLAUDIUS	Hamlet	MALCOLM, King	Macbeth
KING of France	All's Well That Ends Well	MALVOLIO, Olivia's steward	Twelfth Night
KING of France	King Lear	MAMILLIUS	The Winter's Tale
KING PHILIP of France	King John	MARCELLUS	Hamlet
KING SIMONIDES of Pentapolis	Pericles, Prince of Tyre	MARCUS ANDRONICUS, a tribune	Titus Andronicus
LAERTES	Hamlet	MARDIAN, a eunuch	Antony and Cleopatra
LAFEU, an old lord	All's Well That Ends Well	MARGARET	Henry VI Part 1
LANCE	The Two Gentlemen of Verona	MARGARET	Much Ado About Nothing
LANCELOT, a clown	The Merchant of Venice	MARGARETON, a bastard	Troilus and Cressida
LARTIUS, a General	Coriolanus	MARIA	Love's Labour's Lost
LAVATCH, a clown	All's Well That Ends Well	MARIA, a waiting-gentlewoman	Twelfth Night
LAVINIA	Titus Andronicus		
LEAR, King of Britain	King Lear	MARIANA	All's Well That Ends Well
LE BEAU	As You Like It	MARIANA	Measure for Measure
LEGATE	Henry VI Part 1	MARINA	Pericles, Prince of Tyre
LENNOX, a Thane	Macbeth	MARINER	The Winter's Tale
LEONARDO	The Merchant of Venice	MARSHAL	Pericles, Prince of Tyre
LEONATO, governor of Messina	Much Ado About Nothing	MARTEXT, Sir Oliver, a clergyman	As You Like It
		MARTIUS	Titus Andronicus
LEONINE, a murderer	Pericles, Prince of Tyre	MASTER of a ship	Henry VI Part 2
LEONTES, King of Sicily	The Winter's Tale	MASTER of a ship	The Tempest
LEPIDUS	Antony and Cleopatra, Julius Caesar	MASTER GUNNER of Orleans	Henry VI Part 1
LICHORIDA, Thaisa's nurse	Pericles, Prince of Tyre	MATE of a ship	Henry VI Part 2
LIEUTENANT of the Tower	Henry VI Part 3	MAYOR of London	Henry VI Part 1
LIGARIUS	Julius Caesar	MAYOR of Saint Albans	Henry VI Part 2
LINCOLN, Bishop of	Henry VIII	MAYOR of York	Henry VI Part 3
LODOVICO	Othello	MELUN, Count	King John
LONGUEVILLE	Love's Labour's Lost	MENAN	Antony and Cleopatra
LORD CHAMBERLAIN	Henry VIII	MENECRATES	Antony and Cleopatra
LORD CHANCELLOR	Henry VIII	MENELAUS	Troilus and Cressida
LORD CHIEF JUSTICE	Henry IV Part 2	MENENIUS Agrippa	Coriolanus
LORD MARSHAL	Richard II	MENTEITH, a Thane	Macbeth
LORD MAYOR OF LONDON	Henry VIII	MERCADE, a messenger	Love's Labour's Lost
LORD MAYOR OF LONDON	Richard III	MERCHANT OF EPHESUS	The Comedy of Errors
LORENZO	The Merchant of Venice	MERCUTIO	Romeo and Juliet
LOUIS THE DAUPHIN	King John	MESSALA	Julius Caesar
LOUIS, King	Henry VI Part 3	METELLUS CIMBER	Julius Caesar
LOVELL, Sir Thomas	Henry VIII	MICHAEL, Sir	Henry IV Part 1
LUCENTIO, from Pisa	The Taming of the Shrew	MILAN, Duke of	The Two Gentlemen of Verona
LUCETTA, a waiting-woman	The Two Gentlemen of Verona	MIRANDA	The Tempest
LUCIANA	The Comedy of Errors	MONTAGUE, Marquis of	Henry VI Part 3
LUCILIUS, a servant	Timon of Athens	MONTAGUE, Romeo's father	Romeo and Juliet
LUCILLIUS	Julius Caesar		
LUCIO, 'a fantastic'	Measure for Measure	MONTAGUE'S WIFE	Romeo and Juliet
LUCIUS	Titus Andronicus	MONTANO, Governor of Cyprus	Othello
LUCIUS, a flattering Lord	Timon of Athens		
LUCIUS, a servant	Julius Caesar	MONTGOMERY, Sir John	Henry VI Part 3
LUCIUS, an ambassador	Cymbeline, King of Britain	MONTJOY, the French Herald	Henry V
LUCIUS' SERVANT	Timon of Athens	MOPSA, a shepherdess	The Winter's Tale
LUCULLUS, a flattering Lord	Timon of Athens	MOROCCO, Prince of	The Merchant of Venice
		MORTIMER, aka Earl of March	Henry IV Part 1
LUCULLUS' SERVANT	Timon of Athens	MORTIMER, Edmund	Henry VI Part 1
LUCY, Sir William	Henry VI Part 1	MORTIMER, Lady	Henry IV Part 1
LYSANDER	A Midsummer Night's Dream	MORTIMER, Sir Hugh	Henry VI Part 3
		MORTIMER, Sir John	Henry VI Part 3
LYSIMACHUS, Governor of Mytilene	Pericles, Prince of Tyre	MORTON	Henry IV Part 2
MACBETH, Lady	Macbeth	MOTE	A Midsummer Night's Dream
MACBETH, Thane of Glamis	Macbeth		
		MOTE, a page	Love's Labour's Lost
MACDUFF, Lady	Macbeth	MOULDY, Ralph	Henry IV Part 2

Character	Play	Character	Play
MOWBRAY, Thomas, Duke of Norfolk	Richard II	PAROLLES	All's Well That Ends Well
MURELLUS, a tribune	Julius Caesar	PATIENCE, a waiting woman	Henry VIII
MUSTARDSEED	A Midsummer Night's Dream	PATROCLUS	Troilus and Cressida
MUTIUS	Titus Andronicus	PAULINA	The Winter's Tale
MYRMIDONS	Troilus and Cressida	PEASEBLOSSOM	A Midsummer Night's Dream
NATHANIEL, a servingman	The Taming of the Shrew	PEDANT, schoolmaster from Mantu	The Taming of the Shrew
NATHANIEL, Sir, a curate	Love's Labour's Lost	PEMBROKE, Earl of	King John
NELL, a country wench	The Two Noble Kinsmen	PERCY, Earl of Northumberland	Henry IV Parts 1 and 2
NELL, a kitchen-maid	The Comedy of Errors		
NERISSA, a waiting-gentlewoman	The Merchant of Venice	PERCY, Earl of Northumberland	Richard II
NESTOR	Troilus and Cressida	PERCY, Harry	Richard II
NICANOR, a Volscian	Coriolanus	PERDITA	The Winter's Tale
NIM	Henry V	PERICLES, Prince of Tyre	Pericles, Prince of Tyre
NIM	The Merry Wives of Windsor	PETER	Romeo and Juliet
NORFOLK, Duke of	Henry VIII	PETER, a servingman	The Taming of the Shrew
NORFOLK, Duke of	Henry VI Part 3 and Richard III	PETER OF POMFRET, a prophet	King John
NORFOLK, old Duchess of	Henry VIII	PETER THUMP	Henry VI Part 2
NORTHUMBERLAND, Earl of	Henry VI Part 3	PETO	Henry IV Part 2
NORTHUMBERLAND'S WIFE	Henry IV Part 2	PETRUCCIO	Romeo and Juliet
		PETRUCHIO, a gentleman of Verona	The Taming of the Shrew
OBERON, King of the Fairies	A Midsummer Night's Dream	PHILEMON, Cerimon's servant	Pericles, Prince of Tyre
OCTAVIA	Antony and Cleopatra	PHILIP, a servingman	The Taming of the Shrew
OCTAVIUS Caesar	Julius Caesar		
OCTAVIUS CAESAR	Antony and Cleopatra	PHILIP the BASTARD	King John
OLD ATHENIAN	Timon of Athens	PHILO	Antony and Cleopatra
OLDCASTLE, Sir John	Henry IV Part 1	PHILOTUS' SERVANT	Timon of Athens
OLD MAN	Macbeth	PHOEBE, a shepherdess	As You Like It
OLD MAN, Gloucester's tenant	King Lear	PHRYNIA, a whore	Timon of Athens
		PINCH, Doctor, a schoolmaster	The Comedy of Errors
OLIVER	As You Like It		
OLIVIA, a Countess	Twelfth Night	PINDARUS	Julius Caesar
OPHELIA	Hamlet	PIRITHOUS	The Two Noble Kinsmen
ORLANDO	As You Like It	PISANIO, a servant	Cymbeline, King of Britain
ORLÉANS, Duke of	Henry V		
ORSINO, Duke of Illyria	Twelfth Night	PISTOL, Ensign	Henry V
OSRIC	Hamlet		The Merry Wives of Windsor
OSTLER	Henry IV Part 1		
OSWALD, Goneril's steward	King Lear		Henry IV Part 2
OTHELLO, the Moor of Venice	Othello	POET	Julius Caesar
OVERDONE, Mistress, a bawd	Measure for Measure	POET	Timon of Athens
		POINS, Edward	Henry IV Parts 1 and 2
OWAIN GLYNDWR	Henry IV Part 1	POLIXENES, King of Bohemia	The Winter's Tale
OXFORD, Earl of	Henry VI Part 3 and Richard III	POLONIUS, a Lord	Hamlet
PAGE, Anna	The Merry Wives of Windsor	POMPEY (Pompeius)	Antony and Cleopatra
		POMPEY, a clownish servant	Measure for Measure
PAGE, Master George	The Merry Wives of Windsor		
		POPILIUS Laena, a senator	Julius Caesar
PAGE, Mistress Margaret	The Merry Wives of Windsor		
		PORTER	Henry IV Part 2
PAGE, William	The Merry Wives of Windsor	PORTER at Macbeth's castle	Macbeth
PAINTER	Timon of Athens		
PALAMON, a noble kinsman	The Two Noble Kinsmen	PORTER, at the christening	Henry VIII
PANDARUS, a Lord	Troilus and Cressida	PORTIA, an heiress	The Merchant of Venice
PANDER	Pericles, Prince of Tyre	PORTIA, Brutus's wife	Julius Caesar
PANDOLF, Cardinal	King John	POSTHUMUS Leonatus	Cymbeline, King of Britain
PANTHINO, a servant	The Two Gentlemen of Verona		
		PRIAM, King of Troy	Troilus and Cressida
PARIS	Romeo and Juliet	PRIEST	Hamlet
PARIS	Troilus and Cressida	PRIEST	Twelfth Night

SHAKESPEARE

Character	Play	Character	Play
PRINCE EDWARD	Henry VI Part 3 and Richard III	SCALES, Lord	Henry VI Part 2
		SCARUS	Antony and Cleopatra
PRINCE HAL	Henry IV Parts 1 and 2	SCRIVENER	Richard III
PRINCE HENRY	King John	SCROPE, Sir Stephen	Richard II
PRINCE JOHN of Lancaster	Henry IV Part 2	SEBASTIAN	The Tempest
PRINCESS of France	Love's Labour's Lost	SEBASTIAN	Twelfth Night
PROCULEIUS	Antony and Cleopatra	SECOND LORD DUMAINE	All's Well That Ends Well
PROSPERO	The Tempest	SECOND MERCHANT	The Comedy of Errors
PROTEUS, a gentleman of Verona	The Two Gentlemen of Verona	SECOND OFFICER	Twelfth Night
		SELEUCUS	Antony and Cleopatra
PROVOST	Measure for Measure	SEMPRONIUS	Titus Andronicus
PUBLIUS	Titus Andronicus	SEMPRONIUS, a flattering Lord	Timon of Athens
PUBLIUS, a senator	Julius Caesar		
QUEEN, Cymbeline's wife	Cymbeline, King of Britain	SENIOR, Duke	As You Like It
		SENTRY and men of his WATCH	Antony and Cleopatra
QUEEN, wife of Richard II	Richard II		
QUEEN ELEANOR	King John	SERGEANT	Henry VI Part 2
QUEEN ELIZABETH	Richard III	SERJEANT-AT-ARMS	Henry VIII
QUEEN KATHERINE	Henry VIII	SERVANT of Cornwall	King Lear
QUEEN MARGARET	Henry VI Parts 2 and 3	SERVANT of Olivia	Twelfth Night
QUEEN MARGARET	Richard III	SERVANT of the old shepherd	The Winter's Tale
QUICKLY, Mistress	Henry IV Parts 1 and 2		
QUICKLY, Mistress	The Merry Wives of Windsor	SERVILIUS, a servant	Timon of Athens
		SEXTON	Much Ado About Nothing
QUINCE, a carpenter	A Midsummer Night's Dream		
		SEYTON, servant of Macbeth	Macbeth
QUINTUS	Titus Andronicus		
RAMBURES, Lord	Henry V	SHADOW, Simon	Henry IV Part 2
RATCLIFF, Sir Richard	Richard III	SHALLOW, Robert, a country justice	Henry IV Part 2
REGAN	King Lear		The Merry Wives of Windsor
RENÉ, King of Naples	Henry VI Part 1		
REYNALDO, a servant	Hamlet	SHEPHERD, father of Joan	Henry VI Part 1
REYNALDO, a steward	All's Well That Ends Well	SHEPHERD	Henry IV Part 1
RICHARD II, King	Richard II	SHERIFF	King John
RICHARD PLANTAGENET	Henry VI Parts 1, 2 and 3	SHERIFF	Richard III
RICHARD, Duke of Gloucester, afterwards King Richard III	Richard III	SHYLOCK, a Jew	The Merchant of Venice
		SICINIUS Velutus, tribune	Coriolanus
		SILENCE, a country justice	Henry IV Part 2
RICHARD, the young	The Merry Wives of Windsor	SILIUS	Antony and Cleopatra
		SILVIA	The Two Gentlemen of Verona
RIVERS, LORD	Henry VI Part 3		
ROBIN, Sir John's page	The Merry Wives of Windsor	SILVIUS, a young shepherd	As You Like It
		SIMPCOX, Simon	Henry VI Part 2
ROCHESTER, Bishop of	Henry VIII	SIMPCOX'S WIFE	Henry VI Part 2
RODERIGO, a Venetian gentleman	Othello	SIMPLE, Peter, Slender's servant	The Merry Wives of Windsor
ROMEO	Romeo and Juliet	SIWARD, Earl of Northumberland	Macbeth
ROSALIND	As You Like It		
ROSALINE	Love's Labour's Lost	SIWARD, the younger	Macbeth
ROSENCRANTZ	Hamlet	SIX COUNTRYMEN	The Two Noble Kinsmen
ROSS, a Thane	Macbeth	SIX KNIGHTS	The Two Noble Kinsmen
ROSS, Lord	Richard II	SIX SPIRITS	Henry VIII
ROUSILLON, Bertram, Count of	All's Well That Ends Well	SIX WITCHES	Macbeth
		SLENDER, Master Abraham	The Merry Wives of Windsor
ROUSILLON, Countess of	All's Well That Ends Well		
RUGBY, John	The Merry Wives of Windsor	SLY, Christopher, beggar and tinker	The Taming of the Shrew
RUMOUR, the Presenter	Henry IV Part 2	SMITH the WEAVER	Henry VI Part 2
RUSSELL	Henry IV Part 1	SNARE, a sergeant	Henry IV Part 2
RUTLAND, Earl of	Henry VI Part 3	SNOUT, a tinker	A Midsummer Night's Dream
SAINT ASAPH, Bishop of	Henry VIII		
SALERIO	The Merchant of Venice	SNUG, a joiner	A Midsummer Night's Dream
SALISBURY	Henry V		
SALISBURY, Earl of	Henry VI Parts 1 and 2	SOLANIO	The Merchant of Venice
SALISBURY, Earl of	King John	SOLDIER of Alcibiades' army	Timon of Athens
SALISBURY, Earl of	Richard II		
SAMSON	Romeo and Juliet	SOLDIER who has killed his father	Henry VI Part 3
SANDS, Lord	Henry VIII		
SATURNINUS	Titus Andronicus	SOLDIER who has killed his son	Henry VI Part 3
SAWYER	Henry VI Part 2		
SAYE, Lord	Henry VI Part 2	SOLINUS, Duke of Ephesus	The Comedy of Errors

Character	Play	Character	Play
SOMERSET, Duke of	Henry VI Parts 1, 2 and 3	TREBONIUS	Julius Caesar
		TRINCULO, Alonso's jester	The Tempest
SOMERVILLE	Henry VI Part 3	TROILUS	Troilus and Cressida
SOOTHSAYER	Antony and Cleopatra	TUBAL, a Jew	The Merchant of Venice
SOOTHSAYER	Julius Caesar	TUTOR, of Rutland, a chaplain	Henry VI Part 3
SOOTHSAYER, called Philarmonus	Cymbeline, King of Britain	TWELVE COUNTRYMEN	The Winter's Tale
SOUTHWELL, John, a priest	Henry VI Part 2	TYBALT	Romeo and Juliet
		ULYSSES	Troilus and Cressida
SPANIARD	Cymbeline, King of Britain	URSULA, attendant on Hero	Much Ado About Nothing
SPEED	The Two Gentlemen of Verona	VALENTINE, a gentleman of Verona	The Two Gentlemen of Verona
SPIRIT LIKE A CAT	Macbeth	VALENTINE, attending Orsino	Twelfth Night
STAFFORD, Sir Humphrey	Henry VI Part 2		
STAFFORD'S BROTHER	Henry VI Part 2	VALENTINE, kinsman of Titus	Titus Andronicus
STANLEY, Lord, Earl of Derby	Richard III	VALERIA	Coriolanus
STANLEY, Sir John	Henry VI Part 2	VALERIUS, a Theban	The Two Noble Kinsmen
STARVELING, a tailor	A Midsummer Night's Dream	VALTEMAND	Hamlet
		VARRIUS	Antony and Cleopatra
STEFANO, Alonso's drunken butler	The Tempest	VARRIUS, a Lord	Measure for Measure
		VARRUS	Julius Caesar
STEFANO, Portia's servant	The Merchant of Venice	VAUGHAN, Sir Thomas	Richard III
STOKESLEY, Bishop of London	Henry VIII	VAUX, a messenger	Henry VI Part 2
		VAUX, Sir Nicholas	Henry VIII
STRATO	Julius Caesar	VENICE, Duke of	Othello
SUFFOLK, Duke of	Henry VIII	VENICE, Duke of	The Merchant of Venice
SUFFOLK, Earl of	Henry VI Part 1	VENTIDIUS	Antony and Cleopatra
SURREY, Duke of	Richard II	VENTIDIUS	Timon of Athens
SURREY, Earl of	Henry IV Part 2	VERGES, the Headborough	Much Ado About Nothing
SURREY, Earl of	Henry VIII		
TABORER, called Timothy	The Two Noble Kinsmen	VERNON	Henry VI Part 1
TAILOR	The Taming of the Shrew	VERNON, Sir Richard	Henry IV Part 1
		VINCENTIO, Lucentio's father	The Taming of the Shrew
TALBOT, John	Henry VI Part 1		
TAMORA, Queen of the Goths	Titus Andronicus	VINCENTIO, The Duke of Vienna	Measure for Measure
TAURUS	Antony and Cleopatra	VINTNER	Henry IV Part 1
THAISA	Pericles, Prince of Tyre	VIOLA, a lady	Twelfth Night
THALIART, a villain	Pericles, Prince of Tyre	VIRGILIA	Coriolanus
THERSITES	Troilus and Cressida	VOLUMNIA	Coriolanus
THESEUS, Duke of Athens	A Midsummer Night's Dream	VOLUMNIUS	Julius Caesar
		WAITING-GENTLEWOMAN	Macbeth
THESEUS, Duke of Athens	The Two Noble Kinsmen	WART, Thomas	Henry IV Part 2
THIDIAS	Antony and Cleopatra	WARWICK	Henry V
THOMAS, Duke of Clarence	Henry IV Part 2	WARWICK, Earl of	Henry VI Parts 1, 2 and 3
THOMAS, Lord Mowbray	Henry IV Part 2		
THREE APPARITIONS	Macbeth	WARWICK, Neville, Earl of	Henry IV Part 2
THREE FISHERMEN	Pericles, Prince of Tyre	WATCHMEN	Much Ado About Nothing
THREE MURDERERS	Macbeth		
THREE NEIGHBOURS	Henry VI Part 2	WESTMINSTER, Abbot of	Richard II
THREE PRENTICES	Henry VI Part 2	WESTMORLAND	Henry V
THREE QUEENS	The Two Noble Kinsmen	WESTMORLAND, Earl of	Henry IV Parts 1, 2 and 3
THREE STRANGERS	Timon of Athens		
THURIO	The Two Gentlemen of Verona	WHITMORE, Walter	Henry VI Part 2
		WIDOW	The Taming of the Shrew
TIMANDRA, a whore	Timon of Athens	WIDOW CAPILET	All's Well That Ends Well
TIME, as chorus	The Winter's Tale	WILLIAM, a countryman	As You Like It
TIMON of Athens	Timon of Athens	WILLIAM, Lord Hastings	Richard III
TIRREL, Sir James	Richard III	WILLIAMS, Michael	Henry V
TITANIA, Queen of the Fairies	A Midsummer Night's Dream	WILLOUGHBY, Lord	Richard II
		WINCHESTER, Bishop of	Henry VI Part 1
TITINIUS, a Roman officer	Julius Caesar	WITCH, Margery Jordan	Henry VI Part 2
TITUS ANDRONICUS	Titus Andronicus	WOMAN, attending Emilia	The Two Noble Kinsmen
TITUS' SERVANT	Timon of Athens	WOODVILLE, Anthony, Earl RIVERS	Richard III
TOUCHSTONE, a jester	As You Like It		
TRANIO, a servant	The Taming of the Shrew	WOODVILLE, Lieutenant of Tower	Henry VI Part 1
TRAVERS, Northumberland's servant	Henry IV Part 2	WOOER of the jailer's daughter	The Two Noble Kinsmen

S
H
A
K
E
S
P
E
A
R
E

Character	Play	Character	Play
WORCESTER, Earl of	Henry IV Part 1	YORK, Duke of	Richard II
YORK, Duchess of	Richard II	YOUNG CATO	Julius Caesar
YORK, Duchess of	Richard III	YOUNG LUCIUS, a boy	Titus Andronicus
YORK, Duke of	Henry V	YOUNG MARTIUS	Coriolanus
YORK, Duke of	Henry VI Part 2		

First Lines of Shakespearian Sonnets

No.

1 From fairest creatures we desire increase
2 When forty winters shall besiege thy brow
3 Look in thy glass, and tell the face thou viewest
4 Unthrifty loveliness, why dost thou spend
5 Those hours that with gentle work did frame
6 Then let not winter's ragged hand deface
7 Lo, in the orient when the gracious light
8 Music to hear, why hear'st thou music sadly?
9 Is it for fear to wet a widow's eye
10 For shame deny that thou bear'st love to any
11 As fast as thou shalt wane, so fast thou grow'st
12 When I do count the clock that tells the time
13 O that you were yourself! But, love, you are
14 Not from the stars do I my judgement pluck
15 When I consider every thing that grows
16 But wherefore do not you a mightier way
17 Who will believe my verse in time to come
18 Shall I compare thee to a summer's day?
19 Devouring time, blunt thou the lion's paws
20 A woman's face with nature's own hand painted
21 So is it not with me as with that muse
22 My glass shall not persuade me I am old
23 As an unperfect actor on the stage
24 Mine eye hath played the painter, and hath steeled
25 Let those who are in favour with their stars
26 Lord of my love, to whom in vassalage
27 Weary with toil I haste me to my bed
28 How can I then return in happy plight
29 When, in disgrace with fortune and men's eyes
30 When to the sessions of sweet silent thought
31 Thy bosom is endeared with all hearts
32 If thou survive my well-contented day
33 Full many a glorious morning have I seen
34 Why didst thou promise such a beauteous day
35 No more be grieved at that which thou hast done
36 Let me confess that we two must be twain
37 As a decrepit father takes delight
38 How can my muse want subject to invent
39 O, how thy worth with manners may I sing
40 Take all my loves, my love, yea, take them all
41 Those pretty wrongs that liberty commits
42 That thou hast her, it is not all my grief
43 When most I wink, then do mine eyes best see
44 If the dull substance of my flesh were thought
45 The other two, slight air and purging fire
46 Mine eye and heart are at a mortal war
47 Betwixt mine eye and heart a league is took
48 How careful was I when I took my way
49 Against that time – if ever that time come
50 How heavy do I journey on the way
51 Thus can my love excuse the slow offence
52 So am I as the rich whose blessed key
53 What is your substance, whereof are you made
54 O how much more doth beauty beauteous seem
55 Not marble nor the gilded monuments
56 Sweet love, renew thy force. Be it not said
57 Being your slave, what should I do but tend
58 That god forbid, that made me first your slave
59 If there be nothing new, but that which is
60 Like as the waves make towards the pebbled shore
61 Is it thy will thy image should keep open
62 Sin of self-love possesseth all mine eye
63 Against my love shall be as I am now
64 When I have seen by time's fell hand defaced
65 Since brass, nor stone, nor earth, nor boundless sea
66 Tired with all these, for restful death I cry
67 Ah, wherefore with infection should he live
68 Thus is his cheek the map of days outworn
69 Those parts of thee that the world's eye doth view
70 That thou are blamed shall not be thy defect
71 No longer mourn for me when I am dead
72 O, lest the world should task you to recite
73 That time of year thou mayst in me behold
74 But be contented when that fell arrest
75 So are you to my thoughts as food to life
76 Why is my verse so barren of new pride
77 Thy glass will show thee how thy beauties wear
78 So oft have I invoked thee for my muse
79 Whilst I alone did call upon thy aid
80 O, how I faint when I of you do write
81 Or I shall live your epitaph to make
82 I grant thou wert not married to my muse
83 I never saw that you did painting need
84 Who is it that says most which can say more
85 My tongue-tied muse in manners holds her still
86 Was it the proud full sail of his great verse
87 Farewell – thou art too dear for my possessing
88 When thou shalt be disposed to set me light
89 Say that thou didst forsake me for some fault
90 Then hate me when thou wilt, if ever, now
91 Some glory in their birth, some in their skill
92 But do thy worst to steal thyself away
93 So shall I live supposing thou art true
94 They that have power to hurt and will do none
95 How sweet and lovely dost thou make the shame
96 Some say thy fault is youth, some wantonness
97 How like a winter hath my absence been
98 From you have I been absent in the spring
99 The forward violet thus did I chide
100 Where art thou, muse, that thou forget'st so long
101 O truant muse, what shall be thy amends
102 My love is strengthened, though more weak in seeming
103 Alack, what poverty my muse brings forth
104 To me, fair friend, you never can be old
105 Let not my love be called idolatry
106 When in the chronicle of wasted time
107 Not mine own fears nor the prophetic soul
108 What's in the brain that ink may character
109 O never say that I was false of heart
110 Alas, 'tis true, I have gone here and there
111 O, for my sake do you with fortune chide
112 Your love and pity doth th'impression fill
113 Since I left you mine eye is in my mind
114 Or whether doth my mind, being crowned with you

First Lines of Sonnets: Alphabetical Order

SHAKESPEARE

SOVEREIGNS

General Information on Sovereigns of England and Great Britain

William I — Domesday Book of 1086 contained details of the land settlement of England and its purpose was to maximise the land tax yield. It received its name in the 12th century to signify that, like the day of judgement, there could be no appeal from its verdict.

Hereward the Wake ('Watchful One'), a Lincolnshire squire, raided Peterborough Abbey in 1070 as a protest against William's appointment of a Norman abbot. He took refuge on the Isle of Ely and eventually escaped through the Fens.

Bishop Odo of Bayeux was William's half-brother and it was he who commissioned the Bayeux Tapestry (embroidery).

Of William's four sons, Robert became duke of Normandy and Richard died in infancy.

William was Edward the Confessor's cousin by way of his mother Emma, who was the sister of William's grandfather, Count Richard II. Edward the Confessor was Harold II's brother-in-law by way of his marriage to Edith, Harold's sister.

William's invasion forces assembled at the mouth of the Dives river in September 1066 but adverse winds prevented a due-north sailing to the Isle of Wight, so he regrouped at St Valéry on Somme and sailed on 27 September to the south coast of England and took Pevensey and Hastings. unchallenged. Harold was victorious against Tostig and Harald Hardraade at Stamford Bridge, near York, on 25 September and met William at the Battle of Hastings on 14 October. William only had about 7,000 troops but his archers won the day and, when Harold was killed, the English gave up.

William II — William was called Rufus because of his ruddy complexion.

Malcolm III of Scotland (Malcolm Canmore, aka Great Head) became king of Scotland in 1057 on the death of Macbeth, who had killed Malcolm's father, Duncan, in 1040. He invaded England five times between 1061 and 1093 and was killed at Alnwick in Northumberland. Four of his sons succeeded him – Duncan, Edgar, Alexander and David.

Traditionally William was shot by an arrow fired by a Norman knight called Walter Tirel, although many believe that William's younger brother Henry was the instigator.

Henry I — Henry was the only English-born son of William I.

His brother Robert was paid a pension of 3,000 marks to resign his claim to the English throne and concentrate his attentions on Normandy, but in 1105–6 Henry was forced to make war against his brother's maladministration. Robert was defeated at Tinchebrai in 1106, and was kept a prisoner for life.

In 1120, Henry's only legitimate son, William, was drowned on his way from Normandy to England in what is now known as the *White Ship* disaster.

Matilda — Matilda was pledged the throne in 1127 but Stephen became king in 1135. Matilda invaded the kingdom in 1139, landed at Arundel and established a stronghold in the West Country with her half-brother Robert of Gloucester. She captured Stephen at Lincoln and pronounced herself 'Lady of the English'. Her forces were defeated September 14 1141 while besieging the royalist-held Wolvesey Castle in what is known as the 'Rout of Winchester'. Robert Earl of Gloucester was taken prisoner and exchanged for King Stephen. Matilda was never crowned and her six months' reign is often disregarded.

Stephen — Stephen usurped the crown by declaring Matilda illegitimate, as her father had remarried.

Henry II — Henry was the first Plantagenet king of England.

He systematically destroyed the adulterine (unlicensed) castles which had sprung up during the reign of his predecessor.

Henry's conflict with Thomas à Becket was over a written statement made by Henry at Clarendon, near Salisbury, on 30 January 1164 whereby he wanted the benefit of clergy to be lifted and have lay authorities try clerks taking holy orders.

The English pope, Adrian IV, gave Henry authority over the whole of Ireland.

Incited by Queen Eleanor, Prince John and Richard rebelled against Henry and their cause was espoused by the kings of France and Scotland. William the Lion of Scotland was taken prisoner at Alnwick and forced to sign the Treaty of Falaise, 1174, thereby swearing allegiance to Henry.

Henry, the first son of Henry II, died in 1183 and his second son, Geoffrey, was killed in a tournament in Paris in 1185.

Henry's mistress, the fair Rosamond, daughter of Walter Clifford, was said to have borne him two sons – William Longsword, earl of Salisbury, and Geoffrey, archbishop of York – but this is unlikely.

Henry and his two sons were known as Angevin kings, and although Plantagenet was the other name for this royal House, subsequent members are not Angevin. To confuse matters further, although Richard II was traditionally the last king of the House of Plantagenet, the Yorkist Richard III was the last of the direct line.

Henry's second son, Henry (aka FitzHenry), was crowned on 14 June 1170, to rule in association with his father, and was known as Henry III or Henry the Young King; he died of dysentery in 1183.

Richard I

Richard was given the Duchy of Aquitaine aged 11, and was enthroned as duke of Aquitaine at Poitiers in 1172.

He departed for the Holy Land to fight the third Crusade in 1190.

Richard made a truce for three years with Saladin but was captured on his way home by Duke Leopold in December 1192. He was imprisoned at the duke's castle at Durnstein on the Danube and then handed over to Henry VI of Germany. Richard was released in February 1194 after paying a ransom of nearly 150,000 marks.

Richard left Hubert Walter as virtual ruler of England while he was away.

John

John became count of Mortain on Richard's accession in 1189.

When Richard recognised his nephew, Arthur, duke of Brittany, as his heir in October 1190, John broke his oath to Richard not to enter England while he was away at the Crusades.

Richard finally accepted John as his heir in 1196.

John's first marriage to Isabella of Gloucester was dissolved on the grounds of consanguinity, both parties being great-grandchildren of Henry I. John's second marriage, to Isabella of Angoulême, was largely responsible for the loss of many French territories.

Pope Innocent III excommunicated John in November 1209 because of his refusal to accept Stephen Langton as archbishop of Canterbury.

The Barons' War of 1215–17 ensued after John sealed the Magna Carta of 15 June 1215 but did not abide by it. Magna Carta comprises a preamble and 63 clauses. The most famous clauses are (39), guaranteeing every free man security from illegal interference in his person or property, (40), which guaranteed justice to all, and (12), which stated that the king was not to levy taxes without reference to the 'common council'.

Henry III

Henry was 9 years old when he became king, so William Marshal, First Earl of Pembroke and Striguil, acted as his regent for the first three years, followed by Hubert de Burgh for the next eight years.

Henry was forced to agree to the Provisions of Oxford, 1258, which created a council of fifteen barons and formed the first judicial Parliament.

The civil war between Henry III and his barons, led by Simon de Montfort, was called the Second Baron's War (1264–7).

Edward I

Edward won great renown as a knight on the eigth, and last, Crusade of 1270 and did not return home for his coronation until 1274.

He campaigned against Llewelyn ap Gruffud, of Gwynedd, and finally forced him into submission in 1276; and after his death in 1282 the principality was formally annexed to the English Crown by the Statute of Wales, 1284.

In 1289 Edward betrothed his infant son to Margaret, the infant Queen of Scotland (Maid of Norway), in order to unite England and Scotland, but Margaret died the following year.

Edward called the 'Model Parliament' of 1295 to allay discontent at home and the following year marched north, stripped John Balliol of his crown and carried the Stone of Scone back to England.

He had a setback at Stirling Bridge in 1297, but the following year he trounced William Wallace at Falkirk.

Edward II

In 1301 Edward became the first English Prince of Wales.

His favourite was Piers Gaveston, whom he made duke of Cornwall. When Gaveston was executed in 1312, Edward chose Hugh le Despenser and his son as his new favourites, and they aided in the overthrow of Thomas, earl of Lancaster, in 1321.

Edward was defeated by Robert the Bruce at Bannockburn, 24 June 1314.

Edward's wife, Isabella, despised him and took a lover in Roger de Mortimer. In 1326 she landed on the coast of Suffolk, executed the Despensers and forced Edward to abdicate on 25 January 1327, in favour of his son. He was murdered later that year in Berkeley Castle, Gloucestershire, probably by Isabella and Roger de Mortimer. Edward III was crowned in January 1327, eight months before his father died.

Edward III

In 1328 Edward married Philippa of Hainault and two years later put Mortimer to death and banished his mother to Castle Rising.

Charles IV of France died without a son in 1328 and Edward claimed his kingdom by right of his mother, who was Charles's sister. He declared war against Philip VI in 1337, which was in effect the start of the Hundred Years War.

Accompanied by his eldest son, Edward the Black Prince, Edward had a great victory at Crécy in 1346 and another at Poitiers in 1356, where it is said the Black Prince gained his spurs.

Edward's mistress from 1366 onwards was Alice Perrers, his wife's lady-in-waiting, who let the government slip into the hands of Edward's fourth son, John of Gaunt.

The Black Prince died in 1376 and his son by Joan, the Fair Maid of Kent, succeeded Edward III, as Richard II.

Richard II   Although a council of twelve was officially entrusted to govern during Richard's minority, in effect John of Gaunt was the regent.

Poll tax of 1380 created national unrest and led to the Peasants' Revolt of 1381, when rebels under Wat Tyler took Rochester Castle in Kent and then marched on London with fellow radicals from Essex. Richard saw the Essex men at Mile End and made extensive promises, and the next day, 14 June, met Wat Tyler's men at Smithfield. Tyler was struck down by the mayor of London, William Walworth, in revenge for the atrocities of the previous day when the archbishop of Canterbury, Simon of Sudbury, was murdered.

John of Gaunt died in 1399 and his son succeeded him as duke of Lancaster. Richard went to Ireland in May 1399 and on 4 July Henry, duke of Lancaster, landed back in England. Although Richard hurried back to England, he submitted to his cousin at Flint on 19 August and was put in the Tower. On 29 September 1399 he resigned the Crown in favour of Henry and he seems to have been murdered at Pontefract Castle, Yorkshire, early in 1400.

Henry IV   Henry was the first king of the House of Lancaster.

His surname of Bolingbroke came from his birthplace in Lincolnshire.

Henry defeated Harry Hotspur at Shrewsbury on 21 July 1403, when Hotspur was slain.

Henry V   Henry had Richard II's body buried in Westminster Abbey.

Henry thought he had a good claim to the French crown through his great-grandfather, Edward III.

Henry's famous victory at Agincourt was on 25 October 1415.

In 1420 Henry became regent of France via the 'Perpetual Peace' of Troyes.

Henry persecuted the Lollards, would-be Church reformers who had become the first group of English heretics to represent a political threat.

Henry VI   Henry was less than a year old when he became king of England, and on the death of his maternal grandfather, King Charles VI, he became king of France when just over 1 year of age. He was officially crowned king of England in 1429 and of France in 1431.

By 1453 the Hundred Years War was effectively over, with England expelled from all France except Calais.

Cade's Rebellion of 1450 was a revolt by Kentish gentry against the high taxes and alleged corruption in Henry's council. On 18 June Cade defeated a royal army at Sevenoaks and then marched on London. He was eventually killed attempting to evade arrest at Heathfield, Sussex.

Edward IV   Richard, duke of York, became protector while Henry VI suffered temporary madness in 1454. Richard had in fact a better title to the crown than Henry, as he was descended from Lionel, duke of Clarence, third son of Edward III. When Henry recovered, Richard refused to hand back the throne. He defeated Henry at St Albans on 22 May 1455, thereby starting the Wars of the Roses. Although in the ascendant, York did not claim the Crown until 1460, when he became Henry's heir, resulting in Edward Prince of Wales being disinherited. Richard was killed at Wakefield soon after but his son claimed the Crown as Edward IV, after his victory at Mortimer's Cross, and the second battle at St Albans. After a series of victories at Towton, Hedgeley Moor and Hexham, Edward married Elizabeth Woodvillle and the opposition to this family briefly restored Henry VI to the throne in 1470. Undeterred, Edward regrouped and with only 2,000 men, defeated the Lancastrians and killed Warwick at Barnet on 14 April 1471. Edward carried on to Tewkesbury and on 4 May 1471 his decisive victory and the death of Edward, Prince of Wales, effectively ended the Lancastrian resistance. Henry VI was killed soon after in the Tower of London.

Edward V   The 12-year-old King Edward V was escorted from Ludlow by Earl Rivers but Richard, duke of Gloucester, the future Richard III, intercepted him at Northampton, brought him to London on 4 May 1483 and was then made protector. In June, Edward's brother, Richard, duke of York, joined him in the Tower of London and they were never seen again. In 1674 some bones were found and re-interred as theirs in Westminster Abbey.

Richard III   Richard became duke of Gloucester in 1461.

On the death of Edward IV on 9 April 1483, Richard became Protector of the Realm for Edward's son and successor, the 12-year-old King Edward V, whom he imprisoned in the Tower of London along with his younger brother Richard on the premise that Edward IV's marriage was invalid and therefore his sons were illegitimate. Richard was proclaimed king in June 1483.

It is possible that Richard had a hand in the murder of Henry VI in the Tower of London on the night of 21 May 1471.

Richard's chief supporter had been Henry Stafford, 2nd duke of Buckingham, but soon after Richard's coronation he entered into a plot with friends of Henry, earl of Richmond, the future Henry VII. The attempt failed and Buckingham was executed. Henry landed at Milford Haven on 7 August 1485. Richard met him at Bosworth on 22 August, and there lost his kingdom and his life. He was the last British monarch to die in battle.

Henry VII   Henry was the first Tudor monarch of England. His claim to the throne became definite on the deaths of Henry VI's only son, Edward, and Henry VI himself, which made Henry Tudor the last surviving male heir of the House of Lancaster.

S
O
V
E
R
E
I
G
N
S

Henry's victory at Bosworth owed a great deal to his stepfather, Lord Stanley, deserting to him.
Henry united the houses of York and Lancaster by way of his marriage to Elizabeth of York.
In 1487 Lambert Simnel, the son of a baker, under the influence of a priest named William
Symonds, claimed to be Edward Plantagenet, son of George, duke of Clarence. He was crowned
in Dublin in 1487, but his followers were defeated at Stoke and Henry gave Simnel a job in his
kitchens. In 1491 Perkin Warbeck impersonated Richard, duke of York, one of the princes
presumed dead in the Tower. Warbeck invaded south-west England in 1498 but was caught by
Henry and eventually hanged.

Henry VIII
The six wives of Henry VIII were:
Catherine of Aragon (1485–1536), daughter of Ferdinand II of Spain and Isabella I of Castile.
Married 11 June 1509, Chapel of the Observant Friars.
Anne Boleyn (1507–36), marchioness of Pembroke, daughter of Thomas Boleyn. Married 25
January 1533.
Jane Seymour (1509–37), daughter of Sir John Seymour. Married 30 May 1536, Queen's Closet,
York Place, London.
Anne of Cleves (1515–57), daughter of John, duke of Cleves. Married 6 January 1540, Greenwich.
Catherine Howard (1521–42), daughter of Lord Edmund Howard. Married 28 July 1540, Oatlands.
Catherine Parr (1512–48), daughter of Sir Thomas Parr. Married 12 July 1543, Hampton Court.
Henry met Francis I in a field near Calais in June 1520, and although the display of friendship was
short-lived, the lavish ceremonies became known as the Field of the Cloth of Gold.
Henry accused Thomas Wolsey (1475–1530), Lord Chancellor England 1515–29, of high treason
for failing to obtain the pope's permission for the king's divorce from Catherine of Aragon. Wolsey
died on the journey from York to London and was succeeded by Thomas More (1478–1535), who
was executed in 1535 for refusing to swear the oath to the Act of Succession and thereby denying
papal supremacy. Thomas Cromwell now became Henry's most trusted aide. After arranging
Henry's divorce from Catherine in 1533 he organised the dissolution of the monasteries, 1536–9,
but was ultimately executed on a trumped-up charge of treason in 1540.

Edward VI
Edward was 10 years old when he became king and his uncle, Edward Seymour, duke of
Somerset, acted as his first Lord Protector, followed by John Dudley, earl of Warwick.

Lady Jane Grey
Jane was married against her will to the son of the Lord Protector, John Dudley, earl of Warwick,
who connived to put her on the throne because she was the great-granddaughter of Henry VII,
through her mother Lady Frances Brandon, whose own mother was Mary, the younger of King
Henry VIII's two sisters. Jane ruled for only nine days and was beheaded with her husband on 12
February 1554 after her father was found to be involved in the Wyatt Rebellion.

Mary I
Mary was known as Bloody Mary because of her policy of burning heretics.
After she lost Calais in 1554 she was reported to have said that when she died, Calais would be
found writ on her heart.

Elizabeth I
Elizabeth was linked romantically with Robert Dudley, earl of Leicester, and later in life with Robert
Devereux, earl of Essex, whom she was forced to execute for treason.
Two important conspiracies against Elizabeth were the Ridolfi Plot (1571) and the Babington Plot
(1586), which ultimately caused the execution of Mary, Queen of Scots, in 1587.
Elizabeth's chief minister for most of her reign was William Cecil, Lord Burghley.
Elizabeth had a first-class intelligence network which was the envy of Europe; her minister in
charge was Francis Walsingham.

James I
James was also James VI of Scotland (1567–1625), after his mother, Mary, Queen of Scots, was
forced to abdicate.
James's slogan was 'No Bishop, No King', which was used to reassure the people that Elizabethan
Church settlements were to be maintained and that he believed the Anglican Church and the
monarchy to be interdependent.
The leader of the Gunpowder Plot of 5 November 1605 was Robert Catesby, and his fellow
conspirators included Thomas Winter, John Wright and Guido/Guy Fawkes, all staunch Roman
Catholics. The plot was against James's stance on religion, and the aim was to blow up him, his
family and all the lords present. The plot failed when Francis Tresham, a newly enrolled
conspirator, warned his brother-in-law, Lord Monteagle, not to attend parliament that day.
James's parliament of April–June 1614 was called the 'Addled' because it was dissolved without
passing any bills.
Before he became king of England, James was thought to be having a homosexual affair with
Esmé Stuart.
The 'Main' plot of 1603 was an attempt to put Arabella Stuart on the throne.

Charles I
The 'Five Members' that Charles attempted to arrest on 4 January 1642 were John Pym, John
Hampden, Denzil Holles, Arthur Hesilrige and William Strode.
Charles's parliaments were: the 'Short', 13 April–5 May 1640, in which he demanded money for
the Bishops' War against the Scottish covenanters, and the 'Long', in which Charles impeached

Strafford and Laud and which ran from 1640 to 1660 but became the 'Rump' after Pride's purge of about 140 royalist MPs on 6 December 1648.

The Bishops' Wars of 1639–40 were provoked by the attempts of Charles to impose Anglicanism on Scotland. The English prayer book was refused and episcopacy was abolished in Scotland. Charles summoned the Short Parliament in order to obtain supplies for the resumption of the war. After the 'Grand Remonstrance', whereby parliament voiced its dissatisfaction with the monarchy, and the incident of the 'Five Members', civil war was imminent and Charles eventually raised his standard at Nottingham on 22 August 1642. After the indecisive battle of Edgehill, 23 October 1642, Charles was forced to retreat at Turnham Green, London, and for the duration of the Civil War based his capital at Oxford. After many more indecisive battles, the formation of the New Model Army in February 1645, commanded by Fairfax and Cromwell, and the royalist defeat at Naseby, June 1645, spelt the end for Charles.

Charles II
James, duke of Monmouth, was the illegitimate son of Charles II and Lucy Walter.

The incident of Charles hiding up an oak tree to escape capture occurred during the Battle of Worcester in 1651.

General George Monk organised the restoration of the monarchy, and Charles entered London in triumph on his birthday, 29 May 1660, after issuing his Declaration of Breda promising a general amnesty and liberty of conscience.

In 1678 anti-Catholic feeling was stoked to fever-point by the trumped-up revelations of Titus Oates about a supposed Popish plot to murder Charles. In 1683 the Rye House Plot was a conspiracy to murder Charles and his brother James, duke of York, as they travelled from Newmarket races to London past Rye House in Hertfordshire. Monmouth, Algernon, Sidney and several prominent Whigs were implicated.

James II
In 1685 the Monmouth Rebellion was crushed and Judge Jeffreys' Bloody Assizes followed.

James was forced to abdicate because of his Catholic tendencies and was succeeded by the Protestant William of Orange.

Aided by a small body of French troops, James invaded Ireland and made an abortive attempt to reclaim his throne, but was defeated at the battle of the Boyne, 1690, and returned to St Germain.

William III
William landed at Torbay on 5 November 1688, following an invitation from the 'Immortal Seven' noblemen to protect the Protestant religion. When James fled to France, William and Mary were declared joint sovereigns. Jacobite resistance was ended by the battles of Killiecrankie, July 1689, and the Boyne, 1690.

William died after his horse stumbled at seeing a mole run out from his hill, causing him to fall and break his right collarbone. Complications set in when William caught an infection and he died on 8 March 1702.

Anne
Only one of Anne's children survived infancy, William, duke of Gloucester, who died in 1700 at the age of 12.

Sarah Churchill, later duchess of Marlborough, was the lifelong friend and confidante of Anne, and when corresponding they often used the names Mrs Freeman and Mrs Morley. Sarah Churchill's cousin, Abigail Masham, née Hill, later became Anne's favourite.

In 1704 a fund was set up by Anne for the benefit of the poorer clergy and this 'Queen Anne's Bounty' was amalgamated into the Church Commissioners when it was set up in 1948.

George I
The Act of Settlement of 1701 ensured the Crown for George.

George married his cousin Sophia Dorothea of Zell in 1682, but divorced her in 1694 for adultery with a Swedish nobleman and kept her imprisoned in the castle of Ahlden until her death in 1726.

The '15' rebellion (1715) was an attempt by Jacobites to put James Edward Stuart, the Old Pretender (son of James II and Mary of Modena), on the throne.

George's unpopularity was not helped by the fact that he never learnt to speak fluently in English.

George II
George was the last British sovereign to lead an army into battle, in 1743 at Dettingen, which he won.

The '45' rebellion (1745) was an attempt to put Charles Edward Stuart, the Young Pretender (son of James Edward Stuart), on the British throne. It was ruthlessly put down by William Augustus, the duke of Cumberland, the second son of George, at Culloden.

George III
George is said to have had a child by Hannah Lightfoot, a Quaker, and it is possible he even married her, although this is extremely doubtful.

George had long periods of insanity and the Prince of Wales, later George IV, was appointed Regent from 1811 onwards.

George IV
George had a much-publicised affair with an actress, Mrs Robinson, when aged 18; his ceremony of marriage with Mrs Maria Fitzherbert, when aged 23, was deemed unlawful in England.

William IV
William was called the Sailor King.

He lived with an actress, Dorothy Jordan, from 1790 to 1811 and she bore him ten children.

SOVEREIGNS

Victoria   Under Salic law, Victoria could not claim her dominion over Hanover, and this title passed to her uncle, Ernest Augustus, duke of Cumberland.

She became Empress of India in 1876, although officially this title was conferred on her on 1 January 1877.

Victoria published *Leaves from the Journal of our Life in the Highlands (1869)* and *More Leaves (1884)*.

Victoria was the first monarch to live in Buckingham Palace.

Edward VII   Edward's Christian name was Albert but he used his second name in deference to Queen Victoria.

Edward was cited in a divorce scandal of 1870.

George V   George instigated the monarch's Christmas Day broadcasts to the nation in 1932.

Edward VIII   Abdicated to marry a divorcee and became Governor of the Bahamas in WW2.

George VI   George was a keen tennis player and played in the Wimbledon Championships of 1926.

He substituted the title of Head of the Commonwealth for Emperor of India in 1947.

George's Christian name was Albert but he used his fourth name in deference to Queen Victoria.

Elizabeth II   On 13 June 1996, Elizabeth II had ruled longer than Elizabeth I.

Elizabeth was in Kenya when she heard she was Queen.

The Queen's actual birthday is 21 April; her official birthday falls on the second Saturday in June.

NB The list above contains information on sovereigns since the Norman invasion, which tends to be 90 per cent of any school history curriculum; other sovereigns, either of the whole or part of England, are listed below.

House of Wessex

802–839	Egbert (became ruler of all the English kingdoms from 829–30)
839–858	Aethelwulf (son of Egbert)
858–860	Aethelbald (son of Aethelwulf)
860–865	Aethelbert (brother of Aethelbald)
865–871	Aethelred I (brother of Aethelbert)
871–899	Alfred (the Great, brother of Aethelred I)
899–924	Edward (the Elder, son of Alfred)
924–924	Aelfweard (son of Edward)
924–939	Aethelstan (brother of Aelfweard)
939–946	Edmund I (brother of Aethelstan)
946–955	Eadred (brother of Edmund)
955–959	Eadwig (son of Edmund)
959–975	Edgar (the Peaceful, brother of Eadwig)
975–978	St Edward (the Martyr, son of Edgar)
978–1016	Aethelred II (the Unready or Ill-Advised, brother of St Edward)
1013–1014	Swein Forkbeard (deposed Aethelred II in this year)
1016–1016	Edmund II (Ironside, son of Aethelred II)
1042–1066	St Edward (the Confessor, son of Aethelred II)
1066–1066	Harold II (Godwinson)

House of Denmark

1016–1035	Cnut (the Great, son of Swein Forkbeard)
1037–1040	Harold I (Harefoot, son of Cnut)
1040–1042	Harthacnut (brother of Harold)

Kings and Queens of England and Great Britain

	Reign	Date of accession	Born	Died	Marriage(s)
William I aka the Bastard, the Conqueror	1066–1087	25 Dec.	Falaise, France, c. 1028, illegitimate son of Robert I, 6th duke of Normandy, by Herleva/Arlette, daughter of Fulbert the Tanner.	Abdominal injury while riding via Mantes, died 5 weeks later on 9 Sept. 1087 at Rouen. Buried at the Abbey of St Stephen, Caen.	Matilda (died 1083), daughter of Baldwin V, count of Flanders; 4 sons, 5 daughters. Married at Eu c. 1053.
William II Rufus	1087–1100	26 Sept.	Normandy, c. 1056, 3rd son of William I and Matilda.	Arrow wound while hunting in the New Forest, nr Brockenhurst, Hants, 2 Aug. 1100. Buried in Winchester Cathedral.	Unmarried.
Henry I Beauclerc	1100–1135	5 Aug.	Selby, Yorkshire, 1068, 4th son of William I and Matilda. Buried at Reading Abbey. 1 Dec. 1135.	Fever, St Denis-le-Ferment, Grisors. Aged 67,	Edith (aka Matilda), died 1118, daughter of Malcolm III and Margaret. Wed Westminster Abbey, Nov. 1100. Adela, died 1151, daughter of Godfrey VII, count of Louvaine (granddaughter of Edmund Ironside); 1 son, 1 daughter.
Matilda 'Empress Maud'	1141		London, Feb. 1102, only legitimate daughter of Henry I.	Natural causes, Rouen, Normandy. Buried at Fontevraud Abbey church, Anjou.	Henry V, Emperor of Germany, married in 1114, died in 1125. Geoffrey V, count of Anjou; 3 sons. Married 1128, died 1151.
Stephen	1135–1154	22 Dec.	Blois, France, c. 1096, 3rd son of Stephen aka Henry, count of Blois, and Adela, 5th daughter of William I.	Heart attack, St Martin's Priory, Dover, 25 Oct. 1154. Buried at Faversham Abbey.	Matilda, died 1151, daughter of count of Boulogne and Mary, sister of Matilda (wife of Henry I); 3 sons, 2 daughters. Married 1125.
Henry II Plantagenet Fitzempress Curtmantle	1154–1189	19 Dec.	Le Mans, France, 5 March 1133, eldest son of Geoffrey V, count of Anjou, and Matilda, only daughter of Henry I.	Fever, castle of Chinon, Tours, 6 July 1199. Buried at Fontevraud Abbey in Anjou, reburied Westminster Abbey.	Eleanor (1122–1204), daughter of duke of Aquitaine and divorced wife of Louis VII of France; 5 sons, 3 daughters. Married at Bordeaux, 1152.
Richard I aka Lionheart	1189–1199	3 Sept.	Oxford, 8 Sept. 1157, 3rd son of Henry II and Eleanor.	Arrow wound while besieging the castle of Chalus, Limousin, France, 6 April 1199. Buried at Fontevraud Abbey in Anjou, reburied Westminster Abbey.	Berengaria died c:1230, daughter of Sancho VI of Navarre. No issue. Married at Limassol, Cyprus, 1191.
John aka Lackland	1199–1216	27 May	Beaumont Palace, Oxford, 24 Dec. 1167, 5th son of Henry II and Eleanor.	Dysentery, Newark Castle, Notts, Oct. 1216. Buried at Worcester Cathedral.	Isabel, died 1217. Married 1191 at Marlborough, Wilts; no issue. Isabella, died 1246, daughter of count of Angoulême; 2 sons, 3 daughters. Married at Angoulême, Aug. 1200.

	Reign	Date of accession	Born	Died	Marriage(s)
Henry III aka the Builder	1216–1272	28 Oct.	Winchester, 1 Oct. 1207, elder son of John and Isabella of Angoulême.	Natural causes, Westminster, aged 65, 16 Nov. 1272. Buried Westminster Abbey Church.	Eleanor, died 1291, daughter of count of Provence, Raymond Berengar. Married at Canterbury, 1236; 2 sons, 3 daughters.
Edward I aka Longshanks, Hammer of the Scots	1272–1307	20 Nov.	Westminster, 17 June 1239; eldest son (to survive infancy) of Henry III and Eleanor of Provence. Buried at Westminster Abbey.	Natural causes, Burgh-on-the-Sands nr Carlisle, 7 July 1307, aged 68.	Eleanor, died 1290, daughter of king of Castile, Ferdinand III, 4 sons, 7 daughters. Married Las Huelgas, Oct. 1254. Margaret (1282–1317), daughter of King Philip III of France; 2 sons, 1 daughter. Married Canterbury Sept. 1299.
Edward II	1307–1327	8 July	Caernarfon Castle, Wales, 25 April 1284; 4th and only surviving son of Edward I and Eleanor of Castile.	Murdered Berkeley Castle, Sept. 1327. Buried Gloucester Cathedral.	Isabella (1292–1358), daughter of King Philip IV of France; 2 sons, 2 daughters. Married Boulogne, Jan. 1308.
Edward III	1327–1377	25 Jan.	Windsor Castle, 13 Nov. 1312; elder son of Edward II and Isabella.	Natural causes, Sheen, 21 June 1377. Buried at Westminster Abbey.	Philippa (1314–69) daughter of count of Hainault and Holland; 7 sons, 5 daughters. Married at York, 24 June 1328.
Richard II	1377–1399	22 June	Bordeaux, France, 6 Jan. 1367; 2nd but only surviving son of Edward, the Black Prince, and Joan, the Fair Maid of Kent (granddaughter of Edward I).	Neurasthenia, Pontefract Castle. Buried at Westminster Abbey.	Anne of Bohemia (1366–94), daughter of Emperor Charles I. No issue. Wed St Stephens Chapel, 1382. Isabelle (1389–1409), daughter of Charles VI of France. No issue. Wed St Nicholas, Calais, 1396.
Henry IV aka Bolingbroke	1399–1413	30 Sept.	Bolingbroke Castle, Lincolnshire, April 1366; eldest son of John of Gaunt, 4th son of Edward III and Blanche, great-granddaughter of Henry III.	Eczema and gout, Jerusalem Chamber, Westminster. Buried at Westminster Abbey.	Mary de Bohun (1368–94), daughter of Humphrey of Hereford; 5 sons, 2 daughters. Wed Rochford, Essex, 1380. Joan (1370–1437), 2nd daughter of King Charles II of Navarre. No issue. Married Winchester, Feb. 1403.
Henry V aka Harry	1413–1422	21 March	Monmouth, Wales, 16 Sept. 1387; 2nd and eldest surviving son of Henry IV and Lady Mary de Bohun.	Dysentery, Bois de Vincennes, aged 34. Buried in Chapel of the Confessor, Westminster Abbey.	Catherine of Valois (1401–37), daughter of Charles VI of France; 1 son. Wed church of St John, Troyes, 2 June 1420.

	Reign	Date of accession	Born	Died	Marriage(s)
Henry VI	1422–1461	1 Sept.	Windsor, 6 Dec. 1421; only son of Henry V and Catherine of Valois.	Murdered by stabbing, Tower of London, 21 May 1471. Buried at Windsor.	Margaret (1430–82), daughter of René, duke of Anjou; 1 son. Wed Tichfield Abbey, April 1445.
Edward IV	1461–1470	4 March	Rouen, France, 28 April 1442; eldest son of Richard, 3rd duke of York and the Lady Cecily Nevill, daughter of Ralph, earl of Westmorland.	Pneumonia, Westminster, April 1483. Buried at Windsor.	Elizabeth (1437–92), daughter of Sir Richard Woodville; 3 sons, 7 daughters. Wed Grafton, Northants, 1464.
Henry VI	1470–1471	6 Oct.	As above.		
Edward IV	1471–1483	11 April	As above.		
Edward V	1483	9 April	Westminster, 2 Nov. 1470, eldest son of Edward IV and Elizabeth Woodville.	Tower of London?	Unmarried.
Richard III aka Crookback	1483–1485	26 June	Fotheringay, Northants, 2 Oct. 1452; 4th and only surviving son of Richard, 3rd duke of York (the Protector), and Cecily Nevill.	Killed Bosworth 22 Aug.1485. Buried at the Abbey of the Grey Friars, Leicester.	Anne (1456–85), daughter of Richard Nevill, earl of Warwick, and widow of Edward, prince of Wales; 1 son. Married 12 July 1472.
Henry VII	1485–1509	22 Aug.	Pembroke Castle, 27 Jan. 1457; only child of Edmund Tudor, 1st earl of Richmond, and Margaret Beaufort, great-great-granddaughter of Edward III.	Rheumatoid arthritis and gout, 21 April, at Richmond. Buried in his own chapel at Westminster.	Elizabeth (1466–1503), daughter of Edward IV; 3 sons, 4 daughters. Wed Westminster, Jan. 1486.
Henry VIII aka Bluff King Hal, Old Copper Nose	1509–1547	22 April	Greenwich, 28 June 1491; 2nd and only surviving son of Henry VII and Elizabeth.	Sinusitis and periostitis of the leg at Whitehall, 28 Jan. 1547. Buried at Windsor.	See separate entry.
Edward VI	1547–1553	28 Jan.	Hampton Ct, 12 Oct. 1537; only surviving son of Henry VIII by Jane Seymour.	Tuberculosis at Greenwich. Buried in Henry VII's Chapel, Westminster Abbey.	Unmarried.
Jane aka Nine-Day Queen	1553	10 July	Bradgate Park, Leics, Oct. 1537; eldest daughter of Henry Grey, 3rd marquess of Dorset, and Frances, daughter of Mary Tudor, sister of Henry VIII.	Beheaded Tower of London Feb. 1554. Buried St Peter ad Vincula within the Tower.	Guilford Dudley, son of John Dudley, duke of Northumberland. Wed Durham Hse, London, May 1533.
Mary I aka Bloody Mary	1553–1558	19 July	Greenwich, 18 Feb. 1516; only surviving child of Henry VIII and Catherine of Aragon.	Influenza in London. Buried Westminster Abbey.	Philip, son of Emperor Charles V and later king of Spain in 1554.
Elizabeth I aka Virgin Queen	1558–1603	17 Nov.	Greenwich, 7 Sept. 1533; daughter of Henry VIII and Anne Boleyn.	Sepsis from tonsillar abscess at Richmond. Buried Westminster Abbey.	Unmarried.

SOVEREIGNS

	Reign	Date of Accession	Born	Died	Marriage(s)
James I	1603–1625	26 March	Edinburgh Castle, 19 June 1566; son of Mary queen of Scots (daughter of James V) and Henry Darnley.	Bright's disease, Theobalds Park, Herts. Buried Westminster Abbey.	Anne, daughter of Frederick II of Denmark. Married 20 Aug. 1589, by proxy.
Charles I	1625–1649	27 March	Dunfermline Palace, 19 Nov. 1600; only surviving son of James I and Anne of Denmark.	Beheaded at Whitehall, Jan 1649. Buried at Windsor.	Henrietta Maria, daughter of Henry IV of France. Paris, 1 May 1625, by proxy.
Charles II aka Old Rowley	1660–1685	29 May	St James's Palace, 29 May 1630; eldest son of Charles I and Henrietta Maria.	Uraemia and mercurial poisoning, Whitehall. Buried Henry VII's Chapel, Westminster.	Catherine of Braganza, daughter of John. Wed Portsmouth, 21 May 1662.
James II	1685–1688	6 Feb.	St James's Palace, 14 Oct. 1633; only surviving son of Charles I and Henrietta Maria.	Cerebral haemorrhage, St Germain, France. Remains were interred at 5 different venues in France. All are now lost except for those at the parish church at St Germain.	Anne Hyde, daughter of Edward Hyde, Worcester Hse, Strand, 3 Sept. 1660. Mary D'este, daughter of duke of Modena. Wed Modena, 30 Sept. 1673, by proxy.
William III	1688–1702	13 Feb.	The Hague, 4 Nov. 1650; only son of William II, Prince of Orange, and Mary Stuart, daughter of Charles I.	Pleuro-pneumonia following fracture of right collarbone after falling from his horse near Kensington. Buried Henry VII's Chapel, Westminster.	William III.
Mary II	1688–1694	13 Feb.	St James's Palace, 30 April 1662.	Smallpox at Kensington, 28 Dec. 1694. Buried Henry VII's Chapel, Westminster.	William III.
Anne aka Brandy Nan	1702–1714	8 March	St James's Palace, 6 Feb. 1665, daughter of James II and Anne Hyde.	Brain haemorrhage, Kensington. Buried Henry VII's Chapel, Westminster.	George of Denmark (1653–1708), son of Frederick III of Denmark, Chapel Royal, St James's Palace, 1683.
George I	1714–1727	1 Aug.	Osnabrück, 28 May 1660; son of Ernest, duke of Brunswick-Lüneburg and elector of Hanover, and Sophia, daughter of Elizabeth, queen of Bohemia, eldest daughter of James I.	Thrombosis, Ibbenburen. Buried Hanover.	Sophia Dorothea, daughter of George William, duke of Lüneburg-Celle. Wed 21 Nov. 1682, divorced 1694.
George II	1727–1760	11 Jun.	Hanover, 30 Oct. 1683; son of George I and Sophia Dorothea.	Thrombosis, Palace of Westminster. Buried Henry VII's Chapel, Westminster.	Wilhelmina Charlotte Caroline of Ansbach (1683–1737), daughter of John Frederick, margrave of Brandenburg-Ansbach, 22 Aug. 1705.
George III aka Farmer George	1760–1820	25 Oct.	Norfolk House, London, 24 May 1738; son of Frederick Lewis, prince of Wales, and Princess Augusta of Saxe-Gotha.	Senility, Windsor. St George's Chapel, Windsor.	Charlotte Sophia (1744–1818), daughter of Charles Louis Frederick, duke of Mecklenburg-Strelitz, 8 Sept. 1761.

	Reign	Date of Accession	Born	Died	Marriage(s)
George IV	1820–1830	29 Jan.	St James's Palace, 12 Aug. 1762; eldest son of George III and Charlotte.	Stomach rupture and dropsy, Windsor. Buried St George's Chapel, Windsor.	Maria Fitzherbert, 1785, without king's consent and denied by George IV. Caroline of Brunswick, 8 April 1795, Chapel Royal, St James's Palace.
William IV aka Sailor King	1830–1837	26 June	Buckingham Palace, 21 Aug. 1765; son of George III and Charlotte.	Pneumonia/cirrhosis, Windsor. Buried St George's Chapel, Windsor.	Adelaide, daughter of duke of Saxe-Meiningen, 11 July 1818, Kew.
Victoria	1837–1901	20 June	Kensington Palace, 24 May 1819; daughter of Edward duke of Kent, 4th son of George III, and Victoria, daughter of Francis of Saxe-Coburg-Saalfeld.	Senility, Osborne House, IoW. Buried at Frogmore nr Windsor.	Francis Albert (1819–61), 2nd son of Ernest I of Saxe-Coburg-Gotha, 10 Feb. 1840, St James's Palace.
Edward VII aka Denmark, Peacemaker	1901–1910	22 Jan.	Buckingham Palace, 9 Nov. 1841; eldest son of Victoria and Albert.	Bronchitis, Buckingham Palace. Buried at St George's Chapel, Windsor.	Alexandra, daughter of Christian IX of Denmark, 10 March 1863, St George's Chapel.
George V	1910–1936	6 May	Marlborough House, London, 3 June 1865; 2nd son of Edward and Alexander.	Bronchitis, Sandringham. Buried at St George's Chapel, Windsor.	Mary, daughter of Francis, duke of Teck, 6 July 1893, St James's Palace.
Edward VIII aka People's King	1936	20 Jan.	White Lodge. Richmond Park, 23 June 1894; eldest son of George V and Mary.	Throat cancer, Paris, 28 May 1972. Buried at Frogmore, Windsor.	Wallis Simpson née Warfield, 3 June 1937, Château de Candé, near Tours, France
George VI	1936–1952	11 Dec.	York Cottage, Sandringham, 14 Dec. 1895; second son of George V and Mary.	Lung cancer, Sandringham. Buried at St George's Chapel, Windsor.	Elizabeth Bowes-Lyon, daughter of 14th earl of Strathmore and Kinghorne, 26 April 1922.
Elizabeth II	1952–	6 Feb.	17 Bruton St, London, 21 April 1926; elder daughter of George VI and Elizabeth.	Reigned since 6 Feb. 1952.	Philip, son of Prince Andrew of Greece and Princess Alice. Married in Westminster Abbey, 20 Nov. 1947.

British Royalty: Miscellaneous Details

abdicated: first   Edward II (25 January 1327)

Alexandra, Princess   (the Hon. Lady Ogilvy)
full name: Alexandra Helen Elizabeth Olga Christabel
born: 25 December 1936
relationship to Queen: Cousin (sister of Edward, Duke of Kent)
husband: The Rt Hon. Sir Angus Ogilvy (born 14 September 1928)
children: James Robert Bruce Ogilvy (born 29 February 1964)
       Marina Victoria Alexandra Mowatt (born 31 July 1966)
house: Thatched House Lodge, Richmond Park, Surrey

Alexandra Rose Day   inaugurated in 1912 by Queen Alexandra

Andrew, Prince   married Sarah Ferguson in 1986
born: 19 February 1960
full name: Andrew Albert Christian Edward
titles: The Duke of York, Earl of Inverness and Baron Killyleagh
schools: Heatherdown, nr Ascot; Gordonstoun, Morayshire; Lakefield College School, Ontario
children: Beatrice Elizabeth Mary, born 8 August 1988
       Eugene Victoria Helena, born 23 March 1990
houses: Sunninghill Park, Ascot; Buckingham Palace, London

Angevin kings   Henry II, Richard I, John

Anne, Princess   Princess Royal since 1987
born: 15 August 1950
full name: Anne Elizabeth Alice Louise
school: Benenden, Kent
children: Peter Mark Andrew Phillips, born 15 November 1977
       Zara Anne Elizabeth Phillips, born 15 May 1981
marriages: Captain Mark Phillips (1973–92)
       Captain Tim Lawrence (1992–)
attempted kidnapping: by Ian Ball in 1974 in the Mall
house: Gatcombe Park, Gloucestershire

annus horribilis   Queen Elizabeth's name for 1992

anti-smoking tract: published   James I

Babington Plot   Roman Catholic plot against Elizabeth I in 1586

bald as a young woman   Elizabeth I

baldness revealed after execution   Mary, queen of Scots

bathed every three months   Elizabeth I

battle: died in; last sovereign   Richard III

battle: led troops in; last   George II (Dettingen)

bigamist   George IV

Bill of Rights   Act barring Catholics from succession

bodyguard scandal   Commander Michael Trestrail resigned as the Queen's bodyguard (19 July 1982) after admitting to his part in a sexual scandal

breast: extra   Anne Boleyn

Buckingham Palace: first to live in   Queen Victoria
bought by   George III in 1762

burnt the cakes (traditionally)   King Alfred

Cabal   advisers to Charles II: Clifford, Ashley, Buckingham, Arlington and Lauderdale

Cabinet meetings: attended most   Queen Anne

Cavalier Parliament   Charles II (aka Pensionary Parliament) first English Parliament 8 May 1661

Charles II: illegitimate son   Duke of Monmouth, son of Lucy Walter

Charles, Prince   married 1981, divorced 1996
full name: Charles Philip Arthur George
born: 14 November 1948
titles: Duke of Cornwall, Earl of Carrick and Baron Renfrew, Lord of the Isles, Duke of Rothsay, Prince and Great Steward of Scotland
children: William Arthur Philip Louis, born 21 June 1982
       Henry Charles Albert David, born 15 September 1984
Prince of Wales: title bestowed in 1958; inaugurated in 1969
houses: St James's Palace, London and Highgrove, Gloucestershire
Cherry B incident of 1963: Charles bought while under-age, in Outer Hebrides
aka: Lord of the Isles, Steward of Scotland, Duke of Cornwall
children's nanny: Tiggy Legge-Bourke

cherry brandy drinker   George IV

children: most   Henry I (20 acknowledged bastards plus two legitimate)
most legitimate   Edward I (18)

Christian: first   Ethelbert

Clarence, duke of: last   Albert, eldest son of Edward VII

commoner; first to wed   Henry IV

corgis   Princess Elizabeth was given Susan as a present from her parents on her 18th birthday, April 1944. Ten generations of corgis have been descended from Susan and owned by the Queen. In chronological order their names are Sugar, Honey, Bee, Whisky, Sherry, Heather, Buzz, Foxy, Busy, Tiny, Mask, Rufus, Brush, Cindy, Pickles, Tinker, Socks, Geordie, Jolly, Blackie, Edward, Sweep, Smoky, Chipper, Shadow, Piper, Spark, Myth, Fable, Apollo, Diamond, Kelpie, Ranger, Phoenix and Pharos.

crowned: battlefield   Henry VII

crowned: twice   Charles II

Defender of the Faith: first   Henry VIII

deposed   James II

divorced: first   John

dukes: royal   Cornwall, Edinburgh, Gloucester, Kent, York

education   *Prince Charles* Cheam, Gordonstoun, Cambridge. The Prince of Wales also spent the 1966 school year as an exchange student at the Geelong Church of England Grammar School in Melbourne, Australia.
Prince William Mrs Mynors' Nursery School, London, Wetherby School, London, Ludgrove School, Wokingham, Eton College, Berkshire, St Andrews University
Prince Harry Eton College
Princess Beatrice St George's School for Girls, Ascot, Berkshire

Edward, Prince   full name: Edward Antony Richard Louis
born: 10 March 1964
titles: Earl of Wessex, Viscount Severn
marriage: Sophie Helen Rhys-Jones (19 June 1999)
house: Bagshot Park, Surrey
schools: Gibbs Preparatory School, Kensington; Heatherdown Preparatory School, nr Ascot; Gordonstoun, Morayshire; Jesus College, Cambridge

Edward VII: House of Lords speech housing speech given while Prince of Wales

Edward VIII abdication speech written by Walter Monckton

Eleanor Crosses: 12 Marking resting place of Eleanor of Castile's cortege; crosses at Lincoln, Grantham, Stamford, Stratford, Woburn, Dunstable, St Albans, Cheapside, Northampton Geddington and Waltham still standing; last, Charing Cross, is a replica

Elizabeth I: favourite Robert Dudley, Earl of Leicester

Elizabeth II coronation day 2 June 1953
   biographer Sarah Bradford (1996)
   royal arms insignia Dieu et Mon Droit
   aka Lord High Admiral of England
   married 20 Nov. 1947

fattest king George IV

finger: extra Anne Boleyn

Five Members Pym, Hampden, Heselrige, Holles and Strode, whom Charles I attempted to arrest on 4 Jan. 1642, as well as Lord Mandeville

gilded coach used by the new Sovereign during Coronation ceremony

Gloucester, Duke of full name: Richard Alexander Walter George
   born: 26 August 1944
   relationship to Queen: cousin (his father Henry, Duke of Gloucester (1900–74) was the brother of the Queen's father)
   wife: Birgitte Eva Van Deurs (born 20 June 1946)
   children: Earl of Ulster (Alexander Patrick, born 24 October 1974)
      Lady Davina Windsor, born 19 November 1977
      Lady Rose Windsor, born 1 March 1980
   house: Kensington Palace, London

heirs to throne males are heirs apparent; females are heirs presumptive

Henry VIII: fate of wives divorced, beheaded, died, divorced, beheaded, survived

honours: awarded on New Year's Day and the Queen's official birthday

immoral queen Caroline of Brunswick

Irish state coach used by British monarchs for State Opening of Parliaments and by family members at Coronations

jewellers, Crown Garrards

Kent, Duke of full name: Edward George Nicholas Paul Patrick
   born: 9 October 1935
   relationship to Queen: cousin (his father George, Duke of Kent (1902–42), was the brother of the Queen's father)
   wife: Katharine Worsley (born 22 Feb. 1933)
   children: Earl of St Andrews (George Philip Nicholas, born 26 June 1962)
      Lady Helen Taylor, born 28 April 1964
      Lord Nicholas Windsor, born 25 July 1970
   house: Wren House, Palace Green, London

king over the water Jacobite term for pretenders

Lancaster: House of Henry IV, V, VI

Lollards: suppressed Henry V

mad king George III

madness: bouts of Henry VI

Margaret, Princess married 1960 to Anthony Armstrong Jones

married kings of England and France Eleanor of Aquitaine (Louis VII and Henry II)

Michael of Kent, Prince full name: Michael George

Charles Franklin
   born: 4 July 1942
   relationship to Queen: cousin (brother of Edward, Duke of Kent)
   wife: Baroness Marie-Christine Agnes Hedwig Ida von Reibnitz (born 15 January 1945)
   children: Lord Frederick Michael George David Louis Windsor, born 6 April 1979
      Lady Gabriella Marina Alexandra Ophelia, born 23 April 1981
   houses: Kensington Palace, London
      Nether Lypiatt Manor, Gloucestershire

murdered by queen and her lover Edward II

nicknames *Elizabeth II* 'Lilibet' (name originated because she could not pronounce Elizabeth when a child)
   Princess Margaret 'Bud' (coined by her sister Elizabeth as a play on her second name of Rose)

oldest on accession William IV (64)

oldest royal residence Windsor Castle

Parliament: first; in the reign of Henry III

pawned Crown jewels Richard II (to pay for wedding)

Philip, Prince born: 10 June 1921
   titles: Duke of Edinburgh, Earl of Merioneth, Baron Greenwich
   schools: Cheam, Salem School, Germany, Gordonstoun, Morayshire

Plantagenet: first Henry II

last Richard II, although later kings from Plantagenet line

pot-smoking Prince: Prince Harry (sent to drug rehabilitation clinic to warn him of dangers)

Popish Plot fictitious Jesuit plot of Titus Oates and Israel Tonge against Charles II resulting in the execution of Oliver Plunket, primate of Ireland

premier Duke of Scotland Dukes of Hamilton

pretenders: Henry VII's reign Perkin Warbeck (1498), hanged for treason; Lambert Simnel (1487), became kitchen hand

prince of Wales: longest Edward VII (59 yrs)
   last before Charles Edward VIII
   last Welsh Llewellyn

Prince Philip: parents Prince Andrew and Princess Alice of Greece

queen never set foot in England Berengaria, wife of Richard I

Richards all died violently

Ridolfi Plot Catholic plot against Elizabeth I in 1571

Roman Catholic monarch: last James II

royal allowance Civil List

rugby Peter Phillips, son of the Princess Royal, played rugby for Scottish schools

Rye House Plot plot to murder Charles II and his brother on the way home from Newmarket races

Sarah Armstrong-Jones daughter of Princess Margaret, born 1 May 1964, married Daniel Chatto

shortest queen Matilda, wife of William I

spoke little English George I

stammered George VI

St Edward's crown made for Charles II's coronation

toilet: died on George II

two queens: father of James II (Mary and Anne)

urinated in font Ethelred the Unready

USA: first to go to George VI

Victoria's gillie John Brown

Viscount Linley son of Princess Margaret, born 3 November 1961
   married: Hon. Serena Stanhope

SOVEREIGNS

White Ship disaster   William, son of Henry I, drowned at Barfleur, 25 Nov. 1120
wife: met at altar   George III (Charlotte Sophia)
Wimbledon: played at   George VI

wisest fool in Christendom   James I (coined by Henry IV of France)
write name: first to do so   Richard II
York, House of   Edward IV, V, Richard III

Order of Precedence (England and Wales)

The sovereign	Lord President of the Council
The Prince Philip, duke of Edinburgh	Speaker of the House of Commons
The Prince of Wales	Lord Privy Seal
The sovereign's younger sons	Ambassadors and High Commissioners
The sovereign's grandsons	Lord Great Chamberlain
The sovereign's cousins	Earl Marshal
Archbishop of Canterbury	Lord Steward of the Household
Lord High Chancellor	Lord Chamberlain of the Household
Archbishop of York	Master of the Horse
The Prime Minister	Then dukes, marquesses, earls, viscounts, barons

NB The order of precedence has been included in this section purely to show the distinction between order of precedence and succession. Precedence is a traditional ceremonial observation and, although closely following the order of succession in some areas, it is in fact a separate and distinct list.

Order of Succession

1	HRH Prince Charles, The Prince of Wales		11	Viscount Linley, David Armstrong-Jones
2	HRH Prince William of Wales		12	Hon. Charles Armstrong-Jones
3	HRH Prince Henry of Wales		13	Lady Sarah Chatto (née Armstrong-Jones)
4	HRH Prince Andrew, duke of York		14	Samuel Chatto
5	HRH Princess Beatrice of York		15	Arthur Chatto
6	HRH Princess Eugenie of York		16	HRH Richard, duke of Gloucester
7	HRH Prince Edward		17	The earl of Ulster
8	HRH Princess Anne, Princess Royal		18	Lady Davina Windsor
9	Peter Phillips, son of Princess Anne		19	Lady Rose Windsor
10	Zara Phillips, daughter of Princess Anne		20	HRH Edward, duke of Kent

The earl of St Andrews and HRH Prince Michael of Kent, who would usually be in the line of succession at numbers 21 and 29 respectively, forfeited their right through marriage to a Roman Catholic.

Rulers of the British Isles

Kings and Queens of Scotland

House of Alpin

842–858	Kenneth I (MacAlpin)
858–862	Donald I
862–877	Constantine I
877–878	Aed
878–889	Giric and Eochaid
889–900	Donald II
900–943	Constantine II
943–954	Malcolm I
954–962	Indulf
962–966	Duf
966–971	Culén
971–995	Kenneth II
995–997	Constantine III
997–1005	Kenneth III
1005–1034	Malcolm II

House of Dunkeld

1034–1040	Duncan I

House of Moray

1040–1057	Macbeth
1057–1058	Lulach

House of Dunkeld

1058–1093	Malcolm III (Canmore, aka Big Head)
1093–1097	Donald III
1094	Duncan II
1097–1107	Edgar

1107–1124	Alexander I (the Fierce)
1124–1153	David I (the Saint)
1153–1165	Malcolm IV (the Maiden)
1165–1214	William I (the Lion)
1214–1249	Alexander II
1249–1286	Alexander III

House of Norway

1286–1290	Margaret (Maid of Norway)
1290–1292	interregnum (disputed by 13 competitors)

House of Balliol

1292–1296	John Balliol
1296–1306	interregnum

House of Bruce

1306–1329	Robert I (the Bruce)
1329–1371	David II

House of Balliol

1332–1356	Edward (son of John, abdicated)

House of Stewart

1371–1390	Robert II (Stewart)
1390–1406	Robert III
1406–1437	James I
1437–1460	James II
1460–1488	James III

1488–1513	James IV
1513–1542	James V
1542–1567	Mary
1567–1625	James VI

Rulers of the Principality of Wales

Kingdom of Gwynedd

825–844	Merfyn the Freckled
844–878	Rhodri I (the Great)
878–916	Anarawd
916–942	Idwal the Bald
942–950	Hywel I (the Good)
950–979	Iago I
979–985	Hywel II
985–986	Cadwallon
986–999	Maredudd
999–1005	Cynan I
1005–1023	Llywelyn I
1023–1039	Iago II
1039–1063	Gruffydd I
1081–1137	Gruffydd II
1137–1170	Owain
1170–1174	Cynan II
1174–1194	David I (East Gwynedd)
1174–1195	Rhodri II (West Gwynedd)
1174–1200	Gruffydd III (South Gwynedd)
1194–1240	Llywelyn II (The Great)
1240–1246	David II

Principality of Wales

1246–1282	Llywelyn III (ap Gruffydd)
1282–1283	David III

NB Although Llywelyn ap Gruffydd is invariably quoted as the last native prince of Wales, in fact it is true to say that his brother, David ap Gruffydd, was the last native prince of Wales. This confusion arises simply because England did not recognise anyone except Llywelyn as ruler. The Welsh would recognise David as their last prince, and the English Llywelyn. In 1301 the future Edward II became prince of Wales, and subsequently the eldest son of the reigning monarch has been given this title.

The High Kingship of Ireland

House of Ui Néill

445–452	Niall of the Nine Hostages
819–833	Conchobar
1002–1014	Brian Bóruma (king of Munster)
1166–1186	Ruaidri

NB The short list above includes the first and last kings of Ireland and two other famous kings. Many of the other rulers are obscure and were not recognised as such until at least the 9th century.

Other Important Historical Rulers

Israel

1020–1010 BC	Saul
1010–970 BC	David
970–931 BC	Solomon

Kingdom of Judah

930–914 BC	Rehoboam (son of Solomon)

Kingdom of Israel

931–910 BC	Jeroboam I (son of Solomon)

Lydia: last king

560–547 BC	Croesus

Persian Empire

559–530 BC	Cyrus the Great
529–522 BC	Cambyses
522 BC	Smerdis (Bardiya)
521–486 BC	Darius I (The Great)
485–465 BC	Xerxes I
464–424 BC	Artaxerxes I
424 BC	Xerxes II
424 BC	Sogdianus
423–405 BC	Darius II
404–359 BC	Artaxerxes II
358–338 BC	Artaxerxes III
337–336 BC	Arses
335–330 BC	Darius III

Macedonia (selected kings)

399–397 BC	Orestes
359–336 BC	Philip II
336–323 BC	Alexander III (the Great)
179–168 BC	Perseus (the last king)

Visigoth kingdom

395–410	Alaric I (first king of the Visigoths)
711–714	Agila II (last king of the Visigoths)

Anglo-Saxon kingdoms

455–488	Hengest (first ruler of kingdom of Kent)
823–825	Baldred (last ruler of kingdom of Kent)
547–559	Ida (first ruler of Bernicia)
585–592	Hussa (last ruler of Bernicia)
569–599	Aelle (first ruler of Deira)
599–604	Aethelric (last ruler of Deira)
592–616	Aethelfrith (Northumberland: Bernicia and Deira)
913–927	Aldred (last ruler of Northumberland)
633–655	Penda (first ruler of Mercia)
757–796	Offa (kingdom of Mercia)
918–919	Aelfwyn (last ruler of Mercia)
519–534	Cerdic (first ruler of Wessex)
802–839	Egbert (last ruler of Wessex)

Kingdom of France (selected)

Carolingian House

751–768	Pepin the Short (first king of France)
768–814	Charlemagne (Holy Roman Emperor, 800)
840–877	Charles I (the Bald)
877–879	Louis II (the Stammerer)
885–888	Charles II (the Fat)
893–923	Charles III (the Simple)
986–987	Louis V (the Sluggard)

Capetian House

987–996	Hugh Capet
996–1031	Robert II (the Pious)
1108–1137	Louis VI (the Fat)

SOVEREIGNS

1137–1180	Louis VII (the Younger)
1223–1226	Louis VIII (the Lion)
1285–1314	Philip IV (the Fair)
1314–1316	Louis X (the Stubborn)
1316–1322	Philip V (the Tall)
1322–1328	Charles IV (the Fair)

House of Valois

1328–1350	Philip VI
1350–1364	John II (the Good)
1364–1380	Charles V (the Wise)
1380–1422	Charles VI (the Mad)
1422–1461	Charles VII (the Victorious)
1483–1498	Charles VIII

House of Angoulême

1515–1547	Francis I
1547–1559	Henry II
1559–1560	Francis II (husband of Mary of Scots)
1560–1574	Charles IX
1574–1589	Henry III

House of Bourbon

1589–1610	Henry IV (Paris is worth a mass)
1610–1643	Louis XIII
1643–1715	Louis XIV (the Sun King)
1715–1774	Louis XV
1774–1792	Louis XVI

First Empire

| 1804–1814 | Napoleon I (king of Italy, 1805) |

Second Empire

| 1852–1870 | Napoleon III |

Kingdom of Italy

1849–1878	Victor Emmanuel II
1878–1900	Humbert I
1900–1946	Victor Emmanuel III
1946–1946	Humbert II

NB Although Victor Emmanuel III is often thought to be the last king of Italy, in fact, he was the last 'crowned' king. Humbert II (Umberto) was the last incumbent.

Kingdom of Spain (selected)
House of Habsburg

| 1516–1556 | Charles I (Holy Roman Emperor, 1519–58) |
| 1556–1598 | Philip II (husband of Bloody Mary) |

House of Bourbon

| 1700–1724 | Philip V (grandson of Louis XIV of France) |

House of Bonaparte

| 1808–1813 | Joseph Napoleon |

House of Bourbon

| 1975– | Juan Carlos I |

Kingdom of Portugal (selected)

| 1139–1185 | Afonso I |

House of Avis

| 1385–1433 | John I (the Bastard) |
| 1578–1580 | Henry (the Cardinal) |

House of Braganza

1640–1656	John IV
1706–1750	John V (the Magnanimous)
1834–1853	Maria II

House of Saxe-Coburg-Gotha

| 1853–1861 | Pedro V |
| 1908–1910 | Manuel II |

Kingdom of Norway (selected)

858–928	Harald I
1957–1991	Olav V
1991–	Harald V

Kingdom of Denmark (selected)

| 940–986 | Harald I |
| 1972– | Margaret II |

Kingdom of Sweden (selected)

| 980–995 | Erik the Victorious |

House of Vasa

1523–1560	Gustavus I
1560–1568	Erik XIV
1568–1592	John III
1592–1599	Sigismund

House of Bernadotte

| 1818–1844 | Charles XIV |
| 1973– | Charles XVI Gustavus |

Kingdom of Netherlands (selected)

1572–1584	William I (the Silent)
1806–1810	Louis Napoleon
1890–1948	Wilhelmina
1948–1980	Juliana
1980–	Beatrix

Tsars/Tsarinas of Russia

1533–1584	Ivan IV (the Terrible)
1598–1605	Boris Godunov
1462–1505	Ivan III (the Great)
1613–1645	Michael Romanov
1682–1725	Peter I (the Great)
1725–1727	Catherine I (Martha)
1762–1796	Catherine II (the Great, born Sophie of Anhalt)
1894–1917	Nicholas II

Inca Empire

| 1532–1533 | Atauhualpa |
| 1571–1572 | Tupac Amaru |

Aztec Empire

| 1372–1391 | Acamapichtli |
| 1427–1440 | Itzcoatl |

Japanese Empire

0–10 BC	Jimmu
1623–1651	Iemitsu
1713–1716	Ietsugu
1853–1858	Iesada
1867–1868	Keiki (Yoshinobu)

Chinese dynasties

18th–12th cent. BC	Shang
1111–255 BC	Chou
770–221 BC	Tung
221–206 BC	Ch'in
206–220 AD	Han
581–618	Sui
618–907	T'ang

960–1279	Sung	Burma	Thibaw (1878–85)
1206–1368	Yüan	Laos	SavangVatthana (1959–75)
1368–1644	Ming	Cambodia	Sihanouk (1941–55) Monarchy
1644–1912	Manchu (Ch'ing)		re-established on 23 Sept. 1993
		Ethiopia	Asfa Wossen (1974–75)
Last kings/queens of		Madagascar	Ranavalona (1883–96)
Romania	Michael (1940–47)	Zululand	Dinuzulu (1884–87)
Bulgaria	Simeon II (1943–46)	Hawaii	Liliuokalani (1891–93)
Albania	Zog I (1928–39)	Hungary	John Sigismund (1540–70)
Afghanistan	Muhammad Zahir Shah	Poland	Stanislas II Augustus (1764–95)
	(1933–73)	Bohemia	Ferdinand I (1526–64)
Korea	Sunjong (1907–10)		

Holy Roman Emperors

Charlemagne (Charles I)	800–814	William of Holland	1247–1256
Louis I (the Pious)	814–840	Conrad IV	1250–1254
civil war	840–843	great interregnum	1254–1273
Lothair I	843–855	Richard	1257–1272
Louis II	855–875	Alfonso	1257–1275
Charles II (the Bald)	875–877	Rudolf I	1273–1291
interregnum	877–881	Adolf	1292–1298
Charles III (the Fat)	881–887	Albert I	1298–1308
interregnum	887–891	Henry VII	1308–1313
Guido of Spoleto	891–894	Frederick III	1314–1326
Lambert of Spoleto	892–898	Louis IV	1314–1346
Arnulf	898–899	Charles IV	1346–1378
Louis III (the Blind)	901–905	Wenceslas	1378–1400
Conrad I	911–918	Rupert	1400–1410
Berengar	915–924	Jobst	1410–1411
Henry I	919–936	Sigismund	1410–1437
Otto I (the Great)	936–973	Albert II	1438–1439
Otto II	973–983	Frederick III	1440–1493
Otto III	983–1002	Maximillian I	1493–1519
Henry II (the Saint)	1002–1024	Charles V	1519–1556
Conrad II	1024–1039	Ferdinand I	1556–1564
Henry III (the Black)	1039–1056	Maximillian II	1564–1576
Henry IV	1056–1106	Rudolf II	1576–1612
Rudolf	1077–1080	Matthias	1612–1619
Hermann	1081–1093	Ferdinand II	1619–1637
Conrad	1093–1101	Ferdinand III	1637–1657
Henry V	1106–1125	Leopold I	1658–1705
Lothair II	1125–1137	Joseph I	1705–1711
Conrad III	1138–1152	Charles VI	1711–1740
Frederick I (Barbarossa)	1152–1190	interregnum	1740–1742
Henry VI	1190–1197	Charles VII	1742–1745
Philip	1198–1208	Francis I	1745–1765
Otto IV	1198–1214	Joseph II	1765–1790
Frederick II	1215–1250	Leopold II	1790–1792
Henry VII	1220–1235	Francis II	1792–1806
Henry Raspe	1246–1247		

S
O
V
E
R
E
I
G
N
S

Roman Kings

Romulus	753–715 BC	Tarquinius Priscus	616–578 BC
Numa Pompilius	715–673 BC	Servius Tullius	578–534 BC
Tullus Hostilius	673–642 BC	Tarquinius Superbus	534–509 BC
Ancus Marcius	642–616 BC		

NB The traditional seven kings of Rome as listed above are of extremely dubious authenticity and nowadays are only observed as truth in the context of being a very popular quiz question, and to this end the ones to remember are the first, Romulus, and the last, Tarquinius Superbus (Proud Tarquin).

Roman Emperors

Augustus	27 BC–AD 14	Probus	276–282
Tiberius	14–37	Carus	282–283
Caligula	37–41	Numerian (east)	283–284
Claudius	41–54	Carinus (west)	283–285
Nero	54–68	Postumus (Gaul)	260–269
Galba	68–69	Laelian (Gaul)	269
Otho	69	Marius (Gaul)	269
Vitellius	69	Victorinus (Gaul)	269–271
Vespasian	69–79	Tetricus (Gaul)	271–274
Titus	79–81	Diocletian (see below)	284–305
Domitian	81–96	Maximian (see below)	286–305
Nerva	96–98	Constantius I (see below)	305–306
Trajan	98–117	Galerius (see below)	305–311
Hadrian	117–138	Severus (west)	306–307
Antoninus Pius	138–161	Maxentius (west)	307–312
Marcus Aurelius	161–180	Constantine I (west until 324)	307–337
Commodus	180–192	Licinius (Pannonia and east)	308–324
Pertinax	193	Maximinus II (east)	310–313
Didius Julianus	193	Valerius Valens	316–317
Septimius Severus	193–211	Martinian	324
Geta	211	Constantine II (Gaul, Britain, Spain)	337–340
Caracalla	211–217	Constans (west)	337–350
Macrinus	217–218	Constantius II (east)	337–361
Diadumenian	218	Magnentius (west)	350–353
Elagabalus	218–222	Julian the Apostate (Gaul until 361)	360–363
Severus Alexander	222–235	Jovian	363–364
Maximinus the Thracian	235–238	Valentinian I (west)	364–375
Gordian I	238	Valens (east)	364–378
Gordian II	238	Gratian (west)	375–383
Balbinus	238	Valentinian II	375–392
Pupienus Maximus	238	Theodosius I (the Great) (east)	379–395
Gordian III	238–244	Maximus (west)	383–388
Philip I the Arabian	244–249	Victor (west)	387–388
Philip II	247–249	Eugenius (west)	392–394
Decius	249–251		
Herennius Etruscus	251		
Hostilian	251		

After a short interregnum the Empire split into east and west. Selected entries are as follows:

Trebonianus Gallus (co-ruler with Misson Volusian)	251–253	
Volusian	251–253	
Aemilian	253	
Valerian (east)	253–260	
Gallienus (west)	253–268	
Saloninus	260	
Claudius II	268–270	
Quintillus	270	
Aurelian	270–275	
Tacitus	275–276	
Florian	276	

Western Roman Emperors

Honorius	395–423 (the first)
Romulus Augustus	475–476 (the last)

Eastern Roman Emperors

Arcadius	395–408 (the first)
Justinian I (the Great)	527–565
Constantine XI	1449–1453 (the last)

Turkish capture of Constantinople ultimately ended the Byzantine Empire.

NB The names used in the above table are the ones familiarly adopted by history. The full names are complex and can be depicted in an imperial style or in Latin. It became increasingly impractical to rule over the whole of the Roman Empire and although the empire was not officially split until AD 395, many joint emperors divided their territories between east and west, with further subdivisions into Gaul, Britain, Illyria etc. To use the Diocletian tetrarchy as an example, Galerius, residing in Sirmium, administered Illyria, Achaea, and the Danubian provinces; Maximian, residing in Milan, administered Italy, Sicily, and Africa; Constantius I, residing in Trier, governed Gaul, Spain, and Britain; and Diocletian, residing in Nicomedia, watched over Thrace, Asia, and Egypt.

AD 69 is often referred to as the year of the four emperors but in AD 238 there were six emperors. Maximinus became the first soldier who had started from the ranks to become Roman emperor, he was replaced by the aged proconsul Gordian, who ruled jointly with his son. Gordian committed suicide on learning of the death of his son in a battle with Capellianus, governor of Numidia. The Roman Senate then proclaimed two elderly senators Balbinus and Pupienus Maximus joint emperors. The imperial guards murdered the Senate's nominees and the grandson of Gordian became emperor as Gordian III, at the age of 13. Valentinian II was proclaimed emperor in Budapest (Aquincum) at the age of 4, and ruled Italy, Africa, Illyricum, through his mother. He was found dead in his palace at Vienna, probably murdered by agents of Arbogast, the usurper in Gaul. In areas likely to confuse, I have added the administrative area in parenthesis. I have omitted usurpers such as Vetranio (abdicated in AD 351) and Procopius (reigned in Constantinople AD 365–6), as this would only confuse matters further.

American Football

	Superbowl winners			Runners up
1967	Green Bay Packers	NFC	35-10	Kansas City Chiefs
1968	Green Bay Packers	NFC	33-14	Oakland Raiders
1969	New York Jets	AFC	16-7	Baltimore Colts
1970	Kansas City Chiefs	AFC	23-7	Minnesota Vikings
1971	Baltimore Colts	AFC	16-13	Dallas Cowboys
1972	Dallas Cowboys	NFC	24-3	Miami Dolphins
1973	Miami Dolphins	AFC	14-7	Washington Redskins
1974	Miami Dolphins	AFC	24-7	Minnesota Vikings
1975	Pittsburgh Steelers	AFC	16-6	Minnesota Vikings
1976	Pittsburgh Steelers	AFC	21-7	Dallas Cowboys
1977	Oakland Raiders	AFC	32-14	Minnesota Vikings
1978	Dallas Cowboys	NFC	27-10	Denver Broncos
1979	Pittsburgh Steelers	AFC	35-31	Dallas Cowboys
1980	Pittsburgh Steelers	AFC	31-19	Los Angeles Raiders
1981	Oakland Raiders	AFC	27-10	Philadelphia Eagles
1982	San Francisco 49ers	NFC	26-21	Cincinnati Bengals
1983	Washington Redskins	NFC	27-17	Miami Dolphins
1984	Los Angeles Raiders	AFC	38-9	Washington Redskins
1985	San Francisco 49ers	NFC	38-16	Miami Dolphins
1986	Chicago Bears	NFC	46-10	New England Patriots
1987	New York Giants	NFC	39-20	Denver Broncos
1988	Washington Redskins	NFC	42-10	Denver Broncos
1989	San Francisco 49ers	NFC	20-16	Cincinnati Bengals
1990	San Francisco 49ers	NFC	55-10	Denver Broncos
1991	New York Giants	NFC	20-19	Buffalo Bills
1992	Washington Redskins	NFC	37-24	Buffalo Bills
1993	Dallas Cowboys	NFC	52-17	Buffalo Bills
1994	Dallas Cowboys	NFC	30-13	Buffalo Bills
1995	San Francisco 49ers	NFC	49-28	San Diego Chargers
1996	Dallas Cowboys	NFC	27-17	Pittsburgh Steelers
1997	Green Bay Packers	NFC	35-21	New England Patriots
1998	Denver Broncos	AFC	31-24	Green Bay Packers
1999	Denver Broncos	AFC	34-19	Atlanta Falcons
2000	St Louis Rams	NFC	23-16	Tennessee Titans
2001	Baltimore Ravens	AFC	34-7	New York Giants
2002	New England Patriots	AFC	20-17	St Louis Rams
2003	Tampa Bay Buccaneers	NFC	48-21	Oakland Raiders
2004	New England Patriots	AFC	32-29	Carolina Panthers
2005	New England Patriots	AFC	24-21	Philadelphia Eagles

(AFC = American Football Conference. NFC = National Football Conference.)

American Football: General Information

field goals: points score	3
most valuable player award	Jim Thorpe Trophy
players: number	11 a side on pitch at any one time
playing area	grid iron
playing period	60 minutes
rules played	Harvard Rules
safety touch: points score	2
Super Bowl	championship game of the National Football League played by the winners of league's American Football Conference and National Football Conference
touchdown: points score	6
trophy played for	Vince Lombardi trophy
World Bowl 2000 winner	Rhein Fire beat Scottish Claymores 13-10
World League: teams	Barcelona Dragons, London Monarchs, Amsterdam Admirals, Scottish Claymores, Frankfurt Galaxy, Rhein Fire

Angling: British Freshwater Records (as at December 2004)

Barbel	19 lb 6oz	Steve Curtin	Rudd	4 lb 10oz		Simon Parry
Bleak	4oz 9dm	Dennis Flack	Salmon	64 lb		Georgina Ballatine
Bream	18 lb 15oz	Mark Neal	Tench	14 lb 7oz		Gordon Beaven
Carp (Mary)	64 lb 5oz	Jonathan Pack	Natural Trout:			
Carp: Crucian	4 lb 9oz	Martin Bowler	Brown	25 lb 5oz 12dm	A Finlay
Carp: Grass	31 lb	Derek Smith	Cultivated Trout:			
Catfish	62 lb	Rob Garner	Brown	28 lb 1oz		D Taylor
Chub	8 lb 10oz	Peter Smith	Natural Trout:			
Dace	1 lb 4oz 4dm	J. Gasson	Rainbow	36 lb 14oz 8dm	C White
Eel	11 lb 2oz	Steve Terry	Cultivated Trout:			
Golden Orfe	7 lb 14oz 8dm	Mick Pardoe	Rainbow	24 lb 1oz 4dm	J Hammond
Perch	5 lb 9oz	John Shayler	Trout: Sea	28 lb 5oz		J Farrent
Pike	46 lb 13oz	Ray Lewis	Zander	19 lb 5oz 8dm	Dave Lavender
Roach	4 lb 3oz	Ray Clarke				

Angling: Freshwater Champions

	Individual	Team
1959	Robert Tesse (France)	France
1960	Robert Tesse (France)	Belgium
1961	Ramon Legogue (France)	E. Germany
1962	Raimondo Tedasco (Italy)	Italy
1963	William Lane (England)	France
1964	Joseph Fontanet (France)	France
1965	Robert Tesse (France)	Romania
1966	Henri Guiheneuf (France)	France
1967	Jacques Isenbaert (Belgium)	Belgium
1968	Gunter Grebenstein (W. Germany)	France
1969	Robin Harris (England)	Holland
1970	Marcel Van den Eynde (Belgium)	Belgium
1971	Dino Bassi (Italy)	Italy
1972	Hubert Levels (Netherlands)	France
1973	Pierre Michiels (Belgium)	Belgium
1974	Aribert Richter (W. Germany)	France
1975	Ian Heaps (England)	France
1976	Dino Bassi (Italy)	Italy
1977	Jean Mainil (Belgium)	Luxembourg
1978	Jean-Pierre Fourgeat (France)	France
1979	Gérard Heulard (France)	France
1980	Wolf-Rudiger Kremkus (W. Germany)	W. Germany
1981	Dave Thomas (England)	France
1982	Kevin Ashurst (England)	Holland
1983	Wolf-Rudiger Kremkus (W. Germany)	Belgium
1984	Bobby Smithers (Ireland)	Luxembourg
1985	Dave Roper (England)	England
1986	Lud Wever (Netherlands)	Italy
1987	Clive Branson (Wales)	England
1988	Jean-Pierre Fourgeat (France)	England
1989	Tom Pickering (England)	Wales
1990	Bob Nudd (England)	France
1991	Bob Nudd (England)	England
1992	David Wesson (Australia)	Italy
1993	Mario Barros (Portugal)	Italy
1994	Bob Nudd (England)	England
1995	Paul Jean (France)	France
1996	Alan Scotthorne (England)	Italy
1997	Alan Scotthorne (England)	Italy
1998	Alan Scotthorne (England)	England
1999	Bob Nudd (England)	Spain
2000	Jacopo Falsini (Italy)	Italy
2001	Umberto Balabeni (Italy)	England
2002	G Blasco (Spain)	Spain
2003	Alan Scotthorne (England)	Hungary
2004	Tamas Walter (Hungary)	France

World Fly Fishing Champions

	Individual	Team		Individual	Team
1981	C Wittkamp (Netherlands)	Netherlands	1993	Russell Owens (Wales)	England
1982	Viktor Diez (Spain)	Italy	1994	Pascal Cognard (France)	Czechoslovakia
1983	S Fernandez (Spain)	Italy	1995	Jeremy Herrmann (England)	England
1984	Tony Pawson (England)	Italy	1996	Perluigi Coccito (Italy)	Czecholsovakia
1985	Leslaw Frasik (Poland)	Poland	1997	Pascal Cognard (France)	France
1986	Slivoj Svoboda (Czechoslovakia)	Italy	1998	T Starychfolta (Czechoslovakia)	Czechoslovakia
1987	Brian Leadbetter (England)	England	1999	Ross Steward (Australia)	Australia
1988	John Pawson (England)	England	2000	Pascal Cognard (France)	France
1989	Wladislaw Trzebuinia (Poland)	Poland	2001	Vladimir Sedivy (Czechoslovakia)	France
1990	Franciszek Szajnik (Poland)	Czechoslovakia	2002	Jerome Brossutti (France)	France
1991	Brian Leadbetter (England)	NZ	2003	Stefano Cotugno (Italy)	France
1992	Perluigi Coccito (Italy)	Italy	2004	Miroslav Antal (Slovakia)	Slovakia

Archery: Target World Champions

	Men	Team	Women	Team
1931	M Sawicki (Poland)	France	J Kurkowska (Poland)	—
1932	L Reith (Belgium)	Poland	J Kurkowska (Poland)	—
1933	D McKenzie (USA)	Belgium	J Kurkowska (Poland)	Poland
1934	H Kjellson (Sweden)	Sweden	J Kurkowska (Poland)	Poland
1935	A van Kohlen (Belgium)	Belgium	Ina Catani (Sweden)	GB
1936	E Heilborn (Sweden)	Czechoslovakia	J Kurkowska (Poland)	Poland
1937	G de Rons (Belgium)	Poland	Ingo Simon (GB)	GB
1938	F Hadas (Czechoslovakia)	Czechoslovakia	N Weston Martyr (GB)	Poland
1939	R Beday (France)	France	J Kurkowska (Poland)	Poland
1946	E T Holbek (Denmark)	Denmark	N de Wharton Burr	GB
1947	H Deutgen (Sweden)	Czechoslovakia	J Kurkowska (Poland)	Denmark
1948	H Deutgen (Sweden)	Sweden	N de Wharton Burr	Czechoslovakia
1949	H Deutgen (Sweden)	Czechoslovakia	B Waterhouse (GB)	GB
1950	H Deutgen (Sweden)	Denmark	Jean Lee (USA)	Finland
1952	S Andersson (Sweden)	Sweden	Jean Lee (USA)	USA
1953	B Lundgren (Sweden)	Sweden	Jean Richards (USA)	Finland
1955	N Andersson (Sweden)	Sweden	K Wisniowska (Poland)	GB
1957	O Smathers (USA)	USA	C Meinhart (USA)	USA
1958	S Thysell (Sweden)	Finland	S Johansson (Sweden)	USA
1959	J Caspers (USA)	USA	Ann Corby (USA)	USA
1961	J Thornton (USA)	USA	N Vanderheide (USA)	USA
1963	C Sandlin (USA)	USA	V Cook (USA)	USA
1965	M Haikonen (Finland)	USA	M Lindholm (Finland)	USA
1967	Ray Rogers (USA)	USA	M Maczynska (Poland)	Poland
1969	Hardy Ward (USA)	USA	D Lidstone (Canada)	USSR
1971	J Williams (USA)	USA	E Gapchenko (USSR)	Poland
1973	V Sidoruk (USSR)	USA	Linda Myers (USA)	USSR
1975	Darrell Pace (USA)	USA	Z Rustamova (USSR)	USSR
1977	R McKinney (USA)	USA	Luann Ryon (USA)	USA
1979	Darrell Pace (USA)	USA	Kim Jin-ho (Korea)	Korea
1981	K Laasonen (Finland)	USA	N Butuzova (USSR)	USSR
1983	R McKinney (USA)	USA	Kim Jin-ho (Korea)	Korea
1985	R McKinney (USA)	Korea	I Soldatova (USSR)	USSR
1987	V Yesheyev (USSR)	W. Germany	Ma Xiaojun (China)	USSR
1989	S Zabrodskiy (USSR)	USSR	Kim Soo-nyung (Korea)	Korea
1991	S Fairweather (Australia)	Korea	Kim Soo-nyung (Korea)	Korea
1993	Kyung Mo Park (Korea)	France	K Hyo-Jung (Korea)	Korea
1995	Lee Kyung-Chul (Korea)	Korea	N Valeeva (Moldovia)	Korea
1997	Kim Kyung-Ho (Korea)	Korea	Kim Du-Ri (Korea)	Korea
1999	Chil Hong Sung (Korea)	Italy	Lee Eun Kyung (Korea)	Italy
2001	J K Yeon (Korea)	Korea	S H Park (Korea)	China
2003	M Frangilli (Italy)	Korea	Yun Mi-Jin (Korea)	Korea

SPORT&LEISURE

Athletics: Olympic Games 2004

Gold

Men

100m	Justin Gatlin (USA) 9.85
200m	Shawn Crawford (USA) 19.79
400m	Jeremy Wariner (USA) 44.00
800m	Yuriy Borzakovskiy (Rus) 1:44.45
1,500m	Hicham El Guerrouj (Mor) 3:34.18
5,000m	Hicham El Guerrouj (Mor) 13:14.39
10,000m	Kenenisa Bekele (Eth) 27:05:10 (OR)
Marathon	Stefano Baldini (Ita) 2:10:55
110m Hurdles	Xiang Liu (Chn) 12.91 (equals WR)
400m Hurdles	Felix Sanchez (Dom) 47.63
3,000m S/Chase	Ezekiel Kemboi (Ken) 8:05.81
4 x 100m relay	Great Britain 38.07 (Jason Gardener, Darren Campbell, Marlon Devonish, Mark Lewis-Francis)
4 x 400m relay	United States 2:55.91 (Otis Harris, Derrick Brew, Jeremy Wariner, Darold Williamson)
20km walk	Ivano Brugnetti (Ita) 1:19:40
50km walk	Robert Korzeniowski (Pol) 3:38:46
High Jump	Stefan Holm (Swe) 2.36
Long Jump	Dwight Phillips (USA) 8.59
Pole Vault	Timothy Mack (USA) 5.95
Triple Jump	Christian Olsson (Swe) 17.79
Shot Put	Yuriy Bilonog (Ukr) 21.16
*Discus	Virgilijus Alekna (Lit) 69.89
**Hammer	Koji Murofushi (Jpn) 82.91
Javelin	Andreas Thorkildsen (Nor) 86.50
Decathlon	Ramon Sebrle (Cz) 8893pts 100m: 10.85, 894pts Long Jump: 7.84, 1020pts Shot Put: 16.36, 873pts High Jump: 2.12, 915pts 400m: 48.36, 892pts 110m Hurdles: 14.05, 968pts Discus: 48.72, 844pts Pole Vault: 5.00, 910pts Javelin: 70.52, 897pts 1,500m: 4:40.00, 680pts

*Robert Fazekas of Hungary won the discus final (70.93m OR) but was disqualified for subsequently trying to tamper with a sample during a dope test.
**Adrian Annus of Hungary won the hammer final (83.19m) but was disqualified for refusing to take a second drug test despite passing the first.

Women

100m	Yuliya Nesterenko (Blr) 10.93
200m	Veronica Campbell (Jam) 22.05
400m	Tonique Williams-Darling (Bah) 49.41
800m	Kelly Holmes (GBR) 1:56.38
1,500m	Kelly Holmes (GBR) 3:57.90
5,000m	Meseret Defar (Eth) 14:45.65
10,000m	Huina Xing (Chn) 30:24.36
Marathon	Mizuki Noguchi (Jpn) 2:26:20
100m Hurdles	Joanna Hayes (USA) 12.37
400m Hurdles	Fani Halkia (Gre) 52.82
4 x 100m relay	Jamaica 41.73 (Tayna Lawrence, Sherone Simpson, Aleen Bailey, Veronica Campbell)
4 x 400m relay	United States 3:19.01 (DeeDee Trotter, Monique Henderson, Sanya Richards, Monique Hennagan)
20km walk	Athanasia Tsoumeleka (Gre) 1:29:12
High Jump	Yelena Slesarenko (Rus) 2.06
Long Jump	Tatyana Lebedeva (Rus) 7.07
Pole Vault	Yelena Isinbayeva (Rus) 4.91 (WR)
Triple Jump	Francoise Mbango Etone (Cam) 15.30
*Shot Put	Yumileidi Cumba (Cub) 19.59
Discus	Natalya Sadova (Rus) 67.02
Hammer	Olga Kuzenkova (Rus) 75.02 (OR)
Javelin	Osleidys Menendez (Cub) 71.53 (OR)
Heptathlon	Carolina Kluft (Swed) 6952pts 100m Hurdles: 13.21, 1093pts High Jump: 1.91, 1119pts Shot Put: 14.77, 845pts 200m: 23.27, 1052pts Long Jump: 6.78, 1099pts Javelin: 48.89, 839pts 800m: 2:14.15, 905pts

*Irina Korzhanenko of Russia won the women's shot put (21.06m) but was subsequently disqualified after failing a drugs test.

Silver

Men

100m	Francis Obikwelu (Por) 9.86
200m	Bernard Williams (USA) 20.01
400m	Otis Harris (USA) 44.16
800m	Mbulaeni Mulaudzi (SA) 1:44.61
1,500m	Bernard Lagat (Ken) 3:34.30
5,000m	Kenenisa Bekele (Eth) 13:14.59
10,0000m	Sileshi Sihine (Eth) 27:09.39
Marathon	Mebrahtom Keflezighi (USA) 2:11:29
110m Hurdles	Terrence Trammell (USA) 13.18
400m Hurdles	Danny McFarlane (Jam) 48.11
3,000m S/Chase	Brimin Kipruto (Ken) 8:06.11
4 x 100m relay	United States 38.08 (Shawn Crawford, Justin Gatlin, Coby Miller, Maurice Greene)

Women

100m	Lauryn Williams (USA) 10.96
200m	Allyson Felix (USA) 22.18
400m	Ana Guevara (Mex) 49.56
800m	Hasna Benhassi (Mor) 1:56.43
1,500m	Tatyana Tomashova (Rus) 3:58.12
5,000m	Isabella Ochichi (Ken) 14:48.19
10,000m	Ejegayehu Dibaba (Eth) 30:24.98
Marathon	Catherine Ndereba (Ken) 2:26:32
100m Hurdles	Olena Krasovska (Ukr) 12.45
400m Hurdles	Ionela Tirlea-Manolache (Rom) 53.38
4 x 100m relay	Russia 42.27 (Olga Fyodorova, Yuliya Tabakova, Irina Khabarova, Larisa Kruglova)

Men		Women	
4 x 400m relay	Australia 3:00.60 (John Steffensen, Mark Ormrod, Patrick Dwyer, Clinton Hill)	4 x 400m relay	Russia 3:20.16 (Olesya Krasnomovets, Natalya Nazarova, Olesya Zykina, Natalya Antyukh)
20km walk	Francisco Javier Fernandez (Esp) 1:19:45	20km walk	Olimpiada Ivanova (Rus) 1:29:16
50km walk	Denis Nizhegorodov (Rus) 3:42:50	High Jump	Hestrie Cloete (SA) 2.02
High Jump	Matt Hemmingway (USA) 2.34	Long Jump	Irina Simagina (Rus) 7.05
Long Jump	John Moffitt (USA) 8.47	Pole Vault	Svetlana Feofanova (Rus) 4.75
Pole Vault	Toby Stevenson (USA) 5.90	Triple Jump	Hrysopiyi Devetzi (Gre) 15.25
Triple Jump	Marian Oprea (Rom) 17.55	Shot Put	Nadine Kleinert (Ger) 19.55
Shot Put	Adam Nelson (USA) 21.16	Discus	Anastasia Kelesidou (Gre) 66.68
Discus	Zoltan Kovago (Hung) 67.04	Hammer	Yipsi Moreno (Cub) 73.36
Hammer	Ivan Tikhon (Blr) 79.81	Javelin	Steffi Nerius (Ger) 65.82
Javelin	Vadims Vasilevskis (Lat) 84.95	Heptathlon	Austra Skujyte (Lit) 6435pts
Decathlon	Bryan Clay (USA) 8820pts		100m Hurdles: 14.03, 974pts
	100m: 10.44, 989pts		High Jump: 1.76, 928pts
	Long Jump: 7.96, 1050pts		Shot Put: 16.40, 955pts
	Shot Put: 15.23, 804pts		200m: 24.82, 903pts
	High Jump: 2.06, 859pts		Long Jump: 6.30, 943pts
	400m: 49.19, 852pts		Javelin: 49.58, 852pts
	110m Hurdles: 14.13, 958pts		800m: 2:15.92, 880pts
	Discus: 50.11, 873pts		
	Pole Vault: 4.90, 880pts		
	Javelin: 69.71, 885pts		
	1,500m: 4:41.70, 670pts		

Bronze

Men		Women	
100m	Maurice Greene (USA) 9.87	100m	Veronica Campbell (Jam) 10.97
200m	Justin Gatlin (USA) 20.03	200m	Debbie Ferguson (Bah) 22.30
400m	Derrick Brew (USA) 44.42	400m	Natalya Antyukh (Rus) 49.89
800m	Wilson Kipketer (Den) 1:44.65	800m	Jolanda Ceplak (Slo) 1:56.43
1,500m	Rui Silva (Por) 3:34.68	1,500m	Maria Cioncan (Rom) 3:58.39
5,000m	Eliud Kipchoge (Ken) 13:15.10	5,000m	Tirunesh Dibaba (Eth) 14:51.83
10,000m	Zersenay Tadesse (Eri) 27:22.57	10,000m	Derartu Tulu (Eth) 30:26.42
Marathon	Vanderlei de Lima (Braz) 2:12:11	Marathon	Deena Kastor (USA) 2:27:20
110m Hurdles	Anier Garcia (Cub) 13.20	100m Hurdles	Melissa Morrison (USA) 12.56
400m Hurdles	Naman Keita (Fra) 48.26	400m Hurdles	Tatiana Tereshchuk-Antipova (Ukr) 53.44
3,000m S/Chase	Paul Kipsiele Koech (Ken) 8:06.64		
4 x 100m relay	Nigeria 38.23 (Olusoji Fasuba, Uchenna Emedolu, Aaron Egbele, Deji Aliu)	4 x 100m relay	France 42.54 (Veronique Mang, Muriel Hurtis, Sylviane Felix, Christine Arron)
4 x 400m relay	Nigeria 3:00.90 (James Godday, Musa Audu, Saul Weigopwa, Enefiok Udo Obong)	4 x 400m relay	Jamaica 3:22.00 (Novlene Williams, Michelle Burgher, Nadia Davy, Sandie Richards)
20km walk	Nathan Deakes (Aus) 1:20:02	20km walk	Jane Saville (Aus) 1:29:25
50km walk	Aleksey Voyevodin (Rus) 3:43:34	High Jump	Viktoriya Styopina (Ukr) 2.02
High Jump	Jaroslav Baba (Cz) 2.34	Long Jump	Tatyana Kotova (Rus) 7.05
Long Jump	Joan Lino Martinez (Esp) 8.32	Pole Vault	Anna Rogowska (Pol) 4.70
Pole Vault	Giuseppe Gibilisco (Ita) 5.85	Triple Jump	Tatyana Lebedeva (Rus) 15.14
Triple Jump	Danila Burkenya (Rus) 17.48	Shot Put	Svetlana Krivelyova (Rus) 19.49
Shot Put	Joachim Olsen (Den) 21.07	Discus	Irina Yatchenko (Blr) 66.17
Discus	Aleksander Tammert (Est) 66.66	Hammer	Yunaika Crawford (Cub) 73.16
Hammer	Esref Apak (Tur) 79.51	Javelin	Mirela Manjani (Gre) 64.29
Javelin	Sergey Makarov (Rus) 84.84	Heptathlon	Kelly Sotherton (GBR) 6424
Decathlon	Dmitriy Karpov (Kaz) 8725pts		100m Hurdles: 13.44, 1059pts
	100m: 10.50, 975pts		High Jump: 1.85, 1041pts
	Long Jump: 7.81, 1012pts		Shot: 13.29, 747pts
	Shot Put: 15.93, 847pts		200m: 23.57, 1022pts
	High Jump: 2.09, 887pts		Long Jump: 6.51, 1010pts
	400m: 46.81, 968pts		Javelin: 37.19, 613pts
	110m Hurdles: 13.97, 978pts		800m: 2:12.27, 932pts
	Discus: 51.65, 905pts		
	Pole Vault: 4.60, 790pts		
	Javelin: 55.54, 671pts		
	1,500m: 4:38.10, 692pts		

SPORT & LEISURE

Athletics: General Information

Amateur Athletic Association   AAA founded in 1880 from the Amateur Athletic Club of 1866.

decathlon: order of events   100m, Long Jump; Shot; High Jump; 400m; 110m Hurdles; Discus; Pole Vault; Javelin; 1,500m.

discus: weight and dimensions   Men's: 2kg (4 lb 6½ oz),   Women's: 1kg   Circle: 2½m (8 feet 2½ in).

5,000m: first under 13 minutes   Said Aouita (Morocco).

four-minute mile: first   Roger Bannister wearing No. 41 ran 3 mins 59.4 secs at Iffley Rd, Oxford (6 May 1954).

four-minute mile: second   John Landy.

hammer: weight   16 lb.

heptathlon: order of events   100m Hurdles; High Jump; Shot; 200m (first day); Long Jump; Javelin and 800m (second day).

high jump: first to 2m (woman)   Rosie Ackerman (Germany).

first to 6' (man)   Marshall Jones Brooks (1876).

first to 6' (woman)   Iolanda Balas (1958).

first to 7' (man)   Jim Hines (1968).

100m: first (man) under 10 seconds   Armin Hary (1960).

100 yards: first (man) under 10 seconds   J P Tennent (1868).

110 hurdles: first (man) under 13 seconds   Renaldo Nehemiah.

hurdles   men's   110m H: 3' 6" (106.7 cm). Women's 100 H: 2' 9" (83.8 cm). Men's 400 H: 3' high (91.4cm) and 35m between. Women's 400 H: 2' 6" high (26.2cm) 35m between.

javelin: weight and dimensions   Men's: 800 grams (1 lb 12 oz), minimum length 260 cm. Women's: 600 grams (1lb 5oz), minimum length 220 cm.

marathon: distance   26 miles 385 yards.

marathon: origin   distance run by Pheidippides to relay news of battle of Marathon (extra 385 yards added in 1908 Olympics so as to finish race in front of Royal Box).

mile: first man under 3 minutes 50 seconds   John Walker (1975).

mile: first woman under 5 minutes   Diane Leather (1955).

pentathlon: ancient   running, jumping, discus, javelin, wrestling.

pentathlon: modern   riding, fencing, shooting, swimming, cross country run.

pentathlon: women   200m; 100 Hurdles; Shot; High Jump; Long Jump (800m and Javelin added for Heptathlon).

pole vault: first man over 6m   Sergey Bubka (1985).

shot: dimensions   Men's: 7.26 kg (16 lb). Women's: 4kg (8 lb 13 oz). Circle: 2.134m (7 feet).

steeplechase: waterjump   not jumped on first lap so seven times in all.

tattoo   British sprinter Mark Lewis-Francis sports a tattoo of the name of his illegitimate son Romeo (b. 2002) on his left arm.

World Championships: won first six   Sergey Bubka won the first six World Championship pole vault events (1983, 1987, 1991, 1993, 1995, 1997).

world record holders: became MPs   Chris Chataway, Sebastian Coe and Lord Burghley.

world records: five in a day   Jesse Owens (1935).

world records: not broken at Olympics   only the Men's Discus record has never been broken at an Olympic Games.

World Record Holders (as at 31 March 2005)

Men

100m	Tim Montgomery (USA)	9.78
200m	Michael Johnson (USA)	19.32
300m	Michael Johnson (USA)	30.85
400m	Michael Johnson (USA)	43.18
800m	Wilson Kipketer (Ken)	1:41.11
1,000m	Noah Ngeny (Ken)	2:11.96
1,500m	Hicham El Guerrouj (Mor)	3:26.00
Mile	Hicham El Guerrouj (Mor)	3:43.13
2 Miles	Daniel Komen (Ken)	7:58.61
2,000m	Hicham El Guerrouj (Mor)	4:44.79
3,000m	Daniel Komen (Ken)	7:20.67
5,000m	Kenenisa Bekele (Eth)	12:37.37
10,000m	Kenenisa Bekele (Eth)	26:20.31
20,000m	Arturo Barrios (Mex)	56:55.60
1 Hour	Arturo Barrios (Mex)	21,101m
Half Marathon	Paul Tergat (Ken)	59:17
25,000m (road)	Paul Kosgei (Ken)	1:12.45
30,000m (road)	Takayuki Matsumiya (Jpn)	1:28.36
Marathon	Paul Tergat (Ken)	2:04:55
3,000m S/Chase	Saif Saeed Shaheen (Qat)	7:53.63
110m Hurdles	Colin Jackson (GB)	12.91
400m Hurdles	Kevin Young (USA)	46.78
Pole Vault	Sergey Bubka (Ukr)	6.14
High Jump	Javier Sotomayor (Cub)	2.45
Long Jump	Mike Powell (USA)	8.95
Triple Jump	Jonathan Edwards (GB)	18.29

Shot Put	Randy Barnes (USA)	23.12
Discus	Jürgen Schult (Ger)	74.08
Hammer	Yury Sedykh (URS)	86.74
Javelin	Jan Zelezny (Cz)	98.48
Decathlon	Roman Sebrle (Cz)	9026
4x100	USA	37.40
4x200	Santa Monica Track Club	1:18.68
4x400	USA	2:54.20
4x800	GB (Elliott, Cook, Cram, Coe)	7:03.89
4x1500	Germany	14:38.80

Women

100m	Florence Griffith-Joyner (USA)	10.49
200m	Florence Griffith-Joyner (USA)	21.34
400m	Marita Koch (Ger)	47.60
800m	Jarmila Kratochvilova (TCH)	1:53.28
1,000m	Svetlana Masterkova (Rus)	2:28.98
1,500m	Qu Yunxia (Chn)	3:50.46
2,000m	Sonia O'Sullivan (Ire)	5:25.36
Mile	Svetlana Masterkova (Rus)	4:12.56

Women

3,000m	Wang Junxia (Chn)	8:06.11
5,000m	Elvan Abeylegasse (Tur)	14:24.68
10,000m	Wang Junxia (Chn)	29:31.78
20,000m	Tegla Loroupe (Ken)	1:05:26.06
25,000m	Tegla Loroupe (Ken)	1:27:05.90
3,000m S/chase	Gulnara Samitova (Rus)	9:01.59
1 Hour	Tegla Loroupe (Ken)	18,304m
Half Marathon	I. Kristiansen (Nor)	1:06:40
Marathon	Paula Radcliffe (GB)	2:15:25
30,000m	Tegla Loroupe (Ken)	1:45.50
100m Hurdles	Yordanka Donkova (Bul)	12.21
400m Hurdles	Yuliya Pechonkina (Rus)	52.34
Pole Vault	Yelena Isinbayeva (Rus)	4.92
High Jump	Stefka Kostadinova (Bul)	2.09
Long Jump	Galina Chistyakova (URS)	7.52
Triple Jump	Inessa Kravets (Ukr)	15.50
Shot Put	Natalya Lisovskaya (URS)	22.63
Discus	Gabriele Reinsch (Ger)	76.80
Hammer	Mihaela Melinte (Rom)	76.07
Javelin (pre 1999)	Petra Felke (Ger)	80.00
Javelin (post 1999)	Osleidys Menéndez (Cub)	71.54
Heptathlon	Jackie Joyner-Kersee (USA)	7291
4x100	East Germany	41.37
4x200	USA	1:27.46
4x400	Soviet Union	3:15.17
4x800	Soviet Union	7:50.17

NB Marathon and half marathon records are officially 'World Bests' rather than World Records due to the non-standardisation of courses.

Baseball: World Series

	Winners		*Runners-up*
1903	Boston Red Sox (AL)	5–3	Pittsburgh Pirates (NL)
1904	no series		
1905	New York Giants (NL)	4–1	Philadelphia Athletics (AL)
1906	Chicago White Sox (AL)	4–2	Chicago Cubs (NL)
1907	Chicago Cubs (NL)	4–0	Detroit Tigers (AL)
1908	Chicago Cubs (NL)	4–1	Detroit Tigers (AL)
1909	Pittsburgh Pirates (NL)	4–3	Detroit Tigers (AL)
1910	Philadelphia Athletics (AL)	4–1	Chicago Cubs (NL)
1911	Philadelphia Athletics (AL)	4–2	New York Giants (NL)
1912	Boston Red Sox (AL)	4–3	New York Giants (NL)
1913	Philadelphia Athletics (AL)	4–1	New York Giants (NL)
1914	Boston Braves (NL)	4–0	Philadelphia Athletics (AL)
1915	Boston Red Sox (AL)	4–1	Philadelphia Phillies (NL)

	Winners		Runners-up
1916	Boston Red Sox (AL)	4–1	Brooklyn Dodgers (NL)
1917	Chicago White Sox (AL)	4–2	New York Giants (NL)
1918	Boston Red Sox (AL)	4–2	Chicago Cubs (NL)
1919	Cincinnati Reds (NL)	5–3	Chicago White Sox (AL)
1920	Cleveland Indians (AL)	5–2	Brooklyn Dodgers (NL)
1921	New York Giants (NL)	5–3	New York Yankees (AL)
1922	New York Giants (NL)	4–0	New York Yankees (AL)
1923	New York Yankees (AL)	4–2	New York Giants (NL)
1924	Washington Senators (AL)	4–3	New York Giants (NL)
1925	Pittsburgh Pirates (NL)	4–3	Washington Senators (AL)
1926	St Louis Cardinals (NL)	4–3	New York Yankees (AL)
1927	New York Yankees (AL)	4–0	Pittsburgh Pirates (NL)
1928	New York Yankees (AL)	4–0	St Louis Cardinals (NL)
1929	Philadelphia Athletics (AL)	4–1	Chicago Cubs (NL)
1930	Philadelphia Athletics (AL)	4–2	St Louis Cardinals (NL)
1931	St Louis Cardinals (NL)	4–3	Philadelphia Athletics (AL)
1932	New York Yankees (AL)	4–0	Chicago Cubs (NL)
1933	New York Giants (NL)	4–1	Washington Senators (AL)
1934	St Louis Cardinals (NL)	4–3	Detroit Tigers (AL)
1935	Detroit Tigers (AL)	4–2	Chicago Cubs (NL)
1936	New York Yankees (AL)	4–2	New York Giants (NL)
1937	New York Yankees (AL)	4–1	New York Giants (NL)
1938	New York Yankees (AL)	4–0	Chicago Cubs (NL)
1939	New York Yankees (AL)	4–0	Cincinnati Reds (NL)
1940	Cincinnati Reds (NL)	4–3	Detroit Tigers (AL)
1941	New York Yankees (AL)	4–1	Brooklyn Dodgers (NL)
1942	St Louis Cardinals (NL)	4–1	New York Yankees (AL)
1943	New York Yankees (AL)	4–1	St Louis Cardinals (NL)
1944	St Louis Cardinals (NL)	4–2	St Louis Browns (AL)
1945	Detroit Tigers (AL)	4–3	Chicago Cubs (NL)
1946	St Louis Cardinals (NL)	4–3	Boston Red Sox (AL)
1947	New York Yankees (AL)	4–3	Brooklyn Dodgers (NL)
1948	Cleveland Indians (AL)	4–2	Boston Braves (NL)
1949	New York Yankees (AL)	4–1	Brooklyn Dodgers (NL)
1950	New York Yankees (AL)	4–0	Philadelphia Phillies (NL)
1951	New York Yankees (AL)	4–2	New York Giants (NL)
1952	New York Yankees (AL)	4–3	Brooklyn Dodgers (NL)
1953	New York Yankees (AL)	4–2	Brooklyn Dodgers (NL)
1954	New York Giants (NL)	4–0	Cleveland Indians (AL)
1955	Brooklyn Dodgers (NL)	4–3	New York Yankees (AL)
1956	New York Yankees (AL)	4–3	Brooklyn Dodgers (NL)
1957	Milwaukee Braves (NL)	4–3	New York Yankees (AL)
1958	New York Yankees (AL)	4–3	Milwaukee Braves (NL)
1959	Los Angeles Dodgers (NL)	4–2	Chicago White Sox (AL)
1960	Pittsburgh Pirates (NL)	4–3	New York Yankees (AL)
1961	New York Yankees (AL)	4–1	Cincinnati Reds (NL)
1962	New York Yankees (AL)	4–3	San Francisco Giants (NL)
1963	Los Angeles Dodgers (NL)	4–0	New York Yankees (AL)
1964	St Louis Cardinals (NL)	4–3	New York Yankees (AL)
1965	Los Angeles Dodgers (NL)	4–3	Minnesota Twins (AL)
1966	Baltimore Orioles (AL)	4–0	Los Angeles Dodgers (NL)
1967	St Louis Cardinals (NL)	4–3	Boston Red Sox (AL)
1968	Detroit Tigers (AL)	4–3	St Louis Cardinals (NL)
1969	New York Mets (NL)	4–1	Baltimore Orioles (AL)
1970	Baltimore Orioles (AL)	4–1	Cincinnati Reds (NL)
1971	Pittsburgh Pirates (NL)	4–3	Baltimore Orioles (AL)
1972	Oakland Athletics (AL)	4–3	Cincinnati Reds (NL)
1973	Oakland Athletics (AL)	4–3	New York Mets (NL)
1974	Oakland Athletics (AL)	4–1	Los Angeles Dodgers (NL)
1975	Cincinnati Reds (NL)	4–3	Boston Red Sox (AL)
1976	Cincinnati Reds (NL)	4–0	New York Yankees (AL)
1977	New York Yankees (AL)	4–2	Los Angeles Dodgers (NL)
1978	New York Yankees (AL)	4–2	Los Angeles Dodgers (NL)
1979	Pittsburgh Pirates (NL)	4–3	Baltimore Orioles (AL)
1980	Philadelphia Phillies (NL)	4–2	Kansas City Royals (AL)
1981	Los Angeles Dodgers (NL)	4–2	New York Yankees (AL)
1982	St Louis Cardinals (NL)	4–3	Milwaukee Brewers (AL)
1983	Baltimore Orioles (AL)	4–1	Philadelphia Phillies (NL)
1984	Detroit Tigers (AL)	4–1	San Diego Padres (NL)
1985	Kansas City Royals (AL)	4–3	St Louis Cardinals (NL)
1986	New York Mets (NL)	4–3	Boston Red Sox (AL)

	Winners		Runners-up
1987	Minnesota Twins (AL)	4–3	St Louis Cardinals (NL)
1988	Los Angeles Dodgers (NL)	4–1	Oakland Athletics (AL)
1989	Oakland Athletics (AL)	4–0	San Francisco Giants (NL)
1990	Cincinnati Reds (NL)	4–0	Oakland Athletics (AL)
1991	Minnesota Twins (AL)	4–3	Atlanta Braves (NL)
1992	Toronto Blue Jays (AL)	4–2	Atlanta Braves (NL)
1993	Toronto Blue Jays (AL)	4–2	Philadelphia Phillies (NL)
1994	no series		
1995	Atlanta Braves (NL)	4–2	Cleveland Indians (AL)
1996	New York Yankees (AL)	4–2	Atlanta Braves (NL)
1997	Florida Marlins (NL)	4–3	Cleveland Indians (AL)
1998	New York Yankees (AL)	4–0	San Diego Padres (NL)
1999	New York Yankees (AL)	4–0	Atlanta Braves (NL)
2000	New York Yankees (AL)	4–1	New York Mets (NL)
2001	Arizona Diamondbacks (NL)	4–3	New York Yankees (AL)
2002	Anaheim Angels (AL)	4–3	San Francisco Giants (NL)
2003	Florida Marlins (NL)	4–2	New York Yankees (AL)
2004	Boston Red Sox (AL)	4–0	St Louis Cardinals (NL)

(AL = American League.   NL = National League.)

Baseball: General Information

ball: weight   between 5 and 5¼ oz.
bat: dimensions   maximum length of 42 inches, maximum thickness of 2¾ inches.
Black Sox scandal   eight members of the Chicago White Sox were accused of accepting bribes to throw the 1919 World Series. Although subsequently found not guilty the players were suspended for life from the 1921 season onwards.
Black Sox scandal: judge   Kenesaw Mountain Landis.
commissioner: first   Kenesaw Mountain Landis.
Continental League: inaugurated   27 July 1959.
first match under Cartwright Rules (1846)   New York Nine (23) v Knickerbocker Club (1).
Hall of Fame   founded in 1936 in Cooperstown, NY.

innings per game   nine.
inventor of game   Abner Doubleday, a Civil War general, credited with invention in 1839 although it was more likely derived from the game of rounders in the 18th century.
number in team   nine.
playing area   diamond.
rules codified by   Alexander Joy Cartwright (1845).
Ruth: George Herman   nicknamed 'Babe' and 'The Sultan of Swat'.
umpires   four umpires run a game positioned near the home plate and the three bases.
World Series: contestants   winners of the American League and National League.

Boxing Champions (as at 15 June 2005)

International Boxing Federation (IBF), World Boxing Association (WBA),
World Boxing Council (WBC), World Boxing Organization (WBO)

	IBF	WBA	WBC	WBO
Heavyweight	Chris Byrd	John Ruiz	Vitali Klitschko	Lamon Brewster
Cruiserweight (190 pounds)	O'Neil Bell	Jean Mark Mormeck	Jean Mark Mormeck	Johnny Nelson
Light Heavyweight (175 pounds)	Clinton Woods	Fabrice Tiozza	Tomasz Adamek	Zsolt Erdei
Super Middleweight (168 pounds)	Jeff Lacy	Mikkel Kessler	Markus Beyer	Joe Calzaghe
Middleweight (160 pounds)	Bernard Hopkins	Maselino Masoe	Bernard Hopkins	Bernard Hopkins
Junior Middleweight (154 pounds)	Kassim Ouma	Travis Simms	Winky Wright	Daniel Santos
Welterweight (147 pounds)	Zab Judah	Luis Collazo	Zab Judah	Antonio Margarito
Junior Welterweight (140 pounds)	Ricky Hatton	Vivian Harris	Arturo Gatti	Miguel Ángel Cotto
Lightweight (135 pounds)	Julio Diaz	Juan Diaz	Diego Corrales	Diego Corrales
Junior Lightweight (130 pounds)	Robbie Peden	Vincente Mosquera	Marco Antonio Barrera	Jorge Rodrigo Barrios

Featherweight (126 pounds)	Juan Manuel Marquez	Chris John	In-Jin Chi	Scott Harrison
Junior Featherweight (122 pounds)	Israel Vazquez	Mahyar Monshipour	Oscar Larios	Joan Guzman
Bantamweight (118 pounds)	Rafael Marquez	Wladimir Sidorenko	Hozumi Haseqawa	Ratanachai Sor Vorapin
Junior Bantamweight (115 pounds)	Luis Perez	Jose Martin Castillo	Katsushige Kawashima	Fernando Montiel
Flyweight (112 pounds)	Vic Darchinyan	Lorenzo Parra	Pongsaklek Wonjongkam	Omar Narvaez
Junior Flyweight (108 pounds)	Will Grigsby	Roberto Vasques	Eric Ortiz	Hugo Cazares
Strawweight (105 pounds)	Muhammad Rachman	Yutaka Niida	Katsunari Takayama	Iván Calderón

Cricket – Trophy Winners from 1946

	County Championship	Sunday League/ National League	Benson and Hedges Cup	Cheltenham and Gloucester Trophy (C & G) (Gillette Cup 1963–81; NatWest Trophy 1982–2000)
1946	Yorkshire	–	–	–
1947	Middlesex	–	–	–
1948	Glamorgan	–	–	–
1949	Middlesex/Yorkshire	–	–	–
1950	Lancashire/Surrey	–	–	–
1951	Warwickshire	–	–	–
1952	Surrey	–	–	–
1953	Surrey	–	–	–
1954	Surrey	–	–	–
1955	Surrey	–	–	–
1956	Surrey	–	–	–
1957	Surrey	–	–	–
1958	Surrey	–	–	–
1959	Yorkshire	–	–	–
1960	Yorkshire	–	–	–
1961	Hampshire	–	–	–
1962	Yorkshire	–	–	–
1963	Yorkshire	–	–	Sussex
1964	Worcestershire	–	–	Sussex
1965	Worcestershire	–	–	Yorkshire
1966	Yorkshire	–	–	Warwickshire
1967	Yorkshire	–	–	Kent
1968	Yorkshire	–	–	Warwickshire
1969	Glamorgan	Lancashire	–	Yorkshire
1970	Kent	Lancashire	–	Lancashire
1971	Surrey	Worcestershire	–	Lancashire
1972	Warwickshire	Kent	Leicestershire	Lancashire
1973	Hampshire	Kent	Kent	Gloucestershire
1974	Worcestershire	Leicestershire	Surrey	Kent
1975	Leicestershire	Hampshire	Leicestershire	Lancashire
1976	Middlesex	Kent	Kent	Northamptonshire
1977	Kent/Middlesex	Leicestershire	Gloucestershire	Middlesex
1978	Kent	Hampshire	Kent	Sussex
1979	Essex	Somerset	Essex	Somerset
1980	Middlesex	Warwickshire	Northamptonshire	Middlesex
1981	Nottinghamshire	Essex	Somerset	Derbyshire
1982	Middlesex	Sussex	Somerset	Surrey
1983	Essex	Yorkshire	Middlesex	Somerset
1984	Essex	Essex	Lancashire	Middlesex
1985	Middlesex	Essex	Leicestershire	Essex
1986	Essex	Hampshire	Middlesex	Sussex
1987	Nottinghamshire	Worcestershire	Yorkshire	Nottinghamshire
1988	Worcestershire	Worcestershire	Hampshire	Middlesex
1989	Worcestershire	Lancashire	Nottinghamshire	Warwickshire
1990	Middlesex	Derbyshire	Lancashire	Lancashire
1991	Essex	Nottinghamshire	Worcestershire	Hampshire
1992	Essex	Middlesex	Hampshire	Northamptonshire

1993	Middlesex	Glamorgan	Derbyshire	Warwickshire
1994	Warwickshire	Warwickshire	Warwickshire	Worcestershire
1995	Warwickshire	Kent	Lancashire	Warwickshire
1996	Leicestershire	Surrey	Lancashire	Lancashire
1997	Glamorgan	Warwickshire	Surrey	Essex
1998	Leicestershire	Lancashire	Essex	Lancashire
1999	Surrey	Lancashire	Gloucestershire	Gloucestershire
2000	Surrey	Gloucestershire	Gloucestershire	Gloucestershire
2001	Yorkshire	Kent	Surrey	Somerset
2002	Surrey	Glamorgan	Warwickshire	Yorkshire
2003	Sussex	Surrey	Surrey*	Gloucestershire
2004	Warwickshire	Glamorgan	Leicestershire	Gloucestershire

*In 2003 the Benson & Hedges Cup was replaced by the Twenty20 Cup.

Cricket: General Information

ball: weight Between 5½ and 5¾ ounces (159.9–163g).

bat throwing controversy Dermot Reeves (Warks) threw bat away to avoid bat and pad catch.

Benson and Hedges Cup in 1999, the Benson and Hedges Super Cup replaced the old format, but the original format was reverted to in 2000.

best Test Match bowling figures Jim Laker 19 for 90, England v Australia at Old Trafford (1956). (Tony Locke took other wicket).

best Test Match bowling figures in single innings Jim Laker 10 for 53 v Australia at Old Trafford (1956).

Bodyline Series of 1932/3 (Australia v England) the leading bowler was Harold Larwood (33 wickets) and the England captain was Douglas Jardine, who instructed Larwood to bowl at the leg stump and into the batsman's body.

Bosie Aussie name for googly (named after its inventor B J T Bosanquet, father of newsreader Reginald).

brothers: seven played for Worcestershire Foster brothers: Basil, Henry, Maurice, Neville, Reginald, Geoffrey, Wilfrid.

captain of England also Olympic boxing gold medallist J W H T Douglas.

Chinaman googly bowled by a left-hander, i.e. ball that breaks from off to leg.

county captain: longest tenure W G Grace for Gloucester (1871–99).

County Championship officially constituted in 1890, although counties existed prior to that date and claimed a sort of unofficial title. The 1890 championship was contested by eight counties, Gloucestershire, Kent, Lancashire, Middlesex, Nottinghamshire, Surrey, Sussex, and Yorkshire. The title was won in 1890, and the following two seasons, by Surrey. The sponsors since the 2003 season are Liverpool Victoria, branded under their affinity name of Frizzell. Previous sponsors included Schweppes (1977–83), Britannic Assurance (1984–98), PPP Healthcare (1999–2000) and Cricinfo (2001–02). The only two counties to join the championship since World War One are Glamorgan (1921) and Durham (1992). The County Championship was split into two divisions each of nine teams from the 2000 season onwards.

county cricket: grounds Derbyshire – Nottingham Road, Derby; Durham – Riverside Ground, Chester-le-Street; Essex – New Writtle St, Chelmsford; Glamorgan – Sophia Gardens, Cardiff; Gloucestershire – Nevil Road, Bristol; Hampshire – Rose Bowl, Southampton; Kent – St Lawrence Ground, Canterbury; Lancashire – Old Trafford, Manchester; Leicestershire – Grace Road, Leicester; Middlesex – Lord's, London; Northants – Wantage Road, Northampton; Nottinghamshire – Trent Bridge, Nottingham; Somerset – St James's Street, Taunton; Surrey – Foster's Oval, Kennington; Sussex – Eaton Road, Hove; Warwickshire – Edgbaston, Birmingham; Worcestershire – New Road, Worcester; Yorkshire – Headingley, Leeds.

CGU National League nicknames Derbyshire (Scorpions), Durham (Dynamos), Essex (Eagles), Glamorgan (Dragons), Gloucestershire (Gladiators), Hampshire (Hawks), Lancashire (Lightning), Leicestershire (Foxes), Middlesex (Crusaders), Northamptonshire (Steelbacks), Nottinghamshire (Outlaws), Somerset (Sabres), Surrey (Lions), Sussex (Sharks), Warwickshire (Bears), Worcestershire (Royals), Yorkshire (Phoenix).

dismissal: methods bowled, caught, handled the ball, hit the ball twice, hit wicket, leg before wicket (lbw), obstructing the field, run out, stumped, timed out.

double: first to complete (1000 runs and 100 wickets in a season) W.G. Grace.

Douglas, J W H T : nickname Johnny Won't Hit Today. Douglas also won a gold medal for Great Britain in the 1908 Olympics at Middleweight Boxing.

Duckworth/Lewis System used to determine the winning score in rain-interrupted one-day matches.

ECB (England and Wales Cricket Board): chairman Lord MacLaurin of Knebworth.

fifty: slowest first class Trevor Bailey.

googly off break bowled with a leg-break action.

highest scorer in first class cricket Brian Lara 501 not out v Durham.

highest scorer in test cricket Brian Lara 400 not out v England (Antigua, 2003–04).

hundred: first recorded John Minshull, 107 for Duke of Dorset's XI v Wrexham (1769).

last man to take hattrick in Test Match for England Darren Gough v Australia at Sydney (1998–99).

Lords: three locations St John's Wood, London (1814 to present); Marylebone Bank, Regent's Park, London (1811–14); Dorset Fields, London (1787–1811).

monarch made cricket illegal Edward IV in 1477 (revoked in 1748).

Olympic champions Great Britain.

one day internationals: fastest century Shahid Afridi (Pakistan) scored 100 in 37 balls against Sri Lanka in 1997.

run: distance for completion of 58ft (17.68m).

six 6's in over: first Gary Sobers (for Notts v Glamorgan, bowler: Malcolm Nash); Ravi Shastri was the second man to accomplish the feat.

stumps: height 28 inches (71.1cm).

Sunday League CGU National League 1999 and 2000; Norwich Union League 2001 and 2002; ECB National League in 2003; totesport League from 2004. Scotland joined the National Cricket League Division Two in 2003. Under current regulations matches are 45 overs per side.

Sunday League: double century Ally Brown of Surrey.

swearing incident Mike Gatting at umpire Shakoor Rana (1987).

TCCB: name change in 1996 ECB (England and Wales Cricket Board).

Test cricket: oldest player Wilfred Rhodes (52).

Test cricket: youngest English player Brian Close (18).

Test cricket: youngest player Hasan Raza (Pakistan) was 14 yrs 227 days old when he played against Zimbabwe in 1996–97.

Test Match century: fewest balls Viv Richards (56)

against England at St John's in 1985–86.

Test Match double century: fewest balls Nathan Astle (153) for New Zealand against England at Christchurch in March 2002. The first hundred took 114 balls and the second hundred only 39 balls.

Test Match: first Australia v England, Melbourne Cricket Ground 1877.

Test Match: tied Australia v West Indies (1960) and Australia v India (1986).

university grounds Cambridge – Fenner's, Oxford – The Parks.

West Indies: three Ws Weekes, Worrell, Walcott.

Wisden: colour yellow.

World Cup football winner played County Cricket Geoff Hurst.

World Cup winners West Indies beat Australia (1975); West Indies beat England (1979); India beat West Indies (1983); Australia beat England (1987); Pakistan beat England (1991); Sri Lanka beat Australia (1996); Australia beat Pakistan (1999); Australia beat India (2003).

World Cup: defeated West Indies Kenya bowled West Indies out for 93 in group match of 1996 World Cup.

Darts: World Champions

	Winner		*Runner-up*
1978	Leighton Rees (Wal)	11–7	John Lowe (Eng)
1979	John Lowe (Eng)	5–0	Leighton Rees (Wal)
1980	Eric Bristow (Eng)	5–3	Bobby George (Eng)
1981	Eric Bristow (Eng)	5–3	John Lowe (Eng)
1982	Jocky Wilson (Sco)	5–3	John Lowe (Eng)
1983	Keith Deller (Eng)	6–5	Eric Bristow (Eng)
1984	Eric Bristow (Eng)	7–1	Dave Whitcombe (Eng)
1985	Eric Bristow (Eng)	6–2	John Lowe (Eng)
1986	Eric Bristow (Eng)	6–0	Dave Whitcombe (Eng)
1987	John Lowe (Eng)	6–4	Eric Bristow (Eng)
1988	Bob Anderson (Eng)	6–4	John Lowe (Eng)
1989	Jocky Wilson (Sco)	6–4	Eric Bristow (Eng)
1990	Phil Taylor (Eng)	6–1	Eric Bristow (Eng)
1991	Dennis Priestley (Eng)	6–0	Eric Bristow (Eng)
1992	Phil Taylor (Eng)	6–5	Mike Gregory (Eng)
1993	John Lowe (Eng)	6–3	Alan Warriner (Eng)
1994	John Part (Can)	6–0	Bobby George (Eng)
	Dennis Priestley (Eng)	6–1	Phil Taylor (Eng)
1995	Richie Burnett (Wal)	6–3	Ray Barneveld (Ned)
	Phil Taylor (Eng)	6–2	Rod Harrington (Eng)
1996	Steve Beaton (Eng)	6–3	Richie Burnett (Wal)
	Phil Taylor (Eng)	6–4	Dennis Priestley (Eng)
1997	Les Wallace (Sco)	6–3	Marshall James (Wal)
	Phil Taylor (Eng)	6–3	Dennis Priestley (Eng)
1998	Ray Barneveld (Ned)	6–5	Richie Burnett (Wal)
	Phil Taylor (Eng)	6–0	Dennis Priestley (Eng)
1999	Ray Barneveld (Ned)	6–5	Ronnie Baxter (Sco)
	Phil Taylor (Eng)	6–2	Peter Manley (Eng)
2000	Ted Hankey (Eng)	6–0	Ronnie Baxter (Sco)
	Phil Taylor (Eng)	7–3	Dennis Priestley (Eng)
2001	John Walton (Eng)	6–2	Ted Hankey (Eng)
	Phil Taylor (Eng)	7–0	John Part (Can)
2002	Tony David (Aust)	6–4	Mervyn King (Eng)
	Phil Taylor (Eng)	7–0	Peter Manley (Eng)
2003	Ray Barneveld (Ned)	6–3	Ritchie Davies (Wal)
	John Part (Can)	7–6	Phil Taylor (Eng)
2004	Andy Fordham (Eng)	6–3	Mervyn King (Eng)
	Phil Taylor (Eng)	7–6	Kevin Painter (Eng)
2005	Ray Barneveld (Ned)	6–2	Martin Adams (Eng)
	Phil Taylor (Eng)	7–4	Mark Dudbridge (Eng)

NB First named winners are Embassy BDO champions. Second named winners are WDC champions (now called PDC).

Darts: General Information

BDO: stands for	British Darts Organization
News of the World Competition	1991–7 suspended sponsorship
News of the World: best of legs	best of three throughout competition
PDC: stands for	Professional Darts Council
venues: Embassy	Lakeside CC, Frimley Green, Surrey
	Heart of Midlands Club, Notts (1978)
	Jollees Night Club, Stoke (1979–85)
venue: PDC	Circus Tavern, Purfleet
WDC: stands for	World Darts Council
World Champions: nine-dart legs	John Lowe won £102,000 for achieving
	the first nine-dart 501 leg
	Paul Lim (USA) was second man to achieve
	a nine-dart leg

Darts: News of the World Champions

1948	Harry Leadbetter	1960	Tom Reddington	1972	Brian Netherton	1982	Roy Morgan
1949	Jack Boyce	1961	Alec Adamson	1973	Ivor Hodgkinson	1983	Eric Bristow
1950	Dixie Newberry	1962	Eddie Brown	1974	Peter Chapman	1984	Eric Bristow
1951	Harry Perryman	1963	Robbie Rumney	1975	Derek White	1985	Dave Lee
1952	Tommy Gibbons	1964	Tom Barrett	1976	Bill Lennard	1986	Bobby George
1953	Jimmy Carr	1965	Tom Barrett	1977	Mick Norris	1987	Mike Gregory
1954	Oliver James	1966	Wilf Ellis	1978	Stefan Lord	1988	Mike Gregory
1955	Tom Reddington	1967	Wally Seaton		(Sweden)	1989	Dave Whitcombe
1956	Trevor Peachey	1968	Bill Duddy	1979	Bobby George	1990	Paul Cook
1957	Alwyn Mullins	1969	Barry Twomlow	1980	Stefan Lord	1997	Phil Taylor
1958	Tommy Gibbons	1970	Henry Barney		(Sweden)		
1959	Albert Welch	1971	Dennis Filkins	1981	John Lowe		

Football: English League Winners

	Division 1	Division 2	Division 3	Division 3 South
1889	Preston North End	—	—	—
1890	Preston North End	—	—	—
1891	Everton	—	—	—
1892	Sunderland	—	—	—
1893	Sunderland	Small Heath	—	—
1894	Aston Villa	Liverpool	—	—
1895	Sunderland	Bury	—	—
1896	Aston Villa	Liverpool	—	—
1897	Aston Villa	Notts County	—	—
1898	Sheffield United	Burnley	—	—
1899	Aston Villa	Manchester City	—	—
1900	Aston Villa	The Wednesday	—	—
1901	Liverpool	Grimsby Town	—	—
1902	Sunderland	West Bromwich Albion	—	—
1903	The Wednesday	Manchester City	—	—
1904	The Wednesday	Preston North End	—	—
1905	Newcastle United	Liverpool	—	—
1906	Liverpool	Bristol City	—	—
1907	Newcastle United	Nottingham Forest	—	—
1908	Manchester United	Bradford City	—	—
1909	Newcastle United	Bolton Wanderers	—	—
1910	Aston Villa	Manchester City	—	—
1911	Manchester United	West Bromwich Albion	—	—
1912	Blackburn Rovers	Derby County	—	—
1913	Sunderland	Preston North End	—	—
1914	Blackburn Rovers	Notts County	—	—
1915	Everton	Derby County	—	—
1916	not held	not held	—	—
1917	not held	not held	—	—
1918	not held	not held	—	—
1919	not held	not held	—	—
1920	West Bromwich Albion	Tottenham Hotspur	—	—
1921	Burnley	Birmingham City	Crystal Palace	—

	Division 1	Division 2	Division 3 North	Division 3 South
1922	Liverpool	Nottingham Forest	Stockport County	Southampton
1923	Liverpool	Notts County	Nelson	Bristol City
1924	Huddersfield Town	Leeds United	Wolverhampton Wanderers	Portsmouth
1925	Huddersfield Town	Leicester City	Darlington	Swansea Town
1926	Huddersfield Town	The Wednesday	Grimsby Town	Reading
1927	Newcastle United	Middlesbrough	Stoke City	Bristol City
1928	Everton	Manchester City	Bradford Park Avenue	Millwall
1929	The Wednesday	Middlesbrough	Bradford City	Charlton Athletic
1930	Sheffield Wednesday	Blackpool	Port Vale	Plymouth Argyle
1931	Arsenal	Everton	Chesterfield	Notts County
1932	Everton	Wolverhampton Wanderers	Lincoln City	Fulham
1933	Arsenal	Stoke City	Hull City	Brentford
1934	Arsenal	Grimsby Town	Barnsley	Norwich City
1935	Arsenal	Brentford	Doncaster Rovers	Charlton Athletic
1936	Sunderland	Manchester United	Chesterfield	Coventry City
1937	Manchester City	Leicester City	Stockport County	Luton Town
1938	Arsenal	Aston Villa	Tranmere Rovers	Millwall
1939	Everton	Blackburn Rovers	Barnsley	Newport County
1940	not held	not held	not held	not held
1941	not held	not held	not held	not held
1942	not held	not held	not held	not held
1943	not held	not held	not held	not held
1944	not held	not held	not held	not held
1945	not held	not held	not held	not held
1946	not held	not held	not held	not held
1947	Liverpool	Manchester City	Doncaster Rovers	Cardiff City
1948	Arsenal	Birmingham City	Lincoln City	Queen's Park Rangers
1949	Portsmouth	Fulham	Hull City	Swansea Town
1950	Portsmouth	Tottenham Hotspur	Doncaster Rovers	Notts County
1951	Tottenham Hotspur	Preston North End	Rotherham United	Nottingham Forest
1952	Manchester United	Sheffield Wednesday	Lincoln City	Plymouth Argyle
1953	Arsenal	Sheffield United	Oldham Athletic	Bristol Rovers
1954	Wolverhampton Wanderers	Leicester City	Port Vale	Ipswich Town
1955	Chelsea	Birmingham City	Barnsley	Bristol City
1956	Manchester United	Sheffield Wednesday	Grimsby Town	Leyton Orient
1957	Manchester United	Leicester City	Derby County	Ipswich Town
1958	Wolverhampton Wanderers	West Ham United	Scunthorpe United	Brighton & Hove Albion

	Division 1	Division 2	Division 3	Division 4
1959	Wolverhampton Wanderers	Sheffield Wednesday	Plymouth Argyle	Port Vale
1960	Burnley	Aston Villa	Southampton	Walsall
1961	Tottenham Hotspur	Ipswich Town	Bury	Peterborough United
1962	Ipswich Town	Liverpool	Portsmouth	Millwall
1963	Everton	Stoke City	Northampton Town	Brentford
1964	Liverpool	Leeds United	Coventry City	Gillingham
1965	Manchester United	Newcastle United	Carlisle United	Brighton & Hove Albion
1966	Liverpool	Manchester City	Hull City	Doncaster Rovers
1967	Manchester United	Coventry City	Queen's Park Rangers	Stockport County
1968	Manchester City	Ipswich Town	Oxford United	Luton Town
1969	Leeds United	Derby County	Watford	Doncaster Rovers
1970	Everton	Huddersfield Town	Orient	Chesterfield
1971	Arsenal	Leicester City	Preston North End	Notts County
1972	Derby County	Norwich City	Aston Villa	Grimsby Town
1973	Liverpool	Burnley	Bolton Wanderers	Southport
1974	Leeds United	Middlesbrough	Oldham Athletic	Peterborough United
1975	Derby County	Manchester United	Blackburn Rovers	Mansfield Town
1976	Liverpool	Sunderland	Hereford United	Lincoln City
1977	Liverpool	Wolverhampton Wanderers	Mansfield Town	Cambridge United
1978	Nottingham Forest	Bolton Wanderers	Wrexham	Watford
1979	Liverpool	Crystal Palace	Shrewsbury Town	Reading
1980	Liverpool	Leicester City	Grimsby Town	Huddersfield Town
1981	Aston Villa	West Ham United	Rotherham United	Southend United
1982	Liverpool	Luton Town	Burnley	Sheffield United
1983	Liverpool	Queen's Park Rangers	Portsmouth	Wimbledon
1984	Liverpool	Chelsea	Oxford United	York City
1985	Everton	Oxford United	Bradford City	Chesterfield
1986	Liverpool	Norwich City	Reading	Swindon Town
1987	Everton	Derby County	Bournemouth	Northampton Town

	Division 1	Division 2	Division 3	Division 4
1988	Liverpool	Millwall	Sunderland	Wolverhampton Wanderers
1989	Arsenal	Chelsea	Wolverhampton Wanderers	Rotherham United
1990	Liverpool	Leeds United	Bristol Rovers	Exeter City
1991	Arsenal	Oldham Athletic	Cambridge United	Darlington
1992	Leeds United	Ipswich Town	Brentford	Burnley

	Premier League	Division 1	Division 2	Division 3
1993	Manchester United	Newcastle United	Stoke City	Cardiff City
1994	Manchester United	Crystal Palace	Reading	Shrewsbury Town
1995	Blackburn Rovers	Middlesbrough	Birmingham City	Carlisle United
1996	Manchester United	Sunderland	Swindon Town	Preston North End
1997	Manchester United	Bolton Wanderers	Bury	Wigan Athletic
1998	Arsenal	Nottingham Forest	Watford	Notts County
1999	Manchester United	Sunderland	Fulham	Brentford
2000	Manchester United	Charlton	Preston North End	Swansea City
2001	Manchester United	Fulham	Millwall	Brighton & Hove Albion
2002	Arsenal	Manchester City	Brighton & Hove Albion	Plymouth Argyle
2003	Manchester United	Portsmouth	Wigan	Rushden and Diamonds
2004	Arsenal	Norwich City	Plymouth Argyle	Doncaster Rovers
2005	Chelsea	Sunderland	Luton Town	Yeovil Town

For the 2004/5 season the sponsors for the Premiership were Barclays. The former Division One was renamed the Coca-Cola Football League Championship. The former Division Two was renamed the Coca-Cola Football League One. The former Division Three was renamed the Coca-Cola Football League Two.

Football: English League Clubs

Club	League debut	Nickname(s)	Ground	Previous name(s)
Arsenal	1893	Gunners	Arsenal Stadium, Highbury	Dial Square, Royal Arsenal, Woolwich Arsenal
Aston Villa	1888	Villans	Villa Park	none
Barnet	1991	Bees	Underhill	Barnet Alston FC
Barnsley	1898	Tykes, Reds, Colliers	Oakwell	Barnsley St Peter's
Birmingham City	1892	Blues	St Andrew's	Small Heath Alliance, Small Heath, Birmingham
Blackburn Rovers	1888	Rovers	Ewood Park	none
Blackpool	1896	Seasiders	Bloomfield Road	Blackpool St Johns, Blackpool South Shore
Bolton Wanderers	1888	Trotters	The Reebok Stadium	Christ Church FC
Boston United	2002	Pilgrims	York Street Stadium	none
AFC Bournemouth	1923	Cherries	Fitness First Stadium, Dean Court	Boscombe St John's, Boscombe, Bournemouth & Boscombe Athletic
Bradford City	1903	Bantams	Valley Parade	none
Brentford	1920	Bees	Griffin Park	none
Brighton & Hove Albion	1920	Seagulls	Withdean Stadium	Brighton & Hove Rangers, Brighton & Hove United
Bristol City	1901	Robins	Ashton Gate	Bristol South End
Bristol Rovers	1920	Pirates (originally The Purdown Poachers)	Memorial Ground	Black Arabs, Eastville Rovers, Bristol Eastville Rovers
Burnley	1888	Clarets	Turf Moor	Burnley Rovers
Bury	1894	Shakers	Gigg Lane	none
Cambridge United	1970	The 'U's'	Abbey Stadium	Abbey United
Cardiff City	1920	Bluebirds	Ninian Park	Riverside, Riverside Albion
Carlisle United	1928	Cumbrians, Blues	Brunton Park	amalgamation of Shaddongate United and Carlisle Red Rose
Charlton Athletic	1921	Addicks, Valiants, Robins	The Valley	none
Chelsea	1905	Blues	Stamford Bridge	none
Cheltenham Town	1999	Robins	Whaddon Road	none
Chester City	1931	Blues, City	Deva Stadium	King's School Old Boys and Chester Rovers, Chester
Chesterfield	1899	Spireites, Blues	Recreation Ground, Saltergate	Chesterfield Town

Club	League debut	Nickname(s)	Ground	Previous name(s)
Colchester United	1950	The 'U's'	Layer Road	Colchester Town
Coventry City	1919	Sky Blues	Ricoh Arena	Singers FC
Crewe Alexandra	1892	Railwaymen	Alexandra Stadium, Gresty Road	none
Crystal Palace	1920	Eagles	Selhurst Park	none
Darlington	1921	Quakers	Williamson Motors Stadium	none
Derby County	1888	Rams	Pride Park	none
Doncaster Rovers	1901	Rovers	Belle Vue	none
Everton	1888	Toffees	Goodison Park	St Domingo FC
Exeter City (NC)	1920	Grecians	St James Park	amalgamation of St Sidwell's United and Exeter United
Fulham	1907	Cottagers	Craven Cottage	Fulham St Andrew's
Gillingham	1920	Gills	Priestfield Stadium	Excelsior, New Brompton
Grimsby Town	1892	Mariners	Blundell Park	Grimsby Pelham
Halifax Town (NC)	1921	Shaymen	Shay Stadium	none
Hartlepool United	1921	Pool	Victoria Park	Hartlepools United, Hartlepool
Huddersfield Town	1910	Terriers	Alfred McAlpine Stadium, Leeds Rd	none
Hull City	1905	Tigers	Kingston Communications Stadium	none
Ipswich Town	1938	Blues, Town, Tractor Boys	Portman Road	Ipswich Association FC
Kidderminster Harriers	2000	Harriers	Aggborough Stadium	none
Leeds United	1920	United, The Whites, The Peacocks	Elland Road	formed after Leeds City disbanded by FA order
Leicester City	1894	Foxes, Filberts	Walkers Stadium	Leicester Fosse
Leyton Orient	1905	The 'O's'	Leyton Stadium, Brisbane Road	Glyn Cricket & Football Club, Eagle FC, Orient, Clapton Orient
Lincoln City	1892	Red Imps	Sincil Bank	none
Liverpool	1893	Reds, Pool	Anfield	none
Luton Town	1897	Hatters	Kenilworth Road	amalgamation of Luton Town Wanderers and Excelsior
Macclesfield Town	1997	Silkmen	Moss Rose	none
Manchester City	1892	Citizens, Blues	City of Manchester Stadium	Ardwick FC
Manchester United	1892	Red Devils	Old Trafford	Newton Heath
Mansfield Town	1931	Stags	Field Mill	Mansfield Wesleyans
Middlesbrough	1899	Boro	Riverside Stadium	none
Millwall	1920	Lions	New Den, Bermondsey	Millwall Rovers, Millwall Athletic
MK Dons	1977	Dons	National Hockey Stadium, Milton Keynes	Wimbledon Old Centrals, Wimbledon
Newcastle United	1893	Magpies	St James' Park	Stanley, Newcastle East End
Northampton Town	1920	Cobblers	Sixfields Stadium	none
Norwich City	1920	Canaries	Carrow Road	none
Nottingham Forest	1892	Forest, Reds	City Ground	none
Notts County	1888	Magpies	County Ground, Meadow Lane	Notts FC
Oldham Athletic	1907	Latics	Boundary Park	Pine Villa
Oxford United	1962	The 'U's'	Kassam Stadium, Grenoble Road	Headington, Headington United
Peterborough United	1960	Posh	London Road	formed after Peterborough and Fletton disbanded
Plymouth Argyle	1920	Pilgrims	Home Park	Argyle Athletic Club
Portsmouth	1920	Pompey	Fratton Park	none
Port Vale	1892	Valiants	Vale Park	Burslem Port Vale
Preston North End	1888	Lilywhites, North End	Deepdale	none
Queen's Park Rangers	1920	Rangers, 'R's', the Hoops	Rangers Stadium, Loftus Road	St Jude's
Reading	1920	Royals, Biscuitmen	Madejski Stadium	none
Rochdale	1921	Dale	Spotland	none
Rotherham United	1893	Merry Millers	Millmoor	Thornhill United, Rotherham County, Rotherham Town
Rushden and Diamonds	2001	Diamonds	Nene Park	formed from a merger between Rushden Town and Diamonds in 1992
Scarborough (NC)	1987	Boro	McCain Stadium, Seamer Road	Scarborough Cricketers' FC
Scunthorpe United	1950	The Iron	Glanford Park	Scunthorpe & Lindsey United
Sheffield United	1892	Blades	Bramall Lane	none
Sheffield Wdnesday	1892	Owls	Hillsborough	The Wednesday

Club	League debut	Nickname(s)	Ground	Previous name(s)
Shrewsbury Town	1950	Shrews, Town	Gay Meadow	none
Southampton	1920	Saints	St Mary's Stadium	Southampton St Mary's
Southend United	1920	Shrimpers, Blues	Roots Hall	none
Stockport County	1900	County, Hatters	Edgeley Park	Heaton Norris Rovers
Stoke City	1888	Potters	The Britannia Stadium	Stoke
Sunderland	1890	Rokerites, Black Cats	The Stadium of Light	Sunderland and District Teachers Association FC
Swansea City	1920	Swans, Jacks	Vetch Field	Swansea Town
Swindon Town	1920	Robins	County Ground	Spartans and St Mark's Young Men's Friendly Society (amalgamation)
Torquay United	1927	Gulls	Plainmoor	Torquay Town
Tottenham Hotspur	1908	Spurs	White Hart Lane	Hotspur FC
Tranmere Rovers	1921	Rovers	Prenton Park, Birkenhead	Belmont AFC
Walsall	1892	Saddlers	Bescot Stadium	Walsall Town Swifts
Watford	1920	Hornets	Vicarage Road	West Herts
West Bromwich Albion	1888	Throstles, Baggies, Albion	The Hawthorns	West Bromwich Strollers
West Ham United	1919	Hammers, Irons	Boleyn Ground, Upton Park	Thames Ironworks FC
Wigan Athletic	1978	Latics	JJB Stadium	none
Wimbledon	1977	Dons	Selhurst Park	Wimbledon Old Centrals
Wolverhampton Wanderers	1888	Wolves	Molineux	St Luke's
Wrexham	1921	Robins, Red Dragons	Racecourse Ground	none
Wycombe Wanderers	1993	Chairboys, Blues	Causeway Stadium	North Town Wanderers
Yeovil Town	2003	Glovers	Huish Park	Yeovil Casuals
York City	1929	Minstermen	Bootham Crescent	none

(NC) Nationwide Conference

Football: Scottish League Clubs

Club	Ground	Nickname(s)
Aberdeen	Pittodrie Stadium	The Dons
Airdrie United (formerly Airdrieonians)	New Broomfield Park	The Diamonds/Waysiders
Albion Rovers	Cliftonhill Stadium, Coatbridge	The Wee Rovers
Alloa Athletic	Recreation Park	The Wasps
Arbroath	Gayfield Park	The Red Lichties
Ayr United	Somerset Park	The Honest Men
Berwick Rangers	Shielfield Park	The Borderers
Brechin City	Glebe Park	City
Celtic	Celtic Park (formerly Parkhead), Glasgow	The Bhoys
Clyde	Broadwood Stadium, Cumbernauld	The Bully Wee
Clydebank	Cappielow Park	The Bankies
Cowdenbeath	Central Park	Blue Brazil
Dumbarton	Strathclyde Homes Stadium	The Sons
Dundee	Dens Park	The Dark Blues/Dee
Dundee United	Tannadice Park	The Terrors
Dunfermline Athletic	East End Park	The Pars
East Fife	Bayview Park, Methil	The Fifers
East Stirling	Firs Park, Falkirk	The Shire
Elgin City	Borough Briggs	City/Black & Whites
Falkirk	Brockville Park	The Bairns
Forfar Athletic	Station Park	The Loons/Sky Blues
Greenock Morton	Cappielow Park	The Ton
Gretna	Raydale Park	Black and Whites/Borders
Hamilton Academical	New Douglas Park	The Accies
Heart of Midlothian	Tynecastle Park, Edinburgh	The Jam Tarts
Hibernian	Easter Road, Edinburgh	The Hi-Bees
Inverness Caledonian Thistle	Caledonian Stadium, East Longman	Caley/The Jags
Kilmarnock	Rugby Park	The Killies
Livingston	City Stadium	Livi Lions
Montrose	Links Park	The Gable Endies
Motherwell	Fir Park	The Well
Partick Thistle	Firhill Park, Glasgow	The Jags

Peterhead	Balmoor Stadium	Blue Toon
Queen of the South	Palmerston Park, Dumfries	The Doonhamers/Queens
Queen's Park	Hampden Park, Glasgow	The Spiders
Raith Rovers	Stark's Park, Kirkcaldy	The Rovers
Rangers	Ibrox Stadium, Glasgow	The Blues/Gers
Ross County	Victoria Park, Dingwall	County
St Johnstone	McDiarmid Park, Perth	The Saints
St Mirren	St Mirren Park, Love Street, Paisley	The Buddies
Stenhousemuir	Ochilview Park	The Warriors
Stirling Albion	Forthbank Stadium	The Binos/The Albion
Stranraer	Stair Park	The Blues

NB Elgin City are now the most northerly club in the Football League. Airdrie United took over Clydebank (The Bankies) in June 2002 and play in the colours of the former Airdrieonians.

European Nations Championship

Date	Venue	Winners		Runners-up
1960	Paris	Soviet Union	2–1	Yugoslavia
1964	Madrid	Spain	2–1	Soviet Union
1968	Rome	Italy	2–0	Yugoslavia (replay after 1–1 draw)
1972	Brussels	West Germany	3–0	Soviet Union
1976	Belgrade	Czechoslovakia	2–2	West Germany (5–3 on penalties)
1980	Rome	West Germany	2–1	Belgium
1984	Paris	France	2–0	Spain
1988	Munich	Holland	2–0	Soviet Union
1992	Gothenburg	Denmark	2–0	Germany
1996	London	Germany	2–1	Czech Republic (golden goal after 1–1)
2000	Rotterdam	France	2–1	Italy (golden goal after 1–1)
2004	Lisbon	Greece	1–0	Portugal

PFA Young Player of the Year

Kevin Beattie (Ipswich)	1974
Mervyn Day (West Ham)	1975
Peter Barnes (Manchester City)	1976
Andy Gray (Aston Villa)	1977
Tony Woodcock (Notts Forest)	1978
Cyrille Regis (WBA)	1979
Glenn Hoddle (Tottenham)	1980
Gary Shaw (Aston Villa)	1981
Steve Moran (Southampton)	1982
Ian Rush (Liverpool)	1983
Paul Walsh (Luton)	1984
Mark Hughes (Manchester Utd)	1985
Tony Cottee (West Ham)	1986
Tony Adams (Arsenal)	1987
Paul Gascoigne (Newcastle)	1988
Paul Merson (Arsenal)	1989
Matt Le Tissier (Southampton)	1990
Lee Sharpe (Manchester Utd)	1991
Ryan Giggs (Manchester Utd)	1992
Ryan Giggs (Manchester Utd)	1993
Andy Cole (Newcastle)	1994
Robbie Fowler (Liverpool)	1995
Robbie Fowler (Liverpool)	1996
David Beckham (Manchester Utd)	1997
Michael Owen (Liverpool)	1998
Nicolas Anelka (Arsenal)	1999
Harry Kewell (Leeds)	2000
Steven Gerrard (Liverpool)	2001
Craig Bellamy (Newcastle)	2002
Jermaine Jenas (Newcastle)	2003
Scott Parker (Chelsea)	2004
Wayne Rooney (Manchester Utd)	2005

PFA Player of the Year

Norman Hunter (Leeds)	
Colin Todd (Derby County)	
Pat Jennings (Tottenham)	
Andy Gray (Aston Villa)	
Peter Shilton (Notts Forest)	
Liam Brady (Arsenal)	
Terry McDermott (Liverpool)	
John Wark (Ipswich)	
Kevin Keegan (Southampton)	
Kenny Dalglish (Liverpool)	
Ian Rush (Liverpool)	
Peter Reid (Everton)	
Gary Lineker (Everton)	
Clive Allen (Tottenham)	
John Barnes (Liverpool)	
Mark Hughes (Manchester Utd)	
David Platt (Aston Villa)	
Mark Hughes (Manchester Utd)	
Gary Pallister (Manchester Utd)	
Paul McGrath (Aston Villa)	
Eric Cantona (Manchester Utd)	
Alan Shearer (Blackburn)	
Les Ferdinand (Newcastle)	
Alan Shearer (Newcastle)	
Dennis Bergkamp (Arsenal)	
David Ginola (Tottenham Hotspur)	
Roy Keane (Manchester Utd)	
Teddy Sheringham (Manchester Utd)	
Ruud van Nistelrooy (Manchester Utd)	
Thierry Henry (Arsenal)	
Thierry Henry (Arsenal)	
John Terry (Chelsea)	

FIFA World Footballer of the Year

1991	Lothar Matthäus (Germany and Inter Milan)	1998	Zinédine Zidane (France and Juventus)
1992	Marco Van Basten (Holland and AC Milan)	1999	Rivaldo (Brazil and Barcelona)
1993	Robert Baggio (Italy and Juventus)	2000	Zinédine Zidane (France and Juventus)
1994	Romario (Brazil and Barcelona)	2001	Luis Figo (Portugal and Real Madrid)
1995	George Weah (Liberia and AC Milan)	2002	Ronaldo (Brazil and Real Madrid)
1996	Ronaldo (Brazil and Inter Milan)	2003	Zinédine Zidane (France and Real Madrid)
1997	Ronaldo (Brazil and Inter Milan)	2004	Ronaldinho (Brazil and Barcelona)

Football Writers' Player of the Year

1948	Stanley Matthews (Blackpool)	1977	Emlyn Hughes (Liverpool)
1949	Johnny Carey (Manchester Utd)	1978	Kenny Burns (Notts Forest)
1950	Joe Mercer (Arsenal)	1979	Kenny Dalglish (Liverpool)
1951	Harry Johnston (Blackpool)	1980	Terry McDermott (Liverpool)
1952	Billy Wright (Wolves)	1981	Frans Thijssen (Ipswich)
1953	Nat Lofthouse (Bolton)	1982	Steve Perryman (Tottenham)
1954	Tom Finney (Preston North End)	1983	Kenny Dalglish (Liverpool)
1955	Don Revie (Manchester City)	1984	Ian Rush (Liverpool)
1956	Bert Trautmann (Manchester City)	1985	Neville Southall (Everton)
1957	Tom Finney (Preston North End)	1986	Gary Lineker (Everton)
1958	Danny Blanchflower (Tottenham)	1987	Clive Allen (Tottenham)
1959	Syd Owen (Luton)	1988	John Barnes (Liverpool)
1960	Bill Slater (Wolves)	1989	Steve Nicol (Liverpool)
1961	Danny Blanchflower (Tottenham)	1990	John Barnes (Liverpool)
1962	Jimmy Adamson (Burnley)	1991	Gordon Strachan (Leeds)
1963	Stanley Matthews (Stoke City)	1992	Gary Lineker (Tottenham)
1964	Bobby Moore (West Ham)	1993	Chris Waddle (Sheffield Wednesday)
1965	Bobby Collins (Leeds)	1994	Alan Shearer (Blackburn Rovers)
1966	Bobby Charlton (Manchester Utd)	1995	Jürgen Klinsmann (Tottenham)
1967	Jackie Charlton (Leeds)	1996	Eric Cantona (Manchester Utd)
1968	George Best (Manchester Utd)	1997	Gian Franco Zola (Chelsea)
1969	Tony Book (Manchester City) and	1998	Dennis Bergkamp (Arsenal)
	Dave Mackay (Derby County)	1999	David Ginola (Tottenham)
1970	Billy Bremner (Leeds)	2000	Roy Keane (Manchester Utd)
1971	Frank McLintock (Arsenal)	2001	Teddy Sheringham (Manchester Utd)
1972	Gordon Banks (Stoke City)	2002	Robert Pires (Arsenal)
1973	Pat Jennings (Tottenham)	2003	Thierry Henry (Arsenal)
1974	Ian Callaghan (Liverpool)	2004	Thierry Henry (Arsenal)
1975	Alan Mullery (Fulham)	2005	Frank Lampard (Chelsea)
1976	Kevin Keegan (Liverpool)		

European Footballer of the Year

1956	Stanley Matthews (Blackpool)	1980	Karl-Heinz Rummenigge (Bayern Munich)
1957	Alfredo Di Stefano (Real Madrid)	1981	Karl-Heinz Rummenigge (Bayern Munich)
1958	Raymond Kopa (Real Madrid)	1982	Paolo Rossi (Juventus)
1959	Alfredo Di Stefano (Real Madrid)	1983	Michel Platini (Juventus)
1960	Luis Suarez (Barcelona)	1984	Michel Platini (Juventus)
1961	Omar Sivori (Juventus)	1985	Michel Platini (Juventus)
1962	Josef Masopust (Dukla Prague)	1986	Igor Belanov (Dynamo Kiev)
1963	Lev Yashin (Moscow Dynamo)	1987	Ruud Gullit (AC Milan)
1964	Denis Law (Manchester Utd)	1988	Marco Van Basten (AC Milan)
1965	Eusebio (Benfica)	1989	Marco Van Basten (AC Milan)
1966	Bobby Charlton (Manchester Utd)	1990	Lothar Matthäus (Inter Milan)
1967	Florian Albert (Ferencvaros)	1991	Jean-Pierre Papin (Marseille)
1968	George Best (Manchester Utd)	1992	Marco Van Basten (AC Milan)
1969	Gianni Rivera (AC Milan)	1993	Roberto Baggio (Juventus)
1970	Gerd Muller (Bayern Munich)	1994	Hristo Stoichkov (Barcelona)
1971	Johann Cruyff (Ajax)	1995	George Weah (AC Milan)
1972	Franz Beckenbauer (Bayern Munich)	1996	Matthias Sammer (Borussia Dortmund)
1973	Johann Cruyff (Barcelona)	1997	Ronaldo (Inter Milan)
1974	Johann Cruyff (Barcelona)	1998	Zinédine Zidane (Juventus)
1975	Oleg Blokhin (Dynamo Kiev)	1999	Rivaldo (Barcelona)
1976	Franz Beckenbauer (Bayern Munich)	2000	Luis Figo (Real Madrid)
1977	Allan Simonsen (Borussia	2001	Michael Owen (Liverpool)
	Moenchengladbach)	2002	Ronaldo (Real Madrid)
1978	Kevin Keegan (SV Hamburg)	2003	Pavel Nedved (Juventus)
1979	Kevin Keegan (SV Hamburg)	2004	Andriy Shevchenko (AC Milan)

NB From 1955–1994 the award was restricted to Europeans. Since 1995 it is for all players in European clubs regardless of nationality.

SPORT&LEISURE

Football: General Information

Arsenal: unbeaten in League	2003/4 season (played 38, won 26, drew 12)
Arsenal tube station: former name	Gillespie Road (one of the innovative Herbert Chapman's ideas).
artificial turf: 1st team to use	Queen's Park Rangers (1981). Luton followed soon after.
ball: circumference	between 27 and 28 inches (69–71cm).
Black: 1st English international	Viv Anderson (1978).
caps 1st awarded for internationals	1886.
city that never had Premier (Div. 1) team	Hull.
crossbar introduced	1875.
England team from one club	In 1894 Corinthians supplied all eleven players for England v Wales at Wrexham.
England: 1st home loss to foreign side	In 1953 Hungary defeated England 6–3.
England: 1st loss to foreign side	In 1929 Spain beat England 4–3 in Madrid.
European Footballer of the Year: 1st	Stanley Matthews (1956).
FA Charity Shield: contestants	FA Cup winners v League winners.
FA Cup Final: 1st monarch to attend	King George V (1914).
FA Cup: 15 original teams	Barnes, Civil Service, Clapham Rovers, Crystal Palace (not the present one), Donnington School (Spalding), Great Marlow, Hampstead Heathens, Harrow Chequers, Hitchin, Maidenhead, Queen's Park, Reigate Priory, Royal Engineers (Chatham), Upton Park, Wanderers.
FA Cup: 1st floodlit tie	Kidderminster v Brierley Hill (1955).
1st player sent off in final	Kevin Moran of Manchester Utd (1985).
1st replay (Wembley)	1970 (draw at Wembley, replayed at Old Trafford).
1st scorer	M P Betts (a Harrow Chequer) scored the first goal in an FA Cup tie.
broke neck in final	Bert Trautmann of Manchester City (1956).
horse cleared pitch	PC George Storey on a white horse cleared overcrowded pitch at Wembley's first Cup Final (1923).
non-League winner	Tottenham Hotspur (1901).
played every year	Great Marlow (now Marlow) and Maidenhead have played in every FA Cup since 1872.
stolen	1895 (from a Birmingham shop).
floodlit game: 1st	1887.
floodlit: international 1st	England v Spain at Wembley (1955).
Football Association: address	25 Soho Square, London W1D 4FA; tel: 020 7745 4545.
Football Association: set up at	Freemason's Tavern, Lincoln's Inn Fields (1863).
goal nets: used for 1st time	1891 (North v South match).
goal: dimensions	height: 8 feet (2.4m), width: 8 yards (7.3m).
home internationals: 1st played	1883 (Scotland v Ireland was the first match).
home internationals: last played	1984 (Ireland won on goal difference after all four teams finished on 3 points).
international: first official	England v Scotland (1872).
Irish club: lst founded	Cliftonville (1879).
Irish FA: when formed	1880.
League and Cup double: 1st	Preston North End won FA Cup without conceding a goal and League without losing a game (1889).
numbering of players	introduced by Herbert Chapman, manager of Arsenal (1928).
oldest club: when founded	Sheffield (1857).
oldest League club: when founded	Notts County (1862).
oldest Scottish club: when founded	Queen's Park (1867).
Olympic Games: UK victory	White City (1908) and Stockholm (1912).
penalty kick introduced	1891 (at request of the Irish FA).
penalty spot: distance from goal	12 yards (11m).
points: first club to score over 100 in League	York City (101) 1983/4 season.
points: League record	Sunderland (105) 1998/9.
Rangers: won every league match	1898/9 season.
religious support: Glasgow	traditionally Catholics follow Celtic and Protestants follow Rangers.
rules: codified	at Cambridge University (1846).
Scottish FA: when formed	1873.
shinguards introduced	1874.
stadiums: famous world football	Amsterdam Arena, Amsterdam (Ajax); Azteca Stadium, Mexico; Bernabeu, Madrid (Real Madrid); Giuseppe Meazza, San Siro (AC and Inter Milan); Lansdowne Rd, Dublin; Maracana, Rio de Janeiro; Noucamp, Barcelona; Olympic Stadium, Munich (Bayern Munich); Parc des Princes, Paris (St Germain); Stade de France, St Denis; Stadio Delle Alpi, Torino (Juventus); Stadium of Light, Lisbon (Benfica); Windsor Park, Belfast (Linfield).
stadium: largest capacity	Maracana Stadium, Rio de Janeiro.
Sunday football: 1st League game	20 Jan. 1974 (Millwall v Fulham).

televised football: 1st	29 Aug. 1936 (Arsenal v Everton). BBC showed same evening.
televised football: 1st live	30 April 1938, Wembley FA Cup final, shown by BBC.
3 points: 1st played	1981/2 season.
3 points: 1st played Scotland	1994/5 season.
tragedies: Bolton	9 March 1946 (wall and barrier collapsed, 33 killed) Bolton v Stoke.
Bradford	11 May 1985 (3rd Division game between Bradford City and Lincoln City), fire in main stand, 56 died.
Heysel (Brussels)	29 May 1985 (European Cup final Liverpool v Juventus), Liverpool fans on rampage, 41 died.
Hillsborough	15 April 1989 (Notts Forest v Liverpool, FA Cup semi-final), Leppings Lane end, 96 died.
Ibrox	5 April 1902 (stand collapsed, 25 killed) Scotland v England. 2 Jan. 1971 (Celtic v Rangers who equalised in final minute, causing mayhem, 66 died).
transfer: 1st £1,000	A Common from Sunderland to Middlesbrough (1905).
1st £10,000	D Jack from Bolton to Arsenal (1928).
1st £50,000	D Law from Huddersfield to Manchester City (1960).
1st £100,000	D Law from Torino to Manchester Utd (1962).
1st £100,000 (English clubs)	A Ball from Blackpool to Everton (1966) (actual transfer price £110,000).
1st £200,000	M Peters from West Ham to Spurs (1970).
1st £500,000	G McQueen from Leeds to Manchester Utd (1978).
1st £1 million	T Francis from Birmingham to Nottingham Forest (1979).
1st £2 million	P Gascoigne from Newcastle to Spurs (1988).
1st £5 million	C Sutton from Norwich City to Blackburn Rovers (1994).
1st £10 million and £15 million	A Shearer from Blackburn to Newcastle (1996).
1st £30 million	R Ferdinand from Leeds to Manchester Utd (2002)
two-handed throw introduced	1895.
war started by football match	El Salvador v Honduras (1969).
Welsh FA: when formed	1876.
white ball legalised	1950.
World Cup: England 1st played	in 1950 (England were beaten in the qualifying competition in Brazil).
World Cup: most tournaments	Antonio Carbajal, the Mexican goalkeeper (5). Lothar Matthäus, Germany (5).
World Cup: top scorer in single tournament	Just Fontaine of France (13), 1958.

Football Association Cup

Date	Winner		Runner-up
1872	Wanderers	1–0	Royal Engineers
1873	Wanderers	2–0	Oxford University
1874	Oxford University	2–0	Royal Engineers
1875	Royal Engineers	1–1, 2–0	Old Etonians
1876	Wanderers	1–1, 3–0	Old Etonians
1877	Wanderers	2–1 aet	Oxford University
1878	Wanderers	3–1	Royal Engineers
1879	Old Etonians	1–0	Clapham Rovers
1880	Clapham Rovers	1–0	Oxford University
1881	Old Carthusians	3–0	Old Etonians
1882	Old Etonians	1–0	Blackburn Rovers (first appearance of a Northern club in the final)
1883	Blackburn Olympic	2–1 aet	Old Etonians (last appearance of English amateur finalists)
1884	Blackburn Rovers	2–1	Queen's Park
1885	Blackburn Rovers	2–0	Queen's Park
1886	Blackburn Rovers	0–0, 2–0	West Bromwich Albion
1887	Aston Villa	2–0	West Bromwich Albion
1888	West Bromwich Albion	2–1	Preston North End
1889	Preston North End	3–0	Wolverhampton Wanderers
1890	Blackburn Rovers	6–1	The Wednesday
	William Townley scored first-ever Cup Final hat-trick		
1891	Blackburn Rovers	3–1	Notts County
1892	West Bromwich Albion	3–0	Aston Villa
1893	Wolverhampton Wanderers	1–0	Everton
1894	Notts County (first 2nd Division team to win the FA Cup)	4–1	Bolton Wanderers
1895	Aston Villa	1–0	West Bromwich Albion
	trophy was stolen on 11/9/95 and was never recovered		

Date	Winner		Runner-up
1896	The Wednesday	2–1	Wolverhampton Wanderers
	new trophy was an exact replica of the original		
1897	Aston Villa (second team to do 'the double')	3–2	Everton
1898	Nottingham Forest	3–1	Derby County
1899	Sheffield United	4–1	Derby County
1900	Bury	4–0	Southampton
1901	Tottenham Hotspur	2–2, 3–1	Sheffield United
	Tottenham – only non-League team to win the FA Cup since the League started in 1888/9 – also started the tradition of decorating the cup with ribbons in the colours of the winning team		
1902	Sheffield United	1–1, 2–1	Southampton
1903	Bury (record winning margin in FA Cup Final)	6–0	Derby County
1904	Manchester City	1–0	Bolton Wanderers
1905	Aston Villa	2–0	Newcastle United
1906	Everton	1–0	Newcastle United
1907	The Wednesday	2–1	Everton
1908	Wolverhampton Wanderers	3–1	Newcastle United
1909	Manchester United	1–0	Bristol City
1910	Newcastle United	1–1, 2–0	Barnsley
	after this final it was discovered that the trophy had not been copyrighted and it had been copied for another tournament, so the trophy was presented to Lord Kinnaird and a new one was commissioned		
1911	Bradford City	0–0, 1–0	Newcastle United
	first winners of new (present) trophy made by Fattorini & Sons of Bradford		
1912	Barnsley	0–0, 1–0 aet	West Bromwich Albion
1913	Aston Villa	1–0	Sunderland
1914	Burnley	1–0	Liverpool
1915	Sheffield United	3–0	Chelsea
1916	not held		
1917	not held		
1918	not held		
1919	not held		
1920	Aston Villa	1–0 aet	Huddersfield Town
1921	Tottenham Hotspur	1–0	Wolverhampton Wanderers
1922	Huddersfield Town	1–0	Preston North End
1923	Bolton Wanderers	2–0	West Ham United
	first Wembley Final – official crowd figure 126,047 – actual figure 180,000–200,000		
1924	Newcastle United	2–0	Aston Villa
1925	Sheffield United	1–0	Cardiff City
1926	Bolton Wanderers	1–0	Manchester City (1st team to reach the Cup Final and be relegated in same season)
1927	Cardiff City (only non-English team to win the Cup)	1–0	Arsenal
1928	Blackburn Rovers	3–1	Huddersfield Town
1929	Bolton Wanderers	2–0	Portsmouth
1930	Arsenal	2–0	Huddersfield Town
1931	West Bromwich Albion	2–1	Birmingham City
1932	Newcastle United	2–1	Arsenal
1933	Everton	3–0	Manchester City
1934	Manchester City	2–1	Portsmouth
1935	Sheffield Wednesday	4–2	West Bromwich Albion
1936	Arsenal	1–0	Sheffield United
1937	Sunderland	3–1	Preston North End
1938	Preston North End	1–0 aet	Huddersfield Town
1939	Portsmouth	4–1	Wolverhampton Wanderers
1940	not held		
1941	not held		
1942	not held		
1943	not held		
1944	not held		
1945	not held		
1946	Derby County	4–1 aet	Charlton Athletic
	the ball burst during the final – also this was the only season when two-legged matches were played in the FA Cup – prior to the semi-final stage		
1947	Charlton Athletic	1–0 aet	Burnley
	the ball burst again		
1948	Manchester United	4–2	Blackpool
	only time winners have played against a team from top flight in every round		

Date	Winner		Runner-up
1949	Wolverhampton Wanderers	3–1	Leicester City
1950	Arsenal	2–0	Liverpool
1951	Newcastle United	2–0	Blackpool
1952	Newcastle United	1–0	Arsenal
1953	Blackpool	4–3	Bolton Wanderers
	'The Matthews Final' – Stan Mortensen hat-trick – winner scored by Bill Perry		
1954	West Bromwich Albion	3–2	Preston North End
1955	Newcastle United	3–1	Manchester City
1956	Manchester City	3–1	Birmingham City
1957	Aston Villa	2–1	Manchester United
1958	Bolton Wanderers	2–0	Manchester United
1959	Nottingham Forest	2–1	Luton Town
1960	Wolverhampton Wanderers	3–0	Blackburn Rovers
1961	Tottenham Hotspur (3rd team to do 'the double' – first in 20th century)	2–0	Leicester City
1962	Tottenham Hotspur	3–1	Burnley
1963	Manchester United	3–1	Leicester City
1964	West Ham United	3–2	Preston North End
	Howard Kendall was the then youngest finalist in 20th century		
1965	Liverpool	2–1 aet	Leeds United
1966	Everton	3–2	Sheffield Wednesday
1967	Tottenham Hotspur	2–1	Chelsea
	first all-London Wembley final		
1968	West Bromwich Albion	1–0 aet	Everton
1969	Manchester City	1–0	Leicester City
1970	Chelsea	2–2, 2–1 aet	Leeds United
1971	Arsenal (4th team to do 'the double')	2–1 aet	Liverpool
1972	Leeds United	1–0	Arsenal
1973	Sunderland (first 2nd division team to win the Cup since West Brom in 1931)	1–0	Leeds United
1974	Liverpool	3–0	Newcastle United
1975	West Ham United	2–0	Fulham
	Bobby Moore played for Fulham against West Ham		
1976	Southampton	1–0	Manchester United
1977	Manchester United	2–1	Liverpool
1978	Ipswich Town (only team to play in every round of Cup including preliminary)	1–0	Arsenal
1979	Arsenal	3–2	Manchester United
1980	West Ham United (most recent 2nd Division Cup winners)	1–0	Arsenal
	Paul Allen beat Howard Kendall's 20th century record as youngest player		
1981	Tottenham Hotspur	1–1, 3–2	Manchester City
1982	Tottenham Hotspur	1–1, 1–0	Queen's Park Rangers
1983	Manchester United	2–2, 4–0	Brighton & Hove Albion
1984	Everton	2–0	Watford
1985	Manchester United	1–0 aet	Everton
1986	Liverpool	3–1	Everton
1987	Coventry City	3–2 aet	Tottenham Hotspur
1988	Wimbledon	1–0	Liverpool
1989	Liverpool	3–2 aet	Everton
1990	Manchester United	3–3, 1–0	Crystal Palace
1991	Tottenham Hotspur	2–1 aet	Nottingham Forest
1992	Liverpool	2–0	Sunderland
1993	Arsenal	1–1, 2–1 aet	Sheffield Wednesday
	Arsenal also beat Sheffield Wednesday in the League Cup final		
1994	Manchester United (6th team to do 'the double')	4–0	Chelsea
1995	Everton	1–0	Manchester United
1996	Manchester United (1st team to do a second 'double')	1–0	Liverpool
	Eric Cantona 1st foreign player to captain the FA Cup winners		
1997	Chelsea	2–0	Middlesbrough
1998	Arsenal	2–0	Newcastle United
1999	Manchester United (3rd double – also 1st team to do a 'treble' of League, FA Cup and European Champions Cup)	2–0	Newcastle United
2000	Chelsea	1–0	Aston Villa
2001	Liverpool	2–1	Arsenal
2002	Arsenal	2–0	Chelsea
2003	Arsenal	1–0	Southampton
2004	Manchester United	3–0	Millwall
2005	Arsenal	0–0, 5–4 on pens	Manchester United

European Cup Winners' Cup

Date	Winner		Runners-up	Venue
1961	Fiorentina	4–1 on agg.	Glasgow Rangers	Glasgow, Florence
1962	Atletico Madrid	1–1, 3–0	Fiorentina	Glasgow, Stuttgart
1963	Tottenham Hotspur	5–1	Atletico Madrid	Rotterdam
1964	Sporting Lisbon	3–3,1–0	MTK Budapest	Brussels, Antwerp
1965	West Ham United	2–0	Munich 1860	Wembley
1966	Borussia Dortmund	2–1 aet	Liverpool	Glasgow
1967	Bayern Munich	1–0 aet	Glasgow Rangers	Nuremberg
1968	AC Milan	2–0	SV Hamburg	Rotterdam
1969	Slovan Bratislava	3–2	Barcelona	Basle
1970	Manchester City	2–1	Gornik Zabrze	Vienna
1971	Chelsea	1–1, 2–1 aet	Real Madrid	Athens, Athens
1972	Glasgow Rangers	3–2	Dynamo Moscow	Barcelona
1973	AC Milan	1–0	Leeds United	Salonika
1974	Magdeburg	2–0	AC Milan	Rotterdam
1975	Dynamo Kiev	3–0	Ferencvaros	Basle
1976	Anderlecht	4–2	West Ham United	Brussels
1977	SV Hamburg	2–0	Anderlecht	Amsterdam
1978	Anderlecht	4–0	Austria Vienna	Paris
1979	Barcelona	4–3 aet	Fortuna Düsseldorf	Basle
1980	Valencia	0–0, 5–4 on pens	Arsenal	Brussels
1981	Dynamo Tbilisi	2–1	Carl Zeiss Jena	Düsseldorf
1982	Barcelona	2–1	Standard Liège	Barcelona
1983	Aberdeen	2–1 aet	Real Madrid	Gothenburg
1984	Juventus	2–1	FC Porto	Basle
1985	Everton	3–1	Rapid Vienna	Rotterdam
1986	Dynamo Kiev	3–0	Atletico Madrid	Lyon
1987	Ajax	1–0	Lokomotiv Leipzig	Athens
1988	Mechelen	1–0	Ajax	Strasbourg
1989	Barcelona	2–0	Sampdoria	Berne
1990	Sampdoria	2–0	Anderlecht	Gothenburg
1991	Manchester United	2–1	Barcelona	Rotterdam
1992	Werder Bremen	2–0	AS Monaco	Lisbon
1993	Parma	3–1	Royal Antwerp	London (Wembley)
1994	Arsenal	1–0	Parma	Copenhagen
1995	Real Zaragoza	2–1	Arsenal	Paris
1996	Paris St-Germain	1–0	Rapid Vienna	Brussels
1997	Barcelona	1–0	Paris St-Germain	Rotterdam
1998	Chelsea	1–0	VFB Stuttgart	Stockholm
1999	Lazio	2–1	Real Majorca	Birmingham

NB The European Cup Winners' Cup was established in 1960 and was contested by national Cup winners or the runners-up if the winners were in the European Cup. 1999 was the last competition. As from 1999/2000 national Cup winners compete in an expanded UEFA Cup.

European Champion Clubs' Cup

Date	Winner		Runners-up	Venue
1956	Real Madrid	4–3	Stade de Reims	Paris
1957	Real Madrid	2–0	Fiorentina	Madrid
1958	Real Madrid	3–2, aet	AC Milan	Brussels
1959	Real Madrid	2–0	Stade de Reims	Stuttgart
1960	Real Madrid	7–3	Eintracht Frankfurt	Glasgow
1961	Benfica	3–2	Barcelona	Berne
1962	Benfica	5–3	Real Madrid	Amsterdam
1963	AC Milan	2–1	Benfica	London
1964	Inter Milan	3–1	Real Madrid	Vienna
1965	Inter Milan	1–0	Benfica	Milan
1966	Real Madrid	2–1	Partizan Belgrade	Brussels
1967	Celtic	2–1	Inter Milan	Lisbon
1968	Manchester United	4–1, aet	Benfica	London
1969	AC Milan	4–1	Ajax	Madrid
1970	Feyenoord	2–1, aet	Celtic	Milan
1971	Ajax	2–0	Panathinaikos	London
1972	Ajax	2–0	Inter Milan	Rotterdam
1973	Ajax	1–0	Juventus	Belgrade
1974	Bayern Munich	1–1, 4–0	Atletico Madrid	Brussels

Date	Winner		Runners-up	Venue
1975	Bayern Munich	2–0	Leeds United	Paris
1976	Bayern Munich	1–0	St Etienne	Glasgow
1977	Liverpool	3–1	Borussia Moenchengladbach	Rome
1978	Liverpool	1–0	FC Bruges	London
1979	Nottingham Forest	1–0	Malmo	Munich
1980	Nottingham Forest	1–0	SV Hamburg	Madrid
1981	Liverpool	1–0	Real Madrid	Paris
1982	Aston Villa	1–0	Bayern Munich	Rotterdam
1983	SV Hamburg	1–0	Juventus	Athens
1984	Liverpool	1–1, 4–2 on pens	AS Roma	Rome
1985	Juventus	1–0	Liverpool	Brussels
1986	Steaua Bucharest	0–0, 2–0 on pens	Barcelona	Seville
1987	FC Porto	2–1	Bayern Munich	Vienna
1988	PSV Eindhoven	0–0, 6–5 on pens	Benfica	Stuttgart
1989	AC Milan	4–0	Steaua Bucharest	Barcelona
1990	AC Milan	1–0	Benfica	Vienna
1991	Red Star Belgrade	0–0, 5–3 on pens	Marseille	Bari
1992	Barcelona	1–0, aet	Sampdoria	London
1993	Marseille*	1–0	AC Milan	Munich
1994	AC Milan	4–0	Barcelona	Athens
1995	Ajax	1–0	AC Milan	Vienna
1996	Juventus	1–1, 4–2 on pens	Ajax	Rome
1997	Borussia Dortmund	3–1	Juventus	Munich
1998	Real Madrid	1–0	Juventus	Amsterdam
1999	Manchester United	2–1	Bayern Munich	Barcelona
2000	Real Madrid	3–0	Valencia	Paris
2001	Bayern Munich	1–1, 5–4 on pens	Valencia	Milan
2002	Real Madrid	2–1	Bayer Leverkusen	Glasgow
2003	AC Milan	0–0, 3–2 on pens	Juventus	Manchester (Old Trafford)
2004	FC Porto	3–0	Monaco	Gelsenkirchen
2005	Liverpool	3–3, 3–2 on pens	AC Milan	Istanbul

*Marseille were subsequently stripped of title following bribery scandal concerning Bernard Tapié, the club president.

NB The European Cup was established in 1955 and was contested by the respective League champions of the member countries of the Union of European Football Associations (UEFA).

In recent seasons, clubs finishing second, third and fourth in the League of those countries with the highest UEFA points coefficients can qualify for the European Champions Cup.

From 1992/3 season the European Cup changed its format to include a qualifying competition, two group stages and a final knockout phase of quarter-finals, semi-finals, played over two legs, and a single-match final. Since 2003/4 there has been a single group stage, with 16 clubs advancing to the knockout phase. The competition since the rule changes is more properly called the UEFA Champions League.

European Super Cup

1972	Ajax		1989	Milan
1973	Ajax		1990	Milan
1974	not contested		1991	Manchester Utd
1975	Kiev Dynamo		1992	Barcelona
1976	Anderlecht		1993	Parma
1977	Liverpool		1994	Milan
1978	Anderlecht		1995	Ajax
1979	Notts Forest		1996	Juventus
1980	Valencia		1997	Barcelona
1981	not contested		1998	Chelsea
1982	Aston Villa		1999	Lazio
1983	Aberdeen		2000	Galatasaray
1984	Juventus		2001	Liverpool
1985	not contested		2002	Real Madrid
1986	Steaua		2003	AC Milan
1987	FC Porto		2004	Valencia
1988	Mechelen			

NB The European Super Cup was for the winners of the UEFA Champions League and the European Cup Winners Cup. With the demise of the latter trophy the opponents have been the UEFA Cup winners.

Original 12 Football League Clubs

Accrington	Everton
Aston Villa	Notts County
Blackburn Rovers	Preston North End
Bolton Wanderers	Stoke City
Burnley	West Bromwich Albion
Derby County	Wolverhampton Wanderers

Women's World Cup

1991	USA
1995	Norway
1999	USA
2003	Germany

Asian Cup

Date	Winner	Date	Winner	Date	Winner
1956	South Korea	1976	Iran	1996	Saudi Arabia
1960	South Korea	1980	Kuwait	2000	Japan
1964	Israel	1984	Saudi Arabia	2004	Japan
1968	Iran	1988	Saudi Arabia		
1972	Iran	1992	Japan		

African Champions Cup

Date	Winner	Date	Winner
1964	Oryx Douala (Cameroon)	1985	FAR Rabat (Morocco)
1965	not held	1986	Zamalek (Egypt)
1966	Stade Abidjan (Ivory Coast)	1987	Al Ahly (Egypt)
1967	TP Englebert (Zaïre)	1988	EP Setif (Algeria)
1968	TP Englebert (Zaïre)	1989	Raja Casablanca (Morocco)
1969	Al Ismaili (Egypt)	1990	JS Kabylie (Algeria)
1970	Asante Kotoko (Ghana)	1991	Club Africain (Algeria)
1971	Canon Yaoundé (Cameroon)	1992	Wydad Casablanca (Morocco)
1972	Hafia Conakry (Ghana)	1993	Zamalek (Egypt)
1973	AS Vita Kinshasa (Zaïre)	1994	Esperance (Tunisia)
1974	CARA Brazzaville (Congo)	1995	Orlando Pirates (South Africa)
1975	Hafia Conakry (Ghana)	1996	Zamalek (Egypt)
1976	MC Algiers (Algeria)	1997	Raja Casablanca (Morocco)
1977	Hafia Conakry (Ghana)	1998	ASEC Abidjan (Ivory Coast)
1978	Canon Yaoundé (Cameroon)	1999	Raja Casablanca (Morocco)
1979	Union Douala (Cameroon)	2000	Hearts of Oak (Ghana)
1980	Canon Yaoundé (Cameroon)	2001	Al Ahly (Egypt)
1981	JE Tizi-Ouzou (Algeria)	2002	Zamalek (Egypt)
1982	Al Ahly (Egypt)	2003	Enyimba (Nigeria)
1983	Asante Kotoko (Ghana)	2004	Enyimba (Nigeria)
1984	Zamalek (Egypt)		

African Nations Cup

Date	Winner	Date	Winner
1957	Egypt	1982	Ghana
1959	Egypt	1984	Cameroon
1962	Ethiopia	1986	Egypt
1963	Ghana	1988	Cameroon
1965	Ghana	1990	Algeria
1968	Zaïre	1992	Ghana
1970	Sudan	1994	Nigeria
1972	Congo	1996	South Africa
1974	Zaïre	1998	Egypt
1976	Morocco	2000	Cameroon
1978	Ghana	2002	Cameroon
1980	Nigeria	2004	Tunisia

World Club Intercontinental Cup

Date	Winner	Date	Winner
1960	Real Madrid	1983	Gremio (Porto Alegre, Brazil)
1961	Peñarol (Montevideo)	1984	Independiente (Argentina)
1962	Santos (São Paulo)	1985	Juventus (Turin)
1963	Santos (São Paulo)	1986	River Plate (Buenos Aires)
1964	Internazionale (Milan)	1987	FC Porto (Oporto)
1965	Internazionale (Milan)	1988	Nacional (Montevideo)
1966	Peñarol (Montevideo)	1989	AC Milan
1967	Racing Club (Arg)	1990	AC Milan
1968	Estudiantes (La Plata, Argentina)	1991	Red Star Belgrade
1969	AC Milan	1992	São Paulo
1970	Feyenoord (Rotterdam)	1993	São Paulo
1971	Nacional (Montevideo)	1994	Velez Sarsfield (Argentina)
1972	Ajax (Amsterdam)	1995	Ajax (Amsterdam)
1973	Independiente (Argentina)	1996	Juventus (Turin)
1974	Atletico Madrid	1997	Borussia Dortmund
1975	not played	1998	Real Madrid
1976	Bayern Munich	1999	Manchester United
1977	not played	2000	Boca Juniors (Buenos Aires)
1978	Boca Juniors (Buenos Aires)	2001	Bayern Munich
1979	Olimpia (Paraguay)	2002	Real Madrid
1980	Nacional (Montevideo)	2003	Boca Juniors
1981	Flamengo (Rio)	2004	FC Porto
1982	Peñarol (Montevideo)		

NB From 1960 to 1979 the competition was decided on points, not goal difference. From 1980 it was played as a single match in Tokyo. In 2000 the inaugural FIFA Club World Championship took place in Brazil and was won by the Brazilian side Corinthians.

Copa America
South American Championship

Date	Winner	Date	Winner
1910	Argentina	1949	Brazil
1916	Uruguay	1953	Paraguay
1917	Uruguay	1955	Argentina
1919	Brazil	1956	Uruguay
1920	Uruguay	1957	Argentina
1921	Argentina	1959	Argentina
1922	Brazil		Uruguay
1923	Uruguay	1963	Bolivia
1924	Uruguay	1967	Uruguay
1925	Argentina	1975	Peru
1926	Uruguay	1979	Paraguay
1927	Argentina	1983	Uruguay
1929	Argentina	1987	Uruguay
1935	Uruguay	1989	Brazil
1937	Argentina	1991	Argentina
1939	Peru	1993	Argentina
1941	Argentina	1995	Uruguay
1942	Uruguay	1997	Brazil
1945	Argentina	1999	Brazil
1946	Argentina	2001	Colombia
1947	Argentina	2004	Brazil

Copa Libertadores
South American Club Cup

Date	Winner	Date	Winner
1960	Peñarol (Montevideo, Uruguay)	1990	Olimpia (Asunción, Paraguay)
1964	Independiente (Buenos Aires, Argentina)	1991	Colo Colo (Santiago, Chile)
1965	Independiente (Buenos Aires, Argentina)	1995	Gremio (Pôrto Alegre, Brazil)
1969	Estudiantes (La Plata, Argentina)	1996	River Plate (Buenos Aires, Argentina)
1970	Estudiantes (La Plata, Argentina)	1997	Cruzeiro (Belo Horizonte, Brazil)
1972	Independiente (Buenos Aires, Argentina)	1998	Vasco Da Gama (Rio, Brazil)
1974	Independiente (Buenos Aires, Argentina)	1999	Palmeiras (São Paulo, Brazil)
1975	Independiente (Buenos Aires, Argentina)	2001	Boca Juniors (Buenos Aires, Argentina)
1976	Cruzeiro (Belo Horizonte, Brazil)	2002	Olimpia (Asunción, Paraguay)
1985	Argentinos Juniors (Buenos Aires, Argentina)	2003	Boca Juniors (Buenos Aires, Argentina)
1987	Peñarol (Montevideo, Uruguay)	2004	Once Caldas (Manizales, Colombia
1989	Atlético Nacional (Medellín, Colombia)		

NB The competition has been held every year since 1960. Only the winners that did not go on to win the World Club Cup are listed.

Scottish Cup Finals

Date	Winner		Runner-up
1874	Queen's Park	2–0	Clydesdale
1875	Queen's Park	3–0	Renton
1876	Queen's Park	1–1, 2–0	Third Lanark
1877	Vale of Leven	0–0,1–1, 3–2	Rangers
1878	Vale of Leven	1–0	Third Lanark
1879	Vale of Leven	1–1, walkover	Rangers
1880	Queen's Park	3–0	Thornlibank
1881	Queen's Park	3–1	Dumbarton
1882	Queen's Park	2–2, 4–1	Dumbarton
1883	Dumbarton	2–2, 2–1	Vale of Leven
1884	Queen's Park	walkover	Vale of Leven
1885	Renton	0–0, 3–1	Vale of Leven
1886	Queen's Park	3–1	Renton
1887	Hibernian	2–1	Dumbarton
1888	Renton	6–1	Cambuslang
1889	Third Lanark	2–1	Celtic
1890	Queen's Park	1–1, 2–1	Vale of Leven
1891	Hearts	1–0	Dumbarton
1892	Celtic	5–1	Queen's Park
1893	Queen's Park	2–1	Celtic
1894	Rangers	3–1	Celtic
1895	St Bernard's	2–1	Renton
1896	Hearts	3–1	Hibernian
1897	Rangers	5–1	Dumbarton
1898	Rangers	2–0	Kilmarnock
1899	Celtic	2–0	Rangers
1900	Celtic	4–3	Queen's Park
1901	Hearts	4–3	Celtic
1902	Hibernian	1–0	Celtic
1903	Rangers	0–0, 1–1, 2–0	Hearts
1904	Celtic	3–2	Rangers
1905	Third Lanark	0–0, 3–1	Rangers
1906	Hearts	1–0	Third Lanark
1907	Celtic	3–0	Hearts
1908	Celtic	5–1	St Mirren
1909	cup withheld (see below)		
1910	Dundee	2–2, 0–0, 2–1	Clyde
1911	Celtic	0–0, 2–0	Hamilton
1912	Celtic	2–0	Clyde
1913	Falkirk	2–0	Raith Rovers
1914	Celtic	0–0, 4–1	Hibernian
1915	not held		
1916	not held		

Date	Winner		Runner-up
1917	not held		
1918	not held		
1919	not held		
1920	Kilmarnock	3–2	Albion Rovers
1921	Partick Thistle	1–0	Rangers
1922	Morton	1–0	Rangers
1923	Celtic	1–0	Hibernian
1924	Airdrieonians	2–0	Hibernian
1925	Celtic	2–1	Dundee
1926	St Mirren	2–0	Celtic
1927	Celtic	3–1	East Fife
1928	Rangers	4–0	Celtic
1929	Kilmarnock	2–0	Rangers
1930	Rangers	0–0, 2–1	Partick Thistle
1931	Celtic	2–2, 4–2	Motherwell
1932	Rangers	1–1, 3–0	Kilmarnock
1933	Celtic	1–0	Motherwell
1934	Rangers	5–0	St Mirren
1935	Rangers	2–1	Hamilton
1936	Rangers	1–0	Third Lanark
1937	Celtic	2–1	Aberdeen
1938	East Fife	1–1, 4–2	Kilmarnock
1939	Clyde	4–0	Motherwell
1940	not held		
1941	not held		
1942	not held		
1943	not held		
1944	not held		
1945	not held		
1946	not held		
1947	Aberdeen	2–1	Hibernian
1948	Rangers	1–1, 1–0	Morton
1949	Rangers	4–1	Clyde
1950	Rangers	3–0	East Fife
1951	Celtic	1–0	Motherwell
1952	Motherwell	4–0	Dundee
1953	Rangers	1–1, 1–0	Aberdeen
1954	Celtic	2–1	Aberdeen
1955	Clyde	1–1, 1–0	Celtic
1956	Hearts	3–1	Celtic
1957	Falkirk	1–1, 2–1	Kilmarnock
1958	Clyde	1–0	Hibernian
1959	St Mirren	3–1	Aberdeen
1960	Rangers	2–0	Kilmarnock
1961	Dunfermline	0–0, 2–0	Celtic
1962	Rangers	2–0	St Mirren
1963	Rangers	1–1, 3–0	Celtic
1964	Rangers	3–1	Dundee
1965	Celtic	3–2	Dunfermline
1966	Rangers	0–0, 1–0	Celtic
1967	Celtic	2–0	Aberdeen
1968	Dunfermline	3–1	Hearts
1969	Celtic	4–0	Rangers
1970	Aberdeen	3–1	Celtic
1971	Celtic	1–1, 2–1	Rangers
1972	Celtic	6–1	Hibernian
1973	Rangers	3–2	Celtic
1974	Celtic	3–0	Dundee United
1975	Celtic	3–1	Airdrieonians
1976	Rangers	3–1	Hearts
1977	Celtic	1–0	Rangers
1978	Rangers	2–1	Aberdeen
1979	Rangers	0–0, 0–0, 3–2	Hibernian
1980	Celtic	1–0	Rangers
1981	Rangers	0–0, 4–1	Dundee United
1982	Aberdeen	4–1 aet	Rangers
1983	Aberdeen	1–0 aet	Rangers
1984	Aberdeen	2–1 aet	Celtic
1985	Celtic	2–1	Dundee United
1986	Aberdeen	3–0	Hearts

Date	Winner		Runner-up
1987	St Mirren	1–0 aet	Dundee United
1988	Celtic	2–1	Dundee United
1989	Celtic	1–0	Rangers
1990	Aberdeen	0–0, 9–8 pens	Celtic
1991	Motherwell	4–3 aet	Dundee United
1992	Rangers	2–1	Airdrieonians
1993	Rangers	2–1	Aberdeen
1994	Dundee United	1–0	Rangers
1995	Celtic	1–0	Airdrieonians
1996	Rangers	5–1	Hearts
1997	Kilmarnock	1–0	Falkirk
1998	Hearts	2–1	Rangers
1999	Rangers	1–0	Celtic
2000	Rangers	4–0	Aberdeen
2001	Celtic	3–0	Hibernian
2002	Rangers	3–2	Celtic
2003	Rangers	1–0	Dundee
2004	Celtic	3–1	Dunfermline Athletic
2005	Celtic	1–0	Dundee United

NB In 1879 Vale of Leven awarded cup as Rangers failed to appear for replay after 1–1 draw.
In 1881 Dumbarton protested the first result in which Queen's Park won 2–1.
In 1884 Queen's Park awarded the cup after Vale of Leven failed to appear.
In 1889 Scottish FA ordered a replay because of playing conditions after Third Lanark won match 3–0.
In 1892 both teams protested about first game in which Celtic won 1–0.
In 1909 Celtic v Rangers 2–2, 1–1 with riot in extra time – clubs refused to play a third match – cup was withheld by Scottish FA.

World Cup

Date	Winner		Runner-up		Venue
1930	Uruguay	4–2	Argentina		Uruguay
1934	Italy	2–1	Czechoslovakia	after extra time	Italy
1938	Italy	4–2	Hungary		France
1950	Uruguay	2–1	Brazil	deciding match of pool	Brazil
1954	West Germany	3–2	Hungary		Switzerland
1958	Brazil	5–2	Sweden		Sweden
1962	Brazil	3–1	Czechoslovakia		Chile
1966	England	4–2	West Germany	after extra time	England
1970	Brazil	4–1	Italy		Mexico
1974	West Germany	2–1	Holland		West Germany
1978	Argentina	3–1	Holland	after extra time	Argentina
1982	Italy	3–1	West Germany		Spain
1986	Argentina	3–2	West Germany		Mexico
1990	West Germany	1–0	Argentina		Italy
1994	Brazil	0–0	Italy	Brazil won 3–2 on penalties	USA
1998	France	3–0	Brazil		France
2002	Brazil	2–0	Germany		Japan

Inter-Cities Cup (became UEFA Cup in 1972)

Date	Winner		Runner-up
1955–58	Barcelona	8–2 agg.	London
1958–60	Barcelona	4–1 agg.	Birmingham City
1961	AS Roma	4–2 agg.	Birmingham City
1962	Valencia	7–3 agg.	Barcelona
1963	Valencia	4–1 agg.	Dynamo Zagreb
1964	Real Zaragoza	2–1 (in Barcelona)	Valencia
1965	Ferencvaros	1–0 (in Turin)	Juventus
1966	Barcelona	4–3 agg.	Real Zaragoza
1967	Dynamo Zagreb	2–0 agg.	Leeds United
1968	Leeds United	1–0 agg.	Ferencvaros
1969	Newcastle United	6–2 agg.	Ujpest Dozsa
1970	Arsenal	4–3 agg.	Anderlecht
1971	Leeds United	3–3 agg., away goals	Juventus
1972	Tottenham Hotspur	3–2 agg.	Wolverhampton Wanderers

Date	Winner		Runner-up
1973	Liverpool	3–2 agg.	Borussia Moenchengladbach
1974	Feyenoord	4–2 agg.	Tottenham Hotspur
1975	Borussia Moenchengladbach	5–1 agg.	Twente Enschede
1976	Liverpool	4–3 agg.	FC Bruges
1977	Juventus	2–2 agg., away goals	Athletic Bilbao
1978	PSV Eindhoven	3–0 agg.	Bastia
1979	Borussia Moenchengladbach	2–1 agg.	Red Star Belgrade
1980	Eintracht Frankfurt	3–3 agg., away goals	Borussia Moenchengladbach
1981	Ipswich Town	5–4 agg.	AZ67 Alkmaar
1982	IFK Gothenburg	4–0 agg.	SV Hamburg
1983	Anderlecht	2–1 agg.	Benfica
1984	Tottenham Hotspur	2–2 agg., 4–3 on pens	Anderlecht
1985	Real Madrid	3–1 agg.	Videoton
1986	Real Madrid	5–3 agg.	Cologne
1987	IFK Gothenburg	2–1 agg.	Dundee United
1988	Bayer Leverkusen	3–3 agg., 3–2 on pens	Espanol
1989	Napoli	5–4 agg.	Stuttgart
1990	Juventus	3–1 agg.	Fiorentina
1991	Inter Milan	2–1 agg.	AS Roma
1992	Ajax	2–2 agg., away goals	Torino
1993	Juventus	6–1 agg.	Borussia Dortmund
1994	Inter Milan	2–0 agg.	Casino Salzburg
1995	Parma	2–1 agg.	Juventus
1996	Bayern Munich	5–1 agg.	Bordeaux
1997	Schalke 04	1–1 agg., 4–1 on pens	Inter Milan
1998	Inter Milan	3–0 (Paris)	Lazio
1999	Parma	3–0 (Moscow)	Marseille
2000	Galatasaray	0–0, 4–1 on pens	Arsenal
2001	Liverpool	5–4 on golden goal (Dortmund)	Alavés
2002	Feyenoord	3–2 (Rotterdam)	Borussia Dortmund
2003	FC Porto	3–2 on golden goal (Seville)	Celtic
2004	Valencia	2–0	Marseille
2005	CSKA Moscow	3–1 (Lisbon)	Sporting Lisbon

NB The 1998 UEFA Cup in Paris was held over one leg for the first time.
Between 1967 and 1971 the competition was known as the European Fairs Cup.

Football League Cup (currently known as the Carling Cup)

Date	Winner		Runner-up
1961	Aston Villa	3–2 on agg. aet	Rotherham United
1962	Norwich City	4–0 on agg.	Rochdale
1963	Birmingham City	3–1 on agg.	Aston Villa
1964	Leicester City	4–3 on agg.	Stoke City
1965	Chelsea	3–2 on agg.	Leicester City
1966	West Bromwich Albion	5–3 on agg.	West Ham United
1967	Queen's Park Rangers	3–2	West Bromwich Albion
1968	Leeds United	1–0	Arsenal
1969	Swindon Town	3–1	Arsenal
1970	Manchester City	2–1	West Bromwich Albion
1971	Tottenham Hotspur	2–0	Aston Villa
1972	Stoke City	2–1	Chelsea
1973	Tottenham Hotspur	1–0	Norwich City
1974	Wolverhampton Wanderers	2–1	Manchester City
1975	Aston Villa	1–0	Norwich City
1976	Manchester City	2–1	Newcastle United
1977	Aston Villa	0–0, 1–1, 3–2 aet	Everton
1978	Nottingham Forest	0–0, 1–0 aet	Liverpool
1979	Nottingham Forest	3–2	Southampton
1980	Wolverhampton Wanderers	1–0	Nottingham Forest
1981	Liverpool	1–1, 2–1	West Ham United
1982	Liverpool	3–1 aet	Tottenham Hotspur
1983	Liverpool	2–1 aet	Manchester United
1984	Liverpool	0–0, 1–0 aet	Everton
1985	Norwich City	1–0	Sunderland
1986	Oxford United	3–0	Queen's Park Rangers
1987	Arsenal	2–1	Liverpool
1988	Luton Town	3–2	Arsenal
1989	Nottingham Forest	3–1	Luton Town
1990	Nottingham Forest	1–0	Oldham Athletic
1991	Sheffield Wednesday	1–0	Manchester United

Date	Winner		Runner-up
1992	Manchester United	1–0	Nottingham Forest
1993	Arsenal	2–1	Sheffield Wednesday
1994	Aston Villa	3–1	Manchester United
1995	Liverpool	2–1	Bolton Wanderers
1996	Aston Villa	3–0	Leeds United
1997	Leicester City	1–1, 1–0 aet	Middlesbrough
1998	Chelsea	1–0	Middlesbrough
1999	Tottenham	1–0	Leicester City
2000	Leicester	2–1	Tranmere Rovers
2001	Liverpool	1–1, 5–4 on pens.	Birmingham
2002	Blackburn Rovers	2–1	Tottenham
2003	Liverpool	2–0	Manchester United
2004	Middlesbrough	2–1	Bolton Wanderers
2005	Chelsea	3–2 aet	Liverpool

NB In 1982 the League Cup became the Milk Cup following sponsorship by the Milk Marketing Board. Over the next few seasons it became the Littlewoods, Rumbelows, Coca Cola, Worthington Cup, and is now the Carling Cup.

Scottish League Cup

	Winners		Runners-up		Winners		Runners-up
1947	Rangers	4–0	Aberdeen	1978	Rangers	2–1	Celtic
1948	East Fife	1–1, 4–1	Falkirk	1979	Rangers	2–1	Aberdeen
1949	Rangers	2–0	Raith Rovers	1980	Dundee Utd	0–0, 3–0	Aberdeen
1950	East Fife	3–0	Dunfermline	1981	Dundee Utd	3–0	Dundee
1951	Motherwell	3–0	Hibernian	1982	Rangers	2–1	Dundee Utd
1952	Dundee	3–2	Rangers	1983	Celtic	2–1	Rangers
1953	Dundee	2–0	Kilmarnock	1984	Rangers	3–2	Celtic
1954	East Fife	3–2	Partick Thistle	1985	Rangers	1–0	Dundee Utd
1955	Hearts	4–2	Motherwell	1986	Aberdeen	3–0	Hibernian
1956	Aberdeen	2–1	St Mirren	1987	Rangers	2–1	Celtic
1957	Celtic	0–0, 3–0	Partick Thistle	1988	Rangers	3–3, 5–3 on penalties	Aberdeen
1958	Celtic	7–1	Rangers				
1959	Hearts	5–1	Partick Thistle	1989	Rangers	3–2	Aberdeen
1960	Hearts	2–1	Third Lanark	1990	Aberdeen	2–1	Rangers
1961	Rangers	2–0	Kilmarnock	1991	Rangers	2–1	Celtic
1962	Rangers	1–1, 3–1	Hearts	1992	Hibernian	2–0	Dunfermline
1963	Hearts	1–0	Kilmarnock	1993	Rangers	2–1	Aberdeen
1964	Rangers	5–0	Morton	1994	Rangers	2–1	Hibernian
1965	Rangers	2–1	Celtic	1995	Raith Rovers	2–2, 6–5 on penalties	Celtic
1966	Celtic	2–1	Rangers				
1967	Celtic	1–0	Rangers	1996	Aberdeen	2–0	Dundee
1968	Celtic	5–3	Dundee	1997	Rangers	4–3	Hearts
1969	Celtic	6–2	Hibernian	1998	Celtic	3–0	Dundee Utd
1970	Celtic	1–0	St Johnstone	1999	Rangers	2–1	St Johnstone
1971	Rangers	1–0	Celtic	2000	Celtic	2–0	Aberdeen
1972	Partick Thistle	4–1	Celtic	2001	Celtic	3–0	Kilmarnock
1973	Hibernian	2–1	Celtic	2002	Rangers	4–0	Ayr United
1974	Dundee	1–0	Celtic	2003	Rangers	2–1	Celtic
1975	Celtic	6–3	Hibernian	2004	Livingston	2–0	Hibernian
1976	Rangers	1–0	Celtic	2005	Rangers	5–1	Motherwell
1977	Aberdeen	2–1	Celtic				

Scottish League Champions

1892	Dumbarton	1904	Third Lanark	1916	Celtic
1893	Celtic	1905	Celtic	1917	Celtic
1894	Celtic	1906	Celtic	1918	Rangers
1895	Hearts	1907	Celtic	1919	Celtic
1896	Celtic	1908	Celtic	1920	Rangers
1897	Hearts	1909	Celtic	1921	Rangers
1898	Celtic	1910	Celtic	1922	Celtic
1899	Rangers	1911	Rangers	1923	Rangers
1900	Rangers	1912	Rangers	1924	Rangers
1901	Rangers	1913	Rangers	1925	Rangers
1902	Rangers	1914	Celtic	1926	Celtic
1903	Hibernian	1915	Celtic	1927	Rangers

Year	Club	Year	Club	Year	Club
1928	Rangers	1959	Rangers	1983	Dundee Utd
1929	Rangers	1960	Hearts	1984	Aberdeen
1930	Rangers	1961	Rangers	1985	Aberdeen
1931	Rangers	1962	Dundee	1986	Celtic
1932	Motherwell	1963	Rangers	1987	Rangers
1933	Rangers	1964	Rangers	1988	Celtic
1934	Rangers	1965	Kilmarnock	1989	Rangers
1935	Rangers	1966	Celtic	1990	Rangers
1936	Celtic	1967	Celtic	1991	Rangers
1937	Rangers	1968	Celtic	1992	Rangers
1938	Celtic	1969	Celtic	1993	Rangers
1939	Rangers	1970	Celtic	1994	Rangers
1947	Rangers	1971	Celtic	1995	Rangers
1948	Hibernian	1972	Celtic	1996	Rangers
1949	Rangers	1973	Celtic	1997	Rangers
1950	Rangers	1974	Celtic	1998	Celtic
1951	Hibernian	1975	Rangers	1999	Rangers
1952	Hibernian	1976	Rangers	2000	Rangers
1953	Rangers	1977	Celtic	2001	Celtic
1954	Celtic	1978	Rangers	2002	Celtic
1955	Aberdeen	1979	Celtic	2003	Rangers
1956	Rangers	1980	Aberdeen	2004	Celtic
1957	Rangers	1981	Celtic	2005	Rangers
1958	Hearts	1982	Celtic		

Golf: Majors

Year	British Open	US Open	US PGA	US Masters
1860	W Park	—	—	—
1861	T Morris Snr	—	—	—
1862	T Morris Snr	—	—	—
1863	W Park	—	—	—
1864	T Morris Snr	—	—	—
1865	A Strath	—	—	—
1866	W Park	—	—	—
1867	T Morris Snr	—	—	—
1868	T Morris Jnr	—	—	—
1869	T Morris Jnr	—	—	—
1870	T Morris Jnr	—	—	—
1871	not held	—	—	—
1872	T Morris Jnr	—	—	—
1873	T Kidd	—	—	—
1874	M Park	—	—	—
1875	W Park	—	—	—
1876	R Martin	—	—	—
1877	J Anderson	—	—	—
1878	J Anderson	—	—	—
1879	J Anderson	—	—	—
1880	R Ferguson	—	—	—
1881	R Ferguson	—	—	—
1882	R Ferguson	—	—	—
1883	W Fernie	—	—	—
1884	J Simpson	—	—	—
1885	R Martin	—	—	—
1886	D Brown	—	—	—
1887	W Park Jnr	—	—	—
1888	J Burns	—	—	—
1889	W Park Jnr	—	—	—
1890	J Ball	—	—	—
1891	H Kirkcaldy	—	—	—
1892	H Hilton	—	—	—
1893	W Auchterlonie	—	—	—
1894	J Taylor	—	—	—
1895	J Taylor	H Rawlins	—	—
1896	H Vardon	J Foulis	—	—
1897	H Hilton	J Lloyd	—	—
1898	H Vardon	F Herd	—	—
1899	H Vardon	W Smith	—	—
1900	J Ball	H Vardon	—	—
1901	H Kirkcaldy	W Anderson	—	—

Year	British Open	US Open	US PGA	US Masters
1902	A Herd	L Auchterlonie	—	—
1903	H Vardon	W Anderson	—	—
1904	J White	W Anderson	—	—
1905	J Braid	W Anderson	—	—
1906	J Braid	A Smith	—	—
1907	A Massy (France)	A Ross	—	—
1908	J Braid	F McLeod	—	—
1909	J Taylor	G Sargent	—	—
1910	J Braid	A Smith	—	—
1911	H Vardon	J McDermott	—	—
1912	Ted Ray	J McDermott	—	—
1913	J Taylor	F Ouimet	—	—
1914	H Vardon	W Hagen	—	—
1915	not held	J Travers	—	—
1916	not held	C Evans Jnr	J Barnes	—
1917	not held	not held	not held	—
1918	not held	not held	not held	—
1919	not held	W Hagen	J Barnes	—
1920	G Duncan	Ted Ray (GB)	J Hutchison	—
1921	J Hutchison	J Barnes	W Hagen	—
1922	W Hagen	G Sarazen	G Sarazen	—
1923	A G Havers	B Jones	G Sarazen	—
1924	W Hagen	C Walker	W Hagen	—
1925	J Barnes	W McFarlane	W Hagen	—
1926	B Jones	B Jones	W Hagen	—
1927	B Jones	T Armour	W Hagen	—
1928	W Hagen	J Farrell	L Diegel	—
1929	W Hagen	B Jones	L Diegel	—
1930	B Jones	B Jones	T Armour	—
1931	T Armour	B Burke	T Creavy	—
1932	G Sarazen	G Sarazen	O Dutra	—
1933	D Shute	J Goodman	G Sarazen	—
1934	T Cotton	O Dutra	P Runyan	H Smith
1935	A Perry	S Parks Jnr	J Revolta	G Sarazen
1936	A Padgham	T Manero	D Shute	H Smith
1937	T Cotton	R Guldahl	D Shute	B Nelson
1938	R Whitcombe	R Guldahl	P Runyan	H Picard
1939	R Burton	B Nelson	H Picard	R Guldahl
1940	not held	L Little	B Nelson	J Demaret
1941	not held	C Wood	V Ghezzi	C Wood
1942	not held	not held	S Snead	B Nelson
1943	not held	not held	not held	not held
1944	not held	not held	B Hamilton	not held
1945	not held	not held	B Nelson	not held
1946	S Snead	L Mangrum	B Hogan	H Keiser
1947	F Daly	L Worsham	J Ferrier	J Demaret
1948	T Cotton	B Hogan	B Hogan	C Harmon
1949	B Locke	C Middlecoff	S Snead	S Snead
1950	B Locke	B Hogan	C Harper	J Demaret
1951	M Faulkner	B Hogan	S Snead	B Hogan
1952	B Locke	J Boros	J Turnesa	S Snead
1953	B Hogan	B Hogan	W Burkemo	B Hogan
1954	P Thompson	E Furgol	C Harbert	S Snead
1955	P Thompson	J Fleck	D Ford	C Middlecoff
1956	P Thompson	C Middlecoff	J Burke	J Burke Jnr
1957	B Locke	D Mayer	L Hebert	D Ford
1958	P Thompson	T Bolt	D Finsterwald	A Palmer
1959	G Player	W Casper	B Rosburg	A Wall Jnr
1960	K Nagle	A Palmer	J Hebert	A Palmer
1961	A Palmer	G Littler	J Barber	G Player
1962	A Palmer	J Nicklaus	G Player	A Palmer
1963	R Charles	J Boros	J Nicklaus	J Nicklaus
1964	T Lema	K Venturi	B Nicholls	A Palmer
1965	P Thompson	G Player	D Marr	J Nicklaus
1966	J Nicklaus	W Casper	A Geiberger	J Nicklaus
1967	R de Vicenzo	J Nicklaus	D January	G Brewer
1968	G Player	L Trevino	J Boros	B Goalby
1969	A Jacklin	O Moody	R Floyd	G Archer
1970	J Nicklaus	A Jacklin	D Stockton	W Caspar
1971	L Trevino	L Trevino	J Nicklaus	C Coody
1972	L Trevino	J Nicklaus	G Player	J Nicklaus

Year	British Open	US Open	US PGA	US Masters
1973	T Weiskopf	J Miller	J Nicklaus	T Aaron
1974	G Player	H Irwin	L Trevino	G Player
1975	T Watson	L Graham	J Nicklaus	J Nicklaus
1976	J Miller	J Pate	D Stockton	R Floyd
1977	T Watson	H Green	L Wadkins	T Watson
1978	J Nicklaus	A North	J Mahaffey	G Player
1979	S Ballesteros	H Irwin	D Graham (Australia)	F Zoeller
1980	T Watson	J Nicklaus	J Nicklaus	S Ballesteros
1981	W Rogers	D Graham (Australia)	L Nelson	T Watson
1982	T Watson	T Watson	R Floyd	C Stadler
1983	T Watson	L Nelson	H Sutton	S Ballesteros
1984	S Ballesteros	F Zoeller	L Trevino	B Crenshaw
1985	S Lyle	A North	H Green	B Langer (Germany)
1986	G Norman	R Floyd	B Tway	J Nicklaus
1987	N Faldo	S Simpson	L Nelson	L Mize
1988	S Ballesteros	C Strange	J Sluman	S Lyle
1989	M Calcavecchia	C Strange	P Stewart	N Faldo
1990	N Faldo	H Irwin	W Grady (Australia)	N Faldo
1991	I Baker-Finch	P Stewart	J Daly	I Woosnam
1992	N Faldo	T Kite	N Price	F Couples
1993	G Norman	L Janzen	P Azinger	B Langer
1994	N Price	E Els	N Price	J M Olazabal
1995	J Daly	C Pavin	S Elkington	B Crenshaw
1996	T Lehman	S Jones	M Brooks	N Faldo
1997	J Leonard	E Els	D Love III	T Woods
1998	M O'Meara	L Janzen	V J Singh	M O'Meara
1999	P Lawrie	P Stewart	T Woods	J M Olazabal
2000	T Woods	T Woods	T Woods	V J Singh
2001	D Duval	R Goosen	D Toms	T Woods
2002	E Els	T Woods	R Beem	T Woods
2003	B Curtis	J Furyk	S Micheel	M Weir
2004	T Hamilton	R Goosen	V Singh	P Michelson
2005				T Woods

Golf: World Matchplay Championship

	Winner	Runner-up		Winner	Runner-up
1964	Arnold Palmer	Neil Coles	1985	Severiano Ballesteros	Bernhard Langer
1965	Gary Player	Peter Thomson	1986	Greg Norman	Sandy Lyle
1966	Gary Player	Jack Nicklaus	1987	Ian Woosnam	Sandy Lyle
1967	Arnold Palmer	Peter Thomson	1988	Sandy Lyle	Nick Faldo
1968	Gary Player	Bob Charles	1989	Nick Faldo	Ian Woosnam
1969	Bob Charles	Gene Littler	1990	Ian Woosnam	Mark McNulty
1970	Jack Nicklaus	Lee Trevino	1991	Severiano Ballesteros	Nick Price
1971	Gary Player	Jack Nicklaus	1992	Nick Faldo	Jeff Sluman
1972	Tom Weiskopf	Lee Trevino	1993	Corey Pavin	Nick Faldo
1973	Gary Player	Graham Marsh	1994	Ernie Els	Colin Montgomerie
1974	Hale Irwin	Gary Player	1995	Ernie Els	Steve Elkington
1975	Hale Irwin	Al Geiberger	1996	Ernie Els	Vijay Singh
1976	David Graham	Hale Irwin	1997	Vijay Singh	Ernie Els
1977	Graham Marsh	Ray Floyd	1998	Mark O'Meara	Tiger Woods
1978	Isao Aoki	Simon Owen	1999	Colin Montgomerie	Mark O'Meara
1979	Bill Rogers	Isao Aoki	2000	Lee Westwood	Colin Montgomerie
1980	Greg Norman	Sandy Lyle	2001	Ian Woosnam	Padraig Harrington
1981	Severiano Ballesteros	Ben Crenshaw	2002	Ernie Els	Sergio Garcia
1982	Severiano Ballesteros	Sandy Lyle	2003	Ernie Els	Thomas Bjorn
1983	Greg Norman	Nick Faldo	2004	Ernie Els	Lee Westwood
1984	Severiano Ballesteros	Bernhard Langer			

Golf: Ryder Cup

	Winner	Venue		Winner	Venue
1927	USA	Worcester, Massachusetts	1969	tie	Royal Birkdale, Lancashire
1929	GB	Moortown, North Yorkshire	1971	USA	St Louis, Missouri
1931	USA	Scioto, Ohio	1973	USA	Muirfield, Scotland
1933	GB	Southport & Ainsdale, Lancashire	1975	USA	Laurel Valley, Pennsylvania
			1977	USA	Royal Lytham, Lancashire
1935	USA	Ridgewood, New Jersey	1979	USA	Greenbrier, Virginia
1937	USA	Southport & Ainsdale, Lancashire	1981	USA	Walton Heath
			1983	USA	Palm Beach
1947	USA	Portland, Oregon	1985	Europe	Belfry
1949	USA	Ganton, Yorkshire	1987	Europe	Muirfield Village
1951	USA	Pinehurst, North Carolina	1989	tie	Belfry
1953	USA	Wentworth, Surrey	1991	USA	Kiawah Island
1955	USA	Thunderbird G & C, California	1993	USA	Belfry
1957	GB	Lindrick, Yorkshire	1995	Europe	Oak Hill CC
1959	USA	Eldorado CC, California	1997	Europe	Valderrama
1961	USA	Royal Lytham, Lancashire	1999	USA	Boston, Massachusetts
1963	USA	Atlanta, Georgia	2002	Europe	Belfry
1965	USA	Royal Birkdale, Lancashire	2004	Europe	Oakland Hills, Michigan
1967	USA	Houston, Texas			

NB Since 1979 the Ryder Cup has been contested by USA and Europe.
The 2001 event was cancelled due to the terrorist attack of 11 September.

Golf: General Information

British Open: correct title	The Open Championship (as it was the first championship open to the world)
oldest winner	Old Tom Morris (46)
youngest winner	Young Tom Morris (17)
youngest winner 20th century	Seve Ballesteros (22)
clubs: maximum allowed	14
Curtis Cup	Biennial tournament instituted in 1932 and played between amateur ladies' teams from the United States and Great Britain and Ireland. Teams consist of six players, two substitutes and a captain.
golf balls: pimples	332
Ryder Cup: father and sons played	Percy and Peter Alliss, Antonio and Ignacio Garrido
Samuel Ryder: profession	seed-merchant
Solheim Cup	Biennial tournament instituted in 1990 and played between professional ladies teams from the United States and Europe. It takes its name from Karsten Solheim, owner of golf club manufacturer Ping. Teams consist of 12 players and a non-playing captain.
US Masters: oldest winner	Jack Nicklaus (46)
youngest winner	Tiger Woods (21)
US Open: oldest winner	Hale Irwin (45)
youngest winner	John McDermott (19)
US PGA: oldest winner	Julius Boros (48)
youngest winner	Gene Sarazen (20)
US Women's Open: first UK winner	Laura Davies (1987)
Walker Cup	Inaugurated in 1921 and played between amateur teams from the United States and the British Isles. It was proposed by George Walker, the then president of the USGA, as the International Challenge Trophy but took its present name in 1922. It became a biennial event in 1924. Teams consist of eight players, two substitutes and a captain.
yips: coined by	Scottish professional Tommy Armour in the 1920s. Term describing inability to release the putter through the ball.

Greyhound Racing

Derby Winners

Year	Winner	Year	Winner
1980	Indian Joe	1993	Ringa Hustle
1981	Parkdown Jet	1994	Moral Standards
1982	Laurie's Panther	1995	Moaning Lad
1983	I'm Slippy	1996	Shanless Slippy
1984	Whisper Wishes	1997	Some Picture
1985	Pagan Swallow	1998	Tom's the Best
1986	Tico	1999	Chart King
1987	Signal Spark	2000	Rapid Ranger
1988	Hit the Lid	2001	Rapid Ranger
1989	Lartigue Note	2002	Allen Gift
1990	Slippy Blue	2003	Farloe Verdict
1991	Ballinderry Ash	2004	Droopys Scholes
1992	Farloe Melody		

Horse Racing: British Classics and Grand National Winners

	St Leger		Oaks		Derby	
Year	Horse	Jockey	Horse	Jockey	Horse	Jockey
1776	Allabaculia	J Singleton	—	—	—	—
1777	Bourbon	J Cade	—	—	—	—
1778	Hollandaise	G Hearon	—	—	—	—
1779	Tommy	G Lowrey Snr	Bridget	R Goodison	—	—
1780	Ruler	J Mangle	Teetotum	R Goodison	Diomed	S Arnull
1781	Serina	R Forster	Faith	R Goodison	Young Eclipse	C Hindley
1782	Imperatrix	G Searle	Ceres	S Chifney Snr	Assassin	S Arnull
1783	Phoenomenon	A Hall	Maid of Oakes	S Chifney Snr	Saltram	C Hindley
1784	Omphale	J Kirton	Stella	C Hindley	Sergeant	J Arnull
1785	Cowslip	G Searle	Trifle	J Bird	Aimwell	C Hindley
1786	Paragon	J Mangle	Perdita by Tanden	J Edwards	Noble	J White
1787	Spadille	J Mangle	Annette	Fitzpatrick	Sir Peter Teazle	S Arnull
1788	Young Flora	J Mangle	Nightshade	Fitzpatrick	Sir Thomas	W South
1789	Pewett	J Singleton	Tag	S Chifney Snr	Skyscraper	S Chifney Snr
1790	Ambidexter	G Searle	Hippolyta	S Chifney Snr	Rhadamanthus	J Arnull
1791	Young Traveller	J Jackson	Portia	J Singleton	Eager	Stephenson
1792	Tartar	J Mangle	Volante	C Hindley	John Bull	F Buckle
1793	Ninety-three	W Peirse	Caelia	J Singleton	Waxy	W Clift
1794	Beningborough	J Jackson	Hermione	S Arnull	Daedalus	F Buckle
1795	Hambletonian	Boyes	Platina	Fitzpatrick	Spreadeagle	A Wheatley
1796	Ambrosio	J Jackson	Parissot	J Arnull	Didelot	J Arnull
1797	Lounger	J Shepherd	Nike	F Buckle	Brown c by fidget	J Singleton
1798	Symmetry	J Jackson	Bellissima	F Buckle	Sir Harry	S Arnull
1799	Cockfighter	T Fields	Bellina	F Buckle	Archduke	J Arnull
1800	Champion	F Buckle	Ephemera	Fitzpatrick	Champion	W Clift
1801	Quiz	J Shepherd	Eleanor	Saunders	Eleanor	Saunders
1802	Orville	J Singleton Jnr	Scotia	F Buckle	Tyrant	F Buckle
1803	Remembrancer	B Smith	Theophania	F Buckle	Ditto	W Clift
1804	Sancho	F Buckle	Pellisse	W Clift	Hannibal	W Arnull
1805	Staveley	J Jackson	Meteora	F Buckle	Cardinal Beaufort	Fitzpatrick
1806	Fyldener	T Carr	Bronze	W Edwards	Paris	J Shepherd
1807	Paulina	W Clift	Briseis	S Chifney	Election	J Arnull
1808	Petronius	B Smith	Morel	W Clift	Pan	Collinson
1809	Ashton	B Smith	Maid of Orleans	J Moss	Pope	T Goodison
1810	Octavian	W Clift	Oriana	W Peirse	Whalebone	W Clift
1811	Soothsayer	B Smith	Sorcery	S Chifney	Phantom	F Buckle
1812	Ottrington	R Johnson	Manuella	W Peirse	Octavius	W Arnull
1813	Altisidora	J Jackson	Music	T Goodison	Smolensko	T Goodison
1814	William	J Shepherd	Medora	Barnard	Blucher	W Arnull
1815	Filho da Puta	J Jackson	Minuet	T Goodison	Whisker	T Goodison
1816	The Duchess	B Smith	Landscape	S Chifney	Prince Leopold	W Wheatley
1817	Ebor	R Johnson	Neva	F Buckle	Azor	J Robinson
1818	Reveller	R Johnson	Corinne	F Buckle	Sam	S Chifney Jnr
1819	Antonio	J Nicholson	Shoveler	S Chifney	Tiresias	W Clift
1820	St Patrick	J Johnson	Caroline	H Edwards	Sailor	S Chifney Jnr
1821	Jack Spigott	W Scott	Augusta	J Robinson	Gustavus	S Day
1822	Theodore	J Jackson	Pastille	H Edwards	Moses	T Goodison

SPORT & LEISURE

	St Leger		Oaks		Derby	
Year	Horse	Jockey	Horse	Jockey	Horse	Jockey
1823	Barefoot	T Goodison	Zinc	F Buckle	Emilius	F Buckle
1824	Jerry	B Smith	Cobweb	J Robinson	Cedric	J Robinson
1825	Memnon	W Scott	Wings	S Chifney	Middleton	J Robinson
1826	Tarrare	G Nelson	Lilias	T Lye	Lap-dog	G Dockeray
1827	Matilda	J Robinson	Gulnare	F Boyce	Mameluke	J Robinson
1828	The Colonel	W Scott	Turquoise	J B Day	Cadland	J Robinson
1829	Rowton	W Scott	Green Mantle	G Dockeray	Frederick	Forth
1830	Birmingham	P Conolly	Variation	G Edwards	Priam	S Day
1831	Chorister	J B Day	Oxygen	J B Day	Spaniel	W Wheatley
1832	Margrave	J Robinson	Galata	P Conolly	St Giles	W Scott
1833	Rockingham	S Darling	Vespa	J Chapple	Dangerous	J Chapple
1834	Touchstone	G Calloway	Pussy	J B Day	Plenipotentiary	P Conolly
1835	Queen of Trumps	T Lye	Queen of Trumps	T Lye	Mundig	W Scott
1836	Elis	J B Day	Cyprian	W Scott	Bay Middleton	J Robinson
1837	Mango	S Day Jnr	Miss Letty	J Holmes	Phosphorus	G Edwards
1838	Don John	W Scott	Industry	W Scott	Amato	J Chapple
1839	Charles the Twelfth	W Scott	Deception	J B Day	Bloomsbury	S Templeman
1840	Launcelot	W Scott	Crucifix	J B Day	Little Wonder	Macdonald
1841	Satirist	W Scott	Ghuznee	W Scott	Coronation	P Conolly
1842	Blue Bonnett	T Lye	Our Nell	T Lye	Attila	W Scott
1843	Nutwith	J Marson	Poison	F Butler	Cotherstone	W Scott
1844	Foig a Ballagh	H Bell	The Princess	F Butler	Orlando	E Flatman
1845	The Baron	F Butler	Refraction	H Bell	The Merry Monarch	F Bell
1846	Sir Tatton Sykes	W Scott	Mendicant	S Day	Pyrrhus the First	S Day
1847	Van Tromp	J Marson	Miami	S Templeman	Cossack	S Templeman
1848	Surplice	E Flatman	Cymba	S Templeman	Surplice	S Templeman
1849	Flying Dutchman	Marlow	Lady Evelyn	F Butler	Flying Dutchman	Marlow
1850	Voltigeur	J Marson	Rhedycina	F Butler	Voltigeur	J Marson
1851	Newminster	S Templeman	Iris	F Butler	Teddington	J Marson
1852	Stockwell	J Norman	Songstress	F Butler	Daniel O'Rourke	F Butler
1853	West Australian	F Butler	Catherine Hayes	Marlow	West Australian	F Butler
1854	Knight of St George	Basham	Mincemeat	Charlton	Andover	A Day
1855	Saucebox	J Wells	Marchioness	S Templeman	Wild Dayrell	R Sherwood
1856	Warlock	E Flatman	Mincepie	A Day	Ellington	Aldcroft
1857	Imperieuse	E Flatman	Blink Bonny	Charlton	Blink Bonny	Charlton
1858	Sunbeam	L Snowden	Governess	Ashmall	Beadsman	J Wells
1859	Gamester	Aldcroft	Summerside	G Fordham	Musjid	J Wells
1860	St Albans	L Snowden	Butterfly	J Snowden	Thormanby	H Custance
1861	Caller Ou	T Challoner	Brown Duchess	L Snowden	Kettledrum	Bullock
1862	The Marquis	T Challoner	Feu de Joie	T Challoner	Caractacus	J Parsons
1863	Lord Clifden	J Osborne	Queen Bertha	Aldcroft	Macaroni	T Challoner
1864	Blair Atholl	J Snowden	Fille de l'Air	A Edwards	Blair Atholl	J Snowden
1865	Gladiateur	H Grimshaw	Regalia	Norman	Gladiateur	H Grimshaw
1866	Lord Lyon	H Custance	Tormentor	J Mann	Lord Lyon	H Custance
1867	Achievement	T Challoner	Hippia	J Daley	Hermit	J Daley
1868	Formosa	T Challoner	Formosa	G Fordham	Blue Gown	J Wells
1869	Pero Gomez	J Wells	Brigantine	T Cannon	Pretender	J Osborne
1870	Hawthornden	J Grimshaw	Gamos	G Fordham	Kingcraft	T French
1871	Hannah	C Maidment	Hannah	C Maidment	Favonius	T French
1872	Wenlock	C Maidment	Reine	G Fordham	Cremorne	C Maidment
1873	Marie Stuart	T Osborne	Marie Stuart	T Cannon	Doncaster	F Webb
1874	Apology	J Osborne	Apology	J Osborne	George Frederick	H Custance
1875	Craig Millar	T Challoner	Spinaway	F Archer	Galopin	Morris
1876	Patriarch	J Goater	Enguerrande	Hudson	Kisber	C Maidment
1877	Silvio	F Archer	Placida	H Jeffrey	Silvio	F Archer
1878	Jannette	F Archer	Jannette	F Archer	Sefton	H Constable
1879	Rayon d'Or	J Goater	Wheel of Fortune	F Archer	Sir Bevys	G Fordham
1880	Robert the Devil	T Cannon	Jenny Howlet	J Snowden	Bend Or	F Archer
1881	Iroquois	F Archer	Thebais	G Fordham	Iroquois	F Archer
1882	Dutch Oven	F Archer	Geheimnis	T Cannon	Shotover	T Cannon
1883	Ossian	J Watts	Bonny Jean	J Watts	St Blaise	C Wood
1884	The Lambkin	J Watts	Busybody	T Cannon	St Gatien/Harvester	C Wood/Loates
1885	Melton	F Archer	Lonely	F Archer	Melton	F Archer

	St Leger		Oaks		Derby	
Year	Horse	Jockey	Horse	Jockey	Horse	Jockey
1886	Ormonde	F Archer	Miss Jummy	J Watts	Ormonde	F Archer
1887	Kilwarlin	W Robinson	Reve d'Or	C Wood	Merry Hampton	J Watts
1888	Seabreeze	W Robinson	Seabreeze	W Robinson	Ayrshire	F Barrett
1889	Donovan	F Barrett	L'Abbesse de Jouarre	J Woodburn	Donovan	T Loates
1890	Memoir	J Watts	Memoir	J Watts	Sainfoin	J Watts
1891	Common	G Barrett	Mimi	F Rickaby	Common	G Barrett
1892	La Fleche	J Watts	La Fleche	G Barrett	Sir Hugo	Allsopp
1893	Isinglass	T Loates	Mrs Butterwick	J Watts	Isinglass	T Loates
1894	Throstle	M Cannon	Amiable	W Bradford	Ladas	J Watts
1895	Sir Visto	S Loates	La Sagesse	S Loates	Sir Visto	S Loates
1896	Persimmon	J Watts	Canterbury Pilgrim	F Rickaby	Persimmon	J Watts
1897	Galtee More	C Wood	Limasol	W Bradford	Galtee More	C Wood
1898	Wildfowler	C Wood	Airs and Graces	W Bradford	Jeddah	O'Madden
1899	Flying Fox	M Cannon	Musa	O Madden	Flying Fox	M Cannon
1900	Diamond Jubilee	H Jones	La Roche	M Cannon	Diamond Jubilee	H Jones
1901	Doricles	K Cannon	Cap and Bells ll	M Henry	Volodyovski	L Reiff
1902	Sceptre	F W Hardy	Sceptre	H Randall	ard Patrick	J Martin
1903	Rock Sand	D Maher	Our Lassie	M Cannon	Rock Sand	D Maher
1904	Pretty Polly	W Lane	Pretty Polly	W Lane	St Amant	K Cannon
1905	Challacombe	O Madden	Cherry Lass	H Jones	Cicero	D Maher
1906	Troutbeck	G Stern	Keystone ll	D Maher	Spearmint	D Maher
1907	Wool Winder	W Halsey	Glass Doll	H Randall	Orby	J Reiff
1908	Your Majesty	W Griggs	Signorinetta	W Bullock	Signorinetta	W Bullock
1909	Bayardo	D Maher	Perola	F Wootton	Minoru	H Jones
1910	Swynford	F Wootton	Rosedrop	C Trigg	Lemberg	B Dillon
1911	Prince Palatine	F O'Neill	Cherimoya	F Winter	Sunstar	G Stern
1912	Tracery	G Bellhouse	Mirska	J Childs	Tagalie	J Reiff
1913	Night Hawk	E Wheatley	Jest	F Rickaby Jnr	Aboyeur	E Piper
1914	Black Jester	W Griggs	Princess Dorrie	W Huxley	Dubar ll	M MacGee
1915	Pommern	S Donoghue	Snow Marten	Walter Griggs	Pommern	S Donoghue
1916	Hurry On	C Childs	Fifinella	J Childs	Fifinella	J Childs
1917	Gay Crusader	S Donoghue	Sunny Jane	O Madden	Gay Crusader	S Donoghue
1918	Gainsborough	J Childs	My Dear	S Donoghue	Gainsborough	J Childs
1919	Keysoe	B Carslake	Bayuda	J Childs	Grand Parade	F Templeman
1920	Caligula	A Smith	Charlebelle	A Whalley	Spion Kop	F O'Neill
1921	Polemarch	J Childs	Love in Idleness	J Childs	Humorist	S Donoghue
1922	Royal Lancer	R Jones	Pogram	E Gardner	Captain Cuttle	S Donoghue
1923	Tranquil	T Weston	Brownhylda	V Smyth	Papyrus	S Donoghue
1924	Salmon-Trout	B Carslake	Straitlace	F O'Neill	Sansovino	T Weston
1925	Solario	J Childs	Saucy Sue	F Bullock	Manna	S Donoghue
1926	Coronach	J Childs	Short Story	R A Jones	Coronach	J Childs
1927	Book Law	H Jellis	Beam	T Weston	Call Boy	C Elliot
1928	Fairway	T Weston	Toboggan	T Weston	Felstead	H Wragg
1929	Trigo	M Beary	Pennycomequick	H Jelliss	Trigo	J Marshall
1930	Singapore	G Richards	Rose of England	G Richards	Blenheim	H Wragg
1931	Sandwich	H Wragg	Brulette	E C Elliot	Cameronian	F Fox
1932	Firdaussi	F Fox	Udaipur	M Beary	April the Fifth	F Lane
1933	Hyperion	T Weston	Chatelaine	S Wragg	Hyperion	T Weston
1934	Windsor Lad	C Smirke	Light Brocade	B Carslake	Windsor Lad	C Smirke
1935	Bahram	C Smirke	Quashed	H Jelliss	Bahram	F Fox
1936	Boswell	P Beasley	Lovely Rosa	T Weston	Mahmoud	C Smirke
1937	Chulmleigh	G Richards	Exhibitionist	S Donoghue	Mid-day Sun	M Beary
1938	Scottish Union	B Carslake	Rockfel	H Wragg	Bois Roussel	C Elliot
1939	no race held		Galatea ll	R A Jones	Blue Peter	E Smith
1940	Turkhan	G Richards	Godiva	D Marks	Pont L'Eveque	S Wragg
1941	Sun Castle	G Bridgland	Commotion	H Wragg	Owen Tudor	W Nevett
1942	Sun Chariot	G Richards	Sun Chariot	G Richards	Watling Street	H Wragg
1943	Herringbone	H Wragg	Why Hurry	C E Elliot	Straight Deal	T Carey
1944	Tehran	G Richards	Hycilla	G Bridgland	Ocean Swell	W Nevett
1945	Chamossaire	T Lowrey	Sun Stream	H Wragg	Dante	W Nevett
1946	Airborne	T Lowrey	Steady Aim	H Wragg	Airborne	T Lowrey
1947	Sayajirao	E Britt	Imprudence	W R Johnstone	Pearl Diver	G Bridgland
1948	Black Tarquin	E Britt	Masaka	W Nevett	My Love	W Johnstone
1949	Ridge Wood	M Beary	Musidora	E Britt	Nimbus	C Elliot
1950	Scratch ll	W R Johnstone	Asmena	W R Johnstone	Galcador	W R Johnstone
1951	Talma ll	W R Johnstone	Neasham Belle	S Clayton	Arctic Prince	C Spares
1952	Tulyar	C Smirke	Frieze	E Britt	Tulyar	C Smirke
1953	Premonition	E Smith	Ambiguity	J Mercer	Pinza	G Richards

	St Leger		Oaks		Derby	
Year	Horse	Jockey	Horse	Jockey	Horse	Jockey
1954	Never Say Die	C Smirke	Suncap	W R Johnstone	Never Say Die	L Piggott
1955	Meld	W H Carr	Meld	W H Carr	Phil Drake	F Palmer
1956	Cambremer	F Palmer	Sicarelle	F Palmer	Lavandin	W R Johnstone
1957	Ballymoss	T P Burns	Carrozza	L Piggott	Crepello	L Piggott
1958	Alcide	W Carr	Bella Paola	M Garcia	Hard Ridden	C Smirke
1959	Cantelo	E Hide	Petite Etoile	L Piggott	Parthia	W Carr
1960	St Paddy	L Piggott	Never Too Late	R Poincelet	St Paddy	L Piggott
1961	Aurelius	L Piggott	Sweet Solera	W Rickaby	Psidium	R Poincelet
1962	Hethersett	W Carr	Monade	Y Saint-Martin	Larkspur	N Sellwood
1963	Ragusa	G Bougoure	Noblesse	G Bougoure	Relko	Y Saint-Martin
1964	Indiana	J Lindley	Homeward Bound	G Starkey	Santa Claus	A Breasley
1965	Provoke	J Mercer	Long Look	J Purtell	Sea Bird II	T P Glennon
1966	Sodium	F Durr	Valoris	L Piggott	Charlottown	A Breasley
1967	Ribocco	L Piggott	Pia	E Hide	Royal Palace	G Moore
1968	Ribero	L Piggott	La Lagune	G Thiboeuf	Sir Ivor	L Piggott
1969	Intermezzo	R Hutchinson	Sleeping Partner	J Gorton	Blakeney	E Johnson
1970	Nijinsky	L Piggott	Lupe	A Barclay	Nijinsky	L Piggott
1971	Athens Wood	L Piggott	Altesse Royale	G Lewis	Mill Reef	G Lewis
1972	Boucher	L Piggott	Ginevra	A Murray	Roberto	L Piggott
1973	Peleid	F Durr	Mysterious	G Lewis	Morston	E Hide
1974	Bustino	J Mercer	Polygamy	P Eddery	Snow Knight	B Taylor
1975	Bruni	A Murray	Juliet Marny	L Piggott	Grundy	P Eddery
1976	Crow	Y Saint-Martin	Pawneese	Y Saint-Martin	Empery	L Piggott
1977	Dunfermline	W Carson	Dunfermline	W Carson	The Minstrel	L Piggott
1978	Julio Mariner	E Hide	Fair Salinia	G Starkey	Shirley Heights	G Starkey
1979	Son of Love	A Lequeux	Scintillate	P Eddery	Troy	W Carson
1980	Light Cavalry	J Mercer	Bireme	W Carson	Henbit	W Carson
1981	Cut Above	J Mercer	Blue Wind	L Piggott	Shergar	W Swinburn
1982	Touching Wood	P Cook	Time Charter	W Newmes	Golden Fleece	P Eddery
1983	Sun Princess	W Carson	Sun Princess	W Carson	Teenoso	L Piggott
1984	Comanche Run	L Piggott	Circus Plume	L Piggott	Secreto	C Roche
1985	Oh So Sharp	S Cauthen	Oh So Sharp	S Cauthen	Slip Anchor	S Cauthen
1986	Moon Madness	P Eddery	Midway Lady	R Cochrane	Shahrastani	W Swinburn
1987	Reference Point	S Cauthen	Unite	W Swinburn	Reference Point	S Cauthen
1988	Minster Son	W Carson	Diminuendo	S Cauthen	Kayhasi	R Cochrane
1989	Michelozzo	S Cauthen	Snow Bride	S Cauthen	Nashwan	W Carson
1990	Snurge	A Quinn	Salsabil	W Carson	Quest for Fame	P Eddery
1991	Toulon	P Eddery	Jet Ski Lady	C Roche	Generous	A Munro
1992	User Friendly	G Duffield	User Friendly	G Duffield	Dr Devious	J Reid
1993	Bobs Return	P Robinson	Intrepidity	M Roberts	Commander-in-Chief	M J Kinane
1994	Moonax	P Eddery	Balanchine	L Dettori	Erhaab	W Carson
1995	Classic Cliché	L Dettori	Moonshell	L Dettori	Lammtara	W Swinburn
1996	Shantou	L Dettori	Lady Carla	P Eddery	Shaamit	M Hills
1997	Silver Patriarch	P Eddery	Reams of Verse	K Fallon	Benny the Dip	W Ryan
1998	Nedawi	J Reid	Shahtoush	M J Kinane	High Rise	O Peslier
1999	Mutafaweq	R Hills	Ramruma	K Fallon	Oath	K Fallon
2000	Millenary	T Quinn	Love Divine	T Quinn	Sinndar	J Murtagh
2001	Milan	M J Kinane	Imagine	M J Kinane	Galileo	M J Kinane
2002	Bollin Eric	K Darley	Kazzia	L Dettori	High Chaparral	J Murtagh
2003	Brian Boru	J Spencer	Casual Look	M Dwyer	Kris Kin	K Fallon
2004	Rule of Law	K McEvoy	Ouija Board	K Fallon	North Light	K Fallon
2005			Eswarah	R Hiller	Motivator	J Murtagh

	2000 Guineas		1000 Guineas		Grand National	
Year	Horse	Jockey	Horse	Jockey	Horse	Jockey
1809	Wizard	W Clift	—	—	—	—
1810	Hephestion	F Buckle	—	—	—	—
1811	Trophonius	S Barnard	—	—	—	—
1812	Cwrw	S Chifney	—	—	—	—
1813	Smolensko	H Miller	—	—	—	—
1814	Olive	W Arnold	Charlotte	W Clift	—	—
1815	Tigris	W Arnold	Brown foal by Selim	W Clift	—	—
1816	Nectar	W Arnold	Rhoda	S Barnard	—	—
1817	Manfred	W Wheatley	Neva	W Arnold	—	—
1818	Interpreter	W Clift	Corinne	F Buckle	—	—
1819	Antar	E Edwards	Catgut	F Buckle	—	—
1820	Pindarrie	F Buckle	Rowena	F Buckle	—	—
1821	Reginald	F Buckle	Zeal	F Buckle	—	—

		2000 Guineas		1000 Guineas		Grand National	
Year	Horse	Jockey	Horse	Jockey	Horse	Jockey
1822	Pastille	F Buckle	Whizgig	F Buckle	—	—
1823	Nicolo	W Wheatley	Zinc	F Buckle	—	—
1824	Schariar	W Wheatley	Cobweb	J Robinson	—	—
1825	Enamel	J Robinson	Tontine	W Alkover	—	—
1826	Dervise	J B Day	Problem	J Day	—	—
1827	Turcoman	F Buckle	Arab	F Buckle	—	—
1828	Cadland	J Robinson	Zoe	J Robinson	—	—
1829	Patron	F Boyce	B foal by Godolphin	Arnull	—	—
1830	Augustus	P Conolly	Charlotte West	J Robinson	—	—
1831	Riddlesworth	J Robinson	Galantine	P Conolly	—	—
1832	Archibald	Pavis	Galata	Arnull	—	—
1833	Clearwell	J Robinson	Tarantella	Wright	—	—
1834	Glencoe	J Robinson	May-Day	J Day	—	—
1835	Ibrahim	J Robinson	Preserve	E Flatman	—	—
1836	Bay Middleton	J Robinson	Destiny	J Day	—	—
1837	Achmet	E Edwards	Chapeau d'Espagne	J Day	The Duke (Maghull)	Mr Potts
1838	Grey Momus	J B Day	Barcarolle	E Edwards	Sir Henry (Maghull)	T Olliver
1839	The Corsair	Wakefield	Cara	G Edwards	Lottery (Liverpool)	Jem Mason
1840	Crucifix	J B Day	Crucifix	J Day	Jerry	Mr Bretherton
1841	Ralph	J B Day	Potentia	J Robinson	Charity	Mr Powell
1842	Meteor	W Scott	Firebrand	S Rogers	Gaylad	T Olliver
1843	Cotherstone	W Scott	Extempore	S Chifney	Vanguard	T Olliver
1844	The Ugly Buck	J Day Jnr	Sorella	J Robinson	Discount	Crickmere
1845	Idas	E Flatman	Pic-nic	W Abdale	Cure-all	W G Loft
1846	Sir Tatton Sykes	W Scott	Mendicant	S Day	Pioneer	Taylor
1847	Conyngham	J Robinson	Clementina	E Flatman	Matthew	D Wynne
1848	Flatcatcher	J Robinson	Canezou	F Butler	Chandler	Capt Little
1849	Nunnykirk	F Butler	Flea	A Day	Peter Simple	T Cunningham
1850	Pitsford	A Day	Chestnut foal by Slane	F Butler	Abdel Kader	C Green
1851	Hernandez	E Flatman	Aphrodite	J Marson	Abdel Kader	T Abbot
1852	Stockwell	Norman	Kate	A Day	Miss Mowbray	Mr A Goodman
1853	West Australian	F Butler	Mentmore Lass	Charlton	Peter Simple	T Olliver
1854	The Hermit	A Day	Virago	J Wells	Bourton	Tasker
1855	Lord of the Isles	Aldcroft	Habena	S Rogers	Wanderer	J Hanlon
1856	Fazzaletto	E Flatman	Manganese	J Osborne	Freetrader	G Stevens
1857	Vedette	J Osborne	Imperieuse	E Flatman	Emigrant	C Boyce
1858	Fitz-Roland	J Wells	Governess	Ashmall	Little Charley	W Archer
1859	The Promised Land	A Day	Mayonnaise	G Fordham	Half Caste	C Green
1860	The Wizard	Ashmall	Sagitta	Aldcroft	Anatis	Mr Thomas
1861	Diophantus	A Edwards	Nemesis	G Fordham	Jealousy	J Kendall
1862	The Marquis	Ashmall	Hurricane	Ashmall	Huntsman	H Lamplugh
1863	Macaroni	T Challoner	Lady Augusta	A Edwards	Emblem	G Stevens
1864	General Peel	Aldcroft	Tomato	J Wells	Emblematic	G Stevens
1865	Gladiateur	H Grimshaw	Siberia	G Fordham	Alcibiade	Capt Coventry
1866	Lord Lyon	Thomas	Repulse	T Cannon	Salamander	Mr A Goodman
1867	Vauban	G Fordham	Achievement	H Custance	Cortolvin	J Page
1868	Moslem	T Challoner	Formosa	G Fordham	The Lamb	Mr Edwards
1869	Pretender	J Osborne	Scottish Queen	G Fordham	The Colonel	G Stevens
1870	Macgregor	J Daley	Hester	J Grimshaw	The Colonel	G Stevens
1871	Bothwell	J Osborne	Hannah	C Maidment	The Lamb	Mr Thomas
1872	Prince Charlie	J Osborne	Reine	H Parry	Casse Tete	J Page
1873	Gang Forward	T Challoner	Cecilia	J Morris	Disturbance	J M Richardson
1874	Atlantic	F Archer	Apology	J Osborne	Reugny	J M Richardson
1875	Camballo	J Osborne	Spinaway	F Archer	Pathfinder	Mr Thomas
1876	Petrarch	Luke	Camelia	T Glover	Regal	J Cannon
1877	Chamant	J Goater	Belphoebe	H Jeffery	Austerlitz	Mr F G Hobson
1878	Pilgrimage	T Cannon	Pilgrimage	T Cannon	Shifnal	J Jones
1879	Charibert	F Archer	Wheel of Fortune	F Archer	The Liberator	G Moore
1880	Petronel	G Fordham	Elizabeth	C Wood	Empress	T Beasley
1881	Peregrine	F Webb	Thebais	G Fordham	Woodbrook	T Beasley
1882	Shotover	T Cannon	St Marguerite	C Wood	Seaman	Lord Manners
1883	Galliard	F Archer	Hauteur	G Fordham	Zoedone	Count Kinsky
1884	Scot-free	Platt	Busybody	T Cannon	Voluptuary	Mr E P Wilson
1885	Paradox	F Archer	Farewell	G Barrett	Roquefort	Mr E P Wilson
1886	Ormonde	G Barrett	Miss Jummy	J Watts	Old Joe	T Skelton
1887	Enterprise	T Cannon	Reve d'Or	C Wood	Gamecock	W Daniells

	2000 Guineas		1000 Guineas		Grand National	
Year	Horse	Jockey	Horse	Jockey	Horse	Jockey
1888	Ayrshire	J Osborne	Briar-root	W Warne	Playfair	Mawson
1889	Enthusiast	T Cannon	Minthe	J Woodburn	Frigate	T Beasley
1890	Surefoot	Liddiard	Semolina	J Watts	Ilex	A Nightingall
1891	Common	G Barrett	Mimi	F Rickaby	Come Away	H Beasley
1892	Bonavista	W Robinson	La Fleche	G Barrett	Father O'Flynn	Capt Owen
1893	Isinglass	T Loates	Siffleuse	T Loates	Cloister	Dollery
1894	Ladas	J Watts	Amiable	W Bradford	Why Not	A Nightingall
1895	Kirkconnel	J Watts	Galeottia	F Pratt	Wildman From Borneo	J Widger
1896	St Frusquin	T Loates	Thais	J Watts	The Soarer	D Campbell
1897	Galtee More	C Wood	Chelandry	J Watts	Manifesto	T Kavanagh
1898	Disraeli	S Loates	Nun Nicer	S Loates	Drogheda	J Gourley
1899	Flying Fox	M Cannon	Sibola	J T Sloan	Manifesto	G Williamson
1900	Diamond Jubilee	H Jones	Winifreda	S Loates	Ambush II	A Anthony
1901	Handicapper	W Halsey	Aida	D Maher	Grudon	A Nightingall
1902	Sceptre	H Randall	Sceptre	H Randall	Shannon Lass	D Read
1903	Rock Sand	J H Martin	Quintessence	H Randall	Drumcree	P Woodland
1904	St Amant	K Cannon	Pretty Polly	W Lane	Moifaa	A Birch
1905	Vedas	H Jones	Cherry Lass	G McCall	Kirkland	F Mason
1906	Gorgos	H Jones	Flair	B Dillon	Ascetic's Silver	Hon A Hastings
1907	Slieve Gallion	W Higgs	Witch Elm	B Lynham	Eremon	A Newey
1908	Norman III	O Madden	Rhodora	L Lyne	Rubio	H B Bletsoe
1909	Minoru	H Jones	Electra	B Dillon	Lutteur III	G Parfrement
1910	Neil Gow	D Maher	Winkipop	B Lynham	Jenkinstown	R Chadwick
1911	Sunstar	G Stern	Atmah	F Fox	Glenside	J R Anthony
1912	Sweeper II	D Maher	Tagalie	L H Hewitt	Jerry M	E Piggott
1913	Louvois	J Reiff	Jest	F Rickaby Jnr	Covetcoat	P Woodland
1914	Kennymore	G Stern	Princess Dorrie	W Huxley	Sunloch	W J Smith
1915	Pommern	S Donoghue	Vaucluse	F Rickaby Jnr	Ally Sloper	J R Anthony
1916	Clarissimus	J Clark	Canyon	F Rickaby Jnr	Vermouth	J Reardon
1917	Gay Crusader	S Donoghue	Diadem	F Rickaby Jnr	Ballymacad	E Driscoll
1918	Gainsborough	J Childs	Ferry	B Carslake	Poethlyn	E Piggott
1919	The Panther	R Cooper	Roseway	A Whalley	Poethlyn	E Piggott
1920	Tetratema	B Carslake	Cinna	W Griggs	Troytown	J R Anthony
1921	Craig An Eran	J Brennan	Bettina	G Bellhouse	Shaun Spadah	F B Rees
1922	St Louis	G Archibald	Silver Urn	B Carslake	Music Hall	F B Rees
1923	Ellangowan	C Elliot	Tranquil	E Gardner	Sgt Murphy	Capt Bennet
1924	Diophon	G Hulme	Plack	E C Elliott	Master Robert	R Trudgill
1925	Manna	S Donoghue	Saucy Sue	F Bullock	Double Chance	Major Wilson
1926	Colorado	T Weston	Pillion	R Perryman	Jack Horner	W Watkinson
1927	Adam's Apple	J Leach	Cresta Run	A Balding	Sprig	T E Leader
1928	Flamingo	C Elliot	Scuttle	J Childs	Tipperary Tim	W P Dutton
1929	Mr Jinks	H Beasley	Taj Mah	W Sibbritt	Gregalach	R Everett
1930	Diolite	F Fox	Fair Isle	T Weston	Shaun Goilin	T Cullinan
1931	Cameronian	J Childs	Four Course	E C Elliott	Grakle	R Lyall
1932	Orwell	R Jones	Kandy	E C Elliott	Forbra	J Hamey
1933	Rodosto	R Brethes	Brown Betty	J Childs	Kellsboro Jack	D Williams
1934	Colombo	W Johnstone	Campanula	H Wragg	Golden Miller	G Wilson
1935	Bahram	F Fox	Mesa	W R Johnstone	Reynoldstown	F C Furlong
1936	Pay Up	R Dick	Tide-Way	R Perryman	Reynoldstown	F T Walwyn
1937	Le Ksar	C Semblat	Exhibitionist	S Donoghue	Royal Mail	E Williams
1938	Pasch	G Richards	Rockfel	S Wragg	Battleship	Bruce Hobbs
1939	Blue Peter	E Smith	Galatea II	R A Jones	Workman	T Hyde
1940	Djebel	C Elliot	Godiva	D Marks	Bogskar	M Jones
1941	Lambert Simnel	C Elliot	Dancing Time	R Perryman	no race	—
1942	Big Game	G Richards	Sun Chariot	G Richards	no race	—
1943	Kingsway	S Wragg	Herringbone	H Wragg	no race	—
1944	Garden Path	H Wragg	Picture Play	E C Elliott	no race	—
1945	Court Martial	C Richards	Sun Stream	H Wragg	no race	—
1946	Happy Knight	T Weston	Hypericum	D Smith	Lovely Cottage	Capt R Petre
1947	Tudor Minstrel	G Richards	Imprudence	W R Johnstone	Caughoo	E Dempsey
1948	My Babu	C Smirke	Queenpot	G Richards	Sheila's Cottage	A P Thompson
1949	Nimbus	C Elliot	Musidora	E Britt	Russian Hero	L McMorrow
1950	Palestine	C Smirke	Camaree	W R Johnstone	Freebooter	J Power
1951	Ki Ming	A Breasley	Belle Of All	G Richards	Nickel Coin	J A Bullock
1952	Thunderhead II	R Poincelet	Zabara	K Gethin	Teal	A P Thompson
1953	Nearula	E Britt	Happy Laughter	E Mercer	Early Mist	B Marshall
1954	Darius	E Mercer	Festoon	A Breasley	Royal Tan	B Marshall
1955	Our Babu	D Smith	Meld	W H Carr	Quare Times	P Taaffe
1956	Gilles de Retz	F Barlow	Honeylight	E Britt	E.S.B.	D V Dick

Year	2000 Guineas Horse	Jockey	1000 Guineas Horse	Jockey	Grand National Horse	Jockey
1957	Crepello	L Piggott	Rose Royale II	C Smirke	Sundew	F Winter
1958	Pall Mall	D Smith	Bella Paola	S Boullenger	Mr What	A R Freeman
1959	Taboun	G Moore	Petite Etoile	D Smith	Oxo	M Scudamore
1960	Martial	R Hutchinson	Never Too Late	R Poincelet	Merryman II	G Scott
1961	Rockavon	N Stirk	Sweet Solera	W Rickaby	Nicolaus Silver	R Beasley
1962	Privy Councillor	W Rickaby	Abermaid	W Williamson	Kilmore	F Winter
1963	Only For Life	J Lindley	Hula Dancer	R Poincelet	Ayala	P Buckley
1964	Baldric II	W Pyers	Pourparler	G Bougoure	Team Spirit	W Robinson
1965	Niksar	D Keith	Night Off	W Williamson	Jay Trump	T Smith
1966	Kashmir II	J Lindley	Glad Rags	P Cook	Anglo	T Norman
1967	Royal Palace	G Moore	Fleet	G Moore	Foinavon	J Buckingham
1968	Sir Ivor	L Piggott	Caergwrle	A Barclay	Red Alligator	B Fletcher
1969	Right Tack	G Lewis	Full Dress II	R Hutchinson	Highland Wedding	E Harty
1970	Nijinsky	L Piggott	Humble Duty	L Piggott	Gay Trip	P Taaffe
1971	Brigadier Gerard	J Mercer	Altesse Royale	Y Saint-Martin	Specify	J Cook
1972	High Top	W Carson	Waterloo	E Hide	Well To Do	G Thorner
1973	Mon Fils	F Durr	Mysterious	G Lewis	Red Rum	B Fletcher
1974	Nonoalco	Y Saint-Martin	Highclere	J Mercer	Red Rum	B Fletcher
1975	Bolkonski	G Dettori	Nocturnal Spree	J Roe	L'Escargot	T Carberry
1976	Wollow	G Dettori	Flying Water	Y Saint-Martin	Rag Trade	J Burke
1977	Nebbiolo	G Curran	Mrs McArdy	E Hide	Red Rum	T Stack
1978	Roland Gardens	F Durr	Enstone Spark	E Johnson	Lucius	R Davies
1979	Tap on Wood	S Cauthen	One in a Million	J Mercer	Rubstic	M Barnes
1980	Known Fact	W Carson	Quick as Lightning	B Rouse	Ben Nevis	C Fenwick
1981	To-Agori-Mou	G Starkey	Fairy Footsteps	L Piggott	Aldaniti	R Champion
1982	Zino	F Head	On the House	J Reid	Grittar	R Saunders
1983	Lomond	P Eddery	Ma Biche	F Head	Corbiere	B De Haan
1984	El Gran Señor	P Eddery	Pebbles	P Robinson	Hallo Dandy	N Doughty
1985	Shadeed	L Piggott	Oh So Sharp	S Cauthen	Last Suspect	H Davies
1986	Dancing Brave	G Starkey	Midway Lady	R Cochrane	West Tip	R Dunwoody
1987	Don't Forget Me	W Carson	Miesque	F Head	Maori Venture	S Knight
1988	Doyoun	W Swinburn	Ravinella	G Moore	Rhyme 'n Reason	B Powell
1989	Nashwan	W Carson	Musical Bliss	W Swinburn	Little Polveir	J Frost
1990	Tirol	M Kinane	Salsabil	W Carson	Mr Frisk	Mr M Armytage
1991	Mystiko	M Roberts	Shadayid	W Carson	Seagram	N Hawke
1992	Rodrigo De Triano	L Piggott	Hatoof	W Swinburn	Party Politics	C Llewellyn
1993	Zafonic	P Eddery	Sayyedati	W Swinburn	no race	—
1994	Mr Baileys	J Weaver	Las Meninas	J Reid	Minnehoma	R Dunwoody
1995	Pennekamp	T Jarnet	Harayir	R Hills	Royal Athlete	J Titley
1996	Mark of Esteem	L Dettori	Bosra Sham	P Eddery	Rough Quest	M Fitzgerald
1997	Entrepreneur	M J Kinane	Sleepytime	K Fallon	Lord Gyllene	A Dobbin
1998	King of Kings	M J Kinane	Cape Verdi	L Dettori	Earth Summit	C Llewellyn
1999	Island Sands	L Dettori	Wince	K Fallon	Bobbyjo	P Carberry
2000	King's Best	K Fallon	Lahan	R Hills	Papillon	R Walsh
2001	Golan	K Fallon	Ameerat	P Robinson	Red Marauder	R Guest
2002	Rock of Gibraltar	J Murtagh	Kazzia	L Dettori	Bindaree	J Culloty
2003	Refuse to Bend	P Smullen	Russian Rhythm	K Fallon	Monty's Pass	B Geraghty
2004	Haafhd	R Hills	Attraction	K Darley	Amberleigh House	G Lee
2005	Footstepsinthe-sand	K Fallon	Virginia Waters	K Fallon	Hedgehunter	R Walsh

SPORT & LEISURE

Horse Racing: General Information

all weather tracks: UK	Lingfield, Southwell, Wolverhampton
autumn double	Cesarewitch and Cambridgeshire
champion jockey: 13 times in a row	E Flatman (1840–52) and Fred Archer (1874–86)
champion jockey: shot himself	Fred Archer (aged 29)
Cheltenham Gold Cup: won five times in row	Golden Miller (1932–36)
classics: jockey won most	Lester Piggott (30)
crash helmets: made compulsory	1924
Derby: inaugurated by	Sir Charles Bunbury
Derby: longest winning distance	Shergar (10 lengths)
Derby: where run during WW2	Newmarket (1940–45)
flat jockey: champion most times	Gordon Richards (26)
Fred Archer: nickname	The Tinman
French Derby: run	Chantilly

Gary Bardwell: nickname	The Angry Ant
Grand National winner: future monarch owned	Ambush II (King Edward VII in 1900)
Grand National: 1st woman jockey	Charlotte Brew (1977)
Grand National: 1st woman jockey to complete	Geraldine Rees
Grand National: number of fences	30
Grand National: royal horse that collapsed	Devon Loch, ridden by Dick Francis
Grand National: where run during WW1	Gatwick (1916–18) as 'War National Chase' (1917–18), and 'Race Course Association Chase' 1916
Grand National: youngest winning rider	Bruce Hobbs on Battleship in 1938 aged 17
harness racing: gaits	trotting (striding with horse's left front and right rear leg synchronised)
	pacing (moving both legs on one side of body at the same time)
harness racing: vehicle pulled	sulky
Harry Wragg: nickname	The Head Waiter
Irish Classics: run	all at the Curragh
Irish Grand National: run	Fairyhouse
Irish Grand National: woman jockey won	Ann Ferris
jockey: 1st knighted	Gordon Richards
Lester Piggott: 1st winner	The Chase (1948)
Lester Piggott: nickname	The Long Fellow
mare: age filly becomes	five
Melbourne Cup: run	Flemington Park
Oaks: where run during WW2	Newmarket (1940–45)
pacing: US Triple Crown	William H Cane Futurity (1955); Messenger Stake (1957); Little Brown Jug (1946)
racehorse birthdays	1 January (Northern Hemisphere) and 1 August (Southern Hemisphere)
racehorses: maximum letters in name	18
racing colours: Her Majesty the Queen	purple, gold braid, scarlet sleeves, black velvet cap with gold fringe
racing colours: Queen Elizabeth the Queen Mother	blue, buff stripes, blue sleeves, black cap, gold tassel
Scottish Grand National: run	Ayr
spring double	Lincoln and Grand National
stallion: age colt becomes	five
starting stalls: 1st used in UK	Newmarket in 1965 (8 July)
thoroughbred: ancestry	Darley Arabian, Byerly Turk, Godolphin Arabian (aka barb)
trotting: US Triple Crown	Hambleton (commenced 1926); Yonkers Futurity (1958); Kentucky Futurity (1893)
US Triple Crown	Kentucky Derby (1st of the season), Preakness Stakes, Belmont Stakes (last of the season)
virtual racetracks	Portman Park (Flat)
	Steepledown (Jumps)
Welsh Grand National: run	Chepstow

Motor Racing: Formula 1 World Champions

Year	Winning driver	Country	Car	Runner-up	Constructor Championship
1950	Giuseppe Farina	Italy	Alfa Romeo	Juan Manuel Fangio	—
1951	Juan Manuel Fangio	Argentina	Alfa Romeo	Alberto Ascari	—
1952	Alberto Ascari	Italy	Ferrari	Giuseppe Farina	—
1953	Alberto Ascari	Italy	Ferrari	Juan Manuel Fangio	—
1954	Juan Manuel Fangio	Argentina	Maserati/Mercedes	Jose Gonzalez (Argentina)	—
1955	Juan Manuel Fangio	Argentina	Mercedes-Benz	Stirling Moss (GB)	—
1956	Juan Manuel Fangio	Argentina	Lancia-Ferrari	Stirling Moss (GB)	—
1957	Juan Manuel Fangio	Argentina	Maserati	Stirling Moss (GB)	—
1958	Mike Hawthorn	UK	Ferrari	Stirling Moss (GB)	Vanwall
1959	Jack Brabham	Australia	Cooper-Climax	Tony Brooks (GB)	Cooper-Climax
1960	Jack Brabham	Australia	Cooper-Climax	Bruce McLaren (NZL)	Cooper-Climax
1961	Phil Hill	USA	Ferrari	Wolfgang von Trips (W. Germany)	Ferrari
1962	Graham Hill	UK	BRM	Jim Clark	BRM
1963	Jim Clark	UK	Lotus-Climax	Graham Hill	Lotus-Climax
1964	John Surtees	UK	Ferrari	Graham Hill	Ferrari
1965	Jim Clark	UK	Lotus-Climax	Graham Hill	Lotus-Climax
1966	Jack Brabham	Australia	Brabham-Repco	John Surtees	Brabham-Repco
1967	Denny Hulme	New Zealand	Brabham-Repco	Jack Brabham	Brabham-Repco
1968	Graham Hill	UK	Lotus-Ford	Jackie Stewart	Lotus-Ford
1969	Jackie Stewart	UK	Matra-Ford	Jacky Ickx (Belgium)	Matra-Ford
1970	Jochen Rindt	Austria	Lotus-Ford	Jacky Ickx (Belgium)	Lotus-Ford
1971	Jackie Stewart	UK	Tyrrell-Ford	Ronnie Peterson (Sweden)	Tyrrell-Ford
1972	Emerson Fittipaldi	Brazil	Lotus-Ford	Jackie Stewart	Lotus-Ford

Year	Winning driver	Country	Car	Runner-up	Constructor Championship
1973	Jackie Stewart	UK	Tyrrell-Ford	Emerson Fittipaldi	Lotus-Ford
1974	Emerson Fittipaldi	Brazil	McLaren-Ford	Clay Regazzoni (Switzerland)	McLaren-Ford
1975	Niki Lauda	Austria	Ferrari	Emerson Fittipaldi	Ferrari
1976	James Hunt	UK	McLaren-Ford	Niki Lauda	Ferrari
1977	Niki Lauda	Austria	Ferrari	Jody Scheckter	Ferrari
1978	Mario Andretti	USA	Lotus-Ford	Ronnie Peterson (Sweden)	Lotus-Ford
1979	Jody Scheckter	South Africa	Ferrari	Gilles Villeneuve (Canada)	Ferrari
1980	Alan Jones	Australia	Williams-Ford	Nelson Piquet	Williams-Ford
1981	Nelson Piquet	Brazil	Brabham-Ford	Carlos Reutemann (Argentina)	Williams-Ford
1982	Keke Rosberg	Finland	Williams-Ford	J Watson (GB) and D Pironi (France)	Ferrari
1983	Nelson Piquet	Brazil	Brabham-BMW	Alain Prost	Ferrari
1984	Niki Lauda	Austria	McLaren-TAG	Alain Prost	McLaren-TAG
1985	Alain Prost	France	McLaren-TAG	Michele Alboreto (Italy)	McLaren-TAG
1986	Alain Prost	France	McLaren-TAG	Nigel Mansell	Williams-Honda
1987	Nelson Piquet	Brazil	Williams-Honda	Nigel Mansell	Williams-Honda
1988	Ayrton Senna	Brazil	McLaren-Honda	Alain Prost	McLaren-Honda
1989	Alain Prost	France	McLaren-Honda	Ayrton Senna	McLaren-Honda
1990	Ayrton Senna	Brazil	McLaren-Honda	Alain Prost	McLaren-Honda
1991	Ayrton Senna	Brazil	McLaren-Honda	Nigel Mansell	McLaren-Honda
1992	Nigel Mansell	UK	Williams-Renault	Ricardo Patrese (Italy)	Williams-Renault
1993	Alain Prost	France	Williams-Renault	Ayrton Senna	Williams-Renault
1994	Michael Schumacher	Germany	Benetton-Ford	Damon Hill	Williams-Renault
1995	Michael Schumacher	Germany	Benetton-Renault	Damon Hill	Williams-Renault
1996	Damon Hill	UK	Williams-Renault	Jacques Villeneuve	Williams-Renault
1997	Jacques Villeneuve	Canada	Williams-Renault	Michael Schumacher	Williams-Renault
1998	Mika Hakkinen	Finland	McLaren-Mercedes	Michael Schumacher	McLaren-Mercedes
1999	Mika Hakkinen	Finland	McLaren-Mercedes	Eddie Irvine	Ferrari
2000	Michael Schumacher	Germany	Ferrari	Mika Hakkinen	Ferrari
2001	Michael Schumacher	Germany	Ferrari	David Coulthard (UK)	Ferrari
2002	Michael Schumacher	Germany	Ferrari	Rubens Barrichello (Brazil)	Ferrari
2003	Michael Schumacher	Germany	Ferrari	Kimi Raikkonen (Finland)	Ferrari
2004	Michael Schumacher	Germany	Ferrari	Rubens Barrichello (Brazil)	Ferrari

Motor Racing: General Information

circuits: Formula 1
Argentinian – Buenos Aires; Australian – Adelaide, Melbourne; Austrian – A1 Ring, Spielberg; Bahrain – Bahrain International Circuit; Belgian – Spa-Francorchamps, Zolder; Brazilian – São Paolo, Interlagos (pre-1990 Jacarepagua circuit, Rio de Janeiro); British – Silverstone; Canadian – Montreal; Chinese – Shanghai International; Dutch – Zandvoort; European – Nurburgring, Germany; French – Magny Cours, Dijon; German – Hockenheim; Hungarian – Budapest; Italian – Monza; Japanese – Suzuka; Malaysian – Sepang; Mexican – Mexico City; Monaco – Monte Carlo; Portuguese – Estoril; San Marino – Imola; Spanish – Catalunya Montjuich (Barcelona); US – Detroit, Long Beach, Indianapolis.
Nurburgring is no longer used for German GP but has been the venue of the European GP in recent years. Similarly, Aida in Japan is no longer used for its own GP but has been the venue for Pacific GP.

Formula 1: flags
black – disqualification of a driver; black and white chequered – end of race; blue – car about to overtake; red – premature end of race; yellow – danger, no overtaking; yellow and red diagonal stripes – oil on track.

Formula 1: most consecutive wins Alberto Ascari (9).
Formula 1: oldest champion Juan Manuel Fangio (46).
Formula 1: points system For the 2003 season points are awarded for the top eight finishers thus: 10, 8, 6, 5, 4, 3, 2, 1.
Formula 1: posthumous champion Jochen Rindt (1970).
Formula 1: woman driver, first Maria Teresa de Filippis (1958)
fuel: used in Formula 1 pre 1961 nitro-methane, but since 1961 ordinary commercial fuel has been compulsory, although Indianapolis still uses nitro-methane.
Indianapolis 500: first winner Ray Harroun in Marmon Wasp (1911).
Indianapolis 500: laps 200, (although the race is 500 miles in length, hence the name).
Indianapolis 500: Formula 1 winners Jim Clark (1965), Graham Hill (1966), Mario Andretti (1969), E Fittipaldi (1989 and 1993), J Villeneuve (1995).
land speed record: holder Andy Green in Thrust SSC (714 mph).
first over 100 mph: Louis Rigolly in 1904.
Monaco GP: five times winner Graham Hill.
motor cycling: nine championships Giacomo Agostini of Italy (eight consecutive 1965–72 and 1975 in the 500 cc class).

SPORT & LEISURE

speedway championships

UK motor racing circuit: first

raced over four laps, the short track world championships commenced in 1936 and long track in 1971.

Brooklands.

Olympic Games: Venues

1896	Athens, Greece	1960	Rome, Italy
1900	Paris, France	1964	Tokyo, Japan
1904	St Louis, USA	1968	Mexico City
1908	London, UK	1972	Munich, Germany
1912	Stockholm, Sweden	1976	Montreal, Canada
1920	Antwerp, Belgium	1980	Moscow, USSR
1924	Paris, France	1984	Los Angeles, USA
1928	Amsterdam, Holland	1988	Seoul, South Korea
1932	Los Angeles, USA	1992	Barcelona, Spain
1936	Berlin, Germany	1996	Atlanta, USA
1948	London, UK	2000	Sydney, Australia
1952	Helsinki, Finland	2004	Athens, Greece
1956	Melbourne, Australia	2008	Beijing, China

Winter Olympics: Venues

1924	Chamonix, France	1972	Sapporo, Japan
1928	St Moritz, Switzerland	1976	Innsbruck, Austria
1932	Lake Placid, NY, USA	1980	Lake Placid, NY, USA
1936	Garmisch Partenkirchen, Germany	1984	Sarajevo, Yugoslavia
1948	St Moritz, Switzerland	1988	Calgary, Canada
1952	Oslo, Norway	1992	Albertville, France
1956	Cortina, Italy	1994	Lillehammer, Norway
1960	Squaw Valley, California, USA	1998	Nagano, Japan
1964	Innsbruck, Austria	2002	Salt Lake City, USA
1968	Grenoble, France	2006	Turin, Italy

Olympics: General Information

ancient Olympics: in honour of

appearances: most

black power salute

Briton took part in Summer and Winter Olympics

British peer gold medallist

cancelled games: intended hosts

champions: father and son

champion: five times in row

champion: four times in row

cheat: Modern Pentathlon

country contested every games

diplomas awarded to

equestrian: disqualification

equestrian events: 1956

extra lap run in error

father and son rowing gold medallists

flag: colours

gold medals: last given

gold medal: received by post

golds: most in single games

high jump: youngest champion

host country: no golds

IOC: presidents

marathon: barefoot winner

marathon: distance standardised

medal withheld for professionalism

Zeus.

Raymondo d'Inzeo (8).

Tommie Smith and John Carlos 1968. (Other man on rostrum was Peter Norman of Australia.)

Derek Allhusen.

The Marquess of Exeter (Lord Burghley) 1928, 400m Hurdles.

1916 – Berlin; 1940 – Tokyo (then Helsinki); 1944 – London.

Imre Nemeth (Hammer) and Miklos Nemeth (Javelin).

Steve Redgrave (Rowing 1984–2000).

Al Oerter (Discus 1956–68).

Boris Onischenko in Fencing discipline (1976).

UK (both Summer and Winter).

fourth to eighth places.

Cian O'Connor of Ireland was stripped of his gold medal won in the Individual Show Jumping event in 2004 following a positive drug test on his horse, Waterford Crystal.

held in Stockholm.

Steeplechase 1932.

Charles and Richard Burnell.

blue, yellow, black, green, red rings on a white background. (Rings represent the five major continents.)

1912 was the last time solid gold medals were given.

Harold Abrahams (1924).

Mark Spitz (7) (Swimming 1972).

Ulrike Mayfarth (16), who was also the oldest winner aged 28.

Canada (1976).

Dimitrios Vikélas (1894–96); Baron de Coubertin (1896–1925); Henri de Baillet-La Tour (1925–42); J. Sigfrid Edström (1946–52); Avery Brundage (1956–72); Michael Morris, Lord Killanin (1972–80); Juan António Samaranch (1980–2001).

Abebe Bikila (1960).

1924 (although first run as 26 miles 385 yds in 1908).

Jim Thorpe in 1912 (he was reinstated in 1973).

modern Olympics: instigator	Baron Pierre de Coubertin.
Munich massacre	Black September terrorists killing of Israeli athletes (1972).
oldest Briton to win gold medal	Jerry Milner (60 years old in 1908 when winning Shooting gold).
Olympiad: definition	in ancient Greece the time between games was an Olympiad (four years).
Olympic motto	Citius Altius Fortius (Faster, Higher, Stronger).
opening parade	always led by Greece and completed by the host country.
original location	Olympia (776 BC–AD 393, abolished by Emperor Theodosius I).
POW in World War Two	Harold Cassells (1920 Hockey gold medallist).
sex testing: year began	1968.
swimming: first 100m under 1 minute	Johnny Weismuller (1924) (59 seconds).
walkover: champion	Wyndham Halswelle in the 400m (1908).
woman gold medallist: first	Charlotte Cooper (GB) when she won Tennis Singles (1900).
woman: running, throwing, jumping medals	Mildred 'Babe' Didrikson won gold in 80m Hurdles and Javelin and silver medal in High Jump (1932).
Zatopek gold medal treble	In 1952 Emil Zatopek won 5k, 10k and Marathon.

Summer Olympics: British Gold Medal Winners

Name	Date	Sport	Event
Abrahams, Harold	1924	Athletics	4 x 100m Relay
Ainslie, Ben	2000	Sailing	Laser Class
	2004	Sailing	Finn Class
Ainsworth-Davis, Jack	1920	Athletics	4 x 400m Relay
Allhusen, Derek	1968	Equestrian	3-Day Event – Team
Amoore, Edward	1908	Shooting	Small-Bore Rifle Team
Applegarth, Willie	1912	Athletics	4 x 100m Relay
Aspin, John	1908	Yachting	12 Metres Class
Astor, J J	1908	Rackets	Doubles
Atkin, Charles	1920	Hockey	
Attrill, Louis	2000	Rowing	Coxed Eight
Ayton, Sarah	2004	Sailing	Yngling Class
Bacon, Stanley	1908	Wrestling	Middleweight Freestyle
Badcock, Felix	1932	Rowing	Coxless Fours
Bailey, Horace	1908	Football	
Baillon, Louis	1908	Hockey	
Barber, Paul	1988	Hockey	
Barrett, Edward	1908	Tug of War	
Barrett, Frederick	1920	Polo	
Barrett, Roper	1908	Lawn Tennis	Indoor Men's Doubles
Barridge, J E	1900	Football	
Bartlett, Charles	1908	Cycling	100km Track Race
Batchelor, Steve	1988	Hockey	
Beachcroft, Charles	1900	Cricket	
Beesly, Richard	1928	Rowing	Coxless Fours
Belville, Miles	1936	Yachting	6 Metres Class
Bennett, Charles	1900	Athletics	1500m
	1900	Athletics	5000m Team
Bennett, John	1920	Hockey	
Bentham, Isaac	1912	Swimming	Water Polo Team
Beresford, Jack	1924	Rowing	Single Sculls
	1932	Rowing	Coxless Fours
	1936	Rowing	Double Sculls
Beresford, John	1900	Polo	
Berry, Arthur	1908	Football	
	1912	Football	
Bevan, Edward	1928	Rowing	Coxless Fours
Bhaura, Kulbir	1988	Hockey	
Bingley, Norman	1908	Yachting	7 Metres Class
Birkett, Arthur	1900	Cricket	
Blackstaffe, Harry	1908	Rowing	Single Sculls
Boardman, Chris	1936	Yachting	6 Metres Class
Boardman, Chris	1992	Cycling	4000m Pursuit
Bond, David	1948	Yachting	Swallow Class
Bowerman, Alfred	1900	Cricket	
Braithwaite, Bob	1968	Shooting	Clay Pigeon
Brasher, Chris	1956	Athletics	3000m Steeplechase
Brebner, Ron	1912	Football	
Brown, Godfrey	1936	Athletics	4 x 400m Relay
Buchanan, John	1908	Yachting	12 Metres Class

Name	Date	Sport	Event
Buckenham, Claude	1900	Football	
Buckley, George	1900	Cricket	
Bucknall, Henry	1908	Rowing	Eights
Budgett, Richard	1984	Rowing	Coxed Fours
Bugbee, Charlie	1912	Swimming	Water Polo Team
	1920	Swimming	Water Polo Team
Bullen, Jane	1968	Equestrian	3-Day Event Team
Bunten, James	1908	Yachting	12 Metres Class
Burchell, Francis	1900	Cricket	
Burgess, Edgar	1912	Rowing	Eights
Burghley, Lord David	1928	Athletics	400m Hurdles
Burn, Tom	1912	Football	
Burnell, Charles	1908	Rowing	Eights
Burnell, Richard	1948	Rowing	Double Sculls
Bushnell, Bertie	1948	Rowing	Double Sculls
Butler, Guy	1920	Athletics	4 x 400m Relay
Campbell, Charles	1908	Yachting	8 Metres Class
Campbell, Colin	1920	Hockey	
Campbell, Darren	2004	Athletics	4 x 100m Relay
Canning, George	1920	Tug of War	
Carnell, Arthur	1908	Shooting	Small-Bore Rifle
Cassels, Harold	1920	Hockey	
Chalk, Alfred	1900	Football	
Chapman, Frederick	1908	Football	
Christian, Fred	1900	Cricket	
Christie, Linford	1992	Athletics	100m
Clift, Robert	1988	Hockey	
Clive, Lewis	1932	Rowing	Coxless Pairs
Coales, Bill	1908	Athletics	3 Miles Team
Cochrane, Blair	1908	Yachting	8 Metres Class
Coe, Sebastian	1980	Athletics	1,500m
	1984	Athletics	1,500m
Coe, Tom	1900	Swimming	Water Polo Team
Coleman, Robert	1920	Yachting	7 Metres Class
Coode, Ed	2004	Rowing	Coxless Fours
Cook, Stephanie	2000	Modern Pentathlon	Individual Event
Cooke, Harold	1920	Hockey	
Cooper, Charlotte	1900	Lawn Tennis	Women's Singles
	1900	Lawn Tennis	Mixed Doubles
Cooper, Malcolm	1984	Shooting	Small-Bore Rifle, three positions
	1988	Shooting	Small-Bore Rifle, three positions
Corbett, Walter	1908	Football	
Corner, Harry	1900	Cricket	
Cornet, George	1908	Swimming	Water Polo Team
	1912	Swimming	Water Polo Team
Cracknell, James	2000	Rowing	Coxless Fours
	2004	Rowing	Coxless Fours
Crichton, Charles	1908	Yachting	6 Metres Class
Crockford, Eric	1920	Hockey	
Cross, Martin	1984	Rowing	Coxed Fours
Crummack, Rex	1920	Hockey	
Cudmore, Collier	1908	Rowing	Coxless Fours
Cuming, Fred	1900	Cricket	
Currie, Lorne	1900	Yachting	Open Class
	1900	Yachting	0.5–1 Ton Class
Daly, Denis	1900	Polo	
D'Arcy, Vic	1912	Athletics	4 x 100m Relay
Davies, Chris	1972	Yachting	Flying Dutchman Class
Davies, Lynn	1964	Athletics	Long Jump
De Relwyskow, George	1908	Wrestling	Lightweight Freestyle
Deakin, Joe	1908	Athletics	3 Miles Team Race
Dean, Billy	1920	Swimming	Water Polo Team
Dennis, Simon	2000	Rowing	Coxed Eight
Derbyshire, Rob	1900	Swimming	Water Polo Team
	1908	Swimming	4 x 200m Freestyle Relay
Devonish, Marlon	2004	Athletics	4 x 100m Relay
Dines, Joe	1912	Football	
Dixon, Charles	1912	Lawn Tennis	Indoor Mixed Doubles
Dixon, Richard	1908	Yachting	7 Metres Class
Dod, William (brother of Lottie)	1908	Archery	York Round

Name	Date	Sport	Event
Dodds, Richard	1988	Hockey	
Doherty, Laurie	1900	Lawn Tennis	Men's Singles
	1900	Lawn Tennis	Men's Doubles
Doherty, Reggie	1900	Lawn Tennis	Men's Doubles
(brother of Laurie Doherty)	1900	Lawn Tennis	Mixed Doubles
	1908	Lawn Tennis	Men's Doubles
Donne, William	1900	Cricket	
Douglas, Johnny	1908	Boxing	Middleweight
Douglas, Rowley	2000	Rowing	Coxed Eight
Downes, Arthur	1908	Yachting	12 Metres Class
Downes, Henry (Arthur's brother)	1908	Yachting	12 Metres Class
Dunlop, David	1908	Yachting	12 Metres Class
Easte, Philip	1908	Shooting	Clay Pigeon Team
Eastlake-Smith, Gladys	1908	Lawn Tennis	Indoor Women's Singles
Edwards, Jonathan	2000	Athletics	Triple Jump
Edwards, Jumbo	1932	Rowing	Coxless Pairs
	1932	Rowing	Coxless Fours
Eley, Maxwell	1924	Rowing	Coxless Fours
Elliot, Launceston	1896	Weightlifting	One-Handed Lift
Ellison, Adrian	1984	Rowing	Coxed Fours (cox)
Etherington-Smith, Raymond	1908	Rowing	Eights
Exshaw, William	1900	Yachting	2–3 Ton Class
Faulds, Richard	2000	Shooting	Double Trap
Faulkner, David	1988	Hockey	
Fenning, John	1908	Rowing	Coxless Pairs
Field-Richards, John	1908	Motor Boating	8 Metres Class
Finnegan, Chris	1968	Boxing	Middleweight
Fleming, John	1908	Shooting	Small-Bore Rifle, moving target
Fleming, Philip	1912	Rowing	Eights
Fletcher, Jennie	1912	Swimming	4 x 100m Freestyle Relay
Forsyth, Charlie	1908	Swimming	Water Polo Team
Foster, Bill	1908	Swimming	4 x 200m Freestyle Relay
Foster, Tim	2000	Rowing	Coxless Fours
Fox, Jim	1976	Modern Pentathlon	Team Event
Freeman, Harry	1908	Hockey	
Garcia, Russell	1988	Hockey	
Gardener, Jason	2004	Athletics	4 x 100m Relay
Garton, Stanley	1912	Rowing	Eights
George, Rowland	1932	Rowing	Coxless Fours
Gillan, Angus	1908	Rowing	Coxless Fours
	1912	Rowing	Eights
Gladstone, Albert	1908	Rowing	Eights
Glen-Coats, Thomas	1908	Yachting	12 Metres Class
Godfree, Kitty	1920	Lawn Tennis	Women's Doubles
Goodfellow, Fred	1908	Tug of War	
Goodhew, Duncan	1980	Swimming	100m Breaststroke
Gordon-Watson, Mary	1972	Equestrian	3-Day Event Team
Gore, Arthur	1908	Lawn Tennis	Indoor Men's Singles
	1908	Lawn Tennis	Indoor Men's Doubles
Gosling, William	1900	Football	
Grace, Fred	1908	Boxing	Lightweight
Green, Eric	1908	Hockey	
Green, Tommy	1932	Athletics	50km Walk
Gretton, John (serving MP)	1900	Yachting	Open Class
	1900	Yachting	0.5–1 Ton Class
Griffiths, Cecil	1920	Athletics	4 x 400m Relay
Grimley, Martyn	1988	Hockey	
Grinham, Judy	1956	Swimming	100m Backstroke
Grubor, Luka	2000	Rowing	Coxed Eight
Gunn, Dick	1908	Boxing	Featherweight
Gunnell, Sally	1992	Athletics	400m Hurdles
Halswelle, Wyndham	1908	Athletics	400m
Hampson, Tommy	1932	Athletics	800m
Hannam, Edith	1912	Lawn Tennis	Indoor Women's Singles
	1912	Lawn Tennis	Indoor Mixed Doubles
Hanney, Ted	1912	Football	
Hardman, Harry	1908	Football	
Harmer, Russell	1936	Yachting	6 Metres Class
Harrison, Audley	2000	Boxing	Super Heavyweight
Haslam, A	1900	Football	

SPORT & LEISURE

Name	Date	Sport	Event
Haslam, Harry	1920	Hockey	
Hawkes, Robert	1908	Football	
Hemery, David	1968	Athletics	400m Hurdles
Herbert, Garry	1992	Rowing	Coxed Pairs (cox)
Hill, Albert	1920	Athletics	800m
	1920	Athletics	1,500m
Hill, Arthur	1912	Swimming	Water Polo Team
Hill, Bertie	1956	Equestrian	3-Day Event Team
Hillyard, George	1908	Lawn Tennis	Men's Doubles
Hirons, Bill	1908	Tug of War	
Hoare, Gordon	1912	Football	
Hodge, Percy	1920	Athletics	3,000m Steeplechase
Holman, Fred	1908	Swimming	200m Breaststroke
Holmes, Andy	1984	Rowing	Coxed Fours
	1988	Rowing	Coxless Pairs
Holmes, Fred	1920	Tug of War	
Holmes, Kelly	2004	Athletics	800m
	2004	Athletics	1,500m
Horsfall, Ewart	1912	Rowing	Eights
Hoy, Chris	2004	Cycling	1km Sprint
Humby, Harry	1908	Shooting	Small-Bore Rifle Team
Humphreys, Fred	1908	Tug of War	
	1920	Tug of War	
Hunt, Kenneth	1908	Football	
Hunt-Davis, Ben	2000	Rowing	Coxed Eight
Ireton, Albert	1908	Tug of War	
Jacobs, David	1912	Athletics	4 x 100m Relay
Jarvis, John Arthur	1900	Swimming	1,000m Freestyle
	1900	Swimming	4,000m Freestyle
Johnson, Victor	1908	Cycling	One-Lap Race
Johnstone, Banner	1908	Rowing	Eights
Jones, Ben	1908	Cycling	5,000m Track Race
	1908	Cycling	Three-Lap Pursuit
Jones, Ben	1968	Equestrian	3-Day Event Team
Jones, Chris	1920	Swimming	Water Polo Team
Jones, J H	1900	Football	
Keene, Foxhall	1900	Polo	
Kelly, Fred	1908	Rowing	Eights
Kemp, Peter	1900	Swimming	Water Polo Team
Kerly, Sean	1988	Hockey	
Kingsbury, Clarrie	1908	Cycling	20km Track Race
	1908	Cycling	Three-Lap Pursuit
Kinnear, Wally	1912	Rowing	Single Sculls
Kirby, Alister	1912	Rowing	Eights
Kirkwood, Jimmy	1988	Hockey	
Knight, Arthur	1912	Football	
Lambert-Chambers, Dolly	1908	Lawn Tennis	Women's Singles
Lance, Tommy	1920	Cycling	2,000m Tandem
Lander, John	1928	Rowing	Coxless Fours
Larner, George	1908	Athletics	3,500m and 10 Mile Walk
Laurie, Ran	1948	Rowing	Coxless Pairs
Law, Leslie	2004	Equestrian	3-Day Event
Laws, Gilbert	1908	Yachting	6 Metres Class
Leaf, Charles	1936	Yachting	6 Metres Class
Leighton, Arthur	1920	Hockey	
Leman, Richard	1988	Hockey	
Lessimore, Edward	1912	Shooting	Small-Bore Rifle Team, 50m
Lewis, Denise	2000	Athletics	Heptathlon
Lewis-Francis, Mark	2004	Athletics	4 x 100m Relay
Liddell, Eric	1924	Athletics	400m
Lindsay, Andrew	2000	Rowing	Coxed Eight
Lindsay, Robert	1920	Athletics	4 x 400m Relay
Lister, Bill	1900	Swimming	Water Polo Team
Littlewort, Henry	1912	Football	
Llewellyn, Sir Harry (Foxhunter)	1952	Equestrian	Prix des Nations Team
Lockett, Vivian	1920	Polo	
Logan, Gerald	1908	Hockey	
Lonsbrough, Anita	1960	Swimming	200m Breaststroke
Lowe, Douglas	1924	Athletics	800m
	1928	Athletics	800m
McBryan, Jack	1920	Hockey	

Name	Date	Sport	Event
MacDonald-Smith, Iain	1968	Yachting	Flying Dutchman Class
McGrath, George	1920	Hockey	
Macintosh, Henry	1920	Athletics	4 x 100m Relay
McIntyre, Mike	1988	Yachting	Star Class
Mackay, Frank (USA born)	1900	Polo	
McKenzie, John	1908	Yachting	12 Metres Class
MacKinnon, Duncan	1908	Rowing	Coxless Fours
Mackworth-Praed, Cyril	1924	Shooting	Running Deer (double shot)
MacLagen, Gilchrist	1908	Rowing	Eights
McMeekin, Tom	1908	Yachting	6 Metres Class
Macnabb, James	1924	Rowing	Coxless Fours
McNair, Winifred	1920	Lawn Tennis	Women's Doubles
McTaggart, Dick	1956	Boxing	Lightweight
McWhirter, Douglas	1912	Football	
Maddison, W J	1920	Yachting	7 Metres Class
Mallin, Harry	1920	Boxing	Middleweight
(retired undefeated 300 fights)	1924	Boxing	Middleweight
Marcon, Sholto	1920	Hockey	
Martin, Albert	1908	Yachting	12 Metres Class
Martin, Leonard	1936	Yachting	6 Metres Class
Martin, Steve (played 1 minute)	1988	Hockey	
Matthews, Ken	1964	Athletics	20km Walk
Matthews, M K	1908	Shooting	Small-Bore Rifle Team
Maunder, Alex	1908	Shooting	Clay Pigeon Team
Meade, Richard	1968	Equestrian	3-Day Event Team
	1972	Equestrian	3-Day Event and Team
Melvill, Tim	1920	Polo	
Meredith, Leon	1908	Cycling	Three-Lap Pursuit
Merriman, Fred	1908	Tug of War	
Miller, Charles	1908	Polo	
Miller, George (brother of Charles)	1908	Polo	
Millner, Jerry	1908	Shooting	Free Rifle
Mills, Edwin	1908	Tug of War	
	1920	Tug of War	
Mitchell, Harry	1924	Boxing	Light-Heavyweight
Moore, Bella	1912	Swimming	4 x 100m Freestyle Relay
Moore, F W	1908	Shooting	Clay Pigeon Team
Moorhouse, Adrian	1988	Swimming	100m Breaststroke
Morris, Stewart	1948	Yachting	Swallow Class
Morrison, Robert	1924	Rowing	Coxless Fours
Morton, Lucy	1924	Swimming	200m Breaststroke
Murray, Robert	1912	Shooting	Small-Bore Rifle Team
Neame, Philip	1924	Shooting	Running Deer (double shot)
(only man to be awarded Victoria Cross, knighthood and Olympic gold)			
Nevinson, George	1908	Swimming	Water Polo Team
Newall, Queenie	1908	Archery	National Round
Nicholas, J	1900	Football	
Nickalls, Guy	1908	Rowing	Eights
Nickalls, Patteson	1908	Polo	
Nightingale, Danny	1976	Modern Pentathlon	Team Event
Noble, Alan	1908	Hockey	
Noel, Evan	1908	Rackets	Singles
O'Kelly, Con	1908	Wrestling	Heavyweight, Freestyle
Oldman, Albert	1908	Boxing	Heavyweight
Osborn, John	1976	Yachting	Tornado Class
Ovett, Steve	1980	Athletics	800m
Packer, Ann	1964	Athletics	800m
Page, Edgar	1908	Hockey	
Palmer, Charles	1908	Shooting	Clay Pigeon Team
Pappin, Veryan	1988	Hockey	
Parker, Adrian	1976	Modern Pentathlon	Team Event
Parker, Bridget	1972	Equestrian	3-Day Event Team
Pattisson, Rodney	1968	Yachting	Flying Dutchman Class
	1972	Yachting	Flying Dutchman Class
Payne, Ernest	1908	Cycling	Three-Lap Pursuit
(known as the Worcester Wonder, Payne changed sports to become a Manchester Utd footballer)			
Peacock, Bill	1920	Swimming	Water Polo Team
Pennell, Vane	1908	Rackets	Doubles

Name	Date	Sport	Event
Pepe, Joseph	1912	Shooting	Small-Bore Rifle Team, 50m
Percy, Iain	2000	Sailing	Finn Class
Perry, Herbert	1924	Shooting	Running Deer (double shot)
Peters, Mary	1972	Athletics	Pentathlon
Phillips, Mark	1972	Equestrian	3-Day Event Team
Pike, J F	1908	Shooting	Clay Pigeon Team
Pimm, William	1908	Shooting	Small-Bore Rifle Team
	1912	Shooting	Small-Bore Rifle Team, 50m
Pinsent, Matthew	1992	Rowing	Coxless Pairs
	1996	Rowing	Coxless Pairs
	2000	Rowing	Coxless Fours
	2004	Rowing	Coxless Fours
Postans, J M	1908	Shooting	Clay Pigeon Team
Potter, Jonathan	1988	Hockey	
Powlesland, Alfred	1900	Cricket	
Pridmore, Reggie	1908	Hockey	
Purcell, Noel	1920	Swimming	Water Polo Team
(Purcell was also an Irish rugby			
international)			
Purnell, Clyde	1908	Football	
Quash, Bill	1900	Football	
Queally, Jason	2000	Cycling	Kilometre Sprint
Radmilovic, Paul	1908	Swimming	Water Polo Team
	1908	Swimming	4 x 200m Freestyle Relay
	1912	Swimming	Water Polo Team
	1920	Swimming	Water Polo Team
Rampling, Godfrey	1936	Athletics	4 x 400m Relay
Rand, Mary	1964	Athletics	Long Jump
(Mary won the full set of medals with			
silver in Pentathlon and bronze in the relay)			
Rawlinson, Alfred	1900	Polo	
Rawson, Ronald	1920	Boxing	Heavyweight
Redgrave, Steve	1984	Rowing	Coxed Fours
	1988	Rowing	Coxless Pairs
	1992	Rowing	Coxless Pairs
	1996	Rowing	Coxless Pairs
	2000	Rowing	Coxless Fours
Redwood, Bernard	1908	Motor Boating	8 Metres Class
	1908	Motor Boating	Under 60-Foot Class
Rees, Percy	1908	Hockey	
Rhodes, John	1908	Yachting	8 Metres Class
Rimmer, J T	1900	Athletics	4,000m Steeplechase
	1900	Athletics	5,000m Team Race
Ritchie, Major	1908	Lawn Tennis	Men's Singles
Rivett-Carnac, Charles	1908	Yachting	7 Metres Class
Rivett-Carnac, Frances	1908	Yachting	7 Metres Class
(wife of Charles)			
Roberts, Bill	1936	Athletics	4 x 400m Relay
Robertson, Arthur	1908	Athletics	Three Miles Team Race
Robertson, Arthur	1900	Swimming	Water Polo Team
Robertson, Shirley	2000	Sailing	Europe Dinghy Class
	2004	Sailing	Yngling Class
Robinson, Eric	1900	Swimming	Water Polo Team
Robinson, John	1908	Hockey	
Robinson, Sidney	1900	Athletics	5,000m Team Race
Rook, Laurence	1956	Equestrian	3-Day Event Team
Russell, Arthur	1908	Athletics	3,200m Steeplechase
Ryan, Harry	1920	Cycling	2,000m Tandem
Sanders, Terence	1924	Rowing	Coxless Fours
Sanderson, Ronald	1908	Rowing	Eights
Sanderson, Tessa	1984	Athletics	Javelin
Scarlett, Fred	2000	Rowing	Coxed Eight
Searle, Greg	1992	Rowing	Coxed Pairs
Searle, Jonny	1992	Rowing	Coxed Pairs
Sewell, John	1912	Tug of War	
	1920	Tug of War	
Sharpe, Ivan	1912	Football	
Sheen, Gillian	1956	Fencing	Individual Foil
Shepherd, John	1908	Tug of War	
	1920	Tug of War	
Sherwani, Imran	1988	Hockey	

Name	Date	Sport	Event
Shoveller, Stanley	1908	Hockey	
	1920	Hockey	
Smith, Charles	1908	Swimming	Water Polo Team
	1912	Swimming	Water Polo Team
	1920	Swimming	Water Polo Team
Smith, Faulder	1920	Hockey	
Smith, Herbert	1908	Football	
Somers-Smith, John	1908	Rowing	Coxless Fours
Southwood, Dick	1936	Rowing	Double Sculls
Spackman, F G	1900	Football	
Spiers, Annie	1912	Swimming	4 x 100m Freestyle Relay
Spinks, Terry	1956	Boxing	Flyweight
Stamper, Harry	1912	Football	
Stapley, Henry	1908	Football	
Steer, Irene	1912	Swimming	4 x 100m Freestyle Relay
Stewart, Douglas	1952	Equestrian	Prix des Nations Team
(only British man to have competed at Olympic eventing and show jumping competitions)			
Stiff, Harry	1920	Tug of War	
Strode-Jackson, Arnold	1912	Athletics	1,500m
Styles, William	1908	Shooting	Small-Bore disappearing target
Sutton, Henry	1908	Yachting	8 Metres Class
Swann, Sidney	1912	Rowing	Eights
Symes, John	1900	Cricket	
Tait, Gerald	1908	Yachting	12 Metres Class
Taylor, Henry	1908	Swimming	400m Freestyle
	1908	Swimming	1,500m Freestyle
	1908	Swimming	4 x 200m Freestyle Relay
Taylor, Ian	1988	Hockey	
Thomas, Harry	1908	Boxing	Bantamweight
Thompson, Daley	1980	Athletics	Decathlon
	1984	Athletics	Decathlon
Thompson, Don	1960	Athletics	50km Walk
Thomson, Gordon	1908	Rowing	Coxless Pairs
Thorne, Ernie	1920	Tug of War	
Thornycroft, Tom	1908	Motor Boating	8 Metres Class
	1908	Motor Boating	Under 60-Foot Class
Thould, Tom	1908	Swimming	Water Polo Team
	1912	Swimming	Water Polo Team
Toller, Montague	1900	Cricket	
Trapmore, Steve	2000	Rowing	Coxed Eight
Turnbull, Noel	1920	Lawn Tennis	Men's Doubles
Turner, R R	1900	Football	
Tysoe, Alf	1900	Athletics	800m
	1900	Athletics	5,000m Team Race
Vaile, Bryn	1988	Yachting	Star Class
Voigt, Emil	1908	Athletics	Five Miles
Walden, Harry (also music-hall comic)	1912	Football	
Warriner, Michael	1928	Rowing	Coxless Fours
Webb, Sarah	2004	Sailing	Yngling Class
Weldon, Frank	1956	Equestrian	Three-Day Event Team
(born in India, Weldon was the only British Olympic gold medal winner to escape from Colditz)			
Wells, Allan	1980	Athletics	100m
Wells, Henry	1912	Rowing	Eights (cox)
West, Kieran	2000	Rowing	Coxed Eight
White, Reg	1976	Yachting	Tornado Class
White, Wilf	1952	Equestrian	Prix des Nations Team
Whitlock, Harold	1936	Athletics	50km Walk
Whitty, Allen	1924	Shooting	Running Deer (double shot)
Wiggins, Bradley	2004	Cycling	4,000m Pursuit
Wilkie, David	1976	Swimming	200m Breaststroke
Wilkinson, Cyril	1920	Hockey	
Wilkinson, George	1900	Swimming	Water Polo Team
	1908	Swimming	Water Polo Team
	1912	Swimming	Water Polo Team
Williams, Steve	2004	Rowing	Coxless Fours
Wilson, Herbert	1908	Polo	
Wilson, Jack	1948	Rowing	Coxless Pairs
Wodehouse, Lord John	1920	Polo	
Wolff, Freddie	1936	Athletics	4 x 400m Relay

SPORT&LEISURE

Name	Date	Sport	Event
Wood, Arthur	1908	Yachting	8 Metres Class
Wood, Harvey	1908	Hockey	
Woodward, Vivian	1908	Football	
	1912	Football	
Woosnam, Max	1920	Lawn Tennis	Men's Doubles
(also played football for England and golf and cricket for Cambridge)			
Wormald	1912	Rowing	Eights
Wright, Cyril	1920	Yachting	7 Metres Class
Wright, Dorothy	1920	Yachting	7 Metres Class
(wife of Cyril)			
Wright, Gordon	1912	Football	
Zealey, Jim	1900	Football	

Rugby League Challenge Cup Winners

Year	Winners		Runners Up		Venue	Att	Man of Match
1897	Batley	10	St Helens	3	Leeds	13,492	(First awarded in 1946)
1898	Batley	7	Bradford	0	Leeds	27,941	
1899	Oldham	19	Hunslet	9	Manchester	15,763	
1900	Swinton	16	Salford	8	Manchester	17,864	
1901	Batley	6	Warrington	0	Leeds	29,563	
1902	Broughton R	25	Salford	0	Rochdale	15,006	
1903	Halifax	7	Salford	0	Leeds	32,507	
1904	Halifax	8	Warrington	3	Salford	17,041	
1905	Warrington	6	Hull KR	0	Leeds	19,638	
1906	Bradford	5	Salford	0	Leeds	15,834	
1907	Warrington	17	Oldham	3	Broughton	18,500	
1908	Hunslet	14	Hull	0	Huddersfield	18,000	
1909	Wakefield T	17	Hull	0	Leeds	23,587	
1910	Leeds	7	Hull	7	Huddersfield	19,413	
replay	Leeds	26	Hull	12	Huddersfield	11,608	
1911	Broughton R	4	Wigan	0	Salford	8,000	
1912	Dewsbury	8	Oldham	5	Leeds	15,271	
1913	Huddersfield	9	Warrington	5	Leeds	22,754	
1914	Hull	6	Wakefield T	0	Halifax	19,000	
1915	Huddersfield	37	St Helens	3	Oldham	8,000	
1920	Huddersfield	21	Wigan	10	Leeds	14,000	
1921	Leigh	13	Halifax	0	Broughton	25,000	
1922	Rochdale H	10	Hull	9	Leeds	32,596	
1923	Leeds	28	Hull	3	Wakefield	29,335	
1924	Wigan	21	Oldham	4	Rochdale	41,831	
1925	Oldham	16	Hull KR	3	Leeds	28,335	
1926	Swinton	9	Oldham	3	Rochdale	27,000	
1927	Oldham	26	Swinton	7	Wigan	33,448	
1928	Swinton	5	Warrington	3	Wigan	33,909	
1929	Wigan	13	Dewsbury	2	Wembley	41,500	
1930	Widnes	10	St Helens	3	Wembley	36,544	
1931	Halifax	22	York	8	Wembley	40,368	
1932	Leeds	11	Swinton	8	Wigan	29,000	
1933	Huddersfield	21	Warrington	17	Wembley	41,874	
1934	Hunslet	11	Widnes	5	Wembley	41,280	
1935	Castleford	11	Huddersfield	8	Wembley	39,000	
1936	Leeds	18	Warrington	2	Wembley	51,250	
1937	Widnes	18	Keighley	5	Wembley	47,699	
1938	Salford	7	Barrow	4	Wembley	51,243	
1939	Halifax	20	Salford	3	Wembley	55,453	
1941	Leeds	19	Halifax	2	Bradford	28,500	
1942	Leeds	15	Halifax	10	Bradford	15,250	
1943	Dewsbury	16	Leeds	9	Dewsbury	10,470	
	Dewsbury	0	Leeds	6	Leeds	16,000	
	(Dewsbury win 16–15 on aggregate)						
1944	Bradford N	0	Wigan	3	Wigan	22,000	
	Bradford N	8	Wigan	0	Bradford	30,000	
	(Bradford win 8–3 on aggregate)						
1945	Huddersfield	7	Bradford N	4	Huddersfield	9,041	
	Huddersfield	6	Bradford N	5	Bradford	17,500	
	(Huddersfield win 13–9 on aggregate)						

Year	Winners		Runners Up		Venue	Att	Man of Match
1946	Wakefield T	13	Wigan	12	Wembley	54,730	Billy Stott
1947	Bradford N	8	Leeds	4	Wembley	77,605	Willie Davies
1948	Wigan	8	Bradford N	3	Wembley	91,465	Frank Whitcombe
1949	Bradford N	12	Halifax	0	Wembley	95,050	Ernest Ward
1950	Warrington	19	Widnes	0	Wembley	94,249	Gerry Helme
1951	Wigan	10	Barrow	0	Wembley	94,262	Cec Mountford
1952	Workington T	18	Featherstone R	10	Wembley	72,093	Billy Ivison
1953	Huddersfield	15	St Helens	10	Wembley	89,588	Peter Ramsden
1954	Warrington	4	Halifax	4	Wembley	81,841	
replay	Warrington	8	Halifax	4	Bradford	102,569	Gerry Helme
1955	Barrow	21	Workington T	12	Wembley	66,513	Jack Grundy
1956	St Helens	13	Halifax	2	Wembley	79,341	Alan Prescott
1957	Leeds	9	Barrow	7	Wembley	76,318	Jeff Stevenson
1958	Wigan	13	Workington T	9	Wembley	66,109	Rees Thomas
1959	Wigan	30	Hull	13	Wembley	79,811	Brian McTigue
1960	Wakefield T	38	Hull	5	Wembley	79,773	Tommy Harris
1961	St Helens	12	Wigan	6	Wembley	94,672	Dick Huddart
1962	Wakefield T	12	Huddersfield	6	Wembley	81,263	Neil Fox
1963	Wakefield T	25	Wigan	10	Wembley	84,492	Harold Poynton
1964	Widnes	13	Hull KR	5	Wembley	84,488	Frank Collier
1965	Wigan	20	Hunslet	16	Wembley	89,016	Ray Ashby & Brian Gabbitas
1966	St Helens	21	Wigan	2	Wembley	98,536	Len Killeen
1967	Featherstone R	17	Barrow	12	Wembley	76,290	Carl Dooler
1968	Leeds	11	Wakefield T	10	Wembley	87,100	Don Fox
1969	Castleford	11	Salford	6	Wembley	97,939	Mal Reilly
1970	Castleford	7	Wigan	2	Wembley	95,255	Bill Kirkbride
1971	Leigh	24	Leeds	7	Wembley	85,514	Alex Murphy
1972	St Helens	16	Leeds	13	Wembley	89,495	Kel Coslett
1973	Featherstone R	33	Bradford N	14	Wembley	72,395	Steve Nash
1974	Warrington	24	Featherstone R	9	Wembley	77,400	Derek Whitehead
1975	Widnes	14	Warrington	7	Wembley	85,098	Ray Dutton
1976	St Helens	20	Widnes	5	Wembley	89,982	Geoff Pimblett
1977	Leeds	16	Widnes	7	Wembley	80,871	Steve Pitchford
1978	Leeds	14	St Helens	12	Wembley	96,000	George Nicholls
1979	Widnes	12	Wakefield T	3	Wembley	94,218	Dave Topliss
1980	Hull KR	10	Hull	5	Wembley	95,000	Brian Lockwood
1981	Widnes	18	Hull KR	9	Wembley	92,496	Mick Burke
1982	Hull	14	Widnes	14	Wembley	92,147	Eddie Cunningham
replay	Hull	18	Widnes	9	Leeds	41,171	
1983	Featherstone R	14	Hull	12	Wembley	84,969	David Hobbs
1984	Widnes	19	Wigan	6	Wembley	80,116	Joe Lydon
1985	Wigan	28	Hull	25	Wembley	97,801	Brett Kenny
1986	Castleford	15	Hull KR	15	Wembley	82,134	Bob Beardmore
1987	Halifax	19	St Helens	18	Wembley	91,267	Graham Eadie
1988	Wigan	32	Halifax	12	Wembley	94,273	Andy Gregory
1989	Wigan	27	St Helens	0	Wembley	78,000	Ellery Hanley
1990	Wigan	36	Warrington	14	Wembley	77,729	Andy Gregory
1991	Wigan	13	St Helens	8	Wembley	75,532	Denis Betts
1992	Wigan	28	Castleford	12	Wembley	77,286	Martin Offiah
1993	Wigan	20	Widnes	14	Wembley	77,684	Dean Bell
1994	Wigan	26	Leeds	16	Wembley	78,348	Martin Offiah
1995	Wigan	30	Leeds	10	Wembley	78,550	Jason Robinson
1996	St Helens	40	Bradford B	32	Wembley	75,994	Robbie Paul
1997	St Helens	32	Bradford B	22	Wembley	78,022	Tommy Martyn
1998	Sheffield E	17	Wigan W	6	Wembley	60,699	Mark Aston
1999	Leeds R	52	London B	16	Wembley	73,242	Leroy Rivett
2000	Bradford N	22	Leeds R	18	Edinburgh	75,356	Henry Paul
2001	St Helens	13	Bradford B	6	Twickenham	68,250	Sean Long
2002	Wigan W	21	St Helens	12	Edinburgh	62,140	Kris Radlinski
2003	Bradford B	22	Leeds R	20	Cardiff	71,212	Gary Connolly
2004	St Helens	32	Wigan W	16	Cardiff	73,734	Sean Long

SPORT & LEISURE

Rugby League – Man of Steel

1977	David Ward (Leeds)	1991	Gary Schofield (Leeds)
1978	George Nicholls (St Helens)	1992	Dean Bell (Wigan)
1979	Doug Laughton (Widnes)	1993	Andy Platt (Wigan)
1980	George Fairbairn (Wigan)	1994	Jonathan Davies (Warrington)
1981	Ken Kelly (Warrington)	1995	Denis Betts (Wigan)
1982	Mick Morgan (Carlisle)	1996	Andy Farrell (Wigan)
1983	Allan Agar (Featherstone Rovers)	1997	James Lowes (Bradford Bulls)
1984	Joe Lydon (Widnes)	1998	Iestyn Harris (Leeds Rhinos)
1985	Ellery Hanley (Bradford Northern)	1999	Adrian Vowles (Castleford Tigers)
1986	Gavin Miller (HKR)	2000	Sean Long (St Helens)
1987	Ellery Hanley (Wigan)	2001	Paul Sculthorpe (St Helens)
1988	Martin Offiah (Widnes)	2002	Paul Sculthorpe (St Helens)
1989	Ellery Hanley (Wigan)	2003	Jamie Peacock (Bradford Bulls)
1990	Shaun Edwards (Wigan)	2004	Andy Farrell (Wigan Warriors)

Rugby Union Six Nations Championships

1977	France	1992	England
1978	Wales	1993	France
1979	Wales	1994	Wales
1980	England	1995	England
1981	France	1996	England
1982	Ireland	1997	France
1983	France / Ireland	1998	France
1984	Scotland	1999	Scotland (last Five Nations Championship)
1985	Ireland	2000	England
1986	France / Scotland	2001	England
1987	France	2002	France
1988	France / Wales	2003	England
1989	France	2004	France
1990	Scotland	2005	Wales
1991	England		

Tennis: Wimbledon Champions

	Men	Women	Men's Doubles	Women's Doubles
1877	S W Gore (GB)	—	—	—
1878	P F Hadow (GB)	—	—	—
1879	J T Hartley (GB)	—	—	—
1880	J T Hartley (GB)	—	—	—
1881	W Renshaw (GB)	—	—	—
1882	W Renshaw (GB)	—	—	—
1883	W Renshaw (GB)	—	—	—
1884	W Renshaw (GB)	M Watson (GB)	W Renshaw / E Renshaw	—
1885	W Renshaw (GB)	M Watson (GB)	W Renshaw / E Renshaw	—
1886	W Renshaw (GB)	B Bingley (GB)	W Renshaw / E Renshaw	—
1887	H F Lawford (GB)	C Dod (GB)	W Wilberforce / P B Lyon	—
1888	E Renshaw (GB)	C Dod (GB)	W Renshaw / E Renshaw	—
1889	W Renshaw (GB)	B Bingley Hillyard (GB)	W Renshaw / E Renshaw	—
1890	W J Hamilton (GB)	H Rice (GB)	J Pim / F O Stoker	—
1891	W Baddeley (GB)	C Dod (GB)	W Baddeley / H Baddeley	—
1892	W Baddeley (GB)	C Dod (GB)	E W Lewis / H S Barlow	—
1893	J Pim (GB)	C Dod (GB)	J Pim / F O Stoker	—
1894	J Pim (GB)	B Hillyard (GB)	W Baddeley / H Baddeley	—
1895	W Baddeley (GB)	C Cooper (GB)	W Baddeley / H Baddeley	—
1896	H S Mahony (GB)	C Cooper (GB)	W Baddeley / H Baddeley	—
1897	R F Doherty (GB)	B Hillyard (GB)	R F Doherty / L H Doherty	—
1898	R F Doherty (GB)	C Cooper (GB)	R F Doherty / L H Doherty	—
1899	R F Doherty (GB)	B Hillyard (GB)	R F Doherty / L H Doherty	—
1900	R F Doherty (GB)	B Hillyard (GB)	R F Doherty / L H Doherty	—
1901	A W Gore (GB)	C Cooper Sterry (GB)	R F Doherty / L H Doherty	—
1902	L H Doherty (GB)	M E Robb (GB)	S H Smith / F L Riseley	—
1903	L H Doherty (GB)	D K Douglass (GB)	R F Doherty / L H Doherty	—

	Men	Women	Men's Doubles	Women's Doubles
1904	L H Doherty (GB)	D K Douglass (GB)	R F Doherty / L H Doherty	—
1905	L H Doherty (GB)	M Sutton (US)	R F Doherty / L H Doherty	—
1906	L H Doherty (GB)	D K Douglass (GB)	S Smith / F Riseley	—
1907	N E Brookes (Aus)	M Sutton (US)	N E Brookes / A F Wilding	—
1908	A W Gore (GB)	C Sterry (GB)	A F Wilding / M J G Ritchie	—
1909	A W Gore (GB)	D P Boothby (GB)	A W Gore / H Roper Barrett	—
1910	A F Wilding (NZ)	D K Douglass Chambers (GB)	A F Wilding / M J G Ritchie	—
1911	A F Wilding (NZ)	D K Douglass Chambers (GB)	A H Gobert / M Decugis	—
1912	A F Wilding (NZ)	E W Larcombe (GB)	H Roper Barrett / C P Dixon	—
1913	A F Wilding (NZ)	D K Douglass Chambers (GB)	H Roper Barrett / C P Dixon	R J McNair / D P Boothby
1914	N E Brookes (Aus)	D K Douglass Chambers (GB)	N E Brookes / A F Wilding	E Ryan / A M Morton
1915	not held	not held	not held	not held
1916	not held	not held	not held	not held
1917	not held	not held	not held	not held
1918	not held	not held	not held	not held
1919	G L Patterson (Aus)	S Lenglen (Fr)	R V Thomas / P O'Hara Wood	S Lenglen / E Ryan
1920	W T Tilden (US)	S Lenglen (Fr)	R N Williams / C S Garland	S Lenglen / E Ryan
1921	W T Tilden (US)	S Lenglen (Fr)	R Lycett / M Woosnam	S Lenglen / E Ryan
1922	G L Patterson (Aus)	S Lenglen (Fr)	J O Anderson / R Lycett	S Lenglen / E Ryan
1923	W M Johnston (US)	S Lenglen (Fr)	L A Godfree / R Lycett	S Lenglen / E Ryan
1924	J Borotra (Fr)	K McKane (GB)	F T Hunter / V Richards	H Wightman / H N Wills
1925	R Lacoste (Fr)	S Lenglen (Fr)	J Borotra / R Lacoste	S Lenglen / E Ryan
1926	J Borotra (Fr)	K McKane Godfree (GB)	J Brugnon / H Cochet	M K Browne / E Ryan
1927	H Cochet (Fr)	H N Wills (US)	F T Hunter / W T Tilden	H N Wills / E Ryan
1928	R Lacoste (Fr)	H N Wills (US)	J Brugnon / H Cochet	P Saunders / M Watson
1929	H Cochet (Fr)	H N Wills (US)	W L Allison / J Van Ryn	P Saunders Michell/ M Watson
1930	W T Tilden (US)	H N Wills Moody (US)	W L Allison / J Van Ryn	H N Wills Moody/ E Ryan
1931	S B Wood (US)	C Aussem (Ger)	G M Lott / J Van Ryn	P Mudford / D Shepherd-Barron
1932	H E Vines (US)	H N Wills Moody (US)	J Borotra / J Brugnon	D Metaxa / J Sigart
1933	J H Crawford (Aus)	H N Wills Moody (US)	J Borotra / J Brugnon	E Ryan / R Mathieu
1934	F J Perry (GB)	D E Round (GB)	G M Lott / L R Stoefen	E Ryan / R Mathieu
1935	F J Perry (GB)	H N Wills Moody (US)	J H Crawford / A K Quist	F James / K E Stammers
1936	F J Perry (GB)	H H Jacobs (US)	G P Hughes / C R D Tuckey	F James / K E Stammers
1937	J D Budge (US)	D E Round (GB)	J D Budge / G Mako	S Mathieu / B Yorke
1938	J D Budge (US)	H N Wills Moody (US)	J D Budge / G Mako	S Palfrey Fabyan / A Marble
1939	R L Riggs (US)	A Marble (US)	E T Cooke / R L Riggs	S Palfrey Fabyan / A Marble
1940	not held	not held	not held	not held
1941	not held	not held	not held	not held
1942	not held	not held	not held	not held
1943	not held	not held	not held	not held
1944	not held	not held	not held	not held
1945	not held	not held	not held	not held
1946	Y Petra (Fr)	P M Betz (US)	T Brown / J A Kramer	L A Brough / M Osborne
1947	J Kramer (US)	M E Osborne (US)	R Falkenburg / J A Kramer	R B Todd / D J Hart
1948	B Falkenburg (US)	A L Brough (US)	J E Bromwich / F A Sedgman	A L Brough / M E Osborne du Pont
1949	T Schroeder (US)	A L Brough (US)	R A Gonzales / F A Parker	A L Brough / M du Pont
1950	B Patty (US)	A L Brough (US)	J E Bromwich / A K Quist	A L Brough / M du Pont
1951	D Savitt (US)	D J Hart (US)	K B McGregor / F A Sedgman	D J Hart / S J Fry
1952	F Sedgman (Aus)	M Connolly (US)	K B McGregor / F A Sedgman	D J Hart / S J Fry
1953	V Seixas (US)	M Connolly (US)	L A Hoad / K R Rosewall	D J Hart / S J Fry
1954	J Drobny (Cze)	M Connolly (US)	R N Hartwig / M G Rose	A L Brough / M du Pont
1955	M A Trabert (US)	A L Brough (US)	R N Hartwig / L A Hoad	A Mortimer / J A Shilcock
1956	L A Hoad (Aus)	S J Fry (US)	L A Hoad / K R Rosewall	A Buxton / A Gibson
1957	L A Hoad (Aus)	A Gibson (US)	J E Patty / G Mulloy	A Gibson / D R Hard

	Men	Women	Men's Doubles	Women's Doubles
1958	A J Cooper (Aus)	A Gibson (US)	S Davidson / U Schmidt	M E Bueno / A Gibson
1959	A Olmedo (Per)	M E Bueno (Braz)	R Emerson / N A Fraser	J Arth / D R Hard
1960	N A Fraser (Aus)	M E Bueno (Braz)	R H Osuna / R D Ralston	M E Bueno / D R Hard
1961	R G Laver (Aus)	A Mortimer (GB)	R Emerson / N A Fraser	K Hantze / B J Moffitt
1962	R G Laver (Aus)	K Hantze Susman (US)	R A J Hewitt / F S Stolle	B J Moffitt / K Hantze Susman
1963	C R McKinley (US)	M Smith (Aus)	R H Osuna / A Palafox	M E Bueno / D R Hard
1964	R S Emerson (Aus)	M E Bueno (Braz)	R A J Hewitt / F S Stolle	M Smith / L R Turner
1965	R S Emerson (Aus)	M Smith (Aus)	J D Newcombe / A D Roche	M E Bueno / B J Moffitt
1966	M Santana (Spa)	B J Moffitt King (US)	K N Fletcher / J D Newcombe	M E Bueno / N Richey
1967	J D Newcombe (Aus)	B J King (US)	R A J Hewitt / F D McMillan	R Casals / B J Moffitt King
1968	R G Laver (Aus)	B J King (US)	J D Newcombe / A D Roche	R Casals / B J King
1969	R G Laver (Aus)	A Haydon Jones (GB)	J D Newcombe / A D Roche	M Smith Court / J A M Tegart
1970	J D Newcombe (Aus)	M Smith Court (Aus)	J D Newcombe / A D Roche	R Casals / B J King
1971	J D Newcombe (Aus)	E F Goolagong (Aus)	R S Emerson / R G Laver	R Casals / B J King
1972	S R Smith (US)	B J King (US)	R A J Hewitt / F D McMillan	B J King / B Stove
1973	J Kodes (Cze)	B J King (US)	J S Connors / I Nastase	R Casals / B J King
1974	J S Connors (US)	C M Evert (US)	J D Newcombe / A D Roche	E F Goolagong / M Michel
1975	A R Ashe (US)	B J King (US)	V Gerulaitis / A Mayer	A Kiyomura / K Sawamatsu
1976	B Borg (Swe)	C M Evert (US)	B E Gottfried / R Ramirez	C M Evert / M Navratilova
1977	B Borg (Swe)	S V Wade (GB)	R L Case / G Masters	H Gourlay Cawley / J C Russell
1978	B Borg (Swe)	M Navratilova (Cze)	R A J Hewitt / F D McMillan	K Reid / W Turnbull
1979	B Borg (Swe)	M Navratilova (US)	J P McEnroe / P Fleming	B J King / M Navratilova
1980	B Borg (Swe)	E F Goolagong Cawley (Aus)	P McNamara / P McNamee	K Jordan / A E Smith
1981	J P McEnroe (US)	C M Evert Lloyd (US)	J P McEnroe / P Fleming	M Navratilova / P H Shriver
1982	J S Connors (US)	M Navratilova (US)	P McNamara / P McNamee	M Navratilova / P H Shriver
1983	J P McEnroe (US)	M Navratilova (US)	J P McEnroe / P Fleming	M Navratilova / P H Shriver
1984	J P McEnroe (US)	M Navratilova (US)	J P McEnroe / P Fleming	M Navratilova / P H Shriver
1985	B Becker (Ger)	M Navratilova (US)	H P Gunthardt / B Taroczy	K Jordan / E Smylie
1986	B Becker (Ger)	M Navratilova (US)	J Nystrom / M Wilander	M Navratilova / P H Shriver
1987	P Cash (Aus)	M Navratilova (US)	R Seguso / K Flach	C Kohde-Kilsch / H Sukova
1988	S Edberg (Swe)	S Graf (Ger)	R Seguso / K Flach	S Graf / G Sabatini
1989	B Becker (Ger)	S Graf (Ger)	J B Fitzgerald / A Jarryd	J Novotna / H Sukova
1990	S Edberg (Swe)	M Navratilova (US)	R Leach / J Pugh	J Novotna / H Sukova
1991	M Stich (Ger)	S Graf (Ger)	J B Fitzgerald / A Jarryd	L Savchenko / N Zvereva
1992	A Agassi (US)	S Graf (Ger)	J P McEnroe / M Stich	G Fernandez / N Zvereva
1993	P Sampras (US)	S Graf (Ger)	T Woodbridge / M Woodforde	G Fernandez / N Zvereva
1994	P Sampras (US)	C Martinez (Spa)	T Woodbridge / M Woodforde	G Fernandez / N Zvereva
1995	P Sampras (US)	S Graf (Ger)	T Woodbridge / M Woodforde	J Novotna / A Sanchez-Vicario
1996	R Krajicek (Ned)	S Graf (Ger)	T Woodbridge / M Woodforde	M Hingis / H Sukova
1997	P Sampras (US)	M Hingis (Swi)	T Woodbridge / M Woodforde	G Fernandez / N Zvereva
1998	P Sampras (US)	J Novotna (Cze)	J Eltingh / P Haarhuis	M Hingis / J Novotna
1999	P Sampras (US)	L Davenport (US)	M Bhupathi / L Paes	L Davenport / C Morariu
2000	P Sampras (US)	V Williams (US)	T Woodbridge/M Woodforde	V Williams / S Williams

	Men	Women	Men's Doubles	Women's Doubles
2001	G Ivanisevic (Cro)	V Williams (US)	D Johnson / J Palmer	L Raymond / R Stubbs
2002	L Hewitt (Aus)	S Williams (US)	J Bjorkman / T Woodbridge	V Williams / S Williams
2003	R Federer (Swi)	S Williams (US)	J Bjorkman / T Woodbridge	K Clijsters / A Sugiyama
2004	R Federer (Swi)	M Sharapova (US)	J Bjorkman / T Woodbridge	C Black / R Stubbs
2005	R Federer (Swi)	V Williams (US)	S Huss / W Moodie	C Black / L Huber

Tennis: US Open

	Men	Women	Men's Doubles	Women's Doubles
1881	R D Sears (US)	—	C M Clark / F W Taylor	—
1882	R D Sears (US)	—	R D Sears / J Dwight	—
1883	R D Sears (US)	—	R D Sears / J Dwight	—
1884	R D Sears (US)	—	R D Sears / J Dwight	—
1885	R D Sears (US)	—	R D Sears / J S Clark	—
1886	R D Sears (US)	—	R D Sears / J Dwight	—
1887	R D Sears (US)	E Hansell (US)	R D Sears / J Dwight	—
1888	H W Slocum (US)	B L Townsend (US)	O S Campbell / V G Hall	—
1889	H W Slocum (US)	B L Townsend (US)	H W Slocum / H A Taylor	M Ballard / B L Townsend
1890	O S Campbell (US)	E C Roosevelt (US)	V G Hall / C Hobart	E C Roosevelt / G W Roosevelt
1891	O S Campbell (US)	M E Cahill (US)	O S Campbell / R P Huntington	M E Cahill / W F Morgan
1892	O S Campbell (US)	M E Cahill (US)	O S Campbell / R P Huntington	M E Cahill / A M McKinley
1893	R D Wrenn (US)	A M Terry (US)	C Hobart / F H Hovey	A M Terry / H Butler
1894	R D Wrenn (US)	H R Hellwig (US)	C Hobart / F H Hovey	H R Hellwig / J P Atkinson
1895	F H Hovey (US)	J P Atkinson (US)	M G Chace / R D Wrenn	H R Hellwig / J P Atkinson
1896	R D Wrenn (US)	E H Moore (US)	C B Neel / S R Neel	E H Moore / J P Atkinson
1897	R D Wrenn (US)	J P Atkinson (US)	L E Ware / G P Sheldon	J P Atkinson / K Atkinson
1898	M D Whitman (US)	J P Atkinson (US)	L E Ware / G P Sheldon	J P Atkinson / K Atkinson
1899	M D Whitman (US)	M Jones (US)	H Ward / D F Davis	J W Craven / M McAteer
1900	M D Whitman (US)	M McAteer (US)	H Ward / D F Davis	E Parker / H Champlin
1901	W A Larned (US)	E H Moore (US)	H Ward / D F Davis	J P Atkinson / M McAteer
1902	W A Larned (US)	M Jones (US)	R F Doherty / H L Doherty	J P Atkinson / M Jones
1903	H L Doherty (GB)	E H Moore (US)	R F Doherty / H L Doherty	E H Moore / C B Neely
1904	H Ward (US)	M G Sutton (US)	H Ward / B C Wright	M G Sutton / M Hall
1905	B C Wright (US)	E H Moore (US)	H Ward / B C Wright	H Homans / C B Neely
1906	W J Clothier (US)	H Homans (US)	H Ward / B C Wright	L S Coe / D S Platt
1907	W A Larned (US)	Evelyn Sears (US)	F B Alexander / B C Wright	M Wimer / C B Neely
1908	W A Larned (US)	M Barger-Wallach (US)	F B Alexander / H H Hackett	Evelyn Sears / M Curtis
1909	W A Larned (US)	H Hotchkiss (US)	F B Alexander / H H Hackett	H V Hotchkiss / E E Rotch
1910	W A Larned (US)	H Hotchkiss (US)	F B Alexander / H H Hackett	H V Hotchkiss / E E Rotch
1911	W A Larned (US)	H Hotchkiss (US)	R D Little / G F Touchard	H V Hotchkiss / Eleanora Sears
1912	M E McLoughlin (US)	K Browne (US)	M E McLoughlin / T C Bundy	D Greene / MK Browne
1913	M E McLoughlin (US)	M K Browne (US)	M E McLoughlin / T C Bundy	M K Browne / L Williams
1914	R N Williams (US)	M K Browne (US)	M E McLoughlin / T C Bundy	M K Browne / L Williams
1915	W M Johnston (US)	M Bjurstedt (Nor)	W M Johnston / C J Griffin	H V Hotchkiss Wightman / Eleanora Sears
1916	R N Williams (US)	M Bjurstedt (Nor)	W M Johnston / C J Griffin	M Bjurstedt / Eleanora Sears
1917	R L Murray (US)	M Bjurstedt (Nor)	F B Alexander / H A Throckmorton	M Bjurstedt / Eleanora Sears
1918	R L Murray (US)	M Bjurstedt (Nor)	W T Tilden / V Richards	M Zinderstein / E E Goss
1919	W M Johnston (US)	H Hotchkiss Wightman (US)	N E Brookes / G L Patterson	M Zinderstein / E E Goss
1920	W T Tilden (US)	M Bjurstedt Mallory (US)	W M Johnston / C J Griffin	M Zinderstein / E E Goss
1921	W T Tilden (US)	M Mallory (US)	W T Tilden / V Richards	M K Browne / L Williams
1922	W T Tilden (US)	M Mallory (US)	W T Tilden / V Richards	M Zinderstein Jessup / H N Wills
1923	W T Tilden (US)	H N Wills (US)	W T Tilden / B I C Norton	K McKane / P L Howkins Covell

	Men	Women	Men's Doubles	Women's Doubles
1924	W T Tilden (US)	H N Wills (US)	H O Kinsey / R G Kinsey	H Wightman / H N Wills
1925	W T Tilden (US)	H N Wills (US)	R N Williams / V Richards	M K Browne / H N Wills
1926	R Lacoste (Fr)	M Mallory (US)	R N Williams / V Richards	E Ryan / E E Goss
1927	R Lacoste (Fr)	H N Wills (US)	W T Tilden / F T Hunter	K McKane Godfree / E H Harvey
1928	H Cochet (Fr)	H N Wills (US)	G M Lott / J F Hennessey	H Wightman / H N Wills
1929	W T Tilden (US)	H N Wills (US)	G M Lott / J H Doeg	P Watson / P Michel
1930	J H Doeg (US)	B Nuthall (GB)	G M Lott / J H Doeg	B Nuthall / S Palfrey
1931	H E Vines (US)	H N Wills Moody (US)	W L Allison / J Van Ryn	B Nuthall / E Bennett Whittingstall
1932	H E Vines (US)	H H Jacobs (US)	H E Vines / K Gledhill	H H Jacobs / S Palfrey
1933	F J Perry (GB)	H H Jacobs (US)	G M Lott / L R Stoefen	B Nuthall / F James
1934	F J Perry (GB)	H H Jacobs (US)	G M Lott / L R Stoefen	H H Jacobs / S Palfrey
1935	W L Allison (US)	H H Jacobs (US)	W L Allison / J Van Ryn	H H Jacobs / S Palfrey Fabyan
1936	F J Perry (GB)	A Marble (US)	J D Budge / G Mako	M Van Ryn / C A Babcock
1937	J D Budge (US)	A Lizana (Chile)	G Von Cramm / H Henkel	S Palfrey Fabyan / A Marble
1938	J D Budge (US)	A Marble (US)	J D Budge / G Mako	S Palfrey Fabyan / A Marble
1939	R L Riggs (US)	A Marble (US)	A K Quist / J E Bromwich	S Palfrey Fabyan / A Marble
1940	W D McNeill (US)	A Marble (US)	J A Kramer / F R Schroeder	S Palfrey Fabyan / A Marble
1941	R L Riggs (US)	S Palfrey Cooke (US)	J A Kramer / F R Schroeder	S Palfrey Cooke / M E Osborne
1942	F R Schroeder (US)	P M Betz (US)	G Mulloy / W F Talbert	A L Brough / M E Osborne
1943	J R Hunt (US)	P M Betz (US)	J A Kramer / F A Parker	A L Brough / M E Osborne
1944	F A Parker (US)	P M Betz (US)	W D McNeill / R Falkenburg	A L Brough / M E Osborne
1945	F A Parker (US)	S Palfrey Cooke (US)	G Mulloy / W F Talbert	A L Brough / M E Osborne
1946	J A Kramer (US)	P M Betz (US)	G Mulloy / W F Talbert	A L Brough / M E Osborne
1947	J A Kramer (US)	A L Brough (US)	J A Kramer / F R Schroeder	A L Brough / M E Osborne
1948	R A Gonzales (US)	M E Osborne du Pont (US)	G Mulloy / W F Talbert	A L Brough / M E Osborne du Pont
1949	R A Gonzales (US)	M E du Pont (US)	J Bromwich / O W Sidwell	A L Brough / M E du Pont
1950	A Larsen (US)	M E du Pont (US)	J Bromwich / F A Sedgeman	A L Brough / M E du Pont
1951	F A Sedgeman (Aus)	M Connolly (US)	K B McGregor / F A Sedgeman	D J Hart / S J Fry
1952	F A Sedgeman (Aus)	M Connolly (US)	M G Rose / E VSeixas	D J Hart / S J Fry
1953	M A Trabert (US)	M Connolly (US)	R N Hartwig / M G Rose	D J Hart / S J Fry
1954	E V Seixas (US)	D J Hart (US)	E V Seixas / M A Trabert	D J Hart / S J Fry
1955	M A Trabert (US)	D J Hart (US)	K Kamo / A Miyagi	A L Brough / M E du Pont
1956	K R Rosewall (Aus)	S J Fry (US)	L A Hoad / K R Rosewall	A L Brough / M E du Pont
1957	M J Anderson (Aus)	A Gibson (US)	A J Cooper / N A Fraser	A L Brough / M E du Pont
1958	A J Cooper (Aus)	A Gibson (US)	A Olmedo / H Richardson	J M Arth / D R Hard
1959	N A Fraser (Aus)	M E Bueno (Braz)	N A Fraser / R S Emerson	J M Arth / D R Hard
1960	N A Fraser (Aus)	D R Hard (US)	N A Fraser / R S Emerson	M E Bueno / D R Hard
1961	R S Emerson (Aus)	D R Hard (US)	C McKinley / R D Ralston	D R Hard / L Turner
1962	R G Laver (Aus)	M Smith (Aus)	R H Osuna / A Palafox	M E Bueno / D R Hard
1963	R H Osuna (Mex)	M E Bueno (Braz)	C McKinley / R D Ralston	R Ebbern / M Smith
1964	R S Emerson (Aus)	M E Bueno (Braz)	C McKinley / R D Ralston	B J Moffitt / K Hantze Susman
1965	M Santana (Spa)	M Smith (Aus)	R S Emerson / F S Stolle	C A Graebner / N Richey
1966	F S Stolle (Aus)	M E Bueno (Braz)	R S Emerson / F S Stolle	M E Bueno / N Richey
1967	J D Newcombe (Aus)	B J Moffitt King (US)	J D Newcombe / A D Roche	R Casals / B J Moffitt King
1968	A R Ashe (US)	S V Wade / B M Smith Court (Aus)	R C Lutz / S R Smith	M E Bueno / B M Smith Court

	Men	Women	Men's Doubles	Women's Doubles
1969	R G Laver (Aus) / S R Smith (US)	B M Court (Aus)	K R Rosewall / F S Stolle D Crealy / A Stone	F Durr / D R Hard B M Court / S V Wade
1970	K R Rosewall (Aus)	B M Court (Aus)	P Barthes / N Pilic	B M Court / J A M Dalton
1971	S R Smith (US)	B J King (US)	J D Newcombe / R Taylor	R Casals / J A M Dalton
1972	I Nastase (Rom)	B J King (US)	C E Drysdale / R Taylor	F Durr / B Stove
1973	J D Newcombe (Aus)	B M Court (Aus)	O K Davidson / J D Newcombe	B M Court / S V Wade
1974	J S Connors (US)	B J King (US)	R C Lutz / S R Smith	R Casals / B J King
1975	M Orantes (Spa)	C M Evert (US)	J S Connors / I Nastase	B M Court / S V Wade
1976	J S Connors (US)	C M Evert (US)	T S Okker / M C Riessen	L Boshoff / I Kloss
1977	G Vilas (Arg)	C M Evert (US)	R A J Hewitt / F D McMillan	M Navratilova / B Stove
1978	J S Connors (US)	C M Evert (US)	R C Lutz / S R Smith	B J King / M Navratilova
1979	J P McEnroe (US)	T A Austin (US)	J P McEnroe / P Fleming	W M Turnbull / B Stove
1980	J P McEnroe (US)	C M Evert Lloyd (US)	R C Lutz / S R Smith	B J King / M Navratilova
1981	J P McEnroe (US)	T A Austin (US)	J P McEnroe / P Fleming	K Jordan / A Smith
1982	J S Connors (US)	C M Evert Lloyd (US)	K Curren / S Denton	R Casals / W M Turnbull
1983	J S Connors (US)	M Navratilova (US)	J P McEnroe / P Fleming	M Navratilova / P H Shriver
1984	J P McEnroe (US)	M Navratilova (US)	J B Fitzgerald / T Smid	M Navratilova / P H Shriver
1985	I Lendl (Cze)	H Mandlikova (Cze)	K Flach / R Seguso	C Kohde-Kilsch / H Sukova
1986	I Lendl (Cze)	M Navratilova (US)	A Gomez / S Zivojinovic	M Navratilova / P H Shriver
1987	I Lendl (Cze)	M Navratilova (US)	S Edberg / A Jarryd	M Navratilova / P H Shriver
1988	M Wilander (Swe)	S Graf (Ger)	S Casal / E Sanchez	G Fernandez / R White
1989	B Becker (Ger)	S Graf (Ger)	J P McEnroe / M Woodforde	H Mandlikova / M Navratilova
1990	P Sampras (US)	G Sabatini (Arg)	P Aldrich / D Visser	G Fernandez / M Navratilova
1991	S Edberg (Swe)	M Seles (Yug)	J B Fitzgerald / A Jarryd	P H Shriver / N Zvereva
1992	S Edberg (Swe)	M Seles (Yug)	J Grabb / R Reneberg	G Fernandez / N Zvereva
1993	P Sampras (US)	S Graf (Ger)	K Flach / R Leach	A Sanchez-Vicario / H Sukova
1994	A Agassi (US)	A Sanchez-Vicario (Spa)	J Eltingh / P Haarhuis	J Novotna / A Sanchez-Vicario
1995	P Sampras (US)	S Graf (Ger)	T Woodbridge / M Woodforde	G Fernandez / N Zvereva
1996	P Sampras (US)	S Graf (Ger)	T Woodbridge / M Woodforde	G Fernandez / N Zvereva
1997	P Rafter (Aus)	M Hingis (Swi)	Y Kafelnikov / D Vacek	J Novotna / L Davenport
1998	P Rafter (Aus)	L Davenport (US)	S Stolle / C Suk	M Hingis / J Novotna
1999	A Agassi (US)	S Williams (US)	S Lareau / A O'Brien	S Williams / V Williams
2000	M Safin (Rus)	V Williams (US)	L Hewitt / M Mirnyi	A Sugiyama / J Halard-Decugis
2001	L Hewitt (Aus)	V Williams (US)	W Black / K Ullyett	L Raymond / R Stubbs
2002	P Sampras (US)	S Williams (US)	M Bhupathi / M Myrnyi	V Ruano Pascual / P Suarez
2003	A Roddick (US)	J Henin-Hardenne (Belg)	J Bjorkman / T Woodbridge	V Ruano Pascual / P Suarez
2004	R Federer (Swi)	S Kuznetsova (Rus)	M Knowles / D Nestor	V Ruano Pascual / P Suarez

Tennis: Australian Open

	Men	Women		Men	Women
1905	R W Heath (Aus)	—	1919	A R F Kingscote (GB)	—
1906	A F Wilding (NZ)	—	1920	P O'Hara Wood (Aus)	—
1907	H M Rice (Aus)	—	1921	R H Gemmell (Aus)	—
1908	F B Alexander (US)	—	1922	J O Anderson (Aus)	M Molesworth (Aus)
1909	A F Wilding (NZ)	—			
1910	R W Heath (Aus)	—	1923	P O'Hara Wood (Aus)	M Molesworth (Aus)
1911	N E Brookes (Aus)	—			
1912	J C Parke (GB)	—	1924	J O Anderson (Aus)	S Lance (Aus)
1913	E F Parker (Aus)	—	1925	J O Anderson (Aus)	D S Akhurst (Aus)
1914	A O'Hara Wood (Aus)	—	1926	J B Hawkes (Aus)	D S Akhurst (Aus)
1915	F G Lowe (GB)	—	1927	G L Patterson (Aus)	E F Boyd (Aus)
1916	not held	—	1928	J Borotra (Fr)	D S Akhurst (Aus)
1917	not held	—	1929	J C Gregory (GB)	D S Akhurst (Aus)
1918	not held	—	1930	E F Moon (Aus)	D S Akhurst (Aus)

Year	Men	Women	Year	Men	Women
1931	J H Crawford (Aus)	C Buttsworth (Aus)	1970	A R Ashe (US)	M Court (Aus)
1932	J H Crawford (Aus)	C Buttsworth (Aus)	1971	K R Rosewall (Aus)	M Court (Aus)
1933	J H Crawford (Aus)	J Hartigan (Aus)	1972	K R Rosewall (Aus)	V S Wade (GB)
1934	F J Perry (GB)	J Hartigan (Aus)	1973	J D Newcombe (Aus)	M Court (Aus)
1935	J H Crawford (Aus)	D E Round (GB)	1974	J S Connors (US)	E Goolagong (Aus)
1936	A K Quist (Aus)	J Hartigan (Aus)	1975	J D Newcombe (Aus)	E Goolagong (Aus)
1937	V B McGrath (Aus)	N M Wynne (Aus)	1976	M Edmondson (Aus)	E Goolagong Cawley (Aus)
1938	J D Budge (US)	D M Bundy (US)			
1939	J E Bromwich (US)	E Westacott (Aus)	1977 (Jan)	R Tanner (US)	K Reid (Aus)
1940	A K Quist (Aus)	N M Wynne Bolton (Aus)	1977 (Dec)	V Gerulaitis (US)	E Cawley (Aus)
1941	not held	not held	1978	G Vilas (Arg)	C O'Neill (Aus)
1942	not held	not held	1979	G Vilas (Arg)	B Jordan (US)
1943	not held	not held	1980	B Teacher (US)	H Mandlikova (Cze)
1944	not held	not held	1981	J Kriek (SA)	M Navratilova (US)
1945	not held	not held	1982	J Kriek (SA)	C M Evert Lloyd (US)
1946	J E Bromwich (US)	N M Bolton (Aus)			
1947	D Pails (Aus)	N M Bolton (Aus)	1983	M Wilander (Swe)	M Navratilova (US)
1948	A K Quist (Aus)	N M Bolton (Aus)	1984	M Wilander (Swe)	C M Evert Lloyd (US)
1949	F A Sedgman (Aus)	D J Hart (US)			
1950	F A Sedgman (Aus)	L A Brough (US)	1985	S Edberg (Swe)	M Navratilova (US)
1951	R Savitt (US)	N M Bolton (Aus)	1986	not held	not held
1952	K B McGregor (Aus)	T Long (Aus)	1987	S Edberg (Swe)	H Mandlikova (Cze)
1953	K R Rosewall (Aus)	M Connolly (US)	1988	M Wilander (Swe)	S Graf (Ger)
1954	M G Rose (Aus)	T Long (Aus)	1989	I Lendl (Cze)	S Graf (Ger)
1955	K R Rosewall (Aus)	B Penrose (Aus)	1990	I Lendl (Cze)	S Graf (Ger)
1956	L G Hoad (Aus)	M Carter (Aus)	1991	B Becker (Ger)	M Seles (Yug)
1957	A J Cooper (Aus)	S J Fry (US)	1992	J Courier (US)	M Seles (Yug)
1958	A J Cooper (Aus)	A Mortimer (GB)	1993	J Courier (US)	M Seles (Yug)
1959	A Olmedo (Per)	M Carter Reitano (Aus)	1994	P Sampras (US)	S Graf (Ger)
1960	R G Laver (Aus)	M Smith (Aus)	1995	A Agassi (US)	M Pierce (Fra)
1961	R S Emerson (Aus)	M Smith (Aus)	1996	B Becker (Ger)	M Seles (US)
1962	R G Laver (Aus)	M Smith (Aus)	1997	P Sampras (US)	M Hingis (Swi)
1963	R S Emerson (Aus)	M Smith (Aus)	1998	P Korda (Cze)	M Hingis (Swi)
1964	R S Emerson (Aus)	M Smith (Aus)	1999	Y Kafelnikov (Rus)	M Hingis (Swi)
1965	R S Emerson (Aus)	M Smith (Aus)	2000	A Agassi (US)	L Davenport (US)
1966	R S Emerson (Aus)	M Smith (Aus)	2001	A Agassi (US)	J Capriati (US)
1967	R S Emerson (Aus)	N Richey (US)	2002	T Johansson (Swe)	J Capriati (US)
1968	W W Bowrey (Aus)	B J Moffitt King (US)	2003	A Agassi (US)	S Williams (US)
			2004	R Federer (Swi)	J Henin-Hardenne (Belg)
1969	R G Laver (Aus)	M Smith Court (Aus)	2005	M Safin (Rus)	S Williams (US)

Tennis: French Open

Year	Men	Women	Year	Men	Women
1891	H Briggs	—	1913	M Decugis (Fr)	M Broquedis (Fr)
1892	J Schopfer (Fr)	—	1914	M Decugis (Fr)	M Broquedis (Fr)
1893	L Riboulet (Fr)	—	1915	not held	not held
1894	A Vacherot (Fr)	—	1916	not held	not held
1895	A Vacherot (Fr)	—	1917	not held	not held
1896	A Vacherot (Fr)	—	1918	not held	not held
1897	P Aymé (Fr)	C Masson (Fr)	1919	not held	not held
1898	P Aymé (Fr)	C Masson (Fr)	1920	A H Gobert (Fr)	S Lenglen (Fr)
1899	P Aymé (Fr)	C Masson (Fr)	1921	J Samazeuilh (Fr)	S Lenglen (Fr)
1900	P Aymé (Fr)	Y Prévost (Fr)	1922	H Cochet (Fr)	S Lenglen (Fr)
1901	A Vacherot (Fr)	P Girod (Fr)	1923	P Blanchy (Fr)	S Lenglen (Fr)
1902	A Vacherot (Fr)	C Masson (Fr)	1924	J Borotra (Fr)	D Vlasto (Fr)
1903	M Decugis (Fr)	C Masson (Fr)	1925	R Lacoste (Fr)	S Lenglen (Fr)
1904	M Decugis (Fr)	K Gillou (Fr)	1926	H Cochet (Fr)	S Lenglen (Fr)
1905	M Germot (Fr)	K Gillou (Fr)	1927	R Lacoste (Fr)	K Bouman (Ned)
1906	M Germot (Fr)	K Fenwick	1928	H Cochet (Fr)	H N Wills (US)
1907	M Decugis (Fr)	M de Kermel (Fr)	1929	R Lacoste (Fr)	H N Wills (US)
1908	M Decugis (Fr)	K Fenwick	1930	H Cochet (Fr)	H N Wills Moody (US)
1909	M Decugis (Fr)	J Mattey (Fr)			
1910	M Germot (Fr)	J Mattey (Fr)	1931	J Borotra (Fr)	C Aussem (Ger)
1911	A H Gobert (Fr)	J Mattey (Fr)	1932	H Cochet (Fr)	H N Wills (US)
1912	M Decugis (Fr)	J Mattey (Fr)	1933	J H Crawford (Aus)	M C Scriven (GB)

	Men	Women		Men	Women
1934	G von Cramm (Ger)	M C Scriven (GB)	1971	J Kodes (Cze)	E Goolagong (Aus)
1935	F J Perry (GB)	H Sperling (Den)	1972	A Gimeno (Spa)	B J Moffitt King (US)
1936	G von Cramm (Ger)	H Sperling (Den)	1973	I Nastase (Rom)	M Court (Aus)
1937	H Henkel (Ger)	H Sperling (Den)	1974	B Borg (Swed)	C M Evert (US)
1938	J D Budge (US)	S Mathieu (Fr)	1975	B Borg (Swed)	C M Evert (US)
1939	W D McNeill (US)	S Mathieu (Fr)	1976	A Panatta (Ita)	S Barker (GB)
1940	not held	not held	1977	G Vilas (Arg)	M Jausovec (Yug)
1941	not held	not held	1978	B Borg (Swed)	V Ruzici (Rom)
1942	not held	not held	1979	B Borg (Swed)	C M Evert Lloyd (US)
1943	not held	not held	1980	B Borg (Swed)	C M Evert Lloyd (US)
1944	not held	not held	1981	B Borg (Swed)	H Mandlikova (Cze)
1945	not held	not held	1982	M Wilander (Swe)	M Navratilova (US)
1946	M Bernard (Fr)	M E Osborne (US)	1983	Y Noah (Fr)	C M Evert Lloyd (US)
1947	J Asboth (Hung)	P Todd (US)	1984	I Lendl (Cze)	M Navratilova (US)
1948	F A Parker (US)	N Landry (Belg)	1985	M Wilander (Swe)	C M Evert Lloyd (US)
1949	F A Parker (US)	M E Osborne du Pont (US)	1986	I Lendl (Cze)	C M Evert Lloyd (US)
1950	J E Patty (US)	D J Hart (US)	1987	I Lendl (Cze)	S Graf (Ger)
1951	J Drobny (Cze)	S J Fry (US)	1988	M Wilander (Swe)	S Graf (Ger)
1952	J Drobny (Cze)	D J Hart (US)	1989	M Chang (US)	A Sanchez-Vicario (Spa)
1953	K R Rosewall (Aus)	M Connolly (US)			
1955	M A Trabert (US)	M Connolly (US)	1990	A Gomez (Ecu)	M Seles (Yug)
1955	M A Trabert (US)	A Mortimer (GB)	1991	J Courier (US)	M Seles (Yug)
1956	L A Hoad (Aus)	A Gibson (US)	1992	J Courier (US)	M Seles (Yug)
1957	S Davidson (Swe)	S J Bloomer (GB)	1993	S Bruguera (Spa)	S Graf (Ger)
1958	M Rose (Aus)	S Kormoczy (Hung)	1994	S Bruguera (Spa)	A Sanchez-Vicario (Spa)
1959	N Pietrangeli (Ita)	C C Truman (GB)	1995	T Muster (Aut)	S Graf (Ger)
1960	N Pietrangeli (Ita)	D R Hard (US)	1996	Y Kafelnikov (Rus)	S Graf (Ger)
1961	M Santana (Spa)	A S Haydon (GB)	1997	G Kuerten (Braz)	I Majoli (Croat)
1962	R G Laver (Aus)	M Smith (Aus)	1998	C Moya (Spa)	A Sanchez-Vicario (Spa)
1963	R S Emerson (Aus)	L R Turner (Aus)	1999	A Agassi (US)	S Graf (Ger)
1964	M Santana (Spa)	M Smith (Aus)	2000	G Kuerten (Braz)	M Pierce (Fra)
1965	F S Stolle (Aus)	L R Turner (Aus)	2001	G Kuerten (Braz)	J Capriati (US)
1966	A D Roche (Aus)	A S Haydon Jones (GB)	2002	A Costa (Spa)	S Williams (US)
			2003	J C Ferrero (Spa)	J Henin-Hardenne (Belg)
1967	R S Emerson (Aus)	F Durr (Fr)			
1968	K R Rosewall (Aus)	N Richey (US)	2004	G Gaudio (Arg)	A Myskina (Rus)
1969	R G Laver (Aus)	M Smith Court (Aus)	2005	R Nadal (Spa)	J Henin-Hardenne (Belg)
1970	J Kodes (Cze)	M Court (Aus)			

S
P
O
R
T
&
L
E
I
S
U
R
E

Tennis: General Information

Australian Open: venue	Melbourne Park (formerly known as Flinders Park).
Davis Cup: inaugurated	1900.
most wins	USA.
official title	The International Men's Team Championship of the World.
Federation Cup	women's equivalent of the Davis Cup. Inaugurated in 1963. The United States defeated Australia 2–1 in the first final.
'Four Musketeers'	Jean Borotra, Jacques ('Toto') Brugnon, Henri Cochet, René Lacoste.
French Championships: made Open	before 1925 the French Championships were open only to members of French clubs.
French Open: venue	Roland Garros Stadium, Paris, since 1928.
Grand Slam: definition	winning the four major titles consecutively irrespective of calendar year (formerly had to be achieved in the calendar year).
holders	Donald Budge, Maureen Connolly, Margaret Court, Steffi Graf, Rod Laver (twice) and Martina Navratilova.
junior winner	Earl Buchholz won all four junior titles in 1958 followed by Stefan Edberg in 1983.
Hopman Cup	international mixed teams event first held between 28 December 1988 and 1 January 1989, Czechoslovakia beating Australia in the first championship.
net: height in middle	3 feet (91cm).
nicknames: Bounding Basque	Jean Borotra.
Poker Face	Helen Wills Moody.
Rocket	Rod Laver.
The Ghost	Harold Mahony.
The Two Helens	Helen Wills Moody and Helen Jacobs (great rivals and born on the same street in Berkeley, California).

Olympic champions: 2004	Nicolas Massu (Chi) and Justine Henin-Hardenne (Belg).
Olympic Games: ice hockey player	Jaroslav Drobny (Cze, 1948).
tennis challenge: battle of the sexes	Bobby Riggs had beaten Margaret Court but was then beaten by Billie Jean King (and famously presented with a pig).
tennis: original name	sphairistiké.
'Three Musketeers'	Jean Borotra, Henri Cochet, René Lacoste.
US Open: venue	Flushing Meadows, New York, since 1978. Finals showcourt named after Arthur Ashe.
Wimbledon champion: 1st black man	Arthur Ashe (1975).
1st black person	Althea Gibson (1957).
Mixed Doubles: brother and sister	John and Tracy Austin won the 1981 Championship.
man and wife	Mr and Mrs L A Godfree won the 1926 Championship.
boycott year	1973 (due to suspension of Nikki Pilic of Yugoslavia).
champion at first and only attempt	Bobby Riggs (1939) won all three titles on his only appearance at the Championships.
first professional champion	Rod Laver (1968).
last amateur champion	John Newcombe (1967).
longest match	5 hours 12 minutes: Pancho Gonzales beat Charlie Pasarell (22–24, 1–6, 16–14, 6–3, 11–9) in 1969 (this match hastened the need for the tie-break system).
oldest men's champion	Arthur Gore (41).
champion later represented Brazil in Davis Cup	Robert Falkenburg.
unseeded champion	Boris Becker (1985).
unseeded player in two finals	Kurt Nielsen (Den) beaten in 1953 and 1955.
youngest champion	Lottie Dod (GB) aged 15.
youngest men's champion	Boris Becker (Ger) aged 17.

Sporting Trophies

Name	Sport	Details	First held
Admirals Cup	yachting	biennial international competition for sailing yachts	1957
Air Canada Silver Broom	curling	formerly the Scotch Whisky Cup, became Air Canada in 1959	1968
America's Cup	yachting	originally called 100 Guineas Cup and raced around the Isle of Wight	1851
Ashes	cricket	England v Australia test matches (since 1882 called 'Ashes')	1877
Baron Matsui Inter-Club Cup	judo	club competition named after the Japanese Ambassador	1928
Bledisloe Cup	rugby union	New Zealand v Australia	1931
Bologna Trophy	swimming	England v Scotland v Wales speed swimming contest	1929
Borg-Warner Trophy	motor racing	winner of the Indianapolis 500	1932
Bowring Bowl	rugby union	annual Oxbridge Varsity match	1872
Britannia Cup	yachting	for small yachts (under 32ft) of any country to challenge the holder	1951
Britannia Shield	speedway	inter-club challenge competition	1957
Calcutta Cup	rugby union	England v Scotland	1870
Camanachd Cup	shinty	championship of Scotland	1896
Canada Cup	golf	world team championship (two per team)	1953
Cole Cup	fencing	men's sabre	1922
Cowdray Park Gold Cup	polo	international competition	1956
Currie Cup	cricket	South African Provincial competition	1889
Currie Cup	rugby union	South African Provincial Championship	1892
Curtis Cup	golf	amateur women – USA v Great Britain and Ireland	1932
Davis Cup	tennis	The International Lawn Tennis Challenge Trophy	1900
Dewar Cup	rifle shooting	small-bore shooting competition	1909
Diamond Challenge	rowing	blue riband of single sculling	1884
Doggetts Coat & Badge	rowing	sculling contest on the Thames between ex-passenger skiffs	1715
Eisenhower Trophy	golf	biennial international competition	1958
Federation Cup	tennis	women's world amateur team championship	1963
George Hearn Cup	diving	awarded to England's most successful diver	1954
Goldberg-Vass Memorial Trophy	judo	London open competition	1956
Gordon Bennett Trophy	motor racing	forerunner of the Grand Prix	1901
Grand Challenge Cup	rowing	Henley Regatta – eights	1839
Grey Cup	Canadian football	championship game between winners of Eastern and Western Conferences	1909

Name	Sport	Details	First held
G Melville Clark Trophy	diving	awarded to England's most successful diving club	1951
Harry Sunderland Trophy	rugby league	man of the Premiership final. T Fogarty of Halifax first winner	1965
Heisman Memorial Trophy	American football	awarded annually by the Downtown Athlete Club of New York City to the outstanding college football player of the United States	1935
Henry Benjamin Trophy	swimming and water polo	awarded to England's most successful swimming and water polo club	1910
Iroquois Cup	lacrosse	English club championship	1890
Jules Rimet Trophy	football	world cup	1930
King George V Gold Cup	showjumping	men's international competition at Hickstead	1934
Kinnaird Cup	Eton fives	public schools' competition	1926
Lance Todd Award	rugby league	man of the match award in Challenge Cup final	1897
Lapham Trophy	squash	Canada v USA	1921
Leonard Trophy	bowls	World team championship	1966
Liam MacCarthy Cup	Hurling	Awarded to winner of All-Ireland Senior Hurling championship	1921
Londonderry Cup	squash	public schools' Old Boys' competition	1934
Lonsdale Belt	boxing	British title – won outright for winning three title fights at the same weight	1909
Lugano Trophy	walking	world championship of race walking	1961
MacRobertson International Shield	croquet	international competition	1925
Manuel Avilla Camacho Cup	polo	Mexico v USA	1941
Marcel Corbillon Cup	table tennis	women's world table tennis team championships	1934
Marchant Cup	rugby fives	London grammar schools competition	1929
Middleton Cup	bowls	inter-county championship	1911
Philadelphia Gold Cup	rowing	Olympic single sculling trophy	1908
Pilkington Cup	rugby union	English club knockout cup (prev. National Cup)	1972
Powergen Cup	rugby union	English club knockout cup (formerly John Player Cup, Pilkington Cup, Tetley's Bitter Cup)	1972
Presidents Trophy	golf	USA v Rest of World (Men)	1994
Prince of Wales Cup	yachting	international 14 ft dinghy championship	1927
Prince Rainier Cup	fencing	awarded tothe nation with best results in World Championships	1950
Princess Elizabeth Cup	rowing	Henley Regatta – eights for public schools	1946
Queen Elizabeth II Cup	showjumping	women's international competition at Hickstead	1949
Queen's Prize	rifle shooting	open competition first competed for at Wimbledon	1860
Ranfurly Shield	rugby union	NZ rugby trophy for provincial teams	1902
Regal Trophy	rugby league	formerly sponsored by John Player, became Regal Trophy in 1989	1971
Russell-Cargill Trophy	rugby union	Awarded to winner of Middlesex Sevens	1951
Ryder Cup	golf	men – USA v Europe (USA v GB and I before 1979)	1927
Sam MacGuire Trophy	Gaelic football	All-Ireland Men's Senior Football championship	1928
Scottish Tennant's Cup	rugby union	Scottish club knockout cup	1996
Seawanhaka Cup	yachting	For small yachts (under 25ft) of any country to challenge the holder	1895
Silver Goblets & Nickalls Cup	rowing	Henley Regatta: coxless pairs amateur international	1845
Sir William Burton Trophy	yachting	national 12 ft dinghy championship	1936
Solheim Cup	golf	women – USA v Europe	1990
Stanley Cup	ice hockey	North American ice hockey championship	1894
Strathcona Cup	curling	Canada v Scotland international competition	1903
Subalterns' Cup	polo	inter-services competition	1896
Super 12 Trophy	rugby union	Southern Hemisphere provincial championship	1995
SWALEC Cup	rugby union	Welsh club knockout cup (prev. Welsh Cup, Schweppes Cup)	1972
Swaythling Cup	table tennis	men's world table tennis team championships	1927
Talbot Handicap	crown green bowls	Blackpool-based open competition	1882
Thomas Cup	badminton	men's world badminton team championship	1949
Über Cup	badminton	women's world badminton team championships	1957
Val Barker Trophy	boxing	most stylish boxer at an Olympic Games	1904
Vince Lombardi Trophy	American football	superbowl	1967
Volvo World Cup	showjumping	world championship competition	1979
Walker Cup	golf	amateur men – USA v Great Britain and Ireland	1922
Waterloo Cup	coursing	the 'Derby' of coursing, named after a Liverpool hotel	1836

Name	Sport	Details	First held
Waterloo Cup	crown green bowls	Blackpool-based open competition	1907
Webb Ellis Trophy	rugby union	world cup	1987
Westchester Cup	polo	Great Britain v USA	1886
Wheeler-Schebber	motor racing	awarded to the leader of the Indianapolis 500 after 400 miles (160 laps), replaced in 1932 by the Borg-Warner Trophy	
Wightman Cup	tennis	annual team competition between USA and England	1923
Wolfe-Noel Cup	squash	USA v GB women's match	1933
Worrell Trophy	cricket	West Indies v Australia	1931
Wyfold Challenge Cup	rowing	Henley Regatta	1847
Yeaden Memorial Trophy	swimming	awarded to the English swimmer whose performance is adjudged the best	1938
Zurich Premiership Trophy	rugby union	Awarded to winner of English club league championship	1987

NB The inaugural dates given are for the competition; in some cases the trophy has been renamed.

Television Sports Personality of the Year

Chris Chataway	1954	Robin Cousins	1980
Gordon Pirie	1955	Ian Botham	1981
Jim Laker	1956	Daley Thompson	1982
Dai Rees	1957	Steve Cram	1983
Ian Black	1958	Torvill and Dean	1984
John Surtees	1959	Barry McGuigan	1985
David Broome	1960	Nigel Mansell	1986
Stirling Moss	1961	Fatima Whitbread	1987
Anita Lonsbrough	1962	Steve Davis	1988
Dorothy Hyman	1963	Nick Faldo	1989
Mary Rand	1964	Paul Gascoigne	1990
Tommy Simpson	1965	Liz McColgan	1991
Bobby Moore	1966	Nigel Mansell	1992
Henry Cooper	1967	Linford Christie	1993
David Hemery	1968	Damon Hill	1994
Ann Jones	1969	Jonathan Edwards	1995
Henry Cooper	1970	Damon Hill	1996
HRH Princess Anne	1971	Greg Rusedski	1997
Mary Peters	1972	Michael Owen	1998
Jackie Stewart	1973	Lennox Lewis	1999
Brendan Foster	1974	Steve Redgrave	2000
David Steele	1975	David Beckham	2001
John Curry	1976	Paula Radcliffe	2002
Virginia Wade	1977	Jonny Wilkinson	2003
Steve Ovett	1978	Kelly Holmes	2004
Sebastian Coe	1979		

Commonwealth Games: Venues

Hamilton, Canada	1930	Christchurch, NZ	1974
London, England	1934	Edmonton, Canada	1978
Sydney, Australia	1938	Brisbane, Australia	1982
Auckland, NZ	1950	Edinburgh, Scotland	1986
Vancouver, Canada	1954	Auckland, NZ	1990
Cardiff, Wales	1958	Victoria, Canada	1994
Perth, Australia	1962	Kuala Lumpur, Malaysia	1998
Kingston, Jamaica	1966	Manchester, England	2002
Edinburgh, Scotland	1970	Melbourne, Australia	2006

Number of Players in a Team

		Details
polo	4	Up to 8 chukkas of $7^1/_2$ min
basketball	5	4 periods
ice hockey	6	3 periods of 20 min
volleyball	6	Court size: 30ft x 60ft
kabaddi	7	2 halves of 20 minutes each
netball	7	4 periods of 15 min
water polo	7	blue or white caps (red for goalkeepers)
baseball	9	9 innings
rounders	9	2 innings
American football	11	1 hour
football	11	2 halves of 45 min
cricket	11	see relevant section
hockey	11	field size: 100 yd x 60 yd (goal 4 yd x 7 ft high)
		men's, 2 halves of 35 min; women's, 2 of 30 min
stoolball	11	girls' game resembling cricket
lacrosse (men's)	10	4 periods of 15 min
lacrosse (women's)	12	4 periods of 15 min
Canadian football	12	field size: 110 yd x 65 yd
shinty	12	field size: 160 yd x 80 yd
rugby league	13	no wing forwards
rugby union	15	2 halves of 40 min
Gaelic football	15	2 periods of 30 min
hurling	15	women's version called 'camogie'
Australian rules	18	4 periods of 25 min

Sportspeople

Aaron, Hank (US)	**baseball**	Ball, John	**golf**
Abdul-Jabbar, Kareem	**basketball**	Barber, Paul	**hockey**
Ackland, Janet	**bowls**	Barnato, Woolf	**motor racing**
Adams, Neil	**judo**	Barrichello, Rubens (Braz)	**motor racing**
Alexander, Wayne	**boxing**		**(Formula 1)**
Allahgreen, Diane	**athletics**	Barry, Ernest	**rowing**
Allan, Alister	**shooting**	Barton, Pam	**golf**
Allen, Marcus (US)	**American football**	Beamish, George	**rugby union**
Alsop, Fred	**triple jump**	Beck, Margaret	**badminton**
Altwegg, Jeannette	**figure skating**	Bedell-Sivright, Darkie	**rugby union**
Angus, Howard	**rackets and real tennis**	Bell, Diane	**judo**
Aoki, Haruchika (Jpn)	**motor cycling (125cc)**	Beresford, Jack	**rowing**
Appleyard, Bob	**cricket**	Berra, Lawrence 'Yogi' (US)	**baseball**
Armstrong, Gary	**rugby union**	Besford, Jack	**swimming**
Ashton, Eric	**rugby league**	Biaggi, Massimiliano (Ita)	**motor cycling (250cc)**
Aspinall, Nigel	**croquet**	Bickers, Dave	**motocross**
Astbury, Andrew	**swimming**	Bird, Larry (US)	**basketball**
Atkins, Geoffrey	**rackets**	Black, Ian	**swimming**
Atkins, John	**cyclo cross**	Blankers-Koen, Fanny (Ned)	**athletics**
Baddeley, Steve	**badminton**	Blenkinsop, Ernie	**football**
Baddeley, Wilfred and Herbert	**tennis**	Bond-Williams, Louise	**fencing**
Baerlein, Edgar	**rackets and real tennis**	Boocock, Nigel	**speedway**
		Boone, Willie	**rackets**
Baggaley, Andrew	**table tennis**	Bourne, Teddy	**fencing**
Bailey, Bill	**cycling**	Bowman, George	**carriage driving**
Bailey, McDonald	**athletics**	Bradley, Caroline	**show jumping**
Bailey, William James	**cycling**	Bradshaw, Harry	**golf**
Baillieu, Chris	**rowing**	Braid, James	**golf**
Baird, Charlotte	**surfing**	Braithwaite, Bob	**shooting**
Baker, Edwin Percy	**bowls**	Briggs, Johnny	**cricket**
Baker, Philip Noel	**athletics (1959 Nobel Peace Prize)**	Briggs, Karen	**judo**
		Brinkley, Brian	**swimming**
Baker, Zoe	**swimming**	Brittin, Janette	**cricket**
Bakewell, Enid	**cricket**	Brockway, John	**swimming**
Balashov, Alexandr (Rus)	**ice speedway**	Bromfield, Percy	**table tennis**
Balding, Gerald	**polo**	Bullen, Jane	**three-day event**
Balding, Gerald Matthews	**polo**	Burns, Tommy (Can)	**heavyweight boxer**
		Butcher, Don	**squash**

Cacho, Fermin (Esp)	athletics	Doohan, Michael (Aus)	motor cycling (500cc)
Cadalora, Luca (Ita)	motor cycling (250cc and 125cc)	Doyle, Tony	cycling
		Driffield, Leslie	billiards
Caira, Philip Mario	weightlifting	Drummond, Des	rugby league
Callender, Simone	judo	Drummond-Hay, Anneli	show jumping
Calzaghe, Joe	boxing	Duke, Geoff	motor cycling (500cc)
Capirossi, Loris (Ita)	motor cycling (125cc and 250cc)	Dugard, Martin	speedway
		Dundee, Johnny (US)	boxing
Carnill, Denys	hockey	Eastman, Howard	boxing
Cavendish, Mark	cycling	Edwards, Hugh 'Jumbo'	rowing
Cazelet, Victor	squash	Edwards, Margaret	swimming
Chamberlain, Wilt (US)	basketball	Egan, Joe	rugby league
Chambers, Dwayne	athletics	Egg, Oscar (Swi)	cycling
Chapman, Vera	hockey	Elford, Vic	motor racing
Cheape, Leslie	polo	Ellaby, Alf	rugby league
Cheeseborough, Susan	gymnastics	Elliot, Douglas	rugby union
Chester, Frank	cricket	Elliot, Helen	table tennis
Chifney, Sam	horse racing	Elliot, Launceston	weightlifting
Childs, Joe	horse racing	Elwell, Keith	rugby league
Clark, Gillian	badminton	Erhardt, Carl	ice hockey
Clark, Roger	rallying	Erskine, Joe	boxing
Clarke, Chris	croquet	Evans, Mal	bowls
Cobb, John	motor racing	Everts, Stefan (Bel)	motocross
Cobb, Ty (US)	baseball	Ewing, Patrick (Jam)	basketball
Cockett, John	hockey	Fahey, Robert (Aus)	real tennis
Colclough, Maurice	rugby union	Fairbrother, Nicola	judo
Colledge, Cecilia	figure skating	Fairs, Punch	real tennis
Collett, Rebecca	figure skating	Fallon, Craig	judo
Collins, Peter (1931–58)	motor racing	Farndon, Tom	speedway
Collins, Peter (1954–)	speedway	Farr, Judy	walking
Cooke, Nicole	cycling	Ferris, Liz	diving
Cooke, Rebecca	swimming	Ferris, Sam	marathon
Cooper, Charlotte	tennis	Figg, James	boxing
Cooper, Malcolm	shooting	Flockhart, Ron	motor racing
Cotter, Edmond	croquet	Fogarty, Carl	superbike racing
Couch, Jane	boxing	Ford, Bernard	ice dancing
Covey, Fred	real tennis	Ford, Horace	archery
Craven, Peter	speedway	Ford, Trevor	football
Creus, Julian	weightlifting	Fordham, George	football
Cripps, Norwood	rackets and real tennis	Foster, Bob (US)	boxing
		Foster, Jimmy	ice hockey
Cronshey, John Dennis	speed skating	Fox, Jim	modern pentathlon
Crooks, Lee	rugby league	Fox, Neil	rugby league
Crooks, Tim	rowing	Fox, Richard	canoeing
Culvert, David	shooting	Fox-Pitt, William	equestrianism
Cumming, Arthur	figure skating	Foxx, Jimmie (US)	baseball
Curry, Don	boxing	Freeman, Alfred 'Tich'	cricket
Curry, Joan	squash and tennis	Frentzen, Heinz-Harold (Ger)	motor racing (Formula 1)
Curtis, Steve	powerboat racing		
Cutler, David	bowls	Frith, Frederick	motor cycling
Daly, Fred	golf	Fulford, Robert	croquet
Datoo, Camille	fencing	Fulton, Arthur	shooting
Davidge, Chris	rowing	Funnell, Pippa	equestrianism
Davies, Terry	rugby union	Furrer, Carl	trampolining
Davis, Howard	hockey	Galica, Davina	skiing and motor racing
Dawes, Alison	show jumping		
De Beaumont, Charles	fencing	Gallie, Christine	judo
De Wharton Burr, Nilla	archery	Gans, Joe (US)	welterweight boxer
Dear, Jim	rackets, real tennis, squash	Gardner, Jason	athletics
		Gault, Michael	shooting
Deaton, Nicola	table tennis	Gee, Kenneth	rugby league
Dempsey, Jack 'Nonpareil'	boxing	George, Walter	athletics
Denny, Doreen	ice dancing	Giles, Jack	squash
Didrikson, Babe (US)	athletics and golf	Glen Haig, Mary	fencing
Di Maggio, Joe (US)	baseball	Goddard, James	swimming
Disley, John	steeplechaser	Gordon, Winston	judo
Dixon, Charles	tennis	Gower, Lily	croquet
Dixon, Karen	three-day event	Grace, Edward Mills	cricket
Dixon, Robin	bobsleigh	Green, Tommy	walking
Dod, Willie	archery	Greenwood, Giles	weightlifting
Doherty, Reggie	tennis	Guthrie, Jimmy	motor cycling
Donaldson, Walter	snooker	Haining, Peter	rowing

Hale, Jack	**swimming**	Jordan, Tony	**badminton**
Hall, Darren	**badminton**	Kane, Peter	**boxing**
Hallam, Ian	**cycling**	Kanu, Nwankwo (Nig)	**football**
Hallard, Steve	**archery**	Karalius, Vince	**rugby league**
Halliday, Jim	**weightlifting**	Keane, Moss	**rugby union**
Hamill, Billy (USA)	**speedway**	Keenan, Peter	**boxing**
Hancock, Greg (USA)	**speedway**	Kelly, Sean	**cycling**
Hand, Tony	**ice hockey**	Kelly-Hohmann, Margaret	**swimming**
Hann, Quinten (Aus)	**snooker**	Kelsey, Jack	**football**
Harding, Phyllis	**swimming**	Kendall-Carpenter, John	**rugby union**
Hardisty, Alan	**rugby league**	Kerly, Sean	**hockey**
Hardstaff, Joe	**cricket**	Kershaw, Cecil	**rugby union**
Harlow, Greg	**bowls**	King, Norman	**bowls**
Harper, Ernie	**marathon**	King, Shayne (NZ)	**motocross**
Harris, Lord George	**cricket**	Kingpetch, Pone (Thai)	**boxing**
Harris, Reg	**cycling**	Kitchen, Bill	**speedway**
Harrison, Audley	**boxing**	Kluft, Carolina (Swed)	**athletics**
Hart, Marvin (US)	**boxing**	Knight, Billy	**tennis**
Hatfield, Jack	**swimming**	Kocinski, John (USA)	**motor cycling (250cc**
Hathorn, Gina	**skiing**		**and superbikes)**
Hatton, Ricky	**boxing**	Laidlaw, Roy	**rugby union**
Haughton, Colin	**badminton**	Langton, Eric	**speedway**
Havelock, Gary	**speedway**	Larcombe, Ethel	**tennis**
Hawke, Lord Martin	**cricket**	Larner, George	**walking**
Hayles, Rob	**cycling**	Latham, Peter	**rackets and real**
Healey, Donald	**rallying**		**tennis**
Heaney, Julz	**water skiing**	Lawler, Ivan	**canoeing**
Heaney, Nick	**water skiing**	Lawton, Barbara	**high jumper**
Heatley, Basil	**marathon**	Leather, Diane	**athletics**
Heatly, Peter	**diving**	Leden, Judy	**hang gliding**
Helme, Gerry	**rugby league**	Lee, George	**gliding**
Hendren, Patsy	**cricket**	Lee, Michael	**speedway**
Herriott, Maurice	**steeplechaser**	Lee, Norvel (US)	**boxing**
Hicks, Humphrey	**croquet**	Lee, Sidney	**billiards**
Hide, Molly	**cricket**	Legh, Alice	**archery**
Hill, Albert	**athletics**	Leman, Richard	**hockey**
Hiller, Bob	**rugby union**	Lemon, Meadowlark (US)	**basketball**
Hilton, Elliot	**ice skating**	Le Moignan, Martine	**squash**
Hipwood, Julian	**polo**	Lennox, Avril	**gymnastics**
Hocking, Gary (Zim)	**motor cycling**	Lerwill, Alan	**long jumper**
	(500cc)	Lesnevich, Gus (US)	**boxing**
Hodgson, Neil	**superbike racing**	Lessing, Simon	**triathlon**
Holden, Jack	**marathon**	Levinsky, Battling (US)	**boxing**
Holmes, Andrea	**trampolining**	Lewis-Francis, Mark	**athletics**
Holmes, Terry	**rugby union**	Line, Peter	**bowls**
Horgan, Denis	**shot putter**	Lloyd, Emrys	**fencing**
Hoskyns, Bill	**fencing**	Lombardi, Vincent (US)	**American football**
Hoy, Chris	**cycling**	Long, Liz	**swimming**
Howland, Bonzo	**shot putter**	Longo, Jeannie (Fra)	**cycling**
Hume, Donald	**badminton**	Loram, Mark	**speedway**
Inman, Melbourne	**billiards**	Loris, Chris	**speedway**
Ireland, Innes	**motor racing**	Lowe, Samantha	**judo**
Ivy, Bill	**motor cycling (125cc)**	Lucas, Muriel	**badminton**
Jackson, Kanukai	**gymnastics**	Lumb, Margot	**squash**
Jackson, Reggie (US)	**baseball**	Lumley, Penny	**real tennis**
James, Carwyn	**rugby union**	Lunn family	**skiing**
Jameson, Andrew	**swimming**	Lunn, Gladys	**athletics**
Jameson, Tommy	**squash**	Lycett, Randolph	**tennis**
Jarrett, Keith	**rugby union and**	Lydon, Joe	**rugby league**
	league	Lynch, Benny	**flyweight boxer**
Jarvis, John	**swimming**	Mace, Jem	**middleweight boxer**
Jay, Allan	**fencing**	Mack, Curly	**badminton**
Jeeps, Dickie	**rugby union**	Mackey, Mick	**hurling**
Jofre, Eder (Braz)	**boxing**	Mackinnon, Esmé	**skiing**
Johnson, Earvin 'Magic' (US)	**basketball**	Maduaka, Joice	**athletics**
Johnson, Ralph	**fencing**	Maguire, Stephen	**snooker**
Johnson, Tebbs Lloyd	**walking**	Mahoney, Harold	**tennis**
Jones, Cliff (1914–90)	**rugby union**	Male, James	**rackets and real**
Jones, Cliff (1935–)	**football**		**tennis**
Jones, Courtney	**ice dancing**	Mallin, Frederick	**middleweight boxer**
Jones, Mandy	**cycling**	Mallin, Harry	**middleweight boxer**
Jordan, Michael (US)	**basketball**	Mann, Julia	**badminton**

Mannion, Wilf	football	Neville, Tracey	netball (sister of Gary & Phil)
Mansergh, Terence	hockey		
Mantle, Mickey (US)	baseball	Newall, Queenie	archery
Mapple, Andy	water skiing	Newman, Tom	billiards
Marques, David	rugby union	Nicholas, Alison	golf
Marshall, Peter	squash	Nielsen, Hans (Den)	speedway
Martin, Louis	weightlifting	Nieto, Angel (Esp)	motor cycling (125cc)
Martin, Stephen	hockey	Noel, Susan	squash
Matthews, Ken	walking	Norman, Wendy	modern pentathlon
Mays, Willie (US)	baseball	Obolensky, Alex	rugby union
McAuliffe, Jack	lightweight boxer	Obree, Graeme	cycling
		O'Dell, George	motor cycling
McAvoy, Jock	light-heavyweight boxer	O'Keefe, Dan	Gaelic football
		Oliver, Alan	show jumping
McCoig, Robert	badminton	Oliver, Eric	sidecar racing
McConnell, William	hockey	Opie, Lisa	squash
McEvoy, Freddie	bobsleigh	O'Reilly, Wilf	speed skating
McGregor, Yvonne	cycling	Ottley, Dave	javelin
McGwire, Mark (US)	baseball	Paish, Geoff	tennis
McIntyre, Bob	motor cycling	Palmer, Charles	judo
McKechnie, Neil	swimming	Palmer, Thomas 'Pedlar'	bantamweight boxer
McKenzie, George	wrestling	Panis, Olivier (Fra)	motor racing (Formula 1)
McKiernan, Catherina	athletics		
McKinlay, Ken	speedway	Papke, Billy (US)	boxing
McLean, William	hockey	Papp, László (Hung)	boxing
McLeod, Hugh	rugby union	Parke, James	tennis and rugby union
McNeill, Carol	orienteering	Parker, Jack	speedway
McQueen, Delroy	weightlifting	Pastrano, Willie (US)	boxing
McRae, Alister	rallying	Paterson, Alan	high jumper
McRae, Colin	rallying	Pattisson, Rodney	yachting
McRae, Jimmy	rallying	Patton, Peter	ice hockey
McTigue, Mike	boxing	Paul, René	fencing
Meade, Richard	three-day event	Payne, Howard	hammer thrower
Menu, Alain (Swi)	touring cars	Payne, Rosemary	discus thrower
Meredith, Billy	football	Paynter, Eddie	cricket
Meredith, Leon	cycling	Payton, Walter (US)	American football
Miles, Eustace	rackets and real tennis	Peall, W J	billiards
		Peck, Geoff	orienteering
Milford, David	rackets	Pendleton, Victoria	cycling
Millar, David	cycling	Pep, Willie (US)	boxing
Millar, Robert	cycling	Petersen, Jack	light-heavyweight boxer
Miller, David	bowls		
Miller, Sammy	motor cycling	Phelps, Brian	diving and trampolining
Millward, Roger	rugby league		
Minter, Derek	motor cycling	Phelps, Richard	modern pentathlon
Mirra, Dave (US)	BMX	Phelps, Ted	rowing
Mitchell, Abe	golf	Phillips, Mollie	figure skating
Mitchell, Beryl	rowing	Pickering, Jean	long jumper
Mitchell, William	billiards	Pickering, Karen	swimming
Monaghan, Terry	speed skating	Pilch, Fuller	cricket
Montana, Joe (US)	American football	Pinching, Evie	skiing
Montgomerie, Robert	fencing	Platt, Susan	javelin
Moore, Ann	show jumping	Porter, Hugh	cyclist
Moore, Steve	water skiing	Potter, Jon	hockey
Morgan, Janet	squash	Potter, Martin	surfing
Morris, Stewart	yachting	Prenn, John	rackets
Morton, Lucy	swimming	Price, Berwyn	athletics
Moss, Pat	rallying	Price, Sarah	swimming
Mould, Marion	show jumping	Price, Tommy	speedway
Muckelt, Ethel	figure skating	Probyn, Jeff	rugby union
Murphy, Catherine	athletics	Pullin, John	rugby union
Mynn, Alfred	cricket	Queally, Jason	cycling
Namath, Joe (US)	American football	Quixall, Albert	football
Nash, Tony	bobsleigh	Radford, Peter	athletics
Neale, Denis	table tennis	Radmilovic, Paul	swimming and water polo
Nedved, Pavel (Cze)	football		
Neligan, Gwen	fencing	Rainey, Wayne (US)	motor cycling (500cc)
Nettleton, Louise	archery	Randall, Graeme	judo
Netzer, Gunter (Ger)	football	Ray, Ted	golf
Nevett, Bill	jockey	Read, Phil	motor cycling (125cc and 250cc)
Neville, Gary	football		
Neville, Phil	football	Redman, Jim (Zim)	motor cycling (250cc)

Reece, Tom	billiards
Rendle, Sharon	judo
Renshaw, William	tennis
Rhodes, Ronald	canoeing
Rice, Jerry (US)	American football
Richards, Gordon W (1930–98)	horse racing
Richards, Sir Gordon (1904–86)	horse racing
Richards, Tom	marathon
Richardson, Peter	cricket
Richardson, T D	figure skating
Richmond, Ken	wrestling and judo
Ring, Christy	hurling
Ringer, Anthony	shooting
Riseley, Frank	tennis
Ritchie, Margaret	discus
Roberts, John	billiards
Roberts, Karen	judo
Roberts, Philippa	water skiing
Robinson, Brian	cycling
Robinson, Jack (US)	baseball
Robinson, Jem	horse racing
Robinson, Val	hockey
Rodman, Dennis (US)	basketball
Rogers, Iris	badminton
Rogers, Michelle	judo
Ronaldson, Chloe	roller skating
Rooney, Wayne	football
Rose, Justin	golf
Ross, Jonathan	bowls
Round, Dorothy	tennis
Rowe, Arthur	shot putter
Rowe, Diana	table tennis
Rowe, Rosalind	table tennis
Russell-Vick, Mary	hockey
Ruth, Babe (US)	baseball
Rutherford, Monica	gymnastics
Salo, Mika (Fin)	motor racing (Formula 1)
Salvadori, Roy	motor racing
Sandford, Cecil	motor cycling (125cc and 250cc)
Saunders, Vivien	golf
Savage, David	hockey
Saville, Sammy	hockey
Schofield, Garry	rugby league
Schwantz, Kevin (US)	motor cycling (500cc)
Scotland, Ken	rugby union
Scott, Peter	yachting and gliding
Scriven, Peggy	tennis
Seaman, Dick	motor racing
Searle, Greg and Johnny	rowing
Seaton, Paul	water skiing
Segrave, Henry	motor racing
Sekjer, Martyn	bowls
Selby, Vera	snooker
Seligman, Edgar	fencing
Sharpe, Graham	figure skating
Shaw, Norma	bowls
Sheen, Gillian	fencing
Sheil, Norman	cycling
Sheppard, Alison	swimming
Sheridan, Eileen	cycling
Shilcock, Anne	tennis
Shotton, Sue	trampolining
Shoveller, Stanley	hockey
Shrubb, Alf	athletics
Simmers, Max	rugby union
Simmonds, Dave	motor cycling (125cc)
Simmonite, Rachael	rallying
Simmonite, Stephanie	rallying
Simpson, Cyril	rackets
Simpson, Tommy	cycling
Sindelar, Matthias (Aut)	football
Singleton, Georgina	judo
Singleton, Joey	boxing
Sixsmith, Janet	hockey
Slawinski, Kendra	netball
Small, Ruth	bowls
Smith, Charles	water polo
Smith, Lawrie	yachting
Smith, Sydney	tennis
Smithies, Karen	cricket
Snode, Chris	diving
Snow, John	cricket
Snow, Julian	real tennis
Snowball, Betty	cricket
Solomon, John	croquet
Sopwith, Sir Tommy	yachting
Sosa, Samuel (Dom Rep)	baseball
Springman, Sarah	triathlon
Stammers, Kay	tennis
Starbrook, Dave	judo
Steel, Dorothy	croquet
Steele, Mavis	bowls
Stevens, Ray	badminton
Stewart-Wood, Jeannette	water skiing
Stoichkov, Hristo (Bulg)	football
Stoop, Adrian	rugby union
Sturgess, Colin	cycling
Sturgess, William	walking
Surtees, William	rackets
Talbot, Derek	badminton
Tancred, Bill	discus
Tanner, Haydn	rugby union
Tarleton, Nelson	boxing
Tate, Maurice	cricket
Tatum, Kelvin	speedway
Taylor, Ian	hockey
Terry, Simon	archery
Thomas, Neil	gymnastics
Thompson, Don	walking
Thompson, Ian	marathon
Thomson, Andy	bowls
Thorpe, Dave	motocross
Thorpe, Jim (US)	American football and athletics
Tisdall, Bob	400m hurdler
Tomes, Alan	rugby union
Tomlins, Freddie	figure skating
Tortelli, Sébastien (US)	motocross
Towler, Diane	ice dancing
Tredgett, Mike	badminton
Tredgold, Roger	fencing
Trew, Billy	rugby union
Trinidad, Felix (P Rico)	boxing
Troke, Helen	badminton
Tucker, Andrew	shooting
Tucker, Sam	rugby union
Tuckey, Raymond	tennis
Tweddle, Elisabeth	gymnastics
Tyler, Dorothy	high jumper
Ubbiali, Carlo (Ita)	motor cycling (125cc and 250cc)
Uber, Betty	badminton
Ulyett, George	cricket
Usher, Georgina	fencing
Valderrama, Carlos (Col)	football
Verstappen, Jos (Neth)	motor racing (Formula 1)
Vickers, Stan	walking
Viollet, Denis	football

Wagstaff, Harold	**rugby league**	Whiteley, Johnny	**rugby league**
Walker, Stefanie	**ice dancing**	Whitford, Arthur	**gymnastics**
Wallace, Shaun	**cycling**	Whitlock, Harold	**walking**
Warburg, David	**real tennis**	Whittle, Harry	**athletics**
Ward, David	**bowls**	Whyte, Jamie	**ice dancing**
Ward, Pat	**tennis**	Wigg, Simon	**speedway**
Wardrop, Jack	**swimming**	Wilkinson, Diana	**swimming**
Warner, Sir Pelham	**cricket**	Wilkinson, George	**water polo**
Warren, James	**judo**	Williams, Freddie	**speedway**
Waterman, Split	**speedway**	Wills, Philip	**gliding**
Watson, Maud	**tennis**	Wilson, Justin	**motor racing**
Watson, Willie	**cricket and football**	Wonderful Terrific Mons III (USA)	**baseball**
Weah, George (Lib)	**football**		
Webb, Jonathan	**rugby union**	Wooderson, Sydney	**athletics**
Webster, Steve	**motor cycling (sidecars)**	Woodgate, W B	**rowing**
		Woodward, Clive	**rugby union**
Weetman, Harry	**golf**	Woodward, Vivian	**football**
Wells, Billy	**heavyweight boxer**	Wooller, Wilf	**rugby union**
Welsh, Freddie	**boxing**	Woosnam, Max	**tennis and football**
Westwood, Jean	**ice dance**	Yardley, Norman	**cricket**
White, Belle	**diving**	Young, Cy (US)	**baseball**
White, Wilf	**show jumping**	Zale, Tony (US)	**boxing**
Whitehead, Adam	**swimming**		

NB The table above is merely a list of perhaps less well-known sports people, due either to their practising a minority sport or to the time elapsed since their success. A more thorough record of their achievements is beyond the scope of this book. Sportspeople listed are British unless stated otherwise.

Sporting Terms

adolph *trampolining* three-and-a-half front twisting somersault.

airshot *golf* complete missing of ball which constitutes a stroke (unless mulligan awarded).

albatross *golf* score of 3 under par on a particular hole.

appel *fencing* beating or stamping of foot during contest.

apron *golf* grass cut short between fairway and approach to the green.

Arab spring *gymnastics* cartwheel with a quarter turn.

assist *basketball* final pass given to shooter of a basket.

axel *ice skating* a one-and-a-half turn jump from the forward outside edge of one skate to the backward outside edge of the other (named after Norwegian skater Axel Rudolph Paulser).

back alley *badminton* the area at the back of the court.

bai-hou *karate* white crane stance with one knee raised high (popularised in *Karate Kid* films).

balestra *fencing* attack after an appel.

barani *trampolining* front somersault with half twist.

battery *baseball* originally a term for the pitcher but now incorporates the pitcher and catcher.

baulk *billiards* line from which game begins.

ba(u)lk *baseball* illegal action by a pitcher.

beamer *cricket* ball bowled higher than a full toss so endangering the batsman.

Bernouilli effect *hang-gliding* see venturi effect.

besom *curling* type of broom used to sweep the ice to gain more distance.

bib *netball* tie-up over top with player's position labelled.

birdie *golf* score of 1 under par on a hole.

blind side *rugby* short side between scrum and touch line.

block *volleyball* basic return at the net to counter the opponent's spike.

blocking *basketball* illegal personal contact that impedes the progress of an opponent who does not have the ball.

bogey *golf* score of 1 over par on a hole.

bonk *cycling* tiredness caused by lack of food.

bonspiel *curling* term used for an important match.

boom *yachting* long spar or pole hinged at one end, securing the bottom of a ship's sail.

bosey / bosie *cricket* Australian name for a googly (named after B J T Bosanquet 1877–1936, an English cricketer).

Boston crab *wrestling* manoeuvre whereby one fighter sits on the back of the other with legs tucked under his arms.

bouncer *cricket* ball bowled short and fast in order to cause batsman to take evasive action.

bowling crease *cricket* line extended from the stumps sideways and four feet behind the popping crease; the ball must be delivered between these two lines.

brakeman *bobsleigh* person who operates the brakes in the sleigh.

Brill bend *high jumping* named after Debbie Brill, equivalent to the Fosbury flop.

brush *curling* implement for sweeping the ice, thereby causing the stone to travel further.

bunt *baseball* to let the ball hit the bat without swinging at it.

burgee *yachting* ornamental flag which serves no other purpose.

buttonhook *American football* type of pass for the receiver running straight downfield and then doubling back a few steps to receive it.

bye *cricket* extra gained by batting side when the batsmen run or the ball crosses the boundary after no contact with bat has taken place.

calx *Eton wall game* area behind the goal-line.

caman *shinty* stick used for striking.

cannon *billiards* object ball hitting opponent's ball and the red ball (scores 3 points).

capriole *dressage* horse jumps straight upward with its forelegs drawn in, kicking back with its hind legs horizontal.

catch *real tennis* obsolete former name for the game.

catch a crab *rowing* to get an oar trapped

underwater or to miss the water with a stroke.

catenaccio system *football* sweeper system.

checking *ice hockey* legal manoeuvre of physical contact to gain control of puck.

chicane *motor racing* sharp double-bend.

chinaman *cricket* left-handed bowler's googly to a right-handed batsman.

chistera *pelota / jaĩ alaĩ* curved glove with a chestnut or ash frame, aka Cesta.

christiania *skiing* turn in which the skis are kept in parallel, used for stopping short. Aka christie.

Christmas tree *drag racing* starting system.

Christmas tree *football* descriptive formation.

chui *judo* warning with 3 points deducted.

chukka *polo* each of the 7 ½-minute periods into which a game is divided. Also spelt 'chucker' or 'chukker'.

close-hauled *wind surfing* area 45 degrees each side of wind direction.

conversion *Canadian football* method of adding to score after touchdown has been scored.

conversion *rugby* method of adding to score after try has been scored (2 points score).

courbet / curvet *dressage* jump forward at the levade.

cover *cricket* fielding position midway between infield and outfield in which a good fielder may save a single.

cover point *cricket* fielding position on the off side and nearer the batsman than the non-striker.

crampon *curling* device formerly used to enable a steady delivery but now obsolete.

crampon *rock-climbing* frame with 10 or 12 metal spikes, strapped to boots to give a firmer footing.

cross buttock *wrestling* throw in which a wrestler throws an opponent head first over his or her hip.

crosse *lacrosse* stick between 40–72 inches long and 4–10 inches wide.

crucifix *gymnastics (rings)* basic position with the arms held outstretched to the sides.

curve ball *baseball* ball which deviates from the path it would otherwise take, because of the spin imparted by the pitcher.

cut line *squash* line above which a served ball must strike the wall.

dan *martial arts* each of the numbered grades of the advanced level of proficiency in many martial arts.

diamond *baseball* the area formed by the four bases within the infield.

dig *volleyball* defensive motion of digging the ball up from below the net height with two hands to counter a spike.

ditch *bowls* the channel around the rink.

dog-leg *golf* hole that bends sharply to one side, so ensuring a positional shot is played.

domestiques *cycling* team members of tour teams who will sacrifice their position for team leaders.

double eagle *golf* score of 3 under par on a particular hole (US term).

down *American football* each of a fixed number of attempts to advance the ball 10 yards.

drop-kick *rugby* kick made by dropping the ball and kicking it as it rebounds from the ground.

drop-line *angling* weighted fishing-line for fishing near the bottom of a waterway.

drop-out *rugby* a drop-kick made from within the defending team's 22-metre (formerly 25yds) line in order to restart play after the ball has gone dead.

dropped goal *rugby* goal scored with a drop-kick that propels the ball over the crossbar.

dummy, sell a *rugby* to successfully feign a pass.

dunk *basketball* shoot a basket by jumping so that the hands are above the ring and the ball is dunked down through the hoop.

eagle *American football* defensive formation.

eagle *golf* score of 2 under par on a hole.

egg position *skiing* tucked position that ensures a good fast glide.

en garde *fencing* call to a fencer to adopt a defensive stance in readiness for an attack or bout.

end *bowls* division of a match whereby after all woods are bowled the next 'end' is played from the other end of the rink.

end *curling* division of a match whereby after all stones are bowled the next 'end' is played from the other end of the rink.

English *pool* north American term for using 'side' on the cueball.

Eskimo roll *canoeing* a 360-degree roll starting and finishing above water but 180 degrees of which is underwater.

expedite *table tennis* rule whereby a match is brought to a conclusion after a series of long rallies or deuces by setting a limit to the number of strokes per point.

extras *cricket* generic name for all types of byes and penalty runs scored other than by the batsman hitting the ball.

face-off *ice hockey* start of game.

fairway *golf* part of golf course between tee and green in which the grass is cut short to reward accuracy.

feng taidu *kung fu* phoenix stance keeping low on one leg ready to rise.

fine leg *cricket* fielding position between wicket keeper and square leg but deeper.

flèche *archery* obsolete name for an arrow.

flèche *fencing* a running attack.

flic flac *gymnastics* simple back flip.

fliffis *trampolining* double front somersault with twist.

flying mare *wrestling* throw in which one wrestler throws the other over his or her back using the other's arm as a lever.

Fosbury flop *high jumping* technique named after Dick Fosbury, whereby head and shoulders are thrown over the bar first, chest upwards and with legs pulled back to ensure economical clearance.

free throw *basketball* free shot at basket due to an infringement by the opposition.

fukuro shinai *kendo* wooden sword often covered in cloth or leather.

full-nelson *wrestling* two-handed hold whereby the arms are placed under the arms of the opponent and interlocked behind his neck, immobilising the upper body.

gaff *yachting* spar situated on the after side of a mast and supporting the head of a fore-and-aft sail.

garryowen *rugby* another name for an up and under.

genoa *yachting* large jib with a low foot.

gojo-ryu *karate* hard / soft technique.

gokuhi *martial arts* techniques and 'secrets' of masters relayed to gifted students.

googly *cricket* off-break ball bowled with apparent leg-break action.

goosewinged *yachting* square-rigged boats having the topsail spread for scudding under when the wind is strong, the bunt of the sail being hauled up to the yard.

gridiron *American football* the field of play.

gully *cricket* fielding position a little wider than the slips.

gybe *yachting* of a fore-and-aft sail or its boom, to swing from one side of a vessel to the other.

hack *curling* notch made in the ice used to steady the foot when delivering a stone.

hackamore *horse racing* bitless bridle with a hard oval noseband which allows pressure to be exerted on the nose by means of the reins attached just in front of a heavy counterbalancing knot.

half-nelson *wrestling* hold whereby the arm of the opponent is bent behind his back and pushed upwards.

halyard *yachting* rope or tackle for raising or lowering a sail.

hammer grip *table tennis* rarely used method of holding the bat whereby no fingers touch its face.

hand-in *squash* the server.

hand-out *squash* when player loses a point on his service he becomes hand-out.

haute école *dressage* advanced training methods (high school).

head *bowls* the grouping of the woods around the jack.

hecht *gymnastics* dismount from the asymmetric bars head and body first between bars.

held ball *basketball* called when two opponents have one or two hands so firmly upon the ball that neither can gain possession.

herringboning *skiing* method of climbing a slope by walking with the skis pointing outwards.

hikiwake *kendo* a draw in a competitive match.

hog line *curling* line behind which the stone must be delivered.

hog's back *equestrianism* sharp-ridged natural mound for jumping.

honk *cycling* cycling out of the saddle.

hooker *rugby* front row of scrum position player supported between the two props who attemps to hook ball back with his feet to be used by his team.

hoop *basketball* the metal ring of the 'basket'.

hoop *croquet* arch through which the ball must be driven.

house *curling* the round target area of concentric circles.

I formation *American football* offensive formation.

in touch *rugby* out of play.

ippon *judo* full point in Japan (scores 10 points in competition).

Irish whip *wrestling* one-handed throw whereby the arm is whipped back and forth forcing a somersault in the air by the opponent.

jack *bowls* white ball which is the target for the woods.

jib *yachting* triangular staysail stretching from the outer end of the jib-boom to the fore-topmast.

judoka *judo* judo player.

jugogi *judo* judo suit.

jump ball *basketball* method of putting the ball into play whereby the referee tosses it up between two opponents who try to tap it to a teammate.

katame-waza *judo* basic hold.

keikoku *judo* judge's warning with 7 points deducted.

kinsa *judo* 3 point scoring technique.

kip *gymnastics* movement whereby the body is straightened from a piked position by pushing the hips forward and the legs back.

knock-on *rugby* illegal move that knocks the ball forward and on to the ground with hand or arm.

koka *judo* hold between 10 and 20 seconds.

kyu *martial arts* student.

laundry *drag racing* the parachute that slows the cars down.

leg-bye *cricket* run scored after the ball has touched any part of the batsman but his hand.

leg side *cricket* the side of the wicket on which the receiving batsman stands.

levade *dressage* horse raises and draws in its forelegs, standing balanced on its bent hind legs.

line-out *rugby* method of throwing ball back into play between two lines of opposing forwards after it has gone out over the touchline.

lock *rugby* one of two forwards in second row of scrum.

long bomb *roller hockey* long pass from defence to set up sudden counter-attack.

long dong *kung fu* eastern dragon position with one hand in front of forehead (palm out) and the other covering abdomen (palm down).

long hop *cricket* ball that is bowled flat and short so as to almost bounce twice before reaching batsman.

luff *yachting* the edge of a fore-and-aft sail next to the mast or stay (among other definitions it is also a term for obstructing the opposition attempting to pass on the windward side by sailing closer to the wind).

lutz *ice skating* jump in which the skater takes off from the outside back edge of one skate and lands, after full rotation, on the outside back edge of the other.

maiden *cricket* an over in which no runs have been scored.

mallet *croquet* the striking implement used to manoeuvre the ball through the hoops.

mashie *golf* obsolete colloquial name for a no. 5 iron.

mashie-niblick *golf* obsolete colloquial name for a no. 7 iron.

mata *judo* break of a hold.

maul *rugby* distinguished from ruck by ball being held off the ground.

men *kendo* the armour that covers the head and face.

mid-off *cricket* fielding position on the side opposite to where the facing batsman stands; in the case of a right-handed batsman, to the left of the bowler during his run-up.

mid-on *cricket* fielding position on the side where the facing batsman stands; in the case of a right-handed batsman, to the right of the bowler during his run-up.

mid-wicket *cricket* self-explanatory fielding position whereby if an equilateral triangle was plotted using the 22 yards between the stumps, mid-wicket would lie on the apex.

monkey climb *wrestling* move whereby one wrestler climbs up and wraps himself around the other to immobilise him.

mulligan *golf* free stroke awarded informally after a poor shot, usually an air shot.

nage-waza *judo* basic throw.

niblick *golf* obsolete colloquial name for a sand wedge or sometimes a wedge.

night watchman *cricket* lower-order batsman who comes in up the order to protect a key player if a wicket is lost near close of play.

no side *rugby* official name for end of the game, no longer commonly used.

nock *archery* notch at end of bow to run string through.

nocking point *archery* point of a bowstring to which the notch of an arrow is applied.

Notre Dame shift *American football* offensive move whereby the backs move just before the snap of the ball from their T-formation.

nunchaku *kung fu* rice flail used in exhibitions.

nutmeg *football* to play the ball between the legs of a defender and run around him to collect it.

O'Brien shift *shot putting* common gliding technique named after Parry O'Brien.

Oklahoma *American football* defensive formation.

oxer *equestrianism* brush fence with a guard rail on one side.

ozeki *sumo* the second rank after yokozuna (means 'great barrier').

painter *yachting* short rope or chain by which the shank of an anchor is held fast.

parallelogram *Gaelic football* playing area.

parry *fencing* warding off an attack especially with a counter.

passage *dressage* cadenced high-stepping trot.

pebble *curling* another name for a stone.

penholder grip *table tennis* method of holding the bat like a pencil popularised by the Chinese; quick footwork is essential as backhands are impossible to play. Aka eastern grip.

penthouse *real tennis* sloping roof of the corridor or gallery running around three sides of the court.

piaffe *dressage* a trot in place.

pick *basketball* action of a player who, without causing contact, delays or prevents an opponent from reaching his desired position.

pick-up *sprinting* second phase of race after the start during which the head is raised and relaxation starts.

pile-driver *wrestling* up-ending the opponent and driving his head into the canvas.

pinch-hitter *baseball* less technically accomplished player capable of hitting out forcefully.

piste *fencing* total fencing area.

piste *skiing* total skiing area.

pitcher *baseball* specialist thrower of the ball towards the opposing batter.

piton *rock-climbing* eye peg hammered into rock so that a rope can be attached.

pivot *basketball* movement in which a player with the ball steps once or more in any direction with the same foot while the other foot is kept at its point of contact with the floor.

plastron *fencing* padded, leather-covered breastplate.

point *cricket* off-side fielding position wide of gully.

popping crease *cricket* line four feet in front of and parallel to the wicket within which the batsmen must remain unless the ball is dead or they are running.

press *basketball* defensive technique of harassing players into hurried play.

prop *rugby* one of the two forwards in the front row of the scrum who support hooker.

puck *ice hockey* flat rubber disc used in place of ball.

puissance *show jumping* high jump event.

punt *rugby* kick made by dropping the ball and kicking before it hits the ground.

putout *baseball* self-explanatory term meaning to cause a batter or base runner to be out.

quarterback *American football* player stationed behind the centre who directs a team's attacking play.

rack *pool* implement used for setting the red balls at the start of a frame (also the name used for an individual frame).

randolph (randi) *trampolining* two-and-a-half twisting front somersault.

repechage *rowing* a second chance for the best of the losing rowers in eliminating heats to progress to a final.

return crease *cricket* the lines either side of the wicket at right angles to the bowling crease.

riposte *fencing* a lunge or quick thrust after parrying.

rocker *ice skating* a skate with a curved blade.

roquet *croquet* to strike another player's ball with your own.

rover *American football* defensive linebacker assigned to move about to anticipate opponents' plays.

rover *archery* target chosen at random and at an undetermined range (also a mark for long-distance shooting).

rover *Australian rules football* player forming part of the ruck.

rover *croquet* ball that has passed through all the hoops but not pegged out (also a name for a player whose ball has done this).

ruck *rugby* occurs when progress of the ball is checked and two or more players struggle to gain possession. Distinguished from maul by ball being on the ground and legally playable only with the feet.

rush *ice hockey* sudden attack on goal often from a defensive position.

salchow *ice skating* full-turn jump from the inside back edge of one skate to the outside back edge of the other.

schuss *skiing* starting gate or housing.

scissors *high jump* training technique of clearing bar with legs only and no rotation of hips.

scissors *rugby* change of direction of attack by player running in diagonally opposite to the line of attacking play when receiving ball.

screen *basketball* another name for 'pick'.

scrimmage *American football* offense and defense facing each other.

scrum *rugby* formed by eight forwards of each side in three ranks for purpose of gaining possession with the feet. Note: rugby league scrummages contain six players.

serpentine *dressage* series of half-circles alternately to right and left.

shido *judo* judge's warning with no point deducted.

shime-waza *judo* strangulation technique.

shinai *kendo* sword made up of four bamboo sticks bound together.

shobu-ari *kendo* the end of a match.

shopping, going *billiards* potting your opponent's ball.

short leg *cricket* fielding position close to the batsman and on the leg side.

shotgun *American football* offensive formation.

shroud *yachting* set of ropes supporting the mainsail.

shukokai *karate* a karate school.

shuriken *karate* one of various designs of small throwing weapons often eight-sided and sharp.

side *billiards* off-centre striking of the cueball to make false angle in positional play.

silly mid-off *cricket* close fielding position short of mid-off.

silly mid-on *cricket* close fielding position short of mid-on.

sleeper *wrestling* application of pressure on the nerves in the neck which can cause loss of consciousness.

slip *cricket* fielding position next to the wicket-keeper.

snap *American football* put the ball into play on the ground by a quick backward movement.

soigneur *cycling* general dogsbody of team responsible for its physical and mental preparation.

soop *curling* assist the progress of a curling stone by sweeping the ice in front of it.

southpaw *boxing* boxer who leads with his right hand.

space lob *roller hockey* use of end boards to pass to team mates.

spare *ten pin bowling* knocking down all the pins with two successive bowls.

spider *billiards, snooker* implement used when bridging directly over a ball.

spider *darts* wire frame around the board.

spike *volleyball* one-handed attacking shot from above and across the net. Spike serves are common at the higher levels.

spinnaker *yachting* large triangular sail carried forward of or opposite the mainsail.

spinner *angling* real or artificial bait or lure fixed so as to revolve when pulled through the water.

spinnerama *roller hockey* complicated tactical move to deceive opposition.

spinning *cycling* US term for twiddling now commonly used in UK.

split *ten pin bowling* attempt to knock down pins which are wide apart.

split *weightlifting* action of thrusting forward with one foot and backward with the other to aid leverage during lift.

split T *American football* offensive formation.

spoon *angling* artificial bait in the shape of the bowl of a spoon, used in spinning or trolling.

spoon *golf* any club with a slightly concave wooden head, but often refers to a 3 wood specifically.

stealing bases *baseball* reaching bases without the striker hitting the ball.

stone *curling* the heavy 'top' with a handle which is aimed at the house.

straddle *high jump* similar to western roll, but the straddle jumper keeps legs wide apart and body straight.

strike *baseball* complete miss of the ball.

strike *ten pin bowling* knocking all the pins down with one ball.

suicide squad *American football* specialist players who deliberately block attacks.

sulky *harness racing* vehicle used in harness racing.

sweeper *curling* team member who sweeps the ice to gain distance for stone.

swingtime *trampolining* a series of different moves performed between bounces.

switch-hitting *boxing* changing from orthodox to southpaw during a bout.

tack *equestrianism* saddle, bridle and bit.

tack *yachting* zigzag movement of a boat.

tagged out *baseball* self-explanatory term.

tame-shiwari *karate* exercise for toughening using breaking techniques.

taw *marbles* line from which a player shoots; also another name for the actual game and formerly a name for a large marble.

tee *curling* centre point of the house.

tee *golf* small peg on which to rest the ball when driving; also the name for the area where the initial drive is made.

T formation *American football* offensive formation.

third man *cricket* fielding position deep behind the slip area.

tice *cricket* obsolete term for a yorker.

tice *croquet* stroke tempting an opponent to aim at one's ball.

tiger country *golf* deep rough usually on high ground.

tin *squash* the lower line on the wall above which all shots must be played.

tkachyov *gymnastics* one-handed 360-degree swing on horizontal (high) bar.

tolley *marbles* portmanteau word from 'taw' and 'alley'.

touchdown *American football* equivalent of a try in rugby, except that the ball need not touch the ground when carried or received inside the opponents' end zone (6 points score).

touché *fencing* an acknowledgment that a scoring hit has been made in a bout.

toucher *bowls* wood that has touched the jack in its travels.

tram lines *tennis* the outer lines at each side of the court which become part of the court in doubles matches.

trapeze *yachting* sliding support used for outboard balancing on a yacht.

travelling *basketball* running with the ball without bouncing it.

triangle *angling* set of three hooks fastened together so that the barbs form a triangle.

triangle *snooker* implement used for setting the red balls at the start of a frame.

troll *angling* fish by drawing bait along in the water.

try *rugby* scoring method by means of touching the ball down in the opponents' goal area behind their goal line (5 points score).

tsuba *kendo* guard of the sword.

tsuka *kendo* handle of the sword.

tsukahara *gymnastics* vault consisting of a quarter or half turn on to the horse followed by one and half somersaults off.

turkey *ten pin bowling* gaining three strikes in successive bowls.

turnover *basketball* loss of possession of the ball by a team before any member has been able to try for a basket.

twiddling *cycling* pedalling fast in a gear with no pressure asserted.

up and under *rugby* kicking the ball up field high and long to make time for the kicker and attacking players to reach the point where it comes down.

uwate-dashi-nage *sumo* one-handed throw.

uwate-nage *sumo* hip throw using both hands.

veer attack *American football* offensive formation.

Venturi effect *hang-gliding* basis for wing design, explaining that air flowing over the upper part of a wing moves faster than the air on the underside of the wing, so that the pressure underneath is greater and hence creates lift. Aka Bernouilli effect.

volley *volleyball* two-handed shot that may go over the net or to another team member to spike.

vorlage *skiing* position in which the skier leans forward without lifting the heels from the skis. It is also a common name for skiing trousers when pluralized.

vorlaufer *skiing* literally meaning 'run on ahead' in German, it is a term used for the pre-competition skiers who test the safety and degree of difficulty of a ski course.

walkover *horse racing* horse having the formality of walking over the line as it is the only entrant in a race.

wall pass *football* pass from one player to another and back to save having to face a defender (also called one-two).

warner single wing *American football* offensive formation.

wazari-ni-chikai-waza *judo* 5-point score (two make an ippon).

wazari *judo* almost point in Japanese (scores 7 points in competition).

western grip *table tennis* traditional method of holding a bat with fingers on face of bat.

western roll *high jumping* technique, rarely used today, whereby the front leg is thrown high over the bar and the body and other leg roll over and parallel to the bar.

wicket maiden *cricket* an over during which no runs have been scored and a wicket has been taken.

wide *cricket* extra given to batting side due to ball being bowled too wide of the batsman.

wipe out *surfing* tumbling off the board, often due to unforeseen wave.

wired *croquet* prevented from taking a particular course by an intervening hoop or peg.

wishbone *yachting* boom composed of two halves that curve outward from the mast on either side of the sail and in again, the clew of the sail between them being attached to the point where they meet aft.

yamashita *gymnastics* flat handspring over the vaulting horse.

yokozuna *sumo* grand champion.

yori kiri *sumo* strong forward push.

yorker *cricket* ball bowled at feet of batsman whether playing back or forward.

yuko *judo* hold between 20 and 25 seconds.

NB This is far from being an exhaustive listing of sporting terminology. Dictionaries of terms are available on many individual sports and so it would be impossible to catalogue all known terms. What I have tried to do is give a good cross-section of technical terms over many sports. I should also point out that some terms will relate to other sports, e.g. billiards-based sports or running ball sports.

Other Sports: World's Strongest Man

The World's Strongest Man competition has been covered by BBC Television almost since the beginning and is based on all aspects of strength and not just the lifting of weights, although most of the very best competitors have also been champion weight-lifters. Geoff Capes of Great Britain ushered in a new breed of athlete: not only very large but also very fit and very quick. The competitions have had many great personalities over the years, from the great bullish Kazmaier to the very extrovert Sigmarsson (sadly no longer with us), with his 'Viking' chant, and of course the other great Icelander Magnusson.

1977	Bruce Wilhelm (United States)	1991	Magnus Ver Magnusson (Iceland)
1978	Bruce Wilhelm (United States)	1992	Ted Van Der Parre (Holland)
1979	Don Reinhoudt (United States)	1993	Gary Taylor (Great Britain)
1980	Bill Kazmaier (United States)	1994	Magnus Ver Magnusson (Iceland)
1981	Bill Kazmaier (United States)	1995	Magnus Ver Magnusson (Iceland)
1982	Bill Kazmaier (United States)	1996	Magnus Ver Magnusson (Iceland)
1983	Geoff Capes (Great Britain)	1997	Jouko Ahola (Finland)
1984	Jon Pall Sigmarsson (Iceland)	1998	Magnus Samuelsson (Sweden)
1985	Geoff Capes (Great Britain)	1999	Jouko Ahola (Finland)
1986	Jon Pall Sigmarsson (Iceland)	2000	Janne Virtanen (Finland)
1987	*Jon Pall Sigmarsson (Iceland)	2001	Sven Karlssen (Norway)
1988	Jon Pall Sigmarsson (Iceland)	2002	Mariusz Pudzianowski (Poland)
1989	Jamie Reeves (Great Britain)	2003	Mariusz Pudzianowski (Poland)
1990	Jon Pall Sigmarsson (Iceland)	2004	Vasil Virastyuk (Ukraine)

*Competition known as Pure Strength

Other Sports: The Superstars

The World Superstars competition ran for six years on the BBC and made stars of athletes such as Brian Budd, who treated the competition with the same professional approach as his own sport of soccer. Although Brian Hooper won the last of the competitions, the domestic Superstars was won by fine athletes such as Lynn Davies, Andy Ripley, John Conteh, David Hemery, Keith Fielding, and the most famous of all, judo player Brian Jacks, he of the dip-bar records. And who can ever forget the painful demise of Kevin Keegan on a bike. Austin Healey won the 2001 one-off special. The BBC resurrected the British version in 2003, athlete Duaine Ladejo having a comfortable victory. The series was axed again after the next competition in 2005, won by skier Alain Baxter after a close battle with Ladejo. The champions are listed together with their original sport.

1977 Bob Seagren, USA, Pole Vault
1978 Brian Budd, CAN, Soccer
1979 Brian Budd, CAN, Soccer

1980 Brian Budd, CAN, Soccer
1981 Jody Sheckter, RSA, Racing
1982 Brian Hooper, GBR, Pole Vault

Miscellaneous Information: Sport

Acque Minerale and Tamburello	features of Imola and San Marino motor racing circuits.
archery: target colours	gold (centre), red, blue, black, white.
Australian rules football: inventor	George Ligowsky.
backwards: sports where competitors move	back-stroke swimming; rowing; tug of war.
badminton: All-England champion seven successive years	Rudy Hartono (1968–74).
badminton: family won 35 All-England titles	Frank Devlin and his daughters Judy and Sue.
badminton: origin	originally called Shuttlecock and Battledore and named after the country estate of the Duke of Beaufort, where it originated in 1873. It was popularized by army officers in India who played it as an outdoor game.
bagatelle: brief description	similar to bar billiards but board has nine holes and nine balls are used (four red, four white and a black ball that scores double).
bagatelle: variations	cannon game; Mississippi; sans égal.
basketball: court size	50′ × 94′.

basketball: famous US teams	Boston Celtics; Houston Rockets; Los Angeles Lakers; Milwaukee Bucks; New York Knickerbockers; Philadelphia 76ers; Phoenix Suns; Portland Trail Blazers; Seattle Supersonics; St Louis Hawks; Washington Bullets.
basketball: inventor	Dr James Naismith invented basketball at the YMCA training school in Springfield, Mass. (1891).
beard: not allowed	jockeys.
billiards: World Matchplay champion 1998	Mike Russell of England defeated Peter Gilchrist of England 8–5.
boat race: dead heat	1877 (although Oxford are said to have won by about six feet). The actual closest winning margin being the official one foot victory by Oxford in the 2003 race.
boat race: first woman cox	Susan Brown in 1981.
boat race: reserve crews	Cambridge – Goldie, Oxford – Isis.
bowls: first world champion in 1966	David Bryant (Eng).
bowls: invented by	flat green bowls in its modern form began in 1848 when William Mitchell, a Glasgow solicitor, drew up the rules.
boxing: amateur weight limits	light fly – 106lb/48kg; fly – 112lb/51kg; bantam – 119lb/54kg; feather – 126lb/57kg; light – 132lb/60kg; light welter – 140lb/63.5kg; welter – 148lb/67kg; light middle – 157lb/71kg; middle – 165lb/75kg; light heavy – 179lb/81kg; heavy – 201lb/91kg; super heavy – 201lb+/91kg+.
champion at five weights	Sugar Ray Leonard.
first champion	James Figg is generally regarded as the first modern champion when he set up his school in 1719.
first East European professional	Laszlo Papp.
first fight with gloves	Gentleman Jim Corbett defeated John L Sullivan in 1892.
first million dollar gate	Jack Dempsey v Georges Carpentier in 1921.
four main governing bodies	World Boxing Association (WBA), founded 1920; World Boxing Council (WBC), founded 1963; International Boxing Federation (IBF), founded 1983; World Boxing Organization (WBO), founded 1988.
heavyweight champion longest reign	Joe Louis (1937–49).
last bareknuckle champion	John L Sullivan.
oldest and youngest world champions	light heavyweight, Archie Moore (48); light welterweight, Wilfredo Benitez (17).
professional weight limits	straw/mini-fly – 105lb/48kg; light fly/jnr fly – 108lb/49kg; fly – 112lb/51kg; super fly/jnr bantam – 115lb/52kg; bantam – 118lb/54kg; super bantam/jnr feather – 122lb/55kg; feather – 126lb/57kg; super feather/jnr light – 130lb/59kg; light – 135lb/61kg; super light/jnr welter – 140lb/64kg; welter – 147lb/67kg; super welter/jnr middle – 154lb/70kg; middle – 160lb/73kg; super middle – 168lb/76kg; light heavy – 175lb/79kg; jnr heavy/cruiser – 190lb/86kg; heavy – 190lb+/86kg+.
Queensberry Rules: first fight under	Jim Corbett beat John L Sullivan (1892).
initiated by	Jack Broughton devised first rules in 1743, but they were not codified until 1867 by 8th marquess of Queensberry.
undefeated heavyweight champion	Rocky Marciano (49 fights).
undisputed heavyweight champions	John L Sullivan (1882); James J Corbett (1892); Bob Fitzsimmons (1897); James J Jeffries (1899); Marvin Hart (1905); Tommy Burns (1906); Jack Johnson (1908); Jess Willard (1915); Jack Dempsey (1919); Gene Tunney (1926); Max Schmeling (1930); Jack Sharkey (1932); Primo Carnera (1933); Max Baer (1934); James J Braddock (1935); Joe Louis (1937); Ezzard Charles (1949); Jersey Joe Walcott (1951); Rocky Marciano (1952); Floyd Patterson (1956); Ingemar Johansson (1959); Floyd Patterson (1960); Sonny Liston (1962); Cassius Clay (1964); Joe Frazier (1970); George Foreman (1973); Muhammad Ali (1974); Leon Spinks (1978); Mike Tyson (1987).
youngest world heavyweight champion	Mike Tyson.
bullfighting: barbed sticks	banderillas.
cape	muleta (red one side and yellow the other).
term used for a pass	veronica.
terms for fighters	matador – principal fighter appointed to kill the bull; picador – horseman who pricks the bull with a banderilla to weaken it; toreador – stock name for any fighter.
croquet	four balls used; two to a team; red and yellow play against blue and black; six hoops are used.

cycling: oldest British sprint champion
Reg Harris (aged 54).

terms
honking – cycling off the saddle; spinning – turning an easy gear very quickly with no effort.

Tour de France, first non-European winner
Greg Lemond of USA in 1986.

Tour de France, five times winners
Eddie Merckx, Jacques Anquetil, Bernard Hinault.

Tour de France, six times winner
Lance Armstrong of USA (1999–2004).

darts: sponsors
Embassy sponsor the BDO World Championship while Skol sponsor the WDC Championship.

fatalities: sport with highest rate of
angling (fish rather than folk!).

fencing: caught cheating
Boris Onischenko of USSR in Modern Pentathlon (1976).

heaviest weapon
épée.

target areas
foil – body only; épée – no restriction; sabre – over waist.

technical term for guard
coquille.

weapons used by women
traditionally foil only but nowadays championships exist for sabre and épée.

frisbee: two forms of
Ultimate and Guts.

gong: banged for J Arthur Rank
Bombardier Billy Wells (1889–1967), British heavyweight boxing champion, was succeeded by Ken Richmond, the wrestling gold medalist at the 1954 Commonwealth Games.

Greyhound Grand National: triple winner
Sherry's Prince.

greyhound racing: most consecutive wins
Ballyregan Bob (32).

trap colours
red – 1; blue – 2; white – 3; black – 4; orange – 5; black and white striped – 6.

grouse shooting: season
Glorious Twelfth (August) to 10 December.

gymnastics: exercises for men
floor, horizontal bar, parallel bars, pommel horse, rings, vault (lengthwise).

exercises for women
floor, asymmetric bars, beam, vault (widthwise).

first perfect score of 10
Nadia Comaneci in 1976.

London Marathon organisers
John Disley and Chris Brasher organised first London Marathon in 1981.

martial arts: meanings
tae kwon do – way of the foot and fist; judo – gentle way; aikido – way of spirit harmony; karate – way of the empty hand; kyudo – way of the bow; kung fu – leisure time/hobby.

Olympic Games: famous competitors
Philip Noel Baker was an Olympic finalist at 1,500m in 1912 and silver medallist in 1920 before winning the Nobel Peace Prize in 1959. Noel Harrison, who took part in Skiing in 1952, is the actor son of Rex Harrison. Harry Llewellyn, who won gold medal for Equestrianism in 1952, is father of Roddy Llewellyn. Charles Simmons, who took part in Gymnastics 1952, is father of Jean Simmons. John Kelly, who won gold medal for Rowing in 1920, was father of Grace Kelly. Prince Albert of Monaco took part in bobsleigh events in 1988. Godfrey Rampling, who ran in the 4 x 400m Relay in 1936, was the father of Charlotte Rampling. Bill Nankeville who ran in the 1500m in 1948, is the father of Bobby Davro. Ioannis Theodoracopulous, who was a hurdler in 1936, was the father of Taki. Arthur Porritt, who accompanied Harold Abrahams in the 1924 Games, was father of Jonathon Porritt the Green politician.

pelota vasca (jai alai): origins
invented in Italy as 'longue paume' and introduced to France in 13th century. It is the fastest ball game in the world.

pheasant shooting: season
1 October to 1 February.

polo: pitch dimensions
polo has the largest pitch of any sport with a maximum length of 300 yards and width of 200 yards.

racketball: inventors
American racketball devised by Joe Sobek in 1949; British racketball was devised by Ian Wright in 1976.

real tennis: origins
developed from 'jeu de paume' (game of the palm) and played in Australia, England, France, Scotland and USA. First world champion in 1740 was a Frenchman named Clergé. World champion since 1994: Robert Fahey (Aus).

roller skating: first rink opened
Newport, Rhode Island, in 1866.

rowing: skimming of oar across water
feathering.

SPORT & LEISURE

rugby league: nicknames	Australia – Kangaroos; New Zealand – Kiwis; Widnes – Chemics; Warrington – Wires.
rugby union: jersey colours	Australia – gold; Barbarians – black and white hoops; England – white; France – blue; Ireland – green; New Zealand – black; Scotland – blue; Wales – red.
nicknames	Argentina – Pumas; Australia – Wallabies; New Zealand – All Blacks; South Africa – Springboks.
played both codes at same time	Martin Offiah left Wigan August 1996 to play union for Bedford and league for London Broncos.
skiing: Olympic champions who won all titles	Toni Sailer (1956) and Jean-Claude Killy (1968).
piste grading	black – difficult run; red – intermediate run; blue – easy run; green – beginners' slope.
snooker: first televised 147 maximum by	Steve Davis (1982 Lada Classic).
first to make 147 in World Championships	Cliff Thorburn (1983).
world champions at the Crucible	John Spencer (1977), Ray Reardon (1978), Terry Griffiths (1979), Cliff Thorburn (1980), Steve Davis (1981), Alex Higgins (1982), Steve Davis (1983–84), Dennis Taylor (1985), Joe Johnson (1986), Steve Davis (1987–89), Stephen Hendry (1990), John Parrott (1991), Stephen Hendry 1992–96), Ken Doherty (1997), John Higgins (1998), Stephen Hendry (1999), Mark Williams (2000), Ronnie O'Sullivan (2001), Peter Ebdon (2002), Mark Williams (2003), Ronnie O'Sullivan (2004), Shaun Murphy (2005).
softball: inventor	George Hancock invented the indoor version of baseball in 1887 in Chicago.
speedway: laps	four
2004 world champion	Jason Crump of Australia.
squash: origins	Harrow school.
world champion sixteen years running	Heather McKay Blundell of Australia.
stop on line: competitors do not pass finishing line	swimming.
substitutes: allowed while game in play	ice hockey.
suicides: famous sportsmen	Fred Archer (1857–86), champion jockey for 13 years 1874–86, shot himself aged 29. George O'Dell (1945–81), a double world champion in side-car racing, took his own life aged 35. Recent sporting suicides include the Yorkshire cricketer David Bairstow and footballer Justin Fashanu.
table tennis: ball dimensions	from 2001 season ball diameter increased to 40mm.
expedite rule	comes into play in long game and means point must be won within so many strikes or receiver is awarded the point.
ten pin bowling: maximum score in one game	300.
tennis champs: British, venue	Telford.
Vasaloppet	Swedish marathon ski race over 85km between Sälen and Mora, first run in 1922.
volleyball: former name	invented in 1895 by William Morgan of Massachusetts and called 'Mintonette'.
weightlifting: Olympic lifts	clean and jerk, snatch.
weightlifting: power lifts	bench press, dead lift, squat.
wrestling: two styles	freestyle and Greco-Roman.
yachting: famous champion	Peter Scott, son of explorer Robert Falcon Scott, won bronze medal in 1936 Olympics and became British gliding champion in 1963.
Olympic classes	Europe, Finn (solo class), 470, Laser, Mistral, Star, Tornado (catamaran), Soling (three-man crew).

Games: Miscellaneous

baccarat	gambling card game the object of which is to hold cards with values as near to nine as possible.
backgammon	dice number: 5; counters: 15 per player; points on board: 24.
bezique	played with a 64-card double piquet deck, i.e. all cards below 7, except the ace, are removed from two standard 52-card decks.

bingo calls

The origins of Bingo can be traced back to Italy in the year 1530, when a State-run lottery game Lo Giuoco del Lotto d'Italia was originated. 'Le Lotto' migrated to France in the late 1700s in a form similar to the Bingo we know today, with a playing card, tokens and numbers read aloud. Throughout the 1800s these lottery type of games spread quickly throughout Europe and many offshoots of the game were created. In 1929, a game called 'Beano' was played at a carnival near Atlanta, Georgia. A New York toy salesman named Edwin Lowe observed the game, where players exclaimed 'BEANO!' if they filled a line of numbers on their card. Lowe introduced the game to his friends and one of them mistakenly yelled 'BINGO!' in her excitement . 'Lowe's Bingo' was soon very popular and the name stuck.

1 Kelly's eye, Buttered scone, At the beginning, Little Jimmy, Nelson's column, B1 Baby of bingo
2 One little duck, Baby's done it, Doctor Who, Me and you, Little boy blue
3 Dearie me, I'm free, Debbie McGee, You and me, Goodness me, One little flea, Cup of tea
4 The one next door, On the floor, Knock at the door, B4 Crowd says 'and after'
5 Man alive, Jack's alive, Dead alive
6 Tom Mix, Tom's tricks, Chopsticks
7 Lucky seven, God's in heaven, One little crutch
8 Garden gate, Golden gate, Harry Tate, One fat lady
9 Doctor's orders
10 Downing street (UK prime minister's address), Cock and hen (rhyming), Uncle Ben (rhyming), Tony's Den (or whoever is the PM of the day)
11 Legs eleven, Legs – they're lovely, Kelly's Legs Number eleven
12 One dozen, One and two – a dozen, Monkey's cousin (rhymes with 'a dozen')
13 Unlucky for some, Devil's number, Baker's dozen
14 Valentine's day
15 Rugby team, Young and keen
16 Sweet sixteen, She's lovely, Never been kissed
17 Often been kissed, Old Ireland, Dancing queen, The age to catch 'em
18 Key of the door, Now you can vote, Coming of age
19 Goodbye teens
20 One score, Getting plenty, Blind 20
21 Royal salute, Key of the door
22 Two little ducks (suggesting the necks of two swans), Ducks on a pond, Dinky doo, All the twos
23 A duck and a flea, Thee and me, The Lord's My Shepherd (based on 23rd Psalm)
24 Two dozen, Hours from Tulsa
25 Duck and dive
26 Bed and breakfast (traditional price was 2 shillings 6 pence), Half a crown (equivalent to 2 shillings 6 pence), Pick and mix
27 Little duck with a crutch, Gateway to heaven
28 In a state, The old brags, Over weight
29 You're doing fine, Rise and shine
30 Burlington Bertie, Dirty Gertie, Speed limit (in built-up area, UK), Blind 30, Flirty thirty
31 Get up and run
32 Buckle my shoe
33 Dirty knees, All the feathers, All the threes, Gertie Lee, Two little fleas, Sherwood forest (all the trees)
34 Ask for more
35 Jump and jive
36 Three dozen
37 A flea in heaven, More than eleven
38 Christmas cake
39 Those famous steps, All the steps
40 Two score, Life begins at, Blind 40, Naughty 40
41 Life's begun, Time for fun
42 That famous street in Manhattan, Winnie the Poo
43 Down on your knees
44 Droopy drawers, All the fours, Open two doors
45 Halfway house, Halfway there
46 Up to tricks
47 Four and seven
48 Four dozen
49 PC (Police Constable), Copper, Nick nick, Rise and shine
50 Bulls eye, Bung hole, Blind 50, Half a century
51 I love my mum, Tweak of the thumb, The Highland Div[ision]
52 Weeks in a year, The Lowland Div[ision], Danny La Rue
53 Stuck in the tree, The Welsh Div[ision]
54 Clean the floor

S
P
O
R
T
&
L
E
I
S
U
R
E

55 Snakes alive, All the fives
56 Was she worth it?
57 Heinz varieties, All the beans (Heinz 57 varieties of canned beans)
58 Make them wait, Choo choo Thomas
59 Brighton line
60 Three score, Blind 60, Five dozen
61 Bakers bun
62 Tickety boo, Turn of the screw
63 Tickle me
64 The Beatles number, Red raw
65 Old age pension, Stop work (retirement age)
66 Clickety click, All the sixes
67 Made in heaven, Argumentative number
68 Saving grace
69 The same both ways, your place or mine?, Any way up, Either way up, Any way round, Meal for two
70 Three score and ten, Blind 70
71 Bang on the drum
72 A crutch and a duck, Six dozen, Par for the course (golf)
73 Crutch with a flea, Queen B
74 Candy store
75 Strive and strive
76 Trombones
77 Sunset strip, All the sevens, Two little crutches
78 Heaven's gate
79 One more time
80 Gandhi's breakfast, Blind 80, Eight and blank
81 Fat lady and a little wee, Stop and run
82 Fat lady with a duck, Straight on through
83 Fat lady with a flea, Time for tea, Ethel's Ear
84 Seven dozen
85 Staying alive
86 Between the sticks
87 Fat lady with a crutch, Torquay in Devon
88 Two fat ladies, Wobbly wobbly, All the eights
89 Nearly there, All but one
90 Top of the shop, Top of the house, Blind 90, As far as we go, End of the line

canasta   played with two standard decks of 52 cards, plus four jokers, totalling 108 cards. Hands are played until one partnership reaches 5000 points.

Canasta was developed in Uruguay and passed via Argentina to the USA in 1949.

card games: names   beggar my neighbour, boston, briscola, calabrasella, donkey, écarté, imperial, klaberjass, loo, michigan, napoleon, oh hell, old maid, Persian pasha, Pope Joan, skat, vint.

cards: Queen depicted   Elizabeth of York (wife of Henry VII).

charades   parlour game whereby one person mimes and the other players guess the title.

chess: right-hand corner   the right-hand corner square as white sets up is white (important to remember).

chess: world champions   Wilhelm Steinitz (Austria) (1886–94), Emanuel Lasker (Ger) (1894–1921), Jose Capablanca (Cuba) (1921–27), Alexander Alekhine (USSR) (1927–35), Max Euwe (Neth) (1935–37), Alexander Alekhine (USSR) (1937–46), Mikhail Botvinnik (USSR) (1948–57), Vasily Smyslov (USSR) (1957–58), Mikhail Botvinnik (USSR) (1958–60), Mikhail Tal (USSR) (1960–61), Mikhail Botvinnik (USSR) (1961–63), Tigran Petrosian (USSR) (1963–69), Boris Spassky (USSR) (1969–72), Bobby Fischer (US) (1972–75), Anatoly Karpov (USSR) (1975–1985), Garry Kasparov (USSR/Rus) (1985–2000), Vladimir Kramnik (Rus) (2000–present).

chicane   bridge hand without trumps or without cards of any one suit.

Cluedo: characters   Colonel Mustard, Professor Plum, Reverend Green, Mrs Peacock, Miss Scarlet, Mrs White, Dr Black (victim).

      weapons   knife, revolver, spanner, lead pipe, rope, and candlestick.

crambo   game in which a player gives a word or verse line to which each of the others must find a rhyme.

cribbage   developed by poet, Sir John Suckling, in the early 17th century and usually played to 121 points.

dominoes   28 tiles in a set with a total of 168 pips (seven doubles).

El Gordo   Spanish National Lottery (largest in the world).

euchre   played with a 32-card deck (cards below 7 are removed).

fan-tan   chinese gambling game in which players try to guess the remainder after the banker has divided a number of hidden objects into four groups.

faro	gambling card game in which bets are placed on the order of appearance of the cards. This is the game in which Count Rostov lost a fortune in Tolstoy's *War and Peace*.
frisbee: original name	Pluto Platter.
go	Japanese board game using terms: false eyes, eyes and armies. Played on a grid of 19 horizontal and 19 vertical lines forming 361interactions.
jai alai	South American version of pelota played with large curved wicker baskets.
mah jongg	Chinese game using terms: pung, kong and chow. 144 tiles are usually used (36 bamboos, 36 circles, 36 characters, 12 honours, 16 winds, 8 flowers and seasons). The name was coined and copyrighted by Joseph P Babcock.
Monopoly: inventor	Charles Darrow, a heating engineer.
original properties	brown: Old Kent Road (cheapest), Whitechapel; light blue: Angel Islington (pub), Euston Road, Pentonville Road; mauve: Pall Mall, Whitehall, Northumberland Avenue; orange: Bow Street, Marlborough Street, Vine Street (statistically the most 'landed on' square); red: Strand, Fleet Street, Trafalgar Square; yellow: Leicester Square, Coventry Street, Piccadilly; green: Regent Street, Oxford Street, Bond Street; dark blue: Park Lane, Mayfair (most expensive).
stations	King's Cross, Marylebone, Fenchurch Street, Liverpool Street.
corners	Go, Just Visiting, Free Parking, Go to Jail.
USA version	Atlantic City, New Jersey, is used, with 'Boardwalk' the most expensive property.
ombre	card game for three players that was popular throughout Europe in the 17th and 18th centuries.
pall-mall	game in which a ball is driven by a mallet along an alley and through an iron ring.
patzer	poor player at chess.
pelota	Basque and Spanish game played in a walled court with a ball and 'basket-like' rackets attached to the hand. Pelota is thought to be the fastest of ball sports outside golf.
pinochle	pronounced 'pea knuckle', and played with 48 cards (two decks stripped of cards below 9). Within the game, pinochle stands for the Jack of Diamonds and Queen of Spades. The 9 of trumps is called the dix. Winner is player who first reaches 1000 points.
piquet	given the name by Charles I of England to honour Henrietta Maria, his French wife. Piquet deck is 32 cards with all cards below 7 stripped from deck.
poker: best hand	royal flush (ace to 10 in the same suit).
roulette: numbers	European wheels have 37 divisions (0–36), American wheels have 38 including a double zero.
Scrabble: inventor	James Brunot in 1949, first used the name scrabble.
made by	Spear Games.
tile values	highest Q and Z (10), J and X (8), K (5), Y H V W F (4), P M C B (3), D G (2), others 1 point except blank (0).
original name	criss cross (designed by Alfred M Butts, an architect, in 1931).
vigoro	Australian ball game combining elements of cricket and baseball.
Yarborough	whist or bridge hand with no card above a 9. Named afer the earl of Yarborough who died in 1897, and was said to have bet against its occurrence.
tarot	originally 22 cards (the Major Arcana: see below). The Venetians added 56 cards (the Minor Arcana) split into 4 suits: the clubs, symbolising money matters; cups (hearts), symbolising love and friendship; swords (spades), symbolising ill fortune; denari (diamonds), symbolising business and travel.

0	Fool/Joker	11	Fortitude / Strength
1	Magician / Mountebank	12	Hanged Man
2	High Priestess / Popess	13	Death
3	Empress	14	Temperance
4	Emperor	15	Devil
5	Hierophant / Pope	16	Tower
6	Lovers	17	Star
7	Chariot	18	Moon
8	Justice	19	Sun
9	Hermit	20	Judgement
10	Wheel of Fortune	21	World / Universe

NB In some versions of the Major Arcana nos. 8 and 11 are reversed.

SPORT & LEISURE

Stamps: First Issues

Country	Year	Country	Year	Country	Year
Aden	1937	Georgia	1919	Northern Rhodesia	1925
Afghanistan	1870	Germany	1872	Norway	1855
Andorra	1928	Ghana	1875	Orange Free State	1868
Antigua and Barbuda	1862	Gibraltar	1886	Pakistan	1947
Argentina	1858	Great Britain	1840	Palestine	1918
Armenia	1920	Greece	1861	Panama	1878
Ascension	1922	Greenland	1938	Papua	1901
Australia	1902	Grenada	1861	Papua New Guinea	1952
Austria	1850	Guatemala	1871	Paraguay	1870
Azerbaijan	1919	Guyana	1850	Philippines	1854
Bahamas	1859	Haiti	1881	Pitcairn Isles	1940
Bahrain	1933	Hawaii	1851	Portugal	1853
Bangladesh	1971	Heligoland	1867	Queensland	1860
Barbados	1852	Honduras	1866	Rhodesia	1890
Barbuda	1922	Hong Kong	1862	Rhodesia and Nyasaland	1954
Belgium	1849	Hungary	1871	Russia	1857
Belize	1866	Iceland	1873	Sabah (North Borneo)	1883
Bermuda	1865	India	1852	San Marino	1877
Bolivia	1866	Ionian Isles	1859	Sarawak	1869
Bosnia-Hercegovina	1879	Ireland	1922	Saudi Arabia	1916
Botswana	1886	Isle of Man	1973	Serbia	1866
Brazil	1843	Israel	1948	Seychelles	1890
British Indian Ocean	1968	Italy	1862	Sierra Leone	1860
Territory		Jamaica	1860	South Africa	1910
British Solomon Isles	1907	Japan	1871	South Australia	1855
Brunei	1906	Jordan	1920	Southern Rhodesia	1924
Bulgaria	1879	Kenya	1890	South West Africa	1923
Burma/Myanmar	1937	Kiribati	1911	South Yemen	1963
Canada	1851	Latvia	1918	Spain	1850
Cape of Good Hope	1853	Lebanon	1924	Sri Lanka	1857
Cayman Islands	1900	Leeward Isles	1890	St Helena	1856
Channel Isles	1941	Liberia	1860	Sudan	1897
Chile	1853	Liechtenstein	1912	Swaziland	1889
China	1878	Lithuania	1918	Sweden	1855
Cook Isles	1892	Luxembourg	1852	Switzerland	1843
Crete	1900	Malawi	1891	Syria	1919
Cuba	1855	Malaysia	1867	Tasmania	1853
Cyprus	1880	Maldives	1906	Thailand	1883
Czech Republic	1918	Malta	1860	Tokelau Isles	1948
Danish West Indies	1855	Mauritius	1847	Tonga	1886
Danzig	1920	Mexico	1856	Transvaal	1869
Denmark	1851	Monaco	1885	Turkey	1863
Dominica	1874	Mongolia	1924	Uganda	1895
Dominican Republc	1865	Montserrat	1876	Uruguay	1856
Ecuador	1865	Natal	1857	USA	1845
Egypt	1866	Nauru	1915	USA: Confederacy	1861
El Salvador	1867	Nepal	1881	Victoria	1850
Estonia	1918	Netherlands	1852	Western Australia	1854
Ethiopia	1894	New Guinea	1914	Yemen	1926
Faroe Isles	1940	New South Wales	1850	Zambia	1964
Fiji	1870	New Zealand	1855	Zanzibar	1895
Finland	1856	Nicaragua	1862	Zimbabwe	1979
France	1849	Nigeria	1914	Zululand	1888
Gambia	1869	Norfolk Isles	1947		

Programmes

A For Andromeda Julie Christie (Christine/A for Andromeda).

Absolutely Fabulous Jennifer Saunders (Edina Monsoon), Joanna Lumley (Patsy Stone), Julia Sawalha (Saffron), Jane Horrocks (Bubble), June Whitfield (Mother). Shopped at Harvey Nichols and based on Lynne Franks.

Adam Adamant Lives! Gerald Harper (Adam Llewellyn De Vere Adamant), Juliet Harmer (Georgina Jones), Peter Ducrow (the Face). Entombed from 1902 to 1966.

Addams Family, The Carolyn Jones (Morticia), John Astin (Gomez), Jackie Coogan (Uncle Fester Frump), Ted Cassidy (Lurch and Thing), Blossom Rock, sister of Jeanette McDonald (Grandmama). Lived in Cemetery Ridge with assortment of pets including octopus called Aristotle, black widow spider called Homer, man-eating African strangler called Cleopatra.

Adventures of Black Beauty, The Judi Bowker (Victoria Gordon), William Lucas (Dr James Gordon).

Adventures of Robin Hood, The Richard Greene (Robin), Bernadette O'Farrell and Patricia Driscoll (Maid Marian), Archie Duncan and Rufus Cruikshank (Little John), Alexander Gauge (Friar Tuck), Alan Wheatley (Sheriff of Nottingham). Theme sung by Dick James.

Adventures of Tugboat Annie, The Minerva Urecal (Tugboat Annie Brennan, Capt. of *Narcissus*), Walter Sande (Capt. Bullwinkle).

Adventures of William Tell, The Conrad Phillips (Tell), Jennifer Jayne (Hedda), Willoughby Goddard (Landburgher Gessler).

After Henry Prunella Scales (Sarah France), Joan Sanderson (Eleanor Prescott). Originally a BBC radio series, it was transferred to television with the same two stars.

Agony Maureen Lipman (Jane Lucas), Simon Williams (Laurence Lucas). Magazine: *Person Series*. Created by Anna Raeburn and Len Richmond.

Airwolf Jan-Michael Vincent (Stringfellow Hawke, a keen cellist), Ernest Borgnine (Dominic Santini).

Alf Alien Life Form (Michu Meszaros wore furry suit and Paul Fusco was the voice of ALF), Max Wright (Willie Tanner). Home planet: Melmac. Neighbours: Ochmoneks. Tanners' pet cat was called Lucky.

Alias Smith and Jones Pete Duel (Hannibal Heyes/Joshua Smith), Ben Murphy (Jed 'Kid' Curry/Thaddeus Jones). Roger Davis was narrator of first series but took over from Pete Duel after he committed suicide and Ralph Story took over voice-overs.

All Creatures Great and Small Christopher Timothy (James Herriot), Robert Hardy (Siegfried Farnon), Tricki Woo (Pekinese), Peter Davison (Tristan Farnon), Carol Drinkwater and Lynda Bellingham (Helen Alderson/Herriot).

All Gas and Gaiters Derek Nimmo (Rev. Mervyn Noote), William Mervyn (Bishop), Robertson Hare (Archdeacon).

All in the Family Carroll O'Connor (Archie Bunker), Jean Stapleton (Edith 'Dingbat' Bunker), Rob Reiner (Mike 'Meathead' Stivic the Pole), Sally Struthers (Gloria). America's answer to Alf Garnett.

All Our Yesterdays Presenters: James Cameron, Brian Inglis, Bernard Braden.

'Allo 'Allo Gorden Kaye (René Artois), Carmen Silvera (Edith), Vicki Michelle (Yvette), Guy Siner (Lt Gruber), Nicholas Frankou (Flying Officer Carstairs), John D. Collins (Flying Officer Fairfax), Kirsten Cooke (Michelle), Richard Gibson (Herr Flick), Richard Marner (Colonel Von Strohm), Kim Hartman (Helga Geerhart). Created by Jeremy Lloyd and David Croft.

Ally McBeal Calista Flockhart (Ally McBeal), Gil Bellows (Billy Thomas), Courtney Thorne-Smith (Georgia Thomas), Greg Germann (Richard Fish), Peter MacNicol (John Cage), Lucy Liu (Ling Woo).

And Mother Makes Three Wendy Craig (Sally Harrison/Redway). Follow-up series called *And Mother Makes Five*.

Andromeda Breakthrough, The Susan Hampshire (Christine/A for Andromeda). Follow-on series from *A For Andromeda*.

Andy Pandy Created by Freda Lingstrom and Maria Bird. Friends: Teddy and Looby Loo.

Angels Fiona Fullerton (Patricia Rutherford), Julie Dawn Cole (Jo Longhurst), Shirley Cheriton (Kathy Betts), Pauline Quirke (Vicky Smith). Hospital: St Angela's, Battersea.

Animal Hospital Rolf Harris, Shauna Lowry (Hamden Veterinary Hospital in Aylesbury).

Animal Magic Presenters: Johnny Morris, Terry Nutkins.

Antiques Roadshow Presenters: Angela Rippon, Bruce Parker, Arthur Negus, Hugh Scully, Michael Aspel. See *Going For A Song*.

Aquarius Presenters: Humphrey Burton, Russell Harty, Peter Hall.

Are You Being Served? John Inman (Mr Humphries), Mollie Sugden (Mrs Slocombe), Arthur Brough (Mr Grainger), Frank Thornton (Capt. Peacock), Nicholas Smith (Mr Rumbold), Arthur English (Mr Harman), Wendy Richard (Miss Brahms), Mike Berry (Mr Spooner), Trevor Bannister (Mr Lucas). Sequel: *Grace and Favour*.

Army Game, The William Hartnell (CSM Bullimore), Bill Fraser (Sgt Claude Snudge), Michael Medwin (Corporal Springer), Harry Fowler (Corporal 'Flogger' Hoskins), Charles Hawtrey (Pte 'Prof' Hatchett), Bernard Bresslaw (Pte 'Popeye' Popplewell), Alfie Bass (Pte 'Excused Boots' Bisley), Norman Rossington (Pte 'Cupcake' Cook), Frank Williams (Capt. Pocket), Mario Fabrizi (Lance Corporal Ernest 'Moosh' Merryweather), Dick Emery (Pte 'Chubby' Catchpole). Base: Hut 29 of the Surplus Ordnance Depot at Nether Hopping, Staffordshire.

Around the World in 80 Days Michael Palin's reconstruction of Phileas Fogg's journey.

Arthur of the Britons Oliver Tobias (Arthur), Rupert Davies (Cerdig), Jack Watson (Llud), Brian Blessed (Mark of Cornwall), Michael Gothard (Kai).

Ask the Family Brain-teasing quiz between families of four, usually mum and dad and two children.

Robert Robinson was host throughout its original run, 1967–84, Alan Titchmarsh hosted a one-off series on UK Gold in 1999 and the series was revived by the BBC in April 2005 with children's presenters Dick and Dom as hosts.

A-Team, The George Peppard (Col. John 'Hannibal' Smith), Lawrence 'Mr T' Tureaud (Sgt Bosco 'BA' Baracus), Dwight Schultz (Capt. H M 'Howling Mad' Murdock), Dirk Benedict (Lt Templeton 'Faceman' Peck), Melinda Culea (Amy Amanda Allen alias Triple A). 'BA' stood for Bad Attitude.

At Last the 1948 Show John Cleese, Tim Brooke-Taylor, Graham Chapman, Marty Feldman, Aimi Macdonald.

Auf Wiedersehen Pet Tim Healy (Denis Patterson), Jimmy Nail ('Oz' Osbourne), Kevin Whately (Neville Hope), Gary Holton (Wayne), Pat Roach (Bomber), Timothy Spall (Barry Taylor), Christopher Fairbank (Moxey). Gary Holton died during filming of the follow-up series in Spain. Pat Roach died after filming series four and did not appear in the Christmas special in 2004.

Avengers, The Patrick MacNee (John Steed), Honor Blackman (Cathy Gale), Diana Rigg (Emma Peel), Linda Thorson (Tara King), Patrick Newell (Mother). Steed lived at 3 Duchess Mews, London. Originally called *Police Surgeon*, starring Ian Hendry as Dr David Keel.

A J Wentworth, BA Arthur Lowe played the absent-minded teacher.

Bagpuss Bagpuss owned by Emily. Narrator and writer: Oliver Postgate.

Ballykissangel Niall Tobin (Father MacAnally), Gary Whelan (Brendan Kearney), Peter Caffrey (Padraig Kelly), Deirdre Donnelly (Siobhan Mehigan), Birdy Sweeney (Eamon), Victoria Smurfit (Orla), Don Wycherley (Father Aidan), Aine Ni Mhuiri (Kathleen), Joe Savino (Liam), Tina Kellegher (Niamh Egan), Lorcan Cranitch (Sean Dillon), Frankie McCafferty (Donal). Original series starred Stephen Tompkinson (Father Clifford) and Dervla Kirwan (Assumpta Fitzgerald) and the late Tony Doyle.

Banacek George Peppard (Thomas Banacek).

Banana Splits, The Voices: Fleegle (Paul Winchell), Bingo (Daws Butler), Drooper (Allan Melvin), Snorky (Don Messick).

Batman Adam West (Batman/Bruce Wayne), Burt Ward (Robin/Dick Grayson), Frank Gorshin and John Astin (Riddler), Julie Newmar, Eartha Kitt, Lee Meriwether (Catwoman), Vincent Price (Egg Head), Tallulah Bankhead (Black Widow), Burgess Meredith (Penguin), Carolyn Jones (Queen of Diamonds), Liberace (Chandel), Cliff Robertson (Shame), Van Johnson (Minstrel), Shelley Winters (Ma Parker), Ida Lupino (Dr Cassandra), Otto Preminger, George Sanders and Eli Wallach (Mr Freeze), Cesar Romero (Joker), Yvonne Craig (Batgirl alias Barbara Gordon).

Battlestar Galactica Lorne Greene (Commander Adama), Dirk Benedict (Lt Starbuck).

Baywatch David Hasselhoff (Lt Mitch Bucannon), Pamela Denise Anderson (C J Parker), Erika Eleniak (Shauni McLain), Nicole Eggert (Summer Quinn), Yasmin Bleeth (Caroline Holden). Story of Los Angeles County Lifeguards working on Malibu Beach. Spin-off from 1989 TV film *Panic at Malibu Beach*, starring David Hasselhoff.

Beadle's About Popular hidden-camera show starring Jeremy Beadle and still shown regularly on Challenge TV. Little-known fact: Jeremy is a trivia buff par excellence and entered the 2002 British Quiz Championships, placing a very respectable 30th.

Beauty and the Beast Vincent (Ron Perlman), Assistant DA Catherine Chandler (Linda Hamilton), Roy Dotrice (Father), Stephen McHattie (Gabriel).

Beiderbecke Affair James Bolam (Trevor Chaplin), Barbara Flynn (Jill Swinburne). The Beiderbecke of the title was Bix Beiderbecke the jazz great, whose music was played by Kenny Baker. Sequels were *The Beiderbecke Tapes* and *The Beiderbecke Connection*.

Ben Casey Vince Edwards (Ben), Sam Jaffe (Dr David Zorba), Ben Piazza (Dr Mike Rogers). Hospital: County General. Produced by Bing Crosby Productions, which discovered Vince Edwards.

Bergerac John Nettles (Det. Sgt Jim Bergerac), Terence Alexander (Charlie Hungerford), Lisa Goddard (Philippa Vale). Story of an alcoholic policeman in Jersey.

Beverly Hillbillies Buddy Ebsen (Jed Clampett), Irene Ryan (Daisy Moses alias Granny), Donna Douglas (Elly May), Max Baer Jnr (Jethro Bodine and Jethrene Bodine), Nancy Kulp (Jane Hathaway), Sharon Tate (Janet Trego).

Beverly Hills 90210 Shannen Doherty (Brenda Walsh), Jason Priestley (Brandon Walsh). Title is a Zip code.

Bewitched Elizabeth Montgomery (Samantha Stephens), Dick York and Dick Sargent (Darren), Agnes Moorehead (Endora), Marion Lorne (Aunt Clara), David White (Larry Tate).

Big Big Talent Show, The Jonathan Ross hosts the star-spotting talent show.

Big Break Snooker-based game show hosted by Jim Davidson and John Virgo.

Big Brother Launched in July 2000. The original ten housemates were Anna, Andrew, Caroline, Craig, Darren, Melanie, Nick, Nichola, Sada and Thomas. Nick Bateman was evicted for cheating and replaced by Claire Strutton. The three finalists were Craig Philips, Anna Nolan and Darren Ramsey. The winner of the £70,000 first prize was Craig. Marjorie was the pet chicken, Juanita the toy baby, and Davina McCall the presenter. The 2004 winner was Nadia Almada.

Birds of a Feather Pauline Quirke (Sharon Theodopolopoudos), Linda Robson (Tracey Stubbs), Lesley Joseph (Dorien Green), Peter Polycarpou and David Cardy (Chris Theodopolopoudos). Series created by Laurence Marks and Maurice Gran.

Blackadder Various series written by Rowan Atkinson, Richard Curtis and Ben Elton. Characters included Baldrick (Tony Robinson), Queen Elizabeth I (Miranda Richardson), Melchett (Stephen Fry), Captain Darling/Percy (Tim McInnerny).

Blake's 7 Gareth Thomas (Blake), Paul Darrow (Kerr Avon), Sally Knyvette (Jenna Stannis), Michael Keating (Vila Restal), Jan Chappell (Cally from Auron), Josette Simon (Dayna Mellanby), David Jackson (Gan Olag), Steven Pacey (Capt. Del Tarrant), Peter Tuddenham (voice of Zen and Orac), Glynis Barber (Soolin), Jacqueline Pearce (Servalan). Spacecraft: Liberator and Scorpio Penal Colony, Cygnus Alpha. Dictatorship name: The Federation. Creator: Terry Nation. Gan Olag was implanted with a 'Brain Limiter' to stop him killing.

Blooming Marvellous Sarah Lancashire (Liz), Clive Mantle (Jack).

Blott on the Landscape David Suchet (Blott), George Cole (Sir Giles Lynchwood MP), Simon Cadell (Dundridge). Adaption by Malcolm Bradbury of Tom Sharpe's black comic novel. Filmed at Stanage Park, near Ludlow.

Blue Peter Original presenters in 1958: Leila Williams and Christopher Trace. Other presenters include Valerie Singleton, Peter Purves, John Noakes, Lesley Judd, Simon Groom, Sarah Greene, Peter Duncan, Janet Ellis, Michael Sundin, Anthea Turner, Diane-Louise Jordan, Caron Keating, John Leslie, Mark Curry, Yvette Fielding, Tim Vincent, Romana D'Annunzio, Richard Bacon, Katy Hill, Konnie Huq, Simon Thomas, Matt Baker, Zoe Salmon and Liz Barker.

Bonanza Lorne Greene (Ben Cartwright), Michael Landon (Little Joe Cartwright), Dan Blocker (Eric 'Hoss' Cartwright, Norwegian for good luck), Pernell Roberts (Adam), Victor Sen Yung (Hop Sing), Ray Teal (Sheriff Ray Coffee), David Canary (Mr 'Candy' Canaday), Tim Matheson (Griff King). The three sons had different mothers.

Boon Michael Elphick (Ken Boon), Neil Morrissey (Rocky Cassidy).

Boss Cat Cartoon characters include: Benny the Ball, Choo Choo, Spook, The Brain, Fancy-Fancy, Officer Dibble. Series called *Top Cat* outside UK.

Bottom Rik Mayall (Richie Richard), Adrian Edmondson (Eddie Hitler).

Bouquet of Barbed Wire Frank Finlay (Peter Manson), Sheila Allen (Cassie), Susan Penhaligon (Prue), James Aubrey (Gavin Sorenson).

Boyd QC Michael Denison.

Boys from the Blackstuff Bernard Hill (Yosser Hughes), Michael Angelis (Chrissie Todd), Julie Walters (Angie Todd). Written by Alan Bleasdale. Famous catchphrase: Gi's a job.

Boys from the Bush Tim Healy (Reg Toomer), Chris Haywood (Dennis Tontine).

Brains Trust, The Chairmen: Hugh Ross Willliams, Michael Flanders.

Branded Chuck Connors (Jason McCord), only survivor of Indian massacre at the Battle of Bitter Creek in Wyoming and thought therefore to be a coward. Opening court martial scene is memorable.

Brass Timothy West (Bradley Hardacre), Caroline Blakiston (Patience), Geoffrey Hinsliff and Geoffrey Hutchings (George Fairchild). Set in Utterley.

Bread Peter Howitt and Graham Bickley (Joey Boswell), Jean Boht (Nellie), Ronald Forfar (Freddie), Victor McGuire (Jack), Gilly Coman and Melanie Hill (Aveline), Jonathan Morris (Adrian), Nick Conway (Billy), Rita Tushingham (Celia Higgins). Series created by Carla Lane.

Brideshead Revisited Anthony Andrews (Lord Sebastian Flyte), Jeremy Irons (Charles Ryder), Diana Quick (Lady Julia Flyte), Laurence Olivier (Lord Marchmain), John Gielgud (Edward Ryder), Claire Bloom (Lady Ryder).

Brittas Empire, The Chris Barrie (Gordon), Pippa Heywood (Helen), Julia St John (Laura Lancing). Leisure centre: Whitbury Newtown Leisure Centre.

Brothers, The Jean Anderson (Mary Hammond), Glyn Owen and Patrick O'Connell (Edward Hammond), Gabrielle Drake (Jill Hammond), Colin Baker (Paul Merroney), Liza Goddard (April Merroney), Kate O' Mara (Jane Maxwell). Type of business: haulage.

Brush Strokes Karl Howman (Jacko), Mike Walling (Eric), Nicky Croydon (Jean), Howard Lew Lewis (Elmo Putney), Gary Waldhorn (Lionel Bainbridge).

Buck Rogers in the 25th Century Gil Gerard (Buck), Felix Silla (Twiki: voiced by Mel Blanc, Bob Elyea), Henry Silva and Michael Ansara (Kane), Wilfred Hyde-White (Dr Goodfellow), Pamela Hensley (Princess Ardala). Year 2491. Space capsule: Ranger 3, launched in 1987. City: New Chicago. Rivals: Draconians.

Budgie Adam Faith (Budgie Bird), Iain Cuthbertson (Charlie Endell), Lynn Dalby (Hazel), Georgina Hale (Jean Bird), John Rhys-Davies (Laughing Spam Fritter), Rio Fanning (Grogan). Writers: Keith Waterhouse and Willis Hall.

Buffy the Vampire Slayer Sarah Michelle Gellar (Buffy Summers), Alyson Hannigan (Willow Rosenberg), Nicholas Brendon (Xander Harris), Anthony Head (Rupert Giles), Emma Caulfield (Anya), Seth Green (Oz), Marc Blucas (Riley Finn), David Boreanaz (Angel), Charisma Carpenter (Cordelia), James Marsters (Spike).

Bulman Don Henderson (George Bulman). Character first appeared in *The XYY Man* and then in *Strangers*. His quirky nature included his wearing of fingerless gloves, constant use of an inhaler and carrying of a plastic bag whose contents we rarely saw.

Busman's Holiday Presenters: Julian Pettifer, Sarah Kennedy, Elton Welsby.

Butterflies Wendy Craig (Ria Parkinson), Geoffrey Palmer (Ben Parkinson, a dentist), Andrew Hall (Russell Parkinson), Nicholas Lyndhurst (Adam Parkinson). Series created by Carla Lane.

By the Sword Divided Sharon Mughan (Anne Lacey/Fletcher), Julian Glover (Sir Martin Lacey), Tim Bentinck (Sir Thomas Lacey). Plot: a family is torn apart by the English Civil War.

Cagney and Lacey Tyne Daly (Mary Beth Lacey), Meg Foster and Sharon Gless (Christine Cagney).

Call My Bluff Presenters: Robert Robinson, Bob Holness.

Callan Edward Woodward (Callan), Russell Hunter (Lonely), Ronald Radd, Michael Goodliffe, Derek Bond, William Squire (Hunter), Anthony Valentine (Toby Meres), Patrick Mower (Cross). Series started as an Armchair Theatre production, *A Magnum For Schneider*, with Peter Bowles playing Toby Meres.

Camberwick Green Took over Monday *Watch with Mother* slot from 'Picture Box'. Characters included Capt. Snort, Sgt Major Grout, Windy Miller of Colley's Mill, Mickey Murphy the baker, Dr Mopp, Thomas Tripp the milkman, Mrs Dingle the postmistress, Mrs Honeyman, PC McGarry (No. 452).

Campion Peter Davison (Albert Campion), Brian Glover (Magersfontein Lugg, Campion's manservant).

Candid Camera Presenters: Bob Monkhouse, Jonathan Routh, Peter Dulay.

Captain Pugwash Characters included Capt. Horatio Pugwash (Skipper of the *Black Pig*), Able Seamen Barnabas and Willy, Master Mate (occasionally referred to as Master Bate), Tom and Cutthroat Jake. Theme music 'The Hornblower', performed by Tommy Edmondson. Narrator: Peter Hawkins.

Captain Scarlet and the Mysterons Voices: Francis Matthews (Paul Metcalfe/Capt. Scarlet), Donald Gray (Charles Gray/Col. White), Ed Bishop (Adam Svenson/Capt. Blue), Paul Maxwell (Bradley Holden/Capt. Grey), Sylvia Anderson (Magnolia Jones/Melody Angel), Liz Morgan (Juliette

T
E
L
E
V
I
S
I
O
N

Pointon/Destiny Angel), Janna Hill (Karen Wainwright/Symphony Angel), Liz Morgan (Diane Sims/Rhapsody Angel), Lian-Shin (Chan Kwan/Harmony Angel), Donald Gray (Conrad Turner/Capt. Black), Charles Tingwell (Edward Wilkie/Dr Fawn), Gary Files (Patrick Donaghue/Capt. Magenta), Jeremy Wilkin (Richard Frazier/Capt. Ochre), Cy Grant (Seymour Griffiths/Lt Green), Paul Maxwell (World President). Year: 2068. Spectrum base: Cloudbase Angel. Interceptor aircraft codeword: SIG Spectrum is Green.

Casey Jones   Alan Hale Jnr (John Luther 'Casey' Jones). Worked for Illinois Central Railroad. Engine name: Cannonball Express. His faithful dog was called Cinders.

Cathy Come Home   Carol White (Cathy Ward), Ray Brooks (Reg Ward). Written by Jeremy Sandford, directed by Ken Loach. This drama brought Shelter, a campaign for the homeless, to the awareness of many.

Catweazle   Geoffrey Bayldon (Catweazle), Robin Davis (Carrot Bennett). Story of an 11th-century wizard stranded in the 20th century.

Celeb   Harry Enfield (Gary), Amanda Holden (Debs), Leo Bill (Troy), Rupert Vansittart (Johnson). Sit-com set in the home of a rock superstar. Based on a cartoon in *Private Eye* magazine.

Champions   Stuart Damon (Craig Stirling), William Gaunt (Richard Barrett), Alexandra Bastedo (Sharon McCready). Worked for Nemesis, based in Geneva.

Changing Rooms   Hosted by Carol Smillie. Designers include Graham Wynne and Linda Barker. DIY expert: Andy Kane.

Charlie's Angels   Kate Jackson (Sabrina Duncan), Farrah Fawcett-Majors (Jill Munroe), Jaclyn Smith (Kelly Garrett), Cheryl Ladd (Kris Munroe), Shelley Hack (Tiffany Welles), Tanya Roberts (Julie Rogers). Voice of Charlie Townshend: John Forsythe.

Cheers   Ted Danson (Sam Malone), Shelley Long (Diane Chambers), Rhea Perlman (Carla Tortelli/Le Bec), Georg Wendt (Norm the accountant), John Ratzenberger (Cliff the mailman), Kelsey Grammer (Frasier Crane the psychiatrist), Woody Harrelson (Woody), Kirstie Alley (Rebecca Howe).

Chef   Lenny Henry (Gareth Blackstock), Caroline Lee Johnson (Janice), Roger Griffiths (Everton). Chef of Le Château Anglais in the Oxfordshire Cotswolds.

Cheyenne   Clint Walker (Cheyenne Bodie). Replaced for short time by Ty Hardin as Bronco Lane, who eventually gained his own series.

Chigley   Described as a hamlet near Camberwick Green, Trumptonshire. Characters included Mr Clutterbuck the Builder, Chipppy Minton the Carpenter, Lord Belborough, Mr Cresswell the owner of the biscuit factory, Harry Farthing the Potter, Mr Brackett the Butler.

Chinese Detective, The   David Yip (Det. Sgt Johnny Ho).

Chips   Erik Estrada (Francis 'Ponch' Poncherello), Larry Wilcox (Jonathan Baker). Story of two Los Angeles police motorcyclists working for the California Highway Patrol (Chips).

Circus Boy   Notable for the casting of Mickey Braddock (formerly and latterly Dolenz) as Corky.

Cisco Kid, The   Duncan Renaldo (Cisco), Leo Carrillo (Pancho). Cisco's horse: Diablo. Pancho's horse: Loco. Pancho was expert with a whip. Based on stories by O'Henry.

Citizen James   Sid James (Sidney Balmoral James), Bill Kerr (William 'Bill' Kerr), Liz Fraser (Liz Fraser).

Citizen Smith   Robert Lindsay (Walter Henry 'Wolfie' Smith), Mike Grady (Ken), Tony Millan (Tucker), Cheryl Hall (Shirley), Peter Vaughan and Tony Steedman (Charlie Johnson). Leader of the Tooting Popular Front with his catchphrase 'Power to the People'.

Clangers, The   Clangers were the pink and woolly, mouse-like creatures who took their names from the sound made when they battened down their dustbin-lid hatches and retreated underground. Other inhabitants of the planet were the Froglets, Soup Dragon and Iron Chicken.

Cleopatras, The   Actresses who played the Cleopatras included Michelle Newell, Elizabeth Shepherd, Caroline Mortimer, Sue Holderness, Amanda Boxer, Prue Clarke, Pauline Moran.

Colditz   Jack Hedley (Lt Col. John Preston), Robert Wagner (Flt Lt/Major Phil Carrington), David McCallum (Flt Lt Simon Carter), Bernard Hepton (Kommandant), Anthony Valentine (Major Horst Mohn).

Come Dancing   Presenters include McDonald Hobley, Angela Rippon, David Jacobs, Terry Wogan, Rosemarie Ford, Noel Edmonds, Judith Chalmers, Keith Fordyce, Michael Aspel, Peter West and Peter Dimmock.

Compact   Ronald Allen (Ian Harmon), Carmen Silvera (Camilla Hope), Vincent Ball (David Rome). Created by Hazel Adair and Peter Ling of *Crossroads* fame.

Cool For Cats   Britain's first pop music show in 1956 and hosted by Ker Robertson and then Kent Walton.

Cosby Show   Bill Cosby (Heathcliff Huxtable, an obstetrician), Phylicia Ayres-Allen/Rashad (Clair, a lawyer). Their children: Sondra, Rudy, Denise, Theo, Vanessa.

Countdown   Words-and-numbers game hosted by Richard Whiteley and Carol Vorderman. First programme on Channel 4. *Countdown* has the most professional production team of any show on the box – it includes three *Countdown* champions and producer Mark Nyman is a former World Scrabble Champion. The author has happy memories of the show although beaten on the conundrum on his second appearance.

Cracker   Robbie Coltrane (Eddie 'Fitz' Fitzgerald). Created by Jimmy McGovern.

Crackerjack   Hosts: Eamonn Andrews, Leslie Crowther, Michael Aspel, Ed Stewart, Stu Francis. Stooges: Peter Glaze, Don Maclean, Leslie Crowther. Game: Double or Drop.

Crime Traveller   Michael French (David Wicks in *EastEnders*) starred in this time machine series.

Criss Cross Quiz   Popular quiz show hosted by Jeremy Hawk (father of actress Belinda Lang). Derived its format from the American *Tic Tac Dough*.

C.A.T.S. Eyes   Jill Gascoigne (Maggie Forbes), Rosalyn Landor (Pru Standfast), Leslie Ash (Frederica 'Fred' Smith). C.A.T.S. stood for Covert Activities Thames Section.

Dad's Army   Arthur Lowe (Capt. George Mainwaring, a bank manager), John Le Mesurier (Sgt Arthur Wilson), Clive Dunn (L/Corporal Jack Jones, a butcher), John Laurie (Pte James Frazier, an undertaker), James Beck (Pte James Walker, a spiv), Ian Lavender (Pte Frank Pike, a silly boy), Arnold Ridley (Pte Charles Godfrey), Bill Pertwee (ARP Warden William Hodges, a greengrocer), Frank Williams (the vicar), Colin Bean (Pte Sponge), Pamela Cundell (Mrs Fox). Created by Jimmy Perry and David Croft and set in Walmington-on-Sea (supposedly Bexhill).

Dalziel and Pascoe   Warren Clarke (Det. Supt Andrew Dalziel), Colin Buchanan (Det. Insp. Peter Pascoe). Written by Stephen Lowe and based on Reginald Hill's books.

Dangermouse   Voices: Dangermouse (David Jason), Penfold (Terry Scott), Stiletto Mafioso (Brian Trueman), Baron Greenback (Edward Kelsey). Created by Mike Harding and Brian Trueman. Written by Brian Trueman and Angus Allen. Narrated by David Jason.

Darling Buds of May, The   David Jason (Sidney Charles 'Pop' Larkin), Pam Ferris (Ma Larkin), Catherine Zeta-Jones (Mariette Larkin/Charlton), Philip Franks (Cedric 'Charley' Charlton).

Defenders, The   E G Marshall (Lawrence Preston), Robert Reed (Kenneth Preston). Father and son lawyers.

Dempsey and Makepeace   Michael Brandon (Lt James Dempsey), Glynis Barber (Det. Sgt Harriet Makepeace). Dept: S110.

Department S   Peter Wyngarde (Jason King), Joel Fabiani (Stewart Sullivan), Rosemary Nichols (Annabelle Hurst). Department S was a department of Interpol.

Desmond's   Norman Beaton (Desmond Ambrose), Carmen Munroe (Shirley Ambrose), Ram John Holder (Pork Pie). Life in a Peckham barber's shop.

Desperate Housewives   Marcia Cross (Bree Van De Kamp), Teri Hatcher (Susan Mayer), Felicity Huffman (Lynette Scavo), Eva Longoria (Gabrielle Solis), Nicollette Sheridan (Edie Britt), Brenda Strong (Mary Alice Young), Andrea Bowen (Julie Mayer), Ricardo Antonio Chavira (Carlos Solis), Steven Culp (Rex Van De Kamp), James Denton (Mike Delfino), Cody Kasch (Zach Young), Jesse Metcalfe (John), Mark Moses (Paul Young).

Detectives, The   Jasper Carrott (Bob Louis), Robert Powell (Dave Briggs), George Sewell (Supt Frank Cottam).

Dial 999   Robert Beatty (Canadian Mountie Mike Maguire), seconded to London on work experience.

Dick Van Dyke Show, The   Dick Van Dyke (Rob Petrie), Mary Tyler Moore (Laura), Larry Matthews (Ritchie), Rose Marie (Sally Rogers), Carl Reiner (Alan Brady), Morey Amsterdam (Maurice 'Buddy' Sorrell).

Dinnerladies   Victoria Wood (Bren), Thelma Barlow (Dolly), Celia Imrie (Philippa), Maxine Peake (Twinkle), Anne Reid (Jean), Duncan Preston (Stan), Andrew Dunn (Tony), Shobna Gulati (Anita), Julie Walters (Petula), Christopher Greet (Mr Michael), Jane Hazlegrove (Lisa), Sue Devaney (Secretary).

Doctor Finlay   Tannochbrae 20 years on (real-life Auchtermuchty in Fife), with Dr Finlay played by David Rintoul and the character's Christian name changed to John.

Dr Finlay's Casebook   Bill Simpson (Dr Alan Finlay), Andrew Cruickshank (Dr Angus Cameron), Barbara Mullen (Janet). Set in 1920s Tannochbrae (real-life Callander), the base for practice was Arden House. The stories were based on *The Adventures of a Black Bag* by A J Cronin.

Doctor in the House   Barry Evans (Michael Upton), Robin Nedwell (Duncan Waring), Geoffrey Davies (Dick Stuart-Clark), George Layton (Paul Collier). Based on the books by Richard Gordon.

Don't Wait Up   Nigel Havers (Dr Tom Latimer), Tony Britton (Dr Toby Latimer). Writer: George Layton.

Doomwatch   John Paul (Dr Spencer Quist), Simon Oates (Dr John Ridge), Robert Powell (Tobias 'Toby' Wren).

Dotto   Game show hosted by Robert Gladwell, Jimmy Hanley and Shaw Taylor during its two-year run. Based on American show which was taken off as part of the 'Quiz Show Scandal'.

Dr Kildare   Richard Chamberlain (Dr James Kildare), Raymond Massey (Dr Leonard Gillespie). Based on Max Brand books. Richard Chamberlain had a hit with the vocal version of the theme tune, 'Three Stars Will Shine Tonight'. Hospital: Blair General.

Dr Who   First Dr Who was William Hartnell, followed by Patrick Troughton, Jon Pertwee, Tom Baker, Peter Davison, Colin Baker, Sylvester McCoy. Other Dr Who's have included Richard Hurndall, who took William Hartnell's part in *The Five Doctors*, Paul McGann who played the Doctor in a television film, and Peter Cushing, who appeared as the Doctor in two feature films. The original crew were William Russell (Ian Chesterton), Jacqueline Hill (Barbara Wright) and Carole Ann Ford (Susan Foreman, the Doctor's granddaughter). Other assistants included Peter Purves (Steven Taylor), Nicola Bryant (Perpugilliam 'Peri' Brown), Sophie Aldred (Ace), Louise Jameson (Leela), Frazer Hines (Jamie McCrimmon), Janet Fielding (Tegan Jovanka), Elizabeth Sladen (Sarah Jane Smith), Katy Manning (Jo Grant), Sarah Sutton (Nyssa). The Doctor is from the planet Gallifrey. The five actors who played the Master were (1) Roger Delgado (2) Peter Pratt (3) Geoffrey Beevers (4) Anthony Ainley (5) Eric Roberts. Tardis: Time And Relative Dimension In Space. The series was axed in 1989 but resurrected in March 2005, the Doctor being played by Christopher Eccleston and his assistant, Rose Tyler, by Billie Piper. Their first adversaries were the Autons and the series was written by Russell T Davies.

Dragnet   Jack Webb (Joe Friday). Episodes began: 'The story you are about to see is true, only the names have been changed to protect the innocent.' Set in Los Angeles. Badge no.: 714.

Drop the Dead Donkey   Robert Duncan (Gus), Neil Pearson (Dave), Jeff Rawle (George), Stephen Tompkinson (Damien), David Swift (Henry), Victoria Wicks (Sally). Written by Andy Hamilton and Guy Jenkin. Original working title for the show was 'Dead Belgians Don't Count'.

Duchess of Duke Street, The   Gemma Jones (Louisa Trotter), Christopher Cazenove (Charles Tyrrell). Loosely based on the life story of Rosa Lewis, a kitchen maid who became manageress of the Cavendish Hotel in Jermyn Street. Hotel in series: Bentinck.

Dukes of Hazzard, The   Catherine Bach (Daisy Duke), Tom Wopat (Luke Duke), John Schneider (Bo Duke), Sorrell Booke (Jefferson Davis 'Boss' Hogg). The Dukes were the Robin Hoods of Hazzard County, driving around in their 1969 Dodge Charger named The General Lee. Narration and theme tune by Waylon Jennings.

Dustbinmen, The   John Woodvine and Brian Wilde (Bloody Delilah), Bryan Pringle (Cheese and Egg), Graham Haberfield (Winston Platt), Trevor Bannister (Heavy Breathing). Created and produced by Jack Rosenthal. Lorry called Thunderbird Three.

Edge of Darkness   Bob Peck (Ronald Craven), Joanne Whalley (Emma Craven), Joe Don Baker (Darius Jedburgh). Music by Eric Clapton.

TELEVISION

Edward and Mrs Simpson Edward Fox (Edward), Cynthia Harris (Mrs Wallis Warfield Simpson), Peggy Ashcroft (Queen Mary), David Waller (Stanley Baldwin).

Edward the Seventh Timothy West (Edward as an adult), Charles Sturridge (Edward as a teenager), Annette Crosbie (Queen Victoria), Robert Hardy (Prince Albert).

Eggheads Hosted by Dermot Murnaghan. Amateur quizzers take on a professional panel of Kevin Ashman, Daphne Fowler, Chris Hughes, Judith Keppel and C J De Mooi.

Elizabeth R Glenda Jackson (Elizabeth), Robert Hardy (Robert Dudley), Ronald Hines (William Cecil), Daphne Slater (Mary Tudor), Vivian Pickles (Mary, Queen of Scots), John Woodvine (Sir Francis Drake), Nicholas Selby (Sir Walter Raleigh).

Emergency Ward 10 Jill Browne (Carole Young), Charles Tingwell (Dr Alan Dawson), Desmond Carrington (Dr Chris Anderson), John Carlisle (Mr Lester Large), Ray Barrett (Dr Don Nolan), Jane Rossington (Nurse Kate Ford), Paul Darrow (Mr Verity), John Alderton (Dr Richard Moone), Pik-Sen Lim (Nurse Kwai).

Empire Road Norman Beaton (Everton Bennett).

Equalizer, The Edward Woodward (Robert McCall).

ER George Clooney (Dr Douglas Ross), Noah Wyle (Dr John Carter), Eriq La Salle (Dr Peter Benton), Julianna Margulies (Nurse Hathaway), Alex Kingston (Dr Elizabeth Corday), Anthony Edwards (Dr Mark Greene), Paul McCrane (Dr Robert Romano), Ming-Na (Dr Jing-Mai Chen), Michael Michele (Dr Cleo Finch), Maura Tiernay (Nurse Abby Lockheart), Laura Innes (Dr Kerry Weaver), Goran Visnjie (Dr Luka Kovac), Erik Palladino (Dr Dave Malucci). Set in Cook County Hospital, Chicago.

Ever-Decreasing Circles Richard Briers (Martin Brice), Penelope Wilton (Ann Brice), Stanley Lebor (Howard Hughes). Creators: John Esmonde and Bob Larbey.

Expert, The Marius Goring (Dr John Hardy).

Face to Face Presenter: John Freeman.

Fairly Secret Army Geoffrey Palmer (Major Harry Kitchener Wellington Truscott). Army called Queen's Own West Mercian Lowlanders.

Fall and Rise of Reginald Perrin, The Leonard Rossiter (Reginald Iolanthe Perrin/Martin Wellbourne), Pauline Yates (Elizabeth), John Barron (CJ), Sue Nicholls (Joan Greengross), Geoffrey Palmer (Jimmy), John Horsley (Doc Morrissey), Bruce Bould (David Harris-Jones). Created by David Nobbs. Companies: Sunshine Desserts/Grot.

Fame Debbie Allen (Lydia Grant), Erica Gimpel (Coco Hernandez), Gene Anthony Ray (Leroy Johnson), Lori Singer (Julie Miller), Janet Jackson (Cleo Hewitt).

Fame Academy BBC programme showcasing new talent. The first winner in 2002 was David Sneddon, with Ireland's Sinead Quinn runner-up.

Family at War, A Colin Douglas (Edwin Ashton), Barbara Flynn (Freda Ashton), Coral Atkins (Sheila Ashton), John Nettles (Ian McKenzie).

Family Fortunes Presenters include Bob Monkhouse, Max Bygraves and Les Dennis.

Family, The Fly-on-the-wall look at the Wilkins family from Reading.

Fantasy Football Presenters: Frank Skinner and David Baddiel.

Fantasy Island Ricardo Montalban (Mr Roarke), Herve Villechaize (Tattoo).

Far Pavilions, The Ben Cross (Ashton Pelham-Martyn), Amy Irving (Princess Anjuli), Christopher Lee (Kaka-Ji-Rao), Omar Sharif (Koda Dad), John Gielgud (Cavagnari), Rossano Brazzi (the Rana of Bhithor).

Father Dear Father Patrick Cargill (Patrick Glover), Natasha Pyne (Anna Glover), Ann Holloway (Karen Glover), Noel Dyson (Matilda 'Nanny' Harris).

Fawlty Towers John Cleese (Basil), Prunella Scales (Sybil), Andrew Sachs (Manuel), Connie Booth (Polly Sherman), Ballard Berkeley (Major Gowen). Set in Torquay.

FBI, The Efrem Zimbalist Jnr (Inspector Lewis Erskine).

Fifteen to One General knowledge quiz hosted by William G Stewart. Series winners include Jon Goodwin, Anthony Martin, Kevin Ashman, Mal Collier, Thomas Dyer, Andrew Francis, Barbara Thompson, Leslie Booth, Julian Allen, Martin Riley, Ian Potts, Arnold O'Hara, Trevor Montague, Stanley Miller, Glen Binnie, Bill Francis, Mike Kirby, Nick Terry, Doug Griffiths and Bill McKaig. Mal Collier won the Champion of Champions event held at Christmas 1997.

Filthy, Rich and Catflap Nigel Planer (Filthy Ralph), Rik Mayall (Richard Rich), Adrian Edmondson (Eddie Catflap). Written by Ben Elton.

Fire Crackers Joe Baker (Jumbo). Inept local firemen working in Cropper's End.

Fireball XL5 Characters include Colonel Steve Zodiac, Professor Matthew Matic, Venus Commander Zero, Lt 90, Zoonie, Robert the Robot.

Flintstones Characters include Fred, Wilma and Pebbles Flintstone, Barney, Betty and Bamm Bamm Rubble, and Dino the pet dinosaur.

Flipper Luke Halpin (Sandy Ricks), Brian Kelly (Porter Ricks). Last star dolphin of seven, called Bebe, died 4 May 1997, aged 40.

Flowerpot Men, The Characters included Bill and Ben, Little Weed and Slowcoach the Tortoise.

Follyfoot Gillian Blake (Dora), Arthur English (Slugger), Desmond Llewellyn (the Colonel), Steve Hodson (Steve).

Food and Drink Presenters include Chris Kelly, Henry Kelly, Susan Grossman, Jilly Goolden, Michael Barry, Oz Clarke, Paul Heiney.

Footballers' Wives Zöe Lucker (Tanya Laslett), Gary Lucy (Kyle Pascoe), Jessie Birdsall (Roger Webb), Ben Price (Conrad Gates), Laila Rouass (Laila Gates), Jamie Davis (Harley Lawson), Sarah Barrand (Shannon Donnelly), Gillian Taylforth (Jackie Pascoe), Caroline Chikezie (Elaine Hardy), Peter Ash (Darius Fry), Alison Newman (Hazel Bailey), Marcel McCalla (Noah Alexander).

Forsyte Saga, The Kenneth More (Jolyon Forsyte), Eric Porter (Soames Forsyte), Nyree Dawn Porter (Irene Heron/Forsyte).

Fortunes of War Kenneth Branagh (Guy Pringle), Emma Thompson (Harriet Pringle).

Fosters, The Notable for an early performance by Lenny Henry as Sonny Foster.

Four Feather Falls Voice of Tex Tucker: Nicholas Parsons. One feather allowed Tex's dog Dusty to speak; another gave speech to his horse, Rocky; the last two controlled the accuracy of his pistols.

Four Just Men, The Jack Hawkins (Ben Manfred MP), Dan Dailey (Tim Collier), Richard Conte (Jeff Ryder), Vittorio De Sica (Ricco Poccari).

Frasier Kelsey Grammer (Frasier Crane), David Hyde Pierce (Niles Crane), Bebe Neuwirth (Lilith),

John Mahoney (Martin Crane), Jane Leeves (Daphne Moon), Peri Gilpin (Roz Doyle).

Friends   Lisa Kudrow (Phoebe), Matt Le Blanc (Joey), Courtney Cox (Monica), Jennifer Aniston (Rachel Green), David Schwimmer (Ross), Matthew Perry (Chandler). Matt Le Blanc reprised his role in the 2005 spin-off *Joey*.

F Troop   Ken Berry (Captain Wilton Parmenter), Forrest Tucker (Sgt Morgan O'Rourke), Larry Storch (Corporal Randolph Agarn), John Mitchum (Trooper Hoffenmuller).

Fugitive, The   David Janssen (Dr Richard Kimble), Barry Morse (Lt Philip Gerard), Bill Raisch (Fred Johnson alias the one-armed man).

Game for a Laugh   Presenters include Matthew Kelly, Henry Kelly, Sarah Kennedy, Jeremy Beadle, Rustie Lee, Martin Daniels, Debbie Rix, Lee Peck.

Generation Game   Hosts include Bruce Forsyth, Larry Grayson and Jim Davidson.

Gentle Touch, The   Jill Gascoigne (DI Maggie Forbes), Derek Thompson (Det. Sgt Jimmy Fenton).

Get Smart   Don Adams (Maxwell Smart, Agent 86), Barbara Feldon (Agent 99). Cover: salesman for Pontiac Greeting Card Co. Series created by Mel Brooks.

Girl From Uncle, The   Stefanie Powers (April Dancer), Noel Harrison (Mark Slate), Leo G Carroll (Mr Waverly).

Girls on Top   Tracey Ullman (Candice), Dawn French (Amanda), Jennifer Saunders (Jennifer), Ruby Wax (Shelley), Joan Greenwood (Lady Carlton).

Give Us a Break   Robert Lindsay (Mickey Noades), Paul McGann (Mo Morris).

Gladiators   Presenters: John Fashanu, Jeremy Guscott, Ulrika Jonsson.

Gnomes of Dulwich   Terry Scott and Hugh Lloyd continuing their partnership as a big and small gnome. John Clive played the third 'old' gnome.

Going For a Song   Presenter: Max Robertson.

Golden Girls, The   Beatrice Arthur (Dorothy Zbornak), Rue McClanahan (Blanche Devereaux), Betty White (Rose Nylund), Estelle Getty (Sophia Petrillo).

Golden Shot, The   Presenters included Jackie Rae, Bob Monkhouse, Norman Vaughan, Charlie Williams.

Good Afternoon   Channel 5 daytime programme featuring the hospital documentary series Liverpool Mums, Pets Go Public, where contestants have to match pets with their owners, and Cryptogram, a general knowledge and word game of which the author has pleasant memories.

Good Life, The   Richard Briers (Tom Good), Felicity Kendall (Barbara), Penelope Keith (Margo Leadbeatter), Paul Eddington (Jerry Leadbeatter). Goat: Geraldine.

Goodness Gracious Me   Sanjeev Bhaskar, Meera Syal, Kulvinder Ghir, Nina Wadia. Irreverent sketch show that takes a light-hearted look at the Anglo-Asian community.

Goodnight Sweetheart   Nicholas Lyndhurst (Gary Sparrow), Dervla Kirwan (Phoebe Bamford), Victor McGuire (Ron Wheatcroft), Christopher Ettridge (PC Reg Deadman), Michelle Holmes (Yvonne Sparrow). Elizabeth Carling and Emma Amos took over leading female roles.

Good Old Days, The   Transmitted from the Leeds City Varieties Theatre, compered by Leonard Sachs (originally Don Gemmell). Every show ended with a rendition of 'Down at the Old Bull and Bush'.

Grange Hill   Long-running school drama. Transient cast since 1978 include Todd Carty (Peter 'Tucker' Jenkins), Susan Tully (Suzanne Ross), Letitia Dean (Lucinda), Peter Moran (Pogo Patterson), Gwyneth Powell (Bridget McCluskey), Mark Savage (Gripper Stebson), Sean Maguire (Tegs Ratcliffe), Terri Dwyer (Miss Adams), Chris Perry-Metcalf (Patrick 'Togger' Johnson), Edward Baker-Duly (Mr Malachay), Holly Mann (Sammy Lee), Georgia May Foote (Alison Simmons), Reece Noi (Taylor Mitchell), Simon O'Brien (Wally Scott), Kacey Barnfield (Maddie Gilks), Jacqui Boatswain (Mrs Bassinger).

Great Antiques Hunt, The   Host: Jilly Goolden.

Grimleys, The   Brian Conley (Digby), Amanda Holden (Geraldine), Noddy Holder, James Bradshaw.

Gunsmoke/Gun Law   James Arness (Matt Dillon), Amanda Blake (Kitty Russell), Milburn Stone (Dr Galen 'Doc' Adams), Dennis Weaver (Chester Goode), Burt Reynolds (Quint Asper).

Happy Days   Henry Winkler (Arthur Fonzarelli), Ron Howard (Richie Cunningham), Scott Baio (Charles 'Chachi' Arcola), Suzi Quattro (Leather Tuscadero), Robin Williams (Mork).

Hark at Barker   Ronnie Barker (Lord Rustless), David Jason (Dithers).

Harry Enfield Show   Characters include the Slobs: Wayne and Waynetta and children Frogmella and Spudulike.

Hart to Hart   Robert Wagner (Jonathan Hart), Stefanie Powers (Jennifer Hart), Lionel Stander (Max), Freeway the dog. Occupations: businessman and journalist.

Have Gun Will Travel   Richard Boone (Paladin), Kam Tong (Hey Boy), Lisa Lu (Hey Girl).

Have I Got News for You   Hosted by Angus Deayton. Team captains are Paul Merton and Ian Hislop. Following the sacking of Angus Deayton a series of guest presenters were used including William Hague, Charlotte Church, Greg Dyke, Charles Kennedy, Liza Tarbuck and Bruce Forsyth.

Hawaii Five-O   Jack Lord (Steve Garrett), James MacArthur ('Danno' Williams), Kam Fong (Chin Ho Kelly).

Hawkeye and the Last of the Mohicans   John Hart (Nat 'Hawkeye' Cutler), Lon Chaney Jnr (Chingachgook).

Hazell   Nicholas Ball (James Hazell), Roddy McMillan (Choc Minty). Created by Terry Venables and Gordon Williams.

Heartbeat   Nick Berry (PC Nick Rowan), Derek Fowlds (Sgt Oscar Blaketon), Bill Maynard (Claude Jeremiah Greengrass). Set in 1964 Yorkshire.

Hector's House   Adventures of a dog (Hector), a cat (Zaza) and a frog (Mrs Kiki).

Herbs, The   Garden owners: Sir Basil and Lady Rosemary. Other characters include Constable Knapweed, Mr Onion the schoolteacher and his pupils, the Chives, Bayleaf the gardener, Aunt Mint, Sage the owl, Tarragon the dragon, Pashana Bedi the snake-charmer, and Belladonna. The real stars were Dill the dog and Parsley the lion. Gordon Rollings was the narrator and the magic word that opened the gate was 'Herbidacious'.

Here's Lucy   Lucille Ball (Lucy Carter), Gale Gordon (Harrison Carter).

Hergé's Adventures of Tin Tin   Narrator: Peter Hawkins. Characters include Snowy the white fox-terrier, Captain Haddock, the Thompson Twins, Professor Calculus and General Alcazar.

TELEVISION

Hi-De-Hi Paul Shane (Ted Bovis), Ruth Madoc (Gladys Pugh), Simon Cadell (Jeffrey Fairbrother), David Griffin (Squadron Leader Clive Dempster), Jeffrey Holland (Spike Dixon), Su Pollard (Peggy Ollerenshaw). Holiday camp: Maplins at Crimpton-on-Sea.

Highway to Heaven Michael Landon (Jonathan Smith), Victor French (Mark Gordon).

Hill Street Blues Daniel J Travanti (Captain Frank Furillo), Veronica Hamel (Joyce Davenport), Robert Prosky (Sgt Stanislaus Jablonski).

Hitch-Hiker's Guide to the Galaxy, The Simon Jones (Arthur Dent), David Dixon (Ford Prefect), Sandra Dickinson (Trillian), David Learner (Marvin), Stephen Moore (Marvin's voice), Mark Wing-Davey (Zaphod Beeblebrox), Peter Jones (the book voice).

Hogan's Heroes Bob Crane (Colonel Robert Hogan), Werner Klemperer (Colonel Wilhelm Klink), John Banner (Sgt Hans Schulz), Larry Hovis (Sgt Andrew Carter), Ivan Dixon (Corporal James Kinchloe).

Holiday Presenters include Frank Bough, Des Lynam, Cliff Michelmore, Joan Bakewell, Jill Dando, Anneka Rice, Eamonn Holmes.

House of Cards Ian Richardson (Francis Urquhart). Based on Michael Dobbs's novel.

How/How 2 Presenters include Fred Dineage, Jack Hargreaves, Jon Miller, Bunty James, Marian Davies, Carol Vorderman, Gareth Jones.

Howard's Way Maurice Colbourne (Tom Howard), Jan Harvey (Jan Howard), Glyn Owen (Jack Rolfe), Stephen Yardley (Ken Masters), Tony Anholt (Charles Frere), Nigel Davenport (Sir Edward Frere), Kate O'Mara (Laura Wilde). Created by Gerard Glaister and Allan Prior. Yard name: Mermaid.

How Do They Do That? Presenters: Esther McVeigh and Eamonn Holmes.

HR Pufnstuff Jack Wild (Jimmy), Billie Hayes (Witchiepoo).

Huckleberry Hound Show, The Characters included Pixie and Dixie, Jinks the Cat, Yogi Bear and Boo Boo, Hokey Wolf and Ding a Ling. Huckleberry used to sing 'Clementine' constantly.

Human Jungle, The Herbert Lom (Dr Roger Corder), Sally Smith (Jennifer Corder), Mary Yeomans (Nancy Hamilton).

I Claudius Derek Jacobi (Claudius), Siân Phillips (Livia), Brian Blessed (Octavian/Augustus), George Baker (Tiberius), John Hurt (Caligula), Patrick Stewart (Sejanus), Chris Biggins (Nero).

I Love Lucy Lucille Ball (Lucy Ricardo), Desi Arnaz (Ricky Ricardo), Vivian Vance (Ethel Mertz), William Frawley (Fred Mertz). First sit-com to be filmed live in front of a studio audience.

In at the Deep End Chris Searle and Paul Heiney took it in turn to learn new skills.

Inside George Webley Roy Kinnear played the depressive character created by Keith Waterhouse and Willis Hall.

Inspector Alleyn Mysteries, The Patrick Malahide (Chief Insp. Roderick Alleyn). Character created by Ngaio Marsh.

Inspector Morse John Thaw (Chief Insp. Endeavour Morse), Kevin Whately (Det. Sgt Robbie Lewis).

Interpol Calling Charles Korvin (Insp. Paul Duval), Edwin Richfield (Insp. Mornay).

Invaders, The Roy Thinnes (David Vincent, an architect). Narrator: William Conrad.

Invisible Man, The In the original series Dr Peter Brady's voice was that of Tim Turner although no actor was billed. David McCallum played the character of Daniel Westin in the 1975 series.

I Spy Robert Culp (Kelly Robinson, tennis pro), Bill Cosby (Alexander Scott, tennis trainer).

It Ain't Half Hot Mum Windsor Davies (RSM B L Williams), Melvyn Hayes (Bombardier 'Gloria' Beaumont), George Layton (Bombardier Solomons), Michael Bates (Rangi Ram), Don Estelle (Gunner 'Lofty' Sugden).

It Takes a Thief Robert Wagner (Alexander Mundy), Fred Astaire (Alister Mundy).

Ivor the Engine Narrated by David Edwards, Anthony Jackson, Olwen Griffiths and Oliver Postgate, who also wrote the stories. Railway: Merioneth and Llantissily Rail Traction Company. Driver: Jones the Steam. Other characters included Owen the Signal and Dai Station, the man who looked after Llaniog Station. Ivor's boiler was fired by Idris the dragon. Jones always aspired to sing in the choir like his pal Evans the Song. Peter Firmin drew all the pictures.

Jackanory First story told by Lee Montague ('Cap of Rushes'). Most prolific story teller: Bernard Cribbins.

The Jamie Kennedy Experiment Actor/comedian Jamie Kennedy, nicknamed JKX for the purposes of this show, combines hidden-camera pranks with sketch comedy to see how everyday people and celebrities behave in unusual situations. JKX is often disguised, and when the joke has run its course he delivers the immortal tag line 'You've been X-ed'. First aired in January 2002 on Channel 4.

Jane Glynis Barber played the wartime cartoon character in the 1982 television adaption.

Jemima Shore Investigates Patricia Hodge played the TV reporter created by Lady Antonia Fraser.

Jesus of Nazareth Robert Powell (Jesus as an adult), Immad Cohen (Jesus as a boy), Olivia Hussey (Virgin Mary), Anne Bancroft (Mary Magdalene), Ian McShane (Judas Iscariot), Rod Steiger (Pontius Pilate), James Mason (Joseph of Arimathea), Peter Ustinov (Herod the Great), Michael York (John the Baptist), Stacy Keach (Barabbas), Laurence Olivier (Nicodemus).

Jetsons, The Jetsons lived in the 21st century in Orbit City. George Jetson worked at Spacely Space Sprockets. The family pet dog was Astro.

Jewel in the Crown, The Peggy Ashcroft (Barbie Batchelor), Geraldine James (Sarah Layton), Stuart Wilson (Major Clark), Tim Pigott-Smith (Ronald Merrick), Art Malik (Hari Kumar), Susan Wooldridge (Daphne Manners), Charles Dance (Sgt Guy Perron), Josephine Welcome (Mira). Based on Paul Scott's novels.

Joe 90 Joe McClaine, alias Joe 90, worked for WIN, the World Intelligence Network, using his father's invention BIGRAT (Brain Impulse Galvanoscope Record And Transfer).

Joking Apart Robert Bathurst (Mark Taylor), Tracie Bennett (Tracy), Fiona Gillies (Becky Taylor).

Jonathan Creek Alan Davies (Jonathan Creek), Caroline Quentin (Madeline Magellan), Julia Sawahla (Carla Borrego).

Juke Box Jury First panel: Alma Cogan, Susan Stranks, Gary Miller and Pete Murray. The three presenters were David Jacobs, Noel Edmonds and Jools Holland.

Juliet Bravo Stephanie Turner (Insp. Jean Darblay), Anna Carteret (Insp. Kate Longton). Fictional town: Hartley in Lancashire.

Junior Criss Cross Quiz Hosts included Jeremy Hawk, Bob Holness, Mike Sarne, Bill Grundy and Danny Blanchflower.

Just Good Friends Paul Nicholas (Vince Pinner), Jan Francis (Penny Warrender).

Kavanagh QC John Thaw (James Kavanagh QC), Geraldine James (Eleanor Harker QC).

Keeping Up Appearances Patricia Routledge (Hyacinth Bucket), Geoffrey Hughes (Onslow). Created by Roy Clarke.

Knight Rider David Hasselhoff (Michael Knight, formerly Michael Long), William Daniels (voice of Kitt, the Knight Industries Two Thousand).

Kojak Telly Savalas (Lt Theo Kojak), Dan Frazer (Capt. Frank McNeil), Kevin Dobson (Lt Bobby Crocker), George Savalas (Stavros), Mark Russell (Saperstein). Worked in Manhattan South 13th Precinct.

Krypton Factor, The Tough quiz testing both physical and mental faculties. Gordon Burns's name was synonymous with the series.

The Kumars at No. 42 Sanjeev (Sanjeev Bhaskar), Dad (Vincent Ebrahim), Mum (Indira Joshi), Granny Sushila (Meera Syal). Spoof chat show following the pretext that the Kumars have bulldozed their back garden to build a studio on the back of their house to indulge their spoilt son, Sanjeev, who fancies himself as a celebrity chat-show host.

Kung Fu David Carradine (Kwai Chang Caine), Keye Luke (Master Po), Radames Pera (Caine as a boy). Bruce Lee was rejected for the role and died soon after.

KYTV Angus Deayton (Mike Channel), Geoffrey Perkins (Mike Flex), Helen Atkinson Wood (Anna Daptor).

LA Law Richard Dysart (Leland McKenzie), Harry Hamlin (Michael Kuzak), Corbin Bernsen (Arnie Becker), Michael Tucker (Stuart Markowitz), Diana Muldaur (Rosalind Shays).

Laramie John Smith (Slim Sherman), Robert Fuller (Jess Harper), Hoagy Carmichael (Jonesy), Spring Byington (Daisy Cooper).

Larry Sanders Show, The Garry Shandling (Larry Sanders), Rip Torn (Arthur), Jeffrey Tambor (Hank Kingsley).

Last of the Summer Wine Peter Sallis (Norman Clegg), Bill Owen (Compo Seminite), Michael Bates (Blamire), Brian Wilde (Foggy Dewhurst), Michael Aldridge (Seymour Utterthwaite), Kathy Staff (Nora Batty), Jean Alexander (Auntie Wainwright). Filmed in Holmfirth in Yorkshire. Written by Roy Clarke.

League of Gentlemen, The Jeremy Dyson, Mark Gatiss, Steve Pemberton, Reece Shearsmith. Set in Royston Vazey (the real name of comedian Roy 'chubby' Brown).

Life and Loves of a She Devil, The Julie T Wallace (Ruth Patchett), Dennis Waterman (Bobbo Patchett), Patricia Hodge (Mary Fisher).

Likely Lads, The James Bolam (Terry Collier), Bob Ferris (Rodney Bewes), Sheila Fearn (Audrey Collier), Brigit Forsyth (Thelma Ferris). Written by Dick Clement and Ian La Frenais. Sequel: *Whatever Happened to the Likely Lads*.

Little Britain Radio series written and performed by Matt Lucas and David Walliams, transferred to BBC3 in September 2003 and repeated on BBC2, before winning numerous awards. Characters include Vicky Pollard, the incomprehensible teenager from Darkly Noone; Marjorie Dawes, the rotund leader of Fat Fighters; Lou and Andy, a 'helper' (Walliams) and his apparently wheelchair-bound friend (Lucas); Emily Howard, a totally unconvincing transvestite; and Daffyd, a committed 'homosexualist' residing in the Welsh town of Llanddewi Brefi. His catchphrase 'I'm the only gay in the village' was voted best comedy catchphrase ever in a poll of 3,800 television viewers in January 2005.

Little House on the Prairie Michael Landon (Charles Ingalls), Karen Grassle (Caroline Ingalls), Melissa Gilbert (Laura Ingalls/Wilder), Melissa Sue Anderson (Mary Ingalls/Kendall).

Liver Birds, The Polly James (Beryl Hennessey), Nerys Hughes (Sandra Hutchinson/Paynton), Pauline Collins (Dawn, the original flatmate of Beryl), Elizabeth Estensen (Carol Boswell), Mollie Sugden (Mrs Hutchinson), John Nettles (Paul), Jonathan Lynn (Robert).

London's Burning Mark Arden (Roland 'Vaseline' Cartwright), Glen Murphy (George Green), James Hazeldine (Mike 'Bayleaf' Wilson), Richard Walsh (Bert 'Sicknote' Quigley), Gerard Horan (Leslie 'Charisma' Appleby), Ben Onwukwe (Stuart 'Recall' Mackenzie), Heather Peace (Sally 'Gracie' Fields), Edward Peel (John Coleman), Michael Garner (Geoffrey 'Poison' Pearce), Fuman Dar (Ronnie 'Hi-Ho' Silver), Connor Byrne (Rob 'Hyper' Sharpe), Sam Callis (Adam Benjamin), Al Hunter Ashton (Pit bull). Firefighters of Blue Watch B25, Blackwall, created by Jack Rosenthal.

Lone Ranger, The Initially played by Clayton Moore and then by John Hart before he left to play Hawkeye. Jay Silverheels always played the faithful Tonto. Lone Ranger's horse: Silver. (He would often say 'Hi-ho, Silver, away' when in a hurry.) Tonto's horse: Scout. (Tonto would often call his friend Kemo Sabe, which meant Trusty Scout.) The Lone Ranger's real name was John Reid, a Texas Ranger ambushed and left for dead. It is often said that if you can listen to Rossini's 'William Tell Overture' without thinking of the Lone Ranger (same tune) then you are a real classical music aficionado.

Lord Peter Wimsey Ian Carmichael (Lord Peter Wimsey), Glyn Houston (Bunter, his manservant).

Lost in Space Guy Williams (Professor John Robinson), Jonathan Harris (Zachary Smith), Bob May (the robot), Dick Tufeld (voice of the robot). Spaceship: Jupiter 11. Pet space monkey: the Bloop.

Lotus Eaters, The Ian Hendry (Erik Shepherd), Wanda Ventham (Ann Shepherd). Drama set on Crete.

Lou Grant Edward Asner (Lou), Robert Walden (Joe Rossi). Spin-off from the *Mary Tyler Moore Show*. Newspaper: *Los Angeles Tribune*.

Love Hurts Adam Faith (Frank Carver), Zoë Wanamaker (Tessa Piggott), Jane Lapotaire (Diane Warburg), Tony Selby (Max Taplow).

Love Me Do Game show in which three couples vie for the chance to wed. Host: Shane Richie.

Love Thy Neighbour Jack Smethurst (Eddie Booth), Kate Williams (Joan), Rudolph Walker (Bill Reynolds), Nina Baden Semper (Barbie), Keith Marsh (Jacko Jackson). Jacko's famous saying: 'I'll 'ave 'alf.'

Lovejoy Ian McShane (Lovejoy), Dudley Sutton (Tinker Deal), Chris Jury (Eric Catchpole), Phyllis Logan (Lady Jane Felsham). Lovejoy's Morris Minor: Miriam.

Lovers, The Richard Beckinsale (Geoffrey), Paula Wilcox (Beryl).

TELEVISION

Lucy Show, The Lucille Ball (Lucy Carmichael), Gale Gordon (Theodore J Mooney), Vivian Vance (Vivian Bagley).

Lytton's Diary Peter Bowles (Neville Lytton). Incidents in the life of a newspaper diarist.

Magic Roundabout Characters include Dougal (the dog), Ermintrude (the cow), Brian (the snail), Mr Rusty, Mr McHenry, Zebedee, Dylan (the rabbit), Florence. Created by Serge Danot and narrated by Eric Thompson and Nigel Planer.

Magnificent Evans, The Ronnie Barker (Plantagenet Evans), Dyfed Thomas (Home Rule O'Toole), Myfanwy Talog (Bron).

Magnum PI Tom Selleck (Thomas Sullivan Magnum), John Hillerman (Jonathan Quayle Higgins III), Roger E Mosley (Theodore 'TC' Calvin), Orson Welles (voice of Robin Masters).

Magpie Presenters include Susan Stranks, Pete Brady, Tony Bastable, Mick Robertson, Jenny Hanley, Tommy Boyd, Douglas Rae.

Main Chance, The John Stride (David Main), Kate O'Mara (Julia Main). Story of a young, successful lawyer.

Making Out Margi Clarke (Queenie), Shirley Stelfox (Carol May), Tracie Bennett (Norma), Melanie Kilburn (Jill), Keith Allen (Rex), Brian Hibbard (Chunky).

Man About the House Richard O'Sullivan (Robin Tripp), Paula Wilcox (Chrissy Plummer), Sally Thomsett (Jo), Brian Murphy (George Roper), Yootha Joyce (Mildred Roper). Spin-off series were *Robin's Nest* and *George and Mildred*.

Man at the Top Kenneth Haigh (Joe Lampton). Feature film of the same name followed.

Man Called Ironside, A Raymond Burr (Chief Robert T Ironside), Don Galloway (Det. Sgt Ed Brown), Barbara Anderson (Eve Whitfield), Don Mitchell (Mark Sanger), Elizabeth Baur (Fran Belding).

Man From Atlantis Patrick Duffy (Mark Harris; had green eyes), Belinda J Montgomery (Dr Elizabeth Merrill), Victor Buono (Mr Schubert), Robert Lussier (Brent). Submersible name: Cetacean.

Man From Uncle, The Robert Vaughn (Napoleon Solo, agent no. 11), David McCallum (Ilya Kuryakin, agent no. 2), Leo G Carroll (Alexander Waverly, agent no. 1). UNCLE: United Network Command for Law and Enforcement. Secret office: behind Del Floria's Tailor Shop. Enemy: Thrush.

Manhunt Alfred Lynch (Jimmy Porter), Peter Barkworth (Vincent), Cyd Hayman (Nina). Heroic tales of French Resistance in WW2. Theme tune: Beethoven's Fifth Symphony.

Man in a Suitcase Richard Bradford (McGill).

Man in Room 17, The Richard Vernon (Oldenshaw), Michael Aldridge (Dimmock). Criminologists working in an office near the Houses of Parliament.

Marcus Welby MD Robert Young (Welby), James Brolin (Dr Steven Kiley).

Mark Saber Donald Gray (Saber), Michael Balfour (Barny O'Keefe). Story of the one-armed detective.

Marriage Lines Richard Briars (George Starling), Prunella Scales (Kate).

Mary Tyler Moore Show Mary Tyler Moore (Mary Richards), Ed Asner (Lou Grant), Valerie Harper (Rhoda Morgenstern), Cloris Leachman (Phyllis Lindstrom). Based in TV Station WJM-TV.

M.A.S.H. Alan Alda (Capt. Benjamin Franklin 'Hawkeye' Pierce), Wayne Rogers (Capt. 'Trapper John' McIntyre), Loretta Swit (Maj. Margaret 'Hot Lips' Houlihan), Larry Linville (Maj. Frank Burns), Gary Burghoff (Corporal Walter 'Radar' O'Reilly), William Christopher (Father Francis Mulcahy), Jamie Farr (Corporal Maxwell Klinger). Hawkeye's tent known as the Swamp. M.A.S.H.: Mobile Army Surgical Hospital.

Mastermind Ran from 1972 to 1997 with Magnus Magnusson as 'Interrogator' throughout the run. Producer/director David Mitchell. Other producers include Bill Wright, Roger MacKay, Peter Massey, Penelope Cowell Doe. Main researcher: Dee Wallace. Winners: Nancy Wilkinson (1972), Patricia Owen (1973), Elizabeth Horrocks (1974), John Hart (1975), Roger Pritchard (1976), Sir David Hunt (1977), Rosemary James (1978), Dr Philip Jenkins (1979), Fred Housego (1980), Leslie Grout (1981), Sir David Hunt (1982), Christopher Hughes (1983), Margaret Harris (1984), Ian Meadows (1985), Jennifer Keaveney (1986), Dr Jeremy Bradbrooke (1987), David Beamish (1988), Mary-Elizabeth Raw (1989), David Edwards (1990), Stephen Allen (1991), Steve Williams (1992), Gavin Fuller (1993), George Davidson (1994), Kevin Ashman (1995), Richard Sturch (1996), Anne Ashurst (1997). The format transferred to Radio 4 for three years and was hosted by Peter Snow. The winners were Robert Gibson (1998), Rev Kit Carter (1999), Stephen Follows (2000). The Discovery Channel then took over for one season in 2001. The winner was Michael Penrice. The series was revived on the BBC in 2003, the winner being Andy Page. Shaun Wallace became the first black champion in 2004. John Humphrys is the current interrogator.

Maverick James Garner (Brett Maverick), Jack Kelly (Bart Maverick), Roger Moore (Cousin Beau).

May to December Anton Rodgers (Alec Callender), Eve Matheson/Lesley Dunlop (Zoe Angell/Callender).

McCloud Dennis Weaver (Sam McCloud), seconded to New York from Taos, New Mexico.

McMillan and Wife Rock Hudson (Commissioner Stewart McMillan), Susan Saint James (Sally McMillan). Based in San Francisco.

Me and My Girl Richard O'Sullivan (Simon Harrap), Joanne Ridley (Samantha Harrap), Joan Sanderson (Nell Cresset), Tim Brooke-Taylor (Derek Yates). Advertising agency: Eyecatchers. Theme song sung by Peter Skellern.

Meet the Wife Thora Hird (Thora Blacklock), Freddie Frinton (Freddie Blacklock). Stemmed from a Comedy Playhouse production called *The Bed*.

Me Mammy Milo O'Shea (Bunjy Kennefick), Anna Manahan (Mrs Kennefick), Yootha Joyce (Miss Argyll), David Kelly (Cousin Enda), Ray McAnally (Father Patrick).

Men Behaving Badly Martin Clunes (Gary), Neil Morrissey (Tony), Leslie Ash (Deborah), Caroline Quentin (Dorothy). The first series featured Harry Enfield as Dermot but Neil Morrissey replaced him for series two Although originally an ITV series, by series three it was screened on BBC 1. The writer was Simon Nye, who also created Frank Stubbs.

Metal Mickey The robot Mickey was invented by Ken Wilberforce and played by Ashley Knight. This series is best remembered for the fact that Mickey Dolenz was the producer/director.

Miami Vice Don Johnson (James 'Sonny' Crockett), Philip Michael Thomas (Ricardo Tubbs), Edward James Olmos (Lt Martin Castillo), Sheena Easton (Caitlin Davies).

Midnight Caller Gary Cole (Jack 'Nighthawk' Killian).

Millennium Lance Henriksen (Frank Black), Megan Gallagher (Catherine Black), Chris Ellis (Penseyres). Created by Chris Carter of *X Files* fame.

Minder George Cole (Arthur Daly), Dennis Waterman (Terry McMann), Glynn Edwards (Dave), Patrick Malahide (Det. Sgt Albert 'Charlie' Chisholm), Peter Childs (Sgt Rycott). The theme tune, 'I Could Be So Good For You', was sung by Dennis Waterman.

Mind Your Language Barry Evans (Jeremy Brown), François Pascal (Danielle Favre), Pik-Sen-Lim (Chung Su-Lee).

Miss Marple Joan Hickson (Miss Marple).

Mission Impossible Peter Graves (Jim Phelps), Leonard Nimoy (Paris), Barbara Bain (Cinnamon Carter), Martin Landau (Rollin Hand), Greg Morris (Barney Collier), Steven Hill (Daniel Briggs), Lesley Ann Warren (Dana Lambert), Peter Lupus (Willie Armitage). Voice on the tape: Bob Johnson. Catchphrase: 'This tape will self-destruct in five seconds' (occasionally ten seconds).

Mister Ed Alan Young (Wilbur Post). Story of a talking horse.

Mogul Series about an oil company, which later changed its title to *The Troubleshooters*.

Moment of Truth Cilla Black hosted the show in which three contestants have a week to master a given task.

Monkees, The TV Series about a pop group. Micky Dolenz, Mike Nesmith, Peter Tork and Davy Jones.

Monty Python's Flying Circus Messrs Cleese, Idle, Gilliam, Jones, Palin, Chapman and Carol Cleveland.

Moonlighting Bruce Willis (David Addison), Cybill Shepherd (Maddie Hayes). Detective agency: Blue Moon.

Mork and Mindy Robin Williams (Mork from Ork), Pam Dawber (Mindy McConnell), Jonathan Winters (Mearth). Mork gave birth to Mearth, who called Mindy 'Shoe' and Mork 'Mommy'. Series was a spin-off from an episode of *Happy Days*.

Moviedrome Presenters Alex Cox, Mark Cousins.

Mr and Mrs The alternating presenters were Alan Taylor and Derek Batey.

Mr Magoo Voice of Magoo (Jim Backus); Waldo was his nephew.

Mr Pastry Richard Hearne, an actor, acrobat and dancer, invented this character. Popular for over 20 years.

Muffin the Mule Presenter: Annette Mills. Puppeteer: Ann Hogarth.

Munsters, The Fred Gwynne (Herman), Yvonne De Carlo (Lily), Al Lewis (Grandpa), Butch Patrick (Eddie), Beverley Owen/Pat Priest (Marilyn). Lived at: 1313 Mockingbird Lane, Mockingbird Heights.

Muppet Show, The Characters include Miss Piggy Lee, Kermit T Frog, Statler and Waldorf, Animal, Gonzo, Fozzie Bear, Zoot, Swedish Chef, Dr Teeth, Robin the Frog. First seen in *Sesame Street*. Created by Jim Henson and Frank Oz.

My Favorite Martian Ray Walston (Uncle Martin), Bill Bixby (Tim O'Hara).

Nearest and Dearest Hylda Baker (Nellie Pledge), Jimmy Jewel (Eli), Madge Hindle (Lily), Edward Malin (Walter).

Never the Twain Donald Sinden (Simon Peel), Windsor Davies (Oliver Smallbridge), Honor Blackman (Veronica).

New Avengers Joanna Lumley (Purdey), Gareth Hunt (Mike Gambit), Patrick MacNee (John Steed).

New Statesman, The Rik Mayall (Alan Beresford B'Stard), Terence Alexander (Sir Greville), Marsha Fitzalan (Sarah).

Nice Time Germaine Greer, Jonathan Routh and Kenny Everett in wacky sketch show produced by John Birt.

Night Fever Channel 5 karaoke programme hosted by Suggs.

99–1 Leslie Grantham (Mick Raynor), Robert Stephens (Commander Oakwood).

No Hiding Place Sequel to *Crimesheet* and *Murder Bag*. Raymond Francis (Superintendent Lockhart), Eric Lander (Sergeant Baxter), Johnny Briggs (Det. Sgt Russell).

No, Honestly John Alderton (Charles 'CD' Danby), Pauline Collins (Clara Danby).

No Place Like Home William Gaunt (Arthur Crabtree), Martin Clunes (Nigel Crabtree), Patricia Garwood (Beryl).

No – That's Me Over Here Ronnie Corbett (Ronnie), Rosemary Leach (Rosemary), Henry McGee (Henry).

Not in Front of the Children Wendy Craig (Jennifer Corner), Paul Daneman/Ronald Hines (Henry Corner).

Not Only But Also Peter Cook and Dudley Moore.

Not the Nine O'Clock News Rowan Atkinson, Chris Langham (replaced by Griff Rhys-Jones), Mel Smith, Pamela Stephenson.

NYPD Blue Dennis Franz (Det. Andy Sipowicz), Rick Schroder (Det. Danny Sorenson), James McDaniel (Lt. Arthur Fancy), Nicholas Turturro (Det. James Martinez), Sharon Lawrence (Asst. DA Sylvia Costas Sipowicz), Gordon Clapp (Det. Greg Medavoy), Mark-Paul Gosselaar (Det. John Clark Jr), Henry Simmons (Det. Baldwin Jones), Bill Brochtrup (PAA John Irvin), Esai Morales (Lt. Tony Rodriguez), Charlotte Ross (Det. Connie McDowell), Garcelle Beauvais-Nilon (ADA Valerie Haywood), Jacqueline Obradors (Det. Rita Ortiz), Sherry Stringfield (Laura Michaels Kelly). Co-created by Steven Bochco and David Milch. NYPD is New York Police Department.

Office, The Ricky Gervais (David Brent), Martin Freeman (Tim Canterbury), Mackenzie Crooke (Gareth Keenan), Lucy Davis (Dawn Tynsley), Ewan Macintosh (Keith), Ralph Ineson (Chris 'Finchy' Finch), Oliver Chris (Ricky), Joel Beckett (Lee), Sally Bretton (Donna), Patrick Baladi (Neil Godwin), Steve Merchant (Nathan aka The Oggmonster or Oggy). Co-written and directed by Ricky Gervais and Steve Merchant. Theme tune: 'Handbags and Gladrags', written by Mike D'abo and arranged and performed by Big George.

Oh Brother/Oh Father Derek Nimmo (Brother/Father Dominic), Felix Aylmer (Father Anselm).

Oh, Doctor Beeching! Su Pollard (Ethel Schumann), Paul Shane (Jack Skinner), Jeffrey Holland (Cecil Parkin), Stephen Lewis (Harry Lambert), Julia Deakin (May Skinner).

Old Grey Whistle Test/Whistle Test Bob Harris, Anne Nightingale, Andy Kershaw, Mark Ellen, Ian Whitcomb, Richard Skinner.

One Foot in the Grave Richard Wilson (Victor Meldrew), Annette Crosbie (Margaret), Angus Deayton (Patrick).

Onedin Line, The Peter Gilmore (Capt. James

T
E
L
E
V
I
S
I
O
N

Onedin), Jane Seymour (Emma Callon), Jill Gascoigne (Letty Gaunt). First ship: *Charlotte Rose.*

Only Fools and Horses   David Jason (Del Boy Trotter), Nicholas Lyndhurst (Rodney), Lennard Pearce (Grandad), Buster Merryfield (Uncle Albert), Tessa Peake-Jones (Raquel), Gwyneth Strong (Cassandra), Roger Lloyd Pack (Trigger), John Challis (Boycie), Sue Holderness (Marlene). Pub: Nag's Head. Trotters' address: 368 Nelson Mandela House, Peckham. Company name: Trotter's Independent Trading. Transport: features Del's yellow Reliant Regal Van Mk II. Title from the adage 'Only fools and horses work'. Writer: John Sullivan.

Only When I Laugh   James Bolam (Roy Figgis), Peter Bowles (Archie Glover), Richard Wilson (Dr Gordon Thorpe).

On Safari   Presenters Armand and Michaela Denis.

On the Buses   Reg Varney (Stan Butler), Stephen Lewis (Blakey), Anna Karen (Olive), Michael Robbins (Arthur), Bob Grant (Jack). Bus company: Luxtons.

On the Move   Bob Hoskins (Alf), Donald Gee (Bert).

On the Up   Dennis Waterman (Tony Carpenter), Sam Kelly (Sam), Joan Sims (Mrs Fiona Wembley).

Opportunity Knocks   Presenters: Hughie Green, Bob Monkhouse, Les Dawson.

Other 'Arf, The   Lorraine Chase (Lorraine Watts), John Standing (Charles Lattimer), Pat Hodge (Sybil Howarth).

OTT (Over The Top)   Adult version of *TISWAS,* with variations such as the three naked balloon dancers.

Our Man at St Mark's   Leslie Phillips (Rev. Andrew Parker), Donald Sinden (Rev. Stephen Young).

Outside Edge   Robert Daws (Roger Dervish), Brenda Blethyn (Miriam, 'Mim'), Timothy Spall (Kevin Costello), Josie Lawrence (Maggie).

Pallisers, The   Susan Hampshire (Lady Glencora McCluskie/Palliser), Philip Latham (Plantagenet Palliser), Jeremy Irons (Frank Tregear), Anthony Andrews (Earl of Silverbridge), Derek Jacobi (Lord Fawn).

Panorama   Presenters include Pat Murphy, Richard Dimbleby, Malcolm Muggeridge, David Dimbleby.

Paradise Club   Leslie Grantham (Danny Kane), Don Henderson (Frank Kane).

Partridge Family   Shirley Jones (Shirley), David Cassidy (Keith), Susan Dey (Laurie), Danny Bonaduce (Chris).

Peak Practice   Kevin Whately (Dr Jack Kerruish), Amanda Burton (Dr Beth Glover), Gray O'Brien (Tom Deneley), Gary Mavers (Andrew Attwood), Maggie O'Neill (Alex Redman), Joseph Millson (Sam Morgan). Set in Cardale, Peak District.

Pebble Mill at One   Presenters: Bob Langley, Donny MacLeod, Jan Leeming, Anna Ford, Paul Coia, Magnus Magnusson. Pebble Mill was revived after a short break with presenters including Judi Spiers, Alan Titchmarsh, Gloria Hunniford and Ross King.

Pennies From Heaven   Bob Hoskins (Arthur Parker), Cheryl Campbell (Eileen), Gemma Craven (Joan Parker). Written by Dennis Potter.

Perfect Scoundrels   Peter Bowles (Guy Buchanan), Bryan Murray (Harry Cassidy). Series created by its stars.

Perry Mason   Raymond Burr (Perry Mason), Barbara Hale (Della Street), William Hopper (Paul Drake), William Talman (Hamilton Burger), Ray Collins (Lt Tragg). Set in Los Angeles.

Persuaders, The   Tony Curtis (Danny Wilde), Roger Moore (Lord Brett Sinclair), Laurence Naismith (Judge Fulton).

Peter Principle, The   Jim Broadbent (Peter), Claire Skinner (Susan), Stephen Moore (Geoffrey), Tracy Keating (Brenda), David Schneider (Bradley), Daniel Flynn (Dave), Janette Legge (Iris). Tale of inept bank manager.

Petrocelli   Barry Newman (Tony Petrocelli), Susan Howard (Maggie). Set in fictional San Remo.

Peyton Place   Ryan O'Neal (Rodney Harrington), Mia Farrow (Allison McKenzie), Ed Nelson (Dr Mike Rossi), Dorothy Malone (Constance McKenzie), Christopher Connelly (Norman Harrington).

Phil Silvers Show   Phil Silvers (Master Sgt Ernest Bilko), Maurice Gosfield (Pte Duane Doberman), Joe E. Ross (Sgt Rupert Ritzik), Billy Sands (Pte Dino Paparelli), Paul Ford (Colonel John Hall), Allan Melvin (Cpl Henshaw), Harvey Lembeck (Cpl Rocco Barbella), Elizabeth Fraser (Joan). Rocco Barbella was the real name of boxer Rocky Graziano, the casting director.

Phoenix Nights   Peter Kay plays club boss Brian Potter, who was disabled after being crushed by a fruit machine during a flood, as well as doorman Max and Chorley FM's mullet-haired DJ Paul Le Roy. Series developed from one-off *The Club* and other characters include resident compere Jerry St Clair, real name Jerry Dignan (Dave Spikey), Kenny Senior (Archie Kelly), Kenny Junior (Justin Moorhouse), Holy Mary (Janice Connolly). Resident band: Les Alanos with Alan (Steve Edge) on keyboards and Les (Toby Foster) on drums. Written by Peter Kay, Dave Spikey and Neil Fitzmaurice.

Pie in the Sky   Richard Griffiths stars as masterchef and ace detective Henry Crabbe.

Pinky and Perky   Creators: Jan and Vlasta Dalibor.

Plane Makers, The   Patrick Wymark (John Wilder), Barbara Murray/Ann Firbank (Pamela Wilder), Jack Watling (Don Henderson). Aircraft factory name: Scott Furlong. Follow-on series was called *The Power Game.*

Please Sir   John Alderton (Bernard 'Privet' Hedges), Deryck Guyler (Norman Potter), Peter Cleall (Eric Duffy), Joan Sanderson (Doris Ewell), David Barry (Frankie Abbott), Richard Davies (Mr Price), Jill Kerman (Penny Wheeler/Hedges), Spin-off series: *The Fenn Street Gang.*

Poldark   Robin Ellis (Ross Poldark), Angharad Rees (Demelza), Ralph Bates (George Warleggan). Based on novels by Winston Graham.

Police Woman   Angie Dickinson (Sgt Suzanne 'Pepper' Anderson), Earl Holliman (Lt Bill Crowley).

Popstars   Auditions of thousands of young budding pop stars in the quest to put together a five-piece all singing and dancing supergroup. The five winners were Danny Foster, Myleene Klass, Noel Sullivan, Kym Marsh and Suzanne Shaw who became Hear'Say. The show's executive producer was 'Nasty' Nigel Lythgoe.

Porridge   Ronnie Barker (Norman Stanley Fletcher), Richard Beckinsale (Lennie Godber), Fulton MacKay (Mr MacKay), Peter Vaughan (Groutie), David Jason (Blanco), Brian Wilde (Mr Barrowclough), Patricia Brake (Ingrid), Chris Biggins (Lukewarm), Maurice Denham (Judge Rawley), Tony Osoba (McLaren), Sam Kelly (Warren). Prison setting: HMP Slade. Sentence: five years. Sequel: *Going Straight.*

Porterhouse Blue   David Jason (Skullion), Ian Richardson (Sir Godber Evans), Griff Rhys-Jones (Cornelius Carrington).

Postman Pat   Characters include Jess the cat, Mrs Goggins the postmistress and twins Katie and Tom Pottage.

Pot Black   Half-hour snooker programme which popularised the game as a television medium. Ran from 1969 to 1986, Ray Reardon was the first champion and Jimmy White the last. The theme tune was 'Ivory Rag'. *Pot Black* was briefly revived for one series. A *Masters Pot Black* was held in 1997, the winner being Joe Johnson.

Potter   Arthur Lowe (Redvers Potter), replaced by Robin Bailey when Arthur Lowe died between series.

Price is Right, The   Presenters: Leslie Crowther and Bruce Forsyth.

Pride and Prejudice   Colin Firth (Fitzwilliam Darcy), Jennifer Ehle (Elizabeth Bennet), Alison Steadman (Mrs Bennet), Julia Sawalha (Lydia Bennet).

Prisoner, The   Patrick McGoohan (No. 6). Filmed in Portmeirion, Wales.

Professionals, The   Gordon Jackson (George Cowley), Lewis Collins (William Bodie), Martin Shaw (Ray Doyle).

Protectors, The   Robert Vaughn (Harry Rule), Nyree Dawn Porter (Contessa di Contini), Tony Anholt (Paul Buchet).

Quantum Leap   Scott Bakula (Dr Sam Beckett), Dean Stockwell (Al Calavicci).

Quatermass   Reginald Tate/André Morell/John Robinson/John Mills (Professor Bernard Quatermass). Written by Nigel Kneale.

Question of Sport, A   Presenters: David Vine, David Coleman, Sue Barker.

Rab C Nesbit   Gregor Fisher's character first appeared in *Naked Video*. Children are Gash and Burney.

Rag Trade, The   Peter Jones (Mr Fenner), Reg Varney (Reg), Miriam Karlin (Paddy), Sheila Hancock (Carole), Esma Cannon (Little Lil), Barbara Windsor (Judy), Wanda Ventham (Shirley). A revival series starred Anna Karen as the character she played in *On the Buses*.

Randall and Hopkirk (Deceased)   Mike Pratt (Jeff Randall), Kenneth Cope (Marty Hopkirk), Annette Andre (Jean Hopkirk). Revived in the 1990s with Reeves and Mortimer playing Marty and Jeff.

Rawhide   Eric Fleming (Gil Favor), Clint Eastwood (Rowdy Yates), Paul Brinegar (Wishbone), Sheb Wooley (Pete Nolan), James Murdock (Harkness 'Mushy' Mushgrove).

Ready Steady Go   Presenters Keith Fordyce, Cathy McGowan, David Gell, Michael Aldred.

Red Dwarf   Chris Barrie (Arnold J Rimmer BSc, SSC), Craig Charles (Dave Lister), Danny John-Jules (Cat), Norman Lovett/Hattie Hayridge (Holly), David Ross/Robert Llewellyn (Kryten).

Remington Steele   Pierce Brosnan, Stephanie Zimbalist (Laura Holt, the owner of Remington Steele Investigations).

Rhoda   Valerie Harper (Rhoda Morgenstern/Gerard), Julie Kavner (Brenda Morgenstern), Lorenzo Musoc (Carlton the doorman, voice only). Spin-off from the *Mary Tyler Moore Show*.

Rich Man Poor Man   First of the TV 'Best Sellers', based on an Irwin Shaw novel and starring Peter Strauss and Nick Nolte.

Rifleman, The   Chuck Connors (Lucas McCain), Johnny Crawford (Mark McCain).

Right to Reply   Presenters include: Gus MacDonald, Linda Agran, Brian Hayes, Rory McGrath, Sheena McDonald, Roger Bolton.

Rings on Their Fingers   Martin Jarvis (Oliver Pryde), Diane Keen (Sandy Bennett/Pryde).

Rising Damp   Leonard Rossiter (Rigsby), Richard Beckinsale (Allan), Frances de la Tour (Miss Jones), Don Warrington (Philip), Vienna the cat. Based on a one-act play, *The Banana Box*.

Robin Hood   Short-lived series of 1953 in which Patrick Troughton (second Dr Who) took the lead role.

Robin of Sherwood   Michael Praed (Robin of Loxley), Jason Connery (Robert of Huntingdon), Clive Mantle (Little John), Ray Winstone (Will Scarlet), Judi Trott (Maid Marian). Music by Clannad.

Robin's Nest   Richard O'Sullivan (Robin Tripp), Tessa Wyatt (Victoria Nicholls), Tony Britton (James Nicholls), David Kelly (Albert Riddle, the one-armed washer-up), Honor Blackman/Barbara Murray (Marion).

Rock Follies   Charlotte Cornwell, Julie Covington (Devonia Dee Rhoades), Rula Lenska. Group name: The Little Ladies.

Rockford Files, The   James Garner, Noah Beery Jnr (Joseph 'Rocky' Rockford), Joe Santos (Det. Sgt Dennis Becker).

Room 101   Original presenter Nick Hancock, who was followed by Paul Merton.

Roseanne   Roseanne Barr (Roseanne Conner), John Goodman (Dan), George Clooney (Booker Brooks).

Royle Family, The   Caroline Aherne (Denise Best), Ricky Tomlinson (Jim Royle), Sue Johnston (Barbara Royle), Craig Cash (Dave Best), Ralf Little (Anthony Royle), Liz Smith (Norma Speakman).

Rumpole of the Bailey   Leo McKern (Horace Rumpole), Patricia Hodge (Phyllida Trant/Erskine-Brown), Peter Bowles (Guthrie Featherstone), Bill Fraser (Justice Bullingham). Wife: Hilda (She who must be obeyed). Winebar: Pomeroy's. Drink: Château Fleet Street).

Saint, The   Roger Moore (Simon Templar alias the Saint). Car: Volvo P1800S. Inspector: Claude Eustace Teal. Sequel: *Return of the Saint*, starring Ian Ogilvy.

Sea Hunt   Lloyd Bridges (Mike Nelson). Boat: the *Argonaut*.

Secret Army   Jan Francis (Lisa Colbert; codename Yvette), Bernard Hepton (Albert Foiret), Clifford Rose (Sturmbannführer Ludwig Kessler). Underground movement: Lifeline.

Secret Diary of Adrian Mole, Aged 13¾   Gian Sammarco (Adrian), Stephen Moore (Mr Mole), Julie Walters and Lulu (Pauline Mole), Lindsey Stagg (Pandora). Based on the Sue Townsend novels.

Seinfeld   Jerry Seinfeld (Jerry), Jason Alexander (George), Michael Richards (Kramer), Julia Louis Dreyfus (Elaine).

September Song   Michael Williams (Billy Balsam), Russ Abbot (Ted Fenwick), Michael Angelis (Arnie).

77 Sunset Strip   Efrem Zimbalist Jnr (Stuart Bailey), Roger Smith (Jeff Spencer), Ed Byrnes (Kookie). Much of the action took place outside Dean Martin's restaurant, Dino's.

Sex and the City   Sarah Jessica Parker (Carrie Bradshaw), Kim Cattrall (Samantha Jones), Kristin

Davis (Charlotte York), Cynthia Nixon (Miranda Hobbes), John Corbett (Aidan), Christopher Orr (Alexander).

Sexton Blake Laurence Payne (Sexton Blake), Roger Foss (Tinker), Dorothea Phillips (Mrs Bardell). Bloodhound: Pedro. White Rolls Royce nicknamed the Grey Panther.

Shameless David Threlfall (Frank Gallagher), Anne-Marie Duff (Fiona Gallagher), Jody Latham (Lip Gallagher), James McAvoy (Steve), Gerard Kearns (Ian Gallagher), Maxine Peake (Veronica), Dean Lennox Kelly (Kev), Maggie O'Neill (Sheila Jackson), Chris Bisson (Kash). Written by Paul Abbott. Set on the Chatsworth Estate.

Sharpe Sean Bean (Richard Sharpe), Daragh O'Malley (Sgt Pat Harper), Peter Postlethwaite (Hakeswill), Philip Whitchurch (Frederickson), Liz Hurley (Isabella), Assumpta Sema (Teresa, the first Mrs Sharpe), Abigail Cruttenden (Lady Jane, the second Mrs Sharpe), Cecile Paoli (Lucille Dubert, the third Mrs Sharpe), Louise Germaine (Sally Clayton), John Tams (Hagman) also co-wrote the music. Based on novels by Bernard Cornwell.

Shillingbury Tales Robin Nedwell (Peter Higgins), Diane Keen (Sally Higgins), Lionel Jeffries (Major Langton), Bernard Cribbins (Cuffy), Jack Douglas (Jake).

Shine On Harvey Moon Kenneth Cranham/Nicky Henson (Harvey Moon), Linda Robson (Maggie Moon), Nigel Planer (Lou Lewis), Elizabeth Spriggs (Nan), Pauline Quirke (Veronica), Maggie Steed (Rita Moon). Harvey's occupation: professional footballer.

Simpsons, The Characters include: Homer and Marge Simpson and their children Bart, Lisa and Maggie. The pet dog is called Santa's Little Helper. Other characters include Montgomery Burns, Waylon Smithers, Professor John Frink, Millhouse van Houten, Sideshow Bob, Krusty the Clown, and Chief Wiggum and his son Ralph. Series is set in Springfield and started life as a cartoon short on the *Tracy Ullman Show*.

Singing Detective, The Michael Gambon (Philip E Marlow), Joanne Whalley (Nurse Mills/Carlotta), Patrick Malahide (Mark Binney/Mark Finney/Raymond Binney), Jim Carter (Mr Marlow), Alison Steadman (Beth Marlow/Lili). Hospital ward: Sherpa Tensing. Illness: psoriasis. Written by Dennis Potter.

Sir Francis Drake Terence Morgan (Drake), Jean Kent (Queen Elizabeth), Michael Crawford (John Drake).

Six-Five Special Presenters: Pete Murray, Josephine Douglas, Freddie Mills, Jim Dale. Jack Good was the original producer and Adam Faith made his debut on his way to stardom.

Six Million Dollar Man Lee Majors (Steve Austin), Richard Anderson (Oscar Goldman), Lyndsay Wagner (Jaime Sommers). The opening sequence showing Steve Austin's crash in the Mojave Desert was in fact Donald Campbell's fatal accident while attempting the world water-speed record on Coniston Water.

64,000 Dollar Question, The Questions were guarded every week by Detective Fabian. Bob Monkhouse hosted the British version.

Six Wives of Henry VIII, The Keith Michell (Henry), Annette Crosbie (Catherine of Aragon), Dorothy Tutin (Anne Boleyn), Anne Stallybrass (Jane Seymour), Elvi Hale (Anne of Cleves), Angela Pleasance (Catherine Howard), Rosalie Crutchley (Catherine Parr), Patrick Troughton (Duke of Norfolk). Narrator: Anthony Quayle.

Sliders John Rhys-Davies (Maximillian Arturo), Jerry O'Connell (Quinn Mallory), Sabrina Lloyd (Wade Wells), Cleavant Derricks (Rembrandt Brown). Sliding is the term used for entering parallel universes.

Slinger's Day Bruce Forsyth (Cecil Slinger). The untimely death of Leonard Rossiter precipitated the arrival of Bruce Forsyth to take over the role of the put-upon supermarket manager, his name changed from Tripper to Slinger.

Soap Katherine Helmond (Jessica Tate), Cathryn Damon (Mary Dallas Campbell), Billy Crystal (Jodie Dallas), Robert Guillaume (Benson Dubois), Robert Mandan (Chester Tate).

Soldier, Soldier Jerome Flynn (Paddy Garvey), Robson Green (Dave Tucker), David Haig (Mjr Tom Cadman).

Some Mothers Do 'Ave 'Em Michael Crawford (Frank Spencer), Michele Dotrice (Betty). Daughter: Jessica.

Sopranos, The James Gandolfini (Tony Soprano), Edie Falco (Carmela Soprano), Nancy Marchand (Livia Soprano), Lorraine Bracco (Dr Jennifer Melfi), Jamie-Lynn Sigler (Meadow Soprano), Robert Iler (A J Soprano), Aida Turturro (Janice 'Parvati' Soprano), Dominic Chianese (Corrado Soprano), Tony Sirico (Paulie Walnuts), Steve van Zandt (Silvio Dante), John Ventimiglia (Artie Bucco). Theme tune: 'Woke Up This Morning' by Alabama 3.

Sorry! Ronnie Corbett (Timothy Lumsden, a librarian), Barbara Lott (Mrs Phyllis Lumsden).

South Park Adult cartoon series. Characters include Kenny (who is invariably killed), Kyle, Stan, Cartman, Chef, Mr Garrison, Ned, Uncle Jimbo and Officer Barbrady.

Space: 1999 Martin Landau (John Koenig), Barbara Bain (Dr Helena Russell), Catherine Schell (Maya), Barry Morse (Professor Victor Bergman). Crew of Moonbase Alpha stranded in space.

Space Patrol Voices: Capt. Larry Dart (Dick Vosburgh), Husky and Slim (Ronnie Stevens), Gabblerdictum (Libby Morris), Colonel Raeburn (Murray Kash). Ship: Galasphere 347. Year: 2100. The Space Patrol was the active unit of the United Galactic Organization. Libby Morris was Raeburn's super-efficient blonde secretary from Venus; fortunately there is no such thing as a dumb blonde on Venus.

Special Branch George Sewell (Det. Chief Insp. Alan Craven), Patrick Mower (Det. Chief Insp. Tom Haggerty), Derren Nesbitt (Det. Insp. Jordan), Fulton Mackay (Det. Supt Inman).

Spender Jimmy Nail, Sammy Johnson (Stick), Paul Greenwood (Supt Yelland).

Spenser For Hire Robert Urich (Spenser), Avery Brooks (Hawk), Barbara Stock (Susan Silverman).

Spitting Image Created by Peter Fluck, Roger Law and Michael Lambie-Martin.

St Elsewhere Ed Flanders (Donald Westphall), William Daniels (Mark Craig), Ed Begley Jnr (Victor Ehrlich). Hospital: St Elegius, Boston.

Star Trek William Shatner (James Tiberius Kirk), Leonard Nimoy (Mr Spock – his mother is Amanda, an earth woman, his father is Sarek, a Vulcan), De Forest Kelly (Dr Leonard 'Bones' McCoy), James Doohan (Scottie), George Takei (Mr Sulu), Nichelle

Nichols (Lt Uhura), Walter Koenig (Ensign Pavel Chekov), Majel Barrett (Nurse Chapel). Crew size: 430. Decks: 8. Five-year mission to boldly go where no man has gone before. Enterprise no.: NCC 1701A. Shuttle: Galileo. Spock's blood colour: green (T positive).

Star Trek: The Next Generation Patrick Stewart (Captain Jean-Luc Picard), Jonathan Frakes (Commander William Ryker), LeVar Burton (Lt Geordi La Forge), Michael Dorn (Lt Worf), Denise Crosby (Lt Tasha Yar), Gates McFadden (Dr Bev Crusher), Marina Sirtis (Deanna Troi), Brent Spiner (Lt Cmdr Data), Wil Wheaton (Wesley), Diana Muldaur (Dr Katherine Pulaski), Whoopi Goldberg (Guinan). Original *Star Trek* set in the 23rd century; this series was set 78 years later. Enterprise no.: NCC 1701D.

Stars in Their Eyes Presenters: Leslie Crowther, Matthew Kelly, Cat Deeley. 2005 winner: Gordon Hendrix as Elvis Presley ('Suspicious Minds').

Starsky and Hutch David Soul (Ken Hutchinson), Paul Michael Glaser (Dave Starsky), Antonio Fargas (Huggie Bear).

Steptoe and Son Harry H Corbett (Harold), Wilfred Bramble (Albert), Hercules the horse. American spin-off: *Sandford and Son*.

Stingray Troy Tempest, George 'Phones' Sheridan, Atlanta Shore, Titan, Agent X20. Marina was the mute daughter of Emperor Aphony from Pacifica and her pet seal was called Oink. Organisation: WASP, World Aquanaut Security Patrol, in Marineville. Year: 2000.

Streets of San Francisco, The Karl Malden (Det. Lt Mike Stone), Michael Douglas (Insp. Steve Keller).

Strictly Come Dancing Presented by Bruce Forsyth and Tess Daly. Judges: Len Goodman, Arlene Phillips, Bruno Tonioli, Craig Revel Horwood. Series one won by Natasha Kaplinsky and Brendan Cole, series two by Jill Halfpenny and Darren Bennet. Natasha stood in for Tess during the first half of series two while she had a baby. Claudia Winkleman hosted the nightly update show on BBC2.

Sunday Night at the London Palladium Comperes included: Tommy Trinder, Bruce Forsyth, Des O'Connor, Jimmy Tarbuck, Norman Vaughan, Jim Dale, Hughie Green, Alfred Marks, Robert Morley, Dave Allen, Roger Moore, Don Arrol, Arthur Haynes, Dickie Henderson.

Supercar Mike Mercury, Professor Popkiss, Dr Beaker, Masterspy, Mitch the monkey, Zarin.

Supergran Gudrun Ure (Granny Smith), Iain Cuthbertson (Scunner Campbell). Set in Chisleton.

Superman Original series starred George Reeves, who committed suicide after being typecast in this role. The more recent series stars Dean Cain as Superman and Teri Hatcher as Lois Lane.

Surgical Spirit Nichola McAuliffe (Dr Sheila Sabatini), Duncan Preston (Dr Jonathan Haslam). Gillies Hospital.

Sutherland's Law Iain Cuthbertson played Procurator Fiscal Sutherland.

Sweeney, The John Thaw (Det. Inspector Jack Regan), Dennis Waterman (Det. Sgt George Carter).

Sykes Eric Sykes and Hattie Jacques (lived at Sebastopol Terrace), Derek Guyler (Korky), Richard Wattis (Mr Brown).

Sylvania Waters Australian fly-on-the-wall story of the Baker-Donaher family by Paul Watson (*The Family*).

Taggart Mark McManus (Det. Chief Insp. Jim Taggart), Neil Duncan (Det. Sgt Peter Livingstone), Blythe Duff (Det. Sgt. Jackie Reid).

Take Three Girls Angela Down, Liza Goddard, Susan Jameson.

Take Your Pick Presenters: Michael Miles, Des O'Connor. Original man with the gong: Alec Dane.

Taxi Judd Hirsch (Alex Reiger), Jeff Conaway (Bobby Wheeler), Danny de Vito (Louis de Palma), Marilu Henner (Elaine Nardo), Tony Danza (Tony Banta), Andy Kaufman (Latka Gravas), Christopher Lloyd (Reverend Jim 'Iggie' Ignatowski). Cab company: Sunshine Cabs.

Teletubbies Tinky Winky, Dipsy, Laa Laa, Po. Babygros open to reveal televisions. Created by Anne Wood. Looked after by a vacuum cleaner called Noo Noo. Voices include Eric Sykes and Toyah Wilcox.

Tenko Stephanie Beacham (Rose Millar), Stephanie Cole (Dr Beatrice Mason), Bert Kwouk (Yamauchi).

Thank Your Lucky Stars Presenters: Brian Matthews, Jim Dale and Keith Fordyce.

Third Man Michael Rennie (Harry Lime). Popular theme tune played on the zither by Shirley Abicaire.

This Morning Popular daytime magazine hosted live by Richard Madeley and Judy Finnegan.

Thomas the Tank Engine Narrators: Ringo Starr, Michael Angelis. Thomas is a blue engine; Gordon is green. Written by the Reverend Awdry. The Fat Controller became Sir Topham Hat.

Thunderbirds Thunderbird 1 pilot Scott Tracy (usually first at the scene because of its high-speed capability); Thunderbird 2 pilot Virgil (pod carrier for Thunderbird 4 and any special equipment required); Thunderbird 3 pilot Alan (rocket back-up) – Alan manned the Spacestation occasionally; Thunderbird 4 pilot Gordon (underwater machine which had great versatility); Thunderbird 5 pilot John (the stationery Spacestation). Jeff Tracy was the father and co-ordinator and Kyrano was his oriental assistant. GB agent was Lady Penelope Creighton-Ward and her butler was Parker. Her Rolls Royce had the registration FAB1; her yacht was FAB2. Technical expert was Hiram Hackenbacker (Brains). Set in the year 2063. The Hood (Kyrano's half-brother) was the arch-enemy who regularly appeared.

Till Death Us Do Part Warren Mitchell (Alf Garnett), Anthony Booth (Mike), Dandy Nichols (Else), Una Stubbs (Rita), Patrica Hayes (Min Reed). Written by Johnny Speight.

Time Tunnel, The James Darren (Dr Tony Newman), Robert Colbert (Dr Doug Phillips), Lee Meriwether (Dr Ann McGregor).

Tinker Tailor Soldier Spy Alec Guinness (George Smiley), Bernard Hepton (Toby Esterhase), Beryl Reid (Connie Sachs).

TISWAS Today is Saturday, Watch (wear a) and Smile. Presenters included Chris Tarrant, John Asher, Trevor East, Sally James, Lenny Henry, John Gorman, Clive Webb, Sylvester McCoy, Frank Carson, Fogwell Flax and Bob Carolgees and Spit the dog.

Today's the Day Current affairs quiz programme hosted by Martyn Lewis. Your author, with his chum, Andy Curtis, won the 1997 series.

To the Manor Born Penelope Keith (Audrey Fforbes-Hamilton), Peter Bowles (Richard de Vere), Michael Bilton (Ned), Angela Thorne (Marjory Frobisher), John Rudling (Brabinger), Daphne Heard (Mrs Polouvicka).

TELEVISION

Tonight   Presenter: Cliff Michelmore. Catchphrase: The next Tonight will be tomorrow night. Notable reporters included Trevor Philpott, Julian Pettifer, Magnus Magnusson, Alan Whicker and the hugely popular Fyfe Robertson.

Top Gear   Presenters include William Woolard, Angela Rippon, Barrie Gill, Noel Edmonds, Sue Baker, Jeremy Clarkson, Quentin Willson, Tiff Needell, Chris Goffey, Tony Mason, Janet Trewin, Michele Newman.

Triangle   Kate O'Mara (Katherine Laker), Michael Craig (John Anderson), Larry Lamb (Matt Taylor). Company: Triangle Lines. Short-lived soap notable for the bikini-clad posing of its star.

Tripper's Day   Leonard Rossiter (Norman Tripper); see *Slinger's Day*.

Trumpton   Spin-off series from *Camberwick Green* but the action moved from Pippin Fort. Captain Flack's local firemen: Hugh, Pugh, Barney McGrew, Cuthbert, Dibble and Grubb.

Tutti Frutti   Robbie Coltrane (Danny McGlone), Emma Thompson (Suzie Kettles). Band: The Majestics.

TW3   That Was The Week That Was, presented by David Frost and produced by Ned Sherrin.

Twin Peaks   Kyle MacLachlan (Agent Dale Cooper), Michael Ontkean (Sheriff Harry S Truman), Ray Wise (Leland Palmer), Sheryl Lee (Laura Palmer/Madeleine Ferguson), Piper Laurie (Catherine Martell), Dana Ashbrook (Bobby Briggs), Sherilyn Fenn (Audrey Horne). Characters included a dwarf who talked backwards, the Log Lady and Audrey, who tied knots in cherry stalks with her tongue. Killer was Laura's father, Leland, possessed by 'Bob'.

Two Fat Ladies   Jennifer Paterson and Clarissa Dickson Wright. Oversize chefs who ride in a combination motorcycle.

2 Point 4 Children   Belinda Lang (Bill Porter), Gary Olsen (Ben Porter).

Two's Company   Elaine Stritch (Dorothy McNab), Donald Sinden (Robert Hiller).

UFO   Ed Bishop (Commander Edward Straker), George Sewell (Colonel Alec Freeman), Peter Gordeno (Peter Karlin, the captain of the Vipers), Gabrielle Drake (Lt Gay Ellis), Michael Billington (Colonel Paul Foster), Wanda Ventham (Colonel Virginia Lake). Defence unit: SHADO (Supreme Headquarters Alien Defence Organization). Reconnaissance satellite: S.I.D. (Space Intruder Detector). Location: beneath the Harlington-Straker film studios just outside London (and Moonbase).

University Challenge   Began in 1962 with Bamber Gascoigne as the presenter. After he bowed out in 1987 the series was resumed in 1995 with Jeremy Paxman as the new presenter. The highest winning score was in a first-round match in 1987 when University College, Oxford, defeated Reading 520-35. Series winners are as follows: 1963 Leicester, 1964 no series this year, 1965 New College, Oxford, 1966 Oriel College, Oxford, 1967 Sussex, 1968 Keele, 1969 Sussex, 1970 Churchill College, Cambridge, 1971 Sidney Sussex College, Cambridge, 1972 University College, Oxford, 1973 Fitzwilliam College, Cambridge, 1974 Trinity College, Cambridge, 1975 Keble College, Oxford, 1976 University College, Oxford, 1977 Durham, 1978 Sidney Sussex College, Cambridge, 1979 Bradford, 1980 Merton College, Oxford, 1981

Queen's University, Belfast, 1982 St Andrews, 1983 Dundee, 1984 Open University 1985 No series this year, 1986 Jesus College, Oxford, 1987 Keble College, Oxford, 1995 Trinity College, Cambridge, 1996 Imperial College, London, 1997 Magdalen College, Oxford, 1998 Magdalen College, Oxford, 1999 Open University, 2000 Durham, 2001 Imperial College, London, 2002 Somerville College, Oxford, 2003 Birkbeck College, London, 2004 Magdalen College, Oxford. In 2002 a special 40th anniversary series was made featuring previous champions. Sidney Sussex College, Cambridge, were victorious. In 2003 *University Challenge: The Professionals* began, the Inland Revenue being the first winners; 2004 winners were the British Library.

Upstairs Downstairs   Gordon Jackson (Mr Angus Hudson), Angela Baddeley (Mrs Kate Bridges), Jean Marsh (Rose), David Langton (Lord Richard Bellamy), Simon Williams (Capt. James Bellamy), Nicola Pagett (Elizabeth Bellamy/Kirkbridge), Lesley-Anne Down (Georgina Worsley), Jacqueline Tong (Daisy), Christopher Beeny (Edward), Pauline Collins (Sarah), John Alderton (Thomas). Address: 165 Eaton Place. Spin-off series: *Thomas and Sarah*.

V   Marc Singer (Mike Donovan), Jane Badler (Diana: famous scene where she swallowed a mouse), Jenny Beck and Jennifer Cooke (Elizabeth), Michael Ironside (Ham Tyler), Blair Tefkin (Robin Maxwell, who gave birth to Elizabeth).

Very Peculiar Practice, A   Peter Davison (Dr Stephen Daker), David Troughton (Dr Bob Buzzard), Barbara Flynn (Dr Rose Marie), Michael J Shannon (Jack B Daniels). Set at Lowlands University. Written by Andrew Davies.

Vicar of Dibley, The   Dawn French (Geraldine Granger), Emma Chambers (Alice Tinker), Gary Waldhorn (David Horton), James Fleet (Hugo Horton), Roger Lloyd Pack (Owen Newitt), Trevor Peacock (Jim Trott), John Bluthal (Frank Pickle). Written by Paul Mayhew-Archer and Richard Curtis.

Virginian, The   James Drury (Virginian), Doug McClure (Trampas), Lee J Cobb (Judge Henry Garth), Gary Clarke (Steve Hill), John McIntire (Clay Grainger), Stewart Grainger (Alan MacKenzie), Lee Majors (Roy Tate). Series set on the Shiloh Ranch, Medicine Bow, Wyoming.

Vision On   Presenters include Tony Hart, Larry Parker, Sylvester McCoy, Pat Keysell, Ben Benison, Wilf Lunn, David Cleveland.

Voyage to the Bottom of the Sea   Richard Basehart (Admiral Harriman Nelson), David Hedison (Captain Lee Crane). Nuclear submarine: the *Seaview*. Set in the year 1984.

Wacky Races   Eleven cars lined up to win the title 'The World's Wackiest Racer'. Car 1: Boulder Mobile; Rock and Gravel Slag. Car 2: Creepy Coupé; Big and Little Gruesome. Car 3: Ring-a-Ding Convert-a-Car; Prof. Pat Pending. Car 4: Crimson Haybailer; Red Max. Car 5: Compact Pussycat; Penelope Pitstop. Car 6: Army Surplus Special; Gen. Sgt and Private Pinkley. Car 7: Bulletproof Bomb; Clyde and Anthill Mob. Car 8: Arkansas Chugabug; Luke and Blubber Bear. Car 9: Turbo Terrific; All-American Peter Perfect. Car 10: Buzz Wagon; Rufus Ruffcut and Sawtooth. Car 00: Mean Machine driven by Dick Dastardly and his dog Muttley. Spin-off series were *The Perils of Penelope Pitstop* and *Dastardly and Muttley in their Flying Machines*, in which they tried to 'Stop the Pigeon'.

Waltons, The   Ralph Waite (John), Michael Learned

(Olivia), and their seven children: Richard Thomas and Robert Wightman (John Boy), Judy Norton Taylor (Mary Ellen), Jon Walmsley (Jason), Mary Elizabeth McDonough (Erin), David W Harper (J Robert 'Jim Bob'), Eric Scott (Ben), Kami Cotler (Elizabeth). Their grandparents were played by Will Geer (Zeb) and Ellen Corby (Esther).

Washington Behind Closed Doors Jason Robards (President Richard Monckton).

Watch With Mother Original five: Picture Book (Patricia Driscoll), Andy Pandy, Bill and Ben, Rag, Tag and Bobtail, The Woodentops. Ran from 1952 to 1980. Others included Tales of the Riverbank, Pogles Wood, Bizzy Lizzy and Barnaby.

Watchdog Presenters include Nick Ross, Lynn Faulds Wood, John Stapleton, Anne Robinson, Alice Beer.

Water Margin, The Set in the water margins of Lian Shan Po. The hero was Lin Chung who, with his wife Hsiao, warred against evil in 14th-century China.

Weakest Link, The Presenter Anne Robinson's catchphrase of 'You are the weakest link, goodbye' soon became the ultimate put-down. The popular daytime BBC2 quiz show was given a prime-time slot on BBC1 due to its record viewing figures.

West Wing, The Martin Sheen (President Josiah Bartlet), Allison Janney (C J Cregg), Rob Lowe (Sam Seaborn), John Spencer (Leo McGarry), Janel Maloney (Donna Moss), Richard Schiff (Toby Ziegler), Dulé Hill (Charlie Young), Bradley Whitford (Josh Lyman), Stockard Channing (Abigail Bartlet).

Whack-O! Jimmy Edwards (Prof. James Edwards), Arthur Howard and Julian Orchard (Mr Oliver Pettigrew). School name: Chiselbury.

What's My Line Presenters include Eamonn Andrews, Emma Forbes, Penelope Keith, David Jacobs. Original panel: Isobel Barnett, David Nixon, Gilbert Harding, Barbara Kelly.

What the Papers Say Presenters include Kingsley Martin, Brian Inglis and Stuart Hall.

When the Boat Comes In James Bolam (Jack Ford), Susan Jameson (Jessie Seaton).

Whiplash Peter Graves (Christopher Cobb). Set in the outback of Australia with a memorable theme tune.

Who Wants to Be a Millionaire? Presenter Chris Tarrant's catchphrases include 'D'you wanna phone a friend?', '50/50', and 'Ask the audience'. The first winner was Judith Keppel and the first man to win the million was David Edwards.

Whoops! Apocalypse Barry Morse (Johnny Cyclops), Richard Griffiths (Premier Dubienkin), Ed Bishop (Jay Garrick), Alexei Sayle (Commissar Solzhenitsyn), Peter Jones (Kevin Pork), John Cleese (Lacrobat).

Wind in the Willows, The Voices were Michael Hordern (Badger), David Jason (Toad), Peter Sallis (Rat), Richard Pearson (Mole).

Winds of War, The Robert Mitchum (Commander Victor 'Pug' Henry), Victoria Tennant (Pamela Tudsbury), Ali MacGraw (Natalie Jastrow), Jan-Michael Vincent (Byron Henry), Ben Murphy (Warren Henry), Howard Lang (Winston Churchill), Gunter Meisner (Hitler). Written by Herman Wouk.

Winston Churchill – The Wilderness Years Robert Hardy (Winston), Siân Phillips (Clementine), Peter Barkworth (Stanley Baldwin), Eric Porter (Neville Chamberlain).

Win, Lose or Draw Hosts: Danny Baker, Shane Richie, Bob Mills.

WKRP in Cincinnati Gary Sandy (Andy Travis), Gordon Jump (Arthur Carlson, 'Big Guy'), Loni Anderson (Jennifer Marlowe), Tim Reid (Gordon Sims, 'Venus Flytrap'), Howard Hesseman (Johnny Caravella, 'Dr Johnny Fever').

Woodentops, The Characters included Daddy and Mummy Woodentop, their twin children Jenny and Willy, Baby Woodentop, Mrs Scrubbit, Sam (the man who helped out in the garden), Buttercup the cow and Spotty the mischievous dog.

World at War World War Two history researched by Noble Frankland, produced by Jeremy Isaacs and narrated by Laurence Olivier.

World's End Short-lived soap opera set around the Mulberry public house, Chelsea, and starring Harry Fowler, Michael Angelis, Paul Brooke, Neville Smith, Primi Townsend.

Worzel Gummidge Jon Pertwee (Worzel), Una Stubbs (Aunt Sally), Geoffrey Bayldon (the Crowman), Lorraine Chase (Dolly Clothes-Peg), Joan Sims (Mrs Bloomsbury-Barton). Written by Keith Waterhouse and Willis Hall from an adaption of Barbara Euphan Todd novels. Worzel was found in Ten Acre Field on Scatterbrook Farm by John and Sue Peters.

Wyatt Earp, The Life and Legend of Hugh O'Brian (Wyatt Earp), Mason Alan Dinehart III (Bat Masterson, Earp's deputy), Douglas Fowley and Myron Healey (Doc Holliday), Lash La Rue (Sheriff John Behan).

Wycliffe Jack Shepherd (Det. Supt Wycliffe), Helen Masters (Det. Insp. Lane), Jimmy Yuill (Det. Insp. Kersey).

Xena: Warrior Princess Lucy Lawless (Xena), New Zealand-made off-shoot series from *Hercules*.

X Files, The David Duchovny (Fox Mulder), Gillian Anderson (Dana Scully), Mitch Pileggi (Skinner), William B Davis (the Cigarette-Smoking Man [C G B Spender]).

XYY Man, The Stephen Yardley (William 'Spider' Scott, who had an extra 'Y' chromosome which appeared to give him a liking for dangerous pursuits, sometimes criminal), Don Henderson (Det. Sgt George Bulman).

Year in Provence, A John Thaw (Peter Mayle), Lindsay Duncan, Christian Luciani.

Yes Minister/Prime Minister Paul Eddington (Jim Hacker, Minister of Administrative Affairs/Prime Minister), Nigel Hawthorne (Sir Humphrey Appleby), Derek Fowlds (Bernard Wooley). Created by Antony Jay and Jonathan Lynn.

You Rang, M'Lord Paul Shane (Alf Stokes), Su Pollard (Ivy Teesdale), Jeffrey Holland (James Twelvetrees). Title song sung by Paul Shane and Bob Monkhouse.

Young Ones, The Rik Mayall (Rick), Nigel Planer (Neil), Adrian Edmondson (Vyvyan), Christopher Ryan (Mike), Alexei Sayle (Jerzy Balowski, and his family). Saying: For Cliff's sake.

You've Been Framed Presenters include Jeremy Beadle and Lisa Riley.

Z Cars Stratford Johns (Det. Chief Insp. Barlow), Frank Windsor (Det. Sgt John Watt), Brian Blessed (PC William 'Fancy' Smith), Joseph Brady (PC John 'Jock' Weir), James Ellis (Sgt Herbert 'Bert' Lynch), Jeremy Kemp (PC Bob Steele), Terence Edmond (PC Ian Sweet), Colin Welland (PC David Graham), Leonard Rossiter (Det. Insp. Bamber), John Slater (Det. Sgt Tom Stone), Alison Steadman (WPC Bayliss). Theme tune based on folk song 'Johnny Todd'. Spin-off series *Softly Softly*, set in Wyvern.

TELEVISION

Zoo Gang, The John Mills (Tommy Devon), Brian Keith (Stephen Halliday), Barry Morse (Alec Marlowe), Lili Palmer (Manouche Roget).

Zoo Time Presenters were Desmond Morris, Chris Kelly and Harry Watt.

Zorro Guy Williams (Don Diego de la Vega, 'Zorro'), Gene Sheldon (Bernardo). Zorro means fox in Spanish.

Soap Operas: Cast of Characters

Character	Actor
Albion Market	
(set in Manchester; aired between August 1985 and August 1986) ITV	
Alan Curtis	Simon Rouse
Anita Rai	Souad Faress
Carol Broadbent	Barbara Wilshere
Colette Johnson	Nimmy March
Debbie Taylor	Jane Hazlegrove
Derek Owen	David Hargreaves
Geoff Travis	Geoffrey Leesley
Janet Owen	Hetta Charnley
Jaz Sharma	Paul Bhattacharjee
Keith Naylor	Derek Hicks
Larry Rigg	Peter Benson
Lisa O'Shea	Sally Baxter
Louise Todd	Kelly Lawrence
Ly Nhu Chan	Pik-Sen Lim
Lynne Harrison	Noreen Kershaw
Miriam Ransome	Carol Kaye
Morris Ransome	Bernard Spear
Narya Vyas	Rashid Karapiet
Paul O'Donnell	Paul Beringer
Peggy Sagar	Maria Vega
Phil Smith	Burt Caesar
Ralph Friend	David Boyce
Roy Harrison	Jonathan Barlow
Sita Sharma	Seeta Indrani
Ted Pilkington	Anthony Booth
Terry Flynn	Alistair Walker
Tony Fraser	John Michie
Viv Harker	Helen Shapiro
The Bill	
(set in Sun Hill and first aired in 1983) ITV	
ADI Samantha Nixon	Lisa Maxwell
CAD Officer Dean McVerry	Luke Hamill
Chief Insp Cato	Philip Whitchurch
Chief Insp Derek Conway	Ben Roberts
Chief Supt Charles Brownlow	Peter Ellis
DC Alfred 'Tosh' Lines	Kevin Lloyd
DC Danny Glaze	Karl Collins
DC Eva Sharpe	Diane Parish
DC Jo Masters	Sally Rogers
DS Mickey Webb	Chris Simmons
DC Mike Dashwood	Jon Iles
DC Suzie Sim	Wendy Kweh
DC Terry Perkins	Bruce Byron
DC Woods	Tom Cotcher
DCI Jack Meadows	Simon Rouse
Det Chief Insp Kim Reid	Carolyn Pickles
Det Insp Chris Deakin	Shaun Scott
Det Insp Frank Burnside	Christopher Ellison
Det Insp Neil Manson	Andrew Lancel
Det Insp Roy Galloway	John Salthouse
Det Sgt Danny Pearce	Martin Marquez
Det Sgt Don Beech	Billy Murray
Det Sgt Ramani De Costa	Thusitha Jayasundera
Det Sgt Ted Roach	Tony Scannell
DS Debbie McAllister	Natalie Roles
DS Phil Hunter	Scott Maslen

Character	Actor
FDO Roberta Cryer	Moya Brady
Insp Gina Gold	Roberta Taylor
PC Amber Johannsen	Myfanwy Waring
PC Andrea Dunbar	Natalie Robb
PC Barry Stringer	Jonathan Dow
PC Cameron Tait	Daniel MacPherson
PC Cathy Bradford	Connie Hyde
PC Dave Litten	Gary Olsen
PC Dave Quinnan	Andrew Paul
PC Des Taviner	Paul Usher
PC Francis 'Taffy' Edwards	Colin Blumenau
PC Gabriel Kent	Todd Carty
PC Gary Best	Ciaran Griffiths
PC Gemma Osbourne	Jane Danson
PC George Garfield	Huw Higginson
PC Honey Harman	Kim Tiddy
PC Jarvis	Stephen Beckett
PC Jim Carver (former DC)	Mark Wingett
PC Kerry Young	Beth Cordingly
PC Lance Powell	Ofo Uhiara
PC Leela Kapoor	Seema Bowri
PC Luke Ashton	Scott Neal
PC Nick Klein	Rene Zagger
PC Reg Hollis	Jeff Stewart
PC Roger Valentine	John Bowler
PC Robin Frank	Ashley Gunstock
PC Ron Smollett	Nick Stringer
PC Ruby Buxton	Nicola Alexis
PC Sheelagh Murphy	Bernie Nolan
PC Steve Hunter	James Lloyd
PC Steve Loxton	Tom Butcher
PC Timothy Able	Mark Haddigan
PC Tony Stamp	Graham Cole
PC Tony 'Yorkie' Smith	Robert Hudson
PC Yvonne Hemmingway	Michele Austin
Sgt Bob Cryer	Eric Richard
Sgt Craig Gilmore	Hywel Simons
Sgt Dale Smith	Alex Walkinshaw
Sgt June Ackland	Trudie Goodwin
Sgt Matthew Boyden	Tony O'Callaghan
Supt Adam Okaro	Cyril Nri
TDC Brandon Kane	Pal Aron
Viv Martella	Nula Conwell
WPC Cathy Marshall	Lynne Miller
WPC Claire Brind	Kelly Lawrence
WPC Norika Datta	Seeta Indrani
WPC Polly Page	Lisa Geoghan
Brookside	
(set in Liverpool and first aired in 1982; created by Phil Redmond) C4. Final episode 4 November 2003	
Adele Murray	Katy Lamont
Alan Gordon	John Burton
Ali Gordon	Kristopher Mochrie
Annabelle Collins	Doreen Sloane
Anthea Dixon	Barbara Hatwell
Anthony Murray	Raymond Quinn
Barry Grant	Paul Usher
Bel Simpson	Lesley Nightingale
Beth Jordache	Anna Friel
Bev McLoughlin	Sarah White

Billy Corkhill	John McArdle
Bobby Grant	Ricky Tomlinson
Brigid McKenna	Meg Johnson
Chrissy Rogers	Eithne Browne
Christy Murray	Glyn Pritchard
Damon Grant	Simon O'Brien
Dan Morrisey	Matthew Crompton
Dan Simpson	Andrew Butler
David 'Bing' Crosbie	John Burgess
D-D Dixon	Irene Marot
Debbie Gordon	Annette Ekblom
Diane Murray	Bernie Nolan
Diana Spence / Corkhill	Paula Frances
Doreen Corkhill	Kate Fitzgerald
Dr Gary Parr	Ben Hull
Emily Shadwick / O'Leary	Jennifer Ellison
Gabby Parr	Stephanie Chambers
Georgia Simpson	Helen Grace
Heather Huntington / Haversham / Black	Amanda Burton
Jackie Corkhill	Sue Jenkins
Jacqui Dixon / Farnham	Alexandra Fletcher
Jerome Johnson	Leon Lopez
Jimmy Corkhill	Dean Sullivan
Julia Brogan	Gladys Ambrose
Karen Grant	Shelagh O'Hara
Katie Rogers	Diane Burke
Katrina Evans	Ann Marie Davies
Lance Powell	Mickey Poppins
Leanne Powell	Vickie Gates
Leo Johnson	Steven Cole
Lindsay Corkhill	Claire Sweeney
Luke Smith	Callum Giblin
Madge Richmond	Shirley Stelfox
Mandy Jordache	Sandra Maitland
Marty Murray	Neil Caple
Max Farnham	Steve Pinder
Mick Johnson	Louis Emerick
Mike Dixon	Paul Byatt
Nat Simpson	John Sandford
Nicholas Black	Alan Rothwell
Nikki Shadwick	Suzanne Collins
Ollie Simpson	Michael J Jackson
Peter Phelan	Sam Kane
Rachel Dixon	Tiffany Chapman
Ray Hilton	Kenneth Cope
Robbie Moffat	Neil Davies
Rod Corkhill	Jason Hope
Roger Huntington	Rob Spendlove
Ron Dixon	Vince Earl
Ruth Smith	Lynsey McCaffrey
Sean Smith	Barry Sloane
Sheila Grant / Corkhill	Sue Johnston
Steve Murray	Steven Fletcher
Stuart Gordon	David Lyon
Susannah Farnham / Morrisey	Karen Drury
Thomas 'Sinbad' Sweeney	Michael Starke
Tim 'Tinhead' O'Leary	Philip Oliver
Tracy Corkhill	Justine Kerrigan
Trevor Jordache	Brian Murray

Casualty

(set in Holby City Hospital; first aired in Sept 1986) BBC1

Adam Osman	Pal Aron
Amy Howard	Rebecca Wheatley
Anna Paul	Zita Sattar
Baz Fairhead	Julia Watson
Beth Harper	Lynda Rooke
Bex Reynolds	Sarah Manners
Charlie Fairhead	Derek Thompson
Chloe Hill	Jan Anderson
Claire Guildford	Leanne Wilson
Clive King	George Harris
Colette Kierney	Adjoa Andoh
Comfort Jones/Newton	Martina Laird
Dillon Cahill	Dan Rymer
Dr Barbara 'Baz' Samuels Hayes	Julia Watson
Dr Ewart Plimmer	Bernard Gallagher
Dr Mike Barratt	Clive Mantle
Elizabeth Straker	Maureen O'Brien
Ellen Zitek	Georgina Bouzova
Eve Montgomery	Barbara Marten
Finlay Newton	Kwame Kwei-Armah
Guppy Sandhu	Elyes Gabel
Harry Harper	Simon MacCorkindale
Holly Miles	Sandra Huggett
Jack Hathaway	Peter Birch
Jack Vincent	Will Mellor
Jan Goddard	Judy Loe
Jimmy Powell	Robson Green
John 'Abs' Denham	James Redmond
Josh Griffiths	Ian Bleasedale
Jude Korcanik	Lisa Coleman
Lisa 'Duffy' Duffin	Catherine Shipton
Liz Harker	Sue Devaney
Luke Warren	Matthew Wait
Maggie Coldwell	Susan Cookson
Matt Hawley	Jason Merrells
Max Gallagher	Robert Gwilym
Megan Roach	Brenda Fricker
Mel Dyson	Michelle Butterly
Merlin	Orlando Seale
Nikki Marshall	Kelly Harrison
Nina Farr	Rebekah Gibbs
Patrick Spiller	Ian Kelsey
Paul 'Woody' Joyner	Will Thorp
Penny Hutchens	Donna Alexander
Philip Hall	Dominic Guard
Roxanne Bird	Loo Brealey
Ryan Johnson	Russell Boulter
Sam Bateman	Luke Bailey
Sandra Nicholl	Maureen Beattie
Sean Maddox	Gerald Kyd
Selena Manning	Liz Carling
Simon Kaminski	Christopher Colquhoun
Tess Bateman	Suzanne Packer
Tina Seabrook	Claire Goose
Tony Vincent	Lee Warburton
Tony Walker	Eamonn Boland

The Colbys

(spin-off from Dynasty set in Los Angeles; aired between 1985 and 1987) BBC1

Bliss Colby	Claire Yarlett
Constance Colby	Barbara Stanwyck
Fallon Carrington / Colby	Emma Samms
Francesca Scott Colby	Katherine Ross
Jason Colby	Charlton Heston
Miles Colby	Maxwell Caulfield
Monica Colby	Tracy Scoggins
Sable Scott Colby	Stephanie Beacham
Zachary Powers	Ricardo Montalban

Coronation Street

(set in Weatherfield; first aired in 1960) ITV

Aidan Critchley	Dean Ashton
Alan Bradley	Mark Eden
Alan Howard	Alan Browning

TELEVISION

Character	Actor/Actress	Character	Actor/Actress
Alan McKenna	Glenn Hugill	Gary Mallett	Ian Mercer
Albert Tatlock	Jack Howarth MBE	Geena Gregory	Jennifer James
Alec Gilroy	Roy Barraclough	George Barton	Patrick Troughton
Alf Roberts OBE	Bryan Mosley	Gordon Clegg	Bill Kenwright CBE
Alma Halliwell / Sedgewick / Baldwin	Amanda Barrie	Harry Flagg	Iain Rogerson
		Harry Hewitt	Ivan Beavis
Amy Barlow	Rebecca Pike	Hayley Patterson / Cropper	Julie Hesmondhalgh
Andy McDonald	Nicholas Cochrane		
Angela Harris	Kathryn Hunt	Hilda Ogden	Jean Alexander
Angie Freeman	Deborah McAndrew	Himself	Sir Trevor McDonald
Annie Walker	Doris Speed MBE		
Archie Shuttleworth	Roy Hudd	Ian Davenport	Philip Bretherton
Arthur Stokes	Stan Richards	Irma Ogden / Barlow	Sandra Gough
Arthur Watts	Kenneth Waller	Ivy Nelson / Tilsley / Brennan	Lynne Perrie
Ashley Peacock	Steven Arnold	Jack Duckworth	Bill Tarmey
Audrey Potter / Roberts	Sue Nicholls	Jack Walker	Arthur Leslie
Bernard Bulter	Gorden Kaye	Janice Battersby	Vicky Entwistle
Bernard Evans (Dave the Rave)	Paul Shane	Jason Grimshaw	Ryan Thomas
Bet Lynch / Gilroy	Julie Goodyear MBE	Jed Stone	Kenneth Cope
		Jeff Bateman	Peter Dean
Betty Turpin / Williams	Betty Driver MBE	Jerry Booth	Graham Haberfield
Bill Fielding	John Junkin	Jez Quigley	Lee Boardman
Bill Webster	Peter Armitage	Jim McDonald	Charles Lawson
Billy Walker	Ken Farrington	Joe Carter	Jonathan Wrather
Bingo checker	Tim Healy	John Arnley	Paul Warriner
Blanche Hunt	Maggie Jones	Joshua Peacock	Benjamin Beresford
Brian Tilsley	Christopher Quentin	Judy Mallett	Gaynor Faye
		Justine Davenport	Sophie James
Candice Stowe	Nikki Sanderson	Karen Phillips / McDonald	Suranne Jones
Charlie Dickinson	Bill Owen	Katy Harris	Lucy-Jo Hudson
Charlie Stubbs	Bill Ward	Ken Barlow	William Roache MBE
Chesney Brown	Sam Aston		
Chris Collins	Matthew Marsden	Kevin (a lorry driver)	Kevin Whately
Chris Gascoyne	Peter Barlow	Kevin Webster	Michael Le Vell
Ciaran McCarthy	Keith Duffy	Leanne Battersby / Tilsley	Jane Danson
Cilla Brown	Wendi Peters	Len Fairclough	Peter Adamson
Claire Casey / Peacock	Julia Haworth	Leonard Swindley	Arthur Lowe
Concepta Hewitt / Regan / Riley	Doreen Keogh	Les Battersby	Bruce Jones
Craig Harris	Richard Fleeshman	Lillian Spencer	Maureen Lipman
Customer in Sylvia's Separates	Joanne Whalley	Linda Sykes / Baldwin	Jacqueline Pirie
Danny Baldwin	Bradley Walsh	Liz McDonald	Beverley Callard
David Barlow	Alan Rothwell	Lorraine Mason	Samantha Beckinsale
David Platt	Jack P Shepherd		
Deirdre Hunt / Langton / Barlow / Rachid	Anne Kirkbride	Lucille Hewitt	Jennifer Moss
		Lucy Barlow	Katy Carmichael
Dennis Tanner	Philip Lowrie	Maggie Clegg	Irene Sutcliffe
Derek Wilton	Peter Baldwin	Malcolm Nutall	Michael Ball
Des Barnes	Philip Middlemiss	Maria Sutherland	Samia Ghadie
Detective Sergeant Cross	Peter Postlethwaite	Martha Longhurst	Lynne Carol
Dev Alahan	Jimmi Harkishin	Martin Platt	Sean Wilson
Don Brennan	Geoff Hinsliff	Maud Grimes	Elizabeth Bradley
Doreen Heavey	Prunella Gee	Maureen Grimes / Naylor / Holdsworth / Elliot	Sherrie Hewson
Dr Graham	Fulton MacKay		
Duggie Ferguson	John Bowe	Mavis Riley / Wilton	Thelma Barlow
Eddie Yeats	Geoffrey Hughes	Maxine Heavey / Peacock	Tracy Shaw
Eileen Grimshaw	Sue Cleaver	Maya Sharma	Sacha Behar
Eileen Hughes	Prunella Scales	Mickey Malone	Bill Maynard
Elaine Perkins	Joanna Lumley	Mike Baldwin	Johnny Briggs
Elsie Grimshaw / Tanner / Howard	Pat Phoenix	Minnie Caldwell	Margot Bryant
Emily Nugent / Swain / Bishop	Eileen Derbyshire	Mrs Chadwick	Sue Johnston
Emma Watts	Angela Lonsdale	Mrs Snape	Patricia Routledge
Ena Sharples	Violet Carson OBE	Myra Dickenson / Booth	Susan Jameson
Ernest Bishop	Stephen Hancock	Natalie Horrocks / Barnes	Denise Welch
Fiona Middleton	Angela Griffin	Nellie Harvey	Mollie Sugden
Fiz Brown	Jennie McAlpine	Nick(y) Tilsley	Warren Jackson
Florrie Lindley	Betty Alberge		Adam Rickitt
Frank Roper	Paul Shane	Norman 'Curly' Watts	Kevin Kennedy
Fred Elliott	John Savident	Norris Cole	Malcolm Hebden
Fred Gee	Fred Feast	PC Wilcox	Richard Beckinsale
Gail Potter / Tilsley / Platt / Hillman	Helen Worth	Percy Sugden	Bill Waddington
		Peter Barlow	John Heanneau

Character	Actor/Actress	Character	Actor/Actress
	Mark Duncan	Beena Shah	Rebecca Hazlewood
	Linus Roache		
	Christopher Dormerr	Belle Wise	Jessica Fox
	Joseph McKenna	Benny Hawkins	Paul Henry
	David Lonsdale	Betty Waddell	Anne Charleston
	Chris Gascoine	Bradley Clarke	Luke Walker
Phyllis Pearce	Jill Summers	Carlos Raphael	Anthony Morton
Ralph Lancaster	Kenneth Watson	Carol Sands	Joanne Good
Raquel Wolstenholme / Watts	Sarah Lancashire	Caroline Winthrop	Elaine Page
		Chris Hunter	Stephen Hoye
Ravi Desai	Saeed Jaffrey OBE	Cleopatra Samson	Clare Wilkie
Ray Harrison	Kenneth Cranham	Clifford Leyton	Johnny Briggs
Ray Langton	Neville Buswell	Daniel Freeman	Philip Goodhew
Reg Holdsworth	Ken Morley	Dave Stocks	Jim Dunk
Richard Hillman	Brian Capron	David Hunter	Ronald Allen
Rita Littlewood / Fairclough / Sullivan	Barbara Knox	Diane Lawton / Hunter / Parker	Susan Hanson
		Dick Jarvis	Brian Kent
Ron Jenkins	Ben Kingsley	Doris Luke	Kathy Staff
Rosie Webster	Helen Flanagan	Glenda Banks	Lynette McMorrough
Roy Cropper	David Neilson		
Sally Webster	Sally Whittaker	Holly Brown	Stephanie De Sykes
Samantha Failsworth	Tina Hobley		
Samia Ghadie	Maria Sutherland	Hugh Mortimer	John Bentley
Samir Rachid	Al Nedjari	J Henry Pollard	Michael Turner
Sarah Louise Platt	Leah King	Jill Richardson / Harvey / Chance	Jane Rossington
	Lyndsey King	Jim Baines	John Forgeham
	Tina O'Brien	Jimmy Gudgeon	Jimmy Hanley
Sean Tully	Antony Cotton	Jimmy Samson	Graham McGrath
Shelley Unwin	Sally Lindsay	Joe Lacey	Richard Burke
Spider (Geoffrey) Nugent	Martin Hancock	Joe McDonald	Carl Andrews
Stan Ogden	Bernard Youens	Josefina Raphael	Gillian Betts
Stan Potter	Noddy Holder	Kate Loring	Kate Robbins
Stanley Fairclough	Peter Noone	Kate Russell	Jane Gurnett
Steve McDonald	Simon Gregson	Kath Brownlow	Pamela Vezey
Sunita Parekh / Alahan	Shobna Gulati	Kevin Banks	David Moran
Susan Barlow / Baldwin	Katie Heanneau	Kevin McArthur	Vincent Ball
	Wendy Jane Walker	Lady Alice Fox	Kate O'Mara
	Suzy Patterson	Lola Wise	Freema Agyeman
	Joanna Foster	Louise Dixon (aka Sarah Jane)	Joanne Farrell
Tanya Pooley	Eva Pope	Mandy Dobbs	Natasha Marquiss
Ted Sullivan	William Russell	Marilyn Gates / Hope	Sue Nicholls
Terry Duckworth	Nigel Pivaro	Max Samson	Stuart Milligan
Todd Grimshaw	Bruno Langley	Meg Richardson / Mortimer	Noele Gordon
Tommy Harris	Thomas Craig	Miranda Pollard	Claire Faulkenbridge
Tommy Nelson	Thomas Craig		
Toyah Battersby	Georgia Taylor	Myrtle Cavendish	Gretchen Franklin
Tracy Langton / Preston / Barlow	Christabel Finch	Nicola Freeman	Gabrielle Drake
	Holly Chamarette	Oona Stocks	Di Sherlock
	Dawn Acton	Patrick Russell	Neil McCaul
	Kate Ford	Paul Ross	Sandor Elès
Tyrone Dobbs	Alan Halsall	Reg Lamont	Reginald Marsh
Valerie Barlow	Anne Reid	Rocky Wesson	Roger Sloman
Vera Duckworth	Elizabeth Dawn	Rosemary Hunter	Janet Hargreaves
Vera Hopkins	Kathy Staff	Roy Lambert	Steven Pinder
Vicky Arden / McDonald	Chloe Newsome	Ryan Samson	Luke Roberts
Vikram Desai	Chris Bisson	Sam Benson	Norman Bowler
Vinnie Sorrell	James Gaddas	Sandra Gould	Diane Keen
Wally Bannister	Bernard Cribbins	Sandy Richardson	Roger Tonge
Warren Baldwin	Danny Young	Sarah Jane Harvey	Sophie Cook
		Sharon Metcalfe	Carolyn Jones
Crossroads		Shugie McFee	Angus Lennie
(set in Kings Oak, nr Birmingham; 1964–88; 2001–02; short-lived revival in 2003) ITV		Sid Hooper	Stan Stennett
		Stafford Wynter	Paul Shelley
Adam Chance	Tony Adams	Stan Harvey	Edward Clayton
Amy Turtle	Ann George	Stevie	Wendy Padbury
Angel Samson	Jane Asher	Suzie Samson	Emma Noble
Anne-Marie Wade	Dee Hepburn	Tish Hope	Joy Andrews
Anthony Mortimer	Jeremy Sinden	Tom Curtis	Toby Sawyer
Arthur Brownlow	Peter Hill	Tracey Booth	Cindy Marshall-Day
Barbara Brady / Hunter	Sue Lloyd	Valerie Pollard	Heather Chasen
		Vera Downend	Zeph Gladstone

TELEVISION

Character	Actor/Actress	Character	Actor/Actress
Vince Parker	Peter Brookes	Monica Colby	Tracy Scoggins
Virginia Raven	Sherrie Hewson	Prince Michael	Michael Praed
Wally Soper	Max Wall	Sable Colby	Stephanie Beacham
Wedding Car Chauffeur	Larry Grayson	Sammy Jo	Heather Locklear
		Steven Carrington	Al Corley and
			Jack Coleman

Dallas
(main location Southfork Ranch, Dallas; aired from 1978 to 1991) BBC1

Character	Actor/Actress
Ben Stivers / Wes Parmalee	Steve Forrest
Bobby Ewing	Patrick Duffy
Carter McKay	George Kennedy
Clayton Farlow	Howard Keel
Cliff Barnes	Ken Kercheval
Don Lockwood	Ian McShane
Dusty Farlow	Jared Martin
Eleanor Southworth Ewing / Farlow (Miss Ellie)	Barbara Bel Geddes and Donna Reed
Gary Ewing	David Ackroyd and Ted Shackelford
Jenna Wade	Morgan Fairchild, Francine Tacker, Priscilla Presley
Jock Ewing	Jim Davis
John Ross 'JR' Ewing	Larry Hagman
Katherine Wentworth	Morgan Brittany
Kristin Shepard	Colleen Camp and Mary Crosby
LeeAnn De La Vega	Barbara Eden
Lucy Ewing / Cooper	Charlene Tilton
Pamela Barnes / Ewing	Victoria Principal
Ray Krebbs	Steve Kanaly
Stephanie Rogers	Lesley Anne Down
Sue Ellen Ewing	Linda Gray
Valene Ewing	Joan Van Ark
Willard 'Digger' Barnes	David Wayne and Keenan Wynn

Dawson's Creek
(set in Capeside, Massachusetts) C4

Character	Actor/Actress
Andrea 'Andie' McPhee	Meredith Monroe
Audrey Liddell	Busy Philipps
Dawson Leery	James Van Der Beek
Evelyn 'Grams' Ryan	Mary Beth Peil
Gail Leery	Mary-Margaret Humes
Jack McPhee	Kerr Smith
Jennifer 'Jen' Lindley	Michelle Williams
Josephine 'Joey' Potter	Katie Holmes
Mitchell 'Mitch' Leery	John Wesley Shipp
Pacey Witter	Joshua Jackson

Dynasty
(set in Denver, Colorado; aired from 1981 to 1989) BBC1

Character	Actor/Actress
Adam Carrington / Michael Torrance	Gordon Thomson
Alexis Carrington / Colby / Dexter	Joan Collins
Amanda Carrington	Catherine Oxenburg and Karen Cellini
Ben Carrington	Christopher Cazenove
Blake Carrington	John Forsythe
Caress Morell	Kate O'Mara
Dominique Deveraux	Diahann Carroll
Dr Nick Toscanni	James Farentino
Fallon Carrington / Colby	Pamela Sue Martin and Emma Samms
Jeff Colby	John James
Krystle Jennings / Carrington	Linda Evans

EastEnders
(set in Walford, E20; and first aired in 1985) BBC1

Character	Actor/Actress
Aidan Brosnan	Sean Maguire
Alan Jackson	Howard Anthony
Alex Healy	Richard Driscoll
Alfie Moon	Shane Richie
Ali Osman	Nejdet Salih
Andy O'Brien	Ross Davidson
Angel	Goldie
Angie Watts	Anita Dobson
Annie Palmer	Nadia Sawalha
Anthony Trueman, Dr	Nicholas R Bailey
Arthur Fowler	Bill Treacher
Barry Evans	Shaun Williamson
Beppe di Marco	Michael Greco
Bianca Butcher	Patsy Palmer
Big Ron	Ron Tarr
Billy Mitchell	Perry Fenwick
Carol Jackson	Lindsay Coulson
Charlie Slater	Derek Martin
Chrissie Watts	Tracy-Ann Oberman
Cindy Beale	Michelle Collins
Colin Russell	Michael Cashman
Dan Sullivan	Craig Fairbrass
Danny Moon	Jake Maskall
Darren Miller	Charlie G Hawkins
David Wicks	Michael French
Debbie Wilkins	Shirley Cheriton
Demi Miller	Shana Swash
Dennis Rickman	Nigel Harman
Dennis 'Dirty Den' Watts	Leslie Grantham
Derek Harkinson	Ian Lavender
Diane Butcher	Sophie Lawrence
Doris Moisey	Marcia Ashton
Dot Cotton / Branning	June Brown
Eddie Royle	Michael Melia
Ethel Skinner	Gretchen Franklin
Frank Butcher	Mike Reid
Fred Fonseca, Dr	Jimi Mistry
Garry Hobbs	Ricky Groves
George 'Lofty' Holloway	Tom Watt
George Palmer	Paul Moriarty
Gianni di Marco	Marc Bannerman
Gita Kapoor	Shobu Kapoor
Grant Mitchell	Ross Kemp
Gus Smith	Mohammed George
Harold Legg, Dr	Leonard Fenton
Harry Slater	Michael Elphick
Hattie Tavernier	Michelle Gayle
Ian Beale	Adam Woodyatt
Irene Hills / Raymond	Roberta Taylor
Jake Moon	Joel Beckett
James Willmott-Brown	William Boyde
Jamie Mitchell	Jack Ryder
Jane Collins	Laurie Brett
Janine Butcher	Rebecca Michael Alexia Demetriou Charlie Brooks
Jim Branning	John Bardon
Joanne Ryan	Tara Lynne O'Neill
Joe Wicks	Paul Nicholls
Johnny Allen	Billy Murray
Kat Slater	Jessie Wallace
Kate Tyler	Jill Halfpenny

Character	Actor/Actress
Kathy Beale / Mitchell	Gillian Taylforth
Keith Miller	David Spinx
Kelly Taylor	Brooke Kinsella
Kelvin Carpenter	Paul Medford
Laura Dunn / Beale	Hannah Waterman
Lisa Shaw / Fowler	Lucy Benjamin
Little Mo Slater / Mitchell	Kacey Ainsworth
Lorraine Wicks	Jacqueline Leonard
Lou Beale	Anna Wing
Lucy Beale	Melissa Suffield
Lynne Slater / Hobbs	Elaine Lordan
Mark Fowler	David Scarboro and Todd Carty
Martin Fowler	Jon Peyton Price and James Alexandrou
Matthew Rose	Joe Absolom
Melanie Healy / Owen	Tamzin Outhwaite
Michelle Fowler / Holloway	Susan Tully
Mickey Miller	Joe Swash
Minty Peterson	Cliff Parisi
Mo Harris	Laila Morse
Nana Moon	Hilda Braid
Natalie Evans	Lucy Speed
Nick Cotton	John Altman
Nigel Bates	Paul Bradley
Nina Harris	Troy Titus-Adams
Pat Butcher / Evans	Pam St Clement
Patrick Trueman	Rudolph Walker
Paul Trueman	Gary Beadle
Pauline Fowler	Wendy Richard
Peggy Mitchell / Butcher / Mitchell	Jo Warne and Barbara Windsor
Pete Beale	Peter Dean
Phil Mitchell	Steve McFadden
Polly Becker	Victoria Gould
Rick Peterson	Cliff Parisi
Ricky Butcher	Sid Owen
Robbie Jackson	Dean Gaffney
Rosie Miller	Gerry Cowper
Roy Evans	Tony Caunter
Sadie Banks	Isobel Middleton
Sam Mitchell / Butcher / Mitchell	Daniella Westbrook and Kim Medcalf
Sandra di Marco	Clare Wilkie
Sanjay Kapoor	Deepak Verma
Sarah Hills	Daniela Denby-Ashe
Sharon Watts / Mitchell / Watts	Letitia Dean
Simon Wicks	Nick Berry
Sonia Jackson	Natalie Cassidy
Spencer Moon	Christopher Parker
Stacey Slater	Lacey Turner
Steve Owen	Martin Kemp
Sue Osman	Sandy Ratcliff
Terry Hills	Brian Croucher
Terry Raymond	Gavin Richards
Tiffany Raymond / Mitchell	Martine McCutcheon
Tina Stewart	Charlotte Avery
Tom Banks	Colm O Maonlai
Tom Clements	Donald Tandy
Tony Hills	Mark Homer
Trevor Morgan	Alex Ferns
Vicki Fowler	Samantha Crown and Scarlett Johnson
Wellard	Robbie Jackson's Dog
Willy	Ethel Skinner's Dog
Winston	Ulric Browne

Character	Actor/Actress
Zoe Slater	Michelle Ryan

Eldorado
(set in Los Barcos and first aired on 6 July 1992) BBC1

Blair Lockhead	Josh Nathan
Dieter Schultz	Kai Maurer
Drew Lockhead	Campbell Morrison
Gwen Lockhead	Patricia Brake
Joy Slater	Leslee Udwin
Marcus Tandy	Jesse Birdsall
Nessa Lockhead	Julie Fernandez
Stanley Webb	William Lucas
Trish Valentine	Polly Perkins

Emmerdale Farm
(set in Beckindale; first aired 16 October 1972; since 1989 the series has been known as Emmerdale) ITV

Adam Forrester	Tim Vincent
Alan Turner	Richard Thorp
Albert Dingle	Bobby Knutt
Amos Brearly	Ronald Magill
Andy Hopwood / Sugden	Kelvin Fletcher
Angie Reynolds	Freya Copeland
Annie Sugden / Kempinski / Brearly	Sheila Mercier
Ashley Thomas	John Middleton
Belle Dingle	Emily Mather
Bernice Blackstock	Samantha Giles
Betty Eagleton	Paula Tilbrook
Biff Fowler	Stuart Wade
Bob Hope	Antony Audenshaw
Brian Addyman	Martin Reeve
Butch Dingle	Paul Loughran
Cain Dingle	Jeff Hordley
Carl King	Tom Lister
Carlos Diaz	Gary Turner
Charity Tate / Dingle	Emma Atkins
Chloe Atkinson	Amy Nuttall
Christopher Tate	Peter Amory
Danny Daggert	Cleveland Campbell
Dave Glover	Ian Kelsey
Des Bartenshaw	Tony Barton
Diane Blackstock / Sugden	Elizabeth Estensen
Dolly Arcaster / Skilbeck	Katherine Barker and Jean Rogers
Donna Windsor	Sophie Jeffery and Verity Rushworth
Edna Birch	Shirley Stelfox
Emily Wylie / Dingle / Kirk	Kate McGregor
Eric Pollard	Christopher Chittell
Ethan Blake	Liam O'Brien
Frank Tate	Norman Bowler
Gloria Weaver / Pollard	Janice McKenzie
Glynis Hardy	Christine Cox
Henry Wilks	Arthur Pentelow
Jack Sugden	Andrew Burt and Clive Hornby
Jan Glover	Roberta Kerr
Jarvis Skelton	Richard Moore
Jason Kirk	James Carlton
Jerry 'Mack' Mackinley	Rob Dixon
Jimmy King	Nick Miles
Joe Sugden	Frazer Hines
Kathy Bates/Merrick/Tate/Glover	Malandra Burrows
Katie Addyman / Sugden	Sammy Winward
Kelly Windsor / Glover	Adele Silva
Kim Barker / Tate / Marchant	Claire King
Laurel Potts	Charlotte Bellamy
Len Reynolds	Peter Martin
Linda Glover / Fowler	Tonicha Jeronimo

Character	Actor/Actress
Lisa Clegg / Dingle	Jane Cox
Louise Appleton	Emily Symons
Luke McAllister	Noah Huntley
Mandy Dingle / Kirk	Lisa Riley
Marc Reynolds	Anthony Lewis
Marlon Dingle	Mark Charnock
Matt Skilbeck	Jo Kendall
Matthew King	Matt Healy
Ned Glover	Johnny Leeze
Nick Bates	Cy Chadwick
Nicola Blackstock	Nicola Wheeler
Olivia 'Ollie' Reynolds	Vicky Binns
Pat Merrick / Sugden	Helen Weir
Patricia 'Tricia' Stokes	Sheree Murphy
Patrick 'Paddy' Kirk	Dominic Brunt
Paul Lambert	Ashley Bose
Rachel Hughes	Glenda McKay
Rev Ashley Thomas	John Middleton
Rev Donald Hinton	Hugh Manning
Robert Sugden	Karl Davies
Rodney Blackstock	Patrick Mower
Roy Glover	Nicky Evans
Sadie King	Patsy Kensit
Sam Dingle	James Hooton
Sarah Sugden	Alyson Spiro
Scott Windsor	Toby Cockerell and Ben Freeman
Sean Reynolds	Stephen McGann
Seth Armstrong	Stan Richards
Shadrach Dingle	Andy Devine
Sophie Wright	Jane Cameron
Steph Stokes	Lorraine Chase
Steve Marchant	Paul Opacic
Syd Woolfe	Nathan Gladwell
Tamsin Charles	Jenny Gleave
Tara Oakwell / Thornfield / Cockburn	Anna Brecon
Terry Woods	Billy Hartman
Tina Dingle	Jacqueline Pirie
Tom King	Ken Farrington
Vic Windsor	Alun Lewis
Victoria Sugden	Hannah Midgley
Viv Windsor / Hope	Deena Payne
Zak Dingle	Steve Halliwell
Zoe Tate	Leah Bracknell

Falcon Crest

(set in winery in Tuscany Valley, California; aired between 1981 and 1990)

Angela Channing / Stavros	Jane Wyman
Apollonia	Patricia 'Apollonia' Kotero
Chase Gioberti	Robert Foxworth
Diana Hunter	Shannon Tweed
Dr Michael Ranson	Cliff Robertson
Emma Channing	Margaret Ladd
Francesca Gioberti	Gina Lollobrigida
Frank Agretti	Rod Taylor
Greg Reardon	Simon MacCorkindale
Jacqueline Perrault	Lana Turner
Jordan Roberts	Morgan Fairchild
Kit Marlowe	Kim Novak
Lance Cumson	Lorenzo Lamas
Maggie Gioberti / Channing	Susan Sullivan
Nick Hogan	Roy Thinnes
Peter Stavros	Cesar Romero
Phillip Erikson	Mel Ferrer
Tony Cumson	John Saxon

Family Affairs

(aired at launch of C5 in March 1997)

Character	Actor/Actress
Albie Leach	Martin Herdman
Alex Williams	Jake McCarthy
Amir Sadati	Kayvan Novak
Angus Hart	Ian Cullen
Ania Williams	Elizabeth Holmes-Gwillim
Anna Gregory	Martha Cope
Annie Hart	Liz Crowther
Babs Woods	Jan Harvey
Becky Scott	Chandra Ruegg
Ben Galloway	Peter England
Benji McHugh	Mark McLean
Cameron Davenport	Rupert Hill
Cat Webb	Nicola Duffett
Chloe Costello	Leah Coombes
Chris Hart	Ian Ashpitel
Chris Jacobs	Gemma Wardle
Chrissy Costello	Kazia Pelka
Claire Callan / Toomey	Tina Hall (formerly Russell)
Conrad Williams	Simon Merrells
Dan Wilkinson	Charlie Watts
Darren Scott	Ike Hamilton
Dave Matthews	Richard Hawley
David Cash	James Gaddas
Denise Boulter	Claire Perkins
Doug MacKenzie	Gareth Hale
Duncan Hart	Rocky Marshall
Eddie Harris	Tony Scannell
Eileen Day / Callan	Rosie Rowell
Elsa Gates	Delena Kidd
Gary Costello	Gary Webster
Gemma Craig	Angela Hazeldine
Geri Evans	Anna Acton
Ginny Davenport	Joanna Foster
Grace Ellis	Amber and Jade Montague
Graham Parker	Lee Warburton
Holly Hart	Sandra Huggett
Jack Gates	Ken Farrington
Jake Walker	Seb Castang
Jamie Hart	Michael Cole
Jim Webb	Jo Dow
Joe Thorn	Les Dennis
John Stokes	David Michaels
Justin MacKenzie	Ryan Davenport
Karen Ellis	Tanya Franks
Katie Williams	Robyn Page
Kelly Boulter	Carryl Thomas
Kelly Hurst	Nicky Talacko
Kim Davies	Troy Titus-Adams
Les Boulter	Howard Saddler
Lucy Day	Julia Lee Smith
Maria Simons	Annie Miles
Matt Ellis	Matthew Jay Lewis
Melanie Costello	Rebecca Hunter
Melanie Hart	Cordelia Bugeja
Myra Costello	Kate Williams
Nick Trip	Barry McCormick
Nikki Warrington	Rebecca Blake
Olly Taylor	Alex Hardy
Paul Webb	Martin Delaney
Pete Callan	David Easter
Sadie Hargreaves / Lloyd	Barbara Young
Samantha Cockerill	Tessa Wyatt
Tanya Woods	Carol Starks
Tim Webster	Idris Elba
Vince Farmer	Stephen Yardley
Yasmin Matthews / MacKenzie	Ebony Thomas

Character	Actor/Actress	Character	Actor/Actress
Flamingo Road		Roger Sandford	Richard Hope
(set in Truro County, Florida; aired between January		Samantha Kennedy	Colette Brown
1981 and May 1982)		Sandy Harper	Laura Sadler
Claude Weldon	Kevin McCarthy	Stan Ashleigh	Paul Shane
Constance Weldon / Carlyle	Morgan Fairchild	Steve Waring	Peter De Jersey
Elmo Tyson	Peter Donat	Terry Fox	Miles Anderson
Eudora Flowers Weldon	Barbara Rush	Tom Campbell-Gore	Denis Lawson
Fielding Carlyle	Mark Harmon	Tony Vincent	Lee Warburton
Lane Ballou Curtis	Cristina Raines	Victoria Merrick	Lisa Faulkner
Lute-Mae Sanders	Stella Stevens		
Michael Tyronne	David Selby	**Hollyoaks**	
Sam Curtis	John Beck	(set in Hollyoaks, Chester, and first aired in 1995) C4	
Sheriff Titus Semple	Howard Duff	Abby Davies	Helen Noble
Skipper Weldon	Woody Brown	Adam Morgan	David Brown
		Alex Bell	Martino Lazzeri
General Hospital		Andy Morgan	Ross Davidson
(set in Midland General; aired between Sept 1972 and		Anna Green	Lisa M Kay
Jan 1979) ITV		Bazz FM	Toby Sawyer
Dr Gregory Knight	Carl Rigg	Becca Hayton	Ali Bastian
Dr Guy Wallman	Tom Adams	Ben Davies	Marcus Patric
Dr Martin Baxter	James Kerry	Beth Morgan	Elizabeth O'Grady
Dr Matthew Armstrong	David Garth		and Kate Baines
Dr Neville Bywaters	Tony Adams	Bombhead	Lee Otway
Dr Peter Ridge	Ian White	Brian Drake	Jonathon Le Billon
Dr Robert Thorne	Ronald Leigh-Hunt	Carol Groves	Nathalie Casey
Jeffrey Burstall	Ray Lonnen	Chloe Bruce	Mikyla Dodd
Mr William Parker-Brown	Lewis Jones	Cindy Cunningham	Laura Crossley and
Nurse Hilda Price	Lynda Bellingham		Stephanie Waring
Principal Nursing Officer	Kathleen Byron	Craig Dean	Guy Burnet
Ruth Milner		Dan Hunter	Andy McNair
Sister Ellen Chapman	Peggy Sinclair	Darren Osborne	Adam Booth and
Sister Holland	Pippa Rowe		Ashley Taylor
Sister Washington	Carmen Munroe		Dawson
Student Nurse Katy Shaw	Judy Buxton	Dawn Cunningham	Lisa Williamson
		Debbie Dean	Jodi Albert
Holby City (spin-off from *Casualty* and set in the		Ellie Hunter	Sarah Baxendale
same hospital; first aired in January 1999) BBC1		Eve Crawford	Natasha Lund
Adrian Townsend	Ian Ashpitel	Frankie Dean	Helen Pearson
Alex Adams	Jeremy Sheffield	Geri Hudson / Cunliffe	Joanna Taylor
Ben Saunders	David Paisley	Gina Patrick	Danielle Brent
Carole Townsend	Kate Rutter	Gordon Cunningham	Bernard Latham
Chrissie Williams	Tina Hobley	Helen Richardson / Cunningham	Kathryn George
Christian Connolly	Michael	Izzy Cornwell	Elize Du Toit
	Fassbender	Jack Osborne	James McKenna
Damien Weatherall	Matt Dempsey	Jake Dean	Kevin Sacre
Danny Shaughnessy	Jeremy Edwards	Jambo Bolton	Will Mellor
David Keelan	Pascal Langdale	Jamie Nash	Stefan Booth
Deborah Sandford	Tracy Whitwell	Jasmine Bates	Elly Fairman
Diane Lloyd	Patricia Potter	Jason Cunliffe	Alex Thorne
Ed Keating	Rocky Marshall	Jill Patrick / Osborne	Lynda Rooke
Elaine Sandford	Gillian Bevan	Jodie Nash	Kate McEnery
Guy Morton	Paul Blackthorne	Joe Spencer	Matt Milburn
Jan Goddard	Judy Loe	Jude Cunningham	Davina Taylor
Jane Archer	Christine Entwistle	Kate Patrick	Natasha Symms
Jasmine Hopkins	Angela Griffin	Kerry	Sarah Vandenburgh
Jess Griffin	Verona Joseph	Kurt Benson	Jeremy Edwards
Joanne Townsend	Lucy Gaskell	Laura Burns	Lesley Johnston
Karen Gilham	Indra Ove	Lee Hunter	Alex Carter
Kath Shaughnessy	Jan Pearson	Les Hunter	John Graham
Kirsty Shaw	Natalie Blades		Davies
Lisa Fox	Luisa Bradshaw-	Lewis Richardson	Ben Hull
	White	Lisa Hunter	Gemma Atkinson
Mubbs Hussein	Ian Aspinall	Lucy Benson	Kerrie Taylor
Natalie Anderson	Sophie Shaw	Luke Morgan	Gary Lucy
Nick Jordan	Michael French	Mandy Richardson / Hutchinson	Sarah Dunn
Owen Davis	Mark Moraghan	Matt Musgrove	Kristian Ealey
Pam McGrath	Denise Welch	Max Cunningham	Ben Sheriff
Patricia Kennedy	Lois Baxter		and Matt Littler
Paul Eccles	Leroy Liburd	Nick O'Connor	Darren Bransford
Ray Sykes	Ian Curtis	Nikki Sullivan	Wendy Glenn
Ric Griffin	Hugh Quarshie	Norman Sankofa	Jamie Luke

TELEVISION

Character	Actor/Actress
Ollie Benson	Paul Leyshon
Rob Hawthorn	Warren Derosa
Rory 'Finn' Finnegan	James Redmond
Ruth Osborne / Benson	Terri Dwyer
Sally Hunter	Katherine Dow-Blyton
Sam 'OB' O'Brien	Darren Jefferies
Sam Smallwood	Tim Downie
Scott Anderson	Daniel Hyde
Sol Patrick	Paul Danan
Steph Dean	Carley Stenson
Sue Morgan	Eve White
Theo	Andrew Somerville
Toby Mills	Henry Luxemburg
Tom Cunningham	Ellis Hollins
Tony Hutchinson	Nick Pickard
Will Davies	Barney Clevely
Zara Morgan	Kelly Greenwood

Locations include Dan's Pit Stop (a motor accessories shop), Gnosh Village (bistro), The Loft (nightclub) and The Dog in the Pond pub.

Home and Away
(set in Summer Bay nr Sydney) C5

Character	Actor/Actress
Adam Cameron	Mat Stevenson
Ailsa Hogan Stewart	Judy Nunn
Al Simpson	Terence Donovan
Alf Stewart	Ray Meagher
Angel Brooks / Parish	Melissa George
Barry Hyde	Ivar Kants
Beth Hunter	Clarissa House
Blake Dean	Les Hill
Bobby Simpson / Morgan / Marshall	Nicolle Dickson
Brad Cooper	Bruce Samazan
Carly Morris / Lucini	Sharyn Hodgson
Celia Stewart	Fiona Spence
Chloe Richards / Fraser	Kristy Wright
Colleen Smart	Lyn Collingwood
Curtis Reed	Shane Ammann
Damian Roberts	Matt Doran
Dan Baker	Tim Campbell
Dani Sutherland	Tammin Sursok
David Croft	Guy Pearce
Donald 'Flathead' Fisher	Norman Coburn
Emma Jackson	Dannii Minogue
Eric Dalby	Mark Furze
Finlay Roberts	Tina Thomsen
Floss McPhee	Angela Keep
Flynn Saunders	Joel McIlroy
Frank Morgan	Alex Papps
Grant Mitchell	Craig McLachlan
Greg Marshall	Ross Newton
Gypsy Nash	Kimberley Cooper
Hayley Smith	Rebecca Cartwright
Henry Hunter	Tobi Atkins
Irene Roberts	Lynne McGranger
Jack Wilson	Daniel Amalm
Jade Sutherland	Kate Garven
Jesse McGregor	Ben Unwin
Joel Nash	David Woodley
Joey Rainbow	Alex O'Han
Jude Lawson	Ben Steel
Kane Phillips	Sam Atwell
Kim Hyde	Chris Hemsworth
Kirsty Sutherland	Christie Hayes
Lachlan 'Lachie' Fraser, Dr	Richard Grieve
Lance Smart	Peter Vroom
Leah Poulos / Patterson	Ada Nicodemou
Marilyn Chambers / Fisher	Emily Symons

Character	Actor/Actress
Martin Dibble	Craig Thompson
Matilda Hunter	Indiana Evans
Matt Wilson	Greg Benson
Max Sutherland	Sebastian Elmaloglou
Natalie Nash	Angelica La Bozzetta and Antoinette Byron
Natasha Andrews	Isabel Lucas
Neville McPhee	Frank Lloyd
Nick Parrish	Bruce Roberts
Nick Smith	Christopher Egan
Noah Lawson	Beau Brady
Peter 'Tug' O'Neale	Tristan Bancks
Pippa Fletcher	Vanessa Downing
Pippa Fletcher / Ross	Debra Lawrance
Rebecca Fisher	Jane Hall and Danielle Carter
Rebecca Fisher / Nash	Belinda Emmett
Rhyss Sutherland	Michael Beckley
Robbie Hunter	Jason Smith
Ruth 'Roo' Stewart	Justine Clarke
Sally Keating / Fletcher	Kate Ritchie
Sam Nicholls Marshall	Ryan Clark
Sarah Thompson	Laura Vazquez
Scott Hunter	Kip Gamblin
Sebastion 'Seb' Miller	Mitch Firth
Selina Cook / Roberts	Tempany Deckert
Shane Parrish	Dieter Brummer
Shannon Reed	Isla Fisher
Shauna Bradley	Kylie Watson
Shelley Sutherland	Paula Forrest
Simon Fitzgerald	Richard Norton
Sophie Simpson	Rebekah Elmaloglou
Steven Matheson	Adam Willits
Tom Nash	Graeme Squires
Tom Fletcher	Roger Oakley
Travis Nash	Nic Testoni
Vincent 'Vinnie' Patterson	Ryan Kwanten
Will Smith	Zac Drayson

Knots Landing
(spin-off from *Dallas* set in California)

Character	Actor/Actress
Abby Cunningham / Ewing / Sumner	Donna Mills
Charles Scott	Michael York
Gary Ewing	Ted Shackleford
Gregory Sumner	William Devane
Joshua Rush	Alec Baldwin
Karen Fairgate / MacKenzie	Michele Lee
Patrick 'Mack' MacKenzie	Kevin Dobson
Peter Hollister	Hunt Block
Ruth Galveston	Ava Gardner
Valene Ewing / Gibson / Waleska	Joan Van Ark

Neighbours
(set in Erinsborough, Melbourne; first aired in 1986) BBC1

Character	Actor/Actress
Amy Greenwood	Jacinta Stapleton
Annalise Hartman	Kimberley Davies
Anne Wilkinson	Brooke Satchwell
Ben Kirk	Sean Berends
Beth Brennan / Willis	Natalie Imbruglia
Beverly Marshall, Dr	Lisa Armytage and Shaunna O'Grady
Billy Kennedy	Jesse Spencer
Boyd Hoyland	Kyal Marsh
Brad Willis	Scott Michaelson
Bronwyn Davies	Rachel Friend
Caroline Alessi	Gillian Blakeney

Charlene Mitchell / Robinson — Kylie Minogue
Cheryl Stark / Carpenter — Caroline Gillmer
Christina Alessi / Robinson — Gayle Blakeney
Clive Gibbons, Dr — Geoff Paine
Connor O'Neill — Patrick Harvey
Danni Stark — Eliza Szonert
Darcy Tyler — Mark Raffety
David Bishop — Kevin Harrington
Debbie Martin — Mandy Storvik
Des Clarke — Paul Keane
Dione Bliss — Madeleine West
Dorothy Burke — Maggie Dence
Doug Willis — Terence Donovan
Drew Kirk — Dan Paris
Felicity 'Flick' Scully — Holly Valance
Gaby Willis — Rachel Blakely
Gail Lewis / Robinson — Fiona Corke
Hannah Martin — Rebecca Ritters
Harold Bishop — Ian Smith
Helen Daniels — Anne Haddy
Henry Mitchell — Craig McLachlan
Izzy Hoyland — Natalie Bassingthwaighte

Jack Scully — Jay Bunyan
Jane Harris — Annie Hones
Jim Robinson — Alan Dale
Joanna Hartman — Emma Harrison
Joe Mangel — Mark Little
Joe Scully — Shane Connor
Joel Samuels — Daniel Macpherson
Julie Robinson / Martin — Vikki Blanche and Julie Mullins

Karl Kennedy, Dr — Alan Fletcher
Kerry Bishop — Linda Hartley
Lance Hails Wilkinson — Andrew Bibby
Lauren Carpenter — Sarah Vandenbergh
Libby Kennedy / Kirk — Kym Valentine
Liljana Bishop — Marcella Russo
Lou Carpenter — Tom Oliver
Lucy Robinson — Kylie Flinker
Sascha Close
Melissa Bell
Lyn Scully — Janet Andrewartha
Madge Mitchell / Ramsey / Bishop — Anne Charleston
Malcolm Kennedy — Benji McNair
Mark Gottlieb — Bruce Samazan
Max Hoyland — Stephen Lovatt
Max Ramsay — Francis Bell
Melanie Pearson / Mangel — Lucinda Cowden
Michelle Scully — Kate Keltie
Mike Young — Guy Pearce
Nell Mangel / Worthington — Vivean Gray
Oscar Scully — Ingo Dammer-Smith
Pam Willis — Sue Jones
Paul McClain — Jansen Spencer
Paul Robinson — Stefan Dennis
Phoebe Bright — Simone Robertson
Philip Martin — Christopher Milne and Ian Rawlings
Dan Falzon
Rick Alessi — Joy Chambers
Rosemary Daniels — Ailsa Piper
Ruth Wilkinson — Richard Grieve
Sam Kratz — Nicola Charles
Sarah Beaumont — Darius Perkins and Jason Donovan
Scott Robinson — Ben Nicholas
Scott Timmins — Lara Sacher
Serena Bishop — Peter O'Brien
Shane Ramsay

Sindi Watts — Marisa Warrington
Sky Bishop / Mangel — Miranda Fryer
Stephanie McIntosh
Stephanie Scully — Carla Bonner
Stuart Parker — Blair McDonough
Summer Hoyland — Marisa Siketa
Susan Kennedy — Jackie Woodburne
Tadpole 'Tad' Reeves — Jonathon Dutton
Teresa Bell — Krista Vendy
Toadfish Rebecchi — Ryan Moloney
Toby Mangel — Finn Greentree-Keane
Todd Landers — Kristian Schmid
Tom Ramsay — Gary Files

The Newcomers
(set in Angleton; aired from 1965 to 1969) BBC1
Andrew Kerr — Robin Bailey
Ellis Cooper — Alan Browning
Joyce Harker — Wendy Richard
Julie Robertson — Deborah Watling
Maria Cooper — Judy Geeson
Robert Malcolm — Conrad Phillips
Vivienne Cooper — Maggie Fitzgibbon

The Sullivans
(made between 1976 and 1982) ITV (set during World War Two)
Alice Watkins / Sullivan (Maggie's daughter) — Megan Williams
Anna Kauffmann (John's 1st wife) — Ingrid Mason
Bert Duggan (killed in the war) — Peter Hehir
Cara — Kylie Minogue
Caroline Sullivan (Terry's wife) — Genevieve Picot
Christopher Merchant — John Waters
Dave Sullivan — Paul Cronin
Detective Sgt Shearer — Noel Trevarthen
Dr Donovan Sullivan — Keith Eden
Ernest 'Erger' O'Keefe — Peter Harvey Wright
Flynn Errol (flying ace) — Peter Ford
Frank Errol — Damon Herriman
Geoff Johnson/Sullivan (adopted son) — Jamie Higgins
Grace Sullivan (killed in London) — Lorraine Bayly
Harry Sullivan — Michael Caton
Horace 'Orrible' Brown — Nick Waters
Ida Jessup / Pike — Vivean Gray
Jack Fletcher — Reg Gorman
Jim Sullivan (Alice's husband) — Andy Anderson
John Sullivan — Andrew McFarlane
Juliana Sleven — Saski Post
Kate Meredith — Ilona Rodgers
Kitty Sullivan — Susan Hannaford
Leslie 'Magpie' Maddern — Gary Sweet
Lou Sullivan (Harry's 2nd wife) — Annie Byron
Maggie Baker (Norm's 2nd wife) — Vikki Hammond
Maureen Sullivan — Fiona Paul
Melina Baker (Norm's 1st wife) — Chantel Contouri
Norm Baker — Norman Yemm
Patty Spencer / Sullivan (Tom's wife) — Penny Downie
Robbie McGovern (Kitty's husband) — Graham Harvey
Rose Sullivan (Harry's 1st wife) — Maggie Dence
Sally Meredith — Lisa Crittenden
Terry Sullivan — Richard Morgan
Tom Sullivan — Steven Tandy

TELEVISION

Television, Radio and Media Adverts

A diamond is forever De Beer Consolidated Mines

A little dab'll do ya Brylcreem

Aah . . . Bisto

All human life is there News of the World

All the news that's fit to print *New York Times*

And all because the lady loves . . . Milk Tray

Any time, any place, anywhere Martini (coined by Barry Day)

Appliance of science Zanussi

Are you with . . . No, I'm with the Woolwich

Ask the man from the . . . Pru (Prudential Assurance Co. Ltd)

A . . . works wonders Double Diamond

Australians wouldn't give a xxxx for anything else Castlemaine xxxx lager

Bank that likes to say Yes TSB

Beanz meanz . . . Heinz

Beats as it sweeps as it cleans Hoover vacuum cleaners

Because I'm worth it L'oriel

Because life's complicated enough Abbey National

Beer that made Milwaukee famous Schlitz

Bet you can't eat three Shredded Wheat

B . . . O . . . Lifebuoy soap

Bread with nowt taken out Allinson's bread

. . . Brings express relief Settlers

Builds bonny babies Glaxo

Buy some for Lulu Smarties

. . . calling! Avon

Can you tell . . . from butter? Stork margarine

Central heating for kids Ready Brek

Chocolates with the less fattening centres Maltesers

Chocolates? No . . . Maltesers

Cleans a big, big carpet for less than half a crown 1001

Cleans and polishes in one go Pledge

Clunk click, every trip Jimmy Savile's seat belt campaign (from 1971)

Cool as a mountain stream Consulate cigarettes

Cuts cleaning time in half Flash

Does she or doesn't she? Clairol hair colouring (coined by Shirley Polykoff)

Don't ask the price. It's a penny Marks & Spencer (when first opened)

Don't be vague, ask for . . . Haig whisky

Don't leave home without it American Express

Don't say brown, say . . . Hovis

Don't you just love being in control British Gas, and Mrs Merton and her son, Malcolm

Eveninks and morninks I drink . . . Warninks

Everything you want from a store, and a little bit more Safeways

Finger of Fudge is just enough to give your kids a treat

Fingerlickin' good Kentucky Fried Chicken

First truly feminine cigarette Eve

Fly the flag British Airways

For men who don't have to try too hard Old Spice

Forces grey out, forces white in Fairy Snow

Fortifies the over forties Phyllosan

Fresh as the moment when the pod went pop Birds Eye peas

Full of Eastern promise Fry's Turkish Delight

Genuine article Budweiser

Getting there is half the fun Cunard Steamship Line

Gives a meal man appeal Oxo

Good to the last drop Maxwell House coffee

Gordon's gin (first scented advert) Shown in May 1997 when juniper berries could be smelt in cinema

Go to work on an . . . Egg (slogan is often attributed to Fay Weldon)

Graded grains make finer flour Homepride

Great way to fly Singapore Airlines

Hands that do dishes are as soft as your face with mild, green Fairy Liquid

Have a break, bave a . . . KitKat

Helps you work, rest and play A Mars a day (possibly attributed to Murray Walker)

Hold it up to the light, not a stain and shining bright Surf

I dreamed I . . . in my Maidenform bra

I think you probably are Cockburns Port

I was so impressed I bought the company Remington (said by Victor Kiam)

If you see Sid, tell him British Gas slogan during privatisation

I'm only here for the beer Double Diamond

I'm . . . fly me National Airlines

. . . is good for you Guinness

I never knew it had so much in it TV Times

Is it live, or is it . . . Memorex

Is she or isn't she? Harmony hair spray

It could be you National Lottery

It's for yoo-hoo! British Telecom

It's the real thing Coca-Cola

It's what your right arm's for Courage beer

Keep going well, keep going Shell

Keep your schoolgirl complexion Palmolive

Keynsham – spelt K-E-Y-N-S-H-A-M Horace Batchelor's phrase on Luxembourg's pools advisory service

Kills 99% of all household germs Domestos

King of beers Budweiser

Let's face the music and dance Allied Dunbar

Let your fingers do the walking Yellow Pages (Kirsty MacColl's version of 'Days' was popular theme)

Lion goes from strength to strength Peugeot

Liquid engineering Castrol Motor Oil

Listening Bank The Midland

Looks good, tastes good and by golly it does you good Mackeson

Lot less bovver than a hover Qualcast

Loudest noise comes from the electric clock Rolls Royce

Made by robots, driven by humans Nissan

Made in Scotland from girders Irn Bru

Made to make your mouth water Opal Fruits

Make tea bags make tea Tetley's

Make yourself heard Ericsson

Makes exceedingly good cakes Mr Kipling

Means happy motoring   Esso (sign)

Melts in your mouth, not in your hands   Treets

Milk from contented cows   Carnation

Mint with the hole   Polo

Minty bit stronger   Trebor Mints

Naughty but nice   Original advert about cream cakes (Salman Rushdie coined the phrase)

Never knowingly undersold   John Lewis Stores

Nice 'ere 'innit?   Campari (Lorraine Chase)

Nice face, shame about the breath   Listerine mouthwash

Nice one, Cyril   Wonderloaf

Nicole . . . Papa   Renault Clio

99 44/100 % Pure   Ivory soap

Nissan Almira   Parodies of *The Sweeney* and *The Professionals*

Nissan Micra   'No No No' by Nancy Nova

Not everything in black and white makes sense   Guinness

Nothing acts faster than . . .   Anadin

Nuts! Whole hazelnuts   Cadbury's Wholenut

Often a bridesmade – but never a bride   Listerine mouthwash

One degree under? Try . . .   Aspro

Pizza Hut: appeared in adverts   Jonathan Ross, Caprice, Gareth Southgate, Damon Hill, Mikhail Gorbachev, Pamela Anderson

Plink plink fizz   Alka Seltzer

Prevents that sinking feeling   Bovril

Probably the best lager in the world   Carlsberg

Prolongs active life   Pal dog food

Promise her anything, but give her . . .   Arpège (coined by Edouard Cournand, president of Lanvin Perfumes)

Pure genius   Guinness

Put a tiger in your tank   Esso

Puts the 'T' in Britain   Typhoo tea

Refreshes the parts other beers cannot reach   Heineken (coined by Terry Lovelock)

Ring of confidence   Colgate toothpaste

. . . satisfy   Senior Service cigarettes

Schhh . . . you know who   Schweppes

Seven pieces of heaven   Fry's Chocolate Cream

Simply years ahead   Philips

'Singing in the Rain' (rap version)   McDonald's

Snap! crackle! and pop!   Kellogg's Rice Crispies

Solutions for a small planet   IBM

Splash it on all over   Brut

Spreads straight from the fridge   Blueband margarine

Station of the Nation   Radio Caroline

Stays sharp till the bottom of the glass   Harp lager

Stop me and buy one   Wall's ice cream

Sweet you can eat between meals   Milky Way (without spoiling your appetite)

Takes good care of you   BOAC

Tastes as good as it smells   Maxwell House Coffee

Tested by dummies, driven by the intelligent   Volvo

That's the wonder of …   Woollies (Woolworths)

The appetizer   Tizer

The bank that listens   Midland

The bright one, the right one, it's . . .   Martini

The cereal that's shot from guns   Quaker Puffed Wheat

The drive of your life   Peugeot 106

The real smell of . . .   Brut

The shirt you don't iron   Rael Brook Toplin

The soluble aspirin   Disprin

They came in search of paradise   Bounty

They grow on you   Roses chocolates

They're bootiful   Bernard Matthews's turkeys

They're grrrreat!   Frosties

Things go better with . . .   Coke (Coca-Cola)

To fly, to serve   British Airways

Too good to hurry mints   Murray Mints

To our members we're the fourth emergency service   Automobile Association

Top breeders recommend it   Pedigree Chum dog food

Top people read the . . .   Times

Try a little VC 10derness   British Airways

Vorsprung durch Technik   Audi

Watch out there's a Humphrey about   Milk

We never forget you have a choice   British Caledonian

We sell more cars than Ford, Chrysler, Chevrolet and Buick combined   Matchbox toys

We try harder   Avis Car Rentals (coined by Doyle, Dane & Bernbach)

We'll take more care of you   British Airways

Were you truly wafted here from Paradise? Nah! Luton Airport   Campari (Lorraine Chase)

When you fancy a fruity treat, unzip a . . .   Banana

When you've got it, flaunt it   Braniff Airways

Where do you want to go today   Microsoft

Which twin has the Toni?   Toni Home Perms

Why does the man in the mask drink . . .   Metz

Wodka from Warrington   Vladivar

World's favourite airline   British Airways

World's finest blade   Wilkinson Sword

Wot a lot I got   Smarties

Would you give me your last . . .?   Rolo

You know what comes between me and my Calvins?   Calvin Klein jeans (15-year-old Brooke Shields in 1980)

You'll look a little lovelier each day   with fabulous pink Camay soap

You'll wonder where the yellow went . . .   when you brush your teeth with Pepsodent

You make it what it is   BBC

You press the button, we do the rest   Kodak

You too can have a body like mine   Charles Atlas (Angelo Siciliano)

Your country needs you   WW1 army recruitment poster (Kitchener pointing with right hand)

Your flexible friend   Access credit card

You're never alone with a . . .   Strand (coined by John May)

T
E
L
E
V
I
S
I
O
N

Television and Radio: Miscellaneous Information

advertisement: first Gibbs SR toothpaste.

advertisement: shown after death Yul Brynner made anti-smoking advert with the message, 'Hullo, I'm dead; smoking killed me.'

Any Questions/Answers Presenters: Freddy Grisewood, David Jacobs.

Archers First broadcast on BBC on 1 January 1951, although first heard on a local station in the Midlands in 1950. The Archers lived on Brookfield Farm in Ambridge, just south of Borchester, Borsetshire. Many weddings during the series have been recorded at Hanbury Church in Worcestershire. Princess Margaret as President of the NSPCC visited Ambridge for a fashion show (1984). Eddie Grundy famously got drunk in Britt Ekland's dressing room at the Christmas pantomime (1992). Billing: Everyday story of country folk. Local pub: The Bull.

aspect ratio Normal: 4 x 3. Wide screen: 16 x 9.

BAFTA TV Awards: 2004

Best Actress Anamaria Marinca (*Sex Traffic*)

Best Actor Rhys Ifans (*Not Only But Always*)

Best Light Entertainment Performance Paul O'Grady (*The Paul O'Grady Show*)

Best Comedy Performance Matt Lucas and David Walliams (*Little Britain*)

Best Single Drama *Omagh*

Best Drama Serial *Sex Traffic*

Best Factual Series *The Power of Nightmares*

Best Comedy Programme *Little Britain*

Best Situation Comedy *The Office*

Best Soap *Coronation Street*

BBC announcer: first Leslie Mitchell.

BBC Choice First new BBC channel for 34 years (Clive Anderson opened the proceedings on 23 September 1998).

BBC Director General: first Lord Reith.

BBC Director of Radio Jenny Abramsky took over from Matthew Bannister on 19 November 1998.

BBC1 Commenced broadcasting from Alexandra Palace in 1936.

BBC Radio controllers Radio 5 Live – Bob Shennan; Radio 4 – Mark Damazer; Radio 3 – Roger Wright; Radio 2 – Lesley Douglas; Radio 1 – Andy Parfitt.

BBC Television controllers BBC1 – Peter Fincham; BBC2 – Roly Keating; BBC3 – Stuart Murphy; BBC4 – Janice Hadlow.

BBC Television executives Chairman is Michael Grade and Director General is Mark Thompson.

BBC3 Digital station. Commenced 9 February 2003 and launched by Johnny Vaughan.

BBC2 Commenced 20 April 1964; mascots were Hullabaloo and Custard (two kangaroos).

Beyond Our Ken Billed as 'A sort of radio show' and starred Kenneth Horne.

Brain of Britain Hosted by Robert Robinson and produced by Richard Edis. Questions set by Kevin Ashman (Jorkins). Winners: Martin Dakin (1954), Arthur Maddock (1955), Anthony Carr (1956), Rosemary Watson (1957), David Keys (1958), Dr Reginald Webster (1959), Patrick Bowing (1960), Irene Thomas (1961), Henry Button (1962), Ian Barton (1963), Ian Gillies (1964), Robert Crampsey (1965), Richard Best (1966), Lt Cmdr Loring (1967),

Ralph Raby (1968), T D Thomson (1969), Ian Matheson (1970), Fred Morgan (1971), A Lawrence (1972), Glyn Court (1973), Roger Pritchard (1974), Winifred Lawson (1975), Thomas Dyer (1976), Martin Gostelow (1977), James Nesbitt (1978), Arthur Gerard (1979), Tim Paxton (1980), Peter Barlow (1981), John Pusey (1982), Sue Marshall (1983), Peter Bates (1984), Richard Fife (1985), Stephen Gore (1986), Ian Sutton (1987), Paul Monaghan (1988), Barbara Thompson (1989), Jim Eccleson (1990), Chris Wright (1991), Mike Billson (1992), Geoffrey Colton (1993), Ian Wynn-Mackenzie (1994), Ian Kinloch (1995), Kevin Ashman (1996), Daphne Fowler (1997), Guy Herbert (1998), Leslie Duncalf (1999), Mike Smith-Rawnsley (2000), Tom Corfe (2001), Dr David Jones (2002), Dave Steadman (2003), Alan Bennett (2004).

Brains Trust The first panel were Julian Huxley, C E M Joad and Cmdr A B Campbell. The chairman was Donald McCullough, who was replaced by Gilbert Harding.

Breakfast Television Started 17 January 1983 (*BBC Breakfast Time*).

Broadcasting Standards Authority: first chairman Lord Rees Mogg.

BSkyB: controller Elizabeth Murdoch.

Byker Grove: **setting** Newcastle upon Tyne.

Carlton TV: fine Carlton Television was fined £2m for faking the documentary *The Connection*.

Channel 4 Started in 1982 (first programme: *Countdown*).

Channel 4: chief executive Mark Thompson (chairman: Vanni Treves).

Channel 5 Launched on 30 March 1997 by Dawn Airey and the Spice Girls.

Channel 5: chief executive Dawn Airey.

chefs on television Jane Asher, Susan Brooks, Robert Carrier, Fanny Craddock, Anton Edelman, Keith Floyd, Philip Harbin, Ainsley Harriott, Graham Kerr, Anton Mosimann, Jean-Christophe Novelli, Jamie Oliver, Gordon Ramsay, Paul Rankin, Gary Rhodes, Delia Smith, Rick Stein, Brian Turner, Antony Worrall Thompson.

Classic FM: chief executive Roger Lewis.

colour television Started in 1967.

Crookes Tube: function Produced cathode rays.

Desert Island Discs: **first guest** Vic Oliver.

Desert Island Discs: **presenters** Roy Plomley, Michael Parkinson, Sue Lawley.

digital television: advantages Traditional broadcasting is based on electronic signals that rise and fall to represent the shades of black, white and colour in the TV picture. The continuously varying signal is a direct analogue of the image it represents, just as the variations in the grooves of an LP, picked up by the stylus, are an analogue of the music. Analogue broadcasting is spendthrift in its use of the radio spectrum. There is a limited range of frequencies that can be used for TV transmissions, and each analogue station needs a healthy chunk of that space (approx 8 megahertz). Transmitters using the same frequency must be a long way apart, otherwise they interfere with one another, so transmitters closer than a few hundred kilometres to each other must employ different frequencies. As a result, it takes 44 frequencies in the UHF band to provide the four terrestrial channels. Digital broadcasting alters the rules. Instead of representing the image by a continuously variable signal, digital TV encodes it in the same language used by computers, a long stream of binary digits, or 'bits', each of which is either 0 or 1, a pulse or a non-pulse. It takes an enormous number of such bits to encode a TV picture, but it is easier to distinguish a pulse from a non-pulse than it is to discern the varying waveform of an analogue signal. This means that transmitters can be run at a much lower signal strength and still provide a decent picture. This in turn reduces the interference problem for terrestrial broadcasters so that better use can be made of the available frequencies, and picture quality is greatly improved. A full TV picture requires about 216 million bits per second but only the changes from one picture to the next are encoded so as to enable the data to fit into the frequency band.

Hamish Macbeth: setting Plockton, on the west coast of Scotland.

House of Lords: first televised 1985.

iconoscope: inventor Vladimir Zworykin (1923).

ITMA (It's That Man Again) Tommy Handley was the title character and Dorothy Summers played Mrs Mopp.

ITN newscaster: first Chris Chataway.

ITV: managing director David Liddiment.

Just a Minute Chairman Nicholas Parsons. Panellists have included: Kenneth Williams, Derek Nimmo, Peter Jones, Clement Freud, Paul Merton, Graham Norton, Lance Percival and Sheila Hancock. The aim is to talk for one minute on a given topic without Hesitation, Deviation or Repetition.

Life with the Lyons Ben Lyon and Bebe Daniels and their children Barbara and Richard.

local radio stations Aire – Leeds, Arrow – Hastings, Beacon – Wolverhampton, BRMB – Birmingham, The Beach – Lowestoft, Broadland – Norwich, Cat – Cheltenham, Centre – Leicester, Chiltern – Luton/Bedford, City – Liverpool, Dream – Colchester, Hallam – Sheffield, Hereward – Peterborough, Kestrel – Basingstoke, Mercia – Coventry, Mercury – Crawley, Oak – Loughborough, Orwell – Ipswich, Pennine – Bradford, Piccadilly – Manchester, Ram – Derby, Silk – Macclesfield, Trent – Nottingham, 2CR – Bournemouth, Viking – Hull, West – Bristol, Wire – Warrington, Wish – Wigan, Wyvern – Hereford and Worcester.

Men from the Ministry, The Wilfrid Hyde Whyte (Roland Hamilton-Jones), Richard Murdoch (Richard Lamb).

Nielsens US equivalent of BARB showing American audience ratings.

OnDigital TV service 30-channel service launched by Ulrika Jonsson on 15 November 1998.

pirate radio station: first Radio Caroline, from 1964 to 1967.

radio play: caused panic Orson Welles's War of the Worlds broadcast in 1938.

radio stations: formerly called Radio 4 (Home), Radio 3 (Third), Radio 2 (Light). These were the three main stations. Radio 1 commenced in 1967.

radio station: top 2004 BBC Radio 2 received the most listeners in the UK.

Round Britain Quiz Hosted by Nick Clarke.

satellite TV: reception areas Known as Footprints.

S4C: full name Sianel Pedwar Cymru.

SkyDigital Launched on 1 October 1998.

soap opera: first on television The Appleyards ran from 1952 to 1957 and is truly the first example of a televised British soap opera. The first adult British soap opera was The Grove Family (1954–7). The first daily soap opera was Sixpenny Corner (set in the new town of Springwood). This is another controversial area that requires careful attention. The Appleyards was shown fortnightly and was a children's soap, while The Groves was broadcast weekly and was for adults.

soap opera: why called Term derived from the American radio of the 1930s when soap and detergent companies sponsored the 15-minute daily radio programmes. Proctor and Gamble were a leading light in this field.

Steve Coogan creations Alan Partridge, Paul Calf, Pauline Calf, Tony Farino.

stripping Showing of programme at the same time every day of every week.

swear word: first to use Kenneth Tynan was the first to use the 'f' word on television.

Teletext BBC – Ceefax; ITV – Oracle.

television companies Anglia TV, based in Norwich, started in 1959 (logo is a series of triangles in shape of an 'A'). Associated Television (ATV) first broadcast in September 1955, at weekends only. The BBC formed in London in 1922 as a radio station and in 1936 started television broadcasts. BSkyB formed in 1990 by merger of Sky TV and British Satellite Broadcasting. Border Television formed in 1961 (logo is ovoid shape with an inverted 'Y' running through the centre). Carlton Television formed in 1992. Central Television formed in 1982 and is now part of the Carlton Network (logo is a 12-part sphere). Grampian Television formed in 1961 (logo is a saltire cross on a television screen). Granada Television formed in 1955 and is the only original franchise holder still broadcasting. Harlech Television formed in 1968. ITC (Independent Television Corporation) formed as an alternative to the BBC. LWT (London Weekend Television) started in 1967 from Fridays at 6.00 p.m. to Sunday nights. Meridian Television replaced TVS as franchise holder for the south and south-east on 1 January 1993 (logo is a sunny face). Rediffusion started broadcasting on weekdays only in September 1955. Scottish Television formed in 1957. Southern Television formed in 1958. Thames Television formed when ABC merged with Associated Rediffusion in the late 1960s. Tyne Tees formed in 1959 and is now owned by Granada Media. Ulster Television formed in 1959. Westcountry Television formed in 1993 and is owned by Carlton Communications. Yorkshire Television formed in 1968 and is owned by Granada Media.

television: inventor John Logie Baird created his first televisor, a contraption made from a tea-chest, a biscuit box and darning needles, in 1923, and gave a first public demonstration in 1926. In 1928 he produced a crude colour system.

television licences: first Licences were first issued in 1946 at £2 each. Cost of a colour licence at April 2005 is £126.50. Black and white is £42.

test card girl: famous Carol Hersey (billed as the most seen person on television).

TV am: launched by David Frost, Michael Parkinson, Robert Kee, Anna Ford, Angela Rippon.

Twenty Questions: presenters Stewart McPherson, Gilbert Harding, Kenneth Horne, Cliff Michelmore.

TELEVISION

Twenty Questions: mystery voice   Norman
Hackforth.

Ulster TV: chairman   John B McGuckian.

Ulster TV: location   Havelock House, Belfast.

Variety Playhouse: **MC**   Vic Oliver.

weather   Laura Greene (ITV), Ian McCaskill, Bill
Giles, Suzanne Charlton, Helen Young, John Ketley,
Peter Cockcroft, Michael Fish (BBC).

weather: hurricane announcement   Michael Fish
gave us the good news on 15 October 1987 that the
person who rang up saying a hurricane was likely
for tomorrow was completely wrong!

Wogan: **appeared drunk on in 1990**   George Best.

World Service Radio: controller   Mark Byford.

World Service Television   BBC channel launched in
1991.

TRANSPORT: AIRCRAFT

Chronology

1300 Marco Polo reports man-carrying kites in use in China.

1500 Leonardo da Vinci designs helicopters and ornithopters.

1709 A model hot-air balloon demonstrated by Father Laurenço de Gusmao at the court of King John V of Portugal (8 Aug.).

1783 First manned balloon flight by Pilâtre de Rozier and the marquis d'Arlandes in the Bois de Boulogne (21 Nov.). First flight of hydrogen balloon by Professor Jacques Charles (1 Dec.).

1784 First British balloon flight (4 Oct.).

1785 First crossing of the English Channel by balloon piloted by Jean-Pierre Blanchard and John Jeffries (7 Jan.).

1799 Sir George Cayley designs his first glider.

1810 Cayley publishes a paper on the theory of the airplane.

1843 The 'Steam Airplane' patented by William Samuel Henson.

1849 Cayley's 'Boy-Lifter' glider succeeds in lifting a small boy off the ground.

1852 Henri Giffard makes first semi-controlled powered flight in airship (24 Sept.).

1853 Cayley succeeds in making his coachman fly his glider.

1861 Balloons used by Union forces in American Civil War.

1870 Leon Gambetta escapes from a besieged Paris by balloon (7 Oct.).

1890 Clément Ader's *Eole* aircraft makes a short 'hop' near Paris (9 Oct.).

1891 Otto Lilienthal makes his first glider flight.

1894 Sir Hiram Maxim's biplane makes brief uncontrolled ascent (31 July).

1896 Otto Lilienthal dies after glider crash (10 Aug.).

1899 Glider pioneer Percy Pilcher dies following glider crash (2 Oct.).

1900 LZ1 makes first rigid airship flight (Count Zeppelin) (2 July).

1900 Wright brothers begin glider experiments (1 Dec.).

1903 Lebaudy airship makes first fully controlled flight in history (8 May). Samuel Langley's *Aerodrome* aircraft narrowly fails to make first powered flight (7 Oct.). Wright brothers make first powered flight (Orville at the controls) in *Flyer* (17 Dec.).

1906 Alberto Santos-Dumont makes first powered flight in Europe (23 Oct.). French company, Voisin Frères, established for the production of powered aircraft (Nov.).

1907 Breguet gyroplane makes first helicopter 'hop' (19 Sept.). Paul Cornu's helicopter makes first 'hop' (13 Nov.). Lt Thomas W Selfridge becomes first person killed in a plane crash when he and Orville Wright crash at Fort Meyer, Virginia (17 Sept.).

1908 Samuel Cody makes first powered flight in Britain (16 Oct.).

1909 Louis Blériot makes first flight across the English Channel (25 July).

1910 Harry Houdini, the celebrated escapologist and illusionist, makes the first successful flight on the Australian continent in a Voisin biplane (18 March).

1911 Eugene Ely lands Curtiss biplane on USS *Pennsylvania* (18 Jan.). First mail carried by air in UK (9 Sept.). First aerial warfare by Italian Army Aviation Corps over Libya (23 Oct.). Lt Giulio Gavotti makes the first air raid by dropping a 4½ lb bomb on Turks at Ain Zara (1 Nov.). Aircraft used in Mexican Revolution.

1912 Royal Flying Corps (RFC) formed (13 April). Death of Wilbur Wright (30 May). Bulgarian M Popoff becomes first pilot killed in warfare, during a reconnaissance flight (3 Nov.).

1914 Lts V Waterfall and C G G Bayley first British fliers killed in action (22 Aug.). Paris becomes the first capital city to be bombed from the air (30 Aug.). Japanese seaplanes attack the Austro-German fleet at Kiaochow, causing the first ship to be sunk from the air (17 Sept.). HMS *Ark Royal* becomes the world's first aircraft carrier (9 Dec.).

1915 LZ38 airship makes the first air raid on London (31 May). Flt Sub-Lt R A Warneford (VC) downs the LZ37, the first Zeppelin to be shot down (7 June). Katherine Stinson becomes first woman to loop the loop (18 July). Roland Garros is captured in Belgium (20 April). Garros was the first Frenchman to cross the Mediterranean by air, and working with Raymond Saulnier invented deflector plates to enable him to fire a machine gun through the propeller.

1916 Death of Ernst Mach (19 Feb.). Boeing formed as Pacific Aero Products Co (15 July). SL11 airship shot down in North London by Lt W Leefe-Robinson (VC) (2 Sept.). World's first flying bomb, the Hewitt-Sperry, built by Curtiss, is tested (12 Sept.). The airship ace Heinrich Mathy is killed when LZ72 is shot down over Potters Bar (2 Oct.). First British airline, Aircraft Transport & Travel Ltd, registered (5 Oct.).

1917 Baron von Richthofen awarded the 'Pour le Mérite' medal (16 Jan.). Death of Count von Zeppelin (8 March). Billy Mitchell became the first US Army officer to fly over German lines (24 April). Albert Ball killed in France (7 May), awarded posthumous VC (3 June). Sopwith Camel goes into service with Royal Flying Corps (RFC) in France (July). First flight of the Vickers Vimy (30 Nov.).

1918 Air Ministry established and Lord Rothermere is first Sec. of State for Air (2 Jan.). Royal Flying Corps and Royal Naval Air Service combine to create the Royal Air Force (1 April). Baron von Richthofen shot down (21 April). Hermann Goering takes over as leader of

Richthofen's squadron (7 July). HMS *Furious*, adapted from cruiser to aircraft carrier, launched six Sopwith Camels against Zeppelin sheds (19 July). Peter Strasser, German commander of airships, shot down in L70 off Cromer (5 Aug.). Roland Garros killed when his SPAD XIII breaks up during a dogfight (5 Oct.). Handley Page 0/400 becomes first plane to fly from Egypt to India (12 Dec.).

1919 Britain's first scheduled air service inaugurated (10 May). US Navy Curtiss flying boat flown by Lt Cmdr Albert Read becomes first aircraft to fly the Atlantic (in stages) (27 May). Alcock and Brown make first non-stop crossing of the Atlantic in a Vickers Vimy (15 June). German Zeppelin fleet scuttled (23 June). First flight of Junkers F13, the first all-metal monoplane airliner (25 June). London's first airport opens at Hounslow Heath (1 July). British airship R34 makes first two-way Atlantic crossing (13 July). Edward Mannock, Britain's most successful ace, posthumously awarded VC (18 July). First flight over the Canadian Rockies by Capt. Ernest Hoy (7 Aug.). KLM founded (7 Oct.). Handley Page Transport provide first in-flight meals (11 Oct.). Ross and Keith Smith make first flight from Britain to Australia in a Vickers Vimy (10 Dec.) .

1920 First flight from Britain to South Africa (20 March). Croydon Airport begins operations, taking over from Hounslow (29 March). Juan de la Cierva is granted a patent for the Autogiro (27 Aug.). Dayton-Wright RB Racer aircraft flown with retractable landing gear. Qantas (Queensland and Northern Territory Aerial Services) founded (16 Nov.). First British airline disaster: Handley Page 0/400 crashes at Cricklewood, killing four (14 Dec.). Airline AT & T goes into liquidation (15 Dec.).

1921 First free flight of a helicopter since 1907, assisted by a balloon (15 Jan.). Orly aerodrome opened in Paris (1 March). Croydon Airport officially opened (31 March). Vickers Vernon, first troop-carrying aircraft, delivered to RAF (1 Aug.). First aerial crop-dusting takes place in Ohio, USA, by Lt John B Macready in a Curtiss JN6 (3 Aug.). Airship R38 crashes in Hull, killing many of Britain's most experienced airshipmen (24 Aug.).

1922 Formation of RAF reserve announced (9 Feb.). Jack Sanderson became first airline steward (2 April). First mid-air collision, between Farman Goliath and Daimler DH18, over Poix in northern France (7 April). First night flight by Grands Express from Le Bourget to Croydon (9 June). First air crossing of South Atlantic by S Cabral and G Coutinho of Portugal (16 June). Dr Albert Taylor and Leo Young make first successful detections of objects by radio observation (23 Sept.). QANTAS flies its first scheduled service, the first passenger being Mr A Kennedy (2 Nov.). First instance of skywriting 'Smoke Lucky Strikes' (28 Nov.).

1923 First public flight of Juan de la Cierva's Autogyro (9 Jan.). First drop tank used (Boeing MB-3A) (5 March). First air troop-transport took place during Kurdish uprising when 280 Sikhs were flown from Kingarban to Kirkuk (April).

Etienne Ochmichen makes world's first helicopter closed-circuit flight (1 May). Amelia Earhart receives pilot's certificate from NAA, the first woman to do so (16 May). Sabena Airlines formed in Belgium (23 May). Formation of New Zealand Air Force (14 June). First flight of US airship *Shenandoah* (3 Sept.). Dixmunde disaster over the Mediterranean: 52 killed in airship explosion (21 Dec.).

1924 Royal Canadian Air Force formed (1 April). First sustained forward flight of a helicopter made by Etienne Ochmichen (14 April). Fleet Air Arm established (April). Start of first aeroplane flight round the world by Lts L H Smith and Erik Nelson (24 April–28 Sept.). Formation of Imperial Airways (28 April). First circumnavigation of Australia: Goble and McIntyre in a Fairey IIID (19 May). First flight around Japan: Goto and Yonezawa in a Kawanishi K-6 (31 July). First aerial circumnavigation by two Douglas world cruisers of the US Army Air Service: Smith and Arnold in *Chicago*, Nelson and Harding in *New Orleans* (28 Sept.).

1925 First production DH60 Moth delivered (21 July), maiden flight 22 Feb. First flight of M-17 ELLO, the first Messerschmitt aircraft (16 Aug.). *Shenandoah* breaks up in mid-air over Ohio; 29 dead (3 Sept.).

1926 Alan Cobham flies his DH-50 over Victoria Falls on the way to Cape Town (24 Jan.). Robert Goddard launches first liquid-fuelled rocket (16 March). Formation of Deutsche Luft Hansa A.G. (6 April). Richard G Byrd flies over North Pole in Fokker F.VII (9 May). Amundsen makes first flight over North Pole in an airship (14 May). US Army Air Service becomes US Army Air Corps (2 July). First aircraft launched and recovered by submarine, US *S-1* (28 July). Alan Cobham completes epic flight from London to Australia and back (1 Oct).

1927 Lindbergh makes first non-stop solo Atlantic crossing in *Spirit of St Louis* (21 May). Lt Dick Bentley makes first solo flight from Britain to Cape Town (28 Sept.).

1928 Inauguration of Flying Doctor service in Australia (15 May). Nobile's *Italia* airship crashes in the Arctic (25 May). Charles Kingsford Smith flies Pacific in *Southern Cross* (9 June). Amelia Earhart becomes first woman to fly the Atlantic (as passenger 18 June). JAL formed in Japan (30 Oct.).

1929 Formation of LOT in Poland (1 Jan.). First scheduled passenger flight from London to India (6 April). First stowaway on transatlantic flight (journalist Arthur Shreiber, 14 June). *Graf Zeppelin* completes first circumnavigation of the globe (29 Aug.). Schneider Trophy retained by Britain, Flying Officer H R D Waghorn in Supermarine S-6B (7 Sept.). Testing of first wireless guidance system for aircraft (1 Oct.). R101 unveiled at Cardington (2 Oct.). First flight of R100 from Howden (16 Nov.).

1930 Whittle applies for patent for his turbojet (16 Jan.). Jack Northrop flies experimental 'Flying Wing', with tail boom (1 May). Ellen Church, a registered nurse from Iowa, became the first air hostess (15 May). Amy Johnson makes first solo flight to Australia by a woman (24 May). Formation of TWA (16 July). Death of Glen Curtiss (23 July). R101 receives Certificate of Airworthiness (2 Oct.). R101 crashes and explodes at Beauvais, France, on way to India (5 Oct.). First demonstration of Handley Page HP42 (17 Nov.).

1931 Iraqi airforce makes inaugural flight (8 April). Wiley Post makes flight around Northern Hemisphere in Lockheed Vega *Winnie Mae* (1 July). 400 mph barrier broken by Flt Lt George Stainforth in Supermarine SGB (29 Sept.). USS *Akron* aircraft carrier airship commissioned (2 Nov.).

1932 Asian mainland attacked from the air for the first time by Japanese bombers (26 Feb.). Aeroflot formed in Moscow (25 March). Amy Johnson and Jim Mollison announce their engagement (9 May). Amelia Earhart becomes first woman to fly Atlantic non-stop solo (21 May). Santos-Dumont commits suicide (23 July). First flight of Model 17, Beech Aircraft Corporation's first aircraft (4 Nov.).

1933 Maiden flight of Boeing 247 (8 Feb.). Formation of Indian airforce (1 April). French Armée de l'Air created (1 April). First flight over Everest (Westland PV3 piloted by marquis of Douglas and Westland Wallace piloted by David McIntyre (3 April). USS *Akron* crashes into the Atlantic off New Jersey; 70 killed (5 April). USS *Macon* (*Akron*'s replacement) commissioned (23 June). First flight of Douglas DC-1 (1 July). Air France inaugurated (31 Oct.).

1934 Deutsche Luft Hansa becomes Lufthansa (1 Jan.). First flight of Boeing P-26 (10 Jan.). DC-2 goes into service with TWA (11 May). De Havilland Comet wins England–Australia air race (24 Oct.).

1935 Amelia Earhart becomes first woman to fly the Pacific alone (12 Jan.). Death of Hugo Junkers (3 Feb.). USS *Macon* crashes into the sea off California (12 Feb.). Goering named as chief of the new Luftwaffe (10 March). First flight of Messerschmitt BF 109 (28 March). Swissair begins regular scheduled service to London (1 April). First flight of privately funded Bristol 142 (Blenheim) (12 April). Successful radar experiment in Suffolk (24 July). First flight of Boeing 299 (Flying Fortress) (28 July). Deaths of Wiley Post and Will Rogers in Alaskan air crash (15 Aug.). First flight of Hurricane (6 Nov.). Charles Kingsford Smith disappears over Indian Ocean (9 Nov.). First air traffic control centre opens in US (1 Dec.). First flight of Douglas DST (DC-3) (12 Dec.).

1936 Death of Billy Mitchell (19 Feb.). Maiden flight of *Hindenburg* (4 March). Supermarine Spitfire makes first flight piloted by Mutt Summers (5 March). Gatwick Airport officially opened (6 June). First flight of Westlander Lysander (10 June). First flight of Vickers Wellington (by Mutt Summers) (15 June). Formation of RAF Volunteer Reserve (30 July). Death of Blériot (8 Aug.). First Short Empire C-Class flying boat goes into service (30 Oct.). DC-2 crashes at Croydon killing 14 including Juan de la Cierva (9 Dec.).

1937 Saab established (2 April). First trials of Whittle's turbojet (13 April). Guernica bombed (26 April). *Hindenburg* explodes at Lakehurst; 36 killed (6 May). Death of R J Mitchell (11 June). Amelia Earhart disappears over the Pacific while attempting a round-the-world flight (navigator: Fred Noonan) (2 July).

1938 First in-flight refuelling of an airliner (Short Empire Flying Boat) (20 Jan.). Short-Mayo composite aircraft separates in flight for the first time (6 Feb.). First flight of Bell XP-3A Airacobra, the first US fighter to feature a cannon (6 April). First flight of Douglas DC-4 (7 June). Spitfire goes into RAF service (4 Aug.). Japanese aircraft shoot down a Chinese DC-2 airliner, the first civil airliner to be lost to hostile air attack (24 Aug.). First flight of Westland Whirlwind (11 Oct.). Germany launches its first aircraft carrier, *Graf Zeppelin* (8 Dec.). First flight of Boeing Stratoliner, the first pressurised airliner (31 Dec.).

1939 First flight of XP-38, Lockheed Lightning (27 Jan.). First flight of Mitsubishi Zero (1 April). Chain Home radar system goes online (4 April). First flight of Short Stirling (14 May). First flight of Focke-Wulf FW 190 (1 June). First flight of rocket-powered Heinkel He 176 at Peenemünde (20 June). Formation of Women's Auxiliary Air Force (28 June). First flight of Bristol Beaufighter (17 July). Formation of BOAC from British Airways and Imperial Airways (4 Aug.). First flight of jet aircraft, Heinkel He 178 (23 Aug.). RAF mobilised (1 Sept.). German paratroops make first-ever offensive parachute drop in Poland (3 Sept.). First 'bombing' raid (of leaflets) by RAF against Germany (4 Sept.). First 'kills' by RAF against German bombers (16 Oct.). First German bomber brought down on British soil since 1918 (28 Oct.). First flight of Heinkel He 177 (19 Nov.). First flight of Consolidated XB-24, Liberator (29 Dec.).

1940 First flight of Hawker Typhoon (24 Feb.). Sikorsky VS-300 helicopter makes first free flight (13 May). First flight of North American B-25 Mitchell (19 Aug.). First RAF raid on Berlin (25 Aug.). Caproni-Campini N.I. experimental jet makes first flight (28 Aug.). Battle of Britain Day; entire strength of RAF Fighter Command committed against Luftwaffe attack (15 Sept.). Eagle Squadron of RAF formed by US volunteer pilots at Church Fenton (19 Sept.). First flight of North American NA-73 (P-51 Mustang) (20 Oct.). First major Italian air raid on Britain (11 Nov.). Twenty Fairy Swordfish from HMS *Eagle* and HMS *Illustrious* successfully attack Italian fleet at Taranto (12 Nov.). Coventry bombed (14 Nov.). First flight of DH 98 Mosquito (25 Nov.). First test flight of HS-293A guided bomb (18 Dec.).

1941 Death of Amy Johnson when her Airspeed Oxford crashes in Thames Estuary (5 Jan.). First flight of Avro Lancaster (9 Jan.). First flight of the Heinkel He 280, the world's first multi-jet aircraft (2 April). First flight of Republic P-47 Thunderbolt (6 May). Rudolf Hess parachutes into Scotland from a Messerschmitt Me110 (10 May). First British jet aircraft, a Gloster E-28/39, makes its maiden flight (15

T
R
A
N
S
P
O
R
T

A
I
R
C
R
A
F
T

May). Opening of Washington National Airport (16 June). First successful rocket assisted take-off in California (July). Heini Dittmar pilots a Messerschmitt Me 163A Komet at a speed of 623.85 mph (2 Oct.). Japanese attack Pearl Harbor (7 Dec.).

1942 Arthur Harris takes charge of Bomber Command (22 Feb.). First Lancaster mission (3 March). Doolittle raid against Japanese B 25s from USS *Hornet* (21 April). Battle of the Coral Sea (8 May). Battle of Midway (6 June). First flight of Grumman Hellcat (26 June). First flight of Me 262 jet fighter (18 July). First flight of Hawker Tempest (2 Sept.). First flight of B29 Super Fortress (21 Sept.). First flight of Bell XP-59 Airacomet, the first US jet aircraft (1 Oct.). Brabazon Committee (postwar airliners) established (23 Dec.).

1943 First flight of Gloster Meteor, the first British jet fighter (5 March). RAF breaches Mohne and Eder dams using 'bouncing' bomb designed by Barnes Wallis (16 May). Leslie Howard shot down in KLM DC-3 over the English Channel (1 June). First flight of Arado Ar 234, the world's first jet bomber (15 June). *Memphis Belle* becomes first B-17 to complete 25 missions in Europe (19 June). First use by RAF of 'Window', the strips of metal foil dropped to jam radar systems (24 July).

1944 First B29 raid (on Bangkok) (5 June). First V1 hits London (13 June). Marianas Turkey Shoot – Japanese lose 480 aircraft and 3 carriers (20 June). First use of napalm (by Lockheed Lightnings against Coutances, France (17 July). International Civil Aviation conference in Chicago; 52 countries attend. Gives rise to Chicago Convention (1 Nov.–7 Dec.). *Tirpitz* sunk by RAF Lancasters of 617 Squadron (12 Nov.). Glenn Miller disappears in a UC-64 over the English Channel (5 Dec.).

1945 22,000 lb Grand Slam, the heaviest bomb ever dropped, used successfully against the Bielefeld Viaduct (14 March). International Air Transport Association (IATA) formed in Havana (19 April). Atomic bomb tested at Alamogordo (16 July). Atomic bomb 'Little Boy' dropped on Hiroshima by B29 *Enola Gay* (6 Aug.). Atomic bomb 'Fat Man' dropped on Nagasaki by B29 *Bock's Car* (9 Aug.). First flight of turboprop-powered aircraft, a modified Gloster Meteor (20 Sept.). Absolute speed record taken to 606 mph by Gloster Meteor (7 Nov.).

1946 Civil Aviation Act establishes BOAC, BEA and BSAA (British South American Airways), their first commercial departure, made from London Heathrow, a BSAA Lancastrian (1 Jan.). First Pan-Am flight to London from New York (1 June). Air India formed from TATA airlines (29 July). Scandinavian Airline Systems (SAS) formed (31 July). First flight of Convair B-36 (8 Aug.). Aerolinee Italiane Internazionali (Alitalia) established (16 Sept.). Cathay Pacific Airways formed in Hong Kong (24 Sept.). First artificial snowstorm caused by cloud seeding (13 Nov.).

1947 Last DC-3 built by Douglas; it is sold to Sabena but on 2 March 1948 it crashes at Heathrow with loss of 19 lives. First round-the-world air service operated by Pan-Am (12 June).

Kenneth Arnold sees nine aircraft moving 'as a saucer would if you skimmed it over the water' at high speed near Mt Rainier, Washington (24 June). First flight of Boeing Stratocruiser (8 July). Last DC-4 built by Douglas delivered to South African Airways (and still in service) (9 Aug.). USAF established as a separate armed service (18 Sept). Captain Charles Yeager becomes first man to break the sound barrier flying at Mach 1.015 at 42,000' in Bell X-1 (14 Oct.). BEA makes last scheduled flight from Croydon Airport (1 Nov.). Hughes H-4 Hercules (*Spruce Goose*), the largest aircraft in the world, is flown for the first and only time by Howard Hughes, for one mile (2 Nov.).

1948 Death of Orville Wright (30 Jan.). Thirty killed when a Pan-Am Lockheed Constellation crashes near Shannon (15 April). First action by Israeli airforce (20 May). Start of Operation Vittles – the Berlin Airlift (26 June). Thirty-nine killed at Northolt when an RAF Avro York collides with an SAS DC-6 (4 July). First flight of Vickers Viscount (16 July). Idlewild Airport (now JFK) opens in New York (31 July). John Derry breaks sound barrier in UK in a DH 108 (6 Sept.). El Al comes into being (15 Nov.). Wright Flyer goes on display at the Smithsonian Institute (17 Dec.).

1949 Israeli airforce Messerschmitt 109s shoot down four RAF Spitfires near the Egyptian border (7 Jan.). First non-stop round-the-world flight completed by USAF B-50A *Lucky Lady II* (2 March). First flight of English Electric Canberra (13 May). First flight of De Havilland Comet, the world's first jet airliner (27 July). BOAC absorbs BSAA (30 July). First flight of Bristol Brabazon, largest aircraft ever built in Britain (4 Sept.).

1950 World's worst aircrash: 80 killed when Avro Tudor carrying rugby fans crashes in a field near Cardiff (12 March). First glider crossing of the English Channel (Lorne Welch, 12 April). HMS *Ark Royal* launched (3 May). First North Korean aircraft shot down in Korean war by Twin Mustang (27 June). First helicopter rescue of downed pilot behind enemy lines in Korea (4 Sept.). First flight of Lockheed Super Constellation (13 Oct.). Twenty-eight killed as BEA Viking crashes in fog at Heathrow (31 Oct.). World's first jet-against-jet dogfight, F-80 versus Mig-15, the F-80 being successful (8 Nov.). Bell Model 47 helicopters arrive at MASH units in Korea (1 Dec.).

1951 First non-stop unrefuelled crossing of Atlantic by jet, RAF Canberra (21 Feb.). First flight of Vickers Valiant (18 May). First in-flight refuelling under combat conditions in Korea (6 July). First in-flight sweeping of wings – Bell X-5 research aircraft (16 July). JAL reformed in Tokyo (1 Aug.). First flight of Supermarine Swift (5 Aug.). USAF orders nuclear-powered aircraft from Convair (5 Sept.). First mass movement of troops to battlefront by helicopter, in Korea (21 Sept.). Last DC-6 completed and delivered to Braniff Airways (2 Nov.). First flight of Gloster Javelin (26 Nov.). First interception of aircraft by missile at White Sands, New Mexico (27 Nov.). First turbine-engined helicopter,

Kaman K-225, makes its maiden flight (10 Dec.). First airline flight over North Pole by Alaska Air (12 Dec.).

1952 First flight of Bristol type 173 twin rotor helicopter (3 Jan.). De Havilland Comet 1 gets first certificate of airworthiness for a jet airliner (22 Jan.). First flight of B-52 (15 April). First successful landing of an aircraft at the North Pole (USAF C-47) (3 May). First scheduled passenger jet service: BOAC Comet 1 from London (3 May). BOAC begins a weekly service from London to Colombo with Comet 1 (11 Aug.). First flight of Bristol Britannia (16 Aug.). First flight of Avro Vulcan (30 Aug.). John Derry and 28 spectators killed when his DH110 crashes at Farnborough (6 Sept.). First doubts about Comet safety after take-off accident in Rome (26 Oct.). First flight of Handley Page Victor (24 Dec.).

1953 Lufthansa revived in Germany (6 Jan.). BOAC Comet crashes near Calcutta killing 43 (2 May). First flight of DC-7 (18 May). Dan-Air established (21 May). 129 killed when USAF C-124 Globemaster II crashes on take-off in Japan (18 June). Neville Duke breaks absolute speed record (727.48 mph) in Hawker Hunter (7 Sept.).

1954 First flight of Lockheed Starfighter (7 Jan.). BOAC Comet *Yoke Peter* crashes off Elba, killing 35 (10 Jan.). Last operational flight of a RAF Spitfire (1 April). South African Airways Comet crashes off Stromboli (8 April). Churchill orders the grounding of all Comets (12 April). First flight of Jet Provost (26 June). First flight of Boeing Model 367-80, prototype of the 707 (15 July). First flight of the Rolls Royce Thrust Measuring Rig, 'The Flying Bedstead' (3 Aug.). First flight of Lockheed Hercules (23 Aug.). Court of Inquiry into Comet crashes concludes that metal fatigue is to blame (19 Oct.).

1955 Pakistan International Airlines (PIA) established (10 Jan.). First operational departure from the central complex at Heathrow (17 April). Fifty-eight killed when a Lockheed Constellation of El Al is shot down by Bulgarian Airforce Mig-15s near the Greek border (27 July). First flight of Republic Thunderchief (22 Oct.). Forty-four killed aboard a United Airlines DC-6B after it blows up in mid-air. It is subsequently proven that the explosion was caused by a bomb, planted to perpetrate an insurance fraud. (Arthur Hailey's *Airport* was based on this incident) (1 Nov.). First flight of Fokker Friendship (24 Nov.).

1956 Death of Lord Trenchard (10 Feb.). Peter Twiss flies Fairey Delta 2 at 1,131.76 mph to take official airspeed record (10 March). First flight of Dassault Super Mystère (15 May). 128 killed when a United Airlines DC-3 collides with a TWA Constellation over the Grand Canyon (30 June). First flight of Fiat G-91 (9 Aug.). First human flight over 100,000': Iven Kincheloe in Bell X-2 (125,907') (7 Sept.). Luftwaffe re-established (24 Sept.). First flight of Convair B-58 Hustler (11 Oct.). UK's first atomic bomb dropped in Australia (11 Oct.). Last RAF Lancaster retired (15 Oct.). First aircraft landing at the South Pole: US Navy R4D-5

Skytrain *Que Sera Sera* (31 Oct.). First flight of Dassault Mirage III (17 Nov.).

1957 World's first long-haul airliner, Bristol Britannia, enters service with BOAC (1 Feb.). Death of Richard Byrd (12 March). First flight of Short SC-1 (2 April). UK's first hydrogen bomb dropped near Christmas Island (15 May). First flight of Fairey Rotodyne (6 Nov.). First flight of Boeing 707 (production model) (21 Dec.).

1958 Death of Ernst Heinkel (Jan.). Munich air crash: seven Manchester Utd players killed (6 Feb.). First flight of De Havilland Comet 4 (27 April). First flight of Blackburn Buccaneer (30 April). First flight of McDonnell F-4 Phantom (27 May). First flight of DC-8 (30 May). New Gatwick Airport opens (9 June). First flight of Westland Wessex (20 June). Death of Henri Farman (17 July). NASA created (29 July). Last flying boat operations in UK (Aquila Airways: Southampton to Madeira) (30 Sept.). First jet airliner on Atlantic route (BOAC Comet 4: London–New York–London) (4 Oct.). Last DC-6 built delivered to JAT (Jugoslavian Airlines) (17 Nov.). First production Fokker Friendship delivered to Aer Lingus (29 Nov.).

1959 First flight of A.W. Argosy (8 Jan.). First flight of Convair 880 (27 Jan.). Buddy Holly, Richie Valens and the Big Bopper killed when their Beechcraft Bonanza crashes in Mason City, Iowa (3 Feb.). First flight of Alouette III (28 Feb.). First scheduled passenger flight of Sud-Aviation Caravelle (6 May). Last operational flight of RAF Sunderland (15 May). First flight of X-15 (8 June). First flight of Mirage IV A (17 June). First flight of Northrop F-5 (30 July). Jacqueline Auriol becomes first woman to exceed Mach 2 (in Mirage III) (26 Aug.). Croydon Airport closed (30 Sept.). De Havilland merges with Hawker Siddeley (17 Dec.).

1960 First flight of Grumman A-6 Intruder (19 April). Gary Powers shot down in Lockheed U-2 over Siberia (1 May). Captain Joseph Kittinger free-falls from 102,800' to 17,500', the highest parachute jump ever (16 Aug.). First flight of Hawker P-1127 (prototype of Harrier) (21 Oct.). 132 killed when TWA Super Constellation and United DC-8 collide over New York (16 Dec.).

1961 Seventy-three killed when Sabena 707 crashes in Brussels (15 Feb.). VIASA begins operations in Caracas (1 April). Yuri Gagarin becomes first man in space (12 April). X-15 flown at 3,074 mph and 105,100' by Major Robert White (21 April). Alan Shepherd becomes first US astronaut (5 May). First flight across the Channel by VTOL aircraft, Short SC-1 (27 May). First flight of Aviation Traders ATL-98 Carvair (21 June). Air Congo established (28 June). First flight of Handley Page HP-115 (17 Aug.). Mirage III jet slices through a cable car wire killing six at Chamonix (30 Aug.). Dag Hammarskjöld's DC-6B crashes near Ndola, Northern Rhodesia (18 Sept.).

1962 First flight of Hawker Siddeley Trident (9 Jan.). First use of Agent Orange in defoliant raids in SE Asia (12 Jan.). First US helicopter shot down in Vietnam (4 Feb.). 111 killed when British Caledonian DC-7C crashes at Douala,

Cameroon (4 Mar). First flight of Bristol T-188 (14 April). Death of Sir Frederick Handley Page (21 April). First flight of A-12 (prototype of SR-71 Blackbird) (26 April). 130 killed when Air France 707 crashes at Orly (3 June). Air France 707 crashes in Guadeloupe, killing 113 (21 June). X-15A flies at 4,159 mph (27 June). First flight of Vickers VC-10 (29 June). X-15 goes into space: Major Robert White flies it to 314,750', earning himself 'Astronauts' Wings' (17 July). First flight of HS 125 (13 Aug.). First flight of Aerospace Lines 'Pregnant Guppy' (19 Sept.).

1963 First reference to Anglo-French supersonic airliner as 'Concorde', in speech by De Gaulle (13 Jan.). First flight of Boeing 727 (2 Feb.). BEA introduces first stand-by fares (1 April). Last RAF Mosquitoes retired (8 May). First flight of BAC III (20 Aug.). First flight of HS-748 (21 Dec.). Idlewild Airport renamed John F. Kennedy (24 Dec.).

1964 First flight of Short Belfast (5 Jan.). Death of Maurice Farman (25 Feb.). Jerrie Mock completes first solo aerial circumnavigation by a woman (17 April). VC-10 enters airline service (29 April). First flight of BAC 221 (Concorde research aircraft) (1 May). Actor Roger Moore becomes Air France's 8,000,000th passenger (21 May). First flight of North American XB-70 Valkyrie (21 Sept.). First flight of BAC TSR2 (27 Sept.). First flight of General Dynamics F-111 (21 Dec.). First flight of Lockheed SR-71 (22 Dec.).

1965 First flight of Mirage III V-01 (VTOL aircraft) (12 Feb.). First flight of Douglas DC-9 (25 Feb.). TSR2 cancelled by Wilson government (6 April). Death of Sir Geoffrey De Havilland (26 May).

1966 Four hydrogen bombs fall from a B-52 over southern Spain following a collision with KC-135 tanker; all four are recovered (17 Jan.). Laker Airways launched (8 Feb.). France leaves NATO (7 March). Death of Sir Sydney Camm (12 March). North American XB-70 crashes after colliding with a chase aircraft (8 June). Sheila Scott completes first round-the-world solo flight by a British woman (20 June). X-15 flies at 4,250 mph (Mach 6.33) (18 Nov.).

1967 First flight of Saab 37 Viggen (8 Feb.). Wrecked oil tanker the *Torrey Canyon* bombed by RAF and Royal Navy aircraft (18 March). First flight of Boeing 737 (9 April). First flight of HS Nimrod (23 May). DC-4 charter plane crashes in the Pyrenees, killing 88 (3 June). British Midland Argonaut crashes at Manchester, killing 72 (4 June). Six-day war begins with Israeli air strikes against Egypt, Syria and Jordan (5 June). X-15 attains its fastest speed, 4,534 mph (Mach 6.72), flown by Major William Knight (3 Oct.). Concorde rolled out at Toulouse (11 Dec.).

1968 Last Handley Page Hastings retires from RAF (5 Jan.). Yuri Gagarin is killed when his Mig-15 crashes near Moscow (27 March). 121 survive crash of BOAC 707 at Heathrow (8 April). Last Avro Anson retires from RAF after 32 years (28 June). First flight of Sepecat Jaguar (8 Sept.). First flight of TU-144 'Concordski' (31 Dec.).

1969 First flight of Boeing 747 (9 Feb.). First flight of Concorde (001 at Toulouse) (2 March). First flight of Concorde (002 in UK) (9 April). RAF Strike Command formed from Bomber and Fighter Command (30 April). Concorde goes supersonic for the first time (1 Oct.). Nigeria Airways VC-10 crashes in the jungle; 87 killed (20 Nov.).

1970 First wide-bodied airliner landing at Heathrow (Boeing 747 of Pan-Am) (12 Jan.). Death of Mikhail Mil (31 Jan.). Death of Lord Hugh Dowding (15 Feb.). Last Dakota retires from RAF service (4 April). Tullamarine Airport in Melbourne opens (1 July). First flight of McDonnell Douglas DC-10 (29 Aug.). Black September blow up TWA 707, Swissair DC-8 and BOAC VC-10 at Dawson's Field, and a Pan-Am 747 at Cairo (12 Sept.). Concorde 002 lands at Heathrow (13 Sept.). Concorde 001 flies at Mach 2 (4 Nov.). First flight of Lockheed Tristar (16 Nov.). Death of Artem Mikoyan (15 Dec.). Airbus Industrie formally established (18 Dec.). Jeanne M Holm becomes first USAF female general (31 Dec.).

1971 Four members of the Red Arrows killed when two Folland Gnats collide at RAF Kemble (20 Jan.). London Air Traffic Control Centre opens at West Drayton (31 Jan.). First flight of Westland Lynx (21 March). Federal Express founded (17 April). Southwest Airlines begin operations (18 June). 162 killed when ANA Boeing 707 collides with a fighter in Japan (30 July). DC-10 enters airline service (5 Aug.). Civil Aviation Authority established in London (5 Aug.). First flight of Shackleton AEW (30 Sept.). BEA Vanguard breaks up over Belgium; 55 killed (2 Oct.). D B Cooper successfully hijacks a Northwest Boeing 727, demands $200,000 and escapes by parachute (24 Nov.).

1972 President Nixon announces that the space shuttle will be developed (5 Jan.). British Airways Board takes over BOAC, BEA and their subsidiaries (1 April). Lockheed Tristar enters airline service (26 April). First fly-by-wire in the USA: Phantom II (29 April). First flight of Fairchild A-10 (10 May). Japanese terrorists kill 25 at Lod Airport (30 May). 118 killed at Staines when BEA Trident crashes after take-off, Britain's worst air disaster until Lockerbie (18 June). First flight of McDonnell Douglas F15 Eagle (27 July). Ilyushin IL-62 crashes in Berlin; 156 killed (14 Aug.). Prince William of Gloucester is killed when his Piper Cherokee crashes during the Goodwood Trophy air race at Wolverhampton (28 Aug.). Death of Igor Sikorsky (26 Oct.). Death of Andrei Tupolev (23 Dec.).

1973 Libyan Airlines 727 shot down by Israeli fighters over Sinai; 74 killed (21 Feb.). TU-144 crashes at the Paris Air Show following mid-air breakup; 14 killed (3 June). 123 die at Orly when a Varig 707 burns after an emergency landing (11 July). Death of Sir Alan Cobham (21 Oct.). First flight of Dassault-Bregeu Dornier Alpha jet (26 Oct.).

1974 First flight of General Dynamics F-16 (2 Feb.). Last Comet in airline service retires (12 Feb.). World's worst air disaster: 346 killed when a

Turkish Airlines DC-10 crashes near Paris (worst until 27 March 1977) (3 March). Airbus A300 enters airline service (23 May). Death of Charles Lindbergh (26 Aug.). First flight of Panavia Tornado (14 Aug.). Fifty-nine killed when Lufthansa 747 crashes in Nairobi, the first ever 747 crash (20 Nov.). First flight of Rockwell B-1 Bomber (23 Dec.).

1975 Death of Air Chief Marshal Sir Keith Park (6 Feb.). Death of Adrienne Bolland (18 March). First flight of DHC Dash 7 (27 March). US helicopters airlift last personnel from embassy roof in Saigon (30 April). First flight of Boeing 747 SP (4 July). Last Lockheed Constellation in airline service retires (16 July). Concorde becomes first aircraft to make four Atlantic crossings in one day (1 Sept.). Graham Hill killed when his aircraft crashes near Elstree (29 Nov.).

1976 First commercial flight of Concorde (Paris–Rio and London–Bahrain) (21 Jan.). Death of Howard Hughes (5 April). Air France and British Airways Concordes land together at Dulles Airport, Washington (24 May). Israeli commandos rescue over 100 passengers from Palestinian terrorists at Entebbe, Uganda (4 July). Viktor Belenko defects to the West in a Mig-25 in Japan (6 Sept.). Worst ever mid-air collision: 176 killed when BA Trident and Yugoslav DC-9 collide over Croatia (10 Sept.).

1977 Death of Sergei Ilyushin (7 Feb.). World's worst ever air disaster: two 747s (KLM and Pan-Am) collide on the ground in Tenerife, 575 killed (27 March). Death of Werner von Braun (16 June). Rockwell B-1 cancelled by President Carter (30 June). First gliding flight of space shuttle *Enterprise* (released from 747) (13 Aug.). Bryan Allen flies *Gossamer Condor*, the first successful man-powered aircraft (23 Aug.). Freddie Laker launches his Skytrain service from London to New York (26 Sept.). GSG 9 successfully storm a hijacked Lufthansa 737 at Mogadishu; 86 saved (17 Oct.).

1978 213 killed when Air India Boeing 747 explodes in mid-air over Bombay (1 Jan.). British Aerospace takes control of British Aircraft Corporation, Hawker Siddeley and Scottish Aviation (1 Jan.). Narita Airport opens in Tokyo amid environmental protests (22 May). First crossing of Atlantic by balloon: *Double Eagle II* (17 Aug.). Death of German aircraft engineer Willy Messerschmitt (15 Sept.). Collision between Pacific Southwest 727 and Cessna in San Diego; 144 killed (25 Sept.). Icelandair DC-8 crashes in Sri Lanka; 202 killed (16 Nov.).

1979 All DC-10 aircraft grounded following crash at Chicago on 25 May which killed 279 (6 June). Bryan Allen flies man-powered aircraft, *Gossamer Albatross*, across the Channel (13 June). Death of Emile Dewoitine (5 July). Death of Sir Barnes Wallis (30 Oct.). 257 killed in Antarctica when Air New Zealand DC-10 crashes near Mt Erebus (29 Nov.).

1980 Air UK formed from British Island Airways and Air Anglia (16 Jan.). Air Zimbabwe created from Air Rhodesia (18 April). Operation Eagle Claw aborted in Iranian desert following

collision of CH-53 helicopter with Hercules transport. The operation was intended to free US hostages in Tehran (25 April). HMS *Ark Royal* makes its final voyage, to the breakers yard (22 Sept.). Last commercial flight of Comet 4, a round trip for enthusiasts (9 Nov.).

1981 Last Boeing 707 in Pan-Am service retires (3 Jan.). Death of Donald Douglas (1 Feb.). Death of Jack Northrop (18 Feb.). First flight of Rockwell Space Shuttle *Columbia* (12 April). Israeli airforce bombs Iraqi nuclear reactor at Osirak (7 June). Gulf of Sirte/Sidra incident: two US Navy F-14s shoot down two Libyan SU-22s (19 Aug.). First flight of Boeing 767 (26 Sept.). First flight of Hughes Notar helicopter, i.e. No Tail Rotor (17 Dec.).

1982 Eighty killed when Air Florida 737 crashes into the icy Potomac River in Washington, after wings ice up before take-off (13 Jan.). First flight of Boeing 757 (19 Feb.). First flight of Airbus A310 (3 April). RAF Vulcans take part in the longest bombing runs in history (7,860 miles) from Ascension Island against targets in the Falklands (April–May). Braniff International Airlines files for bankruptcy (13 May). Last Boeing 707 in British Airways service retires (24 May). Last Boeing 707 in Air France service retires (28 Oct.). Last British V-Bomber Squadron disbanded (21 Dec.).

1983 269 killed when a Soviet SU-15 shoots down a Korean Airlines 747 over Sakhalin Island (2 Sept.).

1984 Inaugural flight of Virgin Atlantic Airways (22 June). Last Boeing 727 completed (14 Aug.). First flight of ATR 42 feeder airliner (16 Aug.). First flight of Rockwell B-1B (18 Oct.). First flight of MD-83 (17 Dec.).

1985 TWA 727 hijacked in Rome by AMAL guerrillas; all bar one of the hostages are subsequently released (15 June). 329 killed after an Air India 747 explodes over the Atlantic en route to London (23 June). 520 when JAL 747 crashes into a mountain in Japan (13 Aug). Fifty-four killed at Manchester when a British Airtours 737 catches fire (22 Aug.).

1986 Armed police begin patrolling Heathrow Airport (8 Jan.). *Challenger* disaster: all seven crew are killed when space shuttle explodes shortly after launch (28 Jan.). Terminal 4 opens at Heathrow (12 April). USAF F-IIIs execute air strikes against targets in Libya (15 April). Death of Marcel Bloch (18 April). BA privatised (21 Oct.). Forty-five killed when a BA Chinook ferrying oil workers crashes in the Shetlands (6 Nov.). Dick Rutan and Jeana Yeager fly around the world non-stop and unrefuelled, in specially designed aircraft *Voyager* (23 Dec.).

1987 First flight of Airbus A320 (22 Feb.). Last airworthy Bristol Blenheim crashes at Denham (21 June). BAA privatised (16 July). Richard Branson and Per Lindstrand complete first hot-air balloon crossing of the Atlantic (3 July). BA takes over British Caledonian (16 July). BA takes on first female pilots (31 Oct.). London City Airport opens (5 Nov.).

1988 First ever aircraft registration number retired by FAA, i.e. Amelia Earhart's Lockheed Electra

TRANSPORT AIRCRAFT

which vanished in July 1937 (8 Feb.). North Terminal opens at Gatwick Airport (18 March). First flight of 'Super-Jumbo' Boeing 747-400 (29 April). Airbus A320 crashes in trees at Mulhouse air show; four killed (26 June). 290 killed when USS Vincennes shoots down Iranian Airbus (3 July). Thirty-three killed at Ramstein when Frecce Tricolori (Italian National Aerobatic Team) aircraft collide above spectators at air show (28 Aug.). Death of Sheila Scott (20 Oct.). F-117A Stealth aircraft formally unveiled by USAF (10 Nov.). Lockerbie disaster: 270 killed after bomb causes Pan-Am Jumbo to crash on houses; worst air disaster in British history (21 Dec.).

1989 Thirty-two killed when British Midland 737 crashes on to the M1 at Kegworth (8 Jan.). First flight of Northrop B-2 Spirit Flying Wing Stealth Bomber (17 July). 107 killed at Sioux City, Iowa, when United Airlines DC-10 crashes on landing (19 July). Death of Alexander Yakovlev (22 Aug.). Bell/Boeing Vertol V-22 Osprey tilt rotor aircraft makes first transition to level flight (14 Sept.).

1990 First flight of Northrop/McDonnell Douglas YF-23 (subsequently dropped in favour of Lockheed YF-22) (27 Aug.). First flight of

Rockwell/MBB X-31A low-speed experimental aircraft (11 Oct.). United Airlines takes over Pan-Am's London routes (23 Oct.). Osaka Airport opens in Japan (9 Nov.).

1991 First Boeing 727 retires after 27 years with United Airlines (13 Jan.). Air Europe, based at Gatwick Airport, ceases to operate (17 Jan.). Operation Desert Storm makes large-scale use of Stealth aircraft for the first time (Jan.). First scheduled United Airlines flight to London (4 April). Boeing finally ends production of 707 after 37 years (1 Sept.). First flight of McDonnell Douglas C-17 (15 Sept.). First flight of Airbus A-340 (25 Oct.). First MD-11 delivered (to Finnair) (29 Nov.). Pan-Am ceases operations (4 Dec.).

1992 TWA announces that it is bankrupt (11 Jan.). Piper declared bankrupt (1 April). Plans for MD-12 (4-engine, 600-seat airliner) announced (30 April). BAA announces plans for Terminal 5 at Heathrow (12 May).

1995 First Boeing 777 begins operations at Heathrow (United Airlines) (July).

2003 Air France announces it is to chop its fleet of Concordes on 31 May while British Airways closes down its fleet of seven Concordes at the end of October.

Airports: UK

Airport	Location	Airport	Location	Airport	Location
Aldergrove	Belfast	**Heathrow**	London	**Sibson**	Peterborough
Ballasalla	Isle of Man	**John Lennon**	Liverpool	**Silverstone**	Northants
Baltasound	Unst, Shetlands	**(formerly Speke)**		**Southampton**	Hampshire
Barton	Manchester	**Kidlington**	Oxford	**Stansted**	NE London
Benbecula	Hebrides	**Kirkwall**	Orkneys	**Stapleford**	Essex
Birmingham	Solihull	**Leeds Bradford**	West Yorkshire	**Staverton**	Gloucestershire
Blackbushe	Camberley	**Leuchars**	Fife (RAF	**Stornoway**	Hebrides
Booker	Wycombe,		Station)	**Stronsay**	Orkneys
	Bucks	**Linley Hill**	Beverley	**Sumburgh**	Shetlands
Bournemouth	Dorset	**Lulsgate**	Bristol	**Sywell**	Northampton
Brize Norton	Oxford (RAF	**Lydd**	Ashford, Kent	**Teeside**	Cleveland
	Station)	**Manchester**	Manchester	**Tingwall**	Lerwick,
Brough	East Yorkshire	**(formerly Ringway)**			Shetlands
City	Belfast	**Manston**	Kent	**Tiree**	Hebrides
City	London	**North Bay**	Barra, Hebrides	**Tresco**	Scillies
Compton Abbas	Dorset	**North Denes**	Great Yarmouth	**Turnhouse**	Edinburgh
Conington	Peterborough	**North Ronaldsay**	Orkneys	**Unst**	Shetlands
Coventry	West Midlands	**Papa Westray**	Orkneys	**Walney Island**	Barrow,
Dalcross	Inverness	**Port Ellen**	Islay, Hebrides		Cumbria
Dyce	Aberdeen	**Prestwick**	Ayrshire	**West Freugh**	Dumfries
East Midlands	Derbyshire	**Rhoose**	Cardiff	**West Midlands**	Birmingham
Eday	Orkneys	**Robin Hood**	Doncaster	**Westray**	Orkneys
Eglinton	Londonderry	**Roborough**	Plymouth	**Whalsay**	Shetlands
Exeter	Devon	**Ronaldsway**	Isle of Man	**Wick**	Caithness
Fair Isle	Shetlands	**St Angelo**	Enniskillen,	**Wickenby**	Lincolnshire
Filton	Bristol		Fermanagh	**Woodford**	Greater
Flotta	Orkneys	**St Just**	Land's End		Manchester
Gatwick	West Sussex	**St Mary's**	Scilly Isles	**Woodvale**	Merseyside
Glasgow	Glasgow	**Sanday**	Orkneys		(RAF Station)
Glenegedale	Islay	**Sandown**	Isle of Wight	**Yeovilton**	Somerset
Goodwood	Chichester	**Scatsa**	Shetlands		(private airfield)
Grimsetter	Orkney	**Scone**	Perth		
Hatfield	Hertfordshire	**Shoreham**	East Sussex		

Airlines

Name	Country	Name	Country	Name	Country
ACES	Colombia	**Delta Airlines**	USA	**Norontair**	Canada
Aer Lingus	Ireland	**DETA**	Mozambique	**Northwest Airlines**	USA
Aeroflot	Russia	**Dragonair**	Hong Kong	**Olympic**	Greece
Aerolineas	Argentina	**Eastern Airlines**	USA	**Pan-Am**	USA
Air Littoral	France	**El Al**	Israel	**PIA**	Pakistan
Air UK	UK (Stansted)	**Flitestar**	South Africa	**Qantas**	Australia
Alia	Jordan	**Frontie Airlines**	USA	**Republic Airlines**	USA
Alitalia	Italy	**Garuda**	Indonesia	**RyanAir**	Ireland
American Airlines	USA	**Gronlandsfly**	Greenland	**Sabena**	Belgium
ANA	All Nippon Airways	**Iberia**	Spain	**Sansa**	Costa Rica
Augusta Airways	Australia	**Interflug**	East Germany	**SAS**	Denmark, Norway, Sweden
Avianca	Colombia	**JAL**	Japanese Airlines		
Bell-Air	New Zealand	**JAT**	Yugoslavia	**TAP**	Portugal
Britannia	UK (Luton)	**KLM**	Netherlands	**THY**	Turkey
British Airways	UK	**Kyrnair**	Corsica	**Tower Air**	USA
Cathay Pacific	Hong Kong	**Ladeco**	Chile	**Transavia Airlines**	Netherlands
Continental Airlines	USA	**LAP**	Paraguay	**Transworld Airlines**	USA
		Linjeflyg	Sweden	**United Airlines**	USA
CP Air	Canada	**LOT**	Poland	**Varig**	Brazil
Crossair	Switzerland	**Lufthansa**	Germany	**VIASA**	Venezuela
CSA	Czech Republic	**Malev**	Hungary	**Virgin**	UK (Gatwick)
		NFD	Germany	**Western Airlines**	USA

Airport Codes

Code	Airport	Location	Code	Airport	Location	Code	Airport	Location
ABD	Abadan	Iran	**BKO**	Bamako	Mali	**DUS**	Düsseldorf	Germany
ABJ	Abidjan	Ivory Coast	**BLZ**	Blantyre	Malawi	**DXB**	Dubai	UAE
ABS	Abu Simnel	Egypt	**BRN**	Berne	Switzerland	**DYU**	Dushanbe	Tadzhikstan
ABZ	Aberdeen	Scotland	**BSL**	Basle	Switzerland	**EGC**	Bergerac	France
ACE	Arecife	Lanzarote	**BTZ**	Bursa	Turkey	**EVN**	Yerevan	Armenia
ACI	Alderney	Channel Islands	**BUH**	Bucharest	Romania	**EWR**	Newark, NJ	USA
ACK	Nantucket, MA	USA	**BXO**	Bissau	Guinea-Bissau	**EYW**	Key West	Florida
ACT	Waco, Texas	USA	**BZV**	Brazzaville	Congo	**FAO**	Faro	Portugal
ADD	Addis Ababa	Ethiopia	**CAJ**	Cairo	Egypt	**FBU**	Fornebu	Oslo
AGP	Malaga	Spain	**CCS**	Caracas	Venezuela	**FCO**	Fiumicino	Rome
AKL	Auckland	New Zealand	**CCU**	Calcutta	India	**FIE**	Fair Isle	Scotland
			CDG	Charles de Gaulle	Paris	**FIH**	Kinshasa	Dem Rep. of Congo
ALC	Alicante	Spain	**CER**	Cherbourg	France	**FNA**	Freetown	Sierra Leone
ALH	Albany, WA	Australia	**CFN**	Donegal	Eire			
ALP	Aleppo	Syria	**CFR**	Caen	France	**FNC**	Funchal	Madeira Islands
ALY	Alexandria	Egypt	**CFU**	Kerkyra	Greece			
AMA	Amarillo, Texas	USA	**CHC**	Christchurch	New Zealand	**FNI**	Nîmes	France
ANR	Antwerp	Belgium				**FRA**	Frankfurt	Germany
ASD	Andros	Bahamas	**CMN**	Casablanca	Morocco	**GBE**	Gaborone	Botswana
AUH	Abu Dhabi	UAE	**CPT**	Cape Town	South Africa	**GCI**	Guernsey	UK
BBQ	Barbuda	Leeward Isles	**CXI**	Christmas Island	Kiribati	**GNB**	Grenoble	France
						GOA	Genoa	Italy
BEB	Benbecula	Scotland	**DCA**	Washington	USA	**GOH**	Nuuk (Godthaab)	Greenland
BEY	Beirut	Lebanon	**DLH**	Duluth	Minnesota			
BFS	Belfast	N. Ireland	**DOL**	Deauville	France	**GOI**	Goa	India
BGO	Bergen	Norway	**DTM**	Dortmund	Germany	**GPS**	Galapagos Isles	Ecuador
BHX	Birmingham	England	**DUD**	Dunhedin	New Zealand			
BJL	Bangui	Gambia				**HAJ**	Hanover	Germany
BKK	Bangkok	Thailand				**HBA**	Hobart	Tasmania

Code	Airport	Location	Code	Airport	Location	Code	Airport	Location
HDO	Hyderabad	Pakistan	LHR	Heathrow	London	ORD	O'Hare	Chicago
HFA	Haifa	Israel	LIG	Limoges	France	ORK	Cork	Eire
HKT	Phuket	Thailand	LTN	Luton	Bedfordshire	ORN	Oran	Algeria
HLZ	Hamilton	New Zealand	LUN	Lusaka	Zambia	PAP	Port au Prince	Haiti
			LWK	Lerwick	Shetlands	PFO	Paphos	Cyprus
HND	Haneda	Tokyo	LXR	Luxor	Egypt	PGF	Perpignan	France
HYD	Hyderabad	India	MAA	Madras	India	PID	Paradise Island	Bahamas
IAD	Dulles International	Washington	MBJ	Montego Bay	Jamaica	PMO	Palermo	Italy
			MCM	Monte Carlo	Monaco	PNQ	Poona	India
IBZ	Ibiza	Spain	MDL	Mandalay	Burma (Myanmar)	PPG	Pago Pago	American Samoa
IEV	Kiev	Ukraine						
IOM	Isle of Man	UK	MEB	Melbourne	Australia	PRJ	Capri	Italy
IOR	Inishmore	Eire	MFN	Milford Sound	New Zealand	PRY	Pretoria	South Africa
IPC	Easter Island	Chile				RBA	Rabat	Morocco
JDH	Jodhpur	India	MLH	Mulhouse	France	REK	Reykjavik	Iceland
JFK	John F. Kennedy	New York	MMA	Malmö	Sweden	RUH	Riyadh	Saudi Arabia
			MME	Teesside	England			
JNU	Juneau	Alaska	MOW	Moscow	Russia	SEL	Seoul	South Korea
JRS	Jerusalem	Israel	MPM	Maputu	Mozambique	SNN	Shannon	Eire
KEF	Keflavik	Iceland	MRS	Marseille	France	SPK	Sapporo	Japan
KEL	Kiel	Germany	MXL	Mexicali	Mexico	STR	Stuttgart	Germany
KHI	Karachi	Pakistan	NBO	Nairobi	Kenya	THR	Tehran	Iran
KLU	Klagenfurt	Austria	NCE	Nice	France	TIA	Tirana	Albania
KRK	Krakow	Poland	NCL	Newcastle	England	URO	Rouen	France
KTP	Kingston	Jamaica	NDY	Sanday	Scotland	VRN	Verona	Italy
KTW	Katowice	Poland	NQY	Newquay	England	WAW	Warsaw	Poland
LAS	McCarran	Las Vegas	NRT	Narita	Tokyo	WLG	Wellington	New Zealand
LAX	Los Angeles	California	NSI	Nsimalen, Yaoundé	Cameroon			
LCA	Larnaca	Cyprus				YXY	Whitehorse	Canada
LEH	Le Havre	France	NTE	Nantes	France	YYC	Calgary	Canada
LFW	Lomé	Togo	NTY	Sun City	South Africa	YZF	Yellowknife	Canada
LGW	Gatwick	London	ODE	Odense	Denmark	ZAZ	Zaragosa	Spain
LHE	Lahore	Pakistan	OPO	Oporto	Portugal	ZRH	Zurich	Switzerland

NB The airport codes above are a small-cross section of the thousands of abbreviations used internationally. Most of the codes represent the location of the airport but others denote the name.

Airports: International

Name	Location	Name	Location
Abadan	Iran	Barajas	Madrid
Adana	Turkey	Basle-Mulhouse (Euro Airport)	Basle, Switzerland
Agno	Lugano, Switzerland		
Albany County	New York	Bata	Equatorial Guinea
Alexander Hamilton	St Croix, W Indies	Beira	Mozambique
Alfonso Bonilla Aragon	Cali, Colombia	Ben Gurion	Tel Aviv
Amausi	Lucknow	Benina	Benghazi, Libya
Amborovy	Majunga, Madagascar	Benito Juarez	Mexico City
Amerigo Vespucci	Florence	Bierset	Liège, Belgium
Amilcar Cabral	Cape Verde	Bilund	Denmark
Aminu	Kano, Nigeria	Blackburne / Plymouth	Montserrat
Arlanda	Stockholm	Blagnac	Toulouse
Arnos Vale	St Vincent	Blue Danube	Linz
Arrecife	Lanzarote	Bole	Addis Ababa
Arturo Marino Benitez	Santiago, Chile	Bonriki	Kiribati
Atuona	Hiva Oa, French Polynesia	Boukhalef	Tangier, Morocco
Augusto Co Sandino	Managua, Nicaragua	Bourgas	Bulgaria
Balice	Krakow, Poland	Bradley	Hartford, Connecticut
Baneasa	Bucharest	Brnik	Ljubljana
Bangor	Maine	Bromma	Stockholm
Banja Luka	Bosnia	Bulawayo	Zimbabwe
Bankstown	New South Wales	Butmir	Sarajevo

Name	Location	Name	Location
Byrd Field	Richmond, Virginia	Fort Worth	Dallas, Texas
Cairns	Queensland	Frederic Chopin	Warsaw
Calabar	Nigeria	Freeport	Bahamas
Cancun	Mexico	Fua'amotu	Tonga
Canefield	Roseau, Dominica	Fuenterrabia	San Sebastián
Cannon	Reno, Nevada	Fuerteventura	Canary Islands
Canton	Akron, Ohio	Fuhlsbüttel	Hamburg
Capodichino	Naples	Galileo Galilei	Pisa
Cardiff	Rhoose	Gardermoen	Oslo
Carrasco	Montevideo	G'Bessia	Conakry
Carthage	Tunis	General Manuel Marquez de Leon	Mexico
Cebu	Philippines		
Changi	Singapore	General Mitchell	Milwaukee
Charleroi	Belgium	Gillot	Réunion
Charles B Wheeler	Kansas City, Missouri	G. Marconi	Bologna
Charles de Gaulle	Paris	Golden Rock	St Kitts
Charlotte	North Carolina	Grantley Adams	Barbados
Chatarpati Shivaji	Bombay / Mumbai	Gulfport-Biloxi	Mississippi
Chek Lap Kok	Hong Kong (new)	Hahaya	Moroni, Comoros
Chiang Kai Shek	Taipei, Taiwan	Halim Perdanakusama	Djakarta
Chileka	Blantyre, Malawi	Hanan	Niue
Ciampino	Rome	Hancock Field	Syracuse, NY
Cointrin	Geneva	Haneda	Tokyo
Collinstown	Dublin	Hartsfield	Atlanta, Georgia
Congonhas	São Paulo, Brazil	Hato	Curaçao
Coolidge	Antigua	Hellenikon	Athens
Costa Smeralda	Olbia, Sardinia	Henderson Field	Honiara, Solomon Isles
Cotonou	Benin	Heraklion	Crete
Cristoforo Colombo	Genoa	Hewanorra	St Lucia
Crown Point	Scarborough, Tobago	Heydar Aliyev	Baku
Cuscatlan	El Salvador	Hongqiao	Shanghai
Dabolim	Goa	Hopkins	Cleveland, Ohio
Dalaman	Turkey	Indira Gandhi	New Delhi
Deurne	Antwerp	Inezgane	Agadir, Morocco
D F Malan	Cape Town	Ippokratis	Kos
Diagoras	Rhodes	Isla Verde	San Juan, Puerto Rico
Domodedovo	Moscow	Ivanka	Bratislava
Dorval	Montreal	Ivato	Antananarivo, Madagascar
Douala	Cameroon	Izmir	Turkey
Dulles	Washington	Jackson Field	Port Moresby, PNG
Dum Dum	Calcutta	James M Cox	Dayton, Ohio
Eagle Farm	Brisbane	J F Kennedy	La Paz
Ecterdingen	Stuttgart	Jinnah	Karachi
Eduardo Gomes	Manaus, Brazil	Johan Adolf Pengel	Paramaribo, Surinam
El Alto	La Paz, Bolivia	John F Kennedy	New York
El Dorado	Bogotá, Colombia	John Foster Dulles	Washington DC
Elat	Israel	John Paul II	Krakow
Elmas	Cagliari	John Wayne	Los Angeles, California
Eppley Airfield	Omaha, Nebraska	Jorge Chavez	Lima, Peru
Esenboga	Ankara	Jose Martí	Havana, Cuba
Ezeiza	Buenos Aires	Kai Tak	Hong Kong (old)
Faaa	Tahiti	Kamazu	Lilongwe, Malawi
Faleolo	Apia, Samoa	Kastrup	Copenhagen, Denmark
F D Roosevelt	St Eustatius, W Indies	Katunayake	Colombo, Sri Lanka
Ferihegy	Budapest	Keflavik	Reykjavik, Iceland
Findel	Luxembourg	Kent County	Grand Rapids, Michigan
Fiumicino (Leonardo da Vinci)	Rome	Kerkyra	Corfu
		Khon Kaen	Phuket
Flamingo Field	Bonaire	Khoramaksar	Aden
Flesland	Bergen, Norway	Khwaja Rawash	Kabul, Afghanistan
Fontanarossa	Catania, Sicily	Kimpo	Seoul, South Korea
Fornebu	Oslo	King Khaled	Riyadh, Saudi Arabia
Fort Myers	Florida	Kingsford Smith	Sydney, Australia

TRANSPORT AIRCRAFT

Name	Location	Name	Location
Kitsap	Washington, USA	Mercedita	Puerto Rico
Klagenfurt	Austria	Merignac	Bordeaux
Kloten	Zurich	Midway	Chicago
Kota Kinabulu	Sabah, Malaysia	Ministro Pistarini	Buenos Aires
Kotoka	Accra, Ghana	Mirabel	Montreal
Kranebitten	Innsbruck	Mohammed V	Casablanca
Kuching	Sarawak, Malaysia	Monroe County	Rochester, NY
Kungsangen	Norrköping, Sweden	Morelos	Mexico
La Aurora	Guatemala	Münster / Osnabrück	Germany
La Coruña	Spain	Murtala Muhammed	Lagos, Nigeria
La Guardia	New York	Nadi	Fiji
La Mesa	San Pedro Sula, Honduras	Naha	Okinawa (Japan)
Landvetter	Göteborg (Gothenburg), Sweden	Narita	Tokyo
		Narssarsuaq	Greenland
Larnaca	Cyprus	N'Djili	Kinshasa, Congo Democratic Republic
Las Americas	Dominican Republic		
Las Palmas	Gran Canaria	Nejrab	Aleppo, Syria
Lawica	Poznan	Netaji Subhas Chandra Bose	Calcutta / Kolkata
Le Bourget	Paris		
Lech Walesa	Gdansk	Newark	New York
Le Lamentin	Martinique	Newcastle	Nevis Island
Leonardo da Vinci (Fiumicino)	Rome	Ngurah Rai	Denpasar, Bali
		Ninoy Aquino	Manila, Philippines
Le Raizet	Guadeloupe	Nis	Yugoslavia
Les Angades	Oujda, Morocco	Noi Bai	Hanoi
Lesquin	Lille, France	Norman Manley	Kingston, Jamaica
Lester B Pearson	Toronto	Norman Rogers	Kingston, Ontario
Linate	Milan	North Front	Gibraltar
Lindbergh	San Diego, California	Nouadhibou	Mauritania
Logan	Boston, Massachusetts	Oakland	California
Long Beach	California	O'Hare	Chicago
Loshitsa	Minsk, Belarus	Okecie	Warsaw
Louis Botha	Durban	Olaya Herrera	Medellín, Colombia
Lourdes/Tarbes	Juillan, France	Oran	Algeria
Lubbock	Texas	Orebro	Sweden
Lungi	Freetown, Sierra Leone	Orly	Paris
Lupepau'u	Tonga	Osaka	Japan
Luqa	Malta	Osnabrück (Münster)	Germany
M'Poko	Bangui, Central African Republic	Osvaldo Vieira	Guinea Bissau
		Otopeni	Bucharest
Mactan	Cebu, Philippines	Owen Roberts	Grand Cayman
Mahon	Menorca	Palese	Bari, Italy
Mais Gate	Haiti	Paphos	Cyprus
Malmi	Helsinki	Paradisi	Rhodes
Malpensa	Milan	Patenga	Bangladesh
Manas	Bishkek, Kyrgyzstan	Patrick Henry	Norfolk, Virginia
Marco Polo	Venice	Pearson	Toronto
Mariscal Sucre	Quito, Ecuador	Pekoa	Vanuatu
Marsh Harbour	Abaco Island, Bahamas	Peretola	Florence
Matsapha	Manzini, Swaziland	Peshawar	Pakistan
Maturin	Venezuela	Peterson Field	Colorado
Maxglan	Salzburg, Austria	Phillip SW Goldson	Belize
Maya Maya	Brazzaville, Congo	Piarco	Trinidad
McCarran	Las Vegas	Pochentong	Cambodia
McCoy	Orlando, Florida	Point Noire	Congo
McNary Field	Salem, Oregon	Point Salines	Grenada
Meenambakkam	Madras, India	Polonia	Indonesia
Mehrabad	Tehran, Iran	Port Bouet	Ivory Coast
Melbourne	Florida	Port Harcourt	Nigeria
Melita	Djerba, Tunisia	Portland	Maine
Melsbroek	Brussels	Princess Beatriz	Aruba
Melville Hall	Dominica	Prince Said Ibrahim	Moroni, Comoros Islands
Menara	Marrakesh, Morocco	Provence	Marseille

Name	Location	Name	Location
Pula	Croatia	Subang	Malaysia
Pulkovo	St Petersburg	Sunan	North Korea
Punta Raisi	Palermo, Sicily	Sylmet	Dhaka, Bangladesh
Queen Alia	Jordan	Tacoma	Seattle
Queen Beatrix	Aruba	Tamatve	Madagascar
Ras Al Khaimah	United Arab Emirates	Tarbes (Lourdes)	Juillan, France
Rebiechowo	Gdansk, Poland	Tegel	Berlin
Reina Beatrix	Aruba	Tempelhof	Berlin
Reina Sofia	Tenerife	Thalerhof	Graz, Austria
Riem	Munich	Theodore Francis Green	Rhode Island
Robert Mueller	Austin, Texas	Timehri	Georgetown, Guyana
Roberts	Monrovia, Liberia	Toncontin	Tegucigalpa, Honduras
Rochambau	French Guiana	Tontouta	New Caledonia
Roskilde	Copenhagen	Torslanda	Göteborg (Gothenburg)
Ruzyne	Prague	Totegegie	Gambier Island
Sainte Foy	Quebec	Townsville	Australia
Sale	Rabat, Morocco	Treasure Cay	Abaco Island, Bahamas
Salgado Filho	Brazil	Tribhuyan	Nepal
Salote Pilolevu	Tonga	Trivandrum	India
Sangster	Montego Bay, Jamaica	Truax Field	Wisconsin
San Pablo	Seville	Tullamarine	Melbourne
Santa Caterina	Funchal, Madeira	Turku	Finland
Santa Cruz	Bombay	Ulemiste	Estonia
Santa Isabel	Malabo, Guinea	U Michaeli	Haifa, Israel
Santos Dumont	Rio	Unokovo	Moscow
Schipol	Amsterdam	Uplands	Ottawa
Schönefeld	Berlin	VC Bird	Antigua
Schwechat	Vienna	Vagar	Faeroe Islands
Seeb	Oman	Vantaa	Helsinki
Seewoosagur Ramgoolam	Mauritius	Vigie	St Lucia
		Viracopos	São Paulo, Brazil
Senou	Mali	Vnukovo	Moscow
Seretse Khama	Gaborone, Botswana	WA Mozart	Salzburg
Sfax	Tunisia	Wall Blake	Anguilla
Sharjah	United Arab Emirates	Washington	Baltimore, Maryland
Sheremetyevo	Moscow	Wattay	Laos
Silvio Pettirossi	Paraguay	West End	Bahamas
Simon Bolivar	Ecuador	Wichita	Kansas
Simon Bolivar	Caracas, Venezuela	Wickede	Dortmund
Sir Seretse Khama	Botswana	Will Rogers	Oklahoma
Skanes	Morocco	William B Hartsfield	Atlanta, Georgia
Sky Harbour	Phoenix, Arizona	William P Hobby	Houston, Texas
Snilow	Ukraine	Willow Run	Detroit, Michigan
Sola	Stavanger, Norway	WK Kellogg	Battle Creek, Kalamazoo, Michigan
Sondica	Bilbao		
Søndre Srømfjord	Greenland	Yeager	Charleston, West Virginia
Spilve	Latvia	Yoff	Senegal
Spokane	Washington	Yundam	Gambia
Standiford Field	Louisville, Kentucky	Zarsis	Djerba, Tunisia
Stapleton	Denver, Colorado	Zaventem	Brussels
St Thomas	Virgin Islands	Zia	Bangladesh
Sturup	Malmö, Sweden	Zvartnots	Yerevan, Armenia

TRANSPORT AIRCRAFT

TRANSPORT: CARS

Makes and Models

AC Cars Ace, Aceca, Cobra Sportster

Alfa Romeo GTV, 156, Spider

Aston Martin DB5, DB7 (David Brown), V8

Audi A3, 80, Cabriolet, Quattro

Austin A90, Healey, Maestro, Metro

Bentley Arnage Mulsanne, Brooklands, Continental T

BMW 528i, M3, 328i, Z3

Cadillac Allante, Evoq, Fleetwood, La Salle

Citroën Berlingo, Dyane, Mehari, Saxo 2CV, VTS, Xantia, Xsara

Daewoo (Korea) Cielo, Espero, Lanos, Leganza, Matiz, Nexia, Nubira

Daihatsu (Japan) Applause, Cuore, Move

Dodge Charger, Coronet, Power Wagon, Viper

Ferrari Berlinetta, F355, Maranello, 360 Modena, 360 Spider, Testarossa

Fiat Barchetta, Brava, Bravo, Cinquecento, Doblo, Ducato, Fiorino, Marea, Multipla, Punto, Scudo, Seicento, Spider, Stilo, Tempra, Tipo, Ulysse, Uno

Ford Aerostar, Anglia, Aspire, Bronco, Capri, Contour, Cortina, Cougar, Edsel, Escort, Explorer, Fiesta, Focus, Galaxy, Granada, Ka, Maverick, Model T, Mondeo,

Mustang, Pinto, Probe, Ranger, Sapphire, Scorpio, Taurus, Torino, Thunderbird, Victoria

Honda Accord, Aerodeck, Civic, CR-V, J-VX, Legend, Odyssey, Passport, Prelude

Hyundai (Korea) Accent, Avatar, Elantra, Santa Fe, Sonata, Tiburon

Jaguar E-Type, S-Type, XJ12, XK120, XK8

Lada Niva, Riva, Samara

Landrover Defender, Discovery, Freelander

Lincoln Blackwood, Navigator

Lotus Elan, Elise, Esprit, Exige

Maserati Ghibil

Mercedes C180, CLK, Malaya, Necar 3, SLK Roadster, Vision SLR

Mitsubishi Diamante, Eclipse, Mirage, Montero, Salent, Shogun

Nissan Almira, Frontier, Maxima, Micra, Pathfinder, Patrol, Primera, Quest, QX, Serena, Skyline, 300 ZX, Tirano

Peugeot Boxer, 406, Partner, 205

Porsche Boxster, Carrera, 911, 924, Varrera minivan

Proton Perdana, Persona, Satria

Renault Clio, Espace, Extra, Fuego, Kangoo, Laguna, Master, Mégane Alizé, Mégane Scenic, Safranes, Spider, Trafic, Twingo

Rolls Royce Camargue, Corniche, Phantom, Silver Cloud, Silver Dawn, Silver Ghost, Silver Seraph, Silver Shadow, Silver Spirit, Silver Wraith

Rover Ascot, 800, Relax, 200

Saab Carlsson, Sonett

Seat Alhambra, Arosa, Malaga, Marbella

Skoda Felicia

Subaru Justy, Legacy, Loyale

Suzuki Alto, Baleno, Capuccino, Swift, Vitaras

Toyota Avalon, Camry Solara, Celica, Corolla, Highlander, Lexus, Prius, RAV4, Sequoia, Sienna, Supra, Tacoma, Tercel, Tundra

TVR Cerbera, Chimaera

Vauxhall Astra SRi, Belmont SRi, Calibra, Carlton, Cavalier (became Vectra), Chevette, Corsa, Frontera, Monterrey, Nova, Omega, Senator, Tigra Bermuda, Vectra

Vauxhall (van) Arena, Astravan, Brava, Combo, Corsavan

Volkswagen Beetle, Cabrio, Cabriolet, Corrado, Fox, Golf GTi, Jetta, Passat, Polo, Scirocco, Sharan, Thing, Vento

Volvo C70, 850, 340, S60, S80, V40, V70

Yugo 55A GL

Motorways

M1	London to Leeds	M32	Bristol to M4	M66	Manchester to Rochdale
M2	Rochester to Faversham	M40	London to Birmingham	M67	Hyde Bypass
M3	Sunbury to Southampton	M41	London to West Cross	M69	Coventry to Leicester
M4	London to Swansea	M42	Bromsgrove to Measham	M73	Glasgow
M5	Birmingham to Exeter	M45	M1 to A45 (Coventry)	M74	Glasgow to Lesmahagow
M6	Rugby to Carlisle	M50	Ross to Tewkesbury	M77	Ayr
M8	Edinburgh to Erskine Bridge	M53	Chester to Wallasey	M80	Stepps Bypass
M9	Edinburgh to Dunblane	M54	M6 to Telford	M90	Dunfermline to Perth, Bonnybridge to Kincardine Bridge
M10	M1 to St Albans	M55	Preston to Blackpool		
M11	London to Cambridge	M56	Manchester to Queensferry	M180	M18 to Humber Bridge
M18	Rotherham to Goole	M57	Liverpool outer ring road		
M20	Swanley to Folkestone	M58	Liverpool to Wigan	**NB** The first UK motorway was the Preston Bypass in 1958, now part of the M6.
M23	Hooley (Surrey) to Crawley (Sussex)	M61	Manchester to Preston	
M25	London Orbital	M62	Liverpool to Hull	
M26	Sevenoaks to Tonbridge	M63	Manchester south ring road	
M27	Southampton Bypass	M65	Calder Valley from M6	

Vehicle Number Plates

A new registration mark system was introduced on 1 September 2001. The new plates will comprise seven characters: the first two letters to denote the registered office; the next two a numeric age identifier; the final three letters a random element to differentiate vehicles. The age identifier will be subject to change every six months. The tables are reproduced below and the example given by the DVLA is as follows: BD51 SMR where BD indicates the vehicle was registered in the Birmingham office and the 51 indicates a registration date between Sept 2001 and Feb 2002. The typeface was also standardised from 1 September 2001 and only regular block capitals are now allowable.

Letter	Region	Local Offices	DVLA Local Office Identifier
A	Anglia	Peterborough	AA AB AC AD AE AF AG AH AJ AK AL AM AN
		Norwich	AO AP AR AS AT AU
		Ipswich	AV AW AX AY
B	Birmingham	Birmingham	BA – BY
C	Cymru	Cardiff	CA CB CC CD CE CF CG CH CJ CK CL CM CN CO
		Swansea	CP CR CS CT CU CV
		Bangor	CW CX CY
D	Deeside to Shrewsbury	Chester	DA DB DC DD DE DF DG DH DJ DK
		Shrewsbury	DL DM DN DO DP DR DS DT DU DV DW DX DY
E	Essex	Chelmsford	EA – EY
F	Forest & Fens	Nottingham	FA FB FC FD FE FF FG FH FJ FK FL FM FN FP
		Lincoln	FR FS FT FV FW FX FY
G	Garden of England	Maidstone	GA GB GC GD GE GF GG GH GJ GK GL GM GN GO
		Brighton	GP GR GS GT GU GV GW GX GY
H	Hampshire & Dorset	Bournemouth	HA HB HC HD HE HF HG HH HJ
		Portsmouth	HK HL HM HN HO HP HR HS HT HU HV HW HX HY
			(HW will be used exclusively for Isle of Wight residents)
K		Luton	KA KB KC KD KE KF KG KH KJ KK KL
		Northampton	KM KN KO KP KR KS KT KU KV KW KX KY
L	London	Wimbledon	LA LB LC LD LE LF LG LH LJ
		Stanmore	LK LL LM LN LO LP LR LS LT
M	Manchester & Merseyside	Manchester	MA – MY
N	North	Newcastle	NA NB NC ND NE NG NH NJ NK NL NM NN NO
		Stockton	NP NR NS NT NU NV NW NX NY
O	Oxford	Oxford	OA – OY
P	Preston	Preston	PA PB PC PD PE PF PG PH PJ PK PL PM PN PO PP PR PS PT
		Carlisle	PU PV PW PX PY
R	Reading	Reading	RA – RY
S	Scotland	Glasgow	SA SB SC SD SE SF SG SH SJ
		Edinburgh	SK SL SM SN SO
		Dundee	SP SR SS ST
		Aberdeen	SU SV SW
		Inverness	SX SY
V	Severn Valley	Worcester	VA – VY
W	West of England	Exeter	WA WB WC WD WE WF WG WH WJ
		Truro	WK WL
		Bristol	WM WN WO WP WR WS WT WU WV WW WX WY
Y	Yorkshire	Leeds	YA YB YC YD YE YF YG YH YJ YK
		Sheffield	YL YM YN YO YP YR YS YT YU
		Beverley	YV YW YX YY

TRANSPORT CARS

Age Identifiers

Code	Date	Code	Date
		51	Sept 2001 – Feb 2002
02	March 2002 – Aug 2002	52	Sept 2002 – Feb 2003
03	March 2003 – Aug 2003	53	Sept 2003 – Feb 2004
04	March 2004 – Aug 2004	54	Sept 2004 – Feb 2005
05	March 2005 – Aug 2005	55	Sept 2005 – Feb 2006
06	March 2006 – Aug 2006	56	Sept 2006 – Feb 2007
07	March 2007 – Aug 2007	57	Sept 2007 – Feb 2008
08	March 2008 – Aug 2008	58	Sept 2008 – Feb 2009
09	March 2009 – Aug 2009	59	Sept 2009 – Feb 2010
10	March 2010 – Aug 2010	60	Sept 2010 – Feb 2011
11	March 2011 – Aug 2011	61	Sept 2011 – Feb 2012

General Information

Automobile Association founded in 1905; originally formed to warn members of police patrols.

Breathalyser introduced in 1967 by Minister of Transport, Barbara Castle.

car founders and designers: Fiat – Agnelli family; Jaguar – William Lyons; Lotus – Colin Chapman.

driving test initiated in 1935 and L-plates issued in the same year.

Mini introduced in 1959 and designed by Alex Issigonis.

MoT (Ministry of Transport) testing established in 1960 and compulsory for vehicles over three years old.

number plates first issued in 1903, the first being A1 to Lord Russell.

parking meters first seen in the UK in 1958, the same year that London saw its first traffic wardens.

petrol pumps were first used in 1919 in the UK.

Route 66 runs from Chicago (Illinois) to Los Angeles (California).

Royal Automobile Club founded in 1897, the second largest motoring organisation after the AA.

veteran cars are those built up to the end of 1918; contrast Vintage cars, 1919–30.

TRANSPORT: SHIPS

Famous Ships: Miscellaneous

Aaron Manby first iron steamship, launched in 1822.

Achille Lauro formerly *Willem Ruys*, Italian cruise ship dogged by disaster. Collided with a fishing boat 1971, one crew member killed; fire broke out on board 1981, two passengers killed; hijacked between Alexandria and Port Said by the PLO Oct. 1985, one passenger murdered; gutted by fire and sank in the Indian Ocean Nov. 1994, two passengers killed.

Amoco Cadiz super-tanker that ran aground off the coast of Brittany (March 1978) spilling 220,000 tons of crude oil.

Ancon first ship through the Panama Canal.

Andrea Doria Italian ship which collided with a Swedish ship and sank (1956).

Archimedes first large sea-going steamship driven by a screw-propeller, it weighed 237 tons (Nov. 1838).

Argonaut first submarine to navigate extensively in the open sea. Built in 1897 by the US engineer and naval architect Simon Lake, it was fitted with wheels for travel on the bottom of the sea. In 1898 the *Argonaut* travelled from Norfolk, Virginia, to New York, through heavy storms, proving the seaworthiness of this type of submarine construction.

Black Pig vessel captained by Captain Pugwash in the children's series.

Braer oil tanker that ran aground off the Shetlands (Jan. 1993) spilling 85,000 tons of crude oil.

Britannia launched in April 1953, the Royal Yacht *Britannia* was finally laid to rest in December 1997.

Britannic sister ship of the *Titanic*, sank after hitting a mine in 1916 in the Aegean while employed as a hospital ship.

Californian Leyland liner, accused of ignoring *Titanic*'s distress calls but subsequently found to have no radio operator on duty.

Canberra P&O cruise ship, affectionately nicknamed 'The Great White Whale'; entered service 1961; served as a hospital ship in the Falklands 1982; last cruise 1997.

Carnival Destiny largest passenger ship in history: 893' long, 116' wide, gross registered tonnage 101,353 tons and too wide to go through Panama Canal.

Carpathia ship that came to the rescue of the *Titanic* when it sank.

Charlotte Dundas first commercially successful paddle-steamer launched in Scotland, 1802, by William Symington for Lord Dundas.

Charlotte Rhodes James Onedin's ship in the TV series *The Onedin Line*.

Christina Aristotle Onassis' yacht named after his daughter.

Cutty Sark famous tea and wool clipper built in 1869, the name deriving from the witch in Burns's *Tam O'Shanter*. It has been on display at Greenwich since 1957.

Don Juan boat in which Percy Bysshe Shelley was drowned in 1822.

Dona Paz Philippine ferry that collided with the tanker *Vector* in the Sibuyan Sea, 20 December 1987. In the subsequent fire both ships sank and a total of 4,386 people lost their lives, only 24 surviving from the *Dona Paz* and two from the *Vector*. The worst-ever peacetime maritime disaster.

Elise first steamboat to cross the English Channel (1816).

ENZA New Zealand catamaran with eight-man crew led by Peter Blake and Robin Knox-Johnston which won the Jules Verne Trophy for sailing non-stop round the world in a record time of 74 days 22 hrs 17 mins, returning on 1 April 1994.

Estonia Swedish-owned ferry that sank in the Baltic in September 1994 when the bow doors broke open, costing 852 lives.

Exxon Valdez super-tanker that ran aground off Alaskan coast (March 1989) spilling 12,000,000 gallons of crude oil.

Forfarshire steamer wrecked off the Farne Islands in 1838, Grace Darling famously helping in the rescue.

Francis Smith first British steamboat fitted with screw-propellers and built by Francis Pettit Smith, a farmer from Hendon (1836). It was 25' long and weighed 5 tons.

Grand Princess the P&O liner is currently being built in Fincantieri, Italy, and is expected to be 951' long with a gross registered tonnage of 109,000 tons exceeding the *Carnival Destiny* as the largest-ever passenger ship.

Great Britain built by Isambard Kingdom Brunel (1843), it was the first iron-hulled screw-propeller steamship. Since being towed from the Falklands in 1970, where it had been scuttled in 1937, it has been on display in Bristol.

Great Eastern built by Isambard Kingdom Brunel (1858). At 666' long, it was the world's largest ship until 1899. In 1866, it laid the transatlantic cable. Sold for scrap in 1888.

Great Western built by Isambard Kingdom Brunel (1838), it was the first wooden steamship to make regular transatlantic crossings.

Gypsy Moth IV Francis Chichester became the first Englishman to sail single-handed round the world in this yacht (1966/7). Now on display at Greenwich.

Happy Giant formerly named the *Seawise Giant* and with a deadweight tonnage of 564,763 tons, this was the largest ship afloat, but after extensive damage in the Gulf in Dec. 1987 and May 1988 has been refitted and reduced to 420,000 tons.

Helias Fos this steam-turbine oil tanker is the current largest ship afloat at a deadweight tonnage of 550,051 tons.

Herald of Free Enterprise Townsend Thoresen-owned cross-Channel ferry which capsized near the Belgian port of Zeebrugge due to the bow doors being insecure (6 March 1987); 193 lives were lost as a result.

Hispaniola fictional ship in Robert Louis Stevenson's *Treasure Island*, skippered by Captain Smollet and owned by Squire Trelawney.

Lady Ghislaine yacht owned by Robert Maxwell and named after his daughter, from which he went overboard and drowned (Nov. 1991).

Lake Champlain first British liner with ship's radio (1901), it communicated with the SS *Lucania* mid-Atlantic.

Lenin first nuclear-powered ship. This Soviet naval ice-breaker was launched in 1957.

Little Juliana first steamboat fitted with screw-propellers (May 1804).

Lively Lady yacht in which Alec Rose sailed single-handed round the world, returning to Portsmouth after nearly a year (4 July 1968).

Lusitania Cunard liner sunk by German torpedo off the Irish coast (7 May 1915) with the loss of about 1,200 lives. This was a major factor in the USA's entry into the First World War.

Maiden British yacht with all-female crew skippered by Tracy Edwards; won its class in Whitbread Round the World Race (1989).

Marchioness Thames pleasure steamer rammed and sunk by the dredger *Bowbelle* at Southwark (August 1989); 51 lives were lost.

Mary Celeste US brigantine under command of Ben Briggs, found in Atlantic (1872) with no sign of crew or struggle; cargo was secure.

Mauretania sister ship of the *Lusitania*, built in 1907.

Mayflower carried the 102 Pilgrim Fathers from Plymouth to Cape Cod, Massachusetts (1620), to found the first New England colony. Oceanus Hopkins was born on board the *Mayflower*.

Morning Cloud yacht owned and captained by Edward Heath.

Nautilus Captain Nemo's submarine in Jules Verne's novel *20,000 Leagues Under the Sea*.

Normandie passenger liner destroyed by fire in New York harbour in 1941.

Norway longest passenger liner ever built (formerly called *France*): overall length 1035′ 2″.

Olympic sister ship of the *Titanic*.

Pequod whaling ship captained by Captain Ahab and destroyed by Moby Dick in Melville's novel.

Pyroscaphe first practical steamboat. Built near Lyon in 1783, it was a 138′-long paddle steamer and weighed 182 tons.

Queen Anne's Revenge Edward Teach's (Blackbeard) ship captured in the Caribbean in 1717 and used for piracy until Jan. 1718.

Queen Elizabeth built in 1938, the *Queen Elizabeth* (Seawise University) was destroyed in Hong Kong Harbour in Jan. 1972.

QEII built in 1968, it is the largest passenger liner in service between Southampton and New York.

Queen Mary now a floating hotel in Long Beach, California, it was built in 1936 and was the flagship of the Cunard line.

Rainbow Warrior Greenpeace ship which was sunk in Auckland Harbour in July 1985 by French intelligence agents, killing one member of the crew.

Rising Star first ship to cross the Atlantic from east to west (1821/2).

Savannah first steamship to cross the Atlantic (1819).

Savannah first commercially successful nuclear-powered ship, launched 1959.

Sea Empress oil tanker which ran aground off Milford Haven (Feb. 1996) spilling 72,000 tons of crude oil.

Speedwell sister ship of the *Mayflower* which left Southampton for New England but was forced into harbour at Plymouth, Devon.

Suhaili yacht in which Robin Knox-Johnston became first man to circumnavigate the world non-stop and single-handed; he returned in April 1969.

Talitha G motor yacht owned by John Paul Getty.

Thomas W Lawson US schooner; the only seven-masted sailing vessel on record. Designed by Bowdoin B Crowninshield and built by the Fore River Ship and Engine Building Co in 1902 for Coastwise Transportation Co. The seven masts were Fore, Main, Mizzen, Number 4, Number 5, Number 6 and Spanker.

Titanic White Star's unsinkable flagship which hit an iceberg on its maiden voyage on the night of 14 April 1912 and capsized in the early hours of 15 April with the loss of 1,513 lives. Wreck was found in 1985.

Torrey Canyon ran aground off Land's End (March 1967) spilling its cargo of 100,000 tons of crude oil.

Turbinia built and demonstrated by Charles Parsons at Spithead (1897), it was the first ship to use turbine engines.

Victoria and Albert name given to three royal yachts; the first was a paddle-steamer of 1843; the last was built in 1899 and used until replaced by *Britannia*.

Famous Ships: Naval

Agamemnon 64-gun ship launched in 1781, commanded by Nelson from 1793 and his favourite ship. Abandoned in 1809 when it ran aground at Maldonado Bay.

Amethyst frigate which in July 1949 escaped under cover of night along the flooded Yangtze.

Arethusa launched 1849; last Royal Navy ship to go into action entirely under sail, at Sebastopol in 1855. From 1874 to 1933 it was a training ship at Greenhithe.

Argus first aircraft carrier, completed in 1918.

Arizona said to be the first US battleship sunk at Pearl Harbor on 7 Dec. 1941.

Ark Royal many ships have had the name but the most famous were probably the flagship of the British Fleet against the Spanish Armada (1588), although it was only the nickname, the aircraft carrier sunk by an Italian torpedo in November 1941, and the present aircraft carrier which is the Royal

Navy's largest fighting ship.

Association flagship of Sir Cloudesley Shovell, wrecked off the Scilly Isles in 1707 with all hands lost.

Belfast Europe's largest surviving WW2 warship, displacing 11,500 tons. Commissioned 1939, paid off 1971. The cruiser is now on display on the Thames.

Bellerophon Napoleon Bonaparte surrendered to the British aboard this ship (15 July 1815) after the Battle of Waterloo.

Birmingham US light cruiser from which Eugène Ely took off in a 50 hp Curtiss pusher biplane (10 Nov. 1910) while it was at anchor in Chesapeake Bay, so making it the first ship with a temporary flight-deck.

Bismarck German battleship sunk in the North Atlantic after it had sunk the British battle cruiser HMS *Hood* (May 1941).

Bonhomme Richard John Paul Jones's 40-gun

warship, blown in two off Flamborough Head in 1779.

Bounty ship that while carrying breadfruit trees from Tahiti was the scene of a mutiny (28 April 1789) by Fletcher Christian (settled on Pitcairn Island). Captain William Bligh and 18 crew were set adrift in the Pacific.

Captain experimental British turret ship of 1870 designed by Captain Cowper Coles; sank in the Bay of Biscay shortly after commissioning with the loss of 472 lives.

Constitution American ship of the line, launched 1798. Nicknamed 'Old Ironsides'; on display in Boston.

Coventry sister ship of the *Sheffield* and also sunk by an Argentinian Exocet missile during the Falklands War.

Devastation launched 1871; first British capital ship which did not require sails.

Dreadnought British battleship launched 1906 which revolutionised naval warfare in the early decades of the 20th century.

Dreadnought Britain's first nuclear submarine, launched in 1960.

Elizabeth Bonaventure Drake's flagship in the raid on Cadiz in 1587.

Enterprise first nuclear-powered aircraft carrier.

Excellent home to the naval gunnery school established in 1830; since 1891, a shore base on Whale Island, Portsmouth.

Ganges last British ship of the line; launched 1821, paid off 1861. From 1866 a training ship. Name passed to a shore base near Ipswich in 1905; closed 1976.

General Belgrano Argentine cruiser sunk by the British submarine *Conqueror* during Falklands War (2 May 1982).

Graf Spee German pocket battleship scuttled by her captain off Montevideo Harbour after being harried across the River Plate by the cruisers, *Ajax*, *Achilles* and *Exeter* (Dec. 1939).

Henry, Grâce de Dieu Henry VIII's flagship, built 1514 and carried 186 guns.

Hermes aircraft carrier, last of the old-style carriers operated by the Royal Navy, which was flagship during the Falklands War.

Invincible the second aircraft carrier that was sent to the Falklands after the Argentine invasion (2 April 1982).

Lightning first purpose-built torpedo boat (1877).

Long Beach first nuclear warship, launched in Quincy, Massachusetts (14 July 1959).

Maine American armoured cruiser of 1886; blew up in Havana 1898, resulting in the Spanish-American War.

Mary Rose Henry VIII's favourite ship, launched 1509, sank 1545 but was raised in 1982 and is still being restored at Portsmouth.

Merrimack steam frigate scuttled in Norfolk harbour by Union forces, then raised by the Confederates, converted to an ironclad and renamed *Virginia*; fought a draw with the *Monitor* in Hampton Roads in 1862 and destroyed by her own captain shortly afterwards.

Missouri Japanese surrender terms were signed aboard this ship in Tokyo Bay (2 Sept. 1945).

Monarch First British turret-gunned ship, launched 1868.

Monitor US iron-hulled warship with single gun turret, fought *Merrimack* in Hampton Roads 1862; capsized in a gale shortly after.

Nautilus world's first nuclear-powered submarine, launched by the USA in 1954. The name derived from an early submarine designed by Robert Fulton for Napoleon (1800).

Northumberland third-rate ship of the line which took Napoleon Bonaparte to St Helena in 1815.

PT 109 John F Kennedy's torpedo boat during World War II.

Revenge Drake's ship used during the attack by the Spanish Armada (1588). In 1591, captained by Sir Richard Grenville, fought a fifteen-hour battle single-handedly against 53 Spanish ships off Flores.

Royal George 100-gun ship of 1756; carried Hawke's flag at Quiberon Bay in 1759; capsized at Spithead in 1782 with loss of 900 lives.

Royal Oak British battleship sunk at Scapa Flow (Orkneys) by a German torpedo (Oct. 1939) with the loss of 833 lives.

Scharnhorst German battlecruiser which escaped from Brest with the *Gneisenau* and *Prinz Eugen* (Feb. 1942) but was sunk at the Battle of North Cape (Dec. 1943).

Sheffield British destroyer hit by an Exocet missile on 4 May 1982 with the loss of 20 lives.

Squirrel Sir Humphrey Gilbert's ship used during the attack by the Spanish Armada (1588).

Temeraire 98-gun ship launched in 1798; fought at Trafalgar; broken up on the Thames 1838 and immortalised on canvas by Turner.

Tiger the ship used by Harold Wilson and Ian Smith during their UDI discussions (1966).

Tirpitz German battleship sunk by RAF bombers in April 1944.

Trincomalee built 1817, renamed *Foudroyant* in 1892 and a training ship in Portsmouth Harbour until 1987 when she was towed to Hartlepool for restoration and given back her original name.

Vanguard iron-hulled frigate accidentally rammed and sunk by her sister ship *Iron Duke* in 1875.

Vanguard Britain's largest battleship. Decommissioned 1960 and ran aground on leaving Portsmouth to be scrapped.

Vasa flagship of Gustavus Adolphus of Sweden. Sank in harbour in 1628; recovered intact from seabed and now on display.

Victoria launched 1859; last wooden battleship built for the Royal Navy. Paid off 1867; name used by British battleship of 1887 which sank off Tripoli in 1893 when flagship of Admiral George Tryon. It was accidentally rammed by *Camperdown*, flagship of Tryon's second-in-command, Alfred Markham.

Victory launched at Chatham 1765, Horatio Nelson's flagship at the battle of Trafalgar (21 Oct. 1805); flagship of C-in-C Portsmouth since 1835. Drydocked and restored in 1922, the *Victory* is now on display at Portsmouth.

Warrior first iron-hulled battleship (and last surviving); built at Blackwall on the Thames (1859/60). When commissioned in 1861, it made every other naval vessel obsolete. On display in Portsmouth since 1987.

Wilton first plastic warship, launched in Southampton 18 Jan. 1972.

Famous Ships: Voyages of Exploration

Adventure James Cook's consort ship to the *Resolution* during his Antarctic voyage 1772–5; converted from a Whitby collier.

Arktika first ship to reach the North Pole, in 1977.

Beagle Charles Darwin's ship which surveyed South American islands and in particular Galapagos (1831–6). Darwin was the science officer, the captain was Robert Fitzroy.

Calypso most famous survey ship of Jacques Cousteau.

Challenger Royal Navy survey ship, sailed 79,000 miles from 1872 to 1876, adding greatly to knowledge of the seas. Most recent RN ship of that name also an oceanographic vessel.

Discovery Captain James Cook sought the Northwest Passage in 1776–9 with the *Resolution* and the *Discovery*. He was slain on the beach at Kealakekua, Hawaii, by Polynesian natives (1779).

Discovery Robert Falcon Scott's ship used in his British National Antarctic Expedition of 1901–4 in which he was accompanied by Ernest Shackleton. Now on display in Dundee.

Endeavour James Cook's voyage to Australia and New Zealand (1768–71), on which Joseph Banks was chief scientist, was carried out on this converted collier, originally called *Earl of Pembroke*.

Endurance Ernest Shackleton's ship on his Antarctic voyage of 1914–16; sank in the Weddell Sea but since raised and on display in Dundee.

Erebus one of the two ill-fated ships (the other was the *Terror*) used by Sir John Franklin in his search for the Northwest Passage (1845–6).

Fram Norwegian explorer Fridtjof Nansen's ship used on his Arctic explorations (1893–6). Roald Amundsen sailed in *Fram* (which meant 'Forward') on his successful expedition of 1911–12 to the South Pole.

Gjöa Roald Amundsen's ship in which he sailed the Northwest Passage (1902–6) and found the magnetic North Pole.

Golden Hind ship on which Francis Drake became first Englishman to circumnavigate the globe (1580); originally called *Pelican*.

Grenville the schooner that James Cook commanded while surveying the coast of Newfoundland 1763–68.

Kon Tiki Thor Heyerdahl's single-sailed balsa-wood raft on which he crossed the Pacific (1947).

Matthew John Cabot discovered Newfoundland and Nova Scotia (1497) in this 50-ton ship.

Mazurek carried Krystyna Choynowska-Liskievicz on the first female solo circumnavigation of the globe in 1978.

Morning Supply ship that accompanied the *Discovery* in Scott's Antarctic expedition of 1901–4.

Ernest Shackleton was invalided home on this ship.

Nimrod Ernest Shackleton's ship on the voyage (1907–9) in which he located the magnetic South Pole, and climbed Mt Erebus but only came within 97 miles of the South Pole.

Quest ship on which Ernest Shackleton died during his third Antarctic voyage (Grytviken, South Georgia 1922).

RA II Thor Heyerdahl's papyrus raft on which he crossed the Atlantic (1970).

Resolute one of Edward Belcher's ships sent to seek the missing (and already dead) John Franklin in 1852; abandoned in 1854 after being locked in ice off Melville Island; found 1,000 miles away in Davis Strait in 1855, still perfectly seaworthy.

Resolution James Cook's flagship during his voyage to Antarctica 1772–5. Cook sought the Northwest Passage 1776–9 in this ship.

Roebuck William Dampier's ship on his voyage to Australia and New Guinea (1699–1700).

Santa Maria Christopher Columbus's flagship during his expedition to the New World (1492–3), accompanied by the caravels *Niña* and *Pinta*.

Spray Joshua Slocum's boat in which he circumnavigated the Earth, the first man to do so solo (1895–8).

Terra Nova Captain Robert Falcon Scott's ship used on his ill-fated Antarctic expedition 1910–12.

Terror one of the two ships (the other was *Erebus*) used by Sir John Franklin in his search for the Northwest Passage (1845–6).

Theodore Roosevelt Robert Peary's ship used when he became first person to reach the North Pole (6 April 1909). Peary's former friend, Frederick Cook, was found to have fraudulently reported his own earlier reaching of the Pole.

Tigris Thor Heyerdahl's third raft.

Trieste bathysphere submarine which holds the record for the deepest descent (10,916 m) on 23 Jan. 1960.

Vega first ship to achieve the Northeast Passage, in 1878–9, under Nils Nordenskjöld.

Victoria first ship to circumnavigate the globe (1519–22). Although Ferdinand Magellan set out with five ships (the flagship *Trinidad*, *San Antonio*, *Concepción*, *Santiago* and *Victoria*) four were lost and he himself was killed in the Philippines (1521). The circumnavigation was completed by the Basque seaman Juan Sebastián del Cano.

Viking Norwegian explorer Fridtjof Nansen's first exploratory ship (1888) in which he first sailed to Greenland.

Windward British Arctic explorer Frederick Jackson's ship on which Fridtjof Nansen briefly journeyed back to Norway in Aug. 1896.

Ships: General Information

binnacle the casing in which the ship's compass is kept.

box the compass to name the points of the compass in proper order.

breeches buoy life-saving device run on a rope stretched from a wrecked vessel to a place of safety.

bulwark that part of the sides of a ship which rises above the upper deck.

caïque long, narrow, light rowing skiff used on the Bosporus.

clipper ship: first *Rainbow* (1845).

dahabeah/dahabeeyah houseboat used on the Nile (from Arabic: the Golden One).

dhow single-masted ship with a very long yard and a lateen sail, used on the Arabian sea.

diesel-powered ship: first *Petit-Pierre*.

distress signals SOS – Morse (formerly CQD, Come Quickly Danger); Mayday – vocal distress shout.

extremities of ship front – bow; back – stern; left side looking front – port (formerly larboard); right side looking front – starboard.

felucca small vessel used in the Mediterranean, propelled by oars or lateen sails, or both.

flotsam goods lost in shipwreck and found floating.

gondola long, narrow Venetian boat with peaked ends, propelled by one oar.

gunwale upper edge of a ship's side next to the bulwarks.

hull: plank types clinker-built – built with overlapping planks fastened with clinched nails; carvel-built – having the planks flush at the edges.

hydrofoil invented by Comte de Lambert in 1897 and developed by Enrico Forlanini in 1898.

jetsam goods thrown overboard in order to lighten a ship in distress, and subsequently washed ashore.

junk flat-bottomed vessel with lugsails, used in the Chinese seas.

kayak Inuit and Alaskan canoe, made of sealskins stretched on a light wooden framework.

kitchen or cook-house galley.

knot one nautical mile per hour. The British nautical mile was 6,080 feet but in 1970 the International nautical mile of 1,852 metres was adopted. The measurement was devised by Richard Norwood in 1673.

lighthouses: UK authority Trinity House.

lights starboard – green; port – red; top at night – white.

masts: how many sloop and cutter (1); ketch, brig, brigantine, yawl (2); barque (3 or more); schooner (2 or more).

oldest surviving ships *Khufu I* and *Khufu II*, built *c.* 2600 BC and buried in pits outside the Great Pyramid of Khufu in Egypt. *Khufu I*, first to be excavated after discovery in 1954, is plank-built and 43 metres long.

P&O: meaning Peninsular and Oriental.

pipe down naval colloquialism derived from the boatswain's call of this name, meaning 'Hands turn in', i.e. 'Lights out'.

piping the side traditional ceremony of blowing the boatswain's pipe when royalty arrive or depart from battleship.

plimsoll line maximum loading mark on hull of ship, named after Samuel Plimsoll (1824–98), promoter of the Merchant Shipping Act 1876.

ports: famous Athens – Piraeus; London – Tilbury; Rome – Ostia.

ports: general biggest – New York; busiest – Rotterdam; largest inland – Montreal.

PT Boat: meaning Patrol Torpedo Boat.

Q-ship merchant ship with concealed guns, used to decoy enemy ships into the range of its weapons. Q stood for 'Query'.

rudder: invented by Chinese, 1st century BC.

sails lateen – triangular.

ships: register of Lloyd's.

ship: largest oil tanker *Jahre Viking* at 1,504′ long and weighing over 564,000 tonnes.

steam turbine: inventor Charles Parsons (1897).

V-shaped hull: pioneer Uffa Fox (who instructed HRH Prince Philip, the Duke of Edinburgh, in the finer points of yachting).

Venice: water bus vaporetto.

watches at sea first watch – 8pm to midnight; middle watch – midnight to 4am; morning watch – 4am to 8am; forenoon – 8am to midday; afternoon watch – midday to 4pm; first dog watch – 4pm to 6pm; second dog watch – 6pm to 8pm.

xebec/zebec small three-masted Mediterranean vessel with both square and lateen sails, formerly used by Algerian pirates.

yachts: famous *Talitha G* – John Paul Getty; *Saratoga* – Humphrey Bogart; *Saxara* – Mohamed Al Fayed.

TRANSPORT: TRAINS

Railway Tunnels: World's Longest

	Span	Built	Railway	Length (mile)
Seikan	Honshu–Hokkaido	1988	Japan Rail	33.5
Channel	Cheriton–Fréthun	1994	BR/French National	30.7
Daishimizu	Jōmō-Kogen–Echigo	1980	Japan Rail	13.9
Iwate-ichinohe	Morioka–Aomori	2002	Japan Rail	16.1
Simplon No. 2	Brig–Iselle	1922	Swiss Federal	12.4
Simplon No. 1	Brig–Iselle	1906	Swiss Federal	12.3
Shin Kanmon	Honshu–Kyushu	1975	Japan Rail	11.6
Vereina	Lavin–Klosters	1999	Swiss Federal	11.9
Apennine	Florence–Bologna	1934	Italian State	11.5
Rokko	Osaka–Shinkobe	1972	Japan Rail	10.1
Qinling	Qinling Mountains	2002	China Rail (Tube)	11.4
Furka Base	Oberwald–Realp	1982	Furks-Oberalp Switzerland	9.6
Haruna	Jōmō-Kogen–Echigo	1982	Japan Rail	9.5
Gotthard	Göschenen–Airolo	1882	Swiss Federal	9.3
Mt Macdonald	Selkirk Mts–British Columbia	1989	CP Rail, Canada	9.1

Longest railway tunnel on the Indian sub-continent is the Kojak Tunnel at Shelabagh, Pakistan (2½ miles). The Lyttelton Tunnel (1.6 miles) was the first railway tunnel in NZ and the only one through an extinct volcano. Longest overland railway tunnel in the UK is the Severn Tunnel.

Railway Bridges: World's Longest

	Location	Opened	Length (ft)
Huey P Long	New Orleans, USA	1935	23,235
Yangtze River	Nanjing, China	1968	22,218
Hell Gate	New York, USA	1917	19,233
Greenwich	London, England	1836	19,000
Orvieto Viaduct	Paglia River	1980	17,634
Savannah River	S. Carolina, USA	1909	13,000
Lower Zambesi	Mozambique	1934	12,064
Venice Viaduct	Italy	1846	11,821
Tay	Scotland	1887	11,653
Storstrom	Denmark	1937	10,537

World's oldest railway bridge is the Tanfield Arch in County Durham, designed by Ralph Wood and built in 1727. World's highest railway bridge, above water, is the Hanging Bridge above the Arkansas River, Colorado, at 1,053'.

London Underground Stations: Name Changes

Current name	Previous name
Acton Town	Mill Hill Park
Arsenal	Gillespie Road
Becontree	Gale Street Halt
Charing Cross	Strand
Debden	Chigwell Road
Embankment	Charing Cross
Euston Square	Gower Street
Fulham Broadway	Walham Green
Green Park	Dover Street
Kensington (Olympia)	Addison Road
Ladbroke Grove	Notting Hill
Marylebone	Great Central
Moor Park	Sandy Lodge
Oakwood	Enfield West
Ravenscourt Park	Shaftesbury Road
South Woodford	George Lane
St Paul's	Post Office
Tooting Bec	Trinity Road
Tower Hill	Mark Lane
West Kensington	North End (Fulham)
White City	Wood Lane
Woodside Park	Torrington Park, Woodside

Rail Companies: Since BR Privatised

Anglia Railway	Island Line	South Wales and West
Cardiff Railway Co.	LTS Rail (London, Tilbury South)	South West Trains
Central Trains	Mersey Rail	South West Trains (Stagecoach)
Chiltern Railway Co.	Midland Mainline	Thames
Connex South Central	North London Rail	Thameslink
Connex South Eastern	North Western Trains	Virgin West
Eurostar	Regional Railways North East	West Anglia Great Northern
Gatwick Express	Scot Rail	West Coast Railway Co.

Railway Stations: Locations

Anhalter	Berlin	**King's Cross**	London	**Saint Lazare**	Paris
Bank Top	Darlington	**Lime Street**	Liverpool	**Shrub Hill**	Worcester
Buchanan Street	Glasgow	**Liverpool Street**	London	**Snow Hill**	Birmingham
Charing Cross	London	**London Rd**	Leicester	**Spa**	Bath
Citadel	Carlisle	**Low Level**	Wolverhampton	**St David's**	Exeter
Connolly	Dublin	**Marine**	Dover	**St Enoch**	Glasgow
Euston	London	**Midland**	Derby	**Temple Meads**	Bristol
Foregate Street	Worcester	**Mumps**	Oldham	**Thorpe**	Norwich
Forster Square	Bradford	**New Street**	Birmingham	**Trent Valley**	Nuneaton
Gare du Nord	Paris	**Paddington**	London	**Union**	Washington
Grand Central	New York	**Paragon**	Hull	**Victoria**	London,
Harbour	Folkestone,	**Parkway**	Bristol		Manchester,
	Portsmouth	**Piccadilly**	Manchester		Bombay
Haymarket	Edinburgh	**Priory**	Dover	**Waterloo**	London
High Level	Wolverhampton	**Queen Street**	Cardiff,	**Waverley**	Edinburgh
High Street	Swansea		Glasgow	**Yaroslavl**	Moscow

Railways: General Information

accident: first caused by moving train Rt Hon William Huskisson MP was run down by the *Rocket* at the opening of the Liverpool & Manchester Railway 15 Sept. 1830. He was rushed to Eccles Hospital on the *Northumbrian*. A runaway wagon caused the death of two boys in a Tyne coalpit in 1650. Unfortunately numerous incidents of this kind took place but were not really the work of trains in the accepted sense of the word.

air-brake: designer George Westinghouse (1846–1914) developed the air-brake from the simple non-automatic system of 1866 into the fully automatic (i.e. the brakes are automatically applied should any break in the train air pipe occur). System still in use in most countries. Most British railways used the vacuum brake, which had nothing to do with Westinghouse.

APT BR Advanced Passenger Train ran from London to Glasgow in 3 hrs 52 mins 45 secs at an average speed of 103 mph (12 Dec. 1984). This service was abandoned in 1986 due to numerous problems.

British speed records A Eurostar train reached 208mph on a stretch of track between Ashford and Dartford in Kent to create a new UK speed record in July 2003. A Virgin Pendolino tilting train set a record for the non-stop journey between London and Manchester in September 2004. The 184 miles were covered in 1hr 54mins.

broad-gauge railway: last train the *Cornishman* was the last broad-gauge passenger train to run, on 21 May 1892, from Paddington to Penzance.

Chicago rail system nicknamed the 'El', which is short for elevated (several other cities, notably New York, also had elevated railways known as 'Els').

diesel locomotive: first the first diesel locomotive to go into regular service was a Swedish-built metre-gauge Bo Bo type put into operation by Tunisian Railways in 1921.

dining car: first first buffet cars were put into service on the Philadelphia, Wilmington & Baltimore Railroad in 1863.

electric railway: first Brighton seafront, built by Magnus Volk (1851–1937), still known as Volk's Electric Railway.

electrification of railways modern standard system of railway electrification at 25 kV 50 Hz was first used in France in 1950 and in England on the Colchester– Clacton–Walton lines in 1959.

fare-paying customers: first to carry Oystermouth Railway built a railway from Swansea to Mumbles and on 25 March 1807 became first to convey fare-paying passengers. This railway closed in 1960.

father of railways George Stephenson.

father of the locomotive Richard Trevithick.

highest railway station Condor station in Bolivia.

horse-drawn railways Middleton Railway, Leeds, in 1758 was the first to be built under its own Act of Parliament, although other horse-worked railways had been operating in the Tyne coalfield on private land for many years previously.

T
R
A
N
S
P
O
R
T

T
R
A
I
N
S

horse-drawn railways: public the Surrey Iron Railway from Wandsworth to Croydon (opened 26 July 1803) was the first horse-drawn railway opened to the public, inasmuch as it accepted consignments. Passengers were not carried (at least not officially!).

locomotive railway: first Stockton and Darlington, opened in 1825.

locomotive railway: first passenger line Liverpool to Manchester, opened in 1830.

London railway: first Spa Road to Deptford, part of London & Greenwich Railway, opened 8 Feb. 1836.

London Underground: first automatic barrier Stamford Brook.

London Underground: first line Metropolitan Line, from Bishop's Road to Farringdon Street, 10 Jan. 1863.

longest platform in Great Britain Colchester, at 1981'.

longest platform in the world Kharagpur Station, West Bengal at 2,733'.

Mallard LNER 'A4' Class Pacific No. 4468 *Mallard* reached a speed of just over 126 mph for a few seconds on a brake-test trial run between Grantham and Peterborough (3 July 1938). *Mallard* can be seen at the National Railway Museum, York.

monorail: first Charles Lartique's monorail system was used on a short demonstration line in France and then on the Listowel and Ballybunion Railway in Ireland, 1883. It was not a true monorail but comprised a single rail raised about 4' above the ground on an A-frame with two guiding rails about 1' off the ground.

National Railway Museum museum opened in York in 1975 and combining the holdings of the British Transport Commission's museum at Clapham and the LNER museum at York.

nationalisation railways were nationalised from 1 Jan. 1948 and were divided into five regions: 1) Scottish, 2) North Eastern, 3) London Midland, 4) Eastern, 5) Western and Southern. (The Eastern and North Eastern were amalgamated on 1 Jan. 1967.)

platforms: most UK Waterloo main line.

Puffing Billy world's first steam locomotive running on smooth rails instead of the previous rack rails. Designed by William Hedley and first put into operation in 1813 from Wylam colliery in Northumberland to the river Tyne. The *Wylam Dilly* was made at much the same time. Note: Trevithick's Penydarren engine had smooth iron wheels running on smooth cast-iron tram plates!

railcar: designer William Bridges Adams designed the 6-wheeled steam railcar *Fairfield* (named after the road in Bow, London, where he operated from).

railtrack: longest in straight line Nullarbor Plain, Australia.

railway: first private opened in June 1789 by the Loughborough & Nanpanton Railway Co.

railway king George Hudson.

Railways Act 1921 from 1 Jan. 1923 the amalgamation of the railways meant that four major companies were formed: 1) The Great Western Railway, 2) The London, Midland & Scottish Railway, 3) The London and North Eastern Railway, 4) The Southern Railway.

railways: USA operating co. Amtrak.

Rainhill Trials competition held on 6–14 Oct. 1829 near Liverpool to choose the design of locomotive for Liverpool & Manchester Railway. Robert

Stephenson's *Rocket* won the £500 prize by beating Timothy Hackworth's *Sans Pareil* and John Braithwaite and John Ericsson's *Novelty*.

RKB code: meaning the code RKB refers to a single item of rolling stock containing a restaurant seating portion, a buffet counter and a kitchen.

San Francisco rail system BART (Bay Area Rapid Transit).

Schools-Class locomotives introduced by Southern Railway in 1930 and named after famous schools, first being called *Eton*.

Scottish railway: first Kilmarnock and Troon Railway was the first 'proper' railway in Scotland. Opened 6 July 1812.

sleeping cars: European wagons lits.

sleeping car: first the *Chambersburg*, introduced by the Cumberland Valley Railroad on its Pennsylvanian Harrisburg–Chambers route, was the first example of a sleeping car (1836).

standard gauge first used on Willington Colliery wagonway near Newcastle upon Tyne in 1764 and set at 4' 8½" or 1,435 mm, this being an average of the wagon ways in this area. It is thought that the average gauge of between 4' 6" and 4' 9" was the width of the track required for two horses abreast.

station: largest Grand Central, New York.

station: largest UK Clapham Junction.

station: most northerly in Great Britain Thurso.

steam locomotive: first Richard Trevithick built the first locomotive and ran it on the Penydarren Railway, near Merthyr Tydfil, on 6 Feb. 1804.

TGV Train à Grande Vitesse (High-Speed Train); began a regular hourly service between Paris and Lyon, the 265-mile journey taking 2 hrs 40 mins.

third-class travel redesignated as second class by British Rail in 1956. (The old second class had largely fallen out of use by the turn of the century.)

timetable: national *Bradshaw's Railway Companion* was the first national railway timetable in 1839.

underground: British four British cities with underground railways: London, Glasgow, Liverpool and Newcastle (Metro).

most passengers Moscow.

most stations New York.

names Berlin – U Bahn; Rome – Metropolitana; Stockholm – T-Bana; Paris – Métro.

USSR: terms for first and second class Soft and Hard class.

wheel configurations: nicknames Atlantic (4-4-2): name originally applied to a batch of 4-4-2s built by Baldwin of Philadelphia for the Atlantic Coast Railroad in 1894. In the UK, Atlantics were in use for hauling express passenger trains on the Great Northern, North Eastern, North British and London, Brighton & South Coast Railways. It should be borne in mind that the term 'Atlantic' properly describes a 4-4-2 locomotive with a separate tender; thus 4-4-2 tank engines, such as were in widespread use in the UK, are not true Atlantics but are more analogous to a 4-4-0 with an additional axle to support a rear bunker. **Mogul (2-6-0):** first true Mogul, with a leading two-wheel Bissell truck, was built by Baldwin of Philadelphia for the Louisville & Nashville Railroad in 1860. In the UK in the twentieth century Moguls were in extensive use on all four of the post-1923 mainline railways, and after 1948, in all regions of British Railways. The term Mogul properly applies to a 2-6-0 with outside cylinders, so that the inside-cylindered 2-6-0s of the Caledonian,

and Glasgow and South Western Railways were not true Moguls, being essentially large 0-6-0-s with a leading truck for increased front-end stability.
Pacific (4-6-2): name seems to have originated because the engines concerned were obviously bigger than Atlantics. In the UK, Pacifics were in general express service on the LNER from the mid-Twenties, the LMS from 1933 and the Southern Railway from 1941. The Great Western Railway had actually built the first UK Pacific (No. 111 *The Great Bear*) in 1908 but found it something of a white elephant. It was scrapped in 1924, and various mechanical components were incorporated in a new 'Castle' class 4-6-0, No. 111 *Viscount Churchill*.
Baltic (4-6-4): name appears to be of Germanic origin. (To an American, a 4-6-4 is a Hudson.) Only one 4-6-4 tender engine ever ran in the UK. This was Gresley's experimental high-pressure water-tube boiler 4-cylinder compound No. 10000, built for the LNER in 1929. It was rebuilt as a conventional 3-cylinder simple expansion engine and ran until 1959, latterly as British Railways No. 60700. This engine was not a true Baltic, since the rear carrying axles were disposed as a Cartazzi axle and a separate two-wheel radial truck, making the engine technically a 4-6-2-2. Around 1920, however, there was a vogue, particularly on the London Brighton & South Coast, Lancashire & Yorkshire and Glasgow & South Western Railways, for extremely large 4-6-4 tank engines, which, while not true Baltics (*vide supra* under Atlantic), were referred to as Baltics consistently enough to legitimise the usage. **Prairie (2-6-2):** name applied in the American Midwest after first examples were built in 1900 for the Chicago, Burlington & Quincy Railroad. Apart from one curious 8-cylinder experimental engine built as a semi-private venture by Cecil Paget at Derby in 1908, the only 2-6-2 tender engines to run in the UK were Gresley's extremely successful V2-class built from 1936 onwards for the LNER, and his lightweight V4 design of 1941, of which only two examples were built before his death. In the 20th century, several hundred 2-6-2 tank engines were built in the UK, particularly by the Great Western Railway, and, although not true Prairies (being actually Moguls with a rear bunker), they were generally referred to as Prairie tanks. **Consolidation (2-8-0):** name is that carried by the first example of this type, built in 1865 for the Lehigh & Mahanoy Railroad. The name was not much used to describe British 2-8-0s, but it does seem to have attached itself to the 2-8-0 freight locomotives built at Swindon for the Great Western Railway by G J Churchward and his successors. This may be due to Churchward's close following of American locomotive practice resulting in

an essentially American designation attaching itself to his engines of the 2-8-0 type. **Mikado (2-8-2):** so named because the first examples were made in the USA for export to Japan. In the UK, the only 2-8-2 tender engines were built by Gresley for the LNER. First, the two heavy freight engines of class P1, built in 1925. These were mechanically a cross between an A1-class Pacific and an O2-class Consolidation. As a small, non-standard class they were both withdrawn in 1945. Second was the magnificent class P2, six examples of which were built 1934–36, for working express passenger trains to Scotland. They were rebuilt as very mediocre Pacifics after Gresley's death. **Decapod:** a curiosity – to an American, a Decapod is a 2-10-0. The only two classes of engines of this type to run in the UK were the 251 examples of the standard-class 9F, built by British Railways between 1954 and 1960, and 25 examples bought secondhand from the Ministry of Supply after WW2. These, however, were never referred to as Decapods (except, presumably, by Americans!). The Decapod, however, was a huge 0-10-0 tank engine built by the Great Eastern Railway in 1903 as part of an experiment in the drastic acceleration of suburban trains. It did everything which was expected of it, but was far too heavy for the track and bridges. It was broken up shortly afterwards and a few components incorporated in a 0-8-0 goods engine. **NB** The following type names are largely in American use only, generally because no locomotives of the type referred to ever ran in the UK. **American (4-4-0):** applies only to the classic outside-cylindered, bar-framed three-point suspension locomotive familiar from countless Western films. **Ten Wheeler (4-6-0):** strictly an American term only. (Casey Jones was driving Illinois Central ten-wheeler No. 382 when he met his death at Vaughan, Mississippi, on 29 April 1900.) **Mastodon (4-8-0):** there were actually two 4-8-0 tender engines on the narrow-gauge Londonderry & Lough Swilly Railway in Ireland. They were used on the desolate Burtonport extension line in north-west Donegal, where I doubt if anyone ever referred to them as Mastodons. **Berkshire (2-8-4):** pronounced 'BurkSHIRE'. **Mountain (4-8-4) Santa Fe (2-10-2):** introduced by the Atchison, Topeka & Santa Fe Railroad in 1903, for working over the Raton Pass. **Texas (2-10-4):** called this in the USA but called 'Selkirk' in Canada.

world speed record   322mph by a French TGV in 1990.

world's longest railway: Trans-Siberian   running from Moscow (Yaroslavl Station) to Vladivostok (5,801 miles); opened 3 Nov. 1901.

United States

Presidents

	President		Birthplace	Life span	Party	In office
1	Washington	George	Virginia	1732–1799	Federalist	1789–1797
2	Adams	John	Massachusetts	1735–1826	Federalist	1797–1801
3	Jefferson	Thomas	Virginia	1743–1826	Republican	1801–1809
4	Madison	James	Virginia	1751–1836	Republican	1809–1817
5	Monroe	James	Virginia	1758–1831	Republican	1817–1825
6	Adams	John Quincy	Massachusetts	1767–1848	Republican	1825–1829
7	Jackson	Andrew	South Carolina	1767–1845	Democratic	1829–1837
8	Van Buren	Martin	New York	1782–1862	Democratic	1837–1841
9	Harrison	William Henry	Virginia	1773–1841	Whig	1841
10	Tyler	John	Virginia	1790–1862	Whig	1841–1845
11	Polk	James Knox	North Carolina	1795–1849	Democratic	1845–1849
12	Taylor	Zachary	Virginia	1784–1850	Whig	1849–1850
13	Fillmore	Millard	New York	1800–1874	Whig	1850–1853
14	Pierce	Franklin	New Hampshire	1804–1869	Democratic	1853–1857
15	Buchanan	James	Pennsylvania	1791–1868	Democratic	1857–1861
16	Lincoln	Abraham	Kentucky	1809–1865	Republican	1861–1865
17	Johnson	Andrew	North Carolina	1808–1875	Union	1865–1869
18	Grant	Ulysses Simpson	Ohio	1822–1885	Republican	1869–1877
19	Hayes	Rutherford Birchard	Ohio	1822–1893	Republican	1877–1881
20	Garfield	James Abram	Ohio	1831–1881	Republican	1881
21	Arthur	Chester Alan	Vermont	1830–1886	Republican	1881–1885
22	Cleveland	Stephen Grover	New Jersey	1837–1908	Democratic	1885–1889
23	Harrison	Benjamin	Ohio	1833–1901	Republican	1889–1893
24	Cleveland	Grover	New Jersey	1837–1908	Democratic	1893–1897
25	Mckinley	William	Ohio	1843–1901	Republican	1897–1901
26	Roosevelt	Theodore	New York	1858–1919	Republican	1901–1909
27	Taft	William Howard	Ohio	1857–1930	Republican	1909–1913
28	Wilson	Thomas Woodrow	Virginia	1856–1924	Democratic	1913–1921
29	Harding	Warren Gamaliel	Ohio	1865–1923	Republican	1921–1923
30	Coolidge	Calvin	Vermont	1872–1933	Republican	1923–1929
31	Hoover	Herbert Clark	Iowa	1874–1964	Republican	1929–1933
32	Roosevelt	Franklin Delano	New York	1882–1945	Democratic	1933–1945
33	Truman	Harry S	Missouri	1884–1972	Democratic	1945–1953
34	Eisenhower	Dwight David	Texas	1890–1969	Republican	1953–1961
35	Kennedy	John Fitzgerald	Massachusetts	1917–1963	Democratic	1961–1963
36	Johnson	Lyndon Baines	Texas	1908–1973	Democratic	1963–1969
37	Nixon	Richard Milhous	California	1913–1995	Republican	1969–1974
38	Ford	Gerald Rudolph	Nebraska	1913–	Republican	1974–1977
39	Carter	James Earl	Georgia	1924–	Democratic	1977–1981
40	Reagan	Ronald Wilson	Illinois	1911–2004	Republican	1981–1989
41	Bush	George Herbert Walker	Massachusetts	1924–	Republican	1989–1993
42	Clinton	William Jefferson	Arkansas	1946–	Democratic	1993–2001
43	Bush	George Walker	Connecticut	1946–	Republican	2001–

Vice Presidents

Vice President		Birthplace	In office	Vice President to
Adams	John	Massachusetts	1789–1797	Washington
Jefferson	Thomas	Virginia	1797–1801	Adams
Burr	Aaron	New Jersey	1801–1805	Jefferson
Clinton	George	New York	1805–1812	Jefferson/Madison
Gerry	Elbridge	Massachusetts	1813–1814	Madison
Tompkins	Daniel D	New York	1817–1825	Monroe
Calhoun	John Caldwell	South Carolina	1825–1832	Adams/Jackson
Van Buren	Martin	New York	1833–1837	Jackson
Johnson	Richard Mentor	Kentucky	1837–1841	Van Buren
Tyler	John	Virginia	1841	Harrison
Dallas	George Mifflin	Pennsylvania	1845–1849	Polk
Fillmore	Millard	New York	1849–1850	Taylor
King	William Rufus De Vane	North Carolina	1853	Pierce
Breckinridge	John Cabell	Kentucky	1857–1861	Buchanan
Hamlin	Hannibal	Maine	1861–1865	Lincoln
Johnson	Andrew	North Carolina	1865	Lincoln
Colfax	Schuyler	New York	1869–1873	Grant

Vice President		Birthplace	In office	Vice President to
Wilson	Henry	New Hampshire	1873–1875	Grant
Wheeler	William A	New York	1877–1881	Hayes
Arthur	Chester A	Vermont	1881	Garfield
Hendricks	Thomas A	Ohio	1885	Arthur
Morton	Levi Parsons	Vermont	1889–1893	Harrison
Stevenson	Adlai E	Kentucky	1893–1897	Cleveland
Hobart	Garret A	New Jersey	1897–1899	McKinley
Roosevelt	Theodore	New York	1901	McKinley
Fairbanks	Charles Warren	Ohio	1905–1909	Roosevelt
Sherman	James Schoolcraft	New York	1909–1912	Taft
Marshall	Thomas R	Indiana	1913–1921	Wilson
Coolidge	Calvin	Vermont	1921–1923	Harding
Dawes	Charles Gates	Ohio	1925–1929	Coolidge
Curtis	Charles	Kansas	1929–1933	Hoover
Garner	John Nance	Texas	1933–1941	Roosevelt
Wallace	Henry Agard	Iowa	1941–1945	Roosevelt
Truman	Harry S	Missouri	1945	Roosevelt
Barkley	Alben W	Kentucky	1949–1953	Truman
Nixon	Richard Milhous	California	1953–1961	Eisenhower
Johnson	Lyndon Baines	Texas	1961–1963	Kennedy
Humphrey	Hubert H	South Dakota	1965–1969	Johnson
Agnew	Spiro T	Maryland	1969–1973	Nixon
Ford	Gerald Rudolph	Nebraska	1973–1974	Nixon
Rockefeller	Nelson Aldrich	Maine	1974–1977	Ford
Mondale	Walter F	Minnesota	1977–1981	Carter
Bush	George Herbert Walker	Massachusetts	1981–1989	Reagan
Quayle	J Danforth	Indiana	1989–1993	Bush, G H W
Gore	Albert	Washington DC	1993–2001	Clinton
Cheney	Richard B	Nebraska	2001	Bush, G W

Presidents and Vice Presidents: Miscellaneous Information

assassinated Lincoln, Garfield, McKinley, Kennedy.

attempts Jackson (Richard Lawrence 1835), Truman (Griselio Torresola and Oscar Collazo 1950), Ford (5 Sept 1975, Lynette 'Squeaky' Frome; 22 Sept 1975, Sarah Jane More), Reagan (John Hinckley) 1981.

bachelor James Buchanan.

bald Martin Van Buren and Dwight Eisenhower.

bath: got stuck in William Howard Taft.

born in a log cabin Andrew Jackson

broccoli: hated George Bush.

Camelot: nickname of John F Kennedy's regime.

China: first to visit Richard Nixon.

Clinton's cat: named Socks (belonged to daughter Chelsea).

Confederate states: president Jefferson Davis.

cried on television during campaign Edmund Muskie.

Declaration of Independence: drafted by Thomas Jefferson.

Democrat-turned-Republican: first Ronald Reagan.

Democratic Party Headquarters Tammany Hall, New York.

Democratic Party symbol Donkey.

Democratic split during Vietnam War Hawks and Doves.

died in office W Harding, W Harrison, F D Roosevelt, Z Taylor.

divorced: first Ronald Reagan.

duel: killed opponent in Andrew Jackson killed Charles Dickinson in a pistol duel, 30 May 1806.

elected for four terms F D Roosevelt.

elected unanimously by Electoral College George Washington.

elected with one vote against James Monroe.

ex-director of the CIA George Bush.

father and son John Adams and his son John Quincy Adams.

father was UK ambassador John F Kennedy's father Joseph.

fireside chats: radio broadcasts F D Roosevelt.

four freedoms Speech, worship, freedom from fear and want. Roosevelt's basis for UN Charter, San Francisco 1945.

Fourteen Points Woodrow Wilson.

Garfield: assassinated by Charles Guiteau 1881.

Gettysburg Address Lincoln's speech of 1863.

grandfather and grandson William Harrison and Benjamin Harrison.

Grand Old Party (GOP) Republican party nickname.

Great Triumvirate of statesmen John Calhoun, Henry Clay, Daniel Webster.

hospital: first born in Jimmy Carter.

illegitimate child: accused of having Stephen Grover Cleveland.

impeachment: two In 1868 Andrew Johnson was cleared of breaching Tenure of Office Act. Senate vote fell one short of two-thirds majority. In 1999 Bill Clinton was cleared of high crimes and misdemeanours by the Senate vote on both Articles I and II.

imprisoned by British Andrew Jackson (during War of Independence).

Jefferson: holiday retreat Poplar Row.

Kennedy's attorney general Robert Kennedy, his brother.

Kennedy: assassinated by Lee Harvey Oswald, 1963 (shot by Jack Ruby).

kitchen cabinet Andrew Jackson's unofficial advisers.

knighted by Britain Eisenhower.

Lincoln assassinated by　John Wilkes Booth (an actor), 1865. Samuel Mudd jailed for setting Booth's leg. Lincoln died in Peterson House, Washington DC.

longest term　F D Roosevelt, 12 years.

male model: former　Gerald Ford.

McKinley assassinated by　Leon Czolgosz, 1901.

minister to Great Britain: first　John Adams.

Monroe Doctrine: allegedly drafted by　John Quincy Adams.

Monroe: lived　Oak Hill.

New Deal　F D Roosevelt's 1930s recovery plan.

newspaper publisher　Warren Harding – Marion *Star*.

nicknames　J Carter – Hot Shot & Toadsy; G Bush – Wimp; Andrew Jackson – Old Hickory; Clinton – Comeback Kid.

Nobel Peace Prize　Theodore Roosevelt, 1906; Woodrow Wilson, 1919.

not elected as President　Gerald Ford (was also not elected Vice President).

occupation: most common　lawyer.

oldest to take office　Ronald Reagan, aged 69.

pneumonia: died of　William Henry Harrison.

President for the day　David Atchison – Zachary Taylor would not be sworn in on a Sunday.

prison; presidential candidate ran from　Eugene Debs in 1912.

Quakers　Herbert Hoover, Richard Nixon.

qualifications required　native born,14 years' residence, 35 years old.

re-elected: after losing office　Stephen Grover Cleveland.

Republican Party symbol　elephant.

residence　White House.

resigned　Richard Nixon.

resigned as Vice President　Spiro Agnew; income tax evasion charge.

Roman Catholic: first　John F Kennedy.

Roughriders　Roosevelt second in command to Col. Leonard Wood.

Secretary of State　Eisenhower's – John Foster Dulles; Nixon's – Henry Kissinger; Carter's – Cyrus Robert Vance.

shirt advertisement: appeared in　Ronald Reagan.

shortest term　William Henry Harrison, about a month.

slogans: presidential　Full Dinner Pail – McKinley; Great Society – Lyndon Johnson; New Deal – F D Roosevelt; New Frontier – Kennedy.

slogans: other　'Would you buy a used car from this man?' – said by anti-Nixon protesters. 'The buck stops here' – Truman. 'No taxation without representation' – during dispute with Britain over taxation.

State of the Union　presidential speech given annually in January.

stood against　Bush – Michael Dukakis; Clinton – Ross Perot and George Bush; Hayes – Samuel Tilde; Hoover – Al Smith; Truman – Thomas Dewey.

terms limitation　two, under the 22nd Amendment to Constitution.

Vice President: born James Colbath　Henry Wilson.

Crédit Mobilier scandal　Schuyler Colfax.

Confederate general　John Cabell Breckinridge.

killed Alexander Hamilton　Aaron Burr.

letters from London　George Mifflin Dallas.

lives at　Admiralty Building, Washington.

Nobel Peace Prize 1925　Charles Dawes.

treason trial　Aaron Burr.

wrote no. 1 hit single　Charles Dawes ('It's all in the Game').

vice-presidential candidate: first female　Geraldine Ferraro in 1984.

Virginia plan　James Madison.

Washington: lived　Mount Vernon.

Watergate scandal　burglary of Democratic HQ in Washington on 17 June 1972.

White House: architect　James Hoban.

White House: first occupier　John Adams.

wives of presidents　George Washington – Martha Custis; Abraham Lincoln – Mary Todd; F D Roosevelt – Eleanor Roosevelt; J F Kennedy – Jacqueline Bouvier; Ronald Reagan – Nancy Davis; George Bush – Barbara Pierce; Bill Clinton – Hilary Rodham.

youngest elected president　John F Kennedy.

youngest president　Theodore Roosevelt (took office following assassination of McKinley).

States

State	Nickname	Motto	State tree	State bird	State flower	State capital	Zip code
Alabama (Ala.)	Cotton / Yellowhammer / Heart of Dixie	We dare defend our rights	southern pine	yellowhammer	camellia	Montgomery	AL
Alaska (Alas.)	Last Frontier / Land of the Midnight Sun	North to the future	Sitka spruce	willow ptarmigan	forget-me-not	Juneau	AK
Arizona (Ariz.)	Grand Canyon / Apache	God enriches	paloverde	cactus wren	saguaro cactus blossom	Phoenix	AZ
Arkansas (Ark.)	Land of Opportunity / Bear / Wonder	The people rule	pine	mockingbird	apple blossom	Little Rock	AR
California (Cal.)	Golden	I have found it	Californian redwood	Californian valley quail	golden poppy	Sacramento	CA
Colorado (Colo.)	Centennial	Nothing without providence	Colorado blue spruce	lark bunting	Rocky Mountain columbine	Denver	CO
Connecticut (Conn.)	Constitution / Nutmeg	He who transplanted still sustains	white oak	American robin	mountain laurel	Hartford	CT
District of Columbia	DC	Justice for all	scarlet oak	woodthrush	American beauty rose		DC
Delaware (Del.)	First / Diamond	Liberty and independence	American holly	blue hen chicken	peach blossom	Dover	DE
Florida (Fla.)	Sunshine / Peninsular	In God we trust	sabal palm	mockingbird	orange blossom	Tallahassee	FL
Georgia (Ga.)	Empire State of the South / Peach	Wisdom, justice and moderation	live oak	brown thrasher	Cherokee rose	Atlanta	GA
Hawaii (Hi.)	Aloha	The life of the land is perpetuated in righteousness	kukui (candlenut)	nene (Hawaiian goose)	hibiscus	Honolulu	HI
Idaho (Ida.)	Gem / Gem of the Mountains	Let it be perpetual	western white pine	mountain bluebird	syringa	Boise	ID
Illinois (Ill.)	Prairie / Land of Lincoln	State sovereignty – national union	white oak	cardinal	native violet	Springfield	IL
Indiana (Ind.)	Hoosier	Crossroads of America	tulip tree (yellow poplar) / oak	cardinal	peony	Indianapolis	IN
Iowa (Ia.)	Hawkeye / Corn	Our liberties we prize and our rights we will maintain	oak	eastern goldfinch	wild rose	Des Moines	IA
Kansas (Kan.)	Sunflower / Jayhawker	To the stars through difficulties	cottonwood	western meadowlark	native sunflower	Topeka	KS
Kentucky (Ky.)	Blue Grass	United we stand, divided we fall	tulip tree (yellow poplar)	cardinal	goldenrod	Frankfort	KY

UNITED STATES

State	Nickname	Motto	State tree	State bird	State flower	State capital	Zip code
Louisiana (La.)	Pelican Creole Sugar Bayou	Union, justice and confidence	bald cypress	eastern brown pelican	magnolia	Baton Rouge	LA
Maine (Me.)	Pine Tree	I direct	eastern white pine	chickadee	white pine cone and tassel	Augusta	ME
Maryland (Md.)	Free Old Line	Manly deeds, womanly words	white oak	Baltimore oriole	black-eyed Susan	Annapolis	MD
Massachusetts (Mass.)	Bay Old Colony	By the sword we seek peace, but peace only under liberty	American elm	chickadee	mayflower (trailing arbutus)	Boston	MA
Michigan (Mich.)	Wolverine Water Wonderland	If you seek a pleasant peninsula, look about you	white pine	robin	apple blossom	Lansing	MI
Minnesota (Minn.)	North Star Gopher Land of 10,000 Lakes Land of Sky-Blue Waters	The North Star	red, or Norway pine	loon	pink and white lady's slipper	St Paul	MN
Mississippi (Miss.)	Magnolia	By valor and arms	magnolia	mockingbird	magnolia	Jackson	MS
Missouri (Mo.)	Show Me	The welfare of the people shall be the supreme law	dogwood	bluebird	hawthorn	Jefferson City	MO
Montana (Mont.)	Treasure Big Sky Country	Gold and silver	Ponderosa pine	western meadowlark	bitterroot	Helena	MT
Nebraska (Nebr.)	Cornhusker Beef Tree Planters	Equality before the law	cottonwood	western meadowlark	goldenrod	Lincoln	NB
Nevada (Nev.)	Sagebrush Silver Battle Born	All for our country	single-leaf piñon	mountain bluebird	sagebrush	Carson City	NV
New Hampshire (NH)	Granite	Live free or die	white birch	purple finch	purple lilac	Concord	NH
New Jersey (NJ)	Garden	Liberty and prosperity	red oak	eastern goldfinch	purple violet	Trenton	NJ
New Mexico (N. Mex)	Land of Enchantment Sunshine	It grows as it goes	piñon (nut pine)	roadrunner	yucca flower	Santa Fe	NM
New York (NY)	Empire	Ever upward	sugar maple	bluebird	rose	Albany	NY
North Carolina (NC)	Tar Heel Old North	To be rather than to seem	longleaf pine	cardinal	dogwood	Raleigh	NC
North Dakota (N. Dak.)	Flickertail Sioux	Liberty and union, now and forever, one and inseparable	American elm	western meadowlark	wild prairie rose	Bismarck	ND

UNITED STATES

State	Nickname	Motto	State tree	State bird	State flower	State capital	Zip code
Ohio (Oh.)	Buckeye	With God, all things are possible	buckeye	cardinal	scarlet carnation	Columbus	OH
Oklahoma (Okla.)	Sooner	Labor conquers all things	redbud	scissor-tailed flycatcher	mistletoe	Oklahoma City	OK
Oregon (Oreg.)	Beaver	The Union	Douglas fir	western meadowlark	Oregon grape	Salem	OR
Pennsylvania (Pa.)	Keystone	Virtue, liberty, and independence	hemlock	ruffed grouse	mountain laurel	Harrisburg	PA
Rhode Island (RI)	Little Rhody Plantation	Hope	red maple	Rhode Island red	violet	Providence	RI
South Carolina (SC)	Palmetto	Prepared in mind and resources / While I breathe, I hope	cabbage palmetto	Carolina wren	yellow jessamine	Columbia	SC
South Dakota (S. Dak.)	Coyote Sunshine	Under God the people rule	Black Hills spruce	ring-necked pheasant	pasqueflower	Pierre	SD
Tennessee (Tenn.)	Volunteer	Agriculture and commerce	tulip poplar	mockingbird	iris	Nashville	TN
Texas (Tex.)	Lone Star	Friendship	pecan	mockingbird	bluebonnet	Austin	TX
Utah (Ut.)	Beehive	Industry	blue spruce	sea gull	sego lily	Salt Lake City	UT
Vermont (Vt.)	Green Mountain	Freedom and unity	sugar maple	hermit thrush	red clover	Montpelier	VT
Virginia (Va.)	Mother of Presidents Old Dominion Cavalier	Thus always to tyrants	flowering dogwood	cardinal	dogwood	Richmond	VA
Washington (Wash.)	Evergreen Chinook	By and by	western hemlock	willow goldfinch	western rhododendron	Olympia	WA
West Virginia (W. Va.)	Mountain Panhandle	Mountaineers are always free	sugar maple	cardinal	big rhododendron	Charleston	WV
Wisconsin (Wis.)	Badger America's Dairyland	Forward	sugar maple	robin	wood violet	Madison	WI
Wyoming (Wyo.)	Equality	Equal rights	cottonwood	meadowlark	Indian paintbrush	Cheyenne	WY

States: Bordered by

Alabama Tennessee, Georgia, Mississippi, Florida.
Alaska None.
Arizona California, Nevada, Utah, New Mexico, Colorado.
Arkansas Tennessee, Mississippi, Louisiana, Missouri, Texas, Oklahoma.
California Arizona, Nevada, Oregon.
Colorado Utah, Wyoming, Arizona, New Mexico, Nebraska, Kansas, Oklahoma.
Connecticut Massachusetts, Rhode Island, New York.
Delaware Pennsylvania, New Jersey, Maryland.
Florida Georgia, Alabama.
Georgia South Carolina, Florida, Alabama, Tennessee, North Carolina.
Hawaii None.
Idaho Utah, Nevada, Washington, Wyoming, Oregon, Montana.
Illinois Kentucky, Missouri, Indiana, Wisconsin, Iowa.
Indiana Illinois, Michigan, Ohio, Kentucky.
Iowa Nebraska, Missouri, Illinois, Wisconsin, Minnesota, South Dakota.
Kansas Colorado, Oklahoma, Missouri, Nebraska.
Kentucky Tennessee, Illinois, Virginia, West Virginia, Missouri, Ohio, Indiana.
Louisiana Mississippi, Arkansas, Texas.

Maine New Hampshire.
Maryland Pennsylvania, Virginia, West Virginia, Delaware.
Massachusetts Vermont, New Hampshire, Rhode Island, New York, Connecticut.
Michigan Indiana, Ohio, Wisconsin.
Minnesota North Dakota, South Dakota, Iowa, Wisconsin.
Mississippi Louisiana, Arkansas, Tennessee, Alabama.
Missouri Iowa, Illinois, Kentucky, Tennessee, Arkansas, Oklahoma, Kansas, Nebraska.
Montana Idaho, Wyoming, North Dakota, South Dakota.
Nebraska Colorado, Wyoming, Iowa, South Dakota, Kansas, Missouri.
Nevada California, Utah, Arizona, Idaho, Oregon.
New Hampshire Maine, Massachusetts, Vermont.
New Jersey New York, Pennsylvania, Delaware.
New Mexico Colorado, Oklahoma, Texas, Arizona, Utah.
New York Vermont, Massachusetts, Connecticut, New Jersey, Pennsylvania.
North Carolina South Carolina, Virginia, Georgia, Tennessee.
North Dakota Montana, Minnesota, South Dakota.
Ohio Michigan, Indiana, Kentucky, West Virginia, Pennsylvania.

Oklahoma Texas, Arkansas, Kansas, Missouri, New Mexico, Colorado.
Oregon Washington, Idaho, California, Nevada.
Pennsylvania Delaware, New Jersey, New York, Maryland, West Virginia, Ohio.
Rhode Island Connecticut, Massachusetts.
South Carolina North Carolina, Georgia.
South Dakota North Dakota, Minnesota, Iowa, Nebraska, Wyoming, Montana.
Tennessee Kentucky, Alabama, Mississippi, Missouri, Arkansas, Georgia, Virginia, North Carolina.
Texas Louisiana, New Mexico, Oklahoma, Arkansas.
Utah Colorado, New Mexico, Arizona, Nevada, Wyoming, Idaho.
Vermont Massachusetts, New York, New Hampshire.
Virginia Maryland, West Virginia, Kentucky, Tennessee, North Carolina.
Washington Oregon, Idaho.
West Virginia Virginia, Kentucky, Ohio, Pennsylvania, Maryland.
Wisconsin Illinois, Michigan, Minnesota, Iowa.
Wyoming Montana, South Dakota, Nebraska, Colorado, Utah, Idaho.

Statistical Information

Order of Admission to the Union

1st	Delaware (1787)	18th	Louisiana (1812)	35th	West Virginia (1863)
2nd	Pennsylvania (1787)	19th	Indiana (1816)	36th	Nevada (1864)
3rd	New Jersey (1787)	20th	Mississippi (1817)	37th	Nebraska (1867)
4th	Georgia (1788)	21st	Illinois (1818)	38th	Colorado (1876)
5th	Connecticut (1788)	22nd	Alabama (1819)	39th	North Dakota (1889)
6th	Massachusetts (1788)	23rd	Maine (1820)	40th	South Dakota (1889)
7th	Maryland (1788)	24th	Missouri (1821)	41st	Montana (1889)
8th	South Carolina (1788)	25th	Arkansas (1836)	42nd	Washington (1889)
9th	New Hampshire (1788)	26th	Michigan (1837)	43rd	Idaho (1890)
10th	Virginia (1788)	27th	Florida (1845)	44th	Wyoming (1890)
11th	New York (1788)	28th	Texas (1845)	45th	Utah (1896)
12th	North Carolina (1789)	29th	Iowa (1846)	46th	Oklahoma (1907)
13th	Rhode Island (1790)	30th	Wisconsin (1848)	47th	New Mexico (1912)
14th	Vermont (1791)	31st	California (1850)	48th	Arizona (1912)
15th	Kentucky (1792)	32nd	Minnesota (1858)	49th	Alaska (1959)
16th	Tennessee (1796)	33rd	Oregon (1859)	50th	Hawaii (1959)
17th	Ohio (1803)	34th	Kansas (1861)		

Largest: by size

1st	Alaska	18th	North Dakota	35th	Tennessee
2nd	Texas	19th	Oklahoma	36th	Virginia
3rd	California	20th	Missouri	37th	Kentucky
4th	Montana	21st	Washington	38th	Indiana
5th	New Mexico	22nd	Wisconsin	39th	Maine
6th	Arizona	23rd	Georgia	40th	South Carolina
7th	Nevada	24th	Florida	41st	West Virginia
8th	Colorado	25th	Illinois	42nd	Maryland
9th	Wyoming	26th	Iowa	43rd	Vermont
10th	Michigan	27th	Arkansas	44th	New Hampshire
11th	Oregon	28th	New York	45th	Massachusetts
12th	Minnesota	29th	North Carolina	46th	Hawaii
13th	Utah	30th	Alabama	47th	New Jersey
14th	Idaho	31st	Louisiana	48th	Connecticut
15th	Kansas	32nd	Mississippi	49th	Delaware
16th	Nebraska	33rd	Pennsylvania	50th	Rhode Island
17th	South Dakota	34th	Ohio		

Largest: by population

1st	California	18th	Maryland	35th	New Mexico
2nd	New York	19th	Washington	36th	Utah
3rd	Texas	20th	Louisiana	37th	Nebraska
4th	Florida	21st	Minnesota	38th	Maine
5th	Pennsylvania	22nd	Alabama	39th	Hawaii
6th	Illinois	23rd	Kentucky	40th	New Hampshire
7th	Ohio	24th	Arizona	41st	Nevada
8th	Michigan	25th	South Carolina	42nd	Idaho
9th	New Jersey	26th	Colorado	43rd	Rhode Island
10th	North Carolina	27th	Oklahoma	44th	Montana
11th	Georgia	28th	Connecticut	45th	South Dakota
12th	Virginia	29th	Iowa	46th	North Dakota
13th	Massachusetts	30th	Oregon	47th	Delaware
14th	Indiana	31st	Mississippi	48th	Alaska
15th	Missouri	32nd	Kansas	49th	Vermont
16th	Tennessee	33rd	Arkansas	50th	Wyoming
17th	Wisconsin	34th	West Virginia		

UNITED STATES

General Information

Alamo: killed in siege of 1836 Davy Crockett and Jim Bowie. **site of siege** Franciscan Mission Hall in San Antonio, Texas. **dates of siege** 23 February to 6 March 1836. **Mexican leader** Santa Anna. **meaning of** poplar (Spanish) or cottonwood tree.

Alaska: purchased from Russia, 1867; known as Seward's Folly.

America: named after Amerigo Vespucci.

anti-communist witch hunts 1950s Senator Joseph McCarthy.

Back to Africa Movement leader Marcus Garvey.

Bay Area Rapid Transit (BART) San Francisco.

Black Muslims: developed movement Elijah Muhammad 1934.

borders with eight other states Missouri and Tennessee.

Boss Tweed Corrupt leader of Tammany Hall Democrats, New York.

Boston Mountains Arkansas and Oklahoma (Ozarks).

Boston Tea Party: date of 16 December 1773. **reason for destruction of tea** protest against British

tea tax. **owners of tea** British East India Company. **British retaliation** Intolerable Acts (shut down port, pending payment).

Bretton Woods Conference, NH, 1944: formed IMF and International Bank for Reconstruction.

bus boycott of Montgomery, Alabama: caused by Rosa Parks refusing to give up seat in Dec. 1955.

California: largest city Los Angeles.

Californian gold rush: first prospector James Wilson Marshall, 1848.

first major strike J A Sutter, a Swiss settler, 1849.

capital of America before Washington DC Philadelphia, 1783–9.

Central Park: designers Frederick Law Olmstead and Calvert Vaux.

child: first born of English parents Virginia Dare.

civil rights demo: troops called in Selma, Alabama,1956; Autherine Lucy expelled.

Civil War: dates of outbreak and surrender 15 April 1861 to 9 April 1865. **started: where** Fort Sumter in Charleston Harbour, SC, April 1861. **Lee surrender to Grant: where** Appomattox

Court House, Virginia, 9 April 1865. **official ending: on surrender of** Gen. Richard Taylor, 4 May 1865. **first state to secede from Union** South Carolina, December 1860. **second state to secede** Mississippi, January 1861. **antebellum: meaning of** period before the war. **battle above the clouds** Lookout Mountain, Chattanooga, Tennessee. **Confederate capital** Richmond, Virginia.

Colin Powell: autobiography *My American Journey.*

commonwealths: officially called Massachusetts, Kentucky and Virginia.

commonwealth: self-styled Pennsylvania.

Confederate states: antebellum Alabama, Florida, Georgia, Louisiana, Mississippi, South Carolina, Texas. **four joined at outbreak of Civil War** Arkansas, North Carolina, Tennessee, Virginia. **President** Jefferson Davis.

Congress: first woman Jeanette Rankin, 1916.

Constitution of the USA: ratified by New Hampshire's ninth vote, 1788.

constitutional amendments Abolition of Slavery, 13th. Presidential Terms, 22nd. Prohibition, 18th. Votes for Blacks, 15th. Votes for Women, 19th.

coterminous states: high and low point Mt Whitney and Death Valley, both in California.

Coxey's Army unemployed march to Washington DC, 1894.

Dakota: named after Sioux Indian tribe.

Declaration of Independence 4 July 1776.

Delaware: three counties New Castle, Kent, Sussex.

Delaware: largest city Wilmington.

District of Columbia: ceded by Maryland, 1791.

Emancipation proclamation freeing of slaves during Civil War.

Essex Junto: leader Timothy Pickering. **term coined by** John Hancock, 1778. **supported** Alexander Hamilton. **based** Massachusetts.

first state to join Union Delaware, 7 Dec. 1787.

Florida: largest city Jacksonville.

four corners touching Utah, Colorado, New Mexico, Arizona.

Gadsden purchase of land for USA in 1853 land bought from Mexico, now New Mexico and Arizona.

Georgia: marched through during Civil War General Sherman.

gold on land caused rush 1849 John Sutter.

good neighbour policy 1928 Latin American policy of F D Roosevelt.

Grape Workers Union leader led boycott Cesar Chavez, 1968.

Hartford Convention of 1814–15 began demise of Federalist Party.

Hawaii: European discoverer Captain James Cook, 1778.

Hawaii: former name Sandwich Islands.

Haymarket Massacre of 1886 police fire on crowd at May Day Rally in Chicago.

Homestead Act 1862: Lincoln's aim to provide land free to settlers to cultivate.

Honolulu: island situated Oahu.

honorary citizenship Winston Churchill.

Indian chief surrendered to General Miles Geronimo.

Intolerable Acts enforced embargo of Boston until compensation paid.

Irangate scandal: USA accused of arms for Iran in return for funds to Nicaraguan Contras. **famous testimony** Oliver North.

Ivy League: nickname for The top eight universities and colleges of USA. **members** Harvard (1636), Yale (1701), Pennsylvania (1740), Princeton (1746), Columbia (1754), Brown (1764), Dartmouth (1769), Cornell (1853).

Kent State University, Ohio, 1970 National Guard shot dead four students during anti-war demo.

Ku Klux Klan: formed Pulaski, Tennessee, 1866.

Lend-lease Pact: March 1941 Roosevelt signed with Britain for WW2 aid.

Lewis and Clark expedition 1804–6 exploration of western America.

Lewis and Clark: state governors of Louisiana and Missouri Territory respectively.

Los Angeles: name when founded, 1781 the Town of the Queen of the Angels.

Louisiana purchase Mississippi valley bought from France 1803; 828,000 sq miles cost $15 million!

Louisiana: largest city New Orleans.

Louisiana: named in honour of Louis XIV.

Mammoth Cave Kentucky.

Manhattan Island: bought from Indian tribes for trinkets worth 60 guilders.

Manhattan Island: purchaser Peter Minuit.

mapped America Samuel de Champlain, 1605; John Smith, 1614.

Maryland named in honour of wife of Charles I: Henrietta Maria.

Mason–Dixon line: boundaries Pennsylvania–Maryland; border of North and South.

Mason–Dixon line: why drawn disputes of Penn and Calvert families in 1760s.

Mayflower: **sister ship** *Speedwell;* deemed unseaworthy.

Mexican ceded states of 1848 Texas, New Mexico, California.

Mexican ceded states: clerk responsible Nicholas Trist.

Michigan: two land masses joined by Mackinac Bridge (Big Mac), built 1957.

Michigan: borders on Great Lakes all except Ontario.

Mississippi University: first black to enter James Meredith.

Montana: name means mountain (Spanish).

Mormon Church: founded at Fayette, New York, in 1830.

mountain: highest in America Mount McKinley, Alaska, 20,320' (6,194 m).

Nat Turner insurrection 1831 slave uprising in Virginia.

Naval Academy Annapolis, Maryland.

Nebraska: name means flat water.

Nevada: name means snow-clad (Spanish).

New England: named by John Smith, 1614. **six states** Connecticut, Maine, Massachusetts, New Hampshire, Rhode Island, Vermont.

New Hampshire: named after English county of Hampshire, 1629.

New Orleans: same parallel as Cairo, Delhi, Shanghai.

New York named in honour of duke of York, later James II.

New York City: five boroughs Queens, Bronx, Manhattan, Brooklyn, Staten Island.

New York State: capital's former name Fort Orange, 1624; became Albany.

New York: political differences   upstate is Conservative, downstate is Liberal.

North Dakota: largest city   Fargo.

Oklahoma: name means   red people.

oldest American town   St Augustine, Florida, 1565.

Pilgrim Fathers: ship   *Mayflower*. **landed** Provincetown in Massachusetts, November 1620. **first to land**   John Alden. **established** Plymouth Colony. **Indian interpreter**   Squanto. **Indian welcomed them**   Samoset, a Pemaquid from Maine.

Portsmouth, New Hampshire   treaty ended Russo-Japanese war, 1905.

presidential primary: earliest   New Hampshire.

rectangular-shaped states   Wyoming and Colorado.

Rhode Island: official name   The State of Rhode Island and Providence Plantations.

Richmond County: named in honour of   Charles Lennox, duke of Richmond, son of Charles II.

Russia: closest point to   Diomede Islands, Bering Strait.

San Francisco meeting of United Nations   April 1945.

school integration: Federal troops enforced   Little Rock, Arkansas, 1957.

Sea Islands: sub-tropical islands of   South Carolina.

senator: first black   Edward Brooke.

Seneca Falls Convention, 1848   Women's Rights' Movement began.

size of USA doubled by   Louisiana purchase.

slave abolitionist leader   Harriet Tubman, former slave.

slavery: abolished   1863. **escape network to the North**   underground railroad. **last state to abolish** Mississippi.

Spindletop oil well, Texas   blew 1901.

Tammany Hall (New York)   byword for municipal corruption.

Tarpon Springs, Florida   centre for Greek Orthodox religion and sponge industry.

Teapot Dome Affair, aka Elk Hills Scandal   Sec. of Interior Albert Fall jailed for corruption.

territories: overseas   American Virgin Islands, Commonwealth of Puerto Rico, Guam, Samoa.

terrorism: executed 1927 but pardoned 1977 Sacco and Vanzetti.

Texas: annexed by America, in   1845. **former capital**   Houston, until 1839, then Austin. **largest city** Houston.

Townshend Acts 1767   British taxes that sparked revolt.

Vietnam: secret documents   Pentagon papers showed USA involvement. **secret documents revealed by**   Daniel Ellsberg, 1971.

Virginia: named in honour of   Elizabeth I.

War of Independence: started   Lexington, Massachusetts, April 1775. **ended**   Yorktown, Virginia, October 1781. **rode to warn of British approach**   Paul Revere. **traitor for British** Benedict Arnold. **American general**   George Washington. **British general**   Charles Cornwallis. **Washington's ally**   Marquis of Lafayette.

Washington: capital since   1789.

Watts riots   Los Angeles, 1965.

witchcraft trials   Salem, Massachusetts, 1692 (20 executed).

wobblies   Industrial Workers of the World, trade union.

Yellowstone National Park: three states   Wyoming, Montana, Idaho.

NB More detailed information pertaining to rivers, mountains and other geographical features of the USA can be found in the Geography section.

U
N
I
T
E
D

S
T
A
T
E
S

Miscellaneous Items of Interest

Units of Length

link (surveying)	7.92 inches (100th part of chain)
span	9 inches (approx span of hand)
hand	4 inches (horse measurement)
cubit	18 inches (biblical measurement)
pace	30 inches (from the stride)
cable	120 fathoms (720 feet; a fathom equals six feet)
nautical mile	6,080 feet (1 sec of arc at Equator) (now 1,852 metres)

Paper Sizes

A0	841 x 1189 mm	$(33\frac{1}{8} \times 46\frac{3}{4}$ inches)
A1	594 x 841 mm	$(23\frac{3}{8} \times 33\frac{1}{8}$ inches)
A2	420 x 594 mm	$(16\frac{1}{2} \times 23\frac{3}{8}$ inches)
A3	297 x 420 mm	$(11\frac{3}{4} \times 16\frac{1}{2}$ inches)
A4	210 x 297 mm	$(8\frac{1}{4} \times 11\frac{3}{4}$ inches)
A5	148 x 210 mm	$(5\frac{7}{8} \times 8\frac{1}{4}$ inches)
A6	105 x 148 mm	$(4\frac{1}{8} \times 5\frac{7}{8}$ inches)
A7	74 x 105 mm	$(2\frac{15}{16} \times 4\frac{1}{8}$ inches)
A8	52 x 74 mm	$(2\frac{1}{16} \times 2\frac{15}{16}$ inches)
A9	37 x 52 mm	$(1\frac{15}{32} \times 2\frac{1}{16}$ inches)
A10	26 x 37 mm	$(1\frac{1}{32} \times 1\frac{15}{32}$ inches)
Elephant	584 x 711 mm	$(23 \times 28$ inches)

Book Sizes

Crown Quarto	246 × 189 mm
Crown Octavo	186 × 123 mm
Demy Quarto	276 × 219 mm
Demy Octavo	216 × 138 mm
Royal Quarto	312 × 237 mm
Royal Octavo	234 × 156 mm

Morse Code

A dot dash	**H** dot dot dot dot	**O** dash dash dash	**V** dot dot dot dash
B dash dot dot dot	**I** dot dot	**P** dot dash dash dot	**W** dot dash dash
C dash dot dash dot	**J** dot dash dash dash	**Q** dash dash dot dash	**X** dash dot dot dash
D dash dot dot	**K** dash dot dash	**R** dot dash dot	**Y** dash dot dash dash
E dot	**L** dot dash dot dot	**S** dot dot dot	**Z** dash dash dot dot
F dot dot dash dot	**M** dash dash	**T** dash	
G dash dash dot	**N** dash dot	**U** dot dot dash	

Mnemonics

Types of cedars Atlas – Ascending branches, deodar – drooping branches, Lebanon – level branches.

Can Queen Victoria eat cold apple pie? The seven hills of Rome: Capitoline, Quirinal, Viminal, Esquiline, Caelian, Aventine, Palatine.

Did Mary ever visit Brighton Beach? Order of Nobility: Duke, Marquess, Earl, Viscount, Baron, Baronet.

Bless my dear Aunt Sally Order of operations in algebraic expressions: Brackets, Multiply, Divide, Add, Subtract.

BROM 4689 (Duke of Marlborough's Telephone No.) Marlborough's battles: Blenheim (1704), Ramilies (1706), Oudenarde (1708), Malplaquet (1709).

Men very easily make jugs serve useful nocturnal purposes Planets from the sun: Mercury, Venus, Earth, Mars, Jupiter, Saturn, Uranus, Neptune, Pluto.

Spring forward, fall back Mnemonic to remember whether to put clock forward or back.

Virgins are rare Ohm's Law: Volts = Amps × Resistance.

How I want a drink alcoholic of course after the heavy chapters involving quantum mechanics Mnemonic for remembering pi to 14 places: 3.14159265358979.

No plan like yours to study history wisely British ruling houses: Norman, Plantagenet, Lancaster, York, Tudor, Stuart, Hanover, Windsor

Richard of York gave battle in vain Rainbow colours in order: red, orange, yellow, green, blue, indigo, violet

NB This last little section on mnemonics is a reminder in itself that a sound general knowledge base can only be achieved if facts are committed to memory. There is no shortcut to success in the quiz world; of course, a keen interest taken in things going on around you is desirable, as is a basic level of intelligence, but given that most people share those basic requirements then the secret of success is the amount of data consumed and the way that data is processed. The rate at which information is consumed varies depending on the level of commitment of the reader, but the way that information is stored can be the vital edge required to recall that seemingly long-forgotten nugget or that either/or situation so often encountered by quiz buffs. Mnemonics are an invaluable aid to quiz players, and should be used in some form or other when memorising lists. It does not matter how silly, rude, outlandish or downright inarticulate the mnemonic is, all that matters is that it works.

Colours

alabaster	White	elephant	Grey	olive	Greyish-Green
amaranth	Purple	emerald	Green	or	Gold
amber	Yellow	fallow	Yellow	peridot	Green (yellowish-green)
argent	Silver	fawn	Yellowish-Brown		
ash	Pale Grey	flame	Orangey-Red	pillar-box	Bright Red
auburn	Reddish-Brown	foxy	Reddish-Brown	plum	Reddish-Purple
aureate	Golden	gamboge	Yellow	primrose	Pale Yellow
azure	Sky Blue	gentian	Violet	puce	Purple-Brown
bamboo	Yellowish-Brown	gridelin	Grey-Violet	russet	Reddish-Brown
bay	Reddish-Brown	grizzly	Grey	rust	Reddish-Brown
bice	Blue	gules	Red	sable	Black
bistre	Brown	hazel	Reddish-Brown	saffron	Orange-Yellow
bronze	Yellowish-Brown	heliotrope	Mauve (light purple)	sandy	Yellowish-Red
brunette	Dark Brown			sanguine	Blood Red
buff	Pale Yellow	honey	Yellow	sapphire	Blue
cardinal	Red (scarlet)	indigo	Violet Blue	scarlet	Bright Red tinged with Orange
carmine	Red (crimson)	ivory	Creamy-White		
carnation	Rosy Pink	jonquil	Yellow		
celandine	Yellow	jupiter	Blue	sepia	Reddish-Brown
cerise	Red	khaki	Brownish-Yellow	sienna	Yellowish-Brown
cerulean	Blue	lake	Crimson	solferino	Crimson
chestnut	Reddish-Brown	lapis lazuli	Blue	sorrel	Reddish-Brown
chocolate	Brown	lavender	Pale Blue (with a trace of red)	straw	Pale Yellow
chrome	Yellow			tan	Yellowish-Brown
cinereous	Ash-Grey	lilac	Pinkish-Violet	teak	Reddish-Brown
cinnabar	Vermilion	lily	White	teal	Greenish-Blue
cinnamon	Yellowish-Brown	livid	Bluish-Purple	topaz	Yellow
citrine	Lemon Yellow	magenta	Mauve (mauvish-crimson)	turquoise	Greenish-Blue
cobalt	Blue			ultramarine	Blue
cochineal	Scarlet	malachite	Green	umber	Reddish-Brown
cornelian	Reddish-White	maroon	Brownish-Crimson	verd-antique	Green
cornflour	Blue	mazarine	Blue	vermilion	Red
crimson	Purplish-Red	moon	White	violet	Bluish-Purple
damask	Pinkish-Red	murrey	Purplish-Red	viridescent	Green
duck-egg	Blue	nacarat	Orangey-Red	xanthin	Yellow
dun	Greyish-Brown	ochre	Yellow (light browny yellow)		
ebony	Brownish-Black				

M
I
S
C
E
L
L
A
N
E
O
U
S

Angles

	Angles in regular polygon	Total angles	Sides	Formula
triangle	60°	180°	3	$(2 \times 3 - 4) \times 90 = 180$
quadrilateral	90°	360°	4	$(2 \times 4 - 4) \times 90 = 360$
pentagon	108°	540°	5	$(2 \times 5 - 4) \times 90 = 540$
hexagon	120°	720°	6	$(2 \times 6 - 4) \times 90 = 720$
heptagon	129°	900°	7	$(2 \times 7 - 4) \times 90 = 900$
octagon	135°	1080°	8	$(2 \times 8 - 4) \times 90 = 1080$
nonagon	140°	1260°	9	$(2 \times 9 - 4) \times 90 = 1260$
decagon	144°	1440°	10	$(2 \times 10 - 4) \times 90 = 1440$
dodecagon	150°	1800°	12	$(2 \times 12 - 4) \times 90 = 1800$
hendecagon	162°	3240°	20	$(2 \times 20 - 4) \times 90 = 3240$

NB Sum of the interior angles of a polygon = $(2n - 4) \times 90$ degrees where n = the number of sides.

Adjectives

Objects

acicular	needle-like	**hastate**	spear-shaped
acinaciform	scimitar-shaped	**lenticular**	lens-shaped
		ligneous	wood-like
aciniform	grape-like	**linguiform**	tongue-shaped
alaric	wing-shaped		
allantoic	sausage-shaped	**lunate**	crescent-shaped
		marmoreal	marble-like
amygdaloid	almond-shaped	**navicular**	boat-shaped
		oculiform	eye-shaped
annular	ring-shaped	**odontoid**	tooth-shaped
arcuate	bow-shaped	**oviform**	egg-shaped
baculiform	rod-like	**palmate**	palm-shaped
cancroid	crab-like	**pinnate**	feather-like
clavate	club-shaped	**pyriform**	pear-like
cordate	heart-shaped	**reniform**	kidney-shaped
cricoid	ring-shaped	**sagittate**	arrow-shaped
crinoidal	lily-like	**saponaceous**	soap-like
cuneal	wedge-shaped	**scutate**	shield-shaped
cyprinoid	carp-like	**stellate**	star-shaped
decussate	cross-shaped	**toroid**	doughnut-shaped
dendroid	tree-shaped	**trochal**	wheel-shaped
dentoid	tooth-shaped	**unciform**	hook-shaped
ethmoid	sieve-like	**verticillate**	whorl-shaped
falciform	sickle-shaped	**xiphoid**	sword-shaped
ganoid	scale-like		

Animals

anguine	snake-like	**lupine**	wolf-like
anserine	goose-like	**murine**	mouse-like
apian	bee-like	**ovine**	sheep-like
aquiline	eagle-like	**ophidian**	snake-like
asinine	ass-like	**passerine**	sparrow-like
avian	bird-like	**pavanine**	peacock-like
bovine	ox-like	**piscine**	fish-like
canine	dog-like	**porcine**	pig-like
caprine	goat-like	**psittacine**	parrot-like
cervine	deer-like	**saurian**	lizard-like
columbine	dove-like	**simian**	ape-like
corvine	crow-like	**squaloid**	shark-like
equine	horse-like	**taurine**	bull-like
feline	cat-like	**turdine**	thrush-like
hircine	goat-like	**ursine**	bear-like
leonine	lion-like	**vaccine**	cow-like
leporine	hare-like	**vulpine**	fox-like

Alphabets

	No. of characters	Description
Albanian	36	based on the Tosk language since 1945.
Arabic	28	all consonants; written from right to left.
Aramaic	22	all consonants; written from right to left.
Armenian	38	31 consonants and 7 vowels.
Balinese	27	the Latin alphabet is now used in Bali.
Bassa	29	formerly used in Liberia.
Batak	30	20 consonants, 10 vowels, written from bottom to top.
Braille	63	each made up of 1–6 raised dots arranged in six-position matrix.
Buhid	48	used to write the Tagalog language of the Philippines.
Bulgarian	30	adaptation of the Cyrillic alphabet.
Cyrillic	32	nowadays synonymous with the Russian alphabet.
Ethiopic	26	all consonants; 7 variations of each letter.
Etruscan	20	16 consonants, 4 vowels written left to right then right to left.
Gaelic	18	no J, K, Q, V, W, X, Y, Z.
Georgian	33	used by about 3.5 million people.
Gothic	27	original Gothic alphabet had 25 letters.
Grantha	35	30 consonants and 5 vowels; written left to right.
Greek	24	17 consonants and 7 vowels.
Gujarati	41	34 consonants, 7 vowels each having two variants.
Hebrew	22	all consonants; written from right to left.
Latin (Roman)	26	alphabet used by English speakers. J, U, W not in original Roman alphabet.
Mongolian	33	adaptation of the Cyrillic alphabet.
Ogham	29	also known as beth luis, or beth luis nion.
Phoenician	22	no vowels.
Runic	24	also known as fu(th)ark from its first six letters.
Russian	33	adaptation of the Cyrillic alphabet.
Serbian	29	adaptation of the Cyrillic alphabet.
Tamil	36	24 consonants, 12 vowels.
Telugo	51	35 consonants, 16 vowels.
Ugaritic	30	cuneiform alphabet of 27 consonants and 3 vowels.
Ukrainian	33	adaptation of the Cyrillic alphabet.

Roman Roads

Aemilian Way	Rimini to Milan	**Fosse Way**	Lincoln to Exeter
Akeman Street	Alchester to Cirencester	**Icknield Way**	Wash to Salisbury Plain
Appian Way	Rome to Brindisi	**Salarian Way**	Rome to Ancona
Aurelian Way	Rome to Genoa	**Stane Street (1)**	London to Chichester
Casinge Street	Dover to London	**(2)**	Braughing in Hertfordshire to Colchester
Cassian Way	Rome to Florence		
Dere Street	Risingham to Hadrian's Wall	**Watling Street (1)**	London to Wroxeter via St Albans
Ermine Street	London to York	**Watling Street (2)**	Wroxeter to Abergavenny
Flaminian Way	Rome to Rimini		

US Money

All US bills have a portrait of a famous American on the front and a design on the back as follows:

	Front	Back		Front	Back
$1	Washington	Great Seal of USA	$100	Franklin	Independence Hall
$2	Jefferson	Signers of Declaration	$500	McKinley	Ornate Design
$5	Lincoln	Lincoln Memorial	$1,000	Cleveland	Ornate Design
$10	Hamilton	US Treasury	$5,000	Madison	Ornate Design
$20	Jackson	White House	$10,000	Chase	Ornate Design
$50	Grant	US Capitol	$100,000	Wilson	Ornate Design

British Money

Until 1943 there were white bank notes for values of £10, £20, £50, £100, £500 and £1,000 but these ceased to be legal tender in 1945. The old white £5 note issued between 1945 and 1956 ceased to be legal tender in 1961. The £5 note issued between 1957 and 1963 that coincided with the term of office of Harold MacMillan, and bearing a portrait of Britannia, ceased to be legal tender in 1967. The £5 note issued between 1963 and 1971 was the first of the series to bear a portrait of the Queen. The first note with a portrait of the Queen on the front was a £1 note issued in 1960. The 10 shilling note was replaced by the 50p coin in 1969 and ceased to be legal tender in 1970 (they could however be redeemed if presented at the Head Office of the Bank of England). The £1 note was replaced by a coin in 1983 and ceased to be legal tender in 1988, although the Scottish £1 note is still acceptable in Scotland.

The current notes as at April 2005 portray famous people as follows:

£5	Elizabeth Fry (1780–1845)
£10	Charles Darwin (1809–82) and the *Beagle*
£20	Sir Edward Elgar (1857–1934) and Worcester Cathedral
£50	Sir John Houblon (1632–1712) the Bank of England gatekeeper. The current Chief Cashier of the Bank of England is Andrew Bailey, who replaced Merlyn Lowther.

Previous portraits on notes are as follows:

£5	George Stephenson and before him The Duke of Wellington
£10	Charles Dickens and before him Florence Nightingale
£20	Michael Faraday and before him William Shakespeare
£50	Sir Christopher Wren

British coins ceased to be legal tender as follows:

Farthing (¼d)	1960
Pre-decimal halfpenny	1969
Half-crown (2s 6d)	1970
Threepenny bit	1971
Sixpence (6d = 2½p)	1980
Decimal halfpenny	1984

Confusion often arises when one considers which was the first decimal coin brought into circulation. In 1968 the shilling and two shilling coins were replaced by a new 5p and 10p coin. This pre-empted decimalisation in 1971 and was an exercise in the public becoming used to the new system. The coins were of the same value as previously and did not alter the public perception in any way. In 1969 the new 50p coin was introduced, replacing the ten-shilling note which of course was a vastly different form, hence it often being considered as the first decimal coin introduced.

In 1971 the ½p, 1p, and 2p coins were introduced and in 1982 the 20p coin followed. In 1983 the £1 coin replaced the £1 note and in 1986 the first £2 coin was minted. Decimal coins minted before 1982 had their value in 'New' pence.

UK Telephone STD Codes

0121	Birmingham
0131	Edinburgh
0141	Glasgow
0151	Liverpool
0161	Manchester
0191	Newcastle upon Tyne

Recent changes to STD codes

Cardiff was 01222 now 02920
Coventry was 01203 now 02476
London was 0171 now 0207
London was 0181 now 0208
Portsmouth was 01705 now 02392
Southampton was 01703 now 02380

NB All Northern Ireland numbers have been changed to six-digit numbers, all of which begin 028.

and finally

A few well-known people whose name belies their gender:

Colley Cibber (dramatist) male
Wilkie Collins (novelist) male
Richmal Crompton (novelist) female
Keri Hulme (novelist) female
Ngaio Marsh (novelist) female
Julian of Norwich (mystic) female
Harper Lee (novelist) female
Laurie Lee (novelist) male
Marilyn Manson (pop star) male

Joan Miro (painter) male
Nelly (rapper) male
Andrea Palladio (architect) male
Caryl Phillips (novelist) male
Carol Reed (film director) male
Vesta Tilley (music hall star) female
Reese Witherspoon (actress) female
Evelyn Waugh (novelist) male
George Sand (novelist) female

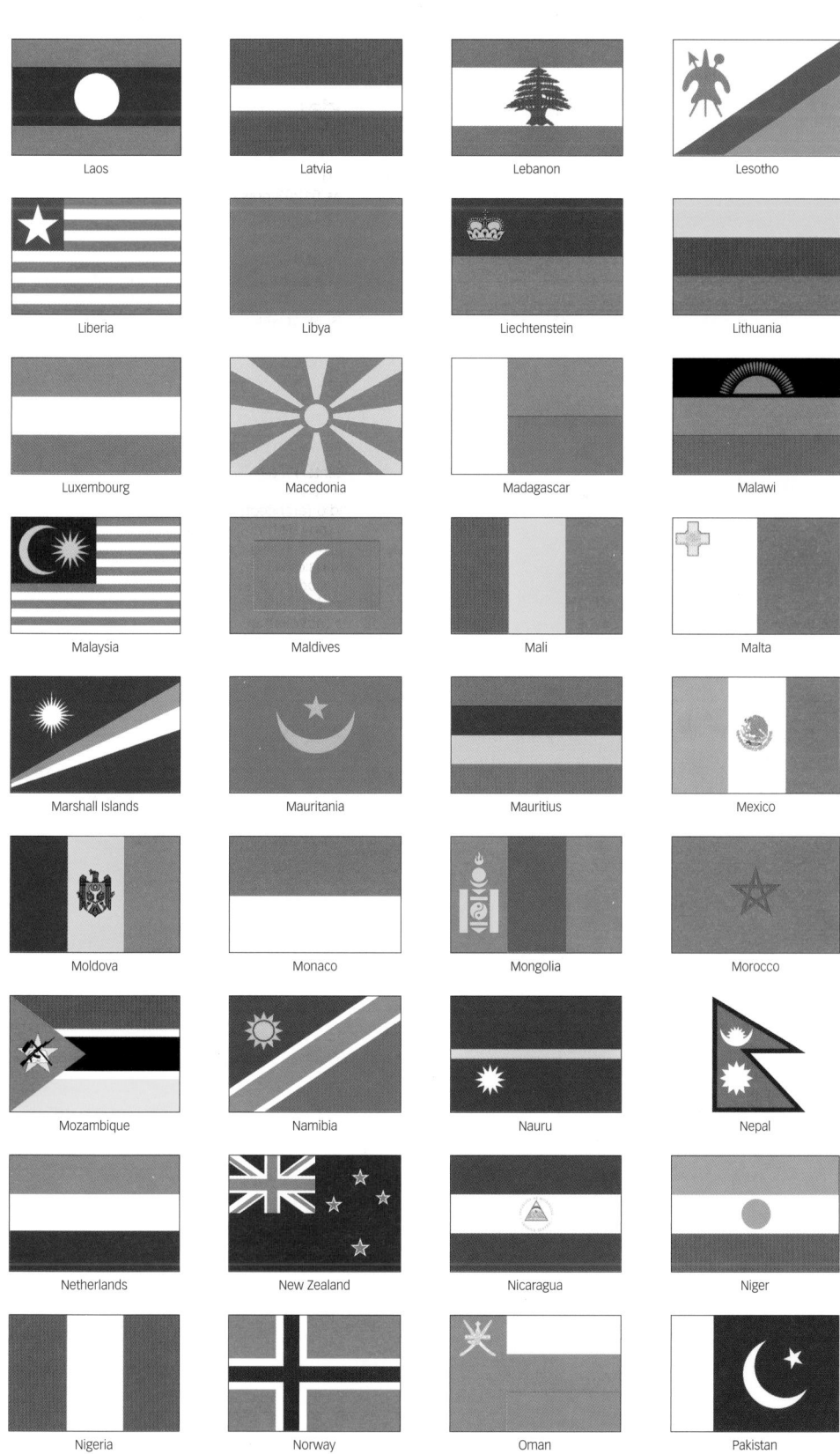

Laos	Latvia	Lebanon	Lesotho
Liberia	Libya	Liechtenstein	Lithuania
Luxembourg	Macedonia	Madagascar	Malawi
Malaysia	Maldives	Mali	Malta
Marshall Islands	Mauritania	Mauritius	Mexico
Moldova	Monaco	Mongolia	Morocco
Mozambique	Namibia	Nauru	Nepal
Netherlands	New Zealand	Nicaragua	Niger
Nigeria	Norway	Oman	Pakistan

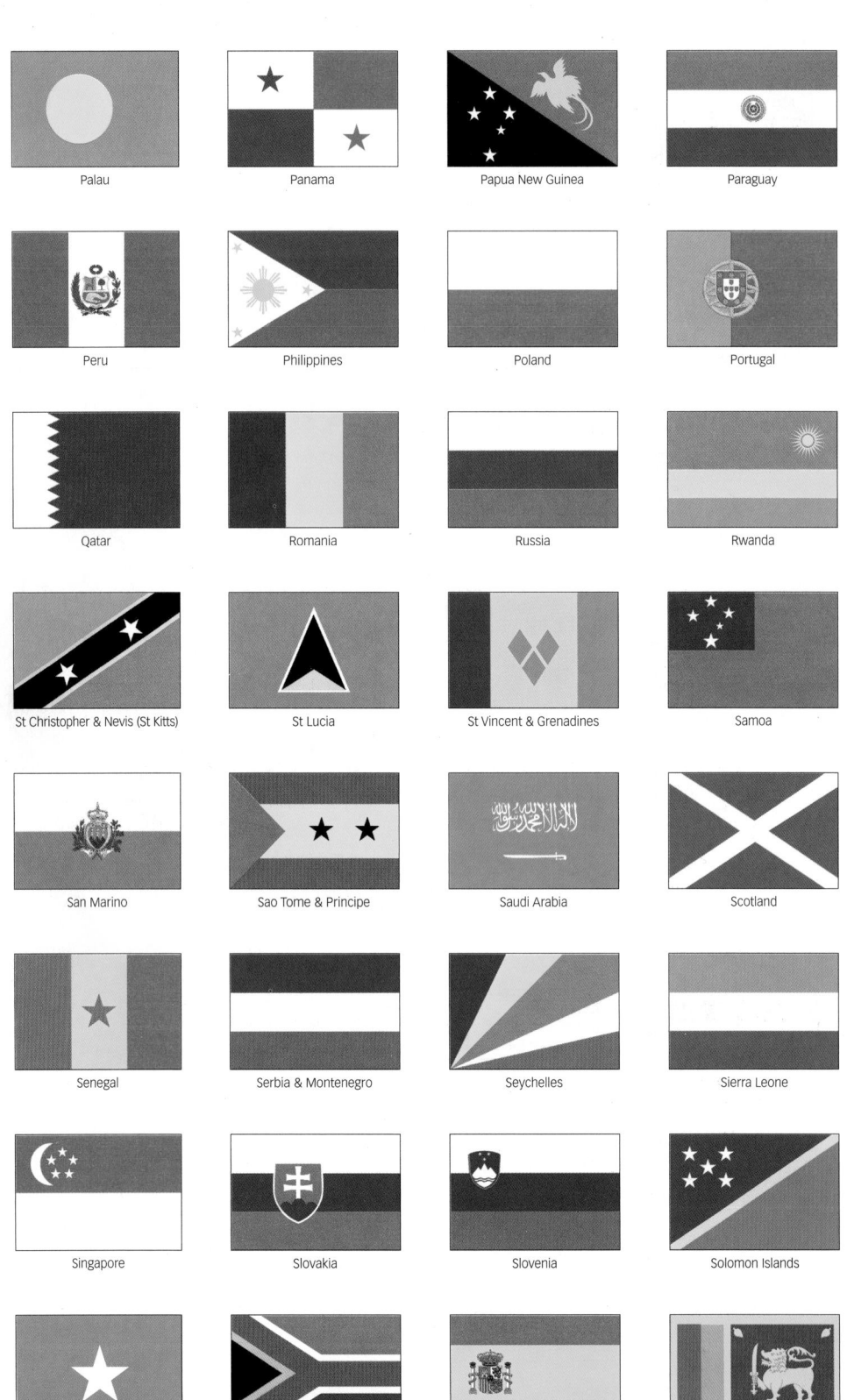

Palau	Panama	Papua New Guinea	Paraguay
Peru	Philippines	Poland	Portugal
Qatar	Romania	Russia	Rwanda
St Christopher & Nevis (St Kitts)	St Lucia	St Vincent & Grenadines	Samoa
San Marino	Sao Tome & Principe	Saudi Arabia	Scotland
Senegal	Serbia & Montenegro	Seychelles	Sierra Leone
Singapore	Slovakia	Slovenia	Solomon Islands
Somalia	South Africa	Spain	Sri Lanka